KU-025-622

OXFORD ILLUSTRATED DICTIONARY

OXFORD ILLUSTRATED DICTIONARY

TEXT EDITED BY

J. COULSON C. T. CARR
LUCY HUTCHINSON DOROTHY EAGLE

ILLUSTRATIONS EDITED BY
HELEN MARY PETTER

OXFORD
AT THE CLARENDON PRESS

Oxford University Press, Ely House, London W. 1
GLASGOW NEW YORK TORONTO MELBOURNE WELLINGTON
CAPE TOWN SALISBURY IBADAN NAIROBI DAR ES SALAAM LUSAKA ADDIS ABABA
BOMBAY CALCUTTA MADRAS KARACHI LAHORE DACCA
KUALA LUMPUR SINGAPORE HONG KONG TOKYO

FIRST PUBLISHED 1962
REPRINTED (WITH CORRECTIONS) 1963
REPRINTED (WITH CORRECTIONS AND ADDENDA) 1965
REPRINTED (WITH CORRECTIONS AND ADDENDA) 1970

PRINTED IN GREAT BRITAIN

PUBLISHER'S NOTE

SOME years before the last war it had become clear that there was a demand for a dictionary which would combine the essential features of an encyclopaedia and of a dictionary in the ordinary sense; that is to say, a work which would deal not only with words and phrases, but also with the things for which these words and phrases stand. The general reader would thus be able to find within a single pair of covers two types of information for which he would ordinarily have to consult at least two different books.

Mrs. J. Coulson was asked to draw up a plan for a reference book on these lines and one where the factual character of much of the information would be emphasized and the exposition aided by a copious use of illustration. The plan and specimens were approved and the work of building up the material was far advanced when towards the end of the war Mrs. Coulson was obliged for family reasons to abandon it. In 1945 Professor C. T. Carr of St. Andrews University took over the task of completing the text and revising it. By 1952, however, his academic duties had become too heavy for him to continue and the late Miss Lucy Hutchinson, who had already been called in to help with the problems of illustration, took over the whole dictionary, and in 1956 Miss H. M. Petter became responsible for the illustrations. When Miss Hutchinson died in 1959, at a tragically early age, the whole book was in galley proof. The task of seeing it through the press was undertaken by Mrs. Dorothy Eagle.

The publishers would like to express their gratitude to all these editors They are grateful also to Mrs. Mary Alden who read the proofs at galley stage and to Mr. J. M. Wyllie who gave much helpful criticism in the early stages of the book's preparation.

It is not possible to make more than a general acknowledgement of help received from many other quarters, but the publishers would like to express particular thanks to the following for help on specialized and technical matters: Miss R. J. Banister, Mr. J. S. P. Bradford, Dr. C. J. Danby, Dr. T. K. Derry, Dr. R. B. Freeman, Commander D. H. Fryer, R.N. (Rtd), Dr. Ll. Hammick, Mr. E. N. Hamnett, Mrs. J. M. Harrison, Dr. B. M. Hobby, Mr. G. T. Hollis, Dr. D. H. Howling, Dr. W. O. James, Dr. R. H. Kay, Professor K. Kirkwood, Mr. G. E. Middleton, Mr. T. A. Morris, Mr. D. Maddison O'Brien, Mr. J. F. R. Peel, Dr. G. Rushworth, Dr. J. Sanders, Professor R. S. Sayers, Mr. W. F. Snook, Dr. J. M. K. Spalding, Dr. J. S. Weiner, Mr. J. S. de Wet, Dr. K. C. Wheare, Mr. M. J. White, Professor B. S. Yamey, Professor O. L. Zangwill.

The publishers would also like to thank the following artists who have made important contributions: G. F. Campbell (nautical subjects), Christine Court (anatomy), R. W. Ford (scientific, mechanical, and botanical subjects),

M. S. Macdonald-Taylor (costume and furniture), H. Russell Robinson (armour and weapons), and K. G. V. Smith (zoology).

They are grateful also to many people who have supplied material from which drawings have been made, including the following: Sir William Arrol & Co. Ltd. (p. 187); the Birmingham Assay Master (p. 365); the Trustees of the British Museum (pp. 63, 567, 723, 747); John Broadwood & Sons Ltd. (pp. 146, 370, 618); J. & P. Coats Ltd. (p. 191); Commonwealth Bureau of Horticulture (p. 350); Controller of H.M.S.O. (pp. 25, 63, 66, 450, 593, 755, 799); Crown Copyright (pp. 592, 828, 878); De Havilland Aircraft Co. Ltd. (p. 12); Director-General of Artillery, Ministry of Supply (pp. 117, 361, 707, 845); East Malling Research Station (p. 324); Educational Productions Ltd. (pp. 42, 51, 60, 72, 134, 190, 386, 463, 550, 803, 835); English Electric Co. Ltd. (pp. 203, 399); C. & J. Hampton Ltd. (pp. 626, 799); Imperial War Museum (p. 511); London School of Weaving (p. 485); Joseph Lucas Ltd. (p. 253); Museum of English Life, Reading (pp. 116, 748, 924, 938); Museum of the History of Science, Oxford (pp. 18, 37, 43, 579, 670, 702); Nuffield Organization (p. 535); Public Record Office, c. 220/15/8/mem. 33 (p. 747); Smiths Clocks and Watches Ltd. (p. 149); Sperry Gyroscope Co. Ltd. (p. 362); R. H. Walker & Son Ltd. (p. 577); Westland Aircraft Ltd. (p. 377). Illustrations have been based on figures from the following books: Léon Bertrand, *The Fencer's Companion*, Gale & Polden (p. 293); I. E. S. Edwards, *The Pyramids of Egypt*, Penguin Books (p. 669); Singer, Holmyard, Hall, and Williams, *A History of Technology*, Clarendon Press (p. 945); J. Z. Young, *The Life of Vertebrates*, Clarendon Press (pp. 29, 572, 638, 650, 763); *The Book of the Motor Car*, Naldrett Press (p. 151).

PREFACE

ACCORDING to the distinction used by H. W. Fowler in the preface to the *Concise Oxford Dictionary*, a dictionary normally takes the uses of words and phrases as such for its subject-matter and is concerned with giving information about the things for which these words and phrases stand only so far as correct use of the words depends upon knowledge of the things. In an encyclopaedia, on the other hand, the emphasis will be much more on the nature of the things for which the words and phrases stand.

This book attempts to combine in a form that can be handled conveniently the essential features of dictionary and encyclopaedia. Where things are more easily explained by pictures or diagrams than by words, illustration has been used to help out definition. As the dictionary thus becomes the first Oxford English dictionary to make use of illustration (apart from the *Oxford Dictionary of Nursery Rhymes* where illustration is used for a different purpose and in a different way), it has been given a title which distinguishes it from the rest of the family by its most conspicuous feature.

VOCABULARY

The general reader for whom the book is intended may not always have another dictionary or encyclopaedia at his ready disposal and so the vocabulary has been chosen with an eye to the needs of one who may require either type of information. Information about words, however, is more often sought by the average user of a reference book than information about things and the vocabulary has therefore been based on that of the *Concise Oxford Dictionary* and the definitions retain its historical ordering. Familiar words are less fully treated, however, and the phrases illustrating such words have been more sparingly used so as to obtain a wider scope for the treatment of things.

The vocabulary should thus be adequate for the reader who consults the book for ordinary dictionary purposes. But it also contains terms in everyday use which would be excluded from an ordinary dictionary because of their technical and scientific character or which would be very briefly dealt with; familiar words in semi-technical use (e.g. *vertical trust*, *combine*, etc.); the names of famous people (e.g. statesmen, explorers, inventors, artists, and writers), historical, contemporary, or fictitious; and the names of important places and events.

Special pains have been taken to ensure that scientific and technical terms are up to date and accurate in selection and in definition and at the same time intelligible to the user, but the present pace of development in science and technology is so swift that no reference book which deals with them in even the most general way can ever be completely up to date: between the time the book is compiled and its publication new words and senses will have come into use and existing words and senses will have acquired fresh shades of meaning or become obsolescent.

In order to keep the book within reasonable compass obsolete words and phrases have been omitted except for a few which some special interest has made it desirable to retain.

ILLUSTRATIONS

So far as possible the illustrations have been planned to support the function of the text and each of them is independent and self-explanatory: each is intended to show the meaning of a word or indicate the character of the thing for which the word stands. To avoid wasteful repetition many subjects have been grouped together, especially where the members of the group help to explain one another: the picture of a machine, for example, will not only illustrate the machine itself but will exhibit the nature of its parts, and their relation to one another and to the whole. In some cases the illustrations demonstrate how things work, but only where this helps to define the words. Historical development may also be indicated where this information is an essential part of the definition, for instance costume may be dated, although it is not the intention to illustrate the history of costume.

The subjects chosen for illustration are those which can be defined more clearly by this means than verbally. Words are often best defined in general terms but a drawing has to be of a particular thing and therefore gives an example of the particular use of the word rather than a generalized statement. Thus the human body has been chosen to show the different bones of the skeleton, although the same terms are used for comparable bones in other vertebrates.

The subjects are limited to those of general interest, but very familiar words are not illustrated. Space has not permitted the illustration of every subject and therefore examples with a wide range of reference have usually been chosen; thus the zoological drawings are intended to illustrate one particular example from each order.

ABBREVIATIONS

Abbreviations in current use appear in their alphabetical place in the body of the text to save a separate alphabet. But there is a separate list of those abbreviations used in the dictionary itself.

ETYMOLOGY

For the sake of space derivations have been omitted with a few exceptions. These occur where the etymology is especially interesting or unexpected (e.g. *penicillin*, *derrick*), or when a thing has been named after its inventor or place of origin (e.g. *Fortin barometer*, *Borstal*). In these cases the etymology is given in square brackets at the end of the entry.

CROSS-REFERENCES

Where a word is given small capitals in a definition, this indicates that reference to the word in its alphabetical place will provide further information (e.g. CEREBRUM in the entry for *brain*) or discuss the term which is given in comparison or contradistinction (e.g. NOBLE or PRECIOUS metals as opposed to *base* metals). Where something is illustrated as part of a composite picture the reference is usually given in round brackets (e.g. *aileron* . . . (ill. AEROPLANE)).

PRONUNCIATION

1. **Accent.** The accentuation mark ʹ is usually placed at the end of the stressed syllable.

2. **Phonetic System.** Where the pronunciation of a word or part of a word cannot be shown by the ordinary spelling and markings, a phonetic spelling is given in round brackets immediately after the black-type word. The phonetic scheme is as follows:

CONSONANTS: b; ch (ch*in*); d; dh (dh*e* = the); g (g*o*); h; j; k; l; m; n; ng (*si*ng); ngg (*fi*ng*er*); p; r; s (s*ip*); sh (sh*ip*); t; th (th*in*); v; w; y; z; zh (*vi*zh*n* = vision).

ṅ indicates French nasalization of preceding vowel.

The symbol χ represents the ch in *lo*ch.

VOWELS: ā ē ī ō ū ōō (mate mete mite mote mute moot)
ă ĕ ĭ ŏ ŭ ŏŏ (rack reck rick rock ruck rook)
ār ēr īr ōr ūr (mare mere mire more mure)
âr êr ôr (part pert port)
ah aw oi oor ow owr (bah bawl boil boor brow bower)

Vowels printed in italic within the brackets indicate vague sounds.
Vowels marked ˘̄ may be pronounced either way, e.g. **vŏ̄lt.**

3. **Pronunciation without Respelling.** As far as possible pronunciation is shown without respelling by placing symbols over the words (e.g. **ā, ĕ, ār, êr, ŏŏ**, etc.) in the black type.

(*a*) The ordinary spelling often coincides with the phonetic system described in paragraph 2.

(*b*) The following additional symbols are used in the black type:
ė = ĭ (nāʹkėd, rėlȳʹ, cŏllʹėge, prĭvʹėt)
îr, ûr = êr (bîrth, bûrn)
ȳ, y̆ = ī, ĭ (ĭmplȳʹ, sŭnnʹy̆)

(*c*) final *e* when unmarked is mute, i.e. not to be pronounced. Thus **ape** is to be pronounced āp. Where final *e* is pronounced, it is marked as in **rĕʹcĭpė.**

(*d*) Unless another pronunciation is indicated, the following letters and combinations have the usual values in English spelling which are shown alongside them:

Vowels

ae = ē (aegis)
ai = ā (pain)
air = ār (fair)
au = aw (maul)
ay = ā (say)
ea, ee = ē (mean, meet)
ear, eer = ēr (fear, beer)
eu, ew = ū (feud, few)
ie = ē (thief)
ier = ēr (pier)
oa = ō (boat)
ou = ow (bound)
oy = oi (boy)

Consonants

c is 'hard' and = k (cob, cry, talc) *but*
c before **e, i, y**, is 'soft' and = s (ice, icy, city)
dg = j (judgement)
g before **e, i, y**, is 'soft' and = j (age, gin, orgy)
n before **k**, 'hard' **c, q, x** = ng (zinc uncle, tank, banquet, minx)
ph = f (photo)
qu = kw (quit)
tch = ch (batch)
x = ks (fox)

Thus in **gĕm** the pronunciation of *g* is not marked because it comes under the rule above: '**g** before **e, i, y**, is "soft" and = j'; but **gĕt** is followed by (g-) to show that here exceptionally **g** before **e** is 'hard' as in *go*.

(*e*) The following terminations have the values shown:

-age = -ĭj (garbage)
-ate = -ĭt or -*a*t (mandate)
-ey = -ĭ (donkey)
-ous = -*u*s (furious)
-sm = -zm (atheism, spasm)
-tion = -sh*o*n (salvation)
-ture = -ch*er* as well as -tūr, esp. in common words

SWUNG DASH (~)

The 'swung dash' or 'tilde' is frequently used to save space in the body of the entry. It represents the headword when this is repeated as a different part of speech or when it is used in combination with another word, either hyphenated or detached (but not when it has become part of a complete new word). For example, in the article **pitch**[1] *n.* we have ~ *v.t.* when the headword becomes a new part of speech, and ~ *black* and ~*-pine* when it is in combination (but *pitchblende* as a whole word). When a word repeated as a different part of speech is spelt the same but is differently accentuated, it is written again, as **trănsfer′** *v.*, **trăns′fer** *n.*

CONTENTS

PRONUNCIATION (part of Preface) vii

ABBREVIATIONS USED IN THE DICTIONARY xiii

DICTIONARY 1

ADDENDA 963

APPENDIXES 965

I. Roman Emperors 965

II. Emperors of the Western (or Holy Roman) Empire 966

III. The Popes since the Seventh Century 966

IV. Rulers of England and of the United Kingdom 968

V. Prime Ministers of Great Britain 969

VI. Presidents of the United States of America 970

VII. States of the United States of America with their Capitals 970

VIII. Counties and County Towns of the United Kingdom 970

IX. The Chemical Elements 972

X. Weights and Measures 974

ABBREVIATIONS USED IN THE DICTIONARY

(*Abbreviations in general use have entries in the main text*)

abbrev./iation etc.
abl./ative
abs./olute
acc./ording
accus./ative
act./ive
adj./ective etc.
adjs., adjectives
adv./erb etc.
advs., adverbs
AF, Anglo-French
Afr./ica(n)
alg./ebra etc.
allus./ive etc.
Amer./ica(n)
anal./ogy etc.
anat./omy etc.
Anglo-Ind./ian
anon./ymous etc.
antiq./uities
anthrop./ology etc.
app./arently
app./endix
Arab./ic
Aram./aic
arbitr./ary
archaeol./ogy etc.
archit./ecture etc.
arith./metic etc.
assim./ilated etc.
assoc./iated etc.
astrol./ogy etc.
astron./omy etc.
at./omic
attrib./utive etc.
augment./ative etc.
Austral./ia(n)
auxil./iary
av./oirdupois

b./orn
back form./ation
bibl./ical etc.
bibliog./raphy etc.
biochem./istry etc.
biol./ogy etc.
Boh./emian
bot./any etc.
Br./itish
Braz./ilian
Brit./ish
Bulg./arian
Burm./ese
Byz./antine

c./entury
c/irca
cap./ital
Celt./ic
cf., compare
Ch./urch
chem./istry etc.
Chin./ese
chronol./ogy etc.
cinemat./ography etc.
cogn./ate
collect./ive(ly)
colloq./uial etc.
com./mon
comb./ination etc.
commerc./ial etc.
comp., compar./ative
compl./ement
conch./ology etc.
confus./ion
conj., conjunction, conjugation
conn./ect etc.
constr./uction etc.
contempt./uous etc.
contr./action etc.
cop./ulative
correl./ative etc.
corresp./onding etc.
corrupt./ion
cryst./allography
cu., cub., cubic

d./ied
Dan./ish
dat./ive

demonstr./ative
deriv./ative etc.
derog./atory etc.
dial./ect etc.
dict./ionary
diff./erent
dim./inutive etc.
diplom./acy
dist./inct
distrib./utive etc.
Du./tch
dub./ious

E., east(ern)
eccles./iastical etc.
econ./omics
Egyptol./ogy
E. Ind., East Indian
elect./ricity etc.
ellipt./ical etc.
embryol./ogy
eng., engin./eering etc.
Engl., England, English
entom./ology etc.
erron./eous(ly)
esp./ecial(ly)
ethnol./ogy etc.
etym./ology etc.
euphem./ism etc.
Eur./ope(an)
exagg./eration etc.
exc./ept
exch./ange
excl., exclamation etc., exclusive etc.
expl./ain etc.
expr./essing etc.

f./rom
facet./ious etc.
fam./iliar etc.
fem./inine etc.
fig./urative etc.
Fl./emish
foll./owing (word)
footb./all
fort./ification
Fr./ench
freq./uent(ly)
frequent./ative(ly)
ft, foot, feet
ut./ure

Gael./ic
gal./lon(s)
gen., general etc., genitive
geog./raphy etc.
geol./ogy etc.
geom./etry etc.
Ger./man
Gk, Greek
govt., government
gram./mar etc.

Heb./rew
her./aldry etc.
Hind./ustani
hist./orical etc., history
hort./iculture etc.

i., intransitive
Icel./andic
ill./ustration
illit./erate etc.
imit./ative etc.
imp., imper./ative
imperf./ect
impers./onal
improp./er(ly)
incl./uding, inclusive
Ind./ia(n)
ind., indicative, indirect
indecl./inable
indef./inite
inf./initive
infl./uence etc.
instr./umental (case)
int./erjection
interrog./ative(ly)
intrans./itive
Ir./ish
iron./ically
irreg./ular(ly)
It., Ital./ian
ital./ics

Jap./an(ese)
Jew./ish
joc./ose, -ular(ly)

L, Latin
lang./uage
Lat./in

LG, Low German
lit./eral(ly)
Lith./uania(n)
LL, late Latin
log./ic etc.

magn./etism etc.
manuf./acture etc.
masc./uline
math./ematics etc.
MDu., Middle Dutch
ME, Middle English
mech./anics etc.
med./icine etc.
med.L, medieval Latin
metaph./or etc.
metaphys./ics etc.
meteor./ology etc.
Mex./ican, Mexico
MG, Middle German
MHG, Middle High German
mil./itary etc.
min./eralogy etc.
MLG, Middle Low German
mod./ern
morphol./ogy etc.
mus./ic etc.
myth./ology etc.

N., north(ern)
n./oun
N. Amer., North America(n)
nat. hist., natural history
naut./ical etc.
nav./al etc.
nec./essary, -essarily
neg./ative(ly)
neut./er
nom./inative
Norm./an
north./ern
Norw./egian, Norway
ns., nouns
N.T., New Testament
num./eral

obj./ect etc.
obl./ique
obs./olete
obsolesc./ent
occas./ional(ly)
OE, Old English
OF, Old French
OHG, Old High German
OIr., Old Irish
OLG, Old Low German
ON, Old Norse
onomat./opoeic etc.
opp., (as) opposed (to), opposite
ord./inary, -inarily
orig./inal(ly)
ornith./ology etc.
O.T., Old Testament

p./age
paint./ing
palaeog./raphy etc.
palaeont./ology etc.
parenth./etic etc.
parl./iament(ary)
part., participle
part. adj., participial adjective
pass./ive(ly)
past part./iciple
past t./ense
path./ology etc.
pedant./ic(ally)
perf./ect (tense)
perh./aps
Pers./ia(n)
pers./on(al)
Peruv./ian
pharm./acy etc.
philol./ogy etc.
philos./ophy etc.
phon., phonet./ics etc.
phot., photog./raphy etc.
phr./ase
phys./ics etc.
physiol./ogy etc.
pl./ural
pluperf./ect
poet./ical etc.
Pol./ish, Poland
pol./itics etc.
pol. econ., political economy
pop./ular etc.
Port./uguese, Portugal
poss./essive
pp., pages

pr./onounced etc.
prec., (the) preceding (word)
pred./icate etc.
pref./ix
prep./osition
pres./ent (tense)
pret./erite
print./ing
prob./able etc.
pron., pronoun etc., pronounced etc., pronunciation
prop./er(ly)
pros./ody etc.
psych., psychol./ogy etc.
psycho-anal./ysis

railw./ay
R.C., Roman Catholic
ref./erence
refl./exive(ly)
rel./ative
repr./esent etc.
rhet./oric etc.
Rom./an
Russ./ia(n)

S., south(ern)
S. Afr., South Africa(n)
Sansk./rit
Sax./on
sb., substantive
Sc., Scotch, Scots, Scottish
Scand./inavia(n)
sculp./ture
sent./ence
Serb./ia(n)
sing./ular
Slav./onic
sociol./ogy etc.
Span./ish
sp./elling
spec./ial(ly)
specif./ic(ally)
sport./ing etc.
St. Exch., Stock Exchange
subj., subject etc., subjunctive
superl./ative
surg./ery etc.
surv./eying etc.
Swed./ish, Sweden
syn./onym

t., tense, transitive
tech./nical(ly)
teleg./raphy etc.
term./ination etc.
Teut./on(ic)
theatr./ical
theol./ogy etc.
thr./ough
trans./itive etc.
transf., in transferred sense
transl./ation etc.
trig./onometry etc.
Turk./ish, Turkey
typ./ography etc.

U.K., United Kingdom
ult./imate(ly)
unexpl./ained
U.S., United States
usu./al(ly)

v./erb
var., variant, various
v. aux., verb auxiliary
vb(s)., verb(s)
vbl, verbal
v.i., verb intransitive
voc./ative
v.r., verb reflexive
v.t., verb transitive
vulg./ar(ly)

W., west(ern)
w./ith
W. Afr., West Africa(n)
wd, word
wds, words
W. Ind., West Indian, Indies

yd(s), yard(s)
yr(s), year(s)

zool./ogy etc.

A

A, a (ā). 1. 1st letter of modern English and Roman alphabet, descended, through Greek and Latin, from first letter, aleph (𐤀), of Hebrew and Phoenician alphabets; representing originally in English a 'low-back-wide' vowel sound, and now a number of vowel sounds. 2. 1st in series, order, or class, esp. (alg.) first known quantity. 3. (mus.) 6th note of 'natural' major scale (C major). 4. (logic) Universal affirmation. 5. **A 1,** applied in Lloyd's Register to ships in first-class condition in respect of both hull (designated by A) and equipment (1); hence, first-class, prime, perfect.

A *abbrev.* Adult (i.e. for exhibition to adults, of cinema picture); air; alto; ampere; *avancer* (on time-piece regulator = to accelerate).

a, an (*a, an*; emphatic, ā, ăn) *adj.* The 'indefinite article'. One, some, any; a certain; each.

a- *prefix.* Without, not, un-, non-; of, on.

A.A. *abbrev.* Anti-aircraft; Automobile Association.

A.A.A. *abbrev.* Amateur Athletic Association; (U.S.) Agricultural Adjustment Administration.

Aach'en (ahχ-). German name of *Aix-la-Chapelle*, ancient city of Germany near Belgian and Dutch borders, scene of coronation of German kings until 16th c.

A.A.G. *abbrev.* Assistant Adjutant-General.

Aaland: see ÅLAND ISLANDS.

A. and M. *abbrev.* (Hymns) Ancient and Modern.

A.A.Q.M.G. *abbrev.* Assistant Adjutant and Quartermaster-General.

aard'vārk (ar-) *n.* S. Afr. ant-eating quadruped (*Orycteropus*

AARDVARK

afra and *O. aethiopicus*) with long extensile tongue. [Du., = 'earth-pig']

aard'-wolf (ard wŏolf) *n.* Carnivorous mammal (*Protelas lalandii*) resembling the hyena.

Aaron (ār'on). Brother of Moses and traditional founder of Jewish priesthood; ~*'s beard* (see Ps. cxxxiii. 2), various plants, esp. St. John's wort; ~*'s rod* (see Numbers xvii. 8), plant with tall flowering stem, esp. great mullein and golden rod.

aasvogel (ahs'fōgl) *n.* Any of several large S. Afr. vultures. [Du., = 'carrion-bird']

ab- *prefix.* Off, away, from.

A.B. *abbrev.* Able-bodied seaman.

ăb'a, abaya (*a*bā'ya) *ns.* Sack-like outer garment worn by Arabs.

abăck' *adv.* Backwards; *taken* ~, (of ship) with square sails pressed back against the mast by the wind; (fig.) surprised, discomfited.

ăb'acus *n.* (pl. *-ci*, pr. -sī). 1. Frame for arithmetical calculation with balls sliding on wires, used before the adoption of the nine figures and zero, and still in China etc. and in elementary teaching. 2. (archit.) Upper member, often a square flat slab, of capital, supporting architrave (ill. ORDER). 3. (mus.) Diagram of pianoforte or organ keyboard.

Abădd'on. Heb. name of APOLLYON (see Rev. ix. 11).

abaft' (-bah-) *adv.* On or towards stern of ship. ~ *prep.* Aft of, behind.

ăbalō'nė *n.* Californian edible mollusc, a gastropod of genus *Haliotis*, with ear-shaped shell lined with mother-of-pearl; sea-ear.

abăn'don *v.t.* Give up, surrender, forsake. ~ *n.* Careless freedom. **abăn'donment** *n.* **abăn'doned** *adj.* (esp.) Profligate, loose.

abăndonee' *n.* Underwriter to whom salvage of wreck is abandoned.

abāse' *v.t.* Humiliate, lower, make base. **abāse'ment** (-sm-) *n.*

abăsh' *v.t.* Put out of countenance, confound.

abāte' *v.* Diminish, make or become less; lower; deduct (part of price); (law) quash (action), end (nuisance). **abāte'ment** (-tm-) *n.*

ăb'atis, abătt'is *n.* (mil.) Obstacle of felled trees with branches pointing outwards.

ăbăttoir (abăt'wahr *or* ăb'-) *n.* Slaughter-house.

Abb'a (ă-). Used (in ~, *father*) in invocations to God; title of bishops in Syriac and Coptic Churches. [Aramaic, = 'father']

ăbb'acy *n.* Office, jurisdiction, or tenure of abbot or abbess.

Abb'as[1] (ă-; *or* abahs') (566–652). Uncle of Mohammed, descent from whom was claimed by **Abbas'ids**, dynasty of caliphs ruling in Baghdad 750–1258.

Abb'as[2] (ă-; *or* abahs') 'the Great'. Shah of Persia; reigned 1587–1628.

abbā'tial (-shl) *adj.* Of an abbey, abbot, or abbess.

ăbb'é (-ā) *n.* Frenchman entitled to wear ecclesiastical dress, esp. without official duties.

ăbb'ĕss *n.* Female superior of community of nuns, in those orders in which monks are governed by abbots.

ăbb'ey (-ĭ) *n.* Body of monks or nuns governed by an abbot or abbess; monastic buildings; church or house once an abbey or part of it.

Abb'ey Theatre. Irish national theatre, located since 1904 in Abbey St., Dublin.

ăbb'ot *n.* Superior of community of monks (now chiefly in Benedictine and Augustinian orders), usu. elected by the monks for life or period of years, and freq. holding certain episcopal rights; ~ *of misrule*: see MISRULE. [Aramaic *abbā* father]

Abb'otsford (ă-). Sir Walter Scott's house, near Melrose on the Tweed.

abbrēv'ĭāte *v.t.* Shorten, contract (esp. word, by writing part for the whole). **abbrēvĭā'tion** *n.*

A B C *n.* Alphabet; rudiments of subject; alphabetical railway time-table; ~ *Powers*, Argentine, Brazil, Chile, the three principal States of S. America.

Abdēr'a (ă-). Ancient Greek city on coast of Thrace whose inhabitants were proverbial for their stupidity. **Abdēr'ite** *adj.* & *n.* (Native, inhabitant) of Abdera; *the* ~, Democritus.

ăb'dicāte *v.* Renounce, relinquish, (esp. crown) formally or by default. **ăbdicā'tion** *n.*

ăbdōm'ėn (*or* ăb'do-) *n.* 1. Belly, lower part of body, containing digestive and other organs. 2. (zool.) Hinder part, not bearing walking limbs, of insects, spiders, etc. **ăbdŏm'ĭnal** *adj.* (*Illustration, p.* 2.)

ăbdū'cent *adj.* (anat., of muscles) Drawing back.

abdŭct' *v.t.* Take away (esp. woman) by force or fraud; (of muscle etc.) draw limb from normal position. **abdŭc'tion, abdŭc'tor** *ns.*

abeam *adv.* On a line at right angles to ship's length (also of aircraft); opposite the middle of ship's side (ill. BEARING).

ābėcėdār'ĭan *adj.* 1. Arranged alphabetically, as the 119th Psalm. 2. Elementary, ignorant. ~ *n.* Pupil learning the alphabet (U.S.).

à Becket, Thomas: see BECKET.

abĕd' *adv.* (archaic, poet.) In bed.

A'bel (ā-). 2nd son of Adam, killed by his brother Cain: see Gen. iv. 1–16.

Abélārd (ăb'ā-), Pierre (1079–1142). French philosopher; lecturer in the schools of Paris; advocate of rational theological inquiry and founder of scholastic theology. See also HÉLOÏSE.

abele (*a*bēl′, ā′bl) *n.* White poplar, *Populus alba.*

Aberdeen′ (ă-). University city and county borough on E. coast of N. Scotland, county town of the county of Aberdeenshire, known as the 'granite city' and humorously credited with extremely 'careful' population; ~ *terrier*, Scotch terrier. **Aberdōn′ian** *adj.* & *n.* (Citizen) of Aberdeen.

ăberdėvīne′ *n.* Bird-fancier's name for siskin.

Fletcher's 'Scornful Lady', the 'waiting gentlewoman' (cf. 1 Sam. xxv. 24–31); hence, waiting-woman, lady's-maid.

abĭl′ĭty *n.* Sufficient power, capacity (*to* do); legal competency (to act); cleverness, talent, mental faculty.

Abĭm′ėlĕch (*a*-, -k). 1. Son of Gideon, one of the judges of Israel: see Judges viii, ix. 2. King of Gerar, southern Palestine: see Gen. xx, xxvi.

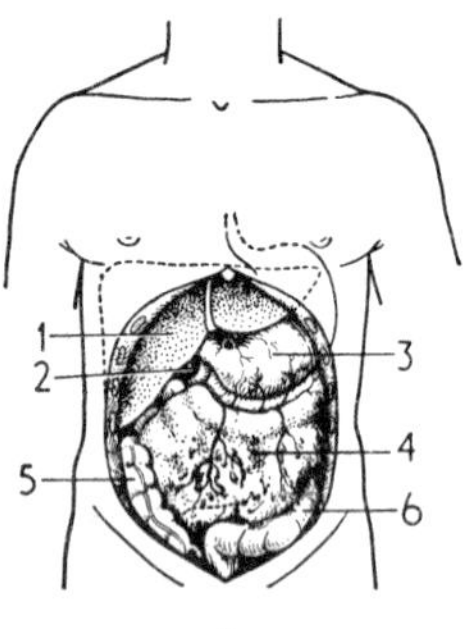

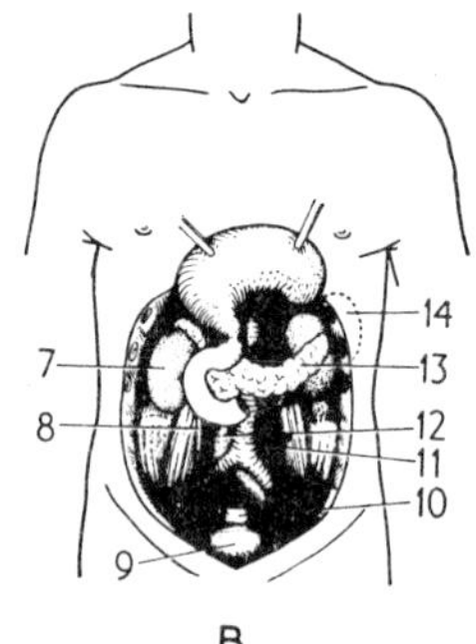

ABDOMEN: VENTRAL VIEW: A. WITH STOMACH AND INTESTINES IN PLACE. B. WITH STOMACH TURNED BACK AND INTESTINES CUT AWAY

A. 1. Liver. 2. Gall bladder. 3. Stomach. 4. Omentum (part of peritoneum). 5. Ascending colon. 6. Descending colon. B. 7. Kidney. 8. Ureter. 9. Bladder. 10. Rectum. 11. Abdominal aorta. 12. Inferior vena cava. 13. Pancreas. 14. Position of spleen

aberglaube (ah′b*e*rglowb*e*) *n.* Superstition, irrational belief. [Ger. wd]

ăbě′rrant *adj.* 1. Wandering, straying from moral standard. 2. (biol.) Diverging from normal type. **ăbě′rrance** *n.*

ăberrā′tion *n.* 1. Mental or moral slip or error; deviation from type. 2. (optics) Non-convergence of rays to one focus. 3. (astron.) Displacement of true position of heavenly body to observer on earth, due to earth's motion and non-instantaneous transmission of light; *planetary* ~, aberration due to motion of the planet itself.

abĕt′ *v.t.* Countenance, incite, assist. **abĕtt′er, abĕtt′or** *ns.*

ăb ĕx′tra *adv.* From outside.

abey′ance (-bā-) *n.* State of suspension, dormant condition (of rights etc.).

abhôr′ *v.t.* Regard with disgust and hatred. **abhŏ′rrent** *adj.* Inspiring disgust, repugnant, detestable. **abhŏ′rrently** *adv.* **abhŏ′rrence** *n.*

abīde′ *v.* (past t. and past part. *abode*). Remain; continue; dwell (archaic); wait for; (with neg.) bear, put up with; ~ *by*, remain faithful to.

ăbīĕ′tĭc *adj.* Of resin; ~ *acid*, the chief constituent of common rosin.

Ab′ĭgail (ă-). 1. Wife of Nabal and subsequently of David (1 Sam. xxv). 2. In Beaumont and

ăb ĭnĭt′ĭō. From the beginning (abbrev. *ab init.*). [L]

ăbiogĕn′ėsĭs *n.* The (supposed) origination of living organisms from lifeless matter; spontaneous generation.

ăb′jĕct *adj.* Brought low, miserable, craven, degraded. **ăb′jĕctly** *adv.*

abjure′ (-oor) *v.t.* Renounce on oath. **ăbjurā′tion** *n.*

abl. *abbrev.* Ablative.

ăblā′tion *n.* 1. Removal (esp. in surgery, of part of body). 2. (geol.) Wastage of a glacier by evaporation and melting.

ăb′latīve *adj.* & *n.* (gram.) Case in (esp. Latin) nouns expressing direction from a place or time, and hence source, agent, cause, etc.; ~ *absolute*, Latin construction of noun and participle (both in ablative case), expressing time, occasion, or circumstances.

ăb′laut (-owt) *n.* (philol.) Systematic vowel permutation (not due to influence of contiguous sounds) in root of word in derivation, as in *sing*, *sang*, *sung*.

ablāze′ *adv.* Blazing; on fire.

ā′ble *adj.* Having the power or ability; talented, clever; ~*-bodied*, physically fit, robust; ~*-bodied seaman*, (abbrev. A.B.) fully trained and qualified sailor with special rating and higher pay than *ordinary seaman*. **ā′bly** *adv.*

ablu′tion (-ōō-, -ū-) *n.* Ceremonial washing; water or wine used in this; (pl.) ordinary personal washing.

ăb′nėgāte *v.t.* Deny oneself (thing), renounce (right, belief). **ăbnėgā′tion** *n.*

abnôrm′al *adj.* Deviating from type, exceptional, irregular. **ăbnormăl′ĭty** *n.*

abnôrm′ĭty *n.* Irregularity; monstrosity.

Ab′ō (ă-) *n.* (Austral.) Aboriginal.

Åbo (ō′bōō). Swedish name of Turku, Finland.

aboard′ (-ōrd) *adv.* & *prep.* On board (ship, railway train, etc.).

abōde′ *n.* Dwelling-place.

abŏl′ĭsh *v.t.* Do away with.

ăbolĭ′tion *n.* Action or fact of abolishing; in 18th and 19th centuries esp. with ref. to Negro slavery and the movement against it. **ăbolĭ′tionĭsm** *n.* **ăbolĭ′tionĭst** *n.* & *adj.*

ăbomās′um *n.* Fourth stomach of ruminant (ill. RUMINANT).

A-bomb *abbrev.* Atomic bomb.

abŏm′ĭnable *adj.* Morally or physically loathsome, detestable, odious, revolting; ~ *snowman*: see YETI. **abŏm′ĭnably** *adv.*

abŏm′ĭnāte *v.t.* Loathe, dislike strongly.

abŏmĭnā′tion *n.* Loathing; object or practice deserving of aversion or disgust; ~ *of desolation*, desecration of the Temple at Jerusalem: see Dan. ix. 27, Matt. xxiv. 15.

ăborĭ′gĭnal *adj.* Indigenous, existing or present at dawn of history or before arrival of colonists or invaders. ~ *n.* Aboriginal inhabitant. **ăborĭ′gĭnēs** (-z) *n.pl.* Aboriginal inhabitants, plants, etc. (also found in sing. **ăborĭ′gĭnė**).

abôrt′ *v.i.* Miscarry; (biol.) become sterile, remain undeveloped.

abôr′tion *n.* Expulsion of foetus from uterus during first 28 weeks of pregnancy, either spontaneous or induced; dwarfed or misshapen creature. **abôr′tionĭst** (-shon-) *n.* One who procures abortion.

abôrt′ĭve *adj.* Premature; fruitless; rudimentary. **abôrt′ĭvely** *adv.* **abôrt′ĭvenėss** *n.*

Abou Ibn Sina: see AVICENNA.

Aboukir (*a*bōō′kēr) **Bay.** Bay on coast of Egypt at one of the mouths of the Nile; scene (1798) of Battle of the Nile, in which Nelson destroyed Napoleon's fleet.

abou′lĭa (-ow-), **abū′lĭa** *n.* Loss of will-power as mental disorder.

abound′ *v.i.* Be plentiful; be rich *in*, teem or be infested *with*.

about′ *adv.* & *prep.* 1. All round from outside or from a centre; somewhere round; here and there; circuitously. 2. Near in number, amount, etc. 3. Facing round. 4. Occupied with; in connexion with. 5. *put* ~, distracted, annoyed; (*v.*, of ship) turn on opposite tack; ~ *turn!* (mil. etc.) turn so as to face in opposite direction; *be* ~ *to* (do), be on the point of (doing).

about'-slĕdge *n.* Largest hammer used by smiths.

above' (-ŭv) *adv.* Higher up, overhead; up-stream; earlier in a book etc. ~ *prep.* Over, higher than, of higher rank, etc., than; in addition to; ~*-board* (*adv.* & *pred. adj.*) without concealment; fair, open, honest.

Abp *abbrev.* Archbishop.

ăbracadăb'ra *n.* Cabbalistic word formerly used as charm, orig. by Gnostics, and believed to have power of curing agues etc. when written in triangular arrangement and worn as amulet; (now) spell, mysterious formula, gibberish.

abrāde' *v.t.* Scrape off, wear away, injure, by rubbing.

A'brahăm (ā-). Jewish patriarch, from whom all Jews trace their descent (Gen. xi. 27–xxv. 10); ~*'s bosom*, heavenly abode of the blessed dead; *Plains of* ~, plateau near Quebec, scaled from St. Lawrence River by English army under WOLFE (1759) and scene of subsequent battle with French under Montcalm which decided fate of Canada.

abrā'sion (-zhn) *n.* Rubbing or scraping off; rough or sore place on skin caused by this; (geol.) wearing away of earth's surface by wind-borne particles of rock or 'sand' (cf. EROSION).

abrā'sĭve *adj.* Tending to produce abrasion. ~ *n.* Any substance, as emery, carborundum, etc., used for grinding or polishing.

ăbrēăc'tion *n.* (psycho-anal.) Removal, by revival and expression, of the emotion associated with an event which has undergone repression in memory.

abreast' (-ĕst) *adv.* On a level and facing the same way; ~ *of*, keeping up with, not behind (times etc.).

abrĭdge' *v.t.* Condense, shorten, curtail. **abrĭdge'ment** (-jm-) *n.* Curtailment; epitome, abstract.

abroad' (-awd), *adv.* In or to foreign lands; broadly, in different directions; (of rumour etc.) current; *from* ~, from foreign countries.

ăb'rogāte *v.t.* Repeal, cancel. **ăbrogā'tion** *n.*

abrŭpt' *adj.* Sudden, hasty; disconnected; steep; (bot.) truncated; (geol., of strata) suddenly cropping out. **abrŭpt'ly** *adv.* **abrŭpt'nĕss** *n.*

abs- *prefix.* Off, away, from.

Ab'salom (ă-). 3rd and favourite son of DAVID, killed while leading rebellion against his father (2 Sam. xiii–xix).

ăb'scess (-sĕs) *n.* Local inflammation of body tissues with deep suppuration caused by bacteria which destroy the cells in the centre of the area and leave a cavity filled with pus.

abscĭss'a (-sĭs-) *n.* (pl. *-sae*) (geom.) Portion of line intercepted between a fixed point within it and an ordinate drawn from a given point without it (ill. GRAPH).

abscĭ'ssion (-sĭshn) *n.* Cutting off (esp. surg.).

abscŏnd' *v.i.* Go away secretly, fly from the law.

ăb'sence *n.* Being away or absent; non-existence, want (*of*); abstracted state.

ăb'sent *adj.* Not present; not existing; abstracted in mind: ~*-minded*, abstracted, preoccupied, whence ~*-mindedly*, ~*-mindedness*. **absĕnt'** *v.t.* Keep (oneself) away, withdraw (oneself).

ăbsentee' *n.* Person not present, one who absents himself from his duties; person (esp. landlord) habitually living away from property. **ăbsentee'ĭsm** *n.*

ăb'sĭnth *n.* WORMWOOD, the plant or its essence; (also *ăb'sĭnthe*) strong greenish-grey liqueur flavoured with wormwood and anise.

ăb'sĭt ōmĕn! May the ominous implication of the words not be realized. [L]

ăb'solute (-ōōt, -ūt) *adj.* Complete, perfect, pure, mere; unrestricted, independent; ruling arbitrarily; not in (the usual) grammatical relation with other words; real, not relative or comparative; unqualified; self-existent and conceivable without relation to other things; ~ *alcohol*, containing at least 99% pure alcohol by weight; ~ *drought*, ~ *humidity*: see these words; ~ *music*, self-dependent instrumental music without literary or other extraneous suggestions (opp. PROGRAMME *music*); ~*pitch*, ability to remember pitch of notes, (also) pitch of a note defined scientifically in terms of vibrations per second; ~ *temperature*, temperature measured on a Centigrade (Celsius) scale which has its zero at absolute zero; ~ *zero*, that temperature (approx. —273·1° C.) at which all substances have lost all their available heat and so can be cooled no further. **ăb'solutely** *adv.*

ăbsolu'tion (-ōō-) *n.* Formal forgiveness, esp. ecclesiastical declaration of forgiveness of sins; remission of penance.

ăb'solutĭsm (-ōōt-) *n.* 1. (theol.) Dogma that God acts absolutely in matter of salvation. 2. (pol.) Principle of absolute government, despotism. **ăb'solutĭst** *n.* Supporter of absolute government; (metaphysics) one who maintains absolute identity of subject and object.

absŏlve' *v.t.* Set or pronounce free from blame etc.; acquit.

absôrb' *v.t.* Swallow up, incorporate; engross the attention of; suck in (liquid); take in (heat, light, etc.).

absôrb'ent *adj.* Having a tendency to absorb; ~ *cotton*, cotton rendered suitable for use as dressing etc. by removal of natural wax. ~ *n.* Absorbent substance.

absôrp'tion *n.* Action of absorbing, fact of being absorbed; natural or medicinal removal of tissues or deposits.

abstain' *v.i.* Keep oneself away, refrain *from*; esp. refrain from alcohol. **abstain'er** *n.* One who abstains from alcohol.

abstēm'ious *adj.* Sparing or moderate in food, drink, etc. **abstēm'iously** *adv.* **abstēm'iousnĕss** *n.*

abstĕn'tion *n.* Refraining or holding back; (parl. etc.) not using one's vote.

abstêr'gent *adj.* Cleansing. ~ *n.* Cleansing substance. **abstêr'sion** *n.* **abstêr'sive** *adj.*

ăb'stinence *n.* Abstaining from food, pleasure, etc.; *total* ~, abstaining from alcohol. **ăb'stinent** *adj.* Practising abstinence.

ăb'străct *adj.* Not concrete; ideal, not practical; (of art) concerned with pure form and pattern, not representing forms of visible world. ~ *n.* 1. (*the* ~), ideal or theoretical way of regarding things. 2. Epitome, summary. 3. Abstraction, abstract term. **abstrăct'** *v.t.* Deduct, remove; steal; disengage (attention etc.); summarize; *abstrăct'ed*, withdrawn in thought, not attending.

abstrăc'tion *n.* Withdrawal; stealing; absent-mindedness; abstract art.

abstruse' (-ōōs) *adj.* Hard to understand, profound. **abstruse'ly** (-sl-) *adv.* **abstruse'nĕss** *n.*

absûrd *adj.* Incongruous, unreasonable, ridiculous, silly. **absûrd'ly** *adv.* **absûrd'ity** *n.*

Abt (ăpt), Franz (1819–85). German song-writer.

abŭn'dance *n.* Plenty, more than enough; affluence, wealth; (physics) amount present. **abŭn'dant** *adj.* Plentiful, rich, in abundance. **abŭn'dantly** *adv.*

abūse' (-z) *v.t.* Make bad use of, misuse; revile; (archaic) deceive. ~ (-s) *n.* Misuse, perversion; unjust or corrupt practice; reviling. **abū'sĭve** *adj.* **abū'sĭvely** (-vl-) *adv.* **abū'sĭvenĕss** *n.*

abŭt' *v.* Have common boundary with; border (*upon*); end *upon*, lean *against*. **abŭt'ment** *n.* (archit.) Support from which arch, vault, etc., springs, and which receives the lateral thrust. **abŭtt'er** *n.* (law) Owner of adjoining property.

Abȳ'dŏs. 1. Ancient city on the Hellespont, whence (Gk myth.) LEANDER swam to Sestos. 2. Ancient ruined city of Upper Egypt.

abȳsm' (poet.), **abȳss'** *ns.* The primal chaos, bowels of the earth, supposed cavity of lower world; bottomless chasm; deep gorge.

abȳs'mal (-z-) *adj.* Bottomless (esp. fig.). **abȳs'mally** *adv.*

abȳss'al *adj.* Of lowest depths of ocean; ~ *rocks*, crystalline igneous rocks, as granite, which have solidified deep below earth's surface; ~ *zone*, strata of sea below 300 fathoms.

Abўssĭn'ia (ă-) *n.* **Abўssĭn'ian** *adj.* & *n.*: see ETHIOPIA.

A.C. *abbrev.* Aircraftman (also **A/C**); Alpine Club; alternating current (also **a.c.**); *ante Christum* (L, = 'before Christ').

a/c *abbrev.* Account.

A.C.A. *abbrev.* Associate of the Institute of Chartered Accountants.

acā'cia (-sha) *n.* 1. Genus of leguminous shrubs or trees (subfamily *Mimoseae*), found in warmer regions of Old World and Australia, some species of which yield gum arabic, catechu, etc. 2. N.-Amer. locust-tree (*Robinia pseudAcacia*, false ~), with sweet-scented pea-like flowers, freq. grown as ornamental tree in England etc.

ăc'adēme *n.* (properly) = ACADEMUS; (used by mistake in poet. style for) the Greek ACADEMY, hence, college, university. [Gk; mistake perh. caused by Milton's 'grove of Academe', i.e. Academus]

ăcadĕm'ĭc *adj.* 1. Of an academy or academician. 2. Of the philosophic school of Plato, sceptical. 3. Scholarly; abstract, cold, merely logical; unpractical. ~ *n.* Member of university; (pl.) academic arguments.

ăcadĕm'ĭcal *adj.* Of college or university. **ăcadĕm'ĭcally** *adv.* **ăcadĕm'ĭcals** *n.pl.* Academical robes, college or university costume.

acădemĭ'cian (-shn) *n.* Member of academy, esp. of Académie française or Royal Academy of Arts.

Académie française (ăkădāmē' frahṅsāz'). French literary academy, founded by Richelieu (1635); membership, limited to 40, is considered the highest distinction for men of letters; among its functions are the compilation and periodical revision of a dictionary of the French language (1st ed. 1694), and of a grammar (1st ed. 1932).

Acadē'mus (ă-). Greek legendary hero who revealed hiding-place of their sister Helen to the Dioscuri when they invaded Attica.

acăd'emy *n.* 1. *A~*, pleasure-garden near Athens (said to have belonged to the legendary hero Academus) in which Plato taught; Plato's followers, the philosophical school founded by him. 2. Place of study (including universities, but generally used pretentiously or ironically of school or of institution between school and university). 3. Place of training in a special art. 4. Society for cultivating literature, art, etc.; *The A~*, usu. the ROYAL ACADEMY (of Arts), or one of its annual exhibitions.

Acā'dĭa (*a*-). Name given by French to district in what is now known as Nova Scotia, first settled by them at end of 16th c. **Acā'dĭan** *adj.* Of Acadia. ~ *n.* Native or inhabitant of Acadia, or descendant of such.

acănthŏpterў'gian *adj.* & *n.* (Fish) of section *Acanthopterygii*, usu. with hard spiny rays in dorsal and anal fins.

acăn'thus *n.* 1. *A~*, genus of herbaceous plants with large, deeply-cut, hairy, shining leaves, natives of southern Europe, Asia, and Africa. 2. Conventionalized leaf of *A. mollis* or *A. spinosus* (with narrower spiny-toothed leaves) used as architectural ornament, esp. on the Corinthian and Composite capitals (ill. ORDER).

ăc'arĭd *n.* A member of the arachnid order *Acarina*, a mite or tick.

acătalĕc'tĭc *n.* & *adj.* (pros.) (Line) not docked of a syllable, complete.

acc. *abbrev.* Account; accusative.

Accad, Accadian: see AKKAD.

accēde' (*a*ks-) *v.i.* Consent, agree (*to*); ~ (*to*), enter upon office or dignity, join party.

accĕlerăn'dō (aks-, ach-) *adv.*, *adj.*, & *n.* (mus.) (Passage performed) with gradual increase of speed. [It.]

accĕl'erāte (*a*ks-) *v.* Make, become, quicker; cause to happen earlier; put on pace; *accelerated motion*, (physics) progressively quicker motion; *accelerating force*, force which causes this.

accĕlerā'tion (*a*ks-) *n.* Accelerating; vehicle's power to accelerate; (physics) rate of increase in velocity of moving body (written, e.g., 10 ft per sec./sec. if body moves 10 ft per second faster in every second).

accĕl'erative (*a*ks-) *adj.* Tending to increase speed.

accĕl'erātor (*a*ks-) *n.* Thing that increases anything's speed; pedal which operates throttle of internal combustion engine (ill. MOTOR); substance added to mixture to reduce time taken by chemical reaction; electrical or magnetic apparatus giving high velocities to free electrons or other atomic particles; ~ *nerve*, any of the cardiac sympathetic nerves, discharges from which quicken and strengthen the heart-beats.

ăc'cent (-ks-) *n.* Prominence given to syllable by stress or pitch; mark used to indicate syllabic pitch, vowel quality, etc. (*acute* ~, ´; *grave* ~, `; *circumflex* ~, ˆ or ˜); individual, local, or national mode of pronunciation; (pl.) speech; (pros.) rhythmical stress; (mus.) stress recurring at intervals. **accĕnt'** *v.t.* Pronounce with accent or stress, emphasize; mark with (written) accents; intensify, make conspicuous.

accĕn'tor (*a*ks-) *n.* Kinds of bird (= WARBLER); esp. (*hedge* ~) the dunnock, *Prunella modularis occidentalis*, usu. but misleadingly called hedge-sparrow.

accĕn'tūal (*a*ks-) *adj.* Of accent; (esp. of verse) in which metre or rhythm results from alternation of strong and weak (not long and short) syllables. **accĕn'tūally** *adv.*

accĕn'tūāte (*a*ks-) *v.t.* Accent (esp. in fig. senses). **accĕntūā'tion** *n.*

accĕpt' (*a*ks-) *v.t.* Consent to receive; answer (invitation etc.) affirmatively; receive as adequate or true; agree to meet (bill of exchange); undertake (office).

accĕpt'able (*a*ks-) *adj.* Worth accepting, welcome, pleasing. **accĕpt'ably** *adv.* **accĕptabĭl'ĭty** *n.*

accĕpt'ance (*a*ks-) *n.* Consent to receive, favourable reception or answer; engagement to meet bill, bill so accepted.

acceptā'tion (ăks-) *n.* Particular sense given to word or phrase; generally recognized meaning.

accĕpt'ed (*a*ks-) *adj.* Generally recognized or believed in.

accĕpt'or (*a*ks-) *n.* One who accepts a bill.

ăc'cĕss (-ks-) *n.* 1. Approach; addition; right or means of approach; being approached. 2. Attack or outburst.

accessary: see ACCESSORY *n.*

accĕss'ĭble (*a*ks-) *adj.* Able to be reached or entered; open to influence (of). **accĕssĭbĭl'ĭty** *n.* **accĕss'ĭbly** *adv.*

accession (aksĕ'shn) *n.* Acceding or attaining (esp. to throne or manhood); joining, addition; (law) addition to property by natural growth or artificial improvement.

accĕss'ory (*a*ks-) *adj.* Additional, subordinately contributive, adventitious. ~ *n.* 1. (correctly spelt *accessary* but *-ory* is now more usual) Person who is privy *to* an (esp. criminal) act or helps in it but is not the chief actor. 2. Accompaniment, adjunct; (pl., commerc.) smaller articles of (esp. woman's) dress, as shoes, gloves, etc.

acciaccatura (achahkatoor'a) *n.* (mus.) Grace-note performed quickly before an essential note of a melody.

ăc'cĭdence (-ks-) *n.* The part of grammar dealing with inflexions, i.e. with the accidents or non-essentials of words; book, or part of one, on this subject.

ăc'cĭdent (ăks-) *n.* 1. Event without apparent cause, the unexpected; unintentional act, chance, misfortune, mishap. 2. Property or quality not essential to our conception of a substance, attribute; mere accessory. **ăccĭdĕn'tal** *adj.* **ăccĭden'tally** *adv.* **ăccĭdĕn'tal** *n.* (mus.) Sharp ♯, flat ♭, or natural ♮ sign occurring not in key signature but before particular note.

acclaim' *v.t.* Welcome or applaud loudly, hail. ~ *n.* Shout of applause or welcome.

ăcclamā'tion *n.* Loud and eager assent; (pl.) shouting in person's honour.

ăcc'lĭmate *v.* (U.S.) = ACCLIMATIZE. **ăcclĭmā'tion** *n.* (biol.) Acclimatization as a natural process of plants or animals, not imposed on them by man.

acclĭm'atīze *v.t.* Habituate to new climate or surroundings. **acclīmatīzā'tion** *n.* Fact, process, of acclimatizing, esp. (biol.) in ref. to transference of plants or animals to a new environment under human management and not by nature (cf. ACCLIMATION).

acclĭv'ĭty *n.* Upward slope.

ăccolāde' (*or* -ahd) *n.* 1. Ceremony of conferring knighthood, usu. by stroke on shoulder with flat of sword. 2. (mus.) Vertical line or brace coupling staves (ill. STAVE).

accŏmm'odāte *v.t.* 1. Adapt (*to*); harmonize; reconcile, settle differences between; compose (quarrel). 2. Equip, supply (*with*); oblige, confer favour on; find lodging for. **accŏmm'odāting** *adj.* Obliging.

accommodā'tion *n.* 1. Adaptation, adjustment; (of eye) adjustment of shape of lens to bring light rays from various distances to focus upon retina; (of sense organs) property which causes the nervous discharges initiated by a stimulus of constant activity to diminish or die out. 2. Settlement, compromise. 3. Serviceable thing, convenience. 4. Lodgings, entertainment. 5. Money loan. 6. ~ *address*, house, shop, etc., where letters are sent for person who has no permanent address or wishes to conceal it; ~ *bill*, bill of exchange given not for value received but for purpose of raising money on credit; ~ *ladder*, ladder up ship's side for entering or leaving small boat.

accom'panĭment (-ŭm-) *n.* Accompanying thing; appendage; (mus.) subsidiary part, esp. instrumental part sustaining voice etc.

accom'panĭst (-ŭm-) *n.* Performer of accompaniment.

accom'pany (-ŭm-) *v.t.* Go with, escort, attend; coexist with; (mus.) support (player, singer, etc.) by performing additional part.

accŏm'plĭce (*or* -ŭm-) *n.* Associate, usu. subordinate, in guilt or crime.

accŏm'plĭsh (*or* -ŭm-) *v.t.* Perform, carry out, succeed in doing. **accom'plĭshed** *adj.* Having accomplishments. **accom'plĭshment** *n.* Achievement, fulfilment; social attainment.

accôrd *v.* 1. Agree, be consistent (*with*). 2. Grant (indulgence, request, etc.). ~ *n.* Consent; mutual agreement; harmonious correspondence in colour, tone, etc.; assent. **accôrd'ance** *n.* Conformity, agreement. **accôrd'ant** *adj.*

accôrd'ĭng *adv.*: ~ *as*, in proportion as, in a manner depending on which of certain alternative is true; ~ *to*, in a manner consistent with; on the authority of. **accôrd'ĭngly** *adv.* Correspondingly; in accordance with what might be expected; in due course; therefore.

accôrd'ion *n.* Small portable musical instrument with bellows and keyboard admitting wind to metal reeds when keys are depressed.

accŏst' *v.t.* Make up to and address; (of prostitute) solicit.

accouchement (ăkōōsh'mahñ) *n.* Lying-in, delivery. ***accoucheur*** (ăkōō'shėr) *n.* Man-midwife. ***accoucheuse*** (-ėrz) *n.* Midwife. [Fr.]

account' *n.* 1. Counting, reckoning; *money of* ~, denominations of money used in reckoning. 2. Statement of money received and expended, with balance; statement of discharge of responsibilities generally, answering for conduct; final account at judgement-seat of God (esp. in *sent, gone, to one's* ~); *current, deposit,* ~: see BANK[2]; *keep* ~*s*, keep statement of expenditure and receipts; *balance, square* ~*s* (*with*), settle account by payment of money due (freq. fig.); *current* ~: see CURRENT *adj.*; *joint* ~: see JOINT *adj.*; *for* ~ *of*, to be sold on behalf of; *give (good)* ~ *of oneself*, be successful, give favourable impression; *on* ~, as interim payment; *on* ~ *of*, in consideration of, because of; *on no* ~, not for any reason, certainly not; *on one's own* ~, for one's own purposes and at one's own risk. 3. Reckoning in one's favour, profit, advantage; *turn to* ~, make useful. 4. Estimation; *make* ~ *of*, value, esteem; *take into, leave out of,* ~, (fail to) take into consideration. 5. Narration, report, description (*of*). ~ *v.* 1. Consider, regard as. 2. ~ *for*, give reckoning for; answer for; explain cause of, serve as explanation of.

accoun'table *adj.* 1. Bound to give account, responsible, liable. 2. Explicable. **accountabĭl'ĭty** *n.*

accoun'tancy *n.* Profession or duties of accountant.

accoun'tant *n.* Professional keeper or inspector of accounts; *chartered* ~, member of professional institute of accountants, authorized to audit accounts, act as trustee, company secretary, etc.

accou'tre (-ōōter) *v.t.* Attire, equip, esp. with special costume (chiefly in past part. *accoutred*). **accou'trement** (-ōōtre-) *n.* (usu. in pl.) Equipment, trappings.

Accra (*a*krah'). W.-Afr. seaport on Gulf of Guinea, capital of Ghana.

accrĕd'ĭt *v.t.* Gain credit for, dispose one to believe; send out with credentials; attribute *to*. **accrĕd'ĭtėd** *adj.* Officially recognized; generally accepted.

accrēte' *v.* Grow together or into one; form round or on *to*; attract (such additions). **accrē'tion** *n.* Growth by organic enlargement; increase by external additions; adhesion of extraneous matter; matter so added, extraneous addition.

accrue' (-ōō) *v.i.* Fall (*to* one) as a natural growth, advantage or result (esp. of interest on invested money).

accū'mūlāte *v.* Heap up, amass, make money; grow numerous, form increasing mass or heap. **accūmūlā'tion** *n.* **accū'mūlatĭve** *adj.*

accū'mūlātor *n.* 1. One who collects. 2. An electric cell (or group of these connected in series) in which the chemical action which produces the current can be reversed by passing an electric current through it in the opposite direction, and which thus constitutes a means of storing electric energy in the form of chemical energy; a storage battery.

ăc'cūrate *adj.* Precise, exact, correct. **ăc'cūrately** (-tl-) *adj.* **ăc'cūracy** *n.*

accûrs'ėd *adj.* Lying under a curse; execrable, detestable.

ăccūsā'tion (-z-) *n.* Accusing, being accused; indictment.

accū's'ative (-z-) *adj.* & *n.* (gram.) (Case of nouns etc.) denoting goal of motion or object of action. **accū's'atively** (-vl-) *adv.*

accūsatôr'ial (-z-) *adj.* ~ *procedure* etc., that in which prosecutor and judge are not the same (opp. to *inquisitorial*).

accū's'atory (-z-) *adj.* Conveying or implying accusation.

accūse' (-z) *v.t.* Charge with fault, indict; blame, lay fault on.

accŭs'tom *v.t.* Habituate. **accŭs'tomed** *adj.* Customary, usual; wonted, used.

āce *n.* 1. The 'one' on dice, cards, etc.; one point at rackets etc. 2. Distinguished airman (orig., one who has brought down ten enemy aircraft); person excelling in any sport or skill; (tennis) service that beats opponent.

Acĕl'dama (*a*-). Field near Jerusalem purchased for cemetery with blood-money received by Judas Iscariot (see Matt. xxvii. 8; Acts i. 19); scene of slaughter or bloodshed.

acĕph'alous (acĕf-) *adj.* Headless; (zool.) having no part of body specially organized as head; (bot.) with head aborted or cut off; (pros.) lacking the regular first syllable.

acêrb'ĭty *n.* Astringent sourness; bitterness of speech, manner, or temper.

acet(o)- *prefix.* (chem.) Derived from, connected with, acetic acid or acetyl.

ă'cėtal *n.* Colourless pleasant-smelling liquid formed by slow oxidation of alcohol; class of complex ethers, derivatives of aldehyde, of which this is the type.

ăcetăl'dėhȳde *n.* Aldehyde.

ăcėtăn'ĭlĭde *n.* White crystalline solid made by action of acetic acid on aniline and used as febrifuge and analgesic.

ă'cėtāte *n.* Salt of acetic acid; ~ *fibre*, textile fibre made of cellulose acetate.

acĕt'ĭc *adj.* Of, producing, vinegar; ~ *acid*, colourless pungent biting organic acid (CH_3COOH) which gives vinegar its characteristic taste.

acĕt'ĭfȳ *v.* Turn into vinegar, make or become sour. **acĕtĭfĭcā'tion** *n.*

ă'cėtōne *n.* Colourless fragrant inflammable liquid ketone (CH_3COCH_3) widely used as an organic solvent and in making chloroform etc.

ă'cėtous (*or* asēt'-) *adj.* Of, producing, vinegar; sour, acid.

ă'cėtȳl *n.* Monovalent radical (CH_3CO) of acetic acid. **acĕt'ȳlēne** *n.* Colourless, nearly odourless (when pure), highly inflammable gaseous hydrocarbon, usu. prepared by adding water to calcium carbide (impurities in which produce the characteristic unpleasant smell), and used for lighting, for welding and cutting metals, etc.

A.C.F. *abbrev.* Army Cadet Force.

Achaea (*a*kē'*a*). 1. District of ancient Greece along S. shore of Gulf of Corinth. 2. Roman province comprising all the southern part of Greece. **Achae'an** *adj.* & *n.* 1. In Homer, apparently = Greek; hence, (one) of the early Greeks; of the early Greek civilization. 2. In classical times, (an inhabitant) of Achaea; ~ *League*, confederation of 12 city-states of Achaea in 3rd c. B.C.

Achates (*a*kāt'ēz). (Gk and Rom. legend) Friend of Aeneas, usu. called *fidus* (faithful) ~; hence, *fidus* ~, a faithful friend.

ache (āk) *v.i.* Suffer continuous or prolonged pain. ~ *n.* Continuous or prolonged pain.

ă'chēne (-k-; *or* -kēn') *n.* (bot.) Small dry one-seeded fruit which does not open to liberate seed (ill. FRUIT).

Ach'eron (ăk-). (Gk myth.) One of the rivers of Hades, over which the dead were carried by Charon's ferry.

Ach'ėson (ăch-), Edward Goodrich (1856–1931). American inventor of carborundum and artificially prepared graphite.

Acheu'lian (*a*shü-). Of the palaeolithic period succeeding the Chellean. [*St. Acheul*, Amiens, France]

achieve' *v.t.* Accomplish; acquire; reach (an end). **achieve'ment** (-vm-) *n.* 1. Completion, accomplishment; thing accomplished. 2. (her.) Escutcheon or ensign armorial commemorating distinguished feat, hatchment (ill. HERALDRY).

Achilles (*a*kĭl'ēz). Greek hero of the Trojan war, son of Peleus and Thetis; quarrelled with Agamemnon and 'sulked in his tent' refusing to fight, until his friend Patroclus was killed by Hector, whom he then slew; was killed by Paris with a poisoned arrow; it pierced his heel where his mother had held him in infancy when she plunged him into the Styx to make him invulnerable; hence, *Achilles' heel*, vulnerable part; ~ *tendon*, tendon in heel by which calf-muscles extend foot (ill. MUSCLE).

ăchromăt'ĭc (-k-) *adj.* Colourless; transmitting light without dispersing it into its constituent colours; ~ *lens*, pair of lenses, e.g. one of crown glass and the other of flint glass, the dispersion of one correcting the dispersion of the other (ill. LENS). **achrōm'atĭsm** *n.* Achromatic quality. **achrōm'atīze** *v.t.*

acĭc'ūlar *adj.* Like a small needle or bristle.

ă'cĭd *adj.* 1. Sour, sharp to taste; (fig.) biting, severe. 2. Having properties of an acid. *n.* One of a class of chemical compounds in which hydrogen may be replaced by metals to form salts: they neutralize alkalis, usu. corrode or dissolve metals, and have sour taste; ~ *salt*, a salt derived from an acid having more than one replaceable hydrogen atom, one at least of which has not been replaced by a metal; ~ *test*, (fig.) severe or conclusive test. **acĭd'ĭfȳ** *v.*

ăcĭdĭm'ėtry *n.* Measurement of quantity of acid.

ăcĭd'ĭty *n.* Acid property.

ăcĭdōs'ĭs *n.* (med.) Pathological condition in which normal alkalinity of blood and reserve alkalinity of body tissues are reduced by excessive production or deficient secretion of acids.

acĭd'ūlāted, acĭd'ūlous *adjs.* Made slightly acid.

A'cĭs (ā-): see GALATEA.

A.C.I.S. *abbrev.* Associate of the Chartered Institute of Secretaries.

ăck-ăck *adj.* & *n.* Anti-aircraft (gun etc.). [from letter A in signallers' former phonetic alphabet]

ăck ĕmm'a. 1. ANTE MERIDIEM. 2. Air mechanic. [names in signallers' former phonetic alphabet of letters A, M]

acknowledge (*a*knŏl'ĭj) *v.t.* Admit the truth of, admit, own; announce receipt of; express appreciation of. **acknowl'edg(e)ment** *n.* Acknowledging; thing given or done in return for service etc.

aclĭn'ĭc *adj.* ~ *line*, magnetic equator, line on which magnetic needle has no dip.

ăc'mė *n.* Highest point or pitch, culmination; (fig.) point of perfection.

ăc'nė *n.* Skin eruption due to inflammation of sebaceous glands, common in adolescence, and characterized by red pimples esp. on face.

ăc'olȳte *n.* Officer of highest of four minor orders in R.C. Church, attending priests and deacons, lighting and carrying candles, etc.; attendant, assistant, novice.

Aconcagua (ăkŏnkah'gw*a*). Extinct volcano and highest peak (23,081 ft) in Andes, near boundary between Argentina and Chile.

ăc'onīte *n.* (Plant of) poisonous ranunculaceous genus *Aconitum*, with five blue or yellow sepals, of which one is helmet-shaped; esp. the common European *A. napellus*, monk's-hood, wolf's-bane; dried root of this plant used in pharmacy and as poison; *winter* ~, (plant of) genus *Eranthis*, esp. winter-flowering *E. hyemalis*, with yellow anemone-like flower springing from whorl of leaves.

acŏn'ĭtine (*or* -ēn) *n.* Bitter white crystalline highly poisonous alkaloid, essential principle of aconite.

ā'corn *n.* Fruit of oak, oval nut growing in shallow woody cup (ill. FRUIT); ~ *barnacle*, sessile barnacle, of many genera (ill. BARNACLE).

acŏtȳlēd'on *n.* (bot.) Plant with no distinct cotyledons or seed-leaves, as fern, moss, etc. **acŏtȳlēd'onous** *adj.*

acous'tic (-ōō-, -ow-) *adj.* Of the sense of hearing; of sound, of acoustics; ~ *mine*, underwater mine designed to be detonated by sound-waves proceeding from ship's propellers. **acous'tĭcs** *n.* Science of sound; properties of building, room, etc., in respect of audibility of sounds. **acous'tĭcal** *adj.* **acous'tĭcally** *adv.*

acquaint' *v.t.* Make aware or familiar, inform; *be acquainted with*, have personal knowledge of. **acquain'tance** *n.* Personal knowledge; person with whom one is acquainted, but not intimate. **acquain'tanceship** *n.*

ăcquiĕsce' (-ĕs) *v.i.* Agree, esp. tacitly; not object. **ăcquiĕs'cence** *n.* **ăcquiĕs'cent** *adj.*

acquīre' *v.t.* Gain, get, come to have; *acquired characteristics*, mental or physical characteristics gained through influence of environment, and not inherited from parents; *acquired taste*, one gained by experience, not innate. **acquīre'ment** (-īrm-) *n.* Acquiring; (pl.) mental attainments.

ăcquisĭ'tion (-z-) *n.* Acquiring; thing acquired, useful or pleasant addition.

acquis'ĭtive (-z-) *adj.* Desirous of, given to, acquiring and retaining. **acquis'ĭtĭvely** (-vl-) *adv.* **acquis'ĭtĭvenėss** *n.*

acquit' *v.t.* Pay (debt); declare not guilty, free from blame; ~ *oneself* (*well*, *ill*, etc.), perform one's part or duty.

acquitt'al *n.* Discharge from debt; performance (of duty); deliverance from a charge by verdict etc.

acquitt'ance *n.* Payment of or release from debt; receipt in full.

acre[1] (āk'*er*) *n.* Land-measure, legally 4840 sq. yds, but varying in some districts; (pl.) lands, fields; *county* (*land*) *of broad* ~*s*, Yorkshire. **acreage** (āk'erĭj) *n.*

Amount of acres, acres collectively.

Acre[2] (āk'*er*) (also *St. Jean d'Arc*, Arab. *Akka*). Seaport on coast of Israel; captured by Christians in 3rd Crusade, 1191; recaptured, the last Christian stronghold in the Holy Land, 1291.

ăc'rid *adj.* Bitterly pungent, irritating; of bitter temper or manner. **ăc'ridly** *adv.* **acrid'ity** *n.*

ăcrimōn'ious *adj.* Marked by acrimony. **ăcrimōn'iously** *adv.* **ăcrimōn'iousnėss** *n.*

ăc'rimony *n.* Bitterness of temper or manner.

Ac'rita (ăk-) *n.pl.* (zool.) Animals with no distinct nervous system.

ăcro- *prefix.* Highest, topmost, terminal.

ăc'robăt *n.* Performer of daring and spectacular gymnastic feats, tumbler, rope-dancer. **ăcrobăt'ic** *adj.* **ăcrobăt'ically** *adv.* **ăcrobăt'ics** *n.*

ăcromĕg'aly *n.* Disease due to over-activity of pituitary gland, resulting in overgrowth of bones esp. of extremities and skull.

ăcrophōb'ia *n.* (psych.) Dread of high places.

acrŏp'olis *n.* Citadel or upper fortified part of ancient Greek city esp. *the A~*, that of Athens, situated on a hill about 250 ft high and richly adorned, esp. in 5th c. B.C., with architecture and sculpture.

across' (-aws *or* -ŏs) *prep.* & *adv.* From side to side (of), to or on the other side (of), forming a cross with.

acrŏs'tic *n.* Poem etc. in which first or first and last letters of lines form word(s); puzzle so made, in which words must be guessed from clues, called 'uprights' for words which must be read vertically, 'lights' for horizontal words.

ăcrotēr'ion *n.* (pl. *-ia*). (archit.) Pedestal for statue or ornament on angle of classical pediment (ill. ORDER).

ăct *n.* 1. Thing done, deed. 2. Decree passed by legislative body, court of justice, etc.; statute; (law) instrument in writing to verify facts. 3. Each of main divisions of dramatic work, in which definite part of whole action is completed. 4. Variety turn. ~ *v.* 1. Represent in mimic action, perform (play); personate, play part of (on stage or fig. in real life); perform on stage. 2. Perform actions, do things; perform special functions; (of things) work, fulfil functions; ~ *as*, perform in character of, serve as; ~ (*up*)*on*, influence, affect; regulate one's conduct by, put into practice.

Actae'on (ă-). (Gk myth.) A hunter who, because he accidentally saw Artemis bathing, was punished by being changed into a stag and killed by his own hounds.

ăct'ing *adj.* (esp., prefixed to title) Temporarily doing duties; doing alone duties nominally shared with others.

Acti'nia (ă-) *n.* Genus of sea anemones.

ăctin'ic *adj.* Of actinism; ~ *rays*, rays possessing actinism, as the green, blue, violet, and ultra-violet rays of sunlight, which have a marked photochemical effect.

ăc'tinism *n.* That property of radiant energy, found esp. in the shorter wave-lengths of the spectrum, by which chemical changes are produced, as in photography.

ăctin'ium *n.* Radio-active element, found in pitchblende; symbol Ac, at. no. 89, principal isotope 227.

ăctinŏm'ėter *n.* Instrument for measuring heat radiation.

ăctinomŏrph'ic *adj.* (biol.) Radially symmetrical. **ăctinomŏrph'ism** *n.*

Actinozō'a: = ANTHOZOA.

ăc'tion *n.* 1. Process of acting, exertion of energy or influence; ~ *committee*, a Communist committee appointed to purge societies and organizations of non-Communist elements. 2. Thing done. 3. Series of events represented (in drama). 4. Mode of acting; mechanism of instruments etc. 5. Legal process; *take* ~, institute legal proceedings; take steps in regard to any matter. 6. Battle, engagement between opposing forces. ~ *v.t.* Bring legal action against. **ăc'tionable** (-shon-) *adj.* Affording ground for action at law.

Ac'tium (ă-). Promontory on W. coast of Greece (opposite modern Preveza on Gulf of Amurakia), near which, in 31 B.C., the fleets of Mark Antony and Cleopatra were decisively defeated by Octavian (Augustus).

ăc'tivāte *v.t.* Make active, esp. (physics) radio-active; render (molecules) capable of reacting chemically. **ăctivā'tion** *n.*

ăc'tive *adj.* 1. Working, acting, operative; consisting in or marked by action; energetic, diligent; ~ *list*, list of officers who are on active service or available for it and who receive full pay; ~ *service*, war service in armed forces. 2. (gram.) The ~ *voice* comprises all forms of intransitive verbs, and those forms of transitive verbs that attribute the verbal action to the person or thing whence it proceeds (the logical subject), as *We punished him*; not, like the forms of the *passive* voice, to the person or thing to whom it is directed (the logical object), as *He was punished by us*. **ăc'tively** *adv.*

ăc'tivist *n.* Member of a Communist ACTION committee.

ăctiv'ity *n.* Exertion of energy; state or quality of being active, energy, diligence, liveliness; active force or operation.

ăc'tor *n.* Dramatic performer; *~-manager*, actor who is also manager of theatre or company.

ăc'trėss *n.* Female actor.

Acts of the Apostles. Book of the N.T. immediately following Gospels, relating early history of Christian Church and dealing largely with the life and work of the apostles Peter and Paul; traditionally ascribed to Luke.

ăc'tūal *adj.* Existing, real, present, current. **ăc'tūally** *adv.* In actual fact, really; even, as a matter of fact.

ăctūăl'ity *n.* Reality, realism.

ăc'tūalize *v.t.* Realize in action, treat realistically.

ăc'tūary *n.* Expert on insurance who calculates risks and premiums. **ăctūār'ial** *adj.*

ăc'tūāte *v.t.* Serve as motive to; communicate motion to. **ăctūā'tion** *n.*

acū'ity *n.* Sharpness, acuteness.

acūl'ėate *adj.* 1. (zool.) Having a sting. 2. (bot.) Prickly, pointed.

acūm'ĕn *n.* Keen discernment, penetration.

acūm'inate *adj.* (biol.) Tapering to a point.

acu'shla (-ōō-) *n.* Darling. [Ir. *ā cuisle* O pulse (of my heart)!]

acūte' *adj.* 1. Sharp, keen, penetrating; clever. 2. (Of disease) coming sharply to a crisis, not chronic. 3. (Of sound) sharp, shrill; having acute accent. 4. ~ *accent*, the accent ', originally indicating a high or rising pitch on the vowel so marked; ~ *angle*, angle less than a right angle (ill. ANGLE); ~ *mixture*, organ stop in which additional pipes, tuned sharp, sound the overtones. **acūte'ly** (-tl-) *adv.*, **acūte'nėss** (-tn-) *n.*

A.C.W. *abbrev.* Aircraftwoman.

ad- *prefix.* To, with sense of motion or direction to, reduction or change into, addition, adherence, increase, or intensification.

A.D. *abbrev. Anno Domini* (L, = 'in the year of our Lord').

ăd'age *n.* Traditional maxim, proverb.

adagio (adahj'yō) *adv.*, *adj.*, *n.* (mus.) Leisurely (passage or movement).

Ad'albĕrt (ă-), St. (*c* 955–97). Missionary in N. Germany and Poland, called 'apostle of the Prussians'; martyred in Bremen, and commemorated 23rd April.

Ad'am[1] (ă-). The first man of Hebrew mythology (see Gen. ii. 4–iii. 24), who lived with his wife EVE in the Garden of Eden, but was driven from it for eating the fruit (traditionally an apple) of 'the tree of the knowledge of good and evil'; *the old* ~, unregenerate condition; *~'s ale*, water; *~'s apple*, projection formed by the thyroid cartilage of the larynx, particularly prominent in males. [Heb., = 'man']

Ad'am[2] (ă-), Robert (1728–92). The best known of a family of Scottish architects; introduced into Britain a neo-Classical style of decoration, furniture, etc., based on ancient Roman and Italian

Renaissance designs. ~, James (1730–94). Architect, brother of Robert Adam.

ăd'amant *n.* Thing impenetrably hard; stubborn or unyielding person; (archaic) fabulous mineral with properties of hardness and attraction. **ădamăn'tīne** *adj*

Ad'amīte (ă-) *n.* 1. Child of Adam, human being; unclothed man. 2. Member of heretical sect in N. Africa (2nd and 3rd centuries), who believed that they enjoyed Adam's original state of innocency, and wore no clothes.

Ad'ams[1] (ă-), John (1735–1826). 2nd president of U.S. 1797–1801; member of committee formed to draft Declaration of Independence.

Ad'ams[2] (ă-), John (*c* 1760–1829) alias Alexander Smith. English seaman, one of the *Bounty*[2] mutineers; founded settlement on Pitcairn Island.

Ad'ams[3] (ă-), John Couch (1819–92). English astronomer, discoverer of NEPTUNE.

Ad'ams[4] (ă-), John Quincy (1767–1848). 6th president of U.S. 1825–9; son of John Adams[1].

Ad'ams[5] (ă-), Samuel (1722–1803). American Revolutionary leader, one of those who signed Declaration of Independence.

Ad'am's Peak (ā-). Mountain in Ceylon, with a hollow on the summit which is said by Moslems to be Adam's footprint and by Buddhists to be Buddha's.

Adanson (ădahṅsawṅ), Michel (1727–1806). French botanist; first exponent of classification of plants into natural orders.

adăpt' *v.* Suit, make suitable, fit (*to, for*); alter, modify, so as to make suitable for new surroundings, purpose, etc. **adăptabil'ity** *n.* **adăpt'able** *adj.*

ădaptā'tion *n.* (esp. biol.) Process, characteristic of living matter, by which organism or species becomes adjusted to its environment; that which is so adapted.

A.D.C. *abbrev.* Aide-de-camp; Amateur Dramatic Club.

ădd *v.* Join by way of increase or supplement; perform arithmetical process of addition; ~ *up*, ~ *together*, find sum of.

ădd'ăx *n.* Large light-coloured antelope (*Addax nasomaculatus*) of N.-Afr. deserts, with spiral horns.

addĕn'dum *n.* (pl. *-da*). Something to be added, addition, appendix.

ădd'er *n.* Small venomous snake, viper (*Vipera berus*), only poisonous snake found in England; *puff* ~, *death* ~, *horned* ~, highly poisonous African and Australian species of *Viperidae*; ~'*s tongue*, a fern (*Ophioglossum vulgatum*); Amer. white- or yellow-flowered dog-tooth violet.

addict' *v.t.* (esp. in pass.) Devote, apply habitually (*to*). **addic'tion** *n.* **ădd'ict** *n.* One addicted to (specified) drug etc.

Add'is Ab'aba (ăd-, ăb-). Capital town and seat of government of Ethiopia.

Add'ison (ă-), Joseph (1672–1719). English essayist and poet; contributor to 'Tatler' and joint-author (with Steele) of 'Spectator'.

Add'ison's disease (ă-). Disease connected with defective functioning of suprarenal glands and freq. characterized by bronzy pigmentation of skin. [First recognized by Dr. Thomas *Addison* (1793–1860), English physician]

addi'tion *n.* Adding; arithmetical process of putting together two or more numbers or amounts into one number or group of numbers; thing added; *in* ~, as well, besides; *reaction*, (chem.) one in which two univalent atoms or radicals are taken up by an unsaturated molecule, the double bond being converted into a single bond. **addi'tional** (-shon-) *adj.* **addi'tionally** *adv.*

ădd'itive *adj.* Of addition; to be added; ~ *process*, process of colour reproduction in which the primary colours are superimposed one upon another. ~ *n.* Substance added to mixture or alloy in order to impart specific qualities to the resulting product.

ădd'le *adj.* (of egg) Rotten, producing no chicken; empty, vain, muddled, unsound. ~ *v.* Make or grow addle; muddle, confuse. **ădd'led** *adj.* Made addle; *A~ Parliament*, that summoned in April 1614 and dissolved in June, without having passed a Bill.

ADDER

1. Poison sac. 2. Fang. 3. Tongue

addrĕss' *n.* 1. Readiness, skill, adroitness. 2. Superscription of letter etc.; place to which letters etc. are directed. 3. Manner, bearing, in conversation; way of addressing person. 4. Discourse delivered to audience; esp., parliamentary reply to Royal Speech at opening of Parliament. 5. (pl.) Courteous approach, courtship. ~ *v.t.* 1. Direct in speech or writing; speak to; send as written message (*to*); write address on outside of (letter etc.). 2. Apply one*self*, direct one's skill or energies (*to*). 3. (golf) ~ *the ball*, take aim, prepare to make stroke.

ăddrĕssee' *n.* Person to whom letter etc. is addressed.

addrĕss'ograph (-ahf) *n.* Machine for addressing letters.

addūce' *v.t.* Cite as proof or instance.

addū'cent *adj.* (anat.) (Of muscles) drawing together certain parts of the body.

addŭct' *v.t.* Draw to a common centre or towards median line or long axis of body. **addŭc'tion, addŭc'tor** *ns.*

Ad'ėlaide (ă-). Seaport and capital of South Australia.

Ad'en (ā-). Seaport and coaling-station in SW. Arabia near entrance to Red Sea; annexed to British India 1839; formerly part of Br. Protectorate; since 1967 capital of SOUTHERN YEMEN.

ăd'ėnoids *n.pl.* Pathological enlargement of lymphoid tissue between back of nose and throat, occurring usu. in children and often obstructing breathing. **ădė-noid'al** *adj.*

adĕpt' *adj.* Thoroughly proficient (*in*). **ăd'ept** *n.* Adept person.

ăd'ėquate *adj.* Proportionate *to* what is necessary; sufficient. **ăd'ėquately** *adv.* **ăd'ėquacy** *n.*

ad fin. *abbrev.* *Ad finem* (L, = 'towards the end').

adhēre' (-h-) *v.i.* Stick fast, cleave (*to*).

adhēr'ent (-h-) *adj.* Sticking; connected with (*to*). ~ *n.* Supporter (*of* party etc.). **adhēr'ence** *n.*

adhe'sion (-hēzhn) *n.* Adhering.

adhēsi've *adj.* & *n.* Adhering; sticky (substance). **adhēs'ively** (-vl-) *adv.*

ăd hōc. Arranged for this purpose; special. [L]

ădiabăt'ic *adj.* (of physical change) Involving neither loss nor acquisition of heat.

ădiăn'tum *n.* Genus of ferns including true maidenhair, with wedge-shaped pinnules on slender black shining stems; (pop.) black maidenhair, a kind of spleenwort (*Asplenium adiantum nigrum*). [Gk *adianton* maidenhair, lit. 'unwetted']

adieu (adū') *int.* & *n.* Good-bye; *make, take,* one's ~, say good-bye. [Fr. *à Dieu* to God]

ăd ĭnfīnĭt'um *adv.* Without limit, for ever. [L]

ad init. *abbrev.* *Ad initium.* [L, = 'at the beginning']

ăd ĭn'terĭm *adv.* & *adj.* For the meantime. [L]

ăd'ipocēre *n.* Greyish fatty or saponaceous substance (chemically a mixture of *margaric, oxymargaric,* and *palmitic acids,* with some ammonia) formed in dead animal bodies by decomposition of body fats when exposed to moisture.

ăd'ipōse *adj.* Of fat, fatty; ~ *tissue,* connective tissue cells in animal body containing large globules of fat. **ădipŏs'ĭty** *n.*

Adirŏn'dăcks (ă-). Group of mountains in New York State, U.S., a holiday resort.

ăd'ĭt *n.* Horizontal entrance to, or passage in, mine (ill. MINE).

Ad'ĭti (ahd-). (In VEDA) impersonation of infinity or of all-embracing nature; (Hindu myth.) mother of the gods.

adjā'cent *adj.* Lying near *to*, contiguous. **adjā'cency** *n.*

ăd'jĕctive *adj.* Additional, not standing by itself, dependent; ~ *law*, subsidiary part of law, procedure. ~ *n.* (gram.) Name of attribute added to name of thing to describe thing more fully or definitely. **ădjĕctīv'al** *adj.* **ădjĕctīv'ally** *adv.*

adjoin' *v.t.* Be contiguous with.

adjourn (ajẽrn') *v.* Put off, postpone; break off; (of persons met together) suspend proceedings and separate; change place of meeting. **adjourn'ment** *n.*; *move the* ~ (in House of Commons), bring motion that the House shall adjourn, esp. in order to discuss a specified matter (which, if the motion is carried, is discussed the same evening).

Adjt *abbrev.* Adjutant.

adjŭdge' *v.t.* Adjudicate upon; pronounce or award judicially; condemn.

adju'dĭcāte (ajōō-) *v.* Decide upon; pronounce; sit in judgement and pronounce sentence; award prizes etc. in competition. **adjudĭcā'tion, adju'dĭcātor** *ns.*

ădj'ŭnct (ăj-) *n.* Subordinate or incidental thing, accompaniment; (gram.) amplification of the predicate, subject, etc.; (logic) non-essential attribute. **adjŭnct'ĭve** *adj.* **adjŭnct'ĭvely** (-vl-) *adv.*

adjure (ajoor') *v.t.* Charge under oath or penalty of curse *to* do; request earnestly. **ădjurā'tion** *n.*

adjŭst' (aj-) *v.t.* Arrange, put in order; harmonize; adapt (*to*). **adjŭst'ment** *n.*

ădj'utant (-ōō-) *n.* 1. (army etc.) Officer assisting commanding officer by communicating orders, conducting correspondence, etc.; *A~-General*, (Brit.) second executive officer of Imperial General Staff of the Army, whose duties are concerned with recruiting, training, etc. 2. ~ (*bird*), large stork of genus *Leptoptilus*, esp. Indian *L. dubius*, walking with stiff-legged gait.

ad lib. *abbrev. Ad libitum.* [L, = 'to the extent desired']

ăd'-lĭb' *v.* (orig. U.S.) Improvise (words etc.) during a broadcast etc.

Adm. *abbrev.* Admiral.

Admēt'us (ă-). (Gk legend) Husband of ALCESTIS.

admin'ĭster *v.* 1. Manage (affairs, estate, etc.); dispense (justice, sacraments, etc.); act as administrator. 2. Tender (oath) *to.* 3. Furnish, give; apply (remedies). 4. Contribute *to* (one's comfort etc.)

administrā'tion *n.* 1. Administering; management; management of public affairs, government; (law) management of deceased person's estate; *letters of* ~, authority to administer intestate estate. 2. Executive part of legislature; the ministry, the Government. **admĭn'istrative** *adj.* Of administration; executive. **admĭn'ĭstrātor** *n.* **admĭn'ĭstrātrix** *n.* (pl. *-trīcēs*). Female administrator (in legal sense).

ăd'mirable *adj.* Worthy of admiration; estimable, excellent.

ăd'miral *n.* 1. Naval officer commanding fleet or subdivision of fleet; (hist.) commander-in-chief of navy (in Britain, his administrative duties are now discharged by the *Lords Commissioners of the* ADMIRALTY, and his judicial functions vested in the *High Court of Admiralty*); *A~ of the Fleet, A~, Vice-A~, Rear-A~*, four highest ranks of British naval officers (ranking with field-marshal, general, lieutenant-general, and major-general in army); *A~ of the Red* (*White, Blue*) *Squadron*, (hist.) British admirals flying red (white, blue) flags. 2. Privileged commander of fishing or merchant fleet. 3. Ship that carries the admiral, flagship. 4. *Red A~, White A~*, two European species of butterfly (*Vanessa atalanta, Limenitis sibylla*). [Arab. *amir* commander]

ăd'miralty *n.* 1. Office, rank, of admiral; (rhet.) command of the seas. 2. (*Board of*) *A~*, British department of State superintending navy, headed by the *Lords Commissioners of A~*, of whom the First Lord is a minister of the government; (*High*) *Court of A~*, part of High Court of Justice concerned with maritime questions and offences.

Ad'miralty Islands. Group of small islands of Bismarck Archipelago N. of New Guinea; since the war of 1914–18 Australian mandated territory.

admīre' *v.t.* Regard with pleased surprise or approval; (colloq.) express admiration of. **ădmirā'tion** *n.* **admīr'er** *n.* One that admires; lover.

admĭ'ssion (-shn) *n.* Admitting, being admitted, fee for this; acknowledgement that something is true.

admĭt' *v.* 1. Allow entrance or access (*to*). 2. Allow, permit; accept as valid or true; acknowledge; ~ *of*, be capable of or compatible with; leave room for. **admĭtt'ance** *n.* **admĭtt'ĕdly** *adv.*

admix' *n.* Add as an ingredient, mingle *with.* **admix'ture** *n.*

admŏn'ish *v.t.* Exhort; give advice; warn; remind, inform. **admŏn'ishment** *n.*

ădmoni'tion *n.* Admonishing; warning, reproof. **admŏn'ĭtory** *adj.*

ăd naus'ĕăm *adv.* To a disgusting extent. [L]

ado (adōō') *n.* Fuss; difficulty.

adō'bē (*or* -ōb') *n.* Sun-dried clay used for building by Indians in Mexico etc.; house made of such clay bricks. [Span., f. *adobar* daub, plaster]

ădolĕs'cent *adj.* & *n.* (Person) between childhood and maturity; between the ages (roughly) of 14 and 20. **ădolĕs'cence** *n.*

Adōnā'ī (*a*-). One of names given in the Old Testament to the Deity. [Heb., = 'my lords']

Adō'nis (*a*-). 1. (Gk myth.) A beautiful youth loved by Aphrodite; he was killed by a boar but restored to life by Persephone on condition that he should spend six months with her and the rest of the year with Aphrodite; yearly festivals were held in his honour. 2. Beau, dandy. 3. (bot.) A genus of the *Ranunculaceae*, including pheasant's eye. 4. (entom.) The butterfly Clifden Blue (*Lysandra bellargus*).

adŏpt' *v.t.* Take into relationship not previously occupied, esp. take as one's own child, assume rights and duties of parent towards; take (idea etc.) from another and use as one's own; take up, choose. **adŏp'tion** *n.* ~ *society*, organization which arranges adoption of orphaned or unwanted infants. **adŏpt'ĭve** *adj.*

adōre' *v.t.* Regard with utmost respect and affection; worship as a deity; (R.C. Ch.) reverence with relative or representative honours. **adōr'able** *adj.* **adōr'ably** *adv.* **ădorā'tion** *n.*

adōr'er *n.* Worshipper; ardent admirer, lover.

adôrn' *v.t.* Add beauty or lustre to; furnish with ornament(s). **adôrn'ment** *n.*

Adrăs'tus (*a*-). (Gk myth.) King of Argos and leader of expeditions against Thebes.

ăd rĕm. To the point; to the purpose.

adrēn'al *adj.* At or near kidney; ~ *glands, adrenals*, the suprarenal glands, two flattened yellowish-brown ductless glands lying on upper anterior surface of kidneys (ill. KIDNEY).

adrĕn'alin *n.* Hormone secreted by adrenal glands and affecting circulation and muscular action; this obtained from these glands in animals and used in medicine as a stimulant.

Ad'rian (ā-). Name of 6 popes: ~ *I*, pope 772–95; ~ *II*, pope 867–72; ~ *III*, pope 884–5; ~ *IV* (Nicholas Breakspear), pope 1154–9, only English pope; ~ *V*, pope in 1276; ~ *VI*, pope 1522–3, most recent non-Italian pope, born at Utrecht.

Adrianō'ple (ā-). (Turk. *Edirne*) Town in European Turkey, named after the Emperor Hadrian;

scene of a battle (A.D. 378) in which Romans were defeated by Visigoths.

Adrĭăt'ic (ā-) *adj.* ~ (*Sea*), arm of Mediterranean lying between Italy and Balkan peninsula; *Marriage of the* ~, (hist.) ceremony symbolizing the sea-power of Venice, during which the Doge dropped a ring into the water from his state barge.

adrift' *adj.* Drifting; at mercy of wind and tide or of circumstances; (colloq.) not at one's post; deficient in knowledge, training, etc.

adroit' *adj.* Dextrous, deft. **adroit'ly** *adv.* **adroit'nĕss** *n.*

ădsciti'tious (-sitĭsh'*us*) *adj.* Adopted from without; supplemental.

adsŏrb' *v.t.* Act as adsorbent of. **adsŏrb'ent** *adj.* & *n.* (Substance) producing adsorption.

adsŏrp'tion *n.* Process by which specific gases, vapours, or substances in solution adhere to exposed surfaces of certain, usu. solid, materials. **adsŏrp'tive** *adj.*

ăd'sŭm. I am here, as answer in roll-call etc. [L]

ăd'ūlāte *v.t.* Flatter basely. **ădūlā'tion** *n.* **ăd'ūlatory** *adj.*

Adŭll'am (*a*-). Cave where all who were distressed, in debt, or discontented came to join David when he fled from Saul: see 1 Sam. xxii. 1–2, applied by John Bright to Liberal M.P.s who voted with Conservatives against Reform Bill of 1866; hence, **Adŭll'amīte**, member of any dissident political group.

adŭlt' (*or* ăd'-) *adj.* & *n.* (One who is) grown-up; mature.

adŭl'terant *adj.* & *n.* (Thing) employed in adulterating.

adŭl'terāte[1] *v.t.* Falsify, corrupt, debase, esp. by admixture of baser ingredients. **adŭlterā'tion** *n.*

adŭl'terate[2] *adj.* Defiled by adultery; spurious, counterfeit.

adŭl'terer, adŭl'terĕss *ns.* Man, woman, guilty of adultery.

adŭl'tery *n.* Voluntary sexual intercourse of married person with one who is not his or her lawful spouse. **adŭlt'erous** *adj.* **adŭl'terously** *adv.*

ăd'umbrāte (*or* adŭm'-) *v.t.* Represent in outline; faintly indicate; typify, foreshadow; overshadow. **ădumbrā'tion** *n.*

ăd valŏr'ĕm. (Of taxes or duties) in proportion to (estimated) value of goods. [L]

advance' (-vah-) *n.* 1. Going forward, progress. 2. Personal approach, overture. 3. Rise in price. 4. Payment beforehand; loan. 5. *in* ~, in front, ahead; beforehand; ~ *copy*, copy of book etc., supplied before publication; ~ *guard*, guard before main body of army. ~ *v.* Move or put forward; bring forward (claims etc.); accelerate (events); pay (money) before it is due; lend; help on, promote; make progress; raise (price), rise (in price). **advanced'** (-st) *adj.* Far on in progress; ahead of times, others, etc. **advance'ment** (-sm-) *n.* (esp.) Promotion, preferment; furtherance, improvement.

advan'tage (-vah-) *n.* Better position, precedence, superiority; favourable circumstance; (at tennis) next point won after deuce (~ *in*, ~ *out*, advantage to server, receiver of service); *mechanical* ~: see MECHANICAL; *take* ~ *of*, avail oneself of (circumstance); overreach (person). ~ *v.t.* Be beneficial to; be an advantage to; further, promote. **ădvantā'geous** (-j*us*) *adj.* **ădvantā'geously** *adv.*

ăd'vent *n.* 1. Arrival, esp. important one. 2. *A*~, season before Christmas, beginning on 4th Sunday before it; coming of Christ; second coming of Christ.

Ad'ventist (ă-) *adj.* & *n.* (Member) of one of various sects believing in imminence of second coming of Christ.

ădventi'tious (-sh*us*) *adj.* Coming from without, accidental, casual; (law, of inheritance) coming from a stranger or by collateral succession. **ădventi'tiously** *adv.*

advĕn'ture *n.* Unexpected or exciting experience; daring enterprise, hazardous activity. ~ *v.* Hazard, imperil; incur risk; dare to go or come *into*, dare to enter (*up*)*on*.

advĕn'turer (-ch*er*-) *n.* One who seeks adventure; soldier of fortune; speculator; one who lives by his wits. **advĕn'turĕss** *n.* Female adventurer; woman on look-out for a position.

advĕn'turous (-ch*er*-) *adj.* Venturesome, enterprising. **advĕn'turously** *adv.*

ăd'vĕrb *n.* (gram.) A 'part of speech', word expressing any relation of place, time, circumstance, causality, manner, or degree, or modifying or limiting attribute or predicate; word qualifying or modifying adjective, verb, or other adverb. **ădvĕrb'ial** *adj.* **ădvĕrb'ially** *adv.*

ăd'versary *n.* Opponent, antagonist, enemy; *the A*~, the Devil.

advĕrs'ative *adj.* (Of words etc.) expressing opposition or antithesis. **advĕrs'atively** *adv.*

ăd'vĕrse *adj.* Contrary, hostile *to*; hurtful, injurious. **ăd'vĕrsely** *adv.*

advĕrs'ity *n.* Condition of adverse fortune; misfortune.

advĕrt'[1] *v.i.* Refer *to*.

ăd'vert[2] *n.* (commerc. abbrev.) Advertisement.

ăd'vertise (-z) *v.* Notify, warn, inform; make generally or publicly known; proclaim merits of; esp., try to encourage sales of (product) by public announcement; ~ *for*, ask for by public notice. **ăd'vertiser** *n.*

advĕrt'isement (-zm-) *n.* Advertising; public announcement (in newspaper, by placards, etc.).

advīce' *n.* Opinion given or offered as to action; information given, news; (pl.) communications from a distance; (commerc.) formal notice of transactions.

advīs'able (-z-) *adj.* To be recommended; expedient. **advīsabil'ity** *n.*

advīse' (-z) *v.* Offer counsel to; (commerc.) announce; recommend. **advīsed'** (-zd) *adj.* Deliberate, considered; judicious. **advīs'ĕdly** *adv.*

advīs'er (-z-) *n.* Counsellor, esp. person habitually consulted; *legal* ~, solicitor.

advīs'orȳ (-z-) *adj.* Giving advice; consisting in giving advice.

ăd'vocacy *n.* Function of advocate; pleading in support *of*.

ăd'vocate *n.* Professional pleader in court of justice, counsel (technical title in Roman law courts and in countries retaining Roman law, as Scotland, France, etc.); one who pleads for another; one who speaks for cause etc.; *Faculty of A*~*s*, Scottish bar; *Lord A*~, principal law-officer of Crown in Scotland; *A*~*s' Library*, library in Edinburgh opened 1689 and presented to nation by Faculty of Advocates, 1924; since 1925 the National Library of Scotland. **ăd'vocāte** *v.t.* Plead for, support (policy etc.).

ădvocāt'us dĭăb'olī. 'Devil's advocate', popular name of officer of Sacred Congregation of Rites at Rome who advances all possible arguments against candidate for beatification or canonization; hence, a deprecator. [L]

advow'son (-z-) *n.* (Engl. law) Right of presentation to benefice.

advt *abbrev.* Advertisement.

ăd'ȳtum (pl. -*ta*) *n.* Innermost part of temple; private chamber, sanctum. [Gk *aduton* not to be entered (*duō* enter)]

ădze *n.* Carpenter's tool for cutting away surface of wood, like

ADZE

axe with arched blade at right angles to handle. ~ *v.t.* Dress or cut with adze.

aed'īle *n.* (Rom. antiq.) Roman magistrate who superintended public buildings, games, shows, etc.

A.E.F. *abbrev.* Allied Expeditionary Force.

Aege'an (ējē'*an*) *adj.* ~ (*Sea*), arm of Mediterranean between Greece and Asia Minor; ~ *Civilization*, the Bronze Age civilization of the coasts and islands of the Aegean Sea, the MINOAN and MYCENAEAN civilizations.

Aegir (ē̆j'ēr). (Scand. myth.)

Chief of the sea-giants, representing the peaceful ocean.

ae'gis *n.* (Gk myth.) Shield of Zeus or Athene; hence (fig.) protection, impregnable defence.

Aegis'thus (ēg-, ēj-). (Gk legend) Nephew of Atreus, whom he murdered, and lover of CLYTEMNESTRA, who helped him murder her husband AGAMEMNON.

aegrōt'ăt (*or* ē'-) *n.* Certificate that candidate is too ill to attend examination etc. [L, = 'he is sick']

Æl'fric (ăl-) (*c* 955–1020). English monk and writer, chiefly of homilies and lives of saints.

Aenē'as. (Gk and Rom. legend) Trojan hero; son of Anchises and Aphrodite; escaped after fall of Troy and after long wandering reached the Tiber; married daughter of King Latinus and became king of the Latins; the Romans regarded him as the originator of their State and the emperors claimed him for their ancestor.

Aenē'id (*or* ēn'ėid). Epic poem by Virgil in 12 books of Latin hexameters relating story of Aeneas after fall of Troy.

Aeō'lian *adj.* 1. Of AEOLIS. 2. Of AEOLUS; caused by, relating to, wind; ~ *deposit*, substance deposited on earth by wind, as desert sand; ~ *harp*, musical instrument consisting of rectangular box on or in which are stretched strings or wires producing musical sounds as the wind passes across them; ~ *mode*, (mus.) ancient Greek MODE (ill. MODE); 9th of eccles. modes, with A as final and E as dominant.

Ae'olis. Coastal district of NW. Asia Minor colonized by Greeks at very early date.

Ae'olus. (Gk myth.) The god of the winds.

ae'on, ē'on *n.* An age of the universe; immeasurable period; eternity.

aepyŏrn'is *n.* Genus of extinct gigantic flightless birds resembling moas and known from remains found in Madagascar.

ā'erāte *v.t.* Expose to mechanical or chemical action of air; charge with carbon dioxide; *aerated bread*, bread raised by being charged by machinery with carbon dioxide (instead of with yeast, which produces carbon dioxide by fermentation); *aerated waters*, sweetened flavoured beverages charged with carbon dioxide. **aerā'tion** *n.*

aer'ial (ār- *or* āēr-) *adj.* Of air, gaseous; ethereal; immaterial, imaginary; atmospheric; existing, moving, happening, in the air; ~ *attack, warfare*, conducted by aircraft. ~ (ār-) *n.* Radiating or receiving wire(s) or rod used in radio communication. **aer'ialist** *n.* Performer on high wire or trapeze.

aerie, aery (ār'ĭ, ēr'ĭ) *n.* Nest of bird of prey (esp. eagle) or of other bird that builds high up; house, castle, stronghold built on high rock or hill.

ā'erifŏrm (*or* ār') *adj.* Of the form of air, gaseous; unsubstantial.

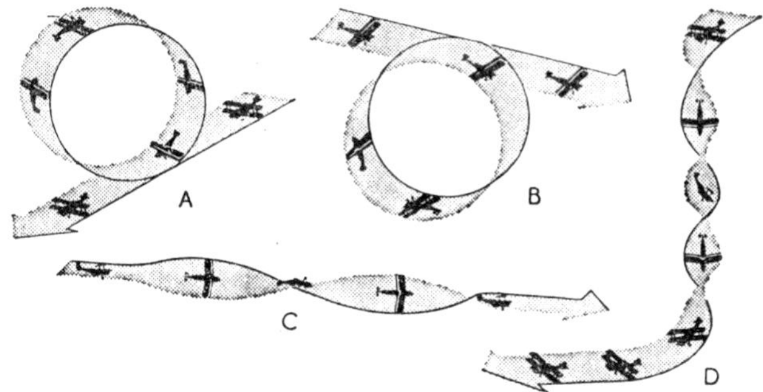

AEROBATICS: A. LOOP. B. BUNT. C. ROLL. D. SPIN

aero- *prefix.* Air-; of aircraft.

aerobăt'ics (ār-) *n.pl.* Feats of expert and often spectacular aviation. **aerobăt'ic** *adj.*

ā'erōbe (*or* ār'-) *n.* Micro-organism capable of living only in the presence of atmospheric oxygen; opp. of ANAEROBE. **āerŏb'ic** *adj.*

aerobiŏl'ogy (ār-) *n.* Study of airborne micro-organisms esp. as agents of infection.

aer'odrōme (ār-) *n.* Taking-off and landing ground for aircraft, together with the runways, hangars, offices, workshops, etc.

aerodynăm'ics (ār-) *n.* Branch of dynamics dealing with the effects produced in air by the motion of solid bodies through it and the effects produced on such bodies by the air through which they pass. **aerodynăm'ic** *adj.* **aerodynăm'icist** *n.*

aer'odyne (ār-) *n.* Heavier-than-air aircraft.

aer'ofoil (ār-) *n.* Any or all of the lift-producing surfaces of an aircraft, as wings, ailerons, tail-plane, fins, etc.

aer'olite, -lith (ār-) *n.* Meteorite.

aerŏl'ogy (āer-, ār-) *n.* Study of the atmosphere.

aer'onaut (ār-) *n.* (obs.) Navigator or pilot of airship or aeroplane. **aeronaut'ic(al)** *adj.* Of, pertaining to, aeronautics. **aeronaut'ics** *n.pl.* Science or practice of flight, aerial navigation.

aer'oplāne (ār-) *n.* Heavier-than-air flying machine with wings. (*Illustration, p.* 12.)

aer'osŏl (ār-) *n.* System of colloidal particles dispersed in a gas, as mist, fog, etc.; container with spraying device (~ *pack* etc.).

aerostăt'ics (ār-) *n.* Physics of gases in equilibrium; science of air navigation. **aerostăt'ical** *adj.*

Aeschylus (ēs'kĭlus) (525–456 B.C.). Athenian poet regarded as founder of Greek tragic drama; he introduced a second actor (where there had previously been only one actor and chorus) and subordinated chorus to dialogue; of his many tragedies only seven are extant: 'The Persians', 'The Seven against Thebes', 'Prometheus Bound', 'The Suppliants', and the Orestes trilogy, 'Agamemnon', 'Choephori', and 'Eumenides'.

Aesculāp'ius. Latin form of *Asklēpios* (Gk myth.), god of medicine, son of Apollo and the nymph Coronis; usu. represented bearing staff with serpent coiled round it. **Aesculāp'ian** *adj.*

Æs'ir (ă-). (Scand. myth.) Collective name of the gods.

Aes'ŏp (6th c. B.C.). Semi-legendary Phrygian teller of fables about animals, said to have been a slave in Samos; the fables attributed to him are prob. compiled from various sources.

aes'thēte *n.* Professed lover of beauty.

aesthĕt'ic *adj.* Of appreciation of the beautiful; having such appreciation; in accordance with principles of good taste. **aesthĕt'ical** *adj.* (rare). **aesthĕt'ically** *adv.* **aesthĕt'icism** *n.* **aesthĕt'ics** *n.* Philosophy of the beautiful; philosophy of art.

aes'tival *adj.* Of summer. **aes'tivāte** *v.i.* Spend the summer, esp. (zool.) in state of torpor. **aestivā'tion** *n.*

aet., ae'tăt. *abbrevs.* of ***aetā'tis***, of or at the age of.

Æthelred: see ETHELRED.

Æthelstan: see ATHELSTAN.

aetiŏl'ogy *n.* Assignment of a cause; philosophy of causation; (med.) science of causes of disease. **aetiolŏ'gical** *adj.* **aetiolog'ically** *adv.*

Aëtius (āĕt'ius) (d. 454). Roman general who, with Theodoric, defeated Attila at Châlons, 451.

Aetōl'ia. District of Greece, N. of Gulf of Corinth.

A.E.U. *abbrev.* Amalgamated Engineering Union.

A.F. *abbrev.* Admiral of the Fleet.

A.F.A. *abbrev.* Amateur Football Association.

afar' *adv.* At, to, a distance; *from* ~, from a distance.

A.F.A.S. *abbrev.* Associate of

the Faculty of Architects and Surveyors.

A.F.C. *abbrev.* Air Force Cross.

ăff'able *adj.* Easy of address, courteous, complaisant. **ăffabĭl'ity** *n.* **ăff'ably** *adv.*

played; full of affectation. **affĕct'ėdly** *adv.*

affĕct'[2] *v.t.* Attack (as disease); move, touch; produce (material effect on). **affĕct'ing** *adj.* Touching, moving. **affĕct'ĭngly** *adv.*

relation, etc.; property, attribute.

affĕc'tionate (-shon-) *adj.* Loving, fond; showing love or tenderness. **affĕc'tionately** *adv.*

affĕc'tive *adj.* Of the affections, emotional.

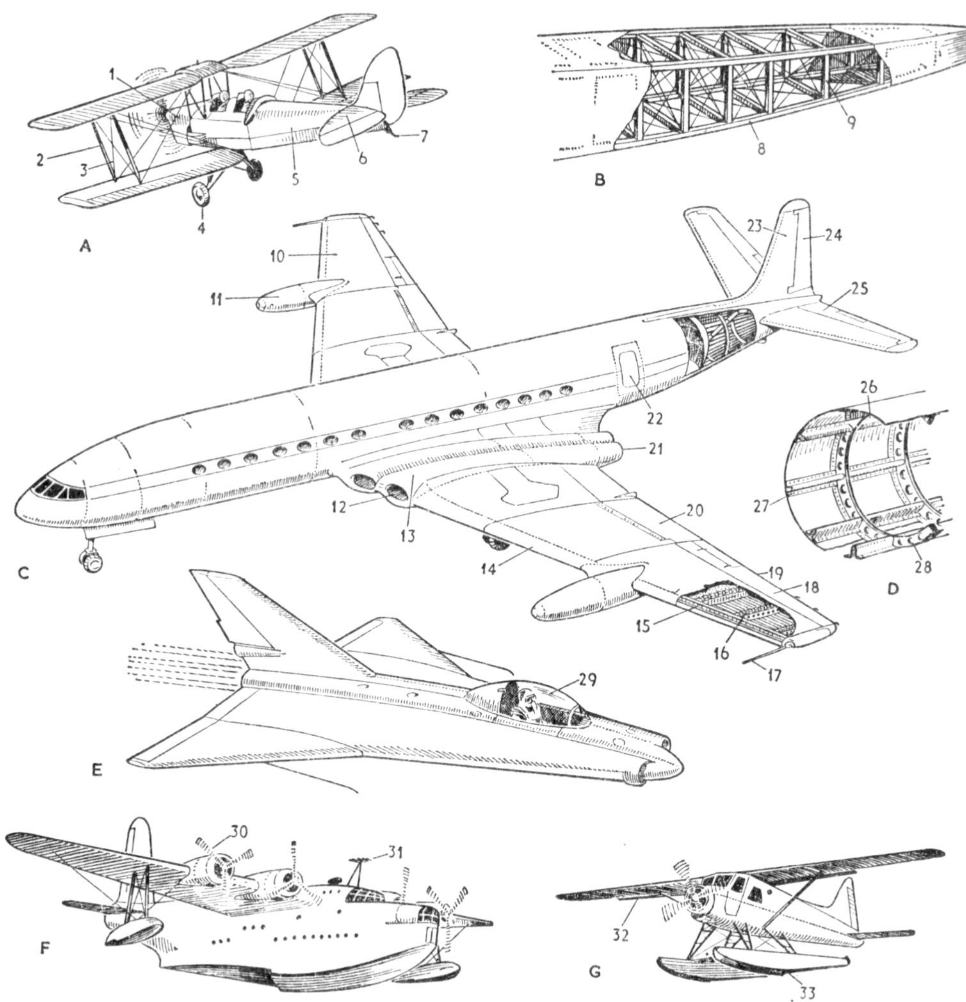

AEROPLANES: A. BIPLANE. B. FABRIC-COVERED WOODEN CONSTRUCTION. C. MONOPLANE WITH PARTS CUT AWAY TO SHOW CONSTRUCTION. D. STRESSED-SKIN CONSTRUCTION. E. DELTA WING. F. FLYING BOAT. G. SEAPLANE

A. 1. Engine cowling. 2. Wing strut. 3. Stay. 4. Undercarriage. 5. Fuselage. 6. Tail-plane. 7. Skid. B. 8. Longeron. 9. Strut. C. 10. Wing. 11. Outboard fuel tank. 12. Air intake for jet engines. 13. Engine nacelle. 14. Leading edge. 15. Spar. 16. Rib. 17. Pitot-tube. 18. Aileron. 19. Trailing edge. 20. Flap. 21. Exhaust tube of jet engines. 22. Passenger door. 23. Fin. 24. Rudder. 25. Elevator. D. 26. Skin. 27. Stringer. 28. Frame. E. 29. Cockpit. F. 30. Airscrew or propeller. 31. Radar aerial. G. 32. Slotted flap. 33. Float

affair' *n.* Business, concern; (colloq.) thing; (pl.) ordinary pursuits of life; public, commercial or professional business or transactions; (*love*) ~: see LOVE; ~ *of honour*, duel.

affĕct'[1] *v.t.* Practise, use; assume (character); pretend to have or feel; pretend (*to* do). **affĕct'ėd** *adj.* Artificially assumed or dis-

ăff'ĕct *n.* (psychol.) Emotion, feeling, as antecedent of action.

ăffĕctā'tion *n.* Studied display *of*; artificiality of manner; pretence.

affĕc'tion *n.* 1. Affecting, being affected. 2. Mental state, emotion; goodwill, kind feeling, love. 3. Bodily state due to any influence; esp. malady, disease. 4. Temporary or non-essential state,

ăff'erent *adj.* (Of blood- and lymph-vessels, nerves, etc.) bringing, conducting, inwards or towards.

affī'ance *v.t.* Promise solemnly in marriage.

ăffĭdāv'ĭt *n.* Written statement, confirmed by oath, to be used as judicial proof. [L, = 'has stated on oath']

affĭl'ĭāte *v.t.* 1. (Of institution) adopt (persons as members, societies as branches); attach *to*, connect *with* (a society). 2. (law) Fix paternity of (illegitimate child) for purpose of maintenance; father (thing) *upon*, trace *to*. **affĭliā'tion** *n.*

affĭn'ĭty *n.* Relationship, relations, by marriage or in general; structural resemblance; similarity of character suggesting relationship; liking, attraction; (chem.) tendency of chemical elements or compounds to react with others.

affîrm' *v.* Assert strongly; make formal declaration or affirmation; state in the affirmative; ratify (judgement). **ăffirmā'tion** *n.* Affirming, esp. (law) solemn declaration by person who conscientiously declines taking oath.

affîrm'ative *adj.* & *n.* Affirming, answering yes; (logic) expressing agreement of the two terms of a proposition; *answer in the* ~, answer yes. **affîrm'atively** *adv.*

affĭx' *v.t.* Fasten, append, attach. **ăff'ix** *n.* Appendage, addition; (gram.) prefix or suffix.

afflăt'us *n.* Divine impulse; inspiration.

afflĭct' *v.t.* Distress with bodily or mental suffering. **afflĭc'tion** *n.* Misery, distress; pain, calamity.

ăff'luent (-lōō-) *adj.* Flowing freely; abounding; wealthy. ~ *n.* Tributary stream. **ăff'luence** *n.* Wealth, abundance.

ăff'lŭx *n.* Flow towards a point; accession.

affōrd' *v.t.* (With *can*) have the means, be rich enough, manage to spare (time etc.); furnish; bestow; yield supply of.

affŏ'rĕst *v.t.* Convert into a forest; plant with trees. **affŏrĕstā'tion** *n.*

affrăn'chīse (-z) *v.t.* Free from servitude or obligation.

affray' *n.* Breach of peace caused by fighting or rioting in public place.

affright' (-īt) *v.t.* (archaic) Frighten. ~ *n.* Alarm, terror.

affront' (-ŭnt) *v.t.* Insult openly; face defiantly. ~ *n.* Open insult.

affū'sion (-zhn) *n.* Pouring on, esp. of water in baptism.

Afghan (ăf'găn) *adj.* & *n.* (Native) of Afghanistan; (strictly) (member) of the Duranni tribe of Pathans who inhabit E. Afghanistan and speak Pashtu; (of) the PASHTU language; ~ *hound*, hunting dog of ancient breed with long silky hair and tuft on head; ~ *Wars*, three campaigns (1839–42, 1879–80, 1919) fought by the British in Afghanistan in order to secure the NW. frontier of India.

Afghăn'ĭstăn (ăfg-). Inland kingdom of SW. Asia bounded on W. by Persia, on S. and E. by Pakistan and on N. by U.S.S.R.; founded in 18th c. by Durrani tribe of Pathans who broke away from Mogul Empire; later under British protection but declared a sovereign state in 1921; inhabited by various chiefly Mohammedan peoples, including Afghans and Tadjiks, speaking several languages of which the principal are Pashtu and Persian (the official language); capital, Kabul.

afĭciona'do (-syonahdō) *n.* Devotee of bull-fighting (or other sport or pastime).

afield' *adv.* On, in, or to the field; away, at a distance.

afīre' *adv.* & *pred. adj.* On fire.

A.F.L. *abbrev.* American Federation of Labour.

aflāme' *adv.* & *pred. adj.* In flames; in a glow of light.

afloat' *adv.* & *pred. adj.* Floating; at sea, on board ship; full of water; out of debt, paying one's way.

A.F.M. *abbrev.* Air Force Medal.

A.F.O. *abbrev.* Admiralty Fleet Order.

afŏŏt' *adv.* & *pred. adj.* On one's feet; astir; in operation or employment.

afōre' *adv.* & *prep.* (naut.) In front (of); (archaic, dial.) previously.

afore- *prefix.* Before, previously.

ā fortiōr'ī. With stronger reason. [L]

afraid' *pred. adj.* Alarmed, frightened.

ăf'reet, -rit, rite (-rēt) *n.* Evil demon in Mohammedan mythology.

afrĕsh' *adv.* Anew, with fresh beginning.

Af'rĭca (ă-). Continent, largest southward projection of the landmass which constitutes the Old World, surrounded by sea except where Isthmus of Suez joins it to Asia, and extending nearly as far southward of equator as northward; its indigenous inhabitants are dark-skinned peoples varying in colour from light copper in N. to black in equatorial and southern parts. It was visited by Portuguese from 15th c. onwards but remained largely unknown, except for limited colonization by the Dutch and British in the Cape region and by the French in Algeria, until mid-19th c.; in the 'scramble for Africa' of the 1880's the leading European nations competed for colonies and the continent was divided between them, Liberia and Ethiopia alone remaining under native rule. **Af'rĭcan** *adj.* Of Africa. ~ *n.* Native of Africa, esp. dark-skinned person as dist. from European or Asiatic settlers or their descendants.

Afridi (*a*frē'dī). Warlike Pathan tribe of mountainous districts of border between Afghanistan and Pakistan.

Afrĭkaans' (ă-, -ahns). Language, derived from Dutch, used in the Republic of South Africa as one of its two official languages, the other being English.

Afrika'ner (ă-, -kah-), *n.* Person born in South Africa of European stock (now usu. one descended from Dutch, not British, settlers). Except in historical use the older spelling **Afrikăn'der** is now reserved to describe specific breed of cattle.

A.F.S. *abbrev.* Army Fire Service; Auxiliary Fire Service.

aft (ah-) *adv.* (naut.) In, to, or towards stern of ship.

af'ter (ah-) *adv.* & *prep.* Behind; in pursuit (of); following in point of time; in view of; next in importance (to); according to; in imitation of; ~ *all*, in spite of everything that has happened, been said, done, etc. ~ *conj.* In or at a time subsequent to that when. ~ *adj.* Later, following; (naut.) nearer stern.

af'terbirth *n.* Placenta and membrane enveloping foetus in womb, extruded after the child.

af'ter-care *n.* Attention bestowed on person(s) after period of treatment or training, e.g. after discharge from hospital or prison.

af'terdamp *n.* Mixture of gases containing lethal amount of carbon monoxide, found in coal-mine after explosion of fire-damp.

af'ter-effect *n.* Delayed effect; effect following after an interval.

af'terglow *n.* Glow in west after sunset.

af'ter-grass *n.* Grass that grows after the first crop has been mown for hay, or among stubble after harvest.

af'ter-image *n.* Image retained by retina and producing visual sensation after the eyes are turned away or closed.

af'termăth *n.* = AFTER-GRASS; (fig.) results, consequences.

af'termost *adj.* (naut.) Farthest aft.

afternoon' *n.* Time between noon and evening.

af'ter-pains *n.pl.* Pains caused by uterine contraction after childbirth.

af'terpiece *n.* Farce or smaller entertainment after a play.

af'ter-taste *n.* Taste remaining or recurring after eating or drinking (freq. fig.).

af'terthought *n.* Reflection after the act; later expedient or explanation.

af'terwards *adv.* Later, subsequently.

A.F.V. *abbrev.* Armoured Fighting Vehicle.

A.G. *abbrev.* Adjutant-General; air-gunner.

ăg'a *n.* Commander or chief officer in Ottoman Empire; *Aga Khan*, title given to Hasan Ali Shah (1800–81), when he fled from Persia and settled in Bombay under British protection, and subsequently held by his successors; as direct descendant of Mohammed's son-in-law Ali, the Aga Khan is spiritual leader (Imam) of the Ismaili sect of Mohammedans. [Turk. *aghā* master, *khan* ruler, king]

Agadir′ (ă-, -ēr). Seaport on Atlantic coast of Morocco, scene of an 'incident' in 1911, when the appearance there of the German gunboat *Panther* nearly caused war between France and Germany.

A′găg (ā-). King of Amalekites, spared by Saul but killed by Samuel: see 1 Sam. xv. 7–33.

again′ (*or* -ĕn) *adv.* Another time, once more; further, besides; on the other hand; in return, in response; *~ and ~*, repeatedly; *as much ~*, twice as much; *half as much ~*, one-and-a-half times as much.

against′ (*or* -ĕnst) *prep.* In opposition to; in contrast to; in anticipation of; into collision with; opposite to (usu. *over ~*). *~ conj.* (archaic) By the time that.

Agamĕm′non (ă-). (Gk. legend) King of Argos, brother of Menelaus, and commander of the Greek host which besieged Troy; murdered on his return from Troy by his wife Clytemnestra and her lover Aegisthus.

Aganipp′ė (ă-). (Gk antiq.) Fountain on Mt. Helicon sacred to the Muses.

agāpe′[1] *adv.* & *pred. adj.* Gaping.

ăg′apē[2] *n.* Love-feast held by early Christians in connexion with Lord's Supper. [Gk, = 'brotherly love']

Agapĕm′onė (ă-) *n.* (= 'abode of love') Institution founded in Somerset (1845) by Henry James Prince (1811–99), where he and his followers lived with property in common, professed certain religious doctrines, and were believed to practise free love. **agapĕm′onīte** *adj.* & *n.* (Member) of this sect.

āg′ar-āg′ar *n.* Gelatinous substance obtained from various seaweeds and used as laxative, as solidifying agent in culture media for bacteria etc., and in East as food. [Malay wd]

ăg′aric *n.* Fungus of family *Agaricaceae*, including common mushroom, with central stalk and umbrella-like cap with radiating gills on lower side.

ăg′ate *n.* 1. Various semi-precious stones, semi-pellucid and variegated, usu. having a banded appearance and consisting largely of silica. 2. (U.S.) Size of printing-type (= Engl. *ruby*).

Agāv′ė *n.* Genus of plants (family *Amaryllidaceae*), including American aloe, with large rosette of spiny leaves and, after a number of years, a gigantic terminal inflorescence bearing numerous flowers once in the plant's life.

āge *n.* 1. Length of life or of existence; a generation; (colloq., esp. in pl.) long time. 2. Duration of life required for a purpose; *come of ~*, *reach* one's *full age*, attain age of 21 years, assume rights and responsibilities of adult; *~ of discretion*, legal term, now rare, for age of 14 years. 3. Latter part of life (also *old ~*). 4. (hist., geol.) Great period, as *Patriarchal A~*, *Ice A~*. *~ v.* 1. (Cause to) grow old. 2. Fix colours and mordants in (printed cloth etc.) by exposing to steam or to warm moist atmosphere. **aged** *adj.* 1. (ājd) Of the age of; (of horses) more than 6 years old. 2. (ā′jĭd) Old. **āge′lėss** *adj.* Never growing old.

ā′gency *n.* Active operation, action; instrumentality; action personified; office of agent; agent's business establishment.

agĕn′da *n.* Things to be done, items of business to be considered at a meeting.

ā′gēne *n.* Nitrogen trichloride used in bread-making for improving, stabilizing, and artificially ageing the flour. **ā′gėnātor** *n.* Apparatus used for this. **ā′gėnīze** *v.t.* Treat with agene.

ā′gent *n.* One who, thing that, exerts power or produces effect; one acting for another in business, law, politics, etc.; natural force acting on matter.

agent prŏvŏcateur′ (ahzhahṅ; -ter). Person employed to detect suspected offenders by tempting them to overt action. [Fr.]

Agēsĭlā′us (*a*-) (444–360 B.C.). King of Sparta, leader of successful campaign against Persians; killed in war against Thebes.

agglŏm′erāte *v.* Collect into a mass. **agglŏmerā′tion** *n.* **agglŏm′erative** *adj.* **agglŏm′erate** *adj.* & *n.* (Collected into) a mass; (geol.) aggregate of angular fragments of rock (of any or of several kinds) that has been shattered by volcanic action and subsequently consolidated into a mass.

agglut′ināte (-lōō-) *v.* 1. Unite as with glue; combine simple words to express compound ideas without important change of form or loss of meaning. 2. Turn into glue. **agglutinā′tion** *n.* **agglu′tinative** *adj.* (Of languages) characterized by the joining of simple roots to express compound ideas without material change of form or loss of meaning.

ăgg′randīze *v.t.* Increase the power, rank, wealth, etc., of; exaggerate. **aggrănd′izement** *n.*

ăgg′ravāte *v.t.* Increase the gravity of; (colloq.) exasperate. **ăggravā′tion** *n.*

ăgg′rėgāte *v.* Collect together; unite; amount to. **ăggrėgā′tion** *n.* **ăgg′rėgate** *adj.* Collected into one body; collective, total; (law) composed of associated individuals; (bot., of fruit) formed from carpels of one flower (as raspberry). *~ n.* Total; assemblage, collection; (physics) mass formed by union of homogeneous particles; (geol.) mass of minerals formed into one rock; (building) material mixed with lime, cement, bitumen, etc., to make concrete.

aggrĕ′ssion (-shn) *n.* Beginning of quarrel; unprovoked attack. **aggrĕss′or** *n.*

aggrĕss′ive *adj.* Of attack, offensive; disposed to attack. **aggrĕss′ively** *adv.* **aggrĕss′ivenėss.** *n.*

aggrieved′ (-vd) *pred. adj.* Distressed, oppressed; injured, having a grievance.

aghast′ (-gah-) *adj.* Terrified; struck with amazement.

ă′gīle *adj.* Quick-moving; nimble, active. **ă′gīlely** *adv.* **agĭl′ity** *n.*

A′gincourt (ăj-). Village of NW. France, scene of victory (1415) of Henry V of England over French.

ā′giō (*or* ă-) *n.* Percentage charged for changing paper money into cash, or one currency into another more valuable; excess value of one currency over another. **ă′giotage** (-ĭj) *n.* Exchange business; speculation in stocks; stock-jobbing.

agĭst′ment *n.* Contract for feeding cattle etc. on pasture-land for money payment; profit from this.

ă′gitāte *v.* 1. Shake, move; disturb, excite. 2. Revolve mentally, discuss, debate; keep up an agitation (*for*).

ăgitā′tion *n.* 1. Shaking. 2. Commotion, disturbance. 3. Debate, discussion; keeping of matter constantly before public; public excitement.

ă′gitātor *n.* 1. Person who creates excitement or disturbance, esp. for political ends. 2. Mechanical device for keeping liquid etc. in motion.

Aglā′ia (-ya). One of the GRACES.

ăg′lėt, ai′glet *n.* Metal tag of a lace; tag or spangle as dress-ornament, esp. (now written *aiguillette*) tagged braid or cord hanging from shoulder in some military or naval uniforms; catkin of hazel, birch, etc.

ăg′nail *n.* Torn skin at root of fingernail; resulting soreness.

ă′gnāte *adj.* Descended from the same male ancestor; of same clan or nation. *~ n.* Agnate person or animal.

Ag′nės (ă-), St. (4th c.). Patron saint of virgins, martyred in the persecution of Diocletian and commemorated 21st Jan.

Agni (ăg′nē). (Vedic myth.) God of fire.

ăgnōm′ĕn *n.* Additional name, esp. (Rom. antiq.) fourth name occas. assumed by Romans.

agnŏs′tic *n.* One who holds that nothing is known, or likely to be known, of the existence of a God or of anything beyond material phenomena. *~ adj.* Pertaining to this theory. [Gk *agnōstos* (*theos*) unknown (god); taken by T. H. Huxley f. Acts xvii. 23]

Ag′nus Dē′ī. Part of the Mass beginning with these words;

figure of lamb as emblem of Christ bearing cross or banner; small disc of wax stamped with this figure and blessed by pope. [L, = 'lamb of God']

agō' *adv.* & *adj.* Past, gone by; since.

agŏg' *adv.* & *pred. adj.* Eager, on the move, expectant.

agŏn'ic *adj.* Making no angle; ~ *line*, line joining places where magnetic compass points to true north.

ăg'onīze *v.* Torture; suffer agony, writhe in anguish; wrestle; make desperate efforts for effect.

ăg'ony *n.* Extreme bodily or mental suffering, esp. the last sufferings of the Saviour before the Crucifixion; death pangs; ~ *column*, in newspaper, column of personal advertisements (for missing friends etc.).

ăgoraphōb'ĭa *n.* Morbid dread of open spaces.

ăgout'ĭ (-ōō-) *n.* Rodent (several species in genus *Dasyprocta*) of Central America and W. Indies, related to guinea-pigs, nocturnal in habit and destructive to sugar-plantations etc.

Agra (ahg'-). City on river Jumna, N. India, capital of Mogul emperors from early 16th c. to mid-17th c.; site of the TAJ MAHAL.

agrār'ĭan *adj.* Of landed property or cultivated land; ~ *movement*, one attempting to procure redistribution of land. ~ *n.* One who favours redistribution of land. **agrār'ĭanism** *n.*

agree' *v.i.* Consent (*to*); concur (*with*); be in harmony (*with*); (gram.) take same number, gender, case, or person.

agree'able *adj.* Pleasing (*to*); (colloq.) well-disposed (*to, to* do); conformable *to*. **agree'ably** *adv.*

agree'ment *n.* Mutual understanding, covenant; (law) contract legally binding on parties; accordance in opinion; (gram.) concord in number, case, gender, person.

agrĕs'tĭc *adj.* Rural, rustic.

Agrĭc'ola (*a*-), Gnaeus Julius (A.D. 40–93). Roman general; governor of Britain for several years from 77 or 78.

ăg'rĭcŭlture *n.* Cultivation of the soil. **ăgrĭcŭl'tural** *adj.* **agrĭcŭl'tur(al)ist** *n.*

ăg'rĭmony *n.* A perennial plant of the rose family, esp. *Agrimonia eupatoria*, which has yellow flowers and hooked clinging fruit; *hemp* ~, see HEMP.

Agrĭpp'a (*a*-), Marcus Vipsanius (*c* 63–12 B.C.). Roman general, son-in-law of the Emperor Augustus.

agrŏn'omy *n.* Rural economy, husbandry. **ăgronŏm'ic(al)** *adjs.* **ăgronŏm'ics, agrŏn'omist** *ns.*

aground' *adv.* & *pred. adj.* On the bottom of shallow water.

ā'gūe *n.* Malarial fever; cold shivering stage of this; shivering fit.

ah *int.* Expressing joy, sorrow, surprise, entreaty, etc.

A.H. *abbrev.* *Anno Hegirae* (= in the year of the HEGIRA).

aha (ahhah') *int.* Expressing surprise, triumph, mockery.

A'hăb (ā-). King of Israel: see 1 Kings xvi–xxii.

Ahasūēr'us (*a*hăz-). See Esther, *passim*; also Ezra iv. 6, Dan. ix. 1; the Persian king mentioned in the Bible by this name is generally supposed to be XERXES.

A'hăz (ā-). King of Judah: see 2 Kings xvi.

ahead (*a*hĕd') *adv.* & *pred. adj.* In advance; in a direct line forward; forward at a rapid pace; in advance *of*.

ahoy' *int.* Nautical call used in hailing.

Ah'rĭman. The principle of evil in the ZOROASTRIAN system.

Ahura-Măz'da (*a*hoor'*a*-). The principle of goodness or light in the ZOROASTRIAN system; = ORMAZD.

ai (ah'-ĭ) *n.* Three-toed sloth (*Bradypus tridactylus*) of S. America. [f. its cry]

A.I. *abbrev.* Admiralty Instruction; artificial insemination (*A.I.D.* by donor, *A.I.H.* by husband).

aid *v.t.* Help, assist, promote. ~ *n.* Help, assistance; (hist.) grant of subsidy or tax to king, exchequer loan; helper; material source of help.

Aid'an, St. (d. 651). A monk of Iona, apostle to Northumbria, and first bishop of Lindisfarne.

aide n. = foll.; assistant.

aide-de-camp (ā'dekahṅ) *n.* (pl. *aides-de-camp*). Officer assisting general by carrying orders etc. [Fr.]

aide-mémoire (ăd'māmwahr') *n.* Manual of formulae etc. to serve as aid to the memory; in diplomatic use, memorandum. [Fr.]

aig'rĕtte (ā-) *n.* = EGRET; long black plumes grown by this in breeding-season; tuft of feathers or hair; spray of gems etc.

aiguille (ā'gwēl) *n.* Sharp peak of rock.

aiguillette (āgwĭlĕt'): see AGLET.

ail *v.* Trouble, afflict; be ill.

ail'ment *n.* Illness, esp. slight one.

ail'eron *n.* One of hinged flaps on trailing edge of wings of aircraft, near the tips, which provide variation of lift on either side and are used to execute the movement known as 'banking' [Fr., = 'little wing, fin', dim. of *aile* wing]

ailūr'ophōbe *n.* Person who is morbidly afraid of cats. **ailūrophōb'ĭa** *n.*

aim *v.* Direct *at*; point (gun etc.); deliver blow, discharge missile (*at*); take aim; form designs. ~ *n.* Direction of or act of directing a missile or weapon towards an object; design, purpose, object. **aim'lėss** *adj.* **aim'lėssly** *adv.* **aim'lėssnėss** *n.*

ainé (ān'ā) *n.* Elder son.

air *n.* 1. The invisible, odourless, and tasteless mixture of gases enveloping the Earth, consisting chiefly of oxygen and nitrogen, with some carbon dioxide and traces of other gases, and breathed by all land animals; atmosphere; unconfined space; breeze; *on the* ~, broadcast(ing) by radio transmission. 2. Appearance; mien; affected manner. 3. (mus.) Melody, tune aria. 4. ~*-ball, -balloon, -bladder, -cushion, -jacket,* etc., containing air or inflated by air; *air'borne*, (of aircraft) having left the ground; in flight; (of troops) carried by aircraft; ~*-brake*, brake operated by piston driven by compressed air; also, brake consisting of flaps or other movable surfaces, normally lying parallel to air-flow, turned through 90° to retard progress of aircraft or car; ~ *bridge*, air transport as a means of surmounting physical or other obstacles between two places; ~*-brush*, fine spray for paint used in commercial art and for retouching photographs; *Air Chief Marshal*, title, rank, of officer in R.A.F., ranking next below a Marshal and above an Air Marshal; ~*-conditioning*, process of cleaning air and controlling its temperature and humidity before it enters a room, building, etc., and in certain manufacturing processes; ~*-cooled* (*adj.*) (of internal-combustion engine) cooled by exposure to stream of air; *air'craft* (pl. same) any kind of flying machine, including aeroplanes, airships, balloons; flying machines collectively; *aircraft carrier*, ship designed to carry aeroplanes with special deck for taking-off and

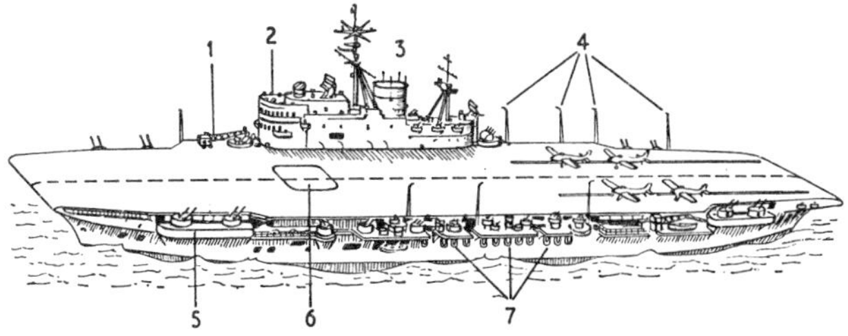

AIRCRAFT CARRIER

1. Mobile crane. 2. Bridge. 3. Island superstructure. 4. Wireless aerial masts. 5. Sponson. 6. Lift. 7. Life-saving rafts

landing; *air'field*, area of land where aircraft are accommodated and maintained and may take off or land; ~ *force*, that branch of armed forces of a country which fights in the air, in aeroplanes or airships, together with the staff necessary to maintain it and its machines etc.; *air'-graph*, photographic reproduction of letter etc. conveyed by air mail in form of microfilm to save weight; *~-gun*, gun from which missile is discharged by compressed air; ~ *hostess*, stewardess in passenger aircraft; *~-lift*, transportation of supplies by air to area cut off from normal communications; ~ *liner*, large passenger aeroplane; *~-lock*, stoppage of flow of liquid in pump or pipe by bubble of air; intermediate chamber between outer air and working chamber of pneumatic caisson (ill. CAISSON); similar intermediate chamber; ~ *mail*, mail carried by aircraft; *air'man*, aviator; *Air Marshal*, title, rank, of officer in R.A.F., equivalent to Lieutenant-General in the army; *~-minded* (*adj.*) interested in, or enthusiastic for, use and development of aircraft; *air'plane*, (orig. U.S.) aeroplane; *~-pocket*, local condition of atmosphere, as a down current or sudden change of wind velocity, which causes aircraft to lose height suddenly; *air'port*, aerodrome for transport of passengers and goods by air; *~-power*, power of offensive and defensive action dependent upon a supply of aircraft; *~-pump*, pump for exhausting vessel etc. of its air; (also) compressor; ~ *raid*, attack by aircraft; *air'screw*, aeroplane propeller (ill. PROPELLER); *~-sea rescue*, applied to the branch of the R.A.F. whose task is to rescue airmen and passengers from the sea, and to such operations; *~-shaft*, passage for ventilating mine or tunnel (ill. MINE); *air'ship*, flying machine lighter than air; a dirigible balloon, usu. cigar-shaped, consisting of gas-bags enclosed in an outer envelope, driven by engines, and carrying passengers, crew, etc., usu. in cars ('gondolas') suspended below the ship; *~-sickness*, kind of nausea, sometimes affecting persons in an aircraft, caused by rapid change of altitude, rolling, and pitching; *~-speed*, speed of aircraft in relation to the air, as dist. from *ground-speed*; *airstrip*, a strip of land prepared for the taking off and landing of aircraft, often for temporary use; *~-tight*, impermeable to air; *Air Training Corps*, organization for the training of cadets for the R.A.F.; *~-umbrella*, force of aircraft used to give air protection to military operation; *~-way*, ventilating passage in mine; route regularly followed by aircraft; *~-worthy*, (of aircraft) in fit condition to be flown. ~ *v.t.* Expose to open air, ventilate; finish drying of (clothes etc.) by warmth; parade (grievances, clothes, etc.).

Aire'dāle (ārd-). Valley of river Aire in Yorkshire; a breed of large terriers with rough reddish-brown coats.

air'lėss *adj.* Stuffy; breezeless, still.

air'y *adj.* Breezy; light, thin; immaterial; sprightly, graceful, delicate; superficial, flippant. **air'ily** *adv.*

aisle (īl) *n.* Division of church, esp. parallel to nave, choir, or transept, and divided from it by pillars (ill. CHURCH); passage between rows of seats, esp. in church. [L *ala* wing]

Aisne (ān). River of N. France; *Battle of the* ~, German offensive of May 1918 directed across the river Aisne and towards the Marne.

ait *n.* Small isle, esp. one in a river.

aitch'bōne *n.* Rump-bone, cut of beef over this bone (ill. MEAT).

Aix-la-Chapĕlle' (ĕx-, sh-). French name of AACHEN.

ajăr' *adv.* (Of a door) slightly open.

A'jăx (ā-). 1. A Greek hero of the Trojan war, son of Telamon king of Salamis; disappointment when the armour of Achilles was awarded to Ulysses drove him mad, and he killed a flock of sheep thinking them the sons of Atreus, and afterwards slew himself. 2. Another Greek, son of Oileus king of Locris, who was killed by lightning on his homeward journey after the fall of Troy.

Ak'bar (ă-). Jellaladin Mohammed (1542–1605), Mogul emperor; enlarged the Mogul Empire in India to its greatest extent.

à Kempis, Thomas: see THOMAS À KEMPIS.

Akhna'ton (ăknah-). 'Glory of the sun', name taken by Amenhotep IV, king of Egypt of 18th dynasty (14th c. B.C.), who tried to replace the worship of the old sun-god Ammon by that of a new sun-god Ra, and built a new capital at El Amarna, away from Thebes where the old priesthood was established.

akim'bō *adv.* (Of the arms) with hands on hips and elbows out.

akin' *pred. adj.* Related by blood; (fig.) of similar character.

Akk'ad, Acc- (ă-). The N. part of ancient Babylonia; also, the city (Agado) founded by Sargon, *c* 3800 B.C. **Akkăd'ian, Acc-** *adj.* & *n.* (Native) of Akkad; (of) the language of this people, the oldest known Semitic language.

Aksakov (ăksah'kof), Sergey Timofey'evich (1791–1859). Russian author of a 'Family History' and other works describing country life.

a.l. *abbrev.* Autograph letter.

à la (ah lah) *prep.* After the manner of. [Fr.]

Ala *abbrev.* Alabama.

Alabama (ă-, -ah'ma, U.S. -ăm'a). An east-south-central cotton-growing State of the U.S.A., admitted to the Union in 1819; capital, Montgomery.

ăl'abaster (-bah-) *n.* A pure granular gypsum rock of white, pink, or yellowish colour, used for statues. ~ *adj.* Of alabaster; resembling it in whiteness or smoothness.

à la carte (ah lah kart). From the bill of fare. [Fr.]

alăc'rity *n.* Briskness, cheerful readiness.

Alădd'in (*a*-). Hero of a story in 'Arabian Nights', who acquired a lamp the rubbing of which brought a genie to do the will of the owner; *~'s lamp*, talisman enabling the owner to gratify any wish.

Al'amein (ă-, -ān). *El* ~, place near the NE. coast of Egypt, where the advance of the German forces into Egypt was halted in July 1942; scene of a battle, in Oct. 1942, in which the Germans were decisively defeated.

à la mode (ah lah mōd). In the fashion, fashionable; *beef* ~, a kind of beef stew. [Fr.]

Å'land Islands (ō-). Group of islands in the Gulf of Bothnia constituting a department of Finland.

āl'ar *adj.* Pertaining to wings; wing-shaped, wing-like; axillary.

Alarcón (ălarkōn'), Pedro Antonio de (1833–91). Spanish poet, dramatist, and prose writer.

Alarcón y Mendoza (ălarkōn' ī mĕndōth'a), Juan Ruiz de (*c* 1581–

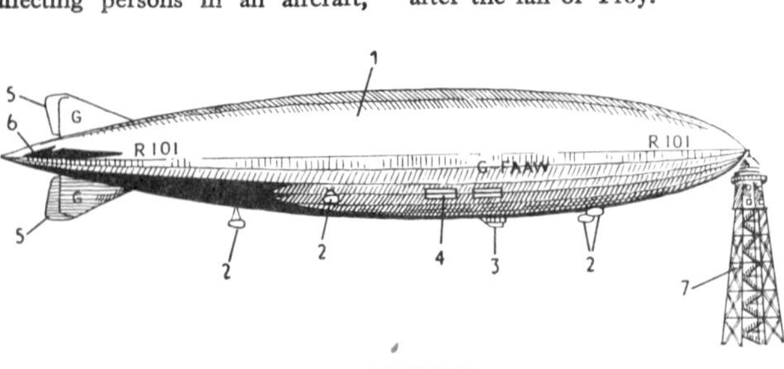

AIRSHIP

1. Envelope 2. Engines. 3. Control cabin. 4. Passenger cabin. 5. Rudder. 6. Elevator. 7. Mooring mast

1639). Mexican-Spanish dramatist.

Al'aric I (ă-) (*c* 370–410). A Visigoth, the first Germanic conqueror of Rome (A.D. 410).

alarm' *n.* Call to arms; warning sound giving notice of danger; warning; excited anticipation of danger; mechanism that sounds alarm. ~ *v.t.* Arouse to sense of danger; disturb, agitate. **ală'rum** *n.* Mechanism that sounds alarm; *alar(u)ms and excursions* (joc.), noise and bustle; *alar(u)m-clock*, one with apparatus that can be set to ring at predetermined time. [It. *all' arme* to arms]

alas' (-ahs) *int.* Expressing grief, pity, concern.

Alas. *abbrev.* Alaska.

Alăs'ka (*a*-). A State of the U.S. in the extreme NW. of N. America, with coasts in Arctic Ocean, Bering Sea, and North Pacific; discovered by Russian explorers (under Vitus Bering) in 1741, and further explored by Cook, Vancouver, and others during the last quarter of 18th c.; the territory was purchased from Russia in 1867 and admitted to the Union in 1959; capital, Juneau.

ălb *n.* White vestment reaching to feet, worn by celebrant at Mass over the cassock and by some consecrated kings (ill. VESTMENT).

Alba, Duke of: see ALVA.

ăl'bacōre *n.* Large species of W. Indian fish (*Thynnus germo*) allied to tunny; other fish of the same genus. [Arab. *al* the, *bukr* young camel, heifer]

Al'ban (awl-) St. (d. *c* 304). The first British martyr, commemorated on 22nd June; martyred at Verulamium, which was afterwards named St. Albans.

Alban. *abbrev.* (Bishop) of St. Albans (replacing surname in his signature).

Albān'ia (ă-). A Balkan State between Greece and Yugoslavia; under Turkish rule from 16th c. until 1912, when disputes arising from the demand for Albanian autonomy nearly caused a European war; in Jan. 1925 the country was proclaimed a republic, which continued until 1928 when it was changed into a monarchy; again proclaimed a republic in 1946; capital, Tirana. **Albān'ian** *adj.* & *n.* (Native, language) of Albania.

Al'bany[1] (awl-). Ancient poetic name, of Gaelic origin, for the N. part of Britain.

Al'bany[2] (ăl-). Capital of New York State, U.S.

Al'bany[3] (awl-). (*The*) ~, house near Piccadilly, London, formerly belonging to Frederick, Duke of York and Albany, converted *c* 1803 into sets of chambers where many famous men of letters have resided.

ăl'batrŏss *n.* Genus (*Diomedea*) of very long-winged oceanic birds allied to petrels, found chiefly in the S. hemisphere; *wandering* ~, (*D. exulans*) one of the largest sea-birds, white when adult, with dark wings and hooked beak. [f. obs. *alcatras* frigate-bird, f. Span. and Port., f. Arab. *al-qadus* the bucket (name for the pelican, from its supposed water-carrying habit)]

albē'ĭt (awl-) *conj.* Though.

Albeniz (ălbānēth'), Isaac (1860–1909). Spanish pianist and composer, famous chiefly for works based on the rhythm of Spanish popular music.

Al'berich (ă-, -ĭχ). (Scand. myth.) King of the elves, guardian of the treasure of the Nibelungs, stolen from him by Siegfried.

Al'bert[1] (ă-), Prince (1819–1861). Prince of Saxe-Coburg-Gotha; cousin and consort (1840) of Queen Victoria; ~ *Hall*, large concert and exhibition hall in Kensington, London, erected in his memory (1867); ~ *Medal* (abbrev. A.M.), awarded since 1866 for 'gallantry in saving life at sea or on land'; ~ *Memorial*, an elaborate monument, designed by Sir Gilbert Scott, erected (1872–6) in Hyde Park, London.

Al'bert[2] I (ă-) (1875–1934). King of the Belgians (1909–34), commander-in-chief of the Belgian army during the war of 1914–18.

ăl'bert[3] *n.* 1. Watch-chain, with cross-bar for insertion in buttonhole of waistcoat, named after Prince ALBERT[1]. 2. Size of writing paper (6 × 4 in.).

Albĕrt'a (ă-). Western prairie province of Canada, bounded on the south by the U.S.A., and on the west by the Rocky Mountains; capital, Edmonton.

Alberti (ălbar̄t'ĭ), Leon Battista degli (1404–72). Italian architect, painter, writer on art, poet, and musician.

Albert Nyăn'za. Large shallow lake in Uganda, part of the Nile system, discovered in 1864 and named after Prince ALBERT[1].

Albĕrt'us Măg'nus (ă-) (1193 or 1206–1280). Swabian Dominican monk, one of the great scholastic philosophers; known as 'Doctor Universalis'.

ălbĕs'cent *adj.* Growing white, fading into white.

Albigenses (ălbĭjĕn'sēz). Various Christian sects living in Provence in the 12th c., whose censure of the corruptions of the papacy led Pope Innocent III to preach a crusade against them on the ground of heresy. **Albigen'sian** *adj.* & *n.* [L, f. town of *Albi*]

ălbī'nō (-bē-) *n.* Animal or human being marked by congenital absence of pigment in skin and hair, which is white, and eyes, which are pink or very pale blue and unduly sensitive to light; plant lacking normal colouring. **ălbĭnŏt'ic** *adj.* **ăl'bĭnism** *n.*

Al'bĭon (ă-). Ancient poetical name for Britain.

Alboin (ălbwăn) (d. 573). King of the Lombards, conqueror and settler of northern Italy (568).

Albuera (ălbwar̄'*a*). Small village in Spain, scene (1811) of a combined English, Portuguese, and Spanish victory over the French under Marshal Soult.

ăl'bum *n.* Blank book for insertion of autographs, photographs, etc.

ălbūm'ėn *n.* White of egg; a constituent of animal cells, milk, etc., found nearly pure in white of egg; (bot.) substance found between skin and embryo of many seeds, usu. the edible part (ill. SEED). **ălbū'mėnīze** *v.t.* Coat (paper) with an albuminous solution. **ălbūm'ĭnōse, ălbūm'ĭnous** *adjs.*

ălbūm'ĭn *n.* Any of a class of water-soluble proteins.

ălbūm'ĭnoid *n.* Any of a class of organic compounds forming chief part of organs and tissues of animals and plants; protein. **ălbūmĭnoi'dal** *adj.*

ălbūmĭnūr'ia *n.* (med.) Condition in which the urine contains proteins, sometimes a symptom of kidney disease.

Al'būquerque (ă-, -kĕrk), Afonso d' (1453–1515). Portuguese navigator, founder of Portuguese power in India.

ălbûrn'um *n.* Recently formed wood in trees, sap-wood.

Alcae'us (ă-, -sē-) (d. *c* 580 B.C.). Greek lyric poet of Mitylene in Lesbos, inventor of the **Alcā'ic** metre, a stanza of four lines:

– – ⏑ – – | – ⏑ ⏑ – ⏑ ⏓
– – ⏑ – – | – ⏑ ⏑ – ⏑ ⏓
– – ⏑ – – – ⏑ – –
– ⏑ ⏑ – ⏑ ⏑ – ⏑ – ⏑

Al'catrăz (ăl-). Island in San Francisco Bay, California; the U.S. federal prison there.

Alcĕs'tĭs (ăls-). (Gk legend) Wife of Admetus, whose life she saved by giving her own; she was brought back from Hades by Hercules.

ăl'chėmy (-k-) *n.* The medieval forerunner of chemistry, primarily the attempt to transmute base metals into gold or silver. **alchĕm'ic, alchĕm'ical** *adjs.* **ăl'chėmist** *n.* [Arab. *al-kimia*, f. *al* the, Gk *khēmeia* transmutation of metals]

Alcibiades (ălsĭbī'*a*dēz) (*c* 450–404 B.C.). Athenian general and politician to whose irresponsibility the defeat of Athens in the Peloponnesian War was partly due.

Alcinous (ălsĭn'ō*u*s). (Gk legend) King of Phaeacia and father of Nausicaa; entertained Ulysses during his journey home from Troy.

Alc'man (ă-), **Alcmae'on** (*c* 630 B.C.). The principal lyric poet of Sparta, a native of Lydia, brought to Sparta as a slave.

Alcmē'nē (ă-). (Gk myth.) Wife of Amphitryon and mother of Hercules by Zeus.

Al'cŏck (awl-), Sir John William (1892–1919). English airman;

made first non-stop flight across the Atlantic, 1919 (Newfoundland to Ireland, 16 hrs 12 m.).

ăl'cohŏl *n.* 1. Colourless volatile inflammable liquid, also called *ethyl* ~ (C_2H_5OH), formed by fermentation of sugars and contained in wine ('spirit of wine'), beer, whisky, etc., of which it is the intoxicating principle; also used in medicine and industry as a solvent for fats, oils, etc., and as a fuel. 2. Any liquor containing alcohol. 3. (chem.) Any of a class of compounds analogous to alcohol in constitution and derived from hydrocarbons by the replacement of hydrogen atoms by hydroxyl groups. **ălcohŏl'ic** *adj.* Pertaining to, containing, alcohol. ~ *n.* Person addicted to alcoholism. [Arab. *al* the, *koh'l* powder (for staining eyelids)]

ăl'coholism *n.* Action of alcohol on the human system; continual heavy drinking of alcoholic liquors.

ălcoholŏm'ėter *n.* Instrument for measuring alcoholic content of liquids.

Alcoran (ălkorahn', ăl'-): see KORAN.

ăl'cōve *n.* Vaulted recess in room-wall; recess in garden-wall or hedge; summer-house. [Arab. *al-qobbah* the vault]

Alcuin (ăl'kwin) or *Albinus*, Engl. name *Ealhwine* (735–804). English theologian and man of letters, Charlemagne's coadjutor in educational reforms, and finally abbot of Tours.

Alcȳ'onė (ă-). (Gk legend) Wife of Ceyx; threw herself into the sea after finding the body of her shipwrecked husband on the shore; the gods changed both into kingfishers, and the sea is said be calm while they are nesting; hence the expression 'halcyon days'.

Ald. *abbrev.* Alderman.

Aldĕb'aran (ă-). A bright, reddish star in the constellation TAURUS. [Arab., = 'the following' (because it follows the Pleiades)]

ăl'dėhȳde *n.* Any of a class of organic compounds containing the group CHO— in their structures, esp. acetaldehyde, CH_3CHO. [abbrev. of L *al*cohol *dehyd*rogenatum (deprived of hydrogen)]

al'der (awl-) *n.* Tree (genus *Alnus*) of birch family, esp. *A. glutinosa*, growing by lakes and streams and in marshy ground; ~ *buckthorn*, shrub (*Frangula alnus*) of buckthorn family growing in damp peaty soils.

al'derman (awl-) *n.* Co-opted member of an English county or borough council, next in dignity to mayor; (hist.) as an Anglo-Saxon title, a noble or person of high rank. **aldermăn'ic** *adj.* **al'dermanship** *n.* **al'dermanry** *n.* Ward, district of a borough having its own alderman; rank of alderman.

Al'derney (awl-). One of the four larger Channel Islands; famous for its dairy cattle (which are of the Guernsey breed).

Al'dershŏt (awl-). Town in Hampshire having a permanent military camp and training centre.

Ald'helm (ă-), St. (*c* 640–709). English churchman and scholar, 1st bishop of Sherborne; author of Latin works in verse and prose.

Al'dīne (awl-) *adj.* Printed by **Aldus Manutius** (Aldo Manuzio, 1449–1515), whose press at Venice issued the first printed editions of many Greek authors, and introduced italics into typography.

Al'dis lamp (awl-). Signalling lamp, used esp. in navy and air force, in which Morse signs are transmitted by rotating a mirror at whose focus the light is located. [inventor, A. C. W. *Aldis*]

āle *n.* Liquor made from an infusion of malt by fermentation, flavoured with hops etc.; beer; (hist.) merry-making at which ale was drunk; ~*-house*, one at which ale is sold.

Alĕc'tō (*a*-). (Gk myth.) One of the Furies.

alee' *adv.* & *pred. adj.* On the lee side of a ship, to leeward.

āle'-hōōf *n.*: see GROUND-ivy.

Aleman (ălėmahn'), Mateo (*c* 1550–1614). Spanish picaresque novelist.

Alembert (ălahṅbār'), Jean le Rond d' (1717–83). French encyclopaedist, philosopher, and mathematician.

alĕm'bic *n.* (hist.) Apparatus used by alchemists for distilling.

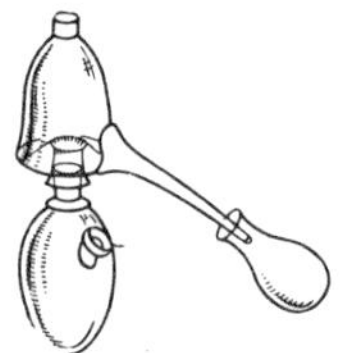

ALEMBIC

[Arab. *alanbig* still, f. Gk *ambix -ikos* cup, cap of a still]

Alençon' (ălahṅsawṅ). Town in NW. France, famous for the manufacture of needlepoint lace (*point d'Alençon*), orig. copied from Venetian lace.

Alĕpp'ō (*a*-). (*Haleb*) Ancient city in Syria, twice besieged (though not taken) during the Crusades.

alert' *adj.* Watchful, vigilant; lively, nimble. ~ *n.* Warning-call, alarm; warning of air-raid, period of warning; *on the* ~, on the lookout. ~ *v.t.* **alert'ly** *adv.* **alert'ness** *n.* [It. *all' erta* to the watch-tower]

Alėxan'der[1] (ăl-, -ahn-). Name of three emperors of Russia; ~ *I* (1777–1825), emperor 1801–25 during the Napoleonic Wars and sponsor of the Holy Alliance; ~ *II* (1818–81), emperor 1855–81, assassinated in St. Petersburg; ~ *III* (1845–94), emperor 1881–94.

Alėxan'der[2] (ăl-, -ahn-) I (*c* 1078–1124), ~ *II* (1198–1249), ~ *III* (1241–85). Kings of Scotland.

Alėxan'der[3] (-ăl-, -ahn-) VI. Pope: see BORGIA, Rodrigo.

Alėxan'der (ăl-, -ahn-) **Nĕv'skĭ** (1220–63). Russian saint and national hero, called 'Nevski' from the river Neva, on the banks of which he defeated the Swedes.

Alėxan'der (ăl-, -ahn-) **the Great** (356–323 B.C.). King of Macedon; son of Philip II of Macedon; educated by Aristotle; became king 336 B.C.; was nominated by the Greek states to conduct the war against Persia, in which he was victorious; he extended his conquests to Egypt (where he founded Alexandria) and India.

Alėxan'dra (ăl-, -ahn-) (1844–1925). Wife of Edward VII and queen of England, daughter of Christian IX of Denmark.

Alėxan'drĭa (ăl-, -ahn-). City and seaport of Egypt, founded by Alexander the Great 332 B.C.; capital of Egypt under the Ptolemies; until the Roman conquest of Egypt it was a centre of Greek culture, and possessed a famous library, part of which was accidentally burnt when Julius Caesar was besieged in the city.

Alėxan'drĭan *adj.* Of Alexandria; ~ *period*, period of Hellenistic literature with Alexandria as its chief centre from end of the time of Alexander the Great to the Roman conquest of Greece, 300–146 B.C. **Alėxan'drĭanism** *n.* Term used of influence of Greek poets of the Alexandrian period on Roman poetry, the chief features of which were artificiality and display of mythological learning.

Alėxăn'drīne (ăl-) *adj.* & *n.* (pros.) (Line) of 6 iambic feet, or 12 syllables; the French heroic verse. [so called either from the French poet Alexandre Paris, or because it was used in early poems on the subject of Alexander the Great]

Alfieri (ălfyār'ĭ), Vittorio, Count (1749–1803). Italian dramatist; author of tragedies on classical and other subjects, satirical comedies, and political works.

Alfŏn'sō (ă-). Name of several kings of Spain, the last of whom, ~ *XIII* (1886–1941), was deposed in 1931 when Spain became a republic.

Al'frėd the Great (ă-) (849–899). King of the West Saxons 871; drove the Danes from his territories; built a navy; composed a code of laws; encouraged the revival of letters in the W. of England, himself translating Latin works into English.

ălfrĕs'cō *adv.* & *adj.* In the open air; open-air.

ăl'ga *n.* (pl. *-gae*). One of the *algae*, a division of primitive cryptogamic plants including green, brown, and red seaweeds, pond-scums, and many microscopic water-plants showing immense diversity of structure.

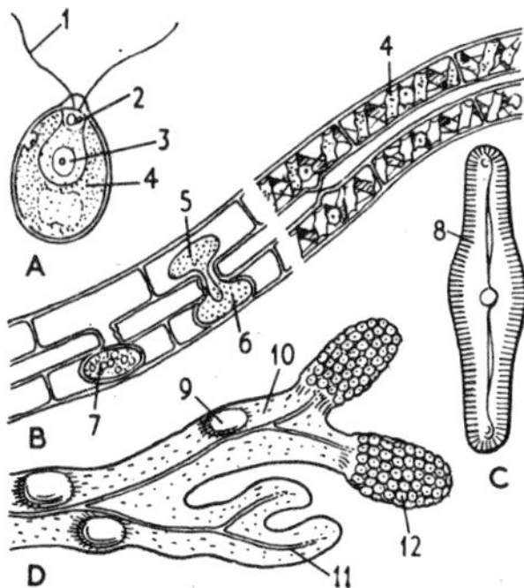

ALGAE: A. *CHLAMYDOMONAS*. B. *SPIROGYRA*. SHOWING METHOD OF REPRODUCTION (LEFT) AND VEGETATIVE STATE (RIGHT). C. DIATOM. D. BLADDERWRACK, A SEAWEED

A. 1. Flagellum. 2. Contractile vacuole. 3. Nucleus. 4. Plastids containing chlorophyll. B. 5. Male gamete. 6. Female gamete. 7. Zygote. C. 8. Frustule. D. 9. Bladder. 10. Thallus. 11. Midrib. 12. Conceptacle

ăl'gėbra *n.* Branch of mathematics dealing with relations and properties of numbers by means of letters and other general symbols. **ălgėbrā'ic(al)** *adjs.* **ălgėbrā'ically** *adv.* **ăl'gėbrāist** *n.* [Arab. *al-jebr* the reunion of fragments]

Algeria (ăljēr'ĭa). Country in N. Africa. Independent 1962. **Alger'ian** *adj.* & *n.*

Algeria (ăljēr'ĭa). Republic in N. Africa. Independent since 1962. **Alger'ian** *adj.* & *n.*

Algiers (ăljērz'). Capital of Algeria.

Algŏnk'ĭn (ă-). The most widespread linguistic family of N.-Amer. Indians (orig. used of one tribe living near Quebec).

ăl'gorism *n.* Arabic (decimal) notation; *cipher in* ~, 0, mere dummy. [med. L *algorismus*, f. Arab. *al-Khowarazmi* the man of Khiva, surname of a mathematician]

Alhăm'bra (ăl-). Palace of the Moorish kings at Granada, built in 13th c. [Arab. *al hamra'* the red house]

Ali (ăl'ĭ). Cousin and son-in-law of Mohammed; regarded by some Mohammedans as the first caliph, his 3 predecessors being considered interlopers.

āl'ias *adv.* & *n.* (Name by which one is or has been called) on other occasions.

Ali Baba (ăl'ĭ bahb'*a*). Hero of a story supposed to be from the 'Arabian Nights'; discovered the magic formula ('Open Sesame!') which opened the cave in which forty robbers kept the treasures they had accumulated.

ăl'ībi *adv.* & *n.* (The plea that when an alleged act took place one was) elsewhere.

Alĭcăn'tė (ă-). City and province of SE. Spain; a red wine (also *Alicănt'*) made there.

ăl'idāde *n.* Movable arm of quadrant etc. carrying the sights and indicating degrees cut off on the arc (ill. ASTROLABE). [Arab. *al-'idadah* the revolving radius (upper arm)]

āl'ien *adj.* Not one's own; foreign; differing in nature (*from*); repugnant (*to*). ~ *n.* Stranger, foreigner. ~ *v.t.* (law) Transfer ownership of. **āl'iėnable** *adj.* **āliėnabĭl'ity** *n.*

āl'iėnāte *v.t.* Estrange, transfer ownership of; divert (*from*). **āliėnā'tion** *n.* Estrangement; transference of ownership; diversion to different purpose; insanity (also *mental* ~).

āl'iėnism *n.* Study and treatment of mental diseases. **āl'iėnist** *n.* (now rare) Specialist in mental diseases.

Alighieri: see DANTE.

alight'[1] (-īt) *v.i.* Dismount, descend (*from*); settle, come to earth (from the air).

alight'[2] (-īt) *pred. adj.* Kindled, on fire, lighted up.

align' (-īn) *v.* Place, lay, in a line; bring into line; form a line. **align'ment** *n.* Act of aligning; formation in a straight line, esp. of soldiers.

alīke' *pred. adj.* Similar, like. ~ *adv.* In like manner.

ăl'iment *n.* Food; mental sustenance. **ălimĕn'tal** *adj.* **ălimĕn'tally** *adv.*

ălimĕn'tary *adj.* Nourishing; performing functions of nutrition; providing maintenance; ~ *canal*, channel in animal body through which food passes, including whole length from mouth, through the intestines to the anus.

ălimentā'tion *n.* Nourishment; maintenance.

ăl'imony *n.* Nourishment (archaic); allowance made to wife from husband's estate after legal separation or divorce.

ăliphăt'ic *adj.* (chem.) Belonging to the group of organic compounds in which the carbon atoms are linked in open chains as opposed to rings.

ăl'iquŏt *adj.* & *n.* (Part) contained by the whole an integral number of times, thus, 6 is an aliquot part of 18; (mus.) overtone, harmonic.

alīve' *pred. adj.* Living; active, brisk; fully susceptible *to*; swarming *with*.

alĭz'arĭn *n.* Red colouring matter of madder. [prob. f. Arab. *al* the, *'açarah* extract]

ăl'kalī *n.* (pl. *-s*, *-es*). (chem.) Any of a number of substances having strongly basic properties; they include the carbonates and hydroxides of the alkali metals and of ammonium and the hydroxides of some other reactive metals; ~ *metal*, any of a group of highly reactive metallic elements including lithium, sodium, and potassium. **ăl'kalīne** *adj.* **ălkalĭn'ity** *n.* [Arab. *al-qaliy* calcined ashes (*qalay* fry)]

ăl'kaloid *n.* Any of a large group of nitrogenous organic substances of vegetable origin having basic or alkaline properties; many, as morphine, strychnine, cocaine, etc., are used as drugs.

ălkāne' *n.* Any member of the paraffin series of hydrocarbons.

ăl'kȳl (*or* ăl'kĭl) *adj.* Derived from, or related to, the paraffin series of hydrocarbons; ~ *radical*, any of the series of radicals derived from paraffin hydrocarbons by removal of a hydrogen atom, e.g. methyl (CH_3), ethyl (C_2H_5).

all (awl) *adj.* The entire; the greatest possible; the entire number of. ~ *n.* All men; the whole, every one, everything; *at* ~, in any way; ~ *one*, just the same. ~ *adv.* Wholly, quite; ~ *right*, safe and sound, in good state; satisfactorily; (as sentence) I consent; all is well; ~ *the same*, just the same; in spite of this, notwithstanding. ~ in phrases etc.; ~-*clear*, signal giving information that there is no danger; esp., signal that hostile aircraft have left the neighbourhood; *A~ Fool's Day*, the first of April, the celebration of which is probably a survival of ancient festivities held

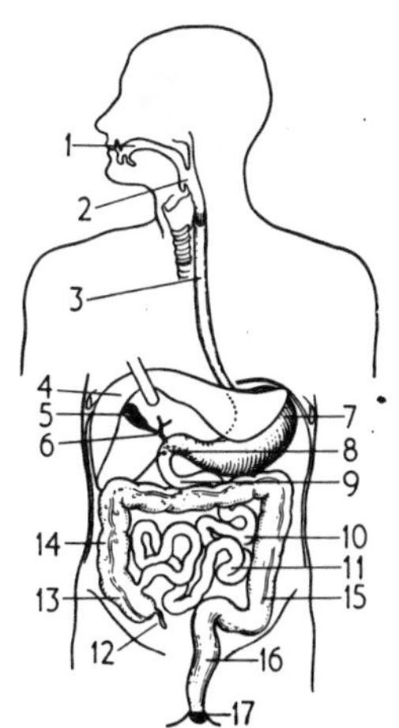

ALIMENTARY CANAL

1. Oral cavity. 2. Pharynx. 3. Oesophagus. 4. Liver (turned back). 5. Gall bladder. 6. Bile duct. 7. Stomach 8. Pylorus. 9, 10, 11. Small intestine (9, duodenum; 10, jejunum; 11, ileum). 12. Vermiform appendix. 13, 14, 15. Large intestine (13, caecum; 14, ascending colon; 15, descending colon). 16. Rectum. 17. Anus

at spring equinox; *on ~-fours*, on hands and knees; *A~ Hallows, A~ Saints' (Day)*, 1st Nov., on which there is a general celebration of the saints; *~-Hallows Eve (Hallowe'en)*, 31st Oct., the last day of the year in the old Celtic calendar, and the night of all the witches; *~-hands*, entire ship's company; *~ in* (orig. U.S.) quite exhausted; *~-in*, (of wrestling) with no restrictions; *~-out*, using or involving all one's (or its) strength or resources; fully extended; at top speed; *~-round*, having ability and skill in all departments, esp. of a game; *~-rounder (n.)*; *A~ Souls (College)*, Oxford college founded 1437; *A~ Souls' (Day)*, 2nd Nov., day on which prayers are offered for the souls of all the faithful deceased; *~ there*, (colloq.) having all one's wits about one; *~-way*, from and to which there is movement in all possible directions.

All'ah (ă-). Moslem name of God. [Arab., f. *al* the, *ilah* god = Heb. *eloah*]

Allăhăbăd' (ă-). Indian city at the confluence of the Jumna with the Ganges; capital of the United Provinces; a place of Hindu pilgrimage.

allay' *v.t.* Put down, repress; alleviate; diminish.

allege' (-ĕj) *v.t.* Affirm, advance as argument or excuse. **ăllėgā'tion** *n.* Alleging; assertion (esp. one not proved).

Allėghan'y Mountains (-ă, -gā-). Ranges of the Appalachian system in eastern U.S.

allē'giance (-jans) *n.* Duty of subject to sovereign or government; loyalty.

ăll'ėgory *n.* Narrative description of subject under guise of another suggestively similar; figurative story. **ăllėgŏ'ric(al)** *adjs.* **ăllėgŏ'rically** *adv.*

ăll'ėgorize *v.* Treat as an allegory, make allegories.

allėgrĕtt'ō *adv.* (mus.) Somewhat briskly. ~ *n.* Passage marked thus. [It.]

allegr'ō (-lā-) *adj., adv.* & *n.* (mus.) Lively, gay (movement) in brisk time.

ăll'ēle, ăll'ėlomŏrph (*or* -lēl'-) *ns.* Gene which occupies the same relative position on homologous chromosomes.

ăllėlu'ia (-lōōya) n. Song of praise to God. [Heb., = 'praise ye Jehovah']

allemande (ăl'mahnd) *n.* Name of several German dances; country-dance figure; (mus.) movement in 4/4 time at the beginning of a suite or after the prelude. [Fr., = 'German (dance)']

All'enby (ă-), Edmund Henry Hynman, Viscount (1861–1936). Commanded the British forces in Egypt and Palestine, 1917–18; High Commissioner for Egypt and Sudan, 1919–25.

ăll'ergy *n.* (med.) Constitutional condition characterized by acute reaction of body tissues to the intake of foreign proteins, resulting in the release of histamine (manifested in, e.g., asthma, hay fever, urticaria). **allĕr'gic** *adj.* Of, possessing, allergy; susceptible *to* (also fig.).

allēv'iāte *v.t.* Mitigate, relieve. **allēviā'tion** *n.* **allēv'iative, allēv'iatory** *adjs.*

ăll'ey *n.* Narrow street; walk, passage; (U.S.) back street; enclosure for skittles etc.; *blind ~*, one closed at one end; (fig.) way that leads nowhere.

Alleyn (alān'), Edward (1566–1626). English actor; built with Henslowe the Fortune Theatre in Cripplegate, London; built and endowed Dulwich College. **Alleyn'ian** *n.* Member of Dulwich College.

allī'ance *n.* Union by marriage; relationship; confederation (esp. between States); *Holy A~*, that formed between Russia and other European States in 1815; *Triple A~*, esp. that formed between Germany, Austria, and Italy in 1882.

ăll'igātor *n.* Crocodilian (genera *Alligator* and *Cayman*) of New World and China, having certain teeth in lower jaw which fit into pits, not into notches as in crocodiles proper; *~-pear*, AVOCADO. [Span. *el lagarto*, f. L *lacerta* lizard]

allīterā'tion *n.* Commencement of two or more words in close connexion with the same letter or sound, esp. as a device in verse. **allĭt'erāte** *v.i.* (Contain words that) begin with the same sound. **allĭt'erative** *adj.* **allĭt'eratively** *adv.*

ăll'ocāte *v.t.* Assign (*to*); locate. **ăllocā'tion** *n.* Apportionment.

allōd'ium *n.* (hist.) Estate held absolutely, without acknowledgement to an overlord. **allōd'ial** *adj.* **allōd'ially** *adv.*

allŏp'athy *n.* Traditional medical practice which aims at curing disease by remedies having opposite effect to that caused by the disease (opp. to HOMOEOPATHY). **ăllopăth'ic** *adj.* **ăllopăth'ically** *adv.* **allŏp'athist** *n.*

allŏt' *v.t.* Assign (*to*), distribute by lot.

allŏt'ment *n.* Apportioning; lot in life; share allotted to one; portion of land let out for cultivation, esp. small plot where occupier produces vegetables and fruit crops for home consumption.

ăll'otrōpe *n.* One form of an element, differing from another or others in crystal form, or in chemical properties, or in molecular complexity, or in all three (as oxygen and ozone; yellow and red phosphorus; graphite and diamond). **ăllotrŏp'ic** *adj.* **ăll'otropy** (*or* -lŏt'-) *n.* Existence of elements in allotropic form.

allow' *v.* Admit; (U.S.) form the opinion (*that*); permit; indulge oneself in; admit *of*; give (limited periodical sum); add, deduct, in consideration of something; *~ for*, take into consideration. **allow'able** *adj.*

allow'ance *n.* Permission; tolerance; limited portion, esp. yearly income; addition to salary to cover special expenses, as *entertainment ~*, *foreign service ~*; *family ~*, allowance paid to employees or State-insured persons in proportion to size of their families; deduction, discount; *make ~ for*, allow for. ~ *v.t.* Make allowance to (person).

allow'ėdly *adv.* Admittedly.

ăll'oy (*or* aloi') *n.* 1. A metallic substance consisting of two or more metallic elements and usu. having more useful properties than its constituents (e.g. brass is an alloy of copper and zinc, type-metal an alloy of lead and tin and antimony). 2. (archaic) A base metal mixed esp. with gold or silver. **alloy'** *v.t.* 1. Form a mixture of two or more metals. 2. Debase.

all'spīce (awl-) *n.* Pimento, supposed to combine flavour of cinnamon, nutmeg, and cloves.

All'ston (awl-), Washington (1779–1843). American Romantic painter.

allude' (-ōōd, -ūd) *v.i.* Refer indirectly or covertly (*to*).

allu'sion (-ōōzhn, -ūzhn) *n.* Indirect, covert, or implied reference.

allus'ive (-ōō-, -ū-) *adj.* Containing an allusion, full of allusions. **allus'ively** *adv.* **allus'ivenėss** *n.*

allūre' *v.t.* Tempt, entice; fascinate, charm. ~ *n.* Personal charm. **allūre'ment** *n.*

allūv'ion (*or* -ōō-) *n.* Wash of sea against shore or of river against banks; flood, matter deposited by flood; (law) formation of new land by action of water.

allūv'ium (*or* -ōō-) *n.* (pl. *-via, -viums*). Deposit of water-borne clay, sand, and gravel laid down on the flood plain of a river. **allūv'ial** *adj.*; *~ cone, fan*, deposit left by swift stream entering a valley or plain. **allūv'ially** *adv.*

allȳ'[1] *v.t.* Combine, unite, for special object; *allied to*, connected with. **allȳ'** (*or* ăl'ī) *n.* Person, State, etc., allied with another.

ăll'ȳ[2] *n.* Choice playing-marble of marble, alabaster, or glass.

Al'ma (ă-). River in the Crimea, scene of first battle in the Crimean War, 1854, in which the French and British defeated the Russians.

Al'măck (awl-), William (d. 1781). Founder of *~'s Assembly Rooms* in St. James's, London, celebrated in the 18th and early 19th centuries as the scene of social functions, and of a gaming-club.

Al'magĕst (ăl-). Arabic version of Ptolemy's astronomical treatise; the name was applied in the Middle Ages to other celebrated textbooks of astrology and alchemy. [Arab. *al* the, Gk *megistē* (*suntaxis*) great (system)]

Al'ma Māt'er (ăl-). Used of one's university or school, 'fostering mother'. [L]

Alma-Tăd'ėma (ăl-), Sir Lawrence (1836–1912). Painter of classical subjects; born in Holland, naturalized as an Englishman.

al'manac(k) (awl-) *n.* Annual calendar of months and days with astronomical and other data.

almighty (awlmīt'ĭ) *adj.* All-powerful; *The A~*, God.

alm'ond (ahm-) *n.* Kernel of stone-fruit of two varieties of *Prunus amygdalus* (*sweet, bitter ~*), allied to plum and peach; the tree; anything almond-shaped.

ăl'moner (*or* ahm'ner) *n.* 1. Official distributor of alms; *Hereditary Grand A~, Lord High A~*, officials in royal household of Gt Britain. 2. Social worker, usu. woman, at hospital or clinic, with duty of helping patients to carry out doctor's advice esp. after discharge from hospital (formerly also responsible for collecting fees).

al'mōst (awl-) *adv.* Very nearly.

alms (ahmz) *n.* Charitable relief of the poor; donation; *~-house*, one founded by charity for reception of poor, usu. old, people; *alms'man*, one supported by alms.

ăl'oe (-ō) *n.* Genus of liliaceous plants with erect spikes of flowers, rosettes of fleshy leaves (often spiny), and bitter juice; (pl.) purgative drug procured from juice of aloes; *American ~*, agave. **ăloĕt'ic** *adj.* (med.) Containing aloes.

alŏft' *adv.* & *pred. adj.* High up; upward; esp. (*go aloft*) in(to) the upper parts of a ship's rigging.

alōne' *pred. adj.* Solitary; standing by oneself; *leave, let, ~* abstain from interfering with; *~ adv.* Only, exclusively.

alŏng' *prep.* & *adv.* From end to end of, through any part of the length of; in company or conjunction *with*; *all ~*, all the time; *get ~*, get on *with*, progress; *alongside*, close to side of ship; *alongside of*, side by side with.

alōōf' *adv.* & *pred. adj.* Away, apart.

ălōpē'cĭa *n.* (med.) Baldness; (pop. used for) *~ areata*, infection of scalp causing temporary bald patches. [Gk *alōpekia* fox-mange f. *alōpēx* fox]

aloud' *adv.* Loudly; not silently or in a whisper.

ălp *n.* Mountain-peak; green pasture-land on (Swiss) mountain-side; *the A~s*, mountain-range extending from Ligurian Sea and Rhône valley through Switzerland to the western Hungarian plain.

ălpăc'a *n.* S. Amer. domesticated camel-like hoofed mammal, bred in Andes for its long woolly hair; its fleece; fabric of alpaca hair mixed with cotton; various silk, cotton or rayon fabrics more or less resembling this. [Arab. *al* the, Peruvian name *paco*]

ăl'pėnstŏck *n.* Staff with iron point used in mountain climbing.

ăl'pha *n.* The Greek letter A (*A*, *α*); (astron.) chief star of constellation; *~ and omega*, first and last letters of Greek alphabet; hence, beginning and end (see Rev. i. 8); *~ plus*, superlatively good; *~ rays*, the first of three types of radiation emitted by radio-active substances, consisting of positively charged particles.

ăl'phabėt *n.* Set of letters (in customary order) used in a language; first rudiments. **ălphabĕt'ĭcal** *adj.* Of the alphabet; esp. in *~ order*. **ălphabĕt'ĭcally** *adv.* [Gk *alpha*, *beta*, first two letters of alphabet]

ăl'pīne *adj.* Of the Alps or other lofty mountains; *~ climate*, (geog.) that of regions above coniferous forests and below line of permanent snow; *~ plants*, plants native to these regions, or (loosely) to mountain districts, or suited to similar conditions. **ăl'pĭnĭst** *n.* Alpine climber.

already (awlrĕd'ĭ) *adv.* Beforehand; by this time, thus early.

a.l.s. *abbrev.* Autograph letter signed.

Alsace (ăl'săs *or* -săs'). French province W. of the Rhine; inhabited by mixed German and Latin stocks; annexed with part of Lorraine (the annexed territory was known as Alsace-Lorraine) by Germany after the Franco-Prussian war of 1870; restored to France by the war of 1914–18.

Alsā'tia (ă-, -sha). Old name of Alsace; cant name of precinct of Whitefriars, London, which, until its privileges (orig. those enjoyed by the Carmelites) were abolished in 1697, was a sanctuary for debtors and law-breakers. **Alsā'tian** *adj.* & *n.* (Native) of Alsace; *~ (wolf-hound)*, the German sheep-dog.

al'sō (awl-) *adv.* In addition, besides *~ ran*, (person, horse, etc.) not in first three.

ălt *n.* (mus.) High note; *in ~*, in the octave (beginning with G) above the treble stave.

al'tar (awl-) *n.* Flat-topped block for offerings to deity; Communion table; *lead to the ~*, marry; *~-cloth*, linen cloth used at Communion or Mass; silk frontal and super-frontal; *~-piece*, painting or sculpture above back of altar.

ALTARS

1. Baldachin. 2. Riddel post. 3. Riddel. 4. Reredos or retable. 5. Gradine. 6. Predella. 7. Frontal

al'ter (awl-) *v.* Change in character, position, etc.; *altered rock*, (geol.) rock which has been metamorphosed by pressure or heat. **alterā'tion** *n.*

al'terative (awl-) *adj.* Tending to alter. *~ n.* Treatment, medicine, that alters processes of nutrition.

al'tercāte (ăl- *or* awl-) *v.i.* Dispute hotly, wrangle. **altercā'tion** *n.*

ăl'ter ĕg'ō *n.* One's other self, intimate friend. [L]

altẽrn'ate (awl-) *adj.* (Of things of two kinds) coming each after one of the other kind; placed on alternate sides (of line, stem, etc.). **altẽrn'ately** *adv.* **al'ternāte** (awl-) v. Arrange, perform, alternately; interchange (one thing) alternately *with*, *by* another; succeed each other by turns; consist of alternate things; *alternating current* (abbrev. A.C. or a.c.), electric current whose direction is regularly reversed; *alternating generations*, (biol.) reproductive cycles in which the offspring differ in structure and habits from their parents but resemble their grandparents; (also, erron.) cycles in which sexual reproduction is preceded and followed by asexual.

altẽrn'atĭve (awl-) *adj.* (Of two things) mutually exclusive. *~ n.* Permission to choose between two things; either of two possible courses; one of more than two possibilities. **altẽrn'atĭvely** (-vl-) *adv.*

al'ternātor (awl-) *n.* Dynamo producing alternating current (ill. DYNAMO).

although (awldhō') *conj.* Though.

ăltĭm'ėter (*or* ăl'timēter) *n.* Aneroid barometer indicating altitude reached, as in aviation.

ăl'tĭtūde *n.* 1. Height. 2. (geom.) Length of perpendicular from vertex to base. 3. (geog.) Height above mean sea-level. 4. (astron., of heavenly body) Angular distance above horizon. 5. High place, (fig.) eminence.

ăl'tō *n.* (pl. *-s*). Highest male voice, produced by falsetto (ill. VOICE); female voice of similar range, contralto; singer with alto voice; musical part for this; *~ clef*, C clef so placed as to indicate that middle C stands on the central line of the stave (ill. CLEF).

ăltocūm'ūlus *n.* (meteor.) Type of cloud, of medium height, in form of thin patches often very close together or almost joined. (ill. CLOUD).

altogĕth'er (awl-, -dh-) *adv.* Totally; on the whole; (*n.*) *in the ~*, completely naked.

ăl'to-rėlie'vo (-lē-) *n.* (Sculpture in) high relief. [It. *alto-rilievo*]

ăltostrāt'us *n.* (meteor.) Continuous veil of cloud, thin or thick, of medium height (ill. CLOUD).

ăl'truism (-rōō-) *n.* Regard for others as a principle of action. **ăltruis'tic** *adj.* **ăltruist'ically** *adv.*

ăl'um *n.* One of series of double sulphates, esp. that of potassium and aluminium; used industrially, esp. in paper-making and leather tanning.

alūm'ina *n.* Aluminium oxide (Al_2O_3), which occurs as ruby, sapphire, etc., and as bauxite from which aluminium is obtained. **alūm'ināte** *n.* A compound of alumina with one of the stronger bases.

ălūmin'ium (U.S. **ălūm'inum**), *n.* A very light silvery white metallic element (symbol Al, at. no. 13, at. wt 26·9815), not found native but very widely distributed in the form of compounds; the metal is obtained by electrolysis and is very widely used esp. in alloys for construction of aircraft etc.

ălūm'inous *adj.* Of the nature of alum or alumina; containing aluminium.

alūm'nus *n.* (pl. *-nī*). (Former) pupil of a school or university. [L, = 'foster-child']

Al'va, Alba (ă-), Fernando Alvarez de Toledo, Duke of (1508–82). Spanish general, Stadholder of the Netherlands, 1567–73.

ălvē'olar *adj.* Of, pertaining to a tooth-socket; ~ *consonant*, one formed with point of tongue against the alveolus behind the upper teeth.

ăl'vėolate (-*a*t) *adj.* Honeycombed, pitted with small cavities.

alvē'olus *n.* (pl. *-lī*). Small cavity, socket of a tooth; structure in roof of mouth behind upper teeth; terminal air-sac of lung in which exchange of gases between lung and blood takes place; cell of honeycomb; conical chamber of belemnite.

always (awl'wāz) *adv.* At all times, on all occasions.

ăm, 1st pers. sing. pres. of BE.

a.m. *abbrev. Anno mundi* (= in the year of the world); *ante meridiem* (= before noon).

A.M. *abbrev.* Air Ministry; Albert Medal; Master of Arts.

Am'adis of Gaul (ăm-). Hero of a Spanish (or Portuguese) 15th-c. romance of chivalry.

amain' adv. (archaic) Vehemently; in all haste.

Amăl'ėkīte (*a*-), *adj.* & *n.* (Member) of a nomadic people often mentioned in the O.T., proverbial for treachery.

amăl'gam *n.* An alloy of a metal or metals, with mercury, freq. plastic and used, e.g., in dentistry.

amăl'gamāte *v.* Combine, unite (esp. of business firms); mix; (of metals) alloy with mercury. **amălgamā'tion** *n.*

amănūĕn'sis *n.* (pl. *-ses*). One who writes from dictation, or copies; literary assistant.

ăm'arănth *n.* Imaginary unfading flower; genus of plants including love-lies-bleeding; purple colour. **ămarăn'thine** *adj.* (freq. poet.) Unfading; purple.

ămarȳll'is *n.* Genus of autumn-flowering bulbous plants comprising only one species, *A. belladonna* from Cape of Good Hope, also called belladonna lily. [Gk *Amarullis* name of a country girl in Theocritus and Virgil]

amăss' *v.t.* Heap together; accumulate.

ămateur' (-tėr, -tūr) n. One who is fond *of*; one who practises a thing, esp. an art or game, as a pastime; freq. opp. to *professional.* **ămateur'ish** *adj.* Like an amateur; imperfect in execution, unskilful. **ămateur'ishly** *adv.* **ămateur'ishnėss, ămateur'ism** *ns.*

Amati (*a*mah'tĭ). Family of violin-makers of Cremona, flourishing *c* 1550–*c* 1700; Nicola ~ (1596–1684) taught Antonio Stradivari.

ăm'ative *adj.* Disposed to loving. **ăm'ativenėss** *n.*

ăm'atŏl *n.* A high explosive, mixture of ammonium nitrate and trinitrotoluene. [*am*(monia) + (trinitro)*tol*(uol)]

ăm'atory *adj.* Pertaining to a lover or sexual love.

amāze' *v.t.* Overwhelm with wonder. ~ *n.* (poet.) Amazement. **amāz'ėdly, amāz'ingly** *advs.* **amāze'ment** (-zm-) *n.*

Am'azon (ă-). 1. One of a fabulous race of female warriors alleged by Herodotus to exist in Scythia; hence, strong or athletic woman. 2. The great river of S. America, flowing into the southern Atlantic on N. coast of Brazil; it bore various other names after its discovery in 1500, and was called the Amazon because of a legend that a tribe of women warriors lived somewhere on its banks. **Amazō'nian** *adj.*

ămbăss'ador *n.* Minister sent by one sovereign or State on mission to another; minister permanently representing sovereign or State at foreign court or government; official messenger. **ămbăssador'ial** *adj.* **ămbăss'adrėss** *n.* Female ambassador; ambassador's wife.

ăm'ber *n.* Yellow translucent fossil resin found chiefly on S. shore of Baltic and valued as ornament. [Fr. *ambre*, f. Arab. *'anbar* ambergris, to which the name originally belonged]

ăm'bergris (-ēs) *n.* Wax-like grey or blackish substance found floating in tropical seas and in intestines of sperm-whale, odoriferous and used in perfumery. [Fr. *ambre gris* grey amber]

ăm'bidĕx'ter *adj.* & *n.* (Person) able to use left hand as readily as right; double-dealing. **ămbidĕxtĕ'rity** *n.* **ămbidĕx'trous** *adj.* Ambidexter. **ămbidĕx'trously** *adv.* **ămbidĕx'trousnėss** *n.*

ăm'biėnt *adj.* Surrounding, circumfused. **ăm'biėnce** *n.*

ămbig'ūous *adj.* Obscure; of double meaning; of doubtful classification; of uncertain issue. **ămbig'ūously** *adv.* **ămbig'ūousnėss** *n.* **ămbigū'ity** *n.* Double meaning; expression capable of more than one meaning.

ăm'bit *n.* Precincts; bounds; compass, extent.

ămbi'tion *n.* Ardent desire for distinction; aspiration *to* (be or do); object of such desire.

ămbi'tious (-sh*u*s) *adj.* Full of or showing ambition; strongly desirous. **ămbi'tiously** *adv.* **ămbi'tiousnėss** *n.* [L. *ambitio* canvassing for votes, f. *ambire* go round]

ămbiv'alent *adj.* Having either or both of two contrary values or qualities; entertaining contradictory emotions (as love and hatred) towards the same person or thing.

ăm'ble *v.i.* (Of horse etc.) move by lifting two feet on one side together; ride, move, at an easy pace. ~ *n.* Pace of an ambling horse; easy pace.

ămblyŏp'ia *n.* Dimness of vision without discernible change in the eye. **ămblyŏp'ic** *adj.* **ămblyŏp'ically** *adv.*

ăm'bō *n.* (pl. *-bōs, -bō'nēs*) Pulpit in early Christian churches (ill. BASILICA).

Amboin'a, Amboyn'a (ă-). Town and island of the Moluccas; ~*-wood*, a very hard ornamental wood (*Pterocarpus indicus*) exported from the Moluccas.

Ambrōse (ă-, -z), St. (*c* 340–97). Bishop of Milan; a Father of the Church; developed the use of music in the church, introducing the *Ambrōs'ian chant.*

ămbrōs'ia (-zi*a*, -zhy*a*) *n.* (myth.) Food of the gods; anything delightful to taste or smell; bee-bread. **ămbrōs'ial** *adj.* **ămbrōs'ially** *adv.* [L, f. Gk, f. *ambrotos* immortal].

ăm'bry *n.* Var. of AUMBRY.

ăm'būlance *n.* Conveyance for sick or wounded persons; moving hospital following army.

ăm'būlatory *adj.* Pertaining to, adapted for, walking, movable; not permanent. ~ *n.* Place for walking; arcade, cloister; esp., aisle round apse at east end of church (ill. CHURCH).

ambury. Var. of ANBURY.

ămbuscāde' *n.* Ambush. ~ *v.* Lie, conceal, in ambush.

ăm'bush (-ōō-) *n.* Concealment of troops, troops concealed, in a wood, etc.; lying in wait. ~ *v.* Lie in wait (for); conceal (troops, only in past part.).

A.M.D.G. *abbrev. Ad majorem Dei gloriam* (L, = 'to the greater glory of God').

âme damnée (ahm dahn'ā). Devoted adherent, tool. [Fr., = 'damned soul']

ameer′, amir′ (-ēr) *n.* Title of various Mohammedan rulers in Sind and Afghanistan. [Arab. *amir* commander]

amēl′iorāte *v.* (Cause to) become better. **amēliorā′tion** *n.* **amēl′iorative** *adj.* **amēl′ioratively** *adv.*

amĕn′[1] (ā- *or* ah-) *int.* So be it (int. used at end of prayer etc.). [Heb. *amen* certainty, certainly (*aman* strength)]

Amen[2]: see AMMON.

amēn′able *adj.* Responsible; liable *to*; capable of being tested by (*to*); responsive, tractable. **amēn′ableness, amēnabil′ity** *ns.* **amēn′ably** *adv.*

amĕnd′ *v.* Abandon evil ways; correct an error in (document), make professed improvements in (measure before Parliament, proposal, etc.); make better. **amĕnd′ment** *n.*

amende honorable (ămahnd ŏnŏrah′bl). Public apology and reparation. [Fr.]

amĕnds′ (-dz) *n.* Reparation, restitution, compensation.

Amĕnhŏt′ĕp or **Amĕnōph′ĭs** (ah-). Name of 4 pharaohs of the 18th dynasty in Egypt; ~ *IV*: see AKHNATON.

amĕn′ity *n.* Quality of being pleasant, agreeable; (characteristic of) situation, climate, disposition, etc., that is agreeable or pleasant (often pl.).

āmėnorrhoe′a (-rē*a*) *n.* (physiol.) Absence of menstruation.

amĕn′tum *n.* (pl. *-ta*). Catkin (ill. FLOWER). **ămĕnta′ceous** (-sh*us*), **ămentĭf′erous** *adjs.*

amĕrce′ *v.t.* Fine; punish. **amĕr′ciable** *adj.* **amĕrce′ment** (-sm-), **amĕr′ciament** *ns.*

Amĕ′rica. The continent of the New World or western hemisphere, consisting of two great land-masses, *North*~ and *South*~, joined by the narrow isthmus of *Central* ~; N. America comprises Canada, the United States, and Mexico; Central and S. America are divided into a number of independent States. N. America was prob. visited by Norse seamen in 8th or 9th c., but for the modern world the continent was discovered by Christopher Columbus, who reached the W. Indies in 1492 and the S. American mainland in 1498. **Amĕ′rican** *adj.* & *n.* Of America; (person) born in or inhabiting the continent of America; (citizen) of the United States of America; ~ *Civil War* (1861–5), war between 11 Southern (Confederate) States and the rest of the Union; the Confederate States asserted their right to leave the Union, disagreeing esp. with the Northern (Federal) States' policy of freeing the Negro slaves imported from Africa to work in the plantations; the Northern States were victorious, and slavery was abolished throughout the U.S.; ~ *cloth* (not U.S.) flexible cotton cloth treated with cellulose nitrates to make it resemble shiny leather; (*North*-) ~ *Indian*, one of the aboriginal inhabitants of N. America, chiefly nomadic tribes of hunters and warriors with red skins and black smooth hair; ~ *organ*, (not U.S.) instrument resembling harmonium but sucking wind inward through pipes instead of expelling it; ~ *War of Independence* (1775–83), also called the ~ *Revolution*, the revolt of the English colonies in N. America which subsequently formed the UNITED STATES. [named after *Amerigo* VESPUCCI]

Amĕ′ricanism *n.* 1. Word or phrase peculiar to or borrowed from U.S. 2. Attachment to, sympathy with, U.S.

America's Cup. A yacht-racing trophy orig. presented by the R.Y.S. for a race round the Isle of Wight (1851), and won by the American schooner *America*; offered as a challenge trophy for a race between English and American yachts, but in spite of many attempts not subsequently regained by an English yacht.

ămericium (-ĭsĭ-, -ĭshĭ-) *n.* (chem.) A metallic radio-active transuranic element not occurring in nature but made artificially; symbol Am, at. no. 95, principal isotope 241. [f. *America* (first made at Berkeley, California)]

Amerigo Vespucci: see VESPUCCI.

ăm′ĕthyst *n.* Purple or violet precious stone, a variety of quartz coloured by manganese. **ămėthy̆s′tine** *adj.* [Gk *amethustos* not drunken (*methu* wine), because the stone was supposed to have the power of preventing intoxication]

Amhă′ric (ă-) *adj.* & *n.* The official and court language of Ethiopia, a Semitic language related to ancient Ethiopic.

ām′iable *adj.* Feeling and inspiring friendship; lovable. **āmiabil′ity** *n.* **ām′iably** *adv.*

ăm′icable *adj.* Friendly. **ămicabil′ity** *n.* **ăm′icably** *adv.*

ăm′ice[1] *n.* Square of white linen worn by celebrant priest about the the neck and shoulders (formerly on head) (ill. VESTMENT).

ăm′ice[2] *n.* Cap, hood, cape, of religious orders; badge worn by French canons on left arm.

A.M.I.C.E. *abbrev.* Associate Member of the Institution of Civil Engineers.

amī′cus cūr′iae. Disinterested adviser. [L, = 'friend of the court']

amid′, amidst′ *prep.* In the middle of; in the course of.

ām′ide *n.* Any of a class of organic compounds containing the group —CO·N< in their structures.

amid′ships *adv.* In the middle of ship.

A.M.I.E.E. *abbrev.* Associate Member of the Institution of Electrical Engineers.

A.M.I.Mech.E. *abbrev.* Associate Member of the Institution of Mechanical Engineers.

Amiens (ămĭăṅ). Town of NE. France; *Battle of* ~ (1918), a successful and important combined British and French offensive of the war of 1914–18.

ām′ine *n.* (chem.) A compound derived from ammonia by replacing one or more of the hydrogen atoms by certain aliphatic or aromatic radicals.

amino- *prefix.* (chem.) Pertaining to, or containing the group NH_2, as ~*-acid.*

amiss′ *adv.* & *pred. adj.* Out of order; wrong(ly); untoward(ly).

ămitōs′is *n.* (pl. *-sēs*). Direct division of a nucleus or cell without mitosis.

ăm′ity *n.* Friendship, friendly relations.

ămm′ėter *n.* Instrument for measuring electric currents. [AMPERE + METER]

Amm′on, Am′ĕn (ă-). The supreme god of the Egyptians in the Theban religion; his worship spread to Greece, where he was identified with Zeus, and to Rome, where he was known as Jupiter Ammon.

ammōn′ia *n.* Colourless gas (NH_3) with pungent smell, very soluble in water, giving alkaline solution; aqueous solution of this gas. [f. Jupiter AMMON, near whose temple sal ammoniac is said to have been prepared]

ammōn′iăc *adj.* Of the nature of ammonia; *sal* ~, ammonium chloride (NH_4Cl), a hard white crystalline salt used in pharmacy, electric batteries, etc. **ămmonī′acal** *adj.* Of or resembling ammonia.

ammōn′iātėd *adj.* Combined with ammonia.

ămm′onīte[1] *n.* Member of an extinct group of cephalopods with chambered shell coiled in a flat spiral, freq. found fossilized in some Mesozoic rocks [L *cornu Ammonis* horn of AMMON]

AMMONITE

Amm′onīte[2] (ă-) *adj.* & *n.* (Member) of a tribe of ancient Transjordania, of Hebrew stock, freq. mentioned in the O.T.

ammōn′ium *n.* (chem.) A

radical (NH_4), which has not been isolated, whose compounds resemble those of the alkali metals.

ămmūnĭ'tion *n.* Military stores (now only of projectiles with their necessary propellants, detonators, fuses, etc.).

ămnēs'ĭa (-z-) *n.* Loss of memory.

ăm'nėsty *n.* Pardon granted by sovereign or State for an offence, esp. one of a political character. ~ *v.t.* Give amnesty to.

ăm'nĭŏn *n.* (physiol.) Membrane lining the cavity which encloses the foetus (ill. EMBRYO). **ămnĭŏt'ic** *adj.* ~ *fluid*, fluid which fills this cavity (the ~ *sac*).

amoeb'a (amēb'*a*) *n.* Primitive microscopic single-celled animalcule perpetually changing shape by protruding portions of its body (pseudopods) and reproducing by fission. **amoeb'ic, amoeb'oid** *adjs.* (ill. PROTOZOA).

amok: see AMUCK.

among', amongst' (-mŭ-) *prep.* In the assemblage or number of; surrounded by, within the limits of; by joint action of; reciprocally.

Amŏntilla'do (-ahdō). One of the principal types of dry sherry, with nutty flavour. [Span., = 'made like (the wine of) *Montilla*' (place in Cordova)]

āmŏ'ral *adj.* Non-moral; outside the sphere of morals.

Am'orīte (ă-) *adj.* & *n.* (Member) of an ancient race inhabiting Canaan before the Israelites.

ăm'orous *adj.* Inclined to love; in love; of or pertaining to love; in a state of sexual excitement. **ăm'orously** *adv.* **ăm'orousnėss** *n.*

amŏr̄ph'ous *adj.* Shapeless; (chem., min.) not crystalline. **amŏr̄ph'ĭsm** *n.* **amŏr̄ph'ously** *adv.* **amŏr̄ph'ousnėss** *n.*

amŏr̄t'īze *v.t.* Alienate in mortmain; extinguish (debt, usu. by sinking-fund). **amŏr̄tīzā'tion** *n.*

Am'os (ā-). Jewish prophet (*c* 760 B.C.); the O.T. book containing his prophecies.

amount' *v.i.* Be equivalent *to*; reach the total (of). ~ *n.* Total, quantity.

amour' (-oor). Love affair, intrigue.

amour-prŏpre (ăm'oor-prŏpr) *n.* Self-esteem. [Fr.]

ămp *n.* = AMPERE.

ămpėlŏp'sĭs *n.* (pl. *-sēs*). Climbing plant of vine family; (erron.) virginia creeper. [Gk, = 'looking like a vine' (*ampelos* vine, *opsis* appearance)]

ămpēr̄'age *n.* Strength of current of electricity measured in amperes.

Ampère (ahṅp'ār̄), André-Marie (1775–1836). French physicist and mathematician; established the relation between magnetism and electricity.

ampere (ăm'pēr̄) *n.* Unit of amount or flow in an electric current, being that produced by one volt acting through a resistance of one ohm. [named after A.-M. AMPÈRE]

ăm'persănd *n.* The sign & (*and*). [f. phrase 'and *per se* (= by itself) and']

ămphĕt'amīne *n.* Powerful synthetic drug which stimulates the heart and respiration, constricts blood-vessels, and induces sleeplessness.

amphi- *prefix.* Both, of both kinds, on both sides, around.

ămphĭb'ĭan *adj.* & *n.* 1. Living both on land and in water; (animal) of the *Amphibia*, a class of vertebrates intermediate between reptiles and fishes and comprising *Anura* (frogs and toads), *Urodela* (newts and salamanders), and *Apoda* (coecilians. 2. (Aeroplane, tank, etc.) able to operate both on land and water. [Gk *amphibios* leading a double life]

ămphĭb'ĭous *adj.* Living both on land and in water, connected with both; ~ *operation*, military operation in which both land and sea forces take part.

ămphĭŏx'us *n.* = LANCELET.

ămphĭp'rostȳle *adj.* (archit.) With portico at both ends (ill. TEMPLE).

ămphĭsbaen'a *n.* 1. Fabulous serpent with head at each end. 2. (*A*~, zool.) Genus of worm-like lizards. [Gk *amphis* both ways, *baino* go]

ăm'phĭtheatre (-ĭater) *n.* Oval or circular building or arena with seats rising in tiers round a central open space; semicircular gallery in theatre; (fig.) scene of a contest.

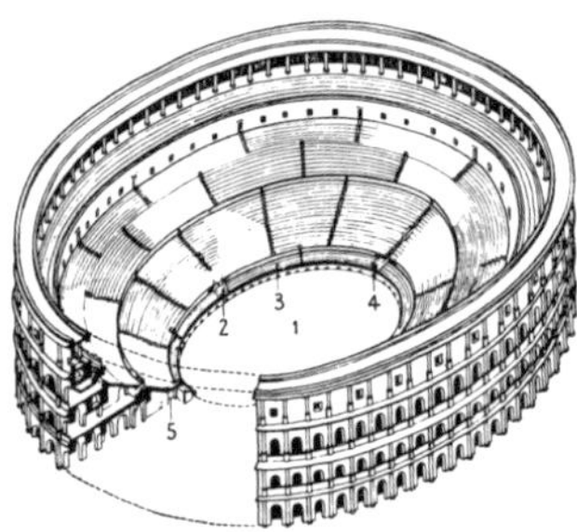

ROMAN AMPHITHEATRE

1. Arena. 2. Emperor's or Consul's box. 3. Podium. 4. Animals' entrance. 5. Animals' dens

Amphĭtrīt'ė (ă-). (Gk myth.) A sea-goddess, the wife of Poseidon.

Amphĭt'rȳon (ă-). (Gk myth.) Husband of Alcmene; while he was absent Zeus impersonated him and became the father of Hercules by Alcmene. In Molière's comedy 'Amphitryon' (iii. 5) a servant, perplexed by the impersonation, exclaims 'Le véritable Amphitryon est l'Amphitryon où l'on dîne'; hence, ~, a generous host or a gastronome.

ăm'phora *n.* (pl. *-rae*). Greek or Roman two-handled vase (ill. VASE).

ămphōtĕ'rĭc *adj.* (chem.) Capable of reacting as either acid or base.

ăm'ple *adj.* Spacious, extensive; abundant; quite enough. **ăm'ply** *adv.*

ăm'plĭfȳ *v.* Enlarge; increase strength of (electric currents, signals, etc.); add details. **ămplĭfĭcā'tion** *n.* **ăm'plĭfīer** *n.* (esp.) Appliance for increasing strength of signals.

ăm'plĭtūde *n.* 1. Breadth; abundance; wide range. 2. (astron.) Distance from due east or west at which celestial body rises or sets. 3. (physics) Maximum displacement from mean position of vibrating body etc. (ill. VIBRATION).

ăm'poule (-ōōl), **ăm'pūle** *n.* (med.) Small sealed glass vessel used for storing sterilized materials prepared for injection.

ămpull'a (-ŏŏl*a*) *n.* (pl. *-ae*). Roman globular two-handled flask; medieval pilgrim's bottle; vessel for holding chrism or oil used in ceremonial anointing.

ăm'pūtāte *v.t.* Cut off (esp. part of animal body). **ămpūtā'tion** *n.*

A.M.S. *abbrev.* Army Medical Staff (*or* Service).

A.M.S.E. *abbrev.* Associate Member of the Society of Engineers.

Am'sterdăm' (ă-). Capital of the Netherlands.

amuck', amok' *adv.* *Run* ~, run about in frenzied thirst for blood; (also fig.) get out of control. [Malay *amog* rushing in frenzy]

ăm'ūlėt *n.* Thing worn as charm against evil.

Am'undsen (ăm'ŏŏ-), Roald (1872–1928). Norwegian explorer; explored North-west Passage 1903–6; reached S. Pole 1911; perished in attempt to rescue the Italian airship expedition to N. Pole under General Nobile.

amūse' (-z) *v.t.* Divert from serious business; tickle the fancy of; entertain. **amūs'ĭng** *adj.* **amūs'ĭngly** *adv.* **amūse'ment** (-zm-) *n.* Pleasant diversion; excitement of risible faculty; pastime.

ăm'ȳl *n.* (chem.) A radical (C_5H_{11}) occurring in the structure of various isomeric alcohols (~ *alcohols*), some of which are constituents of fusel oil; ~ *acetate*, colourless volatile liquid derived from amyl alcohol and acetic acid, with odour of jargonelle pears, used in making artificial fruit essences and as solvent of cellulose acetate. **ămȳl'ĭc** *adj.* [Gk *amulon* fine meal]

ămȳlā'ceous (-sh*us*) *adj.* Of starch, starchy.

ăm'ȳloid *adj.* & *n.* Starchy (food).

an[1] *adj.*: see A.

ăn[2] *conj.* (archaic) If.

ăna- (**an-** before vowel) *prefix.* Up, back, again, anew.

ān'a *n.* (pl. *-s*). Collection of person's sayings; anecdotes, literary gossip, about a person.

-āna *suffix.* Appended to a name with the meaning: sayings of, anecdotes about, publications bearing on, persons or places.

Anabăp'tist (ă-) *n.* & *adj.* (Member) of a sect which arose in Germany in 1521, was heavily persecuted by both Catholics and Protestants, and suppressed; lit. = 'one who baptizes over again' because the Anabaptists held that infant baptism was ineffectual and some of them rebaptized adults; also (opprobriously) = BAPTIST. **ănabăp'tism** *n.*

ănăb'olism *n.* Synthesis by living things of complex molecules from simpler ones.

anăch'ronism (-kr-) *n.* Error in computing time; event or thing which would be incongruous in the period in which it is supposed to have happened or existed. **anăchronis'tic** *adj.*

ănacolūth'on *n.* (pl. *-tha*). Sentence, words, lacking grammatical sequence.

ănacŏn'da *n.* Tropical S. Amer. aquatic and arboreal boa (*Eunectes murinus*).

Anăc'rèon (*a-*) (*c* 563–478 B.C.). Greek lyric poet, of whose poems very few genuine fragments survive. **anăcrèon'tic** *adj.* & *n.* (Poem) in the manner or metre of Anacreon's lyrics; convivial and amatory.

ănacrus'is (-ōō-) *n.* (pl. *-sēs*). (pros.) Unstressed syllable at beginning of verse; (mus.) unstressed note(s) before the first bar-line. [Gk *anakrouō* strike up]

Anadyŏm'ĕnē. (ă-) Epithet of Venus (Aphrodite) as sprung from the sea-foam. [Gk, = 'rising']

anaem'ia *n.* Lack of blood; deficiency of red blood-corpuscles or their haemoglobin; unhealthy paleness. **anaem'ic** *adj.* (freq. fig.).

anā'erōbe (*or* anār-) *n.* Micro-organism which can live and reproduce in the absence of atmospheric oxygen. **anaerōb'ic** *adj.*

ănaesthēs'ia (-zia) n. Insensibility, esp. to pain; *local* ~, anaesthesia induced in a limited area of the body; *spinal* ~, anaesthesia of the spinal cord below the neck.

ănaesthĕt'ic *adj.* & *n.* (Drug etc. as chloroform or ether) inducing local or general anaesthesia, used in surgical operations.

anaes'thètist *n.* One who administers anaesthetics during surgical operation.

anaes'thètize *v.t.* Render insensible; administer anaesthetics to.

ăn'agrăm *n.* Word or phrase formed by transposing letters of another.

ān'al *adj.* Of the anus.

ăn'alĕcts, analĕc'ta *n.pl* Literary gleanings.

ănălgēs'ia (-z-) *n.* Absence of pain; relief of pain. **ănălgĕt'ic, ănălgēs'ic** *adjs.* & *ns.* (Drug) giving analgesia.

ănalŏg'ic *adj.* Of analogy. **ănalŏ'gical** *adj.* According to analogy; expressing an analogy. **ănalŏ'gically** *adv.*

anăl'ogous *adj.* Similar, parallel (to); (biol., of limb or organ) similar in function but not necessarily in structure or position (cf. HOMOLOGOUS). **anăl'ogously** *adv.*

ăn'alogue (-ŏg) *n.* Analogous word or thing.

anăl'ogy *n.* Agreement, similarity; analogue; (math.) proportion; (logic) process of reasoning from parallel cases; (gram.) process whereby words and grammatical forms are built up on the model of others.

ăn'alyse (-z) *v.t.* Examine minutely the constitution of; PSYCHO-ANALYSE; (chem.) ascertain the elements present in a compound or the constituents of a mixture, sample of food, etc.; (gram.) resolve into grammatical elements.

anăl'ysis *n.* (pl. *-sēs*). Resolution into simple elements; PSYCHO-ANALYSIS; *chemical* ~, determination of composition of substances; *qualitative* ~, identification of elements or compounds present; *quantitative* ~, determination of precise amounts of elements etc. present; (*bowling, bowler's*) ~, (cricket), statement of number of balls bowled, wickets taken, runs made, etc. **ăn'alyst** *n.* One skilled in (chemical) analysis. **ănalyt'ic** *adj.* Pertaining to analysis. **ănalyt'ical** *adj.* Employing the method of analysis; (of language) using separate words instead of inflexions; ~ *psychology*: see PSYCHOLOGY. **ănalyt'ically** *adv.*

anān'as (*or* -nahn-) *n.* Pineapple.

Ananī'as (ă-). 1. The Jewish high priest before whom Paul was brought: see Acts xxiii. 2. The husband of Sapphira, struck dead because he 'lied unto God': Acts v.

ăn'apaest *n.* (pros.) Foot consisting of two short (or unstressed) syllables followed by one long (or stressed). **ănapaes'tic** *adj.*

anăph'ora *n.* 1. Eucharistic service in the Greek Orthodox Church. 2. Repetition of words or phrases at beginning of a succession of clauses.

ănaphylăx'is *n.* (med.) Reaction of tissues, already sensitized by an injection, to a subsequent injection of foreign protein.

ăn'archist (-k-) *n.* Advocate of **ăn'archism,** system or theory which conceives of society without government.

ăn'archy (-k-) *n.* Absence of government; disorder, political and social confusion. **anar'chic(al)** *adjs.* Lawless. **anar'chically** *adv.*

anăstigmăt'ic *adj.* Free from astigmatism (used esp. of photographic lenses in which this error is corrected).

anăstomōs'is *n.* (pl. *-ōsēs*). Cross-connexion of arteries, rivers, etc.

anăth'èma *n.* Accursed thing; curse of God; curse of the Church, excommunication; imprecation. **anăth'èmatize** *v.* Curse. [Gk *anathema* thing devoted, (later) accursed thing]

Anatōl'ia (ă-). Asiatic part of Turkey; = ASIA Minor.

ănatŏm'ical *adj.* Belonging to anatomy; structural. **ănatŏm'ically** *adv.*

anăt'omist *n.* Dissecter of bodies; one skilled in anatomy; (fig.) analyser. **anăt'omize** *v.* Dissect; (fig.) analyse.

anăt'omy *n.* (Science of) bodily structure; dissection; analysis.

Anăxăg'orăs (ă-). Greek philosopher and scientist of 5th c. B.C.; acc. to his explanation of the universe, the permanent elements of which it is constituted are unlimited in number, and are combined in bodies in changing proportions, as the result of a system of circulation directed by Spirit or Intelligence, a supreme independent force; he also explained solar eclipses.

ăn'bury, ăm'bury *n.* Soft swelling on horses and cattle; disease of turnips and allied plants.

ăn'cèstor *n.* Any of those from whom one's father or mother is descended, progenitor. **ăn'cestrèss** *n.fem.*

ăncĕs'tral *adj.* Belonging to, inherited from, ancestors.

ăn'cèstry *n.* Ancestral lineage; ancient descent; ancestors.

Anchises (ăngkīs'ēz). (Rom. myth.) Father of Aeneas by Venus.

ănch'or (-k-) *n.* Heavy iron, consisting usu. of long shank and two (curved) barbed arms, used

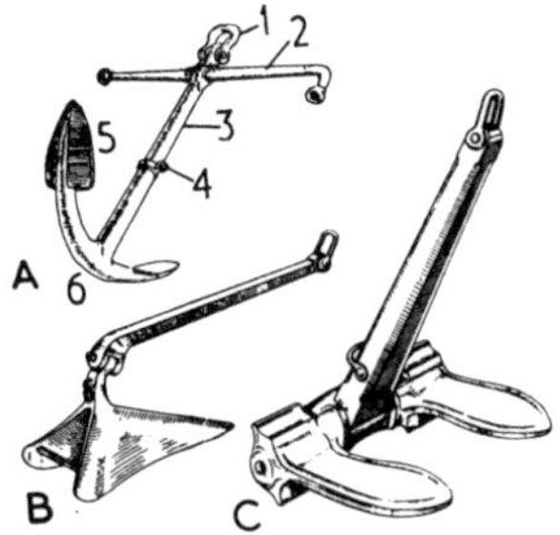

ANCHORS: A. ADMIRALTY PATTERN. B. CQR. C. STOCKLESS

1. Ring. 2. Stock. 3. Shank. 4. Gravity band. 5. Fluke. 6. Crown

for mooring ship to bottom of sea etc.; (fig.) source of confidence; *sheet-*~, *bower-*~, *kedge-*~, largest middle, smallest size of anchor; *~-plate*, heavy piece of metal or timber as point of support for cables of suspension-bridge (ill. BRIDGE). ~ *v.* Secure (ship) with anchor; (fig.) fix firmly; cast anchor, come to anchor.

ănch'orage (-k-) *n.* Anchoring; lying at anchor; anchoring-ground; (fig.) thing to depend upon.

ănch'orėt (now rare), **ănch'orīte** (-k-) *n.* Hermit, recluse. **ănch'orėss, ănc'rėss** *n.fem.* **ănchorĕt'ic** *adj.*

ănchōv'y (*or* ăn'chō-) *n.* Small fish of herring family, esp. the Mediterranean *Engraulis encrasicholus*, esteemed for its rich pungent flavour and used in sauces.

ănchus'a (-chōō- *or* -kū-) *n.* Genus (*A~*) of plants of borage family with blue or purple trumpet-shaped flowers.

anchylosis: ANKYLOSIS.

ancien régime (ahṅ'syăṅ rāzhēm'). Time before French Revolution. [Fr., = 'old rule']

ān'cient[1] (-shent) *adj.* Belonging to times long past; having existed, lived, long; ~ *lights*, window that neighbour may not deprive of light by building. ~ *n.* *The A~ of Days*, God (Dan. vii. 9); *the ~s*, civilized people of antiquity. **ān'ciently** *adv.* **ān'cientnėss** *n.*

ān'cient[2] (-shent) *n.* (archaic) = ENSIGN.

ăn'cillarỹ (*or* ancill'-) *adj.* Subservient, subordinate.

ancon (ăng'kon) *n.* 1. (physiol.) Elbow; *A~ sheep*, race with long bodies and short legs, the forelegs crooked. 2. (archit.) Deep bracket consisting of two reversed volutes, supporting or appearing to support a cornice, console (ill. CONSOLE).

and (and, *emphat.* ănd) *conj.* Connecting words, clauses, and sentences.

Andalusia (ăndalōōz'ĭa). Ancient province of S. Spain. **Andalus'ĭan** *adj.* & *n.*

An'damăn Islands (ă-). Large group of islands in Bay of Bengal; administered (with Nicobar Islands) by the Republic of India.

ăndăn'tė *adv.* & *n.* (mus.) (Movement) in moderately slow time. ***ăndăntinō*** (-tē-) *adv.* & *n.* (Movement) slightly quicker (orig. slower) than *andante*. [It.]

An'dersen (ă-), Hans Christian (1805–75). Danish poet and dramatist, best known for his 'Fairy-tales'.

An'derson (ă-), Mrs Elizabeth Garrett (1836–1917). English physician, a pioneer of the professional education of women.

An'derson shelter (ă-). Small prefabricated arched corrugated-steel air-raid shelter issued to householders in the early years of the war of 1939–45. [Sir John *Anderson*, Home Secretary 1939–40]

An'dēs (ă-, -z). Mountain system running from N. to S. along the whole of the Pacific coast of S. America.

ăn'diron (-īrn) *n.* Stand for supporting logs on hearth, fire-dog (ill. FIRE).

Andŏ'rra (ă-). Semi-independent State (generally regarded as an autonomous republic) in the Pyrenees, on the border between France and Spain; under the joint suzerainty of France and the Spanish bishops of Urgel.

Andrea del Sarto: see SARTO.

Andrea Ferrara: see FERRARA.

An'drew (ă-, -rōō), St. Apostle and patron saint of Scotland, commemorated 30th Nov. *St. ~'s Ambulance Association*, founded 1882; responsible for Red Cross work in Scotland; *St. ~'s Cross*, a cross shaped like the letter X, saltire; as blazoned, a white cross on a blue ground.

An'drewes (ă-, -rōōz), Lancelot (1555–1626). English bishop, one of the translators of the 'Authorized' version of the Bible.

Andreyev (ăndrā'ĕf), Leonid Nicolayevich (1871–1919). Russian novelist and playwright.

An'droclēs (ă-, -z). A runaway slave who extracted a thorn from a lion's paw; when captured, he was condemned to fight with a lion in the arena, but the lion was the same one, and refused to attack him (story told by Gellius, Latin author of 2nd c. A.D.).

ăndroe'cĭum (-rēs-) *n.* (bot.) The stamens collectively (ill. FLOWER).

ăn'drogėn *n.* Any organic compound which promotes development of masculine characteristics.

ăndrŏ'gỹnous (*or* -g-) *adj.* Hermaphrodite; (bot.) with both staminate and pistillate flowers in a cluster (ill. INFLORESCENCE). **ăndrŏ'gỹny** *n.*

Andrŏm'achė (ă-, -k-). (Gk legend) Wife of HECTOR[1].

Andrŏm'ėda (ă-). 1. (Gk legend) Daughter of Cassiopeia. Because her mother had offended Poseidon, she was exposed on a rock to a sea-monster, but was rescued by Perseus, who changed the monster to a stone by showing it Medusa's head. 2. A constellation, conspicuous for its great spiral nebula. **Andrŏm'ėdēs, Andrŏm'ėdĭds** *ns.pl.* System of meteors appearing to radiate from a point in Andromeda and usu. seen in November.

ăn'ėcdōte *n.* Narrative of detached incident; narrative of private details of history. **ănėcdōtage** *n.* Anecdotes; (joc.) garrulous old age. **ăn'ėcdōtist** *n.* **ănėcdŏt'al, ănėcdŏt'ĭc(al)** *adjs.*

anēle' *v.t.* Anoint; give extreme unction to.

anĕm'ograph (-ahf) *n.* Anemometer equipped with recording apparatus (usu. pen and rotating drum). **anĕm'ogrăm** *n.* Record traced by this.

ănėmŏm'ėter *n.* Instrument for measuring speed (sometimes also direction) of wind. **ănėmomĕt'rĭc** *adj.* **ănėmom'ėtry** *n.*

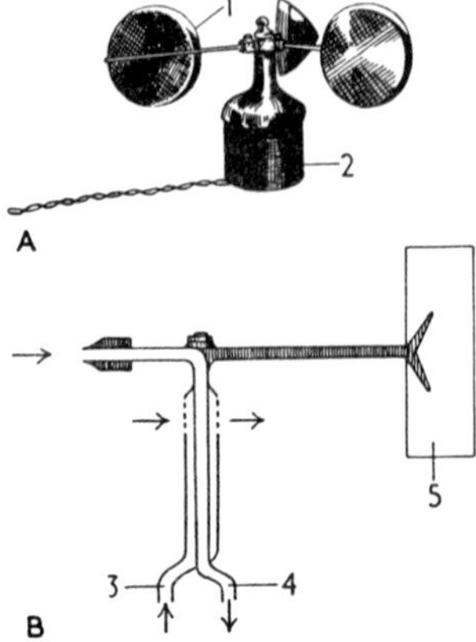

ANEMOMETERS: A. CUP TYPE. B. PITOT-TUBE

A. 1. Hollow metal cup. 2. Generator. B. 3. Suction tube. 4. Pressure tube. 5. Vane. Arrows indicate direction of wind and flow of air in tubes

anĕm'onė *n.* Genus (*A~*) of plants of the buttercup family (*Ranunculaceae*) with flowers of various colours; *wood-~*, wind-flower, a delicate, white, spring flower growing wild in Britain; *sea-~*: see SEA. [Gk, = 'wind-flower']

ănėmoph'ĭlous *adj.* (bot.) Pollinated by wind.

anĕnt *prep.* (archaic) Concerning.

ăn'eroid *adj.* & *n.* (Barometer) that measures air-pressure by its action on the flexible lid of a metal box nearly exhausted of air, not by height of fluid column (ill. BAROMETER).

ăn'eurỹsm, -ĭsm *n.* (path.) Localized dilatation of an artery caused by a weakening in its wall.

anew' *adv.* Again; in a different way.

ăng'ary (-ngg-) *n.* (law) Belligerent's right (subject to compensation) of seizing or destroying neutral property under stress of military necessity.

ān'gel (-j-) *n.* 1. Divine messenger; *orders of ~s*, three hierarchies, each consisting of three orders, to which in 4th c. angels were conceived as belonging, namely: seraphim, cherubim, thrones; dominions, virtues, powers; principalities, archangels, angels. 2. Lovely or innocent being; minister of loving offices. 3. ~ (*-noble*), old English gold coin showing the archangel Michael piercing a dragon, worth from 6*s.* 8*d.* to 10*s.* 4. *~-fish*, S. Amer. freshwater fish (various species of *Pterophyllum*), laterally flattened, with bars of black and silver; *~s on horseback*, savoury dish of oysters wrapped in slices of bacon. [Gk *aggelos* messenger]

ăngĕl′ic (-j-) *adj.* Like an angel; *A~ Doctor*, St. Thomas Aquinas.

ăngĕl′ica (-j-) *n.* Aromatic plant used in cooking and medicine; candied root of this.

Angĕl′icŏ (ă-), Fra (1387–1455). Name given after his death to a Dominican friar, Fra Giovanni da Fiesole, painter of religious subjects, active in Florence and Rome.

ăngė′lus (-j-) *n.* Devotional exercise (beginning *Angelus domini* 'the angel of the Lord') commemorating the Incarnation, said by Roman Catholics at morning, noon, and evening, at sound of bell; bell for this.

ăng′er (-ngg-) *n.* Hot displeasure, rage. *~ v.t.* Make angry, enrage. [ON *angr* affliction]

An′gėvin (ănj-) *adj.* & *n.* (Native) of Anjou; (member) of the ruling house of Anjou; *~ kings*, the PLANTAGENET kings of England (Henry II to Richard II).

ăngīn′a (-j-) *n.* (obs.) Constriction and spasmodic affection of throat and chest, as quinsy, croup, etc.; *~ pectoris*, intense pain in chest and arm, accompanied by sense of suffocation, caused by insufficient blood-supply to heart during sudden exertion.

ăn′giospērm (-j-) *n.* Flowering plant, i.e. one which has ovules enclosed in an ovary; opp. of GYMNOSPERM.

angle[1] (ăng′gl) *n.* Space between two meeting lines or planes; inclination of two lines to each other (*right ~*, angle of 90°; *acute ~*, angle smaller than 90°; *obtuse ~*, greater than 90°; *reflex ~*, greater than 180°); corner, sharp projection; (colloq.) point of view;

ANGLES

1. Right. 2. Acute. 3. Obtuse. 4. Reflex

~-iron, metal plate of L-shaped section (ill. GIRDER). **ăng′led** (-ld) *adj.* *~ deck*, flight deck on aircraft-carrier with landing path inclined to ship's fore-and-aft axis.

angle[2] (ăng′gl) *v.i.* Fish with hook and bait; (fig.) try to gain by artifice or intrigue. **ăng′ler** *n.* 1. Fisherman. 2. (zool.) Fish that preys on smaller fish, attracting them by filaments attached to its head and mouth (various species, of which *Lophius piscatorius* is the commonest).

Angles (ăng′glz), **Ang′lī.** The people of Angul (Angel), a district of Holstein; one of the Low-German tribes that settled in Britain, where they formed the kingdoms of Northumbria, Mercia, and East Anglia, and finally gave their name to England and the English.

Anglesey (ăng′glsī). Island separated from the coast of NW. Wales by the Menai Strait; a county of Wales; known to the Romans as Mona.

Ang′lican (ăngg-) *adj.* & *n.* (Member) of the reformed Church of England; *~ chant*, short harmonized melody in two or more phrases each beginning with a reciting note, for singing to unmetrical words, as psalms, canticles; *~ Communion*, the Church in communion with, and recognizing the leadership of, the see of Canterbury. **Ang′licanism** *n.*

Anglice (ăng′glisē) *adv.* In English. [L]

Anglo- (ăng′glo-) *prefix.* English.

Ang′lo-Căth′olic *adj.* & *n.* (Adherent) of the section of the Church of England which claims that the Reformed Church is the true descendant and national branch of the Catholic Church.

Ang′lo-In′dian *adj.* & *n.* (Person) of British birth but living or having lived long in India (but in Eurasian use = EURASIAN).

Ang′lo-Nōrm′an *adj.* & *n.* (Of) the variety of the Norman dialect of Old French spoken in England after the Norman Conquest.

Ang′lophil(e) *adj.* & *n.* (Person) well disposed towards the English.

Angl′o-Săx′on *adj.* & *n.* English Saxon (as dist. from the Old Saxons of the Continent); Old English (person, language) before the Norman Conquest; of English descent.

Angō′la (ăngg-). Portuguese province of W. Africa, N. of SW. Africa and W. of N. Rhodesia.

Angōr′a (ăngg-). (English name, now less common, for) ANKARA; fabric made from fleece of Angora goat, mohair; *~ cat, goat, rabbit*, varieties of these animals with long silky hair; *~ (wool)*, sheep's wool mixed with hair of Angora rabbit.

Angostūr′a (ăngg-). Former name of Ciudad Bolivar, town in Venezuela on Orinoco; *~ (bark)*, aromatic bitter bark used as tonic and febrifuge, obtained from S. Amer. tree, *Cusparia angostura*.

Angoulême (ahngg̅ōolām′). Town of SW. France; (hist.) French royal duchy.

ăng′ry (-ngg-) *adj.* Enraged, resentful; irritable, passionate; (of wound etc.) inflamed, painful. **ăng′rily** *adv.*

Ångström (ŏng′strērm), Anders Jonas (1814–74). Swedish physicist and astronomer; *~ unit*, the unit used in measuring the wavelengths of light, one hundred-millionth of a cm.; abbreviation Å.U.

ăng′uish (-nggw-) *n.* Severe bodily or mental pain.

ăng′ūlar (-ngg-) *adj.* Having angles; sharp-cornered; placed in, at, an angle; wanting plumpness or suavity; *~ distance* (math.), distance between two points measured in terms of the angle which they make with a third (in astronomy the point of observation).

Ang′us (ăngg-). County of E. Scotland, lying N. of the Tay estuary, formerly Forfarshire.

ănhēd′ral *adj.* & *n.* (of aircraft) Having wings inclined downwards towards the tips; angle between such wings and the horizontal.

ănhȳd′rīde *n.* Substance which chemically combines with water to form an acid.

ănhȳd′rous *adj.* (chem.) Of substances having no water, esp. water of crystallization, in their composition; of substances deprived of their water of crystallization.

ăn′il *n.* The shrub indigo; dye-stuff obtained from it. [Arab. *an-nil* (*an* the, *nil* f. Sansk. *nili* indigo)]

ăn′iline *adj.* & *n.* (Of) phenylamine ($C_6H_5NH_2$), an oily liquid with characteristic smell, made by reduction of nitro-benzene and used in the manufacture of many chemicals, dye-stuffs, drugs, etc.; *~ dye*, (pop.) any synthetic dye-stuff. [formerly got from *anil*]

ăn′ima *n.* (psychol.) The inner aspect of personality, esp. its unconscious facets. [L, = 'breath', 'soul']

ănimadvēr′sion (-shn) *n.* Criticism, censure. **ănimadvert′** *v.i.* Pass criticism or censure *on.*

ăn′imal *n.* Organized being endowed (more or less perceptibly) with life, sensation, and voluntary motion; other animal than man; quadruped; brutish man. *~ adj.* Pertaining to the functions of animals; pertaining to animals as opp. to vegetables; carnal; *~ magnetism*, (old name for) mesmerism; *~ spirits*, natural buoyancy. [L *anima* breath]

ănimăl′cūle *n.* Microscopic animal.

ăn′imalism *n.* Animal activity; sensuality; doctrine that men are mere animals.

ăn′imalīze *v.t.* Convert into animal substance, sensualize.

ăn′imate *adj.* Living, lively.

ăn′imāte *v.t.* Breathe life into; enliven, inspirit; inspire. **ănimā′tion** *n.* **ăn′imātėdly** *adv.*

ăn′imism *n.* Attribution of living soul to inanimate objects and natural phenomena. **ăn′imist** *n.* **ănimis′tic** *adj.*

ănimŏs′ity *n.* Active enmity.

ăn′imus *n.* Animating spirit; animosity.

ăn′īŏn *n.* Ion carrying a negative charge which moves towards the anode (positive electrode) during electrolysis (opp. of CATION). [Gk *ana* up, + ION]

ăn′ise (-is) *n.* Umbelliferous plant (*Pimpinella anisum*) with aromatic fruits.

ăn′iseed *n.* Fruits of anise, used as carminative and for flavouring.

ănisĕtte′ (-z-) *n.* Colourless sweet liqueur flavoured with aniseed.

Anjou (ahṅzhōō′). Old French province on the Loire, W. of Touraine; Henry II of England, as a Plantagenet, was count of Anjou, but it was lost to the English Crown by King John (1204).

Ankara (ăng′k*ara*), less freq. **Angōr′a.** City (in province of same name) of Asia Minor, since 1924 capital of Turkey.

ank′le (ăngkl) *n.* Joint connecting foot with leg (ill. FOOT); slender part between this and calf. **ănk′lėt** *n.* Fetter or ornamental band round ankle.

ănkylōs′ĭs, (rare) **anch-** (ăngkĭ-) *n.* (pl. *-osēs*). Formation of stiff joint by consolidation of articulating surfaces. **ănk′ȳlōse** (-z) *v.* (Of joints, bones) stiffen, unite.

ănn′a *n.* Former Indian and Pakistani coin, sixteenth part of rupee.

ănn′als *n.pl.* Narrative of events year by year; historical records. **ănn′alĭst** *n.* Writer of annals.

Ann′ăm (ă-). Eastern coastal portion of Indo-China. **Annamēse′** (-z) *adj.* & *n.*

Annăp′olis (*a*-). Capital of Maryland, U.S., site of the U.S. Naval Academy.

ănn′ātes (-ts) *n.pl.* (R.C. Ch.) First year's revenue of see or benefice, formerly paid to pope.

Anne[1] (ăn) (1665–1714). Queen of England 1702–14; 2nd daughter of James II; succeeded William, husband of her sister Mary, in 1702, and died without surviving issue; *Queen ~'s Bounty*, Crown revenues from tithes and first-fruits (formerly paid to the pope, and appropriated by the Crown in 1534), granted by her to the Church of England.

Anne[2] (ăn), St. Mother of the Virgin Mary; commemorated 26th July.

anneal (*a*nēl′) *v.t.* Toughen (glass or metals) by gradually diminishing heat; temper.

Anne Boleyn: see BOLEYN.

ănn′ėlĭd *n.* One of the *Annelida*, segmented worms (including earthworms, leeches, etc.).

Anne of Cleves (klēvz) (1515–57). Daughter of John, Duke of Cleves, and 4th wife of Henry VIII of England; the marriage (1540) was annulled after a few months.

annĕx′ *v.t.* Add as subordinate (part); append; take possession of (territory); attach as an attribute, addition, or consequence. **ănnėxā′tion** *n.* **ănn′ĕx(e)** *n.* Addition to document; building added to larger one, esp. to provide extra accommodation.

annī′hĭlāte (-nīĭ-) *v.t.* Demolish, destroy utterly. **annīhĭlā′tion** *n.* Utter destruction; (theol.) destruction of soul as well as body.

ănnivẽrs′ary *n.* Yearly return of a date, celebration of this.

ănn′ō aetat′ĭs sŭ′ae. In the (specified) year of his or her age. [L]

Ann′ō Dŏm′ĭnī (ă-). In the year of our Lord, of the Christian era (abbrev. A.D.); (as *n.*, colloq.) advancing age. [L]

ănn′otāte *v.t.* Furnish with notes. **ănnotā′tion, ănn′otātor** *ns.*

announce′ *v.t.* Proclaim; intimate the approach of. **announce′ment** (-sm-) *n.* **announ′cer** *n.* (esp.) Broadcasting official who announces programme, reads news items, etc.

annoy′ *v.t.* Irritate; molest, harass. **annoy′ance** *n.* Molestation; vexation; disgust.

ănn′ūal *adj.* & *n.* Reckoned by the year; recurring yearly; lasting for one year; (plant) that lives only for a year; (book etc.) published in yearly numbers.

annū′ĭty *n.* Sum payable in respect of a particular year; yearly grant; investment of money entitling investor to series of equal annual sums. **annū′ĭtant** *n.* One who holds an annuity.

annŭl′ *v.t.* Annihilate; abolish; declare invalid. **annŭl′ment** *n.*

ănn′ūlar *adj.* Ring-like; ~ *eclipse*, partial eclipse of sun, during which a ring of the sun's surface can be seen outside the moon's disc; this happens when the distance of the moon from the earth in relation to the distance of the sun from the earth is too great for the eclipse to be total (ill. ECLIPSE).

ănn′ūlate, -ātėd *adjs.* Furnished, marked, with rings; formed of rings.

ănn′ūlėt *n.* Little ring; (her.) small circle (ill. HERALDRY); (archit.) fillet or moulded band encircling a column (ill. ORDER).

ănn′ūlus *n.* (pl. *-lī*). Ring, ring-like body, esp. (bot.) ring of cells round sporangia in ferns (ill. FERN).

annŭn′ciāte (-shĭ-) *v.t.* Announce.

ănnŭnciā′tion (-sĭ-) *n.* Announcement; (*A~*) the announcement of the Incarnation made by the angel Gabriel to the Virgin Mary; festival commemorating this, Lady Day, 25th March.

Annunzio (*a*nōōnt′sĭō), Gabriele d' (1863–1938). Italian poet, airman, and politician.

ăn′ōde *n.* (elect.) Positive pole or terminal (ill. THERMIONIC). [Gk *anodos* way up]

ăn′odȳne *adj.* & *n.* (Medicine, drug) able to assuage pain; (anything) mentally soothing.

anoint′ *v.t.* Apply ointment, oil, to, esp. as religious ceremony at baptism or on consecration as priest or king; *The Lord's Anointed*, Christ; king by divine right.

anŏm′alous *adj.* Irregular, abnormal. **anŏm′alously** *adv.* **anŏm′alousnėss** *n.*

anŏm′aly *n.* Unevenness of motion etc.; irregularity; (astron.) angular distance of planet or satellite from its last perihelion or perigee. **anŏmalĭs′tic** *adj.*; (astron.) ~ *year*, time (365 days, 6 hrs, 13 m., 53·1 sec.) earth takes to pass from perihelion to perihelion; ~ *month*, time (27 days, 13 hrs, 18 m., 33·1 sec.) moon takes to pass from perigee to perigee.

anŏn′ *adv.* Soon, presently; *ever and* ~, from time to time.

anon. *abbrev.* Anonymous.

ăn′ŏnȳm *n.* Person whose name is not revealed; pseudonym. **ănonȳm′ĭty** *n.*

anŏn′ȳmous *adj.* Not named; not bearing author's, painter's, etc., name. **anŏn′ȳmously** *adv.*

Anŏph′elēs (*a*-, -z) *n.* Genus of mosquitoes, comprising numerous species, many of which are carriers of malaria. [Gk, = 'hurtful']

anŏs′mĭa (-z-) *n.* Lack of the sense of smell.

anoth′er (-ŭdh-) *adj.* & *pron.* An additional (one); unnamed additional party to legal action; a counterpart to; a different (one).

anŏx′ĭa *n.* (med.) Lack of oxygen, caused by asphyxiation or high altitude (*direct* ~), or by various diseases which render the blood incapable of conveying enough oxygen to the tissues (*indirect* ~).

Anschluss (ăn′shlōōs) *n.* Annexation, esp. of Austria to Germany. [Ger., = 'union']

An′selm (ă-), St. (1033–1109). Italian monk, a pupil of Lanfranc; became abbot of Bec in Normandy and later (1093) archbishop of Canterbury; commemorated 21st April.

ăn′serīne *adj.* Of, like, a goose; silly.

answer (ahn′s*er*) *v.* Reply; reply to (charge); be responsible *for*; fulfil (purpose), correspond to (expectation); do, succeed; (vulg.) ~ *back*, answer rebuke saucily. ~ *n.* Reply; defence; solution; thing done in return; (mus.) repetition of theme by another voice or instrument, esp. in fugue. **an′swerable** *adj.* Responsible.

ănt *n.* Small hymenopterous insect of family *Formicidae*, with

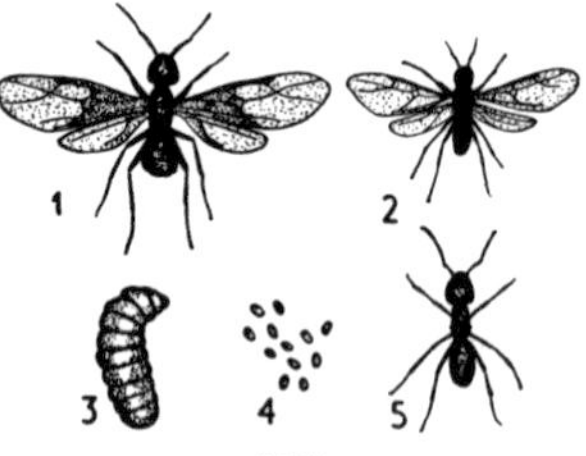

ANT

1. Queen. 2. Male. 3. Larva. 4. Eggs. 5. Worker

complex instincts and social system, proverbial for industry; *~-eater*, various mammals living on ants; *~-heap*, *~-hill*, mound over ants' nest; (loosely) conical nest of termites; (fig.) crowded dwellings swarming with people.

ăn′ta *n.* (pl. *-tae*) Square pilaster on either side of door or at corner of buildings; one of two short walls forming sides of portico; *in antis*, (of portico) having its columns standing between antae (ill. TEMPLE).

ăntă′cĭd *adj.* & *n.* Preventing, preventive of, acidity, esp. in stomach.

Antae′us (ă-). (Gk myth.) A Libyan giant, son of Poseidon and Ge (the earth); when Hercules wrestled with him, Antaeus was only overcome when lifted from the earth, from which he drew new strength whenever he touched it.

ăntăg′onism *n.* Active opposition; opposing principle.

ăntăg′onist *n.* 1. Opponent, **adversary.** 2. (physiol.) Counteracting muscle. **ăntăgonĭs′tic** *adj.*

ăntăg′onīze *v.* Counteract, tend to neutralize (force etc.); evoke hostility in, make into an enemy.

ăntar̂c′tic *adj.* & *n.* Of the south polar regions; *A~ Circle*, the parallel of 66° 32′ S., south of which the sun does not rise at midwinter or set at midsummer (ill. EARTH); *the A~*, the regions (both land and sea) round the S. Pole. [Gk *anti* opposite + ARCTIC (*arktos* bear)]

ăn′tė *n.* (poker etc.) Stake put up before drawing new cards.

ăntė- *prefix.* Before.

ăntėcēd′ent *adj.* Previous; presumptive, *a priori.* ~ *n.* Preceding thing or circumstance; (logic) part of conditional proposition on which other part depends; (gram.) noun, clause, etc., to which following (relative) pronoun or adverb refers; (math.) first term of ratio; (geog., of river) one which has maintained its course in spite of changes in land formation; (pl.) past history.

ăn′tėchāmber *n.* Room leading to chief apartment.

ăn′tėchăpel *n.* Outer part at west end of chapel.

ăntėdāte′ *v.t.* Affix, assign, an earlier than the true date to; precede; anticipate.

ăntėdilūv′ian *adj.* & *n.* Belonging, referring, appropriate, to the time before the Flood; old-fashioned or very old (person).

ăn′tėfix *n.* Ornament above cornice of classical building concealing joint between tiles (ill. TEMPLE), **antėfix′al** *adj.*

ăn′tėlōpe *n.* Any of several cloven-hoofed ruminants (related to deer, goats, and cattle) including the chamois, gazelle, and gnu.

ăn′te mĕrīd′ĭēm. Between midnight and noon (abbrev. a.m.). [L]

ăntėnāt′al *adj.* Previous to birth.

ăntĕnn′a *n.* (pl. *-nae*). 1. Sensory organ found in pairs on heads of insects and crustacea, usually long slender projections like horns, sometimes knobbed (ill. INSECT). 2. Wires or aerials used for transmitting or receiving electric waves in wireless telegraphy or telephony. [L, = 'sail-yard']

ăntĕnn′ūle *n.* (zool.) Minute organ resembling antenna (ill. LOBSTER).

ăntėpĕn′dium *n.* (pl. *-dĭa*). Veil, hanging, for front of altar; frontal.

ăntėpėnŭlt′, ăntėpėnŭl′timate (*-at*) *adjs.* & *ns.* (Syllable) last but two.

ăn′tēr′ior *adj.* More to the front; prior *to.*

ăn′tė-rōōm *n.* Room leading to another, antechamber.

ănthēl′ion *n.* Luminous ring projected on cloud or fog-bank opposite the sun.

ăn′thėm *n.* Composition sung antiphonally; prose composition (usu. from Scriptures or Liturgy) set to sacred music; song of praise.

ănthēm′ion *n.* (pl. *-ia*). (archit.) Ancient Greek ornament of radiating plant forms.

ăn′ther *n.* (bot.) Terminal part of stamen containing pollen in pollen sacs.

ănthŏl′ogy *n.* Collection of small choice poems; literary collection: *the Greek A~*, large collection of epigrams and short poems from Greek writers of 5th c. B.C.–6th c. A.D. [Gk *anthologia*, f. *anthos* flower, *-logia* collection (*legō* gather)]

An′thony[1] (ăn′to-), St. (*c* 250–*c* 350). Born in Egypt, the first Christian monk; ~ *pig*, smallest pig of litter, named after St. Anthony as patron saint of swineherds; *St. ~'s cross*, a cross shaped like the letter T; *St. ~'s fire*, erysipelas, popularly supposed in the Middle Ages to be cured by the intercession of St. Anthony.

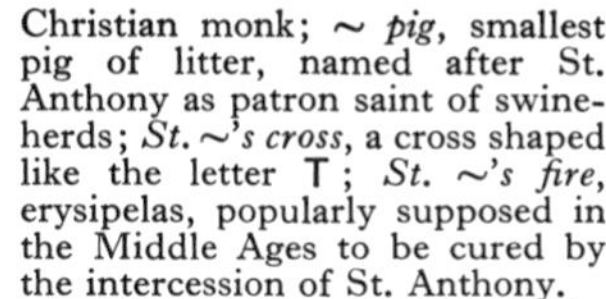

An′thony[2] (ăn′to-) of Padua, St. (1195–1231). Portuguese Franciscan monk, patron saint of Portugal.

Anthozō′a (ă-) *n.pl.* Class of aquatic animals including corals, sea-anemones, etc. [Gk. *anthos* flower, *zōon* animal]

ăn′thracēne *n.* (chem.) An aromatic hydrocarbon ($C_{14}H_{10}$) obtained by distillation of coal-tar and used in manufacture of alizarin and other dyes.

ăn′thracīte *n.* Glossy variety of coal containing much carbon and low percentage of volatile matter, burning with hot smokeless flame and leaving little ash. **ănthracĭt′ic** *adj.*

ăn′thrăx *n.* Disease of sheep and cattle, transmitted to man by infected wool, bristles, etc., and characterized by inflammatory skin lesions; caused by a bacillus *B. anthracis*).

ăn′thropoid *adj.* & *n.* Man-like; (being that is) human in form only; ~ (*ape*), one of those most nearly related to man, i.e. chimpanzees, gibbons, orang-utans, and gorillas (ill. APE).

ănthropŏl′ogy *n.* Science of man; study of man as an animal (*physical* ~) and of human, esp. primitive, societies (*social* ~). **ănthropolŏ′gical** *adj.* **ănthropolŏ′gically** *adv.* **ănthropŏl′ogist** *n.*

ănthropŏm′etry *n.* Measurement of human body. **ănthropomĕt′ric** *adj.*

ănthropomor̂ph′ism *n.* Ascription of human form and attributes to God, or of human attributes to something irrational or impersonal. **ănthropomor̂ph′ic** *adj.*

ănthropomor̂ph′ous *adj.* Having human form. **ănthropomor̂ph′ize** *v.* Regard as anthropomorphous.

anti- *prefix.* Opposite, against, in exchange, instead.

ănti-air′craft (-ahft) *adj.* For shooting down, or for defence against, hostile aircraft (abbrev. A.A.).

ăn′tiar̂ *n.* Upas tree of Java; the poison obtained from it.

ăntibiōs′is *n.* Condition of antagonism between life-forms, esp. micro-organisms (opp. of SYMBIOSIS).

ăntibiŏt′ic *adj.* & *n.* (Substance, drug, as penicillin, streptomycin) obtained from a mould or fungus or other micro-organism and having the power to inhibit the growth of other micro-organisms, e.g. bacteria.

ăn′tibŏdy *n.* (physiol.) Any of various organic substances. formed

ANT-EATERS

1. Spiny ant-eater or echidna (a monotreme). 2. Banded ant-eater (a marsupial). 3. Great ant-eater (an edentate). 4. Scaly ant-eater or pangolin (Order *Pholidota*)

within the body to inactivate other compounds (esp. bacterial toxins and viruses) which are foreign to it, and found in blood-plasma.

ăn'tĭc *n.* (often pl.) Grotesque posture or trick.

An'tĭchrīst (ă-, -k-). The great personal opponent of Christ expected by early Christians to appear before the end of the world; person hostile to Christ and his teaching.

ăntĭchrĭs'tian (-k-) *adj.* Opposed to Christianity.

ăntĭ'cĭpāte *v.t.* Look forward to, expect; forestall; consider etc. beforehand; use in advance. **ăntĭ'cĭpative** *adj.* **ăntĭ'cĭpatively** (-vl-) *adv.* **ăntĭcĭpā'tion** *n.* (esp., mus.) Sounding of single note of chord before chord itself.

ăntĭclĕ'rical *adj.* Opposed to undue influence of clergy, esp. in politics, or to existence of organized clerical hierarchy. **ăntĭclĕ'ricalism** *n.*

ăntĭclī'măx *n.* Lame end to anything promising a climax.

ăn'tĭclīne *n.* (geol.) Arch-like fold in bed(s) of rock (opp. to SYNCLINE, trough-like fold; ill. ROCK). **ăntĭclīn'al** *adj.*

ăntĭcȳc'lōne *n.* Atmospheric system in which barometric pressure is high, and from centre of which air tends to flow spirally outward (clockwise in N. hemisphere, anti-clockwise in S. hemisphere) (ill. WEATHER).

ăn'tĭdōte *n.* Medicine used to counteract disease or poison.

Antiet'am (ăntĭt-). Tributary of the Potomac river, scene of a Confederate victory (1862) in the Amer. Civil War.

ăn'tĭ-freeze *n.* Chemical agent (usu. ethylene glycol) added to water to lower its freezing-point.

ăn'tĭgėn *n.* Substance introduced into blood to stimulate production of antibodies.

Antĭg'onė (ă-). (Gk legend) A daughter of Oedipus; she buried the body of her brother Polynices by night, against the order of King Creon; he condemned her to be buried alive but she took her own life.

Antĭg'ūa (*or* ăntēg'wa). One of the Leeward Islands, in the British West Indies, discovered in 1493 by Columbus and settled by English in 1632.

Antĭ-Jăc'obĭn (ă-) *adj.* & *n.* (One) opposed to the Jacobins (the French revolutionary party, 1789), or to the French Revolution; *The* ~, a journal founded by Canning to combat the subversive principles of philosophy and politics represented by the Jacobins.

Antĭll'ēs (ă-, -z). Group of W. Indian islands; the *Greater* ~ comprise Cuba, Jamaica, Hispaniola (Haiti and Santo Domingo), and Puerto Rico.

ăntĭlŏg'arĭthm (-dhm) *n.* Number to which a logarithm belongs, as 100 *is the* ~ *of* 2.

ăntĭmacăss'ar *n.* Covering on chair-back to protect it from hair-grease or as ornament. [f. *Macassar oil*, pop. as hair-oil in 19th c.]

ăn'tĭmony *n.* A brittle metallic element, bluish-white, of flaky crystalline texture, used in alloys esp. with lead, and in medicine; symbol Sb, at. no. 51, at. wt 121·75.

Antĭnōm'ĭan (ă-) *adj.* & *n.* (Person) holding that the moral law is not binding on Christians on the ground that faith alone is sufficient to salvation; (member) of German sect (*c* 1535) alleged to hold this opinion. **Antĭnōm'ianism** *n.*

ăntĭn'omy *n.* Contradiction in a law, or between laws, principles, etc.

Antinous (ăntĭn'ōus). A Bithynian youth, favourite of the Emperor Hadrian, represented in art as the ideal type of youthful beauty.

An'tĭŏch (ă-, -k). Name of several ancient cities of the Near East, esp. (1) the capital of Syria under the Seleucid kings (now Antakya in Turkey near the Syrian border); (2) 'Antioch towards Pisidia' in the Roman province of Galatia (near the present Yalvaç in SW. Anatolia, Turkey). Both were visited by St. Paul.

Antĭp'ater (ă-) (*c* 398–319 B.C.). Macedonian general; succeeded Alexander as ruler of Macedonia.

ăntĭp'athy *n.* Constitutional or settled aversion (*to, against, between*). **ăntĭpathĕt'ĭc, ăntĭpăth'ĭc** *adjs.*

ăntĭ-pėrsonnĕl' *adj.* (Of aerial bombs) designed to kill or injure human beings.

ăn'tĭphon *n.* Versicle, sentence, sung by one choir in response to another; composition consisting of such passages. **ăntĭph'onal** *adj.* Sung alternately. ~ *n.* Collection of antiphons.

ăntĭph'onary *n.* Antiphonal.

ăntĭph'ony *n.* Antiphon; antiphonal singing.

Antĭp'odēs (ă-, -z) *n.pl.* Places on opposite sides of the earth; esp. region diametrically opposite to our own. **ăntĭp'odal** *adj.* **ăntĭpodē'an** *adj.* & *n.* [Gk, = 'having the feet opposite']

ăn'tĭpōpe *n.* Pope in opposition to one (held to be) canonically chosen.

ăn'tĭpȳrĕt'ĭc *adj.* & *n.* (Drug) allaying or preventing fever **ăntĭpȳr'ĭn** *n.* Trade name of an antipyretic substance derived from coal-tar.

ăn'tĭquary *n.* Student or collector of antiquities. **ăntĭquār'ĭan** *adj.* & *n.* **ăntĭquār'ianism** *n.*

ăn'tĭquātėd *adj.* Out of date, antique.

antique (ăntēk') *adj.* Of or existing from old times; old-fashioned; of the ancients. ~ *n.* Relic of ancient art or of old times.

ăntĭq'uĭty *n.* Ancientness; ancient times, esp. (*classical* ~) the period of the ancient Greek and Roman civilizations; (pl.) customs, practices, etc., of ancient times, objects surviving from them.

ăntĭrrhīn'um (-rī-) *n.* Snapdragon. [Gk *anti* resembling + *rhinos* nose.]

ăntĭscŏrbūt'ĭc *adj.* & *n.* (Medicine etc.) preventing or curing scurvy.

ăntĭ-Sēm'īte *adj.* & *n.* (Person) hostile to Jews. **ăntĭ-Sėmĭt'ĭc** *adj.* **ăntĭ-Sēm'ĭtism** *n.*

ăntĭsĕp'tĭc *adj.* & *n.* (Agent) counteracting putrefaction.

ăntĭsō'cial (-shl) *adj.* Opposed to principles on which society is based.

Antĭs'thėnēs (ă-, -z) (5th c. B.C.). Athenian philosopher, pupil of Socrates and founder of the Cynic school of philosophy.

ăntĭs'trophė *n.* (Lines recited during) returning movement from left to right in Greek choruses. **ăntĭstrŏph'ĭc** *adj.* [Gk, = 'turning about']

ăntĭth'ėsĭs *n.* (pl. *-esēs*). Contrast of ideas marked by parallelism of strongly contrasted words; direct opposite. **ăntĭthĕt'ĭc(al)** *adj.*

ăntĭtŏx'ĭn *n.* Serum or principle serving to neutralize a toxin. **ăntĭtŏx'ĭc** *adj.*

ăn'tĭ-trāde *adj.* & *n.* 1. (Wind) blowing in opposite direction to trade wind in the upper air of the same region. 2. (Wind) blowing in opp. direction to trade wind, but in different region, and on the surface.

ăn'tĭtȳpe *n.* That which a type or symbol represents. **ăntĭtȳp'ĭcal** *adj.*

ăn'tler *n.* Whole or any branch of deer's horns (ill. DEER).

Antonin'us Pī'us (ă-) (A.D. 86–161). Roman emperor; the Roman wall built during his reign from Forth to Clyde is known as the Antonine Wall.

An'tony[1] (ă-), Mark. Marcus Antonius (*c* 82–30 B.C.), Roman general and consul; after Julius Caesar's death tried to make himself sole ruler of the empire; later formed a triumvirate with Octavian and Lepidus; became enthralled by CLEOPATRA; left her to marry Octavian's sister, but returned to her four years later; was deprived of his powers (32 B.C.) by the senate, which declared war on Cleopatra; was defeated in the naval battle of Actium (31 B.C.); committed suicide, mistakenly believing that Cleopatra had done likewise.

Antony[2], St.: see ANTHONY.

ăn'tonȳm *n.* A word of contrary meaning to another.

An'trĭm (ă-). Town and county of Northern Ireland.

ăn'trum *n.* (pl. *-tra*). Cavity in the body, esp. one in the upper jaw-bone.

An'twėrp (ă-). (Fl. Antwerpen, Fr. Anvers) Belgian city-port.

Anūb'is (*a*-). Ancient Egyptian jackal-headeddeity,rulerofthedead, whom he conducts to the shades.

Anūr'a *n.pl.* Order of the class *Amphibia*, containing those amphibians which have no tail or gills as adults, i.e. frogs and toads; = *Batrachia*.

ān'us *n.* End of alimentary canal, opening from the rectum to the exterior (ill. ALIMENTARY).

ăn'vil *n.* Block (usu. of iron) on which metal is worked by smith;

ANVIL

thing resembling this, esp. the INCUS (ill. EAR).

anxī'ėty (ăngz-) *n.* Uneasiness, concern; solicitous desire. **ăn'xious** (-kshus) *adj.* Troubled, uneasy; earnestly desirous; causing anxiety. **ăn'xiously** *adv.*

any (ĕn'ĭ) *adj., pron.,* & *adv.* One, some, no matter which; at all, in any degree.

an'ybŏdy (ĕ-) *n.* or *pron.* Any person.

an'yhow (ĕ-) *adv.* & *conj.* In any way whatever; in any case; at haphazard.

any'thing (ĕ-) *n.* Whatever thing; a thing, no matter which.

an'yway (ĕ-) *adv.* & *conj.* Anyhow.

anywhere (ĕn'ĭwār) *adv.* In any place.

An'zăc (ă-) *adj.* & *n.* (Belonging to, member of) the Australian and New Zealand Army Corps in the 1914–18 war. [initials of name]

A.O.C.(-in-C.) *abbrev.* Air Officer Commanding(-in-Chief).

A. of F. *abbrev.* Admiral of the Fleet.

ā'orist (*or* ār'-) *adj.* & *n.* (Gk & Sansk. gram) ~ (*tense*), one denoting simply occurrence, without limitations as to continuance etc.

āôr't'a *n.* Great artery issuing from left ventricle of heart, carrying blood through its branches to all other parts of body (ill. BLOOD).

à outrance (ah ōōtrahṅs'). To the death. [Fr.]

A.P. *abbrev.* Associated Press.

apāce' *adv.* Swiftly.

Apache *n.* & *adj.* 1. (*a*pǎch'ĭ) (Member) of tribe of N. Amer. Indians fierce and skilful in raiding; ~ *State*, pop. name of Arizona (U.S.), as the home of most of these Indians. 2. (*a*pahsh') Violent street ruffian in Paris.

ăp'anage, ăpp- *n.* Provision for younger children of kings etc.; dependency; perquisite.

apârt' *adv.* Aside, separately.

apârt'heid (-hāt) *n.* Policy of racial segregation in S. Africa. [Afrikaans]

apârt'ment *n.* Single room of a house; (pl. *or* sing.) set of rooms; (sing., chiefly U.S.) flat.

ăp'athy *n.* Insensibility to suffering; indifference; mental indolence. **ăpathĕt'ic** *adj.* **ăpathĕt'ically** *adv.*

ăp'atīte *n.* A native crystallized phosphate of lime.

āpe *n.* (pop.) Monkey; (zool.) = *anthropoid* ~, i.e. gorilla, chimpanzee, orang-utan, or gibbon; *the great* ~*s*, the first 3 of these. ~ *v.t.* Imitate, mimic.

Apĕll'ēs (*a*-, -z). Greek painter of 4th c. B.C.

Ap'ėnnīne(s) (ă-). Mountain range running down the length of Italy.

aperçu (ahp'ārsōō) *n.* Summary exposition, conspectus.

apē'rient (*or* -ēr-) *adj.* & *n.* Laxative.

apéritif (*a*pĕ'ritēf) *n.* Alcoholic liquor taken before meal to stimulate appetite; appetizer.

apĕ'ritive *adj.* & *n.* 1. Laxative, aperient. 2. APÉRITIF.

ăp'erture *n.* Opening, gap; space through which light passes in camera or other optical instrument.

apĕt'alous *adj.* Without petals.

āp'ĕx *n.* (pl. *ā'pĭcēs*, *ā'pĕxes*). Tip, top; vertex (of cone, triangle).

aphās'ia (-z-) *n.* Loss of speech, partial or total, or loss of power to understand written or spoken language as result of cerebral affection.

aphēl'ion *n.* (pl. *-lia*). Point of planet's or comet's orbit farthest from sun.

ăph'ĭs *n.* (pl. *ăph'ĭdēs*). Greenfly; plant-louse, infesting leaves and stems of plants (ill. BUG). **aphid'ian** *adj.*

aphōn'ia *n.* Absence or loss of the power of speech, due to congenital defect or organic disease or functional disturbance.

ăph'orism *n.* Short pithy maxim; definition. **ăphoris'tic** *adj.*

ăphrodis'iăc (-z-) *adj.* & *n.* (Drug) provoking sexual excitement. [f. APHRODITE]

Aphrodīt'ė (ă-). (Gk myth.) Goddess of love and beauty, born of the sea-foam; called Venus by the Romans; her cult was of eastern origin, and she was identified with Astarte, Ishtar, etc.

APES: A. CHIMPANZEE. B. ORANG-UTAN. C. GORILLA. D. GIBBON

āp'iary *n.* Place where bees are kept. **āp'iarist** *n.* Bee-keeper.

ăp'ical *adj.* Belonging to an apex; placed at the tip.

āp'icŭlture *n.* Bee-keeping.

apiece' *adv.* Severally, each.

Ap'is (ah- *or* ā-). An ancient Egyptian deity, the incarnation as a bull of the sun-god Ptah; represented as a bull with the disc of the sun between his horns.

āp'ish *adj.* Like an ape.

aplomb (*a*plŏm') *n.* Self-possession.

A.P.M. *abbrev.* Assistant Provost-Marshal.

Apŏc'alypse. A 'revelation', esp. that made to St. John in the island of Patmos; the book ('Revelation of St. John') recording this. **apŏcalyp'tic(al)** *adjs.* **apŏcalyp'tically** *adv.*

ăpocâr'pous *adj.* (bot.) Having the carpels distinct (ill. FLOWER).

apoc'opė *n.* Cutting off of last sound or syllable of word.

Apŏcr. *abbrev.* Apocrypha.

apŏc'rypha *n.pl.* 1. *The A*~ (of the O.T.), those books which were included in the Septuagint (Greek O.T.) but were not orig. written in Hebrew and not counted genuine by the Jews, and are excluded from the canon. 2. Also applied to other writings which are of doubtful authenticity or spurious; esp. (*New Testament A*~) a number of early Christian writings (Gospels, Epistles, Acts, etc.) some of which were at one time included in the N.T. canon. **apŏc'ryphal** *adj.* Of the Apocrypha; of doubtful authenticity, spurious. [Gk *apokrupha* hidden or secret (writings), i.e. those reserved for the initiated and often falsely ascribed].

Ap'ŏda (ă-) *n.pl.* The coecilians or *gymnophiona*, an order of tropical worm-like animals of the class *Amphibia*.

apŏd'osĭs *n.* (pl. *-sēs*). Concluding clause of sentence; consequent clause in a conditional sentence.

ăp'ogee *n.* Point in orbit of moon or planet farthest from earth; (fig.) highest point.

Apŏll'ō. (Gk myth.) A god, called Phoebus and identified with the sun; he brought back sunshine in spring, sent plagues, and founded cities and colonies; he was the god of music and poetry and could foretell the future.

Appŏll'yon. 'The destroyer', the angel of the bottomless pit (Rev. ix. 11).

apŏlogĕt'ĭc *adj.* Regretfully acknowledging, excusing, fault or failure; of the nature of an apology. **apologĕt'ĭcally** *adv.* **apologĕt'ĭcs** *n.pl.* Reasoned defence, esp. of Christianity. **apŏl'ogist** n. One who defends by argument. **apŏl'ogīze** *v.i.* Make an apology.

ăp'ologue (-ŏg) *n.* Moral fable.

apŏl'ogy *n.* Regretful acknowledgement of offence; excuse; explanation, vindication.

ăp'ophthegm (-ofthĕm; -othĕm) *n.* Terse or pithy saying. **ăpophthegmăt'ĭc** (-ofthĕg-, -othĕg-) *adj.*

ăp'ophȳge (-j) *n.* (archit.) Outward curve at top or bottom of a column (ill. ORDER).

ăpoplĕc'tĭc *adj.* Pertaining to, causing, apoplexy; liable to, suffering from, apoplexy. **ăpoplĕc'tĭcally** *adv.*

ăp'oplĕxy *n.* Seizure caused by blockage or rupture of an artery in the brain, 'stroke'.

ăposiopēs'ĭs *n.* (pl. *-pēsēs*) (rhet.) Breaking off short for effect.

apŏs'tasy *n.* Renunciation of religious vows, faith, party, etc. **apŏs'tate** *n.* & *adj.* (One) guilty of apostasy. **apŏs'tatīze** *v.i.* Become an apostate.

ā pŏsteriōr'ī. (Reasoning) from effects to causes. [L, = 'from what comes after']

apŏs'tle (-sl) *n.* Messenger, esp. any of the twelve sent forth by Christ to preach Gospel (Matt. x. 2); first successful Christian missionary in a country; leader of reform; ~ *spoon*, one with figure of one of the Apostles on the handle; *Apostles' Creed*, simplest and prob. oldest of the Christian creeds, ascribed by tradition to the Apostles. **apostŏl'ĭc** *adj.* Of the Apostles; of the character of an Apostle; of the pope as successor of St. Peter.

apŏs'trophē *n.* Exclamatory address, esp. to absent person or inanimate object; sign (') of omission of letter(s) or of possessive case. **apŏs'trophīze** *v.t.*

apŏth'ecary *n.* (archaic) Druggist, pharmaceutical chemist. [Gk *apothēkē* store-house]

ăpothē'cĭum *n.* (pl. *-cĭa*). (bot.) Cup-shaped fruit body containing asci, freq. brightly coloured, produced by some fungi (ill. LICHEN).

apŏtheōs'ĭs *n.* (pl. *-ōsēs*). Deification; transformation; deified ideal. **apŏth'eosīze** *v.t.*

app. *abbrev.* Appendix; apparent(ly).

appal' (-awl) *v.t.* Dismay, terrify.

Appalăch'ian (ă-) **Mountains.** Mountain system of eastern N. America, which in early days of settlement in America confined English settlers to the eastern coastal belt.

appanage: see APANAGE.

ăpparāt'us *n.* Mechanical requisites, an appliance, for doing something, esp. for scientific experiment; ~ *crit'icus*, materials for critical study of document; variant readings of manuscripts or early editions, usu. printed below text.

appă'rel *v.t.* Dress, attire. ~ *n.* 1. Dress, clothing. 2. (eccles.) Embroidered panel on dalmatic or tunicle.

appă'rent (*or* -ār-) *adj.* Manifest; seeming; *heir* ~, one who cannot be superseded by birth of nearer heir (cf. PRESUMPTIVE). **appă'rently** *adv.*

ăpparĭ'tion *n.* Appearance, esp. of startling kind; ghost.

appă'rĭtor *n.* Officer of civil or ecclesiastical court; herald, usher.

appeal' (-pēl) *v.i.* Call *to* higher tribunal for alteration of decision of lower; call *to* witness for corroboration; make earnest request; ~ *to*, be, prove, attractive to. ~ *n.* Act or right of appealing; *Court of A*~, one hearing cases previously tried in inferior court.

appear' *v.i.* Become visible; present oneself; be published; seem; be manifest. **appear'ance** *n.* Appearing; look, aspect; (pl.) outward show (of prosperity etc.); apparition.

appease' (-z) *v.t.* Pacify, soothe; satisfy. **appease'ment** (-zm-) *n.* (esp.) Policy (orig. that of Neville Chamberlain in 1938–9) of making concessions to an aggressor.

appĕll'ant *adj.* Appealing; concerned with appeals. ~ *n.* One who appeals to higher court. **appĕll'ate** *adj.* Taking cognizance of appeals.

ăppellā'tion *n.* Name, title.

appĕll'atĭve *adj.* (Of words) designating a class (not an individual). ~ *n.* Common noun; appellation.

appĕnd' *v.t.* Attach as an accessory; add, esp. in writing. **appĕnd'age** *n.*

appĕndĭcīt'ĭs *n.* Inflammation of vermiform appendix.

appĕn'dĭx *n.* (pl. *-icēs*, *-ixes*). 1. Subsidiary addition (*to* book etc.). 2. Small process developed from organ, esp. vermiform appendix of the intestine (ill. ALIMENTARY).

ăppertain' *v.i.* Belong, be appropriate, relate, *to*.

ăpp'ĕtīte *n.* Desire, inclination (*for* food, pleasure, etc.); relish. **ăpp'ĕtīzer** *n.* Anything taken to give appetite for a meal. **ăpp'ĕtīzing** *adj.* Rousing appetite.

Appian Way (ă-). Roman highway running SE. from Rome to Brundisium (Brindisi), begun by the censor Appius Claudius Caecus, 312 B.C.

applaud' *v.* Express approval (of), esp. by hand-clapping; praise.

applause' (-z) *n.* Approbation loudly expressed.

ăp'ple *n.* Firm fleshy edible fruit of a rosaceous tree of genus *Malus* (ill. FRUIT); *upset one's* ~*-cart*, spoil one's plans; ~*-jack*, (U.S.) spirit distilled from cider; apple brandy; ~ *of the eye*, pupil, treasured object; ~*-pie bed*, one with sheets, as a joke, so folded as to prevent a person from stretching at full length between them; ~*-pie order*, extreme neatness; ~ *of discord*, the golden apple, inscribed 'to the fairest', introduced by Ate into an assembly of the gods, and contended for by Juno, Minerva, and Venus; hence, cause, subject, of dispute; ~ *of Sodom*, fruit which, acc. to ancient writers, dissolved into smoke and ashes when plucked, Dead Sea apple.

App'leton layer (ăplt-). Layer of the ionosphere at about 300 km. height, now usually termed F_2-layer. (ill. ATMOSPHERE). [Sir E. *Appleton* (1892–1965), British physicist]

applī'ance *n.* Applying; thing applied as means to an end.

ăpp'lĭcable *adj.* Capable of being applied. **ăpplĭcabĭl'ĭty** *n.*

ăpp'lĭcant *n.* One who applies.

ăpplĭcā'tion *n.* Applying; thing applied; request; relevancy, diligence.

appliqué (aplēk'ā) *n.* & *adj.* (Needlework) consisting of pieces of material cut out and applied to the surface of other material of different colour or texture; material so applied. ~ *v.t.* Sew (material) to another as appliqué.

applȳ' *v.* Put close *to*, put in contact; administer (remedy); devote (*to*); refer (*to*); address oneself (*for* help etc.) *to*; make application (*for*); *applied*, put to practical use.

appoggiatura (-ŏjatoor'a) *n.* (mus.) Grace-note. [It.]

appoint' *v.t.* Fix (time etc.); prescribe, ordain; assign *to* office. **appoint'ment** *n.* Engagement, assignation; appointing; office assigned; (pl.) outfit.

appŏrt' (*or* ăp'ŏrt) *n.* Material thing produced, professedly by occult means, at spiritualist séance.

appŏr'tion *v.t.* Assign as share; portion out. **appŏr'tionment** *n.*

ăpp'osĭte (-z-) *adj.* Well put; appropriate. **ăpposĭ'tion** (-z-) *n.* Placing side by side; (gram.) in ~, syntactically parallel; in same case etc.

appraise' (-z) *v.t.* Fix price for; estimate. **apprais'al** (-z-), **appraise'ment** (-zm-) *ns.*

apprē'ciable (-sha-) *adj.* Capable of being estimated; sensible, perceptible. **apprē'ciably** *adv.*

apprē'ciāte (-shĭ-) *v.* Estimate aright; be sensitive to; esteem highly; raise, rise, in value. **apprēciā'tion** (-shĭ-) *n.* **apprē'ciative** (-sha-) *adj.*

ăpprėhĕnd' *v.t.* Seize, arrest; understand; anticipate with fear.

ăpprėhĕn'sĭble *adj.* Perceptible to senses.

ăpprėhĕn'sion (-shn) *n.* Arrest; understanding; dread.

ăpprėhĕn'sĭve *adj.* Relating to sensuous perception, or intellectual understanding; uneasy in mind. **ăpprėhĕn'sĭvely** (-vl-) *adv.* **ăpprėhĕn'sĭvenėss** (-vn-) *n.*

apprĕn'tĭce *n.* Learner of a craft, bound to serve, and entitled to instruction from, his employer for a specified term. ~ *v.t.* Bind as apprentice (*to*). **apprĕn'tĭceshĭp** (-ssh-) *n.*

apprīse' (-z) *v.t.* Give notice *of*, inform.

ăpp'rō *n.* *On* ~ (of goods supplied), on approval, i.e. to be returned if not satisfactory.

approach' *v.* Come nearer (to); make overtures to. ~ *n.* Approaching; access, passage; (golf) shot which is intended to reach green. **approach'able** *adj.* Easy of access; welcoming, friendly to advances.

ăpp'robāte *v.t.* (U.S.) Approve formally, sanction.

ăpprobā'tion *n.* Sanction, approval. **ăpp'robātĭve, ăpp'robātory** *adjs.*

apprō'priate *adj.* Suitable, proper. **apprō'priately** *adv.* **apprō'priāte** *v.t.* Take possession of; devote to special purposes. **apprōpriā'tion** *n.*

approve' (-oov) *v.* Confirm, sanction, commend; ~ *of*, pronounce or consider good; *approved school*, reformatory school, formerly called an industrial school; *approved society*, a benevolent society officially approved and entitled to administer benefits etc. under the National Insurance Act (1911) and subsequent acts. **appro'val** *n.*

appro'ver (-ōōv-) *n.* One who approves; one who turns Queen's (*or* King's) evidence.

apprŏx'ĭmate *adj.* Very near; fairly correct. **apprŏx'ĭmately** *adv.* **apprŏx'ĭmāte** *v.* Bring or come near (*to*). **apprŏxĭmā'tion** *n.*

appûrt'ėnance *n.* Appendage; accessory; belonging. **appûrt'ėnant** *adj.* Belonging, appertaining.

Apr. *abbrev.* April.

āp'rĭcŏt *n.* Succulent orange-pink fruit, with smooth stone, of the rosaceous tree *Prunus armeniaca*; this tree; colour of the fruit.

Ap'rĭl (ā-). 4th month of the modern calendar (2nd of the Roman); ~ *Fools' Day*, 1st April, day on which the unsuspecting are made victims of practical jokes or sent on fool's errands.

ā priōr'ī *adv.* & *adj.* (Reasoning) from cause to effect; deductive(ly). [L, = 'from what is before']

āp'ron *n.* 1. Garment worn in front of body to protect clothes; *tied to* (person's) ~*-strings*, unduly dependent on. 2. Part of ceremonial dress (of bishops, freemasons, etc.). 3. (theatr.) Advanced strip of stage for playing scenes before proscenium arch; ~ *stage*, stage equipped with this (ill. THEATRE). 4. Part of lathe carrying gears and controls. 5. Area near hangars of airfield for accommodation of aircraft manœuvring on ground. 6. Broad strip on inner side of boat's bow strengthening the stem (ill. BOAT).

ăpropos' (-pō) *adv.* & *adj.* To the purpose; in respect *of*.

ăpse *n.* Semicircular or polygonal recess, usu. with vaulted roof, in church or other building (ill. BASILICA).

ăp'sĭdal *adj.* 1. Of the form of an apse. 2. Of the apsides (see foll.).

ăp'sĭs *n.* (pl. *ăp'sĭdēs, ăpsīd'ēs*). Aphelion or perihelion of planet; apogee or perigee of moon.

ăpt *adj.* Suitable, appropriate; quick, ready; inclined (*to*). **ăpt'ly** *adv.* **ăpt'nėss** *n.*

ăp'terous *adj.* Wingless.

ăp'terÿx *n.* New Zealand nocturnal bird with rudimentary wings and no tail, kiwi. [Gk *a-* not, *pterux* wing]

ăp'tĭtūde *n.* Fitness; natural propensity; ability; (psychol.) capacity to acquire skill in a particular field of bodily or mental performance.

Apuleius (ăpūlē'*us*), Lucius (b. *c* A.D. 114). Platonic philosopher, of Madaura in N. Africa; author of the romance known as 'The Golden Ass'.

Apūl'ia. Ancient country and modern region (It. *Puglia*) forming the 'heel' of SE. Italy.

A.Q.M.G. *abbrev.* Assistant Quartermaster-General.

ă'qua-fŏrt'ĭs *n.* (Old term for) nitric acid; *aqua forti* or *a.f.* (on prints), etched by (so-and-so). [L, = 'strong water']

ă'qualŭng *n.* Diver's portable breathing apparatus, consisting of cylinders of compressed air.

ăquamarine' (-ēn) *n.* Bluish-green transparent beryl; colour of this. [L *aqua marina* sea-water]

ă'qua-rē'gĭa *n.* Mixture of concentrated nitric and hydrochloric acids, able to dissolve gold and platinum, which are not attacked by the unmixed acids. [L, = 'royal water']

ăquarĕlle' *n.* (Painting in) transparent water-colour.

aquâr'ĭum *n.* (pl. *-ĭums, -ĭa*). Artificial pond or tank for keeping live aquatic plants, fishes, or animals; place containing such tanks.

Aquâr'ĭus (*a*-). The Water-carrier, a constellation; the 11th sign (♒) of the zodiac, which the sun enters on 21st Jan.

aquăt'ĭc *adj.* & *n.* (Plant, animal) living in or frequenting water; (of sports) conducted in or on water.

ă'quatĭnt *n.* (Colour-) print with finely grained transparent effect, produced by coating a copper plate (or plates) with a porous resin ground, painting the design on it with varnish, immersing it in nitric acid, and inking it, when the protected parts, being less corroded by the acid, will take up less ink; this process. ~ *v.* Work in aquatint; reproduce by this means.

ăquavit' (-vēt) *n.* Colourless or yellowish alcoholic spirit distilled from potatoes or other starch-containing plant; schnapps.

ă'qua-vīt'ae *n.* (obs.) Brandy or other alcoholic spirit. [L, = 'water of life']

ă'quėdŭct *n.* Artificial channel, esp. elevated structure of masonry across valley etc. for conveyance of water.

ROMAN AQUEDUCT
1. Water channel

ā'quėous *adj.* Of water, watery; (geol.) produced by the action of water; ~ *humour* (physiol.) fluid secreted in the eye.

Aquĭlē'gia (ă-, ja) *n.* Botanical name of columbines.

ăq'uĭlīne *adj.* Of an eagle; eagle-like; curved like eagle's beak.

Aquĭn'as, St. Thomas (*c* 1225–74). Italian philosopher, a Dominican friar, whose writings, notably his 'Summa Totius Theologiae', represent the culmination of scholastic philosophy.

Aquĭtaine' (ă-). Ancient province of SW. France, comprising at some periods the whole country from the Loire to the Pyrenees; by the marriage of Eleanor of Aquitaine to Henry II it became one of the English possessions in France.

A.R. *abbrev.* Advice of receipt; annual return.

A.R.A. *abbrev.* Associate of the Royal Academy.

A′rab (ă-). 1. Native of Arabia; the term was originally confined to the pure Semites of Arabia but is now applied to their descendants, many of whom are mixed with native races, in Africa, Palestine, Persia, etc. 2. Arab horse of a breed noted for its graceful build and speed. 3. *street* ~, homeless child.

ărabĕsque′ (-sk) *adj.* & *n.* 1. Arabian; fantastic. 2. (Decoration) of fancifully twisted scroll-work, leaves, etc., orig. devised by Mohammedan artists owing to ban

ARABESQUE

1. Moresque. 2. Renaissance type with grotesques

on images. 3. Musical composition suggestive of this decoration. 4. (ballet) Pose in which dancer stands on one foot with one arm extended in front and the other arm and leg extended behind.

Arāb′ĭa (*a*-). Peninsula of SW. Asia, largely desert, lying between the Red Sea and the Persian Gulf and bounded on the north by Jordan and Iraq; SAUDI ~: see entry; ~ *Deserta*, ancient name for the Syrian desert and parts of the Arabian peninsula; ~ *Felix*, the more fertile SW. mountainous coastal regions of Arabia, including the modern YEMEN, ASIR, and part of Hadhramaut; ~ *Petrae*, the Sinai peninsula.

Arāb′ian (*a*-) *ad*. & *n.* (Native) of Arabia; ~ *camel*, one-humped camel (*Camelus dromedarius*); ~ *Nights* (*Entertainments*), also called the 'Thousand and One Nights', a collection of fairy-stories and fantastic romances written in Arabic, linked together by a framework of Persian origin, though the tales themselves, which were probably collected in Egypt at some time in the 14th–16th centuries, are for the most part not Persian but Arabian in character.

A′rabĭc (ă-) *adj.* Arabian; *gum* ~, gum exuded from various kinds of acacia and used in the manufacture of adhesives, confectionery and in textile printing, pharmacy, etc.; ~ *numerals*, those (1, 2, 3, etc.) now in common use in all western countries, most of which were first used in India and were introduced into the west by the Arabs. ~ *n.* A Semitic language, orig. that of the Arabs, but now spoken in a large part of northern Africa and in Syria and Palestine, as well as in Arabia. **A′rabist** *n.* Student of Arabic civilization, language, etc.

Arabi Pash′a (*a*rahb′ĭ) (*c* 1839–1911). Egyptian soldier and politician of anti-European sympathies, defeated at Tel-el-Kebir (1882) by Sir Garnet Wolseley.

ă′rable *adj.* & *n.* (Land) fit for tillage.

Arăch′nē (*a*-, -k-). (Gk legend) A skilful weaver who challenged Athene to a contest; Athene tore the work in pieces, and Arachne hanged herself, but Athene changed her into a spider.

arăch′nĭd (-k-) *n.* (zool.) Member of the *Arachnida*, a class of wingless arthropods including spiders, scorpions, mites, king-crabs, and others, and distinguished from insects esp. by having eight or more legs and no antennae.

arăch′noid (-k-) *adj.* & *n.* (anat.) (One) of the three membranes surrounding the brain and supporting the blood-vessels.

A′ragon (ă-). Province of Spain, bounded on N. by the Pyrenees and on E. by Catalonia and Valencia.

A.R.A.M. *abbrev.* Associate of the Royal Academy of Music.

Aramā′ĭc (ă-). Language of Aram or Syria; the northern branch of the Semitic family of languages, including Syriac and Chaldee.

A′ran Islands (ă-). Group of three islands off W. coast of Ireland, lying across mouth of Galway Bay.

A′rany (ah-), János (1817–82). Hungarian national epic poet.

A′rarăt (ă-). Two peaks of the Armenian plateau, on which, acc. to Gen. viii. 4, Noah's ark rested after the Flood.

Araucăr′ĭa (ă-) *n.* Genus of evergreen coniferous trees including monkey-puzzle. [*Arauco* district in Chile]

ar̄b′alĕst *n.* Crossbow with mechanism for drawing it.

ar̄b′ĭter *n.* Judge; one appointed by two parties to settle dispute, umpire; one with entire control *of*; ~ *elegantiae*: see PETRONIUS ARBITER.

ar̄bĭt′rament *n.* Decision of dispute by arbiter; authoritative decision.

ar̄b′ĭtrary *adj.* Derived from mere opinion, capricious; despotic; (law) discretionary. **ar̄b′ĭtrarĭly** *adv.*

ar̄b′ĭtrāte *v.* Decide by arbitration. **ar̄bĭtrā′tion** *n.* Settlement of dispute by an arbiter.

ar̄b′ĭtrātor *n.* (now the legal term for) Arbiter.

ar̄b′or *n.* Main support of machine; axle or spindle on which wheel revolves (ill. WHEEL).

ar̄borā′ceous (-sh*u*s) *adj.* Tree-like; wooded.

Arb′or Day (ar̄-). Day set apart annually in U.S., S. Australia, and elsewhere for public tree-planting.

ar̄bōr′ėal *adj.* Of, living in, trees.

ar̄bōr′ėous *adj.* Wooded; arboreal; arborescent.

ar̄borĕs′cent *adj.* Tree-like; branching. **ar̄borĕs′cence** *n.*

ar̄borĕt′ŭm *n.* (pl. -*ta*). Tree-garden.

ar̄b′orĭcŭlture *n.* Cultivation of trees and shrubs. **ar̄borĭcŭl′tural** (-ch*e*r-) *adj.* **ar̄borĭcŭl′turist** *n.*

ar̄b′our (-*er*) *n.* Shady retreat with sides and roof of trees or climbing plants.

Arb′uthnot (ar̄-), John (1667–1735). English physician and writer of political pamphlets and medical works.

arbū′tus (ar̄-) *n.* Genus (*A*~) of evergreens of the heather family (*Ericaceae*) including strawberry-tree.

ar̄c[1] *n.* 1. Part of circumference of circle or other curve (ill. CIRCLE). 2. (elect.) Intense electrical discharge in gas or vapour, a luminous bridge of conducting gas formed between two separate electrical poles; ~-*lamp*, ~-*light*, using this; ~-*welding*, welding by striking an arc between, e.g., an iron electrode and two pieces of iron requiring to be welded together; the heat of the arc fuses the surfaces which are to be welded.

Arc[2], Joan of: see JOAN.

A.R.C.A. *abbrev.* Associate of the Royal College of Art.

ar̄cāde′ *n.* 1. Passage arched

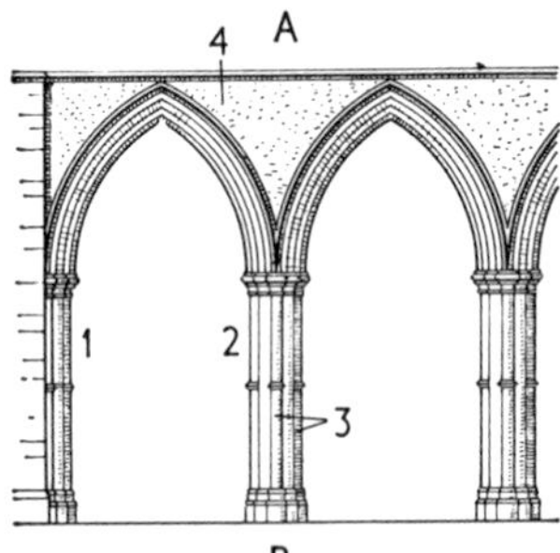

ARCADES:
A. ROMANESQUE BLIND ARCADE
B. GOTHIC NAVE ARCADE
1. Respond. 2. Pier. 3. Shafts. 4. Spandrel

over; any covered walk, esp. one with shops at side(s). 2. (archit.) Series of arches on same plane, supporting, or attached to, a wall.

Arcăd'ĭa (âr-). Mountainous district in the Peloponnese, taken as an ideal region of rustic contentment (in this sense also **Arc'ady**). **Arcăd'ĭan** *adj.* & *n.* Of Arcadia; ideal(ly) rustic.

ârcāne' *adj.* Mysterious, secret.

ârcān'um *n.* (usu. in pl. *-na*). Mystery, secret.

ârch[1] *n.* Structure, usu. curved, consisting of wedge-shaped pieces so arranged as to support one another by mutual pressure, and used to carry weight of roof, wall, etc., or as ornament; any curved structure resembling this in form and function; curve; vault; *archway,* arched passage or entrance. **ârch'wīse** (-z) *adv.* **ârch** *v.* Furnish with, form into, form, an arch; overarch, span.

Archaeozō'ĭc (-k-) *adj.* & *n.* (Of) the geological period before the Palaeozoic (ill. GEOLOGY)

ârchā'ĭc (-k-) *adj.* Primitive, antiquated; no longer in common use. **ârchā'ĭcally** *adv.*

ârch'āĭsm (-k-) *n.* Obsolete word or phrase; retention or imitation of the old or obsolete (esp. in language and art). **ârch'āīze** *v.i.*

ârch'āngel[1] (-k-) *n.* Angel of highest rank. **ârchăngĕl'ĭc** *adj.*

Arch'āngel[2] (ârk-). Arkhangelsk, port of N. Russia, on White Sea.

with bow and arrows. **ârch ery** *n.*

ârch'ėtȳpe (-k-) *n.* 1. Original model, prototype. 2. (Jungian psychol.) Universal symbol; mental image given by inheritance.

ârch'fiend' (-ēnd) *n.* Satan.

ârchidīăc'onal (-kĭ-) *adj.* Of an archdeacon.

ârchiėpĭs'copal (-kĭ-) *adj.* Of an archbishop.

Archĭl'ochus (-kĭl'*okus*) (*fl.* 648 B.C.). Greek poet of Paros, celebrated for satirical iambic verse.

ârchĭmăn'drīte (-k-) *n.* Superior of monastery of Orthodox Church, equivalent to abbot in Western Churches.

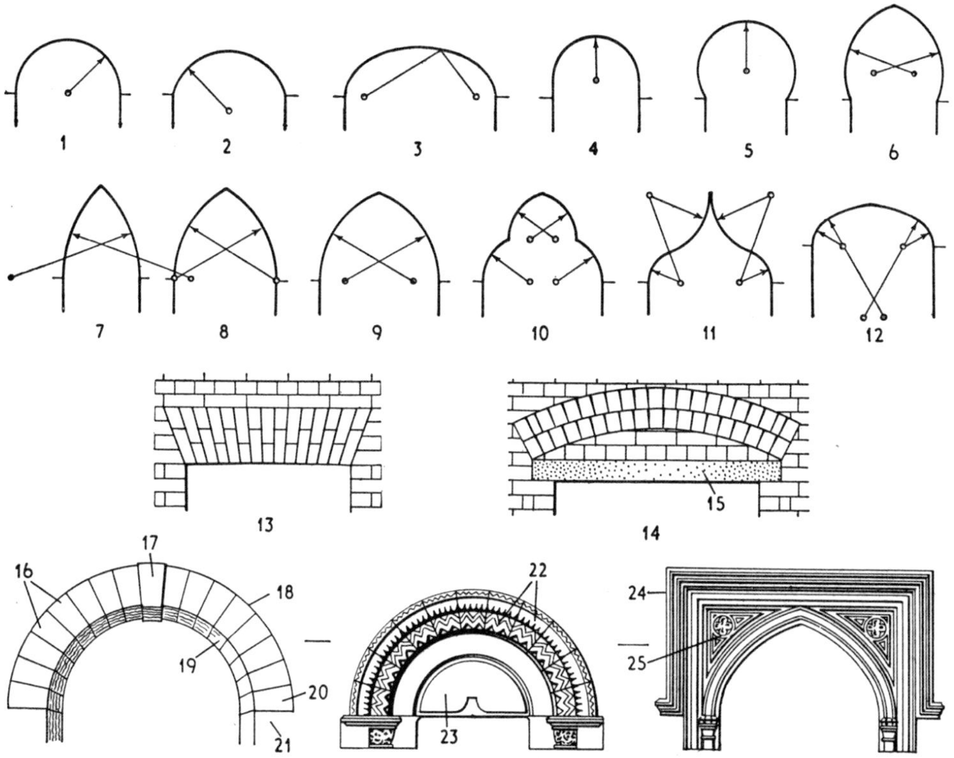

TYPES AND CONSTRUCTION OF ARCHES

1. Semicircular. 2. Segmental. 3. Elliptical. 4. Stilted. 5. Round horseshoe. 6. Pointed horseshoe. 7. Lancet. 8. Equilateral. 9. Drop. 10. Trefoil or cusped. 11. Ogee. 12. Four-centred. 13. Flat arch. 14. Relieving arch. 15. Lintel. 16. Voussoirs. 17. Keystone. 18. Extrados. 19. Intrados, soffit, or archivolt. 20. Springer. 21. Impost. 22. Orders. 23. Tympanum. 24. Hoodmould, dripstone, or label. 25. Spandrel

ârch[2] *adj.* Playfully roguish. **ârch'ly** *adv.* **ârch'nėss** *n.*

ârch- *prefix.* Chief, superior; leading; extreme; first.

ârchaeŏl'ogȳ (-kĭ-) *n.* Study of antiquities or of prehistoric remains. **ârchaeolŏ'gĭcal** *adj.*

ârchbĭsh'op *n.* Chief bishop, metropolitan. **ârchbĭsh'opric** *n.*

ârchdeac'on *n.* Ecclesiastical dignitary next below bishop, superintending rural deans and holding ecclesiastical court. **ârchdeac'onry** *n.*

ârchdī'ocese (-sēs) *n.* Archbishop's see.

ârch'dūke *n.* Prince of imperial house of Austria. **ârchdū'cal** *adj.* **ârchdŭch'ėss, ârchdŭch'y** *ns.*

ârch-ĕn'ėmy *n.* Chief enemy; *the* ~, Satan.

ârch'er *n.* One who shoots

Archĭmēd'ēs (ârk-, -z) (287–212 B.C.). Greek mathematician of Syracuse; said to have made many mechanical inventions, including the screw (named after him) for raising water; *principle of* ~, (physics) the principle

ARCHIMEDEAN SCREW

that when a body is partly or completely immersed in a fluid the apparent loss of weight is equal to the weight of the fluid displaced. **Archimēd'ean** *adj.*

ar̄chĭpĕl'agō (-k-) *n.* (pl. *-s*). Aegean Sea; sea with many islands; group of islands.

ar̄ch'itĕct (-k-) *n.* 1. Designer of buildings who prepares plans and superintends execution. 2. Designer of ship.

ar̄chitĕctŏn'ic (-k-) *adj.* 1. Of architecture. 2. Of the systematization of knowledge.

ar̄ch'itĕcture (-k-) *n.* Science of building; thing built; style of building; construction. **ar̄chitĕc'tural** (-cher-) *adj.* **ar̄chitĕc'turally** *adv.*

ar̄ch'itrāve (-k-) *n.* 1. Main beam resting immediately on two or more columns; lowest part of entablature (ill. ORDER). 2. Moulded frame round doorway, window, or arch (ill. DOOR).

ar̄ch'īve (-k-) *n.* (usu. pl.). Public records; place in which these are kept. **ar̄ch'ivist** *n.* Keeper of archives.

ar̄ch'ivōlt (-k-) *n.* Under-curve of arch (ill. ARCH); mouldings decorating this.

ar̄ch'on (-k-) *n.* One of 9 chief magistrates in ancient Athens; chief magistrate of other ancient Greek cities; ruler, president. **ar̄ch'onship** *n.*

A.R.C.M. *abbrev.* Associate of the Royal College of Music.

A.R.C.O. *abbrev.* Associate of the Royal College of Organists.

A.R.C.S. *abbrev.* Associate of the Royal College of Science.

ar̄c'tic *adj.* Of the N. Pole; northern; intensely cold; *A~ Circle*, the parallel of 66° 32′ N., north of which the sun does not rise at midwinter or set at midsummer (ill. EARTH); *A~ Ocean*, the ocean N. of the Arctic Circle; the *A~*, the regions (both land and sea) round the N. Pole. [Gk *arktos* bear, Ursa Major]

Arctūr'us (ar̄-). Star in the constellation Boötes, one of the highest in N. hemisphere. [Gk *arktos* bear, *ouros* guardian, because of its position in a line with the tail of Ursa Major]

Ard'en (ar̄-). A woodland district of N. Warwickshire, part of an ancient forest formerly covering a great part of the Midlands and W. England.

Ardennes (ar̄dĕn', -ĕnz'). Ancient forest district including parts of Belgium, Luxemburg, and N. France.

ar̄d'ent *adj.* Eager, zealous, fervent; burning. **ar̄d'ently** *adv.*

ar̄d'our (-*er*) *n.* Zeal; warmth.

ar̄d'ūous *adj.* Hard, laborious; strenuous. **ar̄d'ūously** *adv.* **ar̄d'ūousness** *n.*

are (ar̄) pl. pres. ind. of BE.

ar̄'ea *n.* Extent of surface; region; scope, range; sunk court or yard before basement of house (ill. HOUSE); floor of concert-hall etc.

ă'rėca (*or* arēk'*a*) *n.* Genus of tropical Asiatic palms bearing pungent astringent fruit; ~ *nut*, astringent seed of a species of areca; betel.

arēn'a *n.* Central part of amphitheatre, in which combats take place (ill. AMPHITHEATRE); central part of stadium; scene of conflict or action.

ărėnā'ceous (-sh*us*) *adj.* Sandy; sand-like.

Arėŏp'agus (ă-). Hill at Athens where highest judicial tribunal met. **Arėŏp'agīte** (-g-). Member of court of Areopagus. [Gk *Areios pagos* hill of Ares]

Ares (ar̄'ēz). (Gk. myth.) The god of war, son of Zeus and Hera; identified with the Roman MARS.

arête' (-āt) *n.* Sharp ridge of mountain (ill. MOUNTAIN). [Fr.]

Arėthūs'a (ă-, -z-). (Gk legend) A water-nymph who fled from Greece to Ortygia in Sicily, pursued by the river-god Alpheus. The waters of the river Alpheus (in the Peloponnese) were believed to flow unmixed through the sea and emerge mingled with the fountain of Arethusa at Ortygia.

Arėti'nō (ă-, -ēn-), Pietro (1492–1556). Italian author of comedies, satires, and licentious poems.

ar̄'gali *n.* Large Asiatic wild sheep, *Ovis ammon.*

Argand (ar̄g'ahṅ), Aimé (*c* 1750–1803). Swiss inventor of the ~ *lamp* (ar̄g'*a*nd), with a tubular wick, which allows air to reach both inner and outer surfaces of the flame (ill. LAMP); ~ *burner*, a gas-burner constructed on the same principle.

ar̄'gent *n.* & *adj.* Silver (colour, esp. in heraldry; ill. HERALDRY).

ar̄gentif'erous *adj.* Yielding silver.

Argenti'na (ar̄-, -ēn*a*) (also *the Ar'gentīne*). Republic occupying most of S. part of S. America E. of the Andes; first settled by Spaniards (1526 onwards); remained a Spanish colony until a revolt, beginning in 1810, led to the declaration in 1816 of the independence of the *Provincias Unidas del Rio de la Plata* ('United Provinces of the Silver River'); capital, Buenos Aires. **Argentin'ian** *adj.* & *n.* (Native, inhabitant) of Argentina. [L *argentum* silver, because the Rio de la Plata district exported it]

ar̄'gentīne *adj.* Of silver; silvery; *the A~*, ARGENTINA.

ar̄'gil (-j-) *n.* (Potter's) clay. **ar̄gillā'ceous** (-sh*us*) *adj.*

Arg'īve (ar̄g-) *adj.* & *n.* (Native) of ARGOS or Argolis; Greek.

ar̄g'ŏl *n.* Crude tartar; grey or red substance deposited from fermented wines.

ar̄g'ŏn *n.* (chem.) An inert gaseous element, present to extent of about 1 % in the air, discovered *c* 1894 by Lord Rayleigh and Sir William Ramsay; used in 'gas-filled' electric light bulbs etc.; symbol A, at. no. 18, at. wt 39·948.

Arg'onauts (ar̄-). (Gk legend) The heroes who accompanied JASON on board the ship *Argo* on the quest for the Golden Fleece.

Arg'ŏs (ar̄-). An ancient Greek town of the E. Peloponnese, from which the peninsula of **Arg'olis** derived its name.

ar̄g'osy *n.* (hist., poet.) Large vessel (orig. of Ragusa or Venice) carrying rich merchandise; (poet.) ship. [prob. from It. *Ragusea* (*nave*), (ship) of Ragusa]

ar̄g'ot (-ō) *n.* Jargon, slang, esp. of thieves.

ar̄g'ūe *v.* Maintain by reasoning; reason; prove, indicate. **ar̄g'ūable** *adj.*

ar̄g'ūfȳ *v.i.* (colloq.) Argue excessively.

ar̄g'ūment *n.* Reason advanced; debate; summary of subject-matter of book etc. **ar̄gūmĕntā'tion** *n.* Methodical reasoning; debate.

ar̄gūmĕn'tative *adj.* Logical; fond of arguing. **ar̄gūmĕn'tatively** *adv.* **ar̄gūmĕn'tativenėss** *n.*

Arg'us (ar̄-). (Gk myth.) 1. Fabulous person with 100 eyes, slain by Hermes; after his death Hera transferred his eyes to the tail of the peacock. 2. The dog of Ulysses, who recognized his master on his return from Troy after an absence of 20 years. 3. Specific name of certain butterflies. 4. Genus of pheasants, natives of Asia.

Argyl. *abbrev.* Argyllshire.

Argyllshire (ar̄gīl-). County on W. coast of Scotland.

ar̄'ia *n.* Air, song, esp. in opera or oratorio, usu. of formal structure and accompanied by instrument(s); song-like movement in instrumental composition.

Ariăd'nė (ă-). (Gk myth.) Daughter of Minos, king of Crete; helped Theseus to escape from the labyrinth of the Minotaur by providing him with a clue of thread; then became his wife, but he deserted her in the island of Naxos, where she was found and married by Dionysus.

Ar'ian (ar̄-) *adj.* & *n.* (Holder) of the heretical doctrine of *Arius* of Alexandria (4th c.), who denied the consubstantiality of Christ. **Ar'ianism** *n.*

A.R.I.B.A. *abbrev.* Associate of the Royal Institute of British Architects.

ă'rid *adj.* Dry, parched; (geog., of climate or region) having insufficient water to support vegetation. **arid'ity** *n.*

Ar'iel (ar̄-). In Shakespeare's 'The Tempest', a spirit whom the magician Prospero has released from imprisonment by a witch, Sycorax.

Aries (ar̄'ĭēz). The Ram, the first constellation and sign (♈) of the zodiac, which the sun enters at the vernal equinox.

aright′ (-īt) *adv.* Rightly.

ă′ril *n.* (bot.) Extra seed-covering, freq. brightly coloured (e.g. yew, spindle) (ill. YEW).

Arimathea: see JOSEPH[1].

Arī′on (7th c. B.C.). Greek poet and musician of Lesbos; said to have perfected the dithyramb. Acc. to legend, sailors on a ship resolved to murder him, but he begged first to play a tune, did so, and leapt overboard; dolphins were attracted by the music, and one bore him on its back to land.

Ariŏs′tō (ă-), Lodovico (1474–1533). Italian poet, author of the romantic epic 'Orlando Furioso'.

arīse′ (-z) *v.i.* (past t. *arōse′*, past part. *arisen* pr. -ĭzn). Appear, spring up, occur.

Aristârch′us[1] (ă-, -k-) of Samos (*c* 280 B.C.). Astronomer and mathematician; he maintained that the earth revolved round the sun, though he thought that its orbit was a circle (not an ellipse).

Aristârch′us[2] (ă- -k-) of Samothrace (*c* 217–*c* 145 B.C.). Librarian at Alexandria; edited the Greek classics; regarded as the originator of scientific scholarship.

Aristīd′ēs (ă-, -z) (d. *c* 468 B.C.). Athenian general and statesman, called 'the Just'; commanded his tribe at the battle of Marathon; was archon in 489, but was later ostracized and died in poverty.

Aristĭpp′us (ă-). Name of two Greek philosophers: the elder (late 5th c. B.C.), a native of Cyrene and friend of Socrates, is freq. called the founder of the Cyrenaic school, prob. by confusion with the younger, his grandson (fl. *c* 400–365), who taught that immediate pleasure is the only end of action.

ăristŏc′racy *n.* The nobility; supremacy of privileged order; government by nobles.

ă′ristocrăt *n.* Member of aristocracy. **ăristocrăt′ic** *adj.* Belonging to the aristocracy; having distinguished bearing and manners. **ăristocrăt′ically** *adv.*

Aristŏph′anēs (ă-, -z) (*c* 444–*c* 380 B.C.). Athenian comic dramatist; author of comedies (the 'Birds', 'Frogs', 'Wasps', etc.) caricaturing his contemporaries and their attitude to public affairs.

A′ristŏtle (ă-) (384–322 B.C.). Aristoteles, Greek philosopher; pupil of Plato at Athens; became tutor to the young Alexander of Macedon; returned to Athens in 335; there conducted a school which was known as the 'Peripatetic' from his habit of walking up and down (*peripatŏn*) the paths of the LYCEUM while lecturing; wrote the 'Ethics', 'Politics', and 'Poetics', and works on zoology, physics, metaphysics, logic (which he invented), and rhetoric. **Aristotēl′ian** *adj.* & *n.*

arĭth′mĕtic *n.* Science of numbers; computation. **ărithmĕt′ical** *adj.* **ărithmĕt′ically** *adv.* **ărithmĕtĭ′cian** (-shn) *n.*

Arius: see ARIAN.

Ariz. *abbrev.* Arizona.

Arizō′na (ă-). A mountain State of U.S., admitted to the Union in 1912; capital, Phoenix.

ârk *n.* 1. Chest, box; ~ *of the Covenant*, *of Testimony*, wooden coffer containing tables of Jewish law, 'the most sacred religious symbol of early Israel'; ~ *of the Law*; chest or cupboard in Jewish synagogue containing scrolls of the Law. 2. Covered floating vessel in which NOAH was saved at the Deluge.

Ark. *abbrev.* Arkansas.

Arkansas (ârk′*a*nsaw). A west-south-central State of U.S., admitted to the Union in 1836; capital, Little Rock.

Arkwright (ârk′rīt), Sir Richard (1732–92). English engineer, inventor of the spinning-frame.

Arles (ârl). Town of S. France, on the river Rhône, on the site of a Roman city (*Arelate*), the chief residence of Constantine.

ârm[1] *n.* Upper limb of human body; sleeve; branch; arm-like thing; ~-*chair*, chair with supports for arms; *arm′pit*, hollow under arm at shoulder. **ârm′ful** *n.* **ârm′-lĕss** *adj.*

ârm[2] *n.* 1. Particular kind of weapon; (pl.) weapons; *fire-arms*, weapons requiring explosive; *small arms*, portable fire-arms, as rifles, pistols, light machine-guns, sub-machine-guns, etc.; *stand of arms*, set of weapons for one soldier. 2. Each kind of force, as *infantry* ~, *air* ~. 3. (pl.) Heraldic devices (ill. HERALDRY); *coat of arms*, blazon; *King of Arms*, Chief Herald. ~ *v.* Furnish with arms; take up arms; provide, furnish, *with*.

Armada (ârmahd′*a*). (*Spanish*) ~, the fleet sent by Philip II of Spain against England in 1588; it was defeated in the Channel and dispersed by the English fleet under Lord Howard of Effingham and such captains as Drake, Frobisher, and Hawkins; many of the ships were lost in attempting to return round the N. of Scotland.

ârmadĭll′ō *n.* (pl. -*s*). 1. Burrowing, usu. nocturnal, S.-Amer. mammal, protected by bony plates resembling armour. 2. Genus of small terrestrial crustacea allied to wood-louse. [Span. dim. of *armado* armed creature]

ARMADILLO

Armagĕdd′on (âr-, -g-). The place where the kings of the earth are to be gathered together for 'the battle of that great day of God Almighty': see Rev. xvi. 16.

Armagh (ârmah′). County and county town of Northern Ireland.

ârm′ament *n.* Force (usu. naval) equipped for war; military equipment, esp. big guns, on warship; process of equipping for war.

ârm′ature *n.* 1. Arms, armour, defensive covering of animals or plants. 2. Piece of soft iron placed in contact with poles of a magnet to preserve the intensity of magnetization or to support a load; core of laminated iron wound round by coils of insulated copper-wire, that part of a dynamo which rotates in the magnetic field (ill. DYNAMO). 3. Framework of wire, wood, etc., round which sculptor builds clay or plaster model.

Armēn′ia (âr-). One of the constituent Republics of the Soviet Union, lying S. of the Caucasus, part of the larger kingdom of Armenia, most of which was under Turkish rule from the 16th c.; capital, Erivan. **Armēn′ian** *adj.* & *n.* (Native, language) of Armenia.

ârm′iger (-j-) *n.* One entitled to bear heraldic arms.

ârm′illary *adj.* Pertaining to bracelets; ~ *sphere*, skeleton celestial globe consisting of metal rings representing the equator, ecliptic, tropics, etc., revolving on an axis.

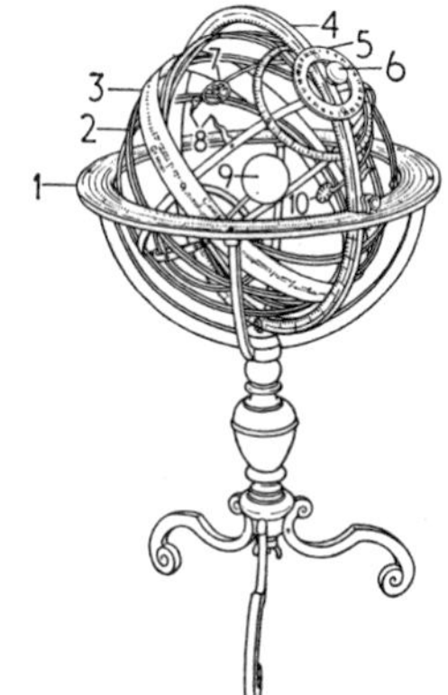

16th-c. ARMILLARY SPHERE

1. Horizon. 2. Equator. 3. Ecliptic. 4. Meridian circle. 5. Time scale. 6. Pole. 7. Moon. 8. Star pointers. 9. Earth. 10. Sun

Armĭn′ius[1] (âr-) (18 B.C.–A.D. 19). Latinized form of Hermann, chief of the German tribe of the Cherusci, leader of the insurrection against the Romans under Varus, who were defeated at the battle of the Teutoburg forest (A.D. 8).

Armĭn′ius[2] (âr-), Jacobus (d. 1609). Latinized form of Harmensen, a Dutch Protestant theologian, with views opposed to those of CALVIN esp. on predestination. **Armĭn′ian** *adj.* & *n.* **Armĭn′ianism** *n.*

ar̂m'ĭstice *n.* Cessation of hostilities by agreement between belligerents; short truce; *A~ Day,* 11th Nov., kept as anniversary of the armistice that ended hostilities in the war of 1914–18 (combined, since war of 1939–45, with REMEMBRANCE Day). [L *arma* arms + *-stitium*, stopping]

ar̂m'lĕt *n.* Band worn round arm.

ar̂mŏr'ial *adj.* Of heraldic arms.

ar̂m'ory *n.* Heraldry.

Armŏ'rica (ar̂-). Roman name of Brittany.

ar̂m'our (-mer) *n.* Defensive covering for body worn in fighting; steel-plates etc. protecting ship, tank, car, etc., from projectiles etc.; tanks and other fighting vehicles equipped with such armour. ~ *v.t.* Furnish with such protective covering; *armoured car, train,* one supplied with protective armour and (usu.) guns; *armoured column, division,* etc., one equipped with armoured cars, tanks, etc.

ARMOUR: A. ARMOUR OF GREEK HOPLITE, 5th c. B.C. B. MAIL, 12th c. C. FIELD ARMOUR, *c* 1470. D. MAIL WITH SURCOAT, 13th c. E. COAT OF PLATES, *c* 1370. F. TABARD, *c* 1420. G. HELM FOR THE TILT, 15th c. H. SALLET AND BEAVER, *c* 1480. I. PIECE OF MAIL OR CHAIN ARMOUR (⅕ size). J. GORGET, *c* 1530. K. CUIRASS WITH LANCE REST AND SUPPORT FOR STEADYING BUTT OF LANCE, *c* 1480

A 1. Helmet. 2. Crest. 3. Cuirass. 4. Sword. 5. Shield. 6. Spear. 7. Greave. B. 8. Casque. 9. Hauberk or habergeon. C. 10. Visor. 11. Beaver. 12. Pauldron. 13. Vambrace. 14. Gauntlet. 15. Tasset. 16. Cuisse. E. 17. Plastron. K. 18. Breastplate. 19. Back-plate

ar̄m'ourer (-mer-) *n.* Manufacturer of arms; one in charge of ship's or regiment's small arms.

ar̄m'oury (-mer-) *n.* Place where small arms are kept; armourer's workshop.

ar̄m'y *n.* Organized body of men armed for war; vast host; ~ *corps*, main subdivision of an army, in the field consisting of two or more divisions and certain technical and administrative units; ~ *list*, official list of commissioned officers.

Arndt (ar̄nt), Ernst Moritz (1769–1860). German patriot, poet, and agitator against Napoleonic domination.

Arne (ar̄n), Thomas (1710–78). English composer of operas, masques (including 'Alfred' which contains 'Rule, Britannia!'), and songs.

ar̄n'ica *n.* (*A*~) Genus of composite plants, largely American, including mountain tobacco; tincture, prepared from root and rhizome of mountain tobacco and used for bruises, sprains, etc

Arn'ō (ar̄-). River of N. Italy, flowing through Florence and Pisa.

Arn'old[1] (ar̄-) of Brescia (d. 1155). Italian Augustinian, an ascetic who vigorously condemned the temporal power and abuses of the clergy and papacy; executed by Adrian IV.

Arn'old[2] (ar̄-), Matthew (1822–88). English poet and critic; son of Thomas ARNOLD[3].

Arn'old[3] (ar̄-), Thomas (1795–1842). Headmaster of Rugby (1828–42), which he raised to the rank of a great public school.

ar̄'oid *adj.* & *n.* (Plant) belonging to *Arum* family.

arōm'a *n.* Fragrance; subtle pervasive quality.

ăromăt'ic *adj.* 1. Fragrant, spicy. 2. (chem.) Of the group of organic compounds in which the carbon atoms are arranged in 6-membered rings (as in benzene).

around' *adv.* & *prep.* On every side; all round; (U.S.) round; (U.S.) here and there; about, enveloping.

arouse' (-z) *v.t.* Awaken; stir up into activity.

A.R.P. *abbrev.* Air-raid precautions.

ar̄peggi'o (-ĕj'ō) *n.* (mus.) Striking of notes of chord in rapid succession; chord so struck. [It., = 'harp-like']

arquebus: see HARQUEBUS.

arr. *abbrev.* Arrives etc.

ă'rrack (*or* arăk') *n.* Alcoholic spirit manufactured in the East, esp. from coco-palm or rice. [Arab. *araq* juice]

arraign' (-ān) *v.t.* Indict, accuse; call in question. **arraign'ment** *n.*

A'rran (ă-). Scottish island at mouth of Firth of Clyde.

arrānge' (-nj) *v.* Put in order; settle; settle beforehand order etc. of; form plans, take steps; (mus.) adapt (composition). **arrānge'ment** (-jm-) *n.*

ă'rrant *adj.* Downright, notorious.

ă'rras[1] *n.* Rich tapestry; hangings of this round walls of room. [f. ARRAS[2]]

Arras[2] (ă'rah). Town in NE. France famous in 13th–16th centuries for tapestry weaving; *Battle of* ~, Allied offensive of April 1917 which resulted in very heavy casualties.

array' *v.t.* Dress, esp. with display; marshal (forces). ~ *n.* Dress; imposing series; martial order.

arrear' *n.* That which is behind; (pl.) outstanding debts; work etc. in which one is behindhand; *in* ~(*s*), behindhand. **arrear'age** *n.* Backwardness; unpaid balance; thing in reserve.

arrĕst' *v.t.* Stop; (law) ~ *judgement*, stay proceedings after verdict; seize (person) esp. by legal authority; catch (attention); catch attention of. ~ *n.* Legal apprehension; stoppage; seizure.

arrĕs'tor *n.* (mech.) Attachment for bringing an object to a stop.

Arrhen'ius (ărān-), Svante August (1859–1927). Swedish physical chemist, awarded Nobel Prize in 1903 for his work on the physical chemistry of electrolytes.

arrière-pensée (ă'rïar̄ pahń'sā) *n.* Ulterior motive; mental reservation. [Fr.]

ă'rris *n.* 1. Sharp edge where two planes or curved surfaces meet (ill. ORDER); ~-*gutter*, V-shaped gutter. 2. (eng.) Raised circle of material left on surface of metal plate when hole is drilled through it.

arrīve' *v.i.* Come to destination or end of journey; be brought; come; establish one's repute or position. **arrīv'al** *n.*

ă'rrogant *adj.* Overbearing, presumptuous. **ă'rrogantly** *adv.* **ă'rrogance** *n.*

ă'rrogāte *v.t.* Claim unduly. **ărrogā'tion** *n.*

arrondissement (arawńdēs'-mahń) *n.* Administrative subdivision of French department.

ă'rrow (-ō) *n.* Missile shot from bow, usu. consisting of straight slender wooden shaft with sharp point or head of stone or metal, and feathers fastened to the butt (ill. BOW[1]); mark like an arrow or arrow-head, often used as indication of direction etc.; *broad* ~: see BROAD; *arrowhead*, water-plant, *Sagittaria sagittifolia*, with arrow-shaped leaves, growing in ponds and slow streams; *arrowroot*, nutritious starch, obtained from rhizomes of *Maranta arundinacea*, and used as food esp. for invalids.

ar̄se *n.* (vulgar) Buttocks, rump.

ar̄s'enal *n.* State establishment where weapons and ammunition are made and stored. [Arab. *dar accinā'ah* house where things are made]

ar̄s'enic *n.* Brittle steel-grey semi-metallic element, symbol As, at. no. 33, at. wt 74·9216; (pop.) white mineral substance (~ trioxide), a violent poison. **ar̄s'enic** (*or* -sĕn'-) *adj.* Of arsenic; (chem.) applied to compounds in which arsenic is pentavalent. **ar̄sĕn'ical** *adj.* [Gk *arsenikon*, f. Arab. *az-zernikh* the orpiment, f. Pers. *zerni* (*zar* gold)]

ar̄sēn'ious *adj.* Containing arsenic in trivalent form.

ar̄s'ine (-ēn) *n.* Colourless inflammable poisonous gas (AsH_3) having an odour like garlic; any of a group of poisonous gases derived from this.

ar̄s'is *n.* (pl. *-sēs*). Accented syllable in English scansion; unaccented part of a foot in Greek and Latin prosody.

ar̄s'on *n.* Wilful setting on fire of houses or other property.

ar̄t *n.* Skill, esp. applied to design, representation, or imaginative creation; human skill as opp. to nature; cunning, stratagem; subject in which skill may be exercised; (pl.) certain branches of learning (*liberal* ~*s*) traditionally serving as preparation for more advanced studies or for life (*Bachelor*, *Master*, *of Arts*, one who has obtained a standard of proficiency in these at a university); *black* ~, magic; *applied*, *decorative* ~*s*, those concerned with the design and decoration of objects in practical use, handicrafts; *fine* ~*s*, (usu.) painting, architecture, sculpture, music, poetry.

Artaxer̄x'es (ar̄-, -ēz). Name of two kings of ancient Persia: ~ *I*, son of Xerxes, reigned 464–424 B.C.; ~ *II*, son of Darius II, reigned 404–358 B.C.

ar̄t'ėfăct, ar̄'tĭ- *n.* (archaeol.) Object, as palaeolithic flint, made by human workmanship; (biol.) something not present in the natural state of an organism but produced while it is being prepared for examination.

Art'ėmis (ar̄-). (Gk myth.) Goddess of chastity and of hunting; twin sister of Apollo, identified with the moon and the Roman Diana.

ar̄tēr'ial *adj.* Belonging to, of the nature of, an artery; ~ *road*, important main road.

ar̄tēr'ialize *v.t.* Convert (venous blood) into arterial blood by impregnating it with oxygen in lungs; furnish with arterial system. **ar̄tērializā'tion** *n.*

ar̄tērioscler̄ōs'is *n.* Hardening of the arteries.

ar̄t'ėry *n.* Muscular-walled blood-vessel conveying the blood impelled by the heart to the small vessels which supply the tissues (ill. BLOOD); something serving as channel of supplies, e.g. main road, river.

ar̄tē'sian (-zhn) *adj.* ~ *well*, perpendicular bore into a curved or slanting water-saturated stratum, penetrating it at a level lower than the source of the water, which rises spontaneously to the surface in a continuous flow (ill. WELL). [f. *Artois*, Fr. province]

ârt'ful *adj.* Cunning, crafty.

ârthrīt'ĭs *n.* Inflammation of joint. **ârthrĭt'ĭc** *adj.*

ârth'rŏpŏd *n.* One of the *Arthropoda*, the largest animal phylum, comprising insects, arachnids, myriapods, crustaceans, and trilobites, and characterized by jointed limbs and a hard jointed external skeleton.

Arth'ur[1] (âr-). King of Britain; historically perh. a 5th- or 6th-c. chieftain or general. Acc. to legend he was the son of Uther Pendragon and Igerne, wife of Gorlois of Cornwall; became king of Britain at age of 15; married Guinevere; held court at Caerleon-on-Usk and established there a company of knights whose seats were at a Round Table so that none had precedence; was mortally wounded at Camelford in battle against his usurping nephew Modred; and was then borne off in a magic boat to Avalon whence he will one day return. **Arthūr'ĭan** *adj.*

Arth'ur[2] (âr-), Prince, Duke of Brittany (1187–1203). Grandson of Henry II of England; declared by his uncle, Richard I, to be heir to the throne, to which his other uncle, John, also laid claim; but during the war between France and Britain he was captured and, prob. by John's orders, murdered at Rouen.

Arth'ur[3] (âr-), Chester Alan (1830–86). American politician, lawyer, and soldier (in Civil War); 21st president of U.S., 1881–5.

Arth'ur's Seat. Saddle-backed hill on E. side of Edinburgh, dominating the city.

ârt'ĭchōke *n.* 1. Plant, *Cynara scolymus* (of which bottom of flower and bases of its scales are edible), allied to thistle. 2. *Jerusalem ~*, species of sunflower with edible tuberous roots. [It. *articiocco*, f. Arab. *alkharshuf*; Jerusalem corrupt. of It. *girasole* sunflower]

ârt'ĭcle *n.* Separate portion of anything written; separate clause, literary composition forming part of magazine etc.; *leading ~*, in newspaper, expressing editorial opinion; particular; particular thing; (gram.) either of the adjs. 'a, an' (*indefinite ~*) and 'the' (*definite ~*), or their equivalents in other languages. ~ *v.t.* Bind by articles of apprenticeship; set forth in articles.

ârtĭc'ūlar *adj.* Of the joints.

ârtĭc'ūlate *adj.* Having joints; distinctly jointed, distinguishable; (of speech) clearly defined; capable of verbal expression. **ârtĭc'ūlāte** *v.* Connect by joints; divide into words, pronounce distinctly; speak distinctly. **ârtĭc'ūlatory** *adj.*

ârtĭcūlā'tion *n.* Articulate utterance, speech; jointing.

ârt'ĭfĭce *n.* Device; cunning; skill. **ârtĭf'ĭcer** *n.* Craftsman.

ârtĭfĭ'cial (-shl) *adj.* Produced by art; not natural; not real; ~ *language*, language constructed from roots of several languages and intended for international use, e.g. Esperanto; ~ *rain*, rain made by dispersal of solid carbon dioxide or other chemical material in suitable cloud, causing the cloud to cool and condense; ~ *respiration*: see RESPIRATION; ~ *silk*: see RAYON. **ârtĭfĭ'cially** *adv.* **ârtĭfĭcĭăl'ĭty** *n.*

ârtĭll'ery *n.* Large mounted fire-arms of calibre greater than small arms; cannon; ordnance; branch of army that uses these; *~-man*, one belonging to the artillery, gunner. **ârtĭll'erist** *n.* Artilleryman.

ârtĭsăn' (-z-) *n.* Mechanic; handicraftsman.

ârt'ĭst *n.* One who practises one of the fine arts, esp. painting; one who makes his craft a fine art; artiste. **ârtĭs'tĭc** *adj.* **ârt'ĭstry** *n.*

ârtiste' (-ēst) *n.* Professional singer, dancer, etc.

ârt'lèss *adj.* Guileless, simple; lacking art, crude. **ârt'lèssly** *adv.* **ârt'lèssnèss** *n.*

Artois (âr'twa). Ancient province of NE. France.

ârt'y *adj.* Having artistic pretensions.

Ar'um (ār-) *n.* Genus of plants including cuckoo-pint (lords and ladies) (ill. INFLORESCENCE); *~-lily*, inflorescence of *Richardia africana* (Arum family) used for decoration esp. on altar.

A.R.W.S. *abbrev.* Associate of the Royal Society of Painters in Water-colours.

Ar'ȳan (ār-) *adj.* & *n.* 1. Applied by some to the family of languages (also called *Indo-European*, *Indo-Germanic*) that includes the Indian, Iranian, Greek, Latin, Celtic, Germanic, and Slavonic groups, by others only to the Indo-Iranian portion of these. 2. Loosely and inaccurately applied to members of races (not necessarily of a common stock) speaking any of these languages; in Nazi Germany esp. contrasted with SEMITE. [Sansk. *arya* noble (in earlier use a national name comprising worshippers of the gods of the Brahmans); the earlier *Arian* is f. L *Arianus*, = 'of Aria' (f. Gk. *Areia* eastern Persia)]

as[1] (ăz, *az*) *adv.* & *conj.* In the same degree; similarly; while, when; since, seeing that.

ăs[2] *n.* Roman copper coin, orig. weighing 12 oz., but finally reduced to ½ oz.

A.S. *abbrev.* Anglo-Saxon.

ăsafoet'ĭda (-fĕt-) *n.* Concreted resinous gum of various Persian plants of genus *Ferula* with strong smell of garlic and bitter taste, used in medicine. [Pers. *aza* mastic, L *foetida* stinking]

Asaph. *abbrev.* (Bishop) of St. Asaph (replacing surname in his signature).

As'aph (ā- *or* ă-), St. (d. *c* 596). Welsh saint, prior of Llanelwy, and first bishop of St. Asaph; commemorated 1st May.

ăsbĕs'tŏs (ăz-) *n.* White or grey fibrous mineral (consisting largely of calcium and magnesium silicates) that can be woven into an incombustible fabric used for fireproof clothing, thermal insulation of pipes, etc., or formed into light sheet material for roofing. [Gk, = 'unquenchable']

ascĕnd' *v.* Go or come up; rise, mount, climb.

ascĕn'dancy, -ency *n.* Dominant control, powerful influence.

ascĕn'dant, -ent *adj.* & *n.* Rising; (astron.) rising towards zenith; (astrol.) (point of ecliptic or degree of zodiac that is) just rising above eastern horizon; predominant.

ascĕn'der *n.* (esp. printing) Limb of letter above x-height (ill. TYPE).

ascĕn'sion (-shn) *n.* Ascent; ascent of Christ into Heaven on fortieth day after resurrection; rising of a celestial body; *A~ Day*, day commemorating Christ's ascension, sixth Thursday after Easter.

Ascĕn'sion Island. Small island in S. Atlantic, discovered by Portuguese on Ascension Day 1501, but uninhabited until a British garrison was placed there in 1815.

ascĕnt' *n.* Ascending, rising; upward path or slope.

ăscertain' *v.t.* Find out. **ăscertain'able** *adj.* **ăscertain'ment** *n.*

ascĕt'ĭc *adj.* Severely abstinent, austere. ~ *n.* One who practises severe self-discipline, esp. (eccles. hist.) one who retired into solitude for this purpose. **ascĕt'ĭcal** *adj.* **ascĕt'ĭcally** *adv.* **ascĕt'ĭcĭsm** *n.*

Ascham (ăs'kam), Roger (1515–68). English scholar and prose-writer, author of 'The Scholemaster', a treatise on the (private) education of boys.

ascĭd'ĭan (*a*sĭd-) *n.* Primitive marine chordate animal of the subphylum *Urochorda* (which comprises principally the sea-squirts); = tunicate. [Gk *askidion* dim. of *askos* wine-skin]

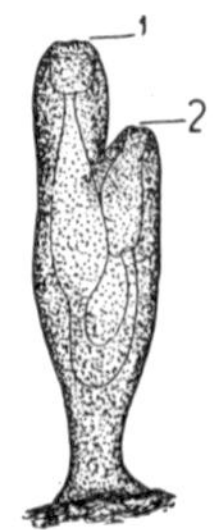

ASCIDIAN: SEA-SQUIRT

1. Mouth. 2. Anus

Asclēp′iadēs (*a*-, -z). Greek lyric poet (*c* 290 B.C.), to whom is attributed the invention of the **asclēp′iăd,** a verse of a spondee, 2 or 3 choriambs, and an iambus.

ascomȳ′cēte (ă-) *n.* Fungus producing ascospores, e.g. cup fungus (ill. FUNGUS).

ascor̄b′ic *adj.* ~ *acid,* Vitamin C, which occurs in fresh foods, esp. fruits and vegetables, and is necessary to obviate scurvy.

ăs′cospōre *n.* Spore developed in an ascus.

As′cot (ă-). (Used for) ~ *Heath,* race-course in Berkshire; ~ *Week,* annual race-meeting there in June, instituted by Queen Anne, 1711.

ascrībe′ *v.t.* Attribute, impute; assign. **ascrip′tion** *n.* Ascribing.

ăs′cus *n.* (pl. *-cī*). (bot.) Round or elongated sac-like body containing spores, in certain fungi (ill. LICHEN).

As′dic (ăz-) *n.* Anti-submarine detector of secret design, kind of hydrophone. [initials of *A*nti-*S*ubmarine *D*etection *I*nvestigation *C*ommittee]

A.S.E. *abbrev.* Associated Society (*or* Associate of the Society) of Engineers.

āsĕp′sis *n.* Absence of putrefactive matter or harmful bacteria; aseptic method in surgery.

āsĕp′tic *adj.* Free from putrefaction or blood-poisoning; sterilized; seeking the absence, rather than counteraction, of septic matter.

āsĕx′ūal *adj.* Not sexual, without sex; ~ *generation* (biol.) any form of reproduction not brought about by the union of gametes.

As′gar̄d (ăz-). (Scand. myth.) The region, in the centre of the universe, inhabited by the gods.

ăsh[1] *n.* Forest-tree of genus *Fraxinus* with silver-grey bark, pinnate leaves, and close-grained wood; wood of this; *mountain* ~, rowan-tree.

ăsh[2] *n.* (usu. pl.). Powdery residue left after combustion of any substance; (pl.) remains of human body after cremation; *the Ashes,* imaginary trophy claimed by winner of each series of cricket matches (Test Matches) between England and Australia (from epitaph in 'Sporting Times' on occasion of first match won by Australia, 1882, lamenting death of English cricket and stating that the ashes would be taken to Australia); *A~ Wednesday,* first day of Lent (from early custom of sprinkling ashes on penitents' heads).

ashāmed′ (-md) *adj.* Abashed, upset, by consciousness of guilt.

Ashăn′tĭ (*a*-) (pl. *-s,* or as sing.). Native of Ashanti, a division of Ghana (Gold Coast).

Ash′down (ă-). Place, possibly near Ashbury in Berkshire, where Alfred with his elder brother Æthelred won his first victory over the Danes (871).

ăsh′en *adj.* Pertaining to an ash-tree; made of ash-wood; pale.

Ash′er (ă-). One of the sons of Jacob (see Gen. xxx. 12, 13); one of the tribes of Israel.

Ashkenazim (ăshkĭnahz′ĭm) *n.pl.* Polish-German Jews (as dist. from SEPHARDIM).

ăsh′lar *n.* Square hewn stone(s); masonry of this (ill. MASONRY).

ăsh′laring *n.* Short upright wall in garrets, cutting off acute angle formed by rafters with floor.

Ash′mōle (ă-), Elias (1617–92). English antiquary, founder of the *Ashmōl′ėan Museum* at Oxford.

ashōre′ *adv.* To or on shore.

Ashtaroth, -oreth: see ASTARTE.

ăsh′y *adj.* Of ashes; ash-coloured; pale.

Asia (āsh′*a*). Continent of N. hemisphere, E. part of the great land-mass formed by the Old World; separated from Europe by the Ural Mountains and the Caspian Sea; home of the oldest known civilizations; ~ *Minor,* westernmost part of Asia, a peninsula bounded by the Black Sea, the Aegean, and the Mediterranean, and comprising most of Turkey; = Anatolia. **A′sian, Asiăt′ic** (āshĭ-) *adj.* & *ns.* (Native) of Asia.

asīde′ *adv.* To or on one side; away, apart. ~ *n.* Words spoken by an actor and supposed not to be heard by other performers.

ăs′inīne *adj.* Of asses; stupid.

Asir (*a*zēr′). Region of SW. Arabia between Hejaz and the Yemen.

ask (ah-) *v.* Call for an answer (to); make a request (for); invite; demand, require.

As′kalon (ă-). Ancient Philistine city of the Palestine coast (near Majdal in modern Israel), destroyed *c* 1270 after several times changing hands in the Crusades.

askănce′ (*or* -ahns) *adv.* Sideways; *look* ~ *at,* view suspiciously.

ăskar̄′i *n.* European-trained African native soldier. [Arab wd]

askew′ *adv.* Obliquely, awry.

aslant′ (-ahnt) *adv.* Obliquely.

asleep′ *adv.* & *pred. adj.* In a state of sleep; (of limbs) benumbed; (of top) spinning without apparent motion.

Aslib *abbrev.* Association of Special Libraries and Information Bureaux.

aslōpe′ *adv.* & *pred. adj.* Sloping, crosswise.

Asmodē′us, -daeus (ăz-). An evil spirit of Jewish legend: see Tobit iii. 8.

Asōk′a (ă-) (272–232 B.C.). Emperor of India 269– ; ruled over the greater part of the peninsula; was converted to Buddhism, did much to propagate it, and is revered by Buddhists.

ăsp *n.* 1. Small viper of S. Europe (*Vipera aspis*). 2. Viper of N. Africa and Arabia (various species of *Cerastes*).

aspă′ragus *n.* (*A~*) Genus of plants of lily family with many-branched fine stems, and leaves reduced to scales; species of this (*A. officinalis*) whose vernal shoots are a table delicacy; ~ *fern,* the species *A. plumosus* used as decoration.

Aspās′ia (-zĭ*a*, -zhĭ*a*) (5th c. B.C.). Famous Greek courtesan, mistress of Pericles.

ăs′pĕct *n.* Way a thing presents itself to eye or mind; side (of building etc.) looking, fronting, in a given direction; appearance.

ăs′pen *n.* Kind of poplar (*Populus tremula*) with leaves tremulous on account of long thin leaf-stalks.

Asper̄′gės (*a*-, -jēz) *n.* (R.C. Ch.) Anthem beginning with this word (L, = 'thou shalt sprinkle') sung before High Mass while altar, clergy, and people are sprinkled with holy water; the rite itself.

ăspĕ′rity *n.* Roughness; severity; harshness.

asper̄se′ *v.t.* Attack the reputation of, calumniate. **asper̄′sion** (-shn) *n.*

ăs′phălt *n.* 1. Solid or plastic pitch derived from petroleum either naturally (as in asphalt lakes of Trinidad and Venezuela) or by distillation. 2. Mixture of this with sand etc. used for surfacing roads etc. ~ *v.t.* Lay (road) with asphalt.

ăs′phodĕl *n.* Hardy liliaceous plants from Mediterranean and India, including classical *Asphodeline lutea* in Greece; (poet.) immortal flower in Elysium.

asphȳx′ia *n.* Defective aeration of blood, caused by blockage of air-passages or paralysis of respiratory muscles or collapse of the lungs, and resulting in death if air-flow fails completely. **asphȳx′iāte** *v.* Kill by asphyxia, suffocate. **asphȳxiā′tion** *n.* [Gk *a*- not, *sphuxis* pulse]

ăs′pic *n.* Savoury jelly, usu. containing cold game, eggs, etc.

ăspidis′tra *n.* Plant of the lily family, with broad taper leaves, freq. grown as a pot-plant, and often regarded as a symbol of dull middle-class respectability. [Gk *aspis* shield]

ăs′pirant (*or* aspīr′-) *n.* One who aspires.

ăs′pirate *n.* & *adj.* (Consonant) pronounced with a breathing, blended with sound of *h*; the sound of *h*. **ăs′pirāte** *v.t.* 1. Pronounce with a breathing. 2. Draw out (gas) from vessel.

ăs′pirātor *n.* Apparatus for drawing gas through tube or through a liquid.

ăspirā′tion *n.* Drawing of breath; desire.

aspīre′ *v.i.* Desire earnestly; (fig.) mount up.

ăs′pirin *n.* Trade-name for acetyl-salicylic acid, used as an analgesic and febrifuge.

asquint′ *adv.* & *pred. adj.* With a squint.

As′quith (ă-), Herbert Henry, first Earl of Oxford and Asquith (1852–1928). English Liberal statesman; Prime Minister of England 1908–16.

A.S.R.S. *abbrev.* Amalgamated Society of Railway Servants.

ăss (*or* ahs) *n.* 1. Quadruped (*Equus onager*, *E. hemippus*, *E. hemionus*, etc.) related to the horse but smaller, with tuft at end of tail and long ears, donkey; domesticated for draft and riding and descended from the *wild* ~ (*Equus asinus* or *E. taeniopus*) of Abyssinia. 2. (fig.) Ignorant or stupid person.

ăssa'i (-ah-ē) *adv.* (mus.) Very. [It.]

assail' *v.t.* Attack, assault. **assail'ant** *n.* One who assails.

Assăm' (*or* ăs'ăm). Former province of NE. India, since 1947 a State of the Republic of India.

assăss'ĭn *n.* One who undertakes to kill treacherously; *A~s*, (hist.) fanatical sect of the Ismaili Moslems in time of Crusades, founded in the 11th c. by the 'Old Man of the Mountains' (Hasan-ben-Sabbah), and notorious for secret murders carried out at the order of their chief. [Arab. *ḥashishiyy* hashish-eater]

assăss'ĭnāte *v.t.* Kill by treacherous violence. **assăssĭnā'tion** *n.*

assault' *n.* Hostile attack; rush against walls of fortress etc.; (law) unlawful personal attack (including menacing words). ~ *v.t.* Make attack upon.

assay' *n.* Testing of an alloy or ore to determine the proportion of a given metal; ~ *mark* (on gold and silver), hall-mark indicating standard of fineness (ill. HALL). ~ *v.* Try the purity of; attempt.

ăss'ègai (-gī) *n.* Slender spear of hard wood tipped with iron, used as missile by S. Afr. tribes. [Fr. *azagaye*, f. Arab.]

assĕm'blage *n.* Collection, concourse.

assĕm'ble *v.* Bring or come together; collect; fit together parts of (machine etc.).

assĕm'bly *n.* 1. Gathering of persons, esp. of deliberative body; *~-room*, large room for social gatherings. 2. (eng.) The assembling of those parts of a machine etc. that form a unit; the parts so assembled.

assĕnt' *v.i.* Agree (*to*), defer (*to*); express agreement. ~ *n.* Concurrence; sanction.

assẽrt' *v.t.* Vindicate a claim to (rights); declare; ~ *oneself*, insist upon one's rights.

assẽr'tion *n.* Insistence upon a right; affirmation, positive statement.

assẽrt'ĭve *adj.* Given to assertion; positive, dogmatic. **assẽrt'ĭvely** (-vl-) *adv.* **assẽrt'ivenėss** (-vn-) *n.*

assĕss' *v.t.* Fix amount of (taxes, fine); fine, tax; estimate value of (esp. for taxation). **assĕss'ment** *n.*

assĕss'or *n.* One who assesses taxes or estimates value of property for purpose of taxation; adviser to judge or magistrate.

ăss'ĕt *n.* 1. (pl., law) Enough goods to enable heir to discharge debts and legacies of testator; property liable to be so applied; effects of insolvent debtor; property that may be made liable for debts; (sing.) item of this in balance-sheet. 2. (loosely) Any possession; any useful quality. [med. L *ad satis* sufficiently]

assĕv'erāte *v.t.* Solemnly declare. **assĕverā'tion** *n.*

ăssĭdū'ĭty *n.* Close attention, persistent application.

assĭd'ūous *adj.* Persevering, diligent. **assĭd'ūously** *adv.* **assĭd'ūousnėss** *n.*

assign' (-īn) *v.t.* Make over formally; allot; appoint; ascribe. ~ *n.* One to whom a property, right, etc., is legally transferred.

ăss'ĭgnăt *n.* Paper money secured on State lands, esp. that issued by French revolutionary government.

ăssĭgnā'tion (-g-) *n.* Assigning; appointment (of time and place).

ăssignee' (-īnē) *n.* One appointed to act for another; assign.

assign'ment (-īn-) *n.* Allotment; legal transference; document effecting this, attribution; task, commission.

assĭm'ĭlāte *v.* Make or become like; absorb, be absorbed into the system. **assĭmĭlā'tion** *n.* **assĭm'ĭlatĭve, assĭm'ĭlatory** *adjs.*

Assisi (*a*sēz'ĭ). Town of Umbria, central Italy; birthplace of St. Francis.

assist' *v.* Help; be present. **assis'tance** *n.*

assis'tant *adj.* Helping. ~ *n.* Helper, subordinate worker.

assīze' *n.* (usu. pl.) Periodical sessions in counties of England and Wales held by judges on circuit for administration of civil and criminal judgement; (hist.) statutory price (of bread and ale).

assoc. *abbrev.* Association.

assō'ciāte *v.* Join; connect in idea; combine; have intercourse (*with*). **assō'ciate** (-sĭ*a*t *or* -shĭ*a*t) *adj.* Joined, allied. ~ *n.* partner, companion; subordinate member of an association; thing connected with another. **assō'ciatĭve, assō'ciatory** *adjs.*

assōciā'tion *n.* Associating; organized body of persons; connexion of ideas; intercourse; *free* ~: see FREE; ~ *football*, kind of football played with round leather ball, which must not be handled, except by the goalkeeper, and with two teams of eleven, each consisting of one goalkeeper, two full-backs, three half-backs, and five forwards, on a field (not exceeding 130 yds in length and 100 yds in breadth, nor less than 100 yds in length and 50 yds in breadth) with a goal at each end.

assoil' *v.t.* (archaic) Absolve from sin, pardon.

ăss'onance *n.* Resemblance of sound between two syllables; rhyming of one word with another in the accented vowel but not in the following consonants (e.g. *sonnet, porridge*). **ăss'onant** *adj.*

assôrt' *v.* Arrange in sorts; suit, harmonize (*with*).

assôrt'ment *n.* Assorting; mixture of various sorts.

Asst *abbrev.* Assistant.

assuāge' (-sw-) *v.t.* Calm, soothe; appease. **assuāge'ment** (-jm-) *n.*

assūme' *v.t.* Take upon oneself; undertake; simulate; take for granted. **assūm'ĭng** *adj.* Taking much upon oneself, arrogant.

assŭm'ption *n.* Assuming; thing assumed; arrogance; *the A~*, reception of the Virgin Mary into heaven; feast in honour of this, 15th Aug.

Ass'ur, Ash'ur (ă-). Local god of the city of that name, the ancient capital of Assyria (on the Tigris at modern Sharqat in N. Iraq); he became the supreme god of the Assyrians, the god of war, and the protector of the people.

assur'ance (*a*shoor-) *n.* Positive assertion; self-confidence; impudence; (life) insurance.

assure' (*a*shoor') *v.t.* Make safe; make certain, ensure; insure (life); make (person) sure (*of*); tell (person) confidently. **assur'ėdly** *adv.*

Assy̆'rĭa (*a*-) The more northerly of the two ancient empires of the region (Mesopotamia) between the Tigris and the Euphrates. The Assyrians, a mixed Semitic race speaking a language closely related to Akkadian, apparently displaced the Sumerians from the city of Assur and made it their capital.

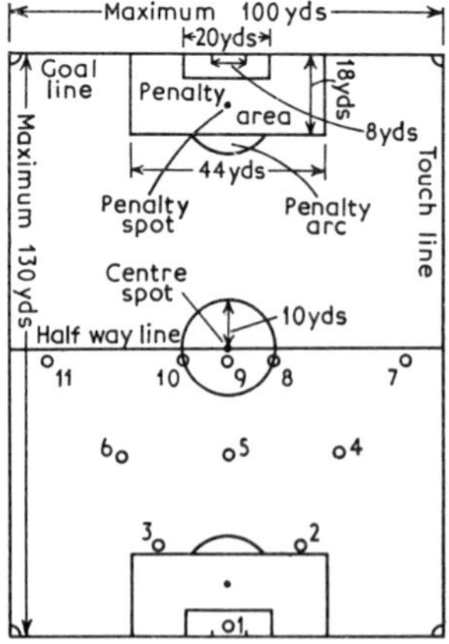

ASSOCIATION FOOTBALL: FIELD AND POSITION OF PLAYERS

1. Goalkeeper. 2. Right full-back. 3. Left full-back. 4. Right half-back. 5. Centre-half. 6. Left half-back. 7. Outside right. 8. Inside right. 9. Centre-forward. 10. Inside left. 11. Outside left. Goal 8 ft. high

Until *c* 1300 B.C. Assyria was under the power of Babylonia, but Shalmaneser I established the supremacy of Assyria in W. Asia though it was often threatened by revolt in Babylon. The 'second' Assyrian Empire, founded by Tigleth-Pileser I, ended soon after the death of Assur-bani-pal (7th c. B.C.), who subdued rebellious Egypt and Elam but left the empire too exhausted to repel the Medes; these finally destroyed Nineveh, the last Assyrian stronghold, in 612 B.C. **Assȳ'rĭan** *adj.* & *n.* 1. (Native, language) of Assyria. 2. (Member) of the NESTORIAN community. [f. ASSUR]

Assȳrĭol'ogist, -gy *ns.* Student, study, of the civilization, language, etc., of Assyria.

Astart'ē, Ash'tarŏth, -orĕth (ă-), **Ish'tar.** The Eastern equivalent of the Greek Aphrodite, the goddess of love and fruitful increase.

ăs'tatīne *n.* (chem.) A radioactive element of short life (symbol At, at. no. 85, principal isotope 211), which does not occur in nature but can be made artificially; the heaviest element of the halogen group. [Gk *astatos* unstable]

ăs'ter *n.* Genus of herbaceous plants, including Michaelmas daisies, with showy radiated flowers of various colours; *China* ~, *Callistephus chinensis* allied to this. [Gk *aster* star]

ăs'terisk *n.* Star (*) used to mark words for reference or distinction, to indicate a hypothetical form or fill up space in a line where something is omitted. ~ *v.t.* Mark with asterisk.

ăs'terism *n.* Cluster of stars; 3 asterisks (⁂) calling special attention to word or passage.

astern' *adv.* In, at, the stern; behind.

astern'al *adj.* ~ *rib*: see RIB.

ăs'teroid *n.* 1. (astron.) Any of the small planets revolving round sun between orbits of Mars and Jupiter (ill. PLANET). 2. (zool.) One of the class of *Asteroidea* or starfishes. **ăsteroid'al** *adj.* [Gk *asteroeidēs* starlike]

ăsth'ma (-sm-) *n.* Disorder, freq. of allergic origin, characterized by paroxysms of difficult breathing.

ăsthmăt'ic (-sm-) *adj.* & *n.* (Person) suffering from asthma. **ăsthmăt'ically** *adv.*

As'tĭ (ă-). Town in Piedmont producing wines, sparkling (~ *spumante*) and still.

astĭg'matism *n.* Structural defect in eye or lens, preventing rays of light from being brought to a common focus, arising from unequal refraction at different points. **ăstĭgmăt'ic** *adj.*

astir' *adv.* In motion; out of bed.

astŏn'ish *v.t.* Amaze, surprise. **astŏnishment** *n.*

astound' *v.t.* Shock with alarm or surprise; amaze.

ăs'tragal *n.* 1. (archit.) Small moulding round top or bottom of column (ill. ORDER). 2. Ring round cannon near mouth.

astrăg'alus *n.* 1. Ball of ankle-joint. 2. (*A*~) Genus of leguminous plants including milk-vetch.

Astrakhan' (ă-, -kăn). Region of the U.S.S.R., on the lower Volga; town at head of the Volga delta, exporting new-born Persian lamb skins, a soft close-curled fur, called **astrakhan.**

ăs'tral *adj.* Connected with, consisting of, stars; ~ *body*, (theosophy) spiritual counterpart of the human body accompanying it in life and surviving its death; ~ *hatch* = ASTRODOME.

astray' *adv.* Out of the right way.

astrīde' *adv.*, *pred. adj.*, & *prep.* In striding position; with legs on each side (*of*).

astrin'gent (-nj-) *adj.* & *n.* Binding, styptic (medicine); severe; austere.

ăs'trodōme *n.* Dome-shaped window in aircraft used for aeronautical observations.

ăs'trolābe *n.* Instrument used to take altitudes and solve other problems of practical astronomy, especially of stars; *prismatic* ~, surveying instrument for determining position by observations to stars at a fixed altitude (45° or 60°).

astrŏl'ogy *n.* Art of understanding the reputed occult influence of the stars on human affairs. **astrŏl'oger** *n.* **ăstrolŏ'gical** *adj.* **ăstrolŏg'ically** *adv.*

ăs'tronaut *n.* One who travels in space.

ăstronaut'ics *n.* Science of navigation in space. **ăstronaut'ic(al)** *adjs.*

astrŏn'omer *n.* One who studies astronomy; *A*~ *Royal*, astronomer in charge of the Royal Observatory, Greenwich, appointed by the Crown (since 1675).

ăstronŏm'ical *adj.* Relating to, concerned with, astronomy; (of numbers, distances, etc.) very big, immense; ~ *unit*, (abbrev. a.u.) mean distance of the earth from the sun as unit of measurement, approx. 93 million miles. **ăstronŏm'ically** *adj.*

astrŏn'omy *n.* Science of the heavenly bodies.

ăs'trophȳsics (-z-) *n.* That branch of physics which deals with the physical or chemical properties of heavenly bodies.

Astur'ĭas (ă-). Principality of Spain; *Prince of the* ~, former title of eldest son of the king of Spain.

astūte' *adj.* Shrewd, sagacious; crafty. **astūt'ely** *adv.* **astūte'nėss** (-tn-) *n.*

asŭn'der *adv.* Apart; to pieces.

Asunción (asōōnsiŏn', -thiŏn'). Capital city of Paraguay.

Asur'as (*a*-). (Hindu myth.) Evil demons, the enemies of the gods; in the Vedas, freq. the gods themselves.

Aswan dam (ăs'wahn). Dam, 1¼ miles long, holding a reservoir, at Aswan in Upper Egypt; completed 1902.

asȳl'um *n.* Sanctuary, place of refuge, esp. for criminals or debtors; shelter; institution for the care of the afflicted or destitute, esp. the insane; *political* ~, protection from arrest or extradition given by one nation to refugee from another.

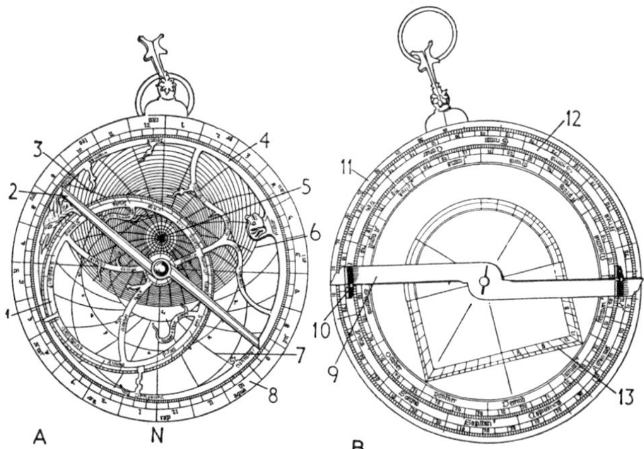

ASTROLABE: A. FRONT. B. BACK

A. 1. Ecliptic ring. 2. Index. 3. Star pointer. 4. Tropic of Capricorn ring. 5. Zenith. 6. Horizon. 7. Unequal hour line. 8. Equal hour scales. B. 9. Alidade. 10. Sight. 11. Scale of degrees. 12. Zodiac/calendar scales. 13. Shadow square.

asȳm'mėtry *n.* Absence of symmetry. **ăsȳmmĕt'rical** *adj.* **ăsȳmmĕt'rically** *adv.*

ăs'ȳmptōte *n.* Line which continually approaches a given curve, but does not meet it within a finite distance.

at (ăt, at), *prep.* expressing exact, approximate, or vague position (*at York*, *at school*, *at dinner*) or time of day (*at one o'clock*); ~ *all*, in any degree, of any kind; ~ *that*, at that estimate, moreover, into the bargain.

A.T.A.(S.) *abbrev.* Air Transport Auxiliary (Service).

Atalăn'ta (ă-). (Gk legend) Daughter of Iasus; she required all her suitors to run a race with her and killed them if they lost; but Milanion (or Hippomenes) won the race by throwing down 3 golden apples from the garden of the Hesperides, given to him by Aphrodite, which were so beautiful that Atalanta stopped to pick them up.

Atatürk (ăt'atĕrk), Kemal (-ahl') (1880–1938). Turkish nationalist leader; first president of the republic 1923–38; known first as Mustapha (mōōs'tafa) Kemal, then as Kemal Pasha; took surname Atatürk, 1934. [*Mustapha*, personal name; *Kemal*, nickname, = 'perfection'; *Atatürk* = 'father-Turk']

ăt'avism *n.* Resemblance to remote ancestors, reversion to earlier type. **ătavis'tic** *adj.* **ătavis'tically** *adv.* [L *atavus* great-grandfather's grandfather]

atăx'ic *adj.* Characterized by ataxy.

atăx'y *n.* Irregularity of animal functions; *locomotor* ~ (or *ataxia*), disease (*tabes dorsalis*) causing loss of control of co-ordinated movement by destruction of the sensory nerves concerned.

A.T.C. *abbrev.* Air Training Corps.

Ate (ăt'ē *or* ah'tē). (Gk myth.) The goddess of evil, who incites men to wickedness and strife.

atelier (ăt'elyā) *n.* Workshop, studio.

Athanā'sian (ă-, -shn) *adj.* Of Athanasius (*c* 296–373), bishop of Alexandria; ~ *Creed*, that beginning 'Quicunque vult' (Whosoever will), prob. composed not by Athanasius but by Caesarius, bishop of Arles in 6th c.

āth'ėism *n.* Disbelief in the existence of a God; godlessness. **āth'ėist** *n.* **āthėis'tic** *adj.*

Ath'elstan (ă-) (*c* 894–939). King of the West Saxons 925–39; grandson of Alfred the Great.

Athėnae'um (ă-). 1. (Rom. antiq.) College of rhetoric and poetry, founded at Rome *c* A.D. 133 by the Emperor Hadrian. 2. ~ (*Club*), a London club, founded 1824 as an association of men of distinction in literature, art, and learning. 3. Literary and artistic review, founded 1828 by James Silk Buckingham; incorporated in 'The Nation and Athenaeum', 1921. [L, f. Gk *Athēnaion* temple of ATHENE]

Athēn'ė (*a-*) Greek goddess of wisdom, industry, and war, identified with the Roman Minerva; she sprang fully grown and armed from the brain of her father, Zeus; her emblem was an owl.

Ath'ėns (ă-). (Gk *Athenai*) Leading city of ancient Greece; capital of modern Greece. **Athēn'ian** *adj.* & *n.* (Native, inhabitant) of Athens.

athîrst' *pred. adj.* Thirsty; eager (*for*).

ăth'lēte *n.* One who competes or excels in physical exercises.

ăthlĕt'ic *adj.* Pertaining to athletes; physically powerful. **ăthlĕt'ics** *n.pl.* Physical exercises; athletic sports (comprising, in organized sport, running, jumping, throwing, walking, hurdling, and steeplechasing). **athlĕt'icism** *n.*

at-hōme' *n.* Reception of visitors within time during which hostess or host or both have announced that they will be at home.

Ath'ŏs (ă-), Mount. A peninsula projecting into the Aegean Sea from Macedonia, occupied since the Middle Ages by various communities of monks.

athwart' (-ôrt) *adv.* & *prep.* Across from side to side (usu. obliquely); ~-*hawse*, (of ship) across stem of another ship at anchor.

Atlăn'ta. Capital of Georgia, U.S.

Atlăn'tic. The great ocean lying between Europe and Africa on E. and America on W.; orig., the sea near the NW. coast of Africa; *Battle of the* ~, prolonged offensive by German naval (esp. submarine) and air forces against Allied Atlantic shipping during the war of 1939–45, which reached its peak from 1941 to 1943); ~ *Charter*, declaration of 8 common principles in the national policies of U.S. and Great Britain, drawn up at a conference in mid-Atlantic in Aug. 1941 by Winston Churchill and President Franklin Roosevelt and endorsed by other nations at war with Germany, Italy, and Japan; ~ *Pact*, pact for mutual defence against aggression signed in April 1949 by various W. European nations and by Canada and U.S.A.; ~ *Wall*, line of fortifications built by Germans to defend the N. and W. coasts of France during the war of 1939–45. [f. ATLAS[2]]

Atlăn'tis. (Gk legend) A fabled island in the ocean W. of the Pillars of Hercules; it was beautiful and prosperous, the seat of an empire which dominated part of Europe and Africa, but was overwhelmed by the sea because of the impiety of its inhabitants.

ăt'las[1] (ă-), *n.* 1. Collection of maps in a volume, so called from the use of a figure of ATLAS[2] supporting the heavens as a frontispiece. 2. Size of drawing-paper (26 × 33 in.). 3. Uppermost vertebra of backbone, supporting the skull (ill. SPINE).

At'las[2] (ă-). (Gk legend) One of the Titans, who was punished for revolting against Zeus by being made to support the heavens with his head and hands. Acc. to another legend Perseus, with the aid of Medusa's head, turned him into a mountain (the ~ *Mountains* of N. Africa).

ăt'mosphēre *n.* Gaseous envelope surrounding a heavenly body, esp. the envelope of air surrounding the earth, which consists of gases (nitrogen, oxygen, argon, carbon dioxide, helium, and others) and water vapour, and is rarer as distance from the earth increases; air (of a place); mental or moral environment. **ătmosphĕ'ric** *adj.* ~ *pressure*, pressure of the weight of a column

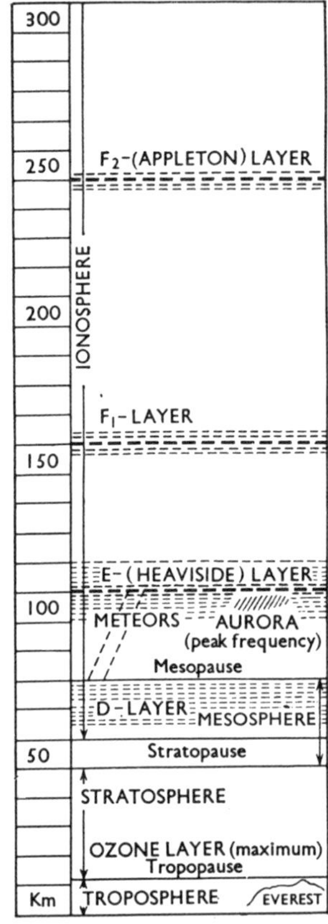

DIAGRAM OF THE ATMOSPHERE

of air above a given point, equivalent on the earth's surface to about 14½ lb. per sq. in., but decreasing with increasing height above the earth. **ătmosphĕ'rics** *n.pl.* Crackling or other sounds in wireless or telephone receiver caused by electrical disturbances in the atmosphere.

atŏll' (*or* ăt'-) *n.* Ring-shaped coral reef enclosing lagoon. [Malay]

ăt'om *n.* 1. Body too small to be divided; minute portion, small thing. 2. (chem. physics) Smallest particle of an element that cannot be further subdivided without destroying its identity; acc. to modern theories, the atom is regarded as consisting of a minute central positively charged *nucleus* in which almost all the mass is concentrated, and a number of negative electrons arranged round the nucleus; ~ *bomb*, = ATOMIC bomb.

atŏm'ĭc *adj.* Of atoms; ~ *bomb*, bomb deriving its destructive power from the fission, and partial conversion into energy, of the atomic nuclei of certain heavy elements such as uranium 235 or plutonium; (also) HYDROGEN bomb; ~ *energy*, the energy which appears when part of the atomic nucleus vanishes; this as source of industrial power; ~ *nucleus*: see ATOM; ~ *number*, (abbrev. at. no.) number of unit positive charges carried by the nucleus of an atom of an element, number determining the position of the element in the periodic table; ~ *pile*, assembly of uranium and graphite (or heavy water) in which fission of nuclei is controlled, used for making plutonium and production of atomic energy; ~ *theory*, theory that elements consist of atoms of definite relative weight and that atoms of different elements unite with one another in fixed proportions; ~ *weight*, for most purposes the weight of an atom expressed as multiple of weight of the hydrogen atom (now more precisely expressed as the ratio between the weight of one atom of an element and $\frac{1}{16}$ of the weight of an atom of oxygen).

ăt'omīze *v.t.* Reduce to atoms.

ăt'omīzer *n.* Instrument for reducing liquids to a fine spray.

ăt'omỳ[1] *n.* Atom, tiny being.

ăt'omỳ[2] *n.* (archaic) Skeleton, emaciated body. [f. ANATOMY]

atōn'al *adj.* (Of music) not written in keys. **ătonăl'ity** *n.*

atōne' *v.i.* Make amends; ~ *for*, expiate. **atōne'ment** (-nm-) *n.* *The A~*, expiation of man's sin by Christ; *Day of A~*: see YOM KIPPUR.

atŏn'ĭc *adj.* Unaccented; (path.) wanting tone. ~ *n.* Unaccented word (esp. in Gk gram.).

ătrabĭl'ious *adj.* Affected by black bile; melancholy; acrimonious. [L *atra bilis* black bile, transl. of Gk *melagkholia* MELANCHOLY]

Atreus (āt'rūs). (Gk legend) King of Argos, who set the flesh of his brother Thyestes' children before their father at a banquet in revenge because Thyestes had seduced his wife; he was himself murdered by Aegisthus.

āt'rium *n.* (pl. *-ia*, *-iums*). 1. Central court of Roman house (ill. HOUSE). 2. Covered portico, esp. before church door. 3. Either of the two upper cavities (*left* and *right* ~) of the heart into which the veins pour the blood (ill. HEART).

atrō'cious (-sh*us*) *adj.* Heinously wicked; very bad. **atrō'ciously** *adv.*

ătrŏ'cĭty *n.* Atrocious deed; bad blunder; (colloq.) hideous object.

ăt'rophy *n.* Wasting away through imperfect nourishment or lack of use. ~ *v.* Waste away.

ăt'ropine (-ēn) *n.* White crystalline alkaloid prepared from *Atropa belladonna* ('deadly nightshade') and used to dilate the pupil of the eye or to relieve pain. [f. ATROPOS]

At'ropŏs (ă-). (Gk myth.) The eldest of the Fates, who cut the thread of human life with her shears. [Gk, = 'inflexible']

A.T.S. *abbrev.* Auxiliary Territorial Service (now W.R.A.C.).

ătt'a *n.* The common wheaten flour or meal of India.

ătt'aboy *int.* (orig. U.S.) Exclamation expressing encouragement or admiration.

attăch' *v.* Fasten, join; attribute (importance etc. *to*); adhere, be incident *to*; seize by legal authority; bind in friendship, make devoted. **attăch'ment** *n.*

attaché (*a*tăsh'ā) *n.* Junior official attached to ambassador's suite; military or naval officer connected with embassy in a foreign country in order to report on military or naval affairs; ~ *case*, small rectangular valise orig. for carrying documents etc.

attăck' *v.t.* Fall upon, assault, assail; act destructively on. ~ *n.* Act of attacking; assault; onset.

attain' *v.* Reach, gain, accomplish; ~ *to*, arrive at. **attain'ment** *n.* Attaining; thing attained; (pl.) personal accomplishments.

attain'der *n.* (hist.) Consequences of sentence of death or outlawry (loss of civil rights, forfeiture of estate, etc.); *bill of* ~, legislative act inflicting results of attainder without judicial trial.

attaint' *v.t.* Subject to attainder (hist.); affect; infect; sully.

ătt'ar *n.* Fragrant essential oil distilled from flowers, esp. roses. [Pers. *'ater* perfume]

attĕm'per *v.t.* Qualify by admixture; modify; temper.

attĕmpt' *v.t.* Try; try to master. ~ *n.* Attempting; endeavour.

attĕnd' *v.* Turn the mind, apply oneself (*to*); be present at; wait upon, accompany.

attĕn'dance *n.* Attending; body of persons present; *dance* ~ *upon*, attend the convenience of.

attĕn'dant *adj.* Waiting on; accompanying. ~ *n.* Servant.

attĕn'tion *n.* Act or faculty of attending; consideration, care; (pl.) ceremonious politeness; courtship, addresses; *at* ~, (mil.) formal attitude of troops standing on parade as dist. from *at* EASE or EASY; ~! order to stand thus.

attĕn'tĭve *adj.* Heedful, observant; polite. **attĕn'tĭvely** (-vl-) *adv.* **attĕn'tĭvenėss** (-vn-) *n.*

attĕn'ūāte *v.t.* 1. Make slender or thin; reduce in force or value. 2. (elect., of circuit) Lose power. **attĕnūā'tion** *n.* **attĕn'ūate** (-*a*t) *adj.* Slender; rarefied.

attĕst' *v.* Testify, certify; put on oath or solemn declaration; *attested*, (of cattle) approved by authority as free from disease. **ăttėstā'tion** *n.*

Att'ĭc[1] (ă-) *adj.* & *n.* Of Attica. ~ (*dialect*), Greek spoken by the Athenians; ~ *salt*, *wit*, refined wit; ~ *order*, square column of any of the five orders (*see* ORDER). **ătt'ĭcism** *n.* Style, idiom of Athens; refined amenity of speech; attachment to Athens.

ătt'ĭc[2] *n.* 1. (archit.) Structure consisting of small order placed above another of greater height. 2. (Room in) highest storey of building, usu. immediately under the roof and not having a flat ceiling (ill. HOUSE). [Fr. *attique* upper part of house, so called from Attic order of architecture]

Att'ica (ă-). District of ancient Greece of which Athens was the capital.

Att'ĭla (ă-) (d. A.D. 453). King of the Huns, known as the 'scourge of God'; ravaged the Eastern Roman Empire (445–50); after making peace with Theodosius invaded the Western Empire and was defeated at Châlons by Aëtius in 451.

attīre' *v.t.* & *n.* Dress, array.

Att'ĭs, At'ȳs (ă-). A Phrygian deity connected with the worship of Cybele; his death was mourned for two days in the spring, and his recovery (when his spirit passed into a pine-tree and violets sprang up from his blood) then celebrated.

ătt'ĭtūde *n.* 1. Posture of body; settled behaviour, as indicating opinion; ~ *of mind*, settled mode of thinking. 2. Angular relation between aircraft's axis and wind.

ăttĭtūd'inīze *v.i.* Practise attitudes; act, speak, etc., affectedly.

Att'lee (ă-), Clement Richard, 1st Earl Attlee (1883–1967). English statesman; Labour Prime Minister 1945–51.

attorn'ey (-tėr-) *n.* One appointed to act for another in business in legal matters; *A~-General*, chief legal officer empowered to act in all cases in which the State is a party (in U.K. usu. a member of the House of Commons, appointed on advice of Government and resigning with it; in U.S. appointed by president).

attrăct' *v.t.* Draw to oneself; excite pleasurable emotions of; draw forth and fix on oneself (attention etc.). **attrăc'tion** *n.* Attracting; thing that attracts. **attrăc'tĭve** *adj.* **attrăc'tĭvely** (-vl-) *adv.* **attrăc'tĭvenėss** *n.*

attrĭb'ūte *v.t.* Ascribe as belonging or appropriate *to*; refer; assign. **ăttrĭbū'tion** *n.* **ătt'rĭbūte** *n.* Quality ascribed to anything; material object regarded as appropriate to person or office;

characteristic quality; (gram.) attributive word.

attrĭb'ūtĭve *adj.* & *n.* Assigning an attribute to a subject; (gram.) expressing an attribute, qualifying; word denoting an attribute. **attrĭbūt'ĭvely** *adv.*

attrĭ'tion *n.* Friction; abrasion; wearing out.

attūne' *v.t.* Bring into musical accord; adapt; tune.

At'wood's machine (ă-). Apparatus, consisting essentially of a nearly frictionless wheel which carries a cord with equal weights suspended from its ends, designed to demonstrate the mechanical law that a body which is not disturbed by force continues to move with uniform speed in a straight line. [named after George *Atwood* (1745–1807), English mathematician]

A.U. *abbrev.* ÅNGSTRÖM unit.

aubade (ōbahd') *n.* (mus.) Dawn-piece. [Fr.]

Auber (ōb'ā), Daniel François Esprit (1782–1871). French musician, composer of operas.

aubergine (ō'berzhēn) *n.* Elongated, usu. purple, fruit of the egg-plant (*Solanum melongena*), used as a vegetable.

Aubrietia (-rē'sha) *n.* Genus of spring-flowering dwarf perennial plants of mustard family. [after Claude *Aubriet* (d. 1743) French painter of flowers and animals]

aub'urn (-ern) *adj.* Golden-brown (usu. of hair).

Aubusson (ōb'ūsawṅ). Town in central France, famous since the 16th c., and esp. in the 18th, for the manufacture of tapestries and carpets.

A.U.C. *abbrev.* *Ab urbe condita* or *anno urbis conditae* (= from, in the year of, the founding of the city, i.e. Rome).

Auck'land. Largest city and chief seaport of New Zealand; also, the province comprising the northern part of North Island.

Auck'land Islands. Uninhabited group in the S. Pacific, S. of New Zealand.

au courant (ō k'ōōrahṅ) *pred. adj.* Acquainted *with* what is going on, well informed. [Fr.]

auc'tion *n.* Public sale at which articles are sold to the highest bidder; *Dutch* ~, sale at which price is reduced until a buyer is found; ~ *bridge*: see BRIDGE². ~ *v.t.* Sell (*off*) by auction.

auctioneer' (-shon-) *n.* One who conducts auctions. ~ *v.i.* Conduct auctions.

audā'cious (-shus) *adj.* Daring, bold; impudent. **audā'ciously** *adv.* **audā'ciousnĕss, audă'cĭty** *ns.*

aud'ĭble *adj.* Perceptible to the ear. **aud'ĭbly** *adv.* **audĭbĭl'ĭty** *n.*

aud'ience *n.* Hearing; formal interview; persons within hearing; assembly of listeners or spectators.

audio-frequency: see FREQUENCY.

aud'ĭt *n.* Official examination of accounts; periodical settlement of accounts between landlord and tenant; ~ *ale*, strong ale brewed in some colleges of Oxford and Cambridge, orig. for use on day of audit. ~ *v.t.* Examine (accounts) officially.

audĭ'tion *n.* Hearing; trial hearing of actor, singer, etc., seeking employment. ~ *v.t.*

aud'ĭtor *n.* One who audits accounts.

audĭtōr'ĭum *n.* Part of building occupied by audience (ill. THEATRE).

aud'ĭtory *adj.* Of hearing. ~ *n.* Hearers, audience; auditorium.

Aud'rey, St. (630?–679). Etheldreda, first abbess of Ely.

Aud'ūbon, John James (1785–1851). American naturalist and painter; his 'Birds of America', engraved in aquatint, was published in London, 1838, and his 'Quadrupeds of North America' in New York, 1848 and 1854.

au fait (ō fā). Conversant, instructed. [Fr.]

au fond (ō fawṅ). At bottom. [Fr.]

Aug. *abbrev.* August.

Augē'an stables. (Gk legend) The cow-byres of Augeas, king of Elis; they had never been cleaned and the task was one of the 'labours' of Hercules, who accomplished it by diverting the course of the river Alpheus through them.

au'ger (-g-) *n.* Tool for boring holes in wood, having a long shank with cutting edge and screw point, and handle at right angles.

AUGER

aught (awt) *n.* Anything.

aug'ment *n.* (gram.) Vowel prefixed to past tenses in the older Indo-European languages. **augmĕnt'** *v.* Increase; prefix augment to; *augmented fourth, fifth, octave*, (mus.) perfect interval widened by a semitone (ill. INTERVAL). **augmentā'tion** *n.*

augmĕn'tatĭve *adj.* & *n.* Increasing; (gram.) (word or affix) increasing in force the idea of the original word; (mus.) lengthening of phrase by increasing the values of the notes.

au grand sérieux (ō grahṅ sĕrēēr'). Quite seriously. [Fr.]

Augs'bûrg (ow-). City of Bavaria; ~ *Confession*, a statement of the Protestant position drawn up by Melanchthon for the Diet of 1530.

aug'ur (-er) *n.* Roman religious official who foretold future events by observing flight or notes of birds etc.; soothsayer. ~ *v.* Forebode, anticipate; ~ *well, ill*, have good (bad) implications or expectations *of, for*. **aug'ūry** *n.* Divination; omen; promise.

augŭst'¹ *adj.* Majestic, venerable. **augŭst'ly** *adv.* **augŭst'nĕss** *n.* [L *augustus* consecrated, venerable]

Aug'ust². 8th month of the year. [named after Rom. emperor AUGUSTUS]

Augŭs'ta. Capital of Maine, U.S.

Augŭs'tan *adj.* Of AUGUSTUS; ~ *Age*, period of literary eminence in the life of a nation, so called because Virgil, Horace, Ovid, etc., all flourished during Augustus' reign; in English literary history, the period of Pope and Addison.

Augŭs'tĭne¹, St. (354–430). Theologian; son of a pagan father and Christian mother (St. Monica); was for a time attracted by Manichaeism, but baptized as a Christian 387; became bishop of Hippo in N. Africa, 391; defended Christianity against ancient religions and philosophies and contemporary heresies in numerous writings, of which the best-known are the 'City of God' ('Civitas Dei') and the autobiographical 'Confessions'.

Augŭs'tĭne², St. (d. 604). First archbishop of Canterbury; led mission to England from Rome and founded a monastery at Canterbury.

Augustĭn'ĭan *adj.* Of St. AUGUSTINE¹ of Hippo; ~ *Canons*, an order of R.C. canons regular, who adopted the 'rule of St. Augustine' (based largely on Augustine's writings but not formulated by him) in the 11th c.; ~ (or *Austin*) *Friars*, a mendicant order founded *c* 1250 and observing the Augustinian rule.

Augŭs'tus (63 B.C. – A.D. 14). Gaius Julius Caesar Octavianus (Octavian), great-nephew and adopted son of Julius Caesar; member of the second TRIUMVIRATE and first Roman emperor; the title of Augustus was conferred on him by senate and people in 27 B.C. and was borne by all subsequent Roman emperors.

auk *n.* Any of the *Alcidae* family of sea-birds, which includes the guillemot, puffin, razor-bill, little auk (*Alle alle*), and the extinct great auk (*Plautus*, or *Alca, impennis*).

aul'ic *adj.* Pertaining to a court; *A~ Council*, official council of the emperor in the Holy Roman Empire, established by Maximilian I in 1499.

Aul'is. Ancient Greek town on Boeotian coast, where (in legend) the Greek fleet was detained by contrary winds before the Trojan War, and where Iphigenia was sacrificed.

aum'bry *n.* Closed recess in wall of church.

au naturel (ō nătūrĕl'). (Cooked) in the simplest way. [Fr.]

aunt (ahnt) *n.* Father's or

mother's sister; uncle's wife; *A~ Sally*, game in which sticks or balls are thrown at wooden skittle-shaped dummy (orig. at pipe in mouth of wooden woman's head); (fig.) any person or institution which becomes a mark of popular attack.

au pair (ō pār). (Of arrangements between two parties) paid for by mutual services (no money passing). [Fr.]

au pied de la lettre (ō pyā' de lah lĕt'r). Literally. [Fr.]

aur'a *n.* 1. Subtle emanation; atmosphere diffused by or attending a person etc. (esp. in mystical use as definite envelope of body or spirit). 2. (path.) Sensation as of cold air rising from part of body to head, premonitory symptom in epilepsy and hysterics. **aur'al**[1] *adj.*

aur'al[2] *adj.* Of, received by, the ear. **aur'ally** *adv.*

Aurēl'ian, Lucius Domitius Aurelianus (*c* A.D. 212–75). Roman emperor, 270–5.

Aur'ėngzēb (1618–1707). Mogul emperor of India, 1658–1707, a period of great wealth and splendour for the empire.

aurē'ola, aur'ėōle *ns.* Celestial crown worn by martyrs, saints, virgins, etc.; pictorial representation of this in form of golden ring or disc painted behind and round head of wearer; halo, esp. that of the sun seen in eclipses. [L *aureola* (*corona*) golden crown]

aurėomȳ'cĭn *n.* An antibiotic substance (*chlortetracycline*), which is produced by micro-organisms of the group *streptomyces* and used in medical treatment, particularly of lung diseases.

au revoir (ō revwâr'). (Goodbye) till we meet again. [Fr.]

aur'ĭcle *n.* 1. External ear of animals (ill. EAR); process shaped like lobe of ear. 2. Small appendage of the ATRIUM, sense 3.

aurĭc'ūla *n.* Species of Alpine primula, so called from shape of leaf.

aurĭc'ūlar *adj.* Pertaining to the ear; pertaining to auricle of the heart; *~ confession*, confession made privately (in the ear of the priest).

aurĭf'erous *adj.* Yielding gold.

Aurīg'a. A northern constellation, the Waggoner.

Aurignā'cian (-shn) *adj.* Of a palaeolithic culture believed to have existed in France *c* 11,500–10,000 B.C. [f. *Aurignac* in Haute-Garonne, SW. France, where flint implements were found]

aur'ĭst *n.* Ear specialist.

aur'ŏchs (-ŏks) *n.* Extinct European wild ox; (improperly) the European bison.

Aurôr'a. Roman goddess corresponding to the Greek Eos, goddess of the dawn; (poet.) the dawn; *~ Australis*, phenomenon similar to Aurora Borealis, seen in southern latitudes; *~ Borealis*, luminous phenomenon, popularly called the *northern lights*, seen in northern latitudes esp. at night; it usually appears as streamers of many colours ascending from above the northern horizon and is supposed to be of electrical origin (ill. ATMOSPHERE).

auscultā'tion *n.* Act of listening, esp. (med.) to movement of heart, lungs, etc. **auscŭl'tatory** *adj.*

aus'pĭce *n.* Observation of birds for purpose of taking omens; (pl.) patronage. **auspĭ'cious** (-shus) *adj.* Of good omen; favourable; prosperous. **auspĭ'ciously** *adv.* **auspĭ'ciousnėss** *n.*

Auss'ie (*or* (ŏz'ĭ) *n.* An Australian, orig. of Australian troops in the war of 1914–18.

Aus'ten, Jane (1775–1817). English author of 6 novels: 'Pride and Prejudice', 'Northanger Abbey', 'Sense and Sensibility', 'Mansfield Park', 'Emma', and 'Persuasion'.

austēre' *adj.* Harsh; stern; stringently moral; severely simple. **austere'ly** (-ērl-) *adv.* **austere'nėss** (-ērn-) *n.* **austĕ'rĭty** *n.* Quality of being austere; severity, austere or ascetic practice; applied esp. during the war of 1939–45 to clothes etc. in which non-essentials were reduced to a minimum as a war-time measure of economy.

Aus'terlĭtz (ow-). Slavkov, town in Moravia, scene in 1805 of Napoleon's defeat of the Austrians and Russians.

Aus'tĭn[1], Alfred (1835–1913). English minor poet, poet laureate from 1896.

Aus'tĭn[2]. Capital of Texas, U.S.

Aus'tin Friars: see AUGUSTINIAN Friars.

aus'tral *adj.* Southern. [L *Auster*, the south wind]

Australā'sia (-sha). Term used loosely to include Australia and the islands scattered over the SW. Pacific. **Australā'sian** *adj.* & *n.*

Austrāl'ia. Continent of S. hemisphere in the SW. Pacific; a Dominion of the British Commonwealth. The existence of a *Terra Australis* ('southern land') was known in Europe in the 16th c.; from 1606 onwards its W. coast was explored by the Dutch and in 1642 Tasman proved that it was an island. It was visited by an Englishman, William Dampier, in 1699. In 1770 Capt. James Cook, on the first of his 3 voyages, landed at Botany Bay on the E. side and formally took possession of New South Wales; British colonization began in 1788 (also the settling of convicts at Port Jackson, discontinued in 1840). In 1901 the 6 colonies (New South Wales, Victoria, Queensland, South Australia, Western Australia, and Tasmania) federated as sovereign states of the *Commonwealth of ~*, which also administers Northern Territory, Capital Territory (site of the federal capital, Canberra), and certain areas outside the continent. **Austrāl'ian** *adj.* & *n.* (Native) of Australia.

Aus'trĭa. German-speaking country of central Europe, which became a republic in 1918; formerly it was the nucleus of the Austro-Hungarian Empire. For much of its earlier history it was a mark (the Ostmark or eastern mark) of the German Empire, an outpost of defence against Slavs and Magyars; it became a duchy in 1156 and later the seat of the Habsburg emperors. In 1918 the empire was divided between Hungary, Poland, Czechoslovakia, Italy, Rumania, Yugoslavia, and Austria itself. In March 1938 Austria was forcibly annexed to the German Empire, but was liberated from Nazi rule in 1945. Capital, Vienna. **Aus'trĭan** *adj.* & *n.* (Native) of Austria.

Aus'trĭa-Hŭng'ary (-ngg-). Name for the Austrian Empire. **Aus'tro-Hungār'ian** *adj.*

aut'archy[1] (-k-) *n.* Absolute sovereignty, despotism. [Gk *autarkhia* (*arkhō* rule)]

aut'archy[2] (-k-), **aut'arky** *ns.* Economic self-sufficiency of a political unit. [Gk *autarkeia* (*arkeō* suffice)]

authĕn'tĭc *adj.* Reliable, trustworthy; of undisputed origin; *~ mode*, (mus., of eccles. modes) having their sounds comprised within an octave from the final (ill. MODE). **authĕn'tĭcally** *adv.* **authĕntĭ'cĭty** *n.*

authĕn'tĭcāte *v.t.* Establish the truth or authorship of: make valid.

auth'or *n.* Originator; writer of book etc. **auth'orėss** *n.fem.* **auth'orshĭp** *n.*

authoritār'ian *adj.* & *n.* (Person) favouring obedience to authority as opp. to individual liberty; of, pertaining to, a dictatorship.

authŏr'ĭtatĭve *adj.* Possessing or claiming authority. **authŏ'rĭtatĭvely** *adv.*

authŏ'rĭty *n.* Power or right to enforce obedience; delegated power; person etc. having authority; personal influence; expert.

auth'orīze *v.t.* Sanction; give ground for; give authority to. *Authorized Version* (of the Bible), the English translation of 1611.

autĭs'tĭc *adj.* (psychol., of thinking) Controlled by wish and affect rather than by logic or fact. **aut'ĭsm** *n.*

auto- *prefix.* Same, self.

autobīŏg'raphy *n.* Writing the story of one's own life; the story so written. **autobīogrăph'ĭc(al)** *adjs.* **autobīŏg'rapher** *n.*

aut'ocâr *n.* (rare) Motor-car.

autŏch'thon (-k-) *n.* (usu. pl.) Original inhabitants. **autŏch'thonous** *adj.*

autŏc'racy *n.* Absolute government.

aut'ocrăt *n.* Absolute ruler; dictatorial overbearing person; *A~ of all the Russias*, (hist.) title of the Tsar. **autocrăt'ic** *adj.* **autocrăt'ically** *adv.*

aut'o-da-fé' (-dah-fā) *n.* Sentence of the Inquisition; execution of this, esp. burning of a heretic. [Port., = 'act of faith']

autogīr'ō *n.* Proprietary name of a type of aeroplane, or gyroplane, deriving its lift mainly from a system of freely rotating horizontal wings and capable of landing in a very small space.

aut'ograph (-ahf) *n.* Author's own manuscript; person's own handwriting, esp. signature; document signed by its author, as dist. from HOLOGRAPH, one wholly written in his hand (freq. *attrib.*, as ~ *letter*). ~ *v.t.* Write one's signature on or in; sign. **autogrăph'ic(al)** *adjs.* **autogrăph'ically** *adv.*

automăt'ic *adj.* Self-acting, working of itself; mechanical; unconscious; ~ *control*, device enabling machine to maintain a predetermined temperature, pressure, speed, etc., without intervention of operator; ~ *pilot*, similar device in aircraft for maintaining a set course or height; ~ *gun, pistol*, fire-arm which, after the first round is exploded, by gas pressure or force of recoil automatically ejects the empty case, loads another into the chamber, fires, and repeats this movement until the ammunition in the mechanism is exhausted or pressure on the trigger is released (ill. PISTOL). ~ *n.* Automatic pistol. **automăt'ically** *adv.*

automā'tion *n.* (eng., orig. U.S.) Completely automatic control of a manufactured product through a number of successive stages.

autŏm'atism *n.* 1. Involuntary action; (psychol.) action performed unconsciously or subconsciously. 2. Doctrine that movements or actions of organic beings are mechanical, not resulting from volition.

autŏm'aton *n.* Mechanical device with concealed motive power; person whose actions are mechanical, following a customary routine.

aut'omobile' (-ēl) *n.* (chiefly U.S.) Motor-car.

autonŏm'ic *adj.* (physiol.) Of that part of the nervous system (~ or *involuntary nervous system*) which functions more or less independently of the will; it comprises the SYMPATHETIC and PARASYMPATHETIC systems and consists of groups of nerve-cells which are situated outside the spinal column and regulate gland-secretions and the muscular activity of the heart, blood-vessels, and hollow organs.

autŏn'omous *adj.* 1. Self-governing. 2. (physiol., path.) Independent of the usual processes which regulate the growth of an organism. **autŏn'omously** *adv.*

autŏn'omy *n.* Right of self-government; freedom of the will; self-governing community.

autŏp'sy (*or* aw'-) *n.* Personal inspection; post-mortem examination. **autŏp'tic(al)** *adjs.*

auto-suggĕs'tion *n.* Hypnotic suggestion proceeding from the subject himself.

aut'otȳpe *n.* Photographic printing process for reproducing in monochrome. ~ *v.t.* Reproduce by this process.

aut'umn (-m) *n.* Season of year between summer and winter, popularly reckoned in N. hemisphere as comprising the months September, October, and November, but astronomically as lasting from autumnal equinox (22nd or 23rd Sept.) to winter solstice (21st or 22nd Dec.); (fig.) season of incipient decay. **autŭm'nal** *adj.* Of autumn; ~ *equinox*, time when sun crosses equator as it proceeds southward (22nd or 23rd Sept.).

Auvergne (ōvārn'). Ancient province of S. central France.

auxĭl'iary (-lya-) *adj.* Helpful; subsidiary; (gram., of verbs) serving to form tenses, moods, voices, of other verbs. ~ *n.* Assistant; (esp. pl.) foreign troops serving with another country in war; (naval) vessel auxiliary to fighting vessels, as tanker, supply ship, etc.

A.V. *abbrev.* Authorized Version (of the Bible).

avail' *v.* Be of use or assistance (to); help, benefit. ~ *n.* Use, profit.

avail'able *adj.* At one's disposal, capable of being used. **availabĭl'ity** *n.*

ăv'alanche (-ahnsh) *n.* Mass of snow, rock, and ice, falling down mountain (also fig.); ~ *cone*, pile of material deposited by an avalanche; ~ *wind*, wind produced by avalanche, freq. causing further destruction.

Av'alon (ă-). In the Arthurian legend, the place to which ARTHUR[1] was conveyed after death; in Welsh myth., the kingdom of the dead.

ăv'arice *n.* Greed of gain, cupidity. **ăvarĭ'cious** (-shus) *adj.* **ăvarĭ'ciously** *adv.*

Av'ar (ā-). Member of a Ural-Altaic race prominent from the 6th to the 9th centuries; in the 7th c. their kingdom extended from the Black Sea to the Adriatic; finally subdued by Charlemagne.

avast' (-ahst) *int.* (naut.) Stop, cease. [Du. *houd vast* hold fast]

Av'atar (ă-). (Hindu myth.) The descent to earth and incarnation of a deity.

avaunt' *int.* (archaic, joc.) Begone.

avdp. *abbrev.* Avoirdupois.

ā'vė (*or* ahv'ā) *int.* & *n.* Welcome; *A~ Maria, A~ Mary* (= Hail, Mary!), the angelic salutation to the Virgin (Luke i. 28), combined with that of Elizabeth (i. 42), used as a devotional recitation, together with a prayer to the Virgin.

Ave'bury (āvb-). Village in Wiltshire, site of a very large stone-circle.

avĕnge' (-j) *v.t.* Inflict retribution on behalf of; exact retribution for.

Av'entīne (ăv-). The most southerly of the seven hills of Rome.

avĕn'tūrine *n.* Brownish glass with copper crystals, first manufactured near Venice; quartz, spangled with mica or haematite, resembling this. [It. *avventura* chance (from its accidental discovery)]

ăv'ėnūe *n.* Way of approach; approach to house bordered by trees; roadway with trees etc. at regular intervals; wide street.

avér' *v.t.* Assert, affirm.

ăv'erage *n.* Arithmetical mean; ordinary standard; generally prevailing degree etc.; apportionment of loss of ship, cargo, or freight among the owners or insurers. ~ *adj.* Estimated by average; of usual standard. ~ *v.t.* Estimate average or general standard of; amount on an average to. [L *averāgium* property, cattle]

Avérn'us. A lake in Campania, Italy, filling crater of an extinct volcano, and regarded by the ancients as the entrance to the infernal regions.

Avĕ'rroës (-rōĕz). Abul Walid Mohammed ben Ahmed ibn Roshd (1126–98), Moslem doctor born at Cordova, philosopher, and author of a famous commentary on Aristotle.

avérse' *adj.* Opposed, disinclined (*to, from*); unwilling.

avér'sion *n.* Dislike, unwillingness; object of dislike.

avért' *v.t.* Turn away; ward off.

Avĕs'ta. The relics of the Zoroastrian priestly writings, in Old Iranian; regarded as scripture by the Parsees. **Avĕs'tan** *adj.* & *n.* (Language) of the Avesta.

ăv'iary *n.* Large cage or building for keeping birds.

aviā'tion *n.* The operation of heavier-than-air aircraft. **ăv'iātor** *n.* **ăv'iāte** *v.i.* (rare).

Avicĕnn'a (ă-, -s-). Abu Ibn Sina (980–1037), Persian physician, philosopher, and commentator on Aristotle.

ăv'id *adj.* Eager, greedy. **av'idly** *adv.* **avĭd'ity** *n.*

Avignon (ăv'ēnyawṅ). City on river Rhône, in S. France, to which Clement V removed the papal seat in 1308; it remained there until 1377, and after the outbreak of the papal schism in 1378, two anti-popes, Clement VII and Benedict XIII, resided there; the latter was expelled in 1408, but the city remained in papal possession until 1791.

ăvoca'dō (-kah-) *n.* Succulent pear-shaped fruit, a drupe with soft-coated seed, borne by the tropical Amer. and W. Indian tree *Persea gratissima.* [Span. *avocado* advocate, corrupt. of Mex. name]

ăvocā′tion *n.* Minor occupation; vocation, calling.

ăv′ocĕt *n.* Long-legged wading bird with long upturned beak (*Recurvirostra avosetta*).

Avoga′drō (ă-, -gah-), Amadeo (1776–1856). Italian physicist; ~*'s law*, hypothesis that equal volumes of all gases at the same temperature and pressure contain equal numbers of molecules; ~*'s number*, the number of molecules in the gram-molecular weight of any gas; value, $6{\cdot}02 \times 10^{23}$.

avoid′ *v.t.* Shun, refrain from; evade, escape; (law) quash. **avoid′able** *adj.* **avoid′ably** *adv.* **avoid′ance** *n.*

avoirdupois (ăverdūpoiz′), *n.* System of weights used in English-speaking countries for all goods except precious metals and stones, and medicine; weight, heaviness. [corrupt. of Fr. *avoir de pois* goods of weight]

Av′on (ā-). River, flowing through Warwickshire, a tributary of the Severn (*Swan of* ~, Ben Jonson's sobriquet for Shakespeare, who was born at Stratford on Avon); also, other English rivers.

avouch′ *v.* Guarantee; affirm; confess.

avow′ *v.t.* Admit, confess. **avow′al** *n.* **avow′ĕdly** *adv.*

avŭnc′ūlar *adj.* Of, resembling, an uncle.

await′ *v.t.* Wait for.

awāke′ *v.* (past t. *awōke*; past part. *awōke*, *awāked*). Cease to sleep; rouse from sleep. ~ *pred. adj.* Not asleep; vigilant. **awāk′en** *v.* Awake.

award′ (-ŏrd) *v.t.* Adjudge; grant, assign. ~ *n.* Judicial decision; payment, penalty, assigned by this.

awāre′ *pred. adj.* Conscious, not ignorant (*of*, *that*).

awash′ (-wŏ-) *pred. adj.* Flush with or washed by the waves.

away′ *adv.* To or at a distance; constantly, continuously.

awe *n.* Reverential fear. ~ *v.t.* Inspire with awe. **awe′some** (aws-) *adj.* **awe′strŭck** (aws-) *adj.* Struck with awe.

awf′ul *adj.* Inspiring awe; solemnly impressive; (colloq.) notable in its kind (usu. of thing or person disliked). **awf′ully** *adv.* (esp. colloq.) Extremely. **awf′ulnĕss** *n.*

awhīle′ *adv.* For a short time.

awk′ward *adj.* Ill-adapted for use; hard to deal with; clumsy. **awk′wardly** *adv.* **awk′wardnĕss** *n.*

awl *n.* Small pointed tool for piercing holes in leather, wood, etc., esp. that used by shoemakers.

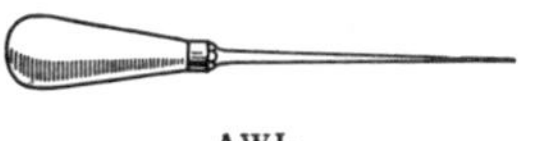

AWL

awn *n.* Stiff bristle-like process terminating grain-sheath of barley, oats, etc. (ill. GRASS). **awned** (-nd) *adj.*

awn′ĭng *n.* Canvas sheet stretched on framework as protection from sun etc., esp. on ship's deck.

A.W.O.L. *abbrev.* Absent without leave.

awry (arī′) *adv.* & *pred. adj.* Crookedly; amiss.

ăxe *n.* Chopping-tool, usu. of iron, with steel edge and wooden handle; drastic reduction of public expenditure. ~ *v.t.* Cut down (personnel, expenses, etc.).

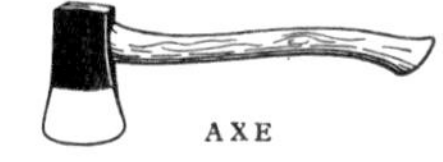

AXE

ăx′ĭal *adj.* Forming, belonging to, an axis. **ăx′ĭally** *adv.*

ăx′ĭl *n.* Upper angle between leaf and stem it springs from, or between branch and trunk (ill. LEAF).

ăx′ĭllary *adj.* 1. Of the armpit. 2. (bot.) In, growing from, the axil.

ăx′ĭom *n.* Self-evident truth; established principle; maxim. **ăxĭomăt′ĭc** *adj.* **ăxĭomăt′ĭcally** *adv.*

ăx′ĭs *n.* (pl. *axēs*). 1. Line about which a body rotates (~ *of equator*, that between N. and S. Poles, round which the earth turns daily); straight line from end to end of a body. 2. (math.) Line dividing a regular figure symmetrically; line by revolution about which a plane is conceived as generating a solid (ill. SYMMETRY). 3. (bot.) Stem or shoot; *floral* ~, that part of a shoot which bears the floral organs, receptacle (ill. FLOWER). 4. (anat.) Second cervical vertebra, on which the head turns (ill. SPINE). 5. (optics) Ray passing through centre of eye or lens or falling perpendicularly on it. 6. *Rome–Berlin A*~, alliance between Germany and Italy, May 1939, later joined by Japan (*Rome–Berlin–Tokyo–A*~); *A*~ *Powers*, these nations.

ă′xle *n.* Spindle on or with which wheel revolves (ill. WHEEL); end of axle-tree; axle-tree; ~*-box*, box closed by detachable cap, in nave of a wheel, through which the ends of axle-tree pass; ~*-tree*, bar connecting wheels of carriage etc.

Ax′mĭnster (ă-). Small town in Devonshire; ~ (*carpet*), carpet of cut pile made by various methods, first made at Axminster, orig. in imitation of hand-knotted oriental carpets.

ă′xolŏtl *n.* Salamander of genus *Amblystoma* of mountain lakes of Mexico and SW. U.S., usu. retaining larval form throughout life. [Aztec]

ăx′on *n.* That part of the nerve which is its conducting element or nerve fibre (ill. NERVE).

ay(e) (ī) *int.* Yes. ~ *n.* (pl. *ayes*). Affirmative answer or vote.

ayah (ī′*a*) *n.* Native Hindu nurse. [Port. *aia* fem. of *aio* tutor]

aye (ā) *adv.* Always; *for* ~, for ever.

aye-aye (ī′ī) *n.* Small tree-climbing animal (*Chiromys*) found in Madagascar, a primate closely related to the lemurs.

Ayles′bury (ālz-). County town of Buckinghamshire; ~ *duck*, duck of white domestic breed.

Ayr′shire (ār-). County of SW. Scotland; breed of dairy cattle, mostly white with reddish or black markings, orig. raised there; kind of bacon cured in Ayrshire.

azāl′ĕa *n.* Various flowering shrubby plants, chiefly natives of N. America and China, included in the genus *Rhododendron.* [mod. L, f. Gk *azaleos* parched, because Linnaeus believed them to grow in dry situations]

Azerbaijan (ăzerbījahn′). 1. One of the constituent republics of the Soviet Union, lying between the Black and Caspian Seas; capital, Baku. 2. Province of N. Persia.

Azĭl′ian (*a*-) *adj.* Of the transitional period between the palaeolithic and neolithic ages. [f. Mas d'*Azil* in Fr. Pyrenees, where remains were found]

ăz′ĭmuth *n.* Arc of the heavens extending from the zenith to the horizon, which it cuts at right angles; ~ *circle*, circle of which this is a quadrant, passing through zenith and nadir (ill. CELESTIAL); *true* ~ of a heavenly body (also called simply *azimuth*), arc of horizon intercepted between north (in S. hemisphere, south) point of horizon and the point where the great circle passing through the body cuts the horizon; *magnetic* ~, arc intercepted between this circle and the magnetic meridian. **ăzĭmūth′al** *adj.*; ~ *projection*: see ZENITHAL projection. **ăzĭmūth′ally** *adv.* [Arab. *al samut* the ways (i.e. directions)]

Azores′ (*a*zōrz′). Group of islands in N. Atlantic, some 800 miles W. of Portugal; in Portuguese possession.

Azov (ăz′ŏf), Sea of. An inland sea of S. Russia, separated from the Black Sea by the Crimea and communicating with it by a narrow strait.

Az′rāel (ă-). (Jewish and Moslem myth.) The angel who at death severs the soul from the body.

Az′tĕc (ă-) *adj.* & *n.* (One) of a native Amer. people first known (*c* A.D. 1100) as inhabitants of the valley of Mexico. They built their capital (on the same site as modern Mexico City) in 1324 and extended their conquests in the 15th c., their most successful leader being Montezuma I (reigned 1440–69). They were conquered by the invading Spaniards under Cortez, early in the 16th c.

ă′zure (-zher, -zhyer) *adj.* & *n.* Sky-blue; unclouded sky; lapis lazuli; (heraldry) blue (ill. HERALDRY). [Arab. *al lazward* (*al* the + Pers. *lazhward* lapis lazuli)]

B

B, b (bē). 1. 2nd letter of the modern English and Roman alphabet, representing a voiced bilabial stop, and derived from the Greek *beta* (β) and Phoenician and Hebrew *beth* (ɓ, ב). 2. *B*, (mus.) 7th note in the 'natural' scale (C major).

b. *abbrev.* Born; (in cricket) bowled, bye.

B. *abbrev.* *Beatus, -a* (L, = 'Blessed'); black (of pencil-lead).

B.A. *abbrev.* Bachelor of Arts; British Academy.

baa (bah) *n.* & *v.* Bleat.

Bā'al (pl. *-im*). God of the ancient Phoenicians and Canaanites; a false god. **Bā'alism** *n.* The worship of Baal, idolatry. [Heb. *ba'al* lord]

Baalbĕk' (bahl-). Site (80 miles from Damascus, in the Lebanese Republic) of the Roman colony of Heliopolis (1st–3rd centuries A.D.), a centre of worship of the sun-god Helios, identified with BAAL.

baas (bahs) *n.* Boss, master; S. Afr. form of address, esp. of native to white man. [Du., = 'master', 'uncle']

baba (au rhum) (bahb'ah ō rōōm), *n.* Small rich sponge-cake soaked in rum.

băb'acōōte *n.* Species of woolly lemur (*Lichanotus brevicaudatus*) found in Madagascar.

băbb'ĭtt *v.* Line with babbitt-metal. ~ *n.* Bearing made of babbitt-metal (ill. BEARING).

băbb'ĭtt-mĕt'al *n.* Soft alloy of tin, copper, and antimony, used for machine bearings. Also *Babbitt's metal.* [I. *Babbitt* (1799–1862), Amer. inventor]

Băbb'ĭtt. Hero of a novel (1922) by Sinclair Lewis; hence, typical business man of U.S. Middle West. **Băbb'ittism, Băbb'ĭttry** *ns.*

băb'ble *v.* Talk half-articulately, incoherently, foolishly or excessively; murmur (of stream etc.). ~ *n.* Foolish or childish talk. **băb'bler** *n.* Chatterer; teller of secrets; long-legged thrush.

bābe *n.* Baby.

Bāb'el. The city of BABYLON; acc. to Hebrew mythology (Gen. xi) its people tried to build a tower which would reach heaven, but God prevented them by 'confounding' their language (so that they could not understand one another) and scattering them abroad; hence, *tower of* ~, visionary scheme. **bāb'el** *n.* Scene of confusion and uproar; noisy assembly.

Bábí: see BAHA'Í.

Băb'ĭngton, Anthony (1561–86). Page to Mary Queen of Scots; executed for conspiring to murder Elizabeth and release Mary from imprisonment.

băbĭru'sa, babyroussa (rōō-) *n.* Wild hog (*Babirusa alfurus*), male of which has long upper canine teeth which pierce the lip and grow upward like horns; found only in islands of Celebes and Buru. [Malagasy, = 'hog deer']

babōōn' *n.* Medium-sized monkey (several species in genus *Papio*) of Arabia and Africa S. and E. of Sahara, living in bands in open rocky country, seldom tree-climbing, characterized by dog-like snout, cheek-prominences, and coloured bare patches on the buttocks; *sacred* ~, species living on Red Sea coasts and formerly in Egypt (*P. hamadryas*).

babouche' (-ōōsh) *n.* Oriental heelless slipper. [Pers. *pa-posh* foot-covering]

Bāb'rius. Author of a collection of fables, in Greek; prob. a Roman of the 2nd c. A.D.

babu (bahb'ōō) *n.* Hindu gentleman; native clerk or official who writes English; (contempt.) Hindu, esp. Bengali, with superficial English education.

Babur (bahb'oor) (1483–1530). The first Mogul emperor, descended from Tamburlaine; he invaded India *c* 1525 and conquered the territory from the Oxus to Patna.

bāb'y *n.* Infant, very young child; childish person; ~*-farmer*, person who keeps babies for payment; ~ *grand*, small grand piano; ~*-sitter*, (colloq.) person who looks after baby when parents go out. **bāb'ўhōōd** *n.* **bāb'ўĭsh** *adj.*

Băb'ўlon. Capital city, on the Euphrates, of the ancient Chaldean Empire; the Jews were brought there in captivity by Nebuchadnezzar (597 and 586 B.C.); its *hanging* (i.e. terraced) *gardens* were one of the Seven Wonders of the ancient world. Babylon was sacked by Cyrus of Persia in 538 B.C. *Whore of* ~, name given by early puritans to Rome, the Papacy (cf. Rev. xvii). **Băbўlōn'ĭa.** The empire of Babylon. **Băbўlōn'ĭan** *adj.* & *n.* **Băb'ўlonĭsh** *adj.* (archaic).

băccalaur'ėate *n.* University degree of bachelor.

băcc'arat (-ah) *n.* Gambling card-game, played against banker by punters staking that their hand will total nine.

băcc'āte *adj.* (bot.) 1. Bearing berries. 2. Berry-shaped.

băcc'hanal (-k-) *adj.* Of Bacchus or his rites. ~ *n.* Priest or votary of Bacchus; reveller.

Băcchanāl'ĭa (-k-) *n.pl.* Festival held in honour of Bacchus; drunken revelry, orgy.

Băcc'hant (-k-), **Bacchăn'tė** (*or* -kănt') *ns.* Priest or priestess of Bacchus, often represented with loose hair garlanded with ivy, and dressed in a leopard-skin; (drunken or noisy) reveller.

băcc'hĭc (-k-) *adj.* Of Bacchus or his worship; riotous, drunken.

Bacchus (băk'*us*). Greek and Roman god of wine: see DIONYSUS.

baccĭf'erous, băcc'ĭfōrm, baccĭv'orous (băks-) *adjs.* Berry-bearing, -shaped, -eating.

băcc'y (-k-) *n.* Colloq. abbrev. for TOBACCO.

Bach (bahχ), Johann Sebastian (1685–1750). German musical composer, the greatest master of contrapuntal music; author of many fugues and other works for organ and other keyboard instruments, a great Mass, and much other choral church-music. Of his 11 sons, several distinguished in music, two of the better-known are Carl Philipp Emanuel ~ (1714–88), who contributed much to the development of the sonata form, and Johann Christian ~ (the 'English Bach', 1735–82), who spent some time in England.

băch'ėlor *n.* Unmarried man; university degree below master; knight serving under another's banner; ~*'s button*, button which can be attached without sewing; ~*'s buttons*, any of various flowers of round or button-like form, orig. the double variety of *Ranunculus acris*; ~ *girl*, unmarried girl living independently.

bacĭll'ary *adj.* Consisting of little rods; connected with bacilli.

bacĭll'ĭfōrm *adj.* Rod-shaped.

bacĭll'us *n.* (pl. *-llī*). Any straight rod-shaped bacterium (ill. BACTERIUM); (loosely and usu. pl.) disease-producing bacteria. [L dim. of *baculus* stick]

băck *n.* Hinder surface of human body, part of this between shoulders and hips; corresponding part of animal's body; hind part of things, side away from spectator; rear; side of hand opposite palm; cover of book's spine; football player stationed behind forwards (ill. ASSOCIATION). ~ *adj.* Situated behind; remote; belonging to past period; inferior. ~ *adv.* To the rear; in(to) an earlier position; to or in remote or retired position. ~ *v.* Put, or be, a back, lining, support, or background to; support with money, argument, etc. (also ~ *up*); bet on; endorse (cheque etc.); ride (horse); (cause to) move back; lay (sail) against the wind; (of wind) change counter-clockwise (cf. VEER); ~ *out of*, withdraw from; *back'er*, one who backs or supports; *back'ing*, support, assistance. **back-** in phrases and compounds: ~*-bench*, ~*-bencher*: see BENCH *n.* 3; *back'bite*, slander; *back'biter* (*n.*); ~*-blocks* (Austral.), the remotest fringe of settlement; *back'bone*, spine; main support; firmness of character; *~-chat*, (slang) impudent retort(s); *~-cloth*, painted cloth hung at the back of scene or stage (ill. THEATRE); *backdoor'*, door at back of house; underhand or secret approach; *~-end*, (colloq.) late autumn; *backfire* (of internal combustion engine) premature ignition in the cylinder during suction stroke; explosion in hot exhaust-pipe of gases escaping when a cylinder has misfired; (also *v.i.*); *~ formation*, making from a supposed derivative (as *burglar*) of the non-existent word (*burgle*) from which it might have come; *back'ground* (*n.*) back part of scene or picture; social surroundings, environment; obscurity, retirement; *back'hand(ed)* (*adjs.*) delivered with the back of the hand, or with the back of hand turned in the direction of the stroke (ill. LAWN); (fig.) ambiguous, equivocal; *back-han'der* (*n.*) back-hand blow; indirect attack: *~-lash (ing)*, irregular recoil of wheels in machinery due to defect or sudden pressure; *back'log* (*n.*) arrears of uncompleted work; *~ number*, out-of-date issue of magazine etc., (slang) out-of-date person or thing; *~ seat*, humble or obscure position; *back'side*, buttocks; *back'sight*, (of gun) that nearer the stock; (surveying) sight taken backwards; *~ slang*, slang in which words are pronounced backwards; *backslide'*, relapse into sin, error, etc.; *back-stairs'*, stairs at the back of a house etc., secondary stairs; (*adj.*) underhand, secret; *back'stays*, ropes from the upper mast-heads to the sides of a ship, supporting the masts under sail (ill. SHIP); *back'stitch*, sew by inserting the needle each time behind the place where it has just been brought out; (*n.*) stitch made thus (ill. STITCH); *back'stroke*, stroke made whilst swimmer is lying on his back; *back'wash*, motion of receding wave, motion of water caused by passage of vessel; *back'-water*, stretch of still water parallel with a stream and fed from it at the lower end; (fig.) place or condition of intellectual stagnation; *back'woods*, remote, only partially cleared forest-land; *back'woodsman*, settler in backwoods, uncivilized person; peer who rarely attends House of Lords.

băckgămm'on *n.* Game for two persons, played by moving pieces like draughtsmen, according to the throw of dice, on a board of two 'tables', each marked off into 12 spaces of alternating colours.

băck'ward(s) *adv.* Back foremost; back towards the starting-point; the reverse way. **băck'-ward** *adj.* Directed to rear or starting-point; reversed; slow in learning or developing. **băck'-wardnėss** *n.* Slowness, dullness.

băckwardā'tion *n.* (Stock Exchange) Percentage paid by seller of stock for right of delaying delivery (cf. CONTANGO).

bāc'on[1] *n.* Back and sides of a pig cured by dry-salting (or pickling in a salt solution) and smoking over a wood fire; *green ~*, unsmoked bacon.

Bāc'on[2], Francis Baron Verulam and Viscount St. Albans (1561–1626). Lord Chancellor of England (1618–20), philosopher who introduced the inductive method into science, and author of famous 'Essays'. **Bācōn'ian** *adj.* & *n.* (Advocate) of the theory that Bacon wrote the plays of Shakespeare.

Bāc'on[3], Roger (1214?–94). English Franciscan, philosopher and student of experimental science (esp. optics) at Paris and Oxford; credited, then and later, with magical powers.

băctērĭŏl'ogy *n.* Study of bacteria, esp. as a branch of medicine. **băctērĭolŏg'ĭcal** *adj.* **băctērĭŏl'ogist** *n.*

băctēr'iophāge (-fāj, -fahzh) *n.* A virus capable of destroying bacteria.

băctēr'ĭum *n.* (pl. *-rĭa*) Any of several types of microscopic or ultra-microscopic single-celled organisms occurring in enormous numbers everywhere in nature, not only in land, sea, and air, but also on or in many parts of the tissues of plants and animals, and forming

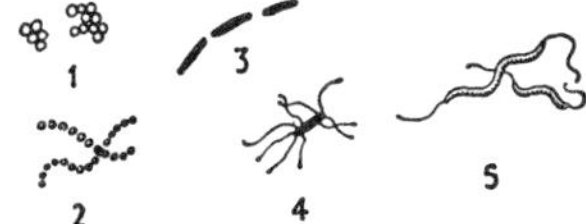

THE MAIN TYPES OF BACTERIA
1, 2. Cocci (1. Staphylococcus, 2. Streptococcus). 3, 4. Bacilli. (3. *B. anthracis*, 4. *B. typhosus*). 5. *Spirilla*

one of the main biologically interdependent groups of organisms in virtue of the chemical changes which many of them bring about, e.g. all forms of decay and the building up of nitrogen compounds in the soil. The activity of some kinds of bacteria is inimical to or destructive of the animal or vegetable organisms in which they live and is then known as disease; see BACILLUS, SPIROCHAETE, etc. **băctēr'ĭal** *adj.* Of or caused by bacteria. [Gk, dim. of *baktron* stick]

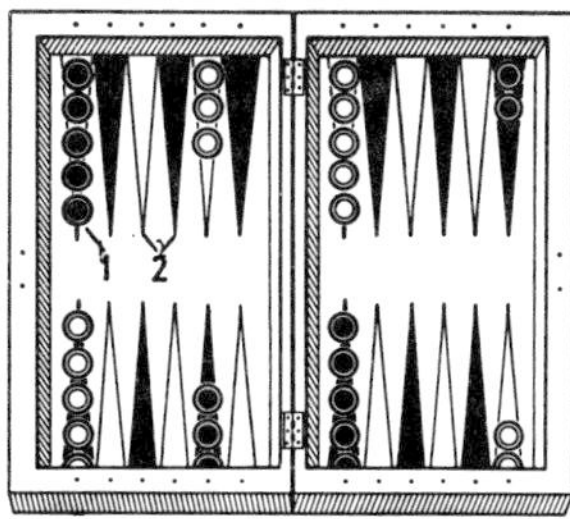

BACKGAMMON BOARD
1. Men. 2. Points

Băc'trĭa. Ancient country of central Asia (now *Balkh* in N. Afghanistan), lying between the Hindu-Kush and the Oxus. **Băc'-trĭan** *adj.* & *n.*; *~ camel*, the two-humped camel of central Asia, *Camelus bactrianus*.

băd *adj.* (comp. *worse*, superl. *worst*). Worthless, inferior, defective, inefficient; not valid; wicked, vicious; painful; ill, in pain; *go ~*, decay; *not ~*, (colloq.) rather good; *~ blood*, ill feeling; *~ coin*, debased or counterfeit coin; *~ debt*, one not recoverable; *~ form*, want of manners; *B~ Lands*, arid rocky regions (esp. those in S. Dakota, U.S.), seamed with deep vertical gullies by occasional heavy rain and thus uncultivable. *~ n.* Ill fortune, ruin; *go to the ~*, go to ruin, degenerate. **bădd'ish** *adj.* **băd'ly** *adv.* **băd'nėss** *n.*

Bădd'ėley (*or* -dlĭ), Robert (1732?–94). English actor, who left money to provide wine and cake (the *~ cake*) on Twelfth Night in the Drury Lane green-room.

Ba'den (bah-). Former State of SW. Germany; now part of the Federal Republic, divided between provinces of S. Baden (capital, Freiburg) and Württemberg-Baden (capital, Stuttgart).

Ba'den-Ba'den (bah-). Health resort, with mineral springs, in Baden, Germany.

Băd'en-Powell (pō'el), Robert Stephenson Smyth, 1st Baron Baden-Powell of Gilwell (1857–1941). English soldier; defended Mafeking, 1900; founded the BOY Scout organization, 1908.

bădge *n.* Distinctive emblem or mark as a sign of office, membership, etc.

bădg'er *n.* Nocturnal plantigrade quadruped (*Meles vulgaris*); intermediate between weasel and bear, with coarse dark-coloured fur and a white blaze on the forehead; it digs a burrow, hibernates, and defends itself fiercely against attack; *B~ State*, popular name of Wisconsin. *~ v.* Pester as dogs worry a badger; tease, torment.

băd'minton *n.* Game like lawn tennis played with shuttlecocks and rackets over a net 5 ft high.

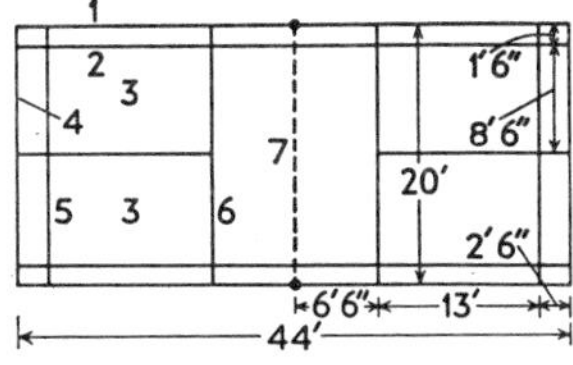

BADMINTON COURT

1. Side line for doubles. 2. Side line for singles. 3. Service court. 4. Back boundary line and long service line for singles. 5. Long service line for doubles. 6. Short service line. 7. net

name of Gloucestershire seat of Duke of Beaufort]

băd'ĭnage (-ahzh) *n.* Banter.

Baed'èker (bād-) *n.* Any of the guide-books issued by Karl ~ (1801–59), German publisher, and his successors; ~ *raids*, reprisal raids undertaken by German air force in April and May 1942 on English cities marked by two stars in Baedeker's guides.

Baer (bār), Karl Ernst von (1792–1876). Estonian biologist; discovered human ovum and made important contributions to embryology.

Baeyer (bī'yer), Johann Friedrich Wilhelm Adolf, Ritter von (1835–1917). German chemist; discovered synthetic indigo; exerted profound influence on development of organic chemistry.

Băff'ĭn, William (1584?–1622). English navigator and explorer; discovered ~ *Land*, a large island off the NE. coast of Canada, and ~ *Bay*, the sea between it and Greenland.

băf'fle *v.t.* Foil, frustrate, perplex; *baffling*, bewildering. ~ *n.* Board (or ~-*board*) surrounding mouth of the cone of a loud-speaker, increasing the sonority and improving the tone by hindering the return of sound-waves to the back of the speaker; plate (~-*plate*) for hindering or regulating passage of gases or fluids through outlet or inlet; one in exhaust-pipe of an internal combustion engine to reduce noise; ~-*wall*, wall parallel with doorway to stop draughts, blast from air-raids, etc.

băff'y *n.* Short wooden golf-club for lofting the ball (ill. GOLF).

baft (-ah-) *adv.* & *prep.* Abaft.

băg *n.* Receptacle of flexible material with an opening usu. at the top; sac in animal body for storing honey, poison, etc.; all a sportsman has shot in one expedition; (pl.) (slang) trousers; ~-*fox*, fox brought out in a bag to be let loose before the hounds; *bag'man*, (colloq.) commercial traveller; ~-*wig*, wig with the back hair tied in a bag (ill. WIG). ~ *v.* Put in a bag; secure (game); (colloq.) take possession of, steal; bulge, hang loosely.

Bagăn'da. Negroid Bantu-speaking people inhabiting kingdom of Buganda, a province of Uganda on the NW. shore of Lake Victoria.

băgatĕlle' *n.* 1. Mere trifle; short unpretentious piece of music. 2. Game played on a table with a semicircular end, the object being to strike balls into numbered holes with a cue.

băgg'age *n.* Portable equipment of an army; luggage; (joc.) saucy girl.

băgg'y (-g-) *adj.* That bags or hangs loosely.

Băghdăd' (-gd-). Ancient city of Mesopotamia, on the Tigris; now the capital of Iraq.

bagnio (băn'yō) *n.* Oriental prison; brothel.

băg'pīpe(s) *n.* Musical instrument consisting of several pipes, including 'drones' or open pipes and a 'chanter' or pipe with finger-

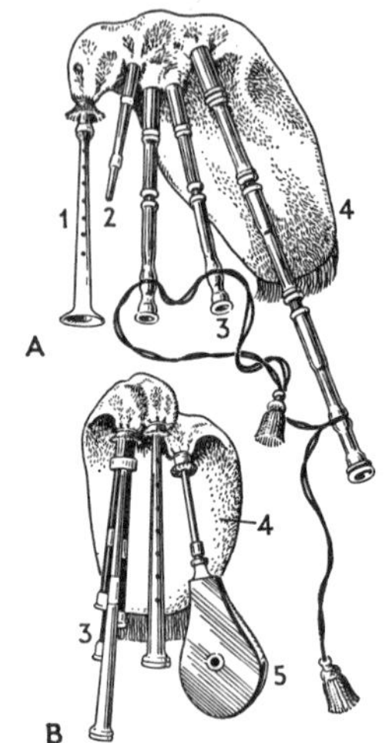

BAGPIPES: A. HIGHLAND PIPES. B. NORTHUMBRIAN SMALL PIPES

1. Chanter. 2. Blow pipe. 3. Tenor and bass bourdons. 4. Bag. 5. Bellows

holes, through which air is forced by pressure on a wind-bag held under the arm; now associated chiefly with Scotland and Ireland, but once popular in England and still played in some places on the Continent, notably Brittany.

B.Agr(ic). *abbrev.* Bachelor of Agriculture.

Bahadur (-hahd'er). Title of respect appended in India to person's name.

Baha'ī (bah'-hī) or **Bábí** (bah'-bī). A sect whose doctrines combine Mohammedan, Christian, Jewish, and Zoroastrian elements; founded in 1844 by a Persian, Mirza Ali Mohammed (1821–50), who became known as the *Bab* (pr. bahb; Pers. *bab ed-din*, 'gate of the faith'); the next leader, Mirza Hosain Ali (1817–92), was known as *Baha* (*baha-Allah*, 'splendour of God') and was believed by his followers to be the son of God.

Baha'mas (-hahmaz). Archipelago of British W. Indies, the first land touched by Columbus in 1492; first colonized by Spaniards and later (in 17th c.) by the English; a British colony since 1783; capital, Nassau.

Bahram V (Barahm') (d. 439). Sassanid king and national hero of Persia, known as *Bahram Gur*, 'the Wild Ass'.

Baikal (bīkahl'), Lake. Large lake in S. Siberia.

bail[1] *n.* 1. Security for a prisoner's appearance for trial. 2. Person who becomes surety. ~ *v.t.* 1. Become bail for, secure the liberation of on bail. 2. Deliver (goods) in trust.

bail[2] *n.* 1. Bar separating horses in an open stable. 2. (cricket) Either of the crosspieces resting on top of the stumps (ill. CRICKET).

bail'er[1] *n.* Ball that hits the bails.

bail[3], **bāle** *v.t.* Throw water out of (boats etc.) with bowls etc.

bail'er[2] *n.* Utensil for bailing.

bailē̄' *n.* Person to whom goods are entrusted.

bail'ey *n.* The open space enclosed by a fortification (ill. CASTLE); *Old B~*, in London, the Central Criminal Court (formerly situated within the ancient bailey of the city wall between Lud Gate and New Gate).

Bail'ey bridge *n.* Prefabricated military pontoon bridge (ill. BRIDGE). [D. C. *Bailey*, inventor]

bail'ie (-lĭ) *n.* Scottish municipal officer corresponding to the English alderman.

bail'ĭff *n.* 1. King's representative in district (now chiefly hist.), esp. chief officer of a hundred. 2. Sheriff's officer who executes writs and processes, distrains, and arrests. 3. Lord of the manor's agent; steward.

bail'ĭwick *n.* District, jurisdiction, of bailie or bailiff.

bail'ment *n.* Delivery of goods in trust; bailing of prisoner.

bail'or *n.* One who entrusts goods to another.

Bain, Alexander (1818–1903). Scottish philosopher: exponent of a system of psychology which traces psychological phenomena to the nerves and brain.

bain-marie (băn-marē') *n.* Vessel for holding hot water in which saucepans are heated.

Bairam (bīrahm'). Each of the two principal festivals of the Mohammedan year, the *Lesser* ~ (lasting 3 days) following the fast of Ramadan, and the *Greater* ~ (lasting 4 days) 70 days later.

bairn *n.* (Sc.) Child.

bait *v.* 1. Worry (animal) by setting dogs at it; worry (person) by jeers. 2. Give (horse etc.) food, esp. on a journey; (of horse) take food thus; (obs.) stop at an inn. 3. Put bait on or in (fish-hook, trap, etc.). ~ *n.* 1. Food etc. used to entice prey; allurement. 2. (obs.) Halt for refreshment.

baize *n.* Coarse woollen usu. green stuff used chiefly for coverings, linings, etc.

bāke *v.* Cook by dry heat, as in an oven; harden by heat; be or become baked; *baked meats*, (obs.) pastry; *bāke'house*, place for baking bread etc.; *bak'ing-powder*, powder consisting of bicarbonate of soda and cream of tartar with a 'filling' of starch or flour, used instead of yeast to make cakes etc. 'rise'.

bakelite (bā'kelīt) *n.* Synthetic plastic material used for insulating, to make moulded articles etc. [L. H. *Baekeland* (1863–1944), Belgian-American inventor]

băk'er *n.* Professional bread-maker; ~*'s dozen*, 13 objects of any kind. **băk'ery** *n.* Bakehouse; trade of baking.

băk'shēēsh *n.* Gratuity, tip. [Pers., = 'present']

Băkst, Leon (1866–1924). Russian stage-designer who worked in Paris for Diaghilev's Russian ballet company.

băk'ū[1] *n.* Fine kind of straw grown in the Philippines and woven in China, and used for hats; hat woven of this.

Băku'[2] (-ōō). Capital of Azerbaijan (U.S.S.R.), on the shore of the Caspian Sea; a centre of the petroleum industry.

Bakunin (-kōōn'ĭn), Mikhail Alexandrovich (1814–76). Russian anarchist, revolutionary leader, and founder of NIHILISM.

BAL. Abbrev. of British Anti-Lewisite, a drug (*dimercaprol*) used to neutralize metallic poisons, e.g. arsenic.

Bāl'aam (-l*a*m). A Gentile prophet: see Numbers xxii–xxiv.

Bălacla'va (-klah-). Crimean village near Sebastopol, scene of battle (1854) of the Crimean War during which occurred the famous Charge of the Light Brigade; ~ *helmet*, a knitted woollen cap covering the whole head and neck, with an opening for the face, worn esp. by soldiers on active service.

Bălakir'ev (-ērĕf), Mily Alexeyevich (1836–1910). Russian composer.

bălalaik'a (-līk*a*) *n.* Russian stringed instrument played by plucking, resembling guitar but with triangular body and 2, 3, or 4 strings.

băl'ance *n.* 1. Weighing apparatus consisting of a beam moving freely on a central pivot with a scale-pan at either end; spring or lever substitute for this. 2. The regulating gear of a clock, watch, etc. (ill. CLOCK). 3. Equilibrium. 4. A preponderating weight or amount. 5. Excess of assets over liabilities or vice versa. 6. Remainder. 7. ~ *of power*, equilibrium of military and political power between several states; ~ *of trade*, difference between total exports and total imports of a country, *favourable* if exports exceed imports, and *adverse* if there is an excess of imports; ~*-sheet*, statement of assets and liabilities, esp. of public company. ~ *v.* 1. Weigh. 2. Equalize, match; bring or come into equilibrium. 3. Find the balance of assets and liabilities in (an account-book).

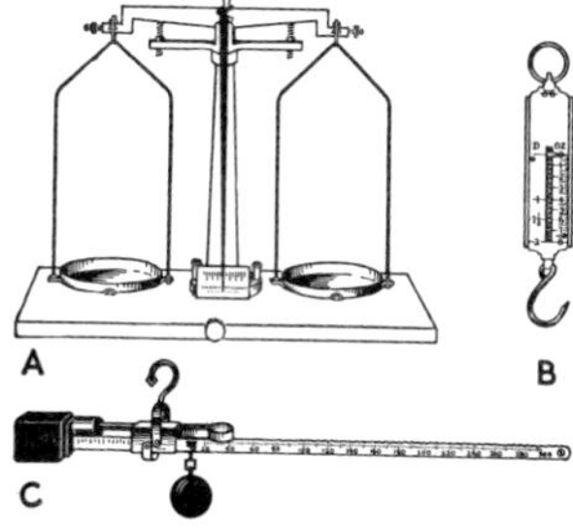

A. BEAM BALANCE OR SCALES. B. SPRING BALANCE. C. STEELYARD

băl'as *n.* Rose-red kind of spinel ruby. [med. L *balascus*, f. Pers. *Badakshān*, district of origin]

băl'ata *n.* Raw material resembling gutta-percha, obtained from the latex of *Mimusops balata* of the W. Indies and S. America, and used as an inferior substitute for gutta-percha.

Bălbō'a[1], Vasco Nuñez de (1475–1517). Spanish explorer, esp. of Central America; first sighted the Pacific Ocean in 1513.

bălbō a[2] *n.* Principal monetary unit of Panama, equivalent of U.S. dollar.

băl'cony *n.* 1. Balustraded platform on the outside of a building with access from an upper-floor window (ill. WINDOW). 2. In a theatre, the seats above the dress or upper circle and below the gallery; in other public buildings, (seats in) a gallery above the ground-floor seats.

bald (bawld) *adj.* 1. Having the scalp wholly or partly hairless; (of animal, bird) without fur, feathers, etc. 2. Bare; meagre; dull. **bald'ly** *adv.* **bald'nėss** *n.*

baldachin, -quin (bawl'd*a*kĭn) *n.* Canopy over an altar, throne, etc., dependent from a ceiling or projecting from a wall (ill. ALTAR). [It., f. *Baldacco* Baghdad]

bald'-cōōt, bald'ĭcōōt (bawl-) *n.* = COOT.

Balder, Baldur (bawl'd*e*r). (Scandinavian myth.) God of the summer sun, invulnerable to all things except mistletoe, with which Loki by a trick induced the blind god Hödur to kill him.

bal'derdăsh (bawl-) *n.* Jumble of words; nonsense, rubbish.

bal'drĭc (bawl-) *n.* Belt for supporting a sword, bugle, etc., worn over one shoulder and under the opposite arm.

Baldwĭn[1] I (bawl'-) (1058–1118). First Christian king of Jerusalem, a leader in the 1st Crusade, and brother and successor of Godfrey of Bouillon.

Baldwĭn[2] (bawl'-), Stanley (1867–1947), 1st Earl Baldwin of Bewdley. English Conservative politician; Prime Minister 1923–4, 1924–9, 1935–7.

bāle[1] *n.* Evil, destruction, woe.

bāle[2] *n.* Large bundle or package, esp. of merchandise, usu. done up in canvas and corded or looped. ~ *v.t.* Make up into bales.

bāle[3] *v.* Erroneous but more usual spelling of BAIL[3] *v.*; ~ *out*, abandon damaged aircraft in air and descend by parachute.

Bāle[4], John (1495–1563). English priest, author of the first English historical play, 'King John'.

Băleăr'ĭc Islands. Group, including Majorca and Minorca, off E. coast of Spain.

balēēn' *n.* Whalebone.

bāle'fīre (-lf-) *n.* (archaic) Great fire in the open, beacon fire.

bāle'ful (-lf-) *adj.* Pernicious, destructive, malignant. **bāle'fully** *adv.* **bāle'fulnėss** *n.*

Băl'four (-foor), Arthur James, 1st Earl of Balfour (1848–1930). Scottish Conservative statesman and philosopher; author of 'A Defence of Philosophic Doubt' (1879); Prime Minister of England 1902–5.

bălĭbŭn'tal *n.* Fine straw of very close weave, used for hats.

Bāl'iol. Surname of several kings of Scotland; John de Baliol (1249–1315) was that claimant to the Scottish throne in 1290 in whose favour Edward I of England decided.

balk, baulk (bawk) *n.* 1. Roughly squared beam of timber; tie-beam. 2. Stumbling-block. 3. The area on a billiard-table (at the bottom end) within which a ball in hand must be placed and out of which it must be played (ill. BILLIARDS). 4. Ridge left unploughed between two furrows. ~ *v.* 1. Thwart, hinder; discourage; foil. 2. Jib, shy.

Bal'kan (bawl-) *adj.* ~ *States*, those occuping the ~ *Peninsula*, the most easterly of the 3 southern prolongations of the continent of Europe, and the home of several racial stocks (Albanians, Vlachs, Greeks, Serbs, Bulgars, and Turks) with differing cultures. From the 3rd to the 7th centuries the peninsula, nominally ruled by the Byzantine emperors, was invaded by successive migrations of Slavs; later, parts of it were conquered by Venice and other States. In 1356 began the Ottoman invasion; Constantinople fell to the Turks in 1453, and by 1478 most of the peninsula was in their power. The subject nations, though largely retaining their languages and religions, did not recover independence until the 19th c. In 1913 the ~ *League* of Greece, Serbia, Bulgaria, and Montenegro attacked and defeated Turkey. During the war of 1914–18 (the immediate cause of which was the assassination of the Austrian Archduke Franz Ferdinand in Serbia) Turkey and Bulgaria sided with Austria and Germany and the other Balkan States with the Allies. By the Treaty of Versailles the peninsula was divided between Greece, Bulgaria, Albania, and Yugoslavia. **Bal'kans** *n.pl.* Balkan States.

ball[1] (bawl) *n.* 1. Solid or hollow sphere, esp. one used in a game; rounded mass (as of snow, string, etc.); ~ *of foot, thumb*, rounded base of great toe, thumb. 2.

(cricket) Single delivery of the ball by a bowler. 3. Missile for cannon, rifles, etc. 4. ~*-bearing*, bearing in which revolving parts of a machine turn upon loose hardened steel balls, which diminish friction (ill. BEARING); ~*-cock*, device for regulating inflow of water, esp. in cisterns, consisting of a floating-ball which rises or falls with the height of the water, thereby shutting or opening a valve through which the water flows in (ill. COCK); ~*-flower*, ornament resembling a round bud, carved in hollow of moulding in Gothic architecture (ill. MOULDING); ~*-point (pen)*, writing instrument having for point a small ball-bearing moistened from a reservoir of semi-liquid ink; ~*-turret*, turret protecting underside of a bomber. ~ *v.* (Of snow etc.) form lumps.

ball² (bawl) *n.* Social assembly for dancing; *ball'room*, large room suitable for this.

Ball³ (bawl), John (d. 1381). English priest, one of the leaders of Wat TYLER's rebellion, for his share in which he was executed.

băll'ad *n.* 1. Narrative poem in short stanzas, telling a popular story. 2. Simple sentimental song (*drawing-room* ~); ~ *metre*: see COMMON metre; ~*-monger*, (contempt.), dealer in ballads. **băll'adry** *n.* Ballad poetry. [Provençal *ballada* dancing-song]

băllade' (-ahd) *n.* A poem of one or more triplets of 7- or 8-lined stanzas, each ending with the same line as refrain, followed by an envoy freq. of 4 lines.

băll'ast *n.* 1. Heavy material, as sand or water, placed in a ship's hold or carried in a balloon or airship for stability. 2. Elements of character which give stability. ~ *v.t.* Furnish with ballast.

bălleri'na (-ēna) *n.* Female ballet-dancer (strictly, dancer who takes one or more of certain classical roles).

băll'et (-lā) *n.* Stage entertainment in which a story is enacted or a dramatic idea expressed by means of dancing to music with the aid of costume and scenery. Ballet in its modern form dates from the late 16th c. and was developed principally in France, Italy, and Russia. *Russian B*~, a company of (orig. Russian) dancers founded in Paris (1909) by DIAGHILEV; it performed in W. Europe and led to the modern revival of ballet there.

băllėtomāne', -mān'ia *ns.* Enthusiast, enthusiasm, for ballet.

Băll'iol College. An Oxford college founded in 1263 by John de Balliol (d. 1269), father of John de BALIOL, king of Scotland.

ballĭs'ta *n.* (pl. *-ae*). Ancient military engine for hurling stones etc.

ballĭs'tĭc *adj.* Of projectiles. **ballĭs'tĭcs** *n.* The science of projectiles.

ballon d'essai (băl'awṅ dĕsā') *n.* Experiment to see how a policy etc. will be received. [Fr., = 'trial balloon']

băll'onĕt *n.* Secondary envelope in a balloon designed to be inflated with air as the buoyant gas is released from the envelope proper.

balloo͞n' *n.* Large air-tight envelope of silk or other light material inflated with gas lighter than air so as to rise in the air, sometimes provided with a basket or 'car' slung beneath from a net enclosing the envelope, used esp. in warfare for making observations and as an anti-aircraft defence; inflatable toy; (colloq.) balloon-shaped outline enclosing speech or thought of character in strip cartoon etc.; ~*-barrage*, anti-aircraft barrier of steel cables supported in an almost vertical position each by a captive balloon; ~*-tyre*, low-pressure motor tyre of large section. ~ *v.t.* Swell out like a balloon (of sails, tyres, etc.).

băll'ot *n.* 1. Secret voting (usu. by placing a voting-paper etc. in a closed ~*-box*). 2. Ball, ticket, or paper used in this. 3. Drawing of lots. ~ *v.i.* Vote by ballot (*for*); draw lots. [It. *ballotta* little ball]

băll'y *adj.* & *adv.* (slang) expressing impatience, disgust, etc.

băllȳhoo͞' *n.* (orig. U.S.) Advance publicity of vulgar or misleading kind; vulgar advertisement; 'eye-wash'.

băll'ȳrăg *v.* Play practical jokes on; indulge in horse-play.

balm (bahm) *n.* 1. Aromatic substance consisting of resin mixed with volatile oils, exuding naturally from various trees. 2. Tree yielding this. 3. The herb *Melissa officinalis*. 4. Aromatic oil or ointment. 5. Healing or soothing influence. **balm'y** *adj.* 1. Of or like balm; fragrant, mild, soothing. 2. Weak-minded, silly, 'simple'. **balm'ĭly** *adv.* **balm'ĭnėss** *n.*

Bălmŏ'ral. Scottish residence in upper Deeside, Aberdeenshire, of the British sovereign. **bălmŏ'ral** *n.* 1. Kind of round cap worn by some Scottish regiments (ill. PLAID). 2. (obs.) Laced walking shoe or boot. 3. (obs.) Kind of striped woollen petticoat.

băl'nėary *adj.* Of baths or bathing.

ba'lsa (bawl-) *n.* Tropical American tree, *Ochroma lagopus*; its wood (~ *wood, cork-wood*), used for life-belts, model aeroplanes, etc., because of its extreme lightness.

ba'lsam (bawl-) *n.* 1. Balm. 2. Aromatic ointment, of various substances dissolved in oil or turpentine. 3. Tree yielding balm. 4. Flowering plant, of genus *Impatiens*, with hooded and spurred coloured sepals and thick succulent stem.

Bălthăz'ar (-t-). Traditional name of one of the three MAGI, represented as king of Chaldea.

Ba'ltĭc (bawl-) *adj.* ~ (*Sea*), an almost landlocked sea in N. Europe, bordered by Sweden, Russia, Germany, Denmark, etc.; *Battle of the* ~: see COPENHAGEN; ~ *languages* see foll. **Balto-Slăv'ic, -Slavŏn'ic** (bawl-) *adj.* & *n.* (Of) the group of Indo-European languages comprising the Baltic branch (Lithuanian, Lettish, and Old Prussian) and the Slavonic branch (Russian, Polish, Czech, Serbian, Bulgarian, etc.).

Bal'tĭmōre (bawl-). Seaport in N. Maryland; ~ *oriole*, bird of the starling family (*Icterus Baltimorii*) found throughout N. America; its colours, black and orange, are like the coat of arms of Lord Baltimore. [Lord *Baltimore*, formerly proprietor of Maryland]

Balu'chĭ (-o͞och-) *n.* Inhabitant of, the Iranian language of, Baluchistan. **Baluchistan'** (-lo͝ok-, -ahn). Province of NW. India, since 1947 part of Pakistan.

băl'uster *n.* Short pillar of circular section and curving outline. [Gk *balaustion* wild-pomegranate flower]

bălustrāde' *n.* Row of balusters with a rail or coping as the parapet of a balcony etc.

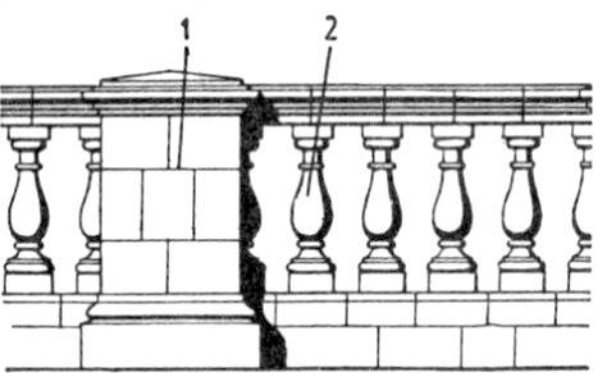

BALUSTRADE

1. Pier. 2. Baluster

Băl'zăc, Honoré de (1799–1850). French realistic novelist, whose 'Comédie Humaine' is a long series of novels intended to depict the whole of contemporary French society.

bămboo͞' *n.* Genus (*Bambusa*) of tropical giant grasses with hollow jointed stems that become woody; the stem of these as a stick or material.

bămboo͞'zle *v.t.* Hoax, mystify.

băn *v.t.* Prohibit, interdict. ~ *n.* Curse, formal prohibition.

băn'al (*or* banahl') *adj.* Commonplace, trite. **banăl'ĭty** *n.*

bana'na (-ahna) *n.* Tropical fruit-tree, *Musa sapientum*; the finger-shaped yellow pulpy fruit of this, growing in clusters or bunches. [Port. or Span., f. native name in Guinea]

Banaras: see BENARES.

Băn'bury. Town in Oxfordshire, formerly noted for the number and zeal of its Puritan inhabitants; ~ *cake*, pastry filled with a currant mixture, made at Banbury.

bănd *n.* 1. Thing that binds, bond (archaic). 2. Flat strip of thin material; hoop of iron, rubber, etc.; belt connecting wheels, pulleys, etc.; strap forming part of garment, esp. binding the neck or waist; (pl.) pair of white linen strips worn at neck as part of legal, ecclesiastical, or academic dress. 3. Body of musicians playing together esp. wind-instrument performers (*brass, dance, military* ~); organized company or group of persons; *B~ of Hope*, association of people pledged to total abstinence from alcoholic drinks. 4. (radio-telephony) Group of frequencies that may be tuned together. 5. *band'-box*, cardboard etc. box for hats (orig. for neckbands); *band'-master*, conductor of a band of musicians; *~-saw*, endless saw running over wheels (ill. SAW); *bands'man*, member of a military or brass band; *band'stand*, (covered, open-air) platform for musicians; *band'wagon*, (orig. U.S.) wagon carrying the band at the head of a procession; *to be on the band-wagon*, to be in the forefront of an enterprise. ~ *v.* Form into band or league; put a band on.

băn'dage *n.* Strip or band of textile material used to bind a wound, sore, etc., or for blindfolding the eyes. ~ *v.t.* Bind up with a bandage.

băndănn'a *n.* Coloured silk or cotton handkerchief with yellow or white spots. [prob. from Hind. *bāndhnū*, a method of dyeing in different colours]

băn'deau (-ō) *n.* Woman's hair-fillet; band inside a woman's hat.

Băndĕll'ō, Matteo (1480–1562). Italian writer of short stories.

băn'derōle *n.* Long narrow flag with cleft end flying from a ship, lance, etc.; ribbon-like scroll; (archit.) feature resembling this and bearing inscription.

băn'dicoot *n.* 1. Genus (*Perameles*) of Australian omnivorous marsupials, somewhat rat-like in appearance. 2. ~ *rat*, large rat (*Nesocia bandicota*), up to 3 ft in length, found in India. [Telugu]

băn'dĭt *n.* (pl. *bandits, banditti*). Outlaw, brigand; lawless and violent robber, esp. member of an organized gang.

băn'dŏg *n.* (archaic) Chained dog; mastiff, bloodhound.

băndoleer', -lier' (-ēr) *n.* Shoulder-belt with loops or pockets for cartridges.

băn'dy *v.t.* Throw or pass to and fro; discuss; exchange. ~ *n.* Hockey; hockey-stick. ~ *adj.* (Of legs) wide apart at the knees.

bāne *n.* Ruin; poison. **bāne'ful** (-nf-) *adj.* Poisonous; pernicious injurious. **bāne'fully** *adv.*, **bāne'-fulnĕss** *n.*

Bănff'shire. County of NE. Scotland.

băng *v.* Strike or shut noisily; make sound as of a blow or explosion; thrash. ~ *n.* Sharp blow; loud noise. ~ *adv.* With a bang, abruptly.

Bang'alōre (-ngg-). City in S. India, capital of Mysore State.

Băngkŏk'. Capital city of Thailand (Siam).

băn'gle (-nggl) *n.* Ring bracelet or anklet.

băn'ian, băn'yan *n.* 1. Hindu trader; (Bengal) native broker to European business house. 2. Indian flannel jacket. 3. ~ (*tree*), the Indian fig, *Ficus religiosa* (or *indica*), whose branches root themselves like new trees over a large area (first applied to a particular tree under which banians had built a pagoda).

băn'ish *v.t.* Condemn to exile; dismiss from one's presence or mind. **băn'ishment** *n.*

băn(n)'ister *n.* Post supporting hand-rail of a staircase (ill. STAIR); (pl.) the posts and hand-rail together. [corrupt. of BALUSTER]

băn'jō *n.* (pl. *-os* or *-oes*). Musical instrument having 4, 5, 6, or 7 strings, head and neck like guitar, and body like tambourine, played

PLECTRUM BANJO

with fingers or with plectrum; introduced into Europe by Amer. Negroes. **băn'jōist** *n.* [Gk *pandoura* 3-stringed mus. instrument]

bănjule'le (-lālĭ) *n.* Musical instrument combining features of banjo and ukulele.

bănk¹ *n.* 1. Raised shelf of ground; artificial slope. 2. Ground at edge of river. 3. (Flat-topped) mass of cloud. ~ *v.* 1. Contain or confine as or with bank(s). 2. Make (road, track) higher at outer edge of a bend to facilitate cornering at high speeds; (aeronaut.) incline (aircraft) laterally in turning so as to avoid a side-slip; ~ *up*, pack tightly (fire, for slow burning).

bănk² *n.* 1. Institution whose debts (*deposits*) are widely accepted in payment of other people's debts. The deposits are the property of the bank's customers and are usu. classified into (*a*) *current accounts* or *demand* or *sight deposits*, freely transferable by cheque or in favour of third parties, and (*b*) *deposit accounts* or *time* or *savings deposits*, transferable nominally only at notice; all deposits are exchangeable into cash. Banks cover their costs and make profits by charging commission to customers and by lending at interest to them, to the Government, and to other financial institutions. *savings* ~, bank which confines itself mainly to savings deposits and lends for purposes more restricted than those applicable to ordinary banks; *central* ~, institution unique in each country, responsible for influencing the conduct of all other banks and other financial institutions in pursuance of the Government's monetary policy; it acts as banker to other banks, usu. also to the Government and sometimes to private customers as well; *~-bill*, bill drawn by one bank on another; (U.S.) bank-note; *~-book*, book showing the state of a customer's account at a bank; ~ *holiday*, day on which banks (and therefore most places of business) are closed by statute; *B~ of England*, London corporation nationalized in 1946, the central bank of England and Wales; ~ *manager*, superintendent of local branch of bank; *~-note*, banker's promissory note payable to the bearer on demand, used as currency as a substitute for coinage; *~-rate*, rate at which the Bank of England is prepared to discount for its customers approved bills of exchange, regarded as an important indicator of money conditions and used as a basis for fixing certain interest rates in other banks. 2. Money before keeper of a gaming-table. ~ *v.* Keep a bank; deposit money at a bank; ~ *on*, count or rely on.

bank³ *n.* Galley-rowers' bench; tier (of oars) in galley; row of organ keys.

bănk'er *n.* 1. Proprietor or director of a BANK²; keeper of money. 2. Keeper of money staked at gaming-table. 3. Card-game in which punters bet that the bottom card of their pile will have a higher value than the bottom card of the banker's pile.

bănkĕt' *n.* Conglomerate rock containing gold, found in Witwatersrand area of S. Africa. [Du., = kind of hardbake (BANQUET)]

bănk'ĭng *n.* The business of a banker or commercial BANK².

bănk'rŭpt *n.* (law) Insolvent person whose effects, on his own or his creditors' petition to the Bankruptcy Court, are administered and distributed for the benefit of all his creditors; (pop.) any insolvent person. ~ *v.t.* Make bankrupt. ~ *adj.* That is a bankrupt; insolvent. **bănk'ruptcy** *n.* [It. *banca rotta* broken bank]

Bănks, Sir Joseph (1743–1820). English explorer and natural historian who accompanied James Cook in his voyage round the world in the *Endeavour*, 1768–71.

bănk'sia *n.* Genus of Australian shrubs with umbellate flowers; ~ (*banksian*) *rose*, Chinese species of climbing rose bearing small white or yellow flowers in clusters. [named after Lady (Joseph) BANKS]

bănn'er *n.* Flag of a king, country, army, etc.; *feast of ~s*, Japanese festival and national holiday in honour of male children, held on 5th May.

bănn'erĕt *n.* Knight with vassals under his banner; one knighted on the field for valour.

bănn'ock *n.* Scottish home-made loaf, usu. of unleavened bread, round and flattish.

Bănn'ockburn. Town in Stirlingshire, Scotland, where the Scots under Robert Bruce defeated Edward II and the English coming to the relief of Stirling in 1314.

bănns *n.pl.* Notice of intended marriage, read three times in church, in order that any objections may be lodged.

bănq'uet *n.* Sumptuous feast; dinner with speeches. ~ *v.* Regale with, take part in, banquet. [Fr., f. It. *banchetto*, dim. of *banco* bench]

bănquĕtte (-kĕt) *n.* Firing-step in trenches.

băn'shee *n.* Spirit supposed by Irish and Highland superstition to wail under the windows of a house in which one of the inmates is about to die. [Ir., = 'fairy woman']

bănt *v.i.* (colloq.) Reduce weight by dieting. [f. W. BANTING[1]]

Băn'tam. Former Mohammedan State in W. Java; seaport, site of the first Dutch settlement on the island. **băn'tam** *n.* 1. Small variety of domestic fowl, of which the cock is a spirited fighter. 2. Member of ~ *battalion* of small-sized soldiers formed during the war of 1914–18; ~*-weight*, boxing-weight not exceeding 8 st. 6 lb.

băn'ter *n.* Humorous ridicule. ~ *v.* Make good-humoured fun of, rally; jest.

Băn'ting[1], William (1797–1878). An English undertaker who advocated a method of reducing weight by dieting. **bănt'ing** *n.* Dieting in order to reduce one's weight.

Băn'ting[2], Sir Frederick Grant (1891–1941). Canadian physiologist, co-discoverer of insulin 1922; was awarded the Nobel Prize for medicine 1923.

bănt'ling *n.* Brat, young child.

Băn'tu (-ōō). Extensive group of negroid races inhabiting the equatorial and southern region of Africa; the language(s) spoken by them.

Banville (bahṅ'vēl), Théodore Faullain de (1823–91). French poet of the Parnassian school.

banyan: see BANIAN (used esp. for the tree).

bā'obăb *n.* African tree, *Adansonia digitata*, naturalized also in India and Ceylon, having extremely thick stem and large woody fruit with edible pulp, known as 'monkey bread'; the fibres of the bark are used for ropes and cloth.

B.A.O.R. *abbrev.* British Army of the Rhine.

băp'tism *n.* Religious rite of immersing in or sprinkling with water in sign of moral or spiritual purification or regeneration, and initiation into the (Christian) church; ~ *of fire*, soldier's first experience of battle. **băptis'mal** (-z-) *adj.*

băp'tist *adj.* & *n.* One who baptizes; JOHN THE B~: see entry; (*B*~), (member) of a Protestant Christian sect, founded early in the 17th c., which holds that baptism should be administered only to believers, not to infants, and by immersion.

băp'tist(e)ry *n.* Part of church (or in early times separate building) used for baptism.

băptize' *v.t.* Administer baptism to; christen; name.

bar[1] *n.* 1. Long-shaped piece of rigid material; straight strip. 2. Strip of silver below clasp of medal as additional distinction (ill. MEDAL). 3. (mus.) Vertical line across stave dividing composition into sections of equal time-value; such a section (ill. STAVE). 4. (her.) Pair of horizontal parallel lines across shield (ill. HERALDRY); ~ *sinister*, erron. for BEND sinister, mark of illegitimacy. 5. Rod or pole used to confine or obstruct; bolt or beam for fastening door etc. 6. Barrier of any shape; bank of sand across mouth of harbour. 7. Barrier with some technical significance, as, in law-court, place at which prisoner stands; *the B*~, the profession of advocate, barristers in general (from bar in Inns of Court separating benchers' seats from rest of hall); *be called to the* ~, be admitted a barrister; *be called within the* ~ (i.e. that in courts within which Q.C.s plead), be appointed Queen's Counsel. 8. (parl.) Rail dividing off space to which non-members may be admitted on business. 9. Plea arresting action or claim at law; moral obstacle. 10. Counter in inn etc. across which alcoholic drinks or other refreshments are handed, space behind this or room containing it; *bar'man*, *bar'maid*, ~*-tender*, attendant at bar. ~ *v.t.* 1. Fasten with bars, keep in or out thus; obstruct, prevent; stay (process or party) by legal objection; exclude from consideration; object to, dislike (person etc.). 2. Mark with stripes. 3. (eng.) Rotate (heavy machinery) by external device.

bar[2] *n.* Unit of barometric pressure equivalent to a pressure of 29·53 in. of mercury at 32° F. in latitude 45°.

Barăbb'as. The notable robber released instead of Jesus: see Matt. xxvii. 16–26.

barb[1] *n.* Beard-like feelers of barbel etc.; chin-piece of nun's head-dress; lateral filament branching from shaft of feather (ill. FEATHER); subordinate recurved point of arrow, fish-hook, etc. ~ *v.t.* Furnish with barb; *barbed wire*, wire used in fencing and as an obstruction in war, with short pointed pieces of wire twisted in at intervals. [L *barba* beard]

barb[2] *n.* 1. Horse of the breed imported from Barbary, noted for speed and endurance. 2. Fancy black or dun-coloured pigeon, orig. introduced from Barbary.

Barbād'os (-ōz). Island in W. Indies, British possession in 1605 and colony in 1625; independent State of British Commonwealth 1966; capital, Bridgetown.

barb'ara *n.* (log.) First word of the scholastic mnemonic lines for figures and moods of the syllogism.

barbar'ian *n.* 1. Foreigner, one differing in language and customs. 2. (hist.) non-Greek; person outside the Roman Empire; person outside the civilization of Christendom. 3. Rude, wild, uncultured or uncivilized person. ~ *adj.* Of or like a barbarian.

barbă'ric *adj.* Rude, rough; of barbarians. **barbă'rically** *adv.*

barb'arism *n.* Absence of culture, ignorance, and rudeness; (use of) words or expressions not in accordance with the classical standard of a language.

barbă'rity *n.* Savage or barbarous cruelty.

barb'arize *v.* Make, become, barbarous.

Barbarossa: see FREDERICK BARBAROSSA.

barb'arous *adj.* Uncivilized, uncultured, savage. **barb'arously** *adv.* **barb'arousness** *n.*

Barb'ary. Old name for the part of N. Africa comprising Morocco, Algeria, Tunisia, and Tripoli; ~ *ape*, large tailless ape of N. Africa and Gibraltar; ~ *sheep*, wild N. Afr. sheep with large horns.

barb'ecue *n.* 1. Framework for smoking or broiling meat above an open fire; hog, ox, etc., cooked thus. 2. (U.S.) (Open-air) social gathering where barbecued meat is served. 3. Open floor for spreading out and drying coffee-beans etc. ~ *v.t.* Dry or cure on barbecue; roast (animal) whole. [Haitian *barbacòa* crate on posts]

barb'el *n.* Large European freshwater fish, *Barbus vulgaris*, with fleshy filaments hanging from mouth; such a filament.

barb'er *n.* One who shaves and trims customers' beards and hair; hairdresser; ~*'s itch*, skin disease affecting face and neck caused by a fungoid organism and communicated by (unsterilized) shaving apparatus; ~*'s pole*, pole painted spirally with red and white stripes, used as barber's sign.

barb'erry *n.* European and N. Amer. shrub, *Berberis vulgaris*, with spiny shoots and small yellow flowers; the oblong, red, sharply acid fruit of this.

barbĕtte' *n.* Platform or mound for mounting guns in a fortification; circular armoured platform with hood protecting heavy guns in warship (ill. BATTLESHIP).

barb'ican *n.* Outer defence to city or castle, esp. double tower over gate or bridge (ill. CASTLE).

barbit'ūrate *n.* (chem.) A salt of barbituric acid; (pharmac.) various hypnotic substances derived from barbituric acid. **barbitūr'ic** *adj.* ~ *acid*, malonyl urea, a crystalline compound obtained by heating alloxantin with sulphuric acid.

Barb'izon (-zawṅ). Village near Fontainebleau, France, frequented in mid-19th c. by the ~ *School*, a colony of painters (T. Rousseau, Millet, Daubigny, and others) who produced naturalistic pictures of landscapes and peasant life.

ba͡rbŏl'a *n.* Decorative work of flowers etc. modelled in a plastic paste and coloured.

A. THREE-MASTED BARK. B. THREE-MASTED BARQUENTINE

Ba͡rb'our (-b*er*), John (1316–95). Author of 'The Bruce' (*c* 1375), a long historical poem; regarded as 'father of Scottish poetry'.

ba͡rc'arōle, -ōlle *n.* Gondolier's song; imitation of this.

Ba͡rcėlōn'a. City and province of Catalonia, NE. Spain; ~ *nuts*, hazel-nuts imported from France and Portugal.

Ba͡rch'ėster. Imaginary cathedral city, county town of Barsetshire, portrayed by Anthony TROLLOPE in a series of novels of which the first, 'Barchester Towers', was published in 1857.

ba͡rd *n.* Celtic minstrel, (in Wales) poet recognized at the Eisteddfod; poet. **ba͡rd'ic** *adj.*

ba͡re *adj.* Unclothed, uncovered; exposed; unadorned; scanty; mere; *bare'back* (*adj.* & *adv.*) on unsaddled horse; *bare'faced*, shameless, impudent; *bare'foot* (*adj.* & *adv.*) with bare feet. **ba͡re'ly** *adv.* Scarcely; only just. **ba͡re'nėss** *n.* **ba͡re** *v.t.* Make bare, strip, expose.

Barebones Parliament (ba͡r'-bōnz). Nickname of Cromwell's 'Little' Parliament (1653), from one of its members, Praise-God Barbon, an Anabaptist leather-seller in Fleet Street.

Ba͡r'ėnts, Willem (d. 1597). Dutch Arctic explorer, after whom is named the ~ *Sea*, the extreme NE. part of the Atlantic Ocean.

ba͡rg'ain (-gĭn) *n.* Agreement on terms of transaction between two parties, compact; thing acquired by bargaining; advantageous purchase; *into the* ~, moreover; *strike a* ~, come to terms. ~ *v.i.* Haggle over terms of transaction; stipulate; ~ *for*, be prepared for, expect.

ba͡rge *n.* Flat-bottomed freight-boat for canals and rivers; large oared vessel for State occasions; house-boat. ~ *v.i.* Lurch or rush heavily *into, against.*

ba͡rge-, in archit. terms, = gable: ~-*board*, board or ornamental screen under edge of gable (ill. GABLE); ~-*couple*, the two beams which meet at the point of a gable; ~-*course*, that part of the roof which projects beyond them; ~-*stones*, those forming the sloping or stepped line of a gable. [med. L *bargus* gallows]

ba͡rgee' *n.* Man in charge of barge; *swear like a* ~, swear fluently and forcibly.

bă'rĭtōne *n.* & *adj.* (Male voice) between tenor and bass (ill. VOICE); singer with this voice.

ba͡r'ium *n.* White metallic element, first separated by Sir Humphry Davy in 1808, occurring as the basis of baryta; symbol Ba, at. no. 56, at. wt 137·34; ~ *sulphate* ($BaSO_4$), a white, very insoluble heavy powder, used as a pigment and to impart opacity to the stomach and intestines when it is desired to make an X-ray photograph of these organs.

ba͡rk[1] *n.* The rind or outer sheath of the trunk and branches of trees (ill. STEM); bark used in tanning. ~ *v.t.* Strip bark from (tree); abrade (shins etc.).

ba͡rk[2], ba͡rque (-k), *n.* Three-masted vessel with fore- and main-masts square-rigged, and mizen fore-and-aft rigged; (poet.) ship, boat.

ba͡rk[3] *v.* (Of dogs etc.) utter sharp explosive cry; make sound like this; speak sharply or petulantly; (slang) cough; *barking deer*, the Indian muntjak, *Cervulus muntjak*, so named from its call. ~ *n.* Sharp explosive cry of dogs, foxes, squirrels, etc.; sound of gunfire; cough.

ba͡rk'er[1] *n.* (esp.) 1. Pistol, gun. 2. Auction-room or side-show tout.

Ba͡rk'er[2], Harley Granville (1877–1946). English dramatic critic, producer, and playwright, author of 'Waste', 'The Madras House', etc.

ba͡rl'ey *n.* Awned cereal (*Hordeum distichon* and *H. vulgare*), used as food and in the preparation of malt; the grain of this; *pearl* ~, white inner kernel of barley; *barleycorn*, a grain of barley; *John Barleycorn*, personification of barley, esp. as the grain from which malt liquor is made; ~-*sugar*, sweetmeat of boiled sugar, usu. in twisted sticks, and formerly made by boiling in decoction of barley; ~-*water*, soothing drink made by the decoction of pearl barley.

ba͡rm *n.* Froth from fermenting malt liquor, used as leaven; yeast.

Ba͡rm'ėcide. Patronymic of a noble Persian family who held high offices at Baghdad under Abbasid caliphs; acc. to the 'Arabian Nights', one of them set a number of empty dishes before a beggar, pretending that they contained a sumptuous banquet; hence, ~'*s feast*, imaginary or illusory benefits.

ba͡rn *n.* Covered building for storing grain (or hay, straw, etc.); ~-*door*, the large door of this; target too big to be easily missed; ~-*door fowls*, domestic poultry; ~-*owl*, the screech-owl, *Strix flammea*; *barn'stormer*, strolling player; ~-*yard*, farm-yard.

Ba͡rn'abas, St. Joseph surnamed Barnabas, an early leader of

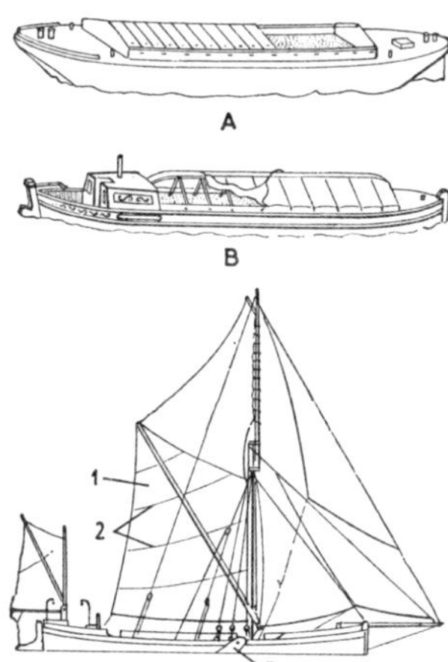

BARGES: A. LIGHTER. B. CANAL BARGE OR NARROW BOAT. C. THAMES SAILING BARGE

1. Spritsail. 2. Brails. 3. Lee-board

the Christian Church and companion of St. Paul on his missionary journeys: see Acts iv, ix, xi, etc.

Bâ̆rn'aby. ~ *bright, long* ~, St. Barnabas's Day, 11th June, in the Old Style reckoned the longest day of the year.

bâ̆rn'acle[1] *n.* (usu. pl.) Pincers put on a horse's nose to keep him still for shoeing etc.

bâ̆rn'acle[2] *n.* 1. An Arctic wild goose, *Anas leucopsis*, visiting the British coasts in winter. 2. Genus of crustaceans (*Cirripedes*) which attach themselves to objects in the water, esp. to ships' bottoms by a long fleshy footstalk.

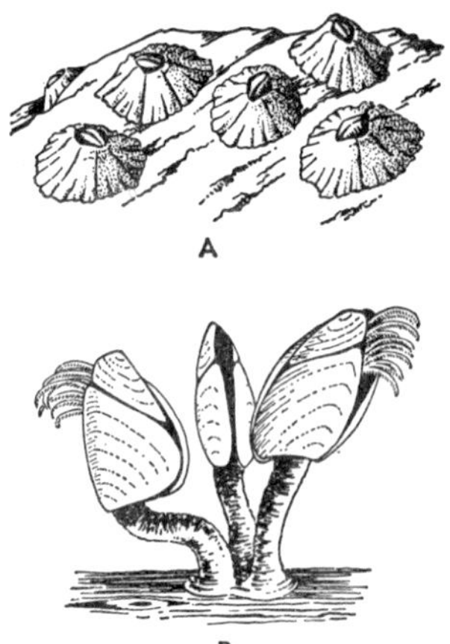

A. ACORN BARNACLES. B. GOOSE OR SHIP'S BARNACLES

Barnâ̆rd'ō, Thomas John (1845–1905). English philanthropist, founder of homes (named after him) for destitute children.

Bâ̆rnes (-nz), William (1801–86). Dorsetshire dialect poet.

Barōd'a. Former State of W. India, now part of the State of Gujerat.

bă'rogrăm *n.* Record of variations in atmospheric pressure.

bă'rograph (-ahf) *n.* Barometer with apparatus (usu. paper roll on drum rotated by clockwork) for making a barogram.

barŏm'ėter *n.* Instrument for measuring atmospheric pressure (and hence for predicting changes in the weather) by means of a tube containing a column of mercury (which rises and falls according to the weight of the atmosphere) or of a vacuum box (see ANEROID ~). **băromĕt'rĭc(al)** *adjs.*, **băromĕt'rĭcally** *adv.*

bă'ron *n.* 1. (hist.) Great noble, noble holding directly from the king by military service; *Barons' War*, revolt (1263–5) of English barons under Simon de Montfort against Henry III. 2. Member of lowest order of nobility in British peerage; holder of foreign title. 3. ~ *of beef*, joint consisting of two sirloins left uncut at backbone.

bă'ronėss *n.* Wife of baron; woman with baronial title in her own right.

bă'ronage *n.* Barons collectively; book with list of barons etc.

bă'ronėt *n.* Member of the lowest hereditary titled order, ranking as a commoner.

bă'ronėtage *n.* List of baronets.

bă'ronėtcy *n.* Baronet's rank or patent.

barōn'ĭal *adj.* Of, belonging to, befitting, a baron.

bă'rony *n.* Baron's rank, domain, or tenure; division of Irish county; large manor in Scotland.

barŏque' (-k), *adj.* 1. Irregularly shaped (of jewels, esp. pearls); grotesque, odd. 2. Of the style of art which, evolved in Italy *c* 1600 out of that of the Renaissance, prevailed in Europe (chiefly in Catholic countries) until *c* 1720, being characterized by massive and complex design in which architecture was combined with painting, sculpture, etc., and esp. by vigorous, restless or violent movement; of the music or literature of this period. 3. Applied loosely to any style which is held to have similar characteristics. ~ *n.* Baroque style. [Fr., f. Span. *barrueco* rough pearl]

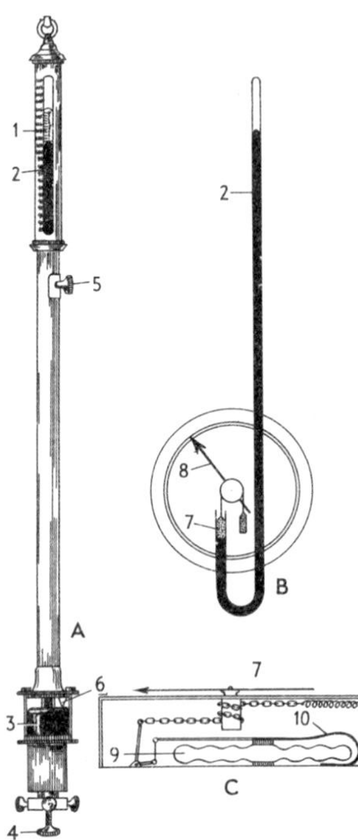

BAROMETERS: A. FORTIN. B. SIPHON. C. ANEROID

1. Vernier scale. 2. Column of mercury, which rises with increase of atmospheric pressure. 3. Mercury cistern. 4. Screw for adjusting level of mercury in cistern. 5. Vernier screw. 6. Fiducial point. 7. Floating weight, which rises with decrease in atmospheric pressure. 8. Dial pointer recording changes in pressure on a dial. 9. Vacuum chamber. 10. Spring, which responds to changes in atmospheric pressure on vacuum chamber and so moves pointer

bărouche' (-ōōsh) *n.* Four-wheeled horse-drawn carriage with a seat in front for the driver, and seats inside for two couples facing each other.

BAROUCHE

barque: see BARK[2], *n.*

barquentine (bâ̆rk'entēn) *n.* Three-masted vessel with foremast square-rigged and main and mizen fore-and-aft rigged (ill. BARK).

bă'rrack *n.* (usu. pl.) Building(s) for lodging soldiers; large building of severely plain, dull, or dreary appearance. ~ *v.t.* Jeer at (side playing a game, speaker, etc.).

bărracud'a (-ōōd-), **-coota, -couta** (-ōōt-) *n.* Large voracious fish of the perch kind, *Sphyraena barracuda*, 6–10 ft long, found in seas of the W. Indies.

bărr'age (*or* bărahzh) *n.* 1. Artificial bar in river or watercourse. 2. (mil.) Obstacle to offensive or defensive action on part of an enemy, usu. in form of a line, area, or volume into which high-explosive shells are fired from a large number of guns either continuously or for pre-arranged periods; *creeping* ~, one laid down in front of an advance of one's own troops and moving with them; *box* ~, one laid down usu. on three lines for the purpose of isolating a particular area; *balloon* ~: see BALLOON.

bă'rrator *n.* One who vexatiously incites to litigation or raises discord.

băr'ratry *n.* 1. Purchase or sale of ecclesiastical preferments or offices of State. 2. Vexatious persistence in or incitement to litigation. 3. Fraud or gross and criminal negligence of ship's master or crew to the prejudice of the owners and without their consent. **bă'rratrous** *adj.*

bă'rrel *n.* 1. Cylindrical wooden vessel of curved staves bound by hoops (ill. CASK); contents or capacity of such a vessel. 2. Revolving cylinder in capstan, watch, etc. (ill. CLOCK). 3. Cylindrical body of object; belly and loins of horse. 4. Metal tube of fire-arm, through which the missile is projected (ill. GUN). 5. ~*-organ*, musical instrument with pin-studded cylinder turned by a handle and operating a mechanism which opens the pipes, the handle also serving to work the bellows; ~*-vault*, vault with uniform concave roof (ill. VAULT).

bă'rren *adj.* Not bearing, incapable of bearing (children, fruit, etc.); waste; unprofitable. ~ *n.* (usu. pl.) Barren land; elevated plains on which grow small trees and shrubs, but no timber. **bă'rrenly** *adv.* **bă'rrennėss** *n.*

Barrès (bă'rĕz), Maurice (1862–1923). French author and Nationalist politician.

Bă'rrett, Elizabeth: see BROWNING[1].

bă'rricāde *n.* (Defensive) barrier, esp. one hastily erected across street etc. ~ *v.t.* Block or defend with a barricade. [Span. *barrica* cask]

Bă'rrie, Sir James Matthew (1860–1937). Scottish writer of comedies and short stories, author of 'Peter Pan', 'Quality Street', 'A Window in Thrums', etc.

bă'rrier *n.* Fence barring advance or preventing access; any obstacle, boundary, or agency that keeps apart, or prevents intercourse, success, etc.; ~ *cream*, ointment forming thin film on skin, used to protect hands from rough work and dirt; ~ *reef*, a high wall of coral rock separated from land by a broad deep channel and with a precipitous face on the seaward side, esp. the *Great B~ Reef*, off E. coast of Australia, some 1,100 miles long and 30 broad.

bă'rrister *n.* Student of law, who, having been called to the bar (see BAR[1] *n.* 7), has the privilege of practising as advocate in the superior courts of law.

bă'rrow[1] (-ō) *n.* Prehistoric grave-mound, tumulus.

bă'rrow[2] (-ō) *n.* Rectangular frame with short shafts for carrying loads on; shallow box with two shafts and one wheel; small two-wheeled handcart.

Bă'rry, Sir Charles (1795–1860). Architect (with A. W. Pugin) of the English Houses of Parliament.

Bar̄'săc. Parish in the Gironde adjoining Sauternes; the white wine produced there, less sweet than most Sauternes.

bar̄se *n.* Common perch (*Perca fluviatilis*).

Bart *abbrev.* Baronet (commonly written after the name of one who holds that rank, to distinguish him from a knight).

bar̄t'er *v.* Exchange (goods, rights, etc.) *for* things of like kind. ~ *n.* Traffic by exchange.

Bar̄thŏl'omew, St. One of the 12 apostles, commemorated on 24th Aug.; *Massacre of St.* ~, massacre of Huguenots throughout France ordered by Charles IX at the instigation of his mother Catherine de Médicis and begun without warning on the feast of St. Bartholomew, 1572; *St. ~'s Hospital*: see BART'S.

bar̄tizăn' *n.* Battlemented parapet, or overhanging battlemented corner turret, at top of castle or church-tower. [Word coined by Sir W. Scott from misunderstanding of an illiterate Sc. spelling of *bratticing* parapet]

Bar̄t'ŏk, Béla (1881–1945). Hungarian composer and collector of Hungarian folk-music.

Bar̄tolommeo (-mā'o) di Pagholo, Fra (1475–1517). Florentine painter.

Bar̄tolozz'i (-lŏtsĭ), Francesco (1727–1815). Italian engraver (after Holbein etc.), active chiefly in England.

bar̄t'on *n.* Farm-yard.

Bar̄t's. Colloq. name of St. Bartholomew's Hospital, London, founded 1123 by the English monk Rahere (d. 1144), prebendary of St. Paul's.

Bar̄'uch (-o͝ok). A book of the Apocrypha, attributed in the text to Baruch, the scribe of Jeremiah (Jer. xxxvi).

bă'ry̆sphēre *n.* The core of the earth, consisting of a very heavy substance, prob. nickel iron.

bary̆t'a *n.* Barium protoxide, an alkaline earth distinguished by its great density.

bary̆t'ēs (-z) (also **bar̄'īte**) *n.* Native barium sulphate, heavy spar, used as a white paint.

bă'ry̆tōne *n.* & *adj.* 1. = BARITONE. 2. Brass wind instrument of saxhorn family, used in military bands. 3. Obsolete stringed instrument resembling viol da gamba. 4. (Greek word) without acute accent on last syllable.

bās'al *adj.* Of or at the base. **bās'ally** *adv.*

basalt (băs'awlt, basawlt') *n.* A dark-coloured fine-grained rock occurring as a lava or as an intrusion, often showing columnar structure, as at the Giant's Causeway in N. Ireland. **basal'tĭc** *adj.*

băs'an (-z-), **băz'an** *n.* Sheepskin tanned in oak- or larch-bark. [Arab. *bitanah* lining]

băs'cūle *n.* Lever apparatus used in ~ *bridge*, kind of drawbridge balanced by a counterpoise which rises or falls as the bridge is lowered or raised, as the Tower Bridge, London (ill. BRIDGE).

bāse[1] *adj.* Morally low, mean, ignoble, debased; menial; ~*-born*, of low birth; illegitimate; ~ *metals*, those which quickly corrode or tarnish (opp. NOBLE or PRECIOUS *metals*). **bāse'ly** (-sl-) *adv.* **base'nėss** *n.*

bāse[2] *n.* 1. That on which anything stands or depends; support, foundation, principle, groundwork, starting-point. 2. (biol.) End at which an organ is attached to trunk. 3. (geom.) Line or surface on which a plane or solid figure is held to stand. 4. (surveying) Known line used as geometrical base for trigonometry. 5. (math.) Starting-number for system of numeration or logarithms (as 10 in decimal counting). 6. (chem.) Antithesis of ACID, substance capable of combining with an acid to form a salt (including, but wider than, ALKALI). 7. (archit.) Part of column between shaft or pedestal and pavement (ill. ORDER). 8. (mil.) Town or other area in rear of an army where drafts, stores, hospital, etc., are concentrated 9. (gram.) The form of a word to which suffixes are attached. 10. One of the four corners of the diamond in BASEBALL (and see ill.). ~ *v.t.* Found or establish *on*.

bāse'ball (-sbawl) *n.* The national field-game of the U.S., played between two teams of 9 players on a field (*diamond*) having four *bases*. The teams field and

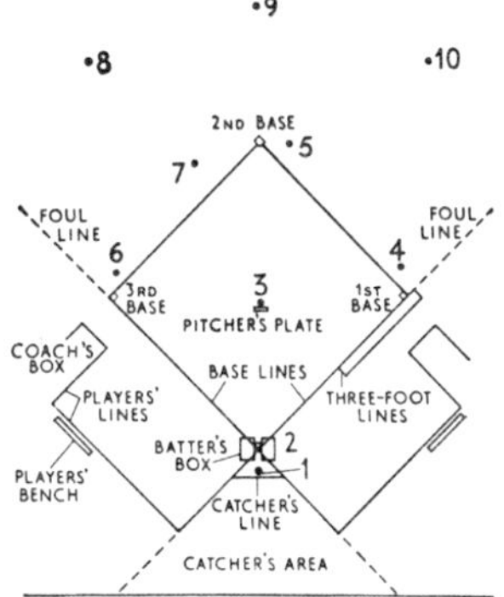

BASEBALL DIAMOND

1. Catcher. 2. Batter. 3. Pitcher. 4. First baseman. 5. Second baseman. 6. Third baseman. 7. Short stop. 8. Left fielder 9. Centre fielder. 10. Right fielder

bat in turn; each batter tries to hit the ball (thrown by the *pitcher*) in such a way that he can run to the next base (and thereby score) before it is returned. Nine innings constitute a game.

bāse'lėss (-sl-) *adj.* Groundless, unfounded.

bāse'ment (-sm-) *n.* Lowest part of a structure; inhabited storey partly or wholly below ground-level.

băsh *v.t.* Strike heavily so as to smash *in*.

Bāsh'ăn. Kingdom beyond Jordan, conquered by Israelites under Moses (Num. xxi. 33), and famous for its cattle (Ps. xxii. 12, Amos iv. 1).

băshaw' *n.* Earlier form of PASHA.

băsh'ful *adj.* Shy, sheepish. **băsh'fully** *adv.* **băsh'fulnėss** *n.*

băshĭ-bazouk' (-o͞ok) *n.* Mercenary soldier of Turkish irregular troops, notorious for lawlessness, plundering, and brutality. [Turk., = 'one whose head is turned']

bās'ic *adj.* 1. Of or forming a base, fundamental. 2. (chem.) Having the chemical properties of a base; ~ *salt*, produced when a base has reacted with fewer than the maximum possible equivalents of acid. 3. (min., of igneous rocks) Having little silica in proportion to the amount of lime, potash, etc. 4. Applied to processes of steel manufacture from phosphoric pig-irons and to the steel thus produced; ~ *slag*, slag from this process, used finely ground as a fertilizer because of its phosphorus and manganese content. 5. *B~ English*, a system of simplified English including only those words (some 850) which are held to be essential to the expression of any idea in English, devised under the auspices of the Orthological Institute, Cambridge, in the first quarter of the present century.

bāsĭ'city *n.* (chem.) The number of equivalents of a base with which one molecule of an acid can react.

basĭdĭomȳ'cēte *n.* Fungus producing basidiospores, e.g. mushroom and toadstool (ill. FUNGUS).

basĭd'ĭospōre *n.* (bot.) Spore borne at the extremity of a basidium (ill. FUNGUS).

basĭd'ĭum *n.* (pl. *-dia*). Spore-bearing structure in some fungi.

băs'ĭl[1] (-z-) *n.* Aromatic herb of the genus *Ocimum*, esp. *sweet ~* (*O. basilicum*) and the dwarf *bush ~* (*O. minimum*), the leaves of which are used for flavouring soups, salads, etc. [L *basilisca* the plant (supposed antidote to basilisk's bite)]

băs'ĭl[2] (-z-) *n.* = BASAN.

Băs'ĭl[3] (-z-), St. (*c* 330–79). Greek Patriarch, founder of a monastic rule which is still the basis of monasticism in the Orthodox Church.

basĭl'ĭca (-z-) *n.* 1. (in ancient Rome) Large oblong building used as exchange or law-court, having an apse at one or each end and freq. side-aisles; colonnaded hall, resembling this, in Roman house.

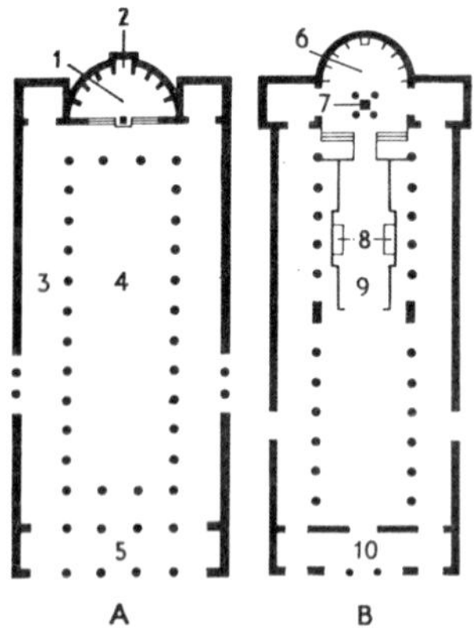

BASILICA: A. ROMAN BASILICA. B. EARLY CHRISTIAN BASILICA

1. Tribune. 2. Judge's seat. 3. Aisle. 4. Nave. 5. Vestibule. 6. Apse. 7. Altar. 8. Ambo. 9. Choir. 10. Narthex

2. Church of similar shape, having a wide nave with aisles, and an apse at one (orig. western) end.

basĭl'ĭcan *adj.* [Gk *basilika* (*oikia*) royal (house), f. *basileus* king]

băs'ĭlĭsk (-z-) *n.* 1. A cockatrice, a fabulous reptile hatched by a serpent from a cock's egg; its breath and even its glance were supposed to be fatal. 2. Small

BASILISK

Amer. lizard of the family *Iguanidae*, with a hollow crest that can be inflated at will. [L *basilicus* kind of lizard, f. Gk *basiliskos* little king]

bās'in (-sn) *n.* 1. Circular or oval vessel of greater width than depth and with sloping or curving sides, for holding water etc.; contents of a basin. 2. Hollow depression; circular or oval valley; tract of country drained by river and its tributaries. 3. Dock with floodgates.

bās'ĭs *n.* (pl. *basēs*). Base; foundation, beginning, determining principle; main ingredient; common ground for negotiation etc.

bask (-ah-) *v.i.* Revel in warmth and light (*in* the sun, firelight, etc.); *basking shark*, one of the largest species of shark, *Cetorhinus maximum*, found in northern seas, so called from its habit of lying near surface of water.

ba'sket (bah-) *n.* Wicker vessel of plaited or interwoven canes, osiers, etc.; contents of this; *basketball*, ball game played with inflated ball which is tossed into baskets

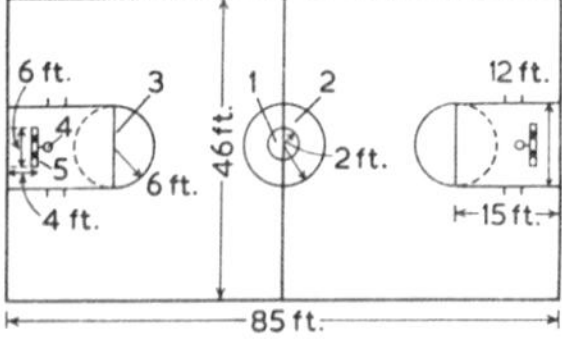

BASKETBALL COURT

1. Centre circle. 2. Restraining circle. 3. Free-throw line. 4. Basket (10 ft above ground). 5. Backboard behind basket

suspended from posts; *~-chair*, one made of wickerwork; *~-work*, interlaced osiers, twigs, etc.

Basle (bahl). Engl. spelling of Basel or Bâle, town and canton of Switzerland.

basque[1] (bahsk) *n.* Short continuation of bodice below waist; bodice having this.

Basque[2] (bahsk) *adj.* & *n.* (Member) of a people inhabiting both slopes of the W. Pyrenees and speaking a non-Indo-European language; (of) this language.

băs-rėlief' (-lēf) *n.* Low relief, carving or modelling in which figures project less than one half of their true proportions from the background.

băss[1] *n.* Any of a large group of perch-like fishes in sea or fresh water including *sea-~* (*Serranidae*), *white ~* (*Roccus chrysops*), *yellow ~* (*Morone interrupta*), etc.

bāss[2] *adj.* & *n.* Deep-sounding; (of, suited to) lowest part in harmonized music; (man with) voice extending $1\frac{1}{2}$ octaves or more below middle C (ill. VOICE); ~ CLARINET, DRUM, FLUTE, see these words; ~ *viol*, viola da gamba.

bass[3]: see BAST.

băss'ėt[1] *n.* Short-legged dog of breed originating in France, used in hunting hares, followed on foot.

băssėt[2] *n.* Obsolete card-game resembling faro.

băssėt-hôrn *n.* A tenor clarinet, of somewhat greater compass than the ordinary clarinet.

băssĭnĕt' *n.* (obs.) Hooded wicker cradle or perambulator.

băss'ō *adj.* & *n.* (mus.) Bass.

bassōōn' *n.* Double-reed musical instrument, the bass of the wood-wind family, having an 8-ft pipe turned back so that the whole instrument measures only 4 ft (ill. WOOD); organ or harmonium stop of similar quality.

Băss Rŏck. Rock 350 ft high, off coast of E. Lothian, Scotland; in 17th c. the site of a prison; now a bird sanctuary.

băst, băss *ns.* Inner bark of lime or linden-tree, which, cut into strips and coarsely plaited, is used for matting etc.; similar fibre obtained from leaf-bases or leaf-stalks of certain palms and used for ropes, brooms, etc.; any flexible or fibrous bark.

băs'tard *n.* & *adj.* (Person) born out of wedlock; hybrid, counterfeit (thing). **băs'tardy** *n.*

băs'tardīze *v.t.* Declare or render bastard.

bāste[1] *v.t.* Sew together loosely, sew with long loose stitches, tack.

bāste[2] *v.t.* 1. Moisten (roasting meat etc.) by pouring over it melted fat, gravy, etc. 2. (colloq.) Thrash, cudgel.

Băstille' (-tēl). (hist.) 14th-c. prison-fortress in Paris, used for political and other prisoners, stormed and destroyed by the mob on 14th July 1789; the anniversary of its fall, as marking the end of absolute monarchy in France and the beginning of the French Revolution, is the national holiday of republican France.

băstĭnā'dō *n.* & *v.t.* (Punish with) caning or cudgelling on the soles of the feet.

băs'tĭon *n.* Mass of masonry or brick- or stone-faced earthwork projecting from fortification in the form of an irregular pentagon.

Basu'tō (-ōō-). (More correctly, *Sotho*~) a Bantu tribe of S. Africa.

Basu'tolănd. Former British protectorate, now Lesotho.

băt[1] *n.* Small nocturnal mammal of the order *Chiroptera*, resembling a mouse, with leather-like wings consisting of a membrane

BAT

stretched from the neck over long spread fingers of forelegs and toes of the hind-feet to the tail.

băt[2] *n.* Wooden implement with handle and striking surface, esp. that used in cricket; long, round stick with handle at one end used in baseball and other games; *bats'man*, player with bat in cricket; man who guides aircraft on to aircraft-carrier by signals made with 'bats' held in the hands. ~ *v.* Use bat, have innings (in cricket etc.).

bata'ta (-ā- *or* -ah-) *n.* The sweet potato, a plant, *Ipomoea batatas*, with edible tuberous roots, prob. native of tropical America.

Batāv'ia. 1. Former name of DJAKARTA. 2. (hist.) Region between Rhine and Waal, inhabited in Roman times by a Celtic tribe, the Batavi. 3. (literary, poet.) The Netherlands. **Batāv'ian** *adj.* & *n.*

bătch *n.* A baking; loaves baked at one time; quantity, number, or set of people or things associated together, esp. in time.

bāte[1] *v.* Let down; restrain (breath); deduct; fall off in force.

bāte[2] *n.* (school slang) Rage.

bateau (băt'ō) *n.* (pl. *bateaux* pr. -ōz). Light river-boat, esp. the long, tapering, flat-bottomed boat used by French Canadians.

bath[1] (-ah-) *n.* 1. Washing; immersion in liquid, air, etc.; water, lotion, etc., for bathing. 2. Vessel, room (also *bath'room*), or (usu. pl.) building for bathing in. 3. Spa resorted to for medical treatment by bathing etc. 4. *Order of the B*~, high order of British knighthood, founded 1725 as revival of the 'Knights of the Bath' first created 1399 at coronation of Henry IV and so named from the ceremonial bath which preceded installation. ~ *v.t.* Subject to washing in bath.

Bath[2] (-ah-). City and county borough of Somersetshire, noted for its hot springs. The Romans built baths and a city (Aquae Sulis) there, but the modern reputation of Bath dates from the 17th c., and in the 18th c. it was a place of fashionable resort. ~*-brick*, calcareous earth moulded into a brick, used for cleaning metal; ~*-bun*, round, spiced currant-bun with sugar-icing; ~*-chair*, wheeled chair for invalids; ~*-chap*, pickled lower half of pig's cheek; ~*-metal*, alloy of zinc and copper; ~ *Oliver*, unsweetened biscuit said to have been invented by William Oliver (1695–1764), a physician of Bath; ~ *stone*, oolite building-stone.

Bath: et Well: *abbrev.* (Bishop) of Bath and Wells (replacing surname in his signature).

bāthe (-dh) *v.* Immerse (in liquid, air, etc.); moisten all over; envelop; take a bath or a bathe; *bāthing-costume*, *-dress*, etc., garment for bathing or swimming in; *bathing-machine*, small hut on wheels, formerly used by sea-bathers for undressing and dressing. ~ *n.* Taking of bath, esp. in sea, river, or swimming-bath. **bā'ther** *n.*

băth'olĭth *n.* Large body of intrusive rock (e.g. granite) such as is found esp. along Pacific coast of America.

bāth'ŏs *n.* Fall from sublime to ridiculous; anticlimax. **bathĕt'ĭc** *adj.*

Băthshēb'a. The wife of Uriah the Hittite (2 Sam. xi); she became one of the wives of David and the mother of Solomon.

băth'ȳscăph(e) *n.* Vessel for deep-sea diving and exploration. [Fr., f. Gk *bathus* deep + *skaphos* ship; coined by A. Piccard]

băth'ȳsphēre *n.* Spherical diving apparatus for deep-sea observation.

băt'ĭk *n.* The Javanese method, practised also in the West, of executing designs on textiles by painting parts of the pattern in wax, dyeing the parts left exposed, and then removing the wax. [Javanese, = 'drawing']

batiste' (-ēst) *n.* Fine light cotton fabric of same texture as cambric, but differently finished; fine smooth woollen fabric. [Fr. *Baptiste* of Cambrai, first maker]

băt'man *n.* (fem. *-woman*). Member of army or air force acting as officer's servant. [orig. man who carried officer's baggage (Fr. *bât* pack-saddle)]

băt'on *n.* 1. Staff of office, esp. *Marshal's* ~; constable's truncheon. 2. (her.) Ordinary like a narrow bend broken off at the extremities, in English heraldry only as ~ *sinister*, the badge of bastardy (see BEND). 3. (mus.) conductor's wand for beating time. ~ *v.t.* Strike with baton or truncheon.

Băt'on Rouge (rōōzh). Capital city of Louisiana, U.S.

batrăch'ian (-k-) *adj.* & *n.* Frog-like (animal); (animal) of the order *Batrachia* (now ANURA).

battăl'ion *n.* Large body of men in battle array; unit of infantry, consisting of four companies and an H.Q. company and forming part of a brigade.

bătt'els *n.pl.* College account at Oxford for board and provisions supplied, or for all college expenses.

bătt'en[1] *n.* 1. Long thin piece of squared timber used for flooring, hanging roof-tiles, etc. (ill. ROOF). 2. (naut.) Strip of wood, esp. used to fasten down edges of hatchway tarpaulin in bad weather. ~ *v.t.* Strengthen, fasten *down*, with battens.

bătt'en[2] *v.i.* Feed gluttonously *on*; grow fat, (fig.) thrive at another's expense.

bătt'er[1] *v.* Strike repeatedly so as to bruise or break; beat out of shape; handle severely; *battering-ram*, heavy beam anciently used for breaching walls, sometimes with ram's-head end. ~ *n.* 1. Mixture of flour and eggs beaten up with liquid for cooking. 2. Defect in printing type or stereotype plate.

bătt'er[2] *v.i.* (of walls etc.) Incline from perpendicular so as to have a receding slope. ~ *n.* Slope of wall etc. from the perpendicular.

bătt'ery *n.* 1. (law) Infliction of blows or the least menacing touch to clothes or person. 2. (mil.) Set of guns with their men, horses, and vehicles; group of guns on a warship; unit of artillery consisting of two troops and forming part of an artillery regiment. 3. Set of similar or connected instruments, utensils, etc.; (elect.) series of cells for generating or storing electricity; (poultry farming) series of individual cages in which laying hens are confined.

băt'tle *n.* Combat, esp. between large organized forces; *line of* ~, troops or ships drawn up to fight; *line-of-*~ *ship*, (obs.) battleship of 74 or more guns; ~*-axe*, kind of long-handled axe used as a medieval weapon; (fig.) termagant;

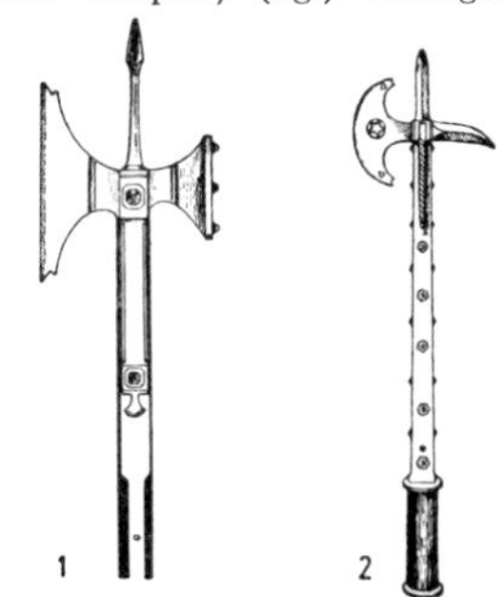

BATTLE-AXES

1. Pole axe, *c* 1470. 2. Horseman's axe, *c* 1520

~*-cruiser*, large, fast, and heavily armed cruiser; ~*-cry*, war-cry; slogan; *battledress*, (formerly) soldier's etc. everyday uniform of belted blouse and trousers, now replaced by *No. 2 dress* of jacket and trousers; *battlefield*, scene of battle; *battleship*, warship of the largest and most powerfully armed class. ~ *v.i.* Struggle *with* or *against*.

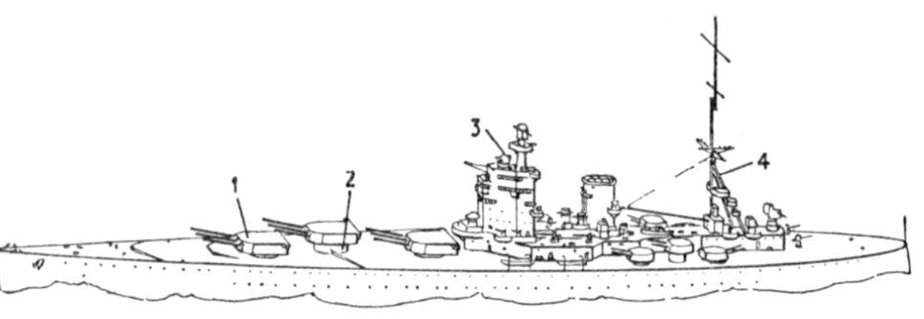

BATTLESHIP
1. Gun turret. 2. Barbette. 3. Director control tower. 4. Tripod mast

Bătt'le Abb'ey. Abbey founded by William the Conqueror (1069) on site of battle of Hastings; ~ *Roll*, document, prob. compiled in 14th c., which purports to show the names of families which came over to England with William; extant versions date from the 16th c.

băt'tledōre *n.* Wooden, stringed, or parchment bat like a small racket for striking shuttlecock; ~ (*and shuttlecock*), the game played with this by two persons who strike the shuttlecock to and fro between them. [prob. f. Span. *batallador* champion]

băt'tlement (-lm-) *n.* Indented parapet at top of wall etc., orig. for purposes of defence against assailants (ill. CASTLE).

Bătt'le of Britain. Series of air battles over London and SE. England between R.A.F. and German Air Force in which British victory ended the threat of German invasion (Aug.–Sept. 1940).

băttūe' (*or* -ōō) *n.* Driving of game from cover towards point where sportsmen are stationed to shoot them; wholesale slaughter, esp. of unresisting crowds.

bau'ble *n.* 1. Showy trinket. 2. Baton surmounted by fantastic head with asses' ears carried by Court fool or jester.

Baudelaire (bōdlār'), Charles Pierre (1821–67). French lyric poet, author of 'Les Fleurs du Mal' (1857).

baux'īte (bŏks-) *n.* A hydroxide of alumina, one of the chief sources of aluminium. [originally found at *Les Baux* near Arles, France]

Bavār'ia. Former State of S. Germany, now a province of the Federal Republic; capital, Munich. **Bavār'ian** *adj.* & *n.*

bawb'ee *n.* (Sc.) Halfpenny.

bawd *n.* Procuress. **bawd'y** *adj.* & *n.* Lewd, obscene (language); ~*-house*, brothel. **bawd'inėss** *n.*

bawl *v.* Shout at the top of one's voice.

Băx, Sir Arnold Edward Trevor (1883–1953). English composer.

bay[1] *n.* 1. Kind of laurel, esp. the sweet bay or bay laurel, *Laurus nobilis*, with deep-green leaves (used to flavour soups etc.) and many dark-purple berries. 2. (usu. pl.) Wreath of bay leaves as a garland for a conqueror or poet. 3. ~ *rum*, a perfume distilled from leaves of *Pimenta acris*.

bay[2] *n.* Part of sea filling wide-mouthed opening of land; *Bay State*, pop. name of Massachusetts.

bay[3] *n.* Division of wall between columns or buttresses (ill. CHURCH). 2. Recess; *sick-*~, part of main deck used as hospital; part of building similarly used. 3. Space added to room by advancing window from wall line; ~*-window*, window in a bay (ill. WINDOW). 4. Railway platform having a cul-de-sac and serving as terminus for a side-line; the cul-de-sac itself; ~*-line*, side-line starting from this.

bay[4] *n.* Bark of large dog or of hounds in pursuit, esp. as they draw near the quarry; *at* ~, in great straits; *stand, be, at* ~, show fight, turn against pursuers. ~ *v.* (of large dog) Bark, bark at.

bay[5] *adj.* & *n.* Reddish-brown (colour); bay horse; *the Bays*, the 2nd Dragoon Guards, who were mounted on bay horses *c* 1767.

bayadère' (-ār) *n.* Hindu dancing-girl.

Bay'ārd, Pierre du Terrail, Seigneur de (1473–1524). French soldier of great valour and generosity, known as the knight 'sans peur et sans reproche'; hence, **bayard** *n.*, gentleman of high courage and honour.

Bayeux tapestry (bāyōō'). Long strip of embroidered linen at Bayeux Cathedral, containing scenes representing the Norman Conquest of England, with which it is usu. held to be nearly contemporary.

Baykal: see BAIKAL.

Bayle, Pierre (1647–1706). Fr. philosopher and sceptic, author of a 'Dictionnaire historique et critique' (1695–7), which had great influence on Voltaire and other 18th-c. French sceptics.

bay'onėt *n.* Stabbing blade which may be attached to rifle muzzle. ~ *v.t.* Stab with bayonet.

bayou (bī'ōō) *n.* (U.S.) Marshy inlet or creek of river or sea in southern states of U.S.

Bayreuth (bī'roit'). Bavarian town in which Wagner festivals are held in a theatre specially built for the production of his operas.

bazaar' *n.* Oriental market-place or permanent market; fancy shop; fancy fair, esp. sale of goods for charities. [Pers. *bāzār* street of shops]

bazook'a (-ōō-) *n.* (U.S.) 1. Crude, pipe-shaped musical instrument. 2. Amer. infantry light tubular projector for armour-piercing (esp. anti-tank) rockets.

BB, BBB *abbrevs.* Double-, treble-, black (of pencil-lead).

B.B. *abbrev.* Boys' Brigade.

B.B.C. *abbrev.* British Broadcasting Corporation.

B.C. *abbrev.* Battery Commander; before Christ; British Columbia.

B.Ch. *abbrev.*: see CH.B.

B.C.L. *abbrev.* Bachelor of Civil Law.

B.Com. *abbrev.* Bachelor of Commerce.

B.D. *abbrev.* Bachelor of Divinity.

bdĕll'ium (d-) *n.* Any of several trees or shrubs, chiefly of the genus *Commiphora*, yielding a gum-resin resembling impure myrrh, of bitter or acrid taste and more or less agreeable smell; the resin itself.

Bdr *abbrev.* Bombardier.

bds *abbrev.* Boards (in bookbinding).

be (bē, bĭ) *v.i.* (past t. *was*, past part. *bēen*). Exist, occur; remain, continue; have a certain state or quality (specified by following noun, adj., etc.); ~*-all* (*n.*) whole being, essence; esp. in *be-all and end-all*, absolutely everything, the whole *of*.

B.E.A. *abbrev.* British Electricity Authority; British European Airways.

beach *n.* Sandy or pebbly shore of the sea (or lake or large river); ~*-comber*, (orig. U.S.) long wave rolling up from the sea; white man in Pacific Islands who lives by pearl-fishing, collecting jetsam, etc.; ~*-head*, fortified position of troops landed on a beach. ~ *v.t.* Run (ship etc.) ashore, haul up.

beach-la-mār *n.* The jargon English used in the W. Pacific. [Port. *bicho do mar* sea-worm]

beac'on *n.* 1. Signal, signal-fire on hill or on pole raised above building. 2. Conspicuous hill suit-

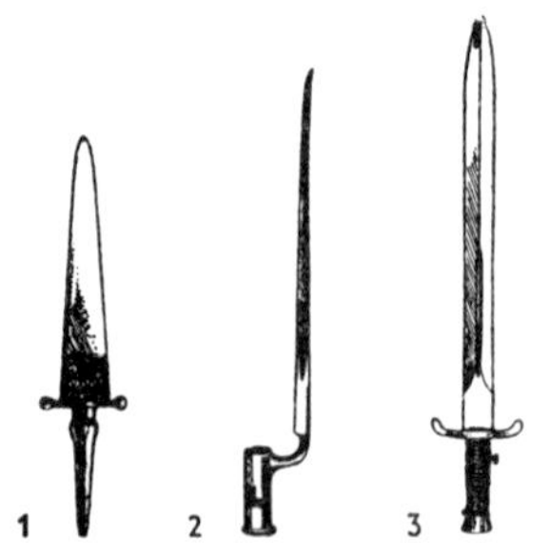

BAYONET
1. Plug bayonet, last quarter of 17th c. 2. Socket bayonet, 18th c. 3. Sword bayonet, 19th c.

able for the lighting of beacons. 3. Lighthouse; conspicuous object, esp. sphere on a pole marking pedestrian crossing-places on highways (see BELISHA BEACON). 4. Radio station enabling ship or aircraft to fix position.

Beaconsfield (bĕk'nzfēld). Town in Buckinghamshire, England; *Earl of* ~: see DISRAELI.

bead *n.* 1. Small perforated ball etc. for threading with others on a string or for sewing on to fabric; small bubble or drop of liquid; (pl.) rosary. 2. Small metal knob forming front sight of gun (*draw a* ~ *on*, take aim at). 3. (archit., also *beading*) Narrow cylindrical moulding sometimes carved to resemble a row of beads (ill. MOULDING). 4. ~*-roll*, list or string of names, catalogue. ~ *v.* Furnish or adorn with beads or a beading. [OE wd meaning 'prayer', from the use of strings of beads for keeping count of the number of prayers said]

bead'ing: see BEAD, 3.

bead'le *n.* 1. (hist.) Inferior parish officer oppointed to keep order in church, punish petty offences, and carry messages, etc. 2. Apparitor or precursor who walks officially in front of dignitaries, mace-bearer (in the Engl. universities usu. spelt *bedel(l)*). **bead'ledom** *n.* Stupid officiousness.

beads'man (-z-) *n.* One who prays for the soul or spiritual welfare of another, one paid to do this; hence, pensioner or almsman, inmate of alms-house. [see BEAD]

bead'y *adj.* (Of eyes) small and bright like beads.

beag'le *n.* Small hound for hunting hares, followed on foot. **beag'ling** *n.* Hunting with beagles.

beak[1] *n.* Bird's bill; extremities, often horny in structure, of mandibles of other animals; hooked nose; projection at prow of ancient ships, esp. war-galleys; spout; *beak'head*, one of a series of grotesque beaked heads carved as ornament on moulding in Romanesque architecture (ill. MOULDING).

beak[2] *n.* (slang) Magistrate; master at public school.

beak'er *n.* 1. Large drinking-cup. 2. Tall wide-mouthed vessel

BRONZE AGE BEAKERS

found in Bronze Age graves; ~ *folk, people*, users of such vessels. 3. Open-mouthed vessel, with lip, used in scientific experiments.

beam *n.* 1. Long piece of squared timber such as is used in house- or ship-building; horizontal support in building. 2. Great timber of plough, to which all other parts of plough-tail are fixed (ill. PLOUGH). 3. Wooden cylinder in loom on which the warp is wound (ill. LOOM). 4. Transverse bar of balances. 5. Transverse horizontal timber of a ship; hence, the greatest breadth of a ship; *on the* ~, at right angle to direction of ship (ill. BEARING); *on the* ~*-ends*, (of a ship) lying on its side and in danger of capsizing; (fig.) extremely hard-up, destitute. 6. Ray or pencil of light, or of electric radiation, etc.; *wireless* ~, wireless waves sent as a beam (i.e. not dispersed or broadcast) in a desired direction by a special aerial system, part of which acts as a reflector; so ~ *system* etc. 7. Radiance, bright look, smile. ~ *v.* Emit (light, affection, etc.); shine, smile radiantly.

bean *n.* 1. Kidney-shaped non-endospermic seed borne in pods of the family *Leguminosae* (ill. SEED), *broad* ~, *Vicia faba*, seed of this; *French* or *haricot* ~, *Phaseolus vulgaris* and its seed; *horse* ~, variety of *Vicia faba* grown for fodder; *kidney* ~, French bean; *scarlet runner* ~, *Phaseolus multiflorus*; *soya* ~, *Glycine soja*, cultivated, esp. in China, for food and many other uses; *tonka* ~: see TONKA BEAN. 2. Similar seed of other plants, as coffee. 3. (slang) Coin, bit of money (in *not a* ~); familiar form of address (in *old* ~); *full of* ~*s*, in high spirits; *give a person* ~*s*, deal severely with him; *spill the* ~*s*, give away information; ~*-feast*, annual dinner given by employers to their workpeople; fête, merry time; *beanstalk*, stem of the bean-plant.

bean'ō *n.* (slang) Bean-feast.

bear[1] (bār) *n.* 1. Heavily-built, thick-furred plantigrade quadruped of the genus *Ursus*. 2. Rough, unmannerly or uncouth person. 3. (Stock Exchange) Speculator for a fall; one who sells stock for future delivery hoping to buy it cheaper in the interval. 4. ~*-garden*, orig. place for baiting bears; scene of strife and tumult; *bear'-skin*, Guards' tall furry cap (ill. INFANTRY); ~ *leader*, travelling tutor to a rich young man. **bear'-ish** *adj.* Rough-mannered, surly.

bear[2] (bār) *v.* (past t. *bōre*, past part. *bōrne* exc. as below). 1. Carry, support. 2. Endure, tolerate. 3. (past part. usu. *born* in passive) Give birth to. 4. Produce, yield. 5. Apply weight; tend, incline; ~ *hard on*, oppress; *bring to* ~, apply. **bear'able** *adj.* Endurable.

bear[3] (bār) *v.* (St. Exch.) Speculate for a fall; cause fall in price of (stocks etc.). ~ *n.* This operation.

beard *n.* Hair upon man's face (now usu. excluding moustache and whiskers); chin tuft of animals; gills of oyster; awn of grasses; (print.) part of type above and below face which allows for ascending and descending letters (ill. TYPE). **beard'less** *adj.* Youthful, immature. **beard** *v.t.* Oppose openly, defy.

Beards'ley (-dzlĭ), Aubrey Vincent (1872–98). English artist and illustrator, chiefly in black and white; art editor of the 'Yellow Book'.

bear'er (bār-) *n.* 1. Bringer of letter etc., presenter of cheque; one who helps to carry coffin; ~ *security, bond*, etc., one not registered, the title to which is vested in its possessor. 2. (eng.) Plate or beam supporting load.

bear'ing (bār-) *n.* (esp.) 1. Behaviour. 2. Heraldic charge or device. 3. Relation, aspect. 4. Part

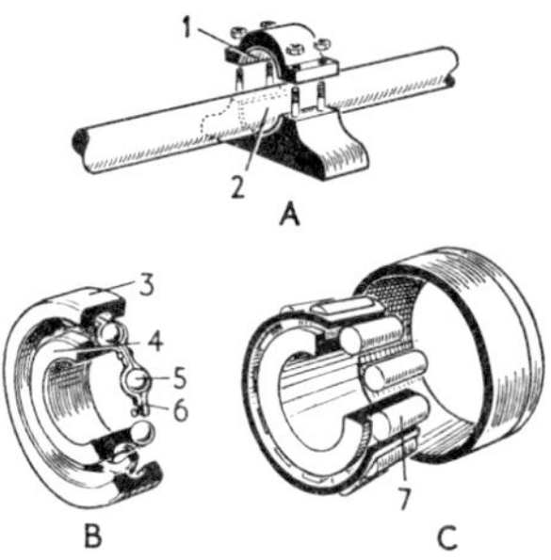

MECHANICAL BEARINGS: A. PLAIN BEARING. B. BALL BEARING. C. TAPER BEARING

1. Bearing shell (made of babbitt-metal). 2. Journal. 3. Outer race. 4. Inner race. 5. Ball. 6. Cage. 7. Taper

of machine that bears the movement. 5. (naut.) The direction of a given object measured as an angle from the vessel's meridian (*take a* ~ *on* e.g. a lighthouse, measure the angle between the line from ship to lighthouse and the line from ship to north); (pl.) relative position

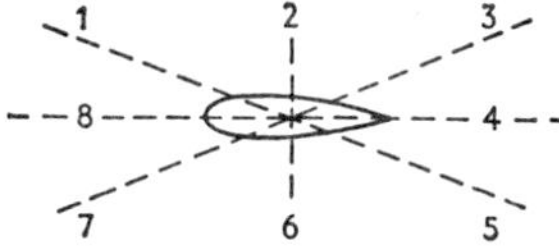

NAUTICAL RELATIVE BEARINGS

1. On the port quarter. 2. Abeam or on the beam. 3. On the port bow. 4. Ahead. 5. On the starboard bow. 6. Abeam. 7. On the starboard quarter. 8. Astern

(also fig.). 6. ~*-rein*, fixed rein from bit to saddle forcing horse to arch its neck.

beast *n.* 1. Animal; quadruped as dist. from birds, man, insects, etc.; bovine animal; animal used for riding, driving, etc. 2. Human being acting like an animal; brutal, savage man; person one dislikes.

beast'ly *adj.* Like a beast or its ways; unfit for human use, dirty; (colloq.) undesirable, unpleasant, annoying. **beast'liness** *n.*

beat *v.* (past. t. *beat*, past part. *beaten* and occas. *beat*). 1. Strike repeatedly; (of sun etc.) strike *upon*. 2. Overcome, surpass; be too hard for, perplex. 3. (Of wings etc.) move up and down; (of heart etc.) pulsate, throb; ~ *time*, mark the time of music by the beat of a wand, tapping with the foot, etc. 4. Shift, drive, alter, deform, or shape by blows. 5. Strike bushes etc. to rouse game. 6. ~ *up*, (naut.) strive or tack against the wind; ~ (person) *up*, (colloq.) attack and injure him by blows and kicks. ~ *n.* 1. Stroke on drum; signal so given; movement of conductor's baton; measured sequence of strokes or sounds; throbbing. 2. Sentinel's or constable's appointed course; habitual round.

beat'en *adj.* (esp.) ~ *track*, *way*, well-trodden way (also fig.); ~ *gold* etc., gold etc. hammered into foil, shaped by the hammer.

beat'er *n.* (esp.) Man employed to rouse game; man who beats gold etc.; implement which beats, as *carpet-beater*, *egg-beater*, etc.

bēatĭf'ĭc *adj.* Making blessed, imparting supreme happiness.

bėăt'ĭfy *v.t.* Make supremely happy or blessed; (R.C. Ch.) declare to be in enjoyment of heavenly bliss (as the first step towards canonization. **bėătĭfĭcā'tion** *n.*

bėăt'ĭtūde *n.* Supreme blessedness; declaration of blessedness, esp. (pl.) those pronounced by Christ in the Sermon on the Mount (Matt. v. 3–11).

Bē'atrĭce. Dante's name for a lady whom he loved, although he never spoke to her; he tells of his few meetings with her in the 'Vita Nuova', and in the 'Divina Commedia' she is his guide through Paradise; she represents for him the type of ideal love.

Beatt'y, David, Earl (1871–1936). Naval officer, commander of the British battle-cruiser fleet at the battle of Jutland, 1916.

beau (bō) *n.* Fop; lady's-man, lover; B~ BRUMMEL, B~ NASH: see these names.

Beaufort Scale (bōf'ert). Scale of numbers used by meteorologists to indicate force of wind (measured at 33 ft above level ground), thus:

0	0 m.p.h.	calm
1	2 m.p.h.	light air
2	5 m.p.h.	light breeze
3	10 m.p.h.	gentle ,,
4	15 m.p.h.	moderate ,,
5	21 p.m.h.	fresh ,,
6	28 m.p.h.	strong ,,
7	35 m.p.h.	near gale
8	42 m.p.h.	gale
9	50 m.p.h.	strong gale
10	59 m.p.h.	storm
11	68 m.p.h.	violent storm
12	78 m.p.h.	hurricane

[devised by Admiral Sir F. *Beaufort* (1774–1857)]

beau geste (bō zhĕst) *n.* Display of magnanimity. [Fr., = 'beautiful (or splendid) gesture']

beau ĭdē'al (bō) *n.* One's highest type of excellence or beauty. [Fr. (*idéal*), = 'the ideal Beautiful', often misconceived in English as a beautiful ideal]

Beaumarchais (bōmărshĕ'), Pierre Auguste Caron de (1732–90). French dramatist, author of two famous comedies, 'Le Barbier de Séville' (1775), 'Le Mariage de Figaro' (1778).

beau monde (bō mawn̄d) *n.* Fashionable society.

Beaumont (bōm'ont), Francis (1584–1616). English playwright, collaborator with John FLETCHER from *c* 1606 to 1616.

Beaune (bōn). Town in the Côte d'Or, France, centre of the wine trade of Burgundy; red wine of Burgundy from this district.

beaut'ėous (būt-) *adj.* (archaic & poet.) Endowed with beauty.

beautician (būtĭsh'n) *n.* (U.S.) One who runs a beauty parlour; beauty specialist.

beaut'ĭful (būt-) *adj.* Having beauty; capital, excellent. **beaut'ĭfully** *adv.* **beaut'ĭful** *n.* *The* ~, beauty in the abstract.

beaut'ĭfȳ (būt-) *v.t.* Make beautiful.

beauty (būt'ĭ) *n.* Combination of qualities (as form, colour, etc.) that delights the eye; combined qualities delighting the other senses, the moral sense, or the mind; beautiful trait or feature; person or thing possessing beauty; ~*-parlour*, place where the business of applying cosmetics, face-massage, and other beauty treatment is carried on; ~ *sleep*, sleep obtained before midnight; ~*-spot*, small patch placed on lady's face as foil to a beautiful complexion; beautiful scene; ~ *treatment*, the use of massage, cosmetics, exercise, etc., in order to improve personal beauty.

beav'er[1] *n.* 1. Amphibious rodent of genus *Castor* with broad, oval, horizontally-flattened tail, webbed hind feet, soft fur, and hard incisor teeth with which it cuts down trees; it is remarkable for the skill and industry with which it constructs dams of wood and mud; *B~ State*, popular name of Oregon. 2. The soft, short, rather woolly light-brown fur of this animal; a hat made from this.

beav'er[2] *n.* Lower portion or faceguard of helmet (ill. ARMOUR).

bėcalm' (-kahm) *v.t.* Make calm; deprive (ship) of wind.

bėcāme' past t. of BECOME.

bėcause' (-ŏz, -awz) *adv.* By reason *of*; *conj.* for the reason that.

Béchamel (bāshamĕl'). ~ *sauce*, a rich white sauce, made of butter, flour, white stock, seasoning, and usu. cream. [f. its inventor, Marquis de *Béchamel*, steward of Louis XIV]

bêche-de-mer (bĕsh, măr) *n.* The sea-cucumber, a marine echinoderm (*Holothuria edulis*), eaten as a luxury by the Chinese.

Bĕchūa'na (-k-, -ahna; *or* -ch-). (more correctly, *Tswana*) Bantu inhabitants of **Bĕchūa'nalănd,** the country of the Tswana, of which part was annexed to the Cape Colony in 1895, and part, a former British protectorate, became the republic of Botswana.

bĕck[1] *n.* (north.) Brook, mountain stream.

bĕck[2] *n.* Significant gesture, nod, etc.; *at the ~ and call of*, entirely dominated by, completely at the service of. ~ *v.* (poet.) Make beck (to).

bĕck'ėt[1] *n.* (naut.) Loop of rope or other simple contrivance for securing loose ropes, tackle, or spars, and for holding or securing the tacks or sheets of sails etc. (ill. SPLICE).

Bĕck'ėt[2], St. Thomas à (1117–70). Archbishop of Canterbury (1162) and Chancellor of England (1158) under Henry II; he successfully opposed Henry's policy in taxation and other matters, and was murdered by Henry's orders, in Canterbury Cathedral; two years later he was canonized, and his shrine became the most famous in Christendom; it was destroyed in 1538.

Bĕck'ford, William (1759–1844). English eccentric; author of 'Vathek', an Oriental novel in French (1787).

bĕck'on *v.* Summon, call attention of, by gesture; make mute signal *to*.

bėcloud' *v.t.* Cover with clouds, obscure.

bėcome' (-ŭm) *v.* (past t. *-cāme*, past part. *-come*). 1. Come into being; begin to be. 2. Suit, befit, look well on. **bėcom'ĭng** *adj.* **bėcom'ĭngly** *adv.*

Becquerel (bĕk'erĕl), Antoine Henri (1852–1908). French physicist; discoverer of radio-activity; ~ *rays*, rays emitted by a radioactive substance.

bĕd *n.* 1. Thing to sleep on; mattress; framework with mattress and coverings; animal's resting-place, litter. 2. Flat base on which anything rests; foundation of road or railway; garden-plot for plants; bottom of sea, river, etc.; stratum (ill. ROCK). 3. ~*-clothes*, sheets, pillows, blankets, etc., of bed; *bed'fellow*, sharer of bed; ~*-pan*, invalid's chamber utensil for use in bed; *-plate*, metal plate forming base of machine (ill. LATHE); ~*-ridden* (*adj.*) confined to bed by infirmity; ~*-rock*, solid rock underlying alluvial deposits etc.; also fig.; *bed'room*, room for sleeping in; ~*-sitting-room*, combined bedroom and sitting-room; *bed'sore*, sore developed by long lying in bed; ~*-spread*, coverlet; *bed'stead*, wooden or other framework of bed; *bed'-straw*, any of the genus *Galium*, plants with slender stems and small clustered flowers. ~ *v.* 1. Put or go to bed; provide bedding for horses etc. 2. Plant *out* in a garden bed. 3. Cover up or fix firmly in something; (eng.) fit accurately. 4.

Arrange as, be or form, a layer.

B.Ed. *abbrev.* Bachelor of Education.

bėdăbb′le *v.t.* Splash with liquid.

bėdaub′ *v.t.* Smear or daub with paint, mud, etc.

bĕdd′ing *n.* (esp.) 1. Mattress and bed-clothes; litter for horses etc. to sleep on. 2. (geol.) Layered structure visible in some rocks resulting from their deposition in water in layers or beds.

Bēde. Baeda, 'the Venerable ~' (673–735), English historian and scholar, a monk of Jarrow; author of a Latin history of the English Church and many other works in Latin.

bėdĕck′ *v.t.* Adorn.

bĕd′ėguar (-gâr) *n.* Kind of gall caused by the puncture of an insect, *Cynips rosae*, and forming a moss-like excrescence on rose-bushes. [Pers. *badawar* brought by the wind]

bedel(l): see BEADLE.

bėdĕv′il *v.t.* Treat diabolically, bewitch. **bėdĕv′ilment** *n.* Possession by devil; maddening trouble, confusion.

bėdew′ *v.t.* Cover with drops of or like dew.

Bĕd′fordshire. East-midland county of England.

bėdim′ *v.t.* Make dim, obscure.

bėdī′zen *v.t.* Deck out gaudily.

Bĕd′lam. (hist.) The hospital of St. Mary of Bethlehem, founded as a priory in 1247 in Bishopsgate, and used as a hospital for lunatics. It was removed to Moorfields, then to Lambeth, and finally to Beckenham. **bĕd′lam** *n.* Lunatic asylum, madhouse; scene of uproar. **bĕd′lamīte** *n.* Lunatic.

Bĕd′lĭngton *n.* ~ (*terrier*), curly-haired, grey terrier with narrow head, short body, and longish legs. [*Bedlington* in Northumberland]

Bĕd′ouin (-ōōēn). Arab of the desert. [Arab. *badāwīn* dwellers in the desert]

bėdrăgg′le *v.t.* Wet (dress etc.) by trailing it, or so that it trails or hangs limp.

Beds. *abbrev.* Bedfordshire.

bee *n.* 1. Hymenopterous 4-winged stinging insect living in societies composed of one *queen* (perfect female), a small number of *drones* (males) and a number of *workers* (undeveloped females),

BEE

1. Worker. 2. Queen. 3. Male (drone)

who produce wax and collect honey, which they store up in wax-cells for winter food. 2. Any of a large group of allied insects. 3. (chiefly U.S.) Meeting of neighbours to unite their labours for the benefit of one of them, gathering or meeting for some object, esp. for a competition in spelling (*spelling-bee*). 4. ~ *in one's bonnet*, eccentric whim, craze on some point; ~-*bread*, honey and pollen eaten by nurse-bees; ~-*hive*, HIVE; ~-*line*, straight line between two points, such as a bee is supposed to make returning to the hive; *bees′wax*, wax secreted by bees for making honeycombs, and used as a polish for wood etc.; *bees′wing*, crust of shiny filmy scales of tartar formed on port and some other wines after long keeping.

beech *n.* Forest-tree of Europe and W. Asia (genus *Fagus*) with fine thin smooth bark, glossy oval leaves, boughs and foliage which form a dense canopy, and three-sided nuts borne in pairs in a rough or prickly involucre; its wood; any of various other trees more or less resembling this; ~-*marten*, marten (*Martes foina*) of Europe and Asia, with white patch on breast and throat, stone-marten; ~-*mast*, beech nuts collectively. **beech′en** *adj.* Of beech or beechwood.

beef *n.* Flesh of ox, bull, or cow used as food; ox, any animal of the ox kind; ~-*eaters*, (f. obs. sense of 'dependants') pop. name of the Yeomen of the Guard, instituted at the accession of Henry VII (1485), and of the Warders of the Tower of London, who wear the same uniform; ~-*steak*, slice of beef cut from hindquarters and suitable for grilling, frying, etc. (ill. MEAT); ~ *tea*, stewed beef juice for invalids. **beef′y** *adj.* Solid, muscular; stolid.

Bėēl′zėbŭb. A god of the Canaanites, mentioned in 2 Kings i. 2 as the 'god of Ekron', and in the N.T. as 'prince of demons'; the devil. [Heb. *ba'alz'būb* fly-lord]

been, past part. of BE.

beer *n.* Alcoholic liquor made from fermented malt flavoured with hops, ale; (in trade usage) any of the liquors brewed from malt, as ale, stout, porter, lager; (pop.) ale as distinct from the others; *small* ~, weak beer, (fig.) trifling matter; ~-*engine*, apparatus for drawing beer from the barrel in the cellar to the tap in the bar of a public house.

Beer′bohm (-bōm), Sir Max (1872–1956). English author and caricaturist.

beer′y *adj.* Of or like beer; betraying its influence.

bees′tings *n.pl.* First milk drawn from a cow after parturition.

beet *n.* Any of several plants with edible roots (varieties of *Beta vulgaris*), including *sugar*-~ (with white root from which sugar is extracted), *garden beet′root* (crimson root used in salads etc.), spinach ~, chard, and mangolds.

Beethoven (bāt′ōven), Ludwig van (1770–1827). German composer of Flemish descent; worked mainly in Vienna; contributed much to the development of the

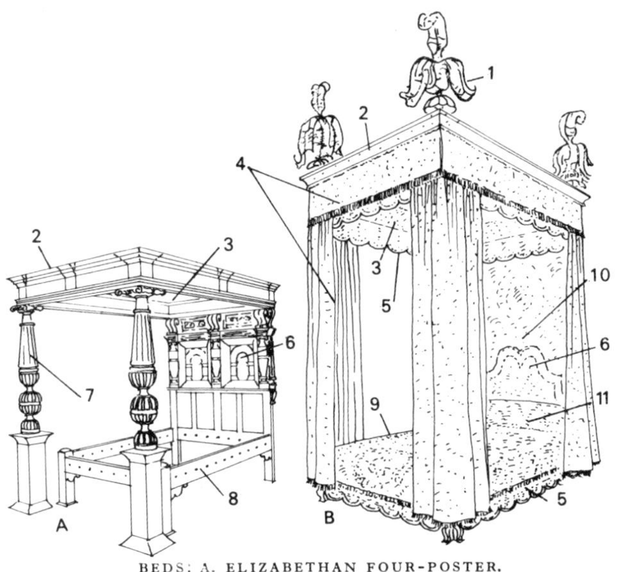

BEDS: A. ELIZABETHAN FOUR-POSTER. B. LATE 17TH-C. FOUR-POSTER

1. Ostrich feather plume. 2. Cornice. 3. Ceiler. 4. Hangings. 5. Valance. 6. Headboard. 7. Bed post. 8. Bedstock. 9. Counterpane. 10. Tester. 11. Bolster

symphony and other musical forms; wrote 9 symphonies, an opera, many pianoforte sonatas, string quartets, and other orchestral and chamber music; during his later years he was stone-deaf.

beet'le[1] *n.* Tool with handle and heavy head for crushing, ramming, etc., mallet; machine for finishing cloth. ~ *v.t.* Beat with beetle; finish (cloth) with beetle.

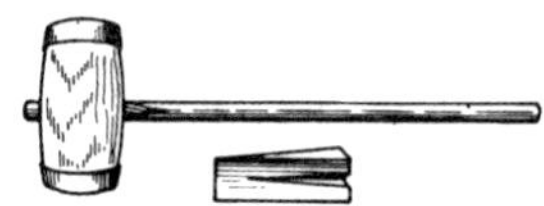

BEETLE OR MAUL AND WEDGE

beet'le[2] *n.* Any coleopterous insect with upper pair of wings converted into hard sheaths or wing-cases which close over the back and protect the lower or true wings; (pop.) insect resembling these, esp. largish black one; *black-~*, cockroach.

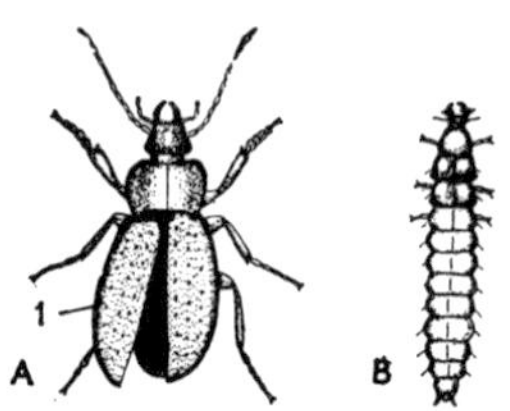

BEETLE: A. ADULT. B. LARVA

1. Wing-case, elytron, or shard

beet'le[3] *v.i.* Overhang threateningly. ~ *adj.* (in ~ *brows*, ~*-browed*) projecting, shaggy, scowling.

Beet'on, Mrs Isabella Mary (1836–65). Author of a famous book of cookery and household management, first published serially 1859–61.

B.E.F. *abbrev.* British Expeditionary Force.

bėfall' (-awl) *v.* Happen, happen to.

bėfit' *v.t.* Be suited to, become.

bėfŏg' *v.t.* Envelop in fog; confuse, obscure.

bėfōōl' *v.t.* Make a fool of, dupe.

bėfōre' *adv.* Ahead; in front; previously, already. ~ *prep.* In front of, ahead of; in the presence of; earlier than. ~ *conj.* Before the time when; rather than.

bėfōre'hănd *adv.* In anticipation, in readiness.

bėfoul' *v.t.* Make foul.

bėfriend' (-rĕnd) *v.t.* Help, favour.

bĕg *v.* 1. Ask for (food, money, etc.) as alms; live by alms. 2. Ask earnestly or humbly, entreat. 3. (Of dog etc.) sit up with forepaws raised expectantly. 4. ~ *the question*, take for granted the matter in dispute, assume by implication what one is trying to prove.

bėgăn', past t. of BEGIN.

bėgĕt' *v.t.* (past t. *bėgŏt'*, past part. *bėgŏtt'en*). Procreate (usu. of father); give rise to, occasion. **bėgĕtter'** *n.*

bĕgg'ar *n.* One who begs, esp. one who lives by begging; poor person; (colloq.) fellow. ~ *v.t.* Reduce to poverty; exhaust resources of; *~-my-neighbour*, simple card-game in which the object of each player is to acquire all the cards.

bĕgg'arly *adj.* Needy, poverty-stricken; mean, sordid, intellectually poor.

bĕgg'ary *n.* Extreme poverty.

Beghard (bĕg'*ard*) *n.* Member of lay brotherhoods which arose (in imitation of the BÉGUINES) in the Low Countries in 13th c.; the name was soon adopted by many who were simply idle mendicants, and from the 14th c. the brotherhoods were denounced by Popes and Councils and persecuted by the Inquisition; in the 17th c. those which survived were absorbed in the Tertiarii of the Franciscans.

bėgĭn' *v.* (past t. *bėgăn'*, past part. *bėgŭn*). Commence, set about; be the first; originate; come into being, arise. **bėgĭnn'er** *n.* (esp.) Tiro, learner. **bėgĭnn'ĭng** *n.* (esp.) Time at which anything begins; source, origin; first part.

bėgĭrd' *v.t.* (past part. *bėgĭrt*). Gird, encircle.

bėgŏne' *v. imper.* Be off, away with you (also occas. as infin.).

bėgōn'ĭa *n.* Genus of tropical under-shrubs and herbaceous plants having flowers with brightly coloured perianths (but no petals) and often richly-coloured foliage; often cultivated as ornamental plants. [Michel *Begon*, Fr. botanist (1638–1710)]

bėgŏt', bėgŏtt'en, past t. & past part. of BEGET.

bėgrime' *v.t.* Make grimy.

bėgrŭdge' *v.t.* Grudge.

bėguile' (-gīl) *v.t.* Delude; cheat; charm, amuse; divert attention from (passage of time etc.). **bėguile'ment** (-lm-), **bėguil'er** *ns.*

Béguine (bāgēn') *n.* Member of certain lay sisterhoods, first founded in the Netherlands in the 12th c., who devoted themselves to a religious life but did not bind themselves by strict vows; small communities still exist in the Netherlands. [f. Lambert *Bègue* (or *le bègue* the stammerer), the founder]

bēg'um *n.* Mohammedan queen or lady of high rank in Hindustan. [Turk. *bīgam*, fem. of *beg* lord]

bėgŭn' past part. of BEGIN.

bėhalf' (-ahf) *n.* Part, account, or interest *of*.

Behar: see BIHAR.

bėhāve' *v.i.* & *refl.* Conduct oneself, act; show good manners.

bėhāv'iour (-*yer*) *n.* Manners, conduct, way of behaving.

bėhāv'iourism (-*yer-*) *n.* Psychological doctrine, based on the 'objective' study of behaviour, that all human actions admit of analysis into stimulus and response. **bėhā'viourist** *n.*

bėhead' (-hĕd) *v.t.* Cut off the head of.

bėhĕld', past t. of BEHOLD.

bėhēm'oth *n.* Enormous creature; in Job xl. 15, prob. the hippopotamus.

bėhĕst' *n.* Command.

bėhīnd' *adv.* & *prep.* In or to the rear (of); hidden (by); past, too late; in concealment; in arrear (with); in support of. ~ *n.* Posterior.

bėhīnd'hănd *adv.* & *pred. adj.* In arrear (*with*); out of date, behind time.

Behn (bān), Mrs Aphra (1640–89). English dramatist and novelist, author of 'Oroonoko'.

bėhōld' *v.t.* (past t. and past part. *bėhĕld'*). See; take notice, attend. **bėhōl'der** *n.*

bėhōl'den *pred. adj.* Under obligation *to*.

bėhōōf' *n.* Benefit, advantage.

bėhōve', bėhōōve' *v.t. impers.* Be incumbent on; befit.

Behring: see BERING.

beige (bāzh) *n.* Fine woollen fabric left undyed and unbleached; the yellowish-grey colour of this. ~ *adj.* Of this colour.

bē'ĭng *n.* (esp.) Existence; constitution, nature, essence; anything that exists; person.

bĕl[1] *n.* Interval of intensity between two sounds, expressed as the common logarithm of the ratio of the two intensities. [A. G. BELL[2]]

Bĕl[2]. Akkadian form of BAAL ('lord'); ~ *and the Dragon*, apocryphal addition to O.T. Book of Daniel.

bėlăb'our (-b*er*) *v.t.* Thrash.

Bela Kun: see KUN.

bėlāt'ėd *adj.* Overtaken by darkness; coming too late.

bėlaud' *v.t.* Load with praise.

bėlay' *v.t.* Coil (running rope) round cleat etc., to secure it; *imp.* (naut.) stop!; *belaying pin*, fixed wooden or iron pin for belaying on.

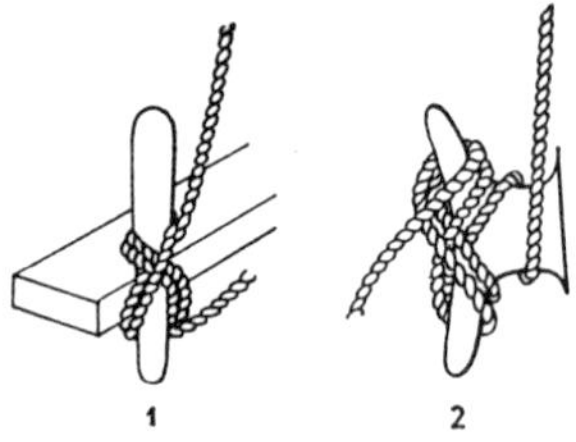

BELAYING

1. Rope belayed to belaying pin.
2. Rope belayed to cleat

bĕl căn'tō *n.* Singing in the Italian manner, characterized by full rich tone and accomplished technique.

bĕlch *v.* Emit wind noisily from throat; utter noisily or drunkenly;

(of gun or volcano) emit (fire, smoke, etc.). ~ *n.* Eructation.

bĕl'cher *n.* Neckerchief with blue ground and large white spots having a dark-blue spot in the centre. [James *Belcher* (1781–1811), English prize-fighter]

bĕl'dam(e) *n.* Old woman, hag; virago.

bėleag'uer (-ger) *v.t.* Besiege.

bĕl'emnīte *n.* Common fossil, occurring in Mesozoic rocks, consisting of the hard part of an ex-

BELEMNITE

tinct marine animal similar to the squid, freq. torpedo-shaped and up to 1 ft in length. [Gk *belemnon* dart]

Bĕlfast' (-ahst). Seaport in Ulster, capital city of N. Ireland; centre of the Irish linen industry.

bĕl'fry *n.* Bell tower; room or storey in which the bells are hung (ill. SPIRE).

Bĕl'ġian (-jan) *adj.* & *n.* (Inhabitant) of Belgium; ~ *Congo*: see CONGO.

Bĕl'ġium (-jum). Small kingdom of N. Europe, the S. part of the Low Countries (see NETHERLANDS, 2), inhabited by people of French and Flemish stock speaking both languages; established in 1831 as an 'independent and perpetually neutral sovereign state'; capital, Brussels. [L, territory occupied by the *Belgae*]

Bĕlgrāde'. Engl. name for Beograd, city on the Danube, capital of Yugoslavia and formerly of Serbia.

Bĕlgrāv'ia. Fashionable residential district of London, S. of Knightsbridge. [f. *Belgrave* Square, named after Belgrave in Leicestershire]

Bē'lial. 'Worthlessness', 'destruction'; but in Deut. xiii. 13 and elsewhere in the O.T. the word is retained untranslated in the phrase 'sons of Belial'; hence, the spirit of evil personified, the devil.

bėlie' *v.t.* Fail to justify or act up to; give false notion of.

bėlief' *n.* Trust, confidence (*in*); acceptance of Christian theology; acceptance as true or existing; thing believed.

bėlieve' *v.* Have faith (*in*), trust word of; accept as true; be of opinion *that.* **bėliev'able** *adj.* **bėliev'er** *n.*

bėlīke' *adv.* (archaic) Probably; perhaps.

Bĕlisār'ius (?505–65). Byzantine general under Justinian; defeated the Vandals, Ostrogoths, and Persians.

Belisha beacon (belēsh'*a*) *n.* Post about 7 ft high surmounted by an amber-coloured globe and erected on pavement at officially recognized pedestrian crossings of the highway, first used in 1934. [Leslie Hore-*Belisha*, Minister of Transport 1931–7]

bėlĭt'tle *v.t.* Disparage, dwarf.

bĕll[1] *n.* Hollow cup-shaped or spherical body of cast metal, emitting clear musical sound when struck by a tongue or clapper suspended inside it or by a hammer

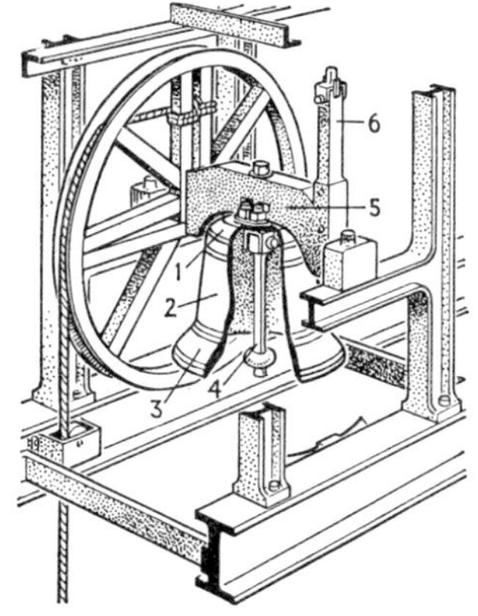

BELL

1. Crown. 2. Waist. 3. Sound-bow. 4. Clapper. 5. Headstock. 6. Stay

impelled by a spring or by electricity, etc.; bell struck on shipboard every half-hour, to indicate the number of half-hours of the watch which have elapsed; bell-shaped object, esp. flower corolla shaped like a bell; ~*-boy,* (U.S.) hotel page-boy; ~*-buoy,* buoy with a bell rung by the motion of the sea; ~*-founder,* caster of bells; ~*-foundry,* place where bells are cast; ~*-glass,* bell-shaped glass used to protect plants; ~*-hop,* (U.S. slang) bell-boy; ~*-man,* crier, town-crier (who attracted attention to his announcements by ringing a bell); ~*-metal,* alloy of copper and tin, with more tin than in ordinary bronze, used for bells; ~*-ringer,* one who rings church-bells, campanologist; ~*-ringing,* art of ringing church-bells, campanology; ~*-tent,* conical tent; ~*-wether,* leading sheep of flock, with bell on neck (also fig.).

Bĕll[2], Alexander Graham (1847–1922). Scottish-American inventor of the telephone.

Bĕll[3], Currer, Ellis, and Acton. Pen-names of Charlotte, Emily, and Anne BRONTË.

bĕlladŏnn'a *n.* Specific name of the deadly nightshade, *Atropa belladonna*; the dried parts of this, containing atropine and related alkaloids, used as a drug which causes marked dilatation of the pupils; ~*-lily,* a S Afr. bulbous plant, *Amaryllis belladonna.* [It., = 'fair lady']

Bĕll'ay, Joachim du (*c* 1524–60). French poet and critic, a member of the PLEIAD (*la Pléaide*) and author of its 'manifesto', 'Deffence et Illustration de la Langue Françoyse' (1549).

bĕlle *n.* Handsome woman; reigning beauty.

Bėllĕ'rophon. Legendary Greek hero, among whose adventures was the slaying of the Chimaera with the help of Pegasus.

belles-lettres (bĕl lĕtr) *n.pl.* Studies, writings, of a purely literary kind; essays, literary criticism, etc., as a division of literature. **bĕllėtrĭs'tic** *adj.*

bĕll'ĭcōse (-s) *adj.* Inclined to war or fighting. **bĕllĭcŏs'ĭty** *n.*

bĕllĭ'ġerent (-j-) *adj.* & *n.* (Nation, party, or person) waging regular war as recognized by the law of nations; of such nation etc. **bĕllĭ'ġerency** *n.*

Bĕllī'nī[1] (-lē-), Giovanni (*c* 1435–1516). Italian painter of the Venetian School; his father Jacopo (*c* 1400–70) and brother Gentile (1429?–1507) were also painters.

Bĕllī'nī[2] (-lē-), Vincenzo (1801–35). Italian composer of operas.

Bĕllōn'a. The Roman goddess of war.

bĕll'ow (-ō) *v.* Roar as a bull; shout, roar with pain; shout loudly and angrily; reverberate, roar. ~ *n.* Bellowing sound.

bĕll'ows (-ōz) *n.pl.* 1. Instrument or machine for driving strong blast of air into fire, organ, etc.; in its simplest form consisting of a pair of boards joined by flexible leather sides, with a valve through which air enters when the boards are moved apart, and a nozzle or tube through which air is forced as they are brought together. 2. Expansible portion of photographic camera (ill. PHOTOGRAPHY).

bĕll'y *n.* Abdomen; stomach; cavity or bulging part of anything. *bellyful,* as much as one wants of anything, esp. fighting; ~ *landing,* landing of aircraft on the under surface of fuselage without use of the undercarriage. ~ *v.* Swell out.

bėlŏng *v.i.* Pertain, be proper, *to.* **bėlŏng'ings** *n.pl.* Person's property, relatives, or luggage.

Bĕlorŭ'ssia (-sha). White Russia, one of the constituent republics of the Soviet Union, including the former provinces of Minsk, Vitebsk, and Mogilov; capital, Minsk. **Bĕlorŭ'ssian** *adj.*& *n.* (Inhabitant, language) of Belorussia; White Russian.

bėloved (-lŭv'ĭd *or* -lŭvd') *adj.* & *past part.* Dearly loved. ~ *n.* Beloved person.

bėlow' (-ō) *adv.* At or to a lower level; in a lower position or rank. ~ *prep.* Lower in position, amount, degree, rank, etc., than; unworthy of, beneath.

Bĕlshăzz'ar. Acc. to the O.T. (Dan. v.), son of Nebuchadnezzar and last king of Babylon, who was killed in the sack of the city by Cyrus (538 B.C.); his doom was foretold by writing which appeared on the walls of his palace at a great banquet. But in inscriptions and documents from Ur, Belshazzar was the son of the last king of Babylon, Nabonidos, and did not himself reign.

bĕlt *n.* 1. Broadish flat strip of leather etc., used to gird or encircle the person, confine some part of the dress, or support various articles; such an article awarded to boxing champion or worn as a mark of rank by knight or earl. 2. Strip of colour etc., line of trees, round or on anything; zone or district; endless strap connecting pulleys in machinery; flexible strip holding machine-gun cartridges and carrying them to firing chamber ~ *v.t.* Put belt round, fasten with belt; thrash with belt.

Bĕl'tāne. Celtic name for 1st May (Old Style), formerly a quarter-day in Scotland, and of the ancient Celtic May Day celebrations, in which bonfires were kindled on the hills.

bĕl'vėdēre *n.* Raised turret or lantern, summer-house, to view scenery from. [It., = 'fine view']

B.E.M. *abbrev.* British Empire Medal.

bėmean' *v.t.* Render mean or base.

bėmīre' *v.t.* Besmirch, befoul.

bėmoan' *v.t.* Lament.

bėmūse' (-z) *v.t.* Make confused or muddled; stupefy.

bĕn[1] *n.* (Sc.) Inner room (usu. of two-roomed cottage); *but and* ~, the outer and inner room, i.e. the whole house.

bĕn[2] *n.* (Sc.) Mountain peak.

Bėnar'ės (-z). Former spelling of **Banaras** (bŭnar'ŭs), city on the Ganges, India, regarded as sacred by the Hindus.

bĕnch *n.* 1. Long seat of wood or stone; thwart of boat. 2. Judge's or magistrate's seat; office of judge, law-court (*King's, Queen's, B*~, a division of the High Court of Justice); judges, magistrates. 3. (parl.) Seats in House of Commons (ill. PARLIAMENT) traditionally appropriated to certain groups, as *back benches*, for members who have never held office, *front benches*, for members of Government and leaders of Opposition, *treasury* ~, front bench on Government side, i.e. on Speaker's right. 4. Working-table in carpenter's shop, laboratory, etc. 5. Level ledge or terrace in masonry, earthwork, hillside, etc.; ~*-mark*, surveyor's mark cut in stone etc. to indicate a point in a line of levels; it consists of a 'broad arrow' with a horizontal line through its apex. ~ *v.t.* Exhibit (dog) at show.

bĕn'cher *n.* (esp.) One of the senior members of the Inns of Court, who form for each Inn a self-elective body managing its affairs.

bĕnd[1] *n.* 1. (naut.) Knot. 2. (her.) Diagonal band from dexter chief to sinister base of shield (ill. HERALDRY); ~ *sinister*, in the opposite direction, a mark of bastardy. 3. Shape in which hides are tanned.

bĕnd[2] *v.* (past t. and past part. *bĕnt*). 1. Force into, receive, curved or angular shape. 2. Tighten up; bring to bear; (pass.) be determined. 3. Attach (sail etc.) with bend or knot. 4. Turn in new direction. 5. Incline from perpendicular; bow, stoop, submit, force to submit. ~ *n.* 1. Bending, curve; bent part. 2. *the bends*, disease with apoplectic and paralytic symptoms incident to those working under high atmospheric pressure, caused by bubbles of dissolved nitrogen emerging from the body fluids, as pressure is reduced, and collecting in joints and blood-vessels.

bĕnd'er *n.* (slang) Sixpenny-bit.

bėneath' *adv.* & *prep.* Below, under, underneath.

bĕnėdī'cĭtė *n.* 1. Blessing invoked; grace at table. 2. One of the Canticles, from the opening words in L, *Benedicite omnia opera.* [L, = 'bless ye']

Bĕn'ėdick. Character in Shakespeare's 'Much Ado about Nothing'; hence, a newly married man.

Bĕn'ėdĭct, St. (*c* 480–543). Italian monk, founder (529) of the first of the monastic orders of the Western Church, for which he built the abbey of Monte Cassino in Campania. **Bĕnėdĭc'tĭne** *adj.* & *n.* 1. (Monk) of this order; ~ *Rule*, the rule written for it by St. Benedict, later adopted by other monastic communities. 2. (-ēn) A liqueur of brandy flavoured with herbs etc., made at Fécamp in Normandy, orig. by the monks of the Benedictine abbey there.

bĕnėdĭc'tion *n.* Utterance of blessing, at end of church service, or at table; *B*~, R.C. service; a blessing, blessedness. **bĕnėdĭc'tory** *adj.*

bĕnėdĭc'tus *n.* 1. 5th movement in the service of Mass, beginning with *Benedictus qui venit.* 2. Hymn of Zacharias (Luke i. 68) used as a canticle in the Church of England. [L, = 'blessed']

bĕnėfăc'tion *n.* Doing good; charitable gift.

bĕn'ėfăctor, bĕn'ėfăctrėss *ns.* Person who has given friendly aid; patron of, or donor to, cause or charity.

bĕn'ėfĭce *n.* Church living. **bĕn'ėficed** (-ĭst) *adj.*

bėnĕf'ĭcent *adj.* Doing good, showing active kindness. **bėnĕf'ĭcence** *n.*

bĕnėfĭ'cial (-shl) *adj.* 1. Advantageous. 2. (law) Of, having, the usufruct of property. **bĕnėfĭ'cially** *adv.*

bĕnėfĭ'ciary (-sha-) *adj.* Holding or held by feudal tenure. ~ *n.* Holder by feudal tenure; holder of living; receiver of benefits.

bĕn'ėfĭt *n.* 1. Advantage. 2. Allowance, pension, etc. to which person is entitled. 3. Exemption from ordinary courts by the privilege of one's order (e.g. ~ *of clergy*). 4. Theatre performance, game, etc., of which proceeds go to particular players or charity. ~ *v.* Do good to; receive benefit.

Bĕn'ėlŭx. Collective name for *Be*lgium, the *Ne*therlands, and *Lux*emburg, esp. with reference to their economic collaboration.

Beneš (bĕn'ĕsh), Eduard (1884–1948). President of Czechoslovakia 1935–8 and 1946–8.

bėnĕv'olent *adj.* Desirous of doing good; charitable. **bėnĕv'olently** *adv.* **bėnĕv'olence** *n.*

B.Eng. *abbrev.* Bachelor of Engineering.

Bengal (bĕnggawl'). District of the Ganges delta, formerly a province of British India, now (since 1947) divided into *West* ~, a state of India, and *East* ~, a province of Pakistan, = East Pakistan; *Bay of* ~, part of Indian Ocean lying between Indian peninsula and Burma; ~ *light*, firework with steady vivid light, used as a signal; ~ *tiger*, the tiger proper, so called from its abundance in lower Bengal.

Benga'lĭ (bĕnggaw-) *adj.* & *n.* (Of the) Indo-European language spoken in Bengal; (native) of Bengal.

bėnight'ėd (-nīt-) *adj.* Overtaken by night; involved in moral or intellectual darkness; ignorant.

bėnign' (-īn) *adj.* Gracious, gentle; fortunate, salutary; (of diseases) mild, not malignant.

benig'nant *adj.* Kind, kindly, to inferiors; gracious; salutary.

benig'nancy, benig'nity *ns.*

bĕn'ison (-zn) *n.* (archaic) Blessing.

Bĕn'jamin. The smallest of the 'tribes of Israel', named after Jacob's youngest and favourite son (see Gen. xxxv. 8, xlii, etc.).

Bĕn Nĕv'is. Mountain in Inverness-shire, the highest peak (4,406 ft) in the British Isles.

bĕnt[1] *n.* Reedy or rush-like stiff-stemmed grass of various kinds; the genus *Agrostis*; stiff flower-stalk, old stalk, of grasses; heath, unenclosed pasture.

bĕnt[2] *n.* Inclination, bias.

bĕnt[3] past t. & past part. of BEND.

Bĕn'tham (-tam), Jeremy (1748–1832). English Utilitarian philosopher, and writer on ethics, jurisprudence, and political economy; prison and poor-law reformer; he believed that the end of life is happiness (which he identified with pleasure) and that the highest morality is the pursuit of the greatest happiness of the greatest number. **Bĕn'thamĭsm, Bĕn'thamīte** *ns.*

bĕn trova'tō (-ah-) *adj.* Well invented, characteristic if not true. [It.]

bėnŭmb' (-m) *v.t.* Make torpid; paralyse.

bĕn'zēne *n.* (chem.) Aromatic hydrocarbon (C_6H_6), a colourless, volatile, and highly inflammable liquid obtained from coal-tar etc., used as a solvent and in the chemical industry; ~ *ring*, the ring-like arrangement of the 6 carbon atoms in the benzene molecule.

bĕn'zine (-ēn) *n.* A mixture of hydrocarbons obtained from petroleum and used as a solvent, for removing grease stains etc.

bĕn'zoĭn *n.* 1. (*gum-*~) Fragrant aromatic resin obtained from various trees of the genus *Styrax* from Sumatra and Siam, and used in perfumery, medicine, etc. 2. (chem.) A constituent of gum-benzoin. **bĕnzō'ic** *adj.* (chem.) Of or derived from benzoin; ~ *acid*, benzene carboxylic acid, C_6H_5COOH. [Fr. *benjoin* f. Arab. *luban jawi* Java frankincense]

bĕn'zŏl, -ōle *n.* Earlier name, still in trade use, of BENZENE.

bĕn'zoline (-ēn) *n.* (Trade-name for) BENZINE.

Bē'owulf (-wo͝o-). Legendary Swedish hero celebrated in the Old English epic poem, 'Beowulf'.

bėqueath' (-dh), *v.t.* Leave by will.

bėquĕst' *n.* Bequeathing; thing bequeathed.

Béranger (bārahṅzhā'), Pierre Jean de (1780–1857). French poet, author of many satirical and political songs of great contemporary influence.

bėrāte' *v.t.* (now chiefly U.S.) Scold.

Bėr̃b'er *adj.* & *n.* (Member) of a fair-skinned aboriginal people of N. Africa.

berceuse (bãrsẽrz') *n.* Cradle-song; composition in style of this.

bėreave' *v.t.* 1. Rob, dispossess *of.* 2. Leave desolate; deprive of relation, wife, etc. **bėreave'ment** *n.*

bėrĕft', past. t. & past part. of BEREAVE in sense 1.

Bĕrėnī'cė[1] (3rd c. B.C.). Egyptian queen, wife of Ptolemy III Euergetes; during his absence on a warlike expedition in Syria, she dedicated her hair as votive offering for his safe return; the hair was stolen, and legend said that it was carried to the heavens, where it became the constellation *Coma Berenices*.

Bĕrėnī'cė[2] (b. *c* A.D. 28). Jewish princess, called Bernice in Acts xxv; daughter of Agrippa I and wife of her uncle Herod, king of Chalcis; after his death she lived with her brother Agrippa II.

beret (bĕ'rā) *n.* Round flat woollen cap, worn by Basque peasantry; similar cap worn esp. as part of sports or holiday costume or as a military cap.

bẽrg *n.* = ICEBERG.

bẽrg'amŏt[1] *n.* 1. Tree of the lemon kind, *Citrus bergamia*; the fragrant oil extracted from the fruit. 2. Various plants of the family *Labiatae*, esp. *Monarda* species. [f. *Bergamo* in Italy]

bẽrg'amŏt[2] *n.* A fine kind of pear. [Turk. *beg-armūdi*, prince's pear]

Bergerăc (bãrzh'-), Cyrano de (1619–55). French soldier and author of comedies.

Bergson (bãrg'sawṅ), Henri (1859–1941). French philosopher who regarded reality as change and movement, 'becoming' rather than 'being'. **Bẽrgsōn'ian** *adj.* & *n.*

bĕ'rĭbĕrĭ *n.* Disease, with symptoms including polyneuritis, oedema, heart failure, etc., caused by deficiency of vitamin B_1 in diet and affecting chiefly tropical and sub-tropical populations whose staple food is rice from which the outer layer of the grain (containing the vitamin) has been polished away. [Sinhalese *beri* weakness]

Ber'ĭng or **Behr'ĭng** (bār-), Vitus Jonassen (1680–1741). Danish navigator and explorer of Arctic Asia; sailed along coast of Siberia from Kamchatka and reached America from the E.; died on an island near Kamchatka subsequently called ~ *Island*; ~ *Sea*, northernmost part of Pacific; ~ *Strait*, strait between Asia and America, connecting Bering Sea with Arctic Ocean.

Berkeley (bãrk'lĭ), George (1685–1753). Irish bishop and idealist philosopher. **Berkelei'an** (-lē'*an*) *adj.* & *n.*

bẽrkēl'ium *n.* (chem.) A metallic radio-active transuranic element not occurring in nature but made artificially; symbol Bk, at. no. 97, principal isotope 243. [*Berkeley*, Calif., where first made]

Berks. *abbrev.* Berkshire.

Berk'shire (bãrk-). Southern inland county of England, on right bank of Thames; breed of black pigs with occas. white markings.

Bẽrlĭn'[1]. Chief city of Germany, on river Spree; formerly capital of Prussia; capital of Germany from 1871; since 1945 divided into *East* ~, capital of Eastern Germany, and *West* ~, an isolated part of Western Germany; ~ *woolwork*, coarse embroidery in coloured wools. **Bẽrlĭn'er** *n.* Native, inhabitant, of Berlin.

bẽrlĭn'[2] *n.* Four-wheeled covered carriage with hooded seat behind, invented in Berlin in 17th c., pop. in France and England in the 18th c.

Berlioz (bãrl'ĭōz), Hector (1803–69). French composer of operas, symphonic works, etc.

bẽrm *n.* Narrow space or ledge (esp., fort.) space between ditch and parapet.

Bermūd'a. ~ *Islands, the Bermudas*, British group in W. Atlantic, discovered early in 16th c. by Juan Bermudez, a Spaniard; ~ *rig*, rig for a yacht, carrying a very high tapering sail (*Bermudian mainsail*) (ill. YACHT). **Bermūd'ian** *adj.* & *n.*

Bernadŏtte' (bãr-), Jean Baptiste (1763–1844). French soldier; one of Napoleon's marshals; was adopted by Charles XIII of Sweden in 1810 and himself became king (as Charles XIV) in 1818, thus founding the present royal house.

Bẽrn'ard[1], St. (1090–1153). French churchman, first abbot of Clairvaux; he reformed the Cistercian Order and preached the 2nd Crusade.

Bẽrn'ard[2], St., of Menthon (923–1008). Founder of the Alpine hospices of the Great and Little St Bernard; *St.* ~ (*dog*), a breed of large and very intelligent dogs, of the mastiff type, usu. light brown and white; orig. bred by the monks of the St. Bernard hospices and trained to search for travellers lost in the snowdrifts of the Alpine passes (ill. DOG).

Bernard[3] (bãrnãr'), Claude (1813–78). French physiologist; famous for his research on the pancreas and the glycogenic function of the liver, and his discovery of the vaso-motor system.

Bernardin de Saint-Pierre (bãrn'ãrdăn), Jacques Henri (1737–1814). French naturalist; author of the novel 'Paul et Virginie'.

Berne (bãrn). Canton and capital city of Switzerland.

Bern'hãrdt (bãr-, -t), Sarah. Name adopted by the French romantic. and tragic actress Rosine Bernard (1845–1923).

Bernini (bãrnēn'ĭ), Giovanni Lorenzo (1598–1680). Italian baroque architect and sculptor; designer of the colonnade of St. Peter's in Rome.

bĕ'rry *n.* 1. Any small, round, or oval juicy fruit without a stone; grain (of wheat etc.). 2. (bot.) Fruit of any size with seed(s) enclosed in pulp (ill. FRUIT). 3. The eggs of a lobster.

bẽrs'erk(er) *n.* Wild Norse warrior fighting with mad frenzy; *go berserk* (usu. berzẽrk', *also* besẽrk', bẽr'serk), behave thus. [Icel., prob. = 'bear-coat']

bẽrth *n.* 1. Convenient sea-room; room for ship to swing at anchor; ship's place at wharf. 2. Sleeping-place in ship, railway-carriage, etc. 3. Situation, appointment. ~ *v.t.* Moor (ship).

bẽrth'a[1], **bẽrthe** *n.* Deep falling collar or small cape on dress.

Bẽrth'a[2]. In the war of 1914–18, a German gun of large bore, esp. (*Big* ~) a long-range gun used to bombard Paris in 1918. [Frau *Berta* Krupp von Bohlen und Halbach, head of the Krupp steel works in Germany]

Bertillon (bĕrtēyawṅ'), Alphonse (1853–1914). French inventor and general anthropologist; advocate of a system of anthropometric measurements for the identification of criminals, and esp. of the use of finger-prints for this purpose.

Berwickshire (bĕ'rĭk-). County of SE. Scotland.

bĕ'rȳl *n.* Transparent precious stone of pale-green colour passing into light-blue, yellow, and white, chemically a beryllium aluminium silicate; mineral species including also the emerald, which differs from the beryl only in its rich green colour, due to traces of chromium.

bėry̆ll'ium *n.* A very light metallic element obtained from beryl; symbol Be, at. no. 4, at. wt 9·0122.

Berzēl'ius, Jons Jakob (1779–1848). Swedish chemist; discovered selenium and other elements, and invented the present system of representing chemical elements by symbols.

Bĕs'ant (-z-), Mrs Annie (1847–1933). English writer and ardent supporter of socialism and agnosticism; she became a theosophist in 1887 and President of the Theosophical Society in 1907; was active in the cause of Indian self-government and in 1917 was President of the Indian National Congress.

bėseech *v.t.* (past t. and past part. *besought*) Ask earnestly for; entreat.

bėseem' *v.t.* Suit, be fitting or suitable to.

bėsĕt' *v.t.* Hem in; assail, encompass.

bėshrew' (-o͞o) *v.t.* (archaic, only in imprecations) Plague take.

bėsīde' *prep.* At the side of, close to; compared with; wide of; ~ *oneself*, out of one's wits.

bėsīdes' (-dz) *adv.* & *prep.* In addition (to); otherwise, else; except.

bėsiege' *v.t.* Lay siege to; assail, crowd round.

bėslăv'er *v.t.* Slaver upon or over; flatter fulsomely.

bėslŏbb'er *v.t.* Beslaver; kiss effusively.

bėsmear' *v.t.* Smear, bedaub.

bėsmīrch' *v.t.* Soil, discolour; sully.

bĕs'om (-z-) *n.* Bundle of twigs tied round stick for sweeping; (colloq.) hussy.

bėsŏt' *v.t.* Stupefy mentally or morally. **bėsŏtt'ėd** *adj.*

bėspătt'er *v.t.* Spatter; asperse.

bėspeak' *v.t.* (past t. *bespōke'*, past part. *bespōk'en*). Engage beforehand; order; speak to (poet.); indicate, be evidence of. **bėspōke'** *adj.* Ordered (now only in *bespoke tailoring, boots,* etc., as opp. to 'ready-made').

bėsprinkle (-ing'kl) *v.t.* Sprinkle.

Bĕss'ėmer, Sir Henry (1813–98). English engineer; inventor of ~ *process* for making steel, a process in which iron is decarbonized by blowing a blast of air through the molten metal.

bĕst *adj.* & *adv.* Of, in, the most excellent kind, way, etc.; ~ *man*, bridegroom's supporter at wedding; ~ *seller* (orig. U.S.), book with large sale. ~ *v.t.* Get the better of.

bėstead' (-ĕd) *v.* Avail, help.

bĕs'tial *adj.* Of, like, a beast; brutish, barbarous; depraved, obscene. **bĕstiăl'ity** *n.* **bĕs'tialize** *v.t.*

bĕs'tiary *n.* Medieval moralizing treatise on beasts.

bėstīr' *v.refl.* Exert, rouse.

bėstow' (-ō) *v.t.* Confer as gift; deposit, lodge. **bėstow'al** *n.*

bėstrew' (-o͞o) *v.t.* (past part. *bestrowed'* or *bestrewn'*). Strew.

bėstrīde' *v.t.* (past t. *bėstrōde*, past part. *bėstrĭdd'en*). Get or sit upon with legs astride; stand astride over.

bĕt *v.* (past t. and past part. *bĕt*). Risk one's money etc. against another's on result of doubtful event. ~ *n.* Money etc. so risked.

bē't'a. 2nd letter of Gk alphabet (B, β), used of the 2nd star in a constellation, and in other classifications; ~ *brass*, compound of zinc and copper with special metallurgical properties; ~ *particles*, fast-moving electrons emitted by radio-active substances, orig. regarded as rays, and having greater penetrating power than alpha particles and less than gamma rays.

bėtāke' *v.refl.* (past t. *bėto͝ok*, past part. *bėtāk'en*). Commit (oneself) *to* some cause or means; turn one's course, go.

bē't'el *n.* Leaf of a shrubby evergreen plant, *Piper betle*, which is wrapped round a few parings of areca nut and chewed by natives of India etc.; hence (erron.) ~ *nut*, the areca nut. [Malay *veṭṭila* simple leaf]

Bĕtelgeuse' (-go͞oz). Yellowish-red variable star, the brightest in the constellation of Orion.

bête noire (bāt nwahr) *n.* (One's) abomination.

Bĕth'el. Village in Palestine, near Jerusalem. **bĕth'el** *n.* Hallowed spot; Nonconformist, esp. Methodist or Baptist, chapel; seamen's church (ashore or floating). [Heb., = 'House of God'; see Gen. xxviii. 17–19]

bėthink' *v.refl.* (past t. and past part. *bethought'*). Reflect, stop to think; remind oneself.

Bĕth'lėhĕm. Town in Palestine (now in Jordan), near Jerusalem, birthplace of Jesus.

Beth'mann-Hŏllweg (bāt-, -vāg), Theobald von (1856–1921). German statesman, Chancellor of the German Empire 1909–17.

bėtīde' *v.i.* Happen, befall.

bėtīmes' (-mz) *adv.* Early; in good time.

bėtōk'en *v.t.* Be token of; presage; indicate.

bĕt'ony *n.* Labiate plant, *Stachys officinalis* (= *S. betonica*) with spike of reddish-purple flowers; *water* ~, *Scrophularia aquatica*, common beside streams.

bėto͝ok', past t. of BETAKE.

bėtray' *v.t.* Give up or reveal treacherously; be disloyal to; lead astray; reveal involuntarily; be evidence or symptom of. **bėtray'-al, bėtrayer** *ns.*

bėtrōth' (-dh) *v.t.* Bind with a promise to marry. **betrōth'al** *n.* **betrōthed'** (-dhd) *adj.* & *n.*

bĕtt'er *adj. adv.* & *n.* Of, in, a more excellent kind or way. ~ *v.* Improve; surpass. **bĕtt'erment** *n.* Improvement.

bėtween' *prep.* In, into, along, or across, an interval, or space bounded by (*lies* ~ *Paris and Rouen*; *happened* ~ *Monday and Friday*); separating; connecting; intermediately in time, place or order (to); shared by, confined to; to and from; reciprocally on the part of; ~*-maid*, servant helping two others, as cook and housemaid; ~ *whiles*, in the intervals. ~ *adv.* Between two points.

bėtwīxt' *prep.* & *adv.* Between.

bĕv'el *n.* 1. Joiner's and mason's tool, a flat rule with movable tongue or arm stiffly-jointed to one end, for setting off angles (ill. SQUARE). 2. Slope from right angle, or from horizontal or vertical, surface so sloped (ill. MOULDING); ~*-wheel*, toothed wheel whose working-face is oblique with the axis (ill. GEAR). ~ *v.* Impart bevel to, slant.

bĕv'erage *n.* Drink.

Bĕv'in boy *n.* Youth selected by lot to do his war-service in a coal-mine. [f. name of Ernest *Bevin*, Minister of Labour and National Service 1940–5]

bĕv'y *n.* Company (esp. of ladies, roes, quails, or larks).

bėwail' *v.t.* Wail over, mourn for.

bėwāre' *v.* (used without inflexions). Be cautious, take heed (*of, lest, how*).

bėwĭl'der *v.t.* Lead astray, confuse, perplex. **bėwĭl'derment** *n.*

bėwĭtch' *v.t.* Affect by magic; charm, enchant.

bey (bā) *n.* Turkish governor of province or district. **bey'lic** *n.* District or jurisdiction of bey. [Turk. *beg* lord]

Beyle, Henri: see STENDHAL.

bėyŏnd' *adv.* & *prep.* At, to, the further side (of), past, besides; out of reach, comprehension or range of. ~ *n.* The future life, the unknown; *the back of* ~, a very remote or out-of-the-way place.

bĕz'ant (*or* bĭzănt') *n.* 1. (hist.) Gold coin current in England in 9th and 10th centuries; later, silver coin. 2. (her.) Roundel or (ill. HERALDRY). [f. *Byzantium*, where orig. struck]

bĕz'el *n.* Sloped edge or face of chisel etc. (ill. CHISEL); oblique sides or faces of cut gem (ill. GEM); groove holding gem or watch-glass in setting.

bezique' (-ēk) *n.* Card-game for two players who score chiefly by holding various sequences and combinations of cards; the combination of queen of spades and knave of diamonds in this game

b.f. *abbrev.* Bloody fool; bold face (type); brought forward.

B.F.B.S. *abbrev.* British and Foreign Bible Society.

b(h)ăng *n.* Leaves of Indian hemp mixed with resin used as intoxicant and narcotic.

b.h.p. *abbrev.* Brake horsepower.

Bhutan (bōōtăhn'). Independent State lying on the SE. of the Himalayas.

bi- *prefix.* Twice-, doubly, having two.

bī'as *n.* 1. (in bowls) Curving course in which bowl runs, shape of bowl causing it to do this. 2. Inclination, predisposition, prejudice, influence. 3. (dressmaking) Diagonal across material, direction in which it stretches. ~ *v.t.* Give bias to, influence, prejudice.

bĭb[1] *v.i.* Drink much or often, tipple.

bĭb[2] *n.* Cloth placed under child's chin to keep dress-front clean; apron-top.

Bī'ble *n.* Old and New Testament, edition or copy of these; sacred book, authoritative textbook; ~ *Belt,* those parts of the (Southern and Middle Western) U.S. reputed to be fanatically puritan or fundamentalist; ~ *Christians,* Protestant sect, existing chiefly in SW. England, founded 1816 by a Wesleyan preacher, William O'Bryan; ~ *oath,* solemn oath taken on the Bible.

bĭb'lical *adj.* Of, in, concerning, the Bible.

bĭblĭŏg'raphy *n.* History of books, their authorship, editions, etc.; book containing such details; list of books of any author, subject, printer, etc. **bĭblĭŏg'rapher** *n.* **bĭblĭogrăph'ical** *adj.*

bĭblĭŏl'ater *n.* Worshipper of books. **bĭblĭŏl'atry** *n.* **bĭblĭŏl'atrous** *adj.*

bĭbliomān'ĭa *n.* Rage for collecting books. **bĭbliomān'ĭăc** *n.* & *adj.*

bĭb'lĭophīle *n.* Book-lover.

bĭb'ūlous *adj.* Addicted to drinking.

bicăm'eral *adj.* With two (legislative) chambers.

bicar̂b'onate *n.* 1. Salt of carbonic acid in which only one hydrogen atom is replaced by a metal. 2. (pop.) Sodium bicarbonate, $NaHCO_3$, used in medicine and as constituent of baking-powder etc.

bice *n.* Dullish blue pigment obtained from smalt; *green* ~, dull green pigment made by adding yellow orpiment to smalt; the colours of these pigments.

bicĕntĕn'ary (*or* bīcĕn'tėn-) *n.* 200th anniversary.

bicĕntĕnn'ial *adj.* Occurring every, lasting for, 200 years. ~ *n.* (U.S.) Bicentenary.

bicĕph'alous *adj.* Two-headed.

bī'cĕps *n.* & *adj.* (Muscle) with two heads or attachments, esp. that on front of upper arm, which bends forearm (ill. MUSCLE).

bĭck'er *v.i.* & *n.* Quarrel, wrangle.

bicŭs'pĭd *adj* & *n.* (Tooth) with two cusps.

bī'cȳcle *n.* Vehicle having two tandem wheels to which the rider, seated astride a saddle, communicates motion by two pedals operating a crank; *motor-~*, similar more heavily built vehicle propelled by internal combustion engine. ~ *v.* Ride this. **bī'cȳclist** *n.*

bĭd *v.* (past t. *băd, bāde, bĭd,* past part. *bĭdd'en, bĭd*). Command to; invite; salute with (greeting etc.); offer (price) for a thing; (at bridge) make a bid. ~ *n.* Offer of price, esp. at an auction; (at bridge) announcement of the number of tricks that a player will undertake to win at no trumps or with a specified suit as trumps

bidd'able *adj.* Obedient; (of a hand at bridge) on which a bid can reasonably be made.

bīde *v.* Abide (archaic except in ~ *one's time*).

bidet (bēd'ā) *n.* Shallow oval basin on low stand used in washing the person.

bīĕnn'ial *adj.* Lasting, recurring every, two years. ~ *n.* Plant which springs from seed one year and flowers, fructifies, and dies the next. **bīĕnn'ially** *adv.*

bier (bēr) *n.* Movable stand on which corpse or coffin is taken to grave.

B.I.F. *abbrev.* British Industries Fair.

bĭff *n.* (slang) Blow, whack. ~ *v.t.* Strike, hit.

bĭff'in *n.* Deep-red variety of cooking-apple. [= *beefing,* f. *beef* (with ref. to the colour)]

bĭf'ĭd *adj.* Divided by a deep cleft into two lobes.

bīfōc'al *adj.* (Of spectacle lenses) having two segments of different focal lengths, the upper for distant, the lower for near, vision. **bīfōc'als** *n.pl.* Bifocal spectacles.

bīfōl'iate *adj.* Of two leaves.

bī'furcāte (-fer-) *v.* Divide into two branches, fork. ~ *adj.* Forked. **bīfurcā'tion** *n.*

bĭg *adj.* & *adv.* Large; grown-up; pregnant; important; boastful(ly); *B~ Ben,* great bell which strikes the hours in Houses of Parliament; ~ *business,* commerce on the grand scale; *the ~ noise,* the most important person; ~ *three, our,* etc., the predominant few; ~ *top,* circus marquee; *big'wig,* person of importance. **bĭg'nėss** *n.*

bĭg'amist *n.* Person living in bigamy.

bĭg'amous *adj.* Guilty of, involving, bigamy. **bĭg'amously** *adv.*

bĭg'amy *n.* Second marriage while first is still valid.

bight (bīt) *n.* Loop of a rope; curve, recess, of coast, river, etc., bay.

bĭg'ot *n.* One who holds irrespective of reason, and attaches disproportionate weight to, some creed or view. **bĭg'otėd** *adj.* **bĭg'otry** *n.*

Bihar̂', Bė-. Former province of British India, now (since 1947) a State of India (capital, Patna); also, a town in the State of Bihar.

bijou (bēzh'ōō) *n.* Jewel, trinket. ~ *adj.* Small and elegant.

bīke *n.* & *v.i.* (colloq.) Bicycle.

bĭki'ni (-kē-) *n.* Scanty two-piece swim-suit for women. [f. name of island in the Pacific]

bīlāb'ĭal *adj.* & *n.* (phonetics) (Consonant) produced by the junction or apposition of both lips. **bīlāb'ĭally** *adv.*

bīlăt'eral *adj.* Of, on, with, two sides; affecting, between, two parties; ~ *symmetry,* symmetry about a plane, such that one half is a mirror-image of the other (as left and right in human body and in all other vertebrate and many invertebrate animals). **bīlăt'erally** *adv.*

bĭl'berry *n.* The small, blue-black edible berry of *Vaccinium myrtillus,* a dwarf hardy shrub of N. Europe abundant on heaths and stony moors and in mountain woods (also *blaeberry, whortleberry,* U.S. *blueberry*).

bĭl'bō *n.* (hist.) Sword noted for its temper and elasticity. [*Bilbao* in Spain]

bĭl'boes (-ōz) *n.* Iron bar with sliding shackles for prisoner's ankles, and a lock to fix one end of the bar to the floor or ground.

bīle *n.* Bitter, brownish-yellow fluid secreted by the liver and poured into the duodenum in the process of digestion; one of the 'four humours' of early physiology; (fig.) anger, peevishness.

bĭlge *n.* Nearly horizontal part of ship's bottom (ill. SHIP); foulness that collects in the bilge; (slang) nonsense, rot; 'belly' of a cask; *~-water,* foul water that collects in ship's bilge. ~ *v.* Stave in the bilge of, spring a leak in the bilge; bulge, swell.

bĭl'iary *adj.* Of the bile.

bīlĭng'ual (-nggw-) *adj.* Having, written in, speaking, etc., two languages. **bīlĭng'ualism, bīlĭng'ualist** *ns.*

bĭl'ious *adj.* Arising from derangement of the bile; liable to, affected by, this. **bĭl'iously** *adv.* **bĭl'iousnėss** *n.*

bĭlk *v.t.* 1. (cribbage) Balk or spoil person's score in his crib. 2. Evade payment of (creditor, esp. taxi-driver, or bill); cheat, give the slip to. **bĭlk'er** *n.*

bĭll[1] *n.* 1. Obsolete weapon, varying from simple concave blade with long wooden handle, to kind of concave axe with spike at the back of shaft terminating in a spear-head (ill. SPEAR). 2. (also *bill'hook*) Implement used for pruning etc., having long blade with concave edge, often ending in a sharp hook, and a wooden handle in line with blade (ill. HOOK).

bĭll[2] *n.* 1. Bird's beak, esp. when slender or flattened; horny beak of platypus. 2. Narrow promontory. 3. (naut.) Point of anchor-fluke. ~ *v.i.* Stroke bill with bill (as doves); (also ~ *and coo*) exchange caresses.

bill[3] *n.* 1. Draft of proposed Act of Parliament. 2. (law) Written statement of (plaintiff's) case; *find a true* ~, (of Grand Jury) send case for trial. 3. Note of charges for goods delivered or services rendered. 4. Poster, placard; programme of entertainment. 5. (~ *of exchange*), written order to pay sum on given date to drawer or named payee. 6. (U.S.) Bank-note. 7. ~ *of fare*, list of dishes to be served; ~ *of health*, certificate regarding infectious disease on ship or in port at time of sailing; ~ *of lading*, ship-master's receipt for goods to consignor, undertaking to deliver them to a specified port; ~ *of sale*, transferring personal property or authorizing its seizure by lender of money if payment is delayed; *bills of mortality*, (hist.) weekly return of deaths in London and district, which began to be published in 1592; *within the bills of mortality*, within the district covered by these bills; ~*-broker*, dealer in bills of exchange; ~*-poster*, man who pastes up placards. ~ *v.t.* Announce, put in the programme; plaster with placards.

bĭll'abŏng *n.* (Austral.) Branch of river that comes to a dead end.

bĭll'ėt[1] *n.* Order requiring householder to board and lodge soldier etc. bearing it; place where such a person is lodged; appointment, situation. ~ *v.t.* Quarter (soldiers etc.) *on* town, householder, etc., *in, at*, place. **bĭllėtee'** *n.* Person billeted. **bĭllėtôr'** *n.* Person who assigns billet; one who receives a billetee into his or her household.

bĭll'ėt[2] *n.* 1. Thick piece of firewood. 2. Small bar of metal. 3. (archit.) Short roll inserted at intervals in hollow moulding (ill. MOULDING).

billet-doux (bĭlĭdōō') *n.* (pl. *billets-doux*). Love-letter (joc.).

bĭll'iards (-lyardz) *n.pl.* Game played with three small solid balls, one red, one plain white, and one spot white, on a horizontal rectangular table, the standard size of which is 12 ft by 6, covered with

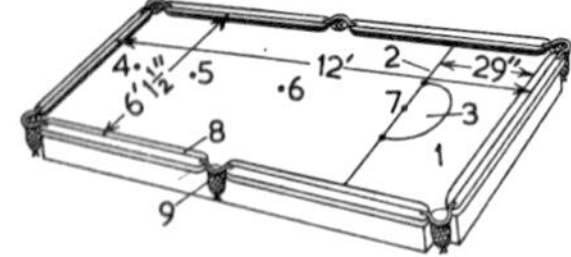

BILLIARD TABLE

1. Balk. 2. Balk line. 3. D. 4. Billiard spot. 5. Pyramid spot. 6. Centre spot. 7. Centre spot of D. 8. Cushion. 9. Pocket

smooth green cloth, surrounded by a cushioned ledge, and provided with six 'pockets' at the corners and in the middle of the long sides. The balls are driven about by means of long leather-tipped tapering sticks called *cues* and points are scored by driving the balls into the pockets and by CANNONS etc.; *billiard-marker*, one (esp. attendant) who marks the score at billiards; *billiard-table*, table on which billiards are played.

Bĭll'ĭngsgate (-z-). Fish-market established at one of the old gates of London on the riverside. **bĭll'ĭngsgate** *n.* Foul language (for which the market was famous in 17th c.).

bĭll'ion (-yon) *n.* A million millions; (U.S.) a thousand millions. **bĭll'ionaire'** *n.* One whose wealth is a billion (dollars, pounds, etc.) or more.

bĭll'on *n.* Alloy of gold or silver with a predominating amount of some base metal.

bĭll'ow (-ō) *n.* Great wave; anything that sweeps along, as sound etc. ~ *v.i.* Rise, move, in billows. **bĭll'owy** (-ōĭ) *adj.*

bĭll'y *n.* (orig. Austral.) Tin can for boiling water etc. in camping.

bĭll'ycŏck *n.* Man's round, low-crowned, hard felt hat; bowler.

bĭll'y-goat *n.* Male goat.

bīlōbed' (-bd) *adj.* Having, or divided into, two lobes.

bĭl'tŏng *n.* Strips of sun-dried lean meat (antelope, buffalo, etc.).

bīmėtăll'ĭc *adj.* 1. Of two metals; ~ *strip*, sensitive element in some thermostats, made of two bands of different metals, one of which expands more than the other when temperature rises, and so causes the strip to bend. 2. Using both gold and silver as currency, at fixed ratio to each other. **bīmĕt'allĭsm, bīmĕtallĭst** *ns.*

bī-monthly (-mŭ-) *adj.* & *n.* (Periodical) produced or occurring every two months.

bĭn *n.* Receptacle (orig. of wicker, now usu. of wood, and fixed) for corn, coal, bottled wine, etc.; receptacle for household rubbish; wine from special bin; canvas receptacle used in hop-picking.

bīn'ary *adj.* Dual, of or involving pairs; ~ *compound*, (chem.) one consisting of two elements; ~ *form*, (mus.) applied to a melody or composition having two sections, the 2nd of which is balanced against the 1st and seems to answer it; ~ *measure*, (mus.) having two beats to a bar; ~ *scale*, (math.) with 2 (not 10) as basis of notation; ~ *stars, system*, two stars revolving round each other, or round a common centre.

bīnd *v.* (past t. and past part. *bound*). 1. Tie, fasten; put in bonds, restrain; fasten or hold together. 2. Be obligatory, impose constraint or duty upon; (pass.) be required by duty; subject to legal obligation; indenture as apprentice. 3. Make costive. 4. Bandage; wreath *with*; edge *with* braid, iron, etc.; fasten (sheets, book) into cover.

bīn'der *n.* (esp.) 1. Book-binder. 2. Long broad band of material to bind round body. 3. Long stone extending through a wall, bond-stone (ill. MASONRY). 4. Reaping-and-binding machine.

bīn'dĭng *adj.* Obligatory (*on*). ~ *n.* (esp.) Book-cover; braid etc. for binding raw edges of textiles.

bīnd'weed *n.* Convolvulus.

bīne *n.* Flexible shoot; stem of climbing plant, esp. the hop.

Binet (bēn'ā), Alfred (1857–1911). French psychologist; experimented in the measurement of intelligence and was the first to devise intelligence-tests.

bĭnge (-nj) *n.* (slang) Heavy drinking-bout; spree.

bĭnn'acle *n.* Box for compass on a ship.

bĭnŏc'ūlar *adj.* Adapted for both eyes; ~ *vision*, type of vision, peculiar to man and some other primates, in which both eyes co-operate in observing the same object and receive a stereoscopic

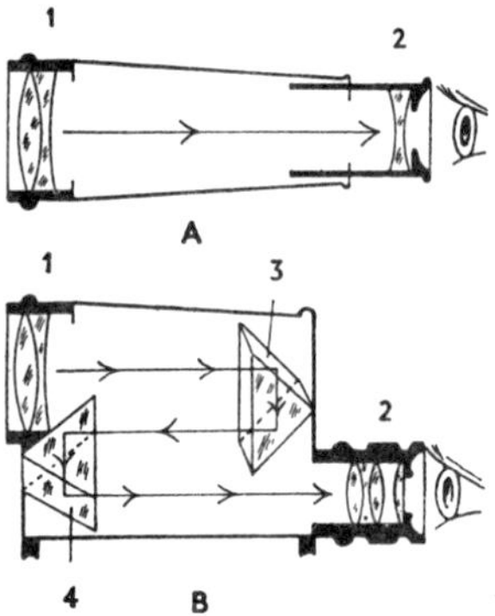

BINOCULARS: A. GALILEAN. B. PRISMATIC

1. Object glass. 2. Eyepiece. 3. Vertical prism. 4. Horizontal prism

impression. ~ *n.* (usu. pl.) Field- or opera-glass for both eyes.

bīnōm'ial *adj.* Consisting of two terms; ~ *theorem*, the general algebraic formula, discovered by Newton, by which any power of a binomial quantity may be found without performing the progressive multiplications. ~ *n.* Algebraic expression consisting of two terms joined by + or −.

bīnŏm'ĭnal *adj.* Of two names; ~ *system*, (biol.) system of nomenclature by genus and species.

bīo- *prefix.* (Course of) life of, concerning, organic life.

bīochĕm'ĭcal (-k-) *adj.* Of biochemistry.

bīochĕm'ĭstry *n.* Science dealing with the chemical properties of the parts of living organisms. **bīochĕm'ĭst** *n.*

bīoclīmatŏl'ogy *n.* Study of climate in relation to life and esp. to human health.

bīogĕn'ėsis *n.* The theory of the descent of living matter from living matter (opp. of ABIOGENESIS).

bīogėŏg′raphy *n.* Study of the distribution of animals and plants.

bī′ograph (-ahf) *n.* Early form of cinematograph, introduced from U.S. and exhibited in London in 1897.

bīŏg′raphy *n.* Written life of a person, branch of literature dealing with such lives. **bīŏg′rapher** *n.* **bīogrăph′ical** *adj.* **biogrăph′ically** *adv.*

bīŏl′ogy *n.* Science of physical life, dealing with the morphology, physiology, origin, and distribution of animals and plants. **bīolŏg′ical** *adj.* Of biology; ~ *control*, control of pests by the use of other organisms which devour or destroy them; ~ *warfare*, distribution of micro-organisms of disease in enemy territory. **bīolŏg′ically** *adv.* **bīŏl′ogist** *n.*

faces, one above the other (ill. AEROPLANE).

bīquadrăt′ic (-kwŏd-) *adj.* Of, raised to, the square of a square (or 4th power) of a number; ~ *equation*, one in which the unknown quantity is biquadratic. ~ *n.* Biquadratic equation; 4th power of a number.

bîrch *n.* 1. Genus (*Betula*) of hardy northern forest-trees with smooth tough bark and slender graceful branches; the wood of this; ~*-bark canoe*, one made of the bark of *Betula papyrifera*. 2. Bundle of birch-twigs used for flogging. ~ *v.t.* Flog with birch. **bîrch′en** *adj.* Made of birch.

bîrd *n.* 1. Any feathered vertebrate animal, member of a class nearly allied to the Reptiles but distinguished by warm blood,

garden on which food is set for birds; ~*-watching*, study of birds in their natural surroundings.

bīr′ēme *n.* Ancient galley with two banks of oars.

bīrĕtt′a *n.* Square cap worn by R.C. and some Anglican clerics.

Bîrk′bĕck College. College of the University of London, originally the London Mechanics' Institution, founded 1823 by Dr. George Birkbeck (1776–1841), a physician and professor of natural philosophy.

Bîrm′ingham (-ng-*a*m). Midland city and county borough, 2nd largest in England, noted for its metal manufactures.

bîrth *n.* 1. Bringing forth of offspring; coming into the world. 2. Origin, beginning. 3. Parentage, descent; noble lineage. 4. ~ con-

BIRD: A. EXTERIOR. B. INTERNAL ORGANS

A. 1. Culmen. 2. Lore. 3. Crest. 4. Ear feathers. 5. Lesser wing coverts. 6. Scapulars. 7. Greater wing coverts. 8. Secondaries. 9. Upper tail coverts. 10. Rectrices. 11. Primaries. 12. Primary coverts. B. 13. Trachea. 14. Syrinx. 15. Lung. 16. Kidney. 17. Testes. 18. Rectum. 19. Cloaca. 20. Intestines. 21. Gizzard. 22. Liver. 23. Crop. 24. Oesophagus

bīŏm′ėtry *n.* Application of mathematics to biology, esp. the study of resemblances between living things by statistical methods. **bīomĕt′rical** *adj.*

Bī′on. Greek pastoral poet of the latter half of the 2nd c. B.C.

bīophўs′ics (-z-) *n.* Science dealing with the mechanical and electrical properties of the parts of living organisms. **bīophўs′ical** *adj.*

bī′oscōpe *n.* = BIOGRAPH; (S. Afr.) cinema.

bīŏt′ic *adj.* (biol.) Relating to life; peculiar to living organisms. **bīŏt′ics** *n.pl.* (Study of) biotic properties.

bīpâr′tisăn′ *adj.* Advocated by two political parties.

bīpâr′t′īte *adj.* Divided into or consisting of two parts; (law, of agreement etc.) drawn up in two corresponding parts, each party delivering a counterpart to the other.

bīp′ĕd *n.* & *adj.* Two-footed (animal).

bīpinn′ate *adj.* (bot.) Having leaflets arranged in two rows on either side of leaf-stalk, the leaflets being themselves subdivided (ill. LEAF).

bīp′lāne *n.* Aeroplane with two planes or main supporting sur-

feathers, and adaptation of the fore-limbs as wings. 2. A game bird. 3. (slang) Girl. 4. (slang) *get the* ~, (of an actor) be hissed; be dismissed, get the sack; so *give the* ~; ~*-bath*, dish of water set in garden for birds' use; ~*-call*, instrument for imitating the notes of birds; ~*-cherry*, species of cherry tree (*Prunus padus*); ~*-lime*, glutinous substance spread on twigs to catch birds; ~ *of paradise*, bird of family *Paradiseidae* native to New Guinea and notable for its brilliant colours and elegant plumes; ~ *of passage*, migratory bird (also fig. of sojourner); ~ *of prey*, member of the group containing hawks, eagles, owls, etc., which hunt mice and small birds for food; ~*-sanctuary*, island or enclosed piece of land where birds are protected by law; ~*-seed*, any of various kinds of seed used esp. for feeding caged birds; ~*'s-eye*, any of several plants, esp. the speedwell, with small round bright flowers; ~*'s-eye maple*, wood of the sugar maple when full of little knots; ~*'s eye view*, view of landscape from above; résumé of a subject; ~*'s nest*, (esp.) the edible nest of certain swallows found in the China Sea; ~*'s nesting*, search for birds' nests usu. in order to collect eggs; ~*-table*, table in

trol, regulation of birth by means of contraceptive methods or devices; *birth′day*, (anniversary of) day of one's birth; *birthday honours*, titles of honour annually conferred by the British sovereign, announced on his or her official birthday; *birthday suit*, (slang) state of nakedness; ~*-mark*, mark on the body from birth; ~*-place*, place at which one was born; ~*-rate*, number of births per 1,000 of population per annum; *birth′right*, rights, privilege, or position to which one is entitled by birth, esp. by being the eldest son.

bĭs *adv.* Twice; (mus.) repeat.

Bĭs′cay, Bay of. Part of N. Atlantic between N. coast of Spain and W. coast of France, notorious for storms.

bĭs′cuit (-kĭt) *n.* 1. Kind of crisp, dry bread more or less hard, variously flavoured, and usu. unleavened, prepared usu. in small flat thin cakes; (U.S.) kind of small leavened cakes resembling scones. 2. Porcelain and other pottery-ware after first firing and before being glazed or painted. 3. Characteristic light-brown colour of biscuit. 4. Small square army mattress, three of which form full-size mattress. ~ *adj.* Of the colour of biscuit.

bīsĕct′ *v.t.* Cut or divide into two (usu. equal) parts. **bīsĕc′tion** *n.* **bīsĕc′tor** *n.* Bisecting line.

bīsĕx′ual *adj.* Of two sexes; having both sexes in one individual, hermaphrodite. **bīsĕxūăl′ĭty** *n.*

bĭsh′op *n.* 1. Clergyman consecrated as ecclesiastical governor of a diocese; *Bishops' Bible*, the English translation prepared by the bishops and printed 1568; ~ *sleeves*, very full sleeves like those worn by bishop. 2. Mitre-shaped chessman moved diagonally (ill. CHESS). 3. Mulled spiced wine. **bĭsh′opric** *n.* Diocese or office of a bishop.

Bĭs′ley (-zlĭ). Village in Surrey, England, where annual meeting of National Rifle Association is held.

Bĭs′marck[1] (-z-), Otto Eduard Leopold, Prince von (1815–98). German statesman; Prussian Prime Minister 1862; Chancellor of N. German Federation 1867; after the war with France, in which the S. German States co-operated, became first Chancellor of the German Empire 1871; resigned, having displeased William II, 1890.

Bĭs′marck[2]. Capital of N. Dakota, U.S.

bĭs′muth (-z-) *n.* Reddish-white brittle metallic element melting at low temperatures; symbol Bi, at. no. 83, at. wt 208·980; some of its salts (esp. ~ *carbonate*) are used as medicines.

bīs′on *n.* 1. Species of wild ox *Bison europaeus*) of heavy build with humped shoulders, formerly prevalent in Europe and still existing in the Caucasus. 2. N. Amer. wild ox (*B. americanus*) formerly roaming in vast herds over the continent, now almost extinct except in protected areas.

bĭsque[1] (-k) *n.* Point given to opponent in certain games, which he may take at any stage, esp. in tennis and golf; (croquet) right of playing extra turn.

bisque[2] (-k) *n.* (pottery) Unglazed white porcelain used for statuettes etc., biscuit.

bĭsque[3] (-k) *n.* Soup made with shellfish etc.

bĭssĕx′tĭle *adj.* & *n.* Leap (-year). [L *bis sextilis* (*annus*) (year) containing the doubled sixth day (because in the Julian calendar the day repeated, 24th Feb., was acc. to the inclusive Roman method of reckoning the 'sixth' before the Calends of March)]

bĭs′tort *n.* Plant (*Polygonum bistorta*) with large twisted rhizome and cylindrical spike of small flesh-coloured flowers, yielding an astringent medicinal drug.

bĭs′toury (-orĭ) *n.* Surgeon's scalpel.

bĭs′tre (-*ter*) *n.* Brown pigment prepared from soot; colour of this.

bĭt *n.* 1. Biting or cutting end or part of tool, as boring-piece of drill (ill. DRILL), cutting-iron of plane, etc.; part of key which engages with levers of lock (ill. LOCK). 2. Mouthpiece of horse's bridle (ill. HARNESS). 3. Something to eat; morsel of food. 4. Small piece of anything; small portion or quantity; small coin. ~ *v.t.* Furnish (horse) with bit; restrain, curb.

bĭtch *n.* Female of dog, fox, wolf; malicious or ill-tempered woman.

bīte *v.* (past t. *bĭt*, past part. *bĭtt′en*). 1. Cut into or off, nip, with teeth; (of insects etc.) sting, suck. 2. (Of fishes) accept bait. 3. Cause glowing, smarting pain to. 4. Corrode. 5. (Of wheels, screw, etc.) grip. ~ *n.* Act of, wound made by, piece detached by, biting; taking of bait by fish; grip, hold.

Bĭthȳ′nia. Ancient name of NW. Asiatic Turkey.

bīt′ing *adj.* (esp.) Pungent, stinging, sarcastic.

bĭtt′er *adj.* Tasting like wormwood, quinine, bitter aloes, etc., obnoxious, irritating, or unfavourably stimulating to the gustatory nerve; unpalatable to the mind, full of affliction; virulent, relentless; biting, harsh; piercingly cold; ~-*sweet*, sweet(ness) with bitter after-taste or element; WOODY nightshade. **bĭtt′erly** *adv.* **bĭtt′erněss** *n.* **bĭtt′er** *n.* 1. Bitterness. 2. Bitter beer; (pl.) liquors impregnated with wormwood etc. taken as stomachics.

bĭtt′ern *n.* Bird of genus *Botaurus*, allied to herons, but smaller; esp. *B. stellaris*, a European marsh-bird noted for its booming cry.

bĭtūm′ĕn (*or* bĭt′ūmĕn) *n.* Mineral pitch, asphalt; any of various kinds of native oxygenated hydrocarbon, as naphtha, petroleum. **bĭtūm′inous** *adj.*

bĭt′ūminize *v.t.* Impregnate, cover, with bitumen.

bīvăl′ent (*or* bĭv′*a*-) *adj.* (chem.) Having a VALENCY of 2.

bīv′ălve *adj.* Having two valves, having two hinged shells. ~ *n.* Mollusc with shell consisting of two halves hinged together by elastic ligament (ill. MUSSEL).

bĭv′ouăc (-ōō-) *n.* Temporary encampment without tents, etc.; improvised ridge tent for two soldiers made with waterproof sheets. ~ *v.i.* Remain, esp. during the night, in open air without tents.

bĭzarre′ (-âr) *adj.* Eccentric, fantastic, grotesque, mixed in style, half barbaric. [Span. *bizarro* brave, handsome]

Bizet (bēz′ā), Georges (1838–75). French composer of 'Carmen' and other operas.

bīzōn′al *adj.* Of or concerning both of two zones.

Björnsen (byêr-), Björnstjerne (1832–1910). Norwegian playwright, novelist, and poet.

B.L. *abbrev.* Bachelor of Law.

blăb *v.* Talk or tell foolishly or indiscreetly, reveal, let out; hence, **blăbb′er** *n.* **blăb** *n.* Blabbing.

blăck[1] *adj.* 1. Opposite to white, colourless from the absence or complete absorption of all light; so near this as to have no distinguishable colour; very dark-coloured. 2. Dark-skinned; dark-clothed; dusky, gloomy; dirty. 3. Deadly, sinister, wicked; dismal; angry, lowering; implying disgrace or condemnation (as ~ *mark* etc.). 4. ~ *and blue*, discoloured with bruise(s); ~ *and tan*, (dog) of these two colours; *B~ and Tans* (from their black and khaki uniform, a mixture of constabulary and military uniforms), an armed force specially recruited in 1921 to combat Sinn Fein in Ireland; ~ *art*, magic; ~ *ball*, black ball put into urn or ballot-box to express adverse vote, whence *black′ball* (*v.t.*) exclude from club, society, etc.; ~-*beetle*, the commonest commensal cockroach (*Blatta orientalis*); (slang) cleric, parson; *black′berry*, the bramble (*Rubus fruticosus*) or its fruit; *black′bird*, a European song-bird (*Turdus merula*, one of the thrushes), the male being black with yellow bill, the female dark brown; (hist.) captive Negro on slave- or pirate-ship; *black′board*, large black-painted board, panel, etc., used in schools and lecture-rooms for writing or drawing on in chalk; ~ *cap*, the cap worn by English judges in full dress, put on when passing sentence of death; *black′cap*, bird, the warbler *Sylvia atricapilla*, which has the top of the head black; ~-*cock*, male of black grouse; *B~ Country*, parts of Staffordshire and Warwickshire grimed and blackened by the fumes and refuse of coal and iron-works; ~ *currant*, the shrub *Ribes nigrum*; its small black fruit; ~ *damp*, the choke-damp of coal-mines, carbon dioxide; *B~ Death*, outbreak of plague, mostly in bubonic form, which spread into Europe from Asia in the 14th c., its most lethal year in England being 1348–9; so called from the symptom of internal haemorrhages which blackened the skin of sufferers; ~ *earth*, dark soil rich in humus; ~-*earth zone*, belt of this in U.S.S.R. from Ukraine to S. Siberia; ~ *eye*, eye with black or very dark iris; (also) discoloration round eye due to bruise; ~-*fellow*, Australian aboriginal; ~ *flag*, black flag used by pirates as ensign, as signal of execution etc.; ~ *friar*, Dominican; ~ *frost*, hard frost without snow or rime; ~ *grouse*, a British species of grouse, *Lyrurus tetrix*; *blackguard* (blăg′ard) (*adj.* & *n.*) scoundrel(ly), foul-mouthed (person); (*v.t.*) revile scurrilously; *blackguardly* (*adj.*); *black′head*, black-headed pimple caused by dirt in pore, comedo; ~ *hole*, any dark hole or deep cell, esp. (hist.) punishment-cell or guard-room in barracks; *B~ Hole of Calcutta*, the punishment-cell of the barracks in Fort William, Calcutta, in which 146 Europeans were confined for a night (1756) by order of Suraj ud Daula and only 23 survived until the morning; ~

jack, pirate's black flag; ~-*jack*, tarred-leather wine-bottle; (U.S.) heavy metal or loaded weapon with

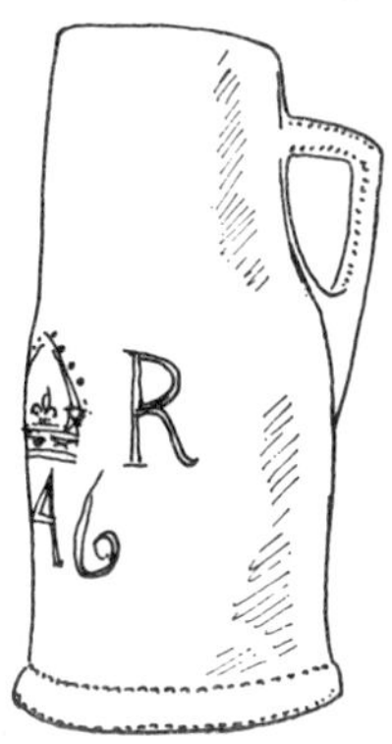

BLACK-JACK

short, pliable shaft used as bludgeon; life-preserver; ~-*lead*, (polish with) graphite; pencil of this material; *black'leg*, swindler (esp. on turf); workman who works for employer whose men are on strike; (*v.*) act as blackleg; ~ *letter*, the 'gothic' type, thus, used by early printers and still occas., esp. in Germany, as dist. from 'roman'; ~-*list*, list of persons against whom charges are made, convictions recorded, etc.; *black'list* (*v.t.*); *black'mail* (*n.*) (hist.) tribute exacted on Scottish and Highland borders by freebooters in return for protection and immunity; hence, payment extorted by threats or pressure, esp. by threatening to reveal discreditable secret; so *black'mail* (*v.t.*); *black'mailer* (*n.*); ~ *Maria*, prison van; during the war of 1914–18, large shell which on bursting emitted masses of black smoke; ~ *market*, surreptitious dealing in rationed or restricted goods; place where these can be obtained; hence, *blackmarketeer*; ~ *mass*, mass for the dead, at which vestments and drapings are black; a travesty of this, used in the cult of Satanism; ~ *monk*, Benedictine (from the colour of his habit); *B*~ *Prince*, 16th-c. name given, for unknown reasons, to Edward (1330–76), the eldest son of Edward III; ~ *pudding*, kind of sausage made of blood and suet; *B*~ *Rod*, gentleman usher to Lord Chamberlain's department, the House of Lords, and the Chapter of the Garter, so called from his ebony rod of office; *B*~ *Sea*, tideless sea between U.S.S.R. and Turkey; ~ *sheep*, scoundrel, unsatisfactory or disreputable member *of* (family etc.); *black'-shirt*, a black shirt as the distinctive mark of the uniform of the Italian Fascisti or of their imitators in other countries; a Fascist; *black'smith*, smith working in iron (as dist. from 'whitesmith' who works in tin etc.); *black'thorn*, the sloe (*Prunus spinosa*), a thorny shrub bearing white flowers before the leaves and small dark-purple fruits; *blackthorn winter*, the time when this thorn blossoms, usu. with cold weather and NE. winds; ~ *velvet*, stout and champagne mixed; *B*~ *Watch*, the Royal Highland Regiment of the British Army, so called from the dark-coloured tartan of their original uniform; *blackwater fever*, tropical fever, originating in malarial infection, characterized by brown or blue-black urine. **blăck'ish** *adj.* **blăck'ly** *adv.* **blăck'nėss** *n.* **blăck** *n.* Black colour, paint, dye, varnish; fungus, smut, in wheat, etc.; particle of soot; black cloth or clothes; Negro. ~ *v.t.* Make black, polish with blacking; ~ *out*, obliterate (printed matter) with printer's ink; obscure (window, street, etc.) so that no light is visible from outside or from the air; ~-*out*, (period of) obscuration of artificial lights during war-time in streets, buildings, ships, etc.; material with which this is done; ban on release of news during an important military operation; temporary loss of vision by pilot etc. of aircraft, occurring when chang-direction at high speeds, and caused by blood being drawn away from the head.

blăck'amoor *n.* Negro; dark-skinned person.

blăck'en *v.* Mark, grow, black or dark; speak evil of.

blăck'ing *n.* (esp.) Paste or liquid for blacking or polishing boots.

Blăck'mōre, Richard Doddridge (1825–1900). English novelist, author of 'Lorna Doone'.

Blăckstone, Sir William (1723–80). English jurist, author of 'Commentaries on the Laws of England' (1765–9).

Blăck'wŏod, William (1776–1834). Scottish publisher; founded 'Blackwood's Magazine' (1817).

blădd'er *n.* 1. Membranous bag in human and other animal bodies, esp. urinary bladder (ill. PELVIS); animal's bladder or part of it prepared for various uses, inflated, etc. 2. Anything inflated and hollow, wordy man, windbag; inflated pericarp or vesicle in plants and seaweeds; ~-*wrack*, species of seaweed (*Fucus vesiculosus*) with air-bladders in substance of fronds (ill. ALGA).

blāde *n.* 1. Flat lanceolate leaf of grass and cereals; (bot.) broad thin expanded part of leaf as opp. to petiole or leaf-stalk (ill. LEAF). 2. Broad flattened leaf-like part of instrument, as oar, paddle, spade, etc., front flat part of tongue; broad flattened bone, esp. scapula (*shoulder-blade*). 3. Thin cutting part of edged tool or weapon. 4. Gallant, free-and-easy fellow.

blaeb'erry (blăb-) *n.* = BILBERRY.

blague (-ahg) *n.* Humbŭg, claptrap.

blain *n.* Inflamed swelling or sore on skin.

Blair, Robert (1699–1746). Scottish poet, author of a melancholy and (in his own time) highly successful blank-verse poem, 'The Grave' (1743).

Blāke[1], Robert (1599–1657). English admiral; fought with distinction against the Dutch and Spanish fleets.

Blāke[2], William (1757–1827). English poet, painter, and mystic; engraved, and sometimes coloured by hand, many of his own works, which included the lyrical 'Songs of Innocence' (1789) and 'Songs of Experience' (1794), and the 'Prophetic Books' (1793–1804).

blāme *n.* Censure; responsibility for bad result. ~ *v.t.* Find fault with; fix responsibility on.

blāme'lėss (-ml-) *adj.* Innocent. **blāme'lėssly** *adv.* **blāme'lėssnėss** *n.* **blāme'worthy** (-mwẽrdhĭ) *adj.*

Blanc (blahṅ), Jean Joseph Charles Louis (1811–82). French socialist and historian; was given by the revolution of 1848 an opportunity to put into practice his theories of the organization of labour; his experiment lasted less than two months and he was forced to flee to England, not returning to France until 1871.

blanch (-ah-) *v.* Make white by withdrawing colour, peeling (almonds), immersing in boiling water (raw meat) or depriving of light (plants); make or grow pale with fear, cold, etc.

blancmange (blamahnzh') *n.* Opaque jelly of isinglass, gelatine, or cornflour boiled with sweetened and flavoured milk.

blănd *adj.* Smooth and suave in manner, gentle; balmy, mild. **blănd'ly** *adv.* **blănd'nėss** *n.*

blănd'ish *v.* Flatter, coax. **blăn'dishment** *n.*

blănk *adj.* 1. Not written or printed on; with spaces left for signature or details. 2. Empty, not filled. 3. Void of interest, incident, result, or expression; unrelieved, sheer. 4. ~ *cartridge*, one without a ball; ~ *cheque*, cheque signed by drawer, with amount left for payee to fill in; hence, full discretionary power; ~ *verse*, (esp.) English unrhymed verse of five-foot iambics. ~ *n.* 1. Void; space left to be filled up in document; dash (—) written in place of omitted letter or word(s); (parl.) provisional words printed in italics in bill. 2. Blank ticket in sweepstake (i.e. one not inscribed with the name of a runner); hence, *draw* ~, elicit no response, fail. 3. Piece of metal ready for stamping as coin, medal, etc.

blănk'ėt *n.* Large woollen sheet used for bed-covering, for horse-cloth, and by primitive people for clothes; *wet* ~, discouraging pe[illegible] by [illegible] warm [illegible], stitch [illegible] used on [illegible] *v.t.* Cover [illegible] keep quiet [illegible] etc.); toss in a [illegible] d from sails of [illegible] g to windward of [illegible]

[illegible] **s'** *n.pl.* (hist.) A body [illegible] n who met at the so-[illegible] lanket Meeting in St. [illegible] Fields, Manchester, in [illegible] n 1817, provided with blan-[illegible] or rugs in order to march to [L]ondon and put their grievances before the Government.

blanquette (blahṅkĕt') *n.* Dish of meat etc. in white sauce.

blāre *v.* & *n.* (Make) sound of trumpet; utter loudly.

Blārn'ey. Village near Cork in S. Ireland; ~ *stone*, inscribed stone, very difficult to reach, in the Castle of Blarney, supposed to confer upon anyone who kisses it 'a cajoling tongue and the art of flattery or of telling lies with unblushing effrontery'. **blārn'ey** *n.* & *v.* (Use, assail with) cajoling talk.

blasé (blahz'ā) *adj.* Cloyed, exhausted, with pleasure.

blăsphēme' *v.* Talk impiously; utter profanity about, revile. **blăsphēm'er, blăs'phėmy** *ns.* **blăs'phėmous** *adj.* **blăs'phėmously** *adv.*

blast (-ah-) *n.* Strong gust of wind; violent gust of air caused by explosion of bomb etc.; blowing or sound of trumpet or other wind-instruments; strong current of air used in smelting etc.; quantity of explosive used in blasting; ~-*furnace*, smelting-furnace into which a blast of compressed heated air is driven by a blowing-engine. ~ *v.t.* 1. Blow up, break, dislodge, with explosives. 2. Wither, shrivel, blight. **blas'tėd** *adj.* (esp.) Damnable. **blas'ter** (-ah-) *n.* (golf) Heavy iron with a lofted face, used for playing from bunkers.

blăs'todērm *n.* External layer and cells formed as a result of cleavage of a yolked egg, characteristic of eggs of reptiles, birds, and, in a different form, insects.

blăs'tūla *n.* (pl. *-lae*). (biol.) Early embryonic stage, usu. a hollow ball of cells, produced by cleavage of an egg (cf. GASTRULA).

blāt'ănt *adj.* Noisy, vulgarly clamorous. **blāt'antly** *adv.* **blāt'ancy** *n.*

Blavăt'sky, Helena Petrovna (1831–91). Russian spiritualist, founder (in U.S.) of the Theosophical Society.

blāze[1] *v.i.* Burn with bright flame; be brilliantly lighted; burn with excitement etc.; show bright colours; emit light. ~ *n.* Bright flame or fire; glow of colour, bright display; *go to blazes*, (slang) go to hell.

blāze[2] *n.* White mark on face of horse or ox; white mark made on tree by chipping off bark, to indicate path, boundary, etc. ~ *v.t.* Mark (tree, path) with blaze.

blāze[3] *v.t.* Proclaim as with trumpet.

blāz'er *n.* (esp.) 1. Unlined (orig. brightly coloured) jacket, usu. with badge on pocket, worn with sports clothes or as part of school uniform. 2. Inner part of chafing-dish.

blāz'on *n.* Heraldic shield, coat of arms, bearings, or banner; correct description of these; record, description, esp. of virtues etc. ~ *v.t.* Describe or paint (arms) heraldically; inscribe with arms etc. in colours; give lustre to; set forth in fitting words; proclaim. **blāz'onry** *n.* (Art of describing or painting) heraldic devices, armorial bearings; brightly coloured display.

bleach *v.* Whiten by exposure to sunlight or chemical process; *bleaching powder*, chemical, such as chloride of lime, used for bleaching. ~ *n.* Bleaching process or substance.

bleak[1] *n.* A small European river-fish, *Alburnus lucidus.*

bleak[2] *adj.* Bare of vegetation; exposed, wind-swept; cold, chilly, dreary; (of person) depressed, lifeless. **bleak'nėss** *n.*

blear *adj.* Dim, filmy, rheumy; misty, indistinct; ~-*eyed* (*adj.*) ~ *v.t.* Dim (eyes) with tears, rheum, etc.; blur. **blear'y** *adj.*

bleat *v.* (Of sheep, goat, etc.) utter characteristic tremulous cry; make sound resembling this, speak feebly or foolishly. ~ *n.* Cry of sheep, goat, etc.; any similar sound.

blĕb *n.* Small blister or bubble.

bleed *v.* (past t. and past part. *blĕd*). 1. Emit blood; suffer wounds or violent death; (of plants) emit sap; (of dyes) come out in water. 2. Draw blood surgically from. 3. Part with money, suffer extortion; extort money from.

bleed'er *n.* (esp.) Person suffering from haemophilia.

bleed'ing *adj.* (esp., vulg. slang) Euphemism for 'bloody'.

blĕm'ish *v.t.* Mar, spoil beauty or perfection of, sully. ~ *n.* Physical or moral defect, stain, flaw.

blĕnch *v.i.* Start aside, flinch, quail.

blĕnd *v.* (past part. occas. *blĕnt*). Mix, mingle (esp. sorts of tea, tobacco, spirits, etc., to produce a certain quality); mingle intimately *with*; mix so as to be inseparable and indistinguishable; pass imperceptibly into each other. ~ *n.* Blending; mixture made by blending.

blĕnde *n.* Native zinc sulphide. [Ger. *blenden* deceive, because although it often resembled galena, it did not yield lead]

Blĕn'heim[1] (-nĭm). Village in Bavaria, scene of the victory (1704) of MARLBOROUGH and Prince Eugene over the French and Bavarians; ~ *Palace*, mansion near Woodstock, Oxfordshire, built by the nation for Marlborough after the battle, and designed by Sir John Vanbrugh; ~ *Orange*, variety of golden-coloured late-ripening eating apple, first grown at Blenheim Palace.

blĕnn'y *n.* Genus (*Blennius*) or family (*Blenniidae*) of small spiny-finned fishes, mostly shore-fishes found in shallow pools.

Blériot (blā'rĭō), Louis (1872–1936). French airman, first man to cross the English Channel in an aeroplane (1909).

blĕss *v.t.* (past part. sometimes *blĕst*). 1. Consecrate (esp. food); sanctify by making sign of cross. 2. Call holy, adore; glorify for benefits received. 3. Pronounce words (held) to confer supernatural favour and well-being upon; make happy or successful; make happy *with* some gift; *bless me!*, *bless you!*, (*God*) *bless my soul!*, *I'm blest!*, etc., exclamations of surprise or indignation.

blĕss'ėd (*or* -blĕst), **blĕst** *adjs.* 1. Consecrated; revered; fortunate; in paradise. 2. Blissful, bringing happiness. 3. (euphem.) Cursed etc. **blĕss'ėdly** *adv.* **blĕss'ėdnėss** *n.*

blĕss'ing *n.* Declaration, invocation, or bestowal, of divine favour; grace before or after food; gift of God, nature, etc., that one is glad of; ~ *in disguise*, misfortune that works for eventual good.

blĕth'er, blăth'er (-dh-) *n.* & *v.i.* (Talk) loquacious nonsense.

Bligh (blī), William (1754–1817). English vice-admiral, who as a lieutenant commanded the *Bounty*[2].

blight (-īt) *n.* 1. Disease of plants caused by fungoid parasites; kind of aphis destructive to fruit-trees. 2. Any obscure or mysterious malignant withering influence. ~ *v.t.* Affect with blight; exert baleful influence on; nip in the bud, mar, frustrate.

blight'er (-īt-) *n.* Anything that blights; (slang) contemptible or annoying person (often merely = 'fellow', 'creature').

Bligh'ty (-īt-) *n.* (army slang) England, home, after foreign service. [Hind. *bilāyatī* foreign, European]

blĭm'ey *int.* Exclamation of surprise, contempt, etc. [f. *Gorblimey* = God blind me!]

blĭmp *n.* 1. Small non-rigid type of airship. 2. (*Colonel*) *B*~, character invented by the cartoonist David Low (1891–1963) representing a muddle-headed, obese, elderly gentleman, pop. interpreted as type of diehard or reactionary. **blĭmp'ery** *n.* **blĭmp'ish** adj.

blīnd *adj.* 1. Without sight. 2. Without foresight, discernment, or moral or intellectual light; reckless; mechanical, not ruled by purpose. 3. Secret, obscure, concealed; without windows or openings; walled up; closed at one end. 4. (slang) Drunk. 5. ~ *alley*, one closed at one end, not leading anywhere (also fig.); ~ *corner*, one on a road round which a motorist etc. cannot see; ~ *man's buff*, game in which blindfolded player tries to catch others; ~ *spot*, point in the retina (ill. EYE) not sensitive to light, where the optic nerve passes through the inner coat of the eyeball (also fig.); ~ *stamping, tooling* (bookbinding), tooling, stamping, without the use of ink or gold-leaf; ~-*worm*, slow-worm. **blīnd'ly** *adv.* **blīnd'ness** *n.* **blīnd** *v.* Deprive of sight permanently or temporarily; rob of judgement, deceive; go blindly or heedlessly. ~ *n.* Obstruction to sight or light; screen for windows, esp. on roller; pretext, stalking-horse; heavy drinking-bout.

blīnd'fōld *adj.* & *adv.* With eyes bandaged; without circumspection. ~ *v.t.* Deprive of sight with bandage.

blĭnk *v.* 1. Move the eyelids, twinkle with the eye or eyelids. 2. Cast sudden or momentary light. 3. Shut the eyes to, evade, ignore. ~ *n.* Momentary gleam or glimpse; shining whiteness on horizon produced by reflection from distant masses of ice.

blĭnk'ers *n.pl.* Leather screens on horse's bridle preventing him from seeing sideways (ill. HARNESS).

blĭp *n.* (In radar) an image of an object as projected on to a screen.

blĭss *n.* Gladness, enjoyment; perfect joy, blessedness; being in heaven. **blĭss'ful** *adj.* **blĭss'fully** *adv.* **blĭss'fulnĕss** *n.*

blĭs'ter *n.* Thin vesicle on skin filled with serum, caused by friction, a burn, etc.; similar swelling on plant, metal, painted surface, etc.; anything applied to raise a blister; ~-*gas*, poison for causing blisters or intense irritation of the skin. ~ *v.* Raise blister on, be or become covered with blisters.

blīthe (-dh) *adj.* (poet.) Gay, joyous. **blīthe'ly** *adv.* **blīthe'some** *adj.*

blĭth'er *v.i.* = BLETHER. **blĭth'ering** (-dh-) *adj.* (esp.) Consummate; despicable, contemptible.

B.Litt. *abbrev.* *Baccalaureus Literarum* (= Bachelor of Letters).

blĭtz *n.* Quick, violent campaign intended to bring speedy victory, intensive air-attack. ~ *v.t.* Damage, destroy, by air-attack. [Ger. *Blitzkrieg*, lightning war]

blĭzz'ard *n.* (orig. U.S.) Blinding snow-storm, esp. one in which powdery snow is swept up from the ground by a high wind.

bloat[1] *v.t.* Cure (herring) by salting and smoking. **bloat'er** *n.* Herring so cured.

bloat[2] *v.* Inflate, swell. **bloat'ĕd** *adj.* Puffed up, esp. with gluttony, overgrown, too big, pampered.

blŏb *n.* Drop of liquid; small roundish mass; (cricket) = nought, a 'duck's egg'.

blŏc *n.* In continental politics, combination of political parties or groups supporting the government; combination of groups, parties, etc., formed to forward some interest; *sterling* ~, group of countries with currencies 'tied' to sterling.

blŏck *n.* 1. Log of wood, tree-stump, large piece of wood for beheading, chopping or hammering on, mounting horse from. 2. Mould for shaping hats on, shape; *barber's* ~, wooden or wax head for wigs. 3. Pulley, system of pulleys mounted in case (ill. PULLEY). 4. Piece of wood or metal engraved for printing. 5. Bulky piece of anything; unhewn lump of rock; prepared piece of building-stone; collection of buildings surrounded by (usu. four) streets; each large plot into which land for settlement is divided; stolid or hard-hearted person. 6. Obstruction; notice that parliamentary bill will be opposed, which prevents its being taken at certain times; jammed vehicles unable to proceed. 7. (cricket) Spot on which batsman blocks ball and rests bat before playing. 8. Number of sheets of paper fastened together at edge(s). 9. ~-*buster*, (slang) large high explosive bomb; *block'head*, dolt; *block'house*, detached fort (orig. one blocking passage), occas. one of connected chain of posts; one-storeyed timber building with loopholes; ~ *letters, writing*, (writing with) detached letters, as in printing, and usu. (in) capitals; ~ *printing*, hand-printing of fabrics with wooden blocks on which design is carved. ~ *v.t.* Obstruct (passage etc.); put obstacles in way of; announce opposition to (bill); (cricket) stop (ball) with bat; shape on block; emboss (book cover); ~ *out*, sketch roughly, plan; *blocked*, (of currency) not freely CONVERTIBLE.

blŏckāde' *n.* Shutting-up of place, blocking of harbour, line of coast, etc., by hostile forces or ships, so as to prevent ingress and egress, the entrance of provisions and ammunition, etc.; *run the* ~, evade the blockading force. ~ *v.t.* Subject to blockade.

Blŏk, Alexander (1880–1921). Russian poet, famous for his poem 'The Twelve', an apologia for the Russian Revolution.

blōke *n.* (slang) Man, fellow.

blŏnd, blŏnde *adj.* (Of hair) light golden brown; (of complexion) fair. **blŏnde** *n.* 1. Person with blond hair and skin. 2. Silk lace of two threads in hexagonal meshes (orig. of raw-silk colour, now white or black).

Blŏn'del de Nesle (nāl) (12th c.). Minstrel who, acc. to legend, discovered the place of captivity of his master Richard Cœur-de-Lion by singing under the window a song they had jointly composed.

blood (-ŭd) *n.* (*Illustration, p.* 78.) 1. The liquid circulating in the veins and arteries of vertebrate animals carrying nourishment and oxygen to all parts of the body and bringing away waste products to be excreted; it consists of a serum or PLASMA in which coloured or colourless cells called corpuscles are suspended; in most vertebrates it is red because certain corpuscles contain a red pigment, haemoglobin. 2. Analogous fluids in invertebrates performing at least some of the same functions. 3. (fig.) Sap, grape-juice, etc. 4. Taking of life, guilt of bloodshed; passion, temperament, mettle. 5. Race, relationship, kin, descent, parentage. 6. Dandy, man of fashion. 7. ~-*ally*, ally (marble) with red veins; ~-*bank*, reserve of blood contributed by blood-donors; ~-*count*, counting of red corpuscles in given volume of blood; ~-*donor*, one who gives part of his blood for transfusion into veins of sick or injured persons; ~-*feud*, feud between families of which one has spilt the other's blood; ~ *group*, one of several types into which human blood may be divided on basis of compatibility of its corpuscles and serum with those of other individuals; ~-*heat*, the normal heat of the blood, 98·4 F. in man; *blood'hound*, large keen-scented dog employed for tracking cattle, criminals, etc.; ~-*letting*, surgical removal of some of patient's blood; ~-*money*, reward to witness for securing capital sentence; compensation for slaughter of relative; ~ *orange*, orange with red-streaked pulp; ~ *poisoning*, condition caused by presence of pathogenic bacteria in the blood; ~-*pressure*, pressure of blood against walls of arteries as it is impelled along them, freq. measured in diagnosis because in certain conditions it may be higher (hypertension) or lower (hypotension) than normal; ~ *relation*, one related by virtue of common descent, not by marriage; *blood'shed*, spilling of blood, slaughter; *blood'shot*, (of eye) suffused, tinged, with blood; *blood'stock*, thoroughbred horses collectively; ~-*stone*, kinds of precious stone spotted or streaked with red, esp. heliotrope; ~-*thirsty*, eager for bloodshed; ~-*vessel*, flexible tube (vein or artery) conveying blood; ~-*worm*, bright red larva of a midge, used as bait in fishing. ~ *v.t.* Remove surgically some of the blood of; allow first taste of blood to (hound); smear face of (novice at hunting) with blood of fox after kill. **blood'lĕss** *adj.* Without blood; unfeeling; pale; without bloodshed.

blood'y (-ŭdĭ) *adj.* 1. Of, like, running or smeared with, blood. 2. Involving, loving, resulting from, bloodshed; sanguinary, cruel. 3. (in foul language) Damned, cursed; bad, deplorable;

infuriating; ~*-minded,* tiresome, cantankerous. ~ *adv.* Confoundedly, very. ~ *v.t.* Make bloody; stain with blood.

bloom[1] *n.* 1. Flower, esp. of plants grown or admired chiefly for the flower, florescence. 2. Prime, perfection; flush, glow; delicate powdery deposit on grapes, plums, etc.; freshness. ~ *v.i.* Bear flowers, be in flower; come into, be in, full beauty; flourish. **bloom'ing** *adj.* (esp. euphemism for) BLOODY (sense 3).

bloom[2] *n.* Mass of puddled iron hammered or squeezed into thick bar. ~ *v.t.* Make puddled iron into a bloom.

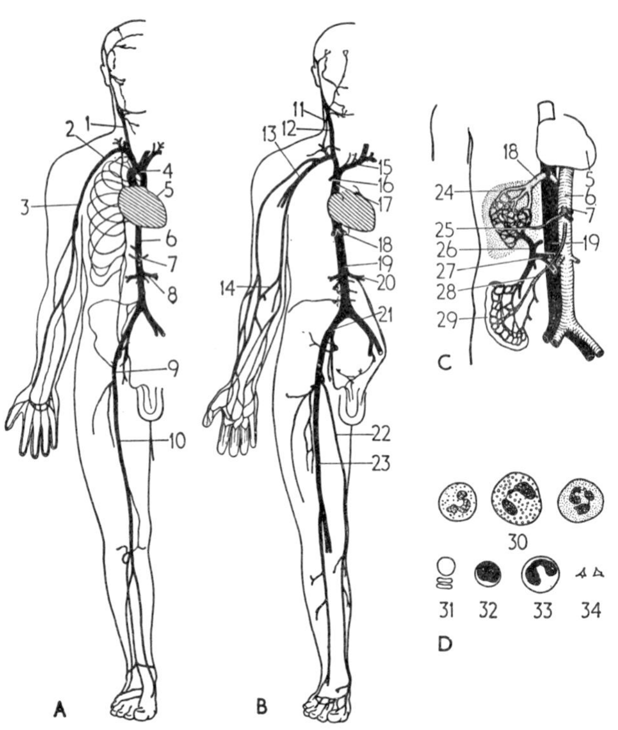

BLOOD: A. ARTERIAL SYSTEM. B. VENOUS SYSTEM. C. PORTAL SYSTEM. D. BLOOD CELLS OR CORPUSCLES

A. 1. Common carotid artery. 2. Right subclavian artery. 3. Brachial artery. 4. Arch of aorta. 5. Heart. 6. Aorta. 7. Coeliac artery. 8. Renal artery. 9. Exterior iliac artery. 10. Femoral artery. B. 11. External jugular vein. 12. Internal jugular vein. 13. Brachial vein. 14. Median basilic vein. 15. Innominate vein. 16. Vena azygos. 17. Superior vena cava. 18. Hepatic vein. 19. Inferior vena cava. 20. Renal vein. 21. Common iliac vein. 22. Long saphenous vein. 23. Femoral vein. C. 24. Liver. 25. Hepatic artery. 26. Portal vein. 27. Splenic vein. 28. Mesenteric artery. 29. Intestine. D. 30. Leucocytes. 31. Erythrocyte. 32. Lymphocyte. 33. Monocyte. 34. Platelets

bloom'er[1] *n.* (slang) Blunder, very bad mistake.

Bloom'er[2], Mrs Amelia Jenks (1818–94). American advocate of 'rational dress' for women; this, which was invented by Mrs E. S. Miller, 'consisted of a small jacket, a full skirt descending a little below the knee, and trousers down to the ankle'. **bloom'ers** *n.pl.* (hist.) The costume introduced by Mrs Bloomer; loose trousers reaching to the knee, knickerbockers, formerly worn by women for gymnastics, cycling, etc.; undergarment of this shape.

Blooms'bury (-zberĭ). District of west-central London containing British Museum and many buildings of London University, formerly a fashionable, and later a literary quarter; (attrib.) intellectual, highbrow, 'precious'.

blŏss'om *v.i.* Open into flower (lit. and fig.). ~ *n.* Flower, mass of flowers on fruit-tree, etc.; early stage of growth, promise. **blŏss'omy** *adj.*

blŏt[1] *n.* Spot or stain of ink etc., dark patch; disfigurement, blemish, defect; moral stain. ~ *v.* 1. Spot or stain with ink, etc.; make blots; sully, detract from; obliterate (writing etc.) with blot, destroy. 2. Dry with *blotting-paper,* absorbent paper for soaking up wet ink-marks.

blŏt[2] *n.* Exposed piece in backgammon; weak point in strategy etc.

blŏtch *n.* Inflamed patch, boil, etc., on skin; large irregular patch of ink, colour, etc. **blŏtched** (-cht), **blŏtch'y** *adjs.*

blŏtt'er *n.* Pad of absorbent paper (blotting-paper) for drying wet ink-marks.

blouse (-owz) *n.* (French) workman's loose linen or cotton garment, usu. belted at waist; woman's loose bodice usu. worn tucked inside skirt at waist; upper part of soldier's or airman's battledress. ~ *v.* Arrange (material, bodice), be arranged, in loose light folds like a blouse.

blow[1] (-ō) *v.* (past t. *blew* pr. bloo, past part. *blown*). 1. Move as wind does, act as current of air; send current of air from mouth; pant, puff; (of whales etc.) eject water and air; cause to pant, put out of breath. 2. Drive, be driven, by blowing; sound (wind instrument, or note *on* or *with* this); (of instrument) sound; direct air-current at; clear, empty, by air-current; break *in* or send flying *off, out, up,* by explosion; ~ *up,* inflate, shatter or be shattered by explosion, reprove violently. 3. (Of flies) deposit eggs in. 4. (Of electric fuse or lamp filament) melt when overloaded. 5. (slang) Curse, confound; squander, spread recklessly. 6. *blow'fly,* flesh-fly, bluebottle; *blow'hole,* each of two holes (containing the nostrils) at top of head in whales etc. through which they blow (ill. WHALE); *blow'out,* (slang) large meal, feast; *blow'pipe,* tube for heating flame by blowing air or other gas into it; tube through which some savage peoples propel arrows or darts by blowing. ~ *n.* Blowing, taste of fresh air; blowing of flute, one's nose, etc.

blow[2] (-ō) *v.i.* (past t. *blew* pr. bloo, past part. *blown*). Burst into, be in, flower. ~ *n.* Blossoming.

blow[3] (-ō) *n.* Hard stroke with fist, hammer, etc.; disaster, shock.

blow'er (-ō'er) *n.* (esp.) 1. Apparatus for increasing draught of fire, esp. sheet of iron held or fixed before grate. 2. (slang) Speaking-tube, telephone.

blow'y (-ō'ĭ) *adj.* Windy, windswept.

blowzed (-zd), **blowz'y** *adjs.* Red- and coarse-faced; dishevelled, frowzy, slatternly.

blŭb *v.i.* (colloq.) Cry, weep.

blŭbb'er *n.* 1. Fatty tissue of aquatic mammals, which keeps them warm; esp. *whale-~,* used as source of oil. 2. Weeping. ~ *adj.* (of lips) Swollen, protruding. ~ *v.* Utter with sobs, weep noisily; wet, disfigure (face) with weeping.

Blü'cher (-ŭχ-), Gebhard Leberecht von (1742–1819). Prussian soldier; led the Prussian army at the battle of WATERLOO.

blu'chers (-ook-) *n.pl.* Old-fashioned low-cut boots. [G. L. von BLÜCHER]

blŭdge'on (-jn) *n.* Short, heavy-headed stick. ~ *v.t.* Strike heavily or repeatedly with or as with bludgeon.

blue (-ōō) *adj.* 1. Coloured like the sky or deep sea, or with darker or paler shades of this colour; livid, leaden-coloured. 2. Affected with fear, discomfort, anxiety, low spirits, etc. 3. Dressed in blue; belonging to a political party (in England usu. Tory) whose badge is blue; (of woman) learned, pedantic; (of talk etc.) indecent, obscene. 4. ~ *baby*, infant suffering from congenital cyanosis; *blue'bell*, (in Scotland) the harebell, *Campanula rotundifolia*, growing on open downs, hills, etc., flowering in late summer, with loose panicle of delicate blue bell-shaped flower on slender stalk; (in S. England etc.) the wild hyacinth (*Endymion non-scriptus*) a bulbous-rooted plant with a nodding raceme of drooping, narrow, bell-like flowers, growing in moist woods and among grass, and flowering in spring; ~ *blood*, high birth; ~ *bonnet*, round flat blue woollen cap formerly generally worn in Scotland; ~ *book*, Parliamentary or Privy Council report, issued in blue paper cover; *blue'-bottle*, blow-fly, meat-fly (*Calliphora vomitoria* and *C. erythrocephala*); blue cornflower (*Centaurea cyanus*); (slang) policeman; ~ *chip* (Stock Exch.) share that is a fairly reliable investment, though less secure than gilt-edged (also attrib.); ~*-coat boy*, scholar of charity school, esp. of Christ's Hospital, whose uniform is a long dark-blue belted gown and yellow stockings; ~ *grass*, species of *Poa*, esp. *P. pratensis* as found in Kentucky and Virginia; ~ *grass country*, the region of blue grass, esp. Kentucky; ~ *ground*, S. Afr. volcanic rock from which diamonds are obtained; ~ *gum*, the *Eucalyptus globulus* of Australia; ~*-jacket*, seaman in Royal Navy; *B~ John*, the blue fluor-spar found in Derbyshire; ~ *law*, (U.S.) severely Puritanical law; ~ *pencil*, pencil making blue mark, used chiefly in making corrections, obliterations, etc.; ~*-pencil* (*v.*) make marks, cuts, or alterations in, censor; *B~ Peter*, blue flag with white square in centre, hoisted by ship before sailing; ~*-point*, (U.S.) small well-flavoured oyster from south shore of Long Island [f. name of headland]; ~*-print*, photographic print of white lines on blue ground or blue lines on white ground, used in copying plans, machine-drawings, etc.; also fig., detailed plan, scheme; ~ *ribbon*, ribbon of the Garter; greatest honour or distinction in any sphere; badge of teetotalism; *blue'-stocking*, woman having or affecting literary tastes and learning [f. *B~ Stocking Society*, name given in 18th c. to meetings for literary conversation etc. at the houses of Mrs Montague and her circle, from the fact that the men attending might wear the blue worsted stockings of ordinary day-time dress instead of the black silk of evening]; ~ *tit*, the blue titmouse, *Parus caeruleus*; ~ *vitriol*, copper sulphate; ~ *water*, deep water, the open sea. **blū'ĭsh** *adj.* **blue'nĕss** *n.* **blue** *n.* Blue colour or pigment; blue powder used in laundering; blue cloth etc.; *the* sky, *the* sea; colour, member, of a political party; (place in team etc. given to) one chosen to represent Oxford University (*dark* ~) or Cambridge (*light* ~) in athletic or sporting contests; (pl.) the dumps; *the Blues*, the Royal HORSE Guards; (also) doleful negro songs; dance resembling slow foxtrot. ~ *v.t.* (pres. part. *blueing* or *bluing*) Make blue; treat with laundering blue; (slang) squander (money).

Bluebeard (blōō'bērd). Hero of a popular tale, who killed several wives in turn because they showed undue curiosity about a locked room; ~*'s chamber*, a repository of mysterious or horrible secrets.

blŭff[1] *adj.* Having perpendicular broad front; abrupt, blunt, frank, hearty. **blŭff'l'y** *adv.* **blŭff'nĕss** *n.* **blŭff** *n.* Headland with perpendicular broad face.

blŭff[2] *v.* (At poker) impose upon (opponent) as to value of one's hand, inducing him to throw up his cards (also transf. of politics, betting, etc.); practise such imposition; assume bold or boastful demeanour in order to disguise one's real strength. ~ *n.* Bluffing.

blŭn'der *v.* Move blindly, stumble; make gross mistake; utter thoughtlessly or stupidly. ~ *n.* Stupid or careless mistake. **blŭn'derer** *n.*

blŭn'derbŭss *n.* Short flintlock gun with large bore, firing many balls or slugs, used esp. in 17th and 18th centuries (ill. MUSKET). [corrupt. of Du. *donderbus* lit. thundergun]

blŭnge (-j) *v.t.* (pottery) Mix (clay, powdered flint, etc.) up with water.

blŭnt *adj.* Dull, not sensitive; without edge or point; plain-spoken. **blŭnt'ly** *adv.* **blŭnt'nĕss** *n.* **blŭnt** *v.t.* Make less sharp or sensitive.

blûr *n.* Smear of ink etc.; dimness, confused effect. ~ *v.* Smear with ink etc.; sully, disfigure; make indistinct; efface; dim.

blûrb *n.* (orig. U.S. slang) Publisher's eulogy or description of book printed on jacket etc.

blûrt *v.t.* Burst *out* with, utter abruptly.

blŭsh *v.i.* Become red with shame or other emotion; be ashamed; be red or pink. ~ *n.* Glance, glimpse; reddening of face in shame etc.; rosy glow, flush of light.

blŭs'ter *v.* Storm boisterously; utter overbearingly. **blŭst'erer** *n.* **blŭs'ter** *n.* Boisterous blowing, noisy self-assertive talk, threats. **blŭs'terous, blŭs'tery** *adjs.*

B.M. *abbrev.* Bachelor of Medicine; British Museum.

B.M.A. *abbrev.* British Medical Association.

B.M.R. *abbrev.* Basal metabolic rate.

B.Mus. *abbrev.* Bachelor of Music.

B.N.C. *abbrev.* Brasenose College (Oxford).

B.O. *abbrev.* Body odour.

bō'a *n.* 1. S. Amer. tropical genus of large non-poisonous snakes killing their prey by constriction or compression (pop. extended to pythons); ~ *constrictor*, large Brazilian species of boa; any great crushing snake. 2. Woman's long round fur or feather wrap for throat.

B.O.A. *abbrev.* British Optical Association.

B.O.A.C. *abbrev.* British Overseas Airways Corporation.

Bōadicē'a (d. A.D. 62). British queen of the Iceni of Norfolk and Suffolk; headed a revolt against the Romans and destroyed Camulodunum and Londinium; when finally defeated by Suetonius Paulinus, took poison.

boar (bōr) *n.* Male uncastrated swine (wild or tame); flesh of this; *wild* ~, the wild swine, *Sus Scrofa*, found in the forests of Europe, Asia Minor, and N. Africa.

board (bōrd) *n.* 1. Thin piece of timber, usu. rectangular, and of greater length than breadth; one or more pieces of this (bare or covered with leather etc.) used in games, for posting notices, etc.; (pl.) the stage; thick stiff paper used in bookbinding etc. 2. Table; table spread for meals; food served, daily meals provided at contract price or in return for services; council-table, councillors, committee. 3. Ship's side (only in certain phrases); *on board*, aboard, in or into ship, train, coach, etc.; (naut.) tack. 4. ~ *foot*, 144 cubic in.; ~*-school*, school under management of a School-board (hist., from Elementary Education Act of 1870 until 1902); *B~ of Trade*, department of British Government dealing with problems of trade; *B~ of Trade unit* (abbrev. B.O.T. *unit*), = KILOWATT-hour; ~*-wages*, those paid to servants while their masters are away from home, including cost of food etc.; ~*-walk* (U.S.) footway of boards or planks. ~ *v.* 1. Cover with boards. 2. Provide with, receive, stated meals at fixed rate; ~ *out*, place (destitute children) in families where they are treated as members. 3. (naut.) Come alongside, force one's way on board; embark on. 4. (naut.) Tack.

board'er (bōr-) *n.* One who boards with someone; boy or girl at boarding-school; one who boards a ship to capture it.

board'ĭng (bōr-) *n.*: *boarding-house*,

house in which persons are boarded and lodged for payment; *boarding-school*, school in which pupils live during term-time, as dist. from day-school.

boast *n.* Vainglorious statement; cause of pride. ~ *v.* Extol oneself, brag *of*, *about*; vaunt, brag of; possess as thing to be proud of. **boast'er** *n.* **boast'ful** *adj.* **boast'fully** *adv.* **boast'fulnėss** *n.*

boat *n.* 1. Small, open oared or sailing vessel; fishing-vessel, mail ment; curtsy. 2. (bell-ringing) Kinds of change in long peals; *treble* ~, one in which the bells, esp. the treble, dodge; ~ *minor, triple, major, royal, maximus*, bobs on 6, 7, 8, 10, and 12 bells. ~ *v.i.* Move up and down, dance, rebound; curtsy; ~ *for*, try to catch (cherries, apples, etc., floating or hanging) with the mouth.

bŏb[3] *n.* *Dry-~*, (at Eton) one who plays cricket; *wet-~*, one who rows. [prob. pet-form of *Robert*]

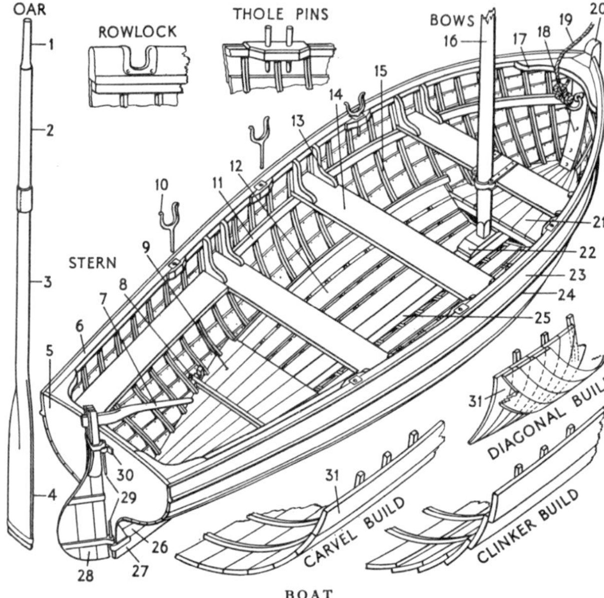

BOAT

Oar: 1. Grip. 2. Loom. 3. Shaft or neck. 4. Blade.

Details of boat: 5. Transom. 6. Gunwale. 7. Tiller. 8. Stretcher. 9. Stern sheets. 10. Crutch (or rowlock). 11. Rising. 12. Bottom boards. 13. Knee. 14. Thwart. 15. Timber or rib. 16. Mast. 17. Breast hook. 18. Apron. 19. Painter. 20. Stem. 21. Fore sheets. 22. Mast step. 23. Top strake. 24. Rubbing piece. 25. Keelson. 26. Garboard strake. 27. Keel. 28. Rudder. 29. Pintle. 30. Gudgeon. 31. Plank or strake

packet, small steamer; occas. large sea-going vessel. 2. Boat-shaped utensil for sauce etc. 3. *~-hook*, long pole with hook and spike; *~-house*, shed at water's edge for keeping boat; *boat'man*, hirer, or rower or sailer of boat for hire; *boatswain* (bō'sn), *bo'sun*, ship's officer in charge of sails, rigging, etc., and summoning men to duty with whistle; ~ *train*, train having connexion with a steamer at a port. ~ *v.* Go in boat; place, carry, in boat.

boat'er *n.* Man's hard straw hat with flat crown and brim.

bŏb[1] *n.* 1. Weight on pendulum, plumb-line, or kite-tail. 2. Knot of hair, tassel-shaped curl; horse's docked tail; woman's bobbed hair. 3. (prosody) Very short line at end of stanza in some old forms of versification. ~ *v.t.* Cut (the hair of woman or girl) to hang short of the shoulders.

bŏb[2] *n.* 1. Jerk, bouncing move-

bŏb[4] *n.* (slang) Shilling.

bŏb[5] *v.* Carry, ride, on a bob-sleigh.

bŏbb'ĭn *n.* 1. Cylinder on which thread, wire, etc., may be wound, reel, spool; ~ *lace*: see LACE. 2. Rounded piece of wood attached to a string, for raising door-latch.

bŏbb'ĭnėt *n.* Machine-made net imitating bobbin lace.

bŏbb'ish *adj.* (slang) Brisk, well.

bŏbb'y *n.* (slang) Policeman. [Pet-form of *Robert*, in allusion to Sir Robert Peel, who was Home Secretary when the Metropolitan Police Act was passed in 1828]

bŏb'olĭnk *n.* A N. Amer. song-bird, the rice-bunting (*Dolichonyx oryzivora*). [orig. *Bob* (*o'*) *Lincoln*; imit. of its call]

bŏb-slĕd, **bob-sleigh** (-slā) *ns.* Sled or sleigh made of two short sleds or sleighs coupled together (ill. SLEDGE).

bŏb'stay *n.* (naut.) Rope holding bowsprit down (ill. SHIP).

bŏb'tail *n.* (Horse or dog with) docked tail; *tag, rag, and* ~, the rabble.

Boccă'ccio (-chĭō), Giovanni (1313–75). Italian novelist, poet, and humanist, author of the 'Decameron', a collection of prose tales.

Boccherini (bŏkerēn'ĭ), Luigi (1740–1805). Italian composer, important chiefly for his works for violoncello.

Bŏche (-sh) *n.* & *adj.* (slang) German.

bŏck *n.* A strong dark-coloured German beer. [Ger., f. *Einbockbier*, beer from *Einbeck*, in Hanover]

bōde[1] *v.* Foresee, foretell (evil); portend, foreshow; promise *well, ill.* **bōde'ful** (-df-) *adj.* Ominous.

Bode[2] (bōd'*e*), Johann Elert (1747–1826). German astronomer; gave currency to an empirical rule, previously formulated by J. D. Titius, but known as *~'s law*, for determining the approximate distances of the planets from the sun.

bodēg'a *n.* Wine-cellar, wine-shop. [Sp., f. L, f. Gk *apothēkē* store]

Bodhisattva (bŏdĭsaht'-) *n.* (Buddhism) Person who is entitled by his good deeds to enter NIRVANA, but who delays doing so out of compassion for human suffering.

bŏd'ĭce *n.* Upper part of woman's dress, down to waist; under-garment for same part of body. [orig. (pair of) *bodies*, stays, corset]

bŏd'ĭlėss *adj.* Incorporeal, separated from the body.

bŏd'ĭly *adv.* In the body, in person; with the whole bulk, as a whole.

bŏd'kĭn *n.* 1. Thick, blunt needle with large eye for threading tape etc. through hem. 2. Dagger (obs.); small pointed instrument for piercing holes in cloth etc.; long pin for the hair. 3. *ride, sit* ~, (colloq.) ride, sit, squeezed between two others.

Bŏdlei'an Library (-lē'*a*n). The library of Oxford University; founded by Humphrey, duke of Gloucester (1391–1447), and re-founded, 1603, by Sir Thomas Bodley (1545–1613), diplomatist and scholar; entitled by statute to a copy of every book published in the U.K. (see COPYRIGHT libraries).

bŏd'y *n.* 1. Physical or material frame or structure of man or any animal; corpse. 2. Trunk, main portion of anything; part of vehicle fitted to receive the load; shank of piece of type (ill. TYPE). 3. Bulk, majority. 4. The person; human being, individual. 5. Corporate body, aggregate of persons or things; society, league, military force; collection. 6. Piece of matter, material thing, quantity; comparative solidity or substantial character; thing perceptible to senses. 7. *~-guard*, guard for the person (esp. of sovereign or dignitary), retinue, escort; *~-line bowl-*

ing, (cricket) fast bowling on the leg side directed or alleged to be directed at the person of the batsman; *the ~ politic*, the State; *~-snatcher*, one who secretly disinters corpses to sell them for dissection. ~ *v.t.* (usu. with *forth*) Give mental shape to; exhibit in outward shape; typify.

Boehme (bêrm'*e*), Jakob (1575–1624). German mystic; held that will is the original force, that every manifestation involves opposition, and that existence is a process of conflict between pairs of contrasted principles, which are ultimately resolved into a new unity.

Boeotia (bēōsh'*ia*). Ancient country of central Greece, whose inhabitants were proverbial for slow-wittedness. **Boeo'tian** *adj.* & *n.*

Bōer (*or* boor). S. Afr. farmer of Dutch origin; ~ *War*, each of two wars fought by Gt Britain: the 1st (1880–1) against Transvaal, which, annexed by Britain in 1877, had proclaimed its independence; the 2nd (1899–1902) against the Transvaal and Orange Free State, resulting in the annexation of these States by Gt Britain.

Bōēth'ĭus, Anicius Manlius Severinus (*c* 475–525). Roman philosopher; consul under Theodoric the Ostrogoth; was suspected of treason and confined to prison, where he wrote 'De Consolatione Philosophiae'; the neoplatonic and stoic ideas of this work had great influence throughout the Middle Ages.

Bŏf'ôrs (-z) *n.* Clip-fed, rapid-firing light anti-aircraft gun. [name of a munition works in Örebro Län, Sweden]

bŏg *n.* (Piece of) wet spongy ground, consisting chiefly of decayed or decaying moss or other vegetable matter; *~-myrtle*, sweet gale, *Myrica Gale*; ~ *oak*, oakwood preserved in a black state in peat-bogs etc.; *~-trotter*, Irishman. **bŏgg'y** *adj.* **bŏgg'inėss** *n.* **bŏg** *v.t.* Submerge in bog.

bō'g(e)y (-gĭ) *n.* (golf) The number of strokes a good player is reckoned to need for the course or for a hole; freq. personified as *Colonel B~*. [app. jocular application of *bogy*, 'something to be afraid of']

bŏg'gle *v.i.* Start with fright, shy; hesitate, demur, *at*; equivocate, fumble.

bō'gie (-gĭ) *n.* Under-carriage with two or more pairs of wheels, pivoted below front part of railway-engine or ends of long railway-carriage, tram-car, etc., to facilitate travelling round curves (ill. LOCOMOTIVE).

bō'gle *n.* (orig. Sc.) Phantom, goblin; bugbear; scarecrow.

bō'gus *adj.* (orig. U.S.) Sham, fictitious, spurious.

bō'gy, bō'gey (-g-) *n.* The Devil; goblin; bugbear.

bohea' (-hē) *n.* Black tea of lowest quality, the last crop of the season (in 18th c., the finest kinds of black tea). [Chin. *Wu-i* district]

Bohêm'ĭa. Slavonic kingdom of central Europe; came under Austrian rule, 1526; by the treaty of Versailles (1919) became a province of Czechoslovakia. **Bohêm'ĭan** *adj.* & *n.* 1. (Native, inhabitant) of Bohemia. 2. (Person, esp. artist or writer) of free-and-easy habits, manners, and sometimes morals (from mistaken belief that gipsies came orig. from Bohemia).

Bohr (bôr), Niels Henrik David (1885–1962). Danish physicist; applied the quantum theory to the problem of atomic structure.

Boiârd'ō, Matteo Maria (1434–94). Italian poet, author of 'Orlando Innamorato' and other poems taking their subject from the Arthur and Charlemagne cycles.

boil[1] *n.* Hard inflamed suppurating tumour.

boil[2] *v.* (Of a liquid) reach or be at that temperature (called the *boiling-point*) where the vapour pressure is equal to the pressure of the atmosphere above its surface and vapour is consequently evolved in bubbles from all parts of the liquid; be agitated by the evolution, rising, and bursting of such bubbles; bring a liquid by the application of heat to this temperature; subject to heat of boiling water, cook, be cooked thus; ~ *over*, bubble up so as to run over sides of vessel; said also of the vessel; *boiled shirt*, (orig. U.S.) dress shirt; *boiled sweets*, sweetmeats made of boiled sugar. ~ *n.* Boiling, boiling-point.

Boileau (bwălō'), Nicolas (1637–1711). French poet and critic, whose 'Art Poétique' greatly influenced French poetic theory and practice.

boil'er *n.* Vessel for boiling, esp. large vessel of riveted wrought-iron plates for making steam under pressure (ill. LOCOMOTIVE); tank, attached to kitchen range, or heated by coke, etc., for heating water for domestic use; *~-iron*, *-plate*, rolled steel up to 2 in. thick; *~-tube*, (in older type of boiler) tube by which heat is diffused through water in boiler; tube (in a water-tube boiler) by which water is carried through heat of a furnace or through hot gases.

boil'ing *n.* (esp.) *The whole ~*, (slang) the whole lot.

bois'terous *adj.* Violent, rough; noisily cheerful. **bois'terously** *adv.* **bois'terousnėss** *n.*

bōld *adj.* Courageous, enterprising, confident; forward, immodest; vigorous, free, well-marked, clear; *~-faced*, impudent; (of type) having a 'thick' or 'fat' face, **thus. bōld'ly** *adv.* **bōld'nėss** *n.*

bōle[1] *n.* Stem, trunk.

bōle[2] *n.* Any of several kinds of fine, compact, earthy, or unctuous clay, usu. yellow, red, or brown with iron oxide.

bolĕc'tion *adj.* & *n.* (Moulding) placed round a panel, which it holds in a groove (ill. MOULDING).

boler'o (-âr- *or* -ēr-) *n.* 1. Lively Spanish dance, music for this. 2. Short jacket coming barely to the waist (ill. COAT).

Bolēt'us *n.* (pl. -*tī*). Genus of fungi having the under surface of the pileus full of pores (instead of gills as in agarics).

Boleyn (bŏŏl'ĭn), Anne (*c* 1507–36). Daughter of Sir Thomas Boleyn; became 2nd wife of Henry VIII of England and mother of Queen Elizabeth; she was beheaded on a charge of unfaithfulness.

Bŏl'ingbroke (-ŏŏk), Henry St. John, Viscount (1678–1751). English Tory statesman and writer on politics and philosophy.

Bŏlivâr'[1]**,** Simon (1783–1830). Venezuelan patriot and statesman, called 'the Liberator'; founded (1819) the republic of Colombia, uniting Venezuela, New Granada (Colombia), and Ecuador; became dictator of Peru; and formed the republic of Bolivia.

bŏlivâr'[2] *n.* (pl. -ârēs). Principal monetary unit of Venezuela, = 100 centimos.

Bolĭv'ĭa. S. Amer. inland republic, formerly part of the Incan Empire, and subsequently of the Spanish possession of Peru; capital, La Paz. **Bolĭv'ĭan** *adj.* & *n.*

bolĭvĭan'ō (-ah-) *n.* (pl. -*s*). Principal monetary unit of Bolivia, = 100 centavos.

bōll *n.* Rounded seed-vessel, as in flax or cotton; *~-weevil*, a weevil, *Anthonomus grandis*, destructive to the cotton-plant in America.

Bŏll'and, John (1596–1665). Flemish Jesuit; began the publication of the 'Acta Sanctorum', legends of saints arranged according to the days of the calendar. The *Bollandists* continued the work until after the dispersal of the Jesuits in 1783; they were re-established in Brussels in 1837.

bŏll'ard *n.* Post on ship or quay for securing ropes to; illuminated post at street-crossing resembling this.

bolŏm'ėter *n.* Electrical instrument for measuring radiant heat. **bŏlomĕt'rĭc** *adj.*

Bŏl'shėvĭk *n.* & *adj.* 1. (Member) of the Revolutionary party led by Lenin, which seized power in Russia in 1917 in the name of the proletariat and based its rule on the ideas of Karl Marx. 2. (loosely, freq. in derisive form *Bol'shie*) Any socialist or person suspected of subversive ideas. **Bŏl'shėvĭst** *adj.* & *n.* **Bŏl'shėvĭs'tĭc** *adj.* **Bŏl'shėvĭsm** *n.* [Russ. *bol'shevik* majority man (i.e. member of majority group in the Social-Democratic party) f. *bol'she* more]

bōl'ster *n.* Long, stuffed (under-) pillow for bed, sofa, etc.; pad or support in many machines and instruments. ~ *v.t.* (usu. with *up*) Support with bolster, prop; aid and abet, countenance; give fictitious support to (something unable to stand of itself); pad.

bōlt[1] *n.* 1. Short heavy arrow of crossbow (ill. BOW). 2. Discharge of lightning. 3. Door-fastening of sliding bar and staple. 4. Sliding part of a service rifle which contains striker and mainspring and which locks the breech. 5. Metal pin with head, for holding things together, usu. secured by riveting or by a nut (ill. SCREW). 6. Length of fabric woven on a loom in one operation. 7. Bundle of osiers or reeds of certain size.

bōlt[2] *v.* 1. Dart off or away; (of horse) break from control, make violent dash; *~-hole*, hole or burrow into which animal bolts for safety (also fig.). 2. Gulp down (food) unchewed. 3. Fasten (door etc.) with bolt; fasten together with bolts. ~ *n.* Sudden start; running away.

bōlt[3] *adv.* ~ *upright*, upright as a BOLT[1], quite upright.

bōlt[4], **boult** (-ō-) *v.t.* Sift; investigate; *bolting-cloth*, stiff transparent silk fabric used esp. for sifting flour. **bo(u)lt'er** *n.* Sieve, boulting-machine.

bōl'tel *n.* Var. of BOWTEL.

bōl'us *n.* Large pill, esp. one administered to an animal; lump of food at moment of swallowing.

bŏmb (-m) *n.* Case filled with explosive, inflammable material, or poison gas, fired from a gun, dropped from aircraft, or thrown by hand; *~-aimer*, airman who releases bombs from an aircraft; *~-bay*, compartment in aircraft for holding bombs; *~-ketch*, (obs.) ketch carrying mortars for bombarding; *~-proof*, strong enough to resist explosion of a bomb; *~-rack*, rack in aircraft to hold bombs; *~-release*, mechanism for releasing bombs from aircraft; *~-shell*, artillery bomb; shell; (fig.) great surprise. ~ *v.* Assail with bombs, throw bombs.

bŏm'bard *n.* 1. Earliest kind of cannon, throwing stone ball or very large shot. 2. Bomb-ketch.

bŏmbard' *v.t.* Batter with shot and shell; assail persistently with abuse, argument, etc.; (physics) subject to a stream of (charged) atoms or sub-atomic particles. **bŏmbard'ment** *n.*

bŏmbardier' (-dēr) *n.* Lowest rank of non-commissioned officer in Royal Artillery; (U.S.) bomb-aimer.

bŏm'bardon *n.* (mus.) Low-pitched brass wind-instrument; organ stop imitating this.

bŏm'basine, -zeen, -zin(e) (*or* bŭm-; -zēn) *n.* Twilled dress-material of worsted, or of silk or cotton with worsted weft, formerly much used for mourning.

bŏm'băst *n.* Turgid language, tall talk. **bŏmbăs'tic** *adj.* **bŏmbăs'tically** *adv.* [orig. = cotton wool, used in 16th c. as padding for clothes; f. Gk *bombux* silk, silk-worm]

Bŏmbay'. City on W. coast of India; ~ *duck*, salted BUMMALO.

bŏmb'er (-mer) *n.* 1. Soldier who throws hand-grenades or bombs. 2. Aeroplane designed to carry bombs.

bōn'a fīd'ė *adj.* & *adv.* Genuine(ly), sincere(ly). ***bōn'a fīd'ēs*** (-z) *n.* Honest intention, sincerity. [L]

bonăn'za *n.* Prosperity, large output (esp. of mines); run of luck, fine weather, good crops, etc. ~ *adj.* Yielding great wealth or a large output. [Sp., = 'fair weather']

Bōn'aparte, Napoleon: see NAPOLEON. ~, Joseph (1775–1844). Brother of Napoleon; king of Naples 1806; king of Spain 1808.

Bŏnavėntūr'a, St. (1221–74), John of Fidanza, Italian Franciscan, scholastic theologian, and mystic; known as the 'seraphic doctor'; commemorated 14th July.

bŏn'-bŏn *n.* Sweetmeat.

bŏnd[1] *n.* 1. Thing restraining bodily freedom, shackle (archaic, chiefly pl.); restraining or uniting force; (chem.) = VALENCY bond. 2. Binding agreement; document by which person binds himself and his heirs etc. to pay a sum to another and his heirs etc.; government's or public company's document undertaking to repay borrowed money; *in* ~, (of goods) stored under charge of Customs in 'bonded warehouse' until importer pays duty (which he pledges himself by bond to do); *~-holder*, person holding bond(s) of another person or of company or government; ~ *(-paper)*, paper of superior quality as used for bonds. 3. Various methods (as *English*, *Flemish*, ~) of holding wall together by making bricks etc. overlap so that vertical joints do not exceed the thickness of one brick (ill. BRICK); *in* ~, arranged thus. ~ *v.t.* Bind together (bricks etc.) in bond; put (goods) into bond; *bonded warehouse*, customs warehouse in which goods in bond are stored.

bŏnd[2] *n.* (Of Dutch-speaking population of S. Africa) league, confederation.

bŏnd[3] *adj.* (archaic) In serfdom or slavery; not free; so *bond'man*, *bond'maid*, *bond'servant*, *bond'-slave*, *bonds'man.*

bŏn'dage *n.* Serfdom, slavery; subjection to some bond, influence, or obligation.

Bŏnd Street. Famous shopping street in London. [named after Sir Thomas *Bond*, who began its construction *c* 1688]

bōne *n.* One of the parts making up the skeleton of a human being or other vertebrate; the substance (mainly calcium phosphate and fibrous protein) of which these consist; article made of this substance; animal's bone as source of nourishment; (pl.) skeleton, bodily frame, body, mortal remains; ~ *to pick*, ~ *of contention*, subject of dispute; *make no ~s of* or *about*, make no objections, scruple, or difficulties about; ~ *china*, fine earthenware containing kaolin and calcined bones, semi-translucent and resembling porcelain; *~-dry*, quite dry; *~-head*, (orig. U.S.) blockhead; *~-idle*, *-lazy*, downright idle, lazy; ~ *lace*, see LACE; *~-setter*, one who sets broken or dislocated bones, esp. without being qualified surgeon; *~-shaker*, bicycle without rubber tyres; *~-spavin*, bony swelling on inside of horse's hock. ~ *v.t.* 1. Take out bones from. 2. (slang) Steal. **bōne'lėss** (-nl-) *adj.*

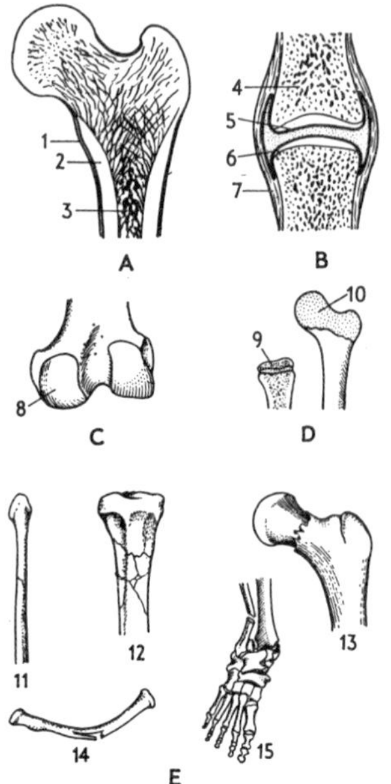

BONE: A. CROSS-SECTION OF HEAD OF FEMUR. B. CROSS-SECTION OF JOINT. C. ARTICULAR SURFACE. D. CHILD'S BONES. E. FRACTURES

A. 1. Periosteum. 2. Compact bone. 3. Marrow. B. 4. Bone. 5. Articular cartilage. 6. Synovial membrane. 7. Capsular ligament. C. 8. Condyle. D. 9. Epiphysis at head of child's ulna. 10. Cartilaginous head of child's femur. E. 11. Simple fracture. 12. Comminuted fracture. 13. Impacted fracture. 14. Greenstick fracture. 15. Pott's fracture

bŏn'fīre *n.* Large fire in the open air.

bŏng'ō (-ngg-) *n.* Large striped African antelope, *Boocercus eurycerus*, related to bushbuck, living in dense forests.

bonhomie (bŏn′ŏmē) *n.* Good nature, good-fellowship. **bŏn′homous** *adj.*

Bŏn′ĭface[1], St. (680–755). Winfrith, English Benedictine, apostle to the Germans under Pope Gregory II; commemorated 5th June.

Bŏn′ĭface[2]. Name of the jovial innkeeper in Farquhar's 'Beaux' Stratagem' (1707); hence, 'mine host', the landlord of an inn.

bon mot (bawṅ mō) *n.* Witty saying.

bŏnn′ĕt *n.* 1. Man's (Scottish) cap; woman's outdoor head-dress with strings and without brim. 2. (naut.) Additional canvas laced to foot of sail. 3. Cowl of chimney etc.; protective cap or cover in various machines; protecting hood over engine of motor-vehicle.

bŏnn′y *adj.* (chiefly Sc.) Comely. **bŏnn′ĭly** *adv.*

bŏn′spiel (-spēl) *n.* Curling-match.

bon ton (bawṅ tawṅ) *n.* Good breeding, the fashionable world.

bō′nus *n.* Something to the good, into the bargain; esp. extra dividend to company's shareholders, distribution of profits to holders of insurance policies, gratuity to employees beyond their wages.

bō′ny *adj.* Of, like, bone; big-boned; with little flesh; ~ *fishes*, those (including most of the common species) which have bones as opp. to cartilage.

bŏnze *n.* (European name for) Japanese or Chinese Buddhist priest.

bŏn′zer *adj.* (Austral. slang). Good, excellent.

boo, *int.*, *n.*, & *v.* (Make) sound of disapproval or contempt; hoot.

boob′y *n.* Silly dull-witted fool, lout; kinds of GANNET; *~-prize*, prize given in derision or fun to player with worst score; *~-trap*, collection of objects balanced on top of door left ajar, so as to fall on head of first person passing through; (mil. colloq.) harmless-looking object concealing an explosive charge, designed to go off when disturbed; hence, *~-trap* (*v.*).

book *n.* 1. Treatise written or printed on a number of sheets which are folded, fastened together hingewise at the folded edges, and protected by a binding or cover; (in antiquity) set of written sheets pasted together to form a roll; literary composition that would fill a book; main division of literary composition or of the Bible; libretto; anything from which one may learn. 2. Blank sheets of paper for keeping accounts, taking notes, etc., fastened together in the shape of a book; anything bound together in this shape, as cheques, stamps, tickets, pieces of flannel for holding needles, etc. 3. Betting-book, record of bets made; (pl.) merchants' accounts. 4. *book′binder*, *book′binding*, binder, binding, of books; *~-case*, case containing bookshelves; *~-ends*, pair of (ornamental) props used to keep row of books upright; *~-hand*, kind of handwriting used in books before the invention of printing; *~-keeper*, *~-keeping*, one who keeps, art of keeping, accounts of merchant, etc.; *~-learned*, *~-learning*, (having) knowledge gained from books not life; *~-maker*,

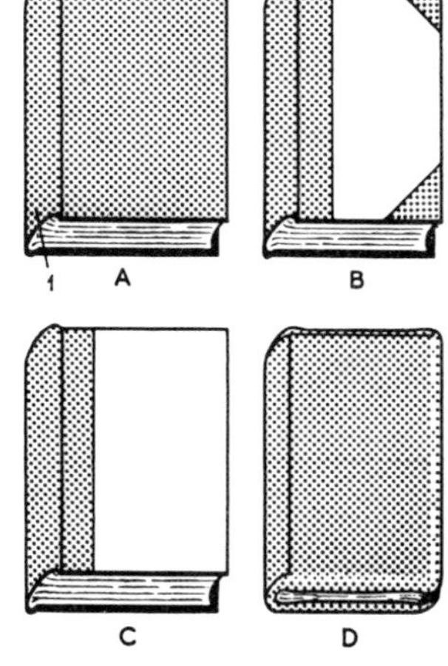

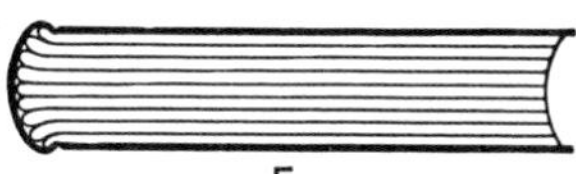

BOOK: A. FULL BOUND BOOK. B. HALF-BINDING. C. QUARTER BINDING. D. YAPP BINDING. E. END VIEW OF FOLDED AND SEWN SECTIONS OF A BOOK IN A BINDING CASE

1. Spine

(esp.) professional betting man; *~-muslin*, fine muslin folded like a book when sold; *~-plate*, label with owner's name, crest, or other device, for pasting into books; ~ *value*, value of a commodity as entered in a firm's books (opp. *market value*); *book′shelf*, shelf for standing books on; *book′worm*, larva of various insects (moths or beetles) which burrows into or destroys pages of books; (fig.) one who is always poring over books. ~ *v.t.* Enter in book or list; engage (seats etc.); enter name of (person engaging seat etc.), issue railway ticket to; take railway ticket; engage (person) as guest etc.

book′ie *n.* (slang) Book-maker.

book′ish *adj.* Literary; addicted to reading books; acquainted only with books. **book′ishly** *adv.* **book′ishnėss** *n.*

boom[1] *n.* Long spar used to keep the bottom of a sail extended (ill. SHIP); obstruction made of heavy pieces of timber fastened together and placed across mouth of a river, entrance to a harbour etc., to prevent entry by enemy ships.

boom[2] *n.* Deep resonant sound; hum, buzz; bittern's cry. ~ *v.* Make, utter with, such sound.

boom[3] *n.* (orig. U.S.) Rapid advance in prices, rush of activity in business or speculation; the effective launching of anything upon the market, or upon public attention; a vigorously worked movement in favour of a candidate or cause. ~ *v.* Burst into sudden activity; make rapid (commercial) progress; advance vigorously; push, puff, write up.

boom′erăng *n.* Australian curved hardwood missile with its convex edge sharp, which may be thrown so as to return to its starting-point, or to hit an object in a different direction from that of projection; (fig.) argument or proposal that recoils on its author.

boon[1] *n.* Request; favour, gift; blessing, advantage.

boon[2] *adj.* 1. (poet.) Gracious, benign. 2. Jolly, convivial (in ~ *companion*).

Boone, Daniel (1735–1820). American pioneer and explorer; played a notable part in the opening up and settlement of Kentucky and Missouri.

boor *n.* Peasant; clumsy or ill-bred fellow. **boor′ish** *adj.* **boor′ishly** *adv.* **boor′ishnėss** *n.*

boost *v.t.* 1. (orig. U.S. slang) Shove, hoist; advance the progress of; praise, extol by puffing. 2. Raise electromotive force in (circuit, battery). ~ *n.*

boot[1] *n.* Good, advantage (now only in *to boot*, as well, in addition). ~ *v.t.* (archaic; usu. impers. & abs.) Do good (*to*), avail. **boot′lėss** *adj.* Unavailing. **boot′lėssly** *adv.* **boot′lėssnėss** *n.*

boot[2] *n.* 1. Outer foot-covering, usu. wholly or partly of leather, and reaching above the ankle; *give* (person) *the* ~, dismiss; *~-ack*, contrivance for pulling off boots; *boot′lace*, string or leather strip for lacing boots; *~-trees*, shaped blocks inserted in boots to keep them in shape. 2. (hist.) Instrument of torture. 3. Luggage receptacle in motor-car (orig., in coach under guard's and coachmans' seat). ~ *v.t.* Kick; (slang) kick (person) *out* (of the house, of employment, etc.); *booted*, wearing boots.

bootee′ *n.* Infant's woollen boot; woman's wool-lined boot.

Boötes (bōōt′ēz). Northern constellation, also called the Wagoner, situated at the tail of the Great Bear. [Gk, = 'ploughman', 'wagoner']

booth[1] (-dh) *n.* Temporary shelter of canvas etc., covered stall in market, tent at fair, etc.; *polling* ~, place where one votes at parliamentary or other election.

Booth[2] (-dh), William (1829–1912). English revivalist preacher, founder and first General of the SALVATION ARMY.

bōōt'lĕg *adj.* (Of alcoholic liquor) illicit, smuggled. ~ *v.t.* Traffic illicitly in. **bōōt'lĕgger** *n.* One who smuggles liquor or sells it illicitly.

bōōts *n.* Hotel servant who cleans boots, carries luggage, etc.

bōōt'y *n.* Plunder or profit acquired in common and to be divided; spoil, prize, plunder.

bōōze *n.* Drink; a drinking-bout. ~ *v.i.* Drink deeply, go on drinking. **bōōz'y** *adj.* Addicted to drink; fuddled.

bō-peep' *n.* Game, played with young child, of hiding and suddenly appearing again.

bortă'cic *adj.* ~ *acid*: see BORIC ACID.

bŏ'rage (*or* bŭ-) *n.* Blue-flowered hairy-leaved plant, *Borago officinalis*, used to flavour claret-cup etc.

borăginā'ceous (-shus) *adj.* Belonging to the order *Boraginaceae* of plants allied to borage.

bor'ate *n.* Salt of boric acid.

bor'ăx *n.* Sodium borate ($Na_2B_4O_7.IOH_2O$), occurring as a native salt, a white crystalline substance giving a slightly alkaline solution; used in the production of optical and hard glasses, ceramic glazes, in laundering, and as a skin lotion. [Arab. *baurag*, prob. f. Pers.]

Bordeaux' (-dō). City and port of SW. France; any of the wines produced in the district round Bordeaux, including Graves, Sauternes, Médoc, and St. Emilion; ~ *mixture*, mixture of blue vitriol (copper sulphate), lime, and water, used for the destruction of fungi.

bord'er *n.* Side, edge, boundary or part near it; frontier of county (*the B~*, the boundary between England and Scotland, and the adjoining districts); continuous bed round garden or part of it, or along path, etc.; distinct edging for strength or ornament or definition round or along anything; *borderland*, land or district on or near a border (also fig.); *borderline*, strip of land along border; (as *adj.*) near the margin of anything. ~ *v.* Put or be a border to; adjoin.

bord'erer *n.* Dweller on or near border, esp. that between England and Scotland.

Bordŏn'e (-ĕ), Paris (1500–71). Venetian painter, pupil of Titian.

bord'ure *n.* (her.) Bearing round the edge of a shield, a fifth part of the field in breadth (ill. HERALDRY).

bore[1] *v.* 1. Make hole in, usu. with revolving tool; hollow out evenly; make by boring, persistent pushing, or excavation. 2. (Of horse) thrust head out; (racing) push (another) out of the course. ~ *n.* 1. Hollow of gun-barrel (ill. CANNON); diameter of this, calibre; inside diameter of tube, esp. in mus. instrument. 2. Small deep hole made in earth to find water, oil, etc.

bore[2] *n.* Nuisance; tiresome person, twaddler. ~ *v.t.* Weary by tedious talk or dullness. **bore'dom** (-ord-) *n.* Being bored, ennui.

bore[3] *n.* Great tide-wave with precipitous front moving up some estuaries.

bor'ėal *adj.* Of the north wind; of the North.

Bor'ėăs. (Gk myth.) The north wind, son of the Titan Astraeus and of Eos the goddess of dawn.

bore'cōle (-ork-) *n.* Kale [prob. f. Du. *boerenkool* peasant's cabbage]

Bor'gia (-jĭa). Italian noble family of Spanish origin: Alonso de Borja, bishop of Valencia, became Pope Calixtus III and gave preferment to his nephew Rodrigo ~ (1431–1503), who became Pope Alexander VI in 1492; Cesare ~ (1475–1507), one of Rodrigo's many illegitimate children, was notorious for his violence and crimes, but an able soldier and an early believer in the unity of Italy; Lucrezia ~ (1480–1519), sister of Cesare, was associated by rumour with his crimes and her 2nd husband, Alfonso of Aragon, was murdered by his direction; she afterwards married Alfonso d'Este, heir of the Duke of Ferrara, and her court became a centre for artists, poets, and scholars.

bor'ic *adj.* ~ *acid* (H_3BO_3), acid occurring in hot springs in some volcanic areas, a mild antiseptic, widely used in the form of an ointment as a dressing for wounds and sores.

Bŏ'rĭs III (1894–1943). King of Bulgaria 1918–43.

Bŏ'rĭs Gŏd'unov (-ōōnŏf) (1552–1605). Tsar of Russia from 1598; an able ruler, but regarded as a usurper and suspected of having contrived the death of the heir, Dmitri; died suddenly during a revolt headed by a pretender, the 'false Dmitri'.

born *past part.* & *adj.* *Be* ~, come into the world by birth; ~ *of*, owing origin to; ~ *fool*, *idiot*, etc., utter, hopeless, fool, etc.

Born'ėo. Large island of Malay archipelago, comprising (1) a region of Indonesia called Kalimantan; (2) North Borneo and Sarawak, formerly Brit. colonies, now parts of MALAYSIA; (3) Brunei, a Brit. protected State.

Bŏ'rodĭn, Alexander Porfyrievich (1834–87). Russian composer.

Bŏrodi'nō (-dē-). Battle, 1812, in which Napoleon defeated the Russians, some 120 miles W. of Moscow.

bor'ŏn *n.* Dark-brown or greenish-brown non-metallic solid element; symbol B, at. no. 5, at. wt 10·811.

borough (bŭ'ro) *n.* Town with corporation and privileges conferred by royal charter or defined by statute; (U.S.) incorporated town or village; *county* ~, borough, usu. with population of 50,000 or more, administered independently of the county authority: *municipal* ~, borough partly dependent on the county authority; *metropolitan* ~, one of the boroughs in the London County Council area; ~ *council*, body responsible for governing a borough, consisting of ~ *councillors* (elected for 3 years), aldermen, and mayor; *pocket* ~, (hist.) borough in which election of member of Parliament was controlled by a private person; *rotten* ~, (hist.) before the Reform Act of 1832, a borough which had so decayed as to have no longer any real constituency; ~ *English*, system of tenure, obtaining in some parts of England, by which youngest son inherits all lands and tenements.

Bŏrromin'ĭ (-mē-), Francesco (1599–1667). Italian baroque architect.

bŏ'rrow[1] (-ō) *v.t.* Obtain or take temporary use of (something to be returned); adopt, use without being the true or original owner or inventor, import from an alien source. **bŏ'rrower** (-ōer) *n.*

Bŏ'rrow[2], George (1803–81). English traveller and linguist; author of 'The Romany Rye' and other books which combine fiction with autobiography and reflect his interest in gipsies.

borsch (-sh) *n.* Soup of beetroot, cabbage, mushrooms, etc., made esp. in Russia and Poland.

Bors'tal. ~ *system*, system in Gt Britain, established 1908, whereby young persons convicted of criminal offences between the ages of 16 and 23 may be sent to a ~ *institution* for a period of reformative training, usu. 3 years, after which they are released subject to further supervision by the ~ *Association*. [f. *Borstal*, village in Kent where first experimental training was carried out]

bort *n.* Coarse diamonds; diamond fragments made in cutting.

borz'oi *n.* A breed of large high-standing dog, called also Russian or Siberian wolfhound, of greyhound type, but with thick silky coat, usu. white with yellow markings. [Russ. *borzoi* swift]

bŏs'cage *n.* Mass of growing trees or shrubs; wooded scenery.

bŏsh *n.* Contemptible nonsense, trash. [Turk., = 'empty', 'worthless' (popularized by Morier's novel 'Ayesha', 1834)]

bŏs'ky *adj.* Wooded, bushy.

Bŏs'nĭa (-z-). Federal unit of Yugoslavia, formerly a province of the Austro-Hungarian Empire.

bosom (bŏŏz'm) *n.* The breast; enclosure formed by breast and arms; breast of dress, space between dress and breast; surface of sea, ground, etc.; the heart, thoughts, desires, etc.; ~ *friend*, specially intimate or beloved friend.

Bŏs'porus, Bŏsph-. Strait connecting the Black Sea and the Sea of Marmora.

bŏss[1] *n.* Protuberance; round metal knob or stud on centre of shield or ornamental work (ill. SHIELD); (archit.) projection, freq. carved, at intersecting point of vault-ribs (ill. VAULT); enlarged part of shaft etc. **bŏss'y**[1] *adj.*

bŏss[2] *n.* Master, person in authority; (U.S.) manager of political organization. ~ *v.t.* Be master or manager of. **bŏss'y**[2] *adj.* (colloq.) Domineering. [orig. U.S., f. Du. *baas* master]

bŏss[3] *adj.* (slang) ~*-eyed*, squint-eyed, cross-eyed; ~*-shot*, a bad shot or aim; an unsuccessful attempt.

Bŏss'uet (-swā), Jacques Bénigne (1627–1704). French divine and theologian, famous for his eloquence, especially in funeral orations.

Bŏs'ton[1]. Capital city and seaport of Massachusetts, U.S., founded *c* 1630 and named after Boston, town in Lincolnshire; ~ *tea-party*, throwing of a cargo of tea into Boston harbour by colonists, 1773, as a protest against tea duties imposed by the English Parliament; it occasioned the general revolt of the American colonies and the War of Independence. **Bŏstō̆n'ian** *adj.* & *n.*

bŏs'ton[2] *n.* Card-game resembling whist, named after the siege of Boston in the American War of Independence, to which the technical terms of the game refer.

bo'sun (bō'sn) *n.* Variant of boatswain (see BOAT).

Bŏs'well (-z-), James (1740–94). A Scotsman, by profession a lawyer, who became a friend of Samuel Johnson and recorded his conversation in a biography published 1791. **Boswĕll'ian** *adj.* **Bŏs'wellīze** *v.i.*

Bŏs'worth (Field) (-zwerth). Scene, near Market Bosworth in Leicestershire, of the last battle of the Wars of the Roses (1485), in which Richard III was defeated and killed.

B.O.T. *abbrev.* Board of Trade.

bŏt(t) *n.* Parasitic maggot or larva of ~*-fly*, genus *Oestrus*; *the botts*, disease of horses, cattle, etc., caused by this.

bŏt'anize *v.i.* Study plants, esp. by seeking them as they grow.

bŏt'any *n.* Science of plants. **botăn'ic, botăn'ical** *adjs.* **botăn'ically** *adv.* **bŏt'anist** *n.*

Bŏt'any Bay. Bay on E. coast of New South Wales (5 miles S. of modern Sydney) where Capt. Cook first landed in 1770; so named because of the variety of its plant life; an English penal settlement was afterwards established there.

bŏtarg'ō *n.* Relish of mullet- or tunny-roe.

bŏtch *n.* Clumsy patch, bungled work. ~ *v.* Patch or mend clumsily or badly; spoil by unskilful work, bungle.

bōth *adj.* & *pron.* The two (and not merely one of them); the pair (of). ~ *adv.* ~ . . . *and* = not only . . . but also.

Bōt'ha (-t*a*), Louis (1862–1919). S. Afr. soldier and statesman, Boer general in the Boer War; conquered German SW. Africa in war of 1914–18.

bŏth'er (-dh-) *n.* Worry, fuss. ~ *v.* Pester, worry; be troublesome; worry oneself, take trouble. ~ *int.* (as mild imprecation) Confound.

bŏtherā'tion (-dh-) *n.* & *int.* Bother.

bŏ'thersome (-dh-) *adj.* Annoying, troublesome.

Bŏth'well, James Hepburn, 4th earl of (*c* 1536–78). 3rd husband of Mary Queen of Scots; implicated in the murder of DARNLEY.

Bŏt'ŏlph, St. (d. 680). English Benedictine monk; commemorated 17th June.

Bŏtticĕll'ī (-chĕl-), Sandro (1447–1510). Alessandro Filipepi, Florentine painter of the Renaissance.

bŏt'tle[1] *n.* Narrow-necked vessel, usu. of glass, but orig. of leather, for storing liquid; the amount of liquid in it; ~*-glass*, coarse dark-green glass; ~*-green*, dark green; ~*-neck*, narrow stretch of road, narrow outlet, esp. one causing congestion of traffic (freq. fig.); ~*-nose*, swollen nose; bottle-nosed whale, a name applied to several of the dolphins and to the whale of the genus *Hyperoödon*; ~*-party*, party to which guests contribute drinks; night-club where drinks ordered in advance may be consumed outside licensed hours; ~*-washer*, factotum, underling. ~ *v.t.* Store in bottles; ~ *up*, conceal, restrain for a time.

bŏt'tle[2] *n.* Bundle (of hay or straw).

bŏtt'om *n.* 1. Lowest part, part on which thing rests; the posterior; seat (of chair). 2. Ground under water of lake etc.; river-basin etc., low-lying land; farthest or inmost point. 3. Less honourable end of table, class, etc., person occupying this. 4. Keel, horizontal part near keel, hull; ship, esp. as cargo-carrier. 5. Foundation, basis, origin; essential character, reality. ~ *adj.* Lowest; last; fundamental. ~ *v.* Put bottom to; base *upon*; touch bottom (of); sound.

bŏtt'omlĕss *adj.* Unfathomable.

bŏtt'omry *n.* System of lending money to shipowner for purposes of voyage on security of ship itself. ~ *v.t.* Pledge (ship).

bŏt'ūlism *n.* Form of poisoning, usu. fatal, caused by food (esp. processed meat) contaminated with the micro-organism *Clostridium botulinum.*

Boucher (bōō'shā), François (1703–70). French painter of elegantly artificial pastorals.

boudoir (bōō'dwâr) *n.* Lady's small private room. [Fr., = 'sulking-place' (*bouder* sulk)]

Bougainville (bōōg'ănvīl), Louis Antoine de (1729–1811). French navigator.

bougainvĭll'aea (bōōg*a*n-) *n.* Tropical climbing plant, with large bright-coloured bracts. [named after BOUGAINVILLE]

bouget (bōōzh'ā) *n.* (her.) Representation of an ancient water-vessel (ill. HERALDRY).

bough (-ow) *n.* Tree-branch.

bought (-awt) past t. & past part. of BUY.

bougie (bōō'zhē) *n.* Wax candle; thin flexible surgical instrument for exploring, dilating, etc., passages of the body. [*Bougie*, Algerian town with wax trade]

bouillabaisse (bōōl'y*a*bās) *n.* Provençal dish of various kinds of Mediterranean fish stewed in water or spiced white wine.

bouillon[1] (bōōl'yawn) *n.* Broth, soup; broth used as medium for culture of bacteria.

Bouillon[2] (bōōl'yawn), Godefroi de, Duke of Lorraine (d. 1100). Leader of the 1st Crusade.

Boulanger (bōōlahnzhā'), Georges Ernest Jean Marie (1831–91). French general; advocated (*c* 1886–9) policy of militarism and revenge against Germany. **Boulăn'gism** (-j-), **Boulăn'gist** *ns.*

boul'der (bōl-) *n.* Large irregular water-worn or weather-worn stone; (geol.) rounded rock fragment about the size of a football or larger; ~ *clay*, mixture of assorted boulders in clay, resulting from a melting glacier.

boulevard (bōōl'vâr) *n.* Wide tree-lined street, esp. in Paris; (U.S.) wide, well-laid-out main street or road.

Boulle (bōōl). Name of a French family of cabinet-makers (esp. André Charles, 1642–1732), noted for ebony furniture inlaid with brass, tortoiseshell, etc., and mounted with gilt bronze; hence, **Boulle, Buhl,** *adj.* & *n.*, (furniture, ornament) of this type.

boul'ter (bōl-) *n.* Long fishing-line with many hooks. ~ *v.i.* Fish with this.

bounce *n.* Rebound; boast, exaggeration, swagger. ~ *v.* Rebound, bound like a ball; throw oneself about; burst *into, out of*, etc.; swagger, talk big; (of cheque) be returned to drawer when there are no funds to meet it; *bouncing*, big and lively, boisterous.

bound[1] *n.* Limit of territory or estate; (pl.) limitation, restriction, limit beyond which schoolchildren, students, soldiers, etc., may not pass. ~ *v.t.* Set bounds to, limit; be boundary of. **bound'lĕss** *adj.* **bound'lĕssly** *adv.* **bound'lĕssnĕss** *n.*

bound[2] *n.* Springy movement upward or forward; recoil (of ball etc.). ~ *v.i.* (Of ball etc.) recoil from wall or ground, bounce; spring, leap, advance lightly.

bound[3] *adj.* Ready to start, having started (*for*).

bound[4] past part. of BIND.

boun'dary *n.* That which serves to indicate bounds or limits of anything; bounds; (cricket) bounds or limits of match enclosure, hit to boundary, runs allowed for this.

boun'den *adj.* Obliged, beholden, indebted, esp. ~ *duty.*

boun'der *n.* (esp. slang) Cheerfully or noisily ill-bred person.

boun'tėous *adj.* Beneficent, liberal; freely bestowed. **boun'tėously** *adv.* **boun'tėousnėss** *n.*

boun'ty[1] *n.* Munificence, liberality in giving; gift, gratuity; subsidy (*~-fed,* subsidized); *Queen Anne's B~*: see ANNE[1]. **boun'tiful** *adj.* Bounteous; *lady ~*, beneficent lady of a neighbourhood (f. *Lady Bountiful* in Farquhar's 'Beaux' Stratagem'). **boun'tifully** *adv.* **boun'tifulnėss** *n.*

Boun'ty[2], Mutiny of the. The crew of H.M.S. *Bounty*, bound from Tahiti to the Cape of Good Hope and the W. Indies, mutinied on 28th April 1789 against their commander, Lieut. BLIGH. He and 18 companions, set adrift in an open boat, succeeded in reaching Timor in the E. Indies, nearly 4,000 miles away. The mutineers returned to Tahiti whence some of them went on to Pitcairn Island, founding a settlement there which was not discovered until 1808; this was eventually adopted by the British Government as a colony.

bouquet (bŏŏk'ā, bŏŏkā') *n.* Bunch of flowers, esp. one presented as a compliment (also fig.); characteristic perfume of wine; bunch of herbs for flavouring.

Bour'bon (boor-). Surname of branch of royal family of France; they became the ruling monarchs when Henry IV succeeded to the throne in 1589. Members of this family became kings of Spain (1700–1931) and of Naples.

Bour'bon whisky (bĕr-). (chiefly U.S.) Whisky distilled from Indian corn and rye, orig. made in County Bourbon, Kentucky.

bour'don(boor-)*n.* Low-pitched (usu. 16-ft) stop in organ; similar stop in harmonium; lowest bell in peal of bells; drone pipe of bagpipe (ill. BAGPIPE). [Fr., = 'drone bee, bass stop in organ']

bourgeois[1] (boor'zhwah) *n.* & *adj.* 1. (orig.) French citizen or freeman of a burgh. 2. (Member) of shop-keeping or mercantile middle class; (person) of humdrum middle-class ideas (now freq. a rather vague term of abuse). **bourgeoisie'** (-zhwăzē) *n.* The middle class.

bourgeois[2] (berjois') *n.* & *adj.* Printing-type between long primer and brevier, approx. 9 point. [Perh. f. a French printer's name]

Bourget (boor'zhā), Paul Charles Joseph (1852–1935). French novelist, whose works are notable for their psychological analysis.

bourn, bourne[1] (boorn) *n.* Small stream, brook, esp. one which dries up intermittently.

bourne, bourn[2] (boorn) *n.* Limit, terminus, boundary, goal.

bourrée (bŏŏrā') *n.* Lively dance, in duple time, of French or Spanish origin; music suitable for or derived from this, esp. as a movement in a suite.

Bourse (boors). French equivalent of the STOCK EXCHANGE.

bout *n.* Spell or turn of work, illness, exercise, etc.; fit of drinking; round at fighting, contest, trial of strength.

bouts *n.pl.* Curves forming waist of violin etc. (ill. STRING).

bōv'īne *adj.* Of, like, an ox; inert, dull.

bow[1] (bō) *n.* 1. Curve; rainbow.

BOWS AND ARROWS: A. BOWMAN WITH LONG-BOW AND SHEAF OF ARROWS IN HIS BELT, *c* 1480. B. CROSSBOW, *c* 1500, AND BOLT OR QUARREL, LATE 15th C.

1. String. 2. Stirrup

2. Weapon for shooting arrows, a strip of flexible wood or other material held in bent position, when in use, by a string stretched between its two ends. 3. Appliance for playing instruments of violin class, rod with a number of horsehairs stretched from end to end, for drawing across the strings (ill. STRING). 4. Slip-knot with double or single loop, ribbon, etc., so tied. 5. *~-compass(es)*, compass with jointed legs (ill. COMPASS); *~-head,* Greenland whale; *~-legged,* bandy; *bow'man,* archer; *~-saw,* saw stretched between ends of bow-shaped handle (ill. SAW); *bow'shot,* distance to which arrow can be shot from bow; *~-window,* curved bay-window. ~ *v.* Play with bow (on violin etc.), use bow.

bow[2] (-ow) *v.* Submit *to*; bend or kneel in sign of submission or reverence, incline head in greeting or assent; express by bowing, usher *in, out,* by bowing; cause to bend. ~ *n.* Bending of head or body in salutation, respect, content, etc.

bow[3] (-ow) *n.* Fore-end of boat or ship from where it begins to arch inwards (often pl.) (ill. BOAT); *on the ~* (of objects) within 45° of the point right ahead (ill. BEARING); ~ (*oar*), oarsman nearest the bow.

Bow bells (bō). The peal of bells of St. Mary-le-Bow, a church in Cheapside near the centre of the City of London; hence, *within the sound of ~*, within the City of London.

Bow chīn'a (bō). Porcelain from the factory at Stratford-le-Bow near London (founded *c* 1745 and active for 20–30 years).

Bowd'ler, Thomas (1754–1825), M.D. of Edinburgh, editor of the 'Family Shakespeare' (1818), an edition 'in which those words and expressions are omitted which cannot with propriety be read aloud in a family'. **bowd'lerīze** *v.t.* Expurgate.

bow'ėl *n.* Division of alimentary canal below stomach, intestine; (pl.) entrails, inside of body; pity, tender feeling; inside of anything, esp. in *~s of the earth.*

bow'er[1] *n.* 1. (poet.) Dwelling, abode; inner room, boudoir. 2. Place closed in with foliage, arbour, summer-house; *~-bird,* Australian bird related to bird of paradise, remarkable for building 'bowers' or 'runs' adorned with feathers, flowers, shells, etc., in courtship. **bow'ery**[1] *adj.*

bow'er[2] *n.* Either of two anchors, or their cables, carried at ship's bow.

bow'er[3] *n.* Each of the two highest cards at euchre, the knave of trumps (*right ~*) and the knave of the other suit of the same colour (*left ~*). [Ger. *bauer* peasant]

Bow'ery[2], The. Street in S. part of New York, formerly notorious as a haunt of criminals. [Du. *bouwerij* husbandry, farm]

bow'ie (-knife) (bō'ĭ) *n.* Large knife with long hollow-ground

AMERICAN BOWIE KNIFE

blade, curved and double-edged near the point. [*Bowie,* name of Amer. inventor]

bowl[1] (bōl) *n.* Basin; drinking-vessel; contents of a bowl; bowl-shaped part of tobacco-pipe, spoon, etc.; tract of country noted for abundance of a particular product, as *wheat-~*.

bowl[2] (bōl) *n.* 1. Wooden ball made slightly out of spherical shape (formerly spherical and weighted on one side) to make it run in a curved course (see BIAS); (pl.) game played on a bowling-green with bowls, the object being to lay the bowls near a smaller one called a 'jack'. 2. Flattened or spherical wooden ball at skittles. ~ *v.* 1. Play bowls; roll (bowl, hoop, etc.); roll like bowl or hoop, move on wheels. 2. (cricket) Deliver ball; dismiss (batsman) by knocking off the bails with the ball; ~ *over*, knock down; disconcert, render helpless.

bowl'er[1] (bōl-) *n.* One who bowls at cricket.

bowl'er[2] (bōl-) *n.* (also ~ *hat*) Hard round felt hat.

bowline (bōl'ĭn) *n.* Rope in ship's rigging from weather side of square sail to bow; ~ (*knot*), simple but very secure knot used in fastening bowline to sail (ill. KNOT).

bowl'ing (bōl-) *n.* ~*-alley*, skittle-alley; ~*-crease*, line from behind which bowler delivers ball; ~*-green*, lawn for playing bowls.

bow'sprit (bōs-) *n.* Spar running out from ship's stem, to which forestays are fastened (ill. SHIP).

Bow Street (bō). Street in London near Covent Garden, in which the principal Metropolitan police court is situated; ~ *Runners*, name in early 19th c. for police officers or detectives, attached to this court before the formation of the London police force.

bow'tĕl (bōt-) *n.* (archit.) Projecting moulding of more or less cylindrical form (ill. MOULDING).

bow'yer (bō'yer) *n.* Maker, seller, of bows.

bŏx[1] *n.* Genus, *Buxus*, of evergreen shrubs or small trees, esp. *B. sempervirens*, with small dark-green leathery leaves, much used in garden borders and hedges; the wood of this (also *box'wood*).

bŏx[2] *n.* 1. Receptacle (usu. lidded, rectangular or cylindrical, and for solids) of wood, cardboard, etc.; quantity contained in this. 2. = CHRISTMAS-box. 3. Driver's seat in vehicle; separate compartment in theatre, tavern, etc., or for horse in stable or railway truck (*loose* ~, in which it can move about); jury-box; witness-box; hut for sentry etc.; small country-house for temporary residence. 4. Protective case for piece of mechanism etc.; (journalism) enclosed space for special news. 5. ~ *barrage*: see BARRAGE; ~*-bed*, bed shut in like large wooden box with hinged shutters or sliding panels in front; ~*-cloth*, thick, coarse, usu. buff-coloured, cloth of which riding-garments are made; ~*-coat*, heavy overcoat such as coachman wears on box; ~*-key*, = box-spanner; ~*-office*, office for booking theatre or cinema seats; ~*-pleat*, double pleat in cloth (ill. PLEAT); ~*-spanner*, *-wrench*, one with a socket-head fitting over nut etc. to be turned (ill. SPANNER). ~ *v.t.* Provide with, put into, confine as in, box; partition *off* from other compartments; ~ *the compass*, (naut.) repeat compass-points in correct order; (fig.) make complete revolution and end where one began (in argument etc.); ~*-haul*, veer ship round on her keel (for want of room).

bŏx[3] *v.* 1. Slap person's *ears*. 2. Fight with fists, usu. in padded gloves; *boxing-gloves*, padded leather gloves used in boxing; *boxing-match*, match between pugilists fighting in boxing-gloves; *boxing-weights*, Heavy (any weight), Light Heavy (not more than 12 st. 7 lb.), Middle (not more than 11 st. 6 lb.), Welter (not more than 10 st. 7 lb.), Light (not more than 9 st. 9 lb.), Feather (not more than 9 st.), Bantam (not more than 8 st. 6 lb.), Fly (not more than 8 st.). ~ *n.* Slap with hand *on the ear*.

Bŏx and Cŏx. Characters in a farce (1847) by J. M. Morton, a printer and a hatter to whom a landlady lets the same room without their knowing it, the one being out at work all night and the other all day; hence, two persons who take turns in sustaining a part.

bŏx-calf (-kahf) *n.* Calfskin tanned with chrome-salts, having a grain of rectangularly crossed lines. [Named after a London bootmaker]

bŏx'er[1] *n.* Person who fights in boxing-match(es), pugilist.

bŏx'er[2] *n.* Smooth-coated brown breed of dog of the bulldog type (ill. DOG).

Bŏx'er Rising. An anti-foreign rising in China (1900) during which the legations at Peking were besieged; it was organized by the *Boxers*, a Chinese secret society. [translation of Chinese word meaning 'fist of harmony']

Bŏx'ing-day *n.* First week-day after Christmas, when Christmas-boxes are given to or expected by postmen, servants, etc.

boy *n.* Male child or youth, son; man retaining boy's character, tastes, etc.; male native servant or labourer; familiarly as term of address; *the* ~, (slang) champagne; *B~ Scout*, member of organization, founded 1908 by Lord BADEN-POWELL, of boys who meet periodically to practise exercises and be trained in duties of a scout; *Boys' Brigade*, organization, founded in Glasgow 1884, of the boys connected with a church or mission, for purposes of drill and instruction.

boy'cott *v.t.* Combine to punish or coerce by systematic refusal of social or commercial relations; abstain from (goods etc.) with this aim. ~ *n.* Boycotting. [f. Captain *Boycott*, an Irish landlord, original victim of this treatment]

boy'hood *n.* Boyish age; boys.

boy'ish *adj.* Of or like boys; **boy'ishly** *adv.* **boy'ishnėss** *n.*

Boyle, Hon. Robert (1627–91). English natural philosopher and chemist, one of the founders of the Royal Society; ~*'s Law*, the law, formulated by him, that the volume of a given quantity of gas varies inversely with the pressure when the temperature is constant.

Boyne. *Battle of the* ~, battle fought across the river Boyne in E. Ireland, 1690; William III and a Protestant (largely English) army defeated the Catholic (Irish and French) army of the exiled James II, who fled to France.

Bŏz. A pseudonym used by Charles DICKENS.

Bp *abbrev.* Bishop.

B.P. *abbrev.* British Pharmacopoeia; British Public.

B.Q.M.S. *abbrev.* Battery Quartermaster-Serjeant.

B.R. *abbrev.* British Railways.

Brabănt' (*or* brăb'*a*nt). Duchy of the Netherlands, now divided between Holland and Belgium.

brāce *v.t.* Strengthen or tighten; make taut; give firmness to, invigorate. ~ *n.* 1. Thing that braces or connects; (pl.) suspenders for trousers; connecting mark in printing or writing ({); strengthening piece of iron or timber in buildings; (naut.) rope attached to yard for trimming sail (ill. SAIL[1]); ~ *and bit*, tool for boring in which the bit is made to revolve by turning the brace etc. (ill. DRILL). 2. Couple, pair, esp. of dogs, hares, pheasants and other game.

brāce'lėt (-sl-) *n.* Ornamental band, chain, etc., for wrist or arm; (pl., slang) handcuffs.

brā'cer *n.* Wrist-guard in archery and fencing.

brăch *n.* Bitch hound.

brăch'ial (-k-) *adj.* Of the arm; like an arm.

brăchycėphăl'ic (-kĭsĭ-) *adj.* Short-headed; (with skull) of which breadth is at least four-fifths of length.

brăck'en *n.* Kind of large fern, *Pteridium aquilinum*, abundant on heaths etc.; mass of this.

brăck'ėt *n.* 1. Flat-topped projection from wall serving as support; shelf with slanting under-prop for hanging against wall; wooden or metal angular support. 2. (freq. pl.) Pair of marks ( ), [ ], { }, used for enclosing words, figures, etc., so as to separate them from the context. 3. (artillery) Specified distance between pair of shots fired beyond target and short of it, in finding range. ~ *v.t.* Enclose in brackets; couple with brace, imply connexion or equality between; (artillery) fire shots beyond and short of target (see above).

brăck'ish *adj.* (Of water) rather salty.

brăct *n.* (bot.) Small modified leaf or scale below flower (ill. INFLORESCENCE).

brăc'tėate *adj.* Bearing bracts. **brăc'tėōle** *n.* (bot.) Small bract on flower-stalk (ill. INFLORESCENCE).

brăd *n.* Thin flattish nail of same thickness throughout (ill. NAIL).

brăd'awl *n.* Small tool consisting of slender stem of steel with chisel edge for making holes for screws, nails, etc.

BRADAWL

Brăd'laugh (-law), Charles (1833–91). English free-thinker, journalist, and politician; was elected M.P. for Northampton in 1880, but unseated, having refused to swear on the Bible.

Brăd'ley, James (1693–1762). English astronomer, discoverer of the aberration of light.

brăd'shaw *n.* 'Bradshaw's Railway Guide', a time-table of all railway trains running in Gt Britain, the earliest form of which was first issued at Manchester in 1839 by George Bradshaw (1801–53), engraver and printer.

brae (-ā) *n.* (Sc.) Steep bank, hill-side.

brăg *v.* Vaunt, talk boastfully. ~ *n.* 1. Boastful talk. 2. Card-game like poker.

Brăgg, Sir William Henry (1862–1942). English physicist, famous for his researches on crystal structure; awarded Nobel Prize for Physics in 1915 with his son Sir William Laurence Bragg (1890–).

brăggadō'cio (-shĭō) *n.* Empty vaunting. [formed by Spenser from *brag* as proper name of personification of vainglory]

brăgg'art *n.* & *adj.* (Person) given to bragging.

Brah'ĕ, Tycho (tĕk'ō), (1546–1601). Danish astronomer; his observations of the sun prepared the way for the discoveries of Kepler (who worked under him); but he did not accept the Copernican system.

brahm'a[1], **brahmapōōt'ra** *n.* Kind of domestic fowl.

Brahm'a[2]. The Supreme God of Hindu mythology, the divine reality, of which the entire universe is only a manifestation.

Brahm'in, -man *n.* Member of the highest or priestly caste among Hindus. **Brahmĭn'ical (-măn-)** *adj.* **Brahm'inism (-man-)** *n.*

Brahms, Johannes (1833–97). German composer of symphonies, chamber music, songs, etc.

braid *n.* 1. Entwined hair, plait; band, etc., entwined with the hair. 2. Woven fabric of silk, linen, etc., in the form of a band. ~ *v.t.* Plait, interweave, arrange in braids; trim, edge, with braid.

brail *v.t.* Haul *up* by means of **brails,** small ropes on sail-edges for trussing sails before furling (ill. BARGE).

Braille (brah-ē), Louis (1809–52). French inventor, himself blind, of the *Braille* (brāl) *system* of printing for the blind; it consists of embossed characters printed on special paper, recognizable by touch, and formed by using varying combinations of 6 dots. ~ *n.* The Braille system, Braille characters. ~ *v.t.* Print in Braille.

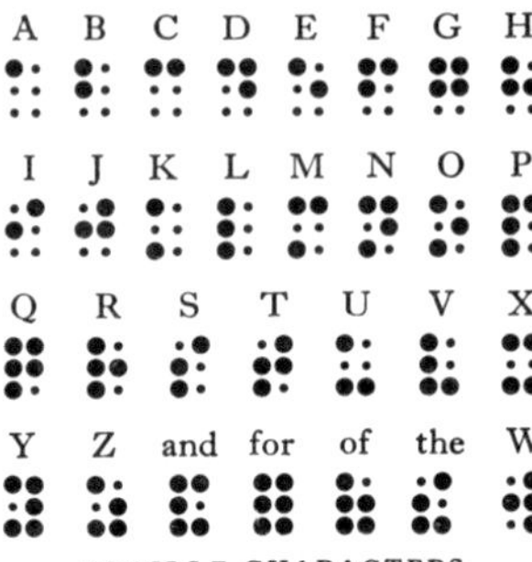

BRAILLE CHARACTERS

brain *n.* 1. Convoluted mass of nervous tissue, contained in the skull, which controls the processes of sensation, learning, and memory in vertebrates and is regarded as the centre of thought and intellectual power in man; its main parts, in primates, are the CEREBRUM or *great* ~, the CEREBELLUM or *lesser* ~, and the MEDULLA oblongata or ~*-stem*; *fore-, mid-, hind-*~, parts which develop from the foremost, middle, hindmost of the 3 main dilatations of the primitive brain. 2. In many invertebrates, that part of the nervous system which corresponds to the vertebrate brain in function and position. 3. ~*-fag*, mental exhaustion; ~*-fever*, inflammation of the brain; ~*-pan*, skull; ~*-storm*, paroxysm of cerebral disturbance; ~ *trust*, (hist.) group of advisers called in by President Franklin Roosevelt; *brains trust*, group of 'experts' assembled to answer questions impromptu; ~*-wash* (*v.*) subject (person) to course of teaching designed to remove his previous opinions (usu. in sinister sense of Communist propaganda); so ~*-washing* (*n.*); ~*-wave*, sudden inspiration, bright thought. **brain'lėss** *adj.* **brain** *v.t.* Dash out brains of.

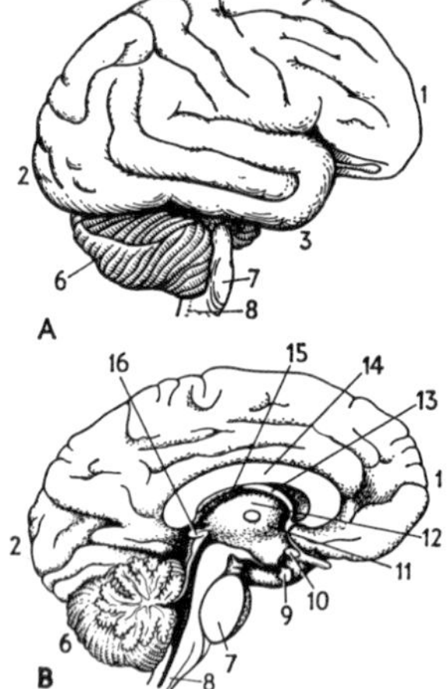

BRAIN: A. SIDE VIEW. B. LONGITUDINAL SECTION

A. 1, 2, 3. Cerebrum (1. Frontal lobe, 2. Occipital lobe, 3. Temporal lobe). 4. Central sulcus. 5. Superior frontal gyrus. 6. Cerebellum. 7. Pons. 8. Medulla oblongata. B. 9. Pituitary or hypophysis. 10. Optic nerve. 11. Third ventricle. 12. Thalamus. 13. Fornix. 14. *Corpus callosum.* 15. Choroid plexus. 16. Pineal body

brain'y *adj.* (colloq.) Clever.

braise (-z) *v.t.* Steam (meat) slowly with vegetables, herbs, etc., in tightly closed pan (prop. with fire above and below).

brāke[1] *n.* Bracken.

brāke[2] *n.* Thicket, brushwood.

brāke[3] *n.* Toothed instrument for braking flax and hemp; ~ (*-harrow*), heavy harrow. ~ *v.t.* Crush (flax, hemp) by beating.

brāke[4] *n.* Frictional apparatus for checking motion of vehicle or machine by pressure, usu. applied to circumference of wheel or to special drum or hub on axle; *brake'(s)man,* man in charge of brake; (U.S.) guard of train; ~*-van,* railway-carriage containing brake, guard's van. ~ *v.t.* Apply brake to (wheel, car, train).

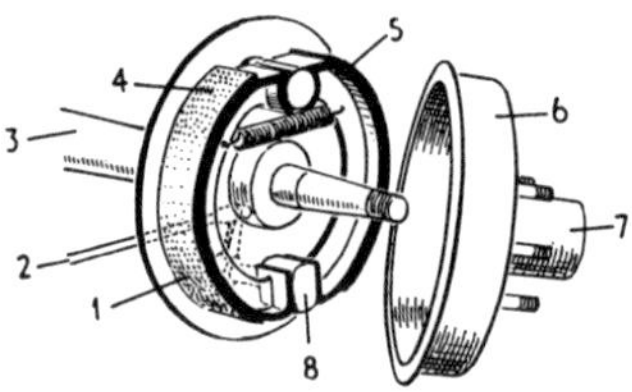

DRUM BRAKE ON NEAR-SIDE WHEEL OF MOTOR-CAR

1. Trailing shoe. 2. Brake rod attached to pedal. 3. Axle. 4. Brake lining. 5. Leading shoe. 6. Brake drum. 7. Hub of wheel. 8. Cam which is turned to apply brake

brāke[5], **break** (brāk) *n.* 1. (usu. *break*) Large carriage-frame with no body, for breaking in young horses. 2. (usu. *brake*) Large wagonette; motor vehicle shaped like van with passenger seats.

Bramăn'tĕ Donato (*c* 1444–1514). Italian High Renaissance architect.

brăm'ble *n.* Rough prickly shrub, esp. the blackberry, *Rubus fruticosus.*

brăm'blĭng *n.* Mountain finch.

brăn *n.* Husks of grain separated from flour after grinding.

branch (-ah-) *n.* Limb of tree etc. growing from stem or bough; lateral extension or subdivision of river, road, family, business, etc.; (U.S.) small stream. **branched** (-sht), **branch'y** *adjs.* **branch** *v.i.* Put branches *out, forth*; spring *out*, spread *forth*, tend *away*, *off*, diverge *into*.

brănch'iae (-kĭē) *n.pl.* Gills. **brănch'ial, brănch'iate** *adjs.*

brănd *n.* 1. Burning or charred piece of wood from hearth. 2. Mark made by burning with hot iron; stigma; trade-mark, goods of particular make or trade-mark; *bran(d)-new*, perfectly new. 3. Iron instrument for branding. 4. (poet.) Sword. ~ *v.t.* Burn with hot iron; impress on memory; stigmatize.

Brăn'denbûrg. (hist.) German electorate which developed into the kingdom of Prussia; (now) province of E. Germany (capital, Potsdam).

brăn'dish *v.t.* Wave about, flourish, in display or threat.

brănd'lĭng *n.* Red worm with rings of brighter colouring, used as bait by anglers.

brăn'dy *n.* Strong alcoholic spirit distilled from wine; ~-*pawnee* [Hind. *pānī* water], brandy and water; ~-*snap*, thin sticky wafer flavoured with brandy and ginger and rolled up. [Du. *brandewijn*, burnt, distilled wine]

brănt(-goose), BRENT(-GOOSE).

Brasenose College (brāz'nōz; abbrev. B.N.C.) College of the University of Oxford, founded 1509 by William Smyth, bishop of Lincoln, and Sir Richard Sutton, Kt., of Prestbury in Cheshire, on the site of *Brasenose Hall*, which had existed at least since 1262. [the name is said to derive from the nose-shaped brass knocker on the orig. door]

brăsh[1] *n.* Loose broken rock or ice; hedge refuse, clippings, etc.

brăsh[2] *adj.* (colloq.) Vulgarly assertive, impudent.

brass (-ahs) *n.* 1. (hist.) Alloy of copper with tin or zinc; (now) yellow alloy of copper and zinc, usu. with about ⅓ total weight of zinc (see BRONZE). 2. Monumental or sepulchral tablet of inscribed brass or similar alloy (usu. latten); musical instruments of brass; (dial.) money. 3. Effrontery, shamelessness. ~ *adj.* Made of brass; ~ *band*, band of musicians with brass instruments; ~ *hat*, (army slang) officer of high rank; ~ *tacks*, (slang) actual details, real business.

brăssard *n.* Badge worn on arm.

brăss'erie (-rē) *n.* Beer-saloon, usu. one in which food is served.

brăss'ière (-ĭār) *n.* Woman's undergarment supporting breasts.

brass'y (-ah-) *adj.* Yellow like brass; sounding or tasting like brass; impudent, shameless. **brass'ie, brass'y** *n.* Wooden golf-club with brass-plate under the head (ill. GOLF).

brăt *n.* (contempt.) Child.

brava'dō (-vah-) *n.* Show of courage, bold front.

brāve *adj.* 1. Courageous. 2. (archaic) Finely dressed; worthy, fine. ~ *n.* Red Indian warrior. **brāve'ly** (-vl-) *adv.* **brāve** *v.t.* Defy, meet with courage.

brāv'ery *n.* Daring; splendour, ostentation, finery.

bra'vo (-ah-) *n.* (pl. *-oes, -os*). Hired assassin; desperado. 2. (also *int.*) Cry of approval, esp. to actors etc.

bravur'a (-oor*a*) *n.* Brilliant execution, attempt at brilliant performance; musical passage requiring great skill and spirit in performance.

brawl *n.* Squabble, noisy quarrel. ~ *v.i.* Engage in brawl; (of stream) run noisily.

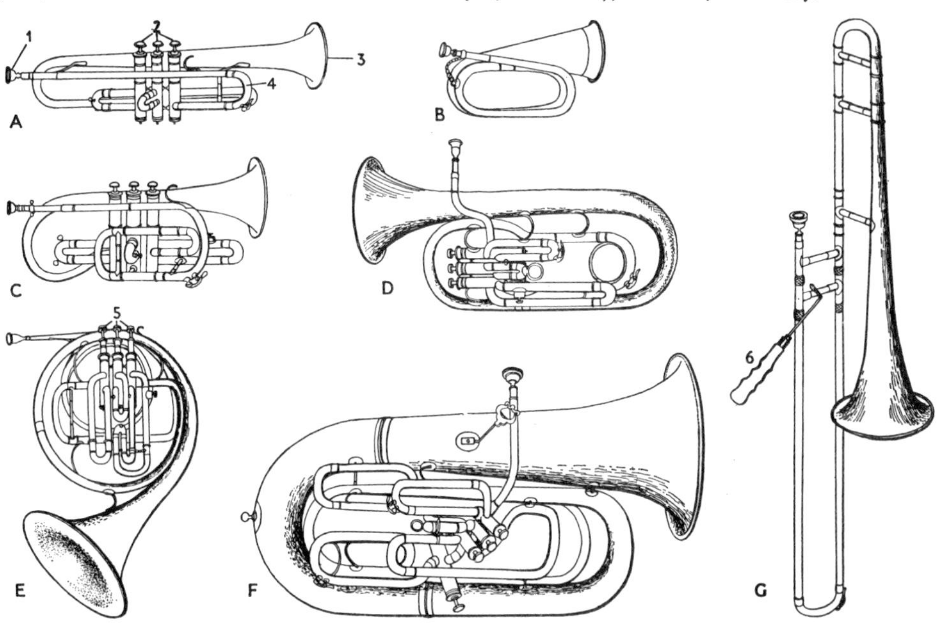

BRASS INSTRUMENTS: A. TRUMPET IN B♭. B. BUGLE IN B♭. C. CORNET IN B♭. D. SAXHORN IN E♭. E. FRENCH HORN IN F. F. BASS TUBA. G. BASS TROMBONE IN G

1. Mouth-piece. 2. Valves. 3. Bell. 4. Tuning slide. 5. Pistons. 6. Slide-handle

brawn *n.* 1. Muscle. 2. Pickled or potted boar's flesh.

brawn'y *adj.* Strong, muscular.

bray[1] *n.* Peculiar cry of some animals, esp. the ass; loud harsh jarring sound resembling this. ~ *v.* Make bray; utter harshly.

bray[2] *v.t.* Pound, usu. in mortar.

Bray[3]. *Vicar of* ~, parson who in an 18th-c. song boasts of having kept his benefice from Charles II's reign to George I's by changing his beliefs to suit the times; possibly based on Symon Symonds who is believed to have remained vicar of Bray in Berkshire from Henry VIII's reign to Elizabeth's.

brāze *v.t.* Solder with alloy of brass and zinc.

brāz'en *adj.* Of brass; strong,

yellow, or harsh-sounding, as brass; shameless. **brāz′enly** *adv.* **brāz′ennėss** *n.* **brāz′en** *v.t.* Adopt impudent, defiant manner under charge or suspicion, esp. ~ *it out.*

brā′zier[1] (-zĭ-, -zh*er*), *n.* Worker in brass.

brā′zier[2] (-zĭ-, -zh*er*) *n.* Large flat pan for holding burning charcoal etc.; iron cage or basket for charcoal fire.

Brazil′. Large S. Amer. Portuguese-speaking State; colonized by Portugal in the early 16th c.; proclaimed a republic, 1889; capital, Brasilia. **brazil′** *n.* 1. (usu. ~-*wood*) Hard brownish-red wood of the E. Ind. sappan-tree, *Caesalpinia Sappan*, from which red dye was obtained; the similar wood of a S. Amer. species, *C. echinata.* 2. ~-*nut*, large three-sided edible nut, the seed of a lofty tree, *Bertholletia excelsa*, which forms large forests in Brazil. [orig. the Span., Port., and Fr. name of the E. Indian wood; transferred to the S. Amer. species, and thence to the country where this was found]

B.R.C.S. *abbrev.* British Red Cross Society.

breach *n.* 1. (naut.) Breaking of waves; (fig.) breaking or neglect (of rule, duty, promise, etc.); breaking of relations, alienation, quarrel. 2. Injury, broken place, gap, esp. made by artillery in fortification; ~ *of the peace*, disturbance of public peace by affray, riot, etc.; ~ *of promise*, breach of promise to marry. ~ *v.t.* Break through, make gap in.

bread (-ĕd) *n.* Flour moistened, usu. leavened, kneaded into dough, and baked in loaves; this as staple article of food; livelihood, means of subsistence; ~ *and butter*, slices of bread spread with butter; livelihood; ~-*and-butter letter*, letter of thanks for hospitality; ~-*crumb*, soft spongy inner part of loaf; small fragment of bread; ~-*fruit*, farinaceous fruit, about the size of a melon, and with whitish pulp like new bread, of *Artocarpus incisa*, the ~-*fruit tree* of the South Sea islands etc.; ~-*winner*, person supporting a family.

breadth (-ĕd-) *n.* 1. Broadness, measure from side to side; piece (of cloth etc.) of full breadth. 2. Extent, distance, room; largeness, liberality, catholicity. **breadth′ways** (-z), **breadth′wīse** (-z) *advs.*

break[1] (brāk) *v.* (past t. *brōke*, past part. *brōk′en* sometimes *brōke*). 1. Divide, disperse, split, separate, otherwise than by cutting; tame, subdue, crush; lay open; fall to pieces; burst, issue, *forth*; ~ *down*, (intrans.) collapse; (trans.) itemize, analyse; ~ *up*, become feeble, dismiss, break small. 2. Make, become, bankrupt. 3. Interrupt, change; transgress, violate. 4. Make a way, come, produce, with effort, suddenness, violence, etc. 5. (Of cricket-ball) deviate from original direction after pitching. 6. *break′down*, collapse, stoppage; failure of health or power; act of disintegrating or analysing a substance; analysis of statistical figures; negro dance; *break′neck*, endangering the neck, headlong; ~-*up*, disintegration, collapse, dispersal; *break′water*, mole etc. built to break force of waves. **break′able** *adj.* **break′age** *n.* **break** *n.* Breaking; breach, gap, broken place; pause in work etc.; deviation of cricket-ball after pitching; (billiards) points scored continuously; (slang) stroke of luck.

break[2] *n.* = BRAKE[5].

break′er[1] (brāk-) *n.* (esp.) Heavy ocean-wave breaking on coast or over reefs.

break′er[2] (brāk-) *n.* (naut.) Small keg.

break′fast (brĕk-) *n.* First meal of the day. ~ *v.i.* Break one's fast, take breakfast.

bream *n.* 1. Yellowish fresh-water fish of genus *Abramis* with high-arched back. 2. Sea-fish of the family *Sparidae*, including many different genera.

breast (-ĕst) *n.* 1. Each of two soft protuberances on woman's thorax, secreting milk for feeding young; corresponding rudimentary organ of man. 2. Upper front part of human body, corresponding part in animals; part of dress, coat, etc., covering this. 3. Heart, emotions, thoughts. 4. ~-*bone*, thin flat vertical bone in chest connecting ribs, sternum (ill. SKELETON); ~ *hook*: see ill. BOAT; *breast′plate*, piece of armour covering breast (ill. ARMOUR); ~-*stroke*, stroke in swimming in which breast is squarely opposed to the water (ill. SWIM); ~-*wheel*, water wheel turned by water flowing in level with the axle (ill. WATER); *breast′work*, temporary defence or parapet a few feet high. ~ *v.t.* Oppose breast to, face, contend with.

breast′sŭmmer (-ĕst-), **brĕss′ŭmmer** *n.* Beam across broad opening, sustaining superstructure (ill. HALF-timber).

breath (-ĕth) *n.* 1. Exhalation as perceptible to sight or smell; slight movement of air; whiff. 2. Air taken into and expelled from lungs; respiration; power of breathing; whisper, murmur. 3. (phonetics) Voiceless expiration of air.

breathe (-dh) *v.* Use the lungs; live, seem alive; take breath, pause; sound, speak, blow, softly; take in (air etc.); utter softly or passionately, exhibit; allow to breathe, rest; force to breathe, exercise.

breath′er (-dh-) *n.* (esp.) Short spell of exercise; spell of rest to recover one's breath after exertion.

breath′ing (-dh-) *n.* (esp. Gk gram.) *rough, smooth,* ~, sign indicating that initial vowel is or is not aspirated; ~-*space*, time to breathe; pause.

breath′lėss (-ĕth-) *adj.* Panting; holding the breath; unstirred by wind. **breath′lėssly** *adv.* **breath′lėssnėss** *n.*

brĕ′ccia (-ch*a*) *n.* (geol.) Composite rock of angular fragments of stone etc. cemented together by some matrix.

Brĕck′nockshire, Brĕc′onshire. County of Wales.

bred: see BREED *v.*

breech *n.* 1. (pl., pron. *brĭch′ĭz*) Short trousers fastened below knee, and now only used for riding, or in court costume, etc.; (loosely) trousers, knickerbockers. 2. Part of cannon behind bore (ill. CANNON); back part of rifle or gun barrel. 3. *Breeches Bible*, the Geneva Bible of 1560 with *breeches* for *aprons* in Gen. iii. 7; ~-*loader*, -*loading*, (gun) loaded at breech, not through muzzle (hist.); (of guns) in which obturation is effected by a specially designed breech and not by a metal cartridge-case; *breeches-buoy*, lifebuoy, slung on a rope, with canvas supports like breeches for the legs. ~ *v.t.* (archaic) Put (boy) into breeches instead of petticoats.

breech′ing (-ĭch-) *n.* 1. Leather strap round shaft-horse's hind-quarters for pushing backwards (ill. HARNESS). 2. (naut.) Rope securing gun to ship's side.

breed *v.* (past t. and past part. *brĕd*). 1. Bear, generate; (make) propagate; raise (cattle etc.); yield produce, result in; arise, spread. 2. Train up; fit for being, adapt *to*, bring up. 3. (physics) Create further fissile material during the nuclear breakdown of a fissile element. ~ *n.* Race, stock, strain; family with hereditary qualities.

breed′er *n.* One who breeds cattle etc.; animal that breeds; ~ (*reactor*), (physics) nuclear reactor in which new fissile material is created during the fission of an element.

breed′ing *n.* (esp.) Result of training, (good) behaviour or manners.

breeze[1] *n.* 1. Gentle wind; wind blowing in from sea during day (*sea*-~), or from land to sea during night (*land*-~). 2. (slang) Quarrel.

breeze[2] *n.* Small cinders, coke, coke-dust, etc., used in burning bricks, and to make ~-*blocks*, flat slabs used for the interior walls of inexpensive buildings.

breez′y *adj.* Wind-swept; pleasantly windy; lively, jovial. **breez′ĭly** *adv.* **breez′inėss** *n.*

Brem′en (brā-). Province of W. Germany; its capital, a seaport on river Weser.

Brĕn′dan, St. (484–577). Irish saint reputed in legend to have made a voyage in search of the earthly paradise, touching at many fabulous islands on the way; commemorated 16th May.

Brĕn gŭn *n.* Light, magazine-fed automatic rifle used in the British Army in the war of 1939–45, noted for its steadiness in action and ease with which barrel can be changed when over-hot. [*Brno*, town in Czechoslovakia where it was orig. made, and first syllable of *Enfield*, town in Middlesex, England, seat of Royal Small-arms factory]

brĕnt(-gōōse), brănt- *n.* Smallest species of wild goose, *Bernicla brenta*, of Arctic origin, visiting Britain in winter.

brẽr *n.* (U.S. negro dial. contraction for) brother.

bressummer: see BREAST-SUMMER.

Brĕst-Lĭtŏvsk′ (-fsk). Polish town on Russian frontier (now in U.S.S.R.), in which was signed the treaty of peace between Germany and Russia in March 1918.

Bret Harte, Francis: see HARTE.

brĕth′rėn (-dh-) *n.pl.* Archaic pl. of *brother*, now used only of fellow members of religious society, or guild, order, or profession; *Elder B~*, the superior members of Trinity House.

Brĕt′on *n.* & *adj.* (Native, language) of BRITTANY.

Breughel: see BRUEGHEL.

brev. *abbrev.* brevet.

brēve *n.* 1. (mus.) Note equal to two semibreves, now rarely used (‖⊖‖). 2. Mark (˘) placed over vowel to show that it is short. 3. (hist.) Letter of authority from sovereign or pope.

brĕv′ėt *n.* Document conferring privilege from sovereign or government, esp. rank without corresponding pay in army. ~ *v.t.* Confer brevet rank on.

brēv′iary *n.* Book containing R.C. Divine Office for each day, to be recited by those in orders.

brėvier′ (-vẽr) *n.* Printing-type size between bourgeois and minion (approx. 8 point).

brĕv′ĭty *n.* Shortness, briefness.

brew (-ōō) *v.* 1. Make (beer etc.) by infusion, boiling, and fermentation, or (tea, punch) by infusion or mixture. 2. Concoct, set in train; foster, gather force. ~ *n.* Brewing; amount brewed; beverage etc. brewed.

brew′er (-ōōer) *n.* (esp.) One who brews malt liquors. **brew′ery** *n.*

Brew′ster (-ōō-), Sir David (1781–1868). Scottish physicist; made discoveries relating to polarization of light.

Brew′ster Sessions (-ōō-). Magistrates' sessions for issuing licences to trade in alcoholic liquors.

Brī′an Boru′ (-ōō) (926–1014). King of Munster; defeated the Danes and in 1002 became high king of Ireland; was killed after a great victory over the Danes at Clontarf.

briar: see BRIER.

Brī′areus (-rōōs). (Gk myth.) Giant with 100 hands and 50 heads, confined under Mt Etna for fighting, with the other giants, against the gods.

brībe *n.* Money etc. offered to procure (often illegal or dishonest) action in favour of the giver. ~ *v.t.* Pervert the action, judgement, etc., of, by gifts or other inducements. **brī′bery** *n.*

brĭc′-à-brăc *n.* Antiquarian or artistic odds and ends.

brĭck *n.* 1. Clay kneaded, moulded, and baked by fire or sun,

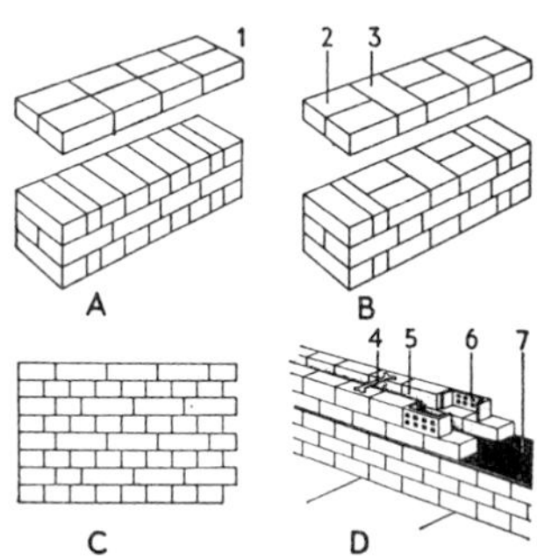

BRICK BONDS: A. ENGLISH BOND. B. FLEMISH BOND. C. DUTCH BOND. D. STRETCHER-BONDED CAVITY WALL

1. Course. 2. Stretcher. 3. Header. 4. Tie. 5. Cavity. 6. Ventilating brick. 7. Damp course

used as a building material; rectangular block of this, usu. about 9 in. × $4\frac{3}{8}$ × $2\frac{5}{8}$. 2. Brick-shaped block, e.g. of tea; child's toy building-block. 3. (slang) Good fellow, warmly-approved-of person. 4. *brick′bat*, piece of brick, esp. as missile (also fig.); *~-field*, piece of ground where bricks are made; *brick′layer* (-lāer), workman who lays bricks in building; *~-red*, the colour of red brick; *~-tea*, tea pressed into small brick and used as medium of exchange. ~ *v.t.* Block *up* with brickwork.

brīd′al *adj.* Of bride or wedding. ~ *n.* (now rare) Wedding-feast.

brīde[1] *n.* Woman on her wedding day and for some time before and after it; *~-cake*, rich highly decorated cake eaten at wedding and sent round to friends.

brīde[2] *n.* Small band or tie-bar connecting motifs of lace (ill. LACE).

Bride[3], St.: see BRIDGET[1].

brīde′grōōm (-dg-) *n.* Man at his marriage or soon before or after it.

brīdes′maid (-dz-) *n.* Unmarried woman or girl attending bride at wedding.

Brīde′well (-dw-). Orig. a royal palace in London near the old well of St. Bride at the mouth of the Fleet river; it was rebuilt by Henry VIII and later became a hospital and then a house of correction. **bride′well** *n.* Prison, gaol.

brĭdge[1] *n.* 1. Structure carrying road or path across river, ravine, etc. 2. (naut.) Platform amidships for officer in command (ill. SHIP). 3. Upper bony part of nose. 4. Movable piece over which strings of violin etc. are stretched (ill. STRING). 5. (billiards) Support for cue formed with left hand; contrivance consisting of a notched or crossed piece at end of a long stick used as a cue-rest. 6. *~-head*, (mil.) fortification, post, at end of bridge or on side of a river nearest enemy; any position established in face of enemy, e.g. by landing force; ~ *passage*, passage connecting principal subjects in musical composition. ~ *v.t.* Span as, with, or as with, a bridge. (*Illustration, p.* 92.)

brĭdge[2] *n.* Card-game, app. of Near-Eastern origin, based upon whist and now superseded by auction and contract bridge. The dealer or his partner (dummy) named trumps or elected to play with no-trumps, dummy's hand was exposed after the lead, and the scoring for tricks over six differed from the modern forms of the game; *Auction B~*, variety of this in which the trump suit (or the playing of the hand in no-trumps) and the person who shall play his partner's (dummy's) hand as well as his own are decided by the players making bids (i.e. undertaking to take a specified number of tricks over six with a specified suit as trump or with no-trumps) or passing (i.e. making no bid) in turn, until a bid is made which none of the other three players bid above, Clubs counting 6 points, Diamonds 7, Hearts 8, Spades 9, and No-trumps 10; 30 points make a game, and two games a rubber; the penalty for under-tricks is 50 'above the line' (i.e. not counting towards game), 100 if doubled, and so on; and further points 'above the line' are awarded for honours in the trump suit; *Contract B~*, a form of auction bridge in which only tricks actually declared count towards game, extra tricks being scored 'above the line'.

Brĭdg′ės (-z), Robert (1844–1930). English poet, poet laureate from 1913.

Brĭdg′ėt[1], **Brĭ′gĭt, Brīde,** St. (453–523). Second patron saint of Ireland, traditionally held to have been born in Louth in the time of St. Patrick; commemorated 1st Feb.

Brĭdg′ėt[2], **Brĭ′gĭd, Bĭrgĭtt′a** (-g-), St. (1304–73). Founder of an order of nuns (Order of the Most Holy Saviour) at Vadstena, Sweden, 1344. **Brĭdg′ėttīne, Brĭ′gĭttīne, Bĭrgĭtt′ine** *adjs.* & *ns.* (Nun) of this order.

brī′dle *n.* 1. Head-gear of harness, including head-stall, bit, and rein (ill. HARNESS); restraint, curb; *~-path*, one fit for horses but not for vehicles. 2. (naut.) Mooring-cable. 3. (physiol.) Ligament or membrane checking motion of a part, or binding one part to another. ~ *v.* Put bridle on, curb, control; express resentment, vanity, etc., by throwing up head and drawing in chin.

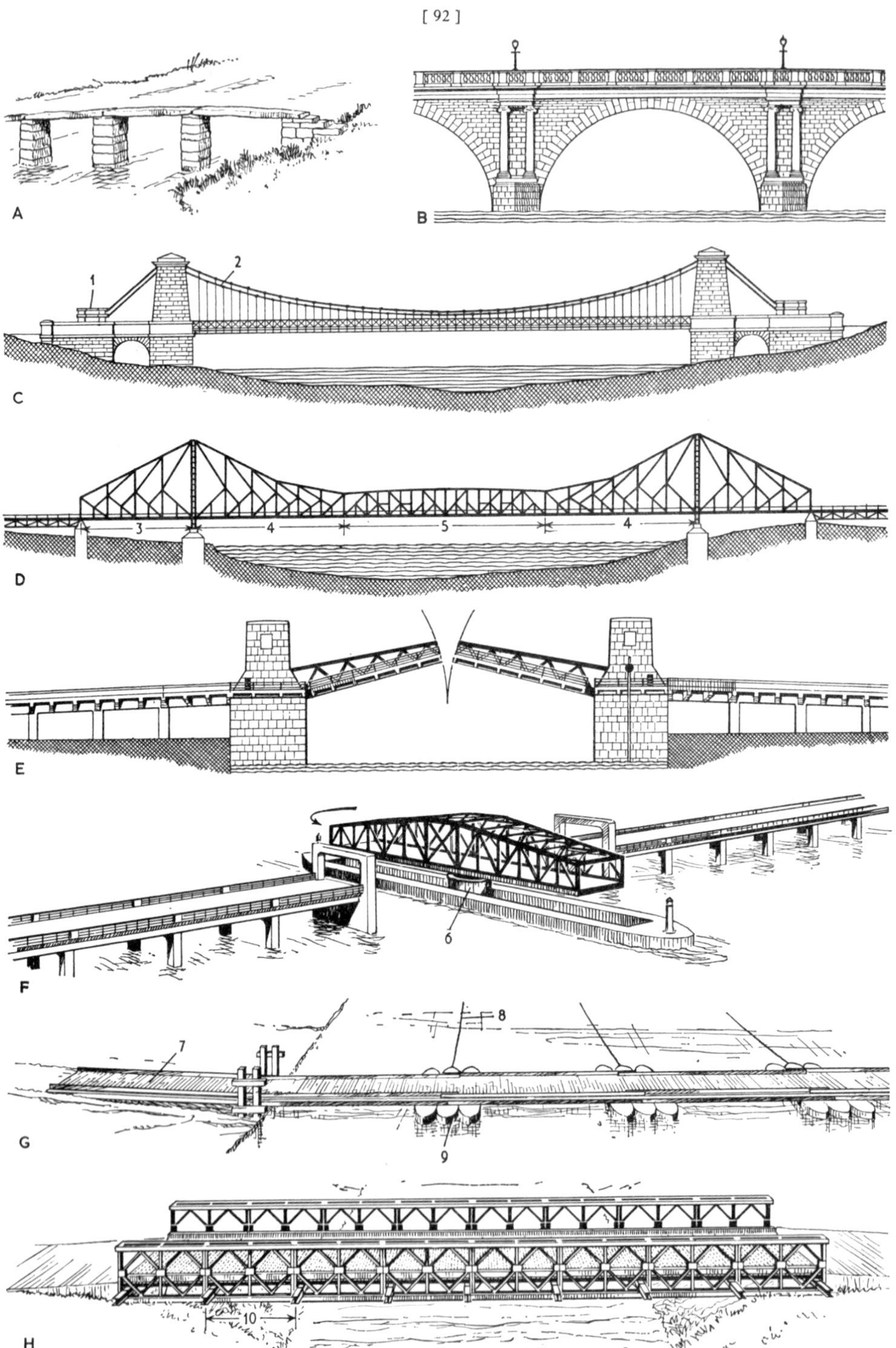

BRIDGES: A. CLAPPER. B. ARCH. C. SUSPENSION. D. CANTILEVER. E. BASCULE. F. SWING. G. PONTOON. H. BAILEY

1. Anchorage. 2. Chains. 3. Anchor plate. 4. Cantilever arm. 5. Suspended span. 6. Turntable. 7. Ramp. 8. Upstream mooring. 9. Pontoon. 10. 10-ft standard section

Brie (brē). District of N. France; the soft cheese produced there.

brief[1] (brēf) *n.* 1. Pope's letter on matter of discipline (less formal than *bull*). 2. (law) Summary of facts and points of law of a case drawn up (usu. by solicitors) for counsel; piece of employment for barrister; *watching-~*, brief of barrister who watches case for a client not directly concerned. ~ *v.t.* Instruct barrister by brief; give (airmen) instructions for operation; give (administrator etc.) necessary facts; *briefing*, airmen's instructions for operational sortie; any set of instructions or facts relating to particular situation.

brief[2] (brēf) *adj.* Short, concise. **brief'ly** *adv.* **brief'ness** *n.*

brief'less (brēf-) *adj.* (Of barrister) without briefs, unemployed.

brī'er[1], **brī'ar**[1] *n.* Prickly bush, esp. wild rose; *sweet ~*, kind of rose with fragrant leaves and flowers; *~-rose*, wild rose, dog-rose.

brī'er[2], **brī'ar**[2] *n.* The white heath, *Erica arborea*, a native of S. France, Corsica, etc.; ~ *pipe*, tobacco-pipe made of its root.

Brieux (brēẽr'), Eugène (1858–1932). French playwright, author of plays dealing with social problems.

brĭg[1] *n.* Two-masted square-rigged vessel having additional lower fore-and-aft sail with a gaff and boom on the mainmast.

Brig.(-Gen.) *abbrev.* Brigadier (-General).

Brigham Young: see YOUNG[4].

bright[1] (-īt) *adj.* Emitting or reflecting much light, shining; lit up with joy etc.; vivid; illustrious; vivacious, quick-witted. **bright'ly** *adv.* **bright'ness** *n.* **bright'en** *v.* **bright** *adv.* Brightly.

Bright[2] (-īt), John (1811–89); English Liberal politician, famous as a leading agitator against the Corn Laws and as an orator.

Bright's disease (-īts). Granular degeneration of the kidneys. [Dr Richard *Bright*, English physician (1789–1858)]

brĭll *n.* European flatfish, *Psetta laevis*, resembling turbot in shape and the quality of its flesh.

brĭll'iant (-lya-) *adj.* Bright, sparkling; illustrious; highly talented; showy. **brĭll'iantly** *adv.* **brĭll'iance, brĭll'iancy** *ns.* **brĭll'iant** *n.* 1. Diamond or other precious stone of finest cut and brilliance; *~-cut*, having two horizontal tables joined by facets (ill. GEM). 2. Very small size of printing-type (approx. 3½ point).

brĭll'iantine (-lyantēn) *n.* Cosmetic for keeping hair smooth and glossy.

brĭm *n.* Edge or lip of cup, bowl, or hollow; projecting edge of hat. *~-full*, full to the brim. ~ *v.* Fill, be full, to the brim.

brĭmm'er *n.* Full cup.

brĭm'stone *n.* (Old name for) sulphur; fuel of hell-fire; ~ *and treacle*, old-fashioned medical concoction; ~ *butterfly*, *moth*, sulphur-coloured species, *Gonepteryx Rhamni* and *Rumia crataegata*.

A. BRIG. B. BRIGANTINE

brĭg[2] *n.* (Sc.) Bridge.

brĭgāde' *n.* Major sub-unit of an army division, commanded by a brigadier, normally consisting, in British Army, of 3 battalions; organized or uniformed band of workers; *Boys' B~*: see BOY.

brĭgadier' (-dēr) *n.* (formerly *~-general*) Army officer ranking immediately above colonel and below major-general.

brĭg'and *n.* Bandit, robber. **brĭg'andage** *n.*

brĭg'antine (-ēn) *n.* Two-masted vessel with square-rigged foremast and fore-and-aft rigged mainmast.

brĭnd'le(d) *adj.* Brownish or tawny with streaks of other colour.

brīne *n.* Water saturated, or strongly impregnated, with salt; the sea; (poet.) tears. ~ *v.t.* Steep or pickle in, wet with, brine. **brīn'y** *adj.* Very salt. ~ *n.* (joc.) The sea.

brĭng *v.* (past t. and past part. *brought* pr. -awt) Cause to come, come with or convey in any fashion; cause, result in; prefer (charge), adduce (argument); cause to become; persuade; ~ *to bear*, apply; ~ *to book*, exact account from; ~ *to mind*, recall; ~ *to pass*, cause to happen; ~ *about*, cause to happen; ~ *down*, kill or wound, cause to fall, cause penalty to alight *on*, abase, lower, continue (record) *to* a point; ~ *forth*, bear, cause; ~ *forward*, carry (sum in accounts) to next page; ~ *in*, produce, introduce; pronounce (*guilty*, *not guilty*, etc.); ~ *off*, rescue from wreck etc., conduct with success; ~ *out*, (esp.) introduce (girl) to society; ~ *round*, restore to consciousness; ~ *to*, bring round, (cause to) come to a stop; ~ *up*, rear, educate, anchor, come to a stop, call attention (*again*) to, continue (accounts etc.) to a further point.

brĭnk *n.* Edge of steep place; border of water, esp. when steep; verge (also fig.).

brĭ'o (-ēō) *n.* Vivacity, dash.

brĭquette' (-kĕt), **brĭ'quet** (-kėt) *n.* Block of compressed coal-dust, usu. with addition of binding substance such as pitch.

Brĭs'bane (-zban). Capital of Queensland, Australia.

Brĭs'ēĭs. (Gk legend) A slave-girl who belonged to Achilles and was taken from him by Agamemnon; this was the cause of the wrath of Achilles and his prolonged inactivity in that part of the 10th year of the Trojan War which is covered by the 'Iliad'.

brĭsk *adj.* Active, lively; enlivening, keen. **brĭsk'ly** *adv.* **brĭsk'ness** *n.* **brĭsk** *v.* Make, become, brisk.

brĭs'kėt *n.* Breast of animals, esp. as joint of meat (ill. MEAT).

brĭs'lĭng *n.* Small Norwegian fish of herring family, resembling a sardine.

brĭ'stle (-ĭsl) *n.* Stiff hair (esp. of hog's back and sides), used for brushes. **brĭs'tly** (-slĭ) *adj.* **brĭs'tle** *v.* (Cause to) stand on end, raise, rise, like bristles; show temper, prepare for fight; be thickly set (*with* difficulties etc.).

Brĭs'tol. City and county port S. of Gloucestershire, port on the

Avon; ~ *board*, fine paste-board for drawing; ~ *cream*, ~*milk*, kinds of sherry first imported at Bristol; ~*-fashion*, (usu. in (*all*) *ship-shape and* ~*-fashion*) in good order.

Brit. *abbrev.* Britain; British.

Brĭt'ain (-an) (also *Great* ~). The whole island containing England, Wales, and Scotland, with their dependencies; *North* ~, (now rare) Scotland.

Brĭtănn'ĭa. Latin name of Britain; (poetic name for) Britain personified, usu. represented (e.g. on coins) as a woman with shield, helmet, and trident; ~ *metal*, an alloy of tin and regulus of antimony, used for tableware etc.

Brĭtănn'ĭc *adj.* (now chiefly in *His, Her* ~ *Majesty*) Of Britain.

Brĭt'ish *adj.* 1. Of Britain, esp. of ancient (or Roman) Britain. 2. Of Gt Britain. 3. In Amer. usage, freq. = English. **Brĭt'isher** *n.* (orig. U.S.) Native of Gt Britain.

British Association for the Advancement of Science. An association of scientists, which first met in 1831, for the promotion and diffusion of scientific knowledge.

British Broadcasting Corporation (abbrev. B.B.C.). Public corporation orig. having the monopoly of broadcasting in Gt Britain, financed by a grant-in-aid from Parliament; established 1927 by royal charter to carry on work previously performed by the British Broadcasting Company.

British Colŭm'bĭa. Province on W. coast of Canada; capital, Victoria.

British Commonwealth of Nations. The association of Great Britain and certain self-governing nations (Canada, Australia, New Zealand, India, Pakistan, Ceylon, Ghana, Nigeria, Cyprus, Sierra Leone, Jamaica, Trinidad and Tobago, Uganda, Kenya, Malaysia, Tanzania, Malawi, Malta, Zambia, The Gambia, Singapore, Swaziland, Guyana, Botswana, Lesotho, Barbados, and Mauritius) together with all her dependencies and theirs; *Commonwealth countries*, all these nations and dependencies; *Members of the Commonwealth*, the self-governing nations.

British Council. Organization established in 1934 at the instance of the Foreign Office to make the culture of the British peoples more widely known abroad.

British Empire. Former name of the BRITISH COMMONWEALTH OF NATIONS, still used, esp. for that part which is not self-governing; *Order of the* ~, mil. and civil award (instituted 1917) for services rendered to Br. Empire.

British Isles. Britain and Ireland, with the islands near their coasts.

brĭt'ishĭsm *n.* Idiom used in Gt Britain but not in U.S.

British Is'rāel (ĭz-). Theory that the Anglo-Saxon peoples are descended from the 'Lost' Tribes of Israel; supporters of this view, who regard John Wilson (d. 1870), a Scotsman, as their founder. **British Is'rāelīte** *n.* One who believes in British Israel.

British Legion: see LEGION.

British Museum. National museum of antiquities etc. in Bloomsbury, London, occupying the site of Montagu House, which was acquired in 1753 to house the library and collections of Sir Hans Sloane; the library has a statutory right to a copy of every book published in the United Kingdom (see COPYRIGHT *libraries*).

British thermal unit: see THERMAL.

Brĭt'on *n.* 1. Inhabitant of Gt Britain. 2. (also *ancient* ~) Inhabitant of the S. part of the island at the Roman invasion.

Britt. *abbrev. Brit(t)an(n)iarum* (= of the Britains, on coins).

Brĭtt'any. Bretagne, NW. district of France, an ancient province and duchy, largely inhabited by a Celtic stock related to that of Britain.

Brĭtt'en, Edward Benjamin (1913–). British composer of operas ('Peter Grimes' etc.) and other music.

brĭt'tle *adj.* Apt to break, fragile. **brĭtt'lenėss** (-ln-) *n.*

broach[1] *n.* 1. Spit for roasting. 2. Church-spire rising from tower without parapet (ill. SPIRE). 3. Boring-bit. ~ *v.t.* Pierce (cask) to draw liquor, begin drawing (liquor), open (bale, box, etc.); begin discussion of (subject).

broach[2] *v.* (usu. ~ *to*) Veer, cause (ship) to veer and present side to wind and waves.

broad (-awd) *adj.* 1. Large across, wide, not narrow; in breadth; extensive. 2. Full, clear, main, explicit; (of humour or speech) coarse, downright; general; tolerant; bold in effect or style. 3. *county, land, of* ~ *acres*, Yorkshire; ~ *arrow*, mark like arrow-head distinguishing British government stores (formerly prison dress etc.); similar sign used as bench-mark (see BENCH *n.*); ~ *Church*, in the Anglican Church, that section favouring comprehension and not pressing doctrines; *broad'cloth*, fine twill-wove woollen cloth, (also) plain-wove cotton cloth (the name now refers rather to quality than to width); *broad'sheet*, large sheet of paper printed on one side only; *broad'side*, ship's side above water between bow and quarter; (discharge of) all guns on one side of ship; (fig.) direct attack; *broad'sword*, broad-bladed cutting-sword (ill. SWORD); *broad'tail* [translating Ger. *breitschwanz*], astrakhan or PERSIAN lamb. ~ *n.* Broad part; *the Broads*, large stretches of fresh water in East Anglia, formed by widening of rivers. **broad'ly** *adv.* **broad'nėss** *n.* (esp. of indelicacy of speech).

broad *adv.* Broadly.

broad'cast (-awdkah-) *adj.* 1. (Of seed) scattered freely, not in drills or rows. 2. (Of information, news, music, etc.) sent or received by broadcasting. ~ *adv.* (Sown, disseminated) in this manner. ~ *n.* Action of broadcasting; broadcast programme etc. ~ *v.* (past t. *-cast* or *-casted*, past part. *-cast*). 1. Sow (seed) broadcast. 2. Disseminate (news, musical performances, etc.) from a transmitting station by radio or television; said also of performer etc. **broad'caster** *n.* Broadcasting company, performer, etc. **broad'casting** *n.* & *adj.*

broad'en (-awdn) *v.* Make, grow, broad.

Broad'moor (-awd-). Asylum in Berkshire for criminal lunatics.

Broad'way (-awd-). Important street in New York, with many theatres etc.

Brŏb'dĭngnăg. In Swift's 'Gulliver's Travels', a country inhabited by giants. **Brŏbdĭngnăg'ĭan** (-g-) *adj.* & *n.*

brocāde' *n.* 1. Fabric, of any weave or yarn, enriched by a design which is formed by additional weft threads, often of metal, running back and forth across each motif only (not from selvage to selvage) 2. Fabric superficially resembling this, produced by Jacquard loom. ~ *v.t.* Enrich (fabric) with design by these means.

brŏcc'olĭ *n.* Cultivated cabbage with edible flower head, hardy variety of cauliflower.

brŏch (-χ) *n.* Prehistoric round stone tower of Orkney and the Shetlands etc.

brŏ'chure (-shoor) *n.* Stitched booklet, pamphlet.

brŏck *n.* Badger.

Brŏck'en. Highest of the Harz Mountains in Saxony, reputed to be the scene of witches' Walpurgis-night revels; *spectre of the* ~, a magnified shadow of the spectator thrown on a bank of cloud in high mountains when the sun is low (first observed on the Brocken).

brŏck'ėt *n.* Stag in its 2nd year, with straight horns like small daggers.

brogue[1] (-ōg) *n.* Rough Irish and Scottish Highland shoe of untanned leather (ill. PLAID); strong shoe for country and sports wear.

brogue[2] (-ōg) *n.* Dialectal, esp. Irish, accent.

broil[1] *n.* Quarrel, tumult.

broil[2] *v.* Cook (meat), be cooked, on fire or gridiron; scorch, make or be very hot.

brōke: var. BROKEN = ruined.

brōk'en *adj.* (past part. of BREAK *v.*). In pieces, shattered; ruined; infirm; incomplete; ~ *English* etc., imperfect English etc.; ~ *ground*, uneven ground; ~*-hearted*, crushed by grief; ~*-winded*, (of horse) unfit for hard work by reason of ruptured air-cells. **brōk'enly** *adv.* Spasmodically, by jerks, with breaks. **brōk'ennėss** *n.*

brōk′er *n.* Dealer in second-hand furniture etc.; middleman in bargains; person licensed to sell or value distrained goods; person acting as agent, esp. one who buys and sells stocks for clients, stock-broker. **brōk′erage** *n.* Broker's fees or commission, esp. on Stock Exchange transactions. [OF *brocheor* 'broacher', retailer of wine]

brōk′ing *n.* Broker's trade, acting as broker.

brŏll′y *n.* (colloq.) Umbrella.

brōm′ide *n.* 1. Compound of bromine with an element or organic radical; ~ *paper*, (phot.) printing-paper coated with an emulsion containing silver bromide. 2. Potassium bromide, KBr, taken as a sedative; (fig., colloq.) conventional and commonplace person or remark.

brōm′ine (-ēn) *n.* A non-metallic element, closely resembling chlorine in its properties and compounds; a dark reddish-black heavy liquid with a strong irritating smell; symbol Br, at. no. 35, at. wt 79·909. [Gk *brōmos* stink]

brōm′oil *n.* (phot.) Process of bleaching a bromide print and restoring the image by applying oily pigment with a brush; print produced by this process.

brŏnc′hī (-ngk-) *n.pl.* (sing. *-us*). The two main divisions of the windpipe (ill. LUNG).

brŏnc′hia (-ngk-) *n.pl.* Ramifications of bronchi in lungs.

brŏnc′hial (-ngk-) *adj.* Of the bronchi or bronchia; ~ *spasm*, asthma.

brŏnchīt′is (-ngk-) *n.* Inflammation of bronchial mucous membrane.

brŏnc′hocele (-ngkosēl) *n.* Swelling of thyroid gland, goitre.

brŏnc′ō (-ngk-) *n.* Wild or half-tamed horse of California or New Mexico; ~*-buster*, (U.S.) one who breaks in broncos.

Brŏn′të (-ĭ), Charlotte (1816–55), Emily (1818–48), and Anne (1820–49). Novelists, daughters of a Yorkshire clergyman of Irish descent; wrote under pseudonyms of Currer, Ellis, and Acton Bell; Charlotte is famous esp. for 'Jane Eyre' (1847) and 'Villette' (1853), Emily for 'Wuthering Heights' (1848) and her poems.

Brŏntosaur′us *n.* Member of jurassic genus of herbivorous quadripedal dinosaurs (order *Saurischia*), among largest terrestrial vertebrates. [Gk *brontē* thunder, *sauros* lizard]

brŏnze *n.* Brown alloy chiefly of copper and tin (as used for British 'copper' coins approx. 95½% copper, 3% tin, and 1½% zinc); work of art made of bronze; colour of bronze; *B~ Age*, that stage of a people's culture (between *Stone Age* and *Iron Age*) during which its weapons etc. were made of bronze. ~ *adj.* Made of, coloured like, bronze. ~ *v.* Give bronze-like surface to; make or become brown, tan. **brŏn′zy** *adj.* [L (*aes*) *Brundisinum* (brass) from Brundisium (Brindisi)]

brooch (-ō-) *n.* Ornamental safety-pin for fastening some part, esp. neck, of dress.

brōōd *n.* Hatch of young birds or other egg-produced animals; (usu. contempt.) human family, children; swarm, crew. ~ *adj.* For breeding. ~ *v.i.* 1. Sit as hen on eggs. 2. Hang close *over*, *on*; meditate, often sullenly or with resentment (*on*, *over*, etc.).

brōōd′y *adj.* (Of hen) inclined to 'sit'.

brŏŏk[1] *n.* Small stream.

brŏŏk[2] *v.t.* Put up with, tolerate.

Brŏŏke, Sir James (1803–68). First English rajah of Sarawak (1841–63); travelling there privately, he found it in revolt against its ruler, the Malay sultan of Brunei; he restored order and was made rajah by the sultan and acclaimed by the people.

brōōm *n.* 1. Yellow-flowered shrub, *Sarothamnus scoparius*, growing on sandy banks, heaths, etc.; genus to which it belongs. 2. Implement for sweeping, orig. of broom twigs fixed to long stick or handle, now of any material; *broom′rape*, genus, *Orobanche*, of brown leafless fleshy-stemmed parasitic plants growing on roots of brooms and other plants; ~*-stick*, handle of broom (on which witches were reputed to fly through the air, and over which parties to a mock-marriage used to jump).

Bros *abbrev.* Brothers.

brŏth *n.* Liquid in which something, esp. meat, has been boiled; thin soup made of this with vegetables, barley, rice, etc.

brŏth′el *n.* House of prostitution, house of ill fame, bawdy-house.

broth′er (-ŭdh-) *n.* 1. Son of the same parents. 2. Fellow, companion, equal. 3. (with pl. *brethren*) Member of religious order, fellow member of church, guild, order, etc. 4. ~*-in-law*, brother of one's husband or wife, husband of one's sister. **broth′erly** *adj.* Of, like, a brother('s), fraternal. **broth′erlĭness** *n.*

broth′erhŏŏd (-ŭdh-) *n.* Fraternal tie; companionship; (members of) association for mutual help etc.

Brougham[1] (brōōm), Henry Peter, Baron Brougham and Vaux (1778–1868). English lawyer (and defender of Queen Caroline), Whig politician, and Lord Chancellor of England.

brougham[2] (-ōōm, -ōō′am) *n.* One-horse 4-wheeled closed carriage; closed electrically-driven carriage for 4 or 5 passengers; limousine with open driver's seat. [f. Lord BROUGHAM[1]]

brought (-awt) past t. & past part. of BRING.

brow *n.* Arch of hair over eye (usu. in pl.); forehead; edge, projection, of cliff, etc., top of hill in road.

brow′beat *v.t.* Bully, bear down, with looks and words.

brown[1] *adj.* 1. Of the colour produced by a mixture of orange and black pigments, or by partial charring of starch or woody fibre, as in toasted bread etc. 2. Dark, dark-skinned; tanned. 3. ~ *bread*, bread of unbolted flour; ~ *coal*, lignite; ~ *paper*, coarse unbleached paper used for parcels etc.; *brown′-shirt*, German Nazi storm-trooper; ~ *sugar*, unrefined or partially refined sugar; ~*-stone*, dark-brown sandstone used in building; ~ *study*, reverie. ~ *n.* Brown colour or pigment; (ellipt. for) brown butterfly, fishing-fly, or clothes; (slang) copper coin. ~ *v.* Make or become brown by roasting, sunburn, or chemical process; *browned off*, (orig. R.A.F. slang) having had too much of something, bored.

Brown[2], John (1800–59). American anti-slavery leader, hanged at Charlestown, Virginia, for a successful armed attack, with only 18 men, on the Federal arsenal at Harper's Ferry, Virginia; hero of the popular marching-song: 'John Brown's body lies a-mouldering in the grave, But his soul goes marching on.'

Brown[3], Lancelot (1716–83). 'Capability Brown', English architect and reviver of the natural style of landscape gardening; laid out gardens at Kew.

Browne, Sir Thomas (1605–82). English physician, author of 'Religio Medici' (1642).

Brown′ian movement. Irregular oscillatory movement of microscopic particles in fluids, due to molecular 'bombardment'. [discovered by Robert *Brown* (1773–1858), Scottish botanist]

brown′ie *n.* 1. Benevolent shaggy goblin haunting house and doing household work secretly. 2. Junior member (aged 8–11) of Girl Guides.

Brown′ing[1], Robert (1812–89). English poet, author of numerous philosophical and dramatic lyrics and of several dramas. ~, Elizabeth Barrett (1806–61). English poetess, wife of Robert Browning.

Brown′ing[2] *n.* ~ (*pistol*), small automatic pistol (ill. PISTOL); ~ *gun*, automatic rifle. [J. M. *Browning* (1884–1926) Amer. inventor]

BROUGHAM

Brown'ĭst *adj.* & *n.* (Member) of an English Puritan sect, followers of Robert Browne (1550–1633), who denounced the parochial system and ordination and is regarded as the founder of Congregationalism.

browse (-z) *v.* Feed *on*, crop (leaves, twigs, scanty vegetation); feed thus; (fig.) read desultorily for enjoyment. ~ *n.* Browsing.

Bruce (-ōōs), Robert de (1274–1329). King of Scotland 1306–29; liberated his country from the English, whom he defeated at the Battle of BANNOCKBURN.

bru'cine (-ōōsēn) *n.* Highly poisonous vegetable alkaloid found in false Angostura bark and in nux vomica.

Bruck'ner (-ŏŏk-), Anton (1824–96). Austrian composer of church music and symphonies.

Brueg(h)el (brügl), **Breughel** (brẽrgl). Surname of a large family of Flemish painters, the most famous of whom is Pieter Bruegel the Elder (*c* 1520–69), painter of lively peasant scenes.

Bruges (brōōzh). Belgian Flemish city, famous for its bells and its many canals.

Bru'in (-ōō-). Name of the bear in the folk-tales about Reynard the Fox; hence, a bear.

bruise (-ōōz) *n.* Injury by blow to body, fruit, etc., discolouring skin. ~ *v.* Injure by blow that discolours skin without breaking it, contuse; dint, batter; pound, bray, grind small; show effects of blow. **bruis'er** *n.* (esp.) Prize-fighter.

bruit (-ōōt) *v.t.* (archaic) Spread *abroad*, *about*, make famous, celebrate.

Brumaire (-ōōmār'). 2nd month in French revolutionary calendar, 22nd Oct.–20th Nov.; *18th* ~, 9th Nov. 1799, day on which Napoleon Bonaparte became First Consul. [Fr. *brume* mist]

Brŭmm'agem (-j-), *adj.* Applied contemptuously to an article of Birmingham manufacture, esp. cheap jewellery etc. [dial. form of *Birmingham*, orig. used of counterfeit coin made there in 17th c.]

Brŭmm'ell, George Bryan (1778–1840). 'Beau Brummell', English dandy, a leader of fashion and favourite of the Prince Regent.

Brunei (-ōōnī). British protected State on NW. coast of Borneo.

Brunel' (-ōōnĕl'), Sir Marc Isambard (1769–1849). French-born engineer; built the Thames tunnel with his son Isambard Kingdom ~ (1806–59), who also built bridges, railways, ships, etc.

Brunĕllĕsc'hĭ (brōō-, -kĭ), Filippo (1377–1446). Italian architect, reviver of the Roman style.

brunĕtte' (-ōō-) *n.* & *ad.* Dark-skinned and brown-haired (woman).

Brun'hĭld (brōō-). In the legend of the Nibelungs, the wife of Gunther, who instigated the murder of Siegfried; in Norse versions, a Valkyrie whom Sigurd wins by penetrating the wall of fire behind which she lies in an enchanted sleep.

Brun'ō[1] (-ōō-), St. (*c* 1035–1101). Founder of the CARTHUSIAN Order.

Brun'ō[2] (-ōō-), Giordano (*c* 1548–*c* 1599). Italian philosopher; regarded God as the unity reconciling spirit and matter; was condemned to death by the Inquisition.

Brŭn'swick (-z-). Braunschweig, city and ancient duchy of N. Germany; ~ *black*, black varnish made of turpentine and asphalt or lamp-black; ~ *green*, a green pigment, oxychloride of copper.

brŭnt *n.* Chief stress of shock or attack.

brŭsh *n.* 1. Brushwood, underwood; thicket; small trees and shrubs. 2. Implement of bristles, hair, wire, etc., set in wood etc. for sweeping or scrubbing dust and dirt from a surface, usu. named acc. to its use, as *clothes-*, *hat-*, *hair-*~; bunch of hairs etc. in straight handle for painting etc.; application of brush, brushing. 3. Tail, esp. of fox; brush-like tuft. 4. (elect.) Brush-like discharge of sparks; strip of conductible material (usu. hardened carbon) for making or breaking contact; fixed contact which bears on slip ring of dynamo (ill. DYNAMO). 5. Short sharp encounter, skirmish. 6. *brush'wood*, undergrowth, thicket; ~*-work*, painter's (style of) manipulation. ~ *v.* Move briskly; sweep or scrub, put in order, remove, with brush; graze or touch in passing; ~ *aside*, *away*, (fig.) ignore, pass over; ~ *up*, furbish, renew one's memory of.

brusque (-ōōsk *or* -ŭsk) *adj.* Blunt, off-hand, abrupt.

Brŭss'els. Bruxelles, capital city of Belgium; ~ *carpet*, a carpet with back of stout linen thread and pile of wool; ~ *lace*, rich pillow-lace of the type first made in Brussels in 18th c.; (also) needlepoint lace made there in same period; ~ *sprouts*, the bud-bearing cabbage, *Brassica oleracea*, producing buds like small cabbages in the axils of its leaves.

brut'al (-ōō-) *adj.* Savagely cruel, rude, coarse, sensual. **brut'ally** *adv.* **brutăl'ĭty** *n.* **brut'alīze** *v.t.*

brute (-ōōt) *n.* & *adj.* 1. (Beast) not gifted with reason. 2. Stupid, sensual, beast-like, cruel, or passionate (person). 3. Unconscious, merely material. 4. Lower animal; lower nature in man. **brut'ĭsh** *adj.* **brut'ĭshly** *adv.* **brut'ĭshnĕss** *n.*

Brut'us[1] (-ōō-), Lucius Junius (d. 508 B.C.). Legendary First Consul of Rome, and leader in the expulsion of the Tarquins.

Brut'us[2] (-ōō-), Marcus Junius (85–42 B.C.). Roman soldier; joined the conspirators who assassinated Julius Caesar in hope of restoring republican government.

Brȳn Mawr (mōr). Women's college in Philadelphia, U.S.

brȳ'ony *n.* Two unrelated climbing plants found esp. in hedgerows: *white*~, *Bryonia dioica*, rough textured and light coloured, with conspicuous coiled tendrils; *black* ~, *Tamus communis*, dark shining green, without tendrils.

B.S.A. *abbrev.* Birmingham Small Arms (Co.); British South Africa.

B.Sc. *abbrev.* Bachelor of Science.

b.s.g.d.g. *abbrev. breveté sans garantie du gouvernement* (= patented without government guarantee).

B.S.I. *abbrev.* British Standards Institution.

B.S.T. *abbrev.* British summer time.

Bt *abbrev.* Baronet.

B.Th.U., B.T.U. *abbrevs.* British thermal unit.

bŭb'ble *n.* 1. Spherical or hemispherical envelope of liquid (or solidified liquid, as glass) enclosing air etc. 2. Unsubstantial or visionary project, enterprise, etc. 3. Sound or appearance of boiling; ~*-and-squeak*, cooked meat, potatoes, and cabbage fried together. ~ *v.i.* Send up, rise in, make the sound of, bubbles.

bŭbb'ly *adj.* Full of bubbles. ~ *n.* (slang) Champagne.

būb'ō *n.* Inflamed swelling in glandular part esp. groin or armpit.

būbŏn'ĭc *adj.* Characterized by buboes; ~ *plague*, disease characterized by these and by fever and prostration, carried by rats and transmitted to man by fleas.

bŭccaneer *n.* Sea-rover, pirate, esp. of Spanish-American coasts; adventurer. ~ *v.i.* Act as buccaneer. [Fr. *boucanier* f. *boucaner* to cure meat on a *boucan* (i.e. barbecue), a Brazilian wd]

bŭc'cĭnātor (-ks-) *n.* Flat thin muscle forming wall of cheek (ill. HEAD). [L = 'trumpeter']

Būcĕn'taur. Italian state barge, esp. that used in Venice in the annual Ascension-Day ceremony called the Marriage of the Adriatic.

Būcĕph'alus. The favourite horse of Alexander the Great.

Buchan[1] (bŭχ'an), Alexander (1829–1907). Scottish meteorologist; ~*'s cold spells*, certain specified periods of cold weather stated by him to occur annually.

Buchan[2] (bŭχ'an), John, 1st Baron Tweedsmuir (1875–1940). Author of novels of adventure (e.g. 'The Thirty-nine Steps', 1915) and historical works.

Būchăn'an (-k-), James (1791–1868). 15th president of U.S., 1857–61.

Būcharĕst' (-k-). Bucuresti, capital city of Rumania.

Buch'manism (bŏŏk-) *n.* Name for the religious movement called the OXFORD Group (see also MORAL Re-Armament). **Buch'manīte** *adj.* & *n.* [Dr Frank N. D. *Buchman*, Amer. founder]

bŭck[1] *n.* Male of fallow-deer, reindeer, chamois, hare, rabbit; dandy; *~-bean*, water plant, *Menyanthes trifoliata*, with pinkish-white flowers; *~-hound*, small staghound; *~-shot*, coarse shot; *buck'skin*, (leather made of) buck's skin; (pl.) breeches of this; *~-tooth*, projecting tooth. ~ *adj.* (slang) Male; of, for, males.

bŭck[2] *v.* (Of horse) jump vertically with back arched and feet drawn together (also *~-jump*); *buck'jumper*, horse given to bucking.

bŭck[3] *v.* (slang) (With *up*) make haste, hurry; become or make vigorous or cheerful.

bŭck[4] *n.* Body of cart; chiefly in combination, as (U.S.) *buck'board*, plank slung upon wheels, light vehicle with body consisting of this.

bŭck[5] *n.* (U.S. slang) Dollar.

bŭck[6] *n.* (U.S. slang) Article placed as a reminder before a person whose turn it is to deal at poker; *pass the ~ to*, shift responsibility to (another).

bŭck'ĕt *n.* 1. Wooden or other vessel for drawing or carrying water. 2. Piston of pump; compartment of water-wheel; scoop of dredger or grain-elevator; vessel hoisted by crane; socket for whip, carbine, etc. 3. *~-seat*, seat with high rounded back; car-seat which tips forward; *~-shop*, (orig. U.S.) office for gambling in stocks, speculating on markets, etc. ~ *v.* Ride hard; (rowing) hurry the forward swing, row hurried stroke.

Bŭck'ingham, George Villiers, 1st Duke of (1592–1628). Favourite of James I of England; assassinated by John Felton. ~, George Villiers, 2nd Duke of (1628–87). English statesman under Charles II and author of satirical verses.

Bŭck'ingham Palace. A royal residence in London, bought 1703 by the Duke of Buckingham and sold 1762 to George III; rebuilt 1825 by the architect John Nash.

Bŭck'inghamshire. Southern English county lying N. of the Thames.

bŭc'kle[1] *n.* Metal (or other) rim with hinged spiked tongue for securing strap, ribbon, etc. ~ *v.* Fasten with buckle; (cause to) give way, crumple up, under pressure; ~ *to*, prepare for, set about; get to work, start vigorously.

Bŭc'kle[2], Henry Thomas (1821–62), English historian, author of two volumes (1857, 1861) of a 'History of Civilization in England'.

bŭck'ler *n.* Small round shield (ill. SHIELD); protection, protector. ~ *v.t.* Shield, protect.

bŭck'ram *n.* Coarse linen or cotton fabric stiffened with gum or paste, used in linings and for binding books.

Bucks. *abbrev.* Buckinghamshire.

bŭck'shee *n.* (army slang) Allowance above the usual amount. ~ *adj.* & *adv.* Gratuitous(ly), free, gratis. [altered f. *baksheesh*]

bŭck'wheat *n.* Cereal plant, *Polygonum fagopyrum*, with seed used for horse and poultry food, and in U.S. for breakfast cakes. [= *beech wheat*, from its three-cornered seeds like beechmast]

būcŏl'ic *adj.* Of shepherds, pastoral, rustic. **būcŏl'ics** *n.pl.* pastoral poems; *the B~*, those of Virgil.

bŭd *n.* 1. Much condensed undeveloped end of a shoot, the rudiment of foliage or flowers (ill. FLOWER); ~ *scale*, altered leaf protecting a bud. 2. (zool.) Asexual reproductive growth attached to parent and developing into new individual esp. in coelenterates (ill. HYDRA). 3. Anything immature or undeveloped; (U.S. colloq.) debutante. ~ *v.* 1. Put forth buds; begin to grow or develop. 2. Graft a bud on to another plant.

Būdapĕst'. Capital city of Hungary, orig. consisting of two towns, Buda on right bank of river Danube and Pest(h) on left.

Buddha (bŏŏd'*a*). 'Enlightened one'; name applied esp. to Siddartha Gautama (*c* 560–*c* 480 B.C.), son of the rajah of the Sakya tribe (hence also called *Sakyamuni*, 'sage of the Sakyas'); as a young man he abandoned his home in Nepal and renounced the world; he practised an extreme asceticism, preached, and became the founder of one of the great Asiatic religions.

Buddhism (bŏŏd'ĭzm) *n.* Religion founded by the Buddha, orig. practised chiefly in India; it was in decline there by the 4th c. A.D. but was diffused over China (which it reached in the 1st c.), Japan, and central and SE. Asia; there are two principal forms, the 'greater vehicle' (*Mahayana*), which became predominant in China, Japan, and Tibet, and the 'lesser vehicle' (*Hinayana*), which survives in Ceylon, Burma, and Siam. Its principal doctrines are: that suffering is inseparable from existence, which is an evil; that the principal cause of suffering is desire; and that the suppression of desire, and consequently of suffering, can be obtained by discipline and ultimately rewarded by *nirvana*, which is extinction of individual existence and absorption into the supreme spirit. **Budd'hist** *adj.* & *n.*

bŭdd'leia (*or* -lē'*a*) *n.* Genus of shrubs and trees of America, Asia, and S. Africa, much grown in gardens, and often having honey-scented flowers. [Adam *Buddle* (d. 1715), botanist]

bŭdd'y *n.* (U.S.) Brother, used as a form of address. [Childish or Negro pronunciation of *brother*]

bŭdge *v.* Move in the slightest degree, stir.

bŭdgerigar' *n.* Grass or zebra parakeet (*Melopsittacus undulatus*), native to Australia, and freq. kept as pet.

bŭdg'ĕt *n.* 1. Contents of a bag or bundle (chiefly fig. of news etc.). 2. Annual estimate of revenue and expenditure, esp. by Chancellor of Exchequer in House of Commons, or by finance minister of other countries. **bŭdg'ĕtary** *adj.* **bŭdg'ĕt** *v.i.* ~ *for*, allow or arrange for in budget.

Buenos Aires (bwĕn'os ar'ĕz). Capital city and chief port of Argentina.

bŭff *n.* 1. Stout velvety dull-yellow leather of buffalo or ox-hide; *in ~*, naked. 2. The dull-yellow colour of this; *The Buffs*, the former East Kent Regiment, orig. so called from the buff-coloured facings on their scarlet uniforms. 3. (path.) Coagulated coating on blood drawn from fever patients. ~ *adj.* Made of, coloured like, buff. ~ *v.t.* Polish (metal) with buff; make (leather) velvety like buff.

bŭff'alō *n.* Kinds of ox, esp. (*a*) *Bos primigenius*, orig. a native of India (where it is tamed), inhabiting most of Asia, parts of S. Europe, and N. Africa; (*b*) *Bos caffer*, the Cape buffalo of S. Africa; and (*c*) (pop.) the Amer. BISON; *~ grass*, a prairie grass, *Sesleria dactyloides*; *~ gnat*, two-winged fly of family *Simuliidae* with humped back and blood-sucking proboscis; *~ robe*, cloak or rug of bison-skin dressed with the hair on.

Bŭff'alō Bĭll. Popular nickname of William Cody (1846–1917), Amer. cattle-herder and scout, credited with legendary exploits against Indians and bandits.

bŭff'er[1] *n.* Apparatus for deadening by springs or padding, or sustaining by strength of beams etc., a concussion, esp. of railway-carriages, engines, etc. (ill. LOCOMOTIVE); *~-state*, State lying between two possible belligerents which serves to make hostilities less easy and probable.

bŭff'er[2] *n.* (slang) Fellow; old-fashioned fellow.

bŭff'ĕt[1] *n.* Blow with the hand; blow of fate etc. ~ *v.* Strike with the hand; knock, hunt, plague; contend (*with* waves etc.).

LATE 16th-C. BUFFET

bŭff'ĕt² *n.* 1. Sideboard, recessed cupboard, for china, glass, etc. (*Illustration, p.* 97.) 2. (bo͝of'ā). Refreshment bar.

bŭf'fle-head (-hĕd) *n.* ~ (*duck*), the Amer. dipper, *Clangula albeola.*

Buffon (bo͝of'awn), George Louis Leclerc, comte de (1707–88). French naturalist, author of 'Histoire Naturelle'.

buffōōn' *n.* (usu. contempt.) Wag, clumsy jester, mocker. **buffōōn'ery** *n.*

bŭg *n.* (also *bed*-~) Flat, ill-smelling blood-sucking insect, *Cimex lectularius*, infesting wooden beds, furniture, etc.; other blood-sucking parasites; (chiefly U.S.) small insect; (colloq.) infection, 'germ'; *big* ~, (slang) person of importance; *plant* ~, member of the order *Hemiptera* including shield-bugs, pond-skaters, water-boatmen, bed-bugs, and aphides; ~-*hunter*, (slang) entomologist.

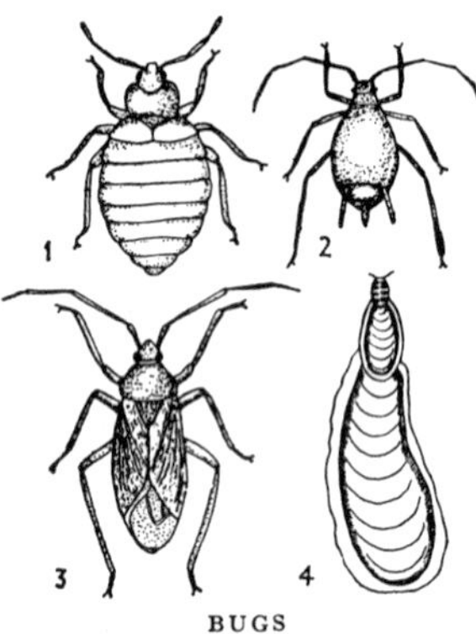

BUGS

1. Bed-bug. 2. Aphis. 3. Shield-bug. 4. Scale-insect (female)

bŭg'abōō *n.* = BUGBEAR.

Bugăn'da (bo͝o-). Kingdom in Uganda inhabited by the BAGANDA people.

bŭg'bear (-bār) *n.* Fancied object of fear; imaginary terror.

bŭgg'er *n.* (law) Sodomite; in very low language, term of abuse, or sometimes merely = fellow. ~ *v.* Commit buggery with; ~ *about*, (slang) interfere with, bother (person), (intrans.) move or act aimlessly or ineffectively. **bŭgg'ery** *n.* (law) Sodomy.

bŭgg'y *n.* Light two-wheeled vehicle; (U.S.) 4-wheeled vehicle, often hooded, drawn by one or two horses.

BUGGY

bū'gle¹ *n.* Brass instrument like small trumpet used for military signals (ill. BRASS). ~ *v.* Sound bugle, sound (call) on a bugle. **bū'gler** *n.*

bū'gle² *n.* Tube-shaped glass bead, usu. black, sewn on dress as ornament.

bū'gle³ *n.* Kinds of plant of the genus *Ajuga.*

bū'glŏss *n.* Kinds of plant allied to borage, esp. (*viper's* ~) *Echium vulgare* and other species of *Echium.* [Gk *bouglōssos* ox-tongued]

buhl: see BOULLE.

build (bĭ-) *v.* (past t. and past part. *built*) Construct by putting parts or material rightly together; be busy making one's house or nest; lay *into* (wall etc.) in building; make gradually; base (*up*)*on*, rely *on*; *built-in*, incorporated in main structure (also fig.); *built up*, constructed of parts, esp. parts separately prepared and afterwards joined together; (of a district, road, etc.), covered with, having a large number of, houses. ~ *n.* Style of construction, make; proportions of human body.

buil'der (bĭ-) *n.* (esp.) Master-builder, contractor for building houses. **build'ĭng** (bĭ-) *n.* (esp.) House, edifice; ~ *society*, limited liability company making mortgage advances to members for building or purchasing a house.

bŭlb *n.* 1. Nearly spherical base of the stem of certain plants, such as lily, onion, etc., consisting of thick fleshy scales and sending roots downwards and leaves etc. upwards; leaf-bud detaching itself from stem and becoming separate plant; (anat.) roundish swelling of any cylindrical organ, as of hair-root. 2. Dilated part of glass tube; glass bulb-shaped container of electric-light filament; bulb-shaped swelling of rubber tube; ~-*exposure*, -*release*, (phot.) method of releasing shutter of camera by pressure on a rubber bulb; also, exposure regulated by the pressure and subsequent release of a rubber bulb, a lever, etc. ~ *v.i.* Swell into bulb(s).

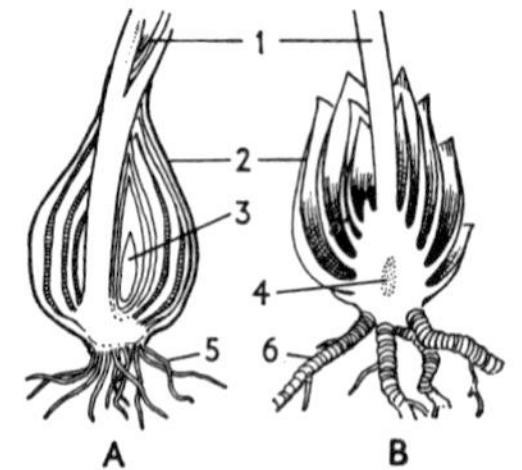

BULB: SECTION OF (A) TULIP, (B) LILY

1. Aerial shoot. 2. Scale. 3. Axillary bud. 4. Core. 5. Adventitious roots. 6. Contractile roots

bŭl'bous *adj.* Of, having, like, springing from, a bulb.

bulbul (bo͝ol'bo͝ol) *n.* Eastern song-thrush of numerous genera; singer, poet.

Bŭlgār'ĭa. Balkan republic (previous to 1946 a kingdom), with a population largely descended from a race related to the Huns and Avars and speaking a Slavonic language; capital, Sofia. **Bŭl'gar, Bŭlgār'ian** *adj.* & *n.* (Inhabitant, language) of Bulgaria; *Bulgarian atrocities*, massacre in S. Bulgaria by Turks and Mohammedan Bulgars (1876) on occasion of rising in Bosnia against Turkey.

bŭlge *n.* Convex part, irregular swelling, tendency to swell out, on surface; specif., outward swell on ship's side below waterline constructed as defence against torpedoes; (fig.) temporary increase in volume or numbers. ~ *v.* Swell outwards irregularly; extend (bag etc.) by stuffing it. **bŭl'gy** *adj.* **bŭl'gĭnėss** *n.* [L *bulga* knapsack]

bŭlk *n.* 1. Cargo; *in* ~, loose, not in packages; (*sell*) *in* ~, (sell) in large quantities, as it is in the hold. 2. Large shape, body, person. 3. Size, magnitude; great size; mass, large mass; *the* greater part or number *of*. ~ *v.* Seem in respect of size or importance.

bŭlk'head (-hĕd) *n.* Upright partition dividing watertight compartments of ship (ill. SHIP); such compartment.

bŭl'ky *adj.* Large, voluminous. **bŭl'kĭnėss** *n.*

bull¹ (bo͝ol) *n.* Papal edict. [L *bulla* seal]

bull² (bo͝ol) *n.* 1. Uncastrated male of ox or other bovine animal; male of elephant, whale, seal, and other large animals. 2. Constellation and sign of Taurus. 3. (Stock Exchange) Speculator who buys low in expectation of a rise in prices or in order to effect such a rise. 4. Bull's-eye of target (see below). 5. ~-*calf*; male calf; *bull'dog*, powerful and courageous large-headed smooth-haired dog formerly used for bull-baiting; university proctor's attendant whose duty it is to chase and apprehend undergraduates suspected of any offence; *bull'-doze*, (U.S. slang) intimidate, coerce (orig. used in elections in

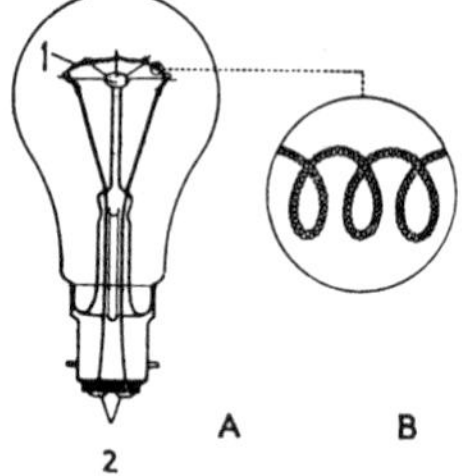

A. ELECTRIC LIGHT BULB. B. DETAIL OF COILED COIL FILAMENT

1. Filament. 2. Terminals

Southern States of U.S. of intimidating voters, esp. Negroes); *bull'dozer*, (orig. U.S.) large mechanical navvy for clearing a way through rubble etc.; *bull'fight*, Spanish spectacle of baiting a bull with horsemen (picadors), footmen (peones), and a swordsman (matador) who finally kills him; similar sport in S. France in which bull is not killed; *bull'finch*, strong-beaked, handsome-plumaged song-bird (*Pyrrhula pyrrhula*); [perh. different wd] high quickset hedge with ditch; *bull'frog*, various large frogs of America and India with loud bellowing note; *bull'head*, small fish with large head, esp. the freshwater miller's thumb, *Cottus gobio*, and the rock-pool species *C. scorpius* and *C. bubalis*; *~-puncher*, (U.S.) cowboy; *bull'ring*, arena for bullfight; *~-roarer*, flat piece of wood with string passed through a hole, which when swung round the head gives a booming sound, used in religious ceremonies by Australian aborigines; a similarly made toy; *bull's-eye*, boss of glass formed at centre of sheet of blown glass; hemispherical piece or thick disc of glass; hemispherical lens; lantern with such a lens; small circular window; central area of target; hit on this part; kind of globular sweetmeat usu. flavoured with peppermint; *~-terrier*, heavily-built smooth-haired usu. white dog, cross between bulldog and terrier (ill. DOG); *bull'trout*, large Amer. salmonid fish, *Salmo eriox*. *~ v.* (Stock Exchange) Speculate for a rise in prices; try to raise price of (stocks).

bull[3] (bo͝ol) *n.* (freq. *Irish ~*) Expression containing contradiction in terms or implying ludicrous inconsistency, as *the hot water is cold and there is none of it*.

Bull[4], John: see JOHN BULL.

bullace (bo͝ol'ĭs) *n.* Wild or semi-wild plum, *Prunus insititia*, larger than the sloe.

Bull'er (bo͞o-), Sir Redvers Henry (1839–1908). Irish soldier; commanded the Natal force during the Boer War; relieved LADYSMITH after 3 unsuccessful attempts; was criticized for his conduct of the campaign and was retired on half-pay for making a public speech in answer to his critics.

bull'ĕt (bo͞o-) *n.* Missile of lead etc., spherical or conical, used in rifles, machine-guns, revolvers, etc. (ill. CARTRIDGE); *~-head*, round head.

bull'ĕtin (bo͞o-) *n.* Short official statement of public event or news or of invalid's condition.

bull'ion[1] (bo͝ol'yon) *n.* & *adj.* Gold and silver before (or as valued apart from) coining or manufacturing; (made of) solid or real gold or silver.

bull'ion[2] (bo͝ol'yon) *n.* Fringe of gold or silver thread.

bull'ock (bo͞o-) *n.* Castrated bull, ox.

Bull Rŭn (bo͝ol). Small river in E. Virginia, U.S., the scene of two important battles (1861 and 1862) in the Amer. Civil War; the Federal side was severely defeated in both.

bull'y[1] (bo͞o-) *n.* 1. Blusterer, tyrant (esp. among boys), coward and tyrant; hired ruffian; prostitute's male protector. 2. Bullying in hockey. *~ v.t.* 1. Persecute, oppress, tease, physically or morally; frighten *into* or *out of*; play the bully. 2. *~* (*off*), (in hockey, of centre-forwards) attempt to secure the ball at beginning of game etc. after each player has hit the ground and then his opponent's stick three times. *~ adj.* (esp. U.S. and colonial) Capital, first-rate.

bull'y[2] (bo͞o-) *n.* Scrummage in Eton football.

bull'y[3] (bo͞o-) *n.* (Also *~-beef*) Tinned beef.

Bülow (bü'lō), Bernhard, Prince von (1849–1929). German statesman and diplomat; imperial Chancellor 1900–9.

bul'rŭsh (bo͞o-) *n.* Kind of tall rush, *Scirpus lacustris*; also the cat's tail or **reed-mace**, *Typha latifolia*; in the Bible, the papyrus of Egypt.

bul'wark (bo͞o-) *n.* 1. Rampart, earthwork, etc.; mole, breakwater; person, principle, etc., that acts as a defence. 2. Ship's side above deck (ill. SHIP).

Bulwer-Lytton, Edward Lytton: see LYTTON.

bŭm[1] *n.* Backside, buttocks (not in polite use); *~-bailiff*, bailiff employed for making arrests; *~-boat*, boat, plying to ships in port or off shore with fresh provisions.

bŭm[2] *n.* (U.S. colloq.) Lazy and dissolute person; loafer, tramp. *~ adj.* Worthless, poor, wretched. *~ v.i.* Wander *around*, loaf; act as a bum.

Bŭm'ble. The beadle in Dickens's 'Oliver Twist', a type of the consequential domineering parish official. **Bŭm'bledom** (-ld-) *n.* Petty officialdom.

bŭm'ble-bee *n.* Large bee, *Bombus*, with loud hum.

bŭm'ble-pŭppy *n.* Old outdoor game resembling bagatelle; game of striking tennis-ball slung to post so as to wind the string round the post; whist played unscientifically.

bŭmm'alō *n.* Small fish, *Harpodon nehereus*, found off coasts of S. Asia; dried and used as relish; when salted, known as 'Bombay duck'.

bŭmmaree' *n.* Middleman at Billingsgate fish-market; (also) independent porter at Smithfield meat-market.

bŭmp *v.* 1. Push, throw down, impinge violently, strike solidly (*against, into, on*). 2. (boat-racing) Overtake and bump into (boat ahead), make a bump. 3. (Of cricket-ball) rise abruptly on pitching, (of bowler) cause (ball) to bump. 4. *~ off*, (slang) Remove by violence, murder. *~ adv.* With a bump, suddenly, violently. *~ n.* 1. Dull-sounding blow, knock, collision; swelling caused by this. 2. (phrenol.) Prominence on skull, faculty supposed to be indicated by it. 3. (In that system of boat-racing in which each competitor starts an equal distance ahead of the next) overtaking and touching of boat by next behind; *~-supper*, supper in celebration of bump(s) in boat-racing. 4. Variation in air-pressure causing irregularity in aircraft's motion. **bŭmp'y** *adj.*

bŭm'per *n.* 1. Brim-full glass of wine etc. 2. (slang) Anything (as harvest, theatre audience) unusually large or abundant. 3. Metal projection on front and back of a motor-car etc. to take the first shock of collision (ill. MOTOR).

bŭmp'kin *n.* Country lout, awkward or bashful fellow.

bŭmp'tious (-shus) *adj.* Self-assertive, offensively conceited.

bŭn *n.* 1. Small soft round sweet cake with currants etc.; (in Scotland) very rich fruit cake; (in parts of Ireland) round loaf of bread; *hot cross ~*, spiced bun marked with cross and eaten on Good Friday. 2. Hair coiled at back of head in bun-shape.

bŭn'a *n.* German synthetic rubber made by the polymerization of BUTADIENE. [Ger. patent name]

Bŭn'bury. In Oscar Wilde's play 'The Importance of Being Earnest', mythical friend whose misfortunes provide the hero with pretexts for absence.

bŭnch *n.* Cluster of things growing or fastened together; lot, collection; (U.S.) company, band. *~ v.* Make into bunch(es), gather (dress) into folds; come, cling, crowd, together. **bŭn'chy** *adj.*

bŭnd *n.* Embankment, causeway, quay.

bŭn'dle *n.* Collection of things fastened together (esp. clothes and odds and ends in handkerchief); set of sticks, rods, etc., bound up; set of parallel fibres, nerves, etc. *~ v.* Tie in, make *up* into, bundle; throw confusedly *in* any receptacle; go, put, or send hurriedly or unceremoniously *out, off*, etc.

bŭng *n.* Stopper, esp. large cork stopping hole in cask; *~-hole*, hole in cask closed with bung (ill. CASK) *~ v.t.* Stop (cask with bung); stop, close, shut up (esp. the eyes); (slang) throw.

bungalow (bŭng'galō) *n.* Lightly built one-storeyed or temporary house. **bŭng'aloid** *adj.* Of or resembling bungalow(s). [Hind. *bangla* of Bengal]

bŭn'gle (-nggl) *n.* Clumsy work, confusion, blunder. *~ v.* Make bungle; blunder over, fail to accomplish.

Bun'ĭn (bo͞o-), Ivan Alexeyevich (1870–1953). Russian novelist and poet; awarded Nobel Prize for Literature in 1933.

bŭn'ion (-yon) *n.* Inflamed swelling on foot, esp. at inside of ball of great toe.

bŭnk[1] *n.* Sleeping-berth, esp. in ship; ~*-house*, (U.S.) house in which miners, lumbermen, etc., are lodged. ~ *v.i.* Sleep in bunk.

bŭnk[2] *v.i.* (slang) Make off, vanish. ~ *n.* (only in *do a* ~, run away).

bŭnk[3] *n.* (orig. U.S.) Humbug, nonsense. [abbrev. for BUNKUM]

bŭnk'er *n.* 1. Large compartment in a ship for storing coal or oil (ill. SHIP); bin for storing domestic fuel. 2. Pit or hollow, forming a hazard on golf-course, in which the natural soil, sometimes top-dressed with sand, is exposed. 3. Reinforced concrete shelter. ~ *v.t.* (pass.) Be hit into bunker, have one's ball in bunker. **bŭnk'ering** *n.* Loading of ships with fuel; provision of fuel for vehicles.

Bŭnk'er Hill. Hill near Boston, Massachusetts; scene of the first battle (1775) of the American War of Independence, in which an English force, after severe fighting and with much loss, compelled the insurgents to withdraw.

bŭnk'um *n.* Humbug, claptrap, sophistry. [*Buncombe* county in N. Carolina; the member for this county is said to have insisted on causing an obstruction to business in Congress by 'making a speech for Buncombe']

bŭnn'y *n.* Childish or pet name for rabbit.

Bun'sen (bōō-), Robert Wilhelm von (1811–99). German chemist, credited with the invention of the ~ *(gas) burner*, which produces a very hot, non-luminous flame by the mixture of air with the stream of gas before it is lighted.

bŭnt[1] *n.* Cavity, baggy part, of fishing-net, sail, etc.

bunt[2] *n.* Aerobatic manœuvre (ill. AEROBATICS).

bŭn'tĭng[1] *n.* Sub-family, *Emberezinae*, of birds allied to finches, including *corn* ~ (*Emberiza calandra calandra*), *reed* ~ (*E. schoeniclus schoeniclus*), *snow* ~ (*Plectrophenax nivalis*), an Arctic bird visiting Britain in winter, and *yellow* ~, the yellow-hammer.

bŭn'tĭng[2] *n.* Worsted or cotton material of open weave used for flags.

Bŭn'yan, John (1628–88). English Nonconformist preacher; author of the allegory 'Pilgrim's Progress' (which he is said to have written while imprisoned for unlicensed preaching), and of other pious works.

buoy (boi) *n.* 1. Anchored wood or metal float marking a channel or indicating position of something, e.g. wreck, reefs. 2. Contrivance (*life-buoy*) for keeping person afloat in water, consisting of belt of cork or one inflated with air. ~ *v.t.* 1. (usu. with *up*) Keep afloat; bring to surface of water; sustain, uplift. 2. Mark with buoy(s).

buoy'age (boi-). System, provision of, buoys.

buoy'ancy (boi-). Capacity for floating, tendency to float in water or air; (fig.) elasticity, recuperative power.

buoy'ant (boi-) *adj.* Apt to float, rise, keep up, or recover; able to keep things up; light-hearted.

B.U.P. *abbrev.* British United Press.

bûr(r) *n.* 1. Clinging hooked fruit or flower head; hence, person hard to shake off. 2. Female catkin of hop before fertilization. 3. Knob or knot in wood; ~*-walnut*, walnut wood containing many knots, used for veneering.

Bûrb'age, Richard (*c* 1567–1619). English actor; part-owner of the Blackfriars and Globe Theatres; acted principal parts in plays by Shakespeare, Jonson, and Beaumont and Fletcher.

bûr'ble *n.* Murmurous noise. ~ *v.* Speak or say murmurously.

bûrb'ot *n.* Eel-like flat-headed bearded freshwater fish, *Lota vulgaris.*

bûrd'en[1] *n.* 1. Load; obligation; bearing of loads; obligatory expense. 2. (freq. *burthen*) Ship's carrying capacity, tonnage. ~ *v.t.* Load; encumber; oppress; tax.

bûrd'en[2] *n.* Refrain, chorus of song; chief theme or gist of poem, complaint, etc. [var. of BOURDON]

bûrd'ensome *adj.* Oppressive, wearying.

bûrd'ock *n.* Coarse weedy plant, *Arctium lappa*, with prickly flower-heads and dock-like leaves.

būreau' (-rō, *or* būr'-) *n.* (pl. *-eaux*, pr. -ōz). 1. Writing-desk with drawers, escritoire (ill. DESK); (U.S.) chest of drawers. 2. Office, government department.

būreauc'racy (-ŏc- *or* -ōc-) *n.* Government by bureaux, centralization; officialism; officials. **būr'eaucrăt** (-ō-) *n.* **būreaucrăt'ic** *adj.*

būrĕtte' *n.* Graduated glass tube with tap at lower end for delivering measured small quantities of liquid in chemical analysis.

bûrg *n.* (U.S. colloq.) Town.

bûrg'age *n.* Ancient tenure by which land and tenements in towns were held of the overlord for a yearly rent.

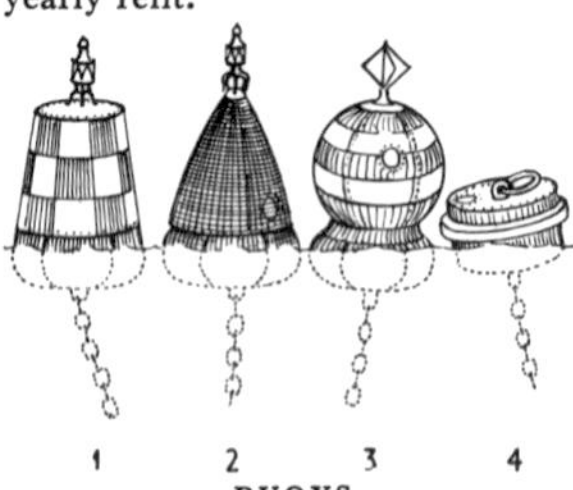

BUOYS

1. Can buoy with light (port hand, red and white). 2. Conical buoy with light (starboard hand, black). 3. Spherical buoy with top-mark (middle ground, red and white). 4. Mooring buoy

bûrgee' *n.* Small swallow-tailed pendant used by yachts etc., usu. as distinguishing flag (ill. FLAG).

bur'geon, bour'geon (bẽr'jn), *v.i.* Put forth, spring forth as, young shoots, bud, begin to grow.

Bürg'er (bûrg-), Gottfried August (1747–94). German writer of lyrics and ballads.

bûr'gĕss *n.* Inhabitant of borough with full municipal rights, citizen; (hist.) member of Parliament for borough, corporate town, or university.

burgh (bŭ'ru) *n.* Scottish town with charter from king (*royal* ~), lord of regality (~ *of regality*) or baron (~ *of barony*).

bûr'gher (-ger) *n.* 1. (archaic) Citizen (chiefly of foreign towns). 2. Citizen of Transvaal Republic or Orange Free State before S. Afr. war of 1899–1902.

Burghley (bûrl'ĭ), William Cecil, first Baron (1521–98). English statesman, Lord Treasurer, and Queen Elizabeth's most trusted councillor and minister.

bûrg'lar *n.* One who breaks into house by night with intent to commit felony. **bûrglār'ious** *adj.* **bûrglār'iously** *adv.* **bûrg'lary** *n.*

bûr'gle *v.* (colloq.) Commit burglary; enter or rob (house) for this purpose.

bûrg'omaster (-mah-) *n.* Mayor of Dutch or Flemish town.

Bûrg'oyne, John (1722–92). 'Gentleman Johnny', English general and playwright; capitulated to the Americans at Saratoga (1777) in the American War of Independence.

Bûrg'undy. Bourgogne, ancient kingdom of SE. France, later an independent duchy, united to France as a province in 1477; any of the wines produced there, of high quality and considerable potency; these include Beaune, Chambertin, Pommard (red), and Chablis and Montrachet (white).

bu'rĭal (bĕ-) *n.* Burying, esp. of dead body.

Bûridan' (-ahn), Jean (*c* 1300–58). French scholastic philosopher and logician, chiefly remembered for the sophism attributed to him (but not found in his works) of the ass dying of hunger between two equally attractive bundles of hay.

bûr'ĭn *n.* Tool for engraving on copper, graver (ill. ENGRAVE).

Bûrke[1], Edmund (1729–97). English Whig statesman, political and philosophical writer, and orator.

Bûrke[2], John (1787–1848). Irish-born genealogical and heraldic writer, first compiler of a 'Peerage and Baronetage' (1826), issued annually since 1847.

Bûrke[3], William (1792–1829). An Irishman who with his accomplice William Hare was executed in Edinburgh for smothering friendless people in order to sell their bodies for dissection to the Edinburgh School of Anatomy.

bûrke[4] *v.t.* Smother (lit. and fig.); hush up, suppress quietly. [BURKE[3]]

bûrl *n.* Knot in wool or cloth, or (U.S.) in wood; overgrown knot in walnut etc., used in veneering.

bûrl'ăp *n.* Coarse canvas of jute, used for sacks.

bûrlĕsque' (-sk) *adj.* Imitating derisively; bombastic, mock-serious; caricaturing, parodying (esp. literary or dramatic work). ~ *n.* Burlesque work or performance; bombast, mock-seriousness; derisive imitation. ~ *v.* Make or perform burlesque (of); caricature, travesty.

Bûrl'ington House. Large building in Piccadilly, London; begun by the 1st earl of Burlington *c* 1664, and bought by the government in 1854; it houses the Royal Academy and various learned societies.

bûrl'y *adj.* Stout, sturdy, massive. **bûrl'inėss** *n.*

Bûrm'a. Republic, established in 1948, occupying the NW. portion of the peninsula projecting southwards from Asia between India and China; formerly a province of British India; capital, Rangoon. **Bûrmēse'** (-z) *adj.* & *n.*

bûrn[1] *n.* (Sc.) Small stream.

bûrn[2] *v.* (past t. and past part. *burnt* or *burned*). Consume, be consumed, waste, by fire; blaze or smoulder; injure by burning; brand; utilize the atomic energy of nuclear fuel; feel intense heat or emotion; *burnt offering*, sacrifice offered by burning. ~ *n.* Sore, mark, made by burning.

Bûrne-Jōnes' (-nz), Sir Edward Coley, Bt (1833–98). English painter and designer of tapestries and stained glass.

bûrn'er *n.* (esp.) That part of lamp etc. from which the flame comes.

bûrn'ėt[1] *n.* Kinds of brown-flowered plant of the genera *Sanguisorba* and *Poterium*; ~*-moth*, greenish-black moth, *Anthrocera filipendulae*, with crimson-spotted wings.

Bûrn'ėt[2], Gilbert (1643–1715). Scottish bishop of Salisbury; author of a 'History of the Reformation in England' and 'History of My Own Times'.

Bûrn'ey, Frances (Madame d'Arblay) (1752–1840). English novelist, originator of the simple novel of home life.

Bûrn'ham scāle (-nam). Graduated scale, adopted in 1924, of salaries and pensions for teachers in English State-aided schools. [Viscount *Burnham*, chairman of committees on teachers' salaries]

bûrn'ing *adj.* That burns; flagrant; hotly discussed, exciting; ~ *bush*, 'the bush that burned and was not consumed' mentioned in Exod. iii; various shrubs or plants with scarlet berries or foliage turning red in autumn etc.; *burning-glass*, lens by which sun's rays may be concentrated on to an object so as to burn it.

bûrn'ish *v.* Polish by friction; take a polish.

bûrnous' (-ōōs) *n.* Arab or Moorish hooded mantle.

Bûrns (-nz), Robert (1759–96). Scottish poet, many of whose poems are written in Lowland Scots; ~ *night*, the evening of 25th Jan. (his birthday), celebrated by many Scots with feasting and drinking.

bûrr *n.* 1. Rough ridge or edge left on metal etc. after cutting, punching, etc.; such ridge on engraved plate, blurred effect obtained by printing from it. 2. (Nebulous) circle of light round moon or star. 3. Silicious rock used for mill-stones; whetstone; kinds of limestone. 4. Rough sounding of letter *r*, esp. rough uvular trill. See also BUR. ~ *v.* Pronounce with burr; speak with rough or indistinct articulation.

burro (bōō'rō) *n.* Small donkey used as pack animal.

bŭ'rrow (-ō) *n.* Hole or excavation in ground in which rabbits, foxes, etc., live. ~ *v.* Make, live in, burrow; make by excavating.

bûrs'a *n.* (pl. *-ae*). (physiol.) Synovial sac between muscles, skin, etc., and bones for lessening friction. **bûrs'al** *adj.*

bûrs'ar *n.* 1. Treasurer, esp. of a college. 2. Student holding bursary in school or university. **bûrsār'ial** *adj.*

bûrs'ary *n.* 1. Treasury; bursar's room in college etc. 2. Endowment given to student in (esp. Scottish) school or university, exhibition.

bûrst *v.* (past t. and past part. *burst*). Fly violently asunder, give way suddenly; explode; rush, move, appear, violently or suddenly; speak, utter, be uttered, explosively; *bursting*, full to overflowing. ~ *n.* Bursting, split; explosion, outbreak; spurt; continuous gallop.

burthen: see BURDEN.

Bûrt'on[1], Sir Richard Francis (1821–90). Traveller, the first Englishman to reach Mecca; Arabic scholar, and translator of the 'Arabian Nights'.

Bûrt'on[2], Robert (1577–1640). English divine, author of the 'Anatomy of Melancholy', a storehouse of curious learning.

bu'ry (bĕ'ri) *v.t.* 1. Deposit in, commit to, earth, tomb, or sea; perform burial rites over; put under ground. 2. Put away, forget; consign to obscurity; hide in earth, cover up, submerge; plunge (head *in* hands, hands *in* pockets, etc.).

bŭs *n.* Omnibus; (slang) motor-car, aeroplane; *busman's holiday*, leisure time spent in same occupation as working hours; ~*-bar*, ~ *conductor*, (elect.) system of conductors in a generating station on which all the power of generators is collected for distribution, or, in a receiving station, on which the power from the generating station is received for distribution (ill. HYDROELECTRIC).

bŭs'by (-z-) *n.* Tall fur cap of hussars etc. (ill. CAVALRY).

bush[1] (bōō-) *n.* Woody plant with numerous stems of moderate length; clump of shrubs; woodland, untilled district (esp. in Australia, N.Z., and S. Africa); luxuriant growth of hair etc.; bunch of ivy formerly used as vintner's sign (chiefly in phr. *good wine needs no* ~); ~*-baby*, galago; *bush'buck*, small African antelope of genus *Tragelaphas*, dwelling in forests and swamps, esp. common bushbuck, *T. scriptus*; *bush'man*, member, language, of aboriginal tribe of S. Africa; (also) dweller, farmer, or traveller in Australian bush; ~*-ranger*, Australian brigand (orig. escaped convict) living in bush; ~*-veld(t)*, veld consisting largely of bush; the 'Low Country' of the Transvaal; ~*-whacker*, backwoodsman. ~ *v.t.* Preserve (trees, land from poachers etc.) by surrounding or strewing with bushes. **bushed** (-sht) *adj.* Lost in the bush.

bush[2] (bōō-) *n.* Metal lining of axle-hole etc.; box or bearing in which shaft revolves; perforated plug. ~ *v.t.* Furnish with bush.

bush'el (bōō-) *n.* Measure of capacity (8 gallons) for dry goods; see Appendix X.

Bushido (bōōsh'ēdō) *n.* The code of honour and morals evolved by the samurai of Japan. [Jap., = 'military knight way']

bush'y (bōō-) *adj.* Abounding in bushes; growing thickly.

business (bĭz'nės) *n.* 1. Task, duty, province; errand; agenda. 2. Serious occupation, work; habitual occupation, profession; trade, commercial transactions; commercial house, firm; ~ *man*, (U.S.) *businessman*, man engaged in commerce. 3. (theatr.) Action, dumb-show. 4. (contempt.) Process, concern, affair, thing. **business-like** *adj.* Systematic, practical, prompt, well-ordered.

bŭsk *n.* Rigid strip stiffening front of stays.

bŭs'ker *n.* Itinerant musician or actor.

bŭs'kin *n.* 1. Boot reaching to calf or knee. 2. Thick-soled boot lending height to Athenian tragic actor; (fig.) tragedy.

Busōn'i (bōō-), Ferruccio (1866–1924). Italian pianist and composer.

bŭst[1] *n.* 1. Sculpture of person's head and chest. 2. Upper front of body, bosom, esp. of woman.

bŭst[2] *v.* (slang) Burst. ~ *adj.* Broke, without money. ~ *n.* Burst, (esp.) spree; ~*-up*, explosion, excitement.

bŭs'tard *n.* Genus, *Otis*, of large, swift-running birds.

bŭs'tle[1] (-sl) *v.* Bestir oneself, make show of activity, hurry *about*; make (others) hurry or work hard. ~ *n.* Excited activity, fuss.

bŭs'tle[2] (-sl) *n.* Pad or framework puffing out top of woman's skirt behind.

BUSTLE AND DRESS WITH BUSTLE, 1870

busy (bĭz'ĭ) *adj.* Occupied, working, engaged, with intention concentrated; unresting, always employed, stirring; fussy, meddlesome, prying; ~*-body*, meddlesome person, mischief-maker. **bus'ĭly** *adv.* **bus'y** *v.t.* Occupy, keep busy. ~ *n.* (slang) Police detective.

bŭt *adv., prep., conj.* Only; except, without, outside of, apart from; unless, if not, yet, still.

būt'adiene (-dēn) *n.* A highly unsaturated hydrocarbon, C_4H_6, gaseous at ordinary temperatures, readily polymerized to rubber-like solid.

būt'āne *n.* A colourless hydrocarbon gas (C_4H_{10}) used compressed in cylinders as an illuminant.

butch'er (bŏŏ-) *n.* Slaughterer of animals for food, dealer in meat; person who causes or delights in bloodshed; ~*-bird*, kind of shrike; ~*'s broom*, a low-growing spiny evergreen, *Ruscus aculeatus*, with stiff stems and spiny leaf-like branches bearing the flower and fruit; ~*'s meat*, meat sold by butchers, as dist. from poultry, bacon, etc. ~ *v.t.* Slaughter in the manner of a butcher (lit. & fig.).

butch'erly (bŏŏ-) *adj.* Fit for, like, a butcher; coarse, cruel, bloody.

butch'ery (bŏŏ-) *n.* Shambles; butcher's trade; needless or cruel slaughter.

Būte'shire. Scottish island county, in the Firth of Clyde.

bŭt'ler[1] *n.* Male servant in charge of wine-cellar, plate, etc., head servant.

Bŭt'ler[2], Samuel (1612–80). English poet and satirist; author of 'Hudibras'.

Bŭt'ler[3], Samuel (1835–1902). English critic and novelist; author of a Utopian novel, 'Erewhon' (1872) and an autobiographical novel, 'The Way of All Flesh', published posthumously in 1903.

bŭtt[1] *n.* Wine or ale cask (holding 108–140 gallons; ill. CASK); any barrel.

bŭtt[2] *n.* 1. Thicker end, esp. of tool or weapon (ill. GUN). 2. Trunk of tree just above ground. 3. Hide of back and flanks of ox etc. reduced to a rough rectangle; leather made from this, sole-leather. 4. Square end of plank meeting a similar end.

bŭtt[3] *n.* 1. Mound behind target; grouse-shooter's stand screened by low turf or stone wall; (pl.) shooting-range; target. 2. End, aim, object *of* (ridicule etc.); object of teasing and ridicule.

bŭtt[4] *v.* Push with the head; ~ *in*, intervene, meddle; meet end to end. ~ *n.* Butting, push with the head.

butte (būt) *n.* Isolated abrupt flat-topped hill in western U.S.

bŭtt'er *n.* Fatty pale-yellow substance made from cream by churning, used for spreading on bread and in cookery; substance of similar consistency or look; fulsome flattery; ~ *bean*, dried seed of white varieties of Lima bean, used as culinary vegetable; *buttercup*, various kinds of ranunculus with yellow cup-shaped flowers, flowering esp. in spring meadows. ~*-fingers*, *-fingered*, (person) unable to hold things, esp. a catch at cricket; ~*-fish*, GUNNEL; *butt'ermilk*, acidulous milk remaining after butter has been churned out; ~*-muslin*, thin, loosely woven fine-meshed fabric used for wrapping butter, carcasses of meat, etc. ~*-nut*, (large oily fruit of) N. Amer. white walnut-tree, *Juglans cinerea*; *butterscotch*, kind of toffee made chiefly of sugar and butter; *butterwort*, violet-flowered fleshy-leaved bog-plant, *Pinguicula vulgaris*. ~ *v.t.* Spread, cook, sauce, with butter; flatter. **bŭtt'ery**[1] *adj.*

bŭtt'erflȳ *n.* Diurnal lepidopterous insect (cf. MOTH) with knobbed antennae, carrying the wings erect when at rest; vain or fickle person.

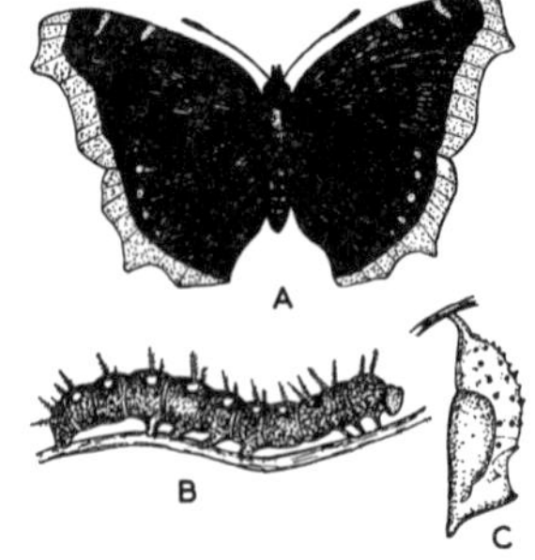

BUTTERFLY (CAMBERWELL BEAUTY): A. IMAGO. B. CATERPILLAR. C. CHRYSALIS

bŭtt'ery[2] *n.* Place in colleges etc. where provisions such as bread, butter, and ale are kept. [AF. *boterie* butt-store, i.e. place for casks]

bŭtt'ock *n.* One of the two protuberances of the rump; (usu. pl.) rump; manœuvre in wrestling in which buttock or hip is used.

bŭtt'on *n.* Knob or disc sewn to garment to fasten it by passing through buttonhole, or for ornament; bud; unopened mushroom; small rounded body; terminal knob (on foil etc.), knob, handle, catch, as in electric bell; *buttonhole*, slit through which button passes; flower(s) for wearing in buttonhole in lapel of coat; (*v.t.*) sew with buttonhole stitch; seize, detain (reluctant listener); *buttonhole stitch*, stitch used for finishing raw edges, blanket stitch, dist. from *tailor's buttonhole stitch* used for edging buttonholes (ill. STITCH); *buttonhook*, small hook for pulling button through buttonhole. ~ *v.* Furnish with button(s); fasten (often *up*) with button(s); enclose (person, thing) within buttoned garment or covering.

bŭtt'ons *n.* Page-boy in livery (from rows of buttons on front of jacket).

bŭtt'rėss *n.* Support built against wall etc., prop; buttress-like projection of hill. ~ *v.* Support with buttress, by argument etc.

BUTTRESS: A. ROMANESQUE PILASTER BUTTRESS. B. GOTHIC BUTTRESS. C. FLYING BUTTRESS

1. Pinnacle. 2. Offset

būtȳ'rĭc *adj.* (chem.) Of, pertaining to, related to, butter; ~ *acid* (C_3H_7COOH), colourless syrupy liquid in rancid butter.

bū'tȳrin *n.* Oily liquid obtained by action of butyric acid on glycerine.

bŭx'om *adj.* Plump, comely. **bŭx'omnėss** *n.*

buy (bī) *v.t* (past t. and past part. *bought* pr. bawt). Obtain in exchange for money or other consideration; gain over by bribery; ~ *in*, buy a stock of; withdraw at auction by naming higher price than the highest offered. ~ *n.* Purchase; *a good* ~, a bargain. **buy'er** *n.* (esp.) One who buys stock for a shop etc.

bŭzz *n.* Hum of bee etc., confused low sound like this; *~-saw*, circular saw. *~ v.* Make humming sound; move, hover, *about* annoyingly like bluebottle; sound confusedly; utter by speaking together; throw hard.

bŭzz'ard *n.* 1. Name of various kinds of hawk belonging to genus *Buteo.* 2. (U.S.) The turkey-buzzard, a species of vulture.

A. BUZZARD. Length 21 in. B. KESTREL. Length 14 in.

bŭzz'er *n.* (esp.) Steam-whistle; electric buzzing machine for sending signals; (army slang) signaller.

B.V.M. *abbrev. Beata Virgo Maria* (= the Blessed Virgin Mary).

B.W.I. *abbrev.* British West Indies.

bȳ *prep.* Near, along, through, via, past; during; through the agency, means, etc., of; as soon as, not later than; according to, after, from; to the extent of. *~ adv.* Near; aside, in reserve; past. **bȳ, bȳe**[1] *adj.* Subordinate, incidental, secondary, side, secret; *~-election*: see ELECTION.

bȳ and bȳ *adv.* Before long, presently. *~ n.* The future.

bȳ'-blow (-ō) *n.* Side blow; bastard child.

bȳe[2] *n.* Something subordinate; (cricket) run scored for ball that passes batsman and wicket-keeper; (in games when competitors are paired off) odd man, position of odd man; (golf) hole(s) remaining unplayed when match is finished.

bȳe'-bȳe[1] *n.* (Nursery word for) sleep, bed.

bȳe-bȳe'[2] *int.* (colloq., vulg.) Good-bye.

bȳ'gŏne *adj.* Past, departed; antiquated. **bȳ'gones** (-gŏnz) *n.pl.* The past, past offences; (in museums) domestic objects of former times.

bȳ'-law, bȳe'-law *n.* Regulation made by local authority or corporation.

bȳ'-nāme *n.* Secondary name, sobriquet.

Bȳng, John (1704–57). English admiral; he was sent to relieve Fort St. Philip in Minorca, which was threatened by the French fleet; he was repulsed, and on his return to England was court-martialled and shot at Portsmouth for neglect of duty; the incident occasioned Voltaire's observation, in 'Candide', that it is a good thing to kill an admiral now and then 'pour encourager les autres'.

bȳ'-pass (-pah-) *n.* 1. Secondary gas-jet alight when main supply is cut off; similar small tube from steam-pipe etc. 2. Road designed to relieve congestion by providing an alternative route for through traffic, esp. round town. *~ v.t.* Furnish with a by-pass; make detour round (town etc.) (also fig.).

bȳ'-path (-ah-) *n.* Retired path.

bȳ'play *n.* Action apart from the main course of events, esp. dumb-show on stage.

bȳ'-prŏduct *n.* Thing produced incidentally in manufacturing something else.

Byrd[1] (bẽrd), Richard Evelyn (1888–1957). Amer. polar explorer; made first flight over N. Pole (1926) and over S. Pole (1929).

Byrd[2] (bẽrd), William (1543?–1623). Composer; the first English madrigalist and the greatest English master of polyphonic music.

bȳre *n.* Cow-shed.

bȳ'-road *n.* Little-frequented road.

Bȳr'on, George Gordon, 6th Baron (1788–1824). English Romantic poet, whose poetry, though much criticized on moral grounds, exerted great influence on the European Romantic movement; he joined the Greek insurgents in 1823, and died of fever at Missolonghi. **Bȳrŏn'ic** *adj.* **Bȳr'onism** *n.*

bȳ'stănder *n.* Spectator.

bȳ'-street *n.* Out-of-the-way street.

bȳ'way *n.* Secluded road or track; short cut; less known department of any subject.

bȳ'word (-wẽrd) *n.* Proverb; person, place, etc., taken as a type of some (usu. bad) quality.

Bȳzăn'tīne *adj.* & *n.* (Inhabitant) of Byzantium or Constantinople; of the style of art and architecture typical of this, characterized esp. by use of the round arch, circle, dome, and cross, and by rich mosaic ornament; *~ Empire*, the Eastern division of the Roman Empire, which had its capital at Constantinople and lasted from the partition of the Roman Empire between the two sons of Theodosius in A.D. 395 to the capture of Constantinople by the Turks in 1453.

Bȳzăn'tium. Original name of CONSTANTINOPLE.

C

C, c (sē). 1. 3rd letter of the modern English and Roman alphabet, deriving its form from Gk *gamma* (Γ). In English the letter represents three or more sounds: (*a*) the 'hard' sound (k) usu. before *a, o, u,* before consonants except *h,* and when final; (*b*) the 'soft' sound (s) usu. before *i, e, y*; (*c*) *ci-* and sometimes *ce-* before another vowel has the sound (-sh-); (*d*) for *ch*: see before the beginning of words in *ch-*. 2. *C, c,* 3rd in serial order. 3. *C,* (mus.) name of the key-note in the 'natural' major scale and the corresponding minor scales; name of these scales. 4. C, Roman numeral, 100 (abbrev. of *centum*). 5. C 3, lowest medical grade in British system of man-power classification in the war of 1914–18; hence, unfit, worthless.

c. *abbrev.* Caught; cent(s); century; chapter; *circa*; *circiter*; colt; cubic.

C. *abbrev.* Centigrade.

C.A. *abbrev.* Chartered accountant (Sc.).

Caaba, K- (kah'*aba*). Moslem sacred building at Mecca, the 'holy of holies', containing the 'black stone' which is supposed to have fallen from Paradise with Adam and been given by the angel Gabriel to Abraham when he was building the Caaba. [Arab. *ka'bah*, = 'square house']

căb *n.* 1. Hackney carriage, esp. of brougham or hansom shape, or taxi; *cab'man*, driver of cab; *~-rank*, row of cabs on *cab'stand*, where cabs are authorized to wait for hire. 2. Driver's shelter on locomotive (ill. LOCOMOTIVE), motor-lorry, etc. *~ v.i.* Go by cab.

C.A.B. *abbrev.* Citizens' advice bureau.

cabăl' *n.* 1. Secret intrigue; clique, faction. 2. (hist.) Under Charles II, the 'Committee for Foreign Affairs', precursor of the modern cabinet; esp. the 5 ministers who signed the treaty of alliance with France for war against Holland in 1672: Clifford, Arlington, Buckingham, Ashley (Earl of Shaftesbury), and Lauderdale. ~ *v.i.* Combine in cabal, intrigue privately. [f. CABBALA, not f. the ministers' initials]

căb'aret (-rā) *n.* 1. French tavern. 2. Entertainment provided in restaurant etc. while guests are at table.

căbb'age *n.* Kinds of green culinary vegetable, esp. some varieties of *Brassica oleracea*, with compact globular heart or head of unexpanded leaves; ~ *lettuce*, variety of lettuce with cabbage-like head; *~-palm*, *-tree*, various trees with edible cabbage-like terminal bud, esp. the W. Ind. *Areca* (*Oreodoxa*) *oleracea*; ~ *rose*, double rose with large round compact flowers, esp. *Rosa centifolia*; *C~ White*, butterfly which feeds on cabbage leaves (*Pieris brassicae*, large white; *P. rapae*, small white).

căb(b)'ala *n.* Jewish oral tradition handed down from Moses to the rabbis of the Mishnah and Talmud, or the pretended tradition of the mystical interpretation of the O.T. 2. Mystery; esoteric doctrine. **căb(b)'alĭsm, căb(b)'alĭst** *ns.* **căb(b)alĭs'tĭc** *adj.* **căb(b)alĭs'tĭcally** *adv.* [Heb. *gabbalah* 'tradition']

căbb'y *n.* (colloq.) Cab-driver.

căb'er *n.* Roughly trimmed young pine-trunk used in Sc. Highland sport of *tossing the ~*. [Gael. *cabar* pole]

căb'ĭn *n.* 1. Small rude dwelling. 2. Room or compartment in ship for sleeping or eating in; officer's or passenger's room; *~-boy*, boy waiting on officers or passengers. **căb'ined** (-ĭnd) *adj.* Confined in small space, cramped.

căb'ĭnėt *n.* 1. Small private room, closet. 2. Case with drawers, shelves, etc., for keeping valuables or displaying curiosities. 3. Private room in which confidential advisers of a sovereign or chief ministers of a State meet; the advisers or ministers collectively. 4. *~-maker*, one whose business is the making of cabinets and the finer kind of joiner's work; *~-making*; *~-photograph*, one of a size larger than a carte-de-visite; *~-pudding*, pudding made of bread or cake, dried fruit, eggs, and milk.

cā'ble *n.* 1. (naut.) Strong thick rope 10 in. or more in circumference, consisting of three hawsers laid left-handed; rope or chain of anchor; as measure, about 100 fathoms. 2. Any insulated conductor of electricity, orig. the conductor of a submarine telegraph. 3. = CABLEGRAM. 4. ~ *moulding*. (archit.) moulding with twisted rope-like ornament (ill. MOULDING); cabled moulding (see CABLE *v.* sense 2); ~ *railway*, funicular railway. ~ *v.* 1. Furnish, fasten with cable. 2. (archit.) Fill lower part of flutings of (column) with convex mouldings. 3. Transmit (message), communicate, by cable.

cā'blegrăm (-lg-) *n.* Telegraph message transmitted by submarine cable.

cā'blėt *n.* Cable-laid rope less than 10 in. in circumference.

cabŏbs' *n.pl.* Oriental dish of meat cooked in small pieces with various seasonings.

căbochon' (-shawṅ) *n.* Precious stone, esp. ruby, sapphire, garnet, or amethyst, polished but not cut into facets (ill. GEM).

caboo'dle *n.* (slang, orig. U.S.) *The whole ~*, the whole lot.

caboose' *n.* 1. Cook-room or kitchen on ship's deck. 2. (U.S.) Workmen's or trainmen's van on freight-train.

Căb'ot, John (*c* 1450–98). Venetian navigator in the service of England; discovered Labrador in 1497 with his son Sebastian (1477–1557).

căb'rĭōle *n.* Kind of curved leg in 17th- and 18th-c. furniture, esp. that of Chippendale type (ill. CHAIR). [orig. = a kind of small arm-chair; see CABRIOLET]

căbrĭolet' (-lā) *n.* Light two-wheeled hooded one-horse chaise. [Fr., f. *cabriole* goat's leap]

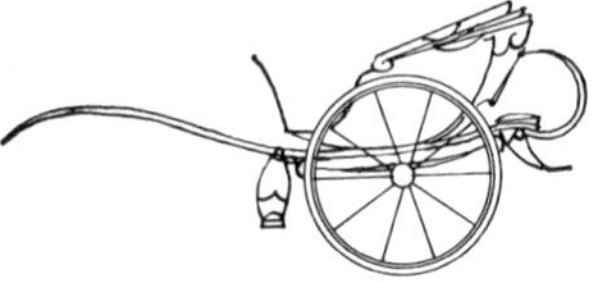

CABRIOLET

ca'cănn'y (kah-) *n.* 'Going slow' at work; deliberate policy of limiting output. [Sc. pron. of *call* + *canny*]

cacā'ō *n.* Seed of a tropical Amer. tree, *Theobroma cacao*, from which cocoa and chocolate are prepared; the tree itself (also *~-tree*).

că'chalŏt (-sh-) *n.* Genus of whales with teeth in lower jaw; *common ~*, the sperm-whale of tropical and sub-tropical seas, from which spermaceti and ambergris are obtained.

căche (-sh) *n.* Hiding-place for treasures, ammunition, provisions, etc., esp. as used by explorers; the stores hidden. ~ *v.t.* Place in cache.

căch'et (-shā) *n.* Stamp (fig.), distinguishing mark.

căc'hĭnnāte (-k-) *v.i.* Laugh loudly. **căchĭnnā'tion** *n.* **căc'hĭnnatory** *adj.*

cach'ou (-shōō) *n.* Pill used by smokers to sweeten the breath. [Malay *kachu*; cf. CATECHU]

cacique' (-sēk) *n.* W. Ind. and Amer. Ind. native chief.

căc'kle *n.* Clucking of hen after laying; glib, noisy, inconsequent talk; loud silly laughter. ~ *v.i.* Make cackle; talk glibly and noisily.

căcodēm'on *n.* Evil spirit; malignant person.

căc'odȳl *n.* (chem.) The radical dimethyl arsenic, $As(CH_3)_2$. [Gk *kakōdēs* stinking]

căcŏēth'es (-ēz) *n.* Itch for doing something unadvisable; esp. ~ *scriben'di*, scribbling-mania.

cacŏg'raphy *n.* Bad handwriting or spelling.

cacŏph'ony *n.* Ill sound, discord. **cacŏph'onous** *adj.*

căc'tŭs *n.* (pl. *-tī*, *-tuses*). Plant of the family *Cactaceae*, flourishing in arid districts of the New World, having a thick fleshy stem adapted for retaining moisture (usu. with spines, rarely with leaves) and bearing brilliantly coloured flowers; ~ *dahlia*, dahlia with ray florets recurved at the edges, orig. from Mexico. **căctā'ceous** (-sh*us*) *adj.*

căd *n.* Vulgar ill-bred person; person guilty of ungentlemanly conduct. **cădd'ĭsh** *adj.*

cadăs'tral *adj.* Of, showing, the extent, value, and ownership of land for taxation.

cadăv'erous *adj.* Corpse-like; deadly pale.

cădd'ie, cădd'y[1] *n.* Golf-player's attendant who carries his clubs etc.; *~-cart*, small two-wheeled trolley for the same purpose. **cădd'y** *v.i.* Act as caddie. [f. CADET[1]]

cădd'ĭs *n.* *~-fly*, feebly flying freq. nocturnal insect living near water; *~-worm*, larva of caddis-fly etc., living in water and making cylindrical case of sticks, stone, shells, etc., used as bait for fishing.

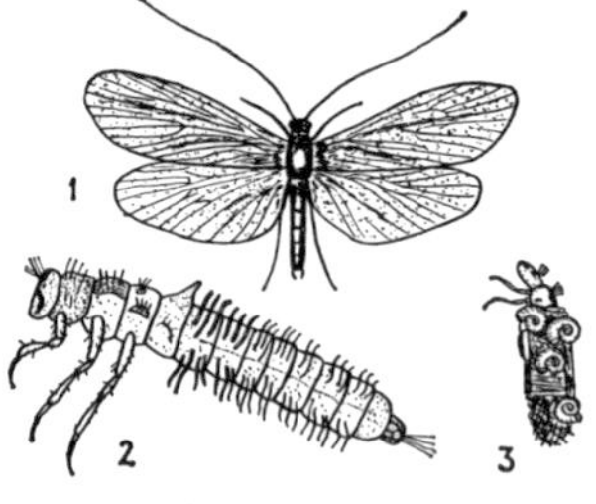

CADDIS-FLY

1. Adult. 2. Larva. 3. Larva in case

cădd'y[2] *n.* Small box for holding tea; *~-spoon*, short-handled spoon for measuring tea from caddy. [Malay *kati*, weight of 1⅓ lb.]

cād'ence *n.* Rhythm; measured movement, esp. of sound; falling tone, esp. of voice at end of period; intonation; (mus.) close of musical movement or phrase.

cadĕn'za *n.* (mus.) Flourish for solo instrument (or, less freq., voice) at close of movement or between two parts of movement, sometimes improvised by performer.

cadĕt′[1] *n.* 1. Younger son or brother. 2. Student in military, naval, or air force college; schoolboy or undergraduate member of ~ *corps*, receiving training as preparation for military service.

cadĕt[2] *n.* (hist.) Member of Russian Constitutional Democratic (or Liberal) Party, formed 1905. [Russ., f. *ka*, *de*, names of initial letters of *K*onstitutsionny *D*emokrat; *t* added for sake of pun on *kadet* CADET[1]]

căḍge *v.* Get by begging; ~ *for*, try to get by begging or 'sponging'.

ca′dī′ (kah-, kā-) *n.* Civil judge, usu. of town, etc., among Turks, Arabs, Persians.

căd′mium *n.* Soft bluish-white metallic element resembling tin, used in a number of alloys and as a protective coating on iron and steel; symbol Cd, at. no. 48, at. wt 112·40; ~ *yellow*, cadmium sulphide, an intense yellow pigment. [Gk *kadmia* CADMEAN (earth)]

Căd′mus. (Gk legend) Founder of Thebes in Boeotia, reputed to have introduced the alphabet into Greece; slew a dragon and sowed its teeth in the earth, from which armed men sprang up and slew one another. **Cădmē′an** *adj.*; ~ *victory*, victory involving one's own ruin.

cadre (kah′dr) *n.* Framework, scheme; (mil.) permanent establishment of regiment forming nucleus for enlargement at need.

cadū′cėus *n.* (pl. *-cĕī*). Ancient Greek or Roman herald's wand; esp. that of Mercury, usu. represented with two serpents twined round it.

CADUCEUS

cadū′cous *adj.* Fleeting, perishable; (biol., of organs and parts) shed when their work is done. **cadū′cĭty** *n.*

caec′um (sē-) *n.* (pl. *-ca*). Any blindly ending tube in the structure of an animal, esp. that arising from the colon and ending at the vermiform appendix in mammals (ill. ALIMENTARY).

Cæd′mon (kăd-) (7th c.). English monk; said by Bede to have received in a vision the power of song and put into English verse passages from the Scriptures, but the only authentic fragment of his work is the first Hymn, which Bede quotes.

Caernârv on (*ker*-). County town of **Caernarvonshire,** a county of N. Wales.

Caesar (sēz′*ar*). Cognomen of the Roman dictator Caius Julius Caesar (see JULIUS CAESAR), used as title by the Roman emperors from Augustus to Hadrian, and subsequently by the emperor's heir-presumptive. **Caesâr′ėan, -ĭan** *adj.* Of Caesar or the Caesars; ~ *operation, section*, delivery of a child by cutting through walls of abdomen, as was done, acc. to Pliny, in the case of Julius Caesar.

cae′sium (sēz-) *n.* A rare alkali-metal element discovered spectroscopically by Bunsen in 1861; symbol Cs, at. no. 55, at. wt 132·905. [L *caesius* bluish-grey, f. the distinctive lines in its spectrum]

caesūr′a (sĭz-) *n.* (In classical prosody) break between words within a metrical foot; (modern prosody) pause about the middle of metrical line.

café (kăf′ā) *n.* Coffee-house, teashop, restaurant; ~ *au lait* (ō lā), coffee taken with about an equal quantity of hot milk; the brownish-cream colour of this; ~ *noir* (nwahr), black coffee, coffee without milk.

căfėtēr′ĭa *n.* (orig. U.S.) Restaurant in which the customer fetches food from the counter.

căff′ėine (-ēn) *n.* Vegetable alkaloid crystallizing in white silky needles, found in leaves and seeds of coffee and tea plants etc. (and hence in these beverages); used in medicine as a cardiac stimulant.

Caffre: see KAFIR.

căf′tan *n.* Long girdled under-tunic worn in Turkey and other eastern countries.

cāge *n.* 1. Fixed or portable prison, of wire or with bars, esp. for birds or beasts; prison. 2. (mining) Frame for hoisting and lowering wagons etc. (ill. MINE); open framework of various kinds. ~ *v.t.* Place or keep in cage.

cā′ġey *adj.* (slang) Wary, non-committal.

Caġliŏs′trō (kălyŏ-), Count Alessandro (1743–95). Name assumed by Giuseppe Balsamo, a notorious charlatan born at Palermo; he was implicated in the *Affair of the* DIAMOND *Necklace*.

caiman: see CAYMAN.

Cain. Eldest son of Adam, and the first murderer (see Gen. iv.); murderer, fratricide; *raise* ~, make a disturbance.

cainozō′ic, k- (kī-), **cen-** (sē-) *adj.* (geol.) Of the series of rock-formations above the Mesozoic; of the animal remains etc. characteristic of this; sometimes = TERTIARY. ~ *n. The C*~, the cainozoic period or formation (ill. GEOLOGY).

caique (ka-ēk′) *n.* Light rowing-boat used on the Bosporus; Levantine sailing-vessel.

Cair′ēne (kīr-) *adj.* & *n.* (Native, inhabitant) of Cairo.

cairn *n.* 1. Pyramid of rough stones as memorial, landmark, etc. 2. ~ (*terrier*), a small terrier (named from being used to hunt among cairns) with longish body, short straight legs, and shaggy coat (ill. DOG).

cairn′ġôrm *n.* Yellow or wine-coloured semi-precious stone, consisting of quartz coloured by iron oxide or titanic acid, named after the mountain in Scotland where it is chiefly found. [Gael. *carn gorm* blue cairn]

Cairo (kīr′ō). Capital city of Egypt, situated on the Nile about 100 miles from its mouths. [Arab. *El-qāhirah* the victorious]

caiss′on (*or* kĭsōōn′) *n.* 1. Ammunition chest or wagon. 2. Large watertight chamber used in laying foundations under water; buoyant chamber attached to side of ship engaged in raising wreck; boat-shaped vessel used as dock gate;

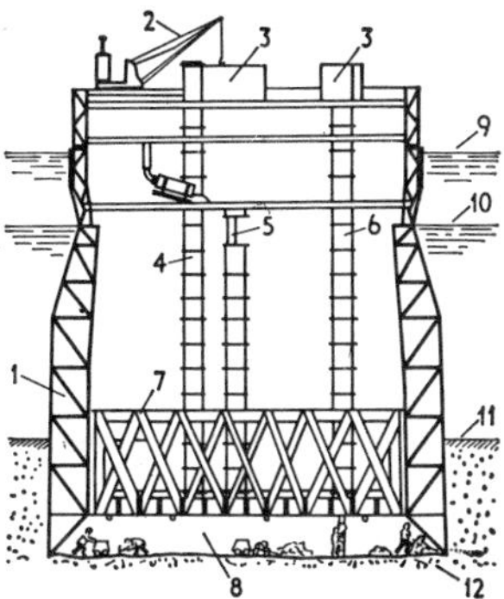

DIAGRAMMATIC SECTION OF CAISSON FOR BRIDGE PIER

1. Wall. 2. Crane for discharging buckets. 3. Air-lock. 4. Shaft for materials. 5. Shaft for concrete. 6. Shaft for men. 7. Girders to keep down roof of working chamber. 8. Working chamber (compressed air). 9. High-water level. 10. Low-water level. 11. Bed of river. 12. Hard rock to take foundations

~ *disease*, disease, also called *bends*, caused by working in atmosphere at high pressure.

Caithnĕss′. County in extreme NE. of Scotland.

cait′iff *n.* & *adj.* (archaic) Base, despicable (person); coward(ly).

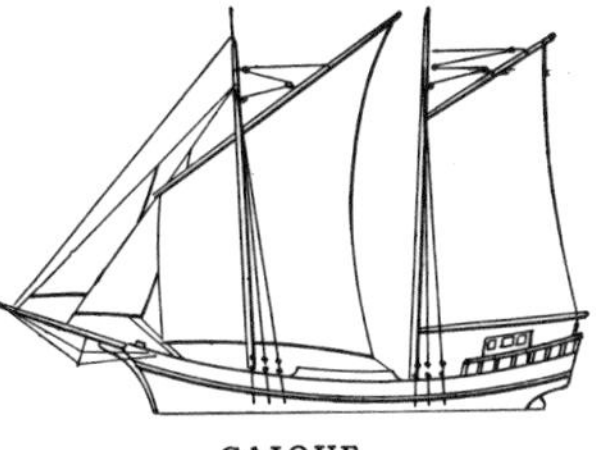

CAIQUE

Caius College (kēz). A Cambridge college (full title Gonville and Caius College), formerly Gonville Hall, founded by Edmund Gonville in 1348; refounded and enlarged by John Caius or Kay (1570–73), scholar and physician to Edward VI and Mary and master of the college 1559–73.

cajōle′ *v.t.* Persuade or soothe by flattery, deceit, etc. **cajōle′ment** (-lm-), **cajōl′ery** *ns.*

căj′upŭt, -apŭt *n.* ~ *oil*, aromatic oil obtained from various species of the E. Ind. tree *Melaleuca*, used as stimulant, antispasmodic, and sudorific. [Malay *kayu* wood, *puteh* white]

cāke *n.* 1. (archaic) Small flattish loaf of bread; (Sc. and northern) thin oaten bread; *land of cakes*, Scotland. 2. Baked sweetened mixture of flour and other ingredients, as butter, eggs, spices, currants, raisins, etc. 3. Flattish compact mass of other food (as fish etc.) or of any compressed substance, as soap, wax, tobacco. 4. *cake′walk*, (orig.) form of entertainment among Amer. Negroes in which a prize of a cake was given for the most graceful steps and figures in walking; popular stage dance developed from these steps. ~ *v.* Form into compact flattish mass.

Cal(if). *abbrev.* California.

Călabar′ bean *n.* Highly poisonous seed of tropical African vine (*Physostigma venenosum*), an extract of which is used to contract the pupil of the eye and in tetanus and strychnine poisoning. [*Calabar* in W. Africa]

căl′abăsh *n.* Various gourds or pumpkins, the shell of which is used for holding liquids etc.; the vessel made from such a shell; ~-*tree*, a tropical Amer. and W. Ind. tree *Crescentia*, bearing a large oval or globular fruit with a hard shell.

călaboōse′ (-z) *n.* (U.S. colloq.) Prison.

călamăn′cō *n.* Glossy Flemish woollen stuff, chequered on one side, much used in 18th c.

călamăn′der *n.* Beautiful, extremely hard, cabinet wood of Ceylon and India, from the tree (related to ebony) *Diospyros quaesita.*

căl′amary *n.* Kinds of cuttlefish (genus *Loligo*) with pen-shaped internal shell, long narrow body and two triangular fins.

căl′amine *n.* A zinc ore (zinc carbonate, $ZnCO_3$), used as emollient in ~ *cream, lotion*, etc.

calăm′ĭty *n.* Adversity, deep distress; grievous disaster. **calăm′ĭtous** *adj.* **calăm′ĭtously** *adv.*

calăsh′ *n.* 1. Light carriage with low wheels and folding hood; Canadian two-wheeled one-seated vehicle with driver's seat on splash-board. 2. Woman's silk hood hooped with cane or whalebone (ill. PANNIER).

călcar′ėous, -ĭous *adj.* Of, containing, calcium carbonate or limestone.

călcėolar′ia *n.* Genus of S. Amer. plants with flowers somewhat resembling a broad-toed slipper.

căl′cėolate *adj.* (bot.) Slipper-shaped.

căl′cĭcōle *n.* Plant inhabiting a soil with free calcium carbonate (or, in wider sense, soils rich in calcium). **călcĭc′olous** *adj.*

călcĭf′erous *adj.* Yielding or containing chalk or calcium carbonate.

căl′cĭfȳ *v.* Convert, be converted, into chalk or calcium carbonate; harden by deposit of calcium salts; petrify. **călcĭfĭcā′tion** *n.*

căl′cīne *v.* Reduce to quicklime or friable substance by heating strongly; desiccate; refine by consuming grosser part; burn to ashes; be calcined. **călcĭnā′tion** *n.* Process of calcining. **călcīn′er** *n.* Machine for calcining.

căl′cīte *n.* (min.) Crystalline calcium carbonate, widely distributed in nature as marble, limestone, etc.

căl′cium *n.* Silver-white malleable light metal, an element in the alkaline earth group (symbol Ca, at. no. 20, at. wt 40·08), widely distributed in nature as limestone or chalk (~ *carbonate*, $CaCO_3$); ~ *car′bide*, produced by intense heating of limestone and coke in an electric furnace and giving acetylene gas on treatment with water; ~ *hypochlorite*, chloride of lime or bleaching powder ($CaOCl_2$), used as disinfectant; ~ *oxide*, quicklime (CaO), made by heating chalk.

călc-spar *n.* (min.) Crystalline form of calcium carbonate (limestone).

căl′cūlable *adj.* That may be reckoned, measured, computed, or relied upon. **călcūlabĭl′ĭty** *n.*

căl′cūlāte *v.* Compute by figures; ascertain beforehand by exact reckoning; plan deliberately; rely upon; suppose, believe (U.S.); (usu. pass.) arrange, adapt, *for, to*; (*past part.*) fit, suitable *to* do. *calculating-machine*, machine that performs arithmetical processes.

călcūlā′tion *n.* (Result got by) calculating; forecast.

căl′cūlātor *n.* (esp.) Set of tables for use in calculating; calculating-machine.

căl′cūlus *n.* 1. (med., pl. *-lī*) Stone, concretion in some part of the body. 2. (math.) Particular method of calculation, esp. DIFFERENTIAL and INTEGRAL calculus. **căl′cūlous** *adj.* Of, suffering from, stone or calculus. [L, = small stone used in reckoning on abacus]

Călcŭtt′a. Largest city in India, capital of W. Bengal; *Black Hole of* ~: see BLACK[1].

Calderón (de la Barca) (kawl-), Pedro (1600–81). Spanish dramatist and poet, author of some 120 plays.

caldron = CAULDRON.

Călėdōn′ia. Roman name of part of northern Britain; in modern times (poet. and rhet.) Scotland, the Scottish Highlands. **Calėdōn′ian** *adj.* & *n.* (Native) of ancient Caledonia or of Scotland; ~ *Canal*, canal from Inverness on the E. coast of Scotland to Fort William on the W. coast.

căl′ėndar *n.* 1. System by which the beginning, length, and subdivision of civil year is fixed, esp. the GREGORIAN ~, used in England since 1752; ~ *month*, one of the 12 months into which year is divided by calendar, as opp. to LUNAR month of 4 weeks; *Jewish* ~: see JEWISH. 2. Table(s) showing months, weeks, and festivals, etc., of a given year or years. 3. Register, list, esp. of canonized saints, prisoners for trial, or documents chronologically arranged with summaries. ~ *v.t.* Register, enter in list; arrange, analyse, and index (documents).

căl′ėnder[1] *n.* Machine in which cloth, paper, etc., is pressed under rollers to glaze or smooth it. ~ *v.t.* Press in calender.

căl′ėnder[2] *n.* Mendicant dervish in Turkey or Persia.

căl′ėnds, k- *n.pl.* 1st day of month in Roman calendar; *Greek* ~, date or occasion which never comes (because the Greeks had no calends).

căl′ėnture *n.* Tropical fever or delirium in which, it is said, sailors etc. fancy the sea to be green fields and desire to leap into it.

calf[1] (kahf) *n.* (pl. *-ves*). 1. Young of bovine animal, esp. domestic cow, for first year; young of elephant, whale, etc. 2. Leather made from skin of domestic calf. 3. (naut.) Floating piece of ice detached from glacier, iceberg, or floe. 4. *sea-*~, seal; *golden* ~: see Exod. xxxii; wealth as an object of worship; ~-*love*, romantic affection between boy and girl; *calf's foot*, dish made of calves' feet boiled and seasoned.

calf[2] (kahf) *n.* Fleshy hinder part of shank of leg; part of stocking covering this.

Căl′ībăn. The 'savage and deformed slave' in Shakespeare's 'Tempest'.

căl′ibrāte *v.t.* Find calibre of; calculate irregularities of (tube, gauge) before graduating; graduate (a gauge) making allowance for irregularities.

căl′ibre (-b*er*, *or* kalē′b*er*) *n.* 1. Internal diameter of gun or any tube; diameter of bullet or shell. 2. Degree of personal capacity or ability, or of merit or importance. [Arab. *qalib* mould]

căl′ĭcō *n.* Plain white unprinted bleached or unbleached cotton cloth; (U.S.) printed cotton cloth.

~ *adj.* Of calico; (U.S.) like printed calico; variegated, piebald. [*Calicut*, town on Malabar coast]

Cālifōrn'ia. State on Pacific coast of U.S., admitted to the Union 1850; capital, Sacramento. **Cālifōrn'ian** *adj.* & *n.*; ~ *poppy*, the genus *Eschscholtzia*.

cālifōrn'ium *n.* TRANSURANIC element; symbol Cf, at. no. 98, principal isotope 244.

Călĭg'ūla, Gaius Caesar. Roman emperor A.D. 37–41; notorious for his cruelty and vices.

căl'ĭpăsh *n.* Part of turtle next upper shell, containing a dull green gelatinous substance.

căl'ĭpee *n.* Part of turtle next lower shell, containing light yellow gelatinous substance.

căl'ĭph *n.* 1. The title assumed by Abu Bakr after the death of Mohammed. 2. In Mohammedan countries, the chief civil and religious ruler, as successor of Mohammed. **căl'ĭphate** *n.* [Arab. *khalifah* successor]

căl'ĭx (pl. *-icēs*) *n.* Cup-like cavity or organ.

calk (cawk) *n.* Sharp iron to prevent horse-shoe or boot from slipping. ~ *v.t.* Provide with calk.

cal'kin (kaw- *or* kăl-) *n.* Turned-down heels of horse-shoe, also turned edge in front, esp. when sharpened in frost; iron pieces nailed on soles of boots or clogs.

call (kawl) *v.* 1. Cry, shout, speak loudly; utter characteristic note; cry *out, to*; read *over* (names of those present); name (suit as trumps, at cards). 2. Summon; summon or nominate by divine authority *into* the Church; ~ *to the bar*, admit as barrister. 3. Name, describe as; consider, regard as. 4. (with preps. etc.) ~ *for*, order; demand; need; go and fetch; ~ *forth*, elicit; ~ *off* (a project), cancel it; ~ *on*, invoke, appeal to; ~ *out*, elicit; challenge to duel; summon (troops) esp. to aid civil authorities; shout or utter loudly; ~ *up*, imagine; ring up (on telephone); summon to serve in army etc.; rouse from sleep. ~ *n.* 1. Shout, cry; special cry of bird etc., imitation, instrument for imitating, this; signal on bugle etc.; roll-call (also ~*-over*). 2. Looking-in on business; short formal visit. 3. Invitation, summons; duty, need, occasion; demand, claim. 4. Telephone conversation. 5. Demand for money, esp. for unpaid capital from company shareholders; (Stock Exchange) option of claiming stock at given date. 6. ~*-box*, small enclosed erection containing public telephone; ~*-boy*, prompter's attendant summoning actors.

căll'a *n.* ~ (*lily*), the S. Afr. white arum, Ethiopian, or trumpet lily, *Richardia aethiopica*.

call'er[1] (kaw-) *n.* (esp.) Person paying a call or visit; person who initiates telephone call.

căll'er[2] *adj.* (Sc.) Fresh (of herrings etc.); fresh, cool (of wind, weather, etc.).

callĭg'raphy *n.* (Beautiful) handwriting. **callĭg'rapher** *n.* **căllĭgrăph'ic** *adj.*

call'ing (kaw-) *n.* (esp.) Occupation, profession, trade; persons following a particular occupation.

Calli'opė. The 9th of the MUSES, presiding over eloquence and heroic poetry. **calli'opė** *n.* (U.S.) Steam-organ. [Gk *kalliope* beautiful-voiced]

căll'iper *adj.* & *n.* 1. ~ *compasses, callipers*, compasses with bowed legs for measuring diameter of convex bodies, or with out-turned points for measuring

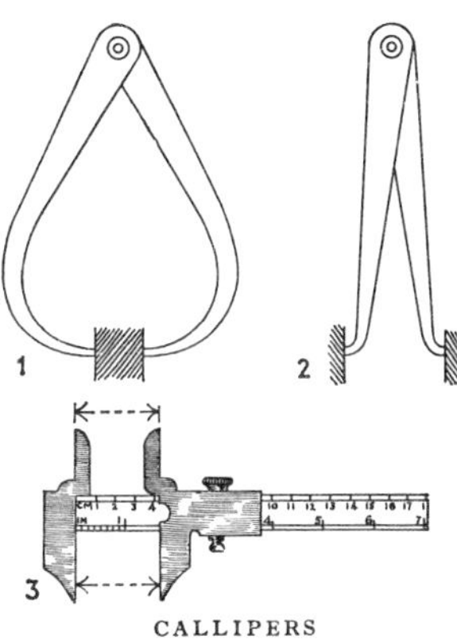

CALLIPERS

1. For outside measurement. 2. For inside measurement. 3. Calliper-square for inside and outside measurement

cavities; ~*-square*, rule with movable cross-heads for taking internal or external diameters. 2. Metal support for weak or injured legs. ~ *v.t.* Measure with callipers. [variant of CALIBRE]

căllĭsthĕn'ic *adj.* Suitable for producing strength and grace. **căllĭsthĕn'ics** *n.* Art and practice of bodily exercises calculated to produce strength and grace.

callŏs'ĭty *n.* Abnormal hardness and thickness of skin; hardened insensible part, lump.

căll'ous *adj.* 1. Hardened, hard (of parts of skin). 2. Unfeeling, insensible. **căll'ously** *adv.* **căll'ousnėss** *n.*

căll'ow (-ō) *adj.* 1. Unfledged; downy like young birds. 2. Raw, inexperienced.

căll'us *n.* Thickened part of skin or soft tissue; bony material formed while bone-fracture heals; (bot.) new tissue, usu. more or less corky, covering a wound.

calm (kahm) *n.* Stillness, serenity; windless period. ~ *adj.* Tranquil, quiet; windless; undisturbed; unabashed, impudent. **calm'ly** *adv.*, **calm'nėss** *n.* **calm** *v.* Make calm; pacify; ~ *down*, become calm.

căl'omĕl *n.* Mercurous chloride (HgCl), a heavy white powder used as a purgative.

căl'orie *n.* 1. (*Great* or *large* ~), standard unit of heat, amount required to raise the temperature of 1 kilogram (1 litre) of water 1 degree centigrade; unit for measuring the heat and other energy produced by the metabolism of food, esp. on a daily basis. 2. (*Lesser* ~), amount of heat required to raise 1 gram (1 cu. cm.) of water 1 degree centigrade.

călorĭf'ic *adj.* Producing heat; ~ *value*, amount of heat, usu. expressed in form of kilogram calories, given out on the complete combustion of a substance.

călorĭm'ėter *n.* An apparatus for measuring heat. **călorimĕt'ric** *adj.* **călorimĕt'rically** *adv.* **călorĭm'ėtry** *n.*

căl'trop *n.* 1. 4-spiked iron ball thrown on ground to maim cavalry horses. 2. Representation of this as heraldic charge (ill. HERALDRY). 3. (usu. pl.) Kinds of plant that catch or entangle the feet.

căl'ūmėt *n.* Amer. Ind. tobacco-pipe with reed stem and clay bowl; used as symbol of peace or friendship (the *pipe of peace*).

calŭm'niāte *v.t.* Slander. **calŭmniā'tion** *n.*

căl'umny *n.* Malicious misrepresentation; false report; slander.

Căl'vary. 1. The hill near Jerusalem on which Jesus was crucified. 2. Representation of the crucifixion, esp. in the open air. [L *calvaria* skull, transl. of GOLGOTHA in Matt. xxvii. 33]

calve (kahv) *v.* Give birth to calf; (of iceberg etc.) throw off masses of ice.

Căl'vĭn, John (1509–64). French theological writer and reformer; settled in Geneva, 1536; wrote 'Institutes of the Christian Religion' (1535), in which he expounded his doctrine of original sin, of predestination and election; his dogma is held by the continental Reformed Churches and forms the basis of Scottish Presbyterianism.

Căl'vĭnĭsm *n.* Tenets and doctrines of CALVIN and his followers and of the Calvinistic Churches. The distinguishing doctrines of this system, usu. called *the five points of* ~, are election or predestination, limited atonement, total depravity, irresistibility of grace, and the perseverance of the saints. **Căl'vĭnĭst** *n.* Follower of Calvin, adherent of Calvinism. **Călvĭnĭs'tic** *adj.* Pertaining to, characteristic of, Calvinism; ~ *Methodists*, section of the Methodists who followed the Calvinistic opinions of WHITEFIELD as opposed to the Arminian opinions of John WESLEY.

cặlx *n.* (pl. *căl'cēs*). (archaic) Powder or friable substance left after heating metal or mineral.

Calўp'sō[1]. In the 'Odyssey', a nymph who kept ODYSSEUS 7 years on her island, Ogygia.

calўp'sō[2] *n.* W. Ind. free-verse narrative chant, freq. topical, with accompaniment on guitar or similar instrument.

căl'ўx *n.* (pl. *-ycēs, -yxes*). (bot.) Whorl of members, often leaf-like, forming outer protective envelope of flower (ill. FLOWER).

căm *n.* Portion of revolving shaft or wheel bearing against, and shaped so as to impart a particular type of motion to, a lever or other movable part of a machine.

cămara'derie (-ahderē) *n.* Intimacy, mutual trust, and sociability, of comrades. [Fr.]

căm'ber *n.* Slight convexity of upper surface, arched form (of road, ship's deck, aeroplane wing, etc.). ~ *v.* Have, give, camber to.

Căm'berwell Beaut'y (bū-). Species of butterfly, *Nymphalis antiopa* (ill. BUTTERFLY). [*Camberwell*, borough of London]

căm'bium *n.* (bot.) Layer of cells from which annual growth of woody tissue and bark takes place (ill. STEM).

Cămbōd'ia. Kingdom of SE. Asia, independent since 1948, established in 1863 as a protectorate forming part of French Indo-China; capital, Phnòm-Penh. **Cămbōd'ian** *adj.* & *n.*

Cambrensis. (Archbishop) of Wales, (replacing surname in his signature).

Căm'bria. Ancient or poetic name for Wales. **Căm'brian** *adj.* & *n.* 1. Welsh(man). 2. (geol.) (Of) the lowest system of the Palaeozoic (ill. GEOLOGY). [Latinized f. *Cymry* Welshman]

cām'bric *n.* Fine white linen or cotton fabric of plain weave. [*Kamerijk*, Fl. name of *Cambrai*, where linen cambric was made]

Cām'bridge[1]. English university city in E. midland county of Cambridgeshire; ~ *blue*, a light blue; ~ *University*: the first historical trace of Cambridge as a university (*studium generale*) is in 1209, its first recognition in a royal writ to the chancellor in 1230, the first papal recognition in 1233.

Cām'bridge[2]. Town in Massachusetts (U.S.), the seat of Harvard University.

Cām'bridgeshire. E. midland county of England; *the* ~ (*Handicap*), a horse-race run annually at Newmarket since 1839.

Cambs. *abbrev.* Cambridgeshire.

căm'el *n.* 1. (*Camelus bactrianus*, or *Bactrian* ~) Large hornless ruminant quadruped with long neck, cushioned feet, and two humps on the back which store food and enable it to go a long time without food or water; native only in Chinese Turkestan, but domesticated from Asia Minor to Manchuria as the chief beast of burden in arid regions; closely related to the dromedary (one-humped *Arabian* ~, *Camelus dromedarius*) and to the llamas and alpacas of S. America; ~('*s*)-*hair*, the hair of this animal, woven into a thick, warm, light-weight, usu. long-piled textile material; imitations of this fabric; ~('*s*)-*hair brush*, artist's paint-brush usu. made of squirrel-hair. 2. Buoyant apparatus for attaching to ship's sides and raising her in the water.

camĕll'ia *n.* Genus of flowering evergreen shrubs of tea family, chiefly natives of China and Japan. [Joseph *Kamel*, Moravian Jesuit who described botany of island of Luzon]

căm'elopârd (*or* camĕl'-) *n.* Giraffe.

Căm'ėlŏt. In the Arthurian legend, the place where King Arthur held his court, stated by Malory to be Winchester.

Căm'embert (-bār). Small rich soft cheese made near the village of Camembert in Normandy; imitations of this.

căm'ėō *n.* (pl. *-s*). Small piece of relief-carving in stone (onyx, agate, etc.), freq. with two layers of different colours, the lower of which serves as background.

căm'era *n.* 1. *In camera* (L), in the judge's private room, not in open court. 2. Apparatus for taking photographs, consisting essentially of a box holding at one end a plate or film which is sensitized so as to retain the image projected through a lens at the other; ~ *lū'cĭda*, a prism which when placed in front of a draughtsman's eye appears to him to project an image upon his paper and thus assists him in copying; so named to distinguish it from the ~ *obscura*, a much older device for tracing images, consisting of a large box, or a room, with a lens at one end and at the other a reflector which throws the image upon a screen or table (L *camera* chamber; *lucida* light, *obscura* dark); variants of this apparatus (the forerunner of the photographic camera) are used for drawing with the microscope; ~-*man*, (films) person responsible for the lighting and for the angles from which shots are taken.

cămerlĭng'ō (-ngg-) *n.* 1. The Pope's chamberlain and financial secretary, highest officer in the papal household. 2. The cardinals' chamberlain, treasurer of the Sacred College.

Căm'eron, Richard (d. 1680). Scottish Covenanter and field preacher who rejected the indulgence granted to non-conforming ministers and formally renounced allegiance to Charles II; his followers afterwards constituted the 'Reformed Presbyterian Church of Scotland'. **Cămerōn'ian** *adj.* & *n.* (Follower) of Richard Cameron; *The* ~*s*, the old 26th Regiment of Foot in the British Army, orig. formed of Cameronians and other Presbyterians who fought at the battle of Killiecrankie.

Cămerōōn. Republic on W. coast of Africa between Nigeria and Congo; from 1884 to 1916 a German protectorate; after war of 1914–18 administered under LEAGUE OF NATIONS (later U.N.) trusteeship by France (*E.* ~) and Great Britain (*Southern* ~*s*); since 1960–1 a Federal Republic comprising *E.* ~ and *W.* ~; capital, Yaoundé.

cămi-knĭck'ers (-n-) *n.* Woman's undergarment combining camisole and knickers.

căm'ion *n.* Low flat 4-wheeled horse or motor truck.

Căm'isard (-âr). Name given to the Calvinist insurgents of the Cévennes during the persecutions which followed the revocation of the Edict of Nantes by Louis XIV in 1685. [L *camisa* shirt]

căm'isōle *n.* Woman's under-bodice, often embroidered or trimmed with lace.

căm'lėt *n.* (archaic) Orig., costly

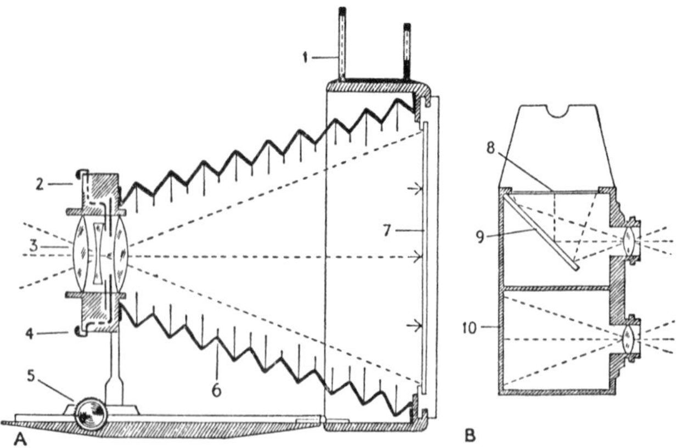

A. FOLDING HAND CAMERA. B. TWIN-LENS REFLEX CAMERA

1. View-finder. 2. Shutter lever. 3. Lens. 4. Iris diaphragm or stop-adjusting lever. 5. Focusing pinion. 6. Bellows. 7. Film or plate on which image is focused. 8. Ground-glass. 9. Mirror. 10. Film

eastern stuff of silk and camel-hair; later, light cloth of various materials for cloaks etc.

Camoëns (kăm'ōens), Luis de (1524–80). Portuguese poet, author of the 'Lusiads', an epic poem on the descendants of Lusus, the legendary hero of Portugal, and on the exploits of Vasco da GAMA.

căm'omile, chăm- (k-) *n.* Aromatic creeping herb, *Anthemis nobilis*, with downy leaves and yellow or white daisy-like flowers of which an infusion is used as a tonic, hair-wash, etc.; *~-tea*, infusion of camomile flowers.

Camŏ'rra. In the 19th c., a secret society of lawless malcontents in Naples and Neapolitan cities. **camŏ'rrist** *n.*

căm'ouflage (-ōōflahzh) *n.* Disguising, disguise, of objects used in war, as guns, ships, camps, factories, etc., by means of smoke-screens, boughs, obscuring outlines by netting and paint of various colours, etc.; deception of any kind whereby an object is made to look like something else or concealed altogether. ~ *v.t.* Conceal by or as by camouflage.

cămp *n.* 1. Place where troops are lodged in tents etc. or received for training. 2. Temporary quarters of nomads, gipsies, travellers; (persons) camping out. 3. (Remains of ancient) entrenched and fortified site within which Roman, Danish, British, etc., army lodged or defended itself. 4. *~-bed, -chair, -stool*, portable folding bed etc.; *~-fire*, fire in camp or encampment, open-air fire; *~-follower*, non-military follower or hanger-on of camp or army; *~-meeting*, religious meeting, esp. in America, held in open air or in a tent and usu. lasting several days. ~ *v.* Encamp, lodge in camp; (also ~ *out*) lodge in tent or in the open, take up quarters; station (troops) in camp.

Cămpagn'a (-ahnya). Rich level district of Italy SE. of river Tiber, extending from the sea on the W. to the Sabine Hills.

cămpaign' (-pān) *n.* 1. Series of military operations in a definite theatre or with one objective or constituting the whole or a distinct part of a war. 2. Organized course of action, esp. in politics, as before an election etc. ~ *v.i.* Serve on a campaign. **cămpaign'er** *n.*

Cămpān'ia. SW. region of Italy.

cămpani'lė (-nē-) *n.* Bell-tower, esp. one detached from main building.

cămpanŏl'ogy *n.* The subject of bells (founding, ringing, etc.). **cămpanŏl'ogist** *n.* **cămpanolŏ'gical** *adj.*

cămpăn'ūla *n.* Genus of herbaceous plants with bell-shaped, usu. blue or white, flowers, including the harebell and Canterbury bells.

Campbell (kăm'bl), Thomas 1777–1844). Scottish poet chiefly remembered for his war-songs 'Hohenlinden', 'Ye Mariners of England', etc.

Campech'ė (-pā-), **-peach'y.** City and State of SE. Mexico, on E. shore of *Gulf of* ~ (S. part of Gulf of Mexico); *Campeachy wood*, log-wood, a red dye-wood yielded by *Haematoxylon campechianum*, orig. exported from Campeachy.

Căm'perdown. Kamperduin, village on coast of Netherlands, off which in 1797 the British fleet defeated the Dutch.

căm'phor *n.* Translucent waxy crystalline substance with strong characteristic smell and bitter taste, obtained from a species of laurel growing in Formosa, also made synthetically from turpentine; used in pharmacy and in manufacture of celluloid etc. **cămphŏ'ric** *adj.*

căm'phorate *n.* Salt of camphoric acid. **căm'phorāte** *v.t.* Impregnate or treat with camphor.

căm'pĭon *n.* Kinds of plant of the genus *Lychnis*, with red or white flowers.

căm'pus *n.* (U.S., first used at Princeton) The grounds of a college or university, open space between or around the buildings. [L, = 'field']

căm'wōōd *n.* The hard red wood of the W. Afr. *Baphia nitida*, used in dyeing, cabinet-making, etc.

căn[1] *n.* 1. Vessel for liquids, usu. of tinned metal, and with handle over top. 2. (orig. U.S.) Tinplate vessel in which meat, fruits, etc., are sterilized and sealed for preservation. ~ *v.t.* Preserve in a can.

căn[2] *v. auxil.* (neg. *cannot, can't*; past t. *could*; defective parts supplied from *be able to*). Be able to; have the right to; be permitted to.

Can. *abbrev.* Canada.

Cān'aan (-nyan, -nan). Ancient name of W. Palestine, promised by God to the Children of Israel. **Cān'aanīte** *adj.* & *n.* (Non-Jewish native) of Canaan. **Cān'aanītish** *adj.*

Căn'ada. State, a member of the British Commonwealth of Nations, occupying the N. part of the N. Amer. continent (with the exception of Alaska and part of the coast of Labrador) from 49° N. to the N. Pole and from the Pacific to the Atlantic Ocean; capital, Ottawa; was discovered by Cabot in 1497, occupied by the French in 1534, and ceded to Gt Britain by the Treaty of Paris in 1763; the Provinces of Canada were united under the title of the Dominion of Canada in 1867; ~ *balsam*, an oleo-resin obtained from the pine *Abies balsamea*, used for mounting microscope slides. **Canād'ian** *adj.* & *n.* (Native, inhabitant) of Canada; ~ *canoe*: see CANOE.

canaille (kanah'-ē) *n.* The rabble.

canăl' *n.* 1. Duct in plant or animal body for food, liquid, air, etc. 2. Artificial watercourse for inland navigation or for irrigation. 3. (zool.) Prolongation of shell for protection of respiratory tube. 4. *Canals of Mars*, faint seasonal markings of doubtful nature on the planet Mars.

căn'alize *v.t.* 1. Furnish with canals; convert (river) into canal by embanking, straightening course, making locks, etc. 2. Direct (energies, wealth, etc.) into a particular course or channel. **cănalīzā'tion** *n.*

căn'apé (-ā) *n.* Small biscuit, piece of pastry, etc., with savoury filling.

canard' (-ar̄, -ar̄d) *n.* Absurd extravagant rumour or report; hoax. [Fr., = 'duck', 'false report']

Canarese: see KANARESE.

Canar̄'y[1]. Island (*Grand* ~, *Gran Canaria*) off NW. coast of Africa; ~ *Islands, Canaries*, the group to which it belongs, in Spanish possession. [L *canaria* (*insula*) (isle) of dogs]

canar̄'y[2] *n.* 1. (also ~ *sack*) A light sweet wine from the Canary Islands, resembling sherry. 2. Singing-bird (*Serinus canarius*), orig. brought from the Canary Islands and commonly kept in captivity; the wild canary, or serin, is greenish above and yellow below, but the cage-breed is mainly yellow (~ *yellow*); *~-creeper*, yellow flowered creeper (*Tropaeolum aduncum*, formerly *T. canariense*); *~-grass*, grass from the Canary Islands (*Phalaris canariensis*) seed of which (*~-seed*) is used for feeding cage-birds.

canăs'ta. Card-game, orig. from Uruguay, for 2–6 persons, played with 108 cards (2 standard 52-card packs and 4 jokers), each card having a numerical scoring value; scoring is made by *melds* (3 or more cards of the same value) and the game is won by the player or partnership first scoring 5,000 points; a *canasta* is a meld of 7 cards. [prob. as CANASTER]

canăs'ter *n.* Tobacco prepared from dried leaves, coarsely broken. [orig. the rush basket container, f. Span. *canastra*, ult. f. Gk *kanastron*]

Căn'berra. Capital of the Commonwealth of Australia, built on land acquired in 1911 from the State of New South Wales.

cancan (kahṅ'kahṅ) *n.* High-kicking dance. [Fr.]

căn'cel *v.* Obliterate, annul, make void, countermand; neutralize, balance, make up for; (print.) suppress and reprint (sheet etc.); (mus., chiefly U.S.) resume natural pitch of note after sharpening or flattening; (arith. etc.) strike out (same factor) from numerator and denominator, from two sides of equation, etc.; ~ (*out*) neutralize or balance each other. **căncellā'tion** *n.* **căn'cel** *n.* (print.) Suppression and reprinting of page or leaf; the suppressed or substituted page or leaf; (mus., chiefly U.S.) sign (♮) for resumption of natural pitch of note after sharpening or flattening (in Engl. usage, a natural).

căn'cer[1] *n.* Malignant tumour in the body, tending to spread indefinitely and to reproduce itself; it proliferates rapidly at the expense of the surrounding tissue and unless treated at an early stage often ends in death. **căn'cerous** *adj.* [L, = 'crab', f. resemblance of swollen veins round tumour to crab's limbs]

Căn'cer[2]. The zodiacal constellation of the Crab, lying between Gemini and Leo; the 4th sign (♋) of the zodiac, which the sun enters at the summer solstice on 21st or 22nd June; *Tropic of* ~, the northern TROPIC, forming a tangent to the ecliptic at the first point of Cancer, about 23° 28′ from the equator (ill. EARTH).

cănc'roid *adj.* Crab-like; like cancer. ~ *n.* Crustacean of crab family; disease like cancer.

c. and b. *abbrev.* Caught and bowled.

căndėla'brum (-lah-) *n.* (pl. *-bra*). Large, usu. branched, candlestick (ill. CANDLE).

căndĕs'cence *n.* Bright glow, as of white-hot metal. **căndĕs'cent** *adj.* Glowing (as) with white heat.

căn'dĭd *adj.* Unbiased; not censorious; frank. **căn'didly** *adv.* **căn'dĭdnėss** *n.* [L *candidus* white]

căn'dĭdacy *n.* (U.S.) Candidature.

căn'dĭdate *n.* One who puts himself or is put forward for appointment to an office or honour; one who undergoes a test or examination; one thought likely to gain any position. [L *candidatus* one aspiring to an office who was clothed in white toga]

căn'dĭdature *n.* Standing for election, being a candidate.

candied: see CANDY[1].

căn'dle *n.* Cylinder of wax, tallow, etc., enclosing wick, for giving light; candle-power; *Roman* ~, firework throwing up luminous coloured balls; *candlelight*, light of candles; any artificial light; *candle-power*, illuminating power of electric lamp etc. measured in terms of the light of a standard candle; *candlestick*, support for candle(s).

Căn'dlemas (-lm-). Feast of the Purification of the Virgin Mary, 2nd Feb.; a quarter-day in Scotland. [Mass celebrated with a great display of candles]

căn'dour (-d*er*) *n.* Fairness, impartiality; openness, frankness.

căn'dy[1] *n.* 1. (also *sugar-*~) Crystallized sugar made by repeated boiling and slow evaporation. 2. (U.S.) Sweetmeat; chocolate, toffee, etc. ~ *v.* Preserve by coating with candy; form into crystals; *candied*, crystallized, preserved by impregnating and coating with sugar. [Fr. *sucre candi*, f. Arab.-Pers. *qand* crystallized sugar-cane juice]

căn'dy[2] *n.* Weight of S. and W. India, averaging about 500 lb.

căn'dȳtŭft *n.* Genus (*Iberis*) of herbaceous cruciferous plants with white, pink, or purple flowers in flat corymbs or 'tufts'. [*Candia* the island of Crete]

cāne *n.* Hollow jointed stem of giant reeds and grasses, or solid stem of slender palms, used as walking-stick or instrument of punishment etc.; stem of raspberry and similar plants; any slender walking-stick; *~-brake*, (U.S.) tract of land thickly overgrown with canes. *~-sugar*, sugar obtained from the sugar-cane as contrasted with beet-sugar. ~ *v.t.* Beat with cane; fit (seat of chair) with (plaited) cane. **cān'ĭng** *n.*

căngue (-ng), **căng**, *n.* Heavy wooden frame or board formerly worn round neck as punishment in China. [Port. *canga* yoke]

căn'īne (*or* kanīn') *adj.* Of, as of, a dog or dogs; ~ *tooth*, one of the four strong pointed teeth between incisors and molars, eye-tooth (ill. TOOTH). ~ *n.* Canine tooth.

căn'ion (-ny*o*n) *n.* (pl., hist.) Close-fitting extensions of short stuffed breeches, covering thighs (ill. DOUBLET).

căn'ĭster *n.* Small case or box, usu. of metal, for tea, shot, etc.; *-shot*, case-shot. [Gk *kanastron* wicker-basket]

cănk'er *n.* 1. Ulcerous disease of animals; disease of fruit-trees; (*-worm*), caterpillar of a moth destroying leaves or buds. 2. Corrupting influence, rotten tendency. **cănk'erous** *adj.* **cănk'er** *v.t.* Consume with canker; infect, corrupt; *cankered*, soured, malignant, crabbed. [as CANCER]

cănn'a *n.* Genus of monocotyledonous plants with bright yellow, red, or orange flowers and ornamental foliage, natives of warm climates.

cănn'abĭs *n.* Hashish.

Cănn'ae. Place in Apulia, SE. Italy (near mouth of modern river Ofanto), scene of a great defeat of the Romans by Hannibal in 216 B.C.

cănn'el *adj.* ~ (*coal*), coal with high gas content which burns with smoky flame and can be lit by a match, formerly an important source of paraffin oil.

cănn'ĭbal *n.* Man who eats human flesh; animal that eats its own species. ~ *adj.* Of, having, these habits. **cănn'ĭbalism** *n.* **cănnibalĭs'tĭc** *adj.* [Span. *Canibales*, variant form of *Caribs*]

cănn'ĭbalīze *v.t.* Utilize one of a number of similar machines to provide spare parts for the others.

cănn'ĭkĭn *n.* Small can.

Cănn'ĭng, George (1770–1827). English statesman and author; foreign secretary under Duke of Portland and prime minister in 1827.

cănn'on[1] *n.* 1. (pl. usu. *cannon*) Piece of ordnance (hist.); gun of the kind that needs mounting (*Illustration, p.* 111); automatic shell-firing gun in aircraft. 2. (mech.) Hollow cylinder moving independently on shaft; watchkey barrel. 3. Smooth round bit (*~-bit*) for horse. 4. (billiards) Hitting of two balls successively by player's ball. 5. *~-ball*, projectile fired by cannon; *~-bone*, large metacarpal or metatarsal bone in leg of horse etc. (ill. HORSE); *~-shell*, shell from aircraft's cannon. ~ *v.i.* Make cannon at billiards; come into collision, run or strike (obliquely) *against, into, with.*

cănn'on[2] *n.* (pl., hist.) Frills worn below breeches.

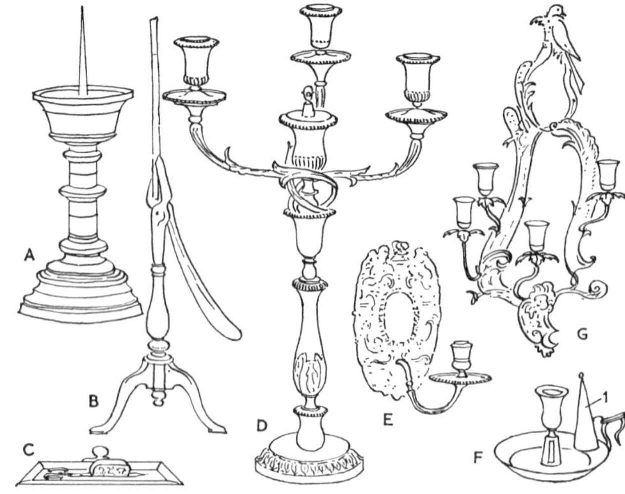

A. PRICKET CANDLESTICK. B. RUSHLIGHT IN HOLDER. C. SNUFFERS AND TRAY. D. CANDELABRUM. E. SCONCE. F. CHAMBER CANDLESTICK. G. GIRANDOLE

1. Extinguisher

cănnonāde' *n.* Continuous gunfire. ~ *v.* Fire continuously; bombard.

CANNON

1. Breech. 2. Touch hole. 3. First reinforce. 4. 'Dolphin' for handling gun. 5. Second reinforce. 6. Bore. 7. Chase. 8. Muzzle. 9. Trunnion

cannot. Ordinary modern way of writing *can not*.

cănn'y *adj.* Shrewd; worldly-wise; thrifty; gentle, circumspect; sly, pawky. **cănn'ĭly** *adv.*

CANOE

1. Irish coracle. 2. Welsh coracle. 3. Canadian birch bark canoe. 4. Eskimo kayak. 5. Ceylon double canoe. 6. Kru dug-out canoe. 7. Ceylon outrigger canoe

canoe' (-ōō) *n.* Small light keelless boat propelled either by paddles with one blade (*Canadian* ~) or by long paddle with blade at either end. ~ *v.i.* Paddle or propel canoe; travel by canoe.

căn'on[1] *n.* 1. Church decree; ~ *law*, ecclesiastical law as laid down in decrees of the pope and statutes of councils. 2. General rule, fundamental principle, axiom; standard of judgement or authority, test, criterion. 3. Collection or list of books of the Bible accepted by the Christian Churches as genuine and inspired; any set of books or works accepted as belonging to a particular author etc. 4. Portion of the Mass between Preface and Pater, containing the words of consecration. 5. (mus.) Composition in which the different parts take up the same subject one after another, in strict imitation. 6. (printing) Large size of type (48 point), equal to 4-line pica. 7. The metal loop or ear by which a bell is hung.

căn'on[2] *n.* 1. (hist.) Clerk living according to rule with others in clergy-house or in a house within the precinct or close of a cathedral or collegiate church. 2. In the Church of England, member of cathedral chapter. **căn'onĕss** *n.* Member of college or community of women living under a rule but not under perpetual vow.

cañon: see CANYON.

canŏn'ical *adj.* 1. Appointed by canon law; ~ *dress*, dress of clergy; ~ *hours*, hours appointed for prayer, for the solemnization of marriage, etc. 2. Included in the canon of Scripture. 3. Authoritative, standard, accepted. 4. (mus.) In canon form. 5. Of a cathedral chapter or a member of it. **canŏn'ically** *adj.* **canŏn'icals** *n.pl.* Canonical dress.

căn'onist *n.* Canon lawyer.

căn'onīze *v.t.* Admit formally to calendar of saints; regard as a saint; sanction by authority of Church. **cănonīzā'tion** *n.*

căn'onry *n.* Benefice, status, etc., of a canon.

canōō'dle *v.* (U.S. slang) Fondle, cuddle.

Canōp'us. 1. (Gk myth.) The helmsman of Menelaus who died in Egypt on the return from Troy. 2. Town in ancient Egypt named after him. 3. Bright star Alpha in the southern constellation Argo.

Canōp'ic *adj.* Of the town of Canopus; ~ *vase*, Egyptian vase with a lid in the form of a human head, used for holding the entrails of embalmed bodies.

căn'opy *n.* Covering suspended or held over throne, bed, person, etc.; the 'umbrella' of a parachute, which fills with air when released from its packing; (fig.) any overhanging shelter; the sky etc. ~ *v.t.* Supply, be, a canopy to. [Gk *kōnōpeion* mosquito net (*kōnōps* gnat)]

canōr'ous *adj.* Melodious, resonant.

Canŏss'a. A castle in Tuscany where in 1077 the Emperor Henry IV submitted to the penance and humiliation imposed on him by Pope Gregory VII; hence, *go to* ~, make a humiliating submission.

cănt[1] *n.* Bevel, oblique face, of crystal, bank, etc.; sloping or tilted position. ~ *v.* 1. Bevel; slope, slant, tilt. 2. Throw, jerk. 3. (naut.) Swing round.

cănt[2] *n.* Jargon of class, profession, sect, etc.; temporary catchwords; words used for fashion without being meant; unreal use of words implying piety; hypocrisy. ~ *v.i.* Use cant; (her.) *canting arms, coat*, etc., arms etc. containing allusion to name of bearer.

can't (kahnt). Colloq. abbrev. of *cannot*: see CAN[2].

Cant. *abbrev.* Canticles.

Căn'tăb *n.*, **Căntabrĭ'ġian** (-j-) *adj.* & *n.* (Member) of Cambridge University.

căntā'bĭlē (-tah-) *adj.* & *n.* (Music) in a smooth flowing style.

căn'taloup (-ōōp) *n.* Small, round, ribbed, delicate-flavoured variety of musk-melon with reddish-orange flesh. [*Cantalupo*, castle near Rome]

căntănk'erous *adj.* Cross-grained, quarrelsome. **căntănk'erously** *adv.* **căntănk'erousnĕss** *n.*

cănta'ta (-ah-) *n.* Choral work, either a short oratorio or a short lyric drama set to music but not intended for acting.

cănteen' *n.* 1. Provision and liquor shop in barracks, camp, etc., refreshment room in factory or office building. 2. Box of cooking and table utensils for camp or expedition; box or case with compartments holding table cutlery 3. Soldier's water-vessel or mess-tin.

căn'ter *n.* Easy gallop. ~ *v.* Go, make (horse) go, at this pace. [shortened f. CANTERBURY gallop]

Căn'terbury. County borough and city in Kent, see of the archbishop and primate of all England; the shrine of Thomas à Becket (St. Thomas of Canterbury), who was murdered in the cathedral, was in pre-Reformation times a favourite object of pilgrimage; ~ *bell*, kind of campanula (f. bells of pilgrims' horses); ~ *trot, gallop, pace*, etc., the easy pace of the mounted pilgrims to Canterbury. **căn'terbury** *n.* Stand with light partitions to hold music etc.

cănthă'rĭdēs (-z) *n.pl.* The dried beetle *Cantharis vesicatoria*, Spanish fly, formerly used in medicine.

căn'ticle *n.* Hymn; one of the hymns, mostly taken from the Scriptures, used in church services, as the *Benedicite, Nunc Dimittis, Te Deum*; *the C~s*, Song of Solomon.

căn'tĭlēver *n.* (archit., eng.) Beam or girder fixed at one end to a pier or wall and free at the other; long bracket; ~ *bridge*, bridge composed of girders projecting from piers and meeting midway between them or carrying intermediate sections (ill. BRIDGE).

căn'tle *n.* Piece, slice, cut off; hind-bow of saddle (ill. SADDLE).

căn'tō *n.* (pl. *-ōs*). Division of long poem.

căn'ton[1] (*or* kăntŏn') *n.* 1. Subdivision of a country; one of the sovereign States of the Swiss federation. 2. (her.) Square division less than a quarter in upper (usu. dexter) corner of shield, flag, etc. (ill. HERALDRY). **căn'tonal** *adj.* **cănton'** *v.t.* 1. (-tŏn') Divide into cantons. 2. (-tōōn') Quarter (troops).

Căntŏn'[2]. City of S. China. **Căntonēse'** (-z) *adj.* & *n.* (Native, dialect) of Canton.

cănton'ment (-ōōn-) *n.* Lodging assigned to troops; in India, permanent military station.

căn'tor *n.* Precentor. **cantōr'ial** *adj.* Of the precentor; of his side of the choir (see foll.).

cantōr'is *adj.* (as mus. direction) To be sung by the precentor's side of the choir (usu. the N.; opp. to DECANI, dean's side).

Cantuar. *abbrev.* (Archbishop) of Canterbury (replacing surname in his signature).

Canŭck' *n.* (U.S.) Canadian, esp. French Canadian; Canadian horse or pony.

Canūte', Cnut (-ōō-). A Danish king of England, 1016–35.

căn'vas *n.* 1. Strong unbleached plain-woven cloth of hemp, flax, or other coarse yarn, for sails, tents, etc.; open kind of this, usu. flax or cotton, for tapestry, embroidery, etc. 2. (*artists'*) ~, canvas prepared for painting on by coating with size, white lead, etc.; hence, a painting, a picture (lit. and fig.). 3. Canvas covering over ends of racing-boat. 4. ~*-back*, a N. Amer. duck, *Fuligula valismeriana*, from the colour of its grey-and-white mottled back feathers.

căn'vass *v.* 1. Discuss thoroughly. 2. Solicit votes, solicit votes from; ascertain sentiments or opinion of; ask custom of. **căn'vasser** *n.* **căn'vass** *n.* Canvassing for votes; (U.S.) scrutiny of votes. [f. CANVAS, the original sense being 'toss in a sheet etc.', and hence 'shake up, agitate', etc.]

canyon, cañon (kăn'yon) *n.* Deep gorge or ravine with steep sides formed by river cutting through soft rock, characteristic of Rocky Mountains, Sierra Nevada, and western plateaux of N. America; *Grand C~*, huge canyon in Colorado, U.S., a mile deep. [Span. *cañon* tube, f. L *canna* reed]

caoutchouc (kowch'ŏŏk) *n.* India rubber (see RUBBER[1], 3). [Fr., f. Carib wd]

căp *n.* 1. Woman's head-dress, esp. one worn indoors. 2. Soft brimless head-dress for out-of-doors. 3. Special head-dress; cap worn as sign of inclusion in football, cricket, etc., team; one who obtains such a cap; *college* ~, black academic head-dress with flat top and tassel; *Scotch* ~, part of Highland dress; ~ *and bells*, jester's insignia; ~ *of liberty*, conical cap given to Roman slave on emancipation, now (esp. French) Republican symbol. 4. Cap-like covering, as of mushroom, toe of shoe, etc. 5. (also *percussion* ~), Cap-shaped piece of copper lined with fulminating composition, for igniting explosive in fire-arms etc.; paper percussion cap of toy pistol. 6. (naut.) Pierced block of wood for joining two masts etc., end to end. 7. (also ~*-money*) Money collected at a hunt from those present who are not hunt-subscribers. 8. ~*-paper*, writing-paper of certain size or kind; packing paper. **căp'ful** *n.* **căp** *v.* 1. Put cap upon; (Sc. universities) confer degree on; confer cap on as symbol of inclusion in team; form or serve as, cover with, cap. 2. Outdo, excel, surpass. 3. Touch or take off one's hat to.

cap. *abbrev. Caput* (= chapter).

căpabĭl'ity *n.* Power *of, for, to*; undeveloped faculty.

căp'able *adj.* 1. Susceptible. 2. ~ *of*, having the power or fitness for; wicked enough for. 3. Able, gifted, competent. **căp'ably** *adv.*

capā'cious (-shus) *adj.* Roomy. **capā'ciously** *adv.* **capā'ciousnėss** *n.*

capă'cĭtance *n.* Ability of an apparatus to store an electric charge.

capă'cĭtāte *v.t.* Render capable; make legally competent.

capă'cĭtor *n.* Device which stores electricity during part of an operation; condenser.

capă'cĭty *n.* 1. Ability to contain or receive; cubic content, volume; *measure of* ~, measure used for liquids, grain, etc. 2. (elect.) = CAPACITANCE. 3. (fig.) Mental power; faculty, talent; capability, opportunity, *to, of*, etc.; relative character (as *in his* ~ *as critic*); legal competency.

căp-à-pie (-pē), *adv.* (*Armed*) from head to foot.

capă'rĭson (-zn) *n.* Horses' trappings; equipment, outfit. ~ *v.t.* Put caparison upon.

cāpe[1] *n.* Short sleeveless cloak, either as separate garment or as fixed or detachable part of cloak or coat. **caped** (kāpt) *adj.*

cāpe[2] *n.* Headland, promontory.

Cāpe[3], The. The Cape of Good Hope, promontory near southern extremity of Africa; ~ *Province* (formerly ~ *Colony*), southernmost province of the Republic of S. Africa; ~ *cart*, two-wheeled horse-drawn vehicle of S. Africa; ~ *Coloured*, S. Africans of mixed black and white descent; ~ *Dutch*, early form of Afrikaans; ~ *gooseberry*, certain species of *Physalis* sometimes grown for their edible fruits; ~ *smoke*, S. Afr. brandy.

Că'pěk (ch-), Karel (1890–1938). Czech writer; author of 'R.U.R.' and other plays etc.

Capěll'a. A star of the first magnitude in the constellation Auriga.

căp'er[1] *n.* Bramble-like S. European shrub, *Capparis spinosa*; (pl.) its flower-buds, pickled for use in sauces; *English* ~*s*, pickled seed-vessels of garden nasturtium (*Tropaeolum majus*).

căp'er[2] *n.* Frisky movement, leap; *cut a* ~, caper. ~ *v.i.* Dance or leap merrily or fantastically; prance as a horse.

căpercaill'ie (-lyĭ) **-kail'zie** *n.* Wood-grouse, *Tetrao urogallus*, the largest European gallinaceous bird, formerly native to the Scottish Highlands, where it was reintroduced from Scandinavia after becoming extinct. [Gael. *capull coille* horse of the wood]

Capérn'āum. City of ancient Israel by the Sea of Galilee.

Căp'et (-ā). French dynasty founded by Hugo Capet in 987, which ruled until 1328, when it was succeeded by the House of Valois; *Louis* ~, name given to Louis XVI when he was tried before the Convention in 1793.

Cāpe Town. The legislative capital of the Union of S. Africa, near the CAPE[3] of Good Hope.

Cāpe Verde Islands (vär'dā). Two groups of islands, Windward and Leeward, off the W. coast of Africa, in Portuguese possession.

capĭll'ary *adj.* 1. Of, or resembling, hair. 2. Having very minute or hair-like internal diameter. 3. Of capillary vessels (see *n.* below). 4. ~ *attraction*, effect of surface tension of liquid that 'wets' material of fine tube in raising liquid inside tube to a level higher than that outside; ~ *repulsion*, corresponding effect of surface tension of liquid that does not 'wet' tube in depressing level inside tube. ~ *n.* One of the extremely minute blood-vessels joining arteries and veins in which the blood is brought into effective contact with the tissues.

căp'ĭtal[1] *n.* Head of pillar or pilaster, wider than the shaft and usu. ornamented (ill. ORDER).

căp'ĭtal[2] *adj.* 1. Involving loss of life; punishable by death. 2. Standing at the head; ~ *letter*, one of the form and size used at beginning of page, sentence, etc., majuscule. 3. Chief; important, leading, first-class; ~ *ship*, battleship or battle cruiser. 4. (colloq.) Excellent, first-rate. 5. Original, principal, of money capital. ~ *n.* 1. Chief town of county, country, etc., usu. the seat of government or administrative centre. 2. Stock of company etc. with which they enter business and on which dividends are paid; (econ.) accumulated wealth of individual, community, etc., used as fund for starting fresh production; wealth of any kind used in producing more wealth; *make* ~ *(out) of*, (fig.) turn to account or advantage, esp. in argument; ~ *levy*, confiscation by the State of a proportion of all property. 3. Capitalists or employers of labour collectively.

căp'ĭtalĭsm (*or* kapĭt'-) *n.* Economic system by which ownership of capital or wealth, the production and distribution of goods, and the reward of labour are entrusted to, and effected by, private enterprise. **căp'ĭtalĭst** (*or* kapĭt'-) *n.* Private owner or holder of capital, esp. in large amounts; one who has capital available for employment in finance or industry. **căp'ĭtalĭst** (*or* kapĭt'-), **căpĭtalĭs'tĭc** *adjs.* **căp'ĭtalīze** (*or* kapĭt'-) *v.t.* Convert into, use as, capital; compute or realize present value of (income). **căpĭtalīzā'tion** *n.*

căpĭtā'tion *n.* (Levying of) tax or fee of so much a head; (attrib.) of so much a head.

Căp'ĭtol. 1. The great national temple of ancient Rome, dedicated to Jupiter Optimus Maximus, on the Saturnian or Tarpeian (afterwards called Capitoline) Hill; the hill itself. 2. The building in Washington occupied by the Congress of the United States; in many States, the state-house, building in which State legislature meets.

Căp'ĭtolīne (Hill). One of the hills of Rome: see CAPITOL, 1.

capĭt'ūlar *adj.* 1. Of a cathedral chapter. 2. (physiol.) Of a terminal protuberance of bone.

capĭt'ūlary *n.* Collection of ordinances, esp. those made on their own authority by the Frankish kings.

capĭt'ūlāte *v.i.* Surrender on terms.

capĭtūlā'tion *n.* 1. Statement of heads of subject, summary. 2. Agreement, conditions. 3. Surrender on terms, agreement containing such terms.

capĭt'ūlum *n.* 1. (physiol.) Protuberance of bone received into a hollow portion of another bone. 2. (bot.) Close head of sessile flowers (ill. INFLORESCENCE). 3. (zool.) The part of a barnacle borne by and forming a head to the peduncle.

cā'pon *n.* Castrated cock. **cā'ponīze** *v.t.*

căp'oral *n.* Kind of French tobacco.

capŏt' *n.* In piquet, winning of all tricks by one player. ~ *v.t.* Score a capot against.

Căppadō'cia (-shĭa). Ancient kingdom of Asia Minor, now part of Turkey. **Căppadō'cian** *adj.*

capriccio (-ĕch'ō) *n.* Lively, usu. short, musical composition. [see CAPRICE]

caprice' (-ēs) *n.* Unaccountable change of mind or conduct; fancy, freak; inclination to these. [It. *capriccio* sudden start, app. f. *capra* goat]

caprĭ'cious (-sh*u*s) *adj.* Guided by whim; inconstant, irregular, incalculable. **caprĭ'ciously** *adv.* **caprĭ'ciousnĕss** *n.*

Căp'rĭcorn. 1. Zodiacal constellation of the Goat, lying between Sagittarius and Aquarius; 10th sign (♑) of the zodiac, into which the sun enters at the winter solstice, 21st or 22nd December; *Tropic of* ~, the southern TROPIC, forming a tangent to the ecliptic at the first point of Capricorn, about 23° 28′ from the equator (ill. EARTH). [L *caper* goat, *cornu* horn]

căp'rīole *n.* 1. Leap or caper. 2. (in manège) Horse's high leap and kick without advancing. ~ *v.i.* Make capriole.

caps. *abbrev.* Capital letters.

căp'sĭcum *n.* Genus of tropical plants with very pungent capsule and seeds; fruit of these, used as condiment and as a digestive stimulant and carminative.

căpsize' *v.* Upset, overturn, esp. on water.

căp'stan *n.* Revolving barrel, worked by men walking round and pushing horizontal levers, or by steam etc., for winding-in cable, hoisting sails, etc. (ill. DOCK).

căp'sūle *n.* 1. (physiol.) Membranous envelope. 2. (bot.) Dry seed-case opening when ripe by parting of valves (ill. FRUIT). 3. (med.) Gelatine envelope enclosing drug or other medicinal substance. 4. (chem.) Shallow saucer formerly used for evaporating etc. 5. Metallic cap for bottle etc. **căp'sūlar** *adj.*

Capt. *abbrev.* Captain.

căp'tain (-ĭn) *n.* 1. Chief, leader; great soldier, strategist, experienced commander. 2. (mil.) Army officer, of rank next below major and above lieutenant, normally commanding company or troop; (nav.) officer of rank between commander and rear-admiral, officer commanding warship; master of merchant-ship. 3. Leader of side in games. **căp'taincy** *n.* **căp'tain** *v.t.* Be captain of; lead.

căp'tion *n.* 1. Legal arrest. 2. (law) Certificate attached to or written on document. 3. (orig. U.S.) Heading of chapter, section, newspaper article, etc., title of picture; title, descriptive passage, dialogue, etc., inserted in (silent) cinema picture.

căp'tious (-sh*u*s) *adj.* 1. Fallacious, sophistical. 2. Fond of taking exception; trying to catch people in their words. **căp'tiously** *adv.* **căp'tiousnĕss** *n.*

căp'tĭvāte *v.t.* Fascinate, charm. **căptĭvā'tion** *n.*

căp'tĭve *adj.* & *n.* (Person, animal) taken prisoner, kept in confinement, unable to escape; (of, like) prisoner; ~ *balloon*, one moored to the ground. **căptĭv'ĭty** *n.* (esp.) *The C~*, that of the Jews in Babylon.

căp'tor *n.*, **căp'trĕss** *n.fem.* One who takes a captive or prize.

căp'ture *n.* Seizing, taking possession; thing or person seized. ~ *v.t.* Take prisoner; seize as prize.

Căp'ūchĭn *n.* 1. Franciscan friar of the new rule of 1528, so called from the sharp-pointed capuche or hood first adopted in 1525. 2. Woman's garment of cloak and hood. 3. ~ *monkey*, Amer. monkey of genus *Cebus*, with black hair like a cowl at back of head; ~ *pigeon*, variety of jacobin pigeon with inverted feathers like a hood or cowl at back of head.

căpўba'ra (-ah-) *n.* Large tailless rodent (*Hydrochoerus capybara*), allied to guinea-pig, living about the rivers of tropical S. America.

car *n.* Wheeled vehicle, (poet.) chariot; (in U.K. now usu. word for) MOTOR-car, automobile; (north.) TRAM-car; (U.S.) any railway carriage or van (so in U.K. but with specification, as *dining-~*, *sleeping-~*); pendant of airship or balloon holding passengers; (U.S.) lift-cage; *car'man*, driver of van, carrier.

cărabĭneer' *n.* Soldier who carries a carbine; *The C~s*, the 3rd (or Prince of Wales') Dragoon Guards, orig. two separate regiments, the 3rd and 6th Dragoon Guards.

că'racal *n.* Kind of lynx, *Felis caracal*, of N. Africa and SW. Asia, with reddish fur and black-tipped ears and tail; pelt of this animal. [Turk. *qarah-qulak* black-ear]

că'racōle *n.* Horseman's half-wheel to right or left, succession of such turns to right and left alternately. ~ *v.i.* Execute caracole(s); caper.

că'racul (-ko͝ol) *n.* Kind of astrakhan fur; cloth imitating this.

carafe' (-ahf) *n.* Glass water-bottle for table etc. [Fr., prob. f. Arab. *gharafa* draw water]

că'ramĕl *n.* 'Burnt sugar', brown substance obtained by heating sugar or syrup and used for colouring spirits etc.; brown colour of this; soft toffee made with caramel.

că'ramĕlīze *v.* Make (sugar) into caramel; (of sugar) turn brown when heated.

că'rapāce *n.* Upper body-shell of tortoises and crustaceans (ill. LOBSTER).

că'rat *n.* 1. Measure of weight, about 3⅓ grains, for precious stones. 2. Measure of $\frac{1}{24}$ in stating the fineness of gold; if e.g. the mass contains 22 parts of gold and two of alloy it is 22 carats fine, or 22-carat gold. [Fr., f. It. *carato*, f. Gk *keration* fruit of carob]

căravăn' (*or* kă'-) *n.* 1. Company of merchants, pilgrims, etc., in the East or in N. Africa, travelling together for security, esp. through desert. 2. Covered cart or carriage; the house on wheels of a gipsy, travelling showman, camping-party, etc. [Pers. *karwan*]

căravăn'serai (-ī *or* -ĭ) *n.* Eastern inn with large courtyard where caravans put up.

că'ravel, car'vel *n.* (hist.) Small light fast ship, chiefly Spanish or Portuguese of 15th–17th centuries; *carvel-built*, (of boat) with planks flush with the side (contrasted with *clinker-built*, where they overlap; ill. BOAT).

că'raway *n.* Umbelliferous plant, *Carum carvi*, with small aromatic carminative fruits called ~-*seeds*, used in cakes, etc.

carb'īde *n.* Compound of carbon with a metal; esp. *calcium* ~, CaC_2, which yields acetylene when moistened, and *iron* ~, Fe_3C, an important constituent of steel.

carb'īne *n.* Kind of short rifle orig. introduced for cavalry use.

carbohȳd'rate *n.* One of a group of compounds of carbon, hydrogen, and oxygen in which the last two elements are present in the same proportions as in water. Carbohydrates include sugars, starches, and cellulose and form an important part of the structure of plant material and of the food of man and other animals. Carbohydrates also comprise other compounds of a different formula but closely related to the above substances, e.g. *rhamnose* ($C_6H_{12}O_5$).

carbol'ic *adj.* ~ (*acid*), PHENOL (C_6H_5OH); colourless deliquescent crystals with pungent smell, obtained from coal-tar; used as an antiseptic and in making certain dyes and plastics.

carb'on *n.* 1. (chem.) An element occurring in two crystalline forms (diamond and graphite) and an amorphous form (charcoal), and in combination in all organic compounds; symbol C, at. no. 6, at. wt 12·01115. 2. (elect.) Rod of carbon used in arc-lamps. 3. Carbon paper (see below), duplicate obtained with this. 4. ~ *dioxide*, CO_2, compound of carbon with oxygen, a colourless odourless gas formed by combustion of carbon, breathed out by animals, formed during fermentation, etc.; ~ *lamp*, electric lamp with a carbon filament; ~ *monoxide*, CO, a highly poisonous inflammable colourless odourless gas formed by the incomplete combustion of carbon or carbon compounds, as in charcoal stoves, petrol engines, etc.; ~ *paper*, thin paper, coated on one side with a coloured wax preparation, which when it is inserted between two sheets of paper causes anything written on the upper sheet to appear also on the lower one; *carbon-14 dating:* see RADIOCARBON.

carbonā'ceous (-shus) *adj.* Of, like, coal or charcoal; consisting of or containing carbon.

Carbonar'ī *n.pl.* Secret republican association formed in the kingdom of Naples during the French occupation under Murat in the early 19th c. [It., = 'charcoal-burners', name of the society]

carb'onate *n.* A salt of carbonic acid. **carb'onāte** *v.t.* Form into a carbonate; aerate.

carbŏn'ic *adj.* Of carbon; ~ *acid*, H_2CO_3, a compound of carbon dioxide and water; ~ *acid gas*, old name for carbon dioxide.

carbonif'erous *adj.* Producing coal; ~ *strata, system, formation*, system of rocks of Upper Palaeozoic, lying above the Devonian and below the Permian, and containing workable coal in at least three continents (ill. GEOLOGY). ~ *n.* (*The C*~), this system, period when it was formed.

carb'onīze *v.t.* Reduce to charcoal or coke by burning off superfluous material. **carbonīzā'tion** *n.*

Carborŭn'dum *n.* Crystalline substance, second in hardness to diamond, a compound of carbon and silicon, SiC; used as a powder or in blocks for polishing and scouring, for grinding tools and as a refractory lining in furnaces. [trade-mark]

carb'oy *n.* Large globular wicker-covered glass bottle for holding acids or other corrosive liquids. [Pers. *qarābah* large flagon]

carb'ŭncle *n.* 1. Red semi-precious stone (formerly, any of several kinds; now, cabochon garnet, an iron-aluminium-silicate, usu. hollowed to allow colour to be seen). 2. (med.) Infective gangrene of subcutaneous tissues caused by invasion of staphylococci; (pop.) red spot or pimple on face. **carbŭnc'ūlar, carb'ŭncled** (-ld) *adjs.*

carbūrā'tion *n.* Process of charging air with hydrocarbon fuel in finely divided liquid form.

carb'ūrėt *v.t.* Combine chemically with carbon.

carbūrĕtt'or, -er *n.* In petrol engines, the apparatus for impregnating air with fine particles of fuel and thus preparing the explosive mixture for the cylinders.

carb'ūrīze *v.t.* Cause carbon to penetrate (surface of solid steel) in order to harden it.

carc'ass, carc'ase *n.* 1. Dead body (of human body now only in contempt or ridicule); (butchering) dead body of beast without head, limbs, or offal. 2. Mere body, dead or alive. 3. Worthless remains; skeleton, framework (of house, ship, etc.)

carcĭnōm'a *n.* (pl. -*ata*). (med.) Cancer.

Card. *abbrev.* Cardinal.

card[1] *n.* Toothed instrument, wire brush, or wire-set rubber or vulcanite strip, for combing wool, flax, cotton, hemp, etc., raising nap on cloth etc. ~ *v.t.* Prepare wool, tow, etc., for spinning by combing out impurities and straightening the fibres with cards; *carding-machine*, machine for carding wool etc.

card[2] *n.* 1. Thin pasteboard; small, usu. oblong, piece of this, or of thin paper, used for various purposes, as for greetings or invitation or programme of race-meeting etc.; see CHRISTMAS-~, POST-~, VISIT*ing*-~. 2. (Also *playing*-~) one of a 'pack' or set of small oblong pieces of pasteboard used in playing games; except for some special games, a pack consists of 52 cards divided into four 'suits' (hearts, diamonds, clubs, spades) each of thirteen cards, ten of which are numbered consecutively, the remaining three (the 'court' or 'picture' cards) having conventional pictures of figures called 'king', 'queen', and 'knave' or 'jack'; *cards*, card-playing, game(s) with cards. 3. Odd, original, or eccentric person; 'character'. 4. *card'-board*, pasteboard for cutting cards from, making boxes, etc.; ~-*case*, case for carrying visiting-cards; ~ *catalogue*, catalogue with items entered on separate cards; ~-*index*, index recorded on separate cards; (*v.t.*) make card-index of; ~-*sharper*, one who makes a trade of cheating at cards; ~-*tray*, tray for holding visitors' cards; ~-*vote*, system by which vote of each delegate to a meeting (e.g. of trade unions) counts for the number of his constituents.

card'amom *n.* Spice consisting of seed-capsules of various species of the E. Ind. and Chinese genera

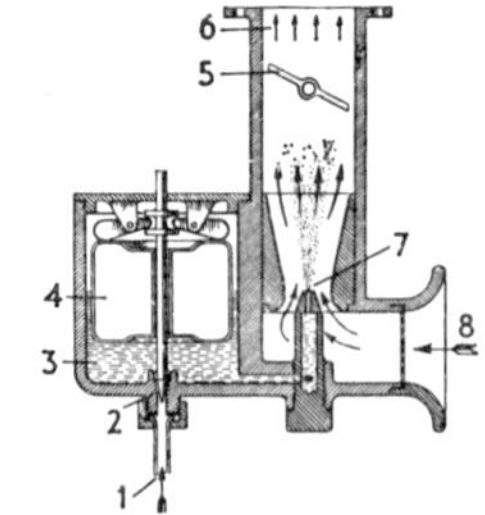

DIAGRAM OF A CARBURETTOR

1. Petrol inlet. 2. Float needle. 3. Float chamber. 4. Float. 5. Throttle valve. 6. Mixture to cylinder. 7. Jet. 8. Air inlet

Amomum and *Elettaria*, used as a stomachic and in curries etc.

cârd'an *adj.* ~ *joint*, (eng.) joint between two shafts enabling one to be driven by the other at varying angles, universal joint; ~ *shaft*, shaft with cardan joint at one or both ends. [Geronimo *Cardano* (1501–76), Italian mathematician]

cârd'ĭăc *adj.* 1. Of the heart; ~ *murmur*, abnormal heart-sound heard in auscultation. 2. (anat.) Of, adjoining, the upper orifice of the stomach. ~ *n.* Heart-stimulant, cordial.

Cârd'iff. Seaport in Glamorgan, and capital city of Wales.

cârd'igan[1] *n.* Knitted woollen over-waistcoat or close-fitting jacket with or without sleeves. [f. 7th Earl of *Cardigan*, distinguished in the Crimean War]

Cârd'igan[2]. County town of **Cardiganshire**, a county on the W. seaboard of Wales.

cârd'inal *adj.* 1. On which something hinges; fundamental, important; ~ *virtues*, in scholastic philosophy, the four 'natural' virtues, justice, prudence, temperance and fortitude, as distinct from the 'theological' virtues, faith, hope and charity; sometimes, the natural and the theological virtues; ~ *number*, a number which answers the question 'how many' (*one*, *two*, *three*, etc.); ~ *points*, the four points of the horizon lying in the direction of the two poles and the two directions at right angles to these: north, south, east and west. 2. Of the colour of a cardinal's robes, scarlet. **cârd'inally** *adv.* **cârd'inal** *n.* 1. (*C*~) One of the ecclesiastical princes of the R.C. Church who constitute the Sacred College, and whose duty it is to elect the Pope. 2. (hist.) Woman's cloak, orig. of scarlet cloth with hood. 3. ~ *bird*, N. Amer. song-bird, *Cardinalis virginianus*, with scarlet plumage; ~*-flower*, N. Amer. flower, the scarlet lobelia; ~ *red*, a bright scarlet-red colour, from the colour of cardinal's robes; ~*'s hat*, the red hat worn by a cardinal, taken as typical of his dignity or office. **cârd'inalate, cârd'inalship** *ns.*

cârdoon' *n.* Composite culinary vegetable, *Cynara cardunculus*, allied to the globe artichoke.

câre *n.* (Occasion for) solicitude, anxiety; serious attention; heed, caution, pains; charge, protection; thing to be done or seen to; *care'free*, free from anxiety; *care'taker*, person hired to take charge, as of house during owner's absence, of school or factory buildings, of empty shop, etc.; *care'worn*, worn by anxiety and trouble. ~ *v.i.* Feel concern or interest *for*, *about*; feel regard, deference, affection *for*, be concerned *whether*, etc.; be willing or wishful *to*; ~ *for*, look after.

careen' *v.* Turn (ship) on one side for cleaning, caulking, etc.; (cause to) heel over. **careen'age** *n.*

career' *n.* 1. Swift course; impetus. 2. Course or progress through life, esp. when publicly conspicuous or successful; development and success of party, principle, etc.; course of professional life or employment, way of making livelihood. ~ *v.i.* Go swiftly or wildly.

career'ist *n.* Person (esp. holder of public or responsible office) who is mainly intent on personal advancement.

câre'ful (-ârf-) *adj.* Painstaking, watchful, cautious; done with, showing, care. **câre'fully** *adv.* **câre'fulness** *n.*

câre'less (-ârl-) *adj.* Unconcerned, light-hearted; inattentive, negligent, thoughtless; inaccurate. **câre'lessly** *adv.* **câre'lessness** *n.*

caress' *n.* Fondling touch, kiss; blandishment. ~ *v.t.* Bestow caress(es) on; pet, make much of.

că'rĕt *n.* Mark (‸) placed below line in writing to indicate place of omission. [L, = 'is wanting']

cârg'ō *n.* Ship's freight.

Că'rib. One of the native race which occupied the southern islands of the W. Indies at their discovery; their language. **Caribbē'an** *adj.* ~ *Sea*, the sea lying between the Antilles and the mainland of Central and S. America.

că'ribou (-ōō) *n.* The N. Amer. reindeer.

că'ricatūre' *n.* Grotesque or ludicrous representation of person or thing by over-emphasis on characteristic or striking features. ~ *v.t.* Represent in caricature. **că'ricatūr'ist** *n.*

câr'ĭēs (-z) *n.* Decay (of teeth or bones). **câr'ious** *adj.* Decayed.

că'rillon (-lyon) *n.* Set of bells that can be played on either from keyboard or mechanically; air played on these; instrument or part of organ imitating bells.

cârk'ing *adj.* Burdensome, oppressive.

cârl(e) *n.* (Sc.) Man, fellow.

cârl'ine *n.* (Sc.) Old woman.

Carliol. *abbrev.* (Bishop) of Carlisle (replacing surname in his signature).

Cârl'ism. Support of Don Carlos, 2nd son of Charles IV of Spain, and his heirs, as the legitimate successors of Ferdinand VII (d. 1833), to the exclusion of Ferdinand's daughter and her heirs. **Cârl'ist** *n.*

Carlovingian: see CAROLINGIAN.

Cârl'ow (-ō). County of Leinster, Eire.

Cârl'ton Club. A London club in Pall Mall, the chief conservative club in England, founded 1831 by the Duke of Wellington and his political associates.

Cârlȳle', Thomas (1795–1881). Scottish literary critic, historian, and writer on social and political problems. **Cârlȳl'ism** *n.*

Carmârth'en (-dh-). County town of **Carmârth'enshire,** a county in S. Wales.

Câ̄rm'ĕl. Mountain in Israel projecting into sea SW. of Haifa; scene of Elijah's contest with the priests of Baal (1 Kings xviii. 19–40), whence its Arabic name Jebel Mar Elias.

Cârm'ĕlīte *adj.* & *n.* (Member) of order of mendicant friars (White Friars) originating in a colony founded in the 12th c. on Mount Carmel by Berthold, a Calabrian; (member) of an order of nuns organized on similar lines.

cârm'inative *adj.* & *n.* (Drug) curing flatulence.

cârm'ine *n.* & *adj.* (Coloured like, colour of) a crimson-red pigment obtained from cochineal.

cârn'age *n.* Great slaughter.

cârn'al *adj.* Sensual; sexual; worldly. **cârn'alism, cârnăl'ity** *ns.* **cârn'ally** *adv.*

cârnā'tion[1] *n.* 1. Light rosy pink or bright red colour. 2. Flesh tints in a painting; the representation of naked flesh. ~ *adj.* Rose-pink.

cârnā'tion[2] *n.* Any of the cultivated kinds of clove-pink derived from *Dianthus caryophyllus.*

Cârne'gie (-nāgĭ), Andrew (1835–1919). Scottish-born American owner of iron and steel works etc., famous for his benefactions for libraries, educational work, etc.

cârnēl'ian *n.* = CORNELIAN.

cârn ival *n.* 1. Last three days or last week before Lent, Shrovetide; festivities usual during this in R.C. countries. 2. Riotous revelry, feasting, merrymaking. [Fr., f. It. *carnevale* Shrovetide, f. L *caro carn-* flesh and *levare* put away]

Cârniv'ora *n.pl.* Large order of mammals including many that eat flesh (cats, dogs, seals, etc.), having usu. sharp teeth and well-developed canines. **cârn'ivōre** *n.* Animal that feeds on flesh; one of the *Carnivora.* **cârniv'orous** *adj.*

că'rob *n.* Evergreen Mediterranean tree (*Ceratonia siliqua*) bearing edible seed-pods whose seeds are said to have been the original carat weight used by goldsmiths.

că'rol *n.* Joyous song, esp. Christmas hymn. ~ *v.* Sing joyfully, sing carols.

Cărolīn'a. (hist.) English colony, named after Charles II, in N. America, from which NORTH and SOUTH CAROLINA were formed. **Cărolīn'ian** *adj.* & *n.* (Native, inhabitant) of Carolina.

Că'rolīne *adj.* Of, pertaining to, Charles (usu. Charles I or Charles II of England); ~ *script*: see CAROLINGIAN.

Cărolin'gian (-j-), **Cârlovin'gian** *adjs.* Of CHARLEMAGNE, king of the Franks; of the line of French kings descended from him (usu. *Carlo-*); ~ *Empire*, empire acquired by Charlemagne early in 9th c. and regarded by him as a revival of the

Roman Empire; at its greatest extent it comprised France (except Brittany), Germany, the Low Countries, N. and central Italy, Bohemia, and Croatia, its capitals being Aix-la-Chapelle (Aachen) and Rome; ~ *Renaissance*, revival of art and letters, imitation of classical antiquity, fostered by Charlemagne; ~ *script*, rounded script adopted in Carolingian period (ill. SCRIPT).

carŏt'ĭd *adj.* & *n.* (Of, near to) one of the two main pairs of arteries in the neck, that which in mammals carries blood to the face and cerebral hemispheres (ill. BLOOD).

că'rotĭn, -ēne *n.* (chem.) Red crystalline hydrocarbon, $C_{40}H_{56}$, contained in carrots, tomatoes, and many other vegetables, important source of vitamin A.

carouse' (-z) *n.* Drinking-bout. ~ *v.i.* Engage in carouse, drink deep. **carous'al** (-zl) *n.* [Ger. *gar aus* (*trinken*) drink to the bottom]

carp[1] *n.* Freshwater fish, *Cyprinus carpio*, commonly bred in ponds; other fish of this genus, which includes gold-fish, silver-fish, etc.

carp[2] *v.i.* Talk querulously, find fault; *carping*, captious.

carp'al *adj.* Of the carpus; ~ *bones*, the 8 small bones which form this.

Carpāth'ĭans. Mountain system between Poland and Czechoslovakia.

carp'el *n.* (bot.) One of the units of which a compound ovary is composed (ill. FLOWER). **carp'ellary** *adj.*

carp'enter *n.* Artificer in woodwork, esp. of rough solid kinds as in ship- or house-building. ~ *v.* Do, make by, carpenter's work. **carp'entry** *n.*

carp'ĕt *n.* Thick fabric for spreading on floor or stair, commonly of wool, freq. patterned in colours, and made by knotting short lengths of yarn on to the warp threads of a fabric during weaving (ill. WEAVE), or by same means as tapestry, or by various mechanical weaving processes; covering or expanse of grass, flowers, etc., resembling a carpet; ~*-bag*, travelling bag, orig. one made of carpet; ~*-bagger*, after the Amer. Civil War, an immigrant from Northern to Southern States whose 'property qualification' was the contents of a carpet-bag; any person interfering with the politics of a locality with which he has no permanent or genuine connexion; ~*-knight*, stay-at-home soldier, ladies' man; ~ *slipper*, slipper with uppers of carpet-like material; ~*-snake*, large Austral. snake with variegated skin, *Morelia variegata*. **carp'ĕtĭng** *n.* **carp'ĕtlĕss** *adj.* **carp'ĕt** *v.t.* Cover with, as with, a carpet.

carp'us *n.* Bones (8 in higher vertebrates) uniting forearm to hand, wrist (ill. HAND); corresponding part of other vertebrates, usu. with fewer bones.

carr *n.* Association of trees and shrubs developing at edges of fens and swamps, as *willow* ~, *alder* ~.

că'rrageen (-g-) *n.* (Also ~ *moss*), a seaweed, *Chondrus crispus*, common on British coasts, yielding when dried and boiled a jelly used for food and in medicine. [*Carragheen* near Waterford in Eire]

că'rrel *n.* Apartment in library for use of one reader.

că'rriage (-rĭj) *n.* 1. Conveying, transport; cost of conveying. 2. Passing, carrying (of motion in committee etc.). 3. Manner of carrying; bearing, deportment. 4. Wheeled vehicle for persons; esp. 4-wheeled private vehicle with two or more horses. 5. Wheeled support of gun (ill. GUN); wheeled framework of vehicle apart from body; (mech.) sliding etc. part of machinery for shifting position of other parts.

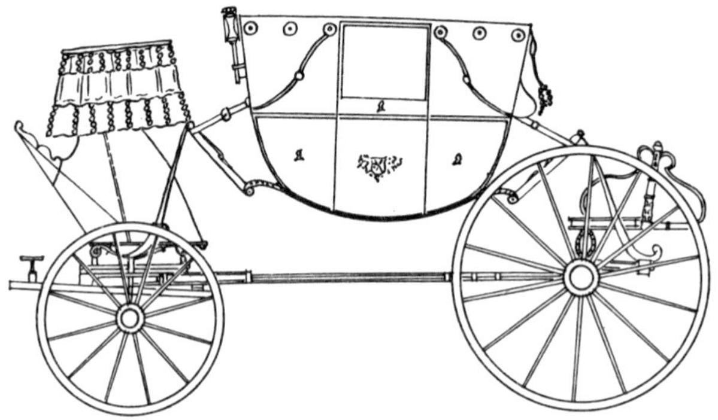

CARRIAGE

că'rrier *n.* 1. One who carries; esp. person plying for hire with cart, van, etc., for conveyance of parcels. 2. Part of bicycle etc. for carrying luggage. 3. Person or animal carrying disease-germs. 4. Aircraft carrier. 5. ~*-pigeon*, breed of pigeon with strong instinct for finding way home, used for carrying letters etc.; ~ *wave*, (teleg., teleph.) high-frequency electrical oscillation used as a basis for multiplex transmission of signals.

că'rrion *n.* Dead putrefying flesh; anything vile, garbage, filth; ~*-crow*, species of crow, *Corvus corone*, smaller than raven and larger than rook, feeding on carrion, small animals, poultry, etc.

Carroll, Lewis: see DODGSON.

cărronāde' *n.* Short large-calibre ship's gun. [*Carron* near Falkirk in Scotland, where orig. cast]

că'rron-oil *n.* Mixture of linseed oil and lime-water, formerly used for treating burns. [Said to have been first used at *Carron* ironworks, near Falkirk, Scotland]

că'rrot *n.* 1. Umbelliferous plant, *Daucus carota*, with large tapering root; the orange-red, fleshy, sweet root of cultivated varieties of this, used as culinary vegetable. 2. (pl., slang), (Person with) red hair. **că'rroty** *adj.*

că'rry *v.* 1. Convey, transport, bear; conduct; be the bearer of; push (process, principle, etc.) to specified point. 2. Support, hold up; hold (oneself etc.) in specified way; have about the person ready for use. 3. Have specified range; (golf etc.) cross, pass over; (make) pitch beyond. 4. Keep (audience) in agreement *with* one; succeed in establishing, passing, electing, etc. 5. Capture, take by storm. 6. (arith.) Transfer (figure) to column of higher notation; ~ *forward*, transfer (figure) to top of new page or column. 7. Have as result or corollary, involve. 8. ~ *away*, inspire, transport, deprive of self-control; (naut.) lose (mast etc.) by breakage; ~ *off*, remove from life; win; make passable; make brave show of (event etc.); ~ *on*, advance (process) a stage; continue; manage; go on with what one is doing; (colloq.) behave strangely, flirt, have amorous intrigue; ~ *out*, put in practice; ~*through*, bring safely out of difficulties; complete. ~ *n.* 1. (mil.) The position of carrying sword. 2. (golf) Ball's flight before pitching. 3. Portage between rivers etc. 4. Range (of gun, sound, etc.).

Cars'on City. Capital of Nevada, U.S.

cart *n.* 1. Strong 2- or 4-wheeled vehicle used in farming and for carrying heavy goods; light 2-wheeled one-horse vehicle for driving in; ~*-horse*, large thickset

FARM CART (TUMBREL)

1. Tailboard. 2. Axle-tree or arbor. 3. Shaft or thill

horse used for heavy work; *cart'-load*, cartful; very large quantity; *cart'road, cart'way*, rough track unsuitable for light or spring-vehicles; *cart'wheel*, wheel of a cart; large coin (as crown or silver dollar); *turn cartwheels*, execute lateral somersaults, as if arms and legs were spokes of a wheel. ~ *v.* Carry in a cart; work with a cart. **cart'er** *n.*

carte *n.* = QUARTE[2].

carte blanche (blahńsh) *n.* Full discretionary power. [Fr., = 'blank card']

carte-de-visite' (-zēt) *n.* Photograph $3\frac{1}{2} \times 2\frac{1}{4}$ in. [Fr., = 'visiting-card']

cart'el *n.* 1. (Written agreement for) exchange or ransom of prisoners. 2. (kartĕl') Manufacturers' union to control production, marketing, and prices; political combination between parties.

cart'elīze *v.i.* Combine to form a business cartel.

Cartē'sian (-zhn) *adj.* & *n.* (Follower) of DESCARTES or his philosophy or mathematical methods.

Carth'age. Ancient city near Tunis on N. coast of Africa; founded by the Phoenicians; destroyed during the PUNIC Wars, and rebuilt by Augustus. **Carthagin'ian** *adj.* & *n.* (Inhabitant) of Carthage; ~ *peace*, a treaty of peace so severe that it means the virtual destruction of the defeated contestant.

Carthūs'ian (-z-) *adj.* & *n.* 1. (Member) of order of monks founded in Dauphiné in 1086 by St. Bruno, and remarkable for the severity of their rule. 2. (Member) of CHARTERHOUSE school. [*Chartrousse*, place of the first monastery]

Cartier' (-tyā), Jacques (1491–1557). French explorer of Canada.

cart'ilage *n.* The elastic flexible tissue which forms the skeleton of young vertebrates and (except for some parts near the joints) changes later into bone (ill. BONE); gristle.

cartilă'ginous *adj.* Of, like, cartilage; ~ *fish*, those having a cartilaginous skeleton.

cartŏg'raphy *n.* Map-drawing. **cartŏg'rapher** *n.* **cartogră-ph'ic(al)** *adjs.*

cart'omancy *n.* Fortune-telling by playing-cards.

cart'on *n.* 1. (Shot striking) white disc in bull's-eye of target. 2. Light cardboard box or case for holding goods; kind of cardboard used for this.

cartōōn' *n.* 1. Drawing on stout paper as design for painting of same size or for tapestry, mosaic, etc. 2. Humorous or topical drawing in newspaper etc.; *strip* ~, series of small drawings depicting events usu. concerning some central character, freq. serial. 3. (also *animated* ~) Film made by photographing a series of drawings.

cartouche' (-ōōsh) *n.* (archit.) Scroll ornament, e.g. volute of Ionic capital; tablet imitating, drawing of, scroll with rolled-up ends, usu. bearing inscription; (archaeol.) oval containing hiero-

CARTOUCHE

glyphic names and titles of Egyptian kings etc.

cart'ridge *n.* Charge of explosive for fire-arms, blasting, or artillery, enclosed in case made of paper, metal, fabric, etc.; *ball* ~, one containing bullet also; *blank*

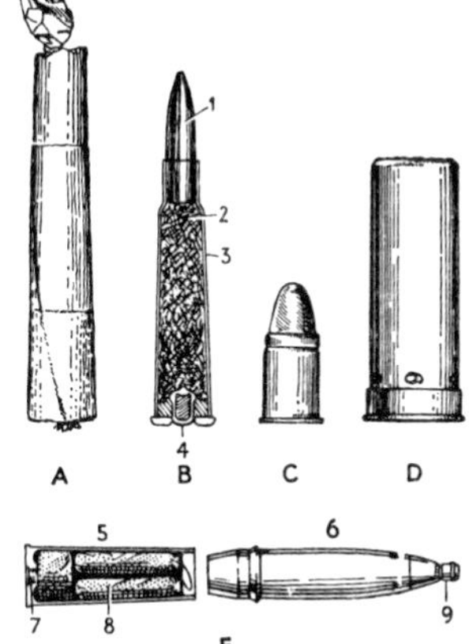

A. BRASS CARTRIDGE, PAPER-COVERED, FOR BREECH-LOADING RIFLE. B. ·303 CARTRIDGE (SECTION). C. REVOLVER CARTRIDGE. D. SHOT-GUN CARTRIDGE. E. QUICK-FIRING SEPARATE-LOADING AMMUNITION FOR GUNS

1. Bullet. 2. Powder. 3. Brass case. 4. Copper detonating cap. 5. Cartridge (section). 6. Projectile. 7. Primer. 8. Propellant. 9. Fuse

~, one for firearm containing explosive only; ~*-belt*, belt with pockets for cartridges; ~*-clip*, device for holding cartridge conveniently for use in magazine-rifle etc.; ~*-paper*, thick rough paper used for making cartridges, and also for drawings and envelopes.

cart'ūlary *n.* Collection or list of charters and records; place where these are kept.

că'rŭncle *n.* 1. Fleshy excrescence, as turkeycock's wattles. 2. Small hard outgrowth formed on seeds of certain plants, e.g. castor-oil plant.

carve *v.* Cut; produce by cutting; change by cutting *into*; cover or adorn *with* cut figures, designs, etc.; cut up meat at or for table; subdivide; *carving*, carved work, carved figure or design; *carving-knife*, long knife for carving meat.

carv'el *n.* = CARAVEL.

carv'er *n.* (esp.) Knife (pl., *knife and fork*) for carving meat.

cărўăt'ĭd *n.* Female figure used as column to support entablature.

CARYATID

[Gk *Caryatis*, a priestess of Artemis at Caryae in Laconia]

cărўŏp'sĭs *n.* (pl. *-sēs*). (bot.) One-seeded indehiscent fruit with pericarp fused to seed-coat, as in wheat and barley.

Căsanōv'a (de Seingalt), Giovanni Jacopo (1725–98). Italian adventurer, author of memoirs, in French, describing his escapades and amours in most countries of Europe.

căscāde' *n.* Waterfall, one section of large broken waterfall; wavy fall of lace etc. ~ *v.i.* Fall in or like cascade.

căscar'a sagra'da (-ahd-) *n.* Bark of a N. Amer. buckthorn, *Rhamnus purshiana*, used as cathartic or purgative. [Span., = 'sacred bark']

cāse[1] *n.* 1. Instance of thing's occurring; actual state of affairs; position, circumstances, plight. 2. (med.) Condition of disease in a person; instance of disease. 3. (law) Cause, suit, for trial; statement of facts in cause drawn up for consideration of higher court; cause that has been decided; *leading* ~, case settling some important point, often cited as precedent; case as presented by one of the parties in a suit; (fig.) ~ *of conscience*, practical question concerning which conscience may be in doubt. 4. (gram.) In inflected languages, form of substantive, pronoun, or adjective expressing its relation to other words in sentence; in uninflected languages, this relation apart from form. 5.

~*-law*, law as settled by decided cases; ~*-work*, social work done by personal study of cases (individuals or families), whence ~*-worker*.

cāse[2] *n.* Thing to contain or hold something else; box, chest, bag, sheath, etc.; outer protection and covering part of anything; box or chest with its contents; (printing) shallow wooden tray for holding type, divided into compartments to take the various letters of the alphabet; *lower* ~, the case usu. holding letters other than capitals; hence, (in) small letters; *upper* ~, case holding large or capital letters etc., hence, (in) capital letters; ~*-bottle*, (square) bottle fitting into case with others; *case'-harden*, harden surface of, esp. give steel surface to (iron etc.) by carbonizing; (fig.) make callous; ~*-knife*, knife worn in sheath; ~*-shot*, bullets in sheet-iron case fired from cannon; shrapnel. ~ *v.t.* Enclose in case; surround (*with*). **cā'sĭng** *n.*

cās'ėin *n.* Protein, one of the constituents of milk, coagulated by acids, and forming the basis of cheese.

cāse'māte (-sm-) *n.* Vaulted chamber in thickness of fortress-wall, with embrasures for defence (ill. CASTLE); (in warships) armoured enclosure in which guns are mounted, with embrasures through which they are fired.

cāse'ment (-sm- *or* -zm-) *n.* Metal or wooden hinged frame with glass, forming window or part of one (ill. WINDOW); (poet.) window; ~ *cloth*, various plain-woven fabrics, mostly cotton, used for curtains etc.

cās'ėous *adj.* Of or like cheese.

cāsh[1] *n.* Ready money; specie and bank-notes; ~*-register*, till for recording and adding amounts put into it. ~ *v.t.* Give or obtain cash for (cheque, money-order, etc.); ~ *in* (*one's checks*), (U.S.) settle accounts in game of poker; (fig.) realize one's assets; (U.S. slang) die.

căsh[2] *n.* (pl. same) Kinds of coin of very small value used in China, E. Indies, etc., esp. the Chinese *le* and *tsien*, coins of alloy of copper and lead, with hole in centre by which they are strung on cord; 1,000 of these made a tael.

căsh'ew (-ōō) *n.* Large tree, *Anacardium occidentale*, of W. Indies etc., cultivated for its kidney shaped edible nut (~*-nut*). [Port. *caju*, f. Tupi (*a*)*caju*]

cashier'[1] *n.* One in charge of cash of bank or other business firm, paying and receiving money etc.

cashier'[2] *v.t.* Dismiss from service, depose; discard.

căsh'mēre *n.* Material woven from fine soft wool found beneath the hair of goats of Kashmir and Tibet; woollen fabric imitating this; ~ *shawl*, richly coloured costly Indian shawl made from cashmere.

casi'nō (-ē-) *n.* (pl. *-os*). 1. Public music or dancing-room; esp. building in continental (esp. French) resort in which gambling takes place, as well as dancing, public entertainments, and other social activities. 2. Card-game in which each player tries to win cards by matching those exposed on the table; points are scored for winning the greatest number of cards, one for the greatest number of spades, two for ten of diamonds (*great* ~) and one for two of spades (*little* ~). [It., = 'little house']

cask (-ah-) *n.* Cylindrical bulging wooden vessel made of staves bound by wooden or iron hoops, used esp. for beer, wine, and cider; cask and its contents.

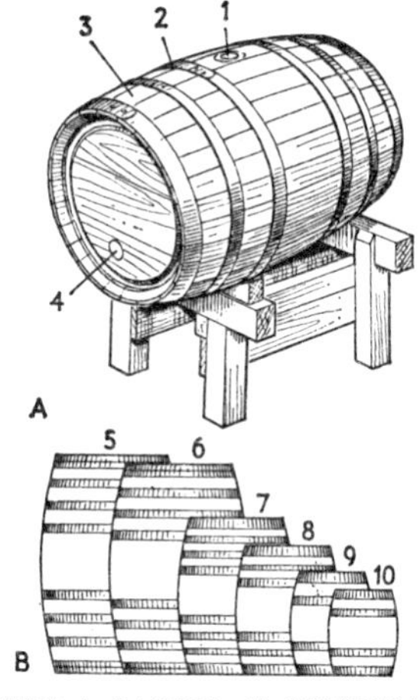

CASK: A. BARREL. B. COMPARATIVE SIZES OF CASKS

1. Bung hole. 2. Hoop. 3. Stave. 4. Tap hole. 5. Brandy puncheon. 6. Butt. 7. Hogshead. 8. Barrel. 9. Kilderkin. 10. Firkin

cas'kėt (-ah-) *n.* 1. Small, often ornamental, box for holding jewels, letters, etc.; *C~ letters*, letters supposed to have passed between Mary Queen of Scots and Bothwell and to have established her complicity in the murder of Darnley. 2. (U.S.) Coffin.

Cās'lon (-z-), William (1692–1766). English typographer; the name is applied to the type-foundry established by him and continued by his son William (1720–78), and to the old-face type cut there, or an imitation of this.

Căsp'ĭan Sea. Inland sea between Europe and Asia.

căsque (-k) *n.* (hist., poet.) Helmet (ill. ARMOUR).

Cassăn'dra. (Gk myth.) A daughter of Priam king of Troy; she was loved by Apollo, who gave her the gift of prophecy and when she deceived him ordained that her prophecies, though true, should not be believed.

cassa'va (-sah-) *n.* 1. The plant manioc, *Manihot utilissima*, widely cultivated in W. Indies, tropical America, and Africa for its fleshy tuberous roots. 2. Nutritious starch obtained from manioc roots, bread made from this.

căss'erōle *n.* Heatproof vessel, usu. of earthenware or glass, in which food is cooked and served. [Fr., = 'stew-pan']

căss'ĭa *n.* 1. Inferior coarse kind of cinnamon, esp. the bark of *Cinnamonum cassia*; this tree. 2. Genus of plants of warm climates, yielding senna-leaves; any medicinal preparation from these.

Cassino: see MONTE CASSINO.

Căssiopei'a (-pēa). 1. (Gk myth.) Wife of Cepheus king of Ethiopia, and mother of Andromeda; she boasted herself more beautiful than the Nereids, thus incurring the wrath of Poseidon. 2. A northern constellation.

căssĭt'erīte *n.* Native stannic dioxide, TIN-stone.

căss'ock *n.* Long close-fitting tunic, usu. black, buttoning up to the neck and reaching to the feet, worn by clergy (ill. VESTMENT).

căss'owary (-*o*-w-) *n.* Genus of large running birds, related to ostrich, found in Australia, New Guinea, etc. [Malay *kasuari*]

CASSOWARY
Height 5 ft

cast (-ah-) *v.* (past t. and past part. *cast*). 1. Throw (archaic and poet. exc. in special uses, as ~ *dice*, *lots*, *fishing-line*, *light*, *shadow*); ~ *an eye*, glance; ~ *adrift*, leave to drift; ~ *anchor*, let it down; ~ *ashore*, leave behind on sea-shore. 2. Throw off, shed, esp. in process of growth; (of horse) lose (a shoe). 3. Form (metal etc.) into desired shape by melting and pouring into a mould; found; ~ *iron*, unpurified unmalleable IRON smelted in blast-furnace; ~*-iron* (*adj.*) made of cast iron; hard, untiring, rigid, unadaptable. 4. Arrange (facts *into* a shape, actors *for* parts in play). 5. ~ *about*, look about, search here and there, *for*; ~ *away*, reject; (pass., of ship, sailor, etc.) be wrecked; *cast'away*, person shipwrecked or cast adrift or rejected; reprobate; ~ *down*, depress; ~ *off*, abandon, throw away; finish off (knitting) by taking stitches off needle and passing each one over the next; (printing) estimate printed length or size of (MS.); *cast-off*, (*n.*) such estimate. ~ *n.* 1. Throw of missile, fishing-line, sounding-lead, etc.; throw of dice, number thrown. 2. Model, shape, made by running molten metal or pressing soft substance into a mould; the mould itself; plaster copy of sculpture made thus. 3. Earth excreted by earth- or lug-worm (*worm-*~); undigested food thrown up by bird. 4. Set of actors taking the parts in a play, distribution of parts among them. 5. Twist, inclination; slight squint. 6. Tinge, hue. 7. Type, quality, stamp.

Căstāl'ĭa. (Gk myth.) Spring on Mount Parnassus, sacred to Apollo and the Muses. **Căstā'lĭan** *adj.*

căstanĕt' *n.* Small concave shell of ivory or hard wood used by Spaniards, Moors, etc., to make

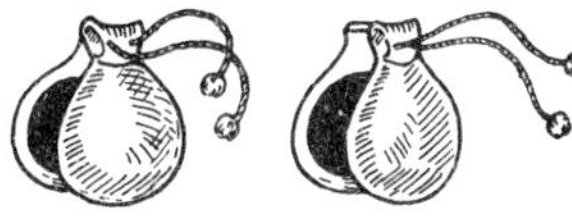

CASTANETS

rattling sound as accompaniment to dancing, a pair being held in the palm of the hand and struck with the middle finger.

caste (-ah-) *n.* 1. Indian hereditary class, with members socially equal, united in religion, and usu. following same trade, having no social intercourse with persons of other castes; hereditary more or less exclusive class elsewhere; this system, the position it confers; *lose* ~, descend in social scale. 2. (zool.) One of the groups into which social Hymenoptera and termites are divided (usu. queens and different types of worker). **caste'lĕss** *adj.*

căs'tellan *n.* Governor or constable of castle.

căs'tellāted *adj.* Built like a castle, having battlements; castle-like.

căs'tĭgāte *v.t.* Chastise, punish. **căstĭgā'tion, căs'tĭgātor** *ns.*

Căstile' (-ēl). Central part of Spain, an ancient kingdom; ~ *soap*, fine hard white or mottled soap made with olive oil and soda. **Căstĭl'ian** *adj.* & *n.* (Inhabitant) of Castile; (of the) language of Castile, literary Spanish.

cast'ĭng (-ah-) *adj.* ~ *vote*, (f. obs. sense of cast = 'turn the scale') vote that decides between two equal parties. ~ *n.* (esp.) Piece of metal or other substance shaped by melting and pouring into a mould; this process of manufacture; DIE-[1], SAND-, PRESSURE-~: see these words.

castle (-ah'sl) *n.* 1. Large fortified building or set of buildings; dwelling that was once fortified. (*Illustration, p.* 120.) 2. *the C*~, (hist.) in Ireland, Dublin Castle as the seat of the viceregal court and administration; the officials who administered the government of Ireland under the viceroy. 3. (hist.) Small wooden tower used in war etc. and borne on elephant's back or ship's deck. 4. (chess) Piece with battlemented top, also called *rook* (ill. CHESS). 5. ~ *in the air*, ~ *in Spain*, day-dream, visionary project or scheme. ~ *v.* (chess) Move king two squares towards one of the castles and (in the same move) this castle to the square next past the king.

Castlereagh (kah'slrā), Robert Stewart, 2nd marquis of Londonderry (1769–1822). Chief secretary for Ireland 1799–1801; secured the passing of the Act of Union by the Irish Parliament; foreign secretary 1812–22; took a leading part in the Congress of Vienna.

cas'tor[1] (-ah-) *n.* 1. Reddish-brown unctuous bitter substance obtained from anal glands of beaver and used in perfumery and formerly in medicine. 2. (slang) Hat (orig. one of beaver or imitation beaver).

cas'tor[2], -er (-ah-) *n.* 1. Small vessel with perforated top for sprinkling pepper, sugar, flour, etc.; ~ *sugar*, finely powdered sugar suitable for use in castor. 2. Small solid wheel and swivel on leg of piece of furniture for moving it without lifting.

Cas'tor[3] (-ah-). 1. (Gk myth.) One of the twin sons (~ *and Pollux*) of Tyndareus and Leda, and half-brother of Helen. 2. The 1st star in the constellation Gemini, Pollux being the 2nd.

cas'tor oil (-ah-) *n.* Pale yellow nauseous acrid oil obtained from seeds of *Ricinus communis* (castor-oil plant), and used as purgative and lubricant.

căstrāte' *v.t.* Remove testicles of, geld; deprive of vigour; expurgate (book). **căstrā'tion** *n.*

căs'ual (-zhŏŏ-, -zū-) *adj.* Accidental; irregular; undesigned, coming by chance or accident; unmethodical, careless; unconcerned, uninterested; ~ *labourer*, one without fixed employment, who does casual or occasional jobs; ~ *pauper, poor*, (one of) those not receiving regular or systematic relief, esp. one admitted to the ~ *ward* of a workhouse, in which were received tramps and others not permanent inmates. **căs'ually** *adv.* **căs'ualnĕss** *n.* **căs'ual** *n.* Casual labourer, casual pauper.

căs'ualty (-zhŏŏ-, -zū-) *n.* 1. Accident, mishap, disaster, esp. (pl.) list or number of persons killed, wounded, and invalided, in a military operation; (sing.) killed, wounded, or injured person; ~ *ward*, hospital ward where accidental injuries are treated.

căsuarī'na (*also* -ēna) *n.* Genus of quickly growing Austral. and E. Ind. trees with jointed leafless branches, like great horse-tails. [f. fancied resemblance to the CASSOWARY]

că'suĭst (-zhŏŏ-, -zū-) *n.* Person, esp. theologian, who studies and resolves cases of conscience or doubtful questions of duty and conduct; sophist, quibbler. **căsuĭs'tĭc(al)** *adjs.* **căsuĭs'tĭcally** *adv.*

căs'uĭstry (-zhŏŏ-, -zū-) *n.* That part of ethics which applies general rules of morality and religion to particular cases, esp. those in which there appears to be a conflict of duties; sophistry, quibbling.

cās'us bĕll'ī. Occasion of war, act justifying or regarded as reason for war.

căt *n.* 1. Small domesticated furry carnivorous quadruped, *Felis domesticus*, kept to destroy mice, and as pet; *wild* ~, *Felis catus*, larger and stronger than the domestic cat, the only feline animal found native in Gt Britain. 2. Any member of the genus *Felis*, which includes lions, tigers, panthers, etc. 3. Cat-like animal of other species, as *civet-cat*, *pole-cat*, etc. 4. Spiteful or back-biting woman. 5. (naut.) Cathead, beam projecting from bows of ship, for raising the anchor, or carrying it suspended, so called because in early times the ring to which the anchor was drawn commonly hung from an ornament, often an animal mask (ill. SHIP). 6. Cat-o'-nine-tails (see below). 7. Piece of wood used in game of tip-cat. 8. ~*-and-dog*, very quarrelsome (life etc.); *C*~*-and-mouse Act*, the Prisoners (Temporary Discharge for Ill-health) Act of 1913, enabling hunger-strikers to be released temporarily; *cat'bird*, an Amer. mocking-bird (*Galeoscoptes carolinensis*) related to wren; also, an Austral. bower-bird (*Aeluredus viridis*); ~*-burglar*, one who enters house by climbing to upper storey; *cat'-call*, shrill whistle expressing disapproval; (*v.*) make catcalls, receive with catcalls; *cat'fish*, any fish of the group *Siluridae*, most of which live in fresh water and have barbels round the mouth; also, the largest of the *Blenniidae*, a fierce carnivorous fish also called *wolf-fish*; *cathead*: see sense 5 above; ~*-ice*, thin ice in shallow places from underneath which water has receded; ~*-lap*, slops, weak tea, etc.; *cat'mint*, aromatic labiate plant with pale-blue flowers, *Nepeta cataria*; ~*-nap*, short light sleep taken sitting in chair etc.; *cat'nip*, (U.S.) catmint; ~*-o'-nine-tails*, whip of 9 knotted cords formerly used in military and naval punishments and still for certain criminal offences; ~*'s-cradle*, child's game with two players lifting intertwined string from each other's fingers in such a way as to form new patterns; ~'*s eye*, precious stone resembling cat's eye with contracted pupil, a hard chalcedonic quartz from Ceylon, Malabar, etc.; faceted glass placed at intervals at centre or side of road so as to reflect light from headlamps of approaching traffic; ~'*s-meat*, horseflesh sold as cats' food; ~'*s-paw*, person used as tool by another; slight breeze rippling water in some places; ~('s) *whisker*, fine adjustable usu. copper wire placed in contact with sensitive spot in crystal wireless receiver; ~'*walk*, narrow bridge or footway giving access to machinery etc. ~ *v.* 1. (colloq.) Vomit. 2. (naut.) Raise (anchor) to cathead.

C.A.T., *abbrev.* College of Advanced Technology.

ca'ta-, cat-, cath- *pref.* Down from, down to, against, in opposition to, mis-.

cătachrē'sis (-k-) *n.* Perversion, improper use, of words.

căt'aclăsm *n.* Violent break, disruption.

căt'aclÿsm *n.* Deluge, esp. 'the Flood'; sudden convulsion or alteration of conditions, political, social, etc., upheaval. **cataclÿs'mal** (-z-), **cataclÿs'mic** *adjs.*

căt'acomb (-ōm) *n.* Subterranean cemetery (orig. that under the basilica of St. Sebastian near Rome, supposed burying-place of Peter and Paul); (pl.) the many subterranean galleries made by Jews and early Christians in and near Rome, with recesses in the sides for tombs; similar works elsewhere (in Paris, worked-out stone quarries with bones from emptied churchyards); wine-cellar. [LL *catacumbas*, name given to the catacomb under St. Sebastian; origin unknown]

cătadiŏp'tric *adj.* Of refraction and reflection (e.g. lens–mirror combination). **cătadiŏp'trics** *n.* Study of this.

catăd'romous *adj.* (Of fish) descending to lower reaches of river, or to sea, to spawn.

căt'afălque (-k) *n.* Decorated stage for coffin or effigy of distinguished person at funeral; open hearse.

Catalan: see CATALONIA.

căt'alāse (-s) *n.* (chem.) Any of various enzymes capable of decomposing hydrogen peroxide.

cătalĕc'tic *adj.* (Of verse) wanting a syllable in last foot.

căt'alĕpsy *n.* Disease characterized by seizure or trance lasting for hours or days, with suspension of sensation and consciousness.

cătalĕp'tic *adj.* & *n.* Of, (person) subject to, catalepsy.

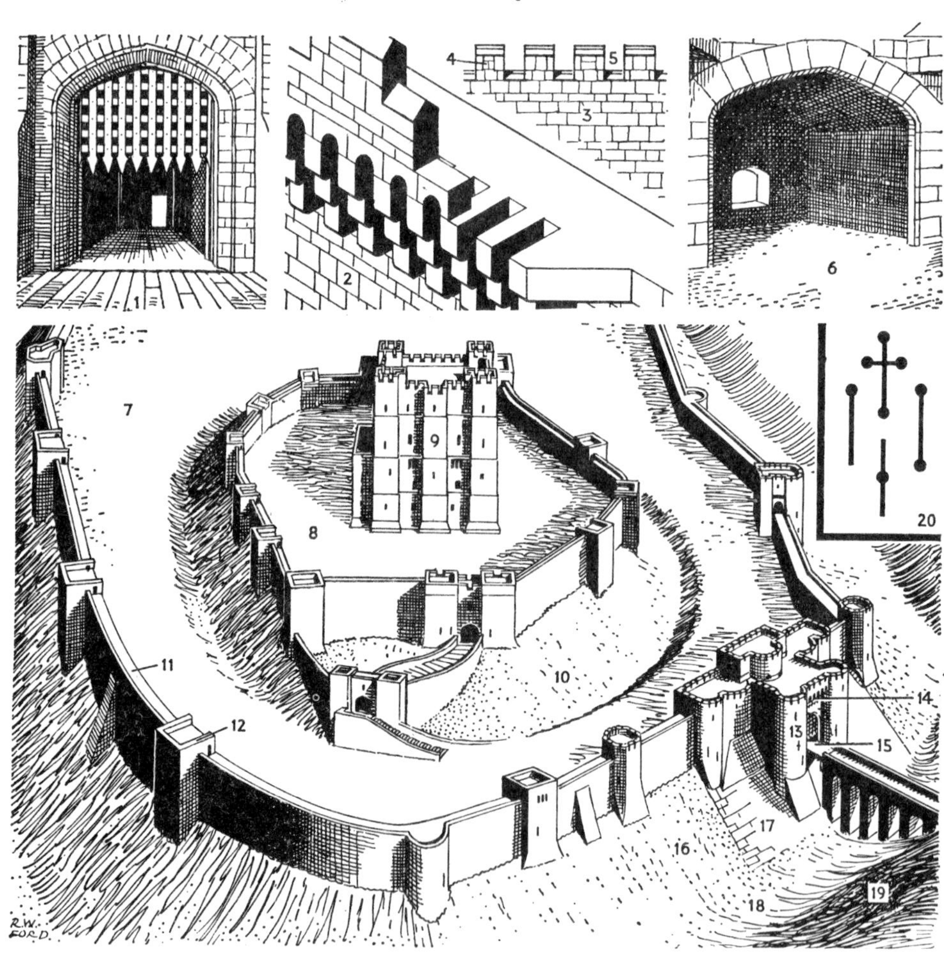

CASTLE

1. Portcullis. 2. Machicolation. 3. Battlements or crenellation. 4. Merlon. 5. Crenel. 6. Casemate. 7. Outer ward or bailey. 8. Inner ward or bailey. 9. Keep or donjon. 10. Motte or mound. 11. Curtain wall. 12. Turret. 13. Gatehouse. 14. Barbican. 15. Drawbridge. 16. Scarp. 17. Revetment. 18. Ditch or moat. 19. Counterscarp. 20. Loopholes

căt'alogue (-ŏg) *n.* Complete list, usu. alphabetical or arranged under headings, and often with descriptive or other particulars; ~ *raisonné* (-nā), (Fr.) descriptive catalogue arranged according to subject etc. ~ *v.* Enumerate, enter, in a catalogue.

Cătalōn'ia. Catalunya, north-easterly part of Spain, formerly a province. **Căt'alan, Cătalōn'ian** *adjs.* & *ns.* (Native) of Catalonia; the dialect of Provençal (or Langue d'Oc) spoken in Catalonia.

catăl'pa *n.* Genus of trees with large simple leaves and trumpet-shaped flowers, natives of N. America, W. Indies, Japan, and China.

catăl'ÿsis *n.* (pl. *-sēs*). The facilitation of a chemical reaction by the presence of an added substance which is itself not consumed in the reaction. **căt'alÿse** (-z) *v.t.* **cătalÿt'ic** *adj.*

căt'alÿst *n.* Substance causing catalysis.

cătamarăn' *n.* 1. E. Ind. raft or float of logs tied together, with longer one in middle; similar W. Ind. craft; raft of two boats side by side used on St. Lawrence etc. 2. Quarrelsome woman. [Tamil *kaṭṭa-maram* tied tree]

căt'amīte *n.* Boy kept for homosexual practices. [L *Catamitus*, corrupt form of *Ganymēdes* Ganymede]

căt'amount *n.* (U.S.) Cougar or other tiger-cat.

căt'aplăsm *n.* Poultice.

căt'apŭlt *n.* 1. Ancient military engine worked with lever and ropes for discharging stones etc. 2. Forked stick with elastic band fastened to two prongs, for shooting small stones etc. 3. Mechanical device for launching aircraft from deck of ship, starting gliders, etc. ~ *v.* Shoot with catapult; hurl as from catapult; launch with catapult.

căt'arăct *n.* 1. Waterfall, esp. large precipitous fall or series of falls; downpour, rush of water. 2. Progressive opacity of lens of eye, resulting, unless treated, in impairment of vision and eventual blindness.

catarrh' (-âr) *n.* Inflammation of mucous membrane, esp. of nose, throat, and bronchial tubes, causing increased flow of mucus. **catârrh'al** (-ral) *adj.*

căt'arrhīne *adj.* & *n.* (Animal) of one of the two divisions of the sub-order *Anthropoidea*; the catarrhine animals are distinguished from the PLATYRRHINE by having the nostrils close together and directed downwards; they include some monkeys, the anthropoid apes, and man.

catăs'trophė *n.* Dénouement of dramatic piece; disastrous end, overthrow, calamitous fate; event subverting order or system of things. **cătastrŏph'ic** *adj.* **cătastrŏph'ically** *adv.*

căt'-boat *n.* Sailing-boat with mast well forward and rigged with one sail.

cătch *v.* (past t. and past part. *caught* pr. cawt) 1. Capture, lay hold of, seize; be entangled, take hold; hit, overtake; intercept (ball etc.) in motion, esp. take hold of (ball thrown) before it reaches ground; (cricket) dismiss (batsman) by intercepting ball from his bat before it touches the ground; be in time for (train etc.); check suddenly. 2. Surprise, detect. 3. Ignite, be ignited. 4. Receive, incur, be infected with. 5. Grasp with senses or mind; arrest, captivate, arrest attention of; take by surprise, trick, deceive. 6. *~-penny*, got up merely to sell; *catch'word*, word so placed as to attract attention, as first word of following page placed at corner of page, word at head of article in dictionary etc., actor's cue-word; word caught up and repeated, esp. in politics etc. ~ *n.* 1. Act of catching; amount of fish caught; chance of, success in, catching ball at cricket; thing or person caught or worth catching. 2. Something designed to deceive or trip up; unforeseen difficulty or awkwardness; hidden trap; surprise. 3. (mus.) = ROUND.

cătch'ing *adj.* (esp.) Infectious; captivating.

cătch'ment *n.* (esp. in ~ *area*) Catching and collection of rainfall over a natural drainage area.

cătch'pōle, -pōll *n.* (hist., contempt.) Petty officer of justice; sheriff's officer, bum-bailiff. [med. L *cacepollus* chase-fowl]

catchup *n.* Misspelling of KETCHUP.

cătch'y *adj.* (colloq.) Attractive; (of tune etc.) readily caught up.

cāte *n.* (archaic; usu. pl.) Choice food.

cătėchĕt'ical (-kĕ-) *adj.* Of, by, oral teaching; according to a catechism; consisting of questions and answers.

căt'ėchism (-k-) *n.* Treatise for instruction by question and answer, esp. on religious doctrine; *Church* ~, that of the Anglican Church in the Book of Common Prayer; *Longer, Shorter*, ~, those of the Westminster Assembly of Divines, used by the Presbyterian churches etc.

căt'ėchīze (-k-) *v.t.* Instruct by question and answer, or by the use of a catechism; put questions to, examine. **căt'ėchist** *n.*

căt'ėchu (-chōō) *n.* (obs.) Various vegetable substances containing tannin. [Malay *kachu*; cf. CACHOU]

cătėchū'mĕn (-k-) *n.* Christian convert under instruction before baptism.

cătėgŏ'rical *adj.* Unconditional, absolute; explicit, direct; ~ *imperative*, (Kantian ethics) the absolute unconditional command of the moral law, a law given by pure reason and universally binding on every rational will. **cătėgŏ'rically** *adv.*

căt'ėgory *n.* 1. Class, division. 2. In Aristotle, one of a possibly exhaustive set of classes among which all things might be distributed (substance, quantity, quality, relation, place, time, posture, possession, action, passion). 3. In Kant etc. the pure *a priori* conceptions of the understanding, applied by the mind to the material received from sense in order to make it an intelligible notion or object of knowledge.

catēn'a *n.* Connected series.

catēn'ary, cătėnār'ian *ns.* & *adjs.* (Like) curve formed by uniform chain hanging freely from two points not in one vertical line.

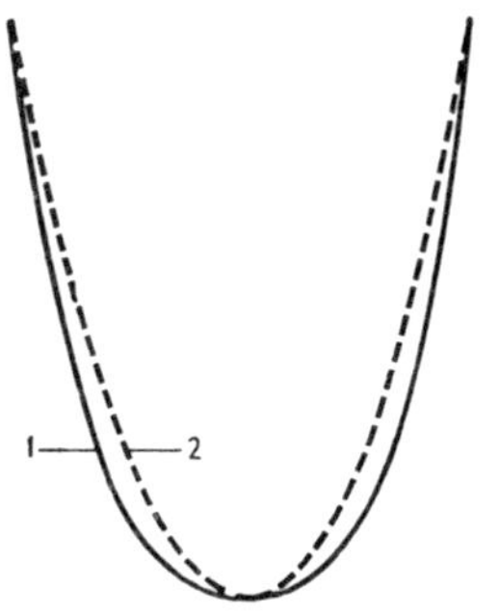

CATENARY

1. Catenary. 2. Parabola for comparison

căt'ėnāte *v.t.* Connect like links of chain. **cătėnā'tion** *n.*

căt'ėnoid *adj.* Catenary. ~ *n.* (math.) Surface formed by revolution of catenary about its axis.

cāt'er *v.i.* Purvey food; provide amusement etc. *for*. **cāt'erer** *n.*

căt'eran *n.* (Sc.) Highland irregular fighting-man, raider, marauder.

căt'erpillar *n.* 1. Larva of butterfly or moth, resembling a worm but possessing several pairs of legs, strong jaws, and short antennae and feeding on leaves, fruit, or other succulent parts of plants (ill. BUTTERFLY). 2. Endless articulated steel bands carrying treads passing round two or more wheels of tractor, tank, or other vehicle required to travel over rough or soft ground (ill. TRACTOR). [OF. *chatepelose* hairy cat]

căt'erwaul *n.* Cry of cat in rut, similar squalling sound. ~ *v.i.* Make caterwaul.

căt'gŭt *n.* Dried and twisted intestines of sheep, horse, etc. (not cat), used for strings of musical instruments, tennis rackets, etc., and for sutures in surgical operations.

cathâr'sis *n.* 1. (med.) Purgation. 2. (with ref. to Aristotle's 'Poetics') Purification of emotions by vicarious experience, esp. through the drama. 3. (psychotherapy) Relieving of neurotic state by re-enacting or relating an experience of strong emotional character which has undergone repression.

cathăr'tĭc *adj.* Effecting catharsis. ~ *n.* Purgative medicine.

Cathay'. (archaic and poet. for) China.

cathēd'ral *n.* Principal church of diocese, containing bishop's *cathedra* or throne. ~ *adj.* Ranking as a cathedral, containing or belonging to a cathedral.

Căth'erĭne, St. (d. 307). Legendary saint and martyr of Alexandria; she was beheaded, after other methods of putting her to death, including that of the wheel, had failed; ~ *wheel*, (orig.) an instrument of torture consisting of 4 wheels armed with knives and teeth turning different ways; now, a kind of firework which rotates while burning; also, a lateral somersault.

Căth'erĭne II (1729–96), 'the Great'. Empress of Russia 1762–96; by birth a German, Princess Sophia of Anhalt-Zerbst; married the Russian heir; 6 months after his accession (as Peter III) he was forced to abdicate and murdered, whereupon Catherine was acclaimed as Empress.

Căth'erĭne de Médicis (1519–89). Wife of Henry II of France and regent of France during the minority of her son, Charles IX; her antagonism to the Protestants led to the Massacre of St. Bartholomew.

Căth'erĭne of Aragon (1483–1536). Daughter of Ferdinand and Isabella of Spain; married Arthur, prince of Wales 1501, and, after his death, his younger brother Henry VIII 1509,; was divorced by Henry 1526, on ground that her 1st marriage made her 2nd invalid.

căth'ėter *n.* Tube for introducing into hollow organs of the body to withdraw excess fluid or sample for analysis, esp. urine from the bladder.

căth'ōde *n.* (elect.) Negative pole (ill. THERMIONIC); ~ *ray*, beam of electrons issuing from cathode of high-vacuum tube under the impulse of an electron field.

căth'olĭc *adj.* 1. Universal, of universal interest or use; all-embracing, of wide sympathies. 2. *C~ Church*, (*a*) the whole body of Christians; (*b*) after the separation of Eastern and Western Churches, the Western or Latin Church; (*c*) after the Reformation, claimed as its exclusive title by that part of the Western Church which remained under Roman obedience, but (*d*) held by Anglicans to include the Church of England as the proper continuation in England of the Ancient and the Western Church. 3. Of or belonging to any of these Churches, esp. = ROMAN CATHOLIC. 4. *His C~ Majesty*, title of kings of Spain; *C~* (and) *Apostolic Church*, the IRVINGITES. ~ *n.* Member of a Catholic church, esp. ROMAN CATHOLIC. **cathŏl'ĭcally, căth'olĭcly** *advs.* **cathŏl'ĭcism, cătholĭ'cĭty** *ns.* **cathŏl'ĭcize** *v.t.*

Căt'ilīne. Lucius Sergius Catilina (d. 63 B.C.), a profligate Roman who formed a conspiracy against his country and was accused by Cicero.

căt'ion *n.* Ion carrying a positive charge which moves towards the cathode (negative electrode) during electrolysis (opp. ANION). [Gk, = 'going down']

căt'kĭn *n.* The hanging inflorescence of willow, birch, etc.; a pendulous spike (ill. FLOWER).

căt'lĭnīte *n.* PIPE-stone.

Cāt'ō, Marcus Porcius (234–149 B.C.). 'Cato the Censor', famous for his opposition to the lax morals and luxury of the Romans and for his insistence that 'Carthage must be destroyed'; author of a treatise 'De Agri Cultura', the oldest extant literary prose work in Latin. ~, Marcus Porcius (95–46 B.C.). Great grandson of Cato the Censor and like him a man of unbending character; chief political antagonist of Julius Caesar.

catŏp'trĭc *adj.* Of mirror, reflector, or reflection. **catŏp'trĭcs** *n.* Part of optics dealing with reflections (cf. DIOPTRICS).

căt'sup *n.* var. of KETCHUP.

cătt'ish, cătt'y *adjs.* Ill-natured, spiteful.

căt'tle *n.* Livestock, esp. oxen; (slang) horses; *~-lifter*, (U.S.) *~-rustler*, marauder who steals cattle; *~-plague*, rinderpest; *~-stop*, ditch across road bridged by open arrangement of logs etc. so that cattle cannot cross it.

cătt'leya (-lēa) *n.* (Member of) orchidaceous genus of Central Amer. and Brazilian plants with handsome violet, pink, or yellow flowers. [William *Cattley*, English patron of botany]

Cătŭll'us, Gaius Valerius (87–54? B.C.). Roman poet and epigrammatist.

Caucā'sian (-shn) *adj.* & *n.* 1. (Native) of the Caucasus. 2. (esp. U.S.) (Member) of the white race, Indo-European (from supposed origin in the Caucasus). **cauc'asĭfōrm** *adj.* Of the white race.

Cauc'asus. Mountain-range between Black Sea and Caspian.

cauc'us *n.* (chiefly in hostile use) Local political party committee for fighting elections, defining policy, etc. (orig. U.S.).

caud'al *adj.* Of, at, like, tail. **caud'ate** *adj.* Tailed.

Caudillo (kowdil'yō), **El.** Title assumed by General FRANCO as head of Spanish State. [Span., = 'leader']

cau'dle *n.* (archaic) Warm thin spiced gruel with wine and sugar, for invalids, esp. women in childbed.

caul *n.* 1. Woman's close-fitting cap or net for the hair (hist.); plain back part of woman's cap. 2. Amnion or inner membrane enclosing foetus; part of this enclosing child's head at birth and superstitiously regarded as lucky omen and preservative against drowning. 3. Omentum.

ca(u)l'dron *n.* Large boiling-vessel (usu.) of deep basin shape, with hoop handle and removable lid.

caul'ĭflower (kŏl-) *n.* Cultivated plant of the genus *Brassica* with young inflorescence forming close white fleshy edible head; ~ *ear*, (pugilist's) ear with lobe thickened and distorted by blows.

caul'īne *adj.* (bot.) Of the stem; (of leaves) growing on an extended stem (ill. LEAF).

caulk (kawk) *v.t.* Stop up seams of (ship), stop up (seams) with oakum and melted pitch (or, in iron ship, by striking junctions of plates with blunt chisel).

caus'al (-z-) *adj.* Of, acting as, expressing, due to, a cause or causes; of the nature of cause and effect. **causăl'ĭty** *n.* Being, having, a cause; relation of cause and effect, doctrine that everything has cause(s).

causā'tion (-z-) *n.* Causing; relation of cause and effect. **caus'ative** (-z-) *adj.* Acting as cause (*of*); (gram.) expressing a cause or causation.

cause (-z) *v.t.* Effect, bring about, produce; induce, make (person *to* do, thing to be done). ~ *n.* 1. What produces an effect, what gives rise to any action, phenomenon, or condition; person or other agent bringing something about; ground or reason for action; motive; *First C~*, original cause or creator of the universe. 2. (law etc.) Matter about which person goes to law; case of one party in a suit; matter in dispute; side of question or controversy expressed by a person or party, militant movement, propaganda; *~-list*, list of causes for trial.

cause célèbre (kōz sālĕb'r) *n.* Law-suit exciting much public interest.

cause'lėss (-zl-) *adj.* Fortuitous; without natural cause; unjustifiable, groundless.

causerie (kōz'erē) *n.* Informal article or talk, esp. on literary subjects.

cause'way (-zwā) *n.* Raised road across low or wet place or piece of water; raised footway at side of road.

caus'tĭc *adj.* 1. Burning, corrosive, destroying organic tissue; ~ *alkalis*, the hydroxides of potassium (~ *potash*, KOH), sodium (~ *soda*, NaOH), and other electropositive metals. 2. Bitter, cutting, sarcastic. 3. (math.) (Of curved surface) formed by intersection of rays from one point reflected or refracted from a curved surface.

~ *n.* 1. Caustic substance; *lunar* ~, silver nitrate in sticks for surgical use. 2. Caustic surface. **caus'tically** *adv.* **causti'city** *n.*

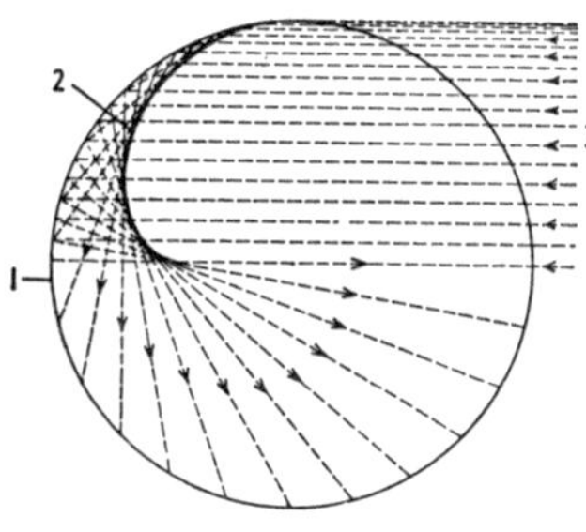

CAUSTIC

1. Reflecting surface. 2. Caustic curve. 3. Rays from distant point

caut'erīze *v.t.* Sear with hot iron or caustic; render callous. **cauterīzā'tion** *n.*

caut'ery *n.* Heated metal instrument for burning or searing organic tissue (*actual* ~); caustic for the same purpose (*potential* ~); cauterizing.

cau'tion *n.* 1. Warning, advice to take heed; warning with reprimand; (slang) extraordinary, strange, person or thing. 2. Heedfulness, taking care, wariness against danger, circumspection. 3. Security, bail, pledge (now Sc. and U.S.); ~ *money*, money deposited as security for good conduct, esp. at university or Inn of Court. ~ *v.t.* Warn; admonish.

cau'tionary (-sho-) *adj.* Conveying a warning or admonition.

cau'tious (-shus) *adj.* Heedful, circumspect, wary. **cau'tiously** *adv.*

căvalcāde' *n.* Company of riders, procession on horseback.

căvalier' *n.* 1. Horseman. 2. Courtly gentleman, gallant, esp. as escorting a lady. 3. One of those who fought for Charles I in the (English) Civil War. ~ *adj.* 1. Careless in manner, off-hand; haughty, supercilious. 2. Royalist. **căvalier'ly** *adv.*

căv'alry *n.* Horse-soldiers, mounted troops; troops formerly mounted but now equipped with mechanical vehicles, as tanks or armoured cars.

Căv'an. County of Ulster, Eire.

căvati'na (-tē-) *n.* (mus.) Short simple song; similar piece of instrumental music, usu. slow and emotional. [Ital. wd]

cāve *n.* Hollow place opening more or less horizontally under the ground; ~*-dweller*, ~*-man*, person (esp. prehistoric man) living in cave; person resembling prehistoric man. ~ *v.* Hollow out, excavate; ~ *in* subside (of earth etc. over hollow place), yield to pressure from outside or above; (fig.) yield to pressure, submit, give in; smash in.

cāv ē *int.* (schoolboy slang) Look out! [L, = 'beware']

cāv'ēăt *n.* 1. (law) Process in court to suspend proceedings. 2. Warning, caution. [L, = 'let him beware']

cāv'ēăt ĕmp'tŏr. Sentence disclaiming responsibility for buyer's disappointment. [L, = 'let the buyer beware']

căv'endĭsh[1] *n.* Tobacco softened, sweetened with molasses, and pressed into cakes.

Căv'endĭsh[2], Henry (1731–1810). English natural philosopher; discovered the constitution of water and atmospheric air; experimented on electricity and the density of the earth. His name is commemorated in the ~ *Laboratory* at Cambridge for physical research, founded in 1874.

căv'ĕrn *n.* (Vast) underground hollow.

căv'ĕrnous *adj.* Full of caverns; as of, huge or deep as, a cavern.

cavĕtt'ō *n.* (archit.) Hollowed moulding whose section is the quadrant of a circle (ill. MOULDING).

căviăr(e)' *n.* Roe of sturgeon and other large fish of eastern European lakes and rivers, pressed and salted, and eaten as relish; ~ *to the general*, (with allusion to 'Hamlet', II. ii.) good thing not appreciated by the ignorant.

căv'ĭl *v.i.* Raise captious objection. ~ *n.* Captious or quibbling objection; cavilling.

căvĭtā'tion *n.* Successive formation and collapse of bubbles behind body moving in stream of fluid.

căv'ĭty *n.* Empty space within solid body, hollow place; ~ *wall*, double wall with internal hollow space (ill. BRICK).

cavŏrt' *v.i.* (orig. U.S. slang) Prance, caper.

Cavour' (-oor), Camillo Benso, Count di (1810–61). Prime minister of Piedmont, 1852–9 and 1860–1, whose statesmanship did much to secure the unification of Italy.

cāv'y *n.* Large rodent of S. Amer. genus *Cavia*, including guinea-pigs. [*cabiai*, native name in Fr. Guiana]

caw *int.* & *n.* Cry of rook, crow, or raven; sound resembling this. ~ *v.i.* Make this sound.

Căx'ton. William (1422?–91). The first English printer; established a press at Westminster, 1477–91, from which he issued about 80 books, many of them translations by himself from French romances; hence, ~ *n.* book printed by Caxton; printing-type in imitation of Caxton's.

cay *n.* Low insular bank or reef of sand, rocks, etc., esp. off coast of Spanish America.

Cayenne (kāĕn'). Chief town of French Guiana; ~ (*pepper*), a very hot and pungent powder made by drying and grinding the seeds of several species of the genus *Capsicum*, and used as a condiment.

caym'an, caim'an *n.* Alligator, esp. of the tropical S. Amer. genus *Caiman*; loosely, any large Amer. saurian. [Carib *acayuman*]

cayūse' (kī-) *n.* Amer. Ind. pony. [Name of Amer. Ind. tribe]

C.B. *abbrev.* Companion of the Bath; confinement to barracks.

C.B.E. *abbrev.* Commander of (the Order of) the British Empire.

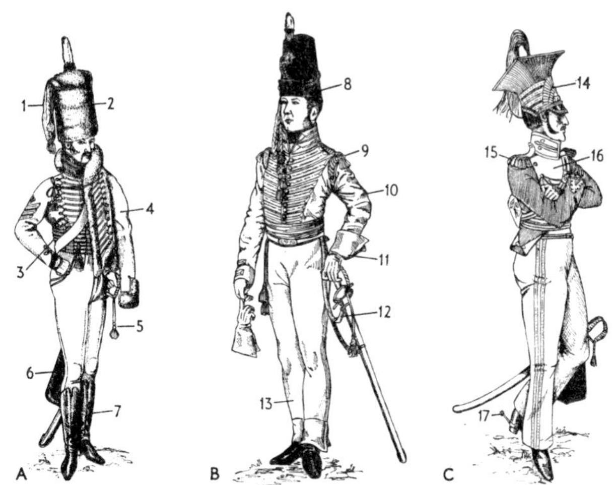

CAVALRY UNIFORMS: A. SENIOR NON-COMMISSIONED OFFICER, 15th HUSSARS, 1808. B. OFFICER, 6th (INNISKILLING) DRAGOONS, 1811. C. OFFICER, 19th LANCERS, 1819

A. 1. Busby bag. 2. Busby. 3. Barrel sash. 4. Pelisse. 5. Sword knot. 6. Sabretache. 7. Hessian boots. B. 8. Shako. 9. Wings. 10. Jacket. 11. Gauntlet. 12. Sword sling. 13. Overalls. C. 14. Lancer cap. 15. Epaulette. 16. Plastron. 17. Spur

c.c. *abbrev.* Cubic centimetre.

C.C. *abbrev.* County Council(lor); cricket club.

C.C.C. *abbrev.* (U.S.) Civilian Conservation Corps; Corpus Christi College (Oxford or Cambridge).

C.D. *abbrev.* Civil Defence; Contagious Diseases (Acts).

c.d., c.div. *abbrevs.* cum dividend.

c.d.v. *abbrev.* *carte-de-visite* (= visiting card).

C.E. *abbrev.* Church of England; Civil Engineer.

cease (-s) *v.* Desist *from*; stop; come, bring, to an end; *~-fire*, (mil.) signal to cease firing. *~ n.* Ceasing (now only in *without ~*, incessantly). **cease'lèss** (-sl-) *adj.* Incessant. **cease'lèssly** *adv.*

Cècĭl'ia, St. (d. A.D. 230). A Christian martyr; through a misinterpretation of a sentence in her Acts she came to be associated with church music and in particular with the organ, which she is supposed to have played; commemorated 22nd Nov.

cēd'ar *n.* Evergreen coniferous tree of genus *Cedrus*, with fragrant fine-grained wood, leaves in fascicles, and erect cones with carpels separating from axis; kinds of tree resembling these; *~-wood*, esp. the wood of *Juniperus bermudiana* and *J. virginiana*, used for lead pencils.

cēde *v.t.* Give up, grant, admit; surrender (territory).

cèdĭll'a *n.* Mark (¸) written under letter *c* to show that it has a sound other than *k*, in French that of *s*, in Span. that of *th*.

cee *n.* The letter *c*; *~-spring*, *C-spring*, spring shaped like letter *c* supporting body of carriage etc.

ceil (sēl) *v.t.* Line roof of (room etc.).

ceilidh (kāl'ĕ) *n.* Informal gathering for song and story in Highlands of Scotland; festive gathering for dancing etc. in Ireland.

ceil'ĭng (sēl-) *n.* 1. Lining of roof, concealing the timbers. 2. (aeronaut.) Altitude beyond which a given aircraft cannot climb and at which only one speed of flight is possible (*absolute ~*) or altitude beyond which the rate of climb falls below 100 ft per minute (*service ~*). 3. Upper limit of prices, wages, etc.

cĕl'adon *n.* & *adj.* Willow-green; *~ wares*, (Chinese) pottery or porcelain with pale grey-green glaze. [Fr., f. name of character in D'Urfé's 'Astrée']

cĕl'andīne *n.* Either of two yellow-flowered plants, the *greater ~*, *Chelidonium majus*, and the *lesser ~*, *Ranunculus ficaria*, also known as pile-wort.

Celebes (sĕl'ebēz *or* selē'-). Island of Indonesia, E. of Borneo.

cĕl'èbrant *n.* Officiating priest, esp. at Eucharist.

cĕl'èbrāte *v.* 1. Perform (religious ceremony etc.) publicly and duly; officiate at Eucharist. 2. Observe, honour (festival, event) with rites, festivities, etc. 3. Publish abroad, praise, extol; *celebrated*, famed, renowned. **cĕlèbrā'tion** *n.*

cèlĕb'rĭty *n.* 1. Being famous. 2. Celebrated person.

cèlĕ'rĭăc *n.* Turnip-rooted variety of garden celery.

cèlĕ'rity *n.* Swiftness.

cĕl'ery *n.* Umbelliferous plant, *Apium graveolens*, cultivated for the use of its blanched stalks as salad and vegetable.

cèlĕs'ta *n.* Musical instrument consisting of metal plates struck with hammers played from a keyboard.

cèlĕs'tĭal *adj.* 1. Of the sky; *~ equator*, great circle of the celestial sphere, formed by a plane cutting through the earth's centre at right angles to its axis; *~ sphere*, the imaginary sphere on which the

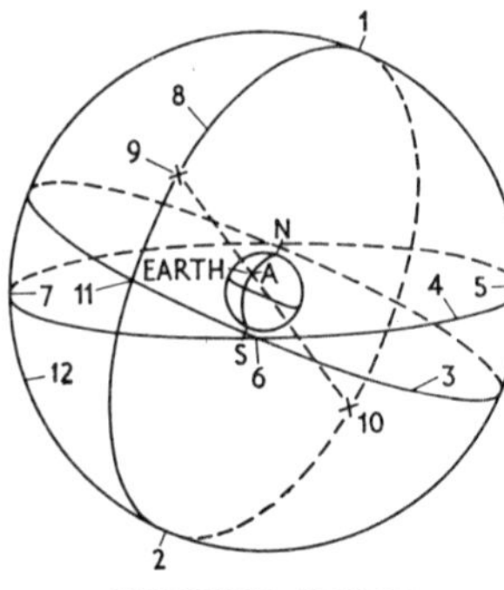

CELESTIAL SPHERE

1. North celestial pole. 2. South celestial pole. 3. Celestial equator. 4. Ecliptic. 5. Summer solstice. 6. Equinox. 7. Winter solstice. 8. Meridian and azimuth circle for point *A* on earth's surface. 9. Zenith for *A*. 10. Nadir for *A*. 11. Node. 12. Colure. *N*. North pole. *S*. South pole

heavenly bodies appear to lie, having its centre at the centre of the earth (or at the point where the observer stands) and an infinite radius. 2. Heavenly, divine; divinely good, beautiful, etc. 3. Chinese; *C~ Empire* (transl. of native title), China. **cèlĕs'tĭally** *adv.* **celĕs'tĭal** *n.* Chinese.

cĕl'ĭbate (-*at*) *n.* & *adj.* Unmarried (person); (person) bound or resolved not to marry. **cĕl'ĭbacy** *n.*

cĕll *n.* 1. Hermit's one-roomed dwelling; (hist.) dependent nunnery or monastery. 2. Single person's small room in monastery etc.; similar room in prison or other place of detention; *condemned ~*, room for prisoner condemned to death. 3. (biol.) Unit of structure of living matter, mass of protoplasm bounded by a membrane (*~-wall*) and containing a nucleus. 4. (zool.) Small container of earth, silk, wax, etc., in which larva or pupa develops, esp. in comb of social insects, e.g. bees. 5. (elect.) Voltaic apparatus with only one pair of metallic elements, unit of battery. 6. (fig.) Small group or single person working in factory, particular district, etc., as nucleus of political, esp. revolutionary, activity.

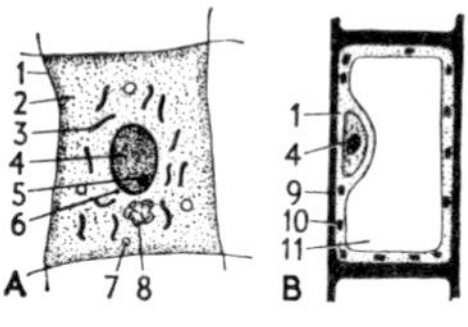

CELL: A. ANIMAL. B. VEGETABLE

1, 2. Cytoplasm (1. Ectoplasm, 2. Endoplasm). 3. Mitochondria. 4. Nucleus. 5. Nucleolus. 6. Centriole. 7. Oil droplet. 8. Golgi bodies. 9. Cell-wall. 10. Plastid. 11. Vacuole

cĕll'a *n.* Principal chamber of classical temple (ill. TEMPLE).

cĕll'ar *n.* Underground room or vault, used for storage, etc.; wine-cellar, stock of wines; *~-book*, book containing account of wines etc. in cellar; *~-kitchen*, basement-kitchen. **cĕll'arage** *n.* Cellar accommodation.

cĕll'arer *n.* Official in monastery etc. in charge of wine and provisions.

cĕllarĕt' *n.* Case or sideboard with compartments for holding wine etc.

Cellini (chĕlēn'ĭ), Benvenuto (1500–71). Florentine goldsmith and sculptor, author of a famous autobiography.

cĕll'ō, 'cĕllō (ch-) *n.* (pl. *-os*). (Short for) VIOLONCELLO. **cĕll'ist** *n.* Violoncellist.

cĕll'ophāne *n.* Proprietary name for glossy transparent material made of cellulose and used as wrapping etc.

cĕll'ūlar *adj.* Of, having, consisting of, cells; porous.

cĕll'ūle *n.* Small cell.

cĕll'ūloid *n.* Solid inflammable material consisting essentially of soluble cellulose nitrate and camphor, used for films and as substitute for ivory, bone, tortoise-shell, etc.

cĕll'ūlōse *n.* (chem.) Carbohydrate which forms chief constituent of cell-walls of all plants and of textiles such as cotton and linen; (pop.) forms of paint or varnish consisting of compounds of cellulose (esp. cellulose nitrate) dissolved in an organic solvent. *~ adj.* *~ acetate*, formed by the action of acetic acid on cellulose, used to make artificial silk (rayon), plastics, etc.; *~ nitrate*, nitrocellulose, guncotton, formed by action of nitric and sulphuric acids on cellulose, a constituent of smokeless gunpowders and of cordite, celluloid, etc.

Cels. *abbrev.* Celsius.

Cĕl'sius, Anders (1701–44). Swedish astronomer; inventor of the centigrade scale for measuring temperature; hence, ~, alternative name for CENTIGRADE.

Cĕlt[1] (k- *or* s-). 1. Member of one of the ancient peoples of W. Europe called by the Greeks *Keltoi* and by the Romans *Celtae*; a Gaul. 2. One of the peoples speaking languages related to those of the ancient *Galli* or Gauls, including Bretons, Cornish, Welsh, Irish, Manx, and Gaels.

cĕlt[2] *n.* Bronze, stone, or iron prehistoric implement used as axe.

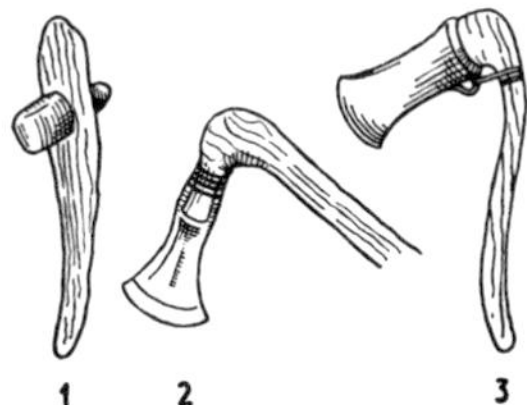

CELTS

1. Stone celt in wooden haft. 2. Bronze palstave in wooden haft. 3. Bronze socketed celt in wooden haft

Cĕl'tĭc (k- *or* s-) *adj.* & *n.* Of the Celts; (of the) branch of the Indo-European family of languages spoken by the ancient Celts or their modern representatives; ~ *fringe*, the Highland Scots, Welsh, Cornish, and Irish, as occupying the outlying edge of the British Isles; ~ *twilight*, the romantic 'fairy-tale' atmosphere supposed to be characteristic of Celtic literature, taken from the title of a collection of stories by W. B. YEATS.

C.E.M.A. *abbrev.* Council for the Encouragement of Music and the Arts (now Arts Council of Great Britain).

cĕm'balō (ch-) *n.* Harpsichord.

cėmĕnt' *n.* Any compound substance, esp. of lime or other stone, ground to powder and mixed with water, which hardens rapidly into stony consistence, used for binding together stones or bricks, covering floors, walls, etc,; similar substance mixed with sand and gravel etc. to form CONCRETE; (physiol.) bony substance forming outer layer of root of tooth; plastic material for filling tooth cavities; any adhesive material used to mend small articles of glass, china, etc.; (fig.) link or bond of union. ~ *v.t.* Unite firmly with or as with cement; coat or line with cement.

cėmĕnt'īte *n.* Hard brittle compound of iron and carbon.

cĕm'ėtery *n.* Place, not being a churchyard, for burying the dead.

cĕn'otaph (-ahf) *n.* Sepulchral monument to person whose body is elsewhere; *the C~*, that erected in Whitehall, London, as a memorial to the British dead of the 1914–18 war, now commemorating the dead of the 1939–45 war also.

cenozoic: see CAINOZOIC.

cĕnse *v.t.* Perfume with incense, burn incense before.

cĕn'ser *n.* Vessel in which incense is burnt.

CENSER

cĕn'sor *n.* 1. Either of two magistrates in ancient Rome who drew up the register or census of citizens and supervised public morals; any person supervising or criticizing the morals and conduct of others. 2. Official inspecting books, letters, newspapers, etc., to ensure that they shall contain nothing immoral, seditious, or unacceptable to military or other authorities. 3. Various university and college officials; at Oxford and Cambridge, official head of non-collegiate students. 4. (psycho-analysis) Power within the mind or personality repressing certain elements in the unconscious and preventing them from becoming conscious. **cĕn'sorshĭp** *n.* **cĕn'sor** *v.t.* Act as censor to; make excisions or changes in.

cĕnsôr'ial *adj.* Of a censor; censorious.

cĕnsôr'ious *adj.* Severely critical, fault-finding. **cĕnsôr'iously** *adv.* **cĕnsôr'iousnėss** *n.*

cĕn'sure (-sher) *n.* Adverse judgement, expression of disapproval, reprimand. ~ *v.t.* Criticize unfavourably; reprove, blame. **cĕn'surable** *adj.*

cĕn'sus *n.* 1. Official numbering of population with various statistics (in Gt Britain normally taken every 10 years); ~*-paper*, form left at every house to be filled up with names, ages, etc., of inmates. 2. In ancient Rome, registration of citizens and property for taxation.

cĕnt *n.* 1. *Per* ~, (often written %), for (in, to) every 100, esp. in stating rates of interest etc. 2. $\frac{1}{100}$ of dollar, gulden, or Ceylon rupee.

cent. *abbrev.* Century.

Cent. *abbrev.* Centigrade.

cĕn'tal *n.* Weight of 100 lb. av., used in measuring corn.

cĕn'taur (-tôr) *n.* 1. (Gk myth.) Fabulous creature with head, trunk, and arms of man joined to body and legs of horse. 2. *C~*, a southern constellation.

cĕn'taury *n.* Various plants, esp. the common centaury of the herbalists, *Erythrea centaurium*, whose medicinal properties were supposed to have been discovered by Chiron the centaur.

cĕntāv'ō *n.* (pl. *-s*). $\frac{1}{100}$ of a peso or similar unit of currency in various republics of S. America.

cĕntėnār'ian *adj.* & *n.* (Person) 100 years old or more.

cĕntēn'ary (also sĕn'tėn-) *adj.* & *n.* (Of) 100 years; (celebration of) 100th anniversary.

cĕntĕnn'ial *adj.* Of, having lived or lasted, completing, 100 years; of the 100th anniversary. ~ *n.* (esp. U.S.) 100th anniversary; *C~ State*, popular name of Colorado, because of its entrance into the Union 100 years after the Declaration of Independence.

cĕn'terĭng *n.* Making central, making two or more centres coincide, esp. setting of lenses with their axes in same straight line; temporary framework of arch or vault.

cĕntĕs'ĭmal *adj.* Reckoning, reckoned, by 100ths.

centes'ĭmo (chĕntāz-) *n.* (pl. *-mi* pr. mē) $\frac{1}{100}$ of a lira.

centi- *prefix.* $\frac{1}{100}$ of (the specified denomination in the metric system).

cĕn'tĭgrāde *adj.* Having 100 degrees; ~ *scale*, temperature scale, invented by CELSIUS, in which the freezing-point and the boiling-point of water are taken as 0 degrees and 100 degrees respectively, used universally in scientific work (for conversion to the Fahrenheit scale see Appendix X).

cĕn'tĭgrăm *n.* Measure of weight, $\frac{1}{100}$ of a gram.

cĕn'tĭlitre (-ēter) *n.* Measure of capacity, $\frac{1}{100}$ of a litre.

cĕntill'ion (-yon) *n.* 100th power of a million (1 with 600 ciphers); (U.S.) 101st power of a thousand (1 with 303 ciphers).

centime (sahn'tēm) *n.* $\frac{1}{100}$ of a franc.

cĕn'tĭmētre *n.* Measure of length, $\frac{1}{100}$ of a metre, or 0·3937 (nearly $\frac{2}{5}$) of an inch; ~*-gram-second system* (abbrev. c.g.s.), system of units of measurement based on the centimetre as the unit of length, the gram as the unit of weight, and the second as the unit of time.

cĕn'tĭmō *n.* (pl. *-s*). $\frac{1}{100}$ of a peseta; $\frac{1}{100}$ of the principal monetary unit in some S. Amer. countries.

cĕn'tĭpēde *n.* Wingless worm-like animal of the order *Chilopoda*, having many joints, and a pair of feet to each segment of the trunk (ill. MYRIAPOD).

cĕn'tō *n.* (pl. *-os*) Composition made up of scraps from other authors.

cĕn'tral *adj.* Of, in, at, from, containing, the centre; leading, principal, dominant; ~ *heating*, heating of building from a central source, as by circulating hot water or steam through pipes or warm air through flues; *C~ Powers*, (before 1914) Germany and Austria-Hungary. **cĕntrăl'ity** *n.* **cĕn'trally** *adv.* **cĕn'tralnėss** *n.*

cĕn'tralism *n.* Centralizing system. **cĕn'tralist** *n.*

cĕn'tralīze *v.* 1. Come, bring, to a centre. 2. Concentrate (administrative powers) in single centre instead of distributing them among local departments; bring (State etc.) under this system. **cĕntralīzā'tion** *n.*

Central Provinces. State of the Republic of India, now officially called Madhya Pradesh; formerly a group of provinces of British India, formed in 1861 out of territory taken from the NW. Provinces and Madras, orig. belonging to the Mahratta kingdom of Nagpur.

cĕn'tre (-*ter*), **cĕn'ter** *n.* 1. Middle point of circle, sphere, line, etc. (ill. CIRCLE); middle point or part of anything; point, pivot, axis, line, upon which a body turns or revolves; in lathe, conical adjustable bearing to hold object being turned. 2. Point of concentration, attraction, or dispersion, nucleus, source. 3. (archit.) Temporary framework supporting arch or dome while building. 4. (mil. etc.) Main body of troops, between the wings; main part of fleet, between van and rear of line of battle, or between weather and lee divisions. 5. In a political assembly, the men of moderate opinions. 6. (football, hockey, etc.) Player whose position is the middle of a line or field of players, esp. = *~-forward*, one occupying central position in forward line (ill. ASSOCIATION). 7. ~ *of attraction*, (physics etc.) point to which bodies tend by gravity etc.; point or object drawing general interest; ~ *of gravity*, point about which all parts of a body exactly balance each other, so that if this point is supported the body remains at rest in any position. 8. *~-bit*, tool with projecting centre-point for making cylindrical holes; *~-board*, (flat-bottomed sailing-boat with) board or plate for lowering through keel in deep water to increase stability and prevent lee-way; *~-forward*: see sense 6; *~-half*, (position of) player at football, hockey, etc., playing from central position among half-backs; *~-punch*, punch for marking centres for holes etc. in metal. **cĕn'treless, cĕn'trĭc(al)** *adjs.* **cĕn'tre** *v.* Be concentrated, have centre, *in*, *on*, *at*, etc.; place in or as in centre; mark with centre; grind (lens) so as to make its optical centre coincide with its geometrical centre; find exact centre of, place in (exact) centre etc.

cĕntrĭf'ūgal *adj.* Flying, tending to fly, from centre; ~ *force*, force in direction away from centre, erron. supposed to be experienced by body moving round it; ~ *machine* etc., one in which rotation about axis results in movement of parts or particles away from the axis. **cĕntrĭf'ūgally** *adv.*

cĕn'trĭfūge *n.* Centrifugal machine, esp. one for separating cream from milk, or for drying objects, by rotary motion.

centring: see CENTERING.

cĕn'triōle *n.* Minute granule found near the nucleus of an animal cell and participating in the processes accompanying its division (ill. CELL).

cĕntrĭp'ėtal *adj.* Tending towards the centre.

cĕn'tūple *adj.* Hundredfold. ~ *v.t.* Multiply a hundredfold. **centūp'lĭcate** *n.* & *v.*

cĕntūr'ĭon *n.* Commander of a century in ancient-Roman army.

cĕn'tūry *n.* 1. (Rom. hist.) Company in army, orig. of 100 men; each of the 193 political divisions by which the Roman people voted. 2. 100, esp. 100 runs at cricket. 3. 100 years, esp. each successive period of 100 years reckoning from a fixed date, e.g. the assumed date of Christ's birth; ~ *plant*, the agave or American aloe, supposed to flower once in 100 years, but often flowering after only 5.

cėphăl'ĭc *adj.* Of, in, the head; ~ *index*, number indicating the ratio of transverse to longitudinal diameter of skull, considered as an indication of race.

cĕph'alopŏd *n.* Animal of the *Cephalopoda*, the most highly organized class of *Mollusca*, characterized by head with 'arms' or tentacles attached and including cuttle-fishes etc.

cĕphalothôr'ăx *n.* (zool.) In some arthropods, part of body formed by fusion of head and thorax (ill. SPIDER).

cėrăm'ĭc *adj.* Of (the art of) pottery. **cėrăm'ĭcs** *n.* Ceramic art. **cĕ'ramĭst** *n.*

Cėrăs'tĭum *n.* Genus of hoary-leaved plants with white flowers.

Cêrb'erus. (Gk myth.) The 3-headed (acc. to Hesiod, 50-headed) watch-dog guarding the entrance to the infernal regions.

cēre *n.* Naked wax-like membrane at base of beak in some birds.

cēr'ėal *adj.* Of corn or edible grain. ~ *n.* (freq. pl.) (Any of) those graminaceous plants cultivated for their seed as human food; an article of food (esp. as breakfast dish) made from cereal. [f. CERES]

cĕrėbĕll'um *n.* The little brain, posterior part of brain, highly developed in mammals and concerned in co-ordination of movement and maintenance of equilibrium (ill. BRAIN).

cĕ'rėbral *adj.* 1. Of the brain or cerebrum; ~ *hemispheres*, the two halves into which the cerebrum is divided longitudinally by a deep fissure; ~ *palsy*: see PALSY. 2. ~ *consonants*, in Sanskrit etc., consonants developed from dentals by retracting tongue and applying its tip to palate.

cĕrėbrā'tion *n.* Working of the brain.

cĕ'rebro- *prefix.* Of the cerebrum; *~-spinal*, of the brain and spinal cord; *~-spinal fluid*, solution of salts and protein filling cavities of brain and spinal cord; *~-spinal meningitis*, inflammation of the meninges of brain and spinal cord.

cĕ'rėbrum *n.* The great brain, a convoluted mass of nervous matter forming the anterior and, in the higher vertebrates, largest part of the brain; in man it fills nearly the whole skull (ill. BRAIN).

cere'cloth (sērk'lŏth, -awth) *n.* Waxed cloth, esp. as winding-sheet; winding-sheet.

cere'ments (sērm-) *n.pl.* Grave-clothes.

cĕrėmōn'ĭal *adj.* With or of ritual or ceremony, formal. ~ *n.* System of rites; formalities proper to any occasion; observance of conventions; book containing the order for rites and ceremonies. **cĕrėmōn'ĭally** *adv.*

cĕrėmōn'ĭous *adj.* Accompanied with rites; according to prescribed or customary formalities; punctilious in observing formalities. **cĕrėmōn'ĭously** *adv.* **cĕrėmōn'ĭousnėss** *n.*

cĕ'rėmony *n.* 1. Outward rite or observance; solemnity; empty form. 2. Usage of courtesy, politeness, or civility; formalities, observance of conventions; *stand upon* ~, insist on punctilious observance of formalities; *Master of Ceremonies*, person superintending forms observed on state or other public occasions.

Cēr'ēs (-z). 1. (Rom. myth.) Goddess of growing vegetation, identified by the Romans with DEMETER and in this later cult worshipped as corn and earth goddess. 2. An asteroid named after the goddess.

ceriph: see SERIF.

cerise' (-ēz *or* -ēs) *n.* & *adj.* Light clear red, cherry-red.

cēr'ĭum *n.* Element of rare-earth group, resembling iron in colour and lustre; symbol Ce, at. no. 85, at. wt 140·12. [discovered in 1803, about the same time as the asteroid CERES and named after it] **cēr'ĭc, cēr'ous** *adjs.*

cēroplăs'tĭc *adj.* Of modelling in wax.

cêrt *n.* (slang) Event or result certain to happen; horse certain to win a race.

cêrt'ain (-tn, -tĭn) *adj.* 1. Settled, fixed, unfailing; unerring, reliable; sure to happen; sure *to* do; indubitable, indisputable. 2. Convinced, confident (*of*, *that*); sure. 3. That might but need not be specified; occas., that it would not be polite to specify; of positive yet restricted amount, degree, etc.; a particular, a definite (person etc.); *for* ~, assuredly.

cêrt'ainly (-tn-) *adv.* 1. Indubitably; infallibly; confidently; admittedly. 2. (in answers) I admit it; of course; no doubt; yes.

cĕrt'ainty (-tn-) *n.* Thing certain or sure; being certain.

cĕrt'ēs (-z) *adv.* (archaic) Assuredly, I assure you.

certif'ĭcate *n.* Document formally attesting a fact, esp. the bearer's status, acquirements, fulfilment of conditions, right to company shares, etc.; *bankrupt's* ~, one stating that he has satisfied legal requirements and may recommence business; *General C~ of Education*, (in U.K.) certificate awarded to successful candidates in examination for school-children of 16 years and over; this examination. **certif'ĭcāte** *v.t.* Furnish with, license by, certificate. **certificā'tion** *n.*

cĕrt'ifȳ *v.t.* 1. Attest formally, declare by certificate; (of doctor etc.) declare by certificate to be insane. 2. Inform certainly, assure. **cĕrtifī'able** *adj.* (esp. of lunatic or lunacy).

cĕrtiorār'ī (-shĭ-) *n.* Writ from superior court, upon complaint that justice has not been done in inferior court, for records of the cause. [L word in original writ]

cĕrt'itūde *n.* Feeling certain, conviction.

cėrul'ėan (-ōō-) *adj.* Deep blue, azure; of the colour of the cloudless sky; ~ *blue*, pigment of this colour prepared from cobalt.

cėrum'ĕn (-ōō-) *n.* The yellow waxy secretion in the external canal of the ear. **cėrum'ĭnous** *adj.*

cēr'use (-ōōs; *or* sėrōōs') *n.* White lead; basic lead carbonate, used as white paint.

Cervăn'tēs (-z), Miguel de (1547–1616). Spanish novelist and dramatist, author of 'Don QUIXOTE' (1605–15).

cĕrv'ical (*or* sĕrvīk'*a*l) *adj.* Of the neck; ~ *vertebrae*, the bones (7 in humans) forming the upper part of the spine (ill. SPINE).

cĕrv'īne *adj.* Of, like, deer.

cĕrv'ix *n.* (pl. *-vīcēs*). (anat.) Neck; neck-like structure.

cesarevitch, -witch[1] = TSAREVICH.

Cėsar'ėwitch[2] (sĭz-). Handicap horse-race of about 2¼ miles, instituted at Newmarket in 1839, and run at the October meeting. [in honour of state visit of the tsarevich who became Alexander II]

cĕss *n.* Tax, levy, rate (now only dial. and in Scotland, Ireland, and India).

cĕssā'tion *n.* Ceasing, pause.

cĕ'ssion (-shn) *n.* Ceding, giving up.

cĕss'pĭt *n.* Midden.

cĕss'pōōl *n.* Well sunk to receive drainage from water-closet etc., retaining solid matter and allowing liquid to escape.

cĕs'toid, -tōde *adj.* & *n.* Ribbon-like (intestinal worm).

Cestr. *abbrev.* (Bishop) of Chester (replacing surname in his signature).

***Cėtā'cėa* n.** Order of marine mammals including whales, dolphins, porpoises, etc. **cėtā'cean** (-shn) *adj.* & *n.* (Member) of the *Cetacea*. **cėtā'ceous** (-sh*u*s) *adj.* [Gk *kētos* whale]

cĕt'erăch (-k) *n.* Genus of ferns with back of fronds thickly covered with scales.

cēt'erĭs pă'rĭbus. Other things being equal. [L]

Cévennes (sāvĕn'). Mountain-range of central France, SE. part of the Massif Central.

Ceylon (sĭlŏn'). Large island in Indian Ocean, near S. point of India; since 1948 a self-governing member of the British Commonwealth; formerly a British colony; capital, Colombo. **Ceylonēse'** (-z) *adj.* & *n.*

Cézanne (sāzăn'), Paul (1839–1906). French painter, central figure of the movement known as Neo-Impressionism.

cf. *abbrev.* Confer (= compare).

C.F. *abbrev.* Chaplain to the Forces.

cg. *abbrev.* Centigram.

C.G. *abbrev.* Coldstream Guards.

C.G.M. *abbrev.* Conspicuous Gallantry Medal.

C.G.S. *abbrev.* Centimetre-gram-second (system of measurement).

C.G.T. *abbrev.* *Confédération Générale du Travail* (= General Confederation of Labour, French equivalent of T.U.C.).

ch, a consonantal digraph, has the sound of *tsh* in native words; of *k* in words taken from Greek; of *sh* in words from mod. French; of (χ), a voiceless postpalatal spirant, in Scottish and Welsh words and in German words after a back vowel; of (ç), a voiceless prepalatal spirant in German words after a front vowel or consonant.

ch., chap. *abbrevs.* Chapter.

C.H. *abbrev.* Companion of Honour.

Chablis (shăb'lē). Small town in Yonne, France; the dry white Burgundy wine made near there.

chaconne (sh*a*kŏn') *n.* Old stately Spanish dance; instrumental composition in 3/4 time with an unchanging ground-bass against which the upper parts are varied (cf. PASSACAGLIA, which it resembles).

Chăd, The. Republic of north-central Africa extending from Lake Chad across the E. Sudan; member of French Community; capital, Fort Lamy.

Chăd'wick, Sir James (1891–). English physicist; famous for his researches on radio-activity and nuclear fission; awarded Nobel Prize for Physics, 1935.

chāfe *v.* 1. Rub (skin etc.) to restore warmth or sensation; rub so as to abrade or injure the surface. 2. Irritate; show irritation, fume, fret. ~ *n.* Rubbing; chafing.

chāf'er *n.* Cockchafer.

chaff (-ah-) *n.* 1. Husks of corn etc. separated by threshing or winnowing; chopped hay and straw for feeding cattle; ~*-cutter*, machine for chopping hay and straw for fodder. 2. Refuse, worthless stuff. 3. Banter, raillery. ~ *v.t.* 1. Chop (straw etc.). 2. Banter.

chăff'er *n.* & *v.* Haggle, bargain.

chăff'inch *n.* Small bird, *Fringilla coelebs*, common in Britain, with blue crown in male and white wing-patches.

chāf'ing-dish *n.* Vessel to hold burning charcoal etc. for heating or keeping warm anything placed upon it; double vessel with outer pan for hot water, used over spirit-lamp etc. for cooking at table.

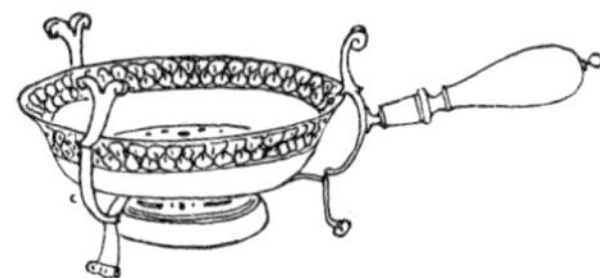

CHAFING-DISH

chagrin (shăgrēn', -ĭn') *n.* Acute disappointment, mortification. ~ *v.t.* Vex acutely, mortify, by thwarting or disappointment.

chain *n.* 1. Strong but flexible string formed of connected series of links. 2. (pl.) Fetters, bonds; confinement, restraint. 3. Personal ornament in form of chain round neck. 4. Connected course, train, or series (of events, objects, mountains, etc.); series of branch businesses. 5. Land-surveyor's measuring rod of 100 jointed iron rods called links; the length of this, 66 ft. 6. (naut.) Contrivance to carry lower shrouds of mast outside ship's side. 7. (chem.) A number of atoms (usu. of carbon) joined in series in a molecule. 8. ~ *armour*, armour of interlaced links or rings, mail (ill. ARMOUR); ~*-bridge*, suspension bridge swung on or by chains; ~*-gang*, gang of convicts chained together at work etc.; ~*-lightning*, (U.S.) forked lightning; ~*-mail*, (erron. for) chain armour; ~*-reaction*, chemical reaction forming intermediate products which react with the original substance and are repeatedly renewed; ~*-shot*, shot consisting of two balls chained together, formerly used in naval warfare to cut ship's rigging; ~*-smoker*, one who lights another cigarette etc. from the stump of the last smoked; ~*-smoking*; ~*-stitch*, embroidery or crochet stitch resembling links of a chain (ill. STITCH); ~ *stores*, series of multiple retail shops belonging to one firm and selling the same goods. ~ *v.t.* Secure, confine, with chain.

chair *n.* 1. Seat for one person; movable, usu. 4-legged, seat with rest for the back, of various forms; ~*-bed*, kind that unfolds to form a bed. 2. Seat, position, of authority, state, or dignity; seat occupied by person presiding at meeting etc.; seat, office, of mayor; seat, office,

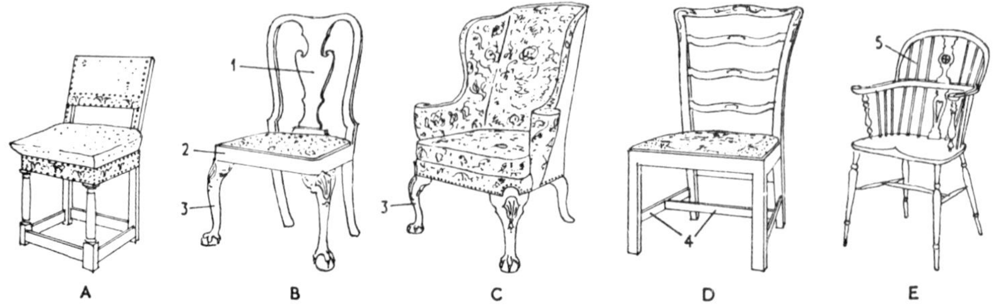

CHAIRS: A. FARTHINGALE. B. QUEEN ANNE. C. WING-CHAIR. D. LADDER-BACK. E. WINDSOR WHEEL-BACK

1. Splat. 2. Seat rail. 3. Cabriole leg. 4. Stretcher. 5. Spindle

of university professor. 3. Iron or steel socket holding rail of railway in place on sleeper (ill. RAIL). 4. (hist.) Sedan. 5. = *electric* ~, chair in which execution by electricity is carried out. ~ *v.* 1. Install in chair of authority. 2. Place in chair etc. and carry aloft in triumph or rejoicing.

chair'man *n.* (fem. *chair'-woman*). 1. Person chosen to preside over meeting, permanent president of committee, board, etc.; *C~ of Committees*, in Houses of Parliament, person presiding instead of Lord Chancellor or Speaker when House is in Committee. 2. (hist.) Wheeler of Bath chair; sedan-bearer. **chair'manship** *n.* Office etc. of chairman of committee.

chaise (shāz) *n.* Pleasure- or travelling-carriage, (esp.) a light open carriage for one or two persons; post-chaise.

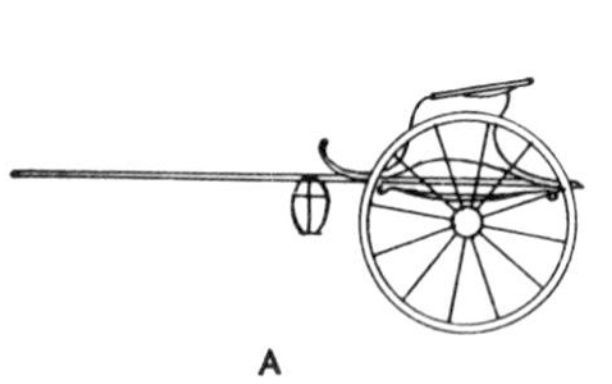

A. CHAISE. B. POST-CHAISE

chaise-longue (shāz-lawngg') *n.* Kind of long low chair with back and arm-rests and seat long enough to support sitter's legs.

chălcĕd'ony (k-) *n.* Precious or semi-precious stone, a cryptocrystalline form of silica with wax-like lustre; including agate, cornelian, onyx, etc.

Chăldē'a (k-). Country of the Chaldeans, freq. identified in the O.T. with Babylonia.

Chăldē'an *adj.* & *n.* (Member) of a race of Semitic Babylonians, originating from Arabia, who settled in the neighbourhood of Ur (Gen. xi. 28) and were later merged with the Babylonians.

Chăldee' (k-) *n.* Term formerly and incorrectly applied to the language of the Aramaic portions of the biblical books of Ezra and Daniel and to the vernacular paraphrases of the O.T. on the assumption that the language was that of the Chaldeans.

chal'dron (kawl-) *n.* Measure for coals, = 36 bushels.

chalet (shăl'ā) *n.* Swiss peasant's wooden house or cottage; villa built in this style; small, usu. wooden, dwelling for holiday-makers.

chăl'ice *n.* Goblet, eucharistic wine-cup; (poet.) flower-cup.

chalk (-awk) *n.* Opaque white soft earthy limestone, consisting largely of calcium carbonate, occurring in deposits of great extent and thickness in SE. England etc., and forming high white cliffs on sea-shore; used for burning into lime, making cement, and for writing, etc. on blackboards or other dark surfaces; coloured preparation of similar texture used for drawing etc.; *by* (*a*) *long* ~(*s*), by far (f. use of chalk to score points in games). ~ *v.t.* Rub, mark, draw, write, etc., with chalk. **chalk'y** *adj.* Abounding in, white as, chalk.

chăll'enge (-j) *n.* 1. Calling to account, esp. sentry's demand for pass-word etc. 2. (law etc.) Exception taken (to a juryman, a vote, etc.). 3. Summons to trial or contest, esp. duel; defiance. ~ *v.t.* 1. Call to account. 2. Take exception to; dispute, deny. 3. Claim (attention, admiration, etc.). 4. Invite to contest, game, or duel; defy. **chăll'enger** *n.*

Châlons (shălawṅ'). Place on the Marne, France, scene of the defeat of the Huns under Attila in A.D. 451 by the Romans and Visigoths.

chalўb'ėate (k-, -*at*) *adj.* (Of spring, mineral water) impregnated with iron salts.

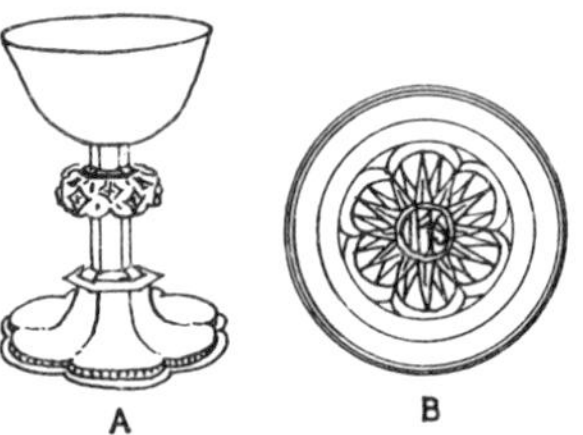

A. CHALICE. B. PATEN

cham (kăm) *n.* *Great C*~, autocrat (used of dominant critic etc., esp. Dr Johnson). [earlier form of KHAN]

chăm'aephȳte (k-) *n.* (bot.) Woody or herbaceous plant with buds less than 25 cm. above soil level.

chām'ber *n.* 1. Room, esp. bedroom (poet. or archaic); (pl.) set of rooms in larger building, esp. an Inn of Court, let separately; (pl.) judge's room for hearing cases etc. not needing to be taken in court. 2. (Hall used by) deliberative or judicial body, one of the houses of a Parliament; ~ *of Commerce*, *Agriculture*, etc.; board formed to protect interests of commerce, agriculture, etc., in district. 3. (also ~*-pot*) Vessel for urine. 4. Cavity in animal body; enclosed space in mechanism, esp. part of gun-bore in which charge is placed; in a revolver, each compartment of breeching containing the charge (ill. PISTOL). 5. *chambermaid*, housemaid in inn etc.; ~*-music*, music fitted for performance in private room, as dist. from concert-room or hall; including music for solo instruments or for small combinations (as quartets, trios, etc.), songs, etc.; *~-concert*, concert of chamber-music; *~ orchestra, organ*, small ones.

chām′berlain[1] (-lĭn) *n.* Officer managing household of sovereign or great noble; officer receiving rents and revenues of corporation or public office; *Lord C~ (of the Household)*, a chief officer of the Royal Household, appointing royal tradesmen, licensing plays for public performance, etc.; *Lord Great C~ of England*, hereditary officer with duties now chiefly ceremonial.

Chām′berlain[2] (-lĭn). Name of a family of English politicians: Joseph ~ (1836–1914), Liberal and Liberal-Unionist, advocate of tariff reform and colonial development; Sir (Joseph) Austen ~ (1863–1937), his son, Liberal-Unionist and Conservative, foreign secretary 1924–9; (Arthur) Neville ~ (1869–1940), half-brother of Austen, Conservative prime minister 1937–40.

chamēl′ėon (k-) *n.* Saurian reptile of the genus *Chamaeleo*, small lizard-like creatures with power of

CHAMELEON

changing colour of skin to suit surroundings, and of living for long periods without food; (fig.) variable or inconstant person. [Gk *khamaileōn*, lit. = 'ground lion']

chăm′fer *n.* Surface produced by bevelling square edge or corner equally on both sides (ill. MOULDING). *~ v.t.* Give chamfer to; channel, flute.

chamois *n.* 1. (shăm′wah) Capriform antelope, *Rupicapra tragus*, found in Alps, Pyrenees, Taurus, and other mountain-ranges of Europe and Asia. 2. (shăm′ĭ) Soft pliable washable leather from skin of goats, sheep, deer, and split hides of other animals.

chăm′omile (k-) *n.* Var. of CAMOMILE.

chămp[1] *v.* Munch (fodder) noisily; bite hard upon (bit); make chewing action or noise.

chămp[2] *n.* Colloq. abbrev. of champion.

champagne (shămpān′) *n.* White wine made in district of Champagne, former province of E. France, esp. the sparkling kind which is bottled before fermentation has ceased.

chăm′paign (-pān) *n.* (Expanse of) open country.

chăm′perty *n.* (law) Offence of assisting a party in a suit in which one is not naturally interested with a view to receiving share of disputed property. **chăm′pertous** *adj.*

chăm′pion *n.* 1. Fighting man, combatant; person who fights, argues, etc., for another or for a cause. 2. Person (esp. boxer, athlete), animal, plant, etc., that has defeated, or been judged superior to, all competitors. **chăm′pionship** *n.* **chăm′pion** *adj.* That is a champion. *~ v.t.* Fight for, maintain the cause of.

champlevé (shahnlevā′) *adj.* & *n.* (Enamel-work) of which the metal ground is hollowed out and the spaces filled with enamel (cf. CLOISONNÉ). [Fr., = 'field removed']

chance (-ahns) *n.* 1. Way in which things fall out; fortune; casual or fortuitous circumstance or occurrence, accident. 2. Possibility, probability, of anything happening. 3. Absence of design or assignable cause, fortuity. 4. *by ~*, as it falls or fell out; without design; *take one's ~*, take what may befall one; seize one's opportunity; *the main ~*, the chance of getting money, one's own interests; *stand a ~*, have a prospect. *~ adj.* Happening by chance, fortuitous. *~ v.* Happen, fall out; (colloq.) risk.

chan′cel (-ah-) *n.* Eastern part of Christian church in which altar stands, reserved for clergy, choir, etc., and freq. screened off from nave (ill. CHURCH). [L *cancelli* lattice-bars]

chan′cellery (-ah-) *n.* Position, staff, department, official residence, of chancellor; office attached to embassy or consulate (now usu. *chancery*).

chan′cellor (-ah-) *n.* 1. *Lord (High) C~, C~ of England*, highest officer of the Crown, presiding in House of Lords, a member of the Cabinet, and the highest judicial functionary in England. 2. *C~ of the Exchequer*, highest finance minister of British Government, who prepares the Budget. 3. *C~ of the Duchy of Lancaster*, representative of king as duke of Lancaster; now, a minister of the Crown, often cabinet minister who does not desire departmental work. 4. *~ of bishop, diocese*, law-officer acting as vicar-general for bishop and holding ecclesiastical courts. 5. *C~ of the Garter* (or other order), officer sealing commissions, mandates, etc. 6. Titular head of a university, usu. honorary, the *Vice-C~* performing the duties. 7. In Germany, Austria, etc., chief minister of State. **chan′cellorship** *n.*

chance-mĕd′ley (-ah-) *n.* (law) Action, esp. homicide, mainly but not entirely unintentional; inadvertency.

chan′cery (-ah-) *n.* 1. The Lord Chancellor's Court, a division of the High Court of Justice, formerly a separate court of equity for cases with no remedy in the common-law courts; (U.S. etc.) a court of equity; office of public records, archives; *in ~*, (boxing) with head held under opponent's arm to be pummelled (from the tenacity with which the old Court of Chancery held anything and the certainty of cost and loss). 2. Office attached to embassy or consulate.

chancre (shănk′*er*) *n.* Venereal ulcer.

chan′cy (-ah-) *adj.* Uncertain, risky.

chăndelier′ (sh-) *n.* Ornamental branched hanging support for a number of candles or other lights.

CHANDELIER

chand′ler (-ah-) *n.* Dealer in candles, oil, soap, paint, and groceries; *corn-~*, dealer in corn etc.; *ship-~*, dealer in cordage, canvas, etc. **chănd′lery** *n.*

chānge (-nj) *n.* 1. Alteration; substitution of one for another; variation, variety. 2. What may be substituted for another of the same kind, esp. in *~ of clothes* etc. 3. Lower coins or notes given for higher one; money returned as balance of that tendered in payment. 4. Arrival of moon at fresh phase (prop. only at new moon). 5. (bell-ringing) Order in which peal of bells is or may be rung; *ring the changes*, go through all the changes in ringing a peal of bells; vary ways of putting or doing thing. 6. *C~*, place where merchants meet, Exchange. *~ v.* 1. Take another instead of; resign, get rid of, *for*; give or get smaller or foreign coin for; put on different clothes; go from one to another; change trains; give and receive, exchange. 2. Make or become different; *~ one's mind*, change one's purpose or opinion; (of moon) arrive at fresh phase, esp. become new moon. 3. *~ up, down*, (in motor driving) change to a higher, lower, gear. **chānge′ful, chānge′lėss** *adjs.*

chānge′able (-j*a*-) *adj.* Irregular, inconstant.

chānge′ling (-jl-) *n.* Thing or child substituted for another by stealth, esp. elf-child thus left by fairies.

chănn'el[1] *n.* 1. Natural or artificial bed of running water; comparatively narrow piece of water joining two large pieces; *the C~*, the English Channel. 2. Tube or tubular passage for fluids. 3. Course in which anything moves, direction; medium of transmission, communication, exchange, etc. 4. Groove; flute. ~ *v.t.* Form channel(s) in, groove; cut out (way etc.).

chănn'el[2] *n.* (naut.) Broad thick plank projecting horizontally from ship's side to broaden base for shrouds.

Chănn'el Islands. A group of islands off the NW. coast of France, of which the largest are Jersey, Guernsey, and Alderney; the only portions of the dukedom of Normandy now belonging to England, to which they have been attached since the Conquest.

Chansons de Geste (shahṅsawṅ' de zhĕst). French historical verse romances, mostly connected with Charlemagne, composed in the 11th–13th centuries.

chant (-ah-) *n.* 1. Song. 2. Short musical passage in two or more phrases each beginning with 'reciting note', for singing to unmetrical words (psalms, canticles). 3. Measured monotonous song, musical recitation of words; singsong intonation. ~ *v.* Sing; utter musically; intone, sing to a chant; ~ *praises of*, praise constantly.

chan'ter (-ah-) *n.* (esp.) Pipe of bagpipe, with finger-holes, on which melody is played (ill. BAGPIPE).

chăn'tĭcleer *n.* The domestic cock.

chant'ry (-ah-) *n.* Endowment for priest(s) to sing masses for founder's soul; priests, chapel, so endowed.

chan'ty (-ah-), **shăn'ty** *n.* Sailors' song, sung while heaving, pulling, etc., with solo by *chantyman* alternating with chorus. [perh. f. Fr. *chantez* sing (imper.)]

chā'ŏs (k-) *n.* 1. Formless void, 'great deep' of primordial matter, abyss from which cosmos was evolved. 2. Utter confusion. **chāŏt'ĭc** *adj.* **chāŏt'ĭcally** *adv.*

chăp[1] *n.* Crack, fissure, in earth etc., esp. fissure in skin caused by exposure to frost, cold wind, etc. ~ *v.* Crack, cause to crack, in fissures.

chap[2], **chŏp** *n.* (pl.) Jaws, esp. of beasts; cheeks; (sing.) lower jaw or half of cheek, esp. of pig as food; ~*-fallen*, with jaw hanging down, dejected, dispirited.

chăp[3] *n.* (colloq.) Man, boy, fellow.

chăparrăl' *n.* (U.S.) Dense tangled brushwood, esp. such as abounds on poor soil in Mexico and Texas.

chăp-bo͝ok *n.* Small pamphlet of popular tales, ballads, tracts, or other specimen of popular literature of the kind formerly hawked by chapmen.

chāpe *n.* 1. Metal plate or mounting of scabbard or sheath, esp. at point (ill. SWORD). 2. Part of buckle by which it is fastened to belt etc.

chăp'el *n.* 1. Place of Christian worship other than parish church or cathedral; esp. one attached to private house or institution; oratory in larger building with altar, esp. compartment or cell of cathedral etc. separately dedicated and with its own altar; place of public worship of established Church subordinate to and dependent on parish church; ~ *of ease*, one built for parishioners living far from parish church. 2. In England and Wales, Nonconformist place of worship. 3. Chapel service, attendance in chapel. 4. Printers' workshop, printing-office; meeting or association of journeyman-printers for keeping order, settling price-disputes, etc.; *father of the* ~, president of this. [L *cappella* dim. of *cappa* cape; first chapel was sanctuary in which St. Martin's sacred cloak was kept]

chăp'elry *n.* District served by chapel.

chăp'erōn (sh-) *n.* Married or elderly woman accompanying young unmarried woman for sake of propriety on public occasions etc. ~ *v.t.* Act as chaperon to. **chăp'eronage** *n.* [Fr., orig. sense 'hood']

chăp'lain (-lĭn) *n.* Priest of chapel, clergyman officiating in private chapel of sovereign or institution, on board ship or for regiment etc. **chăp'laincy** *n.*

chăp'lĕt *n.* 1. Wreath of flowers, leaves, gems, etc., for head. 2. String of beads for counting prayers, one-third of length of rosary; string of beads as necklace. 3. Anything resembling string of beads; (archit.) bead-moulding.

chăp'man *n.* (pl. *-men*). (hist.) Pedlar, hawker.

chăps *n.* Stout leather trousers without seat worn by horsemen in western States of U.S. as protection against thorns and bushes. [Short for Mex. Span. *chaparejos*]

chăp'ter *n.* 1. Main division of a book or treatise (abbrev. *ch.*, *chap.*, *cap.*, or *c.*); Act of Parliament numbered as part of proceedings of one session (thus 5 & 6 Will. IV, cap. 62 = session of 5th and 6th years of William IV's reign, 62nd chapter, i.e. Statutory Declarations Act 1835); (fig.) limited subject, piece of narrative, etc.; ~ *and verse*, exact reference; ~ *of accidents*, series of misfortunes. 2. General meeting or assembly of canons of cathedral or members of religious or knightly order for consultation and transaction of affairs; body of persons constituting this, esp. canons of cathedral; ~*-house*, building attached to cathedral, monastery, etc. for meetings of the chapter (ill. MONASTERY).

chār[1] *n.* (colloq.) Charwoman. ~ *v.i.* Act as charwoman.

chār[2] *v.* Burn to charcoal; scorch; blacken with fire.

chār[3] *n.* Trout of genus *Salvelinus*, found in mountain lakes.

char-à-banc (shă'rabăng) *n.* Long vehicle, with rows of seats looking forward, for holiday excursions; motor-coach.

chă'racter (k-) *n.* 1. Distinctive mark, brand; graphic sign or symbol, esp. graphic symbol standing for sound, syllable, or notion, used in writing or printing; handwriting, printing; cabbalistic sign or emblem. 2. Characteristic, esp. (pl.) distinguishing features of species or genus; sum of distinguishing features of individual etc., mental and moral qualities; such qualities strongly developed or strikingly displayed; reputation, (good) repute. 3. Description or report of person's qualities; esp. formal testimonial given by employer. 4. Personage, personality; imaginary person created by novelist or dramatist or played by actor; status, position; (colloq.) odd or eccentric person; ~ *actor*, one who plays eccentric characters. **chă'racterlĕss** *adj.*

chăracterĭs'tĭc (k-) *adj.* & *n.* 1. Typical, distinctive (trait, mark, quality). 2. (math.) Whole number in logarithm. **chăracterĭs'tĭcally** *adv.*

chă'racterīze (k-) *v.t.* Describe character of; describe *as*; be characteristic of, impart character to. **chăracterīzā'tion** *n.*

charade (sharahd') *n.* Kind of riddle in which each syllable of word to be guessed is enigmatically described or dramatically represented, freq. in dumb show. [Provençal *charrado* chatter]

chār'coal *n.* The black residue of partly burnt wood, bones, coal, etc., porous, capable of reduction to powder, and (when pure) consisting wholly of carbon; ~ *burner*, one employed in manufacture of charcoal by burning wood.

chārd *n.* 1. Seakale beet, variety of beet with large white succulent leaf-stalks used like seakale and leaves used like spinach. 2. (pl.) Late-summer blanched leaves of artichoke or other vegetable.

chārge *n.* 1. Load; quantity of propellant loaded into a gun; quantity of explosive for blasting etc.; quantity of anything which receptacle, piece of mechanism, etc., can receive, bear, etc., at one time. 2. Electrical energy present in a proton or electron; such energy imparted to an object; accumulation of chemical energy in storage battery etc. available for conversion into electrical energy; NEGATIVE, POSITIVE, ~: see these words. 3. (her.) Device, bearing. 4. Figurative load; anything burdensome; responsibility, care, custody; task, duty; thing or person entrusted to another. 5. Pecuniary burden; price for services or goods; expenses; liability to pay money laid upon person or estate. 6. Precept, mandate, order; official instruction by judge to jury, bishop to clergy, etc. 7. Accusation, esp. that upon which prisoner is brought up for trial. 8. Impetuous attack; (mil.) signal for charge. 9. *~-hand*, workman, shop assistant, etc., in charge of others; *~-sheet*, police-station record of persons charged, the charge against them, etc. ~ *v*. 1. Load; fill to full or proper extent; (her.) place bearing on (escutcheon etc.); fill *with*; impart electrical energy to (object), accumulate charge in (battery etc.). 2. Burden, entrust, *with*; command, order, enjoin; exhort or instruct formally or officially. 3. Bring accusation against. 4. Subject or make liable to pecuniary obligation or liability; demand as price or sum (*for*). 5. Make violent onset, attack or assail impetuously.

char̂ge′able (-ja-) *adj*. (esp.) Liable to be made an expense (*to*); proper to be added to (account etc.).

chargé (d'affaires) (shar̂zh′ā dăfar̂′) *n*. Deputy ambassador; ambassador at minor court.

char̂′ger[1] *n*. (esp.) Horse ridden in charging enemy; horse ridden by officer in the field.

char̂′ger[2] *n*. (archaic) Large flat dish.

chă′rĭot *n*. Stately vehicle, triumphal car; 18th-c. light 4-wheeled carriage with back seats

ROMAN CHARIOT

only; low 2-wheeled car used in ancient warfare and racing. **chărioteer′** *n*. **chă′rĭot** *v.t.* Carry or convey in a chariot.

chă′rĭtable *adj*. Liberal in giving to the poor; connected with such giving; inclined to judge favourably of persons, acts, etc. **chă′rĭtably** *adv*. **chă′rĭtableness** *n*.

chă′rĭty *n*. 1. Christian love of fellow men; kindness, affection. 2. Disposition to judge leniently of character, acts, etc., of others. 3. Beneficence, liberality to the poor, almsgiving, alms; bequest, foundation or institution for the benefit of others, esp. the poor or helpless; *C~ Commission(ers)*, board created by Charity Trust Act of 1853 to control administration of charitable trusts.

char̂′ivar̂i (sh-) *n*. 1. Hubbub of various discordant sounds. 2. Name of French comic paper from which the second title of 'Punch' was taken. [Fr. wd for serenade of pans, trays, etc., to unpopular person]

char̂l′atan (sh-) *n*. Impostor in medicine, quack; empty pretender to knowledge or skill, pretentious impostor. **char̂l′atanism, char̂l′atanry** *ns*. [It. *ciarlare* patter]

Charlemagne (shar̂l′emān). Charles the Great (742–814), king of the Franks; crowned by the Pope as emperor of the West, 800 (see also CAROLINGIAN).

Char̂les (-lz). Name of two kings of Gt Britain: *Charles I* (1600–49), succeeded his father James I in 1625; his conflict with Parliament led to the Civil War; beheaded in front of Whitehall, 30th Jan. 1649; *Charles II* (1630–85), son of Charles I, became king at the Restoration, 1660.

Char̂les V (-lz) (1500–58). King of Spain 1516–56 and emperor of the Holy Roman Empire 1519–56 during the Reformation; abdicated the Imperial crown in favour of his brother Ferdinand and the crown of Spain in favour of his son Philip II.

Char̂les XII (-lz) (1682–1718). King of Sweden 1697–1718; a great military commander; defeated Peter the Great at Narva, 1700, but was in turn totally defeated at Poltava, 1709; was killed at Frederikshald in a war with Norway.

Char̂les the Great = CHARLEMAGNE.

Charles's Wain. The constellation *Ursa Major*, the Great Bear, also called the Plough. [*Charles* = CHARLEMAGNE. Orig. called the Wain (i.e. wagon) of Arcturus (a neighbouring star); Arcturus was confused with Arturus, King ARTHUR, who is associated with Charlemagne in legend]

char̂leston (-lz-) *n*. A dance characterized by side-kicks from the knee. ~ *v.i.* Dance this. [*Charleston*, city of S. Carolina]

char̂l′ock *n*. Wild mustard, *Sinapis arvensis*, a yellow-flowered annual weed of arable land.

char̂l′otte (sh-) *n*. Dish of stewed apples or other fruit covered with bread, sponge-cake, etc., and baked; ~ *russe*, whipped cream or custard enclosed in sponge-cake or sponge-biscuits.

char̂m *n*. 1. Word(s), act, or object having or supposed to have magic or occult power or influence; talisman; amulet; trinket worn on watch-chain etc. 2. Quality, attribute, feature, etc., exciting love or admiration; (pl.) beauty. ~ *v.t.* Bewitch, influence, by or as by charm or magic; endow with magic power or virtue; captivate, delight; *charmed*, bewitched; possessed of magic power or influence; protected, fortified, by a spell or charm. **char̂m′er** *n*. (esp.) Beautiful woman (now joc. or archaic). **char̂m′ing** *adj*. Fascinating; very pleasing, delightful. **char̂m′ingly** *adv*.

charmeuse (shar̂mẽrz′) *n*. Soft smooth silk dress-fabric with satin surface.

char̂n′el-house *n*. House or vault in which dead bodies or bones are piled.

Char̂′on (k-). (Gk myth.) The ferryman who conveyed the souls of the dead across the Styx to Hades.

char̂p′oy *n*. Light Indian bedstead.

char̂r *n*. Small red-bellied trout of genus *Salvelinus*, found in lakes and mountain streams of Wales and N. England.

char̂t *n*. 1. Map, esp. one for navigators, showing depth of sea, rocks, channels, coasts, anchorages, etc. 2. Record (by means of curves etc. on graph) of fluctuations of temperature, prices, population, etc.; any sheet with information arranged in tabular form. ~ *v.t.* Make chart of, map.

char̂t′er *n*. 1. Written grant of privileges, rights, etc., by sovereign or legislature, esp. creating or incorporating borough, university, or other corporation. 2. Written instrument, contract, etc., esp. conveying landed property; charter-party. 3. Privilege; publicly conceded right; *Great C~*, see MAGNA CHARTA; *People's C~*, the document published 8th May 1838, embodying demands of the CHARTISTS under 6 headings: adult male suffrage, vote by ballot, annual Parliaments, payment of members of Parliament, equal electoral distribution, and abolition of property qualification; *~-party*, charter between owners and merchants for hire of ships and transportation of cargo. ~ *v.t.* 1. Grant charter to; privilege, license. 2. Hire (ship) by charter-party; hire (vehicle etc.); *chartered accountant*, one qualified under rules of Institute of Accountants, which received royal charter in 1880. **char̂t′erer** *n*.

Char̂t′erhouse. Orig. one of the houses of the Carthusian Order, near Smithfield, London, converted into an alms-house and school by Sir Thomas Sutton; the school, one of the English public schools, has now been removed to Godalming, Surrey. [Fr. *Chartreuse* CARTHUSIAN house]

Char̂t′ist *n*. Member of political reforming body, chiefly of working classes, active 1837–48, whose demands were embodied in the *People's Charter* (see CHARTER). **Char̂t′ism** *n*.

Chartreuse, the Grande (grahn̆d shar̂trẽrz′). The chief Carthusian monastery, near Grenoble. **chartreuse′** *n*. 1. Green or yellow liqueur of brandy and aromatic herbs, made by monks of

Grande Chartreuse. 2. Colour of green chartreuse, pale apple green. [*Chatrousse*, place of the first monastery]

chart'ūlary (k-) *n.* = CARTULARY.

char'woman (-wŏŏ-) *n.* Woman hired by the day or hour for house-work.

char'y *adj.* Cautious, wary; fastidious, shy; careful (*of*); frugal, sparing (*of*).

Charyb'dis (k-). (Gk legend) A dangerous whirlpool in a narrow channel (later identified with the Strait of Messina, where there is no whirlpool), opposite the cave where the sea-monster SCYLLA devoured sailors who tried to pass between.

Chas. *abbrev.* Charles.

chāse[1] (-s) *n.* 1. Pursuit; (*the* sport of) hunting. 2. Hunting-ground; unenclosed park-land (also *chace*). 3. Hunted animal or pursued ship, quarry. 4. (hist.) Chase-guns of a ship; part of ship where chase-ports are (see below). 5. (tennis) 2nd impact of ball opponent has failed or declined to return; this stroke is not scored until opponent has tried to 'better' it by causing his ball to rebound nearer the end-wall. 6. *~-gun*, (hist.) a gun trained through one of the *~-ports*, ports in the bows or through the stern; such guns were of use only when pursuing or being pursued. ~ *v.t.* Pursue; drive *from, out of*, etc. **chās'er** *n.* (esp.) 1. Hunter, pursuer. 2. Horse trained for steeple-chasing. 3. Ship pursuing another; (hist.) chase-gun. 4. (U.S.) Fighter aircraft. 5. Small drink of spirits after coffee, tobacco, etc.; small drink of water or other mild drink after spirits. 6. (colloq.) Letter sent as reminder of previous one.

chāse[2] (-s) *n.* Part of gun enclosing bore (ill. CANNON); groove or trench cut to receive pipe etc.

chāse[3] (-s) *n.* (printing) Iron frame holding composed type for page or sheet (ill. PRINT).

chāse[4] (-s) *v.t.* Engrave (metal), esp. with ornament.

chasm (kăzm) *n.* Deep fissure, cleft, or gap; break, hiatus; wide and profound difference of feelings, interests, etc.

chassé (shăs'ā) *n.* & *v.i.* (Make) gliding sideways step in dancing.

chassepot (shăs'pō) *n.* French army breech-loading rifle of the war of 1870. [inventor's name]

chassis (shăs'ĭs *or* -ē) *n.* (pl. same) Base-frame of gun-carriage; base-frame of motor-vehicle, aeroplane, etc., with its engine, as dist. from the body or coach-work (ill. MOTOR).

chāste *adj.* Pure from unlawful sexual intercourse, virtuous, continent; undefiled, pure; decent; chastened, modest, free from excess, pure in artistic or literary style. **chāste'ly** (-tl-) *adv.* **chās'tity** *n.*

chasten (-āsn) *v.t.* 1. Discipline, correct by suffering. 2. Make chaste in style etc., refine; temper, subdue.

chăstīse' (-z) *v.t.* Punish; beat. **chăs'tisement** (-zm-) *n.*

chăs'ūble (-z-) *n.* Sleeveless vestment worn over alb and stole by celebrant at Mass or Eucharist (ill. VESTMENT).

chăt[1] *n* & *v.i.* (Indulge in) familiar and easy talk. **chătt'y** *adj.* **chătt'ĭly** *adv.* **chătt'inėss** *n.*

chăt[2] *n.* Any of various birds, chiefly warblers; esp. stone-chat and whin-chat.

château (shăt'ō) *n.* (pl. *-x*, pr. -z). Castle, large mansion or country house, in France.

Chateaubriand (shatōbrē'ahṅ), François René, Vicomte de (1768–1848). One of the pioneers of the French romantic movement; author of 'Le Génie du Christianisme' (1802) and several romances.

chăt'ėlaine (sh-) *n.* 1. Mistress of castle or country house. 2. Chain(s) holding keys, watch, scissors, etc., formerly worn hanging from woman's girdle or belt.

Chăt'ham (-*tam*), Earl of: see PITT.

chătt'el *n.* (law) Property of every kind except real estate; (pl.) goods, possessions; (rhet.) slave.

chătt'er *v.i.* 1. (Of birds) utter rapid series of short notes, esp. of sounds approaching those of human voice. 2. (Of persons) talk quickly, incessantly, foolishly, or inopportunely. 3. (Of teeth etc.) rattle together. ~ *n.* Sound of chattering; incessant trivial talk; *chatterbox*, talkative child; *chatterbug*, (orig. U.S. slang) person given to indiscreet talk.

Chătt'erton, Thomas (1752–70). English poet who fabricated a number of poems purporting to be the work of an imaginary 15th-c. Bristol poet, Thomas Rowley.

Chau'cer, Geoffrey (1340?–1400). English poet, author of the 'Canterbury Tales'. **Chaucēr'ian** *adj.* After the manner of Chaucer.

chauffeur (shōf'*er*, shōfēr') *n.*, **chauffeuse'** (-ērz') *n. fem.* Paid driver of private motor vehicle.

chaulmōōg'ra oil *n.* Vegetable oil of nauseous taste obtained from seeds of the Burmese tree *Taraktogenos kurzii*, and used in treatment of leprosy etc.

chautauq'ua *n.* & *adj.* (Of) the system of home study originating with summer schools held at Chautauqua, in New York State; of the organization resulting from this, chartered in 1871: educational or religious meeting of the summer-school type.

chauv'ĭnism (shō-) *n.* Bellicose patriotism. **chauv'ĭnist** *adj.* & *n.* **chauvĭnis'tic** *adj.* [f. Nicolas *Chauvin*, French veteran soldier of First Republic and Empire whose demonstrative loyalty was celebrated and at length ridiculed]

chaw *n.* & *v.* (now vulgar) Chew; *~'-bacon*, (contempt.) country clown, bumpkin.

Ch.B. *abbrev.* *Chirurgiae Baccalaureus* (= Bachelor of Surgery).

Ch. Ch. *abbrev.* Christ Church (Oxford).

cheap *adj.* Inexpensive; costing less than the usual price, rate, etc.; worth more than its cost; costing little trouble, labour, etc.; worthless; made light of, brought into contempt by being made too familiar; *cheap'jack*, hawker at fairs etc., (as adj.) shoddy. **cheap'ly** *adv.* **cheap'nėss** *n.* **cheap** *adv.* At low price, at small expense, cheaply; easily,

cheap'en *v.* Haggle for (archaic); make or become cheap, depreciate.

cheat *n.* 1. Fraud, deception, imposition. 2. Swindler; deceiver, impostor. ~ *v.* Deceive, trick (*out of* something); deal fraudulently; beguile (time, fatigue, etc.). **cheat'ers** *n.pl.* (U.S. slang) Spectacles.

chĕck[1] *n.* 1. (chess) Position of king when exposed to attack by one of opponent's men; if there is no escape from *check* it is *checkmate* and the game is over. 2. Sudden arrest in career or onward course; rebuff, repulse; stop in progress of hounds through failure of scent; sudden stoppage or pause. 3. Restraint on action or conduct; (mus.) part of pianoforte action fixed at back of key to prevent hammer from retouching strings (ill. PIANO). 4. Control securing accuracy, agreement, etc.; token, ticket, of identification for left luggage, coat left in cloakroom, etc.; (U.S.) counter used in card-games; *cash in one's checks*, see CASH. ~ *v.* 1. Threaten opponent's king at chess. 2. Suddenly arrest motion of; (of hounds) stop on losing scent. 3. Restrain, curb. 4. Test (figures etc.) by comparison etc., examine accuracy of. 5. *~-rein*, rein connecting driving-rein of one horse to bit of the other horse; rein preventing horse from lowering head; *~-strap*, strap of helmet etc., under chin; *~-weigher, -weighman*, at collieries, man who in workmen's interest checks weight of coal sent up. [OF. *eschec*, f. Arab., f. Pers. *shāh* king]

chĕck[2] *n.* Pattern of cross-lines forming small squares, like chess-board; fabric woven or printed with this. **chĕcked** (-kt) *adj.*

chĕck[3] *n.* Variant (chiefly U.S.) of CHEQUE.

chĕck'er *n.* & *v.* Var. spelling (chiefly U.S.) of CHEQUER; *checkers*, (pl.) draughts; *~-board*, draught-board.

chĕck'māte' *n.* 1. (chess) Position in which king cannot be extricated from check, move which brings this about. 2. Final defeat; deadlock. ~ *v.t.* Give checkmate to; arrest or defeat utterly, discomfit. [OF. *eschec mat* (see CHECK[1]) f. Arab. *shāh māta* king is dead]

Chĕdd′ar. Village near Mendip Hills, Somerset; kind of cheese orig. made there.

cheek *n.* 1. Side-wall of mouth, side of face below eye; *~-bone*, bone forming lower boundary of eye-orbit. 2. Saucy speech, impudence; cool confidence, effrontery. 3. Side-post of door etc.; (pl.) jaws of vice; side pieces of various parts of machines arranged in lateral pairs. *~ v.t.* (colloq.) Address saucily or impudently.

cheek′y *adj.* Impudent; saucy. **cheek′ĭly** *adv.* **cheek′inėss** *n.*

cheep *v.i.* & *n.* (Utter) shrill feeble note as of young bird.

cheer *n.* 1. Shout of encouragement or applause; *cheers!*, int. used in drinking person's health or saying good-bye; *three cheers*, successive united hurrahs; *~-oh*, said on parting. 2. Frame of mind (only in phrases as *be of good ~*). 3. (archaic) Food. *~ v.* 1. Comfort, gladden; *~ up*, comfort, be comforted. 2. Incite, urge *on*, by shouts etc. 3. Applaud; shout for joy.

cheer′ful *adj.* Contented, in good spirits; pleasant; willing, not reluctant. **cheer′fully** *adv.* **cheer′fulnėss** *n.*

cheer′lėss *adj.* Dull, gloomy, dreary, miserable. **cheer′lėssly** *adv.* **cheer′lėssnėss** *n.*

cheerĭō′ *int.* (slang) Parting exclamation of encouragement.

cheer′lў *adv.* (naut.) Heartily, with a will.

cheer′y *adj.* Lively, in good spirits, genial. **cheer′ĭly** *adv.* **cheer′inėss** *n.*

cheese[1] (-z) *n.* 1. Food made of the curd of milk, separated from the whey and pressed into a close mass; mass of this, usu. wheel-shaped, cylindrical, or globular, with a hardened outer layer or rind. 2. Mass of pomace or apple pulp crushed together like a cheese in cider-making; conserve of fruit of the consistency of cream cheese. 3. Heavy wooden disc used in skittles. 4. *~-cake*, tart of pastry filled with mixture of curds, sugar, etc.; *~-cloth*, thin cotton cloth (of the kind) in which curds are pressed for cheese; *cheese′monger*, dealer in cheese, butter, etc.; *~-paring*, stingy; stinginess; *~-plate*, small plate used for cheese after dinner; *~-straws*, thin strips of pastry flavoured with cheese. **chees′y** *adj.*

cheese[2] (-z) *v.* (slang) *Cheese it!*, stop, have done, cease.

cheet′ah *n.* The hunting leopard, *Cynaelurus jubatus*, tamed and used for hunting antelopes etc. in India [Sansk. *chitraka* speckled]

chĕf (sh-) *n.* Male head cook.

chef-d'œuvre (shādêr′vr) *n.* (pl. *chefs-*, same pr.). Masterpiece.

Cheka (chĕk′*a*, chĕkah′). (hist.) Organization set up in Russia in 1918 for the secret investigation of counter-revolutionary activities; superseded in 1922 by the O.G.P.U. (see G.P.U.). [*che*, *ka*, Russ. names of initial letters of *Ch*rezvychaynaya *K*ommissiya, Extraordinary Commission]

Chekhov (chĕχ′ŏf), Anton Pavlovich (1860–1904). Russian dramatist and novelist, author of 'The Seagull', 'Uncle Vanya', 'The Cherry Orchard', and other plays, and of numerous short stories.

chel′a[1] (chā-) *n.* (Buddhism) Novice qualifying for initiation; disciple; pupil.

chēl′a[2] (kē-) *n.* (pl. *-lae*). The prehensile claw of crabs, lobsters, scorpions, etc.

Chĕll′ėan (sh-) *adj.* Of the earliest palaeolithic period in Europe, as represented by flint implements found at Chelles, Seine-et-Marne, France.

Chĕl′sea (-sĭ). Borough of SW. London associated with artists and men of letters; *Sage of ~*, Thomas CARLYLE; *~ china*, porcelain made at a factory in Chelsea (*c* 1745–84); *~ Hospital*, home for veteran soldiers (*~ Pensioners*) founded by Charles II.

chĕm′ĭcal (k-) *adj.* Of, made by, relating to, chemistry; *~ warfare*, use in war of chemical substances other than explosives, esp. poison gases, for purpose of injuring the enemy. *~ n.* Substance obtained by or used in chemical processes; *heavy ~s*, bulk chemicals used in industry and agriculture (properly only of manufactured chemicals). **chĕm′ĭcally** *adv.*

chemin de fer (shemăn de fâr) *n.* Form of baccarat. [Fr., = 'railway']

chemise (shĭmēz′) *n.* Woman's undergarment worn next skin.

chemisĕtte′ (shĕmĭz-) *n.* Bodice with upper part like chemise; lace etc. insertion at neck of dress.

chĕm′ĭst (k-) *n.* 1. Person skilled in chemistry. 2. Dealer in medical drugs, pharmacist.

chĕm′ĭstry (k-) *n.* Science of the elements and their laws of combination and behaviour under various conditions; *applied* or *practical ~*, art of utilizing this knowledge; *organic ~*, formerly chemistry of substances found in organic structures; now, chemistry of compounds of carbon, whether natural or synthetic; *inorganic ~*, chemistry of the elements other than carbon; *physical ~*, study of the physical aspects of chemistry.

chĕmothĕ′rapy (k-) *n.* Treatment of disease by chemical means.

chenille (shĭnēl′) *n.* Yarn with pile protruding all round it; fabric with weft of this. [Fr., = 'hairy caterpillar']

chĕque (-k), (U.S.) **chĕck** *n.* Written order to banker to pay sum of money on drawer's account to bearer or named person; *crossed ~*: see CROSS, *v.* sense 3; *~ book*, book of stamped and engraved forms for drawing cheques, issued to customer of bank.

chĕq′uer (-k*er*) *n.* 1. (pl.) Chess-board as inn-sign. 2. Chequered pattern. *~ v.t.* Divide or mark like chess-board with squares, esp. of alternating colours; diversify, variegate.

Chĕq′uers (-k*erz*). A Tudor mansion near Princes Risborough, Buckinghamshire, presented to the nation in 1917 by Lord and Lady Lee of Fareham to serve as a country seat of the prime minister of England.

chĕ′rĭsh *v.t.* Foster, nurse; value, keep in the memory or heart, cling to.

Chĕrokee′ *adj.* & *n.* (Member) of a tribe of N. Amer. Indians formerly occupying a large part of southern U.S.

chėrōōt′ (sh-) *n.* Thin, untapered, dark-coloured cigar of the kind made in southern India and Manilla; any cigar open at both ends.

chĕ′rry *n.* A stone-fruit, the pulpy drupe of certain species of *Prunus*, esp. of the cultivated tree, *P. cerasus*; the tree bearing this; cherry-wood; *~ brandy*, dark-red liqueur of brandy in which cherries have been steeped; *~-pie*, garden heliotrope; *~-red*, colour of ripe red cherries. *~ adj.* Cherry-red.

Chêrs′onēse (k-, -s). The Thracian peninsula W. of the Hellespont. [Gk *khersos nēsos* dry island]

chêrt *n.* (geol.) Form of amorphous silica found in several varieties, e.g. flint.

chĕ′rub *n.* 1. (pl. *-im*) One of the 2nd order of angels (next below seraphim), gifted esp. with knowledge. 2. (pl. *-s*) Representation of this in art, usu. as a winged child, or child's head with wings and no body; beautiful or innocent child. **cheru′bĭc** (-ōō-) *adj.* [Heb. *k'rūb*]

chêrv′ĭl *n.* Garden pot-herb, *Anthriscus cerefolium*, with pinnately divided leaves used to flavour salads, soups, etc.

Ches. *abbrev.* Cheshire.

Chĕs′apeake Bay. A large inlet, about 200 miles long, between Maryland and Virginia, U.S.

Chĕsh′ire (-sh*er*). English county of N. Midlands, on Welsh border and Irish Sea; *grin like a ~ cat*, grin broadly (explained as ref. to Cheshire cheeses made in shape of cat, or to lion rampant on *~* inn-signs); *~ cheese*, kind of cheese made orig. in Cheshire; *~ Cheese*, tavern in Mitre Court, Fleet Street, London, famous as the haunt of Dr Johnson.

chĕss *n.* Game played by two persons on chequered board divided into 64 squares, each player having 16 pieces or 'men' (a king, a queen, 2 bishops, 2 knights, 2 castles, and 8 pawns), the object being to CHECKMATE the opponent's king; *~-board*, the board on which this game is played; *chess′man*, one of the pieces used in the game. [see CHECK[1]] *(Illustration, p. 134.)*

chĕst *n.* 1. Large strong box;

box for sailor's belongings. 2. Treasury, coffer, of institution; fund kept in this. 3. Case of some commodity, esp. tea. 4. ~ *of drawers*, frame with set of drawers. 5. Part of human or animal's body enclosed by ribs and breast-bone, and containing heart and lungs; *~-note*, *-voice*, note, voice of lowest register; *~-protector*, flannel etc. worn on chest as protection against cold; *~-register*, the lowest register of the voice.

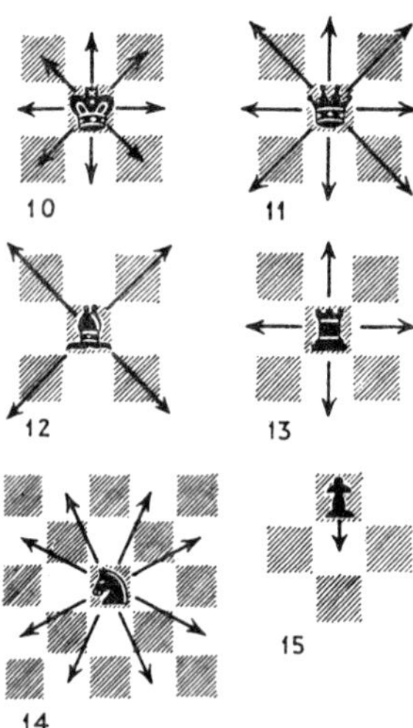

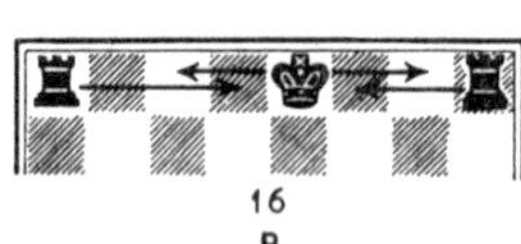

CHESS: A. BOARD AND MEN. B. MOVES

A. 1. Queen's Castle or Rook. 2. Queen's Knight. 3. Queen's Bishop. 4. Queen. 5. King. 6. King's Bishop. 7. King's Knight. 8. King's Castle or Rook. 9. Pawn. B. 10. King. 11. Queen. 12. Bishop. 13. Castle. 14. Knight. 15. Pawn. 16. Castling to left and right

Chĕs'terfield[1], Philip Dormer Stanhope, 4th Earl of (1694–1773). English statesman and diplomatist, chiefly remembered for his 'Letters' to his son.

CHESTS: A. CHEST OR COFFER. B. CHEST OF DRAWERS WITH SERPENTINE FRONT. C. TALLBOY

A. 1. Stile. 2. Rail. 3. Panel. B. 4. Plinth. 5. Canted corner

chĕs'terfield[2] *n.* 1. Kind of overcoat (ill. COAT). 2. Sofa with stuffed (and sometimes cushioned) seat, back, and ends. [f. a 19th-c. earl of *Chesterfield*]

chĕst'nŭt (-sn-) *n.* 1. Tree (also called *Spanish* or *sweet* ~), *Castanea sativa*, native of Asia Minor and S. Europe, bearing a large edible seed or 'nut' enclosed in a prickly pericarp or 'burr'; the nut itself. 2. = HORSE-chestnut. 3. Stale anecdote or joke. 4. Chestnut colour; chestnut-coloured horse. ~ *adj.* Of chestnut-colour, deep reddish-brown.

chėvăl'-glass (sh-, -ahs) *n.* Mirror swung on frame, and long enough to reflect the whole figure.

chĕvalier' (sh-) *n.* 1. Horseman, knight (hist. or archaic); member of certain orders of knighthood, or of French Legion of Honour; soldier cadet of old French noblesse. 2. ~ *of industry*, (Fr. *chevalier d'industrie*) adventurer, swindler. 3. *The C~*, *C~ de St. Georges*, the Old PRETENDER, James Stuart, son of James II of England; *The Young C~*, Charles Edward Stuart, the Young Pretender.

chevaux-de-frise (shevō'defrēz') *n.pl.* 1. Iron spikes set in timber etc., employed in war to check cavalry charges etc. 2. Line of spikes or nails set at angles along top of wall, railing, etc. to prevent persons climbing over. [Fr., = 'horses of Friesland', because first employed by 17th-c. Frisians to compensate for their lack of cavalry]

chevet (shĕv'ā) *n.* Apsidal east end of church with chapels radiating from it (ill. CHURCH).

Chĕv'ĭot (*or* -ē-). ~ *Hills*, *Cheviots*, range of hills on the border between England and Scotland; ~ *sheep*, hardy short-woolled breed thriving there and in mountainous districts. **chĕv'ĭot** *n.* Cheviot sheep; cloth made from its wool.

chĕv'ron (sh-) *n.* Bent bar of inverted V shape as heraldic device (ill. HERALDRY), architectural ornament (ill. MOULDING), etc.; distinguishing mark of this shape on sleeve of non-commissioned officers, policemen, etc., 'stripe'.

chĕv'rotain, -tĭn (sh-) *n.* Small animal of genus *Tragulus*, most primitive of known ruminants, found esp. in India, Malay peninsula, and W. Africa.

CHEVAL-GLASS

chĕv'y, chĭv(v)'y *n.* 1. Chase, pursuit, hunt. 2. The game of prisoners' base. ~ *v.t.* Chase, harry. [prob. f. CHEVY CHASE]

Chĕv'y Chāse. Skirmish, celebrated in a ballad of 15th-c. origin, between Percy, Earl of Northumberland, who had vowed to hunt for 3 days across the Scottish border, and his Scottish neighbour 'the doughty Douglas'; both were killed in the fight.

chew (-ōō) *v.* Work about between teeth, grind to pulp or indent with repeated biting; chew tobacco; turn over in mind, meditate *on* or *over*; ~ *the cud*, (of ruminant animals) bring back half-digested food into mouth for further chewing; *chewing-gum*, preparation of flavoured hardened secretion of spruce-tree, or similar insoluble substance, used for chewing (see also CHICLE). ~ *n.* Act of chewing; quid of tobacco.

Cheyenne (shīĕn'). 1. Capital of Wyoming, U.S. 2. Algonkin tribe of Indians.

Chiăng Kai-shĕk', Generalissimo (1888–). C.-in-c. of the Chinese armed forces in the war against Japan, 1937–45, and president of the Chinese Republic, 1943–9.

Chiăn'tĭ (k-). Dry red or white wine produced in or near the Chianti Mountains in Tuscany.

chiaroscuro (kyârŏskoor'ō) *n.* Treatment of light and shade in painting, esp. when strongly contrasted; light and shade effects in nature; use of contrast in literature etc. [It., = 'bright-dark']

chias'mus (kīăz-) *n.* (rhet. etc.) Inversion in a second phrase of order followed in first, e.g. *I cannot dig, to beg I am ashamed.* [Gk *khiasmos* arrangement like letter khi, χ]

chibouk' (-ōōk) *n.* Long Turkish tobacco-pipe, usu. with amber mouthpiece, long wooden stem, and bowl of baked clay.

chic (shēk) *n.* Skill, effectiveness, style. ~ *adj.* Stylish, in the fashion.

Chicago (shĭkah'gō). Second largest city of U.S., in Illinois.

chĭcāne' (sh-) *n.* 1. Chicanery. 2. In game of bridge, holding of hand without any trumps. ~ *v.* Use chicanery; cheat.

chĭcān'ery (sh-) *n.* Legal trickery, pettifogging, abuse of legal forms; sophistry; quibble, trick, subterfuge.

chĭck *n.* Chicken; young bird before or after hatching; ~*-weed*, any of several weeds of the genus *Stellaria*.

chĭck'ĕn *n.* Young bird, esp. of domestic fowl; flesh of this; youthful person; *Mother Carey's* ~*s*, sailor's name for storm petrels; ~*-hearted*, timorous, cowardly; *chickenpox*, varicella, mild eruptive disease with some resemblance to smallpox, chiefly affecting children.

chĭck-pea *n.* A dwarf pea, *Cicer arietinum.*

chĭc'le (-kl *or* -klē) *n.* Gum-like substance obtained from bully-tree (*Mimusops globosa*) and sapodilla (*Sapota zapotilla*) used for making chewing-gum. [Mex. *tzictli*]

chĭc'ory *n.* 1. (bot.) Any plant of the genus *Cichorium.* 2. Species of this, *C. intybus* (known in U.S. as *endive*), with long smooth blanched leaves eaten as salad; its root, ground and roasted as addition to or substitute for coffee. 3. Another species, *C. endivia* (called *endive* in England but *chicory* in U.S.), varieties of which, with curly or wavy leaves, are eaten as salad.

chīde *v.* (past t. *chĭd*, past part. *chĭdd'en* or *chĭd*). Make complaints, speak scoldingly; scold, rebuke.

chief *n.* 1. (her.) Upper third of shield (ill. HERALDRY). 2. Head, leader, ruler, of body of men, esp. of clan, tribe, etc.; superior officer, head of department, etc., one's superior in office. 3. *in* ~, first in importance, principally, foremost; *tenant in* ~, feudal tenant holding directly from the lord paramount; *Commander-in-C*~, supreme commander of an army; admiral in chief command of naval station. ~ *adj.* Formally the chief or head; first in importance, influence, etc.; prominent, leading. **chief'dom** *n.* **chief'ly** *adv.* Above all; mainly but not exclusively.

chief'tain *n.* Military leader (poet.); captain of robbers; chief of Highland clan or uncivilized tribe. **chief'taincy, chief'tainship** *ns.*

chiel *n.* (Sc.) Fellow, chap.

chĭff'-chăff *n.* Small bird of warbler family, *Phylloscopus collybita.* [f. its note]

chĭff'ŏn (sh-) *n.* Diaphanous plain-woven fabric of fine hard-twisted yarn (silk, nylon, etc.); *attrib.* (in ~ *velvet* etc.) light in weight.

chiffonier' (sh-) *n.* Movable low cupboard with top forming sideboard.

chignon (shē'nyawṅ) *n.* Coil of hair on pad at back of head.

chĭg'ōe *n.* = JIGGER[2].

chĭl'blain *n.* Inflammatory itching swelling on hand, foot, etc., caused by exposure to cold and poor circulation.

chīld *n.* (pl. *chĭld'ren*). Unborn or newly born human being; boy or girl below age of puberty; childish person; son or daughter, offspring; descendant; follower or adherent; *child'bed, child'birth*, parturition. **chīld'lėss** *adj.* **chīld'lėssnėss** *n.*

Chīld'ermas. (archaic) Feast of Holy Innocents, 28th Dec., commemorating the slaughter of the children by Herod (Matt. ii. 16).

chīld'hŏŏd *n.* Child's state; time from birth to puberty; *second* ~, dotage.

chīld'ĭsh *adj.* Of, proper to, a child; puerile, not suited to grown-up person. **chīld'ĭshly** *adv.* **chīld'ĭshnėss** *n.*

chīld'līke *adj.* Having the good qualities of a child, as innocence, frankness, etc.

Chĭl'ė. A S. Amer. Republic lying between the Andes and the south Pacific; the country was discovered by Spanish adventurers in the 16th c. and remained under Spanish rule until 1818; capital, Santiago; ~ *saltpetre*, sodium nitrate $NaNO_3$, found in Chile and Peru, and used as a fertilizer. **Chĭl'ėan** *adj.* & *n.*

chĭll *n.* 1. Cold sensation, lowered temperature of body; feverish shivering. 2. Unpleasant coldness of air, water, etc. 3. Depressing influence; coldness of manner. 4. (eng.) Pieces of solid metal inserted into moulds to effect rapid local cooling. ~ *adj.* Unpleasantly cold; feeling cold; unfeeling, unemotional, abstract. ~ *v.* 1. Make, become, cold; deaden, blast, with cold; keep (meat or other food) at low temperature but without freezing. 2. Depress, dispirit. 3. Harden (molten iron) by contact with cold iron.

chĭll'ĭ *n.* (pl. *-lies*). Dried pod of kinds of capsicum; the pods are acrid, pungent, and of deep red colour, and are used to make Cayenne pepper. [Mexican wd]

chĭll'y *adj.* Rather cold; sensitive to cold; not genial, cold-mannered. **chĭll'ĭnėss** *n.*

Chĭl'tern. ~ *Hills, Chilterns*, range of wooded hills stretching from S. Oxfordshire across Buckinghamshire into Bedfordshire and Hertfordshire. ~ *Hundreds*, 5 hundreds in Oxfordshire and 3 in Buckinghamshire. The manorial rights in these belonged to the Crown, which appointed stewards and bailiffs; these offices have long been obsolete or merely nominal, but the stewardship of the 3 Buckinghamshire hundreds is applied for by members of Parliament wishing to resign. A member cannot resign his seat so long as he is duly qualified, but the holding of an office of profit under the Crown forces him to vacate his seat, and this stewardship is held by a legal fiction to be such an office.

chīme *n.* Set of attuned bells, series of sounds given by this; harmony, melody, rhythm; agreement, correspondence. ~ *v.* 1. Make (bell) sound; ring chimes, ring chimes on; show (hour) by chiming. 2. Harmonize, agree (*with*); ~ *in*, join in harmoniously; break into a conversation.

Chimēr'a, -aera (kī-). (Gk myth.) A fire-breathing monster with lion's head, goat's body, and serpent's tail, killed by Bellerophon. **chimēr'a, -aer'a** *n.* Grotesque monster; bogy; thing of hybrid character, fanciful conception;

(bot., usu. *-aera*) plant in which internal and external tissues are of different origins. **chimĕ'rĭcal** *adj.* **chimĕ'rĭcally** *adv.*

chĭmēre' *n.* Bishop's robe to which lawn sleeves are attached (ill. VESTMENT).

chĭm'ney *n.* Flue carrying off smoke or steam of fire, furnace, engine, etc.; part of flue above roof; glass tube providing draught for lamp-flame; natural vent of volcano etc.; narrow cleft by which cliff may be climbed; *~-corner*, warm seat within old-fashioned

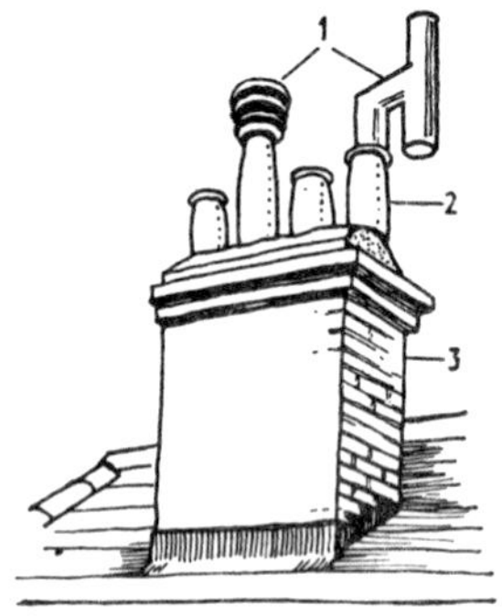

CHIMNEY

1. Cowls. 2. Pot. 3. Stack

fireplace; *~-piece*, mantel; *~-pot*, earthenware or metal pipe at top of chimney; *~-pot hat*, man's tall silk hat; *~-stack*, structure on roof of house etc. containing the vents of several chimneys; *~-sweep*, person whose trade it is to sweep chimneys; *~-sweeper*, chimney-sweep; jointed brush for sweeping chimneys.

chĭmpanzee' *n.* Genus of African apes, *Anthropopithecus*, bearing the closest resemblance to man of any of the surviving anthropoids (ill. APE). [native W. African name]

chĭn *n.* Front of lower jaw; *~-strap*, strap passing under or round chin to hold hat or helmet in place; *~-wag*, (slang) talk, chatter.

Chīn'a[1]. Large country of E. Asia with a civilization dating from the 3rd millennium B.C., governed during most of its history by emperors of numerous (often rival) dynasties of which the most notable are the Han (206 B.C.–A.D. 220), Wei (Tatars; south only; 386–557), Sui (581–618), T'ang (618–906), Sung (960–1279), Yüan (Mongols; 1280–1368), Ming (1368–1644), and Ch'ing (Manchu Tatars, 1644–1912); after a revolution, 1911, a republic was proclaimed, 1912; Communist forces obtained control, 1949; capital, Peking; *~ aster*, any of several garden asters derived from *Callistephus chinensis*; *~ bark*, = CINCHONA; *Chinaman*, native of China (now usu. *Chinese*); *~ orange*, common orange, orig. from China; *~'s Sorrow*: see YELLOW RIVER; *~ tea*, type of tea prepared from a small-leaved variety of tea plant (*Thea sinensis bohea*) grown chiefly in S. China and differing from other kinds of tea chiefly in that it is cured with smoke. [ult. origin unknown; not the native name; found in Sansk. *c* 1st c.]

chīn'a[2] *n.* Very hard fine semi-transparent porcelain of the 'hard-paste' kind orig. manufactured in China and first brought to Europe in 16th c. by Portuguese; manufactured in Europe since beginning of 18th c.; *~-clay*, kaolin. *~ adj.* Of china. [orig. *China-ware*, ware from China]

Chĭn'atown. Part of large town, esp. seaport, in England or U.S., where Chinese live as a colony.

chĭnch *n.* (U.S.) Bed-bug.

chĭnchĭll'a *n.* 1. Genus of small S. Amer. rodents; the fine soft greyish fur of one species, *C. laniger* of Peru and Chile. 2. *~ rabbit*, a long-haired rabbit bred for its fur.

chĭn'-chĭn' *int.* of salutation. [Anglo-Chinese, f. Chin. *ts'ing ts'ing*]

chīne[1] *n.* Deep narrow ravine cut by stream descending steeply to sea (now only in Isle of Wight and Hampshire).

chīne[2] *n.* Backbone; animal's backbone or part of it as joint (ill. MEAT); backbone of bacon-pig after sides are cut off for curing. *~ v.* Remove chine from.

Chīnee' *n.* (slang) Chinaman, Chinese.

Chīnēse' (-z) *adj.* & *n.* (Native, language) of China; *~ copy*, (eng. etc.) precise drawing of structure, apparatus, etc., made from its appearance only without other information; *~ lantern*, collapsible lantern of thin coloured paper; *~ white*, a pigment, zinc oxide.

chĭnk[1] *n.* Crevice; long narrow opening, slit, peep-hole.

chĭnk[2] *n.* Sound as of glasses or coins striking together. *~ v.* Make, cause to make, this sound.

Chĭnk[3] *n.* (slang, orig. U.S.) Chinese.

chĭnk'apin, chin'quapin (-k-) *n.* Dwarf chestnut, *Castanea pumila*, of Virginia and adjacent States. [Amer. Ind. name]

chinoiserie (shĭnwahz'-) *n.* Imitation of Chinese motifs in furniture etc., fashionable in 18th and early 19th centuries.

Chĭnōōk'. N. Amer. Ind. tribe orig. inhabiting region round Columbus river in Oregon. **chĭnōōk'** *n.* 1. Jargon of English, French, Indian, and other words formerly spoken by traders in the Chinook region. 2. Warm usu. south-westerly wind blowing in winter and spring down eastern slopes of Canadian Rockies. 3. *~ (salmon)*, large salmon of NW. coast of N. America, *Salmo schawytscha*.

chĭntz *n.* Orig., painted or stained calico imported from India; now, cotton cloth printed with designs in colour and usu. glazed. [Hind. *chint*, f. Sansk. *chitna* variegated]

chīonodŏx'a (k-) *n.* Blue-flowered genus of liliaceous plants from Crete and Asia Minor, cultivated for its early blooming habit; glory of the snow. [Gk *khiōn* snow + *doxa* glory]

chĭp *n.* 1. Thin piece cut from wood or broken from stone etc.; in gem-cutting, piece chipped off weighing less than ¾ carat. 2. Thin slice of fruit etc., esp. (pl.) stick-shaped slices of potato fried crisp; counter used in games of chance. 3. Wood or woody fibre split into thin strips for making hats, baskets, etc.; basket made of this. 4. Crack or slight fracture caused by chipping. 5. *Chips*, (naut. slang) ship's carpenter; *~-basket*, basket of thin strips of wood roughly joined or interwoven, for packing soft fruit etc.; *~-shot* (golf) short, slightly lofted approach shot; (carry) *a ~ on* one's *shoulder*, (flaunt) a grievance (orig. U.S.; said to be from custom whereby a boy seeking a fight would put a chip on his shoulder and challenge another to knock it off); *~ of the old block*, child resembling father. *~ v.* Cut (wood), break (stone, crockery), at surface or edge; shape thus; cut or break *off*; be susceptible to breakage at edge; make chip-shot.

chĭp'mŭnk, -mŭck *n.* A ground-squirrel, the striped or chipping squirrel of N. America. [Amer. Ind. name]

Chĭpp'endāle. Furniture made by Thomas Chippendale (1718–79), a London cabinet-maker, or in the style of the designs which he published in 'The Gentleman and Cabinet-Maker's Director' (1754); his business was carried on by his son Thomas (1749–1822).

chīr'omancy (k-) *n.* Palmistry.

chīrŏp'odў (k-) *n.* Treatment of feet, corns, toe-nails, etc. **chīrŏp'odĭst** *n.*

chīroprăc'tĭc (k-) *n.* & *adj.* (U.S.) (Of) manipulation of the spinal column as method of curing disease. **chīr'oprăctor** *n.*

chĭrp *n.* Short sharp thin note as of small bird. *~ v.* Utter chirp. **chĭrp'y** *adj.* Lively, cheerful. **chĭrp'inėss** *n.*

chĭr'rup *n.* & *v.i.* (Make) series of chirps, twittering.

chĭs'el (-zl) *n.* Iron or steel cutting-tool with square bevelled end, worked by pressure or by blows of a mallet or hammer; *cold ~*, steel chisel of a temper and strength suitable for cutting cold metal, esp. iron. *~ v.t.* Cut, shape, with chisel; defraud, get (money etc.) *out of*. **chĭs'eller** *n.*

chĭt[1] *n.* Young child, brat; (contempt.) young girl or woman.

chĭt[2] *n.* Written note. [Anglo-Ind. wd]

chĭt'-chăt' *n.* Light conversation; gossip.

chītin (k-) *n.* Organic substance forming horny covering of beetles and crustaceans. **chīt'inous** *adj.*

chĭt'lings, chĭtt'erlings *n.* (usu. pl.). Smaller intestines of beasts, esp. as cooked for food.

chĭv'alrous, -ic (sh-) *adjs.* Of, as of, the Age of Chivalry; of, as of, the ideal knight, gallant, honourable, courteous, disinterested; quixotic. **chĭv'alrously** *adv.*

chĭv'alry (sh-) *n.* 1. Knights or horsemen equipped for battle (archaic); medieval men-at-arms; gallant gentlemen. 2. Knightly skill (archaic); knighthood as rank or order (archaic); knightly system of feudal times with its religious, moral, and social code and usages; *Age of C~*, period of this. 3. The brave, honourable, and courteous character attributed to the ideal knight. [OF. *chevalerie* knighthood (*cheval* horse)]

chīve *n.* Small cultivated herb allied to leek and onion, *Allium schoenoprasum.*

chĭv(v)'y *v.* (colloq.) Chase, harry. [var. of CHEVY]

chlôr'al (kl-) *n.* Trichloroacetaldehyde, an oily liquid with pungent odour, made by action of chlorine on alcohol; it forms white crystals by combination with water (*chloral hydrate*); used as hypnotic and anaesthetic.

chlôr'ate (kl-) *n.* Salt of chloric acid, $HClO_3$.

chlôr'īde (kl-) *n.* Simple compound of chlorine with a metal or organic radical.

chlôr'ine (kl-, -ēn) *n.* Non-metallic element, a yellowish-green, heavy, chemically active gas with irritating smell and powerful bleaching and disinfecting qualities; symbol Cl, at. no. 17, at. wt 35·453. **chlôr'ināte** *v.t.* Treat or act upon with chlorine; sterilize (drinking water) thus. **chlôrinā'tion** *n.*

chlôr'īte (kl-) *n.* Salt of chlorous acid, $HClO_2$.

chlŏ'rofôrm (kl-; *or* klôr-) *n.* Thin colourless liquid with ethereal odour and pungent sweetish taste, the vapour of which inhaled produces insensibility; used as an anaesthetic in surgery. ~ *v.t.* Administer chloroform to.

chlŏr'ophȳll (kl-) *n.* Colouring-matter of leaves and other green parts of plants etc.

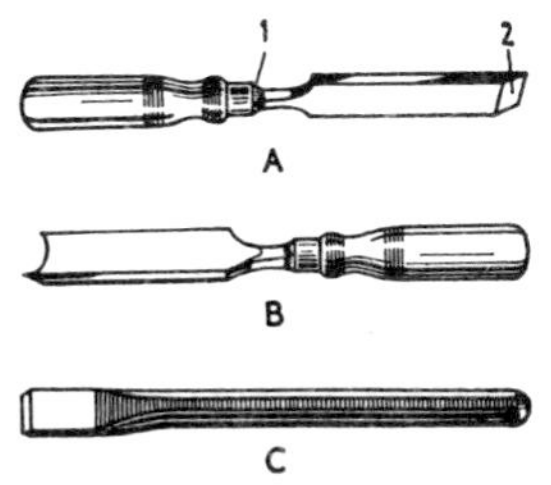

A. CHISEL. B. GOUGE. C. COLD CHISEL

1. Tang. 2. Bevel or bezel

chlorōs'is (kl-) *n.* Green sickness, anaemic disease of girls about age of puberty.

Ch.M. *abbrev. Chirurgiae Magister* (= Master of Surgery).

chŏck *n.* Block of wood, wedge. ~ *v.t.* Make fast, wedge, with chocks; ~ *up*, wedge in tight; encumber. ~ *adv.* Closely, tightly; ~-*a-block*, ~-*full*, stuffed, crammed.

chŏc'olate *n.* Paste or cake of seeds of cacao roasted, ground, sweetened, and flavoured with vanilla etc.; drink made with this; (with pl.) sweetmeat covered with chocolate or made of it; chocolate colour. ~ *adj.* Dark brown, chocolate-coloured; ~-*box*, decorated cardboard box filled with chocolates; (*adj.*) like the (usu. insipid) pictures on chocolate-boxes. [Mexican *chocolatl* (not f. *cacao* or *cocoa*)]

Chŏc'taw. Tribe of N. Amer. Indians.

choice *n.* Act, power, right, etc., of choosing; what is chosen; variety to choose from; pick, best, *élite.* ~ *adj.* Of picked quality, exquisite; carefully chosen.

choir (kwīr) *n.* 1. Band of singers performing or leading in musical parts of church service; choral society, company of singers. 2. Chancel; part of church appropriated to choir (ill. CHURCH). ~ *v.* (rare) Sing in chorus.

choir ôrg'an (kwīr) *n.* One of 3 organs making up a large organ, with its row of keys lowest of the 3, and lighter stops than *great organ* (ill. ORGAN). [orig. *chair* organ]

chōke *n.* 1. Part of tube of firework etc. where it is constricted to form stoppage; choke-bore. 2. Valve for closing the air inlet of petrol-engine (ill. MOTOR). 3. (elect.) Coil having low resistance and large inductance inserted in circuit to impede and smooth out changes in, or change phase of, current. 4. Heart, centre part, of artichoke. 5. ~-*berry*, scarlet fruit of N. Amer. shrub *Pyrus arbutifolia*; the shrub itself; ~-*bore*, bore of fowling-piece narrowing towards muzzle; ~-*cherry*, two N. Amer. astringent cherries, (fruits of) *Prunus borealis* and *P. hyemelis*; ~-*damp*, carbon dioxide in coal-mines, wells, etc. ~ *v.* Suffocate; stop breath of; suffer temporary stoppage of breath; become speechless from anger etc.; smother, stifle; block up wholly or partly. **chōk'er** *n.* (esp.) Clerical or high stand-up collar.

chōk'y *n.* (slang, orig. Anglo-Ind.) Lock-up, prison. [Hind. *chauki* shed]

chŏl'er (k-) *n.* 1. (hist.) One of the four HUMOURS, bile. 2. (poet., archaic) Anger.

chŏl'era (k-) *n.* 1. (also *Asiatic* ~) Infectious and freq. fatal disease with violent vomiting and purging, cramps, and collapse, endemic in India and epidemic elsewhere. 2. Various other diseases esp. *English* ~ or ~ *morbus*, summer diarrhoea.

chŏl'eric (k-) *adj.* Irascible, hot-tempered; (archaic) characterized by choler or bile.

chōl'ĭămb (k-) *n.* Iambic verse with spondee or trochee in last foot, scazon. **chōlĭăm'bĭc** *adj.*

choōse (-z) *v.* (past t. *chōse*, past part. *chōs'en*). Select out of greater number; make choice *between*; select as; decide, think fit, be determined *to* do; (theol.) destine to be saved.

chŏp[1] *v.* Cut by a blow or blows, usu. with axe; cut small, mince; cut short (words etc.); (cricket, tennis, etc.) make short heavy edgeways blow, strike (ball) thus. ~ *n.* Chopping; chopping stroke; slice of meat, esp. mutton or pork, usu. including a rib (ill. MEAT); short broken motion (of waves etc.); ~-*house*, cheap restaurant. **chŏpp'er** *n.* (esp.) Large-bladed short-handled axe, cleaver; axe. **chŏpp'y** *adj.* (Of waves, their motion, etc.) short and broken.

chŏp[2] *n.* Chap, jaw; *chops of the Channel*, entrance to English Channel from Atlantic.

chŏp[3] *v.* 1. ~ (*and change*), change, alter (esp. repeatedly or frequently). 2. (naut., of the wind) Change suddenly. 3. Exchange or bandy words, esp. ~ *logic*, argue, bandy arguments.

Chopin (shŏp'ahṅ *or* shō-), Frédéric François (1809–49). Polish pianist, composer of a large number of pianoforte compositions, études, preludes, nocturnes, etc.

chŏp'sticks *n.pl.* Pair of small sticks of ivory, bone, wood, etc., held between thumb and fingers of one hand and used by Chinese in eating. [Pidgin English (*chop* = quick + *stick*) equivalent of Chin. *k'wai-tsze* 'nimble ones']

chŏp-suey (-sōō'ĭ) *n.* Chinese dish of meat or chicken, rice, onions, etc., fried in sesame-oil. [Chin., = 'mixed bits']

chôr'al (k-) *adj.* Of, sung by, a choir or chorus. **chôr'ally** *adv.*

choral(e) (korahl') *n.* (Metrical hymn set to) simple tune, usu. sung in unison, orig. in Reformed Church of Germany.

chôr'alist (k-) *n.* One who sings in a chorus.

chôrd[1] (k-) *n.* 1. String of musical instrument (poet.); also fig. of mind, emotions, etc. 2. (math.) Straight line joining extremities of arc (ill. CIRCLE). 3. (anat.) (obs. sp. of) CORD.

chôrd[2] (k-) *n.* (mus.) Combination

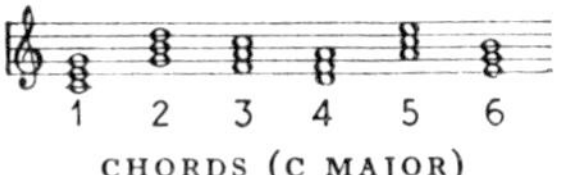

CHORDS (C MAJOR)

Primary triads: 1. Tonic. 2. Dominant. 3. Subdominant. Secondary triads: 4. Supertonic. 5. Submediant. 6. Mediant

of 3 or more (rarely 2) simultaneous notes; *common* ~, note with its major or minor third, perfect fifth, and octave.

chŏr'dāte (k-) *adj.* & *n.* (zool.) (Member) of the phylum *Chordata*; (organism) possessing at some stage in its life-history a notochord, i.e. a rod of tissue lying along the back below the nerve cord.

chōre *n.* (orig. U.S., usu. pl.) House-cleaning, esp. by the day; odd job(s).

chorē'a (k-) *n.* St. VITUS's dance [Gk *khoreia* choral dance]

chŏrēŏg'raphy (k-) *n.* Arrangement of the dancing in a ballet; art of dancing. **chŏrēŏg'rapher** *n.* Designer of the dancing in a ballet. **chŏrēogrăph'ic** *adj.*

chŏ'rĭămb (k-) *n.* Metrical foot of 4 syllables, the first and last long, the others short (– ◡ ◡ –). **chŏrĭăm'bic** *adj.*

chŏr'ic (k-) *adj.* Of, like, CHORUS, sense 1.

chŏr'ion (k-) *n.* Outermost membrane enveloping foetus before birth (ill. EMBRYO).

chŏ'rister (k-) *n.* Member of (usu. male) choir, esp. boy.

chŏr'oid (k-) *adj.* & *n.* ~ *(coat)*, vascular membrane lining eyeball between sclerotic coat and retina, containing numerous dark pigment-cells (ill. EYE).

chŏr'tle *v.i.* Chuckle loudly. [portmanteau wd invented by Lewis Carroll, perh. f. *chuckle*+*snort*]

chŏr'us (k-) *n.* 1. (Gk antiq.) Organized band of singers and dancers in religious festivals and dramatic performances; in Attic tragedy representing 'interested spectators' and employed to explain the action, express sympathy with characters, and draw morals; the song(s) sung by these. 2. Adaptation of this in other drama; in Shakespeare etc. a personage who speaks prologue and explains or comments on happenings in play. 3. Band of singers, choir. 4. Thing sung by many at once, simultaneous utterance; refrain of song, in which audience joins; (mus.) composition, usu. in four parts, for a considerable number of voices. ~ *v.* Sing, speak, say, in chorus.

chose (shōz) *n.* (law) Thing, chattel, piece of property.

chōs'en (-z-) *adj.* Past part. of CHOOSE *v.* used adjectivally; *C~ People*, the Jews.

chou (shōō) *n.* 1. Large ornamental knot of ribbon etc. 2. (pl. -*x*) Small round hollow cake filled with cream etc.; ~ (or *choux*) *paste, pastry*, paste used for éclairs etc., cooked in saucepan before being baked. [Fr., = 'cabbage']

Chouans (shōōahṅ') *n.pl.* Irregular bands in W. France, esp. Brittany, who waged partisan war against Republic and First Empire after 1793, and reappeared in 1832.

Chou En-lai (chō ĕn-lī')(1898–). Chinese revolutionary leader; helped to found the Chinese Red Army; took part in the Communists' 'long march' across China to Shensi province 1934–5; since 1949, prime minister of Chinese People's Republic.

chough (chŭf) *n.* Bird (*Coracia pyrrhocorax*) of crow family, with red feet and bill, usu. frequenting sea-cliffs.

chouse (-s) *n.* & *v.* (slang) Swindle, trick.

chow *n.* 1. (Pidgin English for) Food. 2. Dog of Chinese breed, with short thick coat, usu. black or brown, and black tongue (ill. DOG). 3. (Austral. slang) Chinese.

chow-chow *n.* 1. Mixture or medley, as of pickles or preserves. 2. = CHOW, 2.

chowd'er *n.* Newfoundland and New England dish of fresh fish or clams stewed with bacon, onions, biscuit, etc. [app. orig. in Brittany, in phr. *faire la chaudière* = to supply a pot etc. for cooking a stew]

Chrestien de Troyes (krāt'yahṅ) (12th c.). French author of Arthurian romances.

chrĕstŏm'athy (k-) *n.* Collection of choice passages.

chrism (k-) *n.* Consecrated oil, unguent; anointing, esp. in sacred rites.

Chrīst (k-). The Messiah or Lord's Anointed of Jewish prophecy; (title, now treated as proper name, given to) JESUS of Nazareth as fulfilling this prophecy. [L *Christus* f. Gk *khristos* anointed one (*khriō* anoint) transl. of Heb.; see MESSIAH]

Chrīstadĕl'phĭan (k-) *adj.* & *n.* (Member) of a religious sect, founded in U.S. by a Dr Thomas in 1833, who reject the doctrine of the Trinity. [Gk *Khristos* Christ, *adelphos* brother]

Christ Chûrch. A college of the University of Oxford, begun by Cardinal Wolsey and established by Henry VIII in 1546; also, the (much older) cathedral of Oxford, which is enclosed within the precincts of the college and serves as its chapel.

christen (krĭs'n) *v.* 1. Admit or initiate into Christian Church by baptism; give name to at baptism. 2. Name, dedicate (bell, ship, etc.) with ceremony like baptism; name, give name to.

Christendom (krĭs'ndom) *n.* Christians collectively; Christian countries.

Christian (krĭs'tyan,-s'chan) *adj.* & *n.* (Person) believing, professing, or belonging to, religion of Christ; (person) resembling Christ or following or exemplifying his teaching; ~ *era*, the era reckoned from the supposed date of the birth of Christ (now held to have taken place 4 B.C.); ~ *name*, name given at christening, personal name as dist. from surname or patronymic; ~ *Science, Scientist*, (person believing in) the principles formulated by Mrs EDDY, esp. that matter is an illusion and bodily disease an error of the mind, to be cured by teaching the patient the truth as revealed in the teaching and healing of Christ.

Christia'nia (k-, -ahn-). Former name of the capital of Norway, which reverted in 1925 to its original name OSLO. ~ *n.* (skiing) Kind of 'swing' used for stopping short (ill. SKI).

Christiăn'ity (k-). The Christian faith, doctrines of Christ and his apostles; Christian spirit or character.

Chrĭs'ties (k-). London firm of auctioneers of works of art (now Christie, Manson & Woods), founded in 1766 by James Christie (1730–1803).

Christmas (krĭs'mas). Festival of nativity of Christ, kept on 25th Dec., observed as time of festivity and rejoicing; the days immediately preceding and following this; ~-*box*, small present or gratuity given at Christmas, esp. to postmen, milkmen, etc., in acknowledgement of continuous services not directly paid for by the giver; ~-*card*, ornamental card sent as Christmas greeting (the custom began in England *c* 1867); ~ *Day*, 25th Dec.; ~ *Eve*, 24th Dec.; ~-*rose*, white-flowered winter-blooming species of hellebore, *Helleborus niger*; ~ *pudding*, the plum-pudding eaten at Christmas; ~-*tree*, small tree, usu. a fir, set up in a room and hung with bright ornaments, candles, presents, etc.; a feature of Christmas celebrations in Germany freq. but imperfectly imitated in England since its introduction into Queen Victoria's household early in her reign. **Christmas(s)y** (krĭs'masĭ) *adj.* (colloq.) Of or like Christmas, festive.

Chrīst's College (k-). A college of the University of Cambridge founded by Henry VI in 1448.

Chrīst's Hospital (k-). A 'blue-coat' school, founded in London under a charter of Edward VI as a school for poor children, in buildings that had belonged to the Grey Friars; now removed to Horsham, Sussex.

Chrĭs'ty minstrels (k-). Troupe of 'minstrels' imitating Negroes, originated by George Christy of New York; any similar company with blackened faces, playing banjoes, and singing Negro or pseudo-Negro songs.

chrōm'a (k-) *n.* (painting) Brilliance of hue (= saturation).

chrōm'ate (k-) *n.* Salt of chromic acid.

chromăt'ic (k-) *adj.* 1. Of, produced by, colour; full of bright colour; ~ *aberration*, non-conveyance of coloured constituents of white light to one focus, when refracted through a lens. 2. (mus.)

Including notes which do not belong to the diatonic scale of the prevailing key; ~ *scale*, the full series of notes (12 to an octave, each note differing by a semitone from the next) on which Western music is normally based (ill. SCALE). **chromăt'ically** *adv.*

chrōm'atin (k-) *n.* (biol.) That part of cell-tissue which can be readily stained when immersed in colouring-matter.

chrōm'atism (k-) *n.* = CHROMATIC aberration.

chrōme (k-) *n.* 1. (obs.) Chromium. 2. Yellow pigment and colour obtained from lead chromate, PbCrOI. 3. Potassium dichromate, $K_2Cr_2O_7$, used in dyeing and tanning. 4. ~ *leather*, leather tanned with potassium bichromate; ~*-nickel steel*, stainless steel, alloy of chromium, nickel, and steel; ~ *orange*, *red*, pigments prepared from dibasic lead chromate, $2(PbO)CrO_3$; ~ *steel*, very tough fine-grained alloy of chromium and steel; ~*-tanning*, tanning by treatment with acid solution of potassium bichromate and afterwards with a reducing agent, so that chromic oxide combines with the fibre of the leather and makes it tough and waterproof; ~ *yellow*: see sense 2 above.

chrōm'ic (k-) *adj.* Applied to compounds of chromium in which this element is trivalent; ~ *acid*, CrO_3 (strictly the anhydride of the acid); ~ *oxide*, chromium sesquioxide, Cr_2O_3, a green powder used to give a green colour to glass and porcelain.

chrōm'ium (k-) *n.* Metallic element remarkable for the brilliant red, yellow, or green colour of its compounds; symbol Cr, at. no. 24, at. wt 51·996; it is widely applied in electroplating and in a variety of alloys, the chief being with iron and steel, to which it imparts hardness and stainlessness; ~ *plated*, *-plating*, plated, plating, with chromium; ~*-plate* (*n.* & *v.*).

chrōm'ō (k-) *n.* Colloq. abbrev. of CHROMOLITHOGRAPH.

chrōm'ograph (k-, -ahf) *n.* & *v.t.* (Reproduce with) gelatine copying-apparatus in which aniline dye is used for ink.

chrōmōlith'ograph (k-, -ahf) *n.* Picture printed in colours by LITHOGRAPHY. **chrōmolithŏg'raphy** *n.*

chrōmophōt'ograph (k-, -ahf) *n.* Photograph in natural colours. **chrōmophotŏg'raphy** *n.*

chrōm'osōme (k-) *n.* (biol.) One of the rod-like structures which occur in pairs in the cell nucleus of an animal or plant and hence in every developed cell; they carry the *genes* (hereditary factors) and their number is constant for each species (the human cell nucleus has 23 pairs); they normally take up stains only at cell division.

chrōm'osphēre (k-) *n.* Red gaseous envelope round sun, outside photosphere (ill. SUN). **chrōmosphĕ'ric** *adj.*

chrōm'ous (k-) *adj.* Applied to compounds of chromium in which this element is divalent.

Chron. *abbrev.* Chronicles (O.T.).

chrŏn'ic (k-) *adj.* Of diseases etc. lasting a long time, lingering, inveterate; of invalid having such disease; (transf.) continuous, constant; (vulg.) bad, intense, severe. **chrŏn'ically** *adv.*

chrŏn'icle (k-) *n.* Detailed and continuous register of events in order of time; record, register; *Chronicles*, two of the historical books of the O.T. ~ *v.t.* Enter or record in a chronicle. **chrŏn'icler** *n.*

chrŏn'ogrăm (k-) *n.* Sentence, inscription, in which certain letters express by their numerical values a date or epoch; thus, LorD haVe MerCIe Vpon Vs, printed in lieu of date in a pamphlet of the year 1666 (50+500+5+1,000+100+1+5+5 = 1666). **chrŏnogrammăt'ic** *adj.*

chronŏl'ogy (k-) *n.* Computation of time, assignment of events, etc., to their correct date, arrangement in order of time; chronological table or list. **chrŏnolŏg'ical** *adj.* **chrŏnolŏg'ically** *adv.* **chronŏl'ogīze** *v.t.* Arrange (narrative, list of events) in chronological order.

chronŏm'èter (k-) *n.* Timekeeper adjusted to keep accurate time in all variations of temperature, used for determining position at sea or in the air and for other exact observations. **chrŏnomĕt'ric(al)** *adjs.* Of chronometry. **chronŏm'ètry** *n.* Accurate time-measurement.

chrȳs'alis (k-) *n.* Inactive state into which larva of most insects passes before becoming imago or perfect insect; the hard sheath or case enclosing it at this stage, the cocoon of an insect (ill. BUTTERFLY).

chrȳsăn'thèmum (k-) *n.* 1. Genus of composite plants including ox-eye daisy and corn-marigold. 2. Various cultivated species of this, blooming in autumn.

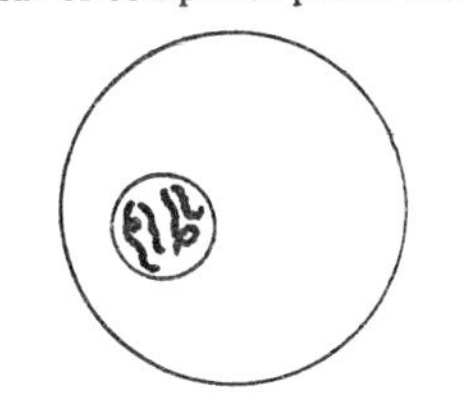

CHROMOSOME: A. DIAGRAM OF CELL SHOWING CHROMOSOMES IN NUCLEUS. B. PORTION OF GIANT CHROMOSOME FROM THE SALIVARY GLAND OF A FLY LARVA

The dark bands indicate the location of genes

chrȳs'ĕlĕphăn'tīne (k-) *adj.* (Of sculpture) covered with ivory and gold.

chrȳsobĕ'rȳl (k-) *n.* Yellowish-green precious stone, an aluminate of beryllium.

chrȳs'olīte (k-) *n.* Precious olivine, a pale yellowish-green silicate of magnesia and iron.

chrȳs'oprāse (k-, -z) *n.* 1. In N.T. etc., golden-green precious stone (prob. a kind of beryl) believed in the Middle Ages to shine in the dark. 2. Apple-green variety of chalcedony.

Chrȳs'ostom (k-), St. John (*c* 345–407). One of the Greek Fathers of the Church, bishop of Constantinople; in his writings he emphasized the ascetic element in religion and the need for personal study of the Scriptures.

chŭb *n.* Thick fat coarse-fleshed European and Caspian river-fish of carp family, *Leuciscus cephalus*, dusky-green above and silvery-white beneath.

Chŭbb lŏck *n.* Patent lock with tumblers and device for fixing bolt immovably if attempt is made to pick the lock. [f. name of inventor, a London locksmith]

chŭbb'y *adj.* Plump, round-faced. **chŭbb'inèss** *n.* [f. CHUB]

chŭck[1] *n.* & *v.i.* (Make) clucking sound like fowl or person calling fowls etc.

chŭck[2] *n.* (archaic) Familiar term of endearment.

chŭck[3] *v.* 1. Give gentle blow *under the chin*. 2. Fling, throw, toss, carelessly or easily (*away*); ~ *up*, (colloq.) give up, give in; ~ *out*, expel (esp. troublesome person from hall, public-house, etc.); *chucker-out*, person engaged to do this; ~ *it*, (slang) stop; ~*-farthing*, game in which the players pitched coins at a mark and then he whose pitch came nearest tossed them all at a hole and won any that fell in; similar games. ~ *n.* Act of chucking; jerk, toss; (colloq.) dismissal.

chŭck[4] *n.* 1. Cut of beef extending from neck to ribs, incl. shoulder-piece (ill. MEAT). 2. Part of lathe etc. that holds rotating work-piece or tool (ill. LATHE, DRILL).

chŭc'kle *n.* & *v.i.* (Make) suppressed and inarticulate sound(s) expressing mirth, exultation, etc.

chŭc'kle-headèd (-hĕd-) *adj.* (dial. or U.S.) Doltish, stupid.

chŭg *n.* & *v.i.* (Make) repeated plunging or explosive sound (esp. of machine); so **chŭg-chŭg** *n.*

chŭkk'er *n.* Each of the periods into which a game of polo is divided. [Hind. *chakar*, f. Sansk. *cakra* wheel]

chŭm *n.* (colloq.) Associate, familiar friend; *new* ~. (Austral.) recent immigrant, greenhorn. ~ *v.i.* Be intimate or familiar *with*; share chambers or rooms *with*. **chŭmm'y** *adj.* Intimate, sociable.

chŭmp *n.* 1. Short thick lump of wood; thick blunt end of anything, esp. of loin of mutton (~-*chop*, chop from chump-end of this, ill. MEAT). 2. (slang) Head. 3. (colloq.) Blockhead.

Chungking′ (chōō-). Town in S. China, the temporary seat of the Chinese Government during the invasion of China by the Japanese (1937–45).

chŭnk *n.* Thick lump cut or broken off anything.

chupătt′y *n.* (Anglo-Ind.) Small flat cake of coarse unleavened bread.

chûrch *n.* 1. Building for public Christian worship, esp. according to the established religion of the country. 2. *C*~, the Christian community; any branch or distinct part of this. 3. The clergy and officers of the Church; the clerical order or profession. 4. Congregation of Christians locally organized for religious worship etc. 5. Public worship in church. 6. *C*~ *Army*, Church of England mission to working classes founded by Preb. Carlile in 1882; *C*~ *Assembly*, the National Assembly of the Church of England established by statute in 1919; *church′man*, member of Church established or recognized in any country; *C*~ *militant*, the Church on earth conceived as warring against evil; *C*~ *of England* (*English* or *Anglican C*~), the English branch of the Western Church, which at the Reformation repudiated the Pope's authority and asserted that of the sovereign over ecclesiastical as well as temporal matters in his dominions; ~ *parade*, attendance at church service as part of military routine etc.; parade of church-goers after morning service on Sunday; *churchward′en*, one of the (usu. two) lay honorary officers of a parish or district church elected annually to assist incumbent in administrative duties, manage various parochial offices, etc.; clay pipe with very long stem; *church′yard*, the enclosed ground round a church, esp. as used for burials. ~ *adj.* Of or connected with the or a church. ~ *v.t.* (usu. pass.) Bring (woman) to church to render thanks for delivery of child.

Chûrch′ill, Sir Winston (Leonard Spencer)(1874–1965). English statesman; under-secretary of state for the colonies 1906–8; president of the Board of Trade 1908–10; home secretary 1910–11; first lord of the Admiralty 1911–15; secretary of state for war 1918–21, for the colonies 1921–2; chancellor of the exchequer (1924–9); prime minister 1940–5, 1951–5.

chûrch′y *adj.* (colloq.) Obtrusive or intolerantly devoted to church or opposed to dissent.

chûrl *n.* Person of low birth; peasant, boor; ill-bred fellow; cross-grained or niggardly person. **chûrl′ish** *adj.* **chûrl′ishly** *adv.* **chûrl′ishnėss** *n.*

chûrn *n.* Vessel or machine for making butter, in which milk or cream is shaken, beaten, or otherwise agitated, so as to separate the globules of milk-fat (butter) from the serous parts. ~ *v.* Shake (milk, cream) in churn into butter, make (butter) thus; make butter; stir (liquid) about, make it froth; (of sea etc.) wash to and fro, seethe.

chute (shōōt) *n.* 1. Smooth rapid descent of water over slope. 2. Sloping channel, slide, for conveying things to lower level, for sliding down into water, etc.

chŭt′ney *n.* Strong pungent condiment of fruits, acids, and herbs, flavoured with chillies, spices, etc. [Hind. *chatni*]

chȳle (k-) *n.* White milky fluid formed by action of pancreatic juice and bile on chyme, and contained in the lymphatics of the intestines. **chȳl′ous** *adj.*

chȳme (k-) *n.* Semi-fluid pulpy acid matter into which food is converted in stomach by action of gastric secretion.

C.I. *abbrev.* Channel Islands; (Order of the) Crown of India.

cibôr′ium *n.* (pl. -*ia*). 1. (eccles. archit.) Canopy, canopied shrine.

A. CIBORIUM. B. MONSTRANCE

2. Covered chalice for reservation of Eucharist.

cĭca′da (-kah-), **cĭca′la, cĭga′la** *ns.* 1. Plant-sucking bug, usu. large and brightly coloured, male of

CICADA

which makes shrill sound from two tympanic structures on the abdomen. 2. A long-horned grasshopper.

cĭc′atrīce, cĭc′atrix *n.* 1. Scar of healed wound; scar on tree bark. 2. (bot.) Mark left by fall of leaf etc.; hilum of seed.

cĭc′atrīze *v.* Heal (wound etc.) by inducing a scar, skin over; (of wound etc.) heal by forming a cicatrice.

cĭ′cėly *n.* Various umbelliferous plants, esp. *sweet* ~, *Myrrhis odorata*, cultivated in herb gardens.

Cĭ′cerō, Marcus Tullius (106–43 B.C.). Roman republican orator and philosopher. **Cicerōn′ian** *adj.* After the style of Cicero, eloquent, classical. ~ *n.* Authority on Cicero.

cicerōn′ė (chĭch-, sĭs-) *n.* Guide who shows and explains antiquities or curiosities of a place. [It., f. CICERO]

Cicestr. *abbrev.* (Bishop) of Chichester (replacing surname in his signature).

Cĭd. Title in Spanish literature of Ruy Diaz, count of Bivar, 11th-c. champion of Christianity against the Moors. [Arab. *sayyid* lord]

C.I.D. *abbrev.* Committee of Imperial Defence; Criminal Investigation Department.

cī′der *n.* Fermented drink made from apple-juice and sugar; ~-*press*, press for extracting juice from crushed apples. [Heb. *shekar* strong drink]

ci-devant (sē devahṅ′) *adj.* That was formerly. ~ *n.* (In the language of the Fr. Revolution) a former person of rank.

C.I.E. *abbrev.* Confédération Internationale des Étudiants; Companion of the Order of the Indian Empire.

c.i.f. *abbrev.* Cost, insurance, and freight.

cĭgâr′ *n.* Compact roll of tobacco-leaves for smoking; ~-*shaped*, cylindrical with pointed end(s).

cĭgarĕtte′ *n.* Small cylinder of cut tobacco (occas. of other herbs) rolled in thin paper for smoking; ~ *card*, *picture*, picture card inserted by makers in packet or box of cigarettes.

C.(I.)G.S. *abbrev.* Chief of (Imperial) General Staff.

cĭl′ia *n.pl.* 1. Eye-lashes; delicate hairs resembling eyelashes on edge of leaf, insect's wing, etc. 2. Hairlike vibrating organs on animal and some vegetable tissues, serving as chief means of locomotion for many lower animals living in water (ill. PROTOZOA). **cĭl′iary, cĭl′iāte** *adjs.*

Cĭliāt′a *n.pl.* Class of Protozoa which move by means of cilia (ill. PROTOZOA).

cill. Var. of SILL.

Cimmer′ian *adj.* Of the Cimmerii, a people fabled by the ancients to live in perpetual darkness; (of darkness etc.) thick, gloomy. ~ *n.* 1. One of the Cimmerii. 2. One of a nomadic people, the earliest known inhabitants of the Crimea, who were expelled and overran Asia Minor in the 7th c. B.C.

C.-in-C. *abbrev.* Commander-in-Chief.

cinch *n.* 1. (U.S.) Saddle-girth used in Mexico etc. 2. (slang)

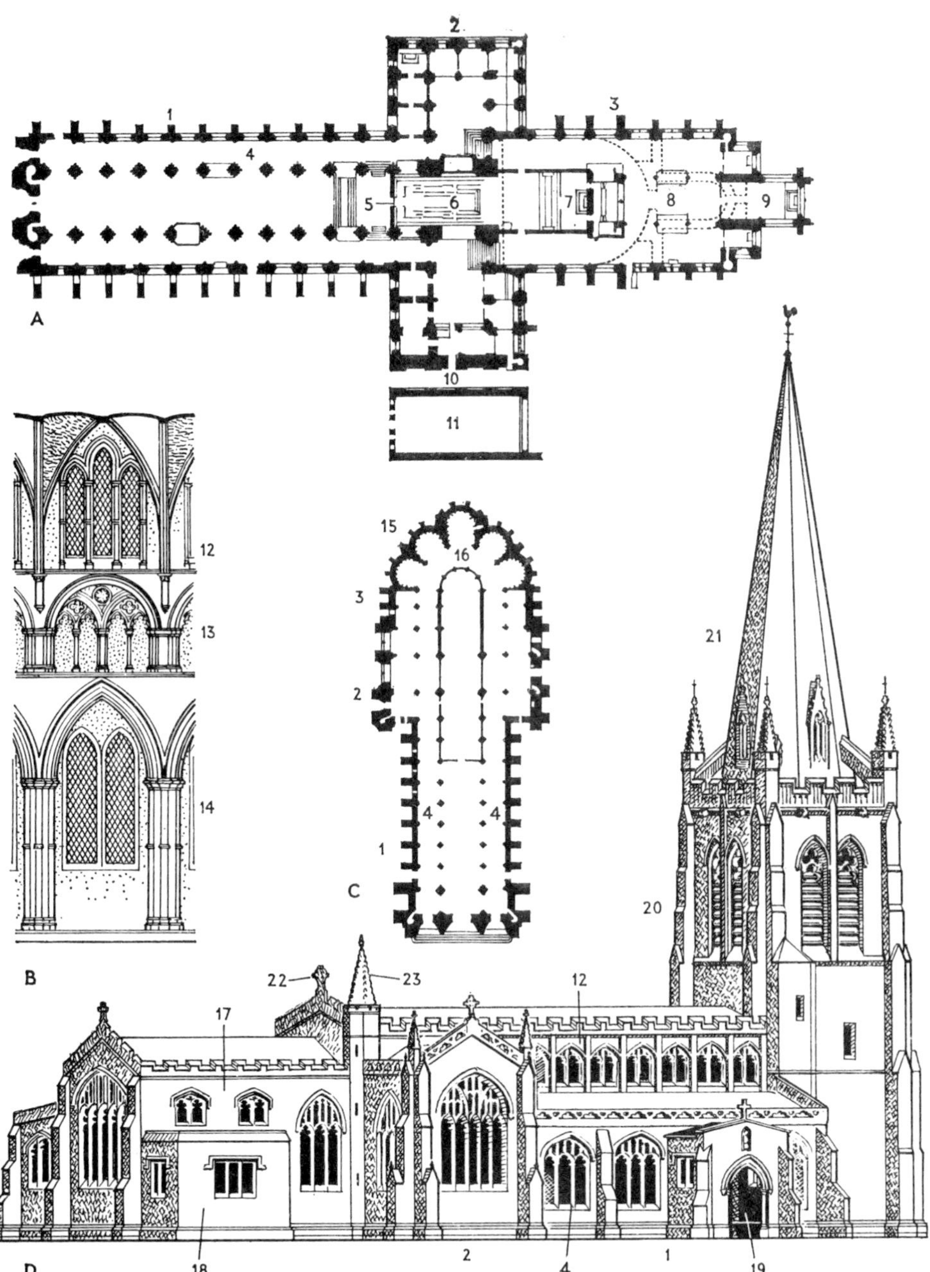

CHURCH: A. PLAN OF WINCHESTER CATHEDRAL. B. BAY OF NAVE OF SALISBURY CATHEDRAL. C. PLAN OF RHEIMS CATHEDRAL. D. TYPICAL ENGLISH PARISH CHURCH

A. 1. Nave. 2. Transept. 3. Choir. 4. Aisle. 5. Choir screen. 6. Crossing. 7. Presbytery or sanctuary. 8. Retrochoir. 9. Lady chapel. 10. Slype. 11. Chapter-house. B. 12. Clerestory. 13. Triforium. 14. Nave arcade. C. 15. Chevet. 16. Ambulatory. D. 17. Chancel. 18. Vestry. 19. Porch. 20, 21. Steeple (20. Tower, 21. Spire). 22. Finial. 23. Pinnacle. The drawings are not on the same scale

Firm hold; safe or easy thing; dead certainty. ~ *v.* 1. Fix saddle securely with girth. 2. Secure a hold on; make certain of.

cĭnchōn'a (-k-) *n.* Genus of S. Amer. trees or shrubs with fragrant white or pink flowers; ~ *bark*, bark of certain species of this containing quinine and other related alkaloids and used as tonic and febrifuge; the drug prepared from it. [named by Linnaeus in honour of countess of *Chinchon* (Spain), who when vice-queen of Peru was cured by cinchona bark in 1638 and brought a supply to Europe in 1640]

Cĭncĭnnāt'us, Lucius Quinctius. A Roman who, acc. to tradition, was called in 458 B.C. from the plough to deliver the Roman army from the peril in which it stood in its conflict with the Aequians; often referred to as a type of old Roman simplicity and frugality.

cĭnc'ture *n.* Girdle, belt, border; ring at top and bottom of column dividing shaft from capital and base. ~ *v.t.* Girdle, gird.

cĭn'der *n.* Slag; residue of coal, wood, etc., that has ceased to flame but has still combustible matter in it; (pl.) ashes; ~-*path*, *track*, foot-path, running- or racing-track, laid with fine cinders. **cĭn'dery** *adj.*

Cĭnderĕll'a. Heroine of a fairy-tale, who, when left at home in the kitchen by her stepmother and step-sisters, was sent by her fairy godmother to the court ball, on the understanding that at midnight her fairy dress would change back into rags, her coach into a pumpkin, and her horses and attendants into rats and mice; hence, person of unrecognized merit or beauty; ~ (*dance*), dance ending at midnight.

cĭn'ė- (in ~-*camera* etc.). Abbrev. of cinema(tograph).

cĭn'ėma *n.* (Abbrev., now more common, for *cinematograph*) Moving photographic pictures, films; the making of these for entertainment or record; theatre where they are exhibited. Hence ~ *adj.*: ~ *camera* (also *cĭn'ė-camera*), apparatus for recording on a long strip of film, in rapid succession, a series of photographs of moving objects; ~ *projector*, apparatus for projecting such photographs successively on a screen, so rapidly as to give the effect of motion.

Cĭn'ėmascōpe, Cĭn'erama (-ah-) *ns.* Types of cinema film using very wide curved screen. [trade-mark]

cĭnėmăt'ic *adj.* Appropriate to the cinema.

cĭnėmăt'ograph (-ahf) *n.* & *adj.* (Of the) cinema. ~ *v.t.* Photograph (scenes) for the cinema. **cĭnėmatogrăph'ic** *adj.* **cĭnėmatogrăph'ically** *adv.* **cĭnėmatŏg'raphy** *n.* Process, art, of producing moving pictures. [Gk *kinēma* movement, *graphō* write, record]

cĭnerār'ia *n.* Genus of plants of aster family, mostly natives of S. Africa, grown chiefly under glass for their bright-coloured flowers (blue or purple in wild forms). [L *cinerarius* of ashes, from the ash-coloured down on the leaves]

cĭn'erary *adj.* Of ashes; ~ *urn*, urn holding ashes of dead after cremation.

Cĭngalēse' (-ngg-, -z). Former spelling of SINHALESE.

cĭnn'abar *n.* Red crystalline form of mercuric sulphide (HgS), esp. as pigment; vermilion.

cĭnn'amon *n.* Yellowish-brown, fragrant, aromatic inner bark of an E. Ind. tree, *Cinnamomum zeylanicum*, dried in the sun and used as a spice; the tree itself. ~ *adj.* Cinnamon-coloured.

cinquecento (chĭnkwĭchĕn'tō) *n.* (Style of art and architecture of) the 16th c. in Italy. **cinquėcen'tist** *n.* Italian artist of the 16th c.

cĭnq(ue)'foil *n.* (sĭnkf-) *n.* 1. Various plants of the genus *Potentilla*, with compound leaves each of five leaflets. 2. (her.) Ornamental design resembling cinquefoil leaf (ill. HERALDRY); (archit.) 5-cusped ornament in an arch or circle.

Cinque Ports (sĭnk). Group of seaports, orig. 5 (Hastings, Sandwich, Dover, Romney, Hythe, to which were added Rye, Winchelsea and several others), on SE. coast of England, with jurisdiction over the whole coast from Seaford in Sussex to Birchington in Kent. In the 13th c. they furnished the chief part of the English Navy and in return received important privileges, most of which they kept until the Reform Act of 1832 and the Corporation Act of 1835. The Lord Wardenship of the Cinque Ports is now chiefly an honorary dignity.

C.I.O. *abbrev.* Congress of Industrial Organizations.

cīph'er, cȳ- *n.* 1. Arithmetical symbol or character (0) of no value by itself, which when placed after any figure (or series of figures) in a whole number increases its value tenfold, and when placed before a figure in decimal fractions decreases its value in the same proportion. 2. Person or thing of no importance or worth, nonentity. 3. Any Arabic numeral. 4. Secret or disguised manner of writing; anything so written; key to this.

CIPHER

5. Device of intertwined initials or other letters, monogram. 6. Continuous sounding of note on organ owing to imperfect closing of pallet or valve. ~ *v.* 1. Use Arabic numerals in arithmetic, do arithmetic; (U.S.) calculate, work *out* in the mind. 2. Put into secret writing. 3. (Of organ-note) go on sounding when not depressed. [Arab. *ṣifr* empty, zero]

cĭr'c'a, cĭr'cĭter *preps.* (abbrev. *c, ca, circ.*) About.

Cĭrcăss'ian *adj.* & *n.* (Member, language) of a group of tribes of the Caucasus, some of whom moved into Turkish territory in 19th c.; the women are remarkable for their physical beauty. [Russ. *Cherkes*, the tribe calling themselves Adighe]

Cĭr'cė. (Gk and Rom. legend.) Enchantress dwelling in island of Aeaea, who transformed all who drank of her cup into swine. **Cĭrcē'an** *adj.* Of, pertaining to, Circe; bewitching.

cĭr'cle *n.* 1. (Line enclosing) plane figure with circumference everywhere equidistant from centre; *square the* ~, find square of same area as given circle (a problem incapable of purely geometrical solution); *great* ~ (*of a sphere*), circle on surface of sphere, whose plane

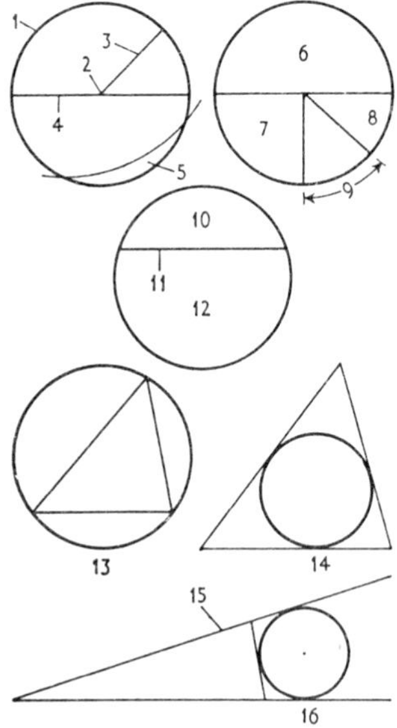

CIRCLE

1. Circumference. 2. Centre. 3. Radius. 4. Diameter. 5. Lune. 6. Semicircle. 7. Quadrant. 8. Sector. 9. Arc. 10. Minor segment. 11. Chord. 12. Major segment. 13. Circumscribed circle. 14. Inscribed circle. 15. Tangent. 16. Escribed circle

passes through centre of sphere (ill. SPHERE); *great* ~ *sailing*, *flying*, navigation along a great circle of the earth. 2. Anything shaped like a circle, ring; curved tier of seats at theatre etc.; *dress* ~, lowest (and most expensive) of these in a theatre (ill. THEATRE); *upper* ~, circle next above dress-circle; (archaeol.) series of stones set up in a ring. 3. Period, cycle, round; completed chain or sequence of events, parts, etc., esp. of consequences which react upon and intensify their causes (often *vicious* ~); (logic) fallacious reasoning, by which a proposition is used to establish a conclusion and is itself proved by means of the conclusion it has established (also *vicious* ~). 4. Persons grouped round centre of interest; set, coterie, class; society. ~ *v.* 1. (poet.) Encompass. 2. Make circuit of; move in a circle.

cîrc'lėt *n.* Small circle; circular band, esp. of gold, jewels, etc., worn on head or elsewhere.

cîrc'uit (-kĭt) *n.* 1. Line enclosing an area, distance round; area enclosed; journey round; roundabout way or journey. 2. Journey of judges etc. through certain appointed areas for purpose of holding courts of justice or performing other specified duties at various places in succession; the judges or barristers making the circuit; district or division through which circuit is made, of which there are 8 in England and Wales—the Northern, North-Eastern, Midland, Western, Oxford, Home or South-Eastern, North Wales and South Wales circuits. 3. Territorial division of Methodist Church, with a number of congregations served by a series of itinerant preachers. 4. Number of theatres etc. under one control. 5. (elect.) Course or path of an electric current; *short* ~, reduction in length or resistance of circuit, esp. when occurring by defective insulation.

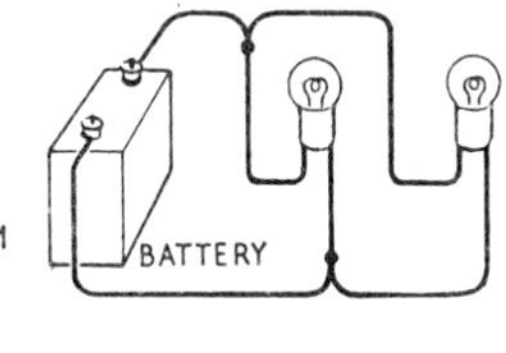

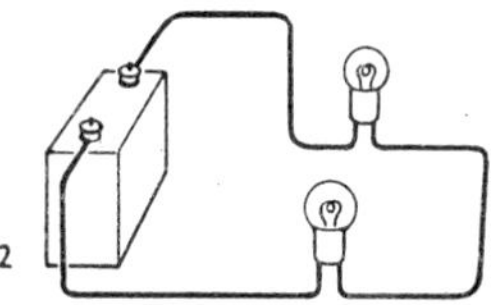

ELECTRIC CIRCUITS

1. Lamps joined in parallel. 2. Lamps joined in series

cîrcū'ĭtous *adj.* Roundabout, indirect. **cîrcū'ĭtously** *adv.* **cîrcū'ĭtousnėss** *n.*

cîrc'ūlar *adj.* Of the form of, pertaining to, moving in, passing over, a circle; ~ *tour* etc., one completed in or near the place of starting; ~ *letter*, letter (notice, advertisement, etc.), sent round in same form to several people, or printed etc. for this purpose; ~ *saw*, saw in form of revolving toothed disc (ill. SAW). **cîrcūlă'rĭty** *n.* **cîrc'ūlarly** *adv.* **cîrc'ūlar** *n.* Circular letter or advertisement. **cîrc'ūlarize** *v.t.* Send circular(s) to.

cîrc'ūlāte *v.* 1. Go round a circuit, circuitous course, system of pipes, etc.; esp. of the blood, flow from heart through arteries and capillaries and back through veins to heart. 2. Pass from place to place, from mouth to mouth, etc.; (of newspaper etc.) pass into hands of readers. 3. Put into circulation, cause to circulate; *circulating library*, library of which books are circulated among subscribers.

cîrcūlā'tion *n.* 1. Movement of blood from and back to heart; similar movement of sap etc.; movement to and fro. 2. Transmission, distribution (of news, books, etc.); no. of copies sold, esp. of newspapers. 3. Currency; coin.

cîrc'ulatory *adj.* Of circulation of the blood, of sap, etc.

circum- *prefix.* Round, about.

cîrcumăm'bĭėnt *adj.* Surrounding (esp. of air or other fluids). **cîrcumăm'bĭence** *n.*

cîrcumăm'būlāte *v.* Walk round, walk about. **cîrcumămbūlā'tion** *n.* **cîrcumăm'būlatory** *adj.*

cîrcumbĕn'dĭbus *n.* (facet.) Roundabout method; circumlocution.

cîrc'umcīse (-z) *v.t.* Cut off foreskin of (as Jewish or Mohammedan rite, or surgically). **cîrcumcĭ'sion** (-zhn) *n.* 1. Act or religious rite of, spiritual purification by, circumcising. 2. (eccles.) Festival of circumcision of Christ, 1st Jan. 3. The Jews, as a circumcised race.

circŭm'ference *n.* Encompassing boundary, esp. of figure enclosed by curve, as circle (ill. CIRCLE); distance round. **cîrcumferĕn'tial** (-shl) *adj.*

circŭm'ferĕntor *n.* 1. (surv.) Instrument with compass for taking sights. 2. Instrument for measuring circumference of a wheel.

cîrc'umflĕx *n.* Circumflex accent. ~ *adj.* 1. ~ *accent*, mark (^, in Greek ~) placed over vowel to indicate contraction, length, or special quality. 2. (anat.) Curved, bending round something else.

circŭm'flūent *adj.* Flowing round, ambient. **circŭm'flūence** *n.*

cîrcumfūse' (-z) *v.t.* Pass round; surround *with*, bathe. **cîrcumfū'sion** (-zhn) *n.*

cîrcumgȳrāte' *v.i.* Turn, wheel, travel, round. **cîrcumgȳrā'tion** *n.*

cîrcumjā'cent *adj.* Situated around.

cîrcumlocū'tion *n.* Use of many words where few would do; evasive talk; roundabout expression; *C~ Office*, government department satirized by Dickens in 'Little Dorrit'. **cîrcumlŏc'ūtory** *adj.*

cîrcumnăv'ĭgāte *v.t.* Sail round. **cîrcumnăvĭgā'tion, cîrcumnăv'ĭgātor** *ns.*

cîrcumpōl'ar *adj.* Around, about, near, a (terrestrial or celestial) pole; (astron., of star etc.) describing its whole diurnal circle above the horizon.

cîrc'umscrībe *v.t.* 1. Draw line round; encompass. 2. Mark out or define limits of; confine within narrow limits, restrict, hem in. 3. (geom.) Describe (figure) about another so as to touch it at certain points without cutting it (ill. CIRCLE). **cîrcumscrĭp'tion** *n.* Circumscribing; inscription round coin, seal, etc. (ill. COIN).

cîrcumsōl'ar *adj.* Situated near, moving round, the sun.

cîrc'umspĕct *adj.* Cautious, wary; taking everything into account. **cîrc'umspĕctly** *adv.* **cîrc'umspĕctnėss, cîrcumspĕc'tion** *ns.*

cîrc'umstance *n.* 1. (pl.) Time, place, manner, cause, occasion, etc., surroundings, of an act; external conditions affecting or that might affect an agent. 2. (pl.) Material welfare, means. 3. Detail in narrative. 4. Formality, ceremony fuss. 5. Incident, occurrence, fact. 6. (U.S.) Comparable or important thing or fact. **cîrc'umstanced** *adj.*

cîrcumstăn'tial (-shl) *adj.* 1. Of or dependent on circumstances; ~ *evidence*, indirect evidence from circumstances affording a certain presumption or capable of only one explanation. 2. Adventitious, accidental. 3. Full of, particular as to, details. 4. Full of circumstance or pomp. **cîrcumstăn'tially** *adv.*

cîrcumvallā'tion *n.* (Making of) rampart or entrenchment.

cîrcumvĕnt' *v.t.* Entrap; overreach, outwit. **cîrcumvĕn'tion** *n.*

cîrc'us *n.* 1. Rounded or oval (freq. temporary) arena lined with tiers of seats for equestrian and other exhibitions; entertainment given in this, consisting usu. of acrobatics, clowning, feats of horsemanship, and performances by animals; travelling show of riders, acrobats, etc., and their equipage. 2. (Rom. antiq.) Large oval or oblong building surrounded with rising tiers of seats for public spectacles and horse or chariot races. 3. Amphitheatre of hills. 4. (Circular) open space in town with streets converging on it.

cîrque (-k) *n.* (poet. and rhet.) Arena, natural amphitheatre; (geol.) = CORRIE.

cirrhos'ĭs (sĭrō-) *n.* Disease of liver, most frequent among habitual spirit-drinkers; chronic interstitial hepatitis, with atrophy of cells and increase of connective tissue. **cĭrrhŏt'ĭc** *adj.*

cirrhus: erroneous but common form of CIRRUS.

cĭ'rrĭpĕd, -pēde *n.* (zool.) Member of the *Cirripedia*, subclass of *Crustacea* comprising chiefly marine animals esp. the barnacles; most have shelly plates strengthening the carapace and feathery legs which are protruded from the shell-valves to collect food.

cirrōcūm'ūlus *n.* (pl. *-lī*). (meteor.) Form of usu. high cloud consisting of roundish fleecy cloudlets in contact with one another, 'mackerel sky' (ill. CLOUD).

cirrōse' (-s), **cĭ'rrous** *adjs.* Of or having cirri; of or like cirrus.

cirrōstrāt'us *n.* (meteor.) Thin usu. high cloud consisting of horizontal or inclined sheets attenuated upwards into light cirri (ill. CLOUD).

cĭ'rrus *n.* (pl. *cirrī*). 1. (zool.) Slender filamentary process or appendage. 2. (meteor.) Form of cloud, usu. high, with diverging filaments or wisps, often resembling curl or lock of hair or wool (ill. CLOUD).

cĭs- *prefix.* On this side of.

Cĭsăl'pīne *adj.* On this (usu. = the Roman) side of the Alps; ~ *Gaul*, northern Italy in ancient times.

cĭss'y, si- *adj.* & *n.* (slang) Effeminate (person). [f. *sister*]

cĭst[1] *n.* (archaeol.) Prehistoric sepulchral chest or chamber of stone or hollowed tree-trunk (also *-grave*); box for sacred utensils in Gk mysteries.

cĭst[2] *n.* Var. of CYST.

Cĭstẽr'cian (-shn). (Member) of the monastic order, observing a stricter form of the Benedictine rule, founded at Cîteaux near Dijon in 1098 by Robert, abbot of Molesme. [L *Cistercium* Cîteaux]

cĭs'tern *n.* Artificial reservoir for storing water, usu. tank in high part of building with pipes supplying taps on lower levels.

cĭs'tus *n.* Genus of handsome shrubs with large spotted red or white short-lived flowers.

cĭt'adel *n.* Fortress, esp. one guarding or commanding a city.

cīte *v.t.* 1. Summon to appear in law-court. 2. Quote in support of a position; mention as example.

cītā'tion *n.* (esp., orig. U.S.) Mention in an official dispatch, recommendation to an honour.

cĭth'er(n), cĭtt'ern *n.* Obsolete musical instrument somewhat like lute but with flat back, with 4 wire strings usu. played with plectrum.

cĭt'izen *n.* 1. Burgess, freeman, inhabitant, of city or town; enfranchised member of a State; ~ *of the world*, cosmopolitan. 2. (hist., as title) Representing Fr. *citoyen*, which at the Revolution took the place of *Monsieur*; so **cĭt'izenĕss**, = *citoyenne*. **cĭt'izenshĭp** *n.*

cĭt'rāte *n.* A salt of citric acid.

cĭt'rĭc *adj.* ~ *acid*, colourless, sharp-tasting crystalline acid found in the juice of oranges, lemons, limes, etc.

cĭt'ron *n.* Ovate acid juicy fruit with pale yellow rind, larger, less acid, and thicker-skinned than lemon; the tree, *Citrus medica*, bearing this.

cĭtronĕll'a *n.* Fragrant grass, *Andropagon nardus*, yielding a fragrant oil much used in perfumery; the oil itself.

cĭt'rous *adj.* Of the Citrus genus.

Cĭt'rus *n.* Genus including citron, orange, lime, lemon, and grape-fruit.

cĭt'y *n.* 1. (loosely) Important town; (strictly, in England) town created city by charter, in early times esp. one containing a cathedral; (in U.S.) town of greater importance, or size, or with wider municipal powers, than those called simply 'towns'; *Holy C~*, Jerusalem; *Celestial C~*, *Holy C~*, *C~ of God*, Paradise; *Eternal C~*, *C~ of the Seven Hills*, Rome; *C~ State*, one of the ancient Greek republics. 2. *The C~*, the *C~ of London*, that part within the ancient boundaries, including the liberties, which is under the jurisdiction of the Lord Mayor and Corporation; esp. the business part of this, near the Exchange and Bank of England, the centre of financial and commercial activity; ~ *article*, financial and commercial article in a newspaper; so ~ *editor*, *page*, etc.; *C~ Company*, one of the corporations historically representing the ancient trade guilds of London; ~ *man*, one engaged in commerce or finance (in the City of London).

cĭv'ĕt *n.* 1. Yellowish or brownish substance, unctuous and smelling strongly of musk, got from anal glands of civet-cat, or other animal of civet genus. 2. Genus of carnivorous quadrupeds yielding this, esp. the central African ~*-cat*, *Vivena civetta*, in size and appearance between fox and weasel.

cĭv'ĭc *adj.* Of, proper to, citizens; of a city, municipal; of citizenship, civil. **cĭv'ĭcs** *n.* Rights and duties of citizenship as part of practical science.

cĭv'ĭl *adj.* 1. Of citizens, of men dwelling together in a community; of the body politic or state. 2. Of, becoming, befitting, a citizen; civilized; 'decently polite', not rude. 3. Non-military; non-ecclesiastical, secular; (law) not criminal or political; ~ *defence*, protection of civil population against effects of aerial attack; *C~ Defence Service*, organization formed in U.K., 1940, co-ordinating the services previously called Air Raid Precautions (A.R.P.); ~ *disobedience*, refusal to obey the laws as part of a political campaign; ~ *engineering*: see ENGINEERING; ~ *law*, the law pertaining to the private rights and remedies of a citizen (cf. CRIMINAL law); the law of Roman citizens; Roman law as a whole, esp. as received in Western Christendom in and after Middle Ages; *C~ List*, amount voted by Parliament from public revenue for household and personal expenses of monarch and for *C~ List pensions*, i.e. those granted by the royal bounty; ~ *marriage*, marriage solemnized as a civil contract, without religious ceremony; ~ *proceedings*, legal proceedings aimed at the redress of wrong; *C~ Service*, all public State departments or services except the army, navy, and air force; *C~ Servant*, official employed in any of these; ~ *war*, war between members of the same community; *the C~ War*, in England, the struggle between Charles I and Parliament in 17th c.; in U.S., the war of Secession, 1861–5. **cĭv'ĭlly** *adv.* **cĭvĭl'ĭty** *n.* Politeness.

cĭvĭl'ian *adj.* & *n.* (Person) not of one of the fighting services.

cĭvĭlīzā'tion *n.* Making or becoming civilized; stage, esp. advanced stage, in social development.

cĭv'ĭlīze *v.t.* Bring out of barbarism; instruct in the arts of life; refine, enlighten.

cĭvv'y *n.* Colloq. abbrev. of CIVILIAN, as in ~ *clothes* (also abbrev. *civvies*), ~ *street*, civilian life.

C.J. *abbrev.* Chief Justice.

cl. *abbrev.* Centilitre; class; classical.

clăck *n.* 1. Sharp sound as of boards struck together; noise or clatter of human tongues. 2. Kind of pump-valve, flap opened by upward motion of fluid (ill. PUMP); locomotive valve closing opening of feed-pump into boiler. ~ *v.i.* Chatter, prate; make clack.

Clăckmănn'anshire. County of central Scotland.

clăd *past part.* & *adj.* Clothed.

clăd'ōde *n.* (bot.) Leaf-like stem (ill. STEM).

claim *v.t.* Demand as one's due; represent oneself as having; demand recognition of the fact that; profess; deserve, call for, demand; (U.S.) contend, assert. ~ *n.* 1. Demand for something as due; right, title, *to*; right to make demand *on*. 2. Piece of land allotted, esp. for mining. **claim'ant** *n.* One who makes or enters a claim.

clairvoy'ance *n.* Faculty of seeing mentally what is out of sight; second sight. **clairvoy'ant** *adj.* & *n.* (Person) having this faculty.

clăm *n.* Various bivalve shellfish, esp. the N. Amer. hard or round ~, *Venus mercenaria*, and soft or long ~, *Mya arenaria*, found abundantly on sandy or muddy shores and esteemed as food; (slang, orig. U.S.) silent, uncommunicative person; ~ *chowder*, see CHOWDER. [orig. *clamshell*; ult. f. Ger. *klam* press or squeeze together]

clăm'ant *adj.* Noisy, insistent, urgent.

clăm'ber *v.i.* Climb with hands and feet; climb with difficulty or labour. ~ *n.* Climbing thus.

clămm'y *adj.* Moist and sticky.

clămm'ĭly *adv.* **clămm'inėss** *n.*

clăm'our (-mer) *n.* Shouting; loud appeal, complaint, or demand; confused noise. ~ *v.i.* Make clamour *for, against*, etc. **clăm'orous** *adj.* **clăm'orously** *adv.* **clăm'orousnėss** *n.*

clămp *n.* Brace, clasp, or band, usu. of iron, for strengthening other materials or holding things together; various appliances or tools with opposite sides connected by screw for holding or compressing. ~ *v.t.* Strengthen, fasten, with clamp or clamps.

clăn *n.* 1. Number of persons descended from same ancestor and associated together, esp. in Scottish Highlands, and also in various parts of the Lowlands with similar social system; *clans'man*, (fellow) member of a clan. 2. Family holding together; coterie, set. **clănn'ĭsh** *adj.* **clănn'ĭshly** *adv.* **clănn'ĭshnėss** *n.*

clăndĕs'tine *adj.* Surreptitious, secret, underhand. **clăndĕs'tinely** *adv.*

clăng *n.* Loud resonant metallic sound. ~ *v.* Make, cause to make, this sound.

clăng'our (-ngger) *n.* Succession of loud metallic ringing noises. **clăng'orous** *adj.*

clănk *n.* Sharp abrupt sound, as of heavy pieces of metal struck together. ~ *v.* Make, cause to make, this sound.

clăn'shĭp *n.* System of clans; clannishness; attachment or loyalty to a clan.

clăp *n.* 1. Loud explosive noise as of thunder; peal. 2. Sound made by striking palms of hands together; act of doing this as applause. ~ *v.* 1. Make clap; make this noise with hands to signify applause, delight, etc.; applaud with claps; shut (door etc.) with clap. 2. Slap with palm of hand, in approval or encouragement; apply, place, set, quickly or energetically; put *in* prison; ~ *eyes on*, catch sight of; ~*-net*, net that can be shut by pulling string.

clăp'board (-bōrd) *n.* & *v.t.* (U.S.) Weatherboard. **clăp'boarding** *n.*

clăpp'er[1] *n.* Tongue or striker of bell (ill. BELL); rattle for scaring birds.

clăpp'er[2] *n.* Rabbit-burrow (obs.); ~ *bridge*, primitive bridge consisting of a series of slabs or planks resting on piles of stones (ill. BRIDGE).

clăp'trăp *n.* Trick or device, language, to catch applause. ~ *adj.* Intended, designed, to draw applause; showy.

claque (klahk) *n.* Body of hired applauders in theatre etc.

clārabĕll'a *n.* Organ stop of flute type. [L *clarus* clear, *bellus* pretty]

Clāre. County of Munster, Eire.

Clāre Cŏll'ege. A college of the University of Cambridge, founded 1326, and re-founded 1342 by Elizabeth, granddaughter of Edward I and sister of Gilbert, Earl of Clare.

clă'rence *n.* Four-wheeled closed carriage with seats for 4 inside and 2 on box. [f. Duke of *Clarence*, afterwards William IV]

Clă'renceux (-sū). The 2nd King of Arms in England, whose office is to marshal and arrange funerals of all baronets, knights, and esquires south of the Trent. [f. *Clarence*, dukedom created for Lionel, 2nd son of Edward III, when he married the heiress of Clare in Suffolk; the Clarence herald was subsequently made a Royal herald and King of Arms]

Clă'rendon[1], Edward Hyde, Earl of (1609–74). English statesman and historian; lord chancellor under Charles II; author of 'The True Historical Narrative of the Rebellion and Civil Wars in England', from the profits of which a new printing-house, which bore his name, was built for the Oxford University Press, also the ~ *Laboratory*, the university physics department, founded in 1872.

Clă'rendon[2], Constitutions of: see CONSTITUTION, 3.

clă'rendon[3] *n.* Thick-faced type of various sizes. [the *Clarendon* Press, Oxford]

Clāres *n.pl.* (also *Poor* ~) Sisterhood instituted at Assisi *c* 1212 by St. Clare, who adopted the Franciscan rule and habit.

clă'ret *n.* Red wine imported from Bordeaux; colour of this, dark reddish-purple; artificial salmon-fly of this colour; (boxing slang) blood. ~ *adj.* Claret-coloured.

clă'rĭfȳ *v.* Make clear; free from impurities, make transparent (liquid, butter, etc.); become or be made clear or pure. **clărĭfĭcā'tion** *n.*

clărĭnĕt' (*or* clă'rĭnĕt) *n.* Woodwind single-reed instrument with compass of about 3½ octaves from C♯ or D below middle C, having cylindrical tube with bell-shaped end, and played by fingers on holes and keys (ill. WOOD); 8-ft organ-stop of similar quality; *bass* ~, instrument like clarinet with range an octave lower.

clă'rĭon *n.* 1. Shrill narrow-tubed trumpet formerly used in war; sound of trumpet, any similar rousing sound; 4-ft organ-stop of similar quality to clarion. ~ *adj.* Loud and clear, like a clarion.

clărĭonĕt' *n.* = CLARINET.

clă'rĭty *n.* Clearness.

clārk'ia *n.* Genus of annual plants with white, pink, or purple flowers, often grown in gardens, natives of N. America. [W. *Clarke*, member of 1st U.S. Government expedition across Rocky Mountains, 1804–5]

clār'ȳ *n.* A pot-herb, *Salvia sclarea*, native of S. Europe, Syria, etc.; various other species of the same genus, including the English wild ~ or vervain, *S. horminoides*, and meadow ~, *S. pratensis.*

clăsh *n.* 1. Loud broken sound as of collision, striking weapons or cymbals, bells rung together. 2. Encounter, conflict; disagreement. ~ *v.* 1. Make clash. 2. Conflict, disagree, be at variance *with*; (of colours) be discordant.

clasp (-ah-) *n.* 1. Contrivance of two interlocking parts for fastening; buckle; brooch; metal fastening of book cover. 2. Embracing, embrace; grasp or joining of hands. 3. Bar of silver bearing name of engagement at which wearer was present, on ribbon of medal commemorating campaign (ill. MEDAL). 4. ~*-knife*, folding knife, esp. large one in which open blade can be rigidly fixed by a catch. ~ *v.* 1. Fasten (clasp), fasten with or as clasp. 2. Encircle, hold closely, embrace; grasp (another's hand); join (hands) by interlocking fingers.

class (-ah-) *n.* 1. Rank, order, of society; *the classes*, the rich or educated (opp. to *the masses*); class system, caste. 2. Division of scholars or students taught together or considered of same standing; their time of meeting, the instruction given to them; (U.S. colleges) all students of the same standing, who enter together, graduate together, etc. (~ *of 1958*, those who graduated in that year); (in conscripted armies) all the recruits of a year. 3. (Methodism) Subdivision of society or congregation meeting regularly under a *class-leader*. 4. Division of candidates or competitors after examination, according to merit; division according to quality. 5. Number of individuals having some character or feature in common; (biol.) division of animals or plants below phylum, subdivided into orders, families, genera, species. 6. ~*-conscious*, conscious of belonging to a particular (esp. working) class, often with implication of hostility to other classes; ~*-consciousness*; ~*-list*, list of competitors in examination arranged in classes; *classman* (Oxford Univ.) one who has taken a 'class' (i.e. an honours degree) as opp. to *passman*. ~ *v.t.* Place in class. **class'lėss** *adj.* (Of a society) not recognizing, not having, social distinctions.

clăss'ĭc *adj.* 1. Of the first class, of avowed excellence. 2. Of the ancient Greek and Latin authors; of Greek and Roman antiquity. 3. (opp. to ROMANTIC) In the classic style, simple, harmonious, proportioned, and finished. 4. Having literary or historic associations. 5. *C~ races*, (in England) the 5 chief horse-races of the year (the 2000 Guineas, 1000 Guineas, Derby, Oaks, and St. Leger). ~ *n.* 1. Writer or artist, work, of acknowledged excellence. 2. Ancient Greek or Latin writer; scholar of

Latin and Greek; (pl.) these studies. 3. Classic race.

clăss'ĭcal *adj.* 1. Standard, first-class, esp. in literature. 2. Of ancient Greek or Latin standard authors or art; learned in, studying, or based on these. 3. In, following, the restrained style of classical antiquity. **clăss'ĭcally** *adv.*

clăss'ĭcism *n.* Following of classic(al) style; classical scholarship; advocacy of classical education. **clăss'ĭcist** *n.*

clăss'ĭfȳ *v.t.* Arrange in classes, assign to a class; *classified*, (of official documents) belonging to a class, e.g. secret or confidential, which only specified persons may see. **clăss'ĭfĭcā'tion** *n.* **clăss'ĭfĭcatory** *adj.*

class'ȳ (-ahs-) *adj.* (slang) Superior; stylish, smart.

clătt'er *n.* Rattling sound, as of many plates struck together; noisy talk, confused din of voices. ~ *v.* Make clatter, cause to rattle.

Claude Lorrain (klawd lorān', klōd lorăṅ'). Name by which Claude Gellée (1600–82), French landscape painter, is generally known.

Claud'ĭan *adj.* 1. Of any of several distinguished Romans of the name of Claudius, or of their gens or family; esp. of the Emperors Tiberius, Caligula, Claudius, and Nero, or their epoch (A.D. 14–68). 2. Of Claude Lorrain.

Claud'ĭus (10 B.C.–A.D. 54). Tiberius Claudius Drusus Nero Germanicus, Roman emperor A.D. 41–54; author of several historical works no longer extant.

clause (-z) *n.* 1. Short sentence; (gram.) subordinate part of sentence including subject and predicate but syntactically equivalent to noun, adjective, or adverb. 2. Single proviso in treaty, law, contract, or other document. **claus'al** *adj.*

claus'tral *adj.* Of the cloister, monastic, narrow.

claustrophō'bĭa *n.* Morbid dread of confined places.

clăv'ĕcĭn *n.* Harpsichord.

clăv'ĭchōrd (-k-) *n.* (hist.) Musical instrument resembling square

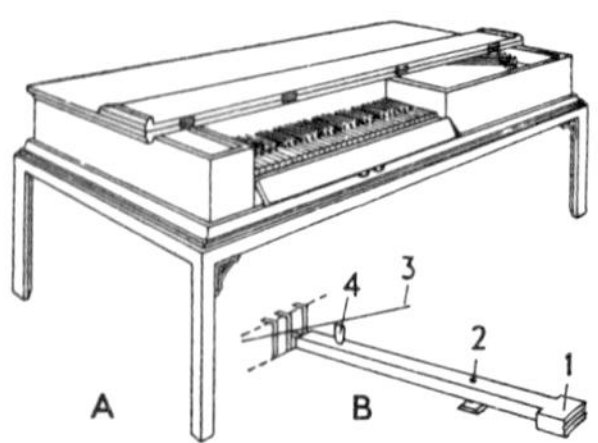

A. CLAVICHORD. B. ACTION

1. Key. 2. Balance. 3. String. 4. Tangent. When the key is depressed the tangent, by striking the string, cuts off the length necessary to form the note by vibration

piano, with keyboard and strings struck by 'tangents' or small brass wedges attached to back of keys; this was the earliest keyboard instrument with strings, and appeared about the middle of the 14th c.

clăv'ĭcle *n.* Collar-bone (ill. SKELETON). **clavĭc'ūlar** *adj.*

claw *n.* Pointed horny nail of beast's or bird's foot; foot so armed, pincers of shell-fish (ill. LOBSTER); (contempt.) hand; mechanical or other contrivance for grappling, tearing, etc.; *~-hammer*, hammer with one end bent and split, for extracting nails (ill. HAMMER); *~-hammer (coat)*, tail-coat of evening dress. ~ *v.* Scratch, tear, seize, pull towards one, with claws or nails; (naut.) beat to windward, esp. ~ *off* (= away from) *shore*.

clay *n.* 1. Stiff viscous earth consisting chiefly of aluminium silicate and forming with water a tenacious paste which may be moulded, or dried and baked into bricks, pottery, tiles, etc.; *~ pigeon*, piece of baked clay jerked up from trap to be shot at. 2. Earth, esp. the earth covering a dead body when buried; earth as the material of the human body, hence, the body. 3. Tobacco-pipe of baked clay. **clay'ey** (-ĭ) *adj.*

clay'mōre *n.* Two-edged broadsword formerly used by Scottish Highlanders. [Gael. *claidheamb mòr* great sword]

clean *adj.* 1. Free from anything contaminating or from dirt; free from weeds, barnacles, etc.; (of paper) blank; (of printer's proof etc.) free from corrections; (of nuclear bombs) not producing fall-out. 2. Free from moral stain; free from ceremonial defilement or of disease; (of beasts etc.) fit for food. 3. Neatly made, not unwieldy, trim; neat; unencumbered, unobstructed; (of wood) free from knots. 4. Entire, complete, total; ~ *sweep*, complete riddance. **clean'ly**[1] *adv.* **clean'nĕss** *n.* **clean** *adv.* Completely; right, outright; altogether; simply, absolutely. ~ *v.* Make clean; make oneself clean; ~ *out*, empty, strip; ~ *up*, clean, make tidy, clear up; (slang) acquire as gain. ~ *n.* Cleaning.

clean'ly[2] (-ĕn-) *adj.* Habitually clean, attentive to cleanness. **clean'lĭly** *adv.* **clean'lĭnĕss** *n.*

cleanse (-ĕnz) *v.t.* Make clean (archaic, or more formal than *clean*); purify; cure (leper etc.).

clear *adj.* 1. Unclouded, transparent, not turbid; lustrous; unspotted. 2. Distinct, unambiguous, intelligible; not confused; manifest. 3. Discerning, penetrating; confident, decided, certain. 4. Easily audible. 5. Without reduction, net; free *of*; whole, complete; open, unobstructed; unengaged, free; not encumbered by debt. ~ *adv.* Clearly; quite; apart, without contact. ~ *v.* 1. Make, become, clear. 2. Free from imputation of guilt. 3. Free or rid *of*; remove; depart; empty, become empty. 4. Free from contact or entanglement; pass without entanglement, contact, or collision. 5. Settle (debt etc.); free from debt; (naut.) free (ship) by paying all dues; (of ship) sail. 6. Make (sum of money) as net gain. 7. ~ *away*, remove, remove meal from table, (of mist etc.) disappear; ~ *off*, get rid of, melt away, (of intruders) go away; ~ *out*, empty, make off; ~ *up*, solve (mystery), make tidy, (of weather etc.) grow clear.

clear'ance *n.* 1. Clearing; removal of obstructions; passing of cheques through Clearing House; (certificate of) clearing of ship at custom-house. 2. Clear space; room to pass. 3. ~ *sale*, shop's sale of goods at reduced prices in order to get rid of superfluous stock.

clear'ĭng *n.* (esp.) Piece of land cleared for cultivation; *C~ House*, bankers' institution in London for exchanging cheques and bills, and settling the balances; similar office (*Railway C~ House*) for settling accounts (for through tickets, freights, etc.) between railways.

clear'ly *adv.* Distinctly; manifestly; undoubtedly.

clear'nĕss *n.* Transparence; distinctness; freedom from obstruction.

cleat *n.* Wedge; projecting piece bolted on spar, gangway, etc., to give footing or prevent rope from slipping; wedge-shaped or other projecting piece of wood or metal for fastening ropes to, etc. (ill. BELAY).

cleav'age *n.* Cleaving; being cleft; way or line in which anything tends to split; property (of minerals and rocks) of splitting readily in certain directions.

cleave[1] *v.* (past t. *clōve* or *clĕft*; past part. *clōv'en* or *clĕft*). Split; chop, break, or come apart, esp. along grain or line of cleavage; make way through (water, air, etc.). **cleav'er** *n.* (esp.) Butcher's chopping-tool for carcasses.

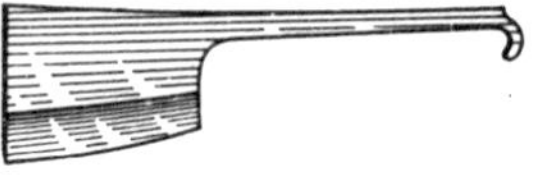

CLEAVER

cleave[2] *v.i.* (past t. *cleaved* or *clave*; past part. *cleaved*). Stick fast, adhere *to* (archaic); be faithful.

cleav'ers, clĭv'ers (-z) *n.* A scrambling weed, *Galium aparine*, also called goose-grass.

cleek *n.* Iron-headed golf-club with straight narrow face and long shaft (ill. GOLF).

clĕf *n.* Symbol placed on line of stave to indicate name and pitch of notes on that line, and hence of those on other lines and spaces; there are three clefs, the *C* ~

(*tenor* , or *alto* : the line of the stave on which the clef is placed represents middle *C* on the piano), the *G* or *treble* ~ (: the 2nd line from the bottom of this stave represents the *G* above middle *C* on the piano), and the *F* or *bass* ~ (or : the 2nd line from the top of this stave represents the *F* below middle *C* on the piano).

clĕft[1] *n.* Fissure, split.

clĕft[2] *past t.* & *part.* of CLEAVE[1] *v.* ~ ***palate***, malformation of palate with longitudinal gap in middle or on either side of roof of mouth; ~ ***stick***, position in which advance and retreat are alike impossible; dilemma, fix.

clĕg *n.* Gad-fly, horse-fly.

cleistogăm'ic (klī-) *adj.* (Of plant) self-pollinating inside a flower which does not open. **cleistŏg'amy** *n.*

clĕm *v.* (north. dial.) Starve.

clĕm'atis *n.* Genus of twining shrubs having flowers with showy calyx and no corolla, and achenes with long feathery appendages; the only species native to Britain is *C~ vitalba*, Traveller's Joy or Old Man's Beard, common in hedgerows on chalk.

Clemenceau (klemahńsō'), Georges (1841–1929). French statesman; prime minister 1906–9 and 1917–20; chairman of the Versailles Peace Conference.

clĕm'ency *n.* Mildness of temper or weather; mercy.

clĕm'ent[1] *adj.* Mild, showing mercy.

Clĕm'ent[2]. Name of several popes and bishops of Rome. **Clĕm'entīne** *adj.* Of, relating to, any of these; ~ *Decretals*, those issued by Clement V, pope 1305–14; ~ *Epistles*, two, probably spurious, Epistles to the Corinthians, attributed to Clement I, a bishop of Rome of the 1st c.; ~ *Vulgate*, revised edition of the VULGATE issued under the direction of Clement VIII, pope 1592–1605.

clĕnch *v.* Fix securely, make fast, as with nails; secure (nail etc.) by hammering point sideways after driving through; set firmly together, close tightly (teeth, fingers); grasp firmly, grip; confirm, drive home, settle conclusively. ~ *n.* Clenching, being clenched.

Clēopăt'ra (*or* -pah-) (68–30 B.C.). Queen of Egypt; daughter of Ptolemy Auletes, king of Egypt; famous for her beauty and charm; exercised these on Julius Caesar, who restored her to her throne in 47 B.C. after her expulsion by Pothinus. Later Mark ANTONY fell in love with her; in the war between Antony and AUGUSTUS the defection of her fleet at the battle of Actium (31 B.C.) hastened Antony's defeat, and to escape being carried captive to Rome by Augustus, Cleopatra took her own life. The granite obelisks known as *~'s Needles* have no connexion with the queen, but were erected at Heliopolis by Thothmes III *c* 1600 B.C.; that which stands on the Thames Embankment was brought to England in 1878.

clere'stōry (-ērs-) *n.* Upper part of wall of nave, choir, and transepts of cathedral or large church above triforium or arches of nave etc., and containing windows clear of the roof of the aisles (ill. CHURCH).

cler'gy *n.* 1. The clerical order; all persons ordained for religious service; clergymen. 2. (hist.) 'Clerkly skill', learning, scholarship. 3. *benefit of* ~, orig. privilege of exemption from trial by secular court, allowed to clergymen arraigned for felony; later, exemption from sentence on first conviction for certain offences claimed by all who could read (ability to read being orig. the test of 'clergy' or clerical position of the accused); ***cler'gyman***, ordained minister, esp. of Established Church.

clĕ'ric *n.* Clerical man, clergyman. [Gk *klērikos* f. *klēros* lot, inheritance; see Acts i. 17]

clĕ'rical *adj.* 1. Of the clergy, a clergyman, or clergymen; of clericalists. 2. Of, made by, a clerk or clerks; ~ ***error***, error in writing anything out. ~ *n.* Cleric; member of a clerical party.

clĕ'ricalism *n.* (esp.) Clerical rule or influence. **clĕ'ricalist** *n.*

clĕ'rihew *n.* Short comic or nonsensical verse, professedly biographical, usu. of two couplets of different length. [Edmund *Clerihew* Bentley (1875–1956)]

clerk (-ark) *n.* 1. Clergyman (archaic & legal); (before the Reformation) member of one of the five 'minor orders', as dist. from higher or 'holy orders'; hence, layman performing similar functions, lay officer of parish church who has charge of building and precincts, leads responses, assists at baptisms, marriages, etc. 2. Officer in charge of records, accounts, etc., of any department, court, corporation, etc. 3. Subordinate employed to make written entries, keep accounts, do mechanical work of correspondence, etc. 4. *C~ of Assize*, officer recording judicial decisions given in assize court; ~ *of the weather*, imaginary functionary supposed to control the weather; *C~ of the Works*, officer superintending erection of building etc. **clerk'ship** *n.* **clerk** *v.i.* (colloq.) Act as clerk.

clerk'ly (-ark-) *adj.* Of a clerk; skilled in penmanship.

Clerk-Măx'well (-ark-), James (1831–79). Professor of experimental physics at Cambridge; contributed to the theory of the conservation of energy and of electricity and magnetism.

Clēve'land (-vl-), Grover (1837–1908). 22nd and 24th president of U.S., 1885–9 and 1893–7.

clĕv'er *adj.* Adroit, dexterous, neat in movement; skilful, talented; ingenious. **clĕv'erly** *adv.* **clĕv'erness** *n.*

clĕv'is *n.* U-shaped piece of iron forming loop for tackle at end of beam etc.

clew (-o͞o) *n.* 1. Ball of thread or yarn; such a ball used as guide through maze or labyrinth (in many mythological or legendary stories). 2. (naut.) Small cords suspending hammock; lower corner of square sail, after corner of fore-and-aft sail, to which are fastened tacks and sheets for extending and securing it (ill. SAIL[1]). ~ *v.t.* (naut.) Draw lower ends of (sails) *up* to upper yard or mast for furling.

cliché (-ēsh'ā) *n.* Stereotype or electrotype block; stereotyped or commonplace phrase or expression.

click *n.* 1. Slight sharp hard non-ringing sound as of dropping latch etc.; ~ *beetle*, adult wireworm or other beetle of family *Elateridae* which when turned over rights itself by jumping with a click. 2. Piece of mechanism, esp. catch falling into notches of ratchet-wheel, acting with this sound. 3. Fault in horse's action, toe of hind hoof striking shoe of forefoot. 4. (phonetics) Class of sharp non-vocal sounds occurring in certain African languages, formed by suction, with sudden withdrawal of tongue from contact with part of mouth. ~ *v.* Make click; (slang) have luck, secure one's object; get on friendly terms *with* person of opposite sex.

clī'ent *n.* 1. (Rom. antiq.) plebeian under protection of noble; (archaic) dependent, hanger-on. 2. One employing services of lawyer; employer of services of any professional or business man; customer.

clī'entēle *n.* 1. Body of clients or dependents. 2. (*also* klēawńtăl') Customers, supporters, professional connexion.

clĭff *n.* Steep rock-face, usu. overhanging sea.

clīmăc'teric (*or* -măctĕ'rĭc) *adj.* Constituting a crisis, critical; esp., occurring at period of life (45–60) at which vital forces begin to decline. ~ *n.* Critical point or period in life; acc. to one superstition, all years denoted by multiples of 7, acc. to another, odd multiples only (7, 21, 35, etc.); *grand* ~, 63rd year, supposed to be specially critical.

clīm'ate *n.* (Region with specified) prevailing conditions of temperature, rainfall, humidity, wind, etc. **clīmăt'ic** *adj.*

clīmatŏl'ogy *n.* Study of climates. **clīmatolŏ'gical** *adj.*

clīm'ăx *n.* Ascending scale; series of ideas or expressions so arranged; last term in these; culmination, apex. **clīmăc'tic** *adj.*

clīmb (-m) *v.* 1. Ascend, mount,

go *up*, esp. with help of hands; ~ *down*, descend similarly; (fig.) retreat from position taken up, give in. 2. (of sun, aeroplane, etc.) Mount upward. 3. (of plants) Creep up by aid of tendrils or by twining. 4. Slope upwards. 5. Rise by effort in social rank, intellectual or moral power, etc. 6. *climbing-irons*, irons strapped to boot to assist in climbing trees etc. or ice-slopes. ~ *n.* Climbing; place climbed or to be climbed.

person. **clĭnk'ĭng** *adj.* & *adv.* (colloq.) Exceedingly (good, fine).

clĭnk[2] *n.* (slang) Prison, lock-up. [proper name of a former prison in Southwark]

clĭnk'er[2] *n.* 1. Very hard pale-yellow Dutch paving-brick; brick with surface vitrified by great heat. 2. Mass of bricks fused by excessive heat; hardened mass formed by fusion of earthy impurities of burned coal, limestone, etc., slag; mass of hardened volcanic lava.

and statesman in the service of the East India Company; avenged the BLACK HOLE of Calcutta by defeating Surâj ud Daula at the battle of Plassey, 1757; became governor of Bengal, 1758.

clōā'ca *n.* (pl. *-ae*) 1. Sewer. 2. Common excrementory cavity at end of intestinal canal in birds, reptiles, etc. (ill. BIRD). **clōā'cal** *adj.*

cloak *n.* Loose usu. sleeveless outer garment; (fig.) covering, pre-

CLOAKS AND CAPES

1. Domino. 2. Cardinal. 3. Pelerine. 4. Mantle. 5. Dolman. 6. Inverness cape. 7. Mob cap. 8. 'Coal-scuttle' bonnet. 9. Bowler hat

clĭmb'er (-mer) *n.* (esp.) Mountaineer; person climbing socially; climbing plant.

clīme *n.* (poet.) Tract, country; climate.

clĭnch *n.* 1. Clinched or clenched nail or bolt; (naut.) way of fastening large ropes with half hitch; clinched part of rope; anything that grips. 2. Struggle or scuffle at close quarters; (boxing) grappling at close quarters. ~ *v.* 1. Clench. 2. Drive home, make conclusive, confirm, establish.

clĭn'cher *n.* (esp.) Remark, argument, that clinches a matter.

clĭng *v.i.* (past t. and past part. *clŭng*). Adhere *together*, remain in one body or in contact, resist separation; stick, adhere *to*; remain faithful *to*; *cling'stone*, ~ *peach*, variety in which flesh adheres to stone.

clĭn'ĭc *n.* 1. Teaching of medicine or surgery at the bed-side; class, institution, so taught or conducted. 2. Institution for giving medical advice or treatment; such advice etc. given regularly at specified time and place.

clĭn'ĭcal *adj.* Of, at, the sick-bed (esp. of lectures, teaching); ~ *medicine*, observation and treatment of patients as distinct from theoretical study of medical science; ~ *thermometer*, one for taking patient's temperature. **clĭn'ĭcally** *adv.*

clĭnk[1] *n.* Sharp, abrupt, clear ringing sound, as of small metallic objects or glasses struck together. ~ *v.* Make clink. **clĭnk'er**[1] *n.* (colloq.) A 'clinking' good thing or

clĭnk'er-built (bĭ-) *adj.* (Of ships etc.) made with external planks overlapping downwards and fastened with clinched copper nails (ill. BOAT).

Clī'ō. The MUSE of epic poetry and history.

clĭp[1] *n.* Appliance for holding things together, or for attachment to objects; set of cartridges held together at base for insertion in magazine rifle. ~ *v.t.* Surround closely; grip tightly, grasp.

clĭp[2] *n.* Clipping, shearing; quantity of wool clipped from sheep, flock, etc.; (U.S.) rate of speed, rapid pace; (colloq.) smart blow. ~ *v.* 1. Cut with shears or scissors; trim, make tidy, thus; cut off part of (hair, wool) thus; remove hair or wool of (sheep etc.) thus; pare edge of (coin); cut short, diminish, curtail. 2. (colloq.) Move quickly, run. 3. (U.S.) Hit smartly.

clĭpp'er *n.* (esp.) 1. Instrument for clipping hair. 2. Swiftly moving horse, ship, etc. 3. Ship with forward-raking bows and aft-raking masts. 4. U.S. transport aircraft for transatlantic service.

clĭpp'ĭng *n.* (esp.) Small piece clipped off, shred of cloth, newspaper cutting, etc.

clique (-ēk) *n.* Small exclusive party, set, coterie. **cliqu'ĭsh, cliqu'(e)y** *adjs.*

clītĕll'um *n.* Raised band encircling the body of earthworms towards the middle (ill. EARTH).

clĭt'orĭs *n.* Erectile female organ, homologue of penis.

Clīve, Robert, Baron Clive of Plassey (1725–74). English soldier

tence, pretext; ~ *-room*, room in which cloaks, hats, luggage, etc., may be left; lavatory. ~ *v.t.* Cover with, wrap in, cloak; conceal, disguise, mask.

clŏbb'er *n.* 1. (slang) Clothes. 2. (slang) Mess, clutter. ~ *v.t.* Patch *up*; esp., add enamelled decoration to (porcelain).

clŏche (-sh) *n.* 1. Kind of bell-glass for protecting plants; frame of sheet-glass or other transparent substance for same purpose. 2. Woman's close-fitting hat with deep crown and small or no brim.

clŏck[1] *n.* 1. Time-measuring instrument consisting of train of wheels set in motion by weights, spring, electro-magnet, etc., actuating and regulated by a pendulum or balance-wheel, and recording hours, minutes, etc., usu. by movement of hands on a dial. 2. Downy seed-head of dandelion etc. (so called from childish game of blowing away seeds to find 'what o'clock it is'). 3. *~-face*, dial of a clock; *~-golf*, game of putting ball into hole not exactly in centre from numbers arranged in circle like those of clock-face; *clock'wise*, moving like hands of a clock, in curve from left to right; *clock'work*, mechanism of clock, mechanism similar to this for driving toys, etc.; (attrib.) regular, mechanical, driven by clockwork; *like clockwork*, regularly, automatically. ~ *v.* Time by the clock; ~ *in, on, out, off*, etc., register arrival, departure, etc., at entrance of factory etc. by means of mechanical device combined with clock; also, arrive, leave, begin, or finish work, regularly or punctually.

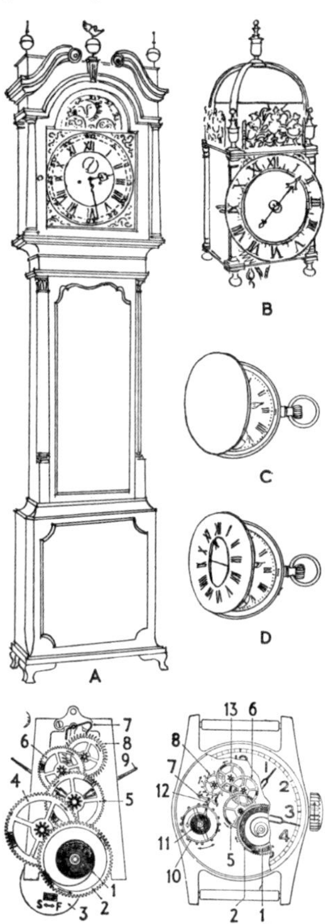

A. LONG-CASE OR GRANDFATHER CLOCK. B. LANTERN CLOCK. C. HUNTER WATCH. D. HALF-HUNTER WATCH. E. MECHANISM OF PENDULUM CLOCK. F. MECHANISM OF WATCH

1. Mainspring. 2. Main wheel (barrel). 3. Pendulum. 4. Intermediate wheel. 5. Centre wheel. 6. Third wheel. 7, 8. Escapement (7. Pallets, 8. Escape wheel). 9. Hour hand. 10. Balance. 11. Hair spring. 12. Lever. 13. Fourth wheel

clŏck[2] *n.* Ornamental pattern on side of stocking or sock near the ankle.

clŏd *n.* 1. Lump of earth etc.; blockhead; *clodhopper*, bumpkin, lout. 2. Cut from neck end of beef (ill. MEAT).

clŏg *n.* 1. Block of wood fastened to leg to impede motion; encumbrance, hindrance. 2. Woman's wooden-soled overshoe for wet ground (archaic; ill. SHOE); shoe with thick metal-rimmed wooden sole; ~ *dance*, step dance performed in clogs. ~ *v.* 1. Fetter or confine with clog; be encumbrance to, burden, impede, hamper. 2. Choke up; fill up with choking matter; stop or act badly from being choked up.

cloisonné (klwahz′ŏnā) *adj.* & *n.* (Enamel) of which different colours have been applied between thin metal plates laid on edge on foundation plaque (cf. CHAMPLEVÉ).

clois′ter *n.* 1. Convent, monastery. 2. Covered walk or arcade in monastery, college, large church, often running round open court of quadrangle with plain wall on outer side and colonnade or windows on inner (ill. MONASTERY). **clois′tered** (-terd) *adj.* Monastic; sheltered. **clois′tral** *adj.*

clōne *n.* 1. (bot.) Group of cultivated plants the individuals of which are transplanted parts of one original seedling or stock. 2. (bot.) Group of individuals produced asexually from a sexually produced ancestor.

clŏn′ic *adj.* Of spasms, in which violent muscular contractions and relaxations occur in rapid succession. **clŏn′us** *n.* Such spasm.

clōse[1] (-s) *adj.* 1. Narrow, confined, contracted; covered, concealed; secret, given secrecy; niggardly; restricted, limited, not open to all. 2. Near; dense, compact, with no or slight intervals or gaps; in or nearly in contact; fitting exactly; near and dear; nearly equal; concentrated. 3. Sultry, stifling, airless, ill-ventilated. 4. (of vowels) Pronounced with tongue near the palate. 5. ~ *borough*, pocket borough (see BOROUGH); ~ *corporation*, corporation which fills its own vacancies; corporation the stock of which is held by a very few persons, usu. officers of the company; ~*-fisted*, *-handed*, niggardly; ~*-hauled*, (naut.) with sail-tacks hauled close, so as to sail as near the wind as possible (ill. SAIL[2]); ~ *order*, (mil.) arrangement of men in line with only slight gaps between them; ~ *quarters*, immediate contact with opponent or enemy; uncomfortable proximity; ~ *season*, *time*, period during which it is unlawful to take certain specified game or fish; ~ *shave*, (fig.) narrow escape from accident; ~*-stool*, chamber-pot enclosed in stool or box; ~*-up*, part of cinema picture taken at short range or with a telephoto lens so as to show persons etc. on large scale. **clōse′ly** (-sl-) *adv.* **clōse′nĕss** *n.* **clōse** *adv.* So as to be close. ~ *n.* Enclosed space; precincts of cathedral; school playground; (in Scotland) entry, passage, esp. one leading from street to inner court or to common stairway of tenement.

clōse[2] (-z) *v.* 1. Shut; (of place of business etc.) declare, be declared, not open; *closed shop*, (orig. U.S.) industrial or other concern in which the employees are obliged to belong to one particular trade union. 2. Be boundary of, conclude; bring or come to an end; complete, settle. 3. Bring or come into contact; close gap(s) in rank, series, etc.; come within striking distance, grapple *with*; (naut.) approach, come alongside of. 4. Express (often eager) agreement *with* (terms, offer, etc.). 5. ~ *down*, close (shop etc.) finally, end business etc.; (of wireless station) cease to broadcast; ~ *in*, enclose, come nearer, (of days) get successively shorter; ~ *up*, block, fill, fill gaps (in), coalesce; move cinema camera nearer subject to make close-up (see *adj.* above). ~ *n.* Conclusion, end.

clŏs′ĕt (-z-) *n.* Private or small room, esp. for private interviews or for study; cupboard; water-closet. ~ *v.t.* Shut up or detain in closet as for private conference etc.

clō′sure (-zher) *n.* 1. Closing, closed condition. 2. In Parliament, decision by vote of House of Commons to put question without further debate. ~ *v.t.* Apply closure to (motion, speakers, etc.).

clŏt *n.* Mass of material stuck together; semi-solid lump of coagulated liquid, esp. blood; (slang) stupid person, blockhead. ~ *v.* Form into clots; *clotted cream*, the thick cream obtained by scalding milk; *clotted nonsense*, utter absurdity.

clŏth (*or* -awth) *n.* 1. (Piece, used for any purpose, of) woven or felted stuff; covering for table, esp. of linen at meals; woollen woven fabric as used for clothes; ~ *of gold*, *silver*, tissue of gold or silver threads interwoven with silk or wool; *American* ~, see AMERICAN. ~*-hall*, hall where sellers and buyers of woollen cloths meet to transact business; ~*-yard*, (hist.) yard of 36 in. (now the statute yard) by which cloth was measured; ~*-yard shaft*, arrow of long bow. 2. Profession, esp. clerical, as shown by clothes; *the* ~, the clergy.

clōthe (-dh) *v.t.* Provide with clothes, put clothes upon; cover like or as with clothes or a cloth.

clōthes (klōz, klōdhz) *n.pl.* Wearing-apparel, dress; bed-coverings; linen etc. to be washed; ~*-bag*, ~*-basket*, bag, basket, for dirty or newly washed linen; ~*-horse*, wooden framework for airing clothes; ~*-line*, rope for hanging washed linen up to dry; ~*-moth*, small buff-coloured moth infesting houses, with larva very destructive to woollen materials, furs, etc.; ~*-peg*, forked peg or clip for fastening linen to clothes-line; ~*-post*, *-prop*, supports for clothes-line.

clōth′ier (-dh-) *n.* Dealer in cloth and men's clothes.

clōth′ing (-dh-) *n.* (esp.) Clothes collectively.

cloud *n.* 1. Visible mass of condensed watery vapour floating in air at some distance above general surface of ground (classifiable as

CIRRUS, CUMULUS, STRATUS, etc.). 2. Unsubstantial or fleeting thing; mass of smoke or dust; local dimness or obscurity in otherwise clear or transparent thing; innumerable body of insects, birds, horsemen, arrows, moving together; obscurity, anything obscuring or concealing; (anything causing) state of gloom, trouble, suspicion, etc.; darkening of countenance; *under a* ~, out of favour. 3. *cloud'berry*, (berry of) *Rubus chamaemorus*, small erect sub-shrub allied to raspberry, growing on high

logy) Amount of sky covered by cloud, measured in figures between 0 (cloudless) and 8 (wholly obscured).

clough (-ŭf) *n.* Ravine.

clout *n.* (archaic & dial.) Patch; cloth; piece of clothing; rap, knock, blow. ~ *v.t.* (archaic & dial.) Mend, patch; cuff heavily.

clōve[1] *n.* One of the small bulbs making up compound bulb of garlic, shallot, etc.

clōve[2] *n.* Dried flower-bud of a tropical tree, *Caryophyllus aromaticus*, orig. native of the Moluccas,

THE CHIEF TYPES OF CLOUD

High clouds, 20,000 ft to 35,000 ft approx. 1. Cirrostratus. 2. Cirrocumulus. 3. Cirrus. Middle clouds, 10,000 ft to 20,000 ft. 4. Cumulonimbus (thundercloud). 5. Altostratus. 6. Altocumulus. Lower clouds, below 10,000 ft. 7. Nimbostratus (rain cloud). 8. Cumulus. 9. Stratocumulus. 10. Stratus

mountains in northern Europe, and bearing one large white terminal flower and large well-flavoured amber-coloured fruit; *~-burst*, violent rainstorm; *~-castle*, castle in the air; *~-cuckoo-land*, name in Aristophanes' 'Birds' of the town built by the birds to separate gods from mankind; hence, fanciful or ideal realm. ~ *v.* Overspread, darken, with clouds, gloom, or trouble; variegate with vague patches of colour or opacity; become overcast or gloomy. **cloud'lèss** *adj.* **cloud'lèssly** *adv.* **cloud'lèssnèss** *n.* **cloud'lèt** *n.* **cloud'y** *adj.* **cloud'ily** *adv.* **cloud'inèss** *n.* (esp., in meteoro-

much used as a pungent aromatic spice; the tree itself; *~-gillyflower*, *~-pink*, a clove-scented species of pink, *Dianthus caryophyllus*, the original of the carnation and other cultivated forms. [Fr. *clou de girofle*; *girofle* was orig. name of the spice; *clou* (L *clavus* nail) was used of it with ref. to its shape; the phrase (in Engl. *clove-gillyflower*) was transferred to the similarly shaped bud of the pink, and later divided into *clove* for the spice and *gillyflower* for the pink]

clōve hitch *n.* Way of fastening rope round spar etc., formed by passing rope round twice in such a way that both ends pass under centre part of loop in front (ill. KNOT). [old past part. of CLEAVE[1] *v.*]

clōv'en *adj.* Divided. Past part. of CLEAVE[1] *v.*; ~ *hoof, foot*, the divided hoof of ruminant quadrupeds; ascribed in pagan mythology to Pan, and thence in Christian mythology to the Devil.

clōv'er *n.* Trefoil, esp. *Trifolium nepens*, white or Dutch ~, and *T. pratense*, red or meadow ~, both largely cultivated for fodder; *live, be, in* ~, live in ease and luxury.

clown *n.* 1. Rustic; ignorant or ill-bred lout. 2. Jester, esp. in pantomime or circus (orig. one of the characters in a harlequinade) with loose baggy white garments, and face painted white. ~ *v.* Play the clown, act like a clown, perform farcically. **clown'ing** *n.*

clown'ish *adj.* Of or like a clown or peasant, rustic, boorish. **clown'ishly** *adv.* **clown'ishnèss** *n.*

cloy *v.t.* Satiate, weary, by richness, sweetness, sameness, or excess.

clŭb *n.* 1. Heavy stick with one thick end, as weapon; *Indian ~s*, pair of special shape swung to develop muscles; stick with crooked (and usu. thickened) end used in hockey etc.; golf-stick; club-shaped knot of hair at back of head, worn by men in 18th c. 2. (transl. Span. *basto*, the 'club' on Spanish cards; the English design is copied from the French *trèfle* or trefoil) Playing-card of the suit bearing a black trefoil; (pl.) this suit. 3. Association of persons with some common interest meeting periodically; body of persons combined for social purposes and having premises for resort, meals, temporary residence, etc. 4. *~-foot*, any of various (usu. congenital) distortions giving foot a stunted lumpy appearance; *~-land*, district round St. James's in London where there are very many clubs; ~ *licence*, (in Britain) licence permitting sale of alcoholic liquors to registered subscribers but not to general public (*country* ~, country inn etc. conducting such trade); *~-moss*, moss (*Lycopodium clavatum*) with club-like upright fertile spikes of spore-cases; any species of *Lycopodium*; *~-root*, disease of cabbages and turnips in which excrescence forms at base of stem. ~ *v.* 1. Beat with club; use butt of (gun) as club. 2. Bring, come, into a mass. 3. Put together into a common stock; combine *together*, or *with* others, in joint action, esp. in making up sum of money *for* some object.

clŭbb'able *adj.* Convivial, sociable.

clŭb-haul *v.* (naut.) Tack ship by dropping lee-anchor as vessel's head comes to the wind; when she then pays off, the cable is cut and the sails trimmed to the other tack; a device for getting off lee-shore when there is not room to wear.

clŭck *n.* Abrupt hollow guttural sound made by hen desiring to sit or calling her brood together; any similar sound. ~ *v.i.* Make cluck.

clue (-ōō) *n.* 1. Clew. 2. Anything which points the way, indicates a solution, or puts one on track of a discovery. **clue'lėss** *adj.* (esp., slang) Stupid.

clŭm'ber *n.* Stocky breed of spaniel with dense silky coat, usu. yellow and white. [f. *Clumber* in Nottinghamshire]

clŭmp *n.* 1. Cluster *of* trees or shrubs. 2. Thick extra sole on shoe, usu. nailed on. ~ *v.* Tread or move heavily and clumsily; plant in clump; keep or mass together.

clŭm'sy (-z-) *adj.* Awkward in movement or shape, ungainly; ill-contrived; tactless. **clŭm'sĭly** *adv.* **clŭm'sinėss** *n.*

Clūny (klūn'ĭ). Monastery near Mâcon in France, from whose rule developed an order which separated from the Benedictines in 11th c. **Clūn'iăc** *adj.* & *n.* (Member) of this order.

clŭs'ter *n.* Group of similar things, esp. such as grow together, bunch; swarm, group, of persons, stars, etc. ~ *v.* Bring, come, into cluster; be in cluster.

clŭtch[1] *v.* Seize eagerly, grasp tightly; snatch *at.* ~ *n.* 1. Tight grasp; (pl.) grasping hands, cruel grasp. 2. (mech.) Device enabling engine or driving parts of machine to be connected or disconnected

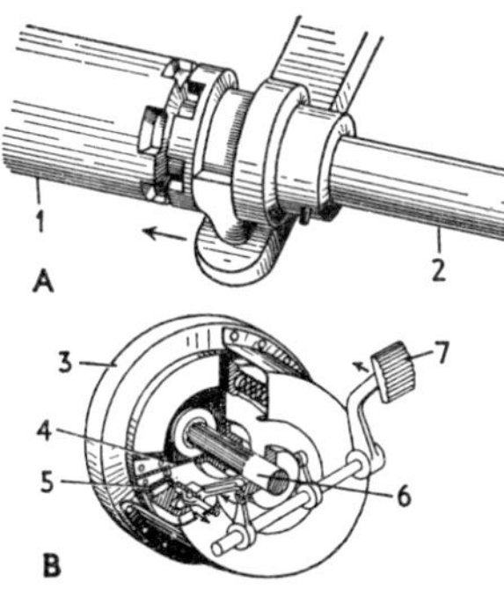

A. DOG CLUTCH. B. PLATE CLUTCH

1. Driving shaft. 2. Driven shaft. 3. Engine fly-wheel. 4. Clutch plate. 5. Clutch lining. 6. Shaft to gearbox. 7. Clutch pedal

with the driven parts; *friction* ~, (used esp. on motor vehicles) one in which this connexion is made between frictional surfaces.

clŭtch[2] *n.* Set of eggs; brood of chickens.

clŭtt'er *n.* Crowded confusion, confused mass. ~ *v.t.* Litter, strew untidily *with*, crowd with disorderly assemblage of things.

Clȳde. River in SW. Scotland, famous for the shipbuilding yards on its banks.

Clȳdes'dāle (-dzd-). One of a breed of heavy draught-horses orig. bred round about the Clyde.

Clȳde'sīde (-ds-). District on bank of Clyde near Glasgow where there are several shipbuilding yards. **Clȳde'sīder** *n.* Native of this area; member of a group of the British Labour Party whose leaders were associated with it.

clȳs'ter *n.* Enema.

Clȳtemnĕs'tra. (Gk legend) Daughter of Tyndareus, king of Sparta, and Leda, and wife of AGAMEMNON. On the return of Agamemnon from the Trojan War, she, with her lover Aegisthus, murdered her husband, and was in turn slain by Orestes, Agamemnon's son.

cm. *abbrev.* Centimetre.

Cmd *abbrev.* Command paper (with series number, as *Cmd 7957*).

Cmdr *abbrev.* Commander.

Cmdre *abbrev.* Commodore.

C.M.F. *abbrev.* Central Mediterranean Forces.

C.M.G. *abbrev.* Companion of (the Order, instituted 1818, of) St. Michael and St. George.

C.M.S. *abbrev.* Church Missionary Society.

cnī'dōblast- (-ah-) *n.* Goblet-shaped cell with an eversible barbed stinging thread, characteristic of *Coelenterates* (ill. JELLY-fish).

c/o *abbrev.* Care of.

Co. *abbrev.* Company; county.

C.O. *abbrev.* Colonial Office; commanding officer; conscientious objector.

co- *prefix.* 1. Jointly, together, mutually; joint, mutual. 2. (in math. terms) Of the complement; complement of.

coach *n.* 1. State carriage. 2. Stage-coach, large 4-wheeled closed carriage with seats inside and on roof, carrying passengers on fixed routes. (*Illustration, p.* 152.) 3. Railway-carriage; (U.S., esp.) passenger carriage of cheaper class. 4. Long-distance single-decked closed motor-bus. 5. (naut. now obs.) Cabin on after part of quarter-deck, usu. occupied by captain. 6. Private tutor preparing candidate for examination; trainer of athletic team etc. 7. *~-work*, wood framework of motor-car or railway coach body. ~ *v.* 1. Travel in, go by, stage-coach. 2. Train, tutor; study with a tutor.

cōăd'jutor (-jōō-) *n.* Helper, assistant, esp. one assisting a bishop and usu. having the right of succession.

cōăg'ūlāte *v.* Convert, be converted, from fluid to more or less solid state; clot, curdle, set. **cōăg'ūlant** *n.* Coagulating agent. **cōăgūlā'tion** *n.* **cōăg'ūable** *adj.*

coaita (kōĭt'a) *n.* Small S. Amer. red-faced spider-monkey of genus *Ateles*, with long coarse glossy black hair.

coal *n.* Black or blackish sedimentary rock consisting mainly of carbonized plant tissue, found in seams or beds and used as fuel; it varies greatly in age and degree of carbonization, the principal types being (1) *lignite* or *brown* ~, which contains the least carbon, (2) *bituminous* ~, which contains more and is used for producing gas, coke, etc., and for domestic purposes, and (3) *anthracite*, which is almost pure carbon and is used esp. for steam-raising; (pl.) pieces of coal; *haul over the coals*, reprimand; *heap coals of fire*, return good for evil (see Rom. xii. 20); *~-black*, completely black; ~ *dust*, powdered coal; ~ *face*, surface of coal seam exposed by mining; *coal'-field*, district with series of coal strata; *~-fish*, the saithe (*Gadus vireus*), a sea-fish allied to cod but smaller, with dusky skin which soils fingers like wet coal; *~-flap*, *-plate*, cover of coal-cellar opening in pavement; *~-gas*, mixture of gases (mainly hydrogen and methane) produced by destructive distillation of coal and used, after removal of impurities such as hydrogen sulphide, for lighting and heating; *~-heaver*, man employed to carry coal; *~-hole*, small coal-cellar; *~-oil*, (U.S.) shale-oil, petroleum; *C~ Measures*, (geol.) the strata in which coal is found, an upper division of the carboniferous system; *~-mine*, mine in which coal is dug, colliery (ill. MINE); *~-owner*, owner or lessee of coal-mine; *~-pit*, coal-mine; *~-sack*, sack for carrying coal; also, any of the patches in the Milky Way distinguished by extraordinary blackness owing to the absence of even dim stars (esp. one near the Southern Cross); *~-scuttle*, receptacle for coals to supply room fire; *~-tar*, thick black viscous liquid, a product of destructive distillation of coal, yielding benzene, creosote, paraffin, aniline dyes, etc.; *~-tit*, (orig. *coalmouse*) small dark-coloured bird (*Parus ater*) with white patch on nape of neck, ~ *v.* Supply (ship etc.) with coal for fuel; take in supply of coal.

coal'er *n.* Ship for supplying others with coal

cōalĕsce' (-s) *v.i.* Come together and form one; combine in coalition. **cōalĕs'cence** *n.* **coalĕs'cent** *adj.*

cōalĭ'tion *n.* Union, fusion; (government by) temporary combination of political parties each retaining its distinctive principles. **cōalĭ'tionist** (-sho-) *n.* & *adj.*

coal'mouse, cōle- *n.* = COAL-tit.

coam'ing *n.* (naut.) Raised border round hatches and scuttles to keep out water (ill. SHIP).

coarse (kōrs) *adj.* Common, inferior; rough, loose, or large in texture, grain, or features; not delicate, unrefined; rude, uncivil, vulgar; obscene. **coarse'ly** (-sl-) *adv.* **coarse'nėss** *n.* **coars'en** *v.* Make, become, coarse.

coast *n.* 1. Border of land near sea, sea-shore; *the ~ is clear*, the danger is over, the way is open. *~-guard*, body of men employed to guard coast, report wrecks, prevent smuggling, etc., whence *coast-guard(sman)*; *coast'line*, configuration of sea-coast. 2. (U.S., Canada) Slope for tobogganing, sliding down this; downhill ride on bicycle etc. without pedalling, or in car etc. with engine not running. **coast'wards** *adv.* **coast'wise** *adj.* & *adv.* **coast** *v.i.* 1. Sail along coast, trade between ports on same coast. 2. Slide downhill on toboggan; ride downhill on bicycle without pedalling, or in car with engine idle.

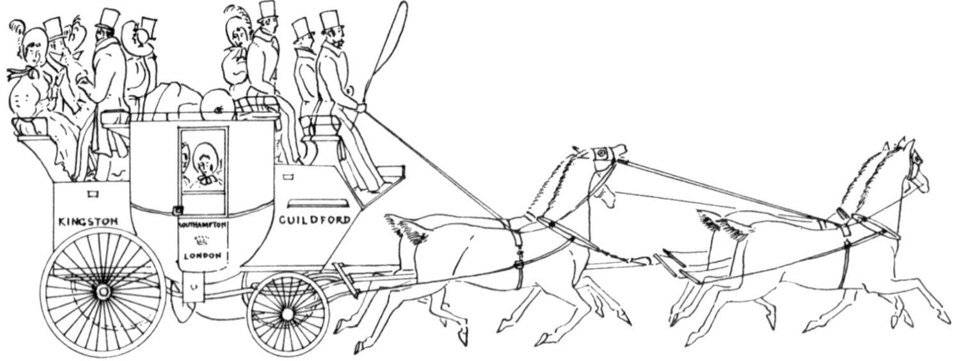

STAGE COACH

coas'tal *adj.* Of, on, pertaining to, the coast; *Coastal Command*, in the war of 1939–45, a command of R.A.F. responsible for co-operation with navy, reconnaissance of enemy's harbours and shipping and for attacking the targets found.

coas'ter *n.* (esp.) Vessel employed in coasting; master or pilot of such a vessel; two-handled wine-cup; low round stand for decanter; wooden stand for cheese.

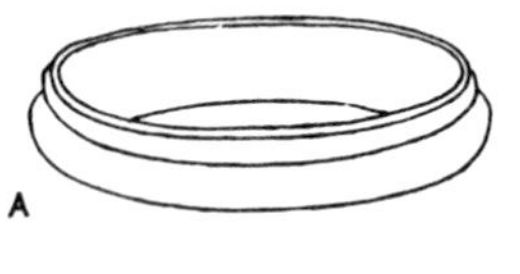

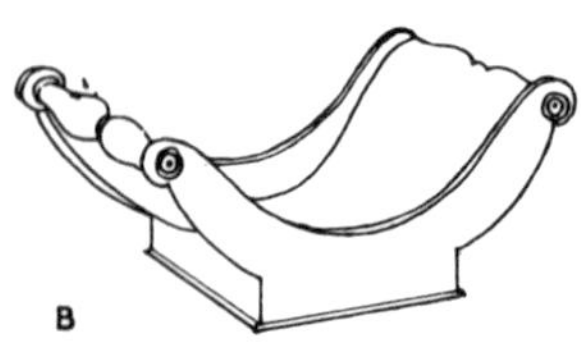

A. WINE COASTER. B. CHEESE COASTER

coat *n.* 1. Man's outer garment, usu. of cloth, with sleeves; woman's outer garment, overcoat or short tailored jacket worn with skirt; (archaic & dial.) petticoat. 2. Coat of arms. 3. Covering compared to garment; beast's hair, fur, etc.; investing membrane etc. of organ; skin, rind, husk; layer of bulb etc.; covering of paint etc. laid on at once. 4. *~-armour*, blazonry, heraldic arms; *~-hanger*, curved wood or metal hanger fitting shoulders of dress or coat; *~ of arms*, (hist.) coat or vest embroidered with heraldic arms, tabard; distinctive heraldic bearings of a gentleman, orig. borne on 'coat of arms'; shield, escutcheon. **coat'less** *adj.* **coat** *v.t.* Provide with coat; cover with surface layer or coating.

coatee' *n.* Close-fitting short coat (ill. INFANTRY).

coat-hâr'die, cōte- *n.* (hist., 14th–15th centuries) Man's or woman's close-fitting tunic-like garment with sleeves.

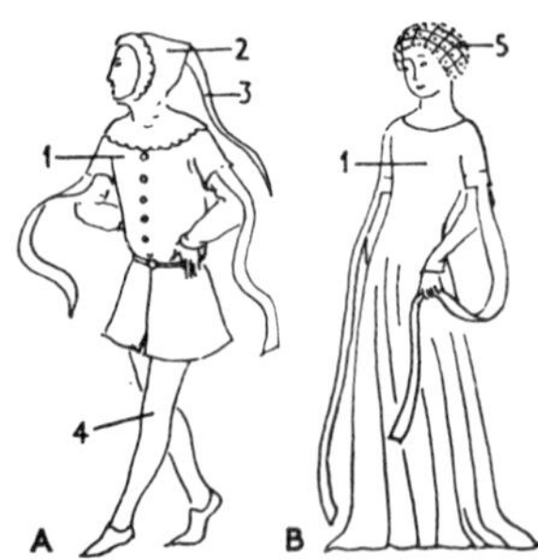

COAT-HARDIE: A. LATE 14TH C. B. 14TH C.

1. Coat-hardie. 2. Hood. 3. Liripipe. 4. Hose. 5. Caul

cōa'tĭ (-ah-) *n.* (also *~-mondi*, *-mundi*) Amer. plantigrade carnivorous mammal (*Nasua*), resembling civet and raccoon, with long flexible snout and long tail.

coat'ing *n.* (esp.) Layer of paint etc.; material for coats.

coax *v.* Persuade by blandishments, wheedle; manipulate (tool etc.) gently.

cōăx'(ĭ)al *adj.* (math.) Having a common axis.

cŏb[1] *n.* 1. Male swan. 2. Stout short-legged riding-horse. 3. Large kind of hazel-nut (also *~-nut*); roundish lump of coal etc.; small roundish loaf. 4. Cylindrical shoot or rachis on which grains of maize grow.

cŏb[2] *n.* Composition of clay, gravel, and straw, used for building walls of cottages etc., esp. in SW. England.

cōb'alt (-awlt) *n.* 1. Silver-white malleable slightly magnetic metallic element, resembling nickel in many ways and used in the alloy *~ steel* for making permanent magnets and in colouring ceramic glazes; symbol Co, at. no. 27, at. wt 58·9332. 2. Deep-blue pigment (*~ blue*), a mixed oxide of cobalt and aluminium. **cobal'tĭc, cobal'tous** *adjs.* [Ger. *kobold* goblin haunting mines]

cōb'altīte (-awl-) *n.* Silver-white mineral with brilliant metallic lustre.

cŏbb'er *n.* (Austral. slang) Pal, mate.

cŏb'ble[1] *n.* Water-worn rounded stone (also *~-stone*), esp. of suitable size for paving; (geol.) rounded fragment of rock bigger than pebble and smaller than boulder; (pl.) pavement of cobbles; (pl.) coals of this size. *~ v.t.* Pave with cobbles.

cŏb'ble[2] *v.t.* Mend, put together, join, roughly or clumsily; patch; mend (shoes), esp. roughly or clumsily.

cŏbb'ler *n.* 1. One whose business is mending shoes; *~'s wax*, resinous substance used by shoemakers for stiffening and preserving thread. 2. Clumsy workman or mender, botcher. 3. Drink of wine (often sherry), sugar, lemon, and pounded ice, drunk through straws.

Cŏb'den, Richard (1804–65). English Liberal statesman, advocate of free trade, peace, and international co-operation, and opposition to Empire. **Cŏb'denĭsm** *n.* **Cŏb'denīte** *adj.* & *n.*

cō-bellĭ'gerent (-ĭj-) *adj.* & *n.* (State) waging war along with another but not accorded full status as ally. **cō-bellĭ'gerency** *n.*

cŏ′ble *n.* Sea fishing-boat of NE. England; an open boat with two side keels, designed for launching from beaches against heavy breakers, formerly with lug-sail, now usually with engine.

cōb′ra *n.* Venomous snake of genus *Naja*, found in S. Asia and Africa, able to dilate its neck into a hood-like shape when excited; esp. the Indian cobra, which has a mark on its hood resembling a pair of spectacles. [Port. *cobra de capello* snake with hood (L *colubra* snake)]

cŏb′wĕb *n.* 1. Web or fine network spun by spider for capture of its prey; single thread of this. 2. Anything frail or flimsy; any musty accumulation, obstruction, etc., which ought to be swept away, like dusty cobwebs in a neglected room; subtly-woven snare. ~ *adj.* Thin, flimsy, delicate. **cŏb′wĕbby** *adj.*

cōc′a *n.* S. Amer. shrub, *Erythroxylon coca*, with leaves which are dried and chewed with powdered lime as masticatory, appeaser of hunger, and nervous stimulant; the dried leaves.

cocaine′ *n.* Alkaloid obtained from coca leaves and young twigs, used as local anaesthetic, stimulant, etc. **cocain′ism** *n.* Chronic condition produced by excessive use of cocaine.

cŏcc′us *n.* (pl. *-cī*). (also *micrococcus*) Minute spherical organism (ill. BACTERIUM).

cŏc′cȳx (-ks-) *n.* Small triangular bone ending spinal column in man and some apes (ill. SPINE); analogous part in birds etc. **coccȳg′ėal** *adj.* [Gk *kokkux* cuckoo (f. resemblance to cuckoo's bill)]

COATS

1. Cocked hat. 2. Steenkirk. 3. Muff. 4. Waistcoat. 5. Breeches. 6. Stockings. 7. Frock. 8. Beaver. 9. Pantaloons. 10. Riding boots. 11. Tail-coat. 12. Chesterfield. 13. Trousers. 14. Spats. 15. Deer-stalker cap. 16. Norfolk jacket. 17. Knickerbockers. 18. Gaiters. 19. Top hat or topper. 20. Frock-coat. 21. Dress coat or 'tails'. 22. Plus-fours. 23. Redingote. 24. Spencer. 25. Parasol. 26. Gown. 27. Paletot. 28. Bolero jacket. 29. Jabot

Cŏch′ĭn-Chīn′a. A former French colony, part of Indo-China; ceded to France by the king of Annam in 1868; see VIETNAM.

cŏch′ineal *n.* Dried bodies of the female of the insect *Dactylopius coccus*, found on cactuses in Mexico etc., used for making red dye.

cŏch′lėa (-k-) *n.* Spiral cavity of internal ear (ill. EAR). [L, = 'snail']

cŏck[1] *n.* 1. Male of common domestic fowl, *Gallus domesticus*; male of other birds. 2. Spout, short pipe, with tap for controlling flow of liquid or gas; lever in firearm raised ready to be released by trigger (ill. MUSKET); *at full* ~, with cock raised ready for firing; *at half* ~, with cock raised off nipple but not drawn up; (fig.) only half-ready; not putting out full effort; cocked position or state; way of cocking hat. 3. *~-and-bull story*, idle invention, incredible tale; *~-crow*, dawn; *~-fighting*, setting cocks to fight as sport; ~ *of the mountain, of the wood*, capercaillie; ~ *of the north*, brambling; (fig.) leader, head, chief person; so ~ *of the walk*; *cock's-comb*, cock's crest;

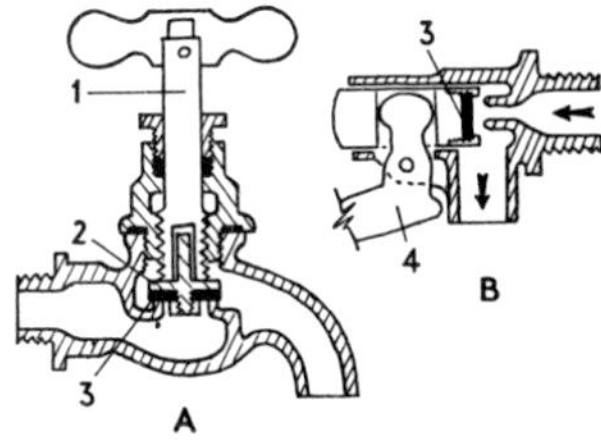

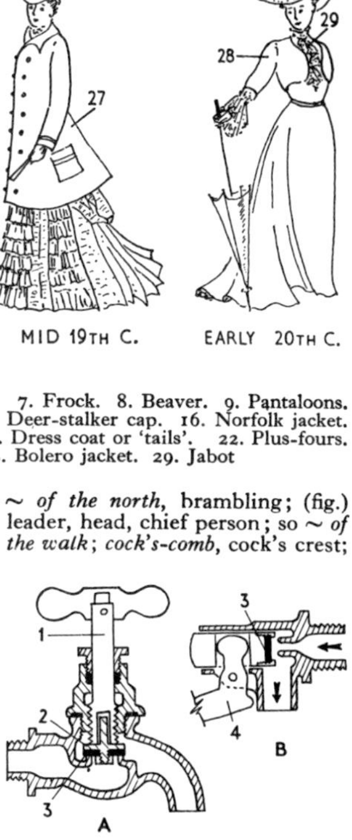

COCK: A. VALVE TAP. B. BALL-COCK

1. Spindle. 2. Valve. 3. Washer. 4. Lever arm to which ball is attached. The arrows indicate the flow of water

fool's cap shaped like this; the yellow rattle, *Rhinanthus Crista-galli*, a common meadow-weed; an ornamental cultivated plant, *Celosia cristata*; various other plants; *cocks'foot*, a strong-growing pasture-grass, *Dactylis glomerata*, with large 3-branched panicle; *~-shot*, *~-shy*, object set up to be thrown at with sticks, stones, etc., as cocks were formerly at Shrovetide; throw at this; *cock'spur*, cock's spur; gas-burner of same shape. ~ *v.* 1. Raise cock or hammer of (gun) in readiness for firing. 2. Erect, stick, or stand *up* jauntily or defiantly; ~ *one's ears*, listen attentively; ~ *the eye*, turn it with knowing look, wink; ~ *one's hat*, set it jauntily on one side; turn up brim of hat; *cocked hat*, hat with very wide brim permanently turned up at front and back, or at both sides, so as to conceal crown completely (ill. COAT).

cŏck[2] *n.* Small conical heap of hay in field. ~ *v.t.* Heap (hay) in cocks.

cockāde' *n.* Rosette etc. worn in hat as badge of office or party, or part of livery. **cockād'ĕd** *adj.*

cŏck-a-hōōp' *adj.* & *adv.* Exultant(ly), crowing with exultation.

Cockaigne' (-ān). 1. Imaginary country of luxury and idleness. 2. (with pun on *Cockney*) London, Cockneydom.

cŏck-a-leek'ie *n.* Scotch soup of cock boiled with leeks.

cŏckatōō' *n.* 1. Various birds of parrot kind, including among others genus *Cacatua*, of Australia and E. Indian islands, with movable crest or tuft of feathers on head. 2. (Austral.) Small farmer, squatter; ~ *fence*, rough fence of logs and saplings. [Malay *kakatua*]

cŏck'atrice (*or* -īs) *n.* = BASILISK.

cŏck'boat *n.* Small ship's-boat.

cŏck'chāfer *n.* Large European pale-brown beetle, *Melolontha vulgaris*, flying by night with loud whirring sound.

cŏck'er[1] *v.t.* Pamper, coddle, indulge.

cŏck'er[2] *n.* (also ~ *spaniel*) One of a breed of spaniels trained to start woodcock and similar game (ill. DOG).

Cŏck'er[3], Edward (1631–75). English arithmetician, reputed author of a popular 'Arithmetick'; *according to* ~, in accordance with strict rule or calculation, exact, correct.

cŏck'erel *n.* Young cock.

cŏck'-eyed (-īd) *adj.* (slang) Squinting; crooked, set aslant, not level.

cŏck'-hôrse *n.* & *adv.* Anything a child rides astride upon; (*a-*) *cock-horse*, astride.

cŏc'kle[1] *n.* Plant, *Lychnis githago*, with reddish-purple flowers and capsules of numerous black seeds, growing in cornfields, esp. among wheat.

cŏc'kle[2] *n.* Genus, *Cardium*, of bivalve molluscs, esp. *C. edule*, common on sandy coasts, and much used for food; the shell or a valve of the shell, of this; (*delight, warm*) *the cockles of the heart*, one's feelings; *~-shell*, shell of cockle; small frail boat.

cŏck'le[3] *n.* Bulge, pucker, on surface that should be flat. ~ *v.* (Cause to) bulge, curl up, pucker.

cŏck'ney *n.* One born in London (strictly, 'within the sound of Bow Bells'); the London dialect. ~ *adj.* Of, characteristic of, cockneys; *C~ school*, contemptuous nickname for set of 19th-c. London writers, of whom Leigh Hunt was supposed to be typical. **cŏck'neydom, cŏck'neyism** *ns.* [orig. meaning 'cock's egg', prob. a small or misshapen egg; later, 'townsman']

cŏck'pĭt *n.* 1. Pit or enclosed area for cock-fights; arena of any struggle. 2. (naut., now obs.) After part of man-of-war's orlop deck, quarters of junior officers, used in action as hospital. 3. Place for pilot, observer, etc., in fuselage of aeroplane.

cŏck'roach *n.* Nocturnal voracious dark-brown beetle-like insect of genus *Blatta* or *Periplaneta*, infesting kitchens etc. (ill. INSECT).

cŏck'-sure (-shoor) *adj.* Absolutely certain *of, about*; self-confident, dogmatic, presumptuous. **cŏck'-surenėss** *n.*

cŏck'tail *n.* 1. Horse with a docked tail; horse of racing stamp but not thoroughbred. 2. (orig. U.S.) Drink of spirit with bitters, fruit juice, flavouring, ice, etc.; *~-shaker*, vessel with cap in which cocktails are vigorously shaken to mix them.

cŏck'y *adj.* Vain, conceited, pert. **cŏck'ĭly** *adv.* **cŏck'ĭnėss** *n.*

cō'cō *n.* (pl. *-os*). Tropical palm-tree, *Cocos nucifera*, producing the *coconut*, a large, ovate, brown hard-shelled fruit with edible white lining enclosing whitish liquid (*coconut milk*); *coconut matting*, matting made of *coconut fibre*, the fibre of the outer husk of the coconut.

cō'coa (-kō) *n.* Powder produced by crushing and grinding cacao seeds; beverage made from this powder; *~-bean*, cacao-seed; *~-butter*, fatty matter obtained from cacao-seed; *~-nib*, cotyledon of cacao-seed; *C~ Press*, nickname of certain free-trade Liberal newspapers owned by cocoa-manufacturers. [corruption of CACAO, confused with COCO]

cocōōn' *n.* Case of silky thread spun by larvae of many insects to protect them in chrysalis state (ill. MOTH), esp. that spun by silk-worm and used as source of silk. ~ *v.t.* Spray with plastic material. [Fr. *cocou*, dim. of *coque* egg-shell]

Cō'cōs Islands. Group of about 20 small coral islands in the Indian Ocean, British from 1857; transferred to Australia 1955; also known as the Keeling Islands.

cŏcŏtte' *n.* Member of the Parisian demi-monde; fashionable prostitute.

cŏd[1] *n.* Large sea-fish, *Gadus morrhua*, of N. Atlantic and connected seas; *~-liver oil*, oil expressed from cod's liver, rich in vitamins A and D and much used in medicine.

cŏd[2] *v.* (slang) Hoax, fool.

C.O.D. *abbrev.* Cash on delivery; Concise Oxford Dictionary.

cō'da *n.* (mus.) More or less independent passage concluding movement or piece of music. [It., f. L *cauda* tail]

cŏdd'le *v.t.* Treat as an invalid in need of careful nourishment and nursing; cook (egg) gently by putting it in hot water which is then allowed to cool, or in cold water which is then brought to the boil.

cōde *n.* 1. One of the systematic collections of statutes made by later Roman emperors, esp. that of Justinian; systematic collection or digest of laws of country etc.; system or collection of rules and regulations. 2. Set of conventional symbols used in transmitting messages by flags, wireless telegraphy, etc.; system, set, of words, figures, groups of letters, etc., used for other words or phrases, to ensure secrecy or brevity in messages or as system of reference. ~ *v.t.* Codify.

cō'deine (-dĭēn, -dēn) *n.* Alkaloid derived from opium, used as a sedative etc. [Gk *kōdeia* poppy-head]

cō'dĕx *n.* (pl. *-ĭcēs*). Manuscript volume, esp. of ancient texts.

cŏdg'er *n.* (colloq.) Fellow, buffer, queer old person.

cŏd'ĭcil *n.* Supplement to will or agreement, altering, explaining, or revoking original contents. **codĭcĭll'ary** *adj.*

cŏd'ĭfȳ (*or* kō-) *v.t.* Reduce to a code or system; write (message etc.) in code. **cŏdĭfĭcā'tion** *n.*

cŏd'lĭn(g)[1] *n.* Immature or inferior apple; variety of cooking apple tapering towards apex; ~ *moth*, moth (*Cydia pomonella*), larva of which feeds on apples.

cŏd'lĭng[2] *n.* Small cod-fish.

coecĭl'ĭan (sĭs-) *adj.* & *n.* (zool.) (Member) of the *Apoda*, tropical worm-like animals, an order of the class *Amphibia*.

cō-ĕd *adj.* (Short for) CO-EDUCATIONAL. ~ *n.* (U.S. colloq.) Girl or woman student in co-educational institution.

cō-ĕdūcā'tion *n.* Education of both sexes together. **cō-ĕdūcā'tional** *adj.* **cō-ĕd'ūcāte** *v.t.*

cōĕffĭ'cient (-shnt) *n.* 1. Joint agent or factor in producing effect or result. 2. (algebra) Number placed before and multiplying known or unknown quantity; (physics) number expressing amount of some change or effect under certain conditions of temperature, pressure, etc.

coel'acănth (sēl-) *n.* Fish of group *Coelacanthini* with fleshy fin-bases and narrow symmetrical tail, extinct since Cretaceous period except for one genus (*Latimeria* or *Malania*) found in SE. Afr. seas.

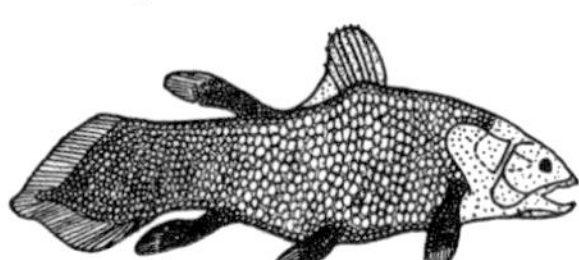

COELACANTH

Coelĕnterāt'a (sēl-) *n.pl.* (zool.) Subdivision of Metazoa, comprising aquatic animals (mostly marine, including jelly-fish, sea anemones, and corals) which have an intestinal canal but no separate true body-cavity; most of them are provided with stinging cells and show radial symmetry. **coelĕn'terate** *adj.* & *n.*

coel'ĭac (sēl-) *adj.* Of the cavity of the abdomen.

Coelŏm'ata (sēl-) *n.pl.* (zool.) Subdivision of Metazoa, comprising animals having a body-cavity or space (**coel'om**) between intestinal canal and body-wall; all higher animals belong to this group. **coelŏm'ate** *adj.* & *n.*

coen'obīte (sēn-) *n.* Member of monastic community. **coenobĭt'ic** *adj.*

cōēq'ual *adj.* & *n.* Equal. **cō-ēq'ually** *adv.*

cōẽrce' *v.* Constrain into obedience etc.; use force, secure by force. **coẽr'cion** (-shn) *n.* Constraint, compulsion, government by force. **coẽr'cionist** (-sho-) *n.* **coẽr'cive** *adj.*

cōėssĕn'tial (-shl) *adj.* Of the same substance or essence.

cōėtẽrn'al *adj.* Alike eternal. **cōėtẽrnally** *adv.*

cōēv'al *adj.* & *n.* (Person) of equal antiquity, of same age; contemporary. **cōēv'ally** *adv.*

cō-ėxist' (-gz-) *v.i.* Exist together or *with*. **cō-ėxis'tence** *n.* (esp. pol.) Peaceful existence side by side of states professing different ideologies.

cōėxtĕn'sive *adj.* Extending over same space or time.

C. of E. *abbrev.* Church of England.

cŏff'ee *n.* Dark-brown, slightly stimulating drink made from the shrub *Coffea arabica* by roasting and grinding its seeds and infusing them in boiling water; these seeds, the powder made by grinding them; the shrub itself, a native of Abyssinia and Arabia, bearing fragrant white flowers and red fleshy berries each containing two seeds (*~-beans*); *~-grounds*, granular sediment in coffee after infusion; *~-house*, refreshment-house selling coffee etc.; in 17th and 18th centuries frequented for political and literary conversation etc.; *~-mill*, contrivance for crushing or grinding roasted coffee beans; *~-pot*, vessel of silver, earthenware, etc., in which the drink coffee is made or served; *~-room*, dining-room of inn or hotel. [Arab. *gahweh* the drink]

cŏff'er *n.* 1. Box, esp. strong-box for valuables etc. 2. (archit.) Sunk panel in ceiling or soffit. 3. (also *~-dam*) Caisson.

COFFERED DOME

cŏff'ĭn *n.* 1. Chest in which corpse is buried. 2. (also *~-ship*) Unseaworthy ship. 3. Whole of horse's hoof below coronet; *~-bone*, small spongy bone in horse's hoof, last phalangeal bone of foot. ~ *v.t.* Enclose in or as in coffin.

cŏg[1] *n.* One of a series of projections on wheel, bar, etc., transmitting or receiving motion by engaging with corresponding projections on another wheel etc. (ill. GEAR); *~-rail*, toothed rail in railways with very steep gradients; *~-wheel*, toothed wheel, wheel with cogs.

cŏg[2] *v.t.* (archaic) Fraudulently control fall of dice; *cogged dice* (by error of mod. writers and dictionaries, now used for) loaded dice.

cō'gent *adj.* Forcible, convincing. **cō'gency** *n.* **cō'gently** *adv.*

cŏ'gĭtāte *v.* Ponder, meditate; devise; (philos.) form conception of. **cŏ'gĭtable** *adj.* Conceivable. **cŏgĭtā'tion** *n.* **cŏ'gĭtative** *adj.*

cognac (kŏn'yăk) *n.* French brandy, strictly the superior kind distilled from Cognac wine. [*Cognac*, town in Charente]

cŏg'nāte *adj.* 1. Descended from a common ancestor, esp., in Roman law, as dist. from AGNATE; akin in origin, allied, related. 2. (of languages) Of the same linguistic stock; (of words) having the same root or origin, representing the same original word. 3. (gram.) ~ *object, accusative*, one of kindred meaning or origin to verb, esp. one used adverbially after intransitive verb (e.g. in *die the death*). ~ *n.* Cognate person; cognate word. **cŏgnā'tion** *n.* Cognate relationship.

cŏgnĭ'tion *n.* (philos.) Action or faculty of knowing (including sensation, conception, etc.) as dist. from feeling and volition. **cŏg'nĭtive** *adj.*

cŏg'nĭzable (kŏn- *or* kŏg-n-) *adj.* Perceptible, recognizable; within jurisdiction of a court etc.

cŏg'nĭzance (kŏn- *or* kŏg-n-) *n.* 1. Being aware; notice. 2. (Right of) dealing with a matter legally or judicially. 3. Distinguishing device or mark. **cŏg'nĭzant** *adj.* Having or taking cognizance; (philos.) having cognition. **cŏgnīze'** (-g-n-) *v.t.* (philos.) Have cognition of.

cŏgnōm'ĕn *n.* 1. Third or family name of Roman citizen, as Caius Julius *Caesar*; additional name or epithet bestowed on individual. 2. Nickname; surname; name.

cŏgnōv'ĭt *n.* (law) Acknowledgement by defendant that plaintiff's case is just. [L, = 'he has acknowledged']

cōhăb'ĭt *v.i.* Live together as husband and wife (freq. of persons not legally married). **cōhăbĭtā'tion** *n.*

coheir (kō'ãr'), **coheir'ėss** *ns.* Joint heir, joint heiress.

cohēre' *v.i.* Stick together, remain united; be consistent, well-knit.

cohēr'ent *adj.* Cohering; consistent, not rambling or inconsequent. **cohēr'ently** *adv.* **cohēr'ence, cohēr'ency** *ns.*

cohēr'er *n.* (elect.) Device of metal filings, wires, or springs in loose contact, used for detecting electric waves.

cohē'sion (-zhn) *n.* Cohering; force with which parts, esp. molecules, cohere; tendency to remain united. **cohēs'ĭve** *adj.*

cō'hŏrt *n.* Division of Roman army, one-tenth of legion; band of warriors.

coif *n.* (hist.) Close cap covering top, back, and sides, of head (ill. SURCOAT).

coiffeur (kwafẽr'), ***coiffeuse'*** (-ẽrz) *ns.* Male, female, hairdresser.

coiffūre' *n.* Way hair is dressed.

coign (koin) *n.* ~ *of vantage*, place affording good view of something. [old spelling of *quoin* preserved in the Shakespearian phrase ('Macbeth', I. vi. 7)]

coil *n.* Length of rope etc. wound continuously round one point; anything arranged thus; such arrangement; one turn of anything coiled; (elect.) wire wound helically. ~ *v.* Dispose, wind, into circular or spiral shape.

coin *n.* Piece of metal of definite weight and value, made into money by being stamped with official device; coined money, money in circulation. ~ *v.t.* 1. Make (money) by stamping metal; make (metal)

COIN

1. Obverse. 2. Milled edge. 3. Reverse. 4. Circumscription. 5. Exergue

into coin. 2. Turn into money, make money by means of. 3. Fabricate, invent, (esp. new word or phrase). [Fr., = 'quoin', 'corner']

coin'age *n.* (Right of) coining; coins collectively, currency; invention, fabrication; coined word.

cōincīde' *v.i.* Fall together and agree in position, (geom.) occupy same portion of space; occur at, occupy, same space of time; be identical, agree exactly.

cōin'cidence *n.* (Instance of) coinciding; notable concurrence of events or circumstances without apparent causal connexion.

cōin'cident *adj.* Coinciding. **cōincidĕn'tal** *adj.* Of coincidence.

coir (koi'er) *n.* Prepared fibre of coconut husk, used for ropes, matting, etc. [Malayalam *kāyar* cord]

cōi'tion *n.* Sexual copulation.

cōke[1] *n.* Compact form of impure carbon obtained from coal by heating out of contact with air, used for smelting metals, for foundry work, and as a fuel esp. for boiler installations etc.; ~*-oven*, plant for converting coal into coke; the modern by-product oven is a horizontal rectangular chamber, closed at each end by cast iron or steel doors, with firebrick lining and heated by gas. ~ *v.t.* Convert (coal) into coke.

cōke[2] *n.* (slang). Cocaine.

cŏl *n.* Marked depression in summit-line of mountain chain (ill. MOUNTAIN). [Fr., = 'neck']

col. *abbrev.* Column.

Col. *abbrev.* Colonel; Colorado; Colossians (N.T.).

cōl'a *n.* Genus of trees, natives of tropical W. Africa; esp. *C. vera*, which has been introduced into W. Indies and Brazil; ~*-nut*, the brownish bitter seed of this, about the size of a chestnut, chewed as mild stimulant. [W. Afr. wd]

col'ander (kŭl-) *n.* Perforated vessel used as strainer in cookery.

Colbert (kŏlbār'), Jean Baptiste (1619–83). French statesman under Louis XIV; reformed French financial administration; developed industry by tariffs; virtually founded the French Navy; founded the French Academies of Literature, Science, and the Fine Arts.

Cōl'chĕster. Town in Essex, England, famous for oysters (~ *natives*).

cŏl'chicum (-kĭ-) *n.* Genus of liliaceous plants including meadow saffron, *C. autumnale*, with purplish mottled crocus-like flower; drug extracted from this, used for gout etc.

Cŏl'chis (-lk-). Country at the E. end of the Euxine or Black Sea, famous in Greek legend as the destination of the ARGONAUTS and the home of MEDEA.

cōld *adj.* 1. Of low temperature, esp. when compared with human body or with usual temperature; relatively without heat, not heated, having been allowed to cool; feeling cold; (of soil) slow to absorb heat, clayey. 2. Without ardour, friendliness, or affection; undemonstrative; apathetic; chilling, depressing. 3. (of colours) Suggesting a cold or sunless day, esp. containing blue or grey. 4. (of hunting scent) Not strong, faint. 5. ~ *blood*, coolness, deliberation; absence of emotion or excitement; ~*-blooded*, (of fishes and reptiles as dist. from other vertebrates) having blood whose temperature varies with that of the external air or water; (of persons, actions) unimpassioned, cool; unfeeling, callous; deliberately cruel; ~ *chisel*: see CHISEL; ~ *cream*, unguent for skin; ~ *feet*, (slang) fear, funk; ~ *front*, (meteorology) line between warm air and advancing cold air (ill. WEATHER); (*give, show, the*) ~ *shoulder*, treat with intentional coldness or indifference, snub, whence ~*-shoulder* (*v.t.*); ~ *snap*, sudden spell of cold weather; ~ *storage*, storage, keeping, preservation of meat, fish, fruit, etc., in refrigerating chambers; building with refrigerating apparatus for this; ~ *war*, use of propaganda, obstruction, intimidation, and subversive political activities to secure advantages such as used to be sought in wars of aggression; ~ *water*, water at its natural temperature; *throw* ~ *water on*, disparage, discourage. **cōld'ly** *adv.* **cōld'nĕss** *n.* **cōld** *n.* 1. Prevalence of low temperature in the atmosphere; sensation produced by loss of heat from the body. 2. Inflammatory condition of mucous membrane of nose and throat, with catarrh and freq. hoarseness and cough (freq. ~ *in the head*).

Cōld'stream Guards. British regiment of guards, first recruited in 1659 by General Monck at *Coldstream* on the Tweed.

cōle *n.* (Now rare exc. in combination) Cabbage, esp. rape; *cole'-seed*, seed of *Brassica napus*, from which rape- or colza-oil is extracted; ~*-slaw*, (U.S.) salad of sliced cabbage; *colewort*, cole, esp. kinds without heart, as kale.

Cŏlēŏp'tera *n.pl.* (zool.) The beetles, a large order of insects having the front pair of wings converted into hard sheaths which cover the other pair when not in use. **cŏlēŏp'terous** *adj.*

cŏlēŏp'tīle *n.* (bot.) Hollow organ produced by germinating cereal grains, inside which the first leaf makes its way to the ground surface.

Cō'leridge, Samuel Taylor (1772–1834). English romantic poet and literary critic; author of 'The Ancient Mariner', 'Kubla Khan', 'Christabel', etc.

Cŏl'ĕt, John (1467?–1519). Dean of St. Paul's and principal English humanist of his day; founded and endowed St. Paul's School, London.

cŏl'ĭc *n.* Severe griping pains in belly. **cŏl'icky** *adj.*

Cŏlisē'um, Cŏlossē'um. Amphitheatre in Rome, begun by Vespasian in A.D. 72; scene of gladiatorial combats and the martyrdom of many Christians.

cŏlīt'is *n.* (med.) Inflammation of membrane of large intestine.

Coll. *abbrev.* College.

collăb'orāte *v.i.* Work in combination (*with*) esp. at literary or artistic production. **collăborā'tion** *n.* In war of 1939–45 esp. applied to traitorous co-operation with the enemy in occupied countries, whence **collăborā'tionist** (-sho-) *n.* **collăb'orātor** *n.*

cŏll'age (-ahzh) *n.* Art form in which materials such as pieces of paper and matchsticks are glued to the pictorial surface.

collăpse' *n.* 1. Falling in, sudden shrinking together, giving way; failure, breakdown. 2. Prostration by loss of nervous or muscular power; breakdown of mental energy, sudden loss of courage, spirits, etc. ~ *v.i.* 1. Fall together, give way, by external pressure, cave in; contract. 2. Fail; break down; come to nothing. **collăp'sible** *adj.* Made to collapse or fold together.

cŏll'ar *n.* 1. Part of garment encircling neck or forming turned-back upper border near the neck; band (often separate) of linen, lace, etc., worn round neck and completing upper part of costume. 2. Ornamental chain forming part of insignia of order of knighthood; band round neck of dog or other animal for identification or ornament; part of harness of draught-animal, leather-covered roll fitting over lower part of neck. 3. Restraining or connecting band, ring, pipe, etc., in machines etc. 4. ~*-beam*, horizontal beam connecting a pair of rafters and preventing them from sagging (ill. ROOF); ~*-bone*, bone connecting breast-bone with shoulder-blade, clavicle (ill. SKELETON); ~*-stud*, stud fastening detachable collar to shirt. ~ *v.t.* Seize (person) by the collar, capture; (football) tackle; (slang) lay hold of, seize, appropriate.

collāte' *v.t.* 1. Compare carefully and exactly (esp. copy of text *with* other or the original); (bookbinding) verify order of sheets of printed book by signatures. 2. (of an Ordinary) Appoint or institute *to* a benefice.

collăt'eral *adj.* 1. Situated or running side by side, parallel; subordinate but from same source; contributory; connected but aside from main subject, course, etc. 2. (opp. to LINEAL) Descended from same stock but in a different line; ~ *security*, property in addition to principal security pledged as guarantee of repayment of money. ~ *n.* Collateral kinsman; collateral security. **collăt'erally** *adv.*

collā'tion *n.* 1. Collating; comparison; description of book or manuscript by signatures, number of quires, list of contents, etc. 2. (R.C. Ch.) light repast on evening of fast-day; any light meal.

cŏll'eague (-ēg) *n.* One of two or more holders of office etc. under same authority, or persons who are members of same profession.

cŏll'ėct[1] *n.* Short prayer in prayer-book, esp. one appointed for particular days or seasons and, in the Anglican Church, read before the Epistle in Morning and Evening Prayer.

collĕct'[2] *v.* Bring or come together, gather, accumulate; gather (money) from a number of people, for charity, as taxes, etc.; make collection of (curiosities, rare books, etc.); regain control of, concentrate, recover (one's faculties etc., also one*self*). **collĕc'tėd** *adj.* (esp.) Not distracted, cool. **collĕc'tėdly** *adv.* **collec'tėdnėss** *n.*

collĕc'tion *n.* 1. Collecting; money collected. 2. Group of things collected and belonging together. 3. (pl.) College terminal examination at Oxford.

collĕc'tive *adj.* Constituting a collection, gathered into one or into a whole, aggregate; of, from, a number of individuals taken or acting together; common; ~ *farm*, in U.S.S.R., farm formed by pooling individual small-holdings; ~ *noun*, singular noun used to denote a collection or number of individuals; so ~ *idea, notion*, etc.; ~ *security*, security for nations, obtained not by arming independently but by trusting in united strength of an international organization for peace or of a group of allied nations. **collĕc'tively** *adv.* **collĕc'tive** *n.* Collective noun. **collĕc'tivism** *n.* Theory or practice of collective ownership or control of all means of production, esp. of land, by the whole community or State. **collĕc'tivist** *adj.* & *n.* **collĕc'tivize** *v.t.*

collĕc'tor *n.* One who collects, esp. scientific specimens, curiosities, works of art, etc.; one who collects money for charities, as taxes, etc.; in India, chief administrative official of district, collecting revenue and usu. holding magisterial powers.

cŏll'een *n.* (Anglo-Ir.) Girl. [Ir. *caile* countrywoman]

cŏll'ėge *n.* 1. Organized society of persons performing certain common functions and possessing special rights and privileges; *Electoral C~*, the princes who elected the emperor of Germany; *Heralds' C~* or *C~ of Arms*, the corporation of Heralds, which records proved pedigrees and grants armorial bearings; *Sacred C~*, the 70 cardinals of the Roman Church who constitute the Pope's council and elect to the papacy. 2. Independent corporation of scholars within, or in connexion with, a university; similar foundation outside a university; (freq., esp. in Scotland and U.S.) university; any institute for higher education, esp. for professional training; also applied to large public secondary school, and pretentiously to private schools; *training ~*, one where teachers are trained. 3. Buildings of a college. 4. *~-living*, benefice in the gift of a college; *~-pudding*, plum-pudding of a size for one person; *C~ Youths*, English society of bell-ringers founded in 1637. **cŏll'eger** *n.* One of the 70 foundation scholars at Eton College. **collē'gian** *n.* Member of a college. **collē'giate** *adj.* Of, constituted as, a college; ~ *church*, church endowed for a body corporate or chapter but with no bishop's see; (Scotland and U.S.) church under joint pastorate.

cŏllĕnchyma (-n-kĭ-) *n.* (bot.) Tissue consisting of cells with local cellulose thickening on their walls, usu. developed near surface of young stems and leaves and affording them mechanical strength.

cŏll'ėt *n.* Encompassing band or ring on rod, spindle, etc.; ferrule; socket; flange or setting of precious stone; horizontal base of a diamond when cut as a brilliant (ill. GEM).

collīde' *v.i.* Come forcibly into contact (*with*), strike or dash together; be in conflict, clash.

cŏll'ie *n.* Sheep-dog of a Scotch breed, with long hair, pointed nose, and bushy tail (ill. DOG).

cŏll'ier (-*yer*) *n.* 1. Coal-miner. 2. (Sailor on) coal-ship. **cŏll'iery̆** *n.* Coal-mine, together with buildings and apparatus belonging to it.

cŏll'imāte *v.t.* Adjust (telescope) so that line of sight is in correct position; place (telescopes, lenses, etc.) with optical axes in same line; (of lens etc.) make (rays of light) parallel. **cŏllimā'tion** *n.*

cŏll'imātor *n.* Small fixed telescope used for collimating astronomical instrument etc.; tube with slit and lens used for limiting to a narrow beam and making parallel light falling on prism or diffraction grating of spectroscope.

Cŏll'ins[1] *n.* Letter of thanks from guest after visit. [letter by Rev. William *Collins* in Jane Austen's 'Pride and Prejudice']

Cŏll'ins[2], William Wilkie (1824–89). English novelist; author of 'The Woman in White' (1860) and 'The Moonstone' (1868), almost the first English novels dealing with the detection of crime.

colli'sion (-zhn) *n.* Colliding; violent encounter of moving body, esp. ship or railway-train, with another; clash, clashing; ~ *bulkhead*, bulkhead protecting against damage by collison; ~ *mat*, mat for covering hole in ship's side caused by collision.

cŏll'ocāte *v.t.* Place together, arrange. **cŏllocā'tion** *n.*

collō̆d'ion *n.* Colourless gummy liquid, a solution of gun-cotton in ether, drying rapidly in air, and used for covering photographic plates, wounds, burns, etc., with a thin skin or film.

collōgue' (-g) *v.i.* Talk confidentially.

cŏll'oid *adj.* Gluey; ~ *substance, tissue*, etc., (path.) gelatinous substance produced in certain forms of tissue-degeneration. ~ *n.* (chem.) Non-crystalline substance with very large molecules, which dissolves to form a viscous, sticky solution, e.g. starch, gelatine, and plastics. **colloid'al** *adj.*

cŏll'op *n.* (Sc.) Slice of meat; (pl.) fried minced meat.

collōq'uial *adj.* Of or in talk, oral; belonging to familiar, not formal or elevated, speech. **collōq'uialism** *n.* **collōq'uially** *adv.*

cŏll'oquy̆ *n.* Converse, conversation; (in Presbyterian churches) judicial and legislative court of pastors and representative elders.

cŏll'otȳpe *n.* Thin plate or sheet of gelatine with sensitized surface etched by actinic rays, so that it can be printed from; print so made, printing by this process.

collu'sion (-ōōzhn) *n.* Fraudulent secret understanding, esp. between ostensible opponents as in a lawsuit. **collus'ive** *adj.* **collus'ively** *adv.*

collȳ'rium *n.* Eye-salve, eye-wash; suppository.

cŏll'ȳwŏbbles *n.pl.* (colloq.) Rumbling in the intestines.

Colo. *abbrev.* Colorado.

cŏl'ocy̆nth *n.* The plant (of the gourd family) bitter-apple, *Citrullus colocynthus*, bearing fruit about size of orange with light spongy extremely bitter pulp; purgative drug prepared from this.

Cologne' (-ōn). Köln, German city on the lower Rhine, famous in the Middle Ages for the shrine of the Wise Men of the East (the *Three Kings of ~*); *Eau* (ō) *de Cologne*, Cologne water, a perfume made of aromatic oils and spirit, first manufactured at Cologne.

Cŏlŏm'bia. A republic lying in the extreme NW. of S. America; capital, Bogotá. It was under Spanish rule until 1819 when a republic was established by Simon BOLIVAR, consisting of the territories now known as Colombia, Panama, Venezuela, and Ecuador; Venezuela and Ecuador seceded in 1830 and Panama in 1903. **Colŏm'bian** *adj.* & *n.*

Cŏlom'bō (-lŭm-). Capital of Ceylon.

cō̆l'on[1] *n.* The greater part of the large intestine, extending from caecum to rectum (ill. ALIMENTARY).

cō̆l'on[2] *n.* Punctuation mark (:), used esp. to mark antithesis or before illustration or quotation.

cō̆l'ŏn[3] *n.* Principal monetary unit of Costa Rica (= 100 centimos) and San Salvador (= 100 centavos).

colonel (kẽr'nl) *n.* Officer in command of a regiment; *C~*

BLIMP, BOGEY: see these words.

colonelcy (kẽr'nlsĭ) *n.*

colŏn'ial *adj.* & *n.* (Inhabitant) of a colony, esp. of a British Crown colony, or (hist.) of the 13 British colonies of America before they became the United States; (of architecture, etc.) of the period during which these States were still colonies; *C~ Office*, department of British Government in charge of colonies; merged with Commonwealth Office 1966, since 1968 combined with FOREIGN OFFICE. **colŏn'iălism** *n.*

cŏl'onist *n.* Settler in, part-founder or inhabitant of, a colony.

cŏl'onize *v.* Establish colony in; establish in a colony; form or establish a colony or settlement. **cŏlonīzā'tion** *n.*

cŏlonnāde' *n.* Row of columns at regular intervals supporting entablature.

cŏl'ony *n.* 1. (Gk hist.) independent city founded by emigrants; (Rom. hist.) settlement of Roman citizens (usu. veteran soldiers) in conquered territory, where they acted as a garrison. 2. Settlement, settlers, in new country remaining subject to or connected with parent State; territory so peopled. 3. Number of people of one nationality or occupation forming a community in a city. 4. (biol.) Aggregate of individual animals or plants forming physiologically connected structure or (more loosely) living close together. 5. Establishment, settlement, for employing or training the unemployed.

cŏl'ophon *n.* Inscription or device at end of book or manuscript, containing title, scribe's or printer's name, date, place of printing, etc.

colŏph'ony *n.* Resin originating from the town of *Colophon* in Lydia; see ROSIN.

Cŏlora'dō (-ah-). Mountain State of U.S. admitted to Union 1876, named from the great ~ *river* which rises there and flows into the Gulf of California; capital, Denver; ~ *beetle*, small beetle (*Leptinotarsa decemlineata*) native to Rocky Mountains and introduced into Europe, yellow with 10 longitudinal black stripes on back, the larva of which is very destructive to the potato.

colo(u)rā'tion (kŭ-) *n.* Colouring; arrangement of colours; natural, esp. variegated, colour of living things.

cŏloratur'a (-ahtoora) *n.* Florid ornament, freq. extempore, in singing; ~ *soprano*, (singer with) high flexible voice capable of this. [It., = 'coloured (music)']

cŏlorĭf'ĭc (*or* kŭ-) *adj.* Producing colour(s).

cŏlorim'ėter (*or* kŭ-) *n.* Instrument for measuring intensity of colour.

colŏss'al *adj.* Of, like, a colossus; gigantic, huge; ~ *order*, (archit.) columns or pilasters on a façade running up past more than one storey. **colŏss'ally** *adv.*

Colosseum: see COLISEUM.

Colŏss'ians, Epistle to. Epistle of N.T., written by St. Paul to the Church at Colossae, a city on the Lycus, near Laodicea.

colŏss'us *n.* (pl. *-ī*, *-uses*). Gigantic statue; huge dominating figure; person or personified empire conceived as standing astride dominions like the statue at Rhodes which was thought to have stood astride the harbour; *C~ of Rhodes*, this statue, in bronze, of the sun-god Helios, said to have been 70 cubits high (over 100 ft); it was shattered by an earthquake in 224 B.C. only 56 years after erection and the fragments, which lay about the harbour for centuries, were regarded as one of the Seven Wonders of the World.

colŏst'omy̆ *n.* (surg.) Formation of an opening from the colon through the abdominal wall.

colour (kŭl'*er*) *n.* 1. Quality or wave-length of light (emitted or) reflected from an object, determined by the physical configuration of the emitting or reflecting surface and the quality of the incident light (if any); sensation produced by stimulation of optic nerve by particular light-vibrations. 2. A particular hue, one of the constituents into which white or 'colourless' light can be decomposed, or any mixture of these; *black*, in which rays of light are wholly absorbed, and *white*, in which they are wholly reflected, may also be included among colours; *primary colours*, (physiol.) red, green, and violet, combinations of which give rise to sensations of all others; (painting) red, blue, and yellow, which may be mixed to produce all others; *secondary colours*, those (as green, purple) produced by mixing two primary colours; *tertiary colours*, grey or greyish hues obtained by mixing secondary colours. 3. The hue of the darker, esp. negro, races of mankind as dist. from 'white'. 4. Complexion, ruddy hue of cheeks, etc. 5. Representation of colour in painting; colouring. 6. (pl.) Coloured ribbon, dress, etc., worn as symbol of party, membership of club, inclusion in athletic team, etc.; flag, ensign, or standard of regiment or ship; *the colours*, the army. 7. Pigment, paint; coloured material etc. 8. Outward appearance, semblance; pretext, show of reason, specious or plausible pretence; tone, character, kind, shade of meaning; (mus.) timbre, variety of expression, etc. 9. *local* ~, see LOCAL; *~-blind*, unable to see, or to distinguish between, certain colours; *~-sergeant*, sergeant with special duty of attending regimental colours in the field (a rank created by the Prince Regent (George IV) in recognition of gallantry of non-commissioned officers in Peninsular War). ~ *v.* Give colour to; paint, stain, dye; disguise; misrepresent; imbue with its own colour; take on colour; blush; *coloured* (*man, person, woman*), not white, wholly or partly of negro descent.

col'ourable (kŭl'*er*-) *adj.* Specious, plausible. **col'ourably** *adv.*

col'ourful (kŭl*er*-) *adj.* Full of colour. **col'ourfully** *adv.* **col'ourfulnėss** *n.*

col'ourĭng (kŭl*er*-) *n.* (esp.) Style in which thing is coloured, or in which artist uses colour; complexion.

col'ourĭst (kŭl*er*-) *n.* Painter skilful in colouring.

col'ourlėss (kŭl'*er*-) *adj.* Without colour; pale; dull; wanting in character or vividness; neutral, impartial, indifferent. **col'ourlėssly** *adv.* **col'ourlėssnėss** *n.*

cŏlporteur' (-tẽr; *or* cŏl'-) *n.* Hawker of books etc., esp. one employed by a religious society.

Col.-S(er)gt *abbrev.* Colour-Sergeant.

cōlt' *n.* Young male of horse (from leaving dam till age of 4, or with thoroughbreds 5); inexperienced person, esp. cricket professional in first season; *cōlts'foot*, common weed in waste or clayey ground, *Tussilago farfara*, with large spreading cordate leaves downy beneath and yellow flowers appearing before the leaves; extract from this used as a household remedy for coughs. **cōl'tĭsh** *adj.*

Cōlt[2] *n.* Kind of revolver (ill. PISTOL). [Samuel *Colt* (1814–62), Amer. inventor]

Colŭm'ba, St. (521–97). Irish monk and missionary who founded the monastery of Iona, Scotland.

cŏlumbār'ium *n.* (pl. *-ia*). 1. Pigeon-house, dove-cot. 2. (Rom. antiq.) subterranean sepulchre with niches for cinerary urns.

Colŭm'bĭa[1]. Poetic name for America; *British* ~, Pacific province of the Dominion of Canada; capital, Victoria. [f. COLUMBUS]

Colŭm'bĭa[2]. Capital of S. Carolina, U.S.

cŏl'umbīne[1] *n.* The plant *Aquilegia vulgaris*, the inverted flower of which, with its horned nectaries, resembles 5 pigeons clustered together. [L *columba* dove]

Cŏl'umbīne[2]. Character in Italian comedy, the mistress of Harlequin; she appears in the harlequinade of English pantomime as a short-skirted dancer.

colŭm'bĭum: see NIOBIUM.

Colŭm'bus[1], Christopher (*c* 1445–1506). A Genoese navigator who prevailed upon Ferdinand and Isabella of Spain to bear the expenses of an expedition of discovery and set out on his 1st voyage in 1492. He first discovered the Bahamas (12th Oct. 1492) and Cuba and on his 3rd voyage (1498) landed near the mouth of the Orinoco in S. America; ~ *Day*, 12th Oct., a legal holiday in most States of U.S., the W. Indies, and some S. Amer. republics.

Colŭm′bus². Capital of Ohio, U.S., named after COLUMBUS¹.

cŏl′umn (-m) *n*. 1. (archit.) Long cylindrical or slightly tapering body usu. supporting entablature or arch or standing alone as monument (ill. ORDER). 2. Natural column-shaped formation, esp. of igneous rock; anything resembling a column in shape or function; upright mass of air, water, mercury, smoke, etc. 3. One of the narrow vertical divisions of a sheet of paper, page of book, etc., used for lists of figures, names, etc., or for convenience in arranging printed matter on a wide page; esp. such a division of a newspaper, the printed matter filling it, a newspaper article. 4. Formation of troops, armoured vehicles, etc., in which the elements are placed one behind the other as dist. from *line* in which they are abreast; (nav.) ships in line ahead.

cŏl′umnar (*or* kolŭm′n*ar*) *adj*. Like a column; in columns.

cŏl′umnist (-*u*mĭst) *n*. Journalist who regularly contributes to a newspaper (or, in U.S., group of newspapers) a column of comment on events.

colūre′ *n*. (astron.) One of two great circles intersecting at right angles at the poles and dividing the equinoctial and ecliptic into 4 equal parts; one passes through the equinoctial points, the other through the solstitial points, of the ecliptic (ill. CELESTIAL).

cŏl′za *n*. *~-oil*, oil expressed from cole-seed, used in lamps.

com- *prefix*. With.

cō′ma¹ *n*. (path.) Prolonged loss of consciousness; (loosely) stupor, lethargy. **cō′matōse** (-s) *adj*. In a state of coma; drowsy, lethargic.

cō′ma² *n*. (astron.) Nebulous envelope surrounding nucleus of comet. [Gk *komē* hair]

comb (kōm) *n*. 1. Strip of bone, metal, etc., with indentations forming series of teeth, or with teeth inserted, used for disentangling, cleaning, and arranging hair, or to keep it in place. 2. Various things of similar appearance or function: instrument with several rows of teeth for carding wool or flax, steel instrument with projecting teeth used for cutting screw-thread, etc. 3. Red fleshy indented or serrated crest or caruncle on head of domestic fowl, esp. male. 4. Honeycomb. *~ v*. Draw comb through (hair), dress (wool, flax) with comb; (of wave) curl over; search or examine closely.

cŏm′bat (*or* kŭm-) *n*. Encounter, fight; struggle; conflict. *~ v*. Do battle; fight with; contend with, oppose.

cŏm′batant (*or* kŭm-) *n*. One who fights. *~ adj*. fighting.

cŏm′bative (*or* kŭm-) *adj*. Pugnacious. **com′batively** *adv*. **com′bativeness** *n*.

combe: see COOMB.

cōmber (-m*er*) *n*. (esp.) Long curling wave, breaker.

cŏmbinā′tion *n*. 1. Combining; combined state; group or set of things combined. 2. Union, association, of persons for a common object, esp. union (formerly illegal) of employers or workmen to further their interests. 3. Chemical union, in which substances combine to form new compounds, product of this. 4. (pl.) Close-fitting undergarment combining vest and drawers. 5. Motor-cycle with side-car attached. 6. *~-room*, in University of Cambridge, senior common-room.

cŏm′binative *adj*. Combining; of combination; (phonetics, of sound-changes in words etc.) due to a combination of sounds or letters.

combīne′ *v*. 1. Join together, unite; come together; unite for common purpose, co-operate; *combined operations*, operations in which military, naval, and air forces are combined. 2. Enter into chemical union (*with*); *combining weight*: see EQUIVALENT. **cŏm′bīne** *n*. Combination of persons in business, politics, etc., esp. to control prices or obstruct course of trade; *~(-harvester)*, machine reaping and threshing in one operation.

cōmb′ings (-mĭ-) *n.pl*. (esp.) Hairs combed off.

combŭst′ible *adj*. & *n*. (Matter, thing) capable of burning; excitable, inflammable.

combŭs′tion (-schn) *n*. Consumption or destruction by fire; development of light and heat accompanying chemical combination; oxidation of organic material; *spontaneous ~*, ignition of mass of organic material, e.g. straw, from heat generated within itself; *internal ~ engine*, engine in which the motive power is produced by the combustion and expansion of a mixture of petrol and oil vapour (or gas) and air inside the cylinders. (*Illustration, p*. 160.)

come (kŭm) *v.i.* (past t. *cāme*, past part. *come*). 1. Move or start towards, arrive at, a point, time, or result; be brought; fall, land (*on*); move relatively by motion of beholder etc., towards one. 2. Occur, fall; happen; issue; be derived, descend; (of time etc.) arrive in due course; become, get to be; turn out to be. 3. (quasi-trans.) Traverse, accomplish (a distance); play or practise (a dodge, trick) *over*; act, perform one's part (*come it strong* etc.); *~ a cropper*, fall. 4. *~ about*, happen; *~ across*, meet with; *~ across with*, hand over; *~ along*, (colloq.) make haste; *~ at*, reach, discover, get access to; *~ back*, recur to memory; *~-back*, retaliation, retort; return, recovery, reinstatement; *~ by*, obtain; *~ down*, extend downwards *to*; be handed down; fall, be humbled; *~ forward*, present oneself before the public etc.; *~ in*, enter house or room; take specified place (in race etc.); come into power or office; be received as income; become seasonable or fashionable; serve a purpose, find a place; *~ in for*, get; *~ into*, receive, esp. as heir; *~ off*, become detached; retire or extricate oneself; come to the issue; succeed; *~ on*, advance; continue to progress, thrive, develop; supervene; come upon the stage or scene; begin to bowl at cricket; *~ out*, go on strike; emerge from contest, examination, etc.; (of sun etc.) emerge from clouds, begin to shine; come into public view, become public, be published; appear or be found by computation etc.; develop, display itself; make debut on stage or in society; *~ out with*, utter; *~ round*, recover from ill temper, swoon, etc.; come incidentally or informally; veer round; *~ to*, revive; (naut.) come to a standstill; *~ up*, come to place regarded as higher, e.g. capital, university; come close *to*; arise as subject of attention, discussion, etc.; rise to level or height of; *~ up with*, overtake.

come-ăt′-able (kŭm-) *adj*. That may be come at, accessible.

comēd′ian *n*. Comic actor; (archaic) writer of comedies.

comédiĕnne′ (-mā- *or* -mē-) *n*. Comedy actress.

comēdiĕtt′a *n*. Short or slight comedy.

comēd′ō *n*. (pl. *-dōnēs*). (med. Skin blemish, blackhead.

cŏm′ėdy *n*. Stage-play of light, amusing, and often satirical character, with a happy conclusion to its plot; that branch of drama which adopts a humorous or familiar style and depicts laughable characters and incidents; life, or an incident in it, regarded as a comic spectacle. **comēd′ic** *adj*. (rare) Comic.

come′ly (kŭm-) *adj*. Pleasant to look at. **come′linėss** *n*.

com′er (kŭ-) *n*. One who comes (usu. *first ~*, *last ~*, etc.); *all ~s*, any who apply, take up challenge, etc.

comĕs′tible *n*. (usu. pl.) Thing to eat.

cŏm′ėt *n*. Celestial body with star-like nucleus and train or 'tail' of light moving about sun in elliptical or parabolic orbit. **cŏm′ėtary, comĕt′ic** *adjs*. [Gk *komētes* long-haired (star)]

com′fit (kŭ-) *n*. Sweetmeat, sugar-plum.

com′fort (kŭ-) *n*. 1. Relief in affliction, consolation; person who consoles one or saves one trouble; cause of satisfaction. 2. Well-being, being comfortable; thing that produces or ministers to enjoyment and content. *~ v.t.* Soothe in grief, console; make comfortable. **com′fortlėss** *adj*.

com′fortable (kŭ-) *adj*. Affording consolation; attended with or ministering to comfort or physical well-being; in a state of tranquil enjoyment and content, at ease. **com′fortably** *adv*. **com′forter** *n*.

1. One who comforts; *the C~*, the Holy Ghost; *Job's ~*, one who depresses while professing or intending to comfort. 2. Woollen scarf; (U.S.) quilted coverlet. 3. India-rubber teat given to baby to suck.

Cŏm'infŏrm. Communist 'Information Bureau' consisting of two representatives from each of nine European countries, established at Belgrade 1947 and dissolved 1956; the successor of the COMINTERN.

command' (-ah-) *n.* 1. Order, bidding. 2. Exercise or tenure of authority, esp. naval or military; body of troops, district, ship, etc. under commander; *high ~*, *higher ~*, general staff, esp. commander-in-chief, of army. 3. Control,

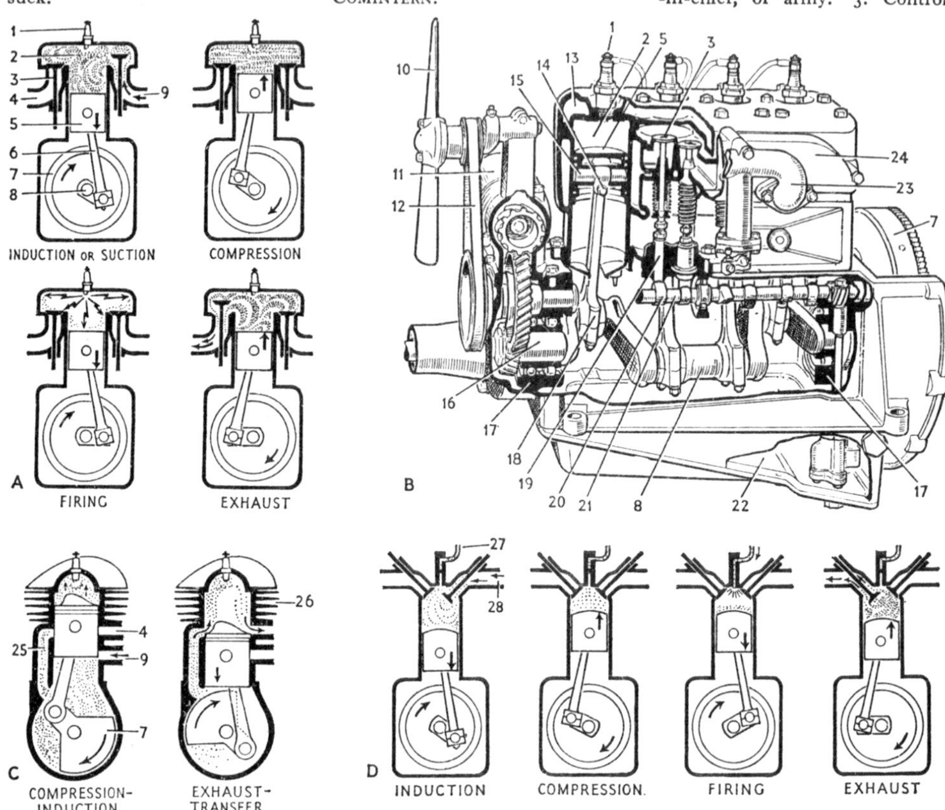

INTERNAL COMBUSTION ENGINES: A. STROKES OF FOUR-STROKE ENGINE. B. FOUR-CYLINDER FOUR-STROKE ENGINE. C. TWO-STROKE ENGINE. D. DIESEL ENGINE

A. 1 Sparking plug. 2. Cylinder. 3. Poppet-valve. 4. Exhaust port. 5. Piston. 6. Connecting rod. 7. Fly-wheel. 8. Crankshaft. 9. Inlet port. B. 10. Fan. 11. Dynamo. 12. Fan belt. 13. Water jacket. 14. Little end of connecting rod. 15. Gudgeon pin. 16. Journal. 17. Main bearings. 18. Big end of connecting rod. 19. Tappet. 20. Cam. 21. Camshaft. 22. Sump. 23. Inlet manifold. 24. Exhaust manifold. C. 25. Transfer port. 26. Cooling fins. D. 27. Oil injector. 28. Air inlet port

com'frey (kŭ-) *n.* Tall ditch-plant, *Symphytum officinale*, with rough leaves and white or purple bell-shaped flowers, the root and leaves of which are used medicinally.

com'fȳ (kŭ-) *adj.* (colloq.) Comfortable.

cŏm'ic *adj.* Of comedy; mirth-provoking, laughable or meant to be so, facetious, burlesque, funny; *~ opera*: see OPERA; *~ strip*, set of drawings, usu. broadly humorous, forming part of a series appearing regularly in a journal. *~ n.* Comic actor or person (colloq.); comic paper; children's magazine or pamphlet consisting largely of stories in pictorial form.

cŏm'ical *adj.* Mirth-provoking, laughable; odd, queer. **cŏmicăl'ity** *n.* **cŏm'ically** *adv.*

Cŏm'intĕrn. The Third Communist INTERNATIONAL, founded at Moscow in Mar. 1919; formally dissolved June 1943.

cŏm'ity *n.* Courtesy; *~ of nations*, friendly and courteous recognition as far as practicable by nations of laws and usages of other nations; (freq., erroneously) the company of nations practising this.

cŏmm'a *n.* Punctuation mark (,) used to separate smallest parts of a sentence, also used to separate figures etc.; (mus.) minute 'interval' or difference of pitch; *inverted ~s*, (' ' or " ") commas raised above line at beginning and end of quotation, the first, or first pair, being inverted; *~ butterfly*, butterfly, *Polygonia comma-album*, with white comma-shaped mark on underside of wings.

mastery, possession; *~ paper*, (abbrev. Cd, Cmd), paper laid by command of Crown before Parliament etc.; *~ performance*, theatrical etc. performance given by royal command. *~ v.* 1. Order, bid. 2. Have authority over or control of, be supreme; be in command (of). 3. Restrain, master; have at disposal or within reach; demand and obtain; dominate (position etc.) from superior height, look down over.

cŏmmandănt' (*or* -ahnt) *n.* Commanding officer, esp. one holding special command, of depot, particular force, fortress, etc.

cŏmmandeer' *v.* Force (men) into, seize (stores) for, military service; take arbitrary possession of.

comman'der (-ah-), *n.* One

who commands; one who has command of a ship, naval officer ranking below captain; *Lieutenant-C~*, naval officer below commander and above lieutenant; *Wing C~*, officer in air force ranking above Squadron-Leader and below Group Captain; *C~-in-Chief*, chief commander of all military land forces of a State; senior naval officer in command of all ships on a station; *C~ of the Faithful*, title of the Caliphs, first assumed by Omar I *c* 640.

comman'dĭng (-ah-) *adj.* Ruling, controlling; nobly dignified; *~ officer*, officer in command.

command'ment (-ah-) *n.* Divine command, esp. one of the divisions of the decalogue, the *Ten C~s* (Exod. xx. 1–17).

comman'dō (-ah-) *n.* (pl. *-s*). Party called out for military purposes; in the Boer War (1899–1902), unit of Boer army composed of militia of an electoral district; in the war of 1939–45, one of several bodies of troops in British Army specially trained for raids on enemy's coasts etc.

comme il faut (kŏmēlfō') *adj. phr.* According to etiquette, correct in deportment or behaviour.

commĕm'orāte *v.t.* Celebrate in speech or writing; preserve in memory by some celebration; be a memorial of. **commĕmorā'tion** *n.* 1. Commemorating; service or prayer commemorating saint or sacred event. 2. At Oxford, annual Trinity Term celebration in memory of the founders and benefactors of the University. **commĕm'orative** *adj.*

commĕnce' *v.* Begin; (archaic) start or set up as; take full degree of Master or Doctor at university. **commĕnce'ment** (-sm-) *n.* Beginning; ceremony of conferring university degrees (in Cambridge and Dublin, those of Master and Doctor, in U.S. universities, all degrees).

commĕnd' *v.t.* Entrust, commit (archaic exc. in, e.g., *~ one's soul to God*); praise, extol; *~ me to* (freq. iron.), give me by choice.

commĕn'dable *adj.* Praiseworthy. **commĕn'dably** *adv.*

commĕn'dăm *n.* Tenure of benefice in absence of regular incumbent, esp. of benefice which bishop etc. might hold along with his own preferment (abolished in England by statute in 1836).

commĕndā'tion *n.* Praise; act of commending person to another's favour.

commĕn'datory *adj.* 1. Commending. 2. Holding, held, in commendam.

commĕn'sal *adj.* & *n.* (Person) eating at same table; (animal or plant) living attached to or as tenant of another, and sharing its food. **commĕn'salism, cŏmmĕnsăl'ity** *ns.*

commĕn'surable (-sher-) *adj.* Measurable by the same standard; divisible without remainder by the same quantity. **commĕn'surably** *adv.* **commĕnsurabĭl'ity** *n.*

commĕn'surate (-sher-) *adj.* Coextensive; proportionate. **commĕn'surately** *adv.*

cŏmm'ĕnt *n.* Explanatory or critical note or remark; expository or critical matter; criticism. *~ v.i.* Write explanatory or critical notes *upon*; make (esp. unfavourable) comments or remarks (*upon*).

cŏmm'entary *n.* Expository treatise; series of running comments on book, speech, performance, etc.; comment, remark; *running ~*, (esp.) broadcast commentary on some public event while it is in progress.

cŏmmentā'tion *n.* Making of comments.

cŏmm'entātor *n.* Maker of comments, writer or speaker of commentary.

cŏmm'ẽrce *n.* 1. Exchange of merchandise, esp. on a large scale between different countries or districts. 2. Intercourse. 3. Card-game in which exchange or barter is chief feature.

commẽr'cial (-shl) *adj.* Of, engaged in, bearing on, commerce; *~ college, school*, college, school, for instruction in commercial subjects; *~ hotel, ~ room*, hotel, room in hotel or inn, for accommodation of commercial travellers; *~ traveller*, agent of manufacturer, wholesale trader, etc., who travels over a district showing samples and soliciting orders. *~ n.* Commercial traveller (vulg.); commercial hotel. **commẽr'cialism** (-shal-) *n.* **commẽr'cialize** *v.t.* **commẽr'cially** *adv.*

cŏmminā'tion *n.* Threatening of divine punishment or vengeance; denunciation; recital of divine threats against sinners, part of an office for Ash Wednesday in the Anglican liturgy. **cŏmm'inatory** *adj.* Threatening, denunciatory.

commĭng'le (-nggl) *v.* Mingle together.

cŏmm'inūte *v.t.* Reduce to minute particles; divide into small portions; *comminuted fracture*: see ill. BONE. **cŏmminū'tion** *n.*

commĭs'erāte (-z-) *v.* Feel, show, express, pity for; condole *with*. **commiserā'tion** *n.* **commĭs'erative** *adj.*

cŏmmissăr' *n.* Official of Communist party or Soviet government.

cŏmmissăr'iat *n.* 1. Department (esp. military) for supply of food etc. 2. Department of Civil Service of U.S.S.R.

cŏmm'issary *n.* 1. Deputy, delegate; representative of bishop in part of his diocese, or of absent bishop. 2. Officer charged with supply of food etc. for body of soldiers; *C~ general*, chief commissary, esp. head of military commissariat.

commĭ'ssion (-shn) *n.* 1. Authoritative charge or direction; authority, esp. delegated authority, body of persons having authority, to act in some specified capacity, investigate some specified question, etc.; *~ of the peace*, authority given, persons authorized, to act as Justices of the Peace; *Royal C~*, body of persons entrusted by British sovereign with duties and powers of holding an inquiry (freq. with power to compel evidence) and issuing a report. 2. Warrant conferring authority, warrant by which officer in army, navy, or air force exercises command; office conferred by such a warrant. 3. Being authoritatively entrusted or given in charge; *in ~*, exercising delegated authority; (of an office) placed by warrant in charge of a body of persons; (of a ship of war) manned, armed, and ready for sea. 4. Charge entrusted to anyone to perform; order given to artist, writer, etc. for a particular piece of work. 5. Authority to act as agent for another in trade or business; system of trading in which dealer acts as agent for another, receiving a percentage as remuneration; the percentage of the amount involved paid to the agent. *~ v.t.* Empower by commission; give (officer) command of ship; order (ship) for active service; assume command of (ship); give (artist etc.) a commission. **commĭ'ssioned** (-nd) *adj.* Authorized; (of officer) holding rank by commission; (of ships) put in commission.

commissionaire' (-shonār) *n.* Member of *Corps of Commissionaires*, an association of pensioned soldiers, orig. established in London in 1859, organized for employment as porters, messengers, etc.; person in uniform who is employed as door porter in hotel, large shop, cinema, etc.

commĭ'ssioner (-shon-) *n.* One appointed by commission; member of permanently constituted commission or government board etc.; representative of supreme authority in district, department, etc.; official at head of various branches of public service etc.; *High C~*, chief representative of British Dominion in England; representative of the sovereign at the General Assembly of the Church of Scotland.

cŏmm'issūre *n.* Joining, seam; joint between two bones; line where lips, eyelids, meet; band or bundle of white or grey nerve-substance connecting hemispheres of brain, parts of cerebrum and cerebellum, two sides of spinal cord, etc.

commĭt' *v.t.* 1. Entrust, consign, for treatment or safe keeping, consign officially *to* custody, prison, etc.; refer (bill etc.) to committee. 2. Perpetrate (crime, blunder). 3. Involve, compromise; engage or pledge by implication (*to*). **commĭt'ment** *n.* (esp.)

Engagement; thing undertaken, responsibility. **commĭtt'al** *n.* Committing, consigning, esp. committing to prison; committing of body to grave at burial; reference to committee; committing of oneself.

commĭtt'ee *n.* Body of persons appointed for special function by (and usu. out of) larger body; *standing* ~, one which is permanent during the existence of the appointing body; *joint* ~, composed of members nominated by two or more distinct bodies; *C~ of the whole House,* the House of Commons sitting as a committee and presided over by a chairman (not the Speaker); *C~ of Supply, C~ of Ways and Means,* financial committees of the House of Commons consisting of all the members.

commĭx' *v.* (archaic, poet.) Mix. **commĭx'ture** *n.*

commōde' *n.* Chest of drawers, chiffonier; close-stool.

commōd'ious *adj.* Roomy. **commōd'iously** *adv.* **commōd'iousnėss** *n.*

commŏd'ĭty *n.* Useful thing; article of trade.

cŏmm'odōre *n.* Naval officer ranking above captain and below rear-admiral (in British Navy a temporary rank); as courtesy-title, senior captain when three or more ships cruise together, captain of pilots, president of yacht-club; senior captain of a shipping line; commodore's ship; *Air C~,* rank in R.A.F. immediately above Group Captain.

cŏmm'on *adj.* 1. Possessed or shared alike by both or all; belonging to more than one; belonging to all mankind alike; general; public. 2. Of ordinary occurrence and quality; usual, frequent; undistinguished, ordinary; of little value, mean, of inferior quality; low-class, vulgar. 3. (math.) Of a number or quantity, belonging equally to two or more quantities. 4. (gram., logic) Of a noun, name, etc., applicable to every individual or species of a class or genus; of either gender or sex. 5. (mus. etc.) (of time, measure) Consisting of two or four beats in a bar, esp. of 4 crotchets in a bar. 6. ~ *carrier,* one recognized by law as bound to serve the public; ~ *chord*: see CHORD[2]; ~ *form,* form of probate in which grant is made by executor's oath without opposition; customary form of words in common-law pleadings; form of words common to documents of like kind; (colloq.) formula etc. of general application; ~ *ground,* basis for argument etc. accepted by both sides; ~ *land*: see *n.* below; ~ *law,* unwritten law of England, administered by sovereign's courts and purporting to be derived from ancient and universal usage, which is embodied in the older commentaries and in reports of adjudged cases; ~ *lodging-house,* one in which any person may obtain a bed for the night, esp. one in which the charge is very low; ~ *metre,* hymn-stanza of four lines, of which the first and third have eight syllables and the second and fourth six (also called 'ballad metre' from its use in Old English ballads); *C~ Pleas,* civil actions at law brought by one subject against another; *Court of C~ Pleas,* until 1875 one of the three superior courts of common law in England; *C~ Prayer,* liturgy or form of public service prescribed by Church of England and first set forth in the *Book of C~ Prayer* of 1549 (the edition now used in England being substantially that of 1662); ~ *recovery*: see RECOVERY; ~*-room* (also *senior* ~*-room*), room in school, university, etc., to which members of staff have common access; esp. at Oxford, room to which fellows of college retire after dinner; similar room (also *junior* ~*-room*) for undergraduates or students; ~ *sense,* normal understanding, good practical sense in everyday affairs; ~ *soldier,* private soldier; ~ *weal,* (archaic) commonwealth; public welfare. ~ *n.* 1. Land belonging to local community as a whole, now esp. the unenclosed waste land remaining to represent this. 2. (law) A man's right in the land or water of another, as of pasturage, fishing, etc. 3. *the* ~, what is common or ordinary (esp. in *out of the* ~); *in* ~, in joint use, shared; *in* ~ *with,* in the same way as, like; *tenants in* ~, tenants holding by distinct titles but 'by unity of possession'. **cŏmm'onnėss** *n.* Vulgarity.

cŏmm'onable *adj.* (Of animals) that may be pastured on common land; (of land) that may be held in common, subject to right of common.

cŏmm'onage *n.* Right of common; land, condition of land, held in common or subject to right of common; commonalty.

cŏmm'onalty *n.* The general body of the community, the common people as dist. from those of rank or in authority; the general or universal body.

cŏmm'oner *n.* 1. One of the common people, one below the rank of a peer. 2. (rare) Member of House of Commons; *the Great C~,* the elder William Pitt. 3. (in some English colleges) One who pays for his commons, i.e. student not on the foundation (see COMMONS *n.pl.*, 2). 4. One who has right of common. **cŏmm'only** *adv.* Usually; to an ordinary degree, meanly, cheaply; vulgarly.

cŏmm'onplāce *n.* Notable passage entered for reference or use in a ~ *book* kept for this purpose; opinion or statement generally accepted; ordinary topic; anything common and trite. ~ *adj.* Lacking originality, trite, trivial, hackneyed.

cŏmm'ons *n.pl.* 1. The common people; third estate in English and similar constitutions, body of people, not ennobled, represented by Lower House of Parliament; the Lower House itself (also *House of Commons*; ill. PARLIAMENT). 2. Provisions shared in common, esp. in monastic house, college, etc.; (at Oxford and Cambridge) definite portion of victuals supplied from college buttery or kitchen at fixed charge; (more widely) daily fare; *short* ~, insufficient fare.

cŏmm'onwealth (-wĕl-) *n.* 1. Body politic, independent community; republican or democratic State. 2. *The C~, C~ countries, members of the C~*: see BRITISH COMMONWEALTH OF NATIONS. 3. *The C~,* (Engl. hist.) the republican Government established in England between the execution of Charles I in 1649 and the Restoration in 1660. 4. *C~ of Australia,* title of the federated States of AUSTRALIA.

commō'tion *n.* Physical disturbance; bustle, confusion; public disorder, tumult, insurrection.

commove' (-o͞ov) *v.t.* Move violently, excite.

cŏmm'ūnal *adj.* Of a commune or the Paris Commune; of or for the community, for common use.

cŏmm'ūnalĭsm *n.* Principle of communal organization of society; theory of government by local autonomy. **cŏmm'ūnalĭst** *n.* **cŏmmūnalĭs'tic** *adj.*

cŏmm'ūne[1] *n.* 1. Smallest French territorial division for administrative purposes, governed by a *maire* and municipal council. 2. *The C~* (*of Paris*), body which usurped municipal government of Paris in 1789 and played a leading part in the Reign of Terror until suppressed in 1794; (also) communalistic government set up for a short time in Paris by an insurrection in 1871.

commūne'[2] (*or* kŏm'ūn) *v.i.* Hold intimate intercourse *with*; (U.S.) receive Holy Communion.

commūn'icant *n.* 1. One who receives Holy Communion, esp. regularly. 2. One who imparts information.

commūn'ĭcāte *v.* 1. Impart, transmit (*to*). 2. Receive, administer, Holy Communion. 3. Hold intercourse, transmit (by speech, writing, etc.). 4. (of spaces, rooms, etc.) Have common door or opening (*with*).

commūnĭcā'tion *n.* Imparting (esp. news); information given; intercourse; access or means of access, passage, connexion by rail, road, telegraph, etc., between places; (mil., pl.) connexion between base and front; ~*-cord,* cord or chain in passenger train which partially brakes it when pulled.

commūn'ĭcative *adj.* Ready to impart; open; talkative.

commūn'ĭcātor *n.* Person, thing, that communicates.

commūn'ion (-yon) *n.* Sharing, participation; fellowship (esp. between branches of Catholic Church); body professing one faith; (*Holy*) *C~*, participation in the Eucharist; *~-rail*, rail in front of Communion table, altar-rail; *~ table*, table used in celebrating Communion.

commūn'iqué (-kā) *n.* Official intimation or report.

cŏmm'ūnism *n.* 1. An order of society in which property is owned in common (*primitive ~*). 2. An order of society in which the means of production, distribution, and exchange are to be owned in common and each member is to work according to his capacity and be paid according to his needs, the State having shed its coercive functions; this as the professed aim of the political parties which derive their doctrines from MARX, ENGELS, and LENIN. 3. The doctrines and activities of these parties regarded as an international movement (*international ~*). 4. The social order established in Russia by the Bolshevik party under Lenin after the revolution of 1917 (*Soviet ~*); similar social orders established more recently elsewhere, as in Mexico and China. **cŏmm'ūnist** *adj.* & *n.* (Advocate) of communism. **cŏmmūnis'tĭc** *adj.*

commūn'ĭty *n.* 1. Joint or common ownership, liability, etc. 2. Identity of character, quality in common. 3. Social intercourse; life in association with others; body of people organized into political, municipal, or social unity; body of men living in same locality, or with common race, religion, pursuits, etc., not shared by those among whom they live. 4. Body of persons living together and practising community of goods. 5. *~ singing*, singing in chorus by large gathering of people.

cŏmm'ūnize *v.t.* Make common property; make communistic.

commūt'able *adj.* Exchangeable, convertible into money value. **commūtabĭl'ĭty** *n.*

cŏmmūtā'tion *n.* Commuting; *~ ticket*, (U.S.) season-ticket; ticket entitling holder to travel an indefinite number of times between two points during a specified time.

commūt'ative *adj.* Relating to or involving substitution or interchange; *~ justice*, justice in performing contracts or undertakings.

cŏmm'ūtātor *n.* Contrivance for altering course of electric current; ring-shaped fitting on dynamo or electric motor providing the brushes with a series of separate connexions with different parts of the armature during each revolution and so enabling a dynamo to generate, or a motor to utilize, a direct current (ill. DYNAMO).

commūte' *v.* 1. Exchange, change, interchange; redeem obligation by money payment; change (punishment etc.) *for* (*to, into*) less severe one, or a fine; change (one kind of payment) *into, for*, another. 2. (orig. U.S.) Buy, use, a season-ticket; travel daily to and from work. **commūt'er** *n.* (esp., U.S.) Season-ticket holder.

cŏm'păct[1] *n.* Agreement or contract between parties.

compăct'[2] *adj.* Closely or neatly packed together; dense, solid; condensed, terse; (archaic) framed, composed *of*. **compăct'ly** *adv.* **compăct'nèss** *n.* **cŏm'păct** *n.* Box, case, of compact powder or rouge. **compăct'** *v.t.* Join firmly together; consolidate; compress, condense; devise, compose.

compăn'ion[1] (-yon) *n.* 1. One who accompanies or associates with another; associate *in*, sharer *of*. 2. Member of lowest grade of order of knighthood. 3. Person (usu. woman) paid to live with another rather as friend or equal than as servant. 4. Thing that matches another (also as *adj.*, as *~ picture*). *~ v.* Accompany; consort *with*. **compăn'ionable** (-nyo-), *adj.* Sociable. **compăn'ionably** *adv.* **compăn'ionablenèss** *n.*

compăn'ion[2] (-yon) *n.* (naut.) Raised frame on quarter-deck for lighting cabins etc. below; companion-way, companion-ladder; *~-hatch*, wooden covering over companion-way; *~ hatchway*, opening in deck leading to cabin; *~-ladder*, ladder from deck to cabin; *~-way*, staircase to cabin. [Du. *kompanje* quarter-deck, corresp. to It. (*camera della*) *compagna* pantry, caboose]

compăn'ionshĭp (-nyo-) *n.* Fellowship; (printing) company of compositors working together.

com'pany (kŭ-) *n.* 1. Companionship; the society *of* others. 2. Number of individuals assembled together, person(s) with whom one usually associates; social party, guests. 3. Body of persons combined or incorporated for a common (esp. commercial) object; medieval trade guild, or a corporation historically representing this. 4. Association formed to carry on some commercial or industrial undertaking; partner or partners not named in title of firm (abbrev. Co.). 5. Party of actors etc.; actors associated together in a play or plays, or in a theatre. 6. (mil.) Subdivision of infantry battalion, usu. commanded by captain or major. 7. (naut.) Entire crew of ship. 8. *~ promoter*: see PROMOTER; *~ sergeant-major*, senior non-commissioned officer of company; *~ union* (U.S.), workers' union within a given company, unconnected with a trade union, and freq. managed by the employers. *~ v.* (archaic) Accompany; consort *with*.

cŏm'parable *adj.* That may be compared (*with*), worthy to be compared (*to*). **cŏmparabĭl'ĭty** *n.*

compă'rative *adj.* 1. Of or involving comparison, esp. of different branches of a study, as *~ anatomy, philology, religion*. 2. (gram., of a derived adjective or adverb, as *higher, faster*) expressing a higher degree of the quality etc., denoted by the simple word. 3. Estimated by comparison; that is such when compared with something else implied or thought of. **compă'ratively** *adv.* **compă'rative** *n.* (gram.) The comparative degree; an adj. or adv. in this degree.

compāre' *v.* Liken, pronounce similar (*to*); estimate the similarity of (one thing *with, to*, another, two things); bear comparison (*with*). *~ n.* Comparison (chiefly in: *beyond, past, without ~*).

compă'rĭson *n.* Comparing; simile, illustration by comparing; (gram.) *degrees of ~*, the positive, comparative, and superlative of adjectives or adverbs.

compârt' *v.t.* Divide into compartments.

compârt'ment *n.* Division separated by partitions, esp. of railway-carriage; water-tight division of ship; (pol.) separate portion of a Bill, or business in hand, for discussion of which a limit of parliamentary time is allowed by Government.

com'pass (kŭ-) *n.* 1. (now usu. pl.) Instrument for taking measurements and describing circles, consisting of two legs connected at one end by movable joint. 2. Circumference, boundary; area, extent; range, esp. range of tones of a voice or musical instrument; (archaic) circular movement, round, detour. 3. Instrument for determining magnetic meridian, or one's direction or position with respect to it, consisting of a magnetized needle turning freely on a pivot; GYRO, PRISMATIC, *~*: see these words; *box the ~*, see BOX; *points of the ~*, the 32 equidistant points marked in a circle on the *~-card*, to which the magnetized needle is attached with

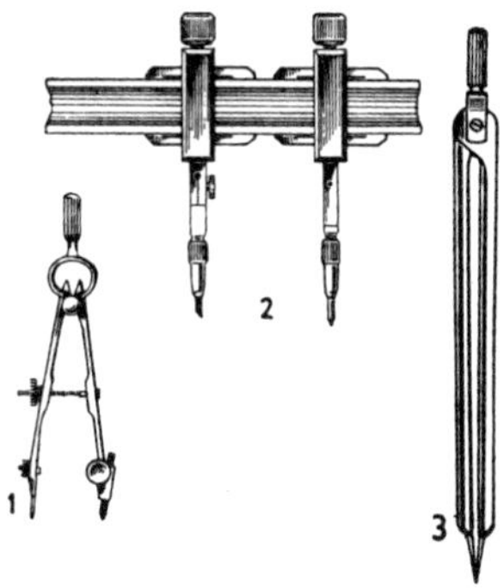

COMPASSES AND DIVIDERS

1. Bow compasses. 2. Beam-compass. 3. Dividers

its pivot at the centre of the circle. 4. ~*-plane*, smoothing-plane with convex sole and iron, for planing concave surfaces; ~*-saw*, narrow saw for cutting curves. ~ *v.t.* 1. Go round; hem in. 2. Contrive, devise; accomplish, achieve.

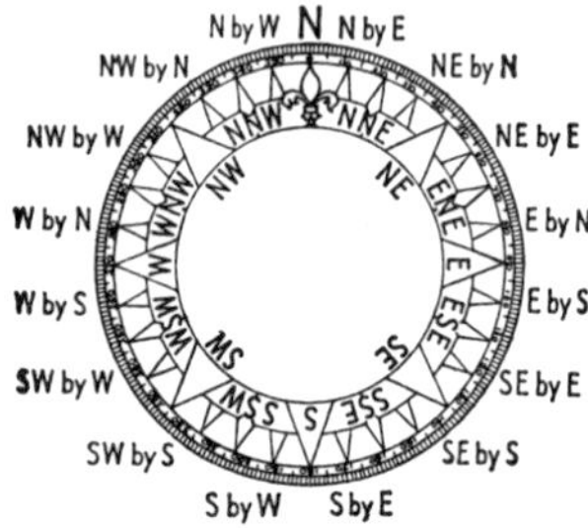

MARINER'S COMPASS

Cardinal points: N., E., S., W. Half-cardinal points: NE., SE., SW., NW. Three-letter points, NNE., ENE., etc. By-points: N. by E., NE. by N., etc.

compă'ssion (-shn) *n.* Pity inclining one to spare or succour. **compă'ssionate** (-sho-) *adj.* Feeling or showing compassion; granted out of compassion. **compă'ssionately** *adv.* **compă'ssionatenėss** *n.* **compă'ssionāte** *v.t.* Regard or treat with compassion.

compăt'ĭble *adj.* Mutually tolerant; accordant, consistent, congruous. **compătĭbĭl'ĭty** *n.*

compăt'rĭot *n.* Fellow countryman.

compeer' *n.* Equal, peer; comrade.

compĕl' *v.t.* Constrain, force; bring about by force.

compĕn'dĭous *adj.* Brief but comprehensive. **compĕn'dĭously** *adv.* **compĕn'dĭousnėss** *n.*

compĕn'dĭum *n.* (pl. *-ĭums, -ĭa*). Abridgement; summary; concise and comprehensive account or treatise.

cŏm'pėnsāte *v.* Counterbalance; make amends; recompense; provide with mechanical compensation, make up for (variations in a pendulum etc.); (elect.) neutralize one electromotive or magnetomotive force by another. **cŏmpėnsā'tion** *n.* Compensating; recompense, remuneration, amends; ~*-balance, -pendulum*, balance-wheel or pendulum in chronometer neutralizing effects of variations of temperature. **compĕn'satĭve, com'pĕnsatory** *adjs.* **cŏm'pėnsātor** *n.*

compère (kŏm'pār) *n.* Organizer of variety entertainment who introduces artists, comments on turns, etc. ~ *v.* Act as compère (to). [Fr., = 'godfather', 'gossip']

compēte' *v.i.* Strive (*with* another, *for* or *in* something), vie (*with*); contend (*for*).

cŏm'pėtence, cŏm'pėtency *ns.* Sufficiency of means for living, easy circumstances; ability (*to* do, *for* a task); (of court, magistrate, etc.) legal capacity, right to take cognizance.

cŏm'pėtent *adj.* Adequate, sufficient; properly or legally qualified; belonging *to*, permissible, admissible. **cŏm'pėtently** *adv.*

cŏmpėtĭ'tion *n.* Act of competing (*for*) by examination etc.; rivalry in market, striving for custom; contest, trial.

compĕt'ĭtĭve *adj.* Of, by, offered for, competition. **compĕt'ĭtĭvely** *adv.*

compĕt'ĭtor *n.* One who competes, rival.

compĭlā'tion *n.* Compiling; thing compiled.

compīle' *v.t.* Collect (materials) into a volume; make up (volume) of such materials; (cricket slang) score (number of runs).

complā'cence, complā'cency *ns.* Tranquil pleasure; self-satisfaction.

complā'cent *adj.* Self-satisfied. **complā'cently** *adv.*

complain' *v.i.* Express dissatisfaction or discontent, murmur; let it be known that one is suffering (from illness etc.); make formal complaint of grievance *to* or *before* competent authority. **complain'ant** *n.* One who complains; plaintiff or prosecutor in Chancery or ecclesiastical courts.

complaint' *n.* 1. Utterance of grievance. 2. Formal accusation; (U.S.) plaintiff's case in civil action. 3. Subject, ground, of complaint. 4. Bodily ailment.

cŏm'plaisance (-plĭz-; *or* kŏmplĭzăns') *n.* Obligingness, politeness; deference. **cŏm'plaisant** *adj.*

cŏm'plėment *n.* 1. What completes; (gram.) word(s) joined to another to complete the sense (esp. of predicate); (math.) ~ *of an angle*, the angular amount which would make up a given angle to 90°. 2. Full quantity or number required, esp. to man a ship. **cŏm'plėmĕnt** *v.t.* Complete; form complement to.

complėmĕn'tal *adj.* Forming a complement, completing. **cŏmplėmĕn'tally** *adv.*

complėmĕn'tary *adj.* Forming a complement, completing; (of two or more things) mutually complementing each other; ~ *angles*, angles which together form a right angle.

complēte' *adj.* Having all its parts; entire; finished; thorough, unqualified; (archaic, of persons) accomplished. **complēte'ly** *adv.* **complēte'nėss** *n.* **complēte'** *v.t.* Finish; make whole or perfect; make up the amount of. **complē'tion** *n.*

cŏm'plĕx *n.* 1. Whole consisting of several parts. 2. (psychol.) Group of related ideas or memories of strongly emotional character which have undergone repression; (loosely) fixed mental tendency or obsession; *inferiority* ~, *Oedipus* ~: see INFERIORITY, OEDIPUS. ~ *adj.* Consisting of parts, composite; complicated; (gram.) ~ *sentence*, one containing subordinate clause(s). **cŏm'plĕxly** *adv.* **complĕx'ĭty** *n.*

complĕx'ion (-kshn) *n.* Natural colour, texture, and appearance of skin (esp. of face); character, aspect. **complex'ioned** (-kshond) *adj.* Having a (specified) complexion.

complī'ance *n.* Action in accordance with request, demand, etc.; base submission; *in* ~ *with*, according to; *out of* ~, (of trade unionist) so far behind with dues as to forfeit membership.

complī'ant *adj.* Disposed to comply, yielding. **complī'antly** *adv.*

cŏm'plĭcacy *n.* Complexity; complicated structure.

cŏm'plĭcāte *v.t.* Mix up *with* in intricate or involved way; make complex or intricate. **cŏmplĭcā'tion** *n.* Involved condition; entangled state of affairs; complicating circumstance.

complĭ'cĭty *n.* Partnership in an evil action.

cŏm'plĭment *n.* Polite expression of praise, act equivalent to this; (pl.) formal greetings. **cŏm'plĭmĕnt** *v.t.* Pay compliment to (person *on* something); present *with* as mark of courtesy. **cŏmplĭmĕn'tary** *adj.* Expressive of, conveying, compliment; (of tickets etc.) presented as a courtesy.

cŏm'plĭn(e) *n.* (eccles.) Last service of day.

cŏm'plŏt *n.* (archaic) Plot, conspiracy.

complȳ' *v.i.* Act in accordance (*with*).

cŏm'pō *n.* Abbrev. of COMPOSITION, esp. = stucco, plaster.

compōn'ent *adj.* Contributing to the composition of a whole. ~ *n.* Component part.

compôrt' *v.* Conduct, behave (oneself); agree, accord, *with*.

compōse' (-z) *v.t.* 1. Make up, constitute. 2. Construct in words; produce in literary form; (mus.) invent and put into proper form; set to music. 3. (print.) Set up (type); set up in type. 4. Put together so as to form a whole; arrange artistically. 5. Settle, arrange; adjust (oneself, one's features, etc.) in specified or understood manner, or for specified purpose; tranquillize. **compōs'ėdly** *adv.* **compōs'ėdnėss** *n.*

compōs'er (-z-) *n.* One who composes (usu. music). **compōs'ĭng** (-z-) *n.* ~*-room*, room in which type is set up; ~*-stick*, compositor's metal or wooden tray of adjustable width in which type is set.

cŏm'posite (-zĭt *or* -zīt) *adj.* 1. Made up of various parts, compound. 2. (archit.) Of the 5th classical order, of Ionic and Corinthian mixed (ill. ORDER). 3. (bot.) Of the natural order *Compositae*, in which what is pop. called the flower is a close head of many small flowers sessile on a common receptacle and surrounded by a common involucre of bracts, as daisy, dandelion, etc. (ill. INFLORESCENCE). **cŏm'posĭtely** *adv.* **cŏm'posĭteness** *n.* **cŏm'posĭte** *n.* Composite thing or plant.

cŏmposĭ'tion (-z-) *n.* 1. Putting together; formation, construction; formation of words into compound. 2. Construction of sentences, art of literary production; act, art, of composing music. 3. Setting up of type. 4. Arrangement (of the parts of a picture etc.); thing composed; piece of music or writing. 5. Agreement, treaty (archaic); compromise; agreement for paying, payment, of sum of money in lieu of other obligation etc., esp. agreement by which creditor accepts portion of debt from insolvent debtor; sum of money paid thus. 6. Compound artificial substance, esp. one substituted for natural substance.

compŏs'ĭtor (-z-) *n.* Typesetter.

cŏm'pŏs (mĕn'tĭs) *adj.* In one's right mind.

cŏm'pŏst *n.* Mixture of various natural fertilizing ingredients, compound manure. ~ *v.t.* Treat with, make into, compost.

compō'sure (-zh*er*) *n.* Tranquil demeanour, calmness.

cŏmpotā'tion *n.* Drinking together, drinking-bout.

cŏm'pōte *n.* Fruit preserved or cooked in syrup.

compound'[1] *v.* 1. Mix; combine (verbal elements) into word; make up (a composite whole). 2. Settle (matter) by mutual concession, (debt) by partial payment, (subscription, obligation) by payment of lump sum etc.; condone (liability, offence) for money etc.; come to terms *with* (person); ~ *a felony*, forbear prosecution for private motive. **cŏm'pound** *adj.* Made up of several ingredients, consisting of several parts; combined, collective; (zool., bot.) consisting of a combination of organisms or simple parts; ~ *eye*, in insects and crustaceans, eye consisting of numerous minute simple eyes bound together; ~ *fracture*, fracture of bone complicated by skin wound; ~ *interest*: see INTEREST; ~ *interval*, (mus.) interval greater than an octave, i.e. consisting of simple interval plus octave. ~ *n.* 1. (mainly fig.) Mixture of elements; compound thing, esp. word. 2. (chem.) Substance which consists of elements chemically united in fixed proportions and has properties different from those of its components.

cŏm'pound[2] *n.* In India, China, etc., enclosure round house, factory, etc. [perh. f. Malay *kampong*]

cŏmprėhĕnd' *v.t.* Grasp mentally, understand; include, take in.

cŏmprėhĕn'sĭble *adj.* That may be understood, or comprised. **cŏmprėhĕn'sĭbly** *adv.* **cŏmprėhĕnsĭbĭl'ĭty** *n.*

cŏmprėhĕn'sion *n.* Understanding; inclusion; ecclesiastical inclusion, esp. of nonconformists within established Church by enlarging terms of ecclesiastical communion.

cŏmprėhĕn'sĭve *adj.* Of understanding; including much; ~ *school*, large secondary school providing courses of various types. **cŏmprėhĕn'sĭvely** *adv.* **cŏmprėhĕn'sĭveness** *n.*

comprĕss' *v.t.* Squeeze together; force into smaller volume, condense. **comprĕss'ĭble** *adj.* **comprĕssĭbĭl'ĭty** *n.* **cŏm'prĕss** *n.* Soft pad of lint etc. for compressing artery etc.; wet cloth applied to relieve inflammation.

comprĕ'ssion (-shn) *n.* Act of compressing or state of being compressed; in internal combustion engines, act of compressing the explosive mixture after admission to the engine and before combustion (ill. COMBUSTION); ~ *ratio*, in internal combustion engines, ratio of volume of charge, when compressed by engine, to its volume at entry.

comprĕss'or *n.* Mechanical device for reducing the volume taken up by a quantity of gas.

comprīse' (-z) *v.t.* Include, comprehend; consist of; condense.

cŏm'promīse (-z) *n.* Settlement of dispute by mutual concession; adjustment of conflicting opinions, courses, etc., by modification of each. ~ *v.* Settle (dispute) by mutual concession; make compromise; bring under suspicion, into danger, by indiscreet action.

cŏmprovĭn'cial (-shl) *adj.* & *n.* (Bishop) of same archiepiscopal province.

comptrōll'er (kont-) *n.* Erroneous spelling of CONTROLLER, retained in some official titles, esp. ~ *of accounts*.

compŭl'sion (-shn) *n.* Constraint, obligation.

compŭl'sĭve *adj.* Tending to compel. **compŭl'sĭvely** *adv.*

compŭl'sory *adj.* Enforced, obligatory; compelling, coercive. **compŭl'sorĭly** *adv.* **compŭl'sorĭness** *n.*

compŭnc'tion *n.* Pricking of conscience; feeling of regret. **compŭnc'tious** (-sh*us*) *adj.* **compŭnc'tiously** *adv.*

compûrgā'tion *n.* Clearing from charge or accusation by the oaths of others. **cŏm'pûrgātor** *n.* (hist.) Witness who swore to innocence or character of the person accused. **compûrg'atory** *adj.*

compūte' *v.t.* Reckon. **compūt'able** (*or* kŏm'-) *adj.* **cŏmpūtā'tion** *n.* **compūt'er** *n.* Person who computes; electronic apparatus for making calculations.

cŏm'rade (*or* kŭm-) *n.* Mate or fellow in work or play or fighting, equal with whom one is on familiar terms; (as title) used by socialists, communists, etc., before surname to avoid such titles as 'Mr'; fellow socialist, communist, etc.

cŏm'stŏckery *n.* Opposition to naked realism in art or literature. [Anthony *Comstock* (d. 1915), U.S. neo-Puritan]

Comte (kawnt), Auguste (1798–1857). French philosopher, founder of the POSITIVIST system. **Comt'ĭsm, Comt'ĭst** *ns.*

cŏn[1] *v.t.* Peruse, scrutinize, learn (by heart).

cŏn[2] *v.t.* Direct steering of (ship) from commanding position on shipboard.

cŏn[3] *n.* (in attrib. use) Confidence, esp. in (U.S.) ~*-game*, *-man*. ~ *v.t.* Swindle, dupe.

con[4]: see CONTRA.

con- *prefix.* With.

cŏn amōr'ė. With enthusiasm.

conā'tion *n.* (philos.) Desire and volition; exertion of will, striving.

cŏn brio (brē'ō). (mus.) With spirit.

concăt'ėnāte *v.t.* Link together (fig.) **concătėnā'tion** *n.*

cŏn'cāve (*or* konkāv') *adj.* Having outline or surface curved like interior of circle or sphere (cf. CONVEX); hollow. **cŏn'cāvely** *adv.* **cŏn'cāve** *n.* Concave surface. **concăv'ĭty** *n.* Being concave; concave surface; hollow, cavity.

cŏncăv'ō- *prefix.* Concavely, concave and . . . , as ~*-concave*, concave on both sides, ~*-convex*, concave on one side, convex the other.

conceal' *v.t.* Keep secret; hide. **conceal'ment** *n.*

concēde' *v.t.* Admit, allow, grant.

conceit' (-ēt) *n.* 1. Personal vanity. 2. Fanciful notion, far-fetched comparison, etc. 3. Favourable opinion, esteem (only in *out of ~ with*); *in one's own ~*, in one's private opinion or estimation. **conceit'ėd** *adj.* Vain. **conceit'ėdly** *adv.*

conceiv'able (-sēv-) *adj.* That can be (mentally) conceived. **conceiv'ably** *adv.*

conceive (-sēv) *v.* 1. Become pregnant (with). 2. Form in the mind, imagine; fancy, think. 3. formulate, express in words, etc.

cŏn'centrāte *v.* Bring to or towards a common centre; focus (attention), keep mind or attention intently fixed (*on*); increase strength of (solution etc.) esp. by evaporation of solvent etc.; *con'centrated*, (fig.) intense. **cŏncentrā'tion** *n.* ~ *camp*, camp in which large numbers of people, esp. political prisoners, are detained by force.

concĕn'tre *v.* Bring, come, to a common centre.

concĕn'trĭc *adj.* Having a common centre. **concĕn'trĭcally** *adv.* **cŏncĕntrĭ'cĭty** *n.*

cŏn'cĕpt *n.* Idea of a class of objects, general notion.

concĕp'tacle *n.* (bot.) Hollow organ of some brown seaweeds, within which sexual organs are formed (ill. ALGA).

concĕp'tion *n.* Conceiving; thing conceived; idea. **concĕp'-**

tional (-sho-) *adj.* Of, like, a conception or idea.

concĕp'tĭve *adj.* Conceiving; of conception.

concĕp'tual *adj.* Of mental conceptions.

concĕp'tūalĭsm *n.* 1. Scholastic doctrine that universals have reality, but only as mental concepts. 2. Psychological doctrine that the mind is capable of forming ideas corresponding to abstract and general terms. **concĕp'tūalĭst** *n.*

concĕrn' *v.t.* Relate to, affect; interest (oneself); *concerned,* involved, taking part; troubled; *concerning, (prep.)* about. ~ *n.* Relation, reference; interest, solicitous regard, anxiety; matter that affects one; business, firm; (colloq.) thing; (pl.) affairs.

concĕrn'ment *n.* Affair, business; importance; being concerned (*with*); anxiety.

cŏn'cert *n.* 1. Agreement; union by mutual agreement; *C~ of Europe,* the chief powers of Europe acting together. 2. Combination of voices or sounds. 3. Musical entertainment; ~ *grand,* grand piano of largest size for concerts; ~ *pitch,* state of unusual efficiency or readiness [f. custom of using a pitch slightly higher than the ordinary at concerts for brilliancy of effect.]

concĕrt' *v.t.* Arrange by mutual agreement. **concĕrt'ĕd** *adj.* Contrived, pre-arranged; done in concert; (mus.) arranged in parts for voices or instruments.

cŏncerti'na (-ēna) *n.* Portable musical instrument consisting of bellows with a set of finger-studs at each end controlling the valves which admit wind to the free metallic reeds. ~ *v.* Shut up like a concertina.

concert'ō (-char-) *n.* (pl. *-os*). Musical composition, usu. in sonata form with 3 or 4 movements, for a solo instrument (or, rarely, more than one) accompanied by orchestra.

concĕ'ssion (-shn) *n.* Conceding; thing conceded; esp. grant of land, trading rights, etc., land or rights so granted, by Government to State, company, or person. **concĕ'ssionary** *adj.*

concĕssionaire' (-shonār) *n.* Holder of concession, grant, etc., esp. of monopoly given by Government to foreigner.

concĕss'ĭve *adj.* Of, tending to, concession; (gram.) expressing concession.

cŏnch (-k *or* -ch) *n.* 1. Shellfish; (now usu.) large gastropod; shell of mollusc, esp. spiral shell of any large gastropod; such a shell used as a trumpet, esp. (Gk myth.) of Triton. 2. (archit.) Domed roof of semicircular apse. 3. External ear, its central concavity (ill. EAR).

cŏnchĭf'erous (-k-) *adj.* Shell-bearing.

cŏnchŏl'ogy (-k-) *n.* Study of shells and shell-fish.

cŏn'chy (-shĭ) *n.* (slang) Abbrev. for 'conscientious objector' to conscription in war.

concierge (kawṅsĭārzh') *n.* In France etc., door-keeper, porter, of block of flats or other building.

concĭl'ĭar *adj.* Of a council (esp. ecclesiastical) or its proceedings.

concĭl'ĭāte *v.t.* Gain (goodwill, esteem, etc.) by acts which pacify, soothe, etc.; gain over, overcome distrust or hostility of, soothe, placate. **concĭlĭā'tion** *n.* Reconcilement; use of conciliatory measures.

concĭl'ĭatĭve, concĭl'ĭatory *adjs.*

concīse' (-s) *adj.* Brief and comprehensive in expression. **concīse'ly** *adv.* **concīse'nĕss** *n.*

concĭ'sion (-zhn) *n.* 1. Mutilation; in Phil. iii. 2 = circumcision. 2. Conciseness.

cŏnc'lāve *n.* Meeting-place, assembly, of cardinals for election of pope; private assembly.

conclude' (-ōōd) *v.* Bring to an end, make an end; come to an end; settle, arrange (treaty etc.); infer; come to a conclusion; resolve.

conclu'sion (-ōōzhn) *n.* Termination; final result; inference; decision; (logic) proposition deduced from previous ones, esp. last of three forming a syllogism; settling, arrangement (*of* peace etc.).

conclus'ĭve (-ōō-) *adj.* Decisive, convincing. **conclus'ĭvely** *adv.* **conclus'ĭvenĕss** *n.*

concŏct' *v.t.* Make up by mixing variety of ingredients; fabricate. **concŏc'tion** *n.*

concŏm'ĭtance, -cy *n.* Being concomitant, coexistence, esp. of body and blood of Christ in each of Eucharistic elements.

concŏm'ĭtant *adj.* Going together, accompanying. ~ *n.* accompanying state, quality, thing, etc. **concŏm'ĭtantly** *adv.*

cŏnc'ŏrd[1] *n.* 1. Agreement, harmony, between persons or things; treaty. 2. (mus.) Combination of notes satisfactory to the ear, requiring no 'resolution' or following chord. 3. (gram.) Formal agreement between words in gender, number, etc.

Cŏnc'ŏrd[2]. Capital of New Hampshire, U.S.; ~ *buggy,* (U.S.) buggy with side-spring suspension; ~ *grape,* large, bluish-black, sweet-flavoured N. Amer. grape.

concŏrd'ance *n.* 1. Agreement, harmony. 2. Alphabetical arrangement of chief words or subjects occurring in a book (esp. the Bible) or in an author's works, with citations of passages concerned.

concŏrd'ant *adj.* Agreeing, harmonious; in musical concord. **concŏrd'antly** *adv.*

concŏrd'ăt *n.* Agreement between pope and secular government for settlement and control of ecclesiastical affairs.

cŏnc'ourse (-ōr-) *n.* 1. Flocking together; crowd, throng, confluence; assemblage. 2. (U.S.) Large main hall, or central open space, of building, or (esp.) railway-station.

cŏnc rēte *adj.* 1. (gram., of noun) Denoting a thing as opp. to a quality, state, or action; not abstract. 2. Existing in material form, real. 3. Made of concrete. **cŏncrētely** *adv.* **cŏnc'rēte** *n.* 1. Concrete thing. 2. Composition of stone chippings, sand, gravel, etc., formed into a mass with cement and used for building, paving, etc.; *reinforced* ~, concrete with iron or steel bars, wire-netting, etc., embedded in it. **concrete** *v.* 1. (konkrēt') Form into a mass, solidify. 2. (kŏnk'rēt) Treat, build, pave, etc., with concrete.

concrē'tion *n.* Coalescence; concrete mass, esp. (path.) hard morbid formation in body, stone; (geol.) mass formed by aggregation of solid particles, usu. round a nucleus. **concrē'tionary** (-sho-) *adj.* (geol.).

concūb'ĭnage (-n-k-) *n.* Cohabiting of man and woman not legally married; being, having, a concubine.

cŏnc'ūbīne *n.* Woman who cohabits with man, not being his wife; (among polygamous peoples) secondary wife.

concūp'ĭscence (-n-k-) *n.* Sexual appetite. **concūp'ĭscent** *adj.* Lustful, eagerly desirous.

concŭr' (-n-k-) *v.i.* Happen together, coincide; co-operate; agree in opinion (*with*). **concŭ'rrence** *n.*

concŭ'rrent (-n-k-) *adj.* 1. Running together, going on side by side, occurring together; meeting in or tending to same point. 2. Co-operating; agreeing. 3. (law) Covering the same ground; having authority or jurisdiction in same matters. 4. ~ *lease,* lease made before another has expired; ~ *insurance, policy,* etc., one of which various companies have accepted definite proportions of the risk on precisely similar terms. ~ *n.* Concurrent circumstance. **concŭ'rrently** *adv.* Unitedly, (operating, running) simultaneously (esp. of legal sentences).

concŭss' (-n-k-) *v.t.* Shake violently, agitate; intimidate, coerce; *be concussed,* (colloq.) suffer concussion of brain etc.

concŭ'ssion (-n-k-) *n.* 1. Violent shaking; shock. 2. Injury caused to brain, spine, etc., by shock of heavy blow, fall, etc.

condĕmn' (-m) *v.t.* 1. Censure, blame; bring about conviction of. 2. Give judicial sentence against, find guilty; sentence (*to* death etc.); (fig., esp. pass.) doom *to* some (unkind) fate or condition. 3. Pronounce forfeited, as smuggled goods, etc.; pronounce unfit for use or consumption. **condĕm'nable** *adj.*

cŏndĕmnā'tion *n.* Censure; judicial conviction; ground for condemning. **condĕm'natory** *adj.*

condĕn'sary *n.* Factory for making condensed milk.

cŏndĕnsā′tion *n.* Condensing; condensed mass; liquid formed by condensed gas or vapour.

condĕnse′ *v.* 1. Increase density of, reduce in volume; compress, thicken, concentrate. 2. Compress into few words. 3. Reduce, be reduced, from form of gas or vapour to liquid.

condĕn′ser *n.* (esp.) 1. Chamber in steam-engine in which steam is condensed on leaving cylinder. 2. Arrangement of two (or two sets of) plates separated by insulating substance for increasing capacity of a conductor or for temporary accumulation of electricity. 3. Lens, system of lenses, for concentrating light (ill. MICROSCOPE).

cŏndėscĕnd′ *v.i.* Deign, stoop; be condescending, waive one's superiority. **cŏndescĕn′ding** *adj.* (esp.) Making a show of condescension, patronizing. **cŏndėscĕn′dingly** *adv.*

cŏndėscĕn′sion (-shn) *n.* Affability to inferiors; patronizing manner.

condign′(-īn) *adj.* (of punishment) Adequate, appropriate. **condign′ly** *adv.*

cŏn′dĭment *n.* Seasoning for food; anything spicy or pungent used as a relish, as mustard, pepper, etc.

condĭ′tion *n.* 1. Stipulation; thing upon fulfilment of which depends that of something else, ~ *precedent*, condition which must be fulfilled before right, title, etc., conferred by will or other legal document can take effect. 2. (pl.) Circumstances, esp. those essential to a thing's existence; state of being; *in* ~, *out of* ~, in good, bad, training and health. 3. (U.S.) Subject in qualifying examination in which student has failed to pass, though he is allowed to proceed to next academic stage if he passes in this subject within a certain time. ~ *v.t.* 1. Stipulate; agree by stipulation (*to*). 2. Subject to as a condition; govern, qualify, limit, as a condition, be the (precedent) condition of; (pass.) be conditional on. 3. (U.S.) Subject to or admit under conditions (sense 3). 4. Bring into (good) condition (*for*). **condĭ′tioned** (-shond) *adj.* (esp. in ~ *reflex*, reflex or reflex action which through habit or training has been induced to follow a stimulus which is not naturally associated with it).

condĭ′tional (-sho-) *adj.* 1. Not absolute; dependent. 2. (gram.) Of a clause, mood, conjunction, phrase, expressing or introducing a condition. **condĭ′tionally** *adv.*

condōle′ *v.i.* Express sympathy (*with* person *upon* loss etc.). **condōl′ence** *n.*

cŏndomĭn′ium *n.* Joint control of a State's affairs vested in two or more other States; territory so governed.

condōne′ *v.t.* Forgive, overlook (offence, esp. violation of marriage vow); cause condonation of. **cŏndonā′tion** *n.*

cŏn′dor *n.* Large S. Amer. vulture, *Sarcorhamphus gryphus*, with blackish plumage and fleshy excrescence falling over bill; *California* ~, the great Californian vulture, *Cathartes californianus*, somewhat resembling this.

cŏndŏttier′e (-tyārĭ) *n.* (pl. *-ri*, pr. -rē). Leader of troop of mercenaries in late Middle Ages.

condūce′ *v.i.* (Usu. of events) lead, contribute, *to*. **condū′cive** *adj.*

condŭct′ *v.* 1. Lead, guide *to*. 2. Command (army); direct (orchestra, concert, etc.); manage (business etc.). 3. Behave (*oneself*). 4. (physics) Of a body, convey (some form of energy, as heat, electricity, etc.) through its particles, transmit. **cŏn′duct** *n.* Manner of conducting (any business etc., or oneself), behaviour; ~*-money*, money paid for travelling-expenses (of witness to place of trial, of seamen for navy to place of embarkation, or (hist.) of men furnished by a hundred to serve in king's army to rendezvous at the coast).

condŭc′tance *n.* (elect.) Conducting power of a specified conductor.

condŭc′tion *n.* Conducting (of liquid through a pipe etc.); transmission (of heat, electricity, etc.).

condŭc′tive *adj.* Having the property of conducting some form of energy, esp. electricity. **cŏnductĭv′ĭty** *n.*

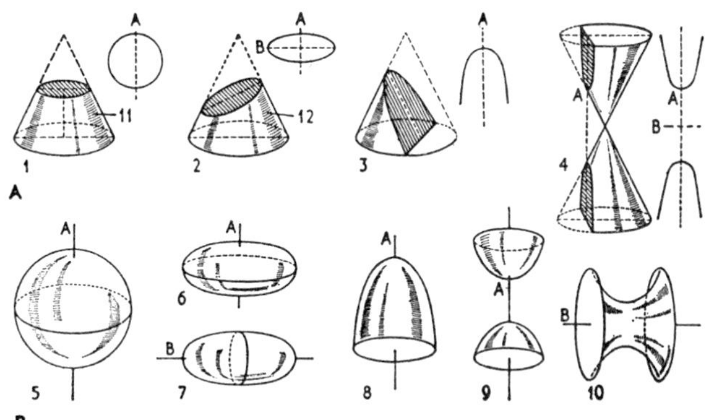

A. CONES SHOWING CONIC SECTIONS. B. CONOIDS: SOLID FIGURES MADE BY THE REVOLUTION OF CONIC SECTIONS

A. 1. Circle. 2. Ellipse. 3. Parabola. 4. Hyperbola. B. 5. Sphere. 6. Oblate ellipsoid or spheroid. 7. Prolate ellipsoid or spheroid. 8. Paraboloid. 9, 10. Hyperboloids (9, Hyperbola revolved about vertical axis; 10, about horizontal axis). 11. Frustum. 12. Ungula. Axes of revolution are marked A and B

condŭc′tor *n.* 1. Leader, guide; manager. 2. Director of orchestra or chorus, who indicates to the performers the rhythm, expression, etc., by motions of a baton or the hands. 3. Official in charge of passengers on omnibus, tram, or (U.S.) train. 4. Thing that conducts or transmits (some form of energy); *lightning-*~, metallic rod at top of building etc., conducting atmospheric electricity to earth; ~*-rail*, in electric traction, rail through which current is supplied.

con′duit (kŭn′dĭt, kŏn′-) *n.* Channel or pipe for conveying water or other liquids; tube or trough for receiving and protecting electric wires; ~*-pipe*, conduit in form of a pipe.

cŏn′dyle (-ĭl) *n.* (anat.) Rounded process at end of bone, forming articulation with another bone (ill. BONE). **cŏn′dўloid** *adj.*

Cŏn′dy's fluid. Solution containing sodium manganate and permanganate, formerly used as disinfectant. [H. B. *Condy*, English physician]

cōne *n.* 1. Solid figure or body of which the base is a circle (or other curved figure) and the summit a point, and every point in the intervening surface is in a straight line between the vertex and the circumference of the base; any conical mass. 2. Fruit of pine or fir, a dry, scaly multiple fruit, more or less cone-shaped, formed by hard persistent imbricated scales covering naked seeds (ill. CONIFER). 3. Other cone-shaped objects: marine shell of genus *Conus* of gastropods; cone-shaped building; cone-shaped mountain-peak, esp. volcanic peak; (meteorol.) cone-shaped vessel hoisted as foul-weather signal or to indicate direction of wind; (physiol.) one of the minute, cone-shaped bodies which form, with 'rods', one of the layers of nerve elements in the retina. 4. *cone′-flower*, garden plants of genus *Rudbeckia*, native in N. America. ~ *v.t.* Catch or trap (aircraft) in a cone of searchlights.

Cŏnėstōg′a. Tribe of N. Amer. Indians formerly inhabiting parts of Pennsylvania and Maryland; ~ *wagon*, heavy, broad-wheeled, covered travelling-wagon. [*Conestoga* (= 'place of muddy water'), Pennsylvania]

cŏn'făb *n.*, **confăb'** *v.* Colloq. shortening of confabulation, confabulate.

confăb'ūlāte *v.i.* Converse, chat. **confăbūlā'tion** *n.*

confĕc'tion *n.* 1. Mixing, compounding. 2. Medicinal preparation compounded with sweetening and preserving agent; prepared dish or delicacy; sweetmeat, comfit. 3. Fashionable or elegant ready-made article of women's dress.

confĕc'tioner (-sho-) *n.* Maker or seller of sweetmeats, pastry, etc. **confĕc'tionery** *n.* Things made or sold by a confectioner; confectioner's shop; confectioner's art.

confĕd'eracy *n.* 1. League, alliance; league for unlawful or evil purpose; conspiracy. 2. Body of allies, esp. union of States; (*Southern*) *C*~, the CONFEDERATE States of America.

confĕd'erate *adj.* Allied; *C*~ *States* (of America), the 11 States and territories which seceded from the Union in 1861 and fought the others (*Federal States*) in the Civil War until defeated by them in 1865; the 11 were N. and S. Carolina, Mississippi, Florida, Alabama, Georgia, Louisiana, Texas, Virginia, Arkansas, and Tennessee. ~ *n.* 1. Ally, esp. in bad sense, accomplice. 2. (*C*~), supporter of the Confederate States of America. **confĕd'erāte** *v.* Bring, come, into alliance (*with*). **confĕderā'tion** *n.* (Union formed by) confederating.

confêr' *v.* 1. Grant, bestow (title, degree, favour, etc., *on*). 2. Converse, take counsel (*with*). **confêr'ment** *n.* Bestowing, granting.

cŏn'ference *n.* Consultation; meeting, for consultation or discussion; annual assembly of Methodist Church, constituting its central governing body.

confĕss' *v.* Acknowledge, own, admit; make formal confession of sins, esp. to a priest; (of priest) hear confession of (a penitent). **confĕss'ėdly** *adv.*

confĕ'ssion (-shn) *n.* Acknowledgement, admission (of fact, guilt, etc.); thing confessed; *C*~ (*of Faith*), formulary in which Church or body of Christians sets forth religious doctrines which it considers essential, a creed.

confĕ'ssional (-sho-) *adj.* Of confession. ~ *n.* Cabinet or stall in which priest sits to hear confession.

confĕss'or *n.* 1. One who makes confession. 2. One who avows his religion in the face of danger and persecution, but does not suffer martyrdom; *the C*~, King EDWARD the Confessor, canonized 1161. 3. Priest who hears confession.

confĕtt'ĭ *n.pl.* Plaster bonbons, little discs of coloured paper, used as missiles in carnival, thrown at bride and bridegroom at weddings, etc. [It., = 'sweetmeats']

cŏnfidănt' *n.* (fem. **-ante** pr. -ănt') Person trusted with private affair.

confīde' *v.* Repose confidence *in*; impart (secret *to*); entrust (*to*).

cŏn'fidence *n.* 1. Firm trust; assured expectation. 2. Boldness, fearlessness; impudence, presumption. 3. Imparting of private matters; thing so imparted; ~ *trick*, *game*, etc., swindle worked by practising on the confidence or trust of a credulous person; ~ *man*, one who practises this trick.

cŏn'fident *adj.* Trusting, fully assured; bold; impudent. **cŏn'fidently** *adv.* **cŏn'fident** *n.* Confidant, sharer of (secret).

cŏnfidĕn'tial (-shl) *adj.* Spoken, written, in confidence; entrusted with secrets; charged with secret service. **confidĕn'tially** *adv.*

configūrā'tion *n.* Mode of arrangement, conformation, outline; (astron.) relative position of planet or other celestial bodies.

config'ure (-ger) *v.t.* Give shape or configuration to.

cŏn'fīne *n.* (usu. pl.). Borderland, boundaries. **confīne'** *v.* Keep *within*, *to*, limits; imprison, immure; (pass.) be in childbed, be brought to bed. **confīne'ment** (-nm-) *n.* Imprisonment; restriction, limitation; childbirth, delivery.

confîrm' *v.t.* 1. Establish more firmly; ratify, sanction; corroborate; establish, encourage (person *in* opinion etc.). 2. Administer religious rite of confirmation to. **confîrm'ative, confîrm'atory** *adjs.*

cŏnfirmănd' *n.* Candidate for confirmation.

cŏnfirmā'tion *n.* 1. Confirming, corroboration. 2. Rite administered to baptized persons in various Christian Churches; in the Church of England, rite in which baptized persons renew and ratify their baptismal vows and are then admitted to the full privileges of the Church.

cŏn'fiscāte *v.t.* Appropriate to the public treasury by way of penalty; seize as by authority, appropriate summarily. **cŏnfiscā'tion** *n.* **confis'catory** *adj.*

cŏnflagrā'tion *n.* Great and destructive fire.

conflāte' *v.t.* Fuse together, esp. two variant readings of a text into a composite reading. **conflā'tion** *n.*

cŏn'flict *n.* Fight, struggle; collision; clashing (*of* opposed principles etc.). **conflict'** *v.i.* Struggle; clash, be incompatible.

cŏn'fluence (-lo͝oens) *n.* Flocking or flowing together, esp. meeting and joining of two or more streams etc.

cŏn'fluent (-lo͝oent) *adj.* Flowing together, uniting; ~ *smallpox*, form in which vesicles run together. ~ *n.* Stream uniting with another (of approximately equal size).

cŏn'flŭx *n.* Confluence.

confôrm' *v.* Form according to a pattern, make similar (*to*); adapt one*self to*; comply with, be conformable (*to*).

confôrm'able *adj.* Similar (*to*); consistent, adapted (*to*); tractable. **conformabil'ity** *n.* **confôrm'ably** *adv.*

confôrm'al *adj.* (math.) Conserving size of all angles in representing one surface upon another.

cŏnformā'tion *n.* 1. Conforming, adaptation. 2. Manner in which thing is formed, structure.

confôrm'ist *n.* One who conforms, esp. to usages of Church of England.

confôrm'ity *n.* Likeness (*to*, *with*); compliance (*with*, *to*).

confound' *v.t.* 1. Defeat utterly, discomfit (archaic); overthrow, defeat (plan, hope); (bibl.) put to shame. 2. Throw into perplexity; throw into disorder; mix up; confuse (in idea). 3. (as mild oath) = 'Bring to perdition' whence **confound'ėdly** *adv.*

cŏnfratêrn'ity *n.* Brotherhood (esp. religious or charitable); body, gang.

confront' (-ŭnt) *v.t.* Meet face to face, stand facing; be opposite to; face in hostility or defiance; oppose; bring (person) face to face *with* (accusers etc.); compare.

Confū'cius (-shĭ-) (*c* 550–478 B.C.). Chinese philosopher whose sayings relating mainly to temporal and secular matters were recorded by his followers. **Confū'cian** (-shn) *adj.* & *n.* (Follower) of Confucius. **Confū'cianism** *n.* A system of cosmology, politics, and ethics evolved in China during the Han dynasty (206 B.C.–A.D. 220). It regarded the emperor and the hierarchy of officials as divinely appointed, and the social relations as governed by the rules of Confucius. [Latinized f. Chin. *K'ung Fû tsze* K'ung the master]

cŏn fuŏc'ō (fw-). (mus.) With fire.

confūse' (-z) *v.t.* Throw into disorder; mix up in the mind; abash, perplex. **confūs'ėdly** *adv.* **confūs'ėdnėss** *n.*

confū'sion (-zhn) *n.* Confusing; confused state; tumult; ~ *worse confounded*, confusion made worse than it was.

confūte' *v.t.* Convict (person) of error by proof; prove (argument) false. **cŏnfūtā'tion** *n.*

congé (kawṅ'zhā, kŏn-) *n.* Dismissal without ceremony.

congeal' (-j-) *v.* Freeze, solidify by cooling; coagulate. **cŏngelā'tion** *n.* Congealing; congealed state; congealed substance.

cŏn'gee (-j-) *n.* = CONGÉ; (archaic) bow at leave-taking etc.

cŏn'gėner (-j-) *n.* Member of same kind or class with another.

cŏngenĕ'rĭc *adj.* Of same genus, kind, race; allied in nature or origin. **congĕn'erous** *adj.* Of same genus or (loosely) family; of same kind; ~ *muscles*, muscles concurring in same action.

congēn'ial (-j-) *adj.* Kindred, sympathetic (*with, to*); suited, agreeable (*to*). **congēniăl'ity** *n.* **congēn'ially** *adv.*

congĕn'ital (-j-) *adj.* Belonging to one from birth (esp. of defects, diseases, etc.). **congĕn'itally** *adv.*

cŏn'ger (-ngg-) *n.* (also ~-*eel*) Large species of eel living in salt water and caught for food; common on European coasts, but rare on Atlantic coast of America.

congĕ'ries (-jĕrĭēz) *n.* (pl. same). Collection; mass, heap.

congĕst' (-j-) *v.* Accumulate to excess; affect with congestion. **congĕst'ed** *adj.* 1. Overcrowded; ~ *district*, area of land too crowded to support its population. 2. (med.) Overcharged with blood.

congĕs'tion (-jĕschon) *n.* Congested or overcrowded condition, as of population, traffic, etc.; (med.) abnormal accumulation of blood in an organ etc.

cŏn'globāte *v.* Form into a ball or rounded mass. ~ *adj.* So formed. **cŏnglobā'tion** *n.*

conglŏm'erate *adj.* Gathered together into more or less rounded mass, clustered; (geol., of rock) formed of rounded water-worn pebbles or gravel cemented together. ~ *n.* Conglomerate rock. **conglŏm'erāte** *v.* Collect into a coherent mass. **conglŏmerā'tion** *n.*

Cŏng'ō (-ngg-). River of W. Africa flowing into Atlantic; area surrounding it; *Republic of the* ~, State of equatorial Africa and member of the French Community; capital, Brazzaville. **Cŏngolēse'** (-z) *adj.* & *n.* (Native) of the Congo; ~ *Republic*, State of equatorial Africa (formerly *Belgian Congo*); capital, Leopoldville; the area, opened up by STANLEY between 1878 and 1882 for Leopold II of Belgium, was named the *Independent State of the Congo* (1885) and administered by the king and his advisers independently of the Belgian Government; but in 1908, in the face of severe criticism, he ceded it to Belgium against compensation; it was proclaimed independent in 1960.

cŏng'ou (-nggōō, -ō) *n.* Kind of black China tea. [Chin. *kung-fu* (*ch'a*) labour (tea)]

congrăt'ūlāte *v.t.* Address (person) with expression of sympathetic joy (*on* something); ~ *oneself*, think oneself fortunate. **congrătūlā'tion** *n.* Congratulating; (pl.) congratulatory expressions. **congrăt'ūlative, congrăt'ūlatory** *adjs.*

cŏng'rėgant (-ngg-) *n.* Member of Jewish congregation.

cŏng'rėgāte (-ngg-) *v.* Collect, gather, into a crowd or mass.

cŏngrėgā'tion (-ngg-) *n.* 1. Collection into a body or mass; assemblage. 2. General assembly of members of a university, or of members possessing specified qualifications. 3. Body of persons assembled for religious worship, or to hear a preacher; body of persons habitually attending a particular place of worship. 4. (R.C. Ch.) community bound together by common rule; any of various permanent committees of College of Cardinals; *special* ~, temporary committee of cardinals etc. to decide etc. some particular matter.

cŏngrėgā'tional (-ngg-, -sho-) *adj.* 1. Of a congregation. 2. (*C*~), of or adhering to Congregationalism.

Cŏngrėgā'tionalism (-ngg-, -sho-) *n.* System of ecclesiastical polity regarding all legislative, disciplinary, and judicial functions as vested in the individual church or local congregation of believers. **Cŏngrėgā'tionalist** *n.*

cŏng'rėss (-ngg-) *n.* 1. Coming together, meeting. 2. Formal meeting of delegates for discussion, esp. of envoys or persons engaged in special studies. 3. *C*~, national legislative body of U.S., or of Southern and Central Amer. Republics; session of this; *Congressman*, member of Congress. **congrĕ'ssional** (-sho-) *adj.* Of a congress; of Congress.

Cŏng'rēve (-ngg-), William 1670–1729). English writer of Restoration comedies; author of 'Love for Love' and 'The Way of the World'.

cŏng'ruence (-nggrōōens) *n.* Agreement, consistency. **cŏng'ruency** *n.* Congruence; (geom.) system of lines in which parameters have a twofold relation, as when each line twice touches a given surface; (math.) relation between two numbers, which when divided by a third (the *modulus*), give the same remainder.

cŏng'ruent (-nggrōō-) *adj.* Suitable; accordant (*with*); (math.) having congruency; (of triangles etc.) equal in all respects, capable of exact superposition.

cŏng'ruous (-nggrōō-) *adj.* Accordant, conformable (*with*); fitting. **cŏng'ruously** *adv.* **congru'ĭty** *n.*

cŏn'ĭc *adj.* Cone-shaped; of a cone; ~ *section*, figure (ellipse, parabola, or hyperbola) formed by section of right circular cone by a plane (ill. CONE). **cŏn'ĭcs** *n.* Branch of geometry treating of cones and conic sections.

cŏn'ĭcal *adj.* Cone-shaped; of or relating to a cone. **cŏn'ĭcally** *adv.*

conĭd'iophōre *n.* (bot.) Specialized hypha bearing conidia.

conĭd'ium *n.* (pl. -*dĭa*). (bot.) One-celled asexual spore in certain fungi.

cōn'ĭfer *n.* Cone-bearing tree or shrub. **conĭf'erous** *adj.*

conjĕc'tural (-kcher-) *adj.* Involving, given to, conjecture.

conjĕc'ture *n.* Inference based on evidence which is not complete, guessing, esp. in textual criticism, of a reading not in the text; a guess. ~ *v.* Guess; propose (a conjectural reading); make a guess.

conjoin' *v.* Join; combine. **conjoint', conjoined'** (-nd) *adjs.* United; associated; ~ *twins*, twins congenitally united by common tissues. **conjoint'ly** *adv.*

cŏn'jugal (-ōō-) *adj.* Of marriage; of husband or wife in their relation to each other. **cŏn'jugally** *adv.* **cŏnjugăl'ĭty** *n.* Conjugal state.

cŏn'jugāte (-ōō-) *v.* 1. (gram.) Inflect (verb) in voice, mood, tense, number, person. 2. Unite sexually, join in conjugation. **cŏn'jugate** (-*at*) *adj.* Joined together; coupled; (gram.) derived from same root; (math.) joined in a reciprocal relation; (bot. etc.) fused. ~ *n.* Conjugate word or thing.

cŏnjugā'tion (-ōō-) *n.* 1. Joining together; (biol.) fusion of two (apparently) similar cells for reproduction. 2. (gram.) Scheme of verbal inflexion.

conjŭnct' *adj.* Joined together; combined; associated, joint. ~ *n.* Conjunct person or thing. **conjŭnct'ly** *adv.*

conjŭnc'tion *n.* 1. Union, connexion; *in* ~, together (*with*). 2. (astron.) Apparent proximity of two heavenly bodies. 3. Combination of events or circumstances. 4. (gram.) Uninflected word used to connect clauses or sentences, or to co-ordinate words in same clause. **conjŭnc'tional** (-sho-) *adj.* **conjŭnc'tionally** *adv.*

cŏnjunctīv'a *n.* Mucous membrane lining inner eyelid and reflected over front of eyeball (ill. EYE). **conjŭnctivī'is** *n.* (med.) Inflammation of conjunctiva.

conjŭnc'tive *adj.* 1. Serving to join or unite. 2. (gram.) Of the nature of, acting as, a conjunction; uniting sense as well as construction (cf. DISJUNCTIVE); (of a mood) used only in conjunction with another verb. ~ *n.* Conjunctive word or mood. **conjŭnc'tively** *adv.*

conjŭnc'ture *n.* Combination of events, posture of affairs.

cŏnjurā'tion *n.* Solemn appeal; incantation.

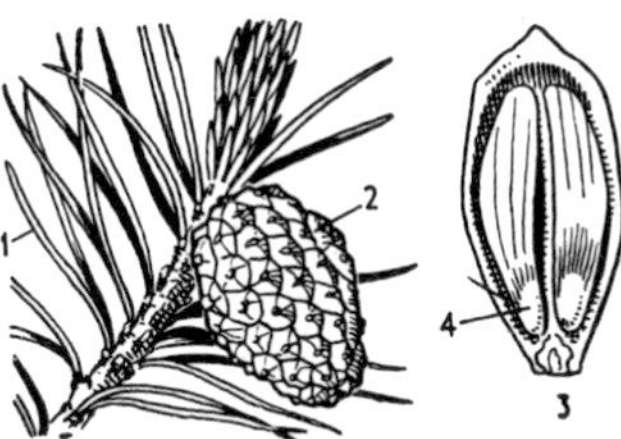

CONIFER

1. Needle. 2. Cone or strobile. 3. Scale of cone. 4. Seed

conjure *v.* 1. (konjoor′) Appeal solemnly or earnestly to. 2. (kŭn′jer) Constrain (spirit) to appear by invocation. 3. (kŭn′jer) Effect, bring *out*, convey *away*, by juggling; juggle; produce magical effects by natural means, perform marvels.

con′jurer, -or (kŭn′jerer) *n.* One who practises legerdemain, juggler.

cŏnk[1] *n.* = CONKER.

cŏnk[2] *v.i.* (slang) Break down, fail, give *out*.

cŏnk′er *n.* (pl.) Boys' game in which a horse-chestnut on a string is alternately struck against, and struck by, that of an opponent, until one of the two is broken; (sing.) a horse-chestnut. [dial. *conker* snail-shell, the game orig. being to press snail-shells point to point until one broke; now associated with *conquer*]

cŏn mōt′ō. (mus.) With spirited movement.

Conn. *abbrev.* Connecticut.

cŏnn′āte *adj.* 1. (Of qualities etc.) born with a person, innate; born together, coeval; cognate. 2. (bot., zool.) Congenitally united, so as to form one compound organ or body.

connă′tural (-cher-) *adj.* Innate, belonging naturally (*to*); of like nature. **connă′turally** *adv.*

connĕct′ *v.* Join; link together in sequence or order; associate in occurrence or action; (pass.) have to do *with*; associate mentally; unite *with* others by family relationship, common aims, etc.; join on (*with*); run in connexion (*with*); *connĕc′ting rod*, rod connecting crank with any other part of machine; in steam- and gas-engines, transmitting motion of piston to crank (ill. COMBUSTION). **connĕc′tėdly** *adv.* **connĕc′tėdnėss** *n.*

Connect′icut (-nĕt-). New England State of U.S.; capital, Hartford.

connĕc′tive *adj.* Serving, tending, to connect; ~ *tissue*, fibrous tissue connecting and supporting organs of the body.

connĕ′xion (-shon), **connĕc′tion** *n.* 1. Connecting, being connected; connecting part or thing; (mech.) joint between members. 2. Relation of thought etc.; personal relation or intercourse; sexual relation. 3. Family relationship; relative. 4. Religious body, esp. Methodist; body of customers etc. 5. Meeting of one means of communication (as railway train) by another at appointed time and place to take on the passengers; train etc. meeting another thus.

cŏnn′ing-tow′er *n.* Pilot-house of warship; superstructure on submarine in which periscope is mounted and from which steering, firing, etc., are directed when the submarine is on or near the surface (ill. SUBMARINE). [CON[2] *v.*]

connīv′ance *n.* Conniving; tacit permission.

connīve′ *v.i.* Wink *at* (what one ought to oppose).

cŏnnoisseur′ (-asẽr) *n.* Critical judge (*of*, *in*, matters of taste). **cŏnnoisseur′ship** *n.*

connōte′ *v.t.* (Of words) imply in addition to the primary meaning; (of facts etc.) imply as a consequence or condition; (logic) imply the attributes while denoting the subject; (loosely) mean. **cŏnnotā′tion** *n.* **connōt′ative** *adj.* **connōt′ātively** *adv.*

connūb′ial *adj.* Of marriage; of husband or wife; married. **connūb′ially** *adv.* **connūbiăl′ity** *n.*

cōn′oid *adj.* Approaching a cone in shape. ~ *n.* Conoid body; (geom.) solid generated by revolution of conic section about its axis (ill. CONE); surface generated by straight line remaining parallel to fixed plane and passing through fixed straight line and fixed curve. **conoid′al** *adj.*

cŏnq′uer (-ker) *v.* Overcome by force; get the better of; acquire, subjugate. **cŏnq′ueror** (-kerer) *n.* One who conquers; horse-chestnut which has broken others in game of conkers; *the C~*, WILLIAM I.

cŏnq′uĕst *n.* Subjugation, conquering; conquered territory; person whose affections have been won; *the C~*, the NORMAN Conquest.

Cŏn′răd, Joseph. Teodor Josef Konrad Korzeniowski (1857–1924), a Polish-born writer in English of novels dealing with seafaring life.

Cons. *abbrev.* Conservative; Consul.

cŏnsănguin′ėous (-nggw-) *adj.* Of the same blood, akin. **cŏnsănguin′ity** *n.* Blood-relationship, kinship.

cŏn′science (-shens) *n.* Moral sense of right and wrong as regards things for which one is responsible; faculty or principle pronouncing upon moral quality of one's own actions or motives; *in all* ~, in reason or fairness; ~ *money*, money sent to relieve conscience, esp. in payment of evaded income-tax; *~-stricken*, overcome with remorse. **cŏn′scienceless** *adj.*

cŏnscien′tious (-shĭensh-) *adj.* Obedient to conscience, scrupulous; ~ *objector*, one whose conscience forces him to object, e.g. to taking an oath or esp. to military service. **cŏnsciĕn′tiously** *adv.* **cŏnsciĕn′tiousnėss** *n.*

cŏn′scious (-shus) *adj.* Aware, knowing; with mental faculties awake or active; selfconscious; (of actions etc.) realized by the actor etc. **cŏn′sciously** *adv.* **cŏn′sciousnėss** *n.* State of being conscious; totality of person's thoughts and feelings, or of a class of these; perception (*of*, *that*).

conscrībe′ *v.t.* Enlist by conscription (now rare; usu. superseded by *conscript*).

cŏn′script[1] *adj.* *~fathers*, (Rom. hist.) collective title of Roman senators.

cŏn′script[2] *n.* Recruit enrolled by conscription. **conscript′** *v.t.* (orig. U.S.) Enlist by conscription. **conscrip′tion** *n.* Compulsory enlistment for State service, esp. for army, navy, or air force.

cŏn′sėcrāte *adj.* Consecrated. ~ *v.t.* Set apart as sacred (*to*); devote *to* (purpose); sanctify.

cŏnsėcrā′tion *n.* Act of consecrating, dedication, esp. of church, churchyard, etc., by bishop; ordination to sacred office, esp. of bishop; devotion *to* (purpose). **cŏn′sėcrātory** *adj.*

cŏnsėcū′tion *n.* Logical sequence; sequence of events; (gram.) sequence (of words, tenses, etc.).

consĕc′ūtive *adj.* 1. Following continuously. 2. (gram.) Expressing consequence; ~ *intervals*, (mus.) intervals of the same kind, esp. octaves or fifths, immediately succeeding one another. **consĕc′ūtively** *adv.* **consĕc′ūtivenėss** *n.*

consĕn′sūal *adj.* Relating to or involving consent. **consĕn′sūally** *adv.*

consĕn′sus *n.* Agreement (*of* opinions etc.).

consĕnt′ *v.i.* Acquiesce, agree (*to*, *that*, etc.). ~ *n.* Voluntary agreement, compliance; permission; *age of* ~, age at which consent, esp. of girl to sexual intercourse, is valid in law; *with one* ~, unanimously; ~ *decree*, (U.S.) agreed verdict, verdict to which parties assent.

cŏnsĕntān′ėous *adj.* Agreeable, accordant; unanimous, concurrent.

consĕn′tient (-shnt) *adj.* Agreeing; concurrent; consenting (*to*).

cŏn′sėquence *n.* 1. Thing or circumstance which follows as a result from something preceding; logical inference. 2. Importance, moment; social distinction, rank. 3. (pl.) A round game in which a narrative (of a meeting and its 'consequences') is concocted by contributions of a name or fact from each player, in ignorance of what has been contributed by the others.

cŏn′sėquent *n.* Event etc. following another (without implication of causal connexion); (logic) second part of conditional proposition, dependent on antecedent; (math.) second of two numbers in a ratio, second and fourth of four proportionals. ~ *adj.* Following as a result (*on*); following logically; logically consistent.

cŏnsėquĕn′tial (-shl) *adj.* 1. Following as a result or inference. 2. Following or resulting indirectly. 3. Self-important. **cŏnsėquĕn′tially** *adv.*

cŏn′sėquently *adv.* & *conj.* As a result; therefore.

consẽrv′ancy *n.* Commission, court, controlling a port, river, etc.; official preservation (of forests etc.).

cŏnservā′tion *n.* Preservation; ~ *of energy*, doctrine that total energy of any system of bodies can be neither increased nor diminished, though it may be changed into various forms, and that the universe is such a system.

consĕrv'ative *adj.* 1. Preservative, keeping or tending to keep intact or unchanged. 2. *C*~, of, belonging to, one of the great English political parties, which believes in the maintenance of existing institutions. 3. (of estimate etc.) Moderate, cautious, low (orig. U.S.). ~ *n.* Conservative person; member of Conservative Party. **consĕrv'atively** *adv.* **consĕrv'atism** *n.*

consĕrv'atoire(-twâr) *n.* Public institution in France, Germany, Italy, etc., for teaching music and declamation.

cŏn'servātor (*or* konsĕrv'*a*-) *n.* Preserver, guardian; official custodian; (U.S.) official guardian of idiot or lunatic; member of conservancy.

consĕrv'atory *n.* 1. (Ornamental) greenhouse for tender or exotic plants. 2. (chiefly U.S.) Female conservator.

cŏnsĕrve' *n.* (usu. pl.). Confection, preserve. ~ *v.t.* Keep from harm, decay, or loss.

consĭd'er *v.* Contemplate mentally; weigh the merits of; reflect, reckon with, make allowance for; be of opinion; regard as.

consĭd'erable *adj.* Worth considering; notable, important; much, no small. **consĭd'erably** *adv.*

consĭd'erate *adj.* Thoughtful for others. **consĭd'erately** *adv.* **consĭd'erateness** *n.*

consĭderā'tion *n.* 1. Considering; meditation; *take into* ~, consider. 2. Fact, thing, regarded as a reason; *in* ~ *of*, in return for, on account of. 3. Compensation, reward; (law) thing given, done, as equivalent by person to whom a promise is made. 4. Thoughtfulness for others. 5. Importance, consequence.

consĭd'ering *prep.* Taking into account, in view of; (ellipt., colloq.) considering the circumstances.

consign' (-īn) *v.t.* Hand over, deliver, *to*; transmit, send by rail etc., *to*; (Sc. law) deposit (money *in* bank, with third party etc.). **consignee', consignor'** (-īn-) *ns.*

cŏnsĭgnā'tion (-g-n-) *n.* Formal payment of money to person legally appointed; consigning goods.

consign'ment (-īn-) *n.* Consigning; goods consigned.

consĭl'ience *n.* Coincidence, concurrence (of inductions drawn from different groups of phenomena). **consĭl'ient** *adj.*

consĭst' *v.i.* Be composed *of*; be comprised or contained *in*; agree, harmonize, *with*.

consĭs'tence *n.* Degree of density, esp. of thick liquids; firmness, solidity. **consĭs'tency** *n.* 1. Consistence. 2. Being consistent.

consĭs'tent *adj.* 1. Compatible (*with*), not contradictory. 2. Constant to same principles of thought or action. **consĭs'tently** *adv.*

consĭs'tory (*or* kŏn'-) *n.* 1. Senate in which pope, presiding over whole body of cardinals, deliberates on affairs of the Church. 2. (Also *C*~ *Court*), in Anglican Church, bishop's court for ecclesiastical causes and offences. 3. In Lutheran Church, supervising clerical board; in Reformed, Genevan, or Presbyterian Church, a court of presbyters. **cŏnsĭstôr'ial** *adj.*

cŏnsolā'tion *n.* Consoling; consoling circumstance; ~ *prize*, *race*, etc., one for unsuccessful competitors.

consŏl'atory (*or* -sōl-) *adj.* Tending or designed to console.

consōle'[1] *v.t.* Comfort in sorrow or mental depression.

cŏn'sōle[2] *n.* 1. (archit.) Tall bracket consisting partly or wholly of volutes and supporting a cornice; ~-*table*, table supported by bracket against a wall. 2. Ensemble of keyboards, stops, etc., of organ, esp. when separate from body of instrument, as in electric organ (ill. ORGAN).

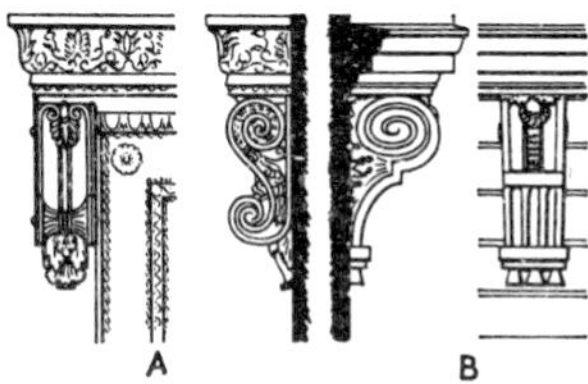

A. GREEK ANCON. B. RENAISSANCE CONSOLE

consŏl'idāte *v.* 1. Solidify, strengthen. 2. Combine (territories, companies, debts, statutes, etc.) into one whole; *consolidated annuities*, Government securities of Great Britain, consolidated in 1751 into a single stock at 3% (later 2½); *Consolidated Fund*, fund, established in 1787, into which main part of revenue is paid, and out of which are paid interest on National Debt and charges other than supply charges, voted annually.

consŏls *n.pl.* Abbrev. of *consolidated annuities* (see CONSOLIDATE, 2).

consŏmm'é (-*ā*) *n.* Clear soup.

cŏn'sonance *n.* Recurrence of same or similar sounds in words or syllables, assonance; (mus.) sounding together of notes in harmony; consonant interval; agreement, harmony.

cŏn'sonant[1] *adj.* Agreeable *to*, consistent *with*; harmonious; agreeing in sound; (mus.) making concord. **cŏn'sonantly** *adv.*

cŏn'sonant[2] *n.* Sound in speech, other than a vowel, produced by a complete momentary stoppage or by partial stoppage or constriction of the air-stream in some part of the mouth-cavity or by the lips as it passes from the lungs; letter or symbol expressing such a sound. **cŏnsonăn'tal** *adj.* [L *consonantem* (*letteram*); the name is due to the erroneous view that a consonant can only be sounded along with a vowel]

cŏn'sôrt *n.* 1. Husband or wife; *king*, *prince* ~, (titles sometimes given to) husband of reigning queen; *queen* ~, king's wife. 2. Ship sailing in company with another. **consôrt'** *v.* Class or bring together, keep company, (*with*); agree, harmonize, (*with*).

conspĕc'tus *n.* General or comprehensive survey; tabulation of details, synopsis.

conspĭc'ūous *adj.* Clearly visible, striking to the eye; attracting notice, remarkable. **cŏnspicū'ity** (rare), **conspĭc'ūousness** *ns.* **conspĭc'ūously** *adv.*

conspĭ'racy *n.* Conspiring; combination for unlawful purpose; plot. **conspĭ'rator** *n.* **conspĭratôr'ial** *adj.* **conspĭratôr'ially** *adv.*

conspīre' *v.* Combine privily for unlawful purpose, esp. treason, murder, sedition; combine, concur (*to* do); plot, devise.

con'stable[1] (kŭn-) *n.* 1. Chief officer of household, court, administration, or military forces of a ruler; *C*~ *of France*, principal officer of household of early French kings, who ultimately became commander-in-chief of army in monarch's absence; *C*~ *of England*, *Lord High C*~, one of chief functionaries of English royal household (since 1521, a title granted only temporarily for special occasions). 2. Governor or warden of royal fortress or castle. 3. Officer of the peace; esp., = *police* ~, policeman of lowest rank; *Chief C*~, officer at head of police force of county or equivalent district; *High C*~, officer of hundred or large administrative district acting as conservator of peace (abolished 1869); *Petty* (*Parish*) ~, similar officer of parish or township (abolished or incorporated in police system, 1872); *special* ~, person sworn in by justices of the peace to assist or replace police on special occasions. [L *comes stabuli* count of the stable]

Con'stable[2] (kŭn-), John (1776–1837). English landscape-painter.

constăb'ūlary *adj.* Of constables; of the police. ~ *n.* Organized body of constables; police force of a district; district under a constable.

cŏn'stancy *n.* Firmness, endurance; faithfulness; unchangingness.

cŏn'stant *adj.* Unmoved, resolute; faithful; unchanging; unremitting. ~ *n.* (math. etc., Quantity which does not vary; numerical quantity expressing relation, property, etc., that remains the same for the same substance under all conditions.

Constăn'tia (-sh*a*). Wine produced on Constantia Farm, near Cape Town, S. Africa.

Cŏn'stantīne (the Great) (274–337). Roman emperor (306–37); converted to Christianity, which he made the State religion; transferred the capital of the empire to Byzantium, which he renamed Constantinople.

Cŏnstăntinō'ple. Turkish city on the Bosporus, the former capital of Turkey; now officially called *Istanbul*; originally the Roman city of Byzantium; renamed ~ by Constantine the Great, who transferred the capital of the empire there (A.D. 328).

cŏn'stantly *adv.* Always; often.

cŏn'stellāte *v.* Form into a constellation; stud, adorn thickly.

cŏnstellā'tion *n.* Number of fixed stars grouped within outline of an imaginary figure as viewed from the earth; group of distinguished persons.

cŏn'sternāte *v.t.* Fill with consternation.

cŏnsternā'tion *n.* Amazement and terror such as to prostrate one's faculties, dismay.

cŏnstĭpā'tion *n.* Condition of bowels in which defaecation is irregular and difficult. **cŏn'stĭpāte** *v.t.* Affect with constipation.

constĭt'ūency *n.* Body of voters who elect a representative member; place, residents in place, so represented.

constĭt'ūent *adj.* Composing, making up, a whole; appointing, electing; able to form or alter a (political) constitution. ~ *n.* 1. Component part. 2. One who appoints another his agent or representative; member of a constituency.

cŏn'stĭtūte *v.t.* 1. Appoint (person) to office, dignity, etc., of; establish, found, give legal form to (assembly, institution, etc.). 2. Frame, form (by combination of elements); make up, be components of.

cŏnstĭtū'tion *n.* 1. Act, mode, of constituting; way in which thing is constituted; esp. character of body in regard to health, strength, vitality, etc.; condition of mind, disposition. 2. Mode in which State is organized; body of fundamental principles according to which a State is governed; esp. (U.S.) the Constitution of the United States framed at Philadelphia in 1787 and ratified 1788, together with subsequent amendments. 3. (hist.) Decree, ordinance; (Rom. law) enactment made by the emperor; *C~s of Clarendon*, propositions drawn up at Council which met at Clarendon in Wiltshire in reign of Henry II (1164), defining limits of civil and ecclesiastical jurisdiction in England.

cŏnstĭtū'tional (-sh*o*-) *adj.* 1. Of, inherent in, affecting, the bodily or mental constitution. 2. Belonging to the very constitution of anything; essential. 3. Of, in harmony with, authorized by, the political constitution; adhering to the political constitution. ~ *n.* (colloq.) Walk taken for health's sake. **cŏnstĭtū'tionalism, cŏnstĭtū'tionalist, cŏnstĭtūtionăl'ĭty** *ns.* **cŏnstĭtū'tionally** *adv.*

cŏn'stĭtūtive *adj.* Constructive, formative; essential; component. **cŏn'stĭtūtively** *adv.*

constrain' *v.t.* Compel; bring about by compulsion; confine forcibly, imprison; *constrained*, forced, embarrassed. **constrain'ėdly** *adv.*

constraint' *n.* Compulsion; confinement; restraint of natural feelings, constrained manner.

constrict' *v.t.* Contract, compress; cause (organic tissue) to contract. **constric'tion** *n.* **constric'tive** *adj.*

constric'tor *n.* 1. Muscle that draws together or narrows a part. 2. Surgical instrument for producing constriction. 3. = BOA-constrictor.

constrĭnge' (-nj) *v.t.* Compress; cause (organic tissue) to contract. **constrĭn'gent** *adj.* Causing constriction. **constrĭn'gency** *n.*

construct' *v.t.* Fit together, frame, build; (gram.) combine (words) syntactically; (geom.) draw, delineate.

construc'tion *n.* 1. Act, mode, of constructing; thing constructed. 2. (gram.) Syntactical connexion between verbs and their objects or complements, prepositions and their objects, etc. 3. Construing, explanation (of words); interpretation. 4. ~ *crew, gang, labourer*, (U.S.), men, man, engaged on construction, esp. of railways; ~ *train*, train carrying materials etc. for making or repairing railways. **construc'tional** (-sh*o*-) *adj.* Of, engaged in, construction; structural.

construc'tionist (-sh*o*-) *n.* One who interprets a law, esp. the Constitution of the U.S., strictly, broadly, or in some other specified manner.

construc'tive *adj.* 1. Of construction; constructing, tending to construct (esp. as opp. to *destructive*). 2. Deduced by construction or interpretation, not directly expressed, inferred. **construc'tively** *adv.*

construc'tor *n.* One who constructs, esp. supervisor of naval construction.

cŏn'strue (*or* konstrōō')*v.* Combine (words) grammatically; analyse (sentence), translate word for word; admit of grammatical analysis; expound, interpret.

cŏnsubstăn'tial (-shl) *adj.* Of the same substance, esp. of the three Persons of the Trinity. **cŏnsubstantiăl'ity** (-shĭăl-) *n.*

cŏnsubstăn'tiāte(-shĭ-)*v.* Unite in one substance. **cŏnsubstăntiā'tion** *n.* Doctrine of real substantial presence of body and blood of Christ together with bread and wine in Eucharist (dist. from TRANSUBSTANTIATION).

cŏn'suėtūde (-sw-) *n.* Custom, esp. as having legal force.

consuėtūd'ĭnary (-sw-) *adj.* Customary. ~ *n.* Treatise containing collection of customs or usages, esp. of monastic house, cathedral, etc.

cŏn'sul *n.* 1. Title of two annually elected magistrates exercising supreme authority in Roman Republic. 2. Title of 3 chief magistrates of French Republic (1799–1804); of these, the *First C~*, Napoleon Bonaparte, had all the real power. 3. Agent of sovereign State residing in foreign port or town to protect interest of its traders and residents there and assist commercial relations between the countries; *~-general*, consul of highest rank.

cŏn'sūlar *adj.* Of a consul; ~ *service*, system of commercial consuls (in Britain now part of the Foreign Service). ~ *n.* (Roman) of consular rank, ex-consul.

cŏn'sūlate *n.* 1. Government of Rome by consuls; office or dignity of consuls. 2. (Period of) consular government in France. 3. Office or establishment of modern commercial consul. **cŏn'sulship** *n.*

consŭlt' *v.* Take counsel (*with*); seek information or advice from; take into consideration; *consulting chemist, engineer*, etc., one who makes a business of giving professional advice to the public or to those practically engaged in his own profession; *consulting physician* etc., physician etc. to whom others may refer their patients for advice. **consŭl'tative** *adj.*

consŭl'tant *n.* Consulting physician etc.

cŏnsultā'tion *n.* Act of consulting; deliberation; conference.

consūme' *v.* Make away with; use up; eat, drink, up; burn up; spend, waste; waste away; *consumed*, eaten up *with*. **consūm'ėdly** *adv.* Excessively.

consūm'er *n.* (esp. econ.) One who uses up an article produced, thereby exhausting its exchangeable value; ~ *goods*, things which directly satisfy human needs and desires, e.g. food and clothing.

consŭmm'ate *adj.* Complete, perfect. **consŭmm'ately** *adv.* **cŏn'summāte** *v.t.* Accomplish, complete (esp. marriage by sexual intercourse). **cŏnsummā'tion** *n.* Completion; desired end, goal; perfection; perfected thing; physical completion of marriage.

consŭmp'tion *n.* 1. Consuming; destruction; waste; amount consumed. 2. Wasting disease, esp. pulmonary tuberculosis.

consŭmp'tive *adj.* 1. Tending to consume. 2. Having a tendency to, affected with, pulmonary tuberculosis, whence ~ *n.*, consumptive person.

cŏn'tăct *n.* State, condition, of touching; (math.) meeting of curves or surfaces so as to have tangents or tangent planes in common; (elect.) junction or touching surface of two conductors or ends of conducting wire through which a current passes; (esp. pl.) friendly relationships, persons with whom one comes into touch; (med.) person who has been exposed to contagious disease; *come into* ~ *with*, come across, meet; *make, break* ~, complete, interrupt electric circuit; ~ *lenses*, small lenses worn on eyeballs instead of spectacles. ~ *v.t.* Get into touch with (person).

cŏntadi'nō (-ahdē-) *n.* (pl. *-ni*). Italian peasant (fem. ***-na***, with pl. *-ne* pr. nā).

contā'gion (-jn) *n.* Communication of disease from body to body by contact; contagious disease; moral corruption; contagious influence.

contā'gious (-jus) *adj.* Communicating disease or corruption by contact; (of diseases) communicable by contact; (fig.) catching, infectious. **contā'giously** *adv.* **contā'giousnėss** *n.*

contain' *v.t.* Have, hold, as contents; comprise, include; (of a measure) be equal to; (geom.) enclose, form boundary of; (of numbers) be divisible by (number) without remainder; restrain; (mil.) hold (enemy force) in position so that it cannot operate elsewhere.

contăm'ināte *v.t.* Pollute, infect. **contăminā'tion** *n.*

contăng'ō (-ngg-) *n.* (Stock Exchange) Percentage paid by buyer of stock to seller for postponement of completion of purchase (cf. BACKWARDATION); ~ *day*, second day before settling-day.

contĕmn' (-m) *v.t.* Despise, treat with disregard.

cŏn'templāte *v.* Gaze upon; view mentally; expect; intend, purpose; meditate. **cŏntemplā'tion** *n.* **cŏn'templātive** (*or* kontĕm'pla-) *adj.* Meditative, thoughtful; (of life or monastic order) devoted to religious contemplation and prayer. **cŏn'tėmplātively** *adv.* **cŏn'templātivenėss** *n.*

contĕmporăn'ėous *adj.* Existing, occurring, at the same time (*with*); of the same period. **contĕmporăn'ėously** *adv.* **contĕmporanē'ity, contĕmporăn'ėousnėss** *ns.*

contĕm'porary *adj.* & *n.* (Person) belonging to the same time; (person) equal in age; (newspaper) published during same period.

contĕm'porīze *v.t.* Make contemporary.

contĕmpt' *n.* Act, mental attitude, of despising; condition of being despised; (law) disobedience or open disrespect to authority or lawful commands of sovereign, Houses of Parliament, or esp. courts of law. **contĕmp'tĭble** *adj.* Deserving contempt, despicable; *Old C~s* (in allusion to an alleged reference by Wilhelm II to 'General French's contemptible little army'), the British Army of regulars and reserves sent to France in autumn of 1914. **contĕmptĭbĭl'ĭty** *n.* **contĕmp'tĭbly** *adv.* **contĕmp'tĭblenėss** *n.*

contĕmp'tūous *adj.* Showing contempt (*of*); scornful; insolent. **contĕmpt'ūously** *adv.* **contĕmpt'ūousnėss** *n.*

contĕnd' *v.* Strive, fight; struggle *with*; compete, be in rivalry; argue (*with*); maintain (*that*).

cŏn'tĕnt[1] *n.* 1. Containing power, capacity; volume; amount contained or yielded. 2. (pl.) What is contained; esp. things contained or treated of in writing or document; *table of* ~*s*, summary of subject-matter of book. 3. Constituent elements of a conception; substance (of art etc., as opp. to *form*).

contĕnt'[2] *n.* Contented state, satisfaction. ~ *adj.* Satisfied; willing (*to* do). ~ *v.t.* Satisfy; ~ *oneself*, be satisfied (*with*). **contĕnt'ėdly** *adv.* **contĕnt'ėdnėss** *n.* **contĕnt'ment** *n.*

contĕn'tion *n.* Strife, dispute, controversy; competition, rivalry; point contended for in argument.

contĕn'tious (-shus) *adj.* Quarrelsome; involving contention. **contĕn'tiously** *adv.* **contĕn'tiousnėss** *n.*

contẽrm'ĭnous *adj.* Having a common boundary (*with*); meeting at their ends; coextensive. **contẽrm'ĭnously** *adv.*

cŏn'tĕst *n.* Debate, controversy; strife; competition. **contĕst'** *v.* Debate, dispute; strive in argument; strive *for*; dispute with arms; contend or compete for (seat in Parliament etc.). **contĕs'table** *adj.*

contĕs'tant *n.* One who contests.

cŏntėstā'tion *n.* Disputation, dispute; competition, conflict; assertion contended for.

cŏn'tĕxt *n.* Whole structure of connected passage in relation to any of its parts; parts immediately preceding and following a passage or word. **contĕx'tūal** *adj.* **contĕx'tually** *adv.*

contĕx'ture *n.* Act, mode, of weaving together; structure; fabric; mode of literary composition.

cŏntĭgū'ĭty *n.* Contact; proximity; (psychol.) proximity of ideas or impressions in space or time, as a principle of association.

contĭg'ūous *adj.* Touching, adjoining; neighbouring. **contĭg'ūously** *adv.*

cŏn'tĭnent[1] *adj.* Temperate, chaste. **cŏn'tĭnently** *adv.* **con'tĭnence, -cy** *ns.*

cŏn'tĭnent[2] *n.* One of the main continuous bodies of land on earth's surface (now usu. reckoned as Europe, Asia, Africa, N. and S. America, Australia); *the C~*, the mainland of Europe as dist. from the British Isles; (U.S.) the continent of N. America. **cŏntĭnĕn'tal** *adj.* Of the or a continent; esp. of the mainland of Europe; of the continent of N. America; (hist.) of the Amer. colonies or States (during and immediately after the War of Independence); *C~ Congress*, assembly of delegates from the revolting colonies meeting at Philadelphia in 1774–6; ~ *drift*, (geol.) supposed slow movement of the continents away from a single land-mass to their present positions; ~ *shelf*, sloping platform round the continents, outside which the ocean bed descends steeply; *C~ System*, system of blockade designed to exclude England from commerce with the continent of Europe instituted by Napoleon in 1806. **cŏntĭnĕn'tal** *n.* 1. Inhabitant of a continent, esp. Europe. 2. Soldier of the (Amer.) Continental army. 3. Currency note issued by the Continental Congress; (hence) something of no value, a whit.

contĭn'gency (-j-) *n.* Uncertainty of occurrence; chance occurrence; thing that may happen hereafter; thing dependent on uncertain event; thing incident to another, incidental expense, etc.

contĭn'gent (-j-) *adj.* 1. Of uncertain occurrence; accidental; incidental *to*. 2. True only under existing conditions; non-essential; conditional, dependent *on* some prior occurrence or condition. **contĭn'gently** *adv.* **contĭn'gent** *n.* 1. Contingent thing. 2. Troops contributed to form part of military or naval force; also fig.

contĭn'ūal *adj.* Always going on, incessant; very frequent. **contĭn'ually** *adv.*

contĭn'ūance *n.* Going on, duration; remaining, stay. **contĭn'ūant** *adj.* & *n.* (Consonant) of which sound can be continued and prolonged as long as breath lasts, as opp. to a STOP.

contĭnūā'tion *n.* 1. Carrying on, resumption. 2. (Stock Exchange) Carrying over of account till next settling-day. 3. That by which anything is continued, continuing addition; ~ *school*, school giving instruction to persons who have finished their regular schooling and are usu. in employment.

contĭn'ūative *adj.* Tending, serving, to continue.

contĭn'ūe *v.* Maintain, keep up (action etc.); retain (person *in* office etc.); take up, resume; (law) adjourn; remain in existence; stay; not cease.

cŏntĭnū'ĭty *n.* 1. Being continous; unbroken series, succession; close relationship, logical sequence, of ideas. 2. Specification of all the details in the sequences required for a film; ~ (*man*), person who notes what is filmed so as to ensure consistency etc.

contĭn'ūous *adj.* Connected, unbroken; uninterrupted in time or sequence; ~ *wave*, (physics) wave motion which continues over a long period so that the beginning and end of the motion can be neglected in mathematical analysis. **contin'ūously** *adv.*

contin'ūum *n.* A whole, the structure of whose parts is continuous and not atomic, as *space-time* ~.

contŏrn'iate *adj.* & *n.* (Medal) with deep furrow round disc, within the edge.

contŏrt' *v.t.* Twist, distort.

contŏr'tion *n.* Twisting; twisted state. **contŏr'tionist** (-sho-) *n.* (esp.) Gymnast who throws his body into contorted postures.

cŏn'tour (-oor) *n.* Outline, line separating differently coloured parts of design; outline of coast, mountain mass, etc.; ~ (*line*), line representing horizontal contour of earth's surface at given elevation (ill. MAP). ~ *v.t.* Mark with contour lines.

cŏn'tra *prep.* & *n.* 1. In *pro and contra* (usu. *con*), for and against; *pros and cons*, arguments for and against. 2. (book-keeping) Opposite side of account, esp. credit side.

contra- *prefix.* Against; in names of mus. instruments and organ-stops, denoting a pitch of an octave below.

cŏn'trabănd *n.* Prohibited traffic, smuggling; smuggled goods; (U.S., during Civil War) negro slave, esp. fugitive or captured slave; ~ *of war*, anything forbidden to be supplied by neutrals to belligerents. ~ *adj.* Forbidden to be imported or exported; concerned with contraband.

cŏn'trabăss *n.* (mus.) Double-bass.

cŏntracĕp'tive *adj.* & *n.* Preventive of uterine conception. **cŏntracĕp'tion** *n.*

cŏn'trăct *n.* 1. Mutual agreement between parties, States, etc., esp. business agreement for supplying goods or performing work at specified price. 2. Agreement enforceable by law; department of law relating to contracts; formal agreement for marriage. 3. (In the game of bridge) undertaking by declarer to make so many tricks; ~ *bridge*: see BRIDGE². **contrăct'** *v.* 1. Enter into business or legal arrangement; ~ (oneself) *out* (*of*), contract for exemption or exclusion from provisions of (law etc.). 2. Form (friendship, habit); incur (disease, liability). 3. Draw together; make smaller; restrict, confine; (gram.) shorten (word) by combination or elision; shrink, become smaller.

contrăc'tile *adj.* Capable of, producing, contraction.

contrăc'tion *n.* Contracting; contracted word.

contrăc'tor *n.* 1. One who undertakes a contract, esp. in building and related trades, or for Government or other public body. 2. Contracting muscle.

contrăc'tūal *adj.* Of (the nature of) a contract.

cŏntradict' *v.t.* Deny (statement); deny words of (person); be contrary to.

cŏntradic'tion *n.* Denial; opposition; statement contradicting another; inconsistency; ~ *in terms*, plainly self-contradictory statement or words.

cŏntradic'tious (-shus) *adj.* Given to contradiction.

cŏntradic'tory *adj.* Making denial; mutually opposed or inconsistent; contradictious. **cŏntradic'torily** *adv.* **cŏntradic'toriness** *n.* **cŏntradic'tory** *n.* Contradictory assertion.

cŏntradistinc'tion *n.* Distinction by contrast.

cŏntradisting'uish (-nggw-) *v.t.* Distinguish by contrast.

cŏntra-in'dicāte *v.t.* (med.) Give indications contrary to (usual treatment, a particular remedy, etc.). **contra-indicā'tion** *n.* **cŏntra-indic'ative** *adj.*

contrăl'tō *n.* (pl. *-ōs*) Lowest female voice (ill. VOICE); singer with such voice; part assigned to it.

cŏntraposi'tion (-z-) *n.* Antithesis, opposition; (logic) mode of conversion in which proposition having contrary of original predicate for its subject is inferred, e.g. *all men are mortal, therefore no non-mortals are men.* **cŏntrapŏs'itive** *adj.* & *n.*

cŏn'traprŏp *n.* Abbrev. of *contra-rotating propellers*, pair of propellers on same axis rotating in opposite directions (ill. PROPELLER).

contrăp'tion *n.* (colloq.) (Queer) contrivance or device.

cŏntrapŭn'tal *adj.* Of, in, counterpoint. **cŏntrapŭn'tist** *n.* One skilled in counterpoint.

cŏntrarī'ety *n.* Opposition in nature, quality, or action; disagreement, inconsistency.

cŏn'trariwise (-z; *or* kontrar'-) *adv.* On the other hand; in the opposite way; perversely.

cŏn'trary *adj.* 1. Opposed in nature or tendency (*to*); (of wind) impeding, unfavourable. 2. (sometimes pr. kontrar'ĭ) Perverse, self-willed. 3. Opposite in position or direction. **cŏn'trarily** *adv.* **cŏn'trariness** *n.* **cŏn'trary** *adv.* In opposition (*to*). ~ *n.* *The* opposite; object, fact, or quality that is the very opposite of something else; *on the* ~, (corroborating a denial expressed or understood) *to the* ~, to the opposite effect (contradicting something that has been said or assumed).

cŏn'trast (-ah-) *n.* Juxtaposition showing striking differences; comparison clearly revealing differences or opposing qualities; person or thing of most opposite qualities. **contrast'** (-ah-) *v.* Set (two things, one *with* another) in opposition, so as to show their differences; show striking difference on comparison *with.*

cŏn'trasty (-ah-) *adj.* (Of photographic negatives or prints) having very marked contrasts of light and shade.

cŏn'tra-suggĕs'tible *adj.* (psychol.) Resistant to suggestion; oppositional; apt to take the opposite view or action to that suggested.

cŏn'trate *adj.* ~ *wheel*, one with teeth set at right angles to its plane (ill. GEAR).

cŏntravallā'tion *n.* Chain of redoubts and breastworks placed by besiegers between their camp and the beleagured place.

cŏntravēne' *v.t.* Infringe (law); dispute (statement); conflict with. **cŏntravĕn'tion** *n.* Infringement, violation (*of*).

contretemps (kawn'tretahn) *n.* Unlucky accident; embarrassing occurrence, hitch.

contrib'ūte *v.* Pay, furnish (*to* common fund etc.), give or pay jointly with others; ~ *to*, have a part or share in producing.

cŏntribū'tion *n.* Contributing; thing, help, literary article, contributed; imposition levied for support of army in the field.

contrib'ūtor *n.* One who contributes (esp. literary work). **contrib'ūtory** *adj.* That contributes; ~ *negligence*, negligence on the part of a person injured that has helped to bring about the injury. ~ *n.* Person bound on the winding up of a joint-stock company to contribute towards payment of its debts.

cŏn'trīte *adj.* Crushed in spirit by a sense of sin, completely penitent; (of action) arising from contrition. **cŏn'trītely** *adv.*

contri'tion *n.* Being contrite, penitence.

contrīv'ance *n.* 1. Contriving. 2. Deceitful practice. 3. Invention; inventive capacity; thing contrived; mechanical device.

contrīve' *v.t.* Invent, devise; bring to pass, manage (thing, *to* do etc.). **contrīv'er** *n.* Deviser, inventor; schemer; (good or bad) manager.

contrōl' *n.* 1. Controlling; function or power of directing and regulating. 2. Restraint; check; standard of comparison for checking inferences from experiment etc. 3. Controller; (spiritualism) personality or 'spirit' alleged to control medium's words and actions. 4. Place where motor-cars, aeroplanes, etc., in race must stop for official examination and where time is usu. allowed for overhaul etc.; section of road etc. over which speed of motor vehicles is checked. 5. Apparatus by means of which machine in operation, esp. aeroplane or motor-car, is controlled. ~ *v.t.* Exercise restraint or direction over; command, dominate, regulate; hold in check; check, verify.

contrōll'er *n.* (esp.) One who controls or checks expenditure, steward, esp. of royal household, mint, navy, etc. **contrōll'ership** *n.*

cŏntrovĕr'sial (-shl) *adj.* Of, open to, given to, controversy

cŏntrovẽr'sialism, cŏntrovẽr'sialist *ns.* **cŏntrovẽr'sially** *adv.*

cŏn'trovẽrsy *n.* Disputation; dispute, contention; discussion (esp. conducted in writing) in which opposite views are advanced and maintained by opponents.

cŏn'trovẽrt (*or* -vẽrt') *v.t.* Dispute about, discuss; dispute, deny.

cŏntūmā'cious (-sh*u*s) *adj.* Insubordinate, disobedient, esp. to order of court. **cŏntūmā'ciously** *adv.* **cŏntūmā'ciousnėss** *n.* **cŏn'tūmacy** *n.*

cŏntūmēl'ious *adj.* Opprobrious, insolent. **cŏntūmēl'iously** *adv.*

cŏn'tūmėly *n.* Insolent, reproachful, language or treatment; disgrace.

contūse' (-z) *v.t.* Injure by blow without breaking skin, bruise. **contū'sion** (-zhn) *n.*

conŭn'drum *n.* Riddle, puzzle.

cŏnûrbā'tion *n.* Group of towns which have become contiguous by expansion and which can be regarded as a single community for certain purposes.

cŏnvalĕsce' (-s) *v.i.* Regain health. **cŏnvalĕs'cence** *n.* Gradual recovery of health after illness. **cŏnvalĕs'cent** *adj.* & *n.* (Person) recovering from illness; ~ *home, hospital*, nursing home, hospital, for such persons.

convĕc'tion *n.* (physics) Conveyance of heat by (usu. upward) movement of heated fluid, e.g. air or water. **convĕc'tional** (-sh*o*-) *adj.*

convenances (kawn'venahns) *n.pl.* Conventional propriety.

convēne' *v.* Assemble; convoke; summon (person *before* tribunal). **convēn'er** *n.* One who convenes, member of a committee etc. who fixes dates, and issues notices, of meetings.

convēn'ience *n.* 1. Suitableness, commodiousness; material advantage; personal comfort or ease; advantage. 2. Useful appliance; water-closet; (pl.) material comforts.

convēn'ient *adj.* Suitable, favourable, commodious; not troublesome; (colloq.) within easy reach, conveniently near. **convēn'iently** *adv.*

cŏn'vent *n.* Religious community (usu. of women, cf. MONASTERY) living together; building occupied by this.

convĕn'ticle *n.* (hist.) Clandestine religious meeting, esp. of nonconformists or dissenters; building used for this.

convĕn'tion *n.* 1. Convening. 2. Formal assembly for deliberation or legislation on important matters; esp. (hist.) certain extraordinary assemblies of Parliament without summons of sovereign, e.g. that of 1660, which restored Charles II; *National C~*, the sovereign assembly which governed France from 21st Sept. 1792 to 26th Oct. 1795. 3. (U.S. etc.) Assembly of delegates or representatives, conference. 4. Agreement; in diplomacy, less formal or less important agreement than treaty. 5. General agreement or consent (often implicit), as foundation of usage etc., rule or practice based on this; accepted usage become artificial and formal; (pl., bridge etc.) standard methods of bidding, leading, etc.

convĕn'tional (-sh*o*-) *adj.* Depending on convention(s), not natural, not spontaneous; (of weapons) other than atomic. **convĕn'tionally** *adv.* **convĕn'tionalism, convĕn'tionalist, convĕntionăl'ity** *ns.* **convĕn'tionalize** *v.t.*

convĕn'tūal *adj.* & *n.* (Member, inmate) of a convent; (member) of the less strict branch of Franciscans, living in large convents.

convẽrge' *v.* (Of lines etc.) tend to meet in a point; approach nearer together; (math.) approximate in sum of its terms toward a definite limit. **convẽr'gence, convẽr'gency** *ns.* **convẽr'gent** *adj.*

convẽrs'able *adj.* Easy, pleasant, in conversation; fit for social intercourse. **convẽrs'ablenėss** *n.* **convẽrs'ably** *adv.*

cŏn'versance, cŏn'versancy *n.* Familiarity, acquaintance (*with*). **cŏn'versant** *adj.* Having frequent intercourse, well acquainted (*with*).

cŏnversā'tion *n.* 1. Talk, interchange of thoughts and words. 2. Sexual intercourse; *criminal* ~ (abbrev. *crim. con.*), adultery. 3. ~ *piece*, painting of group of figures all of which are portraits.

cŏnversā'tional (-sh*o*-) *adj.* Fond of, good at, pertaining to, conversation. **cŏnversā'tionally** *adv.* **cŏnversā'tionalist** *n.*

cŏnversăziōn'ė (-săts-) *n.* Soirée given by learned body or society of arts etc.

convẽrse'[1] *v.i.* Talk. **cŏn'vẽrse** *n.* (archaic) Discourse; intercourse.

cŏn'vẽrse[2] *adj.* & *n.* Opposite, contrary; (logic) converted proposition; statement etc. derived from another by transposition of two important antithetical members, e.g. *he is brave but not good* is the converse of *he is good but not brave*; (math.) proposition which assumes the conclusion and proves the datum of another. **cŏn'vẽrsely** (-sl-) *adv.*

convẽr'sion (-shn) *n.* 1. Transposition, inversion, esp. (logic) of subject and predicate. 2. Bringing over (*to* a faith, opinion, party, etc.); turning of sinners to God. 3. Changing (*to, into*); change (of debentures, stocks, etc.) into others of different character.

convẽrt' *v.t.* Change (*into*); cause to turn (*to* opinion, faith, etc.); turn to godliness; (logic) see CONVERSION, 1; (Rugby football) kick goal from (try). **cŏn'vẽrt** *n.* Person converted, esp. to religious faith or life.

convẽrt'ible *adj.* That may be converted; (of items) equivalent, synonymous; (econ., of a currency) that may be freely converted into gold or dollars at a fixed price. **convẽrtibĭl'ity** *n.* **convẽrt'ible** *n.* (orig. U.S.) Motor-car with collapsible hood, touring-car.

cŏn'vĕx *adj.* Curved like outside of circle or sphere, reverse of CONCAVE. **convĕx'ity** *n.* **cŏn'vĕxly** *adv.*

convey' (-ā) *v.t.* Transport, carry; transmit; impart, communicate (idea, meaning); (law) transfer, make over (property) by deed or legal process.

convey'ance (-vā'*a*-) *n.* 1. Carrying; transmission; communication. 2. (Document effecting) transference of property. 3. Carriage, vehicle. **convey'ancer** *n.* Lawyer who prepares documents for conveyance of property and investigates titles. **convey'ancing** *n.* Drawing of deeds etc. for the transfer of property, branch of law dealing with titles and their transference.

convey'er (-ā'*er*), **-or** *n.* (esp.) Mechanical device (usu. in form of endless belt or band) for conveying goods, esp. those in process of manufacture.

convict' *v.t.* Prove guilty (*of* offence); declare guilty by verdict of jury or decision of judge; impress (person) with sense of error. **cŏn'vict** *n.* Condemned criminal undergoing penal servitude.

convic'tion *n.* 1. Proving or finding guilty. 2. Act of convincing. 3. Settled belief; (theol.) being convinced or convicted of sin.

convince' *v.t.* Firmly persuade (*of, that*); produce in (person) moral conviction (of sin etc.). **convin'cingly** *adv.* **convin'cingnėss** *n.* **convin'cible** *adj.* Open to conviction.

conviv'ial *adj.* Of, befitting, a feast; festive, jovial. **conviv'ially** *adv.* **convivĭăl'ity** *n.*

cŏnvocā'tion *n.* Calling together; assembly; (C. of E.) synod of clergy of province of Canterbury or York; legislative assembly (in Durham and Oxford Universities) of all qualified members holding degree of M.A.; (in other universities) assembly of qualified members for discussing matters connected with university. **cŏnvocā'tional** *adj.*

convōke' *v.t.* Call together; summon to assemble.

cŏn'volūte *adj.* (bot., conch.) Rolled together, coiled. ~ *n.* Coil. **cŏn'volūtėd** *adj.* Coiled, twisted. **cŏnvolū'tion** *n.* Coiling, twisting; coil, twist.

convŏl'vūlus *n.* Genus of plants with usually twining stems and trumpet-shaped white, pink, or blue flowers, bindweed.

cŏn'voy (*or* konvoi') *v.t.* (Of ship of war or aircraft) escort (usu. merchant or passenger vessel);

escort with armed force; (archaic) conduct (guests, lady, etc.). **cŏn'voy** *n.* 1. Convoying; protection; escort. 2. Company, supply of provisions, etc., under escort; number of merchant ships under escort or sailing in company.

convŭlse' *v.t.* Shake violently; throw into convulsions (usu. pass.); cause to be violently seized with laughter (usu. pass.).

convŭl'sion (-shn) *n.* 1. (usu. pl.) Violent irregular motion of limb or body due to involuntary contraction of muscles (esp. as disorder of infants); (pl.) violent fit of laughter. 2. Violent social or political agitation; violent physical disturbance, esp. earthquake or similar phenomenon.

convŭl'sive *adj.* Attended or affected with, producing, resembling, convulsions. **convŭl'sively** *adv.*

cōn'y, cōn'ey *n.* (pl. *-ies, -eys*). 1. Rabbit (now retained only in statutes etc. and as shop name for the fur). 2. Small pachyderm of genus *Hyrax*, living in caves and clefts of rocks in Palestine, Syria, and E. Africa.

coo *v.* & *n.* (Make) soft murmuring sound of, or as of, doves and pigeons; say cooingly; *bill and ~*, converse amorously.

coo'ee', coo'ey *n.* Call adapted as signal by Australian colonists from aborigines. ~ *v.i.* Make this call.

cook[1] *v.* Prepare food, prepare (food) by application of heat; undergo cooking; concoct; (colloq.) tamper with, falsify (accounts etc.); (slang, of exertion etc.) exhaust; *~ person's goose*, do for him, settle his hash. ~ *n.* One whose business it is to cook food, esp. woman-servant employed in private family; *~-book*, (U.S.) cookery-book; *~-general*, servant who does all work of house as well as cooking; *~-house*, camp kitchen; outdoor kitchen in warm countries; galley on ship; *~-housemaid*, female servant who acts as both cook and housemaid, *~-shop*, eating-house; *~-stove*, (U.S.) cooking-stove.

Cook[2], James (1728–79). English navigator and explorer esp. of the S. Pacific islands and Australasia; landed at Botany Bay in 1770 and took formal possession of Australia for the British Crown.

cook'er *n.* 1. Stove or vessel for cooking. 2. Fruit etc. suitable for cooking. 3. One who cooks (accounts etc.). **cook'ery** *n.* Art, practice, of cooking; *~-book*, book of recipes and instructions in cookery.

cook'ie *n.* (Sc.) Plain bun; (U.S. etc.) sweet biscuit.

cool *adj.* 1. Moderately cold. 2. Unexcited, calm; lacking zeal, lukewarm; wanting cordiality. 3. Calmly audacious or impudent. 4. (colloq.) Applied complacently or emphatically to a large sum of money, e.g. *it cost me a ~ thousand.* **cool'ly** *adv.* **cool'ness** *n.* **cool** *n.* Cool air, cool place; coolness. ~ *v.* Make or become cool; *~ one's heels*, be kept waiting.

cool'ant *n.* Liquid applied to edge of a cutting-tool to lessen friction; in motor, cooling medium for cylinders.

cool'er *n.* Vessel in which anything, as wine, butter, is cooled or set to cool; (slang) prison cell.

Cool'idge, Calvin (1872–1933). 30th president of U.S., 1923–9.

cool'ie *n.* Native hired labourer in India, China, etc.

coomb, combe (koom) *n.* Valley or flank of hill; short valley running up from coast.

coon *n.* (U.S.) = (RAC(C)OON); Negro; sly fellow; *gone ~*, one whose case is hopeless.

coon'-căn' *n.* Card-game similar to RUMMY, originating in Mexico; the object is to form sequences of the same suit or sets of the same denomination. [Span. *con quien* with whom?]

coop *n.* Basket or cage placed over sitting or fattening fowl; wickerwork basket for catching fish; narrow place of confinement. ~ *v.* Put in coop; confine narrowly (also ~ *up*).

cō-ŏp' *n.* Colloq. abbrev. of co-operative store or society.

coop'er[1] *n.* Maker of casks and other wooden vessels formed of staves and hoops; one engaged in sampling, bottling, or retailing wine. ~ *v.t.* Make or repair (casks); put or stow in casks. **coop'erage** *n.* Cooper's work or workshop; payment for cooper's work.

Coop'er[2], James Fenimore (1789–1851). Amer. writer of stories dealing esp. with the Red Indians.

cō-ŏp'erate *v.i.* Work together (*with* person *in* a work, *to* an end); concur in producing an effect. **cō-ŏperā'tion** *n.* Working together to same end; co-operative combination.

cō-ŏp'erative *adj.* Of co-operation, co-operating; of industrial co-operation; *~ society*, society or union for production or distribution of goods, in which profits are shared (freq. in form of dividends on purchases) by all contributing members; *~ shop, store*, shop belonging to such a society.

cō-ŏpt' *v.t.* Elect into body by votes of existing members. **cō-ŏptā'tion, cō-ŏp'tion** *ns.* **cō-ŏp'tative, cō-ŏp'tive** *adjs.* Elected by co-option.

cō-ôrd'inate *adj.* Equal in rank, degree, or importance, esp. (gram.) of clauses of compound sentence; consisting of co-ordinate things. **cō-ôrd'inately** *adv.* **cō-ôrd'inate** *n.* Co-ordinate thing, esp. (math.) each of a system of two or more magnitudes used to define position of point, line, or plane, by reference to fixed system of lines, points, etc. (ill. GRAPH). **cō-ôrd'ināte** *v.t.* Make co-ordinate; bring (parts) into proper relation. **cō-ôrdinā'tion** *n.* **cō-ôrd'inative** *adj.*

coot *n.* Any of various swimming and diving birds; now, a bird of the genus *Fulica*, esp. the bald coot, *F. atra*, web-footed bird inhabiting edges of lakes and still

COOT

Length 15 in.

rivers, with base of bill extended to form broad white plate on forehead; (U.S.) the allied *F. Americana.*

cŏp[1] *n.* (spinning) Roll of yarn wound upon spindle in such a way that it needs no support.

cŏp[2] *n.* (slang) Policeman; capture. ~ *v.t.* (slang) Catch, capture.

copai'ba (-pī-) *n.* Aromatic resin of acrid taste obtained from S. Amer. trees or shrubs of the genus *Copaifera* and used in medicine and the arts.

cōp'al *n.* Hard translucent odoriferous resin obtained from various tropical trees and used to make a fine transparent varnish. [Mex. *copalli* incense]

cōpar'cener *n.* (law) One who shares equally with others in inheritance of estate of common ancestor. **cōpar'cenary** *n.* Joint heirship.

cōpart'ner *n.* Partner, sharer, associate. **cōpart'nership** *n.* (esp.) System designed to interest employees in their business by profit-sharing.

cōpe[1] *n.* 1. Vestment like long semicircular cloak without sleeves or arm-holes worn by clergy in procession, at Vespers, etc. (ill. VESTMENT). 2. Vault or canopy (*of heaven* etc.). 3. (founding) Outer portion of mould. ~ *v.* Furnish with cope; cover (wall etc.) with coping; cover as with a vault; project like coping.

cōpe[2] *v.i.* Contend in well-matched struggle *with*; grapple successfully.

C.O.P.E.C., COPEC *abbrevs.* Conference on Politics, Economics, and Citizenship.

cōp'ĕck *n.* $\frac{1}{100}$ of a rouble.

Cōpenhā'gen. København, capital city of Denmark; *Battle of ~*, a naval battle off Copenhagen, 1801, in which the British fleet under Nelson defeated and destroyed the Danish fleet, thus breaking up the Northern Confederacy (Russia, Sweden, and Denmark) against Britain.

cōp'er *n.* Horsedealer.

Copĕr'nicus, Nicolaus. Latinized name of Mikolai Kopernik (1473–1543), Polish astronomer, who demonstrated that the planets, including the earth, revolve on their own axes and move in orbits round the sun. **Copĕrn'ĭcan** *adj.*

cōp'ĭng *n.* Top course of masonry or brickwork in wall, usu. sloping to throw off rain (ill. MASONRY); *~-stone*, stone used in coping; (fig.) finishing touch.

cōp'ĭous *adj.* Plentiful; full of matter; profuse in speech; (of language) having a large vocabulary. **cōp'ĭously** *adv.* **cōp'ĭousness** *n.*

Cŏp'ley, John Singleton (1738–1815). Amer. painter, active also in England.

cŏpp'er[1] *n.* 1. Malleable ductile tenacious metallic element of yellowish-red colour having high electrical conductivity; symbol Cu, at. no. 29, at. wt 63·54. 2. Copper money; the bronze money which has superseded this; bronze coin, penny or halfpenny. 3. Large boiler, orig. of copper, now usu. of iron, for laundry etc. 4. *~-beech*, variety of European beech-tree with copper-coloured foliage; *~-bit*, soldering tool pointed with copper; *~-bottom* (*v.t.*) sheathe bottom of (ship) with copper; *copp'erhead*, N. Amer. venomous snake, *Ankistrodon contortrix*, so called from reddish-brown colour of top of head; *copp'erplate*, polished plate of copper on which design is engraved or etched for printing, print from this; sloping rounded cursive handwriting orig. taught from copy-books printed from engraved copperplates (ill. SCRIPT); *coppersmith*, worker in copper. ~ *v.t.* Cover or sheathe with copper. **cŏpp'ery** *adj.* (esp.) Copper-coloured. [L *cuprum*, f. *Cyprium* (*aes*) Cyprian (metal)]

cŏpp'er[2] *n.* (slang) Policeman.

cŏpp'eras *n.* Ferrous sulphate, $FeSO_4$ hydrated, called also *green ~* and *green vitriol*, used in dyeing, tanning, and making ink.

cŏpp'ice *n.* Small wood of underwood and small trees grown for periodical cutting.

cŏp'ra *n.* Dried kernels of coconut, exported for the expression of coconut oil, used in manufacture of margarine, candles, etc.

cŏp'rolīte *n.* Stony roundish fossil consisting of petrified dung. **cŏprolĭt'ĭc** *adj.*

cŏprŏph'agous *adj.* (of beetles) Dung-eating.

cŏpse *n.* = COPPICE; *copse'wood*, the low trees and underwood of a copse. ~ *v.t.* Treat as copsewood; make a copse of.

Cŏpt. Native Egyptian or Ethiopian Christian of the Jacobite sect of Monophysites. **Cŏp'tĭc** *adj.* & *n.* (Language) of the Copts. [Arab. *quft*, f. Coptic *gyptios*, f. Gk *Aiguptios* Egyptian]

cŏp'ūla *n.* (log., gram.) Part of proposition connecting subject and predicate; the verb *to be* employed as a mere sign of predication; (mus.) short connecting passage. **cŏp'ūlar** *adj.*

cŏp'ūlāte *v.i.* Unite sexually. **cŏpūlā'tion** *n.* 1. Sexual union. 2. Grammatical or logical connexion.

cŏp'ūlatĭve *adj.* Serving to connect; (gram.) connecting words or clauses which are already connected in sense; connecting subject and predicate; relating to sexual union. **cŏp'ūlatĭvely** *adv.* **cŏp'ūlatĭve** *n.* Copulative conjunction or particle.

cŏp'ūlatory *adj.* Of sexual copulation.

cŏp'y *n.* 1. Reproduction (of writing, picture, etc.); imitation; specimen of penmanship written after a model. 2. (law) Transcript of manorial court-roll containing entries of admissions of tenants by manorial custom to land held by tenure, hence called *copyhold.* 3. One of the written or printed specimens of the same writing or work. 4. Original from which a copy is made; esp. specimen of penmanship to be copied; (printing, without *a* or pl.) manuscript or other matter prepared for printing. 5. *~-book*, book containing copies for learners to imitate; (*attrib.*) conventional, commonplace; *~-writer*, one who composes the wording of advertisements. ~ *v.* Transcribe *from* original); make copy of; imitate; *copying-ink*, ink suitable for writing or drawings of which copies by impression are to be made, usu. prepared by adding glycerine to ordinary ink; *copying-pencil*, pencil containing lead made from graphite, aniline blue, and gum arabic, used for same purpose as copying ink. **cŏp'ўĭst** *n.* One who copies or transcribes.

cŏp'ўhōld *n.* Tenure (now obsolete) of land 'at the will of the lord according to the custom of the manor' by COPY (sense 2); land so held. ~ *adj.* Held by this tenure; of copyhold. **cŏp'ўhōlder** *n.*

cŏp'yright (-rīt) *n.* The sole legal right to produce or reproduce a literary, dramatic, musical, or artistic work, by making copies or performance or any other means. Copyright normally belongs to the author of the work or to his heir or assignee. ~ *adj.* Protected by copyright; ~ *libraries*, the British Museum, Bodleian, Cambridge University, National Library of Wales, Scottish National Library, and Trinity College, Dublin, which are entitled by law to a free copy of every book published in the United Kingdom; ~ *union*, international union established by the Berne Convention of 1886, whereby each member country undertakes to give to foreign authors the same rights as its own authors receive. ~ *v.t.* Protect (book etc.) by copyright; secure copyright for.

coquĕt', coquette' (-kĕt) *v.i.* Play the coquette; flirt (*with*); dally, trifle, *with.* **cōq'uĕtry** *n.* Coquettish behaviour or act; coquetting, trifling. **coquette'** *n.* 1. Woman who (habitually) trifles with the affections of men, flirt. 2. Genus (*Lophornis*) of crested humming-birds. **coquĕtt'ĭsh** *adj.* **coquĕtt'ishly** *adv.*

Cor. *abbrev.* Corinthians (N.T.).

cŏ'racle *n.* Small boat of wickerwork covered with pitched canvas (orig. skins) and resembling the Irish curragh, used by ancient Britons and still by Welsh fishermen (ill. CANOE). [Welsh *corwgl*]

cŏ'racoid *adj.* Beaked like a crow; ~ *process*, short projection of the scapula-bone in vertebrates (ill. MUSCLE). ~ *n.* Coracoid process or bone.

cŏ'ral *n.* 1. Hard calcareous substance consisting of the continuous skeleton secreted by many tribes of submarine coelenterate polyps for their support and habitation; found

BRANCHING CORAL SHOWING POLYPS

growing plant-like on sea-bottom or in extensive accumulations called *~-reefs.* 2. Piece of (red) coral as ornament etc.; toy of polished coral (for children cutting teeth). 3. Unimpregnated roe of lobster (so called from colour when boiled). ~ *adj.* Of, of the colour of (red) coral; formed of coral in the mass; *~-island*, island formed by growth of coral; *~-insect*, *-polyp*, one of the individual animals secreting coral; ~ *stitch*: see ill. STITCH.

cŏ'rallĭne *adj.* Coral red; coral-like; ~ *ware*, Italian red-paste pottery of 17th and 18th centuries. ~ *n.* Genus of seaweeds (*Corallina*) with calcareous jointed stem; (pop.) various plant-like compound animals.

cŏ'rallīte *n.* Fossil coral.

cŏ'ralloid *adj.* & *n.* (Organism) like, akin to, coral.

cōr'am *prep.* Before, in the presence of; ~ *populo*, in public.

cōr anglais (ahṅg'glā) *n.* The tenor oboe (ill. WOOD); organ stop of similar tone. [Fr., = 'English horn']

cōrb'el *n.* Projection of stone, timber, etc., jutting out from wall to support weight; short timber laid longitudinally under beam or girder, to shorten its unsupported span; *~-table*, projecting course resting on corbels. ~ *v.* ~ *out*, *off*, (cause to) project on corbels. **cŏrb'elled** (-beld) *adj.* [OF dim. of *corb* crow]

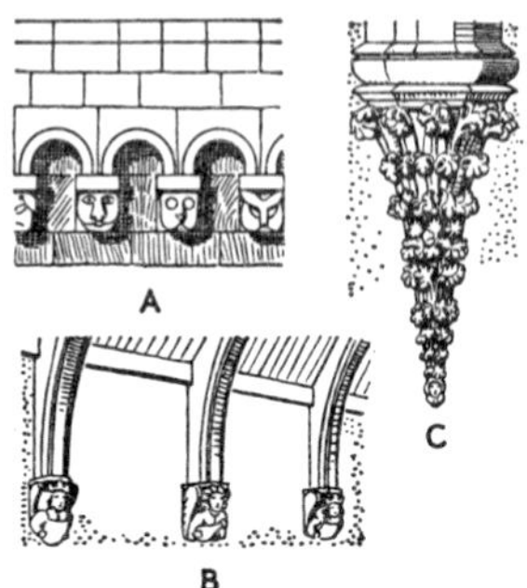

A. ROMANESQUE CORBEL TABLE. B. GOTHIC ROOF CORBELS. C. GOTHIC VAULTING CORBEL

cŏrb'ie *n.* (Sc.) Raven; carrion crow; ~ *steps, stones,* step-like projections on sloping edge of gable (ill. GABLE).

cŏrd *n.* 1. Thin rope, thick string; (anat.) cord-like structure in animal body; SPINAL ~, VOCAL ~: see these words. 2. Raised cord-like rib on cloth, ribbed fabric, esp. corduroy. 3. Measure of cut wood for fuel (usu. 128 cu. ft). ~ *v.t.* Bind or fasten with cord(s).

cŏrd'age *n.* Cords or ropes collectively, esp. in rigging of a ship.

cŏrd'ate *adj.* Heart-shaped.

cŏrd'ėd *adj.* Bound, furnished, with cords; ribbed, twilled.

cŏrdėlier' *n.* 1. Franciscan friar of strict rule (so called from knotted cord worn round waist). 2. Rope-making machine.

cŏrd'ial *adj.* 1. That stimulates the heart. 2. Hearty, sincere; warm, friendly. **cŏrd'ially** *adv.* **cŏrdiăl'ity** *n.* **cŏrd'ial** *n.* Comforting or exhilarating drink; (commercial) aromatized and sweetened spirit.

cŏrdĭller'a (-lyār*a*) *n.* One of series of parallel mountain ridges or chains; (pl.) the parallel chains of the Andes in S. America, Central America, and Mexico.

cŏrd'ite *n.* Smokeless propellant of guncotton, nitroglycerine, and vaseline, usu. pressed into rods of varying length and thickness.

cŏrd'oba *n.* Principal monetary unit of Nicaragua, = 100 centavos.

cŏrd'on *n.* 1. (archit.) String-course, projecting (usu. flat) band of stone on face of wall. 2. Line of troops consisting of men placed at intervals to prevent passage; line or circle of police or other persons; (also ~ *sanitaire* or *sanitary* ~), guarded line between infected and uninfected districts. 3. Ornamental cord or braid worn as badge of honour; ~ *bleu* (blėr), blue ribbon worn formerly by Knights of the Holy Ghost, the highest order under the Bourbons; hence, person of eminence, (esp.) first-class cook. 4. Fruit-tree pruned to grow as single stem (usu. on espalier or wall) (ill. FRUIT).

Cŏrd'ova. City of S. Spain.

cŏrd'uroy *n.* 1. Cotton velvet with ridges in the pile; (pl.) corduroy trousers. 2. Corduroy road (see below). ~ *adj.* Made of corduroy, ribbed like corduroy; ~ *road,* road of tree-trunks laid transversely across swamp or miry ground.

cŏrd'wain *n.* Spanish leather (orig. from Cordova) of goat-skins, or (later) of split horse-hides, used for shoes etc. in Middle Ages.

cŏrd'wainer *n.* Shoemaker (obs. exc. in name of guild). [OF *corduan* of Cordova]

cōre *n.* 1. Dry horny capsule embedded in pulp and containing seeds of apple, pear, etc. (ill. FRUIT). 2. Central portion cut out, as of rock in boring. 3. Central part of different character from what surrounds it; esp. assemblage of soft iron laminae in centre of electro-magnet or induction coil; central strand in hawser-laid rope round which other strands are twisted; central cord of conducting wires in telegraph etc. cable. 4. Innermost part, centre, heart, of anything; *hard* ~, irreducible residuum (esp. of unemployment). ~ *v.t.* Remove core from.

cō-rėlĭg'ionĭst (-jo-) *n.* Adherent of same religion.

cŏrėŏp'sis *n.* Genus of composite plants, cultivated for their handsome yellow or particoloured rayed flowers.

cō-rėspŏn'dent *n.* (law) Person proceeded against together with the RESPONDENT in a divorce suit.

Cŏrf'iōte *adj.* & *n.* (Native, inhabitant) of Corfu.

Cŏrfu' (-ōō). One of the Ionian islands off the W. coast of Greece, anciently called Corcyra.

cŏrg'i, -gy (-g-) *n.* Small Welsh breed of dog (ill. DOG).

cŏriā'ceous (-sh*u*s) *adj.* Like leather.

cŏriăn'der *n.* Annual, *Coriandrum sativum,* of S. Europe, Levant, etc., with compound leaves and globose aromatic fruit (~ *seed*) used as flavouring and as carminative.

Cŏ'rinth. City of Greece, notorious in ancient times for luxury and profligacy. **Corĭn'thian** *adj.* & *n.* 1. (Native) of Corinth. 2. (pl.) The two N.T. Epistles of St. Paul to the Corinthians. 3. (Man) given to elegant dissipation, profligate. 4. ~ *bronze,* an alloy of gold, silver, and copper, used in antiquity in costly ornaments; ~ *order,* (archit.) the most ornate of the Greek orders, with bell-shaped capital adorned with rows of acanthus leaves giving rise to volutes and helices (ill. ORDER).

Cŏriolā̆n'us, Gaius Marcius. Acc. to tradition, a Roman patrician and general of the first half of the 5th c. B.C. who earned the name ~ for the capture of Corioli from the Volscians. He was prosecuted by the tribunes on the charge of aspiring to become tyrant, and exiled; whereupon he joined the Volscians and led them against Rome, but on the entreaties of his mother, Veturia, he spared the town and withdrew to Antium, where he was put to death by the Volscians.

cŏrk[1] *n.* 1. Bark of cork-oak (*Quercus suber*), which grows to a thickness of 1 or 2 in. and is very light, tough, and elastic. 2. Piece of cork used as float for fishing-line, support for swimmer, etc. 3. Cylindrical or tapering piece of cork used as stopper for a bottle, cask, etc.; similar stopper of other substance. 4. (bot.) Tissue forming outer division of bark in higher plants and consisting of close-packed air-containing cells nearly impervious to air and water. 5. *cork'screw,* instrument for drawing corks from bottles, usu. consisting of a piece of steel twisted into a spiral with sharp point and transverse handle; (*adj.*) spirally twisted; (*v.*) twist spirally, (cause to) proceed spirally; *corkwood,* name of various light porous woods (esp. BALSA), and the trees yielding them. ~ *adj.* Made of cork. ~ *v.t.* Stop, stop *up,* with or as with cork; blacken with burnt cork.

Cŏrk[2]. County and county borough of Munster, Eire.

cŏrk'age *n.* Corking, uncorking, of bottles; hotel-keeper's charge for serving wine or spirits, esp. those not supplied by himself.

cŏrked (-kt) *adj.* 1. (of wine) Tasting of the cork, spoiled by an unsound cork into which the wine penetrates. 2. (of face and hands) Blackened with burnt cork.

cŏrk'er *n.* (slang) Something that precludes further discussion, esp. notable lie. **cŏrk'y** *adj.* Like cork; frivolous, lively, buoyant, restive.

cŏrm *n.* (bot.) Swollen base of stem containing food reserves, occurring in some monocotyledonous plants, such as crocus.

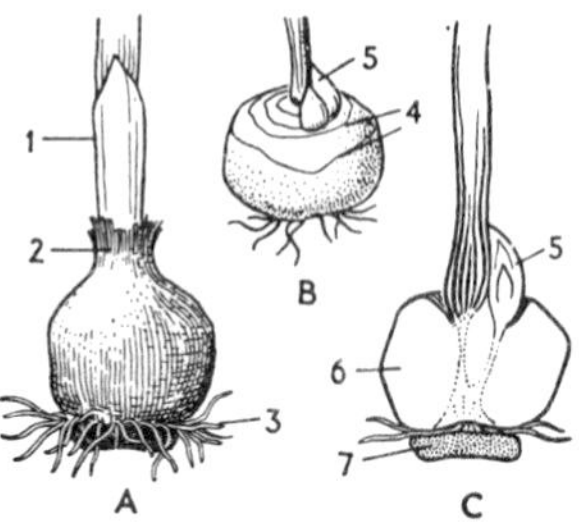

A. CROCUS CORM. B. CORM WITH SCALE LEAVES REMOVED. C. VERTICAL SECTION

1. Aerial shoot. 2. Scale leaves. 3. Roots. 4. Nodes. 5. Lateral bud (next year's corm). 6. Present year's corm. 7. Last year's corm

cŏrm′orant *n.* Large, lustrous-black, voracious sea-bird, *Phalacrocorax carbo*; the genus to which this belongs; (fig.) insatiably greedy or rapacious person. [med. L *corvus marinus* sea-raven]

cŏrn[1] *n.* 1. A grain, seed, esp. of cereals, pepper, etc. 2. Grain; cereal plants, esp. while growing; in England, usu. wheat; in Scotland and Ireland, oats; in U.S., maize or Indian corn, *Zea mays*. 3. *~-chandler*, retail dealer in corn; *~-cob*, elongated woody part of ear of maize to which grains are attached; *~-crake*, the landrail, *Crex pratensis*, which lives among standing corn, etc., and has a harsh grating voice; *~-exchange*, exchange for dealers in corn; *~-factor*, dealer in corn; *~-flour*, meal of Indian corn (occas. of rice etc.) ground very fine; *~-flower*, name of various plants growing among corn, esp. the blue-flowered *Centaurea Cyanus*; *~ laws*, laws regulating trade in corn; esp. (Engl. hist.) laws restricting importation of cereals in force at beginning of 19th c. and repealed in 1846; *~-pone*, (U.S.) kind of bread of Indian corn made with milk and eggs; *~-salad*, lamb's-lettuce, a small annual plant, *Valerianella olitoria*, found wild in cornfields and cultivated as an early salad; *~-silk*, the styles of maize; *~-stalk*, stalk of corn, esp. maize; tall, lithe person; person of European descent born in Australia, esp. New South Wales.

cŏrn[2] *n.* Horny induration of cuticle with hard centre and root sometimes penetrating deep into subjacent tissue, caused by undue pressure, chiefly of boots on feet; *~-cure*, *-plaster*, *-salve*, etc., remedies for corns.

cŏrn[3] *v.* Sprinkle, preserve (meat) with salt; *corned beef*, beef so preserved and canned.

Corn. *abbrev.* Cornwall.

cŏrn′ėa *n.* Transparent horny part of anterior covering of eyeball (ill. EYE). **cŏrn′ėal** *adj.*

Cŏrneille′ (-nā), Pierre (1606–84). French dramatist, famous for his classical tragedies 'Le Cid', 'Horace', 'Polyeucte', 'Rodogune', etc.

cŏrn′el *n.* Common hedgerow shrub, *Cornus sanguinea*, the dogwood.

cŏrnēl′ian, căr- *n.* Deep dull red, flesh-coloured or reddish-white variety of chalcedony, used for seals etc.

cŏrnēl′ian cherry *n.* Variety of cornel.

cŏrn′ėous *adj.* Horny, hornlike.

cŏrn′er *n.* 1. Angular meeting-place of converging sides or edges, projecting angle, esp. where two streets meet; hollow angle enclosed by meeting walls etc.; *drive into a ~*, force into difficult position from which there is no escape. 2. Secluded, secret, or remote place; region, quarter; extremity or end of the earth. 3. Buying up whole of any stock or commodity, so as to compel speculative sellers to buy from one to fulfil their engagements; (loosely) any combination to raise prices by securing monopoly. 4. (Assoc. football) Corner-kick. 5. *~-boy*, one who loafs at street corners; *~-kick*, (Assoc. football) free kick from the corner allowed when opponent has sent ball over his own goal line; *~-man*, corner-boy; end man of row of nigger minstrels, usu. playing bones or tambourine and contributing comic effects; *~-stone*, one of those forming quoin or salient angle of wall; (fig.) indispensable thing or part. *~ v.* Furnish with corners; set in corner; drive into corner (esp. fig.); force (dealers) or control (commodity) by means of corner (sense 3); form corner *in* (stock or commodity).

cŏrn′ėt[1] *n.* 1. Brass musical instrument of trumpet class with valves operated by pistons for producing additional notes (also called *~-à-pistons*; ill. BRASS); cornet-player. 2. Conically-rolled piece of paper for groceries etc.; cone-shaped wafer for holding ice-cream.

cŏrn′ėt[2] *n.* 1. White head-dress of Sisters of Charity. 2. (Formerly) 5th commissioned officer in troop of cavalry, who carried the colours. **cŏrn′ėtcy** *n.* Position or rank of cornet.

cŏrn′ice *n.* (archit.) Horizontal moulded projection crowning or finishing (part of) building, esp. uppermost member of entablature, surmounting the frieze (ill. ORDER); ornamental moulding round wall of room just below ceiling; (mountaineering) overhanging mass of hardened snow at edge of precipice.

Cŏrn′ish *adj.* & *n.* (Language) of Cornwall.

cŏrnūcōp′ia *n.* The horn of plenty, represented as a goat's horn overflowing with flowers, fruit, and corn. **cŏrnūcōp′ian** *adj.* Overflowingly abundant. [L *cornu copiae* = 'horn of plenty', the horn of the goat Amalthea by which the infant Zeus was suckled]

CORNUCOPIA

cŏrnūt′ėd *adj.* Having horns or horn-like projections.

Cŏrn′wall. County in the extreme SW. of England.

cŏrn′y *adj.* (colloq.) Old-fashioned; trite, sentimental.

corŏll′a *n.* (bot.) Whorl of floral leaves (petals) forming inner envelope of flower, and usu. its most conspicuous part (ill. FLOWER).

corŏll′ary *n.* Proposition appended to one already demonstrated, as self-evident inference from it; immediate deduction; natural consequence, result. [L *corollarium* money paid for a chaplet, gratuity]

corōn′a[1] *n.* (pl. *-nae*). 1. Small circle of light (usu. prismatically coloured) round sun or moon; halo of radiating white light seen round the disc of the moon in a total eclipse of the sun (now known to belong to sun) (ill. SUN). 2. Circular candle-holder hung from roof. 3. (archit.) Member of cornice, with broad vertical face, usu. of considerable projection (ill. ORDER). 4. (anat.) Various crown-like parts of body. 5. (bot.) Crown-like appendage on inner side of corolla in daffodil and other flowers (ill. FLOWER).

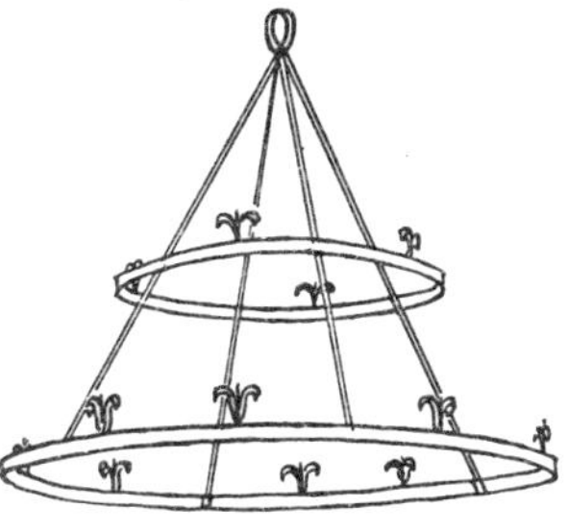

CORONA

Corōn′a[2] *n.* Well-known brand of Havana cigars. [Span. *La Corona*, = 'the crown', proprietary name]

cŏ′ronăch (-χ) *n.* Funeral-song, dirge, in Scottish Highlands and Ireland.

cŏ′ronal[1] *n.* Circlet (esp. of gold or gems) for the head; wreath, garland.

corōn′al[2] *adj.* 1. (anat.) *~ suture*, transverse suture of skull between frontal bones (*~ bone*) and parietal bones (ill. HEAD). 2. (bot.) Of a corona.

cŏ′ronary *adj.* (Of vessels, ligaments, nerves, etc.) encircling parts like a crown; (of parts) connected with these; *~ arteries, veins (vessels)* of the heart, those supplying blood to substance of heart itself; *~ thrombosis, occlusion*, blockage of coronary arteries by a blood-clot.

cŏ'ronate, -ātėd *adjs.* (bot. & zool.) Having a corona or crown-shaped part.

corōnā'tion *n.* Ceremony of crowning sovereign or sovereign's consort; *C~ stone*, stone of Scone (Scotland) on which Scottish kings sat at coronation ceremony, brought to England by Edward I and now preserved in the coronation chair at Westminster Abbey.

cŏ'roner *n.* Officer of county, district, or municipality, orig. for maintaining rights of private property of Crown; now his chief function is to hold inquest on bodies of those supposed to have died by violence or accident. **cŏ'ronership** *n.*

cŏ'ronėt *n.* 1. Small crown, esp. crown denoting dignity inferior to sovereign's, worn by nobility and varying in form according to rank. 2. Decorative fillet or wreath, esp. as part of woman's head-dress; garland for the head. 3. Lowest part of horse's pastern, immediately above coffin (ill. HORSE). **cŏ'ronĕtėd** *adj.* Wearing a coronet; esp., belonging to the peerage.

corōn'oid *adj.* (anat.) Curved like a crow's beak (of processes of bones).

Cŏ'rot (-rō), Jean-Baptiste Camille (1796–1875). French landscape-painter.

Corp. *abbrev.* Corporal.

cor'poral¹ *adj.* Of the human body; personal, bodily. **corporăl'ity** *n.* Material existence; body; (pl.) bodily matters, wants, etc.

cor'poral² *n.*, **cor'poras** *n.* Fine linen cloth on which consecrated elements are placed during Mass.

cor'poral³ *n.* Non-commissioned officer ranking below sergeant; *ship's ~*, petty officer attending to police matters under master-at-arms; *the little C~*, nickname of Napoleon I.

cor'porate *adj.* Forming a body politic or corporation; forming one body of many individuals; of, belonging to, a body politic; *~ town*, town with municipal rights, and corporation; *~ county*, town with its liberties which has been constituted a county independent of the jurisdiction of the historical county within which it is. **cor'porately** *adv.*

corporā'tion *n.* 1. Body corporate legally authorized to act as a single individual; artificial person created by royal charter, prescription, or act of the legislature, with authority to preserve certain rights in perpetual succession. 2. Trade-guild, city company. 3. *municipal ~*, civic authorities of borough, town, or city; mayor, aldermen, and councillors. 4. (U.S.) Business company, firm. 5. (in Fascist Italy) Body representing employers and employees of an industry and responsible to the State for its direction. 6. (colloq.) Abdomen, esp. when prominent. 7. *C~ Act*, act of 1661 requiring all holders of municipal office to acknowledge royal supremacy and subscribe declaration against the Solemn League and Covenant, and making all persons ineligible for office who had not partaken within a year of communion in the Church of England.

CORONETS

1. Duke. 2. Marquis. 3. Earl. 4. Viscount. 5. Baron

cor'porative *adj.* Of a corporation; *~ State*, one with its industrial system organized in corporations (sense 5).

corpor'ėal *adj.* Bodily; material; (law) tangible, esp. *~ hereditament*, hereditament of material objects. **corpor'ėally** *adv.* **corporėăl'ity** *n.*

corporē'ity *n.* Quality of being or having a material body; bodily substance.

cor'posant (-z-) *n.* Luminous electrical discharge sometimes seen on ship during storm, St. Elmo's fire. [It. *corpo santo* holy body]

corps (kor) *n.* (pl. same, pr. korz). 1. = ARMY corps; body of troops for special service. 2. Body of persons in common organization; students' society in German universities; *~ diplomatique*, the ambassadors, attachés, etc., accredited to a particular court or capital; *~ de ballet* (băl'ā), company of ballet-dancers.

corpse *n.* Dead (usu. human) body.

cor'ūlent *adj.* Bulky (of body); fat. **cor'ūlence, cor'ūlency** *ns.*

cor'us *n.* 1. Body, collection, of writings. 2. (physiol.) Structure of special character or function in animal body. 3. *~ juris*, body of law; *~ delicti* (L, = 'body of the crime'), everything that makes a given fact a breach of law.

Cor'us Christī (kr-). Feast of the Blessed Sacrament or body of Christ, the Thursday after Trinity Sunday (regularly celebrated in many places by the performance of 'mystery' or 'miracle' plays or pageants).

Cor'us Christī Cŏll'ege. 1. A college of the University of Cambridge, founded 1352 by a guild of Cambridge townsmen. 2. A college of the University of Oxford, founded 1517 by Richard Fox, bishop of Winchester.

cor'puscle (-sl) *n.* 1. Minute body forming distinct part of organism; esp. (pl.) the minute rounded or disc-like bodies constituting a large part of the blood of vertebrates (ill. BLOOD). 2. (obs.) Electron.

corpŭs'cūlar *adj.* Of corpuscles; *~ theory*, theory that light is emission of streams of imponderable particles from luminous bodies.

corrăl' *n.* Enclosure for horses, cattle, etc. (in U.S. and Span. America); defensive enclosure of wagons in encampment; enclosure for capturing wild animals. *~ v.t.* Form (wagons) into corral; confine in corral.

corrĕct' *adj.* True, accurate; right, proper (of conduct, manners, etc.), in accordance with a good standard (of taste etc.). **corrĕct'ly** *adv.* **corrĕct'nėss** *n.* **corrĕct'** *v.t.* 1. Set right, amend; substitute right for (wrong); mark errors in (proof-sheet etc.) for amendment. 2. Admonish (person); cure (person) of fault; punish (person, fault). 3. Counteract, neutralize, (hurtful qualities). 4. Bring (result of mathematical or physical observation or calculation) into accordance with certain standard conditions; eliminate aberration etc. from lens etc.

corrĕc'tion *n.* 1. Correcting; *under ~*, subject to correction. 2. Thing substituted for what is wrong. 3. Punishment.

corrĕc'titūde *n.* Correctness of conduct or behaviour.

corrĕc'tive *adj.* & *n.* (Thing) serving, tending, to correct or counteract what is harmful. **corrĕc'tively** *adv.*

corrĕc'tor *n.* One who corrects; *~ of the press*, proof-reader.

Corrĕ'ggio (-jiō), Antonio Allegri (1494–1534), called 'Il Correggio' from the place of his birth in Lombardy, an Italian painter famous for his chiaroscuro.

cŏ'rrėlāte *n.* Each of two things so related that one implies or is complementary to the other; each of two related things viewed in reference to the other. *~ v.* Have a mutual relation (*with, to*); bring (thing) into such relation (*with* another). **cŏrrėlā'tion** *n.*

corrĕl'ative *adj.* 1. Having a mutual relation (*with, to*); analogous. 2. (gram., of words) Corresponding with each other and regularly used together each in one member of compound or complex sentence (e.g. *either—or*; *so—as*). *~ n.* Correlative word or thing. **corrĕl'atively** *adv.*

cŏrrėspŏnd' *v.i.* 1. Be congruous, in harmony (*with, to*); be similar, analogous (*to*); agree in amount, position, etc. (*to*). 2. Communicate by interchange of letters (*with*). **cŏrrėspon'dingly** *adv.*

cŏrrėspŏn'dence *n.* 1. Agreement, harmony. 2. Communication by letters; letters.

cŏrrĕspŏn'dent *n.* One who writes letters (to person or newspaper); one employed by newspaper to contribute news and other material from some particular place or on some particular subject; person etc. with regular business relations with another (esp. in foreign country). ~ *adj.* Corresponding. **cŏrrĕspŏn'dently** *adv.*

corri'da (-rē-) *n.* Bull-fight.

cŏ'rridor *n.* 1. Main passage in large building, on which many rooms open; outside passage connecting parts of building; passage in railway carriage, upon which all compartments open. 2. Strip of territory of one State running through another territory to give access e.g. to the sea; *Polish* ~, strip which ran through Prussia from Poland to the Baltic at Danzig, created by the Treaty of Versailles (1919).

cŏ'rrie *n.* (Sc. and geol.) Circular hollow on mountain side, orig. formed by ice, with steep walls and gently sloping floor, freq. containing a lake (ill. MOUNTAIN); cirque. [Gael. *coire* cauldron]

cŏrrigĕn'dum (-j-) *n.* (pl. *-da*). Thing to be corrected (esp. mistake in printed book).

cŏ'rrigible *n.* Capable of being corrected; open or submissive to correction.

corrīv'al *n.* Rival.

corrŏb'orant *adj.* & *n.* Strengthening (medicine); corroborating (fact).

corrŏb'orāte *v.t.* Confirm formally (law etc.); confirm (person, statement) by evidence etc. **corrŏborā'tion** *n.* Confirmation by further evidence. **corrŏb'orative, corrŏb'oratory** *adjs.*

corrŏb'oree *n.* Festive or warlike dance of Austral. aborigines, held at night by moonlight or light of bush fire. [native name in New South Wales]

corrōde' *v.* Wear away, destroy gradually (of rust, chemical agents, etc.); decay. **corrō'sion** (-zhn) *n.*

corrōs'ive *adj.* & *n.* Substance causing corrosion; ~ *sublimate*, mercuric chloride ($HgCl_2$), a highly poisonous white crystalline solid. **corrōs'ively** *adv.* **corrōs'iveness** *n.*

cŏ'rrugate (-o͝o-) *v.* Contract into wrinkles or folds; mark with, bend into, parallel folds or ridges; *corrugated iron*, galvanized sheet iron bent into a series of parallel ridges and grooves, used for roofing etc. **cŏrrugā'tion** *n.*

cŏ'rrugātor (-o͝o-) *n.* Each of two small muscles which contract brows in frowning.

corrŭpt' *adj.* Rotten, putrid, decomposed (archaic); debased in character, depraved, wicked; perverted or influenced by bribery; (of language, texts, etc.) vitiated by errors or alterations; ~ *practices*, (at elections) various illegal forms of direct or indirect bribery. **corrŭpt'ly** *adv.* **corrŭpt'ness** *n.*

corrŭpt' *v.* Infect, taint; bribe. destroy purity of (text, language); become corrupt. **corrŭp'tive** *adj.*

corrŭp'tible *adj.* Liable to corruption, perishable; capable of moral corruption. **corrŭptibil'ity** *n.* **corrŭp'tibly** *adv.*

corrŭp'tion *n.* Decomposition; moral deterioration; use of corrupt practices; bribery etc.; perversion (of language etc.) from original state; (law) ~ *of blood*, affect of attainder on person attainted, by which he and his descendants lost all rights of rank and title, possession of land, etc.

corsage (kōrsahzh', kōr'sĭj) *n.* Bodice of woman's dress; (orig. U.S.) fresh flower or flowers worn on bodice or shoulder.

cōrs'air *n.* Mediterranean privateer, esp. of Barbary; corsair's ship.

cōrse *n.* (archaic, poet.) Corpse.

cōrs'ėt *n.* Tightly fitting undergarment, usu. stiffened and freq. laced to give support round waist and hips, worn esp. by women; stays. **cōrs'ėtėd** *adj.*

Cōrs'ica. Island off the W. coast of Italy, belonging to France. **Cōrs'ican** *adj.* & *n.* (Inhabitant, native) of Corsica; *The* ~, Napoleon Bonaparte, born at Ajaccio in Corsica.

cōrs'lėt, cōrs'elėt (-sl-) *n.* 1. Piece of armour covering body. 2. Garment, usu. tight-fitting, covering body as dist. from limbs; woman's under-garment combining corset and brassière. 3. (zool.) Thorax, part lying between head and abdomen, of insect.

cortège' (kōrtāzh') *n.* Train of attendants; procession.

Cōrt'ēs. Legislative assembly of Spain or Portugal.

cōrt'ĕx *n.* 1. (bot.) Inner bark (ill. STEM). 2. (anat.) Layer of grey matter on surface of brain; outer part of kidney (ill. KIDNEY); outer portion of suprarenal gland. **cōrt'ical** *adj.*

Cortez (kōrt'ĕz), Hernando (1485–1547). Spanish adventurer who conquered Mexico for Spain.

cōrt'icate, -ātėd *adjs.* Having bark or rind.

cōrt'isone (-z-) *n.* Internal secretion of cortex of suprarenal glands, used in treatment of some diseases, e.g. rheumatoid arthritis.

corŭn'dum *n.* Crystallized native alumina (Al_2O_3), translucent mineral of the species which includes sapphire and ruby; the impure forms vary in colour from light blue to smoky grey, brown, and black, and are used as an abrasive in the form of emery. [Tamil *kurundum* ruby]

cŏ'ruscāte *v.i.* Sparkle, flash. **cŏruscā'tion** *n.*

corvée (kōrv'ā) *n.* (hist.) Day's work of unpaid labour owed by vassal to feudal lord; in France, statute labour on public road exacted of peasants before 1776.

cōrvĕtte' *n.* (orig.) Flush-decked warship with one tier of guns; in the war of 1939–45, fast naval escort vessel of 500 to 700 tons used on convoy work.

cōrv'ine *adj.* Of, akin to, raven or crow.

Cŏ'rȳbant *n.* Priest of Phrygian worship of Cybele, which was performed with noisy and extravagant dances. **Cŏrȳbăn'tic** *adj.*

Cŏ'rȳdon. Gk proper name, given by Theocritus and Virgil to a shepherd; hence, typical rustic in pastoral poetry.

cŏ'rȳmb *n.* (bot.) An inflorescence; raceme in which lower flower-stalks are longer, so that flowers form a flat or slightly convex head (ill. INFLORESCENCE).

cŏrȳphae'us (-fē-) *n.* Leader of a chorus.

cŏ'rȳphée (-fā) *n.* Leader of *corps de ballet.*

corȳz'a *n.* (path.) Catarrh of nasal mucous membrane and sinuses.

cŏs[1] *n.* ~ (*lettuce*), kind of lettuce with long leaves and tall head. [introduced from *Cos*, island in Aegean]

cŏs[2] *abbrev.* Cosine.

C.O.S. *abbrev.* Charity Organization Society.

cōsĕc'ant *n.* (abbrev. *cosec*). Secant of complement of given angle (ill. TRIGONOMETRY).

cŏsh *n.* (slang) Bludgeon, heavy-headed stick; ~*-boy*, young gangster. ~ *v.t.* Strike with cosh.

cō-sig'natory *n.* & *adj.* (Person) signing jointly with others.

cōs'ine *n.* (abbrev. *cŏs*). Sine of complement of given angle (ill. TRIGONOMETRY).

cŏsmĕt'ic (-z-) *n.* & *adj.* (Preparation) designed to beautify hair, skin, or complexion.

cŏs'mic (-z-) *adj.* Of the universe or cosmos; ~ *rays*, high-energy radiations originating in the upper atmosphere or outer space. **cŏs'mical** *adj.* **cŏs'mically** *adv.*

cŏs'mism (-z-) *n.* Conception of the cosmos as a self-existent, self-acting whole.

cŏsmŏg'ony (-z-) *n.* (Theory of) the creation of the universe. **cŏsmogŏn'ic(al)** *adjs.* **cŏsmŏg'onist** *n.*

cŏsmŏg'raphy (-z-) *n.* Description, mapping, of general features of universe or earth. **cŏsmŏg'rapher** *n.* **cŏsmogrăph'ic(al)** *adjs.*

cŏsmŏl'ogy (-z-) *n.* Study, philosophy, of the universe as an ordered whole. **cŏsmolŏ'gical** *adj.* **cosmŏl'ogist** *n.*

cŏs'monaut *n.* (esp. in Russian use) ASTRONAUT.

cŏsmopŏl'itan (-z-) *adj.* Belonging to all parts of the world; free from national limitations. ~ *n.* Citizen of the world, one without national attachments or prejudices. **cŏsmopŏl'itanism** *n.*

cŏsmŏp'olite (-z-) *n.* & *adj.* Cosmopolitan.

cŏsmopolit'ical (-z-) *adj.* Belonging to universal polity.

cŏs'mŏs[1] (-z-) *n.* The universe

as an ordered whole; ordered system of ideas etc., sum total of experience; (astron.) all stars in existence, all the galaxies.

Cŏs'mŏs[2] (-z-) *n.* Genus of composite tropical Amer. plants, cultivated for their rose, scarlet, and purple 'flowers' (inflorescences) and elegant foliage.

Cŏss'ack *n.* 1. One of those Russians who sought a free life in the steppes or on the frontiers of imperial Russia and were allowed privileges by the Tsars, including autonomy for their settlements in S. Russia (esp. Ukraine) and Siberia in return for service in protecting the frontiers; one of the descendants of these, still noted for warlike qualities and horsemanship. 2. *cossacks*, (U.S.) Troops used for suppressing strikes etc. (from similar use of Cossacks in imperial Russia). ~ *adj.* Of the Cossacks. [Turk. *quzzāq* seceder, adventurer (first used of an unrelated non-Russian nomadic people of S. Siberia, the Kazakhs)]

cŏss'ĕt *v.t.* Pet, pamper.

cŏst *n.* Price (to be) paid for thing; expenditure of time, labour, etc.; (pl.) law expenses, esp. those allowed by court etc. against losing party; *prime* ~, price at which manufacturer produces; ~ *price*, price at which merchant buys. ~ *v.i.* (past t. and past part. *cost*). 1. Be acquirable at, involve expenditure of; result in the loss of. 2. Estimate or fix cost of production; *costing clerk*, one engaged in fixing costs. **cŏst'lĕss** *adj.*

cŏs'tal *adj.* Of the ribs.

cŏs'tard *n.* Large ribbed variety of apple.

Cŏs'ta Rica (rēk'*a*). A republic of southern Central America, until 1821 part of the Span.-Amer. dominions; capital, San José.

cŏs'tate *adj.* Ribbed, having ribs.

cŏstean', -een *v.i.* (mining) Bore down to rock to find direction of lode. ~ *n.* Bore so made. [Cornish *cothas stean* dropped tin]

cŏs'ter(monger) (-mŭnggər) *n.* Man who sells fruit, fish, etc., from barrow in street (esp. in London).

cŏs'tive *adj.* Constipated. **cŏs'tively** *adv.* **cŏs'tivenĕss** *n.*

cŏst'ly *adj.* Of great value; expensive. **cŏst'linĕss** *n.*

cŏst'mary *n.* Aromatic perennial composite plant, *Chrysanthemum balsamita*, formerly used in medicine and for flavouring ale etc. [Gk *kostos* aromatic plant + (*Virgin*) *Mary*]

cŏs'tūme (*or* kŏstūm') *n.* 1. Mode or fashion of personal attire and dress of a particular nation, class, or period; ~*-piece*, *-play*, dramatic piece in which actors wear costume of some past period. 2. Complete set of outer garments. **cŏs'tūme** *v.t.* Provide with costume.

cŏstūm'ier *n.* Maker of, dealer in, costumes.

cōs'y (-z-) *adj.* Comfortable, snug. ~ *n.* Quilted covering to retain heat in teapot or boiled egg. **cōs'ily** *adv.* **cōs'inĕss** *n.*

cŏt[1] *n.* Small erection for shelter or protection; (poet.) little cottage. ~ *v.t.* Put, keep (sheep) in cot.

cŏt[2] *n.* 1. (Anglo-Ind. etc.) Light bedstead. 2. (naut.) Swinging bed suspended like hammock. 3. Child's small bed; bed in children's hospital. [f. Hind. *khaṭ* bedstead, bier]

cōtăn'gent (-j-) *n.* (abbrev. *cŏt*). Tangent of complement of given angle (ill. TRIGONOMETRY).

cōte *n.* Shed, stall, shelter, esp. for domestic animals.

cote-hardie: see COAT-HARDIE.

cōt'erie *n.* Circle, set, of persons associated by exclusive interests; select circle in society. [Fr., orig. association of country people, f. *cotier* cottar]

cōtĕrm'inous *adj.* = CONTERMINOUS. **cōtĕrm'inously** *adv.*

cothŭrn'us *n.* (pl. *-nī*). Thick-soled boot reaching to middle of leg, worn by Athenian tragic actors to increase height and impressiveness; buskin.

cotill'ion, cotillon (-lyon) *n.* Dance with elaborate series of steps and figures, with giving of favours and changes of partner. [Fr. *cotillon* petticoat]

cotōnēă'ster *n.* Genus of deciduous and evergreen shrubs or small trees with white or pinkish flowers, some with red or orange berries.

Cŏts'wold. ~ *Hills*, *Cotswolds*, range of hills in Gloucestershire, England, noted for their sheep-pastures and for a breed of long-woolled sheep, and formerly for the important woollen trade of the district.

cŏtt'age *n.* 1. Labourer's or villager's small dwelling. 2. Small country or suburban house; (U.S.) summer residence (freq. large and sumptuous). 3. ~ *hospital*, small hospital without resident medical staff; ~ *loaf*, loaf of bread of two rounded masses of dough, the smaller stuck on top of larger; ~ *piano*, small upright piano; ~ *pie*, minced meat covered with potatoes and baked in a pie-dish. **cŏtt'ager** *n.* One who lives in a cottage.

cŏtt'ar, cŏtt'er[1] *n.* 1. (Used to translate *cotarius* of Domesday Book etc.) villein who occupied cottage with attached land (usu. 5 acres), in return for labour service. 2. (Sc.) Peasant occupying cottage on farm and labouring on farm at fixed rate when required. 3. (Irish) cottier.

cŏtt'er[2] *n.* Key, wedge, bolt, for securing parts of machinery etc.; esp. split pin that opens after passing through hole; ~*-pin*, pin to keep cotter in place.

cŏtt'ier *n.* 1. Cottager. 2. Irish peasant cultivating smallholding under obsolete ~ *system*, by which small portions of land were let annually at rents fixed by public competition.

cŏtt'on[1] *n.* White downy fibrous substance clothing seeds of ~*-plant* (*Gossypium*), and used for making thread, cloth, etc.; cotton-plant; thread spun, cloth made, from cotton; *mineral* ~, metallic fibre of fine white threads formed by blowing steam through liquid slag; ~*-grass*, various species of *Eriophorum*, with heads of long white silky hairs; ~*-seed*, seed of ~*-plant*, furnishing oil and cattle-fodder; ~*-spinner*, workman who spins cotton; owner of cotton-mill; *C~ State*, popular name of Alabama; ~*-tail*, the common rabbit, *Lepus sylvaticus*, of U.S., with a white, fluffy tail; *cottonwood*, (U.S.) various species of poplar, with seeds surrounded by cotton-like substance; ~ *wool*, raw cotton, esp. as prepared for wadding etc. **cŏtt'ony** *adj.* [Arab. *qutun*]

cŏtt'on[2] *v.i.* (colloq.) Get *on* together; 'take' *to*, become drawn or attached *to*; agree, fraternize; ~ *on* (*to*), understand (idea etc.).

Cŏtt'on[3], Sir Robert Bruce (1570–1631). English antiquary, collector of coins and of the *Cottonian Library* of ancient manuscripts; this library, transferred to the nation in 1702, suffered badly in a fire at Ashburnham House in 1731, and was removed to Westminster School and in 1753 to the British Museum.

Coty (kōt'ē), René (1882–). French statesman; president of the republic 1953–8.

cŏtylēd'on *n.* 1. Primary leaf in embryo of higher plants, seed-leaf (ill. SEEDLING). 2. Genus of plants with thick succulent peltate leaves, including navelwort or pennywort, *C. umbilicus*. **cŏtylēd'onous** *adj.* Having cotyledons.

cŏt'yloid *adj.* (anat.) Cup-shaped.

couch[1] *n.* 1. Bed, thing one sleeps on; piece of furniture like sofa but with half-back and head-end only. 2. (malting) Bed or layer in which grain is laid to germinate after steeping. ~ *v.* 1. Lay one*self* down (now only in past part.). 2. (Of animals) lie, esp. in lair; crouch, cower; lie in wait. 3. (malting) Lay (grain) on floor to germinate. 4. Lower (spear) to position of attack. 5. (embroidery) Stitch thick thread on surface of material by means of fine thread (ill. STITCH). 6. Remove (cataract) by inserting needle through coats of eye and displacing the opaque crystalline lens below the axis of vision. 7. Express *in* language, words, terms, etc.

couch[2] (*or* kōō-) *n.* (Usu. ~*-grass*) species of grass, *Agropyron repens*, with long creeping underground stems, a common and troublesome weed in cornfields etc. [variant of QUITCH]

couch'ant *adj.* (her., of animals)

Lying with body resting on legs and head lifted (ill. HERALDRY).

Coué (kōō′ā), Émile (1857–1926). French psychologist, advocate of a system of sanguine autosuggestion. **Cou′éism** *n.*

coug′ar (kōō-) *n.* Puma, large Amer. feline quadruped, *Felis concolor.* [Brazilian wd]

cough (kŏf) *v.* Expel air from lungs with violent effort and characteristic noise produced by abrupt opening of glottis, in order to remove obstruction or relieve irritation in air-passages; ~ *down,* silence (speaker) by coughing; ~ *out, up,* eject by, say with, cough; ~ *up,* (slang) bring out, produce (esp. money). ~ *n.* Act of coughing; tendency to cough; condition of respiratory organs resulting in coughing.

coulisse (kōōlēs′) *n.* 1. Side-scene in theatre (ill. THEATRE); space between two of these. 2. Groove in which sluice-gate moves.

couloir (kōōl′wahr) *n.* Steep gully on mountain side (ill. MOUNTAIN). [Fr., = 'strainer']

Coulomb[1] (kōōlawn′), Charles Augustin de (1736–1806). French physicist, inventor of method of measuring the quantity of electricity.

coulomb[2] (kōōlŏm′) *n.* Quantity of electricity conveyed in 1 second by current of 1 ampere. [f. COULOMB[1]]

coul′ter (kōl-) *n.* Iron blade fixed in front of share in plough (ill. PLOUGH).

coum′arin (kōō-) *n.* Aromatic crystalline substance found in tonka bean, woodruff, etc., and used as a perfume. [*cumaru,* native name in Guiana of tonka bean]

coun′cil *n.* 1. Ecclesiastical assembly for regulating doctrine or discipline in church; (N.T.) Jewish Sanhedrim. 2. Advisory or deliberative assembly. 3. Body of men chosen or designated as permanent advisers on matters of state, esp. to advise and assist sovereign etc. (see PRIVY Council); (Sc. hist.) Scottish Privy Council, sitting as *Lords of* ~, for judicial business during vacation of Parliament; (in British Crown colonies and dependencies) body assisting governor in executive or legislative council. 4. Local administrative body of corporate town or city, or (since 1888) of English administrative county or district. 5. *C~ of war,* assembly of military or naval officers called to consult with general etc., usu. in special emergency (freq. fig.). 6. *~-man,* member of town or city council in U.S. or City of London; *~-school,* (free) school supported by town or county council. **coun′cillor.** Official member of a council. **coun′cillorship** *n.*

Council of Trent: see TRENT[2].

coun′sel *n.* 1. Consultation; advice; ~ *of perfection,* one of the advisory declarations (in medieval theology reckoned as twelve) of Christ and the Apostles, not considered universally binding but as a means of attaining greater moral perfection; *keep one's (own)* ~, be reticent about one's intention or opinions. 2. Body of legal advisers in cause; legal adviser, barrister; *King's (Queen's) C~,* barrister(s) appointed (on nomination of Lord Chancellor) as counsel to Crown, taking precedence of ordinary barristers and wearing silk instead of stuff gown. ~ *v.t.* Advise; recommend. **coun′sellor** *n.* Adviser; (also *~-at-law*), barrister, counsel (now only in Ireland); rank given to heads of Departments in Foreign Office, also at larger Embassies abroad, e.g. *C~ (Commercial)* and *C~ (Information)*; in some States of U.S., attorney admitted to practise in all courts.

count[1] *v.* 1. Enumerate, reckon (*up*); repeat numerals in order; include, be included, in reckoning. 2. ~ *out,* count while taking from a stock; bring sitting of (House of Commons) to a close on counting number of members present and finding it less than 40; declare (boxer) to have lost contest by counting 10 seconds before he rises to resume fight; leave out of count or consideration; (children's games) count players with words of formula, the last at each turn being reckoned out of the game. 3. Esteem, account, consider; be reckoned; enter into account or reckoning; ~ *on, upon,* depend or rely on, expect with assurance. ~ *n.* 1. Counting; reckoning; sum total. 2. (boxing) Counting of 10 seconds (time allowed for fallen boxer to rise and resume fighting or be declared loser). 3. (textiles) Number indicating the fineness of yarn, usu. based on the length of yarn which amounts to a given weight. 4. (law) Each charge in an indictment.

count[2] *n.* Foreign title of nobility, corresp. to English *earl*; ~ *palatine*: see PALATINE.

coun′tenance *n.* Expression of face; face; composure; moral support. ~ *v.t.* Sanction; encourage.

coun′ter[1] *n.* 1. Small usu. round piece of metal, ivory, etc., used for keeping account in games of chance, esp. cards; imitation coin. 2. Banker's or money-changer's table; table in shop on which money is counted out and across which goods are delivered; *~-jumper,* (colloq.) shop assistant.

coun′ter[2] *n.* 1. Part of horse's breast between shoulders and under neck. 2. (naut.) Curved part of stern of ship. 3. Depressed part of face of printing type, coin, or medal (ill. TYPE); (also *~-punch*) die used in making counter of type to be engraved on punch. 4. (also *~-rocker, ~-rocking turn*) In skating, rocking-turn with body revolving away from concave of first curve.

coun′ter[3] *n.* 1. (fencing) Circular parry, parry in which hand retains same position while point describes circle. 2. (boxing) Blow delivered as adversary leads off.

coun′ter[4] *n.* (shoemaking) Stiff leather forming back part of shoe or boot round heel.

coun′ter[5] *adj.* Opposed; opposite; duplicate; *~-rocker* etc.: see COUNTER[2]. ~ *adv.* In the opposite direction; contrary.

coun′ter[6] *v.* Oppose, encounter, contradict, controvert; (chess) meet with counter move; (boxing) give return blow while parrying opponent's blow.

counter- *prefix.* Of verbs, nouns, adjectives, adverbs, with sense of: 1. Reciprocation, opposition; frustration, rivalry. 2. Opposite position or direction. 3. Correspondence, match. 4. Duplicate, substitute.

counterăct′ *v.t.* Hinder, defeat, by contrary action; neutralize. **counterăc′tion** *n.* **counterăc′tive** *adj.*

counter-ā′gent *n.* Counteracting agent or force.

coun′ter-approach′ *n.* (mil.) Work constructed by besieged outside permanent fortifications to check besiegers.

coun′ter-attrăc′tion *n.* Attraction of contrary tendency; rival attraction.

coun′terbălance *n.* Weight balancing another. ~ *v.t.* Act as counterbalance to.

coun′terblast (-ah-) *n.* Energetic declaration against something.

coun′tercharge *n.* Charge in opposition to another, or against accuser. ~ *v.t.* Bring countercharge against.

coun′ter-claim *n.* Claim set up against another; claim by defendant in suit. ~ *v.* Claim against plaintiff or prior claim.

coun′ter-ĕs′pionage (*or* -ahzh′) *n.* Spying directed against the enemy's spy system.

coun′terfeit (-fĭt, -fēt) *adj.* & *n.* (Thing) made in imitation, not genuine. ~ *v.t.* Imitate; forge; simulate; resemble closely. **coun′terfeiter** *n.* One who counterfeits, esp. coins, bank-notes.

coun′terfoil *n.* Complementary part of bank cheque, receipt, etc., with note of particulars, retained by drawer.

coun′terfort *n.* Buttress supporting wall or terrace.

counter-ĭ′rritant *n.* (med.) Thing used to produce surface irritation and thus counteract symptoms of disease (also fig.). **counter-ĭ′rritāte** *v.t.* **counter-ĭrritā′tion** *n.*

countermand′ (-ah-) *v.t.* Revoke (command); recall by contrary order; cancel order for. ~ *n.* Order revoking previous one.

coun′termarch *n.* & *v.* (Cause to) march in contrary direction.

coun′termark *n.* Additional mark on bale of goods belonging to several merchants etc.; hall-mark.

coun'termīne *n.* (mil.) Mine made to intercept that of besiegers etc.; submarine mine sunk to explode enemy's mines by its explosion; (fig.) counterplot. ~ *v.* Oppose by countermine; make a countermine.

coun'ter-move (-mōōv) *n.* Move in opposition, contrary move. **coun'ter-movement** *n.*

coun'termūre *n.* Wall within or behind another as additional or reserve defence.

coun'terpane (-ĭn, -ān) *n.* Outer covering of bed, coverlet, quilt.

coun'terpart *n.* Duplicate; person, thing, forming natural complement to another; opposite part of indenture.

coun'terplŏt *n.* Plot contrived to defeat another. ~ *v.* Frustrate by counterplot; devise counterplot.

coun'terpoint *n.* (mus.) Melody added as accompaniment to given melody or plain-song; art of adding one or more melodies as accompaniment to given melody according to certain fixed rules; this style of composition; *double, triple* ~, invertible counterpoint in which melodies may be changed in position above or below one another.

coun'terpoise (-z) *n.* Counterbalancing weight; thing of equivalent force etc. on opposite side; equilibrium. ~ *v.t.* Counterbalance; compensate; bring into, keep in, equilibrium.

coun'ter-rĕformā'tion *n.* Reformation running counter to another; *the C~-R~*, (hist.) reformation in the Church of Rome during the latter part of the 16th c. following on the Protestant Reformation; initiated by the Council of TRENT[2] and largely accomplished by the JESUITS.

coun'ter-rĕvolū'tion *n.* Revolution reversing results of previous revolution. **counter-rĕvolū'tionary** *adj.*

coun'terscarp *n.* (fortif.) Outer wall or slope of ditch, supporting covered way.

coun'tersign[1] (-īn) *n.* Watchword, password, given to man on guard.

countersign'[2] (-īn) *v.t.* Add signature to (document already signed); ratify.

countersink' *v.t.* Bevel off (top of hole) to receive head of screw or bolt; sink (screw-head) in such hole, so as to lie flush with surface.

counter-tĕn'or *n.* (mus.) (Part for, singer with) male voice of tenor quality but alto range.

countervail' *v.t.* Counterbalance; avail against; *countervailing duty*, one put on bounty-fed imports to give home goods an equal chance.

coun'terwork (-ērk) *n.* (mil.) Work raised in opposition to those of enemy; opposing work. ~ *v.* Counteract, frustrate; work in opposition.

coun'tĕss *n.* Wife, widow, of count or earl; lady ranking with count or earl in her own right.

coun'ting-house *n.* Building, room, devoted to keeping accounts; office.

count'lĕss *adj.* Too many to count.

coun'trified (kŭn-, -īd) *adj.* Rural, rustic.

coun'try (kŭn-) *n.* 1. Region; territory of nation; land of person's birth, citizenship, etc., fatherland. 2. Rural districts as opp. to towns; rest of a land as opp. to capital; ~ *club*, (orig. U.S.) club in country surroundings; ~ *cousin*, relation of countrified manners or appearance; ~ *dance*, rural or native dance, traditional dance, folk-dance; ~ *gentleman*, gentleman with landed property in country; ~ *house*, house in country, esp. residence of country gentleman; ~*-seat*, residence of country gentleman; ~*-side*, particular rural district, its inhabitants.

coun'tryman (kŭn-), **-woman** *ns.* 1. Man, woman, of one's own (or a specified) country. 2. Person living in rural parts.

coun'ty *n.* 1. Territorial division of Gt Britain and Ireland; shire; CORPORATE county. 2. Political and administrative division of British colony or dominion, of States of U.S., etc. 3. (Engl. hist.) Periodical meeting under sheriff for transacting business of shire. 4. People of county; esp. county gentry. 5. ~ *borough*, see BOROUGH; ~ *council*, representative governing body of administrative county; ~ *court*, local judicial court, in England for civil actions, chiefly recovery of small debts; in U.S. also for criminal cases; ~ *family*, family of nobility or gentry with seat in county; ~ *palatine*, see PALATINE; ~ *seat* (U.S.), ~ *town*, town which was formerly (but is not necessarily now) the seat of administration of a county: see Appendix VIII.

coup (kōō) *n.* Notable or successful stroke or move; (billiards) holing ball without its striking another; ~ *d'état* (dătah'), sudden and decisive stroke of State policy, esp. violent or illegal change of government by ruling power; ~ *de grâce* (grahs), finishing stroke; ~ *de théâtre* (tāah'tr), dramatically sudden or sensational act or turn.

coupé (kōōp'ā) *n.* 4-wheeled closed carriage with inside seat for 2 and outside seat for driver; end-compartment in railway carriage with seat(s) on one side only; closed 2-seater motor-car.

cou'ple (kŭ-) *n.* 1. Leash for holding two hounds together. 2. Pair, brace, esp. of hunting dogs; wedded or engaged pair; pair of partners in dance; two. 3. One of pair of inclined roof-rafters, meeting at top. 4. (dynamics) Pair of equal and parallel forces acting in opposite directions. ~ *v.* Fasten, link, together (esp. dogs in pairs); connect (railway carriages) by a coupling; unite, bring together; associate in thought or speech; unite sexually. **coup'ler** *n.* (esp.) Contrivance in organ for connecting two manuals, manual with pedals, or two keys an octave apart, so that both can be played by a single motion.

coup'lĕt (kŭ-) *n.* 1. Pair of successive lines of verse, esp. when rhyming together and of same length. 2. (mus.) Two equal notes made to occupy the time of three.

coup'ling (kŭ-) *n.* (esp.) Chain or link connecting two railway carriages etc.; ~ *rod*, rod coupling wheels of locomotive engine (ill. LOCOMOTIVE).

coup'on (kōō-) *n.* Detachable ticket, one of a series entitling holder to periodical payments of interest, services of excursion agency, share of rationed food, etc.; advertiser's token or detachable form to be filled in and forwarded in exchange or part exchange for goods; (politics) party leader's recognition of parliamentary candidate as deserving election.

courage (kŭ'rĭj) *n.* Bravery, boldness.

courāgeous (kurāj'us) *adj.* Brave, fearless. **courā'geously** *adv.* **courā'geousnĕss** *n.*

courante' (kōōrahnt) *n.* Obsolete running dance; (mus.) part of suite, in triple time, usu. following allemande.

cou'rier (kōō-) *n.* 1. Servant employed to make travelling arrangements, esp. on Continent; official of travel agency with similar duties. 2. Official who carries documents, messenger. 3. Title of some newspapers.

course (kōrs) *n.* 1. Onward movement; line or direction taken; career; habitual or ordinary manner of procedure. 2. Pursuit of game, esp. of hares with (grey)-hounds. 3. Ground on which race is run etc.; golf links; line to be taken in race. 4. Channel in which water flows, watercourse. 5. Planned or prescribed series of actions or proceedings, as of lectures, study, diet, etc.; (bell-ringing) successive shifting of order in which bell is struck in series of changes, series of changes in which bells return to former order. 6. Each of successive divisions of meal, consisting of one dish or several. 7. (building) Single continuous layer of bricks, stones, etc., of same height throughout (ill. BRICK); row of slates, tiles, etc. 8. (naut.) Sail attached to lower yards of ship (usu. only fore- and main-sail; ill. SHIP). 9. *of* ~, naturally; *in due* ~, in the natural order; *in the* ~ *of*, during. ~ *v.* Pursue (game) with hounds, esp. hunt (hares) with greyhounds in view (not by scent); run about, run; give (horse) a run; use (hounds) in coursing. **cours'er** *n.* (poet.) Swift horse.

court (kōrt) *n.* 1. Space enclosed by walls or buildings; (Camb.

Univ.) college quadrangle; confined yard opening off street; enclosed quadrangle, open or covered, for games; plot of ground marked off for lawn tennis. 2. Sovereign's residence; his establishment and retinue; the body of courtiers; sovereign and his councillors as ruling power; *C ~ of St. James's*, court of British sovereign. 3. Formal assembly held by sovereign at his residence. 4. Assembly of Parliament (*High C~ of Parliament*); assembly of judges or other persons acting as tribunal to hear and determine any cause; place in which justice is administered; session of judicial assembly. 5. (Meeting of) qualified members of company or corporation; (in some friendly societies) lodge. 6. Attention paid to one whose favour, affection, or interest is sought. 7. *~-baron*, court for freehold tenants of manor, held before lord or his steward; *~-card* (orig. *coat-card*), playing-card bearing picture of king, queen, or knave; *~ circular*, daily report of doings of royal court published in newspapers; *~ cupboard*, massive deep food-cupboard of type made in 16th and 17th centuries

COURT CUPBOARD

with smaller recessed cupboards above it and cornice at top *~ hand*, style of hand-writing used in English law-courts from 16th c. until abolished by statute under George II (ill. SCRIPT); *~-house*, building in which courts of law are held; (southern U.S.) seat of government of a county; *~* LEET, *~ of* RECORD: see these words; *~ martial* (pl. *~s martial*), trial of soldier, sailor, or airman of any rank, conducted by officers, for offences against military law; *~-martial* (*v.t.*) try by court-martial; *~-plaster*, sticking-plaster of silk coated with isinglass formerly used for making face-patches by ladies at court; *~ shoe*, woman's light shoe with low-cut upper and high or highish tapering or curved heel (ill. SHOE); *court'-yard*, open space surrounded by walls or buildings. *~ v.t.* Pay court to; make love to; entice; seek to win (applause etc.); invite (inquiry etc.).

court'ėous (kẽr-, kŏr-) *adj.* Polite, kind, considerate, in manner or address. **court'ėously** *adv.* **court'ėousnėss** *n.*

courtėsan, -zan (kŏrtĭzăn') *n.* Prostitute. [It. *cortigiana*, orig. woman attached to the court]

court'ėsy (kẽr-, kŏr-) *n.* Courteous behaviour or disposition; *by ~*, by favour, not of right; *~ title*, title of no legal validity given by courtesy, esp. that given to eldest son of earl, daughter, or younger son of duke or marquis.

court'ier (kŏr-) *n.* Attendant at, frequenter of, sovereign's court.

court'ly (kŏr-) *adj.* Polished, refined, in manners; obsequious, flattering. **court'linėss** *n.*

Court of International Justice. Court of justice, first provided for in the Covenant of the League of Nations, with its seat at The Hague and having limited jurisdiction in disputes between member-states of the LEAGUE OF NATIONS (or, now, UNITED NATIONS) voluntarily submitted to it.

court'ship (kŏr-) *n.* Courting, wooing, with view to marriage.

couscous (kōōs'kōōs) *n.* N. Afr. dish of granulated flour; sometimes with meat, steamed over broth. [Arab. *kuskus*, f. *kaskasa* bruise, pound small]

cousin (kŭz'n) *n.* Child of one's uncle or aunt (also *first ~*, *~ german*); *second ~*, one's parent's first cousin's child. **cous'inhood, cous'inship** *ns.* **cous'inly** *adj.*

coûte que coûte (kōōt ke kōōt) *adv.* At all costs.

couvade (kōōvahd') *n.* Primitive people's custom by which husband feigns illness when his wife is in childbed.

cōve[1] *n.* Small bay or creek; sheltered recess; (archit.) concave arch, curved junction of wall with ceiling or floor. *~ v.t.* Arch (esp. ceiling at junction with wall); slope (sides of fire-place) inwards.

cōve[2] *n.* (slang) Fellow, chap.

co'ven (kŭ-) *n.* (Sc.) Assembly of witches.

cov'ėnant (kŭ-) *n.* Compact, bargain; (law) contract under seal, clause of this; (bibl.) compact between God and the Israelites; *C~ of the League of Nations*, document constituting the LEAGUE OF NATIONS, incorporated in Treaty of Versailles and other treaties concluding war of 1914–18; (*National*) *Covenant*, protestation signed throughout Scotland in 1638, in which subscribers swore to defend the Protestant religion and to resist all contrary errors; *Solemn League and C~*, (Sc. hist.) bond of agreement between England and Scotland to establish Presbyterianism in both countries, accepted by General Assembly of Church of Scotland in Aug., and by Westminster Assembly of Divines and English Parliament in Sept. 1643. *~ v.* Make covenant with. **cov'ėnanted** *adj.* Bound by a covenant.

cov'ėnanter (Sc. pr. -năn'ter) *n.* One who covenants, esp. (Sc. hist.) adherent of National Covenant of 1638 or of Solemn League and Covenant.

Cŏv'ent Gar'd'en. District of central London, formerly the convent garden of Westminster; site of a fruit and vegetable market, and of the principal English opera-house, opened 1858.

Cŏv'entry (*or* cŭv-). County borough and city in Warwickshire, England; *send (person) to ~*, refuse to associate with or speak to him.

cov'er (kŭ-) *v.t.* 1. Overspread, overlay, (*with*); strew thoroughly (*with*); lie over, be a covering to; extend over, occupy surface of; protect; conceal, screen; *~ (with gun, pistol*, etc.), aim directly at. 2. (mil.) Stand directly behind; (cricket) stand behind (another fielder) so as to stop balls he misses. 3. Include, comprise; get over (ground); be sufficient to defray or meet (expense, loss, etc.); protect by insurance, etc.; (orig. U.S.) report for newspaper. 4. (Of stallion etc.) copulate with. 5. *~-point*, (cricket) fielder behind and a little to bowler's side of point; his position (ill. CRICKET); *covered wagon*, (U.S.) wagon with a tilt, used in travelling; *covering*, (esp.) what covers, a cover; *covering letter*, one sent along with another document to explain it. *~ n.* 1. Thing that covers; lid; binding of book, either board of this; wrapper, envelope, of letter; outer case of pneumatic tyre. 2. Protection from attack; force of aircraft detailed to protect land or sea operation. 3. Hiding-place, shelter; screen, pretence. 4. Woods or undergrowth sheltering game, covert. 5. (commerc.) Funds to meet liability or secure against contingent loss. 6. Plate, napkin, knives and forks, etc., laid for each person at table. 7. = cover-point.

Cŏv'erdāle, Miles (1488–1568). English bishop; translated at Antwerp the Bible and Apocrypha from German and Latin versions; superintended the printing of the 'Great Bible' of 1539.

cov'erlėt, (rare) **cov'erlid,** (kŭ-) *ns.* Counterpane, quilt; covering.

covert[1] (kŭv'*ert*, *-er*) *n.* 1. Shelter, esp. thicket hiding game; *~ coat*, short light overcoat for shooting, riding, etc.; *~ coating*, (usu. waterproof) material for this. 2. (pl.) Feathers covering the bases of a bird's wing and tail feathers (ill. BIRD).

cov'ert[2] (kŭ-), *adj.* Concealed, hidden, secret, disguised. **cov'ertly** *adv.*

cov'erture (kŭ-) *n.* Covering, cover; shelter; condition of married woman under husband's protection.

cov'ėt (kŭ-) *v.t.* Desire eagerly (usu. what belongs to another). **cov'ėtable** *adj.*

cov'ėtous (kŭ-) *adj.* Eagerly desirous (*of*); grasping, avaricious. **cov'ėtously** *adv.* **cov'ėtousnėss** *n.*

cov′ey (kŭ-) *n.* Brood of partridges; family, party, set.

cov′in (kŭ-) *n.* (law) Conspiracy, collusion; (archaic) fraud, deceit, trickery.

cōv′ing *n.* Arched piece of building; (pl.) curved sides of fireplace.

cow[1] *n.* Female of any bovine animal, esp. of the domestic species (*Bos taurus*); female of elephant, rhinoceros, whale, seal, etc.; *cow′boy,* (U.S.) man in charge of grazing cattle on ranch; *~-catcher,* (U.S.) frame fixed in front of locomotive engine etc. to remove cattle and other obstructions; *~-fish,* manatee, sea-cow; fish, *Ostracion quadricorne,* of Indian and Amer. seas, with horn-like spines over eyes; *~-heel,* (dish of) foot of cow or ox stewed to jelly; *cow′herd,* one who tends cows at pasture; *~-hide*(leather, whip, made of) cow's hide; *~-parsley,* umbelliferous plant (wild in Britain), *Anthriscus sylvestris*; *~-parsnip,* large umbelliferous plant (wild in Britain), *Heracleum sphondylium*; *~-pox,* vaccine disease appearing as bluish or livid vesicles on teats of cows; communication of this by vaccination to human subject gives complete or partial immunity from smallpox; *~-puncher,* (U.S. slang) cowboy; *~-shot,* (cricket slang) violent pull made leaning forward on one knee; *~-tree,* S. Amer. tree, *Brosimum galactodendron,* with milk-like juice used as food.

cow[2] *v.t.* Intimidate.

cow′age, cow′itch *n.* Stinging hairs of pod of tropical leguminous plant, *Mucuna pruriens*; the plant or its pods. [perversion of Hind. *kawānch*]

cow′ard *adj.* & *n.* Faint-hearted, pusillanimous (person). **cow′ardly** *adj.* **cowardli′nėss** *n.* [OF *coard,* f. L *cauda* tail]

cow′ardice *n.* Faint-heartedness; *moral ~,* ignoble fear of disapprobation.

cow′er *v.i.* Stand or squat in bent position; crouch, esp. from fear.

cowitch: see COWAGE.

cowl *n.* 1. Monk's hooded garment; hood of this. 2. Hood-shaped covering (freq. turning with wind) of top of chimney or ventilating shaft to assist ventilation (ill. CHIMNEY). **cowled** (-ld) *adj.*

cowl′ing *n.* Covering over or round aeroplane engine.

Cow′per (kōō-), William (1731–1800). English lyric poet and hymn writer.

cowr′ie, cowry *n.* Porcelain-like shell of small gastropod, *Cypraea maneta,* of Indian Ocean, used as money in parts of Africa and southern Asia; the animal itself, or any gastropod (or shell) of the genus, of oval shape, with undeveloped spine and narrow aperture as long as shell. [Hind. *kauri*]

cow′slip *n.* Wild plant, *Primula veris,* growing in pastures etc. and flowering in spring, with drooping umbels of fragrant yellow flowers; *~ tea, wine,* infusion, wine, made from cowslip flowers.

cŏx *n.* Abbrev. of COXSWAIN.

cŏx′a *n.* (pl. *-ae*). Hip (ill. INSECT). **cŏx′al** *adj.*

cŏx′cōmb (-m) *n.* Conceited showy person. **cŏxcōmb′ical** (-mĭ-) *adj.* **cŏx′combry** (-mrĭ) *n.* Foppery, behaviour of a coxcomb. [= *cock's comb*]

coxswain (kŏk′sn, kŏk′swān) *n.* Helmsman of boat; person on board ship permanently in charge of ship's boat and crew. **cŏx′swainlėss** *adj.* [f. *cock* = cockboat + *swain*]

coy[1] *adj.* Shy, (provocatively) modest. **coy′ly** *adv.* **coy′nėss** *n.*

Coy[2] *abbrev.* (mil.) Company.

coyōt′ė (ko-, *also* -ōt) *n.* Prairie-wolf, *Canis latrans,* of western N. America. [Mex. *coyotl*]

coyp′u (-ōō) *n.* S. Amer. aquatic rodent, *Myocastor coypus,* of about size of beaver, with valuable fur called nutria. [S. Amer. name]

coz (kŭ-) *n.* (archaic) Abbrev. of COUSIN.

coz′en (kŭ-) *v.t.* Cheat, defraud, (*of, out of*); beguile (*into*). **coz′enage** *n.*

cp. *abbrev.* Compare.

c.p. *abbrev.* Candle-power.

Cpl *abbrev.* Corporal.

C.P.O. *abbrev.* Chief Petty Officer.

C.P.R. *abbrev.* Canadian Pacific Railway.

C.P.R.E. *abbrev.* Council for the Preservation of Rural England.

C.Q.M.S. *abbrev.* Company Quartermaster-Sergeant.

CQR. Name of a type of stockless anchor with a base like a ploughshare instead of flukes (ill. ANCHOR).

Cr. *abbrev.* Creditor.

C.R.A., C.R.E. *abbrevs.* Commander Royal Artillery, Royal Engineers.

crăb[1] *n.* 1. Various decapod crustaceans, mostly of the tribe *Brachyura,* with abdomen short and bent under thorax, the first legs being pincers; esp. the edible species found on or near sea-coasts (the common European edible crab is *Cancer pagurus,* the U.S. edible or *blue ~* is *Callinectes hastatus*). 2. The zodiacal constellation Cancer (the Crab), between Gemini and Leo; the 4th division of the zodiac, orig. coinciding with the constellation. 3. Machine (orig. with claws) for hoisting heavy weights. 4. (pl.) Lowest throw at hazard, two aces. 5. (rowing) *Catch a ~,* make faulty stroke by which oar-blade becomes jammed under water and handle sometimes sweeps rower off his seat. 6. *~-louse,* parasitical insect, *Pediculus pubis,* infesting human body; *~'s-eyes,* round concretion of carbonate of lime found in stomach of crayfish etc.

crăb[2] *n.* (also *~-apple*) The wild apple, *Malus sylvestris,* or a cultivated variety having similar sour, harsh, astringent quality; *Siberian ~,* the cultivated *Malus baccata.*

crăb[3] *v.* 1. (of hawks) Scratch, claw, fight (with each other). 2. (colloq.) Criticize adversely; interfere with.

crăbb′ėd *adj.* Cross-grained, perverse; churlish, irritable; sour, morose, harsh; difficult to unravel, deal with, make sense of; (of handwriting) ill-formed and hard to decipher. **crăbb′ėdly** *adv.* **crabb′ėdnėss** *n.*

crăck *v.* 1. (Cause to) make sharp or explosive noise; utter (joke). 2. *~ up,* praise, eulogize. 3. Break with sudden sharp report; break without complete separation of parts; come to pieces, collapse, break down; *~ a bottle,* empty, drink, a bottle; *~ a crib,* (slang) break into a house. 4. Render (voice), dissonant, (of voice) become so. 5. Damage, ruin. 6. *Cracked,* (colloq.) crazy, insane. 7. Split up (oil etc.) by heat and catalysts to produce lighter hydrocarbons (as petrol). 8. *~-brained,* crazy; *~-jaw,* (of words) difficult to pronounce. *~ n.* 1. Sudden sharp noise, as of whip, rifle, thunder; sharp blow. 2. Fissure formed by breakage; partial fracture (the parts still cohering). 3. (slang) Brisk talk, chat. 4. (slang, orig. U.S.) Sharp, cutting, or witty remark. 5. Fine player, horse, etc. *~ adj.* (colloq.) First-rate.

crăck′er *n.* Thing, person, that cracks; esp., 1. Kind of firework exploding with sharp report(s); small paper cylinder containing sweets toy, paper cap, or the like, and a fulminant exploding sharply when pulled at both ends. 2. Instrument for cracking, esp. (pl.) nut-crackers. 3. Thin crisp biscuit; (U.S.) biscuit. 4. (southern U.S.) A 'poor white', esp. in Georgia and Florida.

crăck′erjăck *n.* & *adj.* (U.S. slang) Exceptionally fine or splendid (person or thing).

crăc′kle *v.i.* Emit slight continuous cracking sound. *~ n.* 1. Crackling. 2. China-ware with minute cracks all over surface. **crăck′ly** *adj.*

crăck′ling *n.* (esp.) Crisp skin of roast pork.

crăc′knel *n.* Light crisp very dry biscuit of curved or hollowed shape.

crăcks′man *n.* Housebreaker, burglar.

crădge *v.* Shore up (river bank) with soil-filled bags. *~ n.* Bag so used.

crā′dle *n.* 1. Bed, cot, for infant, esp. one on rockers; (fig.) place in which thing is nurtured in earliest stage. 2. Framework resembling cradle, esp. stage suspended from scaffolding for workmen; framework on which ship rests during construction or repairs; light wooden frame attached to scythe to lay corn evenly; protective or supporting framework for injured limb etc.; (mining) trough on rockers in which auriferous earth is shaken in water, to separate the gold; serrated tool (ROCKER) used in mezzotint engraving (ill. ENGRAVE). ~ *v.t.* Place in cradle; contain or shelter as cradle; mow (corn) with scythe fitted with cradle.

crā′dlĭng *n.* (esp. archit.) Wooden or iron or other framework.

craft (-ah-) *n.* 1. Skill; cunning, deceit. 2. Art, trade; members of a craft; *the* ~, the brotherhood of Freemasons. 3. Boat, vessel (pl. ~). **crafts′man** *n.* One who practises a handicraft. **crafts′manshĭp** *n.*

craf′ty (-ah-) *adj.* Cunning, artful, wily. **craft′ĭly** *adv.* **craft′ĭnĕss** *n.*

crăg *n.* 1. Steep or precipitous rugged rock. 2. *C*~, deposit of shelly sand found in Norfolk, Suffolk, and Essex, and used for manure; the pliocene and miocene strata to which these deposits belong. **crăgg′y** *adj.* **crăgs′man** *n.* Skilled climber of crags.

crāke *n.* Corn-crake, or other bird of the same family; corn-crake's cry.

crăm *v.* 1. Fill overfull; force (*into, down*); stuff (*with* food); eat greedily; ~-*full*, as full as cramming can make it. 2. Prepare for examination; learn, get *up*, (subject) for special purpose. ~ *n.* 1. Cramming for examination. 2. (slang) Lie.

crăm′bō *n.* Game in which one player gives word or line of verse to which each of others must find rhyme; *dumb*~, game in which one side announces word rhyming with chosen word, which other side tries to guess by acting one word after another in dumb show. [prob. f. L *crambe repetita* cabbage served up again]

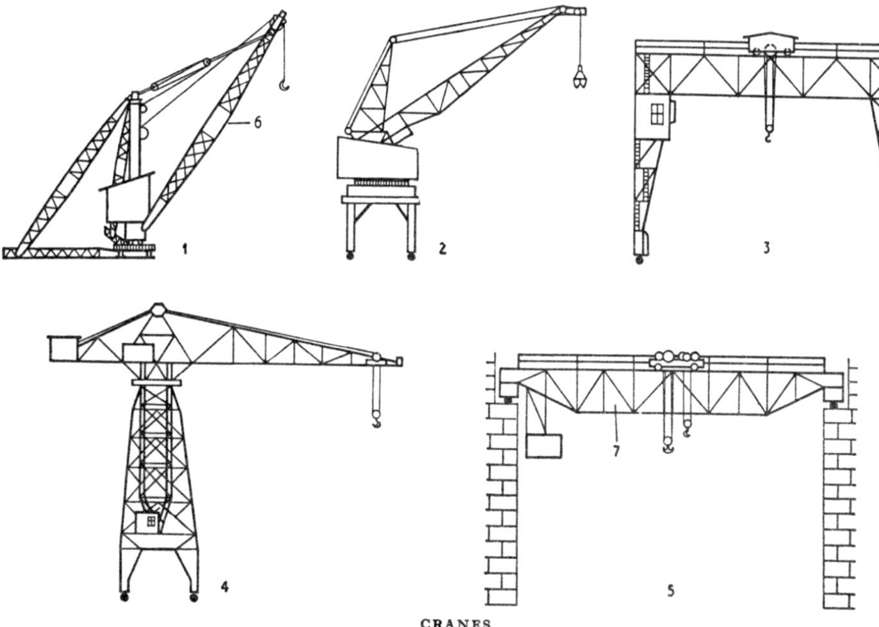

CRANES

1. Derrick. 2. Wharf crane. 3. 'Goliath' crane. 4. Tower crane. 5. Overhead travelling crane. 6. Jib. 7. Gantry

crămm′er *n.* (esp.) 1. One who crams pupils for examination. 2. (slang) Lie.

crămp[1] *n.* Sudden painful involuntary contraction of muscles from chill, slight strain, etc. ~ *v.t.* 1. Affect with cramp. 2. Confine narrowly; restrict.

crămp[2] *n.* Metal bar with bent ends for holding masonry etc. together; portable tool for pressing two planks etc. together for joining; restraint. ~ *v.t.* Fasten with cramp.

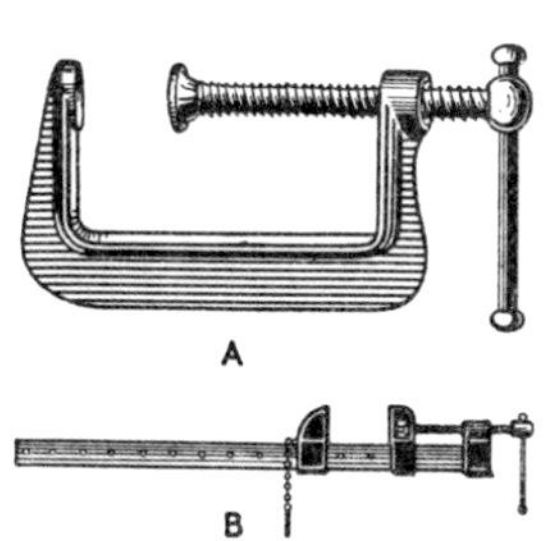

A. CARPENTER'S CRAMP. B. SASH CRAMP

crăm′pon *n.* Metal hook, grappling-iron; iron plate set with spikes for climbing over ice etc.

BOOT WITH CRAMPON

crăn *n.* (Sc.) Measure for fresh herrings (37½ gal., or about 750 fish).

crān′age *n.* Use of crane, dues paid for this.

crăn′berry *n.* Small dark-red acid berry, fruit of dwarf shrub, *Oxycoccus palustris*, growing in turfy bogs in Britain, N. Europe, Siberia, and N. America; the similar but larger fruit of *O. macrocarpus*, native of N. America.

crāne *n.* 1. Large wading-bird with very long legs, neck, and bill, esp. the ashy-grey common European crane, *Grus cinerea*, formerly common in Gt Britain but now extinct. 2. Machine for raising and lowering heavy weights, usu. post rotating on vertical axis with projecting arm or 'jib' over the end of which runs a chain or rope from which the weight may be suspended; overhanging tube for supplying water to locomotive. 3. Bent tube for drawing liquor out of vessel, siphon. 4. ~-*fly*, two-winged long-legged fly of genus *Tipula*, daddy-long-legs; *crane's-bill*, various species of wild geranium (from the long slender beak of the fruit). ~ *v.* Stretch (neck), stretch neck like crane; (colloq., of horse) pull up at obstacle and look over before leaping.

crān'ĭal *adj.* Of the cranium; ~ *index*, ratio of width of skull to its length; ~ *nerves*, 12 pairs of nerves attached to brain and serving regions of head and neck.

crān'ĭum *n.* Bones enclosing brain; less strictly, bones of whole head, skull.

crănk[1] *n.* Part of axis bent at right angles for converting reciprocal into circular motion, or vice versa; ~-*case*, case covering crank-shaft of motor engine; ~-*shaft*, shaft driven by crank (ill. COMBUSTION); ~-*wheel*, wheel acting as crank, esp. one to which connecting rod is attached near circumference. ~ *v.* 1. Bend in shape of crank; attach crank to. 2. ~ (*up*), start (motor engine) by turning crank or starting-handle.

crănk[2] *n.* 1. Fanciful turn of speech; eccentric idea or act. 2. Eccentric person, esp. one enthusiastically possessed by a crotchet or hobby.

crănk[3] *adj.* Weak, shaky (usu. of machinery).

crănk[4] *adj.* (naut.) Liable to capsize.

crănk'y *adj.* Sickly; shaky, crazy; capricious; crotchety, eccentric; full of twists; (naut.) crank.

Crăn'mer, Thomas (1489–1556. Archbishop of Canterbury; propounded views in favour of the divorce of Henry VIII from Catherine of Aragon and maintained the king's claim to be the supreme head of the Church of England; supervised the production of the first prayer-book of Edward VI, 1549, and promulgated in 1552 the 42 articles of religion (afterwards reduced to 39); was condemned for heresy in Queen Mary's reign and burned at the stake at Oxford.

crănn'og *n.* Ancient lake-dwelling in Scotland or Ireland.

crănn'y *n.* Chink, crevice, crack. **crănn'ĭed** (-ĭd) *adj.*

crāpe *n.* Black silk or imitation silk fabric with wrinkled surface, used for mourning dress and funereal trimming and draping; band of this round hat etc. as sign of mourning. ~ *v.t.* Cover, drape, with crape. **crāp'y** *adj.*

crăp(s) *n.* (U.S.) Game of chance played with two dice; *shoot* ~, play this game.

crăp'ūlent *adj.* Given to, suffering from effect of, resulting from, intemperance. **crăp'ūlence** *n.* **crăp'ūlous** *adj.*

crăq'uelure (-ke-) *n.* Small cracks in paint or varnish on surface of picture.

crăsh[1] *n.* Loud noise as of hard body or bodies broken by violent percussion, or of thunder, loud music, etc.; violent percussion or breakage; crashing of aeroplane, motor-car, etc.; (fig.) sudden ruin or collapse, esp. of financial undertaking, credit, etc.; ~-*dive* (*n.* & *v.i.*) (of submarine) to (make) sudden and steep dive; ~-*helmet*, helmet worn as protection in case of crashing; ~-*land*, (of aircraft) land hurriedly with a crash (usu. without lowering under-carriage), whence ~-*landing* (*n*). ~ *v.* Make a crash; move, go, with a crash; (of aircraft) fall, cause to fall, violently to earth; (cause motor-car etc. to) come violently into collision with vehicle or obstacle; fail, esp. financially or in examination; dash in pieces, throw, force, drive, with a crash. ~ *in on*, intrude (into a party etc.).

crăsh[2] *n.* Coarse plain-woven fabric of hand-spun flax, orig. from Russia; various materials resembling this, of linen or cotton freq. combined with jute. [Russ. *krashenina* coloured linen (*kraska* colour, dye)]

crās'is *n.* (Gk gram.). Contraction of vowels of two syllables into one long vowel or diphthong.

crăss *adj.* Thick, gross; (fig.) gross; grossly stupid. **crăss'ly** *adv.* **crăss'nĕss, crăss'ĭtūde** *ns.*

Crăss'us, Marcus Licinius (*c* 112–53 B.C.). Roman consul, member of 1st TRIUMVIRATE.

crāte *n.* Large case or basket of basket-work or light boarding for carrying glass, crockery, fruit, etc. ~ *v.t.* Pack in crate.

crāt'er *n.* 1. Bowl- or funnel-shaped hollow at top or side of volcano from which eruption takes place (ill. VOLCANO); bowl-shaped cavity, esp. that formed by exploding shell or bomb. 2. (Gk antiq.) Large bowl in which wine was mixed with water (ill. VASE).

cravăt' *n.* (archaic) Neckcloth; ornamental band with long flowing ends, or linen or silk handkerchief tied, with bow in front, round neck outside shirt collar (ill. WIG). [Fr. *cravate* f. Croatian *Hrvat* Croat]

crāve *v.* Beg for; long for; beg, long, *for*. **crāv'ĭng** *n.* Strong desire, intense longing.

crāv'en *adj.* & *n.* Cowardly, abject (person). **crāv'enly** *adv.*

craw *n.* Crop of bird or insect.

craw'fĭsh *n.* = CRAYFISH.

crawl[1] *n.* Pen or enclosure in shallow water for fish, turtles, etc. [Colonial Dutch KRAAL]

crawl[2] *v.* Move slowly, dragging body along close to ground, or on hands and knees; walk, move, slowly; creep abjectly; swim with crawl-stroke; (of ground etc.) be alive *with* crawling things; feel creepy sensation. ~ *n.* Crawling; ~(-*stroke*), fast swimming-stroke in which arms execute alternate overarm movements and legs are kicked rapidly, usu. 3, 4, or 5 times to each arm-stroke (ill. SWIM).

crawl'er *n.* (esp. pl.) Infant's overall garment for crawling in.

cray'fĭsh *n.* Small lobster-like freshwater crustacean, *Astacus fluviatilis*; other species of *Astacus* and the allied Amer. genus *Cambarus*; (on English coast) the spiny lobster, *Palinurus vulgaris*.

cray'on *n.* 1. Stick, pencil, of coloured chalk usu. mixed with wax, for drawing; drawing in crayons. 2. Carbon point in electric arc lamp. ~ *v.t.* Draw with crayon(s).

crāze *v.* 1. Render insane (usu. in past part.). 2. Produce small cracks in (glaze of pottery); have such cracks. ~ *n.* Mania, insane or irrational fancy; temporary fashion.

crāz'y *adj.* 1. Full of cracks or flaws; unsound, frail, shaky. 2. Mad, demented; insane; extremely eager. 3. (of pavement, quilt, etc.) Made of irregular pieces fitted together without pattern. **crāz'ĭly** *adv.* **crāz'ĭnĕss** *n.*

creak *v.i.* & *n.* (Make) harsh shrill grating noise, as of ungreased hinge etc. **creak'y** *adj.*

cream *n.* 1. Fatty part of milk, which gathers on top, and by churning is made into butter. 2. Fancy dish, sweet, like or made of cream. 3. Cream-like substance, esp. cosmetic. 4. Best or choicest part of anything. 5. Part of liquid that gathers on top. 6. Cream colour, yellowish-white; cream-coloured horse. 7. ~ *of lime*, pure slaked lime; ~ *of tartar*, purified and crystallized acid potassium tartrate, used as an ingredient of baking-powder and in medicine as a purgative; ~-*bun*, -*cake*, etc.; one filled with cream or creamy custard etc.; ~-*cheese*, soft rich cheese made of unskimmed milk and cream; ~-*laid*, -*wove*, laid, wove (paper) of cream colour. ~ *v.* Form cream or scum; cause (milk) to cream; take cream from (milk); take best part of; add cream to; treat (skin) with cosmetic cream; work (butter etc.) into creamy consistency. **cream'y** *adj.*

cream'er *n.* Flat dish for skimming cream off milk; machine for separating cream. **cream'ery** *n.* Butter (and cheese) factory; shop where milk, cream, etc., are sold.

crease *n.* 1. Line caused by folding; fold; wrinkle. 2. (cricket) Line of whiting (continuing the line of the stumps) from behind which bowler delivers ball (*bowling*-~); line in front of wicket behind which batsman stands to defend wicket (*popping*-~, ill. CRICKET). ~ *v.* Make creases in; fall into creases.

crēāte' *v.t.* Bring into existence, give rise to; originate; invest (person) with rank. **crēāt'ĭve** *adj.* **crēāt'ĭvely** *adv.* **crēāt'ĭvenĕss** *n.*

crē'atine *n.* Amino-acid found in muscles of vertebrates.

creā'tion *n.* 1. Act of creating, esp. of the world; the beginning of things; investing with title, rank, etc. 2. All created things. 3. A production of human intelligence or power, esp. of the imagination.

creāt'or *n.* One who creates; *the C~*, God.

creature (krēch'*er*) *n.* Created thing; animate being; animal (often as distinct from man); human being, person; one who owes his fortune to another; mere instrument.

crèche (krāsh) *n.* Public day-nursery for infants; nursery-school.

Crécy (krĕs'ĭ). Village in Picardy, N. France, scene (1346) of a battle in the Hundred Years War, in which the English under Edward III defeated the French.

crēd'ence *n.* 1. Belief; *letter of ~*, letter of recommendation or introduction. 2. Small side-table or shelf on which Eucharistic elements are placed before consecration (ill. FENESTELLA).

credĕn'tial (-shl) *n.* (usu. pl.). Letter(s) of introduction (also fig.).

crĕd'ĭble *adj.* Believable, worthy of belief. **crĕdĭbĭl'ĭty** *n.* **crĕd'ĭbly** *adv.*

crĕd'ĭt *n.* 1. Belief, trust. 2. Good reputation; power derived from this; acknowledgement of merit; source of commendation or honour. 3. Trust in person's ability and intention to pay at some future time; reputation of solvency and probity in business; (book-keeping) acknowledgement of payment by entry in account, sum entered on credit or right-hand side of account; *letter of ~*, banker's etc. document authorizing person to draw money from writer's correspondent in another place. 4. Kind of distinction awarded in examination to candidate obtaining more than a certain percentage of maximum marks; (U.S.) certificate attesting completion of a certain course of study. ~ *v.t.* 1. Believe. 2. Carry to credit side of account; (fig.) ~ person *with*, give him credit for (quality), ascribe to him.

crĕd'ĭtable *adj.* That brings credit or honour. **crĕd'ĭtably** *adv.*

crĕd'ĭtor *n.* One who gives credit for money or goods; one to whom debt is owing.

crĕd'ō *n.* (pl. *-os*). Creed, esp. APOSTLES' and NICENE which begin in Latin with the word *credo* 'I believe'.

crĕd'ūlous *adj.* Too ready to believe; characterized by or arising from credulity. **credūl'ĭty, crĕd'ūlousness** *ns.* **crĕd'ūlously** *adv.*

creed *n.* Brief formal summary of Christian doctrine, esp. APOSTLES', NICENE, and ATHANASIAN creeds; confession of faith; system of belief.

creek[1] *n.* 1. Narrow inlet of sea-coast or tidal estuary; small harbour. 2. (U.S. etc.) Brook, stream.

Creek[2]. One of a N. Amer. Ind. tribe now settled in Oklahoma. [transl. Algonkin *maskoki*, creeks]

creel *n.* Large wicker basket for fish; angler's fishing-basket.

creep *v.i.* (past t. and past part. *crĕpt*). 1. Move with body prone and close to ground; move timidly, slowly, or stealthily; insinuate oneself *into*, come *in*, *up*, unobserved; proceed, exist, abjectly. 2. (of plants) Grow along ground, wall, etc. 3. (of flesh, skin) Feel as if things were creeping over it (as result of fear, repugnance, etc.). 4. (of metal rails etc.) Move gradually forward under recurrent pressure; (of hot metal) extend slowly under tension; (of salts in solution) spread upwards in crystals on side of vessel from edge of solvent. ~ *n.* Creeping; creeping action of metal etc.; ~ *strength*, maximum stress to which material can be subjected without creeping; *the ~s*, nervous shrinking or shiver of dread or horror.

creep'er *n.* (esp.) Plant that creeps along ground or up wall etc.; small bird that runs or climbs up and down branches, esp. tree-creeper, *Certhia familiaris*; kind of grapnel for dragging ground under water.

creep'y *adj.* Having a creeping of the flesh; producing this; given to creeping; so (colloq.) **creep'y-crawl'y** *adj.*

creese (-s) *n.* = KRIS.

crėmāte' *v.t.* Consume (esp. corpse) by fire. **crėmā'tion** *n.*

crėmāt'or *n.* (esp.) Furnace for cremating corpses or burning rubbish. **crĕmatŏr'ium** (pl. *-s*, *-ia*), **crĕm'atory** (rare) *ns.* Public institution for cremation, esp. of corpses. **crĕm'atory** *adj.* Of cremation.

crème (-ām) *n.* 1. Various syrupy liqueurs; ~ *de menthe* (demahnt), a sweet green liqueur flavoured with peppermint. 2. (cookery) Cream soup; custard.

Crėmōn'a[1]. Town in Lombardy where the craft of violin-making reached its highest perfection in 17th and early 18th centuries; violin made there.

cremōn'a[2] *n.* = CROMORNE.

crēn'ātė(d) *adj.* (bot., zool.) With notched edge or rounded teeth. **crēnā'tion** *n.*

crĕn'ature *n.* Rounded tooth on edge of leaf etc.

crĕn'el (*or* krėnĕl') *n.* Open space or indentation in embattled parapet, orig. for shooting through etc. (ill. CASTLE); representation of this.

crĕn'ellate *v.t.* Furnish with battlements or loopholes. **crĕnellā'tion** *n.*

crē'ōle *n.* 1. Descendant of European or Negro settlers in W. Indies, Mauritius, etc. 2. (U.S.) French-speaking descendant of early French settlers in Louisiana etc. ~ *adj.* Born and naturalized in W. Indies etc., but of European or negro descent; (of animals etc.) bred or grown, but not indigenous, in the W. Indies etc.

crē'osōte *n.* (~ *oil*) Brown oily liquid, a mixture of phenols obtained from coal-tar (formerly from wood tar) having antiseptic properties and used esp. for preservation of timber and in pharmacy.

crêpe (-āp) *n.* Textile fabric with wrinkled surface produced chemically or by twisting the yarn; ~ *de Chine* (deshēn), fine silk crêpe; ~ *paper*, thin crinkled paper; ~ (*rubber*), crude rubber in thin sheets with wrinkled surface.

crĕp'ĭtāte *v.i.* Make crackling sound; (of beetles etc.) eject defensive fluid with sharp report. **crĕp'ĭtant** *adj.* **crĕpĭtā'tion** *n.* Act of crepitating; (med.) grating sound made by ends of bone rubbing together; rattle of breath as heard in pneumonia etc.

crĕp'ĭtus *n.* (med.) Crepitation.

crėpŭs'cūlar *adj.* Of twilight; (zool.) appearing, active, in twilight.

cres. *abbrev.* *Crescendo.*

crėscĕn'dō (-sh-) *adv.*, *n.*, *adj.* (pl. *-os*). (mus.) (Passage to be played) with gradually increasing volume, indicated thus <.

crĕs'cent *n.* 1. Waxing moon, between new moon and full; concavo-convex figure of moon during first or last quarter, esp. when very new or very old (ill. MOON). 2. Representation of this shape, esp. as badge of Turkish sultans; the Turkish power; the Moslem religion. 3. Anything crescent-shaped, esp. row of houses; *C~ City*, New Orleans, Louisiana, from its former shape. ~ *adj.* 1. Increasing; waxing. 2. Crescent-shaped.

crēs'ōl *n.* Any of three isomeric methyl phenols present in wood and coal-tar and forming chief constituents of creosote; used as disinfectants etc.

crĕss *n.* Various cruciferous plants, usu. with pungent edible leaves, esp. *garden ~*, *Lepidium sativum*, and *watercress*, *Nasturtium officinale*.

crĕss'ėt *n.* Metal vessel for holding grease or oil for light, usu. mounted on pole (ill. LAMP); fire-basket for lighting wharf etc.

Crĕss'ĭda. In medieval legends of the Trojan War, the daughter of Calchas, a priest; she was faithless to her lover Troilus, a son of Priam.

crĕst *n.* 1. Comb, tuft, on animal's head; erect plume or other ornament on top of helmet or head-dress. 2. (her.) Device (orig. borne by knight on his helmet) above shield and helmet in coat of arms, or used separately, as on seal, notepaper, etc. (ill. HERALDRY). 3. Top of helmet; helmet, headpiece; summit, top, esp. of hill or mountain. 4. Ridge forming top of anything, esp. of roof or wave; surface line of neck in animals, mane; (anat.) ridge along surface of bone. 5. *~-fallen*, with drooping crest;

abashed, disheartened. ~ *v.* 1. Furnish with crest; serve as crest to; form into crest. 2. Reach crest or summit of.

crĕs'tĭng *n.* Ornamental ridging to wall or roof.

crėtā'ceous (-shus) *adj.* Of (the nature of) chalk; (geol.) of the system or period of rocks at the top of the Mesozoic. ~ *n.* *The C~*, this system (ill. GEOLOGY).

Crēte. Iraklion, an Aegean island belonging to Greece. **Crēt'an** *adj.* & *n.* (Native, inhabitant) of Crete.

crēt'ic *n.* Metrical foot of one short syllable between two long ones (– ◡ –).

crĕt'ĭn (*or* -ē-) *n.* One suffering from cretinism; idiot. **crĕt'ĭnĭsm** *n.* Idiocy combined with physical deformity, stunted growth and freq. goitre, caused by thyroid deficiency; common in Alpine valleys owing to lack of iodine in soil. **crĕt'ĭnous** *adj.* [Swiss Fr. *crestin* Christian, in sense of '(barely) human creature']

crėtŏnne' (*or* krĕt'on) *n.* Stout unglazed cotton or linen fabric with printed pattern.

Creusa (krīōōz'*a*). 1. Daughter of Creon, king of Corinth; when she was about to marry Jason, she put on a garment given her by Medea which was poisoned and set her body on fire. 2. Daughter of Priam, king of Troy, and wife of Aeneas.

crėvăsse' *n.* Deep fissure in ice of glacier (ill. MOUNTAIN).

crĕv'ĭce *n.* Chink, fissure.

crew (-ōō) *n.* Body of men engaged upon particular piece of work, esp. (U.S.) in working railway train; whole body of men manning ship, boat, or aircraft; sometimes, men manning ship, excluding officers; associated body, company, of persons; set, gang, mob.

crew'el (-ōō-) *n.* Thin worsted yarn used for embroidery; *~-needle*, blunt-ended needle for embroidery on canvas etc.; *~-work*, embroidery in crewels.

crĭb *n.* 1. Barred receptacle for fodder, in cow-sheds, yards, fields, etc.; (U.S.) bin etc. with barred or slatted sides for storing Indian corn etc. 2. Cabin, hovel; (thieves' slang) house. 3. Child's small bed with barred or latticed sides. 4. Framework lining shaft of mine; heavy crossed timbers used in foundations in loose soil etc. 5. Wicker salmon-trap. 6. Set of cards given to dealer in cribbage, made up of cards thrown out of other players' hands. 7. (colloq.) Plagiarism; translation of classics etc. for illegitimate use of students. 8. *~-biting*, horse's vicious habit of seizing manger in teeth and at same time noisily drawing in breath. ~ *v.t.* 1. Confine in small space. 2. Furnish (cow-shed etc.) with cribs. 3. Pilfer; copy unfairly or without acknowledgement.

cribb'age *n.* Card-game for 2, 3, or 4 persons, played with pack of 52 cards and a board of 61 holes on which points are scored with pegs; 5 or 6 cards are dealt to each player and the dealer has in addition the 'crib' of cards discarded by other players.

crĭb'rĭfōrm *adj.* (anat., bot.) Perforated with numerous small holes.

Crichton (krīt'*o*n), James (1560–85). Scottish prodigy of intellectual and knightly accomplishments, said to have disputed on scientific questions in 12 languages; *Admirable ~*, nickname given to him; hence, any very versatile person.

crĭck *n.* Painful spasmodic affection of muscles of neck, back, etc., sudden stiffness. ~ *v.t.* Produce crick in.

crĭck'ėt[1] *n.* Orthopterous jumping insect of genus *Acheta* or related genera; esp. the *house-~*, *A. domestica*, living in hearths and other warm places, and producing a characteristic shrill noise by rubbing parts of forewings together.

crĭck'ėt[2] *n.* Open-air game played with bats, ball, and 2 wickets by two sides of 11 players each; the batsman (one at each wicket) defends his wicket against the ball, which is bowled by a player of the opposing side, the other players of this side being stationed about the field in order to catch or stop the ball; scoring is chiefly by runs made by the batsmen between the wickets after the ball has been struck by the bat, and a batsman may be 'out' if the ball strikes his wicket so as to remove the bails when it is bowled, or while he is running, or if it is caught after being struck by the bat, and in various other ways; *not ~*, (colloq., of conduct) unsporting, unfair. ~ *v.i.* Play cricket. **crĭck'ėter** *n.*

crĭck'ėt[3] *n.* (U.S. and local) Low stool.

crĭc'oid *adj.* & *n.* (anat.) Ring-shaped; cartilage of this shape forming lower and back part of larynx (ill. HEAD).

crī'er *n.* (esp.) Officer who makes public announcements in court of justice or (*town ~*), in streets etc. of a town.

crī'key *int.* (slang) Expressing astonishment.

crim. con. *abbrev.* Criminal conversation.

crime *n.* Act (usu. grave offence) punishable by law; evil act, sin; *~-sheet*, record of soldier's offences against regulations. ~ *v.t.* (mil.) Charge with or convict of military offence.

Crīmē'a. Russian peninsula lying between Sea of Azov and Black Sea. **Crīmē'an** *adj.* ~ *War*, inconclusive war in the Crimea, 1854–6, in which Russia fought Turkey, France, and Britain, both sides sustaining heavy losses.

crĭm'inal *adj.* Of (the nature of) crime; concerned with crime or its punishment; guilty of crime; ~ *conversation*, adultery; ~ *law, proceedings*, those aiming at punishment of offenders (cf. CIVIL law). **crĭm'ĭnally** *adv.* **crĭm'ĭnal** *n.* Person guilty or convicted of crime.

crĭm'ĭnāte *v.t.* Charge with crime; prove guilty of crime. **crĭmĭnā'tion** *n.* **crĭm'ĭnatĭve, crĭm'ĭnatory** *adjs.*

crĭmĭnŏl'ogy *n.* Scientific study of crime. **crĭmĭnŏl'ogist** *n.*

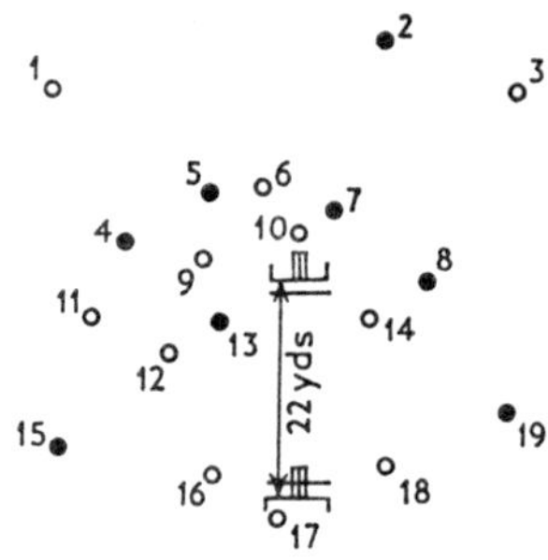

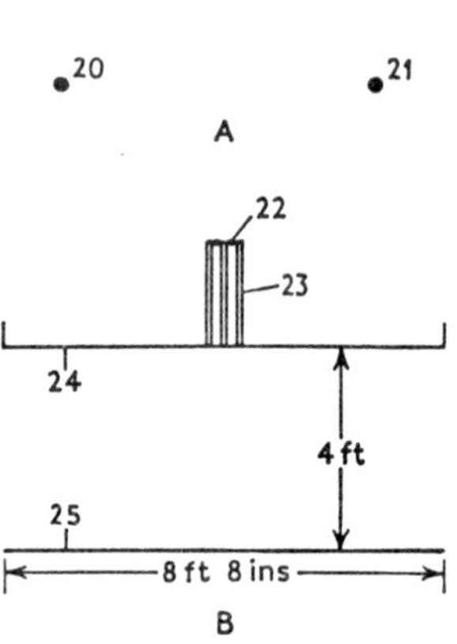

CRICKET: A. POSITIONS OF FIELD. B. WICKET

A. 1. Third man. 2. Deep fine leg. 3. Long leg. 4. Backward point. 5. Second slip. 6. First slip. 7. Short fine leg or leg slip. 8. Square leg. 9. Gully. 10. Wicket-keeper. 11. Cover-point. 12. Short extra cover. 13. Silly mid-off. 14. Forward short leg or silly mid-on. 15. Extra cover. 16. Mid-off. 17. Bowler. 18. Mid-on. 19. Mid-wicket. 20. Long-off. 21. Long-on. The white circles show a typical field; the black ones alternative positions. B. 22. Bails. 23. Stumps. 24. Bowling-crease. 25. Popping-crease

crĭm'ĭnous *adj.* Only in ~ *clerk*, clergyman guilty of crime.

crimp[1] *n.* Agent procuring seamen, soldiers, etc., by seducing, decoying, entrapping, or impressing them. ~ *v.t.* Impress, entrap, thus.

crimp[2] *v.t.* 1. Compress into plaits or folds, frill; wrinkle or crumple minutely. 2. Cause (flesh of newly caught fish) to contract and become firm by gashing. ~ *n.* (chiefly U.S.) Fold, crease.

crĭm'son (-z-) *adj.* & *n.* (Of) deep-red colour inclining towards purple; ~ *rambler*, climbing rose with clusters of crimson flowers. ~ *v.* Make, become, crimson.

crĭnge (-nj) *v.i.* Cower; bow servilely; behave obsequiously. ~ *n.* Fawning obeisance.

crĭngle (-ng'gl) *n.* (naut.) Eye of rope containing thimble for another rope to pass through (ill. SAIL[1]).

crĭn'īte *adj.* (bot., zool.) Hairy.

crĭnkle (-ng'kl) *v.* & *n.* Twist, wrinkle. **crĭnk'ly** *adj.*

crĭnk'um-crănk'um *n.* & *adj.* (Thing) full of twists and turns.

crĭn'oid *adj.* & *n.* (Echinoderm) with stalked and rooted calyx-like body; 'sea lily'.

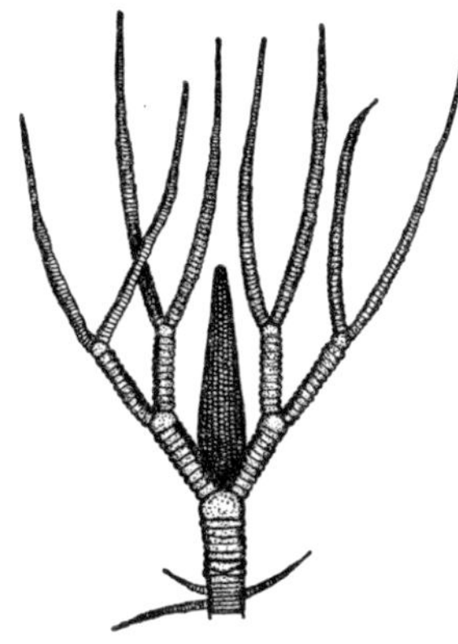

CRINOID

crĭn'olĭne (*or* -lēn) *n.* 1. Stiff fabric of horsehair etc. formerly used for skirts, now for women's hats etc.; petticoat of this, or

CRINOLINE

hooped petticoat, used to expand skirt of woman's dress. 2. Defensive screen of anti-torpedo nets surrounding a stationary ship.

crĭp'ple *n.* Lame person. ~ *v.t.* Lame; disable, impair.

crī'sĭs *n.* (pl. *crī'sēs* pr. -z). Turning-point, esp. of disease; moment or brief period of danger or suspense in politics, commerce, etc.

crĭsp *adj.* Hard or firm but fragile, brittle; bracing; brisk, decisive; (of hair etc.) closely curling. **crĭsp'ly** *adv.* **crĭsp'nĕss** *n.* **crĭsp** *n.* Anything dried or shrivelled by frying, roasting, etc. (chiefly U.S.); (pl.) very thin slices of potato fried crisp and eaten cold. ~ *v.* Make or become crisp. **crĭsp'y** *adj.* Curly; brittle, crisp.

crĭspā'tion *n.* Curling, undulation; slight contraction (esp. of skin in 'goose-flesh').

crĭss-crŏss *n.* Crossing lines, currents, etc.; network of intersecting lines; ~ *row* (archaic), the alphabet (from cross before row of letters in horn-books). ~ *adj.* In crossing lines. ~ *adv.* Crosswise. ~ *v.t.* Mark with criss-cross lines. [orig. *Christ's cross*]

crĭs'tāte *adj.* Crested, like a crest.

critēr'ĭon *n.* (pl. *-ĭa*). Principle, rule, standard, by which thing is judged.

crĭt'ĭc *n.* One who pronounces judgement; censurer; judge of literary or artistic works; one skilled in textual criticism.

crĭt'ĭcal *adj.* 1. Censorious, fault-finding; skilful, engaged, in criticism; belonging to criticism. 2. Relating to crisis; involving risk or suspense. 3. (math., physics) Marking transition from one state, property, condition, etc., to another; ~ *angle*, (optics) largest angle at which light rays passing through a dense medium can strike the face of a rarer medium and pass into it (i.e. be refracted; if the angle exceeds this they will be totally reflected); ~ *point*, temperature for any gas above which it cannot be liquefied by compression (also ~ *temperature*). **crĭt'ĭcally** *adv.*

crĭticăs'ter *n.* Petty or inferior critic.

crĭt'ĭcĭsm *n.* Criticizing; work of a critic; critical essay or remark; science dealing with text, character, composition, and origin of literary documents; *textual* ~, that whose object is to ascertain the genuine text and meaning of an author; *higher* ~, criticism, other than verbal or textual, of the Old and New Testaments.

crĭt'ĭcīze *v.t.* Discuss critically; censure, find fault with.

crĭtique' (-ēk) *n.* Critical essay or notice; criticism.

croak *n.* Deep hoarse sound made by frog or raven; sound resembling this. ~ *v.* 1. Utter croak; utter dismally; forbode evil. 2. (slang) Kill; die. **croak'y** *adj.*

Crō'at. Native of Croatia, descendant of Slavonic tribe which occupied that country in 7th c. **Croā'tia** (-shĭa). District of Yugoslavia. **Croā'tian** *adj.* & *n.* (Language) of Croats.

crō'cēāte *adj.* Saffron, saffron-coloured.

crō'chet (-shĭ) *n.* Kind of knitting done with a single hook; material so made. ~ *v.* Do this work; make of crochet.

CROCHET

A. Double crochet. B. Treble crochet

crŏck[1] *n.* Earthen pot or jar; broken piece of earthenware used for covering hole in flower-pot.

crŏck[2] *n.* (slang) Worn-out or failing person; broken-down horse. ~ *v.* Give way, break down (also ~ *up*); cause to collapse.

crŏck'ery *n.* Earthenware vessels, esp. for domestic use.

crŏck'ĕt *n.* 1. (archit.) Small ornament (usu. bud or curled leaf) on sloping side of pinnacle, pediment, etc. (ill. PINNACLE). 2. Terminal knob on stag's horn.

crŏc'odīle *n.* 1. Large amphibious thick-skinned long-tailed

CROCODILE

saurian reptile of *Crocodilus* or related genera, esp. *C. niloticus*, the crocodile of the Nile. 2. Children walking two and two; any long procession of objects close together. 3. ~*-bird*, Egyptian black-headed plover, *Pluvianus aegyptius*, a small bird with lavender and cream plumage and black-and-white markings, which eats crocodile's insect parasites; ~ *tears*, (from the ancient belief that the crocodile wept while devouring its victim) hypocritical tears.

crŏcodĭl'ian *adj.* & *n.* (Animal) like, closely allied to, the crocodile.

crō'cus *n.* Genus of hardy dwarf plants with corms, natives of S. and central Europe and W. Asia, cultivated for their brilliant, usu. yellow or purple, flowers, appearing in spring or autumn.

Croes'us (krēs-) (6th c. B.C.). King of Lydia, famous for his riches; hence, a very rich man.

croft (-ŏ-, -aw-) *n.* Enclosed piece of (usu. arable) land; small agricultural holding worked by peasant tenant, esp. in Scottish Highlands. **crof'ter** *n.* One who cultivates a croft; joint tenant of divided farm.

Crō-Magnon (măn'yawn̄). Cave in Dordogne, France, where prehistoric remains were discovered in 1868; applied to European neolithic or mesolithic race with very large long heads, low foreheads, very broad faces, deep-set eyes, and tall stature.

Crōme, John (1768–1821). English landscape-painter, founder of the 'Norwich School' of painters.

crŏm'lĕch (-k) *n.* Obsolescent term still current in Wales for a megalithic tomb (DOLMEN) and in France for a prehistoric circle or enclosure of upright stones. [Welsh *crom* crooked, *llech* (flat) stone]

cromōrne' *n.* An organ reed-stop. [Fr., f. Ger. *krummhorn* crooked horn]

Crŏm'well[1], Oliver (1599–1658). Leader of the Parliamentary troops in the Civil War; Lord Protector of England, 1653–8.

Crŏm'well[2], Thomas, Earl of Essex (1485?–1540). Chief adviser to Henry VIII in ecclesiastical matters; negotiated Henry's match with Anne of Cleves. The failure of this match and the policy underlying it led to his downfall and execution.

crōne *n.* Withered old woman; old ewe.

Crŏn'us. (Gk myth.) One of the Titans and father of Zeus, by whom he was dethroned as ruler of the universe.

crōn'y *n.* Intimate friend.

crŏŏk *n.* 1. Shepherd's staff, with one end curved or hooked, for catching sheep's leg; bishop's or abbot's pastoral staff; anything hooked; hook; curve, bend; *~-back(ed)*, hunch-back(ed). 2. (slang) Dishonest person, rogue; esp. professional criminal. ~ *v.* Bend, curve.

crooked *adj.* 1. (krŏŏk'ĭd) Not straight, bent, twisted; deformed; bent with age; not straightforward, dishonest; ~ *cross*, swastika. 2. (krŏŏkt) Of stick etc., having cross handle. **crŏŏk'ĕdly** *adv.* **crŏŏk'ĕdnĕss** *n.*

Crŏŏkes (-ks), Sir William (1843–1919). English physicist; invented the radiometer and a special glass largely opaque to heat rays and ultra-violet light, and discovered the element thallium; ~ *layer*, layer of vapour separating any spheroidal mass or liquid from the surface on which it rests; ~ *space*, the dark space within the negative-pole glow at the cathode of a discharge tube; ~ *tube*, a high-vacuum discharge tube.

crōōn *v.* & *n.* (Hum, sing, mutter, in) low undertone. **crōōn'er** *n.* Singer of sentimental songs in a soft artificial voice.

crŏp *n.* 1. Pouch-like enlargement of gullet in birds, where food is prepared for digestion (ill. BIRD). 2. Stock, handle, of whip; (*hunting*)-~, short whipstock with loop instead of lash. 3. Produce of cultivated plants, esp. cereals; season's total yield (of cereal etc.). 4. Entire hide of animal tanned. 5. Cropping of hair; style of wearing hair cut short; piece cropped or cut off anything. ~ *v.* 1. Cut off; (of animals) bite off (tops of plants). 2. Gather, reap. 3. Cut short. 4. Raise crop on; bear a crop. 5. ~ *up*, turn *up* unexpectedly; come to surface; ~ *out*, appear.

crŏpp'er *n.* (esp.) 1. Plant yielding good etc. crop. 2. (slang) Heavy fall (also fig.).

crŏpp'y *n.* Person with hair cropped short, esp. Irish rebel in 1798, wearing hair very short as sign of sympathy with French Revolution.

crōq'uet (-kĭ) *n.* 1. Game played on lawn, in which wooden balls are driven with wooden mallets through iron arches or 'hoops' fixed in the ground. 2. Croqueting a ball in this game. ~ *v.t.* Drive away (another ball) by striking one's own ball placed in contact with it.

croquette' (-kĕt) *n.* Seasoned and fried ball of rice, potato, meat, etc.

crōre *n.* Ten millions, 100 lakhs (usu. of rupees).

crō'sier, crō'zier (-zhyer) *n.* Pastoral staff or crook of bishop or abbot (ill. VESTMENT).

cross (-ŏ-, -aw-) *n.* 1. Stake (usu. with transverse bar) used by the

CROSSES

1. Greek. 2. Latin. 3. Saltire or St. Andrew's Cross. 4. Maltese. 5. Tau or St. Anthony's Cross. 6. Swastika or fylfot. 7. Cross of Lorraine. 8. Sarcelly. 9. Papal

ancients for crucifixion, esp. that on which Christ was crucified; model of this as religious emblem; sign of cross made with right hand as religious act; staff surmounted with cross and borne before archbishop or in processions. 2. Monument in form of cross, esp. one in centre of town. 3. *The C~*, (fig.) the Christian religion. 4. Trial, affliction; annoyance. 5. Cross-shaped thing or mark; southern constellation (*Southern C~*) within Antarctic Circle, with four bright stars roughly in shape of cross; cross-shaped decoration in orders of knighthood etc.; *crooked ~*, SWASTIKA; *fiery ~*: see FIERY; *Grand C~*, decoration of highest class of order of knighthood, person wearing it; *Greek*, *Latin*, *Maltese*, *St. Andrew's*, *Tau*, ~: see ill.; VICTORIA C~: see entry. 6. Intermixture of breeds; animal etc. resulting from this; mixture, compromise, *between* two things. 7. (slang) Fraud, swindle. 8. *on the ~*, diagonally, obliquely, on the bias. **cross'wise** (-z) *adj.*

cross *v.* 1. Place crosswise. 2. Make sign of cross on or over. 3. Draw line across; write across (what is already written, a letter); draw or stamp two lines across (cheque, which may then be paid only through bank). 4. Go across; bestride; carry, move, across; meet and pass. 5. Thwart. 6. (Cause to) inter-breed; cross-fertilize. ~ *adj.* 1. Passing from side to side, transverse; intersecting. 2. Contrary, opposed. 3. (colloq.) Peevish, out of humour, whence **cross'ly** *adv.*, **cross'nĕss** *n.*

cross- (-ŏ-, -aw-) in combination: *cross'belt*, belt for cartridges etc., from shoulder to opposite hip; *~-bench*, bench at right angles to others, occupied in English Parliament (ill. PARLIAMENT) by independent or neutral members (*~-benchers*); *cross'bill*, bird of genus *Loxia* (one of the finches), with mandibles of bill so curved as to cross each other when bill is closed; found in Europe, America, and Japan; *~-bones* (*n.pl.*), figure of two thigh-bones laid across each other, usu. under skull as emblem of death; *cross'bow*, bow fixed across wooden stock, with groove for missile (arrow, stone, etc.) and mechanism for drawing back and releasing string (ill. BOW); *cross'-bowman* (*n.*); *~'-breed*, breed from individuals of different species or races; *~'-bred* (*adj.*); *~-bun'*, bun marked with cross, usu. eaten on Good Friday; *~-butt'ock* (*n.* & *v.t.*) throw over the hip, in wrestling; *~'-country*, transversely to great highways; across fields etc. instead of following roads; *~'-cut*, diagonal cut, path, etc.; *~-cut saw*, saw for making cross-cut (ill. SAW); *~-examine*, examine by questions designed to check results of previous examination; esp. examine thus in court of law (witness who has already given evidence for other side); *~-examina'tion*, *~-exam'iner* (*ns.*); *~-eyed*, having squint in which eyes are turned inwards; *~-fertilize*, fertilize (plant) with gamete from another; *~-grained*, (of wood) with grain running irregularly or in crossing directions; (fig.) perverse, intractable; *~-hatch*, shade (drawing, engraving, etc.) with intersecting series of parallel lines; *~-head*, bar at end of piston-rod of steam-engine, communicating motion to connecting rod; paragraph-heading printed across page or column in body of article in newspaper etc.; *~-legged*, with legs crossed; with one leg laid across the other; *~-over*, anything arranged with one part crossing another; connexion by which tram, train, etc., may be transferred from one set of rails to another; (*adj.*) that crosses over, having one part crossing another; *cross'patch*, ill-tempered person; ~

purposes, contrary or conflicting purposes; *be at ~ purposes*, misunderstand one another; *~-ques'tion* (*v.t.*) cross-examine; *~-ref'erence* (*n.*) reference from one part of book etc. to another; (*v.t.*) provide with cross-reference(s). *~-road*, road that crosses another or joins two main roads; (also *~ roads*) intersection of two roads; *~-sec'tion*, cutting across; section made by plane cutting anything transversely; typical representation of constituents of a thing or group; *~-stitch*, needlework stitch of two straight stitches crossing each other (ill. STITCH); *~-tie*, transverse connecting piece (of timber etc.); *~-town* (*adj.*) (U.S.) lying, leading, going, across a town; *~ -tree(s)*, horizontal cross-timber(s) bolted to mast of ship (ill. SAIL[1], SHIP); *~ -vault*, vault formed by intersection of two or three simple vaults (ill. VAULT); *~-word* (*puzzle*), puzzle which is solved by filling in words indicated by verbal 'clues' down and across a prescribed chequered pattern so as to fit wherever they cross.

crŏsse (-ŏ-, -aw-) *n.* Implement used in lacrosse for catching and throwing ball, consisting of long shank curved round at end with net stretched across curved part. [Fr.; see LACROSSE]

crŏss'ĭng *n.* (esp.) Intersection of two roads, railways, etc. (ill. RAILWAY); place where street is crossed; part of church where transepts cross nave (ill. CHURCH); *level ~*, intersection of road and railway, or of two railways, at same level; *~-sweeper*, (hist.) person who sweeps street-crossing.

crŏss'lĕt *n.* (her.) Little cross.

crŏtch *n.* (chiefly U.S.) Fork of tree or bough; fork of human body where legs join trunk, crutch; corresponding part of garment.

crŏtch'ĕt *n.* 1. (mus.) Black-headed note with stem (♩ or ♪), of value of half a minim. 2. Whimsical fancy, whence **crŏtch'ĕty** *adj.* **crŏtch'ĕtiness** *n.*

crō't'on *n.* Large genus (*C~*) of mainly tropical plants, the seeds of one species of which, the E. Ind. *C. tiglium*, yield *~ oil*, a drastic purgative. [Gk *kroton* sheep-tick, croton, so called f. shape of seeds]

crouch *v.i.* Stoop, bend, esp. timidly or servilely; (of animals) lie close to ground, when about to pounce on prey, or from fear. *~ n.* Action or position of crouching.

croup[1] (-ōō-) *n.* Inflammatory disease in larynx and trachea of children, marked by hard cough and difficulty of breathing.

croup[2], **-pe** (-ōō-) *n.* Rump, hind quarters, esp of horse (ill. HORSE).

croup'ier (-ōō-) *n.* One who rakes in, and pays out, money at gaming-table; assistant chairman at public dinner. [Fr., orig. = 'one who rides behind on the CROUP[2]']

croûton (krōōt'awṅ) *n.* (cookery) Small piece of fried or toasted bread used for garnishing or served with soup.

crow[1] (-ō) *n.* 1. Bird of genus *Corvus*; in England, usu. the *carrion ~*, a large black bird feeding on carcases, *C. Corone*, or the rook, *C. frugilegus*; in U.S., a gregarious species, *C. americanus*. 2. = *crow'-bar*, an iron bar, usu. with beak-like end, used as lever. 3. *crow-berry*, black insipid fruit of small evergreen heath-like shrub, *Empetrum negrum*, of N. Europe; (U.S.) cranberry; *crowfoot*, various species of *Ranunculus* or buttercup, and other plants; (naut.) arrangement of small ropes for suspending awning; *~'s-foot*, wrinkle at outer corner of human eye; *~'s-nest*, barrel or protected platform fixed at masthead of sailing vessel for look-out man (ill. SHIP); *~ steps*, = CORBIE stones (ill. GABLE).

crow[2] (-ō) *n.* Crowing of cock; joyful cry of infant. *~ v.i.* Utter loud cry of cock; (of child) utter joyful cry; exult loudly.

crowd *n.* Throng, dense multitude; (colloq.) company, set, lot; large number (of things). *~ v.* 1. Collect in a crowd; fill, occupy, cram (*with*); fill (places etc.) as crowd does; force one's way *into*, *through*, etc. (confined space, etc.); *~ out*, exclude by crowding. 2. (naut.) Press or hasten on; *~ (on) sail*, hoist unusual number of sails on ship.

crown *n.* 1. Wreath of flowers etc. worn on head, esp. as emblem of victory. 2. Monarch's head-covering of gold etc. and jewels; (fig.) king or queen, regal power, supreme governing power in a monarchy. 3. Crown-shaped ornament. 4. Various coins orig. stamped with a crown; silver coin of Gt Britain of value of 5*s.*; principal monetary unit of Czechoslovakia; principal monetary unit of Scandinavian countries (see KRONE). 5. Size of paper (orig. with crown watermark): in Gt Britain 20×15 in., in U.S. 19×15 in. 6. Top part, esp. of skull; whole head. 7. Upper part of cut gem above girdle (ill. GEM); highest or central part of arch or arched structure, esp. road; top part of hat; part of tooth projecting from gum. 8. *~-and-anchor*, gambling game played with dice marked with crowns, anchors, and the four card-suits; *C~ colony*, colony with legislation and administration under control of home Government; *C~ Derby*, see DERBY; *~-glass*, kind of thick glass for window-panes, without lead or iron, made in circular sheets by blowing and whirling; *C~ jewels*, jewels forming part of the regalia (in England kept in the Tower of London); *C~ land*, land belonging to the Crown; *C~ law*, criminal law; *C~ lawyer*, lawyer in criminal cases, lawyer in service of Crown; *C~ office*, office transacting common-law business of Chancery; *C~ prince*, heir apparent or designate to sovereign throne, esp. in N. Europe and (hist.) Germany. *C~ princess*, his wife; *~-wheel*, contrate wheel (ill GEAR). *~ v.t.* 1. Place crown on; invest with regal crown or dignity; (fig.) reward. 2. Occupy the head of, form chief ornament to; put finishing touch to; bring (efforts) to happy issue. 3. (draughts) Make (piece) king, by putting another piece on top, or by turning up side marked with crown; (dentistry) protect remains of (tooth) by a gold etc. cap cemented on.

crown'er *n.* (joc. or dial.) Coroner.

croy'don *n.* Kind of 2-wheeled gig introduced *c* 1850. [*Croydon*, town in Surrey]

crozier: see CROSIER.

C.R.T. *abbrev.* Cathode-ray tube.

cru'cial (-ōōshl) *adj.* 1. Decisive, critical. 2. (anat.) Cross-shaped.

cru'cian, -sian, (-ōōshn) *n.* Central European deep-yellow fish, *Carassius carassius*, allied to carp.

cru'ciāte (-ōōsh-) *adj.* (zool., bot.) Cross-shaped.

cru'cĭble (-ōō-) *n.* Vessel (usu. of earthenware) withstanding great heat, and used for fusing metals etc.; hollow at bottom of furnace to collect molten metal; (fig.) severe test or trial.

crucif'erous (-ōō-) *adj.* 1. Wearing, adorned with, a cross. 2. (bot.) Of the family *Cruciferae*, having flowers with four equal petals arranged crosswise.

cru'cĭfix (-ōō-) *n.* Figure of Christ on the Cross; (erron.) cross.

crucĭfix'ion (-ōō-; -kshon) *n.* Crucifying (esp. of Christ); picture of this.

cru'cĭfôrm (-ōō-) *adj.* Cross-shaped, esp. of church with transepts.

cru'cĭfȳ (-ōō-) *v.t.* Put to death by fastening to a cross; (fig.) mortify (passions, sins, flesh).

crŭck *n.* (archit.) In medieval building, one of a pair of tall curving timbers standing on ground or foundations and meeting at apex of roof (ill. HALF-timber).

crude (-ōō-) *adj.* In the natural or raw state; not digested; unripe; (fig.) ill-digested, unpolished, lacking finish; rude, blunt. **crude'ly** (-dl-) *adv.* **crude'nĕss, crud'ity** *ns.*

cru'ĕl (-ōō-) *adj.* Indifferent to, delighting in, another's pain; showing such indifference or pleasure; painful, distressing. **cru'ĕlly** *adv.* **cru'ĕlty** *n.*

cru'ĕt (-ōō-) *n.* Small glass bottle with stopper for vinegar, oil, etc., for table; cruet-stand; small vessel for wine or water in celebration of Eucharist; *~-stand*, stand, freq. of silver, for cruets and castors.

cruise (-ōōz) *v.i.* Sail to and fro on look-out for ships, for protection of commerce in time of war, for plunder, or for pleasure, making for no particular port; (of car etc.) travel at *cruising speed*, economic travelling speed of vehicle, ship, or aircraft, less than top speed; (of taxi) go slowly, looking for fare; *cruising radius*, maximum distance that fuel capacity of warship or aircraft will allow her to go and return at cruising speed. ~ *n.* Cruising voyage.

CRUISER

1. Breakwater. 2. Turret. 3. Upper bridge. 4. Control tower. 5. Crane. 6. Tripod mast

cruis'er (-ōōz-) *n.* Warship adapted for cruising, less heavily armoured but faster than battleship; ~-*weight*, boxing weight, not exceeding 12 st. 7 lb.

crŭll'er *n.* (U.S.) Crisp twisted cake of dough containing eggs, butter, sugar, etc., fried in lard or oil.

crŭmb (-m) *n.* Small fragment, esp. of bread, such as breaks or falls off by rubbing etc.; (fig.) small particle, atom; soft inner part of bread. ~ *v.t.* Cover with crumbs, break into crumbs. **crŭmb'y** (-mĭ) *adj.*

crŭm'ble *v.* Break, fall, into crumbs or fragments. **crŭm'bly** *adj.* Apt to crumble.

crŭmp *n.* Sound of heavy shell or bomb exploding.

crŭm'pėt *n.* Soft cake of flour, egg, milk, etc., baked on iron plate, and eaten toasted with butter; (slang) head.

crŭm'ple *v.* Crush together or *up* into creased state; ruffle, wrinkle; become creased; ~ *up*, give way, collapse.

crŭnch *v.* Crush with teeth, esp. noisily; grind under foot (gravel etc.); make one's way thus. ~ *n.* Crunching; crunching noise. **crŭnch'y** *adj.* Fit for being crunched.

crŭpp'er *n.* Strap buckled to back of saddle and passing under horse's tail (ill. HARNESS); hindquarters of horse.

crur'al (-oor-) *adj.* (anat.) Of the leg.

crusāde' (-ōō-) *n.* 1. One of several military expeditions undertaken by the Christians of Europe in the 11th, 12th, and 13th centuries to recover the Holy Land from the Mohammedans; in the *1st C~* (1096–9) the crusaders captured Jerusalem and set up a kingdom there; the *3rd C~* (1189–91), in which Richard I of England, the Emperor Frederick Barbarossa, and Philip Augustus of France took part, resulted in the capture of Acre and the setting-up of a Latin kingdom in the East; in the *6th C~* (1228–9) Jerusalem was recaptured but finally lost; the other crusades were all unsuccessful. 2. Any war instigated by Church for alleged religious ends; (fig.) aggressive movement against public evil etc.; *Children's C~*, crusade of about 50,000 unarmed children which set out in 1212 from France and Germany to recover the Holy Sepulchre. ~ *v.i.* Engage in crusade. **crusād'er** *n.* 1. One who takes part in a crusade. 2. Kind of tank used by Allies esp. in N. Afr. campaign of the war of 1939–45.

cruse (-ōōz) *n.* (archaic) Pot, jar, of earthenware; *widow's* ~: see 1 Kings xvii. 12–16; hence, inexhaustible supply.

crŭsh *v.* Compress, be compressed, with violence, so as to break, bruise, etc.; crumple (dress etc.); be liable to crumple; pulverize by application of pressure; (fig.) subdue, overwhelm; ~ *out*, extinguish, stamp out. **crŭshed** *adj.* ~ *morocco*, (bookbinding) Morocco leather grained, shaved thin, pressed between iron plates, and polished; ~ *strawberry*, deep rather dull pink colour. **crŭsh** *n.* 1. Act of crushing. 2. Crowded mass (esp. of persons); (colloq.) crowded social gathering; (U.S. colloq.) set, group of people associated together. 3. Drink made of juice of crushed fruit. 4. (slang) *a* ~ *on*, a passionate attachment to (a person); ~ *hat*, hat that can be crushed flat, esp. opera hat.

crusian: see CRUCIAN.

Crusoe, Robinson: see ROBINSON CRUSOE.

crŭst *n.* Hard outer part of bread; similar casing of anything, e.g. harder layer over soft snow; hard dry scrap of bread; pastry covering pie; hard dry formation, scab, on skin; (geol.) outer portion of earth; coating, deposit, on surface of anything; deposit of tartar, etc., on inside of wine-bottle; hard external covering of animal or plant; (fig.) anything superficial. ~ *v.* Cover with, form into, crust; become covered with crust. **crŭs'tėd** *adj.* Having a crust; (of wine) having deposited a crust, as old port etc.; (fig.) venerable, antiquated.

Crŭstā'cea (-sha) *n.pl.* (zool.) Large class of arthropods, including crabs, lobsters, shrimps, etc., mostly aquatic, many with hard shell and many legs. **crŭsta'cean** (-āshn) *adj.* & *n.*

crŭstā'ceous (-shus) *adj.* Crust-like; having a hard covering; belonging to the *Crustacea*.

crŭs'ty *adj.* Crust-like, hard; irritable, curt. **crŭs'tily** *adv.* **crŭs'tinėss** *n.*

crŭtch *n.* Staff (now usu. with crosspiece at top fitting under armpit) for lame person; support, prop; forked rest for leg in a side-saddle; fork of the human body; (naut.) various forked contrivances, as a forked rowlock (ill. BOAT); crosspiece.

Crŭtch'ėd Frī'ars. The *Fratres cruciferi* or *Sanctae Crucis*, a minor order of friars wearing a cross; the order was founded in 1169, confirmed by Pope Innocent IV in 1243, and suppressed in 1656. Hence, the site of their convent in the City of London.

crŭx *n.* Difficult matter, puzzle; point at issue.

cruzeir'ō (krōō-) *n.* (pl. -*s*). Principal monetary unit of Brazil, = 100 centavos.

crȳ *n.* 1. Loud inarticulate utterance of grief, pain, fear, joy, etc.; loud excited utterance of words; appeal, entreaty. 2. Proclamation of wares sold in streets. 3. Public voice, generally expressed opinion; watchword. 4. Fit of weeping; ~-*baby*, one who cries childishly. 5. Yelping of hounds, pack of hounds; *full* ~, full pursuit. ~ *v.* 1. Utter loudly, exclaim; make loud utterance; (of animals, esp. birds) make loud call; (of hounds) yelp. 2. Announce for sale; make public announcement of. 3. Weep. 4. ~ *down*, disparage; ~ *off*, withdraw from agreement, decline to do something; ~*up*, praise. **crȳ'ing** *adj.* (esp., of evils) Calling for notice, flagrant.

crȳ'ogėn *n.* Freezing-mixture. [Gk *kruos* frost]

crȳ'olīte *n.* A fluoride of sodium and aluminium (Na_3AlF_6) found esp. in Greenland and used in production of aluminium and for ceramic glazes. [Gk *kruos* frost]

crȳpt *n.* Underground cell, vault, esp. one beneath church, used as burial place.

crȳp'tic *adj.* Secret, mystical; obscure in meaning; (zool.) adapted for concealment, as ~ *coloration*, animal's resemblance in colour, markings, etc., to its environment or to another animal.

crȳpto- *prefix.* Hidden; secret, as ~-*Communist*, secret sympathizer with Communism.

crȳpt'ogăm *n.* (bot.) Plant having no stamens or pistils and therefore no proper flowers. **crȳptogăm'ic, crȳptŏg'amous**

adjs. **Cry̆ptogăm'ĭa** *n.pl.* Cryptogams as a class, including ferns, mosses, algae, lichens, and fungi.

cry̆p'togrăm, cry̆p'tograph (-ahf) *ns.* Anything written in cipher. **cry̆ptŏg'rapher** *n.* **cry̆ptogrăph'ĭc** *adj.* **cry̆ptŏg'raphy** *n.* Art of writing in, or solving, ciphers.

cry̆ptomēr'ĭa *n.* Evergreen coniferous tree, *C. japonica*, of N. China and Japan; Japanese cedar.

cry̆s'tal *n.* 1. Clear transparent ice-like mineral, esp. pure quartz (*rock-~*); piece of this; piece of natural or artificial mineral used in contact with another or with a thin wire as a simple wireless detector. 2. Glass of very transparent quality, usu. with high proportion of lead oxide; fine cut glass; anything made of this; watch-glass. 3. (chem. etc.) Form in which atoms and molecules of many elements and compounds regularly aggregate, with definite internal structure and external form of solid enclosed by a number of symmetrically arranged plane faces. 4. *~ gazing*, concentrating the gaze on ball of rock-crystal or glass for purpose of inducing a hallucinatory vision of distant or future events. ~ *adj.* Made of, like, clear as, crystal. **cry̆st'allīne** *adj.* Made of, clear as, like, crystal; having crystal form; ~ *heaven*, (in Ptolemaic system) sphere between primum mobile and firmament, assumed to explain precession of equinox and motion of libration; ~ *lens*, transparent body enclosed in membranous capsule behind iris, acting as principal agent in focusing rays of light on retina (ill. EYE).

cry̆s'tallīze *v.* Form into crystals or (fig.) definite or permanent state.

cry̆stallŏg'raphy *n.* Branch of science dealing with structure, classification, and properties of crystals. **cry̆stallŏg'rapher** *n.* **cry̆stallogrăph'ĭc** *adj.*

cry̆s'talloid *adj.* & *n.* (Substance) of crystalline structure, esp. substance capable, in solution, of passing through membranes (as dist. from COLLOID).

Cry̆s'tal Păl'ace. Large building of iron and glass, like a greenhouse, designed by (Sir) Joseph Paxton, gardener to the Duke of Devonshire, for the Exhibition of 1851 in Hyde Park, London, and re-erected at Sydenham; accidentally burnt down in 1936.

csardas (chârd'ahsh) *n.* A Hungarian national dance.

C.S.C. *abbrev.* Conspicuous Service Cross.

C.S.I. *abbrev.* Companion of (the Order of) the Star of India.

C.S.M. *abbrev.* Company Sergeant-Major.

C.T.C. *abbrev.* Cyclists' Touring Club.

cu. *abbrev.* Cubic.

C.U. *abbrev.* Cambridge University (esp. in names of clubs, as *C.U.B.C.*, Boat Club); *C.U.P.*, Cambridge University Press.

cŭb *n.* 1. Young of fox; young of bear or other wild beast; *~-hunting*, hunting young foxes at beginning of season. 2. Unpolished youth. 3. Junior member of Boy Scouts (*wolf-~*); (U.S.) apprentice, beginner, novice. ~ *v.* Bring forth (cubs); hunt fox-cubs.

Cūb'a. Largest of the W. Ind. islands, discovered by Columbus in 1492; formerly a part of the Span.-Amer. dominions; freed from Spanish rule by U.S. forces in 1898 and proclaimed an independent republic in 1902; capital, Havana. **Cūb'an** *adj.* & *n.* (Native) of Cuba; ~ *heel*, a high leather heel without the curve of the French heel.

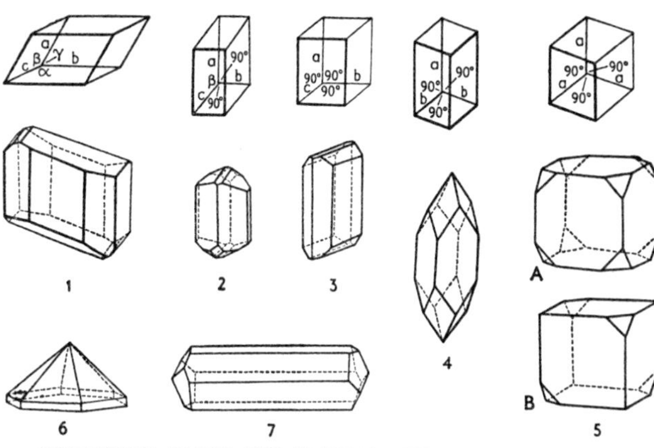

SIMPLIFIED FORMS AND TYPICAL EXAMPLES OF CRYSTAL SYSTEMS

1. Triclinic. 2. Monoclinic. 3. Orthorhombic. 4. Tetragonal. 5. Cubic (A. Holohedral, B. Hemihedral). 6. Hexagonal. 7. Trigonal. α, β, γ = angles; *a, b, c* = sides

cŭbb'y-hōle *n.* Very small confined room, cupboard, etc.

cūbe *n.* 1. Solid figure contained by 6 equal squares and 8 rectangular solid angles (ill. SOLID); anything of this shape. 2. Product of a number multiplied by its square, third power of a quantity. ~ *v.t.* Find cube of (number), find cubic content of.

cūb'ĕb *n.* Pungent spicy berry of Javanese climbing shrub, *Piper cubeba*, used in medicine and cookery.

cūb'ĭc *adj.* Cube-shaped; of three dimensions, solid; involving cube of a quantity; ~ *content*, volume (of solid) expressed in cubic feet, metres, etc.; ~ *foot, inch*, etc., volume of a cube whose edge is one foot, inch, etc.; ~ *measures*: see Appendix X. **cūb'ĭcal** *adj.* **cūb'ĭcally** *adv.*

cūb'ĭcle *n.* Small separate sleeping-compartment in schools etc.; any small partitioned space.

cūb'ifōrm *adj.* Cube-shaped.

cūb'ĭsm *n.* Phase of Post-Impressionist art, initiated *c* 1907 by Picasso and Braque, in which objects were reduced to cubic and other geometrical forms. **cūb'ĭst** *n.* & *adj.* **cūbĭs'tĭc** *adj.*

cūb'ĭt *n.* Ancient measure of length, 18 to 22 in. **cūb'ĭtal** *adj.* 1. Of the length of a cubit. 2. Of the forearm or corresponding part in animals. [L *cubitum* length of forearm (*cubitus* elbow)]

cūb'oid *adj.* Cube-shaped, like a cube; ~ *bone*, one of the bones of the foot, between heel bone and 4th and 5th metatarsal bones (ill. FOOT). ~ *n.* Solid resembling cube, with rectangular faces not all equal; cuboid bone.

cŭck'ĭng-stōōl *n.* (hist.) Chair in which disorderly women etc. were tied and ducked in water as punishment.

cŭck'old *n.* Husband of unfaithful wife. ~ *v.t.* Make a cuckold of. [OF *cucu* cuckoo]

cuck'ōō (kŏŏ-) *n.* Migratory bird (*Cuculus canorus*) with characteristic note or cry, which winters in N. Africa and reaches British Isles in April, depositing its eggs in nests of small birds; *~-clock*, clock in which hours are 'struck' by imitation of cuckoo's call; *~-flower*, lady's smock, *Cardamine pratensis*, meadow-plant with pale lilac flower, blooming in spring; *~-pint*, wild arum, *A. maculatum*; *~-spit*, frothy secretion exuded by and enveloping the nymphs of certain insects (in Gt Britain usu. the frog-hopper

CUCKOO

Length 13 in.

Philaenus spumarius) on leaves, stems, etc., of plants. ~ *adj.* (slang) Crazy. [OF *cuca* imit. of bird's cry]

cūc'ŭmber *n.* 1. Creeping plant, *Cucumis sativus*, native of S. Asia, widely cultivated for its long fleshy fruit; the fruit of this, commonly eaten as salad. 2. (U.S.) (also *~-tree*), the *Magnolia acuminata* and other Amer. species, with fruits resembling small cucumbers.

cūcûrb'it *n.* Gourd. **cūcûrbĭtā'ceous** (-shus) *adj.*

cŭd *n.* Food that ruminating animal brings back from first stomach into mouth and chews at leisure.

cŭd'bear (-bār) *n.* Purple or violet powder for dyeing, prepared from various lichens, esp. *Lecanora tartarea*; this lichen. [named by Dr *Cuthbert* Gordon, 18th-c. patentee]

cŭd'dle *v.* Hug, embrace, fondle; lie close and snug; nestle together; curl oneself *up*. ~ *n.* Hug, embrace. **cŭd'dlesome, cŭdd'ly** *adjs.* Nice to cuddle.

cŭdd'y *n.* Cabin of half-decked boat; (hist.) saloon of large ship; closet; cupboard.

cŭd'gel *n.* Short thick stick used as weapon; *take up cudgels for*, defend vigorously. ~ *v.t.* Beat with cudgel; (fig.) rack (one's brains).

cŭd'weed *n.* Composite plant, *Gnaphalium sylvaticum* or allied or similar plant, with chaffy scales surrounding flower-heads.

cūe[1] *n.* Last word or words of a speech in a play, serving as signal to another actor to enter or speak; similar guide to musical performer; sign or intimation when or how to speak or act; proper or politic course.

cūe[2] *n.* 1. (usu. *queue*) Pigtail. 2. Long straight tapering rod of wood tipped with leather, with which balls are struck in billiards etc.

Cūf'a, Kūf'a. Ancient city near Babylon, residence of caliphs before building of Baghdad, and a seat of Mohammedan learning. **Cūf'ic, Kūf'ic** *adj.* & *n.* Of Cufa; (of, in) an early, angular, form of Arabic writing, found in early copies of the Koran, and much used as decoration.

cŭff[1] *n.* Ornamental part at bottom of sleeve; band, lace, etc., finishing sleeve; separate band of (stiffened) linen worn round wrist; *~ link*, pair of linked buttons for fastening cuff.

cŭff[2] *n.* Blow on head with fist or open hand. ~ *v.t.* Strike thus.

cŭff'ee, cŭff'y *n.* (U.S.) Negro. [Personal name formerly common among Amer. Negroes]

cui bōn'ō? (kī). Who profits by it? (i.e. who is most likely to have brought it about?); (erron., pop.) to what purpose?

cuirăss' (kwĭ-) *n.* Body armour, breastplate and backplate fastened together (ill. ARMOUR). **cuirassier** (kwĭrasēr', kūr-) *n.* Horse-soldier wearing cuirass; heavy cavalryman in some European armies.

cuisine (kwĭzēn') *n.* Kitchen arrangements; style of cooking.

cuisse (kwĭs) *n.* (hist., usu. pl.) Thigh armour (ill. ARMOUR).

Cŭldee'. Member of an ancient Scoto-Irish religious order, found from the 8th c. onwards and brought under canonical rule by the end of the 11th c.

cul-de-săc' (kōō-) *n.* Blind alley.

cŭl'ĭnary *adj.* Pertaining to a kitchen or cooking; fit for cooking.

cŭll *v.t.* Pick (flower etc.); select. ~ *n.* Animal removed from flock (and usu. fattened) as inferior or too old for breeding.

cullender: see COLANDER.

cŭll'ėt *n.* (glass-making) Small pieces of glass at neck of bottle etc. knocked off in blowing the glass; refuse glass with which crucibles are replenished.

Cullŏd'en. Place near Inverness, Scotland, the site of the battle in which in 1746 the Duke of Cumberland defeated the force of the Young PRETENDER.

cŭll'y *n.* Dupe, simpleton; man, fellow.

cŭlm[1] *n.* Coal-dust, esp. of anthracite.

cŭlm[2] *n.* (bot.) Stem of plant, esp. jointed, usu. hollow, stem of grasses (ill. GRASS).

cŭl'mėn *n.* Upper ridge of bird's bill (ill. BIRD).

cŭl'mĭnant *adj.* At, forming, the top; (of heavenly body) on the meridian. **cŭl'mĭnāte** *v.i.* Reach its highest point; (astron.) be on the meridian. **cŭlmĭnā'tion** *n.*

cŭl'pable *adj.* Criminal, blameworthy. **cŭlpabĭl'ĭty, cŭl'pableness** *ns.* **cŭl'pably** *adv.*

cŭl'prĭt *n.* Offender; prisoner at the bar. [orig. in formula *Culprit, how will you be tried*, said by Clerk of Crown to prisoner pleading 'Not Guilty'; prob. abbrev. of Anglo-Fr. *Culpable: prest d'averrer* etc. (You are) guilty: (I am) ready to prove etc.]

cŭlt, cŭl'tus *ns.* System of religious worship; devotion, homage, to person or thing; fad, passing fancy, for some particular thing.

cŭl'tĭvāte *v.t.* 1. Till; break up (ground) with cultivator. 2. Improve, develop (person, mind, etc., esp. in past part.); pay attention to, cherish. **cŭltĭvā'tion** *n.* Cultivating, cultivated state.

cŭl'tĭvātor *n.* 1. Tiller, husbandman, farmer. 2. Agricultural implement for breaking up ground and uprooting weeds between drills of crops.

cŭl'ture *n.* 1. Tillage; rearing, production (of pearls, silk, etc.); artificial development of bacteria etc. in specially prepared media; bacteria etc. so produced. 2. Improvement or refinement of mind, manners, etc., by education and training; condition of being thus trained and refined; particular form or type of intellectual development or civilization. ~ *v.t.* Cultivate (esp. fig., chiefly in past part.). **cŭl'tural** *adj.* **cŭl'turally** *adv.*

cŭl'verĭn *n.* (hist.) Small firearm; large cannon, very long in proportion to its bore, used esp. in 16th and 17th centuries.

cŭl'vert *n.* Channel, conduit, carrying water across or under road, canal, etc.; conduit for electric cable.

cŭm *prep.* With; ~ *grano* (*salis*) (grăn'ō săl'ĭs), with caution or reserve (lit. with a grain of salt); ~ *dividend*, (abbrev. ~ *div.*) including dividend about to be paid. [L]

cum. *abbrev.* Cumulative.

Cumb. *abbrev.* Cumberland.

cŭm'ber *v.t.* Hamper, hinder; burden. **cŭm'bersome** *adj.* Unwieldy, clumsy. **cŭm'bersomely** *adv.* **cŭm'bersomenėss** *n.*

Cŭm'berland[1]. County of NW. England.

Cŭm'berland[2], William Augustus, Duke of (1726–65). 2nd son of George II; in command of the English army at CULLODEN (1746); known as 'the Butcher' on account of the severity with which he stamped out disaffection among the Highlanders.

Cŭm'brĭa. Ancient British northern kingdom, including Cumberland. **Cŭm'brĭan** *adj.* & *n.* (Native) of Cumbria or Cumberland.

cŭm'brous *adj.* Cumbersome. **cŭm'brously** *adv.* **cŭm'brousnėss** *n.*

cum d., cum div. *abbrevs.* Cum dividend.

cŭm'(m)ĭn *n.* Umbelliferous fennel-like plant, *Cummin cyminum*, cultivated in the Levant for its aromatic and carminative seed.

cŭmm'erbŭnd *n.* (Anglo-Ind.) Waist-sash. [Hind. *kamar-band* loin band]

cŭm'ūlāte *v.* Accumulate. **cūmūlā'tion** *n.*

cŭm'ūlatĭve *adj.* Tending to accumulate; increasing in force etc. by successive additions; ~ *vote, voting*, etc., system in which each voter has as many votes as there are representatives, and may give

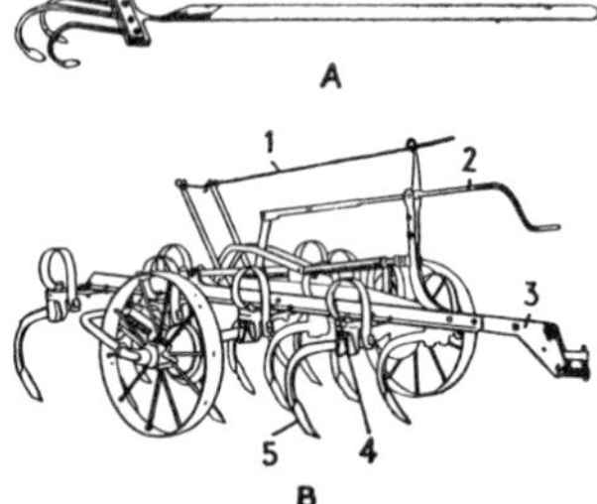

A. HAND CULTIVATOR. B. MECHANICAL CULTIVATOR

1. Trip cord. 2. Depth control lever. 3. Draw bar. 4. Loop spring. 5. Tine

all to one candidate; ~ *preference shares*, shares entitling holder to arrears of interest before other shares receive any for current year. **cūm'ūlatively** *adv.* **cūm'ūlativeness** *n.*

cūmūlonim'bus *n.* (meteor.) Type of low dense cloud, a tall voluminous mass, present in thunderstorms (ill. CLOUD).

cūm'ūlus *n.* (pl. *-lī*). (meteor.) Form of cloud, usu. low, consisting of rounded masses heaped on each other on nearly horizontal base, frequent in summer skies (ill. CLOUD).

Cūnard', Sir Samuel (1787–1865). A native of Nova Scotia who established the first Atlantic steamship service and founded the famous ~ *Line*.

cūn'ėate *adj.* Wedge-shaped.

cūn'ėiform (*or* kūnē'ĭ-) *adj.* & *n.* Wedge-shaped; (character, writing) of ancient inscriptions of

CUNEIFORM CHARACTERS

Assyria, Persia, etc., composed of wedge-shaped or arrow-headed elements.

cŭnn'ing *n.* Skilful deceit, craft, artifice, artfulness; ability, skill, expertness. ~ *adj.* Expert, dextrous; skilful, ingenious; artful, crafty; (U.S. colloq.) quaintly pretty, attractive, taking. **cŭn'ningly** *adv.*

cŭp *n.* 1. Drinking-vessel, with or without handle and stem; ornamental cup or other vessel as prize for race or other contest. 2. Rounded cavity, as socket of certain bones, cup-shaped hardened involucre of an acorn, calyx of flower, cup-shaped blossom, etc. 3. Cupful; (U.S., as measure in recipes) half-pint, 8 fluid ounces; (fig.) something to be partaken of, experience, portion, lot; (pl.) potations, drunken revelry; *in one's ~s*, drunk. 4. Various beverages of wine, cider, fruit juice, etc., sweetened and flavoured, and usu. iced. 5. *~-and-ball*, toy consisting of cup at end of stem, with attached ball to be thrown and caught in cup or on spiked end of stem; *~-and-ring*, kind of mark found cut in megalithic monuments, with circular depression surrounded by concentric rings; *~-bearer*, one who serves wine, esp. officer of royal or noble household; *~-cake*, cake of which ingredients are measured by the cupful, or which is baked in small (paper) cups; *~-moss*, the goblet lichen (*Cladonia pyxidata*), with cup-shaped processes arising from thallus. ~ *v.* 1. (hist.) Bleed (person) by means of *cupping-glass*, a glass vessel with open mouth applied to the skin and forming a partial vacuum. 2. Take or contain as in a cup, make or be cup-shaped. **cŭp'ful** *n.*

cupboard (cŭb'erd) *n.* Shelved closet or cabinet for crockery, provisions, etc.

cūp'el *n.* Shallow absorbent vessel used in assaying the ores of precious metals. ~ *v.t.* Assay or refine in cupel. **cūpellā'tion** *n.*

Cūp'ĭd. The Roman god of love, son of Venus; identified with the Greek Eros; often represented as a beautiful naked boy with wings, carrying bow and arrows with which he wounds his victims; *~'s bow* (upper edge of) upper lip, curved like the double-curved bow of Cupid. [L *cupido* desire, love]

cūpid'ĭty *n.* Greed of gain, avarice.

cūp'ola *n.* 1. Dome, forming the roof of a building or part of a building; diminutive dome above a roof (ill. DOME); ceiling of dome. 2. Furnace for melting metals for casting (formerly with dome leading to chimney, now often without dome). 3. Armour-plated revolving dome protecting guns on warship. 4. (anat., zool.) Dome-like organ or process.

cūprammōn'ĭum *n.* Solution of copper hydroxide in ammonia capable of dissolving cellulose; artificial silk made from this.

cūp'rĭc *adj.* (chem.) Containing copper in bivalent state.

cūp'ro-nĭck'el *n.* Alloy of 75% copper and 25% nickel used in Britain since 1947 for coins formerly made of silver.

cūp'rous *adj.* (chem.) Containing copper in univalent state.

cūp'ūle *n.* (bot., zool.) Cup-shaped organ, receptacle, etc.

cūr *n.* Worthless, low-bred, or snappish dog; surly, ill-bred, or cowardly fellow.

Cūr'açao (-sō). Dutch island in the Caribbean, near coast of Venezuela. **cūr'açao, curaçoa** *n.* Liqueur of spirits flavoured with peel of bitter oranges.

cūr'acy *n.* Curate's office; benefice of perpetual curate.

cūrar'ė *n.* Blackish-brown resinous bitter poisonous substance extracted from *Strychnos toxifera* and other S. Amer. tropical plants, and used by Indians to poison their arrows; it consists of various alkaloids and its chief effect is to block the action of the motor nerves on skeletal muscle. [corrupt. of *wurali*, native Carib name]

cūr'arine (-ēn) *n.* Purified alkaloid extract from curare used medicinally to obtain muscular relaxation.

cūr'assow (-sō) *n.* One of a family of turkey-like birds of Central and S. America. [f. *Curaçao* island]

cūr'ate *n.* Assistant to parish priest in Church of England and in R.C. Church in Ireland; *~-in-charge*, clergyman appointed to take charge of parish during incapacity or suspension of incumbent; *perpetual ~*, incumbent (now ranking as vicar) of chapel of ecclesiastical district forming part of an ancient parish.

cūr'ative *adj.* & *n.* (Thing) tending to cure (esp. disease).

cūrāt'or *n.* 1. Person in charge, manager; keeper, custodian, of museum; member of board managing property or having general superintendence in university. 2. (Rom. and Sc. law) guardian of minor, lunatic, etc. **cūratōr'ial** *adj.* **cūrāt'orship** *n.*

cūrb *n.* 1. Chain, strap, passing under lower jaw of horse, used as check (ill. SADDLE); (fig.) check, restraint. 2. Hard swelling on back of horse's hind leg; disease characterized by this. 3. Frame round top of well; timber or iron plate round top of circular structure; kerb; *~-roof*, mansard roof; *-stone*, kerb-stone. ~ *v.t.* Apply curb to; restrain.

cūrc'ūma *n.* 1. Genus of tuberous plants yielding E. Ind. arrowroot, mango-ginger, turmeric, etc. 2. Turmeric. [Arab. *kurkum* saffron, turmeric]

cūrd *n.* Coagulated substance formed (naturally or artificially) by action of acids on milk, made into cheese or eaten as food; anything resembling this; fatty substance found between flakes of boiled salmon; ~ *soap*, white soap made with tallow and soda. **cūr'dle** *v.* Congeal, form into curd; (fig.) ~ *the blood*, said of effect of horror, fear, etc. **cūrd'y** *adj.* Like curd; (of salmon) full of curd.

cūre[1] *n.* 1. Remedy; course of medical or other treatment (esp. of specified kind); successful medical treatment, restoration to health. 2. Spiritual charge or oversight of parishioners etc.; parish etc. ~ *v.* 1. Restore to health; remedy (an evil). 2. Preserve (meat, fruit, hides) by salting, drying, smoking, etc. **cūr'able** *adj.* **cūrabil'ity** *n.*

cūre[2] *n.* (slang) Odd or eccentric person.

curé (kū'rā) *n.* Parish priest in France etc.

cūrĕtte' *n.* Surgeon's small scoop-like instrument. ~ *v.t.* Scrape with curette. **cūrĕtt'age** (*or* kūr'itahzh) *n.* Process of curetting.

cūrf'ew *n.* Medieval regulation for extinction of fires at fixed hour in evening (orig. for prevention of conflagrations); hour for this, bell announcing it; ringing of bell at fixed evening hour, still surviving in some towns; (under martial law etc.) signal or time after which inhabitants must be indoors.

cūr'ia *n.* 1. One of the ten divisions of each of the three ancient Roman tribes; building belonging to a Roman curia, serving primarily for worship. 2. The senate-house at Rome; senate of ancient Italian towns. 3. Court of justice, esp. under feudal organization. 4. The papal court, government departments of the Vatican. **cūr'ial** *adj.* Of a curia; of the papal court.

Curie[1] (kū'rĭ). Name of two

French chemists and physicists, Marie (1867–1934) and her husband Pierre (1859–1906); discoverers of radium, 1898.

cūr'ie[2] *n*, Standard unit of radium emanation, the quantity in equilibrium with one gram of radium. [f. CURIE[1]]

cūr'iō *n*. Curious object of art.

cūriŏs'ĭty *n*. 1. Desire to know; inquisitiveness. 2. Strangeness; strange or rare object.

cūr'ious *adj*. 1. Eager to learn; inquisitive. 2. Careful, minute. 3. Strange, surprising, odd. **cūr'iously** *adv*. **cūr'iousnėss** *n*.

cūr'ium *n*. (chem.) A radioactive metallic TRANSURANIC element; symbol Cm, at. no. 96, principal isotope 242. [f. CURIE[1]]

cūrl *n*. 1. Spiral or convolute lock of hair; anything spiral or incurved; act of curling; state of being curled; *~-paper*, piece of soft paper twisted into the hair to make it curl. 2. Disease of potatoes etc. in which shoots or leaves are curled up . ~ *v*. 1. Bend, coil, into spiral shape; move in spiral form. 2. Play at CURLING.

cūrl'ew *n*. Wading bird of the genus *Numenius* with long slender

CURLEW
Length 21–22 in.

curved bill and characteristic cry, frequenting estuaries, sea-shores, and moors; *stone-~*, an inland bird, *Oedicnemus*.

cūrl'ing *n*. (esp.) 1. Scottish game played on ice (*~-pond* or other smooth frozen surface) with large stones which are hurled along a defined space (the *rink*) towards a mark (the *tee*); the *~-stones* are of polished granite, cheese-shaped, and not more than 36 in. in circumference or 50 lb. in weight, with an iron or wooden handle on the upper surface. 2. *~-iron*, *~-tongs*, tongs for curling the hair.

cūrl'y *adj*. Having, arranged in, curls. **cūrl'inėss** *n*.

cūrmŭdg'eon (-jn) *n*. Churlish or miserly fellow. **cūrmŭdg'eonly** *adj*.

cŭ'rrach, cŭ'rragh[1] (-r*a*) *n*. Coracle.

cŭ'rragh[2] (-r*aχ*, -r*a*) *n*. Marshy waste ground, in Ireland and Isle of Man; the *C~*, a level stretch of open ground in County Kildare, famous for its race-course and military camp.

cŭ'rrant *n*. 1. Dried fruit of a small seedless variety of grape grown in the Levant, much used in cookery. 2. Small round black, red or white berry of *Ribes nigrum* and *R. rubrum*, natives of N. Europe; these shrubs, or others of the same species, esp. the *flowering ~*, *Ribes sanguineum*, native of N. America, cultivated for its pink or red flowers. [orig. *raisins of Corauntz* (Corinth)]

cŭ'rrency *n*. 1. Time during which thing is current; (of money) circulation; prevalence (of words, ideas, etc.). 2. Money in actual use in a country; SOFT, HARD, ~: see these words; *~ note*, paper money used as currency, esp. English notes for £1 and 10*s*. issued by the Treasury 1918–28.

cŭ'rrent *adj*. In general circulation or use; (of time) now passing; belonging to the current time; *pass*, *go*, etc. ~, be generally accepted as true or genuine; *~ account*, customer's account at bank to meet current expenditure, drawn on by cheque. **cŭ'rrently** *adv*. **cŭ'rrent** *n*. 1. Running stream; water, air, etc., moving in given direction. 2. Course, tendency (of events, opinions, etc.). 3. Transmission of electric force, electric force transmitted, through a body.

cŭ'rricle *n*. Light open 2-wheeled carriage drawn by 2 horses abreast (now obs.).

CURRICLE

cŭrrĭc'ūlum *n*. (pl. *-la*). Course (of study). **cŭrrĭc'ūlar** *adj*.

cŭ'rrier *n*. One who dresses and colours tanned leather.

cūrr'ish *adj*. Like a cur; snappish; mean-spirited. **cūrr'ishly** *adv*. **cūrr'ishnėss** *n*.

cŭ'rry[1] *n*. Dish of meat, fish, fruit, or vegetables, cooked with bruised spices and turmeric, and usu. served with rice; *~-paste*, *-powder*, preparations of turmeric and strong spices for making curries. ~ *v.t.* Make into curry; flavour like curry. [Tamil *kari* sauce]

cŭ'rry[2] *v.t.* 1. Rub down or dress (horse etc.) with comb; dress (tanned leather) by soaking, scraping, beating, colouring, etc.; (fig.) thrash; ~ *favour* (orig. *favel*, f. OF *fauvel* chestnut horse), ingratiate oneself (*with* person) by officious courtesy etc.; *~-comb*, metal comb for currying horses etc.; (*v.t.*) curry.

cūrse *n*. 1. Utterance (by deity or person invoking deity) supposed or intended to consign person or thing to destruction, divine vengeance, etc.; formal ecclesiastical censure, sentence of excommunication. 2. Profane oath, imprecation. 3. Evil inflicted in response to curse; great evil, bane; *~ of Scotland*, the 9 of diamonds in playing-cards (supposed to be so called from its resemblance to the 9 lozenges in the armorial bearings of Lord Stair, who had some share in sanctioning the massacre of Glencoe in 1692 and in the Union of Scotland with England in 1707). ~ *v*. Utter curse against; excommunicate; blaspheme; afflict *with*; utter curses.

cūrs'ėd, cūrst *adj*. (esp.) Damnable, abominable; (archaic) cantankerous; (as *adv.*) cursedly. **cūrs'ėdly** *adv*. **cūrs'ėdnėss** *n*.

cūrs'ive *adj*. & *n*. (Writing) done without lifting the pen, so that the characters are joined together.

cūrs'or *n*. Transparent slide engraved with hair-line forming part of slide-rule etc.

cūrsōr'ial *adj*. (zool., of birds etc.) Having limbs adapted for running.

cūrs'ory *adj*. Hasty, hurried. **cūrs'orily** *adv*. **cūrs'orinėss** *n*.

cūrt *adj*. Discourteously brief; terse, concise. **cūrt'ly** *adv*. **cūrt'nėss** *n*.

cūrtail' *v.t.* Cut short. **cūrtail'ment** *n*.

cūrt'ail-stĕp *n*. Lowest step of stair, with outer end carried round.

cūrt'ain (-tn) *n*. 1. Suspended cloth used as screen round bed, at window, in front of picture, etc.; screen separating stage of theatre from auditorium. 2. Plain wall of fortified place, connecting two towers etc. (ill. CASTLE); piece of plain wall not supporting a roof; partition, cover, in various technical senses; (mil.) barrage. 3. *~-call*, call for actor to appear before curtain after play or scene of play; *iron ~*: see IRON; *~-lecture*, wife's reproof to husband in bed; *~-raiser*, short opening piece performed before principal play in theatre; *~-ring*, one of rings by which curtain is hung, which slide on rod when curtain is drawn; *~-rod*, horizontal rod from which curtain is hung. ~ *v.t.* Furnish, cover, shut *off*, with curtains.

cūrtān'a (*or* -ah-) *n*. Sword without a point borne before sovereign of England at coronation, as emblem of mercy.

cūrt'ilage *n*. (law) Area attached to dwelling-house and forming, or regarded as forming, one enclosure with it.

cūrt's(e)y *n*. Feminine movement of respect or salutation, made by placing one foot behind the other and bending the knees so that trunk is lowered (usu. *make*, *drop*, *a* ~). ~ *v.i.* Make curtsey (*to* person).

cūrv'ature *n*. Curving; curved form; (geom.) amount or rate of deviation (of curve) from straight line or curved surface from plane.

cûrve *n.* Line of which no part is straight, locus traced by moving point the direction of whose motion continuously changes or deviates from a straight line; curved form or thing; (on graph or diagram) line drawn from point to point so as to represent diagrammatically a continuous variation of quantity, force, etc. ~ *v.* Bend or shape so as to form curve.

cûrvĕt′ (*or* kẽrv′ĭt) *n.* Horse's leap with forelegs raised together, and hind legs raised with spring before forelegs reach ground. ~ *v.i.* (of horse or rider) Make curvet.

cûrvilĭn′ėar *adj.* Constrained by, consisting of, curved line(s); ~ *tracery*: see ill. WINDOW. **cûrvilĭnėăr′ĭty** *n.* **cûrvilĭn′ėarly** *adv.*

Cûrz′on, George Nathaniel, first marquess of ~ (1859–1925). English statesman; viceroy of India 1899–1905 and foreign secretary 1918–22; ~ *line*, the eastern boundary of Poland as proposed, but not accepted, at the Peace Conference at Versailles (1919), substantially the same as boundary accepted by the Poles at the Potsdam conference (1945).

cŭs′cŭs *n.* Long fibrous aromatic root of an Indian grass, *Andropogon muricatus*, used for making fans, screens, etc. [Pers. *khas khas*]

cŭsh′at *n.* (Sc. and dial.) Wood-pigeon, ring-dove.

cu′shion (kŏŏshn) *n.* 1. Mass of soft material stuffed into cloth or silk covering, for sitting, kneeling, or reclining on. 2. Pin-cushion; elastic lining or rim of inner side of billiard-table, from which the balls rebound (ill. BILLIARDS); steam or air left in cylinder of steam- or air-engine as buffer to piston. 3. Fleshy part of buttock (of pig etc.); frog of horse's hoof. 4. ~*-tyre*, (bicycle-)tyre of rubber tubing stuffed with shreds of rubber. ~ *v.* Furnish, protect, with cushions; suppress (complaints etc.) quietly; (billiards) place or lean (ball) against cushion; cause ball to rebound off cushion.

cush′y (kŏŏ-) *adj.* (slang; of post, task, etc.) Easy, pleasant, comfortable. [Hind. *khush* pleasant]

cŭsp *n.* Apex, peak; (geom.) point at which two branches of curve meet and stop (ill. ROULETTE); (archit.) projecting point between small arcs in tracery (ill. WINDOW); (bot.) pointed end, esp. of leaf. **cŭsped** (-pt) *adj.*

cŭs′pidal *adj.* Of (the nature of) a cusp. **cŭsp′ĭdate, -āted,** *adjs.*

cŭs′pidôr *n.* (U.S.) Spittoon.

cŭss *n.* (U.S.) Curse; person, creature. **cŭss′ėdnėss** *n.* Perversity.

cŭs′tard *n.* Dish of beaten eggs mixed with milk, freq. sweetened, and baked, or cooked in saucepan and served as sweet sauce; ~*-apple*, fruit of S. Amer. and W. Ind. tree, *Anona reticulata*, with dark-brown rind and yellowish pulp like custard in appearance and flavour; the tree itself, which was introduced into E. Indies in 16th c.; ~ *powder*, preparation of coloured cornflour etc. as substitute for eggs in boiled custard.

cŭstōd′ĭal *adj.* Relating to custody.

cŭstōd′ĭan *n.* Guardian, keeper, esp. of public building etc.

cŭs′tody *n.* Guardianship, care; imprisonment.

cŭs′tom *n.* 1. Usual practice; (law) established usage having the force of law. 2. (pl.) Duty levied upon imports from foreign countries; *the Customs*, department of Civil Service that deals with levying of customs; ~(*s*)*-house*, office (esp. in seaport) at which customs are collected. 3. Business patronage or support; ~ *clothes*, (U.S.) clothes made to measure (so ~*-made*, *-suit*, etc.).

cŭs′tomary *adj.* Usual; (law) subject to, held by, custom (of a manor etc.). **cŭs′tomarily** *adv.* **cŭs′tomarinėss** *n.* **cŭs′tomary** *n.* Written collection of customs of a country.

cŭs′tomer *n.* Buyer, purchaser; (*queer*, *ugly*, etc. ~), person to have to do with.

cŭt *v.* (past t. and past part. *cŭt*). 1. Penetrate, wound, with edged instrument (also fig.); divide with knife etc. (*in*, *into*, pieces etc.); detach by cutting; carve (meat). 2. Cross, intersect; pass *through*, *across*, etc.; (slang) run. 3. Reduce by cutting (hair etc.); reduce (wages, price, time, etc.); shape, fashion, by cutting. 4. Perform, execute, make, as ~ *a caper*, *dash*, *figure*, etc. 5. Divide (pack of cards) to select dealer or partners, prevent cheating, etc. 6. In cricket, hit ball to the off with chopping movement of bat; in lawn-tennis, strike ball across its line of flight so as to impart spin etc. 7. Renounce acquaintance of (person), decline to recognize him; absent oneself from, avoid, renounce. 8. ~ (*tooth*), have it appear through gum. 9. ~ *down*, bring or throw down by cutting; reduce (expenses etc.); ~ *in*, enter abruptly, interpose (in conversation); join in game of cards by taking place of player who cuts out; supersede a partner during a dance; (motoring) obstruct path of vehicle one has just overtaken by returning to one's side of the road too soon; ~ *off*, remove by cutting; bring to an end; intercept, interrupt (supplies, communications); exclude (*from*); ~ *out*, remove by cutting; outdo or supplant (rival); shape by cutting (out of a piece); form, fashion; prepare (*work* to be done); (cards) be excluded from game as result of cutting; (motoring) obstruct path of oncoming vehicle by moving out from one's own side of the road, esp. in order to overtake another vehicle; capture (enemy ship) by getting between it and shore; stop, leave off; disconnect; ~ *up*, cut in pieces; destroy utterly; criticize severely; distress greatly; ~ *up for* (colloq.), leave (specified amount); ~ *up rough*, show resentment. 10. ~*-and-dried*, (of opinions etc.) ready-made, lacking freshness; ~*-away*, (coat) with skirt cut back from the waist; ~*-off*, shorter channel or route cutting off bend etc., (U.S.) by-pass; ~*-out*, contrivance for automatically disconnecting electric circuit; device in motor-car etc. for releasing exhaust gas rapidly without passage through silencer; *cut′purse*, thief; *cut′-throat* (*n.*) murderer; bloodthirsty ruffian; (*adj.*) intensive, merciless; (of card-games) 3-handed; *cut′-water*, knee of head of ship, dividing water before it reaches bow; forward edge of prow; *cut′worm*, caterpillar that cuts off young plants level with ground. ~ *n.* 1. Act of cutting; stroke, blow, with knife, sword, whip; act, speech, deeply wounding the feelings; excision of a part; reduction in rates or prices. 2. Particular stroke in various games (see *v.* above, sense 6). 3. Refusal to recognize an acquaintance. 4. Passage or way across, esp. as opposed to going round about (*short* ~). 5. Style to which garment etc. is cut; fashion, shape, make. 6. Wound made by cutting; incision, slash. 7. Passage or channel cut out; railway cutting. 8. Narrow opening in floor of stage of theatre, by which scenes are moved up and down. 9. Woodcut. 10. Piece, esp. of meat, cut off.

cūtān′ėous *adj.* Of the skin.

cūte *adj.* (colloq.) Clever, shrewd; ingenious; (U.S.) quaint, attractive. **cūte′ly** (-tl-) *adv.* **cūte′nėss** *n.*

cū′tĭcle *n.* Epidermis or other superficial skin; skin at base of finger-nail; (bot.) continuous protective layer of impervious material secreted by cells of epidermis (ill. LEAF). **cūtĭc′ūlar** *adj.*

cū′tĭe *n.* (U.S. slang) Smart attractive young woman.

cū′tĭs *n.* (anat.) True skin or derma.

cŭtl′ass *n.* Short sword with slightly curved blade, esp. that used by sailors (ill. SWORD).

cŭt′ler *n.* One who makes or deals in knives and similar utensils.

cŭt′lery *n.* Trade of cutler; things made or sold by cutlers; collection of knives and similar articles in use in a household.

cŭt′lėt *n.* Neck-chop of mutton; small piece of veal, broiled or fried in bread-crumbs; imitation of mutton-cutlet in minced fish, etc.

cŭtt′er *n.* 1. Person, thing, that cuts; tailor etc. who takes measures and cuts out cloth; cutting-part of machine. 2. Superior kind of brick that can be cut and rubbed.

3. Boat belonging to ship of war, fitted for rowing and sailing; small single-masted vessel rigged like sloop but with running bowsprit (ill. SMACK); (U.S.) small light sleigh, usu. drawn by one horse.

cŭtt'ing *n.* (esp.) 1. Excavation of high ground for railway, road, etc. 2. Paragraph etc. cut from newspaper etc. 3. Piece cut from vegetative part of plant and capable of growing into new plant. ~ *adj.* (esp.) That wounds the mind or feelings. **cŭtt'ingly** *adv.*

cŭt'tle *n.* (usu. *~-fish*) Cephalopod of the genus *Sepia*, esp. *S. officinalis*, which when pursued ejects black fluid from a sac so as to darken water; *~-bone*, internal shell of cuttle-fish used as food for cage-birds and when ground as a polishing powder.

cŭtt'y *adj.* (Sc.) Cut short; abnormally short; *C~ Sark*, (orig. 'short shirt') very fast clipper built at Dumbarton 1869, said to have sailed from Sydney to London in 75 days; *~-stool*, stool in Presbyterian churches where offenders against chastity sat to receive public rebuke during service. ~ *n.* Short pipe.

C.V.O. *abbrev.* Commander of the Royal Victorian Order.

cwm (kōōm) *n.* 1. (Welsh) Valley, coomb. 2. (geog.) Cauldron-shaped hollow, orig. formed by glacier, on mountain-side, corrie (ill. MOUNTAIN).

C.W.S. *abbrev.* Co-operative Wholesale Society.

cwt *abbrev.* Hundredweight.

cÿăn'amīde process *n.* Commercial preparation of ammonia by action of steam on *calcium cyanamide*, $CaCN_2$.

cÿăn'ic *adj.* 1. Blue. 2. (chem.) Containing the group CNO; ~ *acid*, HCNO, a colourless pungent volatile unstable liquid.

cÿ'anīde *n.* Salt of hydrocyanic acid, HCN, compound of cyanide group CN with organic radical; ~ *process*, extraction of gold and silver from ore with dilute solution of sodium cyanide.

cÿăn'ogĕn *n.* A colourless inflammable highly poisonous gas, C_2N_2.

cÿanōs'is *n.* (path.) Blueness of skin caused by presence of large quantities of de-oxygenated blood in its minute vessels. **cÿanŏt'ic** *adj.*

Cÿb'ėlē. Goddess representing the fecundity of nature, worshipped in Phrygia; her cult passed to Greece where she was known as RHEA.

cÿbernĕt'ics *n.* Theory, study of communication and control in living organisms or machines.

cÿc'ăd *n.* (bot.) Plant of the genus *Cycas*, related to conifers, but resembling palms, the trunk of which yields sago. **cÿcadā'ceous** (-shus) *adj.*

Cÿc'ladēs (-z). Circular group of islands in the S. Aegean.

cÿc'lamen *n.* S. European genus of primulaceous plants with fleshy root-stocks, cultivated for their handsome early-blooming flowers.

cÿ'cle *n.* 1. Recurrent period (of events, phenomena, etc.); period of a thing's completion; (physics) one whole excursion of a repetitive phenomenon; one complete oscillation (ill. VIBRATION); esp. (elect.) short for *~-per-second*, the frequency of an alternating current or potential. 2. Complete set or series; series of poems or songs collected round central event, character, or idea. 3. Bicycle, tricycle, or similar machine; *~-car*, light motor-driven vehicle with 3 (rarely 4) wheels. ~ *v.i.* 1. Move in cycles. 2. Ride cycle.

cÿc'lic, -ical *adjs.* 1. Recurring in cycles; belonging to a definite chronological cycle. 2. Of a cycle of mythic and heroic story. 3. (bot., of flower) With its parts arranged in whorls. 4. (math.) Of a circle or cycle.

cÿc'list *n.* Rider of a cycle.

cÿc'loid *n.* Curve traced in space by point in circumference or on radius of a circle as the circle rolls along a straight line (ill. ROULETTE). **cÿcloid'al** *adj.*

cÿclŏm'ėter *n.* 1. Instrument for measuring circular arcs. 2. Apparatus attached to wheel of bicycle etc. for measuring distance traversed.

cÿc'lōne *n.* System of winds rotating around region of low barometric pressure (in N. hemisphere counter-clockwise, in S. clockwise; ill. WEATHER); violent destructive one (*tropical* ~) of limited diameter. **cÿclŏn'ic** *adj.*

cÿclop(a)ed'ia (-pēd-) *n.* = ENCYCLOPAEDIA. **cÿclop(a)ed'ic** *adj.*

Cÿclōpē'an, Cÿclōp'ian *adj.* 1. Of, like, a cyclops; huge. 2. (antiq.) Applied to an ancient style of masonry of immense irregular stones, found in Greece, Italy, etc., and anciently supposed to be the work of the Cyclops.

Cÿc'lŏps *n.* (pl. *-ops, -opses, -ōpēs*). 1. (Gk myth.) One of a race of one-eyed giants who inhabited an island and forged thunderbolts for Zeus. 2. (zool.) Genus of small freshwater crustaceans with an eye in the middle of the front of the head.

cÿclora'ma (-rah-) *n.* Circular panorama; curved back of stage.

cÿclŏs'tomous, cÿclostŏm'atous, *adjs.* Having a round sucking mouth, as a lamprey, or a circular shell-aperture, as some gastropods.

cÿc'lostÿle *n.* Device for multiplying copies of written document from stencil-plate cut by pen with small toothed wheel. ~ *v.t.* Print by cyclostyle.

cÿc'lotrŏn *n.* (physics) Apparatus for accelerating charged atomic particles by passing them repeatedly through the same electro-magnetic field, used in nuclear experiments.

cÿg'nėt *n.* Young swan.

cÿl'inder *n.* 1. (geom.) Solid generated by straight line moving parallel to itself and describing with its ends any fixed curve, esp. circle (ill. PRISM). 2. Roller-shaped body, hollow or solid. 3. Barrel-shaped object of baked clay covered with cuneiform writing and buried under foundations of ancient Babylonian or Assyrian temple; small stone of similar shape used as seal by Babylonians and Assyrians. 4. Cylindrical part of various machines, esp. chamber in which liquids or gases can exert pressure on a moving piston; metal roller used in printing to receive impression, carry printing plates, etc.

cÿlin'drical *adj.* Cylinder-shaped.

cÿl'indroid *adj.* & *n.* (Figure) like a cylinder.

cÿl'ix *n.* Ancient Greek cup with shallow bowl and stem (ill. VASE).

cÿm'a *n.* 1. (archit.) Moulding with double continuous curve; ~ *recta*, ~ *reversa*: see ill. MOULDING. 2. Cyme.

cÿm'bal *n.* One of a pair of concave brass or bronze plates, struck together to make ringing sound.

cÿm'balō *n.* (pl. *-os*). Dulcimer, kind of musical instrument with strings struck by small hammers held in hands.

cÿm'bifōrm *adj.* (anat., bot.) Boat-shaped.

cÿme *n.* (bot.) Inflorescence in which primary axis bears single terminal flower that develops first, system being continued by axes of secondary and higher orders (ill. INFLORESCENCE). **cÿmōse'** *adj.*

Cÿm'ric (k-) *adj.* Welsh. [Welsh *Cymru* Wales, *Cymry* the Welsh]

Cÿn'ėwulf (k-; -ōōlf). A Northumbrian poet of the latter part of the 8th c., the author of 4 poems in Old English contained in the 'Exeter Book' and the 'Vercelli Book'.

cÿn'ic *n.* 1. (*C~*) Philosopher of an ancient Greek sect founded by Antisthenes which showed contempt for ease, wealth, and the enjoyments of life. 2. One who sarcastically discredits the sincerity or goodness of human motives and actions. ~ *adj.* Of, characteristic of, Cynic philosophers; cynical.

cÿn'ical *adj.* Churlish; captious; incredulous of human goodness; sneering. **cÿn'ically** *adv.* **cÿn'icism** *n.* [Gk *kuōn kunos* dog, nickname for cynic]

cÿnocĕph'alus *n.* 1. One of a fabled race of men with dogs' heads. 2. (zool.) Dog-faced baboon.

Cÿnoglŏss'um *n.* Genus of tall flowering herbs of borage family.

cÿn'osūre (*or* -shoor) *n.* 1. The Pole-star; the constellation (Little Bear) containing this. 2. Centre of attraction or admiration. [Gk *kunosoura* dog's tail, Little Bear]

Cÿn'thia. Name for Artemis or

Diana, said to have been born on Mt. Cynthus; the moon. [L *Cynthia* (*dea*) the Cynthian goddess]

cȳph'er *n.* & *v.*: see CIPHER.

cy pres (sēprā') *adv.* (law) As near as possible (to testator's intentions). ~ *adj.* Approximate. ~ *n.* Approximation. [AF, = Fr. *si pres* so near]

cȳp'rĕss *n.* Coniferous tree, *Cupressus sempervirens*, of Persia and Levant, cultivated in Asia, Europe, etc., with hard durable wood and dense dark foliage, formerly used for coffins and hence symbolic of mourning.

Cȳp'rian *adj.* & *n.* 1. (Inhabitant, native) of Cyprus (now usu. *Cypriot*). 2. Licentious (person).

cȳprĭn'oid *adj.* & *n.* (Fish) resembling or allied to carp, of the division *Cyprinoidea*.

Cȳp'rĭot(e) *adj.* & *n.* (Native, language) of Cyprus.

Cȳp'rus. Island in E. Mediterranean famous in ancient times for worship of Aphrodite; captured by the Turks 1570; from 1878 administered by Gt Britain on behalf of Turkey; taken over as British colony 1914; Republic since 1960; capital, Nicosia.

cȳp'sĕla *n.* (pl. *-lae*). (bot.) Achene developed from an inferior ovary, freq. with hairy pappus attached, as in dandelion (ill. FRUIT).

Cȳrēnā'ic *adj.* & *n.* (Philosopher) of the hedonistic school of Aristippus of Cyrene.

Cȳrēnā'ica. District of NE. Libya, N. Africa.

Cȳrēn'ē. Ancient Greek colony in what is now Libya, N. Africa.

Cȳ'ril[1], St. (376–444). Bishop of Alexandria.

Cȳ'ril[2], St. (9th c.). A Greek apostle to the Slavs, for whom he is reputed to have translated with his brother Methodius the Gospels, inventing an alphabet for the purpose.

Cȳrĭll'ic *adj.* Of the ~ *alphabet*, the alphabet, based upon Greek cursive hand of the 9th c., reputedly invented by St. CYRIL[2] and employed by the Slavonic peoples of the Eastern Church (Russians, Ukrainians, and Serbs).

Cȳr'us the Great (d. 529 B.C.). Founder of the Persian Empire; subdued the Greek cities of Asia Minor and conquered the Babylonians.

cȳst, cĭst *n.* (biol.) Hollow organ, bladder, etc., in animal or plant, containing liquid secretion; (path.) sac containing morbid matter, parasitic larva, etc.; cell containing embryo etc. **cȳs'tĭc** *adj.* Of the urinary bladder; of the gallbladder; of the nature of a cyst.

cȳstī'tis *n.* Inflammation of the bladder.

cȳs'toscōpe *n.* (med.) Instrument for visual examination of the bladder.

cȳstŏt'omy *n.* (med.) Operation of cutting open the bladder.

Cȳthēr'a. An island (mod. Gk *Kithira*) off the coast of the Peloponnese, sacred to the goddess Aphrodite, who was thence surnamed Cytherea.

cȳtŏl'ogy *n.* Study of the structure, physiology, and reproduction of cells.

cȳt'oplăsm *n.* The protoplasmic content of a cell other than the nucleus (ill. CELL).

czar, czarina etc.: see **TSAR** etc.

Czech (chĕk, chĕχ) *adj.* & *n.* (Native name for) Bohemian; (loosely) Czechoslovak.

Czechoslovak'ia (chĕk-; -ahk-). Republican State formed by the Treaty of Versailles (1919), including Bohemia, Moravia, and the northern Slavs of the old Austrian Empire; became communist after a revolution, 1948; capital, Prague. **Czĕchoslō'văk** *adj.* & *n.* (Native) of Czechoslovakia.

D

D, d (dē). 4th letter of the modern English and Roman alphabet, corresponding to Greek *delta* (Δ, δ), and Phoenician and Hebrew *daleth* (ד); it represents a voiced dental (or in English rather alveolar) stop consonant; (mus.) *D*, second note of 'natural' major scale (C major); scale or key with D as tonic; D, Roman numeral, = 500; *D*, symbol for day on which a military operation is timed to begin (= *day*, used before date is divulged, preceding days being designated as D–1, D–2, etc.); hence, *D-day*, applied esp. to 6th June 1944, day on which Allies landed in N. France; D, (billiards): see ill. BILLIARDS.

d. *abbrev.* Date; daughter; *dele* (= expunge); denarius (= penny); departs; died.

da: see DAD.

D.A. *abbrev.* (U.S.) District Attorney.

D.A.A.G. *abbrev.* Deputy Assistant Adjutant-General.

dăb[1] *n.* Slight or undecided but sudden blow, tap, peck; brief application of sponge, handkerchief, etc., to surface without rubbing; moisture, colour, etc., so applied. ~ *v.* Strike lightly or undecidedly, hit feebly *at*, tap, peck; press but not rub (surface) with sponge etc.; press (brush etc.) against surface.

dăb[2] *n.* Small flat-fish, *Pleuronectes limanda*, like flounder, common on sandy parts of British coast.

dăb[3] *n.* (colloq.) Expert, adept (*at*).

D.A.B. *abbrev.* Dictionary of American Biography.

dăbb'er *n.* (esp.) Soft rounded mass used to apply ink, colour, etc., to a surface, in printing, painting on china, etc.; brush for pressing damp paper on to type in stereotyping etc.

dăb'ble *v.* 1. Wet intermittently, slightly, or partly; soil, moisten, splash; move (with hands, bill, etc.) in shallow water, liquid, mud, etc., with splashing. 2. Employ oneself *in* (anything) in a dilettante way; work *in, at*, as matter of whim or fancy. **dăbb'ler** *n.*

dăb'chĭck *n.* The little grebe, *Podiceps ruficollis*, a small bird found in fresh water and noted for its diving; (U.S.) another grebe, *Podilymbus podiceps*.

dăb'ster *n.* = DAB[3] *n.*

da ca'pō (dah kah-). (mus. direction). Repeat from beginning (abbrev. D.C.). [It.]

dāce *n.* Small freshwater cyprinoid fish, *Leuciscus leuciscus*.

dachshund (dahks'hoond) *n.* Small dog of German breed with short crooked legs and very long body. [Ger., = 'badger-dog']

dacoit' *n.* Member of Indian or Burmese armed robber band. **dacoit'y** *n.* (Act of) gang-robbery. [Hind. *ḍakait*, f. *daka* gang-robbery]

dăc'tȳl *n.* Metrical foot of one long and two short, or one accented and two unaccented syllables (– ◡ ◡). **dactȳl'ic** *adj.* Of dactyl. ~ *n.* (usu. pl.) Dactylic verse(s). [Gk *daktulos* finger (f. resemblance to its 3 bones)]

dăd, da (dah), **dăd'a, dădd'y** *ns.* (colloq.; childish or familiar) Father (esp. as vocative); *daddy-long'legs*, crane-fly.

Dada (dah'dah) *n.* International movement in poetry and painting, initiated 1916 in Zürich, repudiating tradition, culture, and reason. **Da'daism** *n.* This movement; its doctrine. **Da'daist** *n.* [Fr. *être sur son dada*, ride one's hobby-horse]

dād'ō *n.* 1. Block forming body of pedestal, between base mouldings and cornice (ill. PEDESTAL). 2. Lower part of interior wall, of different material or colour from upper part (ill. WAINSCOT). **dād'ōed** (-ōd) *adj.*

daed'al (dē-) *adj.* (poet.) Skilful, inventive; manifold, complex, mysterious.

Daed'alus (dē-). (Gk myth.) The skilful artisan who constructed the Cretan labyrinth and made wings for himself and his son Icarus. **Daedāl'ian** *adj.* In the manner of Daedalus; intricate, labyrinthine. [Gk *daidalos* cunning one]

daemon, daemonic: see DEMON, DEMONIC.

dăff'odĭl *n.* (also **dăff'odĭlly, dăff'adowndĭll'y** in poetry etc.). The Lent lily, *Narcissus pseudo-narcissus*, yellow-flowered bulbous plant blooming in early spring (alternative to leek as Welsh national emblem); pale yellow colour. ~ *adj.* Pale yellow.

daft (-ah-) *adj.* Foolish, reckless, wild, crazy.

dag. *abbrev.* Decagram.

D.A.G. *abbrev.* Deputy Adjutant-General.

dăgg'er *n.* Short two-edged pointed weapon, like small sword, for thrusting and stabbing; (printing) mark like dagger, obelisk (†); *double* ~ (‡).

DAGGERS

1. Medieval dagger, 14th c. 2. 'Kidney' dagger, 16th–17th centuries. 3. Highland dirk, *c* 1750. 4 Stiletto or poniard, Italian 17th c.

dāg'ō *n.* (contempt., orig. U.S.) Spaniard, Portuguese, or Italian. [app. f Span. *Diego* = James]

Dăg'ŏn. Ancient Philistine national deity, represented as fish-tailed man. [Heb. *dāgōn* dear little fish]

daguĕ'rreotȳpe (-gĕro-) *n.* (Photograph taken by) early photographic process in which image was taken on silver plate sensitized by iodine, and developed by exposure to mercury vapour. ~ *v.t.* Photograph by this process. [name of inventor, Louis *Daguerre* (1789–1851)]

dahabee'yah, -bi'yah (-bē-) *n.* Large lateen-rigged sailing-vessel used on Nile. [Arab. name of gilded state barges of Moslem rulers of Egypt, f. *dhahab* gold]

dah'lĭa (dāl-) *n.* Mexican genus of composite plants widely cultivated for their many-coloured single and double flowers. [f. A. *Dahl*, Swedish botanist (d. 1789)]

Dahōm'ey. Republic in W. Africa, member of the French Community; capital, Porto Novo.

Dáil Eireann (doilyār'*a*n). The Chamber of Deputies or lower house of the Parliament of the republic of Ireland (the upper house being the Senate, *Seanad Eireann*). [Ir., = 'assembly of Ireland']

dail'y *adv.* & *adj.* (Recurring, appearing, done, etc.) every day or week-day; from day to day, constant(ly), often; ~ *bread*, one's necessary food or livelihood; ~ (*help, maid, woman*), one who does domestic work of house but does not sleep there. ~ *n.* Daily newspaper; daily maid.

daim'iō (dī-) *n.* Title of former chief territorial nobles of Japan, vassals of the Mikado. [Jap., f. Chin. *dai* great, *mio* name]

Daim'ler (dīm-), Gottlieb (1834–90). German engineer, a pioneer in the manufacture of motor-cars; original designer of the type (pr. dām-) named after him.

dain'ty *n.* Choice morsel, dish, etc.; delicacy, tit-bit. ~ *adj.* Delicate, choice; tasteful, pretty, of delicate beauty; scrupulously clean; fastidious, of delicate tastes and sensibility. **dain'tĭly** *adv.* **dain'tiness** *n.*

dair'y *n.* Room or building for keeping milk and cream and making butter etc.; shop in which milk, cream, etc., are sold; department of farm or farming concerned with production of milk, butter, and cheese; dairy-farm; ~-*farm*, farm producing chiefly milk, butter, etc.; ~-*maid*, maid employed at dairy; *dair'yman*, dealer in milk etc.

dā'is *n.* Raised platform, esp. at one end of hall, for high table, throne, etc.

dais'y (-zĭ) *n.* 1. Small European composite wild flower, *Bellis perennis*, with small flat flower-heads with yellow disc and white ray (often tinged with pink), which close in the evening; cultivated variety of this; various similar flowers, e.g. (U.S. etc.) the *ox-eye* ~, a common meadow-plant, *Chrysanthemum leucanthemum*, with larger daisy-like flowers on long stiff stalks; ~-*chain*, chain of daisies fastened together; ~-*cutter*, horse lifting feet very little in trotting; (cricket etc.) ball travelling very close to ground. 2. (slang) First-rate specimen.

DAHABEEYAH

dâk (dawk *or* dahk) *n.* (Anglo-Ind.) Post or transport by relays of men or horses; relay; ~-*bungalow*, house for travellers at dak station.

Dak. *abbrev.* Dakota.

Dakōt'a. Former territory of U.S., organized in 1889 into the States of NORTH DAKOTA and SOUTH DAKOTA.

dal. *abbrev.* Decalitre.

Dalai Lama: see LAMA[1].

dāle *n.* Valley (esp. in north of England); *dales'man*, native or inhabitant of dale, esp. in Yorkshire, Cumberland, Westmorland, etc.

dăll'y *v.* Amuse oneself, make sport; toy amorously (*with*); coquet (*with*); be evasive *with* person or business; idle, loiter, delay. **dăll'iance** *n.*

Dălmā'tia (-shĭ*a*). Province of Yugoslavia on the Adriatic coast; formerly (until 1918) province of the Austro-Hungarian Empire. **Dălmā'tian** *adj.* & *n.* ~ (*dog*), large dog with short-haired white coat with black or brown spots, of a breed supposed to have originated in Dalmatia.

dălmăt'ic *n.* Wide-sleeved loose long vestment with slit sides worn by deacons and bishops on some occasions, and by kings and emperors esp. at coronation.

dăl segno (sān'yō). (mus.) Direction to repeat from the point indicated by a sign (usu. 𝄋), abbrev. D.S. [It., = 'from the sign']

Da'lton[1] (dawl-), John (1766–1844). English chemist, who formulated the atomic theory; ~'*s Law*, (chem.) law, discovered by Dalton, that the total pressure of a mixture of gases is equal to the sum of the partial pressures of the constituents. **Dal'tonism** *n.* Congenital colour-blindness, esp. inability to distinguish green from red, so called after John Dalton, who was so affected.

Da'lton[2] (dawl-). Town in Massachusetts, U.S., in the high school of which the educational system (~ *plan, system*) devised by Miss H. Parkhurst was first adopted; the system consists essentially of dividing the year's work into monthly 'assignments', which pupils perform on their own responsibility and with their own discipline.

dăm[1] *n.* Barrier constructed across stream etc. to hold back water and raise its level, form a reservoir, or prevent flooding; barrier constructed in stream by

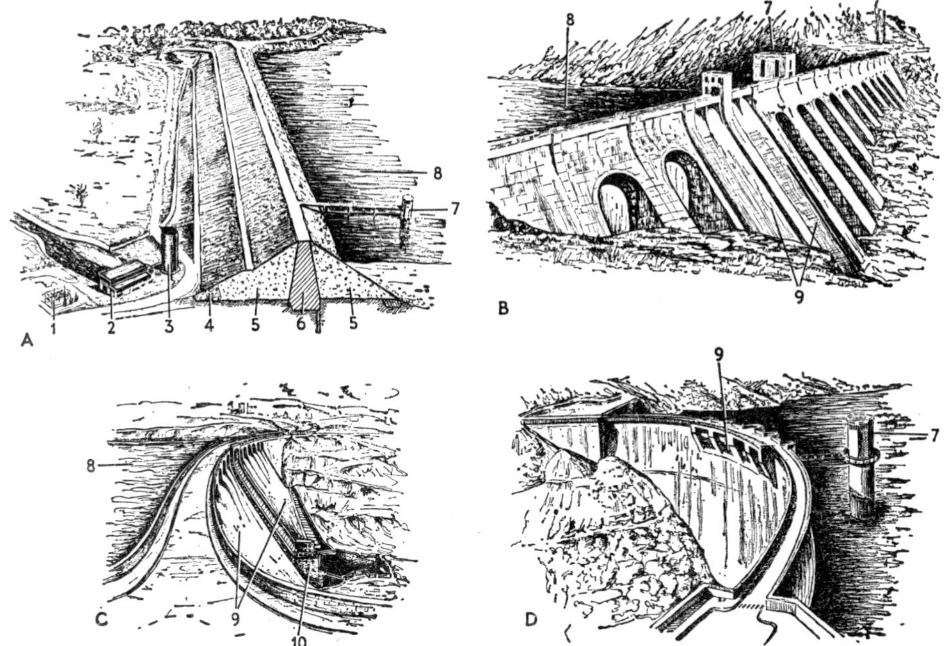

DAMS: A. EARTH DAM. B. BUTTRESS DAM. C. GRAVITY DAM. D. ARCH DAM

1. Switch yard. 2. Power house. 3. Surge tank. 4. Filter. 5. Pervious material. 6. Impervious core. 7. Intake tower. 8. Reservoir. 9. Spillways. 10. Valve house

beavers. ~ *v.t.* Furnish or confine with dam; block *up*, obstruct.

dăm[2] *n.* Mother (usu. of beast).

dam. *abbrev.* Decametre.

dăm'age *n.* 1. Harm; injury impairing value or usefulness. 2. (law, pl.) Sum of money claimed or adjudged in compensation for loss or injury; (slang) cost. ~ *v.t.* Injure (usu. thing) so as to diminish value; detract from reputation of (person etc.). **dăm'ageable** (-ja-) *adj.*

dămascēne', -skeen' *v.t.* 1. Produce watered or striped pattern in (sword, armour, etc.) by hammering on steel in which the iron or carbon particles have separated into patches or bands during cooling. 2. Inlay (steel or iron surface) with designs in gold or silver. [f. DAMASCUS]

Damăs'cus (*or* -mah-). (Arab. *Esh Sham*) Capital of Syria; an ancient city, famous in the Middle Ages for its silks and steel.

dăm'ask *n.* 1. Reversible figured fabric in which the design is executed in a different weave from the background in such a way that the two weaves appear on the face and on the back in exchanged positions; orig. of silk, later of linen, cotton, etc. 2. Steel manufactured at Damascus; combination of iron and steel with wavy pattern on surface (see DAMASCENE). 3. ~ *rose*, species of rose native to Asia Minor (*Rosa damascena*), to which many garden varieties belong; blush-red colour of this. ~ *adj.* Coloured like damask rose; made of or resembling damask fabric or steel. ~ *v.t.* 1. Weave with figured designs. 2. Damascene; ornament with pattern. 3. Make (cheek etc.) red. [f. DAMASCUS]

dāme *n.* 1. (Archaic, poet., or facet. for) lady; mistress of private elementary school (~ *school*) for children (obs.); female part in pantomime, taken by male actor; keeper, male or female, of Eton boarding-house. 2. *D*~, title (used as prefix to name) of woman member of Order of British Empire (also as prefix corresp. *Sir*; ~ *commander*, ~ *Grand Cross* (ranks in O.B.E. and in R.V.O.); title of Benedictine nun who has made her solemn profession; title of higher female member of Primrose League.

dămn (-m) *v.* 1. Condemn, censure; condemn (play etc.) as a failure; bring condemnation on, be the ruin of. 2. Doom to hell; cause damnation of; curse. ~ *n.* Uttered curse; negligible amount (*not worth a* ~, worthless).

dăm'nable (-mn-) *adj.* Subject to, deserving, damnation; hateful, confounded, annoying; **dăm'nably** *adv.*

dămnā'tion (-mn-) *n.* Damning; (condemnation to) eternal punishment in hell.

dăm'natory (-mn-) *adj.* Conveying, causing, censure or damnation.

dămned (-md) *adj.* (esp.) Damnable, infernal, unwelcome; confoundedly, extremely; *the* ~, souls in hell. **dămned'est** (-md-) *n.* *One's* ~, one's very worst or very best.

dăm'nĭfȳ *v.t.* (law) Cause injury to. **dămnĭfĭcā'tion** *n.*

Dăm'oclēs (-z). (Gk legend) A flatterer who extolled the happiness of Dionysius, tyrant of Syracuse; but Dionysius, to show how precarious a ruler's happiness was, seated him at a banquet with a sword suspended over his head by a hair; hence, *sword of* ~, imminent danger, esp. in midst of prosperity.

Dām'ŏn. In classical legend, a Syracusan whose friend Phintias was sentenced to death; Damon went bail for Phintias, who came back at the last moment and saved him; hence, ~ *and Pythias* (erron. for Phintias), faithful friends.

dămp *n.* 1. Moisture in air, on surface, or diffused through solid. 2. Dejection, chill, discouragement. 3. CHOKE-damp; FIRE-damp. 4. ~-*course*, layer of damp-proof material, esp. bituminous felt, in wall just above ground, to prevent damp from rising (ill. BRICK); ~-*proof*, proof against damp. ~ *adj.* Slightly wet; moist, humid. **dămp'ly** *adv.* **dămp'nėss** *n.* **dămp** *v.* 1. Stifle, choke, dull; extinguish; (mus. etc.) stop vibrations of (string etc.), furnish (pianoforte strings) with dampers. 2. Discourage, depress (zeal, hopes). 3. Moisten, make damp.

dăm'pen *v.* (chiefly U.S.) Damp.

dăm'per *n.* 1. Person or thing that depresses. 2. Small cloth- or felt-covered pad in pianoforte resting against string (and thus preventing it from vibrating) except when raised or withdrawn from it when key is struck or 'loud' pedal depressed. 3. Metal plate in flue controlling combustion by regulating or stopping draught. 4. Contrivance for moistening anything. 5. (Austral.) Cake of unleavened bread baked in hot ashes.

dăm'sel (-z-) *n.* (archaic and literary) Young unmarried woman.

dăm'son (-zn) *n.* Small dark-purple plum, *Prunus insititia*, introduced in very early times into Italy and Greece from Syria; tree bearing this; ~ *cheese*, solid conserve of pulped damsons and sugar. [L (*prunum*) *Damascenum* (plum) of Damascus]

Dăn. (O.T.) One of the sons of Jacob; one of the tribes of Israel founded by him; city in the extreme north of land of Canaan; hence, *from ~ to Beersheba*, from one end of the land to the other, Beersheba being in the extreme south of Canaan.

Dan. *abbrev.* Daniel.

Dăn'aē. (Gk. myth.) An oracle foretold that she would bear a son who would kill her father Acrisius, king of Argos; he therefore imprisoned her in a brazen tower, but Zeus visited her there and she conceived PERSEUS, who after many adventures killed Acrisius by accident.

Dăn'āid *n.* (Gk. myth.) One of the 50 daughters of Danaus, king of Argos; all except one, Hypermnestra, murdered their husbands on the wedding-night and were condemned in Hades to carry water in sieves or bottomless vessels.

dance (-ah-) *v.* 1. Move rhythmically with glides, leaps, etc., usu. to music, alone or with partner or in a set; perform (dance); jump about, skip, move in lively way; bob up and down on water etc.; *~ attendance upon*, be kept waiting by; follow about. 2. Dandle, toss up and down (baby etc.). ~ *n.* 1. Dancing motion; definite succession or arrangement of steps and rhythmical movements in dancing; music for this. 2. Dancing party. 3. *D~ of Death*, allegorical representation (common in Middle Ages) of Death leading all sorts and conditions of men in a dance to the grave; *St. Vitus's dance*, chorea (see VITUS). **dan'cer** *n.* (esp.) One who dances professionally in public.

dancett'y, -tee, (dănsĕtt'ĭ) *adj.* (her.) Having a fesse with three indentations (ill. HERALDRY).

dăn'dėlīon *n.* Common composite plant, *Taraxacum officinale*, abundant in meadows, gardens, and waste places, with widely-toothed leaves and large bright-yellow flower on naked hollow stalk, succeeded by globular head of pappose seeds; *~-clock*, the dandelion head of parachute-like fruits, from which children profess to tell the time by blowing away the fruits. [Fr. *dent de lion* lion's tooth]

dăn'der *n.* (colloq., esp. U.S.) Temper, anger, indignation.

Dăn'die Dĭn'mont *n.* Breed of short-legged, long-bodied, rough-coated terrier from Scottish borders. [name of a character in Sir W. Scott's 'Guy Mannering', who kept a special breed of terriers]

dăn'dle *v.t.* Dance (child) on knee or in arms; pet.

dăn'druff *n.* Dead skin in small scales among the hair, scurf.

dăn'dy[1] *n.* 1. Man paying excessive attention to smartness in dress etc., beau, fop. 2. Anything superlatively fine, neat, or dainty. 3. (naut.) Sloop with mizen-lug-sail on jigger-mast aft. 4. Spring-cart used by milkmen etc.; light iron hand-cart (also *~-cart*) for carrying coke to blast-furnace. 5. Small false fire-grate inside ordinary grate for economy. 6. *~-brush*, stiff brush of split whalebone or vegetable fibre for cleaning horses. ~ *adj.* Neat, smart, like a dandy; (U.S.) splendid, first-rate. **dăndī'acal, dăn'dўĭsh** *adjs.* **dăn'dĭfȳ** *v.t.* **dăn'dўĭsm** *n.* [orig. Sc., perh. f. name *Andrew*]

dăn'dy[2] *n.* (Anglo-Ind.) Strong cloth hammock slung from pole, carried shoulder-high by two or more men (a common means of transport in hilly districts). [Hind. *ḍanḍī* (*ḍanḍ* staff)]

Dāne *n.* 1. Native of Denmark. 2. (hist.) Any of the Northmen (VIKINGS) who invaded England between 9th and 11th centuries. 2. *Great ~*, large powerful short-haired breed of dog, of type between mastiff and greyhound.

Dāne'gĕld (-n-g-) *n.* (hist.) Annual land-tax in England in 10th and 11th centuries, orig. imposed to provide funds for protection against Danes.

Dāne'law (-nl-) *n.* (hist.) The part of England occupied by the Danes; the district NE. of Watling Street, ceded to them by the treaty of Wedmore, A.D. 878.

dān'ger (-nj-) *n.* Liability or exposure to harm, risk, peril (*of*); thing that causes peril; position of railway signal directing stoppage or caution. **dān'gerous** *adj.*; ~ *drugs*: see DRUG. **dān'gerously** *adv.*

dăngle (-ng'gl) *v.* Hang loosely, swaying to and fro; hold or carry (thing) swaying loosely; keep (hopes, expectations, etc.) hanging uncertainly (*before* person); hang *after* or *about* a person.

Dăn'iel. Hebrew prophet, captive at Babylon, who interpreted the dreams of Nebuchadnezzar and was delivered by God from the lions' den into which he had been thrown by Darius; a book of the O.T. containing the prophecies of Daniel.

Dān'ĭsh *adj.* & *n.* (Language) of Denmark or the Danes.

dănk *adj.* Soaked, oozy; unpleasantly or unwholesomely damp. **dănk'nėss** *n.*

D'Annunzio, Gabriele: see ANNUNZIO.

Dăn'tė Alĭghieri (ă-, -gyārĭ) (1265–1321). Italian poet, probably born at Florence, author of 'Vita Nuova' and 'Divina Commedia', a philosophical poem comprising the 'Inferno', 'Purgatorio', and 'Paradiso'; in his visit to Hell and Purgatory Dante has for guide the poet Virgil, and there he sees and converses with his former friends or foes; in 'Paradiso' the poet encounters the lady whom he once loved, BEATRICE, now an angel. **Dăn'tĕsque** *adj.* Of, after the manner of, Dante.

Danton (dahṅ'tawṅ), Georges Jacques (1759–94). French statesman of the Revolution; member of the Convention and the first (Dantonist) Committee of Public Safety; he came into conflict with ROBESPIERRE and was guillotined.

Dăn'ūbe. The Donau, a European river about 1,700 miles long, rising in SW. Germany and flowing into the Black Sea. **Danūb'ĭan** *adj.* Belonging to, lying near Danube; ~ *Principalities*, former name for Moldavia and Walachia.

Dăn'zĭg (-nts-). Gdansk, a Baltic city and port of Poland, near mouth of Vistula; ~ *Corridor*: see CORRIDOR.

dăp *v.i.* 1. Fish by letting bait bob on water. 2. Make (ball) bounce, (of ball) bounce, on ground. ~ *n.* Bounce of ball.

Dăph'nė. (Gk myth.) Nymph who was turned into a laurel-bush to save her from the pursuit of Apollo. **dăph'nė** *n.* 1. Genus of flowering shrubs including spurge laurel and mezereon. 2. The 41st of the asteroids.

dăpp'er *adj.* Neat, smart, in appearance or movement.

dăp'ple *v.* Variegate, become variegated, with rounded spots or patches of colour or shade. ~ *adj.* Dappled; *~-grey*, (horse) of grey dappled with darker spots. ~ *n.* Dappled effect; dappled horse etc.

D.A.Q.M.G. *abbrev.* Deputy Assistant Quartermaster-General.

dar̄b'ies (-bĭz) *n.pl.* (slang) Handcuffs.

Dar̄b'y and Joan. Devoted old married couple. [perh. from poem in *Gentleman's Magazine*, 1735]

Dar̄danĕlles' (-lz). Narrow strait between Europe and Asiatic Turkey, anciently called the Hellespont; scene of unsuccessful attack on Turkey by British and French troops in 1915.

dāre *v.* 1. Venture (to), have boldness or courage or impudence (to); attempt, take the risks of. 2. Defy, challenge (person) *to* thing, *to* do. 3. *I ~ say*, I am prepared to believe, do not deny; *~-devil*, reckless (person). **dār'ing** *n.* (esp.) Adventurous courage. ~ *adj.* (esp.) Adventurous, bold. **dār'ingly** *adv.*

Dār'ien. Province, formerly of Colombia, now of Panama; ~ *Scheme*, scheme proposed *c* 1690 for a Scottish settlement on the isthmus of Panama; much Scottish capital was invested in the scheme, which was unsuccessful, and at the Union (1707) compensation was paid by England to Scotland for the losses sustained.

dă'riōle *n.* Savoury dish cooked and served in small mould (*~-mould*).

Darī'us ('the Great'). King of Persia, 521–485 B.C., he extended the Persian Empire and began the great war between the Persians and the Greeks; his army was defeated at MARATHON (490).

dark *adj.* 1. Characterized by (absolute or relative) absence of light; unilluminated; gloomy, sombre. 2. (Of colour) approaching black in hue; deep in shade; (of complexion etc.) brown, not fair. 3. Evil, wicked, foul, atrocious; dismal, sad; sullen, frowning; obscure; secret; little known of; unenlightened. 4. (phonetics, of a consonant, esp. *l*) Having acoustic resemblance to a 'back' vowel (opp. to *clear*). 5. *D~ Ages*, (formerly =) the Middle Ages; (now usu.) approx. 5th–8th centuries A.D., or from fall of Rome to coronation of Charlemagne; *D~ Continent*, Africa; ~ *horse*, horse about whose racing powers little is known; person of unknown capacities; ~ *lantern*, lantern of which light may be concealed; *~-room*, room from which daylight is excluded and which is lighted when desired by a type of coloured light which does not appreciably affect sensitive photographic materials. ~ *n.* Absence of light; nightfall; dark colour; want of knowledge. **dark'ish** *adj.* **dark'ly** *adv.* **dark'ness** *n.*

dark'en *v.* Make or become dark.

dark'ling *adv.* & *adj.* In the dark.

dark'(e)y *n.* (colloq.) Negro.

darl'ing *n.* & *adj.* Loved, best loved, lovable, (person or animal).

darn[1] *v.t.* Mend (esp. knitted fabric) by interweaving yarn with needle across hole; embroider with darning-stitch. ~ *n.* Place so mended. **darn'er** *n.* Darning-needle. **darn'ing** *n.* *~-needle*, long stout needle for darning; *~-stitch*, large running stitch resembling that used in darning, used for embroidering net etc.

darn[2] *n.* & *v.t.* (orig. U.S.) Damn (as imprecation). **darned** (-nd) *adj.* Damned.

darn'el *n.* Grass (now rare in England), *Lolium temulentum*, growing as weed among corn.

dart *n.* 1. Pointed missile thrown by hand, esp. light javelin; arrow; light pointed missile thrown at target; (pl.) game played with darts of this kind. 2. Tapering stitched fold in garment. 3. Sudden rapid motion; act of throwing missile. ~ *v.* 1. Throw (missile). 2. Emit suddenly and sharply, shoot out; spring or start with sudden rapid motion, shoot. **dart'er** *n.* (esp.) 1. Any of the cormorant-like web-footed birds (snake-birds) of the genus *Plotus*, found in tropical Africa and America. 2. Various fishes, esp. the very small and brilliantly coloured fishes of the subfamily *Etheostominae*.

Dart'moor. Moorland district in Devonshire, England; ~ (*Prison*), convict prison near Princetown in this district; ~ *pony*, small shaggy variety living wild on Dartmoor; ~ *sheep*, hardy moorland sheep bred there.

Dart'mouth (-m*u*th). Town and port in Devonshire, England; also the Royal Naval College for training naval officers which is situated there.

Dar'win[1], Charles Robert (1809–82). English naturalist; author of 'The Origin of Species by means of Natural Selection' (1859), in which he propounded the theory that organisms tend to produce offspring varying slightly from their parents, that the process of *natural selection* tends to favour the survival of those best adapted to their environment, and that by the operation of these factors new species may arise widely differing from each other and from their common ancestors. **Darwin'ian** *adj.* & *n.* (Follower) of Darwin or his theories. **Dar'winism** *n.* Darwin's theory of the origin of species; hence, popularly, evolutionism.

Dar'win[2]. Capital city of Northern Territory of Australia.

dăsh *v.* 1. Shatter *to pieces*; knock, drive, throw, thrust, *away*, *off*, etc.; fling, drive, splash, *against*, *upon*, *into*. 2. Bespatter *with* water etc.; dilute, qualify. 3. Frustrate; daunt, discourage, confound. 4. Put *down* on paper, throw *off* (drawing, composition) hastily and vigorously. 5. Damn (as mild imprecation). 6. Fall, move, throw oneself, with violence; come into collision *against*, *upon*; ride, run, drive, *up*, move about, behave, with spirit or display. 7. *dash'board*, board or leather apron in front of vehicle to keep out mud from horses' heels; board in front of driver of motor-car or pilot of aeroplane carrying indicators, gauges, etc. (ill. MOTOR). ~ *n.* 1. Violent blow, impact, or collision; violent throwing and breaking of water, etc., upon anything; sound of dashing. 2. Splash of colour; infusion, touch, tinge. 3. Hasty pen-stroke; horizontal stroke in writing or printing to mark break in sense, parenthesis, omitted letters or words, etc. 4. Rush, onset, sudden advance; (capacity for) vigorous action; showy appearance or behaviour. 5. (slang) Dashboard.

dăsh'er *n.* (esp.) Contrivance for agitating cream in churn.

dăsh'ing *adj.* (esp.) Spirited, lively; showy, given to fashionable and striking display. **dăsh'ingly** *adv.*

dăs'tard *n.* Mean, base, or despicable coward, esp. one who commits malicious or brutal act without endangering himself. **dăs'tardly** *adj.* **dăs'tardliness** *n.*

dāt'a *n.pl.*: see DATUM.

dāte[1] *n.* Fruit of the *~-palm*, *Phoenix dactylifera*, an oblong berry, growing in large clusters, with single hard seed or stone and sweet pulp; an important article of food in W. Asia and N. Africa; the tree itself. [Gk *daktulos* finger]

dāte[2] *n.* Specification in document, letter, book, inscription, of time (and often place) of execution, writing, publication, etc.; precise time at which anything takes place or is to take place; season, period; (colloq., orig. U.S.) appointment, engagement; period to which something ancient belongs; duration, term of life or existence; *out of ~*, obsolete, antiquated; *up to ~*, up to the knowledge, standard, requirements, of the time; *~-line*, line in Pacific Ocean (approx. meridian of 180° from Greenwich) at which calendar day is reckoned to begin and end, so that at places east and west of it the date differs by a day. ~ *v.* Mark (letter etc.) with date; refer (event) to a time; count time, reckon (*from*); bear date, be dated; have origin *from*; be or become recognizable as of a past or particular period; (colloq.) make an appointment with. **dāte'less** (-tl-) *adj.* Undated; endless; immemorial.

dāt'ive *adj.* & *n.* (gram.) (Case in nouns, pronouns, and adjectives) denoting the indirect or remoter object of the verb's action, that to or for which a thing is done or to whom a thing is given.

dāt'um *n.* (pl. *dāt'a*). Thing known or granted, assumption or premiss from which inferences may be drawn; fixed starting-point of scale etc.; *~-line*, horizontal line from which heights and depths are measured in surveying. [L, = '(thing) given']

datur'a *n.* Genus, including thorn-apple, of poisonous plants, with strongly narcotic effects.

daub *v.* 1. Coat (wall etc.) *with* plaster, clay, etc.; smear (surface); lay *on* (greasy or sticky stuff); soil, bedaub. 2. Paint coarsely and inartistically, lay on (colours) crudely and clumsily. ~ *n.* 1. Material for daubing walls etc.; clay or mud mixed with stubble or chaff, daubed on laths or wattle to make walls ect. 2. Patch or smear of grease, colour, etc. 3. Clumsy coarse painting. **daub'er** *n.* **daub'y** *adj.*

Daudet (dōd'ā), Alphonse (1840–97). French novelist, famous as creator of amusing type of Provençal Frenchman, 'Tartarin de Tarascon'.

daught'er (dawt-) *n.* One's female child; female descendant, female member *of* family, race, etc.; a woman as spiritual or intellectual descendant of some person or thing; *~-in-law*, son's wife; *D~s of the American Revolution*, patriotic American women's society formed (1890) to preserve ideals of founders of Amer. independence etc. **daught'erly** *adj.*

daunt *v.t.* Discourage, intimidate. **daunt'lėss** *adj.* Intrepid; persevering. **daunt'lėssly** *adv.* **daunt'lėssnėss** *n.*

dauph'ĭn *n.* (hist.) Orig. title of lords of Vienne; the provinces of the seigneurs of the Viennois were hence called the Dauphiné, and the last lord, Humbert II, on ceding the provinces to Philip of Valois (1349), made it a condition that the title should be borne by the eldest son of the king of France. **dauph'inėss** *n.* Wife of the dauphin.

dăv'enpôrt *n.* 1. Small ornamental writing-table with drawers and hinged writing-slab (ill. DESK). 2. (U.S.) Large sofa. [prob. from maker's name]

Dāv'ĭd[1]. 2nd king of Judah, youngest son of Jesse; in his youth he slew the Philistine giant Goliath (1 Sam. xvii) and on the death of Saul became king of Judah and later of the whole of Israel; *~ and Jonathan*, any pair of devoted friends (see 1 Sam. xviii).

Dāv'ĭd[2], St. (6th c.). Son of a prince of S. Wales, patron saint of Wales; commemorated on 1st March.

David[3] (dahvēd'), Jacques Louis (1748–1825). French painter of classical and historical subjects.

Da Vinci: see LEONARDO DA VINCI.

Dāv'ĭs ăpparāt'us. Device to enable men to escape from a disabled submarine, consisting essentially of a chamber, called the 'escape lock', which is emptied of water by compressed air after each man has left it. [f. name of inventor]

Dāv'ĭs Cup. (lawn tennis) An international challenge cup presented in 1900 by Dwight F. Davis and competed for annually.

dăv'ĭt *n.* Crane at ship's bow for hoisting anchor clear of side; one of pair of uprights curved at top for suspending or lowering ship's boat (ill. SHIP).

Dāv'y[1], Sir Humphry (1778–1829). English chemist, inventor of the miner's safety lamp (*~ lamp*), in which flame is protected by wire-gauze from coming into contact with fire-damp.

dāv'y[2] *n.* (slang) Solemn oath. [short for AFFIDAVIT]

Dāv'y Jōnes (-nz). The spirit of the sea, the sailors' devil; *~'s locker*, bottom of the sea, esp. as grave of those who are drowned or die at sea.

daw *n.* = JACKDAW.

daw'dle *v.* Idle, dally; waste (time). *~ n.* Act of dawdling.

dawk *n.* = DAK.

dawn *n.* First light, daybreak; rise or incipient gleam of anything. *~ v.i.* Begin to appear or grow light; *~ upon*, begin to be perceptible to.

day *n.* 1. Time during which sun is above horizon, interval of light between successive periods of darkness or night; dawn; daylight. 2. Time occupied by earth in one revolution on its axis, 24 hours; *civil ~*, from midnight to midnight; *solar* or *astronomical ~*, from noon till noon; *sidereal ~*, between two meridional transits of first point of Aries, about 4′ shorter than solar day; *natural ~*, = sidereal, also in sense 1 above. 3. Civil day as point or unit of time, date, etc.; specified or appointed day; day of battle; *carry, win, the ~*, be victorious. 4. Period, time, era; lifetime, span of existence; period of power or influence. 5. Part of day allotted for work. 6. *~-bed*, bed to lie on by day, couch (ill. SOFA); *~-book*, book in which commercial transactions of day are entered: *~-boy, -girl*, boy, girl, attending school during day but living at home; *day'break*, dawn; *~-coach* (U.S.), railway passenger carriage other than sleeper; *~-dream*, dream indulged in while awake; *~-fly*, ephemera; *~-labour*, labour hired by the day; *~-labourer*; *~-lily*, genus *Hemerocallis* of liliaceous plants with large yellow or orange flowers lasting only for a day; *~-nursery*, nursery used by children in daytime (as dist. from *night-nursery*); public nursery where children are cared for during day; *~-scholar*, day-boy or -girl; *~-school*, school carried on in daytime (as dist. from *night-* or *evening-school*); school in which there is no provision for boarding pupils; *~-spring*, (poet.) dawn; *~-star*, the sun; the morning star; *~-time*, time of daylight.

day'light (-līt) *n.* Light of day; dawn; openness, publicity; visible interval, as between boats in race, rider and saddle; *~-glass*, glass, coloured blue with cobalt, used with artificial light to give effect of daylight; *~-lamp*, incandescent electric lamp with bulb made of daylight-glass; *~-loading*, (of photographic material) that can be put into camera in daylight, without dark-room; *~ saving*, securing longer period of daylight in evening by putting clock forward (see SUMMER TIME).

dāze *v.t.* Stupefy, bewilder; dazzle. *~ n.* Stupefaction, bewilderment. **dāz'ėdly** *adv.*

dăz'zle *v.t.* Confuse, dim (sight, eye, person) with excess of light, intricate motion, incalculable number, etc.; confound, surprise, by brilliant display. *~ n.* Glitter; bright confusing light; *~-painting*, camouflage, esp. of sea-going vessels, with bright-coloured painted patterns. **dăz'zlement** (-zlm-) *n.* **dăzz'lĭngly** *adv.*

D.B.E. *abbrev.* Dame Commander of (the Order of) the British Empire.

D.C. *abbrev.* *Da capo* (= repeat from the beginning; also d.c.); direct current; District of Columbia.

D.C.L. *abbrev.* Doctor of Civil Law.

D.C.M. *abbrev.* Distinguished Conduct Medal; District Court Martial.

D.D. *abbrev.* Doctor of Divinity; *dono dedit* (= gave as a gift; also d.d.).

D.D.D. *abbrev.* *Dat, dicat, dedicat* (= gives, devotes, and dedicates; also d.d.d.).

D.D.S. *abbrev.* Doctor of Dental Surgery.

D.D.T. *abbrev.* Dichlor-diphenyl-trichlorethane (an insecticide).

de- *prefix.* 1. Down; away; completely. 2. Un- (in this sense a living prefix in English).

deac'on *n.* 1. Kind of minister or officer of primitive Christian church; in Episcopal churches, member of third order of ministry, below bishops and priests, assisting priest in celebration of Eucharist etc. 2. Presbyterian layman attending to secular affairs of congregation; in other Nonconformist churches, one of a body elected to advise and assist pastor, administer charities, and attend to secular affairs of church. 3. One of two inferior officers assisting wardens of lodge of Freemasons. 4. (U.S.) Skin (weighing less than 8 lb.) of new-born or aborted calf. **deac'onshĭp** *n.* **deac'onėss** *n.* Woman in primitive and some modern Christian churches with functions analogous to deacon's, esp. in administering charity.

dead (dĕd) *adj.* 1. That has ceased to live. 2. Benumbed, insensible; without spiritual life; *~ to*, unconscious or inappreciative of, hardened against. 3. Obsolete; past; not effective. 4. Inanimate. 5. Extinct; dull, lustreless; without force; muffled; inactive, motionless, idle. 6. Unconnected to source of electrical power. 7. Abrupt; complete, unrelieved, exact; absolute. 8. *~-alive*, dull, tedious, spiritless; *~ ball*, (football etc.) ball out of play; *~-centre*, position of crank in which it is in direct line with connecting rod, and at which force exerted tends to pull or thrust instead of turning it; centre in lathe which does not revolve; *~ end*, closed end of any passage etc. through which there is no way (also fig.); ~*-eye*, (naut.) round flat three-holed block for extending shrouds; ~*-fall*, (chiefly U.S.) trap for large game with weighted board or heavy log which falls upon the prey; ~*-fire*, St. Elmo's fire: see CORPOSANT, taken as presaging death; ~ *freight*, sum paid in chartering ship for part not occupied by cargo; ~ *hand*, mortmain; ~*-head*, (colloq., orig. U.S.) non-paying theatre-goer, passenger, etc.; ~ *heat*, race in which two or more competitors reach winning-post at same time; ~ *letter*, law, regulation, no longer observed; unclaimed or undelivered letter at post office; *dead'-light*, (naut.) shutter inside porthole to prevent light showing out; ~*-line*, line beyond which it is not permitted or possible to go; fixed limit of time; *dead'lock*, complete stoppage, standstill; state of affairs from which further progress is impossible; ~ *man's* (*men's*) *fingers*, various species of orchis, esp. *O. maculata* and *latifolia*; finger-like divisions of gills in lobster or crab; a zoophyte, *Alcyonium digitatum*, forming lobed fleshy masses; various kinds of orchis and fern; ~ *man's handle*, (in electrically controlled trains) handle which must be pressed down for current to pass, so that train stops if driver releases his grasp; ~ *march*, march-like funeral music; ~ *men*, empty bottles; ~*-nettle*, non-stinging plant of genus *Lamium* with leaves like nettle's; ~*-pan*, (slang) expressionless; ~ *point*, dead centre; ~ *reckoning*, (naut. & aeronaut.) estimation of ship's or aircraft's position from log, compass-courses, etc., and not from observations; ~ *shot*, unerring marksman; ~ *spit*, (colloq.) exact counterpart; ~ *water*, (naut.) eddy-water just behind stern of ship under way; state of tide when there is least rise or fall, slack water; ~ *weight*, heavy inert weight, weight of dead body or lifeless matter. ~ *n.* 1. *The* ~, dead person or persons; all who have ever died. 2. Dead period or time; time of intensest stillness, darkness, cold, etc. (*of* night, winter). ~ *adv.* Profoundly; absolutely, completely; ~ *against*, directly opposite or opposed to; ~*-beat*, tired out.

deaden (dĕd'n) *v.* Deprive of, lose, vitality, force, brightness, feeling, etc.; make insensible *to*.

dead'ly (dĕd-) *adj.* 1. Causing fatal injury; of poisonous nature; implacable, mortal, to the death. 2. (Of sin) entailing spiritual death, mortal. 3. Deathlike; intense. 4. ~ *nightshade*, shrub, *Atropa belladonna*, with dark purple flowers and large round poisonous black berries; (pop., erron.) the woody nightshade, *Solanum dulcamara*, with ovoid scarlet berries. **dead'lĭnėss** *n.* **dead'ly** *adv.* As if dead; extremely.

Dead Sea (dĕd). Lake or inland sea in S. Palestine into which river Jordan flows; it has no outlet, and its waters are intensely salt and bitter; ~ *apple*, *fruit*, apple of Sodom: see APPLE; ~ *scrolls*, large collection of Hebrew and Aramaic manuscripts, including parts of most books of O.T., found (1947–56) in caves NW. of Dead Sea, apparently stored there by a Jewish community which lived at Qumran *c.* 135 B.C.—A.D. 70.

deaf (dĕf) *adj.* 1. Wholly or partly without hearing. 2. Insensible *to*; not giving ear *to*; uncompliant. 3. ~*-adder*, slow-worm; (U.S.) copperhead; various harmless snakes; ~*-aid*, instrument worn or carried by deaf person to improve hearing; ~*-and-dumb alphabet*, *language*, conventional signs made with hands for communication by the deaf; ~*-mute*, deaf and dumb person. **deaf'ly** *adv.* **deaf'nėss** *n.*

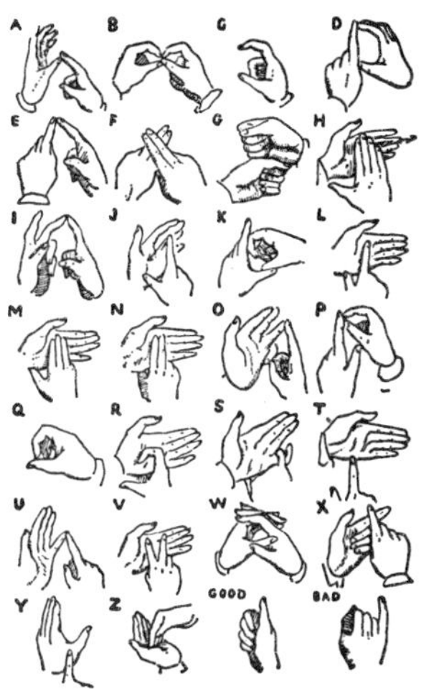

DEAF-AND-DUMB ALPHABET

deaf'en (dĕfn) *v.t.* Deprive of hearing by noise, stun with noise.

deal[1] *n.* *A great* (or *good*) ~, a large (or fairly large) amount; (adverbially) by much, considerably.

deal[2] *n.* Sawn fir or pine wood (in England, 9 in. wide, not more than 3 in. thick, and at least 6 ft long; in N. America, 11 in. wide, 2½ in. thick, and 12 ft long); wood in this form; fir or pine wood.

deal[3] *n.* 1. Distribution, sharing; dealing of cards; turn to deal cards. 2. Business transaction, bargain; (U.S.) secret bargain in commerce or politics; *New D*~, programme of social and economic reform in U.S. planned by the Roosevelt administration from 1932 onwards; *raw* ~, unfair treatment. ~ *v.* (past t. and part. *dealt* pr. dĕlt). 1. Distribute, give *out*, among several; deliver as his share or deserts to person. 2. Distribute cards to players for a game or round; give (card, hand, etc.) to player. 3. Associate *with*; do business (*with* person, *in* goods); occupy oneself, grapple by way of discussion or refutation, take measures, *with*; behave (*well*, *honourably*, *cruelly*, etc., *with* or *by* person). **deal'er** *n.* (esp.) Trader *in* a particular class of goods. **deal'ĭng** *n.*

dean *n.* 1. Head of chapter of collegiate or cathedral church; clergyman invested with precedence or jurisdiction (under bishop or archdeacon) over a division of an archdeaconry (usu. *rural*~); president of convocation in Amer. Episcopal Church; *D*~ *of the Arches*, lay judge of court of Arches, with peculiar jurisdiction over 13 London parishes exempt from authority of bishop of London. 2. At Oxford and Cambridge, resident fellow of a college appointed to supervise conduct and studies of junior members; in continental, Scottish, and modern universities, president of faculty or department of study or administration. 3. Doyen. [L *decanus* one set over ten (monks)]

dean'ery *n.* Office, house, of dean; group of parishes presided over by rural dean.

dear *adj.* 1. Beloved, loved (now often merely polite or ironical, and part of ordinary polite formula at beginning of most letters); precious in one's regard, to which one is attached. 2. High-priced, costly, expensive. ~ *n.* Dear one, darling. ~ *adv.* At a high price, at great cost; dearly. **dear'ly** *adv.* **dear'nėss** *n.* **dear** *int.* ~, ~*!*, ~ *me!*, *oh*~*!*, exclamations expressing surprise, distress, sympathy, etc.

dearth (dẽr-) *n.* Scarcity and dearness of food; scanty supply *of*.

death (dĕth) *n.* 1. Dying; final cessation of vital functions; being dead; cause or occasion of death; *be in at the* ~, be present when fox is killed or (fig.) at end of any enterprise. 2. Being or becoming spiritually dead; end, extinction, destruction; *civil* ~, loss or deprivation of civil rights and privileges, as by banishment, life imprisonment, etc. 3. ~*-bed*, bed on which person dies; ~*-bed repentance*, last-minute change of conduct or policy; ~*-blow*, blow that causes death; ~*-duties*, tax levied on property before it passes to heir; ~*-mask*, cast taken from person's face after death; ~ *penalty*, capital punishment, penalty of death; ~*-rate*, proportion of deaths usu. estimated per 1,000 of population per annum; ~*-rattle*, rattling sound in throat of dying person, caused by partial stoppage of air-passage by mucus; ~*-roll*, list of persons killed (in accident or battle); *death's-head*, (figure or representation of) human skull, esp. as emblem of mortality; *death's-head moth*, large hawk-moth, *Acherontia atropos*, with markings resembling skull on back of thorax; ~-*trap*, place etc. which is unwholesome or dangerous; ~-*warrant*, warrant for execution of death-sentence (also fig.); ~-*watch* (*beetle*), small beetle (*Xestobium rufovillosum*) which bores in old wood and makes noise like watch ticking, formerly supposed to portend death; various insects making similar sound; ~-*wish*, (Freudian psychol.) alleged inborn tendency of organisms to seek death, capable of being directed against the self or others.

death'lėss (dĕ-) *adj.* Immortal. **death'lėssly** *adv.* **death'lėssnėss** *n.*

death'ly (dĕ-) *adj.* Deadly; gloomy, pale, etc., as death. ~ *adv.* To a degree resembling death.

dĕb *n.* Colloq. (orig. U.S.) abbrev. of débutante.

débâcle (dābah'-) *n.* 1. (geol.) Sudden deluge of water, breaking down barriers and carrying stones and other debris with it, esp. the break-up of ice on northern rivers. 2. Sudden and overwhelming collapse, rush, stampede. [Fr., = 'break-up of ice in river']

dēbăg' *v.t.* (colloq.) Remove trousers of.

dėbar' *v.t.* Exclude *from* admission or right.

dėbark' *v.* Disembark. **dēbarkā'tion** *n.*

dėbāse' *v.t.* Lower in quality, value, or character; depreciate (coin) by mixture of alloy or otherwise. **dėbāse'ment** (-sm-) *n.*

dėbāt'able *adj.* Questionable, subject to dispute or debate.

dėbāte' *v.* Contest, fight for (archaic); dispute about, discuss, (question); engage in (formal) argument or discussion (of), esp. in legislative or other assembly; consider, ponder; *debating society*, society whose members meet for practice in debating. ~ *n.* Controversy; discussion; public argument. **dėbāt'er** *n.*

dėbauch' *v.t.* Pervert from virtue or morality; make intemperate or sensual; seduce (woman); vitiate (taste, judgement). ~ *n.* Bout or habit of sensual indulgence. **dėbauchee'** *n.* Viciously sensual person. **dėbauch'ery** *n.*

dėbĕn'ture *n.* 1. (archaic or tech.) Voucher given to person supplying goods to Royal Household or government office, entitling him to payment; custom-house certificate to exporter of amount due to him as drawback or bounty. 2. (Brit.) Sealed bond of corporation or company acknowledging sum on which interest is due till principal is repaid, esp. fixed interest constituting prior charge on assets; (U.S.) promissory note of corporation or company bearing fixed rate of interest, junior to other charges secured by fixed mortgages; ~ *stock*, (Brit.) debentures consolidated into or created as stock, nominal capital of which represents debt of which only the interest is secured by perpetual annuity.

dėbĭl'ĭtāte *v.t.* Enfeeble (constitution etc.).

dėbĭl'ity *n.* Feebleness (of health, purpose, etc.).

dĕb'ĭt *n.* Entry in account of sum owing; side of account (left-hand) in which these entries are made. ~ *v.t.* Charge (person) *with* sum; enter (sum) *against* or *to* person.

dĕbonair' *adj.* Genial, pleasant, unembarrassed.

dėbŏshed' (-sht) *adj.* (Archaic for) debauched.

dėbouch' (-bo͞osh) *v.i.* Issue from ravine, wood, etc., into open ground. **dėbouch'ment** *n.*

Dėbrĕtt'. The 'Peerage of England, Scotland and Ireland', first published by John Debrett in 1802 and now issued annually.

debris (dĕb'rē) *n.* Scattered fragments, wreckage, drifted accumulation.

debt (dĕt) *n.* Money, goods, or service, owing; being under obligation to pay something; ~ *of honour*, debt, usu. of sum lost in gambling, not legally enforceable; ~ *of nature*, necessity of dying, death; *National D*~, debt owing by State to corporations and private individuals who have advanced money to it; *floating* ~, part of National Debt represented by Treasury Bills or by other temporary arrangements with the lenders.

debt'or (dĕt-) *n.* One who owes money, or an obligation or duty; (abbrev. *Dr*) heading of left-hand or debit side of account in book-keeping.

dēbŭnk' *v.t.* Remove the false sentiment from (person, cult, etc.).

dēbŭs' *v.* (mil.) Unload, alight, from motor vehicles.

Debŭss'y (-ē), Claude (1862–1918). French composer of symphonic poems, pianoforte compositions, and one opera 'Pelléas et Mélisande'.

début (dāb'o͞o *or* -ū) *n.* First appearance on stage etc., as performer, or (esp.) in society.

déb'ūtante (dā-, -ahnt) *n.* Girl making first appearance in society, esp. one being presented at Court.

Dec. *abbrev.* December.

dĕc'a- *prefix.* Ten-.

dĕc'ade (*or* dekād') *n.* Set, series, of ten; period of 10 years.

dĕc'adence *n.* Falling away, declining (from former excellence, vitality, prosperity, etc.), esp. of period of art or literature after a culmination.

dĕc'adent *adj.* In a state of decay or decline; of literature, art, etc., belonging to a decadent age. ~ *n.* Decadent writer or artist.

dĕc'agon *n.* Plane figure with 10 sides and 10 angles. **dėcăg'onal** *adj.*

dĕc'agrăm *n.* 10 grams.

dĕcahē'dron *n.* Ten-sided solid. **dĕcahē'dral** *adj.*

dēcăl'cĭfȳ *v.t.* Deprive of lime or calcareous matter. **dēcălcĭfĭcā'tion** *n.*

dĕc'alitre (-lēter) *n.* Measure of capacity, 10 litres.

dĕc'alŏgue (-g) *n.* The Ten Commandments.

Dėcăm'eron. A work by BOCCACCIO, written between 1348 and 1358, containing 100 tales told in 10 days by a party of 7 young ladies and 3 young men who had fled from the plague in Florence.

dĕc'amētre (-ter) *n.* Measure of length, 10 metres.

dėcămp' *v.i.* Break up or leave camp; go away suddenly, take oneself off, abscond. **dėcămp'ment** *n.*

dėcān'al *adj.* Of a dean or deanery; of S. side (on which dean sits) of choir.

dėcān'ī. (mus.) To be sung by decanal side in antiphonal singing (cf. CANTORIS). ~ *adj.* Decanal.

dėcănt' *v.t.* Pour off (clear liquid of solution) by gently inclining vessel without disturbing sediment; pour (wine) similarly from bottle into decanter; pour or empty out.

dėcăn'ter *n.* Stoppered glass vessel in which decanted wine or spirit is brought to table.

dėcăp'ĭtāte *v.t.* Behead. **dėcăpĭtā'tion** *n.*

dĕc'apŏd *n.* Ten-footed crustacean.

dēcarb'onīze *v.t.* Deprive of carbon or carbonic acid; remove carbon deposit from (internal combustion engine). **dēcarbonīzā'tion** *n.*

dĕc'astȳle *adj.* & *n.* Ten-columned (portico or colonnade) (ill. TEMPLE).

dēcă'sualīze (-zho͞o- *or* -zū-) *v.t.* Do away with casual condition of (labour). **dēcăsualīzā'tion** *n.*

dĕcasȳllăb'ĭc *adj.* & *n.* (Metrical line) of 10 syllables. **dĕcasȳll'able** *n.* & *adj.*

dėcay' *v.* Deteriorate; lose quality; decline in power, wealth, beauty, etc.; rot; cause to deteriorate. ~ *n.* Decline, falling off; ruinous state, wasting away; decomposition.

Dĕcc'an, The. Triangular plateau of S. India, bounded by the Malabar and Coromandel coasts, which converge at Cape Comorin, and in the north by the Vindhya mountains.

dėcease' *n.* (Legal or formal for) death. ~ *v.i.* Die. **dėceased'** (-st) *adj.* & *n.* Dead (person).

dėcēd'ent *n.* (U.S.) Deceased person.

dėceit' (-sēt) *n.* Misrepresentation, deceiving; trick, stratagem; deceitfulness. **dėceit'ful** *adj.* **dėceit'fully** *adv.* **dėceit'fulnėss** *n.*

dėceive' (-sēv) *v.* Persuade of what is false, mislead; use deceit; disappoint (hopes etc.). **dėceiv'er** *n.*

dēcĕl'erāte *v.* Decrease speed or velocity of; slow down.

Dėcĕm'ber. 12th and last month of year in modern calendar. [L *decem* ten; orig. 10th month of Roman year]

Dēcĕm′brĭst *n.* One of those who in December 1825 tried to raise revolt against Tsar Nicholas I of Russia.

dēcĕm′vir (-*er*) *n.* 1. (Rom. hist.) Member of board of 10 acting as council or ruling power, esp. two bodies of magistrates appointed 451 and 450 B.C. to draw up code of laws (laws of Twelve Tables). 2. Member of any council or ruling body of 10, as in Venetian Republic. **dēcĕm′virate** *n.*

dē′cency *n.* Propriety of behaviour or demeanour; compliance with recognized notions of modesty or delicacy, freedom from impropriety; respectability; (pl.) decent or becoming acts or observances, outward conditions of decent life.

dēcĕnn′ial *adj.* Of 10-year period; recurring in 10 years. **dēcĕnn′ium** *n.* Period of 10 years.

dē′cent *adj.* 1. Seemly, not immodest, obscene, or indelicate; respectable. 2. Fair, tolerable, passable; (colloq.) kind, not severe or censorious. **dē′cently** *adv.*

dēcĕn′tralīze *v.t.* Divide and distribute (government, organization, etc.) among local centres. **dēcĕntralīzā′tion** *n.*

dēcĕp′tion *n.* Deceiving, being deceived; trick, sham.

dēcĕp′tive *adj.* Apt to deceive, easily mistaken. **dēcĕp′tively** *adv.* **dēcĕp′tivenėss** *n.*

dĕci- *prefix.* One-tenth.

dĕ′cĭbār *n.* (meteorol.) One-tenth of a BAR².

dĕ′cĭbĕl *n.* One-tenth of a BEL; unit for measuring intensity of sound, corresponding to a *phon* in loudness.

dēcīde′ *v.* Settle (question, issue, dispute) by giving victory to one side; give judgement (*between, for, against,* etc.); bring, come, to a resolution or decision. **dēcīd′ėd** *adj.* (esp.) Definite, unquestionable; (of persons) of clear opinions or vigorous initiative; not vacillating. **dēcīd′ėdly** *adv.*

dēcĭd′ūous *adj.* Shed periodically or normally; (of plant) shedding its leaves annually; (fig.) fleeting, transitory; ~ *teeth,* milk-teeth.

dĕ′cĭgrăm *n.* One-tenth of a GRAM.

dĕ′cĭlitre (-ēter) *n.* Measure of capacity, $\frac{1}{10}$ litre.

dēcĭll′ion (-yon) *n.* 1. 10th power of a million (1 followed by 60 ciphers). 2. (U.S.) 11th power of a thousand (1 followed by 33 ciphers).

dĕ′cĭmal *adj.* Of 10th parts, of the number 10; proceeding by tens; ~ *coinage, currency,* monetary system in which value of each denomination is 10 times that of the one next below it; ~ *fraction,* fraction whose denominator is some power of 10, esp. such a fraction expressed by figures written to right of the units figure after a dot (the ~ *point*), and denoting tenths, hundredths, thousandths, etc.; ~ *system,* system of weights and measures in which each denomination is 10 times the value of that immediately below it. ~ *n.* Decimal fraction; *recurring* ~, one in which exact equivalent of fraction can be expressed only by repetition to infinity of one or more decimal figures.

dĕ′cĭmāte *v.t.* Put to death one in 10 of (mutinous or cowardly soldiers); destroy tenth or large proportion of. **dĕcĭmā′tion** *n.*

dĕ′cĭmētre (-ter) *n.* Measure of length, $\frac{1}{10}$ metre.

dēcīph′er *v.t.* Convert (what is written in cipher) into ordinary writing, make out, interpret, by means of key; make out meaning of. **dēcīph′erable** *adj.* **dēcīph′erment** *n.*

dēcĭ′sion (-zhn) *n.* Settlement (*of*), conclusion, formal judgement; making up one's mind, resolve; resoluteness, decided character.

dēcī′sive *adj.* Deciding, conclusive; decided. **dēcī′sively** (-vl-) *adv.* **dēcī′sivenėss** *n.*

Dē′cius (d. 251). Roman emperor, during whose reign (249–51) the Christians were bitterly persecuted. **Dē′cian** *adj.*

dĕck¹ *n.* 1. Platform of planks or wood-covered iron extending from side to side of ship or part of it (in large ships *main, middle, lower* ~*s,* also *upper* or *spar* ~ above main, and *orlop* ~ below lower); floor of tramcar or omnibus; planking of pier, bridge, etc.; ~-*chair,* folding canvas or cane-panelled chair of the kind used on passenger-steamers; ~-*hand,* sailor employed on deck of vessel, ordinary sailor; ~-*house,* room erected on deck of ship. 2. (now chiefly U.S.) Pack of cards.

dĕck² *v.t.* 1. Array, adorn. 2. Cover as or with deck, furnish with deck.

dĕc′kle *n.* Frame in paper-making machine for limiting size or width of sheet; ~-*edge,* rough uncut edge of paper formed by deckle; ~-*edged,* having such an edge, as hand-made paper.

dēclaim′ *v.* Speak or utter rhetorically; recite; deliver impassioned rather than reasoned speech.

dĕclamā′tion *n.* Act or art of declaiming; rhetorical exercise, set speech; impassioned speech, harangue. **dēclăm′atory** *adj.*

dēclār′ant *n.* One who makes legal declaration.

dĕclarā′tion *n.* Stating, announcing, openly, explicitly, or formally; emphatic, solemn or legal assertion or proclamation; public statement as embodied in document, instrument, or public act; (law) plaintiff's statement of claim; simple affirmation sometimes allowed in lieu of oath or solemn affirmation; creation or acknowledgement of trust or use in writing; (cards) in bezique, declaring score by placing certain cards on table; in bridge, naming trump suit or declaring 'as trumps'; *D*~ *of* INDEPENDENCE, *D*~ *of* INDULGENCE: see these words; ~ *of the poll,* public official announcement of numbers polled at election; ~ *of war,* formal announcement by State of commencement of hostilities against another State.

dēclāre′ *v.* 1. Make known, proclaim publicly, formally, or explicitly; pronounce to be; (custom-house) acknowledge possession of (dutiable goods); ~ *dividend,* officially announce dividend to be paid; ~ *for, against,* openly side with, against; ~ *war,* formally proclaim beginning of hostilities. 2. (law) Make declaration. 3. (cricket) Declare innings closed; close innings before ten wickets have fallen. 4. In bezique, claim score by laying certain cards face upwards on table; in bridge, name trump suit or decide to play in 'no trumps'. **dēclă′ratory** *adj.*

dēclār′er *n.* (esp. in bridge) Player who names trumps and plays dummy's hand.

déclăss′é (dā-, -ā) *adj.* (fem. -*ée*). That has lost caste or sunk in social scale.

dēclĕn′sion (-shn) *n.* 1. Declining or deviating from vertical or horizontal position. 2. Deviation from standard; diminution, deterioration, decay. 3. (gram.) Variation of form of noun, adjective, or pronoun, constituting its cases; class in which noun etc. is grouped according to its inflexions; declining. **dēclĕn′sional** (-sho-) *adj.*

dĕclĭnā′tion *n.* 1. Slope, inclination, from vertical or horizontal position. 2. (astron.) Angular distance of heavenly body from celestial equator. 3. Deviation of magnetic needle from true north-and-south line, variation. 4. (U.S.) Declining, refusal.

dēclīne′ *n.* 1. Sinking; gradual loss of vigour or excellence; decay; deterioration; consumption or other wasting disease; downward movement in price or value. 2. Setting, last part of course, of sun, (fig.) of life, etc. ~ *v.* 1. Have downward inclination; bend down, bow down, droop. 2. (Of sun, day, life, etc.) draw to end of its course. 3. Fall off, decay, decrease, deteriorate. 4. Turn away from, refuse, withhold oneself from (discussion, challenge, etc.); not accept, refuse politely. 5. (gram.) Inflect, recite cases of. **dēclīn′able** *adj.* (gram.) That can be declined.

dĕclĭnŏm′ėter *n.* Instrument for measuring astronomical or magnetic declination.

dēclĭv′ĭtous *adj.* Having considerable slope; steep. **dēclĭv′ĭtously** *adv.* **dēclĭv′ĭty** *n.* Downward slope.

dēclŭtch′ *v.i.* Disengage clutch of motor engine.

dēcŏct′ *v.t.* Make decoction of.

dècŏc'tion *n.* (Liquor obtained by) boiling substance in liquid so as to extract soluble parts.

dēcōde' *v.t.* Decipher (coded message).

décolletage (dākŏl'tahzh) *n.* (Exposure of neck and shoulders by) low-cut neck of dress. ***décolleté*** (-ŏl'tā) (fem. *-ée*) *adj.* (Of dress) low-necked; wearing low-necked dress.

dēcol'o(u)rīze (-kŭler-) *v.* Deprive of, lose, colour. **dēcolo(u)rīzā'tion** *n.*

dēcompōse' (-z) *v.* 1. Separate or resolve into constituent parts or elements. 2. Disintegrate, break up; rot. **dēcŏmposi'tion** *n.*

dēcomprĕss' *v.t.* 1. Relieve pressure on (person who has been in compressed air) by means of air-lock. 2. Reduce compression in (motor engine) thus making engine easier to start. **dēcomprĕ'ssion** *n.* ~ *sickness*, symptoms, caused by 'bubbling' of atmospheric nitrogen in the blood, which occur when person is transferred rapidly to conditions of much lower pressure.

dēcontăm'ināte *v.t.* Rid (person, building, etc.) of contamination, esp. that caused by poison gas used in warfare. **dēcontăminā'tion** *n.*

dēcontrōl' *v.t.* Release from (esp. Government) control. ~ *n.* Removal of control, esp. Government control.

décor (dāk'or) *n.* Scenery and furnishings of stage, room, etc.

dĕc'orāte *v.t.* 1. Furnish with ornamental accessories; hang (streets etc.) with flags etc.; paint, paper, etc. (room, house); serve as adornment to. 2. Invest with order, medal, etc. **dĕc'orative** *adj.*

dĕc'orātėd *adj.* (esp., *D*~) Of the second or middle style of English Gothic architecture (prevailing from *c* 1250 to 1350), with increasing use of decoration as part of construction (ill. WINDOW).

dĕcorā'tion *n.* (esp.) 1. (pl.) Flags, wreaths, etc., put up on occasion of public rejoicing. 2. Medal, star, etc., conferred and worn as mark of honour; *D*~ *Day*, (U.S.) annual commemoration (30th Mar.) of soldiers who fell in Amer. Civil War.

dĕc'orātor *n.* (esp.) Tradesman who papers, paints, etc., houses.

dĕc'orous (*or* dĭkōr-) *adj.* Not violating good taste or propriety, dignified and decent. **dėcōr'ously** *adv.*

dėcōr'um *n.* Seemliness, propriety, etiquette; particular usage required by politeness or decency.

dėcoy' *n.* Pond or pool with narrow arms covered with network into which wild duck etc. may be allured and caught; bird or other animal trained to entice others into trap; decoy-duck; enticement, bait, trap; ~*-duck*, duck trained to decoy others; person, esp. swindler's assistant, enticing others into danger or mischief; ~*-ship*, one used to decoy enemy vessels. ~ *v.t.* Entice into place of capture, esp. with aid of decoy; allure *into*, *out of*, *away*, etc., ensnare.

dėcrease' *v.* Lessen, diminish.

dē'crease *n.* Diminution, lessening.

dėcree' *n.* 1. Ordinance or edict set forth by authority; edict or law of ecclesiastical council; one of eternal purposes, will, of God, Providence, Nature, etc. 2. Judgement of court of equity, admiralty, probate, or divorce; in divorce cases, order of court declaring nullity or dissolution of marriage; ~ *nisi*, order for divorce, remaining conditional for a period, after which it is made absolute unless (*nisi*) cause to the contrary is shown. ~ *v.t.* Ordain by decree.

dĕc'rėment *n.* Decrease, amount lost by diminution or waste (opp. to *increment*).

dėcrĕp'it *adj.* Wasted, worn out, enfeebled with age and infirmities. **dėcrĕp'itūde** *n.*

dėcrĕp'itāte *v.* 1. Calcine (mineral or salt) till it ceases to crackle in fire. 2. Crackle under heat. **dėcrĕpitā'tion** *n.*

decrescĕn'dō (dākrĕsh-). (mus.) = DIMINUENDO.

dėcrĕs'cent *adj.* Waning, decreasing (usu. of moon).

dėcrē'tal *n.* Papal decree; (pl.) collection of such decrees, forming part of canon law.

dėcrȳ' *v.t.* Disparage, cry down.

dėcŭm'bent *adj.* (bot. & zool.) Lying along ground, lying flat on surface. **dėcŭm'bently** *adv.*

dĕc'ūple *adj.* & *n.* Tenfold (amount). ~ *v.* Multiply by 10.

dėcŭss'ate *adj.* X-shaped; (bot.) with pairs of opposite leaves etc. each at right angles to pair below. **dėcŭss'āte** *v.* Arrange, be arranged thus; intersect. **dĕcussā'tion** *n.*

dedans (dedăṅ') *n.* Open gallery at end of service side of tennis-court (ill. TENNIS).

dĕd'icāte *v.t.* Devote (*to* God etc.) with solemn rites; give up, devote (*to* person, purpose); inscribe (book, music, etc.) *to* patron or friend. **dĕd'icatory** *adj.* **dĕdicā'tion** *n.* (esp.) Dedicatory inscription.

dėdūce' *v.t.* 1. Trace course of, bring down (record etc.) *from* or *to* particular period; trace derivation or descent of. 2. Derive as conclusion *from* something already known; infer. **dėdūc'ible** *adj.*

dėdŭct' *v.t.* Take away, put aside (amount etc.) *from*.

dėdŭc'tion *n.* 1. Deducting; amount deducted. 2. Deducing; inference by reasoning from generals to particulars (opp. to INDUCTION); thing deduced.

dėdŭc'tive *adj.* Of, reasoning by, deduction. **dėdŭc'tively** *adv.*

deed *n.* 1. Thing done by intelligent or responsible agent; act of bravery, skill, etc., feat, performance, doing. 2. (law) Written instrument purporting to effect some legal disposition, and sealed and delivered by disposing party (in practice now always signed also but not always delivered); ~*-poll*, deed made and executed by one party only (paper or parchment being 'polled' or cut even, not indented). ~ *v.t.* (chiefly U.S.) Convey or transfer by deed.

deem *v.t.* Believe, consider, judge, count.

Deem'ster *n.* One of two justices of Isle of Man, each with jurisdiction over half the island.

deep *adj.* 1. Extending far down from top, or far in from surface or edge. 2. (fig.) Hard to fathom; profound, not superficial, penetrating. 3. Heart-felt; absorbing; absorbed; intense, vivid, extreme; ~ *mourning*, full mourning. 4. Not shrill; low-pitched, full-toned. 5. ~*-sea*, (as *adj.*) of the deeper part of the sea, some way from shore; *D*~ *South*, (U.S.) S. Carolina, Georgia, Alabama, Mississippi, and Louisiana. **deep'ish** *adj.* **deep'ly** *adv.* **deep'nėss** *n.* **deep** *n.* 1. (poet.) *The* sea. 2. Deep part of sea; abyss, pit, cavity; mysterious region of thought or feeling. ~ *adv.* Deeply; far down or in; ~*-laid* (of scheme), secret and elaborate; ~*-rooted*, having deep roots; not easily eradicated (fig.); ~*-seated*, having its seat far below surface, not superficial.

deep'en *v.* Make, become, deep or deeper.

deer *n.* Family (*Cervidae*) of ruminant quadrupeds with deciduous branching horns or antlers; *red*, *roe*, *fallow*, *Japanese* ~, subspecies wild or domesticated in U.K.; ~*-hound*, large rough greyhound of Scottish breed; ~*-lick*, ground impregnated with salt, alum, etc., where deer come to lick; ~*-park*, park where deer are kept; ~*-stalker*, one who stalks deer; cloth cap with peak before and behind (ill. COAT).

RED DEER STAG

1. Antlers. 2. Tine

dėfāce′ *v.t.* Mar appearance or beauty of; disfigure; discredit; make illegible. **dėfāce′ment** (-sm-) *n.*

dē fǎc′tō. In fact, whether by right or not.

defaecate: see DEFECATE.

dĕf′alcāte *v.i.* Commit defalcations; misappropriate property in one's charge.

dēfalcā′tion *n.* 1. Defection, shortcoming. 2. Monetary deficiency through breach of trust by one who has management or charge of funds, misappropriation; amount misappropriated.

dėfāme′ *v.t.* Attack the good fame of, speak ill of. **dēfamā′tion** *n.* **dėfăm′atory** *adj.*

dėfault′ *n.* Want, absence; failure to act or appear; neglect; failure to pay; *judgement by* ~, judgement given for plaintiff on defendant's failure to plead. ~ *v.* 1. Make, be guilty of, default; fail to appear in court; fail to meet money call. 2. Declare (party) in default and give judgement against him. **dėfaul′ter** *n.* One who defaults; one who fails properly to account for money etc. entrusted to him; (mil.) soldier guilty of military offence.

dėfeas′ance (-fēz-) *n.* (law) Rendering null and void.

dėfeas′ĭble (-fēz-) *adj.* Capable of annulment, liable to forfeiture. **dėfeasĭbĭl′ĭty** *n.*

dėfeat′ *n.* Frustration; overthrow in contest, esp. battle. ~ *v.t.* 1. Frustrate, nullify; (law) annul, render null and void; disappoint, defraud, cheat (*of*). 2. Discomfit or overthrow in a contest.

dėfeat′ĭsm *n.* State of mind of one who accepts defeat as inevitable. **dėfeat′ĭst** *n.* & *adj.*

dĕf′ėcāte, -faecāte *v.* Clear of dregs, refine, purify; get rid of, purge away, (dregs, excrement, sin); void faeces. **dĕfecā′tion** *n.*

dėfĕct′ (*or* dē′-) *n.* Lack of something essential to completeness; shortcoming, failing; blemish; amount by which thing falls short. ~ *v.i.* Desert.

dėfĕc′tion *n.* Falling away from allegiance to leader, party, religion, duty; desertion; apostasy.

dėfĕc′tĭve *adj.* Having defect(s); incomplete; faulty; wanting or deficient *in*; (gram.) not having all usual inflexions. **dėfĕc′tĭvely** *adv.* **dėfĕc′tĭvenėss** *n.*

dėfĕnce′ *n.* 1. Defending from, resistance against, attack. 2. Thing that defends; means of resisting or warding off attack; (pl.) fortifications. 3. Justification, vindication; speech or writing used to this end; (law) denial of charge by accused party, defendant's pleading or proceedings. 4. ~ *mechanism*, (psychoanal.) dynamic mental system serving to protect the conscious personality against disruptive unconscious impulses. **dėfĕnce′lėss** (-sl-) *adj.* **dėfĕnce′lėssly** *adv.*

dėfĕnd′ *v.* 1. (archaic) Forbid, avert. 2. Ward off attack from; keep safe; protect (*against*, *from*). 3. Uphold by argument, speak or write in favour of; (law) make defence in court; (of counsel) appear for defendant, conduct defence of.

dėfĕn′dant *n.* Person sued in court of law. ~ *adj.* That is a defendant.

dėfĕn′der *n.* One who defends; holder of championship etc. defending the title; *D*~ *of the Faith* (*fidei defensor*), title borne by English sovereigns since Henry VIII, on whom it was conferred in 1521 by Pope Leo X as reward for writing against Luther.

dėfĕnėstrā′tion *n.* Throwing out of a window; *D*~ *of Prague*, action of Bohemian Protestants who threw two of the emperor's deputy-governors and their secretary out of a window of the royal palace of Prague (21st May 1618) as a protest against Catholic repression; this was the prelude to the Thirty Years War.

dėfĕn′sĭble *adj.* Easily defended (in war or argument); justifiable. **dėfĕnsĭbĭl′ĭty** *n.* **dėfĕn′sĭbly** *adv.*

dėfĕn′sĭve *adj.* Serving, used, done, for defence; protective; not aggressive. **dėfĕn′sĭvely** *adv.* **dėfĕn′sĭve** *n.* State or position of defence.

dėfėr′[1] *v.* Put off, postpone; procrastinate, be dilatory; *deferred bond*, bond on which interest gradually increases to a fixed maximum; (U.S.) deferred share; *deferred payment*, payment by instalments; *deferred* (*share, stock*), share, stock, payment of interest on which is deferred until expiration of fixed time or (usu.) until fixed rate of interest has been paid on ordinary shares. **dėfėrm′ent** *n.*

dėfėr′[2] *v.i.* Submit or make concessions in opinion or action *to* (person etc.).

dĕf′erence *n.* Compliance with advice etc. of one superior in wisdom or position; respect, manifestation of desire to comply, courteous regard; *in* ~ *to*, out of respect for. **dĕferĕn′tial** (-shl) *adj.* **dĕferĕn′tially** *adv.*

dĕf′erent *adj.* 1. (physiol., of ducts etc.) Conveying to a destination (obs.). 2. (rare for) Deferential.

dėfī′ance *n.* Challenge to fight or maintain cause, assertion, etc.; open disobedience; setting at nought.

dėfī′ant *adj.* Openly disobedient; rejecting advances, suspicious and reserved. **dėfī′antly** *adv.*

dėfĭ′ciency (-shn-) *n.* Being deficient; want, lack; thing wanting; amount by which thing, esp. revenue, falls short; ~ *disease*, disease caused by lack in diet of necessary elements (see VITAMIN).

dėfĭ′cient (-shnt) *adj.* Incomplete, defective, wanting *in*; insufficient in quantity, force, etc.; half-witted; **dėfĭ′ciently** *adv.* **dėfĭ′cient** *n.* One who is mentally deficient.

dĕf′ĭcĭt *n.* Amount by which anything, esp. sum of money, is too small; excess of liabilities over assets or of expenditure over income.

dĕfĭlāde′ *v.t.* Secure (fortress) against enfilading fire. ~ *n.* This act or operation (also *defilement*).

dėfīle′[1] (*or* dē′fīl) *n.* Narrow way along which troops can march only in file; narrow pass or gorge. ~ *v.i.* March in file, by files.

dėfīle′[2] *v.t.* Make dirty, befoul; pollute, corrupt; desecrate, profane; make ceremonially unclean. **dėfīle′ment**[1] (-lm-) *n.*

dėfīle′ment[2] (-lm-) *n.* See DEFILADE.

dėfīne′ *v.t.* Settle limits of; make clear, esp. in outline; set forth essence of, declare exact meaning of; characterize, constitute definition of.

dĕf′ĭnĭte *adj.* With exact limits; determinate, distinct, precise, not vague; ~ *article*, (gram.) the demonstrative adjective *the* and its equivalents in other languages; ~ *inflexions*, those of German, OE, etc., adjectives used after the definite article. **dĕf′ĭnĭtely** (-tl-) *adv.* Clearly, plainly; (colloq.) yes indeed. **dĕf′ĭnĭtenėss** *n.*

dĕfĭnĭ′tion *n.* 1. Defining; statement of precise nature of thing or meaning of word. 2. Making or being distinct, degree of distinctness, in outline (esp. of image given by lens or shown in photograph); *high-*~, (television) applied to system securing relatively clear outline in transmitted image by scanning in more than 100 (usu. 240) lines and broadcasting on ultra-short wavelength; *low-*~, applied to system securing less clear outline by scanning in less than 100 (usu. 30) lines and broadcasting on medium wavelength.

dėfĭn′ĭtĭve *adj.* Decisive, unconditional, final. **dėfĭn′ĭtĭvely** *adv.*

dėflāte′ *v.* Let air etc. out of (tyre, balloon, etc.); reduce (inflated currency); practise deflation.

dėflā′tion *n.* Deflating; esp. situation in any country where prices generally are falling relatively to costs of production, giving rise to losses and unemployment. **dėflā′tionary** (-sho-) *adj.*

dėflĕct′ *v.* Bend or turn aside; bend (ray of light) from straight line.

dėflĕ′xion (-kshn), **-ĕc′tion** *n.* Deflecting; (esp.) turning of magnetic needle or recording needle of galvanometer away from its zero.

dēflorā′tion *n.* Deflowering.

dėflow′er *v.t.* Deprive of virginity, ravish; ravage, spoil; strip of flowers.

Defoe (dėfō′), Daniel (*c* 1660–1731). English novelist, author of 'Robinson Crusoe' (1719) etc.

dėfŏ′rėst *v.t.* Clear of forest. **dēfŏrėstā′tion** *n.*

dėfôrm′ *v.t.* Make ugly, deface; put out of shape, mis-shape (esp. in past part.).

dēfŏrmā'tion *n.* Disfigurement; change for the worse; perverted form.

dėfŏrm'ĭty *n.* Being deformed, ugliness, disfigurement; malformation (esp. of body or limb).

dėfraud' *v.t.* Cheat.

dėfray' *v.t.* Settle, discharge by payment. **dėfray'ment** *n.*

dėfrŏck' *v.t.* Unfrock, deprive of ecclesiastical status.

dĕft *adj.* Dextrous, skilful; handling things neatly. **dĕft'ly** *adv.* **dĕft'nėss** *n.*

dėfŭnct' *adj.* Dead; no longer existing.

dėfȳ' *v.t.* 1. Challenge to combat (archaic); challenge *to* contest or trial of skill. 2. Resist boldly or openly, set at nought; (of things) be beyond power of.

deg. *abbrev.* Degree.

Degas (degah'), Hilaire Germain Edgar (1834–1917). French Impressionist painter.

de Gaulle: see GAULLE.

dē-Gauss', dēgauss' (-ows) *v.t.* Demagnetize; esp. render (ship) immune to magnetic mines by fitting round the hull a band of wire (*degaussing belt, girdle*) energized by an electric current which neutralizes ship's magnetism. [see GAUSS]

dėgĕn'erate *adj.* Having lost qualities proper to race or kind, sunk from former excellence, debased, degraded; (biol.) having reverted to lower type. **dėgĕn'eracy** *n.* **dėgĕn'erate** *n.* Degenerate person or animal. **dėgĕn'erāte** *v.i.* Become degenerate.

dėgĕnerā'tion *n.* Becoming degenerate; (path.) morbid disintegration of tissue or change in its structure.

dėglut'ĭnāte (-ōō-) *v.t.* Extract gluten from (flour etc.). **dėglutĭnā'tion** *n.*

dēglutĭ'tion (-ōō-) *n.* Swallowing.

dėgrāde' *v.* 1. Reduce to lower rank; depose as punishment; deprive (ecclesiastic) of orders. 2. Bring into dishonour or contempt; lower in character or quality, debase; tone down, reduce (colour etc.). 3. (biol.) Reduce to lower organic type. 4. (physics) Reduce (energy) to a form less capable of transformation. 5. (geol.) Wear down (rocks etc.) by surface abrasion or disintegration. 6. Degenerate. **dĕgradā'tion** *n.*

dėgrain' *adj.* (Of leather) from which grain has been removed.

dėgree' *n.* 1. Thing placed like step in series, tier, row; stage in ascending or descending scale or process; *by degrees*, gradually. 2. Stage in direct line of descent; (pl.) number of such steps to or from common ancestor, determining proximity of blood of collateral descendants; *prohibited degrees*, those within which marriage is prohibited. 3. Relative social or official rank; relative condition or state. 4. Stage in intensity or amount; (criminal law) relative measure of criminality; (U.S.) distinctive grade of crime (*murder in the first* ~, homicide premeditated or resulting from commission of grave crime; *in the second* ~, unpremeditated, or resulting from commission of lesser crime). 5. Academic rank conferred as mark of proficiency in scholarship or (*honorary* ~) as honour; (freemasonry) each step of proficiency in order, conferring successively higher rank. 6. (gram.) Stage (positive, comparative or superlative) in comparison of adj. or adv. 7. (geom. etc.) Unit of angular measurement (symbol °), angle equal to $\frac{1}{90}$ right angle, arc of $\frac{1}{360}$ circumference of circle; esp. $\frac{1}{360}$ of earth's circumference, = 60 minutes; (thermometry) unit of temperature, varying according to scale employed; (mus.) (interval between) successive notes forming a scale. 8. *third* ~ (orig. U.S.), pressure applied by police to prisoner to extort confession or information. **dėgree'lėss** *adj.*

dėhĭsce' (-s) *v.i.* Gape; (bot., of seed-vessel etc.) burst open. **dėhĭs'cence** *n.* **dėhĭs'cent** *adj.*

Dehm'el (dā-), Richard (1863–1920). German lyric poet, novelist, and dramatist.

dēhūm'anīze *v.t.* Divest of human characteristics.

dēhȳd'rāte *v.* (chem.) Deprive of, lose, water or its constituent elements; dry completely, desiccate (foods). **dēhȳdrā'tion** *n.*

dē-īce' *v.t.* Remove, prevent, formation of ice on wings etc. of aircraft. **dē-ī'cer** *n.* Device or substance for de-icing.

dē'icīde *n.* Killing, killer, of a god.

dē'ĭfŏrm *adj.* Godlike in form or nature.

dē'ĭfȳ *v.t.* Make a god of; make godlike; regard as a god, worship. **dēĭfĭcā'tion** *n.*

deign (dān) *v.* Think fit, condescend (*to*); condescend to give, vouchsafe.

dē'ī grā'tiā (-shĭ-) (abbrev. D.G.) By the grace of God. [L]

dē'ism *n.* Belief in existence of God, with rejection of revelation and supernatural doctrines of Christianity. **dē'ist** *n.* **dēĭs'tĭc** *adj.* **dēĭs'tĭcally** *adv.*

dē'ĭty *n.* Divine status, quality, or nature; a god.

dėjĕct' *v.t.* Dispirit, depress. **dėjĕc'tėdly** *adv.* **dėjĕc'tion** *n.*

déjeuner (dě'zhonā) *n.* Breakfast; lunch, esp. of a ceremonial kind.

dē jure (joor'ĭ) *adj.* & *adv.* Rightful, by right.

Dėkăb'rist *n.* = DECEMBRIST. [Russ. *Dekabr'* December]

Dĕkk'er, Thomas (1570?–1632). English Elizabethan dramatist, author of 'The Honest Whore', 'Patient Grissil', 'The Witch of Edmonton', etc.

dĕkk'ō *n.* (orig. army slang) Look. [Hind. *dekho* look!]

del. *abbrev.* *Delineavit* (= drew this).

Del. *abbrev.* Delaware.

Delacroix' (-krwah), Ferdinand Victor Eugène (1799–1863). French Romantic painter.

dėlaine' *n.* Light dress-fabric, usu. of wool and cotton, and printed.

dėlāte' *v.t.* Inform against; impeach; report (offence). **dėlā'tion, dėlāt'or** *ns.*

Dĕl'awāre. S. Atlantic State of U.S., one of the original 13 States of the Union; capital, Dover.

dėlay' *n.* Delaying; procrastination; hindrance to progress. ~ *v.* 1. Postpone, defer, put off; hinder. 2. Loiter, be tardy; wait.

dĕl cred'erė (-ăd-) *adj.* & *adv.* (commerc.) With the selling agent's guarantee that the buyer is solvent. [It., = 'of belief, of trust']

dĕl'ė. (printing direction) Delete indicated letter, word, etc. (usu. written δ).

dėlĕc'table *adj.* (archaic or iron.) Delightful, pleasant. **dēlĕctā'tion** *n.* Enjoyment.

dĕl'ėgacy *n.* System of delegating; appointment as delegate; bodv of delegates.

dĕl'egate *n.* Deputy, commissioner; elected representative sent to conference. **dĕl'ėgāte** *v.t.* Depute, send as representative; commit (authority etc.) to agent. **dĕlėgā'tion** *n.* Entrusting of authority to deputy; body of delegates; (U.S.) group of members of Congress representing particular State.

dėlēte' *v.t.* Strike out, obliterate (letter, word, passage, etc.). **dėlē'tion** *n.*

dĕlėtēr'ious *adj.* Noxious, harmful. **dĕlėtēr'iously** *adv.* **dĕlėtēr'iousnėss** *n.*

Dĕlft. Town in Holland; kind of pottery (also ~ *ware*) produced there, usu. with white glaze on which a decoration is painted in blue.

Delhi (dĕl'ĭ). Capital of the Republic of India, formerly capital of British India; the State in which it is situated, formerly a province.

Dē'lian (-lyan) *adj.* Of DELOS.

dėlĭb'erate *adj.* Intentional; considered, not impulsive; slow in deciding, cautious; leisurely, not hurried. **dėlĭb'erately** *adv.* **dėlĭb'eratenėss** *n.* **dėlĭb'erāte** *v.* Consider, think carefully; take counsel, consult, hold debate.

dėlĭberā'tion *n.* Careful consideration; discussion, debate; care, avoidance of precipitancy, slowness of movement.

dėlĭb'erative *adj.* Of, appointed for purpose of, deliberation or debate. **dėlĭb'eratively** *adv.*

dĕl'ĭcacy *n.* 1. Fineness of texture, substance, outline, etc., or of feeling or observation. 2. Weakliness; susceptibility to injury or disease; need of care in handling.

3. Refinement, sense of what is becoming or modest; regard for feelings of others. 4. Choice or dainty item of food. 5. Delicate trait; a nicety.

dĕl'ĭcate *adj.* 1. Palatable, dainty (of food); sheltered, luxurious, effeminate (of life, upbringing, etc.). 2. Fine of texture, soft, slender, slight; of exquisite quality or workmanship; (of colour) subdued. 3. Subtle, hard to appreciate. 4. Easily injured; liable to illness. 5. Requiring nice handling; critical, ticklish. 6. Subtly sensitive; finely skilful; avoiding the offensive or immodest, considerate. **dĕl'ĭcately** *adv.* **dĕl'ĭcateness** *n.*

dĕlĭcatĕss'en *n.* (Shop selling) delicacies or relishes for table.

dėlĭ'cious (-shus) *adj.* Highly delightful, esp. to taste, smell, or sense of humour. **dėlĭ'ciously** *adv.* **dėlĭ'ciousnėss** *n.*

dėlĭct' *n.* A violation of law or right, offence.

dėlight' (-īt) *n.* Being delighted; thing affording delight. ~ *v.* Give great pleasure or enjoyment to; rejoice, be highly pleased. **dėlight'ful** *adj.* **dėlight'fully** *adv.* **dėlight'fulnėss** *n.*

Dėlī'lah. The woman who betrayed Samson to the Philistines (see Judges xvi); hence, temptress, false and wily woman.

dėlĭm'ĭt, dėlĭm'ĭtāte, *vbs.t.* Determine limits or territorial boundary of. **dėlĭmĭtā'tion** *n.*

dėlĭn'ėāte *v.t.* Show by drawing or description, portray. **dėlĭneā'tion, dėlĭn'ėātor** *ns.*

dėlĭnq'uency *n.* Being a delinquent; neglect or violation of duty; guilt; act of delinquency, offence, misdeed. **dėlĭnq'uent** *adj.* Defaulting, guilty. ~ *n.* Delinquent person.

dĕlĭquĕsce' (-s) *v.i.* Become liquid, dissolve in moisture absorbed from the air; (fig.) melt away. **dĕlĭquĕs'cence** *n.* **dĕlĭquĕs'cent** *adj.*

dėlĭ'rious *adj.* Affected with delirium, temporarily or apparently mad, raving; wildly excited, ecstatic; betraying delirium or ecstasy.

dėlĭ'rium *n.* Disordered state of mind with incoherent speech, hallucinations, and frenzied excitement; great excitement, ecstasy; ~ *trĕm'ĕns* (abbrev. *d.t.*), form of delirium with terrifying delusions, to which heavy drinkers are liable.

Dĕl'ius, Frederick (1862–1934). English composer of songs, concertos, choral works, etc.

dėlĭv'er *v.t.* 1. Rescue, save, set free (*from*). 2. Assist (female) in giving birth; assist in the birth of; (pass.) give birth to young. 3. Unburden one*self of* opinion, thought, etc., in discourse. 4. Give *up*, *over*, abandon, resign, hand on *to* another; distribute (letters, parcels, etc.) to addressee or purchaser; present, render, (account); (law) hand over formally (esp. deed to grantee or third party). 5. Launch, aim (blow, ball, attack). 6. Utter, enunciate, pronounce openly or formally (judgement, speech, etc.).

dėlĭv'erance *n.* Rescue; emphatically or formally delivered opinion; (in juror's oath) verdict.

dėlĭv'erer *n.* (esp.) Saviour, rescuer.

dėlĭv'ery *n.* 1. Childbirth. 2. Surrender (*of*); handing over (esp. of letters or goods). 3. (law) Formal handing over of property; formal transfer of deed to grantee or third party (formerly essential to its validity). 4. Delivering (missile, blow, etc.), esp. cricket-ball in bowling; action shown in doing this. 5. Uttering of speech etc.; manner of doing this.

dĕll *n.* Small hollow or valley, usu. with tree-clad sides.

Dĕll'a Crŭs'can *adj.* & *n.* 1. (Member) of the Academy della Crusca, a society founded in Florence in 1582 to sift and purify the Italian language, which issued a dictionary in 1612. 2. (Member) of an artificial school of English poets of late 18th c., one of whom, Robert Merry, was elected a member of the Florentine Academy and adopted the signature *Della Crusca*. [It. *della crusca* of the bran (i.e. sifting)]

Dĕll'a Rŏbb'ia, Luca (1400–82). Florentine sculptor famous for his work in terracotta and various sculptures in Florence; the chief characteristic of his terracotta process, which was inherited by the Della Robbia family, is the use of white figures against a usu. blue background.

Dē'lŏs. Island in the Aegean, one of the Cyclades; supposed to have been raised from the sea by Poseidon and anchored to the bottom of the sea by Zeus; an important centre of the worship of Apollo.

dēlouse' *v.t.* Clear of lice.

Dĕl'phī. Ancient Greek town (mod. Dĕl'phī) on slopes of Mt Parnassus, with sanctuary and oracle of Apollo. **Dĕl'phian, Dĕl'phĭc** *adjs.* Of Delphi or the Delphic Apollo; of the Delphic oracle; obscure and ambiguous like the oracle's responses.

Dĕl'phĭn *adj.* Of an edition of Latin classics prepared (1674) for use of the dauphin, son of Louis XIV. [L phrase *ad usum Delphini*, for the use of the dauphin]

dĕlphĭn'ium *n.* Genus of ranunculaceous plants with handsome irregular-shaped blue or pink flowers, including larkspur; esp. a cultivated species or variety of this; the deep blue of some delphinium flowers. [Gk *delphinion* larkspur, dim. of *delphin* dolphin]

dĕl'phĭnoid *adj.* Like or related to a dolphin.

dĕl'ta *n.* 1. 4th letter of Greek alphabet, Δ, δ, corresponding to *d*. 2. Triangular tract of sand, gravel, and silt enclosed and traversed by the diverging mouths of a river. 3. ~ *rays*, rays of low penetrative power emitted by radium, polonium, uranium, etc., consisting of low-velocity electrons knocked from an atom during a collision with some other particle; ~ *wing*, triangular swept-back wing of high-speed aircraft.

dĕl'toid *adj.* Triangular; like river delta; ~ *muscle*, large triangular muscle forming prominence of shoulder and serving to lift upper arm (ill. MUSCLE). ~ *n.* Deltoid muscle.

dėlūde' *v.t.* Impose upon, deceive.

dĕl'ūge *n.* Great flood, inundation; heavy fall of rain; flood of words etc.; *the D~*, the great flood in the time of Noah (Gen. vi–viii). ~ *v.t.* Flood, inundate. [L *diluvium* flood]

dėlu'sion (-o͞ozhn, -ū-) *n.* Imposing or being imposed upon; false impression or opinion, esp. as symptom or form of madness. **dėlū'sional** (-zho-) *adj.*

dėlus'ĭve (-o͞o-, -ū-) *adj.* Deceptive, disappointing, unreal. **dėlus'ĭvely** *adv.* **dėlus'ĭvenėss** *n.*

de lūxe. Luxurious, sumptuous; of superior kind. [Fr.]

dĕlve *v.* Dig (archaic or dial.); (fig.) make laborious research in documents etc.

dēmăg'nėtīze *v.t.* Deprive of magnetic quality.

dĕm'agŏgue (-g) *n.* Leader of popular faction, or of mob; agitator appealing to passions and prejudices of mob; (hist.) popular leader, orator who espoused people's cause against other parties in State. **dĕmagŏg'ĭc** (-gĭk) *adj.* **dĕm'agŏgism, dĕm'agŏgy,** (-g-) *ns.*

dėmand' (-mah-) *n.* 1. Authoritative or peremptory request or claim; what is demanded; legal claim, esp. claim made by legal process to real property. 2. Call for commodity by consumers; urgent or pressing claim or requirement. ~ *v.t.* 1. Ask for with legal right or authority; (law) make formal claim to (real property) as rightful owner; ask for peremptorily or urgently; require, have need of. 2. Ask to know, authoritatively or formally.

dėman'dant (-mah-) *n.* (esp., law) Plaintiff in real action, plaintiff or claimant in any civil action.

dēmarcā'tion *n.* Marking of boundary or limits of anything. **dē'marcāte** *v.t.*

démarche (dāmarsh') *n.* (diplomacy) Political step or proceeding, esp. one involving fresh line of policy. [Fr.]

dēmatēr'ialīze *v.* Make, become, non-material or spiritual.

dėmean'[1] *v.refl.* Behave, conduct, one*self* (in specified way). **dėmean'our** (-ner) *n.* Bearing, outward behaviour.

dėmean'[2] *v.t.* Lower in dignity, reputation, etc.; lower or humble one*self*.

dėmĕn'tėd *adj.* Crazed, mad; infatuated; affected with dementia.

dėmenti (dāmahnt'ī) *n.* Official contradiction of rumour or published statement.

dėmĕn'tĭa (*or* -sha) *n.* Insanity characterized by failure or loss of mental powers and caused by disease in or injury to the brain; ~ *praec'ox*, SCHIZOPHRENIA.

dĕmerar'a *n.* ~ (*sugar*), raw cane-sugar in yellowish-brown crystals, orig. and chiefly from Demerara, a region of British Guiana.

dēmĕ'rĭt *n.* Quality deserving blame or punishment; censurable conduct; want of merit; fault, defect.

dėmesne' (-mān, -mēn) *n.* 1. (law) Possession (of real estate) as one's own; land *held in* ~, land not held by any subordinate tenant; (in modern use) land immediately attached to mansion and held along with it (including park, home farm, etc.). 2. Domain; landed property, estate.

Dēmēt'er. (Gk myth.) Goddess of the corn-bearing earth and of agriculture, the daughter of Cronos and mother of Persephone; identified by the Romans with CERES.

demi- *prefix.* Half, semi-.

dĕm'ĭgŏd *n.* Partly divine being, son of god and mortal, or deified man.

dĕm'ĭjohn (-jŏn) *n.* Large bottle with bulging body and narrow neck, holding 3–10 gal. and usu. cased in wicker-or rush-work. [corrupt. of Fr. *dame-Jeanne* Dame Jane]

dēmĭl'ĭtarīze *v.t.* Do away with military organization of. **dēmĭlĭtarīzā'tion** *n.*

dĕm'ĭlune (-ōōn) *n.* Outwork protecting bastion or curtain.

dĕm'ĭ-mŏnde' *n.* Class of women on outskirts of society, of doubtful reputation and standing. ***dĕmĭ-mŏndaine'*** *n.* Woman of the demi-monde.

dĕm'ĭ-rĕp *n.* Woman of doubtful reputation or suspected chastity. [for *demi-reputable*]

dėmīse' (-z) *v.* 1. Convey, grant, (estate) by will or lease; transmit (title etc.) by death or abdication. 2. Die, decease. ~ *n.* 1. Conveyance or transfer of estate by will or lease; transference of sovereignty, as by death or deposition of sovereign. 2. Decease, death.

dĕm'ĭ-sĕm'ĭ *adj.* Usu. as contemptuous diminutive.

dĕmĭsĕmĭquāv'er (stress variable) *n.* (mus.) Note of half value of semiquaver; symbol for this (𝅘𝅥𝅰, 𝅀).

dėmĭ'ssion (-shn) *n.* Resigning, abdication, *of*.

dėmĭt' *v.* Resign.

dĕm'ĭūrge *n.* (In Platonic philosophy) creator of world; (in Gnostic and other systems) a being subordinate to Supreme Being; occas., author of evil. **dĕmĭūr'gĭc** *adj.* [Gk *dēmiourgos* craftsman (*dēmios* of the people, *-ergos* working)]

dėmŏb' *v.t.* (slang) Demobilize.

dēmōb'ĭlīze *v.t.* Release from mobilized condition; disband (troops, ships, etc.). **dėmōbĭlīzā'tion** *n.*

dėmŏc'racy *n.* 1. Form of government in which sovereign power resides in the people as a whole, and is exercised either directly by them or by their elected representatives; State having this form of government. 2. The common people. 3. (U.S.) Principles, members, of DEMOCRATIC party.

dĕm'ocrăt *n.* 1. Advocate of democracy. 2. (U.S.) Member of DEMOCRATIC party.

dĕmocrăt'ĭc *adj.* 1. Of, like, practising, advocating, democracy. 2. (U.S.) Of the Democratic party; *D~ party*, in U.S., the political party which claims JEFFERSON for its founder and opposes the (present-day) REPUBLICAN party; so called since *c* 1828, but previously known, at various times, as Anti-Federalist, Republican, and Democratic-Republican. **dĕmocrăt'ĭcally** *adv.* **dėmŏc'ratīze** *v.* **dėmŏcratīzā'tion** *n.*

Dėmŏc'rĭtus (5th c. B.C.). Greek philosopher ('the laughing philosopher'), who advanced the theory that the world was formed by the concourse of atoms. **Dėmŏcrĭtē'an** *adj.*

Dēmogōrg'on. (myth.) Mysterious and terrible infernal deity (first mentioned in Latin authors *c* 450).

dēmŏg'raphy *n.* Branch of anthropology dealing with conditions of life in communities of people, as shown in statistics of births, deaths, diseases, etc. **dēmŏg'rapher** *n.* **dēmogrăph'ĭc** *adj.*

dĕmoiselle (-mwazĕl') *n.* (zool.) The Numidian crane, *Anthropoides virgo*, with long feathers and white plumes behind the eyes. [Fr., = 'damsel']

dėmŏl'ĭsh *v.t.* Pull or throw down (building); destroy, make an end of; consume, eat up. **dĕmolĭ'tion** *n.*

dēm'on, dae- *n.* 1. (often *daemon*) In Gk myth., supernatural being, intermediate between gods and men; inferior divinity, spirit, genius, ghost. 2. Evil spirit, devil; cruel, malignant, destructive, or terrible person; evil passion or agency personified. 3. ~ *bowler*, very fast bowler at cricket; ~ *star*, Algol, the β star of Perseus.

dēmŏn'ėtīze (*or* -mŭn-) *v.t.* Withdraw from use as money; deprive of its status as money.

dēmōn'ĭac, dae- *adj.* Possessed by a demon or evil spirit; of demoniacal possession; of or like demons; devilish; frenzied. ~ *n.* One possessed by a demon. **dēmonī'acal** *adj.* Demoniac; ~ *possession*, possession of a man by indwelling demon, formerly held to be cause of some kinds of insanity, epilepsy, etc.

dēmŏn'ĭc, dae- *adj.* 1. Demoniacal, devilish. 2. (usu. *daemonic*) Of or like supernatural power or genius.

dēm'onĭsm *n.* Belief in the power of demons.

dēmonŏl'atry *n.* Worship of demons.

dēmonŏl'ogy *n.* Study of beliefs about demons.

dĕm'onstrable *adj.* Capable of being shown or logically proved. **dĕm'onstrably** *adv.* **dėmŏnstrabĭl'ĭty** *n.*

dĕm'onstrāte *v.* 1. Show, display (feelings etc.). 2. Describe and explain by help of specimens or experiments; act as demonstrator. 3. Establish truth of by argument or deduction; prove. 4. Make, take part in, public demonstration.

dĕmonstrā'tion *n.* 1. Outward exhibition, display, *of*; (mil.) show of military force or offensive movement; public manifestation (usu. mass-meeting or procession) of interest in or sympathy with some cause etc. 2. Demonstrating, clear or indubitable proof, argument(s) proving an assertion etc.; exhibition and explanation of specimens or experiments as method of instruction in science or art.

dėmŏn'strative *adj.* 1. Serving to point out or exhibit; esp. (gram.) of certain adjectives and pronouns. 2. Demonstrating logically or conclusively; serving as proof *of*; evident or provable by demonstration. 3. Given to or marked by outward exhibition or expression of feelings etc. **dėmŏn'stratively** *adv.* **dėmŏn'strativeness** *n.*

dĕm'onstrātor *n.* One who demonstrates; one who teaches by demonstration, esp. assistant to professor of science doing practical work with students; one who takes part in public demonstration.

dėmŏ'ralīze *v.t.* Corrupt morals of, deprave; destroy discipline, courage, powers of endurance, etc., of (esp. troops). **dėmŏralīzā'tion** *n.*

Dēm'ŏs. Personification of populace or democracy.

Dėmŏs'thenēs (-z) (*c* 385–322 B.C.). Athenian orator, famous for his orations delivered to rouse the Athenians to the danger of the subjugation of Greece by Philip of Macedon.

dėmōte' *v.t.* (orig. U.S.) Reduce to lower rank or class. **dėmō'tion** *n.*

dėmŏt'ĭc *adj.* Popular, vulgar; esp. as epithet of popular simplified form of writing used in Egypt after the 6th or 7th c. (as dist. from *hieratic*).

dėmŭl'cent *adj.* & *n.* Soothing (medicine).

dėmūr' *v.i.* Make difficulties, raise scruples or objections *to, at*;

(law) put in a demurrer. ~ *n.* Objecting, objection.

dėmūre′ *adj.* Sober, grave, composed; affectedly or constrainedly grave or decorous; coy, prudish. **dėmūre′ly** *adv.* **dėmūre′nėss** *n.*

dėmŭrr′able *adj.* That may be demurred to; open to objection.

dėmŭrr′age *n.* Compensation for (detention of vessel by freighter beyond time agreed upon); charge for detention of railway trucks; Bank of England's charge for exchanging gold or notes for bullion.

dėmŭrr′er *n.* Legal objection to relevance of opponent's point, which stays action until relevance is determined by court; exception taken to anything.

dėmȳ′ *n.* 1. Size of paper (in printing paper $22\frac{1}{2} \times 17\frac{1}{2}$ in., in writing paper (England) $20 \times 15\frac{1}{2}$ in., (U.S.) 21×16 in.). 2. Foundation scholar at Magdalen College, Oxford (his allowance or 'commons' being orig. half that of Fellow). **dėmȳ′shĭp** *n.* [earlier spelling of *demi-* half]

dĕn *n.* Wild beast's lair; lurking-place of thieves etc.; small room in which person secludes himself to work etc.

dėnār′ius *n.* (pl. *-iī*). Ancient Roman silver coin, orig. of the value of 10 asses (about 8*d.*), whence English abbrev. *d.* for 'penny'.

dēn′ary *adj.* Of ten, decimal.

dēnă′tionalīze (-shon-) *v.t.* Deprive of nationality; destroy independent or distinct nationality of; make (institution etc.) no longer national; transfer (enterprise, industry) from national to private ownership. **dēnătionălīzā′tion** *n.*

dēnăt′uralīze (-cher-) *v.t.* Alter or pervert the nature of, make unnatural; deprive of status and rights of natural subject or citizen. **dēnăturalīzā′tion** *n.*

dēnā′ture *v.t.* Change nature of; render dutiable articles unfit for human consumption so that they may be used for other purposes without duty having to be paid. **dēnā′turant** (-chōō-) *n.* Substance used as denaturing agent. **dēnăturā′tion** *n.*

dēnazĭfĭcā′tion (-ahtsĭ-) *n.* Eradication of Nazi influence in Germany; removal of Nazis from positions of responsibility in German public life. **dēnăz′ĭfȳ** *v.t.*

Dĕn′bighshire (-bĭsh-). County of N. Wales.

dĕn′drīte *n.* 1. (Stone or mineral with) natural tree-like or moss-like marking. 2. Branching process of nerve cell (ill. NERVE). **dĕndrĭt′ic** *adj.*

dĕndrŏl′ogy *n.* Study of trees. **dĕndrŏl′ogist** *n.*

dēne[1] *n.* Deep wooded valley.

dēne[2] *n.* Bare sandy seaside tract; low sand-hill.

dēne-hōle, dāne- *n.* One of a class of ancient excavations (chiefly in Essex and Kent, and in Somme valley in France), consisting of a narrow cylindrical shaft leading to an artificial cave in chalk.

dengue (dĕng′gĭ) *n.* Epidemic infectious eruptive fever of E. Africa, W. Indies, etc., with excruciating pains in joints and great prostration and debility. [prob. orig. Swahili *dinga*, associated with Span. *dengue* prudery, with ref. to stiffness in patient's neck and shoulders]

dėnī′able *adj.* That can be denied.

dėnī′al *n.* Refusal of request; self-denial; contradiction, statement that thing is not true or existent; disowning, disavowal (*of* person); *self-*~, abstinence.

dėnier′ (-nēr) *n.* 1. (archaic) Very small sum or coin. 2. Unit of fineness of silk etc. yarn, estimated by the number of half decigrams which a hank of 450 metres weighs.

dĕn′igrāte *v.t.* Blacken; defame. **dĕnigrā′tion** *n.*

dėnĭm′ (*or* -nēm′ *or* dĕn′ĭm) *n.* Twill-woven cotton fabric used for overalls etc., usu. with blue or brown warp and grey weft. [Fr. (*serge*) *de Nîm* (serge) of Nîmes in S. France]

Dĕn′is, St (d. 280). 1st bishop of Paris and patron saint of France; decapitated on the hill of Montmartre.

dēnī′trāte *v.t.* Remove nitric acid from. **dēnītrā′tion** *n.*

dĕn′izen *n.* Inhabitant, occupant (*of* place); foreigner admitted to residence and certain rights; naturalized foreign word, animal, or plant. ~ *v.t.* Admit as denizen. **dĕn′izenship** *n.*

Dĕn′mārk. Kingdom of N. Europe, consisting of the islands of Zealand, Funen, Lolland, etc., the peninsula of Jutland and the outlying Baltic island of Bornholm; capital, Copenhagen.

dėnŏm′ināte *v.t.* Give name to, call or describe as.

dėnŏminā′tion *n.* 1. Name, designation; esp. characteristic or class name; class, kind, with specific name. 2. Class of units in numbers, weights, money, etc. 3. Religious sect. **dėnŏm′inā′tional** (-sho-) *adj.* Of, like, a religious denomination; sectarian.

dėnŏm′inative *adj.* Serving as, giving, a name; (gram.) formed or derived from noun.

dėnŏm′inātor *n.* (arith. etc.) Number written below line in vulgar fraction, giving value of parts into which integer is divided; *common* ~, denominator common to a number of fractions (freq. fig.).

dēnotā′tion *n.* 1. Denoting; expression by marks or symbols; mark by which thing is made known or indicated; designation. 2. Meaning, signification; (logic) what word denotes, as dist. from *connotation*, aggregate of objects of which word may be predicated.

dėnōt′ative *adj.* Denoting. **dėnōt′atively** *adv.*

dėnōte′ *v.t.* 1. Mark out, distinguish, be the sign of; indicate, give to understand; signify, stand as name for (cf. CONNOTE); (logic) designate, be a name of, be predicated of.

dénouement (dānōōm′ahn) *n.* Unravelling of plot or complications, catastrophe, final solution, in play, novel, etc. [Fr.]

dėnounce′ *v.t.* 1. Prophesy (woe, vengeance), proclaim as threat or warning. 2. Inform against, accuse. 3. Inveigh against. 4. Give notice of termination of (armistice, treaty, etc.). **dėnounce′ment** (-sm-) *n.*

dē nŏv′ō *adv.* Afresh, beginning again. [L]

dĕnse *adj.* 1. Closely compacted in substance; crowded together. 2. Crass, stupid. **dĕnse′ly** (-sl-) *adv.* **dĕnse′nėss** *n.*

dĕn′sity *n.* 1. Closeness of substance; crowded state; (photog.) opaqueness of developed film in negative. 2. Stupidity, crassness. 3. (physics) Degree of consistence of body etc. expressed as weight per unit of volume; ~ *of charge*, (elect.) quantity of electricity per unit of volume or area.

dĕnt *n.* Hollow or impression in surface such as is made by blow with blunt-edged instrument. ~ *v.* Make dent in.

dĕn′tal *adj.* Of tooth, teeth, or dentistry; (of consonant) pronounced with tip of tongue against front upper teeth; ~ *surgeon*, dentist holding recognized university qualification. ~ *n.* Dental consonant.

dĕn′tāte *adj.* Toothed. **dĕntā′tion** *n.*

dĕn′ticle *n.* Small tooth or tooth-like projection. **dĕntĭc′ūlar, dĕntĭc′ūlate** *adjs.* **dĕntĭcūlā′tion** *n.*

dĕn′tifrice *n.* Preparation for cleansing teeth.

dĕn′tĭl *n.* One of the series of small rectangular blocks beneath projecting part of cornice in classical architecture (ill. ORDER).

dĕn′tine (*or* -ēn) *n.* Hard dense tissue forming main part of teeth.

dĕn′tist *n.* One who treats diseases of teeth. **dĕn′tistry** *n.*

dĕntĭ′tion *n.* Teething; characteristic arrangement of teeth in animal.

dĕn′ture *n.* Set of (usu. artificial) teeth.

dėnūde′ *v.t.* Make naked; strip *of*; (geol.) lay (rock etc.) bare by removal of what lies above. **dēnūdā′tion** *n.*

dėnŭnciā′tion *n.* Denouncing; invective. **dėnŭn′ciative, dėnŭn′ciatory** (-sha-) *adjs.* **dėnŭn′ciātor** (-shĭ-) *n.*

Dĕn′ver. Capital city of Colorado, U.S.

dėnȳ′ *v.t.* Declare untrue or non-existent; disavow, repudiate; refuse; ~ *oneself*, practise abstinence.

dē′odănd *n.* (hist.) Chattel which having been immediate cause of death of human being was forfeited to Crown to be applied to pious uses (abolished 1846). [L *deo dandum* that is to be given to God]

dē′odâr *n.* Large cedar (*Cedrus deodara*), native of W. Himalayas. [Hind. f. Sansk. *deva-dara* divine tree]

dēŏd′orīze *v.t.* Deprive of odour, disinfect. **dēŏdorīzā′tion, dēŏd′orīzer, dēŏd′orant** *ns.*

dēŏntŏl′ogy *n.* Science of duty, ethics. **dēŏntolŏg′ical** *adj.* **dēŏntŏl′ogist** *n.* [Gk *deon* duty]

Dē′ō volĕn′tė *adv.* (abbrev. D.V.) God willing.

dep. *abbrev.* Departs.

dėpârt′ *v.* 1. Go away (*from*), set forth, start, leave (chiefly literary); diverge, deviate (*from*). 2. Die; leave by death. **dėpârt′ėd** *adj.* Bygone; deceased. ~ *n.* Deceased person.

dėpârt′ment *n.* 1. Separate division or part of complex whole or organized system; esp. of state or municipal administration; in Gt Britain, a subdivision of one of the great ministries of State; in U.S., one of the (now 10) major branches of the administration; *D~ of State*, the U.S. Foreign Office. 2. In France, one of the administrative districts substituted for the old provinces in 1790. 3. *~ store*, (orig. U.S.) large shop dealing in variety of articles. **dēpârtmĕn′tal** *adj.* **dēpârtmĕn′tally** *adv.*

dėpâr′ture *n.* 1. Departing; going away; deviation (*from* truth etc.). 2. Starting, esp. of train; setting out on course of action or thought. 3. (navigation) Distance which ship etc. moves east or west from given meridian.

dėpas′ture (-pah-) *v.* Graze (upon); put (cattle) to graze; furnish pasturage to (cattle).

dėpĕnd′ *v.i.* 1. Be contingent *on* or conditioned by; *that depends*, (colloq.) that depends on circumstances. 2. Be dependent; rest for maintenance, support, etc. (*on*); rely, reckon confidently (*on*). 3. (Of lawsuit, parliamentary Bill, etc.) be waiting for settlement.

dėpĕn′dable *adj.* That may be depended on. **dėpĕn′dablenėss dėpĕndabil′ity** *ns.* **dėpĕn′dably** *adv.*

dėpĕn′dant, -ent *n.* One who depends on another for support; retainer, servant.

dėpĕn′dence *n.* 1. Depending (*upon*); being conditioned, subordinate, subject. 2. Living at another's cost. 3. Reliance, confident trust; thing relied on.

dėpĕn′dency *n.* Something subordinate or dependent, esp. country or province controlled by another.

dėpĕn′dent *adj.* Depending (*on*); contingent, subordinate, subject; maintained at another's cost; (gram., of clause etc.) in subordinate relation to sentence or word. **dėpĕn′dently** *adv.*

dėpĭct′ *v.t.* Represent in colours, drawing, words, portray, describe. **dėpic′tion** *n.*

dĕp′ilāte *v.t.* Remove hair from. **dĕpilā′tion** *n.* **dėpĭl′atory** *adj.* & *n.*

dėplēte′ *v.t.* Empty out; exhaust. **dėplē′tion** *n.*

dėplōre′ *v.t.* Bewail, grieve over, regret; be scandalized by. **dėplōr′able** *adj.* **dėplōr′ably** *adv.* **dėplōrabil′ity, dėplōr′ablenėss** *ns.*

dėploy′ *v.* (mil.) Spread out from column into line; (nav.) arrange in, take up, battle formation; move strategically. **dėploy′ment** *n.*

dėplume′ (-ōōm) *v.t.* Pluck, strip of feathers.

dēpōl′arīze *v.t.* Deprive of polarity, reverse or destroy effect of polarization.

dėpōne′ *v.* (Sc., law) State or declare upon oath, testify.

dėpōn′ent *adj.* (of Latin or Gk verb) Passive or middle in form but active in meaning (so called from idea that these verbs had laid aside their passive meaning). ~ *n.* 1. Deponent verb. 2. Person making deposition on oath or giving written testimony for use in court etc.

dėpŏp′ūlāte *v.t.* Reduce population of. **dēpŏpūlā′tion** *n.*

dėpôrt′ *v.t.* 1. Bear, conduct, one*self*; behave. 2. Carry away, remove; esp. remove into exile, banish (alien), whence **dēpôrtā′tion, dēpôrtee′** *ns.*

dėpôrt′ment *n.* Bearing, demeanour, manners.

dėpōse′ (-z) *v.* 1. Remove from office; esp. dethrone. 2. Bear witness *that*, testify *to*, esp. on oath in court.

dėpŏs′it (-z-) *n.* 1. Thing stored or entrusted for safe keeping; sum placed in BANK[2]; sum required and paid as pledge for performance of contract, part payment of price etc. 2. Layer of precipitated or deposited matter, natural accumulation. ~ *v.t.* 1. Lay or set down, place in more or less permanent position of rest; lay (eggs); (of water or other natural agencies) leave (matter) lying, form as natural deposit. 2. Store or entrust for keeping (esp. sum at interest in bank); pay as pledge for fulfilment of contract or further payment.

dėpŏs′itary (-z-) *n.* Person to whom thing is committed, trustee.

dĕposi′tion (-z-) *n.* 1. The taking down of the body of Christ from the cross; representation of this in art. 2. Deposing from office; esp., dethronement. 3. (Giving of) sworn evidence; allegation. 4. Depositing.

dėpŏs′itor (-z-) *n.* 1. Person who deposits money etc. 2. Apparatus for depositing some substance. **dėpŏs′itory** (-z-) *n.* 1. Storehouse. 2. = DEPOSITARY.

dĕp′ot (-ō; U.S. dē′pō) *n.* 1. (mil.) Place for stores; headquarters of regiment; station for assembling and drilling recruits; (hist.) place of confinement for prisoners of war. 2. Place where goods are deposited or stored. 3. (chiefly U.S.) Railway station.

dėprāve′ *v.t.* Make bad, deteriorate, pervert, corrupt, esp. in moral character or habits. **dĕpravā′tion** *n.*

dėprăv′ity *n.* Moral corruption, viciousness, abandoned wickedness; (theol.) innate corruption of human nature due to original sin.

dĕp′rėcāte *v.t.* Plead against, express earnest disapproval of. **dĕprėcā′tion** *n.* **dĕp′rėcative, dĕp′rėcatory** *adjs.*

dėprē′ciāte (-shĭ-) *v.* 1. Diminish in value; lower market price of; reduce purchasing power of (money). 2. Disparage, belittle. **dėprē′ciatory** (-sha-) *adj.*

dėprēciā′tion (-sĭ-, -shĭ-) *n.* Depreciating, being depreciated; (allowance made in balance-sheets, valuations, etc., for) wear and tear.

dĕprėdā′tion *n.* (usu. pl.) Spoliation, ravages. **dĕp′rėdātor** *n.* Spoiler, pillager.

dėprĕss′ *v.t.* Push or pull down, lower; bring low, humble; reduce activity of (esp. trade); lower (voice) in pitch; dispirit, deject; *depressed area*, region where trade is bad and unemployment rife.

dėprĕss′ant *adj.* & *n.* (med.) Lowering, sedative (medicine).

dėprĕ′ssion (-shn) *n.* 1. Lowering, sinking; depressed or sunken formation or surface, hollow, low place. 2. (astron. etc.) Angular distance of star or other object below horizontal plane (as opp. to *elevation*, above it). 3. Lowering in quality, vigour, value, or amount; reduction in activity (esp. of trade); lowering in pitch (of voice etc.). 4. Lowering of barometric or atmospheric pressure; (meteorol.) centre of minimum pressure, or system of winds round it. 5. Being depressed in spirits, dejection; (path.) state of reduced vitality.

dėprĕss′or *n.* (esp.) Muscle depressing or pulling down part to which it is attached (also ~ *muscle*); (surg.) instrument for pressing down some part or organ.

dĕprīvā′tion (*or* dēprī-) *n.* Loss, being deprived (*of*); deposition from (esp. ecclesiastical) office.

dėprīve′ *v.t.* 1. Strip, bereave, debar from enjoyment, *of*; *deprived children*, those who lack due parental care. 2. Depose (esp. clergyman) from office. **dėprīv′al** *n.*

dē profŭn′dĭs *n.* & *adv.* (Cry) from the depths (of suffering or sin). [L, first words of Ps. cxxx]

dept *abbrev.* Department.

dĕpth *n.* 1. Being deep; measurement from top down, from front to back, or from surface inwards. 2. Profundity, abstruseness; sagacity; intensity (of feelings, colours, silence, etc.). 3. Deep part of sea or any body of water (usu. pl.); (pl.) lowest part of pit, cavity, etc.; abyss (usu. pl.), lowest or inmost part; middle (of winter, night); deep region of thought, feeling, or being. 4. *Out of one's* ~, in water too deep to stand in; (fig.) engaged in a matter beyond one's understanding; ~ *charge* (*n.*) explosive charge timed to explode at certain depth under water, used in attacking submarines; ~*-charge* (*v.t.*) attack (submarine) with depth charges.

dĕpūtā'tion *n.* Body of persons appointed to go on mission on behalf of others.

dėpūte' *v.t.* Commit (task, authority) to substitute; appoint as one's substitute. ~ *adj.* (Sc.) Deputy.

dĕp'ūtīze *v.i.* Act as deputy or understudy (*for*).

dĕp'ūty *n.* 1. Person appointed to act for another or others, substitute, lieutenant; member of deputation; in City of London, deputy alderman; (U.S.) deputy sheriff. 2. Member of representative legislative assembly; *Chamber of Deputies*, lower house in national assembly of France etc. 3. (coal-mining) Overseer responsible for safety devices, propping, etc. ~ *adj.* Deputed; acting instead of, or as subordinate to; vice-. **dĕp'ūtyship** *n.*

De Quĭn'cey, Thomas (1785–1859). English essayist etc., author of 'Confessions of an English Opium Eater' (1822).

dērā'cināte *v.t.* Tear up by the roots.

dėrail' *v.t.* Cause (train etc.) to leave rails. **dėrail'ment** *n.*

dėrānge' (-nj) *v.t.* Throw into confusion or out of gear, disorganize; cause to act irregularly; make insane; disturb, interrupt. **dėrānge'ment** (-jm-) *n.*

dērāte' *v.t.* Lower or abolish rates upon.

dērā'tion *v.t.* Remove (food etc.) from rationed category.

Der'by (dar-). County borough and county town of DERBYSHIRE; hence: 1. *The D*~, the most famous English horse-race, for three-year-olds, founded 1780 by 12th earl of Derby, and run at Epsom usu. on Wednesday before or second Wednesday after Whitsunday; various important races in other countries, as the *Kentucky* ~ (pr. der-), or run by other animals. 2. Soft-paste porcelain made at Derby *c* 1750–1850; *Crown* ~, variety of this marked with crowned 'D' made from *c* 1784.

der'by *n.* (U.S.) Stiff felt hat with rounded crown and narrow brim, bowler.

Der'byshire (dar-). County of N. Midlands of England; ~ *neck*, variety of goitre, endemic in Derbyshire; ~ *spar*, fluor-spar.

de règle (rā'gl) *pred. adj.* Customary, proper. [Fr.]

dĕ'rėlict' *adj.* & *n.* 1. Abandoned, ownerless (thing, esp. ship at sea). 2. (U.S.) (Person) guilty of dereliction of duty.

dĕrėlic'tion *n.* 1. Forsaking, abandonment; being abandoned; retreat of sea exposing new land. 2. Morally wrong or reprehensible abandonment or neglect (*of* duty etc.); failure in duty, delinquency.

dē'rĕquisĭ'tion *v.t.* Release (house, hotel, etc.) from requisitioning.

dėrīde' *v.t.* Laugh to scorn.

de rigueur (rēger') *pred. adj.* Required by etiquette. [Fr.]

dėrĭ'sion (-zhn) *n.* Ridicule, mockery.

dėrīs'ive, dėrīs'ory *adjs.* Scoffing; mocking; *derisory offer* etc., one so small as to be ridiculous. **dėrīs'ively** (-vl-) *adv.*

dĕrĭvā'tion *n.* Obtaining from a source; extraction, descent; formation of word from word or root, tracing or statement of this.

dėrĭv'ative *adj.* & *n.* (Thing, word, etc.) of derived character or nature, derived from another or from a source, not primitive or original. **dėrĭv'atively** (-vl-) *adv.*

dėrīve' *v.* Get, obtain, (*from* a source); have one's or its origin etc. *from*; gather, deduce, *from*; (pass., refl.) be descended or have one's origin *from*; (pass., of words) be formed *from*; trace, show, assert, descent or origin or formation of (person, thing, word) *from*.

derm, der'ma, der'mis *ns.* (anat.) True skin, layer of tissue lying beneath epidermis (ill. SKIN). **der'mal** *adj.*

dermatī'tis *n.* Inflammation of the dermis.

dermatŏl'ogy *n.* Science of the skin, its nature, diseases, etc. **dermatolŏg'ical** *adj.* **dermatŏl'ogist** *n.*

dĕ'rogāte *v.i.* 1. Detract, make improper or injurious abatement, *from*. 2. Do something unsuited to one's rank or position.

dĕrogā'tion *n.* Lessening or impairment *of* law, position, dignity, etc.; deterioration, debasement.

dėrŏg'atory *adj.* Tending to detract *from*, involving impairment, disparagement, or discredit, *to*; lowering, unsuited to one's dignity or position. **dĕrŏg'atorily** *adv.*

dĕ'rrick *n.* Contrivance for hoisting or moving heavy weights; spar or boom set up obliquely on shipboard, with foot lashed, pivoted, or socketed to deck; kind of crane with jib pivoted to foot of central post, so as to take various angles with perpendicular (ill. CRANE); any outstanding jib or arm with pulley at end; framework over deep bore, as that of an oil well, for supporting boring-tackle and for hoisting or lowering. [orig. = hangman, the gallows, f. surname of hangman at Tyburn *c* 1600]

dĕ'rring-dō' *n.* (pseudo-archaic) Desperate courage. [f. misunderstanding of Chaucer's *In dorryng don that longeth to a knyght* (in daring to do what belongs to etc.)]

dĕ'r(r)inger (-j-) *n.* Small pistol with very large bore. [named after its inventor, H. *Deringer*, a U.S. gunsmith]

dĕ'rrĭs *n.* Genus of tall woody climbing plants, native to the tropics, with a tuberous root from which insecticide is made.

der'vish *n.* 1. Moslem friar vowed to poverty and austerity. 2. One of the fanatical followers of the Sudanese Mahdi. [f. Pers. *darvesh* poor]

dĕs'cănt *n.* 1. Melody extemporized above a plainsong melody; melody, extemporized or written, added in the treble above any song-tune; esp., in hymns, written treble part sung in certain verses by a portion of the choir while the remainder sing the normal melody and harmonies. 2. (obs.) Counterpoint; part-singing; treble part. 3. (fig.) Amplification of a subject, discursive comment on it. **dėscănt'** *v.i.* 1. Talk at large, dwell freely, *upon*. 2. Sing a descant.

Descartes (dāk'art), René (1596–1650). French mathematician, physicist, and philosopher; author of 'Le Discours de la Méthode' (1637), in which he expounded a quasi-mechanical conception of the universe, which he reduced to space, matter, and motion, operating under mathematical laws.

dėscĕnd' *v.* 1. Come or go down, fall, sink; have downward extension, direction, or slope; come or go down (hill, steps, etc.). 2. Make excursion or attack, fall violently *upon*. 3. Come down ideally, mentally, or morally; proceed to something subsequent in time or order, or from generals to particulars; stoop. 4. Be derived by generation, be descended from (rare exc. in pass.); be transmitted by inheritance *from*, pass.

dėscĕn'dant *n.* Person or thing descended (*of*). **dėscĕn'der** *n.* (esp. print.) Limb of letter which descends below x-height (ill. TYPE).

dėscĕnt' *n.* 1. Descending, downward motion; downward slope; way down. 2. Sudden attack. 3. Decline, sinking in scale, fall. 4. Being descended, lineage; transmission of property, title, or quality, by inheritance.

dėscrībe' *v.t.* 1. Set forth in words; recite characteristics of; qualify *as*. 2. Mark out, draw (esp. geom. figure); move in, pass or travel over (a certain course or distance).

dėscrĭp'tion *n.* Describing, verbal portrait or portraiture of person, object, or event, more or less complete definition; sort, kind, class.

dėscrĭp'tive *adj.* Serving to describe; fond of describing. **dėscrĭp'tively** *adv.*

dėscrȳ' *v.t.* Catch sight of, succeed in discerning.

dĕs'ėcrāte *v.t.* Deprive of sacred character; outrage, profane (something sacred). **dĕsėcrā'tion, dĕs'ėcrātor** *ns.*

dēsĕn'sitīze *v.t.* Reduce sensitiveness of (esp. sensitized photographic material).

dėsẽrt'[1] (-z-) *n.* 1. Deserving, being worthy of reward or punishment; (usu. pl.) that in conduct or character which deserves recompense; merit, worth. 2. (usu. pl.) Due reward or recompense (good or evil).

dĕs'ert[2] (-z-) *n.* Uninhabited and uncultivated tract of country; desolate, barren, waterless and treeless region; ~ *rat*, JERBOA; (colloq.) soldier of 7th (British) armoured division, whose divisional sign was a jerboa, and which took part in desert campaign in N. Africa (1941–2). ~ *adj.* Uninhabited, desolate; uncultivated; barren.

dėsẽrt'[3] (-z-) *v.* 1. Abandon, give up (thing); depart from (place, haunt); forsake (person or thing having claims on one); fail. 2. Run away (esp. from service in navy, army, or air force). **dėsẽrt'er, dėsẽr'tion** *ns.*

dėsẽrve' (-z-) *v.* Be entitled by conduct or qualities to (good or bad); have established claim to be *well* or *ill* treated at the hands *of*. **dėsẽrv'ėdly** *adv.* **dėsẽrv'ing** *adj.* 1. Meritorious. 2. Worthy (*of* praise, censure, etc.).

déshabillé (dāzăbē'yā) *n.* = DISHABILLE.

dĕs'iccāte *v.t.* Exhaust of all moisture, dry, dry up (esp. articles of food for preservation). **dĕsiccā'tion, dĕs'iccātor** *ns.* **dĕs'iccative** *adj.*

dėsĭd'erāte *v.t.* (pedant.) Feel the want of. **dėsĭderā'tion** *n.*

dėsĭd'erătive *adj.* (esp. gram., of verb or verbal form), Formed from another verb to express desire of doing act thereby denoted. ~ *n.* Desiderative verb, verbal form, or conjugation.

dėsiderāt'um *n.* (pl. *-ta*). Something wanting and required or desired.

dėsign' (-zīn) *n.* 1. Plan or scheme to be carried out; end in view; purpose, intention; contrivance in accordance with a preconceived plan; scheme of attack *upon*. 2. Preliminary sketch for a work of art; plan for a building, machine, or any composite structure; the combination of parts in a whole; general idea, construction, plot, etc.; faculty of evolving these; pattern, outline of decoration etc.; *industrial* ~, art of making designs for objects which are to be produced by machine. ~ *v.* 1. Form plan or scheme for; contrive; purpose, intend, have in view. 2. Set apart in thought for use *as*, or *for* advantage of; appoint, assign, make over *to* person (Sc. law). 3. Make preliminary sketch for (work of art etc.); plan construction of. **dėsign'ėdly** *adv.* On purpose, intentionally. **dėsign'er** *n.* **dėsign'ing** *adj.* (esp.) Crafty, artful, scheming.

dĕs'ignate (-z-, *-at*) *adj.* (placed after noun) Appointed or nominated but not yet installed. **dĕs'ignāte** *v.t.* Specify, particularize; serve as name or distinctive mark of; style, describe as; appoint to office. **dĕsignā'tion** *n.* Appointing to office; name, description, title.

dėsīr'able (-z-) *adj.* Worthy to be desired. ~ *n.* Desirable thing or person. **dėsīrabĭl'ity, dėsīr'ableness** *ns.* **dėsīr'ably** *adv.*

dėsīre' (-z-) *n.* 1. Feeling or emotion directed to attainment or possession of something expected to give pleasure or satisfaction, longing, craving, wish; sensual appetite, lust. 2. Wish expressed in words, request. 3. Object of desire. ~ *v.t.* Long for, crave, wish; ask for; pray, entreat, command.

dėsīr'ous (-z-) *pred. adj.* Wishful, desiring, (*to* do); ambitious, having the desire, (*of*).

dėsist' (-z-) *v.i.* Cease (*from*).

dĕsk *n.* Fixed or movable piece of furniture for reading or writing at, having as its essential feature a board etc. (often sloping), which serves as a rest for books and papers, and often drawers etc. for writing-materials; (U.S.) editorial subdivision of newspaper office.

dĕs'perate (*-at*) *adj.* 1. Leaving little or no room for hope; extremely dangerous or serious; hopelessly or extremely bad, extreme. 2. Reckless from despair; violent, lawless; staking all on a small chance. **dĕs'perately** *adv.* **dĕs'perateness, dĕsperā'tion** *ns.*

dĕs'picable *adj.* Vile, contemptible. **dĕs'picably** *adv.*

dėspīse' (-z) *v.t.* Look down upon, think scornfully or slightingly of.

dėspīte' *n.* Contempt, disdain (archaic); outrage, injury; settled malice or hatred; *in* ~ *of*, in spite of, notwithstanding the opposition or adverse efforts of. ~ *prep.* In spite of. **dėspīte'ful** (-tf-) *adj.* **dėspīte'fully,** *adv.* (archaic).

dėspoil' *v.t.* Plunder, spoil, rob, deprive. **dėspoil'er, dėspoil'ment, dėspōliā'tion** *ns.*

dėspŏnd' *v.i.* Lose heart, be dejected. ~ *n.* Despondency (archaic; only in *Slough of D~*).

dėspŏn'dency *n.* Condition of having lost heart, dejection. **dėspŏn'dent** *adj.* **dėspŏn'dently** *adv.* **dėspŏn'dingly** *adv.*

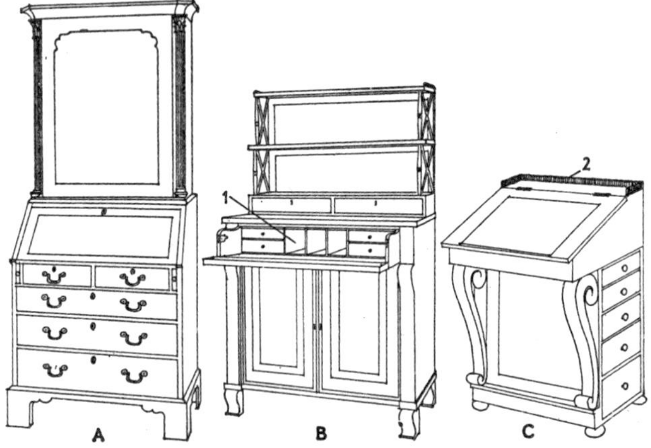

DESKS: A. BUREAU BOOKCASE, *c* 1730. B. REGENCY SECRETAIRE BOOKCASE. C. MID-VICTORIAN DAVENPORT

1. Pigeon-hole. 2. Gallery

Des Moines (dĭmoin'). Capital city of Iowa, U.S., on the Des Moines river.

dĕs'olate *adj.* Left alone, solitary; uninhabited, deserted; dreary, dismal, cheerless; forlorn, wretched. **dĕs'olately** *adv.* **dĕs'olateness** *n.* **dĕs'olāte** *v.t.* Depopulate, devastate; render wretched and comfortless.

dĕsolā'tion *n.* Devastation; dreary barrenness; desolate place, dreary waste or ruin; solitariness; grief, wretchedness.

dėspair' *n.* Loss, utter want, of hope; what causes despair. ~ *v.i.* Lose, be without, hope.

despatch : see DISPATCH.

dĕsperad'ō (-ahd-, -ād-) *n.* Desperate or reckless man; one ready for any violent or lawless deed.

dĕs'pot *n.* Absolute or tyrannical ruler; tyrant, oppressor. **dĕspŏt'ic** *adj.* **dėspŏt'ically** *adv.*

dĕs'potism *n.* Arbitrary rule; despotic state.

dĕs'quamāte *v.i.* Come off in scales. **dĕsquamā'tion** *n.*

dėssẽrt' (-z-) *n.* Course of fruit, sweetmeats, etc., at end of dinner; (U.S.) sweet course; ~*-knife, -fork, -spoon*, etc., those used for dessert (~*-spoon*, one intermediate in size between table-spoon and tea-spoon). [Fr., f. *desservir* clear the table]

dĕstinā'tion *n.* Place to which person or thing is bound.

dĕs'tine *v.t.* Appoint, foreordain, devote, set apart (*to, for*).

dĕs'tiny *n.* 1. What is destined to happen, fate. 2. Power that fore-ordains, overruling or invincible necessity.

dĕs'tĭtūte *adj.* Without resources, in want of necessaries; devoid *of.* **dĕstĭtū'tion** *n.*

dėstroy' *v.t.* Pull down, demolish; undo, reduce to useless form, consume, dissolve, spoil utterly; slay, kill.

dėstroy'er *n.* (esp.) One of a class of small fast warships armed with guns, torpedoes, etc., used for escort-work, attacking submarines, etc., orig. built for attacking torpedo-boats.

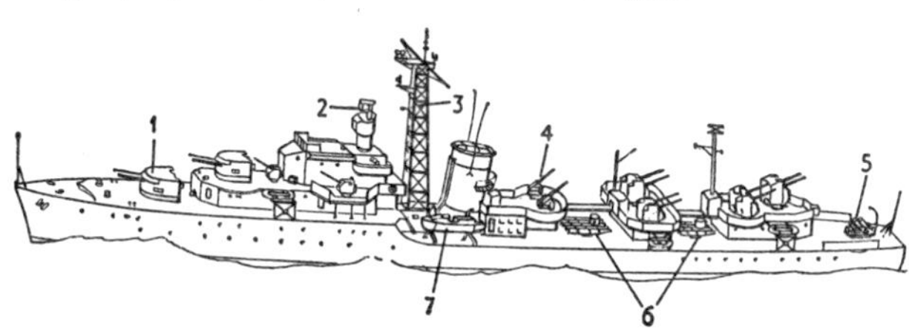

DESTROYER

1. Guns. 2. Control tower. 3. Lattice mast. 4. Anti-aircraft guns. 5. Depth charge throwers. 6. Torpedo-tubes. 7. Motor-boat

dėstrŭc'tĭble *adj.* Able to be destroyed. **dėstrŭctĭbĭl'ĭty** *n.*

dėstrŭc'tion *n.* Destroying, being destroyed; what destroys, cause of ruin.

dėstrŭc'tĭve *adj.* Destroying, causing destruction; (of criticism etc.) negative, not constructive. ~ *n.* Destructive agent, instrument, etc. **dėstrŭc'tĭvely** *adv.* **dėstrŭc'tĭvenėss** *n.* **dėstrŭc'tor** *n.* Furnace for burning refuse.

dēs'uetūde (-swĭ-) *n.* Passing into, state of, disuse.

dĕs'ultory *adj.* Skipping from one thing to another, disconnected, unmethodical. **dĕs'ultorĭly** *adv.* **dĕs'ultorĭnėss** *n.* [L *desultor* circus-rider]

dėtăch' *v.t.* Unfasten and separate (*from*); (mil., nav.) separate and send off (part from main body) for special purpose or mission. **dėtăch'able** *adj.* **dėtăchabĭl'ĭty** *n.*

dėtăched' (-cht) *adj.* Separate; unattached, standing apart. **dėtăch'ėdly** *adv.* **dėtăch'ėdnėss** *n.*

dėtăch'ment *n.* 1. Detaching. 2. Number of troops, ships, etc., detached from main body for employment on separate service, etc. 3. Standing aloof from objects or circumstances, withdrawal from association with surroundings; spiritual separation from world.

dēt'ail *n.* 1. Dealing with things item by item; minute account, number of particulars. 2. Item, small or subordinate particular; minor decoration in building, picture, etc., way of treating this. 3. (mil. etc.) Distribution of orders of the day; telling off, small party told off, for particular service or duty. **dėtail'** *v.t.* 1. Give particulars of, relate or enumerate in detail. 2. (mil.) Tell off for special duty. **dēt'ailed** (-ld) *adj.* Related or described in detail; minute, circumstantial.

dėtain' *v.t.* 1. Keep in confinement or under restraint. 2. Keep back, withhold (esp. what is due); keep from proceeding, keep waiting, stop.

dėtainee' *n.* Person detained in custody (used of those held under Section 18B of the Defence Regulations of 1939).

dėtain'er *n.* (law) (Wrongful) detaining of goods taken for distraint etc.; detaining in custody; writ by which person already arrested may be detained on another suit.

dėtĕct' *v.t.* Find out, discover (person) in possession of some quality or performance of some act; discover presence, existence, or fact of (something apt to elude observation). **dėtĕc'table** *adj.* **dėtĕc'tion** *n.* Detecting, esp. of criminals; detective fiction.

dėtĕc'tĭve *n.* Policeman etc. employed to investigate special cases; private person employed or undertaking to detect criminal etc. ~ *adj.* Employed in, relating to, serving for, detection; ~ *story*, story in which interest is centred in a crime and the detection of the criminal.

dėtĕc'tor *n.* (esp.) Instrument for detecting any thing or action liable to escape observation; (wireless) high-frequency rectifier.

dėtĕnt' *n.* Catch by removal of which a machine is set working; (in clocks etc.) catch which regulates striking.

détente (dāt'ahnt) *n.* (diplomacy) Relaxing of strained relations between two States.

dėtĕn'tion *n.* Detaining, being detained; arrest, confinement; imprisonment by military authorities; (at schools) keeping in as punishment.

dėtĕr' *v.t.* Discourage or restrain by fear or by consideration of danger or trouble. **dėtĕrm'ent, dėtĕ'rrence** *ns.* **dėtĕ'rrent** *adj.* & *n.*

dėtĕr'gent *adj.* & *n.* Cleansing (agent), substance which when dissolved in water causes dirt, grease, etc., to be detached (e.g. soap, but in pop. and trade use freq. distinguished from soap).

dėtēr'iorāte *v.* Make, grow, worse. **dėtērïorā'tion** *n.* **dėtēr'iorative** *adj.*

dėtĕrm'ĭnable *adj.* Capable of being determined; liable to be terminated. **dėtĕrm'ĭnably** *adv.*

dėtĕrm'ĭnant *adj.* & *n.* Determining, decisive, conditioning, defining, (agent, element, word, etc.); (math.) arrangement of quantities in an equal number of rows and columns representing the sum of the products of all possible sets of factors taking one from each row and one from each column, the signs of these products being determined by the direction of the diagonals oining their factors.

dėtĕrm'ĭnate *adj.* Limited, definite, distinct, finite, definitive. **dėtĕrm'ĭnately** *adv.* **dėtĕrm'ĭnatenėss** *n.*

dėtĕrmĭnā'tion *n.* 1. (law) Cessation of estate or interest of any kind. 2. Decision, settlement, (*of* controversy, suit, etc.); conclusion, opinion, sentence. 3. Fixing, delimitation, definition, settlement, (*of* anything); exact ascertainment. 4. Fixed direction, decisive bias; settling of purpose; fixed purpose or intention; resoluteness.

dėtĕrm'ĭnatĭve *adj.* & *n.* (Thing) serving to determine; ideographic sign annexed to word phonetically represented in order to make its meaning clear (ill. HIEROGLYPH). **dėtĕrm'ĭnatĭvely** *adv.* **dėtĕrm'ĭnatĭvenėss** *n.*

dėtĕrm'ĭne *v.* 1. (esp. law) Bring, come, to an end. 2. Settle, decide, as judge or arbiter; come to conclusion, give decision; be decisive factor in regard to. 3. Ascertain precisely, fix. 4. Give an aim to, direct, impel *to*; decide (person) *to* do; resolve. **dėtĕrm'ĭned** (-nd) *adj.* (esp.) Resolute, unflinching.

dėtĕrm'ĭnism *n.* Philosophical doctrine that human action is not free but necessarily determined by motives, regarded as external forces acting on the will. **dėtĕrm'ĭnist** *n.* **dėtĕrmĭnis'tĭc** *adj.*

deterrent etc.: see DETER.

dėtĕrs'ĭve *adj.* & *n.* Cleansing (substance). **dėtĕr'sion** *n.*

dėtĕst' *v.t.* Abhor, dislike intensely. **dėtĕs'table** *adj.* **dėtĕs'tablenėss** *n.* **dėtĕs'tably** *adv.* **dētĕstā'tion** *n.* Abhorrence; detested person or thing.

dėthrōne' *v.t.* Depose. **dėthrōne'ment** (-nm-) *n.*

dĕt'onāte (*or* dē-) *v.* (Cause to) explode with loud report. **dĕtonā'tion** *n.* **dĕt'onatĭve** *adj.*

dĕt'onātor *n.* Detonating contrivance, esp. as part of bomb or shell; railway fog-signal.

détour (dāt'oor, dĭtoor') *n.* Deviation, roundabout way, digression.

dėtrăct' *v.* Take away (*much, something,* etc.) *from*; ~ *from,* diminish, lessen in value, depreciate. **dėtrăc'tion, dėtrăc'tor** *ns.* **dėtrăc'tĭve** *adj.*

dètrain′ *v.* Discharge (troops etc.), alight, from railway train. **dĕtrain′ment** *n.*

dĕt′rīment *n.* Harm, damage. **dĕtrīmĕn′tal** *adj.* Harmful, causing loss or damage. **dĕtrīmĕn′tally** *adv.*

dètrīt′èd *adj.* (geol.) Disintegrated, formed as detritus. **dètrĭ′tion** *n.* Wearing away by rubbing.

dètrīt′us *n.* Matter produced by detrition, esp. gravel, sand, clay, etc., eroded and washed away by action of water. **dètrīt′al** *adj.*

Dètroit′. Chief city of Michigan, U.S., famous for its motor-car industry.

de trop (trō) *pred. adj.* Not wanted, unwelcome, in the way. [Fr.]

dētūmĕs′cence *n.* Subsidence from swelling.

Deucăl′ion. (Gk myth.) Son of Prometheus; married Pyrrha, daughter of Epimetheus. When Jupiter, angered by the impiety of mankind, covered the earth with a deluge, Deucalion and Pyrrha took refuge on the top of Parnassus and after the flood had subsided consulted the oracle of Themis on how to repair the loss of mankind. They were told to throw stones behind them; those thrown by Deucalion became men and those by Pyrrha women.

deuce[1] *n.* 1. Two at dice or cards; *~-ace*, throw that turns up ace with one die and deuce with the other. 2. (tennis, lawn tennis) State of score when the two sides are even, having gained three points or more each, and either must gain two points in succession to win the game.

deuce[2] *n.* Plague, mischief; the devil; *play the ~ with*, spoil, ruin.

deu′cèd *adj.* & *adv.* Confounded(ly); great. **deu′cèdly** *adv.*

dē′us ĕx măc′hĭnā (-k-) *n.* Power, event, that comes in nick of time to solve difficulty, providential interposition, esp. in novel or play. [L, = 'god from the machinery' (by which in ancient theatre gods were shown in the air)]

Deut. *abbrev.* Deuteronomy (O.T.).

deutēr′ium *n.* An isotope of hydrogen, present to extent of about 1 part in 6000 in ordinary hydrogen; symbol D, at. no. 1, at. wt 2·013; ~ *oxide* (D_2O), 'heavy water', used in nuclear fission etc. [Gk *deuteros* second]

deut′ero-canŏn′ical *adj.* Of a second or secondary canon; of those books of the scripture canon, as defined by Council of Trent, accepted later than those of the first canon (including Esther and most of the Apocrypha, Epistle to Hebrews, Epistles of James and Jude).

Deut′ero-Isaiah. The later writer to whom chapters xl–lxvi of Isaiah are attributed.

deut′eron *n.* Nucleus of DEUTERIUM atom.

Deuterŏn′omy. The 5th book of the Pentateuch, containing a repetition, with parenthetic comments, of the Decalogue and most of the laws in Exodus xxi–xxiii and xxiv. [Gk *deuteronomion* 2nd book of law, from a mistranslation of Hebrew words (Deut. xvii. 18) meaning 'a copy or duplicate of this law']

deut′zia (-ū-, -oi-) *n.* Genus of Chinese and Japanese shrubs of the hydrangea family, cultivated for their beautiful flowers (mostly white, pink, or purplish). [f. J. *Deutz*, 18th-c. Dutch botanist]

De′va[1] (dā-). A divinity, one of the good spirits of Hindu mythology. [Sansk., = 'god']

Dēv′a[2]. Latin name of river Dee (Cheshire).

De Valēr′a, Eamon (1882–). American-born Irish statesman, prime minister of Eire 1937–48, 1951–4, 1957–9, president 1959– .

dēvăl′orize *v.t.* Lower the value of (currency etc.).

dēvăl′ūāte *v.t.* Deprive of value. **dēvălūā′tion** *n.* (esp.) Cheapening of a currency in terms of gold or of other currencies. **dēvăl′ūe** *v.t.*

Devanag′arī (dāvanah′-) The formal alphabet in which Sanskrit and the vernacular languages are written throughout northern, western, and central India, Kashmir, and Nepal. [Sanskr.]

dĕv′astāte *v.t.* Lay waste, ravage. **dĕvastā′tion, dĕv′astātor** *ns.*

dèvĕl′op *v.* 1. Unfold, bring out all that is potentially contained in; bring or come forth from latent or elementary condition, make or become manifest. 2. (mus.) Elaborate (a theme), unfold its qualities, reveal its possibilities by modification of melody, harmony, rhythm, etc. 3. (photog.) Render visible (latent image produced by actinic action on sensitive surface) by chemical treatment. 3. Make or become fuller, more elaborate or systematic, more active, bigger; make progress; come or bring to maturity. 4. (U.S.) Bring or come to light; make, become, known.

dèvĕl′oper *n.* (esp.) 1. Chemical agent for developing photographs. 2. Apparatus for developing muscles by exercise.

dèvĕl′opment *n.* Gradual unfolding, growth, evolution; well-grown state; product; more elaborate form, esp. (mus.) in sonata or similar composition, the second section of a movement, containing elaborations on the theme(s) stated in the first section; realization of potentialities of site or territory by building, mining, etc.; fact etc. coming to light. **dèvĕlopmĕn′tal** *adj.* **dèvĕlopmĕn′tally** *adv.*

dē′vĭāte *v.i.* Turn aside, diverge, (*from*); digress.

dēvĭā′tion *n.* (esp.) Deflexion of ship's compass needle by iron in ship etc.; divergence of optic axis from normal position; departure or divergence from orthodox Communist doctrine, whence **dēvĭā′tionist** (-sho-) *n.*

dèvīce′ *n.* 1. (pl.) Fancy, will, desire (only in *leave, left, to one's own devices*). 2. Arrangement, contrivance, expedient; invention. 3. Design, figure; emblematic or heraldic design; motto.

dĕv′il *n.* 1. *The D~*, Satan; in Jewish and Christian theology the supreme spirit of evil, tempter and spiritual enemy of man; represented as a person, usu. with cloven hoofs, horns, and a tail. 2. A demon; heathen god, esp. malignant or evil deity, unclean spirit by which demoniacs were supposed to be possessed; one of the host of Satan, supposed to have their abode in hell. 3. Malignantly wicked or cruel person; energetic, clever, knavish, etc., person; poor wretch, luckless person (usu. *poor ~*). 4. Errand-boy or youngest apprentice (*printer's ~*) in printing office; junior legal counsel doing professional work for a leader; literary hack doing work for which his employer takes credit and (often) payment. 5. Personified evil quality, as *the ~ of greed*; temper, fighting spirit. 6. Tasmanian ~ (see TASMANIAN). 7. Various instruments or machines, esp. with sharp teeth or spikes, for destructive uses. 8. Highly seasoned grilled or fried dish; devilled bones etc. 9. *a ~ of a*, a confounded, very violent; *like the ~*, with the violence, energy, etc., attributed to the devil; *go to the ~*, go to ruin or perdition; *between the ~ and the deep sea*, in an unpleasant dilemma; *the ~ to pay*, much trouble, violence; *~-fish*, the angler, a large pediculate fish (genus *Lophius*); (U.S.) gigantic fish, *Manta birostis*, with expanded sides passing into large pectoral fins like wings; *~-may-care* (*adj.*) wildly reckless; careless and rollicking; *D~'s advocate* (L *advocatus diaboli*), one who urges the devil's plea against canonization of a saint; one who advocates wrong cause, or injures a cause by his advocacy; *~'s-bit*, species of scabious, *Scabiosa succisa*, with blue flowers and thickish root seeming as if bitten off; *~'s-bones*, dice; *~'s coach-horse*, a large cock-tail beetle, *Ocypus olens*, which assumes a rearing attitude when disturbed; *D~'s Own*, the 88th Foot (*the D~'s own Connaught boys*); also, the Inns of Court Volunteers; *~'s tattoo*, restless drumming with the fingers. ~ *v.* 1. Work as lawyer's or author's devil. 2. Grill with strong peppery seasoning.

dĕv′ilish *adj.* Like, worthy of, the devil, damnable. **dĕv′ilishly** *adv.* **dĕv′ilishnèss** *n.*

dĕv′ilment *n.* Mischief, wild spirits; devilish or strange phenomenon.

dĕv′ilry (rarely **-try**) *n.* Diabolical art, magic; the devil and his works; wickedness, cruelty; reckless mischief, daring, or hilarity.

dēv'ious *adj.* Winding or straying, circuitous, erratic; erring. **dēv'iously** *adv.* **dēv'iousnėss** *n.*

dėvīse' (-z) *v.t.* 1. Plan, contrive, invent; plot, scheme. 2. (law) Assign or give (now only real property) by will. ~ *n.* (law) Testamentary disposition of real property, clause in will conveying this. **dėvisee'** *n.* Person to whom property is devised.

dēvīt'alīze *v.t.* Make lifeless or effete. **dēvītalīzā'tion** *n.*

dēvīt'rify̆ *v.t.* Deprive of vitreous qualities; make (glass, vitreous rock) opaque and crystalline. **dēvītrĭfĭcā'tion** *n.*

dėvoid' *adj.* Destitute, empty, *of*.

dĕv'oir (-vwâr) *n.* Dutiful respects, courteous attentions, addresses.

dēv'olute (-ōōt, -ūt) *v.t.* Transfer by devolution.

dēvolu'tion (-lōō-, -lū-) *n.* 1. Descent through a series of changes; descent of property by natural or due succession; lapse of unexercised right to ultimate owner. 2. (biol.) Degeneration (now rare). 3. Deputing, delegation, of work or power (esp. by House of Parliament to its committees).

dėvŏlve' *v.* Throw (duty, work), be thrown, fall, descend, *upon* (deputy, or one who must act for want of others); descend, fall by succession.

Dĕv'on(shire). County of SW. England; *Devon*, one of a breed of cattle noted for the quality of their milk; *Devonshire cream*, thick clotted cream prepared by slow scalding. **Dėvōn'ian** *adj.* & *n.* 1. (Native) of Devonshire. 2. (geol.) (Of) the 4th system of rocks in the Palaeozoic, lying above the Silurian and below the Carboniferous; this system or period (ill. GEOLOGY).

dėvōte' *v.t.* Consecrate, dedicate, give up exclusively *to*; give over to destruction etc. **dėvōt'ėd** *adj.* (esp.) Zealously attached, loyal or faithful; doomed. **dėvōt'ėdly** *adv.*

dĕvotee' *n.* Votary *of*, one devoted *to*; zealously or fanatically pious person.

dėvō'tion *n.* 1. Devoutness; religious worship or observance; (pl.) prayers, worship. 2. Enthusiastic addiction, attachment, or loyalty (*to*). **dėvō'tional** (-sho-) *adj.* **dėvō'tionally** *adv.*

dėvour' (-owr) *v.t.* 1. Eat up voraciously, as a beast of prey, prey upon; eat greedily; eat ravenously or barbarously. 2. Consume recklessly; waste, destroy. 3. Engulf; take in greedily with eyes, ears, etc.; engross the attention of. **dėvour'ingly** *adv.*

dėvout' *adj.* Reverential, religious, pious; earnest, sincere, hearty. **dėvout'ly** *adv.* **dėvout'nėss** *n.*

dew *n.* 1. Vapour condensed in small drops on cool surfaces on or near the ground, when nocturnal radiation has cooled the lower layer of the atmosphere. 2. Freshness, refreshing or gently stealing influence. 3. Any beaded or glistening moisture, esp. tears, sweat. 4. *mountain* ~, illicitly distilled whisky; *~-berry*, fruit akin to blackberry; in Gt Britain, *Rubus caesius*, a low-growing procumbent species with bluish bloom on fruit; in America, *R. canadensis*, of similar habit; *~-claw*, rudimentary inner toe on inside of dog's leg, higher than other toes and not touching the ground; *~-drop*, drop of moisture condensed in form of dew; *~-point*, temperature at which atmosphere becomes saturated with water vapour by cooling; *~-pond*, pond (often artificial) on downs or in other places where there are no springs, fed by dew draining into it from surrounding area. **dew'y** (dū'ĭ) *adj.* **dew'ĭly** *adv.* **dew'inėss** *n.* **dew** *v.t.* Bedew, moisten.

dew'lăp *n.* Fold of loose skin hanging from throat esp. in cattle. **dew'lăpped** (-pt) *adj.*

dĕx'ter *adj.* Of, on, the right-hand side (but in heraldry = on right side of shield from wearer's point of view, i.e. on spectator's left; opp. SINISTER; ill. HERALDRY).

dĕxtĕ'rity *n.* Manual or mental adroitness, skill, neatness of handling.

dĕx'trĭn *n.* (chem.) Gummy substance, used as adhesive, into which starch is converted by dilute acids or alkalis, prolonged heat, etc.

dĕx'tro- *prefix.* (Turning, turned) to the right (opp. LAEVO-): *~-rot'atory*, having the property of causing plane of polarized light to rotate to right.

dĕx'trōse *n.* Dextro-rotatory glucose, i.e. ordinary glucose, grape-sugar.

dĕx'trous, -ter- *adj.* Neat-handed, deft; mentally adroit, clever. **dĕx't(e)rously** *adv.* **dĕx't(e)rousnėss** *n.*

Dey dā). (hist.) Title of commanding officer of Janissaries of Algiers, who in 1710 deposed the pasha or Turkish civil governor and became sole ruler; governor or pasha of Tunis or Tripoli. [Turk. *dāī* maternal uncle]

D.F. *abbrev.* Direction finder (*or* finding).

D.F.C., D.F.M., *abbrev.* Distinguished Flying Cross, Medal.

dg. *abbrev.* Decigram.

D.G. *abbrev.* *Dei gratia* (= by the grace of God); Dragoon Guards.

dhō'ti (dō-) *n.* Loin-cloth worn by Hindus.

dhow (dow) *n.* Lateen-rigged native vessel used on Arabian Sea.

di-[1] *prefix.* Two-, double-.

di-[2], **dia-** *prefix.* Through, thorough(ly), apart, across.

dīabēt'ēs (-z) *n.* Disease (in medicine called *diabetes mellitus*) characterized by excessive discharge of glucose-containing urine, with thirst and emaciation, caused by failure of the pancreas to secrete an adequate amount of insulin and the consequent excessive accumulation of glucose in the blood. **dīabĕt'ic** *adj.* & *n.* Of diabetes; (person) suffering from diabetes.

dīabŏl'ic, dīabŏl'ical *adjs.* Of, having to do with, under the influence of, the devil; devilish, inhumanly wicked. **dīabŏl'ically** *adv.*

dīăb'olism *n.* Sorcery, witchcraft; devilry; worship of the devil.

dīăb'olō *n.* Game with a double-headed spinning-top which is thrown up and caught by means of a string attached to two sticks; the top itself. [mod. fancy formation; older *devil on two sticks*]

dīăc'onal *adj.* Of a deacon. **dīăc'onate** *n.* Office of, term of office as, deacon; deacons collectively.

dīacrĭt'ical *adj.* Distinguishing, distinctive; ~ *signs*, *marks*, those used to indicate different sounds of a letter, as accents, diaeresis, etc.

dīăctĭn'ic *adj.* Transmitting actinic rays of light.

dī'adĕm *n.* Crown; jewelled or plain band or fillet worn round head as badge of royalty; wreath of leaves or flowers etc. worn round head; sovereignty; crowning distinction or glory. **dī'ademed** (-ĕmd) *adj.*

diaerėsis (dīēr'-) *n.* (pl. *-sēs*). Sign (¨) placed over second of two consecutive vowels indicating that they are to be pronounced separately and not as a diphthong.

Diaghilev (dyahg'ĭlĕf), Sergey Pavlovich (1872–1929). Russian impresario; founder (1909) of the 'Russian ballet' company which revived the art of ballet in W. Europe.

dī'agnōse (-z) *v.t.* Determine from symptoms the nature of (a disease).

dīagnōs'is *n.* (pl. *-ses*). Identification of disease by investigation of symptoms and history; formal statement of this.

dīagnŏs'tic *adj.* Of, assisting, diagnosis. ~ *n.* Diagnosis; symptom. **dīagnŏs'tically** *adv.* **dīagnŏstĭ'cian** (-shn) *n.*

dīăg'onal *adj.* Extending, as a line etc., from one angle to a

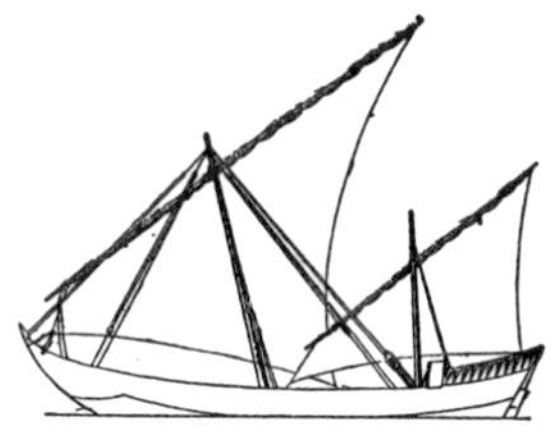

DHOW

It has lateen sails

non-adjacent angle of a rectilineal figure or solid (ill. QUADRILATERAL), or from one corner of anything to the opposite corner; having an oblique direction like the diagonal of a rectangle; marked with diagonal lines. **dīăg'onally** *adv.* **dīăg'onal** *n.* Diagonal line, part, row, etc.

dī'agrăm *n.* (geom.) Figure composed of lines, illustrating definition or aiding in proof etc.; illustrative figure giving the general scheme or outline of an object and its parts; graphic representation of the course or results of an action or process. **dīagrammăt'ic** *adj.* **dīagrammăt'ically** *adv.* **dīagrămm'atīze** *v.t.*

dī'agraph (-ahf) *n.* Instrument for drawing projections, enlarging maps, etc., mechanically, consisting of pencil governed by cords etc. and guided by pointer applied to object to be copied.

dī'al *n.* 1. SUN-dial. 2. Surface of clock or watch bearing graduations and figures marking hours etc.; circular plate marked with figures etc. and fitted with movable index finger; ring of figures on automatic telephone by manipulating which (exchanges and) numbers can be rung up. ~ *v.t.* Measure, indicate (as) with dial; ring up (telephone number) by means of a dial.

dī'alĕct *n.* Form of speech peculiar to a district, class, or person, subordinate variety of a language with distinguishing vocabulary, pronunciation, or idioms. **dīalĕc'tăl** *adj.* **dīalĕc'tally** *adv.* **dīalĕctŏl'ogy** *n.*

dīalĕc'tic *adj.* Logical; of disputation. ~ *n.* 1. (freq. pl.) Art of critical examination into truth of opinion; investigation of truth by discussion; logical disputation. 2. Criticism dealing with metaphysical contradictions and their solutions, esp., in Hegelian philosophy, the stages of thesis, antithesis, and synthesis representing the process of thought developing towards completion. 3. Dialectic philosopher. **dīalĕcti'cian** (-shn) *n.*

dīalĕc'tical *adj.* 1. = DIALECTIC *adj.* 2. Of DIALECTIC *n.* (sense 2); ~ *materialism*, theory propagated by Karl Marx and Friedrich Engels, acc. to which political events are regarded as due to a conflict of social forces (the 'class struggle') produced by man's material needs, and history as a series of contradictions and their solutions (the thesis, antithesis, and synthesis of Hegelian philosophy). 3. = DIALECTAL. **dīalĕc'tically** *adv.*

dīăll'age (-jī) *n.* Figure of speech in which arguments, after being considered from various points of view, are all brought to bear on one point.

dī'alŏgue (-g) *n.* Conversation; literary work in form of conversation between two or more persons; conversational part of novel; conversation written for actors on stage. **dīăl'ogist** (-j-) *n.* Speaker in, writer of, dialogue.

dīăl'ÿsis *n.* (chem., pl. *-sēs*). Separation of soluble crystalloid substances in mixture from colloid by diffusion through parchment membrane. **dī'alÿse** (-z) *v.t.* **dī'alÿser** *n.*

dīamăgnĕt'ic *adj.* (Of substance, as bismuth, zinc, copper, lead, or tin) tending to become magnetized in the presence of a magnetic field so that it lies with its long axis at right angles to the field (cf. PARAMAGNETIC). **dīamăg'netism** *n.*

diamanté (dēamahṅ'tā) *n.* Textile fabric to which sparkling effect is given by powdered glass or crystal, or (paste) brilliants.

dīamăntif'erous *adj.* Diamond-yielding.

dīăm'ėter *n.* (geom.) Straight line passing through centre of circle or sphere and terminated at each end by its circumference or surface (ill. CIRCLE), or through centre of any conic section, or through middle points of system of parallel chords in curve of any order; line passing from side to side of any body through centre; transverse measurement, width, thickness; unit of measurement of lineal magnification of an object. **dīăm'ėtral** *adj.* **dīăm'ėtrally** *adv.*

dīamĕt'rical *adj.* 1. Of, along, a diameter; diametral. 2. (Of opposition, difference, etc.) direct, complete, like that between opposite ends of diameter. **dīamĕt'rically** *adv.*

dī'amond *n.* 1. Very hard and brilliant precious stone, colourless or variously tinted, consisting of pure carbon crystallized in regular octahedrons and allied forms; the most valuable precious stone, and the hardest substance known. 2. Glittering particle or point. 3. Glass-cutting tool of small diamond set in handle. 4. Diamond-shaped figure, rhomb, or square, placed with diagonals vertical and horizontal; playing-card of the suit marked with such figures. 5. (baseball) The figure formed by the 4 bases; the field (ill. BASEBALL). 6. (printing) Third smallest standard size of type ($4\frac{1}{2}$ point). 7. *black* ~, dark-coloured diamond; coal; *rough* ~, diamond before it is cut and polished; person of intrinsic worth but rough manner; *~-cut*, cut with facets like a diamond; *~-drill*, drill set with diamonds, for boring rocks etc.; *D~ Jubilee*, (public celebration in 1897 of) 60th anniversary of Queen Victoria's accession; *D~ Necklace, Affair of the*, plot, successfully carried out in 1783–4, of Jeanne de St. Remy de Valois to get possession from the jewellers of a diamond necklace on the pretence that Queen Marie Antoinette had consented to purchase it; ~ *State*, (U.S.) Delaware, so called on account of its small size; ~ *wedding*, 60th anniversary of wedding. ~ *adj.* Made of, set with, diamond(s); rhomb-shaped. ~ *v.t.* Adorn with or as with diamonds.

dīamōrph'īne *n.* = HEROIN.

Dīăn'a. Ancient Italian moon-goddess, patroness of virginity and hunting; later regarded as identical with Artemis; hence, lady who hunts; ~ *monkey*, W. Afr. species of white-bearded monkey (*Cercopithecus diana*).

dīăn'thus *n.* Genus of flowering plants of the order *Caryophyllaceae*, including pinks and carnations.

dīapās'on (-zn) *n.* 1. Compass of voice or instrument, range, scope; fixed standard of musical pitch (~ *normal*, 'French pitch', that now generally adopted in Britain and U.S.). 2. One of the chief foundation stops in an organ (*open* ~ and *stopped* ~) extending through whole compass of the instrument (ill. ORGAN). [Gk *dia pasōn* (*khordōn*) through all notes of the scale]

dī'aper *n.* 1. Linen fabric woven with small simple diamond pattern; towel etc. of this; baby's napkin; sanitary towel. 2. Ornamental design of diamond reticulations. ~ *v.t.* Ornament surface or background of with small uniform pattern, esp. one based upon diamond reticulations; variegate, adorn with diverse colours.

dīăph'anous *adj.* Transparent.

dīaphorĕt'ic *adj.* & *n.* (Drug, treatment) inducing perspiration.

dī'aphragm (-frăm) *n.* 1. Muscular convex partition separating thorax from abdomen in mammals, which contracts and becomes flatter when air is breathed in, thus increasing the capacity of the thorax (ill. LUNG); (zool., bot.) partition in certain shells, gastropods, plant-tissues, etc. 2. Thin lamina or plate used as partition etc.; vibrating membrane or disc in acoustic instrument (telephone, loud-speaker, etc.); mechanism consisting of set of plates for varying effective aperture of lens of camera etc. (ill. CAMERA). **dīaphragmăt'ic** (-frăg-) *adj.*

dī'ârchÿ, dÿ- (-k-) *n.* Government by two rulers; (hist., usu. *dy-*) system of provincial governments in India established by Government of India Act, 1919. **dīâr'chal, dīâr'chic** *adjs.*

dīarrhoe'a (-rēa) *n.* Excessive looseness of bowels. **dīarrhoe'al, dīarrhoe'ic** *adjs.*

dī'ary *n.* Daily record of events etc., journal; book etc. prepared for this or for noting future engagements. **dī'arīst** *n.* One who keeps a diary. **dī'arīze** *v.* Keep, enter in, a diary.

Dīăs'pora *n.* The dispersion of the Jews, after the Exile, among Gentile nations.

dī'astāse (-s) *n.* (chem.) Enzyme formed in germinating seeds and having property of converting starch into sugar.

dīăs'tolė *n.* Dilatation or relaxation of heart, rhythmically alternating with systole to constitute pulse. **dīastŏl'ic** *adj.*

dīathẽrm'al, dīathẽrm'ic, dīathẽrm'(an)ous *adjs.* Pervious to heat-rays, freely transmitting radiant heat. **dīathẽrm'ancy** *n.*

dī'athẽrmy *n.* Therapeutic use of low-voltage alternating electric currents of very high frequency to produce heat in parts of body below surface.

dīăth'ėsĭs *n.* (pl. *-esēs*). Constitutional predisposition.

dī'atŏm *n.* Microscopic unicellular alga with silicified cell-wall, existing in great numbers in sea and fresh water, and often forming extensive fossil deposits (ill. ALGA). **dīatomā'ceous** (-shus) *adj.*

dīatŏm'ic *adj.* (chem.) Consisting of two atoms; containing two replaceable atoms of hydrogen.

dīăt'omīte *n.* Substance composed of siliceous skeletons of diatoms.

dīatŏn'ic *adj.* (mus.) Of scale, proceeding by notes proper to its key without chromatic alteration (ill. SCALE); (of melody etc.) constructed from such a scale.

dī'atrībe *n.* Piece of bitter criticism, invective, denunciation. [Gk *diatribē* wearing away (of time), discourse]

dīăz'ō-cŏm'pounds *n.* (chem.) Organic compounds, esp. those derived from aromatic hydrocarbons containing the characteristic group —N=N—, and forming the basis of a large group of dye-stuffs (*azo* dyes).

dībās'ic *adj.* ~ *acid*, one which contains two replaceable hydrogen atoms and therefore yields two series of salts.

dĭbb'er, dĭb'ble *ns.* Pointed tool for making holes in ground for seeds, bulbs, or young plants. **dĭb'ble** *v.* Prepare (soil) with this; plant or sow thus; use a dibble.

dĭbs *n.pl.* (slang) Money.

dīce *n.* Pl. of DIE[1]; *~-box*, box, usu. in shape of double truncated cone, from which dice are thrown in gaming. ~ *v.* 1. Gamble with dice, gamble *away*. 2. Cut into small cubes; mark or ornament with pattern of cubes or squares.

dīcĕph'alous *adj.* Having two heads.

dīchŏt'omy (-k-) *n.* 1. Division into two; classification into two groups. 2. (bot.. zool.) Form of branching in which each successive axis divides into two. **dīchotŏm'ic, dīchŏt'omous** *adjs.* **dīchŏt'omīze** *v.*

dīchrō'ic (-kr-) *adj.* Having two colours; esp. (of doubly refracting crystals) showing different colours when viewed in different directions, (of solutions) showing essentially different colours at different concentrations. **dīch'rōism** *n.*

dīchromăt'ic *adj.* Having two colours; esp., of animals, having two different colours in different individuals.

dīchrōm'ic *adj.* Of, including, (only) two colours; esp., of vision of colour-blind persons, including only two of the three primary colours.

dĭck *n.* (U.S. slang.) Detective.

Dĭck'ens[1], Charles John Huffam (1812–70). Popular English novelist, some of whose work, e.g. 'Oliver Twist' and 'Bleak House', exposed social evils; creator, esp. in 'Pickwick Papers', of many humorous characters. **Dĭckĕn'sĭan** (-z-) *adj.* Of, after the manner of, Dickens.

dĭck'ėns[2] *n.* (colloq.) *The* devil, *the* deuce. [app. alliterative substitute for *devil*]

dĭck'er *n.* 1. Ten, half a score, as unit of exchange esp. in hides or skins. 2. (U.S.) Barter, petty bargaining. **dĭck'er** *v.i.* (U.S.) Trade by barter; truck; haggle.

dĭck'y, -ey *n.* 1. Small bird (also *~-bird*). 2. False shirt-front; (U.S.) shirt collar. 3. Seat in carriage for driver; seat at back of carriage or coach for servants, guard, etc.; extra seat at back of two-seater motor-car which can be closed down when not in use. ~ *adj.* (slang) Unsound, shaky, liable to fall.

dīc'līnous *adj.* (bot., of plant) Having stamens and pistils on separate flowers, (of flower) unisexual.

dīcŏtȳlēd'on *n.* Flowering plant with two cotyledons (ill. SEEDLING). **dīcŏtȳlēd'onous** *adj.*

dĭc'taphōne *n.* (Proprietary name for) machine which records words spoken into it and subsequently reproduces them for transcription.

dĭctāte' *v.* 1. Say or read aloud (matter to be written down). 2. Prescribe, lay down authoritatively (terms, things to be done); lay down the law, give orders. **dĭctā'tion** *n.* **dĭc'tāte** *n.* Authoritative direction (usu. of reason, conscience, nature, etc.).

dĭctāt'or *n.* 1. Absolute ruler, usu. temporary or irregular, of a State; person with absolute authority in any sphere. 2. One who dictates for transcription. **dĭctāt'orshĭp** *n.* Rule of dictator.

dĭctatŏr'ial *adj.* Of a dictator; imperious, overbearing. **dĭctatŏr'ially** *adv.*

dĭc'tion *n.* 1. Choice of words and phrases, verbal style, in speech or writing. 2. Manner of speaking, elocution; singer's enunciation of words.

dĭc'tionary (-sho-) *n.* Book dealing, usu. in alphabetical order, with the individual words of a language or some specified subject etc., setting forth their spelling, pronunciation, signification, history, etymology, equivalents in another language, etc., or some of these; also, book of reference on any subject with items arranged in alphabetical order.

dĭc'tograph (-ahf) *n.* (Proprietary name for) telephonic instrument with sound-magnifying device by which it is possible to overhear what is said in a room where the transmitter is stationed or concealed.

dĭc'tum *n.* (pl. *-ums, -a*) 1. Formal saying, pronouncement; (law) expression of judge's opinion on matter of law, not being the formal resolution or determination of a court. 2. Current saying, saw.

dĭd. Past tense of DO.

dĭdăc'tĭc (*or* dī-) *adj.* Meant to instruct; (of persons) too much inclined to instruct, tending to lay down the law. **dĭdăc'tically** *adv.* **dĭdăc'tĭcism** *n.*

dī'dăpper *n.* Small diving-bird, dabchick.

dĭd'dle *v.t.* (slang) Cheat, swindle. **dĭdd'ler** *n.*

Diderot (dēd'erō), Denis (1713–84). French philosopher, dramatist, and critic; one of the founders of the 'Encyclopédie'; author of sentimental comedies.

Dīd'ō. Legendary daughter of a Tyrian king; fled to Africa after the death of her husband Sychaeus and is reputed to have founded the city of Carthage. Virgil makes her a contemporary of Aeneas with whom she falls in love; when, by order of the gods, Aeneas forsakes her, she kills herself.

dīdȳm'ium *n.* A rare metal, formerly supposed to be an element and given symbol Di and subsequently separated into the elements neodymium and praseodymium. [Gk *didumos* twin, from its being always found with lanthanum]

dīe[1] *n.* 1. (pl. *dīce*, freq. used as sing.) Small cube with faces marked with 1–6 spots, thrown from box or hand in games of chance; (pl.) the game played with these; *the ~ is cast*, the decisive step is taken. 2. Small cubical piece of anything. 3. (pl. *dies*) Part of pedestal between base and cornice. 4. Engraved stamp for impressing design etc. upon softer material, as in coining etc.; ~ *casting*, casting obtained from metal mould(s); process of making such castings; *~-sinker*, engraver of dies.

dīe[2] *v.i.* (pres. part. *dying*). 1. Cease to live, expire; (archaic) ~ *the death*, be put to death; ~ *game*, die fighting, not tamely; ~ *hard*, die not without struggle; ~ *in the last ditch*, die desperately defending something, struggle till the end. 2. Suffer spiritual death. 3. Suffer as in death; ~ (*for, to do*), desire keenly or excessively, long greatly; ~ *with laughing*, be exhausted by laughing. 4. Lose vital force, decay; come to an end, cease to exist; (of fire etc.) go out; (also ~ *out*) disappear, be forgotten; (also ~ *away*) fade away. 5. *~-away* (*adj.*), languishing; *~-hard*, one that dies hard, esp. (i) one of the 57th Regiment of Foot (from their stubborn resistance at Albuera); (ii) one of those who were prepared to 'die in the last ditch' in opposition to the Home Rule Bill (1912); hence, stubbornly conservative person, 'crusted Tory'.

dīělěc'trĭc *adj.* & *n.* Insulating, non-conducting (medium or substance).

Dies'el (dēz-), Rudolf (1858–1913). German inventor of an internal combustion engine (~ *engine*), in which air is first drawn into the cylinder and compressed so highly that the heat generated is sufficient to ignite the oil subsequently injected (ill. COMBUSTION); ~*-electric*, of a combination of a Diesel engine driving an electric generator; ~ *oil*, a petroleum fraction used as fuel in Diesel engines, usu. that part distilling below 300°.

dī'ēs īr'ae (-z). 'Day of wrath', first words of Latin hymn on Last Judgement ascribed to Thomas of Celano (*c.* 1250); the hymn itself, sung as part of the Mass for the dead.

dī'ēs nŏn (-z). (Short for *dies non juridicus*), day on which no legal business is transacted, or which is not reckoned in counting days for some particular purpose.

dī'ėt[1] *n.* Conference, congress, on national or international business; meeting of estates of the realm or confederation (esp. as English name for foreign parliamentary assemblies); *D~ of Worms*, that convened in 1521 at Worms, Germany, at which Luther was condemned as a heretic.

dī'ėt[2] *n.* Way of feeding; prescribed course of food, regimen; one's habitual food. ~ *v.* Feed on special food as medical regimen or as punishment.

dī'ėtary *n.* Course of diet; allowance or character of food in hospital, prison, etc. ~ *adj.* Of diet or a dietary.

dīėtět'ĭc *adj.* Of diet, of the regulation of kind and quantity of food, esp. as branch of medical science. **dīėtět'ĭcs** *n.pl.* The part of medicine dealing with regulation of diet.

dīėtĭ'tian, dīėtĭ'cian (-shn) *n.* Person versed in dietetics.

dĭff'er *v.i.* Be unlike, be distinguishable *from*; be at variance, disagree (*with, from*).

dĭff'erence *n.* 1. Being different, dissimilarity, non-identity; point in which things differ; quantity by which amounts differ, remainder after subtraction; *split the* ~, come to compromise. 2. Disagreement in opinion, dispute, quarrel. 3. Characteristic mark distinguishing individual or species; esp. (her.) alteration or addition to coat of arms to distinguish junior member or branch of family; (logic) differentia. ~ *v.t.* Distinguish, serve as distinguishing mark of; make difference in (coat of arms).

dĭff'erent *adj.* Not the same; unlike; of other nature, form, or quality; (slang) out of the ordinary, special, unusual. **dĭff'erently** *adv.*

dĭfferěn'tia (-shĭa) *n.* (logic) Attribute by which a species is distinguished from all other species of same genus; distinguishing characteristic.

dĭfferěn'tial (-shl) *adj.* 1. Of, exhibiting, depending on, a difference; differing according to circumstances; constituting a specific difference, relating to specific differences. 2. (math.) Relating to infinitesimal differences. 3. Relating to, depending on, exhibiting, difference of two (or more) motions, pressures, or other measurable physical quantities. 4. ~ *calculus*, (math.) method of calculation devised by Leibniz (1677), treating of infinitesimal differences between consecutive values of continuously varying quantities; ~ *gear*, arrangement of gears connecting two shafts or axles in the same line and enabling one shaft to revolve faster than the other when required (e.g. in a motor-car, when turning a corner, ill. GEAR); ~ *wage*, higher wage paid in respect of skill; ~ *winding*, method of winding two insulated wires side by side in electric coil, through which currents pass in opposite directions. **dĭfferěn'tially** *adv.* **dĭfferěn'tial** *n.* 1. (math.) Each of the infinitesimal differences of which the differential calculus treats. 2. Differential gear. 3. (wage) ~, agreed sum or proportion by which wages of highly skilled workers are to exceed those of the less skilled.

dĭfferěn'tiāte (-shĭ-) *v.* 1. Constitute difference between; make or become different in process of growth or development, esp. by modification for special function or purpose. 2. Discriminate between, distinguish. **dĭfferěntiā'tion** *n.*

dĭff'ĭcult *adj.* Hard to do, troublesome; obscure, perplexing; unaccommodating, stubborn.

dĭff'ĭculty *n.* Being difficult to accomplish, understand, etc.; difficult thing or question; (usu. pl.) embarrassment of affairs, pecuniary trouble; *make difficulties*, show reluctance, be unaccommodating.

dĭff'ĭdence *n.* Self-distrust, excessive modesty, shyness. **dĭff'ĭdent** *adj.* Wanting in self-confidence, bashful. **dĭff'ĭdently** *adv.*

dĭff'luence (-lōō-) *n.* 1. Flowing apart, dispersion by flowing. 2. Deliquescence. **dĭff'luent** *adj.*

dĭffrăct' *v.t.* (optics) Deflect and break up (beam of light) at edge of opaque body or through narrow aperture or slit. **dĭffrăc'tion** *n.* Breaking up thus of beam of monochromatic light into series of light and dark spaces or bands, or of white or composite light into series of coloured spectra; ~ *grating*, series of close equidistant parallel lines, esp. lines ruled on a polished surface, used for producing spectra by diffraction. **dĭffrăc'tĭve** *adj.* **dĭffrăc'tĭvely** *adv.*

dĭffūse' (-s) *adj.* Spread out, not concentrated; not concise, wordy. **dĭffūse'ly** (-sl-) *adv.* **dĭffūse'nėss** *n.* **dĭffūse'** (-z) *v.* Disperse or be dispersed from a centre; spread widely, shed abroad, disseminate; (of gases or liquids) intermingle by diffusion. **dĭffū'sion** (-zhn) *n.* **dĭffū'sĭve** *adj.* **dĭffū'sĭvely** *adv.* **dĭffū'sĭvenėss** *n.*

dĭg *v.* (past t. and past part. *dŭg*). Turn up (ground) with spade or other tool, or with snout or claws; break up and turn over (soil); excavate; extract by excavation; thrust or plunge (something) *in, into*; stab, prod; give (person) sharp nudge (*in ribs* etc.); ~ *in*, (esp.) excavate defensive trench or pit; ~ *out*, get, find, make, by digging, discover by research; ~ *up*, get out of ground etc. by digging; excavate; break up and loosen soil of. ~ *n.* 1. Piece of digging; (colloq.) archaeological excavation. 2. Thrust, poke; (fig.) gibe. 3. (pl., slang or colloq.) Lodgings.

dĭgămm'a *n.* 6th letter (ϝ, prob. pronounced like English *w*) of original Greek alphabet, later disused (the sound having been lost), but important in philology.

dĭg'amy *n.* Second marriage, remarriage after death of first spouse. **dĭg'amĭst** *n.* **dĭg'amous** *adj.*

dĭgăs'trĭc *adj.* (anat., of muscle) Having two bellies with intervening tendon; of the digastric muscle of the neck. ~ *n.* Muscle of neck used during swallowing (ill. HEAD).

dī'gėst *n.* Methodical compendium or summary, esp. of body of laws; *the D~*, the body of Roman laws compiled from the earlier jurists by order of Justinian. **dĭgėst'** *v.* 1. Reduce into systematic (and usu. condensed) form, classify; arrange methodically in mind, ponder over. 2. Prepare (food) in stomach and intestines for assimilation; (of food) undergo digestion. 3. Brook, endure, stomach, assimilate (insult, opinion); get mental nourishment from. **dĭgėstĭbĭl'ĭty** *n.* **dĭgėst'ĭble** *adj.*

dĭgěs'tion (-sch*o*n) *n.* Digesting of physical or mental food; power of digesting; extraction of soluble constituents of substance by long stewing.

dĭgěs'tĭve *adj.* Of, promoting, digestion. ~ *n.* Substance promoting digestion. **dĭgěs'tĭvely** *adv.*

dĭgg'er *n.* (esp.) 1. One who digs or searches for gold in gold-fields; (colloq.) Australian. 2. Division (*Fossores*) of hymenopterous insects (also ~*-wasps*), most of which build their nests in burrows.

dĭgg'ĭng *n.* (esp.) 1. (pl.) Mine; gold-field. 2. (pl., colloq.) Lodgings, quarters.

dight (dīt) *v.t.* (archaic, chiefly in past part. *dight*). Clothe, array, adorn; make ready.

dĭʹgĭt *n.* 1. (zool., anat., or joc.) Finger or toe. 2. Each numeral below ten (orig. counted on fingers); each Arabic numeral from 0 to 9. 3. (astron.) 12th part of diameter of sun or moon (in expressing magnitude of eclipse). **dĭʹgĭtal** *adj.*

dĭgĭtālʹin *n.* (commerc. chem.) Poisonous substance extracted from foxglove leaves.

dĭgĭtālʹis *n.* 1. (*D~*) Genus, including foxglove, of plants of the order *Scrophulariaceae*. 2. Drug prepared from dried leaves of foxglove, used as heart stimulant, causing heart to beat more strongly and regularly, thus increasing flow of blood and resting heart muscles. [mod. L transl. of Ger. *Fingerhut* thimble, foxglove]

dĭʹgĭtate, -ātėd *adjs.* (zool., bot.) With divided fingers or toes; with deep radiating divisions. **dĭgĭtāʹtion** *n.*

dĭʹgĭtigrāde *adj.* & *n.* (zool.) (Animal) walking on toes, not touching ground with heel.

dĭgʹnĭfȳ *v.t.* Make worthy or illustrious; confer dignity upon; make stately; give high-sounding name or title to. **dĭgʹnĭfied** *adj.* Stately, marked by dignity, majestic.

dĭgʹnĭtary *n.* Person holding high (esp. ecclesiastical) rank or office.

dĭgʹnĭty *n.* 1. Worth, nobleness, excellence; high estate, position, or estimation; high or honourable office, rank, or title. 2. Proper stateliness, elevation of aspect, manner, or style; gravity; *~ ball*, (U.S.) Negro dance (from its elaborate formality).

dĭgʹraph (-ahf) *n.* Group of two letters expressing one sound, as *sh*.

dĭgrĕssʹ *v.i.* Diverge from the track, stray; depart from main subject temporarily in speech or writing. **dĭgrĕssʹion** (-shn) *n.* **dĭgrĕssʹive** *adj.*

dīhēdʹral *adj.* 1. Having two plane faces. 2. (of aeroplane) Having wings inclined upwards (*positive ~*) or downwards (*negative ~*) towards the tips.

dīhȳdʹric *adj.* Having two hydroxyl groups.

dīke, dȳke *n.* 1. Ditch; any water-course or channel. 2. Low wall, esp. of turf; embankment, long ridge, dam, against flooding by sea, rivers, etc.; raised causeway; *~-reeve*, (hist.) officer taking charge of drains, sluices and sea-banks of English fen or marshland. 3. (geol.) Small intrusion usu. of igneous rock cutting across the bedding of older rocks (ill. ROCK). *~ v.t.* Provide, defend, with dike(s).

dĭlăpʹidāte *v.* Bring, come, into disrepair or decay.

dĭlăpidāʹtion *n.* Bringing or falling into, being in, disrepair or decay; impairment of ecclesiastical property belonging to an incumbency, sums charged against incumbent to meet this.

dīlāteʹ *v.* Make or become wider or larger; expand, widen, enlarge; expatiate, speak or write at large. **dīlāʹtion, dīlatāʹtion** *ns.*

dīlātʹor *n.* (anat.) Muscle or nerve which dilates or widens a part; (surg.) instrument for dilating passage etc.

dĭlʹatory *adj.* Tending to, designed to cause, given to, delay. **dĭlʹatorĭly** *adv.* **dĭlʹatorinėss** *n.*

dĭlĕmmʹa (*or* dī-) *n.* Argument forcing opponent to choose one of two alternatives (the *horns* of the dilemma), both unfavourable to him; position involving choice between two evils.

dĭlėttănʹtė *n.* (pl. *-ti* pr. -tē). Lover of the fine arts; (now usu.) one who is interested in an art or science merely as a pastime and without serious study. *~ adj.* Of, like, a dilettante. **dĭlėttănʹtĭsm** *n.*

dĭlʹĭgence[1] (*or* dĭlĭzhahṅsʹ) *n.* (hist.) Public stage-coach (esp. in foreign countries).

dĭlʹĭgence[2] *n.* Persistent effort or work; industrious character.

dĭlʹĭgent *adj.* Hard-working, steady in application, industrious; attentive to duties. **dĭlʹĭgently** *adv.*

dĭll *n.* Umbelliferous annual yellow-flowered herb, *Anethum graveolens*, with carminative fruits; *~-pickle*, pickle flavoured with dill-seeds.

dĭllʹy-dăllʹy *v.i.* (colloq.) Vacillate; loiter.

dĭlʹūent (*or* -ōō-) *adj.* Diluting, esp. making thin the fluids of the body. *~ n.* Solvent, diluting agent; substance increasing proportion of water in body fluids.

dīluteʹ (-ōōt, -ūt) *v.t.* Reduce strength of (fluid) by adding water; water down. *~* (*or* dīʹ-) *adj.* Weakened by addition of water; watery, watered down.

dĭlūʹtion (*or* -ōō-) *n.* 1. Act of diluting; state of being diluted; diluted substance. 2. Introduction of unskilled labour into a body of skilled workmen.

dĭlūvʹial (*or* -ōō-) *adj.* 1. Of a flood, esp. of that recorded in Genesis. 2. (geol.) Explaining geological phenomena by hypothesis of general deluge or periods of catastrophic water-action. **dĭlūvʹialĭst** *n.*

dĭm *adj.* Faintly luminous, not clear, obscure, shadowy; indistinct; dull, faint; not seeing or apprehending clearly or distinctly; (of sound) faint; (fig., of person) inconspicuous, undistinguished. **dĭmʹly** *adv.* **dĭmʹnėss** *n.* **dĭm** *v.* Become, make, dim; becloud; make dim by comparison, outshine; *~-out*, reduced artificial lighting in streets etc. during war-time (as dist. from *black-out*).

dim. *abbrev.* *Diminuendo*; diminutive etc.

dīme *n.* U.S. silver coin of value of $\frac{1}{10}$ dollar, or 10 cents. *~ adj.* (U.S. slang) Cheap, inferior.

dĭmĕnʹsion (-shn) *n.* 1. Measurable extent of any kind; (usu. pl.) measurement, measure, size. 2. Mode of linear measurement, magnitude, or extension, in a particular direction; *the three ~s*, length, breadth, and thickness (or depth); *fourth ~*, imaginary direction in which matter is supposed to extend in addition to the three dimensions of Euclidean geometry. 3. (alg.) Each of the (unknown or variable) qualities contained in a product as factors of it. **dimĕnʹsional** (-sho-) *adj.*

dĭmʹėter *n.* Verse of two measures (a measure having one foot in some metres and two in others).

dĭmĭdʹiate *adj.* Halved, split in two. **dĭmĭdiāʹtion** *n.* (ill. HERALDRY).

dĭmĭnʹĭsh *v.* Make, cause to appear, grow, less or smaller; lessen in importance, estimation, or power; *law of diminishing returns*, fact that expenditure of labour or capital beyond a certain point does not produce proportionate return or that taxation above a certain level fails to produce the desired yield. **dĭmĭnʹĭshed** (-sht) *adj.* (esp., mus.) Of an interval: less by a chromatic semitone than a perfect or a minor interval of the same name.

dĭmĭnūĕnʹdō *adv.* (as mus. direction) With gradually decreasing force or loudness of tone (abbrev. *dim.* and indicated by sign >). *~ n.* (pl. *-s*). Such decrease; passage in which it occurs.

dĭmĭnūʹtion *n.* Diminishing, reduction; (mus.) repetition of a passage in shorter notes than those previously used.

dĭmĭnʹūtive *adj.* 1. Small, minute, tiny. 2. (gram.) Denoting something little, expressing diminution (usu. applied to derivatives or affixes expressing something small of the kind denoted by primitive word). **dĭmĭnʹūtively** (-vl-) *adv.* **dĭmĭnʹūtivenėss** *n.* **dĭmĭnʹūtive** *n.* Diminutive word or term.

dĭmʹĭty *n.* Stout cotton fabric woven with raised stripes, freq. printed, and used for hangings etc.

dīmŏrphʹic *adj.* (bot., zool.) Occurring in two distinct forms in same species, individual, etc.; (chem., min.) occurring in two distinct crystalline forms not derivable from one another. **dīmŏrphʹism** *n.* **dīmŏrphʹous** *adj.*

dĭmʹple *n.* Small hollow or dent in body, esp. in cheek or chin; slight surface depression or indentation resembling this. *~ v.* Mark with dimples, break into dimples or ripples.

dĭn *n.* Continued confused loud noise, stunning or distracting. *~ v.* Make din; utter continuously so as to deafen or weary, repeat *ad nauseam* (*into* person or person's ears).

dīnarʹ *n.* 1. Principal monetary unit of Yugoslavia (= 100 paras) and of Iraq and Jordan (= 1,000 fils). 2. $\frac{1}{100}$ of a Persian rial.

dīne *v.* Take dinner; entertain (persons) at dinner; (of room etc.) provide dining-accommodation for (some number); *dining-car*, railway coach in which meals are served on a journey; *dining-room*, room in private house, hotel, etc., in which the principal meals are taken.

dīn'er *n.* 1. One who dines; *~-out*, one who often dines from home, esp. one whose social qualities make him a welcome guest. 2. Railway dining-car.

dĭng'băt *n.* (U.S. colloq.) Anything used as or suitable for missile; thingumajig.

dĭng-dŏng *adv* & *n.* (With) sound of bell, or alternate strokes of two bells; jingling rhyme. ~ *adj.* Of or like bells or jingling rhyme; downright, desperate; ~ *race*, neck-and-neck race.

dĭng'hy (-nggĭ-) *n.* Small rowing-boat in ship; small pleasure-boat

GUNTER-RIGGED DINGHY

(esp. *sailing-~*); inflatable rubber boat used by airmen who have been forced to bale out over the sea. [Hind. *dingi* small boat]

dingle (dĭng'gl) *n.* Deep dell or hollow, usu. shaded with trees.

dĭng'ō (-ngg-) *n.* Wild or semi-domesticated dog of Australia, *Canis dingo*, usu. reddish-brown and with bushy tail. [Native name]

dĭn'gy (-jĭ) *adj.* Dull-coloured, grimy, dirty-looking. **dĭn'gily** *adv.* **dĭn'giness** *n.*

dĭnk'y *adj.* (colloq.) Pretty, neat, of engaging appearance.

dĭnn'er *n.* Chief meal of day, eaten orig. and still chiefly about middle of day, but now by professional and fashionable classes usu. in evening; formal meal with distinct courses, public repast of this kind; *~-jacket*, less formal dress-coat without tails; *~-pail*, (U.S.) vessel in which workman carries his dinner; *~-wagon*, wheeled trolley with decks for holding dishes. **dĭnn'erless** *adj.*

dīn'osaur *n.* Any of the extinct saurian reptiles (orders *Saurischia* and *Ornithischia*) of the mesozoic age, some of which were of gigantic size. [Gk *deinos* terrible, *sauros* lizard]

dīn'othēre *n.* Member of an extinct genus of quadrupeds resembling the elephant and belonging to the same order (*Proboscidae*). [Gk *deinos* terrible, *therion* wild beast]

dĭnt *n.* 1. *By ~ of*, by force of, through the persistence or vigour of. 2. Mark made by blow or pressure, dent. ~ *v.t.* Make dint or dints in.

dīŏ'cėsan (-zn) *adj.* Of a diocese. ~ *n.* Bishop of diocese; one of the clergy or people of diocese.

dī'ocese (-sēs, -sĭs) *n.* District under pastoral care of a bishop.

Dīoclē'tian (-shn) (245–313). Caius Aurelius Valerius Diocletianus, who became Roman emperor in 284, and abdicated in 305; during his reign the Christians were severely persecuted.

dī'ōde *n.* Electronic valve having two electrodes (ill. THERMIONIC).

dīoe'cious (-ēshus) *adj.* 1. (bot.) Having the unisexual male and female flowers on separate plants (ill. FLOWER). 2. (zool.) Having the two sexes in separate individuals.

Dīŏ'gėnēs (-z) (b. *c* 412 B.C.). Greek Cynic philosopher, who practised at Athens the greatest austerity, taking up his residence, it is said, in a large earthenware jar.

Dīonȳs'us. In Gk myth., the son of Zeus and Semele, a god of the fertility of nature and of wine, who inspires to music and poetry; identified by the Romans with Bacchus. **Dīonȳs'ian** *adj.* Of, pertaining to, Dionysus; Bacchic.

Dīophăn'tus (4th c.). Mathematician of Alexandria, credited with a method of solving problems involving indeterminate equations. **Dīophăn'tīne** *adj.* ~ *analysis*, (math.) indeterminate analysis in the theory of numbers.

dīŏp'ter, -tre *n.* Refractive power of a lens having a focal length of 1 metre (used as unit of refractive power; thus a lens of +5 diopters is a positive lens with a focal length of 20 cm.).

dīŏp'trĭc *adj.* Serving as medium for sight, assisting sight by refraction; of refraction, refractive; of dioptrics. **dīŏp'trĭcally** *adv.* **dīŏp'trĭcs** *n.* Part of optics dealing with refraction (cf. CATOPTRICS).

dīora'ma (-ah-) *n.* Spectacular painting (usu. viewed through an aperture with sides continued towards picture) in which, by changes in colour and direction of light thrown on or through it, atmospheric effects of various kinds are produced. **dīorăm'ĭc** *adj.*

Dīŏs'cūrī. (Gk myth.) The twin sons of Zeus, CASTOR and POLLUX.

dīŏx'īde *n.* (chem.) Oxide of an element in which two atoms of oxygen are united to one of the element.

dĭp *v.* 1. Put or let down temporarily or partially into liquid or the like; dye thus; make (candle) by dipping wick in melted tallow; wash (sheep) in vermin-killing liquor. 2. Obtain or take *up* by dipping. 3. Lower (flag etc.) for an instant; lower (headlights of vehicle). 4. Go under water and emerge quickly. 5. Put hand, ladle, etc., *into* to take something out. 6. Sink or drop down through small space, or below particular level, as if dipping into water; have downward inclination, be inclined to horizon (esp. of magnetic needle). 7. Make investigations; look cursorily or skippingly *into*. ~ *n.* 1. A dipping; quantity dipped up; bathe in sea etc.; amount of submergence. 2. (astron. etc.) Apparent depression of horizon due to observer's elevation; angle made by magnetic needle with horizon; downward slope of surface, esp. of stratum or vein (ill. ROCK); ~ *circle*, instrument for measuring magnetic dip. 3. Hollow depression to which surrounding high ground dips or sinks. 4. Candle made by dipping wick into melted tallow. 5. Preparation in which sheep etc. are dipped.

dĭphthēr'ĭa *n.* Acute, highly infectious disease characterized by inflammation of a mucous surface (usu. that of the throat), and by an

DINOSAURS
1. Brontosaurus. 2. Iguanodon

exudation forming a firm pellicle or false membrane. **dĭphthĕ′rĭc, dĭphtherĭt′ĭc** *adjs.*

dĭph′thŏng *n.* Union of two vowels pronounced as one syllable. **dĭphthŏng′al** (-ngg-) *adj.*

dĭph′thŏngīze (-ngg-) *v.t.* Develop diphthong from single vowel. **dĭphthŏngīzā′tion** *n.*

dĭplo- *prefix* (in scientific terms). Double.

dĭplocŏcc′us *n.* (pl. -ī). Micro-organism of the type which tends to form pairs.

dĭplŏd′ocus *n.* Member of extinct genus of giant herbivorous dinosaurs, remains of which have been found in Colorado and Wyoming. [Gk *diplo-* double, *dokos* beam, from its double-yoked cervical vertebrae]

dĭp′loid *adj.* (biol., of nucleus) Having chromosomes in pairs.

dĭplōm′a *n.* Document granted by competent authority conferring honour, privilege, or licence (as, to teach, practise medicine etc.). [Gk, = 'folded paper', 'letter of recommendation']

dĭplōm′acy *n.* Management of international relations by negotiation; skill in conduct of international intercourse; adroitness, skill, in dealing with others.

dĭp′lomăt *n.* Diplomatist.

dĭplomăt′ĭc *adj.* 1. Of official or original documents, charters, etc.; textual. 2. Of the management of international relations; of diplomacy. 3. Skilled in diplomacy; adroit in negotiations or intercourse of any kind. **dĭplomăt′ĭcally** *adv.* **dĭplomăt′ĭc** *n.* Palaeographic examination of official or original documents.

dĭplōm′atĭst *n.* One officially engaged in diplomacy; adroit negotiator.

dĭplōm′atīze *v.i.* Act as diplomatist; use diplomatic arts.

dĭp′ody *n.* (pros.) A double foot.

dĭp′ōle *n.* (physic. & chem.) Object oppositely charged at two points or poles; molecule in which centre of action of the positive portions (protons) does not coincide with that of the negative portions (electrons). **dīpōl′ar** *adj.* Having two poles, as a magnet.

dĭpp′er *n.* (esp.) 1. Any of various birds which dip or dive in water; water ousel, *Cinclus cinclus*, or other ousels; (U.S.) the buffle-head duck, *Clangula albeola*. 2. (chiefly U.S.) Utensil for dipping up water, esp. long-handled ladle. 3. (U.S.) (*Great, Big*) *D~*, the constellation called in England the Plough or Charles's Wain; *Little D~*, the similar group of seven stars in Ursa Minor. 4. Contrivance for dipping and raising headlights of a motor-car to avoid dazzling an approaching motorist etc.

dĭpp′ĭng-needle *n.* Magnetic needle mounted so as to move in vertical plane about its centre of gravity, and indicating by its dip direction of earth's magnetism.

dĭpp′y *adj.* (slang) Mad, crazy.

dĭpsomān′ia *n.* Morbid craving for alcohol. **dĭpsomān′iăc** *adj.* & *n.*

dĭp′teral *adj.* (archit.) With double peristyle (ill. TEMPLE).

dĭp′terous *adj.* (entom.) Two-winged; (bot.) having two wing-like appendages or processes, as some seeds.

dĭp′tȳch (-k) *n.* 1. Ancient hinged two-leaved writing tablet with inner sides waxed. 2. Painting, esp. altarpiece, of two panels hinged together.

dīre *adj.* Dreadful, calamitous. **dīre′ly** *adv.*

dirĕct′ (*or* -īr-) *v.* 1. Address (letter etc. *to* person or place); utter, write, *to* or to be conveyed *to*. 2. Control; govern the movements of. 3. Turn straight *to* something; tell (person) the way *to*. 4. (Of adviser or principle) guide. 5. Order (person) *to* do (thing) *to be* done; give orders. 6. Assign (workers) to particular industry or employment. *~ adj.* 1. Straight, not devious or crooked; (of light etc.) coming straight from the source, without reflection, refraction, etc.; moving, proceeding, situated, at right angles to given surface etc.; straightforward, uninterrupted; (of succession) in an unbroken line from father to son; *~ current*, electric current flowing through circuit in one direction only; *~ opposite*, what is absolutely or exactly contrary or opposite. 2. Going straight to the point, unambiguous, straightforward; upright, downright. 3. Immediate, without intermediation; (of speech etc.) in form in which it was uttered, not reported in third person. 4. *~ action*, action taking effect without intermediate instrumentality; esp., exertion of pressure on community by strikes, sabotage, demonstrations, etc., rather than through parliamentary representatives; *~ hit*, one right on the target (esp. of bombing); *~ method*, method of teaching a foreign language through conversation, reading, etc., in the language itself without using pupil's native language; *~ speech*: see sense 3 above; *~ tax(ation)*, tax(ation) levied immediately on persons, as dist. from *indirect tax(ation)*, levied upon commodities and included in their purchase price. **dirĕct′nèss** *n.* **dirĕct′** *adv.* Straight in direction or aspect; immediately; absolutely, exactly.

dirĕc′tion (*or* -īr-) *n.* 1. Directing; esp., management, administration; directorate; *~ of labour*: see DIRECT *v.* sense 6. 2. Instruction how to proceed or act, or how to find some person etc.; address, addressing, of letters etc. 3. Course pursued by moving body; point to which one moves or looks; scope, sphere, subject; *~ finder*, radio receiving apparatus so constructed as to indicate direction from which wireless signals are coming.

dirĕc′tional (-sho-; *or* -īr-) *adj.* (esp., wireless) Sending signals in one direction only; detecting, recording, direction from which signals are received.

dirĕc′tĭve (*or* -īr-) *adj.* Giving guidance. *~ n.* Statement setting forth policy etc. for guidance of others, esp. subordinates.

dirĕct′ly (*or* -īr-) *adv.* 1. Straight, undeviatingly; simply, plainly; not obliquely. 2. Entirely, exactly, precisely. 3. Immediately, without intervention of medium or agent. 4. Immediately in time, at once; (as *conj.*, colloq.) as soon as, the moment after.

Dirĕc′toire (-twar̄). Executive body in France during part of the revolutionary period (Oct. 1795–Nov. 1799), consisting of 5 members called directors. *~ adj.* Of, imitating, the dress, furniture, etc., of this period in France, characterized by extravagance of design and imitation of Greek and Roman styles.

dirĕc′tor *n.* (esp.) 1. Superintendent, manager, esp. member of managing-board of commercial company or person responsible for supervising the making of a film. 2. (Fr. hist.) Member of DIRECTOIRE. 3. (eccles.) Priest acting as spiritual adviser to a particular person or society. **dirĕct′rèss** *n.* Female director. **dīrĕctōr′ial** *adj.*

dirĕc′torate *n.* Office of director; board of directors.

dirĕc′tory *n.* 1. Book of rules, esp. for order of public or private worship. 2. Book containing lists of inhabitants of districts, telephone subscribers, members of professions, etc., with various details. 3. (Fr. hist.) The DIRECTOIRE. 4. (U.S.) Directorate, board of directors.

dirĕc′trĭx *n.* 1. Directress. 2. (geom.) Fixed line used in describing curve or surface, esp. straight line the distance of which from any point on a conic section has constant ratio to distance of same point from focus.

dīre′ful (-īrf-) *adj.* Dreadful, terrible. **dīre′fully** *adv.* **dīre′fulnèss** *n.*

dīrge *n.* 1. First word of antiphon at matins in Office for the Dead; used as name for that service, or sometimes for the whole office. 2. Song of mourning or lament for the dead; funeral song. [orig. *dirige*, first word of L antiphon *Dirige, Domine, Deus meus, in conspectu tuo viam meam*, 'Direct, O Lord, my God, my way in thy sight', taken from Ps. v. 8]

dĭ′rĭgible *adj.* Capable of being steered or guided. *~ n.* Dirigible balloon or airship.

dĭ′riment *adj.* Nullifying; *~ impediment*, one rendering marriage null and void from the beginning.

dīrk *n.* Kind of dagger, esp. that worn by a Scottish Highlander (ill. DAGGER). *~ v.t.* Stab with dirk.

dĩrt n. 1. Unclean matter such as soils things by adhering to them; wet mud; anything worthless or unclean. 2. Earth, soil; material from which metallic ore etc. is separated, esp. alluvial deposit from which gold is washed. 3. Dirtiness, foulness in speech or action; *throw, fling*, etc., ~, be scurrilously abusive; *eat* ~, submit to degrading treatment; *~-cheap*, as cheap as dirt, exceedingly cheap; *~-pie*, mud-pie; *~-road*, (U.S.) unmade road, one with natural earth surface; *~-track* (orig. U.S.), race-track with earth surface; track of cinders and brickdust for motor-cycle racing.

dĩrt'y *adj.* 1. Soiled with dirt, foul, muddied; mixed with dirt; that soils or befouls. 2. Morally unclean; dishonourably sordid, base, or corrupt; repulsive, despicable. 3. (Of weather) foul, muddy, (at sea) wet and squally. 4. (Of colour) inclining to, with some tinge of, black, brown, or dark grey. **dĩrt'ily** *adv.* **dĩrt'inėss** *n.* **dĩrt'y** *v.* Make, become, dirty.

dis- *prefix.* Asunder, away, apart or between; un-, not, the reverse of.

dĭsabĭl'ĭty *n.* Thing, want, that prevents one's doing something, esp. legal disqualification; physical incapacity caused by injury or disease; ~ *pension*, pension granted to ex-soldier or employee disabled during service.

dĭsā'ble *v.t.* 1. Incapacitate *from* doing, *for* work, etc.; cripple, deprive of power of acting. 2. Disqualify legally, pronounce incapable; hinder. **dĭsā'blement** *n.*

dĭsabūse' (-z) *v.t.* Undeceive, disillusion.

dĭsaccõrd' *n.* Disagreement, variance. ~ *v.i.* Disagree, be at variance.

dĭsadva'ntage (-vah-) *n.* Unfavourable condition or circumstance; loss or injury to interest, credit, reputation. **dĭsădvantā'geous** (-jus) *adj.* **dĭsădvantā'geously** *adv.*

dĭsaffĕc'tėd *adj.* Estranged, unfriendly, disloyal, esp. to government or constituted authority. **dĭsaffĕc'tion** *n.*

dĭsaffĩrm' *v.t.* (law) Annul, reverse (former decision etc.), repudiate (agreement etc.).

dĭsagree' *v.i.* 1. Differ, be unlike, not correspond; differ in opinion, dissent, quarrel. 2. (Of food etc.) be unsuitable, have bad effects. **dĭsagree'ment** *n.*

dĭsagree'able *adj.* 1. Not to one's taste, unpleasant. 2. Unamiable, bad-tempered. **dĭsagree'ably** *adv.*

dĭsallow' *v.t.* Refuse to sanction, accept as reasonable, or admit; prohibit.

dĭsannŭl' *v.t.* Cancel, annul.

dĭsappear' *v.i.* Cease to be visible, vanish, die away from sight or existence, be lost. **dĭsappear'ance** *n.*

dĭsappoint *v.t.* Not fulfil desire or expectation of; belie, frustrate. **dĭsappoint'ĭng** *adj.* **dĭsappoint'ĭngly** *adv.* **dĭsappoint'ment** *n.* Disappointing; being disappointed; person or thing that disappoints.

dĭsăpprobā'tion *n.* Disapproval.

dĭsapprove' (-o͞ov) *v.* Have, express, unfavourable opinion (*of*). **dĭsappro'val** *n.* **dĭsappro'vĭngly** *adv.*

dĭsārm' *v.* 1. Deprive of weapons; deprive (city, ship) of munitions of war or means of defence; reduce (army, navy), be reduced, to peace footing; abandon or cut down military establishment. 2. Deprive of power to injure; pacify hostility or suspicions of, whence **dĭsārm'ĭng** *adj.* **dĭsārm'ĭngly** *adv.*

dĭsārm'ament *n.* Reduction of nation's military forces and weapons of war.

dĭsarrānge' (-nj) *v.t.* Put into disorder, disorganize. **dĭsarrānge'ment** (-jm-) *n.*

dĭsarray' *n.* Disorder, confusion. ~ *v.t.* 1. Throw into disorder or confusion, rout. 2. (poet.) Dissolve.

dĭsārtĭc'ūlāte *v.* Separate, be separated, at the joints.

dĭsas'ter (-zah-) *n.* Sudden or great misfortune, calamity. **dĭsas'trous** *adj.* **dĭsas'trously** *adv.*

dĭsavow' *v.t.* Refuse to avow, own, or acknowledge, repudiate, disown. **dĭsavow'al** *n.*

dĭsbănd' *v.* Break up, disperse. **dĭsbănd'ment** *n.*

dĭsbār' *v.t.* Deprive of status and privileges of barrister. **dĭsbār'ment** *n.*

dĭsbėlieve' *v.* Refuse credence to; not believe *in.* **dĭsbėlief'** *n.*

dĭsbĕnch' *v.t.* Deprive of status of bencher.

dĭsbûrd'en *v.t.* Relieve of a burden; get rid of (burden).

dĭsbûrse' *v.* Expend; defray; pay out money. **dĭsbûrse'ment** (-sm-) *n.* Money expended.

dĭsc, dĭsk *n.* Thin circular plate; round flat (or apparently flat) object, as *sun's* ~; round flattened part in body, plant, etc.; gramophone record; *~-jockey*, person who selects and introduces gramophone records for radio transmission.

dĭscārd' *v.* 1. Throw out, reject (card) from hand at cards; esp. play (card not of trump suit) when unable to follow suit. 2. Cast aside, give up; dismiss, cashier. **dĭs'cārd** *n.* Discarding at cards; discarded card.

dĭscārn'ate *adj.* Divested of the flesh, disembodied.

dĭscẽrn' *v.* 1. (archaic) Distinguish, perceive difference (between). 2. Recognize, perceive distinctly (with mind or senses). **dĭscẽrn'ĭng** *adj.* Having quick or true insight, penetrating. **dĭscẽrn'ment** *n.*

dĭschārge' *v.* Unload; rid of charge or load; fire off (fire-arm); rid, rid itself, of electric charge; relieve *of*, release *from*, obligation etc.; dismiss from service; release from custody; send away, let go; put forth, emit; let fly, fire off; unload from vessel etc.; give, find, vent; (allow to) escape; cancel (order of court); pay, perform (debt, duty, vow). ~ *n.* Unloading; firing off; omission; release, exoneration, exemption, acquittal, written certificate of these; dismissal; liberation; payment (*of* debt), performance (*of* obligation).

dĭscī'ple *n.* 1. One of Christ's personal followers, esp. one of the Twelve (apostles); any early believer in Christ. 2. Follower, adherent, of any leader of thought, art, etc. **dĭscī'pleshĭp** (-lsh-) *n.* **dĭscĭp'ūlar** *adj.*

dĭscĭplĭnār'ĭan *n.* Maintainer of (esp. strict) discipline.

dĭs'cĭplĭnary *adj.* Of, promoting, discipline; of the nature of mental training.

dĭs'cĭplĭne *n.* 1. Branch of instruction; mental and moral training. 2. Trained condition; order maintained among persons under control or command, as pupils, soldiers, etc.; system for maintenance of order. 3. Control exercised over members of church and their conduct, as by censure, excommunication, etc. 4. Correction, chastisement; mortification of flesh by penance; whip, scourge, esp. for religious penance. ~ *v.t.* Bring under control, train to obedience and order.

dĭsclaim' *v.* 1. Renounce legal claim to; renounce claim. 2. Disown, disavow. **dĭsclaim'er** *n.* Act of disclaiming, renunciation, disavowal.

dĭsclōse' (-z) *v.t.* Remove cover from, expose to view; make known, reveal. **dĭsclō'sure** (-zh*er*) *n.* Disclosing; thing disclosed.

dĭscŏb'olus *n.* (pl. *-lī*). Thrower of discus; *the D~*, statue by Gk sculptor Myron, copies of which survive.

dĭs'coid *adj.* Disc-shaped; (bot., of composite flowers) having disc only, with no ray.

dĭscol'our (-kŭl*er*) *v.* Change or spoil the colour of, stain, tarnish; become stained, tarnished, etc. **dĭscolorā'tion** *n.*

dĭscom'fĭt (-kŭm-) *v.t.* Defeat in battle; thwart, disconcert. **dĭscom'fĭture** *n.*

dĭscom'fort (-kŭm-) *n.* Uneasiness of body or mind; want of comfort. ~ *v.t.* Make uneasy.

dĭscommōde' *v.t.* Put to inconvenience.

dĭscŏmm'on *v.t.* 1. Debar (tradesmen) from serving undergraduates. 2. Enclose (common land). **dĭscŏmm'ons** *v.t.* Deprive (member of college) of commons; discommon (tradesman).

dĭscŏmpōse' (-z) *v.t.* Disturb composure of, ruffle, agitate. **dĭscompō'sure** (-zh*er*) *n.*

disconcẽrt′ *v.t.* Derange, spoil, upset; disturb self-possession of, ruffle, fluster.

disconnĕct′ *v.t.* Sever the connexion of or between. **disconnĕc′tėd** *adj.* (esp., of speech or writing) Incoherent, jerky. **disconnĕc′tėdly** *adv.* **disconnĕc′tėdnėss** *n.* **disconnĕxion, -ction** (-kshn) *n.*

discŏn′solate (-*a*t) *adj.* Forlorn, inconsolable, unhappy, disappointed. **discŏn′solately** *adv.* **discŏn′solatenėss** *n.*

discontĕnt′ *n.* Dissatisfaction, want of contentment; grievance. ~ *adj.* Not content, dissatisfied. ~ *v.t.* (usu. in past part.) Make dissatisfied. **discontĕn′tėdly** *adv.* **discontĕn′tėdnėss, discontĕnt′ment** *ns.*

discontin′ūe *v.* Cause to cease, break off; give up, leave off. **discontin′ūance** *n.*

discontin′ūous *adj.* Not continuous, having interstices or breaks, intermittent. **discontin′ūously** *adv.* **discŏntinū′ity** *n.*

dis′cõrd *n.* 1. Disagreement, variance, strife. 2. Harsh noise, clashing sounds. 3. (mus.) Want of harmony between notes sounded together; chord which by itself is unsatisfactory or unpleasing to the ear, and requires to be 'resolved' by some other chord following; interval between two notes forming a discord (any interval except octave, major and minor third, perfect fourth and fifth, major and minor sixth, and their octaves); note forming discord with another or others. **discõrd′ant** *adj.* **discõrd′antly** *adv.* **discõrd′ance** *n.* **discõrd′** *v.i.* Disagree; be different, inconsistent, or discordant.

dis′count *n.* Deduction from nominal value or price of anything for payment before it is due, or for prompt payment; deduction from amount of bill of exchange etc., by one who gives value for it before it is due; discounting; *at a* ~, below par; (fig.) in low esteem, depreciated. **discount′** *v.t.* 1. Give or receive value (after deduction of discount) of bill of exchange before it is due. 2. Leave out of account; lessen, detract from; part with for immediate but smaller good; allow for exaggeration in; take (news, event) into account beforehand, thus lessening its effect or interest.

discoun′tėnance *v.t.* Refuse to countenance, discourage, show disapproval of.

discou′rage (-kŭ-) *v.t.* Deprive of courage, confidence, or energy; deter *from*; discountenance. **discou′ragement** (-jm-) *n.* **discou′ragingly** *adv.*

dis′course (-õrs) *n.* Talk, conversation (archaic); dissertation, treatise, sermon. **discourse′** *v.* Talk, converse; hold forth in speech or writing on a subject; give forth (music; ref. to 'Hamlet', III. ii. 374).

discourt′ėous (-kẽr-, -kõr-) *adj.* Rude, uncivil. **discourt′ėously** *adv.* **discourt′ėsy̆** *n.*

discov′er (-kŭ-) *v.t.* 1. Disclose, expose to view; reveal, make known; exhibit, manifest, betray. 2. (chess) ~ *check*, put king in check by removing piece or pawn. 3. Find out; obtain sight or knowledge of for first time. **discov′erer** *n.*

discov′ert (-kŭ-) *adj.* (law) Not under the cover, authority, or protection of a husband.

discov′ery (-kŭ-) *n.* Discovering; thing discovered; (law) compulsory disclosure by party to action of facts or documents on which he relies.

discrĕd′it *n.* Loss of repute, thing involving this; doubt, distrust; loss of commercial credit. ~ *v.t.* Refuse to believe; bring disrepute or disbelief upon.

discrĕd′itable *adj.* Bringing discredit, shameful. **discrĕd′itably** *adv.*

discreet′ *adj.* Judicious, prudent, cautious, circumspect. **discreet′ly** *adv.*

discrĕp′ancy *n.* Want of agreement, variance, inconsistency. **discrĕp′ant** *adj.* **discrĕp′antly** *adv.*

discrēte′ *adj.* 1. Separate, individually distinct, discontinuous. 2. (metaphysics) Not concrete; detached from the material. **discrēte′ly** (-tl-) *adv.* **discrēte′nėss** *n.*

discrĕ′tion *n.* 1. Liberty or power of deciding or acting as one thinks fit; (law) power of court etc. to decide, within limits, on punishment, remedy, distribution of costs, etc. 2. Discernment, prudence, judgement; *age, years, of* ~, age at which person is presumed to be capable of exercising discretion (in Engl. law 14). **discrĕ′tionary** (-sh*o*-) *adj.*

discrim′ināte *v.* Constitute, set up, observe, a difference between, distinguish *from, between*; make a distinction; observe distinctions carefully; ~ *against*, distinguish unfavourably. **discrim′ināting** *adj.* Discerning, acute. **discriminā′tion** *n.* **discrim′inative** *adj.* **discrim′inatively** (-vl-) *adv.*

discrown′ *v.t.* Take crown from, depose.

discũrs′ive *adj.* 1. Rambling, digressive, expatiating. 2. Proceeding by reasoning or argument, not intuitive. **discũrs′ively** *adv.* **discũrs′ivenėss** *n.*

dis′cus *n.* Heavy disc of metal etc. used in ancient Greek and Roman athletic exercises and revived in modern times.

discŭss′ *v.t.* 1. Examine by argument, debate. 2. Consume (food) with enjoyment. **discŭ′ssion** (-shn) *n.*

disdain′ *v.t.* Scorn; regard with contempt; consider beneath oneself or one's notice. ~ *n.* Scorn, contempt. **disdain′ful** *adj.* **disdain′fully** *adv.*

disease′ (-zēz) *n.* Morbid condition of body or plant, or some part of it; disorder, illness; any particular kind of this with special symptoms or affecting special organ; deranged, depraved or morbid condition of mind etc. **diseased′** (-zēzd) *adj.* Affected with disease; morbid, depraved.

disėmbãrk′ *v.* Put, go, ashore. **disĕmbãrkā′tion** *n.*

disėmbă′rrass *v.t.* Free from embarrassment, rid or relieve (*of*). **disėmbă′rrassment** *n.*

disėmbŏd′y *v.t.* 1. Separate, free (soul from body, or idea from form in which it is embodied). 2. (obs.) Disband (troops).

disėmbōgue′ (-g) *v.* (of river, lake, etc.) Discharge or empty itself, flow *into*; pour forth (its waters) at the mouth.

disėmbow′ėl *v.t.* Remove entrails of, rip up so as to cause bowels to protrude.

disėmbroil′ *v.t.* Extricate from confusion or entanglement.

disėnchant′ (-ah-) *v.t.* Free from enchantment or illusion. **disėnchant′ment** *n.*

disėncŭm′ber *v.t.* Free from encumbrance.

disėndow′ *v.t.* Deprive or strip (esp. Church) of endowments. **disėndow′ment** *n.*

disėngāge′ *v.t.* Detach, liberate, loosen; come apart, break contact; (fencing) reverse relative position of blades by passing point to opposite side of opponent's sword. ~ *n.* (fencing) Freeing one's blade for a thrust by disengaging it. **disėngāged′** (-jd) *adj.* (esp.) Unoccupied; at liberty, not engaged. **disėngāge′ment** (-jm-) *n.*

disėntail′ *v.t.* Free from entail, break entail of.

disėntăng′le (-nggl) *v.* Extricate, free from complications; unravel, untwist; come clear of tangle. **disėntăng′lement** (-lm-) *n.*

disėntomb′ (-o͞om) *v.t.* Disinter.

disėntwīne′ *v.t.* Disentangle.

disėstăb′lish *v.t.* Deprive of established character; esp. deprive (Church) of State connexion and support, remove from position of national or State Church. **disėstăb′lishment** (-lm-) *n.*

diseur (dēzẽr′), ***diseuse*** (-ẽrz) *ns.* Man, woman, who entertains by speaking monologues. [Fr.]

disfāv′our (-v*er*) *n.* Dislike, disapproval; being disliked.

disfea′ture *v.t.* Disfigure.

disfig′ure (-g*er*) *v.t.* Mar beauty of, deform, deface, sully. **disfigūrā′tion, disfig′urement** *ns.*

disfŏ′rėst *v.t.* Deprive of status or privileges of forest; clear of trees or forest.

disfrăn′chīse (-shīz, -chīz) *v.t.* Deprive of rights and privileges of a free citizen, or of some franchise previously enjoyed; deprive (place) of right of sending, (person) of right of voting for, parliamentary representative. **disfrăn′chisement** (-ĭzm-) *n.*

disfrŏck′ *v.t.* Deprive of clerical garb, and hence of clerical status.

disgôrge′ *v.* Vomit forth (what has been swallowed); give up (esp. what has been wrongfully appropriated); (of river) discharge.

disgrāce′ *n.* 1. Loss of favour, downfall from position of honour; ignominy, shame. 2. Thing involving dishonour; cause of reproach. ~ *v.t.* Dismiss from favour, degrade from position; bring shame or discredit upon, be a disgrace to. **disgrāce′ful** (-sf-) *adj.* **disgrāce′fully** *adv.* **disgrāce′fulnėss** *n.*

disgrŭnt′led (-ld) *adj.* Discontented, displeased.

disguise′ (-gīz) *v.t.* Conceal identity of by changing personal appearance or dress; dress *as* someone, *in* some garb; alter appearance of (anything) so as to mislead or deceive; conceal or cloak real character, state, or identity of. ~ *n.* Use of changed dress or appearance for sake of concealment; disguised condition; garb used to deceive; artificial manner, deception. **disguise′ment** (-gīzm-) *n.*

disgŭst′ *n.* Loathing, nausea, repugnance, strong aversion. ~ *v.t.* Excite loathing, aversion, or indignation in. **disgŭs′ting** *adj.* **disgŭs′tingly** *adv.*

dish *n.* 1. Shallow, flat-bottomed, freq. oval or oblong vessel of earthenware, glass, or metal, for holding food at meals. 2. Food served on or contained in dish; variety or article of food; *standing* ~, one that appears daily or for every meal (also fig.); *made* ~, fancy dish concocted of various ingredients. 3. Dish-shaped receptacle used for any purpose; dish-like concavity, e.g. in wheel. 4. ~*-cover*, cover of metal etc. for keeping food in dish hot; ~*-cloth*, cloth for washing dishes and plates; ~*-water*, water in which dishes have been washed; (pop.) weak tea. ~ *v.* 1. Put (food) into dish ready for serving; ~ *up*, serve, serve meal; (fig.) present (facts, arguments, etc.) attractively. 2. Make concave or dish-shaped; *dished wheel*, concave wheel with spokes at an angle to the hub (ill. WAGON). 3. (of horse) Move forefeet with circular or scooping motion. 4. (slang) Circumvent, outmanœuvre; do for, defeat completely.

dishabille (dĭsabēl′) *n.* Being negligently or partly dressed; undress; undress garment or costume.

dishârm′ony (-s-h-) *n.* Discord, dissonance. **dishârmō′nious** *adj.*

disheart′en (-s-hârtn) *v.t.* Make despondent, rob of courage. **disheart′ening** *adj.* **disheart′enment** *n.*

dishĕv′elled (-ld) *adj.* With disordered hair; (of hair) loose, disordered; (of person) untidy, ruffled. **dishĕv′elment** *n.*

dishon′ėst (dĭsŏ-) *adj.* Fraudulent; knavish; insincere. **dishon′ėstly** *adv.* **dishon′ėsty** *n.* Want of honesty; knavery, deceitfulness, fraud.

dishon′our (-s-ŏner) *n.* State of shame or disgrace, discredit; indignity, insult; cause or source of shame. ~ *v.t.* 1. Treat with indignity; violate honour or chastity of. 2. Bring dishonour or disgrace upon. 3. Refuse or fail to accept or pay (cheque, bill of exchange, etc.).

dishon′ourable (-s-ŏner-) *adj.* Involving disgrace, ignominious; unprincipled, base; against dictates of honour. **dishon′ourablenėss** *n.* **dishon′ourably** *adv.*

dishouse (-s-howz′) *v.t.* Oust or expel from house.

disillu′sion (-lōōzhn) *v.t.* Free from illusion, disenchant. ~ *n.* Freedom from illusion, disenchantment. **disillu′sionize** (-zhon-) *v.t.* Disillusion. **disillu′sionment** *n.*

disinclinā′tion *n.* Want of inclination, willingness, or liking.

disincline′ *v.t.* Make indisposed, averse, or unwilling.

disincôrp′orāte *v.t.* Dissolve (corporate body). **disincôrporā′tion** *n.*

disinfĕct′ *v.t.* Cleanse from infection, destroy germs of disease in. **disinfĕc′tant** *adj.* & *n.* Disinfecting (agent). **disinfĕc′tion** *n.*

disinflā′tion *n.* Policy designed to remove or offset the inflationary elements in a country's economic situation without incurring the bad effects of DEFLATION. **disinflā′tionary** (-sho-) *adj.*

disingĕn′ūous (-j-) *adj.* Insincere, not candid or frank. **disingĕn′ūously** *adv.* **disingĕn′ūousnėss** *n.*

disinhĕ′rit *v.t.* Deprive or dispossess of right to inherit. **disinhĕ′ritance** *n.*

disin′tėgrāte *v.* Separate into component parts; deprive of, lose, cohesion. **disintėgrā′tion** *n.*

disintĕr′ *v.t.* Exhume, unbury; unearth. **disintĕr′ment** *n.*

disin′terėst *n.* Impartiality, disinterestedness; absence of interest. ~ *v.t.* (rare) Rid or divest of interest or concern. **disin′terėstėd** *adj.* Not influenced by interest; impartial, unprejudiced; unbiased by personal interest. **disin′terėstėdly** *adv.* **disin′terėstėdnėss** *n.*

disjĕc′ta mĕm′bra *n.pl.* Fragments, scattered remains. [L, alteration of Horace's *disjecti membra poetae* 'limbs of a dismembered poet']

disjoin′ *v.t.* Separate, disunite, part.

disjoint′ *v.t.* Dislocate; disturb working or connexion of; separate at the joints. **disjoint′ėd** *adj.* (esp. of speech etc.) Incoherent, desultory. **disjoint′ėdly** *adv.* **disjoint′ėdnėss** *n.*

disjŭnc′tion *n.* Disjoining, separation.

disjŭnc′tive *adj.* Disjoining, involving separation; (logic) alternative; involving choice between two statements etc.; (gram., of conjunctions) expressing an alternative, implying adversative relation between the clause they connect. **disjŭnc′tively** *adv.* **disjŭnc′tive** *n.* Disjunctive proposition or conjunction.

disk : see DISC.

dislike′ *v.t.* Not like; have aversion or objection to. ~ *n.* Aversion (*to, of, for*).

dis′locāte *v.t.* Put out of joint; (geol.) make (strata) discontinuous; displace; put out of gear. **dislocā′tion** *n.*

dislŏdge′ *v.t.* Remove, turn out, from position. **dislŏdge′ment** *n.*

disloy′al *adj.* Unfaithful; untrue to allegiance, disaffected to government. **disloy′ally** *adv.* **disloy′alist** *adj.* & *n.* **disloy′alty** *n.*

dis′mal (-z-) *adj.* Depressing, miserable, sombre, dreary; *the* ~ *science*, T. Carlyle's name for political economy. **dis′mally** *adv.* **dis′malnėss** *n.* [orig. noun, = 'unlucky days'; OF *dis mal* f. L *dies mali* ill days (the medieval calendar recognized two of these in each month)]

dismăn′tle *v.t.* Strip *of* covering, protection, etc.; deprive (fortress, ship, factory, etc.) of defences, rigging, equipment. **dismăn′tlement** (-lm-) *n.*

dismast′ (-ah-) *v.t.* Deprive (ship) of mast(s).

dismay′ *n.* Consternation; utter loss of moral courage or resolution in prospect of danger or difficulty. ~ *v.t.* Rouse dismay in; daunt, dishearten.

dismĕm′ber *v.t.* Tear or cut limb from limb; divide into parts or sections so as to destroy integrity, partition (country etc.). **dismĕm′berment** *n.*

dismiss′ *v.t.* 1. Send away, disperse, disband; allow to go; send away from one's presence. 2. Discharge, cashier, from service or office. 3. Put out of one's thoughts. 4. Have done with, bring to an end; treat (subject) summarily. 5. (law) Send out of court, refuse further hearing to; discharge, acquit (accused person). **dismiss′al, dismis′sion** (-shn) (now rare) *ns.*

dismount′ *v.* Alight, cause to alight, from horseback, etc.; unseat, unhorse; remove (thing) from its mount.

disobēd′ience *n.* Being disobedient, withholding of obedience. **disobēd′ient** *adj.* Refusing or failing to obey; stubborn, intractable. **disobēd′iently** *adv.*

disobey′ (-bā) *v.* Disregard orders, break rules; fail or refuse to obey.

disoblige *v.t.* Refuse to consult convenience or wishes of. **disoblīg′ing** *adj.* **disoblī′gingly** *adv.* **disoblī′gingnėss** *n.*

disor'der *n.* 1. Want of order, confusion. 2. Tumult, riot, commotion. 3. Ailment, disease. ~ *v.t.* Disarrange, throw into confusion; put out of health, upset. **disor'derly** *adj.* 1. Untidy, confused. 2. Irregular, unruly, riotous; violating public order or morality; ~ *house*, bawdy house, gaming house, etc. **disor'derliness** *n.*

disor'ganize *v.t.* Destroy system etc. of; throw into confusion. **disorganizā'tion** *n.*

disŏ'rientāte *v.t.* 1. Place (church) with chancel not directly eastwards. 2. Confuse (person) as to his bearings. **disŏrientā'tion** *n.*

disown' (-ōn) *v.t.* Refuse to recognize, repudiate, disclaim; renounce allegiance to.

dispă'rage *v.t.* Bring discredit on, lower; speak slightingly of, depreciate. **dispă'ragement** (-jm-) *n.* **dispă'ragingly** *adv.*

dis'parate *adj.* Essentially different, diverse in kind, incommensurable, without relation. **dis'parately** *adv.* **dis'parateness** *n.* **dis'parate** *n.* (usu. pl.) Thing(s) so unlike that there is no basis for comparison.

dispă'rity *n.* Inequality, difference, incongruity.

dispark' *v.t.* Convert (parkland) to other uses.

dispart'[1] *n.* (gunnery) Difference between semi-diameters of gun at base-ring and at muzzle, to be allowed for in aiming; sight mark on muzzle of gun to make line of sight parallel to axis of bore.

dispart'[2] *v.* Separate, part asunder; go in different directions; distribute.

dispă'ssionate (-shon-) *adj.* Free from emotion, calm, impartial. **dispă'ssionately** (-tl-) *adv.* **dispă'ssionateness** *n.*

dispătch', dės- *v.* 1. Send off to destination or for purpose. 2. Give death-blow to, kill. 3. Get (task, business) promptly done; settle, finish off; eat (food, meal) quickly; (archaic) make haste. ~ *n.* 1. Sending off. 2. Putting to death. 3. Prompt settlement of business; promptitude, efficiency, rapidity. 4. Written message; esp., official communication on State affairs. 5. Agency for conveying goods etc. 6. *~-box, -case*, box, case, for holding or carrying dispatches or other documents; *~-rider*, motor-cyclist, horseman, carrying military messages.

dispĕl' *v.t.* Dissipate, disperse.

dispĕn'sable *adj.* That can be relaxed in special cases; not necessary, that may be done without.

dispĕn'sary *n.* Place, esp. public or charitable institution, where medicines are dispensed; chemist's shop.

dispensā'tion *n.* 1. Distributing, dealing out. 2. Ordering, management, esp. of world by Providence; arrangement or provision of Providence or Nature; special dealing of Providence with community or person; (theol.) religious order or system as part of a progressive revelation adapted to particular nation or age, as *Mosaic* ~. 3. Exemption from penalty or duty laid down in ecclesiastical, etc., law; granting of licence by pope, archbishop, or bishop, to a person to do what is forbidden by ecclesiastical law.

dispĕnse' *v.* 1. Distribute, deal out; administer (sacrament, justice). 2. Make up (medicine) according to prescription or formula. 3. Grant dispensations; release *from* obligation. 4. ~ *with*, relax, give exemption from, (rule); annul binding force of (oath); render needless; do without. **dispĕn'ser** *n.* (esp.) Person who makes up medicines according to medical prescriptions.

dispeo'ple (-pēp-) *v.t.* Depopulate.

disperse' *v.* Scatter; drive, go, throw, send, in different directions; rout, dispel, be dispelled; send to, station at, different points; put in circulation, disseminate; (optics) spread (beam of light) so as to produce spectrum. **disper'sal** *n.* **disper'sėdly** *adv.* **disper'sive** *adj.* **disper'sively** *adv.* **disper'siveness** *n.*

disper'sion *n.* Dispersing; *the D~*, the Jews dispersed amongst Gentiles after the Captivity.

dispi'rit *v.t.* Make despondent, depress. **dispi'ritėdly** *adv.*

displāce' *v.t.* 1. Shift from its place; remove from office. 2. Oust, take the place of; put something else in the place of; replace. 3. *displaced person*, one belonging to racial or other minority who has been obliged to leave his native country and settle elsewhere; orig. civilian deported from a German-occupied country to Germany during the war of 1939–45 for forced labour.

displāce'ment (-sm-) *n.* 1. Displacing, being displaced; amount by which thing is shifted from its place; ousting, replacement. 2. Amount or weight of fluid displaced by body floating or immersed in it.

display' *v.t.* Exhibit, expose to view, show; show ostentatiously; reveal, betray, allow to appear. ~ *n.* Displaying; exhibition, show; ostentation; (printing) selection and arrangement of types to attract attention.

displease' (-z) *v.t.* Offend, annoy, make indignant or angry; be disagreeable to; *be displeased* (*at, with*), disapprove, be indignant or dissatisfied. **displeas'ing** *adj.* **displeas'ingly** *adv.*

displea'sure (-ĕzher) *n.* Displeased feeling, dissatisfaction, disapproval, anger.

displume' (-ōō-) *v.t.* (poet.) Strip of feathers.

disport' *v.* (archaic) Frolic, gambol, enjoy one*self*, display one*self* sportingly. ~ *n.* (archaic) Relaxation, pastime.

dispōs'able (-z-) *adj.* That can be disposed of, got rid of, made over, or used; at disposal.

dispōs'al (-z-) *n.* Disposing of, getting rid of; settling, dealing with; bestowal, assignment; sale; control, management (usu. *at one's* ~); placing, disposition, arrangement.

dispōse' (-z) *v.* 1. Place suitably, in particular order, in proper positions. 2. Bring (person, mind) into certain state; incline, make willing or desirous, *to*; give (thing) tendency *to*. 3. Determine course of events. 4. ~ *of*, do what one will with, regulate; get off one's hands, stow away, settle, finish, kill, demolish; consume (food); sell.

disposi'tion (-z-) *n.* 1. Setting in order, arrangement, relative position of parts. 2. (usu. pl.) Plan, preparations; stationing of troops for attack, defence, etc. 3. Ordinance, dispensation. 4. Bestowal by deed or will. 5. Control, disposal. 6. Temperament, natural tendency; inclination *to*.

dispossĕss' (-zĕs) *v.t.* Oust, dislodge; deprive *of*; rid (person) of evil spirit. **dispossĕs'sion** (-zĕshn) *n.*

dispraise' (-z) *v.t.* Disparage, censure. ~ *n.* Disparagement, censure.

disproof' *n.* Refutation, thing that disproves.

dispropor'tion *n.* Want of proportion. **dispropor'tionate** (-sho-) *adj.* Wanting proportion; relatively too large or too small. **dispropor'tionately** *adv.* **dispropor'tioned** (-shond) *adj.*

disprove' (-ōōv) *v.t.* Prove false, show fallacy of, refute.

dis'pūtable *adj.* Open to question, uncertain. **dis'pūtably** *adv.*

dis'pūtant *adj.* & *n.* (Person) that disputes, engaged in controversy.

dispūtā'tion *n.* Debate, discussion; exercise in which parties formally sustain, attack, and defend a question or thesis, as in medieval schools and universities. **dispūtā'tious** (-shus) *adj.* **dispūtā'tiously** *adv.* **dispūtā'tiousnėss** *n.*

dispūte' *v.* Argue, hold disputation; quarrel, have altercation; discuss; controvert, call in question; resist; contend for, strive to win. ~ *n.* Controversy, debate; heated contention, quarrel, difference of opinion.

disqual'ifȳ (-ŏl-) *v.t.* Unfit, disable; incapacitate legally; pronounce unqualified (esp. to hold place or prize won in sporting contest). **disqualificā'tion** *n.* (esp.) Thing that disqualifies.

disqui'et *v.t.* Deprive of peace, worry. **disqui'etūde** *n.* Anxiety, unrest.

disquisi'tion (-zi-) *n.* 1. (archaic) Investigation, inquiry. 2. Long or elaborate treatise or discourse (*on* subject). **disquisi'tional** (-sho-) *adj.*

Disraeli (dĭzrāl'ĭ), Benjamin, 1st Earl of Beaconsfield (1804–81). English Tory politician, prime minister 1868 and 1874–80; author of 'Coningsby' (1844) and other novels.

dĭsrāte' *v.t.* (naut.) Reduce to lower rank or rating.

dĭsrėgard' *v.t.* Pay no attention to; ignore; treat as of no importance. ~ *n.* Indifference, neglect.

dĭsrĕl'ish *n.* Dislike, distaste, aversion. ~ *v.t.* Regard with disfavour, dislike.

dĭsrėpair' *n.* Bad condition for want of repairs.

dĭsrĕp'ūtable *adj.* Discreditable; of bad repute, not respectable in character or appearance. **dĭsrĕp'ūtablenėss** *n.* **dĭsrĕp'ūtably** *adv.*

dĭsrėpūte' *n.* Ill repute, discredit.

dĭsrėspĕct' *n.* Want of respect, rudeness. **dĭsrėspĕct'ful** *adj.* **dĭsrėspĕct'fully** *adv.* **dĭsrėspĕct'fulnėss** *n.*

dĭsrōbe' *v.* Divest of robe or garment; undress.

dĭsrŭpt' *v.t.* Shatter, separate forcibly. **dĭsrŭp'tion** *n.* Bursting asunder, violent dissolution; rent condition; *the D~*, the split in the Established Church of Scotland in 1843 when owing to the desire of a large part of the Church 451 of its ministers formed themselves into the Free (Protesting) Church of Scotland. **dĭsrŭp'tĭve** *adj.* **dĭsrŭp'tĭvely** (-vl-) *adv.* **dĭsrŭp'tĭvenėss** *n.*

dĭssăt'ĭsfȳ *v.t.* Fail to satisfy, make discontented. **dĭssătĭsfăc'tion** *n.*

dĭssĕct' *v.t.* Cut up, esp., cut up (animal body, plant, etc.) to display position, structure, and relation of internal parts; analyse, examine or criticize minutely. **dĭssĕc'tion** *n.*

dĭsseise', -ze (-sēz) *v.t.* (law) Put out of seisin (*of*); oust, dispossess. **dĭsseis'ee, dĭsseis'or** *ns.* **dĭsseis'ĭn, -zĭn** *n.* Disseising; usu., wrongful possession of lands etc. of another.

dĭssĕm'ble *v.* Cloak, disguise, conceal; conceal one's opinions, intentions, etc., under feigned guise, play the hypocrite. **dĭssĕm'bler** *n.*

dĭssĕm'ĭnāte *v.t.* Scatter abroad, sow in various places. **dĭssĕmĭnā'tion, dĭssĕm'ĭnātor** *ns.*

dĭssĕn'sion *n.* Discord arising from difference in opinion.

dĭssĕnt' *v.i.* Refuse to assent; disagree; think differently, express different opinion (*from*); esp., differ in religious opinion, differ from doctrine or worship of established, national, or orthodox church. ~ *n.* (Expression of) difference of opinion; refusal to accept doctrines of established church, nonconformity; dissenters collectively.

dĭssĕn'ter *n.* (esp.) Member of dissenting church or sect.

dĭssĕn'tient (-shĭ-, -shnt) *adj.* & *n.* (Person) disagreeing with a majority or official view.

dĭssĕp'ĭmėnt *n.* (bot.) Partition, septum.

dĭssertā'tion *n.* Spoken or written discourse treating a subject at length; treatise.

dĭssērv'ĭce *n.* Rendering of ill service or ill turn; injury, detriment.

dĭssĕv'er *v.* Sever, divide.

dĭss'ĭdence *n.* Disagreement, dissent.

dĭss'ĭdent *adj.* Disagreeing, at variance; dissentient. ~ *n.* Dissenter; dissentient.

dĭssĭm'ĭlar *adj.* Unlike (*to*). **dĭssĭmĭlă'rĭty** *n.* **dĭssĭm'ĭlarly** *adv.*

dĭssĭm'ĭlāte *v.* Make, become, unlike. **dĭssĭmĭlā'tion** *n.* (esp.) Differentiation of two identical or similar sounds occurring near each other in a word, by changing one of them (as when older *cinnamom* is changed to *cinnamon*).

dĭssĭmĭl'ĭtūde *n.* Unlikeness.

dĭssĭm'ūlāte *v.* Dissemble (feelings etc.); be hypocritical. **dĭssĭmūlā'tion, dĭssĭm'ūlātor** *ns.*

dĭss'ĭpāte *v.* Dispense, dispel (cloud, vapour, etc.); disappear; dissolve to atoms, bring or come to nothing; squander, fritter away (money, time, etc.). **dĭss'ĭpātėd** *adj.* (esp.) Given to dissipation, dissolute.

dĭssĭpā'tion *n.* 1. Scattering, dispersion, disintegration; wasteful expenditure *of*. 2. Diversion, amusement; distraction of attention; frivolous amusement. 3. Intemperate or vicious living.

dĭssō'ciāte (-shĭ-) *v.t.* Disunite, sunder, cut off from association or society; (chem.) decompose, esp. by heat. **dĭssōciā'tion** (-sĭ-) *n.* (esp.) Disintegration *of* personality or consciousness; pathological state of mind in which two or more personalities exist in the same person. **dĭssō'ciative** (-sh*a*-) *adj.*

dĭss'oluble (-ŏŏbl; *or* -ŏl'ūbl) *adj.* That can be disintegrated, loosed, or disconnected. **dĭssolubĭl'ĭty** *n.*

dĭss'olute (-ōōt, -ūt) *adj.* Lax in morals, licentious. **dĭss'olutely** *adv.* **dĭss'olutenėss** *n.*

dĭssolu'tion (-ōō-, -ū-) *n.* 1. Disintegration, decomposition. 2. Undoing or relaxation of any tie or bond; dismissal, dispersal, of assembly, esp. of a parliament for new election. 3. Death; coming, being brought, to an end; disintegration, disorganization.

dĭssŏlve' (-z-) *v.* 1. Melt; (physics) of a liquid, mix with (a solid, another liquid, or a gas) without chemical action so as to form a homogeneous liquid or solution; of a substance, mix thus *in* a liquid. 2. Bring to nought, undo, destroy, consume; become faint, melt *away*. 3. Disperse; bring (constituted body, esp. Parliament), come, to an end. 4. Cause (cinematograph or magic-lantern picture) to fade *into* another; fade thus. ~ *n.* Dissolving picture, apparatus for producing this. **dĭssŏl'vent** *adj.* & *n.* (Thing) having power to dissolve other things, solvent.

dĭss'onant *adj.* Discordant, harsh-toned, incongruous. **dĭss'onantly** *adv.* **dĭss'onance** *n.*

dĭssuade' (-swād) *v.t.* Advise (person) against; divert *from* course by suasion or influence. **dĭssuā'sion** (-zhn) *n.* **dĭssuās'ĭve** *adj.* **dĭssuās'ĭvely** *adv.* **dĭssuās'ĭvenėss** *n.*

dĭs'taff (-ahf) *n.* Cleft staff about 3 ft long on which wool or flax was wound for spinning by hand; corresponding part of hand spinning-wheel (ill. SPINNING); women's work or occupation; ~ *side*, female branch of family.

dĭs'tal *adj.* (anat., bot.) Away from centre of body or point of attachment, terminal.

dĭs'tance *n.* 1. Being far off, remoteness; extent of space between, interval. 2. Aloofness; *keep* one's ~, avoid familiarity. 3. Distant point; remote field of vision; distant part of landscape; *middle* ~, part between foreground and remote part. 4. Space of time. ~ *v.t.* Place, make seem, far off; leave far behind in race or competition.

dĭs'tant *adj.* 1. Far away (*from*); a specified distance away (*from*); remote, far apart, in position, time, resemblance, etc.; ~ *signal* (railways), signal some distance in advance of home signal and agreeing with it in position. 2. Reserved, cool, not intimate. **dĭs'tantly** *adv.*

dĭstāste' *n.* Dislike, repugnance, slight aversion (*for*). **dĭstāste'ful** (-tf-) *adj.* Disagreeable, repellent (*to*). **dĭstāste'fully** *adv.* **dĭstāste'fulnėss** *n.*

dĭstĕm'per[1] *v.t.* (usu. in past part.) Upset, derange, in health or sanity. ~ *n.* 1. Derangement, ailment, of body or mind. 2. Disease of dogs characterized by catarrh, cough, and loss of strength.

dĭstĕm'per[2] *n.* Method of painting on plaster etc. with powder colours mixed with size or other glue soluble in water, used chiefly in scene-painting and internal decoration of house-walls; the pigment used for this. ~ *v.t.* Paint with distemper.

dĭstĕnd' *v.* Swell out by pressure from within. **dĭstĕn'sĭble** *adj.* **dĭstĕn'sion** (-shn) *n.*

dĭs'tĭch (-k) *n.* Pair of lines of verse, couplet.

dĭstĭl' *v.* 1. Trickle down; issue, give forth, in drops or fine moisture, exude. 2. Vaporize substance by means of heat, and then condense the vapour by cooling it, so as to obtain the substance or part of it in concentrated or purified state; extract essence of, transform or convert, make or produce, drive *off*, by distillation; undergo distillation.

distillā'tion *n.* (esp.) Extraction of spirit or essence of any substance by first converting into vapour and then condensing the vapour; *dry, destructive,* ~, decomposition of substance by strong heat in a retort, and collection of volatile matters evolved; *fractional* ~, separation by distillation of two or more liquids having different boiling-points, utilizing the fact that the first portion or fraction of the distillate has a higher proportion of the more volatile liquid than later fractions. **distill'atory** *adj.*

distill'er *n.* (esp.) 1. One who distils, esp. alcoholic spirit. 2. Apparatus for distilling salt water at sea. **distill'ery** *n.* Establishment for distilling spirits.

distinct' *adj.* 1. Not identical, separate, individual; different in quality or kind, unlike. 2. Clearly perceptible, plain, definite; unmistakable, decided, positive. **distinct'ly** *adv.* **distinct'nėss** *n.*

distinc'tion *n.* 1. Making of a difference; discrimination; the difference made; ~ *without a difference,* merely nominal or artificial distinction. 2. Being different. 3. Thing that differentiates; mark, name, title. 4. Showing of special consideration, mark of honour. 5. Distinguished character, excellence, eminence; individuality.

distinc'tive *adj.* Distinguishing, characteristic. **distinc'tively** *adv.* **distinc'tivenėss** *n.*

distingué (dēstăṅ'gā) *adj.* Of distinguished air, features, manners, etc.

disting'uish (-nggwĭsh) *v.* 1. Class, classify. 2. Mark as different or distinct, differentiate, characterize. 3. Recognize as distinct or different; perceive difference, make or draw distinction, *between.* 4. Perceive distinctly, recognize. 5. Notice specially, honour with special attention; make prominent, remarkable, or eminent in some respect (usu. *pass.* or *refl.*). **disting'uishable** *adj.* **disting'uishably** *adv.*

disting'uished (-nggwĭsht) *adj.* (esp.) Remarkable (*for, by*); eminent, famous, of high standing; *D~ Conduct Medal* (abbrev. D.C.M.), medal awarded to warrant and non-commissioned officers and men in the army and R.A.F. for distinguished conduct in the field, instituted 1862; *D~ Flying Cross* (abbrev. D.F.C.), order bestowed on officers and warrant officers in the R.A.F. and Fleet Air Arm for acts of gallantry when flying in active operations against the enemy, instituted 1918; *D~ Flying Medal* (abbrev. D.F.M.), medal for warrant and non-commissioned officers and men in R.A.F. and Fleet Air Arm for equivalent services as for D.F.C.; *D~ Service Cross* (abbrev. D.S.C.), order bestowed on officers of the R.N. below rank of captain, and for warrant officers; *D~ Service Medal* (abbrev. D.S.M.), medal awarded to members of the services afloat below rank of commissioned officer, instituted 1914; *D~ Service Order* (abbrev. D.S.O.), order of distinction bestowed for especial services in action on British naval, military, and air-force commissioned officers, instituted 1886 (ill. MEDAL).

distort' *v.t.* Put out of shape, make crooked or unshapely; misrepresent. **distort'ėdly** *adv.*

distor'tion *n.* Distorting, being distorted; (in gramophone, wireless receiver, etc.) faulty transmission or reproduction arising from variations in sensitivity under different conditions. **distor'tional** (-sho-) *adj.*

distrăct' *v.t.* Divert, draw away (mind, attention); draw in different directions, divide or confuse the attention of; bewilder, perplex; drive mad, infuriate. **distrăc'tėdly, distrăc'tingly** *advs.*

distrăc'tion *n.* 1. Diversion of mind or attention; something that distracts or diverts; interruption; amusement. 2. Lack of concentration. 3. Confusion, perplexity, internal conflict, dissension; frenzy, madness; *to* ~, to a mad degree.

distrain' *v.* (law) Levy a distress (*upon*), seize chattels of person in order to make him pay debt (esp. rent) or perform obligation, or to obtain satisfaction by selling the chattels; seize (chattels etc.) by way of distress. **distraint'** *n.* Distraining, distress.

distrait' (-trā) *adj.* (fem. *-te* pr. -āt). Absent-minded, not attending.

distraught' (-awt) *adj.* Violently agitated.

distrĕss' *n.* 1. Severe pressure or strain of pain, sorrow, etc., anguish, affliction; damage or danger to ship; exhausted or distressed condition; misfortune, calamity; ~ *signal,* signal of ship in distress. 2. (law) Legal seizure and detention of chattel, distraining. **distrĕss'ful** *adj.* **distrĕss'fully** *adv.*

distrĕss' *v.t.* Subject to severe strain, exhaust, afflict; vex, make anxious or unhappy. **distrĕss'ing** *adj.* **distrĕss'ingly** *adv.*

distrĭb'ūtary *n.* River branch which does not return to main stream after leaving it.

distrĭb'ūte *v.t.* Deal out, give share of to each of a number; spread abroad, scatter, put at different points; divide into parts, arrange, classify; (logic) use (term) in its full extension, so that it includes every individual of the class. **distrĭb'ūtor** *n.*

distribū'tion *n.* 1. Distributing, being distributed. 2. (esp., econ.) Dispersal among consumers effected by commerce; extent to which individuals or classes share in aggregate products of community. 3. Way in which a particular character is spread over members of a class, usually represented graphically by a ~ *curve.* **distribū'tional** (-sho-) *adj.*

distrĭb'ūtive *adj.* 1. Of, concerned with, produced by, distribution; ~ *trades,* all the trades (wholesale and retail) which obtain goods from manufacturers and sell them to consumers. 2. (logic, gram.) Referring to each individual of a class, not to the class collectively. ~ *n.* (gram.) Distributive word. **distrĭb'ūtively** *adv.*

dis'trict *n.* Territory marked off for special administrative purpose; assigned sphere of operations; tract of country with common characteristics, region; division of parish with its own church or chapel and clergyman; urban or rural subdivision of county, having an Urban or Rural District Council. (U.S. etc.) electoral constituency; in some States, subdivision of county, in others, division of State including several counties; ~ *attorney,* (U.S.) local public prosecutor of a district; ~ *commissioner, officer,* representative of Government in a colonial district; ~ *nurse,* nurse employed in a rural or urban district to visit patients in their homes; ~ *visitor,* person working under clergyman's direction in a section of a parish. ~ *v.t.* (chiefly U.S.) Divide into districts.

Dis'trict of Colŭm'bia (abbrev. D.C.). Federal division of U.S., including city of Washington, directly under control of Congress.

distrŭst' *n.* Want of trust, doubt, suspicion. ~ *v.t.* Have no confidence in, doubt, not rely on. **distrŭst'ful** *adj.* **distrŭst'fully** *adv.* **distrŭst'fulnėss** *n.*

distûrb' *v.t.* Agitate, trouble, disquiet, unsettle; perplex.

distûrb'ance *n.* Interruption of tranquillity, agitation; tumult, uproar, outbreak; (law) molestation, interference with rights or property.

dis'tȳle *adj.* & *n.* (Portico) of 2 columns; ~ *in antis*: see ill. TEMPLE.

disŭl'phīde *n.* Sulphide containing 2 atoms of sulphur.

disūn'ion (-yon) *n.* Separation, want of union, dissension. **disūnīte'** *v.t.* **disūn'ity** *n.*

disūse' (-s) *n.* Discontinuance, want of use or practice, desuetude.

disūse' (-z) *v.t.* Cease to use.

disȳll'able, diss- *n.* Word, metrical foot, of 2 syllables. **dis(s)ȳllăb'ic** *adj.* **dis(s)ȳllăb'ically** *adv.*

ditch *n.* Long narrow excavation, esp. to hold or conduct water or serve as boundary; watercourse; (R.A.F. slang) North Sea or English Channel; *~-water,* stagnant water in ditch. ~ *v.* Make or repair ditches; provide with ditches, drain; run, drive (vehicle) into ditch or off track or road; (R.A.F. slang) make forced landing on sea; (slang) leave in the lurch. **ditch'er** *n.* (esp. in *hedger and* ~) One who makes or mends ditches.

dīth'ėism *n.* Religious dualism; esp. belief in two independent antagonistic principles of good and evil.

dĭth'er (-dh-) *v.i.* Tremble, quiver; hesitate. ~ *n.* Dithering; tremulous excitement or apprehension.

dĭth'y̆rămb (-m) *n.* 1. (Gk antiq.) Wild choric hymn (orig. in honour of Dionysus) from which Greek tragedy is believed to have evolved. 2. Vehement or inflated poem, speech, or writing. **dĭthy̆răm'bĭc** *adj.*

dĭtt'any *n.* Perennial herb of genus *Dictamnus*, esp. *D. Creticus*, formerly thought to have medicinal virtues in healing wounds etc., and *D. albus*, the burning bush, which in hot weather gives off inflammable vapours.

dĭtt'ō *adj.* (abbrev. do, d°) The aforesaid, the same (used in accounts and lists, or colloq.). ~ *n.* (pl. -*s*). Duplicate, similar thing; *suit of ditto(s)*, man's suit of one material and colour. [It. *ditto* (now *detto*) said, aforesaid]

dĭttŏg'raphy *n.* (palaeography etc.) Unintentional repetition of letter(s) or word(s) by copyist. **dĭttogrăph'ĭc** *adj.*

dĭtt'y *n.* Short simple song.

dĭtt'y-băg *n.* Sailor's bag for holding odds and ends. **dĭtt'y-bŏx** *n.* Fisherman's box for same purpose.

dīūrēs'ĭs *n.* Passing of urine in large amounts. **dīūrĕt'ĭc** *adj.* & *n.* (Substance) stimulating kidneys to secrete urine.

dīūr'n'al *adj.* Occupying one day (chiefly of apparent motion of heavenly bodies); performed, happening, recurring, every day; of the day as dist. from the night; (zool.) active in day-time. **dīūrn'ally** *adv.*

dĭv'agāte *v.i.* Stray, digress. **dīvagā'tion** *n.*

dīvāl'ent (*or* dĭv'*a*-) *adj.* (chem.) Having a VALENCY of 2, bivalent.

dĭvăn' *n.* 1. Oriental council of State; in Turkey, (hist.) privy council of the Porte, presided over by Sultan or grand vizier; oriental council-chamber, court of justice. 2. (*also* dī'văn) Long seat against wall of room, usu. furnished with cushions to form ~ (*bed*), low bed without head-piece. 3. Smoking-room attached to cigar-shop or bar; cigar-shop. [Pers. *dīwān* account-book, custom-house, court, council, etc.]

dīvă'rĭcāte (*or* dĭ-) *v.i.* Diverge, branch. **dīvă'rĭcate** (-*at*) *adj.*

dīve *v.i.* Plunge, esp. head foremost, into water etc.; go down or out of sight suddenly, dart; (of aeroplane etc.) descend steeply and fast; (of submarine) submerge; plunge hand *into* water, vessel, pocket; plunge *into* subject; *diving-bell*, open-bottomed box or bell in which person can be let down into deep water; *diving-suit*, air- and water-tight garment (with lead-soled boots and glass-fronted helmet, and apparatus for pumping in air) in which person can go down into deep water and remain under water for some time; *diving-helmet*, headgear of diving-dress. ~ *n.* Diving; plunge, header, precipitate fall; (of aeroplane) steep descent; (orig. U.S.) underground or basement room of restaurant, inn, etc. where some speciality as wine, oysters, etc., is sold; ~-*bomb* (*v.t.*) attack from aircraft with bombs released at end of a steep dive; ~-*bomber*, aircraft designed for dive-bombing.

dīv'er *n.* (esp.) 1. One who dives for pearls, to examine and repair sunk vessels or to recover valuable cargo. 2. Water-bird, esp. of the family *Colymbidae*, remarkable for their power of diving and the distance they traverse under water.

dīvĕrge' (*or* dĭ-) *v.* Proceed in different directions from point or from each other; take different courses; deviate; cause (lines, rays) to diverge; (math.) of a series, approach in its sum to an indefinitely great amount when a large number of terms is taken. **dīvĕr'gence** *n.* **dīvĕr'gent** *adj.* **dīvĕr'gently** *adv.*

dīv'ers (-z) *adj.* (archaic) Sundry, several, more than one.

dīvĕrse' *adj.* Unlike in nature or qualities; varied, changeful. **dīvĕrse'ly** (-sl-) *adv.* **dīvĕrse'nĕss** *n.*

dīvĕrs'ĭfy̆ *v.t.* Make diverse, vary, modify, variegate. **dīvĕrsĭfĭcā'tion** *n.*

dīvĕr'sion (*or* dĭ-) *n.* 1. Deflecting, deviation. 2. Diverting of attention; manœuvre to secure this; feint. 3. Recreation, pleasant distraction, pastime.

dīvĕrs'ĭty (*or* dĭ-) *n.* Being diverse, unlikeness; different kind; variety.

dīvĕrt' (*or* dĭ-) *v.t.* Turn aside from (proper) direction or course; deflect; avert, ward off; draw off attention of, distract; entertain, amuse. **dīvĕrt'ĭng** *adj.* **dīvĕrt'ĭngly** *adv.*

divertissement (dēvertēs'mahṅ) *n.* Short ballet or dance given between acts or longer pieces.

Dī'vĕs (-z). Latin word for 'rich man', occurring in Vulgate, Luke xvi, whence commonly taken for the name of the rich man in that parable.

dīvĕst' (*or* dĭ-) *v.t.* Unclothe; strip *of* garment etc.; deprive, rid, *of*. **dīvĕst'ment, dīvĕs'tĭture** *ns.*

dĭvĭ. Colloq. abbrev. of DIVIDEND.

dĭvīde' *v.* 1. Separate into parts or smaller groups, split, break up; mark out actually or mentally into parts; make classification in, distinguish kinds of; sunder, part, cut off (*from*). 2. Cause to disagree; set at variance; distract. 3. Distribute, deal out, (*among*, *between*); share *with* others. 4. (math.) Find how many times a number is contained in another; (of number or quantity) be contained exact number of times in (another). 5. Part (legislative assembly etc.) into two sets in voting; (of assembly) part itself thus. ~ *n.* (U.S. etc.) Watershed; *The Great D~*, watershed of Rocky Mountains; (fig.) dividing line, esp. between life and death.

dĭv'ĭdĕnd *n.* 1. (math.) Number to be divided by another (called the *divisor*). 2. Sum to be divided among a number of persons, payable as interest on loan, profit of joint-stock company, or sum paid to creditors of insolvent estate; amount received by individual holder or creditor as his share; ~-*warrant*, document authorizing shareholder to receive dividend.

dĭvīd'er *n.* (esp., pl.) Compasses having a screw fastened to one leg and passing through the other, used for measuring small intervals, and for dividing straight lines etc. into any desired number of equal parts (ill. COMPASS); simple pair of compasses with steel points.

dĭvĭnā'tion *n.* Divining; insight into or discovery of unknown or future by supernatural means; skilful forecast, good guess.

dĭvīne'[1] *v.* Make out by inspiration, magic, intuition, or guessing; foresee, predict, conjecture; practise divination; *divining-rod*, dowser's rod. **dĭvīn'er** *n.*

dĭvīne'[2] *adj.* Of, from, like, God or a god; ~ *right of kings*, that claimed according to doctrine that (legitimate) kings derive their power from God alone, unlimited by any rights of their subjects. 2. Devoted or addressed to God; sacred; ~ *service*, public worship of God. 3. Superhumanly excellent, gifted, or beautiful. **dĭvīne'ly** (-nl-) *adv.* **dĭvīne'** *n.* Person (usu. cleric) skilled in divinity, theologian.

dĭvĭn'ĭty *n.* 1. Being divine; godhood; a god, deity; godhead. 2. Object of adoration, adorable being. 3. Science of divine things, theology; theological faculty in universities.

dĭv'ĭnīze *v.t.* Deify. **dĭvĭnīzā'tion** *n.*

dĭvĭs'ĭble (-z-) *adj.* Capable of being divided; (math.) ~ *by*, containing (a number) some number of times without remainder. **dĭvĭsĭbĭl'ĭty** *n.*

dĭvĭ'sion (-zhn) *n.* 1. Dividing, being divided; severance, separation; distribution, sharing; ~ *of labour*, division of process of manufacture etc. into parts, each performed by particular person or group. 2. Disagreement, discord. 3. (math.) Process of dividing number by another; *long* ~, method usu. adopted when divisor is greater than 12. 4. (logic) Classification, esp. that based on ordinary knowledge, not on methodical investigation; enumeration of parts; distinction of meaning. 5. Separation of members of legislative body into two parts for counting votes. 6. Dividing line, boundary. 7. Part, section; administrative, judicial, political, or other, division of country, territory, district, etc. 8.

Definite part, under single command, of army or fleet; unit of an army intended to be capable of independent operations, varying greatly in size and composition but usu. consisting of 3 brigades and including infantry, (mechanized) cavalry, artillery, signals, engineers, etc., all under the command of a major-general; (also) specialized arm of military force, as *armoured* ~; (also) a portion of a ship's company appropriated to a particular service; (also, pl.) the parade of a ship's company according to its divisions. 9. (bot.) Major classificatory grouping, = PHYLUM; (zool.) subsidiary category between major groups, e.g. between phylum and class. 10. Any of several grades of civil servants. 11. Any of 3 grades of imprisonment to which judge may sentence offender, the *3rd* ~ being the most severe. **divĭ'sional** (-zho-) *adj.* **divĭ'sionally** *adv.*

dīvīs'or (-z-) *n.* Number by which another (the *dividend*) is to be divided; number that divides another without remainder, factor.

divôrce' *n.* Legal dissolution of marriage; (fig.) complete separation, disunion of things closely connected. ~ *v.t.* Legally dissolve marriage between; separate by divorce *from*; put away, repudiate, obtain divorce from (spouse); dissolve (union); sever. **divôrcee'** *n.* (also *divorcé*, fem. *-cée*) Divorced person. **divôrce'ment** (-sm-) *n.*

dĭv'ot *n.* Turf, sod (Sc.); (golf) piece of turf cut out by player's club when striking the ball.

dīvŭlge' (-j; *or* dĭ-) *v.t.* Let out, reveal. **dīvŭlgā'tion** (-g-), **dīvŭlge'ment** (-jm-), **dīvŭl'gence** *ns.*

dĭvv'y. Colloq. abbrev. of DIVIDEND.

dĭx'ie[1], **dĭx'y** *n.* Iron kettle or pot used by soldiers etc. for making tea or stew. [Hind. *degchi* cooking-pot]

Dĭx'ie[2], **Dixie's Land.** The southern States of U.S., 'the South', the cotton-growing country; also, a popular marching song (prob. composed by Dan Emmett, 1859) sung by Confederate soldiers in the Amer. Civil War. **Dĭx'iecrăt** *n.* Member of the U.S. Democratic party who insists on the maintenance of white superiority over Negroes in the southern States. [origin doubtful; perh. f. *dixie* (Fr. *dix* ten), a 10-dollar note issued in Louisiana before the Civil War; or f. Jeremiah *Dixon*, who with Charles Mason made a survey 1763–7 and drew the MASON AND DIXON LINE which later formed part of the boundary between the slave-owning and free States]

dĭz'en *v.t.* Array with finery, deck *out*, *up*.

dĭzz'y *adj.* Giddy, dazed, unsteady, tottering, confused; making giddy; whirling rapidly. **dĭzz'ily** *adv.* **dĭzz'inėss** *n.* **dĭzz'y** *v.t.* Make dizzy, bewilder.

Djakar̄t'a. City and seaport of NE. Java, capital of Indonesia.

djibbah: see JIBBAH.

dkg., dkl., dkm. *abbrevs.* Decagram, decalitre, decametre.

dl. *abbrev.* Decilitre.

D.L. *abbrev.* Deputy Lieutenant.

D.Lit. *abbrev.* Doctor of Literature; **D.Litt.** Doctor Literarum (= Doctor of Letters).

dm. *abbrev.* Decimetre.

D.M. *abbrev.* Deutsche Mark; Doctor of Medicine.

D.M.I. *abbrev.* Director of Military Intelligence.

D.Mus. *abbrev.* Doctor of Music.

D.N.B. *abbrev.* Dictionary of National Biography.

D.N.I. *abbrev.* Director of Naval Intelligence.

Dniep'er. Russian river flowing from White Russia through Ukraine to Black Sea.

Dnies'ter. River flowing SE. from province of Lwow, between Ukraine and Rumania to Black Sea.

do[1] (do͞o) *v.* (past t. *did*, past part. *done* pr. dŭn). 1. (*v.t.*) Perform, effect, execute; complete; produce, make; operate on, deal with; (colloq.) swindle. 2. (*v.i.*) Act, proceed; perform deeds; fare, get on; be suitable, suffice. 3. Used as auxiliary verb esp. in questions (as *do you know?*), negative or emphatic statements (as *I did not know*; *I do know*), and urgent requests (as *do come!*). 4. Used as substitute for verb just used, to avoid repetition, as *I wanted to see him, and I did* (i.e. saw him). 5. With noun of action as object, = cognate verb of action; e.g. *do writing*, write; *do repairs*, repair things; *do battle*, fight. 6. Phrases and combinations: *to-do*, (*n.*) bustle, fuss; *well-to-do*, comparatively wealthy; *have to do with*, be concerned or connected with, have dealings with; *nothing* etc. *doing*, nothing etc. happening or going on; (colloq.) announcement of refusal, failure, etc.; *done!*, it's a bargain!, I accept!; *it isn't done*, it is bad form, or forbidden by custom or propriety; *done brown*, duped, swindled; *done up*, tired; *do-nothing*, idler, idle; *do away* (*with*), abolish; *do by*, treat, deal with, in specified way; *do down*, overcome, get the better of, bring to grief; *do for*, (colloq.) do house-cleaning for; ruin, destroy, kill; *do in*, (slang) kill; exhaust; *do time*, *do* (10 etc.) *years*, undergo imprisonment; *do to*, *unto*, do by; *do to death*, kill; *do up*, restore, repair; wrap up (parcel); *do with*, get on with, tolerate; find sufficient; *do without*, dispense with; *done in*, *done up*, tired out. ~ *n.* (slang) Swindle, imposture, hoax; entertainment, show. **do'able** *adj.* **do'er** *n.*

dō[2], **dōh** *n.* (mus.) First note of hexachord and keynote of major scale in 'movable-doh' systems; note C in 'fixed-doh' system.

do *abbrev.* DITTO.

dŏbb'in *n.* Draught- or farm-horse. [pet-form of *Robert*]

dŏbb'y *n.* Mechanism attached to loom for weaving small figures.

Dōb'erman pĭn'scher (-sh-). Large terrier with long forelegs and smooth black-and-tan or bluish coat, of breed orig. produced in Thuringia, Germany. [*Dobermann*, name of breeder; Ger. *pinscher* terrier]

Dobru'dja (-bro͞o-). **SE.** part of Rumania between lower Danube and Black Sea.

Docēt'ae *n.pl.* Early sect of Christian heretics who held that Christ's body was not human but a phantom or of celestial substance. **Docēt'ic** *adj.* **Docēt'ism** *n.* [Gk *dokeein* seem, appear]

dō'cīle (*or* (chiefly U.S.) -ĭl) *adj.* Teachable; submissive; easily managed. **docĭl'ity** *n.*

dŏck[1] *n.* Various species of *Rumex*, coarse weedy herbs with panicled racemes of inconspicuous greenish flowers, and large leaves used as popular antidote for nettle-stings.

dŏck[2] *n.* Solid fleshy part of animal's tail (ill. HORSE); crupper of saddle or harness. ~ *v.t.* Cut short (animal in tail, person in hair; or tail etc.); lessen, deprive *of*; put limits on.

dŏck[3] *n.* 1. Artificial basin fitted with flood-gates into which ships are received for loading or unloading, or for repairs; *dry*, *graving*, ~, dock from which water may be pumped out, leaving vessel dry for repairs etc.; *floating* ~, floating structure usable as dry dock; *wet* ~, dock in which water is kept at high-tide level. 2. (pl.) Range of docks with wharves, warehouses, offices, etc.; dockyard. 3. (theatr.) Enclosure at side of stage for scenery. 4. *~-dues*, charges for use of docks; *~-glass*, large glass for wine-tasting; *~-land*, districts about the London docks; *~-master*, superintendent of dock or dockyard; *dock'yard*, enclosure for building and repairing ships, preparing and collecting ships' stores, etc.; esp. Government dockyard for navy. ~ *v.* Bring (ship), come, into dock; furnish with docks. (*Illustration, p.* 236.)

dŏck[4] *n.* Enclosure in criminal court for prisoner on trial; ~ *brief*, brief handed direct to barrister in court by prisoner entitled to legal aid.

dŏck'er *n.* Labourer in DOCK[3].

dŏck'ėt *n.* 1. Abstract, summary (hist.); abstract of contents of proposed letters patent, written upon king's bill authorizing preparation of such letters. 2. (law) Memorandum or register of legal judgements; (U.S.) list of causes for trial or of persons with causes pending. 3. Endorsement on letter etc. indicating contents or subject; label, ticket; (in some govt departments) set of papers on given subject, file. 4. Custom-house warrant certifying payment of duty;

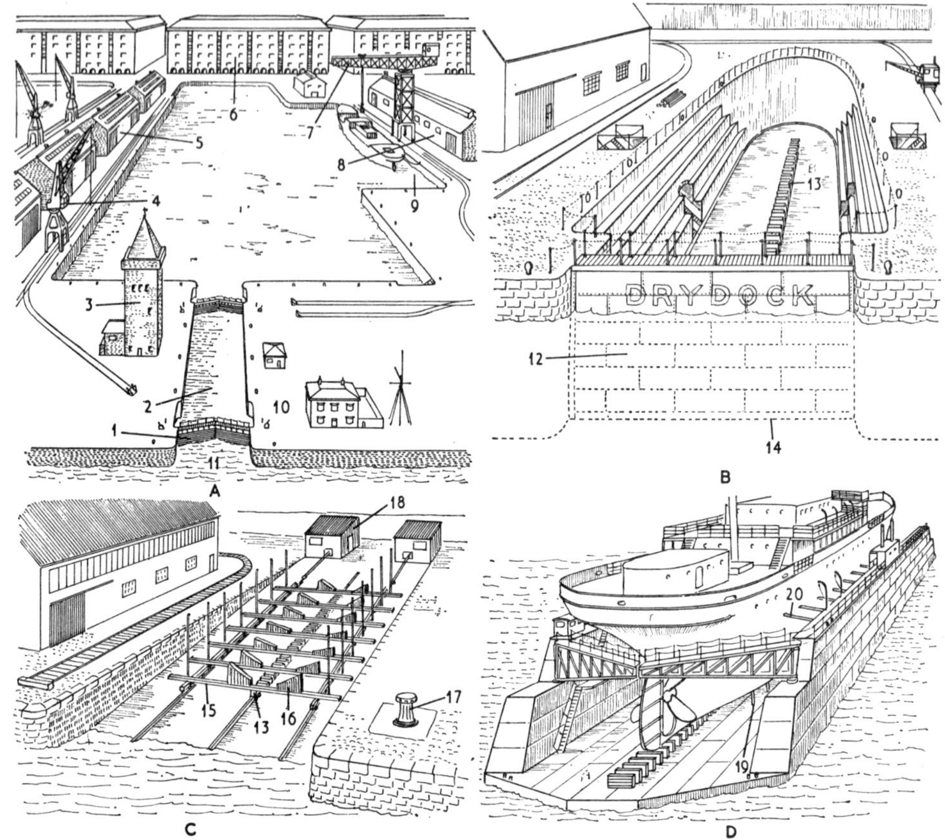

DOCKS: A. WET DOCK. B. DRY DOCK. C. PATENT SLIPWAY. D. FLOATING DOCK

A. 1. Lock gate. 2. Lock. 3. Power house. 4. Travelling dock crane. 5. Dock sheds. 6. Warehouses. 7. Fitting-out crane. 8. Workshops. 9. Fitting basin. 10. Offices. 11. Tidal water. B. 12. Caisson. 13. Keel blocks. 14. Dock sill. C. 15. Travelling cradle on bogies. 16. Adjustable bilge chocks. 17. Capstan. 18. Winch houses. D. 19. Bilge shores. 20. Side shores

certificate of cotton clearing-house entitling presenter to delivery. 5. Workman's record of jobs done during day or week. ~ *v.t.* Make abstract of and enter in docket; endorse (letter etc.) with docket; (U.S.) enter (cause) in docket.

dŏc'tor *n.* 1. Teacher, eminently learned man (archaic). 2. (used as prefix to name, usu. abbrev. Dr) Holder of highest university degree in any faculty; esp., doctor of medicine; (pop.) any medical practitioner. 3. Various mechanical appliances for removing defects, regulating, adjusting, etc. 4. Various local winds which modify extremes of climate. 5. = SURGEON-fish. 6. Ship's cook; cook at lumber-camp etc. 7. *D~s' Commons,* (hist.) common table of former College of Doctors of Civil Law in London; its buildings, the courts held there, where probate and divorce business was transacted; *~'s mandate,* (pol.) commission to administration to prescribe whatever remedies it thinks fit in emergency; *D~s of the Church,* certain early Christian fathers distinguished for their learning and heroic sanctity, esp. Ambrose, Augustine, Jerome, and Gregory in the Western Church, and Athanasius, Basil, Gregory of Nazianzus, and Chrysostom in the Eastern Church. **dŏc'toral, dŏctōr'ial** *adjs.* **dŏc'tor** *v.* Treat medically; castrate; patch up (machinery etc.); adulterate, falsify; *doctoring,* practising as physician.

dŏc'torate *n.* Degree of doctor.

dŏctrĭnaire', -nār'ĭan *ns.* One who holds some doctrine or theory and tries to apply it without allowing for circumstances; pedantic theorist. ~ *adj.* Of, like, a doctrinaire; theoretic, unpractical. **dŏctrĭnair'ism** *n.* [*Doctrinaire,* name of a Fr. political party, 1815]

dŏctrīn'al (*or* dŏc'trĭ-) *adj.* Of, inculcating, doctrine(s). **dŏctrīn'ally** *adv.*

dŏc'trĭne *n.* What is taught, body of instruction; religious, political, scientific, etc., belief, dogma, or tenet; *Monroe D~*: see MONROE. **dŏc'trĭnism, dŏc'trĭnist** *ns.*

dŏc'ūment *n.* Something written, inscribed, etc., which furnishes evidence or information upon any subject, as manuscript, title-deed, coin, etc. ~ *v.t.* Prove or support by documentary evidence; furnish or provide with documents or evidence; keep well informed. **dŏcūmĕn'tary** *adj.* Of documents; *adj.* & *n.* (cinema film) dealing with real happenings or circumstances, not fiction. **dŏcūmĕntā'tion** *n.*

dŏdd'er[1] *n.* Any of the genus *Cuscuta* of slender leafless parasitic plants like masses of twining threads.

dŏdd'er[2] *v.i.* Tremble, nod, with frailty. **dŏdd'erer** *n.* **dŏdd'erĭng** *adj.* Mentally feeble or inept, futile.

dŏdĕca- *prefix.* Twelve-.

dōdĕc'agon *n.* Plane figure of 12 sides.

dōdėcahĕd'ron *n.* Solid figure of 12 faces (ill. SOLID).

Dōdėcanēse' (-z). Group of 12 islands in SE. Aegean occupied by Italy in 1912 during the war with Turkey, and ceded to Greece in 1947.

dōdėcasÿll'able *n.* (prosody) Line of 12 syllables.

dŏdge *v.* 1. Move to and fro, change position, shuffle; move quickly *round, about, behind,* obstacle so as to elude pursuer, blow, etc.; avoid, elude, by change of position, shifts, doubling, etc. 2. (of bell in change-ringing) Be shifted one place in opposite direction instead of following its regular ascending or descending order. ~ *n.* Dodging, quick side-movement, trick, artifice; (colloq.) clever expedient, contrivance, etc.; (change-ringing) act of dodging.

dŏdg'er *n.* (esp.) 1. Artful or elusive person. 2. (colloq.) Screen on ship's bridge as protection from spray etc. 3. (U.S.) Small handbill or circular. 4. (U.S.) small hard cake of Indian meal.

Dŏdg'son, Charles Lutwidge (1832–98). English mathematician, celebrated as author, under his pseudonym Lewis Carroll, of 'Alice's Adventures in Wonderland' (1865) and 'Through the Looking-Glass' (1872).

dōd'ō *n.* (pl. *-oes, -os*). Extinct bird, *Didus ineptus,* with massive

DODO
Length approx. 18 in.

clumsy body and wings too small for flight, formerly inhabiting Mauritius. [Port. *doudo* simpleton]

dōe *n.* Female of fallow deer, hare, or rabbit; *doe'skin,* skin of doe, kind of leather made from this.

dŏff *v.t.* Take off (hat, clothing).

dŏg *n.* 1. Carnivorous quadruped of the genus *Canis,* found wild in various parts of the world, and domesticated or semi-domesticated in almost all countries, in numerous races or breeds varying greatly in shape, size, and colour. (*Illustration, p.* 238.) 2. Male of this animal, or of fox or wolf. 3. (also *gay* ~) gay or jovial fellow; *dirty* ~, (colloq.) despicable person. 4. Each of two constellations, the *Greater* and *Lesser D*~ (*Canis Major* and *Minor*) near Orion; the principal stars of these, Sirius in the Greater Dog (the brightest fixed star) and Procyon in the Lesser Dog. 5. Various mechanical devices, usu. having a tooth or claw for gripping or holding. 6. One of a pair of metal utensils (*fire-*~*s*) placed one at each side of fireplace to support burning wood, or a grate (ill. FIRE); rest for fire-arms. 7. (also *sea-*~) Luminous appearance near horizon, supposed to presage bad weather; *sun-*~, parhelion. 8. Phrases: *to the dogs,* to destruction or ruin; *die like a* ~, die miserably or shamefully; *a dog's chance,* the slightest chance; *a dog's life,* a life of misery, or of miserable subserviency; *a hair of the* ~ *that bit you,* more drink to take off effects of drunkenness; ~ *in the manger,* one who prevents others enjoying what is useless to him. 9. *dog'berry,* fruit of dogwood; ~ *biscuit,* hard biscuit for feeding dogs; ~*-cart,* two-wheeled driving-cart with two transverse seats back to back (the rear one orig. made to shut so as to form a box for dogs); ~*-clutch,* device for coupling two shafts in transmission of power, one member having teeth which engage with slots in another (ill. CLUTCH); ~*-collar,* collar for dog's neck; clergyman's stiff white collar fastening at back of neck; straight high close-fitting collar, esp. jewelled one; ~*-daisy,* the common or (now usu.) the ox-eye daisy; ~*-days,* period during part of July and August about time of heliacal or cosmical rising of Sirius, the dog-star, considered from ancient times the hottest and most unwholesome period of the year; ~*-eared,* (of book) having leaves turned down at corner, or crumpled; ~*-faced baboon,* = CYNOCEPHALUS; ~*-fall,* (wrestling) fall in which both wrestlers touch ground together; ~*-fight,* fight between dogs; general mêlée; mêlée between aircraft; ~*-fish,* various small sharks, esp. *Scyllium catulus* and *S. canicula* of Britain and (U.S.) *Squalus acanthius*; ~ *Latin,* bad Latin, mongrel Latin; ~*-leg,* bent like a dog's hind leg; ~*-nail,* nail with head projecting on one side; ~ *paddle,* method of swimming like dog's (ill. SWIM); ~*-rose,* common wild rose, *Rosa canina,* with pale pink flowers, frequent in hedges; ~*'s-ear,* crumpled corner of leaf of book; *dog'skin,* leather made from dog's skin or sheepskin, used for gloves etc.; ~*'s-meat,* horseflesh, offal, carrion; ~*'s nose,* drink of beer and gin; ~*'s-tail,* genus of grasses, *Cynosurus,* with flowers in each panicle all pointing one way, like dog's tail; ~*-star*: see 4 above; ~*'s-tongue,* the genus *Cynoglossum* of boraginaceous plants, from the shape of the leaves; ~*'s tooth* (*violet*), spring-flowering liliaceous garden-plant, *Erythronium dens-canis,* with spotted leaves and purple flowers, so called from teeth on inner segments of perianth; ~*-tired,* extremely tired, tired out; ~*-tooth,* eye-tooth, canine tooth; (archit.) pointed ornament or moulding frequent in early medieval architecture (ill. MOULDING); ~*-trot,* easy steady trot like a dog's; ~*-violet, Viola canina* and other species of scentless wild violets; ~*-watch,* (naut.) each of the two short watches between 4 and 8 p.m. (of two, instead of four, hours each); *dog'wood,* the wild cornel, *Cornus sanguinea,* or other species of *Cornus*; the close smooth-grained wood of this. ~ *v.t.* Follow closely, pursue, track; (mech.) grip with dog. **dŏgg'ish, dŏg'lėss, dŏg'līke** *adjs.*

dōge (-j) *n.* (hist.) Chief magistrate of republics of Venice and Genoa. **dōg'āte** *n.* Office of doge.

dŏgg'ėd (-g-) *adj.* Obstinate, tenacious, persistent, unyielding. **dŏgg'ėdly** *adv.* **dŏgg'ėdnėss** *n.*

dŏgg'er *n.* Two-masted bluff-bowed Dutch fishing-boat.

Dŏgg'er Bank. Sand-bank in N. Sea between England and Denmark, *c* 150 miles long.

dŏgg'erel (-g-) *adj.* & *n.* Trivial, mean, halting, or irregular (verse).

Dŏgg'ėtt's coat and badge. Rowing competition among Thames watermen, instituted 1716 by Thomas Doggett, English actor and theatre manager.

dŏgg'ō *adv.* (slang) *Lie* ~, lie motionless making no sign.

dŏgg'y, -gie *n.* (nursery) Dog. **dŏgg'y** *adj.* Of dogs; devoted to dogs.

dŏg'ma *n.* Principle, tenet, doctrinal system, esp. as laid down by authority of Church; arrogant declaration of opinion.

dŏgmăt'ic (more rarely, **dŏgmăt'ical**) *adj.* Of dogma(s), doctrinal; based on *a priori* principles, not on experience or induction; authoritative, laying down the law, arrogant. **dŏgmăt'ically** *adv.* **dŏgmăt'ics** *n.* System of dogma; esp. dogmatic theology.

dŏg'matīze *v.* Make positive unsupported assertions, speak authoritatively; express (principle etc.) as a dogma. **dŏg'matism, dŏg'matist** *ns.*

Dō'gra *n.* Member of a warlike Hindu race of NW. India.

doh: see DO².

doil'y *n.* Small ornamental napkin used at dessert, or placed under dishes, decanters, etc. [fabric named f. 17th-c. inventor]

do'ing (dōō-) *n.* (esp., usu. pl.) Performance, deed, act, transaction, proceeding; (slang, pl.) vague term for anything lying about, or wanted.

doit *n.* Small obsolete Dutch coin, worth half a farthing; very small or trifling sum; jot, merest trifle.

dol. *abbrev.* Dollar(s).

dŏl'ce fär nĭĕn'tė (-chā) *n.* Pleasant idleness. [It., = 'sweet doing nothing']

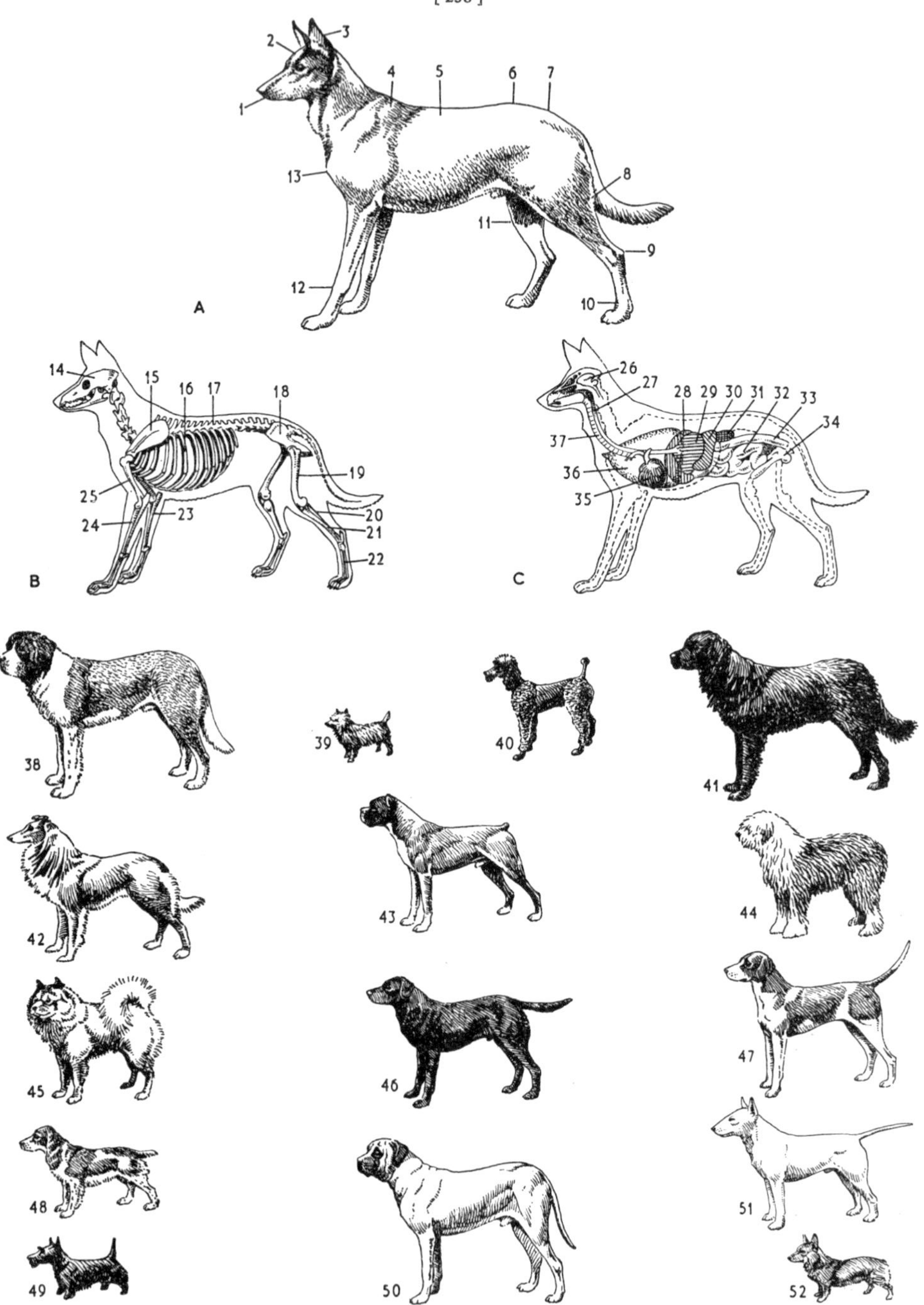

DOGS: A. POINTS. B. SKELETON. C. INTERNAL ORGANS. D. SOME COMMON BREEDS

A. 1. Muzzle. 2. Forehead. 3. Occiput (between ears). 4. Withers. 5. Saddle. 6. Loins. 7. Croup. 8. Stern. 9. Hock. 10. Pastern. 11. Stifle. 12. Knee. 13. Brisket. B. 14. Skull. 15. Scapula. 16. Ribs. 17. Vertebral column. 18. Pelvis. 19. Femur. 20. Fibula. 21. Tibia. 22. Metatarsus. 23. Ulna. 24. Radius. 25. Humerus. C. 26. Brain. 27. Oesophagus. 28. Liver. 29. Stomach. 30. Spleen. 31. Kidney. 32. Intestine. 33. Rectum. 34. Testicles. 35. Heart. 36. Lungs. 37. Trachea. D. 38. St. Bernard. 39. Cairn terrier. 40. Poodle. 41. Newfoundland. 42. Collie. 43. Boxer. 44. Old English sheep-dog. 45. Chow. 46. Labrador retriever. 47. Foxhound. 48. Cocker spaniel. 49. Scotch or Aberdeen terrier. 50. Mastiff. 51. Bull-terrier. 52. Welsh corgi (Pembrokeshire)

dŏl'drums *n.pl.* 1. Dullness, dumps, depression; *in the* ~, (of ship) becalmed. 2. Region near equator where meeting of trade winds produces light baffling winds, sudden storms, and calms (ill. WIND). [prob. f. *dull*, the geog. sense being prob. due to misunderstanding of phrase *in the* ~]

dōle[1] *n.* 1. (archaic) Lot, destiny. 2. Charitable distribution; charitable (esp. sparing, niggardly) gift; portion sparingly dealt out; (colloq.) *the* ~, payment in relief of unemployment. ~ *v.t.* Deal *out* sparingly, esp. as alms.

dōle[2] *n.* (poet.) Grief, woe; lamentation.

dōle'ful (-lf-) *adj.* Dreary, dismal; sad, discontented, melancholy. **dōle'fully** *adv.* **dōle'fulnėss** *n.*

dŏl'erīte *n.* Coarse basaltic rock much used as road-metal. [Gk *doleros* deceptive (because easily confused with true greenstone)]

dŏl'ichocėphăl'ĭc (-kō-) *adj.* Long-headed from front to back; (of skull with breadth less than ⅕ of length; or of tribes having such skulls.)

dŏll *n.* Image of human being used as plaything; toy baby; pretty silly woman. ~ *v.* Dress *up* finely. [shortened pet-form of *Dorothy*]

dŏll'ar *n.* 1. (orig.) English name for the German thaler and also for the Spanish piece of eight (peso) current in Spanish America and used in British N. Amer. colonies before the War of Independence. 2. Principal monetary unit (symbol $) of U.S., Canada, and other countries; ~ *area*, area where the currency is linked to the U.S. dollar. 3. Various foreign monetary units of value more or less approaching Spanish or American dollar, e.g. peso of Mexico and Central and S. Amer. republics. 4. (slang) 5 shillings, crown-piece. [orig. *daler*, f. *Joachimstaler*, coin from silver mine in Joachimstal, Bohemia (Ger. *tal* valley); symbol $ a modification of P[s], Mex. abbrev. for pesos or piastres]

Dŏll'fuss(-ōōs), Engelbert (1892–1934). Austrian statesman; became chancellor and 'dictator' of Austria 1933; assassinated 1934.

dŏll'op *n.* (colloq.) Large quantity; clumsy or shapeless lump.

dŏll'y *n.* 1. (Pet-name for) doll. 2. Various contrivances used in punching, clothes-washing, pile-driving, polishing, etc. 3. ~-*shop*, marine store; ~-*tub*, wash-tub.

Dŏll'y Vârd'en (hat). Large hat with brim drooping at one side, trimmed with flowers etc. [name of character in Dickens's 'Barnaby Rudge']

dŏl'man *n.* 1. Long Turkish robe open in front. 2. Hussar's uniform jacket worn like cape with sleeves hanging loose. 3. Woman's mantle with cape-like sleeves (ill. CLOAK); ~ *sleeve*, loose sleeve like that of dolman, cut in one piece with body of garment (ill. SLEEVE).

dŏl'mėn *n.* Megalithic tomb, large flat stone laid horizontally upon upright ones. [Fr., prob. f. Cornish *tolmên*, lit. 'hole of stone']

DOLMEN

dŏl'omīte *n.* 1. (chem.) Native double carbonate of calcium and magnesium occurring as crystal or in white or coloured granular masses; rock of this. 2. Dolomite mountain, esp. (*The D~s*) those of the southern Tyrol. **dŏlomĭt'ĭc** *adj.* [Sylvain Gratet de *Dolomieu* (1750–1802), French mineralogist]

dŏl'orous *adj.* (usu. poet. or facet.) Distressing, painful; dismal, doleful; distressed. **dŏl'orously** *adv.*

dŏl'our (-ler) (poet.) Sorrow, distress.

dŏl'phĭn *n.* 1. Cetaceous mammal (*Delphinus delphis*) resembling porpoise but with longer and more

DOLPHIN

slender snout. 2. (pop.) A sea-fish, the DORADO (genus *Coryphaena*). 3. A northern constellation (*Delphinus*). 4. Figure of dolphin in heraldry etc.

dōlt *n.* Dull fellow, blockhead. **dōl'tĭsh** *adj.* **dōl'tĭshly** *adv.* **dōl'tĭshnėss** *n.*

D.O.M. *abbrev.* *Deo optimo maximo* (= to God the best and greatest).

Dŏm. 1. Title prefixed to names of R.C. ecclesiastical and monastic dignitaries, esp. Carthusian and Benedictine monks. 2. Portuguese equivalent of DON[1], as title. [L *dominus* master, lord]

domain' *n.* 1. Estate, lands, dominions; district under rule; realm, sphere of influence; scope, field, province, of thought or action; (international and U.S. law) *eminent* ~, lordship of sovereign power over all property in State, with right of expropriation. 2. (physics) In ferro-magnetic materials, an aggregation of atoms or ions which behaves as an elementary magnet, all the ions in a domain having the axes of their permanent magnetic moment aligned in the same direction.

dōme *n.* 1. (poet.) Stately building, mansion. 2. Rounded vault forming roof, with circular, elliptical or polygonal base; natural vault, canopy (of trees, sky, etc.); rounded summit of hill etc. ~ *v.t.* Cover with, shape as, dome. **dōmed** *adj.* Vaulted, dome-like; having a dome or domes. [Fr., f. It. *duomo* cathedral, dome, f. L *domus* house]

Domes'day Bŏŏk (dōōmz-). Record of Great Inquisition of lands of England, their extent, value, ownership, and liabilities, made by order of William the Conqueror in 1086. [popular name (= Doomsday) given to the book as final authority]

domĕs'tĭc *adj.* 1. Of the home, household, or family affairs; of one's own country, not foreign; native, home-made. 2. (Of animals) tame, kept by or living with man. 3. Home-keeping, fond of home, domesticated. ~ *n.* Household servant. **domĕs'tĭcally** *adv.*

domĕs'tĭcāte *v.t.* Naturalize; attach to home and its duties (esp. in past part.); tame and bring under control (animals), accustom to live near men; civilize. **domĕs't'ĭcable** *adj.* **domĕstĭcā'tion** *n.*

dŏmėstĭ'cĭty *n.* Domestic character; home life or privacy; homeliness; (pl.) domestic affairs.

dŏm'ėtt *n.* Soft light fabric of cotton, or wool and cotton, resembling flannel.

dŏm'ĭcīle (*or* -ĭl) *n.* Dwelling-place, home; (law) place of permanent residence, fact of residing; place at which bill of exchange is made payable. ~ *v.* Establish, settle, in a place; make (bill) payable *at* place.

dŏmĭcĭl'ĭary *adj.* Of a dwelling-place; ~ *visit*, medical consultant's visit to patient's home; (also ~ *search*), visit by officials to private dwelling to search or inspect it.

dŏmĭcĭl'ĭāte *v.* Domicile. **dŏmĭcĭlĭā'tion** *n.*

dŏm'ĭnant *adj.* 1. Ruling, prevailing, most influential; occupying commanding position. 2. Of the dominant; (of chord) having dominant for its root. 3. (biol.) Of inherited character: that is a dominant, that is apparent in offspring when the opposite character is also inherited (opp. to RECESSIVE). ~ *n.* 1. (mus.) 5th note of scale in any key (ill. SCALE); reciting note in eccles. modes, usu. 5th from final (ill. MODE). 2. (biol.) That one of a pair of opposite characters which is apparent in the offspring when both are inherited.

dŏm'ĭnāte *v.* Have commanding influence over (also intr. with *over*); be the most influential or conspicuous; (of height) overlook; occupy commanding position. **dŏmĭnā'tion** *n.* 1. Ascendancy, sway, control. 2. (pl.) Angelic order of 4th rank.

dŏmĭneer' *v.i.* Act imperiously, tyrannize (*over*), be overbearing. **dŏmĭneer'ĭng** *adj.* **dŏmĭneer'ĭngly** *adv.*

Dŏm'ĭnĭc, St. Domingo de Guzman (1170–1221), Spanish founder

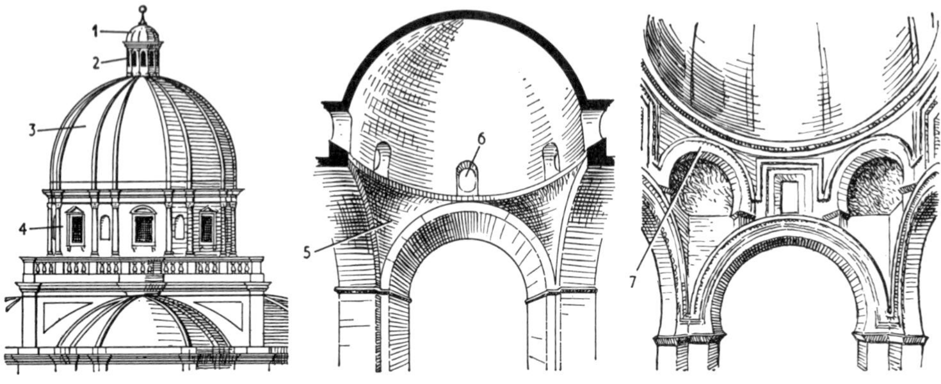

DOME

1. Cupola. 2. Lantern. 3. Dome. 4. Drum. 5. Pendentive. 6. Lunette. 7. Squinch

of an order of preaching friars (*Dominicans*).

domĭn'ical *adj.* Of the Lord (Jesus Christ); of the Lord's Day or Sunday; ~ *letter*, letter denoting Sundays in a particular year (the letters A–G being used to denote first 7 days of the year, and then in rotation the next 7 days, and so on, so that, e.g., if the 3rd Jan. is a Sunday, the ~ letter for the year is C); ~ *year*, the year of our Lord.

Domĭn'ĭcan *adj.* Of St. Dominic or the order of friars (or nuns) founded by him. ~ *n.* Dominican friar, black friar.

Domĭn'ĭcan Rėpŭb'lĭc. A republic (since 1844) occupying the E. part of the W. Indian island of Hispaniola, formerly part of the Spanish Empire; capital, Santo Domingo.

dŏm'inĭe *n.* (Sc.) Schoolmaster.

domĭn'ion (-yon) *n.* 1. Lordship, sovereignty, control; (law) right of possession, ownership. 2. Domains of feudal lord; territory of sovereign or government. 3. (*Self-governing*) ~, term, now rare in official use, applied to certain oversea self-governing nations of the British Commonwealth; ~ *status*, position of these nations as not subject to Gt Britain but associated with her in common allegiance to the crown. 4. *The Old D*~, (U.S.) Virginia.

dŏm'ĭnō *n.* (pl. *-oes*). 1. Loose hooded cloak, app. of Venetian origin, worn at masquerades with small mask over upper part of face (ill. CLOAK); person wearing this. 2. One of a number (usu. 28) of rectangular pieces of ivory, wood, etc., usu. black, and with upper side equally divided into two squares, each either blank or marked with pips, so as to present all possible combinations from double blank to double six; (pl.) game played with these (usu.) by placing corresponding ends in contact.

dŏn[1] *n.* 1. Spanish title prefixed to Christian names; Spanish gentleman, Spaniard; distinguished person. 2. (colloq.) Head, fellow, or tutor of college, esp. at Oxford or Cambridge. [Span., f. L *dominus* lord]

dŏn[2] *v.t.* Put on (garment).

Dŏn[3]. River of S. Russia flowing into Sea of Azov.

dŏn'a(h) (-n*a*) *n.* (slang) Woman, sweetheart. [f. Span. *doña* or Port. *dona* lady]

Dŏnatĕll'o (1386–1466). Italian sculptor, famous esp. for his bronze 'David' in Florence.

donā'tion *n.* Bestowal, presenting; thing presented, gift (esp. money given to institution). **donāte'** *v.t.* (chiefly U.S.) Make donation of; give, grant. **donāt'or** *n.*

Dŏn'atĭst *adj.* & *n.* (Member) of a Christian sect which arose in N. Africa in 311 out of a dispute about the election of the bishop of Carthage; it maintained that it was the only true and pure church, and that baptisms and ordinations of others were invalid.

dŏn'atĭve *n.* Benefice given directly, not involving presentation to or investment by the Ordinary; gift, present, esp. official largess. ~ *adj.* (of benefice) That is a donative.

dŏn'atory *n.* Recipient of donation.

done (dŭn), past part. of DO[1] *v.*

dŏnee' *n.* Recipient of gift.

Dŏnegal' (-awl). County of Eire in extreme NW. of Ireland.

dŏng'a (-ngg-) *n.* (S. Afr.) Ravine, gully.

dŏn'jon *n.* Great tower of castle, keep (ill. CASTLE).

Dŏn Juan (jōō'*a*n). Legendary Spanish nobleman of dissolute life; hence, rake, libertine.

dŏnk'ey *n.* (Usual word for) ass; stupid person; art student's four-legged stool with rest for drawing-board; ~ *engine*, small steam-engine, usu. for subsidiary operations on board ship; ~*-work*, (colloq.) drudgery.

Dŏnne (*or* dŭn), John (1572–1631). Dean of St. Paul's, famous as a preacher and as a 'metaphysical' poet, author of satires, epistles, and elegies.

dŏnn'ĭsh *adj.* Like a university don; pedantic. **dŏnn'ĭshnėss** *n.*

Dŏnn'ybrōōk. Town near Dublin, Ireland; ~ *Fair*, annual fair formerly held there; hence, scene of uproar and disorder, free fight.

dō'nor *n.* Giver; person portrayed in religious picture as having presented it to church etc.; (*blood-*) ~, one who gives his blood for transfusion.

Don Quixote: see QUIXOTE.

dōn't, colloq. contraction of *do not*; as *n.*, prohibition. **dōn't-care** *adj.* Careless, reckless.

dōō'dle *n.* (orig. U.S.) Aimless scrawl made by a person while his attention is engaged. ~ *v.i.* Make a doodle.

dōō'dle-bŭg *n.* 1. (U.S.) Tiger-beetle or its larva. 2. (colloq.) Flying-bomb. 3. (colloq.) Miniature racing car used at fairs.

dōōm *n.* 1. (hist.) Statute, law; decree. 2. (archaic) Decision, sentence, condemnation. 3. Fate, lot, (usu. evil) destiny; ruin, death. 4. The Last Judgement (chiefly in *crack, day, of* ~); (*D*~) representation of this in art; *dooms'day*, the day of judgement; *till doomsday*, to the end of the world, for ever; *Doomsday Book*: see DOMESDAY. ~ *v.* Pronounce sentence against; condemn *to* some fate, *to* do; consign to misfortune or destruction (esp. in past part.).

door (dōr) *n.* 1. Movable barrier of wood or other material, turning on hinges or sliding in groove, and serving to close or open passage into building, room, etc.; doorway; means of entrance or exit. 2. Phrases: *next* ~ *to*, in the next house or room to; very near to, bordering on; *at death's* ~, on the point of dying; *out of doors,* abroad, in the open air; *within doors*, in the house; *lay, lie, at the ~ of*, impute, be imputable, to. 3. *~-bell*, bell within house which may be rung from outside; *~-keeper*, janitor, porter; *~-mat*, mat placed at door for wiping shoes on entering; *~-nail*, large-headed nail with which doors were formerly studded for strength or ornament; *~-plate*, plate on door bearing name of occupant of house or room; *~-post*, either of uprights on each side of doorway, on one of which door is hung; *doorstep*, step at threshold of door; *doorway*, opening or passage which door serves to close or open; *~-yard*, (U.S.) yard or garden about door of house.

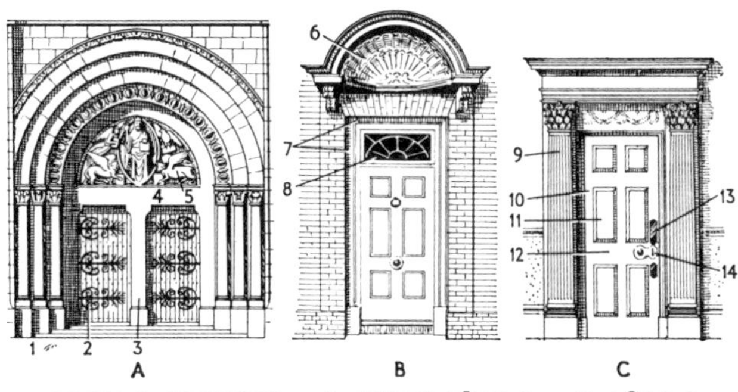

DOOR: A. MEDIEVAL. B. EARLY 18TH C. C. 18TH C. INTERIOR DOOR

1. Jamb. 2. Hinge. 3. Trumeau. 4. Lintel. 5. Tympanum. 6. Shell hood. 7. Architrave. 8. Fanlight. 9. Pilaster. 10. Stile. 11. Panel. 12. Rail. 13. Finger-plate. 14. Escutcheon or scutcheon

dŏp *n.* Cheap S. Afr. brandy made from grape-skins; a dram of liquor. [S. Afr. Du., = 'shell', 'husk']

dōpe *n.* 1. Thick liquid used as food or lubricant; varnish, esp. that applied to cloth parts of aeroplanes etc. to keep them taut and airtight. 2. (slang) Opium or other narcotic, stupefying drink; drug administered to horse etc. before race to improve or spoil its performance; (chiefly U.S.) information, esp. false or deceptive information, or that supplied for newspaper use; fraud, humbug; *~-fiend*, drug-addict. ~ *v.t.* (orig. U.S.) Drug; doctor; apply dope to (aeroplane fabric etc.). **dōp'y** *adj.* (slang) Heavy or stupefied, as if drugged. [app. f. Du. *doop* sauce]

dŏppel-gänger (-gĕng-) *n.* Person's double or apparition seen shortly before or after his death, wraith.

dôr *n.* (also *~-beetle*) Insect flying with loud humming noise, esp. common black dung beetle, cockchafer, and rose-chafer.

Dôr'a. Joc. personification of *D*efence *o*f the *R*ealm *A*ct passed in Aug. 1914, giving Government wide powers during the war. [from initials]

dora'dō (-ah-) *n.* (pl. *-os*). Sea-fish (genus *Coryphaena*), bright blue and silver and very swift, = DOLPHIN sense 2.

Dôrc'as. Woman mentioned in Acts ix. 36 as 'full of good deeds and almsdeeds which she did'; ~ *Society*, ladies' association, connected with a church, for making and providing clothes for the poor.

Doré (dŏrā'), Paul Gustave (1833–83). French artist; famous for his scriptural paintings and illustrations of Dante, Milton, etc.

Dôr'ian *adj.* & *n.* (Native, inhabitant) of Doris; ~ *mode*, (mus.) ancient Greek MODE, reputedly simple and solemn in character; first of eccles. modes, with D as final and A as dominant (ill. MODE).

Dŏ'rĭc *adj.* 1. Dorian. 2. (Of dialect etc.) broad, rustic. 3. (archit.) Built in the ~ *order*, the oldest, strongest, and simplest of the Greek orders of architecture (see ORDER *n.* 6 and ill.). ~ *n.* 1. Doric dialect of ancient Greece. 2. Rustic English. 3. Doric architecture.

Dôr'ĭs, Dôr'ĭa. A small country in ancient Greece, S. of Thessaly, the home of the Dorians.

Dôrk'ĭng *adj.* & *n.* (Fowl) of a white breed of poultry with long squarish body and short legs. [f. *Dorking*, town in Surrey]

dôrm'ant *adj.* Sleeping; inactive as in sleep; with animation or development suspended; not acting, in abeyance; (bot., esp. of seeds and buds) in state of suspended growth; (her., of beast) with head resting on paws. **dôrm'ancy** *n.*

dôrm'er *n.* Projecting vertical window in sloping roof (ill. WINDOW).

dôrm'ĭtory *n.* 1. Sleeping-room with several beds, or divided into cells or cubicles. 2. (U.S.) Hostel, hall of residence, in university.

dôrm'ouse *n.* Small hibernating rodent of family intermediate between squirrels and mice, esp. the British species *Muscardinus avellanarius*.

dôrm'y *adj.* (golf) As many holes ahead of opponent as there are holes still to be played (*~ one, two*, etc.).

dŏ'rothy bag *n.* Woman's handbag with open top drawn up by strings. [name in musical comedy 'Dorothy']

Dŏ'rothy Pẽrk'ĭns. Climbing rose with clusters of pink double flowers.

dôrp *n.* (S. Afr.) Village, small town.

dôrs'al *n.* = DOSSAL. ~ *adj.* (anat., bot., zool.) Of, on, near, the back; ridge-shaped. **dôrs'ally** *adv.*

Dôrs'ėt. County of SW. England.

dôrt'er, -tour (*-er*) *n.* (hist.) Bedroom, dormitory, esp. in monastery (ill. MONASTERY).

dôr'y[1] *n.* (Also *John D~*) European sea-fish, *Zeus faber*, used as food. [Fr. *dorée* gilded]

dôr'y[2] *n.* (U.S.) Small flat-bottomed boat, esp. for fishing.

dōs'age (-s-) *n.* Giving of medicine in doses; size of dose; amount of X-rays etc. applied at one time.

dōse (-s) *n.* Amount of medicine etc. given or prescribed to be given at one time. ~ *v.t.* Give medicine to (person); add spirit to (wine).

dŏss *n.* (slang) Bed, esp. in common lodging-house; sleep; *~-house*, common lodging-house. ~ *v.i.* Sleep, esp. in doss-house; ~ *down*, sleep on makeshift bed.

dŏss'al *n.* Ornamental hanging at back of altar or round chancel.

dŏss'ier (*or* -syā) *n.* Set or bundle of documents relating to a particular person or happening.

Dŏstōĕv'sky (-fs-), Feodor Mikhailovich (1821–81). Russian novelist; author of 'Crime and Punishment', 'The Idiot', 'The Brothers Karamazov', etc.

dŏt[1] *n.* Small spot, speck, roundish pen-mark; period, point over *i* or *j*, point used as diacritical mark; (mus.) point placed after note or rest, lengthening it by half its value; point over or under note indicating that it is *staccato*; *on the ~*, punctually; *~-and-dash*, using dots and dashes, as the Morse alphabet. ~ *v.t.* Mark with dot(s); place dot over (letter *i*, note in music) or after (musical note); diversify as with dots; scatter like dots; ~ *and carry* (*one*), child's formula for remembering to carry in sum; ~ *and go one* (*n., adj.* & *adv.*) limp, limping(ly); *dotted line*, one on a document to carry signature of a party to its contents; hence, *sign on the dotted line*, acquiesce without demur.

dŏt[2] *n.* Woman's marriage portion. [Fr.]

dōt'age *n.* Impaired intellect, esp. through old age; second childhood, senility.

dōt'ard *n.* Man in his dotage.

dōte, doat *v.i.* 1. Be silly,

deranged, infatuated, or feeble-minded, esp. from age. 2. Concentrate one's affections, bestow excessive fondness, (*up*)*on*. **dōt'ingly** *adv.*

dŏtt'(e)rel *n.* Species of plover, *Eudromias morinellus.* [f. DOTE *v.*, from the apparent simplicity with which it allows itself to be taken]

dŏtt'le *n.* Plug of tobacco left unsmoked in pipe.

dŏt'ty *adj.* Dotted about, marked with dots; (colloq.) feeble-minded, half idiotic.

doub'le (dŭ-) *adj.* 1. Consisting of two members, things, or sets combined; twofold; forming a pair; folded, bent; stooping much; having some part double; (of flowers) having number of petals multiplied by conversion of stamens and carpels into petals. 2. Having twofold relation or application; dual; ambiguous. 3. Twice as much or as many (*of*); of twofold or extra size, strength, value, etc. (mus., of instruments etc.) an octave lower in pitch (from the fact that a pipe, string, etc., of double length gives a note an octave lower). 4. Deceitful, hypocritical. ~ *adv.* To twice the amount etc.; two together. ~ *adj.* or *adv. in combination*; ~*-acting*, acting in two ways, directions, etc., esp. of engine in which steam acts on both sides of piston; ~*-barrelled*, (of gun) with two barrels; also fig. of compound surname; ~*-bass*, largest and lowest-pitched instrument of violin class, with 4 strings usu. tuned a fourth apart (ill. STRING); ~ *bed*, bed for two people; ~*-bedded*, with two beds or a double bed; ~*-breasted*, (of coat etc.) having the two fronts overlapping across the breast; ~*-chin*, roll of fat below chin; ~*-cross*, (slang) treachery to both parties, esp. by pretended collusion with each, betrayal of partner in dishonest transaction; (*v.t.*) betray thus; ~*-dealing*, duplicity, deceit; ~*-dealer*; ~*-deck*, (of passenger vehicle) having an upper deck, whence ~*-deck'er* (*n.*); ~*-dyed*, (usu. fig.) deeply stained with guilt; ~ *eagle*, figure of eagle with two heads; (U.S.) twenty-dollar gold piece; ~*-edged*, with two cutting edges; (fig., of argument etc.) telling against as well as for one; ~ *event*, (racing etc.) winning of two races etc. in one meeting or one season; ~*-faced*, insincere; ~ *figures*, number higher than nine and less than a hundred; ~ *first*, (person taking) first-class university honours in two different subjects; ~ (*quick*) *time*, (mil.) regulation running pace; (pop.) very fast speed, short time; ~*-lead'ed* (-lĕd-), (of printed matter) with wide spaces between lines; ~*-lock*, lock by two turns of the key; ~ *meaning*, = DOUBLE ENTENDRE; ~ *pneumonia*, pneumonia affecting both lungs; ~ *star*, two stars really or apparently so close together as to seem one, esp. when forming connected pair; ~*-stopping*, (mus.) simultaneous sounding of notes on two strings of instrument of violin class; ~*-tonguing*, rapid vibratory motion of tongue in producing staccato or rapidly repeated notes on flute, clarinet, etc. **doub'ly** *adv.* **dou'bleness** *n.* **doub'le** *n.* 1. Double quantity; twice as much or as many; ~ *or quits*, game, throw, toss, deciding whether person shall pay twice his debt or nothing; *at the double*, (mil.) running. 2. (bridge) Call by declarer's opponent involving doubling of score for tricks and a bonus to the declarer if he wins. 3. Counterpart of thing or person. 4. Game (at lawn tennis etc.) between two pairs. 5. Sharp turn of river, or in running. 6. Bet on result of two races, the winnings in the first being staked on the result of the second. 7. = Double event, double bed(room), double 'tot' of whisky etc. ~ *v.* 1. Make or become double, increase twofold, multiply by two; amount to twice as much as; (mus.) add same note in lower or higher octave to; call a double (at bridge); ~ *part*, act two parts in same piece. 2. (mil.) Move in double time, run. 3. Put in same quarters with another; share quarters (also ~ *up*). 4. Bend, turn, over upon itself; clench (fist); ~ *up*, (cause to) bend into stooping or curled-up position; become folded. 5. (naut.) Get round (headland). 6. Turn sharply in flight; pursue tortuous course.

double entendre (dōōbl ahṅtahṅ'dr) *n.* Ambiguous expression, phrase with two meanings, one usu. indecent; use of such phrases. [obs. Fr. phrase (now *double entente*)]

doub'lĕt (dŭ-) *n.* 1. (hist.) Men's close-fitting body-garment with or without sleeves and short skirts (14th–18th centuries); ~ *and hose*,

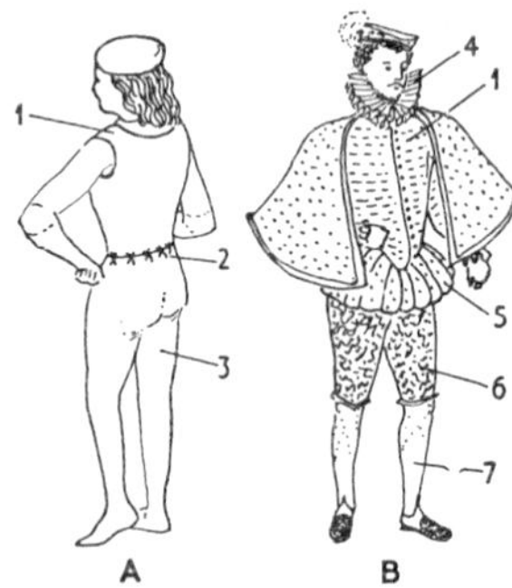

DOUBLET: A. 15TH C. B. LATE 16TH C.

1. Doublet. 2. Points. 3. Hose. 4. Ruff. 5. Trunkhose (bombasted). 6. Canions. 7. Stockings

masculine attire; light attire without cloak. 2. One of a pair, esp. one of two words of same derivation but different form or sense. 3. (pl.) Same number on two dice thrown at once. 4. Combination of two simple lenses; imitation precious stone of two pieces of glass with layer of colour cemented between them, or of thin slice of gem cemented on glass or inferior stone.

dou'bleton (dŭblt-) *n.* (cards) Two cards only of a suit, in one hand.

doublōōn' (du-) *n.* (hist.) Spanish gold coin (orig. two pistoles, 33 to 36 shillings).

doubt (dowt) *n.* Feeling of uncertainty (*about*), undecided frame of mind, inclination to disbelieve; uncertain state of things; *give* (person) *benefit of the* ~, assume innocence rather than guilt when evidence is contradictory or inconclusive; *no* ~, certainly, admittedly; *without* ~, certainly. ~ *v.* Be in doubt or uncertainty (about); call in question; mistrust.

doubt'ful (dowt-) *adj.* Of uncertain meaning, character, truth, or issue; undecided, ambiguous, questionable; uncertain, hesitating. **doubt'fully** *adv.* **doubt'fulnĕss** *n.*

doubt'lĕss (dowt-) *adv.* Certainly; no doubt.

douceur (dōō'sẽr) *n.* Gratuity; bribe.

douche (dōōsh) *n.* Jet of water applied to body externally or internally as form of bathing or medicinally. ~ *v.* Administer douche to, take douche.

dough (dō) *n.* Mass of flour or meal kneaded into paste ready to be baked into bread etc.; any soft pasty mass; (U.S. slang) money; ~*-boy*, boiled flour dumpling, (U.S. slang) infantry soldier; ~*-face*, (U.S.) mask made of dough; pliable or flabby person, esp. (hist.) Northern politician inclined to be unduly compliant to South in questions of slavery etc.; *doughnut*, small spongy cake of dough fried in lard and usu. sprinkled with sugar. **doughy** (dō'ĭ) *adj.*

dought'y (dow-) *adj.* (archaic or joc.) Valiant, stout, formidable. **dought'ily** *adv.* **dought'inĕss** *n.*

Doukhobor: see DUKHOBOR.

dour (-oor) *adj.* (Sc.) Severe, stern, obstinate. **dour'ly** *adv.* **dour'nĕss** *n.*

douse (-s) *v.t.* 1. (naut.) Strike, lower, (sail); close (port-hole). 2. Extinguish (light); ~ *the glim*, (slang) put out the light.

dove (dŭv) *n.* Bird of family *Columbidae* (see PIGEON), esp. the turtle-dove; freq. as type of gentleness or innocence; the Holy Spirit (see Luke iii. 22 etc.); messenger of peace and deliverance (see Gen. viii. 8–12); darling; ~*-colour*, warm grey with tinge of pink or lavender; *-cot(e)*, pigeon-house.

Dōv'er[1]. Seaport of Kent, England; *Strait of* ~, strait at E. end of English Channel between coast of Kent and France.

Dōv′er². Capital of Delaware, U.S.

Dōv′er's powder *n.* (med.) Preparation of opium and ipecacuanha used to produce sweating, a common ingredient of cough mixtures. [Dr. Thomas *Dover* (1660–1742), who prescribed it]

dove′tail (dŭv-) *n.* Tenon shaped like dove's spread tail or reversed wedge, fitting into corresponding mortise and forming joint; such joint (ill. JOINT). ~ *v.* Put together with dovetails; fit together compactly.

dow′ager *n.* Woman with title or property derived from her late husband.

dowd *n.* **dowd′y̆** *adj.* & *n.* (Woman) shabbily, badly, or unfashionably dressed; (of dress) unattractive, unfashionable. **dowd′ily** *adv.* **dowd′inėss** *n.* **dowd′yish** *adj.* **dowd′yism** *n.*

dow′el *n.* Headless pin of wood, metal, etc., fastening together two pieces of wood, stone, etc. ~ *v.t.* Fasten with dowel(s). **dow′elling** *n.* Round wooden rods for cutting into dowels.

dow′er *n.* Widow's share for life of husband's estate; property or money brought by wife to husband, dowry; endowment, gift of nature, talent. ~ *v.t.* Give dowry to; endow *with* talent etc.

dowl′as *n.* Kind of strong coarse calico. [*Doulas* in Brittany]

down¹ *n.* Open high land, esp. (pl.) treeless undulating chalk uplands of S. England; *the D~*, part of sea within Goodwin Sands, off E. coast of Kent, opposite E. end of North Downs, a famous rendezvous for ships. **down′land** *n.* **downs′man** *n.* Native or inhabitant of (Sussex) downs.

down² *n.* First fine soft covering of young birds; bird's underplumage, used for stuffing cushions etc.; fine soft hair, esp. first hair on face; also on fruit etc.; any feathery or fluffy substance.

down³ *adv.* 1. From above, to lower place, to ground; to place regarded as lower; into helpless position; with current or wind; southwards; away from capital or university; (pay, paid) at once, as though on counter; *bear ~*, sail to leeward; *go ~*, (of sun, ship) set, sink; be swallowed, find acceptance; leave university for vacation or at end of university life; *put, take*, etc., ~, write on paper; *send ~*, send away from university as punishment; *up and~*, to and fro. 2. In lower place; not up in capital or university; in fallen posture, prostrate; at low level, in depression, humiliation, etc.; lower in price; *~ in the mouth*, *~-hearted*, dispirited. 3. From higher to lower point in series or order; from earlier to later time; to finer consistence; into quiescence. 4. *Be, come, ~ on*, pounce upon, treat severely, regard with disfavour; *~ east* (U.S.), into, in, the eastern sea-coast districts of New England, esp. Maine; *~ to the ground*, completely; *~ south*, (U.S.) in, into, the southern States; down the Mississippi; *~ at heel*: see HEEL; *~ on one's luck*: see LUCK; *~ and out*, unable to resume the fight in boxing; beaten in the struggle of life, done for; *~ under*, at the Antipodes, in Australia etc. *~ prep.* Downwards along, through or into; from top to bottom of; at a lower part of; with (the wind, current, etc.); *up and ~*, to and fro along; *~ town*, into the (business part of) town from higher or outlying part; (situated) in more central part of town. ~ *adj.* Directed downwards; *~-draught*, downward draught, esp. one down chimney into room; *~ grade*, descending slope in railroad; (fig.) deterioration; *~ train*, train going away from London or other capital (so *~ line, platform*). ~ *v.t.* (colloq.) Put, throw, knock, gulp, etc., down; *~ tools*, cease work; go on strike. ~ *n.* Reverse of fortune; throw in wrestling etc.; (Amer. and Canadian football) pause in attempt to advance ball, when it is declared dead, also, the attempt itself; *have a ~ on*, (colloq.) dislike, be prejudiced against.

Down⁴. County in Northern Ireland.

down′cast¹ (-ah-) *adj.* (of looks) Directed downwards; dejected.

down′cast² (-ah-) **(shaft)** *n.* Intake ventilating shaft in mine (ill. MINE).

down′fall (-awl) *n.* Fall (of rain etc.); fall from prosperity, ruin.

down′hill *adj.* Sloping down; declining. **downhill′** *adv.* In descending direction; on a decline.

Down′ing Cŏll′ėge. College of University of Cambridge, founded 1800 from benefactions made by Sir George Downing.

Down′ing Street. Short street in London running from Whitehall towards St. James's Park and containing official residence of Prime Minister (no. 10) and other government buildings and offices; hence, the British Government.

down′pour *n.* Heavy fall of rain etc.

downright (down′rīt before *n.* etc., downrīt′ after it) *adj.* Plain, definite, straightforward, blunt; out-and-out. ~ *adv.* Thoroughly, positively, quite. **downright-nėss** *n.*

downstairs′ *adv.* **down′stairs** *adj.* Down the stairs; to, on, of, a lower floor.

down′trŏdden *adj.* Crushed by oppression or tyranny.

down′ward(s) *adv.* Towards what is lower, inferior, or later. **down′ward** *adj.*

down′y̆ *adj.* 1. Of, like, covered with, down. 2. (slang) Wide awake, knowing. **down′ily** *adv.* **down′inėss** *n.*

dowr′y *n.* Portion woman brings to her husband on marriage; talent, natural gift.

dows′er (*or* -z-) *n.* Person capable of locating hidden water or minerals by holding in both hands a forked twig which dips abruptly when it is over the right spot. **dows′ing** *n.* Searching for water etc. thus; *~-rod*, forked twig used by dowser, divining-rod.

dŏxŏl′ogy *n.* Liturgical formula of praise to God. **dŏxolŏ′gical** *adj.*

dŏx′y¹ *n.* Beggar's wench, paramour.

dŏx′y² *n.* (joc.) Opinion, esp. in theological or religious matters.

doyen (dwa′-yăń) *n.* Senior member *of* a body, esp. senior ambassador at a court.

Doyle, Sir Arthur Conan (1859–1930). British novelist, famous for his 'Sherlock Holmes' series of detective stories.

doyley: see DOILY.

doz. *abbrev.* Dozen.

dōze *v.i.* Sleep lightly, be half asleep; *~ off*, fall lightly asleep. ~ *n.* Short light sleep.

doz′en (dŭ-) *n.* Twelve; set of twelve; *baker's, long, printer's ~*, thirteen; (*talk*) *nineteen to the ~*, incessantly or very fast.

D.P. *abbrev.* Displaced person.

D.P.H. *abbrev.* Diploma in Public Health.

D.Ph(il). *abbrev.* Doctor of Philosophy.

D.P.I. *abbrev.* Director of Public Instruction.

dr. *abbrev.* Drachm.

Dr *abbrev.* Debtor; Doctor.

D.R. *abbrev.* Dead reckoning.

drăb¹ *n.* Slut, slattern; prostitute. ~ *v.i.* Whore.

drăb² *adj.* & *n.* (Of) dull light brown colour; dull, monotonous.

drăbb′ėt *n.* Drab twilled linen used for smock-frocks etc.

drachm (-ăm) *n.* 1. Apothecaries' weight of 60 grains or $\frac{1}{8}$ oz.; *fluid ~*, apothecaries' fluid measure of 60 minims or $\frac{1}{8}$ fluid oz. 2. = DRACHMA.

drăch′ma (-k-) *n.* (pl. *-mae, -mas*). Principal monetary unit of Greece, = 100 lepta; (Gk antiq.) silver coin, = 6 obols.

Drāc′ō (Gk *Drakon*). Archon at Athens in 621 B.C., said to have established a severe code of laws. **Dracō′nian, Dracŏn′ic** *adjs.* Of Draco or his code of laws; rigorous, harsh, cruel.

draff (-ahf) *n.* Dregs, lees; hog's-wash; refuse of malt after brewing.

draft (-ah-) *n.* 1. (Selection of) detachment of men from larger body for special duty; contingent; reinforcement; member of such detachment; (U.S.) conscription. 2. Drawing of money by written order; bill or cheque drawn, esp. by one branch of bank on another. 3. Sketch of work to be executed. 4. Rough copy of document. 5. (masonry) Chisel-dressing at margin of stone's surface. ~ *v.t.* 1. Draw off (part of larger body, esp.

of troops) for special purpose. 2. Prepare, make rough copy of (document, esp. parliamentary Bill). 3. (masonry) Cut draft on (stone). **draft'er** *n.* 1. One who drafts a document. 2. (U.S.) Draught-horse.

drafts'man (-ah-) *n.* (pl. *-men*). 1. One who drafts documents or parliamentary Bills. 2. One who prepares designs (now usu. DRAUGHTSMAN).

drăg *v.* 1. Pull along with force, difficulty, or friction; allow (feet, tail, etc.) to trail; ~ *anchor*, trail anchor along the bottom, owing to force of wind or current. 2. (mus.) Go too slowly, be wanting in life. 3. Trail, go heavily; ~ *on*, continue tediously. 4. Search bottom of (water) with grapnels, nets, etc. (*for*). 5. Harrow (land). 6. Retard (wheel, vehicle) by applying a drag to it (see *n.* below, 3). ~ *n.* 1. Heavy harrow; rough sledge; four-horsed private vehicle like stage-coach. 2. Net drawn over bottom of water or surface of field to enclose all fish or game (also *~-net*); apparatus for dredging or recovering drowned person etc. from bottom of rivers or pools. 3. Iron shoe for retarding vehicle downhill; obstruction to progress. 4. Strong-smelling lure for hounds in lieu of fox; hunt with hounds following this; club for pursuing this sport. 5. Slow motion; impeded progress. 6. *~-anchor*, floating frame on hawser to check leeway of drifting ship; *~-chain*, chain used to retard vehicle by fixing wheel; *~-hounds*: see sense 4; *~-line*, in excavator, line which pulls bucket towards machine; *~-net*: see sense 2.

dragée (drahzh'ā) *n.* Sweetmeat, esp. one containing drug etc.; chocolate drop.

drăg'gle *v.* Make wet, limp, and dirty, by trailing; hang trailing; *~-tail(ed)*, (woman) with draggled or untidily trailing skirts.

drăg'oman *n.* Interpreter (and guide), esp. in Arabic, Turkish, or Persian. [Arab. *targuman* interpreter]

drăg'on *n.* 1. Mythical monster like crocodile or snake with large claws, usu. winged and often breathing fire; freq. in legends as guardian of treasure, of female chastity, etc.; watchful person, duenna. 2. (bibl.) Whale, shark, serpent, or crocodile; jackal. 3. Lizard of genus *Draco*, with broad wing-like membrane on each flank, able to leap some distance in the air. 4. *~-fly*, insect of order *Odonata* with long body, prominent eyes, and elaborately veined membranous wings, freq. brightly coloured, and capable of rapid darting flight; *~'s-blood*, bright red gum or resin exuded by the fruit of a palm, *Calamus draco*, or obtained from the dragon-tree, used for colouring varnishes etc.; *~'s head, tail*, (astron.) ascending or descending node of the moon or

DRAGON

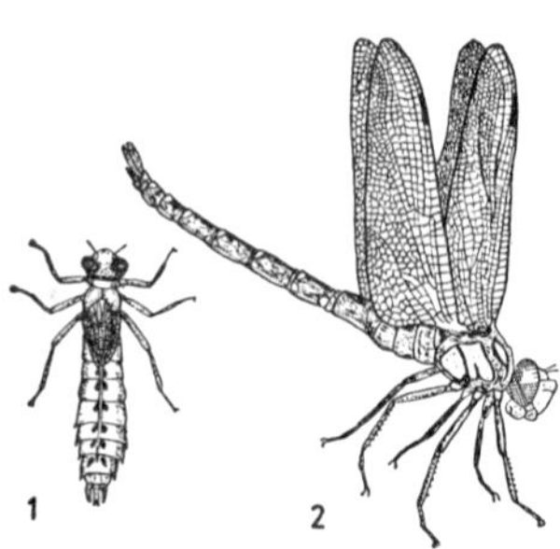

DRAGON-FLY
1. Nymph. 2. Adult

planet, indicated by symbols ☊, ☋; *~-tree*, tree, *Dracaena draco*, of the Canary Islands, bearing panicles of small greenish-white flowers and yielding dragon's-blood.

drăgonnādes' *n.pl.* (hist.) Persecutions of Protestants under Louis XIV by quartering dragoons upon them.

dragōōn' *n.* Cavalryman (ill. CAVALRY) orig. of mounted infantry armed with a kind of carbine called a *dragoon*, now of certain cavalry regiments historically representing these; rough fierce fellow. ~ *v.t.* Set dragoons upon, persecute, oppress; force *into* course by persecution. [Fr. *dragon* carbine, so named as breathing fire]

drail *n.* (U.S.) Fish-hook and line weighted with lead for dragging at depth through water; (Brit.) notched iron on beam of plough to which horses are hitched. ~ *v.i.* Fish with drail.

drain *v.* Draw (liquid) *off, away*, by conduit, drain-pipes, etc.; drink (liquid), empty (vessel), to the dregs; dry (land etc.) by providing channels for the escape of the water in it; (of river) carry off superfluous water of (district); trickle *through*, flow gradually *away*; become rid of moisture by its gradual flowing away; *~-pipe*, large pipe, usu. of earthenware, used for draining; *draining-board*, sloping usu. grooved board on which washed dishes etc. are put to drain; *draining-rack*, rack for same purpose. ~ *n.* Channel carrying off liquid, artificial conduit for water, sewage, etc.; (surg.) tube for drawing off discharge from abscess etc.; constant outlet, withdrawal, demand, or expenditure; small quantity of liquid; (slang) a drink.

drain'age *n.* Draining; system of drains, artificial or natural; what is drained off, sewage.

drāke[1] *n.* Species of *Ephemera* used in fly-fishing; *green* ~, common day-fly, *E. vulgata.*

drāke[2] *n.* Male duck.

Drāke[3], Sir Francis (1540?–96). English admiral; circumnavigated the world in the *Golden Hind*, 1577–81; commanded a division of the English fleet against the Armada; *~'s drum*, sounds, acc. to legend, whenever danger threatens England.

drăm *n.* 1. Avoirdupois weight of $\frac{1}{16}$ ounce. 2. (chiefly U.S.) DRACHM, sense 1. 3. Small draught of spirit etc.; *~-shop*, public-house.

dra'ma (-ah-) *n.* Stage-play; dramatic art, composition and presentation of plays; series of events having the unity and progress of a play and leading to final catastrophe or consummation.

dramăt'ic *adj.* Of, like, drama; theatrical; sudden, striking, impressive. **dramăt'ically** *adv.*

drăm'atĭs pērsōn'ae *n.* (List of) characters in a play.

drăm'atist *n.* Writer of dramas or dramatic poetry.

drăm'atīze *v.* Convert (novel etc.) into play; admit of such conversion; impart dramatic character to. **drăm'atīzā'tion** *n.*

drăm'atûrge, drăm'atûrgist *ns.* Dramatist. **drămatûr'gic** *adj.* **drăm'atûrgy** *n.*

drāpe *v.t.* Cover, hang, adorn, with cloth etc.; arrange (clothes, hangings) in graceful folds. ~ *n.* Fold; (U.S. etc.) curtain.

drāp'er *n.* Retailer of textile fabrics. **drāp'ery** *n.* 1. Cloth, textile fabrics; trade or business of draper. 2. Arrangement of clothing in sculpture etc.; clothing or hangings disposed in folds.

drăs'tic *adj.* Acting strongly, vigorous, violent, esp. (med.) strongly purgative. **drăs'tically** *adv.*

drăt *interj.* Vulgar form of imprecation: confound, curse, bother. **drătt'ĕd** *adj.* ['*od rot* (God rot!)]

draught (-ahft) *n.* (See also DRAFT, a permissible spelling in many senses, and in U.S. the usual spelling.) 1. Drawing, traction; drawing of net for fish etc., catch of fish at one drawing. 2. Single act of drinking, amount so drunk; dose of liquid medicine; *black* ~, purgative of senna, sulphate of magnesia, and liquorice. 3. Depth of water ship draws or requires to float her. 4. (pl.) Game played by two persons on a chess-board with 24 flat wooden discs (*draughtsmen*) of the same value, which are moved diagonally; known as *checkers* in U.S.; ~-*board*, chequered board on which this game is played. 5. Current of air, esp. in confined space, as room or chimney; *feel the* ~, (slang) suffer from adverse conditions. 6. Outline, preliminary drawing, for work of art; (also *draft*) plan of something to be constructed; (usu. *draft*) rough copy, first conception, of document. 7. (usu. *draft*) (Selection of) military detachment, party, reinforcement. 8. (now *draft*) (Written order for) withdrawing of money from fund in bank etc., cheque, bill of exchange. 9. Drawing of liquor from vessel; ~ *beer*, beer drawn from cask, not bottled; *beer on* ~, beer in tapped cask. ~ *v.t.* 1. (now *draft*) Draw off (party for military service etc.) from larger body. 2. (also *draft*) Make plan or sketch of.

draughts'man (-ahft-) *n.* (pl. *-men.*) 1. One who is employed to make drawings, plans, or sketches; one skilled in drawing or designing. 2. Person who drafts document (usu. DRAFTSMAN). 3. One of the pieces in game of draughts. **draughts'manship** *n.* Skill in drawing. **draughts'woman** *n.*

draught'y (-ahftĭ) *adj.* Abounding in draughts or currents of air.

Dravid'ian *adj.* & *n.* (Member) of one of the non-Aryan races of S. India and Ceylon (including Tamils and Kanarese); (of) any of the languages spoken by these people. [f. *Dravida*, old province of S. India]

draw *v.* (past t. *drew*, past part. *drawn*). 1. Pull; pull after one; drag (criminal) on hurdle etc. to execution; contract, distort (features etc.); haul in (net); bend (bow); pull at; pull (curtain, veil) open or shut; (cricket) divert (ball) to 'on' side of wicket with bat; (golf) hit (ball) with a slight 'pull'. 2. Attract, bring to one; take in; attract attention or custom; induce *to* do; be attracted, assemble, *round*, *together*, etc.; bring about, entail. 3. Extract; pull out (sword or other weapon from sheath); draw sword, pistol, etc.; pull or take one from a number of things so as to decide something by chance (esp. in ~ *lots* etc.); obtain by lot; drag (badger, fox) from hole; haul up (water) from well; bring out (liquid, blood) from vessel, body; extract essence of (tea); take, get, from a source; (cards) cause (trumps etc.) to be played; bring (person) out, make him reveal information, talent, irritation, etc.; deduce, infer; extract something from, empty, drain; disembowel; (hunting) search (covert) for game etc.; ~ *blank*, find nothing. 4. Protract, stretch, elongate; make (wire) by pulling piece of metal through successively smaller holes; (naut., of sail) swell out with wind. 5. Trace; delineate, make (picture), represent (object), by drawing lines; use pencil thus; describe in words; practise delineation; frame (document) in due form, compose; formulate, institute (comparisons, distinctions); write out (bill, cheque, draft, *on* banker etc.); make call *on* person, his faith, memory, etc., *for* money or service. 6. Make way, move, *towards*, *near*, *off*, etc.; (racing) get farther *away* to the front, come *level*, gain *on*. 7. (Of ship) require (such a depth of water) to float. 8. End (game, battle) without victory on either side; (abs.) succeed in doing this (freq. ~ *with* the other side). 9. ~ *back*, withdraw from undertaking; ~ *in*, entice, persuade to join; (of day) close in, (of successive days) become shorter; ~ *off*, withdraw (troops); (of troops) withdraw; ~ *on*, lead to, bring about; allure; approach, draw near; ~ *out*, lead out, detach, or array (troops); prolong; elicit; induce to talk; write out in proper form; (of successive days) become longer; ~ *up*, come up *with*, *to*; come to a stand; bring (troops), come, into regular order; compose (documents etc.); ~ *oneself up*, assume stiff attitude. ~ *n.* Act of drawing; esp.: strain, pull; attractive effect; thing that draws custom, attention etc.; drawing of lots; raffle; drawn game; remark etc. meant to elicit information or set person off on pet subject; act of drawing a revolver etc.

draw'băck *n.* 1. Amount paid back from charge previously made, esp. from excise or import duty on goods exported; deduction *from*. 2. Thing that qualifies satisfaction; disadvantage.

draw'bridge *n.* Bridge across moat, river, etc., made to be raised or lowered at one end by chains or pulleys (ill. CASTLE).

drawee' *n.* Person on whom draft or bill is drawn.

draw'er *n.* (esp.) 1. (archaic) Tapster. 2. Box-shaped receptacle sliding in and out of special frame, or of table etc.; *drawers*, *chest of* ~*s*, piece of furniture containing tiers of drawers. 3. (pl.) (Under-) garment for lower part of body and legs, fastening round the waist. **draw'erful** *n.*

draw'ĭng *n.* (esp.) Art of representing by line; delineation by means of pen or pencil or other pointed instrument, esp. with little or no use of colour; product of this, sketch; ~-*block*, block of detachable leaves of drawing-paper adhering at edges; ~-*board*, board for stretching drawing-paper on; ~-*compass(es)*, compasses with pen or pencil substituted for one point; ~-*pin*, flat-headed pin for fastening paper to drawing-board etc. (*Illustration*, *p.* 246.)

draw'ĭng-rŏŏm *n.* 1. Room for reception of company, to which ladies retire after dinner. 2. Levee, formal reception, esp. at court. 3. (U.S.) Section or carriage of railway-train more luxurious or more private than usual. [earlier *withdrawing-room*]

drawl *v.* Speak, utter, with indolent or affected slowness; be so uttered. ~ *n.* Drawling, slow, utterance. **drawl'ĭngly** *adv.*

drawn *adj.* (past part. of DRAW *v.*) ~-*(thread-)work*, ornamental work in textile fabrics done by drawing out threads, with or without addition of needlework.

draw'-tāble *n.* Extensible table with top in three parts, two of which lie under the third and can be drawn out so as to lie level with it.

draw'-wĕll *n.* Well from which water is drawn with rope and bucket.

dray *n.* Low cart without sides for heavy loads, esp. beer-barrels; ~-*horse*, large powerful horse; *dray'man*, driver of brewer's dray.

Dray'ton, Michael (1563–1631). English poet, author of odes, sonnets, satires, and much historical and topographical verse.

dread (-ĕd) *v.* Be in great fear of; shrink from, look forward to with terror; fear greatly; be afraid (*to* do). ~ *n.* Great fear, awe, apprehension; object of fear or awe. ~ *adj.* Dreaded, dreadful; awful, revered.

dread'ful (-ĕd-) *adj.* Terrible, awe-inspiring; troublesome, disagreeable, very bad, horrid; *penny* ~, cheap sensational story of crime and horrors. **dread'fully** *adv.*

dreadnought (drĕd'nawt) *n.* 1. (Cloth used for) thick coat for stormy weather. 2. Name of first British battleship (launched 1906) of a powerful type superior in armament to all its predecessors; hence, a class of battleships having their main armament all of big guns of one calibre (now disused).

dream *n.* Train of thoughts, images, or fancies passing through mind during sleep; conscious indulgence of fancy, reverie, castle in the air; thing of dream-like beauty, charm, goodness, etc. **dream'lĕss, dream'līke** *adjs.* **dream** *v.* (past t. & past part. *dreamt* pr. -ĕmt, or *dreamed*) 1. Have visions etc. in sleep; see, hear, etc., in sleep. 2. Imagine as in a dream; think possible; (with negative) so much as contemplate possibility *of*, have any conception *of*. 3. Fall into reverie; form imaginary visions of; be inactive or unpractical. **dream'er** *n.* (esp.) Unpractical person.

dream'y *adj.* Full of dreams; given to reverie, fanciful, unpractical; dreamlike, vague, misty. **dream'ĭly** *adv.* **dream'ĭnĕss** *n.*

drear (poet.), **drear'y** *adjs.* Dismal, gloomy, dull. **drear'ĭly** *adv.* **drear'ĭnĕss** *n.*

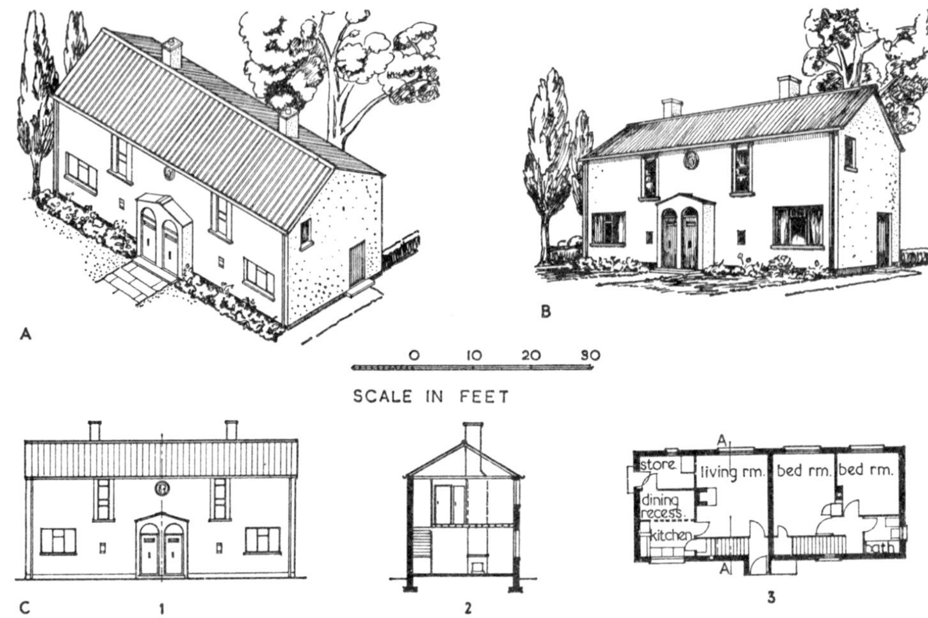

DRAWING: A. ISOMETRIC. B. PERSPECTIVE. C. ORTHOGRAPHIC
1. Elevation. 2. Section at *A–A* on plan. 3. Plan of ground floor and first floor

drĕdge[1] *n.* Apparatus for bringing up oysters, specimens, etc., clearing out mud, etc., from river or sea bottom, or obtaining ores from alluvial deposits. ~ *v.* Bring *up*, clear *away*, *out*, with dredge; clean out (harbour, river) with dredge; use dredge. **drĕdg'er**[1] *n.* One who uses dredge; boat employed in dredging.

drĕdge[2] *v.t.* Sprinkle with flour or other powder; sprinkle (flour etc.) *over*. **drĕdg'er**[2] *n.* Box with perforated lid for sprinkling flour etc.

dree *v.t.* (archaic) Endure (now only in ~ *one's weird*, submit to one's lot).

drĕg *n.* (usu. pl.) Sediment, grounds, lees; worthless part, refuse. **drĕgg'y** *adj.*

drĕnch *n.* 1. Draught or dose administered to animal; (archaic) large, medicinal, or poisonous draught. 2. Soaking; downpour. ~ *v.t.* 1. Make to drink largely; force (animal) to take draught of medicine. 2. Steep, soak. 3. Wet all over with falling liquid. **drĕnch'er** *n.* (esp.) Drenching shower.

Drĕs'den (-z-). German city on the Elbe, capital of Saxony; ~ *china*, English name for porcelain made at MEISSEN near Dresden; ~ *figure*, figurine of this.

drĕss *n.* Clothing, esp. the visible part of it, costume; woman's gown; frock; external covering, outward form; *full* ~, that worn on formal occasions; (*evening*) ~, that worn at dinners or evening parties; *morning* ~, ordinary day-time costume; ~ *circle*, first gallery in theatres, in which evening dress was once required; ~ *coat*, swallow-tailed coat for evening dress; ~*-improver*, bustle; *dress'maker*, woman who makes women's dresses; *dress'making*; ~ *rehearsal*, final rehearsal in costume of play etc. ~ *v.* 1. (mil.) Correct alignment of (companies etc. or men in line); come into correct place in line etc. 2. Array, clothe; provide oneself with clothes; put on one's clothes; put on evening dress; ~ *out*, attire conspicuously; ~ *up*, attire oneself, attire (another), elaborately or in masquerade. 3. Deck, adorn (ship with flags, shop-window with wares etc.); provide (play) with costumes. 4. Treat (wound, wounded person) with remedies; apply dressing to. 5. Subject to cleansing, trimming, smoothing, etc.; brush, comb, do up (hair); curry (horse, leather); finish surface of (textile fabrics, stone for building); prepare, cook (food); manure (ground).

drĕss'age (-ahzh *or*-ĭj) *n.* In horsemanship, type of drill by which horses are trained to execute certain movements with extreme precision and smoothness.

drĕss'er[1] *n.* (esp.) 1. Surgeon's assistant in hospital operations. 2. Person who helps actor to dress for part.

drĕss'er[2] *n.* Kitchen sideboard with shelves for dishes etc.; (U.S.) chest of drawers, dressing-table, in bedroom.

drĕss'ĭng *n.* (esp.) 1. (also ~ *down*) Drubbing, beating; scolding. 2. Seasoning, sauce, etc. used in cooking. 3. Manure etc. spread over land. 4. Remedies, bandages, etc., with which wound is dressed. 5. Glaze, size, or stiffening used in finishing textile fabrics. 6. (pl.) The external parts of a building distinguished from plain walling, as columns, mouldings, cornices, etc. 7. ~*-case*, case containing toilet necessaries; ~*-gown*, *-jacket*, garment worn while making toilet or in dishabille; ~*-room*, room for dressing etc., usu. opening from bedroom; ~*-table*, table with mirror, drawers, etc., for use while dressing.

drĕss'y *adj.* Fond of, smart in,

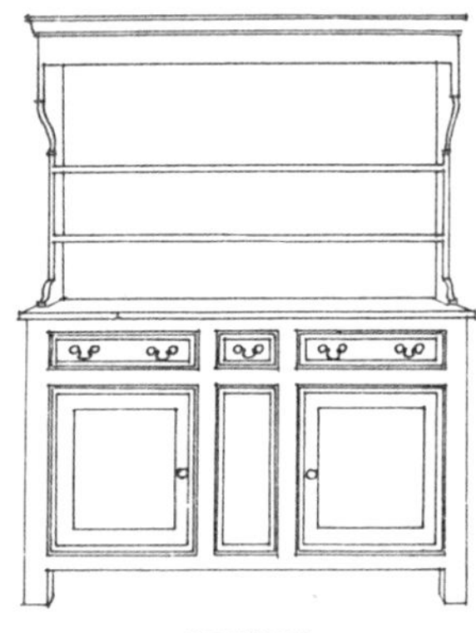

DRESSER

dress; (of clothes) stylish **drĕss'ĭly** *adv.* **drĕss'ĭnĕss** *n.*

drey (drā) *n.* Red squirrel's nest.

Drey'fus (drā-), Alfred (1859–1935). A Jewish officer in the French army, condemned in 1894 to imprisonment on Devil's Island by a secret military tribunal on a charge of divulging military secrets to Germany; evidence of his innocence was found in 1896, but a violent anti-semitic press campaign prevented the reopening of the question; it was not until 1906 that the sentence condemning Dreyfus was finally quashed. **Dreyfusard'** (-âr) *n.* Supporter of innocence of Dreyfus.

drĭb'ble *v.* 1. Flow, let flow, in drops or trickling stream; run at the mouth. 2. (Football, hockey) work (ball) forward with series of short kicks or hits; (billiards) make (ball) just roll, (of ball) just roll, into pocket. ~ *n.* Small trickling or barely continuous stream; act of dribbling.

drĭb'lĕt *n.* Small quantity, petty sum (as instalment etc.).

drī'er *n.* Thing, person, that dries (DRY *v.*); esp., substance mixed with oil paints to expedite drying.

drĭft *n.* 1. Being driven by current; slow course or current; ship's deviation from course due to currents; aeroplane's deviation due to wind etc.; (gunnery) projectile's deviation due to rotation. 2. Natural or unperceived progress, tendency; inaction. 3. Purpose, meaning, tenor, scope. 4. Shower, driving mass; accumulation of snow, sand, etc., heaped up by wind; matter driven by currents of water. 5. (geol.) Anything transported and deposited by wind, water, or ice, esp. the boulder clay left by a glacier. 6. (forest law) Driving of cattle to one place on appointed day to determine ownership etc. 7. = *~-net*, large net for catching herring, pilchards, mackerel, extended by weights at bottom and floats at top and allowed to drift with tide. 8. (mining) Horizontal passage following vein of mineral (ill. MINE). 9. (S. Afr.) Ford. 10. Steel tool for enlarging or shaping hole in metal. 11. (naut.) Length of rope paid out before fastening is made. 12. *~-anchor*, floating frame keeping ship's head to wind in gale or when dismasted; *~-ice*, detached drifting pieces of ice; *~-net*: see sense 7; *drift'wood*, wood drifting on, or cast ashore by, water. ~ *v.* 1. Be carried by or as by current of air or water; (of current) carry; go passively or aimlessly; pile, be piled by wind, into drifts, cover with drifts. 2. Form or enlarge hole with drift. 3. Fish with drift-net. **drĭft'age** *n.*

drĭft'er *n.* (esp.) Boat used in fishing with drift-net.

drĭll[1] *n.* 1. Contrivance (steel tool, machine, etc.) for boring

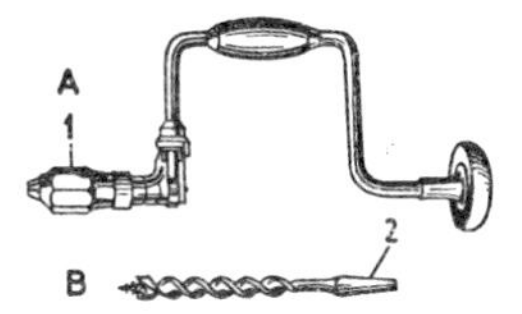

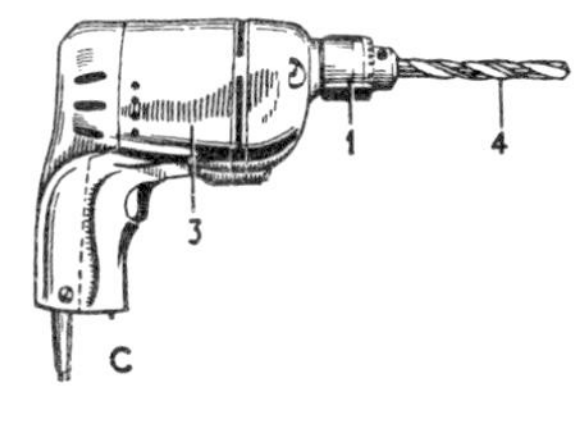

D

DRILLS: A. BRACE. B. BIT. C. ELECTRIC DRILL. D. REAMER

1. Chuck. 2. Fang. 3. Motor. 4. Twist bit

holes in metal, stone, sinking oil-wells, etc. 2. Shell-fish which bores into shells of young oysters. 3. Military exercise or training; physical exercise(s); rigorous discipline, exact routine; *~-instructor, -sergeant*, instructor in drill. ~ *v.* 1. Bore with drill etc. 2. Train in, perform, military movements and exercise; train rigorously and exactly; impart (knowledge etc.) by strict method.

drĭll[2] *n.* 1. Small furrow for sowing seed in; ridge with such furrow on top; row of plants sown in it. 2. Machine for sowing seed in drills. ~ *v.t.* Sow (seed), plant (ground) in drills.

drĭll[3] *n.* W. African species of baboon, *Cynocephalus leucophaeus*, allied to mandrill.

drĭll[4] *n.* Coarse twilled cotton fabric used for uniform, boat sails, etc.

drī'ly. Var. of DRYLY.

drĭnk *v.* (past t. *drănk*, past part. *drŭnk* and poet. *drŭnk'en*). 1. Take (liquid) into stomach, swallow; swallow contents of (cup etc.); swallow liquid; take (*the waters* at spa) medicinally; (of plants, porous substances, etc.) absorb (moisture). 2. Take *in*, esp. with eyes or ears, with eager delight. 3. Drink alcoholic liquor; indulge in alcohol to excess, tipple; spend (money etc.) in drinking; honour (toast etc.) by drinking; *~ to*, pledge, toast. ~ *n.*

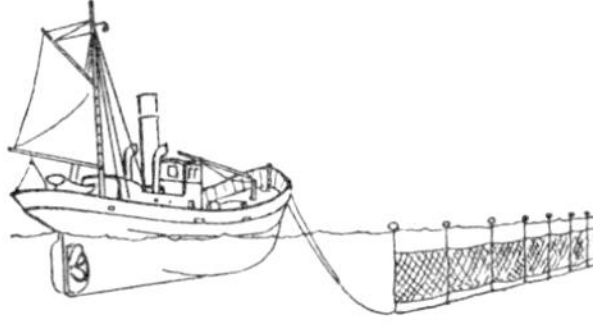

DRIFTER WITH DRIFT-NET

Liquid drunk; beverage; intoxicating liquor; excessive indulgence in this, intemperance; glass or portion of liquor; *the ~*, (R.A.F. slang) the sea; *~-offering*, libation.

drĭnk'able *adj.* & *n.* Fit to drink; (in pl.) things to drink.

drĭp *v.* Fall, let fall, in drops; let drops fall, be so wet (*with* liquid) as to shed drops. ~ *n.* 1. Act of dripping; dripping liquid. 2. (archit., also *~stone*), projecting moulding etc. to throw off rain (ill. WINDOW).

drĭpp'ĭng *n.* (esp.) Fat melted from roasting meat and used for cooking or as food.

drīve *v.* (past t. *drōve*, past part. *drĭv'en*) 1. Urge in some direction, esp. by blows, threats, violence, etc.; chase or frighten (game, wild beasts, etc.) from over large area into small in order to kill or capture; scour (district) thus; (forest law) hold a drift (see DRIFT *n.* sense 6). 2. Direct course of (animal drawing vehicle, vehicle, locomotive, etc.); convey in vehicle; act as driver of vehicle; travel in car or carriage at one's disposal. 3. Impel forcibly, constrain, compel. 4. Impel, carry along, throw, propel, send, (thing) in some direction; (cricket) strike (ball) with upright bat more or less in direction of bowler; (golf) strike (ball), strike ball, with driver; force (stake, nail, etc.) *into* ground etc. with blow. 5. Bore (tunnel, horizontal cavity). 6. Aim blow or missile (*at*). 7. (Of steam or other power) set or keep (machinery) going. 8. Carry on vigorously, effect, conclude; defer. 9. Dash, rush, hasten; work hard. 10. Move along impelled by current, wind, etc.; *~ at*, have for one's drift or aim. ~ *n.* 1. Excursion in vehicle. 2. Driving of game, enemy, etc. 3. Forcible blow or stroke at cricket etc.; (golf) hit with a driver. 4. Energy, push; energetic campaign. 5. Carriage-road, esp. private road to house. 6. WHIST-drive.

drĭv'el *n.* Silly nonsense, twaddle. ~ *v.i.* Run at mouth or nose like child; talk childishly or idiotically. **drĭv'eller** *n.*

drī'ver *n.* 1. One who drives. 2. (golf) Wooden-headed club used to send ball a long distance, esp. from tee (ill. GOLF).

drī'vĭng-wheel *n.* Wheel communicating motion to other wheels in machinery; large wheel of locomotive, to which power is transmitted through connecting rod to crank (ill. LOCOMOTIVE); wheel of vehicle to which driving power is applied.

drĭz'zle *v.i.* Rain in fine, dense, spray-like drops. ~ *n.* Such rain or drops. **drĭz'zly** *adj.*

drōgue (-g) *n.* 1. Buoy at end of harpoon line. 2. Canvas cone open at both ends with a hoop at larger end, used as sea-anchor by seaplanes; lighter form of this towed by aircraft to serve for target practice.

droit *n.* Legal right or perquisite; *~s of Admiralty*, proceeds of seized enemy ships, wrecks, etc., formerly belonging to Court of Admiralty but now paid into Exchequer.

drōll *adj.* Facetious, amusing; queer, odd, surprising. **drōl'ly** (ōl-lĭ) *adv.* **drōll'nėss** *n.* **drōll** *n.* Jester, wag.

drōll'ery *n.* Jesting, waggery; jest; drollness, quaint humour.

drōme *n.* Short for AERODROME.

drŏm'ėdary (*or* -ŭm-) *n.* Light, fleet camel specially reared and trained for riding, esp. the one-humped Arabian camel (*Camelus dromedarius*).

drōne *n.* 1. Male of honey-bee, which does not work (ill. BEE); lazy idler, sluggard. 2. Continued deep monotonous sound, as of humming or buzzing. 3. Bass-pipe of bagpipe, emitting one continuous tone (ill. BAGPIPE); tone emitted by this. *~ v.* Buzz like bee or bagpipe; talk, utter, monotonously.

drōōl *v.* & *n.* Drivel.

drōōp *v.* Hang down, incline, as from weariness or exhaustion; (of eyes) be turned down, with lowered eyelids; languish, flag; become dejected, lose heart; let (head, eyes, etc.) droop. *~ n.* Drooping attitude; loss of spirit, fall of tone. **drōōp'ĭngly** *adv.*

drŏp *n.* 1. Small quantity of liquid that falls, hangs, trickles down, or detaches itself in spherical or pear-shaped form; tear-drop, drop of rain, blood, dew, etc.; (dispensing etc.) smallest quantity of liquid that can be transferred from one vessel to another by pouring through air; minim; (pl.) medicinal preparation to be administered in drops; very small quantity, esp. small quantity of drink. 2. Pendant of metal or precious stone, glass pendant of chandelier, etc.; sweetmeat, sugar-plum. 3. Fall, dropping, descent; abrupt fall in level of surface; depth to which anything sinks; distance through which anything falls, esp. distance through which criminal falls when hanged. 4. Curtain let down before stage between acts or scenes of play etc. (also *~-curtain*). 5. Small platform on gallows which is let fall from under feet of condemned man. 6. *~arch:* see ill. ARCH; *~-kick*, kick at football made by dropping ball and kicking it as it touches the ground; *~-letter*, (U.S.) letter posted for local delivery; *~-scene*, drop-curtain. *~ v.* 1. Fall in drops; give off drops, drip; fall vertically, like a single drop; descend abruptly; fall, sink to ground. 2. Cease, lapse, fall through; fall in direction, amount, degree, etc. 3. Allow oneself to be carried downstream without effort; allow oneself to fall *behind, to the rear*, etc. 4. Come or go casually or unexpectedly; come down *upon* forcibly. 5. Let fall, shed, in drops; let fall like a drop or drops; let fall (words etc.) casually; make (curtsey); post, send (letter etc.); (of animals) give birth to (young); (*slang*) lose, part with (money). 6. Fell, bring down, with blow, shot, etc. 7. Deposit, set down, from ship or vehicle. 8. Omit (esp., letter etc. in pronunciation). 9. Let droop; lower (voice). 10. Obtain (goal) by drop-kick. 11. Break off acquaintance or association with; cease to keep up, end, stop. *~ in*, (esp.) pay casual visit; *~ off*, (esp.) fall asleep; become less numerous etc.

drŏp'lėt *n.* Little drop.

drŏpp'ĭngs *n.pl.* That which drops or falls in drops, as melted wax etc.; dung of animals.

drŏpp'ĭng-wĕll *n.* Well in which water drops or drips from above.

drŏp'sy *n.* Accumulation of watery fluid in serous cavities or connective tissues of body. **drŏp'sĭcal, drŏp'sied** (-sĭd) *adjs.*

drŏs(h)'kў *n.* Russian low 4-wheeled topless carriage; cab in German towns (now obs.).

drŏss *n.* Scum thrown off from metal in melting; foreign matter mixed with any substance; refuse, rubbish, worthless matter. **drŏss'y** *adj.*

drought (-out), (poet.) **drouth** *n.* 1. (archaic) Dryness, lack of moisture; thirst. 2. Continuous dry weather, lack of rain; *absolute ~*, period of 15 days each of which has received not more than 0·01 in. of rain. **drought'y, drouth'y** *adjs.*

drōve *n.* 1. Herd, flock, being driven or moving together; crowd, multitude, large number. 2. Stone-mason's broad-faced chisel.

drōv'er *n.* One who drives animals in droves to market; cattle-dealer.

drown *v.* Suffer death by submersion in water; suffocate by submersion in water; submerge, flood, drench; overcome (grief etc.) with or *in* drink; overpower (sound) by greater loudness.

drowse (-z) *v.* Be heavy or dull with or as with sleep; be half asleep; pass *away* (time etc.) in drowsing. *~ n.* Half-sleep, half-asleep condition.

drows'y (-zĭ) *adj.* Heavy with sleepiness; half asleep, dozing; sleepy; soporific; sluggish, dull, lethargic. **drows'ĭly** *adv.* **drows'ĭnėss** *n.*

drŭb *v.t.* Cudgel, thump, thrash, belabour. **drŭbb'ĭng** *n.*

drŭdge *n.* Servile worker, slave, hack; hard toiler. *~ v.i.* Perform mean or servile tasks; work hard or laboriously, toil. **drŭdg'ery** *n.*

drŭg *n.* Medicinal substance; (*dangerous*) *~*, one which causes euphoria in the taker and predisposes him to addiction, esp. preparation or extract of opium or coca or Indian hemp; narcotic; *~-addict*, person who takes one of these habitually; *~ on the market*, commodity no longer in demand, unsaleable thing; *~-store*, (U.S.) chemist's shop also dealing extensively or mainly in toilet requisites, stationery, newspapers, light refreshments, etc.; *~ traffic*, commercial sale of dangerous drugs, forbidden by law. *~ v.t.* Administer drug to, esp. narcotic; add drug to (food or drink).

drŭgg'ėt (-g-) *n.* Coarse woven fabric for floor coverings etc., usu. of jute and cotton.

drŭgg'ĭst (-g-) *n.* Dealer in drugs, pharmaceutical chemist.

Dru'ĭd (-ōō-) *n.* 1. One of an order of priests (acc. to Caesar) or magicians (acc. to Irish and Welsh legend) among the ancient Celts of Gaul and Britain. 2. Member of Welsh, Cornish, or Breton GORSEDD. 3. Member of *United Ancient Order of Druids*, secret benefit society founded in London in 1781, and having numerous lodges called *groves* in England, America, etc. **Dru'ĭdėss** *n.* **Druĭd'ĭc** *adj.* **Dru'ĭdĭsm** *n.* Religious system of Druids.

drŭm[1] *n.* 1. Percussive musical instrument consisting of hollow cylindrical or hemispherical frame

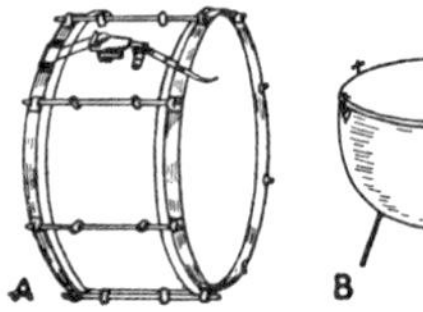

A. BASS DRUM. B. KETTLEDRUM

with tightly stretched membrane at one or both ends, which is struck to produce sound; sound of this; **drum'mer**; *bass ~, tenor ~*, drums struck sideways; *kettledrum*, cauldron-shaped drum which can be tuned to produce note of definite pitch; *side ~*, drum played on upper head, esp. (mil.) carried at side. 2. Hollow part of middle ear, tympanum. 3. Drum-shaped thing; cylinder round which rope or belt passes; (archit.) solid part of Corinthian and Composite capitals; block of stone forming one section of shaft of column; cylindrical structure supporting dome; cylindrical receptacle for oil etc. 4. (archaic) Large evening or afternoon tea party. 5. (also *~-fish*) Any of various Amer. fishes making drumming noise. 6. *~-fire*, rapid heavy gun-fire concentrated on a particular objective; *drum'head*, stretched skin or membrane of drum; membrane across drum of ear; circular top of capstan, into which capstan-bars are fixed; flat-topped kind of cabbage; *drumhead court-martial*, court-martial round upturned drum for summary treatment of offences during military operations; *drumhead service*, religious service round upturned drum; *~-major*, non-commissioned officer commanding drummers of regiment, officer of band etc. leading and conducting it on march; ~-*stick*, stick usu. with padded knob at one end for beating drum; lower part of leg of cooked chicken, so called from its shape. ~ *v.* 1. Play the drum; beat, tap, or thump, continously on something; (of bird, insect) make loud hollow noise with quivering wings. 2. Summon, beat *up*, as by drumming; (colloq.) obtain (custom, customers) by canvassing etc.; (U.S.) solicit orders; drive *out* of regiment etc. publicly by beat of drum, so as to heighten disgrace; din or drive *into* (person, his ears, etc.) by incessant repetition. **drŭmm'er** *n.* 1. Player of drum. 2. (U.S.) Commercial traveller.

drŭm[2], **drŭm'lĭn** *ns.* (geol.) Oval mound of drift or diluvial formation.

drŭnk *pred. adj.* (past part. of DRINK *v.*) Intoxicated, overcome with liquor. ~ *n.* Drinking-bout; drunken person; case of drunkenness. **drŭnk'ard** *n.* Sot; habitually drunken person. **drŭnk'en** *adj.* (usu. attrib.) Intoxicated; given to drinking, often drunk; caused by or exhibiting drunkenness. **drŭnk'enly** *adv.* **drŭnk'ennėss** *n.*

drupe (-ōōp) *n.* Stone-fruit; fleshy or pulpy fruit enclosing stone with kernel, as olive, plum, cherry (ill. FRUIT). **drupā'ceous** (-sh*u*s) *adj.* Bearing drupes.

drup'el(-ōō-), **drupe'lėt**(-ōōpl-) *ns.* (bot.) Small drupe, such as those of which blackberry is composed (ill. FRUIT).

Druse (-ōōz) *n.* Member of Moslem political and religious sect founded 1040, inhabiting region round Mt Lebanon in Syria, believing in transmigration, and holding the 6th Fatimate Caliph, Hakim Biamrillahi, to be a divine incarnation. [Arab. *Durūz*, prob. f. Ismail *al-Darazi* (the tailor), their founder]

drȳ *adj.* 1. Free from moisture, not wet or moist; deficient in rain, not rainy; dried, desiccated, parched; thirsty, causing thirst; not yielding water etc., (of cows etc.) not yielding milk. 2. Not under, in, or on water; not submerged. 3. (Of bread etc.) without butter or the like. 4. Solid, not liquid; (of measures etc.) relating to non-liquids. 5. Of wines etc., not sweet or fruity. 6. Not associated with liquid; favouring or enforcing prohibition of alcoholic liquor. 7. Feeling or showing no emotion; stiff, cold; caustically witty, uttered in, using, matter-of-fact tones without air of pleasantry; meagre, plain, bare. 8. ~ *battery*, electric battery consisting of dry cells; ~-*bob*, at Eton, boy who plays cricket, as opp. to *wet-bob*, one who goes in for rowing; ~-*bulb thermometer*, one of a pair of thermometers in hygrometer of which one has dry and other wet bulb; ~ *cell* (electr.) voltaic cell whose contents are made non-spillable by use of some absorbent substance, esp. cell of Leclanché type, in which, for the sake of portability, sawdust or plaster of Paris, saturated with sal-ammoniac, takes the place of the solution; ~-*clean* (*v.t.*) clean (textiles) without using water, e.g. with spirit; ~-*cooper*, maker of casks for dry goods; ~-*cure* (*v.t.*) cure (meat etc.) without pickling in liquid; ~ *dock*: see DOCK[3]; ~ *farming*, various methods of arable farming designed to conserve moisture in dry areas; ~-*fly*, (fishing) artificial fly which is not immersed in the water, but thrown lightly on the surface and dried by waving in the air before next cast; ~ *goods*, (chiefly U.S.) articles of drapery, mercery, etc., as opp. to groceries; ~ *measure*, measure of bulk, esp. for grain, fruits, etc.; ~-*nurse* (*n.*) nurse who looks after baby without suckling it, as opp. to *wet-nurse*; (fig.) person who looks after another with great care; (*v.t.*) nurse thus; ~ *plate*, photographic sensitized plate coated with a film which does not require immersion in a solution before exposure; ~-*point*, strong pointed tool for scratching design (without use of acid) on copper plate from which prints are taken; process of engraving thus, print so produced; ~-*rot*, decayed condition, caused by various fungi, of unventilated timber, in which it becomes dry, light, and friable; *dry'salter*, dealer in chemicals used in arts, drugs, dyestuffs, etc., sometimes also dealer in oils, sauces, tinned meats, etc.; ~ *shampoo*, kind of shampoo without water; *dry'shod*, without wetting the feet; ~ *spell*, period of little or no rain (in U.K., period of 15 days or more with less than 0·04 in. of rain per day); ~(-*stone*) *wall*, wall built without mortar. **drȳ'ish** *adj.* **drȳ'ly, drī'ly** *advs.* **drȳ'nėss** *n.* **drȳ** *v.* Make or become dry by wiping, evaporation, draining, etc.; cause (cow) to cease giving milk; ~ *up*, make, become, utterly dry; cease to yield water or milk; (colloq.) cease talking; (theatr.) forget one's lines.

drȳ'ăd *n.* Nymph inhabiting tree, wood-nymph.

Drȳd'en, John (1631–1700). English poet, dramatist, critic, and translator of Virgil, Horace, Ovid, etc.

D.S. *abbrev.* *Dal segno* (= repeat from the mark).

D.Sc. *abbrev.* Doctor of Science.

D.S.C., D.S.M., D.S.O. *abbrevs.* Distinguished Service Cross, Medal, Order.

d.t.(s)., D.T. *abbrevs.* Delirium tremens.

D.Th(eol). *abbrev.* Doctor of Theology.

dū'al *adj.* Of two; twofold, divided in two; double; ~ *number*, (gram.) inflected form proper to two persons or things. ~ *n.* Dual number. **dūăl'ĭty** *n.*

dū'alism *n.* 1. Being dual. 2. Theory or system of thought recognizing two independent principles; (philos.) doctrine that mind and matter exist as distinct entities (opp. to MONISM and PLURALISM); doctrine that there are two independent principles, good and evil; (theol.) doctrine that Christ consisted of two personalities (attributed to Nestorius by his opponents). **dū'alist** *n.* **dūalis'tĭc** *adj.*

dŭb[1] *v.t.* 1. Make (person) into a *knight* by striking shoulder with sword. 2. Invest with (new title); name, nickname. 3. Dress (artificial fishing-fly); smear (leather) with grease.

dŭb[2] *v.t.* Add sound effects or new sound-track, esp. in a different language, to (film); insert (sound effects) *in* film or radio or television production.

dŭbb'ĭn(g) *n.* Preparation of grease for softening and waterproofing leather.

dūbī'ėty *n.* Feeling of doubt.

dū'bious *adj.* Doubtful; of questionable or suspected character. **dū'biously** *adv.* **dū'biousnėss** *n.*

dū'bĭtable *adj.* Open to doubt or question. **dūbĭtā'tion** *n.* Doubt, uncertainty, hesitation. **dū'bĭtatĭve** *adj.* Expressing doubt or hesitancy. **dū'bĭtatively** *adv.*

Dŭb'lĭn. County borough and seaport on E. coast of Ireland, capital of the republic and formerly of all Ireland.

dū'cal *adj.* Of, like, bearing title of, duke.

dŭc'at *n.* (hist.) Gold coin of varying value (freq. about 9*s.*) formerly current in most European countries; (hist.) Italian silver coin; (colloq.) coin, (pl.) cash.

Duce (dōōch'ā). Title assumed by Benito MUSSOLINI as head of Italian Fascists and dictator of Italy. [It., = 'leader']

dŭch'ėss *n.* 1. Wife or widow of duke; lady holding in her own right position equal to duke's. 2. (slang) Costermonger's wife (abbrev. *dutch*).

duchesse (dōōshĕs') *n.* ~ (*satin*), *satin* ~, soft kind of satin; ~ *lace*, Brussels pillow-lace worked with fine thread in large sprays; ~ *potatoes*, purée of potato and egg etc. shaped into small cakes and baked; ~ *set*, set of covers for dressing-table.

dŭch'y *n.* 1. Territory of reigning duke or duchess. 2. Each of the two dukedoms of Cornwall and Lancaster (the two earliest in England) vested in the royal family.

dŭck[1] *n.* 1. Any of several kinds of swimming bird found all over the world, esp. domesticated form of mallard or wild duck; female of this (male being DRAKE[2]); flesh of this. 2. Darling. 3. (cricket slang;

also ~'*s egg*) Batsman's score of 0. 4. *Bombay* ~ = BUMMALO; *lame* ~, disabled person or thing; (Stock Exchange slang) defaulter; ~*s and drakes*, game of making flat stone skip over surface of water; *play* ~*s and drakes with*, throw away idly or carelessly, squander; ~-*bill*, ~-*billed platypus*: see PLATYPUS; *duck'-boards*, slatted timbers laid down on muddy ground in trenches or camps; ~-*hawk*, marsh harrier; (U.S.) American variety of peregrine falcon; ~-*shot*, shot of size suitable for shooting wild duck; *duck'weed*, any plant of genus *Lemna*, floating on still water and covering surface like a green carpet.

dŭck[2] *n.* Strong untwilled linen or cotton fabric for small sails and outer clothing, esp. of sailors; (pl.) trousers of this.

dŭck[3] *v.* Plunge, dive, dip head, under water and emerge; bend quickly, bob, to avoid blow etc., or by way of bow or curtsey; plunge (person) momentarily *in*, *under* water; lower (head) suddenly; (bridge) omit to take possible trick at first opportunity. ~ *n.* Quick dip below water in bathing; lowering of head, jerky bow. **dŭck'ing** *n.* Immersion in water, or wetting by submersion; ~-*pond*, pond for ducking of offenders; ~-*stool*, chair in which scolds, dishonest tradesmen, etc., were tied and ducked in water as a punishment.

dŭck[4] *n.* (*colloq.*) Amphibious landing craft. [f. DUKWS, official designation]

dŭck'lĭng *n.* Young duck; *ugly* ~, in one of Hans Andersen's tales, a cygnet hatched with a brood of ducklings and despised for clumsiness until it grew into a swan; hence, despised or unpromising person who turns out brilliantly.

dŭct *n.* Conduit, tube, for conveying liquid; conduit for electric cable; (physiol.) tube or canal conveying secretions or lymph in animal body; (bot.) vessel of plant's vascular tissue holding air, water, etc. **dŭct'lėss** *adj.* (Of gland) having no ducts, containing secretion that passes directly from cells to blood; endocrine.

dŭc'tīle *adj.* 1. (Of metal) malleable, flexible, not brittle; (tech.) capable of being drawn into wire, tough. 2. Plastic; pliable, pliant. **dŭctĭl'ĭty** *n.*

dŭd *n.* (slang) 1. (pl.) Clothes; rags. 2. Scarecrow; shell etc. that fails to explode; futile plan or person. ~ *adj.* That is false or a failure; useless; unsatisfactory.

dūde *n.* (U.S. slang) Exaggeratedly or ridiculously fastidious or foppish person; dandy, swell; ~ *ranch*, cattle ranch converted into holiday centre for visitors, with facilities for riding, hunting, etc.

dŭdg'eon (-jn) *n.* Resentment, feeling of offence.

dud(h)een' (dŏŏ-) *n.* (Ir.) Short clay pipe.

dūe *adj.* 1. Owing, payable, as a debt or obligation; that ought to be given or rendered (*to*); fitting, proper, rightful; adequate, sufficient. 2. To be ascribed or attributed *to* (cause, agent, etc.; the adverbial use for *owing* is incorrect). 3. Under engagement or contract to be ready, be present, or arrive (at defined time). ~ *adv.* (With ref. to points of compass) straight, exactly, directly. ~ *n.* 1. Person's right, what is owed him; what one owes. 2. (usu. pl.) Toll or fee legally demandable.

dū'ėl *n.* Fight with deadly weapons between two persons, in presence of two observers (*seconds*), to settle quarrel; any contest between two parties, persons, animals, causes. ~ *v.i.* Fight duel. **dū'ėllĭst** *n.*

dūĕnn'a *n.* Elderly woman acting as governess and chaperon in charge of girls (orig. and esp. in Spanish family); chaperon.

dūĕt' *n.* Musical composition for two voices or performers. **dūĕtt'-ĭst** *n.*

dŭff[1] *n.* Boiled pudding, dumpling.

dŭff[2] *v.t.* 1. (slang) Fake up (thing) to make it look new or like something which it is not; (Austral.) alter brands on (stolen cattle); cheat (*out of*). 2. (golf) Mis-hit (shot).

dŭff'el, duff'le *n.* Coarse woollen cloth with thick nap; (U.S.) sportsman's or camper's change of clothes or personal effects. [f. *Duffel* in Brabant]

dŭff'er *n.* (colloq.) Inefficient, useless, or stupid person.

dŭg *n.* Udder of female mammal, teat, nipple; (now contempt.) woman's breast.

dug'ŏng (dŏŏ-) *n.* Large aquatic herbivorous mammal (genus *Halicora*) of Indian seas, Red Sea, and Australia. [Malay *duyong*]

dŭg'-out *adj.* Hollowed out by digging. ~ *n.* 1. Canoe made of hollowed-out tree-trunk (ill. CANOE). 2. Underground shelter esp. for troops in trenches; (slang) retired officer etc. recalled to service.

duik'er(bŏk) (dī-) *n.* Small African antelope (genus *Cephalophus*), so called from its habit of diving suddenly into the bush. [Du. *duiker* diver]

dūke *n.* 1. In Gt Britain and some other countries, hereditary noble ranking next below prince; *royal* ~, duke who is a member of royal family, taking precedence of other dukes. 2. In some parts of Europe, sovereign prince, ruler of small State called duchy. 3. (hist.) In late Roman Empire, provincial military commander. 4. (slang) Hand, fist. **dūke'dom** (-kd-) *n.* Duchy; office or dignity of duke.

Dūk'eries (-ĭz). District in Nottinghamshire containing several ducal estates.

Dukh'obŏr, Dou- (dŏŏχo-) *n.* Member of a sect which originated in Russia in second half of 18th c., probably influenced by Anabaptists and Quakers; its members rejected the authority of Church and State and were persecuted for refusing to pay taxes or perform military service; they migrated to Canada in 1899, and settled in Saskatchewan and British Columbia. [Russ., = 'spirit-wrestler']

dŭl'cėt *adj* Sweet, soothing (esp. of sounds).

dŭlcia'na (-ah-) *n.* (mus.) Open organ stop, usu. 8-foot, of soft tone.

dŭl'cĭfȳ *v.t.* Sweeten; make gentle. **dŭlcĭfĭcā'tion** *n.*

dŭl'cĭmer *n.* 1. Musical instrument in which metallic strings of graduated length are stretched over a trapezoidal sounding-board and struck with hammers held in the hands (earliest prototype of pianoforte); similar instrument played by plucking strings, used in Kentucky. 2. (bibl.) Kind of bagpipe.

Dŭlcĭnē'a (*or* -sĭn'ĭa) *n.* Name given by Don QUIXOTE to a village girl whom he idolizes; hence, idealized mistress.

dŭl'cĭtōne *n.* Musical instrument like small pianoforte in which graduated steel tuning-forks are struck by hammers.

dŭll *adj.* 1. Slow of understanding, obtuse, stupid; wanting sensibility or keenness of perception; (of pain etc.) not keen or intense. 2. Slow, heavy, drowsy; stagnant, sluggish; listless, not lively or cheerful, depressed; causing depression or boredom, tedious, uneventful. 3. Not sharp or keen, blunt; not clear, vivid, or intense; obscure, dim, muffled, flat, insipid; (of weather) overcast, gloomy. ~ *v.* Make or become dull, sluggish, inert, etc.; blunt; make or become dim or indistinct. **dŭll'ard** *n.* Dull or stupid person, dunce. **dŭll'ĭsh** *adj.* **dŭl'ly** (-l-lĭ) *adv.* **dŭll'nėss** *n.*

dŭlse *n.* Edible species of seaweed with bright red deeply divided fronds, *Rhodymenia palmata.*

dū'ly *adv.* Rightly, properly, fitly; sufficiently; punctually.

dum'a (dŏŏ-) *n.* (hist.) Russian elective municipal council; elective legislative council of State established in 1905 by ukase of Nicholas II and abolished in 1917.

Dūm'as (-mah), Alexandre (1803–70). 'Dumas *père*', French dramatist and prolific writer of romantic historical novels ('The Three Musketeers', 'Monte-Cristo', etc.). ~, Alexandre (1824–95). His son; novelist and dramatist, author of 'La Dame aux Camélias' etc.

dŭmb (-m) *adj.* 1. Destitute of faculty of speech. 2. Temporarily bereft of speech from astonishment, shock, etc.; remaining persistently silent; refusing to speak; taciturn, reticent. 3. (Of actions) not attended with speech. 4. Not emitting or attended with sound; silent, mute; not having some quality, property, etc., usual in things of the name. 5. (orig. U.S.) Foolish, stupid (prob. after Ger. *dumm*). 6. ~ *barge*, barge without sails or other motive power; (on Thames) lighter travelling up and down with the tide; ~-*bell*, short bar with rounded heavy knob at each end, used in pairs for exercising muscles; object of this shape; ~ *crambo*: see CRAMBO; ~-*iron*, carriage spring of two half-elliptic springs joined at ends; each of forward ends of frame-side members in motor-car chassis to which one end of each front spring is fixed; ~ *show*, part of play represented by action without speech; significant gesture without speech; ~-*waiter*, stand or wagon holding dishes etc., en-

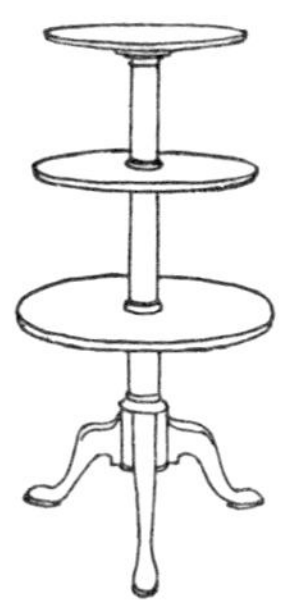

DUMB WAITER

abling waiter to be dispensed with in dining-room. **dŭmb'ly** (-ml-) *adv.* **dŭmb'nĕss** *n.*

Dŭmbârt'on. County town of DUNBARTONSHIRE.

dŭmbfound' (-mf-) *v.t.* Strike dumb, confound, nonplus.

dŭm'dŭm (bullet) *n.* Bullet with soft core uncovered at point, which expands on impact. [*Dum Dum*, military station near Calcutta, with Indian army arsenal]

Dŭmfries'shire. County in SW. Scotland.

dŭmm'y *n.* 1. (whist) Imaginary fourth player whose hand is turned up and played by partner; (bridge) hand of dealer's or declarer's partner, turned up and played by declarer; person holding this hand; *double* ~, (game, problem) with two (or all four) hands exposed. 2. Person taking no real part, or present only for show, figurehead, mere tool. 3. Counterfeit object, sham package, etc.; lay figure; baby's rubber teat; man's figure used as target; imitation ammunition used in training. ~ *adj.* That is a dummy, sham.

dŭmp *n.* Rubbish-heap, place where refuse is deposited; temporary depot, pile, of ammunition, equipment, etc. (also colloq. of town etc.); (pl., colloq.) low spirits. ~ *v.* Shoot, deposit, put down (rubbish); let fall with a bump; send (goods unsaleable at high price in home market) to foreign market for sale at low price.

dŭmp'lĭng *n.* Mass of dough boiled in soup etc. or baked or boiled with fruit inside.

dŭm'py *adj.* Short and stout or thick; ~ *(spirit-)level*, surveyor's instrument for spirit-levelling in which line of sight is adjusted to be perpendicular to vertical axis. ~ *n.* 1. Dumpy animal; esp. one of breed of very short-legged fowls. 2. Woman's short umbrella. 3. Low stuffed seat, humpty.

dŭn[1] *adj.* Of dull greyish-brown colour; (of horse) of light-yellow colour; (poet.) dark, dusky. ~ *n.* Dun colour; dun horse; dun-coloured artificial fishing-fly.

dŭn[2] *n.* Importunate creditor; debt-collector. ~ *v.t.* Importune for payment of debt; pester.

Dŭnbâr', William (1465?–1530?). Scottish poet; author of satires and elegies, etc., of which the 'Lament for the Makaris' is the most famous.

Dŭnbârt'onshire. County in W. Scotland, N. of Firth of Clyde.

dŭnce *n.* One slow at learning, dullard; ~'*s cap*, paper cone put on head of dunce at school. [John DUNS SCOTUS, whose followers were ridiculed by 16th-c. reformers and humanists as enemies of learning]

dŭn'derhead (-ĕd) *n.* Blockhead, stupid person. **dŭn'derheadĕd** *adj.*

Dŭndrear'y *n.* ~ *whiskers*, long side-whiskers worn without a beard. [Lord *Dundreary*, character in T. Taylor's comedy 'Our American Cousin' (1858)]

dūne *n.* Mound or ridge of loose sand on coast.

Dunelm. *abbrev.* (Bishop) of Durham (replacing surname in his signature).

dŭng *n.* Manure; excrement of animals (rarely of man); moral filth; ~-*beetle*, dor-beetle; any of group of beetles (*Coprinae*) which roll up balls of dung; ~-*cart*, cart used for carrying manure; ~-*fly*, two-winged fly of genus *Scatophaga*, feeding on dung; ~-*fork*, pitchfork used to lift or spread dung; ~-*heap*, -*hill*, heap of dung or rubbish; ~-*worm*, worm or larva found in cow-dung, used as bait for fishing. ~ *v.t.* Manure.

dŭngaree' (-ngg-) *n.* Kind of coarse Indian calico; (pl.) trousers or overalls of this.

dŭn'geon (-jn) *n.* 1. Donjon. 2. Strong close cell; subterranean place of confinement.

dun'iwăssal (dōō-) *n.* (Sc.) Highland gentleman of secondary rank.

Dŭnkîrk'. Dunquerque, seaport in NE. France, whence the British Expeditionary Force was evacuated in May 1940; hence, (scene of) evacuation of a defeated army by sea.

dŭn'lĭn *n.* Small reddish-backed migratory wading bird (*Erolia alpina schinzii*), allied to sandpiper, abundant on sea-coasts of Europe; also, an Amer. species or subspecies.

Dŭn'mow Flĭtch (-mō). Acc. to an ancient custom of the manor of Dunmow in Essex (said to have been instituted in 1244) a flitch of bacon is given to any married couple who after 12 months of marriage can swear that they have maintained perfect harmony and fidelity during that time.

dŭnn'age *n.* Light material, as brushwood, mats, etc., stowed under or among cargo to prevent damp and chafing; (colloq. or slang) miscellaneous baggage; tramp's or sailor's clothing.

dŭnn'ock *n.* The hedge ACCENTOR or hedge-sparrow.

Dŭns Scōt'us, John (1265?–1308?). Scholastic theologian, born acc. to tradition at Duns, Berwickshire; called the 'subtle doctor'; his works on theology, logic, and philosophy were university textbooks until the 16th c.

dū'ō *n.* (mus.) Duet.

dūodĕ'cĭmal *adj.* Of twelve or twelfths, proceeding by twelves. ~ *n.pl.* Cross-multiplication, method used for dimensions given in feet, inches, and twelfths of inch, used by quantity surveyors etc.

dūodĕ'cĭmō *n.* (abbrev. 12mo) Book-size in which each leaf is $\frac{1}{12}$ of printing-sheet; book of this size; diminutive thing or person.

dūodēn ary *adj.* Proceeding by twelves, in sets of 12.

dūodēn'um *n.* (anat.) First portion of small intestine immediately below stomach (ill. ALIMENTARY). **dūodēn'al** *adj.* [L *duodeni* twelve at once (from its being about 12 in. long)]

dū'olŏgue (-g) *n.* Conversation between two persons; dramatic piece with two actors.

dūpe *n.* Victim of deception, gull. ~ *v.t.* Cheat, make a fool of. **dūp'ery** *n.*

dū'ple *adj.* (mus., of time) Having two beats in bar; (math., of proportion) in which one quantity is double the other.

dūp'lĕx *adj.* Of two elements; twofold; ~ *burner*, gas-burner having two jets with flames combined into one; ~ *lamp*, lamp with two wicks.

dūp'lĭcate (-*a*t) *adj.* 1. With two corresponding parts; existing in two examples. 2. Doubled; twice as large or as many; ~ *proportion, ratio*, proportion of squares to their radicals. 3. Exactly like thing already existing. ~ *n.* One of two things exactly alike; exact copy; second copy, with equal legal force, of letter or document; synonym; *in* ~, in two exactly corresponding copies or parts. **dūp'lĭcāte** *v.t.* 1. Double, multiply by two. 2. Make in duplicate; make exact copy of; produce copies of; repeat. **dūplĭcā'tion** *n.*

dūp'lĭcātor *n.* Machine for producing copies of hand-written or typewritten documents.

dūplĭ'cĭty *n.* Double-dealing, deceitfulness; doubleness.

dūr'able *adj.* Lasting, not transitory; resisting wear, decay, etc. **dūrabĭl'ĭty, dūr'ableness** *ns.* **dūr'ably** *adv.*

dūrăl'ūmĭn *n.* Trade name of a light hard aluminium alloy containing copper, manganese, and magnesium, used esp. for aircraft.

dūr'a māt'er *n.* Dense tough membrane enveloping brain and spinal cord (ill. SPINE). [med. L. translating Arab. name = 'hard mother', so called because it was supposed to give rise to all membranes of body]

dūrām'ĕn *n.* Dense inner part of tree-trunk, heart-wood.

dūr'ance *n.* Forced confinement, imprisonment (now esp. *in ~ vile*).

dūrā'tion *n.* Continuance in time; time during which thing, action, or state continues.

dŭrb'ar *n.* Court of Indian ruler; audience or levee held by native prince or (hist.) by the British sovereign as Emperor of India or by his deputy.

Dür'er (dü-), Albrecht (1471–1528). German Renaissance engraver and painter; famous for his painting of the four apostles and his numerous line engravings (e.g. 'The Knight, Death, and the Devil') and woodcuts.

dūrĕss(e)' (*or* dūr'ĕs) *n.* Forcible restraint, imprisonment; constraint illegally exercised to force person to perform some act, compulsion.

Durham[1] (dŭ'ram). County in NE. England; city and county town.

Durham[2] (dŭ'ram), John George Lambton, 1st Earl of ~ (1792–1840). British statesman, whose 'Report on the Affairs of British N. America' (1839), usu. called the ~ *Report*, laid down the principles on which self-government was subsequently accorded to the British Dominions.

dur'ĭan (dōōr- *or* dūrē'-) *n.* Large oval or globular prickly fruit of a tree of the Indian Archipelago, *Durio zibethinus*, with hard rind and luscious, civet-smelling, cream-coloured pulp. [Malay *duri* thorn]

dūr'ĭng *prep.* Throughout, at some point in, the continuance of.

dŭrm'ast *n.* Sessile-flowered species of oak, *Quercus petraea*.

dŭrn *v.t.* (U.S.) Darn, confound.

dŭsk *n.* Shade, gloom; darker stage of twilight. ~ *adj.* (poet.) Dusky. ~ *v.* (poet.) Become, look, make, dim or dusky.

dŭs'ky *adj.* Shadowy, dim, dark-coloured. **dŭs'kĭly** *adv.* **dŭs'kĭnėss** *n.*

dŭst *n.* 1. Earth or other solid matter in minute and fine state of subdivision, in particles small and light enough to be easily raised and carried in cloud by wind; a cloud of dust; household refuse; *bite the ~*, fall slain; *in the ~*, humbled, humiliated; *throw ~ in person's eyes*, deceive him. 2. What anything is reduced to by disintegration or decay, esp. mouldered remains of dead body; man's mortal remains; man. 3. Confusion, turmoil, excitement; row, contest also *~-up*). 4. *~-bin*, receptacle for household refuse; *~ bowl*, area denuded of forest and so reduced to desert; *~-cloak, -coat*, coat or cloak worn to keep off dust; *~ cover*, paper jacket of new book; *~ devil*, column-like whirl of dust moving over desert; *dust'man*, man who collects and carts away refuse etc. from dustbins; personification of sleep or sleepiness, SANDman; *~-pan*, utensil for catching dust as it is swept from floor etc. ~ *v.* 1. Sprinkle with dust or powder, (cooking) flour, sugar, etc.; make dusty; sprinkle (dust, powder, etc.). 2. Clear of dust by brushing, wiping, beating, etc.; clear away (dust etc.); clear furniture etc. of dust.

dŭs'ter *n.* 1. Cloth for dusting furniture etc. 2. (U.S.) = DUST-cloak.

dŭs'tĭng *n.* (esp., slang) Thrashing.

dŭs'ty *adj.* Full of dust, strewn with dust; finely powdered like dust; dry as dust, uninteresting; (slang) *not so ~*, fairly good; *~ miller*, the auricula, from the fine powder on the leaves and flowers. **dŭs'tĭly** *adv.* **dŭs'tĭnėss** *n.*

Dŭtch[1] *adj.* 1. Of Holland (the Netherlands) or its language or people; coming from Holland; characteristic of the Dutch. 2. (hist.) Of Germany, German; Teutonic; *High ~*, of the southern Germans, High German; *Low ~*, of the northern Germans, of the northern and north-west parts including the Netherlands and Flanders. 3. ~ *auction*: see AUCTION; *~ barn*, roof over hay, straw, etc., supported on poles; *~ cheese*, round skim-milk cheese made in Holland, esp. kind stained red on outside; *~ courage*, courage due to intoxicants and therefore not lasting; *~ gable*, gable with ogee curve (ill. GABLE); *~ metal*, alloy of copper and zinc made in leaf form in imitation of gold leaf; *~ oven*, device for roasting meat etc. before an open fire consisting of metal box open at one side; *~ supper, treat*, one at which each party pays for or contributes his own share; *talk to one like a ~ uncle*, lecture paternally. ~ *n.* 1. Language of Holland (the Netherlands); a Germanic dialect which has not undergone the High-German consonant-mutation (second sound shift); *Double ~*, gibberish. 2. (obs.) The German language; *High ~* = High German; *Low ~* = Low German; *Pennsylvania ~*, degraded form of High German (orig. from Rhine Palatinate and Switzerland) spoken by descendants of German settlers in Pennsylvania. **Dŭtch'man** *n.* 1. Inhabitant of Holland or the Netherlands. 2. Dutch ship; *Flying ~*, legendary spectral ship condemned with all her crew to sail the seas for ever, and supposed to be seen near the Cape of Good Hope. 3. (hist.) German.

dŭtch[2] *n.* (slang) Cockney costermonger's wife. [abbrev. of *duchess*]

dūt'ėous *adj.* Dutiful, obedient. **dūt'ėously** *adv.* **dūt'ėousnėss** *n.*

dūt'iable *adj.* Liable to customs or other duties.

dūt'ĭful *adj.* Regular or willing in obedience and service. **dūt'ĭfully** *adv.* **dūt'ĭfulnėss** *n.*

dūt'y *n.* 1. Action and conduct due to superior, deference, respect. 2. Payment to public revenue levied upon imports, manufacture of certain goods, transfer and inheritance of property, licence to trade in certain articles, legal recognition of certain documents etc.; *~-paid*, on which customs or excise duty has been paid. 3. Action, act, due in way of moral or legal obligation; what one ought or is bound to do; moral obligation. 4. Business, office, function, performance of or engagement in these (*on, off, ~*, actually so engaged or not); (eccles.) performance of church services; *~ officer*, (mil. etc.) person left in charge when others are absent. 5. Measure of engine's effectiveness in units of work done per unit of fuel.

dūŭm'vir (*-er*) *n.* (Rom. hist.) One of a pair of co-equal magistrates and functionaries in Rome and her colonies. **dūŭm'virate** *n.*

D.V. *abbrev. Deo volente* (= God willing).

Dvořák (dvôr'zhăk), Antonin (1841–1904). Bohemian composer of symphonies, Slav dances, operas, etc.

dwarf (-ôrf) *n.* 1. Person, animal, or plant, much below ordinary size of species; small star of great density, which is believed to have lost a big proportion of the electrons from its atoms. 2. Small supernatural being in Teutonic (esp. Scandinavian) mythology, living underground and skilled in metal-working. ~ *adj.* Undersized; puny, stunted. **dwarf'ĭsh** *adj.* **dwarf'ĭshly** *adv.* **dwarf'ĭshnėss** *n.* **dwarf** *v.t.* Stunt in growth, intellect, etc.; make look small by contrast or distance.

dwĕll *v.i.* (past t. and past part. *dwelt*). 1. Continue, remain, for a time (archaic); have one's abode, live (in house, country, etc.) (now rare). 2. ~ *on*, spend time upon, linger over in action or thought; treat at length. **dwĕll'er** *n.* Inhabitant, resident.

dwĕll'ĭng *n.* (esp.) Place of residence, house; *~-house*, house used as residence, not as office, warehouse, shop, etc.; *~-place*, dwelling.

dwĭn'dle *v.i.* Become smaller,

shrink, waste away; lose importance, decline; degenerate.

dwt *abbrev.* Pennyweight.

dȳ'ad *n.* The number two; group of two, couple.

Dȳ'ăk. Member of one of aboriginal tribes of Borneo; language of this tribe.

dyarchy: see DIARCHY.

dye (dī) *v.* (pres. part. *dyeing*). Colour, stain, tinge; impregnate with colour, fix a colour in the substance of; make (thing) *red, blue,* or other specified colour; ~ *in the wool, in grain,* dye in raw or primitive state, with more permanent result than if thing is dyed after being made up (freq. fig.). ~ *n.* Colour produced by or as by dyeing; tinge, hue; matter used for dyeing, colouring-matter in solution. **dȳ'er** *n.* One who dyes clothes etc.; ~*'s broom, bugloss, oak, weed,* etc., plants yielding dyes.

dȳ'ing *n.* See DIE[2]; (attrib.) connected with death; made at time of death.

dyke: see DIKE.

dyn(am). *abbrev.* Dynamics.

dȳnăm'ic *adj.* Of force producing motion; of force in action or operation, active; potent, energetic, forceful; of dynamics; (philos.) relating to the reason of existence of an object of experience; accounting for matter, or mind, as merely the action of forces; ~ *theory of Kant,* theory conceiving of matter as constituted by two antagonistic principles of attraction and repulsion. ~ *n.* 1. Dynamic theory. 2. (usu. pl. *dynamics,* used as sing.) Branch of physics treating of the behaviour of matter under the action of force; branch of any science considering force or forces; moving forces, physical or moral, in any sphere.

dȳnăm'ical *adj.* 1. Of dynamics; of force or mechanical power actively operative. 2. (theol., of inspiration) Endowing with divine power, not making the medium a mere tool or instrument of his deity; of dynamism. **dȳnăm'ĭcally** *adv.*

dȳn'amĭsm *n.* Philosophical system or theory explaining phenomena of universe by some immanent force or energy. **dȳn'amĭst** *n.* **dȳnamĭs'tĭc** *adj.*

dȳn'amīte *n.* High explosive of nitro-glycerine contained in some absorbent substance, esp. kieselguhr. ~ *v.t.* Blow up with dynamite. **dȳn'amīter** *n.* One who uses explosives for revolutionary purposes. [named by Alfred Nobel, the inventor, f. Gk *dunamis* force]

dȳn'amō *n.* (pl. *-os*). Machine converting mechanical into electrical energy by rotating coils of copper wire in a magnetic field. [short for *dynamo-electric machine*]

dȳnamŏm'ėter *n.* Instrument for measuring energy.

dȳn'ast (*or* dĭ-) *n.* Ruler, member of dynasty. **dȳn'asty** *n.* Line of hereditary rulers. **dȳnăs'tĭc** *adj.* **dȳnăs'tĭcally** *adv.*

dȳne *n.* (physics) Absolute unit of force in the centimetre-gram-second system, force which, acting on a mass of 1 gram, will make it move 1 cm. per second faster in every second.

dys- *prefix.* Bad.

dȳs'entery *n.* Disease with inflammation of mucous membrane and glands of large intestine, and mucous and bloody evacuations. **dȳsentĕ'rĭc** *adj.*

dȳsgĕn'ic *adj.* Exerting detrimental effect on race (opp. to *eugenic*).

dȳslogĭs'tĭc *adj.* Expressing disapprobation or dispraise; having a bad connotation.

dȳspĕp'sĭa *n.* Indigestion. **dȳspĕp'tĭc** *adj.* & *n.* (Person) subject to dyspepsia or the attendant depression.

dȳspnoe'a (-ē'*a*) *n.* (path.) Difficult or laboured breathing. **dȳspnoe'ic** *adj.*

dȳsprōs'ium (-z-) *n.* (chem.) Element of rare-earth group; symbol Dy, at. no. 66, at. wt 162·50. [mod. L, f. Gk *dusprositos* hard to get at]

dȳs'trophy *n.* (path.) Imperfect nutrition.

dzĭgg'etai (-tī) *n.* The Tibetan ass; = KIANG. [Mongolian wd]

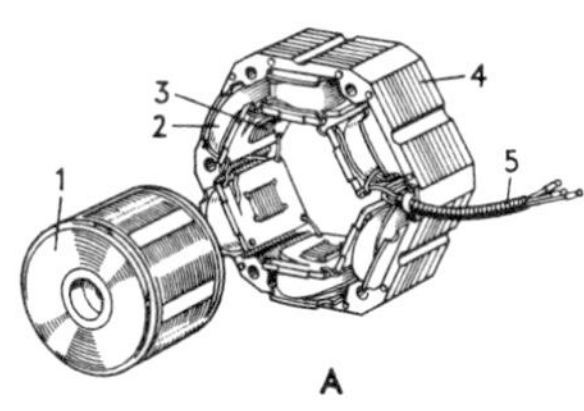

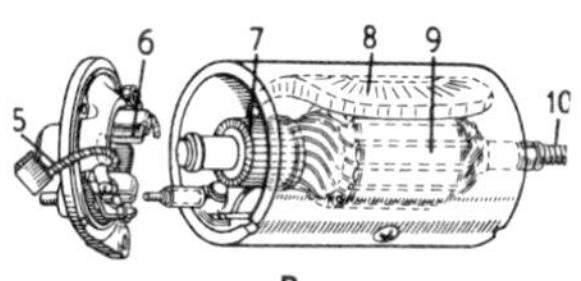

DYNAMOS: A. ALTERNATOR. B. GENERATOR

1. Rotor removed from position in stator. 2. Coils. 3. Pole cores. 4. Stator. 5. Output cable. 6. Brush. 7. Commutator. 8. Field coils. 9. Armature. 10. Driving shaft

E

E, e (ē). 5th letter of modern English and Roman alphabet, representing Semitic ╕, which orig. expressed a sound like that of *h* but was adopted by the Greeks as a vowel; (mus.) third note of 'natural' scale (C major); the scale or key with this for its tonic.

E. *abbrev.* East (as compass point, and as London postal district); Egyptian (in £E); Engineering.

e- *prefix.* Shortened form of EX-.

each *adj.* & *pron.* (Of two or more) every (one) taken separately; ~ *way,* (betting, of horse: backed) for a win or a place.

eag'er (-g-) *adj.* Strongly desirous; keen, impatient. **eag'erly** *adv.* **eag'ernėss** *n.*

ea'gle *n.* 1. Large bird of prey, genus *Aquila,* noted for keen vision and powerful flight; figure of this, esp. as ensign of Roman army, as symbol of the U.S., as lectern in church, or (freq. with two heads) as armorial bearing of the Holy Roman Empire, the Austrian, French, German, and Russian Empires, etc. 2. The northern constellation *Aquila.* 3. (hist.) Coin bearing image of eagle; Amer. 10-dollar gold coin (double ~, 20-dollar). 4. (golf) Score of 2 under par on any hole. 5. ~*-eyed,* keen-sighted; ~*-owl,* large horned owl (*Bubo ignavus*) of Europe and N. Asia. **eag'lėt** *n.* Young eagle.

eagre (ā'*ger,* ē-) *n.* Large tidal wave, esp. in Humber, Trent, and Severn, caused by tide rushing up narrowing estuary.

E. & O.E. *abbrev.* Errors and omissions excepted.

ear[1] *n.* 1. Organ of hearing in man and animals, esp. the external part of this. 2. Sense of hearing; faculty of discriminating sounds, esp. that of recognizing musical intervals; listening, attention. 3. Ear-like object; handle of pitcher etc.; part of bell by which it is hung; projection on side of anything serving as handle, support, etc. 4. ~-*ache*, pain in internal ear; ~-*drum*, DRUM, sense 2; ~-*mark*, mark, usu. a notch, in ear of sheep etc.

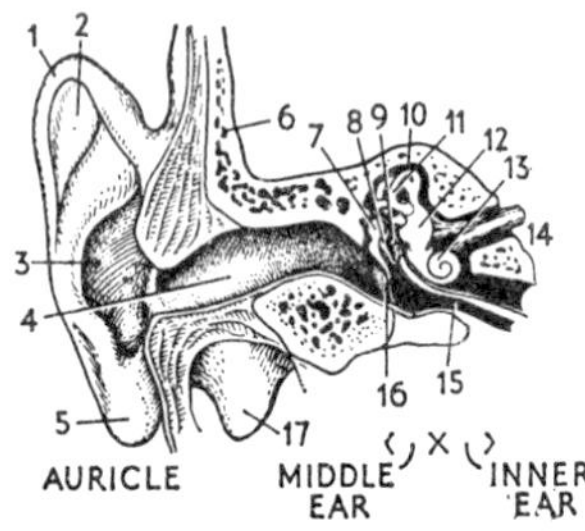

HUMAN EAR

1. Helix. 2. Pinna. 3. Conch or external auditory meatus. 4. Internal auditory meatus. 5. Lobe. 6. Temporal bone. 7, 8, 9. Ossicles (7. Malleus, 8. Incus or anvil, 9. Stapes or stirrup bone). 10. Bony labyrinth. 11. Semicircular canals. 12. Vestibule. 13. Cochlea. 14. Auditory nerve. 15. Eustachian tube or syrinx. 16. Ear-drum or tympanum. 17. Mastoid process

as sign of ownership; (*v.t.*) mark (animals) thus, mark (anything) as one's own, assign (fund etc.) *for* some purpose; ~-*phone*, one of pair of telephone or wireless receivers attachable to listener's ears by band passing over head; small microphone worn in ear by deaf person; ~-*piece*, part of apparatus, esp. of telephone instrument, designed to be fitted to ear; ~-*ring*, ornament worn in lobe of ear; *earshot*, hearing distance; ~-*trumpet*, trumpet-shaped tube held to ear by partly deaf persons to enable them to hear better; ~-*wax*, viscid substance secreted by skin lining external meatus of ear; cerumen.

ear[2] *n.* Spike, head, of corn, containing its flowers or seeds.

ear(r)'ĭng *n.* (naut.) Small rope, one of several fastening upper corner of sail to yard.

earl (ẽrl) *n.* Nobleman ranking in British peerage between marquis and viscount; *E~ Marshal*, high officer of State, formerly deputy of constable as judge of court of chivalry, now president of Heralds' College, with some ceremonial duties (the office is now hereditary in the line of the Dukes of Norfolk). **earl'dom** *n.*

earl'y (ẽr-) *adj.* & *adv.* Absolutely or relatively near to the beginning of a portion of time; of, in, the first part of the morning, the year, etc.; ~ *closing*, system of closing shops etc. for the afternoon once a week; ~-*closing day*; ~-*door*, door at theatre open at specified time before ordinary door at advanced price; *E~ English*, (archit.) first of the pointed Gothic styles of English architecture (*c* 1175–*c* 1275) succeeding the Norman; ~-*Victorian*, of the early years of Queen Victoria's reign.

earn (ẽrn) *v.t.* Obtain as reward of labour or merit. **earn'ĭngs** *n.pl.* Money earned.

earn'ėst[1] (ẽr-) *n.* Money paid as instalment, esp. to confirm contract etc.; foretaste, presage, token (of what is to come).

earn'ėst[2] (ẽr-) *adj.* Serious, zealous, not trifling; ardent. **earn'ėstly** *adv.* **earn'ėstnėss** *n.* **earn'ėst** *n.* Earnestness, seriousness; *in* ~, serious(ly), not jesting(ly).

earth (ẽr-) *n.* (pl. only as below). 1. The ground; (with pl.) soil, esp. as suited for cultivation; mould, dust, clay; the dry land; the planet

EARTH

1. North Pole. 2. North Magnetic Pole. 3. Arctic Circle. 4. Tropic of Cancer. 5. Equator. 6. Tropic of Capricorn. 7. Antarctic Circle. 8. South Pole. 9. South Frigid Zone. 10. Meridian of Greenwich. 11. South Temperate Zone. 12. Torrid Zone. 13. North Temperate Zone. 14. North Frigid Zone

on which we dwell, the world; the present abode of man, as dist. from heaven or hell. 2. (with pl.) Hole or hiding-place of fox, badger, etc. 3. (elect., with pl.) Connexion with the earth, providing return path for current; wire or metal buried in ground to effect this. 4. (chem., with pl.) Any of certain naturally occurring metallic oxides. 5. ~-*closet*, closet, in which dry earth is used to cover and deodorize the contents; ~-*nut*, edible roundish tuber of an umbelliferous plant, *Bunium flexuosum*; pig-nut; ~-*stopper*, person employed by hunt to stop up foxes' earths; *earth'-work*, bank or mound of earth as rampart or fortification; *earth'-worm*, worm (of various genera) that subsists on soil. ~ *v.* 1. Cover (roots of plants) with heaped-up earth. 2. Drive (fox) to earth; (of fox) run to earth. 3. (elect.) Connect (conductor) with earth.

earth'en (ẽr-) *adj.* Made of earth; made of baked clay. **earth'enwāre** *n.* (Vessels etc. made of) baked clay, esp. coarse porous kinds fired at relatively low temperature as dist. from porcelain (also attrib.).

earth'ly (ẽr-) *adj.* Of the earth, terrestrial; *no* ~ *use* etc., (colloq.) no use etc., at all; *not an* ~, (slang) no chance whatever. **earth'lĭnėss** *n.*

earth'quāke (ẽr-) *n.* Convulsion of earth's surface caused by volcanic activity or faults in the earth's crust; (fig.) social or other disturbance or upheaval.

earth'y (ẽr-) *adj.* Like, of, earth or soil; grossly material. **earth'ĭnėss** *n.*

ear'wĭg *n.* Insect, *Forficula auricularia*, or other species of *Forficula*, formerly held to penetrate into head through ear; (U.S.) kind of small centipede.

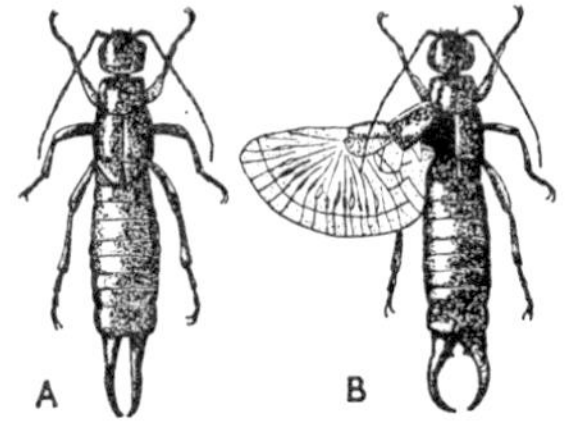

EARWIG: A. FEMALE. B. MALE WITH ONE WING EXTENDED

ease (ēz) *n.* Freedom from pain or trouble; freedom from constraint; relief from pain; facility; *stand at* ~, (mil. etc.) stand in relaxed attitude, with hands behind back and feet apart. ~ *v.* Relieve from pain, trouble, etc.; give mental ease to; relax, adjust (what is too tight); (naut.) slacken (rope, sail, speed, etc.); move gently or gradually; relax or cease one's efforts; ~ *off*, become less burdensome, take things easily.

ease'ful (ēzf-) *adj.* Comfortable, soothing; at rest; slothful. **ease'fully** *adv.* **ease'fulnėss** *n.* **ease'lėss** *adj.*

eas'el (-z-) *n.* Wooden frame to support picture (esp. while artist is at work on it), blackboard, etc. [Du. *ezel* = Ger. *esel* ass]

ease'ment (ēzm-) *n.* 1. (archaic) Advantage, convenience; some-

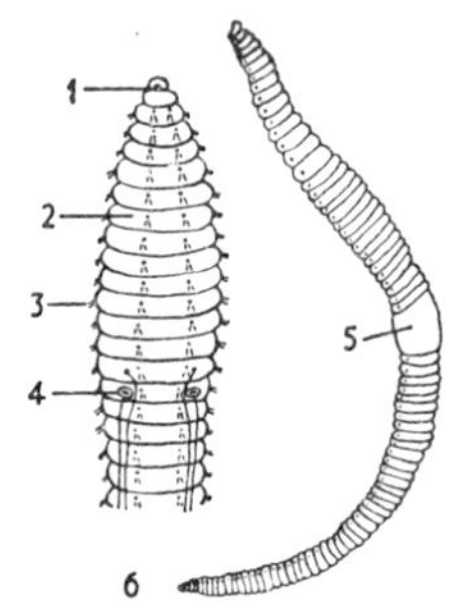

EARTHWORM WITH DETAIL OF FOREPART

1. Mouth. 2. Excretory apertures. 3. Setae. 4. Male reproductive apertures. 5. Clitellum. 6. Anal aperture

thing serving as convenience, as shed, farm building, etc., accommodation in house. 2. (law) Acquired right or privilege of using something not one's own (e.g. right of way).

east *adv.*, *n.*, & *adj.* (Towards, at, near) the point of the horizon where the sun rises at the equinox, or that is 90° to right of north; (towards, in) the eastern part of the world, a country, district, or town; *E~ End*, the eastern part of London; ~ *Side*, the eastern part of New York City, east of Fifth Avenue; ~ *wind*, wind blowing from east. **east'ward** *adv.*, *adj.*, & *n.* **east'wards** *adv.*

East Ang'lĭa (ăngg-). Ancient division of England; now, counties of Norfolk and Suffolk. **East Ang'lĭan** *adj.* & *n.* (Inhabitant) of East Anglia.

Eas'ter. One of the great festivals of the Christian Church, commemorating the resurrection of Christ, and observed by the Western Churches on the 1st Sunday after the calendar full moon falling on or next after 21st March; also, the week commencing with this day; ~ *eggs*, eggs painted in bright colours, or imitations of these, which, by a partial revival of an old custom, are presented to friends at Easter; ~ *eve*, day before Easter; ~ *offering*, voluntary offering of money made by parishioners to incumbent at Easter.

eas'terly *adj.* & *adv.* In an eastern position or direction; (coming) from the east.

eas'tern *adj.* Of, dwelling in, the east part of the world, of the United States, etc.; *E~ Church*, part of the Christian Church (also called *Orthodox* or *Greek*) separated from Catholic Church in 9th c., acknowledging primacy of Patriarch of Constantinople, and consisting chiefly of the Christians of Russia, Greece, and Turkey. **eas'ternmōst** *adj.*

East In'dĭa Company. A company of merchants trading with the East Indies, incorporated in 1600; responsible for the political administration of British territories in India until 1858, when the government of India was assumed by the Crown.

East In'dies (-z). Collective name applied somewhat loosely to the islands off the SE. coast of Asia, formerly including India and the Malay peninsula. **East In'dĭan** *adj.* & *n.* (Inhabitant) of East Indies.

eas'tĭng *n.* (naut.) Course gained to eastward; easterly direction or shifting eastward.

East Lōth'ĭan (-dh-). County of E. Scotland on S. side of Firth of Forth; formerly called Haddington(shire).

East North Central States. Geographical division of the U.S. made by the U.S. Census Bureau, comprising Ohio, Indiana, Illinois, Michigan, and Wisconsin.

East South Central States. Geographical division of the U.S. made by the U.S. Census Bureau, comprising Kentucky, Tennessee, Alabama, and Mississippi.

eas'y (-z-) *adj.* Free from pain, discomfort, annoyance, anxiety, etc., comfortable, luxurious; free from constraint, stiffness, effort, or awkwardness; not hard pressed, not hurried, gentle; fond of ease, not strenuous; indolent, careless, unconcerned; in comfortable circumstances, well off; conducive to ease or comfort; not difficult; not difficult to understand, read, etc.; offering few difficulties or obstructions; easily persuaded, compliant; easily obtained; loosely fitting, not tight; (of burdens, prices, etc.) moderate, not painful or burdensome; (of commodity) not much in demand, (of market) not showing eager demand; ~ *chair*, chair designed for comfort, usu. with arms; *~-going*, taking things easily, inactive, indolent; ~ *money*, money obtained or obtainable without hard work or difficulty; *of ~ virtue*, of woman) unchaste. **eas'ĭly** *adv.* **eas'inèss** *n.* **eas'y** *adv.* In an easy manner, at leisurely pace; *~!*, (move) gently!; ~ *all!*, stop rowing!; *stand ~* (mil.) permission to squad standing at ease to relax attitude further; *take it ~*, proceed comfortably, do no more than one must. ~ *n.* Short rest, esp. in rowing. ~ *v.* (Order to) cease rowing.

eat *v.* (past t. *ate* pr. ĕt, past part. *eat'en*). 1. Take into mouth, masticate, and swallow as food, swallow (soup etc.); consume food, take a meal; *eating-house*, restaurant, cook-shop; ~ one's *dinners*, be studying for the bar students being required to have dined three or more times in the hall of one of the Inns of Court during each of twelve terms before they can be called to the English Bar); ~ one's *words*, retract them in humiliating manner; ~ *out of* person's *hand*, be tamely or completely submissive to him. 2. Devour, consume, prey upon; (of frost, rust, etc.) destroy slowly and gradually; make (hole, passage), make a way, by fretting or corrosion; (U.S. slang) disturb, trouble, vex; ~ one's *heart out*, suffer silently, fret. **eat'able** *adj.* **eat'ables** *n.pl.* Articles of food.

Eat'answĭll (ēt-). In Dickens's 'Pickwick Papers', scene of parliamentary election.

eau (ō) *n.* ~ *de Cologne*: see COLOGNE; ~ *de Javelle*: see JAVELLE; ~ *de Nil*, (of) pale-green colour supposed to resemble Nile water; ~ *de vie*, brandy (Fr., lit. 'water of life').

eaves (ēvz) *n.pl.* (orig. and still occas. sing.) Overhanging edge of roof or thatch (ill. ROOF).

eaves'drŏp (ēvz-) *v.i.* Stand close to walls of house under eaves to listen to secrets; listen secretly to private conversation. **eaves'-drŏpper, eaves'drŏppĭng** *ns.*

E.B., *abbrev.* Encyclopaedia Britannica.

ĕbb *n.* Reflux of tide, return of tide-water towards sea; decline, decay, change to worse state, point of decline or depression. ~ *v.i.* Flow back, recede; flow away; decay, decline.

Eb'ert (ā-), Friedrich (1871–1925). German politician; chancellor of the German Reich 1918–19 and president 1919–25.

Ebĭŏnītes (ĕ'-). Early Jewish Christian sect who held that Jesus was a mere man and that the Mosaic Law was binding upon Christians.

E-boat *n.* Enemy (esp. German or Italian) motor torpedo-boat. [abbrev. from *enemy boat*]

ĕb'on *adj.* & *n.* (poet.) (Made of, black as) ebony.

ĕb'onīte *n.* Hard compound of india-rubber and sulphur, vulcanite.

ĕb'ony *n.* Hard heavy black wood obtained from various tropical trees, esp. various species of *Diospyros* of Ceylon, Madagascar, and Coromandel; tree yielding this. ~ *adj.* Made of, black as, ebony; intensely black.

Ebor. *abbrev.* (Archbishop) of York (replacing surname in his signature). [f. L name *Eboracum*]

ėbrī'ėty *n.* (rare) Drunkenness.

ėbŭll'ient *adj.* Boiling; exuberant, enthusiastic. **ėbŭll'ience, ėbŭll'iency** *nn.*

ĕbullĭ'tion *n.* Boiling; effervescence; sudden outburst (*of* violence, passion, etc.).

E. by N. *abbrev.* East by north.

E. by S. *abbrev.* East by south.

E.C. *abbrev.* East Central (London postal district).

E.C.A. *abbrev.* Economic Cooperation Administration.

écarté (ākar̄t'ā) *n.* Game of cards for two persons, in which cards from 2 to 6 are excluded, and in which certain cards may be discarded and replaced with fresh ones from pack.

Ecce Hōm'ō (ĕk'sĭ). Representation of Christ wearing crown of thorns. [L, = 'behold the man' (John xix. 5)]

ėccĕn'trĭc (-ks-) *adj.* 1. Not concentric to, with axis, point of support, etc., otherwise than centrally placed; not centrally placed or passing through centre; (of orbital motion, curve, etc.) not circular, deviating from a circle; moving in eccentric orbit. 2. Irregular, capricious, odd, whimsical. **ėccĕn'trĭcally** *adv.* **ĕccėntrĭ'cĭty** *n.* **ėccĕn'trĭc** *n.* 1. Eccentric disc on revolving shaft, with connecting rods etc., for changing rotating into backward-and-forward motion, esp. for slide-valve of steam-engine (ill. STEAM). 2. Eccentric person.

Eccles. *abbrev.* Ecclesiastes (O.T.).

Eccles cāke (ĕk'lz) *n.* Round cake of pastry filled with currant mixture. [name of town in Lancashire]

ècclēs'ĭăst (-zĭ-) *n.* 'The Preacher', Solomon considered as author of **Ecclēsiăs'tēs** (-ēz), an O.T. book traditionally ascribed to him and written in his person.

ècclēsiăs'tĭc (-zĭ-) *n.* Clergyman, person in orders.

ècclēsiăs'tĭcal (-zĭ-) *adj.* Of the Church or clergy. **ècclēsiăs'tĭcally** *adv.* **ècclēsiăs'tĭcism** *n.*

Ecclēsiăs'tĭcus (-zĭ-). A book of the Apocrypha, otherwise known as 'The Wisdom of Jesus the son of Sirach', containing moral and practical maxims.

ècclēsiŏl'ogy (-zĭ-) *n.* Science of churches, esp. of church building and decoration. **ècclēsiolŏ'gĭc(al)** *adjs.* **ècclēsiŏl'ogist** *n.*

Ecclus. *abbrev.* Ecclesiasticus.

ĕcdy̆s'is *n.* (pl. *-sēs*) (zool.) Casting of outer skin or shell.

E.C.G. *abbrev.* Electrocardiogram.

e'chelon (ĕsh-) *n.* Formation of troops in parallel divisions, each with its front clear of that in advance; similar formation of ships, aircraft, mechanical parts, etc.; *in* ~, so drawn up. ~ *v.t.* Draw up thus. [Fr. *échelle* ladder]

èchĭd'na (-k-) *n.* The spiny anteater, genus (*E*~) of burrowing nocturnal mammals, toothless but with long extensile tongue for eating ants, living in rocky districts of Australia (ill. ANT-eater).

èchīn'oderm (-k-; *or* ĕk'ĭn-) *n.* Member of the class *Echinodermata* (sea-urchins, sea-cucumbers, starfish, etc.), some species of which have the skin studded with spines or hard plates.

waves; (fig.) repetition or close imitation, enfeebled reproduction; close or obsequious imitator or adherent; ~ *organ*, set of organ pipes enclosed in wooden box to give effect of distance. ~ *v.* (Of place) resound with echo; (of sounds) be repeated by echoes, reverberate, resound; repeat (sound) by or like echo; repeat (another's words), imitate words or opinions of. **ĕch'ōlėss** *adj.*

èchō'ĭc (-k-), *adj.* (Of word etc.) echoing the sound which it denotes or symbolizes; onomatopoeic. **ĕch'ōism** *n.*

Eck'hart (ĕ-), Johannes, known as Meister Eckhart (1260 ?–1327 ?). German philosopher and mystic; regarded as the founder of German mysticism.

éc'lair (ā-) *n.* Small finger-shaped cake of choux pastry filled with cream or custard and iced.

éclaircissement (āklārsēs'-mahṅ) *n.* Clearing up, explanation (of conduct etc.).

ĕclămp'sĭa *n.* (med.) Epileptiform convulsions, esp. during pregnancy or parturition.

éclat (āklah') *n.* Conspicuous success, general applause; social distinction.

èclĕc'tĭc *adj.* & *n.* 1. (Philosopher, esp. of antiquity) not belonging to any recognized school but selecting such doctrines as pleased him in every school. 2. (Person) borrowing freely from various sources, not exclusive in opinion, taste, etc. **èclĕc'tĭcally** *adv.* **èclĕc'tĭcism** *n.*

èclĭpse' *n.* 1. Partial or total interception of light of sun by passage of moon between it and

Great circle of celestial sphere (ill. CELESTIAL); apparent orbit of sun (so called because eclipses happen only when moon is on or very near this line). **èclĭp'tĭcal** *adj.* Of, situated on, the ecliptic.

ĕc'lŏgue (-g) *n.* Short poem, esp. pastoral dialogue.

ēcŏl'ogy, oec- (ē-) *n.* Branch of biology dealing with relations of living organisms to their surroundings, their habits, modes of life, populations, etc. **ēcolŏ'gĭcal** *adj.* **ēcŏl'ogist** *n.*

ēconŏm'ĭc *adj.* Of economics, maintained for profit; practical, utilitarian, adapted to human needs; connected with industrial arts; (of rent) high enough to produce reasonable interest on capital expended or invested. **ēconŏm'ĭcal** *adj.* 1. Saving, thrifty; not wasteful (of). 2. Relating to economics or political economy. **ēconŏm'ĭcally** *adv.* **ēconŏm'ĭcs** *n.* Systematic study of the distribution of scarce resources between alternative uses; condition of country with regard to material prosperity.

ècŏn'omĭst *n.* 1. Manager (*of* money etc.); thrifty person. 2. One expert in economics or political economy.

ècŏn'omīze *v.* Use sparingly; practise economy; turn to best account.

ècŏn'omy *n.* 1. Administration of concerns and resources of any community; art or science of such administration; *Political* ~, former name for ECONOMICS, now applied esp. to analysis of problems of economic policy of governments. 2. Careful management of resources,

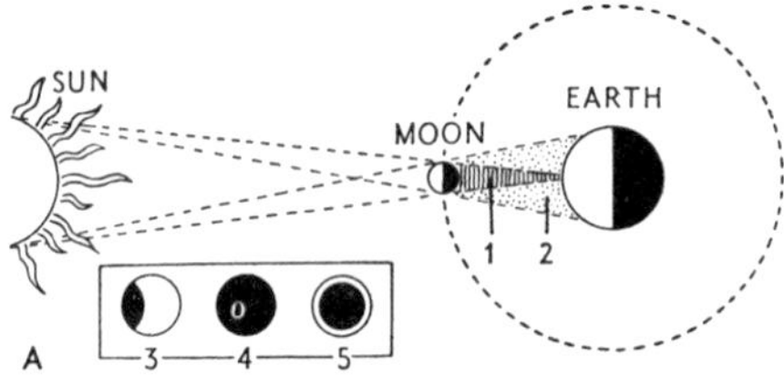

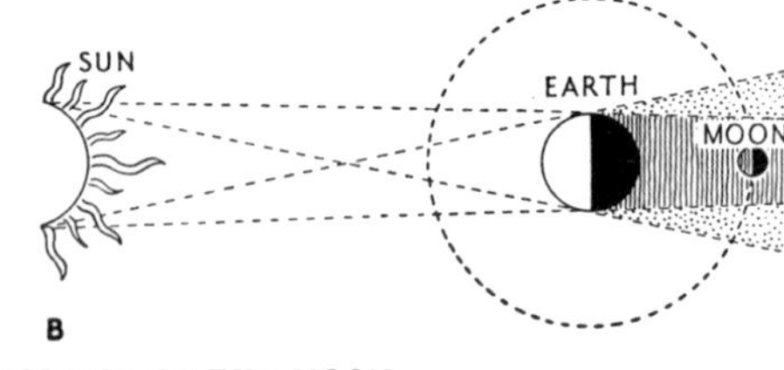

A. ECLIPSE OF THE SUN. B. ECLIPSE OF THE MOON

1. Umbra. 2. Penumbra. 3, 4, 5. Appearance of partial, total, and annular eclipses respectively

èchīn'oid (-k-) *adj.* Resembling the *Echinus*, a genus of sea-urchins. ~ *n.* Any of the sea-urchins (*Echinoidea*), a large group of marine animals with usu. globular or heart-shaped calcareous skeleton of interlocking plates; fossilized member of this group.

èchīn'us (-k-) *n.* 1. (*E*~) A genus of sea-urchins. 2. (archit.) The ovolo moulding next below the abacus of the capital of a column (ill. ORDER).

echo (ĕk'ō) *n.* Repetition of sound produced by reflection of sound-waves from something denser than air, usu. from a rigid and approx. vertical surface; secondary sound constituted by reflected

the earth (~ *of the sun, solar* ~); partial or total obscuration of moon by the earth's shadow (~ *of the moon, lunar* ~); similar obscuration of a satellite by another planet. 2. Temporary or permanent deprivation of light; periodical obscuration of light from lighthouse; obscuration, obscurity, loss of brilliance or splendour. ~ *v.t.* (Of moon) intercept partially or totally the light of the sun from a portion of the earth; usu. pass. (of sun) have light so intercepted, (of moon) be obscured by earth's shadow; intercept (light, esp. of lighthouse); deprive of lustre, outshine, surpass.

èclĭp'tĭc *adj.* Of an eclipse. ~ *n.*

so as to make them go as far as possible; frugality, thrift; a saving. 3. (theol.) Judicious handling of doctrine, presentation of truth etc. in such a way as to suit the needs or conciliate the prejudices of the person addressed. 4. Organization, constitution, of any complex unity; organized body, society, etc.

écorché (ākorsh'ā) *n.* (painting etc.) Figure in which muscular system is displayed. [Fr. *écorcher* flay]

écru (āc'rōō) *adj.* & *n.* (Of) colour of unbleached linen.

ĕc'stasy *n.* Exalted state of feeling, rapture, transport, esp. of delight; state of rapture in contemplation of divine things; poetic frenzy.

ĕcstăt'ic *adj.* Of, producing, subject to, ecstasy. ~ *n.* One subject to (religious) ecstasy.

ecto- *prefix.* Outer, outside.

ĕc'toblast (-ah-) *n.* (physiol.) Outer membrane of a cell.

ĕc'toderm *n.* (embryol.) Outermost of 3 layers of cells formed by embryo at early stage, layer from which skin and nervous system are developed.

ĕctogĕn'ĕsis *n.* (biol.) Production of structures or bodies outside the organism. **ĕctogĕnĕt'ic, ĕctogĕn'ic, ĕctŏ'gĕnous** *adjs.*

ĕc'toplăsm *n.* 1. (biol.) Clear viscid outer layer of cytoplasm in an animal cell (ill. CELL). 2. (spiritualism) Supposed viscid substance believed by some to emanate from body of medium and develop into various forms. **ĕctoplăs'mic, ĕctoplăs'tic** *adjs.*

E.C.U. *abbrev.* English Church Union.

Ec'uador (ĕkw*a*-). Equatorial republic in the NW. of S. America; capital, Quito.

ecumenical: see OECUMENICAL.

ĕc'zēma *n.* (path.) Inflammation of skin, with redness, soreness, and itching papules or vesicles discharging serous fluids. **ĕczĕm'atous** *adj.*

ed. *abbrev.* Edited, edition, editor.

Ed. *abbrev.* Edward.

ėdā'cious (-sh*u*s) *adj.* Of eating; greedy. **ėdă'city** *n.*

Ed'am (ē-) *n.* Round Dutch cheese, usu. of yellow colour with rind dyed red. [name of village in Holland]

ėdăph'ic *adj.* (bot.) Of the soil.

Edd'a (ĕ-). 1. (*Elder, Poetic,* ~), collection (*c* 1200) of ancient Old Norse poems on mythical or traditional subjects. 2. (*Younger, Prose,* ~), miscellaneous handbook to Icelandic poetry, with prosodic and grammatical treatises and quotations and prose paraphrases from old poems; partly written by the Icelandic historian Snorri Sturlason (*c* 1230).

Edd'ington (ĕ-), Sir Arthur Stanley (1882–1944). English physicist; well known for his researches into the motions of stars and for his contributions to the Theory of Relativity.

ĕdd'y[1] *n.* Circular motion in water, small whirlpool; similar unsteady swirling motion of air, wind, fog, dust, etc., moving thus; ~ *current,* (elect.) circulating current induced in a conducting material by a changing magnetic field. ~ *v.* Whirl round, move, in eddies.

Edd'y[2] (ĕ-). Mrs Mary Baker Glover (1821–1910). American founder of the Christian Science movement.

edelweiss (ād'lvīs) *n.* Alpine plant with white flower, *Leontopodium alpinum,* growing in rocky, often inaccessible places, in Swiss mountains. [Ger. *edel* noble, *weiss* white]

Ed'en[1] (ē-). Abode of Adam and Eve at their creation, Paradise; (transf.) delightful abode, state of supreme happiness. [Heb. *'ēden,* orig. = 'delight']

Ed'en[2] (ē-), (Robert) Anthony, 1st Earl of Avon (1897–). English statesman; secretary of state for foreign affairs 1935–8, 1940–5, 1951–5; prime minister 1955–7.

ėdĕn'tate *adj.* & *n.* (Animal) belonging to mammalian order *Edentata* which have no teeth or very simple teeth without enamel (sloths, great ant-eaters, armadillos, aardvarks, etc.).

Ed'gar (ĕ-). King of England 959–75.

ĕdge *n.* 1. Thin sharpened side of cutting instrument or weapon; sharpness given to blade by whetting; (fig.) effectiveness, trenchancy (of speech etc.); *be on* ~, be excited or irritable; *set* person's *teeth on* ~, jar his nerves or sensibilities. 2. Crest of ridge; line at which two surfaces meet abruptly; (skating) *inner* or *outer* edge of skate; (fig.) perilous or critical position or moment. 3. One of narrow surfaces of thin flat object; rim (of vessel); one of the three surfaces of book left uncovered by binding. 4. Boundary of any surface, border, brink (of precipice). 5. ~*-tool,* tool with sharp cutting edge. ~ *v.* 1. Give an edge to, sharpen. 2. Border; furnish with edging. 3. Move edgeways; advance (esp. obliquely) by repeated almost imperceptible degrees; move (thing, oneself) thus; touch (cricket ball) with edge of bat. **ĕdge'lėss** *adj.*

ĕdge'ways, -wise (-jwāz, -jwīz) *advs.* With edge uppermost, foremost, or turned towards spectator; edge to edge; (moving) with edge foremost; *get* (*word*) *in* ~, manage to say it in interval of loquacious person's talk.

ĕdg'ing *n.* (esp.) Border, fringe, etc., on garment, border (of grass etc.) round flower-beds or lawn; lace etc. made to be sewn to edge of garment; ~*-iron,* crescent-shaped tool for cutting verge of turf.

ĕdg'y *adj.* Sharp-edged; irritable, testy.

ĕd'ible *adj.* & *n.* (Thing) fit to be eaten, eatable. **ĕdibĭl'ity** *n.*

ē'dict *n.* What is proclaimed by authority; order issued by sovereign to subjects; *E~ of Nantes*: see NANTES.

ĕd'ifice *n.* Building, esp. large and stately one.

ĕd'ify *v.t.* Benefit spiritually, strengthen, support; instruct, improve. **ĕdĭficā'tion** *n.*

Edin. *abbrev.* Edinburgh.

Ed'inburgh (ĕ-; -b*u*r*u*, -br*u*). County borough and capital city of Scotland, situated to the south of the Firth of Forth.

Edinburgh, Prince Philip, Duke of (1921–). Son of Prince and Princess Andrew of Greece; married (1947) Princess Elizabeth of Gt Britain, afterwards Queen Elizabeth II.

Ed'ison (ĕ-), Thomas Alva (1847–1931). American inventor of the phonograph and (with Sir J. W. Swan, 1828–1914) of the incandescent electric lamp.

ĕd'it *v.t.* Prepare edition of (another's work); collate (material chiefly provided by others) for publication; act as editor of.

ėdi'tion *n.* Form in which literary work is published; whole number of copies of book, newspaper, etc., printed from same set of types and issued at same time.

ĕd'itor *n.* One who prepares work of others for publication; one who conducts newspaper or periodical, or section of newspaper etc. **ĕd'itorship** *n.*

ĕditor'ial *adj.* Of, written by, an editor. ~ *n.* Newspaper article written by or under responsibility of editor. **ĕditor'ially** *adv.*

Edm. *abbrev.* Edmund.

ĕd'ūcāte *v.t.* Bring up (young persons) from childhood, so as to form their habits, manners, intellectual aptitudes, etc.; instruct, provide schooling for; train, discipline, so as to develop some special aptitude, taste, or disposition. **ĕd'ūcable** *adj.* **ĕd'ūcātor,** *n.* **ĕd'ūcatory** *adj.*

ĕdūcā'tion *n.* Systematic instruction, schooling, or training in preparation for life or some particular task; scholastic instruction; bringing up. **ĕdūcā'tional** (-sh*o*-) *adj.* **ĕdūcā'tionally** *adv.* **ĕdūcā'tion(al)ist** *n.* One who studies the science or methods of education.

ĕd'ūcative *adj.* Of education; educating; bearing on, conducive to, education.

ėdūce' *v.t.* Bring out, elicit, develop, from latent, rudimentary, or potential condition; elicit, draw forth, evoke. **ėdŭc'tion** *n.*

ėdŭl'corāte *v.t.* Free from acrid properties or from soluble particles, purify. **ėdŭlcorā'tion** *n.*

Edw. *abbrev.* Edward.

Ed'ward (ĕ-). Name of 6 kings of England since the Conquest and 2 of Gt Britain: *Edward I* (1239–1307), 'the Hammer of the Scots'; son of Henry III; king of England 1272–1307; conquered Wales and attempted the conquest of Scotland; *Edward II* (1284–1327), succeeded his father Edward I in 1307; continued the attempted conquest of Scotland but was defeated by Robert Bruce at Bannockburn (1314); murdered in 1327; *Edward III* (1312–77), son of Edward II, reigned 1327–77; the Hundred Years War against France began in his reign and he gained temporarily the duchy of Aquitaine by the Treaty of Bretigny (1360); *Edward IV* (1442–83), the first 'Yorkist' king; descended from Edward III; reigned 1461–83; defeated the Lancastrians in the

Wars of the Roses; *Edward V* (1470–83), son of Edward IV; king in 1483, in which year he was deposed and murdered in the Tower of London, probably by order of his uncle, Richard, Duke of Gloucester; *Edward VI* (1537–53), son of Henry VIII and Jane Seymour; reigned 1547–53; *Edward VII* (1841–1910), son of Queen Victoria; king of Gt Britain 1901–10; *Edward VIII* (1894–); succeeded his father, George V, on 20th Jan. 1936; abdicated 11th Dec. 1936 and assumed title of Duke of Windsor.

Edward the Confessor. Son of Ethelred the Unready; king of the English 1042–66; canonized 1161.

Edward the Martyr. King of the English 975–9; assassinated by order of his stepmother.

Edwârd'ĭan (ĕ-; *or* -wôr-) *adj.* & *n.* (Person) belonging to or characteristic of reign of Edward VII of Gt Britain.

E.E.G. *abbrev.* Electroencephalogram.

eel *n.* 1. Any member of the family *Anguillidae* of small-finned and soft-finned snake-like fishes, the freshwater forms of which migrate to the Sargasso Sea to spawn; there are many genera including *Anguilla* (the common eel) and *Conger* (conger eel, which is marine). 2. Various other fishes resembling eels in shape. 3. *electric* ~: see ELECTRIC; *~-grass*, marine plant with grass-like leaves, *Zostera marina*; *~-pout*, burbot, (also) blenny; *~-spear*, forked or pronged instrument for catching eels; *~-worm*, any of various worm-like often microscopic animals of the class *Nemathelminthes*, some of which are parasitic on crops.

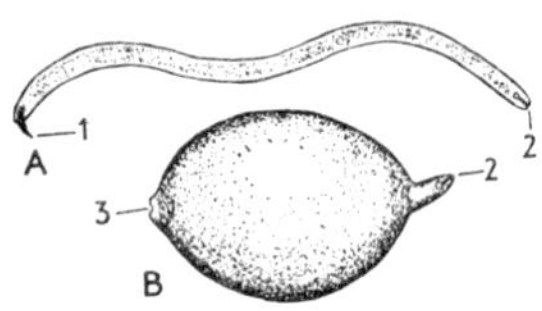

EEL-WORM: A. ADULT MALE. B. ADULT FEMALE (CYST)

1. Copulatory spicule. 2. Mouth. 3. Vulva

e'en, e'er, poet. for EVEN, EVER.

eer'ie, -y *adj.* Gloomy, strange, weird. **eer'ĭly** *adv.* **eer'ĭnėss** *n.*

ėffāce' *v.t.* Rub out; obliterate, wipe out; utterly surpass, eclipse; reduce one*self* to insignificance. **ėffāce'ment** (-sm-) *n.*

ėffĕct' *n.* 1. Result, consequence; efficacy; combination of colour or form in picture, landscape, etc.; (pl.) lighting, appropriate sounds, etc., in play etc.; phenomenon. 2. (pl.) Property, goods. 3. Being operative; operative influence; *give ~ to*, render operative; *take ~*, become operative, come into force. 4. Impression produced on spectator, hearer, etc. 5. *in ~*, virtually, for practical purposes. ~ *v.t.* Bring about, accomplish. **ėffĕc'tĭve** *adj.* 1. Having an effect; that is actually brought to bear on an object; (U.S.) coming into effect, becoming operative; *~ range*, range within which weapon etc. is effective. 2. Powerful in effect; striking. 3. (Of soldiers etc.) fit for work or service. 4. Actual, existing. ~ *n.* Effective soldier, effective part of army. **ėffĕc'tĭvely** *adv.* **ėffĕc'tĭvenėss** *n.*

ėffĕc'tūal *adj.* Answering its purpose; valid; *~ demand*, (econ.) demand sufficient to cause production or bringing to market of goods. **ėffĕc'tūally** *adv.* **ėffĕc'tūalnėss** *n.*

ėffĕc'tūāte *v.t.* Bring to pass, accomplish. **ėffĕctūā'tion** *n.*

ėffĕm'ĭnate *adj.* Womanish, unmanly. **ėffĕm'ĭnately** (-tlĭ) *adv.* **ėffĕm'ĭnatenėss, ėffĕm'ĭnacy** *ns.*

ėffĕn'dĭ *n.* Turkish title of respect, chiefly applied to Government officials and members of learned professions.

ĕff'erent *adj.* (physiol.) Conveying outwards; (of nerves) conveying impulses from central nervous system to muscles and glands.

ĕffervesce' (-ĕs) *v.i.* Give off bubbles of gas, esp. as result of chemical action; bubble. **ĕffervĕs'cence** *n.* **ĕffervĕs'cent** *adj.*

ėffēte' *adj.* Exhausted, worn out; feeble, incapable. **ėffēte'nėss** (-tn-) *n.*

ĕffĭcā'cious (-sh*us*) *adj.* (Of instrument, method, action) producing, sure to produce, intended or appropriate effect. **ĕffĭcā'ciously** *adv.* **ĕffĭcā'ciousnėss, ĕff'ĭcacy** *ns.*

ėffĭ'cient (-sh*e*nt) *adj.* Making, causing to be, productive of effects; effective, operative; skilled, capable. **ėffĭ'ciently** *adv.* **ėffĭ'ciency** *n.* State or quality of being efficient; (physics) ratio of energy or work produced to that expended.

ĕff'ĭgy *n.* Portrait, image.

ĕfflorĕsce' (-ĕs) *v.i.* 1. Burst out into flower (lit. & fig.). 2. (chem., of crystalline substance) Turn to fine powder on exposure to air when water of crystallization evaporates; (of salt) come in solution to surface (of ground, wall, etc.) and there crystallize; (of ground, wall, etc.) become thus covered with powdery crust of saline particles. **ĕfflorĕs'cence** *n.* **ĕfflorĕs'cent** *adj.*

ĕff'luence (-ōō-) *n.* Flowing out, esp. of light, electricity, magnetism, etc.; what flows out, emanation.

ĕff'luent (-ōō-) *adj.* Flowing forth. ~ *n.* Stream flowing from larger stream, reservoir, lake, etc.; outflow from sewage tank etc.

ėffluv'ĭum (-ōō-) *n.* (pl. *-ia*). Exhalation affecting lungs or sense of smell.

ĕff'lŭx *n.* Flowing out (of liquid, air, gas); that which flows out. **ėfflŭx'ion** (-ksh*o*n) *n.*

ĕff'ort *n.* Strenuous exertion; display of power, achievement.

ĕff'ortlėss *adj.* Making no effort, passive; without effort, easy. **ĕff'ortlėssly** *adv.* **ĕff'ortlėssnėss** *n.*

ėffron'tery (-ŭn-) *n.* Shameless audacity.

ėffŭl'gent *adj.* Radiant. **ėffŭl'gently** *adv.* **ėffŭl'gence** *n.*

ėffūse' (-z) *v.t.* Pour forth.

ėffū'sion (-zhn) *n.* Pouring forth; unrestrained utterance, literary outpouring.

ėffūs'ĭve *adj.* Exuberant, demonstrative. **ėffūs'ĭvely** *adv.* **ėffūs'ĭvenėss** *n.*

ĕft *n.* Newt.

ĕftsōōns' *adv.* (archaic) Again; forthwith, soon afterwards.

e.g. *abbrev. Exempli gratia* (L, = 'for example').

ėgăd' *int.* (archaic) By God.

ėgălitâr'ĭan *adj.* & *n.* (Person) asserting equality of mankind.

ĕgg[1] *n.* 1. (pop.) More or less spheroidal body, containing germ of new individual within a shell or membrane, deposited externally (laid) by female of some animals esp. birds, reptiles, fishes, and insects; esp., domestic fowl's egg as article of food. 2. (zool.) Non-motile cell produced by female, capable, usu. after fertilization by a sperm, of developing into a new individual; ovum. 3. *bad ~*, person, scheme, etc., that comes to no good; *~-and-spoon race*, race in which runners carry fowl's egg in spoon; *~ cleavage*, (biol.) process of cleavage in fertilized egg; *~-cup*, cup-shaped vessel to hold egg boiled in shell; *~-flip*, *~-nog*, drink in which white and yolk of eggs are stirred up with hot beer, cider, wine, or spirits; *egg'head*, (U.S. slang) intellectual person, 'high-brow'; *~-plant*: see AUBERGINE; *~-plum*, small, rather hard, egg-shaped yellow plum; *~-shell*, shell of egg; freq. as type of anything frail or fragile; *~-shell china*, extremely thin and delicate porcelain; *~-shell finish*, a paint finish intermediate between flat and glossy; *~-spoon*, small spoon for eating boiled egg; *~-tooth*, protuberance on bill-sheath of embryo bird, reptile, etc., for cracking its shell; *~-whisk*, utensil for beating eggs. ~ *v.t. Egg and* (*bread-*) *crumb*, (cookery) coat with egg or yolk of egg and bread-crumbs. **ĕgg'y** *adj.* Stained with egg.

ĕgg[2] *v.t.* Incite, encourage, urge (*on*).

ĕg'lantīne *n.* Sweet-briar.

ĕg'ō *n.* 1. (metaphysics) Conscious thinking subject as opp. to *non-ego* or object; the self. 2. (psychol.) That part of the mind which is organized and has a sense of individuality (thus used by Freud to distinguish it from the primitive, impersonal, and wholly unconscious part which he called the *id*). [L, = 'I']

ĕgocĕn'trĭc *adj.* Centred in the ego; self-centred, egoistic. **ĕgōcĕn'trĭcally** *adv.* **ĕgocĕntrĭ'cĭty** *n.*

ĕg'ōism *n.* 1. (ethics) Theory which regards self-interest as foundation of morality. 2. Regard to one's own interest, systematic selfishness; selfish aims or purposes; self-opinionatedness. **ĕg'ōist** *n.* **ĕgōis'tĭc(al)** *adjs.* **ĕgōis'tĭcally** *adv.*

ĕgomān'ĭa *n.* Morbid egotism. **ĕgomān'ĭăc** *n.*

ĕg'otĭsm *n.* Obtrusive or too frequent use of 'I' and 'me', practice of talking about oneself; self-conceit, boastfulness; selfishness. **ĕg'otĭst** *n.* **ĕgotĭs'tĭc(al)** *adjs.* **ĕgotĭs'tĭcally** *adv.*

ėgrē'gious (-jus) *adj.* 1. (archaic) Distinguished; striking. 2. Gross, flagrant, outrageous. **ėgrē'giously** *adv.* **ėgrē'giousnėss** *n.* [L *egregius*, lit. 'towering above the flock' (*grex* flock)]

ē'grĕss *n.* (Right or liberty of) going out; (astron.) end of eclipse or transit; outlet. **ėgrĕs'sion** (-shn) *n.* Going out or forth.

ē'grėt *n.* Lesser white heron, aigrette.

E'gypt (ē-). State in NE. Africa formerly part of the Turkish Empire; in 1882 internal disorders led to British military intervention and in 1914 a British Protectorate over Egypt was declared, which was terminated in 1922, since which time Egypt has been independent. **Egyp'tian** (ĭjĭp'shn) *adj.* Of, pertaining to, Egypt. ~ *n.* 1. Native of Egypt. 2. Language of the ancient Egyptians together with its descendant, Coptic, which is still used in the liturgies of the Coptic Church. ~ is one of the Hamitic group of languages and its history is divided into *Old* ~, known from hieroglyphic inscriptions from the 1st Dynasty (*c* 3400 B.C.) onwards; *Middle* ~, represented by remains from the 12th Dynasty; *Late* ~, known from hieratic writings from the 18th Dynasty (*c* 1580 B.C.) to the 21st Dynasty; and *Demotic* ~, from the 8th c. B.C. to the Christian era. 3. ~ *bondage*, oppressive bondage like that of the Israelites in Egypt; ~ *darkness*, darkness such as Moses brought upon Egypt (Exod. x. 22–23); ~ *gum*, gum Arabic.

Egÿptŏl'ogy (ē-) *n.* Study of Egyptian antiquities. **Egÿptŏl'ogist** *n.*

eh (ā) *int.* Ejaculation of inquiry or surprise, or inviting assent.

Ehrlich (ārl'ĭx), Paul (1854–1915). German physician; founder of chemotherapy and discoverer of salvarsan; awarded Nobel Prize for medicine 1908.

eid'er (ī-) *n.* Species of duck (*Somateria mollissima*) resident on N. coasts, the male black and white, the female brown; ~-*down* small soft feathers from breast of eider duck; quilt stuffed with these.

eidĕt'ĭc (ī-) *adj.* (psychol., of visual image) Possessing hallucinatory vividness and circumstantiality. **eidĕt'ĭcally** *adv.*

eidōl'on (ī-) *n.* (pl. *-ons*, *-a*). Spectre, phantom.

Eiffel Tower (īf'-). Iron tower, 300 metres high, built for the Exposition of 1889 by A. G. Eiffel in the Champ de Mars, Paris.

eight (āt) *adj.* & *n.* One more than seven (8, viii, or VIII); figure representing this, anything in this form, esp. skating-figure; crew of 8 in rowing-boat; the *E~s*, boat-races at Oxford between such crews. **eighth** (ātth) *adj.* & *n.* **eighth'ly** *adv.*

eighteen' (āt-) *adj.* & *n.* One more than seventeen (18, xviii, or XVIII); *eighteenmo*, octodecimo. **eighteenth'** *adj.* & *n.*

eight'some (āt-) *adj.* & *adv.* (Sc.) Eight together; ~ *reel*, kind of dance for 8 persons.

eighty (āt'ĭ) *adj.* & *n.* Eight times ten (80, lxxx, or LXXX). **eight'ĭeth** *adj.* & *n.*

Einstein (īn'shtīn), Albert (1879–1955). German-born mathematical physicist; famous for his revolutionary theory of the nature of space and time, known as the Theory of Relativity, which upset the Newtonian conception of the universe.

einstein'ĭum (ī-, -īn-) *n.* TRANSURANIC element, symbol E, at. no. 99, principal isotope 253.

Eire (ār'*e*). A sovereign independent State (since 1921); associated for certain purposes with the British Commonwealth of Nations, and occupying the whole of Ireland with the exception of the six counties which form Northern Ireland; officially called, 1921–37, Irish Free State; 1937–49, Eire; 1949–, Republic of Ireland; capital, Dublin. **Eireann** (ār'*a*n) *adj.*

eirenicon: see IRENICON.

Eis'enhower (īz-), Dwight David (1890–). American general and statesman; C.-in-C. Allied Forces in N. Africa 1942–3; Supreme Commander of Allied Expeditionary Forces in W. Europe 1943–5; North Atlantic Supreme Commander 1950–2; 34th president of the U.S. 1953–61.

eisteddfod (āstĕdh'vod) *n.* Welsh congress of bards prob. of 14th-c. origin; modern revival of this, dating from 19th c., esp. the *National E~*, held annually with competitions in music, poetry, arts and crafts. [Welsh, = 'session' (*eistedd* sit)]

eith'er (īdh-, ē-) *adj.* & *pron.* Each of two; one or other of the two. ~ *adv.* Introducing first of alternatives (*either . . . or . . .*); (in neg. or interrog. sentences) any more than the other, as *if you do not go, I shall not* ~.

ėjăc'ūlāte *v.t.* 1. Utter suddenly. 2. Eject (fluids etc.) from body. **ėjăcūlā'tion** *n.* **ėjăc'ūlatory** *adj.*

ėjĕct' *v.t.* 1. Expel (*from* place, office, etc.); evict *from* property. 2. Throw out from within; dart forth, emit. **ėjĕc'tion, ėjĕct'ment, ėjĕc'tor** *ns.* **ėjĕc'tĭve** *adj.*

ēke[1] *v.t.* ~ *out*, supplement, supply deficiencies of; contrive to make (livelihood) or support (existence) by various makeshifts.

ēke[2] *adv.* (archaic) Also.

ėlăb'orate *adj.* Carefully or minutely worked out; highly finished. **ėlăb'orately** *adv.* **ėlăb'oratenėss** *n.* **ėlăb'orāte** *v.t.* Produce by labour; work out in detail; fashion from raw material. **ėlăborā'tion** *n.* **ėlăb'oratĭve** *adj.*

El Alamein: see ALAMEIN.

El'amīte (ē-) *adj.* & *n.* (Member) of a people inhabiting E. Persia in the Bronze Age, with their capital at Susa (now Shush).

élan (āl'ahṅ) *n.* Vivacity, dash.

ĕl'and *n.* Large heavily built ox-like African antelope, *Oreas canna*, with spirally twisted horns.

ėlăpse' *v.i.* (Of time) pass away.

ėlăs'mobrănch (-z-, -nk) *n.* (zool.) Any cartilaginous fish (shark, dogfish, skate, etc.).

ėlăs'tĭc (*or* -lah-) *adj.* 1. Spontaneously resuming its normal bulk or shape after having been contracted, dilated, or distorted; buoyant, springy; flexible, accommodating. 2. (Of fabric etc.) containing, made of, thin strips or threads of rubber usu. covered with woven material. ~ *n.* Elastic fabric, elastic cord or string. **ėlăs'tĭcally** *adv.* **ėlăstĭ'cĭty** *n.*

ėlāte' *v.t.* Raise spirits of, inspirit, stimulate, excite. **ėlā'tion** *n.*

El'ba (ĕ-). Italian island off the W. coast of Italy, the place of Napoleon's first exile.

Elbe (ĕ-). One of the main rivers of Germany, rising in Czechoslovakia and flowing past Hamburg into the North Sea at Cuxhaven.

ĕl'bow (-ō) *n.* Outer part of joint between fore- and upper arm; elbow-shaped bend or corner in river, road, etc.; short piece of pipe bent at an angle to join two straight pieces; *up to the elbows*, busily engaged *in*; *out at elbows*, ragged, poor; ~-*chair*, (U.S.) arm-chair; ~-*grease*, vigorous rubbing, hard work; ~-*room*, sufficient space to move or work in at one's ease. ~ *v.* Thrust, jostle.

ĕld *n.* (archaic) Old age; the olden time.

ĕl'der[1] *n.* Low tree or shrub, *Sambucus nigra*, with umbel-like corymbs of white flowers, and black berries; other species of this genus, esp. (in N. Amer.) *S. canadensis*; ~-*berry*, fruit of this tree; ~-*berry wine*, wine made from elder-berries.

ĕl'der[2] *adj.* Senior (of relations, or of two indicated persons); *E~ Brethren*: see BRETHREN; ~ *statesmen*, in Japan, body of retired statesmen and nobles acting as emperor's confidential advisers. ~ *n.* 1. (pl.) Persons of greater age.

2. Member of senate, governing body, or class, of men venerable for age (chiefly hist.); in some Protestant churches, one of class or body of laymen assisting in management of church affairs (in Presbyterian churches including also the ministers, called *teaching* ~*s*). **ĕl'dership** *n.*

ĕl'derly *adj.* Getting old.

ĕl'dėst *adj.* First-born or oldest surviving (member of family, son, daughter, etc.).

El Dora'do (ĕl, -ahdō). Fictitious country or city abounding in gold believed by early explorers to exist on Amazon. [Span., = 'the gilded']

ĕl'drĭtch *adj.* (Sc.) Weird, hideous.

Elėăt'ĭc (ĕl-) *adj.* Of, pertaining to, a school of Greek philosophers of the 6th c. B.C. founded by PARMENIDES and his successor Zeno at Elea in Lucania; these philosophers combated the anthropomorphic religion of the ancient poets and maintained that there was a single eternal god not resembling mortals in appearance or thought.

ĕlėcămpāne' *n.* Perennial composite plant, *Inula helenium*, with large yellow radiate flowers and bitter aromatic leaves and root, formerly used as tonic and stimulant; sweet flavoured with this.

ėlĕct' *adj.* 1. Chosen; chosen for excellence or by preference; choice. 2. (theol.) Chosen by God, esp. for salvation or eternal life. 3. (usu. following *n.*) Chosen, elected, to office, dignity, etc., but not yet installed. ~ *v.t.* Choose, choose (person) by vote; (of God) choose (persons) for salvation etc.

ėlĕc'tion *n.* Choosing, esp. by vote; *general* ~, election of representatives to House of Commons or similar body throughout whole country; *by*-~ (U.S. *special* ~), election of member(s) in one constituency only, to fill vacancy caused by death, resignation, etc.

ėlĕctioneer' (-sho-) *v.i.* Busy oneself in political elections. ~ *n.* One who electioneers.

ėlĕc'tĭve *adj.* 1. Appointed or filled by, (of authority) derived from, election; having power of electing by vote; pertaining to, based on, system or principle of election. 2. (orig. chem., now fig. only) ~ *affinity*, tendency of substance to combine with certain particular substances in preference to others. 3. (U.S., of subjects in university etc. course) optional; as *n.*, specially selected or optional course or subject of study.

ėlĕc'tor *n.* Person with right to vote in election; in Gt Britain etc. one legally qualified to vote in election of members of Parliament; in U.S., member of *Electoral College* chosen by the several States to elect the President and Vice-President; *E*~, one of the princes of Germany formerly (911–1803) entitled to take part in election of emperor. **ėlĕc'torshĭp** *n.* **ėlĕc'toral** *adj.* Of electors; being, belonging to, a German Elector; *E*~ *College*: see above.

ėlĕc'torate *n.* 1. State or dignity of German Elector; dominions of an Elector. 2. Whole body of electors.

Elĕc'tra (ĭl-). (Gk myth.) Daughter of Agamemnon and Clytemnestra; urged her brother Orestes to kill Clytemnestra and Aegisthus in revenge for murder of Agamemnon; ~ *complex*, (psycho-anal.) the OEDIPUS complex in females, so called because of Electra's love of her father.

ėlĕc'trėss *n.* Wife of German Elector.

ėlĕc'trĭc *adj.* Of, charged with, worked by, capable of developing, electricity; ~ *blue*, brilliant light blue without tincture of green; ~ *chair*, chair in which persons condemned to death are executed; ~ *charge*: see CHARGE *n.* 2; ~ *circuit*, a system of conductors through which electric energy is conveyed; ~ *current*, flow of electricity through conducting body from positive to negative pole, or from high to low potential; ~ *eel*, large S. Amer. freshwater eel-like fish (*Electrophorus electricus*), capable of giving electric shock; ~ *hare*, in greyhound racing, artificial hare made by electricity to race round a track ahead of the hounds; ~ *ray*: see TORPEDO 1; ~ *shock*, effect on animal body of sudden discharge of electricity; ~ *spark*, luminous discharge over gap in electric circuit; ~ *torch*, portable electric lamp, usu. with dry battery for supply of electric current. **ėlĕc'trĭcal** *adj.* Relating to, connected with, of nature of, electricity. **ėlĕc'trĭcally** *adv.*

ĕlĕctrĭ'cian (-shn) *n.* Person skilled in or dealing with electricity or electrical apparatus.

ĕlĕctrĭ'cĭty *n.* Form of energy present in PROTON or ELECTRON, energy associated with the displacement or movement of CHARGE.

ėlĕc'trĭfȳ *v.t.* 1. Charge with electricity; pass electric current through; subject to electric shock; convert (railway, factory, etc.) to use of electric power. 2. Startle, rouse, excite, as with electric shock. **ėlĕctrĭfĭcā'tion** *n.*

ėlĕc'trō *n.* (pl. *-os*). Colloq. abbrev. of electroplate, electrotype.

ėlĕctrocârd'ĭogrăm *n.* (abbrev. E.C.G.) Record of sequence of electrical waves generated at each beat of heart, used in diagnosis of heart disorders. **ėlĕctrocârd'ĭograph** (-ahf) *n.* Instrument applied to body for taking such records.

ėlĕc'tro-chĕm'ĭstry *n.* The use, or the study of the functions, of electricity in chemistry.

ėlĕc'trocūte *v.t.* Put to death, execute, by powerful electric current; kill by electricity. **ėlĕctrocū'tion** *n.*

ėlĕc'trōde *n.* Either pole or terminal of a source of electricity.

ėlĕctrodȳnăm'ĭc *adj.* Of electrodynamics; of the influence of one electric current on another. **ėlĕctrodȳnăm'ĭcs** *n.* Science of electricity in motion, or of action of electric currents on themselves or one another.

ėlĕc'troĕncĕph'alogrăm *n.* (abbrev. E.E.G.) Record of minute electrical impulses inside the brain. **ėlĕc'troĕncĕph'alograph** (-ahf) *n.* Instrument for taking such records.

ĕlĕctrŏl'ȳsĭs *n.* Chemical decomposition by action of electric current; a method of obtaining a purified deposit of a metal on the cathode, as in electro-plating, and hence of purifying certain metals. **ėlĕc'trolȳte** *n.* Substance which dissolves in water to give a solution capable of conducting an electric current; such a solution. **ėlĕctrolȳt'ĭc** *adj.* **ėlĕctrolȳt'ĭcally** *adv.* **ėlĕc'trolȳse** (-z) *v.t.* Decompose (a liquid) by electricity.

ėlĕc'tro-măg'nėt *n.* Magnet consisting of a piece of soft iron surrounded by coil of wire through which electric current is passed. **ėlĕctro-măgnĕt'ĭc** *adj.* Having both electrical and magnetic character or effects; applied esp. to those waves or radiations which travel with the same velocity as light and whose special character seems to depend entirely on their frequency or wave-length, and which include X-rays, ultra-violet, visible, and infra-red light, radiant heat, radio waves, and other types of radiation. **ėlĕctro-măg'nėtĭsm** *n.* (Study of) magnetic force produced by means of electricity.

ĕlĕctrŏm'ėter *n.* Instrument for detecting and measuring the magnitude of an electric charge, current, or voltage.

ėlĕctromō'tion *n.* Motion of, or produced by, electricity. **ėlĕctromōt'ĭve** *adj.* Of, pertaining to, electromotion; ~ *force*, force set up by difference of potential in an electric circuit, usu. measured in volts (abbrev. e.m.f.).

ėlĕc'trŏn *n.* (physics etc.) The ultimate indivisible unit of the charge of negative electricity, revolving (in numbers constant for each element and equal to the atomic number in the electrically neutral atom) about the positive nucleus of every atom in defined orbits, the nature and number of which determine the chemical properties of the atom; *free* ~, electron freed from its bound state within the atom.

ĕlĕctrŏn'ĭc[1] *adj.* Pertaining to **ĕlĕctrŏn'ĭcs** *n.*, the science of the control of free electrons, esp. in vacuo, and its technological applications; *electronic brain*, (pop. name for) the *electronic computer*, a machine which by means of electronic devices (photo-electric cells, thermionic and crystal valves, cathode-ray tubes, etc.) performs elaborate mathematical calculations much faster than the human brain and can also sort and assess evidence supplied to it with a stated end in view.

ĕlĕctrŏn'ĭc[2] *adj.* (Of mus. instruments) producing sound electrically, without pipes, strings, etc. **ĕlĕctrŏn'ĭcally** *adv.*

ėlĕctrophŏn'ĭc *adj.* = ELECTRONIC[2].

ėlĕc'troplāte *v.t.* Coat (usu. a metallic surface) with a film of another metal (e.g. chromium, silver, or nickel) by electrolysis. ~ *n.* Ware produced by this process.

ėlĕc'troscōpe *n.* Instrument formerly used for detecting presence of electricity, freq. consisting of two pieces of gold leaf suspended together from the end of a conductor; it is now used for detecting and measuring radioactivity, the ionization of air produced by this having the effect of discharging a charged electroscope.

ėlĕctrostăt'ĭcs *n.* That branch of physics dealing with electricity when at rest. **ėlĕctrostăt'ĭc** *adj.*

ėlĕctrotŏn'ĭc *adj.* (of mus. instruments) = ELECTRONIC[2].

ėlĕc'trotȳpe *n.* Printing plate made by electrolytically depositing copper on to a mould of wax or lead. ~ *v.t.* Copy by this method.

ėlĕc'trum *n.* 1. Amber (obs.). 2. Pale-yellow alloy of silver and gold used by ancients. 3. (min.) Native argentiferous gold containing from 20 to 50% of silver.

ĕlėēmŏs'ȳnary (-z-) *adj.* Of, dependent on, alms; charitable; gratuitous.

ĕl'ėgant *adj.* 1. Tastefully ornate in dress; graceful; tasteful, refined; of refined luxury. 2. (chiefly U.S.) Excellent, first-rate. **ĕl'ėgance** *n.* **ĕl'ėgantly** *adv.*

ĕlėgī'ăc *adj.* Appropriate to elegies; mournful; (of metre, couplet) consisting of dactylic hexameter and pentameter. **ĕlėgī'ăcs** *n.pl.* Elegiac verses.

ĕl'ėgy *n.* Song of lamentation, esp. for the dead; poem, poetry, in elegiac metre. **ĕl'ėgīze** *v.* Write elegy, write elegy upon.

ĕl'ėment *n.* 1. Component part; constituent. 2. In ancient and medieval philosophy, one of the four simple substances, earth, water, air, fire, of which all material bodies were held to be compounded; that one of these which is the natural abode of any particular class of living beings; now (pl.) atmospheric agencies or powers; (fig.) person's etc. ordinary range of activity, surroundings in which one feels at home. 3. (chem.) Any of over 100 different substances which cannot themselves be decomposed by chemical means and which alone or in combination constitute all matter; they are distinguished from each other by the number of electrons in their atoms outside the atomic nucleus, and elements corresponding to all the numbers from 1 to 92 of such electrons, except 85 and 87, occur in nature; see PERIODIC law. 4. (pl.) Rudiments of learning; first principles of an art or science; in some English Roman Catholic schools, the lowest class.

ĕlėmĕn'tal *adj.* 1. Of the four elements, earth, air, fire, and water (see ELEMENT, 2), or of any of them; of the powers or agencies of nature; comparable to these. 2. Of the nature of an ultimate constituent, simple, uncompounded; constituent. ~ *n.* (theosophy etc.) Supposed sub-human spirit or entity.

ĕlėmĕn'tary *adj.* 1. Rudimentary, introductory. 2. Simple, not analysable. **ĕlėmĕn'tarĭly** *adv.* **ĕlėmĕn'tarĭnėss** *n.*

ĕl'ėmĭ *n.* Stimulant resin obtained from various trees, as the Brazilian *Icica cicariba*, the Mexican *Elaphrium elemiferum*, etc., used in plasters, ointments, varnish, etc.

ėlĕn'chus (-k-) *n.* (pl. *-chī*). Logical refutation; *Socratic* ~, Socratic method of eliciting truth by short question and answer.

ĕl'ėphant *n.* 1. Huge four-footed thick-skinned mammal with long curving ivory tusks and a prehensile trunk or proboscis (only two species, the Indian and the African, now exist); *white* ~, burdensome or costly possession (from the story that kings of Siam made presents of these animals to those whom they wished to ruin by the cost of their maintenance). 2. Size of drawing- and cartridge-paper, 28 × 23 in. 3. *Sea* ~ or ~ *seal*, species of seal, *Macrorhinus leoninus*, with somewhat prolonged snout in male; ~*-grass*, tall kind of reed-mace, *Typha elephantina*.

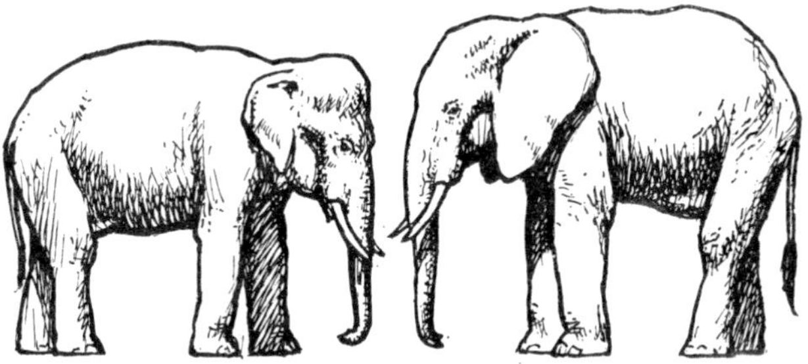

ĕlėphantī'asĭs *n.* Tropical disease, caused by parasites, resulting in gross enlargement of legs etc. and thickening of skin.

ĕlėphăn'tīne *adj.* Of elephants; elephant-like; clumsy, unwieldy.

Eleusĭn'ian (ĕlū-) *adj.* (Gk antiq.) Of Eleusis in Attica; ~ *mysteries*, ancient Greek mysteries celebrated there annually in honour of Demeter and Persephone; probably orig. a feast of purification and fertility.

ĕl'ėvāte *v.t.* Lift up; hold up Host) for adoration; raise (eyes etc.), direct upwards; exalt in rank etc.; raise morally or intellectually; (gunnery) raise axis of (gun etc.). **ĕl'ėvātėd** *adj.* (esp.) 1. Elated, exhilarated; (colloq.) slightly drunk. 2. ~ (*railway, railroad*), railway supported on pillars or arches above street level (U.S. abbrev. *el, L*); ~ *train*, train on such railway.

ĕlėvā'tion *n.* 1. Elevating, being elevated. 2. Swelling; rising ground, eminence. 3. Angle with horizon (esp. of gun); (astron.) angular distance of heavenly body above horizontal plane (as opp. to *depression*, below it). 4. Height above a given level, esp. that of sea; height, loftiness, grandeur, dignity. 5. Drawing of building made in projection on vertical plane, as dist. from ground plan (ill. DRAWING).

ĕl'ėvātor *n.* (esp.) 1. Muscle that raises limb etc. 2. Machine for hoisting corn or flour to upper storey; (orig. U.S.) large building (containing such machines) for storing grain; machine for raising hay etc. on to stack. 3. (U.S.) Apparatus for raising and lowering people or things to other floor of building, lift. 4. (aeronautics) Aerofoil, usu. on tail-plane, for climbing, diving, or keeping the aircraft in level flight.

ėlĕv'en *adj.* & *n.* One more than ten (11, xi, or XI); 11 persons forming side or team at cricket, association football, etc.; *elevens(es)*, (slang) mid-morning refreshments. **ėlĕv'enth** *adj.* & *n.*; ~ *hour*, the latest possible time (see Matt. xx).

ĕlf *n.* (pl. *elves*). One of a class of supernatural beings, in early Teutonic belief supposed to be of dwarfish form and to have formidable magic powers, exercised benevolently or malevolently; mischievous creature; dwarf, little creature; ~*-bolt*, flint arrow-head; ~*-lock*, tangled mass of hair (supposed to be produced by elves),

A   B

A. INDIAN ELEPHANT. B. AFRICAN ELEPHANT

which it was considered unlucky to disentangle. **ĕl'fin** *adj.* Of elves, elf-like; diminutive; fairy-like, full of strange charm. **ĕl'fish** *adj.*

El'gar (ĕ-), Sir Edward (1857–1934). English composer of choral-orchestral works etc.

El'gin (ĕlg-). County of NE. Scotland, also known as Morayshire, lying SE. of Moray Firth; its county town.

El'gin Marbles (ĕlg-). Collection of Greek sculptures chiefly of the school of Phidias and from the Parthenon; acquired by the 7th Earl of Elgin when envoy to the Porte (1799–1803) and sold by him to the British Government; now housed in the British Museum.

El Greco (ĕl grĕk'ō). Domenikos Theotokopoulos (1541–1614), painter, esp. of religious pictures and portraits; born in Crete; was trained in Italy and settled *c* 1577 in Toledo, Spain. [Span., = 'the Greek']

El'ia (ē-). Pseudonym adopted by Charles Lamb in his 'Essays of Elia'.

ėli'cit *v.t.* Draw forth (what is latent or potential); educe (truths etc.) *from* data; extract, draw forth (information, response, etc.) *from* person.

ėlīde' *v.t.* Omit (vowel, syllable) in pronunciation.

ĕl'igible *adj.* Fit to be chosen (*for* offices etc.); desirable, acceptable, suitable (esp. as husband or wife). **ĕligibil'ity** *n.* **ĕl'igibly** *adv.*

Elī'jah (ilīj'*a*). Hebrew prophet in reign of Ahab; he was miraculously fed by ravens at the brook Cherith; raised the dead son of Zarephath; was carried to heaven in a chariot of fire (see 1 Kings xvii. 6–2 Kings ii).

ėlim'ināte *v.t.* Remove, get rid of (esp. waste matter from body or tissues by excretion); expel, exclude; ignore (part of question etc.); (alg.) get rid of (quantities) from equation; get rid of (unknown quantities) in simultaneous equations by combining equations. **ėliminā'tion** *n.*

ėlim'inātor *n.* (esp.) Apparatus eliminating battery from wireless receiver by enabling it to be connected with electric mains.

El'iot (ĕl-), George (1819–80). Pen-name of Mary Ann Cross, *née* Evans, an English novelist; author of 'Adam Bede', 'The Mill on the Floss', 'Silas Marner', etc.

Elish'a (il-). Hebrew prophet; disciple and successor of Elijah.

ėli'sion (-zhn) *n.* Suppression of letter (esp. vowel) or syllable in pronouncing.

élite (ālēt') *n.* Choice part, best (*of*); select group or class.

ėlix'ir (-*er*) *n.* 1. (alchemy) Preparation designed to change baser metals into gold or to prolong life indefinitely; sovereign remedy for disease. 2. Aromatic pharmaceutical solution often containing alcohol and used as flavouring agent in drugs. [Arab. *al-iksir* (*iksir* prob. f. late Gk *xērion* desiccative powder for wounds)]

Eliz'abeth I (il-) (1533–1603). Queen of England 1558–1603; daughter of Henry VIII and Anne Boleyn. **Eliz'abeth II** (1926–). Queen of Gt Britain and Northern Ireland and Head of the Commonwealth 1952– ; succeeded her father, George VI. **Elizabēth'an** *adj.* & *n.* (Person, writer) of the time of Elizabeth I.

ĕlk *n.* Largest existing animal of deer kind, *Alces machlis*, with large palmate antlers, found in N. Europe and N. America, = moose; *~-hound*, Scandinavian breed of dogs with thick weather-resisting grey coat with black tips, and thick tail curled over back.

ĕll[1] *n.* Measure of length (in Engl., 45 in.), now obs. exc. in phr. *give him an inch and he'll take an ell.*

ĕll[2] *n.* (U.S.) = L; L-shaped part of building or room.

ėllipse' *n.* Plane closed curve in which the sum of the distances of any point from the two foci is a constant quantity; figure produced when a cone is cut obliquely by a plane making a smaller angle with the base than the side of the cone makes with the base (ill. CONE). **ėllip'tic(al)**[1] *adjs.*

ėllip'sis *n.* (*pl.* *-sēs* pr. -sēz). (gram.) Omission from sentence of word(s) needed to complete grammatical construction or fully express sense. **ėllip'tical**[2] *adj.* **ėllip'tically** *adv.*

ėllip'soid *n.* Solid formed by rotating an ellipse about an axis through its foci (*prolate ~*) or the perpendicular bisector of this (*oblate~*)(ill. CONE). **ėllipsoid'al** *adj.*

Ell'is Island (ĕ-). Island in New York harbour, belonging to U.S. Government, used until 1954 as an immigrant station.

ĕlm *n.* Large tree of genus *Ulmus*, usually with suckers, esp. in England *U. procera*, tree with small rough doubly serrated leaves and rough bark; in U.S. the white elm, *U. americana.*

El'mō, St. Pop. name for St. Peter González (*c* 1190–1246), Spanish Dominican preacher who became patron saint of seamen. *St. ~'s fire*: see CORPOSANT, interpreted as a sign of his protection, though sometimes of impending disaster (*dead-fire*).

ĕlocū'tion *n.* Manner, style, art, of oral delivery. **ĕlocū'tionary** (-sho-) *adj.* **ĕlocū'tionist** *n.*

Elō'him (ĕ-). Hebrew name of God or gods. **Elō'hist** *n.* Author (or authors) of those parts of the Hexateuch where *Elohim* is used instead of *Yahveh* (Jehovah). **Elōhis'tic** *adj.*

E. long. *abbrev.* East longitude.

ēl'ŏngāte (-ngg-) *v.* Lengthen, prolong; (bot.) increase in length, have slender or tapering form. **ēl'ŏngate** (-*a*t) *adj.* (bot., zool.) Long in proportion to its breadth; slender, tapering.

ēlŏngā'tion (-ngg-) *n.* 1. Lengthening. 2. (astron.) Angular distance of planet from sun, or satellite from its primary.

ėlōpe' *v.i.* (law, of wife) Run away from husband with paramour; (pop., of woman) run away from home with lover to be married. **ėlōpe'ment** (-pm-) *n.*

ĕl'oquence *n.* Fluent, forcible, and apt use of language; rhetoric. **ĕl'oquent** *adj.* **ĕl'oquently** *adv.*

ĕlse *adv.* (Following indef. or interrog. pron.) besides (as *anything ~*, *who ~?*), instead (*what ~ could I say?*); otherwise, if not (*run, ~ you will be late*). **ĕlse'where'** *adv.* In, to, some other place, at some other point.

ėlu'cidāte (-ōō-, -ū-) *v.t.* Throw light upon, clear up, explain. **ėlucidā'tion** *n.* **ėlu'cidatory** *adj.*

ėlude' (-ōōd, -ūd) *v.t.* Escape by dexterity or stratagem (blow, danger, etc.); slip away from (person, pursuit, etc.); evade. **ėlu'sion** (-zhn) *n.* **ėlus'ive** *adj.* **ėlus'ively** *adv.* **ėlus'ivenėss** *n.* **ėlus'ory** *adj.*

ĕl'ver *n.* Young eel, esp. young conger-eel.

ĕl'vish *adj.* Elfish, elfin.

Ely (ēl'ĭ). Cathedral city in the *Isle of ~*, an administrative division of Cambridgeshire, England.

Elysée (ālēz'ā). Official residence in Paris of French President.

Elȳs'ium (ėliz-). (Gk myth.) Abode of the blessed after death; hence, place, state, of ideal or perfect happiness. **Elys'ian** *adj.*; *~ fields*, Elysium.

ĕl'ȳtrŏn *n.* Outer hard wing-case of coleopterous insect (ill. BEETLE). **ĕl'ȳtral, ĕl'ȳtrous** *adjs.*

Elzevir (ĕl'zīv*er*) *adj.* & *n.* (Book) printed by the Elzevier family, numerous members of which were active as printers at Leyden, Amsterdam, Utrecht, and The Hague from 1583, when Louis Elzevier (*c* 1540–1617) issued his first book, to 1712.

ĕm *n.* 1. Name of letter M. 2. (printing) Measure equivalent to 12 points or approx. ⅙ in.; also, the square of any size of type, thus □.

em- *prefix.* Alternative form of EN-.

ėmā'ciāte (-shĭ-) *v.t.* Make lean, waste (esp. in past part.); impoverish (soil). **ėmāciā'tion** (-sĭ-, -shĭ-) *n.*

ĕm'anāte *v.i.* Issue, originate (*from* source, person, etc.); (chiefly of light, gases, etc.) proceed, issue, flow forth (*from*). **ĕm'anative** *adj.*

ĕmanā'tion *n.* (esp.) 1. Something emitted or radiated (*from*); person or thing proceeding from Divine Essence as a source. 2. (chem.) See RADON.

ėmăn'cipāte *v.t.* 1. Set free from control, or from legal, social, or political restraint; esp., set free (slave). 2. (Rom. law) Release (child, wife) from power of *pater familias.* **ėmăn'cipātor** *n.*

ėmăncĭpā′tion *n.* Setting free, esp. from slavery, intellectual or moral fetters, or legal disabilities; *Catholic E~ Act*, Act 10 Geo IV, c. 7 (1829) removing civil disabilities imposed on Roman Catholics by English law; *E~ Day*, (U.S.) 1st Jan. 1863, when slaves of Southern States were declared free by Lincoln's *E~ Proclamation*; anniversary of this. **ėmăncĭpā′tionist** (-shon-) *n.*

ėmăs′cūlāte *v.t.* Castrate; weaken, make effeminate; enfeeble, impoverish (language); weaken (literary composition) by removing what is supposed to be indecorous or offensive. **ėmăscūlā′tion** *n.* **ėmăs′cūlative, ėmăs′cūlatory** *adjs.* **ėmăs′cūlate** (-*at*) *adj.* Castrated; effeminate.

ėmbalm′ (-ahm) *v.t.* Preserve (corpse) from decay by impregnation with aromatic oils and spices; preserve from oblivion; endue with balmy fragrance. **ėmbalm′ment** *n.*

ėmbănk′ *v.t.* Shut in, confine (river etc.) by banks, raised stone structure etc. **ėmbănk′ment** *n.* 1. Mound, bank, etc., for confining river etc.; *the E~*, bank along N. side of Thames in London, public walk along this (freq. with allusion to presence of homeless wanderers, esp. at night). 2. Long earthen bank or mound carrying road or railway over valley etc.

ėmbar̄g′ō *n.* (pl. *-oes*). Order forbidding ships of foreign power to enter, or any ships to leave, ports of a country, usu. issued in anticipation of war; suspension of (branch of) commerce; stoppage, prohibition, impediment. ~ *v.t.* Lay (vessel, trade) under embargo.

ėmbar̄k′ *v.* 1. Put, go, on board ship (*for* destination). 2. Engage *in*, *upon*, undertaking etc.). **ėmbar̄kā′tion** *n.*; ~ *leave*, leave, esp. from armed forces, before being sent overseas.

ėmbă′rrass *v.t.* 1. Encumber, hamper, impede; (pass.) be in difficulties from want of money, encumbered with debts. 2. Perplex, throw into doubt or difficulty; make confused; complicate (question etc.). **ėmbă′rrassĭngly** *adv.* **ėmbă′rrassment** *n.* 1. Embarrassed state or condition; perplexity; constrained feeling or manner arising from bashfulness etc. 2. Impediment, obstruction; (pl.) pecuniary difficulties.

ĕm′bassy *n.* Ambassador's function or office; his residence; deputation to a sovereign etc.

ėmbăt′tle[1] *v.t.* Set (army) in battle array.

ėmbăt′tle[2] *v.t.* Furnish with battlements.

ėmbay′ *v.t.* 1. Lay (vessel) within a bay; (of wind, tide) force (vessel) into a bay. 2. Enclose as in a bay, shut in.

ėmbĕd′, imbĕd′ *v.t.* Fix firmly in surrounding mass; (of mass) surround thus.

ėmbĕll′ish *v.t.* Beautify, adorn; heighten (narrative) with fictitious additions. **ėmbĕll′ishment** *n.*

ĕm′ber[1] *n.* (usu. pl.) Small piece of live coal or wood in dying fire; smouldering ashes.

ĕm′ber[2] *adj.* ~ *days*, days of fasting and prayer appointed by the Church for each of four seasons of year; since Council of Placentia (1095), the Wednesday, Friday, and Saturday following (1) 1st Sunday in Lent, (2) Whitsunday, (3) Holy Cross day, 14th Sept., (4) St. Lucy's day, 13th Dec.

ėmbĕz′zle *v.t.* Divert to one's own use (money etc.) in violation of trust or official duty. **ėmbĕz′zlement** *n.* Fraudulent appropriation of entrusted property.

ėmbĭtt′er *v.t.* Make bitter (now usu. fig.), aggravate (evil); exasperate (person, feeling). **ėmbĭtt′erment** *n.*

ėmblāz′on *v.t.* Inscribe or portray conspicuously, as on heraldic shield; adorn *with* heraldic devices etc.; celebrate, extol. **ėmblāz′onment** *n.* **ėmblāz′onry** *n.* = BLAZONRY.

ĕm′blėm *n.* Symbol, typical representation; type, personification (*of* a quality); heraldic device, or other figured object as distinctive badge of person, family, etc. ~ *v.t.* Symbolize, show forth by emblem.

ĕmblėmăt′ĭc(al) *adjs.* Serving as type or emblem (*of*). **ĕmblėmăt′ĭcally** *adv.*

ĕmblĕm′atĭst *n.* Maker of emblems or of allegories.

ėmblĕm′atīze *v.t.* Serve as emblem of; represent by an emblem.

ėmbŏd′y *v.t.* 1. Invest or clothe (spirit) with body; give concrete form to (what is abstract or ideal); be embodiment or expression of. 2. Cause to become part of body; unite into one body; incorporate; include, comprise (various elements). **ėmbŏd′ĭment** *n.*

ėmbōl′den *v.t.* Make bold, encourage (*to* do).

ĕm′bolĭsm *n.* Blockage of blood-vessel by blood-clot, air-bubble, fat globule, or other foreign body.

embonpoint (ahṅbawṅpwăṅ′) *n.* Plumpness (usu. of women). [Fr. *en bon point*, in good condition]

ėmbo′som (-o͝oz-) *v.t.* Embrace; (chiefly in past part.) enclose, conceal, shelter, *in*, *with*, woods, foliage, mountains, etc.

ėmbŏss′ *v.t.* Carve, mould, in relief; cause figures etc. to stand out on (surface); make protuberant. **ėmbŏss′ment** *n.*

ėmbow′el *v.t.* Disembowel.

ėmbow′er *v.t.* Shelter, enclose, as in bower.

ėmbrāce′ *v.t.* 1. Clasp (person) in arms, usu. as sign of fondness or friendship (also abs.); clasp, enclose. 2. Accept eagerly, avail oneself of (offer, opportunity, etc.); adopt (course of action, party, opinion, etc.). 3. Include, comprise; take in with eye or mind. ~ *n.* Folding in the arms; (euphem.) sexual intercourse. **ėmbrāce′ment** (-sm-) *n.*

ėmbrăng′le (-ngg′-) *v.t.* Entangle; confuse. **ėmbrăng′lement** *n.*

ėmbrā′sure (-zh*er*) *n.* Bevelling off of wall at sides of door or window, so that inside profile of window is larger than that of outside (ill. WINDOW); opening in wall or parapet for gun, widening from within; one of the notches in a battlement.

ĕmbrocā′tion *n.* Liquid used for rubbing bruised etc. part, liniment.

ėmbroid′er *v.t.* Ornament (cloth etc., or abs.) with needlework; work in needlework; embellish (narrative) with rhetorical ornament or fictitious additions. **ėmbroid′ery** *n.*

ėmbroil′ *v.t.* Bring (affairs, narrative, etc.) into state of confusion; involve (person) in hostility (*with* another). **ėmbroil′ment** *n.*

ėmbrown′ *v.t.* (poet.) Make brown.

ĕm′bry̆ō *n.* (pl. *-os*). Offpsring of animal before birth or emergence from egg; rudimentary plant contained in seed; thing in rudimentary stage. ~ *adj.* Undeveloped, immature. **ĕmbry̆ŏn′ĭc** *adj.*

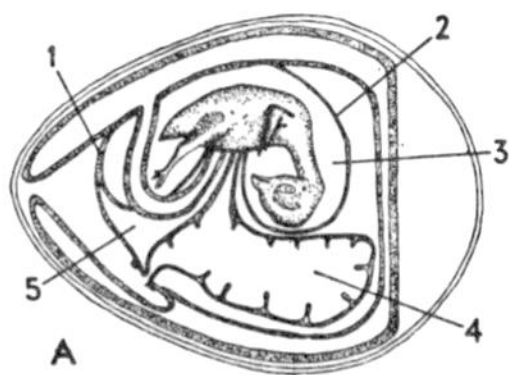

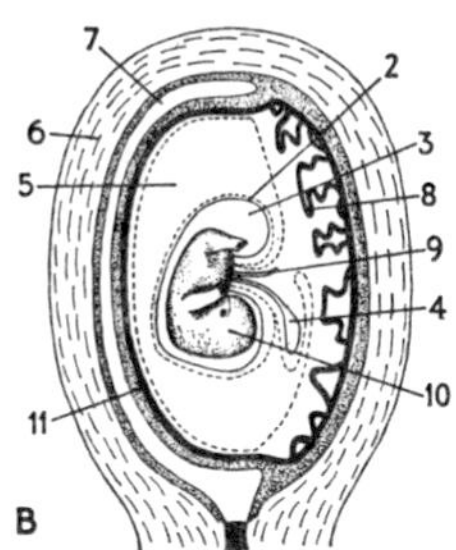

A. EMBRYO OF CHICK.
B. EMBRYO OF MAMMAL

1. Chorion. 2. Amnion. 3. Amniotic cavity. 4. Yolk sac. 5. Extra embryonic coelom. 6. Uterus. 7. Uterine cavity. 8. Placenta. 9. Umbilical cord. 10. Foetus. 11. Trophoblast

ĕmbry̆ŏl′ogy *n.* Science of the embryo. **ĕmbry̆ŏl′ogĭst** *n.* **ĕmbry̆olŏ′gĭcal** (-j-) *adj.*

ėmbŭs′ *v.* (mil.) Put (men, stores, etc.) or get into motor vehicle.

embusqué (ahṅbōōskā′) *n.* One who has escaped service at the front by securing home or base employment. [Fr., f. *embusquer* ambush]

ėmĕnd′ *v.t.* Correct; esp., remove errors from (text of book etc.). **ēmĕndā′tion, ēm′ĕndātor** *ns.* **ėmĕn′datory** *adj.*

ĕm′erald *n.* 1. Bright green precious stone, variety of beryl found chiefly in S. America, Siberia, and India. 2. Size of type (6½ point) larger than nonpareil and smaller than minion. 3. *~-cut*, (of a precious stone) step-cut in square shape; *~ green*, vivid light-green durable pigment of arseniate of copper; colour of this; *E~ Isle*, Ireland (from its greenness).

ėmĕrge′ *v.i.* Come up out of liquid; come into view, issue (*from* enclosed space, state of suffering, etc.); rise into notice (*from* obscurity etc.); (of fact etc.) come out as result of investigation or discussion. **ėmĕr′gence** *n.* **ėmĕr′gent** *adj.*

ėmĕr′gency *n.* Sudden juncture demanding immediate action; urgency, pressing need; (attrib). used, issued, called upon, arising, in an emergency.

ėmĕ′rĭtus *adj.* Honourably discharged from office, retired, as *~ professor*. [L, = 'that has served his time']

ėmĕr′sion (-shn) *n.* Emerging; reappearance of sun, moon, star, after eclipse or occultation.

Em′erson (ĕ-), Ralph Waldo (1803–82). American philosophic writer and essayist.

ĕm′ery *n.* Coarse corundum, used for polishing metals, stones, glass, etc.; *~-cloth, -paper, -wheel*, cloth, paper, wheel, coated with emery-powder; *~-powder*, ground emery.

ėmĕt′ĭc *adj.* & *n.* (Medicine) that causes vomiting.

e.m.f. *abbrev.* Electromotive force.

ĕm′ĭgrāte *v.i.* Leave one's country to settle in another; (colloq.) change one's place of abode. **ĕm′ĭgrant** *adj.* & *n.* **ĕmĭgrā′tion** *n.* **ĕm′ĭgratory** *adj.*

émigré (ām′ēgrā) *n.* Emigrant, esp. royalist who fled from France at French Revolution.

ĕm′ĭnence *n.* 1. Rising ground. 2. Distinguished superiority. 3. Title of honour borne by cardinals.

ĕm′ĭnent *adj.* Exalted, distinguished; (of qualities) remarkable in degree; signal, noteworthy; *~ domain*, sovereign government's power of controlling or confiscating private property for public use, subject to compensation. **ĕm′ĭnently** *adv.*

ĕmir′ (-ēr) *n.* Saracen or Arab prince, governor of province, military commander; a title of Moslem rulers. [Arab. *amīr* commander]

ĕm′ĭssary *n.* Person sent on (usu. odious or underhand) mission, to gain information, adherents, etc. *~ adj.*; *~ veins*, veins which penetrate the skull and connect the veins outside the skull with those in the brain.

ėmĭ′ssion (-shn) *n.* Giving of or out (chiefly of what is subtle or imponderable, light, heat, sounds, etc.); what is emitted. **ėmĭss′ĭve** *adj.* **ēmĭssĭv′ĭty** *n.* (physics) Power of a surface to radiate heat or light.

ėmĭt′ *v.t.* Give out, send forth (light, heat, sound, opinion, etc.).

Emmanuel: see IMMANUEL.

Emmăn′ūel Cŏll′ege. College of the University of Cambridge, founded 1584.

ĕmm′ėt *n.* (dial. or archaic) Ant.

ėmŏll′ient (-lye-) *adj.* & *n.* (Substance) having power of softening or relaxing living animal tissues.

ėmŏl′ūment *n.* Profit from office or employment, salary.

ėmō′tion *n.* Agitation or disturbance of mind, vehement or excited mental state; feeling. **ėmō′tionlėss** *adj.*

ėmō′tional (-sho-) *adj.* Of the emotions; liable to emotion. **ėmō′tionalĭsm, ėmō′tionalist, ėmōtionăl′ĭty** *ns.* **ėmō′tionally** *adv.*

ėmōt′ĭve *adj.* Of, tending to excite, emotion. **ėmōt′ĭvely** *adv.*

ėmpăn′el *v.t.* Enter on panel, enrol.

ĕm′pathy *n.* (psychol., aesthetics) The power of projecting one's personality into (and so fully comprehending) the object of contemplation. [transl. of Ger. *Einfühlung* (*ein-* in, *fühlen* feel)]

Empĕd′ŏclēs (-z) (b. first quarter of 5th c. B.C.). Philosopher and scientist of Agrigentum in Sicily; acc. to one version of his death, threw himself into the crater of Mt Etna.

ĕm′peror *n.* Sovereign (title considered superior in dignity to 'king'); (hist., esp.) sovereign of Roman or Byzantine Empire or head of Holy Roman Empire; *~ (butterfly)* or *purple ~*, butterfly (*Apatura*) of the family *Nymphalidae*, allied to tortoiseshell and peacock butterflies; *~ penguin*, largest known species of penguin of the Antarctic. **ĕm′perorshĭp** *n.*

ĕm′phasis *n.* (pl. *-ses* pr. -sēz). Stress on word or phrase to indicate special significance or importance; vigour, intensity, of expression, feeling, action, etc.; importance assigned to fact, idea, etc.; prominence.

ĕm′phasīze *v.t.* Lay stress on (word, fact, etc.).

ėmphăt′ĭc *adj.* (Of language, tone, gesture) forcibly expressive; (of words etc.) bearing stress; (of person) expressing himself with emphasis; (of actions) forcible, significant. **ėmphăt′ĭcally** *adv.*

ĕmphȳsēm′a *n.* (path.) Abnormal swelling in tissue caused by pressure of air or gas.

ĕm pīre *n.* 1. Supreme and extensive political dominion; absolute sway or control (*over*); government of which sovereign is called emperor. 2. Extensive territory (esp. aggregate of many separate States) under rule of emperor or sovereign State; *The E~*, (esp.) (i) the Holy Roman Empire (see ROMAN); (ii) the BRITISH EMPIRE; (iii) (period of) reign of Napoleon I as Emperor of the French, 1804–15, also called *First E~* to distinguish it from the *Second E~* of Napoleon III, 1852–70. 3. (attrib.), of the or an empire; esp., of, in the style of, the First French Empire, (of furniture) having long straight lines and details from classical and ancient Egyptian art, (of women's dress) having very high waist, low neck, and flowing skirt; (less freq.) of the Second Empire; *E~ City*, (U.S.) New York City; *E~ Day*, Queen Victoria's birthday, 24th May, widely observed as school holiday in British Empire, orig. in commemoration of assistance given by colonies in S. Afr. war of 1899–1902; *E~ State*, (U.S.) popular name of State of New York; *E~ State of the South*, pop. name of Georgia.

ėmpĭ′rĭc *adj.* Empirical. *~ n.* 1. Person relying, in medicine or other sciences, solely on observation and experiment. 2. Untrained practitioner, quack. **ėmpĭ′rĭcĭsm, ėmpĭ′rĭcist** *ns.*

ėmpĭ′rĭcal *adj.* 1. Based, acting, on observation and experiment, not on theory. 2. Without scientific knowledge. 3. *~ formula*, simplest formula of a compound, indicating only the numerical ratios of the atoms present in the molecule of the compound but not necessarily their actual number and not implying its molecular structure. **ėmpĭ′rĭcally** *adv.*

ėmplāce′ment (-sm-) *n.* Situation; placing; platform for mounting heavy guns.

ėmploy′ *v.t.* Apply (thing) to definite purpose, devote (effort, thought, etc.) to object, make use of (time etc.); use services of (person) in professional capacity or for some special business; find work or occupation for (person, his bodily or mental powers). *~ n.* Being employed, esp. for wages; (poet. or archaic) employment, occupation.

ĕmploy′ee *n.* (also ***employé*** pr. ŏmploi′ē, fem. *-ée*). Person employed for wages.

ėmploy′er *n.* (esp.) One who employs servants, workmen, etc., for wages.

ėmploy′ment *n.* (esp.) Regular occupation or business, trade, profession; state of being employed; *~ exchange*, office (esp. under State) enabling employers to find workers and vice versa.

ėmpois′on (-z-) *v.t.* (Chiefly archaic or rhet.) Poison (food, feelings, etc.).

ėmpôr'ĭum *n.* 1. Centre of commerce, mart. 2. (pompously) Large shop, store.

ėmpow'er *v.t.* Authorize, license, (*to* do); enable.

ĕm'prėss *n.* Wife of emperor; woman having rank equivalent to emperor's.

ėmprīse' (-z) *n.* (archaic) Enterprise, esp. of adventurous or chivalrous nature; martial prowess.

ĕmp'ty *adj.* 1. Containing nothing; void, devoid, (*of*); vacant, unoccupied; without anything to carry; (colloq.) hungry. 2. Frivolous, foolish; unsatisfactory, vain; *~-handed*, bringing no gift, carrying nothing away; *~-headed*, frivolous, witless. **ĕmp'tĭly** *adv.* **ĕmp'tĭnėss** *n.* **ĕmp'ty** *n.* Empty truck, wagon, etc.; empty box, bottle, etc., that has contained something. ~ *v.* Remove contents of; transfer (contents of one thing *into* another); (of river etc.) discharge itself (*into*); become empty.

ĕmpûr'ple *v.t.* Make purple, redden.

ĕmpȳēm'a *n.* (path.) Collection of pus in cavity etc., esp. in pleural cavity of lung.

ĕmpȳrē'an *adj.* & *n.* (Of) the highest heaven, as (in ancient cosmology) the sphere of fire, or as the abode of God. **ĕmpȳrē'al** *adj.*

ēm'ū *n.* Australian genus (*Dromaeus*) of fast-running birds, allied to cassowary, with rudimentary wings and long drooping feathers.

ĕm'ūlāte *v.t.* Try to equal or excel; rival; imitate zealously; **ĕmūlā'tion, ĕm'ūlātor** *ns.* **ĕm'ūlative** *adj.*

ĕm'ūlous *adj.* Zealously or jealously imitative (*of*); desirous (*of* renown etc.); actuated by spirit of rivalry. **ĕm'ūlously** *adv.*

ėmŭl'sĭfȳ *v.t.* Convert into emulsion.

ėmŭl'sion *n.* Suspension of an oil or resin in an aqueous liquid, or of an aqueous liquid in an oil, freq. by aid of albuminous or gummy material; this as pharmaceutical preparation, cosmetic, lubricant and paint, etc.

ėmŭl'sive *adj.* That is an emulsion.

ĕn *n.* The letter N; (printing) unit of measure (half an EM) for printed matter.

en-, em- *prefix.* In, into, on.

ėnā'ble *v.t.* Authorize, empower (*to* do); supply with means *to* (do); *enabling act*, legislative enactment enabling person or corporation to take certain action.

ėnăct' *v.t.* Make into legislative act, ordain, decree. **ėnăc'tion, ėnăct'ment** *ns.* **ėnăc'tive, ėnăc'tory** *adjs.*

ėnăm'el *n.* 1. Coloured glass, powdered and fused, used as decoration for gold, silver, or copper (by CLOISONNÉ, CHAMPLEVÉ, or other methods), or for painting. 2. Hard oil paint, freq. containing varnish which renders it glossy; any smooth and lustrous surface colouring. 3. Calcified substance forming glossy coating of teeth. ~ *v.t.* Inlay, encrust, cover, with enamel; variegate like enamelled work, adorn with rich and varied colours.

ėnăm'our (-mer) *v.t.* Inspire with love, make fond (*of*; usu. pass.).

ėnăn'tĭomôrph *n.* Mirror image, form related to another as an object is to its image in a mirror.

en blŏc (ahṅ) *adv.* In a lump, wholesale.

ėncaen'ĭa (-sēn-) *n.* 1. Anniversary festival of dedication of church, esp. of the (Jewish) Temple at Jerusalem. 2. Annual commemoration (in June) at Oxford of founders and benefactors of the university.

ėncāge' *v.t.* Confine (as) in cage.

ėncămp' *v.* (mil.) Settle or lodge in camp; lodge in open in tents etc.

ėncămp'ment *n.* (esp.) Place where troops are encamped; temporary quarters of nomads, travellers, etc.

ėncāse' *v.t.* Put into case; surround as with case.

ėncăsh' *v.t.* Convert (bills etc.) into cash; realize. **ėncăsh'ment** *n.*

ėncaus'tĭc *adj.* Of, produced by, 'burning in'; ~ *brick, tile*, one of red clay inlaid with a design in white clay, glazed, and fired; ~ *painting*, ancient classical method of painting with wax colours and fixing these by heat; painting made thus. ~ *n.* Encaustic painting.

enceinte (ahṅsăṅt') *n.* Enclosure (in fortification). ~ *adj.* (Of woman) pregnant.

ĕncėphăl'ic *adj.* Of the brain.

ĕncĕphalīt'ĭs *n.* (path.) Inflammation of the brain; ~ *lethargica*, 'sleepy sickness', infectious form due to a virus, pandemic during and after the war of 1914–18 and now sporadic.

ėnchain' *v.t.* Chain up, fetter; hold fast (attention etc.).

ėnchant' (-ah-) *v.t.* Bewitch; charm, delight. **ėnchant'er, ėnchant'ment, ėnchant'rėss** *ns.* **ėnchant'ĭngly** *adv.*

ėncîr'cle *v.t.* Surround, encompass; form a circle round.

ėnclasp' (-ah-) *v.t.* Hold in clasp or embrace.

ėnclāve' (*or* ahṅklahv') *n.* Territory surrounded by foreign dominion.

ėnclĭt'ĭc *adj.* & *n.* (gram.) (Word) without accent, or so unemphatic as to be pronounced as part of preceding word, esp. (in Greek) throwing its accent back on preceding word. **ėnclĭt'ĭcally** *adv.*

ėnclōse' (-z) *v.t.* 1. Surround (with walls, forces, etc.) so as to prevent free access; fence in (waste or common land) for cultivation or in order to appropriate it to individual owners; shut up, seclude (now only of monastic seclusion). 2. Shut up in receptacle (esp. something besides letter in envelope); bound on all sides, contain; surround, hem in on all sides.

ėnclō'sure (-zher) *n.* Enclosing (esp. of common land to make it private property); enclosing fence etc.; enclosed place; document etc. enclosed with letter in envelope.

ėnclōthe' (-dh) *v.t.* Clothe.

ėncloud' *v.t.* Envelop in cloud.

ėncōde' *v.t.* Put (message) into code or cipher.

ėncō'mĭăst *n.* Composer of encomium; flatterer. **ėncōmĭăs'tĭc** *adj.*

ėncō'mĭum *n.* Formal or high-flown expression of praise; eulogy, panegyric.

ėncom'pass (-ŭm-) *v.t.* Surround, form circle about. **ėncom'passment** *n.*

encore (ŏngkôr') *n.* & *int.* (Spectator's or auditor's demand for performance to be repeated) again, once more. ~ *v.t.* Demand repetition of (song etc.); summon (performer) for this.

ėncoun'ter *v.t.* 1. Meet as adversary, confront in battle. 2. Meet, fall in with, esp. casually; experience (opposition etc.). ~ *n.* Meeting in combat or casually.

ėncou'rage (-kŭ-) *v.t.* Inspire with courage, embolden; stimulate by assistance, reward, approval, etc.; allow or promote continuance or progress of. **ėncou'ragement** (-jm-) *n.* **ėncou'ragingly** *adv.*

ĕn'crĭnīte *n.* (zool., geol.) Fossil crinoid.

ėncroach' *v.i.* Intrude usurpingly (*on*). **ėncroach'ment** *n.*

ėncrŭst' *v.t.* Cover with crust; overlay (surface) with ornamental crust of precious material.

ėncŭm'ber *v.t.* Hamper *with* clog or burden; burden with obligations, responsibilities, debts, etc.; block up, fill, *with* what is obstructive or useless. **ėncŭm'berment** *n.*

ėncŭm'brance *n.* 1. Burden; annoyance; impediment; *without* ~(*s*), having no children. 2. Claim or liability attached to property; mortgage etc. **ėncŭm'brancer** *n.* Person with encumbrance or legal claim on estate.

ėncȳc'lĭcal *adj.* & *n.* (Letter, esp. issued by pope) intended for extensive circulation.

ėncȳclopaed'ĭa, -ēd'ĭa *n.* Literary work containing extensive information on all branches or one particular branch of knowledge, usu. in alphabetical order; esp. the French encyclopaedia of 'Sciences, Arts, and Trades' (1751–65) by Diderot, d'Alembert, etc. **ėncȳclop(a)ed'ĭc** *adj.* **ėncȳclop(a)ed'ĭst** *n.* [pseudo-Gk *egkuklopaideia*, erron. f. *egkuklios paideia* all-round education, the circle of arts and sciences considered essential to a liberal education]

ėncȳst' *v.t.* Enclose in cyst.

ĕnd *n.* 1. Extremity or outermost part, utmost limit; one of the two extremities of line or of greatest dimension of object; surface bounding thing at either extremity; piece broken off etc., remnant;

(naut.) last length, short length, of rope or cable; (bowls) portion of game played from one 'end' of green to the other; *shoemaker's* ~, length of thread armed with bristle. 2. Limit, close, conclusion, of period of time, action, process, series, discourse, book, etc.; latter or concluding part; termination of existence, destruction; death; ultimate state or condition. 3. Event, issue; intended result, aim, purpose; object for which thing exists or is designed. 4. Phrases etc.: *on* ~, consecutively, without intermission; in an upright position, resting on its end; *world without* ~, (tr. L *in saecula saeculorum*), for ever and ever; ~ *to* ~, with ends in contact, lengthwise; ~ *on*, so as to present end to the eye or to any object; *no* ~, (colloq.) vast quantity or number *of*; immensely, to any extent; *be at, come to, an* ~, be, become, exhausted; be completed; end; *bring to an* ~, exhaust, complete, end; *be at the* ~ *of*, have no more of; *be at one's wits'* ~, be utterly at a loss, perplexed; *put an* ~ *to*, put a stop to, abolish; *make an* ~, finish; *keep one's* ~ *up* (colloq.), acquit oneself well, bear one's part; *at a loose* ~, unoccupied; *make both* ~*s meet*, live within one's income; *be at the* ~ *of one's tether*, be unable to do more. 5. *big* ~, in internal combustion engine, end of connecting rod that connects with crankshaft; *little* ~, end that connects with piston (ill. ENGINE); ~ *game*, (chess) last stage in game when few pieces are left; ~*-mill* (*v.t.*) mill both end and periphery of (piece of metal etc.); ~*-papers*, blank leaves at beginning and end of book, the first and last of which are pasted on to the binding; ~*-play*, (eng.) freedom of shaft of machine to move axially when revolving; ~*-product*, finished article as opposed to raw material; ~*-stopped*, (of blank verse) with pause or stop at end of line(s). ~ *v.* Bring to an end; put an end to, destroy; come to an end; result *in*; ~ *by* (*doing*), come ultimately to (doing); ~ *up*, conclude, finish.

ėndăm'age *v.t.* Damage.

ėndān'ger (-j-) *v.t.* Cause danger to.

ėndear' *v.t.* Render dear (*to*). **ėndear'ingly** *adv.* **ėndear'ment** *n.* (esp.) Action or utterance expressing affection.

ėndeavour (-dĕv'*er*) *v.* Try (*to* do); strive *after*. ~ *n.* Attempt, effort.

ėndĕm'ic *adj.* Regularly found among (specified) people or in (specified) country or district. **ėndĕm'ically** *adv.* **ėndĕm'ic** *n.* Endemic disease.

ĕnd'ing *n.* (esp.) Concluding part (of book, story, etc.); (gram.) inflexional or formative suffix.

ĕn'dīve *n.* 1. Plant of the species *Cichorium endivia* (in U.S. usu. called *chicory*), of which the varieties with frizzled leaves (*curled* ~) or undivided wavy leaves (*Batavian* ~) are eaten as salad. 2. Another species of the same genus, *C. intybus* (called *chicory* in England but *endive* in U.S.), with smooth blanched leaves eaten as salad; root of this, ground and roasted as addition to coffee.

ĕnd'lėss *adj.* Infinite; eternal; incessant; ~ *band, cable, chain*, etc., band etc. with ends joined for continuous action over wheels etc.; ~ *knife, saw*, continuous band of steel with sharp-toothed edge, for similar purpose. **ĕnd'lėssly** *adv.* **ĕnd'lėssnėss** *n.*

endo- *prefix.* Within.

ĕndocar̄d'ium *n.* (pl. *-ia*). (physiol.) Smooth membrane lining cavities of heart. **ĕndocar̄dī'tis** *n.* Inflammation of this.

ĕn'docar̄p *n.* (bot.) Inner layer of pericarp, lining seed chamber (ill. FRUIT); fleshy fruit; often the stone.

ĕn'docrīne (*or* -ĕn) *adj.* & *n.* (Gland) pouring its secretions directly into the blood or lymph, ductless (gland).

ĕn'dodĕrm *n.* 1. (physiol.) Innermost layer of cells of embryo, from which alimentary system is developed. 2. (bot.) = ENDODERMIS.

ĕndodĕr̄m'is *n.* (bot.) Cylinder of tissue one cell thick lying between cortex and conducting tissues (ill. STEM).

ĕndŏg'amy *n.* Custom of marrying only within limits of clan or tribe. **ĕndŏg'amous** *adj.*

ĕn'dogėn *n.* Plant developing new wood in interior of stem. **ĕndŏ'gėnous** *adj.* Growing from within.

ĕndomēt'rium *n.* (pl. *-ia*). (physiol.) Lining tissue of womb.

ĕn'doplăsm *n.* (biol.) Granular fluid cytoplasm contained within ectoplasm in an animal cell (ill. CELL). **ĕndoplăs'mic** (-zm-) *adj.*

ėndor̄se' *v.t.* 1. Write on back of (document), esp. sign one's name (as payee etc.) on back of (bill, cheque, etc.); make (bill, cheque, etc.) payable *to* another by endorsement; write particulars of offence on back of (motorist's driving licence etc.). 2. Confirm, vouch for (statement, opinion); (chiefly U.S.) express approval of (thing, person, etc.). **ėndor̄se'ment** (-sm-) *n.*

ĕn'dospĕr̄m *n.* (bot.) Albumen enclosed with embryo in many seeds (ill. SEED). **ĕndospĕr̄m'ic** *adj.*

ĕndothēl'ium *n.* (pl. *-ia*) Layer of cells lining blood-vessels etc.

ėndow' *v.t.* Give, bequeath, permanent income to (person, institution, etc.); enrich *with* (privileges etc.); furnish *with* (quality, ability, etc.). **ėndow'ment** *n.*; ~ *assurance, insurance, policy*, (policy of) insurance providing for payment of fixed sum at specified date or at death, whichever is earlier.

ėndūe' *v.t.* 1. Put on, assume, as a garment; clothe *with*. 2. Invest *with* power or quality.

ėndūr'ance *n.* Habit, power, of enduring; enduring.

ėndūre' *v.* 1. Undergo (pain etc.); submit to; bear (*to* do); tolerate (thing, person). 2. Last.

ĕnd'ways, -wīse (-z) *advs.* With end towards spectator or uppermost or foremost; end to end.

Endȳm'ion (ĕ-). (Gk myth.) A shepherd, the most beautiful of men, of whom Selene (the Moon) became enamoured.

E.N.E. *abbrev.* East-north-east.

ĕn'ėma (*or* ĕnēm'*a*) *n.* Substance introduced mechanically into rectum; the syringe used for this.

ĕn'ėmy *n.* 1. Hostile person; opponent, antagonist; opposing person, influence, etc.; *the E*~, the Devil. 2. (Member of) hostile army or nation; hostile force; nation, State, at war with another. ~ *adj.* Of a hostile force or nation; hostile.

ĕnergĕt'ic *adj.* Strenuously active; forcible, vigorous; powerfully operative. **ĕnergĕt'ically** *adv.*

ėnĕr̄'gic *adj.* (rare) Energetic.

ĕn'ergism *n.* Ethical doctrine that supreme good lies not in pleasure but in exercise of normal activities. **ĕnergis'tic** *adj.*

ĕn'ergīze *v.t.* Put in operation, infuse energy into, supply with energy.

ĕnergūm'ĕn *n.* Person possessed by a devil, demoniac; enthusiast, fanatical devotee.

ĕn'ergy *n.* 1. Force, vigour (of speech, action, person, etc.); active operation; power actively exerted, (pl.) individual powers in exercise; capacity to produce effect. 2. (physics) Power of doing work possessed at any instant by a body or system of bodies; *actual, kinetic*, ~, power of doing work possessed by moving body by virtue of its motion; *latent, potential*, ~, body's power of doing work by virtue of stresses resulting from its relation to other bodies; *mass-*~, energy which all bodies possess in virtue of their mass, and of which a small portion is released (as radiations etc.) in radio-activity and other types of atomic disintegration; *conservation of* ~, principle that the total energy of any closed system of bodies (including the universe) is invariable.

ĕn'ervāte *v.t.* Weaken physically, impair nervous tone of; destroy capacity of for vigorous effort of mind or will; impair vigour of. **ĕnervā'tion** *n.*

enfant terrible (ahṅ'fahṅ tĕrēbl') *n.* Child who asks awkward questions, repeats what he has heard, etc. [Fr.]

ėnfee'ble *v.t.* Make feeble. **ėnfee'blement** *n.*

ėnfeoff' (-fĕf, -fēf) *v.t.* Invest with fief; put in possession of fee-simple or fee-tail of lands etc. **ėnfeoff'ment** *n.*

En'field (ĕ-). Small town in Middlesex, England, near which is Government small-arms factory; ~ (*rifle*), muzzle-loading rifle made there and used by British Army in Crimean war.

ĕnfĭlāde′ *n.* Fire from guns etc. sweeping line from end to end. ~ *v.t.* Subject (troops etc.) to this.

ėnfōld′ *v.t.* Wrap up (*in, with*); clasp, embrace.

ėnfôrce′ *v.t.* 1. Press home (argument etc.), urge (demand etc.). 2. Compel, constrain, oblige; compel (performance of action, observance of law, etc.) by physical or moral force. **ėnfôrce′ment** (-sm-) *n.*

ėnfrāme′ *v.t.* Set (picture etc.) in frame.

ėnfrăn′chīse (-z) *v.t.* 1. Set free; release from legal liabilities etc.; invest (city etc.) with municipal rights, esp. that of being represented in parliament. 2. Admit to membership of body politic or State; now esp., admit to electoral franchise. **ėnfrăn′chīsement** (-zm-) *n.*

ėngāge′ (-n-g-) *v.* 1. Bind by contract or promise (esp. of marriage); pledge oneself. 2. Hire (employee); bespeak (seats, cab, etc.). 3. (now rare) Gain, win over; persuade, induce; attract, charm. 4. Fasten, attach; (archit., pass., of pillar) be let into wall; (mech.) of part of machinery, interlock *with*, fit into corresponding part. 5. Hold fast, attract (attention etc.); employ, occupy (person, his powers, thought, etc.); embark *in*, enter upon, action, business, etc. 6. Bring, come, into conflict *with* enemy; attack, enter into combat with. **ėngāge′ment** (-jm-) *n.*

ėngā′gĭng (-n-g-) *adj.* (esp.) Winning, attractive. **ėngā′gĭngly** *adv.* **ėngā′gĭngnėss** *n.*

ėngar′land (-n-g-) *v.t.* Put garland upon; wreath (*with*).

Engels (ĕng′lz), Friedrich (1820–95). German socialist writer; with Karl Marx, issued the 'Communist Manifesto', 1848.

ėngĕn′der (-j-) *n.* Beget (now only fig.); give rise to, bring about.

ĕn′gĭne (-j-) *n.* 1. Machine consisting of several parts working together to produce given physical effect; esp., machine consisting of oscillating or reciprocating parts which converts the chemical energy of fuel into mechanical power in a useful form; *~-driver*, driver of engine, esp. locomotive; *~-man*, man having charge of engine, engine-driver; *~-room*, room containing (esp. ship's) engine(s); *~-turned*, ornamented with *~-turning*, engraving of symmetrical patterns on metals by machine. 2. (hist.) Machine used in warfare, esp. of large size (e.g. catapult, battering-ram). ~ *v.t.* Fit (ship etc.) with engines.

ĕngĭneer′ (-j-) *n.* 1. One skilled in the construction and maintenance of works of public utility such as roads, bridges, canals, gasworks, etc. (*civil* ~), or in the design, construction, and maintenance of machines (*mechanical* ~), or in the production and transmission of electrical energy and the manufacture of electrical apparatus (*electrical* ~). 2. One who designs and constructs military works for attack or defence (*military* ~); soldier belonging to branch of army called *Engineers*. 3. One who has charge of steam-engine; (chiefly U.S.) engine-driver. ~ *v.* 1. Act as engineer; construct, manage (bridge, work), as engineer. 2. Contrive, arrange, bring about. **ĕngĭneer′ĭng** *n.* Science, profession, of engineer; work done by engineer.

ėngĭrd′, ėngĭr′dle (-n-g-) *vbs.t.* Surround (as) with girdle.

Eng′land (ĭngg-). Kingdom occupying together with Wales the southern part of Gt Britain. **Eng′lander** *n.* (rare) Native of England; *Little ~*, one who desires to restrict the dimensions and responsibilities of the empire, a term of opprobrium current esp. during the Boer war.

Eng′lĭsh (ĭngg-) *adj.* Of England, the English, or their language. ~ *n.* 1. The people of England. 2. The language of the English, the people of the United States, and the greater part of the British Commonwealth. English, which belongs to the western branch of the Germanic family of languages, was originally the dialect of the Angles and the name was extended to all dialects of the vernacular, whether Anglian or Saxon; *Old ~*, or Anglo-Saxon, is the English language of the period ending *c* 1100; *Middle ~*, the language of the middle period from *c* 1100 to *c* 1500, which is followed by *Modern ~* (*c* 1500–); *American ~*, the variety of English spoken in U.S.; *King's* (*Queen's*) ~, correct grammatical English; (*in*) *plain ~*, (in) plain intelligible words. 3. (typ.) A size of type (14 point). 4. ~ *Channel*, the channel between the S. coast of England and N. coast of France; ~ *horn* = COR ANGLAIS. **eng′lĭsh** (ĭngg-) *v.t.* (archaic, affected) Render into English. **Eng′lĭshman (-woman)** *ns.* Native or citizen of England. **Eng′lĭshry** *n.* (now chiefly hist.) Group of people of English descent, esp. in Ireland.

ėngôrge′ *v.t.* 1. Devour greedily. 2. (pass.) Be crammed; (path.) be congested with blood. **ėngôrge′ment** (-jm-) *n.*

ėngraft′ (-ah-) *v.t.* Graft in; insert (scion of one tree) *into, upon*, another; implant; incorporate *into*.

ėngrail′ *v.t.* Indent edge of, give serrated appearance to; (her.) shape edge of (ordinary etc.) so that it has a continuous series of concave notches (ill. HERALDRY).

ėngrain′, ingrain′ *v.t.* Cause (dye etc.) to sink deeply into a thing (usu. fig.). **ėngrained′** *adj.* Inveterate; thoroughgoing.

ĕn′grăm (-n-g-) *n.* 1. (psychol.) Hypothetical physical memory-trace in the brain, recording a mental experience. 2. (biol.) Permanent and heritable change in cell, due to stimulus. **ėngrăph′ĭc** *adj.* **ėngrăph′ically** *adv.* **ĕn′graphy** *n.*

ėngrāve′ *v.t.* Inscribe, ornament (hard surface) *with* incised marks; carve (design, letters, etc.)

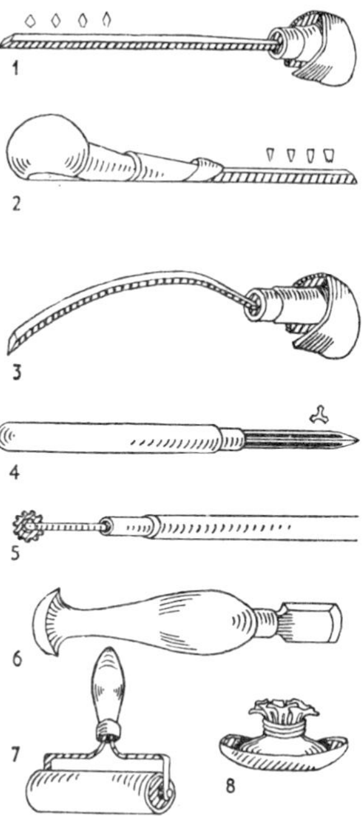

ENGRAVING TOOLS

1, 2. Burin or graver and sections. 3. Stipple graver. 4. Scalper and section. 5. Roulette. 6. Mezzotint rocker. 7. Roller. 8. Dabber

upon surface; cut (design etc.) on metal plate or wood block for printing; (fig.) impress deeply (*upon* memory etc.). **ėngrāv′er** *n.*

ėngrāv′ĭng *n.* (esp.) Print made from engraved plate; copy of painting etc. made by this means; art of imparting designs to plates or blocks in such a way that prints may be taken from them, esp. by incising lines (*line* ~); this and numerous other hand- and mechanical processes collectively.

ėngrōss′ *v.t.* 1. Write in large letters; now chiefly, write in peculiar character appropriate to legal document. 2. Occupy entirely or exclusively, monopolize (person, his attention, etc.); (hist.) buy whole stock of (commodity) in order to retail it at monopoly price. **ėngrōss′ment** *n.*

ėngŭlf′ *v.t.* Plunge into, swallow up (as) in, gulf. **ėngŭlf′ment** *n.*

ėnhance′ (-ah-) *v.* Heighten, intensify (qualities, powers, etc.);

exaggerate; raise (price); increase in price or value. **ènhance'ment** (-sm-) *n.*

ĕnharmŏn'ic *adj.* (mus.) Of, in, the Greek style or scale in which an interval of 2½ tones (5 semitones) was divided into 10 quarter-tones and a major third; of, having, intervals smaller than **semitone** (esp. such intervals as that between G♯ and A♭). **ĕnharmŏn'ically** *adv.*

ĕnĭg'ma *n.* Riddle; puzzling person or thing. **ĕnĭgmăt'ĭc(al)** *adjs.* **ĕnĭgmăt'ĭcally** *adv.*

ènisle' (-īl) *v.t.* Make into, place on, isle; isolate.

ènjămb'ment (-m-m-) *n.* (pros.) Continuation of sentence beyond second line of couplet.

ènjoin' *v.t.* 1. Prescribe, impose (action, conduct, *on* person); command (*to* do); issue instructions (that). 2. Prohibit, forbid, restrain (esp. by legal injunction).

ènjoy' *v.t.* 1. Find pleasure in (festivity, social intercourse, recreation, etc.); ~ one*self*, experience pleasure, be happy. 2. Use, possess, or experience with delight, take delight in; have use or benefit of; occas., experience (something not pleasurable). **ènjoy'able** *adj.* **ènjoy'ably** *adv.* **ènjoy'ment** *n.*

ènkĭn'dle *v.t.* Cause (flame, passions, war, etc.) to blaze up; inflame with passion.

ènlāce' *v.t.* Encircle tightly; enfold; entwine. **ènlāce'ment** (-sm-) *n.*

ènlar̄ge' *v.t.* 1. Make larger, extend limits of, increase size, amount, or number of; (phot.) make copy larger than original negative. 2. Extend range or scope of, widen (ideas, sympathies, etc.); expatiate *upon*. 3. Set at large, release, set free (archaic exc. in U.S.). **ènlar̄ge'ment** *n.* **ènlar̄'ger** *n.* Photographic apparatus for enlarging or reducing negatives or positives.

ènlight'en (-īt-) *v.t.* Instruct, inform (*on* subject); free from prejudice or superstition; (chiefly poet.) shed light on (object), give light to (person). **ènlight'enment** *n.*; *The E~*, (after Ger. *Aufklärung*) an 18th-c. philosophical movement characterized by a reliance on reason and directed to freeing religion and morals from tradition and prejudice.

ènlĭst' *v.* 1. Engage, enrol, for military service (esp. as private soldier or for temporary service). 2. Secure co-operation or support of (*in* enterprise etc.). **ènlĭst'ment** *n.*

ènlī'ven *v.t.* Animate, inspirit; brighten. **ènlī'venment** *n.*

en mȧsse (ahǹ) *adv.* In a mass; all together. [Fr.]

ènmĕsh' *v.t.* Entangle (as) in net. **ènmĕsh'ment** *n.*

ĕn'mĭty *n.* Hatred; state of hostility.

ĕnn'ėad *n.* Set of nine.

ènnō'ble *v.t.* Make (person) a noble; make noble, elevate. **ènnō'blement** (-blm-) *n.*

ennui (ŏn'wē) *n.* Mental weariness from lack of occupation or interest; boredom.

Enoch (ē'n'ok). Patriarch, the father of Methuselah (Gen. v. 24); two apocryphal works, the 'Book of ~' and the 'Book of the Secrets of ~', are ascribed to him.

ènor̄m'ĭty *n.* Monstrous wickedness; crime, monstrous offence.

ènor̄m'ous *adj.* Huge, very large. **ènor̄m'ously** *adv.* **ènor̄m'ousnėss** *n.*

En'osĭs (ĕn-) *n.* Political unification of all Greeks (used esp. of movement to unite Cyprus with Greece).

ènough' (-ŭf) *adj., n., & adv.* Not less than required quantity, number, or degree.

ènounce' *v.t.* Enunciate; pronounce (words). **ènounce'ment** *n.*

ènow' *adj., n., & adv.* (dial. or poet.) Enough.

en passant (ahǹ păsahǹ') *adv.* By the way; *take* (pawn) ~, (chess) take adversary's pawn that has been moved forward two squares with a pawn so advanced that it can threaten the first of these squares, the pawn which takes *en passant* being moved to the threatened square. [Fr.]

ènquire, ènquīry: see INQUIRE, INQUIRY

ènrāge' *v.t.* Make furious.

en rapport (ahǹ răpōr') *adv.* In touch (*with*). [Fr.]

ènrăp'ture *v.t.* Delight intensely.

en règle (ahǹ rāgl) *adv.* In due form. [Fr.]

ènrĭch' *v.t.* Make rich; add to contents of (collection, museum, book); make richer in quality, flavour, etc. **ènrĭch'ment** *n.*

ènrōbe' *v.t.* Put robe upon.

ènrōl' *v.t.* Write (name), inscribe name of (person) on roll or list, esp. of army; incorporate (person) as member (*in* society etc.); enter (deed etc.) among rolls of court of justice, record, celebrate. **ènrōl'ment** *n.*

en route (ahǹ rōōt) *adv.* On the way. [Fr.]

ENSA or **Ensa** *abbrev.* Entertainments National Service Association (a British organization of the war of 1939–45).

ènsăm'ple *n.* (archaic) Example.

ènsăng'uined (-nggwĭnd) *adj.* Blood-stained, bloody.

ènscŏnce' *v.t.* Establish (*in* concealed, secure, comfortable, etc., position).

ensemble (ahǹsahǹbl') *n.* Thing viewed as whole; woman's dress, shoes, hat, etc., as complete whole; (mus.) united performance of voices or instruments in concerted music. [Fr.]

ènshrīne' *v.t.* Enclose (relic etc.) in or as in shrine; serve as shrine for. **ènshrīne'ment** (-nm-) *n.*

ènshroud' *v.t.* Cover completely, hide from view.

ĕn'sign (-sīn; *naut.* -sn) *n.* 1. Conventional sign, emblem; esp., badge or symbol of dignity or office. 2. (chiefly naut.) Standard, banner, flag; esp. (in British use) flag with white, blue, or red field and union in corner; *white* ~, that of Royal Navy and Royal Yacht Squadron (ill. FLAG); *blue* ~, that of naval reserve, ships in service of public offices etc.; *red* ~, that of merchant service. 3. Standard-bearer; formerly, lowest commissioned infantry officer. **ĕn'signcy̆** (-sĭn-) *n.*

ĕn'sĭlage *n.* = SILAGE.

ènsīle' *v.t.* Convert (fodder) into silage. **ĕnsīlā'tion** *n.*

ènslāve' *v.t.* Make slave of, reduce to slavery. **ènslāve'ment** (-vm-) *n.*

ènsnāre' *v.t.* Entrap.

ènsphēre' *v.t.* Encircle, enclose.

ènsūe' *v.* 1. Happen afterwards; result (*from, on*). 2. (bibl.) Seek after.

ènsure' (-shoor) *v.t.* Make safe (*against, from,* risks); make certain; secure (thing *to, for,* person, etc.).

èntăb'lature *n.* (archit.) Part of classical order above column, including architrave, frieze, and cornice (ill. ORDER).

èntā'blement (-blm-) *n.* Horizontal platform supporting statue, above dado and base.

èntail' *n.* Settlement of succession of landed estate, so that it cannot be bequeathed at pleasure by any one possessor; estate so secured; (fig.) inalienable inheritance. ~ *v.t.* 1. Settle (land etc.) by entail; bestow (thing) as inalienable possession. 2. Impose (expense, labour, *on* person); necessitate. **èntail'ment** *n.*

èntă'ngle (-nggl) *v.t.* Catch in snare or among obstacles; involve in difficulties; make tangled or intricate. **èntă'nglement** (-ngglm-) *n.* Act of entangling, state of being entangled; (mil.) barrier of barbed wire etc. to form an obstacle to the enemy.

ĕn'tasĭs *n.* (archit.) Barely perceptible swelling in shaft of column (ill. ORDER).

èntĕl'ėchy (-kĭ) *n.* In Aristotle etc., realization or complete expression of some function, condition in which potentiality has become actuality.

entente (ahǹtahǹt') *n.* (diplom.) Friendly understanding between States; group of States in such relation; *E~ Cordiale*, that formed between Gt Britain and France in 1904; *Little E~*, that between Czechoslovakia, Yugoslavia, and Rumania (1921); *Triple E~*, that between England, France, and Russia (1908). [Fr.]

ĕn'ter *v.* 1. Go, come, in; come upon stage; ~ *for* (race, examination, etc.), undertake to compete in;

~ *into*, engage in, sympathize with, form part of, bind oneself by (contract, treaty, etc.); ~ (*up*)*on*, assume possession of, begin, begin to deal with. 2. Go, come, into; penetrate; begin (period of time). 3. Become member of (society or organized body). 4. Put (name) into list, (fact etc.) into description or record, etc.; insert by name in list of competitors; admit, procure admission for, as pupil, member of society, etc.; ~ *an appearance*, *judgement*, *writ*, etc., (law) enter on record or bring before court in due form; ~ *a protest*, (of minority in deliberative body) record protest in journals or minutes; protest; ~ *up*, enter in regular form, complete series of entries in.

ėntĕ′rĭc *adj.* & *n.* Of the intestines; ~ (*fever*), typhoid. **ĕnterī′tĭs** *n.* (Acute) inflammation of bowels, esp. small intestines.

ĕn′terprīse (-z) *n.* Undertaking, esp. bold or difficult one; courage, readiness to engage in enterprises. **ĕn′terprīsĭng** *adj.* Ready to undertake enterprises. **ĕn′terprīsĭngly** *adv.*

ĕntertain′ *v.t.* 1. Occupy (person etc.) agreeably, amuse. 2. Receive as guest, show hospitality to (also abs.). 3. Admit to consideration, harbour, cherish (idea, opinion, proposal, etc.). **ĕntertain′er** *n.* (esp.) One who gives a public entertainment. **ĕntertain′ĭng** *adj.* (esp.) Amusing. **ĕntertain′ĭngly** *adv.*

ĕntertain′ment *n.* (esp.) Amusement; public performance or exhibition intended to interest or amuse.

ėnthral(l)′ (-awl) *v.t.* Enslave; charm. **ėnthral′ment** *n.*

ėnthrōne′ *v.t.* Place (king, bishop, etc.) on throne, esp. as formal induction. **ėnthrōne′ment** (-nm-), **ĕnthronīzā′tion** *ns.*

ėnthūse′ (-z) *v.i.* (colloq.) Show enthusiasm, gush.

ėnthūs′ĭăsm (-zĭ-) *n.* 1. (archaic) Ill-regulated or misdirected religious emotion; extravagant or false confidence in divine inspiration or favour. 2. Rapturous intensity of feeling *for* a person, cause, pursuit, etc.; passionate eagerness.

ėnthūs′ĭăst (-z-) *n.* One who is full of enthusiasm. **ėnthūsĭăs′tĭc** *adj.* **ėnthūsĭăs′tĭcally** *adv.*

ĕn′thȳmēme *n.* (logic) Syllogism in which one premiss is suppressed.

ėntīce′ *v.t.* Allure, attract, esp. insidiously or adroitly, by offer of pleasure or advantage. **ėntīce′ment** (-sm-) *n.*

ėntīre′ *adj.* Whole, complete; not broken or decayed; not castrated; unqualified; all of one piece, continuous; pure, unmixed. **ėntīre′nėss** (-īrn-) *n.* **ėntīre′** *n.* (hist., and on inn-signs, etc.) Kind of malt-liquor resembling porter.

ėntīre′ly (-īrlĭ) *adv.* Wholly; solely.

ėntīre′ty (-īrtĭ) *n.* 1. Completeness; whole, sum total; *in its* ~, in its complete form, as a whole. 2. (law) Entire or undivided possession of an estate.

ėntī′tle *v.t.* 1. Give (person, book, etc.) the title of. 2. Give (person etc.) a claim (*to* a thing, *to* do).

ĕn′tĭty *n.* 1. A thing's existence, as dist. from its qualities or relations. 2. Something that has a real existence.

ėntomb′ (-ōōm) *v.t.* Place in tomb; serve as tomb for. **ėntomb′ment** (-ōōm-m-) *n.*

ĕntomŏl′ogy *n.* Branch of zoology dealing with insects. **ĕntomolŏ′gĭcal** *adj.* **ĕntomŏl′ogĭst** *n.* **ĕntomŏl′ogīze** *v.i.*

entourage (ŏntoorahzh′) *n.* Persons surrounding or attending on a superior; surroundings. [Fr.]

entr′acte (ŏntrăkt′) *n.* (Performance in) interval between acts of play. [Fr.]

ĕn′trails *n.pl.* Bowels, intestines; inner parts (*of* the earth etc.).

ĕntrain′ *v.* Put, go, into a train.

ĕn′trance[1] *n.* 1. Coming or going in; coming of actor upon stage; entering *into*, *upon* (office etc.). 2. Right of admission; fee paid on admission. 3. Door, passage, etc., one enters by.

ėntrance′[2] (-ah-) *v.t.* Throw into trance; overwhelm (*with* joy, fear); carry away as in trance.

ĕn′trant *n.* One who enters room, profession, etc., or *for* (race etc.).

ėntrăp′ *v.t.* Catch in or as in trap; beguile (*to* destruction etc., *into* doing).

ėntreat′ *v.t.* 1. Ask earnestly (*to* do). 2. (archaic) Treat, deal with, in specified manner. **ėntreat′y** *n.* Earnest request.

entrechat (ahṅ′treshah) *n.* (dancing) Striking together of the heels several times during leap from ground. [Fr.]

entrée (ŏn′trā) *n.* 1. Right or privilege of admission. 2. Made dish served between fish and joint.

ėntrĕnch′ *v.t.* 1. Surround, fortify, with trench (freq. fig.); *entrenching tools*, tools suitable for digging trenches. 2. Encroach, trespass, *upon*. **ėntrĕnch′ment** *n.*

entre nous (ŏn′tre nōō) *adv.* Between you and me. [Fr.]

entrepôt (ŏn′trepō) *n.* Storehouse for deposit; commercial centre for import and export, collection and distribution. [Fr.]

entrepreneur (ŏntreprenẽr′) *n.* Organizer, manager, of (esp. musical) entertainments; manager. 2. One who undertakes an enterprise, esp. contractor acting as intermediary between capital and labour. [Fr.]

entresŏl (ŏn′-) *n.* Low storey between first and ground floor. [Fr.]

ĕn′tropy *n.* A thermodynamic function, a measure of the degree of molecular disorder existing in a system, also determining how much of the system's thermal energy is unavailable for conversion into mechanical work.

ėntrŭst′ *v.t.* Charge (person) *with* (duty, object of care); confide (duty etc. *to* person etc.).

ĕn′try *n.* 1. Coming or going in; coming (of actor) upon stage; ceremonial entrance; beginning, or resumption, of performer's part in concerted music. 2. (law) Taking possession of lands etc. by entering or setting foot on them. 3. Place of entrance; door, gate, entrance-hall, etc. 4. Entering or registering in list, record, account-book, etc.; item so entered; list of competitors (in race etc.); *double* ~, book-keeping in which every credit item of one account in ledger is entered to debit of another.

ent. Sta. Hall *abbrev.* Entered at Stationers' Hall.

ėntwīne′ *v.t.* Interweave; wreathe; embrace.

ėnūc′lėāte *v.t.* 1. Explain, clear up. 2. (surg.) Extract (tumour etc.) from its capsule; remove (eyeball). **ėnūc′lėate** (-at) *adj.* (biol. etc.) Without a nucleus.

ėnūm′erāte *v.t.* Count; mention (number of things or persons) separately; specify. **ėnūmerā′tion** *n.* **ėnūm′erative** *adj.*

ėnŭn′cĭāte *v.t.* Express (proposition, theory) definitely; proclaim; pronounce (articulate sounds). **ėnŭncĭā′tion, ėnŭn′cĭātor** *ns.* **ėnŭn′cĭative** *adj.*

ĕnūrēs′ĭs *n.* (path.) Involuntary passing of urine.

ėnvĕl′op *v.t.* Wrap up (person, thing, subject, etc., *in* garment, flames, mystery, etc.); (mil.) surround. **ėnvĕl′opment** *n.*

ĕn′velōpe (*or* ŏn-) *n.* 1. Wrapper, covering; esp., folded and gummed cover for letter. 2. (bot.) Calyx or corolla, or both together (ill. FLOWER). 3. (math.) Locus of the ultimate intersections of curves in a system of curves.

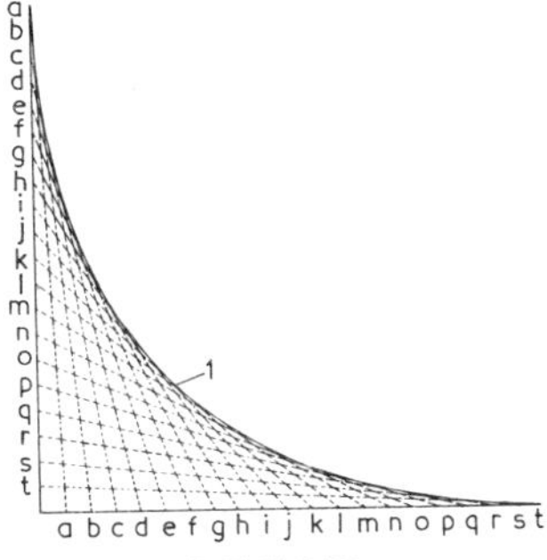

ENVELOPE

1. Envelope formed by lines *a–a*, *b–b*, etc.

ėnvĕn′om *v.t.* Put poison on, taint with poison; infuse venom or bitterness into (actions, words, etc.), embitter; corrupt, vitiate.

ĕn'vĭable *adj.* Calculated to excite envy. **ĕn'vĭably** *adv.*

ĕn'vĭous *adj.* Full of envy; feeling envy *of.* **ĕn'vĭously** *adv.*

ĕnvīr'on *v.t.* Form ring, be stationed, round; encircle, encompass, *with*; surround with hostile or protective intention.

ėnvīr'onment *n.* Surroundings, surrounding objects, region, conditions, or influences. **envīr'onmental** *adj.*

ĕn'virons (*or* ĕnvīr'-) *n.pl.* Outskirts, surrounding districts, of town etc.

ėnvĭ'sage (-z-) *v.t.* Look in the face of; face (danger, facts); contemplate, esp. under particular aspect. **ėnvĭ'sagement** (-jm-) *n.*

ĕn'voy[1], **ĕn'voi** *n.* Concluding part of poetical or prose composition; now esp., short stanza concluding ballade or other archaic forms of poem.

ĕn'voy[2] *n.* Public minister, now esp., diplomatic minister ranking below ambassador and above chargé d'affaires, sent by one sovereign or government to another to transact diplomatic business; messenger, representative. **ĕn'voyship** *n.*

ĕn'vy *n.* Mortification or ill-will or longing occasioned by another's good fortune; object of this. ~ *v.t.* Feel envy of (person, his advantages).

ėnwomb' (-ōōm) *v.t.* Enclose (as) in womb.

ėnwrăp' *v.t.* Wrap, enfold.

ĕn'zȳme *n.* One of a group of complex chemical substances produced by yeast and other living organisms and promoting specific chemical reactions in the organism; their names usu. end in *-ase*, e.g. diastase. **ėnzȳm'ĭc** *adj.*

ē'ocēne *adj.* (geol.) Of the second series of rocks in the tertiary system; of this epoch. ~ *n.* *The E~*, this epoch or formation (ill. GEOLOGY).

ē'olĭth *n.* Flint shaped by nature but used by early man as implement or weapon. **ēolĭth'ĭc** *adj.* Of the earliest age of man represented by implements, of the age preceding the palaeolithic.

eon: see AEON.

ē'osĭn *n.* (chem.) Red dye-stuff produced e.g. by action of bromine on fluorescein; soluble potassium salt of this used as rose-pink dye, as stain in microscopy, red ink, etc.

ēozō'ĭc *adj.* (geol.) (Of strata) showing the earliest indications of animal life.

E.P. *abbrev.* Electroplate.

ē'păct *n.* (also pl.) Number of days constituting excess of solar over lunar year of 12 months; age of moon on 1st Jan.

ĕp'arch (-k) *n.* Governor or bishop of eparchy. **ĕp'archy** (-kĭ) *n.* 1. Subdivision of modern Greece. 2. Diocese of Russian (Gk) Church.

ĕp'aulĕt(te) *n.* Ornamental shoulder-piece of uniform (ill. CAVALRY).

épée (āp'ā) *n.* Sharp-pointed sword used in duelling and (blunted) in fencing.

epergne (ĕpern') *n.* Centre ornament (esp. in branched form) for dinner-table.

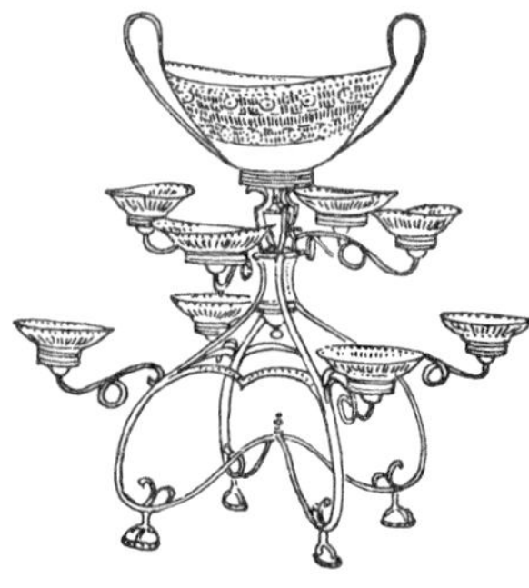

EPERGNE

ĕpĕxėgēs'ĭs *n.* Addition of word(s) to make meaning of preceding word or sentence clearer; word so added. **ĕpĕxėgĕt'ĭc(al)** *adjs.* **ĕpĕxėgĕt'ĭcally** *adv.*

Eph. *abbrev.* Ephesians (N.T.).

ephah (ē'fa) *n.* Hebrew dry measure (see HOMER[2]).

ĕph'ėdrĭne *n.* Drug, resembling adrenalin in its effects.

ėphĕm'era (pl. *-ras*), **-ron** (pl. *-rons, -ra*) *ns.* Commonest of the may-flies (ill. MAY), insect with delicate lacy wings and three long tail-filaments, found near water, and living (in its imago or winged form) only for a day; hence, short-lived thing.

ėphĕm'eral *adj.* 1. (Of diseases) lasting only a day; (of insects etc.) living for a day or a few days. 2. Short-lived, transitory.

ėphĕm'eris *n.* (pl. *-mĕ'rĭdēs*). Table showing predicted positions of heavenly body for every day during given period; astronomical almanac.

ephemeron: see EPHEMERA.

Ephĕmerŏp'tera *n.* Order of insects including may-flies and allied forms.

Ephē'sian (-zhan) *adj.* & *n.* (Native) of Ephesus; *Epistle to the Ephesians*, one of the Pauline Epistles of the N.T.

Eph'ėsus (ĕf-). One of the principal Ionian cities on the coast of Asia Minor; in Roman times, chief city of the province of Asia.

ēph'od *n.* Jewish priestly vestment, sleeveless and slit at sides below armpits, fastened with buckle at shoulders and girdle at waist.

ĕph'or *n.* (Gk hist.) Magistrate in various Dorian States, esp. at Sparta, where 5 annually elected ephors exercised controlling power over kings.

epi- *prefix.* Upon, at, on the ground or occasion of, in addition.

ĕp'ĭblast (-ah-) *n.* (biol.) Outermost layer of cells of a blastoderm or gastrula. **ĕpĭblăs'tĭc** *adj.*

ĕp'ĭc *adj.* Of, in, that species of poetical composition celebrating in continuous narrative achievements of heroic personage(s) of history or tradition; such as is described in epic poetry, of heroic type or scale; ~ *dialect*, dialect in which Greek epic poems were written. ~ *n.* Epic poem; composition comparable to epic poem; subject worthy of epic treatment. **ĕp'ĭcal** *adj.* **ĕp'ĭcally** *adv.*

ĕp'ĭcarp *n.* (bot.) Outermost layer, skin, of fleshy fruit (ill. FRUIT).

ĕpĭcēd'ĭum *n.* Funeral ode.

ĕp'ĭcēne *adj.* 1. (L and Gk gram.) Denoting either sex without change of gender. 2. For, used by, both sexes; having characteristics of both sexes. ~ *n.* Epicene person.

ĕp'ĭcĕntre, ĕpĭcĕn'trum *ns.* Point on earth's surface directly above place where earthquake originates. **ĕpĭcĕn'tral** *adj.*

ĕpĭcŏt'ȳl *n.* (bot.) Seedling shoot above seed-leaves (ill. SEEDLING).

ĕp'ĭcūre *n.* One who is choice and dainty in eating and drinking. **ĕp'ĭcūrism** *n.* [f. EPICURUS].

Epĭcūrē'an (ĕ-) *adj.* & *n.* 1. (Follower) of Epicurus. 2. (Person) devoted to pleasures, esp. refined sensuous enjoyment. **Epĭcūrē'anism** *n.*

Epĭcūr'us (ĕ-) (*c* 300 B.C.). Athenian philosopher who held that pleasure (the practice of virtue) is the highest good.

ĕp'ĭcȳcle *n.* 1. (geom.) Small circle rolling on the circumference of a greater one. 2. (hist., in ancient astronomy) Circle having its centre on the circumference of a greater circle, used in the Ptolemaic system to represent the revolutions of the planets. **ĕpĭcȳc'lĭc** *adj.* Of, like, an epicycle (sense 1); ~ *gear*, gear having pinions in epicyclic arrangement, as in multi-speed gear-box of bicycle (ill. GEAR).

ĕpĭcȳc'loid *n.* Curve traced by point in circumference of a circle rolling round the circumference of another circle (ill. ROULETTE).

ĕpĭdeic'tĭc (-dīk-) *adj.* Meant for display.

ĕpĭdĕm'ĭc *adj.* & *n.* (Disease) spreading rapidly through a community for a period (cf. ENDEMIC). **ĕpĭdĕm'ĭcal** *adj.* **ĕpĭdĕm'ĭcally** *adv.*

ĕpĭdēmĭŏl'ogy *n.* Science of epidemics.

ĕpĭderm'ĭs *n.* 1. (physiol.) Outer non-vascular layer of skin of animals, cuticle (ill. SKIN); outer animal integument of shell. 2. (bot.) Outermost layer of cells in seeds and young stems (sometimes taken to include outermost layer of young root). **ĕpĭderm'al, ĕpĭderm'ĭc, ĕpĭderm'oid** *adjs.*

ĕpĭdĭ'ascōpe *n.* Apparatus for projecting a magnified image of both opaque and transparent objects on to a white screen.

ĕpĭgăs'trium *n.* Part of abdomen immediately over stomach. **ĕpĭgăs'trĭc** *adj.*

ĕpĭgē'al *adj.* (bot.) Carrying seed-leaves above ground in germination.

ĕpĭgĕn'ėsĭs *n.* Formation of organic germ as new product. **ĕpĭgėnĕt'ĭc** *adj.*

ĕpĭglŏtt'ĭs *n.* Erect cartilage at root of tongue, depressed in act of swallowing to cover glottis (ill. HEAD).

ĕp'ĭgōne *n.* One of a later (and less distinguished) generation. **ėpĭg'onal** *adj.*

ĕp'ĭgrăm *n.* Short poem ending in witty or ingenious turn of thought; pointed saying or mode of expression. **ĕpĭgrammăt'ĭc** *adj.* **ĕpĭgrammăt'ĭcally** *adv.* **ĕpĭgrămm'atist** *n.* **ĕpĭgrămm'atize** *v.*

ĕp'ĭgraph (-ahf) *n.* Inscription on stone, statue, coin, etc.; motto. **ĕpĭgrăph'ĭc** *adj.* **ėpĭg'raphy** *n.* Study of (ancient) epigraphs.

ĕp'ĭgȳny (-g-; *or* ĕpĭj'ĭnĭ) *n.* (bot.) Floral structure in which petals and sepals are borne above ovaries (ill. FLOWER). **ĕpĭgȳn'ous** *adj.*

ĕp'ĭlĕpsy *n.* Disorder of nervous system characterized by recurrent attacks of loss of consciousness with convulsive muscular movements and excessive salivation, causing foaming at the mouth. **ĕpĭlĕp'tĭc** *adj.* Of, subject to, epilepsy. ~ *n.* Epileptic person. **ĕpĭlĕp'tĭfōrm** *adj.* Resembling epilepsy.

ĕp'ĭlŏgue (-g) *n.* Concluding part, appendix, of literary work; speech, short poem, addressed by actor to spectators at end of play.

ėpĭph'any *n.* Christian festival commemorating the manifestation of Christ to the Gentiles in the persons of the Magi, observed on 6th Jan.; manifestation of a superhuman being.

ĕpĭphėnŏm'ėnon *n.* (pl. *-na*). Something appearing in addition, secondary symptom; esp., (psych.) consciousness regarded as by-product of material activities of brain and nerve-system.

ėpĭph'ȳsĭs *n.* (pl. *-es* pr. -ēz). 'Cap' at end of long bone (ill. BONE), before maturity separated from the shaft by a pad of cartilage which gradually ossifies, thus allowing for growth.

ĕp'ĭphȳte *n.* Plant growing on another (usu. deriving only support, not nutrition, from it); vegetable parasite on animal body. **ĕpĭphȳt'al, ĕpĭphȳt'ĭc** *adjs.*

ėpĭs'copacy *n.* Government of Church by bishops; the bishops collectively.

ėpĭs'copal *adj.* Of bishop(s); *E~ Church*, Church constituted on principle of episcopacy; esp. (U.S., Scotland, etc.) the Church of England. **ėpĭs'copally** *adv.*

ėpĭscopāl'ĭan *adj.* & *n.* (Adherent) of episcopacy; (member) of Episcopal Church. **ėpĭscopāl'ĭanĭsm** *n.*

ėpĭs'copate *n.* Office, see, tenure, of bishop; the bishops collectively.

ĕp'ĭsōde *n.* 1. Incidental narrative, digression, in poem, story, etc.; incidental happening or series of events in person's life, history of a country, etc. 2. In Gk tragedy, interlocutory (orig. interpolated) parts between two choric songs. **ĕpĭsŏd'ĭc** *adj.*

ĕpĭspăs'tĭc *adj.* & *n.* (med.) Blistering (plaster, substance).

ĕpĭstăx'ĭs *n.* (path.) Bleeding from the nose.

ĕpĭstēmŏl'ogy *n.* Theory of method or grounds of knowledge. **ĕpĭstēmolŏ'gĭcal** *adj.*

ėpĭ'stle (-sl) *n.* Letter; esp., letter from apostle, forming part of canon of Scripture; *the E~*, extract from one of these read in Communion service; literary work, usu. in verse, in form of letter.

ėpĭs'tolary *adj.* Of, carried by, suited to, letters.

ėpĭs'toler *n.* (eccles.) Reader of Epistle in church service.

ėpĭs'trophė *n.* (rhet.) Ending of several sentences or clauses with same word.

ĕp'ĭstȳle *n.* (archit.) Architrave.

ĕp'ĭtaph (-ahf) *n.* Inscription upon tomb; brief composition expressed as if for inscribing on tombstone.

ĕpĭthalām'ĭum *n.* (pl. *-iums*, *-ia*). Nuptial song or poem. **ĕpĭthalām'ĭal, ĕpĭthalăm'ĭc** *adjs.*

ĕpĭthēl'ĭum *n.* (pl. *-ia*). (biol.) Layer of cells which covers the body surface or lines a cavity that communicates with it.

ĕp'ĭthĕt *n.* Adjective expressing quality or attribute; significant appellation. **ĕpĭthĕt'ĭc(al)** *adjs.* **ĕpĭthĕt'ĭcally** *adv.*

ėpĭt'omė *n.* Summary, abstract, of book; condensed account; (fig.) thing representing another in miniature. **ėpĭt'omize** *v.t.*

E.P.N.S. *abbrev.* Electroplated nickel silver.

ĕp'ŏch (-k) *n.* Beginning of era in history, science, life, etc.; date; period in history or life marked by special events. **ĕp'ochal** *adj.*

ĕp'ōde *n.* Kind of lyric poem, invented by Archilochus and used by Horace, in which long line is followed by shorter one; part of lyric ode sung after strophe and antistrophe.

ĕp'onȳm *n.* One who gives his name to a people, place, institution, etc. **ėpŏn'ȳmous** *n.*

ĕp'opee *n.* Epic poem or poetry.

ĕp'ŏs *n.* Early narrative poetry celebrating incidents of heroic tradition; epic poem or poetry.

Ep'som (ĕ-). Town in Surrey, England, famous for the races, esp. the Derby and the Oaks, held on the neighbouring downs; *~ salt(s)*, bitter colourless crystalline salt, magnesium sulphate, used as a purgative, orig. prepared from Epsom mineral waters.

Ep'stein (ĕpshtīn), Jacob (1880–1959). Sculptor of Polish origin, born U.S., settled in London; works include symbolic and religious carvings and portrait bronzes.

E.P.T. *abbrev.* Excess profits tax.

ĕ̄q'uable *adj.* Uniform, even, not easily disturbed. **ĕ̄quabĭl'ĭty** *n.* **ĕ̄q'uably** *adv.*

ēq'ual *adj.* The same in number, size, value, degree, etc.; having strength, courage, ability, etc., adequate *to* (occasion etc.); uniform in operation, action, etc.; evenly balanced. ~ *n.* Person equal to another in rank etc.; (pl.) equal things. ~ *v.t.* Be equal to.

ėqualĭtār'ĭan (-kwŏl-) *adj.* & *n.* (Adherent) of doctrine of equality of mankind. **ėqualĭtār'ĭanĭsm** *n.*

ėqual'ĭty (-kwŏl-) *n.* Condition of being equal; equal footing; *E~ State*, popular name of Wyoming, so called because it was the pioneer in women's suffrage.

ēq'ualīze *v.* Make (thing etc.) equal (to, with); (football etc.) make score equal to opponents'. **ēqualīzā'tion** *n.*

ēq'ually *adv.* In an equal degree; in equal shares; uniformly.

ēquanĭm'ĭty *n.* Evenness of mind or temper; composure; resignation.

ėquāte' *v.t.* State equality of (thing *to*, *with*, another); treat as equivalent.

ėquā'tion *n.* 1. Making equal, balancing; equilibrium, equality. 2. (Amount or process of) compensation for inaccuracy; *personal ~*, time-lag or other error habitually made by individual in making observations, taking readings, etc., and capable of being allowed for when ascertained; *~ of equinoxes*, difference between mean and apparent places of equinoxes, due to their PRECESSION. 3. (math.) Formula affirming equivalence of two quantitative expressions, which are connected by the sign =. 4. (chem.) Expression representing chemical reaction quantitatively by means of symbols. **ėquā'tional** (-sho-) *adj.* **ėquā'tionally** *adv.*

ėquāt'or *n.* (astron.) Great circle of celestial sphere (ill. CELESTIAL) with plane perpendicular to earth's axis (so called because when sun is in equator, day and night are of equal length); (geog.) great circle of the earth equidistant from poles (ill. EARTH); similar circle on any spherical body; *magnetic ~*, irregular line round earth near equator on which the angle of magnetic dip is zero (i.e. magnetic needle lies level).

ĕquatōr'ial *adj.* Of, near, the equator; *~ telescope*, telescope mounted on two axes respectively parallel and perpendicular to earth's polar axis, so that regular rotation about first axis counters apparent motion of star and retains it in field of view. **ēquatŏr'ĭally** *adv.*

ĕq'uerry (*or* ĭkwĕ'rĭ) *n.* Officer of prince or noble charged with care of horses; officer of English royal household with duty of occasional attendance on sovereign. [Fr. *écurie* stable f. OHG *scur* shed; confused in English with L *equus* horse]

ėquĕs'trĭan *adj.* 1. Of, skilled in, horse-riding; mounted on horse; (of statue) representing person on horseback. 2. (Rom. antiq.) Of the order of *Equites* or knights; (hist.) of the 'knightly order' of the Holy Roman Empire. ~ *n.* Rider, performer, on horseback.

ėquĕstrĭĕnne' *n.* Horsewoman; (esp.) female circus rider.

equi- *prefix.* Equal.

ēquĭăng'ūlar (-ngg-) *adj.* Having equal angles.

ēquĭdĭs'tant *adj.* Separated by equal distance(s); parallel.

ēquĭlăt'eral *adj.* Having all the sides equal.

ēquĭlĭb'rate (*or* ĭkwĭl'-) *v.* Cause (two things) to balance; balance; counterpoise. **ēquĭlĭbrā'tion** *n.*

ėquĭl'ĭbrĭst *n.* Rope-walker, acrobat.

ēquĭlĭb'rĭum *n.* State of equal balance between opposing forces or powers; neutrality of judgement etc.

ēquĭmŭl'tĭple *n.* Number having common factor with another.

ēq'uīne *adj.* Of, like, a horse.

ēquĭnŏc'tial (-shl) *adj.* 1. Of equal day and night; happening at or near time of equinox, as ~ *gales*; ~ *line*, celestial EQUATOR. 2. At, near, the equator. ~ *n.* Equinoctial line; (pl.) equinoctial gales.

ēq'uĭnŏx *n.* Time when the sun crosses the equator and day and night are equal, occurring twice yearly, on 20th or 21st March (*vernal* ~) and 22nd or 23rd Sept. (*autumnal* ~); either of the two points at which the sun's path crosses the equator (ill. CELESTIAL).

ėquĭp' *v.t.* Furnish (ship, army, person, *with* requisites); provide (one*self* etc.) for journey etc.

ĕq'uĭpage *n.* Requisites for undertaking; outfit for journey etc.; carriage and horses with attendants. **ėquĭp'ment** *n.* Equipping, being equipped, manner in which person or thing is equipped; outfit, warlike apparatus, necessaries for expedition, voyage, etc.

ĕq'uĭpoise (-z) *n.* Equilibrium; counterpoise, balancing force or thing. ~ *v.t.* Counterbalance; place or hold in equipoise.

ēquĭpŏll'ent *adj.* Equal in power, force, etc.; practically equivalent. ~ *n.* Equivalent. **ēquĭpŏll'ence, -ency** *ns.*

ēquĭpŏn'derāte *v.t.* Counterbalance. **ēquĭpŏn'derant** *adj.*

ēquĭpotĕn'tial (-shl) *adj.* (Of points) in which potential of a force is the same; (of line etc.) in which potential is constant at all points; (of germ, embryo) having equal potentialities in all its parts.

Equisēt'um (ĕ-) *n.* Genus of plants (horsetails) with creeping rhizomes, hollow jointed stems, and inconspicuous leaves.

ĕq'uĭtable *adj.* Fair, just; (of claims etc.) valid in equity as dist. from law. **ĕq'uĭtably** *adv.* **ĕq'uĭtableness** *n.*

ĕquĭtā'tion *n.* Riding on horseback; horsemanship.

ĕq'uĭty *n.* 1. Fairness, impartiality. 2. Recourse to general principle of justice to correct or supplement provisions of law; (in England, U.S., etc.) system of law existing side by side with common and statute law, and superseding these when they conflict with it. 3. Equitable right, right recognizable by court of equity. 4. (chiefly U.S. colloq.) Amount or value of property etc. after all charges etc. are satisfied. 5. (pl.) Stocks and shares not bearing fixed interest. 6. *E*~, name of actors' union in Gt Britain.

ėquĭv'alent *adj.* 1. Equal in value; having equal or corresponding import or meaning; that is virtually the same thing, tantamount; corresponding. 2. (chem.) ~ *weight*, (also *combining weight* or *chemical equivalent*) that amount of an element, by weight, that will combine with or replace one unit weight of hydrogen; *gram*-~ (*weight*), this expressed in grams. ~*n.* Equivalent thing, amount, word, etc.; (chem.) see *adj.* above. **ėquĭv'alence, ėquĭv'alency** *ns.*

ėquĭv'ocal *adj.* Of double meaning, ambiguous; of uncertain nature; undecided; questionable, suspicious. **ėquĭv'ocally** *adv.* **ėquĭv'ocalness** *n.*

ėquĭv'ocāte *v.i.* Use ambiguous words to conceal truth, prevaricate. **ėquĭvocā'tion, ėquĭv'ocātor** *ns.*

ĕq'uĭvōque (-k), **-ōke** *n.* Pun; ambiguity.

E.R. *abbrev.* Elizabeth Regina (= Queen Elizabeth); East Riding (of Yorkshire).

ēr'a *n.* 1. System of chronology starting from some particular point of time (as the *Christian* ~ from the (supposed) date of the birth of Christ, the *Mohammedan* ~ from the year of Mohammed's flight from Mecca, etc.); initial point in such system; memorable or important date. 2. Historical period; period in individual's life, in some continuous process, etc.

E.R.A. *abbrev.* Engine-room artificer.

ėrădĭā'tion *n.* Emission of rays.

ėrăd'ĭcāte *v.t.* Tear up by roots; extirpate, get rid of. **ėrăd'ĭcable** *adj.* **ėrădĭcā'tion** *n.*

ėrāse (-z) *v.t.* Rub out; obliterate. **ėrās'er** *n.* That which erases, esp., preparation of rubber or similar substance for rubbing out writing etc. **ėrā'sure** (-zh*er*) *n.* Process of erasing; word etc. rubbed out.

Eras'mus (ĭrăz-), Desiderius (1466–1536). Dutch humanist; prepared the way for the Reformation by his version of the N.T. and his condemnation of Church abuses in 'Moriae Encomium' (The Praise of Folly).

Erăs'tĭan (ĭ-) *adj.* & *n.* (Adherent) of the doctrine that ecclesiastical power should be subordinated to secular, supposed to have been held by Erastus (Thomas Liebler, 1524–83), a Heidelberg physician who opposed the use of excommunication. **Erăs'tianism** *n.*

ẽrb'ĭa *n.* Erbium oxide, a rose-coloured mineral. **ẽrb'ĭum** *n.* (chem.) Metallic element of rare-earth group, occurring in gadolinite etc.; symbol Er, at. no. 68, at. wt 167·26. [f. *Ytterby* in Sweden, where found]

ere (ār) *prep.* & *conj.* (poet., archaic). Before (in time).

E'rėbus (ĕ-). (Gk myth.) Place of darkness between Earth and Hades.

ėrĕct' *adj.* Upright, not stooping; vertical; (of hair etc.) set up, bristling. **ėrĕct'ly** *adv.* **ėrĕct'nėss** *n.* **ėrĕct'** *v.t.* Raise, set upright; build; constitute or form *into*, invest with rank or character of.

ėrĕc'tīle *adj.* Capable of being erected; ~ *tissue*, tissue in various parts of animals capable of being distended and becoming rigid under excitement.

ėrĕc'tion *n.* Erecting; building, structure.

ėrĕc'tor *n.* Person, thing, that erects; muscle causing erection.

ĕ'rėmīte *n.* Recluse, hermit; esp., Christian solitary of 3rd c. onwards (as dist. from coenobites, who lived in community). **ĕrėmĭt'ĭc(al)** *adjs.*

ĕ'rėthĭsm *n.* (psychol.) Morbid excitability, usu. of sexual manifestation.

ẽrg, ẽrg'on *ns.* (physics) Amount of work done when a force of 1 dyne moves its point of application 1 centimetre in the direction of the force.

ẽrg'ō *adv.* (usu. joc.) Therefore.

ẽrg'ograph (-ahf) *n.* Instrument for measuring and recording work done by muscles.

ẽrgonŏm'ĭcs *n.* Scientific study of the efficiency of workers in their working environment.

ẽrgŏs'terol *n.* A sterol which when exposed to ultra-violet radiation gives a mixture of compounds including vitamin D (the anti-rachitic vitamin); found in yeasts and fungi and present in small quantities in the fats of plants and animals.

ẽrg'ot *n.* 1. Diseased condition of seed of rye and other grasses; the dark-violet hardened mycelium of the fungus (*Claviceps purpurea*) causing this; the dried mycelium, used medically to control haemorrhage or contract uterus. 2. Horny protuberance on inner side of horse's fetlock (ill. HORSE). **ẽrg'otism** *n.* Disease of grasses consisting in formation of ergot; diseased condition of man or animals caused by eating grain or grasses infected with ergot and characterized by muscular cramp and gangrene.

Erie (ẽr'ĭ). Member of an Iroquoian tribe of Red Indians formerly dwelling near *Lake* ~, one of the five great lakes of N. America.

Erin (ĕ'rĭn *or* ẽr-). The ancient name of Ireland, now only poetical.

ėrĭs'tĭc *adj.* Of controversy or disputation. ~ *n.* Controversialist; art of disputation.

Eritrē'a (ĕ-). Former Italian colony on the Red Sea; now mainly self-governing but federated to Ethiopia; capital, Asmara.

ẽrl'-kĭng' *n.* In Danish legend, king of the elves.

ẽrm'ĭne *n.* 1. Animal of weasel tribe, *Putorius erminea*, inhabiting northern countries, with fur reddish-brown above and white beneath in summer and (in northern regions) white in winter, except for black tip of tail; stoat. 2. The fur of this, freq. with the black tails arranged on it, used in official robes of judges, state robes of peers, etc.; (her.) heraldic fur, white marked with black spots (ill. HERALDRY).

ẽrn(e) *n.* Sea eagle (chiefly poet. and in names of pleasure boats).

ėrōde' *v.t.* (of acids, water currents, etc.) Gnaw away, destroy surface of. **ėrō'sion** (-zhn) *n.* Eroding; (geol.) wearing away of earth's surface by wind, water, or ice (cf. ABRASION). **ėrō'sĭve** *adj.*

Eros (ẽr'ŏs, ĕ-). 1. (Gk myth.) The god of love, represented as a youth or young boy, freq. with bow and arrows; in Rom. myth. = CUPID. 2. Asteroid, discovered in 1898, coming at times nearer the earth than any heavenly body except moon.

ėrŏt'ĭc *adj.* Of love, amatory. **ėrŏt'ĭca** *n.pl.* Erotic writings, pictures, etc. **ĕ'rotĭsm** *n.* Sexual excitement.

ėrōtomăn'ĭa *n.* Excessive or morbid erotic desire; preoccupation with sexual passion. **ėrōtomăn'ĭăc** *adj.* & *n.*

ẽrr *v.i.* Make mistakes; be incorrect; sin.

ĕ'rrand *n.* Short journey on which person is sent to carry message etc.; business on which one is sent, object of journey, purpose.

ĕ'rrant *adj.* Roaming in quest of adventure (esp. in *knight* ~); itinerant; wandering; erring in opinion, conduct, etc. **ĕ'rrancy** *n.* **ĕ'rrantry** *n.* Conduct, notions, condition, of a knight-errant.

ĕrrăt'ĭc *adj.* Wandering; (of diseases, pains, etc.) moving from one part to another; irregular or uncertain in movement, having no fixed course, eccentric in conduct, habit, or opinion; ~ *blocks*, (geol.) large pieces of rock carried from a distant source by glaciers. **ĕrrăt'ĭcally** *adv.*

ĕrrā'tum *n.* (pl. *-ta*). Error in printing or writing, esp. (pl.) list of errors attached to book.

ĕrrō'n'ėous *adj.* Mistaken, incorrect. **ĕrrō'n'ėously** *adv.* **ĕrrō'n'ėousnėss** *n.*

ĕ'rror *n.* Mistake; condition of erring in opinion, wrong opinion; transgression; (law) mistake in law appearing on proceedings of court of record; (math. etc.) quantity of deviation from correct or accurate result, determination, etc.

ersatz' (ārz-) *n.* Substitute or imitation; also attrib. [Ger. wd]

Erse (ẽrs) *adj.* & *n.* Irish Gaelic, formerly applied also to the Gaelic of Scotland. [var. of *Irish*]

ẽrst *adv.* (archaic) Formerly, of old. **ẽrst'while** *adv.* Erst. ~ *adj.* former.

ērŭctā'tion *n.* Belching; eruptive action of volcano.

ĕ'rudīte (-rōō-) *adj.* Learned. **ĕ'rudītely** (-tl-) *adv.* **ĕrudĭ'tion** *n.*

ėrŭpt' *v.* Break out or through; (of volcano) emit rocks, lava, ash, or gases, (of geyser) spurt water; (of teeth) break through gums; (of rash) appear on skin.

ėrŭp'tion *n.* Erupting; outbreak of volcano, ejection of hot water from geyser, etc.; breaking out of rash etc.; also (fig.) of war, passion, mirth, etc.

ėrŭp'tĭve *adj.* Bursting forth; tending to burst forth; of, formed by, forced up by, volcanic eruption. **ėrŭp'tĭvely** (-vl-) *adv.* **ėrŭp'tĭvenėss** *n.*

ĕrўsĭp'ėlas *n.* Acute inflammation of lymphatic vessels of the skin, caused by streptococcal infection.

ĕrўthēm'a *n.* Superficial inflammation of skin appearing as rose-coloured patches.

ĕrўth'rocўte *n.* Red blood-cell (ill. BLOOD).

Es'au (ē-). Elder son of Isaac and Rebecca; sold his birthright to his brother Jacob for a mess of pottage (Gen. xxv).

ĕscalāde' *n.* Scaling of walls with ladders. ~ *v.* Scale (wall etc.) thus.

ĕs'calātor *n.* (orig. U.S.) Moving staircase (with stairs moving up or down on endless chain).

ĕscăll'op *n.* (her.) Scallop-shell (ill. HERALDRY).

ĕscal(l)ŏpe' *n.* (cookery) Fish, meat, etc., served in scallop shells; ~ *de veau* (vō), thin round steak of veal called 'collop'.

ĕscapāde' *n.* Breaking loose from restraint; flighty piece of conduct.

ėscāpe' *v.* 1. Gain liberty by flight, get free from detention, control, oppression, etc.; (of fluids etc.) issue, find a way out; (of words etc.) issue unawares from (person, his lips). 2. Get off safely, go unhurt or unpunished; get clear away from (person, his grasp, etc.); avoid; elude notice or recollection of. ~ *n.* Act of escaping; fact of having escaped; leakage (of gas etc.); outlet; FIRE-escape; ~ *clause*, clause in a treaty absolving a contracting party from a particular obligation in specified circumstances.

ėscāpee' *n.* One who has escaped.

ėscāpe'ment (-pm-) *n.* Outlet; mechanism in watch or clock or other timing device, intervening between motive power and regulator, and alternately checking and releasing the train, causing intermittent impulse to be given to regulator (ill. CLOCK).

ėscāp'ĭsm *n.* Tendency to escape from realities of life into fantasy. **ėscāp'ĭst** *n.*

ėscârp', ėscârp'ment *ns.* Steep bank immediately in front of and below rampart; similar natural formation. **ėscârp'** *v.t.* Cut into form of escarp.

ĕschatŏl'ogy (ĕsk-) *n.* Doctrine of death, judgement, heaven, and hell. **ĕschatolŏ'gĭcal** *adj.*

ėscheat' *n.* (law) Reversion of fief to feudal lord when tenant died without leaving successor qualified to inherit; lapsing of land to crown (or State) or lord of manor on owner's dying intestate without heirs; property so lapsing or reverting. ~ *v.* Confiscate; hand over (property) as an escheat; revert by escheat.

ėschew' (ĭs-chōō') *v.t.* Avoid, abstain from.

eschscholtzia (ĭskŏl'sh*a* *or* ĕshŏl'tsĭa) *n.* Californian genus of herbaceous plants of the poppy family, the best-known species being *E. californica*, Californian poppy, which has finely divided glaucous leaves and large bright-yellow flowers with saffron-coloured centre. [J. F. von *Eschscholtz* (1793–1831), Ger. botanist]

ĕs'cŏrt *n.* Body of armed men acting as guard to persons, baggage, etc.; person(s) accompanying another on journey for protection or guidance, or for courtesy's sake; ship(s), aeroplane(s), etc., so employed. **ėscŏrt'** *v.t.* Act as escort to.

ēscrībe' *v.t.* (math.) Describe (circle) so as to touch one side of triangle exteriorly and the other two sides produced (ill. CIRCLE).

ĕscrĭtoire' (-twâr) *n.* Writing-desk with drawers etc. for stationery.

ĕscu'dō (-ōōd-) *n.* (pl. *-s*). Principal monetary unit of Portugal, = 100 centavos.

ĕs'cūlent *adj.* & *n.* (Thing, esp. vegetable) suitable for food.

ėscŭtch'eon (-chon) *n.* 1. Shield with armorial bearings (ill. HERALDRY). 2. Middle of ship's stern where name is placed. 3. Pivoted keyhole-cover (ill. DOOR).

Es'dras (ĕz-). Reputed author of two of the books of the Apocrypha; the first is mainly a compilation from Chronicles, Nehemiah, and Ezra, and the second is a record of angelic revelations.

E.S.E. *abbrev.* East-south-east.

ĕs'kar, -er *n.* (geol.) Long narrow ridge of gravel formed in a tunnel-like channel within a glacier.

Eskimo, Esquimau (ĕs'kĭmō) *n.* & *adj.* (pl. *-moes, -maux*, pr. -mōz). (One) of a N. Amer. race inhabiting Arctic coasts from Greenland to Alaska; the language of these people; ~ *dog*, breed of powerful dog with long usu. greyish hair, used by the Eskimos to draw sledges and for hunting.

Esop: see AESOP.

ĕsotĕ'rĭc *adj.* (Of philosophical doctrine etc.) meant only for the initiated; (of disciples) initiated; private, confidential. **ĕsotĕ'rĭcally** *adv.*

ėspăl'ier *n.* Framework on which fruit-trees or ornamental shrubs are trained; tree so trained (ill. FRUIT).

ėspar̂t'ō *n.* ~ (*grass*), kind of grass, *Stipa tenocissima*, of Spain and N. Africa, used as an ingredient of thick or absorbent paper.

ėspĕ'cial (-shl) *adj.* Pre-eminent, exceptional; particular; belonging chiefly to one case. **ėspĕ'cially** *adv.*

Esperăn'tō (ĕ-) *n.* & *adj.* (Of) an artificial language invented (*c* 1887) for universal use by a Polish physician, Dr Ludovik Lazarus Zamenhof; its vocabulary consists of roots common to the chief European languages, with endings normalized. **Esperăn'tĭst** *n.* [pen-name (= 'hoping-one') of its inventor, f. L *spero* hope]

ėspī'al *n.* Acting as a spy; watching; espying.

ĕspĭonage' (-ahzh; *or* ĕs'pĭonĭj) *n.* Practice of spying or using spies.

ĕsplanāde' *n.* Level piece of ground, esp. one used for public promenade; level space separating citadel of fortress from town.

ėspouse' (-z) *v.t.* 1. (Usu. of man) marry; give (woman) in marriage (*to*). 2. Adopt, support (cause, opinion, etc.). **ėspous'al** (-zl) *n.*

ėsprĕss'ō *n.* Apparatus for making coffee under pressure; coffee-bar equipped with this.

ĕs'prit (-rē) *n.* Sprightliness, wit; ~ *de corps* (kōr̂), regard for the honour and interests of body one belongs to; ~ *fort* (fōr̂), strong-minded person; free-thinker. [Fr.]

ėspȳ' *v.t.* Catch sight of; descry, discern; detect.

Esq. *abbrev.* Esquire.

Esquimau: see ESKIMO.

ėsquīre' *n.* 1. (hist., archaic) Young man of gentle birth attending on knight; squire. 2. Man belonging to higher order of English gentry, ranking immediately below knight, now generally appended (abbrev. *Esq.*) to man's name in addressing letters etc. [L *scutarius* shield-bearer]

ĕss *n.* Name of the letter s; S-shaped thing; *collar of esses*, formerly badge of House of Lancaster, still part of some officials' costume.

ĕss'ay *n.* 1. Attempt (*at*). 2. Literary composition of moderate length (usu. in prose) on any subject. **ĕssay'** *v.* Try, test (person, thing); attempt. **ĕss'ayist** *n.* Writer of essays.

ĕss'ė *n.* 1. *In* ~, in actual existence (as opp. to *in posse*, in potentiality). 2. Essential being or nature. [L *esse* to be]

ĕss'ence *n.* 1. An existence, entity (now usu. spiritual or immaterial). 2. Absolute being, reality underlying phenomena; that by which anything subsists, foundation of being. 3. All that makes a thing what it is; totality of properties etc. without which it would cease to be the same thing; objective character, intrinsic nature as a thing in itself; (loosely) most important indispensable quality or constituent element of anything. 4. Extract obtained by distillation etc. from plant, medicinal, odoriferous, or nutritious substance, etc.; alcoholic solution containing volatile elements to which perfume, flavour, etc., are due; perfume, scent.

Ess'ēne (ĕ-) *n.* Member of an ancient Jewish sect who held property and took meals in common, conformed to rigid rules of purification, and were reputed to heal the sick and work miracles.

ėssĕn'tial (-shl) *adj.* 1. Of, constituting, a thing's essence; that is such in essence; indispensable, necessarily implied; absolutely necessary. 2. That is or is like, an essence or extract; ~ *oil*, volatile oil obtained by distillation and marked by characteristic odour etc. of substance from which it is extracted. ~ *n.* Indispensable element. **ėssĕntiăl'ity** (-shĭăl-) *n.* **ėssĕn'tially** *adv.*

Ess'ėx (ĕ-). County of E. England.

ėstăb'lĭsh *v.t.* Set up on permanent basis; settle; secure permanent acceptance for; place beyond dispute; place (church) in position of national or State Church.

ėstăb'lĭshment *n.* Establishing; Church system established by law, established Church; organized body of men maintained for a purpose, as army, navy, civil service; staff of servants, etc.; public institution, house of business; household; ~ *officer*, in civil service etc., one responsible for staffing. **ėstăblĭshmentār̂'ian** *adj.* & *n.* (Person) adhering to, advocating principle of, an established Church.

estăm'inet (-ēnā) *n.* Unpretentious French café or cottage selling wine, beer, etc.

ėstāte' *n.* 1. (chiefly archaic) State, condition; worldly standing, fortune, etc.; status, degree of rank; *man's, woman's*, ~, manhood, womanhood. 2. Order, class, as part of body politic and as sharing directly or indirectly in government; (*three*) *estates of the realm*, (in England) the lords spiritual, lords temporal, and commons; (erron.) crown, House of Lords, and House of Commons; *third* ~, the English commons; (transl. Fr. *tiers état*), French bourgeoisie before the Revolution; *fourth* ~, (joc.) the press. 4. (law) Person's interest in lands, tenements, etc.; *real* ~, interest in landed property. 5. A landed property (usu. of considerable extent); HOUSING estate; ~ *agent*, steward or manager of landed estate; one whose business is the sale or letting of houses and land; ~ *car*, light saloon motor-car constructed or adapted to carry both passengers and goods (ill. MOTOR). 6. Person's collective assets and liabilities.

ėsteem' *v.t.* Think highly of; consider. ~ *n.* Favourable opinion, regard, respect.

ĕs'ter *n.* Any of a class of organic compounds formed by the interaction of an acid and an alcohol with the elimination of water; esters are volatile liquids or low-melting-point solids and are used as solvents, flavouring essences, and perfumes, and in many chemical processes.

Esther (ĕs'ter). The O.T. book of Esther; its heroine, a Jewess who was chosen on account of her beauty by King Ahasueras to be queen in place of Vashti.

ĕs'tĭmable *adj.* Worthy of esteem.

ĕs'tĭmate *n.* Approximate judgement (of number, amount, etc.); quantity assigned by this; contractor's statement of sum for which he will undertake specified work; judgement of character or qualities; *the Estimates*, accounts presented annually to Parliament showing probable amount of administrative departments' expenditure for current year. **ĕs'tĭmāte** *v.t.* Form estimate of; fix by estimate *at* (so much); form an opinion of. **ĕs'tĭmātor** *n.* **ĕs'tĭmative** *adj.*

ĕstĭmā'tion *n.* Judgement of worth; opinion, judgement; esteem.

estival etc.: see AESTIVAL etc.

ėstoile' *n.* (her.) Charge in form of star with wavy points or rays (ill. HERALDRY).

Est(h)ōn'ia (ĕ-). Country on S. coast of Gulf of Finland, formerly part of the Russian Empire; proclaimed an independent republic 1918; incorporated in the Soviet Union 1940 as a constituent republic; capital, Tallinn. **Est(h)ōn'ian** *adj.* & *n.* (Native, language) of Estonia.

ėstŏp' *v.t.* (law) Stop, bar, hinder; (refl. & pass.) be precluded by one's own previous act or declaration *from* doing, etc. **ėstŏp'pel** *n.* Impediment to action etc. arising from person's own act or declaration.

ėstrade′ (-ahd) *n.* Raised platform, dais.

ėstrānge′ (-j) *v.t.* Alienate (person) in feeling (*from* another). **ėstrānge′ment** (-jm-) *n.*

ėstreat′ *v.t.* Take out record of (fine, bail, etc.) and return it to Court of Exchequer to be prosecuted.

ĕs′tūary *n.* Tidal mouth of large river. **ĕs′tūarĭne** *adj.*

e.s.u. *abbrev.* Electrostatic unit.

ėsūr′ĭent *adj.* (joc.) Hungry; impecunious and greedy. **ėsūr′ience, ėsūr′iency** *ns.*

ēt′a *n.* Name of Greek letter, Η, η, = ē. **et′acism** (ā-) *n.* Pronunciation of Greek ē as English ā.

et al. *abbrev. Et alia* ('and other things'). [L]

ĕt cĕt′era, ėtcĕt′era (abbrev. *etc.*, *&c.*). And the rest, and so on. **ėtcĕt′eras** *n.pl.* Extras, sundries.

ĕtch *v.* Portray by drawing with an *etching-needle* on a metal plate previously coated with a wax-and-resin mixture (the *ground*) and immersing in acid which corrodes the parts laid bare by the needle; make (print) from plate thus prepared; copy (picture) by this process; practise this craft; (of acid) make corrosive markings. **ĕtch′er** *n.* **ĕtch′ing** *n.* Print made from an etched plate; art, process, of etching; *dry-point* (~): see DRY *adj.*; *soft-ground* ~, (print made by) similar process in which the plate is coated with a soft sticky wax mixture and the drawing done with a pencil on thin paper laid over it so that the wax adheres along the lines and comes away when the paper is removed.

ėtērn′al *adj.* Without beginning or end, that always (has existed and always) will exist; (colloq.) incessant, too frequent; *E~ City*, Rome; ~ *triangle*, (emotional relationships in) group of 2 women and a man or 2 men and a woman. **ėtērn′(al)ize** *vbs.t.* **ėtērn′ally** *adv.* **ėtērn′ity** *n.* Being eternal; infinite (esp. future) time; the future life; tediously long time.

Etesian winds (ĭtēzh′an). Strong dry northerly winds blowing in the Mediterranean region in summer.

ĕth′āne *n.* A colourless odourless gas (C_2H_6 of the paraffin series of hydrocarbons) occurring in gas from petroleum deposits.

Eth′elrĕd (ĕ-) the Unready (= 'without counsel') (*c* 968–1016). King of the English 979–1016; son of Edgar and father of Edward the Confessor.

ēth′er *n.* 1. Clear sky, upper regions of space beyond clouds; (hist.) element conceived as filling all space beyond sphere of moon. 2. Substance of great elasticity and subtlety which has been postulated by the wave-theory of light as permeating the whole of space and filling the interstices between particles of air and other matter. 3. (chem.) Colourless volatile liquid ($C_2H_5.O.C_2H_5$), with a characteristic aromatic odour, obtained by distillation of alcohol with sulphuric acid and used as a solvent for the extraction of oils, fats, waxes, etc., and as an anaesthetic; any of a large class of compounds of similar composition. **ēthĕ′rĭc** *adj.*

ėthēr′ėal, -ĭal *adj.* 1. Light, airy; heavenly; of unearthly delicacy of substance, character, or appearance. 2. Of, like, ether. **ėthērėăl′ity** *n.* **ėthēr′ėalize** *v.t.* **ėthēr′ėally** *adv.*

ĕth′ĭc(al) *adjs.* 1. (usu. *-al*) Relating to, treating of, morals or ethics; (esp. U.S.) moral, honourable. 2. *Ethic dative*, dative implying that person other than subject or object has indirect interest in fact stated. **ĕth′ĭcally** *adv.* **ĕth′ĭcs** *n.pl.* Science of morals, study of principles of human duty; treatise on this; moral principles; rules of conduct.

Ethĭōp′ĭa (ē-). In ancient usage, a region on the upper Nile; in modern usage, the official name of *Abyssinia*, an inland kingdom of NE. Africa south-west of Red Sea and Gulf of Aden; converted to Christianity by Syrian missionaries in 4th c., but later cut off from European influences by Mohammedan dominion in N. Africa; rediscovered by Portuguese in 16th c. King Menelik II halted Italian inroads in the battle of Adowa, 1896, and concluded a treaty at his new capital, Addis Ababa; the Italians invaded the country in 1935 and annexed it, but were driven out by British and Imperial troops in 1941 and the emperor Hailé Selassié I was reinstated. **Ethĭōp′ĭan** *adj.* Of, pertaining to, Ethiopia or Abyssinia. ~ *n.* An inhabitant of (ancient or modern) Ethiopia; (hist.) African, blackamoor.

Ethĭŏp′ĭc (ē-) *adj.* & *n.* (Of) an ancient Semitic language (Ge'ez) introduced into Ethiopia by invaders from Arabia and surviving in the liturgical language of the Christian Church of Ethiopia.

ĕth′nĭc, ĕth′nĭcal *adjs.* 1. Pertaining to race; ethnological. 2. Gentile, heathen, pagan. **ĕth′nĭcally** *adv.*

ĕthnŏg′raphy *n.* Scientific description of races of men. **ĕthnŏg′rapher** *n.* **ĕthnogrăph′ĭc(al)** *adjs.* **ĕthnogrăph′ĭcally** *adv.*

ĕthnŏl′ogy *n.* Science of races and peoples, their relations to one another, distinctive physical and other characteristics, etc. **ĕthnolŏ′gĭcal** *adj.* **ĕthnolŏ′gĭcally** *adv.* **ĕthnŏl′ogĭst** *n.*

ēth′ŏs *n.* Characteristic spirit of community, people, or system.

ĕth′ȳl (*or* ēth′ĭl) *n.* 1. (chem.) The alkyl radical having two carbon atoms, C_2H_5. 2. (usu. ~ *fluid*) Lead tetra-ethyl, $Pb(C_2H_5)_4$, one of the substances added to motor fuels to increase their 'anti-knock' rating. 3. ~ *alcohol*, ordinary alcohol or *ethanol*, C_2H_5OH, an inflammable volatile liquid produced by the fermentation of sugars by yeast, used as a fuel, as a solvent, and in the chemical industry; ~ *chloride*, a volatile liquid (C_2H_5Cl), with ethereal odour, used in medicine as anaesthetic.

ĕth′ȳlene *n.* First member of olefine series of hydrocarbons, C_2H_4, an inflammable gas with a faint sweet smell; ~ *glycol*, colourless slightly viscous liquid obtained by treating ethylene with a solution of potassium permanganate, used as anti-freeze in motor engines, for de-icing aircraft, etc.

ēt′ĭolāte *v.t.* Render (plant etc.) pale and colourless by excluding light, blanch; give pale and sickly hue to. **ētĭolā′tion** *n.*

etiology: see AETIOLOGY.

ĕt′ĭquette (-kĕt) *n.* Conventional rules of personal behaviour in polite society; ceremonial of court; unwritten code restricting professional men in what concerns interests of their brethren or dignity of their profession.

Et′na[1] (ĕ-). An active volcano in Sicily.

ĕt′na[2] *n.* Vessel, in form of inverted cone in saucer, for heating small quantity of liquid by burning spirit. [f. ETNA[1]]

Et′on (Cŏll′ege) (ē-). English public school near Windsor, founded 1440 by Henry VI to prepare scholars for King's College, Cambridge; ~ *blue*, a light blue; ~ *collar*, broad stiff white collar worn outside jacket; ~ *crop*, cutting of woman's hair short like boy's; ~ *jacket*, short black jacket (worn by younger boys at Eton) reaching only to waist and worn open in front; ~ *suit*, suit of Eton jacket with black or striped trousers and black waistcoat. **Etōn′ian** *adj.* & *n.* Of Eton; one educated there.

Etrŭs′can (ĭ-) *adj.* & *n.* (Member) of a people of uncertain origin who came to Italy 9th c. B.C., established themselves in what is now Tuscany, and there developed a system of powerful city states and a flourishing civilization.

et seq., et seqq., et sq., et sqq. *abbrevs. Et sequentia* (= 'and what follows'). [L]

E.T.U. *abbrev.* Electrical Trades Union.

étūde′ (ā-) *n.* Short musical composition or exercise.

étui′ (ĕtwē) *n.* Small case for needles, bodkins, etc.

ĕtymŏl′ogize *v.* Give, trace, etymology of; suggest etymology for; study etymology.

ĕtȳmŏl′ogy *n.* Account of, facts relating to, formation and meaning of words; branch of linguistic science concerned with this; part of grammar treating of individual words and their formation and inflexions. **ĕtȳmolŏ′gĭcal** *adj.* **ĕtȳmolŏ′gĭcally** *adv.* **ĕtȳmŏl′ogĭst** *n.*

ĕt'ўmŏn *n.* Primary word which gives rise to derivative.

eu- *prefix.* Well.

eucalўp'tus *n.* Genus of plants including gum-tree of Australia and the neighbouring islands; plant of this genus; (pop.) = ~ *oil*, an essential oil obtained from the leaves of a species of eucalyptus with strong characteristic odour, used as an antiseptic and disinfectant. [Gk *eu kaluptos* well covered, the flower before it opens being protected by a cap]

Eu'charist (-k-) *n.* The Christian sacrament of the Lord's Supper, in which bread and wine are partaken of; the consecrated elements, esp. bread. **Eucharis'tĭ-c(al)** *adjs.*; *Eucharistic Congress*, an international meeting of Roman Catholics, instituted 1908 and held annually in honour of the Blessed Sacrament. [Gk *eukharistia* thanksgiving (*kharizomai* offer willingly)]

eu'chre (-*ker*) *n.* American card-game for 2, 3, or 4 persons, played with pack of 32 cards (the 2, 3, 4, 5, 6, of each suit being rejected), in which, if a player fails to take three tricks, he or his side is said to be 'euchred', and the other side gains two points; the highest cards are the knave of trumps and the other knave of the same colour. ~ *v.t.* Gain advantage over (opponent) by his failure to take three tricks; (fig.) outwit, 'do'.

Euc'lĭd. Eukleides (*c* 300 B.C.), a mathematician of Alexandria, author of a treatise on geometry (the *Elements*); hence, geometry, esp. as school subject; the geometry of ordinary experience, accepting Euclid's axioms as indisputable. **Euclĭd'ėan** *adj.* Of, according to principles of, Euclid; ~ *space*, kind of space for which the axioms of Euclid are valid (in which, e.g. a straight line may be produced to infinity); cf. RELATIVITY.

eudaem'onism, eudē-, *n.* System of ethics basing moral obligation on tendency of actions to produce happiness.

eudiŏm'ėter *n.* Graduated glass tube in which a mixture of an inflammable gas with air or oxygen may be exploded by means of a spark and the volume change measured.

Eugēne', Prince (1663–1736). Austrian general; associated with Marlborough in the War of the Spanish Succession.

eugĕn'ĭc *adj.* Of, adapted to, production of fine (esp. human) offspring. **eugĕn'ĭcs** *n.* Study having this for its object. **eu'gėnĭst** *n.*

eul'ogīze *v.t.* Extol, praise. **eul'ogĭst** *n.* **eulogĭs'tĭc** *adj.* **eulogĭs'tĭcally** *adv.*

eul'ogy *n.* Speech, writing, in commendation or praise.

eun'uch (-*uk*) *n.* Castrated male person, esp. one employed in harem or (in Oriental courts and under Roman Empire) in affairs of State. **eun'uchĭsm** *n.*

euŏn'ўmus *n.* Genus of shrub of which many species are cultivated as ornamental plants. [Gk *euōnumos* well-named, lucky (*onoma* name)]

eu'păd *n.* A dry mixture of calcium hypochlorite and boric acid used as a dry dressing for wounds or mixed with water to form EUSOL. [f. *E*dinburgh *U*niversity *Pa*thological *D*epartment, where first prepared]

eupĕp'tĭc *adj.* Of, having, resulting from, good digestion.

euph'ėmĭsm *n.* Substitution of mild or vague expression for harsher or more offensive one; expression thus substituted. **euphėmĭs'tĭc** *adj.* **euphėmĭs'tĭcally** *adv.* **euph'ėmīze** *v.*

euphŏn'ĭum *n.* Large brass wind instrument, the tenor of the tuba family, used esp. in military bands.

euph'ony *n.* Pleasing sound; quality of having this. **euphŏn'ĭc, euphōn'ĭous** *adjs.* **euphŏn'ĭcally, euphōn'ĭously** *advs.*

euphôr'ĭa *n.* Sense of well-being. **euphŏr'ĭc** *adj.*

euph'rasy *n.* The plant eye-bright (various species of *Euphrasia*).

Euphrāt'ēs (-z). River of SW. Asia, flowing through E. Turkey and Iraq to join the Tigris and thence to the Persian Gulf.

Euphrŏs'ўnē (-z-). One of the GRACES.

euph'ūĭsm *n.* Diction and style like that of John LYLY, characterized by alliterative antithetic clauses, long strings of similes, and a constant endeavour after refinement of expression; loosely, affectedly periphrastic or high-flown style or language. **euph'ūĭst** *n.* **euphūĭs'tĭc(al)** *adjs.* [f. *Euphuēs* (Gk, = 'well-endowed'), chief character in two of Lyly's works]

Eurasian (ūrāsh'*an*) *n.* & *adj.* (Person) of mixed European and Asiatic parentage; of Europe and Asia.

eurēk'a (ūr-) *int.* & *n.* (The exulting exclamation) 'I have found it!'. [Gk *heurēka* (*heuriskein* find) uttered by Archimedes when he discovered means of determining (by specific gravity) the proportion of base metal in Hiero's golden crown]

eurhyth'mĭc (ūrĭth'-) *adj.* 1. In or of harmonious proportion (esp. in architecture). 2. Of eurhythmics. **eurhyth'mĭcs** *n.pl.* System (founded by Émile Jaques-Dalcroze) of expressing musical rhythm in bodily movement.

Eurĭp'ĭdēs (ūr-; -z) (480–406 B.C.). Greek tragedian; author of 'Alcestis', 'Medea', 'The Trojan Women', etc.

Eurōp'a (ūr-). (Gk myth.) Daughter of Agenor, king of Phoenicia; was wooed by Zeus, who took the form of a beautiful bull.

Europe (ūr'op). One of the five continents of the world. **Europē'an** *adj.* & *n.* (Native) of Europe. **Europē'anīze** *v.* **Europē'anĭsm** *n.*

eurōp'ĭum (ūr-) *n.* A rare-earth element; symbol Eu, at. no. 63, at. wt 151·96. [f. EUROPE]

Eurovĭ'sion (ūr-; -zhn) *n.* Television of European range.

Eur'us (ūr-). (Gk and Rom. myth.) God of E. or SE. wind; hence, this wind.

Eurўd'ĭcē (ūr-). (Gk myth.) A nymph beloved by Orpheus; he went down to Hades to recover her and by his music induced Persephone to let her go, but on condition that he should not look back at her as she followed him; he forgot the condition, looked back, and Eurydice vanished for ever.

Eusēb'ĭus (*c* 275–340 A.D.). Bishop of Caesarea in Palestine; a celebrated historian and theologian; his 'History of the Christian Church' earned him the title of 'father of church history'. **Eusēb'ĭan** *adj.*

ĕus'ŏl *n.* An antiseptic solution prepared from calcium hypochlorite and boric acid used as a lotion for wounds. [initials of *E*dinburgh *U*niversity + *sol*(ution); cf. EUPAD]

Eustăch'ĭus (-k-), Bartolommeo (d. 1574). Italian anatomist. **Eustăch'ĭan** *adj.*; ~ *tube*, pharyngo-tympanic tube, passage communicating between the middle ear (tympanic cavity) and the back of the throat (larynx), and serving to equalize air-pressure on both sides of the ear-drum (ill. EAR).

ĕutĕc'tĭc *adj.*; ~ *alloy*, alloy having a lower melting temperature than the other alloys that can be made from the same constituents.

Eutêrp'ė. (Gk myth.) One of the Muses, goddess of music.

euthanās'ĭa (-z-) *n.* Gentle and easy death; bringing about of this, esp. in case of incurable and painful disease.

Euthêr'ĭa *n.pl.* Largest subclass of mammals, comprising those whose young are nourished through an efficient placenta and are born at a relatively late stage.

Eutych'ĭan (-tĭk-) *adj.* Of, pertaining to, doctrine of Eutyches (5th c.), who held that the human nature of Christ was lost in the divine. **Eutўch'ĭanĭsm** *n.*

ėvăc'ūant *adj.* & *n.* (Agent) causing evacuation esp. of stomach, bowels, etc.

ėvăc'ūāte *v.t.* 1. Empty (esp. stomach or bodily organ *of* contents); discharge excrement etc. 2. Withdraw troops, inhabitants, from (place); remove (person) esp. from a place considered dangerous. **ėvăcūā'tion** *n.*

ėvăcūee' *n.* Person evacuated from place of danger etc.

ėvāde' *v.t.* Escape from, avoid (attack, pursuit, etc.); avoid doing (duty etc.), answering (question), yielding to (argument etc.); defeat intention of (law etc.) esp. while complying with its letter; elude, baffle.

ėvă'gĭnāte *v.t.* (physiol.) Turn (tubular organ) inside out. **ėvăgĭnā'tion** *n.*

ėvăl'ūāte *v.t.* Ascertain amount or value of; find numerical expression for. **ėvălūā'tion** *n.*

ĕv'anesce (-ĕs) *v.i.* Fade out of sight; become effaced; disappear. **ĕvanĕs'cent** *adj.* Quickly fading or vanishing away; (math., of diminishing quantity) infinitesimal. **ĕvanĕs'cence** *n.* **ĕvanĕs'cently** *adv.*

ėvăn'gel (-j-) *n.* (archaic) The gospel; one of the four Gospels. [Gk *euaggelion* (reward for bringing) good news]

ēvăngĕl'ĭc (-j-) *adj.* Of, according to, the teaching of the Gospel or the Christian religion. **ēvăngĕl'ical** *adj.* Evangelic; Protestant, Lutheran; esp., of the school of Protestants maintaining that the essence of the Gospel consists in the doctrine of salvation by faith, and denying that either sacraments or good works have any saving efficacy. ~ *n.* Member of this school. **ēvăngĕl'icalism** *n.* **ēvăngĕl'ically** *adv.*

ėvăn'gelism (-j-) *n.* Preaching or promulgation of the Gospel.

ėvăn'gelist (-j-) *n.* 1. One of the writers of the Four Gospels. 2. Preacher of the Gospel; now usu., layman doing home missionary work. **ėvăngelis'tic** *adj.*

ėvăn'gelize (-j-) *v.t.* Preach Gospel to, win over to Christian faith. **ėvăngelizā'tion** *n.*

ėvăn'ish *v.i.* (now rare) Vanish; die away. **ėvăn'ishment** *n.*

ėvăp'orāte *v.* Turn from solid or liquid into vapour; pass away like vapour; remove liquid part of by heating or drying; lose liquid by evaporation. **ėvăporā'tion** *n.* **ėvăp'orātor** *n.* (esp.) Apparatus for evaporating or drying something.

ėvā'sion (-zhn) *n.* Act, means, of evading; shuffling excuse. **ėvās'ĭve** *adj.* Seeking to evade, addicted to evasion; tending to evasion. **ėvās'ĭvely** (-vl-) *adv.* **ėvās'ĭvenėss** *n.*

eve[1] (ēv) *n.* 1. (poet. or archaic) Evening. 2. Evening or day before saint's day or other Church festival, or before any date or event; time immediately preceding.

Eve[2] (ēv). The name given by Adam to his wife (Gen. iii. 20), the first woman.

ėvĕc'tion *n.* Irregularity in moon's orbit due to attraction of sun.

ē'ven[1] *n.* (poet. & archaic) Evening; *evensong*, evening prayer in Church of England; *eventide*, (archaic) evening.

ē'ven[2] *adj.* 1. Level; smooth; uniform in quality; in same plane or line *with*. 2. Equally balanced, impartial; equal in number or amount; *be* ~, be square or quits; have one's revenge. 3. (of temper etc.) Equable, unruffled. 4. (of numbers) Integrally divisible by two; (of sums of money etc.) expressible in integers, tens, etc. (opp. ODD); ~ *money*, equal odds in betting. ~ *v.t.* Make even; (now rare) treat as equal or comparable (*to*). **ē'venly** *adv.* **ē'vennėss** *n.*

ē'ven[3] *adv.* Inviting comparison of an assertion, negation, etc., with a less strong one that might have been made, as *I never ~ opened the book* (much less read it), *Does he ~ suspect* (not to say realize) *the danger?, She sings ~ better than he does* (though he sings very well) etc.; (archaic) exactly, just.

ēve'nĭng (-vn-), *n.* Close of day, esp. time between sunset and bedtime; closing or declining period of life etc.; ~ *dress*, costume prescribed by fashion to be worn in evening; ~ *primrose*, a biennial plant, *Oenothera*, with pale-yellow flowers which open towards evening; ~ *star*, Venus (occas. also Jupiter or Mercury) when seen in the west after sunset.

ėvĕnt' *n.* 1. (Actual or contemplated) fact of a thing's happening; thing that happens, esp. important thing. 2. Any of several possible mutually exclusive occurrences, one of which will happen under stated conditions (*double* ~, combined occurrence of two events, esp. as subject of bets); something on issue of which money is staked; one of the items in a programme of sports. 3. Result, outcome, issue; *in any* ~, *at all events*, in any case. **ėvĕnt'ful, ėvĕnt'lėss** *adjs.*

ėvĕn'tūal *adj.* That will happen in certain circumstances; ultimately resulting. **ėvĕn'tūally** *adv.* **ėvĕntūăl'ĭty** *n.* Possible event.

ėvĕn'tūāte *v.i.* Turn out; result (*in*); (chiefly U.S.) happen, come to pass.

ĕv'er *adv.* 1. Always, at all times; (archaic except in) ~ *after*, ~ *since*, *yours* ~ (letter-ending); *for* ~, for all future time, incessantly; *evermore*, always; (archaic) ~ *and anon*, now and then. 2. (with negatives, or in interrogative hypothetical or conditional sentences) At any time; by any chance, at all. 3. Added for emphasis to *as* (*soon* etc.) *as*, *before*, etc., or following interrogative pronouns, adverbs, etc., to intimate that the speaker has no notion what the answer will be. 4. ~ *so*, (colloq.) very.

Ev'erėst (ĕ-). Highest known mountain of the world 29,028 ft), in the Himalayas on the frontier of Nepal and Tibet; first climbed 1953. [f. Sir George *Everest* (1790–1866), Surveyor-General of India]

ĕv'erglāde *n.* (U.S.) Marshy tract of land mostly under water and covered in places with tall grass, trees, etc.; usu. pl., (with cap.) a large swampy region of Florida.

ĕv'ergreen *adj.* Always green or fresh; (of trees etc.) having green leaves all the year round and in some cases for several years (the leaves of one season remaining on the tree until those of the next are completely formed); ~ *oak*, holm oak, ilex, *Quercus ilex*; *E~ State*, popular name of Washington. ~ *n.* Evergreen tree or shrub.

ĕverlas'tĭng (-ah-) *adj.* Lasting for ever; lasting long; lasting too long, repeated too often; (of plants) keeping their shape and colour when dried. ~ *n.* 1. Eternity. 2. Everlasting flower.

ėvêrt' *v.t.* (med. etc.) Turn inner surface of (eyelid etc.) outwards; turn inside out. **ėvêrs'ĭble** *adj.* **ėvêr'sion** *n.*

every (ĕv'rĭ) *adj.* 1. Each; all taken separately. 2. *everybody*, every person; *everybody else*, every other person; *everyday*, occurring daily, worn or used on ordinary days, commonplace; *every one*, each (*of*); *everyone* (also *every one*), everybody; *everything*, all things, thing of first importance; *everyway*, in every way, in every respect; *everywhere*, in every place.

ėvĭct' *v.t.* 1. (law) Recover (property, title) *of*, *from*, by judicial process or in virtue of superior title. 2. Expel (person) by legal process; (esp.) eject (tenant) from his holding; eject (person) from any position. **ėvĭc'tion** *n.*

ĕv'ĭdence *n.* 1. Being evident, clearness; *in* ~, present; prominent, conspicuous. 2. Indication, mark, sign, (*of* something); ground for belief, testimony or facts tending to prove or disprove something. 3. Information (personal testimony, production of material objects, etc.) given in legal investigation to establish a fact or point in question; statements etc. admissible as testimony in court of law; *turn King's* (*Queen's*) ~, (of accomplice or sharer in crime) offer himself as witness for prosecution against other persons implicated. ~ *v.t.* Serve to indicate; attest.

ĕv'ĭdent *adj.* Obvious to eyes or mind, clear, plain. **ĕv'ĭdently** *adv.* **ĕvĭdĕn'tial, ĕvĭdĕn'tiary** *adjs.* Of, based on, furnishing evidence. **ĕvĭdĕn'tially** *adv.*

ē'vĭl (-vl, -vĭl) *adj.* Bad, harmful, wicked; boding ill; *the E~ One*, the Devil; ~ *eye*, malicious or envious look, once popularly believed to do material harm; supposed faculty of inflicting injury by a look. ~ *n.* Evil thing; sin; harm, mischief. ~ *adv.* In evil manner. **ē'vĭlly** *adv.*

ėvĭnce' *v.t.* Show, indicate (quality etc.); show that one has (quality).

ėvĭs'cerāte *v.t.* Disembowel; (fig.) empty of vital contents. **ėvĭscerā'tion** *n.*

ėvōke' *v.t.* 1. Call up (spirit, feeling, memory, etc.). 2. Summon (cause) from inferior to superior court. **ēvocā'tion** *n.* **ėvŏc'atĭve, ėvŏc'atory** *adjs.*

ĕv'olūte[1] *adj.* & *n.* (math.)

(Curve) which is locus of centres of curvature of another curve (its *involute*), or the envelope of all its normals.

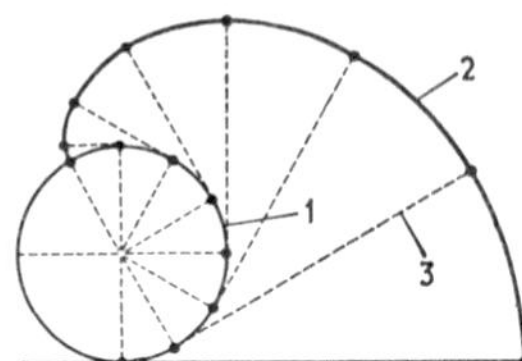

EVOLUTE AND INVOLUTE

1. Evolute of 2. 2. Involute of 1. 3. Normal to 2 and tangent to 1

ĕv'olute[2] (-ōōt, -ūt) *v.* (orig. and chiefly U.S., colloq.) Develop by evolution; evolve.

ėvolu'tion (-lōō-, -lū-) *n.* 1. Opening out (of roll, bud, etc.; usu. fig.); appearance (of events etc.) in due succession. 2. Evolving, giving off (of gas, heat, etc.). 3. Development, detailed working out, of what is implicitly or potentially contained in an idea or principle; development from rudimentary to mature or complete state. 4. Origination of species of animals and plants by process of development from earlier forms. 5. (mil., naut.) Movement, change of position, of body of troops or number of ships. **ėvolu'tional** (-sho-), **ėvolu'tionary** *adjs.* **ėvolu'tionism** *n.* **ėvolu'tionist** *n.* & *adj.* **ĕvolutionis'tic** *adj.*

ėvŏlve' *v.* 1. Unfold, open out; set forth in due sequence; develop, deduce (theory, facts, etc.). 2. Produce, give off (heat etc.). 3. Develop by natural process from rudimentary to more highly organized condition; produce or modify by evolution.

ėvŭl'sion (-shn) *n.* Forcible extraction.

ewe (ū) *n.* Female sheep; ~ *lamb,* most cherished possession (see 2 Sam. xii).

ew'er *n.* Pitcher; large water-jug used in bedrooms.

ĕx *prep.* (commerc.) (Of goods) out of, sold from (*ship, warehouse,* etc.); (of stocks etc.) ~ *dividend,* not including next dividend (abbrev. *ex div., x.d.*).

ex- *prefix.* 1. = L *ex,* forming verbs with sense 'out', 'forth', 'without', 'un-', 'thoroughly'; also as living pref. to nouns with sense 'formerly' (as *ex-chancellor*). 2. = Gk *ek* out (as *exodus*).

ĕxă'cerbāte *v.t.* Aggravate (pain, anger, etc.); irritate. **ĕxăcerbā'tion** *n.*

ėxăct'[1] (-gz-) *adj.* Precise, rigorous; accurate, strictly correct; ~ *sciences,* those which admit of absolute precision in results. **ėxăct'ness, ėxăc'titūde** *ns.*

exăct'[2] (-gz-) *v.t.* Demand and enforce payment of (money etc.); insist upon (act, conduct); require urgently. **ėxăc'table, ėxăc'ting** *adjs.*

ėxăc'tion (-gz-) *n.* Exacting; sum, thing, exacted; illegal or exorbitant demand, extortion; arbitrary and excessive impost.

ėxăct'ly (-gz-) *adv.* (esp. as answer or confirmation) Quite so, just as you say.

exa'ggerāte (ĭgzăj-) *v.t.* Magnify beyond limits of truth; intensify, aggravate; make (physical features etc.) of abnormal size. **ėxă'ggerātėdly, ėxă'ggeratively** *advs.* **ėxăggerā'tion, ėxă'ggerātor** *ns.* **ėxă'ggerative** *adj.*

exalt (ĭgzawlt') *v.t.* Raise, place high in rank, power, etc.; praise, extol; dignify, ennoble. **ĕxaltā'tion** *n.* Raising, lifting up; elation, rapturous emotion.

ėxăm' (-gz-) *n.*: see following.

ėxămĭnā'tion (-gz-) *n.* 1. Investigation by inspection or experiment, minute inspection; investigation. 2. (colloq. abbrev. *exam*) Testing of knowledge or ability of pupils etc. by oral or written questions; ~*-paper,* paper of questions to be answered; candidate's written answers. 3. Formal interrogation, esp. of witness or accused person; statements or deposition thus obtained; ~ *in chief,* that made by party calling the witness. **ėxămĭnā'tional** (sho-) *adj.*

ėxăm'ĭne (-gz-) *v.* Investigate; scrutinize; test, esp. test knowledge or capacity of, by questions; interrogate formally, esp. witness or accused person in court of law; inquire *into.* **ėxămĭnee', ėxăm'ĭner** *ns.*

exam'ple (ĭgzah-) *n.* 1. Typical instance, fact, thing, person, illustrating or forming particular case of general principle, rule, state of things, etc.; specimen of workmanship etc. 2. Warning to others. 3. Precedent. 4. Action or conduct as object of imitation.

ĕx'arch (-k) *n.* 1. (Under Byzantine emperors) governor of distant province. 2. (In Eastern Church) orig., archbishop, patriarch; later, bishop in charge of province and next in rank to patriarch; patriarch's legate. **ĕx'archate** *n.* Office, province, of exarch.

ėxăs'perāte (-gz-) *v.t.* Make worse (ill feeling, disease, pain); irritate; provoke (person). **ėxăs'perā'tion** *n.*

exc. *abbrev.* Except; *excudit* (= engraved this).

Excăl'ĭbur. (myth.) Name of King ARTHUR's magic sword, which he drew easily from a rock where it was held fast, and which was returned on his death to the Lady of the Lake.

ĕx căthĕd'ră *adv.* & *adj.* Authoritative(ly), official(ly); *speak* ~ (of the pope), pronounce an infallible judgement on matter of faith or morals. [L, = 'from the (teacher's) chair']

ĕx'cavāte *v.t.* Make hollow; make (hole etc.) by digging; dig out (soil) leaving a hole; unearth, get out, uncover, by digging. **ĕxcavā tion** *n.*

ĕx'cavātor *n.* 1. Person engaged in excavation. 2. Machine used for excavating.

ėxceed' *v.* Do more than is warranted by (one's commission, rights, etc.); be greater than (quantity, thing, *by* so much); surpass; be pre-eminent; be immoderate in eating etc.; exaggerate. **ėxceed'ĭng** *adj.* & (archaic) *adv.* **ėxceed'ĭngly** *adv.*

ėxcĕl' *v.* Surpass; be pre-eminent.

ĕx'cellence *n.* Surpassing merit; thing in which person etc. excels.

ĕx'cellency *n.* Title of ambassadors, ministers plenipotentiary, governors and their wives, and some other high officers.

ĕx'cellent *adj.* Pre-eminent; very good. **ĕx'cellently** *adv.*

ėxcĕl'sĭor *adj.* Latin motto ('higher') on seal of State of New York, adopted 1778 (it is not clear whether as a blunder for 'upwards' or whether as abbrev. of some grammatically admissible phrase); *E~ State,* New York. ~ quasi-*int.* implying aspiration towards high attainment, as in Longfellow's poem '*E~*' (1841). ~ *n.* (U.S.) Short thin shavings of soft wood for stuffing cushions etc.

ėxcĕpt'[1] *v.* 1. Exclude (thing) from enumeration, statement, etc. 2. Make objection against. **ėxcĕp'tĭve** *adj.*

ėxcĕpt'[2], **ėxcĕpt'ĭng** *prep.* & *conj.* Not including; but, save, with the exception of; (archaic) unless.

ėxcĕp'tion *n.* Excepting; thing excepted, thing that does not follow the rule; (law) objection to ruling of court; *the ~ proves the rule,* the excepting of some cases shows that the rule exists, or that it applies to those not excepted; *take ~,* object *to.* **ėxcĕp'tionable** (-sho-) *adj.* Open to objection.

ėxcĕp'tional (-sho-) *adj.* Forming an exception; unusual. **ėxcĕptionăl'ĭty** *n.* **ėxcĕp'tionally** *adv.*

ĕx'cerpt (*or* iksẽrpt') *n.* Extract from book etc.; article from periodical, transactions of learned society, etc., printed separately for private circulation. **ėxcẽrpt'** *v.t.* Extract, quote, (passage *from* book etc.) **ėxcẽrp'tion** *n.*

ėxcĕss' *n.* 1. (usu. pl.) Outrage. 2. Overstepping limits of moderation; esp., intemperance in eating or drinking. 3. Fact of exceeding; amount by which one quantity exceeds another; exceeding of proper amount or degree; ~ *fare,* payment due for travelling on railway etc. farther or in higher class than ticket warrants; ~ *luggage,* luggage over the weight allowed for free carriage; ~ *profits tax* (abbrev. E.P.T.) tax levied on business profits, orig. during war-time, in excess of average profits of a pre-war standard period. **ėxcĕss'ĭve** *adj.* **ėxcĕss'ĭvely** (-vl-) *adv.*

ėxchānge' *v.* Give, receive, (thing) in place of (*for*) another; interchange (blows, words, glances, etc.); (of coin etc.) be received as equivalent *for*; pass (*from* one regiment or ship *into* another) by exchange with another officer. ~ *n.* 1. Act, process, of exchanging; exchanging of coin, notes, bank deposits, etc., for their equivalent in another country's money; *par of* ~, standard value of one country's monetary unit in terms of another's; (*rate, course, of*) ~, price at which another country's money may be bought; difference between this and par. 2. Building where merchants, stockbrokers, etc., assemble to transact business. 3. TELEPHONE-exchange.

ėxchān'geable (-jabl) *adj.* That may be exchanged (*for*); ~ *value*, value estimated by that of goods for which thing may be exchanged. **ėxchāngeabĭl'ity** *n.*

ėxchĕ'quer (-ker) *n.* 1. Department of public service charged with receipt and custody of revenue; *Chancellor of the E~*, responsible finance minister of United Kingdom. 2. Court of law dealing with matters of revenue etc. converted into division of High Court in 1873 and in 1881 merged in Queen's (King's) Bench Division. 3. Royal or national treasury; money of private person, society, etc. [Fr. *eschequier* f. med. L *scaccarium* chessboard, from use of table with chequered cloth for accounts]

ėxcīse'[1] (-z; *or* ĕk'sīz) *n.* Duty charged on home-produced goods during manufacture or before sale to home consumers; government office collecting this (now *Commissioners of Customs and E~*); ~ *law*, (U.S.) licensing law; *exciseman* (archaic) officer collecting excise duties and preventing infringement of excise laws.

ėxcīse'[2] (-z) *v.t.* Cut out (passage of book, limb, organ, etc.). **ėxcĭ'sion** (-zhn) *n.*

ėxcīte' *v.t.* Set in motion, stir up, rouse (feelings, faculties, etc.); provoke, bring about (action, active condition); promote activity of (bodily organs etc.) by stimulus; move (person) to strong emotion, stir up to eager tumultuous feeling; induce electric or magnetic activity in, set (electric current) in motion. **ėxcīt'able** *adj.* (esp., of persons) Easily excited, unbalanced. **ėxcītabĭl'ity** *n.* **ĕxcĭtā'tion** *n.* **ėxcīt'ative, ėxcīt'atory** *adjs.* **ėxcīt'ėdly** *adv.* **ėxcīte'ment** (-tm-) *n.*

ėxclaim' *v.* Cry out, esp. from pain, anger, delight, etc.; utter thus; ~ *against*, make outcry against, accuse loudly.

ĕxclamā'tion *n.* Exclaiming; words exclaimed; interjection; *note of* ~, ~-*mark*, (!). **ėxclăm'atory** *adj.*

ėxclude' (-lōōd) *v.t.* Shut out (*from* place, society, privilege, etc.); prevent the occurrence of, make impossible; leave out, not include. **ėxclu'sion** (-ōōzhn) *n.*

ėxclus'ĭve (-lōōs-) *adj.* 1. Shutting out; not admitting *of*; desirous of excluding others, (of social circle etc.) chary of admitting others, select; (of news, goods, etc.) not to be had, not published, elsewhere; (of terms etc.) excluding all but what is specified; employed, followed, to the exclusion of all else. 2. (quasi-*adv.*) ~ *of*, not including, not counting. **ėxclus'ĭvely** (-vl-) *adv.* **ėxclus'ĭvenėss** *n.*

ėxcŏ'gĭtāte *v.t.* Think out, contrive. **ėxcŏgĭtā'tion** *n.* **ėxcŏ'gĭtative** *adj.*

ĕxcommūn'ĭcāte *v.t.* (eccles.) Cut off (person) from participation in sacrament, or from all communication with Church. **ĕxcommūnĭcā'tion, ĕxcommūn'ĭcātor** *ns.* **ĕxcommūn'ĭcative, ĕxcommūn'ĭcatory** *adjs.*

ėxcor'ĭāte *v.t.* Remove part of skin of (person etc.) by abrasion etc.; strip, peel off (skin). **ėxcorĭā'tion** *n.*

ĕx'crėment *n.* Waste matter discharged from bowels, dung. **ĕxcrėmĕn'tal, ĕxcrėmĕntĭ'tious** (-shus) *adjs.*

ėxcrĕs'cence *n.* Abnormal or morbid outgrowth on animal or vegetable body (also fig.).

ėxcrĕs'cent *adj.* Growing abnormally, redundant; (gram., of sound or letter) having no etymological value, but developed by influence of euphony.

ėxcrēt'a *n.pl.* Waste expelled from body, esp. faeces and urine.

ėxcrēte' *v.t.* (Of animals, plants, etc.) separate and expel (waste matters) from system. **ėxcrē'tion** *n.* **ėxcrēt'ĭve, ėxcrēt'ory** *adjs.*

ėxcru'ciāte (-ōōshĭ-) *v.t.* Torment acutely (person's senses); torture mentally. **ėxcru'ciātĭngly** *adv.* **ėxcruciā'tion** *n.*

ĕx'culpāte *v.t.* Free from blame; clear (*from* charge etc.). **ĕxculpā'tion** *n.* **ėxcŭl'patory** *adj.*

ėxcur'sion (-shon) *n.* 1. Journey or ramble from any place with intention of returning to it; pleasure-trip, esp. one taken by a number of persons; ~ *train*, train for persons making pleasure excursion, usu. at reduced rates. 2. Sortie, raid (obs. exc. in *alar(u)ms and* ~*s*). 3. (astron.) Deviation from regular path or course. **ėxcur'sionist** (-sho-) *n.* One who makes pleasure excursion.

ėxcurs'ĭve *adj.* Desultory; erratic, digressive. **ėxcurs'ĭvely** (-vl-) *adv.* **ėxcurs'ĭvenėss** *n.*

ėxcurs'us *n.* Detailed discussion of special point in book, usu. in appendix at end.

ėxcūse' (-z) *v.t.* 1. Attempt to clear (person) from blame without denying or justifying his imputed action; seek to remove or extenuate blame of (acknowledged fault); serve as excuse for. 2. Obtain exemption or release for, set free, (person) from task, duty, obligation. 3. Accept plea in exculpation of; admit apology for, overlook, condone; pardon faults of, regard indulgently; dispense with. 4. ~ *me*, used as apology for lack of ceremony, interruption etc. or as polite way of disputing statement. **ėxcūs'able, ėxcūs'atory** *adjs.* **ėxcūs'ably** *adv.* **ėxcūse'** (-s) *n.* Apology offered, exculpation; ground of this; plea for release from duty etc.

ex div. *abbrev.* Ex dividend (see EX).

ĕx'ėăt *n.* Bishop's permission to priest to leave diocese; (in schools etc.) permission for temporary absence. [L, = 'let (him) go out']

ĕx'ėcrable *adj.* Abominable. **ĕx'ėcrably** *adv.*

ĕx'ėcrāte *v.* Express, feel, abhorrence for; utter curses. **ĕxėcrā'tion** *n.* **ĕx'ėcratory** *adj.*

ėxĕc'ūtant (-gz-) *n.* One who executes, performer (esp. of music).

ĕx'ėcūte *v.t.* 1. Carry (plan, command, law, will, judicial sentence) into effect; perform (action, operation, etc.); make (legal instrument) valid by signing, sealing, etc.; discharge (office, function). 2. Carry out design for (product of art or skill); perform (musical composition). 3. Inflict capital punishment on.

ĕxėcū'tion *n.* Executing; excellence in executing (esp. music); effective action (esp. of weapons); seizure of goods or person of debtor in default of payment; infliction of capital punishment. **ĕxėcū'tioner** (-sho-) *n.* One who carries out a capital sentence.

ėxĕc'ūtĭve (-gz-) *adj.* Pertaining to, having function of, executing; concerned with executing laws, decrees, and sentences; ~ *order*, (U.S.) President's order on administrative matter not requiring legislation; ~ *session*, (U.S.) private session of Senate to deal with executive business; hence, private meeting. ~ *n.* 1. Executive branch of government (cf. JUDICATURE, LEGISLATURE). 2. Person holding executive position in business etc.; executive official, esp. President of U.S., Governor of State, or mayor of city.

executor *n.* 1. (ĕk'sĭ-) One who carries out or performs. 2. (ĭgzĕk'-) Person appointed by testator to execute his will; *literary* ~, person entrusted with papers and unpublished works of writer. **ėxĕcūtor'ĭal** *adj.* **ėxĕc'ūtorshĭp** *n.*

ėxĕc'ūtrĭx (-gz-) *n.* (pl. *-trīcēs*). Female executor.

ĕxėgēs'ĭs *n.* Exposition, interpretation, esp. of Scripture. **ĕxėgĕt'ĭc(al)** *adjs.* **ĕxėgĕt'ĭcally** *adv.*

ėxĕm'plar (-gz-) *n.* Model, pattern; type (of a class); parallel instance.

ėxĕm'plary (-gz-) *adj.* Fit to be

imitated; illustrative; (of penalty, damages) serving as a warning. **exĕm'plarĭly** *adv.* **exĕm'plarĭness** *n.*

exĕm'plĭfȳ (-gz-) *v.t.* 1. Illustrate by example; be example of. 2. Make official copy of; make attested copy of (legal document) under official seal.

exĕmpt' (-gz-) *adj.* Freed *from* allegiance or liability to; not liable, exposed, or subject to (danger, disease, charge, duty, etc.). ~ *n.* 1. Exempted person. 2. = EXON. ~ *v.t.* Grant to (person) immunity or freedom *from*. **exĕmp'tion** *n.*

exequāt'ur (-*er*) *n.* Official recognition by foreign government of country's consul or commercial agent; temporal sovereign's authorization of bishop under papal authority, or of publication of papal bulls. [L, = 'he may perform']

ĕx'equies (-kwĭz) *n.pl.* Funeral rites.

ĕx'ercīse (-z) *n.* 1. Employment (of organ, faculty, power, right); practice (of virtues, profession, functions, religious rites). 2. Exertion of muscles, limbs, etc., esp. for health's sake; (pl.) military drill, athletics, etc. 3. Bodily, mental, or spiritual training; task set for this purpose; academical declamation, dissertation, musical composition, etc., required for degree; composition etc. set to pupils at school; piece of music etc. designed to afford practice to learners. 4. Religious observance; public worship. 5. (U.S.) Ceremony on some special occasion. ~ *v.* Employ (faculty, right, etc.); train (person etc.); tax the powers of; perplex, worry; discharge (functions); take, give (horse etc.), exercise.

exergue' (-g; *or* ĕgz'ẽrg) *n.* Small space usu. on reverse of coin or medal for minor inscription, date, etc., below principal device (ill. COIN); inscription there. **exẽr'gual** (-g*a*l) *adj.*

exẽrt' (-gz-) *v.t.* Exercise, bring to bear (quality, force, influence); ~ *oneself*, use efforts or endeavours, strive. **exẽr'tion** *n.* Exerting; vigorous action, effort.

Ex'eter (ĕ-). City of Devonshire, England; ~ *College*, college of the University of Oxford, founded 1314 by Walter de Stapeldon, bishop of Exeter; ~ *Hall*, building in Strand, London, erected 1830–1 and formerly used for religious and philanthropic assemblies.

ĕx'eŭnt. (stage direction) They (two or more actors) leave the stage; ~ *omnes*, all leave the stage. [L, = 'they go out']

exfŏl'ĭāte *v.i.* (Of bones, skin, minerals, etc.) come off in scales or layers; (of tree) throw off layers of bark. **exfōlĭā'tion** *n.*

ĕx gratia (grāsh'*a*). (Done) as a favour.

exhalā'tion (ĕks*a*-) *n.* Evaporation; expiration; what is exhaled, mist, vapour, effluvium.

exhāle' *v.* Give off, be given off, in vapour, evaporate; breathe out.

exhaust' (ĭgzaw-) *v.* 1. Draw off (air); empty (vessel) of contents. 2. Consume entirely; use, account for, the whole of; treat or study subject etc.) so as to leave nothing further to be explained or discovered. 3. Drain (person etc.) of strength, resources, etc.; tire out. **exhaus'tĭble** *adj.* **exhaustĭbĭl'ĭty** *n.* **exhaust'** *n.* (In hydraulic, steam, or internal combustion engines) expulsion or exit of motive fluid, steam, or gaseous products of combustion from cylinder after completion of power-stroke by piston; similar exit of spent fluid or gases from turbine; fluid, steam, etc., expelled thus; ~-*pipe*, pipe for this (ill. COMBUSTION).

exhaustion (ĭgzaws'ch*o*n) *n.* (esp.) Total loss of strength; arriving at conclusion by eliminating alternatives.

exhaus'tĭve (ĭgzaw-) *adj.* (esp.) Comprehensive, exhausting a subject. **exhaus'tĭvely** (-vl-) *adv.* **exhaus'tĭveness** *n.*

exhib'ĭt (ĭgzĭ-) *v.t.* Show, display; submit (document) for inspection; manifest (quality); show publicly; (U.S.) present, declaim (speech, essay) in public. ~ *n.* Document or thing produced in law-court and referred to in written evidence; thing, collection of things, sent by person, firm etc., to exhibition, or on permanant show in museum etc. **exhĭb'ĭtor** *n.* **exhĭb'ĭtory** *adj.*

exhibĭ'tion (ĕksĭ-) *n.* 1. Showing, exhibiting, display; public display (of works of art, manufactured articles, etc.), place where this is held; *Great E~*, the first international industrial exhibition, opened in the Crystal Palace, Hyde Park, 1st Aug. 1851. 2. (U.S.) Public declamation of speeches, performance of music, etc., by pupils of school or college. 3. Fixed sum given to student for term of years from funds of college, school, or university. **exhibitioner** (ĕksĭbĭsh'*o*n-) *n.* One who holds exhibition at university etc.

exhibĭtionism (ĕksĭbĭsh'*o*n-) *n.* Tendency towards display, extravagant behaviour; perverted mental condition characterized esp. by indecent exposure of the person. **ĕxhĭbĭ'tionĭst** *n.*

exhĭl'arāte (ĭgzĭ-) *v.t.* Enliven, gladden (person, spirits). **exhĭlarā'tion** *n.* **exhĭl'aratĭve** *adj.*

exhort (ĭgzŏrt') *v.t.* Admonish earnestly; urge (*to*). **ĕxhŏrtā'tion** *n.* **ĕxhŏrt'atĭve, exhŏrt'atory** *adjs.*

ĕxhūme' *v.t.* Dig out (something buried), unearth. **ĕxhūmā'tion** *n.*

ĕx'ĭgence, ex'ĭgency *ns.* Urgent need; emergency.

ĕx'ĭgent *adj.* Urgent, pressing; requiring much, exacting.

ĕx'ĭgible *adj.* That may be exacted.

ĕxĭg'ūous *adj.* Scanty, small. **ĕxĭgū'ĭty, ĕxĭg'ūousness** *ns.*

ĕx'īle *n.* 1. Penal banishment; long absence from one's country; *the E~*, esp., captivity of Jews in Babylon in 6th c. B.C. 2. Banished person. ~ *v.t.* Banish (*from*).

ĕxĭl'ĭan, ĕxĭl'ĭc *adjs.* Of exile; esp., of the captivity of the Jews.

exĭst' (-gz-) *v.i.* Have objective being; have being in specified place or under specified conditions; occur, be found; live; continue in being.

exĭs'tence (-gz-) *n.* Being, existing; life; mode of existing; all that exists; existing thing.

exĭs'tent (-gz-) *adj.* Existing, actual, current.

ĕxĭstĕn'tial (-gz-, -shl) *adj.* (logic, of a proposition) Predicating existence. **ĕxĭstĕn'tialĭsm** *n.* A 20th-c. anti-intellectualist philosophy of life based on the assumption that reality as existence can only be lived by man as a free and responsible being, but can never become the object of thought. **ĕxĭstĕn'tialĭst** *n.*

ĕx'ĭt. (stage direction) Goes off stage. **ĕx'ĭt** *n.* Departure of player from stage (also fig.); death; going out or forth, liberty to do this; passage to go out by. [L, = 'goes out']

ĕx-lĭb'rĭs *n.* Label with owner's name etc. for pasting into book, book-plate. [L, = 'from the library' (of So-and-so)]

exo- *prefix.* Outside.

Exod. *abbrev.* Exodus (O.T.).

ĕx'odẽrm *n.* Outer layer of blastoderm.

ĕx'odus *n.* Departure, going forth, esp. of body of emigrants; departure of Israelites from Egypt; *E~*, 2nd book of O.T., relating this.

ĕx offĭ'cio (-shĭō) *adv.* & *adj.* In virtue of one's office.

ĕxŏg'amous *adj.* Following the custom compelling man to marry outside his own tribe or group. **ĕxŏg'amy** *n.*

ĕx'ogen *n.* = DICOTYLEDON, with ref. to external growth of stem. **ĕxŏ'genous** *adj.*

ĕx'ŏn *n.* One of four officers who in turn command the Yeomen of the Guard in absence of their superior officers.

Exon. *abbrev.* (Bishop) of Exeter (replacing surname in his signature).

exŏn'erāte (-gz-) *v.t.* Exculpate; free (person) *from* (blame etc.); release (person *from* duty etc.). **exŏnerā'tion** *n.* **exŏn'eratĭve** *adj.*

Exō'nĭan *adj.* & *n.* (Native, inhabitant) of Exeter.

ĕxopăth'ĭc *adj.* (Of disease) originating outside the body.

ĕxŏph'agous *adj.* Not eating members of one's own tribe. **ĕxŏph'agy** *n.*

ĕxophthăl'mus *n.* Protrusion of eyeball. **ĕxophthăl'mĭc** *adj.* Of, characterized by, this.

ĕx′oplăsm *n.* Outermost layer of protoplasm.

exor, exors *abbrevs.* Executor(s).

ėxôrb′ĭtant (-gz-) *adj.* Grossly excessive (of price, demand, ambition, person). **ėxôrb′ĭtance** *n.* **ėxôrb′ĭtantly** *adv.*

ĕx′ôrcīze *v.t.* Expel (evil spirit *from, out of*, person or place) by invocation or use of holy name; clear (person, place, *of* evil spirits). **ĕx′ôrcĭsm, ĕx′ôrcĭst** *ns.*

ėxôrd′ĭum *n.* (pl. *-iums, -ia*). Beginning, introductory part, esp. of discourse or treatise. **ėxôrd′ĭal** *adj.*

ĕxoskĕl′ėton *n.* External skeleton, as of insect, crustacean, tortoise (its shell) or fish (its scales).

ĕxŏsmōs′ĭs *n.* Osmosis outwards, passage of fluid through porous septum or membrane to mix with external fluid.

ĕxotĕ′rĭc *adj.* (Of doctrines, mode of speech, etc.) intelligible to outsiders; (of disciples) not admitted to esoteric teaching; commonplace, ordinary, popular. **ĕxotĕ′rĭcal** *adj.* **ĕxotĕ′rĭcally** *adv.* **ĕxotĕ′rĭcs** *n.pl.* Exoteric doctrines or teachings.

ĕxŏt′ĭc (-gz-) *adj.* (Of plants, words, fashions) introduced from abroad; strange, bizarre. ~ *n.* Exotic plant (also fig.).

ėxpănd′ *v.* 1. Spread out flat or smooth; unfold, open out; swell, dilate, increase in bulk. 2. Expound, write out, in full (what is condensed or abbreviated, algebraical expression, etc.). 3. Become genial or talkative, throw off reserve. **ėxpăn′sĭble** *adj.*

ėxpănse′ *n.* Wide area or extent; expansion.

ėxpăn′sīle *adj.* (Capable) of expansion.

ėxpăn′sion (-shn) *n.* Expanding; increasing, increase, extension (of currency, trade, territory, etc.); increase in bulk. **ėxpăn′sionĭsm** (-sho-), **ėxpăn′sionĭst** *ns.* (Advocate of) policy or theory of expansion, esp. of currency or territory.

ėxpăn′sĭve *adj.* Able, tending, to expand; extensive; comprehensive; (of persons, feelings, speech) effusive. **ėxpăn′sĭvely** (-vl-) *adv.* **ėxpăn′sĭvenėss** *n.*

ĕx pârt′ė *adv.* & *adj.* (law) On, in interests of, one side only; made or said thus.

ėxpā′tiāte (-shĭ-) *v.i.* Speak, write, copiously (*on* subject). **ėxpātiā′tion** *n.* **ėxpā′tiatory** (-sha-) *adj.*

ėxpăt′rĭāte *v.t.* Banish; (*refl.*) withdraw from one's country, renounce one's citizenship. **ėxpătrĭā′tion** *n.* **ėxpăt′rĭate** *adj.* & *n.* Expatriated (person).

ėxpĕct′ *v.t.* Look forward to, regard as likely; look for, anticipate coming of (person or thing); (colloq.) think, suppose.

ėxpĕc′tancy *n.* State of expectation; prospect, esp. of future possession; prospective chance (*of*).

ėxpĕc′tant *adj.* Expecting; having the prospect, in normal course, of possession, office, etc.; (law) reversionary; ~ *mother*, pregnant woman. **ėxpĕc′tantly** *adv.* **ėxpĕc′tant** *n.* One expecting, one entitled to expect something; expectant heir, etc.

ĕxpĕctā′tion *n.* Awaiting; anticipation; ground for expecting; (pl.) prospects of inheritance; being expected; thing expected; degree of probability of occurrence of contingent event; ~ *of life*, length of life normally to be expected by person of given age.

ėxpĕc′tatĭve *adj.* Of reversion of benefices etc., reversionary.

ėxpĕc′torāte *v.t.* Eject (phlegm or other material) from lung airways by coughing; spit. **ėxpĕctorā′tion** *n.* **ėxpĕc′torant** *adj.* & *n.* (Medicine) promoting expectoration.

ėxpēd′ĭent *adj.* (usu. predic.) Advantageous, suitable; politic rather than just. **ėxpēd′ĭently** *adv.* **ėxpēd′ĭence, ėxpēd′ĭency** *ns.* **ėxpēd′ĭent** *n.* Contrivance, device.

ĕx′pėdīte *v.t.* Assist progress of measure, process, etc.); dispatch (business).

ĕxpėdĭ′tion *n.* 1. Warlike enterprise; journey, voyage, excursion, for definite purpose; body of persons, fleet, etc., sent out for warlike or other definite purpose. 2. Promptness, speed. **ĕxpėdĭ′tionary** (-sho-) *adj.*

ĕxpėdĭ′tious (-shus) *adj.* Doing, done, speedily; suited to speedy performance. **ĕxpėdĭ′tiously** *adv.* **ĕxpėdĭ′tiousnėss** *n.*

ėxpĕl′ *v.t.* Eject (*from*) by force; turn out (person *from* community, school, etc.). **ėxpĕll ent** *adj.*

ėxpĕnd′ *v.t.* Spend (money, time, care, etc.); use up; (naut.) use up (rope etc.) by winding it round spar, rope, etc. **ėxpĕn′dable** *adj.* That can be expended or spared.

ėxpĕn′dĭture *n.* Laying out, spending; consuming; amount expended.

ėxpĕnse′ *n.* Expenditure; cost; (pl.) outlay in execution of commission etc., reimbursement of this.

ėxpĕn′sĭve *adj.* Costly. **ėxpĕns′ĭvely** (-vl-) *adv.* **expĕn′sĭvenėss** *n.*

ėxpēr′ience *n.* 1. Actual observation of facts or events; knowledge resulting from this. 2. Event that affects one; fact, process, of being so affected. ~ *v.t.* Meet with, feel, undergo (pleasure, treatment, fate, etc.); learn, find. **ėxpēr′ienced** (-st) *adj.* (esp.) Having experience, wise or skilful through experience.

ĕxpērĭĕn′tial (-shl) *adj.* Of experience; (of philosophy) regarding all knowledge as derived from experience. **ĕxpērĭĕn′tialĭsm** (-shal-), **ĕxpērĭĕn′tialĭst** *ns.* **expērĭĕn′tially** *adv.*

ėxpĕ′rĭment *n.* Action or operation undertaken in order to discover something unknown, test hypothesis, illustrate known fact, etc.; method etc. adopted in uncertainty whether it will answer the purpose. **ėxpĕ′rĭmĕnt** *v.i.* Make experiment (*on, with*).

ėxpĕrĭmĕn′tal *adj.* 1. Based on, derived from, experience. 2. Based on experiment; of, used in, experiments. **ėxpĕrĭmĕn′tally** *adv.* **ėxpĕrĭmĕn′talĭsm, ėxpĕrĭmĕn′talĭst** *ns.* **ėxpĕrĭmĕn′talīze** *v.i.*

ĕx′pērt *adj.* Trained by practice, skilful, (*at, in*). **ĕx′pērtly** *adv.* **ĕx′pērtnėss** *n.* **ĕx′pērt** *n.* Person having special skill or knowledge (freq. attrib.).

ĕxpertise′ (-ēz) *n.* Expertness, esp. in identification of works of art; connoisseurship.

ĕx′pĭāte *v.t.* Pay penalty of, make amends for (sin). **ĕx′pĭable, ĕx′pĭatory** *adjs.* **ĕxpĭā′tion, ĕx′pĭātor** *ns.*

ĕxpirā′tion (-per-) *n.* 1. Breathing out. 2. Termination (of period of time, something made to last a certain time). **ėxpīr′atory** *adj.*

ėxpīre′ *v.* 1. Breathe out. 2. Die; (of fire etc.) die out. 3. (Of period) come to an end; (of law, patent, etc.) become void, reach its term; (of title etc.) cease, become extinct.

ėxpīr′y *n.* Termination (of period, truce, etc.).

ėxplain′ *v.* Give details of; make plain or intelligible; give explanation; interpret; make clear cause, origin, or reason of, account for; ~ *away*, modify, do away with, by explanation; ~ one*self*, make one's meaning clear, give account of one's motives or intentions.

ĕxplanā′tion *n.* Explaining, esp. with view to mutual understanding or reconciliation; statement, circumstance, that explains.

ėxplăn′atory *adj.* Serving, meant, to explain. **ėxplăn′atorĭly** *adv.*

ėxplēt′ĭve *adj.* Serving to fill out; (of words etc.) serving to fill out sentence, metrical line, etc. ~ *n.* Expletive word or phrase, esp. oath or meaningless exclamation.

ĕx′plĭcable (*or* ĭksplĭk′-) *adj.* That may be explained or explicated.

ĕx′plĭcāte *v.t.* 1. Develop (notion, principle, proposition). 2. (archaic) Explain. **ĕx′plĭcatĭve, ĕx′plĭcatory** *adjs.*

ĕx′plĭcĭt[1] *v.* Here ends . . .; (as *n.*) conclusion, finis.

ėxplĭ′cĭt[2] *adj.* Stated in detail, leaving nothing merely implied; definite; (of persons) outspoken; ~ *faith*, (theol.) acceptance of doctrine with distinct apprehension of all that is logically involved in it. **ėxplĭ′cĭtly** *adv.* **ėxplĭ′cĭtnėss** *n.*

ėxplōde′ *v.* 1. Bring into disrepute, expose hollowness of (theory, belief, etc.). 2. (Cause to) go off with loud noise; (of gunpowder etc.) expand violently with loud report under influence of suddenly developed internal energy; (of shell, etc.) burst from similar cause; (of boiler etc.) burst from excessive pressure of steam inside it.

ĕx'ploit[1] *n.* Brilliant achievement.

ėxploit'[2] *v.t.* Work, turn to account, (mine etc.); utilize (person etc.) for one's own ends. **ėxploit'able** *adj.* **ĕxploitā'tion** *n.*

ėxplōre' *v.t.* 1. Investigate (condition, fact); examine, pry into; probe, examine by touch (wound etc.). 2. Search into, examine (country, place, etc.) by going through it; go into, range over, for purpose of discovery. **ĕxplorā'tion, ėxplŏr'er** *ns.* **ėxplŏr'ative, ėxplŏr'atory** *adjs.*

ėxplō'sion (-zhn) *n.* Driving out, issuing forth, going off, with loud noise and violence; the resulting noise, detonation; outbreak, outburst (of anger etc.).

ėxplōs'ive *adj.* Tending to drive something forth with violence and noise; tending to explode or cause explosion; of, like, explosion; (of consonant) produced by explosion of breath, stopped. **ėxplōs'ively** (-vl-) *adj.* **ėxplōs'iveness** *n.* **ėxplōs'ive** *n.* 1. Explosive agent or compound; *high* ~, kinds having very violent and shattering effect and used not as propellents but in shells, bombs, etc. 2. Explosive consonant.

ėxpōn'ėnt *adj.* & *n.* 1. (Person, thing) that sets forth or interprets; executant (of music etc.); type, representative. 2. (alg.) Index; symbol denoting number of times particular quantity is to be taken as factor to produce the power indicated. **ĕxponĕn'tial** (-shl) *adj.* (esp., math.). Involving the unknown quantity as (part of) an exponent.

ėxpōrt' *v.t.* Send out (goods) to another country. **ėxpōrt'able** *adj.* **ĕxpōrtā'tion** *n.* **ĕx'pōrt** *n,* Exported article; (usu. pl.) amount exported; exportation.

ėxpōse' (-z) *v.t.* 1. Leave, place, in unsheltered or unprotected position; abandon (child); lay open, subject (*to* risk etc.). 2. Exhibit, display; offer publicly, put up, *for* sale; disclose (secret, project, etc.); unmask, show up (fault, guilty person, etc.). 3. (photog.) Subject (sensitized surface of plate, film, printing-paper, etc.) to action of actinic rays; make exposure.

exposé (ĕkspōz'ā) *n.* Statement of facts; showing up (of discreditable thing).

ĕxposi'tion (-z-) *n.* 1. Exposure; exhibition. 2. Setting forth, description; explanation; commentary.

ėxpŏs'itive (-z-) *adj.* Descriptive, explanatory.

ĕx pŏst făc'to *adj.* Acting retrospectively. [L, = 'from what is made (i.e. enacted) afterwards']

ėxpŏs'tūlāte *v.i.* Make friendly remonstrance; remonstrate. **ėxpŏstūlā'tion** *n.* **ėxpŏs'tūlatory** *adj.*

ėxpō'sure (-zh*er*) *n.* Exposing, being exposed; (length of) exposing of photographic plate etc.; abandoning (of child); display, esp. of goods for sale; unmasking of error, fraud, etc.

ėxpound' *v.t.* Set forth in detail (doctrine etc.); explain, interpret esp. Scripture).

ėxprĕss'[1] *adj.* 1. (Of likeness) exact; definitely stated, not merely implied. 2. Done, made, sent, for special purpose; ~ *train,* fast train stopping only at a few important stations (orig., train run expressly to convey passengers to a particular place). 3. (Of machinery etc.) having high speed, run at high speed. 4. ~ *delivery,* delivery by special postal messenger (so ~ *letter, fee,* etc.); ~ *rifle,* rifle discharging bullet with high initial velocity and low trajectory. **ėxprĕss'ly** *adv.* **ėxprĕss'** *adv.* With speed; by express messenger or train. ~ *n.* 1. Express train, messenger, or rifle; (U.S.) company for transmitting parcels etc.; ~ *agent,* agent of express company; ~ *car,* railway carriage for carrying goods sent by express. ~ *v.t.* Send by express delivery; (U.S.) send by express.

ėxprĕss'[2] *v.t.* 1. Press, squeeze, or wring out; emit, exude, as if by pressure. 2. Represent by drawing etc. or by figures or other symbols; represent in language, put into words; (*refl.*) put one's thought into words; manifest, reveal, betoken (feelings, personal qualities, etc.).

ėxprĕ'ssion (-shn) *n.* Expressing; wording, diction, word, phrase; (alg.) collection of symbols together expressing algebraical quantity; expressive quality; aspect (of face), intonation (of voice), etc.; manner of musical performance suited to bringing out feeling of passage; (painting etc.) mode of expressing character.

ėxprĕ'ssional (-sh*o*-) *adj.* Of verbal, facial, or artistic expression.

ėxprĕ'ssionism (-sh*o*-) *n.* Movement in art, literature, and music seeking to express emotional experience rather than impressions of the physical world. **ėxprĕ'ssionist** *n.* **ėxprĕssionis'tic** *adj.*

ėxprĕss'ive *adj.* Of expression, serving to express; full of, emphatic in, expression; significant. **ėxprĕss'ively** (-vl-) *adv.* **ėxprĕss'ivenėss** *n.*

ĕxprobā'tion *n.* Reproachful language.

ėxprōp'riāte *v.t.* Dispossess (*from* estate etc.); take away (property). **ėxprōpriā'tion** *n.*

ėxpŭl'sion (-sh*o*n) *n.* Expelling. **ėxpŭl'sive** *adj.* & *n.*

ėxpŭnge (-j) *v.t.* Erase, omit, strike out. **ėxpŭnc'tion** *n.*

ĕx'purgāte (-p*er*-) *v.t.* Purify (book etc.) by removing objectionable matter); clear away (such matter). **ĕxpurgā'tion, ĕx'purgātor** *ns.* **ĕxpûrgatōr'ial, expûrg'atory** *adjs.*

ĕx'quisite (-z-) *adj.* Of consummate excellence or beauty; acute; keen. **ĕx'quisitely** (-tl-) *adv.* **ĕx'quisitenėss** *n.* **ĕx'quisite** *n.* Coxcomb, fop.

exrx *abbrev.* Executrix.

ėxsăng'uine (-nggw-) *adj.* Bloodless.

ėxscind' *v.t.* Cut out, excise.

ėxsêrt' *v.t.* (biol.) Thrust forth or out.

ĕx-sêrv'ice *adj.* Having formerly belonged to one of the fighting services.

ĕx'tant (*or* ĭkstănt') *adj.* Still existing (esp. of documents etc.).

ėxtĕm'porė *adv.* & *adj.* (Spoken, done,) without preparation; offhand. **ėxtĕmporān'ėous** *adj.* **ėxtĕmporān'ėously** *adv.* **ėxtĕmporān'ėousnėss** *n.* **ėxtĕm'porary** *adj.* **ėxtĕm'porarily** *adv.*

ėxtĕm'porize *v.* Compose, produce, extempore; speak extempore; **ėxtĕmporizā'tion** *n.*

ėxtĕnd' *v.* 1. Place (esp. body, limbs, etc.) at full length; write out (contractions, shorthand notes, etc.) at full length. 2. Reach, cause to reach (*to* point, *over, across,* etc., space). 3. Prolong (period); enlarge (scope, meaning, of word, etc.). 4. (mil.) Spread out, cause (line etc.) to spread out, into open order with regular intervals between men. 5. (sport. slang, usu. pass.) Tax powers of (horse, athlete) to the utmost. 6. Stretch forth (hand, arm); accord (kindness, patronage, *to*). 7. (law) Value (land etc.), seize (land etc.) for debt. **ėxtĕn'dible, extĕn'sible** *adjs.* **ėxtĕnsibil'ity** *n.*

ėxtĕn'sile *adj.* Capable of being stretched out or protruded.

ėxtĕn'sion (-shn) *n.* Extending; extent, range; prolongation, enlargement; additional part, building, line, etc. (of railway, plan, theory, etc.); word(s) amplifying subject or predicate; *university* ~, extramural instruction conducted by a university or college.

ėxtĕn'sive *adj.* Large; far-reaching, comprehensive; (of agricultural production etc.) depending on extension of area. **ėxtĕn'sively** *adv.* **ėxtĕn'sivenėss** *n.*

ėxtĕn'sor *n.* Muscle serving to extend or straighten out any part of body (opp. *flexor*) (ill. MUSCLE).

ėxtĕnt' *n.* 1. Space over which thing extends; width of application, scope. 2. (law) Valuation (of land etc.); seizure, writ for seizure, (of lands etc.).

ėxtĕn'ūāte *v.t.* 1. Lessen seeming magnitude of (guilt, offence) by partial excuse. 2. (archaic) Make thin or weak. **ėxtĕnūā'tion** *n.* **ėxtĕn'ūatory** *adj.*

ėxtēr'ior *adj.* Outer, situated or coming from without; relating to foreign affairs; ~ *angle,* that between any side of a polygon and adjacent side produced. **ĕxtēr'ĭorly** *adv.* **ĕxtērĭŏ'rĭty** *n.* **ĕxtēr'ĭor** *n.* Outward aspect or demeanour; (cinema) outdoor scene.

ĕxtēr'ĭorīze *v.t.* Realize (conception) in outward form; attribute external existence *to.* **ĕxtērĭorīzā'tion** *n.*

ĕxtērm'ĭnāte *v.t.* Destroy utterly, root out (species, race, etc.). **ĕxtērmĭnā'tion, ĕxtērm'ĭnātor** *ns.* **ĕxtērm'ĭnative, ĕxtērm'ĭnatory** *adjs.*

ĕxtērn'al *adj.* Situated outside; (of remedies etc.) applied to outside of body; (theol.) consisting in outward acts or appearances; belonging to external world of things or phenomena, considered as outside the perceiving mind; arising, acting, from without; connected with, referring to, what is outside; ~ *evidence,* evidence derived from source independent of the thing discussed. **ĕxtērnăl'ĭty** *n.* **ĕxtērn'ally** *adv.* **ĕxtērn'als** *n.pl.* Outward features or aspect; external circumstances; non-essentials.

ĕxtērn'alīze *v.t.* Give, attribute, external existence to. **ĕxtērnalīzā'tion** *n.*

ĕxtĭnct' *adj.* (Of fire etc.) no longer burning; (of volcano) that has ceased eruption; (of life, hope, etc.) quenched; (of family, class, species) that has died out; (of office etc.) obsolete; (of title of nobility) having no qualified claimant.

ĕxtĭnc'tion *n.* Extinguishing; making, being, becoming, extinct; wiping out (of debt); annihilation. **ĕxtĭnc'tĭve** *adj.*

ĕxtĭng'uĭsh (-nggw-) *v.t.* Put out, quench (light, hope, life, faculties); eclipse, obscure (person) by superior brilliancy; reduce (opponent) to silence; destroy; wipe out (debt); annihilate. **ĕxtĭng'uĭshable** *adj.*

ĕxtĭng'uĭsher (-nggw-) *n.* (esp.) Hollow conical cap for extinguishing light of candle etc.; *fire* ~, apparatus with jet for discharging liquid chemicals to extinguish fire.

ĕx'tĭrpāte *v.t.* Root out, destroy. **ĕxtĭrpā'tion, ĕx'tĭrpātor** *ns.*

ĕxtŏl' *v.t.* Praise enthusiastically.

ĕxtôrt' *v.t.* Obtain (money, promise, etc.) by violence, intimidation, importunity, etc. (*from*); extract forcibly (sense, conclusion, etc., *from* words etc.).

ĕxtôr'tion *n.* Extorting, esp. of money; illegal exaction. **ĕxtôr'tionate** (-sho-) *adj.* Using, given to, extortion; (of prices etc.) exorbitant. **ĕxtôr'tioner** *n.*

ĕx'tra *adj.* Additional; larger than its name indicates; of superior quality. ~ *adv.* More than usually; additionally. ~ *n.* Extra thing, one for which extra charge is made; (cricket) run scored otherwise than off bat; special or additional issue of newspaper; (cinema) actor engaged temporarily as one of crowd etc.

extra- *prefix.* Situated outside of a thing, not coming within its scope.

ĕx'trăct *n.* 1. (chem.) Preparation containing active principle of substance in concentrated form obtained by treatment with a solvent (usu. followed by evaporation of solvent). 2. Passage copied from book etc., excerpt, quotation. **ĕxtrăct'** *v.t.* 1. Copy out (passage in book etc.); make extracts from (book etc.). 2. Take out by force (teeth, anything firmly fixed); draw forth (money, admission, etc.) against person's will. 3. Obtain (juices etc.) by suction, pressure, distillation, etc.); derive (pleasure, comfort, etc., *from*); deduce (principle etc. *from*). 4. (math.) Find (root of a number). **ĕxtrăc'tor** *n.*

ĕxtrăc'tion *n.* 1. Extracting; ~ *rate,* proportion of total weight of unground wheat which is converted into flour, expressed as a percentage of the weight unground. 2. Lineage, as *of Indian* ~.

ĕxtrăc'tĭve *adj.* & *n.* (Thing) of the nature of an extract; ~ *industries,* those dependent on mining and oil.

ĕx'tradīte *v.t.* Give up (fugitive foreign criminal) to the proper authorities.

ĕxtradĭ'tion *n.* Delivery of fugitive criminal to authorities of State in which crime was committed; ~ *treaty,* treaty by which countries bind themselves to extradite criminals who have committed specified offences.

ĕxtrād'ŏs *n.* (archit.) Upper or outer curve of arch (ill. ARCH).

ĕx'trajudĭ'cial (-shl) *adj.* Not belonging to the case before the court; (of opinion, confession, etc.) not made in court; outside ordinary course of law or justice. **ĕxtrajudĭ'cially** *adv.*

ĕxtramŭn'dāne *adj.* Outside of our world or of the universe.

ĕxtramūr'al *adj.* Outside the walls or boundaries of a city etc.; outside the scope of ordinary university teaching or studies.

ĕxtrān'ĕous *adj.* Of external origin; foreign *to* (object to which it is attached, etc.); not belonging (*to* matter in hand, class). **ĕxtrān'ĕously** *adv.* **ĕxtrān'ĕousnĕss** *n.*

ĕx'tra-offĭc'ial (-shl) *adj.* Not pertaining to an office.

ĕxtraord'ĭnary (-trôr-, -tra-ôr-) *adj.* Out of the usual course; exceptional, surprising; unusually great; (of officials etc.) additional, specially employed; *envoy* ~, orig., minister sent on special diplomatic business; now, diplomatic minister of 2nd class, ranking next to ambassador. **ĕxtraord'ĭnarĭly** *adv.* **ĕxtraord'ĭnarĭnĕss** *n.*

ĕx'traparŏch'ĭal (-k-) *adj.* Outside, not concerned with, the parish.

ĕxtraphȳs'ĭcal (-z-) *adj.* Not subject to physical laws.

ĕxtrăp'olāte *v.* (math.) Calculate, from known terms, a series of other terms which lie outside the range of the known terms (also fig.). **ĕxtrapolā'tion** *n.*

ĕxtraspĕc'tral *adj.* Lying outside the visible spectrum.

ĕxtraterrĕs'trĭal *adj.* Outside the earth or its atmosphere.

ĕx'tratĕrrĭtôr'ĭal *adj.* Of the privilege extended to ambassadors of being regarded as outside the territory, and therefore free from the jurisdiction, of the power to which they are sent; of a country's rights of jurisdiction over all its subjects abroad. **ĕx'tratĕrrĭtorĭăl'ĭty** *n.* Such rights and privileges.

ĕxtrăv'agance *n.* Being extravagant; absurd statement or action.

ĕxtrăv'agant *adj.* Immoderate; exceeding the bounds of reason; profuse, wasteful; (of price etc.) exorbitant. **ĕxtrăv'agantly** *adv.*

ĕxtrăvagăn'za *n.* Extravagant or fantastic musical, literary, or dramatic composition; extravagance of language or behaviour.

ĕxtrăv'asāte *v.* Force out (fluid, esp. blood) from its proper vessel; (of fluid) flow out, esp. through walls of blood-vessel etc. **ĕxtrăvasā'tion** *n.*

extravert. Var. of EXTROVERT.

ĕxtrēme' *adj.* 1. Outermost; farthest from centre; situated at either end. 2. Utmost. 3. Last (obs. exc. in ~ *unction,* (R.C. Ch.) anointing of dying person by priest). 4. (Of actions, measures, etc.) severe, stringent; (of opinions, persons, etc.) going to great lengths, not moderate. **ĕxtrēme'ly** (-ml-) *adv.* **ĕxtrēme'nĕss** *n.* **ĕxtrēme'** *n.* 1. *In the* ~, extremely. 2. Thing at either end of anything; esp. (pl.) things as remote or as different as possible; excessive degree. 3. (logic) Subject or predicate in proposition, major or minor term in syllogism; (math.) first or last term of ratio or series.

ĕxtrēm'ĭst *n.* One who holds extreme views or advocates extreme measures. **ĕxtrēm'ĭsm** *n.*

ĕxtrĕm'ĭty *n.* 1. Extreme point; very end; *the extremities,* hands and feet. 2. Extreme adversity, embarrassment, etc.; (usu. pl.) extreme measure(s).

ĕx'trĭcāte *v.t.* Disentangle, release (*from* confinement, difficulty, etc.). **ĕxtrĭcā'tion** *n.*

ĕxtrĭn'sĭc *adj.* Lying outside, not belonging, (*to*); operating from without; not inherent or essential. **ĕxtrĭn'sĭcally** *adv.*

ĕxtrôrse' *adj.* (bot., of anthers) Shedding their pollen outwards (opp. INTRORSE).

ĕx'trovērt *n.* (psychol.) One whose thoughts and activities are directed to things outside the self (opp. to INTROVERT). **ĕxtrovēr'sion** (-shn) *n.*

ĕxtrude' (-ōō-) *v.t.* Thrust out

(*from*). **ėxtru'sion** (-ōōzhn) *n.* **ėxtrus'ĭve** *adj.*

ėxūb'erant (-gz-) *adj.* Luxuriantly prolific; growing luxuriantly; overflowing, abounding; effusive, overflowing with spirits; copious, lavish in ornament. **ėxūb'erantly** *adv.* **ėxūb'erance** *n.*

ėxūb'erāte (-gz-) *v.i.* Be exuberant, abound, overflow.

ėxūde' (-gz-) *v.* Ooze out, give off (moisture etc.) like sweat. **ĕxūdā'tion, ĕx'ūdāte** *ns.* **ėxūd'atĭve** *adj.*

ėxŭlt' (-gz-) *v.i.* Rejoice exceedingly; triumph (*over*). **ėxŭl'tancy, ĕxultā'tion** *ns.* **ėxŭl'tant** *adj.* **ėxŭl'tantly** *adv.*

ėxūv'ĭae *n.pl.* Animal's cast skin, shell, or covering. **ėxūv'ĭal** *adj.* **ėxūv'ĭāte** *v.* Shed exuviae, slough. **ėxūvĭā'tion** *n.*

ĕx vōt'ō *adv.* & *n.* (Offering made) in pursuance of a vow.

eyas (ī'*a*s) *n.* Young hawk taken from nest for training, or not yet completely trained.

eye (ī) *n.* 1. Organ of sight; iris of this; region of the eyes; eye as possessing power of vision; sense of seeing; look, glance, gaze; attention, regard; estimation, opinion, judgement; *up to the* ~*s*, deeply immersed or occupied; *pipe one's* ~, cry; *open person's* ~*s*, enlighten him; *all my* ~, humbug, stuff and nonsense; (*see*) *with half an* ~, at a glance, easily; *make* ~*s at*, look amorously at, ogle; *see* ~ *to* ~, agree entirely (*with*); *in the* ~ *of*, in the direction of (the wind). 2. Thing like eye; spot on peacock's tail, wing of insect etc.; one of three spots at end of coconut; hole in needle for thread etc., hole in tool or implement for insertion of some other object; metal loop used with 'hook' for fastening dress etc.; loop of cord or rope; undeveloped bud of plant; centre of flower; leaf-bud of potato etc.

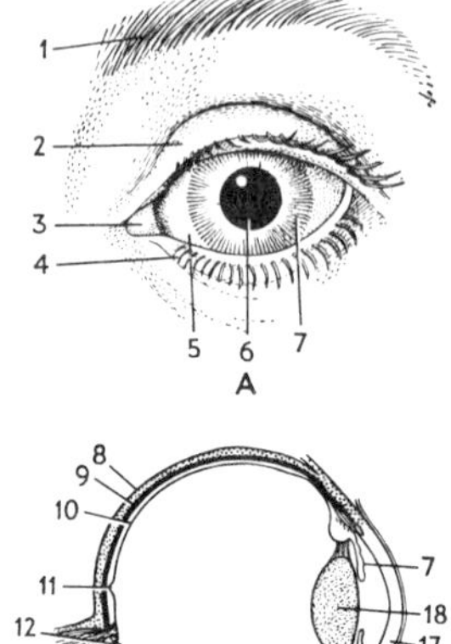

HUMAN EYE: A. EXTERNAL VIEW. B. HORIZONTAL SECTION OF EYEBALL

A. 1. Eyebrow. 2. Eyelid. 3. Nictitating membrane. 4. Eyelash. 5. Eyeball. 6. Pupil. 7. Iris. B. 8. Sclerotic. 9. Choroid or pigmented layer. 10. Retina. 11. Macula lutea. 12. Blind spot or optic disc. 13. Optic nerve surrounding blood-vessels. 14. Retinal artery. 15. Retinal vein. 16. Conjunctiva. 17. Cornea. 18. Crystalline lens

3. *eye'ball*, pupil of the eye; eye within lids and socket; ~ *bath*, -*cup*, small vessel for applying lotion etc. to eye; ~-*bolt*, bolt, bar, with circular hole through head; *eye'bright*, plant (*Euphrasia species*) formerly used as remedy for weak eyes; *eye'brow*, fringe of hair along upper orbit of eye; ~-*glass*, lens for assisting defective sight; monocle; (pl.) pair of these held in position by hand or by spring on nose; *eye'hole*, cavity or socket of eye; hole to look through; *eye'lash*, hair, row of hairs, on edge of eyelid; *eye'lid*, one of movable folds of skin with which eyes are covered or uncovered; ~-*opener*, enlightening or surprising circumstance; (U.S.) alcoholic drink, esp. in morning; *eye'piece*, lens(es) at eye-end of microscope etc.; *eye'sight*, power, faculty, of seeing; *eye'sore*, ugly object, thing that offends the sight; ~-*strain*, strained condition due to excessive or improper use of eyes; ~-*tooth*, pointed tooth just under eye, in upper or lower jaw, canine tooth; ~-*wash*, lotion for eye; (slang) humbug, blarney; ~-*witness*, one who can bear witness from his own observation. ~ *v.t.* Observe, watch. **eye'lėss** *adj.*

eye'lėt (īl-) *n.* Small hole in cloth, sail, etc., for lace, ring, rope, etc.; loophole; small eye.

eyot: see AIT.

eyrie: see AERIE.

Ezēk'ĭel (ĭ-). One of the Hebrew prophets of the 6th c. B.C.; the O.T. books of his prophecies.

Ez'ra (ĕ-). Hebrew scribe and priest of the 5th c. B.C.; O.T. book of Ezra, dealing with the return of the Jews from Babylon and the rebuilding of the Temple.

F

F, f (ĕf). 6th letter of modern English and Roman alphabet, representing Semitic *waw* (= *w*, *u*) and pre-classical Greek Ϝ and pronounced in English as a voiceless labio-dental spirant; (mus.), 4th note of 'natural' scale (C major); scale or key with this note as tonic; *F clef*, bass clef, placed on line of stave appropriate to this note

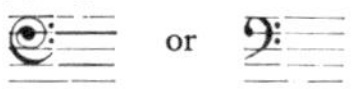

f. *abbrev.* Feet; feminine; filly; folio; foot; *forte* (= loud); franc(s); free; from.

F *abbrev.* Fine (of pencil-lead); French.

F. *abbrev.* Fahrenheit.

F.A. *abbrev.* Football Association.

f.a.a. *abbrev.* Free of all average.

F.A.A. *abbrev.* Fleet Air Arm.

fa(h) *n.* 4th note of hexachord and of major scale in 'movable-doh' systems; note F in 'fixed-doh' system. [see UT]

Fāb'ĭan *adj.* & *n.* 1. Of, like, Quintus Fabius Maximus (d. 203 B.C.) Roman consul and general, surnamed Cunctator ('Delayer') from the tactics he employed against Hannibal in the 2nd Punic War, avoiding battles and weakening the enemy by cutting off supplies and continual skirmishing. 2. (Member) of the ~ *Society*, society of English socialists advocating 'Fabian' policy rather than immediate revolutionary action, founded 1884. **Fāb'ĭanĭsm** *n.*

Fabĭus: see FABIAN.

fā'ble *n.* 1. Story, esp. of supernatural character, not founded on fact; (collect.) myths, legendary tales; idle talk. 2. Short story, esp. with animals for characters, conveying a moral; apologue. ~ *v.* (archaic & poet.) Romance, tell fictitious tales; state fictitiously; *fabled*, celebrated in fable, legendary, fictitious.

făb'liau (-ĭō) *n.* Metrical tale of medieval French poetry, often of a coarsely humorous character.

făb'rĭc *n.* Thing put together; edifice, building; frame, structure; construction, texture, tissue; (freq. *textile* ~) woven material.

făb'rĭcāte *v.t.* 1. Construct, manufacture, esp. (eng.) by welding components together, not by moulding or casting. 2. Invent (fact), forge (document). **făbrĭcā'tion, făb'rĭcātor** *ns.*

făb'ūlĭst *n.* Composer of fables or apologues; liar.

făb'ūlous *adj.* Fond of relating

fables or legends; celebrated in fable; unhistorical, legendary, incredible, absurd, exaggerated. **făb′ūlously** *adv.* **făb′ūlousnėss, făbūlŏs′ĭty** *ns.*

façade′ (-sahd) *n.* Face of building, esp. the principal front; hence, frontal appearance of anything (also fig.).

fāce *n.* 1. Front of head from forehead to chin; ~ *to* ~, confronted; ~ *to* ~ *with*, confronting; *fly in the* ~ *of*, openly disobey; *to* person's ~, openly in his sight or hearing. 2. Expression of countenance; grimace. 3. Composure, coolness, effrontery. 4. Outward show; aspect; surface; front, façade; right side, obverse; dial-plate of clock etc.; working surface of implement etc.; each surface of solid; *on the* ~ *of it*, to judge by appearance; obviously, plainly; *put a new* ~ *on*, alter aspect of; *put good, bold,* ~ *on matter*, make it look well, show courage in facing it; *save one's* ~, save one's credit, good name, or reputation. 5. ~-*ache*, facial neuralgia; ~ *card*, one of a pack of playing-cards on which a human face is represented; the king, queen, or knave; ~-*cloth*, cloth for washing the face; smooth-surfaced woollen cloth; ~-*lifting*, operation of tightening the skin of the face and removing its wrinkles in order to impart a more youthful appearance; ~-*value*, nominal value as stated on coin, note, etc.; (fig.) apparent value. ~ *v.* 1. Meet confidently or defiantly; not shrink from, stand fronting; ~ *the music*, not quail at moment of trial. 2. Present itself to; look, have face or front, in special direction; front towards, be opposite to; (mil.) turn in special direction. 3. Cover part of (garment) with another material, esp. at edge, trim, turn up *with*; cover (surface) with layer of other material; dress surface of.

fā′cer *n.* Blow in the face; sudden difficulty or problem.

fă′cėt *n.* One side of many-sided body, esp. of cut gem (ill. GEM); one segment of compound eye. **fă′cėtėd** *adj.*

facē′tiae (-shĭē) *n.pl.* Pleasantries, witticisms; (in book catalogues) books of a coarsely humorous or obscene character.

facē′tious (-shus) *adj.* Addicted to or marked by pleasantry, waggish. **facē′tiously** *adv.* **facē′tiousnėss** *n.*

fă′cia (-sha) *n.* Plate over shop-front with occupier's name etc. [var. of FASCIA].

fā′cial (-shl) *adj.* Of the face; (colloq., as *n.*) face-massage.

fā′cies (-shĭēz, -shēz) *n.* (pl. same). (geol.) One of two or more different deposits laid down at the same time in the same area (e.g. the sand-banks and mud flats of the Thames estuary, which are contemporaneous).

fă′cĭle *adj.* Easily done or won; working easily, ready, fluent; of easy temper, gentle, flexible, yielding.

fă′cĭlė prĭn′cĕps *pred. adj.* Easily first.

facĭl′ĭtāte *v.t.* Make easy, promote, help forward (action or result). **facilitā′tion** *n.*

facĭl′ĭty *n.* Being easy, absence of difficulty; unimpeded opportunity; ease or readiness of speech etc., aptitude, dexterity, fluency; pliancy.

fā′cĭng *n.* (esp.) Something with which garment is faced, esp. cuffs and collar of military jacket, differently coloured from rest; coating of different material, esp. of stone etc. on wall.

făcsĭm′ĭlė *n.* Exact copy, esp. of writing, printing, picture, etc. ~ *v.t.* Make facsimile of.

făct *n.* 1. Thing certainly known to have occurred or be true; datum of experience; thing assumed as basis for inference; what is true or existent; reality. 2. Evil deed, crime (only in *confess the* ~; *before, after, the* ~).

făc′tion *n.* Self-interested, turbulent, or unscrupulous party, esp. in politics; prevalence of party spirit. **făc′tional** (sho-), **făc′tious** (-shus) *adjs.* **făc′tiously** *adv.* **făc′tiousnėss** *n.*

făctĭ′tious (-shus) *adj.* Designedly got up, not natural, artificial. **făctĭ′tiously** *adv.* **făctĭ′tiousnėss** *n.*

făc′tĭtĭve *adj.* (gram., of verb) Expressing notion of making thing to be of a certain character (either objectively or in thought or representation).

făc′tor *n.* 1. Agent, deputy (now *rare*); merchant buying and selling on commission; (Sc.) land agent, steward. 2. (math.) One of two or more numbers etc. which when multiplied together give a given number, expression, etc. 3. Circumstance, fact, influence, contributing to result. 4. (biol.) Physiological unit held to cause development in offspring of a character present in parent, gene. 5. ~ *of safety*, ratio between the load which a structure or material can support and the load which it is required to support.

făctor′ĭal *adj.* Of a factor or a factorial. ~ *n.* (math.) Product of series of factors in arithmetical progression; product of integer multiplied by all lower integers.

făc′tory *n.* 1. Building or range of buildings with plant for manufacture of goods; *F*~ *Acts*, statutes of 1802, 1833, etc., regulating conduct of factories in interest of employees. 2. Merchant company's foreign trading station.

făctōt′um *n.* Man of all work; servant managing his master's affairs.

făc′tūal *adj.* Concerned with, of the nature of, fact. **făc′tūally** *adv.* **făc′tualnėss** *n.*

făc′ūla *n.* (pl. -*lae*). (astron.) Bright spot or streak on sun.

făc′ultatĭve *adj.* Permissive; optional; contingent; of a faculty.

făc′ulty *n.* 1. Aptitude for any special kind of action; power inherent in the body or an organ; a mental power (e.g. will, reason). 2. One of the departments of learning at a university (esp., one of the traditional *four faculties*, Theology, Law, Medicine, and Arts); masters and doctors (sometimes also students) in any of these; members of a particular profession, esp. medicine; (U.S.) whole teaching staff of college or university. 3. Liberty of doing something given by law or a superior; authorization, licence, dispensation (esp. ecclesiastical).

făd *n.* Pet notion or rule of action, craze. **fădd′ĭsh, fădd′y** *adjs.* **fădd′ĭsm, fădd′ĭst** *ns.*

fāde *v.* Droop, wither, lose freshness and vigour; (of colour etc.) grow dim or pale; cause to lose colour; disappear gradually. ~ *in, out*, cause (cinema picture) to appear or disappear gradually, (transf. of sound films and broadcasting) increase or reduce (sound) from or to inaudibility. ~ *n.* Fading of cinema picture etc. **fāde′lėss** (-dl-) *adj.* **fāde′lėssly** *adv.* **fād′ĭng** *n.* (esp.) Periodic diminution of strength of distant signals in radio reception.

fae′cēs (fē-) *n.pl.* 1. Sediment. 2. Excrement; waste matter discharged from bowels. **faec′al** *adj.*

fā′erĭe *n.* Fairyland; the fairies; the imaginary world portrayed in Spenser's *Faerie Queene*. ~ *adj.* Of faerie; visionary, unreal. [Spenser's archaic variant of *fairy*]

făg *v.* 1. Toil painfully; (of occupation) tire, make weary. 2. (At schools, of seniors) use the service of (juniors), (of juniors) do service for seniors. ~ *n.* 1. Drudgery; unwelcome task; exhaustion. 2. (At schools) junior who has to fag. 3. (slang) Cigarette; ~-*end*, inferior or useless remnant of anything, esp. of cigar or cigarette; extreme end.

făg(g)′ot *n.* 1. Bundle of sticks or twigs bound together as fuel; bundle of iron or steel rods bound together for reheating or welding. 2. (pl.) Dish of chopped liver, lights, etc., made into balls or rolls. 3. ~-*stitch*, stitch used in faggoting (sense 2) (ill. STITCH). ~ *v.* Bind in faggot(s); make faggots; ornament (needlework) with faggoting, join (materials) with faggot-stitch. **făgg′otĭng** *n.* (needlework) 1. Drawn-thread work in which a few cross-threads are fastened together in the middle like faggots. 2. Method of joining two pieces of material together, resembling ~ 1.

fah: see FA.

Fahr′enheit (-hīt), Gabriel Daniel (1686–1736). Prussian physicist; inventor of mercurial thermometer. ~ *adj.* (abbrev. F, Fahr.) According to ~ scale; ~ *thermometer, scale*, etc., with 32° and

212° as freezing- and boiling-points of water.

fai'ble *n.* (fencing) Part of sword-blade nearest point.

faience (fahyahṅs') *n.* Painted and glazed earthenware, majolica. [Fr., = *Faenza*, Italy, site of factory]

fail *n.* *Without* ~ (emphasizing injunction or promise), for certain, irrespective of hindrances. ~ *v.* 1. Be missing or insufficient; not suffice for needs of (person); run short. 2. Neglect, not remember or not choose, *to*. 3. Become extinct, die away; flag, break down; prove misleading, disappoint hopes of. 4. Be insufficiently equipped *in*; not succeed in attainment *of*; not succeed (*in* doing, *to* do); miscarry, come to nothing. 5. Suspend payment; go bankrupt. 6. Be rejected, reject, as candidate.

fail'ĭng *n.* (esp.) Foible, shortcoming, weakness. ~ *prep.* In default of.

fail'ure (-yer) *n.* Non-occurrence, non-performance; running short; breaking down; ill success; insolvency; unsuccessful person, thing, or attempt.

fain *pred. adj.* (archaic) Willing under the circumstances *to*; left with no alternative but *to*. ~ *adv.* Gladly, willingly (as in *would* ~).

faint *adj.* 1. Sluggish; timid; feeble; dim, indistinct, pale. 2. Giddy or languid with fear, hunger, etc., inclined to swoon; *~-heart*, coward; *~-hearted* (*adj.*); *~-heartedly* (*adv.*), *~-heartedness* (*n.*). **faint'ish** *adj.* **faint'ly** *adv.* **faint'nėss** *n.* **faint** *v.* Lose courage, give way, flag (archaic); swoon, lose consciousness. ~ *n.* Swoon.

fair[1] *n.* Periodical gathering for sale of goods, often with shows and entertainments, at place and time fixed by charter, statute, or custom.

fair[2] *adj.* 1. Beautiful; satisfactory, abundant; attractive, pleasing, at first sight or hearing, specious, plausible. 2. (Of complexion etc.) light, not dark. 3. Clean, clear, unblemished; just, unbiased, equitable, legitimate. 4. Of moderate quality; not bad, pretty good. 5. Favourable, promising; gentle; unobstructed. 6. (As *n.*) what is fair; (archaic) a woman. 7. ~ *copy*, copy of document etc. made from rough copy or after final correction; *fair'way*, navigable channel, usual course of vessel(s); (golf) regular track, short-grassed part of course between tee and putting-green; *~-weather*, fit only for fine weather (freq. fig. of friends etc.). **fair'ĭsh** *adj.* **fair'nėss** *n.* **fair** *adv.* *Speak* (person) ~, address him courteously; *write out* ~, clearly; *hit, fight*, ~, according to the rules; *strike, fall*, etc. ~, straight, clean; *bid* ~ *to do*, show promise of doing.

fair'ĭng[1] *n.* Present bought at a fair.

fair'ĭng[2] *n.* (eng.) Shielding round struts of aircraft, supports of bridge, etc., reducing resistance to air- or water-flow; streamlining.

Fair Isle. One of the Shetland Islands; (attrib.) knitted in coloured wools in designs characteristic of the island (alleged to be Moorish and to be traceable to a wrecked ship of the Spanish Armada). [*fair*, Norw., = 'sheep']

fair'ly *adv.* In a fair manner; (also) utterly, completely; rather, tolerably.

fair'y *n.* Small supernatural being with magical powers; ~ *cycle*, kind of child's small bicycle; ~ *lamps, lights*, small coloured lights used in decorative illuminations; *fairy'land*, country of fairies, enchanted land of fancy; ~ *ring*, circular band of darker grass caused by fungi, pop. attributed to fairy dancing; *~-tale*, tale about fairies; unreal or incredible story; falsehood. ~ *adj.* Of fairies; imaginary, fictitious; fairy-like, beautiful and delicate or small.

fait accompli (fāt ăkawṅ'plē) *n.* Accomplished fact.

faith *n.* Reliance, trust, *in*; belief founded on authority; (theol.) belief in religious doctrines, esp. such as affects character and conduct, spiritual apprehension of divine truth apart from proof; system of religious belief; things (to be) believed; warrant; promise, engagement; loyalty, fidelity; *good* ~, honesty of intention; *bad* ~, intent to deceive; *~-cure, -healing*, cure, healing, by power of faith, not drugs etc.

faith'ful *adj.* Loyal, constant (*to*); conscientious; trustworthy; true to fact, the original, etc., accurate; *the* ~, (pl.) true believers, esp. Mohammedans; *Father of the* ~, the caliph. **faith'fully** *adv.* (esp., colloq.) With binding assurances; *yours* ~, customary formula for closing business letter. **faith'fulnėss** *n.*

faith'lėss *adj.* (esp.) Perfidious, false to promises; unreliable. **faith'lėssly** *adv.* **faith'lėssnėss** *n.*

fāke *v.t.* Do *up*; make presentable or specious; contrive out of poor material; tamper with, contrive, in order to deceive. ~ *n.* (freq. attrib.) Piece of faking; faked thing; dodge, sham, cooked report.

fakir *n.* 1. (fah'kēr, fā-) Moslem (or Hindu) religious mendicant, devotee. 2. (fā'ker) (U.S., erron. for) Faker, esp. = pedlar. [Arab. *faqir* poor man]

Făl'angist *adj.* & *n.* (Member) of the Spanish Fascist organization *Falange Española*. [Span. *falange* phalanx]

făl'bala *n.* Flounce, trimming.

făl'cāte *adj.* (anat., bot., zool.) Hooked, sickle-shaped. **făl'cātėd** *adj.* (astron., of moon etc.) Sickle-shaped.

fal'chion (fawl'chon) *n.* Broad curved convex-edged sword (ill. SWORD).

făl'cifōrm *adj.* (anat.) Sickle-shaped.

falcon (faw(l)'kn) *n.* Small diurnal bird of prey, with short hooked beak and powerful claws, esp. one trained to pursuit of other birds or game, usu. the peregrine ~ (*Falco peregrinus*); (in falconry) the female of this. **falc'oner** *n.* Keeper and trainer of hawks; one who hunts with hawks. **falc'onry** *n.* Hawking; breeding and training of hawks.

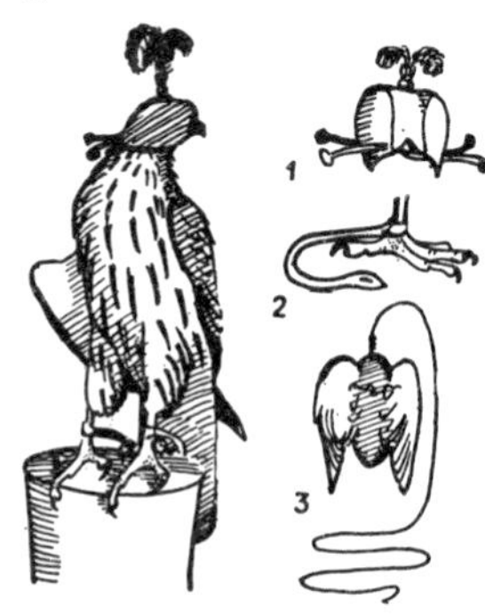

FALCONRY

1. Hood. 2. Jess. 3. Lure.

falc'onėt (fawk-) *n.* (hist.) Light cannon of 15th–17th centuries.

fălderăl' *n.* Gewgaw, trifle. [f. meaningless refrain in songs]

fald'stōōl (faw-) *n.* Armless chair, made to fold up, used by bishop etc. when not occupying throne or when officiating in any but his own church; movable folding stool or desk for kneeling at, esp. one used by sovereign at coronation; small desk from which litany is said.

Falēr'nian *adj.* Of the *ager Falernus* in ancient Campania, Italy, which produced a famous wine. ~ *n.* This wine.

Falkland Islands (fawk-). Group of islands, in British possession, in the S. Atlantic, discovered by John Davis in 1592.

fall (fawl) *v.i.* (past t. *fell*, past part. *fall'en*). 1. Descend freely, drop, lose high position; become detached and drop off; hang down; (of speech etc.) issue from; (of the young of animals) be born. 2. Sink, descend to lower level; decline; slope; subside, ebb, abate, decrease, diminish; (of river etc.) discharge itself *into*; (of face) show sudden dismay; droop; be cast down. 3. Cease to stand; come, be brought, (suddenly) to the ground; (*wicket* ~*s*, in cricket, batsman is out); prostrate oneself; succumb to attack or opposing force; yield to temptation; (of woman) lose chastity; drop down wounded or dead, die by violence; (cards) be captured by higher card; stumble, be drawn or forced, *into* (danger etc.). 4. (Of missile, sight, light, etc.) take direction, be directed, settle; have its situation *in* certain place, *on* certain object etc.; (of choice, lot, etc.) light *upon*; be allotted or apportioned; come as burden or duty. 5. Come by chance into certain position etc.; come naturally. 6. Pass suddenly, accidentally, or in the course of events, into a certain condition, become; ~ *in love*, become enamoured. 7. Come to pass, befall; come in due course; (of season etc.) occur at stated time, within certain limits etc. 8. With preps.: ~ *behind*, be outstripped by; ~ *for*, (colloq., orig. U.S.) be captivated by; ~ *into*, take one's place in (line etc.); engage, enter upon (talk etc.); drop into (habit); ~ *(up)on*, make hostile descent or attack on; ~ *to*, take to, begin; ~ *under*, be classified among; be subjected to (observation etc.). 9. With advs.: ~ *away*, desert, revolt; apostatize; decay, vanish; ~ *back*, retreat, give way; ~ *back (up)on*, have recourse to; ~ *behind*, lag; ~ *foul of*, come into collision with; quarrel with, attack; ~ *in*, (mil.) take, cause to take, places in line; give way inwards; (of debt etc.) become due; (of lease) run out; ~ *in with*, happen to meet; accede to (views); agree with, coincide with, humour; ~ *off*, withdraw, decrease, degenerate; (of ship) refuse to answer helm; ~ *out*, quarrel; come to pass, result *well* etc.; (mil.) leave the ranks; ~*-out* (*n.*) radio-active refuse of a nuclear explosion; ~ *short*, be or become insufficient; (of missile) not go far enough; ~ *through*, miscarry, fail; ~ *to*, begin eating or fighting. 10. *falling sickness*, old name for epilepsy; *falling star*, meteor, shooting star. ~ *n.* Act of falling; also or esp.: 1. Amount of rain etc. that falls. 2. (now chiefly U.S.) Autumn. 3. (freq. pl.) Cataract, cascade; ~*-line*, line joining waterfalls on parallel rivers. 4. Downward trend, amount of descent. 5. Wrestling-bout, throw in this. 6. Rope of hoisting-tackle 7. Amount of timber cut down. 8. Succumbing to temptation; *the F~ (of man)*, Adam's sin and its results.

făll'acy *n.* Misleading argument, sophism; (logic) material or formal flaw which vitiates a syllogism; delusion, error; unsoundness, delusiveness, disappointing quality. **fallā'cious** (-shus) *adj.* **fallā'ciously** *adv.* **fallā'ciousnėss** *n.*

făl-lăl' *n.* Piece of finery.

făll'ible *adj.* Liable to err or be erroneous. **făllibĭl'ity** *n.*

Fallŏp'ian tube. Upper part of oviduct in humans and other mammals (ill. PELVIS). [discovered by G. *Falloppio*, Italian physician (1523–62)]

făll'ow[1] (-ō) *n.* & *adj.* (Ground) ploughed and harrowed but left uncropped for a year. ~ *v.t.* Plough and break up (land) for sowing or to destroy weeds.

făll'ow[2] (-ō) *adj.* Of pale brownish or reddish yellow (now only in ~ *deer*, a species (*Cervus dama*) smaller than the red deer and usu. dappled).

false (fawls, fŏls) *adj.* 1. Erroneous; wrong; incorrect. 2. Lying, deceitful; treacherous, unfaithful *to*; deceptive; spurious, sham, artificial. 3. Improperly so called, pseudo-; subsidiary, supplementary; substituted for, supplementing. 4. ~ *alarm*, alarm given without good cause, either to deceive or under misapprehension of danger; ~ *bottom*, partition built close to bottom as in a box or trunk; ~ *card*, card played contrary to usual custom, in order to mislead opponents; ~ *colours*, flag one has no right to (freq. fig.); ~ *concord*, (gram.) breach of rules for 'agreement' of words in sentence; ~ *dawn*, transient light in east, freq. preceding true dawn by about an hour; ~ *imprisonment*, illegal imprisonment or restraint; ~ *quantity*, incorrect length of vowel in (Latin) verse or pronunciation; ~ *position*, one compelling person to seem inconsistent or act inconsistently with his real character or aims; ~ *pretences*, misrepresentations meant to give false impression; ~ *start*, wrong start in racing; ~ *step*, stumble; transgression; *false'work*, (eng.) temporary supports enabling construction of building etc. to proceed until it is self-supporting. **false'ly** (-sl-) *adv.* **false'nėss, fal'sĭty** *ns.* **false** *adv.* *Play* (person) ~, cheat, betray.

false'hood (fawls-h-, fŏls-) *n.* Falsity; something untrue; contrariety to fact; lying, lie(s).

falsĕtt'ō (fawl-, fŏl-) *n.* 'Head voice' in men, as used by male altos; (fig.) high voice of indignation.

fals'ifȳ (fawl-, fŏl-) *v.t.* Fraudulently alter (document); misrepresent; make wrong, pervert; disappoint (hope, fear, etc.). **falsifĭcā'tion** *n.*

Fal'staff (fawl'stahf, fŏl-), Sir John. A fat, convivial, good-humoured braggart in Shakespeare's 'Henry IV' and 'Merry Wives of Windsor'. **Falstaff'ian** *adj.*

fal'ter (fawl-, fŏl-) *v.* Stumble, stagger, go unsteadily; stammer, speak hesitatingly; waver, lose courage, flinch. **fal'teringly** *adv.*

fāme *n.* Public report, renown; reputation, good reputation; renown, celebrity; *house of ill* ~, brothel. ~ *v.t.* 1. (pass.) Be currently reported. 2. (past part.) Famous, much spoken of.

famĭl'ial *adj.* Of, occurring in, characteristic of (members of) a family.

famĭl'iar (-lyar) *adj.* 1. Extremely friendly, intimate (*with*); closely acquainted *with* (some subject); ~ *spirit*, demon attending and obeying magician etc. 2. Well-known, no longer novel, (*to*); common, current, usual. 3. Unceremonious, free, over-free; amorously or sexually intimate (*with*). **famĭl'iarly** *adv.* **famĭl'iar** *n.* 1. (R.C. Ch.) Person rendering domestic but not menial services in household of pope or bishop; (hist.) officer of Inquisition, chiefly employed in arresting and imprisoning accused. 2. Intimate friend or associate. 3. Familiar spirit.

famĭliă'rĭty *n.* Close intercourse, intimacy *with* (person, subject); amorous intimacy; (pl.) caresses etc.; unceremoniousness, treating of inferiors or superiors as equals.

famĭl'iarīze (-lya-) *v.t.* Make (thing) well known; make well acquainted or at home *with*. **famĭliarīz'ātion** *n.*

famille (fămē') *n.* ~ *rose*, *verte* (vārt), etc., Chinese enamelled porcelain (chiefly 18th-c.) of which the predominant colour is red, green, etc. [Fr., = 'family']

făm'ĭly *n.* Members of household, parents, children, servants, etc.; set of parents and children, or of relations, whether living together or not; person's children; all descendants of common ancestor, house, lineage; race, group of peoples from common stock; group of objects, languages, etc., distinguished by common features; (biol.) grouping above *genus* and below *order*, with Latin name ending in *-idae* for zoological families and usu. in *-aceae* for plant families; ~ *allowance*: see ALLOWANCE; ~ *bible*, large bible with fly-leaves for registering births etc.; ~ *likeness*, that between relations, vague resemblance; ~ *man*, man with family, domestic person; ~ *tree*, genealogical tree; *in the* ~ *way*, pregnant.

făm'ine *n.* Extreme scarcity of food in district etc.; dearth of something specified; hunger, starvation; ~ *prices*, prices raised by scarcity.

făm'ish *v.* Reduce, be reduced, to extreme hunger.

fām'ous *adj.* Celebrated (*for*); well known; (colloq.) capital, excellent. **fām'ously** *adv.*

făm'ūlus *n.* (pl. *-lī*). Attendant on magician.

făn[1] *n.* 1. Winnowing-machine. 2. Instrument, usu. folding and sector-shaped when spread out, on radiating ribs, for agitating air to cool face; anything so spread out, as bird's tail, wing, leaf, kind of ornamental vaulting; rotating apparatus giving current of air for ventilation, etc.; (naut.) (blade of) screw, propeller; (in windmill) small sail for keeping head towards wind (ill. WINDMILL); ~ *belt*, belt driving radiator fan on car engine; ~*-light*, fan-shaped window over door (ill. DOOR); ~ *-tail*, fan-shaped tail or end; kind of pigeon with fan-shaped tail; ~ *tracery*, the elaborate tracery of a fan vault; ~ *vault, vaulting*, vault, vaulting, with ribs diverging like sticks of a fan, characteristic of English architecture of the 15th c. (ill. VAULT). ~ *v.* 1. Winnow (corn); winnow away (chaff). 2. Sweep *away* (as) by wind from fan; move (air) with fan; drive current of air (as) with fan upon, to cool (face etc.) or to kindle (flame); (of breeze) blow gently on, cool. 3. Spread *out* in fan shape, esp. of troops after a break-through **fănn'er** *n.* Winnowing-machine; vane or wheel of this.

făn[2] *n.* (slang) Devotee of specified amusement, or of a particular person or thing. [abbrev. of *fanatic*]

fanăt'ĭc *n.* & *adj.* (Person) filled with excessive and mistaken enthusiasm, esp. in religion. **fanăt'ĭcal** *adj.* **fanăt'ĭcally** *adv.* **fanăt'ĭcism** *n.*

făn'cier *n.* Connoisseur in some article or animal (as *bird-~, rose-~*).

făn'ciful *adj.* Indulging in fancies, whimsical, capricious; fantastically designed, ornamented, etc., odd-looking; imaginary, unreal. **făn'cifully** *adv.* **făn'cifulnėss** *n.*

făn'cy *n.* 1. Delusion; unfounded belief. 2. Faculty of calling up things not present, of inventing imagery; mental image; supposition resting on no solid grounds, arbitrary notion. 3. Caprice, whim; individual taste, inclination; *the* ~, those who have a certain hobby, fanciers, esp. patrons of boxing; ~ *free*, not in love; *~-man*, sweetheart; (slang) man living on prostitute's earnings. ~ *adj.* Ornamental, not plain; (of flowers etc.) particoloured; capricious, whimsical, extravagant; based on imagination, not fact; (of animal) bred for particular 'points' or qualities; ~ *dress*, masquerade costume; ~ *fair*, bazaar for sale of fancy goods; *~-work*, ornamental needlework etc. ~ *v.t.* 1. Picture oneself; conceive, imagine; be inclined to suppose, rather think. 2. (colloq.) Have good conceit of (one*self* etc.); take a fancy to, like. 3. Breed, grow (animals, plants) in order to develop certain conventional points.

fandăng'le (-nggl) *n.* Fantastic ornament, tomfoolery.

făndăng'ō (-ngg-) *n.* Lively Spanish dance in $\frac{3}{4}$ time; tune for this.

fāne *n.* (poet.) Temple.

făn'fāre *n.* Flourish of trumpets, bugles, etc.

fănfăronāde' *n.* Arrogant talk, brag; fanfare.

făng *n.* Canine tooth, esp. of dogs and wolves; serpent's venom-tooth (ill. ADDER); spike of tool held in the stock (ill. DRILL); (prong of) root of tooth.

făn'-tăn' *n.* Chinese gambling game in which a number of small coins are placed under a bowl and the players bet as to what will be the remainder when the pile is divided by four. [Chin. *fan-t'an* repeated divisions]

făntasia (-ā'zĭa, -azē'a, -ah'zĭa) *n.* Musical composition in which form is subservient to fancy.

făn'tăst, ph- *n.* Visionary, dreamer.

făntăs'tĭc *adj.* Extravagantly fanciful, capricious, eccentric; grotesque or quaint in design etc.; (colloq.) incredible. **făntăs'tĭcally** *adv.* **făntăs'tĭcalnėss, făntăstĭcăl'ĭty** *ns.*

făn'tasy, ph- *n.* Image-making faculty, esp. when extravagant or visionary; mental image; fantastic design; fantasia; whimsical speculation.

Făn'tee *n.* Member, language, of a Negro people inhabiting Ghana.

F.A.N.Y. *abbrev.* First Aid Nursing Yeomanry.

F.A.O. *abbrev.* Food and Agriculture Organization.

fär *adv.* At a great distance, a long way off; to a great distance or advanced point; by a great interval, by much; *so* ~, to such a distance; up to now; *how* ~, to what extent; *as* ~ *as*, right to, not short of; *as* ~ *as, so* ~ *as, in so* ~ *as*, to whatever extent; *~-away*, remote, long-past; (of look etc.) absent, dreamy; *~-between*, infrequent; *~-famed*, widely known; *~-fetched*, (of simile, illustration, etc.) studiously sought out, strained; *~-flung*, (rhet.) widely extended; ~ *gone*, advanced; very ill, very drunk, much in debt, etc.; ~ *off*, remote; *~-reaching*, widely applicable; carrying many consequences; *~-seeing*, prescient, prudent; *~-sighted*, far-seeing; seeing distant things more clearly than near ones. ~ *adj.* Distant, remote; *F~ East*, remote eastern regions of Old World, esp. India, China, and Japan; *F~ West*, (U.S.) more remote area to west of earlier U.S. settlements; the States of the U.S. west of the Great Plains. ~ *n.* A distance; *surpass* etc. *by* ~, by a large amount.

fă'rad *n.* Electro-magnetic unit of capacity; capacity of conductor or condenser in which an increase of one coulomb in the charge raises the potential by one volt. [f. FARADAY]

Fă'raday, Michael (1791–1867). English physicist and chemist; famous for his discovery of electric and magneto-electric induction and for his work on electrolysis.

färce[1] *n.* Dramatic work with sole object of exciting laughter; this species of drama; absurdly futile proceeding, pretence, mockery. **fär'cical** *adj.* **fär'cically** *adv.* **färcicăl'ĭty** *n.*

färce[2] *v.t.* (archaic) Season, spice, stuff. ~ *n.* Forcemeat.

fär'cy *n.* Slow chronic disease of oxen etc., caused by a fungus.

färd'el *n.* (archaic) Bundle, burden.

fāre *v.i.* 1. Journey, go, travel (poet.). 2. Happen, turn out; get on *well, ill*, etc., have specified luck. 3. Be entertained, be fed, feed oneself, *well*, etc. ~ *n.* 1. Cost of passenger's conveyance, passage-money. 2. Food provided.

fārewĕll' (-rw-), *int.* Good-bye! ~ *n.* Leave-taking, parting good wishes.

farīn'a *n.* Flour or meal of corn, nuts, or starchy roots; powdery substance; (chem.) starch. **fărinā'ceous** (-sh*us*) *adj.*

fă'rĭnōse (-s) *adj.* Mealy, sprinkled with powder.

färm *n.* Tract of land (orig. one held on lease) used for cultivation; also, tract of water used for breeding oysters etc.; dwelling-place attached to farm; *~-hand*, worker on farm; *farmhouse*, dwelling-house of farm; *~-stead*, farm with buildings on it; *farmyard*, enclosure attached to farmhouse. ~ *v.* 1. Cultivate, till; till the soil, be a farmer. 2. Take proceeds of (tax, office, etc.) on payment of fixed sum; let (*out*) proceeds of (tax etc.) to person for fixed sum; let labour of (persons) for hire. 3. Contract to maintain and care for (persons, esp. children) for fixed sum. **färm'er** *n.* One who farms (esp. land); *~-general*, (hist.) one who, under the French monarchy, farmed the taxes of a particular district.

fär'ō *n.* Gambling card-game in which players bet on the order in which certain cards will appear when taken singly from top of pack. [f. PHARAOH]

Faröe Islands (fär'ō). Group of islands in the N. Atlantic belonging to Denmark; capital, Thorshavn.

farouche' (-ōōsh) *adj.* Sullen, shy.

farrăg'ō (*or* -rah-) *n.* Medley, hotchpotch. [L, = 'mixed fodder' (*far* corn)]

fă'rrier *n.* Shoeing-smith; horse-doctor; N.C.O. in charge of cavalry regiment's horses. **fă'rriery** *n.*

fă'rrow (-ō) *n.* Giving birth to, litter of, pigs. ~ *v.* Produce (pigs); produce pigs.

färth'er (-dh) *adv.* To or at a more advanced point or greater extent or distance; in addition, also, besides, moreover. ~ *adj.* More extended; additional, more; more distant or advanced. ~ *v.t.* (rare) Further. **färth'ermōst** *adj.* **färth'ėst** *adj.* Most distant; *at* (*the*) ~, at the greatest distance, at latest, at most. ~ *adv.* To, at, the greatest distance.

färth'ĭng (-dh-) *n.* Quarter of a penny; bronze coin worth this; least possible amount.

färth'ĭngāle (-dhĭngg-) *n.* Device for making the skirt stand out from the body, worn by women in 16th and 17th centuries, and consisting either of a petticoat with whalebone hoops or of a stiff horseshoe-shaped cushion; ~ *chair*, 17th-c. chair with wide seat, low straight back, and no arms (ill. CHAIR).

FARTHINGALE DRESSES: A. SPANISH. B. FRENCH

f.a.s. *abbrev.* Free alongside ship.

făs'cēs (-sēz) *n.pl.* Bundle of wooden rods with axe in middle, orig. symbol of king's authority in

FASCES

ancient Rome, carried before Roman consul or other high official (6, 12, etc., bundles acc. to rank); this as emblem of Italian FASCISTS. [L pl. of *fascis* bundle]

fă'sci (-shē) *n.pl.* Groups of men organized politically, such as those in Sicily *c* 1895 and those of the FASCISTS.

fascia (făsh'ĭa) *n.* 1. (archit.) Long flat surface of wood or stone under eaves or cornice (ill. ORDER) (cf. FACIA). 2. (anat.) Thin sheet of connective tissue separating muscle layers and ensheathing muscle bundles (ill. MUSCLE). 3. Stripe, band, fillet, belt.

fă'sciātėd (-shĭ-) *adj.* 1. (bot., of contiguous parts) Compressed, growing into one. 2. Striped. **făsciā'tion** *n.*

făs'cĭcle, făs'cĭcūle *n.* 1. One part of book published by instalments. 2. (bot. etc.) Bunch, bundle. **fascĭc'ūlar, fascĭc'ūlate, -ātėd** *adjs.* **fascĭcūlā'tion** *n.*

făs'cĭnāte *v.t.* Deprive (victim) of power of escape or resistance by one's look or presence (esp. of serpents); attract irresistibly, enchant, charm. **făs'cĭnātĭng** *adj.* **făs'cĭnātĭngly** *adv.* **făscĭnā'tion** *n.*

făs'cĭnātor *n.* (esp., hist.) Woman's scarf or hood of soft material worn over hair.

făscine' (-sēn) *n.* Long faggot used for engineering purposes, esp. in war for lining trenches, making batteries, etc.

Făs'cĭsm (făsh-, făs-), ***fascis'mō*** (-shēz-) *n.* Principles and organization of Fascists. **Făs'cĭst** *adj.* & *n.* (Member, supporter) of a body of Italian nationalists organized in 1919 to oppose communism in Italy; as the *Partito Nazionale Fascista* it assumed control of the government in Oct. 1922 and retained it until 1943, its leader Benito MUSSOLINI being dictator; (transf.) (member) of similar organizations in other countries; (person) having fascist sympathies or convictions. [see FASCES]

făsh *v.t.* & *n.* (Sc.) Bother, trouble, inconvenience.

făsh'ion (-shn) *n.* 1. Make, shape; style, pattern, manner; *after, in, a* ~, tolerably, somehow or other, not too well. 2. Prevailing custom, esp. in dress; *the* ~, mode of dress, speech, etc., adopted in society for time being; person, thing, temporarily admired or discussed; *man* etc. *of* ~, person of social standing, moving in and conforming with upper-class society; ~*-plate*, engraved, often coloured picture of person(s) wearing clothes of latest designs. ~ *v.t.* Give shape to, form, mould.

făsh'ĭonable (-shon-) *adj.* Following, suited to, the fashion; characteristic of, treating of, patronized by, persons of fashion. **făsh'ionablenėss** *n.* **făsh'ionably** *adv.*

fast[1] (-ah-) *v.i.* 1. Abstain from all or some kinds of food as religious observance or in sign of mourning. 2. Go without food. ~ *n.* Act of fasting; season or day appointed for fasting; going without food; ~*-day*, day appointed for fasting.

fast[2] (-ah-) *adj.* 1. Firmly fixed or attached; (of friends) steadfast; (of colour etc.) not fading or washing out. 2. Rapid, quick-moving; producing quick movement; (of watch etc.) more advanced than standard time; (of bowler, at cricket) bowling fast balls; (of persons) dissipated (see below). ~ *adv.* 1. Firmly; fixedly; tightly; securely. 2. (archaic & poet.) Close *beside, upon,* etc. 3. Quickly; in quick succession; *live* ~, live in a dissipated way; expend much energy in short time.

fast'en (fah'sn) *v.* 1. Make fast, attach, fix; secure by some tie or bond; become fast. 2. Direct (look, thoughts, etc.) keenly (*up*)*on*; fix (nickname etc.) (*up*)*on*; ~ *upon*, lay hold of, single out for attack, seize upon (pretext). **fast'ener** (fah'sn*er*), **fast'enĭng** *ns.*

făstĭd'ious *adj.* Easily disgusted, squeamish, hard to please. **făstĭd'ĭously** *adv.* **făstĭd'ĭousnėss** *n.*

făstĭ'gĭāte *adj.* (bot.) With conical or tapering outline; with many branches more or less parallel to stem.

fast'nėss (-ah-) *n.* (esp.) Stronghold, fortress.

făt *adj.* 1. Fed up for slaughter, fatted; well-fed, plump; corpulent; thick, substantial (esp. of printing-type). 2. Greasy, oily, unctuous; (U.S., of wood) resinous; (of clay etc.) sticky. 3. Fertile, rich; abundant, plentiful; (slang, of actor's part) offering abundant opportunity for skill, display, etc.; *a* ~ *lot*, (iron.) very little. 4. ~*-head*, (colloq.) dolt; ~*-witted*, (colloq.) stupid. ~ *n.* 1. Fat part of anything; *live on the* ~ *of the land*, have the best of everything. 2. Oily substance composing fat parts of animal bodies; (chem.) one of the organic compounds of which animal fats are composed, glyceryl ester of a fatty acid. 3. (colloq. or slang) Newspaper 'scoop'; actor's part enabling him to appear to advantage, etc. ~ *v.* Fatten; *kill the fatted calf* (see Luke xv), receive returned prodigal with joy. **făt'lėss, fătt'ĭsh** *adjs.* **făt'nėss** *n.*

fāt'al *adj.* 1. Like fate, inevitable, necessary; of, appointed by, destiny; ~ *sisters*, the Fates. 2. Fateful, important, decisive. 3. Destructive, ruinous, ending in death; deadly, sure to kill. **fāt'ally** *adv.*

fāt'alĭsm *n.* Belief that all events are predetermined by arbitrary decree; submission to all that happens as inevitable. **fāt'alist** *adj.* & *n.* **fātalĭs'tĭc** *adj.* **fātalĭs'tĭcally** *adv.*

fatăl'ĭty *n.* 1. Subjection to, supremacy of, fate; predestined liability to disaster; fatal influence. 2. Misfortune, calamity; death by accident, in war, etc.

fāt'alize *v.* Incline to fatalism; subject to government by fate.

Fa'ta Mŏr̄ga'na (fah-, -gah-). The Italian name of Morgan le Fay, ('the fairy'), sister of King ARTHUR, legends of whom are found in Sicily, introduced perh. by Norman settlers there; applied to a mirage seen on S. Italian and Sicilian coasts, which magnifies vertically so that buildings appear like Morgan's fairy palaces.

fāte *n.* 1. Power predetermining events unalterably from eternity; (myth.) goddess of destiny; *the F*~*s*, the three Greek goddesses of destiny, Clotho, Lachesis, and Atropos. 2. What is destined to happen; appointed lot of person etc.; ultimate condition, destiny; death, destruction, ruin. ~ *v.t.* (usu. pass.) Preordain; *fated*, doomed to calamity.

fāte'ful (-tf-) *adj.* Prophetic; fraught with destiny, important, decisive; controlled by, showing power of, fate. **fāte'fully** *adv.*

fa'ther (fahdh-) *n.* 1. Male parent; father-in-law; step-father; one who has adopted a child; progenitor, forefather. 2. Originator, designer, early leader; one who deserves filial reverence; religious teacher or counsellor; ~ *of lies* (see John viii. 44), the Devil; *the F*~*s* (*of the Church*), Christian writers of first five centuries. 3. *The F*~, God; (theol.) first person of the Trinity. 4. (eccles.) Confessor, spiritual director; priest belonging to religious order or congregation;

superior of monastic house; *Right, Most, Reverend F~ in God*, titles of bishop, archbishop; *the Holy F~*, the Pope. 5. Venerable person, god; oldest member, doyen; (pl.) leading men, elders; *Conscript F~s*, senators of ancient Rome. 6. *~-in-law*, father of one's wife or husband; *fatherland*, one's native country; *the Fatherland*, Germany. **fa'therlėss, fa'therlīke, fa'therly** *adjs.* **fa'therhood, fa'therlinėss** *ns.* **fa'ther** *v.t.* Beget, be the father of; originate (statement etc.); pass as, confess oneself, the father, author, of; govern paternally; fix paternity of (child, book, etc.) *upon.*

făth'om (-dh-) *n.* Measure of 6 feet, chiefly used in soundings; quantity of wood 6 ft square in section. ~ *v.t.* Measure with fathom-line, sound (depth of water); (fig.) get to the bottom of, comprehend. **făth'ŏmlėss** *adj.* That cannot be fathomed, of measureless depth. **făth'omlėssly** *adv.*

fathŏm'ėter (-dh-) *n.* Instrument for determining depth of sea by measuring time taken by sound-wave to reach the bottom and return.

fatigue' (-ēg) *n.* 1. Weariness after exertion. 2. Weakness in metals etc. after repeated blows or long strain. 2. Task etc. that wearies; soldier's non-military duty, sometimes allotted as punishment; *~(-party)*, party to which such a duty is assigned. ~ *v.t.* Tire, exhaust, weaken (metal).

Făt'ima. Daughter of Mohammed by his first wife. **Făt'imīte, Făt'imid** *adj.* & *n.* (Person) descended from Fatima and her husband Ali; (member) of Arabian dynasty ruling part of N. Africa, Egypt, and Syria, 908–1171.

făt'lĭng *n.* Young fatted animal.

fătt'en *v.* Make fat (esp. animals for slaughter); grow fat; enrich (soil).

fătt'y *adj.* 1. Like fat, unctuous, greasy. 2. Consisting of fat, adipose; with morbid deposition of fat; ~ *degeneration*, a morbid condition which begins in individual cells and results in deposits of fat in the tissues. 3. (chem.) ~ *acid*, one of a series of acids of the general formula $C_nH_{2n}O_2$, of which some members occur in or are derived from natural fats.

făt'ūous *adj.* Vacantly silly, purposeless, idiotic. **făt'ūously** *adv.* **făt'ūousnėss, fatū'ity** *ns.*

faubourg (fōb'oorg) *n.* Suburb, esp. of Paris.

fau'ces (-sēz) *n.pl.* (anat.) Cavity at back of mouth from which larynx and pharynx open out (ill. HEAD).

fau'cėt *n.* (dial. & U.S.) Tap.

faugh (faw) *int.* of disgust.

fault *n.* 1. Defect, imperfection, blemish, of character, structure, appearance, etc.; *to a ~*, excessively. 2. Transgression, offence; thing wrongly done; (rackets, tennis, etc.) ball wrongly served; *find ~ with*, criticize unfavourably, complain of, whence *fault'finder, fault'finding* (*ns.*). 3. Culpability, responsibility for something wrong; defect causing specified evil. 4. (hunting) Loss of scent; check so caused; *at ~*, puzzled, at a loss. 5. Flaw in ice; (geol.) place where rock-layers have fractured and moved out of alignment (ill. ROCK); ~ *plane*, plane of a fault, surface along which rocks on one side of a fault have moved relatively to those on the other. ~ *v.* (geol.) Cause fault in (strata etc.); show fault; (chiefly U.S.) find fault with. **fault'lėss** *adj.* **fault'lėssly** *adv.* **fault'lėssnėss** *n.* **fault'y** *adj.* **fault'ĭly** *adv.* **fault'ĭnėss** *n.*

faun *n.* One of a class of Latin rural deities represented with horns, pointed ears, and tail of goat, and later also with goat's legs like satyrs, with whom they were associated. [f. FAUNUS]

faun'a *n.* Animals or animal life of a region or epoch. **faun'al** *adj.* [L prop. name of a rural goddess, sister of FAUNUS]

Faun'us. (myth.) Latin god or demigod worshipped by shepherds and farmers and identified with the Gk PAN.

Faust (fowst). A wandering astrologer and necromancer who lived in Germany *c* 1488–1541 and was reputed to have sold his soul to the Devil; hero of dramas by Marlowe and Goethe. **Faust'ĭan** *adj.*

faute de mieux (fōt de myẽr). For want of better.

fauteuil (fōtẽr'ĭ) *n.* Arm-chair; theatre-stall.

faux pas (fō pah) *n.* Act which compromises one's reputation, 'false step', mistake.

fā'vour (-ver) *n.* 1. Friendly regard, goodwill; approval; good graces; kindness beyond what is due, partiality, too lenient or generous treatment; aid, furtherance; *in ~ of*, on behalf or in support of; on the side of; to the advantage or account of. 2. Thing given or worn as mark of favour; knot of ribbons, rosette, cockade, badge. 3. (archaic) Looks, countenance; *well-, ill-*, etc., *favoured*, having handsome, ugly, etc., features. ~ *v.t.* 1. Look kindly upon, approve; treat kindly, countenance; indulge, oblige, *with*. 2. Treat with partiality; be propitious or advantageous to; aid, support. 3. (colloq.) Resemble in face or feature. 4. (journalese) Choose to wear. 5. *Favoured*, having unusual advantages; *most favoured nation clause*, clause in trade agreement giving special advantages with regard to import duties, permission to trade, etc., to a particular nation; hence, *most favoured nation treatment.*

fā'vourable (-ver-) *adj.* Well-disposed, propitious; commendatory, approving; promising, auspicious; helpful, suitable (*to*). **fā'vourably** *adv.* **fā'vourablenėss** *n.*

fā'vourīte (-ver-) *n.* & *adj.* (Person) preferred above others; (person) chosen as intimate by king or superior and unduly favoured; *the ~*, (racing etc.) competitor generally favoured as being most likely to win. **fā'vourītism** *n.*

Fawkes (-ks), Guy (1570–1606). A Yorkshire Catholic, who, with Catesby and other conspirators, planned to blow up the Houses of Parliament on 5th Nov. 1605 (Gunpowder Plot); he was arrested on 4th Nov. and hanged; *Guy ~'s day*, 5th Nov., celebrated with fireworks and burning of Fawkes in effigy.

fawn[1] *n.* 1. Young fallow deer, buck or doe of first year. 2. Colour of this, light yellowish-brown. ~ *adj.* Fawn-coloured. ~ *v.* (Of deer) bring forth fawn.

fawn[2] *v.i.* (Of animal, esp. dog) show affection by tail-wagging, grovelling, etc.; (of persons) behave servilely, cringe. **fawn'ĭng** *adj.* **fawn'ĭngly** *adv.*

fay *n.* Fairy.

F.B.A. *abbrev.* Fellow of the British Academy.

F.B.I. *abbrev.* Federal Bureau of Investigation (U.S.); Federation of British Industries.

F.C. *abbrev.* Football Club.

F.C.A. *abbrev.* Fellow of the Institute of Chartered Accountants.

fcap, fcp *abbrevs.* Foolscap.

F.C.I.S. *abbrev.* Fellow of the Chartered Institute of Secretaries.

F.D. *abbrev.* *Fidei Defensor* (= Defender of the Faith).

fē'alty *n.* Feudal tenant's or vassal's fidelity to his lord; acknowledgement or obligation of this.

fear *n.* Painful emotion caused by impending danger or evil; state of alarm; dread *of, lest, that*; dread and reverence; anxiety for the safety *of*; *for ~ of, lest*, in order to avoid or prevent; *without ~ or favour*, impartially; *no fear!*, it is not likely. ~ *v.* Be afraid; be afraid of; hesitate *to* do, shrink from *doing*; revere (God); apprehend, have uneasy anticipation of; be afraid *that*. **fear'lėss** *adj.* **fear'lėssly** *adv.* **fear'lėssnėss** *n.*

fear'ful *adj.* 1. Terrible, awful; (by exaggeration) annoying etc. 2. Frightened, timid; apprehensive *of, lest*; wanting resolution *to*; reverential. **fear'fully** *adv.* (freq. = very). **fear'fulnėss** *n.*

fear'some *adj.* Appalling, esp. in appearance (usu. joc.). **fear'somely** *adv.* **fear'somenėss** *n.*

feas'ĭble (-z-) *adj.* Practicable, possible; capable of being done or accomplished; (loosely) likely, probable. **feasĭbĭl'ĭty** *n.*

feast *n.* 1. Religious anniversary appointed to be observed with rejoicing; annual village festival (orig. held on feast of saint to whom parish church is dedicated); *movable*

~, feast (as Easter etc.) of which date varies from year to year. 2. Sumptuous meal, esp. one given to number of guests and of public nature; (fig.) gratification, rich treat, to senses or mind. ~ *v.* Partake of feast, fare sumptuously; pass (night etc.) *away* in feasting; regale.

feat[1] *n.* Noteworthy act, esp. deed of valour; act of dexterity or strength, surprising trick.

feat[2] *adj.* (archaic) Adroit, smart, dextrous, neat. **feat'ly** *adv.*

feath'er (fĕdh-) *n.* 1. One of the appendages growing from a bird's skin, usu. consisting of a central horny shaft fringed on either side with a 'vane' or row of thin narrow plates or barbs forming rounded outline at end; (collect.) plumage; feathered game; *birds of a, of the same*, **~**, of the same kind or character; *show the white* **~**, betray cowardice (white feather in game-bird's tail being sign of inferior breeding). 2. Piece(s) of feather attached to

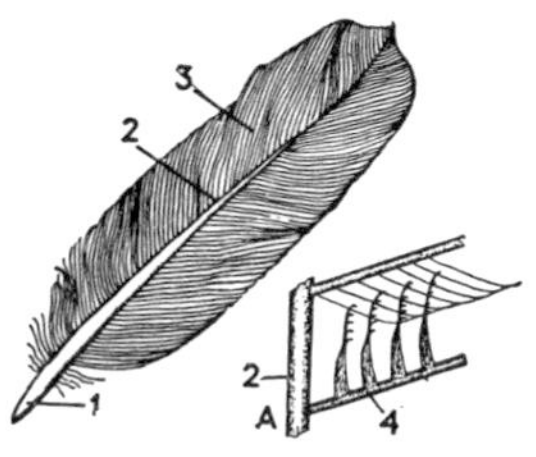

FEATHER: A. ENLARGED DETAIL OF VANE

1. Quill. 2. Rachis or shaft. 3. Vane or web. 4. Barb showing method of interlocking with adjacent barb

base of arrow or dart to direct flight; plume worn in hat etc.; very light object; *Prince of Wales's feathers*, plume of 3 ostrich feathers first adopted as crest by Black Prince; *a ~ in one's cap*, something one may be proud of. 3. Tuft or ridge of upright hair; feather-like flaw in gem. 4. (rowing) Action of feathering. 5. *~-bed*, mattress stuffed with feathers; (*v.t.*) make things easy for, pamper; *~-edge*, fine edge of wedge-shaped board; (*v.t.*) give (board) such an edge; *~-headed, -brained*, silly; *~-stitch*, zigzag embroidery stitch (ill. STITCH); *~-weight*, very light thing or person, esp. boxer of less than 9 stone. **feath'ered, feath'erlėss, feath'ery,** *adjs.* **feath'erinėss** *n.* **feath'er** *v.* 1. Furnish, adorn, line, coat, with feathers; form feather-like covering or adornment for; ~ *one's nest*, enrich oneself. 2. Float, move, wave, like feathers; turn (oar), turn oar, as it leaves water, so that it passes through air edgeways; (hunting, of hound) make quivering motion of body and tail while seeking scent; (shooting) knock feathers from (bird) without killing.

feath'ering (fĕdh-) *n.* (esp.) Plumage; feathers of arrow; feathery structure in animal's coat; feather-like marking in flower.

fea'ture *n.* 1. (usu. pl.) Part(s) of the face, esp. with regard to shape and visible effect. 2. Distinctive or characteristic part of a thing, part that arrests attention; distinctive or prominent article in newspaper; ~ *film*, long fictional film forming chief part of programme; ~ *programme*, (broadcasting) programme in which actual events are re-enacted. **fea'turelėss** *adj.* **fea'ture** *v.t.* Stand as distinctive mark upon; portray, sketch prominent points of; (orig. U.S.) make special feature of, make special attraction of; exhibit as prominent feature in dramatic, esp. cinematographic, piece.

Feb. *abbrev.* February.

fĕb'rifūge *n.* Medicine to reduce fever; cooling drink. **fĕbrĭf'ūgal** *adj.*

fĕb'rīle *adj.* Of fever, feverish.

Fĕb'ruary (-rŏŏ-) *n.* 2nd month of year, containing 28 days except in leap-year, when it has 29. [L *februa*, Roman festival of purification held on 15th of this month]

fec. *abbrev.* *Fecit* or *fecerunt* (= made).

fĕck'lėss *adj.* Feeble, futile, inefficient. **fĕck'lėssly** *adv.* **fĕck'lėssnėss** *n.*

fĕc'ūlent *adj.* Turbid; fetid. **fĕc'ūlence** *n.*

fĕc'und (*or* fē-) *adj.* Prolific, fertile; fertilizing. **fėcŭn'dĭty** *n.*

fĕc'undāte *v.t.* Make fruitful, impregnate.

fĕd past t. and past. part. of FEED; ~ *up*, (slang) surfeited, disgusted (*with*), bored.

fĕd'eral *adj.* 1. (theol.) Based on doctrine of Covenants; ~ *theology*, system based on God's covenant with Adam as representing man, and Christ as representing Church. 2. Of the form of government in which two or more States form a political unity but remain independent in internal affairs; of such political unity, as dist. from the separate States composing it. 3. (U.S. hist.) Favouring strong central government; of the Northern or Union party, or its troops, in the Civil War of 1861–5. **fĕd'eralĭsm, fĕd'eralĭst** *ns.* **fĕderalĭs'tĭc** *adj.* **fĕd'eralīze** *v.t.* **fĕderalīzā'tion** *n.* **fĕd'erally** *adv.*

fĕd'erāte *v.* Bind together in league for some common object; organize on federal basis. **fĕd'erate** (-at), **fĕd'eratĭve** *adjs.* **fĕd'erātor** *n.*

fĕderā'tion *n.* Federating; federated society, esp. federal empire or group of States. **fĕderā'tionist** (sho-) *n.*

fėdōr'a *n.* (chiefly U.S.) Low soft felt hat with curled brim and crown creased lengthways. ['Fédora', title of play by Victor Sardou]

fee *n.* 1. (hist.) Fief; feudal benefice. 2. (law) Estate of inheritance in land; estate held in fee, lordship; *in* **~**, as one's absolute and rightful possession; *~ farm*, tenure of, estate in, land held in fee-simple subject to perpetual fixed rent, without other services; rent so paid; *~-simple*, estate, fee, without limitation to any class of heirs; *in ~-simple*, in absolute possession; *~-tail*, fee limited to some particular class of heirs of person to whom it is granted. 3. Sum payable to public officer for performing his function; sum paid or due to professional man, performer, etc., for occasional service or performance; entrance-money for examination, society, etc.; terminal payment for instruction at school. ~ *v.t.* Pay fee to; engage for a fee.

fee'ble *adj.* Weak, infirm; deficient in character or intelligence; wanting in energy, force, or effect; dim, indistinct. **fee'blenėss** (-bln-) *n.* **fee'bly** *adv.*

feed *v.* (past t. and past part. *fed*). 1. Supply with food; put food into mouth of; graze (cattle); deal out (fodder) to animals; take food, eat; serve as food for. 2. Gratify (vanity, eyes, etc.), comfort (person) *with* hope, etc. 3. Nourish, make grow. 4. Keep (reservoir, fire, etc.) supplied; supply (machine) with material to work on; supply (material) (*on*) *to* machine; (theatr. slang) give (actor) cues, opportunities for jokes, etc. 5. *feed'back*, (wireless) process by which currents in adjacent circuits react on those already flowing, thus strengthening weak signals; *feeding-bottle*, bottle with rubber teat for feeding infants; *feeding-cup*, vessel with spout for feeding invalid; *~-pipe*, pipe conveying material, water, etc., to machine; *~-shaft*, driving shaft for advancing cutting tool of lathe; *~-tank, -trough*, tank holding water for locomotive. ~ *n.* 1. Act of feeding; giving of food; *off one's* ~, with no appetite; *out at* ~, turned out to graze. 2. Pasturage, green crops; horse's allowance of oats etc.; fodder. 3. (colloq.) Meal, feast. 4. Feeding of machine etc., material supplied. 5. (theatr. slang) one who 'feeds' another actor.

feed'er *n.* (esp.) 1. Child's feeding-bottle. 2. Child's bib. 3. Tributary stream. 4. Hopper or feeding-apparatus in machine.

feel *v.* (past t. and past part. *felt*). 1. Explore by touch; search (*about*) with hand *after, for*; try to ascertain by touch *whether, if, how*; ~ *one's way*, find one's way by groping. 2. Perceive by touch; have sensation of touch; *feel one's legs, feet*, find firm standing; be at ease. 3. Be conscious of (sensation, emotion, conviction); be consciously; experience, undergo consciously; be affected by, behave as if conscious of. 4. Be emotionally affected by; have sympathy *with*, compassion *for*; have vague or emotional conviction (*that*). 5. (quasi-pass.) Be realized as; seem, produce impression of being. ~ *n.*

Sense of touch; testing by touch; sensation characterizing something.

feel'er *n.* (esp.) (pop. term for) Organ in certain animals for testing things by touch or searching for food; tentative proposal or hint.

feel'ing *n.* (esp.) 1. Sense of touch; physical sensation. 2. Emotion; (pl.) susceptibilities, sympathies; readiness to feel, tenderness for others' sufferings. 3. Consciousness *of*; conviction not based solely on reason; sentiment. 4. (art etc.) General emotional effect produced. ~ *adj.* (esp.) Sensitive, sympathetic; showing emotion. **feel'ingly** *adv.* **feel'ingness** *n.*

feign (fān) *v.* 1. Invent (excuse, story, accusation); forge (document). 2. (archaic) Represent in fiction; imagine. 3. Simulate, pretend; practise simulation.

feint[1] (fānt) *n.* Sham attack (blow, cut, thrust, etc.) to divert attention or deceive opponent; pretence. ~ *v.i.* Make feint.

feint[2] (fānt) *adj.* & *adv.* Old spelling of FAINT, in ~ *lines, ruled*~.

feldspar: see FELSPAR.

fėli'citāte *v.t.* 1. (rare) Make happy. 2. Congratulate (*on*). **fėlicitā'tion** *n.*

fėli'citous *adj.* Blissful (rare); (of expression, quotation, etc., or person using it) strikingly apt, pleasantly ingenious. **fėli'citously** *adv.*

fėli'city *n.* 1. Being happy, intense happiness; blessing; fortunate trait. 2. Happy faculty in expression, appropriateness; well-chosen phrase.

fē'line *adj.* Of cats; cat-like. ~ *n.* Member of *Felidae* or cat-tribe. **fėlin'ity** *n.*

fĕll[1] *n.* Animal's hide or skin with the hair; thick or matted hair or wool, fleece.

fĕll[2] *n.* Hill, mountain (now only in proper names); wild high stretch of waste or pasture land in N. England and parts of Scotland.

fĕll[3] *adj.* Fierce, ruthless, terrible, destructive.

fĕll[4] *v.* 1. Strike (person, animal) down by blow or cut. 2. Cut down (tree). 3. Stitch down (wider edge left projecting by seam) so that it lies flat over other edge (ill. SEAM). ~ *n.* Amount of timber cut.

fĕll'ah (-*a*) *n.* (pl. *fellaheen, fellahs*). Egyptian peasant. [Arab., = 'husbandman']

fĕll'oe, fĕll'y (usu. pronounced -ĭ and spelt -*oe*) *n.* Outer circle of wheel, attached by spokes (ill. WHEEL); part of this.

fĕll'ow (-ō) *n.* 1. One associated with another, comrade. 2. Counterpart, match; other of pair; equal, one of same class, contemporary. 3. Incorporated member of college or collegiate foundation; one of company or corporation who, with their head, constitute a college; elected graduate holding stipendiary position for term of years on condition of pursuing specified branch of study; ~ *commoner*, (hist.) undergraduate in Oxford, Cambridge, or Dublin, privileged to dine at fellows' table. 4. Member of various learned societies. 5. Man; boy. 6. (attrib.) Belonging to same class; associated in joint action; in same relation to same object; ~-*citizen*, citizen of same city; ~-*countryman*, compatriot, subject of same country; ~-*creature*, person or animal also created by God; ~-*feeling*, sympathy; ~ *traveller*, (also) non-Communist who sympathizes with aims and general policy of Communist party.

fĕll'owship *n.* 1. Participation, sharing, community of interest. 2. (also *good* ~) Companionship, intercourse, friendliness. 3. Body of associates, company; guild, corporation; brotherhood. 4. Dignity or emoluments of college fellow.

fell'y: see FELLOE.

fĕl'ō dė sē *n.* (pl. *felonēs, felos*). Self-murderer; (no. pl.) self-murder. [Anglo-L, = 'felon about himself']

fĕl'on[1] *n.* Small abscess, esp. under or near nail, whitlow.

fĕl'on[2] *n.* One who has committed felony. ~ *adj.* (poet.) Cruel, wicked, murderous. **fėlōn'ious** *adj.* Criminal; (law) of, involving, felony; that has committed felony. **fėlōn'iously** *adv.*

fĕl'onry *n.* The class or body of felons (orig., the convict population of Australia).

fĕl'ony *n.* Grave indictable offence, such as murder, manslaughter, rape, larceny (orig., crime the penalty for which included forfeiture of lands and goods, and corruption of blood).

fĕl'spar, fĕl'dspar *n.* Any of a group of minerals, esp. potassium aluminium silicate, usu. white or flesh-coloured, occurring in crystals and in granite and other primary rocks; used in ceramic and enamelling processes. **fĕl(d)spăth'ic** *adj.*

fĕlt[1] *n.* Fabric made by shrinking and rolling wool, fur, etc. so that the fibres interlock. ~ *v.* Make into felt; mat together, become matted; cover with felt.

fĕlt[2] past t. and past part. of FEEL.

fėlŭcc'a *n.* Small Mediterranean coasting-vessel with oars or lateen sails or both.

fēm'āle *adj.* 1. Of the sex which bears offspring or produces eggs; (of plants or their parts) fruit-bearing. 2. Of women; of female animals or plants. 3. (of part of instrument or contrivance) Adapted to receive corresponding or male part; ~ *screw*, circular hole or socket with spiral thread adapted to receive thread of male screw (ill. SCREW). ~ *n.* Female person or animal; (now contempt.) woman, girl.

feme (fēm) *n.* (law) Wife; ~ *cov'ert* (kŭ-), woman under protection of her husband, married woman; ~*sōle*, spinster, widow, divorced woman; married woman entirely independent of her husband as regards property.

fĕminē'ity *n.* Womanliness; womanishness.

fĕm'inine *adj.* 1. (rare) Female. 2. Of women; womanly; womanish. 3. (gram.) Of gender to which appellations of females belong; (of ending) proper to this gender; (pros.) ~ *rhyme*, in Fr. verse, one ending in 'mute' *e* (a common feminine suffix); hence, rhyme of two syllables of which second is unstressed. **fĕm'ininely** (-nl-) *adv.* **fĕm'inineness, fĕminin'ity** *ns.*

fĕm'inism *n.* Advocacy of extended recognition of claims and achievements of women; advocacy of women's rights. **fĕm'inist** *n.* **fĕminis'tic** *adj.*

fĕm'inize *v.* Make, become, feminine. **fĕminizā'tion** *n.*

femme de chambre (făm de shahnbr) *n.* Lady's maid; chambermaid.

fēm'ur (-*er*) *n.* 1. Thigh-bone (ill. SKELETON). 2. One of upper portions of insect's leg (ill. INSECT). **fĕm'oral** *adj.*

fĕn *n.* Low marshy or flooded tract of land; *the fens*, low-lying districts in Cambridgeshire, Lincolnshire, and adjoining counties; *the* ~-*district*, the fens; *fen'man*, inhabitant of fens; ~-*runners*, long skates used for skating on fens.

fĕnce *n.* 1. Art of fencing; use of the sword. 2. Bulwark (archaic); hedge, wall, railing, etc., keeping out intruders from field etc.; *sunk* ~, one placed along bottom of depression in ground; occas. = ditch; *sit on the* ~, remain neutral in contest, be undecided in opinion. 3. Guard, guide, or gauge, regulating movements of tool or machine. 4. Receiver of, receiving-house for, stolen goods. ~ *v.* 1. Practise sword-play; use sword scientifically; ~ *with*, parry, try to evade (question, questioner). 2. Screen, shield, protect (*from, against*); repel, keep *off* or *out*; surround (as) with fence, enclose, fortify. 3. (of horse) Leap fence. 4. Deal in stolen goods. **fĕn'cer** *n.* (esp.) Swordsman.

fĕnce'lėss (-sl-) *adj.* Unenclosed; (poet.) defenceless, unfortified.

fĕn'cible *n.* (hist.) Soldier liable only for defensive service.

fĕn'cing *n.* 1. See FENCE *v.* 2. Railing; fences; material for fences.

fĕnd *v.* Ward *off*, keep *away*, repel *from*; provide *for* (usu. oneself).

fĕn'der *n.* Thing used to keep something off, prevent collision, etc.; guard; esp. (naut.) piece of old cable, matting, etc., hung over vessel's side; metal frame round hearth to prevent falling coals from rolling into room (ill. FIRE); (U.S.) wing of motor-car.

fĕnestĕll'a *n.* (archit.) Small wall-niche to south of altar containing piscina and often credence.

fenĕs'tra *n.* (pl. *-ae*). Small hole or opening in bone etc., esp. one of two (~ *ovalis* and ~ *rotunda*) in internal ear.

fėnĕs'trate *adj.* Having small perforations or openings like a window. **fėnĕs'trātėd** *adj.* Furnished with windows; pierced with hole(s); perforated.

fĕnėstrā'tion *n.* (esp.) 1. Arrangement of windows in building. 2. (surg.) Operation of making a 'window' in medial wall of middle ear, performed in certain cases of deafness.

Fēn'ĭan *adj.* & *n.* (hist.) (Member) of organization formed among Irish in U.S. and in Ireland in the middle of the 19th c. for promoting revolution and overthrowing English government in Ireland. **Fēn'ĭanism** *n.* [OIr. *féne* the ancient Irish people, confused with *fiann* warriors defending Ireland under Finn and other legendary kings]

fĕnn'el *n.* Fragrant yellow-flowered perennial umbellifer, *Foeniculum vulgare*, used as flavouring in sauces etc.; *oil of* ~, volatile oil extracted from this, used as a carminative.

fĕnt *n.* Remnant, short end (of cloth).

fĕn'ūgreek *n.* Leguminous plant, *Trigonella foenum-graecum*, with seeds used in farriery.

feoff: see FIEF.

feoffee' (fĕf-) *n.* Person to whom freehold estate in land is conveyed by feoffment; ~ (*in, of, trust*), trustee invested with freehold estate in land; esp. (pl.) board holding land for charitable or public purposes. **feoff'ment** *n.* Mode of conveyance (now almost obsolete) of freehold estate in fee. **feoff'er** *n.* One who makes a feoffment.

F.E.R.A. *abbrev.* Federal Emergency Relief Administration.

fēr'al *adj.* Wild, untamed, uncultivated; brutal.

Fērd'ĭnand V (1452–1516). King of Aragon; by marrying Isabella of Castile, 1469, he united the kingdoms of Aragon and Castile and founded the Spanish monarchy.

fĕ'rėtory *n.* Shrine for relics of saint, tomb; bier; chapel in which shrines were deposited.

fēr'ĭal *adj.* (eccles.) (Of day) ordinary, not appointed for festival or fast; (of service etc.) for use on ferial day.

fēr'ĭne *adj.* Feral.

Fĕrĭng'hee (-nggĭ) *n.* (Indian term for) European, now esp. Indian-born Portuguese. [Oriental adaptation of FRANK]

Fērmăn'agh (-*a*). County of N. Ireland.

fērm'ĕnt *n.* 1. Leaven; any fermentative agent. 2. Fermenting, fermentation; agitation, excitement, tumult. **fermĕnt'** *v.* Suffer, subject to, fermentation; (make) effervesce; excite, stir up, foment.

fērmĕntā'tion *n.* Process like that induced by yeast on dough or sugar solutions, with effervescence, evolution of heat, and change of properties; agitation, excitement. **fermĕn'tative** *adj.*

fērm'ium *n.* TRANSURANIC element, symbol Fm, at. no. 100, principal isotope 256.

fērn *n.* Vascular cryptogamous plant, freq. with feathery fronds, of the order *Filicales*; ~*-owl*, the goatsucker, *Caprimulgus europaeus*; the short-eared owl, *Asio brachyotus*; ~*-seed*, the supposed 'seed' (actually spores) of the fern, once pop. believed to be invisible and to render invisible those who carried it. **fērn'y** *adj.* **fērn'ery** *n.* Place where ferns are grown.

ferō'cious (-sh*us*) *adj.* Fierce, savage, cruel. **ferō'ciously** *adv.*

ferŏ'city *n.* Ferocious character or act.

fĕ'rŏx *n.* The great lake trout. [L *Salmo ferox* fierce salmon]

Fĕrra'ra[1] (-ârа). Town in the Po valley, E. Italy. **Fĕrrarēse'** (-z) *adj.* & *n.* (Native, inhabitant) of Ferrara.

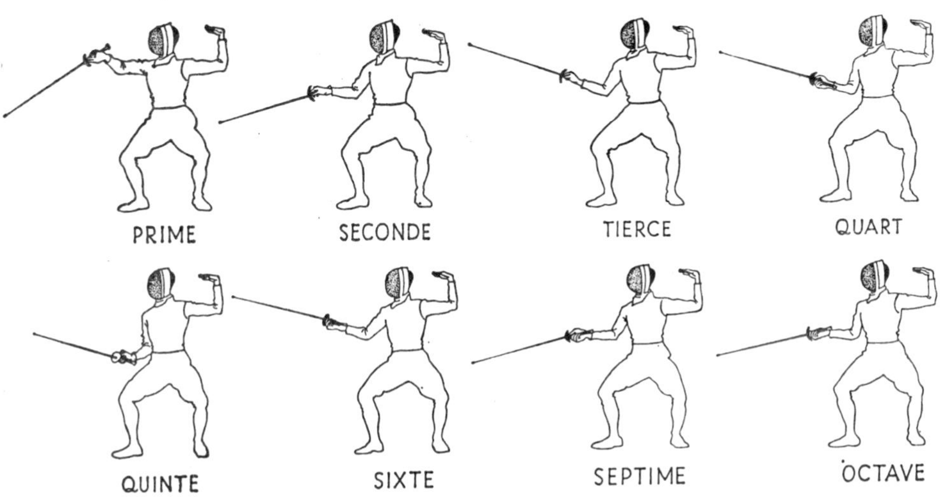

THE EIGHT DEFENSIVE POSITIONS IN FENCING

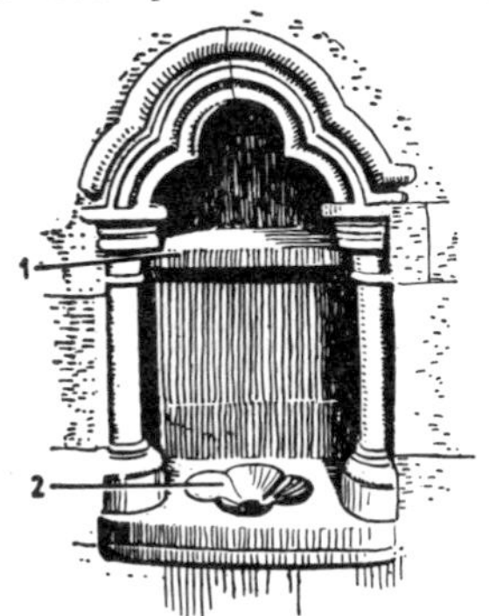

FENESTELLA
1. Credence. 2. Piscina

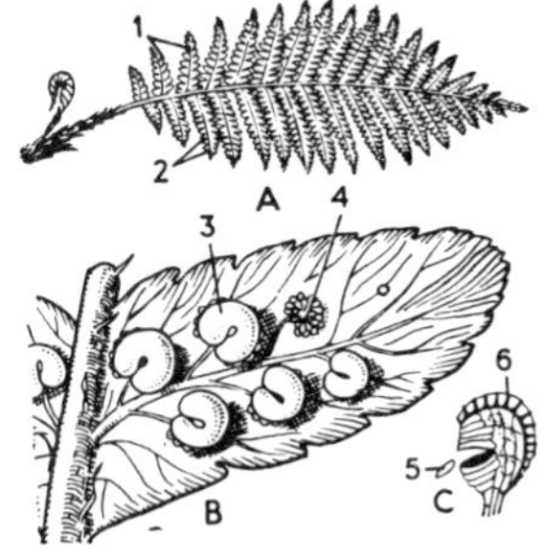

FERNS: A. FROND. B. PINNULE. C. SPORANGIUM
1. Pinna. 2. Pinnule. 3. Sorus. 4. Sporangia. 5. Spore. 6. Annulus

Fĕrra'ra[2] (-ârа), Andrea. Celebrated maker of swords, probably a Venetian, of the 16th c.; hence, ~, a broadsword or claymore.

fĕ'rrāte *n.* (chem.) Salt derived from the hypothetical ferric acid (H_2FeO_4).

fĕ'rrėt[1] *n.* Half-tamed variety of common polecat (*Putorius foetidus*), kept for driving rabbits from burrows, killing rats, etc. ~ *v.* 1. Hunt with ferrets; clear out (holes, ground), take or drive away (rabbits etc.), with ferrets. 2. Rummage, search *about* (*for*); search *out*. **fĕ'rrėty** *adj.* [L *fur* thief]

fĕ'rrėt[2] *n.* Stout cotton or silk tape. [It. *fioretti* floss-silk (L *flos* flower)]

ferri- *prefix.* (chem.) Containing iron in the *ferric* or trivalent state.

fĕ'rriage *n.* Conveyance by, charge for using, ferry.

fĕ'rrĭc *adj.* 1. Of iron. 2. (chem.) Applied to compounds of trivalent iron, e.g. ~ *oxide* (Fe_2O_3).

Fĕ'rrĭs wheel *n.* Giant revolving vertical wheel supporting passenger cars on its rim, an attraction at exhibitions etc. [G. W. G. *Ferris*, Amer. engineer]

fĕ'rrīte *n.* 1. Microstructural constituent of steel, of pure iron or alloy. 2. (chem.) Compound of Fe_2O_3 with the oxide of a bivalent metal, esp., magnetic substances of this formula used as cores for coils in radio apparatus.

ferro- *prefix.* 1. Of, containing, iron. 2. (chem., in names of compounds) Containing iron in the *ferrous* or bivalent state.

fĕrro-cŏnc'rēte *n.* Concrete reinforced by steel bars, netting, etc.

fĕrro-măgnĕt'ĭc *adj.* Of the kind of magnetism shown by iron, cobalt, and nickel and their alloys.

fĕrro-măng'anese (-ngganēz) *n.* Alloy of manganese and iron used in making alloy steels.

fĕ'rrotȳpe *n.* Photographic process producing print on thin iron plate; such photograph.

fĕ'rrous *adj.* (chem.) Containing iron in the bivalent state, e.g. ~ *oxide* (FeO); *non-~*, free from iron (applied to the group of alloys including brass, bronze, duralumin, etc.).

ferru'ginous (-ōōj-) *adj.* Of, containing, iron-rust or iron as chemical constituent; rust-coloured, reddish brown.

fĕ'rrule *n.* Metal ring or cap strengthening end of stick or tube; ring or band giving additional strength or holding parts together.

fĕ'rry *n.* Place where boats pass over river etc., to transport passengers and goods; provision for ferrying; (law) right of ferrying and of levying toll for it; *~-boat*, boat used for ferrying; *ferryman*, man who keeps or looks after ferry. ~ *v.* Convey, pass, in boat, work (boat), (of boat) pass to and fro, over river, canal, or strait; fly (aircraft) from one place to another, esp. from factory to aerodrome.

fẽrt'ile *adj.* Bearing abundantly, fruitful. **fertil'ity** *n.*

fẽr'tilīze *v.t.* Make (esp. soil) fertile or productive; fecundate (individual, organ). **fẽrtilīzā'tion** *n.* Fertilizing; (biol.) fusion of male reproductive cell with female one. **fẽrt'ilīzer** *n.* (esp.) Manure; chemical manure, usu. compound containing nitrogen, phosphorus, or potassium.

fĕ'rule (-ōōl) *n.* Cane, rod, etc., esp. flat piece of wood, used for punishing children; (fig.) school discipline. ~ *v.t.* Strike, beat, with ferule.

fẽrv'ent *adj.* 1. Hot, glowing. 2. Ardent, intense. **fẽrv'ently** *adv.* **fẽrv'ency** *n.*

fẽrv'id *adj.* 1. (poet.) Hot, glowing. 2. Glowing, impassioned.

fẽrv'our (-*ver*) *n.* 1. Glowing condition, intense heat. 2. Vehemence, passion, zeal.

fĕs'cūe *n.* 1. Small stick; pointer. 2. ~ (*grass*), genus (*Festuca*) of grasses, valuable as pasture for sheep.

fĕsse (-s) *n.* (her.) Two horizontal lines as bar across middle of field (ill. HERALDRY).

fĕs'tal *adj.* Of a feast; keeping holiday; gay. **fĕs'tally** *adv.*

fĕs'ter *v.* (Of wound or sore) generate matter, ulcerate; (of poison, disease, grief) cause suppuration, rankle; putrefy, rot; cause festering in. ~ *n.* Festering condition.

fĕs'tĭval *adj.* (not used predic.) Of, befitting, a feast or feast-day. ~ *n.* Time of festive celebration; merrymaking; (periodic) series of performances (of music, drama, films, etc.).

fĕs'tĭve *adj.* Of a feast; joyous; fond of feasting, jovial. **fĕs'tĭvely** (-vl-) *adv.*

fĕstĭv'ity *n.* Gaiety, rejoicing; festive celebration; (pl.) festive proceedings.

fĕstōōn' *n.* Chain of flowers or leaves, or ribbons etc., hung in curve between two points (ill. SWAG). ~ *v.* Adorn (as) with, form into, festoons. **fĕstōōn'ery** *n.*

fĕtch[1] *v.* (Go for and) bring back (person or thing); (now rare) cause to come, draw forth (blood, tears, etc.); ~ *and carry*, run backwards and forwards with things; ~ *up*, vomit. 2. Bring in, realize, sell for (a price). 3. Move the feelings of; delight or irritate. 4. Heave (sigh); draw (breath); deal (blow). 5. ~ *up*, arrive; come to a stand. ~ *n.* 1. (archaic) Far-reaching effort. 2. Dodge, trick. **fĕtch'ĭng** *adj.* Attractive, taking.

fĕtch[2] *n.* (archaic) Double or wraith of living person.

fête (fāt) *n.* Festival; great entertainment; day of saint after whom child is named, observed in R.C. countries like birthday. ~ *v.t.* Entertain, make much of (person).

fête champêtre (fāt shahṅpātr') *n.* Outdoor entertainment, rural festival; picture representing this.

fĕt'ĭd, foet'ĭd *adj.* Stinking. **fĕt'idly** *adv.* **fĕt'ĭdnėss** *n.*

fĕt'ĭsh *n.* Inanimate object worshipped by primitive peoples for its supposed inherent magical powers or as being inhabited by a spirit; anything irrationally reverenced. **fĕt'ĭshĭsm, fĕt'ĭshĭst** *ns.* **fĕtĭshĭs'tĭc** *adj.* [Port. *feitiço* charm, f. L *facticius* factitious]

fĕt'lŏck *n.* Part of horse's leg where tuft of hair grows behind pastern-joint (ill. HORSE).

fĕt'or *n.* Stench.

fĕtt'er *n.* Shackle for feet; bond, (pl.) captivity; check, restraint; *fetterlock*, (heraldic representation of) D-shaped fetter for tethering horse by leg. ~ *v.t.* Bind (as) with fetters; impede, restrain.

Fĕtt'ės. Scottish public school in Edinburgh, founded by Sir William Fettes, opened 1870.

fĕt'tle *n.* Condition, trim (only in *in good, light, fine*, etc. ~). ~ *v.* (eng.) Trim, rectify (rough-edged or warped part).

fetus: see FOETUS.

feu *n.* (Sc. law) Perpetual lease at fixed rent; land so held.

feud[1] *n.* Lasting mutual hostility, esp. between two tribes or families, with murderous assaults in revenge for previous injury.

feud[2] *n.* Fief, feudal benefice; territory held in fee.

feud'al *adj.* Of a feud or fief; of, resembling, according to, the feudal system; ~ *system*, medieval European polity based on relation of superior and vassal arising from holding of lands in feud; system by which land was held of a superior (in England ultimately of the king) in return for services which included military service, homage, etc. **feud'ally** *adv.* **feud'alĭsm, feud'alĭst** *ns.* **feudalĭs'tĭc** *adj.* **feud'alīze** *v.t.* **feudalīzā'tion** *n.*

feudăl'ity *n.* Feudal system or principles; feudal holding, fief.

feud'atory *adj.* Feudally subject *to*; under overlordship. ~ *n.* Feudal vassal.

feuilleton (fẽr'ĭtawṅ) *n.* Ruled-off portion at foot of page of (esp. Fr.) newspapers, devoted to fiction, criticism, light literature, etc.; serial story, article, printed in this portion. [Fr., = 'leaflet']

fēv'er *n.* 1. Reaction of the body to a general infection, characterized by raised temperature, restlessness, panting, thirst, and wasting; any of a group of diseases, each caused by a specific agent, in which this reaction occurs; ~ *heat*, high temperature of body in fever (also fig.); ~ *therapy*, artificial production of state of fever in order to raise body temperature to a point lethal to certain organisms of disease. 2. Nervous excitement, agitation.

fēv'erfew *n.* Feathery-leaved perennial plant, *Chrysanthemum parthenium*, allied to the camomile, formerly used as a febrifuge. [L *febris* fever, *fugare* drive away]

fēv'erĭsh *adj.* Having symptoms of fever; excited, fitful, restless; of or like fever; causing, infested by, fever. **fēv'erĭshly** *adv.* **fēv'erĭshnėss** *n.*

fēv'erous *adj.* Infested with, apt to cause, fever; feverish.

few *adj.* & *n.* Not many; *some* ~, no great number (of); *not a* ~, many; (colloq.) *a good* ~, a fair number (of); *the* ~, the minority, the elect, etc. **few'nėss** *n.*

fey (fā) *adj.* (Sc.) Fated to die, at point of death; disordered in mind (often with over-confidence etc.) like person about to die.

fĕz[1] *n.* Red felt cap like truncated cone, with long black tassel from top, formerly Turkish national head-dress. [Turk., perh. f. FEZ[2]]

Fĕz[2]. Town in Morocco.

ff. *abbrev. Fortissimo* (= very loud).

F.F.A.S. *abbrev.* Fellow of the Faculty of Architects and Surveyors.

F.F.I. *abbrev.* Free from infection.

f.g.a. *abbrev.* Free of general average.

F.G.S. *abbrev.* Fellow of the Geological Society.

F.H. *abbrev.* Fire hydrant.

fiancé (fēahṅ'sā) *n.* (fem. *-ée*). One's betrothed.

Fianna Fail (fē'*a*na foil). Eamon DE VALERA's party in Irish politics, which took the oath and entered the Dail Eireann in Aug. 1927. [Ir. *fianna* warriors and *Fail* gen. of *Fál* Ireland]

fīăs'cō *n.* (pl. *-os*). Failure or breakdown (orig. in dramatic or musical performance); ignominious result. [It., = 'bottle' (significance unknown)]

fī'ăt *n.* Authorization; decree, order; ~ *money*, (U.S.) money without intrinsic or promissory value equal to its nominal value made legal tender by fiat of government. **fī'atism** *n.* (U.S.) Principle or practice of issuing fiat money (e.g. inconvertible paper currency). **fī'atist** *n.* [L *fiat* be it done]

F.I.A.T. *abbrev. Fabbrica Italiana Automobile Torino* (= Italian automobile factory, Turin).

fĭb *n.* & *v.i.* (Tell) venial or trivial falsehood; lie. **fĭbb'er, fĭb'ster** *ns.*

fī'bre (-b*er*) *n.* Thread-like cell or filament forming, with others, animal or vegetable tissue or textile substance; substance consisting of fibres; fibrous structure; fibrous substance fit for textile fabrics; small root or twig. **fī'brelėss, fīb'rĭfŏrm, fīb'rous** *adjs.* **fīb'rously** *adv.* **fīb'ro-** *prefix.*

fīb'rĭl *n.* 1. Small fibre; subdivision of fibre. 2. Ultimate subdivision of root. **fīb'rĭllātėd** *adj.* **fibrĭllā'tion** *n.*

fīb'rĭn *n.* Insoluble protein present in clotted blood or plasma. **fīb'rĭnous** *adj.*

fībrĭn'ogĕn *n.* Soluble protein in blood plasma which is converted into fibrin when the blood clots.

fīb'roid *adj.* (chiefly path.) Resembling fibre or fibrous tissue; (of disease) characterized by formation or inflammation of connective tissue. ~ *n.* Fibroid tumour.

fīb'rōse (-s) *v.i.* (med.) Form fibrous tissues. **fībrōs'ĭs** *n.* (path.) Fibroid degeneration; development of fibrous tissue in organ. **fībrŏt'ĭc** *adj.*

fībrosīt'ĭs *n.* (med.) Inflammation of fibrous tissue.

fīb'ūla *n.* (pl. *-lae*). 1. (antiq.) Clasp, buckle, brooch. 2. (anat.) Slender bone on outer side of leg between knee and ankle (ill. SKELETON). **fīb'ūlar** *adj.*

Fich'tė (-ĭχ-), Johann Gottlieb (1762–1814). German idealist philosopher, also famous for his 'Addresses to the German Nation' delivered at Berlin in 1808 during the French occupation of Prussia.

fī'chu (-shōō) *n.* Woman's small triangular shawl of lace etc. for shoulders and neck.

fĭc'kle *adj.* Inconstant, changeable. **fĭc'klenėss** (-ln-) *n.*

fĭc'tĭle *adj.* Made of moulded earth, clay, etc., by potter; of pottery.

fĭc'tion *n.* 1. Feigning, invention; thing feigned or imagined, invented statement or narrative; literature consisting of such narrative, esp. novels. 2. Conventionally accepted falsehood; *legal* ~: see LEGAL. **fĭc'tional** (-shon-) *adj.*

fĭctĭ'tious (-sh*us*) *adj.* Counterfeit, not genuine; (of name or character) feigned, assumed; imaginary, unreal; of fiction; constituted or regarded as such by (legal or conventional) fiction. **fĭctĭ'tiously** *adv.* **fĭctĭ'tiousnėss** *n.*

fĭc'tĭve *adj.* Creating, created, by imagination.

fĭd *n.* (naut.) Conical wooden pin used to open strands of rope in splicing; square wooden or iron crosspiece for supporting topmast; small thick piece or wedge of anything.

Fid. Def. *abbrev. Fidei Defensor* (= Defender of the Faith).

fĭd'dle *n.* 1. (fam. or contempt. for) Violin; violin-player; *play first, second,* ~, take leading, subordinate, position. 2. (naut.) Rack or other contrivance to keep things from rolling off table. 3. *~-bow*, bow strung with horse-hair with which fiddle is played; *~-case*, case for holding fiddle; *fiddlededee!*, nonsense!; *~-faddle*, trifling talk or action, trivial matters; (*adj.*) trifling, fussy, petty; (*int.*) nonsense! (*v.i.*) fuss, trifle; *fiddlestick*, fiddle-bow; mere nothing, nonsense; *fiddlesticks!*, nonsense! ~ *int.* Nonsense! ~ *v.* 1. Play the fiddle; play (tune) on fiddle. 2. Be idle or frivolous; make aimless movements (*at, with*, etc.); fritter *away*. 3. Cheat, 'wangle'; falsify (accounts); transact black-market business, exchange currency illegally.

fĭdd'ler *n.* 1. Player on fiddle, esp. for hire; *F~'s Green*, sailor's Elysium. 2. Small crab of genus *Gelasimus*.

fiddley (fĭd'lĭ) *n.* (naut.) Iron framework (usu. covered by grating) round hatch leading to stokehole.

fĭdd'lĭng *adj.* (esp.) Petty, futile, contemptible, inconsiderable.

fĭdĕl'ĭty *n.* Faithfulness, loyalty (*to*); strict conformity to truth or fact, exact correspondence to the original.

fĭdg'ėt (-j-) *n.* 1. Bodily uneasiness seeking relief in spasmodic movements (freq. *the* ~*s*); restless mood. 2. Person who fidgets or causes others to fidget. 3. Fidgeting. ~ *v.* Move restlessly (*about*); be uneasy, worry; make (person) uncomfortable, worry. **fĭdg'ėty** *adj.* **fĭdg'ėtĭnėss** *n.*

fĭd'ĭbus *n.* (archaic) Paper spill for lighting pipes etc.

fĭdū'cial (-shl) *adj.* 1. (theol.) Of, of the nature of, trust or reliance. 2. (surveying etc., of line, point, etc.) Assumed as fixed basis of comparison.

fĭdū'ciary (-sh*a*-) *adj.* Of trust or trustee(ship); held or given in trust; (of paper currency) depending for its value on public confidence or on securities. ~ *n.* Trustee.

fie (fī) *int.* Expressing sense of outraged propriety, usu. iron. or to children.

fief (fēf), **feoff** (fĕf) *n.* (feudal law) Estate (in England always heritable) in land held on condition of homage and service to superior lord, by whom it is granted and in whom the ownership remains.

field *n.* 1. (Piece of) ground, esp. one used for tillage or pasture, and usu. bounded by hedges etc.; tract abounding in some natural product, as coal, oil, diamonds. 2. Ground on which battle is fought; scene of campaign or military operations; battle (now rare exc. in *hard-fought* ~ etc.); *hold the* ~, not be superseded or displaced; *leave the* ~ *open*, abstain from interference or competition; *in the* ~, engaged in military operations; *a fair* ~ *and no favour*, equal conditions in contest. 3. Ground for playing cricket, football, etc.; (baseball) ground in which fielders stand. 4. Those who take part in outdoor contest or sport; all competitors in race etc., or all except the favourite; (cricket) fielding side; (cricket and baseball) fieldsmen. 5. Large stretch, expanse, of sea, sky, ice, snow, etc. (also fig.). 6. Surface on which something is portrayed; (her.) surface of escutcheon or of one of its divisions (ill. HERALDRY); ground of flag, picture, etc. 7. Area or sphere of action, operation, investigation, etc.; space or range within which objects are visible through optical instrument; *magnetic* ~, region in which magnetic properties can be detected. 8. attrib.: (of animals etc.) found in the open country, wild; (of crops) grown for feeding to cattle, and covering large area; (of investigation, study, etc.) carried out on the spot, not in laboratory or study or office; ~-*allowance*, allowance to officer etc. on campaign to meet extra expenses; ~-*artillery*, light and mobile ordinance for use on campaign and in battle; so ~-*battery*, -*gun*; ~-*cornet*, minor magistrate of township in Cape Colony; ~-*day*, (mil.) day of exercise for troops in field manœuvres, review; day of brilliant or exciting events; day spent in field by scientific society etc.; ~-*dressing*, wound-dressing for use in field; ~ *events*, events (as high jump, discus-throwing, etc.) in athletic contest, excluding races; ~-*glass(es)*, binocular telescope for outdoor use; that lens of eye-piece of telescope or compound microscope which is nearer to object-glass; ~-*grey*, regulation greenish-grey colour of German army and air force uniform; ~-*hand*, slave working on plantation, farm-labourer; ~ *hospital*, ambulance; temporary hospital near battlefield; *F~ Marshal*, general officer of highest rank; ~-*meeting*, open-air religious meeting; ~-*officer*, army officer above rank of captain and below that of general; ~ *punishment*, (mil.) kinds of punishment for offences on campaign; ~-*sports*, outdoor sports, esp. hunting, shooting, fishing; ~ *telegraph*, *telephone*, movable telegraph, telephone, for use on campaign; ~-*work*: see 8 above; also (mil.) temporary fortification. ~ *v.* Act as fieldsman in cricket, baseball, or rounders; stop (and return) ball. **field'er, field'sman** *ns.* (cricket etc.) One of the side not batting; one who fields the ball.

field'fāre *n.* Species of thrush, *Turdus pilaris*, regular and common autumnal visitor in Britain.

Fiel'ding Henry (1707–54). English novelist; author of 'Tom Jones' (1749) etc.

Field of the Cloth of Gold. The meeting-place of Henry VIII and François I of France, near Calais, in 1520. [f. the magnificence of the display made by the two kings]

fiend (fēnd) *n.* The Devil; evil spirit, demon; person of superhuman wickedness (esp. cruelty or malignity); one excessively addicted (esp. to something injurious or dangerous). **fiend'ish** *adj.* **fiend'ishly** *adv.* **fiend'ishnėss** *n.*

fierce *adj.* Violent in hostility, angrily combative; of formidably violent and intractable temper; raging, vehement; ardent, eager; (of mechanism) violent, not smooth or easy in action. **fierce'ly** (-sl-) *adv.* **fierce'nėss** *n.*

fi'eri fā'ciăs (-shi-) *n.* (abbrev. *fi. fa.*) Writ to sheriff to execute judgement. [L, = 'see that (the sum payable) is made']

fiery (fīr'ĭ) *adj.* 1. Consisting of or flaming with fire; (of arrows etc.) fire-bearing; looking like fire, blazing-red; (of eyes) flashing, ardent; hot as fire; acting like fire, producing burning sensation; (of cricket-pitch) making ball rise dangerously; ~ *cross*, wooden cross with arms charred or dipped in blood, formerly sent among Highland clans as a call to arms. 2. Eager, pugnacious, spirited, irritable; (of horse) mettlesome. **fier'ĭly** *adv.* **fier'ĭnėss** *n.*

fi. fa. *abbrev.* FIERI FACIAS.

fife[1] *n.* Small shrill-toned instrument of flute kind, used chiefly to accompany drum in military music; one who plays this. ~ *v.* Play fife; play (air etc.) on fife. **fīf'er** *n.*

Fīfe[2]. County of E. Scotland.

fīfe-rail *n.* (naut.) Rail round mainmast, with belaying-pins for running rigging.

fĭfteen' (also fĭf'-) *adj.* & *n.* One more than fourteen (15, xv, or XV); (Rugby football) side of 15 players; *the F~*, the Jacobite rising of 1715. **fĭfteenth'** *adj.* & *n.*

fĭfth *adj.* Next after fourth; ordinal numeral belonging to the cardinal five; *under the ~ rib*, (to, in), the heart; *F~ Avenue*, one of the principal streets of New York noted for its fine shops and residences; ~ *column*, orig. the column of supporters which General Mola declared himself to have in Madrid, when he was besieging it in the Spanish Civil War of 1937–9, in addition to the 4 columns of his army outside the city; hence, organized body sympathizing with and working for enemy within a country at war; ~-*columnist*, member of such a body; ~ *monarchy*, last of 5 great empires referred to in prophecy in Dan. ii. 44, in 17th c. identified with millennial reign of Christ; ~-*monarchy man*, 17th-c. believer in immediate second coming of Christ, prepared to assist in establishing his reign by force and meanwhile to repudiate allegiance to any other government; ~ *part*, one of five equal parts of anything. ~ *n.* Fifth part; (mus.) interval of which the span involves 5 alphabetical names of notes, harmonic combination of notes thus separated. **fĭfth'ly** *adv.* In the fifth place.

fĭf'ty *adj.* Five times ten (50, l, or L); large indefinite number. ~ *n.* Set of 50 things or persons; *the fifties*, years between 49 and 60 in life or century; *fifty-fifty*, (colloq.) half-and-half (i.e. 50% each), equally; equal. **fĭf'tiėth** *adj.*

fĭg[1] *n.* 1. (Broad-leaved tree, usu. ~-*tree*, esp. *Ficus carica*, bearing) soft pear-shaped multiple fruit eaten fresh or dried; fig-tree. 2. Anything valueless; ~-*leaf*, device for concealing something shameful or indecorous (see Gen. iii. 7); ~-*wort*, the genus *Scrophularia*, esp. *S. nodosa*.

fĭg[2] *n.* Dress, equipment (only in *in full ~*); condition, form.

fĭg[3] *v.t.* ~ *out, up*, make (horse) lively or spirited; ~ *out*, dress up (person), bedizen.

fig. *abbrev.* Figure.

fight (fīt) *v.* (past t. and past part. *fought* pr. fawt). Contend in battle or single combat (*against, with*); ~ *for*, fight on behalf of (person) or to secure (thing); maintain (cause, suit at law, quarrel) against opponent; contend over (question), win one's *way* by fighting; contend with in battle or duel, or with the fists; set on (cocks, dogs) to fight; manœuvre (ship, troops) in battle; ~ *off*, repel with effort; ~ *out*, settle by fighting; ~ *shy of*, keep aloof from; *fighting chance*, chance of succeeding by great effort; *fighting cock*, game cock trained to fight; *fighting fish*, a Siamese fish, *Betta pugnax*; *fighting line*, that part of an armed force which is engaged in direct combat with the enemy; *fighting-top*, (naut.) high circular platform on warship's mast, on which men and guns can be placed. ~ *n.* Action of fighting; battle; combat, esp. pugilistic or unpremeditated, between two or more persons, animals, or parties; strife, conflict; appetite or ability for fighting; *running ~*, fight kept up while one party flies and one pursues; *sham ~*, fight between troops etc. for practice or display; *stand-up ~*, one in which parties stand up manfully to each other; *show ~*, not yield tamely.

fight'er (fīt-) *n.* One who fights; high-speed aeroplane designed for aerial combat rather than for bombing or carrying passengers; ~-*bomber*, aeroplane combining functions of a fighter and a bomber.

fĭg'ment *n.* Invented statement; thing with no existence except in imagination.

fĭg'ūral *adj.* Of figures; (mus.) embellished with accompaniment resembling a repetitive pattern (see FIGURE *v.*, sense 1).

fĭg'ūrant *n.* (fem. -*ante*) Ballet-dancer; character on stage with little or nothing to say.

fĭgūrā'tion (*or* -ger-) *n.* 1. Determination to a certain form; the resulting form. 2. Allegorical or figurative representation. 3. (mus.) Use of figural or florid counterpoint.

fĭg'ūrative (*or* -ger-) *adj.* 1. Representing by a figure or emblem; of pictorial or plastic representation. 2. (of speech etc.) Using figures or metaphors, metaphorical, not literal; metaphorically so called; abounding in, addicted to, figures of speech. **fĭg'ūratively** *adv.* **fĭg'ūrativenėss** *n.*

fĭg'ure (-*ger*) *n.* 1. External form, shape; (geom.) definite form constituted by line or lines enclosing superficial space, or by surface or surfaces enclosing space of three dimensions; bodily shape; person considered with regard to visible form or appearance; person as contemplated mentally. 2. Conspicuous appearance; (archaic) importance, distinction. 3. Image, likeness; representation of human form in sculpture, painting, etc.; emblem, type. 4. Diagram, illustration; decorative pattern; (dancing) evolution or movement of dance or dancer, division of set dance; (skating) movement, series of movements, beginning and ending at centre. 5. Numerical system, esp. one of the ten Arabic numerals; amount, number, sum, expressed in figures; *double ~s*, number between 9 and 100. 6. (rhet.) Form of expression deviating from normal order or use of words used to give variety, force, etc., e.g. hyperbole, metaphor, etc. (also *~ of speech*); (logic) particular form of syllogism according to position of middle term; (mus.) brief melodic or rhythmic formula out of which longer passages are developed. 7. *~-head*, ornamental carving, usu. bust or full-length figure, over ship's cutwater; nominal leader, president, etc., without real authority or influence. *~ v.* 1. Represent in diagram or picture; picture mentally, imagine; embellish with design or pattern, esp. (mus.) with accompaniment in quicker time. 2. Mark with (numerical) figures; (mus.) write figures over or under (bass) to indicate harmony. 3. Use figures in arithmetic; work *out* (sum); (U.S.) calculate, reckon, estimate; *~ on*, (U.S.) rely on, count on. 4. Make appearance, appear; be conspicuous; *~ as*, pass for, assume character of.

fĭgūrine′ (-ēn) *n.* Small modelled or sculptured figure, statuette.

Fiji (fē′jē). Principal island of Fiji archipelago, a group of about 250 islands in the S. Pacific, in British possession since 1874; capital, Suva.

fĭl′ament *n.* Slender thread-like body (esp., in animal and vegetable structures, one consisting of a row of cells); (bot.) part of stamen supporting anther (ill. FLOWER); fine, not easily fusible metallic conductor in electric lamp or thermionic valve, heated or made incandescent by current (ill. BULB). **fĭlamĕn′tary, fĭlamĕn′tous** *adjs.*

fĭlar′ia *n.* Member of genus *Filaria*, thread-worm. **fĭlar′ial** *adj.*

fĭl′ature (-cher) *n.* (Establishment for) reeling silk from cocoons.

fĭl′bert *n.* (Nut of) cultivated hazel, *Corylus maxima*. [Fr. *noix de filbert*, from being ripe near St. Philibert's day, 22nd Aug. (O.S.)]

fĭlch *v.t.* Steal, pilfer.

file¹ *n.* Instrument usu. of steel with one or more surfaces covered with numerous small raised cutting edges or teeth, for abrading, reducing, or smoothing surfaces. *~ v.t.* Smooth, reduce surface of, with file; *~ away, off*, remove with file.

file² *n.* String or pointed wire on which documents etc. are strung for preservation and reference; folder or other device for holding papers for reference; set of papers so kept, esp. in court of law, referring to a cause; series of issues of newspaper in order. *~ v.t.* Place (papers) on file or among public records.

file³ *n.* 1. (mil.) Front-rank man and the man or men directly behind him; small body of men (now usu. two); *in ~*, one behind the other; *Indian ~*: see INDIAN; *single ~*: see SINGLE; *rank and ~*: see RANK. 2. Row of persons or things one behind the other; (chess) one of the eight lines of squares extending across board from player to player. *~ v.* March in file; order (soldiers) to move *off* by files.

fĭl′ėmŏt *adj.* & *n.* (archaic) (Of) colour of dead leaf, brownish-yellow.

fĭl′ėt *n.* Net with square mesh, used for curtains etc.; *~ lace*, filet net embroidered.

fĭl′ial *adj.* Of, due from, son or daughter. **fĭl′ially** *adv.* **fĭl′ialnėss** *n.*

fĭliā′tion *n.* 1. Being child of specified parent; parentage; descent, transmission, *from*. 2. Formation of branches or offshoots; branch.

fĭl′ĭbĕg *n.* (Sc.) Kilt. [Gael. *feileadh* fold, pleat, *beag* little]

fĭl′ĭbŭster *n.* 1. One who engages in unauthorized warfare against foreign State; (hist.) piratical adventurer pillaging Spanish W. Indian colonies in 17th c.; member of bands of adventurers organizing revolutionary expeditions from U.S. to States in Central America and Spanish W. Indies, 1850–60. 2. (U.S.) Obstructionist, obstruction, in legislative assembly. *~ v.i.* Act as filibuster. [Du. *vrijbuiter* freebooter]

fĭl′ĭgree, fĭl′a- *n.* Ornamental work of fine gold or silver wire formed into delicate tracery; fine metal openwork; anything delicate, light, showy, and frail. **fĭl′ĭgreed** *adj.*

fĭl′ĭng *n.* (esp., usu. pl.) Particle(s) rubbed off by file.

Filipi′nō (-pē-) *n.* (pl. *-os*). Native of Philippine Islands, esp. of Spanish or mixed blood.

fill *v.* 1. Make or become full (*with*); (of wind) cause (sails) to swell; (of sail) become full of wind; stock abundantly; occupy whole capacity or extent of, spread over, pervade; (of dentist) block up (cavity, hollow tooth) with cement etc.; satisfy, satiate; (poker) complete (flush, full house, etc.) by drawing card(s); *~ the bill*, (orig. U.S.) do all that is required, suffice. 2. Hold (position), discharge duties of (office); occupy (vacant time); appoint holder of (vacant post). 3. Adulterate (esp. cotton fabrics). 4. *~ in*, complete (outline); add what is wanted to complete (unfinished document, blank cheque, etc.); *~ out*, enlarge, become enlarged, to proper limit; *~ up*, fill completely; fill tank of motor-car with petrol; supply vacant parts or places or deficiencies in; do away with by filling; grow full. **fĭll′er** *n.* **fill** *n.* Full supply of drink or food (only in *drink, eat, have*, etc., *one's ~*; also fig. in *look* etc. *one's ~*); enough to fill something.

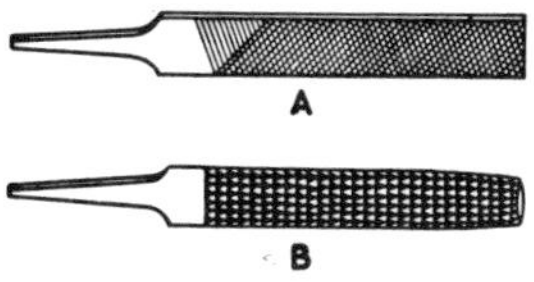
A. FILE. B. RASP

fĭll′ėt *n.* 1. String, narrow band of any material bound round head to confine hair, for ornament, etc.; band, bandage; thin narrow strip of anything. 2. (pl.) Animal's loins; fleshy easily-detached piece of meat near loins or ribs, undercut of sirloin; middle part of leg of veal etc., boned and rolled (ill. MEAT); half of one side of flat fish detached from back-bone; one of thick slices into which fish is easily divided. 3. (archit.) Narrow flat band separating two mouldings (ill. MOULDING); small band between flutes of column; (her.) horizontal division of shield, quarter of CHIEF in depth; raised rim or edge on any surface; (bookbinding) plain line impressed on cover, tool for making this. 4. (eng.) Curve inside an angle serving to prevent concentration of stress. *~ v.t.* 1. Bind (hair etc.) with fillet; encircle with ornamental band; 2. Divide (fish) into fillets.

FILIGREE

fĭll′ĭng *adj.* & *n.* (esp.) Cement etc. inserted into cavity of tooth; *~-station*, place where motorist may fill up with petrol.

fĭll′ip *n.* Sudden release of finger or thumb when it has been bent and checked by thumb or finger; slight smart stroke thus given; stimulus, incentive. *~ v.* Propel (coin, marble, etc.) with a fillip; stimulate; strike slightly and smartly; make a fillip.

fĭll′ister *n.* Rabbeting-plane for window-sashes etc. (ill. PLANE).

Fĭll′mōre, Millard (1800–74). 13th president of U.S., 1850–3.

fĭll'y *n.* Female foal; (slang) young lively girl.

film *n.* 1. Thin skin, plate, coating, or layer; slight veil or covering of haze, mist, etc.; fine thread or filament; morbid growth on eye; growing dimness in eyes of dying person. 2. (phot.) Celluloid etc. coated with light-sensitive emulsion for exposure in camera; piece of this for one exposure, or roll sufficient for a series; story, incident, etc., recorded on such film by cinema camera; (pl.) the cinema; ~ *camera*, camera using roll film; cinematographic camera; ~*-pack*, cut photographic films arranged in pile in case or holder for daylight loading or changing; ~ *star*, star actor in films; ~ *test*, test of would-be film actor. **fĭl'my** *adj.* **fĭl'mĭly** *adv.* **fĭl'mĭnėss** *n.* **film** *v.* 1. Cover, become covered, (as) with film. 2. Reproduce (scene, story, etc.) for the cinema; make cinema film.

fĭl'osĕlle *n.* Floss-silk.

fĭl'ter *n.* Contrivance for freeing liquid from suspended impurities by passing it through stratum of sand, fibre, charcoal, etc.; porous substance used for this purpose; combination of electric circuits designed to suppress unwanted frequencies; (phot.) screen (usu. of coloured glass or gelatine) for absorbing light of certain colours; ~*-bed*, tank or pond with false bottom covered with sand etc., for filtering large quantities of water; ~*-paper*, unsized paper for filtering liquids. ~ *v.* Pass (liquid etc.), flow, through filter; make way *through*, *into*, etc., percolate; (of wheeled traffic) turn off at a controlled junction or cross-roads; (of news etc.) leak *out*, come *through*; obtain by filtering. **fĭl't(e)rable** *adj.*

filth *n.* Loathsome dirt; corruption, pollution, obscenity; foul language. **fĭl'thy** *adj.*; ~ *lucre*, dishonourable gain (see Tit. i. 11); (joc.) money. **fĭl'thĭly** *adv.* **fĭl'thĭnėss** *n.*

fĭl'trāte *n.* Filtered liquor. ~ *v.* Filter. **fĭltrā'tion** *n.*

fĭm'brĭāte, -ātėd *adjs.* (bot., zool., etc.) Fringed, bordered.

fĭn *n.* 1. Organ for propelling and steering, attached to fish, cetaceans, etc., at various parts of body (ill. FISH); (slang) hand. 2. Projecting part; sharp lateral projection on share or coulter of plough; small projecting surface on various parts of aircraft, for ensuring stability.

fin. *abbrev. Ad finem* (= towards the end).

fī'nal *adj.* 1. At the end, coming last, ultimate; putting an end to doubt etc., conclusive, definitive, unalterable. 2. Concerned with end or purpose; ~ *clause*, (gram.) clause expressing purpose or intention. **fī'nally** *adv.* **fī'nal** *n.* Last or deciding heat or game; (sing. or pl.) last of series of examinations; edition of newspaper published latest in the day; (mus.) principal note in any mode (ill. MODE). **fī'nalist** *n.* Competitor in final.

fĭnā'le (-ahlĭ) *n.* (mus.) Last movement of instrumental composition; music bringing act of opera to a close; last scene, closing part, of drama etc., conclusion, end.

fīnăl'ity *n.* 1. Principle of final cause viewed as operative in the universe. 2. Being final; belief that something is final; final act, state, or utterance.

fī'nalīze *v.t.* Approve final form of (scheme, draft, etc.).

fĭnănce' (*or* fī'-) *n.* 1. (pl.) Pecuniary resources of sovereign, State, company, or person. 2. Management of (esp. public) revenue; science of revenue. ~ *v.t.* Furnish with finances, or money; find capital for.

fĭnan'cial (-shl) *adj.* Of revenue or money matters; ~ *year*, annual period for which public accounts are made up. **fĭnăn'cially** *adv.*

fĭnăn'cièr *n.* One skilled in raising and controlling public money; capitalist concerned in financial operations.

fĭnch *n.* Small passerine bird, esp. of genus *Fringilla* (freq. with defining word, as *bullfinch*, *goldfinch*, etc.).

find *v.t.* (past t. and past part. *found*). 1. Come across, fall in with, light upon; meet with, obtain, get (usu. something desirable or needful); gain, recover, use of; perceive, recognize; acknowledge or discover to be; ~ *one's feet*, be able to stand; develop one's powers. 2. Discover by search; discover (game) in hunting (also abs.); recover (something lost); succeed in obtaining; summon up (courage, resolution, etc.); reach, obtain, attain, as if by effort; ascertain, discover, by mental effort, calculation, study, etc.; ~ *one's way*, contrive to reach one's destination; go, be brought, to place, position, etc., in spite of difficulties, or not as matter of course; ~ *oneself*, discover one's vocation (and see below). 3. (law) Determine and declare (person) *guilty* or *innocent*; agree upon (verdict); ascertain validity of (indictment etc.). 4. Supply, provide, furnish; ~ *oneself*, provide for one's own needs. 5. ~ *out*, discover; devise; solve; detect in offence. ~ *n.* Finding, discovery; what is found.

fīn'der *n.* Person, thing, that finds; small telescope attached to large one to find object; contrivance for same purpose in microscope or photographic camera (ill. CAMERA).

fin de siècle (făn de syākl') *adj.* Characteristic of end of 19th c., advanced, modern; decadent.

fīn'dĭng *n.* (esp.) Verdict, decision (of court, jury, etc.); (pl., U.S.) small articles, tools, etc., supplied by workmen, small parts for repairing, etc.

fīne[1] *n.* 1. End (now only in *in* ~, to sum up, finally, in short). 2. Sum of money paid by incoming tenant in consideration of small rent. 3. Sum of money fixed as penalty for offence. ~ *v.* 1. Pay consideration *for* privilege or appointment. 2. Punish by a fine.

fīne[2] *adj.* 1. Of high quality; clear, pure, refined; (of gold or silver) containing specified proportion of pure metal. 2. Delicate, subtle; exquisitely fashioned; (of feelings) elevated. 3. Of slender thread; in small particles; thin; sharp; (of athlete) reduced by training. 4. Capable of delicate perception or discrimination; perceptible only with difficulty. 5. Excellent, of striking merit, good, satisfactory, fortunate, of good effect (often iron.); well conceived or expressed; of handsome appearance or size, dignified; (of weather) bright, cloudless, free from rain; ornate, showy, smart; fastidious, dainty, affecting refinement; (of speech or writing) affectedly ornate; flattering, complimentary. 6. ~ *arts*: see ART; ~*-draw*, sew together so that join is imperceptible; draw out (wire etc.) to a high degree of fineness; ~*-drawn*, subtle; extremely thin; (athletics) trained down in weight; ~ *feathers*, gaudy plumage (freq. fig.); ~ *gentleman*, *lady*, person of fashion; person who thinks himself above work; ~*-spun*, delicate, flimsy; excessively subtle, unpractical. **fīne'ly** (-nl-) *adv.* **fīne'nėss** *n.* **fīne** *adv.* With only a small margin of time or space, as *to cut*, *run*, ~. ~ *n.* Fine weather. ~ *v.* Make (beer) clear; (of liquid) become clear; ~ *away*, *down*, *off*, make, become, finer, thinner, less coarse; (make) dwindle, taper.

fine (champagne) (fēn) *n.* Old liqueur brandy. [Fr. *eau-de-vie fine de la Champagne* fine brandy of Champagne]

fī'nery[1] *n.* Showy dress or decoration; (rare) smartness, stylishness.

fĭn'ery[2] *n.* Hearth where cast iron is made malleable or steel is made from pig-iron.

fĭnĕsse' *n.* 1. Delicate manipulation, subtle discrimination; artfulness, cunning strategy. 2. (whist, bridge) Playing lower card in hope of taking trick, while holding higher card of same suit (not in sequence). ~ *v.* Use finesse; trick *into* etc. by finesse; make finesse, play (card) by way of finesse, in whist or bridge.

fĭng'er (-ngg-) *n.* 1. One of five terminal members of hand, or four excluding thumb (usu. numbered 1st to 4th, starting from that next to thumb, but *fourth* ~ sometimes = ring-finger, that next to little finger); *lay*, *put*, *a* ~ *upon*, touch, however slightly; *lay*, *put one's* ~ *on*, point with precision to; *turn* *twist, round one's* (*little*) ~, cajole; ***have a ~ in,*** have something to do with; *have at one's ~-tips,* (*~-ends*), be versed in, know familiarly. 2. Part of glove made to receive a finger. 3. Measure, breadth of a finger, ¾ inch; small quantity of liquor. 4. Finger-like object or projection. 5. *~-board,* part of neck of violin, guitar, etc., on to which strings are pressed when stopped by fingers (ill. STRING); *~-bowl,* bowl for rinsing fingers after dessert; *~-mark,* mark left on surface by (dirty) finger; *~-plate,* plate fastened on door to prevent finger-marks (ill. DOOR); *~-post,* sign-post; *~-print,* impression of tip of finger, esp. as means of identification; *~-stall,* cover of leather etc. to protect injured finger. ~ *v.t.* Touch with, turn about in, the fingers; play upon (musical instrument) with fingers; (mus.) mark (music) with figures indicating finger with which note is to be played.

fĭng'erĭng[1] (-ngg-) *n.* (esp.) Proper method of using fingers in playing music; marks on music indicating this.

fĭng'erĭng[2] (-ngg-) *n.* Kind of fine wool for knitting stockings etc. [earlier *fingram,* perh. f. Fr. *fin grain* fine grain]

fĭn'ial *n.* (archit.) Ornament finishing off apex of roof (ill. GABLE), canopy, bench-end, etc.; topmost part of pinnacle.

fĭn'ĭcal *adj.* = FINICKING. **fĭn'ĭcally** *adv.* **fĭn'ĭcalnėss** *n.*

fĭn'ĭckĭng *adj.* Over-nice, precise, fastidious; too much finished in details.

fĭn'ĭs *n.* (At end of book) the end; end of anything, esp. life.

fĭn'ĭsh *n.* Last stage, termination, esp. of fox-hunt; what serves to give completeness; accomplished or completed state; (*fight*) *to a finish,* till one party is completely worsted. ~ *v.* Bring to an end, come to the end of, complete; consume, get through, the whole or remainder of; kill, dispatch, overcome completely; perfect, put final or finishing touches to; complete education of; reach the end, cease, leave *off*; end *in* something or *by* doing.

fĭn'ĭsher *n.* (esp.) Workman or machine doing last operation in manufacture.

fī'nīte *adj.* Bounded, limited; not infinite; (gram., of verb) limited by number and person, not infinitive. **fī'nītely** (-tl-) *adv.* **fī'nīteness** *n.*

Fĭn'land. Country of NE. Europe situated on the gulfs of Finland and Bothnia; captured by Russia from Sweden in 1809; since 1917 an independent republic; capital, Helsinki.

Fĭnn[1] *n.* Native of Finland. **Fĭnn'ĭsh** *adj.* & *n.* (Language) of Finland.

Fĭnn[2]**.** The principal hero of a cycle of Irish legends; son of Cumal and father of Ossian; supposed to have lived in the 3rd c. A.D.

fĭnn'an *n.* ~ (*haddock*), Haddock cured with smoke of green wood, turf, or peat. [app. f. name of river *Findhorn,* confused with *Findon,* village in Kincardineshire]

Fĭnno-*prefix.* Finnish; *~-Ugrian languages,* a sub-family of the Ural-Altaic languages spoken in Hungary, Lapland, Finland, and some adjacent parts of Russia.

fĭnn'y *adj.* Having fins; like a fin; of, teeming with, fish.

fiord, fjord (fyôrd) *n.* Long narrow arm of sea between high cliffs, as in Norway.

fĭr *n.* 1. (Also *~-tree*), evergreen coniferous tree of genus *Abies,* or of various other genera with needles arranged singly on the shoots; *silver* ~, (i) *A. alba,* native of mountainous parts of central and S. Europe, with white under leaves; (ii) *A. balsamea* of Canada, small tree furnishing Canada balsam; *Scotch* ~ (or *Scotch pine*), *Pinus sylvestris,* native of arctic Europe and Asia, and perhaps of N. Britain; *spruce* ~ (or *Norway spruce*), *Picea excelsa,* native of N. Europe and mountains of central Europe. 2. Wood of any of these. 3. *~-cone,* fruit of the fir; *~-needle,* leaf of the fir.

fīre *n.* 1. Natural agency or active principle operative in combustion; flame, incandescence; volcanic heat; state of ignition or combustion; *set ~ to, set on* ~, kindle, ignite; *on* ~, ignited, burning; *catch, take,* ~, be ignited. 2. Burning fuel in grate, furnace, etc.; electrical or gas apparatus for heating rooms etc. 3. Destructive burning, esp. of building, forest, etc., conflagration. 4. Luminosity, glow, like that of fire; *St. Elmo's* ~: see CORPOSANT. 5. Burning heat, fever; *St. Anthony's* ~, erysipelas. 6. Burning passion; fervour, enthusiasm; liveliness and warmth of imagination, poetic inspiration. 7. Discharge of fire-arms; *open* ~, begin firing; *line of* ~, path of bullet; *under* ~, being shot at. 8. *~-alarm,* automatic arrangement for giving notice of outbreak of fire; *~-arm,* (usu. pl.) weapon from which missiles are propelled by gunpowder or other explosive; *fire'back,* metal plate at back of open hearth; *~-ball,* large luminous meteor, lightning in globular form; *~-balloon,* balloon made buoyant by heat of combustible burning at its mouth; *~-basket,* framework of metal bars for holding logs or coal in hearth;

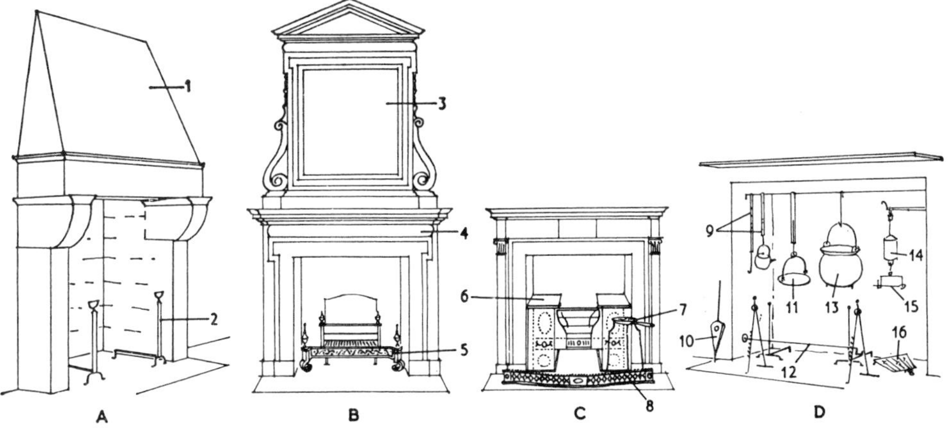

FIRE-PLACE: A. MEDIEVAL. B. EARLY 18TH C. C. LATE 18TH C. D. TRADITIONAL COOKING UTENSILS

1. Hood. 2. Andiron or fire-dog. 3. Overmantel. 4. Mantel. 5. Fire-basket. 6. Hob. 7. Trivet. 8. Fender. 9. Pot-hooks. 10. Bellows. 11. Girdle or griddle. 12. Spit. 13. Cauldron. 14. Jack. 15. Small spit. 16. Gridiron

~*-bomb*, incendiary bomb; ~*-box*, fuel-chamber of steam-boiler; ~*-brand*, piece of burning wood; person or thing kindling strife or mischief; ~*-brick*, brick capable of withstanding great heat, used in furnaces etc.; ~*-brigade*, organized body of firemen; ~*-clay*, clay used for fire-bricks etc.; ~*-control*, system of directing and regulating fire of ship's or fort's guns; ~*-damp*, miners' name for explosive mixture of methane and air formed in coal-mines; ~*-dog*, andiron; ~*-eater*, juggler who eats or pretends to eat flames; one fond of fighting, pugnacious or quarrelsome person; ~*-engine*, vehicle carrying apparatus for extinguishing fires; ~*-escape*, metal stairway on outside of building, movable ladder, or other apparatus for facilitating escape from fire; ~*-extinguisher*, portable metal container from which a chemical liquid can be discharged to extinguish fire; ~*-fighter*, one of a squad of people organized to deal with fires; ~*-fly*, beetle capable of emitting light (any of about 2,000 species); ~*-guard*, metal framework round fire to prevent coals from falling into room, keep children from fire; a fire-watcher; ~*-hose*, hose-pipe for extinguishing fire; ~*-insurance*, insurance against loss by fire; ~*-irons*, implements for tending domestic fire, shovel, tongs, and poker; ~*-light*, light given by fire; ~*-lighter*, small piece of inflammable material used to facilitate the lighting of a fire in a grate; ~*-lock*, (musket with) lock in which sparks were produced to ignite priming; *fire'man*, tender of furnace or fire of steam-engine; (also) one employed to extinguish fires; ~*-place*, grate or hearth for fire in room etc.; ~*-plug*, connexion in water-main for fire-hose; ~*-policy*, policy of insurance against fire; ~*-proof*, proof against fire; strongly resistant to heat; ~*-raising*, arson; ~*-screen*, screen to keep off heat of fire; ~*-ship*, vessel filled with combustibles and set adrift among enemy ships; *fire'side*, space round fire-place; home life; ~*-walk*, ceremony of walking barefoot over hot stones, ashes, etc., as religious rite or ordeal; hence, ~*-walker*; ~*-watcher*, person detailed to detect and report fires caused by aerial bombing; ~*-water*, alcoholic spirit (name orig. used by, or attributed to, N. Amer. Indians); *fire'wood*, wood for fuel; *fire'work*, contrivance or apparatus for producing spectacular effect by use of combustibles, etc., squib, rocket, etc.; (pl.) pyrotechnic display. ~ *v.* Set fire to with intention of destroying; kindle (explosives); catch fire; become heated or excited; redden; bake (pottery, bricks), cure (tea, tobacco) by artificial heat; supply (furnace, engine) with fuel; cause (explosive) to explode; shoot, discharge gun, etc.; (of gun etc.) go off; propel (missile) from gun etc.; (orig. U.S.) expel, dismiss (person); ~ *away*, begin, go ahead; ~ *up*, show sudden anger; ~*-step*, ledge on which soldier in trench stands to fire; *firing-line*, front line of troops (intermittently) engaged in firing upon enemy; *firing-party*, *-squad*, squad of soldiers detailed to shoot condemned man or to fire a volley over grave of soldier buried with military honours.

firk'in *n.* Small cask for liquids, butter, fish, etc.; (as measure) half of kilderkin (ill. CASK).

firm[1] *n.* Partnership for carrying on business, commercial house; team, esp. of doctors and their assistants in hospital; *long* ~, set of swindlers obtaining goods without paying.

firm[2] *adj.* Of solid or compact structure; fixed, stable; steady, not shaking; established, immutable; (of offer etc.) not liable to cancellation after acceptance; steadfast, unflinching, resolute; constant *to*; (of prices, goods) maintaining their level or value. **firm'ly** *adv.* **firm'nĕss** *n.* **firm** *adv.* Firmly (chiefly in *hold* ~, *stand* ~). ~ *v.* Solidify, compact (soil after planting etc., cheese); fix firmly (plants in soil).

firm'ament *n.* Vault of heaven with its clouds and stars.

firm'an *n.* Oriental sovereign's edict, grant, licence, passport.

first *adj.* Earliest in time or order; foremost in position, rank, or importance; coming next after specified or implied time; (*the*) ~ *thing*, as the first thing that is done; *in the* ~ *place*, firstly, first; *F*~ *Lord of the Admiralty*, parliamentary chief of English Navy; *F*~ *Sea Lord*, professional chief of Navy; *F*~ *Lord of the Treasury*, chief minister of Board of the Treasury (usu. prime minister); ~ *aid*, assistance given to injured before medical treatment is procured; ~*-born*, eldest (child); ~*-chop*, first-class; ~ *class*, set of persons or things grouped together as better than others; best accommodation in railway train etc.; highest division in examination list, place in this; ~*-class* (*adj.*) belonging to the first class, of best quality, very good; (*adv.*) by the first class; ~ *cost*, prime cost; ~*-day*, Sunday (esp. among Society of Friends); ~ *floor*, storey next above ground floor; (U.S.) ground floor; ~*-foot*, (Sc.) person who first crosses threshold of a house on New Year's Day; ~ *form*, lowest class in school; ~*-fruit*, (usu. pl.) first products of agriculture for season, esp. as offered to God; first products of work etc.; (hist.) payment to superior by new holder of office; ~*-hand*, direct, without intermediate agency; ~*-night*(*er*), (habitual frequenter of) first performance of play etc.; ~ *offender*, offender against whom no previous conviction is recorded; ~*-rate*, of the highest class; excellent, very well, (naut.) first-rate war-vessel, esp. one of the old three-deckers with 74 to 120 guns. ~ *n.* First day (*of* month); first edition; first-class railway carriage; (holder of) place in first class in examination, etc.; (pl.) best quality (of certain articles of commerce); *the* ~, person or thing first mentioned; *from the* ~, from the beginning; *from* ~ *to last*, throughout; *at* ~, at the beginning; *the F*~, the 1st of September, when partridge-shooting begins; (commerc.) ~ *of exchange*, first of set of bills of exchange of even tenor and date. ~ *adv.* Before anyone or anything else; before some specified or implied event, time, etc., in preference, rather; for the first time; ~ *and last*, taking one thing with another, on the whole; ~ *or last*, sooner or later.

first'lĭng *n.* (usu. pl.). First result of anything, first-fruits; first offspring, first-born of season.

first'ly *adv.* (only in enumerating) In the first place, first.

firth *n.* Arm of sea; estuary.

fisc, fisk *n.* 1. Public treasury of ancient Rome; Roman emperor's privy purse. 2. *fisk*, (Sc. law) Public treasury into which estates lapse by escheat.

fis'cal *adj.* Of public revenue. **fis'cally** *adv.* **fis'cal** *n.* In Italy, Spain, etc., legal official with function of public prosecutor; in Holland etc., magistrate dealing with offences against revenue; (Sc.) short for procurator-fiscal.

fish[1] *n.* (pl. often *fish*). 1. (pop.) Animal living exclusively in water; (strictly) one of class of vertebrate cold-blooded animals having gills throughout life and usu. fins. 2. Flesh of fish as food. 3. (colloq.) Person, fellow, of specified kind, as *poor* ~, *queer* ~. 4. *The Fish*(*es*), zodiacal constellation (*Pisces*) situated between Aquarius and Aries. 5. ~*-glue*, kind of gelatin obtained from fish, isinglass; ~*-hawk*, osprey; ~*-hook*, barbed hook used for catching fish; (naut.) iron hook forming part of tackle for raising anchor; ~*-kettle*, long oval vessel for boiling fish; ~*-knife*, knife, usu. of silver, for eating fish; *fish'monger*, dealer in fish; *fish'pond*, pond in which fish are kept; (joc.) the sea; ~*-pool*, fishpond; ~*-slice*, knife for carving fish; cook's flat implement for turning or taking out fish etc.; ~*-tail*, shaped like fish's tail (esp. of spreading jet of gas from ~*-tail burner*); *fish'wife*, woman selling fish. ~ *v.* Catch or try to catch fish; search *for* something in or under water; collect (pearls, coral) from bottom of sea; try to catch fish in (pool etc.); draw *out of* water, pocket, etc., draw *out*; seek by indirect means or artifice *for* (secrets, compliments, etc.); get (fact, opinion, secret) *out*; ~ *in troubled waters*, make one's profit out of disturbances; (naut.) ~ *the anchor*, draw flukes up to gunwale;

fishing-rod, long tapering usu. jointed rod to which fishing-line is attached.

fĭsh[2] *n.* 1. (naut.) Piece of curved wood, used to strengthen mast or yard. 2. Flat plate of iron, wood, etc., strengthening beam or joint; ~(*-plate*), one of two plates bolted together through ends of two rails on railway to cover and strengthen joint (ill. RAIL[1]). ~ *v.t.* Mend or strengthen (spar etc.), join (rails) with fish.

fĭsh[3] *n.* Small flat piece of bone or ivory used as counter in games.

fĭsh'er *n.* 1. Fisherman (archaic); ~ *of men*, (see Matt. iv. 19), evangelist. 2. Fishing animal. **fĭsh'erman** *n.* Man who lives by fishing; angler; fishing-boat. **fĭsh'ery** *n.* Business or occupation of catching fish etc.; fishing-ground; those engaged in fishing; right of fishing.

fĭsh'y *adj.* 1. Abounding in fish; like fish's (eye, tail, etc.); smelling or tasting like fish; consisting of fish. 2. (slang) Of dubious character, questionable. **fĭsh'ĭly** *adv.* **fĭsh'ĭnėss** *n.*

fisk: see FISC.

fiss'ĭle *adj.* 1. Cleavable, tending to split. 2. Capable of undergoing NUCLEAR fission; ~ *materials*, those (as uranium 235 or plutonium) which break up when bombarded by neutrons liberating atomic energy. **fissĭl'ity** *n.*

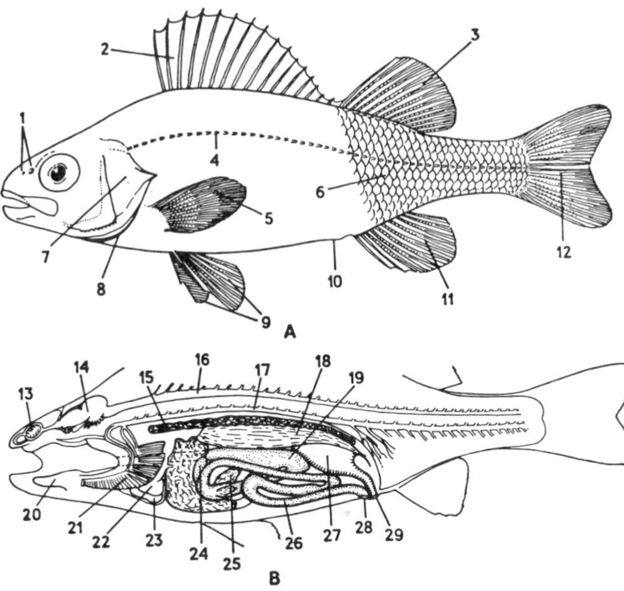

FISH: A. EXTERIOR. B. INTERNAL ORGANS

A. 1. Nostrils. 2. Spinous dorsal fin. 3. Soft dorsal fin. 4. Lateral line. 5. Pectoral fin. 6. Scales. 7. Gill-cover or operculum. 8. Gill-opening. 9. Pelvic fins. 10. Vent. 11. Anal fin. 12. Caudal fin. B. 13. Nasal organ. 14. Brain. 15. Vein. 16. Spinal cord. 17. Artery. 18. Air bladder, swim bladder, or float. 19. Stomach. 20. Tongue. 21. Gills. 22, 23. Heart (22. Auricle, 23. Ventricle). 24. Gall bladder. 25. Pancreas. 26. Intestine. 27. Ovary. 28. Anal-opening. 29. Urogenital sinus

fĭ'ssion (-shn) *n.* 1. (biol.) Division of cell or organism into new cells or organisms, as mode of reproduction. 2. (*Nuclear*) ~: see NUCLEAR. **fĭ'ssionable** (-sh*o*n) *adj.* Capable of undergoing nuclear fission.

fĭ'ssure (-sh*er*) *n.* Cleft made by splitting or separation of parts; (bot., anat.) narrow opening in organ etc., esp. depression between convolutions of brain; cleavage. ~ *v.t.* Split.

fĭst *n.* Clenched hand, esp. as used in boxing; (joc.) hand, handwriting. ~ *v.t.* Strike with fist; (chiefly naut.) handle. **fĭs'tĭc(al)** *adjs.* (joc.) Pugilistic.

fĭs'tĭcŭffs *n.pl.* Fighting with the fists.

fĭs'tūla *n.* 1. Long pipe-like ulcer with narrow mouth; suppurating canal. 2. Natural pipe or spout in whales, insects, etc. **fĭs'tūlar** *adj.* Pipe-like (esp., bot., of pith of hollow stems etc.). **fĭs'tūlous** *adj.*

fĭt[1], **fȳtte** *n.* (archaic) Section of a poem.

fĭt[2] *n.* Paroxysm, or one of recurrent attacks, of periodic or constitutional ailment; sudden transitory attack of some illness; sudden seizure, with loss of consciousness or convulsions, of hysteria, apoplexy, fainting, paralysis, or epilepsy; violent access or outburst (of laughter, rage, etc.), capricious impulse, mood; *by fits and starts*, spasmodically.

fĭt[3] *adj.* Well adapted or suited (*for, to*); good enough *for*; becoming, proper, right; qualified, competent, worthy (*to*); in suitable condition, ready, *to* do, *for*; in good athletic condition or health. **fĭt'ly** *adv.* **fĭt** *v.* Be in harmony with, become, befit; be of right measure, shape, and size for (esp. of dress); fill up, exactly correspond to, make to do this; make suitable, adapt, *for, to*; make competent *for, to*; supply, furnish (ship etc.) *with*; ~ *on*, try on; ~ *out, up*, equip. ~ *n.* Adaptation, adjustment; style in which garment etc. fits.

fĭtch *n.* (Brush made of) polecat's hair.

fĭtch'é, -ee: see FITCHY.

fĭtch'ew *n.* Foumart, polecat.

fĭtch'y, -é, -ee *adj.* (her., of cross) Having its ends sharpened into points (ill. HERALDRY).

fĭt'ful *adj.* Characterized by irregular fits of activity or strength; spasmodic, changing, capricious. **fĭt'fully** *adv.* **fĭt'fulnėss** *n.*

fĭt'ment *n.* Piece of furniture; (pl.) fittings.

fĭt'nėss *n.* Being fit; moral worthiness; propriety.

fĭtt'er *n.* (esp.) 1. Mechanic who fits together parts of engines etc. 2. Tailor or dressmaker engaged in cutting out etc. garments, or altering ready-made garment to fit.

fĭtt'ĭng *n.* (esp., usu. pl.) Fixture(s), apparatus, furniture; ~*-shop*, (eng.) place where parts are put together. ~ *adj.* (esp.) Becoming, proper, right. **fĭtt'ĭngly** *adv.*

FĭtzGĕ'rald, Edward (1809–83). English scholar; famous for his English poetic version of the Rubáiyát of Omar Khayyám.

fīve *adj.* One more than four (5, v, or V); ~*-finger exercise*, piano exercise for practising all fingers, keeping them on same five notes all the time; ~*-o'clock tea*, light afternoon meal; *five'penny*, costing, rated at 5*d.*; ~*-per-cents*, stocks or shares paying 5%; *F~ Nations*, (U.S. hist.) the Iroquois, a powerful confederacy of Indian tribes in western New York, first formed *c* 1570 and consisting of the Seneca, Cayuga, Onondaga, Oneida, and Mohawk tribes; ~*-year plan*, scheme begun in 1928 for the economic development of the U.S.S.R. over a period of 5 years. ~ *n.* The number five; set of 5 things; card, die, or domino with 5 pips; (pl.) gloves, shoes, etc., of fifth size. **fīve'fōld** *adj.* & *adv.*

fīv'er *n.* (colloq.) £5 note; hit for five at cricket.

fīves (-vz) *n.* Game for 2 or 4 persons in which ball is struck by hand in a padded glove or by wooden bat against walls of a court forming three sides of a rectangle. (*Illustration, p.* 302.)

fĭx *v.* 1. Make firm or stable, fasten, secure, implant; direct steadily, set (eyes, attention, etc.) *on, upon*; (of object) attract and hold (attention etc.); make (eyes, features), or become, rigid; deprive of, lose, volatility or fluidity, congeal; make (colour, photographic image) fast; ~ *with one's eyes*, direct steady gaze upon. 2. Place definitely or permanently, station, establish; take up one's position; settle one's choice, decide (*up*)*on*; assign precise position of; refer (thing, person) to definite place or time; determine incidence of (liability etc.); settle, determine, specify (price, date, place); arrest changes or development in, settle permanent form of (language etc.); (chiefly U.S.) arrange, get ready, put in order (also ~ *up*); (U.S.) bring (person) over to one's side, as by bribery, 'square'; (U.S.) ~ *it*, arrange matters. ~ *n.* Dilemma, position hard to escape from; position determined by bearings or astronomical observations.

fĭxā'tion *n.* 1. Fixing, being fixed; process of rendering solid; coagulation; combination of gas with solid. 2. (psychol.) Arrest of emotional development at infantile or immature stage.

fĭx'ative *adj.* Tending to fix. ~ *n.* Liquid with which drawing is coated to prevent chalk etc. from rubbing off; substance applied to hair to keep it tidy.

fixed (-kst) *adj.* (esp., of oil or acid) That cannot be distilled or evaporated without decomposition; ~ *star*, star seeming to keep same relative position to others (opp. to *planet*). **fĭx'ėdly** *adv.* In fixed manner, intently. **fĭx'ėdnėss** *n.* Fixed state, immobility, permanence, steadfastness.

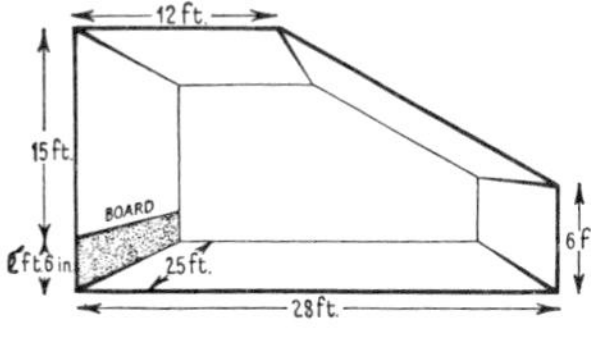

FIVES COURT

fĭx'er *n.* (esp.) Preparation used for fixing dye, photograph, etc.; (phot.) sodium thiosulphate, 'hypo'.

fĭx'ings *n.pl.* (U.S.) Apparatus, equipment; trimming of dress or dish, adjuncts.

fĭx'ĭty *n.* Fixed state; stability, permanence.

fĭx'ture *n.* 1. Thing fixed or fastened in position; (law, pl.) articles of accessory character annexed to houses or lands; person or thing confined to or established in one place. 2. Appointment or date for race, meet, game, etc.; the race, game, etc., itself.

fĭzz *n.* Hissing or spluttering sound; (colloq.) champagne. **fĭzz'y** *adj.* **fĭzz** *v.i.* Make fizz.

fĭz'zle *v.i.* Hiss or splutter feebly; ~ *out*, come to lame conclusion, fail. ~ *n.* Hissing, spluttering; (colloq.) failure, fiasco.

fl. *abbrev.* Florin(s); *floruit* (= flourished).

f.l. *abbrev.* *Falsa lectio* (= false reading).

Fla. *abbrev.* Florida.

flăbb'ergast (-gah-) *v.t.* Dumbfound, overwhelm with astonishment.

flăbb'y *adj.* Hanging loose by its own weight, flaccid, limp, soft; weak, nerveless, feeble. **flăbb'ĭly** *adv.* **flăbb'ĭnėss** *n.*

flabĕll'ate, flabĕll'ĭform *adjs.* Fan-shaped.

flăcc'ĭd (-ks-) *adj.* Hanging or lying loose or wrinkled, limp, flabby; relaxed, drooping; wanting vigour, feeble. **flăccĭd'ĭty** *n.*

flăg[1] *n.* Any of various monocotyledonous plants with bladed or sword-shaped leaves, mostly growing in moist places; esp. one of the genus *Iris*; *sweet*~, *Acorus calamus*, with aromatic rhizome used as a stimulant.

flăg[2] *n.* Flat slab of any fine-grained rock which may be split into flag-stones; (also ~*-stone*) flat stone suitable for paving; (pl.) flagged pavement. ~ *v.t.* Pave with flags.

flăg[3] *n.* (Also ~*-feather*), quill-feather of bird's wing.

flăg[4] *n.* Piece of bunting or other stuff, usu. oblong or square, attached by one edge to staff or

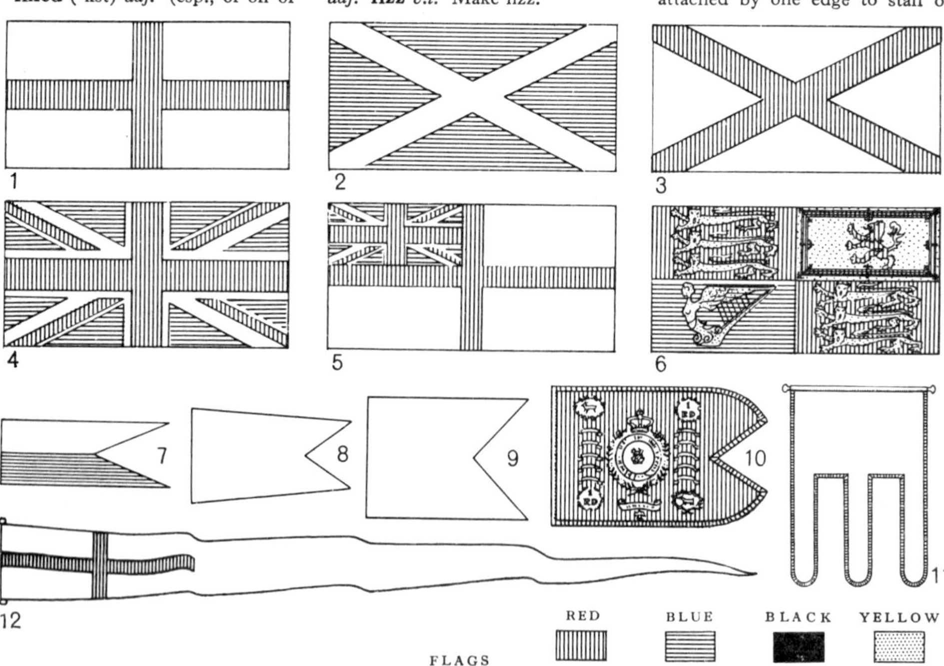

FLAGS

1. Flag of St. George. 2. Flag of St. Andrew. 3. Flag of St. Patrick. 4. Union flag. 5. White ensign, the flag of the Royal Navy. 6. Royal Standard, indicating the Sovereign's presence. 7. Lancers' pennon, a regimental colour. 8. Broad pendant, distinguishes the commodore's ship in a squadron. 9. Burgee, a personal or club flag on yachts. 10. Dragoons' guidon, a regimental standard. 11. Gonfalon, a church banner. 12. Mast-head pendant flown by ships in commission

halyard and used as standard, ensign, or signal; (naut.) flag carried by flagship as emblem of admiral's rank afloat; plate bearing words 'For Hire' attached to meter of taxicab, and lowered to start meter when vehicle is engaged; flag used to indicate start or finish of race; tail of setter or Newfoundland dog; *black* ~, pirate's ensign; also, flag hoisted at prison to announce execution of criminal; *white* ~, ~ *of truce*, white flag raised or carried to indicate desire to parley; *yellow* ~, flag displayed by ship with infectious disease on board, hospital ship, or ship in quarantine; *lower, strike, one's* ~, take it down as salute or sign of surrender; *drop the* ~, give signal for starting race; *hoist, strike, one's* ~, (of admiral) assume, relinquish, command; ~-*boat*, boat serving as mark in aquatic matches; ~-*captain*, captain of flagship; ~-*day*, day on which money is raised for a cause by selling small paper flags or other tokens to be worn as evidence of having contributed; (U.S.) 14th June, anniversary of adoption by Congress of Stars and Stripes as national flag (1777); ~-*flying*, (colloq.) over-bidding at bridge; ~-*lieutenant*, officer acting as aide-de-camp to admiral; ~-*officer*, admiral, vice-admiral, or rear-admiral; *flag'ship*, ship with admiral on board; *flag'staff*, pole on which flag is hoisted; ~-*station*, station where trains stop only if signalled; ~-*wagging*, (mil. slang) signalling with flags held in hands. ~ *v.t.* Place flag on or over; mark out with flags; inform, warn, communicate, by flag-signals.

flăg[5] *v.i.* Hang down, flap loosely; droop, fade, become limp; lag, lose vigour, grow languid; fall off in interest.

flă'gellant (*or* flajĕl'-) *n.* & *adj.* (One) who scourges himself, esp. as religious discipline or penance.

flă'gėllāte[1] *v.t.* Scourge. **flăgėllā'tion, flă'gėllātor** *ns.* **flă'gėllatory** *adj.*

flagĕll'um *n.* (pl. -*la*). (zool., bot.) Microscopic lash-like appendage, esp. one used for locomotion (ill. PROTOZOA). **flă'gėllate**[2] (-*at*), **flagĕll'ĭfôrm** *adjs.*

flăgeolĕt' (-jo-) *n.* Small wind-instrument resembling recorder with mouthpiece at end and 6 holes, 2 of which are at the back for the thumbs; organ-stop with similar tone.

flagĭ'tious (-jĭsh*us*) *adj.* Deeply criminal, atrocious, heinous, villainous. **flagĭ'tiously** *adv.* **flagĭ'tiousnėss** *n.*

flăg'on *n.* Large vessel, usu. with handle, spout, and lid, to hold liquor for table; similar vessel for Eucharist; large bottle for wine, cider, etc., often of flattened globular shape, usu. holding about twice as much as ordinary bottle.

flāg'rant *adj.* (Of offence or offender) glaring, notorious, scandalous. **flāg'rancy** *n.* **flāg'rantly** *adv.*

flail *n.* Hand threshing-implement, wooden staff at end of which a heavy stick hangs swinging. ~ *v.*

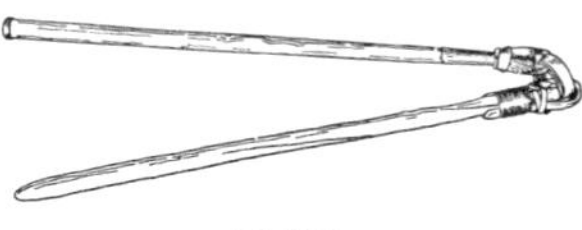

FLAIL

flair *n.* Instinctive discernment, selective instinct for what is good, paying, etc.

flăk *n.* Anti-aircraft fire; ~-*ship*, German anti-aircraft vessel. [Ger., f. initial letters of *Fl*ieger*a*bwehr*k*anone A.A. gun]

flāke[1] *n.* Frame or rack for storing provisions, esp. oat-cakes, or drying produce, esp. fish etc.; small platform hung over ship's side for workmen to stand on.

flāke[2] *n.* Light fleecy tuft, esp. of snow; portion of ignited matter thrown off; thin broad piece peeled off surface; chip of hard stone used in prehistoric times as cutting instrument; natural division of fish's flesh; layer, lamina, stratum; ~-*white*, pigment made from the purest white-lead in form of flakes or scales; *cornflakes* etc., kinds of breakfast cereal. ~ *v.* Fall like, sprinkle as with, snow; take, come, *away, off*, in flakes. **flāk'y** *adj.* (esp., of pastry) Repeatedly folded and rolled with lumps of butter so as to consist when baked of thin delicate flakes or layers.

flăm[1] *n.* Sham story, trick, deception.

flăm[2] *n.* Single stroke on side drum.

flăm'beau (-bō) *n.* Torch, esp. of several thick waxed wicks.

flămboy'ant *adj.* 1. (archit.) Characterized by wavy flame-like lines: of the style prevalent in France in 15th and first half of 16th centuries. 2. Florid, floridly decorated; gorgeously coloured. ~ *n.* Kinds of flame-coloured flower. **flămboy'ance** *n.*

flāme *n.* 1. Vapour heated to point of combustion, ignited gas; portion of this, often spire-like or tongue-like; (pl.) fire; visible combustion. 2. Bright light; brilliant colourings. 3. Passion, esp. of love; (joc.) sweetheart; ~-*thrower* (Ger. *flammenwerfer*), machine of war with reservoir from which long spray of flame can be ejected. ~ *v.* 1. Emit flames, blaze. 2. (of passion) Burst out; (of persons) break *out*, blaze *up*, into anger. 3. Glow like or as with flame; shine brightly. 4. Move as or like flame; send (signal) by fire; subject to action of flame. **flāme'lėss** (-ml-) *adj.* **flām'y** *adj.*

flām'ĕn *n.* (Rom. antiq.) Priest devoted to service of a particular deity.

flamĕn'cō *n.* (pl. -*os*). Spanish gipsy style of singing or dancing; song or dance in this style.

flām'ĭng *adj.* Very hot; bright-coloured; very bright; highly coloured, exaggerated, startling. ~ *onions*, anti-aircraft projectile consisting of balls of fire shot upwards in rapid succession, suggesting a resemblance to ropes of onions.

flamĭn'gō (-ngg-) *n.* Wading bird of a widely distributed family, *Phoenicopteridae*, with scarlet patch on wings, extremely long legs and neck, and heavy bent bill.

flămm'able *adj.* Easily set on fire. **flămmabĭl'ity** *n.*

flăn *n.* Round flat open tart of pastry covered with fruit etc.

flanch (-ah-) *n.* (her.) Sub-ordinary formed on each side of shield by convex line (ill. HERALDRY).

Fla'nders (flah-). Ancient countship now divided between Belgium, France, and Holland; ~ *poppy*, red poppy used as emblem of the soldiers of the Allies who fell in the war of 1914–18; an artificial red poppy made for wearing on REMEMBRANCE Day, sold in aid of disabled soldiers.

flâneur (flahnêr') *n.* Idler, loafer.

flănge (-j) *n.* Projecting flat rim collar, or rib, used to strengthen an object, attach it to another, etc. (ill. GIRDER). ~ *v.t.* Provide with flange.

flănk *n.* 1. Fleshy or muscular part of side between ribs and hip; (leather manuf.) part of hide covering this. 2. Side of building, mountain, etc.; (mil.) extreme left or right side of army or body of troops. ~ *v.t.* Guard, protect, strengthen, on flank; menace or attack flank of; fire sideways upon; be posted or situated at flank of; (pass.) have at flanks or sides.

flănk'er *n.* Projecting part of fortification defending flank of another part, or commanding flank of assailant; (mil., usu. pl.) skirmisher(s) on flank of marching army.

flănn'el *n.* Light soft woollen fabric of plain or twill weave usu. without nap; (pl.) underclothing of flannel; (pl.) garments, esp. trousers, of flannel for games etc.; piece of flannel or other material used in washing hands or face etc., scrubbing floor etc. **flănn'elled** (-ld) *adj.* (esp.) Wearing flannels. **flănn'elly** *adj.*

flănnelĕtte' *n.* Cotton fabric imitating flannel.

flăp *v.* 1. Strike with something broad; drive (flies etc.) *away* or *off*; (of birds) strike with flat of wing. 2. Swing or sway about, flutter, oscillate; move (wings), (of wings) move, up and down; beat the wings. 3. (colloq.) Become agitated or fussed. ~ *n.* 1. Light blow with something broad; motion of something broad and loose, as wing, etc. 2. Broad hanging piece hinged or attached by one side only, as leaf of table, piece of cloth covering opening of pocket, etc.; hinged panel on trailing edge of aircraft's wing, lowered to increase lift of wing. 3. (colloq.) State of agitation or fuss.

flăpdōō'dle *n.* (colloq.) Nonsense, bunkum.

flăp'jăck *n.* 1. Flat round batter-cake cooked on griddle or baked; sweet oat-cake. 2. Vanity-case for face-powder.

flăpp'er *n.* (esp.) 1. Hinged or hanging piece, flap; broad fin; crustacean's tail. 2. Flat instrument for killing flies; broad flat clapper for scaring birds. 3. Young wild duck or partridge. 4. (slang) Girl in her teens, orig. with long hair worn in pigtail.

flāre *v.* 1. (Cause to) widen or spread (gradually) outwards, as the sides of a ship, a skirt, etc. 2. Burn with spreading unsteady flame; shine like such flame; glow as with flame; ~ *up*, burst into sudden blaze or anger; (of part of skin) become inflamed. ~ *n.* 1. Dazzling irregular light; unshaded flame in open air; sudden outburst of flame; combustible material burnt as signal or guide in fog, at night, etc.; bright light dropped from aircraft to illuminate target etc.; ~ *path*, line of lights on air-field etc. to guide aircraft in taking off or landing. 2. (path.) Local inflammation of small blood-vessels in reaction to injury. 3. Gradual widening or spreading of ship's sides, skirt, etc.; piece of garment so cut, whence **flared** (-ārd) *adj.*

flăsh *n.* 1. Sudden quick transitory blaze; time occupied by this, instant; brief outburst, transitory display; superficial brilliancy, ostentation; ~ *in the pan*, ignition of gunpowder in pan of old gun without discharge of missile; (fig.) abortive effort or outburst. 2. Five short pieces of black silk ribbon sewn to back of collar of ceremonial and walking-out dress uniform of 23rd Royal Welch Fusiliers; emblem sewn on shoulder of military uniform indicating unit to which wearer belongs. 3. Preparation of cayenne pepper or capsicum with burnt sugar, for colouring spirits. 4. Rush of water let down weir to take boat over shallows; contrivance for producing this. 5. (orig. U.S. newspaper slang) Very brief newspaper report sent by telegraph or telephone. 6. (cinema) Exposure of a scene. 7. ~-*back*, (cinema) recapitulation of earlier scene, episode beginning with sudden change to an earlier point of time; ~-*lamp*, portable electric lamp producing light by pressure of button; lamp used to give flash-light; ~-*light*, light giving sudden flashes, used for signals, in light-houses etc.; flash of artificial light used in photography in weak light, e.g. at night or indoors; electric torch; *flash'over*, electric spark or arc appearing suddenly across surface of insulating material; ~-*point*, temperature at which vapour given off by oil etc. will ignite. ~ *adj.* Gaudy, showy, counterfeit; cant, slang; connected with thieves, tramps, etc.; knowing, fly. ~ *v.* 1. Break suddenly into flame or light; give out flame or sparks; emit or reflect light, gleam; send, reflect, like a flash or in flashes; cause to flash. 2. Burst suddenly into view or perception; move swiftly. 3. Express or communicate by flash or flashes, esp. by telegraph. 4. (glass-making) Spread out into a sheet; cover (glass etc.) with thin layer of colour etc. 5. (Of water) rush along; send rush of water down (river etc.); ~-*board*, board set up on end on mill-dam to throw more water into mill-race when water is low.

flăsh'ĭng *n.* Strip of metal to prevent flooding or leakage at joint of roofing etc. (ill. ROOF).

flăsh'y *adj.* Brilliant but shallow or transitory; cheaply attractive; showy, gaudy; given to display. **flăsh'ily** *adv.* **flăsh'inėss** *n.*

flask (-ah-) *n.* 1. (usu. *powder*-~) Leather or metal case for carrying sportsman's supply of gunpowder. 2. Italian narrow-necked wicker-covered bottle for oil or wine. 3. Traveller's (usu. flat) bottle of metal, leather-covered glass, etc., for carrying spirit, wine, etc. in pocket; VACUUM flask.

flask'ėt (-ah-) *n.* Long shallow basket (archaic); small flask.

flăt[1] *n.* Floor, storey (now rare); suite of rooms usu. on one floor forming complete residence.

flăt[2] *adj.* 1. Horizontal, level; spread out, lying at full length. 2. Even, smooth, unbroken, without projection; with broad level surface and little depth. 3. Unqualified, plain, downright. 4. Dull, lifeless, monotonous; dejected, without energy; (of drink) that has lost its effervescence or flavour, insipid, stale; (of paint) without lustre. 5. Below the true pitch; *B* ~, *E* ~, etc. (written B♭ etc.; see *n.* below, sense 5), a semitone lower than B, E, etc. 6. (of price, rate, etc.) Unvarying, fixed, uniform; not varying with changed conditions. 7. ~-*boat*, flat-bottomed boat for transport in shallow water; ~-*car*, (U.S.) railway wagon without sides or top; ~-*fish*, a fish of the family *Pleuronectidae*, including sole, turbot, plaice, etc.; ~-*foot*(*ed*), (having) foot not normally arched at instep; hence, (fig.) heavy, clumsy; ~-*head*, one of a tribe (the Salish) of N. Amer. Indians erron. supposed to flatten their children's heads artificially; kind of N. Amer. snake, puff-adder; ~-*iron*, iron for smoothing linen (now usu. of one heated from below, not within); ~ *race*, race over clear and level ground (opp. to hurdle-race, steeplechase); ~ *spin*, kind of spin, which aircraft may enter, in which the controls have little or no effect and aircraft spins round its vertical axis; *flat'worm*, any of the tapeworms, flukes, etc. **flătt'ĭsh** *adj.* **flăt'ways,**

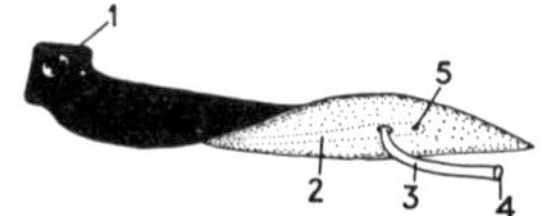

FLATWORM (*PLANARIA*)

1. Head. 2. Pharynx sheath into which pharynx can be withdrawn. 3. Pharynx. 4. Mouth. 5. Generative pore

flăt'wīse (-z) *advs.* **flăt'ly** *adv.* **flăt'nėss** *n.* **flăt** *adv.* Downright, positively, plainly; fully, quite. ~ *n.* 1. What is flat; flat surface or part, esp. broad surface of blade as opp. to edge; inside of open hand; level country; horizontal plane; horizontal bed, stratum, vein, etc.; piece of level ground; low-lying marshy land, swamp; (usu. pl.) level ground over which tide flows, or which is covered by shallow water. 2. Flat-bottomed boat; shallow basket. 3. (theatr.) Section of scenery mounted on frame; *join the* ~*s*, make thing consistent, give unity or coherency to something. 4. (slang) Duffer, dupe. 5. (mus.) Note lowered by a semitone below usual pitch; sign (♭) indicating this lowering, placed before note which is to be flattened or forming part of key-signature; *double* ~ (♭♭), sign indicating that note must be lowered two semitones; *two* ~*s*, *three* ~*s*, etc., key indicated by two, three, etc., flats in key-signature. ~ *v.* Make flat (chiefly in technical language); esp. give (paint) flat or lustreless surface.

flătt'en *v.t.* Make flat; ~ *out*, (esp.) bring (flight of aircraft) parallel with ground after diving.

flătt'er *v.t.* Court, fawn upon; praise or compliment unduly or insincerely; gratify vanity or self-esteem of, make feel honoured or distinguished; inspire with (esp. unfounded) hope; please (usu. one-*self*) with belief, idea, suggestion, *that*; exaggerate good points of, represent too favourably. **flătt'erer, flătt'ery** *ns.* **flătt'eringly** *adv.*

flăt'ūlent *adj.* Generating gas or air in the alimentary canal; caused by, attended with, troubled with, accumulation of this; (fig.) inflated, puffed up, windy, pretentious. **flăt'ūlence** *v.* **flăt'ūlently** *adv.*

flā'tus *n.* Gas, air, in stomach or bowel.

Flaubert (flōbār'), Gustave (1821–80). French realistic novelist; author of 'Madame Bovary' (1856), 'Salammbo' (1862), etc.

flaunt *v.* Wave proudly; display oneself or one's finery; show off, parade. ~ *n.* Flaunting motion. **flaunt'ĭngly** *adv.* **flaunt'y** *adj.*

flaut'ĭst *n.* Flute-player.

flavĕs'cent *adj.* Turning yellow, yellowish.

flāv'ĭn *n.* Any of a group of yellow pigments found in plants and animals and extracted from dyer's oak (*quercitron*) bark for use as dyes and antiseptics.

flāv'our(-ver) *n.* Aroma, mingled sensation of smell and taste; distinctive taste; undefinable characteristic quality. **flāv'orous, flā'vourlėss, flāv'oursome** *adjs.* **flāv'our** *v.t.* Give flavour to. **flāv'ourĭng** *n.* Something used for flavouring food or drink.

flaw[1] *n.* Crack, breach, rent; imperfection, blemish; invalidating defect in legal document or procedure, title, pedigree, etc. ~ *v.* Crack, damage, mar. **flaw'lėss** *adj.* **flaw'lėssly** *adv.* **flaw'lėssnėss** *n.*

flaw[2] *n.* Squall of wind; short storm.

flăx *n.* Blue-flowered plant, *Linum usitatissimum*, cultivated for its seeds (linseed) and for textile fibre obtained from the stem of the plant; dressed or undressed flax fibres; cloth made from these, linen; *~-seed*, linseed. **flăx'en** *adj.* Of flax; (of hair) coloured like dressed flax, pale yellow.

flay *v.t.* Strip off skin or hide of; (fig.) criticize severely; pillage, plunder (person); peel off (skin, bark, peel); pare off (turf).

flea *n.* Small wingless insect of genus *Pulex*, esp. *P. irritans*, well-known for its biting propensities and powers of jumping, feeding on human and other blood; (*go, send*, etc. *away*) *with a ~ in one's ear*, discomfited by stinging or mortifying reproof or repulse; *~-bag*, (joc.) sleeping-bag; *~-bane*, kinds of plants of the genera *Pulicaria* and *Erigeron*, esp. *P. dysenterica*; *~-beetle*, various species of small jumping beetles feeding esp. on root vegetable crops; *~-bite*, (fig.) slight inconvenience or expense, mere trifle; small reddish spot in animal's coloration; *~-louse*, leaping plant-louse of family *Psyllidae*.

fleam *n.* Lancet, esp. for bleeding horses.

flèche (-āsh) *n.* Slender spire, esp. over intersection of nave and transept (ill. SPIRE); one of the 24 points on a backgammon board. [Fr., = 'arrow']

flĕck *n.* Spot in the skin, freckle; patch of colour or light; small particle, speck. ~ *v.t.* Mark with flecks, dapple, variegate.

flĕdge *v.t.* Provide with feathers or plumage, wing for flight; cover as with feathers or down; feather (arrow).

flĕdg(e)'lĭng *n.* Young bird just fledged.

flee *v.* (past t. and past part. *fled*). Run away, seek safety in flight; vanish, cease, pass away; run away from, leave abruptly; eschew, shun.

fleece *n.* Woolly covering of sheep or similar animal; (her.) figure of sheepskin with wool, suspended by a ring; quantity of wool shorn from sheep at one time; rough, abundant, or woolly head of hair; thing like a fleece, white cloud, falling snow, etc.; (carding) thin sheet of cotton or wool fibre. **flee'cy** *adj.* **fleece** *v.t.* 1. (rare) Shear (sheep). 2. Strip of money, property, etc.; plunder, rob heartlessly. 3. Overspread as with fleece.

fleer *v.i.* Laugh impudently or mockingly; gibe, jeer, sneer. ~ *n.* Mocking look or speech.

fleet[1] *n.* Naval armament, number of warships under one commander-in-chief; number of ships or boats sailing in company; number of vehicles or aircraft forming a group or unit; *F~ Air Arm*, the aviation service of the Royal Navy.

fleet[2] *n.* (rare) Creek, inlet.

fleet[3] *adj.* (poet. or literary) Swift, nimble. **fleet'ly** *adv.* **fleet'nėss** *n.*

fleet[4] *adj.* Shallow; (quasi-*adv.*) at no great depth, near the surface.

fleet[5] *v.i.* Glide away, vanish, be transitory; pass rapidly, slip *away;* move swiftly, fly. **fleet'ĭng** *adj.* **fleet'ĭngly** *adv.*

Fleet[6]. *The ~*, a stream (now a covered sewer) flowing into Thames at Blackfriars Bridge; *the ~ (Prison)*, the old prison which stood near it, built by Richard I and serving for a long time as place of imprisonment for those condemned by Star Chamber, but later chiefly as debtors' prison, until demolished in 1848; *~ marriage*, (hist.) marriage performed by clergyman imprisoned in Fleet, without banns or licence (abolished by Marriage Act of 1753); *~ Street*, street in London near the Fleet largely devoted to offices of newspapers and other periodicals; hence, the press, journalism. [f. FLEET[2]]

Flĕm'ĭng[1]. Native of Flanders. **Flĕm'ĭsh** *adj.* & *n.* (Language) of Flanders; *~ bond*, method of brick-laying originating in Flanders; *~ brick*, hard yellow paving brick.

Flĕm'ĭng[2], Sir Alexander (1881–1955). British scientist; the chief discoverer of PENICILLIN.

flĕnch, flĕnse *vbs.t.* Cut up and slice fat from (whale, flayed seal); slice (blubber) from bones of whale; flay (seal).

flĕsh *n.* 1. Soft substance, esp. muscular parts, of animal body between skin and bones; *~ and blood*, the body or its material; mankind; human nature with its emotions and infirmities; (as *adj.*) actually living, not supernatural or imaginary; *one's own ~ and blood*, near relations, descendants; *proud ~*, overgrowth of granulations on wound. 2. Pulpy substance of fruit or plant. 3. Plumpness, fat; *lose, put on, ~*, grow thin, fat. 4. Tissue of animal bodies (excluding fish and sometimes fowls) as food; meat. 5. Visible surface of human body, with ref. to colour or appearance. 6. Whatever has corporeal life; the body (now only in biblical allusions); man's physical nature; the sensual appetites; *in the ~*, in bodily form, in life; *after the ~*, corporeally; *sins of the ~*, unchastity. 7. *~-brush, -glove*, brush, glove, for stimulating circulation by rubbing; *~-colour(ed)*, (of the) colour of flesh (sense 5), yellowish-pink; *~-fly*, one which deposits eggs in dead flesh; *~-pots*, (with ref. to Exod. xvi. 3) high living, luxuries; *~-wound*, one not reaching bone or vital organ. **flĕsh'lėss** *adj.* **flĕsh** *v.t.* Incite (hound etc.) by taste of blood; initiate in bloodshed; inflame by foretaste of success; use (sword etc.) for first time on flesh. **flĕsh'er** *n.* (Sc.) Butcher.

flĕsh'ĭngs *n.pl.* Close-fitting flesh-coloured garment worn on stage etc. to represent natural skin.

flĕsh'ly *adj.* 1. Carnal, lascivious, sensual. 2. Mortal, material; not divine or spiritual; worldly. **flĕsh'lĭnėss** *n.*

flĕsh'y *adj.* Plump, fat; of flesh, without bone; (of fruit etc.) pulpy; like flesh. **flĕsh'ĭnėss** *n.*

Flĕtch'er, John (1579–1625). English dramatist some of whose many plays were written in collaboration with Francis BEAUMONT.

fleur-de-lis (flẽr'de lē') *n.* (pl. *fleurs-*). Iris flower; heraldic lily (ill. HERALDRY); royal arms of France; hence, the French monarchy, France (before 1789).

fleur'ėt (-ūr-) *n.* Ornament like small flower.

fleur'y (-oor-), **flōr'y** *adjs.* (her.) Decorated with fleurs-de-lis (ill. HERALDRY).

flews (-z) *n.pl.* Large chaps of bloodhound or other deep-mouthed dog.

flĕx[1] *n.* Flexible insulated wire used for conveying electric current.

flĕx[2] *v.t.* Bend; esp. bend (joint or limb) by action of flexor muscles.

flĕx'ible *adj.* That will bend without breaking, pliable, pliant; easily led, manageable; adaptable, versatile; supple, complaisant. **flĕxĭbĭl'ity** *n.* **flĕx'ĭbly** *adv.*

flĕx'ile *adj.* (now rare) Supple, mobile; tractable; versatile. **flĕxĭl'ĭty** *n.*

flĕx'ion (-kshn) *n.* 1. Bending, curvature, bent state (esp. of limb or joint); bent part, curve. 2. (gram.) Inflexion; (math.) flexure. **flĕx'ional** (-kshon-), **flĕx'ionlėss** *adjs.* (gram.).

flĕx'or *n.* (also *~ muscle, ~ tendon*) Muscle producing flexion in any part of body (opp. to *extensor*) (ill. MUSCLE).

flĕx'ūous *adj.* Full of bends, winding. **flĕx'ūously** *adv.* **flĕxūŏs'ĭty** *n.*

flĕx'ure (-ksher) *n.* Bending, curvature, bent state; (math.) curving of line or surface; (geol.) bending of strata under pressure, chiefly from below.

flĭbb′ertĭgĭbb′ĕt *n.* Gossiping, flighty, frivolous, or restless person.

flĭck *n.* 1. Light sharp blow with whiplash etc. shot out and withdrawn, or with finger-nail; sudden movement, jerk; quick turn of wrist in bowling or batting; slight sharp cracking sound. 2. (pl., abbrev. of *flickers*). The films, the cinema (slang). ~ *v.t.* Strike with a flick; dash or jerk *away*, *off*; give a flick with; deliver, play (ball) with a flick of the wrist.

flĭck′er[1] *v.i.* Quiver, vibrate; wave to and fro, flutter; flash up and die away alternately; burn fitfully or unsteadily. ~ *n.* Flickering movement; wavering or rapidly fluctuating light or flame. **flĭck′erĭngly** *adv.*

flĭck′er[2] *n.* (U.S.) Woodpecker.

flī′er, flȳ′er *n.* Bird etc. that flies; animal, vehicle, etc., going with exceptional speed; airman (chiefly U.S.); (mech.) moving guide or weight; part of spinning-machine that twists thread as it guides it on to the bobbin (ill. SPINNING).

flīght[1] (-īt) *n.* 1. Action or manner of flying; swift movement, esp. through the air; swift passage (of time); soaring, excursion, sally (*of* wit, fancy, ambition, etc.). 2. Migration, migrating body, flock, of birds or insects; unit of Royal Air Force, of about 6 aeroplanes; volley *of* arrows etc.; *in the first* ~, taking a leading part. 3. Distance that bird, aircraft, or missile, can fly. 4. Voyage in aircraft. 5. Series (*of* stairs etc.) mounting between landings, or without change of direction; set *of* hurdles or rails for racing over. 6. Feather etc. on arrow or dart. 7. Attrib., esp. in titles of various ranks in Royal Air Force, as ~ *lieutenant*, ~ *sergeant*; ~*-deck*, deck of aircraft-carrier for taking-off and landing of aircraft. ~ *v.t.* Shoot (wildfowl) in flight; (cricket) vary trajectory and pace of (ball before pitching).

flīght[2] (-īt) *n.* Running away, fleeing; hasty retreat; absconding; *take to* ~, run away; *put to* ~, rout.

flīght′y (-īt-) *adj.* Guided by whim or fancy, fickle; half-witted, crazy. **flīght′ily** *adv.* **flīght′inėss** *n.*

flĭm′-flăm *n.* Trifle, nonsense, idle talk; piece of humbug, deception.

flĭm′sy (-z-) *adj.* Easily destroyed, frail, slightly put together; paltry, trivial; frivolous, superficial; **flĭm′sĭly** *adv.* **flĭm′sĭnėss** *n.* **flĭm′sy** *n.* Thin kind of paper, reporters' copy; (slang) bank-note(s).

flĭnch *v.i.* Give way, draw back, shrink (*from* something as dangerous, painful, or difficult); wince; blench.

flĭn′ders[1] *n.pl.* Fragments, splinters.

Flĭn′ders[2], Matthew (1774–1814). English navigator and explorer; ~ *bar*, soft iron bar placed vertically near ship's compass to correct deviation due to magnetic induction.

flĭng *v.* (past t. and past part. *flung*). 1. Rush, go angrily or violently. 2. Throw, cast, hurl; throw with violence or hostile intent, hurl as missile; extend (arms) with sudden movement; cast (glance etc.); throw *into* (prison etc.); (of wrestler or ridden horse) throw to the ground; launch (troops etc.) *on* enemy, *against* fortress, etc. ~ *n.* 1. Throw, cast. 2. Gibe, scoff. 3. Vigorous dance in which arms and legs are flung about (esp. *Highland* ~). 4. Spell of indulgence in impulse.

flĭnt *n.* Hard stone of nearly pure silica found in roundish nodules, usu. steely-grey and encrusted with white, and having the property of giving off sparks when struck with steel; piece of this used with steel to kindle flame, fire powder in flint-lock gun, etc.; pebble or nodule of flint flaked or chipped by prehistoric man to form a tool or weapon; *skin a* ~, be miserly or avaricious; ~*-glass*, pure lustrous glass, orig. made with ground flint; ~*-lock*, (gun with) lock in which flint struck against hammer produces sparks which ignite priming (ill. MUSKET), **flĭnt′y** *adj.* **flĭnt′ĭly** *adv.* **flĭnt′ĭnėss** *n.*

Flĭnt′shire. County of N.Wales.

flĭp[1] *n.* Mixture of beer and spirit sweetened and heated with hot iron rod; *egg* ~: see EGG.

flĭp[2] *v.* Put in motion with fillip; fillip; make a fillip; move with flip or jerk; flick. ~ *n.* Smart light blow, fillip, flick.

flĭpp′ant *adj.* Lacking in gravity; treating serious subjects with unbecoming levity, disrespectful. **flĭpp′ancy** *n.* **flĭpp′antly** *adv.*

flĭpp′er *n.* Limb used to swim with; e.g. fore-limb of cetacean, any limb of seal, walrus, turtle; wing of penguin; (slang) hand; (slang) direction indicator of motor-car.

flĭrt *v.* 1. Fillip, send with a jerk; wave or move briskly (fan, bird's tail). 2. Play at courtship *with*, pretend to make love. ~ *n.* 1. Sudden jerk; quick motion quickly checked. 2. Man who pays, or usu. woman who invites or accepts, attentions merely for amusement. **flĭrtā′tion** *n.* **flĭrtā′tious** *adj.*

flĭt *v.i.* 1. Depart, remove; (chiefly north. & Sc.) change one's residence. 2. Pass lightly or softly and (usu.) rapidly; fly lightly and swiftly; make short and swift flights. ~ *n.* Removal.

flĭtch *n.* 1. Side of hog salted or cured, side of bacon. 2. Slice cut lengthwise from tree-trunk, usu. with natural surface as one side; ~(*-plate*), strengthening plate on beam, girder, etc. ~ *v.t.* Cut into flitches.

flĭtt′er *v.i.* Flit about, flutter; ~*-mouse*, bat.

flĭvv′er *n.* (slang, orig. U.S.) Cheap motor-car.

flĭx *n.* Fur of some animals; down of beaver.

float *v.* 1. Rest on surface of liquid; (of stranded vessel) get afloat; move quietly and gently on surface of liquid; be suspended freely *in* liquid; move or be suspended in air as if buoyed up; hover *before* eye or mind. 2. (commerc., of acceptance) Be in circulation, awaiting maturity; launch (scheme, company, etc.), be launched. 3. Cover with liquid, inundate; (of water etc.) support, bear along (object); set afloat; waft through air. ~ *n.* 1. (rare) Floating; *on the* ~, afloat. 2. Floating object; mass of floating weeds, ice, etc.; raft; cork or quill supporting baited fishing-line and dipping when fish bites; cork etc. supporting edge of fishing-net; inflated or hollow organ supporting fish etc. in water (ill. FISH); hollow metallic ball regulating water-level in boiler or tank; device floating in and regulating spirit in carburettor of petrol-motor (ill. CARBURETTOR); watertight structure attached to seaplane to give it buoyancy when resting on surface of water. 3. (pl.) The footlights. 4. One of boards of undershot water-wheel or paddle-wheel (ill. WATER). 5. Kind of low-bodied cart; platform on wheels used for displays etc. 6. Tool for smoothing plaster (ill. TROWEL); single-cut file for smoothing metal. 7. (weaving) Passing of weft-threads over part of warp without being interwoven; thread so passed 8. ~*-board* = sense 4; ~*-grass*, various kinds of grass sedge growing in marshy or swampy ground; ~*-ironed*, ironed with ~ *roll calender*, ironing-machine with sprung and resiliently padded rollers; ~*-plane*, aircraft fitted with floats for alighting on water, seaplane.

float′age *n.* 1. Floating. 2. (Right of appropriating) flotsam; ships etc. afloat on river; floating masses. 3. Part of ship above water-line.

floatā′tion, flōt- *n.* Floating; launching of company or enterprise.

float′er *n.* (esp.) 1. Government stock-certificate, railway bond, etc., accepted as recognized security. 2. (U.S.) Voter not attached to any political party; one who casts a vote to which he is not entitled. 3. (slang) Mistake, bloomer.

float′ĭng *adj.* (esp.) 1. (commerc., of cargo) At sea. 2. Having little attachment, disconnected; (of kidney etc.) displaced, out of the normal position; ~ *rib*, a rib (in man, one of the two lower pairs) not attached to breastbone in front. 3. (commerc.) Not fixed or permanently invested; unfunded. 4. (of population etc.) Fluctuating; variable; not settled in definite state or place. 5. ~ *dock*: see DOCK; ~ *light*, lightship; ~ *vote*, (collectively) persons without definite political views whose votes cannot be relied on by any party.

flŏcc'ōse (-s) *adj.* (bot.) Tufted.

flŏcc'ūle *n.* Small portions of matter like flock of wool.

flŏcc'ūlent, flŏcc'ūlōse, flŏc-c'ūlous *adjs.* Like tufts of wool; in, showing, tufts. **flŏcc'ūlence** *n.*

flŏck[1] *n.* Lock, tuft, of wool, cotton, etc.; (pl.) material for quilting and stuffing made of wool-refuse or torn-up cloth; (pl. or collect. sing.) powdered wool or cloth for making flock-paper; (chem., pl.) precipitate in form of light loose masses like tufts of wool; ~*-bed*, bed stuffed with flocks; ~*-paper*, wall-paper sized and then powdered with flock either all over or in patterns.

flŏck[2] *n.* 1. Large number of people. 2. Number of animals of one kind (now esp. birds) feeding or travelling in company; number of domestic animals (now only sheep or goats) kept together; *flocks and herds*, sheep and cattle. 3. The whole body of Christians; a congregation, esp. in relation to its pastor; (occas.) any body of persons under charge or guidance of another person. ~ *v.i.* Congregate, go in great numbers, troop.

Flŏdd'en (Field). Scene, in Northumberland, of a battle on 9th Sept. 1513, in which the English under the earl of Surrey defeated James IV of Scotland, who was killed in the field.

flōe *n.* Sheet of floating ice.

flŏg *v.t.* 1. Beat with birch, whip, cat, etc.; urge (horse etc.) on with whip; cast fishing-line repeatedly over (stream). 2. (slang) Sell (what is not one's own, esp. official property).

flŏng *n.* Papier-mâché used in stereotyping; mould made of this.

flood (-ŭd) *n.* Flowing in of tide; flowing water, river, stream, sea (poet.); irruption of water over land, inundation (*the F~*, the great deluge recorded in Genesis as occurring in time of Noah); outpouring of water; torrent, downpour (also fig. as ~ *of abuse*); ~*-gate*, gate that may be opened or closed to admit or exclude water, esp. flood-water; lower gate of lock; sluice; ~*-light*, artificial light flooding surface of building etc. more or less uniformly; (*v.t.*) light thus; ~*-tide*, advancing tide. ~ *v.* Inundate, cover with a flood; irrigate; deluge with water; (of rain) fill (river) to overflowing; become flooded; come in floods or great quantities; drive *out* by floods.

floor (-ōr) *n.* 1. Layer of boards, brick, etc., in room on which people tread, lower surface of interior of room; bottom of sea, cave, etc. 2. In legislative assemblies, part of house where members sit and from which they speak; hence, right of speaking. 3. Set of rooms etc. on same level in building, storey. 4. Level area; platform or levelled space for threshing etc.; ~*-cloth*, cloth for washing floors;

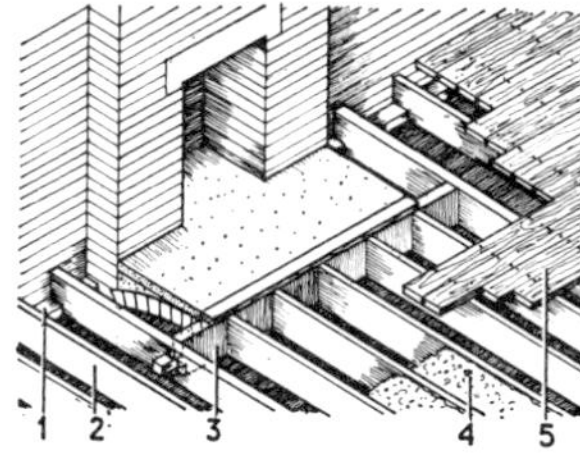

FLOOR

1. Wall plate or torsel. 2. Joist. 3. Trimmer. 4. Sound-proofing. 5. Floor boards

fabric, as oilcloth etc.; ~*-walker* (U.S.) shop-walker. ~ *v.t.* 1. Furnish with floor; pave; serve as floor of. 2. Bring to floor or ground, knock down; confound, nonplus; overcome, get the better of.

flŏp *v.* Sway about heavily and loosely, flap; move clumsily or heavily, or with sudden bump or thud; throw suddenly; (slang) collapse, fail. ~ *n.* Flopping motion, sound made by it; (slang) failure, collapse. ~ *adv.* and *int.* With a flop. **flŏpp'y** *adj.* Inclined to flop.

Flōr'a[1]. Roman goddess of flowers and spring.

flōr'a[2] *n.* (List of) plants of particular region or epoch. **flōr'al** *adj.* Of flora(s); of flower(s). [f. FLORA[1]]

Floréal (flŏrā-ahl'). 8th month (20th Apr.–19th May) in French revolutionary calendar.

Flŏ'rence (It. *Firenze*). Chief city of Tuscany, Italy; ~ *flask*, round or pear-shaped long-necked glass flask, often protected with basket-work, in which olive oil or wine is exported from Italy.

Flŏ'rentīne *adj.* & *n.* (Native, inhabitant) of Florence; ~ *iris*, large white or pale-blue species of iris.

florĕs'cence *n.* Period or state of being in flower. **florĕs'cent** *adj.*

flōr'ĕt *n.* (bot.) One of the small flowers making up a composite flower (ill. INFLORESCENCE); small flower, floweret.

flōr'iāte *v.t.* Decorate with flower-designs.

flōr'icŭlture *n.* Cultivation of flowers. **flōrĭcŭlt'ural** (-cher-) *adj.* **flōrĭcŭlt'urĭst** *n.*

flŏ'rĭd *adj.* Profusely adorned as with flowers, elaborately ornate; ostentatious, showy; (of person) ruddy, flushed, high-coloured. **flŏ'rĭdly** *adv.* **flŏ'rĭdness, florĭd'ĭty** *ns.*

Flŏ'rĭda. South Atlantic State of U.S., admitted to the Union in 1845; capital, Tallahassee; ~ *water*, a perfume resembling eau de Cologne; ~ *wood*, kind of hard boxwood used for inlaying.

florĭf'erous *adj.* Producing many flowers.

flōrĭlē'gĭum *n.* (pl. *-ia*). Anthology.

flŏ'rin *n.* 1. English silver or cupro-nickel two-shilling piece. 2. Principal monetary unit of the Netherlands, guilder (see GULDEN). 3. (hist.) Gold coin first issued at Florence in 1252; English gold coin issued by Edward III; various other coins formerly current in Europe. [OF, f. L *flos flor-* flower, because the orig. florin was stamped with a lily]

flŏ'rĭst *n.* One who deals in, raises, or studies flowers.

flōr'uit (-ōō-) *n.* Period (failing exact dates of birth and death) at which person was alive or worked. [L, = 'he flourished']

flōr'y *adj.*: see FLEURY and ill. HERALDRY.

flŏss *n.* Rough silk enveloping silkworm's cocoon; ~*-silk*, rough silk broken off in winding cocoons, this used in making cheap silk fabrics; untwisted filaments of silk used for needlework; *candy* ~, sweetmeat of fluffy spun sugar, sold on a stick. **flŏss'y** *adj.*

flotation: see FLOATATION.

flotĭll'a *n.* Small fleet; fleet of boats or small ships.

flŏt'sam *n.* Wreckage found floating (cf. JETSAM).

flounce[1] *v.i.* Go with agitated or violent motion, flop, plunge, throw the body about. ~ *n.* Fling, jerk, of body or limb.

flounce[2] *n.* Ornamental strip gathered and sewn by upper edge round woman's skirt etc. and with lower edge hanging. ~ *v.t.* Trim with flounces.

floun'der[1] *n.* Small edible flat-fish, *Pleuronectes flesus*.

floun'der[2] *v.i.* Struggle or plunge (as) in mud or wading; make mistakes, manage affair badly or with difficulty.

flour (-owr) *n.* Finer part of meal (of wheat or other grain) obtained by bolting; wheat meal as dist. from that of other grain; fine soft powder, esp. that obtained by grinding seeds, farinaceous roots, etc. ~ *v.t.* Sprinkle with flour; (U.S.) grind into flour; *flour'ing-mill* (U.S.), mill for making flour (dist. from *grist-mill*). [form of FLOWER; orig. sense 'finest part']

flou'rish (flŭ-) *v.* 1. Grow vigorously; thrive, prosper, be successful; be in one's prime. 2. Embellish with flourishes. 3. Show ostentatiously; wave (weapon) about; throw (limbs) about. ~ *n.* Ornament of flowing curves about letter or word in handwriting; rhetorical embellishment, florid expression; ostentatious waving of weapon etc.; (mus.) fanfare of brass instruments, esp. to announce distinguished person's approach; florid passage, profuse ornamentation; short extemporized sequence of notes as prelude.

flout *v.* Mock, insult, express contempt for by word or act; scoff *at*. ~ *n.* Mocking speech or action.

flow (-ō) *v.i.* 1. Glide along as a stream; (of blood etc.) circulate; (of persons, things) come, go, in numbers; (of talk, literary style, etc.) move easily; (of garment, hair, etc.) hang easily, undulate; result *from.* 2. (math., of numbers) Increase or diminish continuously by infinitesimal quantities. 3. Gush out, spring; (of blood) be spilt; run full, be in flood; (of wine etc.) be poured out without stint; (archaic) be plentifully supplied *with.* ~ *n.* Flowing movement in stream; amount that flows; flowing liquid; outpouring, stream, continuous supply; rise of tide; ~ *of spirits,* habitual cheerfulness.

flow'er (*or* flowr) *n.* 1. (bot.) Reproductive organ in plant containing one or more pistils or stamens or both, and usu. a corolla and calyx; (pop.) coloured (i.e. not green) part of plant from which seed or fruit is later developed; blossom, esp. in regard to beauty or perfume; flowering plant. 2. (pl., chem. etc.) Pulverulent form of substance, esp. powder formed by sublimation; scum formed on wine etc. in fermentation; ~*s of tan,* fungus (*Fulig*) growing on tan heaps. 3. Ornament, esp. in printing (ill. TYPE); (pl.) ornamental phrases (usu. ~*s of speech*); (sing.) *the* pick or choice *of*; *the* best part, essence; *the* choicest embodiment *of.* 4. State of blooming; prime. 5. ~*-de-luce,* archaic and U.S. form of FLEUR-DE-LIS; ~*-girl,* woman who sells flowers, esp. in street; ~*-piece,* picture of flowers; ~*-pot,* pot usu. of red earthenware holding soil in which plant may be set; ~*-show,* competitive or other exhibition of flowers etc. **flow'erless** *adj.* **flow'erėt** *n.* **flow'er** *v.* Produce flowers, bloom, blossom; (gardening) cause, allow, (plant) to flower; embellish with needlework flowers or floral design. **flow'erer** *n.* Plant that flowers at specified time etc. **flow'ering** *adj.*

flow'ery *adj.* Abounding in flowers; full of fine words, compliments, figures of speech, etc.; *F~ Kingdom,* (tr. Chin. *hwa kwo*) China. **flow'erinėss** *n.*

flow'ing (-ōĭ-) *adj.* (esp.) (Of style) fluent, easy; (of lines) smoothly continuous; (naut., of sail) eased off, loosened to wind. **flow'ingly** *adv.*

flown[1] (-ōn) *adj.* (obs. past. part. of *flow*) (archaic) Swollen, puffed up.

flown[2]**:** see FLY[2].

F.L.S. *abbrev.* Fellow of the Linnaean Society.

Flt Lt, Sgt *abbrevs.* Flight Lieutenant, Sergeant.

flŭc'tūāte *v.i.* Vary irregularly, rise and fall, be unstable; vacillate, waver. **flŭctūā'tion** *n.*

flu(e)[1] (-ōō) *n.* (colloq.) (Short for) influenza.

flue[2] (-ōō) *n.* Kind of fishing-net.

flue[3] (-ōō) *n.* Substance formed by loose particles of cotton, down, etc., fluff.

flue[4] (-ōō) *n.* Smoke-duct in chimney; channel for conveying heat, esp. hot-air passage in wall (ill. HYPOCAUST), or tube for heating water in some kinds of boiler; ~*-gas,* mixture of gases in boiler furnace; ~*-pipe,* flue; (also) organ pipe with mouthpiece like whistle (opp. to *reed-pipe*; ill. ORGAN); ~ *stop,* stop controlling this.

flue[5] (-ōō) *v.* Splay, make (opening) widen inwards or outwards.

flu'ency (-ōō-) *n.* Smooth easy flow, esp. in speech; ready utterance.

flu'ent (-ōō-) *adj.* 1. (rare) Flowing; ready to flow, liquid; fluid, not settled, liable to change. 2. (Of motion, curves, etc.) graceful, easy; (of speech, style) copious, coming easily, ready; expressing oneself quickly and easily. 3.

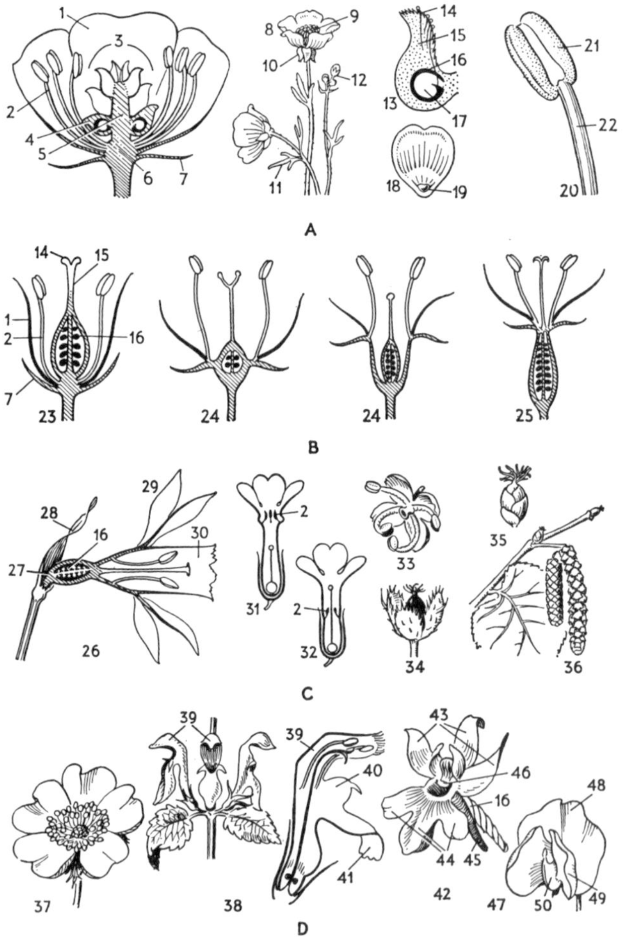

FLOWERS: A. PARTS OF A FLOWER (BUTTERCUP). B. ARRANGEMENT OF PARTS. C. TYPES OF FLOWER. D. FORMS OF FLOWER

A. 1. Petal. 2. Stamen. 3. Apocarpous pistil, or gynaeceum. 4. Carpel. 5. Receptacle or floral axis. 6. Peduncle. 7. Sepal. 8. Corolla consisting of petals. 9. Androecium consisting of stamens. 10. Calyx consisting of sepals. 11. Bracteole. 12. Bud. 13. Carpel. 14. Stigma. 15. Style. 16. Ovary. 17. Ovule. 18. Petal. 19. Nectary. 20. Stamen. 21. Anther containing pollen. 22. Filament. B. 23. Hypogynous arrangement. 24. Perigynous arrangement. 25. Epigynous arrangement. C. 26. Synoecious flower (daffodil). 27. Pedicel. 28. Bract or spathe. 29. Perianth. 30. Corona. 31, 32. Dimorphous flowers (primrose: 31, short-styled; 32, long-styled). 33, 34. Dioecious flowers (stinging nettle: 33, male; 34, female). 35, 36. Monoecious flowers (hazel: 35, female; 36, male catkin or amentum). D. 37. Regular flower (dog-rose). 38, 42, 47. Irregular flowers: 38. White Dead-nettle. 39. Posterior lobe. 40. Lateral lobe. 41. Anterior lobe. 42. Spotted orchid. 43. Outer envelope or upper lip. 44. Labellum or lower lip. 45. Spur. 46. Ovary. 47. Sweet pea. 48. Standard or vexillum. 49. Lateral or wing. 50. Keel

(math.) That flows. **flu'ently** *adv.* **flu'ent** *n.* (math.) Variable quantity in fluxions that is continually increasing or decreasing.

flŭff *n.* Light feathery stuff such as separates from dressed wool, etc.; soft fur; soft downy mass or bunch; (slang) theatrical part imperfectly known. ~ *v.t.* Put soft surface on (flesh side of leather); make into fluff; shake (one*self*, one's feathers, etc.) *up* or *out* into fluffy mass; (slang) blunder in theatrical part, forget one's part; bungle (stroke, catch, etc., in games). **flŭff'y** *adj.* **flŭff'ĭness** *n.*

flu'ĭd (-ōō-) *adj.* Consisting of particles that move freely among themselves and yield to the slightest pressure; moving readily, not solid or rigid, not stable; ~ *ounce*: see OUNCE, and Appendix X. ~ *n.* Fluid substance (gas or liquid); liquid constituent or secretion. **fluĭd'ĭfȳ** *v.t.* **fluĭd'ĭty** *n.*

fluke[1] (-ōō-) *n.* 1. Flat fish, esp. the common flounder. 2. One of a class of parasitic flatworms infesting the liver of sheep and cattle (so called f. resemblance to flounder).

fluke[2] (-ōō-) *n.* Broad flattened barbed extremity of the arm of an anchor (ill. ANCHOR); barbed head of lance, harpoon, etc.; (pl.) whale's large triangular tail.

fluke[3] (-ōō-) *n.* & *v.* (Make) lucky accidental stroke, esp. at billiards; get, hit, etc., by a fluke; (have) unexpected or undeserved success. **fluk'y** *adj.* **fluk'ĭly** *adv.* **fluk'ĭness** *n.*

flume (-ōō-) *n.* (chiefly U.S.) Artificial channel conveying water for industrial use; ravine with stream. ~ *v.* Build flumes; convey down a flume.

flŭmm'ery *n.* Food made by boiling oatmeal down to a jelly (archaic or dial.); kinds of sweet dish made with milk, flour, eggs, gelatine, etc.; empty compliments, trifles, nonsense. [Welsh *llymru*]

flŭmm'ox *v.t.* (slang) Confound, bewilder, disconcert.

flŭmp *v.* Fall or move heavily, set or throw *down*, with dull noise. ~ *n.* Action or sound of flumping.

flŭnk'ey *n.* (orig. Sc.) Liveried servant, footman (usu. contempt.); toady, snob. **flŭnk'eydom, flŭnk'eyĭsm** *ns.*

fluorĕs'cĕin (-ōō-) *n.* Orange-red water-insoluble compound, $C_{20}H_{12}O_5$, used in dyes etc.

fluorĕs'cence (-ōō-) *n.* Coloured luminosity produced in some materials by direct action of (esp. violet and ultra-violet) light-rays, X-rays, and other invisible radiations; property of converting ultra-violet light and other invisible radiations into visible light by absorption and re-emission. **fluorĕsce'** *v.i.* **fluorĕs'cent** *adj.*

flu'orīde (-ōō-) *n.* Salt of hydrofluoric acid, compound of fluorine with another element or organic radical.

flu'orine (-ōō-, -ēn) *n.* Pungent corrosive gaseous element of pale greenish-yellow colour, extremely active chemically; symbol F, at. no. 9, at. wt 18·998.

flu'orīte: see FLUOR-SPAR.

flu'oroscōpe (-ōō-) *n.* Instrument for observing fluorescence, consisting of a box with fluorescent screen.

flu'orspâr *or* **flu'orīte** (flōō-) *n.* Natural calcium fluoride (CaF_2), a transparent or translucent mineral of various colours, crystalline or massive, found esp. in Derbyshire; used as a flux in metallurgy etc.

flŭ'rry *n.* 1. Gust, squall; (chiefly U.S.) sharp sudden shower. 2. Commotion, excitement; nervous hurry, agitation; death-throes of harpooned whale. ~ *v.t.* Confuse by haste or noise, agitate.

flŭsh[1] *v.* Take wing and fly away; cause (birds) to do this, put up. ~ *n.* Number of birds put up at once.

flŭsh[2] *v.* 1. Spurt, rush out; cleanse (drain etc.) by flow of water; flood (meadow). 2. (of plant) Throw out fresh shoots; cause (plant) to do this. 3. (Cause to) glow with warm colour; (of blood) rush into and redden face; (of face) become red or hot, blush; inflame with pride or passion, encourage. ~ *n.* 1. Rush of water; sudden abundance; stream from mill-wheel; cleansing of drain by flushing. 2. Rush of emotion, elation produced by it or by victory etc. 3. Fresh growth of grass etc.; freshness, vigour. 4. Rush of blood to face, reddening caused by this; hot fit in fever.

flŭsh[3] *adj.* 1. Full to overflowing, in flood. 2. (usu. pred.) Having plentiful supply of money etc.; (of money) abundant. 3. Even, in same plane; level *with*; without projections or raised edges. ~ *v.t.* Level; fill in (joint) level with surface.

flŭsh[4] *n.* (cards) Hand of cards all of one suit, or including prescribed number of one suit.

flŭs'ter *v.* Confuse with drink, half-intoxicate; flurry, make nervous; be agitated, bustle. ~ *n.* Flurry, flutter, agitation.

flute (-ōō-) *n.* 1. Musical instrument of wood-wind family (ill. WOOD), a wooden or silver tube without a reed; the modern type is played horizontally and has a mouth-hole at the side and holes stopped by keys, and its range is about 3 octaves above middle C; *bass* ~, flute with range a fourth lower than normal. 2. Organ stop with flute-like tone. 3. Flute-player. 4. Semi-cylindrical vertical groove in pillar (ill ORDER); similar groove or channel elsewhere, e.g. in frills. ~ *v.* 1. Play flute; play on flute; whistle, sing, or speak in flute-like tones. 2. Make flutes or grooves in, whence **flut'ĭng** *n.*

flŭtt'er *v.* 1. Flap wings, flap (wings), without flying or in short flights; come or go with quivering motion; go about restlessly, flit, hover; quiver, vibrate; (of pulse) beat feebly and irregularly; move (flag, fan, etc.) irregularly. 2. Tremble with excitement, be agitated; agitate, ruffle; throw into confusion or agitation. ~ *n.* Fluttering; tremulous excitement; stir, sensation; (slang) gambling venture, speculation.

flut'y (-ōō-) *adj.* Like flute in tone, soft and clear.

fluv'ial (-ōō-) *adj.* Of, found in, river(s). **fluv'iatĭle** *adj.* Of, found in, produced by river(s).

flu'vio-glā'cial (-ōō-) *adj.* (geol., of deposit) Swept off a glacier by the water released by the melting ice; carried by ice, then sorted by running water.

flŭx *n.* 1. Flowing; inflow of tide; flood *of* talk etc. 2. Continuous succession of changes of condition, composition, etc. 3. (math.) Continued motion (of a point). 4. (physics) Rate of flow of fluid across given area; amount of light incident on a given area in a given time; total amount of magnetic or electric field passing through a given area. 5. (archaic) Morbid or excessive discharge of blood or excrement (*bloody* ~, dysentery). 6. Substance mixed with metal etc. to facilitate fusion; substance used to make colours fusible in enamelling etc. ~ *v.* 1. Issue in a flux; flow copiously. 2. Make fluid, fuse; treat with flux.

flŭx'ion (-kshn) *n.* 1. Flowing (rare); continuous change (rare). 2. (math.) Rate or proportion at which flowing or varying quantity increases its magnitude; (*method of*) *fluxions*, the Newtonian calculus. **flŭx'ional** (-shon-), **flŭx'ionary** *adjs.*

flȳ[1] *n.* Two-winged insect, esp. of the family *Muscidae*; insect parasite on plant, plant-disease caused by this; natural or artificial fly used as bait in fishing; ~ *in the ointment*, trifling circumstance that mars enjoyment; ~*-blow*, (*n.*) fly's egg or maggot in meat etc.; (*v.t.*) deposit eggs in, taint; ~*-blown*, so tainted; ~*-book*, case for keeping angler's flies in; ~*-catcher*, trap for flies; plant, insect, bird (usu. of genus *Muscicapa*), that catches flies; ~*-paper*, paper treated with preparation for catching or poisoning flies; ~*-weight*, (boxer having) weight of 8 st. or less.

flȳ[2] *v.* (past t. *flew* pr. flōō, past part. *flown* pr. flōn). 1. Move through air with wings or in aircraft; pilot (aircraft); make (pigeon, hawk) fly; make (kite) rise and stay aloft; (hawking) soar by way of attack *at*; pass or rise quickly through air; jump clear over or *over* fence, etc.; ~ *high*, be ambitious; *high-flown*, exalted, turgid, bombastic; ~ *a kite*, raise money by accommodation bill; try how wind blows, send up *ballon* *d'essai.* 2. (of flag, hair, garment, etc.) Flutter, wave; set or keep (flag) flying. 3. Travel swiftly, rush along, pass rapidly; spring, start, hasten; be driven or forced off suddenly; (of glass etc.) break in pieces suddenly and violently; ~ *at, upon,* attack violently; ~ *out,* burst into violent language or action; *let* ~, discharge (missile); shoot, hit, use strong language, *at.* 4. Run away, flee, flee from. 5. ~*-away,* (of garments) streaming, loose, négligé; (of persons) flighty; ~*-by-night,* one who makes night excursions or decamps by night; *fly'over,* raised crossing, e.g. of one road over another; ~*-past,* procession of aircraft as demonstration. ~ *n.* 1. Flying, distance flown. 2. One-horse hackney carriage. 3. Lap on garment, esp. on front of trousers, to contain or cover button-holes; flap at entrance of tent. 4. Part of flag farthest from staff; breadth of flag from staff to end. 5. (theatr., pl.) Space over proscenium, including upper mechanism and galleries on each side from which it is worked (ill. THEATRE). 6. Speed-regulating device, usu. of vanes on rotating shaft, for regulating striking mechanism of clock etc.; fly-wheel etc. for regulating speed of machinery. 7. ~*-back,* spurious line or trace in cathode-ray tube appearing between end of one cycle and beginning of next; ~*-half* (Rugby football) half-back who stands off from scrum half; ~*-leaf,* blank leaf at beginning or end of book; blank leaf of circular etc.; *flyman,* driver of fly; man stationed in flies of theatre to work ropes etc.; ~*-nut,* nut with wings or projections enabling it to be tightened by hand; ~*-stitch*: see ill. STITCH; ~*-wheel,* wheel with heavy rim on revolving shaft, for regulating motion of machinery or accumulating power (ill. COMBUSTION).

flȳ[3] *adj.* (slang) Knowing, wide awake.

flyer: see FLIER.

flȳ'ing *adj.* 1. That flies. 2. Floating loosely, fluttering, waving; hanging loose. 3. Travelling or passing swiftly; (of a start, race, etc.) in which starting-point is passed at full speed; passing, hasty; temporary; designed for rapid movement. 4. ~*-boat,* seaplane having a boat-like fuselage (ill. AEROPLANE); ~ *bomb,* kind of explosive-carrying, reaction-propelled crewless aeroplane, first used by the Germans against England in June 1944; ~ *buttress,* (archit.) buttress slanting from pier etc. to wall and usu. carried on arch for taking thrust of roof or vault (ill. BUTTRESS); ~ *column,* military force equipped for rapid movement and so supplied as to be capable of operating independently of main force; ~*-fish,* fish of two genera (*Dactylopterus* and *Exocetus*), found in warm seas, which can rise into air by means of enlarged wing-like pectoral fins; ~*-fox,* fruit-eating bat of family *Pteropidae,* found in tropical East and in Australia; ~ *jib,* light sail set before jib on ~ *jib-boom* (ill. SHIP); ~ *jump,* jump with running start; ~ *machine,* machine that can navigate the air; ~ *officer,* officer of Royal Air Force, next in rank below flight lieutenant; ~ *squad,* detachment of police organized for rapid movement; ~ *squirrel,* kinds of squirrel (*Pteromys* and *Sciopterus*) which can glide through air by means of extension of skin connecting fore and hind limbs.

F.M. *abbrev.* Field Marshal.

F.O. *abbrev.* Flying Officer; Foreign Office.

foal *n.* Young of horse, ass, etc., colt or filly. ~ *v.* Give birth to (foal); give birth to foal.

foam *n.* Collection of small bubbles formed in liquid by agitation, fermentation, etc.; froth of saliva or perspiration; (poet.) the sea. ~ *v.i.* Emit foam, froth at the mouth; (of water etc.) froth, gather foam, run foaming *along, down, over,* etc.; (of cup, etc.) be filled with foaming liquor. **foam'y** *adj.*

fŏb[1] *n.* Small pocket for watch etc. formerly made in waistband of breeches. ~ *v.t.* Put in one's fob; pocket.

fŏb[2] *v.t.* Cheat, take in; palm (something inferior) *off upon* person; put (person) *off with* something inferior.

f.o.b. *abbrev.* Free on board.

fō'cal *adj.* Of, situated or collected at, a focus; ~ *distance* or *length,* distance between centre of lens or mirror and its focus (ill. LENS); ~ *plane,* plane parallel with that of lens, passing through the focus; ~ *plane shutter,* (photog.) shutter of roller-blind type placed immediately in front of plate or film.

fō'calīze *v.t.* Focus. **fōcalīzā'tion** *n.*

Foch (fŏsh), Ferdinand (1851–1929). French field marshal; C.-in-C. of the Allied forces in France from April 1918.

fo'c's'le: see FORECASTLE.

fō'cus *n.* (pl. *-ci, -cuses*). 1. (geom.) One of the points from which the distances to any point of a given curve are connected by a linear relation. 2. (optics etc.) Point at which rays meet after being refracted or reflected; point from which rays appear to proceed; point at which object must be situated in order that image produced by lens may be clear and well-defined (ill. LENS); adjustment (of eye or eyeglass) necessary to produce a clear image; (acoustics) point towards which sound-waves converge. 3. Principal seat of disease; centre of activity. ~ *v.t.* Converge, make converge, to a focus; adjust focus of (lens, eye); bring into focus.

fŏdd'er *n.* Dried food, hay, straw, etc., for stall-feeding cattle. ~ *v.t.* Give fodder to.

fōe *n.* (poet. etc.) Enemy, adversary, opponent, ill-wisher; *foe'-man,* (archaic) enemy in war.

foetid: see FETID.

foet'us (fēt-), **fēt'us** *n.* Unborn offspring (used of human embryo after third month of pregnancy; ill. EMBRYO). **foet'al** *adj*; ~ *circulation,* the blood-exchange system of the foetus, including its own blood-vessels and those which connect with the maternal circulation.

fŏg[1] *n.* After-grass; long grass left standing in winter. ~ *v.t.* Leave (land) under fog; feed (cattle) on fog.

fŏg[2] *n.* 1. Thick mist or cloud of minute water-droplets suspended in atmosphere at or near earth's surface; obscurity caused by this, esp. when combined with dust or smoke; (meteor.) atmosphere in which visibility is under 1,100 yds; ~*-bow,* bow, resembling rainbow, sometimes seen opposite sun during fog; ~*-horn,* sounding instrument for warning ships in fog; ~*-signal,* detonator placed on railway-line in fog as signal. 2. (photog.) Opaque cloudy patch on developed negative. ~ *v.t.* Envelop (as) with fog; bewilder, perplex; (photog.) cause fog on (negative).

fŏgg'y *adj.* Thick, murky; of, like, infested with, fog; obscure, dull, confused; beclouded, indistinct. **fŏgg'ily** *adv.* **fŏgg'inėss** *n.*

fō'gle *n.* (thieves' slang) Silk handkerchief.

fōg'(e)y (-g-) *n.* (Usu. *old* ~) old-fashioned fellow; old man behind the times. **fōg'ydom, fōg'yism** *ns.* **fōg'yish** *adj.*

föhn (fėrn) *n.* Hot dry S. wind blowing down N. side of Alps; hot dry wind blowing down leeward slopes of other mountains.

foi'ble *n.* 1. Weak point; weakness of character; quality on which one mistakenly prides oneself. 2. (fencing) Pliant part of sword-blade from middle to point.

foil[1] *n.* 1. (archit.) One of small arcs or spaces between cusps of windows (ill. WINDOW). 2. Metal hammered or rolled into thin sheet; sheet of this formerly placed behind glass of mirror to produce reflection; thin leaf of metal placed under precious stone to increase its brilliance, or under transparent substance to make it look like precious stone. 3. Anything serving to set off another thing by contrast. ~ *v.t.* 1. Set off by contrast. 2. (archit.) Ornament with foils.

foil[2] *v.* 1. (hunting) Run over or cross (scent, ground) so as to baffle hounds; (of deer etc.) spoil the scent thus. 2. Beat off, repulse; frustrate, parry, baffle. ~ *n.* 1. Track of hunted animal. 2. (archaic or literary) Repulse, defeat, check.

foil[3] *n.* Blunt-edged sword used in fencing with button on point to prevent injury.

fois'on (-z-) *n.* (archaic) Plenty.

foist *v.t.* Introduce surreptitiously or unwarrantably *into* or *in*; palm (*off*) *on* or *upon*; father (composition) *upon*.

fol. *abbrev.* Folio.

fōld[1] *n.* Enclosure for sheep; (fig.) church, body of believers. ~ *v.t.* Shut up (sheep etc.) in fold; place sheep in fold(s) on (land) to manure it.

fōld[2] *n.* Doubling of folded object; hollow between two thicknesses; hollow or nook in mountain etc.; (geol.) bend in strata (ill. ROCK); coil of serpent, string, etc.; folding; line made by folding. ~ *v.* 1. Double (flexible thing) over upon itself; ~ *over, together*; bend portion of (thing) *back, down*; become, be able to be, folded; ~ *up*, make more compact by folding; *folding door*, door in two parts (often themselves consisting of hinged leaves which fold up when door is open) hung on opposite jambs, so that edges meet when door is closed. 2. Wind, clasp (arms etc.) *about, round*; lay together and interlace (arms), clasp (one's) hands; swathe, envelop; embrace *in* arms, *to* breast. **fōl′der** *n.* (esp.) Paper-folding instrument; folded circular etc.; folding case for loose papers.

fōliā′ceous (-shus) *adj.* Leaf-like; with organs like leaves; of leaves; laminated.

fō′liage *n.* Leaves, leafage.

fōl′iate *adj.* Leaf-like; having leaves; having specified number of leaflets. **fōl′iāte** *v.* Split into laminae; decorate (arch etc.) with foils; number leaves (not pages) of (volume) consecutively. **fōliā′tion** *n.*

fōl′iō *n.* (pl. -*os*). 1. Leaf of paper, parchment, etc., numbered only on front; (book-keeping) two opposite pages of ledger etc. used concurrently; page of ledger etc. used for both sides of account; page-number of printed book; number of words (in England usu. 72 or 90, in U.S. usu. 100) taken as unit in reckoning length of document. 2. Sheet of paper folded once; volume of the largest size, made up of sheets of paper folded once; *in* ~, (of book) made up of such sheets. ~ *adj.* Formed of sheets or a sheet folded once; folio-sized.

folk (fōk) *n.* 1. (archaic) A people, nation, race. 2. (colloq., now usu. pl.) Men, people in general; (U.S., esp.) respectable people. 3. (attrib.) Of the people; ~-*dance*, (music for) dance of popular origin; ~-*′lore*, traditional beliefs, customs, etc., of the people, study of these; hence, ~-*lorist*; ~-*moot*, (hist.) general assembly of people of town or shire; ~-*song*, traditional song; *folk′ways*, (sociol. etc.) traditional patterns of behaviour common to members of a particular culture or society.

fŏll′icle *n.* 1. (anat.) Small sac; secretory gland of this shape; minute pit in which hair-root grows (ill. SKIN); *Graafian* ~: see GRAAF. 2. Cocoon. 3. (bot.) Fruit which consists of a single carpel and splits open along ventral suture only (ill. FRUIT). **fŏllĭc′ūlar, fŏllĭc′ūlātėd** *adjs.*

fŏll′ow (-ō) *v.* 1. Go or come after (moving thing or person); pursue, chase; go or come after person or thing; go along (path); come after, come next, in order or time; ~ *my leader*, game in which each player must do as leader does; ~ *one's nose*, go straight on; ~ *the plough*, be a ploughman. 2. Accompany, serve, attend upon; go as person's attendant; go after as admirer; be (necessary) accompaniment of, result from, be involved in; result. 3. Strive after, aim at. 4. Treat or take as guide or master, obey, espouse opinions or cause of; conform to, act upon, take as rule; practise (profession etc.); ~ *the sea*, be a sailor. 5. Keep up with mentally; grasp the meaning of; grasp argument, meaning, etc. 6. ~ *after*, follow; ~ *on*, (cricket, of side) be compelled to bat again immediately after first innings, in consequence of having failed to reach the number of runs made by the other side by 150 or more; ~-*on* (*n.*) doing this; ~ *out*, pursue to the end; ~ *through*, (golf) carry stroke through to fullest possible extent after striking ball; ~-*through* (*n.*) this action; ~ *up*, pursue steadily; add another blow etc. to (previous blow etc.); (fig.) prosecute (suggestion etc.) to a conclusion. ~ *n.* (billiards) Stroke causing player's ball to roll on after object-ball, motion so given; (in restaurants etc.) supplementary portion.

fŏll′ower (-ōer) *n.* (esp.) Adherent, disciple; man courting maidservant.

fŏll′owing (-ōi-) *n.* (esp.) Body of adherents, followers. ~ *adj.* (esp.) Now to be mentioned.

fŏll′y *n.* 1. Being foolish, want of good sense, unwise conduct; foolish act, idea, or practice, ridiculous thing. 2. Costly structure (considered) useless or otherwise foolish.

fomĕnt′ *v.t.* 1. Bathe with warm or medicated lotions; apply warmth to. 2. Foster, stimulate, instigate (sentiment, conduct, sedition, etc.). **fōmĕntā′tion** *n.* (Application of) warm or medicated substance for fomenting purposes.

fŏnd *adj.* 1. Infatuated, foolish (archaic); foolishly credulous or sanguine. 2. Over-affectionate, doting; tender, loving; ~ *of*, full of love for, much inclined to. **fŏnd′ly** *adv.* **fŏnd′nėss** *n.*

fŏn′dant *n.* Kind of soft sweetmeat made of flavoured sugar.

fŏnd′le *v.* Caress; toy amorously (*with*).

fŏnt *n.* 1. Receptacle, usu. of stone, for baptismal water; receptacle for holy water; oil-reservoir of lamp. 2. (U.S.) Fount (of type).

fŏn′tal *adj.* 1. Primary, original, of the fountain head. 2. Of the font, baptismal.

fŏntanĕlle′ (-l) *n.* Membrane-covered space in bony vault of skull where union of the bones is incomplete, normally closing in infancy.

fo͞od *n.* Victuals, nourishment, provisions; edibles; particular kind of food; *food′stuff*, material for food; (pl.) articles of food in bulk.

fo͞ol[1] *n.* Silly person, simpleton; dupe; professional jester in medieval great household; *play the* ~, blunder, trifle; indulge in buffoonery; *All Fools' Day*, 1st April; *April* ~, person taken in or sent on fool's errand on that day; ~*'s errand*, fruitless errand; ~*'s mate*: see MATE[1]; ~*'s paradise*, illusory happiness; *fool′proof*, so plain that even a fool cannot misunderstand; (of machines etc.) not liable to be injured by misuse; ~*'s-cap, fools′-cap*, fantastic cap, usu. with bells, worn by medieval jester; dunce's conical paper cap; long folio writing- or printing-paper 15–17×12–13½ in. (from watermark of fool's cap on some old paper). **fo͞ol′ėry** *n.* **fo͞ol′ish** *adj.* **fo͞ol′ishly** *adv.* **fo͞ol′ishnėss** *n.* **fo͞ol** *adj.* That is a fool. ~ *v.* Play the fool, idle, trifle; cheat (person) *out of*; throw *away* foolishly; make a fool of, dupe, play tricks on. [OF *fol* mad f. L *follis* bellows, empty-headed person]

fo͞ol[2] *n.* Stewed crushed fruit mixed with cream or custard.

fo͞ol′hărdy *adj.* Foolishly venturesome, delighting in needless risks. **fo͞ol′hărdinėss** *n.*

fo͞ot *n.* (pl. *feet*). 1. Lowest part of leg beyond ankle-joint; this as

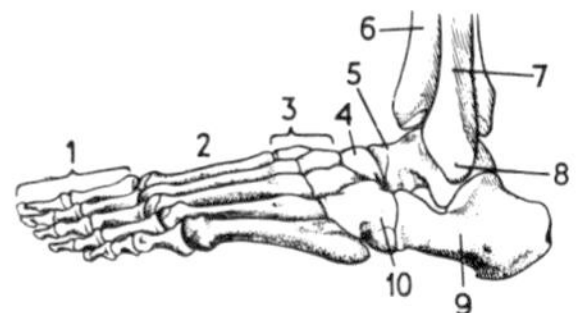

FOOT AND ANKLE

1. Phalanges. 2. Metatarsus. 3, 4, 5, 9, 10. Tarsus. 4. Navicular bone. 5. Talus. 6. Tibia. 7. Fibula. 8. Lateral malleolus. 9. Heel bone. 10. Cuboid bone

organ of locomotion; *carry* one *off his feet*, make him enthusiastic,

15TH-C. FONT

greatly excite; *keep* one's *feet*, not fall; *put* one's ~ *down*, take up firm position (fig.); *put* one's ~ *in it*, blunder; *on* ~, walking, not riding etc.; in motion. 2. Foot-soldiers, infantry. 3. End of bed, grave, etc., towards which feet are placed; part of stocking etc. covering foot. 4. Metrical unit, division of line, with varying number of syllables one of which is accented. 5. Linear measure of 12 inches (see Appendix X). 6. Lower (usu. projecting) part of object, base. 7. (zool.) Organ of locomotion or attachment of some invertebrates, e.g. mussels (ill. SNAIL). 8. Lowest part, bottom, of hill, ladder, wall, list, page, class, etc. 9. (pl. *foots*) Dregs; oil refuse; coarse sugar. 10. ~-*and-mouth* (*disease*), contagious fever, caused by a filtrable virus, of horned cattle and other animals, with ulcerating vesicles in mouth, near hoof, etc.; *foot'ball*, spherical or (in Rugby game) elliptical ball used in game and consisting of inflated rubber ball in leather case; open-air game played with this ball by two sides each trying to kick or carry it over the other's goal-line (see ASSOCIATION and RUGBY football); *foot'board*, footman's platform at back of carriage; sloping board for driver's feet; ~-*bridge*, bridge for foot-passengers; ~-*candle*, a unit of illumination, equal to the illumination of a surface at a uniform distance of 1 ft from a symmetrical point source of 1 candle; *foot'fall*, sound of footsteps; ~-*fault*, (lawn tennis) fault made by overstepping base-line or by running, walking, or jumping, while serving; (*v.*) make foot-fault; record foot-fault against (player); *F~ Guards*, the Brigade of Guards (Grenadier, Coldstream, Scots, Irish, and Welsh Guards); ~-*hill*, (orig. U.S.) lower hill at foot of mountain or mountain-range; *foot'hold*, support for feet, surface for standing on; *foot'lights*, row of screened lights along front of stage on level with actors' feet (ill. THEATRE); ~-*loose*, (U.S.) free, unhampered by ties or obligations; *foot'man*, foot-soldier; liveried servant attending carriage, waiting at table, and answering door; connecting rod between treadle and wheel of spinning-wheel (ill. SPINNING); *foot'mark*, footprint; ~-*muff*, muff for keeping feet warm; *foot'note*, note inserted at foot of page; ~-*pace*, walking pace; *foot'pad*, (hist.) unmounted highwayman; ~-*passenger*, one who walks, not rides, etc.; *foot'path*, path for foot-passengers; *foot'plate*, platform in locomotive for driver and fireman (ill. LOCOMOTIVE); ~-*pound*, work done when weight of one pound is raised a distance of one foot; ~-*poundal*, work done when a force of one poundal moves its point of application one foot in the line of action of the force; *footprint*, impression left by foot; ~-*race*, race between persons on foot; ~-*rot*, inflammatory disease affecting horns and feet of cattle etc.; (also) tinea; ~-*rule*, rigid or folding measure divided off into feet; ~-*slog*, (slang) go on foot, tramp; *foot'sore*, having sore feet, esp. with walking; *foot'stalk*, (bot.) stalk or petiole of leaf; peduncle of flower; (zool.) muscular attachment of barnacle etc.; *foot'step*, tread; footprint; noise made by treading; *foot'stool*, low stool for resting feet on; *foot'wear*, boots and shoes collectively. **fŏŏt'lėss** *adj.* **fŏŏt** *v.* Set foot on, traverse on foot (rare); put new foot to (stocking); add up or *up* (account); pay (bill).

fŏŏt'er *n.* (slang) The game football.

fŏŏt'ĭng *n.* 1. Placing of feet, foothold; surface for standing on, secure position; conditions, relations, position, status, in which person is towards others; entrance on new position, admittance to trade, society, etc. (only in *pay* (*for*) *one's* ~). 2. Projecting course at foot of wall etc.

fōō'tle *v.i.* (slang) Trifle, play the fool. ~ *n.* Twaddle, folly. **fōō'tlĭng** *adj.*

fōō'zle *v.t.* (slang, esp. golf) Do clumsily, bungle, make a mess of. ~ *n.* Clumsy failure.

fŏp *n.* Dandy, exquisite, vain man. **fŏpp'ery** *n.* **fŏpp'ĭsh** *adj.* **fŏpp'ĭshly** *adv.* **fŏpp'ĭshnėss** *n.*

for *prep.* In place of (as in *b. stands ~ born*); in exchange against (*sold ~ 2d.*); in defence of, in favour of (*fought ~ France*); in the interest of, with a view to (*do it ~ her*; *I say this ~ your good*); to get, reach, etc. (*went ~ a taxi*; *sailed ~ India*); as regards (esp. with words implying fitness, as *fit ~ nothing*); because of, on account of (*fear ~ his safety*; *famous ~ wine*); corresponding to (*~ one enemy he has 50 friends*); considering the nature of (*cool ~ a summer day*); during, to the extent of (*wait ~ years*; *walk ~ 3 miles*). ~ *conj.* (Introducing new sentence etc. containing reason for believing what has been previously stated) seeing that, since; because.

f.o.r. *abbrev.* Free on rail.

fŏ'rage *n.* Food for horses and cattle, fodder, esp. that provided for horses in army; ~-*cap*, undress cap of army. ~ *v.* Collect forage from, ravage; search for forage or (fig.) *for* anything, rummage; supply with forage; get by foraging. **fŏ'rager** *n.*

forām'ĕn *n.* Orifice, hole, passage. **forăm'ĭnate, -ātėd** *adjs.*

fŏrasmŭch' as (-az-) *conj.* (archaic) Seeing that, since.

fŏ'ray *n.* Incursion, raid, inroad. ~ *v.i.* Go on, make, foray.

fôrb'ear[1] (-bār) *n.* (usu. pl.) Ancestor(s).

forbear'[2] (-bār) *v.* Abstain or refrain from or *from*; not use or mention; be patient. **forbear'ance** *n.* **forbear'ĭngly** *adv.*

forbĭd' *v.t.* (past t. *-băde*, past part. *-bĭdd'en*). Command not *to* do, not to go to (place); not allow (person etc. something; person or thing to exist or happen); exclude, prevent, make undesirable; *Forbidden City*, Lhasa in Tibet, which foreigners were forbidden to enter; also, innermost part of the northern (Tatar) city of Peking, where under the Manchu dynasty no Chinese might spend a night. **forbĭdd'ĭng** *adj.* Repellent, of uninviting appearance. **forbĭdd'ĭngly** *adv.* **forbĭdd'ĭngnėss** *n.*

forbȳ(e)' *prep.* & *adv.* (Sc. and archaic). Besides; not to mention; in addition.

fôrce[1] *n.* 1. Strength, power, impetus, violence, intense effort; strength exerted on an object, coercion. 2. Military strength; body of armed men, army; (pl.) troops; body of police. 3. Mental or moral strength, influence, controlling power, efficacy; power to convince, vividness of effect; binding power, validity; real import, precise meaning. 4. (physics) Measurable and determinable influence inclining body to motion, intensity of this; (formerly) cause of any class of physical phenomena (e.g. of heat or motion) conceived as inherent in matter; (fig.) agency likened to these. 5. ~-*bill*, (U.S.) coercive measure, esp. one authorizing use of military force; ~-*pump*, pump to raise water etc. by action of piston or plunger (ill. PUMP). ~ *v.t.* 1. Use violence to, ravish. 2. Constrain, compel; put strained sense upon (words); (cards) compel (player) to trump or reveal his strength, compel player to play (certain card); compel (person) *to* do, *into* doing, *into* specified action; strain to the utmost, urge; ~ person's *hand*, compel him to act prematurely or adopt policy unwillingly; ~ *the pace*, adopt high speed in race to tire adversary out quickly; *forced landing*, unpremeditated landing of aircraft owing to engine failure, petrol shortage, etc.; *forced march*, march requiring special effort of troops etc.; *forced move*, (in game) one rendered inevitable by adversary's action or position of piece. 3. Overpower, capture, make way through, break open (stronghold, defences, pass, lock, door) by force; drive by force, propel against resistance; effect, produce, by effort; take by force, extort, wring; impose, press, (thing) *upon* person; ~ *a card*, (in conjuring) make person choose a particular card unconsciously. 4. Artificially hasten maturity of (plant etc.). **fôr'cėdly** *adv.*

fôrce[2] *n.* (northern) Waterfall.

fôrce'ful (-sf-) *adj.* Forcible. **fôrce'fully** *adv.* **fôrce'fulnėss** *n.*

fôrce majeure (mahzhêr') *n.* Irresistible compulsion; war, strike, act of God, etc., excusing fulfilment of contract.

fōrce'meat (-sm-) *n.* Meat chopped, spiced, and seasoned for stuffing; stuffing.

fōr'cĕps *n.* Instrument like pincers, for seizing and holding objects (esp. in surgery); (anat., zool., etc.) organ resembling forceps. **fōr'cipate** *adj.* Formed like a forceps.

fōr'cĭble *adj.* Done by, involving, force; powerful, telling, convincing. **fōr'cibleness** *n.* **fōr'cibly** *adv.*

fōrd[1] *n.* Shallow place where river etc. may be crossed by wading. ~ *v.* Cross (water), cross water, by wading. **fōrd'able, fōrd'lĕss** *adjs.*

Fōrd[2], Henry (1863–1947). Amer. automobile manufacturer, founder of the Ford company at Detroit, U.S.; hence, motor-car made by this company.

fordo' (-ōō) *v.t.* (archaic; past t. *-did*, past part. *-done* pr. dŭn). Kill, destroy, spoil; *fordone*, exhausted, tired out.

fōre[1] *adj.* Situated in front; ~-*cabin*, cabin in fore part of ship, usu. for second-class passengers. ~ *n.* Fore part, bow of ship; *to the* ~, on the spot, ready to hand, available; conspicuous.

fōre[2] *adv.* In front; now only in ~ *and aft*, at bow and stern; backwards and forwards or lengthwise in ship; ~-*and-aft rigged*, having ~-*and-aft sails*, sails set lengthwise, not to yards (ill. SCHOONER).

fōre[3] *int.* (golf) Warning cry to person in line of flight of the ball.

fore- *prefix.* In front; beforehand, in advance; anticipatory, precedent.

forearm[1] (fōr'ārm) *n.* Arm from elbow to wrist or finger-tips.

forearm[2] (fōrārm') *v.t.* Arm beforehand.

forebōde' (*for*b-) *v.t.* Predict (rare); betoken, portend; have presentiment of. **forebō'dĭng** *n.* Presage, omen, presentiment (esp. of evil). **forebōd'ĭngly** *adv.*

forecast (fōrkahst') *v.t.* (past t. and past part. *-cast*). Estimate, conjecture, beforehand. **fōre'cast** (-ahst) *n.* Conjectural estimate of something future, esp. of coming weather.

forecastle (fōk'sl), **fō'c's'le** *n.* Forward part of merchant vessel; crew's quarters in this; (hist.) short raised deck at ship's bow (ill. SHIP); forward part of warship's upper deck (obs.); ~ *in*, with bows under.

foreclose (fōrklōz') *v.* 1. Bar, preclude, prevent; shut out from enjoyment of. 2. (mortgage law) Bar (person entitled to redeem) upon non-payment of money due; bar (right of redemption); take away power of redeeming (mortgage). **foreclō'sure** (-zh*er*) *n.*

foreconscious (fōr'kŏnsh*us*) *adj.* & *n.* (in Freudian psycho-analysis) (Of) a region of the mind containing ideas or memories that can readily be made conscious; preconscious.

forecourt (fōr'kōrt) *n.* Enclosed space before building, outer court.

foredōōm' (*for*-) *v.t.* Doom beforehand; condemn beforehand *to*; foreordain, predestine.

forefather (fōr'fahdh*er*) *n.* (chiefly pl.) Ancestor, progenitor.

forefĭnger (fōr'-, -ngg-) *n.* Finger next thumb, index finger.

forefōōt (fōr'f-) *n.* 1. One of beast's front feet. 2. (naut.) Foremost part of keel; course passing in front of this.

forefront (fōr'frŭnt) *n.* Very front, foremost part, van.

foregō (*for*gō') *v.* (past t. *-went*, past part. *-gone* pr. gŏn *or* gawn). Precede in place or time; *forego'ing*, previously mentioned; *fore'gone conclusion*, decision or opinion formed before case is argued or full evidence known; result that can be or could have been foreseen.

fore'ground (fōrg-) *n.* Part of view, esp. in picture, nearest observer; most conspicuous position.

fore'hănd (fōr-h-) *n.* Part of horse in front of rider. ~ *adj.* (tennis etc.) (Of stroke) made with palm of hand turned forwards (ill. LAWN); (of court, corner, etc.) on side on which forehand stroke is made, i.e. usu. on right-hand side.

fore'hăndĕd (fōr-h-) *adj.* (U.S.) Thrifty; well-to-do, prosperous.

forehead (fŏ'rĕd) *n.* Part of face above eyebrows and between temples.

fŏ'reign (-rĭn) *n.* 1. Belonging to, proceeding from, other persons or things; alien *from* or *to*; irrelevant, dissimilar, inappropriate, *to*; introduced from outside (esp. ~ *body* in the eye, tissues, etc.); situated outside, coming from another district, parish, society, etc. 2. Outside the country, not in one's own land; of, in, characteristic of, coming from, dealing with, some country not one's own. 3. *F~ Legion*: see LEGION; *F~ Office*, department of Secretary of State for Foreign Affairs, building (in Whitehall, London) in which business of this department is carried on. **fŏ'reigner** (-rĭn-) *n.* Person born in foreign country or speaking foreign language; foreign ship, imported animal or article.

foreknow (fōrnō') *v.t.* Know beforehand, have prescience of. **foreknow'ledge** (-nŏlij) *n.*

fŏ'r(r)el *n.* Kind of parchment dressed to look like vellum, used for covering account-books.

foreland (fōr'l*and*) *n.* Cape, promontory.

forelĕg (fōr'l-) *n.* Beast's front leg.

forelŏck[1] (fōr'l-) *n.* Lock of hair growing just above forehead.

forelŏck[2] (fōr'l-) *n.* (chiefly naut.) Wedge put through hole in bolt to keep it in place; linchpin. ~ *v.t.* Secure with forelock.

fore'man (fōrm-) *n.* President and spokesman of jury; principal workman superintending others.

fore'mast (fōrm-) *n.* Forward lower mast of ship (ill. SHIP).

fore'most (fōr'mōst, -*o*st) *adj.* Most advanced in position, front; most notable, best, chief. ~ *adv.* Before anything else in position; in the first place.

forenōōn (fōr'n-) *n.* Part of day before noon.

forĕn'sĭc *adj.* Of, used in, court of law; ~ *medicine*, medical jurisprudence. **forĕns'ĭcally** *adv.*

foreordain' (fōrōr-) *v.t.* Predestinate, appoint beforehand. **foreōrdĭnā'tion** *n.*

fore'peak (fōrp-) *n.* (naut.) Extreme end of hold of a ship in angle of bows (ill. SHIP).

forerŭn' (fōr-r-) *v.t.* (past t. *-răn*, past part. *-rŭn*). Be precursor of, foreshadow. **forerŭn'ner** (*or* (fōr'-) *n.*

fore'sail (fōr'sl, -sāl) *n.* Principal sail on foremast (ill. SHIP); in square-rigged vessel, lowest square sail; in fore-and-aft rigged, triangular sail before mast.

foresee (fōrsē') *v.t.* See beforehand, have prescience of.

foreshădow (fōrshăd'ō) *v.t.* Prefigure, serve as type or presage of.

foresheets (fōr'sh-) *n.pl.* (naut.) Inner part of bows of open boat, fitted with gratings on which bowman stands (ill. SHIP).

fore'shōre (fōr'sh-) *n.* Part of shore between high and low water marks, or between water and land cultivated or built on.

foreshōrt'en (fōrsh-) *v.t.* Show, portray, (object) with the apparent shortening due to visual perspective; (of visual perspective) cause (object) to appear shorter in directions not lying in plane perpendicular to line of sight.

foreshow (fōrshō') *v.t.* Foretell; foreshadow, portend, pre-figure.

foresight (fōr'sīt) *n.* 1. Foreseeing, prevision; care for the future. 2. Front sight of fire-arm (ill. GUN).

foreskĭn (fōr's-) *n.* Prepuce (ill. PELVIS).

fŏ'rĕst *n.* Large tract covered with trees and undergrowth, sometimes intermingled with pasture; trees growing in it; in Gt Britain, district formerly forest, but now more or less under cultivation and often preserved for game; (law, hist.) woodland district, usu. belonging to king, set apart for hunting etc. and having special laws and officers of its own.

forestall (fōrstawl') *v.t.* 1. (hist.) Buy up (goods) in order to profit by enhanced price; prevent sales at (fair, market) thus. 2. Be beforehand with in action, anticipate and so baffle; deal with before the regular time, anticipate.

forestay (fōr's-) *n.* (naut.) Stay from fore mast-head to stem of ship; sail hoisted on this (ill. SHIP).

fŏ′rĕster *n.* 1. Officer in charge of forest, or of growing timber; *F∼*, member of the Ancient Order of Foresters, a friendly society. 2. Dweller in forest; bird or beast of forest.

fŏ′rĕstrȳ *n.* Wooded country, forests; science and art of managing forests.

foretāste (fōr′t-) *n.* Partial enjoyment or suffering (*of*) in advance. **foretāste′** *v.t.* Taste beforehand, anticipate enjoyment etc. of.

foretĕll′ (fōrt-) *v.t.* (past t. and past part. *-told*). Predict, prophesy; presage, be precursor of.

forethought (fōr′thawt) *n.* Previous contriving, deliberate intention; provident care.

foretōk′en (fōrt-) *v.t.* Portend, point to. **fore′tōken** *n.*

foretop (fōr′t-) *n.* (naut.) Top of foremast; *foretop-gall′ant-mast*, mast above foretopmast; *foretop′-mast*, mast above foremast; *foretop′sail*, sail above foresail (ill. SHIP).

forewarn (fōrwōrn′) *v.t.* Warn beforehand.

forewoman (fōr′wŏŏman) *n.* 1. President and spokeswoman of jury. 2. Chief workwoman supervising others.

foreword (fōr′wērd) *n.* Preface; introduction.

foreyard (fōr′yard) *n.* Lowest yard on foremast (ill. SHIP).

Fōr′far(shire). Former name of county of ANGUS.

fōr′feit (-fĭt) *n.* Thing lost owing to crime or fault; penalty for breach of contract or neglect, fine; trivial fine for breach of rules in clubs etc. or in games; article surrendered by player in *game of forfeits* to be redeemed by performing ludicrous task; forfeiture. ∼ *adj.* That has been lost or given up as penalty. ∼ *v.t.* Lose right to, be deprived of, have to pay, as penalty of crime, neglect, etc., or as necessary consequence of something. **fōr′feiture** *n.*

fōrfĕnd′ *v.t.* (archaic) Avert, keep away, prevent.

forgăth′er (-dh-) *v.i.* Assemble, meet together, associate.

fōrge[1] *n.* Smithy; blacksmith's hearth or fire-place with bellows; furnace or hearth for melting or refining metal, workshop containing this. ∼ *v.* 1. Shape by heating in forge and hammering. 2. Fabricate, invent (tale, lie); make in fraudulent imitation, esp. imitate (signature etc.) in writing in order to pass it off as genuine. **fōr′ger** *n.*

fōrge[2] *v.i.* Make way, advance, gradually or with difficulty; ∼ *ahead*, take lead in race etc., get start.

fōr′gery *n.* Forging, counterfeiting, or falsifying, of document; spurious thing, esp. document or signature.

forgĕt′ (-g-) *v.* (past t. *-gŏt*, past part. *-gotten*). Lose remembrance of or *about*; neglect; inadvertently omit to bring, mention, attend to, etc.; put out of mind, cease to think of; disregard, overlook, slight; ∼ *oneself*, neglect one's own interests; act unbecomingly, presumptuously, or unworthily; lose consciousness; ∼*-me-not*, various kinds of *Myosotis*, esp. *M. palustris*, with small yellow-eyed blue flowers. **forgĕt′ful** *adj.* **forgĕt′fully** *adv.* **forgĕt′fulnĕss** *n.*

forgĭve′ (-g-) *v.t.* (past t. *-gāve′*, past part. *-gĭv′en*). Remit, let off (debt etc.); give up resentment against, pardon (offender). **forgĭv′able** *adj.* **forgĭve′nĕss** *n.* **forgĭv′ĭng** *adj.* **forgĭv′ĭngly** *adv.* **forgĭv′ĭngnĕss** *n.*

forgō′ *v.t.* (past t. *-went*, past part. *-gone* pr. gŏn *or* gawn). Abstain from, go without, let go, omit to take or use, relinquish.

forint′ *n.* Principal monetary unit of Hungary, = 100 filler.

fōrk *n.* 1. Pronged agricultural instrument for digging, lifting, carrying, or throwing. 2. Two-, three-, or four-pronged instrument used to hold food while it is cut, convey it to mouth, etc., and in cooking (for types see ill. SPOON). 3. Two-pronged steel instrument giving musical note when struck, tuning-fork. 4. Stake with forked end; forking, bifurcation, e.g. that of human legs, of diverging roads, or of branches; forked part of bicycle frame in which wheel revolves. 5. ∼*-lift*, lifting device with three phases: in the first a fork is pushed under the load; in the the second the load is raised; in the third the load is left in the desired position and the fork is withdrawn. ∼ *v.* Form fork; have or develop branches; lift, carry, dig, throw, with fork; ∼ *out*, (slang) hand over, pay. **fōrked** (-kt) *adj.* With fork or fork-like end, branching, divergent, cleft; two-legged.

forlōrn′ *adj.* Desperate, hopeless; abandoned, forsaken; (poet.) deprived *of*; in pitiful condition, of wretched appearance. **forlōrn′ly** *adv.* **forlōrn′nĕss** *n.*

forlōrn′ hōpe *n.* Storming party; perilous or desperate enterprise. [Du. *verloren hoop* lost troop (*hoop* = heap)]

fōrm *n.* 1. Shape, arrangement of parts, visible aspect (esp. apart from colour); shape of body; body in respect of outward shape and appearance. 2. (philos.) In scholastic philosophy, that which makes anything (*matter*) a determinate species or kind of being; in Kant etc., that factor of knowledge which gives reality and objectivity to the thing known. 3. Mode in which thing exists or manifests itself; species, kind, variety; (gram.) one of various modes of spelling, inflexion, etc., under which word may appear, external characteristics of words, as dist. from their meaning. 4. In schools, one of the numbered classes (of which the sixth is in England usu. the highest) into which pupils are divided. 5. Arrangement and style in literary or musical composition; orderly arrangement of parts. 6. Set or customary method or procedure; set or fixed order of words etc.; formulary document with blanks to be filled up. 7. Formality, mere piece of ceremony; behaviour according to rule or custom; *good, bad*, ∼, behaviour satisfying or offending current ideals. 8. Condition of health and training; good spirits. 9. Long seat without back, bench. 10. (printing; also *forme*) Body of type secured in CHASE[3] for printing at one impression (ill. PRINT). 11. Lair or nest in which hare crouches. ∼ *v.* Fashion, mould; assume shape, become solid; mould by discipline, train, instruct; embody, organize, *into* company etc.); frame, make, produce; articulate (word); conceive (idea, judgement); develop (habit); contract (alliance); be material of, make up, make *one* or *part of*; (mil.) draw up in order, assume specified formation.

fōrm′al *adj.* 1. (metaphys.) Of the form or constitutive essence of a thing, essential; of the outward form, shape, appearance, or external qualities; (logic) concerned with the form, not the matter, of reasoning. 2. That is so in form; that is according to recognized forms, or the rules of art or law; valid in virtue of its form, explicit and definite, not merely tacit. 3. Ceremonial, required by convention; perfunctory, having the form without the spirit; observant of forms, precise, prim; excessively regular or symmetrical, stiff, methodical. **fōrm′ally** *adv.*

fōrmăl′dĕhȳde *n.* Colourless gas (HCHO) with a characteristic pungent odour, used in aqueous solution as disinfectant etc.

fōrm′alin *n.* 40% aqueous solution of formaldehyde.

fōrm′alism *n.* Strict observance of forms; excessive regularity or symmetry. **fōrm′alist** *n.* **fōrmalĭs′tic** *adj.*

fōrmăl′ity *n.* Conformity to rules, propriety; ceremony, elaborate procedure; formal or ceremonial act, requirement of etiquette or custom; being formal, precision of manners, stiffness of design.

fōrm′alīze *v.t.* Give definite shape or legal formality to; make ceremonious, precise, or rigid; imbue with formalism.

fōrm′at (-mah *or* -măt) *n.* Shape and size (of book).

fōrmā′tion *n.* Forming, being formed; thing formed; arrangement of parts, structure; (mil.) disposition of troops, formal stationing or arrangement of number of ships, aeroplanes, etc.; (geol.) assemblage of rocks or series of strata having some common characteristic.

fōrm′ative *adj.* Serving to form, of formation; (gram., of suffixes etc.) used in forming words. ~ *n.* Formative element.

fŏrme: see FORM *n.* 10.

fŏrm'er *adj.* Of the past or an earlier period; *the* ~, the first or first mentioned of two (freq. with ellipsis of *n.*; opp. of LATTER). **fŏrm'erly** *adv.*

fŏrm'ic *adj.* (chem.) ~ *acid*, colourless irritant volatile acid (HCOOH) present in a fluid emitted by ants, used in tanning and electroplating and as reducing agent in dyeing.

fŏrm'idable *adj.* To be dreaded; likely to be hard to overcome, resist, or deal with. **fŏrm'idableness** *n.* **fŏrm'idably** *adv.*

fŏrm'less *adj.* Shapeless, without determinate or regular form. **fŏrm'lessly** *adv.* **fŏrm'lessness** *n.*

Fŏrmōs'a (-*za*). (Chin. *Taiwan*) Island off SE. coast of China, ceded by China to Japan in 1895 and formally relinquished by Japan in 1952; headquarters of Chinese Nationalist Government since 1949. [Port. name, f. L *formosus* beautiful]

fŏrm'ūla *n.* (pl. -*ae*, -*as*). 1. Set form of words in which something is defined, stated, etc., or which is prescribed for use on ceremonial occasion etc.; conventional usage or belief. 2. Recipe; (math.) rule or principle expressed in algebraic symbols; (chem.) expression of constituents of compound in symbols and figures; tabulation of facts etc. in symbols and figures. **fŏrm'ūlarize** *v.t.* **fŏrmūlarīzā'tion** *n.*

fŏrm'ūlary *n.* Collection of formulas; document or book of set forms esp. for belief or ritual; ~ *adj.* In or of formulas.

fŏrm'ulāte *v.t.* Reduce to, express in, a formula; set forth systematically. **fŏrmūlā'tion** *n.*

fŏrm'ūlism *n.* Unintelligent following of rule or conventional usage or belief. **fŏrm'ūlist** *n.* **fŏrmūlis'tic** *adj.*

fŏrn'icāte *v.i.* Commit fornication. **fŏrnicā'tion** *n.* Voluntary sexual intercourse between a man (occas. restricted to unmarried man) and an unmarried woman. **fŏrn'icātor** *n.*

fŏrn'ix *n.* 1. (anat.) An arched formation of the brain (ill. BRAIN). 2. (bot.) A small elongation of the corolla. 3. (conch.) Excavated part of a shell, situated under the umbo.

forsāke' *v.t.* (past *t.* -*sŏŏk*, past part. -*sāken*) Give up, break off from, renounce; withdraw one's help, friendship, or companionship from; desert, abandon.

forsŏŏth' *adv.* (archaic) Truly, in truth, no doubt (chiefly ironically, in parenthesis).

forspĕnt' *adj.* (archaic) Tired out.

forswear' (-wār) *v.t.* (past t. -*swōre*, past part. -*swōrn*). Abjure, renounce on oath; ~ one*self*, swear falsely, perjure oneself; *forsworn*, perjured.

forsȳth'ia *n.* Species of ornamental spring-flowering shrubs with bright-yellow bell-shaped flowers. [W. *Forsyth* (1737–1804), English botanist]

fŏrt *n.* Fortified place, usu. single building or set of connected military buildings; trading-station, orig. fortified, in N. America.

fŏrt'alice *n.* Fortress (archaic and poet.); small outwork of fortification, small fort.

fŏrte[1] *n.* Person's strong point; fencing) sword-blade from hilt to middle.

fŏrt'ĕ[2] (mus. direction, abbrev. *f.*). Loud; *double* ~ (abbrev. *ff.*) very loud; ~ *piano* (abbrev. *fp.*), loud, then immediately soft.

fŏrth[1] *adv.* Forwards (now only in *back and* ~, to and fro); onwards in time (now only in *from this time* ~ etc.); forward, into view; out, away, from home, etc.; *and so* ~, and so on, and the like.

Fŏrth[2]. River of E. Scotland, flowing into the North Sea near Edinburgh.

fŏrthcom'ing (-kŭ-) *adj.* About or likely to come forth; approaching; ready to be produced when wanted.

fŏrth'right (-rīt) *adj.* Going straight, outspoken, unswerving; decisive. ~ *n.* Straight course. **fŏrthright'** *adv.* (archaic) Straight forward; straightway.

fŏrthwith' (-th, -dh) *adv.* Immediately, without delay.

fŏrtificā'tion *n.* 1. Fortifying. 2. Defensive work, wall, earthwork, tower, etc.

fŏrt'ifȳ *v.* Strengthen structure of; impart vigour or physical strength or endurance to, strengthen mentally or morally, encourage; corroborate, confirm (statement); provide (town, army, one*self*) with defensive works; erect fortifications; strengthen (liquors) with alcohol; *fortified bread*, bread made of flour to which vitamins have been added; *fortified wines*, those, esp. port and sherry, to which brandy is added during fermentation.

Fŏr'tin barŏm'ĕter *n.* Type of mercury barometer (ill. BAROMETER). [N. *Fortin* (1750–1831), Fr. maker]

fŏrtiss'imo (mus. direction, abbrev. *ff.*, *ffor.*, *fortiss.*). Very loud. ~ *n.* & *adj.* Very loud (passage).

fŏrt'itude *n.* Courage in pain or adversity.

fŏrt'night (-īt) *n.* Period of two weeks. **fŏrt'nightly** *adj.* & *adv.* (Happening, appearing) once every fortnight.

fŏrt'rĕss *n.* Military stronghold, esp. strongly fortified town fit for large garrison.

fŏrtū'itous *adj.* Due to or characterized by chance, accidental, casual. **fŏrtū'itously** *adv.* **fŏrtū'itousnĕss** *n.* **fŏrtū'ity** *n.* Fortuitousness; a chance occurrence; accident; unstudied or unintended character.

fŏrt'ūnate (*or* -chn*at or* -chŏŏn-) *adj.* Favoured by fortune, lucky, prosperous; auspicious, favourable. **fŏrt'ūnately** *adv.* Luckily, successfully, (now freq. qualifying whole sentence = it is fortunate that).

fŏrt'une (-chŏŏn, -tūn) *n.* 1. Chance, hap, luck, as a power in men's affairs; freq. personified as goddess with wheel, betokening vicissitude, as emblem; *soldier of* ~: see SOLDIER. 2. Luck, good or bad, falling to anyone in life or particular affair; what is to befall in future (chiefly in *tell* ~*s*, *tell person his* ~). 3. Good luck; prosperity, prosperous condition, wealth; large sum of money. *make* (*one's*) ~, become rich, prosper; ~-*hunter*, man seeking rich wife; ~-*teller*, one who professes to foretell the future. ~ *v.i.* (archaic) Chance, occur; come by chance *upon*.

fŏrt'y *adj.* Cardinal number equal to four tens (40, xl, or XL); ~ *winks*, short nap, esp. after dinner. ~ *n.* Age of forty years; *the forties*, years between 39 and 50 of century or one's life; (in British weather forecasts) the sea-area between SW. coast of Norway and NE. coast of Scotland, so called from the 40-fathom line in the N. Sea; *roaring forties*, the part of the S. Atlantic, Pacific, and Indian Oceans between 40° and 50° S. latitude, characterized by exceptionally strong westerly and north-westerly winds (ill. WIND); ~-*five*, revolver of 0·45 calibre; *the Forty-five*, the year 1745, the Jacobite rebellion of that year. **fŏrt'ieth** *adj.* & *n.*

fŏr'um *n.* (Rom. antiq.) Public place or market-place of city; in ancient Rome, place of assembly for judicial and other public business; place of public discussion; court, tribunal (freq. fig.).

fŏr'ward *adj.* 1. (naut.) Belonging to fore part of ship. 2. Lying in front, or in direction of movement; onward or towards the front; (commerc.) prospective, relating to future produce; ~ *play*, (cricket) playing forward. 3. Advanced, progressing to maturity or completion; (of plant, crop, season, etc.) well advanced, early. 4. Ready, prompt, eager; precocious, presumptuous, pert. **fŏr'wardly** *adv.* **fŏr'wardnĕss** *n.* **fŏr'ward** *adv.* 1. Towards the future, continuously onwards; towards the front, in the direction one is facing; with continuous forward motion; in advance, ahead; to the front, into prominence; onward so as to make progress; *play* ~, (cricket) reach forward to play short-pitched ball; *backward and* ~, to and fro; *bring* ~, draw attention to; *carry* ~, (book-keeping) transfer entry to next page or column; *come* ~, offer oneself for task, post, etc.; *put*, *set*, ~, allege; *put oneself* ~, make oneself too conspicuous. 2. (naut.) To, at, in, fore part of ship. ~ *n.* One of first-line players in football, hockey, etc. ~ *v.t.* Help forward, promote; accelerate growth of; send (letter etc.) on to farther destination; (loosely) dispatch (goods etc.). **fŏr'warder** *adj.* & *adv.* Further forward; (freq. in joc. or vulg. form **fŏ'rrarder**, in phr. *get no* ~ etc.). **fŏr'wards** *adv.* = FORWARD *adv.* (esp. to express definite direction viewed in contrast with other directions).

forwear'ied (-ĭd), **forwŏrn'** *adjs.* (archaic) Tired out.

fŏsse *n.* Long narrow excavation, canal, ditch, trench, esp. in fortification; (anat.) groove, depression; *F~ Way*, the Axminster–Lincoln Roman road, so called from the ditch or fosse on each side.

fŏss'ick *v.i.* (slang, Austral.) Rummage, search about.

fŏss'il *adj.* & *n.* Obtained by digging, found buried; now, (thing) found in strata of earth recognizable as remains of plant or animal of former geological period or as showing vestiges of animal or vegetable life of such period; (person or thing) belonging to the past, antiquated, incapable of further growth or progress. **fŏss'ilīze** *v.* **fŏssilīzā'tion** *n.*

fŏssŏr'ial *adj.* (zool.) Burrowing; used in burrowing.

fŏs'ter *v.t.* Tend with affectionate care, cherish, keep warm (in bosom); encourage or harbour (feeling); (of circumstances) be favourable to; *~-child*, child as related to parents who have reared it as their own, or to its wet-nurse and her husband; *~-mother*, woman who brings up another's child (so *~-father*, *-daughter*, *-brother*, *-sister*, *-son*); (also) apparatus for rearing chickens hatched in an incubator. **fŏs'terage** *n.* Fostering; custom of employing foster-mothers. **fŏs'terling** *n.* Foster-child.

foul *adj.* Offensive to the senses, loathsome, stinking; dirty, soiled, filthy; charged with noxious matter; clogged, choked; (of ship's bottom etc.) overgrown with weed, barnacles, etc.; morally polluted, obscene, disgustingly abusive; (of fish at or immediately after spawning) in bad condition; unfair, against rules of game etc.; (of weather) wet, rough, stormy; (of wind) contrary; (naut.) embarrassed, entangled, in collision, etc.; ~ *brood*, disease of larval bees caused by bacillus and characterized by sickly unpleasant smell of hive; *the ~ fiend*, the Devil; ~ *play*, unfair play in games; (fig.) unfair or treacherous dealing (freq. with additional notion of violence); *fall ~ of*, come into collision with. ~ *n.* Something foul; collision, entanglement, esp. in riding, rowing, or running; irregular stroke or piece of play. ~ *adv.* In irregular way, not in accordance with rules. ~ *v.* Become foul, get clogged; make foul or dirty; pollute with guilt, dishonour; cause (anchor, cable) to become entangled, jam or block (crossing, railway line, traffic); become entangled; run foul of; collide with.

foul'ard (fōō-; *or* -ahr) *n.* Thin soft smooth material, usu. twill-woven, of silk or silk and cotton.

foul'ly *adv.* Abominably, cruelly, wickedly; with unmerited insult.

foul'nėss *n.* Foul condition; foul matter; disgusting wickedness.

foum'art (fōō-) *n.* Polecat. [= foul marten]

found[1] *v.* Lay base of (building etc.); be original builder, begin building, of (town, edifice); set up, establish (esp. with endowment), originate, initiate, (institution); construct, base (tale, one's fortunes, rule, etc.) (*up*)*on* some ground, support, principle, etc.; rely, base oneself, (of argument etc.) be based, (*up*)*on.*

found[2] *v.t.* Melt and mould (metal), fuse (materials for glass); make (thing of molten metal, glass) by melting.

foundā'tion *n.* 1. Establishing, constituting on permanent basis, esp. of endowed institution; such institution, e.g. monastery, college, hospital, or its revenues; *on the* ~, entitled to benefit by funds of such institution. 2. Solid ground or base, natural or artificial, on which building rests; lowest part of building, usu. below ground-level; basis, ground-work, underlying principle; body or ground on which other parts are overlaid. 3. *~-muslin*, *-net*, gummed fabrics for stiffening dresses and bonnets; *~-stone*, esp. one laid with ceremony (and freq. inscribed) to celebrate founding of edifice. **foundā'tioner** *n.* One on the foundation of endowed school or college.

found'er[1] *n.* (esp.) One who founds institution(s); *~'s kin*, relatives of founder entitled to election or preference; *~'s shares*, shares issued to founder(s) of public company as part-consideration for business taken over, and separate from ordinary capital. **found'ership, found'rėss** *ns.*

found'er[2] *n.* One who founds metal, glass, etc.

found'er[3] *v.* (Of earth, building, etc.) fall down or in, give way; (of horse) fall from overwork, collapse, fall lame, stick fast in bog, etc.; cause (horse) to break down by overwork; (of ship) fill with water and sink; cause (ship) to do this. ~ *n.* Inflammation of horse's foot from overwork; rheumatism of chest-muscles in horse.

found'ling *n.* Deserted infant of unknown parents; *F~ Hospital*, orphanage for foundlings opened 1741 at Hatton Garden, London, by Capt. Thomas Coram, transferred to Bloomsbury 1745 and to Berkhamstead 1935.

found'ry *n.* Factory where metal, glass, etc., is founded.

fount[1] *n.* (poet. or rhet.) Spring, source, fountain.

fount[2] *n.* Set of type of same face and size.

foun'tain *n.* Water-spring; source *of* river etc.; jet of water made to spout, structure provided for it; public erection with constant supply of drinking-water; soda-fountain; *~-head*, original source; *~-pen*, pen containing reservoir of ink.

four (fōr) *adj.* Cardinal number next after three (4, iv, or IV); *~-ball*, (golf) game in which four balls, one for each player, are used, the best ball on each side counting at each hole; *~-centred arch*: see ill. ARCH; ~ *figures*, one thousand (pounds etc.) or over; *~-flush*, (poker) flush containing only four (instead of five) cards; *~-flusher*, (U.S.) pretender, humbug; *~-foot way*, space (4 ft 8½ in.) between rails on which train runs; *~-handed*, (of card-games) played by four persons; ~ *hundred*, (chiefly U.S.) the most exclusive society of New York (which *c* 1890 was supposed to consist of about this number of people), or of any other place; *~-in-hand*, vehicle with four horses driven by one person; (U.S.) kind of necktie tied in loose knot with long ends hanging straight down; *F~ Last Things*, death, judgement, heaven, and hell; ~ *o'clock*, the plant Marvel of Peru, *Mirabilis jalapa*, with flowers opening about 4 p.m.; *~-post*, (of bed) having four posts (to support canopy and curtains); *~-poster*, four-post bed (ill. BED); *~-pounder*, gun throwing 4-lb. shot; *four'score*, eighty; age of 80 years; *~-square*, square-shaped; solidly based, steady; *F~ Square Gospel*, sect founded 1915 at Belfast by George Jeffreys; *~-stroke*, (of cycle of operations in internal combustion engine) consisting of four strokes, intake, compression, combustion, and exhaust; *~-wheeler*, four-wheeled cab. ~ *n.* The number four; set of four persons or things; card, die, or domino with four pips; four-oared boat and crew; hit etc. at cricket for four runs; *fours*, (pl.) military formation four deep usually facing towards flank for marching; races for four-oared boats; *on all fours*, crawling on hands and knees; (fig.) completely analogous or corresponding. **four'fold** *adj.* & *adv.*

Fourier (fōō'ryā), Charles (1772–1837). French socialist writer. **Four'ierism** *n.* Communistic system for the reorganization of society devised by Fourier; under it the population was to be grouped in *phalansteries*, socialistic groups of about 1,800 persons holding property in common.

four'some (fōr-) *adj.* (Of Scotch reel etc.) performed by four persons together. ~ *n.* Golf match between two pairs of players, each pair sharing a ball; lawn tennis match between two pairs; (colloq.)

company or party of four persons.

fourteen′ (fōr-) *adj.* Four plus ten (14, xiv, or XIV). **fourteenth′** *adj.* & *n.* ~ *of July*, French annual holiday in celebration of fall of Bastille, 1789.

fourth (fōr-) *adj.* Next after third. ~ *n.* 1. Fourth part, quarter. 2. (mus.) Interval of which the span involves four alphabetical names of notes, harmonic combination of two notes thus separated. 3. Fourth day of month; *the Fourth*, (*a*) the fourth of July, anniversary of Declaration of Independence (1776), kept as holiday in U.S.A.; (*b*) the fourth of June, annual commemoration of George III's birthday at Eton College, with 'speeches' (i.e. recitations) and procession of boats on river. **fourth′ly** *adv.* In the fourth place (in enumerations).

fŏv′ĕa *n.* (anat.) Small pit; ~ (*centralis*), small depression in *macula lutea* of retina, spot where vision is most acute.

fowl *n.* 1. Bird (rare); birds (rare exc. in *wild-*~); flesh of birds as food (only in *fish, flesh, and* ~). 2. Domestic cock or hen; its flesh as food; ~-*pest*, acute infectious disease of fowls, caused by a virus. ~ *v.i.* Catch, hunt, shoot, or snare, wild-fowl; *fowl′ing-piece*, light gun used in fowling. **fowl′er** *n.*

fŏx[1] *n.* Flesh-eating quadruped, *Canis vulpes*, with elongated pointed muzzle, long bushy tail, and red fur, preserved in England and elsewhere as beast of chase, and proverbial for cunning; crafty person; ~-*and-geese*, game played on board by two players, one with sixteen pegs, called geese, the other with one, called the fox; *fox′glove*, *Digitalis purpurea*, tall handsome plant, the leaves of which yield digitalis, with purple or white flowers shaped like finger-stall; ~ *hole*, hole in the ground used by soldier for protection against missiles or as firing station; *fox′hound*, kind of hound bred and trained to hunt foxes (ill. DOG); ~-*hunt*, chase, chasing of, fox with hounds; *fox′-tail*, various species of grass with soft brush-like spikes of flowers, esp. *Alopecurus pratensis*; ~-*terrier*, small terrier with smooth or rough (wire-haired) short hair, usu. white with black markings, of a kind bred for unearthing foxes, but kept chiefly as pets; *fox′trot*, ballroom dance in 4/4 time based on slow or quick walking-steps. ~ *v.* 1. Act craftily, dissemble; (colloq.) deceive, (loosely) impede, ruin plans of, etc. 2. Discolour (leaves of book, engraving, etc.) with brownish spots (esp. in past part.).

Fŏx[2], Charles James (1749–1806). English statesman; opposed the policy of PITT; denounced the slave trade; advocated parliamentary reform.

Fŏxe, John (1516–87). English martyrologist, author of 'Actes and Monuments', pop. known as the 'Book of Martyrs'.

fŏx′y *adj.* 1. Fox-like; crafty, cunning. 2. Fox-coloured, reddish brown or yellow; (of painting) having too many reddish tints, over-hot in colouring; spotted, stained, with mildew etc.

foyer (fwah′yā) *n.* Large room in theatre etc. for use of audience esp. during intervals (ill. THEATRE).

fp. *abbrev. forte-piano* (= loud, then soft).

F.P. *abbrev.* Field punishment; fire plug.

fr. *abbrev.* Franc(s).

Fr *abbrev.* Father.

Fr. *abbrev.* French.

Fra Angelico: see ANGELICO.

frăc′as (-ah) *n.* (pl. same). Noisy quarrel, row.

frăc′tion *n.* 1. Breaking or dividing of bread in Eucharist. 2. Numerical quantity that is not an integer, one or more aliquot parts of unit or whole number; small piece or amount, scrap; *vulgar* ~, one in which numerator and denominator are represented by numbers placed above and below horizontal line; *proper* (*improper*) ~, fraction in which numerator is less (greater) than denominator. **frăc′tional** (-shon-) *adj.*; ~ *distillation*: see DISTILLATION.

frăc′tionāte (-shon-) *v.t.* Separate (mixture) by distillation or otherwise into portions of differing properties. **frăctionā′tion** *n.*

frăc′tionīze (-shon-) *v.t.* Break up into fractions.

frăc′tious (-shus) *adj.* Unruly, cross, peevish. **frăc′tiously** *adv.* **frăc′tiousnĕss** *n.*

frăc′ture *n.* 1. Breaking, breakage, esp. of bone or cartilage (ill. BONE). 2. Characteristic appearance of fresh surface of mineral broken with hammer. 3. (phonology) Diphthongization of single vowel, owing to influence of following consonant; diphthong so formed. ~ *v.* Cause fracture in, be fractured; break continuity of.

fraen′um, frē- *n.* (pl. -*na*). (anat.) Small ligament or membranous fold restraining motion of organ to which it is attached. [L, = 'bridle']

frā′gīle (U.S. -ĭl) *adj.* Easily snapped or shattered; weak, perishable; of delicate frame or constitution. **fragĭl′ĭty** *n.*

frăg′ment *n.* Part broken off, detached piece; isolated or incomplete part, remainder of lost or destroyed whole; esp. extant remains or unfinished portion of writing or work of art. **frăg′mentary** *adj.* **frăgmentā′tion** *n.* Separation into fragments; ~ *bomb*, one designed to disintegrate into small fragments on explosion.

frā′grant *adj.* Sweet-smelling. **frā′grance** *n.* Quality of being fragrant; perfume.

frail[1] *n.* Rush basket for packing figs, raisins, etc.; quantity of raisins contained in a frail.

frail[2] *adj.* Fragile; weak, subject to infirmities; morally weak, unable to resist temptation; (euphem., of women) unchaste. **frail′ty** *n.* Liability to err or yield to temptation; fault, weakness, foible.

fraise[1] (-z) *n.* (mil.) Palisade, horizontal or down-sloping, round an earthwork near the berm.

fraise[2] (-z) *n.* Tool for enlarging circular hole in stone, or for cutting teeth in watch-wheel.

F.R.A.M. *abbrev.* Fellow of the Royal Academy of Music.

frămboes′ĭa (-bēz-) *n.* (path.) The YAWS.

frāme *n.* 1. Construction, constitution, build; established order, plan, system. 2. Temporary state (*of* mind). 3. Framed work or structure; human or animal body; skeleton of building; underlying support or essential substructure of anything. 4. Case or border enclosing picture, pane of glass, etc. 5. (gardening) Glazed structure protecting plants from cold. 6. Rigid part of bicycle; skeleton of motor vehicle etc. supporting machinery and body. 7. Structure placed in hive for bees to make honey in. 8. Each small picture on cinematograph film. 9. Single complete picture transmitted in series of 'lines' by television. 10. ~-*house*, house of wooden framework or skeleton covered with boards etc.; ~ *of reference*, characteristic of perception whereby objects are correctly localized in space; standard governing perceptual or logical evaluation; ~-*saw*, thin saw stretched in frame to give it rigidity; ~-*up*, (slang, orig. U.S.) conspiracy, trumped-up case or charge; *frame′work*, frame, substructure, upon or into which anything may be put. ~ *v.* 1. Shape, direct, dispose, to a purpose; adapt, fit, *to*, or *into*; give promise of becoming skilful etc. 2. Construct by combination of parts or adaptation to design; contrive, devise, invent, compose, express; articulate (words); conceive, imagine. 3. Set in frame; serve as frame for. 4. (orig. U.S.) Concoct false charge or accusation against, make victim of frame-up.

frănc *n.* Principal monetary unit of France, Belgium, and Switzerland, = 100 centimes; (hist.) various gold and silver coins. [Fr., perh. f. *Francorum Rex* king of the Franks, legend on earliest coin so called]

France[1] (-ah-). A republic of W. Europe; capital, Paris. The monarchical system of government was overthrown during the French Revolution (1789–93) and the First Republic lasted until Napoleon founded the First Empire in 1804; the monarchy was restored in 1814 and lasted until 1848 when the Second Republic was formed, which became the Second Empire under Napoleon III in 1852; Napoleon was deposed in 1870 and the Third Republic established;

this lasted until the occupation of France by the Germans (1940); after the liberation of France (1945) the republic was restored and the Constitution of the Fourth Republic was in force from 1946 until Oct. 1958; the Constitution of the Fifth Republic, embodying important changes, was adopted on 28th Sept. and Gen. de GAULLE was elected President on 21st Dec., taking office on 8th Jan. 1959.

France[2] (-ahṅs), Anatole. Pseudonym of Jacques Anatole Thibault (1844–1924), French satirical writer.

frăn'chīse (-z) *n.* 1. (chiefly hist.) Legal immunity or exemption from some burden or jurisdiction; privilege or exceptional right, granted to person, corporation, etc. 2. Full membership of corporation or State, citizenship. 3. Right of voting at public elections, esp. for member of legislative body; principle of qualification for this.

Fran'cĭs (-ah-) or **François I** (1494–1547). King of France from 1515 to his death; was involved in many wars against the Emperor Charles V and taken prisoner by him at the battle of Pavia.

Fran'cĭs of Assisi (frah-, *asē'zī*), St. Giovanni Francesco Bernardone (1181?–1226), Italian friar; founded *c* 1209 the *Franciscan Order* of friars whose rules require chastity, poverty, and obedience, and lay special stress on preaching and ministration to the sick. **Francĭs'can** *adj.* & *n.* (Member) of Franciscan Order, Minorite, Grey Friar.

frăn'cium *n.* (chem.) A radioactive metallic element of short life, the heaviest member of the alkali metal series; symbol Fr, at. no. 87, principal isotope 223. [f. *France*, because its existence was first reported by a Frenchwoman, Mlle M. Perey]

Franck (-ahṅk), César Auguste (1822–90). Belgian composer.

Frănc'ō, Generalissimo. Francisco Franco Bahamonde (1892–), Spanish political leader; since 1939 Leader (Caudillo) of the Empire and Chief of the State; head of the Falangist party.

Franco-. French-&, as *~-German*; *Francophil(e)*, *Francophobe*, lover, hater, of the French.

François I: see FRANCIS I.

frănc'olĭn *n.* Bird of genus *Francolinus* found in Persia and N. India, also called 'black partridge'.

frăn'gĭpāne (-j-), **frangĭpăn'ĭ** *n.* 1. Kind of pastry made with almonds, sugar, and cream. 2. Perfume made from flowers of red jasmine or imitation of this. 3. Red jasmine tree, *Plumeria rubra*. [family name *Frangipani*]

frănk[1] *adj.* Ingenuous, open, candid, outspoken; undisguised, avowed. **frănk'ly** *adv.* **frănk'nėss** *n.* [med. L *francus* free, f. *Francus* Frank]

frănk[2] *v.t.* Superscribe (letter etc.) with signature to ensure its being carried without charge, send free of charge (hist.); *franking machine*, an officially authorized machine, first introduced in 1922, for stamping letters etc. and simultaneously recording the cost of postage incurred, this being periodically checked and collected by the Post Office; facilitate coming and going of (person), give social passport to; convey (person) gratuitously. *~ n.* (hist.) Franking signature, franked cover.

Frănk[3]. 1. One of the Germanic nation or coalition of nations that conquered Gaul in 6th c. 2. (in Levant) Person of western nationality. **Frănk'ish** *adj.*

Frănk'enstein (-īn). A romance (1818) by Mary Wollstonecraft Shelley; hero of this, a student who constructs a human monster and endows it with life; hence, *~'s monster*, thing that becomes formidable to its creator or destroys him.

Frănk'fort[1]. (Ger. *Frankfurt*) City in W. Germany on the river Main; *~ black*, pigment made by charring vine-twigs, lees of wine, etc., used in engraving. **frănk'-forter, frănk'furter** *n.* Highly seasoned smoked beef and pork sausage, orig. made at Frankfort.

Frănk'fort[2]. Capital of Kentucky, U.S.

frănk'incĕnse *n.* Aromatic gum resin obtained from trees, chiefly E. African, of genus *Boswellia* and burnt as incense.

frănk'lĭn[1] *n.* (hist.) Landowner of free but not noble birth in 14th–15th centuries.

Frănk'lĭn[2], Benjamin (1706–90). Amer. publicist, popular scientist, and political emissary to Europe; one of the signatories to the peace between the U.S. and Gt Britain after the Amer. War of Independence; inventor of the lightning conductor.

Frănk'lĭn[3], Sir John (1786–1847). Arctic explorer; lost his life in an attempt to discover the North-west Passage; author of two 'Narratives' of voyages to the Polar Sea.

frănk'-plĕdge *n.* (hist.) System in Anglo-Saxon law by which every member of a group of 10 men (called a 'tithing') was responsible for the actions of every other; *view of ~*, court held periodically to ascertain which tithing (or later, which hundred or manor) a man belonged to.

frăn'tĭc *adj.* Wildly excited, beside oneself with rage, pain, grief, etc.; showing frenzy, uncontrolled. **frăn'tĭcally** *adv.*

frăp *v.t.* (naut.) Bind tightly.

frappé (-ăp'ā) *n.* Iced drink, soft water-ice served in glass, etc.

F.R.A.S. *abbrev.* Fellow of the Royal Astronomical Society.

frăss *n.* Excrement of larvae; refuse left behind by boring insects.

frăt *n.* Slang (orig. U.S.) abbrev. of FRATERNITY, FRATERNIZATION.

frāt'er *n.* (hist.) Refectory of monastery (ill. MONASTERY).

fratẽrn'al *adj.* (As) of brothers, brotherly; *~ order*, (U.S.) friendly society, brotherhood; *~ twins*, twins not necessarily of same sex and freq. bearing merely fraternal resemblance, resulting from fertilization of two ova, not one (opp. IDENTICAL).

fratẽrn'ity *n.* 1. Being fraternal, brotherliness; brotherhood. 2. Body or order of men organized for religious or devout purposes; body of men associated by some tie or common interest, or of same class, occupation, etc.; (U.S.) literary or social association of students of college or university.

frăt'ernīze *v.i.* Associate (*with*, together, etc.), make friends, behave as intimates. **frăternizā'tion** *n.*

frăt'rĭcīde *n.* Killing of one's brother or sister; one who commits fratricide. **frăt'rĭcīdal** *adj.*

frau (-ow) *n.* German married woman or widow; (cap.) title, corresponding to *Mrs.*

fraud *n.* 1. Deceitfulness (rare). 2. Criminal deception, using of false representations to obtain unjust advantage or injure another; dishonest trick or stratagem; fraudulent contrivance, spurious or deceptive thing or person; impostor, humbug; *pious ~*, deception for what is considered a good object, esp. advancement of religion.

fraud'ūlent *adj.* Guilty of, of the nature of, characterized or effected by, fraud. **fraud'ūlence** *n.* **fraud'ūlently** *adv.*

fraught (-awt) *adj.* Stored, equipped, *with* (poet.); *~ with*, (fig.) involving, attended with, threatening (danger, woe, etc.); full of (meaning etc.).

fräulein (froi'līn) *n.* German unmarried woman; title, corresponding to *Miss*; German governess in England.

Fraun'hōfer lines (frown-). Dark lines in the solar spectrum, observed from the earth. [J. von *Fraunhofer* (1787–1826), Bavarian optician]

fray[1] *n.* Noisy quarrel, brawl; fight, conflict.

fray[2] *v.* 1. (Of deer) rub velvet off new horns. 2. Wear through by rubbing; ravel *out* edge or end of; become ragged at edge (also fig.).

frăzz'le *n.* (chiefly U.S.) Worn or exhausted state.

F.R.C.M., F.R.C.O., *abbrevs.* Fellow of the Royal College of Music, of Organists.

F.R.C.P.(E.), F.R.C.S.(E.), *abbrevs.* Fellow of the Royal College of Physicians (of Edinburgh), of Surgeons (of Edinburgh).

freak (-ēk) *n.* 1. Caprice, vagary; capriciousness. 2. Product of sportive fancy; eccentric person; (also

~ *of nature*) monstrosity, abnormally developed individual; esp. living curiosity exhibited in show. **freak'ish** *adj.* **freak'ishly** *adv.* **freak'ishness** *n.*

freaked (-kt) *adj.* Oddly flecked or streaked.

frĕck'le *n.* Spotted pigmentation of skin, produced esp. by ultraviolet light, and probably serving as a protection to the tissues; (pl.) number of such spots on various parts of the body, caused by exposure to sun. ~ *v.* Spot, be spotted, with freckles.

Frĕd'erick. Anglicized form of the name, *Friedrich*, of two emperors of the Holy Roman Empire and one German emperor: *Frederick I*: see FREDERICK BARBAROSSA; *Frederick II* (1194–1250), emperor of the Holy Roman Empire from 1220 until his death; *Frederick III* (1831–88), German emperor 1888.

Frĕd'erick Barbarŏss'a (the 'Redbeard') (1121–90). Emperor of the Holy Roman Empire from 1155 until his death; endeavoured unsuccessfully to establish the Hohenstaufen overlordship over Italy; was drowned during the Third Crusade, but legend says that he still sleeps in a cavern in the Kyffhäuser mountains, until the need of his country shall summon him forth.

Frĕd'erick the Great (1712–86). Friedrich II, king of Prussia from 1740 until his death; engaged in wars against Austria and France and by his military talent raised Prussia to the rank of a powerful State.

free *adj.* 1. Not in bondage to another, having personal rights and social and political liberty; (of State, its citizens, etc.) subject neither to foreign dominion nor to despotic government, having national and civil liberty. 2. At liberty, not in custody or confinement; without ties, obligations, or constraint upon one's action; released or exempt from work or duty; unimpeded, unrestricted, unhampered; not constrained or timid; not fettered in judgement; (of literary composition etc.) not observing strict laws of form; (of translation, copy, etc.) not adhering strictly to original; allowable or allowed (*to* do); open (*for* all), open to all competitors; (of space, way) open, unobstructed; clear *of*, *from*; not fixed or fastened; not in contact; (chem.) uncombined; (of power etc.) available for 'work'. 3. Spontaneous, unforced, unearned, gratuitous, willing; lavish, profuse, unstinted, copious; frank, unreserved; forward, impudent, familiar. 4. Released or exempt *from*; possessed of certain exclusive rights or privileges; (of property) freehold; admitted to privileges *of*, invested with rights or immunities *of* (city, chartered company, etc.); allowed use or enjoyment *of* (place etc.); not subject to tax, toll, duty, trade-restrictions, fees, etc. 5. ~-*and-easy*, unconstrained, unaffected, unconventional; (*n.*) convivial gathering for singing etc., smoking concert; ~ *association*, undirected mental activity like that of reverie or dreams; this as a method of psycho-analysis; ~-*board*, the part of ship's side between line of floatation and deck level; ~-*born*, born to the conditions and privileges of citizenship, born free; ~ *church*, church free from State control; nonconformist church; *F~ Church of Scotland*, organization of those who seceded in 1843 from established Presbyterian Church (reunited 1929); ~ *fight*, fight in which all and sundry engage promiscuously; ~-*hand*, (of drawing) done without guiding instruments, measures, or other artificial aid; ~-*handed*, open-handed, generous; *free'hold*, (estate held by) tenure in fee-simple or fee-tail or for term of life; held by freehold; *freeholder*, possessor of freehold estate; ~ *house*, public house not belonging to brewer (opp. *tied house*); ~ *kick*, (football) kick allowed without interference, as penalty for breach of rules by the other side; ~-*lance*, journalist not attached to one periodical, person working for himself and not for an employer; ~ *list*, list of things on which, or persons from whom, payment is not required; ~-*liver*, one who gives free indulgence to his appetites; ~ *love*, sexual relations irrespective of marriage; *free'man*, one who is not a slave or serf, or not subject to tyranny or usurped dominion; one who has freedom of borough, city, etc.; *free'mason*, member of fraternity for mutual help and brotherly feeling, called *Free and Accepted Masons*, having elaborate ritual and system of secret signs (the original *free masons* were probably skilled masons emancipated and moving from place to place for erection of important buildings in and after 14th c., the *accepted masons* being honorary members (orig. supposed to be eminent for architectural or antiquarian learning) who began to be admitted early in 17th c.); *free'masonry*, system and institutions of Freemasons; secret or tacit brotherhood, instinctive sympathy; ~ *on board*, (abbrev. *f.o.b.*) of goods, with all charges paid for delivery when put on board ship or other means of conveyance; ~ *pass*, authority to travel on railway, attend performance, etc., without payment; ~ *place*, place in secondary school awarded free to pupil from primary school; ~ *port*, port open to all traders to load and unload in, (also) port, or zone within a port, where imports and exports are exempt from customs duty; ~ *State*, republic; before Civil War of 1861–5, State of U.S. in which slavery did not exist; *the F~ State*, EIRE; *free'-stone*, fine-grained sandstone or limestone that can easily be cut or sawn; kind of peach or nectarine of which when ripe the stone is loose; ~-*thinker*, one who refuses to submit his reason to control of authority in matters of religious belief, rationalist, deist, etc.; so ~ *thought*; ~ *trade*, trade left to its natural course without customs duties to restrict imports or protect home industries; ~-*trader*, believer in free trade; ~ *verse*: see VERS LIBRE; ~-*wheel*, rear wheel of bicycle designed to be capable of revolving faster than, and independently of, the driving mechanism; the special type of pinion permitting the rear wheel to revolve thus; similar device in motor-cars; (*v.i.*) ride bicycle with pedals stationary; drive motor-car with clutch disengaged; ~ *will*, unconstrained choice; power of directing one's own actions without constraint by necessity or fate. **free'ly** *adv.* **free** *adv.* Freely (now only techn.); without cost or payment. ~ *v.t.* 1. Make free, set at liberty. 2. Relieve *from*, rid or ease *of*; clear, disengage, disentangle; *freed'man*, (esp. in Rom. hist.) emancipated slave.

free'bōōter *n.* Pirate, piratical adventurer.

free'dom *n.* 1. Personal liberty, exemption or release from slavery or imprisonment; civil liberty, independence; liberty of action; power of self-determination, independence of fate or necessity. 2. Frankness, outspokenness; undue familiarity; facility, ease, in action; boldness of conception. 3. (physics) Capability of motion. 4. Exemption *from* defect, disadvantage, burden, etc.; privilege possessed by city or corporation; participation in privileges of membership *of* company etc. or citizenship *of* city; unrestricted use *of*.

free'mârtin *n.* Hermaphrodite or imperfect female of ox kind.

frees'ia (-z-) *n.* Genus, allied to gladiolus, of iridaceous bulbous plants of Cape of Good Hope, cultivated for their ornamental and perfumed flowers. [K. *Frees*, Swed. botanist]

freeze *v.* (past t. *frōze*, past part. *frōzen*). 1. (impers.) *It freezes* etc., the temperature of the atmosphere is such that water becomes ice. 2. Be converted into or covered with ice; become hard or rigid as result of cold; become fastened *to*, *together*, by action of frost; ~ *on to*, (colloq.) take or keep tight hold of. 3. Be affected by, feel, extreme cold; die by frost; be devoid of heat; be chilled by fear etc. 4. Cause to congeal, change (fluid) to solid by diminution of heat, cause ice to form on; congeal (the blood) as if by frost, with terror etc.; chill (feelings etc.), paralyse (powers etc.); stiffen, harden, injure, kill, etc., by chilling; preserve (meat etc.) by refrigeration; make (assets etc.) unrealizable, peg or stabilize (prices, wages, etc.); *freezing mixture*, salt and snow or other mixture used to freeze liquids; *freezing-point*, temperature at which water freezes, temperature at which given liquid freezes; ~ *out*, exclude from business, society, etc., by competition, boycotting, etc. ~ *n.* State, coming, period, of frost.

freez'ing *adj.* (esp.) Very cold; (of manner) chilling; distant. **freez'ingly** *adv.*

freight (-āt) *n.* Hire of ship for transporting goods; transport of goods by water (in U.S. by land also), charge for this; cargo, shipload; load, burden; (U.S.) freight train; ~ *train*, (U.S.) goods train, train for conveyance of goods. ~ *v.t.* Load (ship) with cargo, (wagon etc.) with goods for transport; hire or let out (ship etc.) for carriage of goods and passengers.

freight'age (-āt-) *n.* Hire of ship etc. for conveyance of goods; cost of conveyance of goods; freighting or hiring of ship etc.; cargo.

freight'er (-āt-) *n.* One who (charters and) loads ship; one who owns freight-wagon(s); one who consigns goods for carriage inland; one whose business is to receive and forward freight; cargo-ship, freight-wagon; freight-carrying aircraft.

Frĕnch *adj.* Of France or its people; having the qualities attributed to French people; ~ *bean*, kidney or haricot bean used as culinary vegetable both in unripe sliced pods and in ripe seeds; ~ *bread*, bread made in long loaves with transverse marks on top; ~ *chalk*, finely powdered talc used as dry lubricant and for removing grease-spots etc.; ~ *grey*, grey colour with lavender tint; ~ *horn*: see HORN[1], 3; ~ *knot*, embroiderer's ornamental knot (ill. STITCH); *take* ~ *leave*, go away, do something, without permission or notice; ~ *letter*, (colloq.) a contraceptive sheath; ~ *polish*, coloured solution of shellac and methylated spirit for producing high gloss on wood; ~*-polish* (*v.t.*) polish with this; *F~ Revolution*, revolution, generally regarded as beginning with the meeting of the States General in May 1789, in which the French monarchy was overthrown and the First Republic established; ~ *window*, glazed door, or pair of these, serving as door and window (ill. WINDOW). ~ *n.* Language of France, one of the descendants of Latin.

Frĕnch Community. Association of France, her departments and territories overseas, and various African States (republic of Madagascar and territories of former *Fr. Equatorial Africa* and *Fr. W. Africa*).

Frĕnch'ifȳ *v.t.* Make French in form, character, or manners. **Frĕnchĭfĭcā'tion** *n.*

frenetic: see PHRENETIC.

frenum: see FRAENUM.

frĕn'zy *n.* 1. (rare) Mental derangement; temporary insanity; paroxysm of mania. 2. Delirious fury or agitation; wild folly. ~ *v.t.* (usu. in past part.) Drive to frenzy, infuriate; *frenzied rage*, rage of frenzied person.

frē'quency *n.* 1. Frequent occurrence; being repeated at short intervals. 2. (physiol.) Number of pulse-beats per minute. 3. (physics, acoustics, etc.) Rate of recurrence of a repeated event, e.g. a vibration (ill. VIBRATION); (elect.) number of complete cycles per second of an alternating current or potential; such currents are classified as: *low* ~, (L.F.) 0–*c* 20 cycles per sec.; *audio*-~, (A.F.) *c* 20 cycles–*c* 15 kilocycles per sec.; *radio* ~, (R.F.) *c* 15 kilocycles–*c* 30,000 megacycles per sec.; radio frequency signals are subdivided into: *very low* ~, (V.L.F.), 15–30 kcs.; *low* ~, (L.F.) 30–300 kcs.; *medium* ~, (M.F.), 300 kcs.–3 mcs.; *high* ~, (H.F.) 3–30 mcs.; *very high* ~, (V.H.F.) 30–300 mcs.; *ultra-high* ~, (U.H.F.) 300–3,000 mcs.; *super-high* ~, (S.H.F.) 3,000–30,000 mcs.; ~ *modulation*: see MODULATION. 4. (statistics) Ratio of number of actual to number of possible occurrences of an event.

frē'quent *adj.* Found near together, numerous, abundant; often occurring, common, happening in close succession; (of pulse) rapid; habitual, constant. **frē'quently** *adv.* **frèquĕnt'** *v.t.* Go often or habitually to. **frēquentā'tion, frèquĕn'ter** *ns.*

frèquĕnt'ative *adj.* & *n.* (gram.) (Verb, verbal form, conjugation) expressing frequent repetition of action.

frĕs'cō *n.* (pl. *-oes*, *-os*). Method of painting with powdered pigments by mixing them with water and applying them to wall or ceiling before plaster is dry (also called *true* ~ to distinguish it from *fresco secco*, painting on dry plaster); picture painted thus. ~ *v.t.* Paint thus. [It., = 'fresh']

frĕsh *adj.* 1. New, novel; not previously known, met with, used, etc.; additional, different, further; recent, newly made or arrived; newly come or taken *from*; raw, inexperienced; *fresh'man*, university student (U.S., pupil at school) in his first year. 2. (of food) Not artificially preserved, not salted, pickled, smoked, etc.; (of butter) not salt; (of water) not salt or bitter, fit for drinking; *fresh'water* (*adj.*) of fresh water, not of the sea; (of air etc.) pure, untainted, invigorating, refreshing, cool. 3. Not stale, musty, or vapid; not faded; unsullied, bright and pure in colour; looking healthy or young. 4. Not weary, brisk, vigorous, fit; excited with drink. 5. (slang, prob. infl. by Ger. *frech* impertinent) Presumptuous, amorously impudent, cheeky. **frĕsh'nèss** *n.* **frĕsh'en** *v.* **frĕsh** *adv.* Freshly, newly; ~*-run*, (of salmon) newly come up from the sea. ~ *n.* 1. Fresh part of day, year, etc. 2. Rush of water in river, flood. **frĕsh'nèss** *n.*

frĕsh'er *n.* (slang) = FRESHMAN.

frĕsh'ĕt *n.* Rush of fresh water flowing into sea; flood of river from heavy rain or melted snow.

frĕsh'ly *adv.* Recently; afresh (rare); with unabated vigour; with fresh appearance, odour, etc.

frĕt[1] *n.* Ornamental pattern of continuous combinations of straight

FRET OR MEANDER

lines joined usu. at right angles; ~*-saw*, very thin saw stretched on frame for cutting thin wood in ornamental patterns; ~*-work*, (archit.) carved work in decorative patterns, esp. of intersecting lines; wood cut with fret-saw into ornamental patterns. ~ *v.t.* Variegate, chequer; adorn (esp. ceiling) with carved or embossed work.

frĕt[2] *v.* 1. Gnaw; consume, wear, torment by gnawing; eat *away*; form or make by wearing away. 2. Chafe, irritate, annoy, worry, distress; distress oneself with regret or discontent. ~ *n.* Irritation, vexation, querulousness. **frĕt'ful** *adj.* **frĕt'fully** *adv.* **frĕt'fulnèss** *n.*

frĕt[3] *n.* Bar or ridge on fingerboard of certain stringed instruments fixing positions of fingers to produce required notes (ill. GUITAR).

Freud (froid), Sigmund (1856–1939). Austrian specialist in neurology; founder of psycho-analysis. **Freud'ian** *adj.* & *n.*

Frey or **Freyr** (-*ā*, -ār). (Scand. myth.) The god of fertility and dispenser of rain and sunshine.

Frey'a or **Frey'ja** (frāy*a*). (Scand. myth.) Goddess of love and of the night, the northern Venus.

F.R.G.S. *abbrev.* Fellow of the Royal Geographical Society.

Fri. *abbrev.* Friday.

frī'able *adj.* Easily crumbled. **frīabĭl'ity, frī'ablenèss** *ns.*

frī'ar *n.* Brother or member of certain religious orders founded in 13th c. or after, and esp. the four mendicant orders, Franciscans (*Grey F~s*, *Minorites*), Augustines (*Austin F~s*), Dominicans (*Black F~s*), and Carmelites (*White F~s*); ~*'s balsam*, tincture of benzoin used as application for ulcers and wounds, and, vaporized, as inhalant. **frī'ary** *n.* Convent, fraternity, of friars.

F.R.I.B.A. *abbrev.* Fellow of the Royal Institute of British Architects.

frĭbb'le *v.i.* Trifle, be frivolous. ~ *n.* Trifler.

frĭcandeau' (-dō) *n.* (pl. *-x*, pr. -z). Dish of veal or other meat fried, braised, and served with its sauce. ~ *v.t.* Make into fricandeaux.

fricassee' *n.* Meat cut up, fried or stewed, and served with sauce; esp. ragout of small animals or birds cut in pieces. ~ *v.t.* Make fricassee of.

fric'ative *adj.* & *n.* (Consonant) produced by friction of breath through narrow opening formed in the mouth with the tongue or lips, as *s, f.*

fric'tion *n.* 1. Chafing or rubbing as medical treatment. 2. Rubbing of two bodies, attrition; (physics etc.) resistance body meets with in moving over another; (fig.) clash of wills, temperaments, opinions, etc.; *angle of* ~, maximum angle at which one body will remain on another without sliding; *~-clutch, -cone, -coupling, -disc, -gear(ing)*, contrivances for transmitting motion by frictional contact. **fric'tional** (-shon-) *adj.*

Fri'day (*or* -dĭ) *n.* 6th day of week; *Good* ~, Friday before Easter, commemorating Crucifixion and observed as holiday. [= 'day of (the goddess) Frig' (i.e. FRIGGA), transl. of L *dies Veneris* day of (the planet) Venus]

fridge, frig (-j) *ns.* Colloq. abbrevs. of REFRIGERATOR.

friend (frĕnd) *n.* One (not ordinarily a relative or lover) joined to another in intimacy and mutual benevolence; second in duel; (loosely) acquaintance; stranger towards whom one wishes to express goodwill or kindly condescension; sympathizer, helper, patron; one who is not an enemy, who is on same side; member of Society of Friends; in vocative, ordinary mode of address among Quakers; *my honourable* ~, used in House of Commons by one member to describe another; *my learned* ~, applied in law court by counsel to one another; *a ~ at court*, one who will use his influence in high places to help another; (*Society of*) *Friends*, the QUAKERS as a communion. ~ *v.t.* (poet.) Befriend, help. **friend'lėss** *adj.* **friend'lėssnėss** *n.*

friend'ly (frĕ-) *adj.* Acting, disposed to act, as friend; characteristic of friends, expressing, showing, prompted by, kindness; not hostile, on amicable terms; favourably disposed, ready to approve or help, serviceable, convenient, opportune; ~ *society*, association of members paying fixed contribution in return for pecuniary help in sickness, old age, etc. **friend'lily**(rare)*adv.* **friend'linėss** *n.* **friend'ly** *adv.* (rare) In friendly manner.

friend'ship (frĕ-) *n.* Being friends, relation between friends; friendly disposition felt or shown.

Friesian (frē'zhan), *adj.* & *n.* (Of) a breed of large piebald (usu. black-and-white) dairy cattle orig. imported from Friesland.

Friesland (frē'zland). Province of N. Netherlands.

frieze[1] *n.* Coarse woollen cloth with nap usu. on one side only.

frieze[2] *n.* Member of entablature above architrave and below cornice (ill. ORDER); horizontal broad band of sculpture filling this; any band of painted or sculptured decoration; strip of wallpaper of different pattern or colour from main paper placed below ceiling or cornice of a room. [Fr. *frise* f. L *Phrygium* (*opus*) Phrygian (work)]

frig'ate *n.* 1. In Royal Navy, formerly vessel next in size and equipment to ships of the line, with raised quarter-deck and forecastle (*~-built*, built thus) and from 28 to 60 guns on main deck; later, (loosely) cruiser; in recent use, a large CORVETTE. 2. ~(*-bird*), large swift brown sea-bird (*Fregata aquila*) of tropical regions, with habit of cruising near other species and daringly pursuing them.

Frigg'a. (Scand. myth.) Wife of Odin and goddess of married love and of the hearth.

fright (-īt) *n.* Sudden fear, violent terror, alarm; grotesque- or ridiculous-looking person or thing. ~ *v.t.* (poet.) Frighten.

fright'en (-īt-) *v.t.* Throw into a fright, terrify; drive (*away, out of, into*, etc.) by fright; *frightened at*, affected with fright of.

fright'ful (-īt-) *adj.* Dreadful, shocking, revolting; ugly, hideous; (slang) very great, awful. **fright'fully** *adv.* **fright'fulnėss** *n.* (esp., in war of 1914–18, as transl. of Ger. *Schrecklichkeit*) Policy of terrorizing civilian population as military resource.

fri'gid *adj.* 1. Intensely cold; ~ *zone*, region lying within either polar circle (ill. EARTH). 2. Without ardour, apathetic; (of a woman) sexually irresponsive; formal, forced; chilling, depressing; dull, flat, insipid. **fri'gidly** *adv.* **fri'gidnėss, frigid'ity** *ns.*

frill *n.* Ornamental edging of strip of woven material with one edge gathered and the other left loose so as to give wavy or fluted appearance; similar paper ornament on ham-knuckle, cutlet-bone, etc.; natural fringe of feathers, hair, etc., on bird, animal, or plant; (phot.) irregular puckering of gelatine film at edge of plate etc.; (pl.) airs, affectations; showy accomplishments; unnecessary ornament. ~ *v.* Furnish or decorate with frill; form frill, form frill on. **frill'y** *adj.*

fringe (-nj) *n.* Ornamental bordering of threads of silk, cotton, etc., either loose or formed into tassels, twists, etc.; anything resembling this, border, edging; margin, outer edge; part of front hair brushed forward over forehead and cut short. ~ *v.t.* Adorn or encircle with fringe; serve as fringe to. **fringed** (-jd) *adj.* Having a fringe, formed into a fringe.

fripp'ery *n.* Finery, needless or tawdry adornment, esp. in dress; empty display, ostentation; knickknacks, trifles.

Fris'ian (-z-) *adj.* & *n.* (Native, language) of Friesland.

frisk *v.* 1. Move sportively; gambol. 2. (U.S. slang) Search (person, his clothing) for concealed weapon etc. ~ *n.* Frolic, gambol. **fris'ky** *adj.* **fris'kily** *adv.* **fris'kinėss** *n.*

fris'kėt *n.* (printing) Thin iron frame hinged to tympan, with tapes or paper strips stretched across for keeping sheet in position while printing.

frit *n.* Calcined mixture of sand and fluxes prepared for melting to form glass; vitreous composition from which soft porcelain is made. ~ *v.t.* Make into frit; partially fuse, calcine.

frith *n.*: see FIRTH.

Frith, William Powell (1819–1910). English painter, whose 'Derby Day' and 'The Railway Station' were very popular in their day.

fritill'ary *n.* 1. Plant of the liliaceous genus *Fritillaria*, esp. *F. meleagris*, the snakeshead, found in moist meadows. 2. Kinds of butterfly with spotted markings, esp. of genus *Argynnis*. [L *fritillus* dice-box, with ref. to chequered markings of corolla]

fritt'er[1] *n.* Portion of fried batter, containing slices of fruit, meat, etc.

fritt'er[2] *v.t.* Throw *away* (time, money, energy, etc.) in trifling and wasteful way on various aims.

Fritz. Nickname for the Germans or a German. [Ger., abbrev. of *Friedrich* Frederick]

friv'ol *v.* Be a trifler, trifle; throw *away* foolishly.

friv'olous *adj.* Paltry, trumpery, trifling, futile; given to trifling, not serious, silly. **friv'olously** *adv.* **friv'olousnėss, frivŏl'ity** *ns.*

frizz[1] *v.* Curl, crisp, form into mass of small curls; rub (wash-leather etc.) with pumice-stone or scraping-knife to remove grain, soften surface, and give uniform thickness. ~ *n.* Frizzed state; frizzed hair, row of curls. **frizz'y** *adj.*

frizz[2] *v.i.* Make sputtering noise in frying.

frizz'le[1] *v.* Curl (*up*) in small crisp curls, frizz. ~ *n.* Frizzled hair. **frizz'ly** *adj.*

frizz'le[2] *v.* Fry, toast, or grill, with sputtering noise.

Frl. *abbrev.* FRÄULEIN.

frō *adv.* Away (only in *to and* ~, backwards and forwards).

frŏck *n.* 1. Long habit with large open sleeves, the outer and characteristic dress of a monk; (fig.) priestly character. 2. Smock-frock; sailor's woollen jersey. 3. Child's outer garment of skirt and bodice for indoor wear; woman's dress. 4. Coat with long skirts, frock-coat; *~-coat*, man's double-breasted coat with long square tails or skirts not cut away in front (ill. COAT).

Froe'bel (frẽr-), Friedrich Wilhelm (1782–1852). German founder of the KINDERGARTEN system of education. **Froebēl'ian** *adj.* & *n.* **Froebēl'ianism, Froe'belism** *ns.*

frŏg[1] *n.* Tailless amphibious animal of order *Anura*, esp. the common frog (genus *Rana*) with

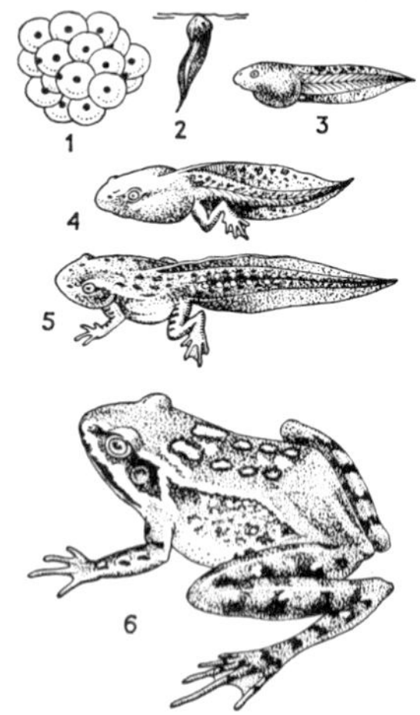

COMMON FROG

1. Spawn. 2–5. Tadpole (2, at 2 weeks. 3, at 6 weeks. 4, at 10 weeks. 5, at 12 weeks). 6. Full-grown frog (not to scale)

smooth shiny skin and long powerful web-footed hind legs with which it swims and leaps; (contempt. for) Frenchman (as eating frogs; also ~-*eater*); ~-*fish*, various fishes, esp. the angler (*Lophius piscatorius*); ~ *in the throat*, hoarseness; *frog'man*, underwater swimmer with long rubber shoes like frog's hind feet; ~-*march*, carrying of prisoner face downwards by four men each holding a limb; (*v.t.*) carry thus; ~-*spawn*, eggs of frog; kinds of freshwater algae.

frŏg[2] *n.* Elastic horny substance in middle of sole of horse's foot.

frŏg[3] *n.* Attachment to waist-belt to support sword, bayonet, etc.; military coat-fastening of spindle-shaped silk-covered button and loop whence **frŏgged** (-gd) *adj.*

frŏg[4] *n.* Grooved piece of iron at place in railway where tracks cross (ill. RAILWAY).

Froissart (frwăs'ar̃), Jean (1337?–1410). French chronicler, whose 'Chroniques' deal chiefly with the affairs of France and England during the period 1325–1400.

frŏl'ic *adj.* (archaic) Joyous, mirthful, sportive, full of pranks. ~ *v.i.* Play pranks, gambol. ~ *n.* Outburst of gaiety; prank; merriment, merrymaking; gay party. **frŏl'icsome** *adj.* **frŏl'icsomely** *adv.* **frŏl'icsomeness** *n.*

from (from, frŏm) *prep.* expressing separation etc. and introducing: place etc. whence motion or action proceeds (*walked* ~ *the town*; *called* ~ *the window*); starting-point (~ *the beginning*; ~ *2nd July*); first-named limit (~ *10 to 20 men*); object etc. whence distance or remoteness is reckoned (*10 miles* ~ *the station*; *am far* ~ *saying*); source (*water* ~ *the well*); giver, sender (*a present* ~ *Ann*); thing or person got rid of, avoided, removed, etc. (*dissuade* ~ *folly*; *release* ~ *engagement*); state changed for another (~ *being attacked became the aggressor*); thing distinguished (*know black* ~ *white*); adverbs or adverbial phrases of place or time, or prepositions (~ *long ago*; ~ *under the bed*).

frŏnd *n.* (bot.) Leaf of certain flowerless plants, esp. ferns (ill. FERN); (zool.) leaf-like expansion in certain animal organisms. **frŏn'dage** *n.* **frŏndōse'** *adj.* Leafy.

Fronde (-awnd). In France, party that rose in rebellion against Mazarin and the court during minority of Louis XIV; hence, a malcontent party. [Fr., orig. = 'sling']

front (-ŭ-) *n.* 1. Forehead (poet.); face; (now rare) effrontery, impudence. 2. (mil.) Foremost line or part of army etc.; line of battle; part of ground towards enemy; scene of actual fighting; direction towards which line faces when formed. 3. Organized body of political forces, as *popular* ~ etc. 4. (archit.) Any face of building, esp. that containing main entrance. 5. (meteor.) Plane on which warm-air and cold-air masses meet (ill. WEATHER). 6. Fore part of anything; (theatr.) part of theatre where audience sits; part of seaside resort fronting sea, promenade; band of false hair, set of false curls, worn over woman's forehead; breast of man's shirt; dicky. 7. (with preps.) Forward position or situation; *in* ~ *of*, before, in advance of; confronting. ~ *adj.* Of the front; situated in front; (phonetics, of sound) in which forepart of tongue touches or is raised towards front of hard palate; ~ *bench*: see BENCH *n.* 3; ~ *door*, principal entrance-door of house. ~ *v.* 1. Face, look *to*, *towards*, (*up*)*on*; face, stand opposite to; have front on side of (street etc.). 2. Confront, meet, oppose. 3. Furnish with front. 4. (mil.) Turn to the front. 5. (phonetics) pronounce with tongue in front position.

fron'tage (-ŭ-) *n.* 1. Land abutting on street or water, land between front of building and road; extent of front; front of building. 2. Ground occupied by troops in camp or on parade. 3. Fronting in certain direction; exposure, outlook.

fron'tal[1] (-ŭ-) *n.* Movable covering for front of altar (ill. ALTAR); façade of building.

fron'tal[2] (-ŭ-) *adj.* 1. Of the forehead; ~ *bone*: see ill. HEAD; ~ *lobes*, foremost region of cerebral hemispheres, situated immediately behind forehead, presumed location of intellectual faculties of brain (ill. BRAIN). 2. Of the front; (of portrait, painted figure, etc.) facing spectator; (of building, sculpture, etc.) intended to be seen from the front; ~ *attack*, direct attack on enemy's front. **frontăl'ity** *n.*

fron'tier (-ŭ-, -ŏ-) *n.* Boundary of a state where its territory abuts upon that of another state; (U.S.) border of settled or inhabited regions of country; *front'iersman*, (U.S.) one who lives on frontier of country, or on extreme edge of settled or inhabited districts. ~ *adj.* Of, on, the frontier.

Frŏn'tignac (-ïnyăk) *n.* Muscat wine from Frontignan, Hérault, France.

fron'tispiece (-ŭ-) *n.* 1. (archit.) Principal face of building; decorated entrance; pediment over door etc. 2. Illustration facing title-page of book or one of its divisions. 3. (slang) Face.

front'lėt (-ŭ-) *n.* Band worn on forehead; phylactery; animal's forehead; cloth hanging over upper part of altar frontal.

fron'ton (-ŭ-) *n.* (archit.) Pediment.

frōre *adj.* (poet.) Frozen, frosty.

frŏst (*or* -aw-) *n.* 1. Freezing; temperature of atmosphere when it is below freezing-point of water; (also *white* ~), frozen dew or vapour, rime; *black* ~, frost without rime; ~-*bite*, inflamed or gangrenous state of skin and adjacent parts produced by exposure to severe cold; ~-*bitten*, affected with this. 2. (slang) Failure. ~ *v.t.* 1. Nip, injure (plants etc.), with frost. 2. Cover (as) with frost; cover (cake) with icing, ice. 3. Give roughened or finely granulated surface to (glass, metal). 4. Turn (hair) white. 5. Arm (horse's shoes) against slipping by nails, roughening, etc. **frŏst'ing** *n.* (esp.) Icing for cakes.

frŏst'y (*or* -aw-) *adj.* Affected with frost, ice-cold; chilling, frigid, lacking in warmth of feeling; covered, looking as if covered, with hoar-frost.

frŏth (*or* -aw-) *n.* Aggregation of small bubbles in liquid, caused by agitation, fermentation, effervescence, etc.; impure matter rising to surface of liquids, scum; unsubstantial or worthless matter, idle talk. ~ *v.* Emit, gather, froth; cause (beer etc.) to foam. **frŏth'y** *adj.* **frŏth'ily** *adv.* **frŏth'iness** *n.*

frou'-frou (-ōō, -ōō) *n.* Rustling, esp. of dresses.

frow (-ow) *n.* Dutchwoman. [Du. *vrouw*]

frō'ward *adj.* (archaic) Perverse, refractory. **frō'wardly** *adv.* **frō'wardness** *n.*

frown *n.* Vertically furrowed state of brow; look expressing severity, disapproval, or deep thought. ~ *v.* Knit brows, esp. to express displeasure or concentrate attention; (of things) present gloomy aspect; express disapprobation (*at*, (*up*)*on*); express (defiance etc.) with frown. **frown'ĭngly** *adv.*

frowst *n.* Close and fusty atmosphere of overcrowded or unventilated room. ~ *v.i.* Remain in, enjoy, such atmosphere. **frowst'y** *adj.*

frowz'y *adj.* Ill-smelling, fusty, musty, close; slatternly, unkempt, dingy. **frow'zĭnėss** *n.*

frōz'en *adj.* (past part. of FREEZE). Congealed; (of credits etc.) not realizable.

F.R.P.S. *abbrev.* Fellow of the Royal Photographic Society.

F.R.S. *abbrev.* Fellow of the Royal Society.

F.R.S.A., F.R.S.E. *abbrevs.* Fellow of the Royal Society of Arts, of Edinburgh.

F.R.S.G.S. *abbrev.* Fellow of the Royal Scottish Geographical Society.

F.R.S.L. *abbrev.* Fellow of the Royal Society of Literature.

F.R.S.S. *abbrev.* Fellow of the Royal Statistical Society.

frŭctĭf'erous *adj.* Bearing fruit.

frŭctĭfĭcā'tion *n.* (bot.) Reproductive parts of plant, esp. of ferns and mosses.

frŭc'tĭfȳ *v.* Bear fruit; make fruitful, impregnate.

frŭc'tōse (-s) *n.* (chem.) Fruit sugar, a sugar found with glucose, which it closely resembles, in honey and the juice of sweet fruits.

frŭc'tūous *adj.* Full of, producing, fruit.

frug'al (-ōō-) *adj.* Careful, sparing (*of*); economical, esp. as regards food; sparingly used or supplied; costing little. **frugăl'ĭty** *n.* **frug'ally** *adv.*

fruit (-ōōt) *n.* 1. (now usu. pl.) Vegetable products fit for food. 2. Edible product of plant or tree, consisting of seed and its envelope, esp. when this is juicy or pulpy; (bot.) ripe seeds and structure surrounding them. 3. (chiefly bibl.) Offspring. 4. What results from action, effort, cause, etc.; issue, consequence; advantage, profit; (pl.) products, revenues. 5. *~-cake*, cake containing currants, raisins, etc.; *~-knife*, knife for cutting fruit, with blade of some material (e.g. silver) not affected by the acids; ~ *salad*, mixture of various fruits served in their syrup; ~ *sugar*: see FRUCTOSE; *~-tree*, tree cultivated for its fruit. (*Illustration, p.* 324.) ~ *v.* Bear, make bear, fruit.

fruitār'ian (frōōt-) *n.* & *adj.* (Of) one who lives on fruit.

fruit'er (frōōt-) *n.* Tree producing fruit; fruit-shop.

fruit'erer (frōōt-) *n.* Dealer in fruit.

fruit'ful (frōōt-) *adj.* Productive, fertile, causing fertility; productive of offspring, prolific; beneficial, remunerative. **fruit'fully** *adv.* **fruit'fulnėss** *n.*

fruition (frōōĭ'shn) *n.* Enjoyment, attainment of thing desired, realization of hopes, etc.

fruit'lėss (frōōt-) *adj.* Not bearing fruit; yielding no profit; ineffectual, useless, empty, vain. **fruit'lessly** *adv.* **fruit'lėssnėss** *n.*

fruit'y (frōōt-) *adj.* Of or like fruit; (of wine) tasting of the grape; (fig.) of rich or strong quality, spicy.

frum'enty (-ōō-), **fûrm'ėty** *n.* Dish of hulled wheat boiled in milk and seasoned with cinnamon, sugar, etc.

frŭmp *n.* Old-fashioned dowdily-dressed woman. **frŭm'pĭsh, frŭm'py** *adjs.*

frŭstrāte' *v.t.* Balk, baffle; counteract; defeat, foil. **frŭstrā'tion** *n.* **frŭs'trāte** *adj.* (archaic) Frustrated.

frŭs'tūle *n.* Silicious two-valved shell of diatom (ill. ALGA).

frŭs'tum *n.* (pl. *-ta*, *-tums*). (math.) Portion of regular solid left after cutting off upper part by plane parallel to base (ill. CONE); portion between 2 planes either parallel or inclined to each other.

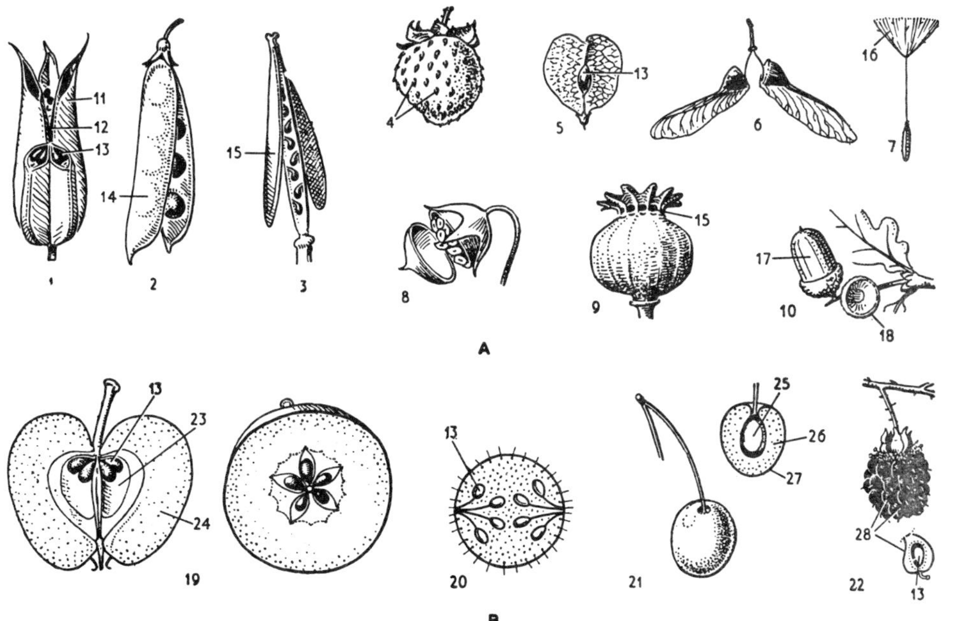

A. DRY FRUITS. B. SUCCULENT FRUITS

A. 1. Collection of follicles (columbine). 2. Legume (pea). 3. Siliqua (wallflower). 4, 5, 6, 7. Achenes: 4. Pips or achenes (strawberry); 5. Samara (elm); 6. Samara (maple); 7. Cypsela (dandelion). 8. Pyxidium (scarlet pimpernel). 9. Capsule (opium poppy). 10. Nut (oak). 11. Follicle. 12. Ventral suture. 13. Seed (part of follicle cut away). 14. Pod or hull. 15. Valve. 16. Pappus. 17. Acorn. 18. Bracteole. B. 19. Longitudinal and transverse sections of pome (apple). 20. Berry (gooseberry). 21. Drupe (cherry). 22. Syncarp (blackberry). 23. Core or carpels. 24. Flesh (receptacle). 25. Endocarp. 26. Mesocarp. 27. Epicarp. 28. Drupels and section of drupel

frut′icōse (frōō-) *adj.* Shrub-like.

fry̆[1] *n.* Young fishes just produced from spawn; young of salmon in 2nd year; young of other creatures produced in large numbers, as bees, frogs; *small* ~, young or insignificant beings, children, etc.

fry̆[2] *v.* Cook in boiling fat; *frying-pan*, shallow pan with long handle for frying. ~ *n.* Fried meat; various internal parts of animals, usu. eaten fried.

Fry̆[3], Elizabeth (1780–1845). Quaker reformer; celebrated for her efforts to improve the state of English prisons and of convicts on their voyage to Australia.

F.S. *abbrev.* Fleet Surgeon.

F.S.A. *abbrev.* Fellow of the Society of Antiquaries, of Arts.

F.S.E. *abbrev.* Fellow of the Society of Engineers.

F.S.R. *abbrev.* Field Service Regulations.

ft *abbrev.* Feet, foot.

fŭb′sy (-zĭ) *adj.* Fat or squat.

fuchsia (fūsh′*a*) *n.* Genus of ornamental shrubs with drooping, usu. red, flowers. [L. *Fuchs*, 16th-c. German botanist]

fuch′sine (fōōk-) *n.* Rosaniline salt, iridescent green crystals soluble in water and forming deep red stain. [f. resemblance to colour of FUCHSIA flower]

fū′cus *n.* Genus of brown seaweeds with flat leathery fronds.

fŭdd′le *v.* Tipple, booze; intoxicate; stupefy, confuse. ~ *n.* Spell of drinking; intoxication; confusion.

fŭdge *int.* Nonsense! ~ *n.* 1. Nonsense. 2. (orig. U.S.) Sweetmeat like soft toffee, made by boiling together sugar, butter, milk, etc. 3. Deceit; piece of fudging. ~ *v.* Fit together, patch, make up, in a makeshift or dishonest way, cook, fake; practise such methods.

fū′el *n.* Material for fires, combustible matter; (fig.) something that feeds passion, excitement, etc. ~ *v.* Provide (ship etc.) with fuel; (of ship etc.) take in fuel; *fuelling station*, port where this is done.

fŭg *n.* Stuffy atmosphere (as) of overcrowded or badly ventilated room. **fŭgg′y** *adj.*

fūgā′cious (-sh*us*) *adj.* Fleeting, evanescent, hard to capture or keep. **fūgă′city** *n.*

fū′gal *adj.* Of the nature of a fugue. **fū′gally** *adv.*

fugato (fōōgah′tō) *n.* (mus.) Passage in fugue style in composition other than a fugue.

fū′gitive *adj.* 1. Fleeing, running away; that has taken flight (from duty, an enemy, master, etc.). 2. Flitting, shifting; evanescent, of short duration, quickly fading; (of literature) of passing interest, ephemeral, occasional. ~ *n.* One who flees from danger, an enemy, an owner, justice, etc.; exile, refugee.

fū′gleman *n.* (rare) Soldier placed in front of regiment, etc., while drilling to show the motions and time; leader, spokesman. [Ger. *flügelmann* leader of file, f. *flügel* wing]

fūgue (-g) *n.* 1. (mus.) Polyphonic composition in which a short melodic theme ('subject') is introduced by one of the parts or 'voices' and successively taken up by others, thereafter forming the main material of the texture; *double* ~, fugue on two themes starting together. 2. (psychol.) State of alteration of consciousness combined with an impulse to wander away from accustomed environment.

Führ′er (fūr-) *n.* Title assumed by Adolf HITLER as head of the German Reich. [Ger., = 'leader']

Fu-kiĕn′ (fōō-). Maritime province of SE. China.

fŭl′crum *n.* (pl. *-ra*). (mech.) Point against which lever is placed to get purchase or on which it turns or is supported (ill. LEVER). [L, = 'post of couch']

fulfil′ (fōō-) *v.t.* Bring to consummation, carry out (prophecy, promise), satisfy (desire, prayer); perform, execute, do, (command, law); answer (purpose), comply with (conditions); bring to an end, finish, complete (period, work). **fulfil′ment** *n.*

fŭl′gent *adj.* (poet. & rhet.) Shining, brilliant.

fŭl′gūrāte *v.i.* Emit vivid flashes like lightning. **fŭlgurā′tion** *n.*

fŭl′gūrīte *n.* 1. (geol.) Tube-like body of sand-grains fused together, formed where a ray of lightning has discharged. 2. Explosive of nitro-glycerine mixed with coarsely ground farinaceous substance.

Fulham (fōōl′*a*m). London borough; ~ *Palace*, official residence of the Bishop of London.

fūlĭ′ginous *adj.* Sooty, dusky.

full[1] (fōōl) *adj.* 1. Containing all it will hold, having no space empty, replete; containing abundance *of*, charged, crowded; abounding (in); replete with food. 2. ~ *of*, engrossed with, absorbed in. 3. Abundant, copious, satisfying, complete; answering in every respect to a name or description; reaching the specified or usual limit; (of moon) having disc completely illuminated; (of face etc.) entirely visible to spectator; ~ *brother*, *sister*, one born of same father and mother; ~ *age*, age attained after minority; *at* ~ *length*, lying stretched out; in full. 4. (of light) Intense; (of colour) deep; (of motion etc.) vigorous. 5. Swelling, plump, protuberant; (of dress) containing superfluity of material arranged in gathers or folds. 6. ~*-back*, football player stationed behind half-backs, his position; ~*-blooded*, vigorous, hearty, sensual; ~*-bodied*, esp. of wine, with much body; ~*-bottomed*, (of wig) long behind (ill. WIG); ~ *dress*: see DRESS; ~*-dress debate*, formal or prearranged debate on important subject; ~ *hand*, (poker) hand containing three of a kind and a pair; also called ~ *house*; ~ *pitch*, (cricket) ball bowled to reach wicket without first touching ground; ~ *score*, (mus.) complete score, comprising music for all performers. ~ *n.* Whole; point or state of greatest fullness; entire amount or range; *in* ~, without abridgement; *to the*

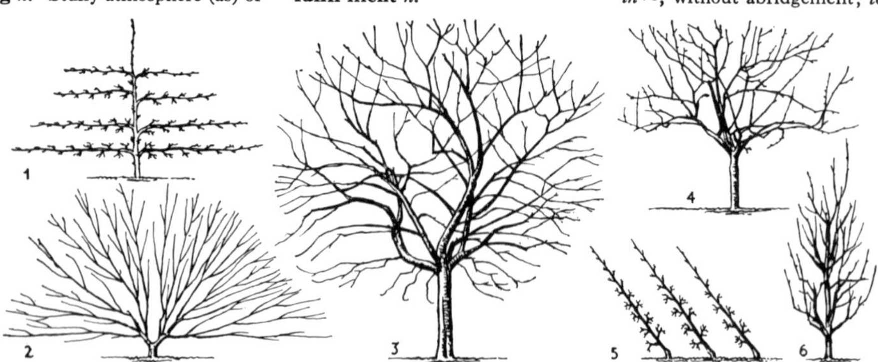

SHAPES OF FRUIT TREES

1. Espalier. 2. Fan. 3. Standard. 4. Bush. 5. Cordon. 6. Dwarf pyramid

~, to the utmost extent, quite. ~ *adv.* Very (chiefly poet.); quite, fully; exactly; more than sufficiently; ~*(fully)-fashioned*, (of garment) shaped to fit without tightness or dragging; ~*-grown*, having reached maturity. **ful(l)'ness** *n.*

full[2] (fŏŏl) *v.t.* Tread or beat (cloth) to cleanse and thicken it; cleanse and thicken (cloth etc.). **full'er**[1] *n.*; ~*'s earth*, absorbent clay containing hydrated silica and alumina, used in cleansing cloth and purifying oils and fats.

full'er[2] (fŏŏl-) *n.* Grooved tool on which iron is shaped by being driven into the grooves (ill. SWAGE); groove made by this. ~ *v.t.* Stamp with fuller.

full'y (fŏŏl'ĭ) *adv.* Completely, without deficiency; quite.

ful'mar (fŏŏ-) *n.* Arctic sea-bird, *Fulmarus glacialis*, of shearwater kind, about size of gull, noted for its easy gliding flight by sea cliffs.

fŭl'mĭnant *adj.* Fulminating; (path., of diseases) developing suddenly.

fŭl'mĭnāte *v.* 1. Flash like lightning; explode, detonate. 2. Thunder forth, utter or publish, (censure); issue (usu. official) censures *against*. **fŭlmĭnā'tion** *n.* **fŭl'mĭnatory** *adj.* **ful'minate** (-*at*) *n.* Salt of fulminic acid; ~ *of mercury*, $Hg(ONC)_2$, very sensitive explosive used in detonators.

fŭl'mĭne *v.* (poet.) Send forth (lightning, thunder); thunder.

fŭlmĭn'ic *adj.*; ~ *acid*, an isomer of cyanic acid, forming explosive salts with some metals.

ful'some (fŏŏ-, fŭ-) *adj.* (of flattery, servility, etc.) Cloying, excessive, disgusting by excess. **ful'somely** *adv.* **ful'someness** *n.*

fŭl'vous *adj.* Reddish-yellow, tawny.

fūm'arōle *n.* Hole in earth's crust through which gases and vapour issue.

fŭm'ble *v.* Use the hands awkwardly, grope about; handle or deal with awkwardly or nervously. ~ *n.* Bungling attempt. **fŭm'bler** *n.*

fūme *n.* Odorous smoke, vapour, or exhalation; watery vapour; noxious vapour supposed to rise from stomach to brain, esp. as result of drinking alcoholic liquors; fit of anger. ~ *v.* 1. Fumigate; perfume with incense; expose (wood, esp. oak etc.) to fumes of ammonia to darken tints; emit fumes. 2. Be pettish; chafe, fret. **fūm'y** *adj.*

fūm'ĭgāte *v.t.* Apply fumes to; disinfect or purify with fumes; perfume. **fūmĭgā'tion, fūm'ĭgātor** *ns.*

fūm'itory *n.* Plant of genus *Fumaria*, esp. *F. officinalis*, formerly used in medicine as an antiscorbutic. [med. L *fumus terrae* earth-smoke]

fŭn *n.* Sport, amusement; jocularity, drollery; *make ~ of, poke ~ at*, ridicule.

fūnăm'bŭlist *n.* Rope-walker.

fŭnc'tion *n.* 1. Activity proper to anything, mode of action by which it fulfils its purpose; duty of office-holder, employment, profession, calling. 2. Social meeting of formal or important kind. 3. (math.) Variable quantity regarded in relation to other(s) in terms of which it may be expressed or on whose value its own depends. ~ *v.i.* Fulfil a function, operate, act.

fŭnc'tional (-shon-) *adj.* 1. (rare) Official, merely formal. 2. (physiol.) Of, affecting, only the functions of an organ etc., not structural or organic (esp. of diseases). 3. (math.) Of a function. 4. (of building etc.) Shaped, constructed, with regard only to its function, not to traditional or other theories of design, whence **fŭnc'tionalism** *n.* **fŭnc'tionally** *adv.*

fŭnc'tionary (-shon-) *n.* One with certain functions or duties to perform, official. ~ *adj.* = FUNCTIONAL 1, 2.

fŭnd *n.* Permanent stock of something ready to be drawn upon; stock of money, esp. one set apart for a purpose; (pl.) pecuniary resources; *in ~s*, in possession of money; *the ~s*, stock of national debt, considered as mode of investment. ~ *v.t.* Convert (floating debt) into more or less permanent debt at fixed interest; invest (money) in the funds.

fŭn'dament *n.* The buttocks.

fŭndamĕn'tal *adj.* 1. Of the groundwork, going to the root of the matter, serving as base or foundation; essential, primary, original; from which others are derived. 2. (mus., of a note) That is the 'root' or lowest note of a chord; (of a chord) with the root as the lowest note; (of a tone) that is produced by the vibration of the whole of a sonorous body (as dist. from *harmonics*). **fŭndamĕn'tal, fŭndamĕntăl'ity** *ns.* Principle, rule, article, serving as groundwork of system (usu. pl.); (mus.) fundamental note or tone. **fŭndamĕn'tally** *adv.*

fŭndamĕn'talism *n.* Strict adherence to traditional orthodox (Protestant) tenets (e.g. the literal inerrancy of Scripture), held to be fundamental to Christianity; adherence to traditional beliefs of any kind. **fŭndamĕn'talist** *n.*

fŭn'dus *n.* (physiol.) Lowest part of stomach or other hollow organ, part farthest removed from its opening; ~ *oculi*, interior region of back of eyeball; ~ *uteri*, interior region of womb farthest removed from cervix.

fūn'eral *adj.* Of, used, carried, etc., at burial or cremation of the dead; ~ *pile, pyre*, pile of wood, etc., on which corpse is burnt; ~ *urn*, urn holding ashes of cremated body. ~ *n.* Burial of the dead with its ceremonies etc., obsequies; burial procession; (U.S.) funeral service.

fūn'erary *adj.* Of funeral.

fūnēr'ėal *adj.* Appropriate to funeral, gloomy, dismal, dark. **fūnēr'ėally** *adv.*

fŭn'gĭble (-j-) *adj.* (legal) That can serve for, or be replaced by, another answering to the same description (of goods etc. contracted for, when an individual specimen is not meant).

fŭn'gĭcīde *n.* Fungus-destroying substance.

fŭng'oid (-ngg-) *adj.* Fungus-like.

fŭng'ous (-ngg-) *adj.* Of fungi, having nature of a fungus; springing up like a mushroom, transitory.

fŭng'us (-ngg-) *n.* (pl. -*gi* pr. gī *or* -jī, -*uses*). 1. Mushroom, toadstool, or one of the allied plants,

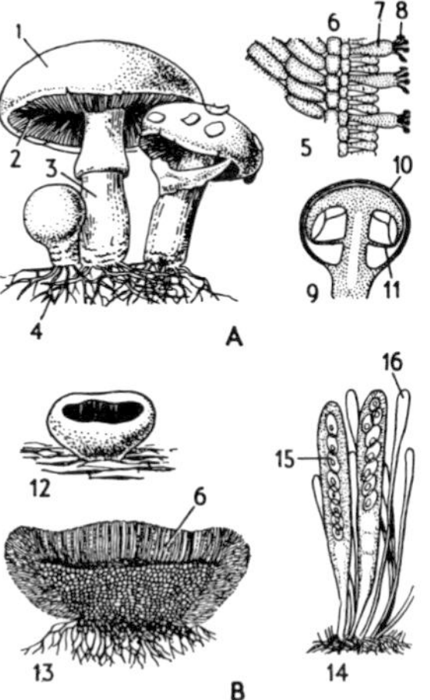

FUNGUS: A. BASIDIOMYCETE (MUSHROOM). B. ASCOMYCETE (CUP FUNGUS)

A. 1. Pileus or cap. 2. Gills. 3. Stipe or stem. 4. Mycelium or thallus. 5. Section across gill. 6. Hymenium. 7. Basidium. 8. Basidiospore. 9. Section through young stage. 10. Volva. 11. Velum. B. 12. Whole plant on decaying tree trunk. 13. Section. 14. Detail of hymenium. 15. Ascospore. 16. Hypha

including the various moulds; (bot.) cryptogamous plant without chlorophyll deriving its substance from organic matter. 2. (path.) Spongy morbid growth or excrescence. **fŭng'al** *adj.*

fūnĭc'ūlar *adj.* Of a rope or its tension; depending on or worked by a rope; ~ *railway*, one worked by cable and stationary engine, cable railway.

fŭnk *n.* (slang) Fear, panic; coward; *blue* ~, terror. ~ *v.* Flinch, shrink, show cowardice; fight shy of, (try to) evade; be afraid of.

fŭnn'el *n.* 1. Diminishing tube, cone-shaped vessel with tube at apex, for conducting liquid, powder, etc., into small opening. 2. Lighting or ventilating shaft;

metal chimney of steam-engine, ship, etc. (ill. SHIP); funnel-shaped lower part of chimney.

fŭnn′y[1] *adj.* Affording fun, comical; curious, queer, perplexing, hard to account for; ~ *bone*, part of elbow over which ulnar nerve passes (from peculiar sensation experienced when it is struck). **fŭnn′ĭly** *adv.* **fŭnn′inėss** *n.*

fŭnn′y[2] *n.* Narrow clinker-built pleasure-boat for one pair of sculls.

fûr *n.* 1. Trimming or lining made of dressed coat of certain animals (as ermine, beaver, fox, etc.); coat of such animals as material for trimming, lining, etc.; (usu. pl.) garment(s) of or trimmed with fur; short fine soft hair of certain animals as distinct from the longer and coarser hair; (pl.) skins of such animals with the fur; (collect.) furred animals. 2. (her.) Tincture representing tufts on plain ground, or patches of different colour supposed to be sewn together. 3. Crust of mould, deposit from wine, etc., adhering to surface like fur; coating formed on tongue in some diseased conditions of body; coating of carbonate of lime formed by 'hard' water in kettle, boiler, etc. **fûrr′y** *adj.* **fûr** *v.* 1. Trim, line, cover, with fur (only in past part.); coat (tongue, kettle, etc.), become coated, with fur. 2. (carpentry) Fix strips of wood to (floor-timbers, rafters, etc.), level them thus.

fur. *abbrev.* Furlong.

fûrb′ėlow (-ō) *n.* Flounce, pleated border of skirt or petticoat (ill. SACK); (pl. contempt.) showy ornament or trimming. ~ *v.t.* Adorn with furbelows.

fûrb′ĭsh *v.t.* Remove rust from, polish *up*, burnish; give new look to, renovate, revive.

fûrc′āte (*or* -*a*t) *adj.* Forked, branched. **furcāte′** *v.i.* Form a fork, divide.

fūr′ĭous *adj.* Full of fury, raging, frantic, violent; *fast and* ~, (of mirth etc.) uproarious, eager. **fūr′ĭously** *adv.*

fûrl *v.* Roll up and tie (sail) on yard or boom; roll or gather up, close, fold up; become furled; roll away like clouds.

fûrl′ŏng *n.* Measure of length, ⅛ mile or 220 yards. [OE *furlang*, f. *furh* furrow and *lang* long]

fûrl′ough (-lō) *n.* Leave of absence, esp. to soldier. ~ *v.t.* Grant furlough to.

furmety: see FRUMENTY.

fûrn′ace (-ĭs) *n.* Apparatus containing chamber for combustibles in which minerals, metals, etc., may be subjected to continuous action of intense heat; closed fireplace for heating water to warm building etc.; (fig.) hot place; (fig.) severe test.

fûrn′ĭsh *v.t.* Provide *with*; fit up (house, room) with all necessary appliances, esp. movable furniture; provide, afford, yield; *furn′ishing* (*n.*, esp. pl.) articles of furniture or other things required to furnish a house etc.

fûrn′iture *n.* Movable contents of house or room, tables, chairs, etc.; contents of receptacle (now rare); harness, trappings, etc., of horse (archaic); rigging, stores, tackle, etc., of ship.

fūrōr′ė *n.* Enthusiastic admiration, rage, craze.

fŭ′rrier *n.* Dealer in, dresser of, furs. **fŭ′rriery** *n.*

fûrr′ing *n.* (esp.) Doubling of planks on ship's side, timber used for this.

fŭ′rrow (-ō) *n.* Narrow trench made in earth with plough; ship's track; rut, track, groove, long indentation; deep wrinkle; ~*-slice*, slice of earth turned up by mould-board of plough. ~ *v.t.* Plough; make furrows, grooves, etc., in; mark with wrinkles.

fûrth′er (-dh-) *adv.* To or at more advanced point in space or time; to greater extent, more; (also *furth′ermore*), in addition, moreover, also; at greater distance. ~ *adj.* Going beyond what exists or has been dealt with, additional; more distant. ~ *v.t.* Help on, promote, favour. **fûrth′erance** *n.* **fûrth′ermōst** *adj.*

fûrth′ėst (-dh-) *adj.* & *adv.* = FARTHEST.

fûrt′ĭve *adj.* Done by stealth, clandestine, meant to escape notice; sly, stealthy; stolen, taken secretly. **fûrt′ĭvely** *adv.* **fûrt′ĭvenėss** *n.*

fūr′uncle *n.* Boil, tumour. **fūrŭnc′ūlar, fūrŭnc′ūlous** *adjs.*

fūr′y *n.* 1. Fierce passion, wild anger, rage; fierce impetuosity or violence; (now rare) inspired frenzy, as of one possessed. 2. (Gk myth.) One of snake-haired goddesses (Allecto, Megaera, Tisiphone) sent from Tartarus to avenge wrong and punish crime; (fig.) avenging or tormenting spirit. 3. Virago, angry or malignant woman.

fûrze *n.* Spiny evergreen yellow-flowered shrub (*Ulex europaeus*) growing abundantly on waste lands throughout Europe, gorse, whin. **fûrz′y** *adj.*

fŭs′cous *adj.* Sombre, dark in colour.

fūse[1] (-z) *v.* Melt with intense heat; blend, amalgamate, into one whole (as) by melting; (of electric light etc.) be put out of action by melting of fuse; cause fuse(s) of (electric circuit) to melt. ~ *n.* Strip of wire or easily-fused metal in electric circuit which melts and so interrupts the circuit if current increases beyond a certain limit. **fūs′ĭble** *adj.* **fūsĭbĭl′ĭty** *n.*

fūse[2] (-z), **fūze** *n.* Tube, casing, cord, etc., filled or saturated with combustible matter for igniting blasting-charge, bomb, etc.; component screwed into shell, mine, etc., designed to detonate explosive charge either after an interval (*time*-~) or on impact, or when subjected to magnetic, vibratory, or other stimulation. ~ *v.t.* Fit fuse to.

fūsee′ (-z-) *n.* 1. Conical pulley or wheel, esp. wheel in watch or clock on which chain is wound and which equalizes power of main-spring. 2. Large-headed match for use in wind.

fūs′ėlage (-z-, -ahzh; *or* -ĭj) *n.* Body or framework of aeroplane.

fūs′el-oil (-z-) *n.* Mixture of several alcohols, chiefly amyl, sometimes produced, usu. in small amounts, during fermentation of alcoholic liquor and making it harmful or poisonous. [Ger. *fusel* or Du. *foezel* bad spirit]

fūs′ĭfôrm (-z-) *adj.* Shaped like spindle, tapering towards each end.

fūs′ĭl (-z-) *n.* Obsolete light musket or firelock.

fūsĭlier′ (-z-) *n.* (usu. pl.) (Man of) certain British infantry regiments (now 5 in number) formerly armed with fusils.

fūsĭllāde′ (-z-) *n.* (Wholesale execution by) continuous discharge of fire-arms. ~ *v.t.* Assault (place), shoot down (persons), by fusillade.

fū′sion (-zhn) *n.* Fusing; fused mass; blending of different things into one; coalition.

fŭss *n.* Bustle, excessive commotion, ostentatious or nervous activity; treatment of trifles as important; abundance of petty detail; (colloq.) person who is always making a fuss (also ~*-pot*). ~ *v.* Make fuss; busy oneself restlessly with trifles; move fussily *about*, etc., agitate, worry (person). **fŭss′y** *adj.* **fŭss′ĭly** *adv.* **fŭss′inėss** *n.*

fŭstanĕll′a *n.* Stiff full white skirt worn by men in Albania and some parts of modern Greece.

fŭs′tian *n.* 1. Thick twilled cotton cloth with short nap, resembling velveteen, usu. dyed in dark dull colours. 2. Turgid speech or writing, bombast. ~ *adj.* Made of fustian; bombastic, worthless, sorry, pretentious.

fŭs′tĭc *n.* Either of two woods yielding yellow dye: *Chlorophora tinctoria* of America and the W. Indies, and (*young* or *Zante* ~) the Venetian sumach, *Rhuo cotinus*; dye from these. [Arab. *fustuq* f. Gk *pistakē* pistachio]

fŭs′tĭgāte *v.t.* (joc.) Cudgel.

fŭs′ty *adj.* Stale-smelling, musty, mouldy; close, stuffy; antiquated, old-fashioned. **fŭs′tinėss** *n.*

fŭtch′el(l) *n.* One of timbers supporting shafts, pole, or axle-bar, of carriage.

fūt′īle (*or*, esp. U.S., -ĭl) *adj.* Useless, ineffectual, vain, frivolous. **fūtĭl′ĭty** *n.* **fūt′īlely** *adv.*

fŭtt′ock *n.* One of middle timbers of ship's frame, between floor and top timbers; ~*-plate*, iron plate across top of a lower mast to which the dead-eyes of the topmast rigging and the upper ends of the ~-shrouds are secured; ~*-shroud*, short, usu. iron, shroud securing ~-plates of topmast rigging to band round lower mast (ill. SAIL[1]).

fū'ture *adj.* About to happen; that will be hereafter; of time to come; (gram., of tense) relating to time to come. ~ *n.* Time to come; what will happen in the future; person's, country's, etc., prospective condition; (gram.) future tense; (commerc., pl.) goods and stocks sold for future delivery, contracts for these. **fū'tureless** *adj.*

fū'turist (-cher-) *n.* 1. (theol.) (One) believing that prophecies of Apocalypse etc. are still to be fulfilled. 2. (Adherent) of **fū'turism,** artistic and literary movement begun *c* 1909 in Italy, marked by violent departure from traditional methods and attempting to represent nature not in a static but a dynamic state. **fūturis'tic** *adj.*

fūtūr'ity *n.* Future time; future events; future condition, existence after death; ~-*stakes,* (U.S.) stakes to be raced for long after the nominations or entries are made.

fuze: see FUSE[2].

fŭzz *n.* Loose volatile matter, fluff; fluffy or frizzed hair. **fŭzz'y** *adj.* Frayed, fluffy; blurred, indistinct; frizzed; ~-*wuzzy,* (soldier's slang) Sudanese warrior.

f.w.b. *abbrev.* Four-wheel brakes.

fȳl'fot *n.* = SWASTIKA (ill. CROSS).

F.Z.S. *abbrev.* Fellow of the Zoological Society.

G

G, g (jē). 7th letter of the modern English and Roman alphabet, orig. differentiated form of C, representing in modern English a voiced postpalatal stop (*hard g*) except in some words, chiefly of French, Latin, or Greek origin, before *e* or *i*, where it is equivalent to the composite sound (*j*); (mus.) 5th note of 'natural' scale (C major); scale or key with this note for tonic; *G clef,* treble clef placed on line in stave used for note G.

gā'ble *n.* Vertical triangular upper part of wall at end of ridged roof, from level of eaves upwards; (also ~-*end*) gable-topped end wall of building; gable-shaped canopy over window or door.

găd'olinite *n.* (min.) Black or brown vitreous mineral containing silicates of yttrium, terbium, erbium, etc.; a source of rare-earth elements. [J. *Gadolin* (1760–1852), Finnish mineralogist]

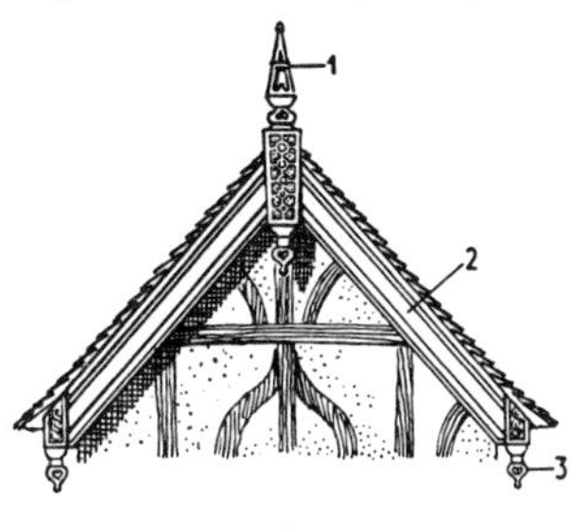

A. HALF-TIMBERED GABLE. B. DUTCH GABLE. C. GABLE WITH CORBIE STONES OR CROW STEPS
1. Finial. 2. Barge-board. 3. Pendant

g. *abbrev.* Guinea, gram(s).

Ga. *abbrev.* Georgia.

găb *n.* (fam.) Talk, prattle, twaddle; *gift of the* ~, talent for speaking; loquacity.

găb'ardine (-ēn) *n.* Twill-woven cloth, usu. of fine worsted.

găb'ble *v.* Talk volubly or inarticulately; read aloud too fast; utter too fast. ~ *n.* Voluble confused unintelligible talk.

găb'brō *n.* Dark-coloured coarsely crystalline igneous rock made up of plagioclase felspar, pyroxene, and magnetite.

gabĕlle' *n.* Tax; esp. salt-tax in France before Revolution.

găb'erdine (-ēn) *n.* 1. Long loose upper garment worn by Jews, almsmen, etc. 2. = GABARDINE.

gā'bion *n.* Cylinder of wicker or woven metal bands to be filled with earth for use in fortification or engineering. **gābionāde'** *n.* Line of gabions.

gaboon' *n.* Fine-grained wood, resembling mahogany, of African tropical tree, *Entandrophragma pierrei.* [f. GABON]

Gabon, Gaboon (gă'bon, gaboon'). W. African republic, formerly a territory of French Equatorial Africa; became independent in 1960; capital, Libreville. **Gabonēse'** *adj.* & *n.*

Gā'briel. (Heb. myth. etc.) One of the 7 archangels, employed as messenger to man.

gā'by *n.* Simpleton.

găd *v.i.* Go about idly, rove, wander. ~ *n.* (only in) (*up*)*on the* ~, on the move, going about.

găd'about *adj.* & *n.* (Person) given to gadding.

găd'-flȳ *n.* Fly which bites and goads cattle, esp. one of the genera *Tabanus* (horse-fly) or *Oestrus* (bot-fly); (fig.) irritating or worrying person.

gădg'ĕt *n.* (orig. naut.) Small fitting, contrivance, or piece of mechanism; dodge, device.

Gadhel'ic (-dĕ-) *adj.* & *n.* Gaelic (in other applications than that to Gaels of Scotland).

găd'oid *adj.* & *n.* (Fish) of the cod family (*Gadidae*).

gădolin'ium *n.* (chem.) Metallic element of rare-earth group, found in gadolinite etc.; symbol Gd, at. no. 64, at. wt 157·25.

gadroon' *n.* Convex fluting as ornament on silverware etc. ~ *v.t.* Decorate with this.

GADROON

Gaek'war (gīk-). (hist.). Title of ruler of Baroda, India. [Marathi, = 'cowherd']

Gael (gāl *or* găl). Scottish or Irish Celt. **Gael'ic** *adj.* & *n.* (Language) of the Celtic inhabitants of Scottish highlands, or of the branch of Celts including Scottish, Irish, and Manx Celts.

găff[1] *n.* 1. Barbed fishing-spear; stick with iron hook for landing large fish. 2. (naut.) Spar used to extend fore-and-aft sails which are not set on stays (ill. SAIL[1]). ~ *v.t.* Seize (fish) with gaff.

găff[2] *n.* (slang) *Blow the* ~, let out plot or secret.

găff[3] *n.* (slang) Public place of amusement, esp. (usu. *penny* ~) low theatre or music hall.

găffe *n.* Blunder, indiscreet act or remark, *faux pas.*

găff'er *n.* 1. Elderly rustic, old fellow. 2. Foreman of gang of workmen. [contr. of *godfather, ga-* by assoc. w. *grandfather*]

găg *n.* 1. Thing thrust into mouth to prevent speech or outcry, or to hold it open for operation, etc.; (parl.) closure, GUILLOTINE. 2. (theatr.) Actor's interpolations in dramatic dialogue. ~ *v.* Apply gag to; silence, deprive of free speech; (of actor) make gag.

găg'a (*or* gah'gah) *n.* Senile, doting; silly, inane, fatuous.

gāge[1] *n.* Pledge, thing deposited as security; (glove thrown down as, any symbol of) challenge to fight. ~ *v.t.* Stake, pledge, offer as guarantee.

gāge[2] *n.* = GREENGAGE.

găg'gle *n.* Flock (of geese). ~ *v.i.* (of geese) Make clucking sound.

Gaia: see GE.

gai'ety *n.* Being gay, mirth; merrymaking, festivity; bright or showy appearance.

gaillar̄d'ia *n.* Genus of showy-flowered composite plants. [*Gaillard* de Marentonneau, Fr. botanist]

gaily: see GAY.

gain *n.* Increase of possessions, advantage, etc., of any kind; profit, advance, improvement; acquisition of wealth, lucre, pelf; (pl.) sums acquired by trade etc., emoluments, winnings; increase in amount. ~ *v.* Obtain, secure (desired or advantageous thing); win (sum) as profits etc.; earn; make a profit, be benefited, improve or advance *in* some respect; be enhanced *by* comparison or contrast; reclaim (land) from sea etc.; win (battle, victory); bring over to one's interests or views, persuade, prevail upon; reach, arrive at (desired place), (of sea) encroach (*up*)*on* land; ~ *time*, obtain delay by pretexts or slow methods; ~ *ear of*, get favourable hearing from; ~ *the upper hand*, be victorious; ~ *ground*, progress, advance, encroach (*up*)*on*; ~ (*ground*) (*up*)*on*, get closer to (person or thing pursued).

gain'ful *adj.* Lucrative, remunerative; (of occupation etc.) paid. **gain'fully** *adv.*

gainsay' *v.t.* (past t. and past part. -*said* pr. -ĕd). Deny, contradict.

Gains'borough (-bro), Thomas (1727–88). English painter; famous esp. for portraits.

gait *n.* Manner of walking; bearing or carriage as one walks.

gait'er *n.* Covering of cloth, leather, etc., for ankle, or ankle and lower leg.

gal. *abbrev.* Gallon(s).

Gal. *abbrev.* Galatians (N.T.).

gal'a (gah-, gā-) *n.* Festive occasion, fête.

galăc'tic *adj.* (astron.) Of the Galaxy or Milky Way.

găl'ăctōse *n.* A sugar, $C_6H_{12}O_6$, obtained by hydrolysis of lactose and having properties very similar to those of glucose.

galāg'ō *n.* (pl. -*gos*). Genus of small Afr. nocturnal tree-climbing animals, with large eyes and ears and long tail, closely related to lemurs and lorises, bush-baby.

găl'antine (-ēn) *n.* Dish of white meat boned, cut up, boiled, and served cold in jelly.

galăn'ty show *n.* Shadow pantomime made by throwing shadows of puppets on screen.

Gălatē'a[1]. (Gk myth.) A sea-nymph; the Cyclops Polyphemus, who loved her, found his rival, Acis, in her arms and crushed him with a rock.

gălatē'a[2] *n.* Strong twilled cotton material, freq. striped (orig. used for children's sailor suits). [f. H.M.S. *Galatea*]

Galā'tia (-sha). (hist.) Roman province of Asia Minor. **Galā'tian** *adj.* & *n.* Of Galatia; one of its inhabitants, believed to have been Gauls who settled there in the 3rd c. B.C.; (pl.) the N.T. Epistle of St. Paul to the Galatians.

găl'axy *n.* The more distant parts of the island universe which contains the solar system, as seen from the earth, forming a faintly luminous band, irregularly encircling the sky, of innumerable stars indistinguishable to the naked eye; the Milky Way; (fig.) brilliant company or assemblage (*of*). [Gk *gala* milk]

găl'banum *n.* Gum resin obtained from stem and root of a Persian species of *Ferula*, used in medicine chiefly as a stimulant in plasters.

gāle[1] *n.* Bog-myrtle, *Myrica gale* (also called *sweet* ~).

gāle[2] *n.* Strong wind; (naut.) storm; (meteor.) wind of velocity between 34 and 40 knots (force 8 on the BEAUFORT scale); ~ *warning*, notice of probability of gales (force 8 or more) issued by Meteorological Office.

gāle[3] *n.* Periodical (payment of) rent; *hanging* ~, rent due at previous gale-day; ~-*day*, rent-day.

gāl'ea *n.* (zool.) Structure like helmet in shape, function, or position; esp., outer lobe of insect's maxilla.

Gāl'en. Claudius Galenus (129–199), Greek physician; born at Pergamum, Asia Minor; practised in Rome; physician to emperor Marcus Aurelius; author of many treatises of which some survive. **Galĕ'nic, Galĕ'nical** *adjs.* Of, according to, Galen; (of remedies) made of vegetable, not chemical, components.

galēn'a *n.* (min.) Native lead sulphide, the common lead-ore PbS).

Gali'cia[1] (-ēshĭa). Province of NW. Spain. **Gali'cian** *adj.* & *n.*

Gali'cia[2] (-ĭshĭa). Former Austrian crown-land, now part of Poland.

Găl'ilee[1]. Northern province of Palestine, now in Israel. **Gălilē'an**[1] *adj.* & *n.* (Native) of Galilee; Christian; *the* ~, Jesus Christ.

găl'ilee[2] *n.* Porch or chapel at entrance of church. [f. GALILEE[1]]

Găliléo (-ā'ō *or* -ē'ō) **Găliléi** (-ā'ē) (1564–1642). Italian astronomer and physicist; discovered Jupiter's satellites, the libration of the moon, etc.; his observations brought him into conflict with the Inquisition and he was compelled to repudiate the Copernican theory. **Găliléan**[2] *adj.* (Of telescope) of the form invented by Galileo, a refracting telescope with concave eyepiece (ill. BINOCULAR).

găl'ingāle (-ngg-) *n.* 1. Aromatic root of E. Ind. plant of genera *Alpinia* and *Kampferia*, formerly much used in medicine and cookery. 2. English species of sedge, *Cyperus longus*, with root of similar properties. [Arab. *Khaulinjān*, perh. ult. f. Chin. *ko-liang-kiang* 'mild ginger from Ko' (in Canton)]

găl'ipŏt *n.* Turpentine or resin exuding from and hardening on stem of certain pines.

gall[1] (gawl) *n.* Bitter, greenish secretion of the liver, bile (now only of lower animals); gall-bladder and its contents; type of bitterness; asperity, rancour; (U.S.) impudence, 'nerve', effrontery; ~-*bladder*, vessel containing the gall or bile (ill. ALIMENTARY); ~ *stone*, morbid calculous formation in gall-bladder.

gall[2] (gawl) *n.* Painful swelling, pustule, blister, esp. in horse; sore produced by chafing; mental soreness or irritation; something galling or exasperating; place rubbed bare; bare spot in field or coppice; (southern U.S.) place where soil is washed away or exhausted. ~ *v.* Rub sore, injure by rubbing; vex, annoy, harass, humiliate. **gall'ing** *adj.*

gall[3] (gawl) *n.* (also ~-*nut*) Excrescence produced on trees by deposition of the eggs of mites or insects, e.g. oak-apple (*oak*-~) used in manufacture of ink and tannin and in dyeing etc.; ~-*fly*, insect causing galls.

GALL

1. Rose-gall. 2. Gall-fly. 3. Oak-apple gall

Găll'a *n.* One of a group of partially civilized Hamitic tribes of equatorial Africa, allied to Abyssinians in language and origin.

găll'ant *adj.* 1. Showy, finely dressed (archaic); (of ship, horse, etc.) grand, fine, stately. 2. Brave, chivalrous (also parl., as conventional epithet of member belonging to armed forces, as *the honourable and ~ member*). 3. (freq. pron. galănt') Markedly attentive to women; concerned with love, amatory. **găll'antly** *adv.* **găll'ant** (*or* -ănt') *n.* (archaic or rare) Man of fashion, fine gentleman; ladies' man, lover, paramour. **gallănt'** *v.* Play the gallant, flirt (with); escort, act as cavalier to.

găll'antry *n.* 1. Bravery, dashing courage. 2. Courtliness, devotion to women; polite or amorous act or speech; conduct of a gallant, amorous intrigue or intercourse.

găll'ėon *n.* (hist.) Vessel shorter but higher than galley; ship of war

GALLEON OF 1588

(esp. Spanish); large Spanish ship used in trade with America.

găll'ery *n.* 1. Covered space for walking in partly open at side, portico, colonnade; balcony; long narrow passage in thickness of wall or supported on corbels, open towards interior of building. 2. Platform projecting from inner wall of church, hall, etc., providing extra room for audience or reserved for musicians, reporters, strangers, etc.; highest of such balconies in theatre, containing cheapest seats (ill. THEATRE); persons seated there, least refined part of audience; group of spectators at golf-match or other game; *play to the ~*, appeal to lower taste, use claptrap. 3. Long narrow room, passage, corridor; room or building used for showing works of art. 4. (mil., mining) Underground horizontal or nearly horizontal passage. 5. Ornamental parapet or railing along edge of table, shelf, etc. (ill. DESK). ~ *v.t.* Provide, pierce, etc., with gallery or galleries.

găll'ey *n.* 1. (chiefly hist.) Low flat single-decked sea-going vessel using sails and oars, and usu. rowed by slaves or criminals (*~-slaves*). 2. Greek or Roman warship with one or more banks of oars. 3. Large open row-boat, e.g. that used by captain of man-of-war. 4. Ship's kitchen. 5. (print.) Oblong tray to which type is transferred from composing-stick; corresponding part of composing machine; *~-proof*, proof in slip form from type in galley.

găll'iard *n.* (hist.) Quick and lively 16th- and 17th-c. dance in triple time; music for this.

găll'ĭc[1] *adj.* (chem.) ~ *acid*, white crystalline substance present in oak-gall, tea, and other vegetable products, used in the manufacture of inks.

Găll'ĭc[2] *adj.* 1. Of the Gauls or Gaul, Gaulish. 2. French. **găll'ĭcism** *n.* **găll'ĭcize** *v.*

Găll'ĭcan *adj.* & *n.* Of the ancient Church of Gaul or France; (adherent) of the school of French Roman Catholics which maintained the right of the French Church to be in certain respects free from papal control (opp. ULTRAMONTANE). **Găll'ĭcanĭsm** *n.*

găllĭgăs'kĭns *n.pl.* Wide hose or breeches of 16th–17th centuries; (joc.) breeches, trousers. [Fr. *garguesque*, f. It. *grechesca* Greek]

găllĭmauf'ry *n.* Heterogeneous mixture, jumble, medley.

găllĭnā'ceous (-sh*us*) *adj.* (zool.) Of the order *Galliformes*, including domestic poultry, pheasants, partridges, turkeys, guinea-fowl, etc.

găllĭnāz'ō *n.* American turkey buzzard, *Cathartes aura*, allied to vulture.

Găll'ĭō. The proconsul of Achaia who refused to try St. Paul when the Jews of Corinth accused him (Acts xviii); hence, person, esp. official, who avoids responsibility of dealing with matters outside his province; an indifferent easy-going person.

găll'iot *n.* Dutch cargo-boat or fishing-vessel; small (usu. Mediterranean) galley.

Gallip'olĭ. Peninsula between the Dardanelles and the Aegean where Allied troops were landed on 25th April 1915 (~ *Day*).

găll'ĭpŏt *n.* Small earthen glazed pot used for ointments etc. [prob. f. GALLEY, as brought in galleys from the Mediterranean]

găll'ium *n.* Rare bluish-white metallic element found in some zinc and aluminium minerals, remarkable for its extremely low melting-point (29° C.); symbol Ga, at. no. 31, at. wt 69·72. [L *gallus* cock, transl. of *Lecoq* de Boisbaudran, its discoverer, 1875]

găllĭvănt' *v.i.* Gad about.

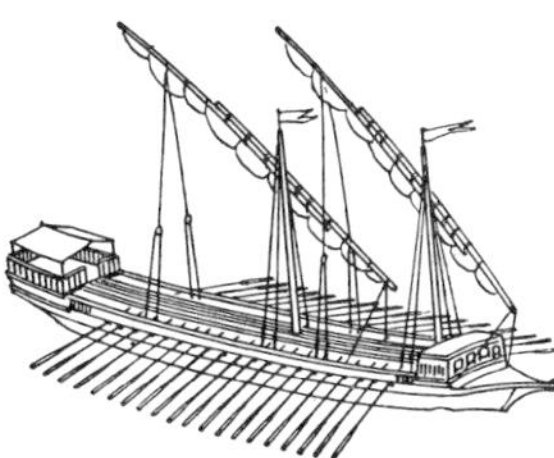

18TH-C. MEDITERRANEAN GALLEY

găll'on *n.* Measure of capacity for liquids, corn, etc.; *imperial ~*, the standard gallon in Gt Britain, approx. 277¼ cu. in.; *wine-~*, the standard in U.S., 231 cu. in.; see Appendix X.

gallōōn' *n.* Narrow close-woven braid for binding dresses etc., of gold, silver, silk, or cotton.

găll'op *n.* Horse's or other quadruped's fastest pace, with all feet off ground together in each stride; a ride at this pace; track or ground for galloping horses. ~ *v.* Go at a gallop; make (horse etc.) gallop; read, talk, say, etc., very fast; move or progress rapidly.

găllopāde' *n.* Lively dance of Hungarian origin.

găll'oper *n.* (esp., mil.) Aide-de-camp; light field-gun, formerly attached to regiments.

găll'ophĭl(e), găll'ophōbe *ns.* One who loves, hates, the French.

Găll'o-Rō'man *adj.* & *n.* (Inhabitant) of Gaul when it formed part of Roman Empire.

Găll'oway[1] (-owā). District of SW. Scotland, shires of Wigton and Kirkcudbright. [Welsh *Gallwyddel*, Ir. *Gallgaidhil*, foreign Gaels]

găll'oway[2] *n.* Small strong horse bred in Galloway.

găll'ows (-ōz) *n.pl.* (usu. treated as sing.) Structure, usu. of two uprights and cross-piece, on which criminals are hanged; similar structure for other uses; punishment of hanging; *~-bird*, person fit to be hanged; *~-tree*, gallows.

Găll'up pōll. A vote on some matter of current interest taken from a cross-section of the inhabitants of a country or region in order to ascertain public opinion on that topic. [after G. H. *Gallup*, Amer. statistician]

găl'op *n.* Lively dance in $\frac{2}{4}$ time. ~ *v.i.* Dance a galop.

galōre' *adv.* & *n.* (In) abundance. [Ir. *go leór* to sufficiency]

galŏsh' *n.* Over-shoe usu. of rubber to keep shoes clean or dry; piece of leather etc. round lower part of boot or shoe above sole.

Galsworthy (gawlz'wẽrdhĭ), John (1867–1933). English novelist and playwright; author of 'The Forsyte Saga' etc.

Gal'ton (gawl-), Sir Francis (1822–1911). English scientist, whose work on the markings of finger-tips led to the adoption of finger-print identifications of criminals.

galŭmph' *v.i.* Go prancing exultantly. [coined by Lewis Carroll, perh. f. *gallop*, *triumph*]

Gălva'ni (-vahnē), Luigi (1737–98). Italian scientist; discoverer of electricity produced by chemical action.

gălvăn'ic *adj.* Of, produced by, suggestive of, galvanism; *~ battery*, battery of primary cells used in galvanism.

găl'vanism *n.* (hist.) 1. Electricity, usu. from a primary battery, used to produce muscular contractions and other effects. 2. The therapeutic effect of applying such electricity to the tissues of the body.

găl'vanīze *v.t.* 1. Stimulate by or as by electricity, rouse by shock or excitement. 2. Coat with metal by electrolysis (rare); coat iron with zinc (usu. without the use of electricity) to protect it from rust. **gălvanīzā'tion** *n.*

gălvanŏm'ėter *n.* Apparatus for detecting and measuring strength of electric currents.

Gal'way (gawl-). County of Connaught in W. Ireland.

Ga'ma (gah-), Vasco da (*c* 1469–1524). Portuguese navigator, who first doubled the Cape of Good Hope (1497) and sailed to India.

găm'ba *n.* Organ-stop of string tone. [short for *viola da gamba*]

gambāde', gambād'ō (pl. *-os, -oes*) *n.* Horse's leap or bound; fantastic movement, freak, escapade.

Găm̆bĕtt'a, Leon (1838–82). French statesman; came into prominence during the siege of Paris, in 1871; became president of the Chamber in 1879; and premier of France in 1881.

Găm'bĭa. W. African state lying on the banks of the river Gambia; former Brit. colony and protectorate; independent, 1965; capital, Bathurst.

găm'bĭer *n.* Astringent extract of Eastern plant, *Uncaria gambir*, used in tanning etc. [Malay *gambir*, the plant]

găm'bĭt *n.* Chess-opening in which player sacrifices pawn or pieces to obtain some advantage over opponent; opening move in discussion etc. [It. *gambetto* tripping up (*gamba* leg)]

găm'ble *v.* Play games of chance for money, esp. for high stakes, (freq. fig.); ~ *away*, lose by gambling. ~ *n.* Gambling; risky undertaking or attempt. **găm'bler** *n.*

gămboge' (-ōōzh) *n.* Gum-resin from various Cambodian, Siamese, etc., trees of genus *Garcinia*, used as pigment giving bright-yellow colour. [f. *Cambodia*]

găm'bol *n.* & *v.i.* Caper, frisk.

gāme[1] *n.* 1. Jest (only in *make ~ of*); diversion, pastime; piece of fun. 2. Contest played according to rules and decided by skill, strength, or luck; (pl., Gk and Rom. antiq.) athletic, dramatic, and musical contests, gladiatorial etc. shows; (pl.) organized athletics in school, etc. 3. Scheme, undertaking, etc., followed up like a game; policy, plan of action; (pl.) dodges, tricks. 4. Single round in some contests, e.g. whist or tennis; winning score in game; state of game. 5. Person's normal standard of play; *on, off, one's* ~, in, out of, form. 6. Object of chase, animal(s) hunted; object of pursuit; (collect.) wild animals or birds hunted for sport or food, flesh of these. 7. ~ *act, law*, act, law, regulating killing and preservation of game; *~-bag*, bag for holding game killed by sportsman; *~-ball*, state of game in tennis etc., at which one side requires only one point to win; ~ *book*, book in which landowner etc. keeps detailed records of all game killed on estate; *~-cock*, cock bred and trained for fighting, or of breed suitable for cock-fighting; *game'keeper*, man employed to take care of game, prevent poaching etc.; *~-licence*, licence to kill or deal in game. ~ *adj.* Like a game-cock, spirited; having the spirit *to, for*. **gāme'ly** (-ml-) *adv.* **gāme'nėss** *n.* **gāme** *v.* Play at games of chance for money, gamble; throw *away* in gambling; *gaming-house*, house frequented for gambling; so *gaming-table*.

gāme[2] *adj.* (Of leg, arm, etc.) lame, crippled.

gāme'some (-ms-) *adj.* Sportive. **gāme'somely** *adv.* **gāme'someness** *n.*

gāme'ster (-ms-) *n.* Gambler.

găm'ēte *n.* Protoplasmic body capable of uniting with another to form new individual; mature sexual cell (ill. ALGA). **gamĕt'ĭc** *adj.*

gamin (gămăn') *n.* Street arab, neglected boy.

gămm'a *n.* 1. 3rd letter of Greek alphabet (Γ, γ), used in enumerations etc. 2. Moth, *Plusia gamma*, with γ-shaped silver marking on front wings. 3. ~ *rays*, electro-magnetic radiations of very short wave-length emitted by radio-active substances, orig. regarded as the 3rd and most penetrating kind of rays emitted by radium (see ALPHA, BETA) but now known to be identical with very short X-rays.

gămm'er *n.* (Rustic name for) old woman. [contraction of *godmother*, ga- by assoc. w. *grandmother*]

gămm'on[1] *n.* 1. Bottom piece of flitch of bacon including hind leg (ill. MEAT). 2. Smoked or cured ham; ~ *and spinach*, humbug (with pun on GAMMON[3]). ~ *v.t.* Cure (bacon) by salting and smoking.

gămm'on[2] *n.* At backgammon, victory scoring two 'hits' or games, when one player removes all his men before his opponent removes any. ~ *v.t.* Beat (adversary) thus.

gămm'on[3] *n.* Humbug, deception; (int.) nonsense! ~ *v.* Talk plausibly; feign; hoax, deceive.

gămm'on[4] *v.t.* (naut.) Lash (bowsprit) to stem of vessel. ~ *n.* Rope, chain used for gammoning.

gămm'y *adj.* (slang) Game (of limb).

gămp *n.* (joc.) Umbrella. [Mrs *Gamp*, monthly nurse who carried a large cotton umbrella, in Dickens's 'Martin Chuzzlewit']

găm'ut *n.* 1. (hist.) Lowest note in medieval music (modern G on lowest line of bass stave). 2. (hist.) The 'great scale' of 7 hexachords, consisting of all the recognized notes used in medieval music, and extending from Γ *ut* to E *la* (E in highest space of treble stave). 2. The whole series of notes recognized by musicians; full range of notes of voice or instrument; (fig.) whole range or scope of anything. [*gamma*, the Gk letter Γ (G), as name of lowest note in medieval music; and *ut*, name of the first note of the hexachord; see UT]

gām'y *adj.* Abounding in game; having flavour or scent of game kept till it is high.

găn'der *n.* Male goose; fool, simpleton.

Gandhi (gahn'dĭ), Mohandas Karamchand, called 'Mahatma' (1869–1948). Indian nationalist leader; originator of 'passive resistance' as a form of political action.

găng[1] *n.* Company of workmen, or of slaves or prisoners; band of persons acting or going about together, esp. for criminal purpose or one disapproved of by speaker.

găng[2] *v.i.* (Sc.) Go.

găng-board, -plank *ns.* Plank, usu. with cleats on it, for walking into or out of boat.

gănge (-j) *v.t.* Protect (fish-hook, part of fishing-line) with fine wire.

găng'er *n.* Foreman of gang of workmen.

Găn'ges (-jēz). River of India, held sacred by the Hindus, flowing from the Himalayas to the Bay of Bengal. **Găngĕt'ĭc** *adj.*

găng'lĭon (-ngg-) *n.* (pl. *-lĭa*). 1. Enlargement or knot on nerve forming centre for reception and transmission of impulses (ill. SPINE). 2. (path.) Cyst-like swelling on tendon. **găng'lĭonātėd, gănglĭŏn'ĭc** *adjs.*

găng'rēne (-ngg-) *n.* Local death of body-tissue caused by obstruction of the blood circulation. ~ *v.* Become affected, affect, with gangrene. **găng'rėnous** *adj.*

găng'ster *n.* Member of gang of criminals. **găng'sterĭsm** *n.*

găngue (-ng) *n.* Earthy or stony matter in mineral deposit, matrix in which ore is found; earthy matter in the charge of a blast furnace.

găng'way *n.* Passage, esp. between rows of seats; in English House of Commons, cross-passage half-way down giving access to back benches; passage etc. on ship, esp. platform connecting quarter-deck and forecastle; opening in bulwarks by which ship is entered or left, bridge laid across from this to shore etc.

gănn'ėt *n.* Any of several large white sea-birds of family *Sulidae*, with black-tipped wings and wedge-shaped tail.

găn'oid *adj.* (Of fish-scales) having many superficial layers of enamel-like substance and therefore shiny. ~ *n.* Fish having such scales.

găn'try *n.* Four-footed wooden stand for barrels; structure supporting travelling crane, railway signals, etc. (ill. CRANE).

Găn'ўmēde. 1. (Gk myth.) Trojan youth, so beautiful that Zeus (Jupiter) caused an eagle to carry him up to heaven and made him his cup-bearer. 2. Largest satellite of the planet Jupiter.

gaol (jāl), **jail** *n.* (*g-* in official use, *g-* and *j-* indifferently in literary use, *j-* in U.S.). Public prison for detention of persons committed by process of law; confinement in this; *~-bird*, prisoner, habitual criminal, rogue; *~-delivery*, clearing of gaol esp. at assizes by trying all prisoners awaiting trial; *~-fever*, virulent typhus formerly endemic in gaols. ~ *v.t.* Put in gaol. **gaol'er, jail'er** *n.* Man in charge of gaol or prisoners.

găp *n.* Breach in hedge or wall; gorge, pass; unfilled space or interval, blank; break in continuity; wide divergence in views, sympathies, etc. **găpped** (-pt), **găpp'y** *adjs.*

gāpe *v.i.* Open mouth wide; open or be open wide, split, part asunder; stare, gaze curiously, *at*; yawn. ~ *n.* Yawn; open-mouthed stare; expanse of open mouth or beak, part of beak that opens; *the gapes*, disease of poultry and some wild birds constituted by the presence of *gape-worm* (*Syngamus trachea*) in the trachea, the obstruction caused by which makes the birds gape or gasp for breath. **gāp'er** *n.* (esp.) Kind of bird, the broad-bill (*Calyptomena viridis*); kinds of fish, esp. the sea-perch (*Serranus cabrilla*); kinds of bivalve mollusc with shell open at one or both ends.

gar *n.* ~ *pike*, N. Amer. freshwater fish of the ganoid genus *Lepidosteus* with lozenge-shaped scales, bony pike; ~ *pike, garfish*, the unrelated *Belone*, allied to flying fish; *alligator* ~, large species of *Lepidosteus* living in rivers of southern U.S. with head resembling alligator's.

gă'rage (-ahzh *or* -ahzh') *n.* Building or shed for storing or repair of vehicles, esp. motor-cars. ~ *v.t.* Put (motor-car etc.) into a garage.

Gă'ramond, Claude (d. 1561). French type-founder; hence, style of type resembling his.

garb *n.* Dress, costume, esp. of distinctive kind; way one is dressed. ~ *v.t.* Attire, put (esp. distinctive) clothes upon.

garb'age (-ĭj) *n.* Offal, esp. entrails, used for food; refuse; filth.

gar'ble *v.t.* Make (usu. unfair or malicious) selections from (facts, statements, etc.), mutilate in order to misrepresent. [Arab. *gharbala* sift, select]

garb'oard (-berd) *n.* ~ (*strake*), first range of planks laid on boat's or ship's bottom next keel (ill. BOAT); corresponding plates in iron ship.

Garcia Lorca (garthē'*a* lork'*a*), Federico (1899–1936). Spanish poet and dramatist.

gard'en *n.* Piece of ground devoted to growing flowers, fruit, or vegetables; (pl.) ornamental grounds for public resort; region of special fertility (*the ~ of England*, Kent, Worcestershire, etc.); ~ *city*, town laid out systematically with open spaces, lawns, trees, etc., between the buildings; *~-party*, social meeting on lawn or in garden; *G~ State*, (U.S.) popular name of New Jersey; ~ *suburb*, suburb laid out like garden city. ~ *v.i.* Cultivate, work in, a garden. **gard'ener** *n.* One who gardens; servant employed to tend garden.

gardēn'ia *n.* Genus of (often spring) trees and shrubs of Cape of Good Hope and tropical Asia and Africa, bearing large white or yellow, usu. fragrant, flowers; flower of one of these. [Alexander *Garden* (d. 1791), vice-president of Royal Society]

gare'fowl (-rf-) *n.* The great auk, *Alca impennis*, a large sea-bird related to the razorbill, formerly inhabiting the N. Atlantic but now extinct.

Gar'field, James Abram (1831–1881). 20th president of U.S. (1881).

garfish: see GAR.

gargăn'tūan *adj.* Enormous, gigantic. [*Gargantua*, large-mouthed voracious giant in Rabelais]

garg'ėt (-g-) *n.* Inflamed state of head or throat in cattle, pigs, or poultry; inflammation of cow's or ewe's udder.

gar'gle *v.* Wash (throat or mouth) with liquid held suspended in throat and kept in motion by breath; wash mouth or throat thus. ~ *n.* Liquid used for gargling.

garg'oyle *n.* Grotesque spout usu. with human or animal mouth, head, or body, projecting from gutter of (esp. Gothic) building to carry water clear of wall.

15TH-C. GARGOYLE

garial: see GHARIAL.

Gărĭbăl'dĭ[1], Giuseppe (1807–82). Italian general and patriot; hero of the RISORGIMENTO; commanded a volunteer force on the Sardinian side in the campaign of 1859 against Austria; organized expeditions by which he conquered Sicily; expelled Francis II from Naples; and finally marched (unsuccessfully) against Rome, 1860–2.

gărĭbăl'dĭ[2] *n.* 1. Kind of woman's (orig. bright red) loose blouse in imitation of the red shirts of Garibaldi's followers. 2. ~ (*biscuit*), a biscuit with a layer of currants.

gar'ish *adj.* Obtrusively bright, showy, gaudy, over-decorated. **gar'ishly** *adv.* **gar'ishnėss** *n.*

garl'and *n.* Wreath of flowers, leaves, etc., worn on head or hung on something as decoration; distinction, palm, prize, for victory etc.; representation of garland in metal etc.; (archaic) anthology, miscellany. ~ *v.t.* Crown with garland; deck with garlands; serve as garland to.

garl'ĭc *n.* Plant of genus *Allium* (usu. *A. sativum*) with strong-smelling pungent-tasting bulbs used as flavouring in cookery. **garl'ĭcky** *adj.*

garm'ent *n.* Article of dress, esp. gown or cloak; (pl.) clothes; outward and visible covering of anything.

garn'er *n.* (poet. & rhet.) Granary. ~ *v.t.* (rhet.) Store, deposit, collect.

garn'ėt *n.* Vitreous mineral, occurring as a 12-sided crystal of which the deep-red transparent variety is used as a gem. [med. L *granatum* pomegranate (f. resemblance to its seeds)]

garn'ĭsh *v.t.* 1. Decorate, embellish (esp. dish for table). 2. Serve notice on (person) for purpose of attaching money belonging to debtor; summon (person) as party to litigation already in process between others. ~ *n.* Things used to decorate dish for table. **garnĭshee'** *n.* Person in whose hands money belonging to debtor or defendant is attached at suit of creditor or plaintiff. **garn'ĭsher, garn'ĭshment** *ns.*

garn'ĭture *n.* Appurtenances, accessories; adornment, trimming, esp. of dish; costume.

gă'rrėt[1] *n.* Room on top floor, room partly or entirely in roof, attic. **gărrėteer'** *n.* Dweller in garret, esp. poor literary hack.

gă'rrėt[2] *v.t.* (building) Insert small pieces of stone in joints of (coarse masonry).

Gă'rrĭck, David (1717–79). Famous actor-manager of Drury Lane, London.

gă'rrĭson *n.* Troops stationed in fortress, town, etc., to defend it; ~ *town*, town having garrison. ~ *v.t.* Furnish with, occupy as, garrison; place (troops, soldier) on garrison duty.

gă'rron *n.* Small inferior horse bred in Scotland and Ireland.

gar(r)ŏtte' *n.* Spanish method of capital punishment by strangulation; instrument used in it, formerly with apparatus for strangling, now with brass collar fitted with a sharp point which pierces the spinal cord; highway robbery performed by throttling victim. ~ *v.t.* Execute by strangulation; throttle in order to rob. **gar(r)ŏtt'er** *n.*

gă'rrulous (-rōō-) *adj.* Given to talk, loquacious, wordy; (of bird, stream, etc.) chattering, babbling. **gă'rrulously** *adv.* **gă'rrulousnėss, garrul'ĭty** (-rōō-) *ns.*

gar't'er *n.* Band worn above or below knee to keep stocking up or as ornament; *the G~*, badge (dark-blue velvet ribbon edged and buckled with gold, worn below knee) of highest order of English knighthood, instituted by Edward III *c* 1344; membership of this order, the order itself; *G~ King of Arms*, principal King of Arms of England; *~-stitch*, the pattern produced by knitting plain to and fro (ill. KNIT). ~ *v.t.* Fasten (stocking), encircle (leg), with garter.

garth *n.* (archaic & dial.) Close, yard, garden, paddock, open space within cloisters (ill. MONASTERY).

găs[1] *n.* 1. Any aeriform or completely elastic fluid (used chiefly of those that do not become liquid or solid at ordinary temperatures, other gases being usu. called *vapours*). 2. Gas, esp. coal-gas, of a kind suitable to be burnt for lighting or heating purposes; (coal-mining) explosive mixture of fire-damp with air; nitrous oxide gas (*laughing ~*), used as anaesthetic, esp. by dentists; hydrogen or other gas used to inflate balloon etc.; any of various gases, liquids, or solids, dispersed in warfare in the form of gases, vapours, or smoke, (*poison gases*), and causing irritation, blistering, or poisoning to those who inhale or come in contact with them (see CHLORINE, MUSTARD gas, PHOSGENE, LEWISITE, etc.). 3. Empty talk, boasting, humbug, windbag eloquence. 4. *~-bag*, bag for holding gas; empty talker; airship's gas-container; (contempt.) balloon or airship; *~-bracket*, gas-pipe with burner(s) projecting from wall; *~-coal*, bituminous coal from which gas can be made; *~-coke*, residuum of coal when gas has been made from it; *~-engine, -motor*, internal combustion engine, usu. of large size, using a mixture of gas and air; *~-fire*, fire in which heat is supplied by gas; *~-fitter*, tradesman or workman providing house with apparatus for heating or lighting with gas (~-fittings); *~-helmet, -mask*, kind of appliance including respirator worn as defence against poison gases; *~-holder*, = GASOMETER; *~-light*, light from an incandescent mantle; *~-light paper, print*, photographic paper suitable for, print made by, artificial light; *~-mantle*, device for increasing the illuminating power of gas, consisting of cellulose fabric impregnated with a mixture of thorium and cerium nitrates, which becomes incandescent when heated by the gas flame enclosed by it; *~-meter*, apparatus registering amount of gas consumed; *~-proof*, impermeable to gas, esp. poison gas; *~-ring*, hollow iron ring with perforations or jets, supplied with gas from pipe and used for cooking, etc.; *~-shell*, shell charged with poison gas and little or no explosive; *~-tar*, coal-tar produced in making gas; *~-trap*, trap to prevent sewer-gas from coming up pipe; *~-turbine*, gas-driven turbine, esp. one used to drive air-compressor in jet-propelled aircraft (ill. TURBINE); *~-works*, manufactory of (coal-) gas. ~ *v.* 1. Supply (room, railway carriage, etc.) with gas. 2. Project poison-gas upon (enemy, place); (pass.) be poisoned with gas. 3. Pass (thread, lace) through gas-flame to remove loose fibres. 4. Talk emptily or boastfully. **gās'ėous** *adj.* [wd invented by Van Helmont, Du. chemist, after Gk *khaos* chaos]

găs[2] *n.* (U.S. colloq.) Abbrev. of GASOLENE; *tread, step, on the ~*, accelerate motor-engine by pressing pedal controlling the throttle; (fig.) put on speed, hasten.

Găs'con *adj.* & *n.* (Native) of **Găscony,** former province of SW. France; braggart, boaster.

găsconāde' *n.* Boasting. ~ *v.i.* boast.

găsėlier' *n.* Gas-lamp with several burners often on branches. [after *chandelier*]

găsh *n.* Long and deep slash, cut, or wound; cleft such as might be made by slashing cut; act of making such cut. ~ *v.t.* Make gash in; cut.

Găs'kell, Mrs Elizabeth Cleghorn (1810–65). English novelist; author of 'Mary Barton', 'Cranford', etc.

găs'kėt *n.* Small cord for securing furled sail to yard; (strip) of hemp, yarn, asbestos, etc., used for packing piston, forming water- or gas-tight joint in pipe, internal combustion engine, etc.

găs'kĭn *n.* Hinder thigh of horse (ill. HORSE).

găs'olēne, -ine (-ēn) *n.* Volatile inflammable liquid distilled from crude petroleum and used for heating, lighting, etc.; (U.S.) petrol.

gasŏm'ėter *n.* 1. (chem.) Vessel for holding gas. 2. Large vessel in which coal-gas is stored for distribution by pipes, gas-holder.

gasp (-ah-) *v.* Catch breath, strain *for* air or breath, with open mouth as in exhaustion or astonishment; utter with gasps. ~ *n.* Convulsive catching of breath; *at one's last ~*, at point of death (also fig.). **gasp'ĭngly** *adv.*

gasp'er (-ah-) *n.* (esp., slang) Cheap cigarette.

găss'y *adj.* Of, full of, like, gas; (of talk etc.) empty, verbose.

găs't(e)ropŏd *n.* One of the *Gasteropoda*, a class of molluscs having the locomotive organ placed ventrally (snails, limpets, etc.).

găs'trĭc *adj.* Of the stomach; ~ *juice*, thin clear acid nearly colourless fluid secreted by certain stomach-glands and acting as chief agent of digestion. **gastrī'tĭs** *n.* Inflammation of the stomach.

gastro- *prefix.* Stomach; *~-enterī'tis*, inflammation affecting both stomach and bowel.

găstrŏl'ogy *n.* Science of cookery. **găstrŏl'oger, găstrŏl'ogĭst** *ns.*

găs'tronōme *n.* Connoisseur of cookery. **găstrŏn'omy** *n.* Art and science of good eating. **găstrŏn'omer, -mĭst** *ns.* **găstronŏm'ĭc(al)** *adjs.* **găstronŏm'ĭcally** *adv.*

găs'trula *n.* (biol.) Stage in development of embryo (typically a double-layered sac) produced by migration of cells of BLASTULA into new positions.

găt *n.* (slang) Revolver or other fire-arm. [short for GATLING]

gāte *n.* 1. Opening in wall of city or enclosure, made for entrance and exit and capable of being closed with barrier; means of entrance or exit. 2. Barrier closing opening of wall, wooden or iron framework, solid or of bars or gratings, hung on hinges, turning on pivots, or sliding; contrivance regulating passage of water. 3. Number entering by payment at gates to see football match etc., amount of money thus taken. 4. H-shaped arrangement of slots through which gear-lever of internal combustion engine is moved to engage different gears. 5. *~-bill*, (at Oxford and Cambridge) record of undergraduate's returns to college after hours; fines imposed for these; *~-crash* (*v.i.*) (slang) gain entrance to party, reception, etc., without invitation or ticket of admission; hence, *~-crasher* (*n.*); *gatehouse*, lodge of park etc.; (hist.) room over city gate often used as prison; room over gate of castle (ill. CASTLE); *~-leg, -legged, table*, folding table with leaves supported on gate-shaped structure which may be swung back to allow them to hang down (ill. TABLE); *~-post*, post on which gate is hung or on which it shuts; *gate'way*, = sense 1; frame of or structure built over gate. ~ *v.t.* (Oxford and Cambridge) Confine (undergraduate) to college, entirely or after certain hours.

gath'er (gădh-) *v.* 1. Bring or come together; cause to assemble; congregate; form a mass; receive additions; *be gathered to one's fathers*, die. 2. Acquire by collecting, amass; cull, pluck; collect (grain etc.) as harvest; pick *up* from ground; sum *up* (scattered facts); infer, deduce (*that*); ~ *way*, (of ship) begin to move. 3. Summon up (energies); gain or recover (breath); summon *up* (thoughts, strength, etc.) for an effort. 4. Draw (garment, brow) together in folds or wrinkles; esp. pucker (part of dress) by running thread through; draw *up* (limbs, person) into smaller compass. 5. Come to a head, develop purulent swelling. ~ *n.* (usu. pl.) Gathered part of dress. **găth'erĭng** *n.* (esp.) 1.

Purulent swelling. 2. Assembly; meeting.

Găt'ling *n.* ~ (*gun*), machine-gun with cluster of barrels, first used in Amer. Civil War. [R. J. *Gatling* (1818–1903), inventor]

gauche (gōsh) *adj.* Tactless; without ease or grace, socially awkward. ***gaucherie'*** (-rē) *n.* Gauche manners; a gauche action.

gauch'ō (gow-, gaw-) *n.* Mounted herdsman of S. Amer. pampas, of mixed Eur. and Ind. descent.

gaud *n.* Something gaudy, showy ornament, gewgaw; (pl.) showy ceremonies, gaieties.

gaud'y[1] *adj.* Tastelessly or inappropriately fine, showy, or brilliant. **gaud'ĭly** *adv.* **gaud'ĭness** *n.*

gaud'y[2] *n.* Grand feast or entertainment, esp. annual college dinner to old members etc.

gauffer: see GOFFER.

gauge (gāj) *n.* 1. Standard measure to which things must conform, esp. measure of capacity or contents of barrel, diameter of bullet, or thickness of sheet metal; distance between rails of railway, tramway, etc. 2. (naut., usu. spelt *gage*) Relative position in respect to wind; *have the weather ~ of*, be to windward of. 3. Graduated instrument measuring force or quantity of rainfall, stream, tide, wind, etc.; contrivance attached to vessel to show height of its contents; instrument for testing and verifying dimensions of tools, wire, etc.; carpenter's adjustable tool for marking parallel lines; (print.) strip regulating depth of margin etc.; means of estimating, criterion, test. ~ *v.t.* Measure exactly (esp. objects of standard size, as wire, bolts; depth of liquid content; fluctuating quantities or forces, as rainfall, wind); find capacity or content of (cask etc.) by measurement and calculation; estimate, take measure of (person, character); make uniform, bring to standard size or shape. **gau'ger** *n.* (esp.) Exciseman.

Gaul. 1. A Roman province of W. Europe; *Cisalpine* ~ included N. Italy, and *Transalpine* ~ the present France, Switzerland, Belgium, and the Netherlands. 2. Native or inhabitant of ancient Gaul; (joc.) Frenchman. **Gaul'ish** *adj.* Of ancient Gaul; (joc.) French. ~ *n.* Celtic language of this region.

Gauleiter (gow'līter) *n.* Political official controlling a 'Gau' or district under the Nazi régime.

Gaulle (gōl), Charles Joseph de (1890–). French general; head of the 'Free French' movement after the occupation of France by the Germans in 1940 and of the French Provisional Government 1944–5; premier of France 1958–9; president 1959–69.

gaunt *adj.* Lean, haggard; grim or desolate looking. **gaunt'nĕss** *n.*

gaunt'lĕt[1] *n.* 1. (hist.) Glove worn as part of armour, usu. of leather covered with steel plates (ill. ARMOUR); *fling, throw, down the* ~, issue challenge; *pick, take, up the* ~, accept challenge. 2. Stout glove with long wrist for driving, fencing, wicket-keeping, etc.; wide part of glove covering wrist. **gaunt'lĕtĕd** *adj.*

gaunt'lĕt[2] *n.* *Run the* ~, pass between rows of persons who strike one with sticks, cords, etc., as military, naval, or school punishment; (fig.) be subjected to criticism. [Swed. *gatlopp* (*gata* lane, *lopp* course)]

Gauss (gows), Karl Friedrich (1777–1855). German mathematician and natural philosopher.

gauss *n.* Unit of intensity of magnetic field: the magnetic induction at a point is 1 gauss when the maximum electromotive force that can be induced in a conductor 1 cm. long moving through the point with a velocity of 1 cm. per sec. is 1 c.g.s. unit of electromotive force. **Gauss'ĭan** *adj.*

Gauta'ma (-tah-). Family name of the BUDDHA.

Gautier (gōtyā'), Pierre Jules Théophile (1811–72). French Romantic poet and novelist.

gauze *n.* Thin transparent fabric of silk, cotton, wire, etc.; slight haze. **gauz'y** *adj.* **gauz'ĭnėss** *n.*

găv'el *n.* Auctioneer's or chairman's hammer.

găv'elkīnd *n.* Land-tenure, esp. in Kent, involving equal division of deceased man's property among his sons.

gavŏtte' *n.* An 18th-c. dance, like minuet but more lively; music for this, in common time, each phrase beginning on 3rd beat of bar, freq. forming part of suite.

gawk *n.* Awkward or bashful person. **gawk'y** *adj.* & *n.* Awkward, ungainly, bashful (person). **gawk'ĭnėss** *n.*

gay[1] *adj.* Full of, disposed to, indicating, mirth; light-hearted, sportive; airy, off-hand; showy, brilliant, bright-coloured, finely dressed; (euphem.) dissolute, immoral, living by prostitution. **gail'y** *adv.*

Gay[2], John (1685–1732). English playwright; author of 'The Beggar's Opera'.

Gay-Lussac (lūsahk'), Joseph Louis (1778–1850). French chemist; *~'s Law*, the statement that when gases react together there is always a simple numerical relationship between their volumes and that of the products, if gaseous; ~ *tower*, part of plant for making sulphuric acid by lead chamber process.

gāze *v.i.* Look fixedly. ~ *n.* Intent look.

gazēb'ō *n.* Structure whence a view may be had, belvedere, lantern, turret, balcony, etc.

gazĕlle' *n.* Small, graceful, soft-eyed, delicately formed kinds of antelope, found in Asia and Africa. [Arab. *ghazal*]

gazĕtte' *n.* News-sheet, periodical publication giving current events (hist.); one of three official journals (*London, Edinburgh, Belfast*, ~), issued by authority twice a week with lists of government appointments, names of bankrupts, and other public notices; (in names of newspapers) newspaper. ~ *v.t.* Publish in official gazette.

găzetteer' *n.* Geographical index or dictionary. [f. an early work of this kind, 'The Gazetteer's or Newsman's Interpreter']

găz'ogēne, gas- *n.* Apparatus for making aerated waters.

G.B. *abbrev.* Great Britain.

G.B.E. *abbrev.* Knight (*or* Dame) Grand Cross (of the Order) of the British Empire.

G.C. *abbrev.* George Cross.

G.C.B. *abbrev.* Knight Grand Cross (of the Order) of the Bath.

G.C.E. *abbrev.* General Certificate of Education (replaced LOCAL examinations 1951).

G.C.F. *abbrev.* Greatest common factor.

G.C.I.E. *abbrev.* Knight Grand Commander (of the Order) of the Indian Empire.

G.C.M. *abbrev.* Greatest common measure.

G.C.M.G. *abbrev.* Knight Grand Cross (of the Order) of St. Michael and St. George.

G.C.S.I. *abbrev.* Knight Grand Commander (of the Order) of the Star of India.

G.C.V.O. *abbrev.* Knight Grand Cross of the Royal Victorian Order.

Ge (gē), **Gaia** (gī'a). (Gk myth.) Personification of the Earth.

gean (jē'an, jēn) *n.* The wild cherry tree (*Prunus avium*), freq. confused with bird-cherry (*P. padus*).

gear (g-) *n.* 1. Equipment, apparel, etc. (archaic); harness of draught animals; apparatus, appliances, tackle, tools. 2. Combination of wheels, levers, etc.; wheels working on one another by teeth etc.; mechanical arrangement connecting motor with its work, usu. effecting a change of relative speed of revolution between driving and driven parts; (in bicycles) number of inches in diameter of rear wheel multiplied by ratio of driving to driven gear wheels; *in, out of*, ~, in, out of, connexion with motor; working, not working; *high, low*, ~, by which driven part of vehicle etc. revolves faster, slower, relatively to driving part. 3. Rigging. 4. Goods; household utensils. 5. *~-box*, in motor-vehicle, the part containing the gear-changing mechanism (ill. MOTOR); *~-case*, in bicycle, case containing driving and driven gear-wheels and the chain; *~-wheel*, cog-wheel, esp. that in bicycle driven immediately by the pedals. ~ *v.* Harness (draught animal); put (machinery) in gear; provide with gear; (of cog-wheel) fit exactly *into*, be in gear *with*; adjust or modify, e.g. production of one factory to meet the requirements of a larger group or organization. **gear'ing** *n.* Manner in which a machine is

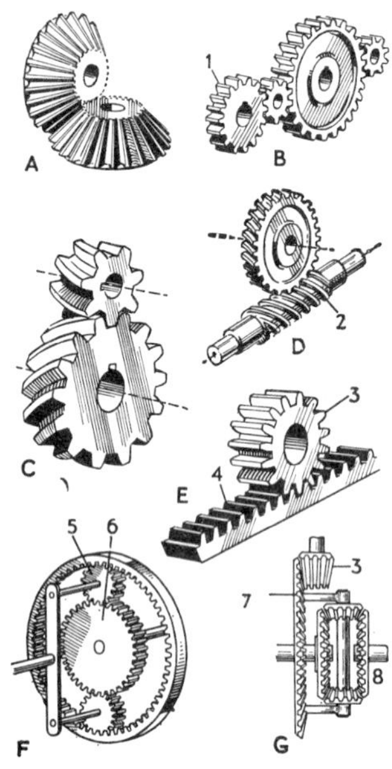

GEARS: A. BEVEL GEARS. B. GEAR TRAIN. C. HELICAL GEARS. D. WORM GEAR. E. RACK AND PINION. F. SUN-AND-PLANET OR EPICYCLIC GEARING. G. DIFFERENTIAL GEAR

1. Cog- or gear-wheel. 2. Worm. 3. Pinion. 4. Rack 5. Planet wheel. 6. Sun-wheel. 7. Crown or contrate wheel. 8. Differential unit

geared; apparatus for transmission of motion or power from one part of a machine to another, esp. a train of toothed wheels.

gĕck'ō (g-) *n.* (pl. *-os, -oes*). Any of numerous species of lizard (family *Geckonidae*), found in warm climates, with peculiar cry and (in some species) adhesive discs on the feet enabling them to climb walls. [Malay *gekoq*, imitating its cry]

gee[1], **gee-gee** *ns.* (colloq., orig. child's word) Horse.

gee[2] *int.* Word of command to horse etc. to go on, go faster, (in some dialects) turn to right. So **gee-(h)ŭp, gee-hō**, etc.

gee[3] *int.* (U.S.) of asseveration, discovery, etc. So **geewhill'ikins, gee-whiz'.**

Gē'ĕz (g-): see ETHIOPIC.

geez'er (g-) *n.* (slang) Old person, old creature.

Gėhĕnn'a (g-). Hell; place of burning, torment, or misery. [Heb. *gehinnom* valley near Jerusalem where children were burnt in sacrifice to Baal or Moloch]

Geig'er coun'ter (gīg-). Instrument for detecting and counting ionizing particles, used for measuring radio-activity esp. in connexion with the release of atomic energy. [Hans *Geiger* (1882–1945), German physicist]

geish'a (gā-) *n.* Japanese girl trained as singer, dancer, and entertainer.

Geiss'ler tūbe (gī-) *n.* Sealed tube filled with rarefied gas which becomes incandescent when an electric current is passed through it. [Heinrich *Geissler* (1814–79), German physicist]

gĕl *n.* Semi-solid colloidal solution. ~ *v.i.* Form or become a gel.

gĕl'atin(e) (or -ēn) *n.* Amorphous brittle yellowish transparent substance consisting essentially of protein, extracted from animal skins and bones, used in making soups, jellies, etc., in many photographic processes, and as the principal constituent of glue; *blasting* ~, gelatin-like explosive solution of collodion cotton in nitro-glycerine; ~ *dynamite*, thin blasting gelatin mixed with other substances to reduce violence of explosion. **gėlăt'inous** *adj.* Jelly-like in consistency etc.; of gelatin.

gĕld (g-) *v.t.* Deprive (usu. male animal) of generative power, castrate, excise testicles or ovaries of. **gĕl'ding** *n.* Gelded horse or other animal.

gĕl'id *adj.* Icy, ice-cold; chilly, cool.

gĕl'ignīte *n.* Variety of gelatin dynamite.

gĕlsēm'ium *n.* Genus of woody vines containing two Asiatic species and one (*G~ sempervirens*) of the southern U.S., from the dried rhizome and roots of which a respiratory poison, used in the treatment of neuralgia etc., is obtained.

gĕm *n.* Precious stone, esp. when cut and polished; object of great beauty or worth, choicest part *of*, prized possession; precious or semi-precious stone with engraved design; *Gem State*, (U.S.) popular name of Idaho. ~ *v.t.* Adorn (as) with gems.

Gėmâr'a (g-). Later part of the Talmud, commentary on the older part (Mishna).

gĕm'inate *adj.* Combined in pairs. **gĕm'ināte** *v.t.* Double, repeat; arrange in pairs. **gĕminā'tion** *n.*

Gĕm'inī. The constellation also called 'Castor and Pollux'; 3rd sign [♊] of zodiac, formerly identical with this, entered by sun about 21st May. [L, = 'twins']

gĕmm'a *n.* (pl. *-ae*). 1. (bot.) Leaf-bud; small cellular body that separates from mother-plant and starts new one. 2. (zool.) Bud-like growth on animal of low organization becoming detached and developing into new individual.

gĕmm'ate *adj.* Having buds, reproducing by gemmation. **gĕmmāte'** *v.i.* Put forth buds, propagate by gemmation. **gĕmmā'tion** *n.* Act, manner, of budding; arrangement of buds, reproduction by gemmae, formation of new individual by protrusion and separation of part of parent.

gĕmmip'arous *adj.* Of, propagating by, gemmation. **gĕmmip'arously** *adv.*

gĕmm'ūle *n.* Asexual reproductive body in sponges.

Gen. *abbrev.* General; Genesis (O.T.).

gend'ârme (zhŏṅ-) *n.* Soldier employed in police duties, esp. in France. **gendârm'erie** (-rē) *n.* Force of gendarmes.

gĕn'der[1] *n.* Each of the three (or in some langs. two) grammatical kinds, corresponding more or less to distinctions of sex and absence of sex ((*masculine, feminine, neuter*), into which nouns are divided according to the modification they may require in words syntactically connected with them; property (in a *n.*) of belonging to or (in other parts of speech) of having the appropriate form to concord with, a specified one of these kinds; division of words into genders as principle of grammatical classification; (joc.) sex.

gĕn'der[2] *v.t.* (archaic & poet.) Engender.

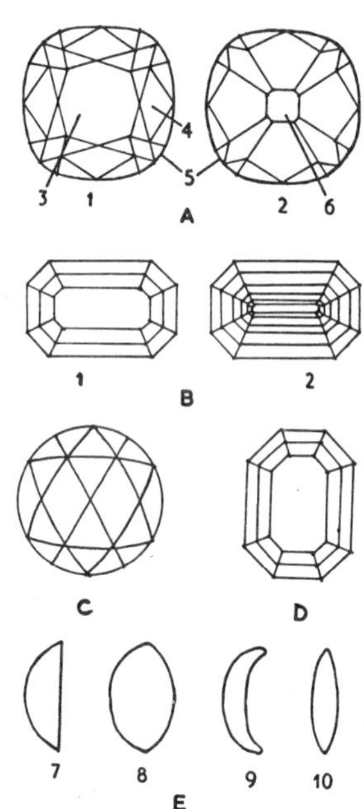

GEM CUTTING: A. BRILLIANT-CUT. B. TRAP-CUT. C. ROSE-CUT. D. TABLE-CUT. E. SECTIONS OF CABOCHONS

1. Crown. 2. Pavilion. 3. Table. 4. Bezel (one of the facets). 5. Girdle. 6. Collet. Cabochons: 7. Simple. 8. Double. 9. Hollowed. 10. Tallow-drop

gēne *n.* Member of any of the pairs of factors or physiological units in the germ-cell which cause the development in offspring of certain characters, one member of each pair being transmitted from each parent; each gene is carried on a chromosome in a fixed position relative to other genes, the pairs of genes being on pairs of chromosomes.

gĕnėalŏ'gĭcal *adj.* Of genealogy; tracing family descent; ~ *tree*, table showing descent of family or of animal species in shape of tree with branches. **gĕnėalŏ'gĭcally** *adv.*

gĕnėăl'ogīze *v.* Trace genealogy of; draw up genealogies. **gĕnėăl'ogĭst** *n.*

gĕnėăl'ogy *n.* Account of descent from ancestor by enumeration of intermediate persons; pedigree; investigation of pedigrees; plant's or animal's line of development from earlier forms.

gĕn'era, pl. of GENUS.

gĕn'eral *adj.* Completely or approximately universal; including or affecting all or nearly all parts or cases or things; not partial or particular; prevalent, widespread, usual; including points common to individuals of a class and neglecting differences; not restricted, not specialized; roughly corresponding or adequate, sufficient for practical purposes; vague, indefinite; (mil., of officer) above rank of colonel; (appended to titles) chief, head, with unrestricted authority or sphere; *in* ~, generally; in all ordinary cases, barring special exceptions, for the most part; *G~ Assembly*, deliberative and legislative council of the Church of Scotland, represented by its ministers, meeting annually and presided over by a Moderator; *G~ Council*, ecclesiastical council called together by invitation to Church at large, and claiming to speak in name of whole Church; ~ *election*, one in which representatives are elected by every constituency; ~ *headquarters* (abbrev. G.H.Q.), headquarters of commander-in-chief; ~ *hospital*, hospital not restricted to those suffering from a particular disease; military hospital receiving patients from a field hospital; *G~ Post Office* (abbrev. G.P.O.), head post office (in town or area); ~ *strike*, concerted strike by workers of all or most important trades or industries. ~ *n.* 1. *The* ~, (archaic) the public. 2. (pl.; now rare) General principles, notions, or rules. 3. Chief of religious order, e.g. of Jesuits, Dominicans; head of Salvation Army. 4. (mil.) Officer next below Field Marshal (also used, by courtesy, of *lieutenant-general* and *major-general*); commander of army; tactician, strategist, of specified merit. 5. (colloq.) General servant.

gĕneralĭss'ĭmō *n.* (pl. *-os*). Commander of combined military and naval force, or of several armies.

gĕnerăl'ĭty *n.* 1. Being general, applicability to whole class of instances. 2. Vagueness. 3. General point, principle, law, or statement. 4. Main body, bulk, majority, *of*.

gĕneralīzā'tion *n.* (Forming of) general notion or proposition obtained by induction.

gĕn'eralīze *v.* 1. Reduce to general laws, form into a general notion, give a general character to, call by a general name; infer (law, conclusion) by induction; base general statement upon (facts etc.); (math., philos.) throw into general form, extend application of; form general notions by abstraction; (painting) render only the typical characteristics of. 2. Make vague or indefinite; use generalities, speak vaguely. 3. Bring into general use. 4. *Generalized*, (zool., of organ or structure) suitable for general use, not specialized (e.g. reptile's forelimb as distinct from bird's wing); (of animal) having generalized organs etc.

gĕn'erally *adv.* 1. For the most part, extensively; in a general sense, without regard to particulars; not specially; as a general rule, commonly.

gĕn'eralshĭp *n.* Office of a general; strategy, military skill; skilful management, tact, diplomacy.

gĕn'erāte *v.t.* Bring into existence, produce, evolve; (math., of point, line, surface, conceived as moving) make (line, surface, solid).

gĕnerā'tion *n.* 1. Procreation, propagation of species, begetting or being begotten; production by natural or artificial process. 2. Offspring of same parent or parents, regarded as single step in descent or pedigree; whole body of persons born about same time; time covered by lives of these; in reckoning historically, interval of time between birth of parents and that of their children (usu. reckoned at about 30 years).

gĕn'erative *adj.* Of procreation; able to produce, productive.

gĕn'erātor *n.* Begetter; apparatus for producing gases, steam, etc.; machine for converting mechanical into electrical energy, dynamo (ill. DYNAMO).

gėnĕ'rĭc *adj.* Characteristic of a genus or class; applied to (any individual of) a large group or class; general, not specific or special; ~ *name*, (biol.) Latin name (written with capital) indicating the genus to which an animal or plant belongs and preceding the *specific name* which indicates the species. **gėnĕ'rĭcally** *adv.*

gĕn'erous *adj.* Magnanimous, noble-minded, not mean or prejudiced; free in giving, munificent; (of soil) fertile; ample, abundant, copious; (of wine, colour, etc.) rich and full. **gĕn'erously** *adv.* **gĕnerŏs'ĭty** *n.*

Gĕn'ėsĭs. First in order of books of O.T., containing account of creation of the world. **gĕn'ėsĭs** *n.* Origin; mode of formation or generation. [Gk, = 'origin', 'creation']

gĕn'ėt *n.* (Fur of) kind of civet-cat, *Genetta vulgaris*, native of S. Europe, Africa, and W. Asia.

gėnĕt'ĭc *adj.* Of, in, concerning, origin; of genetics. **gėnĕt'ĭcally** *adv.* **gėnĕt'ĭcs** *n.pl.* The branch of biology dealing with the resemblances and differences between organisms related by descent, and the nature and distribution of the genes. **gėnĕt'ĭcĭst** *n.*

gėnēv'a[1] *n.* Spirit, made in Holland, distilled from grain and flavoured with juniper berries; Hollands. [Du. f. L *juniperus* juniper]

Gėnē'va[2]**.** City of Switzerland, where meetings of Council and Assembly of League of Nations were held; hence, the League of Nations; ~ *bands*, strips of lawn suspended from the front of the neck, worn esp. by the Calvinist and Presbyterian clergy; ~ *Bible*, English translation of the Bible prepared by Protestant exiles at Geneva and printed there in 1560, the 'Breeches' bible; ~ *cross*, a red Greek cross on a white ground displayed by hospitals, etc. in time of war, more commonly called the *red cross*; ~ *gown*, clergyman's black gown like that worn by Calvinist clergy when preaching. **Gėnēv'an** *adj.* Of Geneva; (esp.) Calvinistic. **Gėnėvēse'** (-z) *adj.* & *n.* (Native, inhabitant) of Geneva.

Genghis Khan (jĕn'gĭz) (1162–1227). The great Mongol conqueror, whose empire extended from the shores of the Pacific to the northern shores of the Black Sea.

gēn'ial[1] *adj.* 1. (now rare) Nuptial; generative. 2. Conducive to growth; (of climate, warmth, etc.) pleasantly warm, mild. 3. Cheering, enlivening; jovial, kindly, sociable. **gēn'ially** *adv.* **gēniăl'ĭty** *n.* **gēn'ialīze** *v.t.*

gėnī'al[2] *adj.* (anat.) Of the chin.

gėnĭc'ūlate, -ātėd *adjs.* (nat. hist.) Having knee-like joints.

gēn'ie (-ĭ) *n.* (pl. usu. *geniī*). Sprite or goblin of Arabian demonology, jinnee.

gėnĭs'ta *n.* Leguminous genus of flowering shrubs including dyer's broom and petty whin.

gĕn'ĭtal *adj.* Of animal generation. **gĕn'ĭtals** *n.pl.* External organs of generation.

gĕn'ĭtive *adj.* & *n.* ~ (*case*), grammatical form of nouns, pronouns, or adjectives, chiefly denoting relation as source, possessor, or the like. **gĕnĭtīv'al** *adj.*

gēn'ius *n.* 1. (pl. *-iuses, -iī*). Tutelary spirit of person, place, or institution; *good, evil,* ~, two mutually opposed spirits by whom every person was supposed to be attended; hence, person powerfully influencing another for good or evil. 2. (pl. -*iī*). Demon, supernatural being. 3. (pl. -*iuses*). Prevalent feeling, opinions, taste, of nation, age, etc.; character, spirit, drift, method, of language, law, etc.; associations, inspirations, *of* a place. 4. Natural ability, special mental endowments; exalted intellectual power, instinctive and extraordinary imaginative, creative, or inventive capacity; person having this.

Gĕn'oa (j-) (Ital. *Genova*). City and seaport of NW. Italy; ~ *cake*, a rich fruit cake with almonds and other nuts on the top. **Gĕnoēse'** (-z) *adj.* & *n.* (Native, inhabitant) of Genoa.

gĕn'ocīde *n.* Extermination of a race.

gĕn'otȳpe *n.* (biol.) Genetic constitution of an organism (cf. PHENOTYPE).

genre (zhahṅr) *n.* Kind, esp. of art or literature; ~(-*painting*), portrayal of scenes from ordinary life, esp. that of a particular class, e.g. peasants.

gĕns (-z) *n.* (pl. *gentēs*). 1. (Rom. antiq.) Clan, sept. 2. (anthrop.) Line of descent through father.

gĕnt *n.* Abbrev. of *gentleman* (now only vulg. or facet.).

gĕnteel' *adj.* (usu. iron.; vulg. in serious use.) Appropriate to, characteristic of, belonging to, the upper classes; stylish, fashionable, well-dressed, elegant. **gĕnteel'ly** *adv.*

gĕn'tian (-shĭan, -shn) *n.* Plant of the genus *Gentiana*, usu. with conspicuous blue flowers, common in Alpine meadows; ~ (*root*), (pharm.) dried rhizome and roots of *G. lutea* used as a tonic and stomachic; ~ *violet*, dye, used as antiseptic, esp. in treatment of burns. [L, f. *Gentius* king of Illyria]

gĕn'tīle *adj.* & *n.* (Person) not of Jewish blood; heathen, pagan; (in Mormon use) non-Mormon.

gĕntĭl'ĭty *n.* 1. (now rare) Gentle birth, status of gentleman or lady. 2. (usu. iron.) Being genteel; social superiority, good manners, upper-class habits.

gĕn'tle *adj.* 1. Well-born; (her.) having right to bear arms (now only in ~ *and simple*); (of birth, blood, etc.) honourable, belonging to or fit for the class of gentleman. 2. (archaic) Generous, noble, courteous. 3. Tame, quiet; easily managed; not stormy, rough, or violent; mild; moderate, gradual; kind, tender. ~ *n.* (f. obs. sense *soft* of *adj.*) Maggot, larva of flesh-fly or bluebottle, used as bait by anglers. ~ *v.t.* Break in or handle (horse) gently. **gĕn'tlefolk** (-tlfōk) *n.pl.* Persons of good position and family.

gĕn'tleman (-tlm-) *n.* 1. Man of gentle birth or entitled to bear arms but not included in nobility (chiefly hist.); man of gentle birth attached to household of sovereign or great person; ~-*at-arms*, one of sovereign's bodyguard. 2. Man of chivalrous instincts, fine feelings, and good breeding; man of good social position, man of wealth and leisure; (courteous synonym for) man; (law) man who has no occupation; *the old* ~, (joc.) the devil; *gentleman's* ~, valet; ~*'s agreement, bargain*, agreement not enforceable at law, and binding only as matter of honour; ~-*commoner*, one of former class of privileged undergraduates at Oxford and Cambridge; ~-*usher*, gentleman acting as usher to great person. **gĕn'tlemanlīke** *adj.* Appropriate to, resembling, a gentleman. **gĕn'tlemanly** *adj.* Feeling, behaving, or looking like a gentleman; befitting a gentleman. **gĕn'tlemanlinėss** *n.*

gĕn'tlenėss (-ln-) *n.* Kindliness, mildness; freedom from severity, violence, suddenness, etc.

gĕn'tlewoman (-tlwŏŏman) *n.* Woman of good birth or breeding, lady.

gĕn'tly *adv.* Quietly, moderately, softly, slowly; mildly, tenderly, kindly; ~ *born*, of gentle birth.

gĕn'try *n.* People next below nobility in position and birth; (contempt.) people.

gĕn'ūflĕct *v.i.* Bend the knee, esp. in worship. **gĕn'ūflĕctor, gĕnūflĕ'xion** (-kshn) *ns.* **gĕn'ūflĕctory** *adj.*

gĕn'ūine *adj.* Of the original stock, pure-bred; really proceeding from its reputed source or author; having the supposed character, not counterfeit, properly so called. **gĕn'uinely** (-nl-) *adv.* **gĕn'ūinenėss** (-n-n-) *n.*

gēn'us *n.* (pl. *gĕn'era*). (logic) Class of things including subordinate kinds, or species; (zool., bot.) group (usu. containing several species) of animals or plants having common structural characteristics distinct from those of all other groups; (loosely) kind, class, order, tribe.

Geo. *abbrev.* George.

gēocĕn'trĭc *adj.* Considered as viewed from the earth's centre; having or representing the earth as centre. **gēocĕn'trĭcally** *adv.*

gē'ōde *n.* Cavity in an igneous rock which has been partly filled with minerals in well-shaped crystals. **gėŏd'ic** *adj.*

gėŏd'ėsy *n.* Branch of mathematics dealing with figure and area of the earth or large portions of it. **gēodĕs'ĭc, gēodĕt'ĭc** *adjs.* Of geodesy; ~ *line*, shortest possible line joining two points on a surface. **gēodĕt'ĭcal** *adj.* **gēodĕt'ĭcally** *adv.*

gēogrăph'ic(al) *adjs.* Of geography; *geographic latitude*, angle made with plane of equator by perpendicular to surface of earth at any point; *geographic(al) mile*, 1 minute of longitude measured along the equator, 6087·2 ft. **gēogrăph'ĭcally** *adv.*

gėŏg'raphy *n.* Science of the earth's surface, form, physical features, natural and political divisions, climate, productions, population, etc.; subject-matter of geography; treatise or manual of geography; features, arrangements, *of* place. **gėŏg'rapher** *n.*

gē'oid *n.* (geog.) The surface constituted by the mean sea-level of the open sea, conceived as extending under the continents at the level to which the sea would rise if admitted by small frictionless impervious canals.

gēolŏ'gĭcal *adj.* Of geology; ~ *map*, one showing the formations of rock exposed at, or underlying, the surface of a region; ~ *survey*, service, institution, which reports on the geological problems of a country or area, as water supply, mines, quarries, etc. **gēolŏ'gĭcally** *adv.*

gėŏl'ogīze *v.* Devote time to examining places geologically, collecting specimens, etc.; examine (place) thus.

gėŏl'ogy *n.* Science of the formation of the earth, the strata of its crust, and their relations and changes; geological features *of* a district. **gėŏl'ogist** *n.*

gē'omăncy *n.* Divination from figure given by handful of earth thrown down, and hence from figures given by dots made at random. **gē'omăncer** *n.* **gēomăn'tĭc** *adj.*

gėŏm'ėter *n.* 1. Person skilled in geometry. 2. One of a family of moths, caterpillars of which move by alternately humping and stretching body, as if measuring ground.

gēomĕt'rĭc(al) *adjs.* Of, according to, geometry; ~ *progression*, progression in which each term is a fixed multiple of the preceding one, as 1, 3, 9, 27; ~ *proportion*, proportion involving equal ratios in its two parts, as 1:3::4:12; ~ *tracery*: see ill. WINDOW. **gēomĕt'rĭcally** *adv.*

gėŏm'ėtrīze *v.* Work, form, by geometrical methods.

gėŏm'ėtry *n.* Science of properties and relations of magnitudes in space, as lines, surfaces, solids.

gēomŏrphŏl'ogy *n.* Study of the present surface of the earth in relation to its past history of denudation.

gėŏph'agy (-jĭ) *n.* Dirt-eating. **geŏph'agist** *n.*

gēophys'ĭcs (-fĭz-) *n.* Study of the physical constants of the earth, i.e. its specific gravity, elasticity, and internal structure. **gēophys'ĭcal** *adj.*

gēopŏl'ĭtics *n.* Study of politics of a country as determined by its geographical position. **gēopolĭt'ĭcal** *adj.*

George[1] (jŏrj), St. (d. 303). Martyr under Diocletian; in legend,

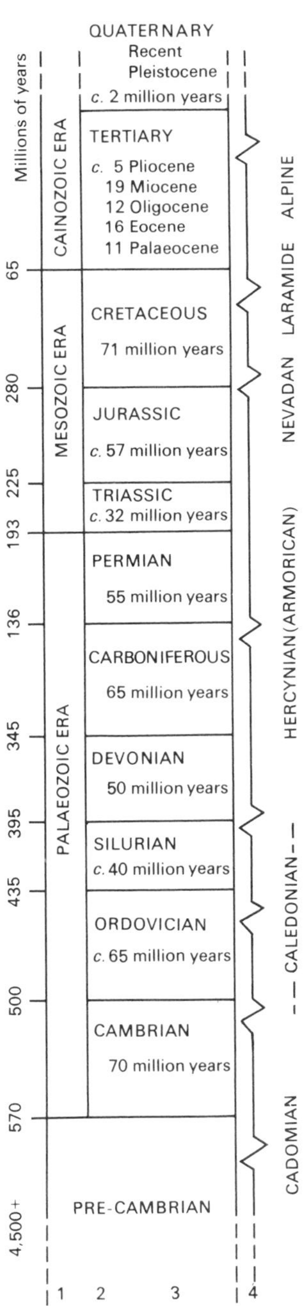

DIAGRAM OF GEOLOGICAL HISTORY

1. Eras. 2. Periods of rock formation. 3. Epochs. 4. Main episodes of mountain building

slayer of a dragon; patron saint of England from time of Edward III, who chose him as patron of Order of the Garter; hence, jewel forming part of Garter insignia; *St. ~'s cross*, vertical and horizontal bars crossing in centre, red on a white ground; *St. ~'s day*, 23rd April.

George[2] (jŏrj). Name of 6 kings of Gt Britain: *George I* (1660–1727), son of the 1st Elector of Hanover and great-grandson of James I, reigned 1714–27; *George II* (1683–1760), his son, reigned 1727–60; *George III* (1738–1820), grandson of George II, reigned 1760–1820; *George IV* (1762–1830), son of George III; Prince Regent 1811–20; reigned 1820–30; *George V* (1865–1936), son of Edward VII, reigned 1910–36; *George VI* (1895–1952), son of George V, reigned 1936–52; *the four Georges*, George I–IV.

George[3] (gā'ŏrge), Stefan (1868–1933). German symbolist poet.

George[4] (jŏrj) *n.* (R.A.F. slang) Automatic pilot of an aircraft.

George Cross, Medal. Decorations, intended primarily for civilians, for gallantry; instituted by George VI, 24th Sept. 1940 (ill. MEDAL).

georgette' (jŏr-) *n.* Thin semi-transparent crêpe of fine twisted yarn (silk, rayon, nylon, etc.). [f. name of French dressmaker]

Geor'gia[1] (jŏrj-). South Atlantic State of U.S., orig. an English colony founded in 1733 and one of the original 13 States; capital, Atlanta. [f. name of *George II* of England]

Geor'gia[2] (jŏrj-). (Russ. *Gruziya*) District of Caucasus, a constituent republic of the Soviet Union; capital, Tbilisi (Tiflis).

Geor'gian[1] (jŏrj-) *adj.* Of the time of the four Georges (George I–IV); of the time of George V–VI of Gt Britain.

Geor'gian[2] (jŏrj-) *adj.* & *n.* (Inhabitant, language) of Georgia in the Caucasus or of Georgia, U.S.

Geor'gic (jŏrj-). One of the 4 books of Virgil's poetical treatise on husbandry. [Gk *geōrgos* farmer]

gēosўn'clīne *n.* Long trough or furrow in earth's surface, usu. under the sea, filling up gradually with shallow deposits.

gēŏt'ropism *n.* Relation of plant-growth to gravity; *positive ~*, tendency (of roots etc.) to grow towards centre of earth; *negative ~*, tendency (of stems etc.) to grow away from centre of earth. **gēotrŏp'ic** *adj.* **gēotrŏp'ically** *adv.*

Ger. *abbrev.* German.

gerān'ium *n.* 1. Genus of herbaceous plants or undershrubs of temperate regions, with fruit like crane's bill; crane's-bill. 2. Cultivated plant of the S. African genus *Pelargonium*; scarlet colour of well-known kind. [Gk *geranos* crane]

gēr'falcon (-awkn, -awl-) *n.* Any large northern falcon, esp. the Icelandic.

gĕriăt'ric (g-, j-) *adj.* Of, concerning, the health of old people. **gĕriă'trics** *n.pl.* Branch of medicine, or of social science, dealing with this.

gĕrm *n.* 1. Portion of organism capable of developing into a new one; (fig.) seed, rudiment, elementary principle. 2. Micro-organism or microbe, esp. one of those capable of causing disease. 3. *~-cell*, cell in body of an organism which is specialized for the purpose of reproduction, and which, when united to one of the opposite sex, forms a new individual; gamete; *~-plasm*, that nuclear part of the germ-cell by which, according to Weismann's theory, hereditary characteristics are transmitted.

-gĕrm'an[1] *adj.* In the fullest sense of relationship; *brother-~*, brother having the same parents, 'own' brother; similarly *sister-~*; *cousin-~*, child of one's father's or mother's 'own' brother or sister.

Gĕrm'an[2] *adj.* Of, pertaining to, Germany, the Germans, their language, etc. *~ n.* Native of Germany; the language of the Germans, one of the Germanic or Teutonic group of languages, subdivided into *High ~*, the group of dialects spoken in south and part of central Germany, now the standard language of the whole of Germany, and *Low ~*, the dialects of North Germany; *~ Empire*, (1) the Holy Roman Empire (962–1806); (2) modern Germany from the time of the unification of the German states under the leadership of Prussia in 1871 to the end of the war of 1914–18; *~ measles*, rubella, a mild contagious disease resembling measles; *~ Ocean*, the North Sea; *~ sausage*, large kind stuffed with spiced and partly cooked meat; *~ script*, the angular form of handwriting sometimes used for writing German, derived from the Merovingian script based on Roman cursive; *~ silver*, a white alloy of nickel, zinc, and copper; *~ text*, (printing) the modern German type, a modification of this used in English printing for ornamental headings, black letter. **Gĕrm'anism, Gĕrm'anist** *ns.*

gĕrmăn'der *n.* Any plant of the genus *Teucrium* esp. *T. chamaedrys*, wall germander; *~ speedwell*, the blue-flowered *Veronica chamaedrys*.

gĕrmāne' *adj.* Relevant, pertinent, *to* the matter or subject. [var. of GERMAN[1]]

Gĕrmăn'ic *adj.* Of, pertaining to, the Germans; of, pertaining to, the Teutons or their language. *~ n.* The language of the Teutons, esp. in its earliest form, *Primitive ~*; the Germanic group of languages is subdivided into *North ~*, Danish, Norwegian, Swedish, and Icelandic; *East ~*, Gothic and some almost lost languages as Burgundian and Vandal; *West ~*, German, English, Frisian, and Dutch.

germān'ium *n.* Rare metallic element of greyish-white colour found in some minerals and in flue dusts from burning certain coals; symbol Ge, at. no. 32, at. wt 72·59. [L *Germania* Germany]

Germ'any. A central European State, since 1919 a republic; formerly, a confederation of German-speaking States, which in 1871 were united under the leadership of the Hohenzollern king of Prussia, who became German emperor. The *Second Empire*, regarded as the successor to the Holy Roman Empire (962–1806), lasted from 1871 until the abdication of William II in 1918; it was followed by the Weimar Republic, which was in turn succeeded by the *Third Empire* under the leadership of Adolf Hitler, 1933–45; since then the country has been divided between the *Federal Republic of* ~ in the W. (capital, Bonn) and the *German Democratic Republic* in the E. (capital, Berlin).

germ'icide *n.* & *adj.* (Substance) having power to destroy (esp. disease-)germs. **germicid'al** *adj.*

germ'inal[1] *adj.* Of germs, of the nature of a germ; in the earliest stage of development. **germ'inally** *adv.*

Germinal[2] (zhārmĭnahl') *n.* The seed month, that from 21st March to 19th April in the French Revolutionary calendar.

germ'ināte *v.* Sprout, bud, put forth shoots; cause to shoot, develop, produce. **germinā'tion, germ'inātor** *ns.* **germ'inative** *adj.*

germ'on *n.* Albacore, fish of genus *Germo*, related to tunny.

gĕrŏntŏc'racy (g-, j-) *n.* Government by, governing body of, old men.

gĕrontŏl'ogy (g-, j-) *n.* Study of old age, esp. conditions affecting the health of the aged. **gĕrontŏl'ogist** *n.*

gĕ'rrymănder (g-) *v.t.* Manipulate (constituency etc.) unfairly so as to secure disproportionate influence at election for some party or class. ~ *n.* Such manipulation. [orig. U.S., f. *Gerry*, governor of Massachusetts]

gĕ'rund *n.* 1. Form of Latin verb capable of being construed as noun but able to govern like verb. 2. English verbal noun in *-ing* when used rather as part of verb than as noun. 3. In Russ. grammar, indeclinable form of verbal participle. **gerŭn'dial** *adj.*

gerŭn'dive *adj.* Of, like, the gerund. ~ *n.* Latin verbal adjective, with same suffix as gerund, expressing idea of fitness or necessity.

gĕss'ō *n.* Plaster of Paris, gypsum, prepared for use in modelling or as ground for painting.

Gestalt (geshtahlt') *n.* (psychol.) A shape or structure which as an object of perception forms a specific whole and has properties which cannot be completely deduced from a knowledge of the properties of its parts; chiefly attrib. as ~ *psychology*, ~ *theory*. [Ger., = 'form', 'shape']

Gesta'po (gĕshtah'pō) *n.* The secret police of the Nazi régime. [Ger., initial letters of *Ge*heime *Sta*ats*po*lizei secret state police]

gĕstā'tion *n.* Carrying or being carried in womb between conception and birth; this period.

gĕstatōr'ial *adj.* ~ *chair*, chair in which Pope is carried on certain occasions.

gĕstĭc'ulāte *v.* Use expressive motion of limbs or body with or instead of speech; express thus. **gĕstĭculā'tion, gĕstĭc'ūlātor** *ns.* **gĕstĭc'ūlative, gĕstĭc'ūlatory** *adjs.*

gĕs'ture *n.* 1. Significant movement of limb or body; use of such movements as expression of feeling or rhetorical device. 2. (after Fr. *geste*) Step or move calculated to evoke response from another or convey (esp. friendly) intention. ~ *v.* Gesticulate.

gĕt (g-) *v.* (past t. *gŏt*; past part. *got*, in U.S. *gott'en*). 1. Obtain, procure, by effort or contrivance; earn, gain, win; learn *by heart* or *rote*; obtain as result of calculation; receive as gift, wages, etc.; extract by prayer, demand, inquiry, etc.; come to have; contract; have inflicted on one; receive as one's lot or penalty; procure, provide; catch (fish etc.); bring in, carry home (crop); (colloq.) corner, puzzle, catch in argument; (colloq.) understand, as *I* ~ *it, do you* ~ *me?*; (colloq., in perf.) have; (of animals) beget; succeed in bringing, placing, etc.; bring into some state; suffer injury etc. to some part of one; induce, prevail upon (person) *to* do; ~ *the best of it*, be victorious; ~ *religion*, be converted; ~ *on the brain*, be obsessed by; ~ *on one's nerves*, be irritated by; ~ *it*, be punished, scolded, etc.; *have got to*, must. 2. (intrans.) Succeed in coming or going *to, from, over, here*, etc.; (slang) be off, clear out; (with infin.) acquire habit; come to be do*ing*; become; ~ *across, over*, (slang) reach audience, be effective; ~ *better, well*, recover from illness; ~ *there*, (slang) succeed. 3. (with preps.) ~ *at*, reach, get hold of, ascertain; (slang) tamper with, bribe, etc.; (slang) attack, banter, try to impose upon; ~ *into*, (colloq.) put on (boots, clothes); ~ *off*, dismount from; obtain release from (engagement etc.); not remain on; ~ *on*, mount (horse etc.); rise on one's *feet* or *legs* to speak in public; ~ *over*, surmount (difficulty); show (evidence, argument) to be unconvincing; recover from (illness) or from surprise at; accomplish (distance, task, etc.); (slang) circumvent; ~ *round*, cajole; evade; ~ *through*, bring to an end; (of Bill etc.) be passed by (Commons, Lords, etc.); while away (time); ~ *to*, begin (business etc.); ~ *upon*, get on. 4. (with advs.) ~ *about*, go from place to place; begin to walk (after illness etc.); (of rumours etc.) be circulated; ~ *abroad*, (of rumours etc.) get about; ~ *along*, advance, meet with success, fare *ill, well*, etc.; manage *without* something; live harmoniously *together, with*; ~ *along with you!*, (colloq.) be off; nonsense; ~ *away*, escape; start; (imper.) be off!; ~ *back*, come home etc.; recover (lost thing); ~ *one's own back*, have one's revenge; ~ *down*, dismount; ~ *in*, be elected; enter carriage etc.; bring home (crop), collect (debts etc.); fit (work etc.) into given time; succeed in placing (blow); ~ *one's hand in*, become at home with some operation; ~ *off*, escape; start; go to sleep; be acquitted or pardoned, be let off *with* or *for* specified penalty; procure pardon, acquittal, or slight penalty for (person); (slang) become friendly *with* one of opposite sex; ~ *on*, don; display (pace); advance, make progress; prosper, fare; manage *without*; agree or live sociably *with*; *be getting on for*, be approaching (age etc.); ~ *out!* (imper.) be off!; nonsense!; transpire; elicit; succeed in uttering, publishing, etc.; ~ *out of*, issue or escape from; abandon (habit) gradually; evade do*ing*; elicit (information), obtain (money) from (person); ~ *out of hand*, break from control; ~ *over*, bring (troublesome task etc.) to an end; ~ *through*, bring to, reach, destination; succeed in examination; (of Bill etc.) be passed in Parliament etc.; ~ *together*, collect; ~ *under*, subdue (fire); ~ *up*, rise, esp. from bed; mount, esp. on horseback; (of fire, wind, sea) begin to be violent; (of game) rise from cover; organize, set on foot; (of laundress) dress (linen); make presentable, arrange the appearance of; make rise; produce; work up (emotion etc.); ~ *up steam*, produce enough to work engine etc.; (fig.) work oneself up into action or energy; ~ *the wind up*, (slang) begin to feel afraid. **gĕtt'able** *adj.*

gĕt-ăt'-able *adj.* (colloq.) Capable of being reached.

gĕt'-away (-*a*-w-) *n.* Getting away; esp. escape of thieves etc.

gĕtt'er *n.* (esp.) Substance inserted into vacuum to absorb stray gases exuded into it after sealing.

Gĕtt'ysburg (g-, -z-). Place in Pennsylvania, U.S., scene of a decisive battle (1863) in the Amer. Civil War, in which the Federals under Meade defeated the Confederates under Lee; ~ *Address*, brief speech by Abraham LINCOLN at dedication of the battlefield as a national cemetery, containing the phrase 'government of the people, by the people, for the people'.

gĕt-ŭp' *n.* Style of equipment or costume; style of production of book etc.

gē'um *n.* Genus of rosaceous plants, including herb bennet, *G. urbanum.*

gew'gaw (g-) *n.* Gaudy plaything or ornament, bauble; paltry showy trifle.

gey (gā) *adv.* (Sc.) Very, considerably.

geys'er[1] (gāz-, gēz-) *n.* 1. Hot spring (usu. in volcanic area) which spouts water at more or less regular intervals. 2. Apparatus for rapidly heating water for bath etc. [*Geysir*, name of a hot spring in Iceland]

geys'er[2] *n.* = GEEZER.

G.G. *abbrev.* Grenadier Guards.

Gha'na (gah-). W. African State comprising the former Gold Coast Colony, Ashanti, the Northern Territories (of the Gold Coast Region), and Transvolta–Togoland; became independent State of Ghana and member of the British Commonwealth in 1957; capital, Accra. **Gha'naian** (*or* gahnā'-), **-nian** *adj.* & *n.*

g(h)ar'ial *n.* Large harmless fish-eating saurian (genus *Garialis*), resembling alligator and crocodile but with more elongated muzzle, found in Ganges. [Hind. *ghariyāl* fish-eater]

ghast'ly (gah-, gă-) *adj.* Horrible, frightful, shocking; deathlike, pale, wan, lurid; (of smile etc.) painfully forced. ~ *adv.* (chiefly with adjs.) Ghastlily. **ghast'lily** *adv.* **ghast'liness** *n.*

gha(u)t (gawt) *n.* (Anglo-Ind.) 1. *Eastern, Western, Ghauts,* two mountain chains along E. and W. sides of S. Hindustan. 2. Mountain pass, defile. 3. Passage or flight of steps leading to river-side; landing-place. 4. (*burning* ~), Hindu funeral pyre.

Gha'zi (gah-). Mohammedan anti-infidel fanatic.

ghee (gē) *n.* Indian buffalo-milk butter clarified to resemble oil.

gherk'in (gĕr-) *n.* Young green cucumber, or small cucumber, used for pickling.

ghĕtt'ō *n.* (pl. *-os*). Quarter of city to which Jews were restricted.

Ghib'elline (gi-), *adj.* & *n.* (Member) of emperor's faction in medieval Italian States (opp. GUELPH). [It., perh. f. Ger. *Waiblingen* estate belonging to Hohenstaufen emperors]

ghōst (gō-) *n.* 1. Soul or spirit, as principle of life (now only in *give up the* ~, die); Spirit (of God), Holy Ghost. 2. Soul of dead person appearing to living; apparition, spectre; emaciated person; shadowy outline or semblance. 3. (optics) Bright spot or secondary image in field of telescope due to defect of lens; (television) faint duplicated image not coinciding with the intended one. 4. Artistic or literary hack doing work for which his employer takes credit. 5. ~*-fish*: see WRY-mouth; ~*-word*, historically bogus word arising from printer's error or popular etymology. ~ *v.i.* Act, write, as ghost (sense 4). **ghōst'ly** *adj.* 1. (archaic) Spiritual; incorporeal; concerned with sacred or incorporeal matters; ~ *father, director,* etc., confessor. 2. (As) of a ghost, spectral. **ghōst'liness** *n.*

ghoul (gōōl, gowl) *n.* Spirit supposed in Mohammedan countries to prey on corpses. **ghoul'ish** *adj.* **ghoul'ishly** *adv.*

G.H.Q. *abbrev.* General Headquarters.

ghyll (gi-) *n.* Var. of GILL[2] *n.*

G.I. *abbrev.* (U.S.) Government issue; (colloq.) enlisted man.

gī'ant *n.* 1. Being of human form but superhuman stature; (Gk myth.) one of the race of beings, sons of Gaia (earth) and Uranus (Heaven) or Tartarus (Hell) who warred against and were destroyed by the gods. 2. Agency of enormous power; abnormally tall or large person, animal, or plant; person of extraordinary ability, courage, strength, etc. 3. Large diffuse star, as dist. from DWARF. 4. *G~'s Causeway,* group of basaltic columns formed in Tertiary period on coast of Antrim, N. Ireland, once believed to be part of a road made by a legendary giant to Staffa in Western Isles of Scotland where there is a similar formation; ~*('s) stride,* gymnastic apparatus of upright pole with revolving head and hanging ropes, enabling user to take huge strides round pole. **gī'antėss** *n.*

gī'antism *n.* Pathological condition characterized by abnormal growth esp. of the bones.

giaour (jowr) *n.* (Turkish contemptuous name for) infidel, esp. Christian.

Gib. colloq. abbrev. of Gibraltar.

gibb'er (j-, g-) *v.i.* Speak fast and inarticulately, chatter like an ape. ~ *n.* Such speech or sound.

gibb'erish (g-) *n.* Unintelligible speech, meaningless sounds, jargon; blundering or ungrammatical talk.

gibb'ėt *n.* (orig.) Gallows; (later) upright post with arm on which bodies of executed criminals were hung up; death by hanging. ~ *v.t.* Put to death by hanging; expose on gibbet; hang up as on gibbet; hold up to infamy or contempt.

gibb'on[1] (g-) *n.* Long-armed tailless ape of genus *Hylobates,* found in SE. Asia (ill. APE).

Gibb'on[2] (g-), Edward (1737–94). English historian; author of 'History of the Decline and Fall of the Roman Empire'.

gibb'ous (g-) *adj.* Convex, protuberant; (of moon or planet) having bright part greater than semicircle and less than circle (ill. MOON); humped, hunch-backed. **gibb'ously** *adv.* **gibbŏs'ity** *n.*

gībe, jībe *v.* & *n.* Flout, jeer, mock. **gīb'er** *n.* **gīb'ingly** *adv.*

gib'lėts *n.pl.* Parts of goose or other fowl taken out or cut off before cooking, as liver, gizzard, feet.

Gibral'tar (-awl-). Fortified town and headland on S. coast of Spain, British possession since 1704. **Gibraltār'ian** *adj.* & *n.* (Native) of Gibraltar. [Arab. *gebel-el-Tarik,* hill of Tarik (a Saracen commander of the 8th c.)]

gib'us (j-) *n.* Opera or crush hat. [maker's name]

gidd'y (g-) *adj.* Dizzy, disposed to fall, stagger, or spin round; making dizzy; circling with bewildering speed; mentally intoxicated, incapable of attention; excitable, frivolous, inconstant, flighty. **gidd'ily** *adv.* **gidd'iness** *n.* **gidd'y** *v.* Make or become giddy.

gift (g-) *n.* 1. Giving; (law) voluntary transference of property without consideration. 2. Thing given, present, donation; faculty miraculously bestowed, virtue looked upon as given by heaven etc.; natural endowment, talent; ~ *coupon,* coupon issued with certain commodities a certain number of which entitles the holder to a free gift. ~ *v.t.* Endow with gifts; present *with* as gift; bestow as gift. **gift'ėd** *adj.* (esp.) Naturally endowed with gifts, talented.

gig[1] (g-) *n.* 1. Light two-wheeled one-horse carriage; ~*-lamps,* (slang)

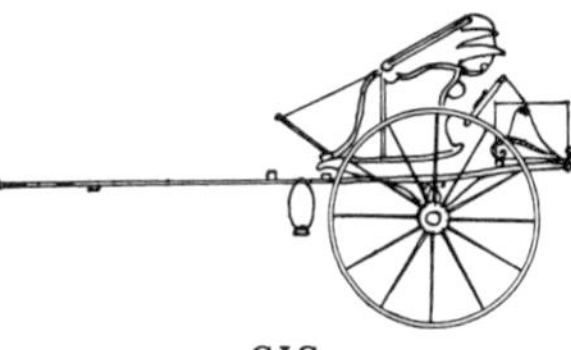

GIG

spectacles. 2. Light narrow clinker-built ship's boat for oars or sails; rowing-boat chiefly used for racing.

gig[2] (g-) *n.* Kind of fish-spear. [short for *fizgig,* f. Span. *fisga* harpoon]

gigăn'tic *adj.* Giant-like in size, stature, etc.; abnormally large, huge. **gigăn'tically** *adv.*

gig'gle (g-) *v.i.* Laugh continuously, not uproariously but in manner suggesting foolish levity or uncontrollable amusement. ~ *n.* Such laugh.

gig-mill (g-) *n.* Machine for raising nap on cloth; building in which these stand.

gig'olō (j-, zh-) *n.* (pl. *-s*). Male professional dancing-partner.

gigue (zhēg) *n.* (mus.) = JIG.

gil'bert[1] (g-) *n.* (physics) The unit of magnetomotive force in the C.G.S. system, equivalent to $10 \div 4\pi$ ampere turns. [W. *Gilbert* (1544–1603), English physician]

Gil'bert[2], Sir Humphrey (1539?–83). English navigator and discoverer; founded (1583) in Newfoundland the first British colony in N. America.

Gil'bert[3], Sir William Schwenck (1836–1911). Librettist of light satiric operas for which Arthur Sullivan composed the music. **Gĭlbĕrt'ĭan** *adj.* Of the humorously topsy-turvy kind characteristic of these operas.

gĭld[1] (g-) *v.t.* (past part. *gilded* or *gilt*). Cover with thin layer of gold laid on as gold leaf or otherwise; make reputable or attractive by supplying with money; tinge, adorn, with golden colour or light; give specious brilliance to by fair words; ~ *the pill*, soften or tone down something unpleasant; *gilded* or *gilt spurs*, emblem of knighthood; *gilded youth*, young men of fashion and wealth; *gilt-head*, various marine fishes with heads marked with gold spots or lines; striped tunny, golden wrasse, etc. **gĭld'ĭng** *n.*

gild[2] *n.*: see GUILD.

gĭll[1] (g-) *n.* (usu. pl.) 1. Respiratory organ(s) in fishes and other water-breathing animals, so arranged that venous blood is exposed to aerating influence of water (ill. FISH); ~*-cover*, bony case protecting fish's gills. 2. Wattles or dewlap of fowls. 3. Vertical radiating plates on underside of mushrooms etc. (ill. FUNGUS). 4. Flesh below person's jaws and ears. ~ *v.t.* Gut (fish); cut off gills of (mushroom).

gĭll[2] (g-) *n.* Deep, usu. wooded, ravine; narrow mountain torrent.

gĭll[3] (j-) *n.* Quarter-pint (in some districts half-pint) liquid measure.

gĭll'ĭe (g-) *n.* Highland chief's attendant; man or boy attending deerstalker or fisherman in Scotland. [Gael. *gille* lad, servant]

gĭll'ȳflower *n.* (now rare) Clove-scented pink; other similarly scented flowers, as wallflower, white stock. [OF *girofle*, ult. f. Gk *karuophullon* (*karuon* nut, *phullon* leaf)]

gĭlt (g-) *adj.* Past part. of GILD[1]. ~ *n.* Gilding; ~*-edged securities, stocks*, etc., securities etc. of finest quality, reliable, safe (not touched by market fluctuations), orig. Government stock (from being printed on gilt-edged paper); (fig.) something dull but dependable.

gĭm'bal *n.* (pl. exc. in combination as ~*-ring* etc.) Contrivance, usu. of rings and pivots, for keeping objects such as compass or chronometer horizontal at sea (ill. GYROSCOPE).

gĭm'crăck *n.* Trumpery article, knick-knack, useless ornament. ~ *adj.* Showy and flimsy, worthless, trumpery. **gĭm'crăckery** *n.*

gĭm'lĕt (g-) *n.* Small boring-tool usu. with wooden crosspiece as handle and worm at pointed end.

GIMLET

gĭmp (g-) *n.* Silk, worsted, or cotton twist with cord or wire running through it; trimming made of this; fishing-line of silk etc. bound with wire; (lace-making) coarser thread outlining design.

gĭn[1] *n.* 1. Snare, net, trap 2. Hoisting apparatus, crane; now usu. tripod with winch for winding rope; (mining) windlass, drum, etc., for hoisting, pumping, etc. 3. Machine for separating seeds from cotton. ~ *v.t.* Separate seeds of cotton with a gin.

gĭn[2] *n.* Spirit distilled from grain or malt and flavoured with juniper or some substitute; ~*-palace*, gaudily decorated public-house; ~*-shop*, dram-shop, esp. for gin; ~ *sling*, Amer. cold drink of flavoured and sweetened gin etc. [abbrev. of GENEVA[1]]

gĭn'ger (jĭnj-) *n.* 1. (Tropical plant, *Zingiber officinale*, with) hot spicy root used in cookery and medicine, and preserved in syrup or candied as sweetmeat; *black* ~, unscraped root, from E. Indies; *white* ~, scraped root, from Jamaica; *green* ~, undried root, usu. in preserve. 2. Mettle, spirit; stimulation. 3. Light reddish-yellow colour. 4. ~*-ale*, *-beer*, kinds of aerated drink flavoured with ginger; *gingerbread*, cake made with treacle and flavoured with ginger; *ginger(bread)-nut*, small round cake or biscuit of gingerbread; ~*-pop*, (colloq.) ginger-beer; ~*-race*, a root of ginger; ~*-wine*, wine of fermented sugar, water, and bruised ginger. ~ *adj.* Ginger-coloured; sandy-haired. ~ *v.t.* Flavour with ginger; put mettle or spirit into, stir or rouse *up*; ~ *group*, in Parliament, group urging Government to more decided action. **gĭn'gery** *adj.*

gĭn'gerly (jĭnj-) *adv.* & *adj.* With, showing, extreme caution so as to avoid making a noise or injuring oneself or what is touched or trodden on.

gingham (gĭng'am) *n.* Plain-woven cotton fabric of dyed yarns, often striped or checked. [Malay *ginggang* striped]

gĭngĭv'al (jĭnj-) *adj.* Of the gums.

gĭngĭvī'tis (jĭnj-) *n.* Inflammation of the gums.

gĭng'lȳmus (jĭngg-) *n.* (anat.) Hinge-like joint (e.g. elbow), with motion restricted to one plane.

gĭnk'gō (g-) *n.* (pl. *-es*). The maidenhair tree (*Ginkgo biloba*) native to China and Japan and cultivated elsewhere, with wedge-shaped leaves and yellow flowers, the only living species of the order *Ginkgoales* which flourished in the mesozoic era. [Jap., f. Chin. *yinhing* silver apricot]

gĭn'sĕng *n.* (Root of) medicinal plant (*Aralia*) found in N. China, Nepal, Canada, and eastern U.S. [Chin. *jên shên* image of man (from forked shape of root)]

Giorgione (jŏrjōn'ĕ). Giorgio da Castelfranco (1477–1510), Venetian painter.

Giotto (jŏt'tō). Giotto di Bondone (1266?–1337), Florentine painter and architect.

gĭp'sȳ, gȳ- *n.* Member of tawny-skinned black-haired wandering race (called by themselves *Rŏm'any*), perhaps orig. from India, living by basket-making, fortune-telling, horse-dealing, etc., and speaking a language related to Hindi; ~ *rose*, scabious; ~ *table*, light round three-legged table. [earlier *gipcyan* for *Egyptian* (because when the race first appeared in England in 16th c. it was believed to have come from Egypt)]

giraffe' (-ahf, -ăf) *n.* African ruminant quadruped with remarkably long neck and fore-legs, and skin spotted like panther's.

gĭ'randōle *n.* 1. Revolving firework, discharge of rockets from revolving wheel; revolving jet of water. 2. Branched bracket or other support for lights (ill. CANDLE). 3. Ear-ring or pendant with large central stone surrounded by smaller ones.

gĭ'rasŏl(e) *n.* Variety of opal with reddish glow in bright light. [It., f. *girare* turn, *sole* sun (orig. = sunflower)]

gîrd[1] (g-) *v.t.* (poet. or rhet.; past t. and past part. *girded* or *girt*) Encircle (waist, person as to waist) with belt etc., esp. to confine clothes; equip *with* sword in belt; fasten (sword etc.) on with belt; secure (clothes) on body with girdle or belt; put (cord etc.) *round*; encircle (tower etc.) *with* besiegers etc.; encircle; ~ one*self*, (*up*) one's *loins*, prepare for action.

gîrd[2] (g-) *v.i.* Jest, gibe, *at*. ~ *n.* Jest, gibe.

gîr'der (g-) *n.* Beam supporting joists of floor; iron or steel beam for like use; latticed or other compound structure of steel etc. forming span of bridge, roof, etc.

gîr'dle[1] (g-) *n* 1. Belt or (now usu.) cord used to gird waist; (orig. U.S.) corset. 2. Something that surrounds like girdle; part of cut gem dividing crown from base and embraced by the setting (ill. GEM); (anat.) bony support for upper and lower limbs (*shoulder* ~, *pelvic* ~); ring round tree made by removal of bark. ~ *v.t.* Surround with girdle; kill (tree) or make it more fruitful by removing bark in ring round trunk.

gîr'dle[2] (g-) *n.* (Sc. & north.) Circular iron plate hung over fire for baking cakes or scones, griddle (ill. FIRE).

gîrl (g-) *n.* Female child; young unmarried woman; maidservant; (colloq.) man's sweetheart (also (*best* ~); *G~ Guide*, member of an organization for girls based on principles of the Boy Scouts. **gîrl'hood** *n.* **gîrl'ish** *adj.* **gîrl'ishly** *adv.* **gîrl'ishnėss** *n.*

Gironde (zhĭrawnd'). Department of SW. France; chief city, Bordeaux. **Gĭrŏn'dĭst** *n.* & *adj.* (Member) of the moderate republican party in the French Assembly. 1791–3, whose leaders were deputies from the Gironde.

gîrt past t. & past part. of GIRD[1].

gîrth (g-) *n.* 1. Leather or cloth band tightened round body of horse etc. to secure saddle etc. (ill. HARNESS). 2. Measurement round any more or less cylindrical thing. ~ *v.t.* Secure (saddle etc.) with girth.

Gîrt'on Cŏll'ege (g-). A Cambridge college for women, opened at Hitchin in 1869 and transferred to Girton, village on outskirts of Cambridge, in 1873.

gĭst (j-) *n.* Real ground or point, substance or pith of a matter.

gĭtt'ern (g-) *n.* Gut-stringed instrument, kind of early guitar.

gĭve (g-) *v.* (past t. *gāve*, past part. *gi'ven*). 1. Bestow gratuitously, hand over as present; confer ownership of with or without actual delivery; render (benefit etc.) without payment; bestow alms or donations (*to*); confer, grant (favour, honour, etc.); accord (affection, confidence, etc.); (of God) grant; bequeath; sanction marriage of (daughter etc.). 2. Deliver, hand over, without reference to ownership; put (food etc.) before one; administer (medicine); deliver (message etc.); commit, consign, entrust; pledge, assign as guarantee (one's *word* etc.). 3. Make over in exchange or payment, pay, sell *for* price. 4. Devote, dedicate; addict. 5. Put forth (some action or effort) to affect another; deliver (judgement etc.) authoritatively; provide (ball, dinner, etc.) as host; (past part., of document) dated. 6. Present, offer, expose, hold out, show; read, recite, sing, act, perform (piece etc.). 7. Make partaker of; impart, be source of. 8. Allot, assign, ascribe; grant; assume. 9. Yield as product or result. 10. Cause or allow to have. 11. Collapse; lose firmness, yield to pressure, become relaxed; make room, shrink. 12. (of window etc.) Look, lead, (*up*)*on*, *into*. 13. ~ *birth to*, bring forth; ~ *chase*, start in pursuit; ~ *ear*, listen; ~ *ground*, retreat; ~ *place*, make room; yield precedence, be succeeded or superseded (by); ~ *rise to*, occasion; ~ *tongue*, (of dog) bark, esp. on finding scent; ~ *way*, retire; fail to resist; be superseded; be dislodged; break down; make concessions; abandon oneself *to* grief etc. 14. (with advs.) ~ *away*, transfer by gift; hand over (bride) to bridegroom; betray or expose to ridicule or detection; distribute (prizes); ~ *back*, restore; ~ *forth*, emit; publish; report; ~ *in*, yield, cease fighting or arguing; hand in (document) to proper official; ~ *off*, emit (vapour etc.); ~ *out*, announce; emit; distribute; cease or break down from exhaustion etc.; run short; ~ *over*, cease from do*ing*; abandon (habit etc.); desist; hand over; ~ *up*, resign, surrender, part with; deliver (fugitive etc.) into hands of pursuers etc.; abandon one*self to* a feeling etc.; cease to have to do with; cease from effort; devote or addict *to*; divulge (names of accomplices etc.); pronounce incurable or insoluble, renounce hope of. **gĭv'er** *n.* **gĭve** *n.* Yielding to pressure, elasticity; ~ *and take*, mutual concession, compromise, exchange of talk.

gĭzz'ard (g-) *n.* Bird's second or muscular stomach for grinding the food after it has been mixed in the first with gastric juice (ill. BIRD); thickened muscular stomach of some molluscs; *fret* one's ~, worry; *stick in* one's ~, be unwelcome or unpalatable.

glāb'rous *adj.* (anat. etc.) Free from hair or down, smooth-skinned.

glacé (-ah'sā) *adj.* 1. (Of cloth, leather, etc.) smooth, finished with a high gloss. 2. (Of fruits etc.) iced, sugared.

glā'cial (*or* -āshĭal *or* -āshl) *adj.* Of ice; icy; (geol.) characterized, produced, by the presence or agency of ice; (chem. of certain compounds) resembling ice; ~ *acetic acid*, pure acetic acid; ~

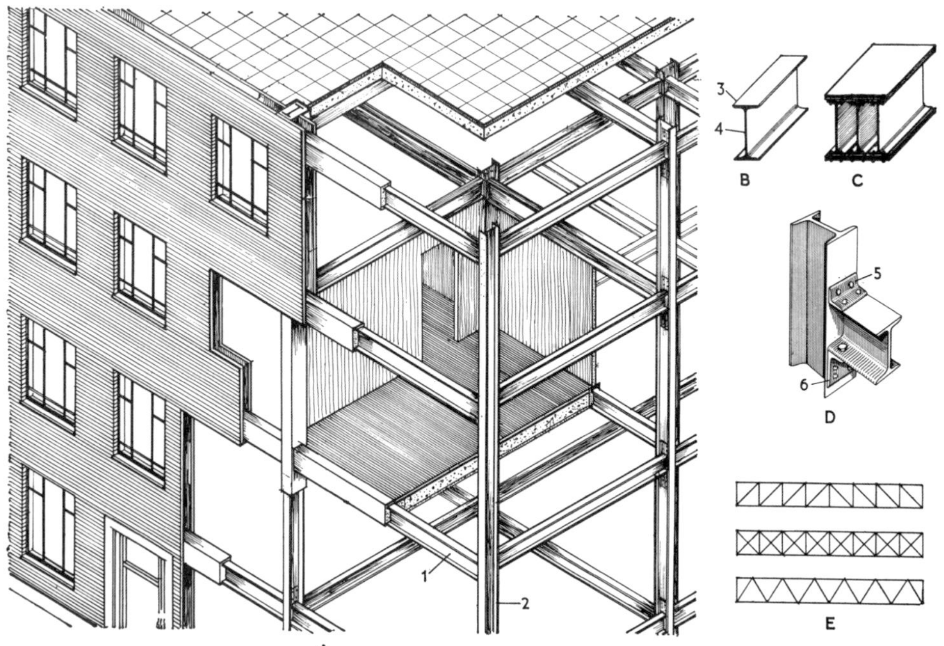

GIRDER: A. DIAGRAM OF STEEL CONSTRUCTION. B. SIMPLE GIRDER. C. COMPOUND GIRDER. D. JOINT. E. LATTICE GIRDER FORMS

1. Girder. 2. Stanchion. 3. Flange. 4. Web. 5. Angle-iron riveted to girder and bolted to stanchion. 6. Angle-iron riveted to stanchion and bolted to girder

deposit, formation laid down by the action of ice (e.g. boulder clay, moraine, kame); ~ *epoch, era, period*, geological period during which greater part of northern hemisphere was covered with an ice-sheet. **glā'cially** *adv.*

glă'ciāted (-s- *or* -sh-) *adj.* Marked or polished by ice-action; covered with glaciers or ice-sheet; **glāciā'tion** *n.*

glă'cier *n.* Slowly moving mass or river of ice in high mountain valley formed by accumulation and gradual consolidation of snow on higher ground (ill. MOUNTAIN).

glă'cis *n.* Bank sloping down from fort, on which attackers are without cover from gunfire.

glăd *adj.* Pleased; marked by, filled with, expressing, joy; giving joy; (of nature etc.) bright, beautiful; ~ *eye*, (slang) amorous glance, ogle; ~ *rags*, (slang) best clothes, esp. evening dress. **glăd'ly** *adv.* **glăd'nėss** *n.* **glăd** *v.t.* (archaic) Make glad. **glădd'en** *v.t.* **glăd'some** *adj.* (poet.). **glăd'somely** (-ml-) *adv.* **glăd'somenėss** *n.*

glāde *n.* Clear open space or passage between forest trees.

glăd'iātor *n.* Man trained to fight with sword or other weapon at ancient Roman shows. **glădiatōr'ial** *adj.*

glădiōl'us *n.* (pl. *-lī, -luses*). Plant of iris family with sword-shaped leaves and spikes of brilliant flowers; many varieties are natives of S. Africa. [L, = 'little sword']

Glăd'stone, William Ewart (1809–98). English Liberal statesman; prime minister 1868–74, 1880–5, 1886, and 1892–4; ~ (*bag*), a light leather portmanteau, hinged so as to open flat into two approx. equal compartments. **Glădstō'nian** *adj.* Of, pertaining to, Gladstone or his policy, esp. with reference to his efforts to obtain Home Rule for Ireland.

Glăgolĭt'ic *adj.* ~ *alphabet*, ancient Slavonic alphabet, largely superseded by Cyrillic but still used in service-books of Dalmatian Roman Catholics etc. [Slav. *glagol* word]

glair *n.* White of egg; kinds of adhesive preparation made from it; any similar viscous substance. ~ *v.t.* Smear with glair. **glair'ėous, glair'y** *adjs.*

glaive *n.* (archaic & poet.) Broadsword, sword.

Glam. *abbrev.* Glamorgan.

Glămōr'gan. County of S. Wales.

glăm'our (-mer) *n.* Magic, enchantment; delusive or alluring beauty or charm. ~ *v.t.* Affect with glamour, bewitch, enchant. **glăm'orous** *adj.* [variant of *grammar* in old sense of magic or necromancy]

glance (-ah-) *v.* 1. (Of weapon) glide off object instead of striking it full; (of talk etc.) pass quickly *over*, glide *off* or *from*, subject; ~ *at*, make passing (and usu. sarcastic) allusion to. 2. (Of bright object or light) flash, dart, gleam; (of eye etc.) cast momentary look, give brief look *at*; ~ *over*, read cursorily. ~ *n.* 1. Swift oblique movement or impact; (cricket) stroke with bat's face turned slantwise to ball. 2. (Sudden movement producing) flash or gleam; brief look.

glănd[1] *n.* Organ in animal body secreting the chemical compounds required for a particular function

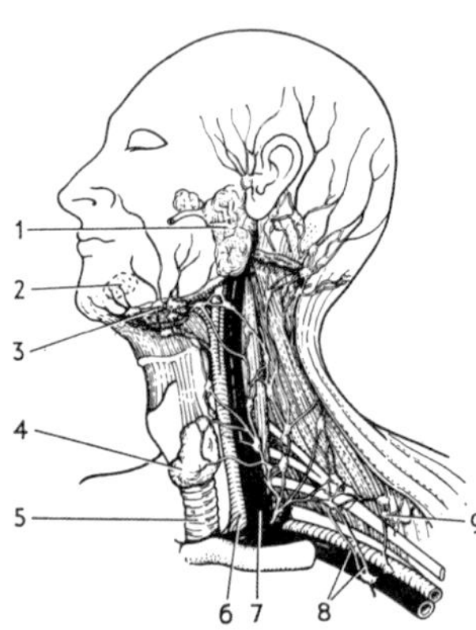

HEAD WITH MUSCLES CUT AWAY TO SHOW GLANDS

1, 2, 3. Salivary glands (1. Parotid, 2. Sublingual, 3. Submaxillary). 4. Thyroid, an endocrine gland. 5. Trachea. 6. Common carotid artery. 7. Jugular vein. 8. Lymphatic ducts. 9. Lymphatic gland

and discharging them (usu. through a duct, but cf. ENDOCRINE ~) into the body or outside it; similar organ in plant. **glăn'dūlar, glănd'lėss** *adjs.*

glănd[2] *n.* (mech.) Sleeve used to press a packing tight on a piston-rod (ill. STEAM).

glăn'ders *n.pl.* Contagious disease of horses, mules, etc., characterized by formation of nodules in lungs, liver, etc., ulceration of mucous membrane, and skin lesions; same disease communicated to man. **glăn'dered** (-erd), **glăn'derous** *adjs.*

glăndĭf'erous *adj.* Bearing acorns.

glāre *v.* 1. Shine dazzlingly or disagreeably; be over-conspicuous or obtrusive. 2. Look fixedly or fiercely (*at, upon*); express (hate etc.) by look. **glār'ing** *adj.* **glār'ingly** *adv.* **glāre** *n.* Strong fierce light, oppressive unrelieved sunshine; tawdry brilliance; fierce or fixed look. **glār'y** *adj.*

Glas'gow (glahz'gō *or* glă-). Large city in W. Scotland, situated on the banks of the Clyde; famous for its shipbuilding and engineering industries.

glass (-ah-) *n.* 1. Non-crystalline solid substance, usu. transparent, lustrous, hard, and brittle, made by fusing sand (silica) with soda or potash, or both, and usu. with other ingredients, as lead oxide; ornaments, utensils, windows, greenhouses, etc., made of this. 2. Glass vessel esp. for drinking, amount of liquid contained in this, drink; sand-glass, hour-glass; carriage etc. window; plate of glass covering picture; glazed frame for plants; looking-glass; eye-glass, (pl.) spectacles; glass disc covering watch-face; telescope, field-glass, opera-glass, microscope; barometer, weather-glass. 3. ~-*blower*, one who fashions hollow and other glassware by blowing molten glass; ~ *case*, case chiefly of glass for exhibiting or protecting objects; ~-*cloth*, linen cloth for drying glassware; cloth covered with powdered glass, used like sand-paper for smoothing or polishing; ~-*cutter*, tool for cutting glass, glazier's diamond; ~ *eye*, false eye made of glass; ~-*house*, greenhouse; (army slang) military prison; ~-*paper*, paper covered with powdered glass, for polishing etc.; *glass'ware*, articles made of glass; ~ *wool*, glass in form of fine fibres for packing and insulation; *glass'-wort*, various plants (esp. *Salicornia herbacea* and *Salsola kali*) containing large quantity of alkali, formerly burnt to provide potash for glass-making. ~ *v.t.* Fit with glass, glaze, (rare); mirror, occasion reflection of. **glass'ful** *n.* **glass'lėss** *adj.*

glass'y (-ah-) *adj.* Having properties of, resembling, glass; (of eye etc.) lacking fire, dull, fixed; (of water) lustrous and transparent, or smooth, as glass. **glass'ĭly** *adv.* **glass'ĭnėss** *n.*

Glas'tonbury (glah-). Town in Somerset, associated with Arthurian legend; site of a ruined medieval abbey; the first church at Glastonbury was supposed to have been built by JOSEPH[1] of Arimathea, whose staff, when planted in the ground, sprouted and became the ~ *thorn*, flowering at Christmas.

Glăswē'gian (-zwējan) *adj.* & *n.* (Inhabitant) of GLASGOW.

Glaub'er (-aw- *or* -ow-), Johann Rudolf (1604–68). German chemist; ~'s *salt(s)*, sodium sulphate, used medicinally as an aperient.

glaucōm'a *n.* Eye-disease characterized by increased tension and hardness of eyeball causing gradual impairment or loss of sight. **glaucōm'atous** *adj.*

glauc'ous *adj.* Of dull greyish green or blue; (bot.) covered with bloom as of grapes.

glāze *v.* 1. Fit (window, picture) with glass; furnish (building) with glass windows. 2. Cover (pottery etc.) with vitreous substance fixed by fusion; fix (colour) *on* pottery thus; overlay (cloth, leather, pastry, etc.) with smooth lustrous coating; cover (eye) with a film; cover (painted surface) with thin coat of transparent colour to modify tone;

give glassy surface to; become glassy. ~ *n.* Vitreous composition for glazing pottery etc.; anything used to produce glazed or lustrous surface; smooth and glossy surface; thin transparent coat of colour laid over another colour. **glāz'ing** *n.* ~ *bar*, bar between panes of glass (ill. WINDOW).

glā'zier (-zĭ-, -zher) *n.* One whose trade is to glaze windows etc.

G.L.C. *abbrev.* Greater London Council (1963).

gleam *n.* Subdued or transient light; faint, temporary, or intermittent show *of* some quality etc. ~ *v.i.* Emit gleams, shine with subdued or interrupted brightness.

glean *v.* Gather ears of corn left by reapers; strip (field etc.) thus; gather (such ears); collect in small quantities, scrape together (news, facts, etc.). **glean'er, glean'ing** *ns.*

glēbe *n.* Earth, land, a field (poet.); portion of land attached to clergyman's benefice.

glee *n.* 1. Musical composition for several voices (one voice to each part), usu. unaccompanied, each part being a more or less independent melody. 2. Mirth; lively and manifest delight. **glee'ful** *adj.* **glee'fully** *adv.*

gleep *n.* Graphite Low Energy Experimental Pile, used in atomic energy research.

gleet *n.* Thin morbid discharge from wound, ulcer, etc., or from the urethra.

glĕn *n.* Narrow valley.

Glĕncōe'. Valley in Argyllshire, Scotland; memorable for the massacre of the inhabitants (Macdonalds) in 1692, carried out by Campbell of Glen Lyon under the orders of William III of England.

glĕngă'rry *n.* A cloth cap, of which the two sides are stiffened and meet in a point in front, usu. adorned with ribbons at the back, originating from the Highlands of Scotland (ill. PLAID). [*Glengarry*, Inverness-shire]

glēn'oid *adj.* (anat.) ~ *cavity*, *fossa*, *surface*, shallow cavity on bone (esp. scapula and temporal bone) receiving projection of other bone to form joint.

glĭb *adj.* (Of surface etc.) smooth, (of movement) unimpeded, easy (rare); (of speaker, speech, etc.) fluent, ready, more voluble than sincere or thoughtful. **glĭb'ly** *adv.* **glĭb'nĕss** *n.*

glīde *v.* Pass, change place, by smooth continuous motion; go quietly or stealthily; pass gently and imperceptibly; pass gradually, shade off insensibly *into*; cause to glide; (of aircraft) fly without engines. ~ *n.* Act of gliding; (mus., phonet., etc.) succession of sounds, sound, made in passing from one note to another, or from one speech-sound to another. **glīd'er** *n.* Engineless aeroplane.

glĭm *n.* (slang) Lamp, or other artificial light.

glĭmm'er *v.i.* Shine faintly or intermittently. ~ *n.* Feeble or wavering light; faint gleam *of* hope etc.; glimpse, half view. **glĭmm'ering** *n.*

glĭmpse *n.* Faint and transient appearance; momentary or imperfect view *of*. ~ *v.t.* Catch glimpse of, see faintly or partly.

glĭnt *v.* & *n.* (Make) flash, glitter, sparkle.

glĭssade' (-ahd, -ād) *n.* Sliding down steep slope (esp. of ice or snow); dancing step consisting of glide to right or left. ~ *v.i.* Perform glissade.

glĭssăn'dō *adv.*, *n.*, & *adj.* (Effect produced by) sliding tip or back of finger over pianoforte keys or harp-strings, or along fiddle-string, or by 'scooping' the voice. [mock-Italian, f. Fr. *glisser* slip]

glis'ten (-ĭsn) *v.i.* Shine fitfully; glitter, sparkle. ~ *n.*

glĭs'ter *v.i.* & *n.* (archaic) Sparkle, glitter.

glĭtt'er *v.i.* Shine with brilliant tremulous light, gleam, sparkle; be showy or splendid (*with* jewels etc.). ~ *n.*

gloam'ing *n.* (chiefly Sc. or poet.) Evening twilight.

gloat *v.i.* Feast eyes or mind lustfully, avariciously, malignantly, etc., (*up*)*on* or *over*. **gloat'ingly** *adv.*

glōb'al *adj.* Of the whole of a group of items, categories, etc.; of, extending over, the whole world.

glōbe *n.* Spherical body; *the* earth; spherical chart of the earth (*terrestrial* ~) or the constellations (*celestial* ~); golden orb as emblem of sovereignty; (anat.) eyeball; approximately spherical glass vessel, esp. lampshade or fishbowl; ~ *artichoke*, = ARTICHOKE 1; ~*-fish*, tropical fish (various species of *Tetrodon*) able to inflate itself into globular shape; ~*-flower*, ranunculaceous plant, *Trollius europaeus*, with round yellow flowers; ~ *lightning*, fire-ball; ~ *trotting*, hurried travelling through foreign countries for sightseeing; hence, ~*-trotter*. ~ *v.* Make, become, globular. **glōb'oid** *adj.* & *n.* **glōbōse'** *adj.* **glōbŏs'ĭty** *n.*

Glōbe Theatre. Theatre where many of Shakespeare's plays were produced, erected at Southwark, London, in 1598.

glŏb'ūlar *adj.* Globe-shaped, spherical; composed of globules. **glŏbūlă'rity** *n.* **glŏb'ūlarly** *adv.*

glŏb'ūle *n.* Small spherical body, esp. of liquid; drop, pill.

glŏb'ūlin *n.* Protein found in animal or plant tissue.

glŏck'enspiel (-shpēl) *n.* Musical instrument, series of tuned metal bars played with hammers, or tubes played from a keyboard. [Ger., = 'bell-play']

glŏm'erule (-ōōl) *n.* (now rare) Clustered flower-head; (former word for) **glomĕ'rulus** *n.* Cluster of small organisms, tissues, blood-vessels, etc., esp. of capillary blood-vessels of kidney.

glōōm *n.* Darkness, obscurity; melancholy, despondency. ~ *v.* Look sullen, frown, be melancholy; (of sky etc.) lower, be dull or threatening; appear darkly or obscurely; cover with gloom, make dark or dismal.

glōōm'y *adj.* Dark, unlighted; depressed, sullen; dismal, depressing. **glōōm'ily** *adv.* **glōōm'inĕss** *n.*

glōr'ia *n.* 1. (Short for) ~ *Patri*, doxology, beginning 'Glory be to the Father'; ~ *tibi*, response 'Glory be to thee, O Lord', following announcement for gospel in Mass etc.; ~ *in excelsis*, the hymn 'Glory be to God on high' forming part of Mass etc., music for this. 2. Aureole, nimbus. [L]

glōr'ifȳ *v.t.* 1. Make glorious, exalt to the glory of heaven; invest with radiance; transform into something more splendid, invest (common or inferior thing) with charm or beauty. 2. Extol, laud. **glōrĭfĭcā'tion** *n.*

glōr'iōle *n.* Aureole, halo.

glōr'ious *adj.* Possessing glory, illustrious; conferring glory, honourable; splendid, magnificent, intensely delightful. **glōr'iously** *adv.*

glōr'y *n.* 1. Exalted renown, honourable fame; subject for boasting, special distinction, ornament, pride. 2. Adoring praise and thanksgiving. 3. Resplendent majesty, beauty, or magnificence; effulgence of heavenly light; imagined unearthly beauty; bliss and splendour of heaven. 4. State of exultation, prosperity, etc. 5. Circle of light round head or figure of deity or saint, aureole, halo. 6. ~*-hole*, (slang) untidy room, drawer, cupboard, etc. ~ *v.i.* Exult, pride oneself, *in*. **glōr'ȳingly** *adv.*

Glos. *abbrev.* Gloucestershire.

glŏss[1] *n.* Word inserted between lines or in margin to explain word in text; comment, explanation, interpretation, paraphrase; misrepresentation of another's words; glossary, interlinear translation, or set of notes. ~ *v.* Insert glosses in (text etc.); write glosses; make comments esp. of unfavourable sort; read different sense into, explain away.

glŏss[2] *n.* Superficial lustre; deceptive appearance, fair outside. ~ *v.t.* Make glossy; give specious appearance to (freq. *over*). **glŏss'y** *adj.* **glŏss'ily** *adv.* **glŏss'inĕss** *n.*

glŏss'al *adj.* (anat.) Of the tongue, lingual.

glŏss'ary *n.* Collection of glosses; list and explanations of abstruse, obsolete, dialectal, or technical terms, partial dictionary. **glŏssār'ial** *adj.* **glŏss'arist** *n.*

glŏssāt'or *n.* Commentator, esp. medieval commentator on Civil and Canon Law.

glŏssīt'is *n.* Inflammation of the tongue.

glŏtt'al *adj.* Of, produced in, the glottis; ~ *stop*, sound produced by sudden explosive release of breath from behind the closed glottis.

glŏtt'ĭs *n.* Opening at upper part of windpipe and between vocal chords, affecting modulation of voice by contracting or dilating (ill. HEAD).

Gloucester (glŏs'ter). City and county town of **Gloucestershire,** county of SW. England; *single, double,* ~, kinds of cheese made in Gloucestershire.

Gloucestr. *abbrev.* (Bishop) of Gloucester (replacing surname in his signature).

glove (-ŭv) *n.* Covering of leather, cotton, silk, wool, etc., for the hand, usu. with separated fingers; padded glove for boxing; *throw down, take up, the* ~, make, accept, a challenge; *fight with the ~s off,* contend in earnest. ~ *v.t.* Provide with gloves. **glov'er** (-ŭv-) *n.* Maker or seller of gloves.

glow (-ō) *v.i.* Be heated to incandescence, throw out light and heat without flame; shine like thing intensely heated; show warm colour; burn with bodily heat or emotional fervour; *~-worm,* beetle (*Lampyris noctiluca*) which emits shining green light from ventral surface of abdomen. ~ *n.* Glowing state; brightness and warmth of colour; ardour, passion. **glow'-ĭngly** *adv.*

glow'er (*or* -owr) *v.i.* Stare, scowl (*at*). **glow'erĭngly** *adv.*

glŏxĭn'ĭa *n.* American tropical plant with large bell-shaped flowers. [B. P. *Gloxin,* Ger. botanist]

glōze *v.* Palliate, explain away, extenuate; talk speciously, use fair words, fawn.

Gluck (-ŏŏk), Christopher Willibald von (1714–87). Bavarian composer of operas, of which 'Orpheus and Eurydice' is the most famous.

glu'cōse (glōō-) *n.* Dextrose, grape-sugar ($C_6H_{12}O_6$), found in some fruits, in honey, and in the blood.

glu'cosīde (glōō-) *n.* Class of vegetable substances yielding glucose on treatment with dilute acids or alkalis etc.

glue (-ōō) *n.* Hard brittle brownish gelatin, obtained from the hides, bones, and other waste parts of animals by boiling with suitable solvents, and used with water as cement; any similar substance; *~-pot,* pot in which glue is melted by heat of water in an outer vessel. ~ *v.t.* Fasten or join (as) with glue; attach tightly or closely. **glu'ey** *adj.*

glŭm *adj.* Sullen, looking dejected or displeased. **glŭm'ly** *adv.* **glŭm'nėss** *n.*

glume (-ōō-) *n.* (bot.) Chaff-like bract in spikelet of grasses etc. (ill. GRASS); husk of grain. **glumā'ceous** (-ōō-, -shus) *adj.* Of, bearing, glumes; belonging to the *Glumaceae* or glume-bearing plants, including grasses and sedges. **glu'mōse** *adj.*

glŭt *v.t.* Feed (person, stomach) or indulge (appetite, desire) to the full, overload with food; satiate, cloy; choke up, fill to excess; overstock (market) with goods. ~ *n.* Full indulgence; one's fill, surfeit; supply in excess of demand.

glutē'al (glōō-) *adj.* ~ *muscle,* one of the three large muscles (*glutaeus maximus, medius, minimus*) forming buttock and serving to move thigh in man (ill. MUSCLE).

glu'tėn (glōō-) *n.* 1. Sticky substance (rare); viscid animal secretion. 2. Nitrogenous part of flour, remaining as viscid substance when starch is washed out. **glu'tĭnīze** *v.t.* Make viscous. **glutĭnŏs'ĭty** *n.* **glu'tĭnous** *adj.* **glu'tĭnously** *adv.* **glu'tĭnousnėss** *n.*

glŭtt'on *n.* 1. Excessive eater, gormandizer; (fig.) person with excessive appetite *for* some activity etc. 2. Voracious animal, *Gulo luscus,* of weasel family but much larger, native of N. Europe, Asia, and N. America; wolverene. **glŭtt'onīze** *v.i.* **glŭtt'onous** *adj.* **glŭtt'onously** *adv.* **glŭtt'ony** *n.*

glȳ'cerīde *n.* (chem.) Ester of glycerine.

glȳ'cerĭn(e) *n.* Colourless sweet viscous liquid obtained as a by-product in the conversion of animal and vegetable oils and fats into soap; used as ointment, as vehicle for drugs, in manufacture of explosives, etc. **glȳ'cerĭnāte** *v.t.* Treat with glycerine.

glȳ'cerŏl *n.* (Name preferred in scientific use for) glycerine.

glȳ'cerȳl *n.* (chem.) Trivalent radical of GLYCERINE.

glȳc'ogėn *n.* The reserve carbohydrate $(C_6H_{10}O_5)_n$ of the animal cell, into which sugar is converted by insulin. **glȳcogĕn'ĭc** *adj.*

glȳc'ŏl *n.* Any aliphatic dihydric alcohol, esp. ethylene glycol (see ETHYLENE).

glȳcŏl'ysĭs *n.* The breakdown of sugar in the body tissues.

glȳcŏn'ĭc *adj.* & *n.* (Gk & L prosody) (Line, metre) consisting of three trochees and dactyl, the dactyl variously placed; esp. the form –⏑|–⏑⏑|–⏑|⏓ (the last trochee being cut short). [*Glukōn,* Gk lyric poet]

glȳcosūr'ĭa *n.* (path.) Condition in which abnormal proportion of sugar appears in the urine. **glȳcosūr'ĭc** *adj.*

glȳp'tĭc *adj.* Of carving, esp. on precious stones.

glȳp'todŏn *n.* Extinct S. Amer. quadruped allied to armadillos, of size of an ox, covered with carapace, and having fluted teeth.

glȳptŏg'raphy *n.* Art or study of gem-engraving.

gm. *abbrev.* Gram(s).

G.M. *abbrev.* George Medal.

G-man *n.* (U.S.) A Federal criminal investigation officer. [G = 'government']

G.M.C. *abbrev.* General Medical Council.

G.M.T. *abbrev.* Greenwich mean time.

gn(s). *abbrev.* Guinea(s).

gnarled (nârld), **gnâr'ly** (n-) *adjs.* (Of tree) covered with protuberances; twisted, rugged, knotted, like an old tree.

gnăsh (n-) *v.* Grind (teeth), grind teeth; (of teeth) strike together.

gnăt (n-) *n.* (pop.) Small two-winged biting or irritating fly; (zool.) = MOSQUITO.

gnăth'ĭc (n-) *adj.* Of jaws.

gnaw (n-) *v.* Bite persistently, wear away thus; (of pain etc.) corrode, waste away, consume, torture. **gnaw'ĭngly** *adv.*

gneiss (gnīs *or* n-) *n.* (geol.) A coarse-grained metamorphic rock in which the mineral grains are arranged in roughly parallel bands, usu. containing felspar and a dark mineral and sometimes quartz.

gnōm'ē[1] (n-; *also* nōm) *n.* Maxim, aphorism. **gnōm'ĭc** *adj.* Of, consisting of, using, gnomes; sententious.

gnōme[2] (n-) *n.* Dwarfish spirit of subterranean race guarding treasures of the earth (see also SYLPH, SALAMANDER); goblin, dwarf. **gnōm'ĭsh** *adj.* [f. mod. L *gnomus* invented by Paracelsus]

gnōm'on (n-) *n.* 1. Pillar, rod, pin, or triangular plate of sundial, showing time by its shadow on marked surface (ill. SUN); column etc. used in observing sun's meridian altitude. 2. (geom.) Part of parallelogram left when similar parallelogram is taken away from one of its corners. **gnōmŏn'ĭc** *adj.* ~ *projection,* geographical projection in which points are projected on to a tangent plane from the centre of the sphere.

gnōs'ĭs (n-) *n.* Knowledge of spiritual mysteries; Gnosticism.

gnŏs'tĭc (n-) *adj.* 1. Relating to knowledge, cognitive. 2. Having esoteric spiritual knowledge; of the Gnostics, occult, mystic. **Gnŏs'tĭc** *n.* (hist.) Member of a heretical sect of early Christians claiming to have superior knowledge of things spiritual, and interpreting sacred writings by a mystic philosophy. **Gnŏs'tĭcism** *n.*

gnu (nū) *n.* S. Afr. quadruped of genus *Connochaetes,* of antelope family but resembling ox or buffalo.

gō *v.* (past t. *went,* past part. *gone* pr. gŏn, gawn). 1. Start, depart, move, continue moving, from some place, position, time, etc. (often not specified if obvious); begin motion; travel, proceed, make one's way. 2. (Of line etc.) lie, point, in certain direction. 3. Be habitually in specified state. 4. Be moving, acting, in working order. 5. Make specified motion. 6. (Of bell) strike (hour). 7. (Of time) pass, elapse. 8. (Of coin, story, etc.) be current. 9. (Of document etc.) have specified tenor. 10. (Of verse etc.) be adaptable *to* a tune. 11. (Of events) turn out *well, ill,* etc.

12. Get away *free*, *unpunished*, etc. 13. Be sold *for* sum. 14. (Of money) be spent *in* or *on* goods. 15. Be relinquished, abolished, or lost; die (esp. in past part.); fail, give way, succumb. 16. Be kept or put in certain place. 17. Reach, extend, penetrate. 18. Be allotted; contribute, tend. 19. (Of number) be capable of being contained in another either without remainder or simply. 20. Pass into a (esp. undesirable) condition. 21. Bid, declare. 22. Phrases: ~ *it*, act vigorously or furiously; *going to*, preparing or intending to; about to; *gone*, dead, lost, undone; *gone on*, (colloq. or vulg.) infatuated with; *far gone*, in advanced stage (of disease etc.), deeply engaged or entangled; ~ *west*, (colloq.) die, be killed. 23. (With preps.): ~ *about*, set to work at; ~ *at*, attack, take in hand energetically; ~ *behind*, re-examine grounds of (decision etc.); ~ *by*, be guided by; ~ *for*, go to fetch; pass for, be accounted as; strive to attain; (colloq.) attack; ~ *into*, enter (profession etc.); frequent (society); take part in; investigate; ~ *over*, inspect details of; rehearse, retouch; ~ *through*, discuss in detail; scrutinize; perform (ceremony etc.); undergo; (of book) be published successively in (so many editions); ~ *with*, be concomitant of, be associated with; take same view as; harmonize with, match; follow the drift of; ~ *without*, not have, put up with want of. 24. (With advs.): ~ *about*, move from place to place; endeavour *to* do; ~ *ahead*, proceed without hesitation; ~ *by*, pass; ~ *down*, (of ship) sink; be continued *to* specified point; fall *before* conqueror; be recorded in writing; be swallowed; (colloq.) find acceptance *with*; ~ *in*, enter as competitor; (cricket) take or begin innings; (of sun etc.) be obscured; ~ *in for*, take as one's object, pursuit, style, etc.; ~ *off*, leave the stage; begin; explode; die; gradually cease to be felt; deteriorate; become unconscious in sleep, faint, etc.; be got rid of by sale; succeed *well*, *badly*, etc.; ~ *on*, continue, persevere; proceed as next step *to* do; conduct oneself; (colloq.) rail *at*; appear on stage; begin bowling; take one's turn to do something; (imper., colloq.) don't talk nonsense; *going on for*, approaching (time, age, etc.); ~ *out*, leave room or house; be extinguished; (of Government) leave office; cease to be fashionable; depart *to* colony etc.; (esp. of girls) leave home for employment (*as*); mix in society; (of workmen) strike; ~ *over*, change one's party or religion; ~ *round*, pay informal visit *to*; be long enough to encompass; (of food etc.) suffice for whole party etc.; ~ *through with*, complete, not leave unfinished; ~ *under*, fail, sink, succumb. 25. ~*-ahead*, enterprising; ~*-as-you-please*, unfettered by rules; ~*-between*, intermediary, negotiator; ~*-by*: *give the ~-by to* (person), outstrip, elude, or ignore him; ~*-cart*, kind of perambulator; ~*-getter*, (orig. U.S.) active pushing person; ~*-off'*, start. ~ *n.* 1. Act of going. 2. Mettle, dash, animation. 3. (colloq.) Turn of affairs, unexpected course of things. 4. Turn at doing something; attempt *at*. 5. (colloq.): *it's no ~*, nothing can be done; *all the ~*, in fashion; *on the ~*, in motion.

Gō'a. Territory on the west coast of India.

Gōanēse' (-z) *adj.* & *n.* (Native) of Goa.

goad *n.* Spiked stick used for urging cattle; thing that torments, incites, or stimulates. ~ *v.t.* Urge with goad; irritate; instigate, drive (*on*), by annoyance.

goal *n.* 1. Point marking end of race; object of effort or ambition; destination. 2. Posts between which ball is to be driven at football and other games; points won by doing this; *goalkeeper*, player stationed to protect goal; ~*-line*, line (at either end of playing-field) in centre of which goal-posts are placed. **goal'ie** *n.* (football, colloq.) Goalkeeper.

goat *n.* Hardy lively wanton strong-smelling usu. horned and bearded ruminant quadruped (genus *Capra*); zodiacal sign Capricorn; licentious person; fool; ~*-god*, Pan; *goat'herd*, one who tends goats; *goat's-beard*, the plant Jack-go-to-bed-at-noon, allied to salsify (*Tragopogon*); *goat'skin*, (garment, bottle, made of) skin of goat; *goat'sucker*, any of several nocturnal birds of family *Caprimulgidae*, e.g. nightjar (*Caprimulgus europaeus*), formerly believed to suck the milk of goats. **goat'ish** *adj.* **goat'ishly** *adv.* **goat'y** *adj.*

goatee' *n.* Chin-tuft like goat's beard.

gŏb *n.* (vulg.) Clot of slimy substance, e.g. spittle; (slang) mouth; hence, ~*-stopper*, large sticky sweet. ~ *v.i.* (vulg.) Spit.

gōbăng' *n.* Japanese game played on chequer-board, on which the two players alternately place counters and endeavour to get five in line. [Jap. *goban* f. Chin. *k'i pan* chess-board]

gŏbb'ėt *n.* (archaic) Piece, lump, esp. of raw flesh or food; lines extracted from a text for translation or comment in examination.

gŏb'ble[1] *v.* Eat hurriedly and noisily. **gŏbb'ler**[1] *n.*

gŏb'ble[2] *v.i.* (Of turkeycock) make characteristic sound in throat; make such sound when speaking, from rage, etc. **gŏbb'ler**[2] *n.* Turkeycock.

gŏbb'ledўgŏŏk *n.* (U.S. slang) Pretentious and unintelligible jargon.

Gŏb'elins (-ăn *or* -ĭn). French State tapestry factory in Paris; orig. a court furniture factory established 1667 by Louis XIV's minister Colbert in workshops previously owned by a dyer named Gobelin; first directed by Charles Le Brun; famous esp. in 17th and 18th centuries, and still functioning on the same site; *Gobelin tapestry*, tapestry made there; imitation of this.

gŏb'lėt *n.* (Archaic) metal or glass drinking-cup, bowl-shaped and without handles, sometimes

GOBLET

1. Knop

with foot and cover; glass with foot and stem, as distinct from TUMBLER, 3.; (poet.) drinking-cup.

gŏb'lin *n.* Mischievous and ugly demon.

gŏb'y *n.* One of genus (*Gobius*) of small acanthopterygian fishes with ventral fins joined into disc or sucker.

G.O.C.(-in-C.) *abbrev.* General Officer Commanding(-in-Chief).

gŏd *n.* 1. Superhuman being worshipped as having power over nature and human fortunes, deity; ~ *of fire*, Vulcan; ~ *of love*, *blind* ~, Cupid; ~ *of war*, Mars; ~ *of wine*, Bacchus. 2. Image, animal, or other object, worshipped as symbolizing, being the visible habitation of, or itself possessing, divine power; an idol; adored, admired, or influential person. 3. (pl., theatr.) (Occupants of) gallery. 4. *God*, supreme being, creator and ruler of universe; *God the Father*, *Son*, *Holy Ghost*, persons of the Trinity; *God knows*, it is beyond mortal or my knowledge, I don't know; (also) I call God to witness; *God willing*, if circumstances allow. 5. *Godfather*, *godmother*, sponsor at baptism; so *godchild*, *-son*, *-daughter*; ~-fearing, sincerely religious; ~*-forsaken*, devoid of all merit; forlorn, dismal; *god'send*, unexpected welcome event or acquisition; ~*-speed*, usu. in *wish* or *bid* person ~*-speed*, wish him success in journey, undertaking etc. **gŏd'-like** *adj.*

gŏdd'ėss *n.* Female deity; ~ *of love*, Venus; ~ *of wisdom*, Minerva.

gō'det (-ā; *or* -ĕt') *n.* Triangular piece inserted in skirt, glove, etc.

godē'tia (-sha) *n.* Genus of free-flowering hardy annuals, natives of America, with large heads of cup-shaped flowers. [C. H. *Godet*, Swiss botanist]

gŏd'head (-ĕd) *n.* Being God or a god, divine nature, deity; *the G~*, God.

Gŏdīv'a. Wife of Leofric, earl of Mercia; acc. to legend, her husband had imposed a tax on the inhabitants of Coventry which he jestingly promised to remit if she would ride naked through the streets at noonday. She took him at his word, directed the people to keep within doors and shut their windows, and complied with his condition.

gŏd'lĕss *adj.* Without a god; not recognizing God; impious, wicked. **gŏd'lĕssnĕss** *n.*

gŏd'ly *adj.* Religious, pious, devout. **gŏd'lĭnĕss** *n.*

gōdown' *n.* Warehouse in India and other parts of E. Asia. [Malay *godong*]

Gŏd'wĭn Aus'ten. Himalayan peak, also known as K2.

gŏd'wĭt *n.* Large wading bird (*Limosa*) like curlew but with bill slightly curved upwards.

Goebb'els (gẽr-), Paul Josef (1897–1945). German Minister for Propaganda under the Nazi régime.

Goethe (gẽr'te), Johann Wolfgang von (1749–1832). Germany's greatest poet, also scientist and statesman in the duchy of Weimar; author of many lyric poems, dramas, and novels, of which 'Faust', a dramatic poem, and the novels 'The Sorrows of Young Werther' and 'Wilhelm Meister' are the most famous.

goff'er, goph'er, gauff'er (gō-, gŏ-) *v.t.* Make wavy, flute, crimp (edge, trimming, etc.) with heated irons. ~ *n.* Iron used for goffering; ornamental frilled edging for bonnets etc.

gŏg'gle *v.* Squint, roll eyes about; (of eyes) project, roll about; turn (eyes) sideways or from side to side. ~ *adj.* (Of eyes) protuberant, full and rolling. **gŏg'gles** (-glz) *n.pl.* Spectacles for protecting eyes from glare, dust, etc., often with coloured glasses etc.; (slang) round-lensed spectacles.

Gōg'ol, Nikolai Vasilievich (1809–52). Russian novelist; best known for his 'Dead Souls', a picaresque romance satirizing provincial Russian society.

Goid'el. Gael, person belonging to Celts of Ireland and the Scottish Highlands. **Goidĕl'ic** *adj.* & *n.* (Language) of the Goidels.

gō'ĭng *n.* (esp.) Condition of ground for walking, riding, etc.; *goings-on*, behaviour; *in ~ order*, in condition for working properly. ~ *adj.* ~ *concern*, one in actual operation.

goi'tre (-t*er*) *n.* Morbid enlargement of thyroid gland, often visible as swelling in neck. **goit'red** (-t*er*d), **goit'rous** *adjs.*

Gŏlcŏn'da. Old name of Hyderabad, formerly celebrated for diamonds; hence, mine of wealth.

gōld *n.* Metallic element, malleable, ductile, of yellow colour and high specific gravity, occurring in the free state, not attacked by most acids, but dissolved by aqua regia, regarded as a precious metal, and used as a standard of value and as the international medium of exchange; symbol Au, at. no. 79, at. wt 196·967; coins made of this, money in large sums, wealth; the metal used for coating surface or as pigment, gilding; colour of the metal; (fig.) brilliant, beautiful, or precious things, stuff, etc.; *old ~*, (coloured) a dull brownish-golden yellow; *~ amalgam*, plastic alloy of gold and mercury; *~-beater*, one who beats gold out into gold leaf; *~-beater's skin*, membrane used to separate leaves of gold during beating, and formerly as covering for slight wounds; *~ brick*, (U.S.) something with only surface appearance of value, fraud, sham; *~-digger*, one who digs for gold; (slang, orig. U.S.) woman attaching herself to man merely for gain; *~-dust*, gold in fine particles, as often found; *~-field*, district in which gold is found; *gold'finch*, bright-coloured song-bird (*Carduelis carduelis*) with patch of yellow on wings; *gold'fish*, small golden-red Chinese fish (*Carrasius auratus*) of carp family, kept for ornament; *~ foil*, gold beaten into thin sheet; *~ leaf*, sheet of beaten gold, thinner than gold foil; *~-mine*, place where gold is mined; source of wealth; *~ plate*, vessels made of gold; *~-rush*, rush to new gold-field; *gold'smith*, worker in gold; *~ standard*, financial system of a country in which paper, silver money, etc., is redeemable on demand in gold at a fixed weight and fineness; *G~ Stick*, (bearer of) gilt rod borne on State occasions by colonel of Life Guards or captain of Gentlemen-at-arms. ~ *adj.* Wholly or chiefly of, coloured like, gold; (of money of account) reckoned at full undepreciated value according to some gold standard established at an earlier date.

Gōld Coast: see GHANA.

gōl'den *adj.* Made, consisting, of gold; abounding in, yielding, gold; coloured, shining, like gold; precious, excellent, important; *~ age*, (in Gk and Rom. poetry etc.) first and best age of world, in which mankind was ideally prosperous and happy; *G~ Bull*, medieval charter sealed with gold, esp. that issued by the Emperor Charles IV in 1356 settling precedence amongst the Electoral princes; *~ eagle*, large eagle of Northern hemisphere with golden yellow feathers on head and neck; *~ eye*, duck of genus *Glaucionetta* with black-and-white plumage in male and gold-coloured iris of the eye; *G~ Fleece*, (Gk legend) fleece of gold taken from the ram that bore Phrixus through the air to Colchis; it was placed in a sacred grove by Aeëtes, king of Colchis, where it was guarded by a sleepless dragon, until it was won by JASON; *Order of the G~ Fleece*, order of chivalry instituted by Philip the Good, Duke of Burgundy, in 1429; *G~ Gate*, entrance of San Francisco bay; *G~ Horde*, (trans. of Tatar name, from richness of Batu Khan's tent) Tatar horde which overran Eastern Europe in 13th c. under Batu Khan, grandson of Genghiz, and kept Russia in subjection until 1486; *G~ Horn*, curved inlet of Bosporus, forming harbour of Constantinople; *G~ Legend*, 13th-c. collection of saints' lives by Jacobus de Voragine, archbishop of Genoa; *~ mean*, avoidance of excess in either direction; *~ number*, number of any year in Metonic lunar cycle of 19 years (found by adding 1 to remainder after dividing number of year by 19); so called because of its usefulness in calculating date of Easter; *~ oak*, (U.S.) canyon live-oak, *Quercus chrysolepis*; (of furniture) made of light-coloured oak; *~ rain*, firework forming shower of golden sparks; *~-rod*, plant of genus *Solidago*, esp. *S. virgaurea*, with rod-like stem and spike of bright-yellow flowers; *~ rule*, the rule, *do to others as you would be done by*, the popular form of the precept in Matt. vii. 12; *~ section*, division of a straight line into two parts so that the ratio of the whole line to the larger part is the same as the ratio of the larger part to the smaller; *~ section rectangle*, rectangle whose long side is in this ratio to its short side; *~ spur*, the papal order of St. Sylvester; *G~ State*, (U.S.) popular name of California; *~ syrup*, (trade name for) pale-coloured treacle; *~ wedding*, 50th anniversary of wedding.

A B C

GOLDEN SECTION

The line is divided at *B* so that $AC/AB = AB/BC$

gōl'dĭlŏcks *n.* One who has golden hair; various yellow-flowered plants, esp. a species of buttercup, *Ranunculus auricomus*.

Gōld'smĭth, Oliver (1730–74). Irish writer; author of the novel 'Vicar of Wakefield' and the comedy 'She Stoops to Conquer'.

gŏlf (*or* gŏf) *n.* Game (usu. for two persons or two couples) in which small hard rubber-cored ball is struck with clubs over surface of course (*~-links*) into series of small holes on smooth greens, the aim being to hit the ball with the fewest possible strokes into any one hole or all holes successively; *~-club*, society for playing this game; one of the sticks with wooden or iron heads with which it is played; *~-course, -links*, the ground on which the game is played, usu. of 9 or 18 'holes' arranged at intervals on stretch of roughish ground, freq. with artificial obstacles (bunkers etc.) added. ~ *v.i.* Play golf. **gŏlf'er** *n.*

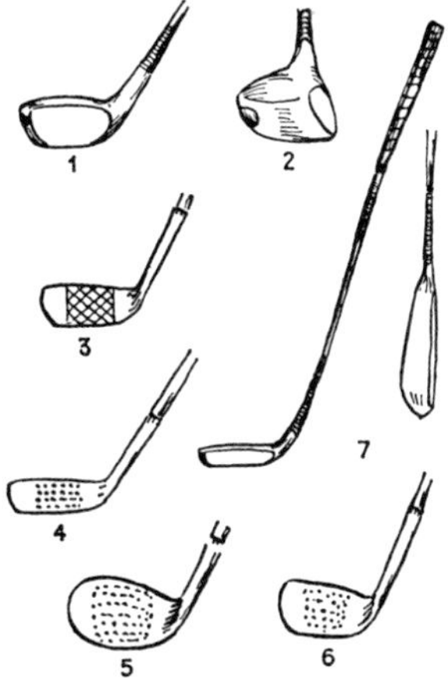

GOLF-CLUBS

1. Driver or brassy. 2. Spoon or baffy (equivalent to Nos. 3 or 4 wood). 3. Mid-iron (equivalent to No. 2 iron). 4. Cleek. 5. Niblick (equivalent to No. 8 iron). 6. Mashie (equivalent to No. 5 iron). 7. Wooden putter

Gŏl'gi body, apparatus *n.* Globule enclosed in a fatty substance, usually present in clumps in the cells of most animals and some plants and thought to be concerned with secretion and excretion (ill. CELL). [It. physician, Camillo *Golgi* (1844–1926)]

Gŏl'gotha. The hill of the Crucifixion near Jerusalem; hence, burial place, cemetery. [Heb. *gulgōleth* skull]

Golī'ath. Philistine giant slain by David: see 1 Sam. xvii.

gŏll'y *int.*, substituted for *God* in oaths or exclamations.

gŏll'ywŏg *n.* Black-faced grotesquely-dressed male doll with shock of fuzzy hair.

golosh: see GALOSH.

golŭp'tious (-shus) *adj.* (joc.) Luscious, delightful.

G.O.M. *abbrev.* Grand old man (usu. in ref. to Gladstone).

gombeen' *n.* (Anglo-Ir.) Usury; ~*-man, -woman*, money-lender.

Gomŏ'rrah (-*a*). Town of Palestine, which, along with Sodom, was destroyed by the Lord on account of the godlessness of its inhabitants (see Gen. xviii and xix); hence, (type of) wicked town.

gŏn'ăd *n.* (biol.) Sexual gland (ovary or testes or ovo-testis). **gonăd'ial, gonăd'ic** *adjs.*

Goncourt (gawnkoor'), Edmond Huot de (1822–96) and his brother Jules (1830–70). French literary critics; wrote several novels and plays in collaboration; founded a prize (*Prix* ~), awarded annually for the best imaginative work in prose.

gŏn'dola *n.* Light flat-bottomed boat with cabin amidships and high point at each end, worked by one oar at stern, used on Venetian canals; boat-shaped car suspended from airship; (U.S.) flat roofless railway car with low sides. **gŏndolier'** *n.* Rower of gondola.

GONDOLA

Gŏndwa'nalănd (-dwah-). Prehistoric land-mass that included what is now Africa, India, and Australia. [named f. *Gondwana system*, geological formation in Central Provinces of India (Gondwana, former kingdom of Gonds)]

gone (gŏn, gawn) *adj.* (past part. of GO). (esp.) Lost, hopeless; past, bygone; ~ *on*, (vulg.) infatuated with. **gŏn'er** *n.* (slang). One who is dead or undone.

gŏn'falon *n.* Banner, often with streamers, hung from cross-bar, esp. as standard of some Italian republics (ill. FLAG). **gŏnfalonier'** *n.* Standard-bearer; (hist.) chief magistrate in some Italian republics.

gŏng *n.* Metal disc with turned rim giving resonant note when struck with drumstick, used esp. to summon household for meals, and occas. in orchestra; saucer-shaped bell struck with hammer or tongue, used as alarm-bell etc.; (mil. slang) medal. ~ *v.t.* (slang, of motorized police) Order (motorist) to stop by striking gong. [Malay]

gŏng'orism (-ngg-) *n.* An affected type of diction and style introduced into Spanish literature by the poet Don Luis de Gongora y Argote (1561–1627), akin to EUPHUISM in England.

gōniŏm'ėter *n.* 1. Instrument for measuring angles in solids such as crystals etc. 2. Instrument for measuring angle of rotation of the aerial in a wireless direction finder, thus indicating direction of radio waves.

gŏnocŏc'cus *n.* (pl. -*ci*). Micro-organism causing gonorrhoea.

gŏnorrhoe'a (-*orēa*) *n.* Venereal disease characterized by inflammatory discharge of mucus from urethra or vagina. **gŏnorrhoe'al** *adj.*

Gonville and Caius College: see CAIUS COLLEGE.

good *adj.* Having the right qualities, adequate; commendable; right, proper; expedient; morally excellent, virtuous; kind, benevolent; (esp. of child) well behaved, not giving trouble; agreeable, favourable, advantageous, beneficial; wholesome; adapted to an end, suitable, efficient; reliable, safe; valid, sound; considerable; not less than (as in *a* ~ *3 miles* etc.); *as* ~ *as*, practically, almost; *have a* ~ *mind to*, be much inclined to; *have a* ~ *time*, enjoy oneself; *make* ~: see MAKE: *say a* ~ *word for*, commend, defend; *take in* ~ *part*, not be annoyed at; ~ *afternoon, day, morning, night*, forms of salutation at meeting or parting; ~ *breeding*, correct or courteous manners; ~ *fellow*, sociable person, agreeable companion; ~*-fellowship*, conviviality, sociability; ~ *for*, beneficial to; having good effect on; in condition to undertake or pay; (of draft) drawn for (so much); ~ *for nothing*, worthless, useless; ~*-for-nothing*, ne'er-do-well; *G~ Friday*: see FRIDAY; ~ *humour*, cheerful mood or disposition, amiability; ~*-humoured* (*adj.*), ~*-humouredly* (*adv.*); *a* ~ *life*, (esp.) one likely to last long, such as insurance office will accept; ~*-looking*, handsome; ~ *looks*, personal beauty; ~ *luck*, being fortunate, happy chance; *good'man*, (archaic) head of household, husband, father, etc.; ~ *nature*, kindly disposition, willingness to humour others or permit encroachment on one's rights; ~*-natured* (*adj.*), ~*-naturedly* (*adv.*); ~ *people*, the fairies; ~ *sense*, practical wisdom; ~ *temper*, freedom from irritability; ~*-tempered* (*adj.*), ~*-temperedly* (*adv.*); ~ *turn*, kind action; *good'wife*, (now chiefly Sc.) mistress of house etc. ~ *n.* 1. What is good or beneficial, well-being, profit, advantage; desirable end or object; *be any* ~, be of any use (similarly *some* ~, *no* ~); *do* ~, act philanthropically, show kindness *to*, benefit; *for* ~ *and all*, finally, permanently; *to the* ~, as balance on right side, something extra etc.; *up to no* ~, bent on mischief. 2. *The* ~, virtuous persons. 3. (pl.) Movable property, merchandise, wares; things for transmission by rail etc. (opp. *passengers*), whence ~*s station*, ~*s train*, etc. **good'ish** *adj.*

good-bye' *int.* & *n.* (Saying of) farewell. [contraction of *God be with you!* with *good* substituted on analogy of *good-night* etc.]

good'ly *adj.* Comely, handsome; of considerable size etc. **good'liness** *n.*

good'nėss *n.* Virtue; excellence; benevolence, kindness, generosity, what is good in a thing, its essence or strength; (in exclamations substituted for) God.

goodwill' *n.* Kindly feeling towards person, favour; cheerful acquiescence, heartiness, zeal; privilege granted by seller of business of trading as recognized successor, connexion of customers as part of saleable value of business.

Good'wood. Race-meeting on

course near Goodwood Park, Sussex.

gŏŏd'y[1] *n.* (archaic) Elderly woman of lower class. [for *goodwife*]

gŏŏd'y[2] *n.* (obs.) Sweetmeat, bonbon.

gŏŏd'y[3], **gŏŏd'y-gŏŏd'y** *adjs.* Primly, pretentiously, inopportunely, obtrusively, weakly, or sentimentally virtuous.

gōōf *n.* (slang) Silly or stupid person. **gōōf'y** *adj.*

gōō'gly *n.* (cricket) Ball breaking from the off, though bowled with leg-break action.

gōōn *n.* (U.S. slang) Fool; (slang) N. Korean in Korean War; (slang) German guard in P.O.W. camps (1939–45).

gōōsăn'der *n.* Duck (*Mergus merganser*) with sharply serrated bill and (in the male) glossy green-black head and back and pale pink underparts.

gōōse *n.* (pl. *geese* pr. gēs). 1. Large web-footed bird (of genus *Anser* or sub-family *Anserinae*), usu. between duck and swan in size; female of this; its flesh as food. 2. Simpleton. 3. Tailor's smoothing-iron (with handle like goose's neck). 4. *~-flesh*, rough bristling state of skin produced by cold or fright; *~-foot*, plant of genus *Chenopodium* (from shape of leaves); *~-grass*, silver-weed (*Potentilla anserina*); cleavers (*Galium aparine*); *~-neck*, pipe, piece of iron, etc., curved like goose's neck; *~-quill*, quill-feather of goose, esp. used as pen; *~-step*, balance step, practised esp. in the German army in marching on ceremonial parades, in which the legs are alternately advanced without bending the knees.

gŏŏse'berry (-zb-) *n.* (Edible berry of) any thorny species of *Ribes*; *play ~*, act as chaperon, play propriety, for pair of lovers; *~ fool*, dish of stewed gooseberries sieved and mixed with cream or custard.

gōph'er[1] *n.* 1. Amer. burrowing rodent of genus *Geomys* or *Thomomys*; *G~ State*, (U.S.) Minnesota, from prevalence of these. 2. Nocturnal burrowing land-tortoise (*Testudo carolina*) of southern U.S. 3. Large burrowing snake, *Spilotes corais*, of southern U.S. 4. Small Amer. ground-squirrel, *Citellus*. *~ v.i.* (U.S.) (mining) Dig small or haphazard holes (*~-holes*).

gōph'er[2] *n.* Tree of wood of which Noah's ark was made, supposed to be cypress.

goph'er[3] *v.*: see GOFFER.

gōr'al *n.* An Indian antelope, *Nemorrhaedus goral*.

Gōrd'ĭan *adj.* *~ knot*, intricate knot tied by Gordius, king of Gordium in Phrygia; an oracle declared that whoever loosened it should rule Asia, and Alexander the Great, unable to undo it, cut it with his sword; hence, a difficult problem or task; *cut the ~ knot*, solve problem by force or by evading conditions.

Gōrd'on, Charles George (1833–85). 'Chinese Gordon'; an officer of the Royal Engineers who commanded the Chinese forces against the Taiping rebels in 1863–4; governor-general of the Sudan, 1877–80, where he put down the slave trade; was sent by the British Government in 1884 to rescue the Egyptian garrisons in the Sudan, was besieged at Khartoum and there killed.

gōre[1] *n.* Blood shed and thickened or clotted. **gōr'y** *adj.* **gōr'ily** *adv.*

gōre[2] *n.* Wedge-shaped piece in garment; triangular or lune-shaped piece forming part of balloon, umbrella-covering, dome, etc.; (U.S.) wedge-shaped strip of land. *~ v.t.* Shape, narrow, with gore.

gōre[3] *v.t.* Pierce with the horn or (rarely) tusk.

gōrge *n.* 1. (rhet.) Internal throat. 2. What has been swallowed, contents of stomach; act of gorging; surfeit; one's *~ rises at*, one is sickened or disgusted by. 3. (fort.) Neck of bastion or other outwork; rear entrance to a work. 4. Narrow opening between hills, rocky ravine, usu. with stream. 5. Solid object meant to be swallowed as bait by fish. *~ v.* Feed greedily; satiate, glut; swallow, devour greedily; fill full, distend, choke up.

gōr'geous (-jus) *adj.* Richly coloured, sumptuous, magnificent. **gōr'geously** *adv.* **gōr'geousnėss** *n.*

gōr'gėt[1] *n.* (hist.) Piece of armour for throat (ill. ARMOUR); (hist.) woman's wimple (ill. KIRTLE); collar of beads, shells, etc., necklace; patch of colour on throat of bird etc.; *~ patch*, distinguishing mark on the collar of a military uniform.

gōr'gėt[2] *n.* (surg.) Channel-shaped steel instrument.

Gōrg'on. (Gk myth.) One of 3 sisters, Stheno, Euryale, and Medusa, with snakes for hair, whose look turned the beholder to stone; the only mortal one, Medusa, was slain by Perseus, and her head fixed on Athena's shield; hence **gōrg'on** *n.* Terrible or ugly person, repellent woman. **gōrgōn'ian** *adj.*

gōrgōn'ĭa *n.* Sea-fan, sea-plume, a kind of polyp colony, allied to corals.

Gōrgonzōl'a. Rich strong ewe-milk cheese, with veinings of bluish mould, made at Gorgonzola near Milan, Italy.

gorĭll'a *n.* Large powerful ferocious arboreal anthropoid ape, native of western equatorial Africa (ill. APE); (U.S. slang) thief using violence. [Afr. wd, = 'wild man']

Gör'ĭng (gẽr-), Hermann Wilhelm (1893–1946). German field marshal; premier of Prussia, president of the Reichstag, and Minister for Aviation under the Nazi régime.

Gōrk'y, Maxim (1868–1936). Pseudonym of Alexei Maximovich Peshkov, Russian writer and revolutionary; famous for his realistic short stories, dealing principally with thieves, tramps, and other outcasts.

gōrm'andīze *v.* Eat voraciously or gluttonously. **gōrm'andīzer** *n.*

gōrse *n.* Prickly yellow-flowered shrub, *Ulex europaeus*, common on moors, commons, etc., whin, furze.

Gōrs'edd (-ĕdh) *n.* Assembly of poets and other writers in Wales, Cornwall, and Brittany, meeting esp. during the National EISTEDDFOD.

gŏsh *int.* By God.

gŏs'hawk (-s-h-) *n.* Large short-winged hawk.

Gōsh'en. Place of light or plenty (Gen. xlv. 10 etc., Exodus viii. 22, ix. 26).

gŏs'lĭng (-z-) *n.* Young goose.

gŏs'pel *n.* 1. Glad tidings (of kingdom of God) preached by Christ; religious doctrine of Christ and his apostles, Christian revelation. 2. Record of Christ's life in books of four evangelists; any of these books; portion from one of them read at Communion service. 3. Thing that may safely be believed; principle that one acts upon, believes in, or preaches. 4. *~ oath*, oath sworn on the gospels; *~-shop*, Methodist chapel; *~ side*, north side of altar, at which gospel is read; *~-truth*, truths contained in gospel; something as true as gospel. [OE *god-spel* (*god* good, *spell* tidings)]

gŏs'peller *n.* Reader of gospel in Communion service; *hot ~*, zealous puritan, rabid propagandist.

gŏss'amer *n.* Light filmy substance, the webs of small spiders, floating in calm air esp. in autumn, or spread over grass; a thread of this; something flimsy; delicate gauze. *~ adj.* Light and flimsy as gossamer. **gŏss'amery** *adj.* [ME *gossomer*, = 'goose-summer', St. Martin's summer, i.e. early November, when geese were customarily eaten and gossamer is abundant]

gŏss'ĭp *n.* 1. (archaic) Familiar acquaintance; (esp. woman) friend. 2. Idle talker, newsmonger, tattler (esp. of woman). 3. Idle talk, groundless rumours, tittle-tattle; easy unconstrained talk or writing, esp. about persons or social incidents; hence *~-column*, column devoted to this in newspaper. **gŏss'ĭpy** *adj.* **gŏss'ĭp** *v.i.* Talk idly or lightly, tattle; write in gossipy style. [orig. = sponsor at baptism, f. *God*+*sib* akin, related]

gossōōn' *n.* (Anglo-Ir.) Lad. [Fr. *garçon*]

gŏt, past t. and past part. of GET; *~-up*, artificially produced, adorned, etc., with a view to effect or deception.

Gŏth *n.* One of a Germanic tribe who in 3rd, 4th, and 5th centuries invaded both the Eastern and Western Roman Empires and founded kingdoms in Italy, France, and Spain; hence, rude, uncivilized, or ignorant person, esp. one who destroys works of art.

Gŏt'ham (-tam). 1. Village (perh. the one of this name in Nottinghamshire) proverbial for folly of its inhabitants (*wise men of* ~). 2. (joc.) The city of New York, a name first given to it in 'Salmagundi', a humorous work by Washington Irving, William Irving, and J. K. Paulding, because its inhabitants were reputed to be wiseacres; hence, **Gŏt'hamīte** *n.* New Yorker.

Gŏth'ĭc *adj.* 1. Of, like, the Goths; hence (fig.) barbarous, rude, uncouth. 2. (archit.) Of the style of architecture prevalent in Western Europe from the 12th to the 16th century, including in England the Early English, Decorated, and Perpendicular, characterized by ribbed vaults, pointed arches, clustered pillars, etc.; of the art of this period; (printing) of the black-letter type, commonly used for printing German (ill. TYPE). 3. ~ *line*, a fortified line constructed by the Germans in Italy in 1944, extending from Pesaro westwards; ~ *Revival*, the revival in England of Gothic architecture in the mid-18th and esp. the 19th c. ~ *n.* 1. Gothic architecture. 2. The now extinct language of the Goths, one of the East GERMANIC group of languages, known from the 4th-c. translation of parts of the Bible made by Bishop Wulfila and other scattered remnants.

gŏtt'en, archaic and U.S. past part. of GET.

gouache (gōō'ahsh) *n.* (Painting in) opaque water-colour.

Goud'a (-ow-). Flat round cheese with yellow rind, made at Gouda in Holland.

gouge (-owj, -ōōj) *n.* Concave-bladed chisel used in carpentry and surgery (ill. CHISEL). ~ *v.t.* Cut with gouge; cut *out* (as) with gouge; force (*out*, esp. person's eye with thumb) (as) with gouge; force out eye of.

goul'ash (gōōl'ahsh) *n.* 1. Hungarian ragout of steak and vegetables seasoned with paprika. 2. (bridge) Deal with unshuffled cards after hands have been thrown in without bidding. [Magyar *gulyás-hús* (*gulyas* herdsman, *hus* meat)]

Gounod (gōōn'ō), Charles François (1818–93). French composer of a number of operas, of which the best known are 'Faust' and 'Roméo et Juliette'.

gourd (gōrd, goord) *n.* (Large fleshy fruit of) trailing or climbing plants of family *Cucurbitaceae*, esp. *Lagenaria vulgaris*; rind of the fruit dried and used as vessel; *bitter* ~, colocynth.

gourmand (goor'mand *or* -mahṅ) *n.* Lover of delicate fare; greedy feeder, glutton.

gourmet (goor'mā) *n.* Connoisseur of table delicacies, esp. of wine.

gout *n.* 1. Paroxysmal disease with painful inflammation of smaller joints, esp. that of great toe, and formation of chalk-stones. 2. Drop, esp. of blood; splash, clot. **gout'y** *adj.* **gout'ily** *adv.* **gout'ĭnèss** *n.* **gout'y** *n.* Kind of boot covering ankle, snow-boot.

gov'ern (gŭ-) *v.* 1. Rule with authority; conduct policy, actions, and affairs of (State, subject) despotically or constitutionally; regulate proceedings of (corporation etc.); be in military command of (fort, town); exercise function of government in person; sway, rule, influence, regulate, determine; be the predominating influence; conduct one*self*; constitute law, rule, principle, etc., for, serve to decide (case); *governing body*, managers of hospital, school, etc. 2. (gram., esp. of verb or prep.) Have (noun, case) depending on it; be necessarily followed by (a certain case).

gov'ernance (gŭ-) *n.* Act, manner, fact, or function, of governing; sway, control.

gov'ernèss (gŭ-) *n.* Female teacher, instructress, esp. of children in private household; ~ *cart*, light two-wheeled vehicle drawn by pony or donkey, with seats at sides, face to face.

gov'ernment (gŭ-) *n.* 1. Act, manner, fact, of governing; portion of country ruled by a governor, province; system of governing, form of polity. 2. Body or successive bodies of persons governing a State; the State as an agent; an administration or ministry; *form a* ~, (of prime minister) select colleagues; *G*~ *house*, official residence of governor; *G*~ *bonds, securities*, etc., bonds, exchequer bills, etc., issued by government.

governmĕn'tal *adj.* **governmĕn'tally** *adv.*

gov'ernor (gŭ-) *n.* 1. One who governs, ruler; official appointed to govern province, town, etc., representative of Crown in dominion (*G*~ *General*) or colony; executive head of any State of U.S.; officer commanding fortress or garrison; head, or member of governing body, of institution. 2. (slang) One's employer; one's father; sir. 3. (mech.) Automatic regulator of supply of gas, steam, etc., to machine, ensuring even motion; device for keeping clock-work or similar machine at constant speed. 5. ~ *general*, governor with deputy- or lieutenant-governors under him. **gov'ernorship** *n.*

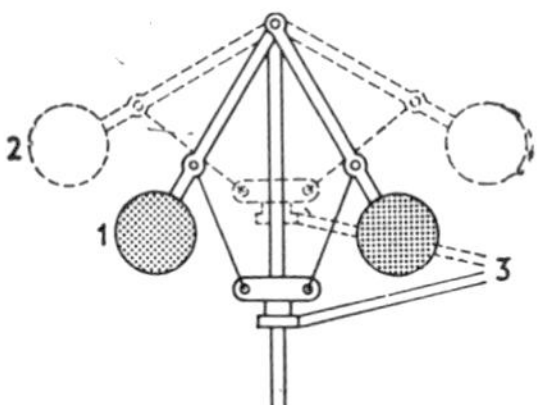

WATT'S CONICAL PENDULUM GOVERNOR

1. Slow-speed position of rotating weights. 2. High-speed position. 3. Link to control power

gow'an *n.* (Sc.) Daisy.

gowk *n.* Cuckoo (dial.); awkward or half-witted person, fool.

gown *n.* Loose flowing upper garment, esp. woman's dress (usu. one with pretensions to elegance), frock; ancient Roman toga; official or uniform robe of various shapes worn by alderman, judge, lawyer, clergyman, member of university, school, college, etc.; *town and* ~, non-members and members of university at a university town; *gownsman*, member of university. ~ *v.t.* (chiefly in past part.) Attire in gown.

Goy'a (y Lucientes) (ē lōōthĭĕn'tĕz), Francisco de (1746–1828). Spanish painter esp. of portraits; etcher of the 'Disasters of War' and other series of macabre and satirical prints.

G.P. *abbrev.* General practitioner (doctor).

G.P.D.S.T. *abbrev.* Girls' Public Day School Trust.

G.P.I. *abbrev.* General paralysis of the insane.

G.P.O. *abbrev.* General Post Office.

G.P.U. (ge-pā-ōō, jē-pē-ū). (hist.) The Soviet-Russian secret police organization which superseded the O.G.P.U.; its activities are now controlled by the M.V.D. (Ministry of Internal Affairs). [f. initials of Russ. (Obedinennoe) Gosudarstvennoe Politicheskoe Upravlenie (United) State Political Directorate]

gr. *abbrev.* Grain(s); grammar.

G.R. *abbrev.* General reserve; *Georgius Rex* (= King George).

Graaf (-ahf), Regnier de (1641–73). Dutch anatomist; *Graaf'ian follicle, vesicle*, one of the small sacs in the ovary of mammals in which the ova are matured.

grăb *v.* Seize suddenly, appropriate rapaciously; capture, arrest; make snatch *at*. ~ *n.* 1. Sudden clutch, grasp, seizure, or attempt to seize; practice of grabbing, rapacious proceedings, esp. in politics or commerce; *have the* ~ *on*, (slang) have great advantage of. 2. (mech.) Device for clutching or gripping, esp. hinged double bucket lowered by crane. 3. Children's card-game in which cards of like value may be snatched from the table and added to player's hand. **grăbb'er** *n.*

grăb'ble *v.i.* Grope about, feel for something; sprawl on all fours.

grāce *n.* 1. Pleasing quality, attractiveness, charm, esp. that belonging to elegant proportions or ease and refinement of movement, action, expression, or manner; becomingness; air with which something is done; attractive feature, accomplishment, ornament; *with a good* ~, as if willing; *with a bad* ~, reluctantly, ungraciously; *airs and graces*, behaviour put on with a view to effect or attraction. 2. (mus.) Embellishment of additional note(s) (~-*note*) not essential to harmony or melody. 3. (Gk myth.) *the (three) Graces*, beautiful sister-goddesses (Aglaia, Thalia, Euphrosyne), bestowers of beauty and charm. 4. Favour, benignant regard or its manifestation, on part of superior; unconstrained goodwill as ground of concession; boon; (in university) permission of Congregation, or of College or Hall, to take degree, dispensation from statutes; *be in person's good ~s*, enjoy his favour or liking; *act of ~*, privilege, concession, that cannot be claimed as right; *by the ~ of God*, formula appended to royal titles. 5. (theol.) Unmerited favour of God; divine regenerating, inspiring, and strengthening influence; condition (also *state of ~*) of being so influenced; a divinely given virtue or excellence, etc.; *year of ~*, year as reckoned from birth of Christ (archaic). 6. Favour shown by granting delay; mercy, clemency; *days of ~*, time allowed by law for payment of bill of exchange or insurance premium after it falls due, in England three days, *Act of ~*, formal, esp. general, pardon by Act of Parliament. 7. Short thanksgiving before or after meal. 8. *His, her, your, G~*, forms of address or description for duke, duchess, or archbishop. ~ *v.t.* Add grace to, adorn, set off *with*; confer honour or dignity on, honour *with* title etc.; do credit to. **grāce'ful** (-sf-) *adj.* Full of grace (sense 1). **grāce'fully** *adv.* **grāce'fulnėss** *n.*

grāce'lėss (-sl-) *adj.* Unregenerate, depraved; without sense of decency, unabashed; without charm or elegance. **grāce'lėssly** *adv.* **grāce'lėssnėss** *n.*

grā'cile *adj.* Slender, thin, lean. **gracĭl'ity** *n.*

grā'cious (-sh*us*) *adj.* Agreeable, pleasing (archaic); kindly, benevolent, courteous (chiefly poet.); condescending, indulgent, and beneficent to inferiors; (of God) dispensing grace, merciful, benignant. **grā'ciously** *adv.* **grā'ciousnėss** *n.* **grā'cious** *int.* (Ellipt. for ~ *God*, as) *good ~!*, *~ me!*, exclamations of surprise.

grăc'kle *n.* Various birds orig. included in genus *Graculipica* (allied to starlings etc.).

gradāte' *v.* (Cause to) pass by imperceptible degrees from one shade of colour to another; arrange in steps or grades.

gradā'tion *n.* 1. Stage(s) of transition or advance (usu. pl.); series of degrees in rank, merit, divergence, etc.; (pl.) such degrees; arrangement in such degrees; (fine arts) insensible passing from one shade, tone, etc., to another. 2. (philol.) Ablaut. **gradā'tional** (-shon-) *adj.* **gradā'tionally** *adv.*

grāde *n.* 1. Degree in rank, proficiency, value, etc.; class of persons or things alike in these; (U.S.) class at school in relation to advancement. 2. (cattle-breeding) Variety produced by crossing native stock with superior breed. 3. (zool.) Group supposed to have branched from common stem at about same stage of development. 4. (philol.) Position of vowel or root in ablaut-series. 5. (esp. U.S.) Gradient, slope; rate of ascent or descent; *make the ~*, (orig. U.S.) reach the proper standard, be up to the mark. 6. (math.) Hundredth part of right angle. ~ *v.t.* Arrange in grades, class, sort; blend so as to affect grade of; colour with tints passing into each other; reduce (road, canal, etc.) to easy gradients; (cattle-breeding) cross with better breed.

grāde'ly (-dlĭ) *adj.* (dial.) Excellent; handsome, comely; real, true, proper.

grā'dient *n.* Amount of slope, inclination to horizontal, in road etc., measured as the ratio of the difference in elevation between two points to the horizontal distance between them (so that a slope rising 1 ft per 10 ft of horizontal distance has a gradient of 1 in 10); proportional rise or fall of thermometer or barometer in passing from one region to another; ~ *post*, post beside railway line indicating gradient.

grād'in(e) (*or* gradēn'), *n.* One of series of low steps or tiers of seats; ledge at back of altar (ill. ALTAR).

grăd'ūal[1] *n.* Respond sung in the service of the Mass between Epistle and Gospel; book containing this and other music for the Mass. [so called because sung at altar-steps or while deacon mounted steps of ambo; f. L *gradus* steps]

grăd'ūal[2] *adj.* Taking place by degrees, slowly progressive; not rapid, steep, or abrupt. **grăd'ūally** *adv.* **grăd'ūalnėss** *n.*

grăd'ūate *n.* One who holds an academic degree; one who has graduated; ~ *nurse*, (U.S.) trained nurse. **grăd'ūāte** *v.* 1. Take academic degree; (chiefly U.S.) admit to academic degree; (U.S.) pass examination on completing course at high school or other educational institution; qualify or perfect oneself *as*. 2. Mark out in degrees or portions; arrange in gradations, apportion incidence of (tax) according to a scale. 3. Pass *away* by degrees; change gradually *into*. **grădūā'tion, grăd'ūātor** *ns.*

grăd'us *n.* Dictionary of Latin prosody used in schools to help in writing Latin verse. [L, short for *gradus ad Parnassum* step to Parnassus]

Grae'cĭsm *n.* Greek idiom, esp. as imitated in another language; Greek spirit, style, etc., imitation of these. **Grae'cīze** *v.* Give Greek cast, character, or form to; favour, imitate, the Greeks.

Graeco- *prefix.* Greek, as ~-*Roman.*

graffi'tō (-fē-) *n.* (pl. -*tĭ*). Drawing or writing scratched on wall etc. esp. on ancient walls as at Pompeii; decoration by scratches through plaster showing different-coloured under-surface.

graft[1] (-ah-) *n.* Plant consisting of shoot or scion inserted into a stock, from which it receives sap;

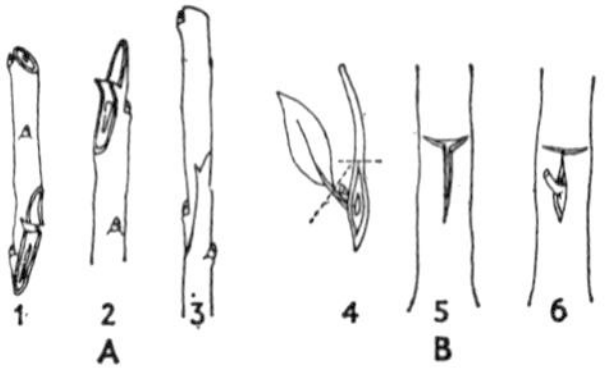

A. GRAFTING. B. BUDDING

1. Scion. 2. Root-stock. 3. Scion and root-stock joined. 4. Bud with shield of bark. 5. Root-stock with bark cut. 6. Bud inserted in slit in bark of root-stock

(surg.) piece of transplanted living tissue; process of grafting; place where graft is inserted. ~ *v.* Insert (scion) as graft; insert graft(s) upon (stock); insert graft(s); (surg.) transplant (living tissue); insert or fix *in* or *upon* so as to produce vital or indissoluble union.

graft[2] (-ah-) *n.* Depth of earth that may be thrown up at once with spade, spit.

graft[3] (-ah-) *n.* (orig. U.S.) Illicit spoils in connexion with politics or municipal business; practices intended to secure these. ~ *v.i.* Seek, make, graft. **graft'er** *n.*

Graham (grā'*a*m), Sylvester (1794–1851). Amer. advocate of vegetarianism; ~ *biscuit, bread, flour*, biscuit, bread, (made from) unbolted wheat flour. **Gra'hamism, Gra'hamite** *ns.*

grail[1] *n.* = GRADUAL[1] *n.*

grail[2] *n.* (Also *holy ~, saint ~, sangreal*). In medieval legend, the platter which Christ used at the Last Supper and in which Joseph of Arimathaea received Christ's blood at the Cross; he, acc. to one version, brought it to Glastonbury, and medieval romances tell how it was sought for by Arthur's knights.

grail[3] *n.* Comb-maker's file for smoothing and finishing teeth.

grain *n.* 1. A fruit or corn of a cereal (ill. SEED); (collect. sing.) wheat or the allied food-grasses or their fruit, corn; a particular species of corn. 2. (pl.) Refuse malt left after brewing or distilling; (also *~s of Paradise*) capsules of the W. African *Amomum meleguetta* used as spice and in medicine. 3. Small hard usu. roundish particle of sand, gold, salt, gunpowder, etc. 4. Smallest unit of weight, 1/5760 of lb. troy, 1/7000 of lb. av.; smallest possible quantity. 5. (hist.) Kermes, cochineal, or dye made from either of these; (poet.) dye, colour; *dye in ~*, (orig.) dye in kermes; dye in fast colour, in fibre, or thoroughly; *in* ~, fast dyed; downright, by nature, genuine, thorough. 6. Granular texture, roughness of surface, mottling; texture, arrangement and size of constituent particles, in flesh, skin, wood, stone, etc.; lines of rays in wood, often giving a pattern; lamination or planes of cleavage in coal, stone, etc.; (fig.) nature, temper, tendency. 7. *against the* ~, contrary to inclination; *~-leather*, leather dressed with grain-side outwards; *~-side*, (opp. *flesh-side*) side of skin on which hair grew. ~ *v.* Form into grains; dye in grain; give granular surface to; remove hair from (hides); paint in imitation of grain of wood or marble. **grain'er** *n.* **grain'less, grain'y** *adjs.*

grains (-z) *n.* Forked fish-spear or harpoon.

grallatōr'ial *adj.* (zool.) Of the *grallatores* or long-legged wading-birds (e.g. cranes). [L *grallator* stilt-walker (*grallae* stilts)]

grăll'och (-*oχ*) *n.* Dead deer's viscera. ~ *v.t.* Disembowel (deer). [Gael. *grealach*]

grăm[1] *n.* Chick-pea; any pulse used as horse-fodder.

grăm[2], **grămme** *n.* Unit of mass in metric system, weight of one cubic centimetre of distilled water at maximum density, weighed *in vacuo*; = 15·432 grains.

Gram[3] (grahm), Hans Christian Joachim (1853–1938). Danish biologist; ~, used attrib. to designate Gram's method of staining bacteria for microscopical examination; *~-positive*, *~-negative*, (of organism) that does, does not, stain by Gram's method.

gra'ma (-rah-), **grămm'a** *n.* (also ~ *grass*) Various low pasture grasses abundant in western and south-western U.S.

gramēr'cy *int.* (archaic) Thank you. [OF. *grant merci* (God give you) great reward]

grāminā'ceous (-sh*us*), **graminĕous** *adjs.* Of, like, grass; grassy.

grămm'alŏgue (-g) *n.* (shorthand) Word represented by single sign; letter or character standing for word.

grămm'ar *n.* 1. Department of language study dealing with inflexional forms or other means of indicating relation of words within sentence, and with rules for employing these (in early English use *grammar* meant only *Latin grammar*); treatise or book on grammar; person's manner of using grammatical forms; speech or writing regarded as good or bad by the rules of grammar, what is correct according to those rules; body of forms and usages in a language; elements, rudiments, of an art or science; *historical* ~, study of historical development of the grammar of a language; *comparative* ~, study of relation between grammars of two or more languages. 2. Lowest class in certain Jesuit schools and colleges. 3. ~ *school*, one of a class of (usu. endowed) English schools founded in or before 16th c. for teaching Latin, now secondary schools with a 'liberal' curriculum including languages, history, literature, and the sciences; (since Education Act of 1947) any secondary school with similar curriculum as dist. from *technical* or *modern* schools; (U.S.) department or school between primary and high schools.

grammār'ian *n.* One versed in grammar, philologist.

grammăt'ical *adj.* Of grammar; conforming to rules of grammar or to formal principles of an art; ~ *gender*, gender (found in most Indo-Eur. and Semitic languages) not determined by real or attributed sex. **grammăt'ically** *adv.*

gramme: see GRAM[2].

grăm'ophōne *n.* 1. An instrument for the mechanical recording of sounds, primarily on a wax disc, consisting essentially of a turntable (with the necessary mechanism, either clock-work or an electric motor, for turning it, and governor for keeping the speed of revolution constant) and a recording-box with needle attached held over it by a movable arm. The sounds to be recorded are conveyed to the recording-box either mechanically (i.e. in the form of sound waves) or electrically (i.e. through the medium of a microphone) and corresponding vibrations are conveyed to the needle either mechanically or by means of electro-magnets, and a record of them is thus traced on the revolving disc. 2. An instrument for reproducing sounds from 'records' (i.e. replicas in a harder material of the records made by the above instrument), consisting essentially of the same parts as the above, but having a sound-box connected with an amplifying horn or an electric 'pick-up' connected to a loud-speaker, in place of the recording-box. **grămophŏn'ic** *adj.*

grăm'pus *n.* (Popular name for) the killer whale, *Orca gladiator*, one of the *Odontoceti* or toothed whales; (also applied to) another of these, *Grampus griseus*, known as Risso's dolphin; hence, person who puffs and blows.

grănadill'a, grĕn- *n.* Various tropical species of passion-flower, esp. *Passiflora quadrangularis* or its fruit, much esteemed as dessert fruit.

grăn'ary *n.* Storehouse for threshed grain.

grănd *adj.* 1. (In official titles) chief over others, of highest rank; *G~ Duke, Duchess*, ruler of certain European countries (called *Grand Duchies*); (also, hist.) child of Tsar of Russia; *G~ Master*, head of military order of knighthood, as Hospitallers, Templars, etc.; head of order of Freemasons or province of this order, or of other societies, as Oddfellows etc.; *G~ Vizier*, chief minister of a Moslem country, esp. formerly of Turkish Empire. 2. (law) Great, principal, chief, (opp. *petty*); ~ *jury*: see JURY. 3. Of most or great importance; final, summing up minor constituents; main; (mus.) full, of full dimensions, for full orchestra, in full classical form; (in Fr. phrases or imitations) great; ~ *opera*, opera on serious theme, with music continuous throughout. 4. Conducted with solemnity, splendour, etc.; fine, splendid, gorgeous; belonging to high society, distinguished; imposing, impressive, great and handsome; dignified, lofty in conception, treatment, or expression; morally imposing, noble, admirable; (colloq.) very satisfactory; ~ *manner, style*, style and manner fitted for great subjects; *G~ Old Man* (G.O.M.), W. E. GLADSTONE; *G~ Old Party* (G.O.P.), the Republican party (U.S.). 5. (in names of relationships) In the second degree of ascent or descent, as *granddaughter, grandson*, one's child's daughter, son; *grandfather, grandmother*, one's parent's father, mother; so *grandchild, grandparent*, etc. 6. *G~ Army*, (= Fr. *Grande Armée*), Napoleon's army, esp. that which invaded Russia in 1812; *G~ Army (of the Republic)*, U.S., association of veterans of Union army or navy of Civil War, formed at Decatur, Illinois, in 1866; *G~ Canyon*, a great canyon, 217 miles long, and 5–15 miles wide, and in places 6,000 ft deep, formed by Colorado River in Arizona, U.S.; (geol.) proterozoic series between Archean and Cambrian in the Grand Canyon of the Colorado; *grandfather clock*, long-case clock, 8–day clock of kind formerly in common use, with weight-and-pendulum movement and tall wooden case (ill. CLOCK); *G~ Fleet*, during war of 1914–18, main British North Sea fleet; *G~ Monarch*, (= Fr. *Grand Monarque*), Louis XIV of France; *G~ National*, steeplechase established in 1839 and run over 4-mile course at Aintree, Liverpool, in first week of flat-racing season; ~ *piano*, large wing-shaped horizontal piano of full tone; *grand'sire*, grandfather; method of ringing changes on ring of bells; ~ *slam*: see SLAM; *~-stand*, principal stand for spectators at races etc.; ~ *tour*, tour of principal cities etc. of Europe, formerly supposed essential to education of young men of good birth or fortune. **grănd'ly** *adv.* **grănd'nĕss** *n.* **grănd** *n.* 1. Grand piano; *baby* ~, small grand piano; *upright* ~, large upright piano. 2. (U.S. slang) 1,000 dollars.

grăn'dăm(e) *n.* (archaic) Grandmother; ancestress; old woman.

grăndee' *n.* Spanish or Portuguese nobleman of highest rank;

(iron.) person of high rank or eminence.

grăn′deur (-jer, -dyer) *n.* Great power, rank, or eminence; great nobility of character; sublimity, majesty, of appearance or effect; conscious dignity; splendour.

Grand Guignol (grahṅ gēnyŏl′). Theatre in Montmartre, Paris, specializing in one-act and two-act sensational plays; hence, dramatic entertainment in which short pieces of a sensational type are played successively. [f. assoc. with *Guignol*, pop. hero of Fr. puppet theatres, and perh. f. affinity with *guignon* evil]

grăndĭl′oquent *adj.* Pompous in language; given to tall talk. **grăndĭl′oquently** *adv.* **grăndĭl′oquence** *n.*

grăn′dĭōse *adj.* Producing, intended or trying to produce, an impression of greatness; planned on a magnificent scale; pompous. **grăn′dĭōsely** (-sl-) *adv.* **grăndĭ-ŏs′ĭty** *n.*

Grăndĭsō′n′ĭan *adj.* Resembling the hero of Richardson's novel 'Sir Charles Grandison' in stately courtesy and chivalric magnanimity.

grand mal (grahṅ mahl). The major form of epilepsy.

Grand Prix (grahṅ prē). An international horse-race for 3-year-olds, run annually at Longchamps near Paris; also various motor races, as *British* ~, *Le Mans* ~, etc.

grānge (-nj) *n.* Barn (archaic); country house with farm-buildings attached.

grān′gerīze *v.t.* Illustrate (book etc.) by addition of prints etc., esp. those cut from other books. [f. James *Granger* who published in 1769 a 'Biographical History of England' with blank leaves to receive portraits or other illustrations]

granĭf′erous *adj.* Producing grain or grain-like seed.

grăn′ĭte *n.* Granular crystalline rock of quartz, orthoclase-felspar, and mica, very abundant and used in building because of its hardness and durability; *G~ City*, Aberdeen, Scotland, so called because of its many granite buildings; *G~ State*, (U.S.) popular name of New Hampshire; ~ *ware*, speckled pottery imitating granite; kind of speckled enamelled ironware.

granĭv′orous *adj.* Grain-eating.

grănn′om, grăn′am *n.* Kind of water-fly; angler's imitation of this.

grănn′y *n.* (Familiar, affectionate, or contempt. for) grandmother; ~ (*knot*), reef-knot crossed the wrong way (ill. KNOT).

grănolĭth′ĭc *adj.* & *n.* (Of) concrete made with crushed granite.

grant[1] (-ah-) *v.t.* Consent to fulfil (request etc.); concede as indulgence; allow (person) to have; bestow formally, transfer (property) legally; concede (proposition) as basis for argument; *take for granted*, assume. ~ *n.* Granting; formal conferment, legal assignment; thing, esp. sum of money, granted; conveyance by written instrument; ~-*in-aid*, sum granted, esp. by government to society or institution. **grantee′, grantŏr′** *ns.* Person to whom, by whom, thing is legally granted.

Grant[2] (-ah-, -ă-), Ulysses Simpson (1822–85). Amer. general; fought on the Federal side during the Amer. civil war; 18th president of U.S., 1869–77.

grăn′ūlar *adj.* Of, like, grains; with granulated surface or structure. **grăn′ūlarly** *adv.* **grănūlă′rĭty** *n.* **grăn′ūlous** *adj.*

grăn′ūlāte *v.* Form into grains; roughen surface of; (of wound etc.) develop small prominences as beginning of healing or junction. **grăn′ūlāted** *adj.* (of metals, sugar, etc.) Formed into or consisting of granules or grain-like bodies. **grănūlā′tion, grăn′ūlātor** *ns.*

grăn′ūle *n.* Small grain.

grāpe *n.* Green or purple berry growing in clusters on vine, eaten as fruit or used in making wine; *the* ~, wine; ~-*fruit*, small variety of shaddock (*Citrus decumana*), having a bitter yellow rind and acid juicy pulp, so called as growing in clusters; ~-*shot*, small cast-iron balls joined together as charge for cannon; ~-*sugar*, dextrose or glucose; ~-*vine*, vine bearing grapes; (colloq., orig. U.S.) routes by which rumours pass.

grăph (*or* -ahf) *n.* Diagram representing the relation between two variable quantities by the distance of a series of points (or a curve or other line joining these) from axes of reference, which are usu. at right angles to each other; the abscissa of any point corresponding to the value of one variable and the ordinate to that of the other. [abbrev. of *graphic formula*]

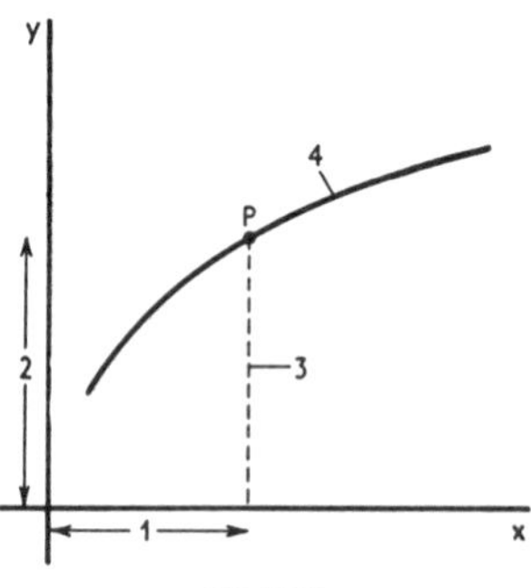

GRAPH

1. x coordinate or abscissa. 2. y coordinate. 3. Ordinate of point *P*. 4. Graph

grăph′ĭc *adj.* Of drawing, painting, engraving, etching, etc.; vividly descriptive, lifelike; of writing; (of minerals) showing marks like writing on surface or in fractures; of diagrams, linear figures, or symbolic curves; ~ *arts*, the reproductive arts of engraving, etching, woodcut, lithography, etc. **grăph′ĭcal** *adj.* (rare). **grăph′ĭcally** *adv.*

grăph′īte *n.* A crystalline allotropic form of carbon, used in pencils, as solid lubricant etc.; black lead, plumbago. **graphĭt′ĭc** *adj.*

graphŏl′ogy *n.* 1. System of graphic formulae, notation for graphs. 2. Study of, art of, inferring character from, handwriting, whence **graphŏl′ogist** *n.* **grăpholŏ′gical** *adj.*

grăp′nel *n.* Iron-clawed instrument thrown with rope to seize object, esp. enemy's ship; small anchor with several flukes, used for boats and balloons.

grăp′ple *n.* Clutching-instrument, grapnel; hold or grip (as) of wrestlers, close contest. ~ *v.* Seize, fasten, (as) with grapnel; take hold of, grip, with the hands, come to close quarters with; contend in close fight, struggle *with*; ~ *with*, try to overcome, accomplish, or deal with; *grappling-iron*: = GRAPNEL.

grăp′tolīte *n.* Marine organism of an extinct group whose remains are found in Lower Palaeozoic rocks and resemble primitive writing.

grasp (-ah-) *v.* Clutch *at*, try to seize; seize and hold firmly with hand; get mental hold of, comprehend. ~ *n.* Fast hold, grip; control, mastery; mental hold, comprehensiveness of mind. **grasp′ing** *adj.* (esp.) Greedy, avaricious. **grasp′ingly** *adv.*

grass (-ah-) *n.* Herbage in general, blades or leaves and stalks of which are eaten by horses, cattle, etc.; a kind of this, plant belonging to the order *Gramineae* (in bot. use including, in popular use excluding, the cereals, reeds, and bamboos); grazing, pasture; pasture land; grass-covered ground, lawn, grass border; ~-*cloth*, fine light linen-like cloth of fibres of inner bark of ~-*cloth plant*, *Boehmeria nivea*; thick vegetable-fibre cloth of Canary Islands; *grass′hopper*, orthopterous insect (of families *Tettigoniidae* and *Locustidae*) with remarkable powers of leaping and producing a shrill chirping noise by rubbing the fore-wings with the hind-legs; *grass′lands*, areas where light rainfall allows grass to grow but not forest; ~-*snake*, harmless common ringed snake, *Tropidonotus natrix*; common green snake of U.S. (*Tropidonotus ordinatus*); ~ *widow*, married woman whose husband is absent. **grass′lėss, grass′y** *adjs.* **grass** *v.t.* Cover with turf; lay (flax etc.) on grass to bleach; knock down, fell (opponent); bring (fish) to bank, (shot bird or animal) to ground.

grāte[1] *n.* Grating (now rare);

frame of metal bars for holding fuel in fire-place or furnace (ill. FIRE); fire-place.

grāte[2] *v.* Reduce to small particles by rubbing on rough surface; have irritating effect (*up*)*on*; grind (teeth); rub with harsh scraping noise *against*, (*up*)*on* something else; sound harshly or discordantly; (of hinge etc.) creak. **grāt'er** *n.* Utensil for grating cheese, vegetables, etc. **grāt'ĭngly** *adv.*

grāte'ful (-tf-) *adj.* Acceptable, comforting, refreshing; thankful, feeling or showing gratitude. **grāte'fully** *adv.* **grāte'fulnėss** *n.*

grăt'ĭfȳ *v.t.* 1. (archaic) Remunerate; make present to; bribe. 2. Please, satisfy, oblige, delight; please by compliance, assent to wish of; give free course to, indulge in (desire, feeling, impulse). **grătĭfĭcā'tion** *n.* **grăt'ĭfȳĭng** *adj.* **grăt'ĭfȳĭngly** *adv.*

grătin (-tăṅ) *n.* Dish baked with covering of bread-crumbs, grated cheese, etc.; *au gratin*, so prepared. [Fr.]

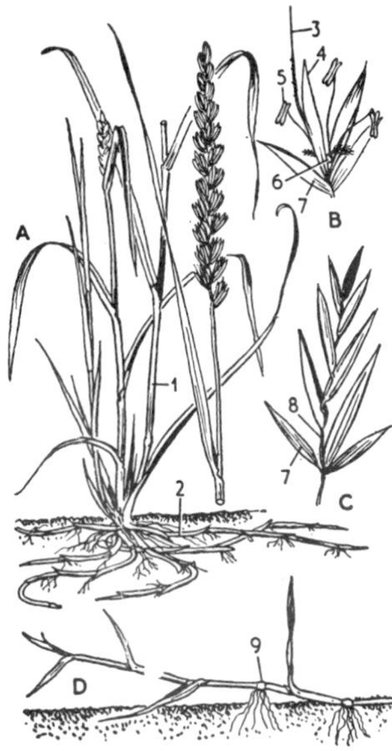

GRASS: A. COUCH-GRASS. B. FLOWER. C. 7-FLOWERED SPIKELET. D. STOLON

1. Culm. 2. Rhizome. 3. Awn. 4. Palea. 5. Anther. 6. Ovary. 7. Glume. 8. Rachis. 9. Node

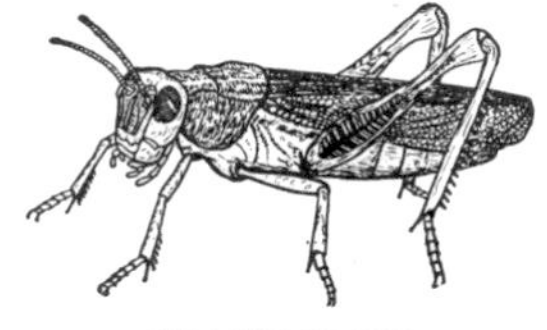

GRASSHOPPER

grāt'ĭng *n.* Framework of parallel or crossed wooden or metal bars; (optics) arrangement of parallel wires, surface of glass, etc., ruled with parallel lines, for producing spectra by diffraction.

grāt'is *adv.* & *adj.* Gratuitous(ly), (given, done) for nothing, without charge, free.

grăt'ĭtūde *n.* Being thankful, appreciation of and inclination to return kindness.

gratū'ĭtous *adj.* Got or given free, not earned or paid for; uncalled for, unwarranted, motiveless, done or acting without good or assignable reason. **gratū'ĭtously** *adv.* **gratū'ĭtousnėss** *n.*

gratū'ity *n.* Money present (amount depending on inclination of giver), in recognition of services of inferior, tip; bounty given to soldiers on discharge, retirement, etc.

grăt'ūlatory *adj.* Expressing joy at another's success etc., congratulatory.

gravām'ĕn *n.* (pl. *-mina*). 1. Grievance; (eccles.) memorial from Lower House of Convocation to Upper on disorders or grievances of Church. 2. Essence, worst part, *of* accusation.

grāve[1] *n.* Excavation to receive corpse, mound or monument over it; being dead, death, Hades; receptacle of or for what is dead; ~-*clothes*, wrappings in which corpse is buried; *grave'stone*, stone over grave, inscribed stone at head or foot of grave; *grave'yard*, burial ground. ~ *v.t.* (past part. *-n*, *-d*) 1. (archaic) Bury. 2. Carve, sculpture, engrave (archaic); (fig.) fix indelibly (*on*, *in*, mind etc.); *graven image*, idol.

grāve[2] *adj.* 1. Important, weighty, needing serious thought; (of faults, responsibilities, difficulties, etc.) serious, formidable; dignified, solemn, slow-moving, not gay; sombre, plain, not showy. 2. (Of sounds) low in pitch, deep in tone; ~ *accent*: see ACCENT. **grāve'ly** (-vl-) *adv.* **grāve** *n.* Grave accent.

grāve[3] *v.t.* Clean (ship's wooden bottom) by burning off accretions and tarring while aground or in *graving-dock* or dry dock.

grăv'el *n.* 1. Coarse sand and small water-worn stones, freq. with slight intermixture of clay, much used for laying paths and roads; (geol.) unconsolidated deposit of pebbles. 2. (path.) (Disease with) aggregations of urinary crystals recognizable as masses by naked eye. **grăv'elly** *adj.* **grăv'el** *v.t.* 1. Lay, strew, with gravel. 2. Perplex, puzzle, nonplus.

grāv'er *n.* (esp.) Engraving tool, burin (ill. ENGRAVE).

Graves (grahv). Light usu. white wine from Graves district. [Fr., gravelly sandy parts of Bordeaux country]

Grāves' disease. (med.) Exophthalmic goitre (primary thyrotoxicosis), disease characterized by enlargement of the thyroid gland and protrusion of the eyeballs; also called Basedow's disease. [R. J. *Graves* (1796–1853), Irish physician]

grăv'ĭd *adj.* Pregnant.

grăv'ĭtāte *v.* Move or tend by force of gravity *towards* a body; sink (as) by gravity, tend to low level, settle down; cause to sink by gravitation, esp. in diamond-digging, manipulate (gravel) after washing so that heavy stones sink to bottom; (transf.) be strongly attracted *to*(*wards*) some centre of influence.

grăvĭtā'tion *n.* Falling of bodies to earth, or sinking to lowest level, moving or tending to centre of attraction; tendency of every particle of matter towards every other particle, of which fall of bodies to earth is an instance; *law of* ~, law (formulated by Sir Isaac Newton) according to which the attractive force of bodies varies directly as their masses and inversely as the square of the distance between them. **grăvĭtā'tional** (-shon-) *adj.*

grăv'ĭty *n.* 1. Being grave, solemnity; importance, seriousness; staidness, sobriety, serious demeanour. 2. Weight; *specific* ~, relative weight of any kind of matter, expressed by ratio of weight of given volume to weight of equal volume of some substance taken as standard (usu. water for liquids and solids, hydrogen or air for gases). 3. Attractive force by which all bodies tend to move towards centre of earth, degree of intensity with which body in given position is affected by this, measured by amount of acceleration produced; degree of intensity with which any body is similarly attracted by any other.

gravūre' *n.* (Short for) PHOTOGRAVURE.

grāv'y *n.* Fat and juices exuding from flesh during and after cooking; dressing for meat etc. made from these with condiments etc.; ~-*boat*, boat-shaped vessel for gravy.

gray[1]**:** see GREY.

Gray[2], Thomas (1716–71). English poet; author of 'Elegy in a Country Churchyard', 'On a Distant Prospect of Eton College', etc.

gray'lĭng *n.* 1. Silver-grey freshwater fish (*Thymallus*) of salmon family, with long high dorsal fin. 2. Common butterfly (*Eumenes semele*) with grey underside to wings.

graywacke: see GREYWACKE.

grāze[1] *v.* Feed (esp. cattle, or *v.i.* of cattle) on growing grass etc.; feed on (grass etc.); tend grazing cattle; pasture cattle.

grāze[2] *v.* Touch lightly in passing; abrade (skin etc.) in rubbing past; suffer slight abrasion of (part of body); go with passing contact *against*, *through*, *by*, etc. ~ *n.* Grazing; abrasion caused by grazing.

grā'zier (-zher) *n.* One who feeds cattle for market.

grease (-s) *n.* Fat of deer or other game; melted fat of dead animals, esp. when soft; oily or fatty matter, esp. as lubricant; oily matter in wool, uncleansed wool; *~-gun*, kind of pump for lubricating parts of machinery with grease; *~-paint*, composition for painting actors' faces etc. ~ (-s *or* -z) *v.t.* Anoint, soil, or lubricate, with grease; *~ palm of*, bribe; *like greased lightning*, (slang) very fast.

greas'er (*or* -z-) *n.* (esp.) Ship's fireman; one who cleans and lubricates machinery etc. with grease; (U.S. colloq.) native Mexican, Spanish-American.

greas'y (*or* -zĭ) *adj.* Smeared or covered with, containing, made of, like, with too much, grease; (of wool) uncleansed; slimy or slippery with mud, moisture, etc.; (of manners or expression) disagreeably unctuous. **greas'ily** *adv.* **greas'iness** *n.*

great (grāt) *adj.* 1. Large, big, (usu. with implied surprise, contempt, indignation, etc.; freq. preceding partly synonymous adj., as *~ big*, *~ thick*, etc.); (of animal etc., species or variety) larger than others; (of letter) capital; (of part of building etc.) main, principal; (of qualities, emotions, etc.) beyond the ordinary in degree or extent; *the ~ majority*, much the larger part. 2. Important, elevated, distinguished, *the* chief, pre-eminent; *the ~ world*, high society; *the Great* (following proper name), the most famous of the name, one of the great men of history. 3. Of remarkable ability, genius, intellectual or practical qualities, loftiness or integrity of character; fully deserving the name of, (with agent-nouns) doing the act much or on a large scale, as *a ~ fiasco*, *a ~ scoundrel*; (colloq. & U.S.) highly satisfactory, fine, magnificent; (predic.) having much skill *at* or information *on*. 4. (with terms denoting kinship, esp. with compounds of *grand*) One degree farther removed in ascending or descending relationship; a *~-aunt*, father's or mother's aunt; *~-grandmother*, grandmother's or grandfather's mother; *great-great-grandfather*, mother's or father's great-grandfather. 5. *G~ Assize*, Day of Judgement; *G~ Bible*, Coverdale's English version (1539); sometimes also, revised versions of this, esp. Cranmer's (1540); *G~ Britain*, England, Scotland, and Wales; *~ circle*: see CIRCLE; *great'-coat*, large heavy overcoat, top-coat; *the G~ Commoner*, the elder William PITT; *~ Dane*, very large smooth-haired dog, allied to the mastiff; *G~ Divide*, the watershed of the Rocky Mountains; *G~ Elector*, Frederick William, Elector of Brandenburg (1620–88); *G~ Fire*, the fire which in Sept. 1666 destroyed most of London; *~ house*, chief house in village etc.; *G~ Lakes*, the large lakes (Superior, Michigan, Huron, Erie, and Ontario), which, except for Michigan, which is in U.S., lie along the frontier between Canada and U.S.; *~ organ*: see ORGAN; *G~ Plague*: see PLAGUE; *~ power*, one of the States exerting through political and military power the chief influence in international relations; *~ primer*, size of type, between English and canon (18-point); *G~ Rebellion*, (Engl. hist.) the Civil War (1642–9), *G~ Seal*: see SEAL². *G~ Spirit*, supreme deity of N. Amer. Indians; *~ stave*: see STAVE; *~ toe*, big toe; *G~ War*, war which began on 28th July 1914 with hostilities between Austria-Hungary and Serbia, ultimately involved most of the nations of the world, and was suspended by armistice 11th Nov. 1918. **great'ness** *n.* **great** *n.* 1. (sing.) What is great; (pl.) great persons. 2. *Greats*, B.A. examination at Oxford, esp. that for honours in classical studies and philosophy (Lit. Hum.).

great'ly (grāt-) *adv.* 1. Much, by much. 2. Nobly, loftily.

greave *n.* (usu. pl.) Piece(s) of armour for shin(s) (ill. ARMOUR).

greaves (-vz) *n.pl.* Fibrous matter or skin found in animal fat, forming sediment on melting and used for feeding dogs etc., or as fish-bait; tallow-refuse; cracklings.

grēbe *n.* Kinds of short-bodied almost tailless diving-birds (of genus *Podiceps* or family *Podicepedidae*), with flattened and lobed

GREAT CRESTED GREBE
Length 17 in.

feet set far behind; *great crested ~*, largest European species, *P. cristatus*.

Grē'cian (-shn) *adj.* Greek, Hellenic (rare except of architecture and facial outline); *~ bend*, stooping attitude, supposed to imitate that of Venus de Milo, affected by some women in the late 19th c.; *~ knot*, woman's coiffure with coil at back of head; *~ nose*, nose straight in profile, continuing forehead line without a dip; *~ slippers*, trade name for oriental slippers. *~ n.* Greek scholar; boy in highest class at Christ's Hospital.

Greece. Maritime kingdom in SE. Europe, bounded on the N. by Albania, Yugoslavia, and Bulgaria, on the S. and W. by the Ionian Sea, and on the E. by the Aegean and Turkey; capital, Athens. *Ancient* or *classical ~*, earliest great civilization of Europe which developed round the shores of the Aegean and reached its peak in 5th c. B.C., having no unified government but consisting of a number of city states of which Athens and Sparta became the most powerful. Wars between these two powers during the following 400–500 years resulted in the ruin of classical Greek civilization. In 146 B.C. Greece became part of the E. Roman (Byzantine) Empire. Overrun by Serbia during the 13th c., conquered by Turkey in the 14th–15th centuries, she remained under Turkish rule until, after years of fierce warfare, she won her independence in 1821.

greed *n.* Insatiate longing, esp. for wealth.

greed'y *adj.* Ravenous, voracious, gluttonous; avaricious, covetous, rapacious; eager, keen, intensely desirous (*to* do); **greed'ily** *adv.* **greed'iness** *n.*

Greek *adj.* Of, pertaining to, Greece, its inhabitants or their language; *~ calends*: see CALENDS; *~ Church*, the ORTHODOX Church; *~ cross*, upright cross with limbs of equal length, **+**; *~ fire*, a combustible composition of naphtha, nitre, and sulphur, used by the Byzantine Greeks for setting fire to an enemy's ships or works; *~ gift*, one given with intent to harm (see Virgil, 'Aeneid', ii. 49). *~ n.* 1. Member of the Hellenic race or nation; inhabitant of Hellas or Greece; member of the Greek Church. 2. The language of the Greeks, esp. of the classical Greeks, a member of the Indo-Germanic family of languages, represented in classical times by four main dialects, Ionic, Attic, Aeolic, and Doric. Modern Greek, which dates from the 15th c., is divided into *Romaic*, the common speech, and *Neo-Hellenic*, which seeks to preserve classical forms and idioms.

Greek'less *adj.* Ignorant of Greek.

green' *adj.* 1. Of the colour between blue and yellow in the spectrum, coloured like grass, sea-water, emerald, etc.; covered with herbage, verdant, in leaf; (of complexion) pale, sickly-hued, as in fear, jealousy, sickness, etc.; (fig.) jealous, envious. 2. (Of fruit etc.) unripe, young and tender, flourishing, not dried; full of vitality, not withered or worn out; immature, undeveloped, inexperienced, gullible; not dried, seasoned, or tanned; (of wound etc.) fresh, not healed. 3. *Green'back*, U.S. Treasury note; *~-blind*, having retina insensitive to green rays; *~ cheese*, unripened cheese; whey cheese; cheese coloured green with sage; (*Board of*) *G~ Cloth*, Lord Steward's department of Royal Household; *~-eyed*, jealous; *~ fat*, green gelatinous portion of turtle, highly esteemed by epicures; *green'finch*, common European bird with gold and green plumage (*Chloris chloris*); *green'fly*, aphis or plant-louse; *green'gage*, roundish green fine-flavoured plum [f. name of Sir W. *Gage*]; ~ *goose*, goose killed under four months old and eaten without stuffing; *green'grocer*, retail dealer in fruit and vegetables; *green'grocery*; *green'heart*, various W. Indian trees, esp. large tree of Guiana, *Ocotea rodiaei*, furnishing very hard timber; this timber used for fishing-rods, in shipbuilding, etc.; *green'horn*, ignoramus, raw hand, simpleton; *green'house*, glass-house for rearing delicate plants; ~ *manure*, growing plants ploughed into soil; *G~ Mountain State*, (U.S.) popular name of Vermont; ~*-room*, room in theatre accommodating actors and actresses when off stage (ill. THEATRE); *green'sand*, sand or sandstone containing hydrated iron silicate; geol. formation largely of this; *green'shank*, large kind of sandpiper, *Tringa nebularia*; ~ *sickness*, chlorosis; *green'stick*, bone-fracture, esp. in children, in which one side of bone is broken and one only bent (ill. BONE); *green'stone*, kinds of eruptive rock containing felspar and hornblende; kind of jade; *greenstuff*, vegetation; green vegetables; *green'sward*, turf; ~ *tea*, tea dried and fired immediately, as opp. to *black tea*, which is fermented or oxidized before firing; *green'wood*, woodlands in summer, esp. as scene of outlaw life. **green'ly** *adv.* **green'nėss** *n.* **green'ish** *adj.* **green'y** *adj.* (usu. in comb., as ~*-grey*). **green** *n.* 1. What is green; green part of anything; green colour; green dye. 2. Vigour, youth, virility. 3. Verdure, vegetation, greenery; (pl.) green vegetables, esp. (in England) small or young cabbages. 4. Piece of public or common grassy land; grass-plot used for special purpose. ~ *v.* Become green, esp. with verdure; dye green; soil etc. with green.

green'ery *n.* Verdure; green branches or leaves as decoration.

green'ing *n.* Kind of apple, green when ripe.

Green'land. Island lying to the NE. of N. America, part of the Kingdom of Denmark. **Green'lander** *n.* **Green'landic** *adj.*

Greenwich (grĕn'ij, grĭn-). Metropolitan borough of SE. London; ~ *Hospital*, built by Wren, orig. for naval pensioners, now occupied by the Royal Naval College for officers; ~ *Observatory*, the Royal Astronomical Observatory, founded 1675 for the purpose of calculating longitude (its work was transferred 1950 to Herstmonceux, Sussex); ~ (*mean*) *time*, (abbrev. G.M.T.) mean solar time of the meridian of Greenwich, adopted as standard time in Gt Britain and used as a basis for calculation in other countries; ~ *meridian*, the meridian which passes through Greenwich Observatory, recognized by most nations as the prime meridian, or 0° longitude.

greet[1] *v.t.* Accost with salutation; salute *with* words or gestures, receive on meeting or arrival *with* speech or action; (of sight etc.) meet (eye, ear). **greet'ing** *n.*

greet[2] *v.i.* (Sc.) Weep.

grėgār'ious *adj.* Living in flocks or communities; fond of company; of flocks or crowds. **grėgār'iously** *adv.* **grėgār'iousnėss** *n.*

grege (-āzh) *n.* & *adj.* (Of) colour between beige and grey. [Fr. *grège* raw (silk)]

Grėgōr'ian *adj.* Pertaining to, originated by, some person named Gregory, esp. one of the popes of that name; ~ *calendar*, the modified calendar, also known as the 'New Style', introduced by Pope Gregory XIII in 1582 and adopted in Gt Britain in 1752; it is a modification of the JULIAN calendar, adapted to bring it into closer conformity with astronomical data and to rectify the error contracted by its use. In order to correct this error, which was due to the fact that the Julian year of 365¼ days was 11 min. 10 sec. too long, 10 days were suppressed in 1582 and in Gt Britain 11 in 1752, and to prevent future displacement Gregory provided that of the centesimal years (1600, 1700, etc.) only those exactly divisible by 400 should be counted as leap years; ~ *chant*, the system of ritual music, otherwise known as plain-chant or plain-song, founded on the 'Antiphonarium', of which Pope Gregory I is presumed to have been the compiler; ~ *telescope*, the earliest type of reflecting telescope, invented by James Gregory (1638–75), a Scottish mathematician; ~ *tones*, 8 plain-song melodies prescribed for psalms in R.C. Church.

Grĕg'ory. Name of 16 popes. *Gregory I*, pope 590–604, a zealous propagator of Christianity and reformer of clerical and monastic discipline; sent AUGUSTINE to England; is presumed to have originated the GREGORIAN chant; *Gregory VII*, pope 1073–85, a Benedictine monk, before his election called Hildebrand; attempted to extend the temporal power of the papacy and came into conflict with the emperor Henry IV, whom he obliged to do penance at CANOSSA; *Gregory XIII*, pope 1572–85, introduced the GREGORIAN calendar.

grĕg'ory-powd'er *n.* Compound powder of rhubarb, magnesia, and ginger used as aperient. [J. *Gregory* (1753–1821), Sc. physician]

grĕm'ial *n.* Silk apron placed on bishop's lap at Mass or ordination.

grĕm'lin *n.* (R.A.F. slang) A mischievous sprite imagined to frequent aeroplanes and to cause mishaps.

grėnāde *n.* Small explosive shell thrown by hand or fitted with tail-rod and shot from rifle-barrel by means of a blank cartridge; glass receptacle thrown to disperse chemicals for extinguishing fires, testing drains, etc. [Span. *granada* pomegranate]

grĕnadier' *n.* 1. (orig.) Soldier who threw grenades (orig. 4 or 5 men in each company, later, a company of the tallest and finest men in each regiment; ill. INFANTRY); (now) *G~ Guards*, *Grenadiers*, first regiment of household infantry. 2. S. Afr. weaver-bird, *Pyromelaena oryx*, with vivid red-and-black plumage.

grĕn'adin(e)[1] *n.* Open silk or silk-and-wool dress-fabric.

grĕn'adine[2] (-ēn) *n.* French cordial syrup of pomegranates.

grĕn'adine[3] *n.* 1. Fricandeau of veal or poultry, filleted and glazed. 2. Kind of strongly scented carnation.

Grĕn'ville, Sir Richard (1541?–91). Elizabethan sea-captain; with his one ship, the *Revenge*, he engaged 15 Spanish ships off Flores, fought them for 15 hours, and was mortally wounded in the engagement.

Grĕsh'am's law. (econ.) The tendency, when two or more coins of equal nominal value but different intrinsic value are in circulation, for the one having the least intrinsic value to remain in circulation and for the other to be hoarded. [Sir Thomas *Gresham*, Engl. financier, founder of the Royal Exchange]

grĕssōr'ial *adj.* (zool.) Walking, adapted for walking.

Grĕt'na Green. Village in Dumfriesshire, just inside Scotland, where English runaway couples contracted 'irregular' marriages valid by Scottish law, by making a declaration before a witness; the blacksmith acted as witness and also read the marriage service to them for sentiment's sake; the practice began after 1754 when English law made hasty marriage difficult, and lapsed after 1857 when Scottish law prescribed certain conditions for 'irregular' marriages, though it recognized such marriages until 1939.

grey (-ā), **gray** *adj.* Intermediate between black and white, coloured like ashes or lead; between light and dark, dull, clouded, depressing, dismal; (of person, his hair, etc.) turning white with age etc.; ancient, immemorial; belonging to old age, experienced, mature; ~*-back*, various birds, esp. hooded crow (*Corvus cornix*), scaup duck (*Fuligula marila*); *grey'beard*, old man; ~*-coat*, (esp.) Cumberland yeoman; ~ *friar*, Franciscan, from the colour of the habit; ~ *goose*, *grey'lag* (*goose*), common European wild goose (*Anser anser*); *greyhound*, slender long-legged keen-sighted swift dog used in coursing hares etc.; swift steamship; *greyhound racing*, sport in which mechanical hare is chased round track by greyhounds; ~ *matter*: see MATTER; ~ *squirrel*, common squirrel of U.S. (*Sciurus carolinensis*), now naturalized in Europe. **grey'ish** *adj.* **grey'ly** *adv.* **grey'nèss** *n.* **grey** *n.* Grey clothes; cold sunless light; grey colour, grey pigment; grey horse; *the Greys, Scots Greys*, the 2nd Dragoons, a regiment raised in 1681, orig. wearing grey uniform, later mounted on grey horses, now equipped with tanks and forming part of Royal Armoured Corps. ~ *v.* Become, make, grey.

greywăcke, gray- (grā'wăke) *n.* (geol.) Sandstone containing about 30% or more of a dark mineral.

grĭd *n.* 1. Grating, frame of parallel bars; strong iron framework for carrying luggage on back of motor-car; gridiron. 2. Network of lines, esp. system of numbered squares printed on map and forming basis of map-reference. 3. Network of overhead wires for distributing electric current or of pipes for distributing gas to towns and villages. 4. (wireless) Wire spiral or wire gauze auxiliary electrode between filament and plate of electrode valve; ~ *bias*, (usu. negative) potential applied to grid of thermionic valve to adjust anode current or to prevent this flowing into grid; ~*-leak*: see LEAK.

gridd'le *n.* 1. Circular iron plate for baking pancakes etc. on (see also GIRDLE[2]). 2. Miner's wire-bottomed sieve or screen. ~ *v.t.* Screen with griddle.

grĭd'iron (-īrn) *n.* Barred metal cooking utensil, usu. on short legs, for supporting food to be boiled or grilled; (naut.) frame of parallel beams for supporting ship in dock; naval manœuvre in which vessels' paths suggest form of gridiron; (theatr.) plank structure over stage supporting mechanism for drop-scenes etc.; (U.S.) football field (from the parallel lines marking out field of play for American form of football); ~ (*pendulum*), compensation pendulum of parallel rods of different metals.

grief *n.* Deep or violent sorrow, keen regret; *come to* ~, meet with disaster, fail, fall.

griev'ance *n.* Real or fancied ground of complaint.

grieve *v.* Give deep sorrow to; feel grief.

griev'ous *adj.* Bringing serious trouble, injurious; (of pain etc.) severe; flagrant, heinous; exciting grief. **griev'ously** *adv.* **griev'ousnèss** *n.*

grĭff'ĭn[1] *n.* (Anglo-Ind.) European newly arrived in India or the East, novice, greenhorn.

grĭff'ĭn[2], **grĭff'on**[1], **grȳph'on** *n.* Fabulous creature with eagle's head and wings and lion's body; (her.) representation of this creature as charge or crest; (fig.) vigilant guardian, esp. duenna or chaperon; *griffon vulture*, large species of vulture (*Gyps fulvus*) found in S. Europe and N. Africa.

GRIFFIN

grĭff'on[2] *n.* Kind of coarse-haired terrier-like dog of continental breed; *Brussels* ~, small variety of this, formerly kept as a pet.

grĭg *n.* Small eel; grasshopper or cricket.

grĭll[1] *v.* Broil on gridiron (also fig. of torture or great heat); (orig. U.S.) question (prisoner etc.) closely, put through severe examination. ~ *n.* 1. Grilled dish; grill-room; ~*-room*, room in restaurant where meat etc. is grilled and served. 2. Gridiron.

grĭll'age *n.* Heavy framework of cross-timbering used as foundation for building on treacherous soil.

grille, grĭll[2] *n.* Grating, latticed screen, esp. in door for observing callers, in convent separating nuns from visitors etc.; (tennis) square opening in end wall on hazard side of court, near main wall.

grilse *n.* Young salmon that has been only once to the sea.

grĭm *adj.* Stern, unrelenting, merciless, severe; of forbidding or harsh aspect; sinister, ghastly, unmirthful. **grĭm'ly** *adv.* **grĭm'nèss** *n.*

grimāce' *n.* Wry face expressing annoyance etc. or meant to raise a laugh; affected look; affectation. ~ *v.i.* Make wry face.

grimăl'kĭn *n.* Old she-cat; spiteful old woman.

grīme *n.* Soot, dirt, ingrained in some surface, esp. the skin. ~ *v.t.* Blacken, befoul. **grīm'y** *adj.* **grīm'inèss** *n.*

Grĭmm, Jacob Ludwig Carl (1785–1863) and Wilhelm Carl (1786–1859). Two brothers, famous for their researches into German language, literature, and antiquities and for their collection of fairy-tales; ~*'s Law*, the statement, formulated by Jacob Grimm in 1822, of the regular changes which certain consonants of the primitive Indo-Germanic consonant system have undergone in the Germanic languages.

Grĭmm'elshausen (-howzen), Hans Jacob Christoph von (1625?–76). German novelist; author of the picaresque novel 'Simplicissimus'.

grĭn *v.* Show teeth in cheerful or unrestrained or forced smile, or in sign of pain or fatuity; express (contempt, satisfaction) by grinning. ~ *n.* Act of grinning.

grīnd *v.* (past t. & past part. *ground*). 1. Reduce to small particles or powder by crushing between millstones, teeth, etc.; produce (flour) by grinding; work (handmill); turn handle of (hurdy-gurdy), produce (music) from hurdy-gurdy etc.; (quasi-pass.) admit of being ground. 2. Sharpen or smooth by abrasion; ~ *in, on*, fix (valves etc.) to their seatings by grinding. 3. Oppress, harass with exactions; toil monotonously, study hard; teach (subject, pupil) laboriously. 4. Rub gratingly *on, into, against*; rub (teeth) hard together. 5. *grind'stone*, thick revolving stone disc for grinding, sharpening, and polishing; kind of stone used for these.

n. Grinding; hard monotonous work or task; walk for exercise; steeplechase; (U.S.) student who works hard.

grīn'der *n.* Thing, person, that grinds; molar tooth; grinding-machine; upper millstone.

grīn'dery *n.* Materials, tools, etc., of shoemakers and other leather-workers.

grĭng'ō (-ngg-) *n.* (contempt.) Among Spanish-Americans, a foreigner, esp. an Englishman or an American of U.S.

grĭp *n.* Firm hold, tight grasp or clasp, grasping power; way of clasping hands; control, mastery, intellectual hold; power of arresting attention; part in machinery etc. that clips, part of weapon etc. that is held; (U.S.) gripsack. ~ *v.* (past t. & past part. *gripped*). Seize, grasp, or hold, tightly; take firm hold; compel attention of; *grip'sack*, (U.S.) traveller's handbag.

grīpe *v.* Clutch, grip; oppress, pinch; affect with colic pains; (naut., of ship) come up into wind in spite of helm; secure with gripes. ~ *n.* 1. Act of griping, clutch; hold, control; handle of implement or weapon; (naut., pl.) lashings securing boat in its place. 2. (pl.) Colic pains.

grĭppe (*or* grēp) *n.* Influenza.

grĭsaille' (-zāl, -zīy) *n.* Method of painting in grey or greyish monochrome, freq. representing figures in relief.

grĭsĕtte' (-z-) *n.* French working-class girl (formerly dressed in grey).

grĭs'kĭn *n.* Lean part of loin of bacon pig.

grĭs'ly (-z-) *adj.* Causing horror, terror, or superstitious dread. **grĭs'linèss** *n.*

grĭst[1] *n.* Corn for grinding; malt crushed for brewing.

grĭst[2] *n.* Size or thickness of yarn or rope.

grĭs'tle (-sl) *n.* Whitish tough flexible tissue in vertebrates, cartilage. **grĭs'tly** (-slĭ) *adj.*

grĭt *n.* Small particles of stone or sand, esp. as causing discomfort or clogging machinery etc.; (also *gritstone*), coarse sandstone, esp. kind used for millstones etc.; (geol.) coarse-grained sand or sandstone in which many of the particles are larger than $\frac{1}{10}$ in. in diameter and less than $\frac{1}{2}$ in.; grain or texture of stone; (colloq.) strength of character, pluck, endurance. ~ *v.* Produce, move with, grating sound; grind (teeth). **grĭtt'y** *adj.* **grĭtt'ĭnėss** *n.*

grĭts *n.pl.* Husked but unground oats; coarse oatmeal.

grĭzz'le *v.i.* (colloq.) Whimper, cry fretfully.

grĭzz'led (-zld) *adj.* Grey (-haired).

grĭzz'ly *adj.* Grey, greyish, grey-haired; ~ *bear*, large fierce bear, *Ursus horribilis*, of mountain districts of western N. America. ~ *n.* Grizzly bear.

grm. *abbrev.* Gram.

groan *n.* Deep inarticulate sound expressing pain, grief, or disapproval. ~ *v.* Utter groan; utter with groans; be oppressed or loaded *under*, *beneath*, *with*. **groan'ĭngly** *adv.*

groat *n.* (hist.) English silver coin worth 4*d.*, first coined in 1351–2 and current until 1662. [MDu. *groot* great, thick (penny)]

groats *n.pl.* Hulled (sometimes also crushed) grain, esp. oats.

grō'cer *n.* Dealer in spices, dried fruits, sugar, and miscellaneous domestic stores. **grō'cery** *n.* Trade of grocer; goods sold by grocer (freq. pl.); (U.S.) grocer's shop.

grŏg *n.* Drink of spirit (orig. rum) and water; ~*-blossom*, pimple or redness on nose supposed to be caused by excessive drinking. [reputedly f. *grogram*, nickname (from his cloak) of Admiral Vernon, who first had grog served out in navy instead of neat rum]

grŏgg'y *adj.* Drunk(en); bibulous; (of horse) weak in forelegs, tottering; unsteady, shaky. **grŏg'ĭly** *adv.* **grŏgg'ĭnėss** *n.*

grŏg'ram *n.* Coarse fabric of silk or mohair and wool, often stiffened with gum. [Fr. *gros grain* large grain]

groin *n.* 1. Depression between belly and thigh. 2. (archit.) Edge formed by intersecting vaults, fillet covering this (ill. VAULT). ~ *v.t.* Build with groins. **groin'ĭng** *n.*

grŏm'well *n.* Any plant of genus *Lithospermum*, with hard stony seeds formerly used in medicine.

groom *n.* 1. One of certain officers of English Royal Household, chiefly in Lord Chamberlain's department. 2. Servant having care of horses. 3. Bridegroom; *grooms'man*, unmarried friend attending bridegroom at wedding, best man. ~ *v.t.* Curry, feed, tend, etc. (horse); give neat or attractive appearance to; prepare as political candidate, film star, etc.

groove *n.* Channel or hollow, esp. one made to direct motion or receive corresponding ridge; routine, undeviating course, rut. ~ *v.t.* Make groove(s) in.

grōpe *v.i.* Feel about as in dark (*for*, *after*); search blindly; ~ *one's way*, find way by feeling, proceed tentatively. **grōp'ĭngly** *adv.*

grōs'beak *n.* Any of various finches with large strong beak.

grosch'en (-ōshn) *n.* 1. $\frac{1}{100}$ of an Austrian SCHILLING. 2. (hist.) Small German silver coin.

grosgrain (grō'grān) *n.* Corded fabric or ribbon of silk etc.

grōss[1] *n.* Twelve dozen.

grōss[2] *adj.* 1. Luxuriant, rank; overfed, bloated, repulsively fat; flagrant, glaring. 2. Total, without deductions, not net. 3. Dense, thick, solid; coarse, dull; coarse in manners or morals, unrefined, indecent. 4. (abs.) *in* (*the*) ~, in a general way, on the whole (now rare); in bulk, in large quantities (opp. to *by retail*). **grōss'ly** *adv.* **grōss'nėss** *n.*

grŏt *n.* (poet.) Grotto.

grotĕsque' (-sk) *n.* Decoration with fantastic interweaving of human and animal forms with foliage (ill. ARABESQUE); (pop.) comically distorted figure or design. ~ *adj.* (archit.) In the grotesque style; distorted, bizarre; ludicrous from incongruity, absurd. **grotĕsque'ly** (-klĭ) *adv.* **grotĕsque'nėss** *n.* [It. *grottesca* antique work, prob. because *grotta* (grotto) was used of excavated ancient Roman houses, in which such paintings were found]

Grō'tius (-shus), Hugo (1583–1645). Dutch statesman and jurist; famous for his treatise on international law, the 'De jure Belli et Pacis', published in 1625.

grŏtt'ō *n.* Picturesque cave; artificial ornamental cave; room etc. adorned with shells etc. in imitation of cave, as cool retreat; (geog.) cave formed by underground stream; *the* ~, London street-boys' grotto-like structure of oyster-shells on 5th Aug. in celebration of close-time for oysters.

grouch *n.* (U.S.) Grumbling; complaint; sulky, grumbling mood; grumbler. **grouch'y** *adj.* **grouch'ĭly** *adv.* **grouch'ĭnėss** *n.* **grouch** *v.i.* Grumble.

ground[1] *n.* 1. Bottom of sea; bottom where water becomes too shallow for vessel etc. to float; (pl.) dregs, esp. of coffee. 2. Base, foundation, motive, valid reason. 3. Substratum, underlying part; surface worked upon in embroidery, painting, etc.; undecorated part; prevailing colour or tone; (painting) preparation spread over canvas, panel, etc., to isolate it from paint layer; (etching) wax mixture spread on metal plate and cut through with needle where acid is to act. 4. Surface of earth; position, area, or distance, on earth's surface; area of special kind or use; portion of land forming person's property; space on which person etc. takes his stand (freq. fig.); (pl.) enclosed land for ornament or recreation attached to house; *fall*, *be dashed*, *to the* ~, (of scheme, hope) be abandoned, fail; *down to the* ~, (colloq.) in all respects; *above* ~, alive; *stand*, *shift*, *one's* ~, maintain, change, one's argument or intention; *gain* ~, advance; *lose*, *give*, ~, retreat, decline; *forbidden* ~, subject that must be avoided; *classic* ~, historic place. 5. (elect., U.S.) Earth (see EARTH, sense 3). 6. Attrib. etc.: (in names of birds) terrestrial, (of beasts) burrowing in or lying on ground, (of plants) dwarfish or trailing; ~ *bait*, bait thrown to bottom of intended fishing-ground to attract fish; ~ *bass*, (mus.) theme in bass constantly repeated with varied melody or harmony above; ~ *floor*, rooms etc. nearest to level of outside ground; *get in on the* ~ *floor*, be admitted to company etc. on same terms as promoters; ~ *frost*, frost on surface of ground but not above it; ~*-hog*, aard-vark; American marmot (*Arctomys*); ~ *ice*, ice formed at bottom of water; ~ *ivy*, ale-hoof, common labiate plant (*Nepeta glechoma*) with bluish-purple flowers and kidney-shaped leaves; ~ *landlord*, owner of land leased for building; ~ *nut*, pod of *Arachis hypogaea* containing two or three seeds which are buried by downward curvature of the flower-stalks; pea-nut; earth-nut; ~ *pine*, herbaceous plant (*Ajuga chamaepitys*) with resinous smell; club-moss; ~ *plan*, plane drawing of divisions of building on the ground level or ground floor; outline, general design, of anything; ~*-rent*, rent paid to ground landlord; *ground'sheet*, waterproof sheet for spreading on ground as protection against damp; *grounds'man*, man employed to keep esp. cricket-ground in order; ~ *speed*, the horizontal component of an aircraft's velocity relative to the earth; ~ *squirrel*, terrestrial squirrel-like rodent, as chipmunk, gopher, etc.; ~ *staff*, staff of groundsmen; non-flying personnel of an air-station employed in servicing aircraft; ~ *swell*, heavy sea-swell as result of distant storm; ~ *water*, water lying below earth's surface in springs and in pores of rock; *ground'work*, foundation or basis (usu. fig.); chief ingredient; general surface of thing showing where not overlaid with embroidery or other ornament. ~ *v.* Base, establish, *on* some fact or authority; instruct thoroughly (*in* elements of subject); prepare ground of (embroidery etc.); lay (esp. arms) on ground; alight on ground; keep on the ground, prevent (aircraft) from taking off; run ashore, strand; (elect., U.S.) connect with the ground, earth.

ground[2], past part. of GRIND; ~ *glass*, glass made non-transparent by grinding or other means.

groun'dage *n.* Duty on ship lying on beach or entering port.

ground'ing *n.* (esp.) Instruction in elements of subject.

ground'less *adj.* Without foundation, authority, or support, unfounded. **ground'lessly** *adv.* **ground'lessness** *n.*

ground'ling *n.* Creeping or dwarf plant; (archaic) frequenter of pit of theatre; hence, spectator or reader of inferior taste.

ground'sel *n.* Plant of genus *Senecio*, esp. *S. vulgaris*, common European weed used as food for cage-birds.

group (-ōōp) *n.* In fine arts, two or more figures or objects forming complete design or distinct part of one; number of persons or things standing near together, knot, cluster; number of persons or things belonging or classed together; ~ *captain*, officer of Royal Air Force, ranking between air commodore and wing commander; (*Oxford*) *Group*: see MORAL Re-Armament. ~ *v.* Form into a group, place in a group *with*; form into well-arranged and harmonious whole; classify. **group'er**[1] *n.* (colloq.) Member of the Group.

group'er[2] (-ōō-) *n.* Various marine food-fishes, esp. the sea-perch or gaper (*Serranus cabrilla*) of W. Atlantic.

grouse[1] *n.* (pl. *grouse*). Gallinaceous bird with feathered feet; (in pop. use restricted to) reddish-coloured game-bird (*Lagopus scoticus*) of British Isles; *black* ~, black game; *great* ~, *wood* ~, capercaillie; *white* ~, ptarmigan.

grouse[2] *v.i.* & *n.* (slang) Grumble. **grous'er** *n.*

grout[1] *n.* Thin fluid mortar for filling interstices. ~ *v.t.* Fill up or finish with grout or cement.

grout[2] *v.* (Of pigs) turn up earth, turn up (earth etc.) with snout.

grŏve *n.* Small wood; group of trees, esp. one with open space in centre.

grŏv'el *v.i.* Lie prone, humble oneself. **grŏv'elling** *adj.* Abject, low, base. **grŏv'ellingly** *adv.*

grow (-ō) *v.* (past t. *grew* pr. grōō, past part. *grown*). 1. Develop or exist as living plant; germinate, sprout, spring up, be produced, come naturally into existence, arise. 2. Increase in size, height, quantity, degree, power, etc.; become gradually; ~ *on*, acquire more and more influence over, gain more and more of (person's) liking or admiration; *growing-pains*, pains prob. of a rheumatic character popularly attributed to growth; *growing season*, season (longest near equator) when rainfall and temperature permit plants to grow; ~ *up*, advance to maturity; emerge *from* soil; reach full size; (of custom) arise, become common. 3. Produce by cultivation; bring forth; let (beard etc.) grow; (pass.) be covered (*over*, *up*) with some growth. **grow'er** *n.* (esp.) Person growing produce; plant that grows in specified way. **grow'ingly** *adv.*

growl *n.* Guttural sound of anger; rumble; angry murmur, complaint. ~ *v.* Utter growl, rumble, murmur angrily; utter with a growl. **growl'ingly** *adv.*

growl'er *n.* (esp.) 1. (slang or colloq.) Four-wheeled cab, esp. of the type formerly used in London. 2. Small iceberg.

grown (-ōn), past part. of GROW; ~*-up*, (*adj.*) mature, adult; (*n.*) grown-up person, adult.

growth (-ō-) *n.* Growing, development, increase; cultivation *of* produce; what has grown or is growing; (path.) morbid formation.

groyne *n.* Timber framework or low broad wall run out into sea to check drifting of beach and so stop encroachment of sea; similar structure in river. ~ *v.t.* Supply (beach) with groynes.

grŭb *n.* 1. Larva of insect, caterpillar, maggot. 2. (cricket) Ball bowled along ground. 3. (slang) Food, a feed. ~ *v.* 1. Dig superficially; clear (ground) of roots and stumps; clear away (roots etc.); fetch *up* or *out* by digging; search, rummage. 2. Plod, toil, *on*, *along*, *away*. 3. (slang) Feed; provide (boarder etc.) with food.

grŭbb'y *adj.* 1. Of, infested with, grubs. 2. Dirty, grimy, slovenly. **grŭbb'iness** *n.*

Grŭb Street. Street (now Milton Street) near Moorfields, London, inhabited in 17th c. by needy authors and literary hacks; hence, such writers; attrib. of these.

grŭdge *v.t.* Be unwilling to give, grant, or allow (*to*); be unwilling *to* do. **grŭdg'ingly** *adv.* **grŭdge** *n.* Feeling of resentment or ill will.

gru'el (grōō-) *n.* Liquid food chiefly for invalids of oatmeal etc. boiled in milk or water; (colloq.) *have*, *take*, *one's* ~, be punished; get killed. ~ *v.t.* Exhaust, disable. **gru'elling** *adj.* & *n.*

grue'some (-ōōs-) *adj.* Grisly, disgusting. **grue'somely** *adv.* **grue'someness** *n.*

grŭff *adj.* Surly, laconic, rough-mannered, rough-voiced. **grŭff'ly** *adv.* **grŭff'ness** *n.*

grŭm'ble *n.* Dull inarticulate sound, murmur, complaint. ~ *v.* Utter grumble, murmur, growl faintly; rumble; complain; utter complainingly. **grŭm'bler** *n.* **grŭm'blingly** *adv.*

grume (grōōm) *n.* (med.) Clot of blood, clotted blood; viscous fluid. **grum'ous** *adj.*

grŭmm'ĕt *n.* (naut.) Ring usu. of twisted rope as fastening, row-lock, gun-wad, etc.

grŭm'py, grŭm'pish *adjs.* Ill-tempered, surly. **grŭm'pily** *adv.* **grŭm'piness** *n.*

Grŭn'dy, Mrs. In Thomas Morton's play 'Speed the Plough' (1798), a neighbour who never appears but is constantly referred to ('What will Mrs. Grundy say?'); hence, symbol of conventional propriety or prudery. **Grŭnd'yish** *adj.* **Grŭnd'yism** *n.*

grŭnt *n.* Low gruff sound characteristic of hogs, any similar sound. ~ *v.* Utter grunt; express discontent, dissent, fatigue, etc., by this; utter with grunt. **grŭn'ter** *n.* (esp.) 1. Pig. 2. Various Amer. fishes (chiefly of genus *Haemulon*) which make grunting noise when caught.

gruyère (grōō'yār) *n.* Pale firm cow's-milk cheese with many cavities, made at Gruyères, Switzerland; French imitation of this.

grys'bŏk *n.* Small grey S. Afr. antelope (*Raphiceros*).

gs *abbrev.* Guineas.

G.S. *abbrev.* General service.

G.S.O. *abbrev.* General Staff Officer.

Gt Britain *abbrev.* Great Britain.

guai'acŏl (gwī-) *n.* A colourless liquid or white crystalline solid with strong smell, obtained by distilling guaiacum resin or wood-tar creosote, and used in medicine.

guai'acum (gwī-) *n.* Genus of W. Indian trees and shrubs; (also **guai'ac**) hard heavy brownish-green wood of *G. officinale* and *G. sanctum*, lignum vitae; resin obtained from these, drug made from it used as a remedy for rheumatism, gout, lumbago, etc.

Guam (gwahm). Largest and southernmost of the Mariana Islands; ceded to U.S. by Spain in 1898 and now a U.S. naval station; capital, Agana.

guan (gwahn) *n.* Kinds of S. Amer. gallinaceous bird allied to curassow.

gua'na (gwah-) *n.* Iguana; large lizard.

guanaco: see HUANACO.

gua'no (gwah-) *n.* Excrement of sea-fowl found esp. on sea-coasts of islands about Peru, rich in phosphates and ammonia and used as manure; artificial manure, esp. that made from fish. ~ *v.t.* Fertilize with guano.

Guara'ni (gwarah-). One of the two main divisions of the Tupi-Guarani, widespread ethnical and linguistic family of S. Amer. Indians; language of this people.

guara'ni *n.* Principal monetary unit of Paraguay, = 100 centimos.

guarantee' (gă-) *n.* Person making guaranty or giving security; guaranty; thing given or existing as security for fulfilment of conditions or permanence etc. of something; person to whom guaranty is given. ~ *v.t.* Be guarantee for, answer for due fulfilment of (contract etc.) or genuineness etc. of (article); assure permanence etc. of; engage *that* something has happened or will happen; secure possession of *to* person; secure *against* or *from* (risk etc.) or *in* (possession etc.). **guă'rantor** (*or* -ôr') *n.*

guă'ranty (gă-) *n.* Undertaking, esp. written, to answer for payment of debt or performance of obligation by another person liable in first instance; ground or basis of security. ~ *v.t.* (now rare) Guarantee.

guard (gârd) *n.* 1. Defensive posture or motion in fencing, boxing, etc.; watch, vigilant state; *keep ~, be on ~*, act as sentry etc.; *on, off, one's ~*, prepared, unprepared, against attack, surprise, etc. 2. Protector, defender, sentry; (U.S.) prison warder; official in charge of stage-coach or train. 3. Body of soldiers etc. serving as protectors of place or person, escort, separate portion of army etc.; (pl.) selected bodies of troops normally for escort or ceremonial duties with a sovereign, e.g. in Brit. Army the Household troops, which comprise the LIFE *G~s*, *Royal* HORSE *G~s*, and *Foot G~s*; *Brigade of G~s*, the Foot Guards, consisting of 5 regiments, the Grenadier, Coldstream, Scots, Irish, and Welsh Guards; *mount, relieve, ~*, take up, take others' place in, sentry duty. 4. Contrivance of metal, wood, etc., to prevent injury or accident; e.g. part of sword-hilt protecting hand from injury, fire-guard, trigger-guard, etc. 5. *~-boat*, boat going rounds of fleet in harbour to see that good watch is kept; official harbour-boat enforcing quarantine or customs regulations; *~-chain*, chain securing watch, brooch, etc.; *~-house*, building for accommodation of military guard or keeping of prisoners under guard; *~-rail*, hand- or other rail to prevent falling, etc.; short rail to keep wheel on line at railway switches, crossings, etc.; *~-room*, room for keeping prisoners under guard, or for military guard; *~-ship*, warship protecting harbour, for directing shipping, and for receiving seamen till they can join their ships; *guards'man*, soldier, esp. officer, of Guards. ~ *v.* Keep safe, stand guard over, keep (door etc.) so as to control passage; protect, defend; secure by explanations or stipulations etc. from misunderstanding or abuse; keep (thoughts, speech) in check; use a fencing guard; take precautions *against*; (chess) protect (piece, pawn) with another. **guard'ĕdly** *adv.* Cautiously, in guarded language.

guard'ant (gâr-) *adj.* (her.) (Of a beast) having the full face towards the spectator (ill. HERALDRY).

guard'ian (gâr-) *n.* Keeper, defender, protector; (law) one having custody of person or property, or both, of minor, idiot, etc.; superior of Franciscan convent; (also ~ *of the Poor, Poor-law ~*), one of board elected to administer poor laws in a particular parish or district (in England abolished by the Poor Law Act, 1927); ~ *angel*, spirit watching over person or place. **guard'ianship** *n.* Office of guardian, legal tutelage; keeping, guard.

Guarnĕr'ĭ(us) (gw-). Name of 17th- and 18th-c. family of famous Italian violin-makers of Cremona; violin made by one of this family.

Guatemala (gwahtĭmah'la). The most northerly republic of Central America, bordering on Mexico; capital, Guatemala.

gua'va (gwah-) *n.* (Tree of tropical Amer. genus *Psidium* of family *Myrtaceae*, esp. *P. guajava*, yielding) acid fruit used for making jelly etc. [Span. *guayaba*, prob. f. native Amer. name]

gūbernatôr'ial *adj.* Of a governor.

gŭdg'eon[1] (-jon) *n.* Small European freshwater fish, *Gobio gobio*, used as bait; credulous person.

gŭdg'eon[2] (-jon) *n.* Pivot at end of beam, axle, etc., on which bell, wheel, etc., works; ring of gate turning on hook of post; socket in which rudder works (ill. BOAT); pin holding two blocks of stone etc. together; ~ *pin*, (esp.) that holding piston and connecting-rod together.

guel'der rōse (gĕ-; -z) *n.* Small tree, *Viburnum opulus*, bearing round bunches of white flowers, snowball tree. [f. *Guelders*, town in Prussia, or *Guelderland*, province of Holland]

Guĕlph (gw-) 1. (Member) of medieval Italian party supporting the pope against the emperor (cf. GHIBELLINE). 2. Princely family of Swabian origin from which the British royal house is descended through George I; the name is often given as the surname of the house of Hanover (although D'Este is equally accurate). [It. *Guelfo* f. MHG. *Welf*, name of the founder of the family, said to have been used at the battle of Weinsberg (1140) as a war-cry by the partisans of the Duke of Bavaria, who fought against the Emperor Conrad III]

guerd'on (gêr-) *n.* & *v.t.* (poet.) Reward, recompense.

Guernsey (gêrn'zĭ). Second largest of the Channel Islands; ~ *flower* or *lily*, S. African plant (*Nerine sarniensis*) with bright-red umbellate flowers, naturalized in Guernsey. **guern'sey** *n.* 1. A thick knitted closely-fitting vest or shirt, usu. made of blue wool, worn by seamen. 2. (cap.) One of a breed of usu. fawn-and-white dairy cattle, orig. raised in Guernsey.

guer(r)ĭll'a (ge-) *n.* (Also ~ *war(fare)*) irregular war waged by small bodies of men acting independently; man engaged in this. [Span. *guerrilla* little war]

guess (gĕs) *v.* Estimate without measurement or detailed calculation; think likely; think one divines nature of; form hypothesis as to, conjecture, hazard opinion about; conjecture (answer to riddle etc.) rightly, divine; *I ~* (chiefly U.S.) I feel sure, I know well. ~ *n.* Rough estimate, conjecture, hypothesis; *by ~*, at haphazard; *~-work*, (procedure based on) guessing.

guest (gĕst) *n.* Person entertained at another's house or table; person lodging at hotel, boarding-house, etc.; animal or vegetable parasite; *paying ~*, boarder; *~-chamber*, room kept for guests; *~-house*, superior boarding-house; *~-night*, one on which guests are entertained at club, college, etc.

guffaw' *n.* Coarse or boisterous laugh. ~ *v.* Make, say with, guffaw.

Guiana (gĭah'na). Region in NE. of S. America, including Guyana, French Guiana, and Surinam; ~ *bark*, CINCHONA bark.

guid'ance (gīd-) *n.* Guiding, direction.

guide (gīd) *n.* 1. One who shows the way; hired conductor of traveller or tourist, esp. climber; adviser; directing principle or standard; (mil.) one of company formed for reconnoitring etc.; *right, left, ~*, (mil.) subalterns of company superintending, marking pivots, etc., in evolutions; (naut.) ship by which rest of fleet regulate their movements; *Girl G~*: see GIRL. 2. Book of rudiments, manual; (also *~-book*), book to inform tourists about city, cathedral, museum, etc. or whole district or country. 3. (mech.) Bar, rod, etc., directing motion of something; gauge etc.; controlling tool; thing marking a position or guiding the eye. 4. ~ *dog*, one trained to guide blind person; *~-post*, signpost; *~-rope*, guy; rope trailing from balloon etc. to anchor or ballast it. ~ *v.t.* Act as guide to, go before, lead, direct course of; arrange course of (events); be principle, motive, or ground, of; conduct affairs of (State etc.).

guid'on (gē-) *n.* Pennant narrowing to point at free end (ill. FLAG); this used as standard of dragoons.

guild, gild (gĭ-) *n.* Society for mutual aid or prosecution of common object, esp. medieval trade- or craft-association, acting as benefit society, promoting common trade-interests of members etc. and freq. developing into municipal corporations; *~-hall*, hall in which medieval guild met; town-hall; *the Guildhall*, hall of Corporation of City of London, used for State banquets etc.; ~ *socialism*, system by which resources, methods, and profits of each industry should be controlled by a council of its members.

guil'der (gĭl-) *n.* 1. The GULDEN or florin of the Netherlands. 2. (obs.) The Austrian florin.

guile (gīl) *n.* Treachery, deceit; cunning devices. **guīle'ful** (-lf-) *adj.* **guīle'fully** *adv.* **guīle'fulnĕss** *n.* **guīle'lĕss** (-l-l-) *adj.*

guīle′lėssly *adv.* **guīle lėssnėss** *n.*

guill′ėmot (gĭl-) *n.* Various sea-birds of genus *Uria.*

guilloche (gĭlōsh′) *n.* (archit.) Ornament imitating braided ribbons.

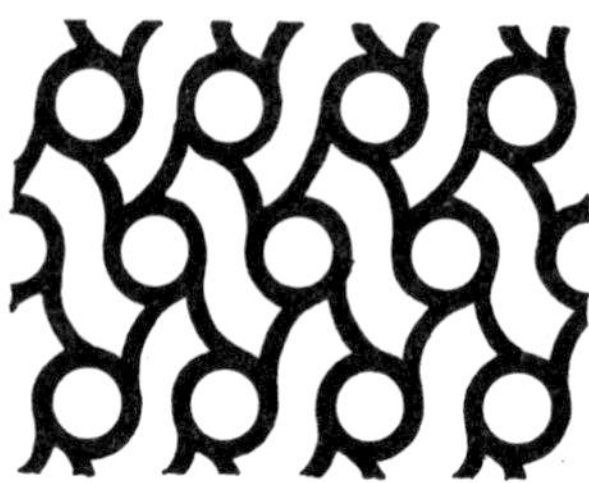

GUILLOCHE

guillotine (gĭlotēn′, gĭl′-) *n.* 1. Instrument used in France (esp. during the Revolution) and elsewhere for beheading, consisting of heavy knife-blade sliding between grooved posts. 2. Surgical instrument for excising uvula, tonsil, etc. 3. Machine for cutting paper, book-edges, etc. 4. (parl.) Method of shortening discussion of Bill by fixing times at which parts of it must be voted on. ~ *v.t.* Use guillotine upon. [I. *Guillotin* (1738–1814), French physician, who advocated its use in 1789]

guilt (gĭ-) *n.* The having committed a specified or implied offence; criminality, culpability.

guĭlt′lėss (gĭ-) *adj.* Innocent (*of*). **guĭlt′lėssly** *adv.* **guĭlt′lėssnėss** *n.*

guĭl′ty (gĭ-) *adj.* Criminal, culpable; conscious of, prompted by, guilt; having committed a particular offence; ~, *not* ~, pleas, verdicts, in criminal trials. **guĭl′tĭly** *adv.* **guĭl′tĭnėss** *n.*

Guinea (gĭn′ĭ). Part of W. coast of Africa extending from Sierra Leone to Benin. **guin′ea** *n.* English gold coin (not coined since 1813) first struck in 1663, orig. of gold from Guinea and for trade with Guinea, of fluctuating value, orig. nominally 20*s.*, fixed in 1717 at 21*s.*; 21*s.* as unit for professional fee, subscription to society, etc., price of racehorse, painting, etc.; ~-*fowl*, -*hen*, gallinaceous bird (*Numida*, esp. *N. meleagris*) with slate-coloured white-spotted plumage, domesticated in Europe; ~-*pig*, (origin of name doubtful) S. Amer. rodent (*Cavia porcellus*) now half-domesticated in Europe etc. as pet, and also as subject for laboratory experiments (hence, *human* ~-*pig*); person receiving guinea fees, esp. company director or deputy clergyman; ~ *worm*, tropical parasitic nematoid worm (*Filaria medinensis*) infesting skin of man and horse, esp. in legs and feet, and causing sores.

guipure (gēp′oor) *n.* Heavy lace made by cutting out pieces of linen and joining them with openwork embroidery.

guise[1] (gīz) *n.* Style of attire, garb (archaic); external appearance; semblance, assumed appearance, pretence.

Guise[2] (gēz). Name of a branch of the princely house of Lorraine, of which the best-known member is Henri de Guise (1550–88), one of the authors of the massacre of St. BARTHOLOMEW and a leader of the *Ligue* which attempted to depose Henri III.

guitar′ (gĭ-) *n.* Musical instrument played esp. in Spain, of lute class, with 6 strings plucked by fingers of right hand, and fretted finger-board for left hand; *English* ~, a kind of cither.

GUITAR

1. Fret

Gujerat′, Gujarat′ (gōō-, -aht). State of W. India formed 1960 from N. part of former Bombay State.

gŭlch *n.* (U.S.) Ravine, esp. one with gold deposit.

gul′den (gōō-) *n.* Principal monetary unit of the Netherlands, guilder, florin, = 100 cents. [Du. & Ger., = 'golden' (orig. name of various gold coins)]

gūles (-lz) *n.* & *adj.* (her.) Red (ill. HERALDRY).

gŭlf *n.* 1. (geog.) Portion of sea partially enclosed by sweep of coast, and usu. narrower at mouth than bay. 2. Deep hollow, chasm, abyss; (poet.) profound depth (in river, ocean); impassable dividing line.

Gŭlf Stream. Great oceanic current of warm water flowing from Gulf of Mexico parallel with Amer. coast to Newfoundland, and thence (under the name of N. Atlantic Drift) towards Europe and round the British Isles.

gŭll[1] *n.* Kinds of long-winged web-footed sea-bird (family *Laridae*), usu. white with mantle varying from pearl-grey to black, with bright-coloured bill and harsh cry; *black-backed*, *black-headed*, *common*, and *herring* ~*s*, species found in Britain. **gŭll′ery** *n.* Colony of sea-gulls; place where these collect.

gŭll[2] *n.* & *v.t.* Dupe, fool. **gŭll′ĭble** *adj.* Easily cheated or duped. **gŭll′ĭbly** *adv.* **gŭllĭbĭl′ĭty** *n.*

Gŭll′ah (-*a*) *n.* One of a group of Negroes, descendants of slaves from W. Africa, inhabiting coastal regions of Carolina, Georgia, and Florida.

gŭll′ėt *n.* Food-passage from mouth to stomach, oesophagus; throat.

gŭll′y *n.* Water-worn ravine; deep artificial channel, gutter, drain, sink; (cricket) part of the field lying between point and the slips (ill. CRICKET). ~ *v.t.* Make gullies in, form (channels) by water-action.

gŭlp *v.* Swallow (usu. *down*) hastily, greedily, or with effort; perform act of swallowing with difficulty, gasp, choke. ~ *n.* Act of gulping; effort to swallow; large mouthful. **gŭlp′ĭngly** *adv.*

gŭm[1] *n.* (usu. pl.) Firm fleshy integument of jaws and bases of teeth; *gum′boil*, small abscess on gum.

gŭm[2] *n.* 1. Viscous secretion of certain trees and shrubs hardening when dry but usu. soluble in water, used as mucilage, to stiffen linen, etc.; sticky secretion collecting in inner corner of eye; viscid or waxy substance surrounding filaments of natural silk; hardish tough sweetmeat made of gelatine; (U.S.) chewing-gum. 2. (also ~-*tree*) Any tree that exudes gum, esp. eucalyptus, various species of the N. Amer. genus *Nyssa* etc.; (U.S.) hollowed-out log, usu. from gum-tree, serving as beehive, water-trough, etc. 3. (U.S.) India-rubber; (pl.) rubber boots. 4. ~ *arabic*: see ARABIC; ~ *dragon*, TRAGACANTH; ~ *juniper*, SANDARAC; ~-*tree*: see 2 above; *up a* ~-*tree*, in a fix, in difficulties. ~ *v.* Stiffen, smear, with gum; fasten *down*, *together*, *up*, etc., with gum; exude gum. **gŭmm′y** *adj.* Viscid, sticky abounding in, exuding, gum.

Gŭm′bō *n.* 1. The okra plant or its pods (*Hibiscus esculentus*); soup thickened with the pods of this plant. 2. A Creole patois in French W. Indies, Louisiana, etc. [Negro patois]

gŭmm′a *n.* (path.) Morbid growth of tissue in late stage of syphilis. **gŭmm′atous** *adj.*

gŭmp′tion *n.* (colloq.) Resource, enterprising spirit, go, ready practical sense.

gŭn *n.* Metal tube for aiming or projecting missiles utilizing the explosive force of gunpowder or some other propellant; piece of ordnance, cannon, musket, fowling-piece, rifle, carbine; insecticide spray; (U.S.) revolver; member of shooting-party; *sure as a* ~, certainly, beyond question; *stick to one's guns*, maintain one's position; *blow great* ~*s*, blow violently, blow a gale; *gun′boat*, small warship carrying heavy gun(s); armed vessel of light draught, esp. for use on rivers; ~-*cotton*, cotton-like explosive made by steeping cotton in mixture of nitric acid and sulphuric acids; cellulose trinitrate; *gun′man*, (esp., U.S. slang) armed robber; ~-*metal*, alloy of copper and tin or zinc (formerly used for guns); *gun′powder*, explosive of saltpetre, sulphur, and charcoal; *Gunpowder Plot*, plot to blow up Houses of Parliament on 5th Nov. 1605, while King, Lords, and Commons were assembled there; *gunpowder (tea)*, fine kind of green tea with leaves rolled up giving granular appearance; ~-*room*, room in private house where guns and sporting equipment are kept; compartment in warship fitted up for junior officers or as lieutenants' mess-room; ~*-runner*, *-running*, (person engaged in) illegal introduction of fire-arms into country; *gun'smith*, maker and repairer of small fire-arms. ~ *v.i.* (chiefly U.S.) Shoot with gun; ~ *for*, go in search of with gun; (slang) 'have it in for (person)'. [perh. f. *Gunna* petform of ON *Gunnhildr* woman's name used as nickname for ballistae and cannon]

gŭnn'el[1] *n.* Butter-fish, small eel-shaped fish (*Pholis gunnellus*) of N. Atlantic, female of which protects her eggs by rolling them into a ball and coiling herself round them.

gŭnnel[2] *n.*: see GUNWALE.

gŭnn'er *n.* Officer or man of artillery (as official term, private); (naut.) warrant officer in charge of battery, magazine, etc.

gŭnn'era *n.* Prickly rhubarb, ornamental foliage plant with gigantic leaves. [J. E. *Gunner* (1718–73), Norw. botanist]

gŭnn'ery *n.* Construction and management of large guns; firing of guns.

gŭnn'y *n.* Coarse sacking, sack, usu. of jute fibre.

gŭn'ter *n.* 1. (also *Gunter's scale*) Flat 2-ft rule with scales etc. on one side, and scales of logarithms on other side, used for mechanical solution of surveying and navigation problems. 2. Topmast, or its sail, sliding up and down lower mast on rings (from resemblance to sliding Gunter's scale; ill. DINGHY). [Edmund *Gunter* (1581–1626), English mathematician]

gunwale (gŭn'l), **gŭnn'el** *n.* Upper edge of ship's or boat's side (ill. BOAT).

gŭp *n.* Gossip; silly talk (orig. Anglo-Ind.).

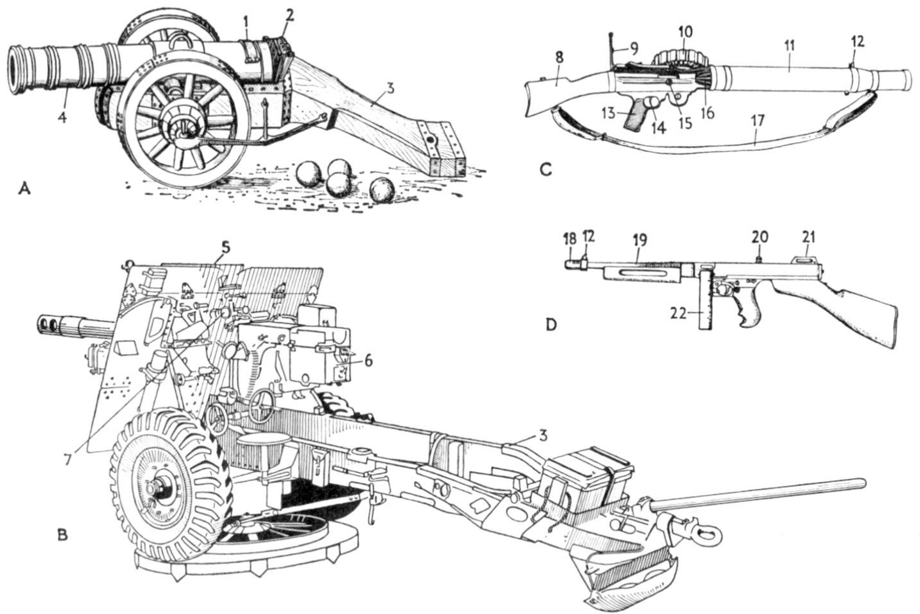

A. FIELD GUN ON CARRIAGE, GERMAN, *c* 1510. B. 25-POUNDER GUN ON CARRIAGE. C. LEWIS MACHINE-GUN. D. THOMPSON SUB-MACHINE-GUN ('TOMMY GUN', MODEL OF 1928)

A. 1. Touch-hole cover. 2. Breech-wedge. 3. Trail. B. 4. Barrel. 5. Gun-shield. 6. Breech. 7. Sight. C. 8. Butt. 9. Adjustable backsight. 10. Magazine for 47 rounds. 11. Casing of cooling system. 12. Foresight. 13. Pistol grip. 14. Trigger 15. Cocking handle. 16. Rear of cooling fins. 17. Sling. D. 18. Recoil-reducer and flash-eliminator. 19. Barrel. 20. Cocking lever. 21. Backsight. 22. Magazine to hold 20 cartridges

gûrgitā'tion *n.* Surging, bubbling motion or sound.

gûrg'le *n.* Bubbling sound as of water poured from bottle or running over stones. ~ *v.* Make gurgle; utter with gurgle(s).

gûrj'un *n.* Large E. Ind. tree (*Dipterocarpus turbinatus*) yielding viscous balsamic liquid (~ *balsam* or *oil*) used medicinally and as varnish.

Gurkha (goork'*a*) *n.* One of a military race, of mixed Aryan-Mongol blood, who settled in the province of Gurkha, Nepal, in the 18th c. and made themselves supreme; they enlisted in specific (*Gurkha*) regiments of the British Indian Army.

gûrn'ard *n.* Marine fish of genus *Trigla* with large spiny head, mailed cheeks, and 2 or 3 pairs of finger-shaped processes used as feelers. [OF *gournart*, lit. = 'grunter']

gŭ'rry *n.* Small Indian fort.

guru (gōō'rōō) *n.* Hindu spiritual teacher or head of religious sect. [Sansk., = 'grave', 'dignified']

gŭsh *n.* Sudden or copious stream (often fig. of speech etc.); effusiveness, sentimental affectation. ~ *v.* Issue in, send forth, gush; emit (water etc.) copiously; speak, behave, with effusiveness. **gŭsh'er** *n.* (esp.) Oil-well spouting oil profusely without pumping. **gŭsh'ingly** *adv.* **gŭsh'y** *adj.*

gŭss'ėt *n.* 1. Triangular piece let into garment to strengthen or enlarge some part. 2. Iron bracket strengthening angle of structure. **gŭss'ėtėd** *adj.*

gŭst[1] *n.* Sudden violent rush of wind; burst of rain, fire, smoke, sound, etc. **gŭst'y** *adj.* **gŭst'ily** *adv.*

gŭst[2] *n.* (archaic & poet.) Sense of taste; keen relish; flavour.

gŭstā'tion *n.* Tasting. **gŭs'tative, gŭs'tatory** *adjs.*

Gŭstāv'us Adŏl'phus (1594–1632). King of Sweden 1611–32; invaded Germany in 1630 and led the forces in opposition to the emperor in the Thirty Years War; defeated Wallenstein at Lützen, but was killed in this battle.

gŭs'tō *n.* Zest, enjoyment with which something is done.

gŭt *n.* 1. (pl.) Bowels or entrails (esp. of animals); (fig. & colloq.) energy, courage, force of character, pluck; (sing.) particular part of lower alimentary canal, intestine;

blind ~, caecum. 2. Material for violin strings made from intestines of animals; material for fishing-lines made from unspun silk-substance in silk-worms. 3. Narrow water-passage, sound, straits; defile, narrow lane or part of street. ~ *v.* Take out guts of, clean, (fish); remove or destroy internal fittings of (house etc.); extract essence of (book etc.).

Gut'enberg (gōō-), Johann (*c* 1398–1468). Printer in Mainz, Germany; inventor of movable printing types.

gŭtt'ae *n.pl.* Drops in a row as ornament esp. in Doric architecture (ill. ORDER).

gŭtt'a-pĕrch'a (*or* -*ka*) *n.* Greyish rubber-like substance obtained from juice of various Malayan trees, esp. *Isonandra gutta*, used in electrical insulations and in the manufacture of golf-balls. [Malay *getāh* gum, *percha* name of tree]

gŭtt'āte *adj.* (biol.) Having drop-like markings.

gŭtt'er *n.* Shallow trough below eaves, channel at side of street, carrying off rain-water; open conduit for outflow of fluid; groove; *in, out of, the* ~, in, out of, low, disreputable, or poverty-stricken surroundings; ~ *press*, newspapers catering for depraved or vulgar taste; ~-*snipe*, street arab. ~ *v.* Furrow, channel; flow in streams; (of candle) melt away by becoming channelled so that wax etc. runs down.

gŭtt'le *v.* Eat gluttonously. **gŭtt'ler** *n.*

gŭtt'ural *adj.* Of the throat; (of sounds) produced in throat, or by back of tongue and palate. ~ *n.* Guttural sound or letter. **gŭtt'uralism** *n.* **gŭtt'uralize** *v.t.* **gŭtt'urally** *adv.*

gŭtt'y *n.* (golf) Gutta-percha ball.

guy[1] (gī) *n.* Rope, chain, etc. to guide and steady thing being hoisted or lowered, or to secure or steady anything liable to shift, or to hold tent etc. in place. ~ *v.t.* Secure with guy(s).

guy[2] (gī) *n.* Effigy of Guy FAWKES burnt on 5th Nov.; grotesquely dressed person, fright; (U.S.) man, fellow. ~ *v.t.* Exhibit in effigy; ridicule, make fun of.

Guy's (Hospital) (gīz). London hospital, founded by Thomas Guy (1645?–1724), a London bookseller and one of the Oxford University printers.

gŭzz'le *v.* Drink, eat, greedily; consume (money etc.) in guzzling. **gŭzz'ler** *n.*

Gwăl'iŏr. The premier Mahratta State of Central India; now called officially Madhya Bharat; capital, Gwalior.

gwȳn'iăd *n.* White-fleshed fish of salmon kind (*Coregonus clupeoides*), found in some lakes of Br. Isles.

gȳbe (j-) *v.* (Of fore-and-aft sail or boom) swing across, make (sail) do this, in wearing or running before wind; (of ship, crew, etc.) change course so that this happens (ill. SAIL[2]).

gyle (g-) *n.* Quantity of beer brewed at once; fermenting wort; fermenting-tun.

gȳm (j-) *n.* (colloq.) Gymnasium, gymnastics; ~-*slip*, -*tunic*, girl's or woman's short sleeveless belted garment worn for gymnastics or games, esp. as school uniform.

gȳmkha'na (j-; -kah-) *n.* (orig. Anglo-Ind.) Public place with facilities for athletics; display of athletic sports; horse and pony meetings, for races, competitions, etc. [mixture of *gymnastics* and Hind. *gend-khāna* ball-house (racquet-court)]

gȳmnās'ium (j-; -z-) *n.* 1. Place, room, or building, with appliances for practice in gymnastics. 2. Continental, esp. German, school of highest grade providing humanistic education.

gȳm'năst (j-) *n.* Expert in gymnastics.

gȳmnăs'tic (j-) *adj.* Of gymnastics; involving bodily or (rarely) mental exercise, discipline, effort, or activity. **gȳmnăs'tically** *adv.* **gȳmnăs'tic** *n.* 1. Course of instruction regarded as discipline. 2. (pl.) Exercises developing the muscles, esp. such as are performed in gymnasium.

gȳmnŏs'ophist (j-) *n.* One of ancient Hindu philosophic sect going nearly naked and given up to contemplation. **gȳmnŏs'ophy** *n.*

gȳm'nospĕrm (j-) *n.* (bot.) Plant having its seeds unprotected by seed-vessels (opp. ANGIOSPERM). **gȳmnospĕrm'ous** *adj.*

gȳnaecē'um (g-, j-) *n.* 1. (Gk & Rom. antiq.) Women's apartments in house. 2. (bot., often incorrectly -*oecium*) Female organs of a flower, the carpels collectively (ill. FLOWER).

gȳnaecŏl'ogy (g-) *n.* Science of diseases of women. **gȳnaecolŏ'gical** *adj.* **gȳnaecŏl'ogist** *n.*

gȳnăn'drous (g-, j-) *adj.* (biol.) Of mixed sex; (bot.) with stamens and pistil united in one column as in orchids.

gynoe'cium: see GYNAECEUM, 2.

gȳp[1] (j-) *n.* Male college servant at Cambridge or Durham. [perh. for obs. *gippo* scullion, orig. man's short tunic, f. obs. Fr. *jupeau*]

gȳp[2] (j-) *n.* (slang) *Give* (someone)~, punish, thrash, treat roughly.

gȳpsŏph'ĭla (j-) *n.* Genus of plants of family *Caryophyllaceae* with small delicate pink or white flowers. [Gk *gupsos* chalk, *philos* loving]

gyp'sum (j-) *n.* Hydrated calcium sulphate, mineral from which plaster of Paris is made by dehydration. **gȳp'sėous, gȳpsĭf'erous, gȳp'sous** *adjs.*

gypsy: see GIPSY.

gȳrāte' (j-) *v.i.* Go in circle or spiral; revolve, whirl. **gȳrā'tion** *n.* **gȳr'atory** *adj.*

gȳr'e (j-) *v.i.* (poet.) Gyrate.

gȳr'ō (j-) *n.* Gyroscope; ~ *compass*, gyroscope made to serve as compass, now fitted in modern ship instead of magnetic compass, points to true north.

gȳr'ograph (j-, -ahf) *n.* Instrument recording revolutions.

gȳr'on (j-) *n.* (her.) Triangular ordinary forming the lower half of an upper quarter (ill. HERALDRY).

gȳr'oplane (j-) *n.* Flying machine in which the lift is mainly provided by vanes rotating freely in a more or less horizontal plane.

gȳr'oscōpe (j-) *n.* Instrument to illustrate dynamics of rotating bodies, solid rotating wheel mounted in ring, with axis free to turn in any direction (the tendency of the wheel, free from disturbing forces, being to maintain rotation in fixed plane); form of this attached to vessels, flying-machines, etc., to maintain equilibrium, act as check on or substitute for mariner's compass, keep torpedo etc. on straight course etc. **gȳroscŏp'ic** *adj.* **gȳroscŏp'ically** *adv.*

GYROSCOPE

1. Gimbals. 2. Fly-wheel. If the fly-wheel is rotated in the direction of the arrow, then a downward force *T* will result in a motion in the direction *P*

gȳr'ostăt (j-) *n.* Form of gyroscope in which the wheel is fixed in a case.

gȳr'us (j-) *n.* (pl. -*rī*). (anat.) Fold, convolution, esp. of brain-surface (ill. BRAIN).

gȳve (j-) *n.* (usu. pl.) & *v.t.* (poet.) Shackle, fetter.

H

H, h (āch). 8th letter of modern English and Roman alphabet, representing historically Semitic 𐤇 (laryngal or guttural spirant, or rough aspirate), Greek H; in modern English usu. standing (except in combination with *c, g, s, t, w*) for simple aspiration or breathing, with just enough narrowing of glottis to be audible before vowel.

h. *abbrev.* Hour(s).

H *abbrev.* Hard(ness).

ha (hah) *int.* Expressing surprise, joy, suspicion, triumph, etc.

H.A.A. *abbrev.* Heavy anti-aircraft.

Hab. *abbrev.* Habakkuk.

Habăkk'uk (7th or 6th c. B.C.). Hebrew prophet; book of O.T. containing his prophecies.

hāb'ėăs cŏrp'us *n.* Writ requiring the body of a person to be brought before a judge or into court, esp. to investigate whether it has been lawful to hold him in custody; ~ *Act*, the Act 31 Chas. II (1679), whereby the granting and enforcing of this writ was much facilitated. [L, = 'you must have the body']

hăb'erdăsher *n.* Dealer in small articles of dress etc., as tape, ribbons, etc. **hăb'erdăshery** *n.*

hăb'ergeon (-jn) *n.* (hist.) Sleeveless coat of mail (ill. ARMOUR).

habĭl'iment *n.* Attire, dress; (pl.) dress suited to particular office or occasion.

habĭl'itāte *v.* 1. Furnish (mine) with working capital. 2. Qualify for office (esp. in German university). **habĭlitā'tion** *n.*

hăb'it *n.* 1. Settled tendency or practice; mental constitution (esp. ~ *of mind*); bodily constitution; (bot., zool.) mode of growth. 2. Dress, esp. of religious order; (also *riding-*~) lady's riding-dress. ~ *v.t.* 1. Clothe. 2. (archaic) Inhabit.

hăb'itable *adj.* That can be inhabited. **hăbitabĭl'ity, hăb'itablenėss** *ns.* **hăb'itably** *adv.*

hăb'itant *n.* 1. Inhabitant. 2. (ăbētahṅ') Native of Canada or Louisiana of French descent.

hăb'ităt *n.* Natural home of plant or animal; habitation. [L, = '(it) inhabits']

hăbitā'tion *n.* Inhabiting; place of abode.

habĭt'ūal *adj.* Customary; constant, continual; given to (specified) habit. **habĭt'ūally** *adv.* **habĭt'ūalnėss** *n.*

habĭt'ūāte *v.t.* Accustom (*to*). **habĭtūā'tion** *n.*

hăb'itūde *n.* Mental or bodily constitution; custom, tendency.

habĭt'ūé (-ā) *n.* Habitual visitor or resident.

Hăbs'bûrg. German family (named after the castle of Habsburg near Aarau in Switzerland) to which belonged the rulers of Austria and many of the Holy Roman Emperors from 1273 to 1918; a Spanish branch of the family ruled Spain fiom 1516 to 1700.

H.A.C. *abbrev.* Honourable Artillery Company.

hăchures' (-shūr) *n.pl.* In map-drawing, short lines of shading indicating differences of slope (close together for steep slopes, wider apart for gradual ones; ill. MAP).

hacĭĕn'da (ăsĭ-, ahthĭ-) *n.* Estate, plantation, with dwelling-house, in Spain, or (former) Spanish colonies.

hăck[1] *n.* Mattock; miner's pick; gash, wound, esp. from kick with toe of boot. ~ *v.* Cut, notch, mangle; kick shin of (opponent at football); deal cutting blows (*at*); emit short dry coughs; *hacking cough*, short dry frequent cough; ~*-saw*, saw with narrow blade set in a frame, for cutting metal (ill. SAW).

hăck[2] *n.* Board on which hawk's meat is laid; frame for drying bricks.

hăck[3] *n.* 1. Horse let out for hire; jade; horse for ordinary riding; (U.S.) hackney carriage. 2. Common (esp. literary) drudge, mere scribbler. ~ *v.* Make common, hackney; ride (horse), ride on horseback, on road at ordinary pace; use hired horses.

hă'ckle *n.* 1. Steel comb for dressing raw silk, flax, etc. 2. Long feathers on neck of domestic cock and other birds; angler's artificial fly dressed with hackle; *with hackles up*, (of cock, dog, etc.) angry, ready to fight. ~ *v.t.* Dress (flax, silk, fly) with hackle.

hăck'ney *n.* Horse of middle size and quality for ordinary riding; drudge, hireling; ~*-carriage, -coach*, etc., vehicle plying for hire. ~ *v.t.* Make common or trite by repetition (esp. in past part. *hackneyed*).

Hădd'ĭngton(shire). Former name of EAST LOTHIAN.

hădd'ock *n.* Fish (*Gadus aeglifinus*) allied to cod but smaller, common in N. Atlantic etc. and much used for food.

hāde *n.* (geol., mining). The angle which a fault plane makes with the vertical plane. ~ *v.i.* (of fault plane) Incline from vertical.

Hā'dēs (-z). (Gk myth.) Oldest name of Pluto; kingdom of Hades, abode of departed spirits or shades; hence, hell, sheol.

Hăd'hramaut (-owt). Part of the E. Aden Protectorate.

Hăd'ĭth. Body of traditions relating to Mohammed, now forming supplement to Koran (the *Sunna*).

Hădj'ĭ, Hăjj'ĭ *n.* (Title of) Mohammedan pilgrim who has been to Mecca.

Hād'rian. Publius Aelius Hadrianus (A.D. 76–138), Roman emperor 117–38; ~*'s Wall*, wall from Solway Firth to mouth of the Tyne, built by Hadrian to protect Roman Britain from the tribes of the north.

haem'al *adj.* Of the blood.

haemăt'ĭc *adj.* Of or containing blood. ~ *n.* Medicine acting on blood.

haem'atĭn *n.* (chem.) Bluish-black amorphous substance with metallic lustre, constituent of haemoglobin.

haem'atīte, hĕm'- *n.* Natural ferric oxide, Fe_2O_3, a red, brown, or blackish iron ore.

haem'atoid, hĕm'- *adj.* Like blood; characterized by presence of blood.

haematūr'ĭa *n.* (path.) Presence of blood in urine.

haemoglōb'ĭn *n.* The oxygen-carrying pigment contained in the red blood-cells of vertebrates.

haemŏl'ȳsis *n.* (physiol., med.) Loss of haemoglobin from red blood-cells. **haemolȳt'ĭc** *adj.*

haemophĭl'ĭa *n.* Constitutional, usu. hereditary, incapacity of blood to clot quickly or at all when shed, involving danger of bleeding to death even from a slight injury.

haemorrhage, hem- (hĕm'-erij) *n.* Escape of blood from blood-vessels; bleeding, internal or external.

haemorrhoids, hem- (hĕm'-eroidz) *n.pl.* Swollen varicose veins of the anus, popularly called piles.

ha'fĭz (hah-) *n.* Mohammedan who knows the Koran by heart. [Arab. *ḥāfiẓ* guardian, observer]

hăf'nium *n.* Rare metallic element (symbol Hf, at. no. 72, at. wt 178·49) usu. found with zirconium and resembling it in properties. [*Hafnia*, L name of Copenhagen]

haft (-ah-) *n.* Handle (of dagger, knife, etc.). ~ *v.t.* Furnish with haft.

hăg[1] *n.* 1. Ugly old woman; witch; (formerly) evil spirit in female form; ~*-ridden*, afflicted by nightmare. 2. (also ~*-fish*) Round-mouthed eel-like fish (*Myxine glutinosa*) allied to lamprey and living on dead or dying fish.

hăg[2] *n.* (Sc.) Piece of soft bog in moor or morass; firm turfy or heathery ground in peat bog.

Hag. *abbrev.* Haggai.

Hagga'dah (-gah'da) *n.* Legendary part of the Talmud, anecdote, parable, etc., introduced to illustrate a point of the Law; Jewish ritual for first two nights of Passover.

Hăgg'āī (6th c. B.C.). Hebrew prophet; book of O.T. containing his prophecies.

hăgg'ard *adj.* Wild-looking (esp. as result of fatigue, privation, worry, etc.); (of hawk) caught in her adult plumage, untamed. **hăgg'ardly** *adv.* **hăgg'ardnėss** *n.* **hăgg'ard** *n.* A haggard hawk.

hăgg'is *n.* Heart, lungs, and liver, of sheep etc., with salt, pepper, onions, suet, etc., and oatmeal, boiled like large sausage in the animal's maw.

hăgg'le *n.* & *v.i.* Dispute, wrangle (esp. *over* or *about* prices or terms).

hagiŏg'rapha (hăg-) *n.pl.* Books of Hebrew Scriptures not included under Law and Prophets. **hăgiŏg'rapher** *n.* Writer of any of these, or of saints' lives. **hăgiogrăph'ic** *adj.* **hăgiŏ'graphy** *n.* Writing of lives of saints.

hagiŏl'atry (hăg-) *n.* Worship of saints.

hagiŏl'ogy (hăg-) *n.* Literature treating of lives and legends of saints.

hag'ioscōpe (hăg-) *n.* = SQUINT (archit.).

Hague (hāg), The. ('s-Gravenhage) Seat of government of the Netherlands; seat of the Court of International Justice.

ha ha (hah hah) *int.* representing laughter.

ha-ha (hah'hah) *n.* Sunk fence bounding park or garden.

Haig (hāg), Douglas, first Earl Haig of Bemersyde (1861–1928). British field-marshal; C.-in-C. British Expeditionary Force in France, 1915–18.

hail[1] *n.* Pellets of condensed and frozen vapour falling in shower, as *~-storm*; shower *of* missiles, questions, etc. ~ *v.* 1. *It hails*, hail falls. 2. (fig.) Pour down (words, blows, etc.), come down, violently.

hail[2] *int.* of greeting; ~ *fellow* (*well met*), familiar, intimate, too intimate, *with*. ~ *v.* Salute; greet (*as*); call to (ship, person) to attract attention; (of ship, person) be come *from* (place). ~ *n.* Salutation; *within* ~, near enough to be hailed. *H~ Mary*: = AVE Maria.

Haileybury (hāl'ĭberĭ). Haileybury and Imperial Services College, a boys' public school in Hertfordshire; Haileybury Coll. founded 1862, I.S.C. founded 1912; the two amalgamated 1942.

hair *n.* One or (collect. sing.) all of the fine filaments growing from skins of animals, esp. from human head (ill. SKIN); (of plants) cells growing from epidermis; hair-like thing; jot, tittle; *to a ~*, exactly; *split hairs*, make fine or cavilling distinctions, be over-precise; *keep one's ~ on*, (slang) keep calm; *get* (person) *by the short hairs*, hold so that escape is painful; have complete control over; *not turn a ~*, show no sign of exhaustion or discomposure; *hair's-breadth*, minute distance; *hair's-breadth escape*, very narrow escape; *hair'brush*, toilet brush for hair; *hair'cloth*, cloth made of hair, for tents, shirts of penitents, etc.; *hair'dresser*, one whose business is to dress and cut hair; *~-line*, line or rope of hair; up-stroke in writing, thin line in (printed) letters (ill. TYPE); *~-net*, *-oil*, *hair'pin*, net, oil, pin, used for the hair; *hair'pin bend*, very sharp bend where road etc. doubles back; *~-raising*, enough to make hair stand on end through fear or excitement; ~ *shirt*, ascetic's or penitent's shirt of haircloth; *~-slide*, horn, tortoiseshell, or metal clip for keeping hair in place; *~-space*, narrowest space between words in printing; *~-splitting*, over-subtle(ty); *~-spring*, fine spring in watch, regulating balance-wheel (ill. CLOCK); *~-stroke*, fine up-stroke in writing; ~ *trigger*, secondary trigger releasing main one by very slight pressure. **hair'iness** *n.* **hair'lėss, hair'līke, hair'y** *adjs.*

Hait'ĭ (*or* hī-). Independent republic (since 1820) occupying western part of island of Hispaniola, W. Indies; capital, Port au Prince. **Hait'ian** *adj.* & *n.*

hāke[1] *n.* Cod-like edible seafish (*Merluccius vulgaris*).

hāke[2] *n.* Wooden frame for drying cheeses, bricks, etc.

hakeem', hakim[1] (-ēm') *n.* In India and Mohammedan countries, physician. [Arab. *ḥakīm* wise, physician]

hakenkreuz (hahk'enkroits) *n.* Swastika, used in Germany and Austria from 1918 onwards as symbol of anti-Semitism or as emblem of the Nazi party. [Ger., = 'hooked cross']

ha'kīm[2] (hah-) *n.* In India and Mohammedan countries, judge, ruler, governor. [Arab. *ḥākim* judge]

Hăk'luyt (-lo͞ot), Richard (1552?–1616). English clergyman; collected and published accounts of English explorations.

halā'tion *n.* (phot.) Spreading of light beyond its proper boundaries on a developed plate.

hăl'berd *n.* (hist.) Combined spear and battle-axe (ill. SPEAR). **hălberdier'** *n.* Man armed with halberd.

hăl'cyŏn *n.* 1. Bird fabled by the ancients to breed in floating nest on sea at winter solstice, and to charm wind and waves into calm for the purpose; kingfisher. ~ *adj.* Calm, peaceful, quiet; ~ *days*, 14 days of calm weather anciently believed to occur about winter solstice.

hāle[1] *adj.* Robust, vigorous.

hāle[2] *v.t.* (archaic) Drag, draw, forcibly.

half (hahf) *n.* (pl. *halves* pr. hahvz). One of two equal or corresponding parts into which thing is divided; (colloq.) half-pint, half-mile, half-back, half-holiday; school term (the school year being formerly divided into two portions); *better ~*, wife; *go halves*, share equally (*with* person *in* thing). ~ *adj.* Forming a half. ~ *adv.* To the extent of half; (loosely) to a considerable extent; *not ~*, (slang) to the greatest possible extent. **half-** in phrases: *half-and-half*, (what is) half one thing and half another, esp. mixture of ale and porter; *~-back*, (football etc.) position, player, immediately behind forwards (ill. ASSOCIATION); *~-baked*, (fig.) not thorough, not earnest, half-witted; *~-bound*, (of book) with leather back and corners, cloth or paper sides (so *~-calf*, *-morocco*, etc.); *~-blood*, person having one parent in common with another, this relationship; person of mixed race; *~-breed*, half-blooded person of mixed race; *~-brother*, brother by one parent only (so *~-sister*); *~-caste*, half-breed; esp. (child) of European father and Indian mother; ~ *cock*: see COCK; *~-crown*, silver or cupro-nickel coin worth 2*s.* 6*d.*; (usu. ~ *a crown*), this sum; *~-hearted*, lacking courage or zeal; so *~-heartedly*, *~-heartedness*; ~ *hitch*: see HITCH; *~-holiday*, day of which (the latter) half is taken as holiday; *~-landing*, landing half-way up flight of stairs (ill. STAIR); *~-length*, portrait of upper half of person; *~-mast*: *at ~-mast*, *~-mast high*, (of flag) lowered to half height of mast as mark of respect for the dead or on other occasions of mourning; ~ *measures*, compromise, half-and-half policy etc.; *~-moon*, moon of which only half is illuminated; anything of this shape; ~ *mourning*, black relieved by grey, lavender, etc., worn as transition from full mourning to ordinary dress; *~(-) nelson*, wrestling hold in which one arm is thrust under corresponding arm of opponent, generally from behind, and the hand pressed on the back of his neck, as opp. to *full nelson* in which both arms and hands are so placed; *~-pay*, reduced allowance to army, navy, or

HALF-TIMBER BUILDING
1. Breastsummer. 2. String-piece. 3. Brick nogging. 4. Stud. 5. Lath and plaster. 6. Wattle and daub. 7. Cruck

air force officer when not in actual service, or after retirement at prescribed time; *~-seas-over*, half drunk; *~ sole*, sole of boot or shoe between shank and toe; *~-timber(ed)*, (archit.) having walls made of timber frame with spaces filled with bricks or plaster; *~-time*, (esp.) interval between two halves of play at football etc.; *~-timer*, (formerly) child who attended school for half usual time, earning money at some employment in other half; *~-title*, title of a book printed at head of first page of text, or title of a section of a book printed on the recto of the leaf preceding it; *~-tone*, (mus.) = SEMITONE; (art) tone intermediate between the extreme lights and extreme shades; photo-mechanical illustration printed from a block in which the tones are broken up into small or large dots by the interposition of a glass screen, ruled with fine cross-lines, between the camera and the object; this process; *~-truth*, statement that conveys only part of the truth, omitting some relevant facts; *~-uncial*, a style of writing intermediate between uncial and minuscule (ill. SCRIPT); *~-volley* (*n.*) (cricket, lawn-tennis, etc.) ball hit or returned as soon as it touches the ground; (*v.*) play (ball) thus; *~-way*, equidistant from two ends; *~-way house*, inn midway between two towns etc.; (fig.) compromise; *~-witted*, imbecile; *~-yearly*, (occurring) every half-year.

halfpenny (hāp'nĭ) *n.* (pl. *halfpence* pr. hāp'ens of amounts, *halfpennies* of coins as such). Bronze coin worth half a penny; this amount, written ½*d.*; *halfpennyworth* (hāp'ath), *ha'p'orth*, as much as a halfpenny will buy.

hăl'ibut *n.* Large flat fish (*Hippoglossus vulgaris*) abundant in northern seas and much used for food. [*haly* holy, *butt* flat fish (because eaten on holy days)]

hăl'īde *n.* A salt derived from a halogen.

hăl'idom *n.* (archaic) Holy thing, anything regarded as sacred, esp. (as oath) *by my ~*.

hălieut'ic *adj.* Of fishing. **hălieut'ics** *n.pl.* Art of fishing.

Hăl'ifăx¹. County borough of West Riding, Yorkshire.

Hăl'ifăx². Capital city of Nova Scotia, Canada.

hălitōs'is *n.* (med.) Foul breath.

hall (hawl) *n.* 1. Large public room in mansion, palace, etc.; principal living-room of medieval house (ill. HOUSE); (in English colleges etc.) common dining-room, dinner in this; large room for public business, entrance-passage of house etc.; (U.S.) any corridor or passage in building; *servants' ~*, room in which servants dine. 2. Residence of landed proprietor; building of guild; (universities) institution governed by head without fellows; building for students having or not having university privileges. 3. *~ church*, type of medieval church having aisles as high as nave; *~-way*, (U.S.) entrance-hall or corridor in building.

hallelujah: see ALLELUIA.

Hăll'ey, Edmund (1656–1742). English astronomer, publisher of Newton's 'Principia'; *H~'s comet*, comet with a periodicity of 76 years, the return of which in 1758 was predicted by Halley.

halliard: see HALYARD.

hall'mârk (hawl-) *n.* Impression stamped on gold or silver article without which it may not legally be sold (in U.K. stamped at one of the 4 official Assay Offices and consisting of 4 marks indicating the standard of fineness, the Assay Office where the article was assayed, the year of assay, and the maker's initial). *~ v.t.* Stamp thus (often fig.). [f. Goldsmiths' *Hall*, London and elsewhere]

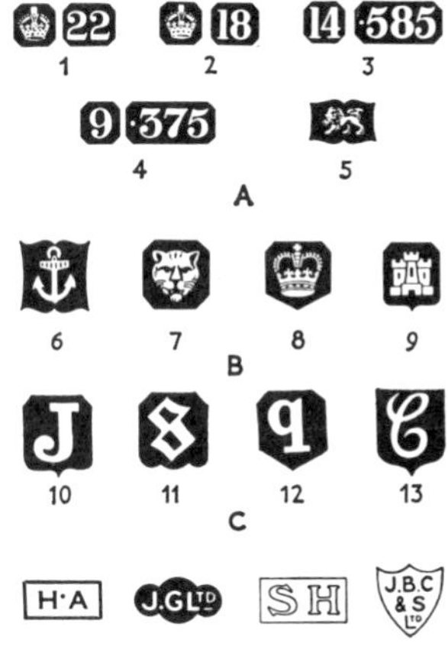

GOLD AND SILVER HALLMARKS: A. STANDARD MARKS. B. OFFICE MARKS. C. DATE LETTERS FOR 1933–4. D. MAKER'S MARKS.

1. 22-carat gold. 2. 18-carat gold. 3. 14-carat gold. 4. 9-carat gold. 5. Sterling silver. 6, 10. Birmingham. 7, 11. London. 8, 12. Sheffield. 9, 13. Edinburgh.

hallō', halloa' (-ō) *int.* calling attention or expressing surprise (e.g. on meeting someone). *~ v.i.* Cry 'hallo!'. *~ n.* The cry.

hallōō' *int.* inciting dogs to the chase, calling attention, or expressing surprise. *~ n.* The cry 'halloo!'. *~ v.* Cry 'halloo!', esp. to dogs; urge on (dogs etc.) with shouts; shout to attract attention.

hăll'ow¹ (-ō) *n.* Holy person, saint, (now only in *all hallows*, *hallowmas*, feast of All-hallows, All Saints' Day; *hallowe'en*, (Sc.) eve of this). *~ v.t.* Make holy; honour as holy.

hăll'ow² (-ō) *v.* Chase with shouts; incite with shouts; shout to incite dogs etc.

Hallstatt civilization (hăl'shtăt *or* -stăt). Prehistoric civilization in Central Europe, named after the finds at Hallstatt in Upper Austria, dated *c* 1000–400 B.C. and characterized by remains showing the transition from bronze to iron culture, usually associated with the Celtic or Alpine race.

hallu'cĭnāte (-lōō-) *v.t.* Produce false impressions in mind of (person). **hallucĭnā'tion** *n.* Illusion; apparent perception of external object not actually present. **hallu'cĭnatory** *adj.*

hăl'ma *n.* Game for two or four persons played on chequer-board of 256 squares with 19 or 13 men placed in one corner of board for each player, the men being moved towards opposite corner with leaps over intervening men into vacant squares beyond.

hăl'ō *n.* Circle of light round luminous body, esp. sun or moon; circle, ring; disc of light surrounding head of saint, nimbus; (fig.) ideal glory investing person etc. *~ v.t.* Surround with halo.

hăl'ogėn *n.* (chem.) Any of the four non-metallic elements fluorine, chlorine, bromine, and iodine.

hăl'oid *adj.* Salt-like.

hăl'ophȳte *n.* Plant inhabiting salty soils.

Hăls, Frans (*c* 1584–1666). Dutch portrait painter; worked at Haarlem; painter of the so-called 'Laughing Cavalier'.

halt¹ (hawlt) *n.* Temporary stoppage on march or journey; small railway-station without usual accommodation or staff, where local trains stop. *~ v.* Make a halt; (mil.) bring to a stand.

halt² (hawlt) *adj.* (archaic) Lame; crippled. *~ v.i.* Walk hesitatingly; hesitate (*between*); (of speech, argument, verse, etc.) be defective; (archaic) be lame. **halt'ingly** *adv.*

ha'lter (hawl-) *n.* Rope, strap, with noose or headstall for horses or cattle; rope with noose for hanging person; death by hanging. *~ v.t.* Fasten with halter; hang (person) with halter.

halve (hahv) *v.t.* Divide into halves; share equally; reduce to half; (golf) reach (hole) in same number of strokes as opponent; fit (crossing timbers) together by cutting out half thickness of each.

hăl'yard, hăll'iard, haul'yard *n.* (naut.) Rope, tackle, for raising or lowering sail, yard, etc. (ill. SAIL¹).

hăm¹ *n.* Back of thigh; thigh and buttock; (formerly) bend of the knee; thigh of hog salted and dried in smoke or otherwise cured for food; (esp. radio) amateur; (slang) ineffective or over-emphatic actor (also attrib.); *~-fisted*, having large or clumsy hands, heavy-handed.

hăm² *n.* (hist.) Town, village.

hămadrȳ'ăd *n.* 1. (Gk myth.) Nymph living and dying with the tree she inhabited. 2. (zool.) King cobra, large, very venomous hooded serpent (*Hamadryas elaps*) of India. 3. (zool.) Large Arabian baboon (*Cynocephalus hamadryas*), held sacred by ancient Egyptians.

hămamēl'ĭs *n.* Genus of shrubs of which the N. Amer. species (*H. virginica*) is the witch hazel.

Hăm'bûrg. 1. City of N. Germany on the Elbe, forming a province of the Federal Republic. 2. Small variety of domestic fowl. 3. Black variety of hothouse grape (*black Hamburg*). 4. ~ (*steak*), chopped beef, spiced and flavoured, formed into a cake and fried. **Hăm'bûrger** (-g-) *n.* 1. Citizen of Hamburg. 2. Hamburg steak.

hāmes (-mz) *n.pl.* Two curved pieces of wood or metal fastened over collar of draught horse, used to attach the traces (ill. HARNESS).

Hămĭl'car. Hamilcar Barca (3rd c. B.C.), Carthaginian general of 1st Punic War; father of HANNIBAL.

Hăm'īte. (Supposed) descendant of Ham, second son of Noah; member of Egyptian or other African race. **Hamĭt'ĭc** *adj.* Of Hamites; esp. of the group of African languages including ancient Egyptian, Berber, Galla, etc.

hăm'lĕt¹ *n.* Small village, esp. one without church.

Hăm'lĕt². Legendary prince of Denmark, hero of a tragedy by Shakespeare; ~ *without the Prince*, entertainment etc. from which chief personage is absent.

hămm'er *n.* Instrument for beating, breaking, driving nails, etc., with hard solid (usu. metal)

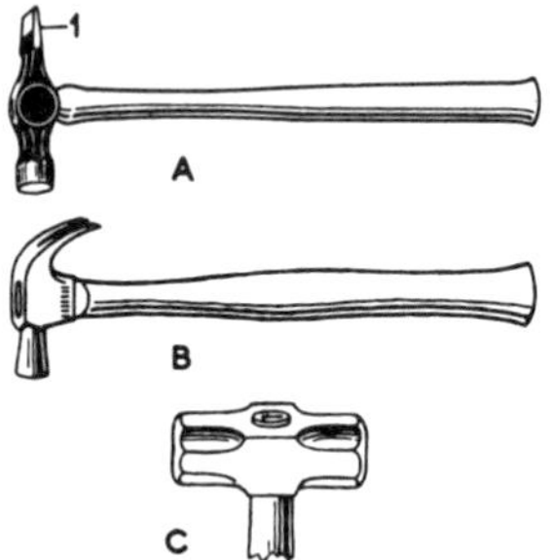

A. JOINER'S HAMMER. B. CLAW HAMMER. C. SLEDGE-HAMMER

1. Pane

head at right angles to handle; machine with metal block serving same purpose; similar contrivance, as for exploding charge in gun, striking string of piano, etc.; auctioneer's mallet used to indicate by rap that article is sold; *come under the* ~, be sold by auction; *throwing the* ~, athletic contest of throwing heavy hammer; ~ *and tongs*, with might and main; ~ *beam*, beam projecting from wall at foot of principal rafter (ill. ROOF); ~-*cloth*, cloth covering driver's seat in coach; ~-*head*, head of hammer; kind of shark with great lateral expansions of head; kind of African bird, shadow-bird (*Scopus umbretta*); ~-*lock*, (wrestling) position in which a wrestler is held with one arm bent behind his back; ~-*toe*, toe deformed by being bent inwards. ~ *v.* Strike, beat, drive, (as) with hammer; (colloq.) inflict heavy defeat(s) on in war or games; work hard *at*; (St. Exch.) declare (person) a defaulter with 3 taps of hammer.

hămm'ock *n.* Hanging bed of canvas or netting suspended by cords at ends, used esp. on board ship.

Hămm'ond ôrg'an. Pipeless organ in which sound is produced by electric lamps. [*Hammond* Electric Co. of Chicago]

Hămp'den (-md-), John (1594–1643). English M.P.; famous for his resistance to Charles I's 'ship-money' tax; killed in the Civil War.

hăm'per¹ *n.* Basketwork packing-case.

hăm'per² *v.t.* Obstruct movement of (person etc.) with material obstacles; (fig.) impede, hinder. ~ *n.* (naut.) Necessary but cumbrous part of equipment of vessel.

Hămp'shire. Southern county of England.

Hăm'pton Court. Palace on the Thames west of London, built by Cardinal Wolsey and ceded by him to Henry VIII; now preserved as a museum and partly occupied by persons of rank in reduced circumstances; ~ *Conference*, conference held there in 1604 to settle points of dispute between the Church party and the Puritans.

hăm'shăckle *v.t.* Shackle (horse etc.) with rope connecting head and foreleg.

hăm'ster *n.* Small rat-like hibernating rodent (*Cricetus frumentarius*), with short tail, and cheek-pouches for carrying grain.

hăm'strĭng *n.* (In man) one of 5 tendons at back of knee; (in quadrupeds) great tendon at back of hock in hind leg, corresponding to that of heel in man. ~ *v.t.* (past t. & past part. -*strung*). Cripple by cutting hamstring(s).

hăm'ūlŭs *n.* (anat., zool.) Hook-like process.

Hăn. Chinese dynasty, 206 B.C. to A.D. 220, when Chinese bureaucracy was developed and Buddhism introduced.

h. & c. *abbrev.* Hot and cold (water).

hănd *n.* 1. Terminal part of human being's or monkey's arm beyond wrist; forefoot of quadruped. 2. Possession, charge, authority, disposal; agency, instrumentality; share in the doing of something; pledge of marriage, bestowal in marriage. 3. Side (right or left), direction, quarter. 4. Person, source, from which thing comes; person who does something, person in relation to action or in reference to skill in doing something; workman, manual worker; (pl.) ship's crew; *all hands*, the whole crew. 5. Skill; style of workmanship; turn, innings, at cricket, billiards, etc.; style of writing; signature. 6. Hand-like thing, esp.

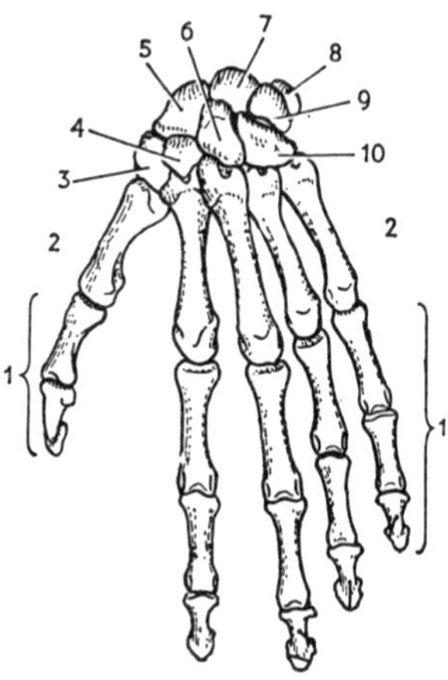

HAND AND WRIST

1. Phalanges. 2. Metacarpus. 3–10. Wrist or carpus. 3. Trapezium. 4. Trapezoid. 5. Scaphoid bone 6. *Os capitatum.* 7. *Os lunatum.* 8. Pisiform bone. 9. *Os triquetrum.* 10. *Os hamatum*

pointer of clock or watch; fixed quantity of various commodities, e.g. bundle of tobacco leaves. 7. Lineal measure of horse's height, = 4 inches. 8. (cards) Cards dealt to a player; player holding these; single round of game; game (of cards etc.). 9. *at* ~, close by; about to happen soon; *by* ~, by physical (as opp. to mechanical) labour; (*live*) *from* ~ *to mouth*, improvidently; *in* ~, held in the hand; at one's disposal; under control; receiving attention; *off* ~, without preparation, then and there; *on* ~, in one's possession; *on one's* ~*s*, resting on one as a responsibility; *on all* ~*s*, to, from, all quarters; *out of* ~, at once, extempore; out of control; *to* ~, within reach, (commerc.) received; *to one's* ~, ready for one without exertion on one's own part; *bear a* ~, take part *in*; *come to* ~, turn up, be received; *do a* ~*'s turn*, make the slightest effort; *lay* ~*s on*, touch, seize; *take in* ~, undertake; *change* ~*s* (of property) pass from one person to another; *with a heavy* ~, oppressively; *with a high* ~, boldly, arrogantly; *have, keep, one's* ~ *in*, be in practice; (*win*) ~*s down*, easily, without effort; ~*s off!*, do not touch; ~*s up!* (direction to persons to hold up their hands as sign of assent etc., or to preclude resistance); ~ *over hand* or *fist*, with each hand successively passing over the other, as in climbing rope; (fig.)

with steady or rapid progress; ~ *to hand*, (of conflict etc.) at close quarters; ~ *in* (or *and*) *glove*, intimate (*with*). 10. *hand-* = made, etc. by hand and not by machinery; *~-ball*, ball for throwing with hand; game played with this between two goals; *hand'-bell*, bell rung by hand, esp. one of set for musical performance; *hand'bill*, printed notice circulated by hand; *hand'book*, short treatise, manual, guide-book; *~-canter*, gentle canter; *~-cart*, cart pushed or drawn by hand; *hand'cuffs*, pair of metal rings joined by short chain, for securing prisoner's hands; *hand'-cuff* (*v.*) secure (person) with these; *~-gallop*, easy gallop; *~-glass*, magnifying-glass held in hand; small mirror with handle; *hand'hold*, something for the hands to grip on (in climbing etc.); *hand'maid*(*en*), (archaic, exc. fig.) female servant; *~-organ*, barrel-organ with crank turned by hand; *~'-out*, (U.S.) what is handed out, e.g. alms; (orig. U.S.) matter handed out to the newspaper press; *~-rail*, railing along edge of stairs etc.; *hand'shake*, shake of person's hand with one's own, as greeting; *hand'spike*, lever for shifting heavy objects, as guns, by hand; spoke of capstan or windlass: *~-spring*, *turn ~-springs*, turn somersaults; *hand'writing*, writing by hand, esp. of particular person. ~ *v.t.* Help (person) with the hand (*into*, *out of*, carriage etc.); (naut.) take in (sail); deliver, transfer by hand or otherwise; ~ *off*, (Rugby football) push (opponent) off with the hand; ~ *it to*, acknowledge superiority of.

Hăn'del (orig. *Haendel*), George Frederick (1685–1759). German-born composer of operas and oratorios; settled in England in 1712 and became court composer; famous for his 'Messiah', 'Samson', 'Judas Maccabaeus', etc.

hănd'ful (-ŏŏl) *n.* Quantity that fills the hand; small number (of men etc.); (colloq.) troublesome person or task.

hăn'dĭcăp *n.* Race, for horses or men, or any contest of skill or strength, in which in order to equalize chances of winning, some artificial disadvantage, in time, weight, score, etc., is imposed on a superior competitor, or some similar advantage is given to an inferior competitor; the advantage given or the disadvantage imposed; (fig.) disability of any kind which puts a person at a disadvantage compared with his fellows. ~ *v.t.* Impose handicap on (competitor); (fig., of circumstances) place (person) at disadvantage. **hăn'dĭcăpper** *n.*

hăn'dĭcraft (-ahft) *n.* Manual skill; manual art or trade, as weaving, pottery, etc.; *hand'icraftsman*, man who exercises a handicraft.

hăn'dĭwork (-wẽrk) *n.* Work done, thing made, by the hands or by anyone's personal agency.

handkerchief (hăng'kerchĭf) *n.* Square of linen, silk, etc., carried in pocket (*pocket-~*) for wiping nose etc. or worn about neck.

hăn'dle[1] *n.* That part of thing which is made to hold it by; fact that may be taken advantage of (*against* person); ~ *to one's name*, title; *~-bar*, (of bicycle etc.) steering-bar with handle at each end.

hăn'dle[2] *v.t.* Touch, feel, with the hands; manipulate; manage (thing, person); treat; treat of; deal in (goods).

hăn(d)'sel *n.* Gift at beginning of New Year, or on entering on new circumstances; earnest-money; foretaste. ~ *v.t.* Give handsel to; inaugurate; be the first to try.

hănd'some (-ns-) *adj.* Of fine form or figure; (of conduct etc.) generous; (of price, fortune, etc.) considerable. **hănd'somely** *adv.* **hănd'somenėss** *n.*

hăn'dy *adj.* Ready to hand; convenient to handle; clever with the hands; *~-man*, man useful for all sorts of odd jobs; sailor.

hăng *v.* (past t. and past part. *hung*, exc. as below). 1. Suspend, attach loosely (*from*, *to*); suspend (meat, game) to dry or become tender or high; place (picture) on wall; attach (wall-paper); suspend floating in space; rest (door on hinges, coach on springs, etc.) in free swinging position; let droop; remain, be, suspended; decorate *with* (things suspended). 2. (past t. and past part. *hanged*) Suspend, be suspended, by the neck on gallows as capital punishment; ~ *oneself*, commit suicide by suspension by the neck. 3. ~ *about*, loiter, linger, about; ~ *back*, show reluctance to act or move; ~ *fire*, (of fire-arm) be slow in going off (freq. fig.); ~ *heavy*, (of time) pass slowly; ~ *on*, depend, rely, on; attend carefully to (words etc.); stick closely (*to*); ~ *out*, suspend from window etc.; protrude downwards; (slang) reside; ~ *together*, be coherent, be associated; ~ *up*, suspend; end telephone conversation by hanging up receiver, ring off; (fig.) put aside, postpone indefinitely; *~-dog*, base and sneaking (fellow); *hang'man*, executioner; *~-nail*, AGNAIL; *~-over*, (U.S.) survival, remainder; (slang) unpleasant after-effects of dissipation. ~ *n.* Downward droop or bend; way a thing hangs; *get the ~ of*, get the knack of, understand.

hăng'ar *n.* Shed for housing aircraft.

hăng'er[1] *n.* (esp.) Loop etc. by which thing is hung; chain, rod, to which pot is hung in fire-place by pot-hook; stroke with double curve in writing (ʅ); short sword, orig. hung from belt; *~-on*, follower, dependant.

hăng'er[2] *n.* Wood on side of steep hill.

hăng'ĭng *n.* (esp., pl.) Drapery with which walls etc. are hung: ~ *committee*, committee deciding on choice of pictures for exhibition; *a ~ matter*, action etc. resulting in capital punishment.

hănk *n.* Circular loop or coil, esp. as definite length of cotton yarn (840 yds), worsted (560 yds), etc.; (naut.) ring of rope, iron, etc., for fixing staysails to stays.

hănk'er *v.i.* Crave, long, *after*. **hănk'erĭng** *n.*

hănk'y *n.* Nursery abbrev. of handkerchief.

hănk'y-pănk'y *n.* Jugglery; underhand dealing.

Hănn'ĭbal (3rd c. B.C.). Carthaginian general; fought against Rome in 2nd Punic War; crossed the Alps into Italy and defeated the Romans at Lake Trasimene (217 B.C.) and Cannae (216 B.C.); was eventually forced to withdraw from Italy and was defeated by Scipio at Zama, N. Africa, in 202 B.C.

Hăn'over (Ger. *Hannover*). N. German town, capital of Lower Saxony; formerly capital of the country of Hanover which was an Electorate of the Empire and subsequently a province of Prussia; in 1714 the Elector of Hanover (Georg Ludwig) became King George I of England; *House of ~*, British royal dynasty from 1714 to the death of Queen Victoria in 1901. **Hănovēr'ian** *adj.* & *n.* 1. (Inhabitant) of Hanover. 2. (Member) of House of Hanover.

Hăn'sard. Official report of proceedings and debates in British Houses of Parliament; compiled by Messrs. Hansard 1774–1892, now published by H.M. Stationery Office.

Hăn'se (-*e*). Company or guild of merchants, esp. political and commercial league (*Hanseatic League*) of Germanic towns, which flourished in the 14th and 15th centuries and maintained a house in London. **Hănsėăt'ic** *adj.* Of the German Hanse.

hăn'som *n.* ~ (*cab*), two-wheeled cabriolet for two inside, with driver

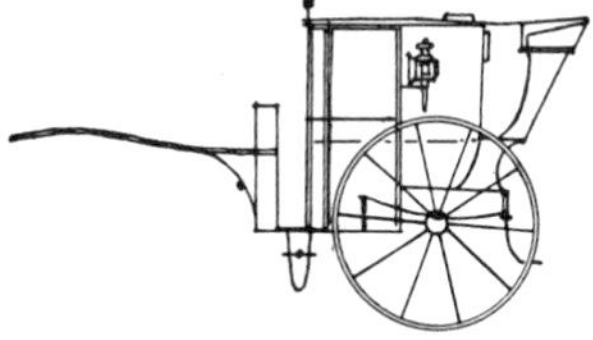

HANSOM

mounted behind and reins going over roof. [J. A. *Hansom* (1803–82), Engl. inventor]

Hants *abbrev.* Hampshire.

hăp *n.* (archaic) Chance, luck, lot; chance occurrence. ~ *v.i.* Come about by chance; happen (*to* do).

hăp'ăx lėgŏm'ėnon *n.* Word of which only one use is recorded. [Gk, = 'once said']

hăp'hăz ard (-p-h-) *n.* Mere chance. ~ *adj.* & *adv.* Casual(ly).
hăp'lėss *adj.* Unlucky. **hăp'lėssly** *adv.*
hăplŏg'raphy *n.* Mistake of writing once what should be written twice, e.g. *philogy* for *philology*.
hăp'loid *adj.* (biol.) (of germ-cell) Having half the characteristic number of chromosomes.
hăp'ly *adv.* (archaic). By chance; perhaps.
ha'p'orth: see HALFPENNY.
hăpp'en *v.i.* Come to pass (by chance or otherwise); chance, have the fortune, *to* (do); come *upon* by chance. **hăpp'ening** *n.*
hăpp'y *adj.* (Of person or circumstance) lucky, fortunate; contented or pleased with one's lot; successful, apt, felicitous; ~ *family*, animals of different kinds in a cage or trained to live together; ~ *families*, game played with cards, each depicting one member of family of four, the aim being to make as many complete families as possible; ~ *dispatch*, HARA-KIRI; ~*-go-lucky* (*adj.*), haphazard. **hăpp'ily** *adv.* **hăpp'inėss** *n.*
Hapsburg: see HABSBURG.
hara-kĭ'rĭ (hah-) *n.* Suicide by disembowelment, as practised by upper classes in Japan when in disgrace or sentenced to death. [Jap. *hara* belly, *kiri* cut]
harangue' (-ăng) *n.* Speech to an assembly; loud or vehement address. ~ *v.* Make harangue (to).
hă'rass *v.t.* Vex by repeated attacks; trouble, worry. **hă'rassment** *n.*
har̄b'inger (-nj-) *n.* 1. (formerly) One sent to purvey lodgings for army, royal train, etc. 2. One who announces another's approach, forerunner. ~ *v.t.* Announce approach of.
har̄b'our (-b*er*) *n.* Place of shelter for ships, esp. where they may lie close to and sheltered by shore, piers, etc.; shelter. ~ *v.* Give shelter to, foster, cherish (evil thoughts); come to anchor in harbour. **har̄b'ourage** *n.* (Place of) shelter.
har̄d *adj.* 1. Firm, unyielding to touch, solid; (of lawn-tennis court) made of asphalt, gravel, etc., not of grass; (of porcelain) made of hard paste; (of sauce) not liquid. 2. Difficult (*to* do); difficult to understand or explain; ~ *of hearing*, somewhat deaf. 3. Difficult to bear; unfeeling, harsh; involving undue or unfair suffering; stingy; harsh, unpleasant, to eye or ear; (of market prices) high, unyielding; strenuous; (U.S. of liquor) spirituous, strong, intoxicating. 4. (phonetics) applied to: (*a*) the letters *c*, *g* when they have their original guttural sounds, as in *can*, *get*, as dist. from the palatal and sibilant sounds, as in *centre*, *gin*; (*b*) to voiceless as dist. from voiced consonants, as *th* in *think* compared with *th* in *this*. ~ *adv.* Strenuously, severely; with difficulty; *be ~ put to it*, be in difficulties; *go* ~, fare ill (*with*); ~ *by*, close by; ~ (*up*)*on*, too severe in criticism or treatment; (of circumstances) bearing with undue severity on; ~ *upon*, close to. ~ *adj.* or *adv.* in combination; ~ *and fast*, (of rules) strict; ~*-bake*, almond toffee; ~*-bitten*, tough in fight, stubborn; *hard'board*, stiff board made from wood waste and used as a substitute for wood; ~ *boiled*, (of eggs) boiled until white and yolk are solid; hardened, callous, hard-headed, sophisticated; ~ *cash*, (orig.) specie as opp. to paper currency, (now) cash as opp. to credit; ~ *coal*, anthracite; ~ *core*, stones, clinker, etc., used as foundation for a road; (fig.) an irreducible nucleus or residuum; ~ *currency*, currency of any country with which another has an adverse balance of payments, with the consequence that difficulties arise in maintaining a supply of it (cf. SOFT); ~*-favoured*, *-featured*, with harsh or ugly features; ~*-fern*, any fern of the genus *Lomaria*; ~*-headed*, practical, not sentimental; ~*-hearted*, unfeeling; ~*-hit*, severely troubled; ~ *labour*, (now only hist. in Britain) orig., labour as work at tread-wheel, stone-breaking, etc., imposed on certain classes of criminals during their term of imprisonment; later (in Britain until the prison reforms of 1938), deprivation of privileges or amenities of ordinary prison life during the first fortnight of imprisonment; ~*-laid*, (of string, fabric, etc.) tightly twisted or woven; ~ *mouthed*, (of horse) not easily controlled by bit (also fig.); ~*-pan*, firm subsoil of clayey, gravelly, or sandy detritus; hard unbroken ground; ~ *rubber*, EBONITE; ~*-shell*, having a hard shell, as ~*-shell crab*, one that has not recently moulted; (U.S. fig.) rigid and uncompromising in religious orthodoxy (esp. *H~-shell Baptists*); ~ *swearing*, swearing (as witness) persistently and tenaciously to one effect regardless of perjury; ~ *tack*, ship-biscuit; hence, ordinary sea-fare; ~*-up*, in want, esp. of money; at a loss *for*; (naut., of tiller) as far as possible to windward; *hard'ware*, ironmongery; ~ *water*, water containing mineral, esp. calcareous, salts which decompose soap, thus making the water unsuitable for washing etc., and cause incrustations in boilers; *hard'wood*, wood of deciduous trees as opp. to pines and firs; in Australia, various kinds of teak-like timber. ~ *n.* 1. Firm beach or foreshore; sloping roadway across foreshore. 2. (slang) Imprisonment with hard labour. **har̄d'en** *v.* Make or become hard, callous, or robust.
Har̄d'enberg (-ar̄g), Friedrich Leopold von (1772–1801). German romantic poet and novelist; author, under the pseudonym 'Novalis', of the mystic 'Hymns of Night' and the novel 'Heinrich von Ofterdingen'.
har̄d'ihŏŏd *n.* Boldness audacity.
Har̄d'ing, Warren Gamaliel (1865–1923). 29th president of U.S., 1921–3.
har̄d'ly *adv.* In a hard manner; with difficulty; harshly; scarcely.
har̄d'nėss *n.* 1. Quality or state of being hard. 2. (min.) Degree of resistance of a mineral to abrasion or scratching; the hardness of a mineral is expressed in terms of the following scale, known as MOHS' scale: (i) talc; (ii) gypsum; (iii) calcite; (iv) fluorite; (v) apatite; (vi) orthoclase; (vii) quartz; (viii) topaz; (ix) sapphire (corundum); (x) diamond; thus, in the description of a mineral, 'H. 7·5' means that it is harder than quartz, but softer than topaz. 3. Quality of water containing dissolved salts of calcium and magnesium; bicarbonates causing temporary hardness, i.e. removable by boiling, and sulphates and chlorides causing permanent hardness, i.e. not removable by boiling; the degree of hardness of water is determined by the amount of standard soap solution sufficient to produce a lather and is expressed in terms of grains of calcium carbonate (*grains of hardness*) per gallon of water.
har̄ds, hūrds *n.pl.* Coarser part of flax or hemp separated in hackling.
har̄d'ship *n.* Hardness of fate or circumstance; severe suffering or privation.
har̄d'y[1] *adj.* 1. Bold, audacious. 2. Robust, capable of endurance; (hort., of plants) able to grow in the open air all the year; *half* ~, requiring shelter in winter only; ~ *annual*, annual that may be sown, or that sows itself, in the open; (fig.) subject that comes up yearly. **har̄d'ily** *adv.* **har̄d'inėss** *n.*
har̄d'y[2] *n.* Blacksmith's bar of hard iron for cutting metal on etc.
Har̄d'y[3], Thomas (1840–1928). English novelist and poet; author of many novels of 'Wessex' life, including 'Tess of the D'Urbervilles' (1891), 'Jude the Obscure' (1896), etc.
hāre *n.* Rodent quadruped (*Lepus*), resembling a rabbit, but larger, with long ears and hind legs, short tail, and divided upper lip, noted for timidity and swiftness; the two species common in Europe are *L. europaeus*, the brown hare, and *L. timidus*, the blue or mountain hare, which changes to white in winter in snowy places; *hold* (*run*) *with the ~ and run* (*hunt*) *with the hounds*, keep in with both sides; ~ *and hounds*, paper-chase; *hare'bell*, round-leaved bell-flower (*Campanula rotundifolia*) with pale-blue flower and very slender stalk; ~*-brained*, rash, wild; ~*-lip*, fissure of upper lip caused by arrested development of upper lip or jaw;

hare's-foot, hare's foot used for applying rouge etc. to face; species of clover (*Trifolium arvense*) with soft hair about flowers; corkwood tree. ~ *v.i.* Run or move with great speed.

hâr'em (*or* hâr'ēm) *n.* Women's part of Moslem dwelling-house; its occupants, female members of Moslem family, esp. wives and concubines.

hâre'wŏŏd *n.* Stained sycamore-wood, used in cabinet-making.

Hâr'greaves (-grāvz), James (1720–78). Lancashire-born mechanic who invented the SPINNING JENNY.

hă'ricot (-kō) *n.* Ragout (usu. of mutton); ~ (*bean*), kidney- or French-bean (*Phaseolus vulgaris*), esp. the dried seeds of some varieties.

hârk *v.* Listen; (as call to hounds) go *forward, away*, etc.; ~ *back*, (of hounds) retrace course to find scent; recall (hounds); (fig.) revert (*to* subject).

hârl(e) *n.* Flax or hempen fibre; barb of a feather.

Hârlei'an (-lē-) *adj.* Of the library or MS. collections (in the British Museum) of Robert Harley, Earl of Oxford (1661–1724) and his son Edward.

Hârl'ėm. District of Manhattan borough, New York City; the chief Negro quarter of New York.

hârl'ėquin (-kwĭn) *n.* Character in Italian comedy; in English pantomime, mute character, invisible to clown and pantaloon, in parti-coloured bespangled tights and visor, and carrying wooden sword or lath as magic wand; ~ (*duck*) northern species of duck (*Histrionicus minutus*) with fantastically variegated plumage. **hârlėquināde'** *n.* Part of pantomime (now usu. omitted) in which harlequin and clown play principal parts.

Hârl'ey Street. London street associated with eminent or fashionable physicians and surgeons; hence, medical specialists.

hârl'ot *n.* Prostitute. **hârl'otry** *n.*

hârm *n.* Damage, hurt; mischief, injury; *out of ~'s way*, in safety. ~ *v.t.* Do harm to; damage, injure. **hârm'ful** *adj.* **hârm'fully** *adv.* **hârm'fulnėss** *n.* **hârm'lėss** *adj.* Doing no harm. **hârm'lėssly** *adv.* **hârm'lėssnėss** *n.*

hârmătt'an *n.* Parching land-wind (with red dust-fog) on coast of upper Guinea in December, January, and February.

hârmŏn'ĭc *adj.* Harmonious, concordant; relating to harmony; (math., of quantities) with reciprocals in arithmetical progression; ~ *conjugates*, (math.) the 1st and 3rd of 4 points that divide a line harmonically in relation to the 2nd or 4th or vice versa; ~ *division*, (math.) division of a line at 4 points so that the distances of the 2nd, the 3rd, and the 4th point from the 1st are in harmonic proportion; ~ *minor*, (mus.) scale with minor 6th and major 7th both ascending and descending (ill. SCALE); ~ *motion*, the motion of the point where a perpendicular to a diameter from a point on the circumference moves round the circumference at a constant speed; any similar motion, e.g. that of the piston of a steam-engine, or any part of a vibrating system; ~ *pencil*, (math.) a set of 4 lines passing through one point and lying in the same plane which divide any other line in that plane harmonically; ~ *progression*, (math.) series of numbers whose reciprocals are in arithmetical progression, as $\frac{1}{2}$, $\frac{1}{3}$, $\frac{1}{4}$, or 12, 15, 20; ~ *stop*, (in organ) stop in which each pipe has small hole in middle, so as to give note corresponding to half its length; ~ *tones*, tones produced by vibration of sonorous body in aliquot parts of its length. **hârmŏn'ically** *adv.* **hârmŏn'ĭc** *n.* Secondary tone produced by vibration of aliquot parts of sonorous body, usu. accompanying primary or fundamental tone produced by vibration of body as a whole, but sometimes produced independently, as in stringed instrument by light pressure on the string at various points etc.; (elect.) one of the component frequencies of a wave or alternating current which is an integral multiple of the fundamental frequency.

HARMONIC TONES OF THE FUNDAMENTAL NOTE G (1)

hârmŏn'ĭca *n.* Various kinds of musical instrument, esp. mouth-organ, with row of free reeds arranged in a case so as to give different notes by expiration and inspiration.

hârmō̆n'ious *adj.* Concordant, forming a consistent or agreeable whole; free from dissent; sweet-sounding; singing, playing, tunefully. **hârmōn'iously** *adv.*

hârm'onist *n.* Person skilled in harmony; collater of parallel narratives; harmonizer. **hârmonis'tic** *adj.*

hârmōn'ium *n.* Keyboard musical instrument, resembling a portable organ, in which the keys operate metal reeds, and a bellows, worked by the player's feet, supplies the wind.

hârm'onize *v.* Bring into, be in, harmony (*with*); make, be, agreeable in artistic effect; add notes to (melody) to form chords. **hârmonizā'tion** *n.*

hârm'ony *n.* 1. Combination or arrangement of parts to form consistent and orderly whole, agreement, congruity; agreeable effect of apt arrangement of parts. 2. Combination of musical notes to produce pleasing effect; combination of (simultaneous) notes to form chords, part of music dealing with formation and relation of chords. 3. Collation of parallel narratives, passages on same subject etc., esp. of the four Gospels.

hârn'ėss *n.* Gear of draught horse or other animal; (fig.) working equipment; apparatus in loom

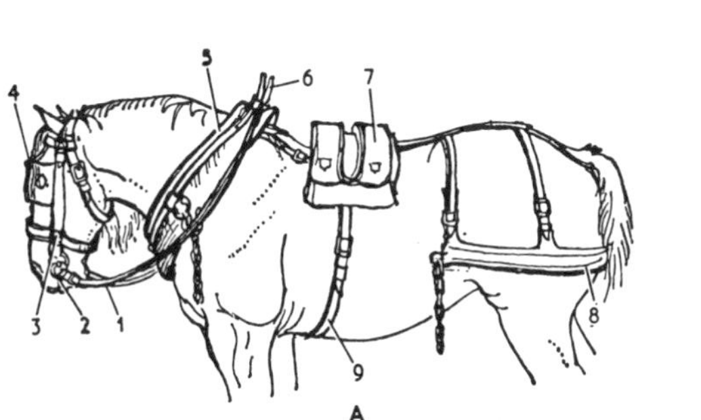

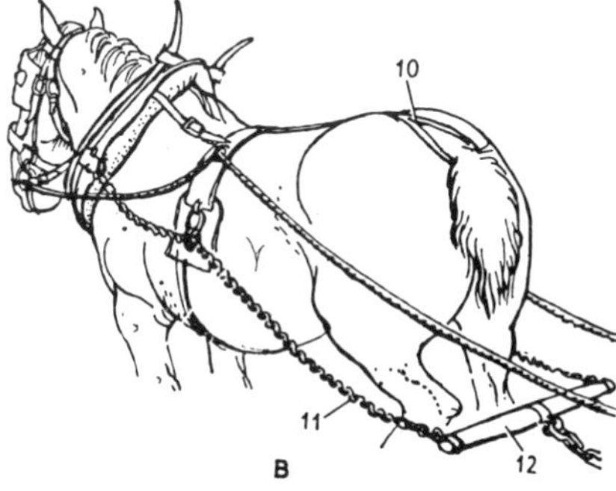

HARNESS: A. CART GEAR. B. PLOUGH GEAR

1. Reins. 2. Bit. 3. Bridle. 4. Blinkers. 5. Collar. 6. Hames. 7. Saddle. 8. Breeching. 9. Girth. 10. Crupper. 11. Trace. 12. Swingle-tree

for shifting warp-threads; (hist.) defensive armour; *in* ~, in the routine of daily work; ~-*cask*, (naut.) cask with rimmed cover for keeping salt meat for current consumption. ~ *v.t.* Put harness on (horse etc.); (fig.) utilize (river, waterfall, natural forces) for motive power.

Hă'rold II. King of England in 1066; killed in that year at the battle of Hastings.

Haroun'-al-Raschid (-rōōn, răsh'ēd) (763–809). 'Haroun the Just', caliph of Baghdad, who figures in many of the tales of the 'Arabian Nights'.

hârp *n.* Stringed musical instrument, roughly triangular, with strings of graduated lengths played with fingers, and with pedals for raising tone of strings by one or two semitones. ~ *v.i.* Play on harp; dwell tediously *on* (subject). **hârp'ĭst** *n.*

with crested head and fan-shaped tail.

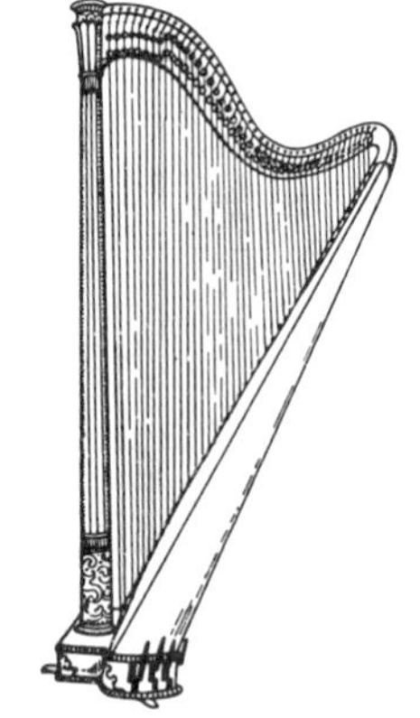

HARP

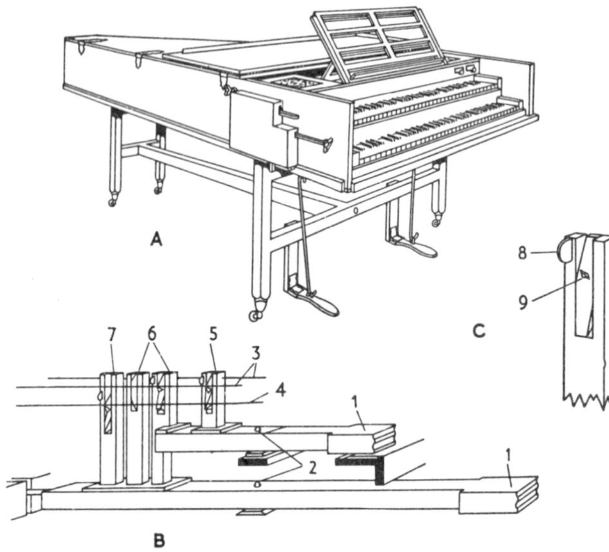

A. TWO-MANUAL HARPSICHORD. B. ACTION. C. DETAIL OF JACK

1. Keys. 2. Balance. 3. Strings. 4. Octave string. 5. Lute jack. 6. Unison jacks. 7. Octave jack. 8. Damper. 9. Plectrum

hârpōōn *n.* Barbed spear-like missile with rope attached, for catching whales and large fish; ~-*gun*, gun for firing harpoon. ~ *v.t.* Strike, spear, with harpoon.

hârp'sichôrd (-k-) *n.* Keyboard musical instrument resembling in shape and construction the grand piano (which partly superseded it) but producing notes by means of quill or metal points (plectra) which pluck the strings.

hârp'y *n.* 1. (Gk & L myth.) Rapacious monster with woman's face and body and bird's wings and claws; rapacious person. 2. ~ (-*eagle*), S. Amer. large powerful bird of prey (*Thrasaëtus harpyia*),

HARPY

hârq'uėbus, âr- (-kw-) *n* (hist.) Early type of portable gun,

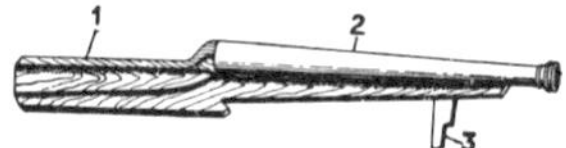

EARLY HARQUEBUS (OR ARQUEBUS) WITHOUT LOCK, GERMAN, *c* 1510

1. Stock. 2. Barrel. 3. Recoil block or hook

supported on tripod by hook or on forked rest. **hârquėbusier'** *n.*

hă'rrĭdan *n.* Haggard old woman, vixen.

hă'rrĭer[1] *n.* One who harries.

hă'rrĭer[2] *n.* 1. Hound used for hunting hare; (pl.) pack of these with huntsman; hare-and-hounds club. 2. Kind of falcon (of *Circus* and related genera); ~ *eagle*, any of several genera of *Accipitrinae* esp. *Circaetus gallicus*; ~-*hawk*, hawk of Amer. genus *Micrastur*, related to goshawk.

Hă'rrĭs[1]. District forming together with Lewis the largest island in the Outer Hebrides; ~ *tweed*, hand-woven tweed made there.

Hă'rrĭs[2], Mrs. In Dickens's 'Martin Chuzzlewit', the mythical friend of Mrs Gamp; hence, non-existent person.

Hă'rrĭson[1], Benjamin (1833–1901). 23rd president of U.S., 1889–93.

Hă'rrĭson[2], William Henry (1773–1841). Amer. general; 9th president of U.S., 1841.

Harrōv'ĭan *adj.* & *n.* (Member) of Harrow School.

hă'rrow[1] (-ō) *n.* Frame with tines or discs which when dragged over soil stirs it up, breaks clods, covers seed, etc. ~ *v.t.* Draw harrow over (land); lacerate, wound. **hă'rrowing** *adj.* (*Illustration, p.* 371.)

hă'rrow[2] (-ō) *v.t.* Harry, spoil (chiefly in phr. ~ *hell*, of Christ freeing the souls of the just when he descended into hell). **hă'rrowing** *n.*

Hă'rrow[3] **(School)** (-ō). English public school at Harrow-on-the-Hill, Middlesex; founded and endowed by John Lyon under a charter (1572) granted by Queen Elizabeth.

hă'rry *v.t.* Ravage, waste, spoil (land); despoil (person); harass, worry.

hârsh *adj.* Rough to the touch, taste, eye, or ear; repugnant to feelings or judgement; cruel, unfeeling. **hârsh'ly** *adv.* **hârsh'nėss** *n.*

hârt *n.* Male of (esp. red) deer, esp. after fifth year; *hart's-tongue*, fern (*Phyllitis scolopendrium*) with long undivided fronds.

hârt'al *n.* Closing of shops for a day in India as sign of mourning or as political gesture.

Hārte, Francis Bret (1836–1902). American writer of short stories and humorous verse.

hārt'ėbeest *n.* Common S. Afr. antelope, *Alcelaphus caama*, of reddish colour, with long doubly curved horns and long skull.

Hārt'ford. Capital city of Connecticut, U.S.

Hārtley, David (1705–57). English physician and philosopher; regarded as the founder of the English (associationist) school of psychologists. **Hārtlei'an** (-ēan) *adj.*

Hārt'mann von Aue (owe) (early 13th c.). German epic writer and minnesinger; author of 'Erec', 'Iwein', etc.

hăsh *n.* Dish of hashed, esp. cooked, meat; old matter served up in new form; medley; *make a* ~ *of*, spoil in dealing with; *settle* a person's ~, make an end of, do for, him. ~ *v.t.* Cut (meat etc.) in small pieces.

Hăsh'imīte *adj.* & *n.* (Member) of an Arab princely family claiming descent from Hashim, an uncle of Mohammed; ~ *Kingdom of the Jordan*: see JORDAN², 2.

hăsh'ish, -eesh *n.* Top leaves and tender parts of common hemp, dried for smoking or chewing as narcotic; liquor prepared from this. [Arab., = 'dry herb']

hās'lėt, hārs- (-z-) *n.* Piece of meat to be roasted, esp. pig's fry.

rash, inconsiderate; quick-tempered; ~ *pudding*, pudding of flour, oatmeal, or Indian meal, stirred in boiling milk or water to consistency of thick batter. **hās'tily** *adv.* **hās'tinėss** *n.*

hăt *n.* Man's or woman's outdoor head-covering, esp. with brim; *top, high, chimney-pot,* ~, man's cylindrical silk hat; *opera* ~, collapsible top hat worn in evening; *cardinal's, red,* ~, (fig.) office of cardinal; *send round the* ~, solicit contributions; *talk through one's* ~, exaggerate, make unsupported assertions; *bad* ~, (slang) immoral or dishonourable person; *hat'band*, band of ribbon etc. round hat; ~*-block*, block for moulding hat

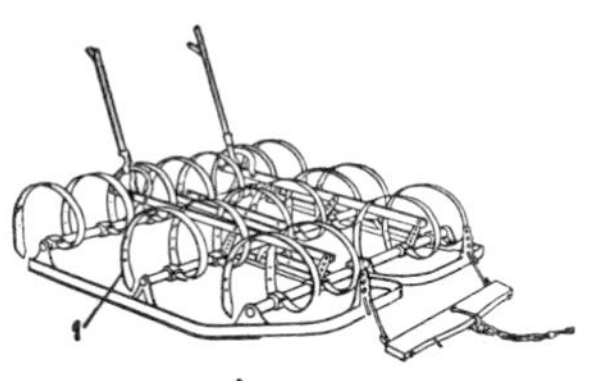

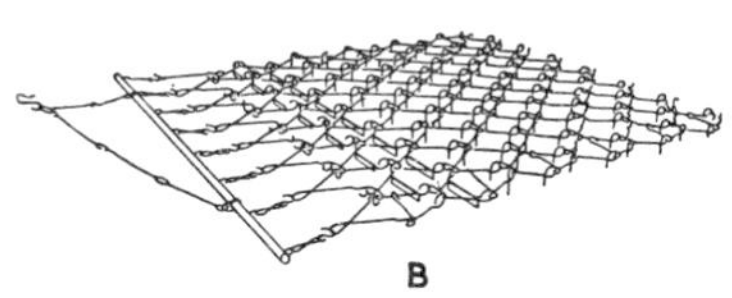

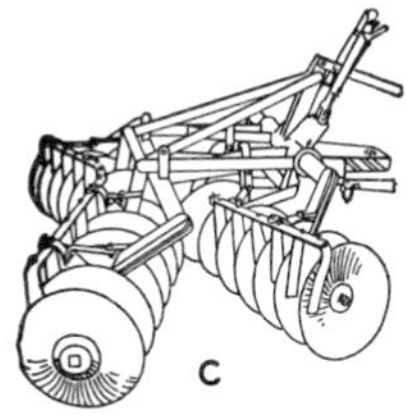

A. SPRING-TINED HARROW. B. CHAIN HARROW. C. DISC HARROW

1. Tine

hārts'hōrn (-s-h-) *n.* Substance got by rasping, slicing, or heating harts' horns, formerly the source of ammonia; (*spirit of*) ~, archaic term for aqueous solution of ammonia; *salt of* ~, archaic term for ammonium carbonate, smelling salts.

hār'um-scār'um *adj.* & *n.* Reckless (person, conduct).

Hārv'ard. American university at Cambridge, Massachusetts; endowed by John Harvard (1607–38), an English settler and graduate of Cambridge University.

hārv'ėst *n.* (Season for) reaping and gathering in of grain or other products; corn-crop; season's yield of any natural product; (fig.) product of any action; ~ *bug*, red larva of mite (*Trombicula autumnalis*) biting man at harvest time; ~ *festival*, thanksgiving service for harvest, at which church is usu. decorated with grain, fruit, etc.; ~ *home*, close of harvesting, festival in celebration of this; ~ *moon*, moon which is full within a fortnight of autumn equinox (22nd or 23rd Sept.) and is popularly supposed to help in ripening the corn; ~ *mouse*, very small mouse (*Micromys minutus*) nesting amongst stalks of growing grain. ~ *v.t.* Reap and gather in (crop); lay up, husband. **hārv'ėster** *n.* 1. Reaper. 2. Reaping-machine (esp. reaper-and-binder). 3. Harvest-bug.

Hārv'ey, William (1578–1657). English physician; discoverer of circulation of the blood.

hăs'-been (-z-) *n.* (colloq.) Person or thing whose career or efficiency belongs to the past.

hasp (-ah-) *n.* Fastening contrivance, esp. clasp passing over staple and secured by padlock or toggle. ~ *v.t.* Fasten with hasp.

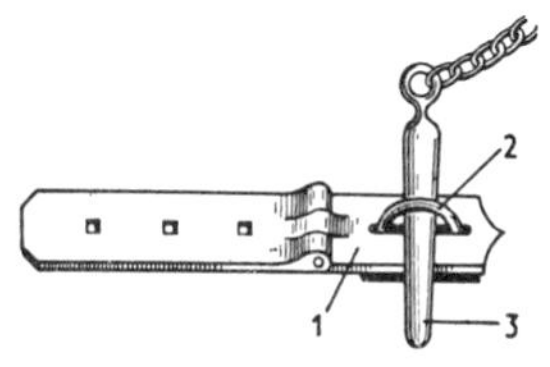

HASP

1. Hasp. 2. Staple. 3. Toggle

hăss'ock *n.* 1. Cushion for kneeling. 2. Tuft of matted grass etc. 3. Soft calcareous limestone separating beds of ragstone in Kent.

hăs'tāte *adj.* (bot. & zool.) Spear-shaped (ill. LEAF).

hāste *n.* Urgency of movement, hurry, precipitancy; *make* ~, be quick. ~ *v.i.* Make haste. **hā'sten** (-sn) *v.* Cause (person) to make haste; accelerate (work etc.); make haste; come or go in haste.

Hās'tings¹. Town on coast of Sussex, England; scene of the battle (1066) in which William of Normandy defeated the English under Harold II, who was killed in the battle.

Hās'tings², Warren (1732–1818). First governor-general of British India; was impeached on the ground of corruption and cruelty in his administration, but acquitted after a trial lasting 7 years (1788–95).

hās'ty *adj.* Hurried; speedy;

on; ~ *trick*, (cricket) the same bowler taking three wickets with three successive balls; (football) the same man scoring three goals in one match; ~ *v.t.* Cover, furnish, with hat. **hăt'ful, hătter** *ns.* **hăt'lėss** *adj.*

hătch¹ *n.* Lower half of divided door; aperture in door, wall, floor, or deck; (naut.) (also *hatch'way*) opening in ship's deck for lowering cargo, trap-door covering this (ill. SHIP); floodgate; *under hatches*, (naut.) below deck; (fig.) down out of sight, brought low.

hătch² *v.* Bring forth (young birds etc.) from egg; incubate (egg); emerge from egg; (of egg) produce young; contrive and develop (plot etc.). ~ *n.* Hatching; brood hatched. **hătch'ery** *n.* Place for hatching eggs, esp. of fish.

hatch³ *v.t.* Engrave, draw, (usu. parallel) lines on (surface) as means of shading drawing etc. ~ *n.* Engraved line, esp. in shading.

hătch'ėt *n.* Light short-handled axe; *bury the* ~, make peace, compose a quarrel; ~*-face*, narrow sharp-featured face.

hătch'ment *n.* Escutcheon; tablet with deceased person's armorial bearings, formerly affixed to front of his house or over his tomb.

hāte *n.* (chiefly poet.) Hatred. ~ *v.t.* Have strong dislike of; bear malice to. **hāte'ful** (-tf-) *adj.* Exciting hatred. **hāte'fully** *adv.* **hāte'fulnėss** *n.*

Ha'thor (hah-), Egyptian goddess of love, freq. represented with cow's head or ears.

hāt'rėd *n.* Active dislike; enmity, ill-will.

hau'berk, haw'berk *n.* Medieval coat of mail (ill. ARMOUR).

haught'y (haw-) *adj.* Proud, arrogant; dignified. **haught'ily** *adv.* **haught'iness** *n.*

haul *v.* Pull, drag, forcibly; pull *at, upon* (rope etc.); transport by cart etc., cart; (naut.) turn ship's course; (of wind) shift; ~ *upon the wind*, bring ship round to sail closer to wind. ~ *n.* Hauling; (fig.) amount gained, acquisition. **haul'age** *n.*

haul'ier *n.* One who hauls (esp. tubs in coal-mine to bottom of shaft); jobbing carter.

ha(u)lm (hawm, hahm) *n.* Stalk, stem; (collect. sing.) stems, stalks, of peas, beans, potatoes, etc., without the pods etc.

haunch *n.* 1. Part of body (of man and quadrupeds) between last ribs and thigh; leg and loin of deer etc. as food. 2. Side of arch between crown and piers.

haunt *v.* 1. Frequent (place); frequent company of (person); (of thoughts etc.) visit (person) frequently; stay habitually. 2. (of ghosts etc.) Visit frequently with manifestations of their presence and influence; (past part.) visited, frequented, by ghosts. ~ *n.* Place of frequent resort; usual feeding-place of animals.

Haupt'mann (how-), Gerhart (1862–1946). German dramatist and novelist; awarded the Nobel Prize 1912.

Haus'a (how-). Widespread negroid race of French Sudan and N. Nigeria, of Bantu family with some Hamitic mixture; the Hamitic language of these people, used, esp. in commerce, over much of W. Africa.

Hauss'mann (hows-), Georges Eugène (1809–91). French administrator; directed the modernization of the streets of Paris. **Hauss'mannīze** *v.t.* Improve (streets etc.) by widening and straightening.

hautboy (hō'boi *or* ō'boi) *n.* 1. (Old name for) OBOE; oboe-player; reed-stop in organ with tone like oboe. 2. Musky-flavoured strawberry (*Fragaria elatior*) of tall growth.

Haut-Brion (ōbrēawn'). (in full, *Château* ~) Claret from commune of Pessac, near Bordeaux.

haute école (ōt ākŏl'). An elaborate method of training and riding horses, practised esp. at Saumur, France, and in Vienna.

hauteur (ōtẽr') *n.* Haughtiness of manner.

Havăn'a. Capital city of Cuba; cigar made at Havana or in Cuba.

hăve *v.* (past t. and past part. *had*). 1. Possess as property or at one's disposal; possess as relative, adjunct, appendage, attribute, function, right, etc.; experience, suffer. 2. Possess as duty; be obliged. 3. Retain; entertain in the mind; show, exhibit (sentiment etc.) in action; carry on, engage in (proceeding etc.); esteem or account as (archaic); ~ *in mind*, remember; ~ *a care*, be careful, be cautious. 4. Express (*it*); assert, maintain; *will not* ~ *it*, refuses to admit. 5. Come into possession of, obtain, get; get into one's power or at a disadvantage; (colloq.) nonplus, put into fix (in argument etc.); (slang) deceive, take in, 'do'. 6. Get into specified condition, procure or oblige (to be done etc.). 7. ~ *it*, win, have the superiority; *let* (person) ~ *it*, give it to him; punish or reprimand him; ~ (person) *up*, cause him to go before court of justice to answer charge; ~ *at*, go or get at, esp. in hostile way. 8. As auxiliary verb, with past part. of another verb, forming compound or perfect tenses of that verb: (*a*) pres. t. of *have* forms present of complete action or '(present) perfect'; (*b*) past t. of *have* forms past of completed action, or 'pluperfect'. ~ *n.* 1. (slang) Swindle, take-in. 2. One who *has*, one belonging to wealthier classes (usu. in pl., opp. to *have-nots*).

hā'ven *n.* Harbour, port; refuge.

hā'ver *v.i.* (chiefly Sc.) Talk foolishly, babble. ~ *n.* (usu pl.) Foolish talk, nonsense.

hăv'ersăck *n.* (Soldier's, traveller's) stout canvas bag for provisions, carried on back or over shoulder. [Ger. *habersack* (*haber* oats)]

hăv'ildar *n.* Indian non-commissioned officer corresponding to sergeant.

hăv'oc *n.* Devastation, destruction; *cry* ~, give signal to army to seize spoil (now only fig.).

haw[1] *n.* (Fruit of) hawthorn; *haw'buck*, country bumpkin; *haw'-finch*, common grosbeak.

haw[2] *n.* Third eyelid of horse, dog, etc., cartilage within inner corner of eye.

Hawai'i (-wī'ē). One of a chain of islands (*Hawaii* or *Sandwich Islands*) in N. Pacific; discovered by Capt. Cook, 1778; annexed by U.S., 1898; admitted to the Union in 1959; capital, Honolulu. **Hawai'ian** (-wī'an) *adj.* & *n.*

haw-haw *int.* & *n.* Boisterous laugh.

hawk[1] *n.* Any of the diurnal birds of prey belonging to the family *Falconidae*, except the very large species, known as *eagles*, and vultures, formerly extensively used in falconry; in zool. restricted to a bird of the subfamily *Accipitrinae*, including the European sparrow-hawk and goshawk, with rounded and shortish wings and low flight; rapacious person; ~*-eyed*, keen-sighted; *Hawkeye State*, popular name of Iowa; ~ *moth*, sphinx-moth (from its hovering and darting flight); ~*-nosed*, with aquiline nose; *hawk's-bill*, species of turtle (*Eretmochelys imbricata*) with mouth like hawk's beak, inhabiting Indian Ocean and warmer parts of Atlantic, source of tortoiseshell; *hawk'weed*, yellow-flowered composite perennial plant of genus *Hieracium*. ~ *v.* Attack as hawk does; (of swallows etc.) hunt insects.

hawk[2] *v.t.* Carry (goods) about for sale (often fig.).

hawk[3] *v.* Clear the throat noisily; bring (phlegm etc.) *up* from throat.

hawk[4] *n.* Plasterer's square board with handle underneath.

hawk'er *n.* Person who sells goods in the street; itinerant vendor, legally distinguished from a *pedlar* by his use of a beast of burden or other means of carrying his wares.

hawse (-z) *n.* Part of ship's bows containing ~*-pipes* for cables; space between head of anchored vessel and anchors; situation of cables before ship's stern when moored with two anchors out from forward, one on starboard, other on port bow.

haws'er (-z-, -s-) *n.* (naut.) Large rope, small cable, now freq. of steel.

haw'thorn *n.* Thorny shrub or small tree, *Crataegus*, with white, red, or pink blossom and small dark-red berry, whitethorn, may-tree; ~ *china, jar, pattern*, (china, jar, with) decoration of flowering branches of Japanese plum-tree in white on dark-blue ground.

Haw'thorne, Nathaniel (1804–64). American novelist; author of 'The Scarlet Letter' etc.

hay[1] *n.* Grass grown or mown and cured or dried for fodder; *make* ~, cure mown grass; *make* ~ *of*, throw into confusion; *make* ~ *while the sun shines*, seize opportunities; ~*-box*, air-tight box stuffed with hay in which heated food is left to continue cooking, the hay acting as an insulator of heat; *hay'cock*, hay piled into a conical heap in the process of haymaking to permit of easy dissipation of heat during the first stages of fermenting and so to lessen the risk of the hay taking fire in the stack; ~ *fever*, summer disorder with catarrhal and freq. asthmatic symptoms, caused by pollen, dust, etc.; ~*-fork*, fork for turning over or loading hay; *hay'maker*, one who lifts, tosses, and spreads hay after mowing; instrument for shaking and drying hay; (slang) swinging blow; *hay'rick, hay'stack*, regular pile of hay with pointed or ridged top; *hay'seed*, (U.S.) rustic, bumpkin; *hay'wire*, wire used to bind a bale of hay; straw, etc.; (U.S.) anything tangled; *go haywire*, (orig. U.S.) become excited or distracted; become tangled. ~ *v.* Put (land) under hay; make into hay; make hay.

hay[2] *n.* Country dance, or movement in dance, of winding or serpentine kind.

Hay'dn (hī-), Franz Josef (1732–1809). Austrian-born composer of many symphonies, concertos, cantatas, etc.; has been described as 'the father of modern instrumental music'.

Hayes (hāz), Rutherford Birchard (1822–93). American lawyer and soldier; 19th president of U.S., 1877–81.

Hay'market. Street in London between Pall Mall and Piccadilly Circus, famous as a theatre centre.

hay'ward (-ŏrd) *n.* Officer of parish, manor, etc., in charge of fences and enclosures.

hăz'ard *n.* 1. Game at dice with chances complicated by arbitrary rules; chance; danger; *at all ~s*, at all risks. 2. Each of winning openings in tennis-court; billiards-stroke by which a ball is driven into a pocket; (golf) bunker, water, roadways, or any kind of 'bad ground' on which certain restrictions are imposed on the player in playing a stroke; *winning ~*, (billiards) striking object ball into pocket; *losing ~*, pocketing own ball off another; *~ side*, (tennis) side of court from which ball is served (ill. TENNIS). *~ v.t.* Expose to hazard; run the hazard of; venture on (action, statement, guess).

hăz'ardous *adj.* Risky; dependent on chance. **hăz'ardously** *adv.* **hăz'ardousnėss** *n.*

hāze[1] *n.* Obscuration of atmosphere near earth caused by presence of visible droplets of water in the air above wet ground or by a mixing of ascending hot air and descending colder air above hot ground; (fig.) mental obscurity or confusion.

hāze[2] *v.t.* (naut.) Harass with overwork; (U.S.) bully, subject to cruel horseplay.

hā'zel *n.* Bush or small tree (*Corylus*) bearing nuts; (stick of) its wood; reddish-brown colour of ripe *~-nut* (esp. of eyes); *~-rod*, *-wand*, stick of hazel used in water-divining.

Hăz'litt, William (1778–1830). English critic and essayist; author of 'Table Talk, or Original Essays on Men and Manners', 'English Comic Writers', etc.

hā'zy *adj.* Misty, vague, indistinct; slightly drunk. **hā'zĭly** *adv.* **hā'zĭnėss** *n.*

HB *abbrev.* Hard black (of pencil-lead).

H.B.M. *abbrev.* His (*or* Her) Britannic Majesty.

H-bomb *abbrev.* Hydrogen bomb.

H.C.(B.) *abbrev.* House of Commons (Bill).

H.C.F. *abbrev.* Highest common factor.

H.C.S. *abbrev.* Home Civil Service.

hē *pron.* The male person in question. *~ n.* Male; *~-man*, (orig. U.S.) masterful or virile man.

H.E. *abbrev.* High explosive; His Excellency.

head (hĕd) *n.* 1. Anterior part of body of animal, upper part of human body, containing mouth, sense-organs, and brain; seat of intellect or imagination; life; headache (colloq.); image of head, esp. on one side of coin; person; individual, esp. of cattle. 2. Thing like head in form or position, e.g. cutting or striking part of tool, knobbed end of nail, part of long bone next to joint, flat end of barrel or cask etc.; rounded or compact part of plant, e.g. compact mass of leaves in cabbage or lettuce, leaf-stalks in celery, flower-buds in cauliflower, etc.; foam on top of liquor, cream on top of milk; top (of mast, staircase, page, etc.); maturated part of boil etc.; upper end; end of lake at which river enters it; end of bed etc. towards which head lies; source of river or stream; (height of) body of water kept at height for supplying mill etc., force of its fall; pressure (per unit of area) of confined body of steam etc.; front (of procession, army, etc.); front part of plough, holding the share; bows of ship; promontory; underground passage for working coal in mine. 3. Ruler, chief; master of college; headmaster of school; position of command; main division in discourse; category; culmination, crisis. 4. *off one's ~*, crazy; *out of one's own ~*, from one's own invention; *put out of one's ~*, (cause to) forget; *over one's ~*, above one; (of danger etc.) impending; beyond one's comprehension; (of promotion etc.) passing over one who has prior right, claim, etc.; *by the ~ and ears*, forcibly, violently; *over ~ and ears*, completely immersed, deeply involved; *from ~ to foot*, all over; *~ of hair*, hair on head, esp. when long or thick; *~ over heels*, topsy-turvy; *by ~ and shoulders*, = by head and ears; (*taller* etc.) by measure of head and shoulders; *keep one's ~*, keep calm; *keep one's ~ above water*, (fig.) keep out of debt; *lose one's ~*, be beheaded; become confused, lose presence of mind; *make ~*, press forward; *make ~ against*, resist successfully; *~ first*, *~ foremost*, (of plunge etc.) with the head foremost; (fig.) precipitately. 5. *headache*,

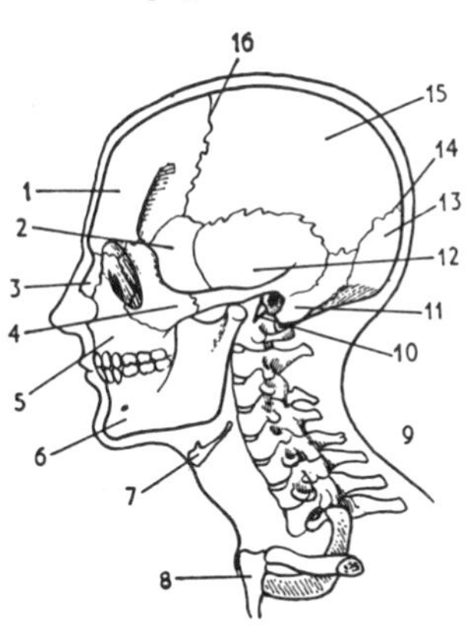

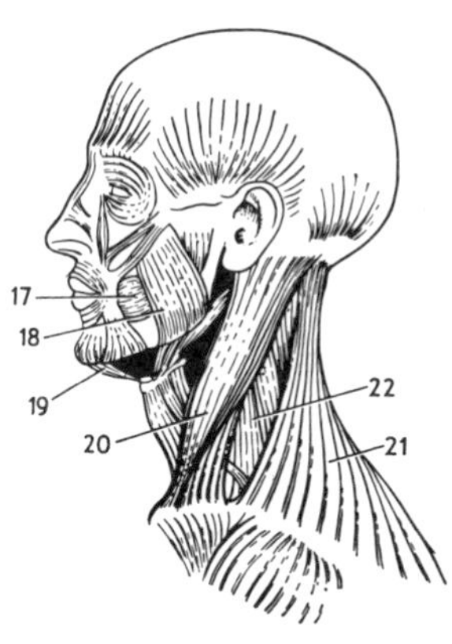

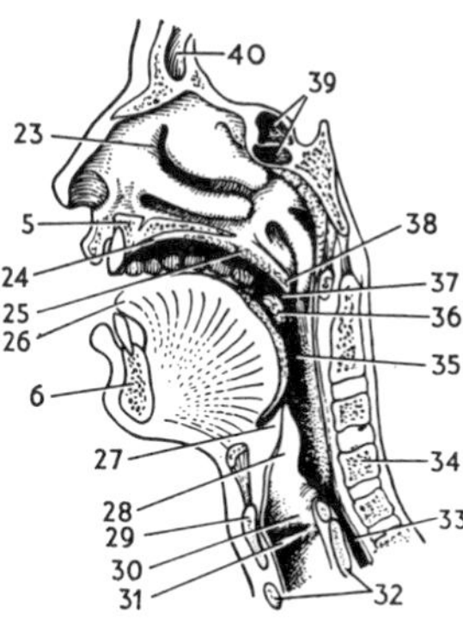

HEAD AND NECK: A. SKULL. B. MUSCLES. C. SECTION OF NOSE, MOUTH, AND THROAT

A. 1. Frontal bone. 2. Sphenoid bone. 3. Nasal bone. 4. Zygoma. 5. Maxilla or upper jaw bone. 6. Mandible or lower jaw bone. 7. Hyoid bone. 8. Sternum. 9. Cervical vertebrae. 10. Styloid process. 11. Mastoid process. 12. Temporal bone. 13. Occipital bone. 14. Lambdoidal suture. 15. Parietal bone. 16. Coronal suture. B. 17. Buccinator. 18. Masseter. 19. Digastric. 20. Sterno-mastoid. 21. Trapezius. 22. Scalenus. C. 23. Middle meatus of nose. 24. Hard palate. 25. Soft palate or velum. 26. Tongue. 27. Epiglottis. 28. Glottis. 29. Thyroid cartilage. 30. Larynx. 31. Vocal cords. 32. Cricoid cartilage. 33. Oesophagus. 34. Vertebra. 35. Pharynx. 36. Tonsil. 37. Fauces. 38. Uvula. 39. Sphenoid sinus. 40. Frontal sinus

continuous pain in head; (colloq.) troublesome or annoying thing; *head'band*, band worn round head; *head'borough*, (hist.) petty constable; *~-dress*, covering, esp. woman's ornamental attire, for the head; *head'fast*, rope at head of vessel to make her fast to wharf etc.; *~-gear*, hat, cap, head-dress; machinery etc. at head of mine-shaft; *~-lamp*, head-light; *headland*, promontory; strip left unploughed at end of field; *~-light*, powerful light at front of locomotive, car, aeroplane, or at mast-head of vessel; *headline*, line at top of page containing title etc.; title or sub-title in newspaper; (pl.) summary of a B.B.C. news broadcast; *headmaster*, *headmistress*, principal master, mistress, of school; *~-on*, (of collision etc.) with head or front of vehicle pointed directly towards or running full against something, esp. front of another vehicle; *~-phone*, in wireless or ordinary telephony, pair of receivers that can be held against listener's ears by band passing over head; *~-piece*, helmet; intellect, man of intellect; ornamental engraving at head of chapter etc. in book; *headquarters*, (mil. etc.) commander-in-chief's residence, place whence commander's orders are issued; centre of operations; *~ room*, overhead space; *~-stall*, part of bridle or halter that fits round head; *head'stock*, bearings of revolving parts in machine, e.g that part of a lathe which carries the mandrel or live stock (ill. LATHE); *head'stone*, gravestone; *head'way*, progress; rate of progress; (archit.) height of arch etc.; *~ wind*, wind meeting one directly in front; *~-work*, mental work. ~ *v.* Furnish with head; lop off head of (plant, tree); be, form, the head of; place (name etc.), be placed, at head of (chapter, list, etc.); come to a head, develop; be, put oneself, at the head of (a company etc.); lead; excel; oppose; go round the head of; front (in specified direction); (of ship etc.) make *for* (place, point); strike (football) with head; ~ *back*, *off*, get ahead of so as to turn back, aside. **head'lèss** *adj.*

head'age (hĕd-) *n.* ~ *money*, reward paid to one who slaughters pests (e.g. rabbits), reckoned per head of animals killed.

head'er (hĕd-) *n.* 1. One who puts heads on casks etc. 2. Brick, stone, laid at right angles to face of wall (ill. BRICK). 3. Head-first plunge. 4. (football) Stroke made with head.

head'ĭng (hĕd-) *n.* (esp.) Title etc. at head of page etc., headline; horizontal passage in preparation for tunnel.

head'lŏng (hĕd-) *adv.* & *ajd.* Head foremost; precipitate(ly); impetuous(ly).

head'mōst (hĕd-) *adj.* Foremost.

heads'man (hĕd-) *n.* Executioner; man in command of whaling boat.

head'strŏng (hĕd-) *adj.* Violently self-willed; **head'strŏngnèss** *n.*

heady (hĕd'ĭ) *adj.* Impetuous, violent; (of liquor etc.) apt to intoxicate.

heal *v.* Restore to health; cure (*of*); (of wound) become sound or whole. **heal'er** *n.*

health (hĕl-) *n.* Soundness of body, mind, etc.; that condition in which functions of body and mind are duly discharged; general condition of body, as *good*, *bad* ~; toast drunk in person's honour.

health'ful (hĕl-) *adj.* Health-giving; conducive to moral or spiritual welfare. **health'fully** *adv.* **health'fulnèss** *n.*

health'y (hĕl-) *adj.* Having good health; conducive to good health. **health'ĭly** *adv.* **health'ĭness** *n.*

heap *n.* Group of things lying one on another; (colloq.) large number or amount; *struck all of a ~*, (colloq.) mentally prostrated, dumbfounded. ~ *v.t.* Pile in a heap; load (*with*); accumulate (insults etc. *upon*).

hear *v.* (past t. and past part. *heard* pr. hẽrd) Perceive (sound etc.), perceive sound(s), with the ear; listen, give audience, to; listen judicially to (case, plaintiff, etc.); grant (prayer); be informed; entertain notion *of*; receive letter or message *from*; ~ *tell of*, (archaic) be told about; *~! ~!*, (form of applause, often iron.). **hear'able** *adj.* **hear'er** *n.*

hear'ĭng *n.* Perception by ear; listening to evidence and pleadings in a court of law; trial of a cause, esp. trial before a judge without a jury; *hard of ~*, rather deaf; *within*, *out of*, ~, near enough, too far off, to be heard; *give fair ~*, listen impartially *to*.

heark'en (hâr-) *v.i.* Listen (*to*).

hear'say *n.* What one hears (but does not know to be true), gossip.

hearse (hẽrs) *n.* Vehicle for conveying body to grave; (formerly) framework supporting pall at funeral, often adapted for carrying tapers.

heart (hârt) *n.* 1. Hollow muscular organ which by rhythmic contraction and relaxation drives the blood round the vascular system; it consists in mammals and birds of 4 chambers, of which the two anterior ones, called *atria* force the blood, received from the veins, into the two posterior ones, called *ventricles*, which then contract and force the blood into the arteries; the return of the blood into the atria and ventricles is prevented by valves. 2. Breast; mind; soul; seat of the emotions, esp. of love; sensibility, tenderness, feeling; courage; enthusiasm, energy. 3. Central part of anything, centre, pith, core; solid central part of tree without sap or alburnum; *~ of oak*, (man of) stout courageous spirit. 4. Vital part or principle; (of land etc.) fertility; *in ~*, in good or sound condition. 5. Heart-shaped thing, esp. conventional symmetrical figure of two similar curves meeting in point at one end and cusp at the other; playing-card marked with heart(s), (pl.) suit of these. 6. *at ~*, in one's inmost feelings; *by ~*, in, from, memory; *from (the bottom of) one's ~*, sincerely; *in one's ~*, secretly; *in ~*, in good spirits; *near(est) one's ~*, dear(est) to one; *out of ~*, in low spirits; *with all one's ~*, sincerely,

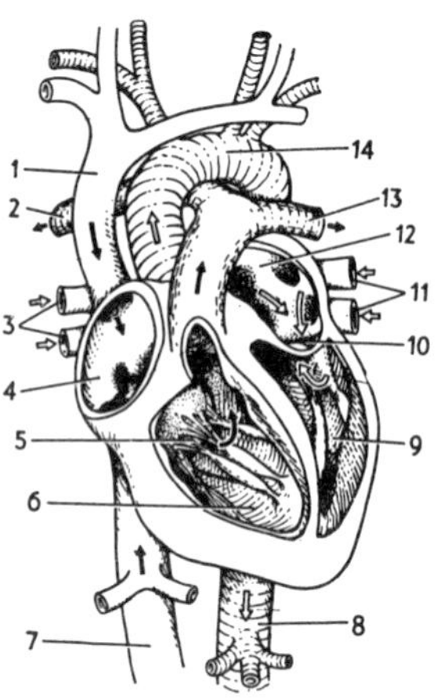

HEART

The black arrows show the direction of flow of venous blood, the white arrows show that of arterial blood. 1. Superior Vena Cava. 2. Right pulmonary artery taking venous blood to lung. 3. Right pulmonary veins taking arterial blood to heart. 4. Right atrium. 5. Tricuspid valve. 6. Right ventricle. 7. Inferior Vena Cava. 8. Aorta. 9. Left ventricle. 10. Mitral valve. 11. Left pulmonary veins. 12. Left atrium. 13. Left pulmonary artery. 14. Arch of aorta

with the utmost goodwill; *find in one's ~*, prevail on oneself (*to*); *have at ~*, be deeply interested in; *lay to ~*, think over seriously; *take to ~*, be much affected by; *~-to-~*, frank, sincere; *break* person's ~, overwhelm him with sorrow; *cry one's ~ out*, cry violently; *eat one's ~ out*, pine away; *have a ~!* (colloq.) protesting appeal for sympathy; *have the ~*, be hard-hearted enough (*to*); *in one's ~ of ~s*, in one's inmost feelings; *have one's ~ in one's mouth*, be violently alarmed or startled; *take ~ of grace*, pluck up courage; *~-ache*, mental anguish; *~-beat*, pulsation of heart; *~('s)-blood*, life-blood, life; *~ block*, (path.) condition of interference with normal rhythmic contraction of chambers of heart; *heart'break*, overwhelming distress; *heart'broken*, having a broken heart; overwhelmed by grief; *heart'burn*, burning sensation in lower part of chest, due to putrefactive fermentation of food in stomach; ~ *burning*, jealousy, grudge; ~ *failure*, (med.) any derangement of heart's mechanism, not necessarily fatal; (pop.) cessation of heart-beat causing death; ~*-felt*, sincere; ~*-rending*, distressing; *hearts'ease*, pansy, esp. small wild form; ~*-sick*, despondent; ~ *sounds*, sounds of closure of heart's valves, contraction of its chambers, etc., heard in auscultation; ~*-strings*, (fig.) heart, deepest affections; ~*-wood*, dense inner part of tree-trunk, affording the hardest timber (ill. STEM); ~*-whole*, with the heart or affections unengaged.

heart'en (hâr-) *v.* Inspirit, cheer; cheer *up*.

hearth (hâr-) *n.* Floor of fire-place; floor of reverberatory furnace, of smith's forge, etc.; *hearth'-rug*, rug laid before fire-place; *hearth'stone*, stone forming hearth; soft kind of stone, rubbed with water over hearth, doorstep, etc. to whiten them.

heart'ĭly (hâr-) *adv.* With goodwill, courage, or appetite; very.

heart'lėss (hâr-) *adj.* Unfeeling, pitiless, cruel. **heart'lėssly** *adv.* **heart'lėssnėss** *n.*

heart'y (hâr-) *adj.* Cordial, genial; (of feelings) sincere; vigorous; (of meals) abundant. ~ *n.* Hearty fellow; (at British universities) one more interested in sports etc. than in art, literature, etc.

heat *n.* 1. Hotness, high temperature; sensation, perception, of this; one of the primary sensations produced by contact with or nearness to fire or any body at a high temperature; (physics) form of energy arising from the random molecular motion of a substance and capable of transmission by conduction or radiation. 2. Hot weather; inflamed state of body; pungency of flavour. 3. Warmth of feeling; anger; violent stage (of debate etc.). 4. Receptive period of the sexual cycle in female mammals. 5. Single effort, stroke; single course in race or other contest (*trial* ~, course the winners of which compete in *final* ~). 6. *latent* ~, heat required to convert solid into liquid or vapour, or liquid into vapour (so called because it does not show its presence by an increase in temperature); *prickly* ~, skin disease (*Lichen tropicus*) common in hot climates and caused by inflammations of the skin round the sweat ducts; *red*, *white*, ~, heat at which metals etc. are red-hot, white-hot; *specific* ~, heat required to raise temperature of unit mass of given substance to given extent (usu. one degree), calculated relatively to some standard, usu. water; ~ *of formation*, thermal change which occurs when substances chemically combine; ~ *lightning*, summer lightning; ~*-spot*, red spot on skin popularly supposed to be caused by heat; (physiol.) small area on skin sensitive to heat stimuli; ~*-stroke*, affection of nervous system, freq. fatal, caused by exposure to excessive heat; ~ *unit*, = lesser calorie (see CALORIE, 2); ~*-wave*, uninterrupted period of very hot weather extending over many days, regarded as passing from place to place; (physics) electro-magnetic wave constituting radiant heat. ~ *v.* Make hot; inflame (blood etc.); inflame with passion; become hot. **heat'ėdly** *adv.* Vehemently, angrily.

heat'er *n.* (esp.) Any contrivance for warming up food, room, etc.

heath *n.* Barren flat waste tract of land, esp. if covered with low herbage and dwarf shrubs; plants and shrubs found on heaths, esp. undershrubs of genus *Erica*, heather, ling; ~*-bell*, bell-shaped flower of heath; ~*-cock*, black-cock; in N. America, Canada grouse. **heath'y** *adj.*

heath'en (-dh-) *adj.* & *n.* (One who is) neither Christian, Jewish, nor Moslem; unenlightened (person). **heath'endom, heath'enism** *ns.* **heath'enish** *adj.* **heath'enishly** *adv.* **heath'enishnėss** *n.* **heath'enīze** *v.*

hea'ther (hĕdh-) *n.* Various species of genus *Erica*, esp. the common heather (*E.* (now *Calluna*) *vulgaris*), growing on moors and heaths, and bearing purple bell-shaped flowers in autumn; ~*-bell*, (flower of) species of *Erica*; ~ *mixture*, (fabric, esp. tweed) of mixed or speckled hue supposed to resemble heather. **hea'thery** *adj.*

heave *v.* (past t. and past part. *heaved* or *hove*) 1. Lift (heavy thing); (of vein or stratum) displace (another); utter (groan, sigh) with effort; (naut. & colloq.) throw; (naut.) haul up, haul, by rope; pull (*at* rope etc.); ~ *down*, turn (ship) over on one side for cleaning etc.; ~ *to*, bring (vessel) to standstill with head to wind; ~ *in sight*, become visible. 2. Rise, swell up; rise with alternate falls, as waves; pant; retch. ~ *n.* Heaving; horizontal displacement of vein or stratum; (pl.) disease of horses, broken wind.

hea'ven (hĕ-) *n.* Sky, firmament (in prose now usu. pl.); region of atmosphere in which clouds float, winds blow, and birds fly; (formerly) each of the heavenly spheres; supposed habitation of God and his angels, usu. placed beyond sky; God, providence; place, state, of supreme bliss; *seventh* ~, highest of seven heavens recognized by Jews, state of supreme bliss. **hea'venward** *adj.* **hea'venward(s)** *adv.*

hea'venly (hĕ-) *adj.* Of heaven, divine; of the sky; of superhuman excellence. **hea'venlĭnėss** *n.*

heav'ier-than-air' (hĕv-) *adj.* (Of flying-machine) with weight greater than that of air it displaces, as distinct from balloons and dirigible airships.

Hea'viside layer (hĕv-). A layer of the ionosphere, some 100 km. above the earth, now usually termed the E-layer (ill. ATMOSPHERE); also known as *Kennelly–Heaviside layer*. Transparent to short-wave radio waves, it reflects back long-wave ones. [Oliver *Heaviside* (1850–1925), British physicist]

hea'vy (hĕ-) *adj.* 1. Of great weight; of great specific gravity; weighty because abundant; (of bread etc.) that has not risen properly, compact, dense; laden *with*; (of ordnance etc.) large; (mil.) carrying heavy arms or equipment. 2. Striking or falling with force or violence; (of ground etc.) clinging, difficult to travel over, dig, etc.; (of food) difficult of digestion; (of horse) ~ *in* (*on*) *hand*, bearing or hanging on bit (also fig.). 3. Grave, severe; overcast, gloomy; clumsy in appearance or effect; (of persons) intellectually slow; unwieldy; dull, tedious; oppressive, grievous; sad; despondent; doleful; drowsy; (theatr., of part etc.) sober, serious, tragic. 4. ~*-handed*, clumsy, laden; ~*-hearted*, melancholy, doleful; ~ *hydrogen*, = DEUTERIUM; ~ *oil*, (*a*) the last fraction obtained before the pitch point in the distillation of coal-tar; creosote oil; (*b*) petroleum and other (esp. fuel) oils which have a flash-point above 75° F.; ~ *spar*, native barium sulphate; barytes; ~ *water*, deuterium oxide (D_2O), with the same chemical properties as ordinary water, but density about 10% greater; ~*-weight*, jockey, rider, etc., of more than average weight; boxer over 12 st. 7 lb. **hea'vĭly** *adv.* **hea'vĭness** *n.* **hea'vy** *n.* *Heavies* (pl.), *the* Dragoon Guards; heavy artillery. ~ *adv.* Heavily.

Heb. *abbrev.* Hebrew; Hebrews (N.T.).

Hĕbb'el, Friedrich (1813–63). German dramatist and poet.

hĕbdŏm'adal *adj.* Weekly; *H~ Council*, representative board of University of Oxford, meeting weekly.

Hĕb'ė. 1 (Gk myth.) Goddess of youth and spring, daughter of Zeus and Hera, and cup-bearer of Olympus. 2. (astron.) The 6th asteroid, discovered 1847.

hĕb'ėtāte *v.* Make, become, dull.

Hēbrā'ĭc *adj.* Of, pertaining to, the Hebrews, or Hebrew. **Hēbrā'ĭcally** *adv.*

Hēb'rāĭsm *n.* Quality or attribute of the Hebrews; Hebrew system of thought or religion; Hebrew idiom or expression. **Hēbrā'ĭst** *n.* Hebrew scholar; adherent of Hebrew thought or religion. **Hēbrāĭs'tĭc** *adj.* **Hēbrāĭs'tĭcally** *adv.*

Hēb'rāīze *v.* Translate into Hebrew; make, become, like a Hebrew.

Hĕb'rew (-ōō) *n.* 1. Person belonging to Semitic tribe or nation descended from Abraham, Isaac, and Jacob; Israelite, Jew. 2. The Semitic language spoken by the Hebrews, and in which most of the books of the O.T. were written; (colloq.) unintelligible speech. ~ *adj.* Belonging to the Hebrews, Jewish; ~ *alphabet*, a Semitic alphabet of 22 letters, the vowels being indicated by a system of points; ~ *calendar*: see JEWISH. **Hĕb'rews** *n.pl.* (Abbreviation of) the Epistle of St. Paul to the Hebrews, a book of the N.T. [Aramaic *'ebrai*, = Heb. *'ibri* one from the other side]

Hĕb'rīdēs (-z). Two groups of islands (*Inner* and *Outer* ~) off the NW. coast of Scotland. **Hĕbridē'an** *adj.* & *n.* (Native) of the Hebrides.

Hĕc'atė. (Gk myth.) Goddess, said to be of Thracian origin, daughter of Perses and Asteria; in later times more or less identified with Artemis or Persephone, and hence regarded as presiding over witchcraft and magical rites.

hĕc'atomb (-ŏm, -ōōm) *n.* (Gk antiq. etc.) Great public sacrifice (prop., of a hundred oxen).

hĕck[1] *n.* 1. Frame obstructing passage of fish in river. 2. One of the sets of perforated pins which guide warp-threads in the process of reeling and form the lease.

hĕck[2] *int.* (dial. and U.S.) Euphemism for *hell.*

hĕck'ėlphōne *n.* Kind of baritone oboe. [W. *Heckel*, German inventor, *c* 1905]

hĕck'le *v.t.* 1. Dress (flax etc.) with hackle. 2. Harass (esp. candidates for Parliament etc. in public) with interruptions, awkward questions, etc. **hĕck'ler, hĕck'ling** *ns.*

hĕc'tare (-âr), -ār) *n.* (In metric system) superficial measure of 100 ares (2·471 acres).

hĕc'tĭc *adj.* 1. ~ *fever*, that which accompanies consumption and similar diseases, attended with flushed cheeks and hot skin; consumptive; morbidly flushed. 2. (slang) Stirring; wild, impassioned; feverishly excited or active. **hĕc'tĭcally** *adv.*

hecto- *prefix.* A hundred.

hĕc'togrăm *n.* Measure of weight, 100 grams (abbrev. *hg.*).

hĕc'tograph (-ahf) *n.* Apparatus for multiplying copies of writing. ~ *v.t.* Multiply with this.

hĕc'tolitre (-lēter) *n.* Measure of capacity, 100 litres (abbrev. *hl.*).

hĕc'tomētre (-t*er*), **-mēter** *n.* Measure of length, 100 metres (abbrev. *hm.*).

Hĕc'tor[1]. (Gk legend) A Trojan warrior, son of Priam and Hecuba and husband of Andromache; killed by Achilles, who dragged his body 3 times round the walls of Troy.

hĕc'tor[2] *n.* & *v.* Bluster(er), bully. [f. HECTOR[1]]

Hĕc'ūba. (Gk legend) Wife of Priam, king of Troy, and mother of Hector, Paris, and Çassandra, among other children.

hĕdd'les *n.pl.* In loom, small cords or wires with loops for suspending the warp threads and separating them into two sets so as to allow passage of shuttle (ill. LOOM).

hĕdge *n.* Fence of bushes or low trees, or of turf, stone, etc.; line of things or persons forming barrier; (fig.) barrier; (betting) act, means, of hedging; ~-*hop*: see HOP[2]; ~-*priest*, (hist.) illiterate priest of low status; *hedge'row*, row of bushes forming hedge; ~-*school*, (hist.) low-class school; (formerly) open-air school esp. in Ireland; ~-*sparrow*, common European bird, one of the warblers (*Accentor modularis*). ~ *v.* 1. Surround with hedge; fence *off*; hem *in*; make, trim, hedges. 2. Secure oneself against loss on (bet, speculation, etc.) by compensating transactions on the other side; avoid committing oneself. **hĕdg'er** *n.* One who makes and trims hedges.

hĕdge'hŏg (-jh-) *n.* Insectivorous quadruped (*Erinaceus*) with pig-like snout, armed above with very many spines and able to roll itself into a ball with these bristling in every direction; various animals armed with spines, as the sea-urchin etc.; prickly seed-vessels or burrs of some plants, the plants themselves; person hard to get on with; fortified position 'bristling' with guns pointing in all directions, esp. one left behind after the main body of troops has retreated.

hēdŏn'ĭc *adj.* Of pleasure. **hēdŏn'ĭcs** *n.pl.* Doctrine of pleasure.

hēd'onĭsm *n.* Doctrine or ethical theory that pleasure is the chief good, or the proper end of action. **hēd'onĭst** *n.* **hēdonĭs'tĭc** *adj.*

hee'bie-jee'bies *n.pl.* (slang) 'Blues', state of nervous depression; dance tunes of a mournful kind, originating among the Negroes of southern U.S.; the dances themselves.

heed *v.t.* (Sc. & literary) Concern oneself about, take notice of. ~ *n.* Careful attention; esp. in *take* ~, *give, pay*, ~, *to.* **heed'ful** *adj.* **heed'fully** *adv.* **heed'fulnėss** *n.* **heed'lėss** *adj.* **heed'lėssly** *adv.* **heed'lėssnėss** *n.*

hee'-haw' *n.* Ass's bray; loud laugh.

heel[1] *n.* 1. Hinder part of human foot below ankle; corresponding part of hind limb in quadruped, often raised above ground; (pop.) hinder part of quadruped's hoof, (pl.) hind feet; ~ *of Achilles*, vulnerable spot (see ACHILLES); *at, on, the* ~*s of*, close behind, in close pursuit; *to* ~, (of dog) close behind, under control; ~*s over head*, (usu.) *head over* ~*s*, upside down, (turn) a somersault; *kick one's* ~*s*, stand waiting; *take to one's* ~*s*, *show a clean pair of* ~*s*, run away; *turn on one's* ~, turn sharply round; (*fair*) ~ *and toe*, walking, not running. 2. Part of stocking that covers heel; part of boot or shoe that supports or raises heel (ill. SHOE); *down at* ~, (of shoes) with heel part crushed down, or heel worn down; (of person) wearing such shoes, slovenly, destitute; *out at* ~*s*, with stockings or shoes worn through at heel; shabby, destitute. 3. Thing like heel in shape or position, as handle end of violin bow, crook in head of golf-club, after end of ship's keel; bottom crust of loaf, rind of cheese. 4. (U.S. slang) Untrustworthy person, 'rotter'. 5. ~-*ball*, shoemaker's polishing mixture of hard wax and lamp black, also used for taking rubbings of monumental brasses, inscriptions, etc.; ~-*tap*, a thickness of leather in heel; liquor left at bottom of glass after drinking. ~ *v.* Touch ground with heel, e.g. in dancing; furnish (boot etc.) with heel; chase or follow closely; (Rugby football) pass ball *out* at back of scrummage with heels; (golf) strike (ball) with heel of club; ~ *in* (tree, plant), cover roots temporarily with earth before planting finally; *heeled* (U.S.) armed, esp. with revolver, supplied with money, etc.

heel[2] *v.* (Of ship etc.) lean over owing to pressure of wind or uneven load; cause (ship) to do this. ~ *n.* (naut.) Inclination of heeling ship.

hĕft *n.* (dial. and U.S.) Weight. ~ *v.t.* (dial. and U.S.) Lift, esp. to judge weight.

hĕf'ty *adj.* Heavy; sturdy, stalwart.

Hegel (hāg'l), Georg Wilhelm Friedrich (1770–1831). German philosopher, in whose system of Absolute Idealism pure being is regarded as pure thought, the universe as its development, and philosophy as its dialectical explication. **Hėgēl'ian** *adj.* & *n.* (Follower) of Hegel or his philosophy. **Hėgēl'ianĭsm** *n.*

hegemŏn'ĭc (hĕjĭ-, hēgi-) *adj.* Ruling, supreme.

hēgĕm'ony (-g-; *also* hĕj'ė-) *n.* Leadership, esp. of one State of a confederacy.

Hegira, Hejira (hĕj'ĭ-; erron. hĭjīr'*a*). Flight of Mohammed from Mecca to Medina in A.D. 622, from which the Moslem chronological era is reckoned. [Arab. *hijrah* departure from one's country]

Hei'delberg (hī-). German university city on the river Neckar in Württemberg; ~ *jaw*, a human lower jaw, found near Heidelberg, regarded as belonging to an extinct species of man (~ *man*) allied to Neanderthal man, and living in the Early Pleistocene period (*c* 400,000 years ago).

hei'fer (hĕf-) *n.* Young cow that has not had a calf, or one that has only recently had her first.

heigh (hā) *int.* expressing encouragement or inquiry; ~-*ho* (*int.*) expressing boredom, disappointment, etc.

height (hīt) *n.* Measurement from base to top; elevation above ground or recognized level, esp. that of sea; considerable elevation; high point; top, highest point or degree; rising ground.

height'en (hīt-) *v.t.* Make high(er); intensify; inflate (description, story).

Heine (hī'ne), Heinrich (1799–1856). German-Jewish lyric poet and witty essayist; famous for his sentimental and ironic verse in the 'Buch der Lieder'.

hei'nous (hān-) *adj.* (Of crime or criminal) odious, atrocious. **hei'nously** *adv.* **hei'nousness** *n.*

heir (ār) *n.* Person receiving or entitled to receive property or rank as legal representative of former owner, esp. upon death of the latter; ~ *apparent*: see APPARENT; ~-*at-law*, heir by right of blood; ~ *of the body*, heir who is direct descendant; ~ *in tail*, heir to entailed estate; ~ *male*, male heir tracing descent wholly through males; ~ *presumptive*: see PRESUMPTIVE. **heir'less** *adj.* **heir'ess** *n.* Female heir.

heir'loom (ār-) *n.* Chattel that follows devolution of real estate; piece of personal property that has been in family for generations.

Hĕjăz'. Region of Arabia on the Red Sea coast, forming with Nejd and Asir the Kingdom of Saudi Arabia.

Hejira: see HEGIRA.

hĕld, past t. and past part. of HOLD².

Hĕl'ĕn. (Gk legend) The most beautiful woman of her time, daughter of Zeus and Leda and wife of Menelaus, king of Sparta. She was carried off to Troy by Paris, son of Priam, and to get her back Menelaus assembled the Greek princes to make war on Troy.

Hĕl'ĕna¹, St. Mother of the Emperor Constantine; said to have discovered (*the Invention of the Cross*) the cross on which Christ was crucified; *Island of St.* ~ (pr. helē'na), in the S. Atlantic, the place of Napoleon's captivity (1815–21).

Hĕl'ĕna². Capital of Montana, U.S.

hēlī'acal *adj.* Pertaining to, near, the sun; solar; ~ *cycle*, solar cycle; ~ *rising*, (of star) when it first emerges from sun's rays and becomes visible before sunrise; ~ *setting*, (of star) when it is last visible after sunset before being lost in sun's rays.

hēliăn'thus *n.* Genus of plants including sunflower.

hĕl'ĭcal *adj.* Of or like a helix; ~ *agitator*, kind of stirrer with series of curved plates fitted to a shaft so that they form a helix, serving to convey liquid from the bottom to the top of a vessel and so producing thorough and rapid agitation; ~ *gearing*, gearing in which cogs are cut slant-wise, so that several engage at once and so secure smoother and less noisy running (ill. GEAR). **hĕl'ĭcally** *adv.*

hĕl'icoid(al) *adjs.* Shaped like a helix; resembling a snail-shell; *helicoidal saw*, endless band of twisted wire used to cut through marble and other stone.

Hĕl'ĭcon. Mountain in Boeotia, sacred to the Muses, where rose the fountains of Aganippe and Hippocrene; hence, source of poetic inspiration. **Hĕlĭcōn'ĭan** *adj.* **hĕl'ĭcon** *n.* Large brass wind instrument of spiral form, made so as to be carried round the body while being played.

hĕl'ĭcŏpter *n.* Aircraft lifted by airscrew(s) revolving horizontally.

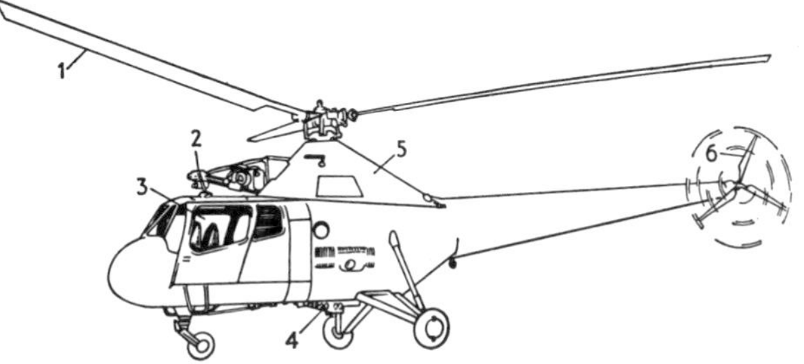

HELICOPTER

1. Main rotor-blade. 2. Winch hoist. 3. Cabin. 4. Freight carrier. 5. Engine housing. 6. Tail rotor

hēliocĕn'trĭc *adj.* As viewed from centre of sun; taking sun as centre.

Hēliogăb'alus, Ēlagăb'alus. Adopted name of Varius Avitus Bassianus, Roman emperor A.D. 218–22, famed for folly and profligacy. [Latinized f. *Elagabal*, Syro-Phoenician sun-god]

hĕl'iogrăm *n.* Message transmitted by heliograph.

hĕl'iograph (-ahf) *n.* Instrument for measuring intensity of sunlight; apparatus for signalling with movable mirror reflecting flashes of sunlight to a distance.

hēliolĭth'ĭc *adj.* (Of civilization) characterized by megaliths and sun-worship.

hēliŏm'ĕter *n.* Astronomical instrument for determining angular distance between stars (orig. for measuring diameter of sun).

hĕl'iotrōpe *n.* 1. Plant of genus *Heliotropium* of herbs or shrubs with small clustered purple flowers, esp. *H. arborescens*, cultivated for its fragrance; colour or scent of heliotrope. 2. Blood-stone, green quartz with spots or veins of red jasper.

hēliotrŏp'ĭc *adj.* (Of plants) turning in particular direction under influence of light.

hēl'ium *n.* Chemical element, an inert gas occurring in small quantities in the atmosphere and in certain natural gases, and produced during radio-active decay; used, on account of its lightness and non-inflammability, in balloons and airships; symbol He, at. no. 2, at. wt 4·0026.

hē'lĭx *n.* (pl. -*ĭcēs*). 1. Spiral or coil like corkscrew (ill. SPIRAL); (archit. etc.) spiral ornament. 2. (anat.) Curved fold or prominence forming rim of external ear (ill. EAR). 3. (zool.) Genus of land molluscs with spiral shells, including the common snail (*H. aspersa*).

hĕll *n.* Abode of the dead; abode of devils and condemned spirits, figured as place of torment; place, state, of wickedness or misery; gaming-house; place under tailor's shop-board where cut-off pieces or shreds of cloth are thrown; *a* ~ *of a*, an infernal, a very bad, great, loud, etc.; ~-*for-leather*, at breakneck speed; ~-*bent*, (U.S.) hell-for-leather; ~-*cat*, spiteful or furious woman; ~-*fire*, the fire of hell; *hellfire club*, club of reckless or abandoned young men at beginning of 18th c.; ~-*hound*, fiend. **hĕll'ish** *adj.* **hĕll'ishly** *adv.* **hĕll'ishnėss** *n.*

Hellăd'ĭc *adj.* ~ *period*, the Bronze Age of the Greek mainland.

Hĕll'ăs. Greece; orig. the name of a district in Thessaly, but applied by the ancient Greeks to the whole of their country.

hĕll'ėbōre *n.* Ancient name of various plants supposed to cure madness; (bot.) species of ranunculaceous genus *Helleborus* including Christmas rose (*black hellebore*).

Hĕll'ēne. A Greek, ancient or modern. **Hellēn'ĭc** *adj.* & *n.* (Language) of the Greeks; (pl.) writings on Greek subjects.

Hĕll'ėnism *n* Greek idiom or construction; Greek character or culture, esp. that represented by ideals of the classical Greeks; Greek nationality. **Hĕll'ėnist** *n.* 1. Greek scholar. 2. One of the Byzantine Greeks who contributed to the revival of learning in Europe in the 15th c. 3. One who used the Greek language but was not a

Greek, applied esp. to the Jews of the Dispersion. **Hĕllĕnis'tic** *adj.* 1. Of, pertaining to, the Hellenists. 2. Of, pertaining to, Greek history, language, and culture after Alexander the Great.

Hĕll'ĕnīze *v.* Make Greek in character; adopt Greek customs, speech, etc.

Hĕll'ĕspŏnt. Ancient name of the DARDANELLES, named after the legendary Helle, who fell into that part of the sea from the back of a ram with golden fleece and wings, which was carrying her and her brother Phrixus from Thebes to Colchis (see also GOLDEN FLEECE).

hĕll'grammīte *n.* (U.S.) Larva (used as bait for black bass) of the dobson fly, an aquatic neuropterous insect (*Corydalus cornutus*).

hĕll'ion *n.* (U.S.) Mischievous or naughty child.

hĕllō' = HALLO.

hĕlm[1] *n.* (archaic) Helmet (ill. ARMOUR); ~(*-cloud*), cloud forming over mountain before or during storm (local name in Cumberland and Westmorland); *~-wind*, violent wind rushing down escarpment of Pennines near Cross Fell, when a helm-cloud lies over summit.

hĕlm[2] *n.* Tiller, wheel, by which rudder is managed (ill. SHIP); space through which helm is turned; (fig.) government, guidance; *down* (*with the*) ~, *up* (*with the*) ~, place helm so as to bring rudder to windward, to leeward; *weather, lee*, ~, helm put up, down; *helmsman*, steersman.

hĕl'mĕt *n.* Defensive head-cover of soldiers, firemen, etc.; felt or pith hat for hot climates; upper part of retort; shell of mollusc of genus *Cassis*; (bot.) arched upper part of corolla in some flowers, esp. labiates and orchids; *~-shell*, mollusc of genus *Cassis*. **hĕl'mĕtĕd** *adj.*

Hĕlm'hŏltz, Hermann Ludwig Ferdinand (1821–94). German physicist and physiologist; inventor of the ophthalmoscope; ~ *coils*, (physics) two equal circular coils placed coaxially at a distance apart equal to their radius and traversed by the same current.

hĕl'minth *n.* Worm (usu. intestinal). **hĕlmĭn'thic, hĕlmĭn'thoid,** *adjs.* **hĕlmĭnthŏl'ogy** *n.*

Hĕlōise'(-ēz)(1101–63). Learned Frenchwoman, renowned for love affair with ABÉLARD which ended in tragic separation.

hĕl'ot *n.* In ancient Sparta, a descendant of the original (chiefly Messenian) inhabitants who were conquered by the Spartans and used by them as serfs (*drunken* ~, one made drunk as a warning to young Spartans); hence, serf, bondman.

hĕlp *v.t.* Aid, assist, as ~ *me*, ~ *me to lift it*, ~ *me over the stile*, ~ *me out* (of a difficulty); ~ (person) *on with his coat*, help him to put it on; ~ (person) *to*, serve him with (food); distribute (food at meal); remedy, prevent, as *it can't be helped, he couldn't* ~ *being late*; (with neg.) avoid doing, as *I can't* ~ *hoping that* —; ~ *oneself to*, (colloq.) steal. ~ *n.* 1. Assistance; domestic servant; *lady* ~, assistant and companion to mistress of house; *mother's* ~, superior nursemaid. 2. Remedy or escape.

hĕlp'ful *adj.* (of person or thing) Useful, serviceable. **hĕlp'fully** *adv.* **hĕlp'fulnĕss** *n.*

hĕlp'ing *n.* (esp.) Portion of food served.

hĕlp'lĕss *adj.* Lacking help; unable to help oneself. **hĕlp'lĕssly** *adv.* **hĕlp'lĕssnĕss** *n.*

hĕlp'māte *n.* Helpful companion or partner, usu. husband or wife.

hĕlp'meet *n.* Helpmate (f. misunderstanding of Gen. ii. 18, 20).

Hĕlsink'ĭ. (Helsingfors) Capital city of Finland.

hĕl'ter-skĕl'ter *adv., adj.,* & *n.* (In) disordered haste; ~ (*n.*) lighthouse-shaped structure in fair etc., with external spiral track down which people may slide on a mat.

hĕlve *n.* Handle of weapon or tool.

Hĕlvē'tian (-shn) *adj.* & *n.* Swiss. [L *Helvetii*, a people of SE. Gaul]

hĕm[1] *n.* Border, edge, of cloth etc., esp. border made by turning in edge and sewing it down; *hem'-stitch* (hem *cloth* etc. with) kind of ornamental stitch producing open-work effect by drawing together threads of material (ill. STITCH). ~ *v.t.* Turn in and sew down edge of (cloth etc.); ~ *in, about, round,* enclose, confine.

hĕm[2] *int.* calling attention or expressing hesitation. ~ *n.* Utterance of this. ~ *v.i.* Utter this sound; clear throat; hesitate in speech.

hemi- *prefix.* Half-, affecting one half, etc.

hĕm'ĭcȳcle *n.* Half-moon figure.

hĕmĭhē'dral *adj.* (chem., of crystal) Having half the number of planes required by the highest degree of symmetry belonging to its system (ill. CRYSTAL).

hĕmĭmĕtăb'olous *adj.* Of insects whose young closely resemble adult, without larval or pupal stages (cf. HOLOMETABOLOUS).

hĕmĭplē'gia *n.* Paralysis of one side of body.

hĕm'ĭsphēre *n.* Half sphere; half the celestial sphere, esp. as divided by equator; (anat.) each half of cerebrum of brain; (geog.) half the earth, esp. as divided by the equator (into *Northern* and *Southern* ~*s*), or (loosely) one of those containing Europe, Asia, and Africa (*Eastern* ~), and America (*Western* ~), respectively; *land* ~, hemisphere with centre in N. Europe, containing about $\frac{6}{7}$ of the land surface of the globe; *water* ~, corresponding hemisphere with centre in the Antipodes. **hĕmĭsphĕ'ric(al)** *adjs.*

hĕm'ĭstich (-k) *n.* Half of line of verse, as divided by caesura etc.

hĕm'lŏck *n.* 1. Poisonous umbelliferous plant (*Conium maculatum*) with stout branched purple-spotted stem, finely divided leaves, and small white flowers, used as powerful sedative; poisonous potion obtained from this (believed to be the poison by which Socrates was put to death). 2. N. Amer. evergreen tree of genus *Tsuga*, esp. *T. canadensis*, from resemblance of branches to hemlock-leaves.

hemorrhage etc.: see HAEM-.

hĕmp *n.* Annual herbaceous plant, *Cannabis sativa* or *indica*, native of W. and Central Asia, cultivated esp. for its cortical fibre; this fibre, used for making cordage and woven into stout fabrics; any of several narcotic drugs, as bhang, hashish, marijuana, obtained from hemp; various other plants yielding useful fibre; ~ *agrimony*, perennial plant (*Eupatorium cannabinum*) of the daisy family, with pale-purple flowers and hairy leaves. **hĕmp'en** *adj.*

hĕn *n.* Female of common domestic fowl; female of various other birds, or of any bird, hen-bird; *hens* (pl.) domestic fowls; *hen'bane* (drug extracted from) plant (*Hyoscyamus niger*) of Europe and northern Asia, growing on waste ground, with dull-yellow purple-streaked flowers, viscid stem and leaves, unpleasant smell, and narcotic and poisonous properties; *~-coop*, coop for keeping poultry in; *~-crab, -lobster*, female crab, lobster; *~-harrier*, European bird of prey, blue hawk, *Circus cyaneus*; *~-pecked*, (of husband) domineered over by wife; *~-roost*, place where fowls roost at night.

hĕnce *adv.* 1. (archaic) From here, from this; *henceforth', hencefor'ward*, from this time forward; *five years* ~, in five years' time from now. 2. As a result from this; as an inference from this; therefore.

hĕnch'man *n.* Squire, page of honour (now only hist.); chief attendant of Highland chief; trusty follower; political supporter.

hendeca- *prefix.* Eleven.

hĕndĕc'agon *n.* Plane rectilineal figure of 11 sides.

hĕndĕcasȳllăb'ic *adj.* & *n.* (Verse) of 11 syllables. **hĕndĕcasȳll'able** *n.* Such a verse.

hĕndī'adȳs *n.* Expression of a single complex idea by two words coupled with *and* (e.g. *in goblets and gold* for *in golden goblets*). [Gk *hen dia duoin* one by means of two]

Hĕng'ist (-ngg-) (d. 488) **and Hŏrs'a** (d. 455). Brothers, natives of Jutland, who landed at Ebbsfleet; Hengist afterwards founded the kingdom of Kent and so began the Anglo-Saxon conquest of Britain.

Hĕn'ley. The Henley Regatta, held annually at Henley-on-Thames, Oxfordshire.

hĕnn'a *n.* Egyptian privet

(*Lawsonia inermis*); shoots and leaves of this used as yellowish red dye for parts of body, hair, etc.

hĕn'othēism *n.* Belief in one god without asserting that he is the only God.

Henri: see HENRY².

Hĕn'ry¹. Name of 8 kings of England: *Henry I* (1068–1135), younger son of William I, reigned 1100–35; conquered Normandy; *Henry II* (1133–89), grandson of Henry I, reigned 1154–89; added Anjou and Aquitaine to the English possessions; established his rule in Ireland, and forced the king of Scotland to acknowledge him overlord of that kingdom; restricted the legal privileges of the Church by the Constitutions of Clarendon (1164); *Henry III* (1207–72), son of John, reigned 1216–72; *Henry IV* (1367–1413), grandson of Edward III, deposed Richard II and became first of the Lancastrian kings, 1399–1413; *Henry V* (1387–1422), son of Henry IV, reigned 1413–22; defeated the French at Agincourt, became regent of France and heir to the French throne; *Henry VI* (1421–71), son of Henry V, reigned 1422–61; during his reign the French possessions were lost and the Wars of the Roses, leading to his deposition by the Yorkists, begun; *Henry VII* (1457–1509), descended from Edward III; the first of the Tudor line; succeeded Richard III after defeating him at Bosworth Field; reigned 1485–1509; *Henry VIII* (1491–1547), son of Henry VII, reigned 1509–47; his quarrels with the pope resulted in the establishment of the Reformation in England; notorious for his matrimonial exploits.

Hĕn'ry². Name (*Henri*) of 4 kings of France: *Henry I* (d. 1060), reigned 1031–60; *Henry II* (1519–59), son of Francis I, reigned 1547–59; *Henry III* (1551–89), son of Henry II and Catherine de Médicis, reigned 1574–89; *Henry IV* (1553–1610), king of Navarre, first Bourbon king of France, reigned 1589–1610.

hĕn'ry³ *n.* The practical c.g.s. electro-magnetic unit of inductance, the inductance of a circuit in which the variation of current at the rate of one ampere per second induces an electromotive force of one volt. [Joseph *Henry* (1797–1878), Amer. physicist]

hėpăt'ic *adj.* Of, good for, the liver; liver-coloured, dark brownish-red.

Hėphaes'tus. (Gk myth.) God of fire; identified by the Romans with Vulcan.

Hepplewhite (hĕp'lwīt), George (d. 1786). English cabinet-maker; author of 'The Cabinet-Makers' and Upholsterers' Guide', published 1788; ~ *furniture*, furniture made by Hepplewhite or according to the designs in this book.

hepta- *prefix.* Seven.

hĕp'tachôrd (-k-) *n.* Seven-stringed musical instrument; system of 7 tones, formed of two conjunct tetrachords.

hĕp'tăd *n.* Set, group, of 7.

hĕp'tagon *n.* Plane rectilineal figure of 7 sides. **hĕptăg'onal** *adj.*

hĕptahĕd'ron (-*a*-h-) *n.* Solid of 7 faces.

hĕp'târchy (-k-) *n.* Government by 7 rulers; the 7 kingdoms supposed to have been established by the Angles and Saxons in Britain.

hĕp tastȳle *adj.* & *n.* (Portico) of 7 columns (ill. TEMPLE).

hĕptasȳllăb'ĭc *adj.* Of 7 syllables.

hĕp'tateuch *n.* First 7 books of Old Testament.

her¹ *pron.* Objective case of SHE.

her² *pron.* & *adj.* Possessive case of, and adj. corresponding to, SHE, with absolute form *hers.*

Hēr'a. (Gk myth.) Daughter of Cronos and Rhea; sister and wife of Zeus; worshipped as queen of the heavens and goddess of power and riches; identified by the Romans with Juno.

Hĕ'raclēs. Gk form of HERCULES.

Hĕraclīt'us. Greek philosopher, of Ephesus; wrote a work 'Concerning Nature' (*c* 513 B.C.), in which he maintained that all things were in a state of flux and that fire, the type of this constant change, was their origin; his melancholy views on the changing character of life led to his being known as the 'weeping philosopher'. **Hĕraclīt'ėan** *adj.* & *n.*

hĕ'rald *n.* 1. Officer who made State proclamations, bore messages between princes, officiated in the tourney, arranged various State ceremonials, regulated use of armorial bearings, settled questions of precedence, and recorded names and pedigrees of those entitled to armorial bearings; *Heralds' College*, royal corporation founded 1483, consisting of Earl Marshal, kings of arms, heralds, and poursuivants, exercising jurisdiction in armorial matters, and now recording proved pedigrees and granting armorial bearings; *Heralds' Office*, office of this corporation. 2. Messenger, envoy (freq. as title of newspaper); forerunner. ~ *v.t.* Proclaim the approach of; usher in.

herăl'dĭc *adj.* Of heraldry.

hĕ'raldry *n.* Science of a herald, esp. art of blazoning armorial bearings and settling right of persons to bear arms or certain bearings; armorial bearings; heraldic pomp. (*See Illustration, p.* 380.)

hērb *n.* Plant whose stem is not woody or persistent but dies down after flowering; plant of which leaves etc. are used for food, medicine, scent, flavour, etc.; ~ *beer*, drink made from herbs; ~ *bennet*, yellow-flowered species of geum; ~ *Robert*, common wild species of *Geranium* (*G. robertianum*) with divided leaves and light-reddish-purple flowers; ~-*tea*, -*water*, medicinal infusion of herbs. **hērbā'ceous** (-sh*us*) *adj.* Of (the nature of) herb(s); ~ *border*, garden border of perennial flowering plants.

hērb'age *n.* Herbs collectively, esp. grass and other low-growing plants covering large extent of ground and used as pasture etc.; green succulent parts of herbaceous plants; (law) right of pasture on another's ground.

hērb'al *adj.* & *n.* (Book with descriptions) of herbs. **hērb'alist** *n.* One skilled in herbs or plants (now used of early botanical writers); dealer in medicinal herbs.

hērbār'ium *n.* (Book, case, room, containing) collection of dried plants.

Hērb'ert, George (1593–1633). English clergyman; author of 'The Temple', a collection of poems of a religious character.

hērbĭf'erous *adj.* Producing herbs.

hērbĭv'orous *adj.* (Of animals) feeding on living plants. **hērb'ĭvōre** *n.*

hērb'orīze *v.i.* Gather herbs, botanize. **hērborīzā'tion, hērb'orist** *ns.*

hērb'y *adj.* Abounding in herbs; of the nature of a herb.

Hercegovina: see HERZEGOVINA.

Hērcūlān'ėum. Ancient town in Campania, buried with Pompeii in eruption of Vesuvius, A.D. 79.

Hērcŭl'ėan (*also* -ē'an) *adj.* Of Hercules; strong as Hercules; difficult as his labours.

Hērc'ūlēs (-z). 1. (Gk & Rom. myth.) Hero of prodigious strength, who performed twelve immense tasks or 'labours' imposed on him by Eurystheus, and after death was ranked among the gods; *Pillars of* ~, the rocks Calpe (Gibraltar) and Abyla (Ceuta) on either side of Strait of Gibraltar, thought to have been set up by Hercules and to be supports of western boundaries of the world. 2. A northern constellation, figured as a man kneeling on his right knee. 3. ~ (*beetle*), S. Amer. lamellicorn beetle (*Dynastes hercules*) about 5 in. long.

Hērc'ūlid *n.* (astron.) Meteor belonging to a shower with radiant point in constellation Hercules.

hērd¹ *n.* Company of animals, esp. cattle, feeding or travelling together; (contempt.) large number of people (esp. *the common* or *vulgar* ~); *the* ~ *instinct*, gregariousness and mutual influence as psychological factor; ~-*book*, pedigree-book of cattle or pigs; *herds'-man*, keeper of herds. **hērd²** *n* Herdsman. ~ *v.* Go in a herd (*together, with* others); tend (sheep, cattle).

Her'der (hār-), Johann Gottfried (1744–1803). German poet and critic; precursor of the Romantic movement; famous for his work on German folk-song and for his philosophy of history.

HERALDRY

Marshalling: 1. Impalement. 2. Quartering. 3. Dimidiation. 4. In pretence.
Points of the shield: 1. Dexter chief. 2. Middle chief. 3. Sinister chief. 4. Honour point. 5. Fesse point. 6. Nombril point. 7. Dexter base. 8. Middle point. 9. Sinister base.
An achievement of arms: 1. Crest. 2. Wreath. 3. Helm. 4. Mantling. 5. Scroll with motto. 6. Shield or escutcheon. 7. Field. 8. Charges. 9. Supporter.
Positions of beasts: 1. Rampant. 2. Sejant. 3. Passant. 4. Rampant regardant. 5. Couchant. 6. Rampant guardant.
Ordinaries and sub-ordinaries: 1. Fesse. 2. Bar. 3. Chevron. 4. Bend. 5. Bend sinister. 6. Pale. 7. Cross. 8. Saltire. 9. Chief. 10. Flanches. 11. Bordure. 12. Quarter. 13. Canton. 14. Pile. 15. Label. 16. Orle. 17. Tressure. 18. Fret. 19. Annulet. 20. Lozenge. 21. Mascle. 22. Gyron.
Divisions of the field, furs, and tinctures: 1. Party. 2. Per Fesse. 3. Quarterly. 4. Per bend. 5. Per saltire. 6. Per chevron. 7. Gyronny. 8. Paley. 9. Barry. 10. Barry wavy. 11. Bendy. 12. Checky. 13. Lozengy. 14. Chevonry. 15. Vair. 16. Ermine. 17. Fleury or flory. 18. Or. 19. Gules. 20. Azure. 21. Argent. 22. Sable. 23. Vert. 24. Purpure.
Some typical charges: 1. Billet. 2. Bouget. 3. Caltrap. 4. Escallop. 5. Estoile. 6. Mullet. 7. Martlet. 8. Fleur-de-lis. 9. Cinquefoil. 10. Cross crosslet fitchy. 11. Cross paty. 12. Bezant. 13. Pellet.
Lines used in parting the field: 1. Engrailed. 2. Embattled. 3. Potent. 4. Invected. 5. Indented. 6. Dancetty. 7. Undy. 8. Nebuly. 9. Raguly. 10. Dovetailed. 11. Rayony

hēre *adv.* In this place; in this country, region, etc.; present to the sight or mind; in this life, on earth; at this juncture, at this point in action, speech, etc.; in the matter before us or in question; (with verbs of coming or bringing) to or towards this place; *~'s (a health) to*, formula in drinking toasts; *~ and there*, in various places; *~, there, and everywhere*, everywhere, all about; *neither ~ nor there*, not to the point, of no importance; *~ goes!* (colloq. excl. announcing commencement of bold act); *here'about(s)*, somewhere near here; *hereaf'ter*, in future, later on; in the world to come; ~ (*n.*) the future, the world to come; *hereat'*, (archaic) at this; *hereby'*, by this means, as a result; *herein'*, in this point, book, etc.; *hereinaf'ter*, below (in document etc.); *hereof*, (archaic) of this; *hereto'*, (archaic) to this matter; *heretofore'*, formerly; *hereun'der*, below (in book etc.); *hereupon'*, after this; in consequence of this; *herewith'*, with this (esp. of enclosure in letter etc.). ~ *n.* This place or point.

hėrĕd'ĭtable *adj.* That may be inherited. **hėrĕdĭtabĭl'ĭty** *n.*

hĕrėdĭt'ament (*or* herĕd'-) *n.* Property that can be inherited; real property; inheritance.

hėrĕd'ĭtary *adj.* Descending by inheritance; transmitted from one generation to another; like, the same as, that one's parents had; of, holding position by, inheritance. **hėrĕd'ĭtarĭly** *adv.* **hėrĕd'ĭtarinėss** *n.*

hėrĕd'ĭty *n.* Tendency of like to beget like; property of organic beings by which offspring inherit nature and characteristics of parents or other ancestors; organic relation between successive generations; germinal constitution.

Hĕ'rėford. City and county town of **Herefordshire**, county in W. England; breed of beef cattle originating there (red and white, with white faces).

hėrĕs'ĭarch (-k) *n.* Leader, founder, of a heresy.

hĕ'rėsy *n.* Opinion or doctrine contrary to the orthodox doctrine of the Christian Church, or to the accepted doctrine on any subject.

hĕ'rėtĭc *n.* Holder of an unorthodox opinion (orig. in matter of religion). **hėrĕt'ĭcal** *adj.*

hĕ'rĭot *n.* (Engl. law) Render of best live beast or dead chattel, or fixed money payment, to lord on decease of tenant (now an incident of manorial tenures only).

hĕ'rĭtable *adj.* That passes to heirs-at-law (opp. to movable property); transmissible from parent to child; capable of inheriting. **hĕ'rĭtably** *adv.*

hĕ'rĭtage *n.* What is or may be inherited; inherited lot or portion; (fig.) portion allotted to anyone.

hĕ'rĭtor *n.* One who inherits; (Sc. law) proprietor of a heritable subject.

hėrmăph'rodīte *n.* Human being, animal, combining characteristics of both sexes; (zool.) animal having normally both male and female sexual organs; (bot.) plant in which same flower has both stamens and pistils; person, thing, combining opposite qualities; sailing-ship having characters of two kinds of craft, esp. one square-rigged like brig forward and schooner-rigged aft. ~ *adj.* Combining both sexes or opposite characteristics. **hėrmăphrodĭt'ic(al)** *adjs.* **hėrmăph'rodītism** *n.* [Gk *Hermaphroditos*, son of Hermes and Aphrodite, who became one with the nymph Salmacis]

hėrmėneut'ĭc *adj.* Of interpretation. **hėrmėneut'ĭcs** *n.pl.* Interpretation, esp. of Scripture. **hėrmėneut'ĭcal** *adj.*

Hėrm'ēs (-z). 1. (Gk myth.) Son of Zeus and Maia; represented as messenger of the gods, god of science, commerce, eloquence, etc., identified by the Romans with Mercury, and represented as a youth with winged rod (*caduceus*), brimmed hat (*petasus*), and winged shoes (*talaria*). 2. ~ *Trismegistus* ('thrice-greatest'), name given by Neo-platonists etc. to Egyptian god Thoth, regarded as author of all mysterious doctrines and esp. of secrets of alchemy.

hėrmĕt'ĭc *adj.* Of Hermes Trismegistus; of alchemy, magical, alchemical; ~ *seal, sealing*, airtight closure of vessel, esp. glass vessel, by fusion, soldering, or welding. **hėrmĕt'ĭcally** *adv.*

hėrm'it *n.* One who from religious motives has retired into solitary life, esp. early Christian recluse; person living in solitude; *~-crab*, crab of family *Paguridae*, living in mollusc's cast-off shell to protect soft shell-less hinder parts.

hėrm'ĭtage *n.* 1. Hermit's abode; solitary abode. 2. French wine from a hill near Valence with ruined hermit's cell on top. 3. *The H~*, museum of art in Leningrad, containing collections begun by Catherine the Great in 1765 and inheriting its name from the 'retreat' in which she displayed them to her friends.

hėrn'ĭa *n.* (path.) Tumour formed by the displacement of part of an organ so that it protrudes through the walls of its containing cavity; rupture. **hėrn'ĭal, hėrn'ĭary** *adjs.*

hėrn'shaw *n.* (now dial.) Heron.

hēr'ō[1] *n.* (pl. *-es*) 1. (Gk antiq.) Man of superhuman strength, courage, or ability, favoured by the gods; later regarded as intermediate between gods and men, and immortal. 2. Illustrious warrior; man of extraordinary bravery, fortitude, or greatness of soul. 3. Man forming subject of epic; chief male character in poem, play, or story; *~-worship(per)*, worship(per) of the ancient heroes or of some great man or men.

Hēr'ō[2]. (Gk legend) A beautiful priestess of Aphrodite at Sestos on the European shore of the Hellespont; beloved of Leander, a youth of Abydos on the opposite shore; Leander used to swim the strait nightly to visit her; one stormy night he was drowned and Hero in grief threw herself into the sea.

Hĕ'rod the Great. King of Judaea 40–4 B.C.; acc. to Matt. ii he ordered the slaughter of all the children of Bethlehem from 2 years old and under, in order that the infant Jesus should be destroyed. **Herō'dian** *adj.* Of, pertaining to, Herod the Great, or members of his family. ~ *n.* (hist.) One of a Jewish party, mainly political, who were partisans of the Herod dynasty, and lax in their Judaism.

Hėrŏd'otus (5th c. B.C.). Greek historian; author of 9 books of 'Histories', the main theme of which is the enmity between Asia and Greece.

hėrō'ĭc *adj.* 1. Of, fit for, a hero; having the qualities of a hero; ~ *age*, period of Greek history before the return from Troy. 2. Describing the deeds of heroes, epic; (of metre) used in heroic poetry (in Greek and Latin, the hexameter, in French, the Alexandrine, in English, German, and Italian, iambic of five feet or ten syllables); (of language) grand, high-flown. 3. Bold or daring, attempting great things. **hėrō'ĭcally** *adv.* **herō'ĭc** *n.* Heroic verse (chiefly pl.); (pl.) high-flown language or sentiments.

hĕ'rōĭn (*or* hĕrō'ĭn) *n.* Drug, also called diacetylmorphine or diamorphine, prepared from morphine; used by addicts, and in medicine as a hypnotic and analgesic. [Ger. trade name]

hĕ'roĭne *n.* Heroic woman; chief woman in poem, novel, etc.

hĕ'roĭsm *n.* Heroic conduct or qualities.

hĕ'ron, hėrn *n.* One of the long-necked long-legged wading-birds of genus *Ardea* in family *Ardeidae*, esp. the common European grey species, *A. cinerea.* **hĕ'ronry** *n.* Place where herons breed.

hėrp'ēs (-z) *n.* Two forms of virus affection, ~ *zoster*, 'shingles', an infection of the cutaneous nerves resulting in severe pain and outbreaks of small blisters related to the distribution of the nerves, and ~ *simplex*, painless form in which the blisters have no relation to the nerves of the skin.

hėrpėtŏl'ogy *n.* Zoology of reptiles. **hėrpėtŏl'ogist** *n.*

Herr (hār) *n.* German equivalent of *Mr*; German gentleman.

Hĕ'rrĭck, Robert (1591–1674). English poet; author of 'Hesperides' (1648), a collection of some 1,200 mostly idyllic nature poems

hĕ'rrĭng *n.* Edible fish, *Clupea harengus*, of N. Atlantic, coming near coast in large shoals to spawn; *kippered* ~, kipper; *red* ~: see RED; ~-*bone*, (of kind of stitch) in which threads are set obliquely on opposite sides of a line, or crossing each other (ill. STITCH); (of masonry, paving) in which stones or tiles are set in zigzag pattern; (of cloth etc.) woven in zigzag pattern; ~-*bone* (*v.t.*) work with herring-bone stitch, mark with herring-bone pattern; ~-*gull*, large white gull of N. Atlantic, with black tips to wings; ~-*pond*, (joc.) *the* N. Atlantic.

Herr'nhuter (hărrnhōō-). One of the 'United Brethren' or MORAVIANS. [f. *Herrnhut* 'the Lord's keeping', their first German settlement, in Saxony]

hers: see HER.

Hĕr'schel (-sh-), Sir William (1738–1822). German-born astronomer, who settled in England and became court astronomer to George III; discoverer of the planet Uranus. **Hĕrschē'lian** *adj.* Of, pertaining to, Sir W. Herschel or his son, Sir John Herschel (1792–1871); ~ *telescope*, a form of reflecting telescope with a concave mirror slightly inclined to the axis, exhibited, but not invented, by Sir W. Herschel.

hersĕlf' *pron.* Emphatic and reflexive form corresponding to SHE.

Hert'ford (hārf-). County town of **Hertfordshire,** one of the Home counties of England.

Hert'ford Cŏl'lege (hārf-). College of the University of Oxford, re-founded in 1740, and again in 1874, on site of Hart Hall, founded in 13th c. by Elias de Hertford.

Herts. *abbrev.* Hertfordshire.

Hertz (hārts), Heinrich Rudolph (1857–94). German physicist; *Hertzian waves*, electromagnetic waves, first demonstrated by Hertz in 1888, and subsequently utilized for wireless telegraphy.

Herzėgōvin'a (hĕrts-, -vē-). Province S. of Bosnia, now part of Yugoslavia.

Hēs'iod (8th c. B.C.). Greek poet; author of 'Works and Days', descriptive of agricultural life in Boeotia, and probably of the 'Theogony', containing a mythical account of the origin of the world and the genealogy of the gods, and of a 'Catalogue of Women', who, being beloved of the gods, became the mothers of heroes. **Hēsiŏd'ic** *adj.*

hĕs'itant (-z-) *adj.* Hesitating, irresolute. **hĕs'itance, hĕs'itancy** *ns.*

hĕs'itāte (-z-) *v.i.* Show, speak with, indecision; scruple; be reluctant, *to* (do). **hĕs'itātingly** *adv.* **hĕsitā'tion** *n.* **hĕs'itative** *adj.*

Hĕspĕr'ian *adj.* (poet.) Western.

Hĕspĕ'rides (-z). (Gk myth.) Three, four, or seven nymphs, daughters of Hesperus; they were guardians, with the aid of a watchful dragon, of the garden in which golden apples grew, in the Isles of the Blest, at the western extremity of the earth.

Hĕs'perus. The evening star, Venus.

Hĕss'e (-*e*). Former State of SW. Germany, now a province of the Federal Republic; capital, Wiesbaden.

Hĕss'ian (*or* -shn) *adj.* Of Hesse; ~ *boot*, high boot, with tassels in front at the top, first worn by Hessian troops (ill. CAVALRY); ~ *fly*, midge (*Mayetiola destructor*) with larva very destructive to wheat (erroneously supposed to have been carried to America by Hessian troops). ~ *n.* 1. Native of, soldier from, Hesse; (U.S.) military or political hireling, mercenary (from the Hessian mercenaries used by British Government during Amer. War of Independence). 2. (without cap.) Strong coarse cloth of mixed hemp and jute used for packing bales etc.

hĕst *n.* (archaic) Behest.

hĕt *adj.* (late ME past part. of HEAT, now dial. and U.S.) Heated; ~ *up*, (orig. U.S., colloq.) excited, agitated.

hetae'ra (-ēra), **hetair'a** (-īra) *n.* Courtesan, harlot. **hetaer'ism, hetair'ism** *n.* Open concubinage; communal marriage in a tribe.

hĕt'ero- *prefix.* Other, different.

hĕt'eroclite *adj.* & *n.* Irregularly declined (noun).

hĕt'erodŏx *adj.* Not orthodox. **hĕt'erodŏxy** *n.*

hĕt'erodȳne *n.* Apparatus for, process of, converting a high-frequency wireless wave to one of an audible frequency by superimposing another high-frequency wave of nearly the same period and so producing a pulsation. ~ *v.i.* Produce this effect.

hĕterŏg'amy *n.* (biol.) Alternation of differently organized generations of animals or plants, as where sexual generation alternates with parthenogenesis; condition of having, or union of, gametes of different size and structure. **hĕterŏg'amous** *adj.*

hĕterogēn'ėous (*or* -ĕn-) *adj.* Diverse in character; composed of diverse elements or substances; (math.) incommensurable because of different kinds. **hĕterogēn'ėously** *adv.* **hĕterogēn'ėousnėss, hĕterogėnē'ity** *ns.*

hĕterogĕn'ėsis *n.* Birth of a living being otherwise than from parent of same kind, esp. supposed spontaneous generation from inorganic matter; alternation of generation. **hĕterogenĕt'ic** *adj.* Descended from different ancestral stock.

hĕteromŏrph'ism *n.* Quality of existing or occurring in different forms. **hĕteromŏrph'ic** *adj.*

hĕterosĕx'ūal *adj.* Of the normal relation of the sexes (opp. to HOMOSEXUAL); of the opposite sex. **hĕt'erosĕxūal'ity** *n.*

hĕterospŏr'ous *adj.* (bot.) Having spores of two different sizes (opp. to HOMOSPOROUS).

hĕterozȳg'ōte *n.* Zygote resulting from fusion of unlike gametes; Mendelian hybrid containing dominant and recessive characters and therefore not breeding true. **hĕterozȳg'ous** *adj.* Bearing two dissimilar alternative genetical factors.

hĕt'man *n.* Polish military commander (retained as title among Cossacks). [Polish, f. Ger. *hauptmann* head man, captain]

heuris'tic *adj.* Serving to find out or discover.

hew (hū) *v.t.* Chop, cut (*down, away, asunder*, etc.) with axe, sword, etc.; cut into shape; fell or cut (wood); cut (coal) from the seam. **hew'er** *n.* One who hews; man who cuts coal from seam.

hexa- (before vowels etc. **hex-**) *prefix.* Six.

hĕx'achŏrd *n.* Series of 6 consecutive notes with semitone between 3rd and 4th, regarded (in medieval music) as unit for purpose of singing at sight, at three pitches, beginning G, C, F respectively and with notes of each named Ut-re-mi-fa-sol-la.

hĕx'ăd *n.* Group of 6.

hĕx'agon *n.* Six-sided figure. **hĕxăg'onal** *adj.*

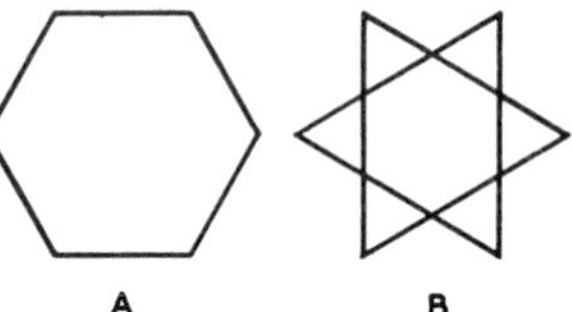

A. HEXAGON. B. HEXAGRAM

hĕx'agrăm *n.* Figure formed by 2 intersecting equilateral triangles (the angular points coinciding with those of a hexagon); figure of 6 lines.

hĕxahĕd'ron *n.* Figure with 6 faces. **hĕxahĕd'ral** *adj.*

hĕxăm'ėter *n.* Line of 6 metrical feet, esp. the *dactylic* ~ of Latin and Greek epic poetry, in which the first 4 feet may be dactyls or spondees, the 5th is a dactyl, and the 6th a spondee or less commonly a trochee, thus: –⏖ | –⏖ | –⏖ | –⏖ | – ⏑ ⏑ | – ⏓ |.

hĕx'apla *n.* Sixfold text in parallel columns, esp. of Old or New Testament.

hĕx'astȳle *adj.* & *n.* (Portico) of 6 columns (ill. TEMPLE)

hĕx'ateuch *n.* First 6 books of Old Testament.

hey (hā) *int.* calling attention, or of joy, surprise, or interrogation; ~ *presto*, conjurer's phrase of command, hence used to announce surprising transformation etc.

hey'-day (hā-) *n.* Full bloom, flush, (of youth, vigour, prosperity, etc.).

heyduck (hī'dŏŏk) *n.* In Serbia etc., robber, brigand; in Hungary, special body of foot-soldiers to whom noble rank and a territory were given in 1605; in Poland, liveried personal follower or attendant of noble.

hf bd *abbrev.* Half-bound.

hf cf *abbrev.* Half-calf.

hg. *abbrev.* Hectogram.

H.G. *abbrev.* High German (also HG); His (*or* Her) Grace; Holy Ghost; Home Guard; Horse Guards.

HH *abbrev.* Double hard (of pencil lead).

H.H. *abbrev.* Heavy hydrogen; His (*or* Her) Highness; His Holiness (the Pope).

hhd *abbrev.* Hogshead.

hī *int.* calling attention.

hīāt'us *n.* Break, gap, esp. in a series, account, or chain of proof; break between word ending, and another beginning, with a vowel.

hī'bernāte *v.i.* Spend the winter (of animals) in torpid state, (of persons) in mild climate; (fig.) remain inactive. **hīb'ernant** *adj.* **hībernā'tion** *n.*

Hībêrn'ia. Latin name of Ireland. **Hībêrn'ian** *adj.* & *n.* (Native) of Ireland.

hĭbĭs'cus *n.* Large, chiefly tropical, genus of malvaceous plants, with large bright-coloured flowers; rose-mallow.

hicc'up, hicc'ough (-kŭp) *n.* Involuntary spasm of respiratory organs, with sudden closure of glottis and characteristic sound. ~ *v.* Make hiccup; say, bring *out*, with hiccup(s).

hĭc jăcĕt *n.* Epitaph. [L, = 'here lies']

hĭck *n.* (colloq., esp. U.S.) Countryman, farmer, provincial.

hĭck'ory *n.* N. Amer. tree (*Carya*) closely allied to walnut, with tough heavy wood, used esp. for golf-clubs, and bearing drupes (usu. with hard woody rind) enclosing frequently edible nuts (pecans); wood, stick, of this; hickory-nut; *Old H~*, nickname of President Andrew JACKSON[1]; *~-elm*, Amer. elm, *Ulmus racemosa*; *~-nut*, nut of the hickory.

hĭd, hĭdden, past t. and past part. of HIDE[3].

hidăl'gō *n.* Spanish gentleman by birth. [Span. *hijo dalgo* son of a 'somebody']

hīde[1] *n.* Animal's skin, raw or dressed; (joc.) human skin; *hide'-bound*, (of cattle) with skin clinging closely to back and ribs as result of bad feeding; (fig.) bigoted, rigidly conventional.

hīde[2] *n.* (hist.) Medieval measure of land, of varying extent; orig., the amount required by one free family and its dependants, or as much as could be tilled with one plough in a year.

hīde[3] *v.* (past t. *hĭd*, past part. *hĭdd'en, hĭd*). Put, keep, out of sight; keep (fact) secret (*from*); keep from view, obstruct the view of (without implication of intention); conceal oneself; *~-and-(go)-seek*, children's game in which one or more players hide and the others look for them (also fig. of dealings with evasive person or thing). ~ *n.* Place of concealment for observation of wild animals; cache; *hide-out*, hiding-place.

hĭd'ėous *adj.* Frightful, repulsive, revolting, to senses or mind. **hĭd'eously** *adv.* **hĭd'ėousnėss** *n.*

hīd'ĭng[1] *n.* *Be in ~*, remain hidden; *~-place*, place of concealment.

hīd'ĭng[2] *n.* Thrashing.

hīe *v.i.* (pres. part. *hy'ing*). (poet.) Go quickly (*to* etc.).

hī'erârch (-k) *n.* Chief priest; archbishop.

hī'erârchy (-k-) *n.* 1. Each of three divisions of angels (each comprising three orders) in the system of Dionysius the Areopagite; the angels. 2. Priestly government; organized priesthood in successive grades; any graded organization. **hīerârch'ĭc(al)** *adjs.*

hīerăt'ĭc *adj.* Of the priests (esp. of ancient Egyptian cursive writing intermediate between hieroglyphic and demotic); priestly; of traditional styles of art (e.g. Egyptian, Byzantine) in which earlier types and methods are conventionally retained.

hī'eroglўph *n.* 1. Figure of an object, used to represent a word or sound or syllable in any of the pictorial systems of writing, esp. the ancient Egyptian; it may be (*a*)

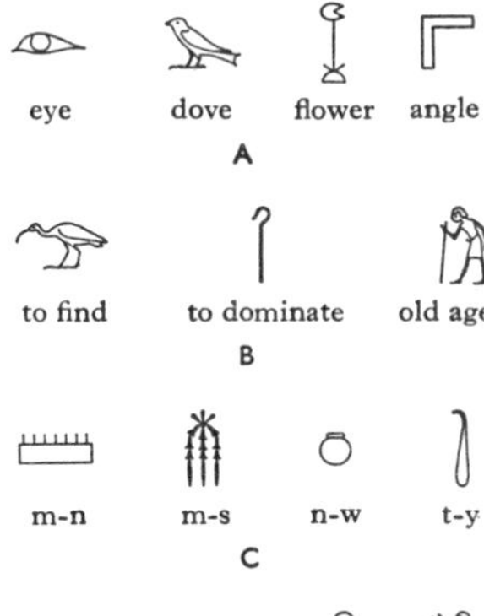

HIEROGLYPHS: A. PICTOGRAPHS. B. IDEOGRAPHS. C. PHONOGRAMS. D. DETERMINATIVES

D. 1. Heaven, sky, what is above. 2. Night sky with star, darkness, night. 3. God or divine person. 4. Pray, worship, praise

a *pictograph*, standing for the object itself (e.g. figure of an eye standing for 'eye'), or (*b*) an *ideograph*, standing for an idea associated with the object, or (*c*) a *phonogram*, standing for a sound or syllable or whole word (e.g. figure of a house, 'pr' in Egyptian, standing for the sounds *pr*), or (*d*) DETERMINATIVE. 2. Secret symbol; writing difficult to make out. **hīeroglўph'ĭc** *adj.* Of, written in hieroglyphs; symbolic. **hīeroglўph'ĭcs** *n.pl.* Hieroglyphs. **hīeroglўph'ĭcal** *adj.* **hīeroglўph'ĭcally** *adv.*

Hīerŏn'ўmīte. (eccles. hist.) Hermit of any of the orders of JEROME.

hī'erophănt *n.* Official expounder of sacred mysteries or religious ceremonies, esp. in ancient Greece; initiating priest. **hīerophăn'tĭc** *adj.*

hĭgg'le *v.i.* Dispute about terms; chaffer.

hĭgg'ledў-pĭgg'ledy (-gldĭ) *adv., adj.,* & *n.* (In) utter confusion.

high (hī) *adj.* 1. Of great or specified upward extent; situated far above ground, sea-level, etc., upper, inland; (of physical actions) extending to or from, performed at, a height; (of vowel sound), produced with (part of) tongue raised. 2. Of exalted rank, position, or quality; important, weighty; (of officers etc.) chief. 3. Great, intense, extreme; (of latitude) at great distance from equator; (of time) far advanced; ~ *colour*, fresh complexion, flush. 4. (Of meat, esp. game) slightly tainted. 5. (Of sounds) acute in pitch, shrill. 6. Extreme in opinion; having High-Church principles (see below). 7. *With a ~ hand*: see HAND; *on the ~ horse*: see HORSE; ~ *altar*, chief altar of church; ~ *and dry*, (of ship) out of the water; (fig.) out of the current of events; ~ *and low*, people of all conditions, (*adv.*) everywhere; ~ *and mighty*, arrogant; *high'ball*, (U.S.) whisky and soda-water served in tall glass with ice; *high'brow*, (person) of intellectual interests; *H~ Church*, (party, principles) giving a high place to authority of episcopate and priesthood, saving grace of sacraments, and ritual; hence *H~ Churchman*; *H~ Court*, supreme court of justice; ~ *day*, festal day; *H~ Dutch*, (archaic) = High German; ~ *explosive*, (abbrev. H.E.) explosive detonating very rapidly and with powerful effect; *~-falutin(g)*, bombast(ic); ~ *farming*, extensive use of fertilizers in cultivation; ~ *frequency*: see FREQUENCY; *H~ German*: see GERMAN; *~-handed*, overbearing, arbitrary; ~ *jinks*: see JINKS; *high'lander, high'lands*: see separate entry; ~ *life*, that of the aristocracy; ~ *light(s)*, brightest part of (subject of) painting, photograph, etc.; *~-lows*, (archaic) boots reaching over ankles; *H~ Mass*: see MASS[1]; *~-minded*, of morally lofty character; *~-pitched*, (of sound) acute in pitch; (of roof etc.) steep; *~-pressure*, (of engine, machine, etc.) having, driven by, high pressure of steam, air, etc.; (fig.) urgent, intense, as *high-pressure salesmanship*; ~ *priest*, chief priest, esp. of Jews; ~ *relief*, *alto-rilievo*, sculpture in which figures etc. project more than half their thickness from background; ~ *road*, main road; ~ *school*, secondary school; ~ *seas*, the seas, ocean, outside territorial waters; ~-*spirited*, of lofty or courageous spirit; pleasurably excited; (of horse) mettlesome, frisky; ~-*stepper*, horse that steps high; social climber; ~ *table*, table raised above others at public dinner, esp. that of president and fellows in college; ~ *tea*, tea at which meat is served; ~ *tide*: see TIDE; ~ *treason*: see TREASON; ~ *water*, state of tide when water is highest; time when tide is at the full; ~-*water mark*, level reached at high water; highest point of flood; highest point of intensity, excellence, prosperity, etc., attained; *high'way*, public road, esp. main or principal road; main route by land or water; (fig.) ordinary direct course (of action etc.); *high'wayman*, (hist.) man (usu. mounted) who robbed passengers on highway; ~'-*wing* (of monoplane) with wings set near top of fuselage. ~ *adv.* Far up aloft; in, to, a high degree; at a high price; for high stakes; (of sounds) at, to, a high pitch; *run* ~, (of sea) have strong current with high tide; ~-*born*, of noble birth; ~-*flown*, extravagant, bombastic; ~-*flyer*, -*flier*, (fig.) ambitious person; one who has high-flown notions. ~ *n.* High place; high level; (meteor.) region of high atmospheric pressure; *on* ~, in a high place, in heaven.

high'lands (hī-) *n.pl.* Mountainous or elevated country, esp. (*H*~) N. part of Scotland. **high'land** *adj.* **high'lander** *n.* Inhabitant of highlands, esp. (*H*~) those of Scotland.

high'ly (hīʹlĭ) *adv.* In a high degree; ~-*strung*, in high state of vigour or sensitiveness; at a high price or rate; honourably, favourably (as ~ *recommended*).

high'nĕss (hī-) *n.* 1. Used for *height* where *height* is not idiomatic, as *the* ~ *of his character*. 2. (*H*~) Title of various British and other princes etc., as *His*, *Her*, (*Royal*, *Serene*, *Imperial*) *H*~.

hight (hīt), past part. of obs. *hight*. (archaic, poet., joc.) Called, named.

H.I.H., H.I.M. *abbrevs.* His (*or* Her) Imperial Highness, Majesty.

hī'jăcker *n.* (U.S. slang) Person who preys on bootleggers, appropriating and profiting by their illicit liquor.

Hijra = HEGIRA.

hīke *v.i.* & *n.* (colloq., orig. dial. and U.S.) Walk (undertaken) vigorously or laboriously, tramp, esp. for pleasure or exercise. **hīk'er** *n.*

hilār'ious *adj.* Mirthful, joyous, boisterously merry. **hilār'iously** *adv.* **hilār'iousnĕss** *n.* **hilă'rity** *n.*

Hĭl'ary, St. (d. 367). Hilarius, bishop of Poitiers and doctor of the church; commemorated 13th Jan.; ~ *term*, legal or university term beginning in January.

Hĭl'dĕbrănd. Pope GREGORY VII.

hill[1] *n.* Natural elevation of earth's surface, small mountain; heap, mound, of sand, earth, etc.; *the* ~*s*, (esp.) highlands of northern and interior India; *hillbilly*, (U.S.) rustic mountaineer; *hillbilly* (*song*), song of simple ballad type popular among such people. ~ *v.t.* Form into hill; bank *up* (plants) with soil. **hĭll'y** *adj.* **hĭll'inĕss** *n.*

Hill[2], Octavia (1838–1912). Social reformer, esp. of housing conditions.

hillo(a)' (-lō)) *int.* used to hail distant person or to express surprise at meeting.

hĭll'ock *n.* Small hill or mound.

hilt *n.* Handle of sword or dagger (ill. SWORD); handle of other weapon or tool; (*prove* etc.) *up to the* ~, completely. ~ *v.t.* Furnish with hilt.

hī'lum *n.* (bot.) Mark at point of attachment of seed to seed-vessel (ill. SEED).

him *pron.* Objective case of HE.

Himalay'a(s) (*or* hĭmah'-). System of mountains N. of the Indian sub-continent, containing highest summits in the world. **Himalay'an** *adj.*

Himm'ler, Heinrich (1900–45). German politician; Minister of the Interior during the Nazi régime, and head of the S.S. and Gestapo.

himsĕlf' *pron.* Emphatic and reflexive form corresponding to HE.

hīnd[1] *n.* Female of (esp. red) deer, esp. in and after third year.

hīnd[2] *n.* Farm servant, esp. (in Scotland and northern England) married and skilled farm-workman with responsible part in working of farm, and provided with cottage on farm; steward; rustic, boor.

hīnd[3] *adj.* Situated at the back, posterior (less usual than *hinder* exc. as opp. to *fore*, of things existing in pairs); *hind'sight*, backsight of a rifle; perception after the event (opp. to *foresight*).

Hĭn'denbûrg, Paul von (1847–1934). German field marshal; 2nd president of the German Republic (1925–34); ~ *line*, in the war of 1914–18, a line of defence established by the Germans in 1916 in NE. France from Lille to Metz.

hīnd'er[1] *adj.* See HIND[3].

hĭn'der[2] *v.t.* Impede, obstruct, prevent.

Hĭn'di (-ē). Great Indo-European vernacular language of N. part of Indian peninsula, spoken from frontiers of Bengal to those of the Punjab, and from the Himalayas to the Deccan.

hīnd'mōst *adj.* Farthest behind; most remote.

hĭn'drance *n.* Obstruction, prevention; obstacle.

Hĭndu' (-ōō), **Hindoo'.** One who practises Hinduism. **Hĭn'duism** (-ōō-). Religion of the majority of the Indian people, with a social system based on caste distinctions.

Hĭndustan' (-ahn). Lit. = 'place of the Hindus'; the Persian name of India; in the stricter sense, India N. of the Deccan exclusive of Bengal and Bihar.

Hĭndusta'ni (-ahnē). Language resulting from Moslem conquest of Hindustan, form of Hindi with large admixture of Arabic, Persian, etc., current as a lingua franca over much of the peninsula (also called *Urdu*). ~ *adj.* Of Hindustan or its people; of Hindustani.

hĭnge (-j) *n.* Movable joint or mechanism like that by which door is hung on side post (ill. DOOR); natural joint doing similar work, as that of bivalve shell; (fig.) central principle, critical point, on which all turns. ~ *v.* Attach (as) with hinge; (of door etc. or fig.) hang and turn *on* (post, principle, etc.). **hĭnged** (-jd), **hĭnge'lĕss** (-jl-) *adjs.*

hĭnn'y *n.* Offspring of she-ass by stallion.

hĭnt *n.* Slight indication; covert or indirect suggestion. ~ *v.* Suggest slightly; ~ *at*, give hint of.

hĭnt'erlănd *n.* District behind that lying along coast or river-bank; area served by a port.

hĭp[1] *n.* Projection of pelvis and upper part of thigh bone at each side of body in man and quadrupeds; (archit.) arris of roof from ridge to eaves (*hipped roof*: ill. ROOF); ~-*bath*, portable bath in which one can sit immersed to the hips; ~-*disease*, disease of hip-joint characterized by inflammation, fungous growth, and caries of the bones; ~-*flask*, flask for spirits etc. carried in hip-pocket; ~-*pocket*, pocket in trousers just behind hip.

hĭp[2] *n.* Fruit of (esp. wild) rose.

hĭp[3] *n.* Morbid depression of spirits, the blues. ~ *v.t.* Make low-spirited. [f. *hypochondria*]

hīpe *v.t.* (wrestling) Throw (antagonist) by placing knee between his thighs. ~ *n.* Such throw.

hĭpp'ō *n.* (colloq.) Hippopotamus.

hippo- *prefix.* Horse.

hĭppocămp'us *n.* 1. (myth.) Sea-horse, with two forefeet, and body ending in fish's tail. 2. Genus of small fishes with horse-like head. 3. (anat.) Each of two elongated eminences (~ *major* and *minor*) on floor of each lateral ventricle of brain.

hĭpp'ocrăs *n.* Wine flavoured with spices. [Fr., f. L *Vinum Hippocraticum*, prob. so-called because filtered through conical bag called *Hippocrates' sleeve*]

Hĭppŏc'ratēs (-z) (b. *c* 460 B.C.). The most celebrated physician of Greek antiquity. **Hippocrăt'ic** *adj.* Of Hippocrates or the school of medicine named after him; applied to the shrunken and livid aspect of the countenance immediately before death, so called because described by Hippocrates; ~ *oath*, oath embodying the code of medical ethics, preserved in Hippocrates' writings (though prob. of still earlier date), and still taken, in various modified forms, by those who qualify as doctors of medicine.

Hĭpp'ocrēne. Fountain on Mount Helicon, sacred to the Muses. [Gk, = 'fountain of the horse', because fabled to have been produced by stroke of Pegasus' hoof]

hĭpp'odrōme *n.* (Gk and Rom. antiq.) Course for chariot races etc.; (high-sounding name for) circus; theatre used for various stage entertainments.

hĭpp'ogrĭff, -grÿph *n.* Fabulous griffin-like creature with body of horse.

hĭppopŏt'amus *n.* (pl. *-muses*, *-mī*). Large African quadruped (*H. amphibius*) with thick heavy hairless body, large muzzle and tusks, and short legs, inhabiting rivers, lakes, etc. [Gk *hippos* horse, *potamos* river]

hīr'cīne *adj.* Goat-like.

hīre *n.* Payment by contract for use of thing or for personal service; engagement on these terms; (fig.) reward; *~-purchase (system)*, system by which hired thing becomes hirer's after certain number of payments; purchase by instalments. ~ *v.t.* Employ (person) for wages; procure, grant, temporary use of (thing) for stipulated payment; *hired girl, man, woman, help*, etc., (U.S.), free man, woman, etc., engaged as servant (the word *servant* formerly including slaves).

hire'lĭng (-īrl-) *n.* (usu. contempt.) One who serves for hire.

hīr'sūte *adj.* Hairy, shaggy; untrimmed.

his (-z) *adj.* & *pron.* Possessive case of, and adj. corresponding to, HE.

Hĭspăn'ĭc *adj.* Of, pertaining to, Spain, its people or their language. **Hĭspăn'icism** *n.* Spanish idiom or mode of speech. [L *Hispania* the Iberian peninsula]

hĭs'pĭd *adj.* (bot., zool.) Shaggy; bristly.

hiss *n.* Sharp continuous spirant sound such as is made by geese and serpents, and in pronunciation of 's'; this sound uttered in disapproval or scorn. ~ *v.* Make this sound, esp. as expression of disapproval or derision; express disapproval of thus; utter with angry hiss.

hist *int.* used to call attention, enjoin silence, or incite dog etc.

his'tamīne *n.* Substance naturally present in the body, responsible for complex physiological phenomena esp. in connexion with work of blood-vessels.

hĭstogĕn'ėsis, hĭstŏ'gėny (-j-) *ns.* Production of organic tissues. **hĭstogėnĕt'ĭc** *adj.*

hĭstŏl'ogy *n.* Study of the minute structure of organic tissues. **hĭstolŏ'gical** *adj.* **hĭstŏl'ogĭst** *n.*

hĭstor'ian *n.* Writer of history.

hĭstor'iātėd *adj.* (Of ornamental letter etc.) decorated with figures of men or animals.

hĭstŏ'rĭc *adj.* 1. Noted in history. 2. (Gk and L grammar, of tenses of verb) used in narration of past events; ~ *present*, present tense used instead of past in vivid narration. **hĭstŏ'rĭcal** *adj.* Of history; belonging to history, not legend; in connexion with history, from the historian's point of view; belonging to the past, not of the present; (of novel, picture, etc.) dealing with historical events. **hĭstŏ'rĭcally** *adv.*

hĭstorĭ'cĭty *n.* Historic quality or character.

hĭstorĭŏg'rapher *n.* Writer of history, esp. official historian of court etc. **hĭstorĭŏg'raphy** *n.* Writing of history. **hĭstorio-grăph'ĭc(al)** *adjs.*

hĭs'tory *n.* 1. Continuous methodical record, in order of time, of important or public events; study of formation and growth of communities and nations; whole train of events connected with particular country, person, thing, etc.; past events in general, course of human affairs; *ancient* ~, history usu. reckoned as ending with fall of Roman Empire, A.D. 476; (joc.) thing that is out of date, or long past. 2. Systematic account of set of natural phenomena (*rare* exc. in *natural* ~).

hĭstrĭŏn'ĭc *adj.* Of actors or acting; stagy, hypocritical. **hĭstrĭŏn'ĭcally** *adv.* **hĭstrĭŏn'ĭcs** *n.pl.* Theatricals, theatrical act; play-acting for effect.

hĭt *v.* 1. Strike with blow or missile; direct blow *at*; (of moving body) strike; strike *against, upon*; deliver (blow, person etc. a blow); (fig.) affect sensibly, wound; *~-and-run raid*, raid by a few bombers and of short duration; ~ *out*, deal vigorous blows. 2. Fall in with, suit; ~ (*upon*), light upon, get at, (thing aimed at); ~ (*off*) imitate to a nicety; ~ *it off*, agree (*with, together*). ~ *n.* Blow, stroke; stroke of sarcasm etc. (*at*); stroke of good luck; successful attempt; success.

hĭtch *v.* 1. Move (thing) with jerk; shift; ~ *up*, lift, pull up, with jerk. 2. Fasten with loop, hook, etc.; become so fastened. 3. ~ (*-hike*), (orig. U.S.) travel by means of lifts in vehicles. ~ *n.* 1. Jerk, abrupt pull or push. 2. (naut.) Noose, knot, of various kinds, by which rope is caught round or temporarily made fast to something, as *half* ~, one formed by passing end of rope round its standing part and then through the bight (ill. KNOT). 3. Temporary stoppage; impediment.

hĭth'er (-dh-) *adv.* To, towards, this place; ~ *and thither*, in various directions, here and there; *hitherto'* -tōō), up to this time; *hith'erward*, (archaic) in this direction. ~ *adj.* Situated on this side; *the* nearer (of two).

Hĭt'ler, Adolf (1889–1945). Austrian-born head of the Nazi party; chancellor of the German Reich 1933; president and dictator (Führer) 1934–45; C.-in-C. of the German armed forces in the war of 1939–45; ~ *Youth*, a Nazi paramilitary youth organization for boys from 14 to 18 years of age. **Hĭt'lerism** *n.*

Hĭtt'īte *n.* 1. Member of an ancient people who flourished in Anatolia *c* 2000–1230 B.C. and acquired an empire controlling N. Syria and other parts of the Near East. 2. In the Bible, the people of N. Syria, possibly descended from the Hittites of Anatolia or akin to them. 3. Language of the Hittites of Anatolia, known from Babylonian cuneiform inscriptions, related to the Indo-European family of languages. ~ *adj.* Of the Hittites.

hīve *n.* Artificial habitation for bees; hiveful of bees; (fig.) busy swarming place; swarming multitude. ~ *v.* Place (bees) in hive, house (persons etc.) snugly; enter hive, live together like bees; store, hoard up (honey etc.) in hive.

hīves (-vz) *n.pl.* (Popular term for) various physical disorders, as skin eruptions, laryngitis, etc.

H.K. *abbrev.* House of Keys (Isle of Man).

hl. *abbrev.* Hectolitre.

H.L. *abbrev.* House of Lords.

H.L.I. *abbrev.* Highland Light Infantry.

hm. *abbrev.* Hectometre.

H.M. *abbrev.* His (*or* Her) Majesty.

H.M.A.S., H.M.C.S. *abbrevs.* His (Her) Majesty's Australian, Canadian, Ship.

H.M.I.(S.) *abbrevs.* His (Her) Majesty's Inspector (of Schools).

H.M.S., H.M.T. *abbrev.* His (Her) Majesty's Ship, Trawler.

hō *int.* expressing surprise, admiration, triumph, derision, calling attention, etc.; freq. added to other interjections, as *heigh-ho, what ho*, etc., or (naut.) to name of destination etc., as *westward* ~.

ho. *abbrev.* House.

H.O. *abbrev.* Home Office; hostilities only.

hoar (hōr) *adj.* Grey-haired with age; greyish white; (of things) grey with age; *~-frost*, white frost; (meteor.) ice crystals formed by condensation of water vapour below freezing-point. ~ *n.* Hoariness; hoar-frost.

hoard (hōrd) *n.* Stock, store (esp. of food, money) laid by; amassed stock of facts etc. ~ *v.t.* Amass (food, money, etc., or abs.) and put away, store *up*; treasure up in the heart.

hoard'ĭng (hōrd-) *n.* Temporary fence of boards round building during erection or repairs, often used for posting bills; any boarding for posting bills.

hoar'hound: see HOREHOUND.

hoarse (hōrs) *adj.* (Of voice) rough, husky, croaking; having such a voice. **hoarse'ly** *adv.* **hoarse'ness** *n.* **hoars'en** *v.* Make, become, hoarse.

hoar'y (hōr'ĭ) *adj.* (Of hair) grey, white, with age; having such hair, venerable; (bot., entom.) covered with short white hairs. **hoar'iness** *n.*

hoax *v.t.* Deceive, take in (person) by way of joke. ~ *n.* Humorous or mischievous deception.

hŏb[1] *n.* 1. Part of casing of fireplace having surface level with top of grate, forming stand for kettle, pan, etc. (ill. FIRE). 2. Peg or pin as mark or target in games, esp. quoits.

hŏb[2] *v.t.* (eng.) Cut (gears) by means of shaped revolving cutter.

Hŏbb'ėma, Meindert (1638–1709). Dutch landscape painter.

Hŏbbes (-bz), Thomas (1588–1679). English philosopher; expounded his political philosophy, according to which man is a naturally selfish unit, in the 'Leviathan' (1651).

hŏbb'le *v.* Walk lamely, limp; (of verse) have halting rhythm; cause to hobble; tie together legs of (horse etc.) to prevent it from straying etc.; tie (legs) thus. ~ *n.* Uneven or infirm gait; awkward situation; rope, clog, etc., for hobbling horse etc.; ~ *skirt*, skirt so narrow at foot as to impede wearer in walking.

hŏbb'ledėhoy *n.* Awkward youth, between boyhood and manhood.

hŏbb'y[1] *n.* 1. (archaic) Small horse. 2. Favourite subject or occupation that is not one's main business; ~-*horse*, wicker figure of horse fastened about waist of one of performers in morris-dance etc.; stick with horse's head which children bestride as toy horse; rocking-horse; horse on merry-go-round; (now rare) hobby.

hŏbb'y[2] *n.* Small falcon (*Falco subbuteo*).

hŏb'gŏblĭn *n.* Mischievous imp; bogy; bugbear. [*Hob* (for *Robin*) *goblin*]

hŏb'nail *n.* Heavy-headed nail for boot-soles. **hŏb'nailed** *adj.* Furnished or set with hobnails; ~ *liver*, cirrhotic liver, studded with projections like nail-heads.

hŏb'-nŏb *v.i.* Drink together, hold familiar intercourse (*with*).

hŏb'ō *n.* (pl. -*s*). (U.S.) Wandering workman; tramp.

Hŏb'son (d. 1631). A Cambridge carrier who let out his horses in rotation without allowing his customers to choose among them; hence, ~'*s choice*, necessity of taking what one can get.

hŏck[1] *n.* Joint of quadruped's hind leg between true knee and fetlock (ill. HORSE).

hŏck[2] *n.* German white wine, properly that of Hochheim on the Main.

hŏck[3] *n.* (U.S. slang) *In* ~, in prison; in pawn; in debt; ~-*shop*, pawn-shop. ~ *v.t.* Pawn.

hŏck'ey *n.* Outdoor field-game played with a small hard ball and with sticks hooked or curved at one end between two teams of eleven players on each side having the same positions as in Association football, the object being to drive the ball through the opponents' goal; in *ice*-~, played on an ice-rink by players on skates, there are 6 players on each side and instead of a ball a disc (called the *puck*) of vulcanized rubber is used.

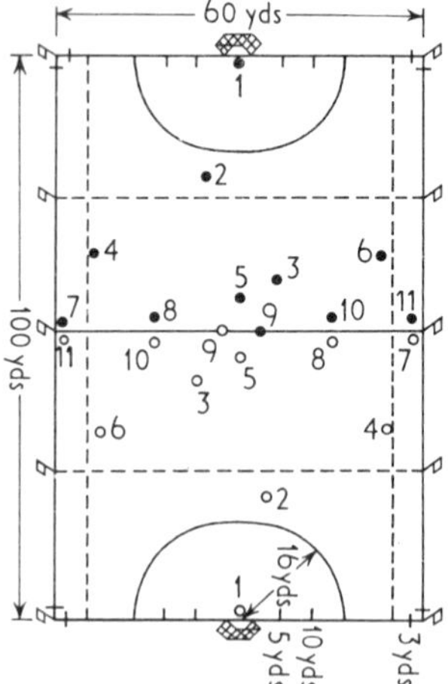

HOCKEY FIELD WITH THE POSITIONS OF PLAYERS

1. Goalkeeper. 2. Right back. 3. Left back. 4. Right half. 5. Centre half. 6. Left half. 7. Outside right. 8. Inside right. 9. Centre forward. 10. Inside left. 11. Outside left

Hŏck'tīde *n.* Time of *hock-days* (*Hock Monday* and *Tuesday*), second Monday and Tuesday after Easter Day, on which in pre-Reformation times money was collected for church and parish purposes, with various festive and sportive customs; kept for some time after Reformation as festive season, with traditional customs, still surviving in some places.

hōc'us *v.t.* Take-in, hoax; stupefy (person) with drugs; drug (liquor).

hōc'us-pōc'us *n.* Jugglery, deception; typical conjuring formula. ~ *v.* Play tricks on; juggle.

hŏd *n.* 1. Builder's light open trough on staff for carrying mortar etc.; *hod'man*, labourer who carries hod; (fig.) mechanical worker, literary hack. 2. Receptacle for coal etc.

hŏdd'en *n.* (Sc.) Coarse woollen cloth; ~ *grey*, grey hodden, typical rustic garb.

Hŏdġe *n.* Typical English agricultural labourer. [f. *Roger*]

hŏdġe-pŏdġe *n.* = HOTCHPOTCH.

hŏdiērn'al *adj.* Of the present day.

hŏdŏm'ėter *n.* Instrument for measuring distance travelled by wheeled vehicle, consisting of indicator attached to wheel or bearing to record number of revolutions; surveyor's instrument, large light wheel trundled along by handle, for measuring distances.

hoe (hō) *n.* Tool consisting of thin iron blade fixed transversely on long handle, for loosening soil, scraping up weeds, etc.; *Dutch* ~, kind pushed forward by user (*illustration, p.* 387); ~-*cake*, (U.S.) coarse bread (orig. baked on broad thin blade of cotton-field hoe) of Indian meal, water, and salt. ~ *v.* (pres. part. *hoeing*). Weed (crops), loosen (ground), dig *up*, cut *down*, with hoe; use hoe.

Hōf'er, Andreas (1767–1810). Tyrolese patriot; led an insurrection against Bavarian rule, and was captured and executed at Mantua in 1810.

Hŏff'mann, Ernst Theodor Amadeus (1776–1822). German novelist of the Romantic school, whose life provided the inspiration for Offenbach's 'Tales of Hoffmann'.

Hŏf'mannsthal (-tahl), Hugo von (1874–1929). Austrian poet and dramatist; a pioneer of the new romantic movement in German drama.

hŏg *n.* Swine, esp. castrated male reared for slaughter; (dial.) young sheep before first shearing; (fig.) coarse, gluttonous, or filthy person; road-hog; *go the whole* ~, do the thing thoroughly; ~-*back*, ~'*s-back*, sharply crested hill-ridge, steep on each side and sloping gradually at each end; ~-*fish*, fish (*Scorpaena*) with bristles on head; (also) porpoise; manatee; ~-*mane*, horse's mane cut short; ~-*plum*, (fruit of) species of *Spondias*, esp. *S. lutea* of W. Indies and Brazil, used as food for hogs; ~'*s pudding*, hog's entrail stuffed with oatmeal, suet, tripe, etc., or with flour, currants, and spice; ~-*tie*, (U.S.) secure by tying together animal's four feet or person's hands and feet; *hog'wash*, kitchen swill etc. for hogs; *hog'weed*, coarse weed of parsnip family with leaves esteemed by many animals. ~ *v.* Raise (back etc.), rise, archwise in centre; cut (mane) short; (slang) appropriate selfishly. **hŏgg'ish** *adj.* Pig-like, swinish; coarsely self-indulgent or gluttonous. **hŏgg'ishly** *adv.* **hŏgg'ishnėss** *n.*

Hŏg'ărth, William (1697–1764). English painter and engraver of social and political caricature; his work includes 4 famous series, 'The Harlot's Progress', 'The Rake's Progress', 'Marriage à la Mode', and 'The Election'.

hŏgg'ėt *n.* Yearling sheep.

hŏgg'in *n.* Mixture of screened or sifted gravel and sand, used in making filter-beds etc.

hŏg'manay *n.* (Sc.) Last day of year; gift of cake etc. demanded by children on that day.

hŏgs'head (-z-hĕd) *n.* Large cask (ill. CASK); liquid measure, 52½ imperial gallons; measure (varying from 100 to 140 gal.) of other commodities, e.g. tobacco.

Hohenlin'den (hōĭn-). Place in Bavaria, Germany, where the French revolutionary general, Moreau, defeated the Austrians in 1800.

Hohenstau'fen (hōĭnshtow-). German princely family of Swabian origin, from which came Holy Roman Emperors from 1138 to 1254.

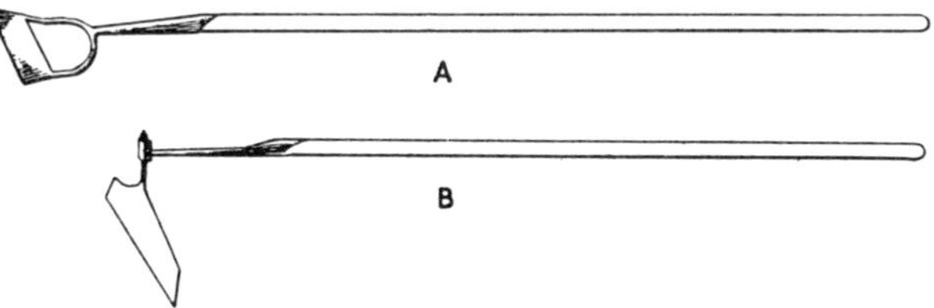

A. DUTCH HOE. B. DRAW HOE

Ho'henzoll'ern (hōĭntsŏl-). German princely family of Swabian origin, from which came the kings of Prussia from 1701 to 1918 and German emperors from 1871 to 1918.

hoi(c)k *v.* Force (aeroplane) to turn abruptly upwards; hoick aeroplane; lift or hoist, esp. with jerk or rapid movement.

hoick(s) *int.* used to incite hounds.

hoi pŏll'oi *n.* The majority, the masses. [Gk, = 'the many']

hoist[1] *v.t.* Raise aloft (esp. flags); raise by means of tackle etc. ~ *n.* Hoisting, shove up; elevator, lift, esp. for things; (eng.) fixed crane.

hoist[2] *past part.* of obs. *hoise*, hoist; ~ *with his own petard*, blown up by his own bomb, ruined by his own devices against others.

hoit'y-toit'y *adj.* (now rare) Frolicsome; haughty, petulant. ~ *int.* expressing surprised protest at undue assumption etc.

hōk'ey-pōk'ey *n.* (now rare) Cheap ice-cream sold by street vendors.

hōk'um *n.* (orig. U.S., theatr. slang) Stage-properties, action, etc., designed to have sentimental or melodramatic appeal; bunkum. [perh. blending of *hocus-pocus* and *bunkum*]

Hŏl'bein (-bīn), Hans (1497–1543). German portrait painter; became court-painter to Henry VIII of England, 1536; called 'the younger' to distinguish him from his less famous father.

hōld[1] *n.* Cavity in ship below deck, where cargo is stored (ill. SHIP).

hōld[2] *v.* (past t. and past part. *held*). 1. Keep fast, grasp; keep (one*self*, one's head, etc.) in particular attitude. 2. Possess, be owner or holder or tenant of; (of vessel) contain; (mil.) keep possession of (place); occupy (place, person's thoughts, etc.); engross (person, his attention). 3. Keep (person etc.) in specified place, condition, etc.; make (person) adhere *to* (terms, promise). 4. Observe, celebrate, conduct (festival, meeting, conversation). 5. Restrain. 6. Think, believe; (of judge or court) lay down, decide (*that*); entertain specified feelings towards; ~ *dear*, regard with affection. 7. Remain unbroken, not give way; keep going; (of laws etc.; also ~ *good, true*) be valid, apply; (archaic) stop, wait; ~ *by, to*, adhere to (choice, purpose, etc.); ~ *with*, approve of. 8. ~ one's *hand*, forbear; ~ one's *head high*, behave proudly; ~ *up* one's *head*, not be downcast or ashamed; ~ one's *ground*, one's *own*, not give way; ~ *water*, (fig.) be sound, bear examination. 9. ~ *aloof*, avoid communication with persons etc.; ~ *back*, restrain; hesitate, refrain *from*; ~ *down*, (U.S.) continue to occupy (a place or post); retain (a job); ~ *forth*, (usu. contempt.) speak publicly; ~ *hard!*, stop!; ~ *in*, confine, keep in check; ~ *off*, delay; ~ *on*, keep one's grasp on something; keep telephone line open; (colloq., imper.) stop; ~ *out*, stretch forth; offer (inducement etc.); endure, persist; ~ *out for*, refuse to accept anything but (specified terms etc.); ~ *over*, postpone; ~ *together*, (cause to) cohere; ~ *up*, support, sustain; exhibit, display (esp. *to* derision etc.); arrest progress of, obstruct; (orig. U.S.) stop and rob on highway etc.; (of horse) keep up, not fall. 10. ~*-all*, portable case for clothes etc.; *hold'fast*, firm grasp; staple or clamp securing object to wall etc.; ~*-up*, robbery by 'holding up'; stoppage or check in progress. ~ *n.* Grasp (esp. in *take, get, keep,* ~ *of*); opportunity of holding, thing to hold by; means of exerting influence *on, over*.

hōld'er *n.* (esp.) Temporary occupant of office etc.; contrivance for holding something, as a pen, cigarette, etc.

Höl'derlin (hērl-), Friedrich (1770–1843). German lyric poet and novelist.

hōld'ing *n.* (esp.) Tenure of land; land held; stocks etc. held. ~ *adj.* ~ *company*, trading company possessing whole or controlling interest in share capital of other(s).

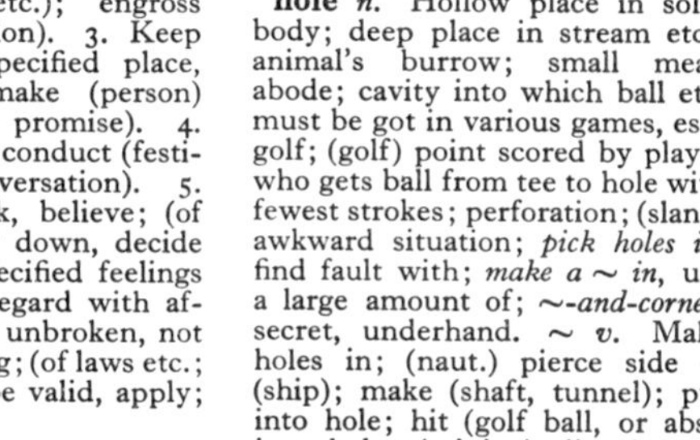

hōle *n.* Hollow place in solid body; deep place in stream etc.; animal's burrow; small mean abode; cavity into which ball etc. must be got in various games, esp. golf; (golf) point scored by player who gets ball from tee to hole with fewest strokes; perforation; (slang) awkward situation; *pick holes in*, find fault with; *make a* ~ *in*, use a large amount of; ~*-and-corner*, secret, underhand. ~ *v.* Make holes in; (naut.) pierce side of (ship); make (shaft, tunnel); put into hole; hit (golf ball, or abs.) into hole; (mining) dig through from one working to another.

hŏl'iday (-dĭ *or* -dā) *n.* 1. Day of cessation from work or of recreation; (usu. pl.) period of this, vacation. 2. Holy day.

hōl'ĭly *adv.* In a holy manner.

hōl'ĭnėss *n.* Sanctity; (with possessive) title of Pope.

hŏl'ism *n.* (philos.) Tendency in nature to produce wholes (bodies or organisms) from ordered grouping of unit structures. **holis'tic** *adj.* **holis'tically** *adv.*

hŏll'a *int.*: see HOLLO.

Hŏll'and[1]. Name of province of the Northern Netherlands, now usu. extended by foreigners to the kingdom of the NETHERLANDS. **Hŏll'ander** *n.*

hŏll'and[2] *n.* Linen fabric, freq. unbleached (*brown* ~).

hŏll'andaise (-āz) **sauce** *n.* Sauce for fish etc. of butter, eggs, vinegar, etc. [Fr., = 'Dutch']

hŏll'ands *n.* Grain spirit manufactured in Holland, Dutch gin. [f. Du. *hollandsch genever* (also ~ *gin*)]

hŏll'ō *int.* calling attention. ~ *n.* The cry 'hollo!'. ~ *v.* Shout; call to hounds.

hŏll'ow (-ō) *adj.* Having a hole, cavity, or depression; not solid, empty inside; empty, hungry; (of sound), not full-toned; (fig.) empty, insincere, false; *holl'ow ware*, trade name for hollow utensils, pots, pans, etc. **hŏll'owly** *adv.* **hŏll'ownėss** *n.* **hŏll'ow** *n.* Hollow place; hole; valley, basin. ~ *adv.* (*beat*) ~, thoroughly, completely, out-and-out. ~ *v.t.* Bend into hollow shape; (also ~ *out*), excavate.

hŏll'y *n.* Evergreen shrub (*Ilex*, esp. *I. aquifolium*) with dark-green tough glossy leaves, having indented edges with sharp stiff prickles at the points, bearing bright red berries; much used for decorating houses etc. at Christmas.

hŏll'y̆hŏck *n.* Tall plant (*Althaea rosa*) of China and southern Europe, with stout stem bearing numerous large flowers of many varieties of colour on very short stalks. [*holy*+*hock* mallow]

Hŏll'ywŏŏd. A suburb of Los Angeles, California; one of the principal centres of the cinema industry.

holm(e)[1] (hōm) *n.* Islet, esp. in river or near mainland; flat ground by river, submerged in time of flood.

holm[2] (hōm) *n.* (Usu. ~-*oak*) evergreen oak, ilex.

Holmes (hōmz), Sherlock. A private detective, the chief character in a number of detective stories by Conan Doyle.

hŏl'mĭa *n.* (chem.) Rare earth of yttria group occurring in gadolinite; oxide of holmium. **hŏl'mĭum** *n.* (chem.) Element of yttrium-cerium group found in gadolinite; symbol Ho, at. no. 67, at. wt 164·930. [f. Stock*holm*, near which yttria-bearing minerals are found]

hŏl'ocaust *n.* Whole burnt-offering; wholesale sacrifice (fig.) or destruction.

hŏl'ograph (-ahf) *adj.* & *n.* (Document) written wholly by person in whose name it appears (cf. AUTOGRAPH).

hŏlohĕd'ral *adj.* (Of crystal) having full number of planes required for highest degree of symmetry belonging to its system (ill. CRYSTAL).

hŏlomĕtăb'olous *adj.* Of insects whose young differ in form from adults, with larval and pupal stages (cf. HEMIMETABOLOUS).

hŏlothūr'ĭan *adj.* & *n.* (Animal) of the *Holothuroidea*, class of echinoderms including sea-cucumber and bêche-de-mer, characterized by elongated form, tough leathery integument, and a ring of tentacles round the mouth.

Hōlst, Gustav Theodore (1874–1934). English musical composer.

Hŏl'stein (-shtīn). 1. Former Danish duchy; later (after 1866) part of the province of Schleswig-Holstein, Prussia. 2. Breed of black-and-white dairy cattle, orig. raised in Friesland.

hōl'ster *n.* Leather case for pistol, fixed to saddle or worn on belt.

hōlt[1] *n.* (poet.) Wood, copse; wooded hill.

hōlt[2] *n.* Animal's lair, esp. otter's or badger's.

hōl'y *adj.* Consecrated, sacred; morally and spiritually perfect; belonging to, commissioned by, devoted to, God; of high moral excellence; *H~ Alliance*, that formed in 1815, after fall of Napoleon, between Russia, Austria, and Prussia, ostensibly for preserving peace and justice in Europe, but used to suppress revolutionary tendencies and demands for constitutional government; *~ cross*, the cross of Christ; *~-cross day*, festival of exaltation of cross, 14th Sept.; *~ day*, religious festival; *H~ Family*, the infant Christ and the Virgin, attended by sacred personages as St. Joseph, St. John the Baptist, St. Elizabeth, etc., as represented in pictures; *H~ Father*: see FATHER; *H~ Ghost, Spirit*, the third person of the Trinity; *~ grail*: see GRAIL[2]; *H~ Island*: see LINDISFARNE; *~ Joe*, (naut. slang) clergyman, pious person; *H~ Land*, W. Palestine, Judaea, as scene of life and death of Jesus Christ, or of development of Jewish and Christian religions; *~ name*, name of Jesus as object of formal devotion; *~ officer*: see OFFICE; *~ orders*: see ORDER; *H~ Roman Empire*: see ROMAN; *~ rood*: see ROOD; *H~ Saturday*, the Saturday in Holy Week; *~ terror*, (slang) formidable person, embarrassing child; *H~ Thursday*, the Thursday in Holy Week; (in the Anglican Ch.) Ascension Day; *~ water*, water dedicated to holy uses and used for ritual purification; water blessed by priest and used in various rites and devotional acts; *H~ Week*, week preceding Easter Sunday; *~ Willie*, hypocritically pious person; *H~ Writ*, holy writings collectively, esp. the Bible. *~ n. ~ of holies*, inner chamber of sanctuary in Jewish temple, separated by veil from outer chamber or 'holy place'; innermost shrine.

hōl'ystōne *n.* & *v.t.* (Scour with) soft sandstone used for scrubbing decks.

hŏm'age *n.* (In feudal law) formal and public acknowledgement of allegiance to feudal superior; acknowledgement of superiority, dutiful reverence.

Hŏm'burg. Town in Prussia; *~ (hat)*, man's soft felt hat with narrow brim and dented crown.

hōme[1] *n.* 1. Dwelling-place, fixed residence of family or household; members of family collectively; (U.S. etc.) private house; *long, last, ~*, the grave. 2. Native land; place where thing is native or most common. 3. Institution of refuge or rest for destitute or infirm persons. 4. (in games) Goal. 5. *At ~*, in one's own house or native land; at one's ease; familiar *with, on, in* (subject etc.); accessible to callers. *~ adj.* Of, connected with, home; carried on at home; proceeding from home; in the neighbourhood of home; carried on, produced, in one's own country, as *~ trade, markets*; treating of domestic affairs; that comes home to one, as *~ truth, thrust*; (in games) of, near, 'home'; reaching, enabling player to reach, home; *~ affairs*, internal affairs of nation; *~-brewed*, (beer etc.) brewed at home; *~-coming*, arrival at home; *H~ Counties*, English counties lying round London: Middlesex, Surrey, Kent, Essex, and sometimes Hertford and Sussex; *~ farm*, farm attached to residence of the occupier of an estate; *H~ Guard*, citizen armed force organized in 1940 for the defence of Great Britain and Northern Ireland against possible invasion, orig. called *Local Defence Volunteers*; *~-keeping*, stay-at-home; *~ land*, native land; (used by Britons abroad, inhabitants of British colonies and dominions etc. for) Great Britain, the mother country; *~-made*, made at home or for home consumption; *H~ Office*, (in Great Britain) department of Secretary of State for Home Affairs; building in which its business is carried on; *~ Rails*, (Stock Exchange) the shares of British Railways; *H~ Rule*, government of country, colony, etc., by its own citizens; esp. the movement in British politics, begun *c* 1870 to obtain self-government for Ireland; *H~ Secretary*, (in Great Britain) Secretary of State for Home Affairs, cabinet minister responsible for administration of internal affairs; *H~ Service*, main general radio service of B.B.C.; *~-sick*, depressed by absence from home, longing for home; *home'spun*, (cloth made of yarn) spun at home; (anything) plain, homely; *home'-work*, work done at home; esp. lessons and exercises to be done by schoolchild at home. *~ adv.* To one's home or country, as *come, go, ~*; arrived at home; to the point aimed at, as *the thrust went ~*; to the goal; *bring charge ~ to person*, convict him of it; *come ~ to*, be realized emotionally by. **hōme'lĕss** (-ml-), **hōme'līke** *adjs.* **hōme** *v.* 1. Go home (esp. of pigeons). 2. Bring in (aircraft) by radio; *homing device*, automatic device for guiding aircraft and missiles.

Home[2], (hūm), Sir Alec Douglas (1903–). Prime minister of Gt Britain 1963–4.

hōme'ly (-ml-) *adj.* Simple, plain; primitive; unpretending; (of persons or features) uncomely, plain. **hōme'linĕss** *n.*

hōm'er[1] *n.* Homing pigeon.

hōm'er[2] *n.* Hebrew measure of capacity, containing 10 ephahs (prob. *c.* 80 gal.). [Heb. *khōmer* heap]

Hōm'er[3]. Greek epic poet, of uncertain birthplace and date; the probable author of the 'ILIAD' and the 'ODYSSEY'. **Hōmĕ'rĭc** *adj.* Of, in the style of, Homer or the poems attributed to him; *~ laughter*, uproarious laughter (like that of Homer's gods as they watched lame Hephaestus hobbling).

hōme'stead (-mstĕd) *n.* House with outbuildings; farm; (U.S.) lot of land adequate for maintenance of a family, esp. lot of 160 acres granted to settlers by *Homestead Act* of Congress, 1862. *~ v.* (U.S.) Take up and occupy as homestead. **hōme'steader** *n.* (U.S.).

hōme'ward (-mw-) *adv.* & *adj.* (Going, leading) towards home; *~ bound*, (esp. of ship) preparing to go, on the way, home. **hōme'wards** *adv.*

hŏm'icīde *n.* 1. One who kills a human being. 2. Killing of a human being, intentionally or accidentally, with or without justification; *felonious ~*, either MANSLAUGHTER or MURDER; *justifiable ~*, killing of a person in the performance of a legal duty, as in the execution of a death sentence; *excusable* ~, killing without criminal intent, as by accident or in self-defence. **hŏmĭcīd'al** *adj.* Having a tendency to homicide; murderous.

hŏmĭlĕt'ĭc *adj.* Of homilies. **hŏmĭlĕt'ĭcs** *n.pl.* Art of preaching.

hŏm'ĭly *n.* Sermon; tedious moralizing discourse.

hōm'ĭng *adj.* That goes home; (of pigeons) trained to fly home from a distance; (of beacon, wireless signal, etc.) guiding (aircraft) homewards.

hŏm'ĭnĭd *n.* A member of the *Hominidae*, a family of mammals represented by the single genus *Homo*; a man (zoologically considered).

hŏm'ĭny *n.* Coarsely ground maize boiled with water or milk.

Hōm'ō[1] *n.* (zool.)The genus Man, including various extinct species; *H~ sapiens*, the species now existing.

hōm'ō[2] *n.* (colloq.) Homosexual.

homo- *prefix.* Same. [Gk *homos*]

hŏmocĕn'trĭc *adj.* Having same centre.

hŏm'oeopăth (-mĭo-) *n.* One who practises homoeopathy. **hŏmoeopăth'ĭc** *adj.* (freq. joc., = minute). **hŏmoeopăth'ĭcally** *adv.* **hŏmoeŏp'athy** *n.* System (founded *c* 1796 by Hahnemann of Leipzig) of treatment of disease by drugs (usu. in minute doses) that in a healthy person would produce symptoms like those of the disease.

hŏmogĕn'ėous *adj.* Of the same kind; consisting of parts all of the same kind, uniform. **hŏmogĕn'ėously** *adv.* **hŏmogėnē'ity, hŏmogĕn'ėousness** *ns.*

hŏmogenĕt'ĭc *adj.* Having common descent or origin. **homŏ'geny** *n.* Similarity due to common descent.

homŏ'gėnīze *v.t.* Treat (milk) so that fat globules emulsify and cream does not separate.

homŏ'genous *adj.* = HOMOGENETIC.

hŏmoious'ĭan (-ows-) *adj.* & *n.* (One who held that Father and Son in the Godhead were) of like but not identical substances (cf. HOMOOUSIAN).

homŏl'ogāte *v.t.* (Sc.) Acknowledge, admit; confirm. **homŏlogā'tion** *n.*

homŏl'ogīze *v.* Be homologous, correspond; make homologous.

homŏl'ogous *adj.* Having the same relation or relative position; corresponding; (biol., of limb or organ) similar in position and structure but not necessarily in function (cf. ANALOGOUS). **hŏm'olŏgue** (-g) *n.* Homologous thing.

homŏl'ogy *n.* Correspondence, sameness of relation. **hŏmolŏ'gical** *adj.* **hŏmolŏ'gically** *adv.*

hŏmomôrph'ĭc, -môrph'ous *adjs.* Of same or similar form.

homŏn'omous *adj.* Having same law of growth.

hŏm'onȳm *n.* Word of same form as another but different sense, as *pale* 'stake' and *pale* 'wan'; namesake. **hŏmonȳm'ĭc, homŏn'ȳmous** *adjs.*

hŏmŏous'ĭan, hŏmous'ĭan *adj.* & *n.* (One who held the persons of the Trinity to be) of the same substance (cf. HOMOIOUSIAN).

hŏm'ophōne *n.* 1. Word having same sound as another, but of different meaning or origin, as *sew* and *sow*. 2. Symbol denoting same sound as another. **hŏmophŏn'ĭc** *adj.* (mus.) Of same pitch, in unison. **homŏph'onous** *adj.* (Of music) in unison; (of symbols) denoting same sound. **homŏph'ony** *n.* Unison.

hŏmoplăs'tĭc *adj.* Similar in structure.

hŏmosĕx'ūal *adj.* Of, characterized by, sexual propensity for one's own sex. ~ *n.* Homosexual person. **hŏmosĕxūăl'ity** *n.*

hŏmospôr'ous *adj.* (bot.) Having spores of one size only (opp. HETEROSPOROUS).

hŏm'otype *n.* Part, organ, like another in structure.

hŏmozȳg'ōte *n.* Zygote of like gametes. **hŏmozȳg'ous** *adj*

homŭnc'ūle, homŭncle' *n.* Little man, manikin.

hōm'y *adj.* Suggesting home, home-like.

Hon. *abbrev.* Honorary; Honourable.

Hōnăn'. Province of central China.

Hŏndūr'ăs (*or* -răs'). 1. A republic of Central America with a seaboard on the Caribbean Sea, formerly (until 1821) part of the Spanish American dominions; capital, Tegucigalpa. 2. *British* ~, British Crown Colony in Central America; capital, Belize.

hōne *n.* Whetstone, esp. for razors; various stones as material for this. ~ *v.t.* Sharpen on hone.

Honegger (ŏn'ĕgār), Arthur (1892–1955). French musical composer; author of tone-poems and choral-orchestral works, notable for their novelty of conception.

hon'ėst (ŏn-) *adj.* Fair and upright in speech and act, not lying, cheating, or stealing; sincere; (of act etc.) showing uprightness; (of gain etc.) earned by fair means; (of things) unadulterated, unsophisticated; good, worthy; (archaic, of woman) chaste, virtuous; *make an ~ woman of*, marry (seduced woman); ~ *Injun*: see INJUN. **hon'ėstly** *adv.*

hon'ėsty (ŏn-) *n.* 1. Uprightness, truthfulness. 2. *Lunaria annua*, cruciferous plant with large purple (or white) flowers and flat round semi-transparent fruits.

hon'ey (hŭn'ĭ) *n.* Sweet viscid yellow fluid, nectar of flowers collected and worked up for food by bees and other insects; (fig.) sweetness; (chiefly Ir. and U.S.) sweet one, sweetheart, darling; *~-bee*, common hive-bee; *~-buzzard*, bird of prey (*Pernis*, esp. *P. apivorus*) feeding chiefly on larvae of bees and wasps; *~-dew*, sweet sticky substance, secreted by aphides, found on leaves and stems; ideally sweet substance; tobacco sweetened with molasses; *~-guide*, small African or Asiatic bird of the genus *Indicator*, which guides men and animals to nests of bees; *hon'eysuckle*, woodbine (*Lonicera periclymenum*), climbing shrub with fragrant yellowish trumpet-shaped flowers, frequent in woods; other plants of this genus. **hon'eyed** (hŭn'ĭd) *adj.*

honeycomb (hŭn'ĭkōm) *n.* 1. Bees' wax structure of hexagonal cells for honey and eggs. 2. Cavernous flaw in metal, esp. of guns. 3. Ornamental or other work hexagonally arranged. 4. RETICULUM (ill. RUMINANT). ~ *v.t.* Fill with cavities; undermine; mark with honeycomb pattern.

hon'eymōōn (hŭ-) *n.* Holiday spent together by newly married couple. ~ *v.i.* Spend honeymoon (*in, at*, place).

Hŏng Kŏng. British Crown Colony, consisting of a number of islands and a part of the mainland; situated off the SE. coast of China at the mouth of the Canton river; first occupied by Great Britain 1841 and formally ceded by Treaty of Nanking 1842; the capital, Victoria, is situated on the island of Hong Kong.

Hŏn'iton (*or* hŭn-). Town in Devonshire, England; type of pillow-lace formerly made there.

hŏnk *n.* Wild goose's cry; sound of motor horn. ~ *v.i.* Emit or give honk.

honorār'ium (ŏn-, hŏn-) *n.* Fee for professional services.

hŏn'orary (ŏn-) *adj.* Conferred as an honour (without the usual requirements, functions, etc.); holding honorary title or position; (of obligations) depending on honour, not legally enforceable; ~ *secretary*, *treasurer*, etc., secretary etc. serving without pay.

honorĭf'ĭc (ŏ-) *adj.* & *n.* (Expression) implying respect (esp. of Oriental forms of speech).

honour (ŏn'*er*) *n.* 1. High respect; glory; reputation, good name. 2. Nobleness of mind; allegiance to what is right or to conventional standard of conduct; (of woman) chastity, reputation for this. 3. Exalted position; (with possessive) title for holder of certain offices, esp. County Court judges. 4. Person, thing, that reflects honour on (*to*) another; thing conferred or done as token of respect or distinction; position or title of rank, dignity; *Companion of H~* (abbrev. C.H.), member of British order, of limited membership, founded in 1917; (golf) right of driving off first as having won last hole; (pl.) civilities rendered to guests etc.; *last, funeral, ~s*, observances of respect at funeral; *military ~s*, marks of respect paid by troops at burial of officer, to royalty etc.; *~s of war*, privileges granted to capitulating force, as that of marching out with colours flying etc. 5. pl. (in whist) Ace, king, queen, and knave of trumps (in bridge the ten also). 6. (pl.) Special distinction for proficiency beyond that required to pass examination; course of higher or more specialized studies than is required for pass degree. 7. *in ~ of*, in celebration of; *in ~ bound*, bound as a moral duty (*to* do); *be on one's ~*, be under moral obligation; *upon my ~*, (colloq.) *~ bright*, forms of asseveration; *code of ~*, rules forming conventional or personal standard of conduct. *~ v.t.* Respect highly; confer dignity upon; (commerc.) accept, pay (bill) when due.

hŏn'ourable (ŏn'er-) *adj.* 1. Worthy of honour; bringing honour to its possessor; consistent with honour; upright. 2. Title (abbrev. *Hon.*) of younger sons of earls and children of peers below rank of earl, Maids of Honour, Justices of High Court, Lords of Session, members of Government or Executive Councils in India and Colonies; *Most ~*, title of marquises, members of Order of the Bath and Privy Council; *Right ~*, title of peers below rank of marquis, Privy Councillors, and others. **hon'ourably** *adv.*

hōōch *n.* (slang, orig. U.S.) Alcoholic liquor, spirits, esp. of inferior or harmful kind. [abbrev. of Alaskan *hoochinoo* spirit]

hŏŏd *n.* Covering for head and neck, whether part of cloak etc. or separate; (universities) garment, varying in material, colour, and shape, worn over gown etc. to indicate degree; leather covering for hawk's head (ill. FALCONRY); thing like hood in shape or use, esp. waterproof (folding) top or cover of motor-car, perambulator, etc.; (U.S.) part covering engine of motor-car, bonnet; *~-mould*, moulding over head of door, window, etc. (ill. WINDOW). *~ v.t.* Cover with hood. **hŏŏd'ĕd** *adj.* (esp.) *~ crow*, *Corvus cornix*; *~ snake*, snake with power of distending elastic skin of neck in shape like hood or cowl; esp. Indian cobra (*Naja tripudians*).

hŏŏdie (-crow) *n.* (Sc.) Hooded crow.

hŏŏd'lum *n.* (U.S.) Street rowdy, young ruffian.

hōō'dōō *n.* & *adj.* (U.S.) Voodoo; malignant spell; (person or thing) bringing bad luck, unlucky. *~ v.t.* Bewitch; bring bad luck to. [Alteration of VOODOO]

hŏŏd'wink *v.t.* Deceive, humbug; blindfold.

hōō'ey *n.* (U.S. slang) Nonsense, humbug.

hōōf *n.* (pl. *-fs*, *-ves*). Horny casing of foot of ruminants, horses, swine, and allied animals, anatomically a development of the toe-nail (ill. HORSE); *cloven ~*: see CLOVEN; *~-pad*, pad to prevent one foot of horse from striking the other; *~-pick*, hook for picking stones from horse's hoof. *~ v.* Strike with hoof; (slang) go on foot; (slang) kick (person) *out* etc.

hŏŏk *n.* Piece of metal or other material bent back or having sharp angle, for catching hold or for hanging things upon; bent piece of wire, usu. barbed, for catching fish; hooked stroke in cricket or golf; (boxing) short swinging blow with elbow bent and rigid; curved cutting-instrument, esp. *reaping-hook*; sharp bend, e.g. in river; projecting point of land; (fig.) trap, snare; *~ and eye*, small metal hook and loop as dress fastening; *by ~ or by crook*, by fair means or foul; *on one's own ~*, (colloq.) on one's own account; *sling, take, one's ~*, (slang) hook it; *~-nose(d)*, (having) aquiline nose; *~-worm*, various nematoid worms infesting man and some beasts, with hook-like ribs or spines in male; disease caused by these. *~ v.* Grasp with hook; secure with hook(s); attach with hook (*on, in, up*, etc.); catch (fish) with hook; (golf) drive (ball) widely to left or (in the case of a left-handed player) to the right; (cricket) play (ball) round from off to on side without hitting it at the pitch; (Rugby football) secure (ball) in scrum with foot; *~ it*, (slang) make off, run away; *~-up*, (orig. U.S.) interconnexion of broadcasting stations for special transmissions.

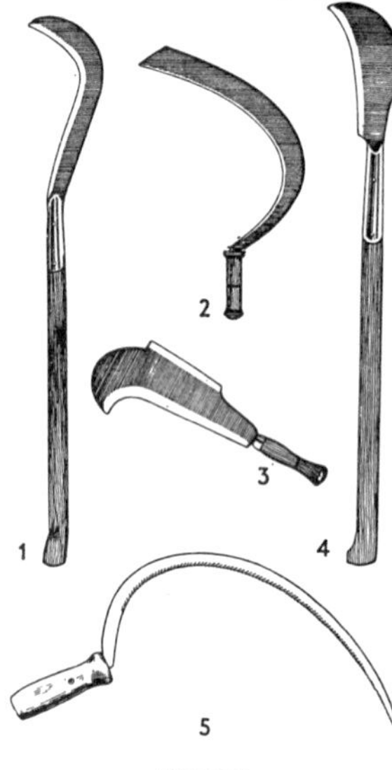

HOOKS

1. Brushing hook. 2. Bagging hook. 3. Billhook. 4. Slasher billhook. 5. Reaping-hook or sickle

hŏŏk'ah *n.* Oriental tobacco pipe with long flexible tube, smoke being drawn through water in vase to which tube and bowl are attached; narghile. [Arab. *huqqah* casket, hookah-bottle]

Hŏŏke, Robert (1635–1703), English mathematician; physicist and philosopher; *~'s Law*, (physics) an approximate empirical law of elasticity, which states that the ratio of the stress to the strain is constant.

hŏŏk'er[1] *n.* (esp., Rugby football) Player in front row of scrum who endeavours to secure ball by hooking it.

hŏŏk'er[2] *n.* Two-masted Dutch coasting or fishing vessel; one-masted fishing smack like hoy on Irish and SW. English coasts.

hōō'lee, hōli (-lē) *n.* Great Hindu festival or carnival in honour of Krishna and the Gopīs or milkmaids, near vernal equinox.

hōōl'ĭgan *n.* Young street rough; member of street gang. **hōōl'ĭganism** *n.*

hōōp[1] *n.* Circular band of metal, wood, etc., esp. for binding staves of casks (ill. CASK); wooden or iron circle trundled along by child; circle of flexible elastic material for expanding woman's skirt; hoop petticoat; circle, ring, arc; one of iron arches through which balls must be driven in croquet; *~ petticoat*, petticoat expanded by hoops. *~ v.t.* Bind with hoops; surround as hoop does.

hōōp[2] *v.t.* Utter the cry *hoop*; *hooping-cough*, variant spelling of WHOOPING-COUGH. *~ n.* The cry *hoop*; sound heard in whooping-cough.

hōōp'-la (-ah) *n.* Game at fairs etc. in which prizes may be won by encircling objects on a board with rings thrown from some distance.

hōō'poe (-pōō) *n.* Bird, esp. S. Eur. *Upupa epops*, with conspicuous variegated plumage and large erectile crest.

hōōse'gow (-z-) *n.* (U.S. slang) Prison. [Span. Amer. *juzgas* tribunal, f. L *judicatum* judged]

hōōsh *n.* (slang) Kind of thick soup, esp. in Arctic travel.

Hōō'sier (-zher) *n.* (U.S. nickname for) native of Indiana, popularly called the *~ State*. [U.S. slang = 'boorish', 'rustic']

hōōt *v.* Make loud sounds, esp. of disapproval (*at*); assail (person etc.) with derisive shouts; drive (person) *out, away*, etc., by hooting; (of owl) utter characteristic cry; sound motor horn, train-whistle, etc.; (of horn etc.) sound. *~ n.* Inarticulate shout, esp. of derision or disapprobation; owl's cry; *don't care a ~*, (slang) don't care at all; *not worth a ~*, worthless.

hōōt'er *n.* (esp.) Siren, steam whistle, esp. as signal for work to begin or cease.

hōōt(s) *int.* (Sc. and north.) expressing dissatisfaction or impatience.

hōōve *n.* Disease of cattle, with inflation of stomach, usu. caused by green fodder.

Hoo̅v'er, Herbert Clark (1874-). Amer. mining engineer, 31st president of U.S., 1929–33.

hŏp[1] *n.* Ripened 'cones' of female hop-plant, used for giving bitter flavour to malt liquors, and as tonic and soporific (usu. pl.); climbing perennial plant (*Humulus lupulus*) with rough lobed leaves, cultivated for green 'cones' of broad scales borne by female; *~-bind, -bine*, climbing stem of hop; *~-garden*, field for cultivation of hops; *~-picker*, labourer, machine, employed to pick hops; *~-pillow*, pillow stuffed with hops to produce sleep; *~-pocket*, sack as measure of hops (168 lb.); *~-pole*, pole on which hop-plant is trained. ~ *v.* Flavour with, bear, hops; gather hops.

hŏp[2] *v.* Spring (of person) on one foot, (of birds and animals) with both or all feet at once; hop over (ditch etc.); (of aircraft) pass low over physical features in a series of movements resembling hops, hence, *cloud-, hedge-, wave-hopping*; (U.S.) jump on to (train etc.); ~ (*it*), (slang) go away; *~-o'-my-thumb*, dwarf, pygmy; *hop'-scotch*, child's game of hopping on one foot and with it pushing flat stone etc. over *scotches* (lines) marked on ground. ~ *n.* Hopping; spring; (colloq.) dance; distance traversed in aircraft at one stretch, one stage of long-distance flight; ~, *skip* (or *step*), *and jump*, exercise consisting of these three movements in sequence; (fig.) short distance.

hōpe *n.* Expectation and desire combined (*of, that*); feeling of trust; ground of hope, probability; person, thing, that hope centres in. ~ *v.* Look with expectation and desire (*for*); expect and desire.

hōpe'ful (-pf-) *adj.* Feeling hope; inspiring hope, promising. ~ *n.* 'Hopeful' boy or girl (chiefly iron.). **hōpe'fully** *adv.* **hōpe'fulnėss** *n.*

Hopei (hōpā'). Province of E. China, formerly called Chihli.

hōpe'less (-pl-) *adj.* Feeling no hope; admitting no hope. **hōpe'lėssly,** *adv.* **hōpe'lėssnėss** *n.*

hŏp'lite *n.* Heavy-armed foot-soldier of ancient Greece (ill. ARMOUR).

hŏpp'er[1] *n.* 1. One who hops; hopping insect, esp. flea or cheese maggot; young locust at wingless stage. 2. Inverted pyramid or cone (orig. with hopping or shaking motion) through which grain etc. passes in mill; similar contrivance in various machines; barge carrying away mud etc. from dredging-machine and discharging it through collapsible bottom; railway truck with similar device.

hŏpp'er[2] *n.* Hop-picker.

hŏpp'le *v.t.* Fasten together legs of (horse etc.) to prevent it from straying; hobble. ~ *n.* Apparatus for this.

hŏp'săck *n.* (Coarse material of hemp and jute for making) sack in which hops are packed; woollen dress-fabric of coarse weave with threads in pairs (ill. WEAVE).

Hŏ'race. Quintus Horatius Flaccus (65–8 B.C.), Latin poet; his work includes the 'Satires', 'Odes', 'Epodes', 'Epistles', and 'Ars Poetica'. **Horā'tian** (-shn) *adj.*

hōr'ary *adj.* Of the hours; occurring every hour.

hōrde *n.* Tribe of Tatar or kindred Asiatic nomads, dwelling in tents or wagons and migrating for pasturage or for war or plunder; gang, troop (usu. contempt.); *Golden H~*: see GOLDEN. [Turk. *ordā* (also *ordū, urdū*) camp]

hore'hound, hoar- (-ōr-) *n.* Labiate herb (*Marrubium vulgare*) with stem and leaves covered with white cottony pubescence, and aromatic bitter juice used as remedy for coughs etc.; other allied herbs.

horīz'on *n.* Line at which earth and sky appear to meet; (fig.) limit of mental perception, experience, interest, etc.; *apparent, sensible, visible,* ~, circle of contact with earth's surface of a cone whose vertex is the observer's eye; *celestial, rational, true,* ~, great circle of celestial sphere, plane of which passes through centre of earth and is parallel to that of sensible horizon of a plane.

hŏrizŏn'tal *adj.* Of, at, the horizon; parallel to the plane of this, at right angles to the vertical; level, flat; (of machinery etc.) having its parts working in horizontal direction; ~ *combine, trust*, combine of concerns engaged in the same stage of manufacture or distribution of a product (as opp. to VERTICAL *combine, trust*). **hŏrizŏn'tally** *adv.* **hŏrizŏn'tal** *n.* Horizontal line, bar, etc.

hōrm'ōne *n.* (physiol.) Substance formed in an organ and carried by the blood stream to another which it stimulates; most of the known hormones, except *insulin*, which is secreted by the pancreas, and the *sex hormones*, formed in the testis and ovary, are secreted by the ductless glands. **hōrmŏn'ic** *adj.*

Hormuz: see ORMUZ.

hōrn[1] *n.* 1. Non-deciduous excrescence, freq. one of a *pair*, often curved and pointed, consisting of epidermal sheath about a bony core, on head of cattle, sheep, goats, and other mammals; projection on head of other animals, e.g. tentacle of snail or slug, crest of feathers on horned owl's head etc.; *draw in one's ~s*, restrain one's ardour, draw back. 2. Substance of which horns consist, article made of this, as shoe-horn, powder-flask, drinking-horn; ~ *of plenty*, cornucopia. 3. Wind instrument orig. made of horn and more or less resembling horn in shape; esp. the modern brass instrument (also called *French~*), which has an 11-ft tube coiled in a circle and a system of valves for producing intermediate notes, is pitched usu. in F and has a compass of *c* 3½ octaves (ill. BRASS); *basset-~*: see BASSET-HORN; *English ~*: see COR ANGLAIS. 4. Funnel- or trumpet-shaped part of gramophone etc. for amplifying sound by resonance. 5. Instrument for sounding warning signal. 6. Horn-shaped projection; extremity of moon or other crescent; arm, branch, of bay, river, etc.; either alternative of a dilemma. 7. *horn'beam*, small tough-wooded European tree (*Carpinus betulus*) used in hedges etc.; related Amer. species (*C. americana*); *horn'bill*, bird (of family *Bucerotidae*) with hornlike excrescence on bill; *~-book*, (hist.) leaf of paper containing alphabet etc. mounted on wooden tablet with handle and protected by thin plate of horn; *~-rimmed*, (of spectacles) rimmed with horn or tortoiseshell; *horn'-stone*, chert. ~ *v.* Furnish with horns; gore with the horns; adjust (frame of ship) at right angles to line of keel; *horned frog, toad*, (U.S.) lizard (*Phrynosoma*) with head and back covered with spikes; *horned* OWL, POPPY: see these words.

Hōrn[2], Cape. The southernmost point of America, on an island of the Fuegian archipelago; discovered by the Dutch navigator Schouten in 1616, and named after Hoorn, his birthplace.

hōrn'blĕnde (-d) *n.* Dark-brown, black, or greenish-black mineral, constituent of granite and many rocks, composed chiefly of silica, magnesia, and lime, and occurring in numerous varieties.

hōrn'er *n.* Maker of horn spoons, combs, etc.; one who blows a horn.

hōrn'ėt *n.* Large insect of wasp family (esp. Eur. *Vespa crabro* and Amer. *V. maculata*), inflicting serious sting.

hōrn'pīpe *n.* 1. Obsolete wind instrument (said to have had bell and mouthpiece of horn). 2. Lively dance, usu. by single person, associated esp. with merrymaking of sailors; music for this.

hōrn'ȳ *adj.* Of, like, horn; abounding in horns; hard as horn, callous. **hōrn'inėss** *n.*

hŏ'rolŏge (-j) *n.* Timepiece, dial, clock. **horŏl'oger, horŏl'ogist** *ns.* **horŏl'ogy** *n.* Art of measuring time or making clocks. **hŏrolŏ'gical** *adj.*

horŏp'ter *n.* The aggregate of all the points that are seen single in binocular vision in any given position of the eyes.

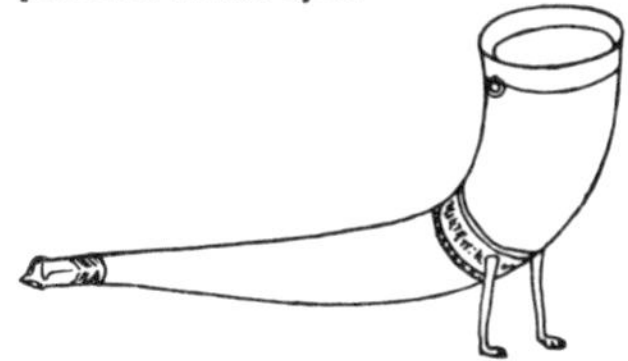

DRINKING HORN

hŏ'roscōpe *n.* (astrol.) Observation of sky and planets at certain moments, esp. at person's birth; zodiacal plan showing disposition of heavens at particular moment. **hŏroscŏp'ic(al)** *adjs.* **horŏs'copy** *n.*

hŏ'rrent *adj.* (poet.) Bristling.

hŏ'rrible *adj.* Exciting, fit to excite, horror; hideous, shocking; (colloq.) excessive, unpleasant. **hŏ'rribleness** *n.* **hŏ'rribly** *adv.*

hŏ'rrid *adj.* Terrible, frightful; (poet., archaic) rough, bristling; (colloq.) unpleasant, very bad, objectionable. **hŏ'rridly** *adv.* **hŏ'rridness** *n.*

hŏ'rrify *v.t.* Excite horror in; shock; scandalize. **horrif'ic** *adj.* **horrif'ically** *adv.*

hŏ'rror *n.* Terrified shuddering; intense dislike (*of*); (med.) shuddering, as symptom of disease; horrifying thing; *the ~s*, fit of horror or depression, esp. as in delirium tremens; *Chamber of H~s*, place full of horrible sights (orig. room of criminals etc. in Tussaud's waxwork exhibition); *~-struck, -stricken*, shocked, horrified.

hors (ōr) *adv.* & *prep.* Outside; as *~ concours*, (of exhibit) not competing for prize; hence, without a rival, unequalled; *~ de combat*, out of fight, disabled; *~-d'œuvre* (pl. usu. *-s*), extra dish served as relish at beginning or in interval of meal.

hŏrse *n.* 1. Solid-hoofed quadruped (*Equus caballus*) with flowing mane and tail, used as beast of burden and draught, and for riding on; (esp.) adult male horse, stallion or gelding; (collect. sing.) cavalry; *light ~*, lightly armed mounted soldiers; ***mount, ride, the high ~***, put on airs; ***on horseback***, mounted on a horse; ***straight from the ~'s mouth***, (of information) from authoritative source. 2. Vaulting-block in gymnasium; frame, often with legs, on which something is supported, as *clothes-~*; (naut.) rope, bar, in various uses, esp. for supporting or guiding; (mining) obstruction in vein. 3. *~-block*, small platform of stone or wood for mounting horse; *~-box*, closed box for taking horse by rail etc.; *~-breaker*, one who breaks in horses; *~-chestnut*, large ornamental tree (*Aesculus hippocastanum*), native of Albania, Greece, and Persia, introduced into England *c* 1576, with large digitate leaves, upright conical clusters of showy flowers, and fruit consisting of soft thick prickly husk enclosing one or two large hard smooth shining brown seeds of coarse bitter taste; fruit of this; *~-cloth*, cloth used to cover horse, or as part of trappings; *~-coper*: see COPER; *~-flesh*, flesh of horse, esp. as food; horses collectively; *~-fly*, insect (of various kinds) troublesome to horses; *H~ Guards*, cavalry brigade of British Household troops, i.e. Life Guards and Royal Horse Guards; esp. the Royal Horse Guards (the Blues), now an armoured-car regiment providing a mounted squadron for ceremonial purposes; headquarters of such troops, esp. building in Whitehall, London, now part of the War Office; *~-hair*, hair from mane or tail of horse, esp. as used in upholstery; *~ latitudes*, belt of calms at N. and S. edges of trade winds; *~-laugh*, loud coarse laugh; *~-leech*, large leech (*Aulastomum*); insatiable person; *daughters of the ~-leech*: see Prov. xxx. 15; *~-mackerel*, various fishes allied to mackerel, esp. the scad (*Caranx trachurus*); *horse'man*, (skilled) rider on horseback; *horse'manship*, art of riding, skill in riding, on horseback; *~-mushroom*, coarse but edible variety with hollow stem; *~-play*, rough or boisterous play; *~-pond*, pond for watering and washing horses; *~-power*, unit for measuring rate of doing work (usu. = 550 foot-pounds per second); *~-race*, race between horses (with riders); *~-radish*, cruciferous plant (*Cochlearia armoracia*) with white flowers and broad rough leaves, whose pungent root is scraped or grated as condiment; *~-sense*, (colloq., orig. U.S.) plain rough sagacity, common sense; *horse'shoe*, iron shoe for horse (now usu. narrow iron plate bent to outline of horse's hoof); thing of this shape; *horseshoe arch*, in Spanish and Islamic architecture: see ill. ARCH; *horsetail*, tail of horse (used in Turkey as standard, or as ensign denoting rank of pasha); cryptogamous plant (*Equisetum*) with hollow jointed stem and whorls of slender branches at joints; *~-whip*, whip for horse; (*v.t.*) chastise (person) with this; *horse'woman*, woman who rides on horseback. ~ *v.* Provide (person, vehicle) with horse(s); carry (person) on one's back; place (person) on man's back to be flogged; mount, go, on horseback. **hŏrse'lėss** (-sl-) *adj.*

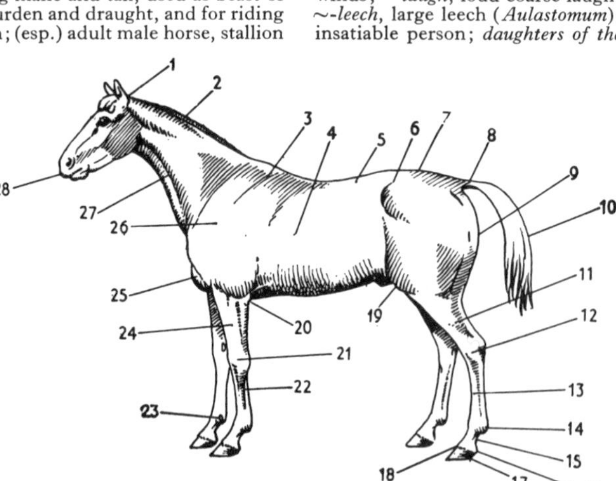

HORSE

1. Poll. 2. Crest. 3. Withers. 4. Chest. 5. Loins. 6. Hip. 7. Croup. 8. Dock. 9. Hindquarters. 10. Tail. 11. Gaskin. 12. Hock or hough. 13. Cannon bone. 14. Fetlock. 15. Pastern. 16. Heel. 17. Hoof. 18. Coronet. 19. Stifle. 20. Elbow. 21. Knee. 22. Splint bone. 23. Ergot. 24. Forearm. 25. Breast. 26. Shoulder. 27. Jugular groove. 28. Muzzle

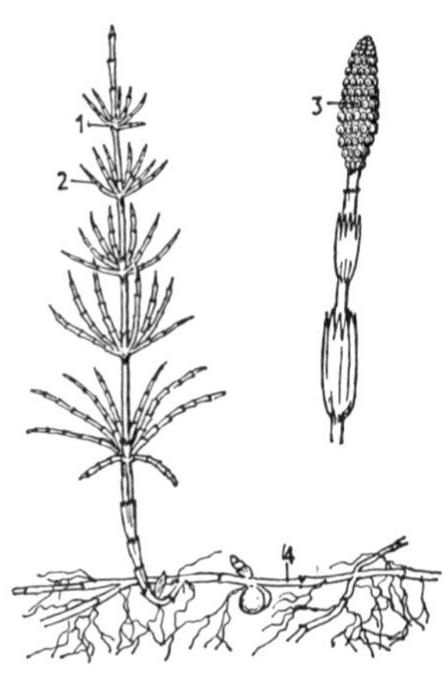

HORSETAIL

1. Node. 2. Scale leaves. 3. Strobile. 4. Rhizome

hŏrs'(e)y *adj.* Concerned with, addicted to, horses or horse-racing; affecting dress and language of groom or jockey. **hŏrs'ily** *adv.* **hŏrs'inėss** *n.*

hŏrst *n.* (geol.) Long ridge of land, often forming a range of hills, between two parallel faults which slope away from each other (ill. ROCK).

hŏrt'ative, hŏrt'atory *adjs.* Tending, serving, to exhort.

hŏrt'ĭcŭlture *n.* Art of garden cultivation. **hŏrtĭcŭl'tural** *adj.* **hŏrtĭcŭl'turist** *n.*

hŏrt'us sicc'us *n.* Arranged collection of dried plants. [L, = 'dry garden']

Hōr'us. Egyptian god of light, represented with hawk's head.

Hos. *abbrev.* Hosea (O.T.).

hōsănn'a (-z-) *n.* Cry of *hosanna*, shout of adoration. [Heb. *hosha'na*, for *hoshi'ahnna* save, pray!]

hōse (-z) *n.* 1. (collect. as pl.) Stockings; (obs.) breeches, drawers (esp. in *doublet and* ~; ill. DOUBLET). 2. (with pl. *hoses*) (also ~ *pipe*) Flexible tube for conveying liquid for watering plants, putting out fires, etc. ~ *v.t.* Provide with hose; drench or water with hose.

Hōsē'a (-z-) (8th c. B.C.). Hebrew prophet; the O.T. book of his prophecies.

hō'sier (-zh*er*) *n.* Dealer in hose and knitted or woven underwear. **hō'siery** *n.*

hŏs'pice *n.* House of rest for travellers, esp. one kept by religious order; home for the destitute or sick.

hŏs'pĭtable *adj.* Giving, disposed to give, welcome and entertainment to strangers or guests. **hŏs'pĭtably** *adv.*

hŏs'pĭtal *n.* 1. Institution for care of the sick or wounded; ~ *ship, train*, one equipped for transporting the sick or wounded. 2. Charitable institution (obs. exc. in legal use and as proper name, e.g. in *Greenwich* ~, orig. a home for superannuated seamen); charitable institution for education etc. of young (now only Sc. and in proper names, as CHRIST'S ~); (hist.) hospice, esp. establishment of Knights Hospitallers.

hŏs'pĭtal(l)er *n.* Member of charitable religious order; (in some London hospitals, orig. religious foundations) chaplain; (*Knights*) *Hospitallers*, the Order of St. John of Jerusalem (also called *Knights of Rhodes* or *Knights of Malta*), a military religious order founded 1099, which provided a hostel for pilgrims at Jerusalem, defended Acre, took Rhodes and held it for 200 years, and was given the island of Malta by the emperor Charles V in 1530 and governed it until 1798; the order still maintains numerous hospitals in Italy and elsewhere and is connected with the R.C. Church; in Gt Britain, where it is not so connected, it controls the St. John Ambulance Association.

hŏspĭtăl'ity *n.* Friendly and liberal reception of guests or strangers.

hŏs'pĭtalīze *v.t.* Admit (sick person, wounded soldier) to hospital.

hōst[1] *n.* Large number (*of*); (archaic) army; *Lord* (*God*) *of* ~*s*, frequent title of Jehovah in some O.T. books.

hōst[2] *n.* One who lodges and entertains another in his house; landlord of inn; (biol.) animal, plant, having parasite or commensal.

hōst[3] *n.* Bread consecrated in the Eucharist.

hŏs'tage *n.* Person handed over to enemies or allies as pledge for fulfilment of any undertaking or one seized by enemy to induce compliance with demands; pledge, security.

hŏs'tel *n.* Inn (archaic); house of residence for students or other special class.

hŏs'telry *n.* (archaic) Inn.

hōs'tess *n.* Woman who entertains guests; mistress of inn.

hŏs'tīle *adj.* Of an enemy; unfriendly; opposed. **hŏs'tīlely** *adv.* **hŏstĭl'ity** *n.* Enmity; state of warfare; opposition; (pl.) acts of warfare.

hos'tler (ŏsl-) *n.* = OSTLER.

hŏt *adj.* 1. Of a high temperature; very warm; communicating or feeling heat; producing the sensation of heat; (of pepper etc.) pungent, biting. 2. Ardent, passionate; angry; excited; exciting; (of dance music) played elaborately and with virtuosity. 3. (hunting, of scent) Strong; (fig., of news etc.) fresh, recent; (slang, of stolen jewellery, bank-notes, etc.) easily identifiable and so difficult to dispose of. 4. ~ *air*, (slang) excited or boastful talk; *hot'bed*, bed of earth heated by fermenting manure; (fig.) place very favourable to growth *of* (vice etc.); ~ *blast*, blast of heated air forced into furnace; ~*-blooded*, (fig.) ardent, passionate; ~*-brained, -headed*, excitable; ~ *cockles*, (hist.) rustic game in which blindfolded person guessed who struck him; ~ *dog*, (orig. U.S. colloq.) hot sausage sandwiched in roll of bread; ~*-foot*, in hot haste; ~*-gospeller*, revivalist preacher; *hot'head*, impetuous person; *hot'house*, heated building with glass roof and sides for growing plants out of season or in colder climate; *hot'pot*, mutton, beef, with potatoes etc., cooked in oven in tight-lidded pot; ~*-press*, press of glazed boards and hot metal plates for smoothing paper or cloth; (*v.t.*) press (paper etc.) in this; ~*-short*, (of iron) brittle in its hot state; ~ *stuff*, (slang) person of high spirit, vigour, skill, or strong will or passions; ~ *water*, (fig.) trouble, disgrace, scrape; ~ *well*, spring of naturally hot water; reservoir in condensing steam-engine. **hŏt'ly** *adv.* **hŏt'nèss** *n.* **hŏt** *adv.* Hotly, eagerly, angrily. ~ *v.t.* (vulg.) Heat, warm *up*.

hŏtch'pŏtch, -pŏt *n.* Dish of many mixed ingredients, esp. mutton broth with vegetables; (law) blending of properties for purpose of securing equal division (esp. of property of intestate parent); mixture, medley.

hōtĕl' (*or* ō-) *n.* House for entertainment of travellers etc.; (usu. large) inn.

Hŏtt'entŏt. Member of a short stocky people of SW. Africa, the Cape, and Bechuanaland, related to Bushmen; (fig.) person of inferior intellect or culture; ~ *bread*, S. Afr. plant, *Testudinaria elephantipes*, with large corky base; ~ *fig*, fleshy-leaved plant, *Mesembryanthemum edule*, with edible pulpy fruit. [Du., perh. = 'stammerer']

hough (hŏk) *n.* = HOCK[1]. ~ *v.t.* Hamstring.

hound *n.* Dog for chase, esp. one hunting by scent, of various breeds, as *blood-, fox-, grey-, otter-, wolf-hound*; player who follows scent in hare and hounds; despicable man; *the* ~*s*, pack of foxhounds; ~*'s-tongue*, genus (*Cynoglossum*) of plants allied to borage, with disagreeable smell. ~ *v.t.* Chase (as) with hound; set (hound, person) *at* (quarry etc.); urge (person) *on*.

houppe'lănde (hōōpl-) *n.* (hist., 14th–15th c.) Man's or woman's garment, close-fitting above with sleeves and skirt very full.

hour (owr) *n.* 1. 24th part of day, 60 minutes; short time; (pl.) time of occupation or duty; *the* time of day; (pl.) habitual time of getting up or going to bed; appointed time, occasion; *small* ~*s*, early hours after midnight. 2. (pl.) (Prayers or offices to be said at) 7 stated times of day; book containing such offices. 3. (astron., geog.) Angular measure of right ascension or longitude, 24th part of great circle of sphere, 15 degrees; ~*-circle*, great circle of celestial sphere passing through poles; graduated circle on equatorial telescope parallel to plane of equator, for observing hour-angle of star. 4. ~*-glass*, sand-glass running for one hour (ill. SAND); ~ *hand*, hand on clock etc. showing hour.

houri (hoor'ĭ, howr'ĭ) *n.* Nymph of Mohammedan paradise; voluptuously beautiful woman. [Pers., f. Arab. *ḥawira* be black-eyed like gazelle]

hour'ly (owr-) *adj.* & *adv.* (Occurring, done, reckoned) every hour.

house (-s) *n.* (pl. pr. -zĭz). 1. Building for human habitation or (usu. with defining prefix) occupation; inn, tavern; building for keeping animals or goods; (place of abode of) religious fraternity; college in university; (boys in) boarding-house forming part of school; (building used by) legislative or deliberative assembly; (audience in) theatre, cinema, etc.; performance at particular time in theatre, cinema, etc., as *first, second house*; household; family, dynasty; mercantile firm; team of doctors resident in hospital; *the House*, (pol.) House of Commons or Lords; (colloq.) Stock Exchange; (euphem.) workhouse; (Oxford Univ.) Christ Church. 2. (transf.) Habitation of any animal; shell of snail, tortoise, etc., in which the animal lives or into which it retires. 3. (astrol.) 12th part of heavens as divided by great circles through north and south points of horizon; sign of zodiac considered as seat of greatest influence of a particular planet. 4. (usu. *housey (-ie)-housey*) Form of lotto played in Army as gambling game, with special cards and checks. 5. *~ of call*, house where carriers call for commissions, where person may be heard of, etc.; *~ of cards*, house built of playing-cards; (fig.) insecure thing; *~ of God*, church, place of worship; *~ of ill fame*, brothel; *~ and home*, (emphat.) home; *~-to-house*, carried on from house to house; *keep ~*, maintain, manage affairs of, a household; *keep, make, a ~*, ensure that enough members attend the House of Commons to form a quorum or support the chosen speakers of a party; *keep open ~*, provide general hospitality; *keep the ~*, not go outdoors; *like a ~ on fire*, vigorously, fast. 6. *attrib.* etc. (of animals) kept in, frequenting, infesting, the house; *~-agent*, agent for sale and letting of houses; *~ arrest*, detention in one's house in protective custody; *~-boat*, boat fitted up for living in; *house'breaker*, person entering another's house by day with felonious intent; man employed in demolishing old houses; *~-dog*, dog kept to guard house; *~-flag*, firm's flag flown by ship; *~-flannel*, coarse flannel for washing floor etc.; *~-fly*, common fly, *Musca domestica*, infesting houses; *house'keeper*, woman managing affairs of household; person in charge of house, office, etc.; *house'keeping*, domestic economy; *houseleek*, succulent herb (*Sempervirum tectorum*) with pink flowers, thick stem, and dense rosette of leaves close to root, growing on walls and roofs; *house'maid*, female servant in charge of reception and bedrooms; *house'maid's knee*, inflammation of the bursa over the knee-cap due to kneeling; *~-martin*, common martin (*Delichon urbica*); *house'master*, master in charge of school boarding-house; *H~ of Keys*, representative branch (of 24 members) of Manx legislature; *~-parlourmaid*, servant combining duties of housemaid and parlourmaid; *~ party*, party of guests staying at country house; *~-place*, living-room in farmhouse etc.; *~-proud*, proud of one's house, desirous of keeping it beautiful; *~-room*, accommodation in house; *~-surgeon, -physician*, surgeon, physician, residing in hospital; *~-top*, (esp. in *proclaim from the ~-tops*, give wide publicity to); *~-warming*, celebration of entrance into new house; *house'work*, cleaning, cooking, etc. *~* (-z) *v.* Receive (person etc.), store (goods), in house or as house does; (naut.) place (gun etc.) in secure position, lower (upper masts); take shelter (as) in house; provide houses for (population).

house'hōld (-s-h-) *n.* Inmates of house; domestic establishment; spec., the royal or imperial household; (pl.) second quality of flour; *~ gods*, (Rom. antiq.) Lares and Penates; (fig.) essentials of home life; *~ troops*, troops employed to guard sovereign's person (in Gt Britain, 1st and 2nd Life Guards, Royal Horse Guards, and Grenadier, Coldstream, and Scots Guards); *~ word*, familiar saying or name. **house'holder** *n.* One who occupies house as his own dwelling (esp. formerly, one thus qualified for franchise); head of household.

housewife *n.* 1. (hows'wīf) Mistress of family; domestic economist. 2. (hŭz'ĭf) Case for needles, thread, etc. **house'wīfelȳ** *adj.* **house'wifery** (-wĭfrĭ) *n.* Domestic economy, housekeeping.

hous'ing[1] (-z-) *n.* 1. Houses collectively; provision of houses; storage, shelter; *~ estate*, residential district planned by one owner or local authority. 2. (naut.) Covering for ship when laid up or under stress of weather. 3. (naut.) Part of lower mast between heel and upper deck, or of bowsprit between stem and knight-heads.

hous'ing[2] (-z-) *n.* Horse's cloth covering for protection or ornament.

Hous'man (-z-), Alfred Edward (1859–1936). English classical scholar and lyric poet; author of 'A Shropshire Lad' etc.

Houyhnhnm (hwĭ'nĭm). One of a race of horses with human characteristics described by Jonathan Swift in 'Gulliver's Travels'. [imit. of horse's neigh; made by Swift]

Hōv'a *n.* Member of dominant race of Madagascar, or of middle class as dist. from nobles and slaves; language of this race.

hŏv'el (*or* hŭ-) *n.* Open shed, outhouse; mean dwelling; conical building enclosing kiln.

hoveller (hŏv'ler, hŭ-) *n.* Unlicensed pilot or boatman, esp. one who goes out to wrecks.

hŏv'er (*or* hŭ-) *v.* (Of bird etc.) hang in the air (*over, about*, spot); loiter *about* (person, place); *~-fly*, fly of family *Syrphidae* which hovers with rapidly beating wings. *~ n.* Hovering, state of suspense.

how *adv.* In what way; to what extent; (in indirect statement, rhet. for) that; (in relative clause) in whatever way, as; *~ are you?, ~ do you do?*, what is your state of health? (freq. as form of greeting); *~-d'ye'-do*, (colloq.) embarrassing situation; *~'s that?* (cricket, formula addressed to umpire), is he out or not out?; *~ now?*, what is the meaning of this?; *howbē'ĭt*, (archaic) nevertheless; *howev'er*, in whatever way; to whatever extent; nevertheless; (archaic) in any case; *howsoever, how — soever*, in whatsoever manner; to what extent soever.

how'dah *n.* Seat for two or more, usu. with canopy, on elephant's back. [Arab. *haudaj* litter]

how'ĭtzer *n.* Short gun for high-angle firing of shells at low velocities. [Ger. *haubitze*, f. Czech *houfnice* catapult]

howl *v.* (Of animals) utter long loud doleful cry; (of persons) utter long cry of pain, derision, etc.; utter (words) with howling; (of wireless receiver) make howl. *~ n.* Long doleful cry of dog, wolf, etc.;

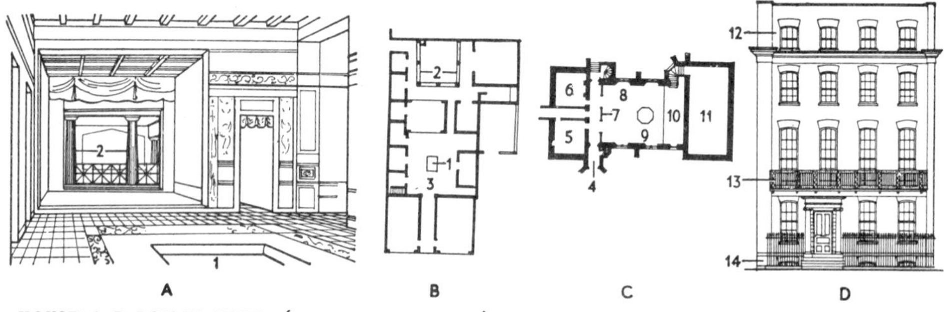

HOUSE: A, B, ROMAN HOUSE (A. ATRIUM, B. PLAN). C. PLAN OF MEDIEVAL HALL. D. FAÇADE OF GEORGIAN HOUSE

A, B. 1. *Impluvium.* 2. Peristyle. 3. Atrium. C. 4. Porch. 5. Buttery. 6. Pantry. 7. Screen. 8. Hall. 9. Hearth. 10. Dais. 11. Solar above. D. 12. Attic. 13. Balcony. 14. Basement with area in front

loud cry of pain; yell of derision; loud noise like animal's howl in wireless receiver, usu. due to low-frequency oscillation.

howl'er *n.* (esp.) 1. S. Amer. monkey of genus *Mycetes.* 2. (slang) Glaring blunder.

howl'ĕt *n.* (dial.) Owl.

howl'ing *adj.* That howls; (bibl., of wilderness) filled with howling, as of wild beasts or wind, (freq. merely) dreary; (slang) glaring.

hoy¹ *n.* Small vessel, usu. rigged as sloop, carrying passengers and goods esp. for short distances.

hoy² *int.* used to call attention, drive beasts etc., and (naut.) hail or call aloft.

hoyd'en *n.* Boisterous girl. **hoy'denish** *adj.* **hoy'denism** *n.*

h.p. *abbrev.* Half-pay; high pressure; hire-purchase; horse-power.

H.Q. *abbrev.* Headquarters.

hr *abbrev.* Hour.

H.R.H. *abbrev.* His (or Her) Royal Highness.

hrs *abbrev.* Hours.

H.S.E. *abbrev. Hic sepultus est* (= here is buried).

H.S.H. *abbrev.* His (Her) Serene Highness.

h.t. *abbrev.* High tension.

ht wt *abbrev.* Hit wicket.

huana'co (hwanah-), **gua-** (gwa-) *ns.* S. Amer. wild llama, *Auchenia huanacos*, with reddish-brown wool.

hŭb *n.* Central part of wheel, rotating on or with axle, and from which spokes radiate (ill. WHEEL); nave; (fig.) centre of interest etc.

hŭbb'le-bŭbble *n.* Form of hookah; bubbling noise; confused talk.

hŭbb'ŭb *n.* Confused din; disturbance, riot; confused yelling of war-cry.

hŭbb'y *n.* (colloq.) Husband.

hū'bris *n.* Overweening pride and insolence. **hūbris'tic** *adj.*

hŭck'abăck *n.* Stout linen or cotton fabric with figured weave and rough surface, for towels etc. (ill. WEAVE).

hŭ'ckle *n.* Hip; haunch; *~-back(ed)*, hump-back(ed); *~-bone*, hip-, haunch-, bone; knuckle-bone of quadruped.

hŭck'leberry (-klb-) *n.* (Fruit of) common N. Amer. species of genus *Gaylussacia* of low berry-bearing shrubs.

hŭck'ster *n.* Pedlar, hawker; mercenary person. *~ v.* Bargain, haggle; carry on petty traffic in; adulterate. **hŭck'ster-er, -ĕss** *ns.*

hŭd'dle *v.* Heap together confusedly; crowd (things etc.) promiscuously *together, up, into*, etc.; coil one*self up*; hurry *over, through*, botch *up*, (work etc.); nestle closely *together*. *~ n.* Confused mass; confusion, bustle; (orig. U.S. slang) consultation, discussion; *go into a ~*, confer.

Hūdibrăs'tic *adj.* In the metre or manner of Samuel Butler's mock-heroic satirical poem 'Hudibras' (1663–78).

Hŭd'son, Henry (d. 1611). English navigator; discoverer of Hudson River and Hudson Bay, Canada; *~'s Bay Company*, joint-stock company, chartered in 1670 by Charles II and given territory and exclusive trade rights in Canada; most of its territory was transferred to the Dominion of Canada in 1869.

hūe¹ *n.* Colour, tint; variety of colour caused by admixture of another. **-hued** *adj.*

hūe² *n.* *~ and cry*, clamour of pursuit or assault; outcry (*against*); proclamation for capture of criminal.

hŭff *v.* Bully, storm at; bully (person *into, out of*); offend; take offence; (draughts) remove (opponent's man) from board as forfeit for neglecting opportunity to take piece with it. *~ n.* Fit of petulance or offended dignity; (draughts) act of huffing. **hŭff'ish** *adj.* **hŭff'ishly** *adv.* **hŭff'ishnĕss** *n.* **hŭff'y** *adj.* **hŭff'ily** *adv.* **hŭff'inĕss** *n.*

hŭg *v.t.* Squeeze tightly in one's arms, usu. with affection; (of bear) squeeze between its forelegs; delight in, cling to (prejudices etc.); exhibit fondness for (person); congratulate one*self* (*on, for*); keep close to (shore etc.); *~-me-tight*, knitted woollen sleeveless wrap. *~ n.* Strong clasp; squeezing grip in wrestling.

hūge *adj.* Very large; enormous; (of immaterial things) great. **hūge'ness** *n.* **hūge'ly** (-jlĭ) *adv.* Enormously, very much.

hū'geous (-jus) *adj.* (usu. joc.) Huge. **hū'geously** *adv.* **hū'geousness** *n.*

hŭgg'er-mŭgg'er *n.* Secrecy; confusion. *~ adj.* & *adv.* Secret(ly); confused(ly). *~ v.* Conceal, hush *up*; proceed in secret or muddled fashion.

hŭgg'ery *n.* Practice (on part of barrister etc.) of courting attorney etc. for employment.

Hū'gō, Victor-Marie (1802–85). French poet, novelist, and dramatist; leader of the French Romantic movement; author of 'La Légende des Siècles', of the dramas 'Ruy Blas', 'Hernani', etc., and the novels 'Notre Dame de Paris', 'Les Misérables', 'Les Travailleurs de la Mer', etc.

Huguenot (hū'genō *or* -nŏt). French Protestant, member of the Calvinistic or Reformed communion of France whose liberty of worship, at first denied, was defined in the Edict of Nantes (1598) and again withdrawn when the Edict was revoked (1685) by Louis XIV; to escape persecution many Huguenots then emigrated to Protestant countries esp. England and America. [assimilation of Ger. *eidgenosz* confederate to Fr. personal name *Hugues*]

hul'a (hōō-) *n.* (Also *hula-hula*), Hawaiian women's dance.

hŭlk *n.* Body of dismantled ship, used as store vessel, etc., or (pl., hist.) as prison; unwieldy vessel; (fig.) big person or mass. **hŭlk'ing** *adj.* Bulky; clumsy.

hŭll¹ *n.* Outer covering of fruit, esp. pod of peas and beans (ill. FRUIT); (fig.) covering. *~ v.t.* Remove hull of.

hŭll² *n.* Frame of ship (ill. SHIP); *~ down*, far away, so that hull is invisible. *~ v.t.* Strike (ship) in hull with cannon shot.

Hŭll³ (Kingston upon Hull). English seaport; city and county borough of E. Riding of Yorkshire.

hŭllabalōō' *n.* Uproar.

hullō', -loa (-lō) *int.* used to call attention, express surprise, etc., or answer call, esp. on telephone.

hŭm¹ *v.* Make continuous murmuring sound, as of bee, spinning top, etc.; make low inarticulate vocal sound, esp. (usu. *~ and ha*) of hesitation; sing with closed lips; (colloq.) be in state of activity or bustle. *~ n.* Humming sound, esp. of hesitation, applause, surprise, etc.

hŭm² *int.* Expressing hesitation, dissent, etc.

hūm'an *adj.* Of, belonging to, man; that is a man or consists of men; of man as opp. to God; having, showing, qualities distinctive of man. *~ n.* (joc.) Human being.

hūmāne' *adj.* Benevolent, compassionate; (of branches of study) tending to refinement, elegant; *~ killer*, implement for painless slaughtering of cattle; *Royal H~ Society*, society founded 1774 for rescue of drowning persons. **hūmāne'ly** (-nl-) *adv.* **hūmāne'nĕss** *n.*

hūm'anism *n.* 1. Devotion to human interests; system of thought or action concerned with merely human interests (as dist. from divine) or with those of human race in general (as dist. from individual). 2. Literary culture, esp. that of the Humanists. **hūm'anist** *n.* Student of human nature or human affairs; one versed in the humanities; (*H~*) one of the scholars who at the revival of learning in 14th–16th centuries devoted themselves to study of language, literature, and antiquities of Greece and Rome; later disciple of same culture. **hūmanis'tic** *adj.*

hūmănitār'ian *n.* One who holds that man's duty consists in advancement of welfare of human race; one who devotes himself to welfare of mankind at large, philanthropist. *~ adj.* Holding, concerned with, views of humanitarians. **hūmănitār'ianism** *n.*

hūmăn'ity *n.* 1. Human nature; (pl.) human attributes. 2. The human race. 3. Humaneness, benevolence; (pl.) benevolent acts. 4. *The humanities*, learning or literature concerned with human culture, as grammar, rhetoric, poetry, and esp. the Greek and Latin classics.

hūm'anīze *v.* 1. Make human, give human character to; prepare (cow's milk) to resemble human milk. 2. Make, become, humane.

hūm'ankind *n.* Mankind.

hūm'anly *adv.* In a human manner; by human means; from human point of view; with human feeling.

hŭm'ble *adj.* Having, showing, low estimate of one's own importance; of lowly condition; of modest pretensions, dimensions, etc., *eat ~ pie*, make humble apology, submit to humiliation. ~ *v.t.* Make humble; bring low, abase. **hŭm'bly** *adv.* **hŭm'bleness** (-bln-) *n.*

hŭm'ble-bee *n.* Bumble-bee.

Hum'bōldt (hŏŏm,-lt), Friedrich Heinrich Alexander von (1769–1859). German traveller and scientist; author of the 'Kosmos', a physical description of the universe.

hŭm'bŭg *n.* 1. Fraud, sham; deception; impostor; (as *int.*) nonsense! 2. Lump of peppermint toffee. ~ *v.* Delude (person); be, behave like, a humbug.

hŭm'drŭm *adj.* & *n.* Commonplace(ness); dull(ness). ~ *v.i.* Proceed in humdrum way.

Hūme, David (1711–76). Scottish philosopher; author of 'Treatise of Human Nature' and 'Enquiry concerning Human Understanding'; in his system of philosophical scepticism human knowledge is restricted to experience of ideas and impressions and ultimate verification of their truth or falsehood is impossible.

hūm'erus *n.* (anat.) Bone of upper arm in man (ill. SKELETON); corresponding bone in other vertebrates. **hūm'eral** *adj.*

hūm'īd *adj.* Moist, damp. **hūmĭd'ĭfy** *v.t.* **hūmĭd'ĭty** *n.* Moisture, dampness; degree of moisture, esp. in atmosphere; *absolute ~*, the amount of water vapour in a given volume of air (usu. in grams per cubic metre); *relative ~*, the ratio between the amount actually present and the amount which would be present if the air were saturated at the same temperature.

hūm'idŏr *n.* Box, cabinet, room, for keeping cigars or tobacco moist.

hūmĭl'ĭāte *v.t.* Lower the dignity or self-respect of; mortify. **hūmĭl'ĭātĭng** *adj.* **hūmĭlĭā'tion** *n.*

hūmĭl'ĭty *n.* Humbleness, meekness, humble condition.

hŭmm'ĭng *adj.* That hums; ~ *bird*, any bird of Amer. (chiefly tropical) family *Trochilidae*, of very small size, and usu. brilliantly coloured, making humming sound by rapid vibration of wings; *~-top*, top which hums when it spins.

hŭmm'ock *n.* Hillock, knoll; rising ground, esp. in marsh; hump or ridge in icefield. **hŭmm'ŏcky** *adj.*

hūm'oral *adj.* Of the bodily humours (see HUMOUR, 4); now chiefly in ~ *pathology*, the pathology of early medicine which ascribed disease to a disordered state of the humours.

hūmorĕsque' (-sk) *n.* (mus.) Composition of light capricious character.

hūm'orist *n.* Facetious person; humorous talker, actor, or writer. **hūmoris'tic** *adj.*

hūm'orous *adj.* Full of humour; facetious, funny. **hūm'orously** *adv.* **hūm'orousnėss** *n.*

hūm'our (hūm'*er or* ū-) *n.* 1. State of mind, mood; inclination (as *in the ~ for fighting*); *out of ~*, displeased. 2. Faculty of perceiving the ludicrous; jocose imagination (less intellectual but more sympathetic than WIT); comicality; facetiousness. 3. Transparent fluid or semifluid part of eye; *aqueous ~*, that in front of iris; *vitreous ~*, that filling most of space between iris and retina. 4. (hist.) In ancient and medieval physiology, one of four chief fluids of the body (blood, phlegm, choler, and melancholy or black choler, called the *cardinal ~s*) which by their relative proportions were supposed to determine a person's physical and mental qualities. ~ *v.t.* Gratify, indulge, (person, taste, temper, etc.); adapt oneself to, make concessions to. **hūm'ourlėss** *adj.* Lacking a sense of the ridiculous.

hūm'oursome (-m*er*-) *adj.* Capricious, peevish. **hūm'oursomenėss** *n.*

hŭmp *n.* Protuberance, esp. on back, formed by curved spine or fleshy excrescence, as natural feature in camel, bison, etc., or deformity in man; rounded boss of earth etc.; (slang) fit of depression or vexation; *~-back*, (person having) back with a hump; *humpback (whale)*, whale of genus *Megaptera*, so called because of the low hump on the back; *~-backed*, having such a back. ~ *v.t.* Make humpbacked; annoy, depress; (Austral.) hoist up, shoulder (pack or swag); (U.S.) exert one*self*. **hŭmped, hŭmp'lėss, hŭmp'y** *adjs.*

humph (hmf) *int.* expressing doubt or dissatisfaction.

hŭmp'ty *n.* Low padded cushion seat.

hŭmp'ty-dŭmp'ty *n.* Short dumpy person; (in nursery-rhyme) egg.

hūm'us *n.* Vegetable mould; the characteristic organic constituent of the soil formed by the decomposition of plant materials.

Hŭn. 1. One of the Asiatic race of warlike nomads who invaded Europe *c* A.D. 375 and overran much of it under Attila in middle of 5th c. 2. (contempt.) German soldier, German (first used in a speech of the Emperor William II on the German expedition to China in 1900 and adopted derisively by the German Social Democrats and during the war of 1914–18 by the British). **Hŭnn'ĭsh** *adj.* [app. f. *Ḥun-yü*, name of a Turkic tribe]

Hunăn' (hōō-). Province of S. China.

hŭnch *v.t.* Bend, arch, convexly; thrust *out, up*, to form a hump. ~ *n.* 1. Hump; thick piece, hunk; *~-back(ed)*, humpback(ed). 2. (colloq.) Hint, tip; presentiment, premonition. **hŭnch'y** *adj.*

hŭn'drėd *n.* & *adj.* 1. Cardinal number equal to ten times ten (100, c, or C); also as ordinal when followed by other numbers; large number; hundredweight; £100; *(great, long) ~*, (in sale of herrings, mackerel, etc.) 120; *a ~ per cent.*, entire(ly), complete(ly). 2. (chiefly hist.) Subdivision of county or shire with its own court, in England and Ireland; division of county in British Amer. colonies or provinces of Virginia, Maryland, Delaware, and Pennsylvania (still existing in State of Delaware); CHILTERN *H~s*: see CHILTERN. 3. *hundreds and thousands*, very small coloured comfits; *hun'dredweight* (abbrev. *cwt*), 112 lb. avoirdupois; (in U.S.) 100 lb. 4. *H~ Days*, period between return of Napoleon I to Paris (20th Mar. 1815) and his 2nd abdication (22nd June); *H~ Years War*, intermittent war between England and France (1337–1453), arising out of English kings' claim to French crown. **hŭn'drėdfōld** *n.* & *adv.* **hŭndrėdth** *adj.* & *n.*; *Old H~*, metrical version, beginning 'All people that on earth do dwell', of Ps. c, or its tune.

hŭng past t. and past part. of HANG.

Hŭng'ary (-ngg-). Country of central Europe, forming until 1918 eastern division of Austro-Hungarian Empire; declared an independent republic in 1918; reconstituted as a kingdom, the functions of the monarch being exercised by a Regent, in 1920; again declared a republic in 1946; capital, Budapest. **Hŭngār'ian** *adj.* & *n.* (Native, language) of Hungary; the MAGYAR language.

hŭng'er (-ngg-) *n.* Uneasy sensation, exhausted condition, caused by want of food; (fig.) strong desire; *~-march*, march of unemployed etc. to call attention to their needs; *~-strike*, refusal to take food (esp. by prisoner trying to force compliance with his demands). ~ *v.i.* Feel hunger; have craving *(for, after)*; *hungered*, (archaic) hungry.

hŭng'ry (-ngg-) *adj.* Feeling hunger; showing hunger; inducing hunger; (fig.) eager, greedy; (of soil) poor, barren; *the ~ forties*, the decade 1840–9 in England, a period of great distress among the poor. **hŭng'rĭly** *adv.* **hŭng'rĭnėss** *n.*

hŭnk *n.* Large piece cut off; clumsy piece.

hŭnk'ers *n.pl.* The hams (esp. in phrase *on* one's ~, in a squatting position).

hŭnks *n.* Close-fisted man, miser.

Hŭnn'ĭsh *adj.*: see HUN.

hŭnt[1] *v.* 1. Pursue wild animals or game; chase (these) for food or sport; pursue with force, violence, or hostility; seek *after*, *for*; drive *away*, *out*; scour (district) in pursuit of game; use (horse, hounds) in hunting; ~ *down*, bring to bay; ~ *out*, track out, find by search; ~ *up*, search for. 2. (change-ringing) Alter position of (bell) in successive changes so as to shift it from first place to last (*hunting up*) or last to first (*hunting down*). 3. (elect. and mech.) Be in a state of instability, oscillate, jump backwards and forwards, as governor when its action is more than is needed to adjust speed or as clutch of arc-lamp, which moves rapidly with variations of current. ~ *n.* Hunting (lit. and fig.); persons hunting with a pack; hunting district; (elect. and mech.) see-sawing or oscillating movement; ~ *ball*, ball given by members of hunt.

Hŭnt[2], James Henry Leigh (1784–1859). English poet, politician, and essayist; imprisoned for libelling the Prince Regent; while in prison wrote his chief poetical work, 'The Story of Rimini'.

Hŭnt[3], William Holman (1827–1910). English PRE-RAPHAELITE painter; famous for his 'Light of the World', an allegorical picture symbolizing Christ knocking at the door of the human soul.

hŭn'ter *n.* 1. One who hunts; ~'s *moon*, full moon next after harvest moon. 2. Horse ridden for hunting. 3. Watch with hinged metal cover to protect glass (ill. CLOCK); *half*-~, similar watch with circular opening in cover. **hŭn'trĕss** *n.*

hŭn'tĭng *n.* Action of person or animal that hunts; chase, pursuit; ~-*box*, small house used during hunting season; ~-*ground*, place where one hunts (freq. fig.); *happy* ~-*grounds*, those expected by Amer. Indians in world to come (also fig.); ~-*watch*: see HUNTER 3.

Hŭn'tĭngdon[1]. County town of **Hŭn'tĭngdonshire,** East Midland county of England.

Hŭn'tĭngdon[2], Selina, Countess of (1707–91). Founder of Calvinistic religious association called the Countess of Huntingdon's Connexion, whence **Hŭntĭngdō'nĭan** *adj.* & *n.*

Hunts. *abbrev.* Huntingdonshire.

hŭnts'man *n.* Hunter; man in charge of (esp. fox-) hounds.

Hupeh (hōōpā'). Province of central China.

hûr'dle *n.* Portable rectangular frame strengthened with wooden bars or withes, for temporary fence etc.; wooden frame to be jumped over in ~-*race*; (pl.) hurdle-race; (hist.) frame on which traitors were dragged to execution. ~ *v.* Fence *off*, etc., with hurdles; run in hurdle race. **hûrd'ler** *n.* One who makes hurdles or runs in hurdle-races.

hûrd'y-gûrdy *n.* 1. Musical instrument resembling lute or guitar, with strings (two or more tuned to produce a drone) sounded by rosined wheel turned with right hand and keys to 'stop' strings played with left hand. 2. Any droning instrument played by turning a handle, as barrel-organ.

hûrl *v.t.* Throw violently from some position; throw (missile etc.). ~ *n.* Hurling, violent throw.

hûrl'ey *n.* Irish game resembling hockey; stick used in this.

hûrl'y-bûrl'y *n.* Commotion, tumult.

Hūr'on. Indian of a confederation of Iroquoian tribes, formerly occupying the region between Lakes Huron, Erie, and Ontario; *Lake* ~, one of the five great lakes of Canada. **Hūrō'nĭan** *adj.* Belonging to a division of the archaean series of rocks as found in Canada.

hurrah' (hu-, hōō-) *int.* expressing exultation or approbation. ~ *n.* This cry. ~ *v.i.* Shout hurrah.

hŭ'rrĭcane (-kan) *n.* 1. Violent W. Indian wind-storm, cyclone with air moving rapidly (up to 130 miles an hour) round central calm space, which with whole system advances in straight or curved track. 2. Any storm in which wind blows with terrific violence; (meteor.) wind of 75 miles per hour (strength 12 in BEAUFORT Scale). ~-*bird*, frigate-bird; ~-*deck*, light upper deck or platform on river steamer; ~ *force*, speed of wind above 75 m.p.h. (Beaufort Scale 12); ~ *lamp*, lamp so made as not to be extinguished by violent wind.

hŭ'rry *n.* Undue haste; eagerness to get thing done quickly; eagerness (*to* do, *for* thing); (with neg. or interrog.) need for haste; *not . . . in a hurry*, not very soon; ~-*call*, (U.S.) call for help in emergency; ~-*scurry*, (in) disorderly haste; proceed thus. ~ *v.* Carry, drive (person *away*, *along*, *into*, etc.) with undue haste; move, act, with great or undue haste; ~ *up*, make haste. **hŭ'rriedly** (-ĭd-) *adv.* **hŭ'rriedness** *n.*

hûrst *n.* Hillock; sandbank in sea or river; wooded eminence; wood.

hûrt *n.* Wound, material injury; harm, wrong. ~ *v.* Cause bodily injury or pain to; damage; inflict injury upon; distress, wound (person, his feelings, etc.); (colloq.) suffer injury or pain. **hûrt'ful** *adj.* **hûrt'fully** *adv.* **hûrt'fulness** *n.*

hûr'tle *v.* Strike together, against something else; hurl swiftly; strike *against*; move with clattering sound; come with a crash.

hŭs'band (-z-) *n.* Man joined to woman by marriage; (archaic) economist. ~ *v.t.* 1. Manage thriftily, economize; (archaic) till (ground), cultivate (plants). 2. (poet., joc.) Provide with husband.

hŭs'bandman (-z-) *n.* Farmer.

hŭs'bandrȳ (-z-) *n.* Farming; (*good*, *bad*) economy; careful management.

hŭsh *n.* Stillness; silence; ~-*money*, money paid to prevent disclosure or hush up something discreditable. ~ *v.* Silence, quiet; be silent (esp. as int. *hush!*). **hŭsh'abȳ** *int.* used to lull child. **hŭsh-hŭsh** *adj.* (colloq.) Highly confidential, very secret.

hŭsk *n.* Dry outer integument of some fruits or seeds; (fig.) worthless outside part of anything. ~ *v.t.* Remove husk from.

hŭs'ky *adj.* 1. Of, full of, husks; dry as a husk; (of voice or person) dry, hoarse. 2. (U.S. etc.) Tough and strong (like husk of Indian corn), big, strong, and vigorous. **hŭs'kĭly** *adv.* **hŭs'kĭnĕss** *n.* **hŭs'ky**[1] *n.* Strong stoutly-built vigorous-looking person.

hŭs'ky[2] *n.* Eskimo dog. [app. corrupt. of *Eskimo*]

Hŭss, John (1373–1415). Bohemian religious reformer; convicted of heresy by the Council of Constance and burnt alive. **Hŭss'ite** *n.* Follower of Huss.

hussâr' (-z-) *n.* One of a body of light horsemen organized in Hungary in 15th c.; soldier of light cavalry regiment elsewhere (ill. CAVALRY). [O.Serb. *husar*, f. It. *corsars* corsair]

hŭss'y (-z-) *n.* Woman of light or worthless character; pert girl. [f. *housewife*]

hŭs'tĭngs *n.* 1. Court held in Guildhall of London by Lord Mayor, Recorder, and Sheriffs (or Aldermen), formerly for common pleas, probate, appeals against sheriffs' decisions, etc., now only for considering and registering gifts made to City; platform on which Mayor etc. sat for this court (obs.). 2. Platform from which (before 1872) candidates for Parliament were nominated; election proceedings.

hŭs'tle (-sl) *v.* Push roughly, jostle; thrust (person *into*, *out of*, etc.); impel unceremoniously; push roughly *against*; push one's way; hurry, bustle. ~ *n.* Hustling.

hŭt *n.* Small mean house of rude construction, esp. such as is inhabited by savages or built for temporary use; (mil.) temporary wooden etc. house for troops. ~ *v.* Place (troops etc.) in huts; lodge in hut.

hŭtch *n.* Box-like pen for rabbits etc.; hut, cabin, small house; box-like truck used in mining etc.; (hist.) chest, coffer.

hŭt'ment *n.* Encampment of huts.

Hŭx'ley, Thomas Henry (1825–95). English physician and agnostic philosopher; supported Darwinism in his many popular scientific writings.

Huyghens (hī'genz *or* hoi-), Christian (1629–95). Dutch mathematician and astronomer; ~*'s principle*, (physics) a principle of wave propagation, according to which every point on an advancing wave front acts as a source of disturbance and sends out smaller waves, the resultant effect of which constitutes the propagation of the wave as a whole.

huzza' (-ah) *int.* of exultation, encouragement, or applause. ~ *n.* & *v.* (Make, greet with) the cry *huzza!*

H.W.M. *abbrev.* High-water mark.

Hy *abbrev.* Henry.

hȳ'acinth *n.* 1. Precious stone (in ancient times a blue gem, prob. sapphire); now, reddish-orange variety of zircon (occas. also of garnet and topaz). 2. Genus (*Hyacinthus*) of bulbous plants with bell-shaped flowers of various colours, esp. purplish-blue. **hȳacinth'ine** *adj.* Of colour of hyacinth (trad. rendering of Homeric epithet applied to hair—perh. meaning dark and glossy).

Hȳacin'thus. (Gk myth.) A beautiful youth, beloved by Apollo and Zephyrus; as Apollo was playing at quoits with Hyacinthus, Zephyrus blew a quoit thrown by Apollo so that it struck the boy and killed him. From his blood Apollo caused the flower that bears his name to spring up.

Hȳ'adēs (-z) *n.pl.* 1. (Gk myth.) Nymphs, daughters of Atlas, placed by Zeus among the Pleiades. 2. (astron.) Cluster of stars in the constellation of Taurus, anciently supposed to indicate rainy weather when they rose simultaneously with the sun.

hyaena: see HYENA.

hȳ'aline *adj.* Glass-like, glassy, vitreous.

hȳ'alite *n.* Colourless variety of opal.

hȳ'aloid *adj.* & *n.* (chiefly anat.) Glassy; ~ (*membrane*), thin transparent membrane enveloping vitreous humour of eye.

hȳb'rid *n.* Offspring of two animals or plants of different species or varieties; person of mixed nationality; (fig.) thing, word, composed of incongruous elements. ~ *adj.* Crossbred, mongrel; heterogeneous. **hȳb'ridism** *n.* Fact, condition, of being hybrid; cross-breeding. **hȳbrid'ity** *n.*

hȳb'ridize *v.* Subject (species etc.) to cross-breeding; produce hybrids; interbreed. **hȳbridizā'tion** *n.*

hȳd'atid *n.* (path.) Cyst containing watery fluid, occurring as morbid formation in animal tissues; esp. one formed by and containing larva of a special variety of tapeworm.

Hȳde Park. A Crown park in London, a fashionable resort and the scene of many political and other demonstrations.

Hȳd'erabăd. Former State of India, in the Deccan; its capital.

hȳd'ra *n.* 1. (Gk myth.) Many-headed snake of marshes of Lerna, whose heads grew again as they were cut off, killed by Hercules; (fig.) thing hard to extirpate. 2. water-snake; southern constellation represented as water-snake or

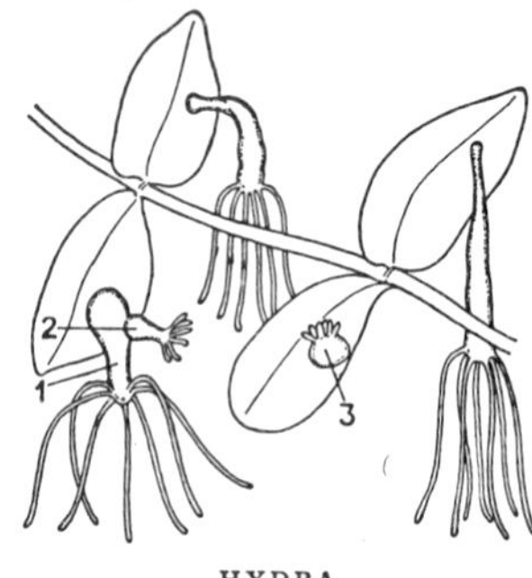

HYDRA

1. Adult polyp. 2. Bud. 3. Detached bud

sea-serpent. 3. Genus of hydrozoa, freshwater polyps of simple structure, with tubular body and mouth surrounded by ring of tentacles with stinging thread-cells.

hȳdrăn'gea (-*ja*) *n.* Genus of shrubs, natives of temperate regions of Asia and America, with white, blue, or pink flowers in large globular clusters.

hȳd'rant *n.* Pipe with nozzle to which hose can be attached, for drawing water directly from main, esp. in street.

hȳd'rate *n.* (chem.) Compound of water with another compound. **hȳdrāte** *v.t.* Combine chemically with water. **hȳdrā'tion** *n.*

hȳdraul'ic *adj.* Of water (or other liquid) as conveyed through pipes or channels, esp. mechanically; (of machine or other device) operated by resistance offered when water, oil, or other liquid is forced through a pipe or orifice, as ~ *brake, crane, lift*, etc.; (of cement etc.) hardening under water; ~ *press*, hydrostatic press. **hȳdraul'ically** *adv.* **hȳdraul'ics** *n.pl.* Science of conveyance of liquids through pipes, etc., esp. as a motive force.

hȳd'ria *n.* (Gk antiq.) Large jar or pitcher for carrying water, with 2 or 3 handles (ill. VASE).

hȳd'rō *n.* (colloq.) Hydropathic.

hydro- *prefix.* 1. (In miscellaneous terms) having to do with water. 2. (In names of diseases) affected with accumulation of serous fluid, dropsical. 3. (In chem. terms) combined with hydrogen.

hȳdrocarb'on *n.* Chemical compound containing hydrogen and carbon only; member of the many series of compounds, including paraffins, benzenes, and olefines, that constitute the subject-matter of organic chemistry.

hȳdrocĕphăl'ic *adj.* Afflicted with, characteristic of, **hȳdrocĕph'alus**, disease of brain, esp. in young children, with accumulation of serous fluid in cavity of cranium and consequent weakness of mental faculties, 'water on the brain'.

hȳdrochlor'ic *adj.* ~ *acid*, hydrogen chloride (HCl), a colourless gas which fumes in moist air, is very soluble in water, and has strongly acid taste and pungent irritating odour; (in ordinary use) a solution of this in water, spirit of salt.

hȳdrocȳăn'ic *adj.* ~ *acid*, (HCN) highly poisonous volatile liquid with smell like bitter almonds, solution of which in water is *prussic acid.*

hȳdrodȳnăm'ic(al) *adjs.* Of the forces acting on or exerted by liquids. **hȳdrodȳnăm'ics** *n.* Science of the motion, energy, and pressure of moving fluids.

hȳdro-ėlĕc'tric *adj.* Of the utilization of water-power for the production of electricity. (*Illustration, p.* 399.)

hȳd'rogėn *n.* The lightest of the elements, a colourless odourless gas which burns with pale-blue very hot flame in oxygen (or air) forming water (H_2O); symbol H, at. no. 1, at. wt 1·00797; ~ *bomb*, kind of ATOMIC bomb in which hydrogen atoms are condensed to form helium, a process accompanied by tremendous release of energy; ~ *fluoride* (HF), colourless, highly corrosive gas, anhydride of *hydrofluoric acid*; ~ *peroxide* (H_2O_2), in its pure anhydrous state, a clear colourless syrupy liquid, used in aqueous solution as an oxidizing and bleaching agent and an antiseptic and disinfectant. **hȳdrŏ'genous** *adj.*

hȳdrŏ'gėnate *v.t.* Charge, cause to combine, with hydrogen; esp. convert coal by this means into a mixture of oils, as a stage in the production of petrol from coal; also, improve heat-resisting qualities of lubricating oil thus. **hȳdrŏgėnā'tion** *n.* **hȳdrŏ'genize** *v.t.*

hȳdrŏg'raphy *n.* Scientific description of the waters of the earth. **hȳdrŏg'rapher** *n.* **hȳdrogrăph'ic(al)** *adjs.*

hȳd'roid *adj.* & *n.* (zool.) (Animal) like, allied to, the hydra (polyp).

hȳdrŏl'ogy *n.* Study of water, esp. its distribution and control.

hȳdrŏl'ȳsis *n.* Splitting of a compound substance by interaction with water. **hȳdrolȳt'ic** *adj.*

hȳd'romĕl *n.* Mixture of honey and water.

hȳdrŏm'ėter *n.* Instrument for determining specific gravity of liquids, commonly a graduated stem with a hollow bulb and a weight at lower end, floated upright in liquid, of which specific gravity is indicated by depth to which stem is immersed. **hȳdromĕt'rĭc** *adj.* **hȳdrŏm'ėtry** *n.*

hȳdropăth'ĭc *adj.* Of, concerned with, hydropathy. ~ *n.* Hydropathic establishment. **hȳdrŏp'athy** *n.* Medical treatment by external and internal application of water.

hȳd'rophāne *n.* Opaque or partly translucent opal that absorbs water on immersion and becomes transparent.

hȳdrophōb'ĭa *n.* Aversion to water, esp. as symptom of rabies in man; rabies, esp. in man. **hȳdrophōb'ĭc** *adj.*

hȳd'rophōne *n.* Instrument for the detection of sound-waves in water.

hȳd'rophȳte *n.* Aquatic plant, esp. alga.

hȳdrŏp'ĭc *adj.* Dropsical.

hȳd'roplāne *n.* 1. Fin-like device enabling submarine to submerge or rise (ill. SUBMARINE). 2. Seaplane.

hȳdropŏn'ĭcs *n.pl.* Cultivation of plants without soil, in water containing dissolved nutrients.

hȳdroquĭnōne' *n.* A phenolic substance prepared from quinone by reduction with sulphur dioxide, used as a photographic developer.

hȳd'rosphēre *n.* The waters of the earth's surface.

hȳd'rostăt *n.* Electrical device for detecting presence of water.

hȳdrostăt'ĭc *adj.* Of the equilibrium of liquids and the pressure exerted by liquids at rest; (of instruments etc.) involving pressure of liquid as source of power or otherwise, hydraulic. **hȳdrostăt'ĭc(al)** *adjs.* **hȳdrostăt'ĭcally** *adv.* **hȳdrostăt'ĭcs** *n.pl.* Branch of mechanics concerned with the pressure and equilibrium of liquids at rest.

hȳdrothĕrapeut'ĭc *adj.* Hydropathic. **hȳdrothĕ'rapy** *n.* Hydropathy.

hȳd'rous *adj.* (chem. and min.) Containing water.

hȳdrŏx'ȳl *n.* (chem.) The radical OH, which occurs in the structures of many chemical compounds. **hȳdrŏx'y-** *prefix.*

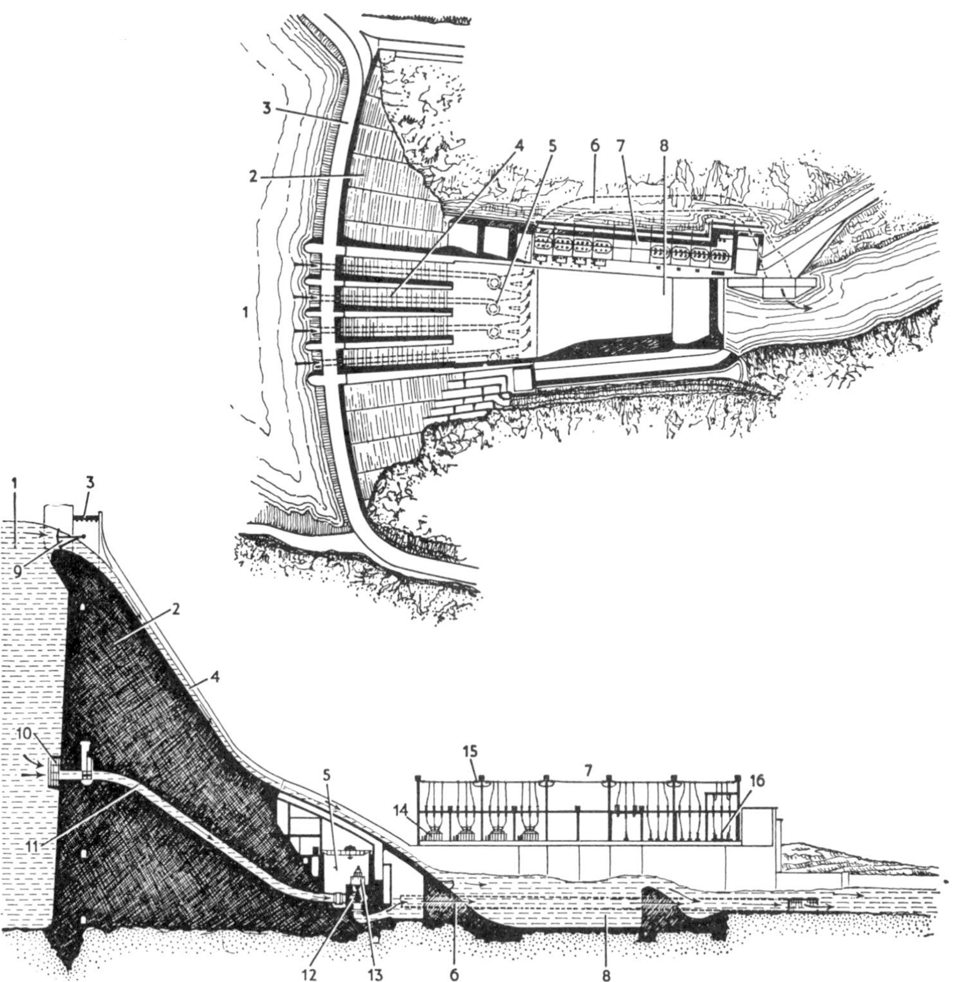

VIEW FROM ABOVE AND SECTION OF HYDRO-ELECTRIC POWER STATION

1. Reservoir. 2. Dam. 3. Dam crest and roadway. 4. Spillway. 5. Power station. 6. Turbine tail-race tunnel. 7. Sub-station. 8. Stilling basin. 9. Radial gates. 10. Intake. 11. Penstock. 12. Turbine. 13. Generator. 14. Generator transformers. 15. Overhead bus-bars. 16. Circuit breakers

Hȳdrozō'a *n.pl.* A class of coelenterate animals, chiefly marine, and simple or compound, including jellyfish and the freshwater hydra. **hȳdrozō'an** *adj.*

hȳēn'a, hȳaen'a *n.* Carnivorous quadruped allied to dog tribe, with powerful jaws, neck, and shoulders, but low and comparatively poorly developed hind quarters; cruel, treacherous, or rapacious person; *laughing* ~, hyena (either *striped* ~, *H. striata*, of Asia and northern Africa, or *spotted* ~, *Crocuta maculata*, of southern Africa) with howl resembling fiendish laughter.

Hȳgei'a (-jēa) (Gk myth.) Goddess of health and daughter of Aesculapius. **hȳgei'an** (-ēan) *adj.*

hȳ'giēne (*or* -jēn) *n.* Principles of health; sanitary science. **hȳgiēn'ic(al)** *adjs.* **hȳgiēn'ically** *adv.* **hȳgiēn'ics, hȳgiēn'ist** *ns.*

hygro- *prefix.* Wet, fluid.

hȳgrŏm'ėter *n.* Instrument for measuring humidity of air or gas. **hȳgromĕt'ric** *adj.* **hȳgrŏm'ėtry** *n.*

hȳg'roscōpe *n.* Instrument indicating but not measuring humidity of air. **hȳgroscŏp'ic** *adj.* Of the hygroscope; (of chem. substances) tending to absorb water esp. from the air.

Hȳk'sōs. Asiatic dynasty of 'shepherd kings' which conquered Egypt *c* 2000 B.C. and ruled until driven out by the 18th dynasty.

hȳl'ic *adj.* Of matter, material.

hȳm'ĕn[1] *n.* Fold of mucous membrane stretched across and partially closing external orifice of vagina of virgin female.

Hȳm'ĕn[2]. (Gk and Rom. myth.) God of marriage; represented as a young man carrying torch and veil.

hȳmėnē'al *adj.* Pertaining to marriage. ~ *n.* Marriage-song. **hȳmėnē'ally** *adv.*

hȳmēn'ium *n.* (pl. *-nia*). Spore-bearing surface in fungi (ill. FUNGUS).

hȳmenŏp'tera *n.pl.* Large order of insects, including ants, bees, etc., with four membranous wings. **hȳmenŏp'teral, hȳmenŏp'terous** *adjs.*

hȳmn (-m) *n.* Song of praise or prayer to God or other divine being, esp. metrical composition sung in religious service; song of praise. ~ *v.* Praise (God etc.) in hymns, express (praise etc.) in hymn; sing hymns.

hȳm'nal *adj.* Of hymns. ~ *n.* hymn-book. **hȳm'nary** *n.* Hymn-book, collection of hymns.

hȳ'mnody *n.* Singing of hymns; composition of hymns; hymns collectively. **hȳm'nodist** *n.*

hȳmnŏg'rapher *n.* Composer of hymns.

hȳmnŏl'ogy *n.* Composition, study, of hymns; hymns collectively. **hȳmnolŏ'gic** *adj.* **hȳmnŏl'ogist** *n.*

hȳ'oid *adj.* & *n.* ~ (*bone*), tongue-bone, between chin and thyroid cartilage; in man, horseshoe-shaped and embedded horizontally in root of tongue (ill. HEAD).

hȳ'oscīne, hȳoscȳ'amīne *ns.* (chem.) Alkaloid, an isomer of atropine, obtained from certain plants (esp. *Hyoscyamus niger* and *Atropa belladonna*) and used as sedative, or, with morphia, to produce partial anaesthesia; = scopolamine.

hȳoscȳ'amus *n.* (bot.) Genus of solanaceous plants of which British species is henbane, *H. niger*.

hȳpaeth'ral *adj.* Open to the sky, roofless; open-air.

hȳpăll'agė (-jĭ) *n.* (gram.) Reversal of natural relations of two elements in a proposition (e.g. *apply the wound to water* for *apply water to the wound*).

hyper- *prefix.* Over, above, exceeding, excessive.

hȳperaem'ia *n.* (path.) Engorgement of the tissues with blood.

hȳperaesthēs'ia (-z-) *n.* (path.) Morbid sensitiveness of nerves; excessive sensibility. **hȳperaesthĕt'ic** *adj.*

hȳpėr'b'aton *n.* Inversion of normal order of words, esp. for sake of emphasis.

hȳpėr'b'ola *n.* (geom.) One of the conic sections (ill. CONE), a plane curve consisting of two separate, similar, equal, and infinite branches, formed by the intersection of a cone by a plane making a larger angle with the base than the side of the cone makes. **hȳperbŏl'ic** *adj.*

hȳpėr'b'olė *n.* (rhet.) Exaggerated statement not meant to be taken literally. **hȳperbŏl'ical** *adj.* **hȳperbŏl'ically** *adv.* **hȳpėr'b'olism, hȳpėr'b'olist** *ns.*

hȳpėr'b'oloid *n.* (geom.) A solid or surface of the second degree, some of whose plane sections are hyperbolas, the others being ellipses or circles (ill. CONE).

hȳperbôr'ėan *adj.* Of the extreme north of the earth. ~ *n.* Inhabitant of extreme north of earth; (Gk myth.) one of a race living in a land of sunshine and plenty beyond the north wind.

hȳpercătalĕc'tic *adj.* (Of verse) having extra syllable after last complete dipody.

hȳpercrit'ical *adj.* Too critical, esp. of small faults.

hȳperglȳcaem'ia (-ĭsēm-) *n.* (path.) Excess of sugar in the blood.

Hȳpēr'ion. (Gk myth.) One of the Titans, the father of Aurora, the Sun, and the Moon; in later myth. identified with the Sun itself.

hȳpermĕt'ric(al) *adjs.* (Of verse) having a redundant syllable; (of syllable) redundant.

hȳpermėtrō'pia *n.* Morbidly long sight. **hȳpermėtrŏp'ic** *adj.*

hȳperphȳs'ical (-z-) *adj.* Supernatural.

hȳpersŏn'ic *adj.* (Of speed) greatly in excess of the speed of sound, i.e. faster than *supersonic*.

hȳp'ersthēne *n.* (min.) Greenish-black or greenish-grey mineral closely allied to hornblende, a silicate of iron and magnesium.

hȳpertĕn'sion (-shn) *n.* Extreme tension; (path.) raised blood-pressure.

hȳperthȳr'oidism *n.* (path.) Condition resulting from over-activity of thyroid gland; = GRAVES' DISEASE.

hȳpėr't'rophy *n.* Excessive development, morbid enlargement, of organ etc. (opp. of ATROPHY). **hȳpertrŏph'ic, hȳpėr't'rophied** (-ĭd) *adjs.*

hypethral *adj.* = HYPAETHRAL.

hȳph'a *n.* (pl. *-phae*). Vegetative filament of a fungus (ill. FUNGUS).

hȳph'en *n.* Sign (-) used to join two words together, to join separated syllables of word broken at end of line, or to divide word into parts. ~ *v.t.* Join (words) with hyphen; write (compound word) with hyphen. **hȳph'enāte** *v.t.* Hyphen; *hyphenated* (U.S., of persons etc.) of nationality designated by hyphenated form, e.g. *Irish-American*.

hȳpnogĕn'ėsis *n.*, **-gėnĕt'ic** *adj.* Induction of, inducing, hypnotic state.

hȳpnŏl'ogy *n.* Science of phenomena of sleep.

hȳpnōs'is *n.* Artificially produced sleep, esp. that induced by hypnotism.

hȳpnŏt'ic *adj.* Of, producing, hypnotism. ~ *n.* Thing that produces sleep; person under influence of hypnotism.

hȳp'notism *n.* (Artificial production of) state resembling deep sleep, in which subject acts only on external suggestion or direction, to which he is involuntarily and unconsciously obedient. **hȳp'notist** *n.* **hȳp'notīze** *v.t.*

hȳp'ō *n.* Sodium thiosulphate, $Na_2S_2O_3.5H_2O$ (incorrectly called sodium hyposulphite), used in fixing photographic negatives and prints.

hypo- *prefix.* Below, under, slightly; (chem.) formerly used to prefix names of oxygen compounds containing less oxygen than other compounds in the same series.

hȳp'oblăst *n.* Inner layer of cells in blastoderm.

hȳp'ocaust *n.* (Rom. antiq.) Hollow space under floor in which heat from furnace was accumulated for heating house or bath. (*Illustration, p.* 401.)

hȳpochŏn'dria (-k-) *n.* (med.) Morbid state of depression for which there is no real cause; (in lay usage) needless or excessive anxiety about one's health. **hȳpochŏn'driac** *adj.* Of, affected by, hypochondria. ~ *n.* Hypochondriac person. **hȳpochondrī'acal** *adj.* **hȳpochondrī'acally** *adv.*

hȳpocoris'tic *adj.* Of, like, a pet-name; tending to use endearing or euphemistic terms.

hўpocŏt'ўl *n.* (bot.) Axis of seedling below seed leaves, forming anatomically a transition zone between stem and root (ill. SEEDLING).

hўpŏc'rĭsў *n.* Simulation of virtue or goodness; dissimulation, pretence.

hўp'ocrite *n.* Person guilty of hypocrisy; dissembler, pretender. **hўpocrit'ical** *adj.* **hўpocrit'ically** *adv.* [Gk *hupokritēs* actor]

hўpocўc'loid *n.* (geom.) A curve traced by a point in the circumference of a circle which rolls round the interior circumference of another circle (ill. ROULETTE).

hўpoderm'ic *adj.* (med., of drugs etc.) Introduced beneath the skin; (anat.) lying under the skin. **hўpoderm'ically** *adv.*

hўpogăs'trium *n.* Lowest region of abdomen. **hўpogăs'tric** *adj.*

hўpogī'al *adj.* Underground.

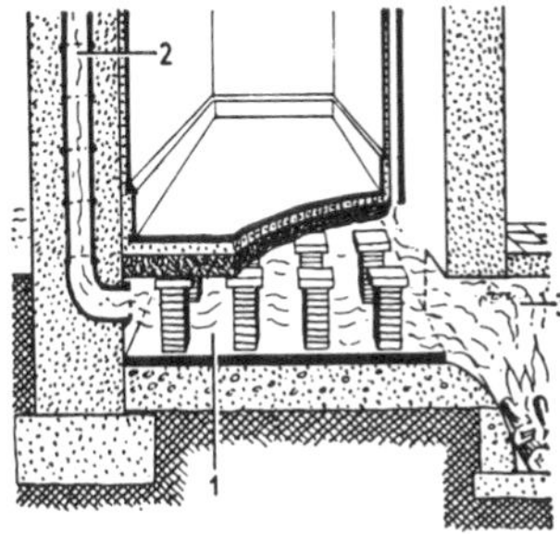

HYPOCAUST

1. Hypocaust. 2. Flue. 3. Stokehole

hўpoglўcaem'ia (-isēm-) *n.* (path.) Deficiency of sugar (glucose) in the blood.

hўpophўs'is (*or* -ŏf'isis) *n.* ~ (*cerebri*), the PITUITARY body.

hўpŏs'tasis *n.* (pl. *-es* pr. ēz). 1. (path.) Passive congestion of an organ or part; deposit of blood in dependent part of body. 2. (metaphys.) Underlying substance, opp. to attributes or to what is unsubstantial; (theol.) personality (of Christ), person (of the Godhead). **hўpostăt'ic(al)** *adjs.* **hўpostăt'ically** *adv.*

hўpŏs'tasize, hўpŏs'tatize *vbs. t.* Make into or treat as substance; personify.

hўpotĕn'sion (-shn) *n.* Lowered blood-pressure.

hўpŏt'ėnūse *n.* Side of right-angled triangle opposite the right angle (ill. TRIANGLE).

hўp'othėc *n.* (Rom. and Sc. law) Security established by law over thing belonging to debtor. **hўpŏth'ėcary** *adj.*

hўpŏth'ėcāte *v.t.* Pledge, mortgage. **hўpothėcā'tion** *n.*

hўpŏth'ėsis *n.* (pl. *-thėsēs*). Supposition made as basis for reasoning, without reference to its truth, or as starting-point for investigation; groundless assumption. **hўpothĕt'ic(al)** *adjs.* **hўpothĕt'ically** *adv.*

hўpŏth'ėsize *v.* Frame a hypothesis; assume.

hўpotrachēl'ium (-k-) *n.* (pl. *-lia*). (Gk antiq.) Groove round shaft of column just below capital (ill. ORDER).

hўpsŏg'raphy *n.* Description of contours of earth's surface; delineation of these in a map.

hўpsŏm'ėter *n.* Instrument for measuring altitudes, by determining the boiling-points of liquids. **hўpsomĕt'ric(al)** *adjs.* **hўpsŏm'ėtry** *n.*

Hўr'ax *n.* Genus of small quadrupeds, the conies, pachyderms distantly related to the elephant and having plantigrade feet with hooves; they include the Syrian rock-rabbit and the S. Afr. rock-badger.

hўs'on *n.* Kind of green tea from China. [Chin. *hsi-ch'un*, lit. = 'bright spring']

hўss'op *n.* Small bushy aromatic herb of genus *Hyssopus*, esp. *H. officinalis*, formerly used medicinally; (bibl.) plant whose twigs were used for sprinkling in Jewish rites, bunch of this used in purification.

hўsterēs'is *n.* (physics) Lagging or retardation of an effect when the forces acting on a body are changed, esp. lagging of magnetic induction behind the magnetizing force (*magnetic* ~); ~ *loss*, the energy loss per cycle involved in taking a magnetic material through a complete magnetic cycle.

hўstēr'ia *n.* 1. (med., psych.) Functional disturbance of nervous system, of psychoneurotic origin. 2. Morbid excitement. **hўstĕ'rical** *adj.* **hўstĕ'rically** *adv.* **hўstĕ'rics** *n.pl.* Hysterical fits or convulsions.

hўs'terŏn prŏt'erŏn *n.* (gram.) Figure of speech in which what should come last is put first; inversion of natural order. [Gk *husteron proteron* latter former]

I

I[1], **i** (ī). 9th letter of modern English and Roman alphabet, in which it was orig. used as symbol both of *i* vowel and of a consonant (orig. *y*, later, in Romanic, developing into 'soft g' (j)). Differentiation was finally made between these two (in England *c* 1630–40), the consonant being expressed by the character J, j, orig. merely a variant form of I, i. In modern English spelling *i* represents chiefly two sounds: a short high front wide vowel (in this dictionary written ĭ) and a diphthong (as in *eye*; in this dictionary written ī). In Roman numerals, I, i = 1.

I[2] (ī) *pron.* Subjective case of 1st pers. pron. ~ *n. The I*, the ego, subject or object of self-consciousness.

I. *abbrev.* Idaho; Island(s).

Ia *abbrev.* Iowa.

I.A. *abbrev.* Indian Army.

ī'ămb *n.* = IAMBUS.

iăm'bic *adj.* Of, containing, based on, iambuses. ~ *n.* Iambic verse.

iăm'bus *n.* (pl. *-buses, -bī*). Metrical foot of short followed by long syllable, or of unaccented followed by accented syllable.

Iăp'ėtus (ī-). 1. (Gk myth.) A Titan, father of Atlas, Prometheus, and Epimetheus, and grandfather of DEUCALION; hence regarded as progenitor of mankind. 2. 8th satellite of Saturn.

ib., ibid. *abbrevs. Ibidem.*

Ibañ'ez (ēbăn'yāth), Vicente Blasco (1867–1928). Spanish novelist.

Ibēr'ia (ī-). 1. Ancient name for country comprising Spain and Portugal, and forming peninsula of extreme SW. of Europe. 2. Ancient name of GEORGIA[2]. **Ibēr'ian** *adj.* Of Iberia. ~ *n.* 1. Inhabitant of ancient Iberian peninsula; member of short dark neolithic race, with long heads, who buried their dead and are thought to have built the cairns, dolmens, etc., found in N. Africa, Spain, France, and Gt Britain. 2. Language of ancient Iberia, supposed to be represented by modern Basque.

ī'bĕx *n.* Various species of wild goat (genus *Capra*), with large scimitar-like horns, now rare in Alps but found in Mongolia and Abyssinia.

ibīd'ĕm *adv.* (abbrev. ib., ibid.) In the same book, chapter, passage, etc. [L, = 'in same place']

īb'is *n.* (pl. *ibis* or *ibises*). Any of a group of birds, widely distributed in warm climates, superficially resembling curlew but larger and with stouter bill and legs; *sacred* ~, white ibis, common in the Nile basin, venerated by the ancient Egyptians.

Ibn-batu'ta (ĭ-, -tōōta) (1304–78). Arabian traveller, who visited Mecca, Asia Minor, Russia, India, China, Ceylon, Spain, Central Africa, etc.

Ibn Saud (ĭ-, -owd) (*c* 1880–1954). King of Saudi Arabia 1932–54.

Ib'sen (ĭ-), Henrik (1828–1906). Norwegian poet and author of plays ('A Doll's House', 'Ghosts', 'Hedda Gabler', etc.) examining and criticizing social conventions. **Ib'senism** *n.*

Ib'ȳcus (ĭ-) (6th c. B.C.). Greek lyric poet. Acc. to legend, robbers attacked him while a flock of cranes was passing and he died crying 'Those cranes will avenge me'; later one of the robbers, seeing some cranes overhead, remarked 'There go the avengers of Ibycus'; this was overheard and the murder was revealed.

i/c *abbrev.* In charge.

Ic'arus (ī- *or* ĭ-). (Gk myth.) Son of DAEDALUS; his father made wings so that both could escape from Crete where they were imprisoned by Minos, but Icarus flew so near the sun that the wax attaching his wings was melted and he fell into the Aegean Sea.

ice *n.* 1. Frozen water; water made solid by exposure to low temperature, a transparent, crystalline, brittle, almost colourless substance; frozen surface of body of water; *break the* ~, (fig.) make a beginning, break through reserve or stiffness. 2. Frozen confection, ice-cream, water-ice; *coconut* ~, sweetmeat esp. of icing-sugar mixed with coconut. 3. ~*-age*, period during the Pleistocene, when large parts of the earth were covered by ice; ~*-axe*, axe used by mountain climbers to cut footholds

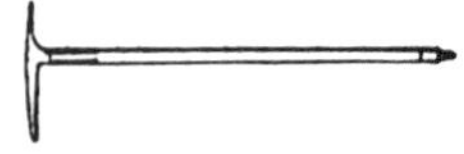

ICE AXE

in ice-slopes; *ice'berg*, floating mass of ice, detached portion of polar ice-sheet or glacier, often travelling great distances in ocean currents before it melts completely; about $\frac{1}{8}$ of the iceberg, which is often of great height above water, projects above sea-level; ~*-blink*, luminous appearance on horizon, caused by reflection from ice; ~*-box*, (chiefly U.S.) refrigerator; ~*-breaker*, boat with reinforced bow for breaking channel through ice of river, harbour, etc.; ~*-cap*, mass of thick ice covering continent, island, or other region; ~ *cream*, flavoured and sweetened cream or custard or some substitute for these, frozen in a refrigerator or congealed by stirring in vessel surrounded by ice or a freezing-mixture; ~*-fall*, steep part of glacier like frozen waterfall; ~*-field*, extensive sheet of floating ice; ~*-floe*, flattish free mass of floating ice, smaller than an ice-field; ~*-foot*, belt or ledge of ice extending along the coast, esp. in Arctic regions, between high and low water marks; ~*-hockey*, form of hockey played on ice with flat disc (*puck*) instead of ball (see also HOCKEY); ~*-house*, building, often partly or wholly underground, for storing ice; ~*-plant*, plant (*Mesembryanthemum crystallinum*) of S. Africa, Canary Is., etc., with leaves covered with pellucid watery vesicles; ~ *point*, the freezing-point of water (0° C.); ~*-run*, artificial tobogganing track of frozen snow; ~*-water*, iced water; ~*-wool*, kind of glossy wool used in crochet etc. ~ *v.t.* Freeze; cover (as) with ice; cool (wine) in ice; cover (cake etc.) with concretion of sugar.

Ice'land (īsl-). Large sparsely inhabited island in N. Atlantic; colonized by Scandinavians after 850; united with Norway 1262–4; on the union of Norway and Denmark (1381) the rule of Iceland was transferred to Denmark, which conceded home rule to Iceland in 1874 and recognized it as a sovereign State, in union with Denmark, in 1918; the union was dissolved in 1944 when Iceland became an independent republic; capital, Reykjavik; ~ *moss*, species of edible lichen (*Cetraria islandica*), having medicinal properties; ~ *poppy*, yellow- or red-flowered perennial poppy (*Papaver nudicaule*) of Arctic origin; ~ *spar*, particularly transparent variety of calc-spar used in optical instruments. **Icelăn'dĭc** *adj.* Of Iceland. ~ *n.* Language of Iceland, in its oldest form practically identical with Old Norse, which it still closely resembles; the sagas, poems, etc., of Old Icelandic (11th–13th centuries) are almost the only source of knowledge of the life and institutions of the old Scandinavians.

Icē'ni (ī-). Ancient British tribe inhabiting a district roughly corresponding to modern Norfolk and Suffolk; conquered, with their queen BOADICEA, by the Romans *c* A.D. 62.

ich'abŏd (ĭk- *or* ĭk-) *n.* (As exclamation of regret, =) 'the glory has departed'; see 1 Sam. iv. 21, in ref. to the taking of the ark by the Philistines.

ĭchneum'on (-k-) *n.* 1. The N. African and Iberian mongoose, *Herpestes ichneumon*. 2. ~ (*fly*), any member of a group of insects related to bees and wasps, all parasitic, mostly on Lepidoptera. [Gk *ikhneumōn* spider-hunting wasp (*ikhneuō* track)]

īch'ôr (īk-) *n.* 1. (Gk myth.) Ethereal fluid flowing like blood in veins of gods. 2. (path.) The thin fetid discharge from an ulcer. **ich'orous** *adj.*

ĭch'thȳoid (ĭk-) *adj.* Fish-like. ~ *n.* Vertebrate of fish type.

ĭchthȳŏl'ogy (ĭk-) *n.* Study of fishes. **ĭchthȳolŏ'gical** *adj.* **ĭchthȳŏl'ogist** *n.*

ĭchthȳŏph'agous (ĭk-) *adj.* Fish-eating.

Ichthȳôrn'is (ĭk-) *n.* Genus of extinct toothed birds.

Ichthȳosaur'us (ĭk-) *n.* Genus of extinct marine reptiles with superficial resemblance to the modern dolphin.

I.C.I. *abbrev.* Imperial Chemical Industries.

ī'cicle *n.* Tapering ice-formation, produced by freezing of successive drops trickling from the point of attachment.

ī'cily *adv.* In an icy manner (lit. and fig.). **ī'cĭnėss** *n.*

ī'cing *n.* (esp.) 1. Coating of sugar and water or white of egg etc. for cakes etc.; ~ *sugar*, finely ground sugar for icing. 2. Formation of ice on aircraft.

Ick'nield (-nēld) **Way.** Ancient pre-Roman track crossing England in wide curve from Cornwall to Norfolk.

ī'con *n.* Image, statue; (Eastern Church) painting, mosaic, etc., of sacred personage, itself regarded as sacred. **īcŏn'ic** *adj.* Of (the nature of) an image or portrait; (of statues) following a conventional type.

īcŏn'oclăsm *n.* Breaking of images. **īcŏn'oclăst** *n.* Breaker of images, esp. one who took part in movement in 8th and 9th centuries against use of images in religious worship in Eastern Church; (fig.) one who assails cherished beliefs. **īcŏnoclăs'tic** *adj.*

īconŏg'raphy *n.* 1. Description of a subject by drawings or figures; book containing this. 2. The subject-matter of art; study of this. **īconŏg'rapher** *n.* 1. Person who illustrates a subject. 2. Student of iconography. **īconogrăph'ic(al)** *adjs.*

īconŏl'atry *n.* Worship of images. **īconŏl'ater** *n.*

īconŏl'ogy *n.* 1. The study of icons. 2. Symbolical representation, symbolism. **īconolŏ'gical** (-j-) *n.* **īconŏl'ogist** *n.*

īconŏs'tasis *n.* (pl. *-asēs*). (Eastern Church) screen, on which icons are placed, separating sanctuary from main body of church.

īc'osahĕd'ron (-*a*-h-) *n.* (geom.) Solid contained by 20 plane faces; *regular* ~, one contained by 20 equilateral triangles (ill. SOLID).

I.C.S. *abbrev.* Indian Civil Service.

Ictīn'us (ĭ-) (5th c. B.C.). Gk architect of Hall of Mysteries at Eleusis and (with Callicrates) Parthenon at Athens.

ĭc'tus *n.* (pros.) Rhythmical or metrical stress.

ī'cȳ *adj.* Abounding in, covered with, ice; very cold.

ĭd *n.* In Freudian psycho-analysis, that part of the mind which comprises the inherited instinctive impulses of the individual together with memories and phantasies evolved in early infancy (cf. EGO).

id. *abbrev. Idem* (= the same).

Id'a (ī-). 1. Mountain range in S. Phrygia, near Troy, from whose summit Zeus was supposed to have watched the progress of the Trojan War; scene of the rape of GANYMEDE and the home of PARIS and OENONE. 2. Ancient name of chief mountain (Mt. Psiloriti) in Crete, where Zeus is said to have been brought up.

Id'ahō (ī-). Mountain State in north-western U.S., bounded on north by British Columbia; capital, Boise.

Idāl'ĭum (ī-). Ancient town in Cyprus where Aphrodite was worshipped.

I.D.B. *abbrev.* Illicit diamond buying.

ĭddy-ŭmp'ty. Conventional verbal representation of dots and dashes of morse code.

īde *n.* Cyprinoid freshwater fish of N. Europe, *Leuciscus idus*.

īdē'a (*or* -ĭa) *n.* 1. Archetype, pattern, as dist. from its realization in individuals; in Platonic philosophy, eternally existing pattern of which individual things in any class are imperfect copies. 2. Conception of standard or principle to be recognized or aimed at; plan of action. 3. Notion conceived by the mind; way of thinking; vague belief, fancy. 4. (In Descartes, Locke, etc.) immediate object of thought or mental perception; (in Kant etc.) conception of reason transcending all experience; (in Hegel etc.) absolute truth of which all phenomenal existence is expression.

īde'al (-ĭal, -ēal) *adj.* 1. Relating to, consisting of, (Platonic) ideas. 2. Answering to one's highest conception; perfect or supremely excellent in its kind. 3. Embodying an idea; existing only in idea; visionary. ~ *n.* Perfect type; actual thing as standard for imitation. **īde'ally** *adv.*

īdē'alism *n.* 1. (philos.) System of thought in which object of external perception is held to consist of ideas (in various senses). 2. Idealizing, tendency to idealize; representation of things in ideal form; imaginative treatment. **īdē'alist** *n.* **īdėalis'tic** *adj.*

īdėăl'ity *n.* Quality of being ideal; imaginative faculty.

īdē'alīze *v.* Represent in ideal form or character, exalt to ideal perfection or excellence. **īdėalīzā'tion** *n.*

īdē'āte *v.* Imagine, conceive; form ideas. **īdėā'tion** *n.* **īdėā'tional** (-shon-) *adj.*

id'ée fixe (ēdā fēks) *n.* Idea that dominates the mind, monomania. [Fr., = 'fixed idea']

id'em *n.* or *adv.* (abbrev. id.) (In) the same author (ī-); the same word (ī-).

īdĕn'tĭc *adj.* (In diplomacy, of notes etc. directed by two or more powers to another) in precisely the same form.

īdĕn'tĭcal *adj.* (Of one thing etc. viewed at different times) the very same; (of different things) agreeing in every detail (*with*); (logic, math.) expressing an identity; ~ *twins*, twins resulting from fertilization of single ovum and consequently alike in all respects including sex. (opp. FRATERNAL). **īdĕn'tĭcally** *adv.*

īdĕn'tĭfȳ *v.* 1. Treat (thing) as identical (*with*); associate oneself inseparably *with*. 2. Establish identity of. **īdĕntĭfĭcā'tion** *n.* ~ *parade*, parade of persons from whom a suspect is to be identified; ~ *plate*, registered number plate of motor vehicle.

īdĕn'tĭty *n.* 1. Absolute sameness; oneness; (algebra) equality of two expressions for all values of the literal quantities, equation expressing this. 2. Condition or fact that person or thing is itself and not something else; individuality, personality; ~ *card, disc, plate*, etc., one serving to identify bearer.

ĭd'ėogrăm, ĭd'ėograph (-ahf) *ns.* Character in pictorial writing (e.g. Chinese) symbolizing an idea by representing an object or objects with which the idea is associated (not, as in a phonetic system, by expressing the sounds which make up its name) (ill. HIEROGLYPH).

ĭd'ėolŏgue (-g), **īdėŏl'ogĭst** *ns.* Idealist, theorist, visionary.

īdėŏl'ogy *n.* Visionary speculation; (pol. jargon) scheme of ideas at basis of some political or economic theory or system, manner of thinking characteristic of a class or individual (e.g. *bourgeois* ~). **īdėolŏ'gĭcal** *adj.* **īdėolŏ'gĭcally** *adv.*

īdes (īdz) *n.pl.* (Rom. antiq.) 8th day after nones (15th Mar., May, July, Oct., 13th of other months); ~ *of March*, day, according to tradition, predicted as that of the murder of Julius Caesar; hence, inauspicious day.

ĭd ĕst (abbrev. i.e.) That is.

ĭd'ĭocy *n.* The mental condition of an IDIOT; extreme imbecility, utter foolishness.

ĭd'ĭom *n.* Language of a people or country; specific character of this; form of expression peculiar to a language. **ĭdĭomăt'ĭc** *adj.* Characteristic of a particular language; vernacular, colloquial. **ĭdĭomăt'ĭcally** *adv.*

ĭdĭomŏrph'ĭc *adj.* (min.) Having its own characteristic form, esp. its characteristic crystallographic faces.

ĭdĭŏp'athy *n.* (path.) Disease not preceded or occasioned by another. **ĭdĭopăth'ĭc** *adj.* **ĭdĭopăth'ĭcally** *adv.*

ĭdĭosȳnc'rasy *n.* Mental constitution; view, feeling, mode of expression, peculiar to a person; (med.) physical constitution peculiar to a person. **ĭdĭosȳncrăt'ĭc** *adj.*

ĭd'ĭot *n.* Person so deficient in mind as to be permanently incapable of rational conduct and having a mental development not exceeding that of an average normal child of two years old (the lowest grade of mental deficiency, next below IMBECILE); utter fool. **ĭdĭŏt'ĭc** *adj.* **ĭdĭot'ĭcally** *adv.*

ī'dle *adj.* 1. (Of action, words, etc.) ineffective, worthless, vain; baseless, groundless; (of things) useless. 2. Unoccupied; lazy, indolent; (of things) not moving or in operation; ~ *wheel*, intermediate wheel transmitting motion between two geared wheels; (of money) not in circulation. **ī'dleness** *n.* **ī'dly** *adv.* **ī'dle** *v.* Be idle; pass (time etc.) *away* in idleness; (of engine etc.) run at low speed without doing any work. **īdler** *n.*

Ido (ēd'ō) *n.* Artificial language, a simplified form of Esperanto, selected by 'Delegation for Adoption of Auxiliary International Language' (founded at Paris, 1901), and made public in 1907. [Esperanto, = 'offspring']

ī'dol *n.* Image of deity used as object of worship; false god; person, thing, that is object of excessive devotion; (logic) false mental image or conception; ~*s of the tribe, cave, market-place, and theatre*, four classes of fallacies (Bacon, 'Nov. Org.' I. xxxix) referable respectively to limitations of human mind, prejudices of idiosyncrasy, influence of words, philosophical and logical prepossessions.

īdŏl'ater *n.* Worshipper of idols; devoted admirer (*of*). **īdŏl'atrėss, īdŏl'atry** *ns.* **īdŏl'atrous** *adj.* **īdŏl'atrously** *adv.*

ī'dolīze *v.* Make an idol of; venerate, love, to excess; practise idolatry. **īdolīzā'tion** *n.*

īdōl'um *n.* Mental image, idea; (logic) idol.

Idūmae'a (ī-). Edom, an ancient kingdom between Egypt and Palestine. **Idumae'an** *adj.* & *n.*

Idun(a) (ē'do͞o-). (Scand. myth.) A goddess, wife of Bragi; she kept the apples which restored the youth of the gods.

ĭd'yll *n.* Short description in verse or (*prose* ~) in prose of picturesque scene or incident, esp. in rustic life; episode suitable for such treatment. **īdȳll'ĭc** *adj.* **īdȳll'ĭcally** *adv.*

i.e. *abbrev. Id est* (= that is).

I.E. *abbrev.* (Order of the) Indian Empire.

ĭf *conj.* On the condition or supposition that; whenever; whether; *as if*, as the case would be if, as though. ~ *n.* Condition, supposition.

Igerne: see IGRAINE.

ĭg'lo͞o *n.* Eskimo dome-shaped house, esp. one built of blocks of compact snow. [Eskimo = 'house']

Ignatius (ĭgnā'sh*us*), St. Bishop of Antioch, martyred at Rome early in 2nd c.

Ignatius Loyōl'a (ĭgnā'sh*us*), St. (1491–1556). Spanish founder of the Society of Jesus (see JESUIT). **Ignā'tian** (-sh*an*) *adj.* & *n.* (Follower) of Ignatius Loyola, Jesuit.

ĭg'nėous *adj.* Of fire, fiery; produced by volcanic agency.

ĭg'nĭs făt'ūus *n.* Will-o'-the-wisp, phosphorescent light (now rarely) seen on marshy ground, supposedly due to the ignition of marsh gas (CH_4) by traces of phosphorous compounds; delusive hope, aim, etc. [med. or mod. L, = 'foolish fire']

ĭgnīte' *v.* Make intensely hot, (chem.) heat to point of combustion or chemical change; set fire to; take fire. **ĭgnĭ'tion** *n.* (esp.) Starting combustion of mixture in cylinder of internal combustion engine, mechanism for doing this.

ĭgnŏ'ble *adj.* Of low birth, position, or reputation; mean, base, dishonourable. **ĭgnō'bleness** *n.* **ĭgnō'bly** *adv.*

ĭg'nominy *n.* Dishonour, infamy; infamous conduct. **ĭgnomĭn'ious** *adj.* (now usu. = humiliating). **ĭgnomĭn'iously** *adv.*

ĭgnorām'us *n.* (pl. *-muses*). Ignorant person. [L, = 'we do not know']

ĭg'norance *n.* Want of knowledge. **ĭg'norant** *adj.* Lacking knowledge; uninformed (*of, in*). **ĭg'norantly** *adv.*

ĭgnorā'tio ėlĕn'chi (-shĭō, -kī) *n.* (logic) Argument that appears to refute opponent while actually disproving something not advanced by him.

ĭgnōre' *v.t.* Refuse to take notice of; (of Grand Jury) reject (bill) as unfounded.

ĭgnōt'um pĕr ĭgnōt'ius *n.* Explanation obscurer than the thing it is meant to explain. [L, = 'the unknown by the still less known']

Igraine', Igĕrne', Ygĕrne' (ĭ-). (Arthurian legend) Wife of Gorlois of Cornwall and mother (by Uther Pendragon) of Arthur.

ĭgua'na (-gwah-) *n.* Large arboreal lizard (esp. of genus *Iguana*) of W. Indies and S. America.

ĭguăn'odon (-wăn-) *n.* Huge amphibious herbivorous lizard found as fossil, with teeth and bones resembling those of the iguana (ill. DINOSAUR).

i.h.p. *abbrev.* Indicated horse-power.

IHS. First 3 letters of Gk ΙΗΣΟΥΣ (*Iēsous*) Jesus; often taken as initials of *J*esus *H*ominum *S*alvator 'Jesus saviour of men', or *I*n *H*oc *S*igno (vinces) 'in this sign (thou shalt conquer)', or *I*n *H*ac (cruce) *S*alus 'in this (cross) is salvation'.

Île-de-France (ēl). Old district of France, with Paris as capital, between rivers Seine, Oise, Marne, and Aisne.

ĭl'ėum *n.* (pl. *-ea*). (anat.) 3rd and terminal portion of small intestine, opening into large intestine (ill. ALIMENTARY).

ĭl'ĕx *n.* Holm-oak; (bot.) large genus of trees and shrubs having small flowers and berry-like fruits, the hollies.

ĭl'iac *adj.* Of the flank or flank-bone (ILIUM); (but orig. of or affecting the ILEUM, whence ~ *passion*, painful affection due to intestinal obstruction).

Il'iad (ĭ-). Greek epic poem by Homer, describing incidents in the 10th and last year of the siege of Troy by the Greeks, and in particular 'the wrath of Achilles'. [Gk *Ilion* Troy]

Iliss'us (ĭ-). River of Attica with source on Mount Hymettus.

ĭl'ium[1] *n.* (pl. *-ia*). (anat.) Hip-bone, the anterior or superior bone of the pelvis (ill. PELVIS).

Il'ium[2] (ĭ-). L form of Gk name (Ilion) of Troy.

ilk *adj.* (Sc.) *Of that* ~, of the same; as *Guthrie of that* ~, Guthrie of Guthrie; (vulg. or trivial) that family, class, or kind.

ĭll *adj.* Out of health, sick; (of health) unsound, disordered; morally bad; harmful; wretched, disastrous; faulty, unskilful; (of manners or conduct) improper; (archaic) difficult. ~ *n.* Evil, the opposite of good; harm, injury; misfortune, calamity, adversity. ~ *adv.* Badly; unfavourably; imperfectly, scarcely; ~ *at ease*, embarrassed, uneasy; *~-advised*, imprudent; *~-advi'sedly*; *~-affected*, not well disposed; *~-bred*, badly brought up, rude; ~ *breeding*, bad manners; *~-conditioned*, of evil disposition; in bad condition; *~-disposed*, disposed to evil, malevolent; unfavourably disposed (*towards*); *~-fated*, destined to, bringing, bad fortune; *~-favoured*, uncomely; displeasing, objectionable; *~-gotten*, gained by evil means; *~-humoured*, bad-tempered; *~-judged*, unwise; *~-mannered*, unmannerly, rude; *~-na'tured(ly)*, churlish(ly); *~-omened*, attended by bad omens; *~-timed*, unseasonable; *~-treat*, *-use*, treat badly.

Ill. *abbrev.* Illinois.

ĭllā'tion *n.* Deduction, conclusion; thing deduced.

ĭllăt'ive *adj.* (Of words) stating, introducing an inference, as ~ *particles* (e.g. *because, then, therefore*); inferential. **ĭllăt'ively** *adv.*

ĭllēg'al *adj.* Not legal; contrary to law. **ĭllēg'ally** *adv.* **ĭllėgăl'ity** *n.*

ĭllĕ'gĭble *adj.* Not legible. **ĭllĕgĭbĭl'ity** *n.* **ĭllĕ'gĭbly** *adv.*

ĭllėgĭt'ĭmate *adj.* 1. Not authorized by law; irregular, improper. 2. Not born in lawful wedlock, bastard. 3. Not correctly deduced or inferred; abnormal. **ĭllėgĭt'ĭmately** *adv.* **ĭllėgĭt'ĭmacy** *n.*

ĭllėgĭt'ĭmāte *v.t.* Declare illegitimate. **ĭllėgĭtĭmā'tion** *n.*

ĭllĭb'eral *adj.* Not befitting a free man; without liberal culture; vulgar, sordid; narrow-minded, stingy. **ĭllĭb'erally** *adv.* **ĭllĭberăl'ity** *n.*

ĭllĭ'cĭt *adj.* Unlawful, forbidden; ~ *process*, (logic) the fallacy in which a term not distributed in the premisses of a syllogism is distributed in the conclusion. **ĭllĭ'cĭtly** *adv.*

ĭllĭm'ĭtable *adj.* Boundless. **ĭllĭm'ĭtableness, ĭllĭmĭtabĭl'ity** *ns.* **ĭllĭm'ĭtably** *adv.*

Illinois' (-oi, -oiz). 1. East North Central State of U.S., bounded on N. by Wisconsin; the 'Prairie State'; capital, Springfield. 2. Indian of confederacy of Algonkin tribes formerly living in Illinois and parts of Iowa and Wisconsin.

ĭllĭt'erate *adj.* Ignorant of letters; unlearned; unable to read. ~ *n.* Illiterate person. **ĭllĭt'erateness, ĭllĭt'eracy** *ns.*

ĭll'ness *n.* Unhealthy condition of body; disease, ailment, sickness.

ĭllŏ'gĭcal *adj.* Devoid of, contrary to, logic. **ĭllŏ'gĭcally** *adv.* **ĭllogĭcăl'ity** *n.*

ĭllūme' *v.t.* (poet.) Light up, make bright.

ĭllum ināte (-ū-, -ōō-) *v.t.* Light up; give spiritual or intellectual light to; throw light upon (subject); shed lustre upon; decorate (buildings etc.) profusely with lights as sign of festivity; decorate (initial letter in manuscript etc.) with gold, silver, and brilliant colours. **ĭllumĭnā'tion** *n.* Act or process of illuminating; state of being illuminated; (optics) surface light density per unit area on an intercepting surface (see FOOT-CANDLE, LUMEN, LUX, PHOT); coloured decorations in a manuscript. **ĭllum'ĭnātor** *n.* **ĭllum'ĭnative** *adj.*

ĭllumĭnāt'ī (-ōō-, -ū-; *also* -ahtē) *n.pl.* 1. Secret society, founded (1776) in Bavaria by Professor Adam Weishaupt, holding deistic and republican principles, and with organization like freemasonry. 2. Persons claiming to possess special enlightenment. **ĭllum'ĭnism, ĭllum'ĭnist** *ns.*

ĭllum'ĭne (-ū-, -ōō-) *v.t.* Light up; enlighten spiritually; brighten.

ĭllu'sion (-lōōzhn, -lū-) *n.* Deception, delusion; sensuous perception of an external object involving a false belief.

ĭllu'sionist (-zhon-) *n.* 1. One who disbelieves in objective existence. 2. One who produces illusions, esp. conjurer.

ĭllu'sive (-ōōs-, -ūs-) *adj.* Deceptive. **ĭllu'sively** *adv.* **ĭllu'siveness** *n.*

ĭllu'sory (-lōō-, -lū-) *adj.* Having the character of an illusion. **ĭllu'sorĭly** *adv.* **ĭllu'sorĭness** *n.*

ĭll'ustrāte *v.t.* Make clear, explain; make clear by examples; elucidate (description etc.) by drawings; ornament (book, newspaper etc.) with pictures etc. **ill'ustrātor** *n.* **illustrā'tion** *n.* Illustrating; example; drawing etc. illustrating book or article in paper.

ill'ustrative (*or* illŭs'-) *adj.* Serving as explanation or example (*of*). **ill'ustratively** *adv.*

illŭs'trious *adj.* Distinguished, renowned. **illŭs'triously** *adv.* **illŭs'triousness** *n.*

Illy̆'ria (ĭ-). Ancient region, with landward boundaries never clearly defined, extending along Balkan coast of Adriatic from Fiume to Durazzo, and including modern Dalmatia, Bosnia, Herzegovina, Montenegro, and part of Albania. **Illy̆'rian** *adj.* Of Illyria. ~ *n.* One of inhabitants of ancient Illyria; the Indo-European language (closely related to modern Albanian) spoken by them.

I.L.O. *abbrev.* International Labour Organization.

I.L.P. *abbrev.* Independent Labour Party.

Il'us (ī-). Legendary founder of Troy (Ilion) and grandfather of Priam.

im- *prefix.* = IN-[1, 2] before *b*, *m*, *p*.

im'age (-ĭj) *n.* 1. Artificial imitation of external form of an object, e.g. statue; esp. figure of saint or divinity as object of religious veneration. 2. Optical appearance or counterpart of object produced by rays of light reflected from a mirror or refracted through any transparent medium (ill. LENS); *real* ~, one formed at the point at which light, originating in the object-point, is finally converged after traversing an optical system, as e.g. on a photographic plate; *virtual* ~, one formed at the point from which light, originating in the object-point, and having traversed an optical system, appears to be diverging, as e.g. one seen in a plane mirror. 3. Mental picture, idea, conception. ~ *v.t.* Make an image of, portray; reflect, mirror; picture; describe vividly; typify.

im'agery *n.* Images; statuary, carving; figurative illustration.

imă'ginable *adj.* That can be imagined. **imă'ginably** *adv.*

imă'ginal *adj.* (entom.) Of an insect imago.

imă'ginary *adj.* Existing only in imagination; (math.) having no real existence, but assumed to exist for a special purpose, e.g. the square root of a negative quantity. **imă'ginarily** *adv.*

imăginā'tion *n.* Imagining; mental faculty forming images of external objects not present to the senses; fancy; creative faculty of the mind.

imă'ginative *adj.* Of, given to using, having or showing in a high degree, the faculty of imagination. **imă'ginatively** *adv.* **imă'ginativeness** *n.*

imă'gine *v.t.* Form mental image of; conceive; guess; suppose, be of opinion; take into one's head.

im'agism *n.* Movement in poetry, originating in 1912 and represented by Ezra Pound, Amy Lowell, and others, aiming at exact use of visual images. **im'agist** *n.*

imā'gō *n.* (pl. *-gos* or *-ginēs*). 1. (entom.) Final and perfect stage of insect after it has undergone all its metamorphoses (ill. BUTTERFLY). 2. (psycho-analysis) Conception of the parent retained in the unconscious and elaborated by child phantasies.

imam', imaum' (-ahm) *n.* 1. In Mohammedan communities, name given to the person who is regarded as taking Mohammed's place as leader of the church, esp. any of 12 successive heads of Islam, beginning with Ali and his sons, recognized by the Shiites; hence, any great spiritual leader. 2. The official who leads the prayers in a mosque. **imam'ate** *n.* Office, title, of imam. [Arab. *amma* go before]

imbăl'ance *n.* (psychol., path.) Disturbance of mental or bodily equilibrium (also fig.).

im'bècile (*or* -ēl) *adj.* Mentally weak, stupid. ~ *n.* Adult person whose intelligence is equal to that of the average normal child between the ages of 3 and 7 years, or between 25 and 50 per cent. of that of the average normal adult (see also IDIOT, MORON); person of weak intellect. **imbecil'ity** *n.*

imbĕd': see EMBED.

imbībe' *v.t.* Drink in, assimilate, (ideas etc.); drink (liquid); inhale (air etc.); absorb (moisture etc.). **imbibi'tion** *n.*

im'bricāte *v.* Arrange (leaves, scales of fish, etc.), be arranged, so as to overlap like tiles. **im'bricāted** *adj.* **imbricā'tion** *n.*

imbro'glio (-ōlyō) *n.* Confused heap; complicated or confused (esp. political or dramatic) situation.

imbrue' (-ōō) *v.t.* Stain (*in*, *with*, blood, slaughter, etc.).

imbūe' *v.t.* Saturate (*with*); dye (*with*); permeate, inspire (*with* feelings etc.); imbrue.

Im'hotĕp (ĭ-) (*c* 3000 B.C.). Ancient Egyptian architect and physician, afterwards revered as god of medicine.

im'itable *adj.* Capable of being imitated. **imitabil'ity** *n.*

im'itāte *v.t.* Follow example of; mimic; be like. **imitā'tion** *n.* Imitating; copy; counterfeit (freq. attrib.); (mus.) repetition of melody etc. usu. at different pitch, in another part or voice. **im'itātor** *n.*

im'itative *adj.* Following model or example (*of*); characterized by, consisting in, imitation; fictitious, counterfeit. **im'itatively** *adv.* **im'itativeness** *n.*

immăc'ūlate (-*at*) *adj.* Pure, spotless; faultless; (nat. hist.) not spotted; *I~ Conception*, doctrine that the Virgin Mary was conceived free from taint of original sin (in 1854 declared an article of faith of R.C. Church). **immăc'ūlately** *adv.* **immăc'ūlacy** *n.*

im'manent *adj.* Indwelling, inherent (*in*); (of God) permanently pervading the universe (opp. to TRANSCENDENT). **im'manence, im'manency** *ns.*

Immăn'ūėl (ĭ-). Name given to Christ as deliverer of Judah prophesied by Isaiah (Isa. vii. 14, viii. 8; Matt. i. 23). [Heb., = 'God with us']

immatēr'ial *adj.* Not material, incorporeal; unimportant. **immatēr'ialism** *n.* Doctrine that matter does not exist in itself apart from perception. **immatēr'ialist** *n.* **immatēriăl'ity** *n.*

immatūre' *adj.* Not mature. **immatūr'ity** *n.*

immea'surable (-mĕzher-) *adj.* Not measurable, immense. **immea'surableness, immea'surabil'ity** *ns.* **immea'surably** *adv.*

immēd'iate *adj.* (Of person or thing in its relation to another) not separated by any intervening medium; (of relation or action) direct, without intervening medium; nearest, next; occurring at once, without delay; (logic) ~ *inference*, inference from single premiss, without intervention of middle term. **immēd'iately** *adv.* **immēd'iateness, immēd'iacy** *ns.*

immemōr'ial *adj.* Ancient beyond memory; very old. **immemōr'ially** *adv.*

immĕnse' *adj.* Vast, huge; **immĕnse'ly** (-sl-) *adv.* In an immense degree; (colloq.) very much. **immĕn'sity** *n.*

Imm'ermann (ĭ-), Karl Lebrecht (1796–1840). German romantic novelist and playwright.

immerse' *v.t.* Dip, plunge (*in* liquid); put over head in water, esp. baptize thus; bury, embed, (*in*); involve deeply, absorb, (*in* debt, difficulties, thought, etc.).

immer'sion (-shn) *n.* Immersing; baptism by plunging whole person in water; absorption (*in* thought etc.); (astron.) disappearance of celestial body behind another or in its shadow; ~ *heater*, electrical element, usu. thermostatically controlled, immersed in water for heating it.

imm'igrāte *v.* Come as settler (*into* foreign country); bring in (person) as settler. **imm'igrant** *adj.* & *n.* **immigrā'tion** *n.*

imm'inent *adj.* (Of events, esp. dangers) impending, soon to happen. **imm'inently** *adv.* **imm'inence** *n.*

immis'cible *adj.* That cannot be mixed. **immiscibil'ity** *n.* **immis'cibly** *adv.*

immit'igable *adj.* That cannot be softened or toned down. **immit'igably** *adv.*

immōb'ile *adj.* Immovable; not mobile; motionless. **immobil'ity** *n.*

ĭmmŏb'ilīze *v.t.* Fix immovably; render immobile or stationary; withdraw (specie) from circulation, holding it against bank-notes. **ĭmmŏbilīzā'tion** *n.*

ĭmmŏd'erate *adj.* Excessive, wanting in moderation. **ĭmmŏd'erately** *adv.*

ĭmmŏd'ėst *adj.* Indecent, indelicate; forward, impudent. **ĭmmŏd'ėstly** *adv.* **ĭmmŏd'ėsty** *n.*

ĭmm'olāte *v.t.* Kill (victim) as sacrifice; (fig.) sacrifice (thing etc. *to* another). **ĭmmolā'tion, ĭmm'olātor** *ns.*

ĭmmŏ'ral *adj.* Opposed to morality; morally evil; vicious, dissolute. **ĭmmŏ'rally** *adv.* **ĭmmorăl'ĭty** *n.*

ĭmmôrt'al *adj.* Undying; divine; unfading, incorruptible; famous for all time. **ĭmmôrt'ally** *adv.* **ĭmmôrt'al** *n.* Immortal being, esp. (pl.) gods of antiquity; person, esp. author, of enduring fame; *the Immortals*, the 40 members of the French Academy (so called because each member's place is filled as soon as he dies); picked body of 10,000 infantry forming ancient Persian royal bodyguard, whose number was kept constantly full. **ĭmmôrtăl'ĭty** *n.*

ĭmmôrt'alīze *v.t.* Confer enduring fame upon; endow with endless life; perpetuate. **ĭmmôrtalīzā'tion** *n.*

ĭmmôrtelle' (-ĕl) *n.* Composite flower of papery texture (esp. *Helichrysum orientale*) retaining colour and shape after being dried.

ĭmmov'able (-mōō-) *adj.* That cannot be moved; motionless; not subject to change; steadfast, unyielding; emotionless; (law, of property) consisting of land, houses, etc. **ĭmmov'ablenėss, ĭmmovabĭl'ĭty** *ns.* **ĭmmov'ably** *adv.* **ĭmmov'ables** *n.pl.* Immovable property, as land etc.

ĭmmūne *adj.* Having immunity; serving to develop immunity.

ĭmmūn'ĭty *n.* 1. Freedom (from); (law) exemption (*from* taxation, jurisdiction, etc.). 2. (physiol.) That property of a living organism by which infection is resisted and overcome; *active* ~, increased resistance to an invading microbe or its products, developed in response to infection (whether a natural infection or one introduced artificially), as distinct from *passive* ~, temporary resistance acquired prenatally or by injection of antibody; *acquired* ~, immunity of an organism that manufactures, or is injected with, antibodies.

ĭm'mūnīze *v.t.* Render immune (*against* infection). **ĭmmūnīzā'tion** *n.*

ĭmmūnŏl'ogy *n.* Study of immunity from disease and the conditions governing it.

ĭmmūre' *v.t.* Imprison; shut oneself up. **ĭmmūre'ment** (-ūrm-) *n.*

ĭmmūt'able *adj.* Unchangeable; not subject to variation in different cases. **ĭmmūtabĭl'ĭty** *n.* **ĭmmūt'ably** *adv.*

ĭmp[1] *n.* Child of the devil; little devil; mischievous child.

ĭmp[2] *v.t.* (falconry) Ingraft feathers in wing of (bird) to strengthen flight.

ĭm'păct[1] *n.* Striking, collision (freq. fig.).

ĭmpăct'[2] *v.t.* Press, fix, closely or firmly (*into, in*). **ĭmpăc'tion** *n.* (esp., surg.) Fracture in which broken parts are driven together so as to become locked (ill. BONE).

ĭmpair' *v.t.* Damage, weaken. **ĭmpair'ment** *n.*

ĭmpāle' *v.t.* 1. Transfix (body etc. *upon, with,* stake, etc., esp. as form of capital punishment). 2. (her.) Combine (two coats of arms) by placing side by side on one shield separated by vertical line down middle (ill. HERALDRY). **ĭmpāle'ment** (-lm-) *n.*

ĭmpăl'pable *adj.* Imperceptible to the touch; not easily grasped by the mind; intangible. **ĭmpălpabĭl'ĭty** *n.* **ĭmpăl'pably** *adv.*

ĭmpărisyllăb'ic *adj.* & *n.* (Gk and L gram.) (Noun) not having same number of syllables in all cases.

ĭmpârt' *v.t.* Give share of; communicate (news etc. *to*).

ĭmpâr'tial (-shal) *adj.* Not partial, unprejudiced, fair. **ĭmpâr'tially** *adv.* **ĭmpârtiăl'ĭty** (-shiăl-) *n.*

ĭmpârt'ĭble *adj.* (Of estate) not divisible.

ĭmpass'able (-pah-) *adj.* That cannot be traversed. **ĭmpass'ablenėss, ĭmpassabĭl'ĭty** *ns.*

ĭmpasse' (-ahs) *n.* Blind alley; position from which there is no escape.

ĭmpăss'ĭble *adj.* Incapable of feeling or emotion; incapable of suffering injury; not subject to suffering. **ĭmpăss'ĭblenėss, ĭmpassĭbĭl'ĭty** *ns.* **ĭmpăss'ĭbly** *adv.*

ĭmpă'ssion *v.t.* Stir the passions of, excite strongly (chiefly in past. part.).

ĭmpăss'ĭve *adj.* Deficient in feeling or emotion; serene; without sensation; not subject to suffering. **ĭmpăss'ĭvely** *adv.* **ĭmpăss'ĭvenėss, ĭmpassĭv'ĭty** *ns.*

ĭmpăs'tō *n.* (paint.) Laying on of colour thickly; (ceramics) enamel colours on slip standing out in relief from surface of ware.

ĭmpā'tient (-shent) *adj.* Not enduring with composure; intolerant *of*; restlessly desirous (*for* thing, *to* do). **ĭmpā'tiently** *adv.* **ĭmpā'tience** *n.*

ĭmpeach' *v.t.* Call in question, disparage (character etc.); accuse (person) *of*, charge *with*; find fault with; accuse of treason or other high crime before competent tribunal. **ĭmpeach'ment** *n.* Calling in question; accusation and prosecution of a person for treason or other high crime or misdemeanour before a competent tribunal; judicial process in which House of Commons (in U.S., House of Representatives) are prosecutors and House of Lords (in U.S., Senate) are judges.

ĭmpĕcc'able *adj.* Not liable to sin; (of things) faultless. **ĭmpĕccabĭl'ĭty** *n.* **ĭmpĕcc'ably** *adv.*

ĭmpėcū'nious *adj.* Having little or no money. **ĭmpėcūniŏs'ĭty** *n.*

ĭmpĕd'ance *n.* (elect.) Total virtual resistance to the flow of electric current, esp. to alternating current, arising from the ohmic resistance and the reactance of the conductor.

ĭmpēde' *v.t.* Retard, hinder.

ĭmpĕd'ĭment *n.* Hindrance, obstruction; esp. (~ *in speech*) stammer, stutter.

ĭmpĕdĭmĕn'ta *n.pl.* Baggage, esp. of army.

ĭmpĕl' *v.t.* Drive, force; drive forward, propel. **ĭmpĕll'ent** *n.*

ĭmpĕnd' *v.i.* Hang, be suspended, (*over*); (fig., of danger) hang threateningly (*over*); be imminent. **ĭmpĕn'dence, ĭmpĕn'dency** *ns.* **ĭmpĕn'dent** *adj.*

ĭmpĕn'ėtrable *adj.* That cannot be penetrated; inscrutable, unfathomable; impervious; (nat. philos.) having that property in virtue of which two bodies cannot occupy same place at same time. **ĭmpĕn'ėtrablenėss, ĭmpĕnėtrabĭl'ĭty** *ns.* **ĭmpĕn'ėtrably** *adv.*

ĭmpĕn'ėtrāte *v.t.* Penetrate deeply.

ĭmpĕn'ĭtent *adj.* Not penitent. **ĭmpĕn'ĭtently** *adv.* **ĭmpĕn'ĭtence, ĭmpĕn'ĭtency** *ns.*

ĭmpĕ'rative *adj.* 1. (gram.) Of verbal mood, or form belonging to it: expressing command, request, or exhortation. 2. Commanding, peremptory; urgent; obligatory. **ĭmpĕ'ratively** *adv.* **ĭmpĕ'rativenėss** *n.* **ĭmpĕ'rative** *n.* Imperative mood. **ĭmpĕratĭv'al** *adj.*

ĭmpercĕp'tĭble *adj.* That cannot be perceived; very slight, gradual, or subtle. **ĭmpercĕp'tĭbly** *adv.*

ĭmpercĭp'ĭent *adj.* Lacking perception.

ĭmpêrf'ĕct *adj.* 1. Not fully formed or done, incomplete; faulty. 2. (gram. of tense) Implying action going on but not completed (e.g. *he is, he will be, singing,* but usu. of past time, as *he was singing*). **ĭmpêrf'ĕctly** *adv.*

ĭmperfĕc'tion *n.* Incompleteness; faultiness; fault, blemish.

ĭmperfĕc'tĭve *adj.* & *n.* (Slav. gram.) (Aspect of verb) expressing action (whether in past, present, or future) without reference to its completion (opp. of PERFECTIVE).

ĭmpêrf'orate *adj.* Not perforated, esp. (anat.) lacking normal opening; (of sheet of postage stamps, or single stamp) without perforations.

ĭmpêr'ĭal *adj.* Of an empire or sovereign State ranking with an empire; of Great Britain, as distinct from its constituent kingdoms etc.; (of weights and measures) appointed by statute for use throughout United Kingdom; (of paper) 30×22 in. **impēr′ially** *adv.* **impēr′ial** *n.* 1. Small beard or tuft below lower lip (after the Emperor Napoleon III). 2. Trunk for luggage adapted for roof of coach. 3. Gold coin of Tsarist Russia, worth 15 (orig. 10) silver roubles.

Imperial Institute. Institute in S. Kensington, London, founded 1893 as national memorial to Queen Victoria, with exhibits illustrating resources, industries, scenery, etc., of British dominions and colonies.

impēr′ialism *n.* Rule of an emperor; principle or spirit of empire, advocacy of what are held to be imperial interests. **impēr′ialist** *n.* Adherent of an emperor, esp. (1600–1800) of German Emperor; advocate of imperial rule, esp. adherent of Bonaparte family; advocate of (British) imperialism. **impērialis′tic** *adj.*

impĕ′ril *v.t.* Bring into danger.

impēr′ious *adj.* Overbearing, domineering; urgent, imperative. **impēr′iously** *adv.* **impēr′iousnėss** *n.*

impĕ′rishable *adj.* That cannot perish. **impĕ′rishablenėss, impĕrishabil′ity** *ns.* **impĕ′rishably** *adv.*

impĕ′rium (*or* -ēr-) *n.* Absolute powers; empire. [L, = 'command, dominion']

impērm′anent *adj.* Not permanent. **impērm′anence, impērm′anency** *ns.*

impērm′ėable *adj.* That cannot be passed through: that does not permit passage of fluids. **impērmėabil′ity** *n.*

imperscrip′tible *adj.* Not backed by written authority.

impērs′onal *adj.* 1. (gram., of verbs) Used only in 3rd person singular without referring to a person or definite subject; hence, used without a subject or with a merely formal one, as Engl. *it*. 2. Having no personality or personal reference or tone. **impērs′onally** *adv.* **impērsonăl′ity** *n.*

impērs′onāte *v.t.* Represent in bodily form, personify; play the part of, personate; act (character). **impērsonā′tion, impērs′onator** *ns.* **impērs′onative** *adj.*

impērt′inent *adj.* 1. Irrelevant (now chiefly in law); out of place, absurd. 2. Intrusive, presumptuous; insolent, saucy. **impērt′inently** *adv.* **impērt′inence** *n.*

impertūrb′able *adj.* Not excitable, calm. **impertūrb′ablenėss, impertūrbabil′ity** *ns.* **impertūrb′ably** *adv.*

impērv′ious *adj.* Not affording passage (*to*); (fig.) impenetrable, not affording entrance *to* (argument, feeling, etc.). **impērv′iously** *adv.* **impērv′iousnėss** *n.*

impėtĭg′ō *n.* Acute inflammatory disease of skin caused by streptococcal and staphylococcal organisms, characterized by pustules chiefly on face and hands.

im′pėtrāte *v.t.* (chiefly theol.) Obtain by request or entreaty. **impėtrā′tion** *n.*

impĕt′ūous *adj.* Moving violently or rapidly; acting with rash or sudden energy. **impĕt′ūously** *adv.* **impĕt′ūousnėss, impĕtūŏs′ity** *ns.*

im′pėtus *n.* Force with which a body moves; (fig.) moving force, impulse.

im′peyan (-pĭan) *adj.* ~ *pheasant*, pheasant of S. Kashmir (*Lophophorus impeianus*), with crested head and, in male, brilliant plumage. [discovered by Sir Elijah *Impey*, 1787]

im′pi *n.* Body of Kaffir warriors, army.

impī′ėty *n.* Ungodliness; want of dutifulness or reverence.

impinge′ (-j) *v.* Make impact (*on, upon*); (archaic) make (thing) do this. **impinge′ment** (-jm-) *n.*

im′pious *adj.* Not pious, wicked, profane. **im′piously** *adv.*

imp′ish *adj.* Of, like, an imp. **imp′ishly** *adv.* **imp′ishnėss** *n.*

implăc′able (*or* -āk-) *adj.* That cannot be appeased. **implăcabil′ity** *n.* **implăc′ably** *adv.*

implant′ (-ah-) *v.t.* Insert, infix (*in*); instil (*in* mind etc.); plant. **implantā′tion** *n.*

im′plėment¹ *n.* 1. (pl.) Things serving as equipment or outfit, as household furniture, ecclesiastical vessels or vestments, etc. 2. Tool; (pl.) apparatus, set of utensils, instruments, etc.

im′plėmĕnt² *v.t.*. Complete (contract etc.); fulfil (engagement); fill up, supplement. **implėmĕntā′tion** *n.*

implē′tion *n.* Filling; fullness.

im′plicāte *v.t.* Entwine, entangle; involve, imply, as inference; involve (*in* charge, crime, etc.). **implicā′tion** *n.* **im′plicātive** *adj.*

impli′cit *adj.* Implied though not plainly expressed; virtually contained (*in*); ~ *faith*, faith in spiritual matters, not independently reached by individual but involved in general belief of Church; absolute, unreserved, faith. **impli′citly** *adv.* **impli′citnėss** *n.*

implōre′ *v.t.* Beg earnestly for; entreat. **implōr′ingly** *adv.* **implōr′ingness** *n.*

implū′vium (-plōō-) *n.* (Rom. antiq.) Square basin in middle of atrium receiving rain-water from open space in roof (ill. HOUSE).

imply′ *v.t.* Involve the truth of (thing not expressly asserted); mean; insinuate, hint.

impōld′er *v.t.* Make a POLDER of; reclaim from sea.

impolīte′ *adj.* Uncivil, rude. **impolīte′ly** (-tl-) *adv.* **impolīte′nėss** *n.*

impŏl′itic *adj.* Not politic; inexpedient. **impŏl′iticly** *adv.*

impŏn′derable *adj.* 1. Having no weight; very light; (fig.) that cannot be estimated. 2. Not to be estimated by physical weight. ~ *n.* Imponderable thing.

impōrt′ *v.t.* 1. Bring, introduce (esp. goods from foreign country *into*). 2. Imply, indicate, mean; express, make known. 3. Be of consequence. **impōrtā′tion** *n.* Bringing in, introducing. **impōrt′er** *n.* One who imports goods. **im′pōrt** *n.* 1. What is implied, meaning, importance. 2. Importation; (usu. pl.) commodity imported.

impōrt′ance *n.* Being important; weight, significance; personal consequence, dignity; pompousness.

impōrt′ant *adj.* Carrying with it great consequence (*to*), weighty, momentous; consequential, pompous. **impōrt′antly** *adv.*

impōrt′ūnate *adj.* Persistent, pressing, in solicitation; (of affairs) urgent. **impōrt′ūnately** *adv.* **importūn′ity** *n.*

impōrt′ūne (*or* -tūn′) *v.t.* Solicit pressingly.

impōse′ (-z) *v.* 1. (archaic) Place (thing) *upon*; (print.) lay (pages of type) in proper order and secure them in a chase. 2. Lay (tax, duty, charge, *upon*). 3. Palm off (thing *upon* person). 4. Exert influence (*on* person) by striking character or appearance; ~ *upon*, take advantage of (person); practise deception upon. **impōs′ingly** *adv.* **impōs′ingnėss** *n.*

imposi′tion (-z-) *n.* (esp.) 1. Laying on *of hands* (in ordination etc.). 2. (print.) Imposing or arranging of pages of type in form. 3. Impost, tax, duty, (fig.) burden. 4. Piece of deception or overcharge. 5. Work set as punishment at school.

impŏss′ible *adj.* Not possible; (loosely) not easy, not convenient; (colloq.) outrageous, intolerable. **impŏssibil′ity** *n.* **impŏss′ibly** *adv.*

im′pōst¹ *n.* (archaic) Tax, duty, tribute.

im′pōst² *n.* Upper course of pillar, bearing arch (ill. ARCH).

impŏs′tor *n.* One who assumes a false character or passes himself off as someone else; swindler.

impŏs′ture *n.* Fraudulent deception.

im′pŏt *n.* (school slang) Imposition.

im′potent *adj.* Powerless; helpless, decrepit; (of males) wanting in sexual power. **im′potently** *adv.* **im′potence, im′potency** *ns.*

impound′ *v.t.* Shut up (cattle) in pound; shut up (person, thing) as in pound; take legal possession of; confiscate.

impŏv′erish *v.t.* Make poor; exhaust strength of. **impŏv′erishment** *n.*

imprăc′ticable *adj.* Impossible in practice; unmanageable; (of roads etc.) impassable. **imprăc′ticablenėss, imprăcticabil′ity** *ns.* **imprăc′ticably** *adv.*

ĭmprăc'tical *adj.* (now chiefly U.S.) Unpractical; impracticable. **ĭmprăc'tĭcăl'ĭty** *n.*

ĭm'prĕcāte *v.t.* Invoke, call down, (evil *upon* person etc.). **ĭmprĕcā'tion** *n.* (esp.) Spoken curse. **ĭm'prĕcatory** *adj.*

ĭmprĕg'nable *adj.* (Of fortress etc.) that cannot be taken by arms; (fig.) proof against attack. **ĭmprĕgnabĭl'ĭty** *n.* **ĭmprĕg'nably** *adv.*

ĭmprĕg'nate *adj.* Pregnant; permeated (*with*). **ĭm'prĕgnāte** (*or* ĭmprĕg'-) *v.t.* Make (female) pregnant; (biol.) fecundate (female reproductive cell or ovum); fill, saturate, (*with*); imbue, fill, (*with* feelings, moral qualities, etc.). **ĭmprĕgnā'tion** *n.*

ĭmprĕsar'ĭō (-z-) *n.* (pl. *-s*). Organizer of public entertainments, esp. manager of operatic or concert company.

ĭmprĕscrĭp'tĭble *adj.* Not subject to prescription, that cannot be legally taken away.

ĭm'prĕss[1] *n.* Stamping; mark made by seal, stamp, etc.; (fig.) characteristic mark. **ĭmprĕss'** *v.t.* Apply (mark etc.) with pressure, imprint, stamp, (*on*); imprint, enforce, (idea etc. *on* person, his mind); mark (thing *with* stamp etc.); affect, influence; affect (person) strongly (*with* idea etc.). **ĭmprĕss'ĭble** *adj.* **ĭmprĕssĭbĭl'ĭty** *n.*

ĭmprĕss'[2] *v.t.* Force (men) to serve in army or navy; seize (goods etc.) for public service; enlist, make use of, (thing) in argument etc. **ĭmprĕss'ment** *n.*

ĭmprĕ'ssion (-shn) *n.* 1. Impressing (of mark); mark impressed. 2. Individual print taken from type or engraving. 3. Number of copies of book printed at one time, printing of these; unaltered reprint from standing type or plates, as opp. to EDITION. 4. Effect produced (esp. on mind or feelings); notion, (vague) belief, impressed on the mind.

ĭmprĕ'ssionable (-shon-) *adj.* Susceptible of impressions, easily influenced. **ĭmprĕssionabĭl'ĭty** *n.*

Imprĕ'ssionĭsm (-shon-) *n.* Method of painting initiated *c* 1870 by a school of French painters (including Manet, Monet, Pissarro, Renoir, and Degas), whose aim was to paint the momentary or transitory appearance of things, and esp. the effects of light and atmosphere, rather than form or structure; method of writing resembling this. **Imprĕ'ssionĭst** *n.* & *adj.* **ĭmprĕssionĭs'tĭc** *adj.* **ĭmprĕssionĭs'tĭcally** *adv.*

ĭmprĕss'ĭve *adj.* Able to excite deep feeling, making deep impression on mind or senses. **ĭmprĕss'ĭvely** (-vl-) *adv.* **ĭmprĕss'ĭvenėss** *n.*

ĭm'prĕst *n.* Money advanced to person to be used in State business.

ĭmprĭmā'tūr *n.* Official licence to print (now usu. of works sanctioned by R.C. Ch.); (fig.) sanction. [mod. L, = 'let it be printed']

ĭmprī'mĭs *adv.* In the first place. [L, = *in primis* among the first things]

ĭmprĭnt' *v.t.* Stamp (figure etc. *on*); impress (idea etc. *on, in* mind etc.); impress (quality etc. *on, in*); stamp (thing *with* figure). **ĭm'prĭnt** *n.* Impression, stamp; name of printer or publisher, date and place of printing or publication, at foot or back of title-page or at end of book etc.

ĭmprĭs'on (-zn) *v.t.* Put into prison; confine, shut up. **ĭmprĭs'onment** *n.*

ĭmprŏb'able *adj.* Not likely to be true or to happen. **ĭmprŏbabĭl'ĭty** *n.* **ĭmprŏb'ably** *adv.*

ĭmprŏb'ĭty *n.* Wickedness; dishonesty.

ĭmprŏmp'tū *adv.* & *adj.* (Spoken, done) without preparation, extempore. ~ *n.* Improvised or extempore performance or composition; musical composition having character of improvisation. [L, *in promptu* in readiness].

ĭmprŏp'er *adj.* Inaccurate, wrong; unseemly, indecent; ~ *fraction*, fraction with numerator greater than denominator. **ĭmprŏp'erly** *adv.*

ĭmprō'prĭāte *v.t.* Annex (ecclesiastical benefice) to corporation or person as property; place (tithes, ecclesiastical property) in lay hands. **ĭmprōp'rĭate** (-at) *adj.* **ĭmprōprĭā'tion** *n.* **ĭmprōp'rĭātōr** *n.* One to whom benefice is impropriated.

ĭmproprī'ėty *n.* Incorrectness; unfitness; indecency.

ĭmprov'able (-ōō-) *adj.* That can be improved; adapted for cultivation. **ĭmprov'ablenėss, ĭmprovabĭl'ĭty** *ns.*

ĭmprove' (-ōō-) *v.* Make, become, better; make good use of (occasion etc.); preach on (*the occasion*) with a view to edification; ~ *away*, get rid of by improvements; ~ *upon*, produce something better than. **ĭmprove'ment** *n.*

ĭmprov'er (-ōōv-) *n.* (esp.) One working at trade for low wage or none to improve his skill; chemical substance added to flour to improve texture etc. of bread.

ĭmprŏv'ĭdent *adj.* Unforeseeing; heedless; thriftless. **ĭmprŏv'ĭdently** *adv.* **ĭmprŏv'ĭdence** *n.*

ĭm'provīse (-z) *v.t.* Compose, utter, (verse, music, etc.) without preparation; provide, get up, extempore. **ĭmprovīsā'tion, ĭm'provīsātor** *ns.* **ĭmprovīsatōr'ial, ĭmprovīs'atory** *adjs*

ĭmprud'ent (-rōō-) *adj.* Rash, indiscreet. **ĭmprud'ently** *adv.* **ĭmprud'ence** *n.*

ĭm'pūdent *adj.* Shamelessly forward; unblushing; insolently disrespectful. **ĭm'pūdently** *adv.* **ĭm'pūdence** *n.*

ĭmpūdĭ'cĭty *n.* Shamelessness, immodesty.

ĭmpugn' (-ūn) *v.t.* Assail by word, call in question, (statement, action). **ĭmpugn'ment** *n.*

ĭm'pŭlse *n.* 1. Impelling, push; (dynamics) indefinitely larger force acting for an inappreciably short time but producing finite momentum; momentum thus produced; product of average value of force multiplied by time during which it acts. 2. Mental incitement; sudden tendency to act without reflection; impetus.

ĭmpŭl'sion (-shn) *n.* Impelling, push; mental impulse; impetus.

ĭmpŭl'sĭve *adj.* 1. Tending to impel. 2. (Of persons, conduct, etc.) apt to be moved, prompted, by sudden impulse. **ĭmpŭl'sĭvely** (-vl-) *adv.* **ĭmpŭl'sĭvenėss** *n.*

ĭmpūn'ĭty *n.* Exemption from punishment; exemption from injury as consequence of act.

ĭmpūre' *adj.* Dirty; unchaste; mixed with foreign matter, adulterated; (of colour) mixed with another colour. **ĭmpūre'ly** (-ūrl-) *adv.* **ĭmpūr'ĭty** *n.*

ĭmpūte' *v.t.* Attribute, ascribe, (fault etc. *to*); (theol.) ascribe (another's righteousness or guilt *to* person). **ĭmpūtā'tion** *n.* **ĭmpūt'atĭve** *adj.* **ĭmpūt'atĭvely** *adv.*

I.M.S. *abbrev.* Indian Medical Service.

ĭn *prep.* Expressing inclusion or position within limits of space, time, circumstance, etc., as ~ *Europe*, ~ *London*, ~ *a box*, ~ *the day*, ~ *the army*; ~ *itself*, apart from all else, absolutely; *not* ~ *it*, not in the running, not a serious competitor; *nothing, little, not much*, ~ *it*, (orig. racing slang) no decided advantage yet gained by any competitor. ~ *adv.* expressing position bounded by certain limits or motion to a point enclosed by them; on the inside, within; in office; (of fire etc.) burning, lighted; (of player or side) having the turn or right to play (esp. to bat in cricket); ~ *for*, committed to (a course of action); in competition for; ~ *for it*, certain to meet with punishment or something unpleasant; ~ *with*, on friendly terms with. ~ *adj.* Internal, living, etc., inside; ~*-patient*, one who remains in hospital while under treatment. ~ *n.* (pl.) Political party in office; *ins and outs*, turnings to and fro (usu. fig.), details (*of* procedure etc.).

in-[1] **(il-, im-, ir-)** *prefix.* In, on, into, towards, against.

in-[2] **(il-, im-, ir-)** *prefix.* Prefixed to adjs. and their derivatives to express negation.

in. *abbrev.* Inch(es).

ĭnabĭl'ĭty *n.* Being unable; lack of power or means.

ĭnaccĕss'ĭble (-ks-) *adj.* That cannot be reached; not open to advances, unapproachable. **ĭnaccessĭbĭl'ĭty** *n.* **ĭnaccĕss'ĭbly** *adv.*

ĭnăcc'ūrate *adj.* Not accurate. **ĭnăcc'ūrately** *adv.* **ĭnăcc'ūracy** *n.*

ĭnăc'tion *n.* Absence of action; sluggishness, inertness. **ĭnăc'tive** *adj.* **ĭnăc'tively** (-vl-) *adv.* **ĭnăctiv'ity** *n.* **ĭnăc'tivāte** *v.t.*

ĭnăd'ėquate *adj.* Not adequate; insufficient. **ĭnăd'ėquately** *adv.* **ĭnăd'ėquacy** *n.*

ĭnadmiss'ible *adj.* That cannot be admitted or allowed. **ĭnadmissibil'ity** *n.* **ĭnadmiss'ibly** *adv.*

ĭnadvert'ent *adj.* Not properly attentive; negligent; (of actions) unintentional. **ĭnadvert'ently** *adv.* **ĭnadvert'ence, ĭnadvert'ency** *ns.*

ĭnāl'ienable *adj.* Not alienable. **ĭnālienabil'ity** *n.* **ĭnāl'ienably** *adv.*

ĭnămora'tō (-rah-) *n.* (fem. *-ta*) Lover.

in-and-in *adv.* Farther and farther in; (esp., of breeding) always within a limited stock, between near relatives.

ĭnāne' *adj.* Empty, void; silly, senseless. **ĭnāne'ly** (-nl-) *adv.* **ĭnăn'ity** *n.* **ĭnāne'** *n.* *The ~*, vacuity, infinite space.

ĭnăn'imate *adj.* Destitute of life; not endowed with animal life; spiritless, dull. **ĭnăn'imately** *adv.* **ĭnăn'imatenėss** *n.*

ĭnani'tion *n.* Emptiness, esp. from want of nourishment.

ĭnăppėtence, -ency *ns.* Want of appetite or desire.

ĭnăpp'licable *adj.* Not applicable, unsuitable (*to*). **ĭnăpplicabil'ity** *n.* **ĭnăpp'licably** *adv.*

ĭnăpp'osite (-z-) *adj.* Not apposite, out of place. **ĭnăpp'ŏsitely** *adv.*

ĭnapprē'ciable (-sha-) *adj.* Imperceptible, not worth reckoning; that cannot be appreciated. **ĭnapprē'ciably** *adv.*

ĭnapprēciā'tion *n.* Failure to appreciate. **ĭnapprē'ciative** *adj.*

ĭnapprō'priate *adj.* Not appropriate. **ĭnapprō'priately** *adv.* **ĭnapprō'priatenėss** *n.*

ĭnăpt' *adj.* Unfit, unskilful. **ĭnăpt'ly** *adv.* **ĭnăpt'nėss, ĭnăp'titūde** *ns.*

ĭnartic'ūlate *adj.* 1. Not jointed. 2. Not articulate; unable to speak distinctly; dumb; unable to express one's ideas. **ĭnartic'ūlately** *adv.* **ĭnartic'ūlatenėss** *n.*

ĭn arti'cūlō mort'is. In the instant of death.

ĭnartifi'cial (-shl) *adj.* Lacking in art, inartistic; artless, natural; **ĭnartifi'cially** *adv.*

ĭnartis'tic *adj.* Not following the principles of art; unskilled in art. **ĭnartis'tically** *adv.*

ĭnasmŭch' (-az-) *adv.* *~ as*, since, because; (archaic) in so far as.

ĭnattĕn'tion *n.* Want of attention, heedlessness; neglect to show courtesy. **ĭnattĕn'tive** *adj.* **ĭnattĕn'tively** (-vl-) *adv.* **ĭnattĕn'tivenėss** *n.*

ĭnaud'ible *adj.* That cannot be heard. **ĭnaudibil'ity** *n.* **ĭnaud'ibly** *adv.*

ĭnaug'ūral *adj.* (Of ceremony) inaugurating; (of speech etc.) given by person who is being inaugurated. *~ n.* Inaugural speech or lecture.

ĭnaug'ūrāte *v.t.* Admit (person) to office etc. with ceremony; enter with ceremony upon (undertaking etc.); initiate public use of (building etc.). **ĭnaugūrā'tion, ĭnaug'ūrātor** *ns.* **ĭnaug'ūratory** *adj.*

ĭnauspi'cious (-shus) *adj.* Not of good omen; unlucky. **ĭnauspi'ciously** *adv.* **ĭnauspi'ciousnėss** *n.*

ĭn'board (-ōrd) *adv.* & *adj.* (naut.) (Situated) within sides or towards centre of ship.

ĭn'bōrn *adj.* Implanted by nature.

ĭn'brĕd (*or* ĭnbrĕd') *adj.* 1. Innate, inherent by nature. 2. Born of closely related parents.

ĭn'-breeding *n.* Breeding from animals or persons closely related.

Inc. *abbrev.* Incorporated.

Inc'a (ĭ-) *n.* Member of Amer. Indian Quichua-speaking people who at the time of the Spanish expedition in 1533 had a highly developed civilization and ruled a large region of S. America with centre at Cuzco, Peru; member of its ruling class, supposedly descended from the sun; *the ~*, the emperor or chief ruler of the Incas. **Inc'an** *adj.* & *n.*

ĭncăl'cūlable *adj.* Too great for calculation; that cannot be reckoned beforehand; uncertain. **ĭncălcūlabil'ity** *n.* **ĭncăl'cūlably** *adv.*

ĭncandĕsce' (-ĕs) *v.* (Cause to) glow with heat. **ĭncandĕs'cent** *adj.* Glowing with heat; shining brightly; (of gas or electric light etc.) produced by glowing of mantle or filament raised to white heat by flame of burning gas or passage of electricity. **ĭncandĕs'cence** *n.*

ĭncăntā'tion *n.* (Use of) magical formula; spell, charm.

ĭncăp'able *adj.* Not capable (*of*; freq. = too honest etc. to do); not susceptible (*of* improvement etc.); disqualified; without ordinary capacity or natural ability. **ĭncăpabil'ity** *n.* **ĭncăp'ably** *adv.*

ĭncapă'citāte *v.t.* Render incapable or unfit. **ĭncapăcitā'tion** *n.*

ĭncapă'city *n.* Inability; disability; legal disqualification.

ĭncar'cerāte *v.t.* Imprison. **ĭncarcerā'tion, ĭncar'cerātor** *ns.*

ĭncarn'adine *adj.* & *v.t.* (poet.) (Dye) flesh-coloured, crimson.

ĭncarn'ate *adj.* Embodied in flesh, esp. in human form. **ĭncarn'āte** *v.t.* Embody in flesh; put (idea etc.) into concrete form, realize; be living embodiment of (quality). **ĭncarnā'tion** *n.* Embodiment in (esp. human) flesh, esp. *the I~* (of Christ); impersonation, living type (*of* quality etc.).

ĭncau'tious (-shus) *adj.* Rash. **ĭncau'tiously** *adv.* **ĭncau'tiousnėss** *n.*

ĭncĕn'diary *adj.* Of, guilty of, the malicious setting on fire of property; (mil.) used for setting on fire enemy's property, esp. *~ bomb*, aerial bomb, usu. containing thermite and magnesium and igniting on impact; (fig.) tending to stir up strife, inflammatory. *~ n.* Incendiary person, incendiary bomb. **ĭncĕn'diarism** *n.*

ĭn'cĕnse[1] *n.* Aromatic gum or other vegetable product, giving sweet smell when burned; smoke of this, esp. in religious ceremonial; (fig.) praise, flattery. *~ v.t.* Fumigate with incense; burn incense to (deity etc.); suffuse with fragrance.

ĭncĕnse'[2] *v.t.* Enrage, make angry.

ĭn'cĕnsory *n.* Vessel for burning incense, censer.

ĭncĕn'tive *adj.* Tending to incite. *~ n.* Incitement, provocation, motive; (in industry) system of payments rewarding workers for greater output.

ĭncĕpt' *v.* 1. (formerly at Camb. Univ.) Enter formally upon office of Master or Doctor. 2. (biol.) Take in.

ĭncĕp'tion *n.* Beginning; (Camb. Univ.) incepting.

ĭncĕp'tive *adj.* Beginning; initial; (gram.) expressing beginning of an action. *~ n.* Inceptive verb.

ĭncert'itūde *n.* Uncertainty.

ĭncĕss'ant *adj.* Unceasing, continual, repeated. **ĭncĕss'antly** *adv.* **ĭncĕss'antnėss** *n.*

ĭn'cĕst *n.* Sexual intercourse between persons related within degrees within which marriage is prohibited. **ĭncĕs'tūous** *adj.* Involving, guilty of, incest. **ĭncĕs'tūously** *adv.*

inch[1] *n.* (abbrev. *in.*) 12th part of foot in British and Amer. measures of length (see Appendix X); (as unit of rainfall) quantity that would cover horizontal surface to depth of 1 in.; (of atmospheric or other pressure) amount that balances weight of column of mercury 1 in. high in mercurial barometer; small amount; (pl.) stature; *by inches*, bit by bit; *every ~*, entirely. *~ v.* Move by inches, edge *in*, *forward*, etc.

inch[2] *n.* Small (esp. Sc.) island.

ĭn'chōate (ĭn-kōat) *adj.* Just begun; undeveloped. **ĭn'chōāte** *v.t.* Begin, originate. **ĭnchōā'tion** *n.* **ĭn'chōative** (*or* ĭn-kō'-) *adj.* (esp., of verbs) Inceptive.

ĭn'cidence *n.* 1. Falling on, contact with, a thing; range, scope, extent, of influence; (of tax) persons on whom it falls; (of disease)

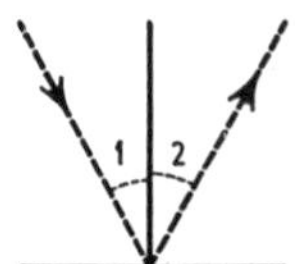

1. ANGLE OF INCIDENCE.
2. ANGLE OF REFLECTION

rate, scale, frequency, of occurrence in a community. 2. (math., physics) Falling of a line, or a thing moving in a line, upon a surface; *angle of* ~, angle which the incident line, ray, etc., makes with the perpendicular to the surface at the point of contact.

in'cident[1] *adj.* 1. (of light etc.) Falling, striking, (*upon*). 2. Apt to occur, naturally attaching, (*to*); (law) attaching as privilege, burden, etc., *to* office, position, etc.

in'cident[2] *n.* 1. Subordinate or accessory event; event, occurrence; detached event attracting general attention; distinct piece of action in play etc. 2. (law) Privilege, burden, etc., attaching to estate etc.

incidĕn'tal *adj.* 1. Casual, not essential; ~ *images, colours*, those perceived as consequence of impressions no longer present; ~ *music*, music interpolated in spoken play. 2. Liable to happen *to*. **incidĕn'tally** *adv.*

incin'erāte *v.t.* Reduce to ashes; consume by fire. **incinerā'tion** *n.* **incin'erātor** *n.* (esp.) Apparatus for outdoor combustion of rubbish.

incip'ient *adj.* Beginning; in an initial stage. **incip'iently** *adv.* **incip'ience, incip'iency** *ns.*

in'cipit. (Here) begins (book etc.).

incise' (-z) *v.t.* Make a cut in; engrave. **inci'sion** (-zhn) *n.* Cutting into a thing; cut, gash, notch.

incis'ive (-s-) *adj.* Cutting, penetrating; mentally sharp; acute, trenchant. **incis'ively** (-vl-) *adv.* **incis'iveness** *n.*

incis'or (-z-) *n.* Cutting-tooth, any front tooth in either jaw, between canine teeth, having sharp edge and single fang (ill. TOOTH).

incite' *v.t.* Urge, stir up (person etc. *to*). **incite'ment** (-ītm-), **incitā'tion** *ns.*

incivil'ity *n.* Rudeness, discourtesy,

in'-clearing *n.* Cheques etc. collectively payable by a bank and received through clearing-house for settlement.

inclĕm ent *adj.* (of weather etc.) Severe, esp. cold or stormy. **inclĕm'ency** *n.*

inclin'able *adj.* Inclined, disposed; favourable.

inclinā'tion *n.* 1. Leaning, slope, slant; difference of direction of two lines, esp. as measured by angle between them; (astron.) angle between plane of a planet's orbit and that of the ecliptic. 2. Disposition, propensity (*to, for*); liking, affection (*for*).

incline' *v.* 1. Bend (head etc.) forward or downward; lean, cause to lean, from vertical etc.; ~ *one's ear*, listen favourably. 2. Dispose (person, mind, etc., *to*); be disposed; tend (*to*). 3. *Inclined plane*, one of the mechanical powers, material plane surface inclined at acute angle to horizon. **incline'** (*or* in'-) *n.* Inclined plane; slope.

inclinŏm ėter *n.* 1. Instrument for measuring vertical component of earth's magnetic field, by means of a magnetic needle free to rotate in a vertical plane. 2. Instrument for measuring the steepness of slopes.

include' (-o͞od) *v.t.* Comprise, embrace, as part of a whole; treat, regard, as so comprised. **inclu'sion** (-o͞ozhn) *n.*

inclus'ive (-o͞os-) *adj.* Including, enclosing, comprehending; comprising; ~ *of*, embracing, comprising (something specified); (quasi- *adv.*), the term or terms named being included. **inclus'ively** (-vl-) *adv.* **inclus'iveness** *n.*

incog. *abbrev.* Incognito.

incŏg'nito *adj.* & *n.* (Person) unknown or concealed under disguised character. ~ *adv.* With one's name, character, etc., concealed.

incŏg'nizable (-kŏgn-, -kŏn-) *adj.* That cannot be apprehended by senses or intellect. **incŏg'nizant** *adj.* Unaware, unconscious *of*. **incŏg'nizance** *n.*

incōhēr'ent *adj.* Not coherent. **incōhēr'ently** *adv.* **incōhēr'ence** *n.*

incōhēs'ive *adj.* Not cohesive.

incombŭs'tible *adj.* That cannot be consumed by fire. **incombŭstibil'ity** *n.*

in'come (-ŭm) *n.* Periodical (usu. annual) receipts from one's business, lands, work, investments, etc.; ~*-tax*, tax levied on this.

in'coming (-kŭ-) *n.* Entrance, arrival; (usu. pl.) revenue, income. ~ *adj.* Succeeding; immigrant; (of profit) accruing.

in commĕn'dăm. As a charge or trust (of benefice pending appointment of regular incumbent, or of its revenue enjoyed by layman etc.).

incommĕn'surable (-sher-) *adj.* Having no common measure integral or fractional (*with* another magnitude); irrational, surd; not comparable in respect of magnitude; not worthy to be measured *with*. **incommĕnsurabil'ity** *n.* **incommĕn'surably** *adv.*

incommĕn'surate (-sher-) *adj.* Out of proportion, inadequate, (*with, to*); incommensurable. **incommĕn'surately** (-tl-) *adv.* **incommĕn'surateness** *n.*

incommōde' *v.t.* Trouble, annoy, hinder.

incommōd'ious *adj.* Not affording good accommodation, uncomfortable. **incommōd'iously** *adv.* **incommōd'iousness** *n.*

incommūn'icable *adj.* That cannot be shared; that cannot be told. **incommūn'icableness, incommūnicabil'ity** *ns.* **incommūn'icably** *adv.*

incommūnicad'ō (-kah-) *adj.* Having no means of communication; in solitary confinement.

incommūn'icātive *adj.* Not communicative. **incommun'icatively** (-vl-) *adv.* **incommūn'icativeness** *n.*

incŏm'parable *adj.* Matchless; not to be compared (*to, with*). **incŏm'parableness** *n.* **incŏm'parably** *adv.*

incompăt'ible *adj.* Opposed in character, discordant; inconsistent (*with*). **incompătibil'ity** *n.*

incŏm'pėtent *adj.* Not qualified or able (*to do*); not legally qualified. **incŏm'pėtently** *adv.* **incŏm'pėtence, incŏm'pėtency** *ns.*

incomplēte' *adj.* Not complete. **incomplēte'ly** (-tl-) *adv.* **incomplēte'nėss** *n.*

incŏmprėhĕn'sible *adj.* That cannot be understood; (archaic, chiefly in allusion to Athanasian Creed) that cannot be contained within limits, boundless, infinite. **incŏmprėhĕn'siblenėss, incŏmprėhĕnsibil'ity** *ns.* **incŏmprėhen'sibly** *adv.* **incomprėhĕn'sion** (-shn) *n.* Failure to understand.

incomprĕss'ible *adj.* That cannot be compressed. **incomprĕssibil'ity** *n.*

inconceiv'able *adj.* That cannot be imagined. **inconceivabil'ity** *n.* **inconceiv'ably** *adv.*

inconclus'ive (-lo͞os-) *adj.* (Of argument etc.) not decisive or convincing. **inconclus'ively** (-vl-) *adv.* **inconclus'ivenėss** *n.*

incŏng'ruous (-nggro͞o-) *adj.* Disagreeing, out of keeping, (*with*); out of place, absurd. **incŏng'ruously** *adv.* **incŏng'ruousnėss, incongru'ity** (-gro͞o-) *ns.*

incŏn'sėquent *adj.* Not following naturally, irrelevant; wanting in logical sequence; disconnected. **incŏn'sėquently** *adv.* **incŏn'sėquence** *n.* **incŏnsėquĕn'tial** (-shl) *adj.* **incŏnsėquĕn'tially** *adv.*

inconsid'erable *adj.* Not worth considering; of small size, value, etc.

inconsid'erate *adj.* Thoughtless, rash; lacking in regard for feelings etc. of others. **inconsid'erately** (-tl-) *adv.* **inconsid'eratenėss** *n.*

incŏnsis'tent *adj.* Not in keeping, discordant, incompatible, (*with*); having inconsistent parts; acting at variance with one's own principles or former conduct. **inconsis'tently** *adv.* **inconsis'tency** *n.*

inconsōl'able *adj.* That cannot be consoled. **inconsōl'ably** *adv.*

inconspic'ūous *adj.* Not conspicuous; not readily seen or noticed; (bot., of flowers) small, pale, or green. **inconspic'ūously** *adv.* **inconspic'ūousnėss** *n.*

incŏn'stant *adj.* Fickle, changeable; variable, irregular. **incŏn'stantly** *adv.* **incŏn'stancy** *n.*

incontĕs'table *adj.* That cannot be disputed. **incontĕs'tably** *adv.*

incŏn'tinėnt *adj.* Wanting in self-restraint (esp. in regard to sexual appetite); unable to hold in something. **incŏn'tinence** *n.*

incŏn'tinent(ly) *advs.* (archaic) At once, immediately.

incŏntrovẽrt'ible *adj.* Not to be disputed. **incŏntrovẽrt'ibly** *adv.*

inconvēn'ience *n.* Want of adaptation to personal requirement or ease; instance of this. ~ *v.t.* Put to inconvenience, incommode. **inconvēn'ient** *adj.* Unfavourable to ease or comfort, troublesome, awkward. **inconvēn'iently** *adv.*

inconvẽrt'ible *adj.* Not convertible; esp., of paper money, that cannot be converted into specie. **inconvẽrtibil'ity** *n.* **inconvẽrt'ibly** *adv.*

incōōrdinā'tion *n.* Want of coordination.

incorp'orate *adj.* (Of company etc.) formed into a corporation; (of persons) united in a corporation. **incorp'orāte** *v.* 1. Unite; combine (ingredients) into one substance. 2. Constitute as a legal corporation; become incorporated (*with*). **incorporā'tion, incorp'orātor** *ns.*

incorpor'ėal *adj.* Not composed of matter, immaterial; of immaterial beings; (law) having no material existence. **incorpor'ėally** *adv.*

incorrĕct' *adj.* Not in conformity with recognized standard, or with fact; improper; erroneous. **incorrĕct'ly** *adv.* **incorrĕct'nėss** *n.*

incŏ'rrigible *adj.* Incurably bad or depraved. **incŏrrigibil'ity** *n.* **incŏ'rrigibly** *adv.*

incorrōd'ible *adj.* Incapable of being corroded.

incorrŭp'tible *adj.* That cannot decay; eternal; that cannot be corrupted, esp. that cannot be bribed. **incorrŭptibil'ity** *n.* **incorrŭp'tibly** *adv.* **incorrŭp'tion** *n.* (archaic, bibl.).

increase' (-s) *v.* Become greater; grow in numbers, esp. by propagation; advance (*in* quality, attainment, etc.); make greater or more numerous; intensify (quality). **increas'ingly** *adv.* **in'crease** *n.* Growth, enlargement; growth in numbers, multiplication; increased amount; (archaic) crops; *on the* ~, increasing.

incrĕd'ible *adj.* That cannot be believed; (colloq.) hard to believe or realize. **incrĕdibil'ity** *n.* **incrĕd'ibly** *adv.*

incrĕd'ūlous *adj.* Unbelieving. **incrĕd'ūlously** *adv.* **incrĕd'ūlousnėss, incrėdūl'ity** *ns.*

in'crėment *n.* Increase; amount of this; profit; (math.) small amount by which variable quantity increases; *unearned* ~, increased value of land due to external causes, not to owner's labour or outlay.

incrim'ināte *v.t.* Charge with crime; involve in accusation. **incriminā'tion** *n.* **incrim'inatory** *adj.*

Incroyable (ăṅkrwa-yahbl'). Affected and extravagantly dressed fop of French Directoire period. [Fr., = 'incredible']

incrŭstā'tion *n.* Encrusting, being encrusted; crust, hard coating, esp. of fine or costly material over rough or common substance; calcareous or crystalline concretion or deposit; scab.

in'cūbāte *v.* Sit on eggs, brood; hatch (eggs) thus or by artificial heat; subject (micro-organisms) to warmth for a period. **incūbā'tion** *n.* (esp., path.) Early phase of disease after micro-organisms have invaded the host and before symptoms of infection appear. **in'cubātive, in'cubātory** *adjs.*

in'cūbātor *n.* Apparatus for hatching birds, rearing infants born prematurely, or developing micro-organisms.

in'cūbus *n.* Evil spirit supposed to descend on sleeping persons; nightmare; person, thing, that oppresses like nightmare.

in'cŭlcāte *v.t.* Urge, impress, persistently (*upon, in,* person, mind). **incŭlcā'tion, in'cŭlcātor** *ns.*

in'cŭlpāte *v.t.* Accuse, blame; involve in charge. **incŭlpā'tion** *n.* **incŭl'patory** *adj.*

incŭm'bency *n.* Office, tenure, sphere, of an incumbent. **incŭm'bent**[1] *n.* Holder of ecclesiastical benefice or (rare) of any office.

incŭm'bent[2] *adj.* Lying, pressing, (*on*); resting (*up*)*on* (person) as duty.

incūn'able *n.* Early printed book, esp. one produced before 1500. ***incūnăb'ūla*** *n.pl.* Incunables. [L *incunabula* swaddling-clothes, (fig.) origin, beginning (*cunae* cradle)]

incûr' *v.t.* Fall into, bring on oneself (danger, blame, etc.).

incûr'able *adj.* & *n.* (Person) that cannot be cured. **incûr'ablenėss, incūrabil'ity** *ns.* **incûr'ably** *adv.*

incûr'ious *adj.* Devoid of curiosity; heedless, careless; uninteresting. **incûr'iously** *adv.* **incūriŏs'ity** *n.*

incûr'sion *n.* Hostile invasion; sudden attack. **incûr'sive** *adj.*

incûrve' *v.t.* Bend into a curve; curve inwards. **incûrvā'tion** *n.*

inc'us *n.* Middle small bone of ear (between malleus and stapes) to which sonorous vibrations are conveyed from malleus (ill. EAR). [L, = 'anvil']

incūse' (-z-) *adj.* (Of impression on coin etc.) hammered or stamped in. ~ *n.* Such impression. ~ *v.t.* (esp. in past part.) Impress (figure etc.) by stamping; mark (coin etc.) with such figure.

Ind (archaic and poet. for) INDIA.

Ind. *abbrev.* India(n); Indiana.

in'damine *n.* (chem.) Any of a series of organic compounds that form bluish or greenish salts.

indebt'ėd (-ĕt-) *adj.* Owing money (*to*); owing gratitude (*to*). **indĕbt'ėdnėss** *n.*

indē'cent *adj.* Unbecoming; immodest, obscene. **indē'cently** *adv.* **indē'cency** *n.*

indėcid'ūous *adj.* Not deciduous.

indėciph'erable *adj.* That cannot be deciphered.

indėci'sion (-zhn) *n.* Want of decision, hesitation.

indėcis'ive *adj.* Not decisive; undecided, irresolute. **indėcis'ively** (-vl-) *adv.* **indėcis'ivenėss** *n.*

indėclin'able *adj.* (gram.) Having no inflexions.

indėcor'ous (*or* indĕk'-) *adj.* Improper; in bad taste. **indėcor'ously** *adv.* **indėcor'ousnėss** *n.* **indėcor'um** *n.* Lack of decorum.

indeed' *adv.* In truth, really (freq. placed after a word to emphasize it).

indėfăt'igable *adj.* Unremitting, unwearying. **indėfătigabil'ity** *n.* **indėfăt'igably** *adv.*

indėfeas'ible (-z-) *adj.* That cannot be forfeited or done away with. **indėfeasibil'ity** *n.* **indėfeas'ibly** *adv.*

indėfĕc'tible *adj.* Unfailing, not liable to defect or decay; faultless.

indėfĕn'sible *adj.* Admitting of no defence. **indėfĕnsibil'ity** *n.* **indėfĕn'sibly** *adv.*

indėfin'able *adj.* That cannot be defined. **indėfin'ably** *adv.*

indĕf'inite *adj.* 1. Vague, undefined; unlimited. 2. (gram., of adjs., pronouns, etc.) Not determining the person, thing, time, manner, etc., to which they refer; (of tenses of verbs) denoting an action without specifying whether it is continuous or complete. **indĕf'initely** (-tl-) *adv.* **indĕf'initenėss** *n.*

indėhis'cent *adj.* (bot.) Not dehiscent; (of fruit) not splitting open when mature, but liberating seed by decay.

indĕl'ible *adj.* That cannot be blotted out or effaced. **indĕlibil'ity** *n.* **indĕl'ibly** *adv.*

indĕl'icate *adj.* Coarse, unrefined; immodest; tactless. **indĕl'icately** *adv.* **indĕl'icacy** *n.*

indĕm'nify *v.t.* Protect, secure (*from, against,* harm or loss); secure (person) against legal responsibility (*for* actions); compensate (*for* loss, expenses incurred, etc.). **indĕmnificā'tion** *n.*

indĕm'nity *n.* Security against damage or loss; legal exemption from penalties etc. incurred; compensation for loss; sum paid for this, esp. sum exacted by victorious belligerent as one condition of peace.

indėmŏn'strable *adj.* That cannot be proved (esp. of primary truths).

indĕnt'[1] *v.* 1. Make tooth-like notches in; form deep recesses in (coast-line etc.); (her.) shape edge of (ordinary etc.) so that it has a series of straight-sided pointed teeth (ill. HERALDRY). 2. Divide (document drawn up in duplicate) into two halves with zigzag line; draw up (document) in exact duplicate. 3. (print.) Set back (beginning of line) farther from margin to mark new paragraph. 4. Make requisition (properly, written order with duplicate) *upon* (person *for* thing); order (goods) by an indent. **ĭn'dĕnt** *n.* Indentation; indenture; official requisition for stores; order for goods.

indĕnt'[2] *v.t.* Make a dent in; impress (mark etc.). **ĭn'dĕnt** *n.* Dent, depression.

indĕntā'tion *n.* Indenting; cut, notch; zigzag; recess in coast line etc.

indĕn'tion *n.* Indenting of line in printing; indentation.

indĕn'tor *n.* (commerc.) One who makes a requisition.

indĕn'ture *n.* Indented document; any sealed agreement or contract, esp. that which binds apprentice to master; formal list, certificate, etc.; indentation. ~ *v.t.* Bind (person) by indenture, esp. as apprentice.

indėpĕn'dence *n.* Being independent; independent income; *Declaration of I~*, public act by which American Continental Congress, on 4th July 1776, declared N. Amer. colonies to be free and independent of Gt Britain; *I~ Day*, this day, observed in U.S. as annual holiday. **indėpĕn'dency** *n.* 1. Independent State. 2. (chiefly hist.) Congregationalism.

indėpĕn'dent *adj.* Not depending on authority of another, autonomous, free; not depending on something else for its validity, efficiency, etc.; not needing to earn one's livelihood; (of income etc.) sufficient to make one independent; unwilling to be under obligation to others; (chiefly hist.) Congregational; *I~ Labour Party* (abbrev. I.L.P.), political organization in Gt Britain for support of socialist parliamentary candidates, founded 1893 by Keir Hardie, later forming the extreme left wing of the Labour party. **indėpĕn'dently** *adv.* **indėpĕn'dent** *n.* 1. Person who acts (in politics etc.) independently of any party. 2. Congregationalist.

indėscrīb'able *adj.* Vague, indefinite; too great, beautiful, bad, etc., to be described. **indėscrībabĭl'ĭty** *n.* **indėscrīb'ably** *adv.*

indėstrŭc'tĭble *adj.* That cannot be destroyed. **indėstrŭctibĭl'ĭty** *n.* **indėstrŭc'tĭbly** *adv.*

indėtẽrm'ĭnable *adj.* That cannot be definitely fixed or ascertained; that cannot be settled.

indėtẽrm'ĭnate *adj.* Not fixed in extent, character, etc.; vague; left doubtful; (math., of quantity) not limited to fixed value(s). **indėtẽrm'ĭnately** *adv.* **indėtẽrm'ĭnateness** *n.* **indėtẽrmĭnā'tion** *n.* Want of determination; being indeterminate.

ĭn'dĕx *n.* (pl. *-es*, *-ĭcēs*) 1. Forefinger; (on instruments) pointer showing measurement etc.; sign, token, indication (*of* something). 2. Alphabetical list, usu. at end of book, of names, subjects, etc., with references. 3. (short for ~ *librorum prohibitorum*) List, formerly published by authority (abolished 1966), of books which Roman Catholics were forbidden to read or might read only in expurgated editions; ~ *expurgatorius*, authoritative specification of passages to be expunged in books otherwise permitted. 4. (alg.) Exponent; ~ *number*, (in statistics) a number used in comparing the value of an attribute at a certain time with its value at a standard time. ~ *v.t.* 1. Furnish (book) with index; enter (word etc.) in index. 2. (mech., of automatic tools) Move in a succession of equal angular steps.

In'dia (ĭ-). 1. Large peninsula of S. central Asia, bounded on N. by Himalayas; inhabited by many brown-skinned races following Hindu, Moslem, and other religions and speaking over 200 languages, esp. Hindi and Bengali in N. and Tamil and Telugu in S. British interest began in early 17th c. with formation of East India Company, which in 1765 acquired the right to administer Bengal (after Clive's victory at Plassey in 1757) and afterwards other parts; in 1858 after the Indian Mutiny the Crown took over the Company's authority; in 1877 Queen Victoria was proclaimed Empress of India; in 1947 the 15 provinces (*British* ~) and numerous native States under British protection were divided between 2 new States, India (see 2 below) and PAKISTAN. 2. The *Republic of* ~, a predominantly Hindu State constituted in 1950 as a member of the British Commonwealth and comprising much of the N. and all the S. and central part of the peninsula; capital, Delhi. 3. ~ *Office*, (hist.) department of British Government dealing, until 1947, with Indian affairs; ~ *paper*, (i) soft absorbent cream or buff paper from China, used for proofs or first impressions of engravings, whence ~ *proof*; (ii) very thin tough opaque printing-paper made by Oxford University Press; *Star of* ~, high order of British knighthood, instituted 1861 in commemoration of Queen Victoria's assumption of style and title of Empress of India. [Gk *Indos* Indus, f. Pers. *hind* = Sansk. *sindhu* river]

In'dĭaman (ĭ-) *n.* (hist.) Ship engaged in trade with India, esp. large vessel belonging to East India Company.

In'dĭan (ĭ-) *adj.* 1. Of India or the E. Indies; of Indian manufacture, material, or pattern. 2. Of the original inhabitants of America and the W. Indies. ~ *n.* 1. Native of India or E. Indies. 2. Member of any aboriginal race of America or W. Indies (usu. excluding Eskimos, Patagonians, and Fuegians); *Red* ~, member of aboriginal race of N. America, with coppery-coloured skin. 3. Language of American Indians. 4. ~ *club*, heavy bottle-shaped club used in gymnastic exercises; ~ *corn*, maize, a N. Amer. graminaceous plant (*Zea mays*) cultivated by Indians before discovery of America; ripened ears or seeds of this; ~ *file*, single file (so called because N. Amer. Indians march thus); ~ *hemp*, common HEMP, esp. as source of narcotics; (also) N. Amer. perennial herb (*Apocynum cannabinum*) of dog-bane family with milky juice and tough fibrous bark; ~ *ink* (also *India ink*), black pigment of lamp black or ivory black mixed with gum etc. and dried, brought chiefly from China and Japan in sticks or cakes; colloidal suspension of this in water; ~ *Mutiny*, revolt (1857–8), beginning at Meerut, of Sepoys in Bengal army of East India Company against British authority; ~ *National Congress*, representative national organization, founded 1885 to obtain self-government and dominion status for India; ~ *Ocean*, ocean to S. of India, extending from E. coast of Africa to Malay Archipelago; *Order of the* ~ *Empire*, high order of British knighthood, instituted 1877 (cf. *Star of* INDIA); ~ *summer*, period of calm dry mild weather with hazy atmosphere, occurring in late autumn, esp. in northern U.S.

Indĭăn'a (ĭ-; *or* -ah'na). East North Central State of U.S. **Indĭanăp'olĭs.** Capital city of Indiana.

ĭn'dia-rŭbb'er *n.* Rubber; see RUBBER[1], 3.

ĭn'dĭcāne *n.* (chem.) A glucoside occurring in plants yielding indigo.

ĭn'dĭcāte *v.t.* Point out, make known, show; state briefly; be a sign of, betoken; (med.) suggest, call for, (treatment). **ĭndĭcā'tion** *n.*

indĭc'ative *adj.* 1. (*also* in'dĭcā-) Suggestive, giving indications, *of*. 2. (Gram., of verbal mood) stating something as objective fact, not as conception, wish, etc., of speaker. **indĭc'atively** (-vl-) *adv.* **indĭc'ative** *n.* Indicative mood.

ĭn'dĭcātor *n.* Person, thing, that points out or indicates; mechanical device indicating condition of apparatus etc. to which it is attached; board etc. in railway station etc. giving times and platforms of trains etc.; (chem.) substance which marks a stage in a chemical reaction by a change of colour.

indīct' (-īt) *v.t.* Accuse (person), esp. by legal process. **indīct'able** *adj.* Liable, rendering one liable, to be indicted. **indīct'ment** *n.* Formal accusation; (formerly) legal process in which this is preferred to and presented by Grand Jury; document containing charge; *bill* *of* ~, written accusation as preferred to Grand Jury.

ĭndīc'tion *n.* Fiscal period of 15 years instituted in A.D. 313 by Constantine and reckoned from A.D. 312; assessment of property-tax by Roman emperors at beginning of each 15 years; this tax.

Indies (ĭn'dĭz). *The* ~, old collective term for India and adjacent regions and islands; see also EAST INDIES, WEST INDIES.

ĭndĭff'erence *n.* Absence of interest or attention (*to, towards*); neutrality; unimportance.

ĭndĭff'erent *adj.* Impartial, neutral; having no inclination for or against; neither good nor bad; rather bad; neutral in chemical, electrical, or magnetic quality; unimportant. **ĭndĭff'erently** *adv.* **ĭndĭff'erent** *n.* Neutral or indifferent person, esp. in religion or politics.

ĭndĭff'erentĭsm *n.* Spirit of indifference, professed or practised, esp. in religious matters. **ĭndĭff'erentĭst** *n.*

ĭn'dĭgēne *n.* Native.

ĭndĭ'gėnous *adj.* Native, belonging naturally (*to* soil etc.). **ĭndĭ'gėnously** *adv.*

ĭn'dĭgent *adj.* Needy, poor. **ĭn'dĭgence** *n.*

ĭndĭgĕs'tĭble *adj.* Not digestible. **ĭndĭgĕstĭbĭl'ĭty** *n.* **ĭndĭgĕs'tion** (-schon) *n.* Difficulty in digesting food, dyspepsia; undigested condition. **ĭndĭgĕs'tĭve** *adj.* Suffering from, tending to, indigestion.

ĭndĭg'nant *adj.* Moved by mingled anger and scorn or feeling of injured innocence. **ĭndĭg'nantly** *adv.*

ĭndĭgnā'tion *n.* Anger excited by meanness, injustice, wickedness, or misconduct.

ĭndĭg'nĭty *n.* Unworthy treatment, slight, insult.

ĭn'dĭgō *n.* Blue dye obtained from plants of genus *Indigofera*; plant from which this is obtained; colour (lying between blue and violet in spectrum) yielded by indigo; *~-bird*, N. Amer. painted finch (*Cyanospiza cyanea*) with head etc. of rich indigo-blue; *~-blue*, blue colour of indigo. [Gk *indikon* Indian]

ĭndĭrĕct' *adj.* 1. Not straight; not going straight to the point; not directly aimed at; *~ rule*, (in colonial administration) government through native institutions (e.g. chiefs, tribal councils); *~ tax*, one paid by consumer in form of increased price for the taxed goods. 2. (gram.) *~ object*, person, thing, affected by action of verb but not primarily acted on (e.g. *him* in *give him the book*); *~ passive*, passive having for subject the indirect object of the active (e.g. *I* in *I was told it*); *~ speech*, reported speech, with necessary changes of pronouns, tenses, etc. (e.g. direct, *I will help you*; indirect, he said *he would help me*). **ĭndĭrĕct'ly** *adv.* **ĭndĭrĕct'nėss** *n.*

ĭndĭscĕrn'ĭble *adj.* & *n.* (Thing) that cannot be discerned or distinguished from another; *identity of ~s*, doctrine that things cannot exist together as separate entities unless they have different attributes. **ĭndĭscĕrn'ĭbly** *adj.*

ĭndĭs'cĭplĭne *n.* Want of discipline.

ĭndĭscreet' *adj.* Injudicious, unwary. **ĭndĭscreet'ly** *adv.*

ĭndĭs'crēte *adj.* Not divided into distinct parts.

ĭndĭscrĕ'tion *n.* Injudicious conduct; accidental or (*calculated ~*) supposed accidental revelation of official secret etc.; imprudence; transgression of social morality.

ĭndĭscrĭm'ĭnate *adj.* Confused, promiscuous; making no distinctions. **ĭndĭscrĭm'ĭnately** *adv.* **ĭndĭscrĭm'ĭnatenėss** *n.* **ĭndĭscrĭminā'tion** *n.* **ĭndĭscrĭm'ĭnatĭve** *adj.*

ĭndĭspĕn'sable *adj.* That cannot be dispensed with, necessary; (of law, duty, etc.) that cannot be set aside. **ĭndĭspĕn'sablenėss, ĭndĭspĕnsabĭl'ĭty** *ns.* **ĭndĭspĕn'săbly** *adv.*

ĭndĭspōse' (-z) *v.t.* Render unfit or unable; make averse; (esp. in past part.) put out of health. **ĭndĭsposĭ'tion** (-z-) *n.* Ill health, ailment, (esp. of passing kind); disinclination; aversion.

ĭndĭs'pūtable *adj.* That cannot be disputed. **ĭndĭs'pūtablenėss, ĭndĭspūtabĭl'ĭty** *ns.* **ĭndĭs'pūtably** *adv.*

ĭndĭss'ŏlūble (*or* ĭndĭsŏl'-) *adj.* Lasting, stable; that cannot be dissolved or decomposed. **ĭndĭssŏlūbĭl'ĭty** *n.* **ĭndĭssŏl'ūbly** *adv.*

ĭndĭstĭnct' *adj.* Not distinct; confused, obscure. **ĭndĭstĭnct'ly** *adv.* **ĭndĭstĭnct'nėss** *n.*

ĭndĭstĭng'uishable (-nggwish-) *adj.* Not distinguishable. **ĭndĭstĭng'uishably** *adv.*

ĭndīte' *v.t.* Put into words, compose, (poem, speech, etc.); (usu. joc.) write (letter etc.).

ĭn'dĭum *n.* Rare silver-white soft metallic element, occurring in association with zinc etc.; symbol In, at. no. 49, at. wt 114·82. [L *indicum* INDIGO, from two blue lines in the metal's spectrum]

ĭndĭvĭd'ūal *adj.* Single; particular, special; having distinct character; of a single person or thing, characteristic of an individual. ~ *n.* Single member of a class, group, or number; single human being (opp. to society, the family, etc.); (vulg.) person.

ĭndĭvĭd'ūalĭsm *n.* 1. Self-centred feeling or conduct, egoism. 2. Social theory advocating free and independent action of individual (cf. SOCIALISM). **ĭndĭvĭd'ūalĭst** *n.* **ĭndĭvĭdūalĭs'tĭc** *adj.*

ĭndĭvĭdūăl'ĭty *n.* Separate existence; individual character, esp. when strongly marked.

ĭndĭvĭd'ūalīze *v.t.* Give individual character to; specify. **ĭndĭvĭdualīzā'tion** *n.*

ĭndĭvĭd'ūally *adv.* Personally, in an individual capacity; in a distinctive manner; one by one, not collectively.

ĭndĭvĭs'ĭble (-z-) *adj.* Not divisible. ~ *n.* Infinitely small particle or quantity. **ĭndĭvĭsĭbĭl'ĭty** *n.* **ĭndĭvĭs'ĭbly** *adv.*

Indo- *prefix.* Indian.

Indo-Ar'ȳan (ĭ-, ār-) *adj.* & *n.* (Of) Indo-European languages of India; (of) Indian native races of Indo-European speech or descent.

In'do-Chīn'a (ĭ-). 1. The region in SE. Asia occupied by VIETNAM, CAMBODIA, and LAOS; formerly a dependency of France known as French Indo-China. 2. The whole peninsula occupied by Burma, Thailand, Malaya, and French Indo-China. **In'do-Chinēse'** (-z) *adj.* & *n.* Of Indo-China; (of the) family of languages, mostly of the isolating type but orig. agglutinative, spoken over an area including N. India, Malay peninsula, China, and most of central and E. Asia (but not Japan).

ĭndŏ'cīle *adj.* Not docile. **ĭndocĭl'ĭty** *n.*

ĭndŏc'trĭnāte *v.t.* Imbue with learning, *with* doctrine, idea, etc.; instruct *in*. **ĭndŏctrĭnā'tion** *n.*

Indo-Europē'an (ĭ-) *n.* (also *Indo-Germanic, Indo-Aryan*) The great family of languages spoken over most of Europe and in Asia as far as N. India, including esp. the Indo-Iranian, Balto-Slavonic, Hellenic, Italic, Celtic, and Germanic groups; member of race or people speaking one of these languages. ~ *adj.* Of this family of languages or any of the peoples speaking one of these languages.

Indo-Gĕrmănĭc = INDO-EUROPEAN.

Indo-Iranian *adj.* & *n.* (Of) the Indo-European languages spoken chiefly in N. India and Persia, and including Sanskrit and its modern derivatives, Persian, Pushtu, etc.

ĭn'dolent *adj.* Slothful, lazy; (med., of tumour etc.) causing no pain. **ĭn'dolently** *adv.* **ĭn'dolence** *n.*

ĭndŏm'ĭtable *adj.* Unyielding; stubbornly persistent. **ĭndŏm'ĭtably** *adv.*

Indonē'sĭa (ĭ-; -sh*a* *or* -sĭa). Republic of SE. Asia, comprising Sumatra, Java, S. and E. Borneo, Celebes and other islands; formerly belonging to the Netherlands; independent since 1949; capital, Djakarta. **Indone'sĭan** *adj.* Of Indonesia, esp. of Sumatra, Java, and Bali; of one of the vast number of SE. Asian languages spoken in Malay Peninsula and Archipelago. ~ *n.* Member of race forming chief pre-Malay population of Malay archipelago, and combining Polynesian and Mongoloid characteristics; member of the Republic of Indonesia.

in'door (-dōr) *adj.* Situated, carried on, within doors or under cover; within workhouse. **indoors'** *adv.* Within a house; under cover.

Indōre'. Former native State of central India, now part of the State of Madya Bharat in the Republic of India.

indorsā'tion *n.* (chiefly Sc.) Endorsement.

In'dra (ĭ-). (Vedic myth.) Chief god of air, rain-giver, type of beneficent heroic power struggling against evil demons, represented as golden in colour, with 4 arms, and riding in golden car; later subordinated to Brahma, Vishnu, and Shiva, and regarded as sensuous deity in celestial paradise, freq. represented riding the elephant Airavata (rain-cloud).

in'draught (-ahft), **-draft** *n.* Drawing in; inward flow or current.

indūb'itable *adj.* That cannot be doubted. **indūb'itably** *adv.*

indūce' *v.t.* 1. Prevail on, persuade (*to*); bring about, give rise to. 2. (elect.) Produce (current) by induction. 3. Infer, derive as an induction. **indūce'ment** (-sm-) *n.* What induces; attraction that leads one on (*to*).

indŭct' *v.t.* Introduce formally into possession (*to* benefice); install (*into*).

indŭc'tance *n.* The setting up of a magnetic field or flux by induction; the coefficient of magnetic or electric self-induction.

indŭc'tion *n.* 1. Inducting; introduction (rare); (archaic) preamble, prologue. 2. Production (*of* facts) to prove general statement; inferring of general law from particular instances; *mathematical* ~, method of proving universal truth of law by showing (i) that if true in a particular case it is true in the next case, (ii) that it is true in a particular case. 3. (elect. etc.) Bringing about of electric or magnetic state in a body by proximity (without contact) of electrified or magnetized body; production of electric current in conductor by motion of magnet near it, or by changes in the magnetic field in which it lies due to other causes; esp. generation of electric current in a conductor by changes in current in a neighbouring conductor; *self-~*, the reaction of a current in a circuit upon itself; *~-coil*, apparatus for producing electric currents by induction, consisting normally of a soft-iron core, surrounded by a coil of wire (the *primary coil*), which is in turn surrounded by a second and usu. much longer coil (the *secondary coil*); when the current in the primary coil is interrupted, a current of much higher voltage than the original one is induced in the secondary coil; by using very long coils enormous voltages suitable for producing X-rays and conducting many physical and other experiments can be induced. 4. (med.) Various procedures for bringing on birth or terminating pregnancy.

indŭc'tive *adj.* 1. (Of reasoning etc.) of, based on, induction. 2. Of electric or magnetic induction. **indŭc'tively** (-vl-) *adv.*

indŭc'tor *n.* 1. Person who inducts to an ecclesiastical benefice. 2. Part of electric apparatus which produces induction.

indŭlge' (-lj) *v.* Gratify (person, one*self*, *in* wish, matter, etc.); gratify (person *with* thing given); give free course to, entertain, (desire etc.); take one's pleasure freely *in*; partake (too) freely of intoxicants. **indŭl'gent** *adj.* **indŭl'gently** *adv.*

indŭl'gence *n.* 1. Indulging; (*self-*)~, habitual indulging of one's desires. 2. Privilege granted; R.C. Ch.) remission of temporal punishment still due for sins whose eternal punishment has been remitted by sacramental absolution; *Declaration of I~*, proclamation of certain religious liberties as special favours, but not as legal rights, esp. those of Charles II in 1672 and James II in 1687. **indŭl'genced** (-nst) *adj.* (R.C. Ch., of prayers, material objects, etc.) Procuring an indulgence to the user.

indŭlt' *n.* (R.C. Ch.) Pope's licence for thing not sanctioned by common law of Church.

in'dūrāte *v.* Make, become, hard; make callous or unfeeling; become inveterate. **indūrā'tion** *n.* (esp. geol.) Hardening of sedimentary rocks by heat or other process. **in'dūrative** *adj.*

In'dus (ĭ-). One of the 3 great rivers of the Indian peninsula, rising in Himalayas of W. Tibet, flowing NW. for some 600 miles, and then SW. through Pakistan to Arabian Sea.

indŭs'trial *adj.* Of industries; engaged in, connected with, industry; having highly developed industries; *I~ Revolution*, rapid development of industry through employment of machinery which took place in England in late 18th and early 19th c.; ~ *school*, (hist.) school where neglected or delinquent children were taught a trade besides ordinary subjects, since the Children and Young Persons Act of 1933 called an approved school; *I~ Workers of the World* (abbrev. I.W.W.), labour organization founded at Chicago in 1905, advocating syndicalism and international socialism. **indŭs'trially** *adv.* **indŭs'trialism, indŭs'trialist** *ns.* **indŭs'trialize** *v.t.*

indŭs'trious *adj.* Diligent, hard-working. **indŭs'triously** *adv.*

in'dustry *n.* 1. Diligence; exertion, effort; systematic work; habitual employment in useful work. 2. Branch of trade or manufacture, esp. one employing much labour and capital; manufacturing in general.

indwĕll *v.* Inhabit, occupy; be permanently present *in*.

Ine, Ina (ēn'*e*) (d. *c* 728). King of Wessex, remembered for code of Anglo-Saxon laws bearing his name.

inē'briate *adj.* Drunken. ~ *n.* Inebriate person, esp. habitual drunkard. **inē'briāte** *v.t.* Make drunk, intoxicate. **inēbriā'tion** *n.* **inēbrī'ėty** *n.* (Habit of) drunkenness.

inĕd'ible *adj.* Not edible. **inĕdibil'ity** *n.*

inĕd'itėd *adj.* Not published; published without editorial alterations.

inĕff'able *adj.* Unutterable, too great for words. **inĕff'ably** *adv.*

inėffāce'able (-s*a*bl) *adj.* That cannot be effaced. **inėffāceabil'ity** *n.* **inėffāce'ably** *adv.*

inėffĕc'tive *adj.* Not producing the desired effect; lacking artistic effect; (of person) inefficient. **inėffĕc'tively** *adv.* **inėffĕc'tiveness** *n.*

inėffĕc'tual *adj.* Without effect, fruitless. **inėffĕc'tūally** *adv.* **inėffĕc'tūalnėss** *n.*

inėffi'cient (-shnt) *adj.* Not fully capable, not well qualified; ineffective. **inėffic'iently** *adv.* **inėffi'ciency** *n.*

inėlăs'tic *adj.* Not elastic; unadaptable, unyielding. **inėlăsti'city** *n.*

inĕl'ėgant *adj.* Ungraceful; unrefined; unpolished. **inĕl'ėgantly** *adv.* **inĕl'ėgance** *n.*

inĕl'igible *adj.* Not eligible. **inĕligibil'ity** *n.* **inĕl'igibly** *adv.*

inėlŭc'table *adj.* That cannot be escaped from.

inĕpt' *adj.* Out of place; absurd, silly. **inĕpt'ly** *adv.* **inĕpt'nėss, inĕp'titūde** *ns.*

inėqual'ity (-kwŏl-) *n.* Want of equality in magnitude, quality, rank, etc.; variableness; (of surface) irregularity; (astron.) deviation from uniformity in motion of heavenly body.

inĕq'uitable *adj.* Unfair, unjust. **inĕq'uitably** *adv.* **inĕq'uity** *n.*

inėrăd'icable *adj.* That cannot be rooted out. **inėrăd'icably** *adv.*

inĕ'rrable *adj.* Not liable to err. **inĕrrabil'ity, inĕ'rrancy** *ns.* **inĕ'rrably** *adv.*

inērt' *adj.* Without inherent power of action, motion, or resistance; sluggish, slow; (chem., of gases) chemically inactive; esp., belonging to the group of gases comprising helium, neon, argon, krypton, xenon, and radon. **inērt'ly** *adv.* **inērt'nėss** *n.*

inēr'tia (-sh*ia*) *n.* 1. (physics) Property of matter by which it continues in its existing state of rest or uniform motion in a straight line unless that state is changed by an external force. 2. Inertness, sloth.

inėscăp'able *adj.* Not to be escaped.

in ĕs'sė. In actual existence.

inĕs'timable *adj.* Too great,

intense, precious, etc., to be estimated. **ĭnĕs'tĭmably** *adv.*

ĭnĕv'ĭtable *adj.* Unavoidable, sure to happen. **ĭnĕv'ĭtablenėss, ĭnĕvĭtabĭl'ĭty** *ns.* **ĭnĕv'ĭtably** *adv.*

ĭnexăct' (-gz-) *adj.* Not exact. **ĭnexăct'ly** *adv.* **ĭnexăct'nėss, ĭnėxăc'tĭtūde** *ns.*

ĭnėxcūs'able (-z-) *adj.* That cannot be justified. **ĭnėxcūs'ably** *adv.*

ĭnėxhaus'tĭble (-ĭgzaw-) *adj.* That cannot be exhausted. **ĭnėxhaustĭbĭl'ĭty** *n.* **ĭnėxhaus'tĭbly** *adv.*

ĭnĕx'orable *adj.* Relentless. **ĭnĕxorabĭl'ĭty** *n.* **ĭnĕx'orably** *adv.*

ĭnėxpē'dĭent *adj.* Not expedient. **ĭnėxpē'dĭency** *n.*

ĭnėxpėn'sĭve *adj.* Cheap. **ĭnėxpĕn'sĭvely** (-vl-) *adv.* **ĭnėxpĕnsĭvenėss** *n.*

ĭnėxpēr'ĭence *n.* Want of experience. **ĭnėxpēr'ĭenced** (-st) *adj.*

ĭnėxpērt' (*or* ĭnĕx'-) *adj.* Unskilled. **ĭnėxpērt'ly** *adv.*

ĭnĕx'pĭable *adj.* That cannot be expiated. **ĭnĕx'pĭably** *adv.*

ĭnĕx'plĭcable (*or* -plĭk'-) *adj.* That cannot be explained or accounted for. **ĭnėxplĭcabĭl'ĭty** *n.* **ĭnĕx'plĭcably** *adv.*

ĭnėxprĕss'ĭble *adj.* That cannot be expressed in words. **ĭnėxprĕss'ĭbly** *adv.*

ĭnėxpŭg'nable *adj.* Impregnable, invincible.

ĭn ėxtĕn'sō. At full length.

ĭnėxtĭng'uĭshable (-nggw-) *adj.* Unquenchable.

ĭn ėxtrēm'ĭs. At the point of death.

ĭnĕx'trĭcable (*or* -trĭk'-) *adj.* That cannot be unravelled or solved. **ĭnĕx'trĭcably** *adv.*

inf. *abbrev. Infra* (= below).

ĭnfăll'ĭbĭlism *n.* Principle of the pope's infallibility. **ĭnfăll'ĭbĭlist** *n.*

ĭnfăll'ĭble *adj.* Incapable of erring; unfailing. **ĭnfăll'ĭbly** *adv.* **ĭnfăllĭbĭl'ĭty** *n.* (esp. as attribute of the pope speaking *ex cathedra*, defined 1870 by Vatican Council).

ĭn'famous *adj.* Of ill fame, notoriously vile; abominable; (law) deprived of all or some rights of citizen on account of infamous crime. **ĭn'famously** *adv.* **ĭn'famy** *n.*

ĭn'fancy *n.* Early childhood, babyhood; (law) minority (to end of 21st year); early stage of development.

ĭn'fant *n.* Child during earliest period of life; child under 7 years of age; minor (under 21); ~ *school*, school for children, usu. under 7.

ĭnfăn'ta *n.* Daughter of king and queen of Spain or Portugal (usu. eldest daughter who is not heir to throne). ***ĭnfăn'tė*** *n.* Son (usu. 2nd son) of king and queen of Spain or Portugal who is not heir to throne.

ĭnfăn'tĭcīde *n.* 1. Murder of infant after birth, esp. with mother's consent; custom of killing newborn infants. 2. One who kills an infant. **ĭnfăntĭcīd'al** *adj.*

ĭn'fantīle *adj.* Of, as of, infants; in its infancy; childish, silly; ~ *paralysis*, (pop. but imprecise term for) acute anterior POLIOMYELITIS.

ĭnfăn'tĭlism *n.* Mentally or physically undeveloped state.

ĭn'fantīne *adj.* Pertaining to, of the nature of, infants.

ĭn'fantry *n*; Foot-soldiers; *ĭn'fantryman*, soldier of infantry regiment.

INFANTRY UNIFORMS: A. SERGEANT OF GRENADIER COMPANY OF THE LIVERPOOL REGIMENT, 1827. B. CORPORAL, LINE INFANTRY, 1813

1. Bearskin. 2. Coatee. 3. Wing. 4. Spontoon. 5. Shako. 6. Shoulder strap. 7. Spatterdashes

ĭn'fārct *n.* (path.) Area of dead tissue caused by the blocking of an artery which normally nourishes it.

ĭnfăt'ūāte *v.t.* Affect (person) with extreme folly; inspire with extravagant passion. **ĭnfăt'ūātėdly** *adv.* **ĭnfătūā'tion** *n.*

ĭnfĕct' *v.t.* Contaminate, pollute (air etc.); implant disease-forming micro-organisms in (person, animal, plant, etc., or environment); imbue (person *with* opinion etc.). **ĭnfĕc'tĭve** *adj.* **ĭnfĕc'tĭvenėss** *n.*

ĭnfĕc'tion *n.* Communication of disease; moral contamination; diffusive influence of example, sympathy, etc.

ĭnfĕc'tious (-sh*u*s) *adj.* Infecting with disease, pestilential; (of disease) such that the infecting agent can be communicated to the environment; (of emotions etc.) apt to spread, catching. **ĭnfĕc'tiously** *adv.* **ĭnfĕc'tiousnėss** *n.*

ĭnfėlĭ'cĭtous *adj.* Not felicitous. **ĭnfėlĭ'cĭty** *n.* Unhappiness; misfortune; inaptness of expression etc.

ĭnfēr' *v.t.* Deduce, conclude; imply.

ĭn'ference *n.* Inferring; esp., in logic, the forming of a conclusion from premisses either by induction or deduction; thing inferred. **ĭnferĕn'tial** (-shl) *adj.* **ĭnferĕn'tially** *adv.*

ĭnfēr'ĭor *adj.* 1. Situated below; (of planets etc.) whose orbit lies within that of the earth; (bot., of calyx) below ovary, (of ovary) below calyx; (print., of small letters or figures) placed lower than ordinary letters, e.g. H_2, C_n. 2. Lower in rank, quality, etc. (*to*); of poor quality. **ĭnfēr'ĭorly** *adv.* **ĭnfēr'ĭor** *n.* Person inferior to another, esp. in rank. **ĭnfērĭŏ'rĭty** *n.*; ~ *complex*, unconscious feeling of inferiority to others, freq. manifested in self-assertive behaviour; (pop.) sense of inferiority.

ĭnfērn'al *adj.* Of hell; hellish, fiendish; (colloq.) abominable, confounded; ~ *machine*, apparatus (usu. disguised) for producing explosion destructive of life or property. **ĭnfērn'ally** *adv.*

ĭnfērn'ō *n.* (pl. *-s*). Hell (*The I~*, first part of Dante's *Divine Comedy*); scene of horror.

ĭnfērt'īle *adj.* Not fertile. **ĭnfērtĭl'ĭty** *n.*

ĭnfĕst' *v.t.* Haunt, swarm in or about, (place). **ĭnfĕstā'tion** *n.*

ĭnfeudā'tion *n.* Enfeoffment; ~ *of tithes*, granting of tithes to laymen.

ĭn'fĭdel *n.* Disbeliever in religion; disbeliever in the true religion (esp. from Jewish or Mohammedan point of view); (hist.) adherent of religion opposed to Christianity; (gen.) unbeliever. ~ *adj.* Unbelieving; of unbelievers.

ĭnfĭdĕl'ĭty *n.* 1. Disbelief in Christianity. 2. Disloyalty, esp. to husband or wife.

ĭn'field *n.* 1. Farm land around or near homestead; arable land; land regularly manured and cropped. 2. (baseball) Part of field enclosed within baselines; the four fielders placed on boundaries of infield. **ĭn'fielder** *n.* (baseball) One of the infield. **ĭn'fieldsman** *n.* (cricket) One fielding close to wicket.

ĭn'-fīghtĭng (-fīt-) *n.* Boxing at closer quarters than arm's length.

ĭnfĭl'trāte *v.* Introduce (fluid) by filtration; permeate by filtration (also fig.). **ĭnfĭltrā'tion** *n.* (esp.) Gradual penetration into territory by small groups of settlers, or into enemy ground by small parties of troops; dissemination of ideas by small group working inside political party etc.

ĭn'fĭnĭte *adj.* Boundless, endless; very great; innumerable, very many; (math., of quantity or magnitude) greater than any assignable quantity or magnitude; (of series) that may be continued indefinitely without ever coming to an end. **ĭn'fĭnĭtely** (-tl-) *adv.*

ĭnfĭnĭtĕs'ĭmal *adj.* & *n.* Infinitely or very small (amount); ~ *calculus*, the differential and integral calculuses conceived as one. **ĭnfĭnĭtĕs'ĭmally** *adv.*

ĭnfĭn'ĭtĭve *adj.* & *n.* (gram.) (Verb-form) that expresses the verbal notion without predicating it of any subject (e.g. *see*, *to see*). **ĭnfĭnitĭv'al** *adj.*

ĭnfĭn'ĭtūde *n.* Infinity.

ĭnfĭn'ĭty *n.* Boundlessness; boundless number or extent; (math.) infinite quantity (symbol ∞).

ĭnfîrm' *adj.* Physically weak, esp. through age; (of person, mind, judgement, etc.) weak, irresolute. **ĭnfîrm'ly** *adv.* **ĭnfîrm'ĭty** *n.*

ĭnfîrm'ary *n.* Hospital; sick-quarters in school, workhouse, etc.

ĭnfĭx' *v.t.* Fix (thing *in* another); impress (fact etc. *in* mind); (gram.) insert (formative element) in body of word. **ĭn'fĭx** *n.* (gram.) Formative element inserted in body of word.

ĭn flăgrăn'tĕ dĕlĭc'to. In the very act of committing an offence.

ĭnflāme' *v.* 1. Set ablaze; catch fire; light up (as) with flame. 2. Excite passionately; become excited; aggravate. 3. Cause inflammation in (body etc.); become affected with inflammation.

ĭnflămm'able *adj.* Easily set on fire; easily excited. ~ *n.* (usu. pl.) Inflammable substance. **ĭnflămmabĭl'ĭty** *n.*

ĭnflammā'tion *n.* Inflaming; condition of living tissue marked by heat, swelling, redness, and usu. pain, arising from the action taken by the organism to repair damaged tissues or destroy or remove invading organisms; the normal response of healthy tissue to damage or infection.

ĭnflămm'atory *adj.* Tending to inflame with desire or passion; of, tending to, inflammation of the body.

ĭnflāte' *v.t.* Distend with air or gas; puff up (*with* pride etc.); resort to inflation of (currency); raise (price) artificially; *inflated*, (of language) bombastic.

ĭnflā'tion *n.* Inflating; (econ.) inordinate rise in prices; (formerly) inordinate increase in the supply of money regarded as the cause of such a rise. **ĭnflā'tionary** (-sho-) *adj.*

ĭnflĕct' *v.t.* 1. Bend inwards, curve. 2. (gram.) Vary termination of (word) to express grammatical relation. 3. Modulate (voice etc.); (mus.) flatten, sharpen (notes). **ĭnflĕc'tion** *n.* = INFLEXION. **ĭnflĕ'ctive** *adj.* Of, characterized by, inflexion.

ĭnflĕx'ĭble *adj.* Unbendable; (fig.) unbending, rigid. **ĭnflĕxĭbĭl'ĭty** *n.* **ĭnflĕx'ĭbly** *adv.*

ĭnflĕx'ion (-kshon) *n.* 1. Inflecting, bending; (geom.) change of curvature from convex to concave or conversely. 2. Modification of word to express grammatical relationship; inflected form of word; inflexional suffix or element. 3. Modulation of voice; change in pitch or tone. **ĭnflĕx'ional** (-kshon-) *adj.*

ĭnflĭct' *v.t.* Lay on (stroke, wound, *upon*); impose (suffering, penalty, etc., *upon*). **ĭnflĭc'tion** *n.*

ĭnflorĕs'cence *n.* (bot.) Arrangement of flowers of plant in relation to axis and to each other; collective flower of plant; flowering.

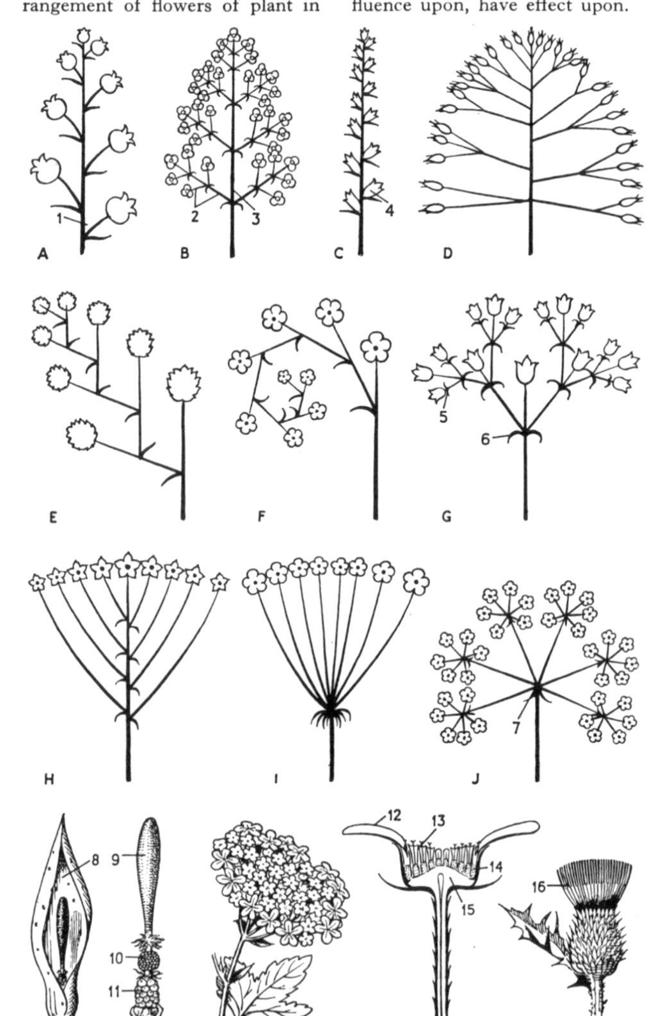

INFLORESCENCES. A. SIMPLE RACEME. B. COMPOUND RACEME. C. RACEMOSE SPIKE. D. RACEMOSE PANICLE. E, F, G. CYMES. H. RACEMOSE CORYMB. I. CYMOSE CORYMB AND SIMPLE UMBEL. J. COMPOUND UMBEL. K. WILD ARUM. L. ANDROGYNOUS FLOWER (GUELDER ROSE). M, N. COMPOSITE FLOWERS (M. SECTION OF DAISY, N. THISTLE)

1. Axil. 2. Pedicel. 3. Peduncle. 4. Sessile flower. 5. Bracteole. 6. Bract. 7. Involucre. 8. Spathe. 9. Spadix. 10. Male flowers. 11. Female flowers. 12–15. Capitulum (12. Ligulate ray florets. 13. Disc florets. 14. Ovary. 15. Receptacle). 16. Tubular florets

ĭn'flow (-ō) *n.* Flowing in.

ĭn'fluence (-lo͞o-) *n.* 1. Action insensibly exercised (*upon*); ascendancy, moral power (*over*, *with*); thing, person, exercising (usu. non-material) power. 2. (astrol.) Supposed flowing from stars of ethereal fluid affecting character and destiny of man. ~ *v.t.* Exert influence upon, have effect upon.

ĭn'fluent (-lo͞o-) *adj.* Flowing in. ~ *n.* Tributary stream.

ĭnfluĕn'tial (-lo͞oĕn'shal) *adj.* Having great influence. **ĭnfluĕn'tially** *adv.*

ĭnfluĕn'za (-lo͞o-) *n.* Infectious febrile disorder, caused by a virus, with rapid prostration and severe catarrh, occurring usu. in widespread epidemics.

ĭn'flŭx *n.* Flowing in, esp. of persons or things (*into* place etc.).

infôrm' *v.* 1. Inspire, imbue (person, thing, *with* quality, principle, etc.). 2. Tell (person *of* thing, *that*, *how*, etc.). 3. Bring charge (*against*). **infôrm'ant** *n.* (esp.) One who tells or gives information.

infôrm'al *adj.* Not according to due form; without formality. **infôrm'ally** *adv.* **informăl'ity** *n.*

in fôrm'a paup'erĭs. As a poor person not liable to costs.

informā'tion *n.* 1. Informing, telling; thing told, knowledge, items of knowledge, news. 2. (law) Charge, complaint, lodged with court or magistrate (*against*). **informā'tional** (-shon-) *adj.*

infôrm'ative *adj.* Giving information, instructive. **infôrm'atory** *adj.*; ~ *double*, (bridge) double meant only to give information to partner.

infôrmed' (-md) *adj.* Instructed, knowing the facts, educated, intelligent.

infôrm'er *n.* One who informs against another; *common* ~, one who detects offenders and lays information against them for reward.

ĭn'fra *adv.* Below, lower down, farther on (in book).

infra- *prefix.* Below.

infrăc'tion *n.* Infringement, violation.

infra dĭg. *pred. adj.* Beneath one's dignity, unbecoming. [abbrev. L *infra dignitatem*]

infralăpsār'ian *n.* Calvinist who held that God's election of some was consequent to his prescience of the Fall, or that it contemplated man as already fallen. ~ *adj.* Of, holding, these views.

infrăn'gĭble *adj.* Unbreakable; inviolable.

ĭn'fra-rĕd' *adj.* (physics) Situated below or beyond the red in the spectrum of ordinary light; ~ *rays*, heat rays, electro-magnetic radiations which, having a wavelength longer than that of red light, are invisible, but can be detected by photographic and other means and can penetrate haze and fog.

infra-rēn'al *adj.* Below the kidneys.

infra-scăp'ūlar *adj.* Below the shoulder-blade.

infra-stĕrn'al *adj.* Below the breast-bone.

ĭn'frastrŭcture *n.* Collective term for the fixed installations necessary to support military operations, as airfields, naval bases, training establishments, supply works, etc.

infrē'quent *adj.* Not frequent. **infrē'quently** *adv.* **infrē'quency** *n.*

infrĭnge' (-j) *v.t.* Transgress, violate (law, oath, etc.). **infrĭnge'ment** (-jm-) *n.*

infŭndĭb'ūlar *adj.* Funnel-shaped.

infŭndĭb'ūlum *n.* (anat.) Funnel-shaped cavity or structure.

infūr'iāte *v.t.* Fill with fury, enrage.

infūse'(-z) *v.* 1. Pour (*into*); instil (*into*). 2. Steep (herb etc.) in liquid to extract its soluble properties; undergo infusion.

infūs'ĭble (-z-) *adj.* That cannot be fused or melted. **infūsĭbĭl'ĭty** *n.*

infū'sion (-zhn) *n.* Infusing; liquid extract thus obtained; infused element, admixture.

infūsôr'ia *n.pl.* 1. (obs.) General name for minute animals found in infusions of decaying organic matter. 2. A class of Protozoa (now more commonly termed Ciliata). **infūsôr'ial** *adj.* **infūsôr'ian, infūs'ory** *adjs.* & *ns.*

ingĕm'ināte (-j-) *v.t.* Repeat, reiterate.

ingēn'ious (-j-) *adj.* Clever at contriving; cleverly contrived. **ingēn'iously** *adv.* **ingēn'iousnėss** *n.*

ingénue (ăṅzhānū'), *n.* Artless girl, esp. of the type represented on the stage.

ingėnū'ĭty *n.* Skill in contriving.

ingĕn'ūous (-j-) *adj.* Open, frank; innocent, artless. **ingĕn'ūously** *adv.* **ingĕn'ūousnėss** *n.*

ingĕst' (-j-) *v.t.* Take in (food) to the stomach. **ingĕs'tion** (-schon) *n.* **ingĕs'tive** *adj.*

ingle (ing'gl) *n.* Fire burning on hearth. ~*-nook*, chimney-corner.

inglôr'ious (ĭn-g-) *adj.* Shameful, ignominious; obscure. **inglôr'iously** *adv.*

ĭng'ot (-ngg-) *n.* Mass (usu. oblong) of cast metal, esp. of gold, silver, or steel.

ingrain (ĭn'-grān *before n.*, ĭn-grān' *after n. or in predicate*) *adj.* Dyed in grain; inherent, inveterate, thorough; ~ *carpet*, reversible carpet without pile, in which two or more cloths of different colours are interwoven to form pattern.

ingrained (ĭn'-grānd *before n.*, -ānd' *elsewhere*) *adj.* Deeply rooted, inveterate; thorough.

ingrāte' (ĭn-g-) *adj.* & *n.* (archaic) Ungrateful (person).

ingratiāte (ĭn-grā'shĭ-) *v.t.* Bring one*self* into favour *with*.

ingrăt'ĭtūde (ĭn-g-) *n.* Want of gratitude.

ingrēd'ient (ĭn-g-) *n.* Component part, element, in a mixture.

Ingres (ăṅgr), Jean Auguste Dominique (1781–1867). French classical painter.

in'grĕss (ĭn-g-) *n.* Going in; right of entrance.

in'growing (ĭn-grōĭ-) *adj.* Growing inwards, esp. (of nail) growing into the flesh.

ing'uinal (-nggw-) *adj.* Of the groin.

ingûr'gĭtāte (ĭn-g-) *v.t.* Swallow greedily. **ingûrgĭtā'tion** *n.*

inhăb'ĭt *v.t.* Dwell in, occupy (region, town, house, etc.). **inhăb'ĭtant** *n.*

inhăb'ĭtancy *n.* Residence as inhabitant, esp. during specified period, so as to acquire rights etc.

inhāl'ant *n.* (esp.) Medicinal preparation for inhaling.

inhāle' *v.t.* Breathe in (air, gas, etc.); take (esp. tobacco-smoke) into the lungs. **inhalā'tion** *n.*

inhāl'er *n.* (esp.) Apparatus for introducing medicated liquids or vapours into breathing passages, or for administering anaesthetic.

inharmŏn'ic *adj.* (mus.) Not forming part of a HARMONIC series.

inharmōn'ious *adj.* Not harmonious. **inharmōn'iously** *adv.*

inhēre' *v.i.* (Of qualities etc.) exist, abide, *in*; (of rights etc.) be vested *in*. **inhēr'ence** *n.* **inhēr'ent** *adj.* **inhēr'ently** *adv.*

inhĕ'rĭt *v.t.* Receive by legal descent or succession; derive (quality etc.) from one's progenitors; (abs.) succeed as heir. **inhĕ'rĭtance** *n.* Inheriting; what is inherited. **inhĕ'rĭtor, inhĕ'rĭtrėss, inhĕ'rĭtrix** *ns.*

inhē'sion (-zhn) *n.* Inhering.

inhĭb'ĭt *v.t.* Hinder, restrain (action, process); forbid, prohibit (*from*; esp. in eccles. law); forbid (ecclesiastic to exercise clerical functions). **inhĭbĭ'tion** *n.* (esp., psychol.) Blocking of thought or action by emotional resistance.

inhĭb'ĭtor *n.* Thing that inhibits; (physiol.) substance which represses a normal physiological process or antagonizes an abnormal one; nerve which inhibits; (chem.) substance which slows down or suppresses a chemical change; negative catalyst. **inhĭb'ĭtory** *adj.*

inhŏs'pĭtable *adj.* Not hospitable; (of region etc.) not affording shelter etc. **inhŏs'pĭtably** *adv.* **inhŏs'pĭtablenėss, inhŏspĭtăl'ĭty** *ns.*

inhūm'an *adj.* Brutal, unfeeling, barbarous; not of the ordinary human type. **inhūm'anly** *adv.* **inhūmăn'ĭty** *n.*

inhūme' *v.t.* Bury. **inhūmā'tion** *n.*

inĭm'ĭcal *adj.* Hostile; harmful. **inĭm'ĭcally** *adv.*

inĭm'ĭtable *adj.* That defies imitation. **inĭm'ĭtablenėss** *n.* **inĭm'ĭtably** *adv.*

inĭq'uĭty *n.* Unrighteousness, wickedness; gross injustice. **inĭq'uĭtous** *adj.* **inĭq'uĭtously** *adv.*

Inisfail' (ĭ-). (Poetical name of) Ireland.

inĭ'tial (-shl) *adj.* Of, existing or occurring at, the beginning; ~ *letter*, letter standing at beginning of word. **inĭ'tially** *adv.* **inĭ'tial** *n.* (esp. pl.) First letter(s) of person's name and surname. ~ *v.t.* Mark, sign, with initials.

inĭ'tiāte (-shĭ-) *v.t.* 1. Begin, set going, originate. 2. Admit (person), esp. with introductory rites or forms (*into* society, office, secret, *in* mysteries, science, etc.). **initiā'tion** *n.* **inĭ'tiatory** *adj.* **inĭ'tiate** (-shĭat) *adj.* & *n.* (Person) who has been initiated.

inĭ'tiative (-shya-) *n.* First step,

origination; power, right, or function of originating something; esp., right of citizen(s) outside legislature to initiate legislation (as in Switzerland); *take the* ~, take the lead. ~ *adj.* Beginning, originating.

injĕct' *v.t.* Drive, force (fluid, medicine, *into* cavity etc.) as by syringe; fill (cavity etc.) by injecting.

injĕc'tion *n.* Injecting; liquid or solution injected.

injudi'cious (-jōōdĭsh'*us*) *adj.* Unwise, ill-judged. **injudi'ciously** *adv.* **injudi'ciousness** *n.*

In'jun *n.* Colloq. and dial. U.S. form of INDIAN 2; *honest* ~, honour bright.

injŭnc'tion *n.* Authoritative admonition or order; judicial process restraining person from wrongful act, or compelling restitution etc. to injured party.

in'jure (-*jer*) *v.t.* Do wrong to; hurt, harm, impair. **in'jured** (-*jerd*) *adj.* Wronged; hurt; showing sense of wrong, offended.

injur'ious (-oor-) *adj.* Wrongful; (of language) insulting, calumnious; hurtful. **injur'iously** *adv.* **injur'iousness** *n.*

in'jury *n.* Wrongful action or treatment; harm, damage.

injŭs'tice *n.* Want of equity, unfairness; unjust act.

ink *n.* 1. Coloured (usu. black or blue-black) fluid used for writing with pen on paper etc. or for printing; writing-inks are fluids containing a colouring matter (in the modern blue-black ink, iron gallate) in suspension (see also COPYING, INDIAN, ink); printer's inks are pigments of various colours mixed with oil or varnish, the ordinary black variety being made from carbon blacks and usu. linseed oil. 2. Black inky liquid secreted by cuttle-fish etc. and ejected to cloud water and assist escape. 3. *~-horn*, small vessel of horn formerly used for holding writing-ink; *ink'pot*, small pot for holding writing-ink; *~-slinger*, (contempt.) professional writer, esp. reckless writer in newspapers; *ink'stand*, stand for one or more ink bottles or inkpots; *~-well*, inkpot fitted into hole in desk. ~ *v.t.* Mark (*in*, *over*, etc.) with ink; cover (types) with ink. **ink'y** *adj.*

Ink'erman (ĭ-). Battle (5th Nov. 1854) of Crimean War, in which part of the allied British and French armies repulsed, with heavy losses, an attack by the Russian army.

ink'ling *n.* Hint, slight knowledge or suspicion, (*of*).

in'land *n.* Interior of country. ~ *adj.* Placed in interior of country, remote from sea or border; carried on within limits of a country; ~ *revenue*, part of national revenue consisting of taxes and of duties on inland trade. **inlănd'** *adv.* In, towards, the interior.

in-law' *n.* (colloq.) Relative by marriage.

inlay' *v.t.* (past t. and past part. *inlaid*). Embed (thing *in* another) so that their surfaces are even; ornament (thing) with another inlaid; mount (illustration or damaged leaf of book) in larger sheet so that both sides are visible. **in'lay** (*or* inlay') *n.* Inlaid ornament, esp. furniture or woodwork.

in'lĕt *n.* 1. Way of admission, entrance. 2. Small arm of sea, creek.

in'lier *n.* (geol.) Outcrop of older strata within a girdle of younger ones (opp. to OUTLIER).

in lŏc'ō parĕn'tĭs. In place of a parent.

in'lў *adv.* (poet.) Inwardly, in the heart; intimately.

in'māte *n.* Occupant (*of* house, institution, etc.), esp. along with others.

in mĕd'ĭās rēs. Into the midst of things; into the middle of a narrative.

in mĕmŏr'ĭăm. In memory of.

in'mōst *adj.* Most inward.

inn *n.* 1. Public house for lodging etc. of travellers; *inn'-keeper*, one who keeps an inn. 2. *Inns of Chancery*, buildings in London formerly used for residence of law students; societies occupying these; *Inns of Court*, buildings in London belonging to 4 legal societies (Inner Temple, Middle Temple, Lincoln's Inn, Gray's Inn); these societies, which have the exclusive right of admitting persons to practise at the English bar.

innāte' (*or* in'-) *adj.* Inborn, natural. **innāte'ly** (-tl-) *adv.* **innāte'ness** *n.*

innăv'igable *adj.* Not navigable.

inn'er *adj.* Interior, internal; *the* ~ *man*, man's soul or mind; (joc.) stomach; ~ *reserve*, secret reserve not disclosed in a balance-sheet; *I~ Temple*: see INN 2; ~ *tube*, separate inflatable rubber tube inside cover of a pneumatic tyre. **inn'ermōst** *adj.* **inn'er** *n.* Division of target next outside bull's-eye, shot that strikes this.

innĕrv'āte *v.t.* (physiol.) Connect (muscle, organ) to nervous system, supply it with nerve-fibre. **innĕrvā'tion** *n.*

inn'ing (U.S.), **inn'ings** *n.* (cricket, baseball, etc.) Portion of game played by either side while 'in' or batting, play of one batsman during his turn (also freq. fig.).

inn'ocent[1] *adj.* Free from moral wrong, sinless; not guilty (*of* crime etc.); simple, guileless; harmless. **inn'ocently** *adv.* **inn'ocent** *n.* Innocent person, esp. young child; simple person; idiot; (*Holy*) *Innocents' Day*, 28th Dec., observed as church festival in commemoration of Slaughter of the Innocents by Herod (Matt. ii. 16). **inn'ocence, inn'ocency** *ns.*

Inn'ocent[2] (ĭ-). Name of 13 popes; *Innocent III*, pope 1198–1216; champion of supremacy of spiritual over temporal authority; proclaimer of 4th crusade and initiator of 'crusades' against ALBIGENSES; he excommunicated King John of England (1209) when John refused to acknowledge his nomination of Stephen Langton as archbishop of Canterbury, but after signing of Magna Carta he supported John against the barons; *Innocent IV*, pope 1243–54; canon lawyer, extreme supporter of papal claims to temporal authority; first bestower of red hat on Roman cardinals.

innŏc'ūous *adj.* Not injurious, harmless. **innŏc'ūously** *adv.* **innŏc'ūousness, innocū'ity** *ns.*

innŏm'inate (-*a*t) *adj.* Unnamed; (anat.) ~ *bone*, hip-bone, a union of three original bones (ilium, ischium, and pubis).

inn'ovāte *v.i.* Bring in novelties; make changes *in.* **innovā'tion, inn'ovātor** *ns.* **inn'ovātory** *adj.*

in nū'bĭbus. In the clouds, vague, speculative.

innūĕn'dō *n.* Oblique hint, insinuation, allusive remark (usu. depreciatory). ~ *v.i.* Make innuendoes. [L, = 'by nodding at, pointing at, meaning' (*innuere* nod at, mean)].

innŭm'erable *adj.* Countless.

inŏc'ūlāte *v.t.* Impregnate (person or animal) *with* agent of disease to induce milder form of it and so safeguard against further attacks. **inŏcūlā'tion** *n.* **inŏc'ūlative** *adj.*

inōd'orous *adj.* Having no odour.

inoffĕn'sive *adj.* Unoffending; not objectionable. **inoffĕn'sively** (-vl-) *adv.* **inoffĕn'siveness** *n.*

inoffi'cious (-sh*us*) *adj.* Without office or function; (law) not in accordance with moral duty.

inŏp'erable *adj.* That cannot be operated; not curable by operation.

inŏp'erative *adj.* Not working or taking effect.

inŏpp'ortūne *adj.* Unseasonable, untimely, tactless. **inŏpp'ortūnely** (-nl-) *adv.* **inŏpp'ortūneness** *n.*

inŏrd'inate *adj.* Immoderate, excessive; intemperate; disorderly. **inŏrd'inately** (-tl-) *adv.*

inŏrgăn'ic *adj.* 1. Having no organized physical structure; not existing by natural growth, extraneous. 2. (chem.) Belonging to any class of substance other than ORGANIC compounds; ~ *chemistry*, the chemistry of the elements other than carbon, and their compounds.

inŏs'cūlāte *v.* (Of blood-vessels etc.) join, have terminal connexion (*with*); (of fibres etc.) unite closely, be interwoven; unite (fibres etc.) closely. **inŏscūlā'tion** *n.*

in părt'ĭbus (infĭdēl'ĭum). (Of R.C. titular bishop) in a heretical country.

in pŏs'sĕ. Potentially.

in prŏp'rĭa persōn'a. In his (her) own person.

in pūr'ĭs nătūrăl'ĭbus. Stark naked.

ĭn'quĕst *n.* Legal or judicial inquiry to ascertain matter of fact; (*coroner's*) *inquest*, inquiry held by coroner's court to ascertain cause of person's death; (also fig.).

inquī'ėtūde (ĭn-kw-) *n.* Uneasiness of mind or body.

inquīre', en- (ĭn-kw-) *v.* Make search (*into* matter); seek information (*of* person, *about*, *after*, thing etc.); ask *for* (person, goods in shop, etc.), ask to be told. **inquīr'ĭngly** *adv.*

inquīr'y, en- (ĭn-kw-) *n.* Asking; question; investigation; *court of* ~, (mil.) investigation of charge against officer or soldier.

inquisĭ'tion (ĭn-kwĭz-) *n.* 1. Search, investigation; judicial or official inquiry. 2. (R.C. Ch.) Ecclesiastical tribunal (the *Holy Office*) set up in 13th c. under Innocent III for the suppression of heresy and punishment of heretics, notorious esp. in Spain in 16th c. for its severities. **inquisĭ'tional** (-shon-) *adj.*

inquĭs'ĭtive (ĭn-kwĭz-) *adj.* Inquiring, curious; prying. **inquĭs'ĭtively** (-vl-) *adv.* **inquĭs'ĭtivenėss** *n.*

inquĭs'ĭtor (ĭn-kwĭz-) *n.* Official investigator; officer of the Inquisition; *Grand I*~, director of court of Inquisition in some countries; *I~ General*, head of Inquisition in Spain.

inquisĭtōr'ial (ĭn-kwĭz-) *adj.* Of, like, an inquisitor; offensively prying. **inquisĭtōr'ially** *adv.*

I.N.R.I. *abbrev. Iesus Nazarenus Rex Iudaeorum* (= Jesus of Nazareth, King of the Jews).

ĭn'road *n.* Hostile incursion, raid; (fig.) forcible encroachment.

ĭn'rŭsh *n.* Rushing in.

insăl'ivāte *v.t.* Mix (food) with saliva. **insălivā'tion** *n.*

insalub'rious (-lōō-) *adj.* (Of climate etc.) unhealthy. **insalub'rĭty** *n.*

ĭnsāne' *adj.* Mad; senseless. **ĭnsāne'ly** (-nl-) *adv.* **ĭnsăn'ĭty** *n.*

ĭnsăn'ĭtary *adj.* Not sanitary.

ĭnsā'tiable (-sha-) *adj.* That cannot be satisfied; inordinately greedy. **ĭnsātiabĭl'ĭty** *n.* **ĭnsā'tiably** *adv.*

ĭnsā'tiate (-shyat) *adj.* Never satisfied.

ĭnscrībe' *v.t.* 1. Write (words etc. *in*, *on*); enter name of (person) on list; mark (sheet, tablet, etc. *with* characters); (esp. in past part.) issue (loan) in form of shares with registered holders. 2. (geom.) Trace (figure) within another so that some particular points of it lie on the boundary of that other (ill. CIRCLE).

ĭnscrĭp'tion *n.* Words inscribed, esp. on monument, coin, etc.; inscribing (*of* loan).

ĭnscrut'able (-ōō-) *adj.* That cannot be penetrated, wholly mysterious. **ĭnscrut'ablenėss, ĭnscrutabĭl'ĭty** *ns.* **ĭnscrut'ably** *adv.*

ĭn'sĕct *n.* (pop.) Small animal with body divided into segments; (zool.) arthropod of the class *Insecta* which breathe through tracheae and have a body divided into 3 regions (head, thorax, and abdomen) and usu., in the adult, 3 pairs of legs and 2 pairs of wings; (fig.) insignificant or contemptible person or creature.

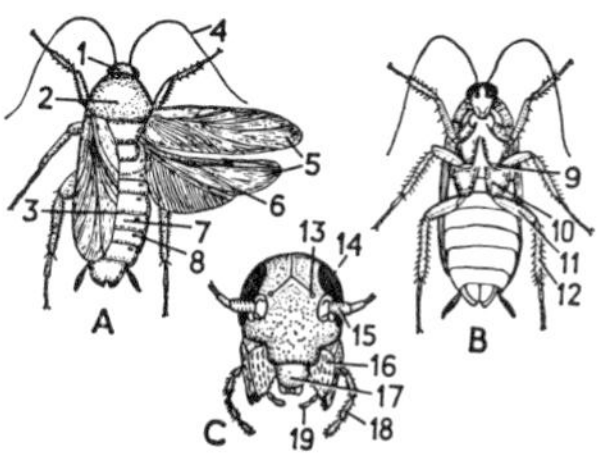

INSECT (COCKROACH): A. DORSAL VIEW. B. VENTRAL VIEW. C. HEAD

1. Head. 2. Thorax. 3. Abdomen. 4. Antenna. 5. Wings. 6. Veins or nervures. 7. Segment. 8. Spiracle. 9. Trochanter. 10. Coxa. 11. Femur. 12. Tarsus. 13. Ocellus. 14. Compound eye. 15. Scape. 16. Mandible. 17. Labrum. 18. Maxillary palp. 19. Labial palp

ĭnsĕc'tĭcīde *n.* Insect-killer, esp. preparation used for killing insects. **ĭnsĕctĭcī'dal** *adj.*

Insĕctĭv'ora *n.pl.* An order of primitive mammals, most members of which (e.g. shrew, hedgehog) feed on insects. **ĭnsĕc'tĭvōre** *n.* Insect-eating animal; member of the *Insectivora*. **ĭnsĕctĭv'orous** *adj.* Insect-eating; (of plant) having special structures for trapping and digesting insects.

ĭnsĕctŏl'ogy *n.* (now rare) Study of insects, entomology.

ĭnsėcūre' *adj.* Unsafe; (of ice, ground, etc.) liable to give way. **ĭnsėcūre'ly** (-ūrl-) *adv.* **ĭnsėcūr'ĭty** *n.*

ĭnsĕm'ĭnāte *v.t.* Sow (seed etc.) *in* (lit. and fig.); (biol.) introduce spermatozoa into female reproductive system, or into the eggs of those animals (e.g. frogs) which fertilize externally. **ĭnsĕmĭnā'tion** *n.*

ĭnsĕn'sate *adj.* Without sensibility, unfeeling; stupid; mad; without physical sensation. **ĭnsĕn'sately** (-tl-) *adv.*

ĭnsĕnsĭbĭl'ĭty *n.* Lack of mental feeling or emotion; indifference (*to*); unconsciousness, swoon.

ĭnsĕn'sĭble *adj.* Too small or gradual to be perceived; inappreciable; unconscious; unaware. **ĭnsĕn'sĭbly** *adv.*

ĭnsĕn'sĭtive *adj.* Not sensitive (*to*); emotionless, callous. **ĭnsĕn'sĭtivenėss** *n.*

ĭnsĕn'tient (-shĭ-) *adj.* Inanimate.

ĭnsĕp'arable *adj.* That cannot be separated; ~ *prefix*, (gram.) prefix found only in combination and incapable of being used as separate word. **ĭnsĕparabĭl'ĭty** *n.* **ĭnsĕp'arably** *adv.*

ĭnsĕrt' *v.t.* Place, fit, thrust, (thing *in*, *into*, another etc.); introduce (letter, article, etc., *in*, *into*, written matter, newspaper, etc.); hence **ĭn'sĕrt** *n.* **ĭnsĕr'tion** *n.* Inserting; thing inserted, esp. in writing or print; ornamental needlework etc. inserted into plain material; (anat.) place or manner of attachment of muscle, organ, etc.

ĭn'sĕt *n.* Extra page(s) inserted in sheet or book; small map etc. inserted within border of larger; piece let into dress; pair of white strips worn as edging to waistcoat opening. **ĭnsĕt'** *v.t.* Put in as an inset.

ĭn'shōre' *adv.* & *adj.* Close to shore; ~ *of*, nearer to shore than.

ĭnsīde *n.* 1. (ĭn'sīd') Inner side or surface; (of path) side next to wall or away from road; inner part, interior. 2. (insīd') Stomach and bowels (colloq.); *the* ~ (middle part) *of a week*; *in'side out*, so that inner side becomes outer. ~ *adj.* (ĭn'sīd) Situated on or in, derived from, the inside; ~ *information*, information not accessible to outsiders. ~ *adv.* (insīd') On or in or to the inside; ~ *of* (colloq.) in less time than. ~ *prep.* (ĭn'sīd) On or to the inner side of, within.

ĭnsīd'er *n.* One who is in some society, organization, etc.; one who is in the secret.

ĭnsĭd'ious *adj.* Treacherous, crafty; proceeding secretly or subtly. **ĭnsĭd'iously** *adv.* **ĭnsĭd'iousnėss** *n.*

ĭn'sight (-īt) *n.* Penetration (*into* character, circumstances, etc.) with the understanding.

ĭnsĭg'nĭa *n.pl.* Badges, distinguishing marks (*of* office, honour, etc.).

ĭnsĭgnĭf'ĭcant *adj.* Unimportant, trifling; contemptible; meaningless. **ĭnsĭgnĭf'ĭcantly, ĭnsĭgnĭf'ĭcance** *ns.*

ĭnsĭncēre' *adj.* Not sincere, disingenuous. **ĭnsĭncēre'ly** *adv.* **ĭnsĭncĕ'rĭty** *n.*

ĭnsĭn'ūāte *v.t.* Introduce gradually or subtly; convey indirectly, hint obliquely. **ĭnsĭn'ūātĭngly** *adv.* **ĭnsĭnūā'tion, ĭnsĭn'ūātor** *ns.* **ĭnsĭn'ūative** *adj.*

ĭnsĭp'ĭd *adj.* Tasteless; wanting in flavour; lifeless, dull, uninteresting. **ĭnsĭp'ĭdly** *adv.* **ĭnsĭp'ĭdnėss, ĭnsĭpĭd'ĭty** *ns.*

ĭnsĭst' *v.* Dwell long or emphatically (*on*); maintain positively; make a stand *on* as essential. **ĭnsĭs'tence, ĭnsĭs'tency** *ns.* **ĭnsĭs'tent** *adj.* **ĭnsĭs'tently** *adv.*

ĭn sĭt'ū. In its (original) place.

ĭnsobrī'ėty *n.* Intemperance, esp. in drinking.

ĭnsolā'tion *n.* Exposure to sun's rays (for purpose of bleaching etc., or as medical treatment, or as cause of disease); (geol.) flaking of rock when exposure to sun alternates with rapid cooling at night.

ĭn'sōle *n.* 1. Inner sole of boot

or shoe (ill. SHOE). 2. Flat piece of material worn inside shoe for warmth or comfort.

ĭn'solent *adj.* Offensively contemptuous, insulting. **ĭn'solently** *adv.* **ĭn'solence** *n.*

ĭnsŏl'ūble *adj.* 1. That cannot be solved. 2. That cannot be dissolved. **ĭnsŏl'ūbleness, ĭnsŏlūbĭl'ity** *ns.* **ĭnsŏl'ūbly** *adv.*

ĭnsŏl'vent *adj.* & *n.* (Debtor) unable to pay debts. **ĭnsŏl'vency** *n.*

ĭnsŏm'nĭa *n.* Sleeplessness.

ĭnsomŭch' *adv.* To such an extent *that.*

ĭnsou'cĭant (-sōō-) *adj.* Careless, unconcerned. **ĭnsou'cĭance** *n.*

ĭnspăn' *v.t.* (S. Afr.) Yoke (oxen etc.) in team to vehicle; harness (wagon).

ĭnspĕct' *v.t.* Look closely into; examine officially. **ĭnspĕc'tion** *n.*

ĭnspĕc'tor *n.* (esp.) Police officer ranking next below superintendent; *I~ General,* (esp.) head of U.S. military department concerned with discipline, supply, accounts, etc. **ĭnspĕc'toral, ĭnspĕctōr'ial** *adjs.* **ĭnspĕc'torshĭp** *n.*

ĭnspĕc'torate *n.* Office of inspector; body of inspectors; district under inspector.

ĭnspĭrā'tion *n.* 1. Drawing in of breath. 2. Inspiring; divine influence, esp. that under which books of Scripture are supposed to have been written, whether *verbal* ~ (dictating every word), *plenary* ~ (covering all subjects treated), or *moral* ~ (confined to moral and religious teaching). 3. Thought etc. inspired, prompting; sudden happy idea. 4. Inspiring principle. **ĭnspĭrā'tional** (-shon-) *adj.*

ĭnspīre' *v.t.* 1. Breathe in, inhale. 2. Infuse thought or feeling into (person); animate (person etc. *with* feeling); infuse (feeling *into* person etc.), create (feeling *in*); suggest or prompt expression of a particular opinion etc., prompt writer or speaker to such expression. **ĭnspīr'atory** *adj.*

ĭnspĭ'rĭt *v.t.* Put life into, animate; encourage.

ĭnspĭss'āte (*or* in'-) *v.t.* Thicken, condense. **ĭnspĭssā'tion** *n.*

inst. *abbrev.* Instant (= of the current month).

ĭnstabĭl'ĭty *n.* Lack of stability.

ĭnstall' (-awl) *v.t.* Place (person *in* office or dignity) with ceremonies; establish (*in* place, condition, etc.); place (apparatus) in position for use. **ĭnstallā'tion** *n.* (Ceremony of) installing; apparatus installed.

ĭnstal'ment (-awl-) *n.* Each of several parts, successively falling due, of a sum payable; each of several parts supplied etc. at different times; part of serial story printed in one issue.

ĭn'stance *n.* Fact illustrating a general truth, example; particular case; (law) process, suit; *for* ~, for example; *at the* ~ *of,* at the request or suggestion of; *court of first* ~, court of primary jurisdiction; *in the first* ~, in the first place, at the first stage of a proceeding. ~ *v.t.* Cite as an instance; (usu. pass.) exemplify.

ĭn'stancy *n.* Urgency.

ĭn'stant[1] *adj.* 1. Urgent, pressing. 2. Immediate; (abbrev. *inst.*) of the current calendar month.

ĭn'stant[2] *n.* Precise (esp. the present) point of time, moment; short space of time, moment. **ĭn'stantly** *adv.* At once.

ĭnstantān'ėous *adj.* Occurring, done, in an instant; immediate; existing at a particular instant. **ĭnstantān'ėously** *adv.* **ĭnstantān'ėousnėss** *n.*

ĭnstăn'ter *adv.* (now usu. joc.) Immediately, at once.

ĭn'stār *n.* (zool.) Stage in life-history of certain animals, esp. arthropods, between successive moultings of the cuticle.

ĭn stăt'ū pūpĭllăr'ī. Under guardianship; under scholastic discipline; (of member of a university) not having the degree of Master.

ĭn stăt'ū quō. In the same state (as formerly).

ĭnstaurā'tion *n.* Restoration, renewal.

ĭnstead' (-ĕd) *adv.* As a substitute or alternative; in place *of.*

ĭn'stĕp *n.* Upper surface of foot between toe and ankle; part of shoe, etc., fitting this; instep-shaped thing.

ĭn'stĭgāte *v.t.* Urge on, incite (person *to*); bring about by persuasion. **ĭnstĭgā'tion, ĭn'stĭgātor** *ns.*

ĭnstĭl(l)' *v.t.* Put in (liquid) by drops; infuse (feeling, idea, etc.) gradually. **ĭnstĭllā'tion** *n.*

ĭn'stĭnct[1] *n.* Innate propensity to certain seemingly rational acts performed without conscious design; innate impulse; intuition, unconscious skill; (zool.) inborn and usually rigid pattern of behaviour in animals, often in response to certain simple stimuli. **ĭnstĭnc'tĭve** *adj.* **ĭnstĭnc'tĭvely** *adv.*

ĭnstĭnct'[2] *pred. adj.* Imbued, charged (*with*).

Institut de France (aństĭtū', frahń). Union of the 5 French Academies (French Academy; Academy of Inscriptions and Belles-Lettres; Academy of Moral and Political Sciences; Academy of Science; Academy of the Fine Arts); founded 1795.

ĭn'stĭtūte *n.* 1. Society, organization, for promotion of scientific or other object; building used by this. 2. (pl.) Digest of elements of a subject, esp. of jurisprudence. ~ *v.t.* Establish, found; set on foot (inquiry etc.); appoint.

ĭnstĭtū'tion *n.* 1. Instituting; establishment (*of* person) in cure of souls. 2. Established law, custom, or practice; (colloq., of person etc.) familiar object. 3. Organization for promotion of some public object, religious, charitable, reformatory, etc.; building used by this; (esp. pop.) building used by benevolent or educational institution. **ĭnstĭtū'tional** (-shon-) *adj.* (esp. of religion) Organized into institutions (churches, priesthood, ritual, etc.) or finding expression through these; (U.S., of church etc.) including educational, charitable, etc., organizations among its activities. **ĭnstĭtū'tionalĭsm** *n.*

ĭnstrŭct' *v.t.* Teach (person etc. *in* subject); inform; direct, command; (of client, solicitor) give information to (solicitor, counsel). **ĭnstrŭc'tor, ĭnstrŭc'trėss** *ns.*

ĭnstrŭc'tion *n.* 1. Teaching. 2. (pl.) Directions, orders. 3. (pl.) Directions to solicitor or counsel. **ĭnstrŭc'tional** *adj.*

ĭnstrŭc'tĭve *adj.* Tending to instruct, conveying a lesson.

ĭn'strument (-rōō-) *n.* 1. Thing used in performing an action; person so made use of; tool, implement, esp. for delicate or scientific work. 2. (*musical* ~), contrivance for producing musical sounds. 3. Formal, esp. legal, document. ~ (*or* -mĕnt') *v.t.* Arrange (music) for instruments.

ĭnstrumĕn'tal (-rōō-) *adj.* 1. Serving as instrument or means (*to, in*). 2. Of, arising from, an instrument. 3. (Of music) performed on instruments. 4. (gram., of case) Denoting the instrument, or means. **ĭnstrumĕn'tally** *adv.*

ĭnstrumĕn'talĭst (-rōō-) *n.* Performer on musical instrument.

ĭnstrumĕntăl'ĭty (-rōō-) *n.* Agency, means.

ĭnstrumĕntā'tion (-rōō-) *n.* Study of character, power, pitch, etc., of various musical instruments; (loosely) orchestration.

ĭnsubōr'dĭnate *adj.* Disobedient, rebellious. **ĭnsubōrdĭnā'tion** *n.*

ĭnsubstăn'tial (-shl) *adj.* Not real; lacking solidity or substance. **ĭnsubstăntĭăl'ĭty** (-shĭăl'-) *n.*

ĭnsŭff'erable *adj.* Unbearably arrogant, conceited, etc.; intolerable. **ĭnsŭff'erably** *adv.*

ĭnsuffĭ'cient (-shent) *adj.* Not sufficient, inadequate. **ĭnsuffĭ'ciently** *adv.* **ĭnsuffĭ'ciency** *n.*

ĭn'sufflāte *v.t.* Blow, breathe, (air, gas, etc.) into cavity of body etc.; treat (nose etc.) thus. **ĭnsufflā'tion** *n.* Blowing on or into; breathing on person as rite of exorcism. **ĭn'sufflātor** *n.* Apparatus for insufflating.

ĭn'sūlar *adj.* Of (the nature of) an island; of, like, islanders, esp. narrow-minded. **ĭn'sūlarly** *adv.* **ĭn'sūlarĭsm, ĭnsūlă'rĭty** *ns.*

ĭn'sūlāte *v.t.* 1. Make (land) into an island. 2. Detach (person, thing) from surroundings, isolate. 3. Isolate (thing) by interposition of non-conductors, to prevent passage of electricity, heat, or sound. **ĭnsūlā'tion** *n.*

ĭn′sūlātor *n.* That which insulates, esp. a non-conducting substance, as porcelain or glass, for insulating electric wires, or asbestos, for insulating heat.

ĭn′sūlin *n.* Hormone secreted by the islets of LANGERHANS in the pancreas of vertebrates, accelerating the passage of glucose from the blood to the tissues and promoting its storage as glycogen in the liver and muscles.

ĭnsŭlt′ *v.t.* Treat with scornful abuse, offer indignity to; affront. **ĭnsŭlt′ĭngly** *adv.* **ĭn′sŭlt** *n.* Insulting speech or action, affront.

ĭnsūp′erable *adj.* That cannot be surmounted or overcome. **ĭnsūperabĭl′ĭty** *n.* **ĭnsūp′erably** *adv.*

ĭnsuppôrt′able *adj.* Unbearable. **ĭnsuppôrt′ably** *adv.*

ĭnsur′ance (-shoor-) *n.* Insuring; sum paid for this, premium; *National* ~: see NATIONAL.

ĭnsur′ant (-shoor-) *n.* Person to whom insurance policy is issued.

ĭnsure′ (-shoor) *v.t.* Secure payment of sum of money in event of loss of or damage to property (esp. by casualty at sea, fire, burglary, etc.), or of the death or disablement of a person, in consideration of the payment of a premium and observance of certain conditions; *the insured*, person to whom such payment is secured. **ĭnsur′er** (-shoor-) *n.* One who insures property in consideration of premium, underwriter.

ĭnsûr′gent *adj.* Rising in active revolt. ~ *n.* Rebel. **ĭnsûr′gency** *n.*

ĭnsurmoun′table *adj.* Not to be surmounted. **ĭnsurmoun′tably** *adv.*

ĭnsurrĕc′tion *n.* Rising in open resistance to established authority; incipient rebellion. **ĭnsurrĕc′tional** (-shon-), **ĭnsurrĕc′tionary** *adjs.* **ĭnsurrĕc′tionist** *n.*

ĭnsuscĕp′tĭble *adj.* Not susceptible. **ĭnsuscĕptĭbĭl′ĭty** *n.*

ĭntăct′ *adj.* Untouched; entire; unimpaired.

ĭntagl′iated (-ăl-) *adj.* Carved on the surface.

ĭntaglio (-tah′lĭō) *n.* (pl. -*s*). Engraved design; incised carving in hard material; gem with incised design (opp. CAMEO); *in* ~, having the design incised (opp. *in* RELIEF); ~ *print*, one made from an incised plate on which the paper is impressed so that the ink is taken up from the furrows, as in etching, photogravure, etc. (ill. PRINT). ~ *v.t.* Engrave (material, design) thus.

ĭn′tāke *n.* Place where water is taken into channel or pipe from river etc.; airshaft in mine; way in; taking in, amount taken in; (chiefly north.) land reclaimed from moor, etc.

ĭntăn′gĭble (-j-) *adj.* That cannot be touched; impalpable; that cannot be grasped mentally. **ĭntăngĭbĭl′ĭty** *n.* **ĭntăn′gĭbly** *adv.*

int. comb. *abbrev.* Internal combustion.

ĭn′tėger *n.* Whole number, undivided quantity; thing complete in itself.

ĭn′tėgral *adj.* Of, necessary to the completeness of, a whole; whole, complete; (math.) of, denoted by, an integer, involving only integers; ~ *calculus*, branch of infinitesimal calculus dealing with integrals of functions; used also to include solution of differential equations, parts of theory of functions, etc. **ĭn′tėgrally** *adv.* **ĭntėgrăl′ĭty** *n.* **ĭn′tėgral** *n.* (math.) Quantity of which given function is differential or differential coefficient; equation or system of equations from which given equation or system can be derived by differentiation.

ĭn′tėgrant *adj.* (Of parts) component, making up a whole.

ĭn′tėgrate *adj.* Made up of parts; whole, complete. **ĭn′tėgrāte** *v.t.* Complete (imperfect thing) by addition of parts; combine (parts) into a whole; (math.) find the integral of; indicate mean volume or total sum of (area, temperature, etc.). **ĭntėgrā′tion** *n.* **ĭn′tėgrātive** *adj.*

ĭntĕg′rity *n.* Wholeness; soundness; uprightness, honesty.

ĭntĕg′ūment *n.* Skin, husk, rind, or other (usu. natural) covering. **ĭntĕgūmĕn′tary** *adj.*

ĭn′tėllĕct *n.* Faculty of knowing and reasoning; understanding; person, persons collectively, of good understanding.

ĭntėllĕc′tion *n.* Action, process, of understanding, esp. as opp. to *imagination*. **ĭntėllĕc′tĭve** *adj.*

ĭntėllĕc′tūal *adj.* Of, appealing to, requiring the exercise of, intellect; possessing a good understanding, enlightened; given to mental pursuits. **ĭntėllĕc′tūally** *adv.* **ĭntėllĕctūăl′ĭty** *n.* **ĭntėllĕc′tūalīze** *v.* **ĭntėllĕc′tūal** *n.* Intellectual person.

ĭntėllĕc′tūalism *n.* Doctrine that knowledge is wholly or mainly derived from pure reason. **ĭntėllĕc′tūalist** *n.*

ĭntĕll′ĭgence *n.* 1. Intellect, understanding; quickness of understanding, sagacity; rational being; ~ *quotient* (abbrev. I.Q.), ratio of person's intelligence to average normal intelligence of persons of the same age; ~ *test*, test designed to ascertain intelligence or mental age, rather than acquired knowledge, of examinee. 2. Information, news; obtaining of (esp. secret) information, persons employed in this; secret service.

ĭntĕll′ĭgencer *n.* (archaic) Bringer of news, informant; secret agent, spy.

ĭntĕll′ĭgent *adj.* Having or showing (usu. a high degree of) understanding. **ĭntĕll′ĭgently** *adv.*

ĭntĕllĭgĕnt′sia, -zia (-jĕn- *or* -gĕn-) *n.* Class (esp. in Russia) to which culture, superior intelligence, and advanced political views are attributed.

ĭntĕll′ĭgĭble *adj.* That can be understood, comprehensible *to*; (philos.) that can be apprehended only by the intellect, not by the senses. **ĭntĕllĭgĭbĭl′ĭty** *n.* **ĭntĕll′ĭgĭbly** *adv.*

ĭntĕm′perate *adj.* Immoderate, unbridled, violent; excessive in indulgence of an appetite; addicted to drinking. **ĭntĕm′perately** *adv.* **ĭntĕm′perance** *n.*

ĭntĕnd′ *v.t.* Purpose, design; design, destine, for a purpose; mean.

ĭntĕn′dant *n.* Superintendent, manager, of public business etc. (chiefly as foreign title).

ĭntĕn′dėd *n.* (colloq.) Fiancé(e); person one hopes to marry.

ĭntĕnd′ment *n.* True meaning as fixed by law.

ĭntĕnse′ *adj.* Existing in a high degree, violent, vehement; having some quality in high degree; eager, ardent; feeling, apt to feel, intense emotion. **ĭntĕnse′ly** *adv.* **ĭntĕnse′nėss, ĭntĕns′ĭty** *ns.*

ĭntĕn′sĭfȳ *v.* Render, become, intense; (phot.) increase opacity of the deposit in a negative by chemical or other means. **ĭntĕnsĭfĭcā′tion** *n.*

ĭntĕn′sion (-shn) *n.* Intensity, high degree, of a quality, opp. to *extension*; strenuous exertion of mind or will; (logic) connotation of a term, sum of the attributes, qualities comprised in a concept.

ĭntĕn′sĭve *adj.* Of, relating to, intensity as opp. to extent; producing intensity; making intense, esp. (gram.) giving force or emphasis; concentrated, directed to a single point, area, or subject; (econ.) serving to increase production of given area. **ĭntĕn′sĭvely** *adv.*

ĭntĕnt′[1] *n.* Intention, purpose; *to all* ~*s and purposes*, practically, virtually.

ĭntĕnt′[2] *adj.* Resolved, bent (*on*); sedulously occupied (*on*); earnest, eager. **ĭntĕnt′ly** *adv.* **ĭntĕnt′nėss** *n.*

ĭntĕn′tion *n.* 1. Intending; thing intended, purpose; ultimate aim; (pl., colloq.) purposes in respect of proposal of marriage. 2. (med.) *first* ~, healing of lesion or fracture by immediate reunion of severed parts, without granulation; *second* ~, healing by granulation after suppuration. 3. (logic) Conception; *first* ~*s*, primary conceptions of things, formed by direct application of mind to the things themselves; *second* ~*s*, secondary conceptions formed by application of thought to first intentions in their relations to each other. 4. (theol.) *special, particular* ~, special purpose for which Mass is celebrated, prayers are offered up, etc. **ĭntĕn′tional** (-shon-) *adj.* Done on purpose. **ĭntĕn′tionally** *adv.*

ĭntêr′ *v.t.* Deposit (corpse etc.) in earth, tomb, etc.; bury.

in'ter- *prefix*. Expressing mutual or reciprocal act or relation, or with sense 'among', 'between'.

in'ter ăl'ia. Amongst other things.

in'ter-allied' (*or* ăl'-) *adj*. Existing or constituted between allies.

interăct' *v.i.* Act reciprocally, act on each other. **interăc'tion** *n*. **interăc'tive** *adj*.

interbreed' *v*. (past t. and past part. *-bred*). Cross-breed; (of animals of different race or species) breed with each other.

intêr'calary *adj*. (Of day or month) inserted in calendar to harmonize calendar with solar year, as the odd day (29th Feb.) in a leap year; (of year) having such additions; interpolated, intervening; (bot.) interpolated at regions other than the apex.

intêr'calāte *v.t.* Insert (intercalary day etc.); interpose (anything out of usual course, esp. in past. part., of strata). **intêrcalā'tion** *n*.

intercēde' *v.i.* Interpose on behalf of another, plead (*with* one person *for* another).

intercĕpt' *v.t.* Seize, catch (person, enemy aircraft, etc.) on the way from place to place; pick up (esp. enemy's) wireless signal; cut off (light etc. *from*); check, stop; (math.) mark off (space) between two points etc. **intercĕp'tion** *n*. **intercĕp'tive** *adj*. **in'tercĕpt** *n*. Intercepted wireless signal; (math.) part intercepted.

intercĕp'tor *n*. (esp.) Aircraft having task of intercepting enemy raiders.

intercĕ'ssion (-shn) *n*. Interceding, esp. by prayer. **intercĕss'ory** *adj*.

in'terchānge *n*. Reciprocal exchange (*of* things) between two persons etc.; alternation. **interchānge'** *v.t.* (Of two persons) exchange (things) with each other; put each of (two things) in the other's place; alternate. **interchānge'able** (-jabl) *adj*. **interchānge'ably** *adv*. **interchāngeabil'ity** *n*.

in'tercŏm *n*. System of internal communication by telephone, wireless, etc., between units of an organization e.g. tanks, aircraft, etc.

intercommūn'icāte *v.i.* Have mutual intercourse; have free passage to each other. **intercommūnicā'tion** *n*.

intercommūn'ion (-yon) *n*. Intimate intercourse; mutual action or relation, esp. reciprocal spiritual relations and ministrations between different religious bodies.

in'tercourse (-ōrs) *n*. Social communication, dealings, between individuals; communion between man and God; communication for trade purposes etc. between different countries etc.; sexual connexion.

intercŭ'rrent *adj*. (Of time or event) intervening; (of disease) occurring during progress of another; recurring at intervals.

interdepĕnd' *v.i.* Depend on each other. **interdepĕn'dence, interdepĕn'dency** *ns*. **interdepĕn'dent** *adj*. **interdepĕn'dently** *adv*.

in'terdict *n*. Authoritative prohibition; (Sc. law) injunction; (R.C. Ch.) sentence debarring place or person from ecclesiastical functions and privileges. **interdict'** *v.t.* Prohibit (action); forbid use of; restrain (*from*); forbid (thing *to* person). **interdic'tion** *n*. **interdic'tory** *adj*.

in'terėst *n*. 1. Legal concern, title right, (*in* property); pecuniary stake (*in* commercial undertaking etc.). 2. Advantage, profit. 3. Thing in which one is concerned; principle in which a party is concerned; party having a common interest. 4. Selfish pursuit of one's own welfare; *make* ~, bring personal interest to bear (*with* person). 5. Concern, curiosity, or quality exciting them. 6. Money paid for use of money lent or for forbearance of debt; *simple* ~, interest reckoned on principal only, and paid at fixed intervals; *compound* ~, interest reckoned on principal and on accumulations of interest. ~ *v.t.* Cause (person) to take personal interest or share (*in*); excite curiosity or attention of; (past part.) having a private interest, not impartial or disinterested. **in'terėstėdly** *adv*. **in'terėsting** *adj*. **in'terėstingly** *adv*.

interfā'cial (*or* -shl) *adj*. Included between two plane faces or surfaces, esp. of angles of crystals.

interfēre' *v.i.* Come into collision or opposition (*with*); meddle; intervene, take part, (*in*); (physics, of waves of usu. similar light proceeding from two or more coherent sources or of electro-magnetic radiations from the same source travelling by different paths) combine with a difference of phase, so that each cancels the other partially or completely and the result is a periodic pattern of light and dark.

interfēr'ence *n*. 1. Interfering. 2. (wireless) 'Fading' of received signals due to waves arriving at receiving set by different paths or arriving out of phase from different transmitters; (pop.) intrusion of electrical disturbances, which interfere with the waves it is desired to receive. 3. (Of light) partial or complete obliteration of light, usu. of a particular wave-length, by the superposition of a component which is not in the same phase.

interfūse' (-z) *v*. Intersperse, mix; blend together; blend with each other. **interfū'sion** (-zhn) *n*.

in'terim *adv*. (archaic) Meanwhile. ~ *n* Intervening time. ~ *adj*. Intervening; provisional, temporary; ~ *dividend*, dividend paid between two annual etc. balances and not in pursuance of published balance-sheet.

intēr'ior *adj*. Situated within; inland, remote from coast or frontier; internal, domestic (opp. to *foreign*) existing in mind or soul, inward. **intēr'iorly** *adv*. **intēr'ior** *n*. Interior part, inside; inland region; inside of building or room, picture of this; inner nature, soul; (department dealing with) home affairs of a country, as *Minister of the I~*.

interjā'cent *adj*. Lying between, intermediate.

interjĕct' *v.t.* Throw in, interpose (remark etc.) abruptly; remark parenthetically. **interjĕc'tory** *adj*.

interjĕc'tion *n*. Ejaculation, exclamation; natural ejaculation viewed as part of speech. **interjĕc'tional** (-shon-) *adj*. **interjĕc'tionally** *adv*.

interlāce' *v*. Bind together intricately, entangle; interweave;

CELTIC INTERLACING PATTERN

mingle; cross each other intricately. **interlāce'ment** (-sm-) *n*.

interlârd' *v.t.* Mix (writing, speech, etc., *with*).

in'terleaf *n*. Extra leaf between leaves of book. **interleave'** *v.t.* Insert leaves between leaves of (book); *interleaved copy* (of book), one bound with blank leaves between the printed ones.

interline' *v.t.* Insert words between lines of (document etc.); insert (words) thus. **interlin'ėar** *adj*. Written, printed, between the lines. **interlinėā'tion** *n*.

interlŏck' *v*. Engage with each other by overlapping etc.; lock, clasp, within each other; (railw.) connect (levers for signals, switches, etc.) so that they cannot be operated independently of each other.

interlŏc'ūtor *n*. One who takes part in dialogue or conversation. **interlocū'tion** *n*. **interlŏc'ūtory** *adj*.

in'terlōper *n*. Intruder, one who (esp. for profit) thrusts himself into others' affairs; (hist.) unauthorized trader. **interlōpe'** *v.i.*

in'terlūde (*or* -lood) *n*. 1. Pause between acts of play; what fills this up; (mus.) instrumental piece played between verses of hymn etc., in intervals of church service etc. 2. (hist.) Dramatic or mimetic representation between acts of mystery plays or moralities.

intermă'rriage (-rij) *n*. Marriage between members of different families, tribes, etc., or (loosely) between near relations.

intermă'rry *v.i.* Become connected by marriage (*with*).

intermĕdd'le *v.i.* Concern oneself (*with, in*, esp. what is not one's business).

intermēd'iary *adj.* Acting between parties, mediatory; intermediate. ~ *n.* Intermediary person or thing, esp. mediator.

intermēd'iate *adj.* Coming *between* two things, in time, place, or order. **intermēd'iately** *adv.* **intermēd'iate** *n.* Intermediate thing; (chem.) compound manufactured from a substance obtained directly from raw materials, and used as a basis for the synthesis of another product. **intermēd'iāte** *v.i.* Act between others, mediate (*between*). **intermēdiā'tion, intermēd'iātor** *ns.*

intermēd'ium *n.* Intermediate thing, medium.

intẽrm'ent *n.* Burial.

intermĕzz'o (-dzō) *n.* (pl. *-zi, -zos*). Short, light, dramatic or musical performance between acts of drama or opera; short movement connecting main divisions of large musical work.

intẽrm'inable *adj.* Endless; tediously long. **intẽrm'inableness** *n.* **intẽrm'inably** *adv.*

interming'le (-nggl) *v.* Mix together; mingle (*with*).

intermi'ssion *n.* Pause, cessation; (U.S.) interval.

intermit' *v.* Suspend, discontinue; stop for a time (esp. of fever, pain, etc., or pulse). **intermitt'ence** *n.* **intermitt'ent** *adj.* **intermitt'ently** *adv.*

intermix' *v.* Mix together.

intẽrn'[1] *v.t.* Oblige to reside within limits of country etc.; confine (esp. enemy aliens and prisoners of war) within prescribed limits. **intẽrnee'** *n.* Person interned. **intẽrn'ment** *n.*

in'tẽrn[2] *n.* (U.S.) Advanced student or recent graduate residing in hospital and acting as assistant physician or surgeon.

intẽrn'al *adj.* Of, situated in, the inside of a thing; of the inner nature of a thing, intrinsic; of the domestic affairs of a country; of the mind or soul, inward, subjective; ~ *combustion engine*, one in which the motive power is obtained by combustion or explosion of a mixture of air and gas or gas or vaporized oil in engine cylinder (ill. COMBUSTION); ~ *evidence*, evidence derived from what is contained in the thing itself. **intẽrn'ally** *adv.*

internă'tional (-shon-) *adj.* Existing, carried on, between different nations; of the International Working Men's Associations (founded in London by Karl Marx in 1864 for promoting joint political action of working classes in all countries, and dissolved in Philadelphia in 1876); ~ *law*, body of rules regarded by the nations of the world as being binding on them in their relations with each other, in peace and war, also called *public ~ law*, in distinction from *private ~ law*, which deals with the rights and obligations of private citizens in a foreign country. **internă'tionally** *adv.* **internă'tional** *n.* 1. One who takes part in international (usu. athletic) contests. 2. Member of First, Second, Third, or Fourth International; *Communist I~*, Third International; *First I~*, the International Working Men's Association (see above); *Second I~*, organization founded at Paris 1889 to celebrate 100th anniversary of French Revolution; *Third I~*, founded at Moscow 1919 by delegates from 12 countries to promote communism and support the Russian Revolution, dissolved 1943; *Fourth I~*, founded 1936 by followers of Trotsky.

Internătionale' (-shonahl) *n.* Revolutionary hymn composed by Eugène Pottier in 1871 and adopted by Socialists.

internă'tionalist (-shon-) *n.* One who advocates community of interests between nations; one versed in international law. **internă'tionalism** *n.*

internă'tionalize (-shon-) *v.t.* Make international; esp. bring (territory etc.) under combined protection etc. of different nations. **internătionalizā'tion** *n.*

internĕ'cine *adj.* Mutually destructive; (orig.) deadly.

in'ternōde *n.* (bot.) Length of stem between one leaf or whorl of leaves and the next (ill. LEAF).

in'ter nōs. Between ourselves.

internŭn'cio (-shĭō) *n.* Ambassador of Pope when or where no nuncio is employed; (hist.) minister representing (esp. Austrian) Government at Ottoman Porte.

interpĕll'āte *v.t.* (In foreign, esp. French, chamber) interrupt order of day by demanding explanation from (Minister concerned). **interpĕllā'tion** *n.*

interpĕn'ėtrāte *v.* Penetrate thoroughly, pervade; penetrate reciprocally; penetrate each other. **interpĕnėtrā'tion** *n.*

interplăn'ėtary *adj.* Situated between the planets.

in'terplay *n.* Reciprocal play; operation of two things on each other.

interplead' *v.i.* Litigate with each other in order to settle point in which a third party is concerned.

In'terpŏl (ĭ-). The International Criminal Police Commission, with headquarters in Paris.

intẽrp'olāte *v.t.* Make insertions in (books etc.), esp. so as to give false impressions as to date etc.; introduce (words) thus; (math.) insert (intermediate term) in series. **intẽrpolā'tion** *n.*

interpōse' (-z) *v.* Insert, make intervene, (*between*); put forth, introduce, (veto, objection, authority, etc.) by way of interference; intervene (between disputants etc.); say as an interruption; make an interruption. **interpōs'al** *n.*

intẽrposi'tion (-z-) *n.* Interposing; thing interposed; interference.

intẽrp'rėt *v.* Expound the meaning of (abstruse words, writings, etc.); make out the meaning of; bring out the meaning of, render, by artistic representation or performance; explain, understand, in specified manner; act as interpreter. **intẽrprėtā'tion** *n.* **intẽrp'rėtative** *adj.*

intẽrp'rėter *n.* One who interprets; one whose office it is to translate orally in their presence the words of persons speaking different languages. **intẽrp'rėtership** *n.*

interrĕg'num *n.* (pl. *-na, -nums*). Period during which State has no normal ruler, esp. between end of king's reign and accession of successor; interval, pause.

interrėlā'tion *n.* Mutual relation. **interrėlā'tionship** *n.*

intĕ'rrogāte *v.t.* Ask questions of, esp. closely or formally. **intĕrrogā'tion** *n.* Asking questions; interview for close questioning; question; *point, mark, note, of ~*, symbol (?) used in printing or writing (usu. at end of sentence, to indicate question).

interrŏg'ative *adj.* Of, having the form or force of, a question; of inquiry; (gram., of words) used in asking question. **interrŏg'atively** *adv.* **interrŏg'ative** *n.* Interrogative pronoun etc.

interrŏg'atory *adj.* Of inquiry. ~ *n.* Question, set of questions, esp. (law) one formally put to accused person etc.

interrŭpt' *v.t.* Break in upon (action, speech, person speaking, etc.); obstruct (view etc.); break the continuity of. **interrŭp'tėdly** *adv.* **interrŭp'ter, interrŭp'tion** *ns.* **interrŭp'tory** *adj.*

intersĕct' *v.* Divide (thing) by passing or lying across it; (of lines etc.) cross, cut, each other. **intersĕc'tion** *n.* Intersecting; point, line, common to intersecting lines, planes. **intersĕc'tional** (-shon-) *adj.*

interspẽrse' *v.t.* Scatter, place here and there (*between, among*); diversify (thing) *with* (others so scattered). **interspẽr'sion** *n.*

in'terstāte *adj.* (U.S.) Existing, carried on, between States.

intẽrs'tice *n.* Intervening space; chink, crevice. **intersti'tial** (-shl) *adj.* Of, forming, occupying, interstice(s).

intertwīne' *v.* Entwine; become entwined. **intertwīne'ment** (-nm-) *n.*

in'terval *n.* 1. Intervening time or space; pause; break, gap; *at ~s*,

MUSICAL INTERVALS

Perfect: 1. Fourth. 2. Fifth. 3. Octave. Major: 4. Second. 5. Third. 6. Sixth. 7. Seventh. 8. Augmented fourth. 9. Minor sixth. 10. Diminished fourth

here and there, now and then. 2. (mus.) Difference of pitch between two sounds in melody or harmony. 3. Distance between persons or things in respect of qualities. **intervăll'ic** *adj.* [L *intervallum* space between ramparts (*vallum* rampart)]

intervēne' *v.i.* Come in, as something extraneous; occur in the meantime; lie, be situated, between; (of person or thing) come between, interfere, so as to prevent or modify result etc.; (law) interpose in lawsuit to which one was not an original party (esp. of Queen's (King's) Proctor in divorce cases). **intervēn'er, intervĕn'tion** *ns.* **intervēn'ient** *adj.*

in'terview (-vū) *n.* Meeting of persons face to face, esp. for purpose of conference; meeting between representative of press and person from whom he seeks to obtain statements for publication; meeting between candidate for appointment and prospective employer etc. ~ *v.t.* Have interview with (person), esp. with view to publication of statements etc. **in'terviewer** (-vūer) *n.*

in'ter vīv'ōs. Between the living (esp. of gift as opp. to legacy).

interweave' *v.t.* (past t. *-wove*, past part. *-woven*). Weave together, interlace; blend intimately.

intĕs'tate *adj.* Not having made a will; not disposed of by will. ~ *n.* Person who dies intestate. **intĕs'tacy** *n.*

intĕs'tine *n.* (Usu. pl.) Lower part of alimentary canal from pyloric end of stomach to anus (ill. ALIMENTARY); *large* ~, caecum, colon, and rectum; *small* ~, duodenum, jejunum, and ileum. **intĕs'tinal** (*or* -īn'-) *adj.*

intĕs'tine² *adj.* (Of wars etc.) internal, domestic, civil.

in'timate¹ *adj.* & *n.* (Person) close in acquaintance, familiar; essential, intrinsic; closely personal. **in'timately** *adv.* **in'timacy** *n.*

in'timāte² *v.t.* Make known, state; imply, hint. **intimā'tion** *n.*

intim'idāte *v.t.* Inspire with fear, cow, esp. in order to influence conduct. **intimidā'tion** *n.*

intim'ity *n.* Inwardness; privacy.

in'to (ĭn'tōō, ĭn'te) *prep.* Expressing (1) motion or direction to a point within a thing, as *come ~ the house, inquire ~ the problem*; (2) change, condition, result, as *water turns ~ ice, collect them ~ heaps.*

intŏl'erable *adj.* That cannot be endured. **intŏl'erableness** *n.* **intŏl'erably** *adv.*

intŏl'erant *adj.* Not tolerant (*of*). **intŏl'erantly** *adv.* **intŏl'erance** *n.*

intonā'tion *n.* (mus.) Opening phrase of plainsong melody, sung by priest alone or by one or a few of the choristers; intoning, reciting in singing voice; utterance, production, of musical tones; modulation of voice in speaking.

intōne' *v.t.* Recite (esp. psalm, prayer, etc.) in singing voice; sing opening phrase of plainsong.

in tōt'ō. Completely.

intŏx'icant *adj.* & *n.* Intoxicating (liquor).

intŏx'icāte *v.t.* Make drunk; excite, exhilarate, beyond self-control. **intŏx'icāting** *adj.* **intŏxicā'tion** *n.*

intra- *prefix.* On the inside, within.

intrăc'table *adj.* Not docile, refractory; (of things) not easily dealt with. **intrăc'tableness, intrăctabil'ity** *ns.* **intrăc'tably** *adv.*

intrăd'ōs *n.* (archit.) Interior curve of arch (ill. ARCH).

intramŭs'cūlar *adj.* Within or going into a muscle.

intrăn'sigent (-z-) *adj.* Uncompromising (esp. in politics). ~ *n.* Uncompromising republican.

intrăn'sitive *adj.* & *n.* (Verb) that does not take a direct object. **intrăn'sitively** *adv.*

intravēn'ous *adj.* Within or going into a vein.

intrĕp'id *adj.* Fearless, brave. **intrĕp'idly** *adv.* **intrepid'ity** *n.*

in'tricate *adj.* Perplexingly entangled; involved; obscure. **in'tricately** *adv.* **in'tricacy** *n.*

in'trig(u)ant (-gant) *n.* (fem. *-ante* pr. -ahnt', -ănt') Intriguer.

intrigue' (-ēg) *v.* 1. Carry on underhand plot; employ secret influence (*with*); have a liaison (*with*). 2. Excite the interest or curiosity of. ~ *n.* Underhand plotting or plot; secret amour, liaison.

intrin'sic *adj.* Belonging naturally, inherent, essential. **intrin'sically** *adv.*

intro- *prefix.* To the inside.

introdūce' *v.t.* 1. Bring in; place in, insert; bring into use (custom, idea, etc.); usher in, bring forward, begin. 2. Make known, esp. in formal manner (person *to* another); present formally, as at court or in an assembly; make acquainted with, draw attention of (person) *to*; bring (Bill etc.) before Parliament. **introdŭc'tory** *adj.*

introdŭc'tion *n.* Introducing; preliminary matter prefixed to book; introductory treatise; formal presentation.

intrō'it *n.* (eccles.) Psalm, antiphon, sung while priest approaches altar to celebrate Mass or Holy Communion.

introjĕc'tion *n.* (psycho-anal.) Unconscious process by which an image representing an external object is incorporated into a person's psychic equipment.

intromit' *v.t.* (archaic) Let in, admit (*into*); insert. **intromi's-sion** (-shn) *n.* **intromitt'ent** *adj.*

intrŏrse' *adj.* (bot., of anthers) Opening to release pollen towards axis of flower (opp. EXTRORSE).

introspĕct' *v.i.* Examine one's own thoughts and feelings. **introspĕc'tion** *n.* **introspĕc'tive** *adj.* **introspĕc'tively** *adv.* **introspĕc'tiveness** *n.*

introvĕrt' *v.t.* 1. Turn (mind, thought) inwards upon itself. 2. (zool.) Withdraw (organ etc.) within its own tube or base, like finger of glove. **introvĕr'sion** *n.* **in'trovĕrt** *n.* 1. (psych.) Person given to introversion (opp. to EXTROVERT). 2. (zool.) Part or organ that may be introverted.

intrude' (-ōōd) *v.* Thrust, force, (thing *into*); force (thing *upon* person); come uninvited, thrust oneself in (*into* company, place, etc., *upon* person etc.). **intrud'er** *n.* One who intrudes; aircraft that invades enemy's air space to interfere with his operations.

intru'sion (-ōōzhn) *n.* Intruding, forcing in; forcing oneself in; (law) thrusting oneself into vacant estate or ecclesiastical benefice to which one has no title or claim; settlement of minister of Church of Scotland without consent of congregation; (geol.) body of rock, usu. of volcanic origin, which has been pushed while molten into or through other rocks (ill. ROCK).

intrus'ive (-ōōs-) *adj.* Intruding, tending to intrude. **intrus'ively** *adv.* **intrus'iveness** *n.*

in'tūbāte *v.t.* (med.) Insert tube into (larynx etc.) to keep it open. **intūbā'tion** *n.*

in'tūit *v.* Know by intuition.

intūi'tion *n.* Immediate apprehension by the mind without reasoning; immediate apprehension by sense; immediate insight. **intūi'tional** (-shon-) *adj.*

intūi'tionalism (-shon-) *n.* Doctrine that perception of truth is by intuition.

intūi'tionism (-shon-) *n.* 1. Doctrine that in perception external objects are known immediately, without the intervention of a vicarious phenomenon. 2. Intuitionalism.

intū'itive *adj.* Of, possessing, perceived by, intuition. **intū'itively** *adv.* **intūi'tiveness** *n.*

intū'itivism *n.* Doctrine that ethical principles are matters of intuition.

intūmĕs'cent *adj.* Swelling up. **intūmĕs'cence** *n.*

intussuscĕp'tion *n.* (path.) Telescoping of one portion of intestine within another.

inŭnc'tion *n.* Smearing, rubbing, with oil.

in'undāte *v.t.* Overflow, flood (*with* water etc.; also fig.). **inundā'tion** *n.*

inūre' *v.* Accustom, habituate; come into operation, take effect. **inure'ment** (-ūrm-) *n.*

inŭrn' *v.t.* Put (ashes of cremated body) in an urn.

inv. *abbrev. Invenit, invenerunt* (= designed this work).

invāde' *v.t.* Make hostile inroad into; assail; encroach upon (rights etc.). **invād'er** *n.*

invă'gināte *v.t.* Put in a sheath; introvert (tubular sheath). **invăginā'tion** *n.*

in'valid¹ (-ēd) *n.* & *adj.* (Person) enfeebled or disabled by illness or injury. **invalid′** (-ēd; *or* in′-) *v.* Lay up, disable, (person) by illness; treat as an invalid, remove from active service (usu. ~ *out*), send *home* etc., as an invalid. **in′validism** (-ēd-) *n.*

invăl′id² *adj.* Not valid; esp., having no legal force. **invalid′ity** *n.*

invăl′idāte *v.t.* Make invalid. **invălidā′tion** *n.*

Invalides (aṅvălēd′), **Hôtel des.** Institution in Paris, founded 1670 by Louis XIV for superannuated or disabled soldiers; Napoleon I is buried in the chapel under its dome and part of the building is now a military museum.

invăl′ūable *adj.* Above price, priceless.

invār′iable *adj.* Unchangeable; always the same; (math.) constant, fixed. ~ *n.* (math.) An invariable quantity, a constant. **invār′iableness, invāriabil′ity** *ns.* **invār′iably** *adv.*

invā′sion (-zhn) *n.* Invading; encroachment.

invĕc′ted *adj.* (her.) Bordered by or consisting of a series of small convex lobes (ill. HERALDRY).

invĕc′tive *n.* Violent attack in words; abusive oratory.

inveigh′ (-vā) *v.i.* Speak violently, rail loudly, *against.*

invei′gle (-vē-, -vā-) *v.t.* Entice, seduce (*into*). **invei′glement** (-gelm-) *n.*

invĕnt′ *v.t.* Devise, originate; produce or construct by original thought etc.; fabricate (false story etc.). **invĕn′tion** *n.* 1. Inventing; thing invented, contrivance, (law) any new manufacture the subject of letters patent. 2. Inventiveness. 3. Fictitious story. 4. *I~ of the Cross*, finding of the Cross in 326 by Helena, mother of the Emperor Constantine; festival commemorating this, 3rd May. **invĕn′tive** *adj.* **invĕn′tively** *adv.* **invĕn′tiveness** *n.* **invĕn′tor** *n.*

in′ventory *n.* Detailed list (of goods, furniture, etc.); stock of goods in this. ~ *v.t.* Enter (goods etc.) in inventory; make inventory of.

Invernĕss′ (ĭ-). County town, at mouth of river Ness, of Scottish highland county of Inverness-shire; ~ *cloak, coat*, man's cloak or coat with removable cape (ill. CLOAK).

invĕrse′ (*or* in′-) *adj.* Inverted in position, order, or relations; ~ *ratio, proportion*, that between two quantities one of which increases at the same rate as the other decreases, esp. when the product of the two remains constant. **invĕrse′ly** *adv.* **in′vĕrse** *n.* Inverted state; thing that is the direct opposite (*of* another).

invĕr′sion *n.* Turning upside down; reversal of position, order, or relation, esp. (gram.) of order of words; (mus.) transference of lower note of interval to that an octave higher; reversal of a ratio. **invĕrs′ive** *adj.*

invĕrt *v.t.* Turn upside down; reverse position, order, or relation, of; change relative position of notes of (chord, interval) by placing lowest note higher, usu. an octave higher; modify (phrase, subject) by inverting intervals between successive notes; (chem.) change dextro-rotatory into laevo-rotatory substances, or vice versa; *inverted comma*: see COMMA. **in′vĕrt** *n.* 1. Inverted arch, as at bottom of sewer. 2. (psychol.) Person whose sexual instincts are inverted, homosexual.

invĕrt′ebrate *adj.* Not having a backbone; (fig.) wanting in firmness; (zool.) belonging to the *Invertebrata*, a classification of convenience which comprises all animals other than the *Vertebrata*; it includes principally those animals which have no notochord in any stage of development, but also a few which do have a notochord (e.g. the tunicates). ~ *n.* Invertebrate animal or (fig.) person.

invĕst′ *v.* 1. Clothe (person etc. *in, with*); cover as garment; clothe, endue, (person etc. *with* qualities, insignia of office etc.). 2. Lay siege to. 3. Employ (money in stocks etc.); ~ *in*, put money into (stocks); (colloq.) lay out money on. **invĕs′tor** *n.*

invĕs′tigāte *v.t.* Examine, inquire into. **invĕstigā′tion, invĕs′tigātor** *ns.* **invĕs′tigatory** *adj.*

invĕs′titure *n.* Formal investing of person (*with* office), esp. ceremony at which sovereign or his deputy confers honours; enduing (*with* attributes).

invĕst′ment *n.* 1. Investing of money; money invested; property in which money is invested. 2. Investiture; clothing.

invĕt′erate *adj.* Long-established; deep-rooted, obstinate. **invĕt′erately** *adv.* **invĕt′eracy** *n.*

invid′ious *adj.* (Of conduct etc.) giving offence, esp. by real or seeming injustice etc.; (of thing) likely to excite ill feeling against the possessor. **invid′iously** *adv.* **invid′iousness** *n.*

invi′gilāte *v.i.* Watch over candidates at examination. **invigilā′tion, invi′gilātor** *ns.*

invig′orāte *v.t.* Make vigorous; animate. **invig′orative** *adj.*

invin′cible *adj.* Unconquerable. **invincibil′ity** *n.* **invin′cibly** *adv.*

invi′olable *adj.* Not to be violated; to be kept sacred from infraction, profanation, etc. **inviolabil′ity** *n.* **invi′olably** *adv.*

invi′olate *adj.* Not violated; unbroken; unprofaned. **invi′olately** *adv.* **invi′olateness, invi′olacy** *ns.*

invis′ible (-z-) *adj.* That cannot be seen; not to be seen at a particular time; too small to be seen; ~ *exports*, shipping services, foreign investments, and other items that account for apparent excess of country's imports over exports; ~ *ink*, an ink that requires heat, vapour, or the like to make visible what is written in it; *I~ League*: see KU KLUX KLAN. **invisibil′ity, invis′ibleness** *ns.* **invis′ibly** *adv.* **invis′ible** *n.* The unseen world, God.

invite′ *v.* Request courteously to come (*to* dinner, *to* one's house, etc.); request courteously (*to* do); solicit courteously; bring on, tend to bring on (thing) unintentionally; (of thing) present inducements, attract. **in′vite** *n.* (colloq.) Invitation. **invit′ing** *adj.* **invit′ingly** *adv.* **invit′ingness, invitā′tion** *ns.*

invocā′tion *n.* Invoking, calling upon God etc. in prayer; appeal to muse for inspiration or assistance in poem. **invŏc′atory** (*or* in′-) *adj.*

in′voice *n.* List of goods shipped or sent, with prices and charges. ~ *v.t.* Make an invoice of (goods).

invōke′ *v.t.* Call on (God etc.) in prayer or as witness; appeal to (person's authority etc.); summon (spirit) by charms; ask earnestly for (vengeance, help, etc.).

in′volūcre (-ker) *n.* Covering, envelope (esp. anat.); (bot.) whorl of bracts surrounding inflorescence (ill. INFLORESCENCE).

invŏl′untary *adj.* Done without exercise of the will, unintentional; ~ *nervous system*: see AUTONOMIC. **invŏl′untarily** *adv.* **invŏl′untariness** *n.*

in′volūte *adj.* Involved, intricate, curled spirally; (bot.) rolled inwards at the edges. ~ *n.* (geom.) Curve traced out by point on flexible inextensible string as it is unwound from, or wound upon, another curve called the *evolute* (ill. EVOLUTE).

involū′tion *n.* Involving; entanglement; intricacy; curling inwards; part so curled; (math.) raising of quantity to any power.

invŏlve′ *v.t.* Wrap (thing *in* another); wind spirally; entangle (person, thing, *in* difficulties, mystery, etc.); implicate (*in*); include (*in*); imply, entail. **invŏlve′ment** (-vm-) *n.* Involving; financial embarrassment; complicated affair.

invŭl′nerable *adj.* That cannot be wounded or hurt; (at contract bridge) that has not made a game towards rubber and is therefore not liable to the increased penalties prescribed for the side that has made one game towards rubber (see VULNERABLE). **invŭlnerabil′ity** *n.* **invŭl′nerably** *adv.*

in′ward *adj.* Situated within; mental, spiritual; directed towards the inside. **in′wardly** *adv.* Of the inside; not aloud; in mind or spirit. **in′wardness** *n.* Inner nature, essence; quality of being inward; spirituality. **in′ward(s)** *adv.* Towards the inside; within mind or soul. **in′wards,** (dial. and vulg.) **in′nards** *n.pl.* Entrails.

in′wrought (-rawt *or* inrawt′)

adj. (Of fabric) decorated (*with* pattern); (of pattern) wrought (*in*, *on*, fabric); (fig.) intimately blended (*with*).

inya′la, nya′la (-ahl*a*) *n.* Large S. Afr. antelope (*Tragelaphus angasi*), one of the bush-bucks.

ī′odīde *n.* Compound of iodine with another element or radical.

ī′odīne (*or* -ēn) *n.* Non-metallic element widely diffused in nature but never in the free state, obtained from the ashes of seaweeds and from the mother-liquor of Chile saltpetre, used in medicine as an antiseptic and in photography and dyeing; symbol I, at. no. 53, at. wt 126·904; tincture or solution of this in alcohol. **iŏd′ĭc** *adj.*

ī′odĭsm *n.* (med.) Morbid state produced by the use of iodine or its compounds, characterized by palpitation and emaciation.

ī′odīze *v.t.* Treat with, expose to fumes of, iodine.

iŏd′ofōrm *n.* Yellow, crystalline, volatile compound of iodine (CHI_3), formerly much used as an antiseptic dressing for wounds.

I. of M., I. of W. *abbrevs.* Isle of Man, Isle of Wight.

I.O.G.T. *abbrev.* International Order of Good Templars.

I.O.M. *abbrev.* Isle of Man.

ī′on *n.* (physics.) 1. Electrified particle formed when a neutral atom or group of atoms loses or gains one or more electrons; if electrons are lost, the particle is positively electrified and is called a *cation*; if electrons are gained, the particle is negatively electrified and is called an *anion*. 2. A gaseous particle electrically charged by action of Röntgen or other rays. [Gk *ion* (thing) going]

Iōn′a (ī-). Island of Inner Hebrides, where St. Columba founded a monastery *c* 563; centre of Celtic missions.

Iōn′ĭa (ī-). Ancient Greek colony on W. coast of Asia Minor. **Iōn′ĭan** *adj.* & *n.* (Native, inhabitant) of Ionia; ~ *Islands*, Greek islands in the Ionian Sea; ~ *mode*, (1) ancient Greek MODE, reputedly soft and effeminate in character; (2) 11th of eccles. modes, with C as final and G as dominant, corresponding to the modern major key of C (ill. MODE); ~ *Sea*, part of Mediterranean, between Greece and S. Italy.

iŏn′ĭc[1] *adj.* Of or pertaining to ions.

Iŏn′ĭc[2] (ī-) *adj.* Of Ionia; ~ *dialect*, the most important of the three main branches of ancient Greek, of which ATTIC was a development; ~ *order*, (archit.) one of the three Greek orders (Doric, Ionic, and Corinthian), characterized by two lateral volutes of the capital (ill. ORDER); ~ *school*, earliest school of Greek philosophers, including Thales, Anaximander, Anaximenes, and Heraclitus. ~ *n.* (Gk and L pros.) Name of a foot consisting of two long syllables followed by two short, – – ⏑ ⏑ (~ *a majore*) or two short syllables followed by two long, ⏑ ⏑ – – (~ *a minore*).

iōn′ĭum *n.* Obsolesc. name for the isotope of THORIUM, one of the products of the radio-active decay of uranium; now usu. called thorium-230.

ī′onīze *v.* (of an electrolyte) Split into ions; (of X-rays, cathode rays, etc.) produce ions in a gas and so make it a conductor. **īonīzā′tion** *n.*

iōn′osphēre *n.* The ionized region that exists in the upper atmosphere (ill. ATMOSPHERE).

iōt′a *n.* Greek letter (I, ι, = I); insignificant part, jot, atom.

iōt′acĭsm *n.* Excessive use of the Greek letter ι; tendency in Greek to level a number of originally different vowels and diphthongs under the sound (ē).

I O U (ī ō ū′) *n.* Signed document bearing these letters followed by specified sum, constituting formal acknowledgement of debt. [= I owe you]

I.O.W. *abbrev.* Isle of Wight.

I′owa (ī-). West North Central State of U.S.; capital, Des Moines.

ĭpĕcăcūăn′ha (-n*a*) *n.* Root of S. Amer. herbaceous or shrubby plant (*Cephaëlis ipecacuanha*), which possesses emetic, diaphoretic, and purgative properties, a common ingredient of cough mixtures.

Iphĭgĕnī′a (ī-). (Gk legend) A daughter of Agamemnon and Clytemnestra. When the Greeks on their way to the Trojan War were detained by contrary winds at Aulis, she was offered by her father as a sacrifice to Artemis, whose stag he had killed; she was snatched from the altar by the goddess and borne away to Tauris, where she became a priestess.

ĭp′sė dĭx′ĭt *n.* Dogmatic statement, assertion, dictum. [L, = 'he himself said it']

ĭpsĭlăt′eral *adj.* (physiol.) Belonging to the same side.

ĭp′sō făc′tō *adv.* By that very fact.

i.q. *abbrev.* *Idem quod* (= the same as).

I.Q. *abbrev.* Intelligence quotient.

ir- (ĭ-r) *prefix.* = IN-, before *r*.

I.R.A., I.R.B. *abbrevs.* Irish Republican Army, Brotherhood.

ĭra′dė (-ah-) *n.* (hist.) Written decree of Sultan of Turkey.

Iran′ (ĭrahn). The Persian name for PERSIA. **Irān′ian** *adj.* & *n.* (Native) of Iran; one of the two Asiatic families of Indo-European languages, comprising Zeud and Old Persian, from which modern Persian is descended.

Iraq (ĭrahk′). Formerly known as Mesopotamia, a republic extending from Kurdistan on N. and NE. to the Persian Gulf on the S. and SE. and from Iran in E. to Syria and the Arabian Desert on W.; freed from Turkish rule during the war of 1914–18 and placed under a British mandate, which was terminated in 1932. Iraq was a kingdom from 1921 until assassination of Faisal II in 1958 when it became a republic; capital Baghdad. **Iraq′i** *adj.* & *n.* (Native) of Iraq; modern Arabic dialect spoken in Iraq.

īrăs′cĭble (*or* ĭ-; -sĭ-). Irritable, hot-tempered. **īrăscĭbĭl′ĭty** *n.*

īrāte′ *adj.* Angry.

īre *n.* (poet.) Anger. **īre′ful** (īrf-) *adj.* **īre′fully** *adv.*

Ire′land (īrl-). An island in the Atlantic Ocean, to W. of Gt Britain; made subordinate to the English legislature in 1494 by the Statutes of Drogheda; in 1916 an insurrection against British rule took place (the 'Easter rising'); in 1920 an Act was passed by the British Parliament dividing Ireland into two parts: (1) Southern Ireland, which was later recognized as an independent democratic State and became known as the Irish Free State or EIRE; and (2) NORTHERN IRELAND (the 'six counties'), which forms part of the United Kingdom.

īrē′nĭc(al) *adjs.* Tending towards, promoting, peace; pacific.

īrĕn′ĭcŏn *n.* Proposal designed to promote peace.

īrĭdā′ceous (-sh*u*s) *adj.* (Of plants) of the iris kind.

ĭrĭdĕs′cent *adj.* Showing colours like those of rainbow; changing in colour as light falls from different angles. **ĭrĭdĕs′cence** *n.*

īrĭd′ĭum *n.* Hard white brittle element of platinum group, mainly used in the form of its alloys with platinum or osmium for various purposes requiring very hard and incorrodible materials; symbol Ir, at. no. 77, at. wt 192·2.

īr′ĭs[1] *n.* 1. Circular pigmented diaphragm in anterior chamber of eye, with central aperture (the *pupil*) which admits light to the lens and contracts or expands according to intensity of light (ill. EYE); ~ *diaphragm*, mechanical device, resembling the iris, for controlling the diameter of a circular orifice by means of movable overlapping shutters (ill. PHOTOGRAPHY). 2. (bot.) Genus of plants with tubers or bulbs, sword-shaped leaves, and showy flowers. 3. Kind of rock-crystal reflecting prismatic colours.

Ir′ĭs[2] (īr-). (Gk myth.) Goddess who acted as the messenger of the gods, and displayed as her sign the rainbow.

Ir′ĭsh (īr-) *adj.* 1. Of Ireland; ~ *bull*: see BULL; ~ *Free State*: see IRELAND and EIRE; *Irishman*, *Irishwoman*, man, woman, of Irish descent; ~ *point*, needlepoint lace made in Ireland; ~ *Republican Army*, (abbrev. I.R.A.) terrorist organization aiming at a united independent Ireland; ~ *Sea*, the sea between Ireland and England; ~ *stew*, mutton cutlets stewed with potatoes and onions; ~ *terrier,* breed of terrier with rough wiry coat of reddish-brown colour; ~ *whiskey*: see WHISKY; ~ *wolfhound,* very large hound resembling a wolfhound but larger and stronger. 2. Of the branch of the Celtic languages spoken in Ireland. ~ *n.* 1. (pl.) *The* Irish people. 2. The Irish language.

Ir'ĭshĭsm (īr-) *n.* Idiom characteristic of the Irish language, or of English as spoken in Ireland.

îrk *v.t.* (archaic) Disgust, tire, bore. **îrk'some** *adj.* Tedious, tiresome. **îrk'somely** *adv.* **îrk'someness** *n.*

iron (īrn) *n.* 1. Abundant metallic element, widely distributed in form of ores (oxides and salts) and found in free state only in meteorites, silver-white in colour, and characterized by great tensile strength, ductility, and magnetic susceptibility; symbol Fe, at. no. 26, at. wt 55·847; the most extensively used of all metals because of its many properties; when purified and alloyed with small quantities of other materials, known as STEEL; *cast* ~, iron obtained by smelting from ores, silvery grey when clean, hard, brittle, crystalline in structure, and containing 2–5% of carbon and smaller quantities of sulphur, phosphorus, and silicon; *pig-*~, cast iron as first obtained from the smelting furnace, cast in long blocks (pigs) for convenience; *wrought* ~, highly malleable iron obtained by stirring pig-iron when molten (puddling), nearly pure but always containing some slag in the form of filaments and thus showing a fibrous structure. 2. Tool, implement, instrument, made of iron, as *curling-*~, *grappling-*~; tool or apparatus with smooth flat surface which can be heated for smoothing out linen (*flat* ~, lighter kind heated from below); golf club with iron head laid back for lofting the ball (ill. GOLF); (usu. pl.) fetters, shackles. 3. Preparation of iron used in medicine as a tonic. 4. (fig.) Type of hardness, as *man of* ~, *rod of* ~. 5. Phrases: *strike while the* ~ *is hot,* act promptly and at a good opportunity; *have* (*too*) *many irons in the fire,* have many undertakings afoot at the same time, have many expedients. ~ *adj.* Made of iron; firm, unyielding, merciless; ~ *age,* period in the history of a people, following the bronze age, characterized by use of iron implements and weapons; ~-*bark,* any species of *Eucalyptus* with solid bark; ~-*bound,* bound with iron; (fig.) inflexible, unyielding; (of coast) rugged, rocky; *iron'clad* (*adj.*) covered with, protected by, iron, as a field magnet; (*n.*, obs.) warship protected by iron plates; *I*~ *Cross,* German military decoration; ~ *curtain,* (fig.) barrier to passage of persons and information at western boundary of Russian sphere of influence in Europe; any similar barrier to spread of ideas etc.; *I*~ *Duke,* Duke of WELLINGTON[1]; ~-*grey,* of the colour of newly broken iron; ~ *lung,* rigid box enclosing the body of a patient (leaving the head free), used, in the treatment of paralysing diseases, for administering prolonged artificial respiration by means of mechanical pumps; (erron.) any apparatus used for the same purpose; *iron'master,* manufacturer of iron articles and appliances; *iron'monger,* dealer in iron and other metal goods, whence *iron'mongery*; ~-*mould,* stain made on textiles by iron-rust; ~ *rations,* (esp. soldier's) emergency rations; *iron'sides,* man of great bravery; (esp.) Cromwell's troopers in the Civil War; *iron'stone,* name of various hard iron-ores; *iron'ware,* generic name for all light articles made of iron; hardware; *iron'work,* iron parts of a structure; casting, mouldings, etc., made of iron; *iron'works,* place where iron is smelted or iron goods made. ~ *v.t.* Furnish, cover, with iron; shackle with irons; smooth (linen etc.) with a hot iron.

īrŏn'ic(al) *adjs.* Of, using, said in, addicted to, irony. **īrŏn'ĭcally** *adv.*

iron'ing (īrn-) *n.* Process of smoothing (linen etc.) with a heated iron; linen etc. to be ironed; ~-*board,* smooth, cloth-covered board on which clothes etc. are spread for ironing.

īr'ŏnist *n.* One who uses irony.

īr'ony[1] *n.* Figure of speech in which the intended meaning is the opposite of that expressed by the words used, usu. taking the form of sarcasm or ridicule in which laudatory expressions are used to imply condemnation or contempt; course of events, combination of circumstances, the result of which is the direct opposite of what might be expected as though due to the malice of fate, as in *life's ironies, irony of fate*; use of language that has an inner meaning for a privileged audience and an outer meaning for the persons addressed or concerned, as in *tragic* ~; *Socratic* ~, assumption of ignorance as means of confuting an opponent in dispute.

irony[2] (īr'nĭ) *adj.* Of, like, iron.

I'roquois (ĭ-; -kwoi *or* -kwah). Indian of a powerful confederacy of tribes formerly inhabiting central New York and known as the Five Nations.

ĭrrăd'ĭant *adj.* Shining brightly, luminous. **ĭrrăd'ĭance** *n.*

ĭrrăd'ĭāte *v.t.* Shine upon; subject to radiation, esp. of X-rays or ultra-violet rays; (fig.) throw light on (subject); light up (face etc. *with* joy etc.). **ĭrrădĭā'tion** *n.* Shining, illumination (lit. and fig.); (physics) apparent enlargement of edges of illuminated object seen against dark background.

ĭrrăd'ĭatĭve *adj.* Having property of irradiating; illuminating.

ĭrră'tional (-shon-) *adj.* Unreasonable, illogical, absurd; not endowed with reason; (math., of roots etc.) not rational, not commensurable with ordinary quantities, not expressible by an ordinary (finite) fraction, proper or improper. ~ *n.* Irrational person; (math.) irrational number or quantity; surd. **ĭrrătionăl'ĭty** *n.* **ĭrră'tionalīze** *v.t.* **ĭrră'tionally** *adv.*

Irrawadd'y (ĭ-; -wŏdĭ). Principal river of Burma, flowing into the E. of the Bay of Bengal.

ĭrrėclaim'able *adj.* Not to be reclaimed or reformed. **ĭrrėclaim'ably** *adv.*

ĭrrĕc'oncīlable *adj.* Implacably hostile; (of ideas etc.) incompatible. ~ *n.* Implacable opponent of political measure etc. **ĭrrĕconcīlabĭl'ĭty, ĭrrĕc'oncīlableness** *ns.* **ĭrrĕc'oncīlably** *adv.*

ĭrrėcov'erable (-kŭ-) *adj.* That cannot be recovered or remedied. **ĭrrėcov'erably** *adv.*

ĭrrėcūs'able (-z-) *adj.* That must be accepted.

ĭrrėdeem'able *adj.* Not to be redeemed, irreclaimable; (of govt. loans, etc.) not to be terminated by repayment; (of paper currency) for which issuing authority does not undertake to pay coin.

ĭrrėdĕn'tĭst *n.* (It. politics) Advocate of recovery to Italy of all Italian-speaking districts; member of other country who holds similar views. **ĭrrėdĕn'tĭsm** *n.* [It. (*Italia*) *irredenta* unredeemed Italy]

ĭrrėdū'cĭble *adj.* That cannot be brought (*to* desired condition); not capable of being reduced; ~ *minimum,* smallest amount, lowest degree, to which anything can be reduced, or point beyond which further reduction would be useless or unacceptable.

ĭrrĕf'ragable *adj.* (Of statement, argument, person) indisputable, unanswerable. **ĭrrĕf'ragably** *adv.*

ĭrrėfrăn'gĭble *adj.* Inviolate; (optics) not capable of being refracted.

ĭrrĕf'ūtable (*or* -rėfūt'-) *adj.* Not to be refuted. **ĭrrėfūtabĭl'ĭty** *n.* **ĭrrĕf'utably** *adv.*

ĭrrĕg'ūlar *adj.* Not regular, contrary to rule, abnormal; not of symmetrical form; (of surface) uneven; disorderly; uneven in duration, order, etc.; (gram.) not inflected in the usual way, pop. applied in English to the strong verb; (of troops) not in regular service. ~ *n.* Member of irregular military force. **ĭrrĕgūlă'rĭty** *n.* **ĭrrĕg'ularly** *adv.*

ĭrrĕl'atĭve *adj.* Unconnected, unrelated, (*to*); having no relations, absolute. **ĭrrĕl'atĭvely** *adv.*

ĭrrĕl'ėvant *adj.* Not to the point; not applicable (*to* matter in hand). **ĭrrĕl'ėvance, ĭrrĕl'ėvancy** *ns.* **ĭrrĕl'ėvantly** *adv.*

ĭrrėlĭ'gion (-jn) *n.* Hostility to,

disregard of, religion. **irreli'gious** (-jus) *adj.* **irreli'giously** *adv.*
irremed'iable *adj.* That cannot be remedied. **irremed'iably** *adv.*
irremiss'ible *adj.* Unpardonable; unalterably binding. **irremiss'ibly** *adv.*
irremo'vable (-moo-) *adj.* That cannot be removed, esp. from office. **irremovabil'ity** *n.* **irremo'vably** *adv.*
irrep'arable *adj.* (Of injury, loss, etc.) that cannot be rectified or made good; **irrep'arableness** *n.* **irrep'arably** *adv.*
irreplace'able (-sa-) *adj.* Of which the loss cannot be supplied.
irrepress'ible *adj.* Not to be repressed or restrained. **irrepress'ibly** *adv.*
irreproach'able *adj.* Free from blame, faultless. **irreproachabil'ity** *n.* **irreproach'ably** *adv.*
irresis'tible (-zis-) *adj.* Too strong, convincing, charming, etc., to be resisted. **irresistibil'ity** *n.* **irresis'tibly** *adv.*
irres'olute (-zoloot, -ūt) *adj.* Undecided, hesitating; wanting in resolution. **irres'olutely** *adv.* **irres'oluteness, irresolu'tion** *ns.*
irresol'vable (-zŏl-) *adj.* That cannot be resolved into parts; (of problem) that cannot be solved.
irrespec'tive *adj.* ~ *of*, not taking into account, without reference to. **irrespec'tively** *adv.*
irrespon'sible *adj.* Not responsible for conduct; acting, done, without due sense of responsibility. **irresponsibil'ity** *n.* **irrespon'sibly** *adv.*
irrespon'sive *adj.* Not responsive (*to*). **irrespon'siveness** *n.*
irreten'tion *n.* Failure to retain (esp. the urine). **irreten'tive** *adj.* Not retentive. **irreten'tiveness** *n.*
irretriev'able *adj.* That cannot be retrieved. **irretrievabil'ity** *n.* **irretriev'ably** *adv.*
irrev'erent *adj.* Wanting in reverence. **irrev'erently** *adv.* **irrev'erence** *n.*
irrevers'ible *adj.* Unalterable; not reversible. **irreversibil'ity** *n.* **irrevers'ibly** *adv.*
irrev'ocable *adj.* Unalterable; gone beyond recall. **irrevocabil'ity** *n.* **irrev'ocably** *adv.*
i'rrigate *v.t.* (Of streams etc.) supply land with water; water (land) by system of artificial channels, ditches; (med.) wash, moisten (wound etc.) with constant flow of liquid. **i'rrigable, i'rrigative** *adjs.* **irriga'tion** *n.*
i'rritable *adj.* Quick to anger, touchy; (physiol., of muscles, nerves) capable of being excited to vital action by physical stimulus; (of parts of body, wounds, etc.) excessively sensitive to stimuli; inflamed, sore; (bot.) capable of responding to external stimulus. **irritabil'ity** *n.* **i'rritably** *adv.*
i'rritancy[1] *n.* Irritation, annoyance.
i'rritancy[2] *n.* (law) Making, being, null and void.

i'rritant *adj.* Causing (usu. physical) irritation. ~ *n.* Substance causing irritation (also fig.).
i'rritate *v.t.* Excite to anger, annoy; excite, inflame, make sore (part of body etc.); (physiol.) stimulate (organ) to activity. **i'rritating** *adj.* **i'rritatingly** *adv.* **irrita'tion** *n.*
irrup'tion *n.* Invasion; violent entry.
Irv'ing[1] (er-), Sir Henry (1838–1905). English actor.
Irv'ing[2] (er-), Washington (1783–1859). American historian, essayist, and novelist; author of 'The Sketch-Book', which includes his 'Rip van Winkle'.
Irv'ingite (er-). Member of a religious body called by its members the Catholic Apostolic Church, founded *c* 1835 on basis of principles promulgated by Edward Irving (1792–1834), a minister of the Church of Scotland.
is, 3rd pers. sing. pres. of BE.
Is. *abbrev.* Isaiah (also **Isa.**); Island.
Isaac (īz'ak). A Hebrew patriarch, son of Abraham and Sarah and father of Jacob and Esau.
isabell'a (iz-) *adj.* & *n.* Greyish yellow. **isabell'ine** *adj.* Isabella-coloured.
isagog'ic (-jĭk) *adj.* Introductory. **isagog'ics** *n.pl.* Study of literary and external history of the Bible.
Isaiah (īzī'a). One of the major Hebrew prophets, who ministered in Judah in 8th c. B.C. and attacked corruption in the national life; the O.T. book of his prophecies.
is'atin *n.* Reddish-yellow crystalline substance obtained by oxidizing indigo and used in the preparation of vat dyes.
is'chium (-k-) *n.* One of the bones of the pelvis (ill. PELVIS). **ischiat'ic** *adj.*
Ish'mael (ish-). Son of Hagar, of whom it was predicted, 'His hand will be against every man, and every man's hand against him' (Gen. xvi. 12); hence, an outcast, one at war with society. **Ish'maelite** *n.* An Ishmael.
Ishtar: see ASTARTE.
Is'idore (iz-) **of Seville** (*c* 560–636). Bishop of Seville, an encyclopaedic writer. **Isidor'ian** *adj.* ~ *Decretals*, a collection of decretals (the author of which took the name of Isidore of Seville) made in the 9th c., containing spurious documents supporting the papal claim to temporal power.
isinglass (īz'ingglahs) *n.* Semi-transparent substance, form of gelatine, got from viscera of certain fishes, esp. the sturgeon, and used in making jellies, glue, etc., and for clarifying alcoholic beverages. [obs. Du. *huisenblas* sturgeon's bladder]
Is'is[1] (ī-). Egyptian deity, the sister and wife of OSIRIS, and mother of HORUS, regarded as a nature-goddess.

Is'is[2] (ī-). The river Thames from its source to its junction with the Thame, below Oxford. [prob. f. false etymology of L *Tamisis* as *Tam*+*Isis*]
Islam (islahm' *or* iz'lăm). The religion revealed through the Prophet Mohammed; the Moslem world. **Islam'ic, Islamit'ic** *adj.* **Is'lamism, Is'lamite** *ns.* [Arab. = 'resignation']
isl'and (īl'-) *n.* Piece of land surrounded by water; (fig.) anything detached or isolated; (naut.) ship's bridge or superstructure; (physiol.) detached portion of tissue or group of cells; ~*s of Langerhans*: see LANGERHANS; *Islands of the Blessed*, (Gk and Rom. myth.) islands of the Western Ocean, where favourites of the gods dwell after death. ~ *v.t.* Make into an island; isolate, dot as with islands.
isl'ander (īl'-) *n.* Native or inhabitant of an island.
isle (īl) *n.* Island, esp. poetical or in proper names, and usu. of small island.
isl'et (īl-) *n.* Little island, isolated tract or spot; (physiol.) small detached mass of tissue within tissue of a different kind.
Ismaili (iz'maēl'i). Member of a Moslem sect which seceded from the Shiah in 9th c. after the rejection of the claim of Isma'il, a descendant of Mohammed's son-in-law Ali, to be leader (imam) of Islam; the sect were very powerful in 10th c. when the Fatimids were in power; in 12th c. they were responsible for a terrorist movement (the Assassins); they now survive mainly in India, Persia, and E. Africa, and regard the Aga Khan as their imam.
iso- *prefix.* Equal.
I.S.O. *abbrev.* Imperial Service Order.
is'obar *n.* 1. Line on map (ill. WEATHER) connecting places at which atmospheric pressure is the same (at given time or on the average). 2. One of two or more elements having the same atomic weight but different chemical properties. **isobar'ic** *adj.*
isocheim'al (-kī-), **isochim'enal** (-kī-) *adjs.* & *ns.* (Line on map) connecting places of same mean winter temperature.
isoch'ronous (*or* is-; -kr-) *adj.* Occupying equal time, vibrating uniformly, as a pendulum.
isodynam'ic *adj.* & *n.* (Line on map) connecting places at which the total magnetic intensity of the terrestrial field has the same magnitude.
isogon'ic *adj.* & *n.* (Line on map) connecting places where the declination of the magnetic needle is the same.
is'olable *adj.* Capable of being isolated.
is'olate *v.t.* Place apart or alone; (chem.) free substance from its

compounds; subject (person etc.) to quarantine, separate (infectious patient) from others; (elect.) = INSULATE. **isolā'tion** *n.*

isolā'tionist (-shon-) *n.* One who favours (political or national) isolation (esp. in U.S. politics). **isolā'tionism** *n.*

is'omer *n.* (chem.) One of two or more substances composed of molecules having the same kind of atoms and in the same proportions, but which, by reason of a difference in arrangement of the atoms, have different chemical and physical properties. **isomě'ric** *adj.* **isŏm'erism** *n.*

isŏm'erous *adj.* (bot.) (Of a flower) having the same number of parts in each whorl.

isomět'ric(al) *adjs.* Of equal measure or dimensions; ~ *drawing*, engineer's or architect's drawing in which the 3 dimensions are represented by 3 sets of lines 120° apart and all measurements are on same scale (i.e. not in perspective; ill. DRAWING).

is'omorph *n.* Substance or organism isomorphous with another. **isomorph'ic, isomorph'ous** *adjs.* Having the property of crystallizing in the same or closely related geometric forms; (math., of groups) corresponding to each other in form and in the nature and product of their operations. **isomorph'ism** *n.*

is'opŏd *n.* Crustacean of large group (including, e.g., wood-lice) varying greatly in form and often parasitic.

isŏs'celēs (-selēz) *adj.* (of triangle) Having two sides equal (ill. TRIANGLE).

isoseis'mal (-sīz-) *adj.* & *n.* (Line on map) connecting places at which an earthquake-shock is of the same intensity.

isŏs'tăsy *n.* (geol.) Theory which postulates that the earth's crust is in a state of equilibrium and that every process that disturbs this state is followed by a readjustment (e.g. when the ice-cap disappeared from Scandinavia the land rose slightly to compensate for the loss of load). **isostăt'ic** *adj.* In static equilibrium, esp. as applied to theory of isostasy.

is'otherm *n.* Line on map connecting places having the same mean annual or monthly temperature. **isotherm'al** *adj.* & *n.*

is'otōpe *n.* One of two or more forms of an element having the same atomic number and the same chemical properties and occupying the same place in the periodic table, but differing in atomic weight and in nuclear properties such as radio-activity. **isotŏp'ic** *adj.*

Is'raěl (ĭz-). 1. The people descended from Jacob (*children of* ~); the Jewish or Hebrew nation or people. 2. An independent Jewish republic in Palestine, established 1948; capital, Jerusalem. **Israā'ėli** *n.* Inhabitant of modern Israel. **Is'raėlīte** *n.* One of the people of Israel; Hebrew; Jew. [Heb. = 'he that strives with God', a symbolic name conferred on Jacob, Gen. xxxii. 28]

Is'rafěl (ĭz-). In Mohammedan tradition, angel of music, who will sound the trumpet on the Day of Judgement.

iss'ūe *n.* 1. Outgoing, outflow; (med.) discharge of blood etc., incision to procure this. 2. Termination, end. 3. Way out, outlet; mouth of river. 4. Progeny, children. 5. Result, outcome. 6. Point in question, esp. (law) between contending parties in action; *at* ~, at variance; in dispute; *join* ~, proceed to argue (*with* person *on* point agreed upon as basis of dispute); (law) submit an issue jointly for decision; (of one party) accept the issue tendered by the other. 7. Giving out, issuing, (*of* bills of exchange, stamps, etc.); number of coins, notes, copies of newspaper or book etc. issued at one time; ~ *v.* 1. Go or come out; emerge from a condition; be derived, spring, (*from*); result (*from*); end, result, (*in*). 2. Come out, be published; send forth; publish, put into circulation (notes, newspaper, book, etc.). 3. (mil.) Supply (soldier) *with* article of equipment etc. **iss'ūable** *adj.* **iss'ūance** *n.*

iss'ūant *adj.* (her.) Emerging from bottom of a chief, or rising from another bearing etc. (esp. of beast of which upper part alone is visible).

Istanbul' (ĭ-; -ōōl). Turkish name of CONSTANTINOPLE.

is'thmus (-sm-, -sthm-, -stm-) *n.* Narrow portion of land connecting two larger bodies of land, neck of land; (anat., bot., zool.) narrow part connecting two larger parts. **is'thmian** *adj.* Of an isthmus; esp. of the Isthmus of Corinth or the *I*~ *Games*, national festival of ancient Greece held at Corinth in alternate years.

Is'tria (ĭ-). Mountainous rocky peninsula projecting into Adriatic east of Trieste; formerly part of the Austrian duchy of Carinthia; assigned to Italy after war of 1914–18; now part of Yugoslavia.

it[1] *pron.* 1. The thing in question; the person in question; as subject of impersonal verb, expressing action or condition of things without reference to agent; as subject of verb, anticipating deferred virtual subject in apposition; as antecedent to relative of either number and any gender, separated by predicate; as indefinite object with transitive or intransitive verb. 2. In children's games, player who must catch or find others; (slang) the *ne plus ultra*, the acme; 'sex appeal'.

it[2] *n.* (in *gin-and-it*) Short for *Italian vermouth.*

I.T.A. *abbrev.* Independent Television Authority.

it'acism (ē-) *n.* Pronunciation of Greek *e* like English *ee*; substitution in MS. of Gk iota (ι) for other vowels or diphthongs.

it(al). *abbrev.* Italic (type).

Ităl'ian (ĭ-) *adj.* Of Italy; ~ *cloth*, kind of cloth with satin face used for linings etc.; ~ *hand*, kind of handwriting developed in Italy and resembling italic printing (opp. GOTHIC); ~ *warehouse*, shop where dried fruits, olive oil, etc., are sold. ~ *n.* 1. Native of Italy. 2. Language of Italy, one of the modern descendants of Latin. **Ităl'ianate** *adj.* Of Italian form or character.

Ităl'ic[1] (ĭ-) *adj.* 1. Of ancient Italy or its tribes; of the Greek colonies in southern Italy; ~ *languages*, Indo-European languages of ancient Italy (Latin, Oscan, Umbrian) as a group.

ităl'ic[2] *adj.* & *n.* (type), *italics*, kind of printing type introduced by Aldus Manutius (1501), in which letters slope towards the right (now usu. employed to emphasize word(s) or distinguish word(s) from others in same context; ill. TYPE). **ităl'icize** *v.t.* Print in italics; (in writing) underline.

It'aly (ĭt-). The peninsula running southward into Mediterranean from the mass of central Europe; formerly divided among various mercantile city states or under foreign domination until unified in 19th c. by the efforts of Mazzini, Cavour, and Garibaldi; a monarchy from 1861 (when Vittorio Emmanuele II of Sardinia was proclaimed king of Italy and the first parliament met) until 1946 when a republic was declared; capital, Rome.

itch *n.* Uneasy sense of irritation in skin; scabies, contagious disease accompanied by itching and caused by the ~-*mite*, small parasitic arachnid (*Sarcoptes scabiei*) which burrows in skin; restless desire, hankering. ~ *v.i.* Feel irritation in skin; crave uneasily. **itch'y** *adj.*

it'ěm *n.* Article, unit, included in enumeration; entry of this in account etc.; detail of news etc. in newspaper etc. ~ *adv.* Likewise, also, (introducing mention of item). **it'ėmize** *v.t.* Set down by items; specify items of (account etc.). [L, *item* in like manner, also]

it'erāte *v.t.* Repeat (quoted words etc.); make (charge, assertion, etc.) repeatedly. **it'erance, iterā'tion** *n.*

it'erative *adj.* (esp. gram., of verb) Denoting repetition of action, frequentative.

Ith'aca (ĭ-). 1. Small island W. of Greece, adjoining Cephallenia; called by modern Greeks *Thiaki.* 2. The island described by Homer as the kingdom of Odysseus (ULYSSES); traditionally identified with Thiaki, but thought by some to be the neighbouring larger island of Leukas.

ĭthȳphăll'ĭc *adj.* Of the phallus carried in Bacchic festivals; in the metre used for Bacchic hymns (trochaic dimeter brachycatalectic, - ∪ - ∪ - -) ~ *n.* Poem in this metre; licentious poem.

ĭtĭn'erant *adj.* Travelling from place to place; (of justices) travelling on circuit; (of Wesleyan ministry) preaching in a circuit. ~ *n.* **ĭtĭn'eracy, ĭtĭn'erancy** *ns.*

ĭtĭn'erary *n.* Route; record of travel; guide-book. ~ *adj.* Of travelling, of roads.

ĭtĭn'erāte *v.i.* Travel from place to place; (of Wesleyan) preach within circuit.

ĭts *poss. adj.* of IT[1] *pron.*

ĭtsĕlf' *pron.* Emphatic and reflexive form corresp. to IT[1]; *by* ~, automatically; apart from its surroundings; *in* ~, apart from its surroundings; viewed in its essential qualities etc.

Ivan (ēvahn'). Name of several rulers of Russia: *Ivan I* (d. 1341), grand duke of Vladimir 1328–, during whose reign the Metropolitan see was transferred from Vladimir to Moscow; *Ivan II* (d. 1359), grand duke of Vladimir; *Ivan III* 'the Great' (1440–1505), grand duke of Muscovy 1462–; *Ivan IV* 'the Terrible' (1530–84), first tsar of Muscovy 1533–; a successful ruler, who limited the power of the boyars and favoured the merchant classes; conquered Kazan and Astrakhan and added Siberia to his dominions; was subject to fits of rage in one of which he killed his son; completely destroyed the city of Novgorod, 1569, because of a reported conspiracy; *Ivan V* (1666–96), associated as tsar from 1682 with his half-brother Peter the Great; *Ivan VI* (1740–64), emperor of Russia 1740–1; kept in imprisonment from 1742 until his death.

Ives (īvz), St. (*also* **Yves** pr. ēv). Ivo of Chartres (*c* 1040–1116), French churchman, bishop of Chartres.

Iviza (ēvē'th*a*). *Ibiza*, Mediterranean island forming part of BALEARIC group.

Ivo of Chartres: see IVES.

īv'ory *n.* 1. Hard white fine-grained substance (dentine of exceptional hardness) composing main part of tusks of elephant, hippopotamus, walrus, narwhal, and (*fossil* ~) mammoth; *vegetable* ~, hard endosperm of seed (~ *nut*) of the palm *Phytelephas*; *black* ~, African Negro slaves; ~ *black*, black pigment from calcined ivory; ~ *tower*, condition of seclusion from the world, shelter from the crudities of life. 2. Colour of ivory, ivory-white. 3. (slang, pl.) Teeth; dice, billiard-balls, piano-keys.

Iv'ory Coast (ī-). Republic of W. Africa, between Liberia and Ghana; member of French Community; capital, Abidjan.

Ivry (ēvrē'). Battle (1590) fought about 40 miles W. of Paris between Huguenots under Henry IV and Catholic League under Mayenne, in which Henry was victorious.

īv'y *n.* Climbing evergreen shrub (*Hedera helix*) with dark-green shining leaves, usu. five-angled.

I.W. *abbrev.* Isle of Wight.

I.W.T.(D.) *abbrev.* Inland Water Transport (Department).

I.W.W. *abbrev.* Industrial Workers of the World.

ĭx'ĭa *n.* Genus of S. Afr. iridaceous plants with large showy flowers.

Ixī'on (ĭ-). (Gk myth.) King of Thessaly, father of the Centaurs; tried to seduce Hera, and was condemned to be bound to a fiery wheel revolving unceasingly through the underworld.

ĭzz'ard *n.* (archaic) The letter z.

J

J, j (jā). 10th letter of modern English alphabet, a late modification of I; in form, i with a tail (i was freq. written thus in MSS. when final); in modern English representing a voiced composite sound (*dzh*), corresponding to the voiceless *tsh*; *J(-pen)*, broad-pointed pen stamped with letter J.

J. *abbrev.* Judge; Justice.

J.A. *abbrev.* Judge Advocate.

jăb *v.t.* Poke roughly; stab; thrust (thing) abruptly (*into*). ~ *n.* Abrupt stabbing blow with pointed thing or fist.

jăbb'er *v.* Speak volubly and with little sense; utter (words) rapidly and indistinctly; chatter, as monkeys etc. ~ *n.* Jabbering, gabble, gibberish.

jăb'ĭru (-ōō) *n.* One of the largest storks (*Mycteria americana*); found in tropical America; related genera found in Australia and India.

jăborăn'dĭ *n.* Dried leaflets of Brazilian plant (*Pilocarpus microphyllus*) with salivant, diuretic, and sudorific properties.

jabot (zhăb'ō) *n.* Ornamental frill on front of woman's bodice (ill. COAT); (hist.) frill on man's shirt-front.

jacana (jăs'*a*nah) *n.* Any of several birds found in S. America with very long toes enabling them to walk over floating plants; various birds of same group found elsewhere.

jă'cĭnth *n.* Reddish-orange gem, variety of zircon.

jăck[1], **Jack** *n.* 1. (*J*~) Familiar by-form of name *John*, esp. as type of common people; (also ~ *tar*) familiar name for sailor; labourer, man who does odd jobs etc.; cheap-jack; steeple-jack; figure striking bell on outside of clock; *every man* ~, every individual. 2. (cards) Knave of trumps in game of all-fours; any knave. 3. Machine for turning spit in roasting meat (ill. FIRE); machine for lifting heavy weights by force from below; machine for raising and supporting axle while removing or cleaning wheel etc.; BOOT-jack; parts of various machines; in spinet, harpsichord, etc., wooden upright fixed to back of key-lever and fitted with quill for plucking string (ill. HARPSICHORD). 4. (elect.) Device for connecting one set of wires to a corresponding set by the insertion of a single plug (used esp. in manual telephone exchanges). 5. (bowls) Smaller bowl as mark for players to aim at. 6. Pike, esp. young or small one. 7. Money. 8. *jack'ass*, male ass; dolt; blockhead; *laughing jackass*, Australian giant kingfisher (*Dacelo gigas*), from its loud discordant cry; *~-boot*, large boot coming above knee; *jack'daw*, daw (*Corvus monedula*), thievish small crow haunting old buildings etc., easily tamed and taught to imitate sound of words; *J~ Frost*, frost personified; *J~ in office*, fussy (esp. petty) official; *~-in-the-box*, toy figure that springs out of box when opened; kind of firework; *J~-in-the-green*, man or boy enclosed in framework covered with leaves in May-day sports; *J~ Ketch*, (f. name of common executioner 1663–86), common hangman; *~-knife*, large pocket clasp-knife; ~ *of all trades*, one who can turn his

SCREW JACK

hand to anything; ~ *o'lantern*, will-o'-the-wisp; ~-*plane*, long heavy plane for coarse work (ill. PLANE); *jack'pot*, (in poker) pool which cannot be opened until some player has two jacks or better in his hand; cumulative stakes or prize in lottery etc.; ~-*pudding*, buffoon, clown; ~-*rabbit*, (U.S.) large prairie-hare with very long ears and legs; ~-*snipe*, small species of snipe (*Scolopax gallinula*); ~ *tar*, common sailor; *J~ the Ripper*, undiscovered murderer of women in London (1888–91), who mutilated his victims; ~-*towel*, endless towel hung from roller. ~ *v.t.* Hoist (*up*) with mechanical jack.

jăck[2] *n.* Ship's flag, smaller than ensign, esp. one flown from jackstaff at bow, indicating nationality; single flag flown on foremast as signal for pilot; *Union J~*: see UNION; *jackstaff*, short staff at bow of ship on which the jack is flown (ill. SHIP).

jăck[3] *n.* (archaic) 1. Foot-soldier's sleeveless padded tunic. 2. (also *black* ~) Vessel for liquor, usu. of waxed leather coated with tar (ill. BLACK).

jăck'al (-awl) *n.* 1. Any of several members of the dog family found wild in Asia and Africa, living on carrion and small animals. 2. Person who does subordinate preparatory work or drudgery for another (because jackals were formerly believed to hunt up lion's prey for him). ~ *v.i.* Act as jackal (*for*). [Turk. *chakāl*]

jăck'anāpes (-ps) *n.* 1. (archaic) (Tame) ape or monkey. 2. Pert fellow; coxcomb; pert child.

jăck'ėt *n.* Sleeved outer garment for man or woman; outer covering round boiler etc. to protect it or keep in heat; loose paper cover or wrapper round book; any outer coat or covering, as skin of potatoes, animal's coat. ~ *v.t.* Cover with jacket.

Jăck'son[1], Andrew (1767–1845). 'Old Hickory', American soldier and statesman; 7th president of U.S. 1829–37.

Jăck'son[2], Thomas Jonathan (1824–63). 'Stonewall Jackson', American general; commander (as Lee's chief assistant) of Southern forces in Amer. Civil War, accidentally killed by the fire of his own men at Chancellorsville.

Jăck'son[3]. Capital city of Mississippi, U.S.

Jāc'ob. (O.T.) Son of Isaac and Rebecca, younger twin brother of Esau, father of Joseph, and traditional founder of Israel (Gen. xxv–lx); ~*'s ladder*, the ladder between earth and heaven, with angels ascending and descending, which Jacob saw in a dream at Bethel (Gen. xxviii. 12); hence, rope-ladder with wooden rungs for ascending ship's rigging; also, blue-flowered perennial plant (*Polemonium caeruleum*) with closely pinnate leaves giving ladder-like appearance; ~*'s staff*, cross-staff; 3-ft long square rod with cursor, as instrument for measuring distances and heights; pointed iron-shod rod for supporting surveyor's circumferentor instead of tripod.

Jăcobē'an *adj.* Of the reign of James I of England (1603–25); of the style of building or furniture in England in early 17th c.; (commerc., of stain, varnish, etc.) of the colour of dark oak. [L *Jacobus* James]

jăc'obĭn[1] *n.* Pigeon with reversed feathers on back of neck, suggesting cowl. [Fr. *jacobine*, fem. of *jacobin* (friar)]

Jăc'obĭn[2]. 1. Friar of order of St. Dominic, esp. French member of the order, from their first convent near church of St. Jacques in Paris. 2. Member of French political club founded 1789 in the old Jacobin convent in Paris to maintain the principles of extreme democracy and absolute equality, and responsible, under Robespierre, for the 'Reign of Terror'; dissolved 1799; sympathizer with principles of Jacobins in French Revolution, extreme radical or revolutionary.

Jăc'obīte[1]. Member of a Syrian sect named from Jacobus Baradaeus, bishop of Edessa (6th c.), who revived the EUTYCHIAN heresy that Christ's nature is not both human and divine, but divine only.

Jăc'obīte[2]. Adherent of James II of England after his abdication, or of the Old or Young Pretender; supporter of Stuarts after revolution of 1688.

Jac'obsen (yahk-), Jens Peter (1847–85). Danish novelist and poet.

jacōb'us *n.* (hist.) English gold coin struck in reign of James I, worth 20–24*s*.

jăc'onėt *n.* 1. Plain white cotton fabric resembling cambric. 2. Dyed cotton fabric, freq. glazed on one side.

Jacquard (jăk'ârd), Joseph Marie (1752–1834). French inventor, improver of the loom; ~ *loom*, loom for mechanically weaving figured patterns by means of an endless belt of cards punched with holes arranged to form the required pattern.

jacquerie (zhăk'erē) *n.* Rising of peasantry, esp. that of 1357–8 in N. France. [Fr., f. *Jacques* James, peasant]

jăctitā'tion *n.* (law) ~ *of marriage*, offence of falsely claiming to be person's wife or husband.

jāde[1] *n.* Inferior, wearied, or worn-out horse; (in reprobation, usu. playful) woman. ~ *v.t.* Exhaust with hard work; make tired or dull. **jād'ėd** *adj.*

jāde[2] *n.* 1. Nephrite, a hard translucent light-green, bluish, or whitish stone used for ornaments etc.; a silicate of calcium and magnesium. 2. Jadeite, a silicate of sodium and aluminium, closely resembling nephrite in appearance. 3. Carved piece of jadeite or nephrite. 4. (also ~-*green*) a light green. [Span. (*piedra de*) *ijada* (stone of) the colic, f. L *ilia* flank]

jād'eite (-dīt) *n.* See JADE, 2.

Jā'ĕl. (O.T.) Woman who murdered SISERA, her guest, by driving a tent-nail through his temples (Judges iv, v).

Jăff'a. Modern (Arabic) name of Joppa, an ancient seaport of Palestine; ~ (*orange*), large oval seedless orange grown in gardens E. of Joppa.

jăg[1] *n.* Sharp projection, e.g. point of rock. ~ *v.t.* Cut, tear, break, in uneven manner, make indentations in. **jăgg'ėd** *adj.* **jăgg'ėdly** *adv.* **jăgg'ėdnėss** *n.* **jăgg'y** *adj.*

jăg[2] *n.* (dial. and U.S.) Small load; (U.S. slang) drinking-bout; 'load' of drink.

J.A.G. *abbrev.* Judge Advocate-General.

Jag(g)anath: see JUGGERNAUT.

jăgg'ery *n.* Coarse dark-brown sugar made in India from palm-sap; any crude sugar. [Indo-Port. *jagara* sugar]

jăg'ūar (*or* -gwar) *n.* Large carnivorous spotted quadruped of cat kind (*Felis onca*), inhabiting wooded parts of America from Texas to Paraguay.

Jah. Jehovah. [repr. Heb. *Yah*]

jail: see GAOL.

Jain (jīn). Member of non-Brahminical Hindu sect established in 6th c. B.C., with doctrines closely resembling those of Buddhism. **Jaīn'ĭsm** *n.* [Sansk. *jina* a Buddha (*ji* conquer, overcome)]

Jaipur (jīpoor'). A former Indian native State; its capital city, now capital of the State of Rajasthan, India.

Jaisalmēr' (jī-). A former Indian native State, now part of the State of Rajasthan, India.

Jakarta: alternative spelling of DJAKARTA.

jăl'ap *n.* (Purgative drug got from roots of) Mexican climbing plant, *Ipomaea Purga*, with salver-shaped purplish flowers. [f. *Jalapa*, Mexican city (Aztec *Xalapan* sand by the water)]

jalŏp(p)'ȳ *n.* (orig. U.S.) Dilapidated motor-car; (transf.) battered old aircraft.

jalousie (zhăl'oozē) *n.* Blind, shutter, with slats sloping upwards from without. [Fr., = 'jealousy']

jăm[1] *v.* Squeeze (thing) between two surfaces; cause (part of machine) to be fixed so that it cannot work; squeeze (things) together in compact mass; thrust (thing) violently (*into* space); block, fill up, (passage etc.) by crowding into it; become tightly wedged; (wireless) cause interference with (signal or station). ~ *n.* Crush, squeeze; stoppage (of machine etc.) due to this; crowded mass, esp.

accumulation of logs in river or traffic in street etc.; (colloq.) awkward situation, a 'fix'.

jăm[2] *n.* Conserve of fruit made by boiling it with sugar to a thick consistency.

Jam. *abbrev.* Jamaica; James (N.T.).

Jamaic'a. Island in the Carribean Sea; discovered by Columbus in 1494 and ruled by Spain until captured by England in 1655; in 1962 it became an independent State within the British Commonwealth; capital, Kingston.

jămb (-m) *n.* Side post of doorway, window, etc. (ill. DOOR).

jămboree' *n.* (orig. U.S.) Noisy revel; carousal or spree; esp., large gathering of Boy Scouts.

Jāmes[1] (-mz). Name of several persons in N.T. 1. The son of Zebedee and elder brother of John the Evangelist (Mark iii. 17); one of the 12 apostles and the first to be martyred; called *St. ~ the Greater*; commemorated 25th July; patron saint of Spain. 2. The 'brother' of Jesus, traditionally regarded as the author of the N.T. 'Epistle of James'; usu. identified with 'James the son of Alphaeus' who was one of the 12 apostles (Mark iii. 18) and with 'James the less' or 'little' (Mark xv. 40); called *St. ~ the Less* or *the Just*; commemorated 1st May, with St. Philip. 3. The father of Judas (i.e. of Jude; Luke vi. 16, where 'brother' is a mistranslation).

Jāmes[2] (-mz). Name of 7 Stuart kings of Scotland: *James I* (1394–1437); son of Robert III; reigned 1406–, but was held captive in England till 1424; *James II* (1430–60), his son, reigned 1437–; *James III* (1451–88), his son, reigned 1460–; *James IV* (1473–1513), his son, reigned 1488–; married Margaret Tudor, daughter of Henry VII of England; invaded England, 1513, and was killed at Flodden Field; *James V* (1512–42), son of James IV and father of Mary Queen of Scots; reigned 1513–; *James VI* and *VII*: see next entry.

Jāmes[3] (-mz). Name of two Stuart kings of England and Scotland: *James I* of England and *VI* of Scotland (1566–1625), son of Lord Darnley and Mary Queen of Scots, and, through her, great-great-grandson of Henry VII; on her abdication, 1567, became king of Scotland, and on Elizabeth I's death, 1603, king of England; *James II* of England and *VII* of Scotland (1633–1701), son of Charles I and grandson of James I; succeeded his brother, Charles II, 1685; had Catholic sympathies; fled to France, and was succeeded, 1688, by his Protestant son-in-law William of Orange.

Jāmes[4] (-mz) (1688–1766). James Francis Edward Stuart, son of JAMES[3] II: see Old PRETENDER.

Jāmes[5], Epistle of. Book of N.T. traditionally ascribed to James, brother of Jesus (see JAMES[1], 2).

James[6] (-mz), Henry (1843–1916). American novelist; settled in Europe from 1875; naturalized as a British subject, 1915.

James[7], William (1842–1910). American philosopher and psychologist, elder brother of Henry JAMES[6]; formulator of theory of PRAGMATISM.

Jameson Raid (jām'sn). March into the Transvaal, 1895, of 600 troops led by the administrator of Rhodesia, Dr (later Sir) Leander Starr Jameson (1853–1917); the force was captured by the Boers at Doornknop and handed over by President Kruger to the Br. Government for punishment; the raid, intended to support a projected rising of Uitlanders in Johannesburg, was unauthorized, though Cecil Rhodes, premier of the Cape, was implicated and resigned forthwith; the incident was one of those leading to the Boer War.

Jāmes'town (-mst-). Ruined village in Virginia, U.S.A., site of first permanent English settlement in America (1607); *~-weed*, jim(p)son weed.

Jami (jahmē') 1414–92). Persian classic poet.

Jammes (zhahm), Francis (1868–1938). French mystical poet and novelist.

Jămshid' (-eed). (Persian myth.) Legendary early king of Persia, reputed inventor of arts of medicine, navigation, iron-working, etc.; he was king of the peris, condemned to assume human form for boasting of his immortality, and ruled Persia for 700 years.

Jan. *abbrev.* January.

jăng'le (-ngg-) *v.* Make harsh metallic noise; cause (bell etc.) to do this; speak, utter, in discordant or noisy way. *~ n.* Discordant sound or clang, harsh noise.

jăn'itor *n.* Doorkeeper; (U.S.) caretaker of building, charged with heating and cleaning it.

jăn'izary, jăn'issary (jă-, yă-) *n.* 1. (hist.) One of body of Turkish infantry forming sultan's guards and main fighting force of Turkish army, orig. (14th c.) personal slaves of sultan, later slaves, conscripts, and sons of subject Christians; abolished after revolt, in which many were killed, 1826. 2. Any Turkish soldier; (fig.) personal instrument of tyranny. [Turk. *yeni tsheri* new soldiery]

Jăn'sen (*or* yahn-), Cornelius (1585–1638). R.C. bishop of Ypres in Flanders and professor at Louvain. **Jăn'senism** (j-) *n.* Religious system based on Jansen's digest of the teaching of St. Augustine; maintaining that the natural human will is perverse and incapable of good, that the capacity for the love of God can be attained only by 'conversion', and that God converts whom He pleases. Jansenism was strongly opposed by the Jesuits and condemned by several popes esp. Clement X; it flourished chiefly in France (17th and 18th centuries), where the nunnery of PORT-ROYAL, near Paris, was its headquarters. **Jăn'senist** *n.*

Jănūār'ius, St. (3rd c.). Bishop of Benevento; martyred under Diocletian; patron saint of Naples; commemorated 19th Sept.

Jăn'ūary. 1st month in modern calendar, having 31 days. [L (*mensis*) *Januarius* (month) of JANUS]

Jān'us. (Roman myth.) Ancient Italian deity, guardian of gates and doorways and esp. of the State in time of war; represented with two faces, one at front and one at back of his head.

Jăp. Colloq. abbrev. of JAPANESE; *~ silk*, light-weight silk fabric, orig. woven in Japan, from which the gum is boiled away after weaving.

japăn'[1] *n.* Hard varnish, esp. that made from asphalt and linseed oil in imitation of Japanese lacquer and used for producing black gloss on metal etc. *~ v.t.* Cover with japan; make black and glossy as with japan.

Japăn'[2]. Empire of Eastern Asia, occupying long group of islands in Pacific, roughly parallel with E. coast of Asiatic mainland; capital, Tokyo. **Jăpanēse'** (-z) *adj.* Of Japan; *~ cherry*, hybrid flowering cherry (*Prunus*) with pink or white, usu. double, flowers; *~ print*, colour-print printed in water-colour from wood-blocks; *~ silk*: see JAP silk; *~ vellum*, stiff smooth yellowish hand-made paper orig. made in Japan from mulberry bark; imitations of this. *~ n.* 1. Native or inhabitant of Japan; one of a yellow-skinned, dark-haired race of small stature, with oblique 'Mongolian' eyes. 2. The language of Japan, which is agglutinative, contains many Chinese loan-words, and is written in Chinese ideographs with characters of a syllabary called *kana* for the agglutinative and inflectional endings. [Chinese *Jih-pun* sunrise (*jih* sun, *pun* origin)]

jāpe *n.* & *v.i.* Jest.

Jāph'ĕth. (O.T.) One of the sons of Noah, supposed ancestor of the peoples living round Mediterranean. **Japhĕt'ic** *adj.* Of or descended from Japheth; sometimes applied to Indo-European peoples.

japŏn'ic *adj.* Japanese.

japŏn'ica *n.* Various ornamental plants supposed to have originated in Japan; esp. the Japanese quince, cultivated in Japan but native in China.

Jaques-Dălcrōze' (zhahk), Émile (1865–1950). Swiss musician; originator of EURHYTHMICS.

jar[1] *n.* Sound, vibration, esp. harsh one; thrill of nerves or feelings, shock; want of harmony, disagreement; quarrel. *~ v.* 1. Sound discordantly, make grating impression (*upon* person, his ear, etc.); strike with grating sound (*upon*, *against*, object); vibrate, resound, discordantly; cause (thing) to jar; send shock through (nerves). 2. Be at variance, disagree (*with*); dispute, wrangle. **jăr'ringly** *adv.*

jăr[2] *n.* Pottery or glass vessel with or without handle(s), usu. cylindrical.

jardinière (zhardĭnyār') *n.* 1. Ornamental pot or stand for display of growing flowers. 2. Dish of mixed vegetables served alone or as garnish with meat.

jarg'on[1] *n.* Unintelligible words, gibberish; barbarous or debased language; mode of speech full of unfamiliar terms or peculiar to a class or profession; twittering of birds.

jarg'on[2], **jargoon'** *n.* Translucent, colourless, or smoky variety of zircon found in Ceylon.

jargonĕlle' *n.* Early-ripening variety of pear.

jarl (y-) *n.* (hist.) Scandinavian or Danish chieftain.

jarv'ey *n.* Hackney-coachman; driver of Irish jaunting-car. [by-form of surname *Jarvis*]

Jas. *abbrev.* James.

jăs'mĭn(e) (-z-), **jĕss'amĭn(e)** *n.* Genus of shrubs with white or yellow salver-shaped flowers, esp. *common* or *white* ~ (*Jasminum officinale*), climbing shrub with fragrant white flowers. [Pers. *yasmin*]

Jās'on. (Gk legend) Son of Aeson, king of Iolcos; his father's throne was usurped by Pelias, who promised to surrender it if Jason would fetch for him the magical golden fleece from Colchis; Jason sailed in the ship Argo with a crew of heroes (the Argonauts), found the fleece guarded by a dragon, and obtained it, aided by the daughter of the king of Colchis, MEDEA.

jăs'per *n.* Opaque variety of quartz, usu. red, yellow, or brown.

Jat (jaht). Member of a people widely distributed in NW. India, esp. Punjab, and varying in religion and occupation.

jaun'dĭce (jaw-) *n.* Yellow discoloration of skin and normally white part of eyeball due to the presence of pigments in the blood which are normally excreted in the bile, often caused by an obstructed bile-duct; this condition; disordered or discoloured vision as characteristic of this. ~ *v.t.* Affect with jaundice; (fig., esp. in past part.) affect (person etc.) with envy or jealousy.

jaunt (jaw-) *v.i.* & *n.* (Take) excursion, journey, esp. for pleasure; *jaunting-car*, light two-wheeled vehicle with seats back to back, formerly common in Ireland.

jaun'tў (jaw-) *adj.* Having or affecting easy sprightliness, airy self-satisfaction. ~ *n.* (naut. slang) Head of ship's police.

Jaurès (zhōrĕs'), Auguste Marie Joseph Jean (1858–1914). French socialist leader; assassinated at outbreak of war of 1914–18.

Jav'a (jah-). Large island of Malay archipelago, first settled by Dutch in 17th c. and now part of Indonesia; ~ *man*, *Pithecanthropus erectus*; ~ *skull*, skull found at Trinil, Java, with other bones of *Pithecanthropus*; ~ *sparrow*, kind of weaver-bird (*Amadira oryzivora*).

jav'a *n.* (U.S. slang) Coffee.

Javanēse' (-z) *adj.* & *n.* (Native, Malayan language) of Java.

jăv'elin (-vl-) *n.* Light spear thrown with the hand.

Javĕlle' (zha-). *Eau de* ~, ~ *water*, solution of potassium chloride and hypochlorite used as bleacher, antiseptic, or disinfectant. [named f. chemical works in the Quai de *Javelle*]

jaw *n.* 1. One of the bones or sets of bones forming the framework of the mouth and carrying the teeth in vertebrates (ill. HEAD); in sing. usu. = lower jaw rather than upper; (pl.) bones etc. of mouth including teeth; mouth; (fig.) grip, e.g. ~ *of death*; (colloq., sing.) loquacity. 2. (pl.) Structure in invertebrates analagous to vertebrates' jaws. 3. (pl.) Seizing members of machine, e.g. vice. 4. (pl.) Narrow mouth of channel, valley, etc. 5. ~*-bone*, each of the two bones forming lower jaw in most mammals; these two combined into one in others; ~*-breaker*, (colloq.) word hard to pronounce. ~ *v.* (colloq.) Speak, esp. at tedious length; scold, lecture (person).

jay *n.* Any of several related birds forming a group of the crow family, esp. the noisy chattering European bird *Garrulus glandarius* which has plumage of vivid blue with jet-black bars and patches of white; (fig.) impertinent chatterer; simpleton; ~*-walker*, (orig. U.S.) pedestrian who crosses street without care or without observing regulations.

jăzz *n.* Syncopated dance-music, of U.S. Negro origin, with characteristic harmony and RAGTIME rhythm; ~*-band*, orchestra playing jazz-music. ~ *adj.* Discordant, loud or fantastic in colour etc. ~ *v.* Dance to, play, jazz-music; arrange (music) as jazz; arrange (pattern etc.) in vivid or grotesque form; brighten, liven, *up*. **jăzz'ў** *adj.*

J.C. *abbrev.* Justice Clerk.

jeal'ous (jĕl-) *adj.* 1. Solicitous for preservation *of* (rights etc.); (bibl., of God) intolerant of unfaithfulness; (of inquiry etc.) suspiciously vigilant. 2. Apprehensive of being displaced in the love or goodwill *of* (wife, lover, friend, etc.; also *of* supposed rival); envious (*of*). **jeal'ously** *adv.* **jeal'ousy** *n.* Quality, state, of being jealous.

jean (jēn, jān) *n.* Heavy twilled cotton fabric; (pl., orig. U.S.) garment, esp. overalls or trousers, of this. [prob. f. Fr. *Gênes* Genoa]

Jĕb'usīte (-z-). Member of Canaanite tribe inhabiting Jerusalem before Jews; 17th-c. nickname for Roman Catholic, esp. Jesuit.

jeep *n.* Small, short, powerful, four-wheeled car having an emergency four-wheel drive. [said to have been f. *g p*, initials of *general purposes*]

jeer[1] *n.* (naut., usu. pl.) Tackle for hoisting and lowering lower yards.

jeer[2] *v.* Scoff derisively (*at*); deride. ~ *n.* Gibe, taunt.

Jĕff'eries, Richard (1848–87). English naturalist and novelist.

Jĕff'erson, Thomas (1743–1826). American liberal statesman, 3rd president of U.S. 1801–09). **Jĕffersōn'ian** *adj.*

Jĕff'erson City. Capital of Missouri, U.S.

Jĕff'reys, George (1648–89), 1st Baron. 'Judge Jeffreys', English lawyer; lord chancellor of England; notorious for his conduct of 'bloody assizes' in the west after suppression of Monmouth's rebellion (1686).

jehad: see JIHAD.

Jėhoi'achin (-kĭn). (O.T.) King of Judah, son of Jehoiakim; taken captive to Babylon after reign of a few months (2 Kings xxiv).

Jėhoi'akim. (O.T.) King of Judah, son of Josiah (2 Kings xxiii, xxiv).

Jėhōr'am, Jōr'am. (O.T.) 1. King of Israel, son of Ahab; killed by Jehu (2 Kings i, iii). 2. King of Judah, son of Jehoshaphat (2 Kings viii, 2 Chron. xxi).

Jėhŏsh'aphăt. (O.T.) King of Judah; son of Asa (1 Kings xxii; 2 Chron. xx).

Jėhōv'ah (-va). Principal and personal name of God in O.T.; ~*'s Witnesses*, a name for the Watch Tower Bible and Tract Society, a religious community founded *c* 1879 by Charles Taze Russell, an American. **Jėhōv'ist** *n.* Author(s) of those non-Deuteronomic parts of the Hexateuch in which the divine name is rendered 'Jehovah'; opp. to ELOHIST. **Jēhōvĭs'tĭc** *adj.* [repr. Hebr. *Yahwe(h)*]

Jē'hū. (O.T.) King of Israel, son of Jehoshaphat, famous for furious driving of chariot (2 Kings ix); hence, fast or furious driver; coachman, driver.

jėjune' (-ōōn) *adj.* Meagre, scanty; barren; unsatisfying to mind. **jėjune'ly** *adv.* **jėjune'nėss** *n.*

jėjun'um (-jōō-) *n.* (anat.) Part of small intestine between duodenum and ileum (ill. ALIMENTARY).

Jĕk'ўll, Henry. Hero of R. L. Stevenson's story 'The Strange Case of Dr Jekyll and Mr Hyde' (1886); handsome and well-respected, he transforms himself by a potion into the dwarfish and detestable Edward Hyde in whom is embodied only the evil side of

Jekyll; hence, *~-and-Hyde character*, dual personality.

Jĕll'ĭcōe, John Rushworth (1859–1935), first Earl. English admiral in command of Grand Fleet at battle of JUTLAND; First Sea Lord, 1916–17.

jĕll'ȳ *n.* Soft stiffish substance, usu. semi-transparent, made of a liquid in which gelatin (or some other gel) has been dissolved; this as food, esp. made with meat or fruit juices; anything of similar consistency; *~-bag*, muslin etc. bag for straining the juice from fruit pulp in preparing jelly; *~-fish*, pop. name of medusa or sea-nettle. ~ *v.* (Cause to) set as jelly, congeal.

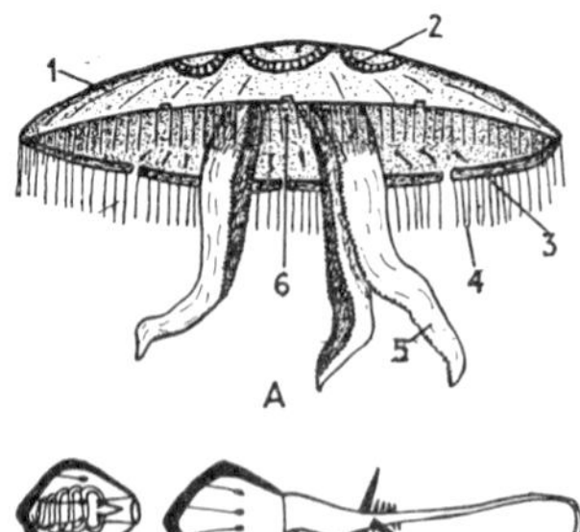

A. JELLY-FISH. B. CNIDOBLASTS WITH NEMATOCYST COILED AND EJECTED

1. Umbrella. 2. Gonad. 3. Circular canal. 4. Tentacles. 5. Oral arm. 6. Mouth

jĕll'ȳgraph (-ahf) *n.* Apparatus, of which essential part is a sheet of jelly, for multiplying copies of writing etc. ~ *v.t.* Copy with this.

jĕmm'y *n.* Crowbar or case-opener used by burglars, usu. made in sections. [fam. form of *James*]

Jena (yān'*a*). German university town in Thuringia, scene of battle in which Napoleon defeated the Prussians, 1806; ~ *glass*, superior kind of glass made there.

je ne sais quoi (zhe ne sā kwah) *n.* An indescribable something. [Fr., = 'I know not what']

Jenghiz Khan: see GENGHIS KHAN.

Jĕnk'ĭns' Ear. In 1738 Robert Jenkins, a master mariner, produced to a committee of the House of Commons what he declared to be his ear, cut off by a Spanish captain at Havana in the exercise of the right of search claimed by the Spaniards to prevent English trade with Spanish America. The incident precipitated a war between England and Spain in 1739 (*War of ~*).

Jĕnn'er, Edward (1749–1823). English physician and pioneer of vaccination.

jĕnn'ėt *n.* Small Spanish horse.

jĕnn ėtĭng *n.* Kind of early apple.

jĕnn'y *n.* 1. Spinning-jenny. 2. Locomotive crane which runs backwards and forwards. 3. *creeping ~*, moneywort, *Lysimachia nummularia*. 4. ~ *wren*, (pop. and nursery name for) wren; (U.S.) herb robert, *Geranium Robertianum*. [fam. form of *Jane* or *Janet*]

jeop'ardīze (jĕp-) *v.t.* Endanger.

jeop'ardy (jĕp-) *n.* Danger. [OF *ieu parti* divided (i.e. even) game]

Jĕph'thah (-tha). (O.T.) A judge of Israel, son of Gilead; sacrificed his daughter in consequence of a vow that if victorious against the Ammonites he would sacrifice the first living thing that met him on his return (Judges xi, xii).

Jer. *abbrev.* Jeremiah (O.T.).

jėrbō'a *n.* Member of family of rodents of which the desert rat (*Dipus*) of N. Africa with very long hind legs and tail is typical; ~ *rat*, certain rodents of the genus *Conilurus* found in Australia. [Arab. *yarbu'*]

jĕrėmī'ăd *n.* Lamentation, doleful complaint. [f. *Jeremiah*]

Jĕrėmī'ah (-ia) (*c* 650–*c* 585 B.C.). Major Hebrew prophet, who saw the fall of Assyria, the vassalage of Judah in turn to Egypt and Babylon, and the destruction of Jerusalem; (*book of*) ~, the O.T. book containing his prophecies; hence, doleful person, denouncer of the times.

Jerez (de la Frontera) (hĕ'rĕth, frŏntā'ra). Town in Andalusia, Spain, centre of sherry-making industry.

Jĕ'rĭcho (-kō). Ancient city in Dead Sea Valley, now in Jordan; first Canaanite city attacked and taken by Israelites (Joshua vi).

jėrk[1] *n.* Sharp sudden pull, twist, etc.; involuntary spasmodic contraction of muscle; (pl.) spasmodic movements of limbs or face, esp. in religious excitement; (*physical*) *jerks*, (colloq.) motions practised in physical training. ~ *v.* Pull, thrust, twist, etc., with a jerk; throw with suddenly arrested motion; move with a jerk. **jėrk'y** *adj.* **jėrk'ĭly** *adv.* **jėrk'ĭnėss** *n.*

jėrk[2] *v.t.* Cure (esp. beef) by cutting in long slices and drying in sun. [Peruv. *ccharqui* dried flesh]

jėrk'ĭn *n.* (hist.) Man's close-fitting jacket, often of leather; sleeveless jacket.

Jĕrobō'ăm (O.T.). 1. First king of northern Israel (10th c. B.C.; 1 Kings xi–xiv); 'a mighty man of valour', 'who made Israel to sin'. 2. King of Israel (8th c. B.C.; 2 Kings xiv). **jĕrobō'ăm** *n.* Wine-bottle of about 4 times normal size. [from the 1st Jeroboam]

Jĕ'rome (*or* jėrōm'), St. (Hieronymus) (*c* 340–420). Latin Father of the Church; born in Dalmatia; made the 'Vulgate' translation of the Bible; commemorated 30th Sept.

jĕ'rry *n.* 1. (Also *~-shop*) low beer-shop. 2. (slang) Chamber-pot. 3. (army slang) German soldier. 4. *~-builder, -building*, builder, building, of unsubstantial houses with bad materials; *~-built*, so built.

Jėrs'ey (-zĭ). Largest of CHANNEL ISLANDS; one of a breed of small usu. buff-coloured dairy cattle, producing milk of high fat content, originating on the island.

jėrs'ey *n.* Close-fitting knitted woollen tunic; knitted fabric.

Jerus'alem (-rōō-). Ancient capital of Judaea, the holy city of the Jews, sacred also to Christians and Mohammedans; capital of modern Israel; *the New ~*, the Heavenly City, the abode of God and the saints; *New ~ Church*, the followers of SWEDENBORG.

Jerus'alem ârt'ĭchōke (-rōō-) *n.* Species of sunflower (*Helianthus tuberosus*) of tropical America, cultivated for edible tuberous roots resembling artichoke in flavour. [prob. corrupt. of It. *girasole articiocco* sunflower artichoke]

jĕss *n.* Short strap of leather, silk, etc., round legs of hawk used in falconry (ill. FALCON). ~ *v.t.* Put jesses on (hawk).

jess'amine: see JASMINE.

Jĕss'ė. (O.T.) Father of David, hence represented as first in genealogy of Jesus Christ; *tree of ~*, (in medieval MSS. etc.) tree representing genealogy of Christ from 'root of Jesse'.

jĕst *n.* Piece of raillery or banter; taunt, jeer; joke; fun; object of derision. ~ *v.i.* Joke, jeer; speak, act, in trifling manner. **jĕst'ingly** *adv.*

jĕs'ter *n.* One who jests, esp. professed maker of amusement (formerly) maintained in court or noble household.

JERKIN: A. LATE 16TH C. B. 17TH C.

1. Ruff. 2. Jerkin. 3. Doublet. 4. Breeches. 5. Falling band. 6. Cloak

Jĕs'ŭit (-z-) *adj.* & *n.* (Member) of the Society of Jesus, an order of priests founded 1534 in Paris by Ignatius Loyola, Francis Xavier, and others, to defend the R.C.

Church against opposition and propagate its faith among the heathen; it is strictly organized and governed by a 'General' responsible only to the Pope; became the chief instrument of the Counter-Reformation and very powerful politically in 17th c.; sent missions to all parts, esp. S. America. Its members, learned and rigorously trained, are bound to poverty, chastity, and obedience, with duties of preaching, educating, and hearing confession. **Jĕsūĭt'ical** *adj.* 1. Of the Jesuits. 2. Having character ascribed to Jesuits; dissembling, practising equivocation or mental reservation of truth. **Jĕs'ŭitry** *n.*

Jēs'us (*c* 4 B.C.–*c* A.D. 30). Source of the Christian religion, accepted by Christians as son of God, second person of the Trinity, and saviour of mankind; born of Mary, wife of Joseph, a carpenter of Nazareth in Galilee; began his public life at about 30; for some 3 years wandered about Palestine, chiefly Galilee, with a band of followers or disciples, teaching and healing; was then arrested in Jerusalem at the time of Passover, handed over by the Jewish high court to the Roman authorities, and condemned to death by crucifixion; the Christian doctrine is that after three days he rose from the dead. *Society of ~*: see JESUIT.

Jēs'us College. 1. College of University of Cambridge, founded 1496. 2. College of University of Oxford, founded 1571.

Jēs'us the son of Sirach: see ECCLESIASTICUS.

jĕt[1] *n.* & *adj.* Hard black lignite taking brilliant polish; (of) colour of this, deep glossy black (also *~-black*).

jĕt[2] *n.* 1. Stream of water, steam, gas(es), etc., ejected from small opening; spout, nozzle, for emitting water etc. thus. 2. In aircraft, stream of gas ejected from rearward-facing nozzle causing a reaction on the aircraft which propels it forward; aircraft propelled thus; hence *~-plane*, *~-propelled*, *~-propulsion*, etc. *~ v.* Spout forth in jets.

jĕt'sam *n.* Goods thrown overboard from ship to lighten it, and (in mod. use) washed ashore.

jĕtt'ed *adj.* (tailoring, of pocket) Having no flap, but an outside seam (*jetting*) on either edge.

jĕtt'ison *n.* Throwing of goods overboard, esp. to lighten ship in distress. *~ v.t.* Throw (goods) overboard thus.

jĕtt'on *n.* Counter with stamped or engraved device.

jĕtt'y[1] *n.* Mole running out to protect harbour or coast; landing-pier.

jĕtt'y[2] *adj.* Jet-black.

jeu d'esprit (zhẽr dĕsprē') *n.* Witty or humorous (usu. literary) trifle.

jeune premier (zhẽrn premyā') *n.* Actor playing part of young hero.

jeunesse dorée (zhẽrnĕs' dŏrā') *n.* The gilded youth, young swells.

Jew (joo) *n.* Person of Hebrew race or religion; orig., Hebrew of kingdom of Judah, as opp. to those of ten tribes of Israel; *Wandering ~*: see WANDERING; *~-baiting*, systematic persecution of Jews; *jews' harp, jew's-harp*, simple musical instrument consisting of elastic steel tongue affixed at one end to lyre-shaped metal frame, played by holding frame between teeth and striking free end of metal tongue with finger. **Jew'ĕss** *n.*

jew'ĕl (jōō-) *n.* Ornament containing precious stone(s), worn for personal adornment; precious stone; highly prized person or thing. *~ v.t.* Adorn, furnish, with jewels; fit (watch) with jewels for the pivot-holes. **jew'eller, jew'ellery, jew'elry** *ns.*

Jew'ish (jōō-) *adj.* Of the Jews; *~ calendar*, complex ancient calendar in use among the Jews, a lunar calendar adapted to the solar year by various expedients, having normally 12 months, but 13 months in leap years which occur 7 times in every cycle of 19 years. The years are reckoned from the Creation (3761 B.C.); the months are Nisan (normally March–April), Iyar (April–May), Sivan (May–June), Tammuz (June–July), Ab (July–Aug.), Elul (Aug.–Sept.), Tishri (Sept.–Oct.), Cheshvan (Oct.–Nov.), Kislev (Nov.–Dec.), Tebeth (Dec.–Jan.), Shebat (Jan.–Feb.), Adar (Feb.–March), 2nd Adar (intercalary month); New Year occurs in the autumn, 1st and 2nd Tishri.

Jewry (joor'ĭ) *n.* The Jews; Jewish quarter in town etc.

Jĕz'ĕbel. (O.T.) Daughter of Ethbaal, king of Tyre and priest of Astarte; wife of Ahab, king of Israel; denounced by Elijah for introducing worship of Baal; killed when Jehu triumphed over Ahab; hence, **jezebel** *n.*, wicked or abandoned woman.

jĭb[1] *n.* Triangular stay-sail from outer end of jib-boom to fore-topmast head in large ships (ill. SHIP), from bowsprit to masthead in smaller ones; *cut of person's jib*, his personal appearance; *~-'boom*, spar run out from end of bowsprit; projecting arm of crane (ill. CRANE). *~ v.* Pull (sail, yard) round from one side of ship to the other; swing round thus.

jĭb[2] *v.i.* (Of horse etc.) stop and refuse to go on, move backwards or sideways instead of going on; (fig.) refuse to proceed in some action; *~ at*, show repugnance to (course, person).

jĭbb'a(h) (-ba), **ju-, dj-** *n.* Mohammedan's or Parsee's long cloth coat, open in front, with sleeves nearly to wrist.

jībe *v.* & *n.* See GIBE.

Jĭbut'i (-bōō-). (*Djibouti*). Chief port and capital of French Somaliland.

jiff'(y) *n.* (colloq.) Very short time.

jĭg *n.* 1. Lively dance; music for this, usu. in $\frac{3}{4}$ or $\frac{6}{8}$ time. 2. (eng.) Device for holding parts in appropriate position for drilling or assembling. 3. Contrivance for jigging ore. *~ v.* Dance a jig; move up and down rapidly and jerkily; separate coarser and finer portions of (ore) by shaking it under water in box with perforated bottom; *~-saw*, (U.S.) machine-fretsaw; *~-saw puzzle*, picture pasted on board etc. and cut in irregular pieces with jig-saw or fretsaw.

jĭgg'er[1] *n.* 1. (naut.) Small tackle consisting of a double and single block with rope. 2. Small sail rigged out on mast and boom from stern of cutter etc.; small smack with such sail. 3. Various mechanical contrivances, used in many trades; (slang) contrivance, gadget.

jĭgg'er[2] *n.* Small flea, *Dermatophilus penetrans*, of W. Indies and S. America, the female of which burrows into skin of human foot. [f. W. Ind. wd]

jĭgg'er[3] *v.t.* (only in pass.) Used as vague substitute for oath (*I'm jiggered* etc.).

jigger[4] *n.* Woman's short outdoor coat.

jĭgg'erȳ-pō'kerȳ *n.* (colloq.) Trickery, underhand dealing.

jĭgg'le *v.t.* Rock or jerk lightly.

jĭhad' (-ahd) *n.* Religious war of Mohammedans against unbelievers; (fig.) campaign against a doctrine, policy, etc.

jilt *n.* Woman who capriciously casts off lover after giving him encouragement; (rarely) man who treats woman thus. *~ v.t.* Play the jilt with, be faithless to.

Jĭm Crow (-ō) *n.* (U.S.) Negro; *~ car*, railway carriage for Negroes.

jĭm'jăms *n.pl.* (colloq.) Delirium tremens; 'creeps', fidgets; fit of depression.

Jĭmm'y. *~ the One* (naval slang), First Lieutenant. [pet form of *James*]

jĭmp *adj.* (Sc.) Slender, graceful; scanty.

jĭm(p)'son weed *n.* (U.S.) Jamestown-weed or thorn-apple, *Datura stramonium*.

jĭn'gle (-ngg-) *n.* 1. Mingled noise like that of small bells, links of chain, etc.; repetition of same or similar sounds in words, esp. if designed to catch the attention; words intended to have pleasing or striking sound without regard to sense. 2. Covered two-wheeled car in Australia and S. Ireland. *~ v.* Make, cause (keys etc.) to make, a jingle; (of writing) be full of alliterations, rhymes, etc.

jĭn'gō (-ngg-) *int.* & *n.* 1. *By ~*, vigorous form of asseveration. 2. (from use of *by jingo* in popular music-hall refrain of 1878) Supporter of Lord Beaconsfield in sending British fleet into Turkish waters in 1878 to resist advance of

Russia; supporter of bellicose policy, blustering patriot; such policy or patriotism. **jĭng'ōĭsm** *n.* **jingōĭs'tic** *adj.*

jinks *n.* *High* ~, boisterous sport, merrymaking.

jĭnn *n.* (prop. pl.) In Mohammedan demonology, order of spirits lower than angels, with supernatural power over men; freq. as sing., one of these. **jĭnnee'** *n.* One of the jinn.

jĭnrĭck'sha *n.* Light two-wheeled hooded vehicle drawn by man or men, first used in Japan *c* 1870. [Jap. *jin-riki-sha* (*jin* man, *riki* strength, power, *sha* vehicle)]

jinx *n.* (U.S. colloq.) Bringer of bad luck, exerciser of evil influence.

jĭtt'er *v.t.* Be nervous, act nervously; *jitt'erbug,* (colloq.) person who dances to hot-rhythm music; nervous person; (*v.i.*) dance thus. **jĭtt'ers** *n.pl.* (colloq.) Extreme nervousness. **jĭtt'ery** *adj.*

jiu-jitsu: see JU-JITSU.

jive *v.i.* = JITTERbug.

jn. *abbrev.* Junction.

Jno. *abbrev.* (obs.) John.

Joachim (yōahχ'ĭm), Joseph (1831–1907). Hungarian violinist.

Joan, Pope: see POPE[1].

Joan of Arc, St. (1412–31). Jeanne d'Arc, French peasant girl who became a national heroine; inspired by 'voices' of St. Catherine and St. Michael, she led the French armies against the English, relieved Orleans, and stood beside Charles VI at his coronation; was captured by the Burgundians and handed over to the English; was tried and condemned for heresy and burnt in the market-place at Rouen; canonized 1919.

jŏb[1] *n.* Piece of work, esp. small definite one done for hire or profit; (colloq.) paid position of employment; transaction in which duty is sacrificed to private advantage; anything one has to do; *bad, good,* ~, unfortunate, fortunate, state of affairs, occurrence, etc.; ~ *lot,* miscellaneous lot of goods bought as speculation; any miscellaneous lot of persons or things; *job'master,* one who lets out horses and carriages by the job; ~*-work,* work done and paid for by the job. **jŏb'lėss** *adj.* Out of work. **jŏb** *v.* 1. Do jobs; hire (horse, carriage) for definite time or job, let out or hire thus; *jobbing carpenter, gardener,* etc., one employed in odd or occasional pieces of work. 2. Buy and sell (stock, goods) as broker; deal in stocks; sell (stock of books) at scrap price to bookseller, who sells it as he can. 3. Turn position of trust to private advantage; deal corruptly with (matter), whence **jŏbb'er, jŏbb'ery** *ns.*

Jōb[2]. Book of O.T., prob. written in 4th c. B.C.; its hero, a wealthy and prosperous man, whose patience and exemplary piety are tried by dire and undeserved misfortunes, and who, in spite of his bitter lamentations, remains finally confident in the goodness and justice of God; hence, a type of patience under misfortune; ~*'s comforter,* one who, like Job's friends, aggravates distress under the guise of administering comfort.

jōbā'tion *n.* (colloq.) Reprimand, esp. lengthy one.

Jocăs'ta. (Gk legend) Mother and wife of OEDIPUS.

Jŏck *n.* (army slang) Scottish, esp. Highland, soldier.

jŏck'ey *n.* Professional rider in horse-races; *J~ Club,* club established 1750 at Newmarket, now the authority controlling all horse-racing in England; ~*-club,* kind of scent in which rose and jasmine are important ingredients. ~ *v.* Outwit; cheat; get (person etc.) *away, out, in,* etc., by trickery; cheat (*into, out of*); ~ *for position,* try to gain advantageous position (esp. by manœuvring in yacht-racing). [f. Sc. *Jock,* Jack]

jocōse' *adj.* Playful, waggish. **jocōse'ly** *adv.* **jocōse'nėss, jocŏs'ity** *ns.*

jŏc'ūlar *adj.* Mirthful; humorous. **jŏc'ūlarly** *adv.* **jŏculă'rity** *n.*

jŏ'cund *adj.* Merry, sprightly; pleasant. **jŏ'cundly** *adv.* **jocŭn'dity** *n.*

jodel: see YODEL.

Jodhpur (jōdpoor'). Former native State in Rajputana, India, now part of the State of Rajasthan.

jodhpurs (jŏd'perz) *n.pl.* Riding-breeches reaching to the ankle, full above and tight below the knee.

Jō'ėl (date disputed; 5th or possibly 9th c. B.C.). Minor Hebrew prophet; the O.T. book bearing his name.

Jōe Mĭll'er. Stale joke, chestnut. [f. *Joe Miller's Jests,* a jest-book (1739) by John Mottley; named after Joseph Miller (1684–1738), comedian at Drury Lane theatre]

jō'ey *n.* Young kangaroo; young animal.

Joffre (zhŏfr), Joseph Jacques Césaire (1852–1931). Marshal of France; commander-in-chief of French armies, 1914–16.

jŏg *v.* 1. Shake with push or jerk; nudge (person), esp. to arouse attention; stimulate (memory). 2. Move up and down with unsteady motion; ~ (*along, on*), proceed laboriously, trudge; go on one's way, depart; ~ *along, on,* proceed, get through the time; ~*-trot,* slow regular trot; (fig.) monotonous progression. ~ *n.* Shake, push; nudge; slow walk or trot.

jŏgg'le[1] *v.* Shake, move, (as) by repeated jerks. ~ *n.* Slight shake.

jŏgg'le[2] *n.* Joint of two pieces of stone or timber, contrived to prevent their sliding on one another; notch in one piece, corresponding projection in the other, or small piece let in between both, for this purpose. ~ *v.t.* Join by means of a joggle.

Jōhănn'ėsbûrg (*or* yō-). Largest city of the Republic of South Africa.

Jōhănn'ĭne *adj.* Of the apostle John.

Johănn'ĭsbĕrger (-g-). Fine white wine from Johannisberg, village in the Rheingau, Germany.

John[1] (jŏn), St. Apostle, called *St. ~ the Evangelist* or *St. ~ the Divine*; son of Zebedee, a Galilean fisherman, and brother of James; the 'beloved disciple' of Jesus; credited since very early time (prob. erron.) with authorship of fourth Gospel and APOCALYPSE, and of 3 N.T. epistles; commemorated 27th Dec.; *Order of St. ~*: see HOSPITALLER; *St. ~'s wort,* herbs and shrubs of genus *Hypericum,* with oval leaves and bright-yellow flowers.

John[2] (jŏn). Name of 23 popes or antipopes: *John VIII,* pope 872–82; much involved in imperial politics; crowned and supported Charles the Bald and Charles the Fat; *John XXI* (should be XX, but there is an error in the numbering), pope 1276–7; identified with Petrus Hispanus, author of medical and philosophical works, and freq. referred to by chroniclers as a magician; *John XXII,* pope at Avignon, 1316–34; involved in unsuccessful struggle against Ludwig of Bavaria; accused of heresy; *John XXIII,* antipope, 1410–15, swore at Council of Constance to abdicate if the rival popes Benedict XIII and Gregory XII would also do so, but subsequently fled and was deposed; *John XXIII* (Angelo Giuseppe Roncalli, 1881–1963), pope 1958–63.

John[3] (jŏn). Name of several Byzantine emperors: *John I* Tzimisces, reigned 969–76; *John II* Comnenus, 'the Good', reigned 1118–43; *John III* Ducas Vatatzes, reigned 1222–54; *John IV* Lascaris, reigned 1258–61; *John V* Palaeologus, reigned 1341–91; *John VI* Cantacuzene, reigned 1341–54 (first as rival to John V, then jointly with him); *John VII,* reigned 1390; *John VIII* Palaeologus, reigned 1425–48.

John[4] (jŏn) (1167–1216). King of England; called 'Lackland' because as youngest son of Henry II he had no apanage in the continental provinces; succeeded his brother Richard Cœur de Lion, 1199; quarrelled with Pope Innocent III over appointment of Stephen LANGTON; alienated barons and people by bad administration and heavy taxation; was forced by barons to sign MAGNA CARTA.

John[5] (jŏn). Name of two kings of France: *John I* (1316), lived only 7 days; *John II* (1319–64), taken prisoner at Poitiers by Black Prince, returned to captivity in England when he could not raise ransom money agreed upon, and died in London.

John[6] (jŏn). Name of 6 kings of Portugal: *John I* 'the Great', reigned 1385–1433; *John II* 'the Perfect', reigned 1481–95; encouraged exploration of sea-route to India (in his reign Diaz rounded Cape of Good Hope) but refused to help Columbus; *John III*, reigned 1521–57; *John IV* 'the Fortunate', reigned 1541–56; founder of Braganza dynasty; *John V*, reigned 1707–50; *John VI*, reigned 1816–26.

John[7] (jŏn). Masculine proper name used in various collocations; ~ *Barleycorn*, personification of malt liquor; ~ *Bull* (from name of character representing English nation in Arbuthnot's satire 'Law is a Bottomless Pit', 1712), personification of English nation, typical Englishman, represented as a stoutish red-faced farmer-like man in top-hat and high boots; ~ *Chinaman*, a Chinese; ~ *Collins*, (U.S.) drink of gin, soda-water, lemon, sugar, and ice; ~ *Company*, humorous name for East India Company, from the name *Jan Kompanie* by which the Dutch East India Company, and later the Dutch Government, was known in the East; ~ *Doe*, (law) fictitious lessee acting as plaintiff in (now obs.) common-law action of ejectment; fictitious name for party to any transaction or proceeding; ~ *Dory*, European sea-fish (*Zeus faber*), having a laterally flattened oval body with a dark spot on each side, and long dorsal spines, used for food; a similar Australian fish; ~ *o' Groat's*, house, said to have been built by a Dutchman, John Groot, in 16th c., on extreme NE. point of Scottish mainland.

John[8] (jŏn), Augustus Edwin (1879–1961). British painter.

John[9] (jŏn), Don (1545–78), of Austria. Natural son of emperor Charles V; commanded fleet at victory of LEPANTO over Turkish fleet; governor-general of Netherlands 1576–. **John,** Don (1629–79) of Austria. Natural son of Philip IV of Spain.

John Chrysostom, St.: see CHRYSOSTOM.

johnny (jŏn'ĭ) *n.* Fellow, esp. fashionable idler; *J~ Armstrong*, (naut. slang) hand-power; *~-cake*, (U.S.) cake of maize-meal, baked in pan or (in southern States) toasted before fire; (Austral.) cake of wheat-meal baked in ashes or fried in pan; *J~ Raw*, novice; *J~ Reb*, (U.S.) northern name for Confederate in Amer. Civil War. [pet form of *John*]

John of Gaunt (jŏn) (1340–99), Duke of Lancaster. English soldier; 4th son of Edward III and father of Henry IV.

John of Lănc'aster (jŏn) (1389–1435), Duke of Bedford. 3rd son of Henry IV and brother of Henry V, after whose death (1422) he was Protector of England, Henry VI being still a minor.

John of Nĕp'omuk (jŏn, -o͝ok), St. (d. 1393 *or* 1383). Patron saint of Bohemia; martyred by Wenceslaus IV for refusing to reveal what he had heard in confession from Wenceslaus's wife Jane.

John of Salisbury (jŏn, sawl'-zbrĭ) (*c* 1115–80). English ecclesiastic and author; bishop of Chartres; supported Becket and was present at his murder.

John of the Cross (jŏn), St. (1542–91). Spanish mystical poet and Carmelite friar; friend of St. Theresa; canonized 1726.

John'ian (jŏn-) *adj.* & *n.* (Member or student) of St. John's College, Cambridge.

Johns Hŏp'kins (jŏnz). University at Baltimore, Maryland, U.S., founded 1876 with money bequeathed by a Baltimore merchant, Johns Hopkins.

John Sōbieski (jŏn, -byĕs'-) (1624–96). National hero of Poland; elected king, as John III, 1674; recovered the greater part of Ukraine from the Turks.

John'son[1] (jŏn'sn), Andrew (1808–75). Amer. Democratic statesman, 17th president of U.S. 1865–9.

John'son[2] (jŏn'sn), Cornelius. Cornelis Jonson van Ceulen (1593–1664?), portrait painter of Flemish origin, born in England.

John'son[3] (jŏn'sn), Lyndon Baines (1908–). Vice-president of the U.S. 1961–3; 36th president 1963–9.

John'son[4] (jŏn'sn), Dr Samuel (1709–84). English man of letters and lexicographer; famous esp. for his conversation recorded by his friend James Boswell. **Johnsōn'ian** *adj.* Of Dr Johnson; esp., of an English prose style abounding in words derived or made up from Latin, or characterized by weighty and well-balanced sentences.

John the Băp'tist (jŏn), St. (N.T.) 'Forerunner' of Jesus; preached in the 'wilderness' and baptized in the Jordan; was executed by order of Herod Antipas.

Jŏhōre'. Constituent State of Malaysia, situated at S. end of Malay peninsula.

joie de vivre (zhwa de vēvr) *n.* Healthy enjoyment of life.

join *v.* 1. Put together, fasten, unite; connect (two points) by straight line; unite in marriage, friendship, alliance, etc.; come together, be united. 2. Take part with others (in); come into company of (person); become member of (club etc.); take, resume, one's place in (regiment, ship, company, etc.); come into connexion with; ~ *up*, enlist in army. 3. ~ *battle*, begin fighting; ~ *hands*, clasp one's hands together, clasp each other's hands; (fig.) combine in action or enterprise; ~ *issue*: see ISSUE. ~ *n.* Point, line, of junction.

join'er *n.* (esp.) 1. One who makes furniture, house fittings, and other woodwork lighter than carpenter's. 2. (U.S. colloq.) One who joins many clubs, societies, etc. **join'ery** *n.* Joiner's work.

joint[1] *n.* 1. Place at which two things are joined together; structure in animal body by which two bones are fitted together; part of stem from which leaf or branch grows; point at which, contrivance by which, two parts of artificial structure are joined, rigidly or so

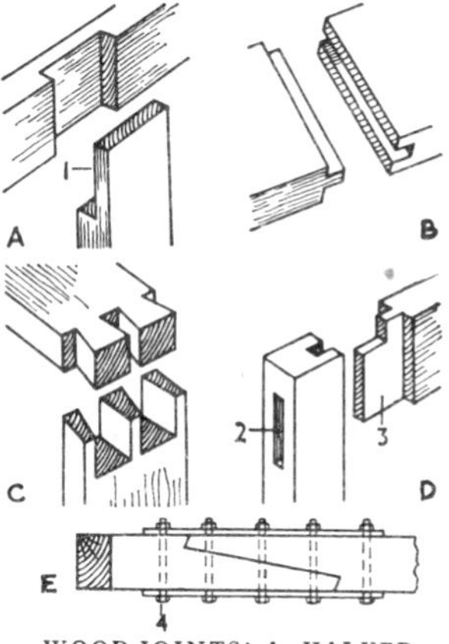

WOOD JOINTS: A. HALVED. B. TONGUE AND GROOVE. C. DOVETAIL. D. MORTISE AND TENON. E. SCARF

1. Rabbet. 2. Mortise. 3. Tenon. 4. Bolt

as to allow of movement; exterior of book-hinge; (geol.) fracture in rock, esp. one along which there has been little or no movement. 2. One of the parts of which body is made up; one of the parts into which butcher divides carcass, esp. as served at table. 3. (chiefly U.S.) Place of meeting or resort, esp. low or illicit drinking-saloon, opium den, etc. ~ *v.t.* 1. Connect by joints; fill up joints of (masonry etc.) with mortar etc., point; prepare (board etc.) for being joined to another by planing its edge; *~-stool*, (hist.) stool made of parts fitted by joiner (orig. *joined stool*), as dist. from one of clumsier workmanship. 2. Divide (body, member) at joint or into joints. **joint'er** *n.* (esp.) Plane for jointing, mason's tool for pointing.

joint[2] *adj.* Held or done by, belonging to, two or more persons etc. in conjunction; (of persons) sharing (*with* others in possession, action, state, etc.); ~ *stock*, capital divided into shares, common fund; *~-stock* (attrib.) holding, formed on basis of, a joint stock. **joint'ly** *adv.*

join'trĕss *n.* Widow who holds jointure.

join'ture *n.* Sole estate limited to wife, to be employed by her after husband's death for her life. ~ *v.t.* Provide (wife) with jointure.

Joinville (zhwăṅvēl'), Jean, Sire de (1224–1319). French seneschal of Champagne; friend and biographer of Louis IX.

joist *n.* One of parallel timbers stretched on edge from wall to wall for ceiling laths or floor boards to be nailed to (ill. FLOOR).

jōke *n.* Thing said or done to excite laughter; witticism, jest; ridiculous circumstance; *practical* ~, trick played on person in order to have laugh at his expense. ~ *v.* Make jokes; poke fun at, banter. **jōk'ingly** *adv.*

jōk'er *n.* 1. One who jokes; (slang) fellow, chap. 2. (cards) Extra card, often blank or with picture of jester, counting in some games (e.g. euchre) as a trump, in others (e.g. poker) as any card the holder chooses to make it. 3. (U.S.) Clause unobtrusively inserted in legislation and affecting its operation in some way not immediately apparent.

jokul, *jökull* (yōk'ōōl, yêr-) *n.* Snow-mountain in Iceland.

jŏll'ify *v.* Make merry, esp. tipple; make jolly; **jŏllificā'tion** *n.*

jŏll'ity *n.* Merrymaking, festivity.

jŏll'y *adj.* Joyful; slightly drunk; festive, jovial; (colloq.) very pleasant, delightful. ~ *adv.* (colloq.) Very. ~ *n.* (nav. slang) Royal marine. ~ *v.t.* (orig. U.S.) Treat (person) pleasantly or agreeably, in order to keep him in good humour or obtain a favour; chaff.

jŏll'y-boat *n.* Clinker-built ship's boat, smaller than cutter.

jōlt *v.* Shake (person etc.) with jerk from seat etc., esp. in locomotion; (of vehicle) move along with jerks, as on rough road. ~ *n.* Such jerk; surprise, shock. **jōlt'y** *adj.*

Jon. *abbrev.* Jonathan.

Jōn'ah (-*a*). (O.T.) Minor Hebrew prophet; acc. to the O.T. book bearing his name he fled when bidden by God to go to Nineveh and prophesy; God then sent a storm to wreck his ship, and the seamen, holding him responsible, threw him overboard; he was swallowed by a great fish and lived in its belly for 3 days before being cast out on dry land. Hence, a person who brings ill luck or is sacrificed lest he do so.

Jŏn'athan. 1. (O.T.) Son of Saul and friend of David, killed at battle of Mount Gilboa (1 Sam. xiii, xiv, xviii–xx, xxxi). 2. *Brother* ~, personified people of U.S.; typical American citizen. **jŏn'athan** *n.* Amer. variety of red autumn dessert apple.

Jōnes[1] (-nz), Henry Arthur (1851–1929). Playwright, of Welsh origin; author of some 60 plays.

Jōnes[2] (-nz), In'igō (in-), (1573–1651). English architect and masque-designer.

jongleur (zhawnglêr) *n.* (hist.) Itinerant minstrel.

jŏn'quil *n.* Species of narcissus (*N. jonquilla*) with long linear leaves and clusters of fragrant white-and-yellow flowers.

Jŏn'son[1], Ben(jamin) (1574–1637). English poet and dramatist; author of 'Every Man in his Humour', 'Every Man out of his Humour', 'Volpone', 'The Devil is an Ass', etc.

Jŏnson[2], Cornelis: see JOHNSON[2].

Jŏpp'a. Ancient name of JAFFA.

Jordaens (yôrd'ahns), Jacob (1593–1678). Flemish painter.

jôrd'an[1] *n.* (not in polite use). Chamber-pot.

Jôrd'an[2]. 1. River flowing southward from Anti-Lebanon mountains through Sea of Galilee and into Dead Sea. 2. The Hashimite Kingdom of the Jordan, an independent Arab State, formerly part of PALESTINE, bordered by Israel, Syria, Iraq, and Saudi Arabia; divided by the river into Eastern Jordan (formerly called TRANSJORDAN) and Western Jordan; capital, Amman. **Jôrdān'ian** *adj.* & *n.*

Jôrd'an alm'ond (ahm-) *n.* Fine almond, esp. from Malaga. [Fr. or Sp. *jardin* garden]

Jôrdan'ēs (-dah-), (6th c.). Historian of the Goths, an inhabitant of lower Danube basin.

Jŏ'rrocks, John. Character in the novels of R. S. Surtees (1805–64); 'a great city grocer of the old school', and a natural sportsman.

jôr'um *n.* Large drinking-bowl; its contents, esp. punch.

Jos. *abbrev.* Joseph.

Jōs'ėph[1] (-z-). Name of several persons in the Bible, esp.: 1. (O.T.) Son of Jacob and Rachel; sold by his brothers into captivity in Egypt, where he attained high office. 2. (N.T.) A carpenter of Nazareth, husband of Mary the mother of Jesus. 3. ~ *of Arimathea*, (N.T.) the Jew who buried Jesus in a rock-hewn tomb; acc. to legend he afterwards led a mission to England and built the first Christian church at GLASTONBURY.

Jōs'ėph[2] (-z-). Name of two Holy Roman Emperors: *Joseph I* (1678–1711), reigned 1705–; *Joseph II* (1741–90), eldest son of Marie Theresa; reigned 1765–.

Jōs'ėphine (-z-, -ēn). Marie Rose Joséphine Tascher de la Pagerie (1763–1814), a Creole of Martinique; wife of Vicomte Alexander Beauharnais (guillotined in 1794) and subsequently (1796) of Napoleon Bonaparte; empress of the French from 1804 until divorced 'for reasons of state' in 1809.

Jōsēph'us, Flā'vius (*c* 37–*c* 95). Jewish statesman and soldier who became a Roman citizen; wrote, in Greek, a history of the Jews.

Josh. *abbrev.* Joshua (also O.T.).

Jŏsh'ūa. (O.T.) Successor of Moses in leadership of Israel; *Book of* ~, 6th book of Bible, telling how he conquered the land of Canaan.

Josī'ah (-*a*) (647–*c* 608 B.C.). (O.T.) king of Judah; carried out complete religious reform based on a book of law (app. Deuteronomy) found in the Temple.

jŏs'kin *n.* Country bumpkin, dolt.

jŏss *n.* Chinese idol; ~-*house*, Chinese temple; ~-*stick*, stick of fragrant gum mixed with clay, burned as incense in Chinese temples. [app. f. Port. *deos* f. L *deus* god]

jŏss'er *n.* (slang) Fool; fellow.

jŏs'tle (-sl) *v.* Knock, push, *against*; struggle *with*; push against, elbow; push (*away, from*, etc.). ~ *n.* Jostling; encounter.

jŏt[1] *n.* (usu. with negative) Small amount, whit. [Gk *iota*, letter i, smallest in alphabet]

jŏt[2] *v.t.* Write (*down*) briefly or hastily. **jŏtt'er** *n.* Memorandum-pad.

Jŏt'un (yŏ-). (Scand. myth.) The giants, enemies of the gods. **Jŏt'unheim,** mountainous region of S. Norway, legendary abode of the Jötun.

Joule[1] (jowl), James Prescott (1818–89). English physicist, who established the universal constant of proportionality between mechanical work and heat.

joule[2] (jowl, jōōl) *n.* Electrical unit of work, energy expended in one second by electric current of one ampere flowing through resistance of one ohm, equal to 10 million c.g.s. units or ergs. [f. JOULE[1]]

jounce *v.* Bump, bounce, jolt.

journ'al (jêr-) *n.* 1. (In bookkeeping by double entry) book in which each transaction is entered, with statement of accounts to which it is to be debited and credited. 2. Daily record of events, diary; record of daily transactions of public body or association; (naut.) log-book; daily newspaper, other periodical. 3. Part of shaft or axle that rests on bearings (ill. BEARING); ~-*box*, box enclosing journal and bearings.

journ'alēse (jêr-, -z) *n.* Newspaper-writers' English.

jour'nalist (jêr-) *n.* One whose business it is to edit or write for a newspaper or other public journal. **jour'nalism** *n.* **journalis'tic** *adj.*

journ'alize (jêr-) *v.* Enter in journal; record in, keep, private journal.

journey (jêrn'i) *n.* Distance travelled in specified time; expedition to some distance, round of travel (usu. by land). ~ *v.i.* make a journey.

journ'eyman (jêrni-) *n.* Qualified mechanic or artisan who works for another; (fig.) mere hireling; (astron.) ~ (*clock*), secondary clock in observatory, used as intermediary in comparison of standard clocks; in electric time-circuit, clock controlled by master-clock.

joust (*or* -ōō-), **jŭst** *v.i.* & *n.* (Engage in) combat between two knights etc. on horseback with lances.

Jōve: = JUPITER.

jōv'ial *adj.* Merry; convivial; **jōv'ially** *adv.* **jōviăl'ity** *n.* [L *jovialis* of Jupiter]

Jow'ėtt (jō-), Benjamin (1817–93). English classical scholar;

master of Balliol College and regius professor of Greek at Oxford.

jowl *n.* Jawbone, jaw, cheek; external throat or neck when prominent, dewlap of cattle, crop of bird; head and shoulders of salmon and other fish.

joy *n.* Vivid emotion of pleasure, gladness; thing that causes delight; *~-ride*, (slang) stolen or other pleasure-ride in motor-car etc.; *joy'-stick*, (slang) control-lever of aeroplane. ~ *v.* (chiefly poet.) Rejoice, gladden. **joy'ful** *adj.* **joy'fully** *adv.* **joy'fulnĕss** *n.* **joy'lĕss** *adj.* **joy'lĕssly** *adv.* **joy'lĕssnĕss** *n.* **joy'ous** *adj.* **joy'ously** *adv.* **joy'ousnĕss** *n.*

Joyce, James (1882–1941). Irish poet and novelist; principally known for his novel 'Ulysses' (1922), which gives a microscopically detailed picture of a single day's life of two middle-class Irishmen, Stephan Dedalus and Leopold Bloom, and is marked by eccentricities of form and frankness of language.

J.P. *abbrev.* Justice of the Peace.

jr *abbrev.* Junior.

Jū'an Fernăn'dĕz. Small group of islands in S. Pacific, off coast of Chile, discovered 1563 by a Spanish pilot, Juan Fernandez; Alexander SELKIRK was marooned there in 1704.

Jub'al (jōō-). (O.T.) Son of Lamech and Adah and 'father of all such as handle the harp and organ' (Gen. iv).

jub'ĭlāte (jōō-) *v.i.* Exult, make demonstrations of joy. **jub'ĭlance, jubĭlā'tion** *ns.* **jub'ĭlant** *adj.* **jub'ĭlantly** *adv.*

jub'ĭlee (jōō-) *n.* 1. (Jewish hist.) Year of emancipation and restoration, kept every 50 years, according to Lev. xxv; (R.C. Ch.) year of remission from penal consequences of sin, granted formerly at various intervals, now at any time. 2. 50th (or occas. 25th) anniversary as occasion for rejoicing; season of rejoicing; exultant joy; *Diamond J~*, 60th year of reign of Queen Victoria. [Heb. *yobel* ram, ram's horn trumpet, jubilee]

Jud. *abbrev.* Judith (Apocr.).

Judae'a (jōō-). Graeco-Roman name for S. part of Palestine.

Jud'ah (jōō-). 1. (O.T.) Youngest son of Jacob and Leah, ancestor of one of the most important of the 12 tribes of Israel. 2. (O.T.) Southern district of Palestine, including Jerusalem, forming one of the two kingdoms of the Jews; constantly at war with the northern kingdom (Israel).

Judā'ĭc (jōō-) *adj.* Jewish.

Jud'āize (jōō-) *v.* Follow Jewish customs or rites; make Jewish. **Jud'āism, Jud'āist** *ns.*

Jud'as (jōō-). 1. ~ *Iscariot*, (N.T.) the disciple who betrayed Jesus to the Jews for 30 pieces of silver and afterwards (acc. to Matt. xxvii) repented and hanged himself; hence, **jud'as** *n.*, infamous traitor; (also) peephole in door; *~-coloured*, red; ~ *kiss*, act of betrayal (from kiss which Judas gave to Jesus as a signal to his captors); *~-tree*, (from legend that Judas hanged himself on tree of this kind) leguminous S. European and Asiatic tree, *Cercis siliquastrum*, with abundant purplish-pink flowers appearing in spring before the leaves; any tree of genus *Cercis*. 2. See JUDE.

jŭdd'er *v.i.* (Of machine etc.) shake noisily, shudder; (of voice in singing) make rapid changes in intensity during emission of a tone, owing to involuntary variations in vocal tension. ~ *n.*

Jude (jōōd), St. (N.T.) One of the 12 apostles, usu. supposed to be Judas the brother of Jesus; called also Lebbaeus in Matthew, Thaddaeus in Mark; martyred in Persia with St. Simon; commemorated with St. Simon, 28th Oct.; *Epistle of ~*, last epistle of N.T., written acc. to tradition by St. Jude, but prob. much later in date.

Judg. *abbrev.* Judges (O.T.).

jŭdge *n.* 1. Public officer appointed to hear and try cases in court of justice; (of God) supreme arbiter; person appointed to decide dispute or contest; person who decides a question; person who is qualified to decide on merits of thing or question; *J~ Advocate General*, civil officer in supreme control of courts martial. 2. (Heb. hist.) Officer having temporary authority in Israel in period between Joshua and the kings; (*Book of*) *J~s*, 7th book of O.T., containing history of this period. ~ *v.* Pronounce sentence on (person) in court of justice; try (cause); decide (question); decide, decree; form opinions about, estimate, criticize, censure; conclude, consider, suppose; act as judge; form a judgement (*of*).

jŭdgemăt'ĭc(al) *adjs.* (colloq.) Judicious, discerning. **jŭdgemăt'ĭcally** *adv.*

jŭdg(e)'ment *n.* 1. Sentence of court of justice; misfortune viewed as sign of divine displeasure; *the last ~*, final trial of subjects of God's moral government at end of world; *~-day*, day of this; ~ *debt*, debt for payment of which a judgement has been given; ~ *debtor*, debtor against whom judgement has been given; ~ *summons*, summons for failure to pay judgement debt; *~-seat*, judge's seat; tribunal. 2. Criticism; opinion, estimate; critical faculty, discernment; good sense.

jud'ĭcature (jōō-) *n.* Administration of justice; judge's (term of) office; body of judges; court of justice; *Supreme Court of J~ in England*, that constituted by Acts of 1873 and 1875 and uniting Courts of Chancery, Queen's (King's) Bench, Common Pleas, Exchequer, Admiralty, etc.

judicial (jōōdĭsh'*al*) *adj.* Of, done by, proper to, a court of law; (theol.) inflicted as a divine judgement; having the function of judgement; of, proper to, a judge; expressing a judgement, critical; impartial; ~ *murder*, legal but unjust sentence of death. **judĭ'cially** *adv.*

judiciary (jōōdĭsh'*arĭ*) *n.* Judges of a State collectively.

judicious (jōōdĭsh'*us*) *adj.* Sensible, prudent; sound in discernment. **judi'ciously** *adv.* **judi'ciousnĕss** *n.*

Jud'ĭth (jōō-). A rich Israelite widow who saved the town of Bethulia from Nebuchadnezzar's army by captivating the besieging general Holofernes and cutting off his head while he slept; *Book of ~*, book of O.T. Apocrypha recounting this.

jud'ō (jōō-) *n.* Modern development of JU-JITSU. [Jap. *jiu dō*, f. Chin. *jiu tao* soft way]

Jud'y (jōō-). Wife of PUNCH in 'Punch and Judy'. [dim. of JUDITH]

jŭg[1] *n.* Deep vessel for holding liquids, with handle and usu. spout; (slang) prison. ~ *v.t.* Stew (hare, rabbit) in jug or jar (usu. in past part.); (slang) imprison. **jŭg'ful** *n.*

jŭg[2] *v.i.* (Of nightingale etc.) utter sound *jug*. **jŭg-jŭg** *n.*

Jŭgg'ernaut (-g-). (Hindu myth.) Jagannath, title of KRISHNA; idol of Krishna at Puri, Orissa, annually dragged in procession in an enormous car under whose wheels, it is said, devotees used to throw themselves; hence, (fig.) institution, notion, to which persons blindly sacrifice themselves or others.

jŭgg'ins (-gĭnz) *n.* (slang) Simpleton.

jŭgg'le *v.* Play tricks of magic or sleight-of-hand; conjure; cheat; practise artifice or deceit *with*; bring, get, change (*away*, *into*, etc.) by trickery. **jŭgg'ler, jŭgg'lery** *ns.*

Jugoslav(ia): see YUGOSLAV(IA).

jŭg'ūlar (*or* jōō-) *adj.* 1. Of the neck or throat; ~ *veins*, 4 great veins at sides of neck, an *external* pair conveying blood from superficial parts of head and an *internal* pair from inside of skull (ill. BLOOD). 2. (Of fish) having the ventral fin in front of the pectoral. ~ *n.* Jugular vein.

Jugur̄th'a (d. 104 B.C.). King of Numidia, captured by Romans in *Jugurthine War* and killed at Rome.

juice (jōōs) *n.* Liquid part of vegetables or fruits; fluid part of animal body or substance; (fig.) essence, spirit, of anything; (slang) electricity, electric current; petrol used in motor-engine. **juice'lĕss** *adj.*

jui'cy (jōō-) *adj.* Full of juice, succulent; (colloq.) of rich intellectual quality, interesting. **jui'cinĕss** *n.*

ju-jĭt'su (jōō-, -sōō), *n.* Japanese system of wrestling etc., characterized by special holds or tricks. [Jap. *jūjutsu*, f. Chin. *jiu shu(t)* soft art]

ju-ju (jōō'jōō) *n.* W. Afr. charm or fetish; supernatural power attributed to this.

ju'jube (jōō'jōōb) *n.* Edible acid berry-like drupe of certain plants; thorny plant (*Zizyphus*) of S. Europe and Asia bearing this; lozenge of gelatin etc. flavoured with or imitating this.

jul'ĕp (jōō-) *n.* Sweet drink, esp. as vehicle for medicine; (U.S.) mixture of spirit with sugar, ice, and flavouring, usu. mint. [Pers. *gulab* (*gūl* rose, *ab* water)]

Jul'ĭan (jōō-) (332–63). Flavius Claudius Julianus, Roman emperor 361–3; called Julian the Apostate because, though brought up as a Christian, he reverted to the worship of the old gods and tried to revive it.

Jul'ĭan calendar (jōō-). Reformed calendar, introduced (46 B.C.) by Julius Caesar and slightly modified under Augustus, in which ordinary year has 365 days, and every 4th year is a leap year of 366 days; the order and names of the months and the number of days in each are retained in the modern (GREGORIAN) calendar with some modifications introduced to bring it into closer conformity with astronomical data.

juliĕnne' (zhū-) *n.* Soup of shredded carrots and other vegetables cooked in meat broth.

Jul'ĭĕt (jōō-). Heroine of Shakespeare's play 'Romeo and Juliet'; ~ *cap*, small network skull-cap, usu. adorned with pearls.

Jul'ĭus (jōō-). Name of 3 popes: *Julius I*, St., pope 337–52, upholder of Athanasius against Arians; *Julius II* (Giuliano della Rovere, 1443–1513), pope 1503–13, statesman and patron of art; laid foundation-stone of St. Peter's; restored papal states to the Church; suppressed nepotism and carried out many reforms; *Julius III* (Giovanni Maria del Monte, 1487–1555), pope 1550–5.

Jul'ĭus Caesar (jōō-, sēz'*ar*). Gaius Julius Caesar (prob. 101–44 B.C.), Roman general and statesman; became quaestor in Spain, 68; formed 1st triumvirate with Pompey and Crassus, 59; conducted the Gallic Wars from 58 to 49 and invaded Britain 55 and 54; after the death of Crassus he crossed the RUBICON in defiance of the Senate in 49, and defeated Pompey in civil war, thus becoming dictator; he was murdered on the Ides of March 44 by a group of nobles, among them BRUTUS[2]. Among his administrative reforms was the introduction of the JULIAN CALENDAR; his writings include the accounts of the Gallic Wars and the civil war ('De Bello Gallico' and 'De Bello Civili').

Julȳ' (jōō-). 7th month of modern (5th of ancient Roman) calendar, with 31 days; *July monarchy*, (Fr. hist.) that of Louis Philippe; *July revolution*, (Fr. hist.), revolution in July 1830 against Charles X, who fled into exile and was succeeded by Louis Philippe. [f. *Julius* Caesar]

jŭm'bal, jŭm'ble[1] *n.* (U.S.) Thin crisp sweet cake, flavoured with lemon or almonds and usu. ring-shaped.

jŭm'ble[2] *v.* Move about in disorder; mix *up*, confuse. ~ *n.* Confused assemblage; muddle; jolting; ~-*sale*, sale of miscellaneous cheap or second-hand articles.

jŭm'bō *n.* Big clumsy person, animal, or thing; esp. (*J*~) elephant in London Zoological Gardens, famous for its size, sold in 1882 to Barnum.

Jŭm'na. River of N. India, rising in Himalayas and flowing into Ganges below Allahabad.

jŭmp *n.* Leap, bound, spring from ground; start caused by shock or excitement; abrupt rise in amount, price, value, etc.; sudden transition, gap in series, argument, etc.; *the* ~*s*, (colloq.) state of nervous excitement; delirium tremens. ~ *v.* 1. Spring from ground etc. by flexion and sudden muscular extension of legs or (of fish) tail; move suddenly with leap or bound; start with sudden jerk from excitement, shock, etc.; rise suddenly in price, etc.; come *to*, arrive *at* (conclusion) hastily; ~ *at*, accept (offer, bargain) eagerly; ~ (*up*)*on*, attack (offender etc.) crushingly with word or act. 2. Agree, coincide (together, one *with* another). 3. Pass over (gate etc.) by leap; (of railway carriage etc.) spring off, leave (line); help (child etc.) to jump *down* etc.; cause to jump; startle (person, nerves); (U.S.) get on or off (train etc.) by jumping, esp. without permission. 4. Pounce upon thing); steal a march upon; take summary possession of (claim abandoned or forfeited by former occupant). 5. Flatten, thicken, etc., end of iron rail or bar by endwise blows; drill (rock etc.) with jumper. **jŭmp'y** *adj.* (esp.) Of nervous temperament. **jŭmp'ily** *adv.* **jŭmp'iness** *n.*

CHINESE JUNK

jŭmp'er[1] *n.* (esp.) Heavy drill worked by hand or with hammer, for making blasting-holes in rock etc.

jŭm'per[2] *n.* Loose outer jacket of canvas etc. worn by sailors etc.; upper part of naval rating's uniform; woman's knitted upper garment not opening in front and reaching to waist or hips.

jun., junr, *abbrev.* Junior.

jŭnc'tion *n.* Joining; joint, meeting-place; esp., station where railway lines meet and unite.

jŭnc'ture *n.* Joining; place where things join; concurrence of events, state of affairs.

June (jōōn). 6th month of modern calendar, with 30 days. [L, prob. orig. f. goddess *Juno*]

Jung (yŏŏng), Carl Gustav (1875–1961). Swiss psychologist; orig. a follower of Freud; later founded school of 'analytical psychology', differing from psychoanalysis in its use of the concepts of unconscious and libido and in its advocacy of a complex classification of types of personality. **Jung'ĭan** *adj.*

Jungfrau (yŏŏng'frow). Mountain in Swiss Alps. [Ger., = 'maiden']

jŭng'le (-ngg-) *n.* Land overgrown with underwood or tangled vegetation, esp. in India, or as home of wild beasts; wild tangled mass; ~-*fever*, severe form of malarial fever. [Hind. *jangal* desert, forest]

jun'ĭor (jōō-) *adj.* The younger (esp. of son having same name as father); of less standing, of lower position; (U.S.) belonging to year below *senior* or last year of course. ~ *n.* Junior person (in U.S., freq. quasi-prop. name for son having same name as father). **juniŏ'rity** *n.*

jun'ĭorate (jōō-) *n.* (In Society of Jesus) two years' course attended by junior members before entering priesthood.

jun'ĭper (jōō-) *n.* Genus of coniferous evergreen shrubs, esp. common European species (*Juniperus communis*), a hardy spreading shrub with prickly leaves and dark purplish berries of pungent taste, yielding volatile oil (*oil of* ~) used in medicine as diuretic etc. and in manufacture of gin, varnish, etc.

Jun'ĭus (jōō-). Pseudonym of author of series of letters (1769–71) in the 'Public Advertiser', bitterly and abusively attacking many public men, esp. the Duke of Grafton, Lord North, the Duke of Bedford, and Lord Mansfield, and actively supporting WILKES.

jŭnk[1] *n.* Old cable cut up for oakum etc.; discarded material, worthless rubbish; (naut.) salt meat; ~-*shop*, marine store, shop of dealer in junk.

jŭnk[2] *n.* Flat-bottomed sailing vessel of China seas, with square prow, prominent stem, and lugsails. [app. f. Javanese *djong*]

junk'er (yŏŏngk-) *n.* Young German noble; narrow-minded, overbearing member of (Prussian) aristocracy.

jŭnk'ĕt *n.* Dish of sweetened and flavoured curds, freq. with scalded cream on top; feast, outing. ~ *v.i.* Feast, picnic.

Jun'ō (jōō-). 1. (Rom. myth.) Chief Roman goddess, consort of Jupiter; worshipped esp. by women; identified with the Greek HERA. 2. The 3rd of the asteroids. **Junōĕsque'** (-k) *adj.* Resembling Juno in stately beauty.

jŭn'ta *n.* Deliberative or administrative council in Spain or Italy; (also *jŭn'tō*), clique, faction, political or other combination of persons.

Jup'iter (jōō-). 1. (Rom. myth.) Orig. a sky-spirit, associated with lightning and thunderbolt; later, the chief of the Roman gods, giver of victory, identified with the Greek ZEUS. 2. Largest planet in solar system, revolving in orbit between those of Mars and Saturn, and with 4 large and several smaller satellites (ill. PLANET).

Jura[1] (joor'*a*). System of mountain ranges between rivers Rhine and Rhône forming the frontier between France and Switzerland.

Jura[2] (joor'*a*) Island, one of the inner Hebrides, on W. coast of Argyllshire, Scotland.

jur'al (joor-) *adj.* Of law; of (moral) rights and obligations.

jurăss'ic (joor-) *adj.* Of the system of rocks in the middle of the Mesozoic. ~ *n.* (*The J~*), this system or period (ill. GEOLOGY). [f. *Jura*[1] Mountains]

jur'at (joor-) *n.* Municipal officer (esp. in Cinque Ports) like alderman; in Jersey and Guernsey an honorary judge; in Alderney, an honorary magistrate.

jurid'ical (joor-) *adj.* Of judicial proceedings; legal.

jur'isconsŭlt' (joor-) *n.* One learned in law, jurist.

jurisdic'tion (joor-) *n.* Administration of justice; legal or other authority; extent of this, territory it extends over. **jurisdic'tional** (-shon-) *adj.*

jurisprud'ence (joor-, -prōō-) *n.* Science, philosophy, of human law; skill in law. **jurisprud'ent, jurispruděn'tial** (-shl) *adjs.*

jur'ist (joor-) *n.* One versed in law; legal writer; student of, graduate in, law. **juris'tic(al)** *adjs.* Of jurist(s); legal, created by law. **juris'tically** *adv.*

juror (joor'*er*) *n.* Member of jury; one who takes an oath.

jury (joor'ĭ) *n.* 1. Body of persons sworn to render verdict on question submitted to them in court of justice; *grand* ~, (formerly) jury appointed to inquire into indictments before they are submitted to trial jury (abolished 1933, exc. in certain cases in London and Middlesex); *trial, common, petty,* ~, jury of 12 persons who try final issue of fact in civil or criminal cases and pronounce their decision in a verdict on which court gives judgement; *coroner's* ~, jury of persons who pronounce decision at coroner's inquest; ~ *of matrons,* jury of discreet women empanelled to inquire into alleged pregnancy; *~-box,* enclosure for jury in court; *jur'yman,* member of jury. 2. Body of persons selected to award prizes in competition.

jury-mast (joor'ĭmahst) *n.* Temporary mast in place of broken or lost one.

jŭss'ĭve *adj.* (gram.) Expressing a command.

jŭst[1] *n.*: see JOUST.

jŭst[2] *adj.* Equitable, fair; deserved; well-grounded; right in amount etc., proper. **jŭst'ly** *adv.* **jŭst'nĕss** *n.*

jŭst[3] *adv.* Exactly; barely; exactly at that moment; (loosely) not long before; (colloq.) positively, quite; ~ *now,* at this moment; a little time ago.

jŭs'tice *n.* 1. Just conduct; fairness; exercise of authority in maintenance of right; judicial proceedings; *poetic(al)* ~, ideal justice as shown in poem etc.; *do* ~ *to,* treat fairly; show due appreciation of; *do oneself* ~, perform worthily of one's abilities. 2. Judge, esp. (in Engl.) of Supreme Court of Judicature; *~-Clerk,* vice-president of Scottish Court of Justiciary; *J~ of the Peace,* (abbrev. J.P.) lay magistrate appointed to preserve peace in county, town, etc.

jŭsti'ciable (-shĭa-) *adj.* Subject to jurisdiction.

jŭsti'ciar (-shyar) *n.* Chief political and judicial officer under Norman and early Plantaganet kings.

jŭsti'ciary (-shya-) *adj.* & *n.* 1. (Of the) administration of justice; judicature. 2. Administrator of justice; justiciar.

jŭs'tifȳ *v.t.* 1. Show the justice or rightness of; vindicate, be such as to justify; make good (statement etc.); adduce adequate grounds for. 2. (theol.) Declare (person) free from penalty of sin on ground of Christ's righteousness or (R.C. Ch.) of the infusion of grace. 3. (print.) Adjust (line of type) to fill a space neatly. **jŭstifī'able, jŭs'tificātive, jŭs'tificātory** *adjs.* **jŭs'tifiably** *adv.* **jŭstificā'tion** *n.*

Jŭs'tin I (450–527). Eastern Roman emperor 518–27; left administration almost entirely to his quaestor Proclus and his nephew JUSTINIAN. **Jŭs'tin II** (d. 578). E. Roman emperor 565–78; nephew and successor of JUSTINIAN I.

Jŭstin'ian I (483–565). Eastern Roman emperor 527–65; reorganized and codified Roman law; built church of St. Sophia at Constantinople; his great general Belisarius recovered Africa from Vandals, occupied Rome, and overthrew the Gothic kingdom in Italy. **Jŭstin'ian II** (669–711). E. Roman emperor 685–95 and 704–11.

Jŭs'tin Martyr, St. (*c* 100–*c* 165). Syrian Christian apologist; martyred in Rome; commemorated 14th April.

jŭt *n.* Projection; protruding point. ~ *v.i.* Project (freq. *out, forth*).

jute[1] (jōōt) *n.* Fibre from bark of plants *Corchorus capsularis* and *C. olitorius,* imported chiefly from Bengal, used for cordage, canvas, etc. [Sansk. *juṭa, jaṭa* braid of hair]

Jute[2] (jōōt) *n.* Member of a Low German tribe that invaded Britain in 5th c. and settled in Kent, Isle of Wight, and parts of Hampshire. [Icel. *Iótar* people of Jutland]

Jŭt'land. The peninsula which forms the continental part of Denmark; *Battle of* ~, inconclusive battle in the North Sea W. of Jutland, May 1916, between the British Grand Fleet under Jellicoe and the German High Seas Fleet under Scheer.

Juv'ĕnal (jōō-). Decimus Junius Juvenalis (*c* A.D. 60–*c* 130), Roman satirist and poet.

juvenĕs'cence (jōō-) *n.* (Transition from infancy to) youth. **juvenĕs'cent** *adj.*

ju'venīle (jōō-) *adj.* Young, youthful; suited to, characteristic of, youth; ~ *lead,* (theatr.) youthful hero's part in play; actor who takes this. ~ *n.* 1. Young person. 2. (trade, usu. pl.) Book for children. **juvenĭl'ity** *n.*

juvenĭl'ia (jōō-) *n.pl.* Literary or artistic works produced in youth.

jŭx'tapōse (-z) *v.t.* Place (things) side by side. **jŭxtaposi'tion** *n.* Placing, being placed, side by side.

K

K, k (kā). 11th letter of modern English alphabet, taken from Gk κ (*kappa*), orig. ꓘ, from Phoenician and general Semitic ꓘ (*Kaph*); pronounced in modern English as a voiceless stop consonant; in early Latin orthography *c* was used for this sound, and *k* fell largely into disuse. In modern English, *k* is used in native words before *e, i, y* (when *c* would normally be pronounced as *s*), and *n,* and medially and finally after a consonant or long vowel.

K2. Peak of the W. Himalayas,

28,250 ft high; believed to be the second highest in the world; also known as Godwin Austen.

Ka (kah) *n.* Ancient Egyptian name for second self or double, surviving with soul after death.

Kaaba: see CAABA.

Kabul (kahb'ōōl). Capital city and province of Afghanistan; ~ *River*, chief river of Afghanistan, flowing into Indus.

Kabyle' (-bīl). Berber of Algeria or Tunis. [Arab. *qabāīl* (pl.)]

Kădd'ĭsh *n.* (Jewish ritual) The doxology recited at the close of the synagogue service. [Aramaic *'qaddish* holy]

kadi: see CADI.

Kăf(f)'ir[1], **Caffre** (-fer). Term originally used by Arabs and Europeans for Bantu inhabitants of southern Africa, but now regarded as term of opprobrium and no longer officially used. ~ *bread*, farinaceous pith of a bread-fruit (*Encephalartos caffer* and related species); the plant itself; ~ (*corn*), kind of sorghum native to E. Africa and cultivated in south-western U.S. and other dry regions for grain and forage; ~ *lily*, S. Afr. herbaceous plant (*Clivia miniata*) with showy flowers. [Arab. *kafir* infidel]

Kaf'ir[2] (kahf'ēr). Native of Kafiristan; one of a small group of tribes, prob. of Iranian origin, speaking an Indo-European language. **Kafiristan** (kahfēristahn'). Mountainous province of Afghanistan S. of Hindu Kush.

kail(yard): see KALE.

kainozoic: see CAINOZOIC.

Kais'ar-i-Hind (kīs-). (hist.) Title of British sovereign as ruler of India. [Pers. *qaysari hind* emperor of India]

Kais'er[1] (kīz-) *n.* Emperor; (hist.) German emperor; emperor of Austria; head of Holy Roman Empire.

Kais'er[2] (kīz-), Georg (1878–1939). German expressionist dramatist; author of 'Die Bürger von Calais', 'Von Morgens bis Mitternachts', etc.

kăkėmōn'ō *n.* Japanese silk wall-picture mounted on rollers. [Jap. *kake* hang, *mono* thing]

kăl'a-āz'ar *n.* Disease found in tropical and subtropical areas, due to the protozoan parasite *Leishmania donovani.*

Kălahăr'ĭ Desert. Large high barren plateau of S. Africa, north of Orange River; mainly in Bechuanaland.

kāle, kail *n.* Cole, cabbage; esp. borecole, variety with wrinkled leaves not forming compact head (*Brassica oleracea acephala*); broth made with Scotch kale; (Sc.) vegetable broth; *curly* ~, ordinary borecole, with very much curled green leaves; *Scotch* ~, variety of borecole with purplish, less wrinkled leaves; *kaleyard*, (Sc.) kitchen-garden of cottage etc.; *kaleyard school*, writers of fiction describing common life in Scotland, with much use of vernacular, e.g. J. M. Barrie, 'Ian Maclaren', and S. R. Crockett.

kaleid'oscōpe (-lī-) *n.* Tube through which are seen symmetrical figures, produced by reflections of pieces of coloured glass, and varied by rotation of tube; (fig.) constantly changing group of bright objects. **kaleidoscŏp'ĭc(al)** *adjs.*

kalends: see CALENDS.

Kalevala (kahl'ĭvahl*a*). Finnish national epic, compiled from popular lays of great antiquity transmitted orally until 19th c. [Finnish, = 'land of heroes']

kăl'ĭ[1] *n.* Prickly saltwort, glasswort (*Salsola kali*), from which potash was obtained.

Kali[2] (kahl'ē). (Hindu myth.) Form of Durga, the bloodthirsty wife of Siva, represented with black body, four arms, necklace of human heads, and protruding bloodstained tongue.

Kalidasa (kahlēdahs'*a*) (prob. 3rd c. A.D.). Indian poet and dramatist of second epoch of Sanskrit literature.

Kalin'in (-lē-), Mikhail Ivanovich (1875–1946). Russian peasant statesman, president of U.S.S.R. 1923–46.

Kăl'mŭck. 1. Member of Buddhist Mongol race of central Asia who invaded Russia in 16th and 17th centuries and settled along lower Volga; many migrated to Chinese Turkestan in 18th c., but descendants of Kalmucks of the western Volga still inhabit western steppes; ~ *Autonomous Province*, autonomous area of the Russian Socialist Federal Soviet Republic, mostly on right bank of lower Volga between Ergeni Hills and Caspian Sea. 2. Language of the Kalmucks, one of the Ural-Altaic family.

kal'ŏng (kah-) *n.* Malay flying-fox or fruit-bat (*Pteropus edulis*), the largest of the bats, having a wing-spread of over 2 ft.

kăl'pa *n.* (Hindu cosmology) A great age of the world; the period beginning with the origin of a world and extending beyond its dissolution to the origin of a new world.

Kam'a (kah-), **Kamadev'a** (-dā-). (Hindu myth.) God of love, represented as a beautiful youth riding on a sparrow and armed with bow and arrows.

Kămchăt'ka. Peninsula of NE. Asia running southwards between Bering Sea and Sea of Okhotsk; province of the Far Eastern Region of U.S.S.R.

kāme *n.* Ridge of sand and gravel built up of debris carried by water from a decaying glacier and deposited near its edge.

kămerad' (-ahd) *int.* 'Comrade', German soldier's appeal for quarter; hence (joc.) plea for mercy.

Kamerun: see CAMEROON.

Kan. *abbrev.* Kansas.

kăn'aka *n.* Native of South Sea Islands, esp. one formerly shipped for forced labour to Australia. [Hawaiian, = 'man']

Kăn'arēse' (-z) *adj.* & *n.* (Native, Dravidian language) of Kanara in W. India.

Kăndahăr'. City of S. Afghanistan, on trade-route between Quetta and Kabul.

Kăn(g)chėnjŭng'a (*or* kĭn-; -ngg-). Himalayan peak, 28,146 ft high; believed to be third highest in the world.

kăngarōō' (-ngg-) *n.* Marsupial of genus *Macropus* with strongly developed hind-quarters and great leaping-power, native of Australia,

KANGAROO

Tasmania, etc.; ~ *closure*, form of Parliamentary closure by which some amendments are selected for discussion and others excluded; *~-rat* or *rat* ~, small Austral. marsupial belonging to any of several genera, esp. *Potorous* and *Bettongia*; also, Amer. pouched rodent (*Dipodomys*) of SW. States and Mexico.

Kăn'sas (-z-). West North Central State of U.S.; capital, Topeka; ~ *City*, large city on right bank of river Missouri, divided between States of Missouri and Kansas; ~ *River*, river draining N. part of Kansas State and flowing eastwards into river Missouri. **Kăn'san** (-z-) *adj.*; ~ *age*, second epoch of glacial period in N. America, deposits of which are found in Kansas State.

Kansu (kahn'sōō'). Extreme NW. province of China.

Kănt, Immanuel (1724–1804). German metaphysician, founder of school of transcendantal philosophy, of which one of the fundamental principles is that knowledge of the external world depends upon sense-impressions co-ordinated or synthesized by the reason, employing such 'categories' or laws of thought as quality, quantity, causation, etc. **Kăn'tian** *adj.* & *n.*

kā'olĭn *n.* China clay, a fine white clay formed by the decomposition and weathering of felspar in granite, in Gt Britain found esp. in Cornwall; used in making porcelain, as a filler for paper and textiles, in medical treatment, etc. [Chin. *kao-ling* high hill (mountain where orig. obtained)]

kapĕll'meister (-mī-) *n.* Conductor of orchestra or choir.

kāp'ŏk (*or* kah-) *n.* Fine short-stapled cottonwool surrounding seeds of kapok-tree (*Eriodendron anfractuosum*) of Java, Ceylon, etc., used for stuffing cushions etc. [Malay *kapog*]

kăpp'a *n.* Greek letter κ (k).

Kapur'thala (-poort-). Former native State of Punjab; now part of the Patiala and E. Punjab Union, India.

kaput' (-pŏŏt) *adj.* (slang) Finished, done for. [Ger.]

Karach'ĭ (-ahch-). Sea- and airport of Sind, on an inlet of the Arabian Sea; former capital of PAKISTAN.

Karad'žić (-ahzh'ĭch), Vuk Stefanović 1787–1864). Serbian author, grammarian, and lexicographer; 'father' of modern Serbian literature.

Karageorge, Karadjordje (kah'rajôrj'ē), Czerny George (*c* 1766–1817). Serbian peasant and patriot; leader of Serbs in struggle against Turkey and founder of *Karageorgevich* dynasty of Serbia.

Kar'aite, Qaraite. Member of Jewish sect, chiefly of Crimea etc., founded 8th c., rejecting rabbinical tradition and basing its tenets on literal interpretation of scriptures. [Heb. *q'raim* (*qara* read)]

Karakor'am, Qarakorum. Mountain region lying to the N. of the W. end of the Himalayas.

karakul: see CARACUL.

Kar'a Kum (kōōm). Flat desert region of Turkmenistan, Asiatic Russia.

Kăramzin' (-ahmzēn'), Nikolay Mikhailovich (1765–1826). Russian historian and novelist.

Kar'a Sea. Shallow part of Arctic Ocean between Novaya Zemlya and Siberian mainland.

Karēl'ia. Area of NW. Russia between Finnish border and White Sea. **Karēl'ian** *adj.* & *n.*

Karēl'o-Fĭnn'ish *adj.* Of Karelia and Finland; ~ *Soviet Socialist Republic*, a constituent republic of the Soviet Union formed in 1940, comprising Karelia and those areas ceded to Russia by Finland after the Russo-Finnish war.

Karls'bad (-baht). German name of *Karlovy Vary*, town in Czechoslovakia; ~ *salts*, aperient salts obtained from its mineral springs.

karm'a *n.* (Buddhism, Hinduism) Sum of person's actions in one of his successive states of existence viewed as deciding his fate in the next; destiny.

Karn'ak. Village of Upper Egypt, on Nile near Luxor, containing magnificent ruins of temple of Ammon on site of ancient Thebes.

Kar(r)ōō' *n.* Elevated barren plateau of clayey soil in S. Africa, waterless in dry season.

Karst. Barren limestone plateau in N. Yugoslavia, with abrupt ridges, caverns, and underground streams; (geog.) any region of this type.

kartell': see CARTEL.

Kăshmir' (-mēr) Himalayan territory with chiefly Moslem, light-complexioned inhabitants of Aryan stock; capitals, Srinagar and Jammu. **Kăshmir'ĭ.** The Indo-European language of Kashmir, much influenced by Sanskrit.

katăb'olism *n.* Phase of metabolism which consists in breaking down complex compounds into simpler ones.

kăt'a-thermŏm'ėter *n.* Instrument which records the rate of cooling of air and evaporation of moisture from the body.

Kăt'rine, Loch. Freshwater lake in Scotland, E. of Loch Lomond.

Kătt'ėgăt'. Channel between Denmark and Sweden, running from Skagerrak southwards towards Baltic Sea.

kăt'ydid *n.* (U.S.) Any of several large green orthopterous insects, related to grasshoppers and crickets, producing characteristic noise by stridulation; common in central and eastern States of America. [imit.]

Kauff'mann (kow-), Angelica (1741-1807). Painter, of Swiss origin, active in England.

Kaun'as (kow-). City of Lithuania.

kau'ri (kow-) *n.* Coniferous tree of New Zealand (*Agathis australis*), furnishing valuable timber and a resin (~-*gum*).

kav'a (kah-) *n.* (Intoxicating beverage prepared from macerated roots of) Polynesian shrub, *Piper methysticum.*

kay'ak (kī-) *n.* Eskimo one-man canoe of light wooden framework covered with sealskins (ill. CANOE).

Kazakh (-ahk', -ahχ') *adj.* & *n.* 1. (Member) of a Turkic people of S. Siberia. 2. (also *Kazakhstan*, pr. -ahn') Area inhabited by these, a constituent republic of the Soviet Union; capital, Alma-Ata.

K.B. *abbrev.* King's Bench.

K.B.E. *abbrev.* Knight Commander (of the Order) of the British Empire.

kc. *abbrev.* Kilocycle(s).

K.C. *abbrev.* King's College; King's Counsel; Knight(s) of Columbus.

K.C.B., K.C.I.E., K.C.M.G., K.C.S.I., K.C.V.O., *abbrevs*, Knight Commander (of the Order) of the Bath, (of the Order) of the Indian Empire, (of the Order) of St. Michael and St. George, (of the Order) of the Star of India, of the (Royal) Victorian Order.

K.E. *abbrev.* Kinetic energy.

kea (kā'*a*) *n.* Green parrot (*Nestor notabilis*) of a group peculiar to the New Zealand region, normally living on fruit, grubs, and carrion, but attacking sheep when pressed by hunger.

Kean, Edmund (1787–1833). English tragic actor.

Keats, John (1795–1821). English lyric poet; author of 'Endymion', the odes 'On a Grecian Urn', 'To a Nightingale', 'To Autumn', etc.

kėbabs' (-ahbz) *n.* = CABOBS.

Kēb'le, John (1792–1866). English divine; a founder of the Oxford or TRACTARIAN movement; writer of sacred verse.

Kēb'le College. Oxford college founded 1870 as memorial to John Keble.

kĕck *v.i.* Make sound as if about to vomit.

Kēd'ar. (O.T.) Son of ISHMAEL (Gen. xxv. 13), whose descendants were a tribe of nomads identified in later Jewish literature with the Arabs.

kĕdge *v.* (naut.) Change position of ship by winding in hawser attached to small anchor at some distance; (of ship) move thus; move (ship) thus. ~ *n.* (also ~-*anchor*) Small anchor for this purpose.

kĕdg'eree *n.* Indian dish of rice, split pulse, onions, eggs, etc.; European dish of fish, rice, eggs, and condiments.

keel[1] *n.* Lowest longitudinal timber of vessel, on which framework of whole is built up (ill. BOAT); combination of iron plates serving same purpose in iron vessel; (poet.) ship; (in aircraft) vertical fin extending longitudinally underneath; ~-*blocks*, blocks on which keel rests in building etc.; ~'-*haul*, haul (person) under keel as punishment. ~ *v.* Turn (ship) keel upwards; ~ *over*, turn, be turned, over, upset, capsize.

keel[2] *n.* Flat-bottomed vessel, esp. of kind used on Tyne etc. for loading colliers; amount carried by this.

Keeling Islands: see COCOS ISLANDS.

keel'son, kĕl- *n.* Set of timbers or plates fastening ship's floor-timbers to keel (ill. BOAT).

keen[1] *n.* Irish funeral song accompanied with wailing. ~ *v.* Utter the keen; bewail (person) thus; utter in wailing tone.

keen[2] *adj.* Having sharp edge or point; sharp; (of sound, light, etc.) penetrating, vivid, strong; (of cold) intense; (of pain etc.) acute, bitter; (of person, desire, interest) eager, ardent (colloq. *on*); (of eyes etc.) sharp, highly sensitive; intellectually acute. **keen'ly** *adv.* **keen'nėss** *n.*

Keene, Charles Samuel (1823–91). English black-and-white artist, illustrator in 'Punch' etc.

keep[1] *v.* (past t. and past part. *kĕpt*). 1. Pay due regard to, observe, stand by, (law, promise, faith, etc.); observe, solemnize (feast etc.). 2. Guard, protect (person, fortress, goal at football etc.); have charge of; maintain in proper form and order; provide for sustenance of, maintain, support; own and manage (animals etc.); maintain (woman) as mistress; have (commodity) habitually on sale. 3. Retain possession of, not lose; maintain, remain, in proper or specified condition; reserve, admit of being reserved, (*for* future time etc.); hide, conceal (secret etc.). 4. Detain (person *in prison* etc.); restrain (*from*); refrain *from*. 5. Continue to follow (way, course); remain in (one's bed, room, house); retain one's place in (the saddle, one's ground, etc.) against opposition; remain (indoors etc.); (colloq., esp. Camb. Univ.) reside. 6. ~ *house*: see HOUSE; ~ *one's feet*, not fall; ~ *at*, work persistently at; ~ *away*, avoid coming; prevent from coming; ~ *back*, hold back, retard progress of, conceal; ~ *down*, hold in subjection; keep low in amount; ~ *in*, confine, restrain, (feelings etc.); confine (schoolboy) after hours; keep (fire) burning; remain indoors; remain on good terms *with*; ~ *one's hand in*: see HAND; ~ *off*, ward off, avert; stay at a distance; ~ *on*, continue to hold, use, show, etc.; continue (do*ing*); ~ *oneself to oneself*, avoid society; ~ *out*, not allow to enter; ~ *to*, adhere to, confine oneself to; ~ *to oneself*, refuse to share with others; ~ *together*, remain, cause to remain, together; ~ *under*, hold in subjection; ~ *up*, prevent from sinking; maintain; keep in repair; carry on (correspondence etc.); cause (person) to sit up at night; bear up, not break down; proceed at equal pace *with*; ~ *it up*, not slacken; ~ *wicket*, (cricket) act as wicket-keeper.

keep[2] *n.* 1. (hist.) Tower, stronghold. 2. Maintenance, food required for this. 3. *for ~s*, (orig. U.S.) in permanence.

keep'er *n.* (esp.) Game-keeper; lunatic's attendant; ring that keeps another (esp. wedding-ring) on finger.

keep'ing *n.* (esp.) 1. Custody, charge. 2. Agreement, harmony. 3. (attrib.) Fit for keeping.

keep'sāke *n.* Thing kept for sake, or in remembrance, of giver; name of various 19th-c. illustrated literary annuals.

keeshond (kās'hŏnd) n. Dutch dog with thick curly hair, like large Pomeranian, kept on barges etc.

kĕg *n.* Small barrel, usu. of less than 10 gallons.

Kékulé (kā'kōōlā) von Stradonitz, Friedrich August (1829–96). German organic chemist, formulator of ring structure of benzene.

kelleck: see KILLICK.

Kĕll'er[1], Gottfried (1819–90). German-Swiss novelist and poet; author of 'Die Leute von Seldwyla', 'Der Grüne Heinrich', etc.

Kĕll'er[2], Helen Adams (1880–). American author, born in Alabama; became blind and deaf in infancy; was taught to speak, read, and use a typewriter; has written several books including the story of her life, travelled extensively, and done much for the education of those similarly handicapped.

Kĕll'ogg Păct. Treaty renouncing war as an instrument of national policy; signed at Paris, 1928, by representatives of 15 nations. [F. B. *Kellogg* (1856–1937), U.S. Secretary of State 1924–9]

Kĕlls, Book of. Illuminated MS. of the gospels, now at Trinity College, Dublin; made perh. by Irish monks in Iona in 8th or early 9th c. [f. *Kells*, town in Co. Meath, Eire, where it was formerly kept]

Kĕlm'scŏtt Press. Printing-press founded and operated (1891–8) by William Morris.

kĕlp *n.* Large seaweeds, which are burnt for the potash, iodine, etc., they contain; calcined ashes of these, formerly used in making soap and glass.

kĕlp'ie, -y *n.* (Sc.) Water-spirit, usu. in form of horse, reputed to take delight in, or bring about, the drowning of passers-by.

kelson: see KEELSON.

kĕlt[1] *n.* Salmon that has spawned.

Kelt[2]: see CELT.

Kĕl vĭn[1], Lord (William Thomson) (1824–1907). Irish-born physicist, professor of Natural Philosophy at Glasgow, who advanced the science of thermodynamics and electricity, improved the system of electrical units, and invented several scientific instruments; ~ *scale* (*absolute scale*), scale of absolute temperature, in which the zero is the temperature at which a perfect gas would occupy zero volume if it could be cooled indefinitely, without liquefaction or solidification; this zero corresponds roughly to −273° C.

kĕl'vĭn[2] *n.* The kilowatt-hour, the ordinary commercial unit of electrical energy. [f. KELVIN[1]]

Kemal Pasha: see ATATÜRK.

Kĕm'ble, Charles (1775–1854). English actor. ~, Frances Anne (Fanny) (1809–93). Actress, daughter of Charles. ~, John Philip (1757–1823). Actor, brother of Charles. ~, Roger (1721–1802). Actor and manager, father of John and Charles and of Mrs Siddons.

kĕmp *n.* Coarse hair in wool. **kĕmp'y** *adj.*

Kempis, Thomas à: see THOMAS À KEMPIS.

kĕn *n.* Range of sight or knowledge. ~ *v.t.* (now Sc.) Recognize at sight; know.

Kĕn'dal. Town in Westmorland, England; ~ *green*, green woollen cloth formerly made there.

Kĕn'ilworth (-wĕrth). Market town in Warwickshire, England, containing ruins of castle begun *c* 1120 and given by Queen Elizabeth to Earl of Leicester.

Kĕnn'ėdy, John Fitzgerald (1917–63). Senator for Massachusetts (Democrat) 1953; 35th president of U.S., 1961–3.

kĕnn'el[1] *n.* House, hut, for shelter of house-dog or hounds; mean dwelling. ~ *v.* Live in, go to, kennel; put into, keep in, kennel.

kĕnn'el[2] *n.* Gutter.

Kĕnn'ėth. Name of two Scottish kings, *Kenneth I MacAlpin* (d. *c* 860), traditional founder of kingdom of Scotland, and *Kenneth II* (d. 995).

kĕnn'ing *n.* Periphrastic expression used instead of simple name of thing in OE, ON, etc., poetry.

Kĕnn'ington. District in borough of Lambeth, S. London, containing ~ *Oval*, Surrey County Cricket Club's ground.

kėnōs'is *n.* (theol.) Renunciation of divine nature, at least in part, by Christ in incarnation.

Kĕn'sington (-z-). Borough of W. London; ~ *Gardens*, orig. gardens of Kensington Palace, thrown open to public in 18th c.; ~ *Palace*, built by Heneage Finch, lord chancellor in reign of Charles II, and bought by William III; a royal residence until death of George II; *South ~ Museum*, the British Museum (Natural History); (also, occas.) the Victoria and Albert Museum.

Kĕn'sit, John (1853–1902). English protestant agitator, a violent opponent of ritualism. **Kĕn'sitīte** *adj.* & *n.* (Follower) of Kensit.

Kĕnt[1]. County of SE. England, between S. bank of Thames estuary and E. end of English Channel; a kingdom of Anglo-Saxon England traditionally founded by Hengist and Horsa; *man of ~*, one born E. of the Medway (as dist. from *Kentish man*, born W. of it). **Kĕnt'ish** *adj.* Of Kent; ~ *man*: see above; ~ *rag*, hard compact limestone found in Kent used for paving and building.

Kĕnt[2], Edward Augustus, Duke of (1767–1820). 4th son of George III and father of Queen Victoria.

Kĕnt[3], William (1684–1748). English painter, sculptor, architect, and landscape-gardener; architect of Horse Guards, Whitehall, and Devonshire House, Piccadilly.

Kĕn'tigĕrn, St. (*c* 518–603). British prince; preached Christianity in Strathclyde and became bishop of Cumbria; also called Mungo. [Gael., = 'chief lord' *Mungo* 'dear one']

kĕnt'ledge (-lĭj) *n.* (naut.) Pig-iron used as permanent ballast.

Kĕntŭck'y. East South Central State of U.S.; capital, Frankfort; ~ *Dĕrby*, horse-race for 3-year-olds run annually at Louisville, Kentucky, founded 1875.

Kĕn′ya. Country of E. Africa between Ethiopia and Tanganyika, former British colony and protectorate; became independent in 1963; capital, Nairobi; *Mt* ~, volcanic mountain in Kenya, just S. of Equator, one of the highest in Africa.

kep′ĭ (kā-, kĕ-) *n.* French military cap with horizontal peak.

Kĕp′ler, Johann (1571–1630). German astronomer, whose three laws of planetary motion provided the basis for much of Newton's work.

Kĕ′rala. State of SW. India, constituted 1956; capital, Trivandrum.

kĕ′ratin *n.* Protein or group of proteins found in skin, hair, nails, horns, hoofs, and feathers.

kĕ′ratōse *adj.* Having horn-like substance (characteristic of a group of sponges, the *Keratosa*).

kẽrb *n.* Stone edging to pavement or raised path; ~-*stone*, one of stones forming this; ~(-*stone*) *market*, stock-exchange business done in street after closing of exchange.

kẽr′chief (-ĭf) *n.* Cloth used to cover head; (poet.) handkerchief.

Kĕrĕn′skȳ, Alexander Feodorovich (1881–). Russian liberal politician; prime minister of 2nd Provisional government until Bolshevik revolution.

kẽrf *n.* Slit made by cutting, esp. with saw; cut end of felled tree.

Kẽrg′uelėn (-gė-). Desolation Island, uninhabited subantarctic island, belonging to France, in Southern Ocean SE. of Cape of Good Hope and SW. of Australia; discovered (1772) by a Breton navigator, Yves-Joseph de Kerguélen-Trémarec; ~ *cabbage*, cabbage-like plant (*Pringlea antiscorbutica*) peculiar to this island.

kẽrm′es (-ĭz) *n.* Female of insect *Kermes ilicis*, formerly supposed to be a berry, gathered from species of evergreen oak in S. Europe and N. Africa and used in dyeing; red dye-stuff prepared from dried bodies of these; ~ (*oak*), evergreen oak, *Quercus coccifera*, on which these insects live.

kẽrn[1] *n.* (printing) Part of a metal type projecting beyond the body or shank, as the curled head of *f* and tail of *j*, etc. (ill. TYPE).

kẽrn(e)[2] *n.* (hist.) Light-armed Irish foot-soldier; peasant, boor.

kẽrn′el *n.* Softer (usu. edible) part within hard shell of nut or stone fruit; whole seed within husk etc., e.g. grain of wheat; nucleus, centre of formation (freq. fig.).

kĕ′rosēne, -ine *n.* Fuel-oil obtained by distillation of petroleum, or from coal or shale, and consisting of mixture of liquid hydrocarbons; paraffin.

Kĕ′rry. Western county in Munster, Eire; cow of Kerry breed, very small black dairy cattle native to Ireland and still produced in Kerry; ~ *blue*, Irish breed of terrier, with characteristics of Irish terrier and Irish wolfhound, and silky blue-grey coat.

kẽrs′ey (-zĭ) *n.* Kind of coarse narrow cloth, usu. ribbed, woven from long wool. [perh. f. *Kersey* in Suffolk]

kẽrs′eymēre (-zĭ-) *n.* Twilled fine woollen cloth; (pl.) trousers of this. [corrupt. of *cassimere* CASHMERE, by association with prec.]

kĕs′trel *n.* Species of small falcon (*Falco tinnunculus*) with habit of remaining in same place in air with head to the wind; windhover (ill. BUZZARD).

Kĕs′wick (-zĭk). Town in Cumberland, England; ~ (*codlin*), ribbed green cooking-apple.

kĕtch *n.* Small two-masted or cutter-rigged coasting vessel (ill. YACHT).

Ketch, Jack: see JACK.

kĕtch′up *n.* Sauce of tomatoes, mushrooms, or walnuts, etc., with vinegar, raisins, spices, etc., used as condiment. [prob. f. Chin. *kôe-chiap* brine of pickled fish]

kĕt′ōne *n.* (chem.) One of a group of organic compounds containing carbonyl group (CO) doubly united with carbon, usu. colourless volatile liquids with pungent ethereal smell, used esp. as solvents. [Ger. *keton*, modification of *acetone*]

kĕtt′le *n.* Vessel for boiling water, usu. of metal with spout, lid, and handle; fish-kettle; *pretty ~ of fish*, awkward state of affairs; ~-*drum*, percussion instrument, hollow brass or copper hemisphere over edge of which parchment is stretched and tuned to definite note (ill. DRUM); ~-*holder*, piece of cloth etc. to protect hand from heat of kettle handle. **kĕtt′leful** *n.*

kĕv′el *n.* (naut.) Peg or cleat, usu. one of pair, to which certain ropes are belayed.

Kew. ~ *Gardens*, the Royal Botanic Gardens, principal English national botanical gardens, at Kew, Surrey, 9 miles W. of London on the Thames; orig. laid out in 18th c. by Lord Capel, extended by George III, and adopted as national establishment in 1840; ~ *Palace*, the 'Dutch House' in Kew Gardens, sold to a Dutch merchant, Sir Hugh Portman, in 16th c., and bought 1781 by George III as nursery for royal children.

key[1] (kē) *n.* 1. Instrument, usu. of iron, for moving bolt of lock forwards or backwards. 2. What gives or precludes opportunity for or access to something; (chess) first move in problem game. 3. (pl., with allusion to Matt. xvi. 19) Ecclesiastical authority held to be transmitted to pope as successor of St. Peter (*St. Peter's ~s*, cross keys borne on papal arms). 4. Solution, explanation; translation of book or exercise in foreign tongue; book of solutions of mathematical problems etc. 5. (mus.) System of tones definitely related to each other and based on *key-note*, according to (*in*) which a piece of music is written; (fig.) tone, style, of thought or expression. 6. Piece of wood or metal inserted between others to secure them; part of first coat of wall or ceiling plaster passing between laths and so securing the rest. 7. Lever pressed by finger in playing organ, piano, flute, concertina, etc.; similar lever in typewriter etc. 8. Instrument for grasping screws, pegs, nuts, etc., esp. one for winding clock or watch. 9. *key′board*, set of keys in piano, organ, typewriter, etc.; ~-*bugle*, bugle fitted with keys to increase number of its sounds; *key′hole*, hole by which key is put into lock; ~ *industry*, one essential to the carrying on of others; ~ *move*: see 2; ~-*note*: see 5; (fig.) prevailing tone or idea; ~-*ring*, ring for keeping keys on; *key′stone*, stone at summit of arch locking the whole together (ill. ARCH); (fig.) central principle etc. on which all depends; *Keystone State*, (U.S.) Pennsylvania. **key′lėss** *adj.* **key** *v.t.* Fasten (*in*, *on*, etc.) with pin, wedge, bolt, etc.; regulate pitch of strings of (piano etc.); ~ *up*, (fig.) stimulate; raise tone or standard of; brace up.

key[2] (kē) *n.* Low island, sand-bank, or reef, of kind common in W. Indies or off coast of Florida.

Keynes (kānz), John Maynard, 1st Baron (1883–1946). English economist; financial adviser to the British Government.

Keys (kēz), **House of.** Body of 24 members forming elective branch of Legislature of Isle of Man.

kg. *abbrev.* Kilogram.

K.G. *abbrev.* Knight (of the Order) of the Garter.

kha′ki (kah-) *adj.* Dull brownish yellow. ~ *n.* Khaki fabric of twilled cotton or wool used in army for field-uniforms. [Hind., = dusty (*khak* dust)]

khăl′ĭfa, khălĭfăt *ns.* = CALIPH(ATE).

khăm′sĭn (kă-) *n.* Oppressive hot S. or SE. wind blowing in Egypt for about 50 days in March, April, and May. [Arab. *khamsūn* 50]

khan[1] (kahn) *n.* (hist.) Title of successors of Genghis Khan, supreme rulers of Turkish, Tatar, and Mongol tribes and emperors of China, in Middle Ages; title of rulers, officials, and men of rank of central Asia, Afghanistan, etc. **khan′ate** *n.* [Turk., perhaps f. *khāqān* king]

khan[2] (kahn) *n.* Caravanserai. [Arab., = 'inn']

Khart(o)um (kãrtōōm′). Capital of SUDAN, on Blue Nile just above junction with White Nile; besieged 1885 and captured by the MAHDISTS after a gallant defence by General GORDON; recaptured by the British under KITCHENER, 1898.

Khayyám, Omar: see OMAR KHAYYÁM.

K.H.C.,K.H.P.,K.H.S. *abbrevs.* Honorary Chaplain, Physician, Surgeon, to the King.

Khedive (kĭdēv′) *n.* (hist.) Title of viceroy or governor of Egypt, accorded to Ismail Pasha by Turkey in 1867.

khi (kī) *n.* Greek letter X, χ (kh).

khĭd′mutgar *n.* Male servant who waits at table (in India). [Hind. *khidmat* service]

khĭl′âfăt *n.* = CALIPHATE; ~ *agitation*, Moslem anti-British movement in India, 1919–24.

Khmer (χmār). 1. Ancient kingdom of Cambodia, French Indo-China; reached peak of its power in 11th c.; was destroyed by Siamese conquests in 12th and 14th centuries. 2. (One of) the people of this kingdom, from whom some modern Cambodians are descended. 3. Monosyllabic language of this people, of Mon-Khmer group of Austro-Asiatic family.

Khōj′a *n.* 1. Mohammedan professor, schoolmaster, or scribe. 2. Indian member of the Ismaili sect.

khor (kor̄) *n.* Watercourse, ravine.

Khrushchev (χrōōshchŏf′), Nikita Sergeyevich (1894–). Soviet Communist leader; in the struggle for power after Stalin's death he emerged as victor, and was 1st secretary of the Communist party of the Soviet Union from 1953 to 1964, and head of the Government from 1958 to 1964; denounced Stalin at party congresses in 1956 and 1961; associated with internal reform and advocacy of 'peaceful co-existence' with the Western powers.

Khyb′er Pass (kī-). Important pass between Afghanistan and Pakistan.

kiăng′, kyang *n.* The Tibetan ass or dziggetai (*Equus hemionus*), with thick dark furry coat, found at altitudes of 15,000 ft and upwards.

Kiangsi (kyăng′sē′). Province of SE. China.

Kiang-su (-sōō). Coastal province of E. China at outlet of Yangtze Kiang.

kĭb′ble *n.* Iron hoisting-bucket used in mines.

kībe *n.* Ulcerated chilblain, esp. on heel.

kĭbĭt′ka *n.* 1. Tatar's circular tent covered with felt; Tatar household. 2. Russian hooded sledge.

kĭb′ŏsh *n.* (slang) *Put the ~ on*, put an end to, dispose of finally.

kĭck *n.* Act of kicking; (colloq.) power of reaction, resilience; recoil of gun when discharged; (U.S. slang) complaint, criticism; (slang, orig. U.S.) sharp stimulant effect, thrill; *~-off*, (football) kick with which game is started; *~-starter*, foot-operated lever for starting engine, esp. of motor-cycle. ~ *v.* Strike out with the foot; show annoyance, dislike, etc. (*against, at*); strike with foot; drive, move, (thing) by kicking; (football) score (goal) by a kick; drive forcibly and contemptuously (*out* etc.); ~ *against the pricks*, resist to one's own hurt; ~ *the bucket*, (slang) die; ~ *off*, throw off (shoes) by kicking; (football) start game by giving first kick; ~ *up*, raise (dust); create (fuss, noise).

Kĭck′apōō. N. Amer. Indian of Algonkin linguistic stock, orig. found in S. Wisconsin.

kĭck′er *n.* (esp.) Horse given to kicking.

kĭck′shaw *n.* Fancy dish in cookery (usu. contempt.); toy, trifle. [Fr. *quelque chose* something]

kĭd[1] *n.* Young of goat; leather from skin of this, used for gloves and boots; (slang) child, young person; *~-glove, (adj.)* over-dainty, fastidious. ~ *v.* Give birth to (kid), give birth to kid. **kĭdd′y** *n.* (slang) Little child.

kĭd[2] *v.t.* & *n.* Hoax, humbug.

kĭd[3] *n.* Small wooden tub, esp. sailor's mess-tub.

Kĭdd, William (*c* 1645–1701). 'Captain Kidd', English privateer and pirate; hanged for piracy, 1701.

Kĭdd′ermĭnster. Town in Worcestershire, England, where carpets have been made since 1735; hence, kind of ribbed carpet without pile, in which two or more cloths of different colours are interwoven to form pattern (also called ingrain carpet; now seldom made).

kĭd′dle *n.* Barrier in river with opening fitted with nets etc. to catch fish; arrangement of stake-nets on sea-beach.

kĭd′năp *v.t.* Steal (child); carry off (person) by illegal force. **kĭd′năpper** *n.*

kĭd′ney *n.* One of a pair of glandular organs in abdominal cavity of vertebrates, serving mainly to excrete nitrogenous matter from the blood; analogous organ in other animals; kidney of sheep, cattle, and pigs, as food; temperament, nature; ~ (*potato*), oval kind of potato; *~-bean*, dwarf French bean (*Phaseolus vulgaris*).

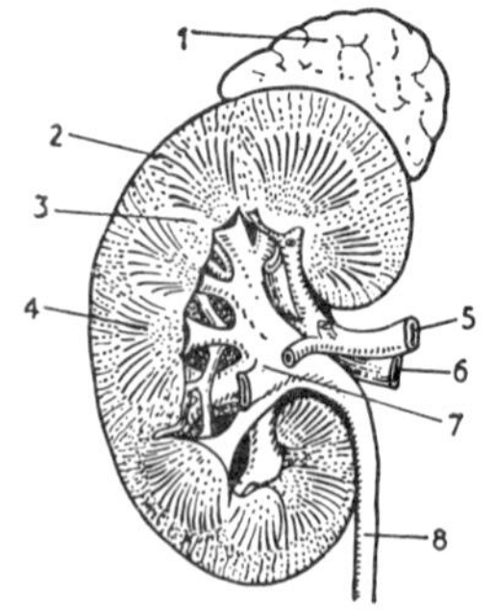

KIDNEY

1. Adrenal. 2. Cortex. 3. Medulla. 4. Pyramid. 5. Renal vein. 6. Renal artery. 7. Pelvis of ureter. 8. Ureter

Kiel Canăl′ (kēl). Canal joining German Baltic naval port, Kiel, with North Sea at Brunsbüttel on mouth of River Elbe; opened 1895.

kier (kēr̄) *n.* Vat in which cloth is boiled for bleaching etc.

Kierkegaard (kēr̄k′eyor̄), Sören Aaby (1813–55). Danish philosopher and theological writer.

kieselguhr (kē′zlgoor) *n.* Porous diatomite (i.e. earth composed of siliceous remains of minute sea-plants), used as abrasive and in dynamite as absorbent for nitro-glycerine.

Kiev (kē′ėf). City of U.S.S.R., capital of Ukraine.

Kĭku′yu (-kōōyōō). (Member of) an agricultural negro people, the largest Bantu tribe in Kenya; their language.

Kĭldār̄e′. County and town of Leinster, Eire.

kĭl′derkĭn *n.* Cask for liquids etc. containing 16 or 18 gal. (ill. CASK); this as measure.

Kĭl′ham (-lam), Alexander (1762–98). English founder of 'Methodist New Connexion'.

Kĭl′ian, St. (7th c.). Irish missionary bishop; apostle of eastern Franconia; martyred at Würzburg.

Kĭlĭmănjār′ō. Mountain in N. Tanganyika, E. Africa, highest known mountain in Africa (19,340 ft).

Kĭlkĕnn′y. County and city of Leinster, Eire; ~ *cats*, cats said proverbially to have fought until nothing but the tails remained, taken as type of combatants who fight until they annihilate each other; *Statute of ~*, laws of 1366 designed to strengthen English authority in Ireland, and forbidding marriage between English settlers and the native Irish.

kĭll *v.* 1. Put to death, slay; cause the death of; perform act of killing, do execution; ~ *off*, get rid of (number of persons etc.) by killing; ~ *two birds with one stone*, effect two purposes at once. 2. Destroy vitality of; destroy, put an end to; neutralize (colours etc.) by contrast; consume (time) for the sake of doing so; overwhelm (person) with admiration, amusement, etc.; strike (ball in lawn-tennis) so that it cannot be returned; stop (ball in football) dead; totally defeat (Bill in Parliament); ~ *with kindness*, destroy or fatally harm with mistaken or excessive kindness; *~-joy*, one who throws gloom over social enjoyment, one who destroys pleasure. ~ *n.* Act of killing; animal killed, esp. by sportsman; destruction or putting out of action of submarine, aircraft, etc.

Killār̄n′ey (-nĭ). Town of County Kerry, Eire, near lakes of Killarney, famous for beauty of landscape.

kĭll′dee(r) *n.* Largest N. Amer. species of ring-plover, *Charadrius vociferous.* [imit.]

kill er *n.* Person, thing, that kills; murderous ruffian; *humane* ~: see HUMANE; ~ (*whale*), grampus (*Orca gladiator*) and other ferocious cetaceans.

kill'ick, -ock, kĕll'ĕck *n.* Heavy stone used by small craft as anchor; small anchor.

Killiecrănk'ie. Pass in Perthshire, Scotland; *battle of* ~, that in which Jacobites under Claverhouse defeated Royalists under Mackay, 1689.

kill'ing *n.*; ~-*bottle*, bottle containing poison for killing captured insects etc. ~ *adj.* (esp., colloq.) Overwhelmingly attractive; overwhelmingly funny. **kill'ingly** *adv.*

kiln *n.* Furnace, oven, for burning, baking, or drying, esp. for calcining lime, baking bricks or drying hops; ~-*dry*, (*v.t.*) dry in kiln.

kilo- *prefix.* A thousand.

kil'ocycle *n.* 1,000 cycles, as unit in measuring frequency of electromagnetic waves (abbrev. kc.).

kil'ogrăm *n.* Standard measure of weight in metric system, equivalent to 1,000 grams (abbrev. kg.); see Appendix X.

kil'olitre (-lēter) *n.* Measure of capacity, 1,000 litres (abbrev. kl.); see Appendix X.

kil'omētre (-ter) *n.* Measure of length, 1,000 metres (abbrev. km.); see Appendix X. **kilomĕt'ric** *adj.*

kil'owatt (-ŏt) *n.* Unit of (esp. electric) power, 1,000 watts (abbrev. kw.); ~-*hour*, unit of electrical energy, energy used when a rate of 1 kilowatt is maintained for 1 hour; = Board of Trade unit.

kilt *v.t.* Tuck up (skirts) round body; gather in vertical pleats (esp. in past part.). ~ *n.* Part of modern Highland dress, skirt, usu. of tartan cloth, heavily pleated round back and sides, reaching from waist to knee (ill. PLAID). **kilt'y** *n.* Highland soldier.

Kim'berley (-lĭ). Diamond mine, district, and town in Griqualand West, Cape Province, S. Africa. [1st earl of *Kimberley*, Colonial Secretary (1871) when gold-mines were taken under protection of Gt Britain]

Kimm'eridge. Village on coast of Dorsetshire, England, where are extensive beds of Upper Oolite; ~ *clay*, bed of clay in Upper Oolite containing bituminous shales; ~ *coal*, shale of Kimmeridge clay containing so much bitumen that it can be burnt as coal. **Kimmerĭdg'ian** *adj.*

kimōn'ō *n.* (pl. -*s*). Long Japanese robe with sleeves; one of these, or similar robe, worn as woman's dressing-gown etc.

kin *n.* 1. Ancestral stock, family; one's relatives; *kith and* ~: see KITH; *of* ~, akin, related by blood ties or character; *near of* ~, closely related; *next of* ~, see NEXT. 2. (*predic., passing into adj.*) Related. **Kin'lĕss** *adj.*

Kincard'ineshire. County on E. coast of Scotland.

kin'chin *n.* (cant) Child; ~ *lay*, practice of stealing money from children sent on errands. [prob. f. Ger. *kindchen* little child]

kin'cŏb (-ngk-) *n.* Rich Indian stuff embroidered with gold or silver.

kind[1] *n.* Race, natural group, of animals, plants, etc.; class, sort, variety; character, quality; (archaic) nature in general; (archaic) way, fashion, natural to person, etc.; ~ *of*, (colloq.) to some extent, in some degree; *in* ~, (of payment) in goods or natural produce, not in money; (of repayment) in something of the same kind as that received.

kind[2] *adj.* Of gentle or benevolent nature; friendly in one's conduct *to*; (archaic) affectionate. **kind'ly** *adv.* **kind'nĕss** *n.*

kin'dergarten *n.* School for young children, esp. one using FROEBEL method of developing intelligence by object-lessons, toys, games, etc. [Ger., = 'children's garden']

kin'dle *v.* Set on fire, light; inflame, inspire, (passion etc.); stir up (person *to*); catch fire, burst into flame; become animated, glow with passion, etc.; make, become, bright; (cause to) glow. **kind'ling** *n.* (esp.) Small wood for lighting fires.

kind'ly *adj.* Kind; pleasant, genial. **kind'lily** *adv.* **kind'linĕss** *n.*

kin'drĕd *n.* Blood relationship; resemblance in character; one's relatives. ~ *adj.* Related by blood; allied, connected, similar.

kine. Archaic pl. of cow.

kin'ĕma etc.: see CINEMA etc.

kinĕmăt'ic *adj.* Of motion considered abstractly without reference to force or mass. **kinĕmăt'ics** *n.pl.* Science of this.

kinĕt'ic *adj.* Of, due to, motion; ~ *energy*: see ENERGY; ~ *theory of heat, of gases*, theory that heat, gaseous state, is due to motion of particles of matter. **kinĕt'ics** *n.pl.* Science of relations between the motions of bodies and the forces acting on them.

king *n.* 1. Male sovereign (esp. hereditary) ruler of independent State; *K~ Emperor*, (hist.) King of United Kingdom and Emperor of India; *K~ of Kings*, God; title assumed by many Eastern kings; *K~ of Terrors*, Death; *the three kings*, wise men who came from the East to worship the new-born Christ (sometimes called *three kings of Cologne* from the belief that their bodies were preserved there). 2. Great merchant etc.; best kind (*of* fruits, plants, etc.); ~ *of beasts*, lion; ~ *of birds*, eagle. 3. (chess) Piece which must be protected against checkmate (ill. CHESS); (draughts) piece which has been 'crowned'; (cards) one card in each suit bearing representation of king, and usu. ranking next below ace; ~'*s bishop, knight, rook*, chess pieces on king's side of board at beginning of game; ~'*s pawn*, pawn in front of king at beginning of game. 4. ~-*bird*, kind of bird of paradise, *Paradisea regia*; Amer. tyrant fly-catcher (usu. *Tyrannus carolinensis*); ~-*bolt*, main or large bolt in mechanical structure; *K~ Charles spaniel*, English black-and-tan toy spaniel with long silky coat and pendulous ears; *K~ Charles's head*, fixed idea, inescapable obsession (from 'David Copperfield,' chap. xiv); ~-*cobra*, the Hamadryad; ~-*crab*, large arachnid with horseshoe-shaped carapace; ~-*cup*, marsh marigold; *king'fisher*, small European bird (*Alcedo ispida*) with long beak and brilliant plumage, feeding on fish it captures by diving; other birds of same family; ~-*maker*, one who sets up kings, esp. Earl of Warwick in reigns of Henry VI and Edward IV; *K~ of Arms*, any of three chief heralds of College of Arms (Garter, Clarenceux, Norroy and Ulster), or Lyon King of Arms of Scotland; ~ *penguin*, large species of penguin (*Aptenodytes patagonica*); ~-*pin*, (U.S.) king-bolt; most important person in organization etc.; ~-*post*, upright post from tie-beam to rafter-top (ill. ROOF); ~'*s* BENCH, COUNSEL, ENGLISH, EVIDENCE: see these words; ~'*s evil*, a prob. tubercular disease formerly held to be curable by king's touch, scrofula; ~'*s friends*, (hist.) political party supporting George III in attempts to increase powers of crown; ~'*s pattern*, type of 19th-c. spoon- or fork-handle (ill. SPOON); ~'*s* PIPE, PROCTOR, SHILLING: see these words. **king'like** *adj.* **king'ship** *n.* **king** *v.* Act the king, govern; make into a king.

king'dom *n.* Organized community with king as its head; monarchical state; territory subject to a king; spiritual reign of God, sphere of this (esp. ~ *of heaven*); domain; province of nature (esp. *animal, vegetable, mineral*, ~); ~ *come*, (slang) the next world; *Middle K~*, imperial State of HONAN under Chan dynasty.

King'lāke, Alexander William (1809–91). English traveller and historian; author of 'Eothen'.

king'lĕt *n.* 1. Petty king. 2. Golden-crested wren.

king'ly *adj.* Fit for, appropriate to, a king; kinglike, majestic. **king'linĕss** *n.*

King of Rome. Title given at his birth to Napoleon François Charles Joseph (1811–32), son of Napoleon I and Marie Louise.

Kings, 1st and 2nd Books of. Two historical books of O.T., following the two books of Samuel, and covering Jewish history, esp. that of kingdom of Judah, from death of David to destruction of the Temple (586 B.C.).

King's Cŏll'ege. 1. A college of the University of Cambridge, founded 1441 by Henry VI and completed by Henry VII and Henry VIII. 2. A college of the University of London, founded 1829.

King's Coun'ty. Former name of OFFALY.

Kings'ley (-zlĭ), Charles (1819–75). English clergyman, novelist, and poet; author of 'Alton Locke', 'Westward Ho!', 'Water Babies', 'Hereward the Wake', etc. ~, Henry (1830–76). Younger brother of Charles Kingsley; novelist. ~, Mary Henrietta (1862–1900). Niece of Charles and Henry Kingsley; traveller (chiefly in W. Africa), author and ethnologist.

Kings'ton. Chief port and capital of JAMAICA.

kĭnk *n.* Back-twist in wire, chain, or rope, such as may cause obstruction or a break; (fig.) mental twist, crotchet. ~ *v.* Form a kink; cause (rope) to do this. **kĭnk'y** *adj.*

kĭnk'ajou (-ōō) *n.* Carnivorous arboreal mammal (*Cercoleptes caudivolvulus*) of Central and S. America, allied to racoon, with prehensile tail.

kĭnnĭkĭnĭc' *n.* Mixture of dried sumach leaves, inner bark of willow, etc., as substitute for tobacco, or for mixing with it; any plant used for this. [Algonkin]

kin'ō (kē-) *n.* Gum of various trees, resembling catechu, used in medicine and tanning as astringent.

Kinrŏss'. County town of Kinross-shire, county of central Scotland.

kĭns'folk (-z-; -ōk) *n.pl.* (literary) Relations by blood. **kĭns'man, kĭns'woman** *ns.*

kĭn'shĭp *n.* Blood relationship; similarity, alliance, in character.

kiŏsk' *n.* Light open pavilion in Turkey and Persia; (kē'ŏsk) structure like this for sale of newspapers etc., esp. in France and Belgium; structure in street etc. containing a public telephone.

kĭp[1] *n.* Hide of young or small beast as used for leather.

kĭp[2] *n.* (slang) Common lodging-house; lodging; bed. ~ *v.i.* Go to bed; sleep.

Kĭp'lĭng, Rudyard (1865–1936). English novelist and poet; born in India; famous for short stories about India, and for children's books. **Kĭplĭngēse'** (-z) *n.* Style like Kipling's; patriotic and imperialistic sentiment characteristic of his writings.

kĭpp'er *n.* Male salmon in spawning season; kippered fish, esp. herring. ~ *v.t.* Cure (salmon, herring, etc.) by splitting open, cleaning, rubbing with salt, pepper, etc., and drying in open air or smoke.

Kirg(h)iz (kẽrgēz') *adj.* & *n.* (Member) of a Turkic, mainly Mohammedan, people of central Asia; (of) their language, one of the Ural-Altaic family. **Kirg(h)iz'ia, Kirg(h)izstan'** (-ahn). A constituent republic of the Soviet Union, on the Chinese frontier; capital, Frunze.

kĩrk *n.* (Sc. and north.) Church; ~ *session*, lowest court in Established Church of Scotland and other Presbyterian churches, composed of minister and elders of congregation or parish.

Kirkcudbright (kẽrkōōb'rĭ-). County town of the *Stewartry of Kirkcudbrightshire*, a county of SW. Scotland N. of the Solway Firth.

kirsch(wasser) (kẽrsh'văser) *n.* Spirit distilled from fermented liquor of wild cherries.

kĩr'tle *n.* (archaic) Woman's gown or outer petticoat; man's tunic or coat.

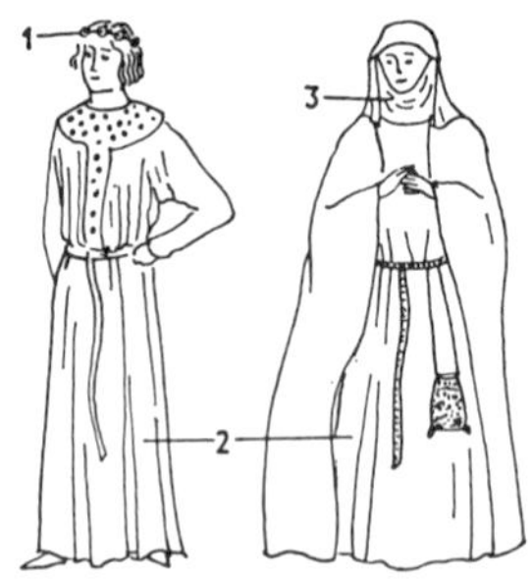

MAN AND WOMAN *c.* 1300

1. Chaplet. 2. Kirtle. 3. Wimple or gorget

Kĭs'falŭdy (kĭsh-), Károly (1788–1830). Hungarian dramatist and author.

Kish[1]. Ancient city of Sumer and Akkad, on old bed of Euphrates.

Kish[2]. (O.T.) Father of Saul (1 Sam. ix. 1; x. 21).

kĭskadee' *n.* Large tyrant-bird of tropical America, esp. *Pitangus sulphuratus*. [imit.]

kĭs'mĕt *n.* Destiny. [Arab. *qasama* divide]

kiss *n.* Caress given with lips; kind of sweetmeat; (billiards) impact between moving balls. ~ *v.t.* Touch with the lips, esp. in sign of affection, greeting, or reverence; (billiards etc. of ball) touch another lightly, esp. after having struck it once; ~ *away*, remove (tears etc.) with kisses; ~ *the book*, kiss Bible in taking oath; ~ *the dust*, yield abject submission; be slain; ~ *the ground*, prostrate oneself in token of homage; (fig.) be brought low; ~ *one's hand to*, wave a kiss to; ~ *hands*, kiss hand of sovereign etc. as ceremonial salutation or on appointment to office; ~ *the rod*, accept chastisement humbly; ~-*curl*, small curl on forehead, in front of ear, or at nape of neck; ~-*in-the-ring*, game for young people in which one pursues and kisses another of opposite sex. **kiss'ĭng** *n.* & *adj.*; ~-*crust*, soft crust where loaf has touched another in baking; ~-*gate*, gate hung in U- or V-shaped enclosure.

kĭt[1] *n.* 1. Wooden tub for various purposes. 2. (Articles carried in) soldier's valise or knapsack; personal equipment, esp. as packed for travelling; workman's, esp. shoemaker's, outfit; ~-*bag*, bag, usu. cylindrical, for carrying soldier's or traveller's kit.

kĭt[2] *n.* (now rare) Small fiddle used by dancing-master etc.

kĭt'-căt *n.* Artist's canvas 36 × 25 in.; portrait of this size, i.e. resembling the portraits painted by Sir Godfrey Kneller for the *Kit-cat Club*, a dining-club of Whig politicians and men of letters founded towards end of 17th c. and orig. meeting in a tavern near Temple Bar, London. [*kit-cat*, members' name for the mutton-pies provided by Christopher Catling, the tavern-keeper]

kĭtch'ėn *n.* Part of house where food is cooked; ~ *garden*, garden for fruit and vegetables for table; ~-*maid*, maid employed in kitchen, usu. under cook; ~ *physic*, good and plentiful food. **kĭtch'ėner**[1] *n.* 1. Cooking-range. 2. Person in charge of monastery kitchen.

Kĭtch'ener[2], Horatio Herbert, Earl Kitchener of Khartoum (1850–1916). British soldier; retook Khartoum with Anglo-Egyptian force 1898; commander-in-chief in Boer War, 1900–2, and in India; secretary of state for war, 1914–16; drowned in the *Hampshire*, which struck a mine on the way to Russia.

kĭtchėnĕtte' *n.* Small alcove etc. used as kitchen (esp. in modern flat).

kīte *n.* 1. Large bird of falcon family (esp. the common European *Milvus ictinus*) with long wings and usu. forked tail; (fig.) rapacious person, sharper. 2. Toy consisting of light wooden frame, usu. in triangular form with circular arc as base, with paper or other thin material stretched over it, flown in strong wind by string; similar contrivance of box-shape (*box*-~) with open sides, used esp. for meteorological observations; (in mine-sweeping) steel frame, similar to a box-kite, for keeping sweep-wire at required depth; (R.A.F. slang) aeroplane; (pl.) highest sails of ship, set only in light wind; *fly a* ~, (fig.) make experiment to gauge public opinion etc. 3. (commerc. slang) Accommodation bill; *fly a* ~, raise money by this. ~ *v.* (Cause to) soar like kite.

kĭth *n.* ~ *and kin*, orig., country and kinsfolk; later, friends and relatives; now freq., kinsfolk.

kĭtt'en *n.* Young of cat; skittish young girl. **kĭtt'enish** *adj.* **kĭtt'en** *v.* Bring forth kittens.

kĭtt'ĭwāke *n.* Smallest of the strictly marine gulls (*Rissa tridactyla*) of Arctic and N. Atlantic Oceans, with black markings on usu.

white plumage, very long wings, and very short hind toe. [imit.]

kĭt'tle *adj.* (orig. Sc.) Ticklish, difficult to deal with.

kĭttul' (-ōōl), **kĭtōōl'** *n.* Kind of palm; strong black fibre from leaf-stalks of this.

kĭtt'y[1] *n.* Pet name for kitten.

kĭtt'y[2] *n.* Pool or joint fund in games etc.

Kĭwan'ĭs (-wah-). International organization (founded at Detroit, 1915) of business and professional men, with clubs chiefly in U.S. and Canada.

ki'wi (kē-) *n.* = APTERYX; (slang) non-flying member of Air Force; (slang) New Zealander.

Kĭzĭl' Kum (kōōm). Desert region in Kazakhstan, Asiatic Russia, SE. of Aral Sea.

K.K.K. *abbrev.* (U.S.) Ku Klux Klan.

kl. *abbrev.* Kilolitre.

Klaip'eda (klīpā-). Lithuanian name of MEMEL.

Klăp'rōth (-t), Martin Heinrich (1743–1817). German chemist; discoverer of several metallic elements.

klăx'on *n.* (Electric) motor-horn. [name of manufacturing company]

Klĕber (klābar'), Jean-Baptiste (1753–1800). French soldier; general in Revolutionary army.

Kleist (klī-), Heinrich von (1777–1811). German dramatist and novelist.

klĕpht *n.* One of the Greeks who after Turkish conquest of Greece in 15th c. maintained independence in mountains; brigand. [mod. Gk *klephtes* (Gk *kleptēs* thief)]

klĕptomān'ĭa *n.* Irresistible tendency to theft in persons not driven to it by needy circumstances. **klĕptomān'ĭăc** *n.*

Klieg light (-ēg) *n.* Kind of arc-light emitting light rich in actinic rays, used in cinema photography. [f. name of inventors, *Kliegl* brothers]

Klŏn'dȳke, -dike. District in Yukon, NW. Canada, where gold was discovered in 1896; ~ *River*, tributary of Yukon River. **klŏn'dȳke** *n.* 1. Mine, quarry, of valuable material. 2. An Amer. card-game. 3. The herring fishery off the W. coast of Scotland. ~ *v.* Export (fresh herring) by fast steamer to the Continent.

klōōf *n.* Ravine, deep narrow valley, in S. Africa. [Du., = 'cleft']

Klŏp'stŏck (-sht-), Gottlieb Friedrich (1724–1803). German epic and lyric poet; famous for his religious epic 'Messias'.

km. *abbrev.* Kilometre.

knăck (n-) *n.* Acquired faculty of doing a thing adoitly; ingenious device, trick, habit, of action, speech, etc.

knăck'er (n-) *n.* One who buys and slaughters useless horses; one who buys old houses, ships, etc., for the materials.

knăg (n-) *n.* Knot in wood, base of a branch.

knăp[1] (n-) *n.* Crest of hill, rising ground.

knăp[2] (n-) *v.* Break (flints for roads) with hammer; (bibl., dial.) knock, rap, snap asunder.

knăp'săck (n-) *n.* Soldier's or traveller's canvas or leather bag, strapped to back and used for carrying necessaries. [Low Ger.]

knăp'weed (n-) *n.* Species of *Centaurea*, esp. *C. nigra*, a common weed with tough stem and light-purple flowers on dark globular head.

knar (n-) *n.* Knot in wood, esp. protuberance covered with bark on trunk or at root of tree.

knāve (n-) *n.* 1. Unprincipled man, rogue. 2. (cards) Lowest court-card of each suit, bearing representation of soldier or court page. **knāv'ery** *n.* **knāv'ĭsh** *adj.* **knāv'ĭshly** *adv.* **knāv'ĭshnėss** *n.*

knead (nēd) *v.t.* Work up (moist flour or clay etc.) into dough or paste by drawing out and pressing or squeezing together; make (bread, pottery) thus; operate on (muscles etc.) as if kneading, massage; *kneading-trough*, wooden trough for kneading dough.

knee (n-) *n.* Joint between thigh and lower leg in man; corresponding joint in animals; part of garment covering the knee; thing like knee in shape or position, esp. piece of wood or iron with angular bend (ill. BOAT); *on one's* ~*s*, kneeling, esp. in supplication, worship, or submission; *on the* ~*s of the gods*, yet uncertain; *bring* (person) *to his* ~*s*, reduce him to submission; ~-*breeches*, breeches reaching down to or just below knee; ~-*cap*, convex bone in front of knee-joint, patella (ill. SKELETON); ~-*deep*, -*high*, so deep or high as to reach the knees; ~-*hole* (*table*), (writing-table with) hole between drawer pedestals to admit knees; ~-*pan*, knee-cap. ~ *v.t.* Touch with the knee; fasten (framework etc.) with knees.

kneel (n-) *v.i.* Fall, rest, on the knee(s), esp. in prayer or reverence (*to*).

knĕll (n-) *n.* Sound of bell, esp. of one rung solemnly after death or at funeral; (fig.) anything regarded as omen of death or extinction. ~ *v.* (archaic) (of bell) Ring, esp. at death or funeral; give forth doleful sound; proclaim as by a knell; (fig.) sound ominously.

Knĕll'er (n-), Sir Godfrey (1648–1723). English portrait-painter of German birth; appointed court painter by Charles II.

Knĕss'ėt(h). The Israeli parliament.

knĭck'erbŏcker (n-) *n.* 1. Descendant of original Dutch settlers of New Netherlands in America; New Yorker. 2. (pl.) Loose-fitting breeches gathered in at knee (ill. COAT); knickers. [*Knickerbocker*, pretended author of W. Irving's 'History of New York']

knĭck'ers (n-) *n.pl.* Woman's drawers, either closed or open at knee.

knĭck'-knăck (n-), **nĭck-năck** *n.* Light dainty article of furniture, dress, or food; trinket, gimcrack.

knīfe (n-) *n.* Blade with sharpened longitudinal edge fixed in handle either rigidly or with hinge, used as cutting instrument or as weapon; sharpened cutting-blade forming part of machine, as in turnip-cutter etc.; *the* ~, surgical operation(s); *war to the* ~, fierce or relentless war; *get, have, one's* ~ *in*(*to*) (person), persecute, show malicious or vindictive spirit towards; ~-*board*, board on which knives are cleaned; ~-*edge*, edge of knife; steel wedge on which pendulum etc. oscillates; arête; ~-*grinder*, itinerant sharpener of knives etc.; ~-*machine*, machine for cleaning knives; ~-*pleats*, overlapping pleats about the width of table-knife blade (ill. PLEAT); ~-*rest*, metal or glass support for carving knife or fork at table. ~ *v.t.* Cut, stab, with knife.

knight (nīt) *n.* 1. (hist.) Military follower, esp. one devoted to service *of* (lady) as attendant or champion in war or tournament; (hist.) person, usu. one of noble birth who had served as page and squire, raised to honourable military rank by king or qualified person; one on whom corresponding rank is conferred as reward for personal merit or services to crown or country; (hist.) ~ (*of the shire*), person representing shire or county in parliament. 2. (Rom. antiq.) One of the class of *equites*, orig. cavalry of Roman army, later a wealthy and politically important class; (Gk antiq.) citizen of second class at Athens in constitution of Solon. 3. Piece in game of chess, usu. with horse's head; for move, see ill. CHESS. 4. ~-*errant*, medieval knight wandering in search of chivalrous adventures; (fig.) person of chivalrous or quixotic spirit; ~-*errantry*, practice, conduct, of a knight-errant; ~-*heads*, two large timbers rising from keel behind stem and supporting bowsprit; ~-*service*, military service rendered by knight in return for lands, tenure of land by military service. 5. *K~ of the Round Table*, one of King ARTHUR's knights; *K~ of the Rueful Countenance*, Don QUIXOTE; *K~s Bachelor*, simple knights not belonging to a special order; *K~s of Columbus*, Amer. R.C. society for men, founded 1882; *K~s Commander*: see COMMANDER; *K~s Companion*: see COMPANION[1], sense 2; *K~s of the Garter*: see GARTER; *K~s of the Golden Circle*, semi-military secret society of Northern sympathizers with South in Amer. Civil War; *K~s Hospitallers*: see HOSPITALLER; *K~s of Labour*,

Amer. labour organization founded as secret society 1869, of great influence in labour disputes after 1881, when it ceased to be secret, and dissolved 1917; *K~s of Malta, K~s of Rhodes*, Knights Hospitallers; *K~s of St. Patrick*: see PATRICK; *K~s Templars*: see TEMPLAR; *K~s of the Thistle*: see THISTLE; *K~s of Windsor*: see WINDSOR. ~ *v.t.* Confer knighthood on. **knight'hood** *n.* Rank, dignity, of a knight. **knight'like, knight'ly** *adjs.*

knight'age (nīt-) *n.* Whole body of knights; list and account of knights.

knit (n-) *v.* Form (close texture) by interlooping successive series of

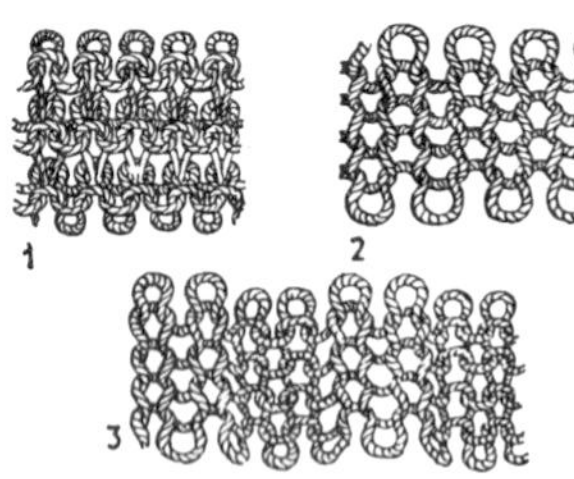

KNITTING

1. Garter stitch. 2. Stocking stitch. 3. Rib (2 plain, 2 purl)

loops of yarn or thread; make (garments etc.) of this; contract (brow) in wrinkles; make, become, close or compact; unite intimately by means of common interests, marriage, etc.; ~ *up*, repair by knitting; *knitwear*, knitted garments.

knitt'ing *n.* (esp.) Work in process of knitting; *~-needle*, slender rod of metal, wood, plastic, etc., two or more of which are used together in knitting.

knitt'le (n-) *n.* (naut.) Small line made of yarn.

knŏb (n-) *n.* Rounded protuberance, esp. at end or on surface of thing; handle of door or drawer; small lump (of sugar, coal, etc.); *knob'kerrie*, short thick stick with knobbed head as weapon of S. Afr. tribes. **knŏbb'y** *adj.* **knŏbb'iness** *n.* **knŏb** *v.* Furnish with knobs; bulge *out*. **knŏbb'le** (n-) *n.* Small knob. **knŏbb'ly** *adj.*

knŏck (n-) *v.* 1. Strike with hard blow; strike door, strike *at the door*, to gain admittance; drive (thing) *in, out, off*, etc., by striking; (of internal combustion engine etc.) make knocking or thumping noise; ~ *on the head*, stun, kill, by blow on the head; put an end to (scheme etc.); ~ *one's head against*, (fig.) come into unpleasant collision with (unfavourable facts or conditions); ~ *into the middle of next week*, send (person) flying; ~ *the bottom out of*, render (argument etc.) invalid. 2. ~ *about*, strike repeatedly, treat roughly; wander, lead irregular life; ~ *(up) against*, collide with, come across casually; ~ *down*, strike to ground with blow; cause to succumb; dispose of (article *to* bidder at auction) by knock with hammer; ~ *off*, strike off with blow; leave off work, leave off (work); (colloq.) dispatch (business) or rapidly compose (verses etc.); deduct (sum from price etc.); ~ *on*, (Rugby footb.) propel ball with hand or arm towards adversary's goal; ~ *out*, empty (tobacco-pipe) by tapping; disable (pugilist) so that he cannot respond to call of 'Time'; (fig.) vanquish; (colloq.) make (plan etc.) hastily; ~ *together*, put hastily together; ~ *up*, drive upwards with blow; make or arrange hastily; score (runs) at cricket; arouse (person) by knocking at door; exhaust, become exhausted. 3. *~-about*, boisterous, noisy (performance in music-hall etc.); wandering irregularly; (of clothes) suitable for rough use; *~-down*, (of blow) overwhelming; (of price at auction) reserve, minimum); *~-knees*, knees that knock together in walking; *~-kneed*, having knock-knees; *~-out*, (blow) that knocks boxer out; (athletic competition) in which defeated competitors in each round are eliminated; one of group who join at auction to buy goods at low price, afterwards reselling among themselves; this practice, such sale; *~-up*, practice or casual game at cricket, tennis, etc. ~ *n.* Blow; rap, esp. at door; thumping noise in engine etc.; (slang) innings at cricket.

knŏck'er (n-) *n.* (esp.) Appendage, usu. of iron or brass, so hinged to door that it may be struck against metal plate to call attention.

knōll[1] (n-) *n.* Small hill, mound.

knōll[2] (n-) *v.* (archaic) Ring (bell); (of bell) sound; toll out (hours); summon by sound of bell.

knŏp (n-) *n.* 1. Knob (now rare exc. in ref. to glassware and silverware; ill. GOBLET). 2. Flower-bed. 3. Loop or tuft formed in strand of yarn for ornament.

Knŏss'os. Ancient city of Crete, where, acc. to classical tradition, King Minos ruled and kept the Minotaur in a labyrinth; historically, the centre of the Minoan civilization, where excavations in 20th c., 3 miles S. of Candia, revealed the ruins of a vast labyrinthine palace (18th–14th centuries B.C.).

knŏt (n-) *n.* 1. Intertwining of parts of one or more ropes, strings, etc., to fasten them together; ribbon etc. so tied as ornament or adjunct to dress; difficulty, problem; central point in problem or plot of story etc. 2. (naut.) Unit of speed of one nautical mile per hour (orig. measured by knots on log-line). 3. Hard lump in animal body; (hard mass formed in trunk at insertion of branch, causing) round cross-grained piece in board, which may fall out, leaving *~-hole*; node on stem of plant. 4. Group, cluster, of persons or things. 5. (usu. *porter's* ~) double shoulder-pad used for carrying loads. 6. *~-grass*, common weed (*Polygonum aviculare*) in waste ground, with intricately-branched creeping stems and small pale-pink flowers. ~ *v.* Tie (string etc.) in knot; make knots for fringes, make (fringe) thus; unite closely or intricately; entangle. **knŏtt'y** *adj.* Full of knots; (fig.) puzzling, hard to explain.

knout (nowt *or* nōōt) *n.* & *v.t.* (Flog with) scourge formerly used as instrument of punishment in Russia, often fatal in its effects.

know (nō) *v.* (past t. *knew* pr. nū, past part. *known* pr. nōn). Recognize, identify; be able to distinguish; be acquainted with (*by sight, to speak to*, etc.); have personal experience of; be on intimate terms with; be aware of, be aware (*that, how*, etc.); be versed in; ~ *about*, have information about; ~ *better than*, be too well informed of the facts to believe; be too discreet (*to* do); ~ *of*, be aware of; ~ *one's own mind*, not vacillate; *~-nothing*, ignorant person; *~-how* (*n.*) (orig. U.S.) practical knowledge of methods. ~ *n.* (colloq.) *In the* ~, knowing (about) the thing in question or what is not generally known. **know'able** *adj.*

know'ing (nōĭ-) *adj.* (esp.) Cunning, wide-awake; (colloq.) smart, stylish. **know'ingness** *n.* **know'ingly** *adv.* In a knowing manner; consciously, intentionally.

knowledge (nŏl'ĭj) *n.* Knowing, familiarity gained by experience, (*of*); person's range of information; theoretical or practical understanding (*of*); the sum of what is known; *to my* ~, as far as I know. **know'ledgeable** (nŏl'ija-) *adj.* (colloq.) Well-informed, intelligent.

Knowles (nōlz), James Sheridan (1784–1862). Irish actor and playwright.

Knŏx (n-), John (1505–72). Scottish Protestant reformer and historian.

Knt *abbrev.* Knight.

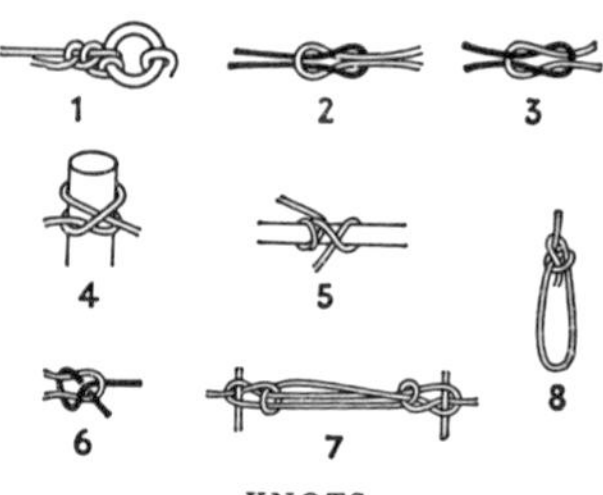

KNOTS

1. Round turn and two half hitches. 2. Reef. 3. Granny. 4. Clove-hitch. 5. Rolling hitch. 6. Sheet bend. 7. Sheepshank. 8. Bowline.

knŭ'ckle (n-) *n.* Bone at finger-joint, esp. at root of finger; projection of carpal or tarsal joint of quadruped; joint of meat consisting of this with parts above and below it; *~-bone*, bone forming knuckle; limb-bone with ball-like knob at joint-end, this part of animal's leg as joint of meat; metacarpal or metatarsal bone of sheep, etc.; (pl.) game played by tossing up and catching these bones in certain way; *~-bow*, guard on sword-hilt to cover knuckles (ill. SWORD); *~-duster*, metal instrument to protect knuckles from injury in striking and increase harmfulness of blow. ~ *v.* Strike, press, rub, with knuckles; place knuckles on ground in playing at marbles; ~ *down, under*, give in, submit.

knūr(r) (n-) *n.* Hard excrescence on trunk of tree; hard concretion; wooden ball in north-country game of ~ *and spell*, in which ball is jerked by club-ended stick out of container and struck as far as possible while in the air.

knūrl (n-) *n.* Knot, knob; bead or ridge in metalwork. **knūrled** (-ld) *adj.*

knŭt (n-). Joc. spelling of NUT, showy or fashionable young man.

K.O. *abbrev.* Knock-out.

koal'a (kōah'-) *n.* (also ~ *bear*) A tailless arboreal marsupial (*Phascolarctos cinereus*) of the Australian region, feeding almost exclusively on the leaves of the gum-tree (*Eucalyptus*).

kōb'ōld *n.* (German folk-lore) Brownie; underground spirit haunting mines or caves, gnome.

Kŏch (-χ), Robert (1843–1910). German bacteriologist and physician, famous for his work on the bacillus of tuberculosis; *~'s postulates*, rules as to conditions which must be satisfied before bacteriologists ascribe a disease to a specific micro-organism.

kōd'ăk *n.* Proprietary name of kind of portable camera. ~ *v.t.* Photograph with kodak.

Kodály (kodī'ė), Zoltán (1882–1967). Hungarian composer.

koh'-i-noor (kōĭ-) *n.* Famous Indian diamond of great size, one of the treasures of Aurungzebe, with history going back to 14th c.; a British Crown jewel since annexation of Punjab, 1849. [Pers. *kōh-i-nūr*, mountain of light]

kohl (kōl) *n.* Preparation, based on powdered sulphide of lead or sulphide of antimony, used to darken eyelids etc. [Arab. *koh'l*]

kohlra'bĭ (kōlrah-) *n.* Cabbage with turnip-shaped stem, used in England as cattle-food, elsewhere as vegetable. [Ger., f. It. *cavoli rape* (pl.), cole-rape]

kola[1] *n.*: see COLA.

Kōl'a[2]. Peninsula of NW. Russia between Barents Sea and White Sea.

Kolchak' (-ahk), Alexandr Vasilevich (1875–1920). Russian admiral; commanded White army against Bolsheviks in 1917; was named supreme ruler of Russia, 1918, by Siberian Government at Omsk; executed by Bolsheviks.

kolĭn'sky *n.* Fur of Siberian mink. [Russ., f. KOLA[2]]

kŏl'khoz (-kŏz) *n.* A collective farm in U.S.S.R.

komōd'ō dragon, lizard *n.* Very large monitor lizard (*Varancus komodoensis*) with heavy powerful body, sometimes as long as 15 ft. [*Komodo*, island in Malay Archipelago]

koodoo: see KUDU.

kōōkabŭ'rra *n.* The laughing jackass (*Dacelo gigas*), a kingfisher of S. Australia; related species.

kopec(k): see COPECK.

kŏp'je (-pĭ) *n.* (S. Afr.) Small hill. [Du., dim. of *kop* head]

Koran (korahn' *or* kōr'an). Sacred book of Islam, in Arabic, consisting of 114 chapters of revelations orally delivered by Mohammed, collected in writing and put in order after his death by Abu Bakr. The four chief duties that it enjoins are prayer, the giving of alms, fasting, and the pilgrimage to Mecca. [Arab. *qur'ān* recitation]

Korē'a. (Chin. *Tai Han*, Jap. *Chōsen*) Country of E. Asia consisting principally of a mountainous peninsula running southward from Manchuria; in Japanese possession 1910–45; in 1945 occupied by troops of U.S.A. (for the United Nations) and the U.S.S.R. respectively S. and N. of the 38th parallel; the *Republic of* ~ (capital, Seoul) was proclaimed in S. Korea in July 1948 and the (Communist) *Korean People's Republic* (capital, Pyongyang) in N. Korea in Sept. 1948; a war between the two States (and their supporters) lasted 1950–3. **Korē'an** *adj.* & *n.* Of Korea; native of Korea, member of a mixed race of Mongol type; (of) the agglutinative language of Korea, which is related to Japanese.

Kō'rĭn, Ogata (1657–1716). Japanese painter and lacquer decorator.

Kōrnil'ov (-nēlo-), Lavr Georgevich (1870–1918). Russian general, appointed commander-in-chief by Kerensky; led an army, which was repulsed by Bolsheviks, against Petrograd after November revolution.

Kŏrolĕn'ko, Vladimir Galaktionovich (1853–1921). Russian short-story writer.

K.O.S.B. *abbrev.* King's Own Scottish Borderers.

Kosciuszko (kŏs-chōōsh'ko) (1746–1817). Polish national hero, soldier, and liberal statesman; served in America under Washington; after the 2nd partition of Poland, 1793, he led a patriotic rising against Russia which failed and was followed by the 3rd partition between Russia, Prussia, and Austria.

kōsh'er *adj.* (of food, or shop where food is sold or used) Fulfilling requirements of Jewish law. [Heb. *kasher* right]

Kŏss'uth (-ōōth, kŏsh'ōōt), Lajos (Louis) (1802–94). Hungarian national hero and liberal statesman.

Kŏtz'ėbue (-bōōė), August Friedrich Ferdinand von (1761–1819). German dramatist, author of a large number of sentimental plays. ~, Otto von (1787–1846). Son of August Friedrich; navigator and explorer; discoverer of ~ *Sound*, inlet of NW. Alaska.

ko(w)tow' *n.* Chinese custom of touching ground with forehead as sign of worship or absolute submission. ~ *v.i.* Make a kowtow; act obsequiously (*to*). [Chin. *k'o t'ou* knock head]

kou'mĭss (kōō-) *n.* Fermented liquor prepared from mare's milk, used as beverage by Tatars and other Asiatic nomads.

kour'băsh (koor-) *n.* Whip of (esp. hippopotamus) hide as instrument of punishment in Turkey and Egypt.

Kŏv'nō. Lithuanian name of KAUNAS.

K.O.Y.L.I. *abbrev.* King's Own Yorkshire Light Infantry.

K.P. *abbrev.* Knight (of the Order) of St. Patrick.

K.R. *abbrev.* King's Regulations.

kraal (-ahl) *n.* S. Afr. village of huts enclosed by fence; enclosure for cattle or sheep. [colonial Du., f. Port. *corral*]

Krafft-Eb'ĭng (-ŭft-āb-), Richard von (1840–1902). German physician and psychologist.

kraft (-ah-) *n.* ~ (*paper*), strong smooth brown wrapping-paper made from unbleached soda pulp.

Krăkatō'a. Small volcanic island of Dutch Indies in Sunda Strait between Java and Sumatra, scene of a great eruption in 1883.

kra'ken (-ah-, -ā-) *n.* Mythical sea-monster appearing off coast of Norway.

krans (-ah-) *n.* (S. Afr.) Precipitous or overhanging wall of rocks. [Du., = 'coronet']

Kreis'ler (krīs-), Fritz (1875–1962). Austrian violinist.

Krem'er (krā-), Gerhard: see MERCATOR.

Krĕm'lĭn. Fortified enclosure or citadel within Russian town or city; esp. that of Moscow, containing the old imperial palace and many public buildings; now the political and administrative centre of the U.S.S.R.; hence, *the* ~, the Russian Government.

kreut'zer (kroi-) *n.* Small silver and copper coins formerly current in Germany and Austria. [Ger. *kreuz* cross]

Kreu'tzer (kroits-) **Sonata.** Sonata (op. 47) by Beethoven for violin and piano, dedicated to Rodolphe Kreutzer (1766–1831), a French violinist and composer.

kriegspiel (krēg'spēl) *n.* War-game in which blocks, flags, etc., representing troops etc. are moved about on maps.

Kriem'hĭld (krē-, -t). In the NIBELUNGENLIED, a Burgundian princess, wife of Siegfried and later of Etzel (Attila), whom she marries in order to be revenged on her brothers for the death of Siegfried.

Krĭmm'er (lamb) *n.* Grey or black fur from skins of young Crimean lambs.

krĭs, creese, crease *n.* Malayan dagger with wavy blade.

Krĭsh'na. In later Hindu mythology, a great deity or deified hero, worshipped as incarnation of Vishnu.

krōm'ėsky (*or* kromēs'-) *n.* Small roll of bacon stuffed with minced meat or fish and fried. [Russ. *kromochki* (*kroma* slice)]

krona: see KRONE.

krōn'e (-e) *n.* (pl. *-ner*). 1. (abbrev. *kr.*) Principal monetary unit of Denmark and Norway and (*krona*, pl. *-nor*) of Sweden, crown, = 100 öre. 2. (hist.) Austrian silver coin. 3. (hist.) German 10-mark gold piece. [Ger. and Dan., = 'crown']

Krŏn'stadt (-stăt). Russian fortress and naval base on Kotlin Island in Gulf of Finland, protecting approach to Leningrad.

Kroō, Kru, Kroō'boy, Kroō'-man. One of a Liberian coastal Negro people, skilful as boatmen and seamen.

Kropōt'kĭn, Petr Alexeivich, Prince (1842–1921). Russian geographer, author, and anarchist.

K.R.R.C. *abbrev.* King's Royal Rifle Corps.

Krug'er (kreeher), Stephanus Johannes Paulus (1825–1904). 'Oom Paul', Afrikaans soldier and statesman; president of Transvaal republic 1883–99.

Krupp (kroŏp), Alfred (1812–87). German metallurgist, founder of steel and armament works at Essen.

Krȳlŏv' (-f), Ivan Andreyevich (1768–1844). Russian writer of fables in verse.

krȳp'ton *n.* (chem.) Chemical element, one of the inert rare gases of the atmosphere (1 part in 670,000); symbol Kr, at. no. 36, at. wt 83·80. [Gk *krupton* hidden]

K.S. *abbrev.* King's Scholar.

Kshatri, Kshatriya (kshaht'rē-). Member of 2nd of the 4 Hindu castes, the military caste. [Sansk., f. *kshatra* rule]

K.S.L.I. *abbrev.* King's Shropshire Light Infantry.

Kt *abbrev.* Knight.

K.T. *abbrev.* Knight (of the Order) of the Thistle; Knight Templar.

Kuan Yĭn, Kwan Yin (kwahn). Female divinity worshipped by Chinese Buddhists as incarnation of mercy or compassion. [Chin., = 'regard sound', i.e. listen to human cries]

Kub'la(i) Khan (koōb'lī) (1216–94). Mongol conqueror and emperor, grandson of GENGHIS KHAN; founder of Mongol dynasty (the Yüan) in China.

kūd'ŏs *n.* (slang) Glory, renown.

kudu (koō'doō), **koō'doō** *n.* Antelope of S. Africa and Somaliland (genus *Strepsiceros*), with vertical white stripes on body and, in the male, twisted horns.

Kuen-lun, Kwen- (kwĕn'loōn), **Kun-lun** (koōn-). Asiatic mountain system of N. Tibet, extending from Pamirs eastward into W. China.

Kufa, Kufic: see CUFA, CUFIC.

Ku Klŭx Klăn (koō). 1. Secret society formed *c* 1865 in southern States of U.S. after Amer. Civil War; also called White Empire or Invisible League; aimed at protecting white interests by instilling fear into the newly freed Negroes; committed acts of terrorism, the members covering themselves and their horses with white sheets; suppressed by law 1871. 2. Similar but more widespread organization which originated in Georgia in 1915; militantly patriotic, anti-Catholic, anti-Jewish, and anti-liberal; influential after the war of 1914–18; revived 1945, but suppressed 1946. [Gk *kuklos* circle (*klan* added for effect)]

kuk'rĭ (koō-) *n.* Curved knife broadening towards point, used by Gurkhas of India.

kul'ăk (koō-) *n.* Well-to-do Russian peasant, farmer, or trader, esp. (under Soviet) peasant-proprietor tilling land for his own profit. [Russ., = 'fist']

kultur (koōltoor') *n.* Civilization as conceived by the Germans.

kultur'kămpf *n.* Conflict between German imperial government and papacy for control of schools and church appointments (1872–87).

kümm'el (kū-) *n.* Sweet liqueur flavoured with caraway seed, orig. made in Riga.

Kun, Bela (bāl'*a* koōn) (1886–1945). Hungarian-Jewish communist leader; head of Hungarian communist government which ruled for a few months in 1919.

Kuomintăng' (koōō-). Chinese nationalist radical party, founded 1905 by Sun Yat-Sen and led, after his death in 1925, by Chiang Kai-Shek; it led the revolution of 1911; was at first aided by the communists but fought them intermittently from 1927 onwards; gained control over most of China and set up a government at Nanking, 1927; in 1949 it was driven out by the communists and its government withdrew to Formosa. [Chin., = 'national people's party']

Kuprin (koōprēn'), Alexandr Ivanovich (1870–1938). Russian novelist.

Kûrd *n.* One of a tall, fair-haired, long-headed pastoral and predatory race, of Aryan stock with Turkish admixture, inhabiting Kurdistan and parts of Persia and Caucasia. **Kûrd'ĭsh** *adj.* & *n.* Of the Kurds; (of) the language of these people, a dialect of Iranian.

Kûrdĭstan' (-ahn, -ăn). 1. Mountainous province of NW. Persia, inhabited chiefly by Kurds. 2. In wider use, the whole area inhabited by the Kurds, including parts of E. Turkey, Armenia, and NE. Iraq, as well as the province of Kurdistan.

Kur'ĭle (koor-) **Islands.** Chain of small islands stretching northwards from Japan to Kamchatka; ceded by Russia to Japan, 1875; regained by Russia, 1945.

kursaal (koor'zahl) *n.* Building for use of visitors at (esp. German) health-resort or watering-place; casino.

Kut'(-ĕl-Amâr'a) (koōt). Small town on left bank of Tigris in which 10,000 British and Indian troops were besieged by the Turks for 143 days before surrendering (April 1916).

Kutuz'ov (-toō-, -f), Mikhail Ilarionovich (1745–1813), Prince of Smolensk. General who commanded Russian troops at Austerlitz (1805) and Borodino (1812) and forced Napoleon to retreat from Moscow.

kV *abbrev.* Kilovolt.

kvăss *n.* Russian fermented beverage made from infusion of rye-flour or bread with malt.

kW *abbrev.* Kilowatt.

Kwăngsi' (-sē). Province of S. China.

Kwăngtung'[1] (-ōōng). Coastal province of S. China.

Kwăn'tung'[2] (-ōōng). Territory of S. Manchuria forming S. part of Liaotung peninsula.

Kwan Yin: see KUAN YIN.

Kwei'chow' (kwā-). Province of SW. China.

Ky *abbrev.* Kentucky.

kyang: see KIANG.

kyăt *n.* Principal monetary unit of Burma, Burma rupee, = 100 pyas.

Kȳd, Thomas (*c* 1558–95). English playwright; author of 'The Spanish Tragedy' etc.

kȳle *n.* (Sc.) Narrow channel between island and mainland, or between two islands, in W. of Scotland.

kȳl'ōe (-ō) *n.* One of a herd of small long-horned cattle of Scottish Highlands and western islands.

kȳm'ograph (-ahf) *n.* Instrument recording variations of pressure, pulsations, sound-waves, etc.

kȳmogrăph'ic *adj.*

Kyrie (eleison) (kēr'iī ĭlā'ĭson; *or* kĭr'ĭ) *n.* Words of short petition used in Eastern and Roman Churches, esp. at beginning of Mass; musical setting of these; response to commandments in Communion Service in Anglican Church. [Gk *kurie eleēson* Lord have mercy]

L

L, l (ĕl). 12th letter of modern English and 11th of ancient Roman alphabet, representing Gk *lambda* (Λ λ), and Semitic *lamed* (of which earliest known forms are 2 and ȣ). The English sound represented by this letter is a voiced consonant formed by emission of breath at sides, or one side, of oral passage, with point of tongue in contact with gums or palate. 1. Thing shaped like L; rectangular joint of pipes etc. 2. Roman numeral symbol for fifty. 3. (U.S.) abbreviation for *elevated* (*railway*).

l. *abbrev.* Left; *libra*(*e*) = pound(s); line; lira; lire; litre(s).

L *abbrev.* Latin; learner (on motor vehicle).

L. *abbrev.* Liberal.

£ *abbrev.* *Libra*(*e*) (= pounds sterling); **£A**, pounds Australian; **£E**, pounds Egyptian; **£T**, pounds Turkish.

La *abbrev.* Louisiana.

la(h) (lah) *n.* (mus.) 6th note of hexachord and of the major scale in 'movable-doh' systems; note A in 'fixed-doh' system. [see UT]

L.A.A. *abbrev.* Light anti-aircraft.

laag′er (lahg-) *n.* Camp, encampment, esp. in circle, of wagons; park for armoured vehicles. ~ *v.* Form (vehicles) into laager; encamp (persons) in laager; encamp.

lăb *n.* (colloq. abbrev. of) Laboratory.

Lab. *abbrev.* Labour; Labrador.

lăb′arum *n.* Standard, said to have been devised by Constantine the Great in 312 after a vision, consisting of a spear converted by a transverse bar into a cross and surmounted by a wreath enclosing the Christian monogram ☧ (Gk *kh* and *r*, first two letters of *Christos*); variants of this, used in Byzantine Empire.

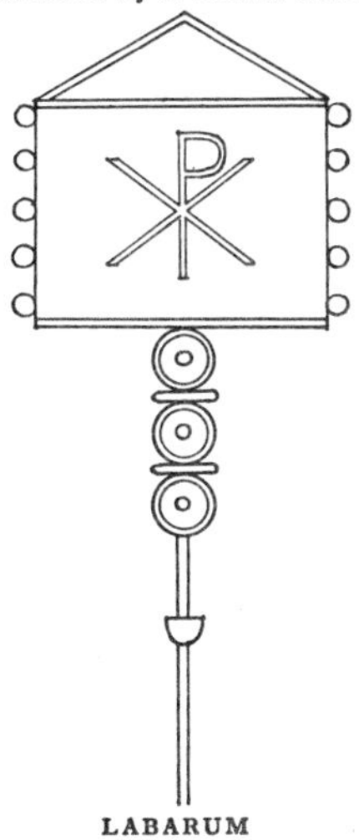

LABARUM

lăb′danum *n.* = LADANUM.

lăbėfăc′tion *n.* Shaking, weakening, downfall.

lā′bel *n.* 1. Slip of paper, card, linen, metal, etc., for attaching to object and indicating its nature, owner, name, destination, etc.; adhesive stamp; (fig.) short classifying phrase or name applied to persons etc. 2. (archit.) Dripstone. 3. (her.) One of the sub-ordinaries (ill. HERALDRY). ~ *v.t.* Attach label to; assign to category.

labĕll′um *n.* (pl. *-la*). (bot.) Lower division or lip of orchidaceous corolla (ill. FLOWER).

lā′bĭal *adj.* 1. Of the lips; (anat., zool.) of, like, serving as, a lip, labial part, or labium; ~ *palps*, sensitive lobes near mouth of certain molluscs; jointed appendage on insect labium (ill. MOTH); ~ *pipe*, (mus.) organ-pipe furnished with lips, flue-pipe. 2. (phonetics, of sounds) Formed by complete or partial closure of lips, e.g. *m*, *b*, *f*. ~ *n.* Labial sound. **lā′bĭalīze** *v.t.* **lā′bĭalism, lābĭalīzā′tion** *ns.*

lā′bĭate *adj.* (bot.) With corolla or calyx divided into two parts suggesting lips; (bot., zool.) like lip or labium. ~ *n.* Labiate plant.

lă′bīle *adj.* (chem. etc.) Unstable, liable to displacement or change.

lā′bĭo-dĕn′tal *adj.* & *n.* (Sound) formed between the lower lip and the teeth, e.g. *f*, *v*.

lā′bĭum *n.* (pl. *labia*). 1. (anat., usu. in pl.) Lip(s) of female pudendum (ill. PELVIS). 2. (zool.) Lower part of insect's mouth, the fused second maxillae. 3. (bot.) Lip, esp. the lower, of labiate corolla.

labŏ′ratory (*or* lăb′-) *n.* Room or building used for experiments in natural science, esp. chemistry, or for chemical etc. examination of manufactured products.

labôr′ious *ad*. Hard-working; toilsome; showing signs of toil, not facile or fluent. **labôr′iously** *adv.* **labôr′iousnėss** *n.*

Labouchère (lăbōōshār′), Henry du Pré (1831–1912). British radical politician, journalist, and wit, known as 'Labby'; founder (1876) of 'Truth', a weekly paper for the exposure of abuses and impostures.

lā′bour (-ber) *n.* 1. Bodily or mental toil, exertion; task; toil tending to supply wants of community; body of those who contribute by toil to production, labourers, the working classes as a political force; *hard* ~: see HARD; ~ *of love*, task one delights in; ~ *of Hercules*, task needing enormous strength etc. 2. Pains of childbirth, travail. 3. *Labor Day*, (U.S.) legal holiday on first Monday in September; ~ *Exchange*: see EMPLOYMENT exchange; ~*-market*, supply of unemployed labour with reference to demand for it; *L~ Party*, political party representing workers, esp. (in England) one formed in 1906 by federation of trade unions and advanced political bodies to secure parliamentary representation of labour. ~ *v.* Exert oneself, work hard; strive (*for, to*); advance with difficulty; be troubled or impeded; suffer *under* mistake etc.; (of ship) roll or pitch heavily; (archaic or poet.) till (ground); elaborate, work out in detail, treat at length; *laboured*, showing signs of labour, not spontaneous.

lā′bourer (-ber-), *n.* (esp.) Man doing for wages work that requires strength rather than skill.

lā′bourīte (-ber-) *n.* Member, adherent, of Labour Party.

Lă′bradôr. Eastern coastal part of large peninsula of extreme NE. America, between Hudson Bay and Atlantic; formerly a dependency of Newfoundland, but since 1944 part of Canada; ~ *Current*, cold ocean current moving southwards from Arctic Ocean along part of E. coast of N. America; ~ (*dog, retriever*), black- or golden-coated breed related to spaniels and setters and used for retrieving game (ill. DOG); ~ *tea*, either of two evergreen shrubs of the order *Ericaceae* (*Ledum latifolium* and *L. palustre*) of N. Amer., the leaves of which are used as a substitute for tea.

lă′bradorīte *n.* Kind of triclinic felspar showing brilliant variety of colour when turned in the light.

lā′brėt *n.* Ornament, usu. piece of bone, shell, or wood, inserted in a hole pierced through the lip.

lā′brum *n.* (pl. *-bra*). Ventral lobe of front of insect's head, covering the mouth parts (ill. INSECT).

La Bruyère (-yār′), Jean de (1645–96), French moralist, whose 'Caractères', on the model of Theophrastus, convey a vivid satirical picture of Parisian society.

labûr′num *n.* Genus of small leguminous trees with poisonous seeds, of which the commonest species, *L. anagyroides*, has racemes of bright-yellow flowers.

lă′by̆rinth *n.* Complicated irregular structure with many passages hard to find way through or about without guidance, maze; intricate or tortuous arrangement; (anat.) complex cavity of internal ear (ill. EAR). **lăby̆rĭn′thīne** *adj.*

lăc[1] *n.* 1. Resinous incrustation produced on certain trees in E. Indies by the insect *Tachardia lacca* and used as varnish or as substitute for true lacquer; known, when melted and formed into thin plates, as shellac. 2. Scarlet dye obtained from females of same insect. 3. (loosely) Lacquer, lacquer ware.

lac[2]: see LAKH.

L.A.C. *abbrev.* Leading aircraftman; London Athletic Club.

Lăcc'adīve Islands. Group of circular coral reefs in Indian Ocean about 200 miles W. of Malabar coast of India; administered by State of Madras.

lăcc'olīth *n.* (geol.) Dome-shaped intrusion of igneous rock into bedded deposits which as a result are arched up (ill. ROCK).

lāce *n.* 1. Cord or leather strip for fastening or tightening opposite edges of boots, stays, etc., by help of eyelets or hooks. 2. Braid for trimming men's coats etc. (usu. *gold* or *silver* ~). 3. Open-work ornamental patterned fabric of fine, usu. linen, thread, either composed of needlework stitches

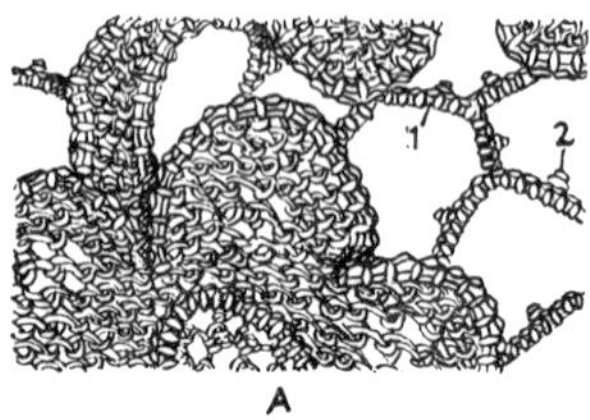

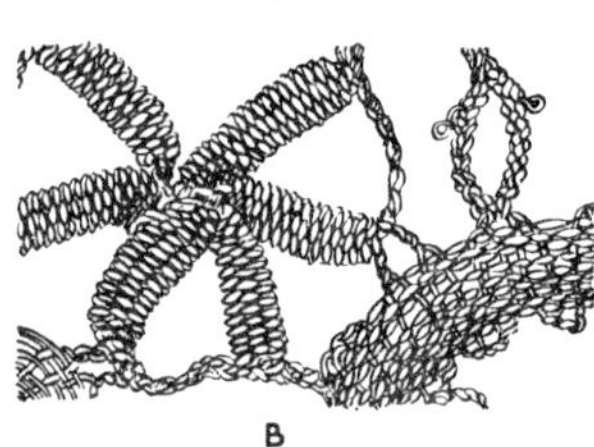

LACE: ENLARGED DETAILS OF (A) NEEDLEPOINT, (B) PILLOW LACE

1. Bride. 2. Picot

(*needlepoint* ~), or plaited with the aid of bobbins on a pillow (*bobbin, pillow,* or *bone* ~); imitations of these, consisting of hand-embroidered net, or made by machine; *~-bark tree,* W. Indian tree (*Lagetta lintearia*) with inner bark of lace-like fibres; *lacewing,* name given to various insects of order *Neuroptera.* **lā'cy** *adj.* **lāce** *v.* Fasten, tighten, compress, trim, with lace(s); compress one's waist; embroider (*with* thread etc.); pass (cord etc.) through; diversify (*with* streaks of colour. 3. Flavour, fortify (beverage) *with* spirit. **lā'cing** *n.*

Lăcėdaem'on. The rich central plain of ancient LACONIA, watered by River Eurotas; Laconia itself. **Lăcėdaemōn'ian** *adj.* & *n.* (Native, inhabitant) of Lacedaemon, Spartan.

lă'cerāte *v.t.* Mangle, tear, (esp. flesh or tissues); afflict, distress, (heart, feelings). **lăcerā'tion** *n.*

lacĕrt'ian, lacĕrt'īne *adjs.* Of lizards; lizard-like.

La Chaise shĕz), François d'Aix de (1624–1709). French Jesuit, father confessor of Louis XIV; the chief cemetery of Paris, Père-la-Chaise, occupies the site of his garden.

lăch'es (-ĭz) *n.* (law) Negligence in performing a legal duty; delay in asserting right, claiming privilege, etc.; culpable negligence.

Lăch'ėsis (-k-). (Gk myth.) One of the three Fates, who with her spindle spun out the course of human life.

Lach'mann (lŭχ-), Karl Konrad Friedrich Wilhelm (1793–1851). German philologist; helped to establish the principles of textual criticism, and maintained that the 'Iliad' and 'Nibelungenlied' consisted of lays by various poets.

lăch'ry̆ma Chris'tī (lăk-) *n.* Strong sweet red wine of S. Italy. [L, = 'Christ's tear']

lăch'ry̆mal (-k-) *adj.* Of, for, tears; ~ *gland,* (anat.) gland beneath upper eyelid secreting tears, which drain from inner corner of eye through ~ *duct* to nose; ~ *vase,* vase intended to contain tears. ~ *n.* Lachrymal vase; (pl.) lachrymal organs.

lăchry̆mā'tion (-k-) *n.* Shedding of tears.

lăch'ry̆mātor (-k-) *n.* Substance distributed in form of smoke or vapour, irritating the eyes and causing tears, tear-gas.

lăch'ry̆matory (-k-) *adj.* Of, for tears; (of 'gas', bomb, etc.) causing eyes to water. ~ *n.* Small phial of kind found in Roman tombs and thought to be tear-bottles.

lăch'ry̆mōse (-k-) *adj.* Tearful, given to weeping. **lăch'ry̆mōsely** *adv.*

lacĭn'iate, -ātėd *adjs.* (bot., zool.) Cut into deep irregular segments, slashed, jagged, fringed.

lăck *n.* Deficiency, want, need, *of*; *for* ~ *of,* owing to want or absence of. ~ *v.* Be wanting (only in part. forms, as *money was lacking*); be without, not have, be deficient in; *~-lustre,* (of eye etc.) dull.

lăckadais'ĭcal (-z-) *adj.* Languidly superior, affected; feebly sentimental. **lăckadais'ĭcally** *adv.* **lăckadais'ĭcalnėss** *n.* [archaic *lackaday, -daisy,* alack]

lăck'ey, lăc'quey (-kĭ) *n.* Footman, man-servant (usu. liveried); obsequious person, parasite. ~ *v.t.* Dance attendance on, behave servilely to.

Lacōn'ĭa. Ancient territory of SW. Greece, now a department, its ancient capital, Sparta, being still the administrative centre. **Lacōn'ĭan** *adj.* & *n.*

lacŏn'ĭc *adj.* Brief, concise, sententious; given to such speech or style. **lacŏn'ĭcally** *adv.* **lacŏn'ĭcĭsm** *n.* [Gk *Lakōn* Laconia, from character of inhabitants]

lăcq'uer (-ker) *n.* 1. (*true* or *far eastern* ~) Natural sap of *~-tree* (*Rhus vernicifera*), used since ancient times in China and Japan as protective and decorative varnish (usu. applied in thin layers to wooden objects or inlaid on metal wares) or, when solidified, as medium for sculpture. 2. Varnish imitating this, invented in Europe in 17th c. and prepared from resin lac or shellac (see LAC[1], sense 1). ~ *v.t.* Coat with lacquer.

lacquey: see LACKEY.

lacrim-, lacrym-: see LACHRYM-.

lacrŏsse' (*or* -kraws) *n.* Ball-game (orig. of N. Amer. Indians) with 12 players on each side; the ball is flung by and carried in the crosse, a bent stick with net stretched across bent end, the object being to throw the ball through the opponents' goal. [Fr., so named by Jesuit missionaries f. resemblance of stick to crosier]

lăc'tate *n.* Salt of lactic acid.

lăctā'tion *n.* Suckling; secretion of milk.

lăc'tėal *adj.* Of milk; conveying chyle or other milky fluid. **lăc'tėals** *n.pl.* Lymphatic vessels of mesentery, conveying chyle to thoracic duct.

lăctĕs'cence *n.* Milky appearance; milky juice. **lăctĕs'cent** *adj.* Milky; yielding milky juice.

lăc'tĭc *adj.* (chem.) Of milk; ~ *acid* (*hydroxypropionic acid*), formed by the fermentation of sugars etc. and present in sour milk; used in the dyeing of wool and the tanning of leather.

lăctĭf'erous *adj.* Yielding milk or milky fluid.

lăctŏm'ėter, lăc'toscōpe *ns.* Instruments for testing milk.

lăc'to-prōt'ėin *n.* Albuminous constituent of milk.

lăc'tōse *n.* Milk sugar, a substance somewhat similar to cane sugar, present in milk, and manufactured by the evaporation of whey.

lacūn'a *n.* (pl. *-ae*). Hiatus, blank, missing portion, empty part; cavity in bone, tissue, etc. **lacūn'al, lacūn'ar(y)** *adjs.*

lacŭs'trīne *adj.* Of, dwelling or growing in, lake(s).

lăd *n.* Boy, youth, young fellow; fellow; *~'s love,* southernwood. **lădd'ĭe** *n.*

lăd'anum *n.* Gum resin exuding from plants of genus *Cistus,* used in perfumery etc.

lădd'er *n.* Set of bars (*rungs*) inserted usu. in two uprights of wood or metal or in two cords to serve as (usu. portable) means of ascending building etc.; (in stocking etc.) ladder-like vertical flaw caused by breaking of thread; (fig.) means of rising in the world or attaining object; *~-back* (*chair*), chair with back formed of horizontal bars (ill.

CHAIR); ~*-dredge*, dredge with buckets carried round on ladder-like chain; ~*-stitch*, cross-bar stitch in embroidery. ~ *v.* (Of stocking etc.) develop ladder.

lāde *v.t.* (past part. *lăd'en*). Put cargo on board (ship); ship (goods) as cargo. **lăd'en** *adj.* Loaded (*with*); painfully burdened *with*. **lăd'ing** *n.* *Bill of* ~: see BILL.

la-di-da (lahdĭdah') *n.* (Person given to) swagger or pretension in manners and pronunciation. ~ *adj.* Pretentious in this way. [imit. of pronunciation used, f. comic song of 1880]

Ladin', Ladin'o (-ēn, -ēnō): see RHAETIC.

Lăd'islaus (-ows). Name of several kings of Hungary: *Ladislaus I*, St. (1040–95), king of Hungary 1077–95; introduced Catholicism into Croatia, which he secured for Hungary; *Ladislaus IV* (1262–90), king of Hungary 1272–90; killed after two years of civil war following declaration of crusade against him by Pope Nicholas IV; *Ladislaus V* (*Posthumene*) (1440–57), king of Hungary and Bohemia.

lād'le *n.* 1. Large spoon, with cup-shaped bowl and long handle, for transferring liquids. 2. (In foundry) receptacle for molten metal. ~ *v.t.* Lift out (liquid) with ladle.

Lad'oga (lah-). Largest European lake, in U.S.S.R., near Finnish border.

lād'y *n.* 1. Woman ruling over subjects, or to whom obedience or homage is due (archaic or poet. exc. in ~ *of the manor*). 2. Woman to whom man is devoted, mistress. 3. *Our L*~, the Virgin Mary. 4. Woman belonging to, or fitted by manners, habits, and sentiments for, the upper classes; ~ *of the bedchamber*, ~*-in-waiting*, lady attending sovereign. 5. (Courteously for) woman. 6. (Title used as less formal prefix for) marchioness, countess, viscountess, baroness; (prefixed to Christian name of) daughter of duke, marquis, or earl; (prefixed to husband's Christian name of) wife of holder of courtesy title *lord*; (prefixed to surname of) wife of baronet or knight; ~ *Mayoress*, wife of Lord Mayor; *my* ~, form of address used chiefly by servants etc. to holders of title *lady*. 7. Wife (archaic or vulg. exc. of those who hold the title *lady*). 8. *Painted* ~, kind of butterfly (*Vanessa cardui*); *ladies' chain*, figure in quadrille etc.; *Ladies' gallery*, gallery in House of Commons reserved for ladies; *L~-altar*, altar in Lady-chapel; *ladybird*, any of a family of beetles (*Coccinellidae*), many of which are conspicuously coloured; ~*-bug*, (U.S.) ladybird; *L~ Bountiful*, (from character in Farquhar's 'Beaux' Stratagem') lady playing the part of Providence in village etc.; *L~-chapel*, chapel in large church usu. E. of high altar and dedicated to Virgin (ill. CHURCH); *L~-Day*, Feast of Annunciation, 25th Mar., one of the quarter-days; ~ *help*, lady employed as domestic; ~*-killer*, man devoting himself to making conquests of ladies; ~*-love*, sweetheart; ~*'s companion*, small case containing needles, cottons, etc.; *L~'s cushion*, mossy saxifrage; ~*'s finger*, finger-shaped sponge-cake; ~*'s-maid*, lady's personal maid, in charge of toilet etc.; ~*'s* (*ladies'*) *man*, man fond of female society; *L~'s-mantle*, the rosaceous herb (*Alchemilla vulgaris*); ~ (*'s*) *-smock*, cuckoo-flower; ~*'s slipper*, orchidaceous plant, *Cypripedium* species; cultivated calceolaria; bird's-foot trefoil; garden balsam; ~*'s tresses*, kind of orchid (*Spiranthes*). **lād'y-hŏod** *n.*

lād'ȳfȳ *v.t.* Make lady of; call lady; *ladyfied*, having the airs of a fine lady.

lād'ylīke *adj.* With manners etc. of a lady; befitting a lady; (of man) effeminate.

Lady Margaret Hall. Women's college of the University of Oxford, founded 1878; named after Margaret Beaufort, Countess of Richmond, mother of Henry VII.

Lady of the Lake. In Arthurian legend, a supernatural being (Morgan le Fay, Vivien, Nimue), who gave Arthur the sword Excalibur, and was one of the three queens in the ship that bore him away to Avalon.

Lady of the Lamp. A name given to Florence NIGHTINGALE, in allusion to her visits at night to hospital wards during the Crimean War.

lād'ȳship *n.* Being a lady; *her, your*, ~, *their* ~*s*, (in respectful mention of or address to titular lady) she, you, they.

Lād'ysmith. Town in Natal, S. Africa, besieged by Boers on outbreak of 2nd Boer War and relieved 4 months later (28th Feb. 1900) by British force under Sir Redvers Buller. [named after *Lady Smith*, wife of colonial governor]

laev'o-cŏm'pound *n.* Chemical compound which is LAEVO-ROTATORY.

laev'o-gȳr'ous *adj.* = LAEVO-ROTATORY.

laev'o-rōt'atory *adj.* (Of chemical substance) having the property of causing the plane of polarization of a ray of polarized light to rotate to left.

laev'ūlōse *n.* (chem.) Laevo-rotatory form of glucose, fruit-sugar.

La Fayĕtte'[1], Marie Joseph Paul Yves Roch Gilbert du Motier, Marquis de (1757–1834). French general and politician; fought in American army in Amer. War of Independence; vice-president of French National Assembly (1789); commander of National Guard (1789, and again in 1830); imprisoned in Austria (1792–7) but released by Napoleon.

La Fayĕtte'[2], Marie-Madeleine Pioche de le Vergne, Comtesse de (1634–92). French novelist; author of 'La Princesse de Clèves'.

La Fŏntaine', Jean de (1621–95). French poet and fabulist.

lăg[1] *v.* Go too slow, not keep pace, fall *behind*. ~ *n.* (Amount of) retardation in current or movement, esp. delay in the phase of current maxima behind the corresponding electromotive force maxima in an alternating-current circuit; delay in time; ~ *of tide*, interval by which tide-wave falls behind mean time in 1st and 3rd quarters of moon. **lăgg'ard** *n.* & *adj.* **lăgg'ing**[1] *adj.*

lăg[2] *v.t.* Send to penal servitude; apprehend, arrest. ~ *n.* Convict; *old* ~, one who has been convicted more than once.

lăg[3] *n.* (Piece of the) non-conducting cover of boiler etc. ~ *v.t.* Encase with lags. **lăgg'ing**[2] *n.*

lăg'an *n.* (law) Goods or wreckage lying on bed of sea.

Lā'găsh. Ancient Sumerian city in Mesopotamia, excavation of which proved that the Babylonians inherited their culture and the art of writing from the Sumerians.

lag'er (beer) (lahg-) *n.* Light, orig. German, beer, distinguished from other kinds by longer fermentation at lower temperature. [Ger. *lagerbier* beer brewed for keeping]

Lagerlöf (lahg'-), Selma Ottiliana Louisa (1858–1940). Swedish novelist; author of 'Gösta Berling's Saga'; first woman to receive Nobel Prize for literature (1909).

lagōōn' *n.* Shallow stretch of salt water partly or wholly separated from sea by narrow strip of land or low sand-bank or coral reef; enclosed water of atoll.

Lāg'ŏs. 1. Former British colony and protectorate on W. coast of Africa, since 1914 part of NIGERIA. 2. Capital and chief port of Nigeria.

lah: see LA.

Lahōre'. City, till 1947 capital of the Punjab in India, now capital of West Punjab province and second city of Pakistan; home of the Punjab University, and centre of Moslem culture and of commerce.

lā'ic *adj.* Non-clerical, lay; secular, temporal. ~ *n.* Layman. **lā'ical** *adj.* **lā'ically** *adv.*

lā'icīze *v.t.* Make lay; commit (school etc.), throw open (office), to laymen. **lāicīzā'tion** *n.*

lair *n.* 1. Wild beast's lying-place. 2. Shed or enclosure for cattle on way to market. ~ *v.* Go to, rest or place in, lair.

laird *n.* Landed proprietor in Scotland. **laird'ship** *n.*

Lā'ĭs. Name of two celebrated Greek courtesans of 5th and 4th centuries B.C. respectively. The elder was probably a native of Corinth; the younger (b. *c* 420 B.C.) was brought from Sicily to Corinth at the time of the Athenian expedition to Sicily.

laissez-aller (lĕs'ā ăl'ā) *n.* Unconstrained freedom, absence of constraint.

laissez-faire (lĕs'ā fãr) *n.* Freedom from government interference in economic or industrial affairs, esp. by tariffs, restrictions on individual enterprise, etc.

lā'ĭty *n.* Being a layman; body of religious worshippers as distinguished from clergy; unprofessional people.

lāke[1] *n.* Large body of water entirely surrounded by land; *the Great Lakes*; see GREAT; ~ *country, district, ~-land, the L~s*, region of English lakes in Westmorland, Cumberland, and Lancashire; *~-dweller*, inhabitant of *~-village*, in new Stone Age built on piles driven into bed of lake, in late Bronze Age on artificial island of timber and brushwood; ~ *poets*, Coleridge, Southey, and Wordsworth, who lived in Lake district. **lāke'lėss** (-kl-) *adj.* **lāke'lėt** *n.*

lāke[2] *n.* Reddish pigment, orig. made from lac; pigment made from animal, vegetable, or coal-tar colouring matter combined with metallic oxide or earth; (dyeing) any insoluble substance resulting from the chemical combination of soluble colouring matter with a mordant.

lăkh (-k), **lăc** *n.* A hundred thousand (usu. *of rupees*).

Lăkshmi' (-ē). (Hindu myth.) Wife of Vishnu and goddess of fortune or prosperity.

Lăll'ans. The vernacular speech of the Lowlands of Scotland, Lowland Scots; this as a literary language.

lăllā'tion *n.* LAMBDACISM.

Lalo (*lalō'*), Édouard Victor Antoine (1823–92). French composer.

lăm *v.* (slang) Thrash, hit hard with cane etc.

Lam. *abbrev.* Lamentations (O.T.).

lam'a[1] (lah-) *n.* Tibetan Buddhist monk. Two abbots of great monasteries, incarnations of Buddhist deities, are the *Dalai* (dăl'ī) *L~* at Lhasa, and the *Tashi L~* at Tashi Lhumpo (western Tibet), also called the *Panchen L~*. **Lam'aism** *n.* Type of monasticism practised by the lamas; their form of Buddhism, = Tantrism. **lam'aist** *n.* **lamas'ery** (-mah-) *n.* Monastery of lamas. [Tibetan *blama* (silent *b*)]

lama[2]: see LLAMA.

Lamarck', Jean-Baptiste Pierre Antoine de Monet, Chevalier de (1744–1829). French botanist and zoologist, who among others anticipated Darwin in conceiving the idea of organic evolution, but accounted for it by a theory, not now generally held to be valid, that characteristics acquired by organisms in response to changed conditions of life etc. can be inherited by their offspring. **Lamarck'ian** *adj.* & *n.* **Lamarck'ism** *n.* A theory of the inheritance of acquired characteristics.

Lamartine (-ēn'), Alphonse de (1790–1869). French Romantic poet and politician; author of 'Méditations poétiques' etc.

lămb[1] (-m) *n.* Young of sheep; its flesh as food; young member of church flock; innocent, weak, or dear person; *the L~ (of God)*, Christ; *lamb'skin*, skin of lamb with wool on, used as fur; *~'s lettuce*, corn-salad; *~'s tails*, hazel catkins; *~'s-wool*, the soft fine wool of lambs used for hosiery etc.; drink of spiced and sugared hot ale mixed with pulp of roasted apples. ~ *v.* Bring forth lamb, yean; tend (lambing ewes); (pass., of lambs) be brought forth. **lămb'kin** *n.* **lămb'līke** *adj.*

Lămb[2] (-m), Charles (1775–1834). English essayist and critic; author of 'Essays of Elia'.

lămbāste' *v.t.* (dial.) Beat, thrash.

lămb'da (-md-) *n.* Greek letter (Λ λ).

lă(m)b'dacĭsm (-md-, -bd-) *n.* Pronunciation of *r* as *l*.

lămb'doid, lămbdoid'al (-md-) *adjs.* Shaped like lambda; ~ *suture*, (anat.) suture connecting the two parietal bones with occipital (ill. HEAD).

lăm'bent *adj.* (Of flame etc.) playing on surface without burning it, with soft radiance; (of eyes, sky, etc.) softly radiant; (of wit, etc.) gently brilliant. **lăm'bently** *adv.* **lăm'bency** *n.*

lăm'bert *n.* A unit of brightness, equal to that of a perfectly diffusing surface radiating or reflecting light at the rate of one LUMEN per square centimetre. [J. H. *Lambert* (1728–77), German physicist]

Lăm'bėth. Metropolitan borough of London S. of Thames; ~ *Palace*, palace in Lambeth, since 1197 residence of archbishop of Canterbury; ~ *Conference*, one of the periodical assemblies at Lambeth Palace of bishops of the whole Anglican Communion; ~ *walk*, dance characterized by a walk and gestures regarded as characteristic of Lambeth.

lăm'brėquin (-kĭn) *n.* (U.S.) Short piece of drapery over top of door or window, or hung from mantel-shelf; (her.) flowing drapery or scrollwork displayed on either side of helmet; mantling.

lāme *adj.* Crippled by injury or defect in a limb, esp. foot or leg; limping or unable to walk; (of argument, story, etc.) imperfect, unsatisfactory; (of metre) halting; ~ *duck*: see DUCK[1]. **lāme'ly** *adv.* **lāme'nėss** *n.* **lāme** *v.t.* Make lame, cripple.

lamé (lah'mā) *n.* & *adj.* (Material) with gold or silver or other metal thread inwoven.

lamĕll'a *n.* (pl. *-ae*). Thin plate, scale, layer, or film, esp. of bone or tissue. **lamĕll'ar, lăm'ellate, -ātėd, lamĕll'ōse** *adjs.*

lamĕll'icorn *adj.* & *n.* (Beetle) having club-shaped antennae.

lamĕnt' *n.* Passionate expression of grief; elegy, dirge. ~ *v.* Express or feel grief for or about; be distressed at, regret; *lamented*, mourned for (esp. conventionally of the dead); *the late lamented*, (freq. iron.) the deceased.

lăm'entable *adj.* Mournful (archaic); deplorable, regrettable. **lăm'entably** *adv.*

lămentā'tion *n.* Lamenting, lament; *L~s (of Jeremiah)*, O.T. poetical book on destruction of Jerusalem by Chaldeans.

lā'mĭa *n.* (Latin myth.) Monster with head and breasts of a woman and body of a serpent preying on human beings and sucking children's blood.

lăm'ĭna *n.* (pl. *-ae*). 1. Thin plate, scale, layer, or flake, of metal, bone, membrane, stratified rock, etc. 2. (bot.) Blade of leaf (ill. LEAF). **lăm'ĭnar, lăm'ĭnate, lăm'ĭnōse** *adjs.*

lăm'ĭnāte *v.* Beat or roll (metal) into thin plates; split into layers or leaves; overlay with metal plates; manufacture by placing layer on layer. **lămĭnā'tion** *n.*

Lămm'as. 1st August, formerly observed as English harvest festival, at which loaves made from first ripe corn were consecrated; in Scotland, one of the quarter-days. [OE. *hlafmæsse* loaf mass]

lămm'ergeyer (-gī-) *n.* Bearded vulture (*Gypaetus barbatus*), largest European bird of prey. [Ger. *lämmer* lambs, *geier* vulture]

lămp *n.* Vessel with oil and wick for giving light; glass vessel enclosing candle, gas-jet, incandescent

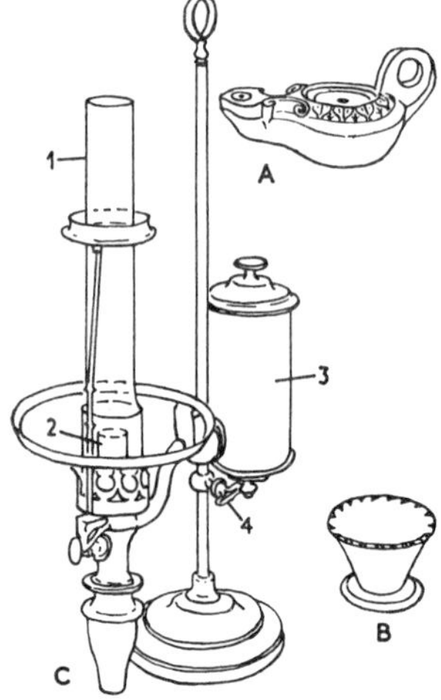

LAMP: A. ROMAN. B. MEDIEVAL CRESSET. C. ARGAND OIL LAMP

1. Chimney. 2. Wick. 3. Fuel-container. 4. Screw to adjust position of lamp on stand

wire, or other illuminant; (fig.) sun, moon, star; source of spiritual or intellectual light, hope, etc.;

smell of the ~, betray nocturnal study, be laborious in style, etc.; ~*-black*, pigment consisting of finely divided almost pure carbon, made from soot of burning oil or gas; ~*-chimney*, glass cylinder making draught for lamp-flame; ~*-holder*, device for holding lamp, esp. electric bulb; *lamp'light*, light given by lamp(s); ~*-lighter*, man who lights street-lamps; ~*-post*, post usu. of iron or concrete supporting street-lamp. ~ *v.* Shine; supply with lamps; illuminate; (U.S. slang) look at.

lăm'pas[1] *n.* Horse-disease with swelling in roof of mouth.

lăm'pas[2] *n.* (orig.) Oriental flowered silk; (now) furnishing material woven on jacquard loom and resembling brocade, with figured design in satin-like warp threads contrasting with corded ground.

lăm'pĭon *n.* Pot of usu. coloured glass with oil and wick used in illuminations.

lămpōōn' *n.* Virulent or scurrilous satire on individual. ~ *v.t.* Write lampoon(s) against. **lămpōōn'er, lămpōōn'ist** *ns.*

lăm'prey *n.* Any of several eel-shaped aquatic vertebrates (genera

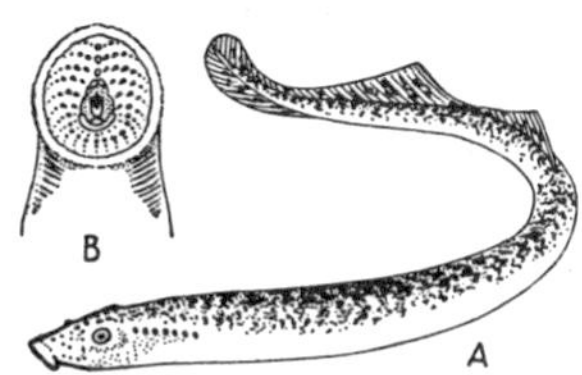

A. LAMPREY. B. MOUTH, FROM BELOW

Lampetra and *Petromyzon*) resembling fishes but without scales or jaws and having sucker-like mouth.

Lăn'arkshire. County of S. central Scotland, containing city of Glasgow and the Clyde valley.

Lănc'ashire. County of NW. England.

Lănc'aster[1]. City and county town of Lancashire.

Lănc'aster[2], Duchy of. Estates, etc. in various parts of England and Wales attached to the Crown since 1399, under a charter of Henry IV; the *Chancellor of the Duchy of* ~ is by tradition a member of the Government.

Lănc'aster[3], House of. English royal family descended from John of GAUNT; Henry IV, Henry V, and Henry VI were reigning monarchs of this house, and in the Wars of the ROSES the house of Lancaster and its supporters were the party of the red rose.

Lăncăs'trian *n.* & *adj.* 1. (Native) of Lancashire. 2. (Adherent, supporter) of house of LANCASTER[3].

lance (lah-) *n.* Weapon with long wooden shaft and pointed steel head used by horseman in charging (ill. SPEAR); similar implement for spearing fish or killing harpooned whale; ~*-corporal*, non-commissioned officer of lowest rank, below corporal; ~*-sergeant*, corporal acting as sergeant; ~*-wood*, tough elastic kinds of W. Indian wood used for fishing-rods etc. ~ *v.t.* 1. (poet.) Fling, launch. 2. (poet.) Pierce (as) with lance; (surg.) prick, cut open, with lancet.

lance'lĕt (lahnsl-) *n.* Small marine animal (*Amphioxus*), one

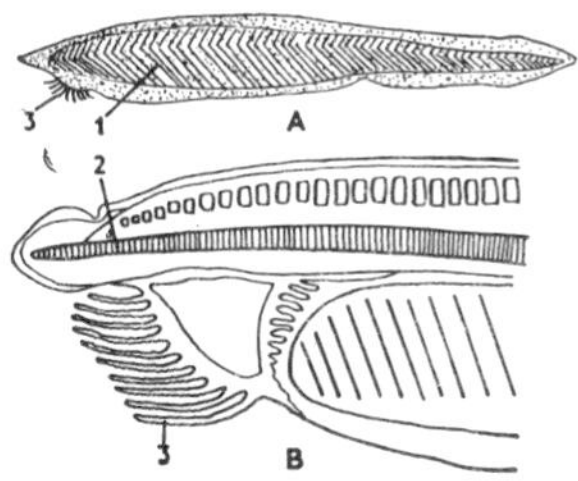

A. LANCELET. B. SECTION OF ANTERIOR PART

1. Myotomes. 2. Notochord. 3. Cirri

of the lowest forms of chordate, about 2 in. long, found in sand of shallow waters throughout the world.

Lance'lot of the Lake (lahns'-lot). (Arthurian legend) Son of King Ban of Brittany; brought up by the LADY OF THE LAKE; most famous of Arthur's knights, and lover of Queen Guinevere.

lăn'cĕolate *adj.* Shaped like spear-head, tapering to each end.

la'ncer (lah-) *n.* 1. Soldier of cavalry regiment orig. armed with lances. 2. (pl.) Square dance, variant of quadrille, for 8 or 16 pairs, derived from cavalry displays and in vogue from *c* 1850 to war of 1914–18; music for this.

la'ncĕt (lah-) *n.* 1. Fine pointed double-edged surgical knife. 2. ~ (*window, arch*), high narrow pointed window or arch in 12th- and 13th-c. Gothic architecture (ill. WINDOW).

la'ncĭnātĭng (lah-) *adj.* (Of pain) acute, shooting.

Lancret (lahṅcrā'), Nicolas (1660–1743). French rococo painter.

Lancs. *abbrev.* Lancashire.

lănd *n.* 1. Solid part of earth's surface; ground, soil, expanse of country; country, nation, State; landed property, (pl.) estates; strip of plough or pasture land parted from others by water furrows. 2. Any of the divisions between rifling-grooves of guns. 3. ~*-agent*, steward of estate; agent for sale etc. of estates; ~*-bank*, bank issuing notes on security of landed property; ~*-breeze*, breeze blowing seaward from land; ~*-crab*, various species of crabs that live on land but breed in sea; *land'fall*, approach to land esp. for first time in voyage or flight; ~*-force(s)*, military, not naval, force(s); ~*-girl*, girl or woman doing farm work, usu. in war-time, esp. member of Women's Land Army; ~*-grabber*, (esp.) man who took Irish farm after eviction of tenant; *land'holder*, proprietor or (usu.) tenant of land; ~ *hemisphere*, that part of the globe, mainly N. of equator, in which about $\frac{6}{7}$ of earth's surface is contained; ~*-hunger*, eagerness to acquire land; *land'lady*, woman keeping inn, boarding-house, or lodgings; woman having tenants; ~*-law(s)*, law(s) of landed property; *L~ League*, Irish association (1879–81) for reducing rents, introducing peasant proprietorship, etc.; ~*-locked*, almost or quite enclosed by land; *land'lord*, person of whom another holds any tenement; keeper of inn, lodgings, etc.; *land'lordism*, system by which land is owned by landlords receiving fixed rent from tenants (esp. in Ireland); ~*-lubber*, (naut.) person ignorant of the sea and ships; *land'mark*, object marking boundary of country, estate, etc.; conspicuous object in district etc. (orig.) esp. as guide in navigation; object, event, etc., marking stage in process or turning-point in history; ~*-mine*, explosive mine laid in, or dropped by parachute on, land; *land'owner*, owner of land; *land'rail*, = CORNCRAKE; *land'slide*, (orig. U.S.) landslip; overwhelming majority of votes for one side, esp. in election; *land'slip*, sliding down of mass of land from cliff or mountain; *lands'man*, non-sailor; ~*-tax*, tax on landed property; ~*-wind*, land-breeze. **lănd'lĕss** *adj.* **lănd'ward** *adj.* & *adv.* **lănd'wards** *adv.*

lănd *v.* Set or go ashore; disembark (*at*); set down from vehicle or aircraft; (of aircraft) come down to ground or surface of water; bring to, reach, find oneself in, a certain place, stage, or position; deal (person blow etc.); alight after jump etc.; bring (fish) to land; (fig.) win (prize etc.).

lăn'dau *n.* Four-wheeled carriage with top of which front and back halves can be independently

LANDAU

raised and lowered. **lăndaulĕt'** *n.* Small landau; motor-car with movable hood over rear seats. [*Landau*, town in Germany]

Landav. *abbrev.* (Bishop) of Llandaff (replacing surname in his signature).

lăn'dĕd *adj.* Possessed of land; consisting of land.

lănd'grāve *n.* (hist.) Title of certain German princes; orig., count having jurisdiction over territory, and with inferior counts under him. **lănd'gravine** (-ēn) *n.* (hist.) Wife of landgrave; woman landgrave.

lăn'dĭng *n.* (esp.) Place for disembarking (also *~-place*); platform between two flights of stairs; *half-~*, small one part-way up flight (ill. STAIR); floor, passage at top of staircase on to which rooms open; *~ craft*, boat, often flat-bottomed and with collapsible side, for

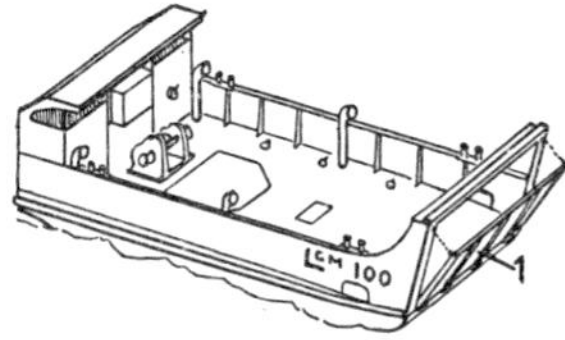

LANDING CRAFT FOR MECHANIZED VEHICLES (L.C.M.)
1. Ramp

carrying troops, armoured vehicles, etc., in amphibious operations; *~-net*, net for landing large fish when hooked; *~-stage*, platform, often floating, on which passengers and goods are disembarked.

Lăn'dŏr, Walter Savage (1775–1864). English critic, essayist, and poet, whose principal prose work is his 'Imaginary Conversations'.

lănd'scāpe (*or* -ns-) *n.* Picture etc. or part of one representing inland scenery; actual piece of such scenery; *~ architecture*, design and lay-out of large spaces, parks, suburbs, etc.; *~ gardening*, landscape architecture, esp. that aiming at pictorial but apparently natural effects. **lănd'scāpist** *n.* Painter of landscapes.

Lănd'seer, Sir Edwin Henry (1802–73). English painter of animals.

Lănd's End. Rocky promontory in Cornwall forming westernmost point of England.

lāne *n.* Narrow road usu. between hedges, narrow street; passage made or left between rows of persons, or marked out for runners in race, streams of traffic, etc.; regular route of ships or aircraft; channel of water in ice-field.

Lăn'frănc (*c* 1005–89). Italian prelate and scholar; archbishop of Canterbury 1070–; rebuilder of Canterbury cathedral.

Lăng, Andrew (1844–1912). Scottish scholar, journalist, and poet; collector of fairy-tales, and, with others, author of prose translations of Homer.

Lăng'erhăns, Robert (1849–88). German pathologist; *islands* (*islets*) *of ~*, groups of small granular cells in the pancreas which secrete INSULIN.

Lăng'land, William (*c* 1330–*c* 1400). English poet, author of 'Piers Plowman'.

Langobard: see LOMBARD.

lăng'rage, -idge (-ngg-) *n.* Case-shot with irregular pieces of iron formerly used to damage enemy's rigging in a sea-battle.

lăng sȳne *adv.* & *n.* (In) the old days. [Sc., = 'long since']

Lăng'ton, Stephen (1151–1228). English cardinal, archbishop of Canterbury, theologian, historian, and poet; a leader of the barons in their conflict with King John which culminated in Magna Carta.

Lăng'trȳ, Emily Charlotte (1853–1929). English actress; known as Lillie Langtry or 'the Jersey Lily'.

lăng'uage (-nggwij) *n.* Whole body of words and methods of combination of words used by nation, people, or race; method of expression; words and their use; faculty of speech; person's style of expressing himself; professional or sectional vocabulary; literary style, wording; *bad ~*, oaths and abusive talk; *strong ~*, speech expressing vehement feelings; *~-master*, teacher of (usu. modern foreign) language(s).

langue d'ŏc (lahṅg). Romance dialects of S. provinces of France.

Langu'edŏc. Old province of S. France stretching from W. bank of Rhône to Pyrenees and including Cévennes and valleys of upper Loire. [Fr. *langue* language, *oc* Provençal form of *oui* yes]

langue d'oïl (lahṅg dōēl). Romance dialects of France other than those of S. France (cf. LANGUE D'OC). [Fr. *langue* language, OF *oïl* yes]

lăng'uid (-nggw-) *adj.* Inert, lacking vigour, indisposed to exertion; spiritless, apathetic, dull; sluggish, slow-moving; faint, weak. **lăng'uidly** *adv.* **lăng'uidnėss** *n.*

lăng'uish (-nggw-) *v.i.* Grow or be feeble, lose or lack vitality; live *under* enfeebling or depressing conditions; droop, pine (*for*); affect languor or sentimental tenderness. **lăng'uishingly** *adv.* **lăng'uishment** *n.*

lăng'uor (-ngger) *n.* Faintness, fatigue; inertia, want of alertness; soft or tender mood or effect; slackness, dullness, drooping state. **lăng'uorous** *adj.* **lăng'uorously** *adv.*

langur (-nggoor') *n.* Long-tailed monkey of India, *Semnopithecus entellus* or Hanuman, held sacred by many Hindus; one species of the catarrhine division of monkeys; other species of same genus.

lăn'iary *adj.* & *n.* (Tooth) adapted for tearing, canine.

lanĭf'erous, lanĭ'gerous *adjs.* Wool-bearing.

lănk *adj.* Shrunken, spare; tall and lean; long and flaccid; (of hair) straight and limp, not wavy.

lănk'y *adj.* Ungracefully lean and long or tall. **lănk'inėss** *n.*

lănn'er[1] *n.* Mediterranean species of falcon, *Falco lanarius*; the female of this. **lănn'erėt** *n.* Male of lanner.

Lănn'er[2], Joseph Franz Karl (1801–43). Austrian composer of dance music, esp. waltzes.

lăn'olin *n.* Fatty matter extracted from sheep's wool, used as basis of ointments and toilet preparations.

Lăn'sĭng. Capital of Michigan, U.S.

lăns'quenėt (-ke-) *n.* 1. (hist.) One of class of mercenaries in German and other continental armies, 17th–18th centuries. 2. Card-game of German origin, in which players bet on single cards. [Fr., f. Ger. *landsknecht*, lit. servant of the country]

lăn'tern *n.* 1. Transparent case protecting flame of candle etc. 2. (also *magic ~*) Optical apparatus for projecting enlarged image of glass picture (*~-slide*) on white screen in dark room; projector. 3. Light-chamber of lighthouse. 4. Superstructure, usu. more or less cylindrical, on dome, tower, or roof, open below and admitting light at sides (ill. DOME). 5. *~ clock*, clock enclosed in metal case like lantern (ill. CLOCK); *~-fly*, one of several species of bugs of family *Fulgoridae*, erron. supposed to be light-producing; *~ jaws*, long thin jaws giving hollow look to face, whence *~-jawed*; *~-slide*, photog. print or drawing on glass plate, used in magic lantern; *~-wheel*, gear-wheel shaped like lantern.

lăn'thanum *n.* One of the rare-earth elements, found in a number of rare minerals and in monazite sand; symbol La, at. no. 57, at. wt 138·91. [Gk *lanthanō* hide]

lăn'yard *n.* Short rope made fast to something (naut.); cord attached to knife, whistle, etc., to hold it or serve as handle.

Lāŏc'ōōn. (Gk legend) Trojan priest of Apollo; crushed to death with his two sons by two serpents which emerged from the sea as he was sacrificing to Poseidon; this was held to be his punishment for profaning the temple of the god and warning the Trojans against the WOODEN horse.

Lāodĭcē'a. Name of several Greek cities of Asia and Asia Minor; esp. *~ ad Lycum*, inland city of W. Asia Minor, site of one of the earliest Christian churches. **Lāodĭcē'an** *adj.* & *n.* (Person) having the fault for which the Church of Laodicea is reproached in Rev. iii. 15, 16, 'lukewarm, neither cold nor hot', indifferent in religion, politics, etc.

Laoighis: see LEIX.

Laos (lows). Kingdom of SE. Asia, independent since 1949, formerly part of Fr. Indo-China; capital, Vientiane. **Laō'tian** (-shn) *adj.* & *n.*

Lao-tse (lah'-ō-tsē'), **Lao'tzu** (-ōō) (6th c. B.C.). Chinese philosopher and metaphysician; reputed founder of TAOISM and contemporary of Confucius.

lăp[1] *n.* Hanging part or flap of garment, saddle, etc.; front part of skirt held up to contain something; front part of body from waist to knees of seated person, considered with dress as place on which child is nursed or object held; *lap'dog*, small pet dog; *~-robe*, (U.S.) rug to cover knees of person seated in vehicle, carriage-rug; *lap'stone*, shoemaker's stone held in lap to beat leather on.

lap[2] *v.* 1. Coil, fold, wrap (garment etc. *about, around*); enfold, swathe, *in*; surround, encircle, enfold caressingly. 2. Make overlap; project *over* something; *~ over*, overlap. 3. (racing etc.) Travel over (distance) as lap; pass (competitor) by one or more laps. *~ n.* Amount of overlapping, overlapping part; layer or sheet (of cotton etc. being made) wound on roller; single turn of rope, silk, thread, etc., round drum or reel; one circuit of race-track.

lăp[3] *n.* Rotating disc for polishing gems or metal. *~ v.t.* Polish with lap.

lăp[4] *v.* Drink by scooping with tongue; drink (*up* or *down*) greedily; (of water) move, beat upon (shore), with sound of lapping. *~ n.* Liquid food for dogs; (slang) weak beverage; single act of lapping, amount taken up by it; sound of wavelets on beach etc.

lăparŏt'omy *n.* Cutting through abdominal walls into abdominal cavity.

La Paz (pahz). Capital city of Bolivia.

lapĕl' (or lăp'-) *n.* Part of front of coat folded back towards shoulder.

lăp'idary *adj.* Concerned with stones; engraved on stone; (of style) suitable for inscriptions, monumental. *~ n.* Cutter, polisher, or engraver, of stones.

lăp'is lăz'ūlī *n.* (min.) A sodium aluminium silicate containing sulphur, used as bright blue pigment; colour of this. [L, = 'stone of azure']

Lăp'ith *n.* (Gk myth.) One of the Lapithae, a race akin to the Centaurs, inhabiting Thessaly; when the Centaurs tried to carry off Hippodamia, bride of their king Peirithous, the Lapiths fought and defeated them.

Lăp'land. Region inhabited by Lapps, most northerly part of Scandinavia, stretching from Norwegian coast to White Sea. **Lăp'lander** *n.* Lapp.

Lăpp *n.* Member of a dwarfish Mongoloid race, largely nomadic, inhabiting Lapland. **Lăpp'ish** *adj.* & *n.* (Of) the language of the Lapps, one of the Finno-Ugrian family.

lăpp'ėt *n.* Flap, fold, loose or overlapping piece, of garment, flesh, membrane, etc.; lobe of ear etc.; streamer of lady's head-dress.

lăpse *n.* Slip of memory etc., slight mistake; weak or careless deviation from right, backsliding; decline to lower state; gliding, flow (of water etc.); passage or interval *of* time; (law) termination of right or privilege through disuse; *~ rate*, (meteor.) rate of change in temperature of atmosphere with height (generally taken as approx. 3° F. per 1,000 ft), called *positive* when temperature decreases as height increases, and *negative* when, more rarely, temperature decreases with height. *~ v.i.* Fail to maintain position or state for want of effort or vigour; fall *back, away*; glide, flow, subside, pass *away*; (of benefice, estate, title, etc.) fall in, pass away, become void, revert *to* someone, by failure of conditions, heirs, etc.

lăp'sus *n.* (pl. *-ūs*). Slip; *~ linguae* (-nggwē), slip of the tongue; *~ cal'amī*, slip of the pen.

Lapūt'a. In Swift's 'Gulliver's Travels', a flying island inhabited by learned men who are absorbed in philosophical and scientific speculation. **Lapūt'an** *adj.* & *n.*

lăp'wing *n.* Bird of plover family, *Vanellus vanellus*, common in temperate parts of Old World; peewit.

lar[1] *n.* (pl. *lār'ēs*). Ancient Roman household deity; *lares* (lār'ēz) *and penates* (-āt'ēz), household gods, the home.

lar[2] *n.* White-handed gibbon (*Hylobates lar*) of SE. Asia.

larb'oard (-berd) *n.* & *adj.* (naut.) Left side of ship looking forward (now replaced, to avoid confusion with *starboard*, by *port*).

lar'cėny *n.* (law) Felonious taking away of another's personal goods with intent to convert them to one's own use; theft; *petty ~*, (formerly) larceny of property below value of 12*d.* **lar'cėnous** *adj.* **lar'cėnously** *adv.*

larch *n.* Bright-foliaged and deciduous coniferous tree, *Larix decidua*, yielding Venetian turpentine, tough timber, and bark used in tanning; any tree of genus *Larix*.

lard *n.* Internal fat of abdomen of pigs etc., esp. when rendered and clarified for use in cooking and pharmacy. *~ v.t.* Insert strips of bacon in (meat etc.) before cooking; smear (as) with lard; (fig.) garnish (talk, writing) *with* particular words, expressions, etc. **lard'y** *adj.*

lardā'ceous (-shus) *adj.* (med.) Lard-like (esp. of degeneration of tissue).

lard'er *n.* Room or cupboard for storing provisions.

lard'on, lardoon' *n.* Strip of bacon or pork used to lard meat.

lares: see LAR[1].

large *adj.* Of considerable or relatively great magnitude; wide in range or capacity, comprehensive; (archaic) liberal, generous. *~ n. At ~*, at liberty, free; (of narration etc.) at full length, with details; as a body or whole; without particularizing, without definite aim; (U.S., of representative etc.) representing State etc. as a whole, not merely a district of it. **large'nėss** -jn-) *n.* **lar'gish** *adj.*

large'ly (-jl-) *adv.* (esp.) To a great or preponderating extent.

lar'gĕss(e) *n.* (archaic) Money or gifts freely bestowed, esp. by great person on occasion of rejoicing; generous or plentiful bestowal.

larg'o *adv.* & *n.* (mus.) (Passage, piece of music) to be rendered in slow time and with broad, dignified treatment.

lă'rĭat *n.* Rope with running noose for picketing horses etc.; lasso.

lark[1] *n.* Any bird of the family *Alaudidae*, in which the hind claw is usu. greatly elongated; (pop.) the skylark (*Alauda arvensis*), small sandy-brown bird which nests in ground and sings continuously while soaring; also, various birds unrelated to these, as *meadow-~* (U.S.; *Sturnella magna*), *tit-~* (= pipit), *wood-~* (*Lullula arborea*); *lark'spur*, plant of the *Delphinium* genus, having a spur-shaped calyx.

lark[2] *n.* Frolic, spree; amusing incident. *~ v.i.* Play tricks, frolic.

La Rochefoucauld (rŏshfōōkō'), François de Marsillac, duc de (1613–80). French writer of maxims, embodying a cynical philosophy that finds in self-love the prime motive of action.

Larousse (lahrōōs'), Pierre Athanase (1817–75). French lexicographer and encyclopaedist.

lă'rrikin *n.* (Usu. young) street rowdy, hooligan.

Lars. In ancient Etruria, honorary appellation prefixed usu. to name of first-born son.

larv'a *n.* (pl. *-ae*). Insect from time of leaving egg till transformation into pupa (ill. MOSQUITO); grub; immature form of other animals that undergo metamorphosis. **larv'al** *adj.* [L, = 'ghost, mask']

lărўngĕc'tomy *n.* Surgical removal of the larynx.

lărўngīt'is *n.* Inflammation of lining membrane of larynx.

lărўngŏl'ogy (-ngg-) *n.* Branch of medicine dealing with diseases of throat. **lărўngŏl'ogist** *n.*

lărўng'oscōpe (-ngg-) *n.* Mirror apparatus for inspecting larynx.

lărўngŏt'omy (-ngg-) *n.* Cutting into larynx from without, esp. to provide breathing-channel.

lă'rўnx *n.* Cavity in upper part of windpipe with cartilaginous walls which when moved by muscles vary the tension of the vocal cords and hence the quality of the sound produced (ill. HEAD). **larўn'gėal** *adj.*

La Salle[1] (sahl), René Robert Cavelier, Sieur de (1640–87). French explorer of the Ohio and Mississippi rivers.

La Salle[2] (sahl), Saint-Jean Baptiste de (1651–1719). French churchman and educationist;

founder of teaching order of 'Brothers of the Christian Schools'; canonized 1900.

Lăs'car *n.* Oriental, esp. E. Indian, sailor, employed on European ships. [perh. incorrect use of Hind. *lashkar* army]

Las Casas (cahs'-), Bartolomé de (1474–1566). Spanish historian and missionary among Indians in Spanish American colonies.

lascĭv'ious *adj.* Lustful, wanton; inciting to lust. **lascĭv'iously** *adv.* **lascĭv'iousnėss** *n.*

lăsh *v.* 1. Make sudden movement of limb, tail, etc.; pour, rush, vehemently; strike violently *at*; hit or kick *out*; break *out* into excess, strong language, etc. 2. Beat with lash, flog; (of waves) beat upon; castigate in words, rebuke, satirize; urge as with whip. 3. Fasten (*down, on, to,* etc.) with cord etc.; *~-up*, temporary connexion of apparatus for experiment or in an emergency. *~ n.* 1. Stroke given with thong, whip, etc.; flexible part of whip; thong; goading influence; *the ~*, punishment of flogging. 2. Eye-lash. **lăsh'lėss** *adj.*

lăsh'er *n.* (esp.) (Water rushing over) weir, pool below weir.

lăsh'ings *n.pl.* (colloq.) Abundance *of*.

lăsque (-k) *n.* Flat or irregular diamond. [perh. Pers. *lashk* piece]

lăss (*or* lahs) *n.* Girl. **lăss'ie** *n.*

Lassalle' (-sahl), Ferdinand (1825–64). German-Jewish socialist, founder of a trade union in Leipzig.

lăss'itūde *n.* Weariness, languor; disinclination to exert or interest oneself.

lăss'ō (*or* lasōō') *n.* Long noosed rope of untanned hide for catching cattle etc.

last[1] (-ah-) *n.* Shoemaker's wooden or metal model for shaping shoe etc. on.

last[2] (-ah-) *n.* Commercial measure of weight, capacity, or quantity, varying with place and goods.

last[3] (-ah-) *adj.* After all others, coming out or belonging to the end; latest up to now; lowest, of least rank or estimation; only remaining; latest *to be*; least likely or willing or suitable; definitive; utmost, extreme; *the four ~ things*, death, judgement, heaven, hell; *~ day*, Day of Judgement, end of the world. *~ n.* Last-mentioned person or thing; last day or moments, death; last performance of certain acts; last mention; *at (long) ~*, in the end, after much delay. *~ adv.* After all others; on the last occasion before the present; in the last place, finally. **last'ly** *adv.*

last' (-ah-) *v.* Go on, remain unexhausted or adequate or alive; suffice; *~ out*, continue (esp. in vigour or use) at least as long as.

last'ĭng (-ah-) *adj.* Enduring, permanent; durable. **last'ingly** *adv.* **last'ĭngnėss** *n.* **last'ĭng** *n.* Strong twill fabric with double warp and single weft threads, used for the uppers of shoes etc.

lăt *n.* Unit of gold currency established in Latvia, 1912.

lat. *abbrev.* Latitude.

Lat. *abbrev.* Latin.

Lătaki'a (-kē-). Seaport of Syria, the ancient Laodicea ad Mare; fine kind of Turkish tobacco shipped from there.

lătch *n.* Door or gate fastening made of small bar falling into catch and lifted by lever etc. from outside; small spring-lock of outer door catching when door is closed and worked by *~-key* from outside; *on the ~*, fastened by latch only, not locked. *~ v.t.* Fasten with latch.

lătch'ėt *n.* (archaic) Thong for fastening shoe.

lāte *adj.* 1. After the due or usual time; backward in flowering, ripening, etc.; far on in day or night, or in time; far on in a period, development, etc. 2. No longer alive; no longer having specified status etc. (as *the ~ prime minister*, dead or resigned); of recent date. **lāte'nėss** (-tn-) *n.* **lāte** *adv.* After proper time; far on in time; (poet.) recently, lately; (as *n.*) *of ~*, recently.

lateen' *adj.* *~ sail*, triangular sail on long yard at angle of 45° to mast (ill. DHOW); (of ship etc.) so rigged. [Fr. (*voile*) *latine* 'Latin sail', because common in Mediterranean]

lāte'ly (-tl-) *adv.* Not long ago, in recent times.

La Tène (tĕn). Archaeological site at E. end of Lake of Neuchâtel, Switzerland; *~ culture*, that of second Iron Age of central and W. Europe, so called because objects characteristic of it were first identified at La Tène.

lāt'ent *adj.* Concealed; dormant; existing but not developed or manifest; *~ heat*: see HEAT. **lāt'ently** *adv.* **lāt'ency** *n.*

lăt'eral *adj.* Of, at, towards, from, the side(s); side-; *~ branch* (of family), branch descended from brother or sister of person in direct line; *~ consonant* (phon.) one formed by partial closure of the air-passage by the tongue, which is, however, so placed as to allow the air to escape at one or both sides of the point of contact, as e.g. *l*; *~ inversion*, that produced by a plane mirror; *~ line*, part of nervous system of fish, enabling it to feel water disturbances and locate the objects that cause them (ill. FISH). **lăt'erally** *adv.* **lăt'eral** *n.* Side part, member or object, esp. lateral shoot or branch; lateral consonant.

Lăt'eran. Site in Rome containing the basilica of St. John the Baptist (*St. John ~*) cathedral church of Rome, and the *~ Palace*, where the popes resided until 14th c.; *~ Councils*, 5 general ecclesiastical councils or synods of the western Church, held in St. John Lateran (1123, 1139, 1179, 1215, 1512–17); *~ Treaty*, concordat between kingdom of Italy and Holy See, signed 1929 in Lateran Palace, and recognizing as fully sovereign and independent a new (papal) State called Vatican City.

lăt'erīte *n.* (geol.) Superficial deposit rich in iron and aluminium oxides, red or yellow in colour, developed by weathering of rocks in some wet tropical climates.

lāt'ĕx *n.* Milky fluid of a number of plants, exuding from cut surfaces and sometimes coagulating rapidly on exposure, used as the raw material of several commercial products, esp. rubber. [L, = 'liquid']

lath (lah-) *n.* (pl. pr. -dhz). Thin narrow strip of wood esp. for use as support for slates or plaster or as material for trellis or Venetian blind; *~ and plaster*, material for face of walls, ceilings, partitions, etc. (ill. HALF) *~ v.t.* Provide (wall, ceiling) with laths.

lāthe[1] (-dh) *n.* One of (now 5) administrative districts in Kent.

lāthe[2] (-dh) *n.* Machine for turning wood, metal, ivory, etc., by rotating the article to be turned against tools which cut it to the required shape; machine with horizontal revolving disc for throwing and turning pottery.

lăth'er (-dh-) *n.* Froth made by agitation of mixture of soap, or other detergent, and water; frothy sweat of horse. **lăth'ery** *adj.* **lăth'er** *v.* 1. Cover (esp. chin etc. for shaving) with lather; (of horse) become covered with lather; (of soap etc.) form lather. 2. Beat, thrash.

lathi (laht'ĭ) *n.* (Anglo-Ind.) Long heavy stick, usu. of bamboo bound with iron, used as weapon.

lātĭfŭn'dia *n. pl.* 1. (Rom. hist.) Large mainly pastoral estates, mostly in Calabria, Apulia, and N. Africa, worked by slaves or poor tenants. 2. Any large agricultural estates.

Lăt'imer, Hugh (*c* 1485–1555). English bishop, one of the leaders in the English Reformation; burnt at the stake at Oxford with Ridley during Mary I's reign.

Lăt'in *n.* 1. Indo-European language of ancient Latium and of the Romans; until modern times the language of school, Church, and State in Western Europe; its history comprises: *Old ~*, before *c* 75 B.C.; *Classical ~*, the literary language from *c* 75 B.C. to *c* A.D. 175; *Late ~*, post-classical literary language to *c* A.D. 600; *Low* or *Vulgar ~*, the popular speech in the post-classical period; *Medieval ~*, from *c* 600 to *c* 1500; *New* or *Modern ~*, the Latin of modern times, employed chiefly in scientific descriptions and classifications. 2. Inhabitant or native of ancient Latium. 3. (hist.) During the Crusades, member of western nations of Europe (as dist. from 'Greeks'). *~ adj.* 1. Of Latium or the ancient

Latins; of, written in, the Latin language. 2. Of that branch of the Christian Church which acknowledges the primacy of the bishop of Rome (the pope) and uses the Latin language in its rites and formularies. 3. Of the European peoples speaking languages descended from Latin. 4. ~ *America*, all Spanish-, Portuguese-, or French-speaking parts of America. ~ *Church*: see 2; ~ *cross*, plain cross with lower member longer than the other three (ill. CROSS); ~ *League*, (Rom. hist.), confederation of cities of Latium, merged in Roman State 338 B.C.; ~ *Quarter*, district of Paris on left or S. bank of Seine, where students and artists live and principal university buildings are situated; ~ *square*, a square conceived as consisting of *n* letters, *a*, *b*, *c*, ..., *n*, arranged in a square lattice of n^2 compartments, all the compartments being occupied so that no letter occurs twice in the same row or in the same column.

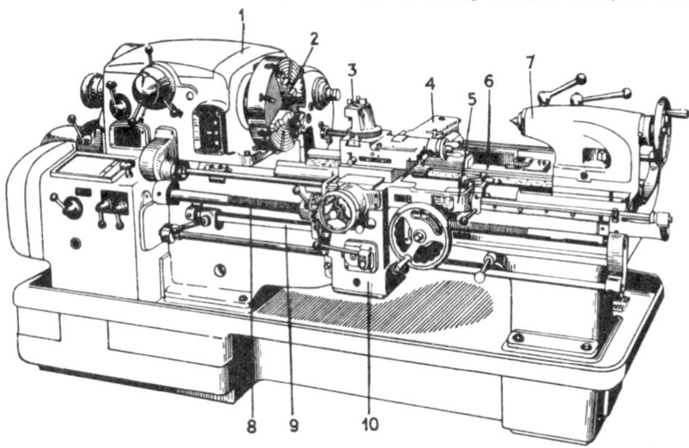

LATHE

1. Headstock. 2. Chuck. 3. Tool-post. 4. Cross-slide. 5. Saddle. 6. Bed-plate. 7. Tail-stock. 8. Leadscrew. 9. Feed-shaft. 10. Apron

Lăt'inism *n.* Idiom characteristic of Latin, esp. one used in another language; conformity in style to Latin models. **Lăt'inist** *n.* Latin scholar. **Latin'ity** *n.* Manner of speaking or writing Latin.

lăt'inize *v.* Give Latin form to.

Lăt'inless *adj.* Ignorant of Latin.

Latin'us. (Rom. legend) Eponymous hero of Latins, son of Faunus and the nymph Marica, king of Latium and father of Lavinia, whom Aeneas married.

lăt'itūde *n.* 1. Breadth, width (now only joc.); scope, full extent (rare). 2. Freedom from narrowness; liberality of interpretation; tolerated variety of attitude or opinion. 3. (geog.) Angular distance on a meridian (ill. PROJECTION); place's angular distance on its meridian, N. or S. of equator, measured from the earth's centre; (usu. pl.) regions, climes (esp. with ref. to temperature; (astron.) angular distance of heavenly body from ecliptic. **lătitūd'inal** *adj.*

lătitūdinār'ian *adj.* Tolerating, characterized by, latitude of opinion, esp. in religious matters. **lătitūdinār'ianism** *n.*

Lā'tium (-shĭ-). Ancient name of district of central Italy lying S. of Apennines and E. of Tiber.

Latō'na (Greek **Leto**). (Gk and Rom. myth.) Daughter of a Titan; mother, by Zeus, of Artemis and Apollo.

latrine' (-ēn) *n.* Privy, esp. in camp, barracks, hospital, etc.

lătt'en *adj.* & *n.* (Of) a yellow alloy of copper, zinc, lead, and tin, used for monumental 'brasses', church candlesticks, etc.

lătt'er *adj.* Later, second (archaic); belonging to end of period, world, etc.; second-mentioned (opp. to *former*); ~*-day*, modern; ~*-day saints*, MORMONS; ~ *end*, death. ~ *n.* Second-mentioned thing or person.

lătt'erly *adv.* Towards the end of life or some period; nowadays, of late.

lătt'ice *n.* 1. Framework of wood or other material made of laths crossed diagonally so as to form a net-like structure serving as screen, door, etc.; ~ (*-work*), laths, etc., so arranged. 2. Arrangement of points representing the relative position of corresponding atomic or molecular centres in the structure units of a crystal. 3. ~ *frame, girder*, girder made of 2 flanges connected by iron lattice-work (ill. GIRDER); ~ *window*, one having lattice; one with small panes set in diagonally crossing strips of lead (ill. WINDOW). **lătt'iced** (-st) *adj.*

Lăt'via. Area on the E. and S. shore of the Gulf of Riga; formerly a Baltic province of the Russian Empire; proclaimed an independent republic in 1918; incorporated in the Soviet Union in 1940 as a constituent republic; capital, Riga. **Lăt'vian** *adj.* & *n.*

laud[1] *n.* 1. Praise, hymn of praise (rare). 2. (pl.) First of day-hours of Church. ~ *v.t.* Praise, celebrate. **laudā'tion, laudāt'or** *ns.* **laud'ative, laud'atory** *adjs.*

Laud[2], William (1573–1645). English churchman; archbishop of Canterbury 1633–45; supported Charles I in his struggle with Parliament; was impeached for treason by Long Parliament, 1640, condemned, and beheaded.

laud'able *adj.* Commendable, praiseworthy. **laudabil'ity** *n.* **laud'ably** *adv.*

laud'anum (lŏdn-) *n.* Tincture of opium. [name given by Paracelsus to a costly medicament, later transferred to preparations containing opium]

laudāt'ōr těm'porĭs ăc'tī *n.* One who prefers the good old days. [L, = 'praiser of time past'.]

laugh (lahf) *v.* Make the sounds and the movements of face and sides by which lively amusement, sense of the ludicrous, exultation, and scorn, are instinctively expressed; have these emotions; utter laughingly; get (person) *out of* habit, belief, etc., by ridicule; (of inanimate objects) be lively with play of movement or light; ~ *up one's sleeve*, be secretly amused; ~ *out of court*, deprive of a hearing by ridicule; ~ *at*, make fun of, ridicule; ~ *away*, dismiss (subject) with a laugh; while away (time) with jests; ~ *down*, silence with laughter; ~ *off*, get rid of (embarrassment etc.) with a jest. ~ *n.* Sound or act of laughing; *have, get, the* ~ *of*, turn the tables on assailant. **laugh'able** *adj.* Exciting laughter, amusing. **laugh'ably** *adv.*

laugh'ing (lahf-) *n.* (esp.) *no* ~ *matter*, serious thing, not a fit subject for laughter; ~*-gas*, nitrous oxide, used as anaesthetic, and producing exhilarating effects when inhaled; ~*-stock*, person or thing exciting general ridicule. **laugh'ing** *adj.* ~ *hyena*: see HYENA; ~ *jackass*: see JACKASS; **laugh'ingly** *adv.*

laugh'ter (lahf-) *n.* Act, sound, of laughing.

launce (lahns) *n.* Sand-eel.

Launcelot: see LANCELOT.

launch[1] (law-, lah-) *v.* 1. Hurl, discharge, send forth (missile, blow, threat, etc.); burst (*out*) *into*

LAUNCHING A SHIP

1. Slipway. 2, 3. Launching cradle (2. Fore poppets, 3. Aft poppets). 4, 5. Launching ways (4. Sliding ways, 5. Standing ways)

expense, strong language, etc.; ~ *out*, spend money freely, expatiate in words; *launching-pad*, platform from which rocket or guided missile is launched. 2. Set (vessel) afloat, cause to slide from land or stocks into water; send off, start, on a course; go *forth, out*, on an enterprise. ~ *n.* Process of launching ship.

launch[2] (law-, lah-) *n.* Man-of-war's largest boat, rather flat-bottomed and usu. sloop-rigged; large electric or steam or motor boat for passengers, pleasure trips, etc.

laun'der (law-, lah-) *v.* Wash and iron (linen etc.); (of fabric) bear laundering (*well* etc.)

laun'dress (law-, lah-) *n.* Woman who launders; caretaker of chambers in Inns of Court.

laun'dry (law-, lah-) *n.* Room or establishment for washing linen; batch of clothes etc. sent to or from laundry.

Laur'a. Subject of love-poems of PETRARCH, by tradition Laura de Noves (*c* 1308–48), wife of Count Hugues de Sade.

laur'ėate *adj.* Wreathed with, (of wreath) consisting of, laurels; worthy of laurels as poet, orator, etc.; *poet* ~, poet receiving stipend as officer of British Royal Household, writer of poems for State occasions. ~ *n.* Poet laureate. **laur'ėateship** *n.*

lau'rel (lŏ-) *n.* 1. Bay-tree, *Laurus nobilis* (rare); foliage of this as emblem of victory or poetic merit; *rest on one's* ~, cease to strive for further glory; *look to one's* ~*s*, beware of losing pre-eminence. 2. Various trees and shrubs with leaves resembling those of bay, esp. *Cerasus laurocerasus* (cherry-~); ~*-magnolia* (U.S.) sweet magnolia, sweet bay, *Magnolia virginiana*; ~ *oak* (U.S.) N. Amer. species of oak. ~ *v.t.* Wreathe with laurel.

Lau'rence (lŏ-), St. (3rd c.). Roman Christian martyr; usu. represented with a gridiron, the instrument of his martyrdom.

Laurĕn'tian (-shan) **Library.** Library in Florence founded by Lorenzo de' Medici in 15th c. and housed in building partly designed by Michelangelo.

laurustīn'us *n.* Evergreen flowering shrub, *Viburnum tinus*.

la'va (lah-) *n.* Molten rock which flows down sides of volcano (ill. VOLCANO); solid substance this cools into; kind, bed, of lava.

lavāb'ō *n.* Ritual washing of celebrant's hands at offertory (accompanied in Roman rite by saying of Ps. xxvi); towel or basin used for this; washing-trough in some medieval monasteries. [L, = 'I will wash', first wd of Ps. xxvi]

Lavăl', Pierre (1883–1945). French politician, several times prime minister of France, 1930–6; head of the VICHY Government, 1942–4; condemned and shot for treason, 1945.

La Vallière (vălyār'), Louise Françoise de (1644–1710). Mistress of Louis XIV.

Lavat'er (-vah-), Johann Kaspar (1741–1801). Swiss poet, theologian, and student of physiognomy.

lăv'atory *n.* Room etc. for washing hands and face (rare); (now usu. euphem.) water-closet, urinal.

lāve *v.t.* (poet.) Wash, bathe; wash against, flow along.

lăv'ėnder *n.* Small lilac-flowered narrow-leaved shrubs, *Lavandula* species, native in S. Europe and N. Africa, extensively cultivated for their perfume; flowers and stalks of this laid among linen etc.; pale-blue colour with trace of red; *French* ~, *L. spica*; *sea* ~, *Limonium vulgare*; ~*-water*, perfume of distilled lavender, alcohol, and ambergris. ~ *v.t.* Put lavender among (linen).

lāv'er[1] *n.* Kinds of marine algae, esp. the edible species.

lāv'er[2] *n.* (bibl.) Large brazen vessel for Jewish priests' ablutions; (archaic) washing or fountain basin, font.

lăv'erock (-vr-) *n.* (Chiefly Sc.) LARK[1].

Lavīn'ia. (Rom. legend) Daughter of Latinus, king of Latium, and wife of Aeneas.

lăv'ish *adj.* Giving or producing without stint, profuse, prodigal; very or too abundant. **lăv'ishly** *adv.* **lăv'ishnėss** *n.* **lăv'ish** *v.t.* Bestow or spread profusely.

Lavoisier (-vwahzyā'), Antoine Laurent (1743–94). French chemist; laid the foundations of modern chemistry by giving a correct explanation of the part played by oxygen in combustion; discovered animal metabolism.

law[1] *n.* 1. Body of enacted or customary rules recognized by a community as binding; one of these rules; their controlling influence, law-abiding state of society (freq. ~ *and order*); the laws as a system or science, jurisprudence; binding injunction(s); one of the branches of the study of law, laws concerning specified department; statute and common law (opp. EQUITY); the legal profession; legal knowledge; judicial remedy, law-courts as providing it, litigation; *the* ~ (*of Moses*): see MOSAIC law; ~ *of the Medes and Persians*, unalterable law (see Dan. vi. 12); *lay down the* ~, talk authoritatively, hector; *be a* ~ *unto oneself*, take one's own line, disregard convention; *international* ~, ~ *of nations*, law regulating relations between states; *take the* ~ *into one's own hands*, redress one's wrong by force. 2. Rule of action or procedure, esp. in an art, department of life, or game; (also ~ *of nature*), correct statement of invariable sequence between specified conditions and specified phenomenon; laws of nature, regularity of nature. 3. Allowance, start, given to hunted animal or competitor in race; time of grace, respite. 4. ~*-abiding*, obedient to law; ~*-calf*, unstained calf used for binding law-books; ~*-court*: see COURT; the *L*~ *Courts*, (esp.) the Royal Courts of Justice, building in Strand, London, in which the superior courts of law and appeal are held; ~ *French*, Anglo-Norman terms used in law-books and law; *law'giver*, one who makes (esp. code of) laws; ~*-hand*, handwriting used in legal documents; ~ *Latin*, barbarous Latin of early English statutes; ~*-lord*, member of House of Lords qualified to assist in its legal work, as being one of the Lords of Appeal in Ordinary or as having held high judicial office; ~ *merchant*, laws regulating trade and commerce, differing in some respects from common law; ~*-officer*, legal functionary and adviser of the Government, esp. Attorney- or Solicitor-General; ~*-stationer*, one selling stationery needed by lawyers and taking in documents to be engrossed; *law'suit*, prosecution of claim in law-court; ~*-term*, period appointed for sitting of law-courts.

law[2], **lawk(s)**, **laws**, *int.* (vulg.) expressing astonishment.

Law[3], Andrew Bonar (1858–1923). Canadian-born Conservative politician, of Scottish origin; Prime Minister of Gt Britain 1922–3.

Law[4], John (1671–1729). Scotsman, who became controller-general of French finance; established (1716) 'Banque Générale', first bank of any kind in France; initiated 'Mississippi Scheme' by which in return for exclusive trading-rights with Louisiana he undertook to pay off French national debt; the failure of the scheme and the ruin of many speculators caused him to flee from France.

Law[5], William (1686–1761). Nonjuror and spiritual writer. Author of 'A Serious Call to a Devout and Holy Life', 1728.

law'ful *adj.* Permitted, appointed, qualified, recognized, by law; not illegal or illegitimate. **law'fully** *adv.* **law'fulnėss** *n.*

law'lėss *adj.* Without law, not regulated by law; regardless of, disobedient to, uncontrolled by, law; unbridled, licentious. **law'lėssnėss** *n.*

lawn[1] *n.* Very fine material of plain weave, made orig. of linen, now usu. of cotton. [prob. f. *Laon* in France].

lawn[2] *n.* (Extent of) grass-covered land; close-mown turf-covered piece of pleasure-ground or garden; ~*-mower*, machine with revolving spiral blades for mowing lawn; ~ *tennis*, modification of tennis played (usu. out of doors) on lawn or other prepared ground between two (*singles*) or four (*doubles*) players, with rackets and felt-covered, hollow, india-rubber balls.

Law'rence[1] (lŏ-), David Herbert (1885–1930). English novelist, poet, critic, and writer of travel books.

Law'rence[2] (lŏ-), Sir Thomas (1769–1830), English portrait-painter.

Law'rence[3] (lŏ-), Thomas Edward (1888–1935). British soldier and scholar; one of the leaders, in war of 1914–18, of Arab revolt and guerrilla warfare against Turks, described by him in the 'Seven Pillars of Wisdom'.

law'yer *n.* Member of legal profession, esp. attorney, solicitor; person versed in law.

lăx[1] *n.* Swedish or Norwegian salmon.

lăx[2] *adj.* Loose, relaxed, not compact, porous (rare); negligent, careless, not strict, vague. **lăx'ly** *adv.* **lăx'ĭty** *n.*

lăx'ative *adj.* & *n.* (Medicine) tending to loosen the bowels.

lay[1] *n.* Short lyric or narrative poem meant to be sung; (loosely) song, poem.

lay[2] *adj.* Non-clerical, not in orders; of, done by, layman or laity; non-professional, not expert (esp. with ref. to law or medicine); ~ *brother, sister*, person who has taken habit and vows of religious order but is employed in manual labour and excused other duties; ~ *clerk*, singing man in cathedral or collegiate church; parish clerk; *lay'man*, one of the laity; non-expert in regard to some profession, art, or science; ~ *reader*, layman licensed to conduct religious services.

lay[3] *adj.* ~ *figure*, jointed wooden figure of human body used by artists, in absence of human model, for arranging drapery on etc.; hence, unimportant person, non-entity; unreal character in novel etc. [Du. *led* joint].

lay[4] *v.* (past t. and past part. *laid*). Place on a surface or in horizontal position; spread, apply (paint etc.); cause to subside (ghost, dust, storm, etc.); impose (obligation etc.); beat down (crops); set (trap) in readiness; aim (cannon); wager (stake); produce (egg); make (rope) by twisting yarn; ~ *an information*, bring legal indictment; ~ *at the door of*, attribute to; ~ *by*, store; ~ *by the heels*, imprison; ~ *down*, relinquish (office etc.), formulate (principle), store (wine) in cellar; ~ *hands on*, attack or seize, (of bishop) confirm or ordain; ~ *off* (employee), dismiss temporarily owing to shortage of work; ~ *on*, provide for supply of (water, electricity, etc.); (slang) arrange, organize; ~ *out*, prepare (corpse) for burial; (slang) kill, knock down, exhaust, (person); dispose, arrange, (grounds etc.); ~ *papers*, put them on table in House of Commons for M.P.s' information; ~ *table, breakfast*, etc., prepare for meal; ~ *to the charge of*, impute to; ~ *up*, save, store, (pass.) be incapacitated by illness; *laid paper*, paper having ribs (*laid lines*) on surface caused by wires of cylinder on which it is dried. ~ *n.* (slang) Line of business, job; pursuit; direction or amount of twist in rope-strands; way, position, or direction in which something (esp. country) lies; lie; ~-*out*, arrangement of ground, printed page, advertisement, etc.; plan or drawing indicating this.

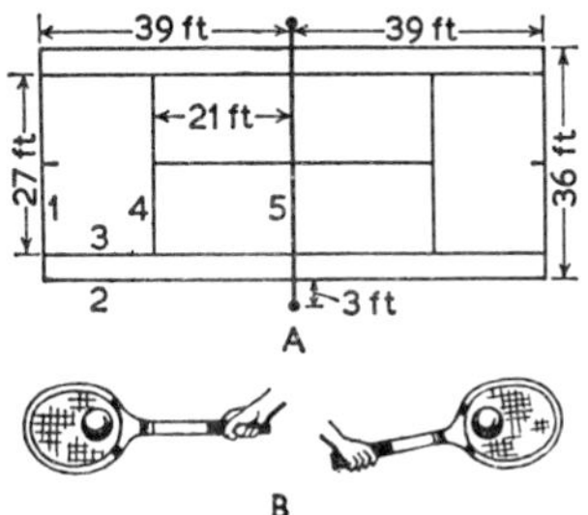

LAWN TENNIS: A. COURT. B. RACKETS SHOWING FORE-HAND AND BACKHAND STROKES

1. Base-line. 2. Doubles side-line. 3. Singles side line. 4. Service-line. 5. Net

lay'-bȳ *n.* Slack part of river in which barges are laid by out of use; railway siding; roadside recess in which vehicles can stop without obstructing the traffic.

Lay'amon (*c* 1200). Middle English poet; author of an alliterative verse chronicle of England, the first known account in English of the stories of Arthur, Lear, and Cymbeline.

lay'er *n.* (esp.) 1. Stratum, thickness of matter (esp. one of several) spread over surface. 2. (gardening) Shoot fastened into earth to strike root while attached to parent plant. 3. Oyster-bed. ~ *v.t.* Propagate by layers.

layĕtte' *n.* Clothes, toilet articles, and bedding, needed for new-born child.

lay'stall (-awl) *n.* Refuse heap.

lăz'ar *n.* Poor and diseased person, esp. leper; ~-*house*, lazaretto. [f. LAZARUS]

lăzarĕt'(tō) *n.* Hospital (chiefly in foreign countries) for diseased poor, esp. lepers; building or ship for performance of quarantine; after part of ship's hold used for stores.

Lăz'arus. (N.T.) 1. Brother of Martha and Mary of Bethany, restored to life by Jesus after 4 days in the tomb. 2. The beggar in the parable of the rich man and the beggar (Luke xvi. 19–25).

lāze *v.* (colloq.) Be lazy; pass (time) *away* in laziness. ~ *n.* Lazy time.

lāz'y *adj.* Averse to labour, slothful; appropriate to, inducing, indolence; ~-*bones*, lazy person; ~-*daisy*, kind of quickly worked embroidery stitch producing long loop with end held down by small stitch; ~-*tongs*, arrangement of several pairs of levers crossing and pivoted at centre like scissors, for picking up objects at a distance, **lāz'ily** *adv.* **lāz'inėss** *n.*

lb. *abbrev.* *Libra(e)* = pound(s) in weight.

l.b. *abbrev.* Leg-bye (in cricket).

l.b.w. leg before wicket.

L.C. *abbrev.* Left centre (of stage).

L.C.(T.) *abbrev.* Landing Craft (Tank).

l.c. *abbrev.* *loco citato* (= in the passage already quoted); lower case (of print).

L.C.C. *abbrev.* London County Council.

L.C.J. *abbrev.* Lord Chief Justice.

L.C.M. *abbrev.* Lowest common multiple; Landing Craft for Mechanized Vehicles.

L.C.P. *abbrev.* Licentiate of the College of Preceptors.

L.-Cpl *abbrev.* Lance-Corporal.

Ld *abbrev.* Limited; Lord.

L.D.S. *abbrev.* Licentiate in Dental Surgery.

lea[1] *n.* (poet.) Tract of open ground, esp. grass land.

lea[2] *n.* (spinning) Measure of length, varying acc. to type of yarn.

leach *v.t.* Make (liquid) percolate through some material; subject (bark, ore) to action of percolating fluid; purge (soluble matter) *away* etc. by such means. **leach'ing** *n.* (esp.) Washing of organic and mineral salts into lower layer of soil by percolating rain-water.

lead[1] (lĕd) *n.* 1. Heavy soft easily fusible metallic element of dull bluish-grey colour, usu. obtained from ~ *sulphide* (the principal ore, PbS) by roasting in a furnace; being malleable it may be rolled into sheets or foil or drawn into tubes or pipes; it is used in building, for tanks, for sheathing electric cables, for storage batteries, etc.; symbol Pb, at. no. 82, at. wt 207·19; *red* ~, red oxide of lead, used as pigment and in glass-making; *white* ~, mixture of lead carbonate and lead hydroxide, used as pigment; ~ *wool*, lead in fibrous state used for jointing water-pipes. 2. Lump of lead used in sounding depth of water; *cast, heave, the* ~, make sounding with this; *swing the* ~, (slang) malinger. 3. (print.) Metal strip for spacing out lines or letters of type. 4. (pl.) Strips of lead used to cover roof; piece of (esp. horizontal) lead-covered roof; lead frames holding glass of lattices or painted window. 5. Graphite (only in ref. to ~ *pencil*, thin stick of prepared graphite encased in wood or inserted in holder). 6. *black*-~, graphite; ~ *poisoning*, form of poisoning caused by absorption of lead into the system, plumbism; *leads'man*, sailor who takes soundings with the lead. ~ *v.t.* Cover, weight, frame (panes etc.) with lead; (print.) separate lines or letters of (type) with leads. **lead'lėss** *adj.*

lead[2] (lēd) *v.* (past t. and past part. *lĕd*). 1. Conduct, guide, esp. by going in front; (of commander) direct movements of; ~ *captive*, take away as prisoner; ~ one *a dance*, give him much trouble to secure his end; ~ *the way*, go first. 2. Conduct (person) by the hand or contact, (animal) by halter etc.; guide by persuasion; guide actions or opinions of, induce *to* do; ~ *astray*, esp. tempt to sin etc.; ~ *by the nose*, induce to do unconsciously all one wishes. 3. (Of road etc.) conduct (usu. abs.) *to* place; (fig.) have as result. 4. Make (rope, water, etc.) go through pulley, channel, etc. 5. Pass, go through, spend, (life etc.). 6. Have first place in; go first; be first at some point in race; direct by example; set (fashion); be official director or spokesman of (party, esp. in Houses of Parliament); act as leading counsel in (legal case, or abs.); have chief role in play etc. 7. (Cards) play as first card, be first player, in trick; play one of (suit) when leading; ~ *away from*, play when leading one of same suit as (ace etc.); ~ *up to*, play so as to elicit (specified card). 8. ~ *away*, (usu. in pass.) induce to follow unthinkingly; ~ *off*, begin (dance, conversation, etc.); ~ *on*, entice into going farther than was intended; ~ *up to*, form preparation for, serve to introduce, direct conversation towards, (subject). 9. Ply (witness) with leading questions. ~ *n.* 1. Direction given by going in front, example; leading place, leadership; (theatr.) (player of) chief part; (cards) act or right of playing first; *give person a* ~, encourage him by doing thing, esp. leaping fence in hunting, first. 2. Artificial watercourse, esp. leading to mill; (elect.) connecting-wire to or from an electric device (~*-in*, wire connecting external aerial to wireless receiver); channel in ice-field. 3. Strap, strip of leather, etc., for leading dog.

leaden (lĕd'n) *adj.* (As) of LEAD[1]; heavy slow, burdensome; inert, deadening; lead-coloured.

Lead'enhall (lĕd'nhawl). Meat and poultry market in City of London. [f. hall with lead roof which stood at corner of Gracechurch St]

lead'er (lēd-) *n.* (esp.) 1. Counsel who leads in case; Q.C.; senior counsel of circuit. 2. *L~ of House* (*of Commons*), member of Government with official initiative in business. 3. (mus.) Chief violin-player in orchestra, string quartet, etc.; (U.S.) conductor. 4. Front horse in team or tandem. 5. Shoot growing at apex of stem or principal branch. 6. LEADING article. 7. (print.) Line of dots or dashes to guide eye. **lead'erless** *adj.* **lead'ership** *n.*

leaderĕtte' *n.* Short editorial paragraph in same type as leading article.

lead'ing (lēd-) *n.* (esp.) *Men of light and* ~, men of deserved influence; ~*-rein*, rein to lead horse with; ~ *strings*, straps or strings for supporting and guiding young children learning to walk; *in* ~*-strings*, in a state of pupilage. ~ *adj.* (esp.) ~ *article*, article in newspaper etc. in prominent position and expressing editorial opinion; (commerc.) article of trade sold at low price to attract custom for other things; ~ *case*, (law) case serving as precedent for deciding others; ~ *edge*, foremost edge of wing, tail, or fin of an aeroplane; ~ *lady*, *man*, actor taking chief part in play etc.; ~ *note*, 7th note in ascending scale, leading the ear to expect the tonic (ill. SCALE); ~ *question*, question that suggests the answer the questioner wishes to receive.

leadscrew (lēd'-) *n.* (eng.) Screw parallel to bed of lathe, which moves the saddle carrying tool for cutting screw threads (ill. LATHE).

leaf *n.* 1. Expanded organ (usu. green) of plant springing from side of stem or branch or directly from root; (pop.) petal (esp. *rose*-~); foliage; in ~, with leaves out; *fall of the* ~, autumn. 2. Leaves of plant cultivated for commercial purposes, e.g. tobacco, tea. 3. Single thickness of folded paper, esp. in book; very thin sheet of metal, esp. gold or silver, or horn, marble, etc.; *turn over new* ~, mend one's ways. 4. Hinged part or flap of door, shutter, table, bridge, etc.; slab inserted in expansible table. 5. (dial. and U.S.) Layer of fat round pig's kidneys; inside fat of other animals. 6. ~ *brass*, brass foil; ~*-mould*, mould mixed with decaying leaves, used as fertilizer. **leaf'age** *n.* **leaf'lèss** *adj.* **leaf'lèssnèss** *n.* **leaf'y** *adj.* **leaf'inèss** *n.*

leaf'lèt *n.* 1. (bot.) One division of compound leaf; young leaf. 2. Small leaf of paper, or sheet folded but not stitched, with printed matter, esp. for gratuitous distribution.

league[1] (lēg) *n.* (archaic) Measure of road-distance, usu. about 3 miles.

league[2] (lēg) *n.* Compact for mutual protection and assistance or prosecution of common interests; parties to such compact; *in* ~ *with*, allied with; ~ *football*, *cricket*, etc., football, cricket, etc., in which clubs forming a league play each other for championship. ~ *v.* Join in league.

League of Nations. Association of self-governing States, colonies, and dominions created by covenant in 1919 peace treaty 'in order to promote international co-operation and to achieve international peace and security'; superseded (1945) by the UNITED NATIONS.

leag'uer[1] (-ger) *n.* Member of league.

leag'uer[2] (-ger) *n.* (archaic) Camp, esp. for purpose of siege; siege.

Lē'ah (-*a*). (O.T.) Elder daughter of Laban and wife of Jacob (Gen. xxix, xxx).

leak *n.* Hole caused by injury, wear, etc., through which liquid makes way into or out of vessel that is immersed in or contains it; water passing through such a hole into a ship; liquid, steam, or gas, escaping through a flaw in a receptacle; escape of electric charge from an incompletely insulated conductor; (*grid*) ~, (wireless) high resistance placed in parallel with a grid condenser to prevent an over-accumulation of negative charge on the grid. ~ *v.i.* Let liquid out or in through a leak; (of liquids, steam, gases) pass into, or out of, a receptacle etc. through a flaw, crack, etc.; ~ *out*, (of secrets etc.) become known improperly through carelessness or treachery. **leak'age** *n.* What leaks out or in; transpiring of secrets; unexplained continuous disappearance of money pointing to embezzlement etc.

leak'y *adj.* Having leak(s); given to letting out secrets; **leak'inèss** *n.*

leal (lēl) *adj.* (Sc. and literary) Loyal, honest; *land of the* ~, heaven.

lean[1] *adj.* Thin, not plump; meagre, of poor quality, innutritious; unremunerative; (of meat) consisting chiefly of muscular tissue, not of fat; ~ *years*, years of scarcity. ~ *n.* Lean part of meat.

lean[2] *v.* (past t. and past part. *leaned* or *leant* pr. lĕnt). Incline one's body against something for support; be or put in sloping position, *against*, *on*; incline body *back*, *forward*, etc.; stand obliquely, out of the perpendicular; rely or depend (*up*)*on*; have tendency *to*, be partial *to* cause, opinion, person, etc.; ~*-to*, building with rafters resting against side of another, pent-house. ~ *n.* Inclination, slope.

Lèăn'der: see HERO[2].

Lèăn'der Club. Oldest English rowing club, founded early in 19th c. and reorganized 1862; now mainly composed of university men.

leap *v.* (past t. and past part. *leapt* pr. lĕpt). Jump (still in poet., literary and dignified use); ~*-frog*, game in which players vault over, by placing hands upon, bent back or shoulders of others. ~ *n.* Jump; thing to be jumped; ~ *in the dark*, hazardous attempt of doubtful issue; *by* ~*s and bounds*, with startlingly rapid progress; ~*-year*, year in which an extra day (~*-day*, 29th Feb.) is inserted to make civil year conform with *tropical year* of 365·242 days (in Gregorian calendar it occurs every 4th year, i.e. whenever date is divisible by 4, but not in century years unless divisible by 400); ~*-year proposal*, proposal of marriage made by woman to man, traditionally allowable only in leap-year.

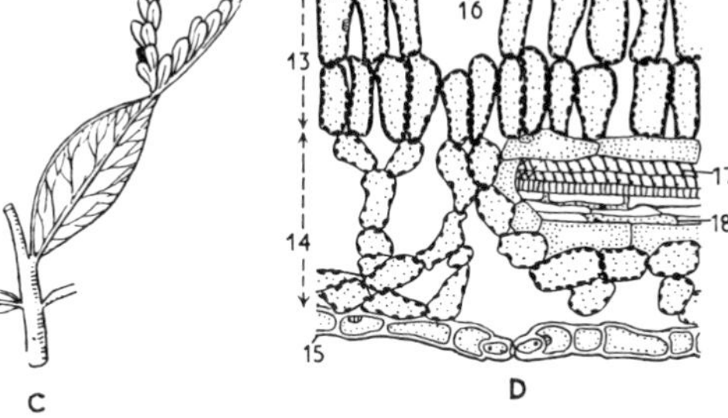

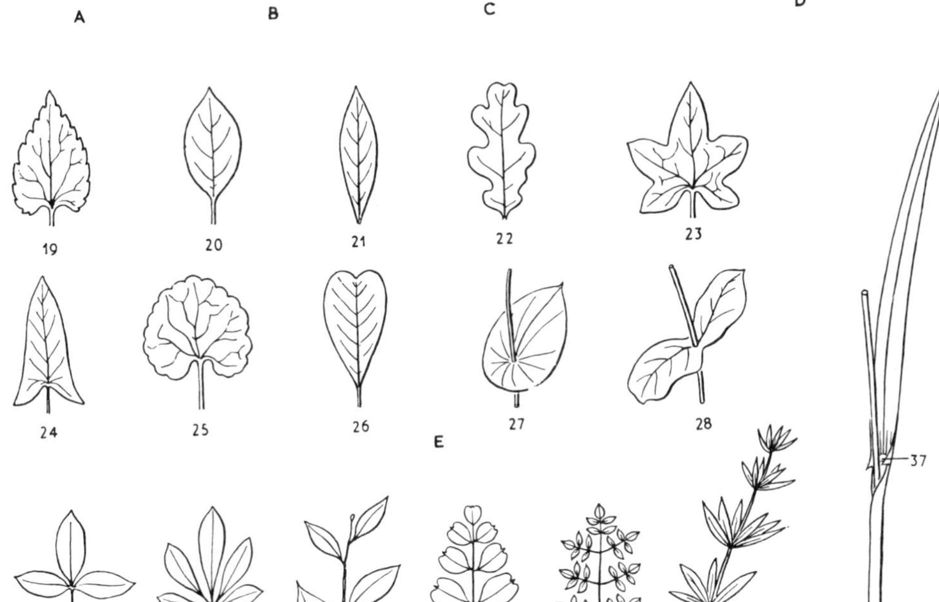

LEAVES: A. LEAF GROWTH. B. PARTS OF LEAF. C. PHYLLODE. D. MAGNIFIED SECTION OF LEAF. E. SIMPLE LEAVES. F. COMPOUND LEAVES (EXCEPT 34 AND 36)

A. 1. Cauline (sessile). 2. Radical. 3. Node. 4. Internode. B. 5. Axil. 6. Stipule. 7. Petiole. 8. Rachis. 9. Blade or lamina 10. Midrib. 11. Vein or nervure. D. 12. Epidermis. 13, 14. Mesophyll (13. Palisade, 14. Spongy parenchyma). 15. Cuticle. 16. Stoma. 17. Xylem. 18. Phloem. E. 19. Cordate, serrate, 20. Ovate, acuminate. 21. Lanceolate. 22. Sinuate. 23. Palmately lobed. 24. Hastate. 25. Reniform, crenate. 26. Obtuse. 27. Perfoliate. 28. Connate. F. 29. Trifoliate. 30. Palmate. 31. Alternate. 32. Pinnate, opposite, with mucronate leaflets. 33. Bipinnate. 34. Whorled. 35. Pinna. 36. Monocotyledonous leaf. 37. Ligule. (All except 36 are dicotyledonous.)

Lear[1]. Legendary British king, a supposed descendant of Aeneas; subject of one of Shakeapeare's tragedies.

Lear[2], Edward (1812–88). English artist, traveller, and writer of nonsense verse; author and illustrator of 'The Book of Nonsense' (1846), which popularized the LIMERICK.

learn (lẽrn) *v.* (past t. and past part. *learnt* or *learned*). Get knowledge of or skill in by study, experience, or being taught; commit to memory (esp. ~ *by heart* or *rote*); become aware *that*, *how*, etc., be informed of, ascertain; receive instruction; (archaic, joc., or vulg.) teach.

learn'ėd (lẽr-) *adj.* Deeply read, erudite; showing profound knowledge; (in conventional use in House of Commons, law-court, etc.) learned in the law; (of language, profession, etc.) pursued or studied by, (of words) introduced by, learned men. **learn'ėdly** *adv.*

learn'ing (lẽr-) *n.* (esp.) (Possession of) knowledge got by study, esp. of language or literary or historical science; *the new* ~, studies, esp. of Greek, introduced into England in 16th c., renaissance.

lease[1] (-s) *n.* Contract by which lessor (landlord), usu. in consideration of rent, conveys land or tenement to lessee (tenant), either for specified time or for a period terminable at the will of either party; *lease'hold*, (real property) held by lease. ~ *v.t.* Grant or take lease of; ~*-lend*, applied orig. in 1941 to an arrangement whereby sites in British possessions overseas were leased to U.S. in exchange for the loan of destroyers; later extended to the arrangement under the Lease-Lend Act, signed by President Roosevelt on 11th Mar. 1941, whereby military equipment and war supplies of U.S. were lent or leased to the governments of the allied nations, also known as *lend-lease*; *reverse lease-lend*, similar aid rendered to U.S. by the United Kingdom.

lease[2] (-s) *n.* Crossing of warp-threads in loom; LEASH, sense 2.

leash *n.* 1. Thong in which hounds or coursing-dogs are held; set of three hounds, hares, etc. 2. (weaving) Cord with eye to receive warp-thread extending between parallel laths of loom-heddle. ~ *v.t.* Connect, hold in, with leash.

leas'ing (-z-) *n.* (bibl.) Lying, lie.

least *adj.* Smallest, slightest; *the* ~ (esp. after neg.) any however small. ~ *n.* Least amount; *to say the* ~ *of it*, to put the case moderately; *at* ~, at all events, even if a wider statement is disputable; at the lowest computation; (*in*) *the* ~, in the smallest degree, at all. ~ *adv.* In the least degree.

least'ways (-z) (vulg.), **least'wīse** (-z) (rare) *advs.* Or at least, or rather.

leat *n.* Open water-course conducting water to mill etc.

leath'er (lĕdh-) *n.* Skin prepared for use by tanning or similar process; article, or part of one, made of leather, piece of leather for polishing, thong; (slang) cricket-ball or football; (pl.) leggings or breeches; *patent* ~, leather with fine black varnished surface; ~-*back*, large soft-shelled turtle, *Sphangis coriacea*; *leath'ercloth*, strong fabric coated to resemble leather and used for upholstery etc.; ~-*jacket*, tough-skinned larva of crane-fly, injurious to roots of grass, cereals, etc. **leath'ern, leath'ery** *adjs.*

leave[1] *n.* Permission; ~ (*of absence*), permission to be absent from duty, period for which this lasts; *on* ~, absent thus; *take* ~ (*of*), bid farewell (to); *take* ~ *of one's senses*, go mad; *ticket of* ~: see TICKET.

leave[2] *v.t.* (past t. and past part. *lĕft*). 1. Cause to or let remain, depart without taking; bequeath. 2. Abstain from consuming or dealing with, (pass.) remain over; let remain in specified state; commit, refer, *to* another agent etc. than oneself; allow *to* do something without interference; deposit, entrust (thing etc.) to be dealt with, station (person) to discharge function, in one's absence. 3. Quit, go away from; depart; pass (object) so as to put it in specified relative direction; cease to reside at, belong to, or serve; abandon, forsake; ~ *alone*, not interfere with; ~ *behind*, go away without; leave as consequence or trace; pass; ~ *go*, (vulg.) relax one's hold; ~ *off*, cease to wear; discontinue; come to, make, an end; ~ *out*, omit; ~ *over*, let stand over for the time. ~ *n.* (billiards) Position in which player leaves the balls.

leav'en (lĕvn) *n.* Substance added to dough to produce fermentation, esp. fermenting dough reserved from previous batch for this; (fig.) spreading and transforming influence (f. Matt. xiii. 33), tinge or admixture *of* some quality. ~ *v.t.* Ferment (dough) with leaven; permeate and transform, modify *with* tempering element.

leav'ings *n.pl.* What is left.

Lĕb'anon. 1. Mountain-range of SW. Syria, famous in ancient times for its cedars. 2. (*Great*) ~ or *Lebanese Republic*, State in French mandated territory in Syria, proclaimed by French Government in 1920 and in 1941 declared an independent State; capital Beirut. **Lĕbanēse'** (-z) *adj.* & *n.*

lebensraum (lāb'enzrowm) *n.* The area claimed by the Germans for their due development (also fig.). [Ger., = 'living-space']

Leblanc (leblahṅ'), Nicolas (1742–1806). French chemist; inventor of a process for manufacturing soda from common salt.

Le Bourget (boor'zhā). French airport near Paris.

Le Brun (-ērṅ), Charles (1619–90). French decorative painter; court painter to Louis XIV and arbiter of taste at his court.

lĕch'er *n.* (archaic) Fornicator, debauchee. **lĕch'erous** *adj.* **lĕch'erously** *adv.* **lĕch'ery** *n.*

lĕ'cithin *n.* Complex phosphorus-containing compound extracted from soya beans etc. and used as emulsifying agent in manufacture of margarine, ice cream, and other foods.

Lĕck'y, William Edward Hartpole (1838–1903). Irish historian; author of 'History of Rationalism', 'History of European Morals from Augustus to Charlemagne', etc.

Leconte' de Lisle' (-kawṅt, lēl), Charles Marie René (1818–94). French poet; founder of the PARNASSIAN school.

lĕc'tern *n.* Reading- or singing-desk in church, esp. that for the lessons.

LECTERN

lĕc'tionary (-shon-) *n.* Book containing, list of, portions of Scripture appointed to be read at divine service.

lĕc'ture *n.* Discourse before audience or class on given subject, usu. by way of instruction; admonition, reproof. ~ *v.* Deliver lecture(s) (*on* subject); instruct or entertain by lecture; admonish, reprimand. **lĕc'turer** (-kche-) *n.* (esp., in some universities) One who assists professor in department or performs professorial duties without corresponding rank or title. **lĕc'tureship** *n.*

lĕ'cythus *n.* (pl. -*thī*). (Gk antiq.) Narrow-necked vase or flask (ill. VASE).

lĕd *adj.* ~ *horse*, spare horse led by groom etc. (past part. of LEAD[2]).

Lē'da. (Gk legend) Wife of Tyndareus, king of Sparta; was loved by Zeus, who took the form of a swan; among her children were Castor and Pollux and Helen (all by Zeus), and Clytemnestra.

lĕdge *n.* Narrow horizontal surface projecting from wall etc.; shelf-like projection on side of rock or mountain; ridge of rocks, esp. below water; (mining) stratum of metal-bearing rock.

lĕdg'er *n.* 1. Principal book of the set used for recording trade transactions, containing debtor-and-creditor accounts. 2. Horizontal timber in scaffolding, parallel to face of building (ill. SCAFFOLD). 3. Flat gravestone. 4. ~-*blade*, stationary blade in cloth-shearing machine acting with revolving spiral blade. ~ *adj.* (mus.) ~ (or *leger*) *line*, short line added above or below stave to extend its compass (ill. STAVE).

lee[1] *n.* Shelter given by neighbouring object; ~ (*side*), sheltered side, side away from wind (opp. *weather side*); (attrib.) belonging to ship's lee side or to leeward of other object; ~-*board*, plank frame fixed to side of flat-bottomed sailing vessel and let down into water to diminish leeway (ill. BARGE); ~ *shore*, shore to leeward of ship; *lee'way*, lateral drift of ship to leeward of course; *make up leeway*, (fig.) make up for loss of time or retardation of progress.

Lee[2], Robert Edward (1807–70). American soldier, commander-in-chief of Southern armies in Amer. Civil War.

leech[1] *n.* (archaic, poet., or joc.) Physician, healer.

leech[2] *n.* Kinds of mainly aquatic blood-sucking worm of the

LEECH

1. Anterior sucker. 2. Posterior sucker

class *Hirudinea*, esp. that formerly used medicinally for bleeding (*Hirudo*); person who sucks profit out of others.

leech[3] *n.* Free edge of a sail (ill. SAIL[1]).

Lee-Enfield. Type of rifle used by British Army in S. Afr. War and, modified, in war of 1914–18. [J. P. *Lee*, Amer. designer and *Enfield*, site of British small-arms factory]

leek *n.* Culinary herb (*Allium porrum*) allied to onion but with cylindrical bulbous part and broad flat leaves; this as Welsh national emblem.

leer[1] *v.i.* & *n.* Glance (esp. sideways) with sly, lascivious, or malign expression. **leer'ingly** *adv.*

leer[2], **lehr** *n.* Annealing-furnace for glass.

leer'y *adj.* (slang) Knowing, sly; (U.S.) suspicious.

lees (-z) *n. pl.* Sediment of wine etc.; basest part, refuse.

leet[1] *n.* (hist.) Yearly or half-yearly court of RECORD holdable by lords of certain manors; jurisdiction or district of this.

leet[2] *n.* (chiefly Sc.) List, esp. list of candidates for an office.

leeward (lū'*ard*) *adj.* & *adv.* On, towards, the sheltered side. ~ *n.* This direction. **lee'wardly** *adj.* (Of ship) apt to fall to leeward.

Leeward Islands (lū'*ard*). Most northerly group of Lesser Antilles, in W. Indies; a British colony.

Le Fanu (lĕf'*anū*), Joseph Sheridan (1814–73). Irish novelist; specialized, in his 'Uncle Silas' etc., in descriptions of the mysterious and terrible.

lĕft *adj.* 1. Belonging to the side of a person's body that has normally the less-used hand, that side which is westward when he faces N.; having corresponding relation to front of any object; ~ *bank* of river, that which is left as one faces its mouth; ~ *hand*, region or direction nearer the left hand; ~ *turn*, turn that brings one's front to face as one's left side did before. 2. Of the left in politics (see *n.* below); ~*-wing*, *-winger*, (politician) of extreme left. ~ *adv.* On or to the left side. ~ *n.* 1. Left hand. 2. In continental legislatures, members on left side of chamber, traditionally the more liberal or democratic (cf. RIGHT); hence, more advanced or innovating section of any group, esp. in politics. **lĕft'ward** *adj.* & *adv.* **lĕft'wards** *adv.*

lĕft-hăn'dĕd *adj.* 1. Having left hand more serviceable than right, using it by preference; awkward, clumsy. 2. Ambiguous, double-edged, of doubtful sincerity or validity; (of marriage) morganatic, (occas.) fictitious; (archaic) ill-omened, sinister. 3. Adapted for use of left hand, (of blow) delivered with it. **lĕft-hăn'dĕdly** *adv.* **lĕft-hăndĕdness** *n.* **lĕft-hăn'der** *n.* Left-handed person or blow.

lĕf'tism *n.* The political views of the left (LEFT *n.* 2). **lĕf'tist** *n.*

lĕg *n.* 1. Organ of support and locomotion in animal body; (in human) part of this from hip to ankle. 2. Leg of animal as food. 3. (archaic) Obeisance made by drawing back one leg. 4. Support, pole, prop, of machine etc.; support of chair, table, bed, etc. 5. One branch of forked object; side of triangle other than base; (naut.) run made on single tack. 6. (cricket) Part of the field to the left of a right-handed batsman or to the right of a left-handed one, esp. the part to the rear of this (ill. CRICKET). 7. Part of garment covering leg. 8. Artificial leg. 9. *pull* one's ~, (colloq.) befool him; *give a* ~ *up*, help to mount (horse etc.) or get over obstacle (also fig.) *shake a* ~, dance; *show a* ~, get out of bed; *stretch* one's ~*s*, take walking exercise; *take to* one's ~*s*, run away; *on* one's (*hind*) ~*s*, standing, esp. to make a speech; *without a* ~ *to stand on*, unable to support thesis by any facts or sound reasons; *on* one's *last* ~*s*, near death or end; *walk person off his* ~*s*, tire him out in walking; *feel*, *find*, one's ~*s*, get power of standing or walking; *long*, *short*, *square* ~, (cricket) fielders variously posted in leg part of field; ~ *before wicket* (abbrev. *l.b.w.*), illegal stopping by batsman's leg of ball which would otherwise have bowled him; ~*-of-mutton sleeve*, *sail*, etc., sleeve, sail, etc., shaped like leg of mutton; ~*-guard*, pad for ankle, shin, and knee, in cricket; ~*-rest*, support for leg of seated person; ~ *theory*, (cricket) bowling to ~ with fieldsmen massed on that side. ~ *v.i.* ~ *it*, walk or run hard.

lĕg'acy *n.* Sum of money or article bequeathed by will; material or immaterial thing handed down by predecessor.

lēg'al *adj.* Of, based on, falling within province of, occupied with, law; required or appointed by law; recognized by law as distinct from equity; lawful; (theol.) of the Mosaic law, of salvation by works not faith; ~*fiction*, statement which is probably fictitious but admitted as true in order to enable some useful purpose, as redress of wrong etc., to be accomplished; ~ *tender*: see TENDER[2]. **lēg'ally** *adv.*

lēg'alism *n.* Exaltation of law or formula, 'red tape'; (theol.) preference of the Law to the Gospel, doctrine of justification by works. **lēg'alist** *n.*

lėgăl'ity, *n.* Lawfulness; legalism.

lĕg'ate[1] (-*at*) *n.* Ecclesiastic deputed to represent pope (~ *ā lăt'ĕrĕ*, one of highest class and full powers); (archaic) ambassador, delegate. **lĕg'atine** *adj.* **lĕg'ateship** *n.*

lėgāte'[2] *v.t.* Bequeath. **lėgāt'or** *n.*

lĕgatee' *n.* Recipient of legacy.

lėgā'tion *n.* Sending of legate or deputy; body of deputies; diplomatic minister and his suite (esp. when he does not rank as ambassador), his official residence; legateship.

lėga'to (-ah-). (mus.) Smooth(ly) and connected(ly), without breaks between successive notes; (skill in performing) such passage.

lĕ'gend *n.* 1. Collection of lives of saints or similar stories; traditional story popularly regarded as historical, myth; such literature or tradition; *Golden L*~: see GOLDEN. 2. Inscription or motto, esp. on coin or medal. **lĕ'gendary** *adj.*

lĕ'ger[1] *adj.*: see LEDGER.

Lĕ'ger[2]: see ST. LEGER.

lĕ'gerdėmain' *n.* Sleight of hand, conjuring tricks, juggling; trickery, sophistry. [Fr. *léger de main* light of hand]

lĕgg'ing (-g-) *n.* (usu. pl.) Outer covering of leather etc. for leg up to knee.

lĕgg'y (-g-) *adj.* Having disproportionately long legs.

Lėghorn[1](-gôrn'). (Ital. *Livorno*) City and seaport of Tuscany, Italy.

lėghorn[2] (-gôrn') *n.* 1. Straw for hats etc. imported from Leghorn, made of stems of a Mediterranean wheat (*Triticum sativum turgidum*) cut green and bleached. 2. Small hardy breed of domestic poultry.

lĕ'gible *adj.* Clear, easily read. **lĕgibil'ity** *n.* **lĕ'gibly** *adv.*

lē'gion (-jn) *n.* Division of 3,000–6,000 men, including complement of cavalry, in ancient Roman army; vast host or multitude; *American L*~, national association of ex-service men, founded 1919; *British L*~, similar association founded 1921 and incorporated by Royal Charter 1925; *Foreign L*~, body of foreign volunteers in modern (esp. French) army, serving in colonies or on distant expeditions; ~ *of Honour*, (Fr. *légion d'honneur*), French order of distinction conferred for civil or military services etc., founded by Napoleon I in 1802.

lē'gionary (-jo-) *adj.* Of legion(s). ~ *n.* Soldier of a legion.

légionnaire' (lēzh-) *n.* Member of legion, esp. French Foreign Legion or Legion of Honour.

lĕ'gislāte *v.i.* Make laws. **lĕgislā'tion** *n.* (Enacting of) laws. **lĕ'gislative** *adj.* **lĕ'gislatively** *adv.*

lĕ'gislātor *n.* Lawgiver; member of legislative body.

lĕ'gislature *n.* Law-making body of a State.

lėgit'imate *adj.* Born in lawful wedlock; lawful, proper, regular, conforming to standard type; logically admissible; (of sovereign's title) based on strict hereditary right; ~ *drama*, body of plays having recognized theatrical and literary merit; so ~ *actor*, *stage*, etc. **lėg'itimately** *adv.* **lėgit'imāte** *v.t.* Make legitimate by decree, enactment, or proof; justify, serve as justification for. **lėgitimā'tion** *n.* **lėgit'imacy** *n* **lėgit'imatize** *v.t.*

lėgit'imism *n.* Adherence to sovereign or pretender whose claim is based on direct descent (esp. in Span. and Fr. politics). **lėgit'imist** *n.*

lėgit'imize *v.t.* Make legitimate. **lėgitimizātion** *n.*

lĕg'ūme, lėgūm'ĕn *n.* Fruit,

edible, part, pod of leguminous plant (ill. FRUIT); vegetable used for food.

lėgūm'ĭnous *adj.* (bot. etc.) Of the order *Leguminosae*, including peas, beans, and other pod-bearing plants.

lehr: see LEER[2].

Leib'nĭz (lī-, -tz), Gottfried Wilhelm (1646–1716). German mathematician and philosopher; discoverer of differential calculus; founder of Society (later Academy) of Sciences at Berlin; in his philosophical writings he regarded matter as a multitude of monads, each a microcosm of the universe, and assumed a 'pre-established harmony' between spirit and matter, established by God, the supreme monad and perfect exemplar of the human soul. **Leibnĭz'ĭan** *adj.* & *n.*

Leicester[1] (lĕs'ter). City and county borough, county town of **Leicestershire,** midland county of England.

Leicester[2] (lĕs'ter), Robert Dudley, Earl of (*c* 1532–88). English statesman, favourite of Queen Elizabeth.

Leics. *abbrev.* Leicestershire.

Leiden: see LEYDEN.

Leif Ericsson (līf, ĕ'-): see VINLAND.

Leight'on (lāt-), Frederic, Baron Leighton of Stretton (1830–96). English painter and president of Royal Academy.

Leins'ter (lĕn-). Province of middle and SE. Eire.

Leip'zĭg (lī-). Commercial and university city in Saxony, E. Germany, centre of publishing trade; ~ *Fair,* annual fair held there since 12th c.

leis'ter (lē-) *n.* Pronged salmon-spear. ~ *v.t.* Spear with this.

leisure (lĕzh'er) *n.* (Opportunity *to* do, *for,* afforded by) free time, time at one's own disposal; *at* ~, not occupied; deliberately, without hurry; *at one's* ~, when one has time. **lei'sured** *adj.*

leisurely (lĕzh'er-) *adj.* Having, acting or done at, leisure, deliberate. ~ *adv.* Deliberately, without haste.

leit-motiv (lī'tmōtēf') *n.* (mus.) Theme associated throughout work with some person, situation, or sentiment.

Leit'rĭm (lē-). County of Connaught, Eire.

Leix, Laoi(gh)is (lēsh). County in province of Leinster, Eire; formerly Queen's County.

lĕk *n.* Principal monetary unit of Albania, = 100 qintar.

Lēl'y, Sir Peter (1618–80). Portrait-painter of Dutch origin, active in England.

lĕm'an *n.* (archaic) Lover, sweetheart; unlawful lover or mistress.

Lĕm'bĕrg. Ger. name for Lvov, a city formerly Polish but now in Ukraine, U.S.S.R.

lĕmm'a *n.* Assumed or demonstrated proposition used in argument or proof; argument or subject of literary composition; head-word of dictionary article; motto appended to picture etc.

lĕmm'ĭng *n.* Small rodent of family *Muridae* inhabiting arctic and sub-arctic regions, one species, the Norway lemming (*Lemmus lemmus*) being remarkable for migrations in which large numbers swim out to sea and are drowned.

Lĕm'nŏs. Large Greek island in N. Aegean. **Lĕm'nĭan** *adj.*

lĕm'on[1] *n.* Tree (*Citrus limonia*), native of Indian Himalayas, now cultivated in Mediterranean countries, bearing oval-seeded fruit with pale-yellow skin and acid juice; fruit of this; pale-yellow colour; ~*-drop,* boiled sweet flavoured with lemon; ~ *squash,* drink of sweetened lemon-juice and water or soda-water; ~*-squeezer,* instrument for pressing out lemon-juice.

lĕm'on[2] *n.* (Usu. ~ *dab, sole*), kind of plaice or flounder resembling sole, but inferior in taste and texture.

Lĕm'on[3], Mark (1809–70). English journalist; one of founders and first editor (1841–70) of 'Punch'.

lĕmonāde' *n.* Drink of lemon-juice, sugar, and water; synthetic substitute for this.

lĕmpir'a (-pēr-) *n.* Principal monetary unit of Honduras, = 100 centavos.

lēm'ur *n.* (zool.) Genus of nocturnal mammals allied to monkeys but with pointed muzzle, found chiefly in Madagascar. **lĕm'ūrīne, lĕm'ūroid** *adjs.* [L. *lemures* spirits of the dead]

RING-TAILED LEMUR

Lēn'a. River rising W. of Lake Baikal, most easterly of 3 great Siberian rivers flowing to Arctic Ocean; famous for the gold-fields in its basin.

Lenclos (lahṅklō'), Anne de, known as Ninon de, (1620–1705). French beauty and wit.

lĕnd *v.t.* (past t. and past part. *lĕnt*). Grant (person) use of (thing) on understanding that it or its equivalent shall be returned; let out (money) at interest, (books etc.) for hire; bestow, contribute (something of temporary service or effect); accommodate one*self to* some policy or purpose; ~ (*an*) *ear, one's ears,* listen; ~ *a* (*helping*) *hand,* help; *lending-library,* one that lends books, esp. for hire; ~*-lease*: see LEASE-lend. **lĕn'der** *n.*

lĕngth *n.* Thing's measurement from end to end, greatest of body's three dimensions; extent in, of, or with regard to, time; distance thing extends; (pros.) quantity of syllable or vowel; (cricket) distance from wicket at which ball pitches; long stretch or extent; piece of cloth etc. of certain length; *at* ~, in detail or without curtailment; at last or after a long time; *at full* ~, (also) lying with body fully extended; ~*-man,* railway employee charged with maintenance of a section of the permanent way. **lĕngth'ways** (-z) *adv.* **lĕngth'wīse** (-z) *adv.* & *adj.*

lĕng'then *v.* Make or become longer; (pros.) make (vowel) long.

lĕng'thȳ *adj.* Of unusual length, prolix, tedious. **lĕng'thĭly** *adv.* **lĕng'thĭnėss** *n.*

lēn'ĭent *adj.* Tolerant, gentle, indisposed to severity; (of punishment etc.) mild. **lēn'ĭently** *adv.* **lēn'ĭence, lēn'ĭency** *ns.*

Lĕn'ĭn. Assumed name of Vladimir Ilyich Ulyanov (1870–1924), Russian revolutionary, exponent of doctrines of Marx, and founder of Bolshevik party; after imprisonment and exile left Russia 1900; returned there in disguise and took part in revolution of 1905; escaped 1907 and directed revolutionary operations from abroad until 1917 when he returned to Russia and became head of the new Government; was severely injured by a would-be assassin in 1918. **Lĕn'ĭnĭsm** *n.* **Lĕn'ĭnĭst** *adj.* & *n.*

Lĕn'ĭngrăd (*or* -ahd). Russian city on an inlet of the Gulf of Finland, founded 1703 by Peter the Great and until 1918 capital of Russia; known as St. Petersburg before the revolution and as Petrograd from 1917 until 1924, when it was renamed after LENIN.

lĕn'ĭtĭve *adj* & *n.* Soothing (drug, appliance); palliative.

lĕn'ĭty *n.* Mercifulness; mercy shown.

Le Nôtre (nōtr), André (1613–1700). French landscape-gardener, designer of gardens of palace of Versailles.

lĕns (-z) *n.* Piece of glass etc. with two curved surfaces, or one plane and one curved, causing regular convergence or divergence of rays of light passing through it, commonly used, either singly or combined, in optical instruments, as a camera, telescope, eyeglasses, etc.; (anat.) = CRYSTALLINE lens (ill. EYE); one facet of compound eye.

Lĕnt. In western Christian Churches, period from Ash Wednesday to Easter Eve, of which the 40 weekdays are devoted to fasting and penitence in commemoration of the fasting of Jesus in the wilderness; ~ *lily,* the daffodil; ~ *races* (at Cambridge), boat-races held during Lent term; ~ *term,* university term in which Lent falls, spring term. **lĕn'ten** *adj.* Of, in, appropriate to, Lent.

lĕn'tĭcĕl *n.* (bot.) Aeration pore penetrating the young cork of stems and some roots (ill. STEM).

lĕntic'ūlar *adj.* Shaped like lentil or lens (esp. ~ *cloud*), double convex; of the lens of the eye.

lĕn'til *n.* (Seed of) leguminous plant, *Lens esculenta*, grown for food.

lĕn'titūde *n.* Sluggishness.

lĕn'tō *adj.* & *adv.* (mus.) Slow(ly).

lĕn'toid *adj.* Lens-shaped.

Lē'ō[1]. The Lion, zodiacal constellation between Cancer and Virgo; in mythology, orig. the Nemean lion killed by Hercules; 5th sign (♌) of zodiac, entered by sun about 21st July.

Lē'ō[2]. Name of 13 popes; *Leo I*, 'the Great', pope 440–61, a doctor of the Church, obtained (445) recognition of the primacy of the popes in the Christian Church; *Leo IV*, pope 847–55, built the LEONINE City; *Leo X* (Giovanni de' Medici, 1475–1521), pope 1513–21, excommunicated Luther and bestowed on Henry VIII of England title of 'Defender of the Faith'.

Lē'ō[3], Johannes (*c* 1494–1552). 'Leo Africanus', a Spanish Moor; travelled, and wrote a 'Description of Africa'; was captured by pirates *c* 1520 and given as a slave to Pope Leo X.

Lē'ō[4] **(the Isaur'ian)** (ĭ-). Leo III, Byzantine emperor 718–41; famous for his edict proscribing the veneration of images, which was repudiated by Pope Gregory II.

León[1] (lāōn'). Province (in Middle Ages a kingdom) of NW. Spain.

León[2] (lāōn'). Fray Luis Ponce de (1527–91). Spanish Augustinian friar and religious poet.

Leonar'do (lā-) **da Vĭn'ci** (-chĭ) (1452–1519). Italian painter, sculptor, architect, engineer, man of science, and writer of prose and verse.

Leoncavăll'ō (lā-), Ruggiero (1858–1919). Italian composer, famous for his opera 'I Pagliacci'.

Lē'onĭd. One of a shower of

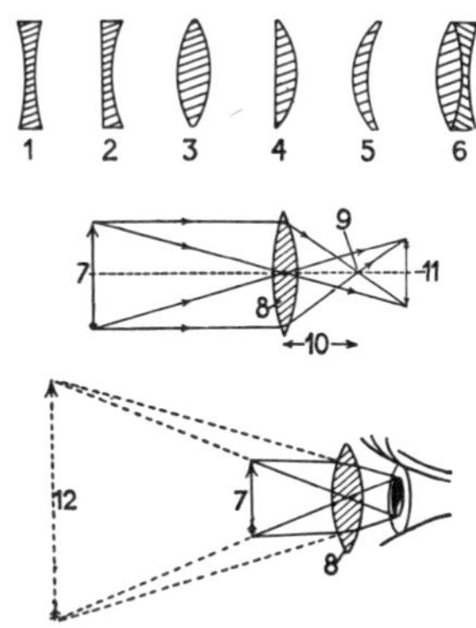

LENSES

1. Concave. 2. Plano-concave. 3. Convex. 4. Plano-convex. 5. Meniscus. 6. Achromatic. 7. Object. 8. Lens. 9. Focus. 10. Focal length. 11. Real image. 12. Virtual image

meteors radiating from a point in the constellation Leo, observable every November but brightly visible only once in 33 years when their orbit is close to the earth's.

Lėŏn'idās. King of Sparta 491–480 B.C.; hero of defence of pass of Thermopylae against invading army of Xerxes, 480 B.C.

lē'onīne[1] *adj.* Lion-like, of lions.

Lē'onīne[2] *adj.* Of, made by, a person (esp. a pope) named Leo; ~ *City*, part of Rome in which Vatican stands, walled and fortified by Leo IV; ~ *verse*, *Leonines*, medieval form of Latin verse in hexameters or alternate hexameters and pentameters, in which final word rhymes with that immediately before the caesura; English verse in which middle and last syllables rhyme.

leop'ard (lĕp-) *n.* 1. Large chiefly nocturnal carnivore (*Felis pardus*) of cat family, with long tail and usu. dark-spotted yellowish-fawn coat, found in Africa and S. Asia, panther; *American* ~, jaguar; *black* ~, variety found in S. India etc.; *hunting* ~, cheetah; *snow* ~, ounce; ~*'s bane*, name given to several herbaceous perennial plants of family *Compositae*. 2. (her.) Lion passant guardant as in arms of England.

Leopar'dĭ (lā-), Giacomo (1798–1837). Italian poet and scholar, whose poetry is noted for its melancholy and pessimism.

Lē'opōld[1]. Name of two Holy Roman Emperors: *Leopold I* (1640–1705), emperor 1658–1705; *Leopold II* (1747–92), emperor 1790–92.

Lē'opōld[2]. Name of 3 kings of the Belgians: *Leopold I* (1790–1865), 4th son of Francis, Duke of Saxe-Coburg-Saalfeld and uncle of Queen Victoria of England; elected king of the Belgians 1831; *Leopold II* (1835–1909), king of the Belgians 1865–1909; *Leopold III* (b. 1901) king of the Belgians from 1934 until his abdication in 1951.

lē'otard *n.* Close-fitting body-garment worn by acrobats, ballet-dancers, etc. [f. J. *Léotard*, 19th-c. Fr. trapeze performer]

Lėpăn'tō, Strait of. Entrance to Gulf of Corinth or Lepanto, Greece; scene (1571) of naval battle in which Turkish fleet was almost completely destroyed by forces of Holy League (Pope Pius V, Venice, Spain, Genoa, Savoy, and other Italian States) under Don John of Austria.

lĕp'er *n.* Person with leprosy.

Lĕpĭdŏp'tera *n.pl.* Order of insects, comprising butterflies and moths, with 2 pairs of membranous wings covered with flattened scales often forming striking colour patterns. **lĕpĭdŏp'-terist** *n.* Student of *lepidoptera*. **lĕpĭdŏp'terous** *adj.* [Gk *lepis* scale, *pteron* wing]

Lĕp'ĭdus, Marcus Aemilius (d. 13 B.C.). Roman politician; member of the 2nd TRIUMVIRATE (with Mark Antony and Octavian) after death of Julius Caesar.

lĕp'orīne *adj.* Of the hare kind.

lĕp'rėchaun (-kawn *or* -χawn) *n.* Irish sprite in form of a wizened old man.

lĕp'rosy̆ *n.* 1. Chronic endemic bacterial disease characterized by thickening and ulceration of skin with loss of sensation, and, in severe cases, deformity and blindness; it now occurs chiefly in tropical and eastern countries but was more widely distributed in the Middle Ages. 2. (bibl.) Various diseases not necessarily identical with leprosy in sense 1. **lĕp'rous** *adj.* Having, like, (as) of, leprosy.

Lerm'ontov (lyār-, -f), Mikhail Yurevich (1814–41). Russian poet and novelist, of Scottish descent (ancestors' name Learmont).

Le Sage (sahzh), Alain René (1668–1747). French dramatist and novelist, author of the picaresque novel 'Gil Blas'.

Lĕs'bian (-z-) *adj.* Of Lesbos; of homosexuality in women (from the association of the island with Sappho, who was accused of this vice). **Lĕs'bian** *n.* Homosexual woman. **Lĕs'bianism** *n.*

Lĕs'bŏs. Island in Aegean Sea, off NW. coast of Asia Minor, inhabited from an early date by Aeolians; birthplace of Alcaeus and Sappho.

lèse-majesté (lāz măzh'ĕstā) *n.* Affront to sovereign or ruler; presumption. **lese-măj'ėsty** (lēz-) *n.* (hist., civil law) Treason. [Fr., f. L *laesa majestas* injured majesty (of the sovereign people)]

lē'sion (-zhn) *n.* Damage, injury; esp. (path.) morbid change in functioning or texture of organs.

lĕss *adj.* Smaller; of smaller quantity, not so much, not so much of; of lower rank etc. (rare); (preceding numeral etc.) minus, not including. ~ *n.* Smaller amount, quantity, or number. ~ *adv.* To smaller extent, in lower degree.

lĕssee' *n.* Holder of, tenant under, lease. **lĕssee'ship** *n.*

lĕs'sen *v.* Decrease, diminish.

Lĕssĕps', Ferdinand Marie, Vicomte de (1805–94). French diplomat and engineer; designed the Suez Canal.

lĕss'er *attrib. adj.* Not so great as the other or the rest, minor, smaller.

Lĕss'ing, Gotthold Ephraim (1729–81). German dramatist and critic, whose influence was of importance in freeing German literature from conventions of French classical school.

lĕss'on *n.* 1. Portion of Scripture etc. read at divine service; now chiefly portion of O.T. (*first* ~) and N.T. (*second* ~) read in Church of England at morning and evening prayer. 2. Thing to be learnt by pupil; amount of teaching given at one time, time assigned to it;

occurrence, example, rebuke, etc., serving as encouragement or warning; (pl.) systematic instruction *in* subject. ~ *v.t.* Admonish, rebuke, discipline.

lĕss'ôr *n.* Person who lets on lease.

lĕst *conj.* In order that . . . . not, for fear that; (after *fear* etc.) that.

lĕt[1] *v.t.* (archaic; past t. and past part. *lett'ed* or *let*) Hinder, obstruct. ~ *n.* Stoppage, hindrance (archaic); (fives, lawn tennis, etc.) obstruction of ball or player in certain ways, on account of which ball must be served again.

lĕt[2] *v.t.* & *auxil.* (past t. and past part. *let*). 1. Allow (confined fluid) to escape; ~ *blood*: see BLOOD. 2. Grant use of for rent or hire; *to* ~, offered for rent. 3. Allow to, suffer to; cause to (only in ~ one *know*, inform him). 4. ~ *alone*, not interfere with, not attend to or do; (imper.) not to mention; ~ *be*, let alone; ~ *down*, lower; fail (friend) at need; disappoint; ~ *fall*, drop; (geom.) draw (perpendicular) from outside point (*up*)*on* line; ~ *go*, release, set at liberty; lose hold of, lose or relinquish hold *of*; dismiss from thought; cease to restrain; ~ *in*, admit, open door to; insert into surface of something; ~ *in for*, involve in difficulty; ~ *into*, admit to; insert into surface of; make acquainted with (secret etc.); ~ *loose*, release, unchain; ~ *off*, discharge (gun etc.); not punish or compel; punish *with* light penalty; allow or cause (fluid etc.) to pass away; ~ *on*, (slang) reveal secret; ~ *out*, open door for exit to; allow to escape; make (garment) looser; put out to hire, esp. to several tenants; divulge; ~ *slip*, loose from leash; miss (opportunity); ~ *up*, (orig. U.S.) cease, relax one's efforts. 5. *v.auxil.* (followed by inf.) supplying 1st and 3rd persons of imperative in exhortations, commands, assumptions, and permissions. ~ *n.* Letting for hire or rent.

lēth'al *adj.* Causing, sufficient or designed to cause, death; ~ *chamber*, chamber for killing animals painlessly. **lēthăl'ĭty** *n.*

lēth'alīze *v.t.* Destroy in lethal chamber.

lĕth'argy *n.* Morbid drowsiness, prolonged and unnatural sleep; torpid, inert, or apathetic state, want of interest and energy. **lėthar'gĭc** *adj.* **lėthar'gĭcally** *adv.*

Lēth'ē. (Greek and Latin myth.) One of the rivers of the underworld, whose water when drunk had the power of making the souls of the dead forget their life on earth. **Lēthē'an** *adj.* [Gk *lēthē* oblivion]

Lē'tō. Greek name of LATONA.

Lĕtt *n.* One of a people closely related to Lithuanians, inhabiting Latvia.

lĕtt'er *n.* 1. Character representing one or more of the elementary sounds used in speech, one of the alphabetic symbols; (print.) type, fount of type; (pl.) lettering, inscription (now only in *proof before* ~*s*), proof taken from engraved plate before lettering is inserted. 2. Missive, epistle; (pl.) epistle of legal or formal kind for various purposes; ~*s patent*: see PATENT. 3. Precise terms of statement etc., strict verbal interpretation. 4. (pl.) Literature; acquaintance with books, erudition; *man of* ~*s*, scholar, (now usu.) writer, author; *profession of* ~*s*, authorship. 5. ~*-book*, book in which copies of correspondence are kept; ~*-box*, box in which letters are posted or deposited on delivery; ~*-card*, folded card with gummed edges for use as postal missive; ~*-case*, pocket-book for holding letters; *letterpress*, matter printed from letters or types, as distinguished from what is printed from plates or blocks. ~ *v.t.* Impress title etc. on (book-cover); inscribe in letters, *with* name, etc.

lĕtt'ered (-*erd*) *adj.* (esp.) Literate, educated. **lĕtt'ering** *n.*

Lĕttish. *adj.* & *n.* (Of) the language of the Letts, one of the Baltic group of Indo-European languages, closely related to Lithuanian.

lettre de cachet (lĕtr, kăsh'ā) *n.* (Fr. hist.) Letter signed by king of France containing order emanating directly from the king himself, esp. one containing arbitrary order of imprisonment, exile, etc. [Fr., = 'sealed letter']

lĕtt'uce (-tĭs) *n.* Garden herb of genus *Lactuca* with crisp leaves much used as salad.

leu *n.* Principal monetary unit of Rumania, = 100 bani.

Leucĭpp'us (5th c. B.C.). Greek philosopher; regarded, with Democritus, as founder of the 'atomistic' theory that the universe is composed of a vast number of indivisible particles moving and combining in space.

leuc'ocȳte *n.* Colourless corpuscle in blood, lymph, etc. (ill. (BLOOD).

leucorrhoe'a (-rē*a*) *n.* (path.) Whitish purulent mucous discharge from vagina and uterine canal.

leucŏt'omy *n.* (surg.) Cutting of certain white tissue-fibres of the brain (esp. in *frontal* or *prefrontal* ~, operation performed for psychiatric reasons).

Leuc'tra. Village of Boeotia, scene of a battle (371 B.C.) in which Thebans under Epaminondas defeated Spartans, ending the period of Spartan hegemony in Greece.

leukaem'ĭa *n.* Blood disease characterized by excess of white corpuscles.

Lev. *abbrev.* Leviticus (O.T.).

lĕv *n.* Principal monetary unit of Bulgaria, = 100 stotinki.

lėvănt'[1] *v.i.* Abscond, bolt.

Lėvănt'[2]. Eastern part of the Mediterranean with its islands and neighbouring countries. **lėvănt'er** *n.* Strong Mediterranean easterly wind. **Lėvănt'īne** *n.* Native, inhabitant, of the Levant, esp. one descended from European settlers. ~ *adj.* Of, trading to, the Levant. [Fr. *levant* sunrise, east]

lĕv'ee[1] (-vĭ) *n.* (Formerly) reception of visitors on rising from bed; assembly held (in afternoon) by sovereign or his (or her) representative at which men only are received; assembly of visitors.

levee[2] (lĕvē', lĕv'ĭ) *n.* (U.S.) Natural embankment of alluvium built up by rivers on either side of their channels; artificial embankment raised to prevent inundations.

lĕv'el *n.* 1. Instrument giving line parallel to plane of horizon for testing whether things are horizontal. 2. Horizontal line or plane; plane or standard in social, moral, or intellectual matters; plane of rank or authority, e.g. *consultation at cabinet level*; *on a* ~ *with*, in same horizontal plane as; *on the* ~, (U.S. colloq.) straightforward(ly), honest(ly). 3. More or less level surface; flat country. ~ *adj.* 1. Horizontal, perpendicular to the plumb-line; on a level or equality (*with*); ~ *crossing*, place where railway and road or two railways cross at same level. 2. Even, equable, uniform, well balanced, in quality, style, judgement, etc.; *one's* ~ *best*, (colloq.) one's very best; ~*-headed*, mentally well balanced. **lĕv'elly** *adv.* **lĕv'elnėss** *n.* **lĕv'el** *v.t.* 1. Make level, even, or uniform; place on same level, bring *up* or *down* to a standard. 2. Raze, lay low; abolish (distinctions). 3. Aim (missile), lay (gun), direct (satire, accusation, etc.) *at*, *against*.

lĕv'eller *n.* (esp.) Person who would abolish social distinctions, advocate of equality, esp. *L*~ (Engl. hist.), one of a party of extreme radical dissenters arising in army of Long Parliament (*c* 1647) and advocating levelling of all ranks and completely democratic form of republican government.

Lēv'en, Loch. Lake of Kinross, Scotland; on the largest of its 7 islands Mary, Queen of Scots, was imprisoned and signed her abdication.

lēv'er[1] *n.* Bar used to prize up heavy or fixed object; (mech.)

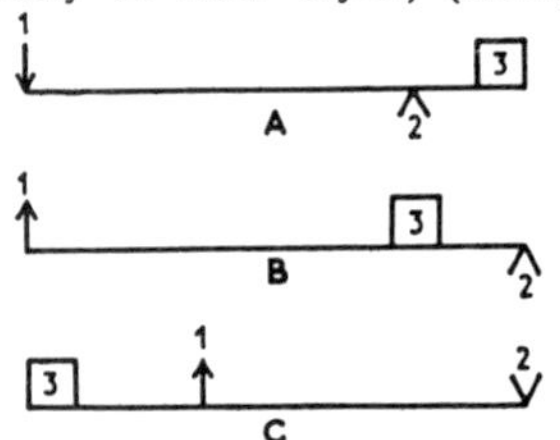

LEVERS: A. FIRST ORDER. B. SECOND ORDER. C. THIRD ORDER

1. Lifting force. 2. Fulcrum. 3. Object lifted. In A and B the mechanical advantage is greater than 1, and in C less than 1

straight bar or other rigid structure of which one point (*fulcrum*) is fixed, another is connected with the force (*weight*) to be resisted or acted upon, and a third is connected with the force (*power*) applied; ~ *escapement*, watch with connexion between pallet and balance made by two levers (ill. CLOCK); ~ (*watch*), watch with lever escapement. ~ *v.* Use lever; lift, move, act on, with lever.

Lēv'er[2], Charles James (1806–72). Irish author of novels describing the military life and fox-hunting Irish society of his day.

lēv'erage *n.* Action of, way of applying, lever; set or system of levers; power, mechanical advantage gained by use, of lever; means of accomplishing a purpose, power, influence.

lĕv'erĕt *n.* Young (esp. first-year) hare.

Leverrier (-vĕ'ryā), Urbain Jean Joseph (1811–77). French astronomer; discoverer of planet Neptune.

Lēv'ī. (O.T.) 3rd son of Jacob and Leah.

lĕvī'athan *n.* Sea-monster (bibl.); huge ship; anything very large of its kind.

lĕv'igāte *v.t.* Reduce to fine smooth powder; make smooth paste of. **lĕvigā'tion** *n.*

lĕv'in *n.* (poet.) (Flash of) lightning.

lĕv'irate *n.* Ancient Jewish custom by which dead man's brother or next of kin had to marry his widow; also practised by some other nations, e.g. of America and Asia. **lĕvirăt'ic(al)** *adj.*

lĕv'itāte *v.* (Make) rise and float in air (esp. in spiritualist language). **lĕvitā'tion** *n.*

Lēv'īte *n.* One of the tribe claiming descent from LEVI; some of its members were dedicated in remote times to religious service and were priests or teachers of the law or aided the priests in caring for the tabernacle, the sacred vessels, and the temple.

Lĕvĭt'ical *adj.* 1. Of the Levites. 2. Of the book of Leviticus.

Lĕvĭt'icus. In the Bible, 3rd book of the Pentateuch, containing details of the law and ritual of the Levites.

lĕv'ĭty *n.* Want of thought, frivolity, unseasonable jocularity, inconstancy; light behaviour.

levulose: see LAEVULOSE.

lĕv'y *n.* Collecting of assessment, tax, etc.; enrolling of men for war etc.; amount or number levied, body of men enrolled; *capital* ~, appropriation by State of fixed proportion of all the wealth in the country. ~ *v.t.* Raise (contribution, taxes), impose (rate, toll); raise (sum) by legal execution or process *on* person's goods; extort; enlist, enrol (soldiers, army); collect men and munitions for, proceed to make (war; usu. *upon, against*).

lewd *adj.* Base, worthless (bibl.); lascivious, unchaste, indecent; **lewd'ly** *adv.* **lewd'nĕss** *n.*

lew'ĭs[1] (lōō-) *n.* Iron contrivance for gripping heavy blocks of stone for lifting.

Lew'ĭs[2] (lōō-). N. part of most northerly island (Lewis-with-Harris) of Outer Hebrides, Scotland.

Lew'ĭs[3] (lōō-), Matthew Gregory (1775–1818). English author of novels and plays of terror, author of the novel 'The Monk'.

Lew'ĭs[4] (lōō-), (Harry) Sinclair (1885–1951). American novelist, whose 'Babbitt' (1922) satirized the ruthless American big-business man; first American to gain Nobel Prize for literature, 1930.

Lew'ĭs gŭn (lōō-) *n.* Light magazine-fed, gas-operated, air-cooled machine-gun (ill. GUN). [Col. I. N. *Lewis* of U.S. Army, inventor]

lew'isīte (lōō-) *n.* Highly irritant and vesicant persistent poison 'gas' (β-chloro-vinyl-dichloro-arsine) a heavy oily liquid. [W. L. *Lewis*, Amer. chemist]

lĕx'ĭcal *adj.* Of the vocabulary of a language; (as) of a lexicon. **lĕx'ĭcally** *adv.*

lĕxĭcŏg'raphy *n.* Dictionary-making. **lĕxĭcŏg'rapher** *n.* **lĕxĭcogrăph'ĭcal** *adj.*

lĕx'ĭcon *n.* Dictionary, esp. of ancient Greek, Hebrew, Syriac, or Arabic.

lĕxĭg'raphy *n.* System of writing in which each character represents a word.

Lĕx'ĭngton. Name of several towns and cities of U.S., esp.: 1. ~, Massachusetts, scene of the 1st battle (1775) of the Amer. War of Independence. 2. ~, Missouri, a centre of military operations during 1st year (1861) of Amer. Civil War.

lĕx tāliō'n'ĭs. Law of retaliation, an eye for an eye.

ley (lā) *n.* Land temporarily under grass; ~ *farming*, system of crop rotation in which pasture land is ploughed up and arable land sown with grass and clover, usu. at intervals of 3–4 years.

Leyd'en (lī-), **Leiden.** City of S. Holland, the Netherlands; when besieged 1573–4 by the Spaniards it was relieved by William the Silent, who cut the dikes and rescued the citizens by ship; ~ *University*, founded 1575 after the siege; ~ *jar*, device (invented 1745 at that university) for storing electric charge, consisting of a glass jar coated inside and outside with tinfoil, the electric energy being stored in the glass dielectric (non-conducting substance) between the tinfoil electrodes.

L.F. *abbrev.* Low FREQUENCY.

L.F.A.S. *abbrev.* Licentiate of the Faculty of Architects and Surveyors.

L.G. *abbrev.* Life Guards.

Lhasa (lahs'a). Capital city of Tibet.

līabĭl'ity *n.* Being liable; what one is liable for; (pl.) debts, pecuniary obligations; *limited* ~, being responsible only to limited amount for debts of trading company.

lī'able *adj.* 1. Legally bound; answerable *for*; subject or amenable *to* tax or penalty; under obligation *to* do. 2. Exposed or open *to*, apt *to* do or suffer, something undesirable; (U.S.) likely.

liaise' (-āz) *v.i.* (Service slang) Make liaison *with.*

liais'on (-zn) *n.* 1. Illicit intimacy between a man and a woman. 2. Sounding of ordinarily silent final consonant before vowel or mute *h* in French. 3. (mil.) Connexion, touch, between units on battlefield etc.; ~ *officer*, officer concerned with liaison of units or acting as go-between for allied forces.

liane' (-ahn) *n.* Woody climbing, twining, or scrambling plant which uses another as support in reaching light, esp. in tropical forest.

lī'ar *n.* Teller (esp. habitual) of lie(s).

lī'as *n.* Blue limestone rock occurring in some SW. English counties; (geol.) *L*~, lower, oldest, strata of jurassic system, blue argillaceous limestone rich in fossils. **līăss'ĭc** *adj.*

Lib. *abbrev.* Liberal.

lībā'tion *n.* (Pouring of) drink-offering to god; (joc.) potation.

lĭb'el *n.* 1. (civil & eccles. law) Plaintiff's written declaration; (Sc. law) form of complaint or ground of charge in prosecution. 2. (law) Published statement damaging to person's reputation, act of publishing it; (pop.) false and defamatory statement; (transf.) thing that brings discredit *on.* ~ *v.t.* Defame by libellous statements, accuse falsely and maliciously; (law) publish libel against; (eccles. etc. law) bring suit against. **lĭb'ellous** *adj.* **lĭb'ellously** *adv.*

Lī'ber. (Rom. myth.) Ancient Roman god of wine and fruitfulness, identified with Dionysus or Bacchus. **Lī'bera.** Female counterpart of Liber.

lĭb'eral *adj.* 1. Fit for a gentleman (now rare exc. in ~ *culture, education*, etc., education etc. directed to general enlargement of mind, not professional or technical). 2. Generous, open-handed, not sparing *of*; ample, abundant. 3. Not rigorous or literal, open-minded, candid, unprejudiced; (of political party etc., esp. in England) favourable to constitutional changes and legal or administrative reforms tending in direction of freedom or democracy. **lĭb'erally** *adv.* **lĭb'eral** *n.* Member of, sympathizer with, (esp. the British) Liberal Party. In British politics the Liberals, who inherit, with considerable modifications, the traditions of the WHIGS, were formerly one of the two great parties in the State, and in opposition to the

Tories, or *Conservatives*. **lĭb′eralism** *n.*

lĭberăl′ĭty *n.* Free giving, munificence; freedom from prejudice, breadth of mind.

lĭb′erāte *v.t.* Set at liberty; release *from*; (in war of 1939–45) free (occupied territory) of the enemy; (iron.) subject to new tyranny; (chem.) set free from combination. **lĭberā′tion** *n.* **lĭb′erātor** *n.*

Lībēr′ia. W. African Negro republic between Ivory Coast (French W. Africa) and Sierra Leone; settled by freed Negro slaves from America from early part of 19th c.; proclaimed an independent republic 1847; capital, Monrovia.

lĭbertār′ian *n.* & *adj.* (Person) believing in free will; advocate of liberty.

lĭb′ertine *n.* 1. Free-thinker on religion; antinomian; (transf.) one who follows his own inclinations. 2. Licentious or dissolute man. ~ *adj.* Free-thinking; licentious, dissolute. **lĭb′ertinage, lĭb′ertinism** *ns.*

lĭb′erty *n.* 1. Being free from captivity, imprisonment, slavery, or despotic control; right or power to do as one pleases or *to* do something; freedom from despotic rule personified; (pl.) privileges, immunities, or rights, enjoyed by prescription or grant; ~ *of conscience*, system allowing all members of State to follow what form of religion seems good to them; ~ *of the press*, system by which anyone may print and publish what he pleases without previous permission; *at* ~, free; having the right *to* do; disengaged; *within the liberties* (of city), within district which is subject to control of municipal authorities; *the liberties* (of a prison, esp. the Fleet and Marshalsea), limits outside prison within which prisoners were sometimes allowed to live. 2. Setting aside of rules, licence; *take the* ~, presume or venture; *take liberties*, be unduly familiar *with*; deal freely *with*; ~ *boat*, (naut.) boat carrying liberty men; ~ *hall*, place where one may do as one likes; ~ *man*, sailor with leave to go ashore; *L~ ship*, medium-sized Amer. cargo vessel used for carrying supplies to Europe etc. during the war of 1939–45; *Statue of L~*, colossal bronze figure of a woman holding up a torch ('Liberty Enlightening the World'), gift of French people to U.S. to commemorate centenary of Amer. independence, erected on high granite pedestal on Bedloe Island, New York harbour, 1885.

lĭbĭd′ĭnous *adj.* Lustful. **lĭbĭd′ĭnously** *adv.*

lĭbī′dō *n.* (psychol.) Sexual drive; in Freudian psycho-analysis the motive force of all human activity. **lĭbĭd′ĭnal** *adj.*

Lī′bra. The Scales, zodiacal constellation between Virgo and Scorpio; 7th sign (♎) of zodiac, into which sun enters at autumnal equinox.

lībrār′ian *n.* Custodian of library. **lībrār′ianshĭp** *n.*

lī′brary *n.* Room or building containing books for reading or reference; writing- and reading-room in house; collection of books, esp. one for use by the public, some part of it, or members of some society, public institution charged with care of such collection; series of books issued by publisher in similar bindings as connected in some way; *free* ~, library used by public without payment, esp. one maintained by municipality out of rates; *circulating* ~, one letting out books for profit; *L~ of Congress*, U.S. national library, at Washington, which receives a copy of every book copyrighted in the U.S.

lībrāte′ *v.i.* Oscillate like beam of balance. **lībrā′tion** *n.* Librating; (astron.) real or apparent motion of oscillating kind; ~ *of moon*, apparent irregularity of moon's motion making part near edge of disc alternately visible and invisible.

lĭbrĕtt′ō *n.* (pl. *-ti* pr. -tē). Text of opera or other long vocal composition. **lĭbrĕtt′ĭst** *n.*

Lĭb′yă. 1. Ancient Greek name for the N. part of Africa W. of Egypt. 2. An independent federal kingdom between Egypt and Tunisia, set up in Dec. 1951; formerly an Italian colony; capital, Tripoli. **Lĭb′yan** *adj.* & *n.* ~ *Desert*, E. part of Sahara, bounded eastwards by River Nile and extending from Mediterranean to Sudan.

lī′cence *n.* 1. Leave, permission; formal, usu. printed or written, authority from constituted authority to marry, publish book, produce play, drive motor-car, carry on some trade (esp. that in alcoholic liquor), etc.; university certificate of competence in some faculty. 2. Liberty of action, esp. when excessive; abuse of freedom, disregard of law or propriety; licentiousness; writer's or artist's singularity in metre, perspective, etc. (usu. *poetic* ~). **lī′cense, lī′cence** *v.t.* Allow (rare); grant licence to; authorize use of (premises) for certain purpose; authorize publication of book etc., performance of play etc.; (in past part.) allow complete freedom to. **līcensee′** *n.*

lī′censer *n.* (esp.) ~ *of the press*, *of plays*, officials licensing publication or performance when satisfied that law, morals, and decency are not outraged.

lĭcĕn′tiate (-shĭat) *n.* Holder of university licence or attestation of competence from collegiate or examining body; licensed preacher not yet having appointment (esp. in Presbyterian Church).

lĭcĕn′tious (-shus) *adj.* (Now rare) disregarding accepted rules, esp. of grammar or style; lascivious, libertine, lewd. **lĭcĕn′tiously** *adv.* **lĭcĕn′tiousnėss** *n.*

lĭch, lȳch *n.* Corpse (obs.); ~-*gate*, roofed gateway of churchyard where coffin is placed to await clergyman's arrival; ~-*owl*, screech-owl.

LICH-GATE

lī′chen (-k-) *n.* Plant organism composed of fungus and an alga in association, freq. grey or yellow and growing on rocks, trees, etc.; some species are edible, others used in manufacture of dyes, perfumes, and cosmetics.

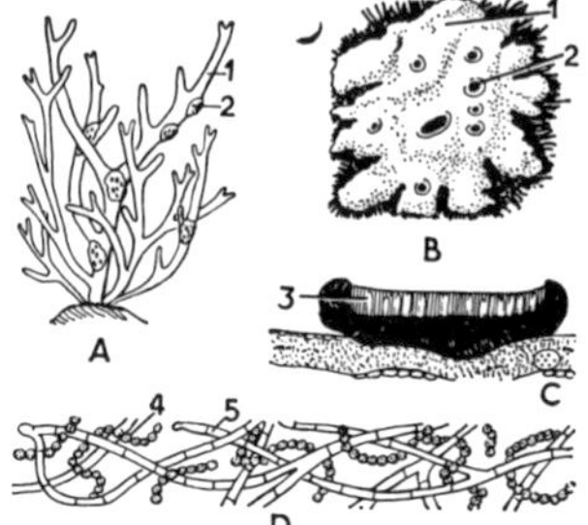

LICHEN: A. FRUTICOSE LICHEN. B. CRUSTACEOUS LICHEN. C. SECTION OF APOTHECIUM. D. SECTION OF THALLUS

1. Thallus. 2. Apothecium. 3. Asci. 4. Algae. 5. Fungal hypha

lĭ′cĭt *adj.* Lawful, not forbidden. **lĭ′cĭtly** *adv.*

lĭck *v.* Pass tongue over to taste, moisten, clean, etc.; take *up* or *off*, make *clean*, by licking; (of waves, flame, etc.) play lightly over; (of flame) swallow *up* in passing; (slang) beat, thrash; (slang) surpass comprehension of; (slang) go, hasten; ~ *into shape*, mould, make presentable or efficient; ~ *person's shoes*, show servility to him; *lick′-spittle*, toady. ~ *n.* Act of licking with tongue; place to which animals resort for salt (also *salt-*~); (slang) rapid pace.

lĭc′tor *n.* (Rom. antiq.) Officer

attending magistrate, bearing fasces as emblems of office and executing sentence on offenders.

lĭd *n.* Hinged or detached cover for aperture, esp. for opening at top of vessel; eye-lid; (bot., conch.) operculum.

Lĭdd'ell, Henry George (1811–98). English scholar; author, with Robert Scott, of the standard 'Greek–English Lexicon'.

Lid'ō (lē-). 1. Chain of sandy islands separating lagoon of Venice from Adriatic Sea, a fashionable bathing-resort. 2. Public open-air pleasure-beach or swimming-pool.

līe[1] *n.* Intentional false statement; imposture, false belief, mistaken convention; *tell a* ~, make intentionally false statement; *white* ~, lie excused or justified by its motive; *give the* ~ *to*, belie, serve to show falsity of; ~*-detector*, instrument indicating physiological changes, esp. in skin-resistance, which occur under stress of emotion. ~ *v.i.* (pres. part. *lȳ'ing*). Speak falsely, tell lie(s); take *away*, get *into*, *out of*, by lying; (of things) deceive; *lying*, deceptive.

līe[2] *v.i.* (pres. part. *lȳ'ing*, past t. *lay*, past part. *lain*). 1. (Of persons or animals) have one's body in more or less horizontal position along ground or surface; have sexual intercourse *with*; (of the dead) be in the grave *at*, *in*; assume lying position (esp. ~ *down*); be kept, remain, in specified state. 2. (Of things) be at rest, usu. more or less horizontally, on surface; be stored up in specified place; remain in specified state; be situated; be spread out to view; (of road) lead *through*, *by*, etc.; (of ship) float in berth or at anchor; exist, be found, reside, be arranged or related, in some position or manner; (law) be admissible or sustainable; ~ *heavy*, be a weight *on* one's stomach or conscience; *as far as in me lies*, to the best of my power. 3. ~ *by*, be unused; keep quiet or retired; *lying down*, behaving in abject manner, not standing up to opponent, etc.; ~ *in*, be brought to bed in childbirth; ~ *off*, (naut.) stand some distance from shore or other ship; ~ *over*, be deferred; ~ *to*, (naut.) come almost to a stop with head near wind by backing or shortening sail; ~ *up*, go into, be in, retirement; take to one's bed; (of ship) go into dock, be out of commission. ~ *n.* Way, direction, or position in which thing lies; place where beast, bird, or fish, is accustomed to lie; (golf) angle of club-head with shaft (*flat*, *upright*, ~).

Lieb'ĭg (lē-), Justus von, Baron (1803–73). German chemist; founder of agricultural chemistry; ~*'s extract*, a concentrated preparation made from beef, containing the salts and extractive principles of the meat, without the albumen, gelatin, or fat.

Lieb'knecht (lēbknĕχt), Karl (1871–1919). German socialist leader, murdered after failure of SPARTACIST revolt.

Liech'tenstein (lĭχ'tenshtīn). Small independent principality in Rhine valley between Austria and Switzerland; capital, Vaduz.

lied (lē-) *n.* (pl. *lieder*). German song or poem of ballad kind.

lief (lēf) *adv.* (archaic) Gladly, willingly.

liege (lēj) *adj.* (Of superior) entitled to receive, (of vassal) bound to give, feudal service or allegiance; ~ *lord*, feudal superior, sovereign. ~ *n.* Liege lord; vassal, subject.

lien (lē'en) *n.* (law) Right to keep possession of property till debt due in respect of it is discharged.

lĭerne' *n.* Short rib connecting bosses and intersections of principal ribs in Gothic vaulting (ill. VAULT).

Lies'ėgăng rings (lē-). Bands of a precipitate formed when a precipitant diffuses in a gel (in contrast with the evenly distributed precipitate in an aqueous solution). [f. L. E. *Liesegang*, Ger. chemist]

lieu (lū) *n.* *In* ~, in the place, instead, *of*.

Lieut. *abbrev.* Lieutenant; **Lieut.-Col., -Gen., -Gov.** Lieutenant-Colonel, -General, -Governor.

lieutĕn'ant (lĕft-, in navy let-; U.S. lo͞ot-, lūt-) *n.* 1. Deputy, substitute, vicegerent, acting for a superior; ~ *of the Tower*, acting commandant of Tower of London; *Lord L*~: see LORD; ~*-governor*, governor's deputy; in British colonies, actual governor of district or province under governor-general; (U.S.), deputy governor of a State. 2. (mil.) Officer next in rank below captain; (navy) junior officer; (U.S.) officer of police-force next in rank below captain; ~*-colonel*, army officer of rank next below colonel's, having actual command of a regiment; ~*-commander*, officer in navy of rank next below commander's and above lieutenant's; ~*-general*, officer in army of rank next below general's and above major-general's; (U.S.) officer in supreme command of army, under President (a title very rarely held). **lieutĕn'ancy** *n.*

līfe *n.* (pl. *lives*). 1. Condition or fact of being living; that state of ceaseless change and functional activity which constitutes the essential difference between living organisms and dead or non-living matter; continuance of animate existence (opp. *death*); energy, liveliness, vivacity, animation; vivifying influence; living things; the living form or model, life-size figure, etc.; (*a matter* etc.) *of* ~ *and death*, (something) on which it depends whether a person shall live or die, of vital importance; *for one's*, *for dear* ~, (as if) to escape death; *as large as* ~, life-size; *to the* ~, with fidelity to the original. 2. Period from birth to death, birth to present time, or present time to death; person considered with respect to expectation of life; ~ *sentence*, *rent*, *annuity*, sentence etc. to continue for rest of person's life; *expectation of* ~, average period that person at specified age may expect to live; *good*, *bad*, ~, person likely to pass, fall short of, this average; *have the time of one's* ~, enjoy oneself as never before. 3. Individual's actions and fortunes, manner of existence; written story of these, biography; active part of existence, business and pleasures of the world; *this* ~, that on earth; *the other*, *future*, *eternal*, *everlasting*, ~, state of existence after death; *see* ~, mix freely with others; *high*, *low*, ~, social customs of upper, lower, classes. 4. ~*-belt*, belt of buoyant material to support human body in water; ~*-blood*, blood necessary to life; vitalizing influence; ~*-boat*, boat of special construction for saving life in storms (ill. SHIP); ~*-buoy*: see BUOY; ~*-cycle*, (biol.) series of changes undergone by an organism from the union of gametes that produced it until its death (but in some animals and plants the life-cycle includes the life and death of successive individuals); ~ *estate*, property that one holds for life but cannot dispose of further; ~ *force*, vital energy, force conceived as striving for survival of individual and race; *L*~ *Guard(s)*, (member of) body-guard of soldiers, formerly (in British army) two regiments of household cavalry, which are now combined in one Armoured Corps regiment but still provide a squadron for ceremonial duties; ~*-guard*, (U.S.) person watching against accidents to bathers; ~ *interest*, right to life estate; ~*-line*, rope used for life-saving, e.g. that attached to life-buoy; diver's signalling line; ~*-office*, office for life-assurance; ~*-preserver*, short stick with heavily loaded end; ~*-table*, statistics of expectation of life; *life'time*, duration of person's life; ~*-work*, task pursued through one's whole life. **līfe'lėss** (-fl-) *adj.* Dead; lacking animation, energy, etc. **līfe'lėssly** *adv.* **līfe'lėssnėss** *n.* **līfe'līke** *adj.* Resembling life; exactly like real person or thing.

līf'er *n.* (slang) One sentenced to, sentence of, penal servitude for life.

Lĭff'ey. Irish river flowing from Wicklow Mountains to Dublin Bay.

lĭft *v.* 1. Raise to higher position, take up, hoist; rise from ground; elevate to higher plane of thought or feeling; give upward direction to; hold or have on high; hit (cricket-ball etc.) into air; (of ship etc. afloat) rise on wave; (of cloud, fog, etc.) rise, disperse; ~ *one's hand against*, strike. 2. Steal (esp. cattle). ~ *n.* 1. Lifting. 2. Help (esp. given to walker by taking him some distance in vehicle). 3. One layer of leather in boot-heel. 4. Apparatus for raising and lowering people or things from one floor or level to another, elevator, hoist. 5. Transport by air; persons or supplies so transported.

lĭg'ament *n.* (anat.) Short band of tough flexible fibrous tissue binding the two bones at a joint (ill. BONE); (loosely) any membranous fold keeping organ in position; similar part in lower organisms. **lĭgamĕn'tal, lĭgamĕn'tary, lĭgamĕn'tous** *adjs.*

lĭg'ature *n.* 1. Thing used in tying, esp. (surg.) cord or band used to tie off blood-vessels to stop haemorrhage or obstruct blood flow. 2. Thing that unites, bond; (mus.) group of two or more notes sung to one syllable, slur, tie; (print. etc.) two or more letters joined together in one character as *æ, fi.* ~ *v.t.* Bind with ligature.

light[1] (līt) *n.* 1. Visible form of electromagnetic radiation produced by energy changes within the atoms of a substance, esp. when excited by intense heat; that which evokes functional activity of organ of sight; natural agent emanating from sun; medium or condition of space in which vision is possible; appearance of brightness; amount of illumination in a place, one's fair or ordinary share of this; daylight; vivacity in person's eyes; favouring aspect; (slang, pl.) eyes; *stand in person's* ~, (fig.) prejudice his chances; ~ *of person's countenance*, his favour, approving presence, or sanction; *see the* ~, be born; *come, bring, to* ~, be revealed, reveal. 2. Object from which brightness emanates; sun or other heavenly body; ignited candle, lamp, or the like; (collect.) lamps etc. illuminating place; beacon lamp, esp. of ship or lighthouse; lighthouse; (fig.) eminent person or luminary; ~*s out*, (mil.) the last bugle call of the day, signal for all lights to be put out. 3. Mental illumination, illumination of soul by divine truth or love etc.; elucidation, enlightenment; fact or discovery serving to explain subject; (pl.) natural or acquired mental powers; (sing.) aspect in which thing is viewed; (in acrostic puzzles) one of the words whose initial and final letters make up the answer; *by the* ~ *of nature*, without aid of revelation or teaching; *see the* ~, (U.S.) become enlightened or convinced; *place in a good (bad)* ~, represent (un)favourably. 4. Window or opening in wall for admission of light; perpendicular division of mullioned window; glazed compartment of side or roof in greenhouse. 5. (paint. etc.) Illuminated surface, part of picture represented as lighted up. 6. (law) Light falling on windows, the obstruction of which by neighbour is illegal *Ancient L~s*, inscription giving notice of this). 7. Flame or spark serving to ignite; thing used for igniting, spill, taper, match; *strike a* ~, produce light with match etc. 8. ~ *due, duty*, toll on ships for maintenance of lighthouses and lightships; *light'house*, tower or other structure containing beacon light(s) for warning or guiding ships at sea; *light'ship*, ship, moored or anchored, containing similar lights; ~*-year*, (astron.) distance which light travels in one year (approx. $5{\cdot}88 \times 10^{12}$ miles), as unit in measuring interstellar distances. **light'lėss** *adj.*

light[2] (līt) *adj.* Well-provided with light, not dark; pale-coloured, pale.

light[3] (līt) *v.* (past t. & past part. *lit* or *lighted*). Set (lamp, fire, etc.) burning; (of fuel etc.) take fire, begin to burn; give light to; brighten with animation; show (person his) way or surroundings with a light; ~ *up*, begin to smoke pipe etc.; kindle lights in street, room, etc., at dusk; light brightly, make conspicuous by light.

light[4] (līt) *adj.* 1. Of little weight, not heavy; deficient in weight; of small specific gravity; having or intended for small load; (of ship, cart, etc.) made lightly for small loads and quick movement; (of building) not looking heavy, graceful, elegant. 2. Acting gently, applied delicately, not violent; not dense or tenacious; porous, friable; easy of digestion; (of wine etc.) not strong; (of syllable) unemphatic; not important, slight, trivial, venial, not grave, jesting, thoughtless, frivolous; wanton, unchaste; nimble, quick-moving; fickle, inconstant. 3. Easily borne or done; aimed or aiming at entertainment merely; (of sleep) easily disturbed, not profound. 4. Free from sorrow, cheerful, sanguine (only in ~ *heart, -hearted*); delirious (now only in ~*-headed*). 5. ~ *engine*, railway engine with no train attached; ~*-fingered*, thievish, given to stealing; ~*-foot*, springy, nimble; ~*-handed*, having a light hand; managing tactfully; ~ *horse*, light-armed cavalry; ~ *marching order*, that in which only arms and ammunition are taken; ~*-minded*, frivolous, thoughtless; ~ *oil*, distillate of coal tar, distilling below 195° F. and consisting mostly of aromatic hydrocarbons; ~*-o'-love*, fickle woman, harlot; *L~ Programme*, (in U.K.) radio service of B.B.C. providing more entertainment than HOME Service; ~ *railway*, one for light traffic; ~*-weight*, (man or animal) below average weight; boxer of not more than 9 st. 9 lb. **light'ly** *adv.* **light'nėss** *n.* **light** *adv.* In light manner.

light[5] (līt) *v.* 1. (naut.) Lift (rope etc.) along, lend a hand in hauling ropes, etc. 2. Alight, descend, come down (archaic); chance, come by chance (*up*)*on*.

light'en[1] (lītn) *v.* Shed light upon, make bright; grow bright, shine, flash; emit lightning.

light'en[2] (lītn) *v.* Reduce load of (ship etc.), (of ship) have load reduced; relieve (heart etc.), be relieved, of weight; reduce weight of; mitigate; grow lighter.

light'er[1] (līt-) *n.* (esp.) Instrument for producing a light, consisting usu. of a reservoir containing petrol, which can be ignited by friction of metal wheel on a flint.

light'er[2] (līt-) *n.* Boat, usu. flat-bottomed, for unloading and loading ships not brought to wharf and for transporting goods in harbour (ill. BARGE). ~ *v.t.* Remove (goods) in lighter. **light'erage, light'erman** *ns.*

light'nĭng (līt-) *n.* Visible electric discharge between clouds or cloud and ground; *forked, chain(ed)*, ~, lightning-flash in form of zigzag or divided line; *sheet* ~, lightning-flash of diffused brightness; *summer, heat*, ~, sheet lightning without audible thunder, result of distant storm; *like* ~, with greatest conceivable speed; ~*-conductor, -rod*, metal rod or wire fixed to exposed part of building or to mast to divert lightning into earth or sea; ~ *strike*, sudden strike taking place without warning.

lights (līts) *n.pl.* Lungs of sheep, pigs, bullocks, etc., used as food esp. for cats and dogs.

light'some (līt-) *adj.* Light, graceful, elegant, in appearance; light-hearted, merry; nimble. **light'somely** *adv.* **light'somenėss** *n.*

light'wŏŏd (līt-) *n.* 1. Various trees with light wood; in Australia chiefly *Acacia melanoxylon.* 2. (chiefly U.S.) Wood used in lighting fire, esp. resinous pine-wood; various trees burning with bright flame.

lign-ăl'ōes (līn-, -z) *n.* The drug aloes; aloes-wood, an aromatic Mexican wood. [L, = 'wood of the aloe']

lĭg'nėous *adj.* Woody (esp. of plants).

lĭg'nĭn *n.* (bot.) Hardening material impregnating cell-walls of woody tissues.

lĭg'nīte *n.* Brown coal, a deposit formed usu. after the carboniferous age, showing visible traces of its plant structure and containing much carbon; the oldest approximates to bituminous coal, the newest to peat.

lĭg'num vī'tae *n.* = GUAIACUM. [L, = 'wood of life']

lĭg'ūlate *adj.* Strap-shaped; (bot.) with strap-shaped florets.

lĭg'ūle *n.* (bot.) Thin appendage at base of leaf-blade, esp. in grasses (ill. LEAF); ligulate corolla in composites.

Lĭgūr'ĭa. Territorial division of N. Italy, once forming the republic of Genoa or *Ligurian Republic*, formed 1797 after Napoleon's Italian campaign, annexed to France 1805, and subsequently merged in kingdom of Italy; also, the more extensive region inhabited by the ancient Ligurians. **Ligūr'ian** *adj.* & *n.* (Native, inhabitant) of Liguria; (member) of an ancient race (*Ligures*) inhabiting NW. Italy, Switzerland, and SE. Gaul and speaking a pre-Italic Indo-European language; ~ *Sea*, part of Mediterranean between Corsica and NW. coast of Italy round Genoa.

līke[1] *adj.* Similar, resembling something, each other, or the original; resembling, such as; characteristic of; in promising state or right mood for do*ing*; (archaic) likely (*to*); *what is he* ~?, what sort of person is he?; ~ *that*, of the kind just seen or referred to; *look* ~, have the appearance of being; give promise, indicate the presence, of; ~*-minded*, having same tastes, views, etc. ~ (*quasi*) *prep.* In the manner of, to the same degree as; ~ *a shot*, without demur, willingly, regardless of consequences. ~ *adv.* In the same manner *as* (archaic); probably (now only in *very* ~, ~ *enough*); (vulg.) so to speak; ~ *as we lie*, (golf) position when both sides have played same number of strokes. ~ *conj.* (vulg. & colloq.) As. ~ *n.* Counterpart, equal, like thing or person; (golf) stroke that equalizes number of strokes played by each side; thing(s) of the same kind; *the* ~ *of*, (colloq.) such a person or thing as; *and the* ~, etcetera.

līke[2] *v.* 1. Be pleasing to (archaic, chiefly impers.). 2. Find agreeable, congenial, or satisfactory; feel attracted by; wish for. ~ *n.* (usu. pl.) Liking, predilection. **līk'(e)able** *adj.* **līk'(e)ableness** *n.*

līke'lihood (-kl-) *n.* Being likely, probability.

līke'ly (-klĭ) *adj.* Probable; such as might well happen, or be or prove true, or turn out to be the thing specified; to be expected *to*; promising, apparently suitable *for*, *to*; capable-looking. ~ *adv. Most* or *very* ~, probably.

līk'en *v.t.* Find or point out resemblance in (thing) *to*.

līke'ness (-kn-) *n.* 1. Being like, resemblance. 2. Representation, copy, portrait; person or thing having exact appearance of another.

līke'wise (-kwīz) *adv.* & *conj.* Similarly (bibl.); also, moreover, too.

līk'ing *n.* What one likes, one's taste; regard, fondness, taste, fancy, *for*.

lĭl'ac *n.* Genus of deciduous shrubs and trees of family *Oleaceae*, commonest of which (*Syringa vulgaris*) has fragrant, usu. pale pinkish-violet, blossoms; colour of these. ~ *adj.* Of lilac colour.

lĭliā'ceous (-shus) *adj.* Of lilies or the order *Liliaceae*; lily-like.

Lilienthal (lēl'yentahl), Otto (1848–96). German aeronautical inventor; constructed a practicable glider.

Lĭl'ĭth. In Jewish folk-lore, a female demon or vampire; in Rabbinical literature, the first wife of Adam, dispossessed by Eve.

Lĭllĭburlēr'ō. Name and part of refrain of a song ridiculing the Irish, popular at end of 17th c. esp. among soldiers and supporters of William III during revolution of 1688.

Lĭll'ĭput. In Swift's 'Gulliver's Travels', a country peopled by pygmies 6 inches high. **Lĭllĭpū'tian** (-shn) *adj.* Of Lilliput; of diminutive size; petty.

lĭlt *v.t.* Sing melodiously or rhythmically. ~ *n.* (Song with) marked rhythmical cadence or swing.

lĭl'y *n.* 1. (Flower of) genus *Lilium* of bulbous herbs bearing large showy white, reddish, or purplish flowers, freq. spotted, on tall slender stem, esp. *L. candidum*, the white or madonna lily; various other plants of allied genera; *African* ~, agapanthus, liliaceous plant with showy blue flowers; *lent* ~, yellow daffodil; *tiger-*~: see TIGER; ~ *of the valley*, spring flower, *Canvallaria majalis*, with (usu.) two longish leaves and racemes of fragrant white bell-shaped flowers; *water-*~: see WATER. 2. Heraldic fleur-de-lis; *the* (*golden*) *lilies*, arms of French monarchy, the Bourbon dynasty. 3. (attrib.) Delicately white; pallid; ~*-livered*, cowardly; ~*-pad*, (U.S.) broad flat leaf of water-lily lying on water; ~*-white*, white as a lily.

Lim'a (lē-). Capital city of Peru; *līm'a bark*, CINCHONA; *līm'a bean*, kind of bean (*Phaseolus lunatus*) native to tropical America, with flat, usu. white, seeds.

lĭmb[1] (-m) *n.* Leg, arm, or wing; main branch of tree; one of four branches of cross; spur of mountain; ~ (*of the devil*, *of Satan*), mischievous child. ~ *v.t.* Disable limb of; dismember. **lĭmb'less** *adj.*

lĭmb[2] (-m) *n.* Edge of surface; graduated edge of quadrant etc.; edge of sun, moon, etc.; expanded part of petal, sepal, or leaf.

lĭm'bate *adj.* (biol.) Having distinct or different-coloured border.

lĭm'bĕck *n.* (archaic) = ALEMBIC.

lĭm'ber[1] *n.* Detachable front of gun-carriage (two wheels, axle, pole, and ammunition-box). ~ *v.t.* Attach limber to (gun), fasten together two parts of gun-carriage (usu. *up*).

lĭm'ber[2] *n.* (naut.) One of the holes cut in floor-timbers for drainage to pump-well.

lĭm'ber[3] *adj.* Flexible; lithe, nimble. ~ *v.t.* Make limber, pliant, or supple (freq. *up*).

lĭm'bō *n.* Region on border of hell, supposed abode of just men who died before Christ's coming and of unbaptized infants; prison, durance; condition of neglect or oblivion. [L *in limbo* at the edge]

Lĭm'bourg (-boorg), **-būrg.** 1. Ancient duchy of the Low Countries. 2. (spelt *-bourg*) Province of NE. Belgium, part of the old duchy. 3. (spelt *-burg*) Province of extreme SE. Holland, including another part of the old duchy.

Lim'būrger (-g-) *adj.* & *n.*; ~ *cheese*, soft white compressed cheese orig. from Limbourg, Belgium, with characteristic smell.

līme[1] *n.* 1. Sticky substance made from holly bark for catching small birds (usu. *bird-*~). 2. White caustic alkaline substance, quicklime (calcium oxide, CaO), made by heating chalk or limestone and used for making mortar; (pop., in *carbonate*, *chloride*, etc., *of* ~) calcium; (theatr.) limelight. 3. ~*-burner*, maker of lime; ~*-kiln*, kiln for burning limestone; *lime'light*, intense white light got by heating lime in oxyhydrogen flame, formerly used in theatres to light up important figures etc.; (fig.) glare of publicity; ~*-pit*, limestone quarry; pit for steeping hides to remove hair; ~*-twig*, twig smeared with bird-lime; *lime'stone*, rock consisting chiefly of calcium carbonate; *lime'water*, solution of calcium hydroxide, $Ca(OH)_2$, used medicinally as an antacid. ~ *v.t.* Smear (twigs), catch (bird), with bird-lime; treat, dress (land) with lime; steep (skins) in lime and water; treat (wood, esp. oak) with lime.

līme[2] *n.* Round fruit of *Citrus medica*, smaller and more acid than lemon; ~*-juice*, juice of this used as beverage and as antiscorbutic; ~*-juicer*, (U.S.) British ship or sailor (because use of lime-juice as anti-scorbutic is enforced in British navy).

līme[3] *n.* (also ~*-tree*) Ornamental tree (*Tilia*, esp. *T. europaea*) with heart-shaped leaves and small fragrant yellowish blossom.

Līme'house (-mhows). Wharf-district of E. London, N. of Thames, with large number of Chinese residents. ~ *v.i.* Make fiery political speeches as David Lloyd George did at Limehouse in 1909.

lĭm'ĕn *n.* (psych.) Limit below which given stimulus ceases to be perceptible, minimum intensity of stimulus required to produce sensation. **lĭm'ĭnal** *adj.* [L, = 'threshold']

Lĭm'erĭck[1]. County of Munster, Eire, town and port at head of estuary of River Shannon.

lĭm'erĭck[2] *n.* Jingle, now usu. epigrammatic and freq. indecent, consisting of 5 lines (2 of 3 ft, 2 of 2 ft, and 1 of 3 ft) with rhymes *aabba*; first found *c* 1820, and popularized by Edward Lear in his 'Book of Nonsense', 1846. [said to be f. chorus 'Will you come up to Limerick?' sung after extempore verses contributed by each member of party]

lĭm'ey (-mĭ) *n.* (U.S. slang) English sailor; Englishman. [f. *lime-juicer*; see LIME[2]]

lĭm'ĭt *n.* Bounding line, terminal point, bound that may not or cannot be passed; *without* ~, unlimited; *the* ~, (slang) the last straw, the worst, etc., conceivable; ~ *man*, competitor receiving longest start in handicap. ~ *v.t.* Confine within limits, set bounds to, restrict *to*; serve as limit to. **lĭm'ĭtlėss** *adj.*

lĭm'ĭtary *adj.* Subject to restriction; of, on, serving as, limit.

lĭmĭtā'tion *n.* Limiting; limited condition, disability or inability; limiting rule or circumstance; legally specified period beyond which action cannot be brought, estate or law is not to continue, etc.; *statute of* ~*s*, one fixing such period.

lĭm'ĭted *adj.* Circumscribed, narrow; scanty; ~ *company*, limited liability company (see LIABILITY); ~ (*express* or *train*), (U.S.) train carrying limited number of passengers (usu. paying extra fare); ~ *monarchy*, one in which powers of monarch are restricted by the constitution.

lĭmn (-m) *v.t.* (archaic) Paint (picture); depict, portray. **lĭm'ner** *n.*

lĭmnŏl'ogy *n.* Study of fresh waters and their inhabitants.

Lĭmoges' (-mōzh). City of W. central France, famous in 16th and 17th centuries for enamel work and later for porcelain.

Limousin (lēmōōzăṅ'). Former province of W. central France.

lĭm'ousine (-ōōzēn) *n.* Motor-car with closed body and partition behind driver. [Fr., f. LIMOUSIN]

lĭmp[1] *v.i.* Walk lamely; (of verse) halt; (of ship) proceed slowly and with difficulty because of damage. ~ *n.* Lame walk. **lĭmp'ĭngly** *adv.*

lĭmp[2] *adj.* Not stiff, flexible; wanting in energy; (of book-bindings) not stiffened with mill-board. **lĭmp'ly** *adv.* **lĭmp'nėss** *n.*

lĭm'pėt *n.* Gasteropod mollusc (*Patella*) with low conical shell found adhering tightly to rocks.

lĭm'pĭd *adj.* Pellucid, clear, not turbid. **lĭm'pĭdly** *adv.* **lĭm'pĭdnėss, lĭmpĭd'ĭty** *ns.*

Lĭmpōp'ō. River of SE. Africa, flowing into Indian Ocean, and for a large part of its course forming N. boundary of Transvaal.

Lĭn'acre (-ėker), Thomas (*c* 1460–1524). English physician and classical scholar; a principal founder and first president of the Royal College of Physicians.

lĭn'age *n.* Number of lines in printed matter; payment according to this.

lĭnch'pĭn *n.* Pin passed through axle-end to keep wheel on (ill. WHEEL).

Lĭnc'oln[1] (-kon). County town of Lincolnshire, England; ~ *green*, (hist.) bright-green cloth made there, formerly worn by, and associated with, hunters in Sherwood Forest.

Lĭnc'oln[2] (-kon). Capital city of Nebraska, U.S.

Lĭnc'oln[3] (-kon), Abraham (1809–65). American statesman; political leader of Northern States in Amer. Civil War, and 16th president of U.S., 1860–5; assassinated by John Wilkes Booth.

Lĭnc'oln Cŏll'ege (-kon). A college of the University of Oxford, founded 1429 by Richard Fleming, bishop of Lincoln.

Lĭnc'olnshire (-kon-). An eastern county of England.

Lĭnc'oln's Inn (-konz). Since 1310, an Inn of Court in London, named after Henry de Lacy, 3rd Earl of Lincoln, who had a house there in reign of Edward I.

Lincs. *abbrev.* Lincolnshire.

Lĭnd, Johanna Maria (1820–87). 'Jenny Lind', Swedish soprano singer.

Lĭnd'bĕrgh (-g), Charles Augustus (1902–). American aviator, first to fly the Atlantic alone.

lĭn'den *n.* Lime-tree.

Lĭn'dĭsfârne (Holy Island). Small island off coast of Northumberland, site of church and monastery founded by St. AIDAN, 635: ~ *Gospels*, illuminated Vulgate manuscript of the four gospels, *c* 700, interlined with an Old English paraphrase of the 10th c.

līne[1] *n.* Fine long flax separated from the tow.

līne[2] *n.* (Order of main senses: 1. Cord; 2. Long narrow mark; 3. Row; 4. Series; 5. Direction). 1. Piece of rope (esp. naut.); wire or cable for telegraph or telephone, route traversed by this; cord bearing fish-hook(s); cord for measuring, levelling, etc.; (pl.) one's lot in life; *hard* ~*s*, ill luck, bad fortune. 2. Long narrow mark traced on surface; use of these in draughtsmanship; (games) mark limiting court or ground or special parts of them; thing resembling traced mark, band of colour, seam, furrow, wrinkle, fold in palm of hand supposed to indicate fate, character, etc.; (math.) continuous extent (straight or curved) of length without breadth or thickness, curve connecting all points having a common property; *the* equator; straight line; contour, outline, lineament; limit, boundary; (as measure) $\frac{1}{12}$ in.; one of the very narrow sections in which televised scenes are photographed and reproduced; (pl.) plan or draft (esp. of ship) in horizontal, vertical, and oblique sections; (pl.) manner of procedure; *hung on the* ~, (of picture) exhibited with its centre level with spectator's eye; ~ *block*, photo-mechanically prepared metal-faced block from which drawing may be printed in conjunction with letterpress; ~ *drawing*, drawing done with pen or similar instrument; ~ *engraving*, incising of lines on metal plate with burin, print taken from such plate. 3. Row of persons or things; direction indicated by them (*get a* ~ *on*, gain a clue to); (mil.) double row (front and rear ranks) of men ranged side by side; (mil.) trench, (pl.) connected series of field-works; row of words in page or newspaper column; short letter; single verse of poetry, (pl.) piece of poetry; (pl.) specified amount of usu. Latin verse to be written out as school punishment; (pl.) certificate of marriage; (pl.) words of actor's part; (naut.) ~ *abreast*, number of ships ranged on line crossing keels at right angles; ~ *ahead*, ships following in one another's wake; ~ *of battle*: see BATTLE; (mil.) *the* ~, (in British army) regular and numbered troops as dist. from guards and auxiliary forces; (U.S.) regular fighting force of all arms; *all along the* ~, at every point; *read between the* ~*s*, discover meaning or purpose not expressed or not obvious. 4. Series or regular succession of steamers, omnibuses, aircraft, etc., plying between certain places; connected series of persons or things following one another in time, esp. several generations of family; family, lineage, stock. 5. Direction, course, track; (railw.) single track of rails, one branch of system, whole system under one management; course followed in riding to hounds; course of procedure, conduct, thought, etc.; department of activity, province, branch of business; (commerc.) class of goods, order for stock of this. ~ *v.* Mark *in*, *off*, *out*, with lines on paper etc.; cover with lines; draw *up* in line; come *up*, spread *out*, in lines; post troops etc. along (road etc.), (of troops) form line along; (of things) stand at intervals along (wall etc.); ~ *out*, (Rugby football, of forwards) form line opposite opponents at right angles to touch-line when ball is thrown in from touch; ~*-out*, *n.*

līne[3] *v.t.* Apply layer of (usu. different) material to inside of (garment, box, etc.); fill (purse, pocket, stomach, etc.); serve as lining for. **lī'nĭng** *n.*

līne[4] *v.t.* Copulate with, cover (bitch).

lĭn'ėage *n.* Lineal descent, ancestry, pedigree.

lĭn'ėal *adj.* In the direct line of descent or ancestry; (rare) of, in, line(s), linear. **lĭn'ėally** *adv.*

lĭn'ėament *n.* (Usu. pl.) distinctive feature(s) or characteristic(s), esp. feature(s) of face.

lĭn'ėar *adj.* 1. Of, in, line(s); (of work of art) conceived or expressed in lines rather than masses. 2. Long, narrow, and of uniform breadth. 3. (math., physics) Involving measurement in one dimension only. **lĭn'ėarly** *adv.*

lĭnėā'tion *n.* Drawing of, marking with, arrangement of, lines.

lĭn'ėn *adj.* Made of flax. ~ *n.* Cloth woven from flax; particular kind of this; (collect.) garments etc.

orig. of linen, now of other materials; undergarments, bed-linen, table-linen; *~-draper*, dealer in linen, calico, etc.; *lin′enfold*, decorative wooden panel carved to represent vertical folds or pleats (ill. WAINSCOT); *~ tester*, small folding magnifying glass for counting warp and weft threads in square inch etc. of fabric.

lĭn′er[1] *n.* Ship belonging to line

LINER

of passenger-ships; aircraft belonging to a regular line, esp. for passenger transport.

lĭn′er[2] *n.* Removable metal lining to prevent wear and tear in guns or other machinery.

lines′man (-nz-) *n.* 1. Soldier of line regiment. 2. (lawn tennis, football) Official assisting umpire or referee by deciding whether or where ball touches or crosses line. 3. Man employed to test safety of railway lines.

lĭng[1] *n.* Long slender N. European sea-fish (*Molva vulgaris*) used (often salted or split and dried) for food.

lĭng[2] *n.* Various heather or ericaceous plants, esp. *Callusa vulgaris.*

lĭng′er (-ngg-) *v.i.* Put off departure, esp. from reluctance to go; stay about, not depart or arrive at expected or right time; dally *round* place, *over*, (*up*)*on*, subject; drag *on* a feeble existence; be protracted; be tardy, delay; (quasi-trans.) throw (time) *away* in delays. **lĭng′erĭngly** *adv.*

lingerie (lă′ṅzhrē) *n.* Women's underclothes.

lĭng′ō (-ngg-) *n.* (contempt.) Foreign language; language belonging to special subject or class of people. [corrupt. of LINGUA (FRANCA)]

lĭng′ua frănc′a (-nggwa) *n.* 1. Mixture of Italian, French, Greek, and Spanish, used in Levant. 2. Any language spoken or understood by various peoples over a wide area. [It. = 'Frankish tongue']

lĭng′ual (-nggw-) *adj.* Of the tongue; of speech or languages.

lĭng′uĭfŏrm (-nggw-) *adj.* (bot., anat., zool.) Tongue-shaped.

lĭng′uĭst (-nggw-) *n.* Person skilled in (foreign) languages. **lĭnguĭs′tĭc** *adj.* Of the study of languages; of language. **lĭnguĭs′tĭcally** *adv.*

linhay (lĭn′ĭ) *n.* (dial.) Shed etc. open in front, usu. with lean-to roof.

lĭn′ĭment *n.* Embrocation, usu. made with oil.

lĭnk[1] *n.* One ring or loop of chain; as measure, $\frac{1}{100}$ of surveying chain, 7·92 in.; CUFF[1]-link; connecting part, thing or person that unites others, filler of gap, member of series; *missing ~*: see MISSING. *~ v.* Connect, join *together*, *to*, or *up*; clasp (hands); hook (arms, arm *in* or *through* another's); attach oneself *on*, *in*, to system, company, etc.

lĭnk[2] *n.* Torch of pitch and tow formerly used for lighting people along streets and carried by *link′man* or *link′boy.*

lĭnk′age *n.* (esp. biol.) Relative inseparability of two or more heritable characteristics, due to their factors being in the same chromosome.

lĭnks *n.pl.* Level or undulating sandy ground near sea-shore, with turf and coarse grass (Sc.); ground on which golf is played, often resembling this (freq. as sing.).

Lĭnlĭth′gowshire (-gō-). Former name of WEST LOTHIAN.

lĭnn *n.* Linden or lime; wood of this.

Linn. *abbrev.* Linnaeus.

Linnae′us. Carl von Linné (1707–78). Swedish naturalist; founder of modern systematic botany. **Lĭnn(a)ē′an** *adj.* Of Linnaeus or his system; *~ system*, system of botanical binomial classification introduced by him; it divided all plants into 24 classes, most of which were based on the number or arrangement of stamens; it has been superseded by the 'natural' system founded by Jussien in 1789; *Linne′an Society*, English society publishing journals and transactions on matters of natural history, founded 1788 in honour of Linnaeus.

lĭnn′ĕt *n.* Common brown or warm-grey song-bird, *Carduelis cannabina*; *green ~*, greenfinch. [Fr. *lin* flax, seeds of which are its food]

lĭn′ō *n.* Abbrev. of LINOLEUM; *~-cut*, (print from) design cut in relief on block of linoleum.

lĭnōl′ĕum *n.* Floor-covering of canvas coated with oxidized linseed-oil and usu. pigments.

lĭn′otȳpe *n.* Machine that casts a slug or line of type from a line of assembled and justified matrices at a single operation of casting. [= *line o′ type*]

lĭn′săng *n.* Member of a purely oriental genus (*Linsang*) of civet-cats resembling the true cats in several features.

lĭn′seed *n.* Seed of flax; *~-cake*, linseed pressed into cake in process of extracting oil, and used as cattle food; *~-oil*, oil obtained by pressure from linseed; *~ poultice*, poultice of linseed.

lĭn′sey-wŏŏl′sey (-zĭ, -zĭ) *n.* Dress-material of cotton (orig. linen) warp and wool weft.

lĭn′stŏck *n.* (hist.) Staff with forked end to hold lighted match, used for applying fire to touch-hole of a cannon.

lĭnt *n.* Soft material for dressing wounds, obtained by ravelling or scraping linen cloth; fluff of any material; raw cotton fibre. **lĭn′ter** *n.* (U.S.) Machine for stripping off short-staple cotton-fibre from cotton-seed after ginning; (pl.) these fibres.

lĭn′tel *n.* Horizontal timber or stone over door or window (ill. DOOR).

Lī′nus. (Gk myth.) Hero whose untimely death was celebrated in a dirge sung annually at harvest-time; perhaps orig. a corn-spirit.

lī′on *n.* 1. Large member of cat family, a powerful tawny carnivore, *Felis leo*, with tufted tail and (in the male) a mane, now native only in Africa and S. Asia. 2. Courageous person. 3. (pl. archaic) Sights worth seeing in town etc. (from custom of showing country visitors the lions formerly kept in Tower of London). 4. Person of literary or other celebrity much sought after for social gatherings. 5. National emblem of Gt Britain. 6. The constellation and zodiacal sign LEO[1]. 7. (*American*) *mountain ~*, puma or cougar; *~ and unicorn*, supporters of English royal arms; *~-hearted*, courageous; *~-hunter*, person who makes much of celebrities; *L~ of Lucerne*, lion carved in rock at Lucerne, Switzerland, as monument to Swiss Guards who fell defending Louis XVI of France in attack on Tuileries, 1792; *L~ of St. Mark*, winged lion as emblem of St. Mark (from traditional interpretation of Ezek. i. 4–12), esp. that in Piazzetta of Venice, of which city he is patron saint; *L~ of the North*, Gustavus Adolphus, king of Sweden; *~'s mouth*, perilous position; *~'s share*, largest or best part. **lī′onĕss** *n.*

lī′onīze *v.t.* Treat (person) as lion or celebrity; see or show sights of (place).

lĭp *n.* 1. One of the fleshy edges of the opening of the mouth; edge of cup, vessel, cavity, wound, etc.; (slang) saucy talk, impudence; *bite one's ~*, show vexation; repress emotion; *smack one's ~s*, express relish for food; (fig.) express delight; *hang on person's ~s*, listen to him with rapt attention. 2. (attrib.) From the lips only, professed, not heartfelt or sincere; (phon.) formed or produced by lips; *~-reading*, apprehension (esp. by deaf person) of what another says by watching movements of his lips; *~ salve*, ointment for sore lips; (fig.) flattery; *lipstick*, stick of cosmetic for colouring lips. *~ v.t.* Touch with lips, apply lips to; (of water) lap.

Lĭp′arĭ Islands. Group of volcanic islands, in Italian possession, N. of Sicily; the ancient Aeolian Islands.

lĭp′ĭd *n.* (chem.) Substance which has the general properties of fats but is not necessarily a glyceride.

Li (Tai) Pō (lē, tī) (*c* 701–62). One of the greatest Chinese poets.

Lĭpp'ĭ, Fra Filippo or Lippo (1406–69). Florentine painter of early Renaissance. ~, Filippo, or Filippino (1457–1504). His natural son, also a painter.

lĭquāte' *v.t.* Separate or purify (metals) by liquefying. **lĭquā'tion** *n.*

lĭ'quėfȳ *v.* Reduce to liquid condition; become liquid. **lĭquėfā'cient** (-sh*e*nt) *adj.* **lĭquėfăc'tion** *n.*

lĭquĕs'cent *adj.* Becoming, apt to become, liquid.

lĭqueur' (-kūr, -kêr) *n.* Strong sweet drink with base of brandy or other spirit and flavouring of aromatic substances, taken in small quantities usu. after meals; mixture of sugar and certain wines, or sugar and alcohol, used to flavour champagne; *~-brandy*, brandy of special quality for drinking as liqueur; *~-glass*, very small glass for liqueurs. ~ *v.t.* Flavour (champagne) with liqueur.

lĭq'uĭd *adj.* In that condition (the normal condition of water, oil, etc.) in which particles move freely over each other but do not tend to separate like those of gases, fluid; watery; having the transparency, translucence, or brightness, of water or wine; (of sounds) flowing clear, fluent, pure, not grating or discordant, not guttural, vowel-like; not fixed, unstable; (of assets, securities, etc.) easily convertible into cash; ~ *air*, air reduced to the liquid state under high pressure and low temperature, used as a refrigerant. **lĭq'uĭdly** *adv.* **lĭq'uĭdnėss, lĭquĭd'ĭty** *ns.* **lĭq'uĭdīze** *v.t.* **lĭq'uĭd** *n.* 1. Liquid substance. 2. (phon.) Sound of one of the letters *l*, *r* (and sometimes *m*, *n*).

lĭq'uĭdāte *v.* Pay, clear off, (debt); wind up, ascertain liabilities and apportion assets of, (company, firm); go into liquidation; put an end to, stamp out, wipe out. **lĭquĭdā'tion** *n. go into* ~, (of company) have its affairs wound up, become bankrupt.

lĭq'uor (-k*er*) *n.* 1. Liquid part of secretion or product of chemical operation; liquid used as wash etc; water used in brewing; liquid contained in oysters. 2. Liquid (usu. fermented or distilled) for drinking. 3. (lī'kwor) (pharm. etc.) Solution of specified drug in water.

lĭq'uorĭce (-ker-), **lĭc'orĭce** *n.* (Black substance used in medicine and as sweetmeat, extracted from) root of a leguminous plant, *Glycyrrhiza glabra*; this plant.

lĭq'uorĭsh (-ko-) *adj.* Fond of, indicating fondness for, alcoholic liquor. **lĭq'uorĭshly** *adv.* **lĭq'uorĭshnėss** *n.*

lira (lēr'*a*) *n.* (pl. *lire* pr. -rā). Principal monetary unit of Italy.

lĭ'rĭpīpe *n.* (hist.) Long tail of medieval hood (ill. COAT-HARDIE).

Lĭs'bon (-z-). Capital city and port of Portugal.

lisle thread (līl thrĕd) *n.* Fine smooth thread (orig. linen, now cotton) used in manufacture of stockings etc. [former spelling of *Lille* in France]

lĭsp *v.* Substitute sound approaching that of English *th* for sibilants in speaking; (of child) speak with imperfect pronunciation. ~ *n.* Lisping pronunciation; rippling of water, rustle of leaves, etc. **lĭsp'ĭngly** *adv.*

lĭss'om(e) *adj.* Lithe, supple, agile.

lĭst[1] *n.* 1. Selvage or edge of cloth, usu. of different material; such edges used for slippers, cushions, etc. 2. (pl.) Palisades enclosing tilting-ground; tilting-ground; (fig.) scene of contest.

lĭst[2] *n.* Roll or catalogue of names, of persons or things belonging to a class, of articles with prices, of things to be done etc.; *active* ~, list of military officers liable to be called on for service; *civil* ~: see CIVIL; *free* ~, list of persons to be admitted free to theatre etc., or of duty-free articles. ~ *v.* 1. Enter in list. 2. (now rare or vulg.) Go as soldier, enlist.

lĭst[3] *v.t.* (archaic) Be pleasing to; desire, choose (*to* do, or abs.).

lĭst[4] *n.* Inclination of ship etc. to one side (owing to leak, shifting cargo, etc.). ~ *v.i.* Lean over to one side.

lĭst[5] *v.* (archaic) Listen, listen to.

lĭ'sten (-sn) *v.* Make effort to hear something, hear with attention, give ear *to*; yield *to* temptation or request; ~ *in*, tap telephonic communication; listen to speech, music, etc., transmitted by wireless. **lĭs'tener** (-sn-) *n.*

Lĭs'ter, Joseph, 1st Baron Lister (1827–1912). English surgeon; founder of the antiseptic method in surgery.

lĭst'lėss *adj.* Languid, indifferent, uninterested, disinclined for exertion. **lĭst'lėssly** *adv.* **lĭst'lėssnėss** *n.*

Liszt (lĭst), Franz (1811–86). Hungarian pianist and composer, whose best-known compositions are his 'Hungarian Rhapsodies'.

lĭt'any *n.* Series of petitions for use in church services or processions, recited by clergy and responded to usu. in recurring formula(s) by people.

litchi (lēchē') *n.* Edible nut with fleshy extra coat to the seed; tree bearing this, *Litchi chinensis*, orig. from China, now grown in Bengal.

lĭt'eracy *n.* Ability to read and write.

Literae Humaniores: see LIT. HUM.

lĭt'eral *adj.* Of, in, expressed by, letter(s) of alphabet; following the letter, text, or exact or original words; taking words in their usual or primary sense without mysticism, allegory, or metaphor; (of persons) prosaic, matter-of-fact; so-called, so described, without exaggeration. **lĭt'erally** *adv.* **lĭt'eralnėss, lĭt'eralism, lĭterăl'ĭty** *ns.*

lĭt'erary *adj.* Of, constituting, occupied with, literature, polite learning, or books and written records esp. of the kind valued for form; (of word etc.) uncolloquial, affected by writers; ~ *man*, man of letters; ~ *property*, property consisting in written or printed compositions; exclusive right of publication as recognized and limited by law. **lĭt'erarĭly** *adv.* **lĭt'erarĭnėss** *n.*

lĭt'erate *adj.* Having some acquaintance with literature; (now usu.) able to read and write. ~ *n.* 1. Literate person. 2. Man admitted to Anglican orders without university degree.

lĭterāt'ī *n.pl.* Men of letters; the literate or learned class.

lĭterāt'ĭm *adv.* Letter for letter, textually, literally.

lĭt'erature *n.* Literary culture (archaic); literary production, the literary profession; realm of letters; writings of a country or period; writings whose value lies in beauty of form or emotional effect; *the* books etc. treating *of* a subject; (colloq.) printed matter.

lĭth'ârge (-j) *n.* Lead monoxide (PbO), a hard yellowish-red crystalline substance, prepared by prolonged heating of lead in air, used in the paint and varnish industry and in the manufacture of lead glazes.

līthe (-dh) *adj.* Flexible, supple. **līthe'nėss** (-dhn-) *n.* **līthe'some** *adj.*

lĭth'ĭa *n.* Lithium monoxide (Li2O); ~ *water*, mineral water containing lithium salts.

lĭth'ĭc[1] *adj.* Of the stone or calculus; of stone.

lĭth'ĭc[2] *adj.* (chem.) Of lithium.

lĭth'ĭum *n.* Soft, silver-white metallic element, the lightest of the alkali metals, occurring in small quantities in various minerals; symbol Li, at. no. 3, at. wt 6·939.

lĭth'ograph (-ahf) *n.* Print taken from stone block which, after design is traced on it with greasy chalk, is so treated with acid, gum, and water that the unchalked parts reject ink and make no impression; print produced (from stone or metal) by variants of this process. ~ *v.* Produce print, copy design, by these means. **lĭthogrăph'ĭc** *adj.* **lĭthŏg'raphy** *n.* A modern high-speed printing process based on the old method of producing a lithograph but using flexible metal plates instead of stones. See also PHOTOLITHOGRAPHY.

lĭthŏl'ogy *n.* 1. Science of the nature and composition of stones and rocks. 2. Department of medical science dealing with calculus. **lĭtholŏ'gĭcal** *adj.*

lĭth'ophȳte *n.* 1. (zool.) Polyp whose skeletal substance is calcareous, as some corals. 2. (bot.) Plant that grows on stone.

lĭth'osphēre *n.* (geol.) The outer crust of the earth, consisting of soil and rock, as distinct from the BARYSPHERE, which it encloses, and the HYDROSPHERE, through which it projects to form the continents.

lĭthŏt'omy *n.* Operation of cutting into the bladder and removing stone.

Lĭthūān'ĭa. Area between Latvia and Poland, formerly a Baltic province of the Russian Empire; declared an independent republic in 1918; incorporated in 1940 in the Soviet Union, of which it is a constituent republic; capital, Vilnius (Vilna). **Lĭthūān'ĭan** *adj.* & *n.* 1. (Native) of Lithuania. 2. (Of) the language of the Lithuanians, one of the highly inflected Baltic group of Indo-European languages.

Lit. Hum. Abbrev. of *Literae Hūmăniōrēs* (-z), 'the more humane letters', as name of final honour school in classical studies and philosophy at Oxford University, colloq. called 'Greats'.

lĭt'ĭgāte *v.* Go to law, be party to lawsuit; contest (point) at law. **lĭt'ĭgant** *n.* & *adj.* **lĭtĭgā'tion** *n.*

lĭtĭ'gious (-jus) *adj.* Given to litigation, fond of going to law; disputable at law, offering matter for lawsuit; of lawsuits. **lĭtĭ'giously** *adv.* **lĭtĭ'giousnėss** *n.*

lĭt'mus *n.* Blue colouring matter got from lichens, esp. orchil, that is turned red by acids and restored to blue by alkalis; *~-paper*, unsized paper stained with litmus, as test for acids etc.

lĭt'otēs (-z) *n.* Ironically moderate form of speech, esp. expression of affirmative by negative of its contrary, as *not bad* for *good*.

litre (lēt'*er*) *n.* Unit of capacity in metric system, equivalent to the volume of one kilogram of pure water at its maximum density (4° C.), about 1·76 pints.

Litt.D. *abbrev. Literarum doctor* (= Doctor of letters).

lĭtt'er *n.* 1. Vehicle containing bed shut in by curtains and carried on men's shoulders or by beasts; framework with couch for transporting sick and wounded. 2. Straw, rushes, etc., as bedding esp. for animals; straw and dung of farmyard. 3. Odds and ends, leavings; state of untidiness; disorderly accumulation of papers etc. 4. The young (of sow, bitch, etc.) brought forth at a birth. ~ *v.* 1. Provide (horse etc.) with litter as bed; spread litter or straw on (floor, stable). 2. Make (place) untidy; scatter and leave lying. 3. (of animals) Bring forth (young).

littérateur (lētĕrahtẽr') *n.* Literary man.

lĭt'tle *adj.* Small (freq. with emotional implications not present in *small*); not great or big; of smaller or smallest size etc.; young; short in stature, distance, or time; trivial, unimportant; mean, paltry, contemptible; not much; ~ *finger, toe*, the smallest; *the ~ people*, fairies; *a ~*, some though not much, even a small amount of; *in ~*, on a small scale; *L~ Bear*, Ursa Minor; *L~ Corporal*, Napoleon; *L~ Englander*: see ENGLANDER; *L~ Entente*: see ENTENTE; *~-go*, (colloq.) first examination for pass B.A. degree at Cambridge University; *L ~ Russian*, Ukrainian; branch of Russian language spoken in Ukraine and southern Poland; ~ *theatre*, a small theatre, esp. (chiefly U.S.) an amateur repertory theatre. ~ *n.* Not much, only a small amount, a mere trifle; a certain but no great amount; (for a) short time or distance; ~ *or nothing*, hardly anything; *a ~*, rather, somewhat; ~ *by ~*, by degrees. ~ *adv.* To a small extent only; not at all.

Little Rock. Capital of Arkansas, U.S.

lĭtt'oral *adj.* Of, on, near, the shore. ~ *n.* Region lying along the shore, esp. land lying between high and low tide levels.

Littré (lētrā'), Maximilien Paul Émile (1801–81). French philosopher and lexicographer, author of an authoritative dictionary of the French language.

lĭt'urgy *n.* 1. Communion office of Eastern Church. 2. Form of public worship, set of formularies for this. 3. (Gk antiq.) Public office or duty performed gratuitously by rich Athenian. **lĭtûr'gĭcal** *adj.* **lĭtûr'gĭcally** *adv.*

Liv. *abbrev.* Livy.

līve[1] *adj.* That is alive, living; full of power, energy, or importance, not obsolete or exhausted; (of combustibles) glowing; (of shell, bomb, etc.) unexploded, unkindled; (of wire) charged with electricity; (of parts of machinery etc.) moving or imparting motion; (of broadcast) heard, viewed, during its occurrence, not recorded; ~ *bait*, living fish or worm as fishing-bait; *~-oak*, American evergreen tree, *Quercus virens*, of southern Atlantic States; *livestock*, domestic animals kept or dealt in for use or profit; ~ *weight*, weight of animal etc. before being killed; ~ *wire*, (fig.) person full of energy.

lĭve[2] *v.* 1. Be alive, have animal or vegetable life; subsist (*up*)*on*; depend (*up*)*on* for subsistence; get livelihood *by* (one's wits etc.); (fig.) sustain one's position or repute (*upon*). 2. Conduct oneself, arrange one's habits, expenditure, feeding, etc., in specified way; spend, pass, experience (life, day, etc.); wear *down* (scandal, prejudice, &c.) by blameless course of life; express in one's life; ~ *a double life*, sustain two different characters, act two different parts, in life. 3. Enjoy life intensely. 4. Continue alive, have one's life prolonged; (of things) survive; (of ship) escape destruction. 5. Dwell; spend daytime *in* room; ~ *in*, (of servant, shop-assistant) reside on premises where one works. **lĭv'able** *adj.* Fit to live in; that can be lived, bearable; easy to live with, companionable.

līve'lĭhood (-vl-) *n.* Means of living, sustenance.

līve'lŏng (-vl-) *adj.* (poet., rhet., of time) Whole length of (with implication of weariness or delight).

līve'ly (-vl-) *adj.* Lifelike, realistic; full of life, energetic, brisk, interesting; (of colour) bright, gay; (of boat etc.) rising lightly to waves; (joc.) exciting, dangerous, difficult. **līve'lĭly** (-vl-) *adv.* **līve'lĭnėss** *n.*

līv'en *v.* Brighten, cheer, (usu. *up*).

lĭv'er[1] *n.* Large dark-red organ in abdomen of vertebrates, the chief site of metabolic reactions, also functioning as a gland, secreting bile (ill. ABDOMEN); organ of similar function in other animals; flesh of animals' liver used as food; colour of liver, dark reddish brown; diseased state of liver; (archaic) liver as seat of emotion; *lily, white*, ~, cowardice; *~-fluke*, flatworm parasitic in the liver, esp. (*Faserola hepatica*) in liver of sheep; ~ *of sulphur*, mixture of sulphur compounds used as insecticide and fertilizer; ~ *wing*, right wing of cooked fowl, under which liver is tucked; *liverwort*, primitive seedless

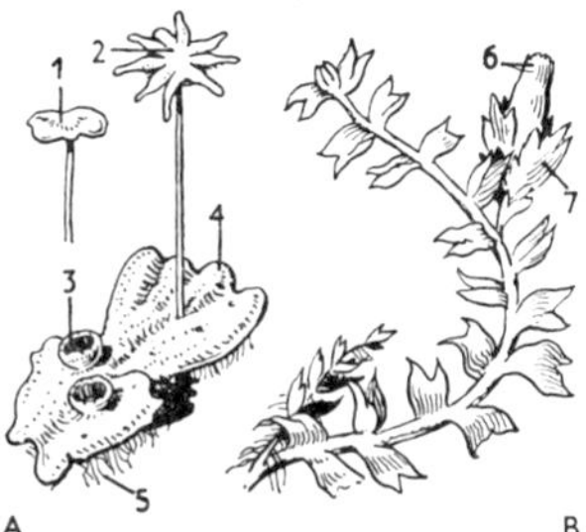

LIVERWORT: A. *MARCHANTIA POLYMORPHA*. B. *CEPHALOZIA BICUSPIDATA*

1, 2. Sporangia (1. Female, 2. Male). 3. Gemma cup. 4. Thallus. 5. Rhizoids. 6. Perianth. 7. Bract

plant allied to mosses. **lĭv'erish** *adj.* Having symptoms of disordered liver.

lĭv'er[2] *n.* One who lives in specified way.

Lĭv'erpōōl. City and seaport of SW. Lancashire, England.

lĭv'ery[1] *n.* 1. Allowance of food or clothing provided for retainers etc. (hist.); allowance of provender for horses; *at ~*, (of horse) kept for owner and fed and groomed for fixed charge. 2. Distinctive clothes worn by member of City Company or person's servant; membership of City Company; *take up one's ~*, become liveryman. 3. (law) Legal delivery of property, writ allowing this; ~ *company*, one of London City Companies that had formerly distinctive costume; ~ *cupboard*, (hist.) box-like food cupboard usu. with ventilation holes in doors; ~ *fine*, payment for becoming member of livery company; *liv'eryman*, member of livery company; keeper of or attendant in livery stable; ~ *stable*, stable where horses are kept at livery or let out for hire.

lĭv'ery[2] *adj.* Of the consistence or colour of liver; (of soil) tenacious; having a disordered liver, feeling out of sorts, irritable.

Lĭv'eyer, -vēre. Permanent inhabitant of Labrador coast. [f. phrase *live here*]

Liv'ia (58 B.C.–A.D. 29). Roman empress; wife of Tiberius Claudius Nero and mother by him of the Emperor Tiberius; married Octavian (Augustus) after her divorce from her first husband.

lĭv'ĭd *adj.* Of bluish leaden colour; discoloured as by bruise; colloq.) furiously angry. **lĭv'idly** *adv.* **lĭvĭd'ĭty** *n.*

lĭv'ĭng *n.* (esp.) 1. Livelihood, maintenance; ~-*room*, room for general day use; ~ *space*, translation of LEBENSRAUM; ~ *wage*, one on which it is possible to live. 2. (eccles.) Benefice. ~ *adj.* (esp.) 1. Contemporary, now existent; *the* ~, those now alive; *in the land of the* ~, alive; *within* ~ *memory*, within memory of persons still living. 2. (Of likeness) exact. 3. (Of rock) native, in native condition and site, as part of earth's crust.

Lĭv'ĭngstone, David (1813–73). Scottish missionary in Central Africa; explored the course of the Zambesi and the sources of the Nile.

Lĭv'ĭngstone Mountains. Range of high land in Tanganyika.

Lĭvōn'ĭa. (hist.) Baltic territory E. of gulf of Riga, a Russian province until war of 1914–18, after which it was divided between Estonia and Latvia. **Lĭvōn'ĭan** *adj.* & *n.* 1. (Native) of Livonia. 2. (Of) the almost extinct Finno-Ugrian language of the Livonians.

Lĭv'y. Titus Livius (59 B.C.–A.D. 17), Roman historian; author of a history of Rome ('Annales') from the foundation of the city to the death of Drusus (9 B.C.); of the 142 books of this history 35 and epitomes of most of the rest are extant.

lĭxĭv'ĭāte *v.t.* Separate (substance) into soluble and insoluble constituents by percolation of water. **lĭxĭvĭā'tion** *n.*

lĭz'ard *n.* Reptile of sub-order *Lacertilia*, related to snakes but distinguished by having (usu.) 4 legs, movable eyelids, eardrums, and fleshy tongue.

L.J. *abbrev.* Lord Justice (pl. L.JJ.).

ll. *abbrev.* Lines.

lla'ma, lama (lah-) *n.* S. Amer. mammal (*Lama glama*) related to the camel but smaller, humpless, and woolly-haired, used as beast of burden; (material made of) its wool; *the* ~*s*, (in zool. usage) group of camel-like S. Amer. mammals including, besides the llama, the alpaca, huanaco, and vicugna.

lla'nō (lah-, lyah-) *n.* (usu. in pl. *llanos*). Treeless grassland of Orinoco basin and Guiana highlands in S. America.

LL.B. *abbrev. Legum baccalaureus* (= Bachelor of Laws).

LL.D. *abbrev. Legum doctor* (= Doctor of Laws).

Llewĕl'ȳn (lōō-). Name of two Welsh princes: ~ *ab Iorwerth* (d. 1240) and ~ *ab Gruffydd* (d. 1282), his nephew, last Welsh prince of Wales.

Lloyd (loid) **George,** David, 1st Earl Lloyd George of Dwyfor (1863–1945). British Liberal politician; coalition prime minister 1916–22.

Lloyd's (loidz). London association of underwriters (orig. meeting in coffee-house opened by Edward Lloyd 1688) and agency for arranging insurance (formerly marine insurance only, but now nearly all kinds); it also issues daily shipping intelligence, as ~ *List* etc.; ~ *Register of Shipping*, independent society which surveys ships to ensure compliance with standards of strength and maintenance; its annual classified list of such ships.

L.M.S. *abbrev.* London Missionary Society.

lō *int.* (archaic) Look!, see!, behold!

loach *n.* Any of several small edible European freshwater fishes of the sub-family *Cobitidinae*.

load *n.* What is (to be) carried, burden; amount usu. carried, recognized unit in measure or weight of certain substances; material object or force acting as weight or clog, resistance of machinery worked to motive power, pressure of superstructure on arch etc., total amount of electric current supplied at given time by dynamo or generating station; burden of responsibility, care, grief, etc.; (pl., colloq.) plenty, superabundance, heaps, lots, *of*; (*river*) ~, solid matter carried along by river; *take a* ~ *off* one's *mind*, relieve him of anxiety; ~-*shedding*, the cutting-off of the electricity supply to an area of the country as a means of avoiding excessive loading of generating plant; *load'stone, lode'stone*, magnetic oxide of iron, piece of it used as magnet, thing that attracts; ~(-*water*) *line*, ship's floatation line when loaded, plimsoll mark (ill. PLIMSOLL MARK). ~ *v.* 1. Put load on or aboard, take load aboard, etc.; place (load, cargo) aboard ship, on vehicle, etc.; add weight to, be burden upon, oppress *with*; weight with lead; supply in excess or overwhelming abundance *with*; adulterate with something to increase weight or (of wines) strength. 2. Charge (fire-arms). 3. (Stock Exch.) Buy heavily of stock; (life-insurance) add extra charge to (premium) for special reasons.

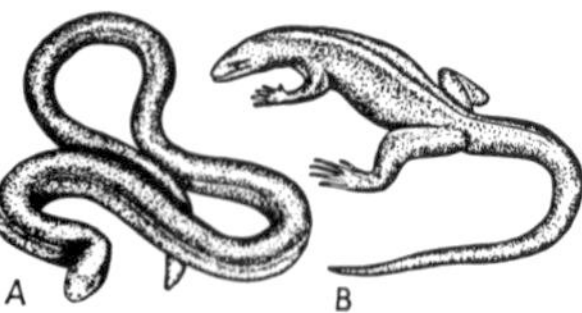

LIZARDS: A. SLOW-WORM. B. MONITOR

load'er *n.* (esp.) Attendant loading sportsman's guns; gun loaded in specified way.

loaf[1] *n.* (pl. *loaves* pr. lōvz). Piece of bread baked alone or as separate or separable part of batch, usu. of some standard weight; (*sugar-*)~, conical moulded mass of sugar; solid roundish head of cabbage or lettuce; ~-*sugar*, sugar in form of loaf or cut into lumps. **loaf, loave** *v.i.* (Of cabbage etc.) form loaf or head.

loaf[2] *v.* Spend time idly; saunter; ~ (time) *away*, spend in loafing. **loaf'er** *n.* **loaf** *n.* Loafing.

loam *n.* 1. Fertile soil chiefly of clay and sand with admixture of decayed vegetable matter; (geog.) deposit of mixed sand, silt, and clay. 2. Paste of clay and water; composition of moistened clay and sand with chopped straw etc., used in making bricks. **loam'y** *adj.*

loan *n.* 1. Thing, esp. sum of money, lent to be returned with or without interest; word, custom, etc., adopted by one people from another; lending or being lent. 2. Money contribution (formerly often forced) from individuals or public bodies to State expenses acknowledged as debt; arrangement or contract by which a government receives advances of money usu. for stipulated interest. 3. ~-*collection*, collection of pictures etc. lent by owner(s) for exhibition; ~-*society*, society of periodical subscribers to fund from which members may have loans. ~ *v.t.* (now chiefly U.S.) Grant loan of.

lo(a)th *adj.* Disinclined, reluctant, unwilling.

loathe (-dh) *v.t.* Regard with disgust, abominate, detest. **loath'ing** *n.* **loath'ĭngly** *adv.*

loath'some (-dh-, -th-) *adj.* Exciting nausea or disgust, offensive to the senses, sickening, repulsive, odious. **loath'somely** *adv.* **loath'somenĕss** *n.*

lŏb *v.* Walk, run, or move, heavily, clumsily, or slowly; toss, bowl, strike, (ball) with slow or high-pitched motion. ~ *n.* Ball bowled underhand at cricket or sent high in air at lawn tennis.

Lōbachĕv'sky, Nikolai Ivanovich (1793–1856). Russian mathematician; pioneer of non-Euclidean geometry.

lōb'ate *adj.* (biol.) Having lobe(s). **lōbā'tion** *n.*

lŏbb'y *n.* Porch, anteroom, entrance-hall, corridor; (in House of Commons etc.) large hall open to public used esp. for interviews between members and outsiders; (*division*) ~, one of two corridors to which members retire to vote. ~ *v.* Influence (member of legisature), get (Bill etc.) *through*, by lobby interviews etc.; frequent lobby of legislature, solicit members' votes. **lŏbb'yist** *n.*

lōbe *n.* Roundish and flattish projecting or pendulous part of an organ, often one of two or more such parts divided by fissure; ~ *of ear*, lower soft pendulous external part (ill. EAR). **lōbed** (-bd), **lōbe'lėss** *adj.*

lobēl'ia *n.* Genus of herbaceous (rarely shrubby) plants with blue, scarlet, purple, or white flowers having deeply cleft corolla without spur; dried leaves of *L. inflata*, used as an ingredient of asthma powder, also known as *Indian tobacco* or *emetic weed*. [M. de *Lobel* (1538–1616), Flemish botanist and physician to James I]

lŏblŏll'y (pine) *n.* (U.S.) Tree (*Pinus taeda*) growing in swamps in southern U.S.

lŏb'scouse (-s) *n.* (naut.) Dish of meat stewed with vegetables and ship's biscuit.

lŏb'ster *n.* Large marine crustacean (esp. *Homarus vulgaris* and *H. americana*), a decapod having a

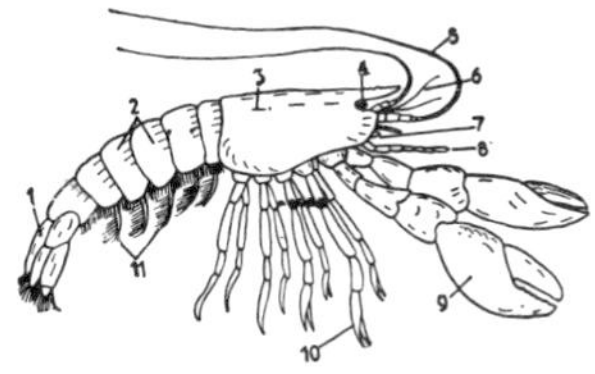

LOBSTER

1. Telson. 2. Somites. 3. Carapace. 4. Eye. 5. Antenna. 6. Antennule. 7. Mandible. 8. Maxilliped. 9. Claw. 10. Legs. 11. Swimmerets

pair of heavy pincer-like claws and stalked eyes, which is eaten as a delicacy and turns from bluish black to bright red when boiled; its flesh as food; ~-*eyed*, with protruding eyes; ~-*pot*, basket in which lobsters are trapped.

lŏb'ūle *n.* Small lobe. **lŏb'ūlar** *adj.*

lŏb'worm (-wẽrm) *n.* Large earthworm used as fishing-bait; lugworm.

lōc'al *adj.* 1. Of, concerned with, place; in regard to place. 2. Belonging to, existing in, or peculiar to, certain place(s); ~ *colour*, details characteristic of the scene or time represented in novel or other literary work inserted to give actuality (see also sense 3 below); ~ *examination*, examination of boys and girls formerly held in various places under university board, see G.C.E. ~ *government*, administration of town etc. by inhabitants, decentralization; ~ *option*, system by which inhabitants of district may prohibit sale of liquor in it; ~ *preacher*, Methodist layman authorized to preach in his own district; ~ *time*, time measured from sun's position over place, identical for places on same meridian but 4 minutes earlier for each degree of longitude eastwards. 3. Affecting, of, a part and not the whole (~ *disease, pain, remedy*); ~ *colour*, (in picture) that natural to particular objects as distinct from that seen by painter or chosen for sake of colour-scheme (but see sense 2 above). 4. (math.) Of a locus. 5. (on cover of letter) For delivery in this town or district. **lōc'ally** *adv.* **lō'cal** *n.* Inhabitant of, professional man practising in, particular district; local preacher; (item of) local news in newspaper; postage-stamp current in limited district; train serving stations of district; (colloq.) public house in near neighbourhood; (pl.) local examination(s); (U.S.) branch of trade union.

local(e)' (-ahl) *n.* Scene or locality of operations or events.

lōc'alism *n.* Attachment to a place; limitation of ideas, etc., resulting; favouring of what is local; local idiom, custom, etc.

locăl'ity *n.* Position of something, place where it is, site or scene of something; faculty of remembering and recognizing places, finding one's way, etc.

lōc'alīze *v.t.* Invest with characteristics of particular place; restrict to particular place; attach to districts, decentralize; concentrate (attention) *upon*.

Locãrn'ō. Town at N. end of Lake Maggiore, Switzerland; *Pact of* ~, series of agreements for peace and arbitration between Germany, France, Belgium, Great Britain, Italy, Poland, and Czechoslovakia, drawn up at Locarno, 1925; they included a treaty of mutual guarantee between Germany, Belgium, France, Great Britain, and Italy, guarantees of the boundaries of Germany and Belgium and Belgium and France, and two treaties of guarantee between France and Czechoslovakia and France and Poland.

locāte' (lo-, lō-) *v.* Establish in a place; (pass., orig. U.S.) be situated; state locality of; discover exact place of; (U.S.) take up residence, settle. **locā'tion** *n.* (esp.) Place, other than studio, chosen for photographing scene of film.

lŏc'atĭve *adj.* & *n.* (gram.) (Case) denoting place where.

loc. cit. *abbrev.* *Loco citato* (= in the passage already quoted).

lŏch (-x) *n.* Scottish lake or narrow or landlocked arm of the sea.

lŏck[1] *n.* One of portions into which hair, beard, etc., naturally divides itself, tress; (pl.) hair of head; tuft of wool or cotton.

lŏck[2] *n.* 1. Appliance for fastening door, lid, etc., with bolt that requires key of particular shape to work it; appliance to keep wheel

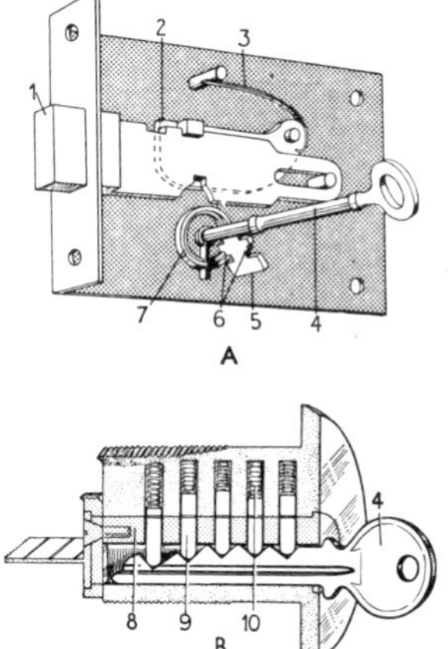

A. MORTISE LOCK. B. CYLINDER LOCK

A. 1. Bolt. 2. Tumbler (mostly behind bolt) which is raised by key to free bolt. 3. Spring keeping tumbler in place. 4. Key. 5. Bit. 6. Wards on key 7. Wards on keyhole. B. 8. Cylinder. 9. One of pins in two parts so that split corresponds with edge of cylinder when key is inserted, thus allowing it to turn. 10. Spring

from revolving or slewing; mechanism for exploding charge of gun (ill. MUSKET); *under* ~ *and key*, locked up; ~, *stock, and barrel*, whole of thing, completely. 2. Portion of canal or river shut off by folding gates provided with sluices to let the water in and out and thus raise or lower boats from one level to another; antechamber to chamber in which engineering work is done in compressed air. 3. Interlocking; extent to which plane of fore wheels can be made to cross that of rear wheels. 4. ~(-*hospital*), hospital for venereal disease; ~ *fast*, secured with lock; ~-*keeper*, *lock'sman*, keeper of lock on canal or river; *lock'smith*, maker and mender

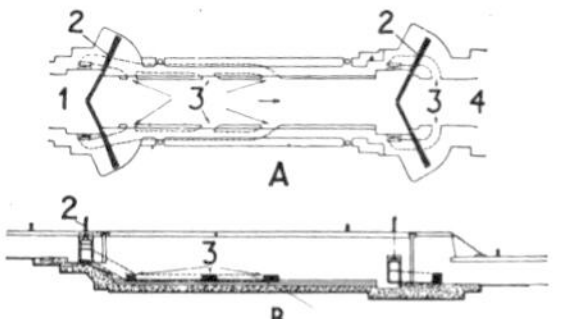

CANAL LOCK: A. PLAN. B. SECTION

1. Head water. 2. Lock gate. 3. Sluices. 4. Tail water

of locks. ~ *v.* 1. Fasten with lock, shut *up* by fastening doors etc. with lock and key; admit of being so fastened; shut *up, in, into*; (of land, hills, etc.) hem in (usu. pass.); (fig.) store *up, away,* inaccessibly; imprison; keep *out* by locking door (esp. of employer coercing workmen by refusing them work). 2. Come or bring into rigidly fixed position; engage, (make) catch, fasten by interlacing or fitting of corresponding parts; entangle, (past part.) joined in hostile or other embrace; (mil., of rear rank) march so close to front rank that feet overlap; (of vehicle etc.) (have fore wheels that) admit of passing askew under body of carriage. 3. Provide canal with locks; convey (boat) *up, down,* through lock; go through lock. 4. *~-chain,* chain for locking wheels of vehicle; *~-jaw,* (pop. name for) trismus, a variety of tetanus, tonic spasm of muscles of mastication causing jaws to remain rigidly closed; *~-nut,* extra nut screwed over another to prevent its becoming slack; *~-out,* locking out of workers by employer; *~-stitch,* sewing- or knitting-machine stitch by which two threads or stitches are firmly locked together; *~-up* (time of) locking up school etc. for night; unrealizable state of invested capital, amount of capital locked up; house or room for temporary detention of prisoners; (attrib.) that can be locked up.

lŏck'age *n.* Amount of rise or fall effected by locks on canal or river; toll for use of lock; use or number of locks.

Lŏcke, John (1632–1704). English empirical philosopher; had great influence on 18th-c. philosophy; author of 'Essay concerning the Human Understanding' and several works on education, government, and religious toleration. **Lŏck'ian** *adj.*

lŏck'er *n.* (esp.) Small cupboard, esp. one of many reserved each for individual's use in public room; (naut.) chest or compartment for clothes, stores, ammunition, etc.

lŏck'ėt *n.* Metal plate or band on scabbard (ill. SWORD); small gold or silver case holding portrait, lock of hair, etc., and usu. hung from neck.

Lŏck'hârt, John Gibson (1794–1854). Scottish author, biographer of Sir Walter Scott.

lōc'o(-weed) *n.* (U.S.) Various leguminous plants of W. and SW. parts of U.S., producing brain-affecting disease in cattle. **lō'co** *adj.* (U.S.) Insane, mad. [Span. *loco* insane]

lōcomō'tion (-shn) *n.* (Power of) motion from place to place; travel, means (esp. artificial) of travelling.

lōc'omōtive (*or* -mōt'-), *adj.* Of locomotion, (joc.) of travel; having power of or given to locomotion, not stationary; effecting locomotion; ~ *engine,* one that goes from place to place by its own power, esp. steam-engine for drawing train along rails. ~ *n.* Locomotive engine (*illustrations,* p. 483); locomotive animal.

lōc'omōtor *adj.* Of locomotion; ~ *ataxia*: see ATAXY. ~ *n.* Locomotive person or thing. **lōc'mōtory** *adj.* Of, having, locomotion.

Lō'cris. Central district of ancient Greece.

lŏc'ūlus *n.* (anat., bot., zool.) One of a number of small separate cavities.

lōc'um tēn'ĕns, (colloq.) **lōc'um** *n.* Deputy acting esp. for clergyman or doctor. **lōc'um-tēn'ency** *n.* [L, = 'holding place']

lōc'us *n.* (pl. *loci* pr. -sī). Locality or exact place of something; (math.) curve etc. made by all points satisfying particular equation of relation between coordinates, or by point, line, or surface, moving according to mathematically defined conditions; ~ *classicus,* best known or most authoritative passage on a subject; ~ *standi,* recognized position, right to intervene, appear in court, etc.

lōc'ust *n.* 1. Various kinds of short-horned grasshopper which migrate in swarms and consume vegetation of whole districts; person of devouring or destructive propensities. 2. Fruit of carob-tree; cassia-pod; ~*(-tree),* various trees, esp. carob and pseudo-acacia.

locū'tion *n.* Style of speech; word or phrase considered in regard to style, idiom.

lŏc'ūtory *n.* Conversation-room in monastery; grille for interviews between inmates of monastery and outsiders.

lōde *n.* 1. Watercourse; open drain in fens. 2. That part of a vein from which ore can profitably be extracted (ill. MINE). 3. *lode'-star, loadstar,* star that is steered by, esp. pole-star; guiding principle, object of pursuit; *lode'stone*: see LOAD.

lŏdge[1] *n.* 1. Small house (archaic). 2. Cottage at gates of park or grounds of large house, occupied by gardener or other servant. 3. Porter's room at gate of college, factory, block of flats, etc. 4. (freemasonry etc.) (Place of meeting for) members of branch; *grand* ~, governing body of freemasons and societies imitating them. 5. Residence of head of college at Cambridge. 6. Beaver's or otter's lair. 7. N. Amer. Indian's tent or wigwam.

lŏdge[2] *v.* 1. Provide with sleeping quarters; receive as guest or inmate; establish as resident *in* house or room(s), (pass.) be *well, ill,* etc., accommodated in regard to house-room. 2. Serve as habitation for, contain, (pass.) be contained *in.* 3. Leave *in* place or *with* person for security. 4. Deposit in court or with official a formal statement of (complaint, information); (pop.) allege (objection etc.). 5. Place (power etc.) *in, with,* etc. 6. (Of wind) lay (crops) flat. 7. (Make, let) stick or remain in place without falling or going farther. 8. Reside, be situated; be inmate paying for accommodation in another's house, whence **lŏdg'er** *n.*

Lŏdge[3], Sir Oliver Joseph (1851–1940). English physicist; pioneer in psychic research.

lŏdg(e)'ment *n.* Firm position gained, foothold; accumulation of matter intercepted in fall or transit; (mil.) temporary defensive work on captured part of enemy's works; (law) deposit(ing) of money.

lŏdg'ĭng *n.* (esp.) Accommodation in hired rooms; dwelling-place, abode, (pl.) room(s) hired elsewhere than in hotel for residing in; *~-house,* house in which lodgings are let; *common ~-house,* usu. one with dormitory in which bed can be had for the night; ~ *turn,* occasion when a railway employee has to lodge at his place of destination.

lō'ĕss (*or* lẽrs) *n.* Light-coloured fine-grained deposit formed by wind-blown dust, very fertile when irrigated, found esp. in Mississippi basin, Rhine valley, and N. China.

Lōfōt'en and Vĕst'eraalen (-awl-) **Islands.** Group off NW. coast of Norway.

lŏft (*or* law-) *n.* Attic; room over stable; pigeon-house, flock of pigeons; gallery in church or hall; (now U.S.) upper floor; (golf) lofting stroke; club with face sloped backwards from vertical. ~ *v.t.* (golf) Hit (ball) into air, over obstacle, etc.; keep (pigeons) in loft.

lŏft'er (*or* law-) *n.* Golf-club for lofting.

lŏft'y (*or* law-) *adj.* Of imposing height, towering, soaring; haughty, consciously superior or dignified; exalted, distinguished, high-flown, elevated, sublime. **lŏft'ĭly** *adv.* **lŏft'ĭnėss** *n.*

lŏg[1] *n.* 1. Unhewn piece of felled tree or similar rough mass of wood. 2. Apparatus for gauging speed of ship (also *~-chip* or *ship, ~-line*), float attached to knotted line wound on a reel, obs. form of log; (*patent ~*) modern form which measures distance instead of speed; (also *~-book*) book in which all particulars of a ship's voyages are entered, including hourly readings of the log. 3. Table by which journeyman-tailor's work-time is assessed. 4. *~-cabin,* cabin built of logs; *~-rolling,* (f. phrase *roll my ~ and I'll roll yours*) mutual help, esp. unprincipled combination in politics or puffing of each other's works by author-reviewers; *log'wood,* Amer. tree (*Haemotoxylon Campechianum*) used in dyeing. ~ *v.t.* Cut into logs; enter in ship's log-book, (of ship) make (distance); enter (seaman's name, with offence committed) in log-book, fine (offender).

lŏg[2] LOGARITHM (prefixed to number or algebraic symbol).

log. *abbrev.* Logic.

lōg'anberry *n.* Hybrid between raspberry and American blackberry. [raised by Judge *Logan* in California, 1883]

lŏg'an(-stōne) *n.* Poised heavy stone rocking at a touch, rocking-stone.

lŏgaoed'ĭc (-*aē*-) *adj.* & *n.* (Line) in metre composed of dactyls and trochees.

lŏg'arĭthm *n.* One of a class of arithmetical functions tabulated for use in abridging calculation; the sum of the logarithms of any numbers is the logarithm of their product; hence a table of logarithms enables one to substitute addition and subtraction for multiplication and division, and multiplication and division for involution and evolution. **lŏgarĭth'mĭc** *adj.* **lŏgarĭth'mĭcally** *adv.*

Lŏgg'an, David (*c* 1635–92). Engraver, born at Danzig; noted for his series of architectural prints of the colleges of Oxford (1675) and Cambridge (1690).

lŏgg'erhead (-hĕd) *n.* 1. Blockhead (archaic). 2. Iron instrument with ball at end heated for melting pitch etc.; post built into boat for catching turn of rope to. 3. Large-headed species of turtle (*Caretta caretta*). 4. *At ~s* (with), disagreeing or disputing (with).

loggia (lŏj'ya) *n.* Gallery or arcade having one or more of its sides open to the air

lŏ'gĭc *n.* Science of reasoning, proof, thinking, or inference; particular scheme of or treatise on this; chain of reasoning, correct or incorrect use of argument, ability in argument, arguments; means of convincing or converting. **logĭ'cian** (-shn) *n.*

lŏ'gĭcal *adj.* Of logic or formal argument; not contravening the principles of logic, correctly reasoned; following as reasonable inference or natural consequence; capable of correct reasoning; ~ *positivism*, (philos.) form of positivism in which symbolic logic is applied. **lŏ'gĭcally** *adv.* **lŏgĭcăl'ity** *n.*

lō'gie (-gĭ) *n.* Zinc ornament looking like jewel, used in theatres.

lŏg'ion (-g-) *n.* (pl. -*ia*) Saying of Christ not recorded in Gospels but preserved elsewhere.

logĭs'tĭcs *n.* Science and practice of moving, lodging, and supplying troops.

lŏg'ogrăm *n.* Sign or character representing word in shorthand.

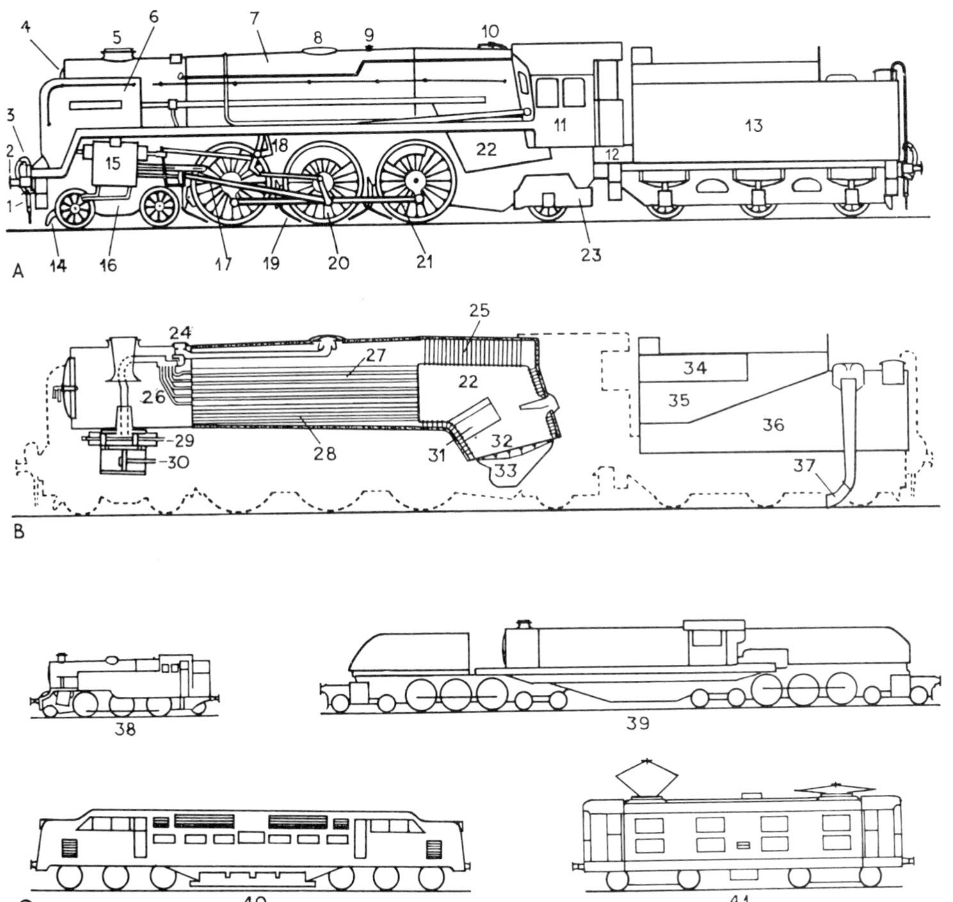

LOCOMOTIVES: A. EXTERIOR. B. SECTION. C. TYPES

A. 1. Coupling links. 2. Buffer. 3. Vacuum-brake connexion. 4. Smoke-box door. 5. Chimney. 6. Smoke deflector ('blinker plate'). 7. Boiler. 8. Steam dome. 9. Safety valves. 10. Whistle. 11. Cab. 12. Footplate. 13. Tender. 14. Guard iron. 15. Cylinder. 16. Leading bogie. 17. Connecting rod. 18. Valve gear. 19. Sand pipe. 20. Driving wheels. 21. Coupling rod. 22. Fire-box. 23. Trailing truck. B. 24. Snifting-valve. 25. Roof stays. 26. Superheater header. 27. Superheater flues. 28. Flue tubes. 29 Valve rod. 30. Piston. 31. Arch. 32. Grate. 33. Ash pan. 34. Tool store. 35. Coal bunker. 36. Water tank. 37. Water scoop. C. 38. Tank (steam). 39. Articulated (steam). 40. Diesel. 41. Electric

logŏg'rapher *n.* (Gk antiq.) Writer of traditional history in prose; professional speech-writer.

lŏg'ogriph *n.* Kind of anagrammatic word-puzzle.

logŏm'achy (-kĭ) *n.* Dispute about words, controversy turning on merely verbal points.

lŏg'os *n.* (theol.) The Word, the Second Person of the Trinity.

lŏg'otȳpe *n.* (print.) Type containing word, or two or more letters, cast in one piece but not as ligature.

Lōh'ėngrĭn. In German legend, son of Parsifal; he was summoned from the temple of the Grail and borne in a swan-boat to Antwerp to defend Elsa of Brabant against Frederick of Telramund, who claimed to marry her; Lohengrin himself married Elsa but was carried away again in the swan-boat when she asked his name.

loin *n.* (pl.) Part of body on both sides of spine between false ribs and hip-bones; (sing.) joint of meat including vertebrae of loins (ill. MEAT); (pl., bibl.) this part of body regarded as part that should be covered by clothing, or as seat of physical strength and generative power; *~-cloth*, cloth worn round loins.

Loire (lwâr). River rising in S. central France and flowing N. and then W. to the Atlantic.

loit'er *v.* Linger on the way, hang about; travel indolently and with frequent pauses; pass (time etc.) *away* in loitering.

Lōk'ĭ. (Norse myth.) Spirit of evil and mischief, who contrived the death of BALDER.

Lōl'a Mŏn'tėz. Stage-name of Marie Dolores Eliza Rosanna Gilbert (1818–61), an English dancer; she became mistress of Ludwig I of Bavaria and exercised for a time full control over the government of that country.

lŏll *v.* Hang (tongue) *out*, (of tongue) hang (*out*); stand, sit, recline, in lazy attitude; let (head, limbs) rest lazily on something.

Lŏll'ard. One of the English 14th-c. heretics who were followers of Wycliffe or held opinions similar to his on the necessity for the Church to aid men to live a life of evangelical poverty and imitate Christ. **Lŏll'ardĭsm, Lŏll'ard(r)y** *ns.*

lŏll'ĭpŏp *n.* Large boiled sweet on a stick; also **lŏll'y**; *iced ~* water-ice etc. on a stick; (slang) money.

Lom'bard (lŭm-, lŏm-). One of a Germanic people from the lower Elbe who invaded Italy in A.D. 568 and founded a kingdom (overthrown by Charlemagne, 774) in the valley of the Po. **Lŏmbâr'd'ic** *adj.* Of Lombardy or the Lombards; esp. of the round-arched style of architecture prevailing in N. Italy from 7th to 13th c.; of a type of handwriting developed from Roman cursive found in Italian MSS. of the same period.

Lom'bard Street (lŭm-, lŏm-). Street in City of London, so called because orig. occupied by Lombard bankers, and still containing many of the principal London banks; hence, the money market of London; *all ~ Street to a china orange*, very long odds.

Lŏm'bardy. Territorial division of N. Italy, lying roughly between the Alps and the river Po; *~ poplar*, tall columnar variety of the black poplar (*Populus nigra italica*).

Lŏmbrōs'ō (-z-), Cesare (1836–1909). Italian criminologist; originator of a theory that criminals are a special type marked by recognizable physiological and psychological characteristics.

lōm'ĕnt(um) *n.* (bot.) Legume which is contracted in spaces between seeds, breaking up when mature into one-seeded joints. **lōmentā'ceous** (-sh*u*s) *adj.*

Lōm'ond, Loch. The largest Scottish lake, in W. Scotland N. of the Clyde; *Ben ~*, mountain in Stirlingshire overlooking the lake.

Lŏmonŏs'ov (-f), Mikhail Vasilyevich (*c* 1711–65). Russian poet, man of letters, and grammarian.

Londin., London. *abbrevs.* (Bishop) of London (replacing surname in his signature).

Lo'ndon (lŭ-). Capital of the United Kingdom, a port on the river Thames,comprising the ancient CITY of London, the city of WESTMINSTER, the royal borough of KENSINGTON, and numerous other boroughs; *County of ~*, area administered by London County Council; *Greater ~*, London and its environs; *~ Bridge*, bridge across Thames about ½ mile above the *Tower of ~*, ancient fortress and prison; *~ clay*, geological formation belonging to lower division of Eocene tertiary, in SE. England, esp. at and near London; *~ Library*, a circulating library founded in 1840; *~ particular*, (joc.) one of the 'pea-soup' fogs characteristic of London esp. in 19th and early 20th centuries; *~ pride*, a pink-flowered saxifrage (*Saxifraga umbrosa*); *~ University*, largest university in Britain, comprising numerous colleges and special schools, constituted 1836 orig. as an examining body. **Lo'ndoner** *n.* Native, inhabitant, of London.

Lo'ndonderry (lŭ-). County of Northern Ireland; its county town (colloq. *Derry*), besieged by James II in 1689 for 105 days before being relieved.

lōne *adj.* Solitary, companionless, single (poet. or rhet. exc. in *~ hand*, (person playing) hand played against the rest at euchre or quadrille; also fig.); *L~ Star State*, Texas, from the single star in its arms and flag.

lōne'ly (-nl-) *adj.* Solitary, companionless, isolated; unfrequented. **lō'nelinėss** *n.*

lōne'some (-ns-) *adj.* Lonely. **lōne'somely** *adv.* **lōne'somenėss** *n.*

lŏng[1] *adj.* Measuring much from end to end in space or time; (colloq.) tall; far-reaching, acting at a distance, involving great interval or difference; having specified length or duration; of elongated shape; remarkable for, distinguished by, concerned with, length or duration; prolix, tedious; lasting, going far back or forward; (phonet., pros., of vowel or syllable) having the greater of the two recognized durations; *~-and-short stitch*: see ill. STITCH; *~-and-short work*, (archit.) alternation of tall quoins with flat slabs (ill. MASONRY); *~-bill*, kinds of bird, esp. snipe; *~-boat*, sailing ship's largest boat; *~-bow*, bow drawn by hand (as dist. from *crossbow*) and discharging long feathered arrow (ill. BOW); *draw the ~-bow*, tell exaggerated or invented stories; *~ butt*, cue used for reaching billiard-ball at long range; *~-case clock*, large clock with pendulum and weights, in tall case, 'grandfather' clock (ill. CLOCK); *~ chance*, one involving much risk; *long'cloth*, kind of calico made in long pieces; *~ clothes*, clothes of baby in arms; *~ distance*, (telephone) of trunk call, line, etc.; (of weather report) made several days in advance; *~ drink*, one served in tall glass; *~ face*, dismal countenance; *~ field*, (cricket) long off or on; part of ground behind bowler; *~ firm*, see FIRM[1]; *~ figure*, one having many ciphers, large sum; *~-hand*, ordinary writing (opp. SHORTHAND); *~ hop*, short-pitched ball in cricket; *~-horn*, long-horned ox or cow: *~ hundred*: see HUNDRED; *~ jump*, jump (as athletic competition) measured along ground; *~ measure*, lineal measure, measure of length; *~ metre*, hymn-metre of four eight-syllabled lines; *~ odds*, (in betting) very uneven chances; *~-off*, *-on*, cricketer fielding behind and to left, right, of bowler (ill. CRICKET); *L~ Parliament*, English Parliament which sat from Nov. 1640 to Mar. 1653, and was restored in 1659 and finally dissolved in 1660; *~ pig*, sailors' translation of cannibals' name for human flesh; *~ primer*, a size of printing type (10-point) between bourgeois and small pica, commonly used in book printing; *~ robe*, legal attire (*gentlemen of the ~ robe*, lawyers); *in the ~ run*, in the end, ultimately; *~ ship*, (ancient) ship of war for large number of rowers, galley; *~ shot*, shot fired at great distance from target; wild guess; (cinemat.) shot which includes figures or scenery at a distance; *~ sight*, defect of sight by which only distant objects are seen distinctly; *~ stop*, (cricket) man fielding directly behind wicket-keeper; *~ suit*, (cards) suit in which more than three cards are held; (fig.) one's strong point; *~-term*, (of plan, policy, etc.) designed to meet the circumstances of a long time ahead; ~ *tongue*, loquacity; ~ *vacation*, summer vacation of law-courts and universities; ~ *wave*, wireless wave of more than 800 metres; ~ *wind*, capacity for running far without rest; ~-*winded*, tedious, prolix. **lŏng'ĭsh** *adj.* **lŏng'ways** (-z), **lŏng'wīse** (-z) *advs.* **lŏng** *n.* (usu. colloq.) Long interval or period; long syllable; long vacation; *the ~ and the short of it*, all that need be said.

lŏng[2] *adv.* For a long time; by a long time; throughout specified time; *as* or *so ~ as*, provided that, if only; (comp. *longer*, with *no*, *any*, etc.) after implied point of time; ~-*ago*, (belonging to) the distant past; ~-*drawn* (-*out*), unduly prolonged; ~-*standing*, that has long existed; ~-*suffering*, bearing provocation patiently.

lŏng[3] *v.i.* Yearn, wish vehemently (*for*, *to*). **lŏng'ĭng** *n.* & *adj.* **lŏng'ĭngly** *adv.*

long. *abbrev.* Longitude.

lŏnganĭm'ĭty (-ngg-) *n.* Long-suffering, forbearance.

lŏn'geron (-j-) *n.* (usu. in pl.) Longitudinal member of aeroplane fuselage.

lŏngēv'al, -gaev'al (-j-) *adj.* Long-lived. **lŏngĕv'ĭty** (-j-) *n.* Long life.

Lŏng'fĕllow (-ō), Henry Wadsworth (1807–82). American poet, author of 'Hyperion', 'Hiawatha', and a number of popular poems, including 'The Wreck of the Hesperus', 'Excelsior', 'The Village Blacksmith'.

Lŏng'ford. Inland county of Eire.

lŏn'gĭcŏrn (-j-) *n.* Beetle of the family *Cerambycidae* with very long antennae.

Lŏngīn'us[1] (-jī-), Dionysius Cassius (*c* 220–73). Greek rhetorician and philosopher; probably not the author of the work 'On the Sublime' usu. ascribed to him, which appears to belong to the 1st or 2nd c. A.D.

Lŏngīn'us[2] (-jī-). The traditional name of the Roman soldier who pierced with his spear the side of our Lord at the crucifixion.

Lŏng Island. Island of New York State, U.S., separated from mainland of Connecticut by ~ *Sound*, an arm of the Atlantic Ocean, and having the Brooklyn and Queens boroughs of New York City on its W. end.

lŏn'gĭtūde (-j-) *n.* (geog.) Angular distance along equator E. or W. from standard meridian, as that of Greenwich, to meridian of any place (ill. PROJECTION); (astron.) angular distance eastward on ecliptic from vernal equinoctial point to foot of circle of latitude of body or point.

lŏngĭtūd'ĭnal (-j-) *adj.* Of or in length; running lengthwise; of longitude. **lŏngĭtūd'ĭnally** *adv.*

Long'obard: see LOMBARD.

lŏng'-shōre *adj.* Existing, found, or employed, on the shore, frequenting the shore; *long'shoreman*, landsman employed in loading ships, shore-fishing, etc.

lŏngueur' (-nggẽr) *n.* Over-lengthy tedious passage in book etc.; long tedious stretch (of time).

Lŏnk. A breed of sheep belonging to the moorlands of N. Lancashire and the W. Riding of Yorkshire. [var. of *Lank*, short for *Lancashire*]

lōō *n.* Round card-game, played with 3 or 5 cards, with penalties paid to the pool; (having to pay) such penalty; *unlimited ~*, game in which penalty is equivalent of whole amount in pool; ~-*table*, kind of round table.

lōōb'y *n.* Silly fellow.

lōōf'ah *n.* Fibrous pod of plant (*Luffa aegyptiaca*) used as flesh-brush. [Arab. *lufah* (name of plant)]

lŏŏk *v.* 1. Use one's sight; turn eyes in some direction, direct eyes *at*; stare, show surprise; contemplate, examine; express, threaten, show, by one's looks; ascertain or observe by sight; (fig.) make mental search, inquire, aim one's attention *at* and consider; take care or make sure *that*, expect *to* do; *to ~ at*, judging by the looks of; *will not ~ at*, refuses to take, rejects, scorns; ~ *here!*, (imper.), formula for demanding attention or expostulating; ~ *sharp*, orig., keep strict watch; now, lose no time, bestir oneself. 2. (Of things) face, be turned, have or afford outlook, in some direction; tend, point; have certain appearance, seem; seem to be; ~ *alive*, make haste; ~ *as if*, suggest by appearance the belief that; ~ *like*, seem to be, threaten or promise. 3. (with preps.) ~ *about one*, examine one's surroundings, take time to form plans; ~ *after*, follow with the eye; seek for; attend to, take care of; ~ *for*, expect, hope or be on the watch for; search for; ~ *into*, examine the inside of; dip into (book); investigate; ~ *on*, regard *as*, regard *with* some feeling; ~ *over*, inspect; overlook or pardon; ~ *through*, direct eyes through (window etc.); penetrate (veil etc.) with sight, or (pretence, pretender) with insight; be visible through; glance through (book etc.); ~ *to*, consider, take care of, be careful about; keep watch over; rely on *for*; expect, count upon; aim at; ~ *towards*, (colloq.) drink health of; ~ *upon*, regard *with* specified feeling, regard *as*. 4. (with advs.): ~ *about*, be on the watch, be in search *for*, let one's eyes rove; ~ *back*, be half-hearted about enterprise one has begun; turn one's thoughts *upon* or *to* something past; cease to progress; ~ *down upon*, consider oneself superior to; ~ *forward to*, anticipate (usu. with pleasure); ~ *in*, make short visit or call; ~ *on*, be mere spectator; ~ *out*, direct eyes or put head out of window etc.; be vigilant; keep one's eyes open *for*, be prepared *for*; select by inspection; have or afford outlook *on*, *over*, etc.; ~ *over*, inspect one by one or part by part; ~ *through*, survey with searching glance; inspect exhaustively or successively; ~ *up*, (esp. commerc.) improve in price or prosperity; search for (esp. word in dictionary, fact in book of reference); call on (person); raise eyes; ~ *up to*, respect, venerate. 5. ~-*in*, informal call or visit; chance of success; *look'ing-glass*, mirror, quicksilvered glass for mirrors etc.; ~-*out*, watch, looking out; post of observation; man, party, etc., stationed to look out; view over landscape; prospect of luck; person's own concern; ~-*see*, (slang) telescope; periscope; *have a ~-see*, have a look. ~ *n.* Act of looking, direction of eyes, glance; appearance (of things etc.); (sing. or pl.) appearance of face, expression, personal aspect; *good ~s*, beauty.

lŏŏk'er *n.* (esp., local) Overseer, inspector (of cloth etc.); ~-*on*, spectator, eye-witness; one who merely looks on, without taking part.

lōōm[1] *n.* 1. Hand-operated or power-driven apparatus (*hand-~*, *power-~*) for weaving threads into fabric by crossing lengthwise threads (*warps*) with transverse ones (*wefts*), by means of a device which parts the warps so that the shuttle carrying the weft can pass between them. 2. (Inboard part of) shaft of oar (ill. BOAT).

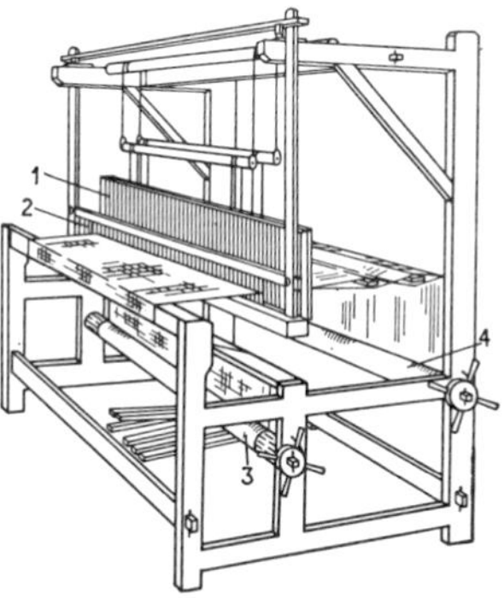

HAND-LOOM

1. Heddles. 2. Reed. 3. Cloth beam. 4. Warp beam

lōōm[2] *v.i.* Appear indistinctly, be seen in vague and often magnified or threatening shape. ~ *n.* Indistinct and exaggerated appearance of object first coming into view, esp. at sea.

loom[3]**:** see LOON[2].

lōōn[1] *n.* (Sc. & archaic) Scamp, idler, boor; lad.

lōōn[2], **lōōm** *n.* Name applied to certain birds all remarkable for their clumsy gait on land, commonly used for the genus *Colymbus* (the divers), also for the great crested grebe (*Podicips cristatus*) and the little grebe or dabchick (*P. fluviatilis*).

lōō n′y *adj.* & *n.* (slang) Lunatic.

lōōp[1] *n.* Doubling or return into itself of string, thong, etc., so as to leave an aperture between the parts, portion so doubled; stitch in knitting; ring or curved piece of metal as handle etc.; railway or telegraph line that diverges from main line and joins it again; circuit in centrifugal railway etc. along top of which passenger travels head downwards, similar path described by aeroplane; (skating) curve crossing itself made on single edge. ~ *v.* Form into loop(s); enclose (as) with loop; fasten (*up, back*) or join (*together*) with loops; ~ *the loop*, (of airman or his machine) describe loop in air (ill. AEROBATICS).

lōōp[2] *n.* (rare) LOOP-HOLE.

lōōp′er *n.* 1. Caterpillar of geometrid moths, progressing by arching itself into loops. 2. Contrivance in sewing-machine etc. for making loops.

lōōp′-hōle *n.* Narrow vertical slit in wall for shooting or looking through, or to admit light or air (ill. CASTLE); outlet, means of evading rule, etc. ~ *v.t.* Make loop-holes in.

lōōp′y *adj.* (slang) Crazy.

Loos (lōōs). Town of NE. France; *Battle of* ~, series of engagements in which the town was captured by British in Allied offensive in autumn of 1915.

lōōse (-s) *adj.* 1. Released from bonds or restraint; detached or detachable from its place; (chem). free, uncombined; hanging partly free; not rigidly fixed, apt to shift; slack, relaxed, not tense or tight; not compact, dense, or serried; (of bowels) relaxed; *at a* ~ *end*, without definite occupation; *with a* ~ *rein*, (fig.) indulgently; ~ *box*: see BOX[2] *n.* 3; ~ *change*, money kept or left unsecured for casual use; ~*cover*, removable cover for chair etc.; ~ *game, play*, (in football) play in which players do not lock together; ~*-leaf*, (of ledger etc.) with each leaf separate and detachable; ~ *tongue*, one given to blabbing. 2. (Of statements, ideas, etc.) inexact, indefinite, vague, incorrect; (of translation) not close or faithful; (of style) ungrammatical. 3. Morally lax, dissolute, wanton in speech or act. **lōōse′ly** (-sl-) *adv.* **lōōse′nėss** *n.* **lōōse** *v.t.* Release, set free, free from constraint; untie, undo; detach from moorings; discharge (arrow), discharge gun (*at*); relax (hold). ~ *n.* Vent, free expression.

lōōs′en *v.* Make or become less tight or compact or firm: loose (person's tongue); relieve (bowels) from costiveness or (cough) from dryness; relax (discipline etc.).

lōōse′strīfe (-s-s-) *n.* Two common tall herbaceous plants growing on margins of ditches or streams: *golden* or *yellow*~, flowering in July, with racemes of golden-yellow flowers (*Lysimachia vulgaris*), and *red* or *purple* ~, summer-flowering, with beautiful showy spikes of purple-red flowers (*Lythrum salicaria*).

lōōt *n.* Goods taken from enemy, spoil, booty; illicit gains. ~ *v.* Plunder, sack: carry off as booty. **lōōt′er** *n.*

lŏp[1] *n.* Smaller branches and twigs of trees. ~ *v.* Cut off branches and twigs of (tree); strip tree of (branches etc.); cut off (person's limb or head); make lopping strokes *at*. **lŏpp′ings** *n.pl.* Branches lopped from tree.

lŏp[2] *v.* Hang limply; let (ears) hang; slouch, dawdle, hang *about* (archaic); ~*-ears*, drooping ears; ~*-ear*, kind of rabbit with lop-ears. ~ *n.* Lop-eared rabbit.

lŏp[3] *v.i.* (Of water) break in short lumpy waves. ~ *n.* Such motion of water.

lōpe *v.i.* & *n.* (Run with) long bounding stride (esp. of animals).

Lope de Vega: see VEGA CARPIO.

Lōp′ėz, Carlos Antonio (1790–1862). President of Paraguay 1844–62 and virtual dictator. ~, Francisco Solano (1827–70). His eldest son, president and dictator of Paraguay; defeated and killed in 'War of the Triple Alliance' (1865–70) against Argentina, Uruguay, and Brazil.

Lóp′ėz de Aya′la (lō-; -yah-), Don Pedro (1332–1407). Spanish statesman, chronicler, and poet.

lŏphobrăn′chĭate (-k-) *adj.* & *n.* (Fish) with gills disposed in tufts.

lŏph′odŏnt *adj.* & *n.* (Animal) with transverse ridges on crowns of molars.

lŏp-sīd′ėd *adj.* With one side lower or smaller than the other, unevenly balanced. **lŏp-sīd′ėdly** *adv.* **lŏp-sīd′ėdnėss** *n.*

loq. *abbrev.* *Loquitur* (='speaks', with speaker's name added, as stage-direction or notice to reader).

loquā′cious (-shus) *adj.* Talkative; chattering, babbling. **loquā′ciously** *adv.* **loquā′ciousnėss, loquă′city** *ns.*

lō′quat (-ŏt) *n.* (Small reddish fruit of) Chinese and Japanese tree, *Eriobotrya japonica*, introduced into S. Europe, India, Australia, etc. [Chin. *luh kwat* rush orange]

loral: see LOREAL.

lôr′cha *n.* Ship with hull of European shape but Chinese rig.

lôrd *n.* 1. Master, ruler, chief, prince, sovereign; (poet.) owner; magnate in some trade; feudal superior; (poet. & joc.) husband; (astrol.) dominant planet; ~*s of creation*, mankind. 2. God; (usu. *the* or *our* L~) Christ; *in the year of our* L~, Anno Domini; *L~'s Day*, (esp. among Nonconformists) Sunday; *L~'s Prayer*, prayer taught by Christ to his disciples (Matt. vi. 9–13); *L~'s Supper*, Eucharist. 3. Nobleman, peer of the realm or person entitled by courtesy to prefix *Lord* as part of his ordinary style; member (whether peer or not) of board performing duties of high state office put in commission; forming part of many official titles, as *L~ Chamberlain, L~ Chancellor*, etc.; *the Lords, House of Lords*, temporal and spiritual peers of Parliament, forming upper legislative chamber of United Kingdom; committee of specially qualified members of this appointed as ultimate judicial court of appeal; *First L~ (of the Admiralty)*, civilian president of the Admiralty board; *Civil L~*, civilian member of Admiralty board; *L~s of Session*, judges of Scottish Court of Session (see SESSION); *L~ Justice General, L~ Justice Clerk*, president, vice-president, of Scottish Court of Justiciary; *L~ Lieutenant*, viceroy of Ireland (till 1922); chief executive authority and head of magistracy in each county; *L~ Rector*, honorary head of Scottish University Court elected triennially by matriculated students; *L~ Mayor*, mayor of London, York, and other cities; *L~ Mayor's day*, 9th Nov., when Lord Mayor of London goes in procession with aldermen etc. to Westminster to receive from Lord Chancellor assent of the Crown to his election; *L~ Mayor's show*, procession on this day. 4. (As prefixed title, part of customary appellation of) marquis, earl, viscount, or baron; (followed by Christian and family name) younger son of duke or marquis; *my L~*, respectful or polite formula for addressing nobleman below rank of duke, or bishop, lord mayor, or judge of supreme court. 5. ~*s and ladies*, wild arum. **lôrd′lĭng** *n.* Young or unimportant lord (usu. contempt.). **lôrd** *v.* Play the lord *over*; ennoble, confer title of *lord* upon.

lôrd′ly *adj.* Haughty, imperious, lofty, disdainful; grand, magnificent, fit for or belonging to a lord; **lôrd′lĭnėss** *n.*

lôrdōs′ĭs *n.* (path.) Anterior curvature of spine, producing convexity in front.

Lôrd's. Cricket ground in St. John's Wood, London, headquarters of the Marylebone Cricket Club. [f. Thomas *Lord*, who removed here at the end of 18th c. from a cricket ground that he had previously opened near Regent's Park]

lôrd′shĭp *n.* Dominion, rule, ownership *of* or *over*; domain, estate, manor; personality of lord; *your*~, respectful form of address to noblemen (except dukes), bishops, and judges.

lôre[1] *n.* Doctrine (archaic); erudition, scholarship (archaic); body of traditions or knowledge relating to some subject

lôre[2] *n.* (zool.) Space between bird's eye and upper mandible (ill. BIRD), or between reptile's eye and nostril.

lôr′(ė)al *adj.* (zool.) Of the LORE[2].

Lōr'ėlei (-lī). Rock or cliff on river Rhine with remarkable echo; in German legend the home of a siren whose song lured boatmen to destruction.

Lōr'ĕntz, Hendrik Anton (1853–1928). Dutch physicist; noted for his researches into the relations between light, magnetism, and matter; awarded Nobel Prize for physics 1902.

Loreto (-āt'ō). Town in Marches of E. Italy, to which, acc. to legend, angels brought the house of the Virgin Mary (*Holy House of* ~).

Lorĕtt'ō. Scottish public school in Musselburgh, about 5 miles E. of Edinburgh; so called because it stands on site of a chapel of Our Lady of LORETO.

lorgnette (lōrnyĕt') *n.* Pair of eyeglasses held in hand, usu. by long handle; opera-glass.

lŏ'ricate *adj.* & *n.* (zool.) (Animal) having defensive armour of bone, plates, scales, etc.

lōr'is *n.* Any of several slender stump-tailed nocturnal arboreal primates found in Africa and

LORIS

tropical Asia, related to the lemurs, and including *slender* ~ (*Loris tardigradus*), *slow* ~ (*Nycticebus coucang*), and potto.

lōrn *adj.* (poet. & joc.) Desolate, forlorn.

Lorraine'. Medieval kingdom on W. bank of Rhine, extending from North Sea to Italy, and divided into two duchies, Upper and Lower Lorraine, in 10th c.; Upper Lorraine (S. of Ardennes) as a province of France, passed to the French crown in 1766; part of Lorraine was acquired with Alsace by Germany in 1871 but was restored to France after war of 1914–18; *Cross of* ~, cross having two transoms (ill. CROSS), adopted as emblem of the Free French movement in the war of 1939–45. [med. L *Lotharingia*, f. *Lothair*, name of king]

lŏ'rry *n.* Long low flat sideless wagon; motor truck; truck used on railways and tramways.

lōr'y *n.* Various bright-plumaged parrots of SE. Asia and New Guinea.

Lŏs Ang'ėlēs (ăngg- *or* ănj-). City on coast of S. California, U.S., with a large suburb, Hollywood, which is the centre of the American cinema industry.

lose (lōōz) *v.* (past t. and past part. *lost* pr. lŏ- *or* law-). 1. Be deprived of, cease by negligence, misadventure, separation, death, etc., to possess or have; suffer loss or detriment, incur disadvantage, be the worse off in money or otherwise *by* transaction etc.; become unable to find, fail to keep in sight or follow or mentally grasp; spend (time, opportunities, pains) to no purpose, waste; fail to obtain, catch, see, or hear; forfeit (stake), be defeated in (game, battle, lawsuit, etc.); fail to carry (motion); cause person the loss of, cost; ~ *patience, one's temper*, become impatient, angry; ~ *ground*, fail to keep position, recede, decline; ~ *interest*, cease to be interested; cease to interest; *losing game*, one in which defeat seems inevitable. 2. (pass.) Disappear, perish, die or be dead; (refl. and pass.) go astray; become merged or engrossed (*in*); be obscured in; *lost soul*, damned soul. **los'er** *n.*

lŏss (*or* laws) *n.* Losing or being lost; person, thing, or amount lost; detriment, disadvantage, resulting from loss; *at a* ~, puzzled, at fault.

lŏt[1] *n.* 1. One of set of objects used to secure a chance decision in dividing goods, selecting officials, etc. (now only in *draw, cast*, ~*s*, and *throw in one's* ~ *with*, share fortunes with); this method of deciding, choice resulting from it; what falls to a person by lot, share; person's destiny, fortune, condition. 2. Plot or portion of land assigned by State to particular owner, piece of land set apart for particular purpose (now chiefly U.S.); plot or portion of land offered for sale. 3. Article or set of articles offered separately at sale, item at auction; *bad* ~, disreputable or vicious person. 4. Number or quantity of persons or things of same kind or somehow associated; (colloq.) considerable number or amount, *a* good or great deal; *the* ~, the whole number or quantity. ~ *v.t.* Divide (land *out*, or goods for sale) into lots.

Lŏt[2]. (O.T.) Son of Abraham's brother Haran and legendary ancestor of the Palestinian peoples Moab and Ammon; his wife, fleeing with him from the destruction of Sodom and Gomorrah, looked back, and was turned into a pillar of salt (Gen. xix).

Lōth'air. Name of two Holy Roman Emperors: *Lothair I* (795–855), eldest son of Louis I; his disputes with his brothers over the partition of the Empire led to the treaty of Verdun (843), by which he received the imperial title and Italy and a territory along valleys of Rhine and Rhône stretching from North Sea to Mediterranean; *Lothair II* (or *III*) 'the Saxon' (*c* 1070–1137), duke of Saxony, emperor and German king in succession to Henry V.

Lothār'ĭo. Name of a character in Rowe's play 'The Fair Penitent', freq. qualified as 'gay'; hence, a libertine, gay deceiver, rake.

Lōth'ĭan (-dh-). District of Scotland, formerly all the E. part of the Lowlands from the Forth to to Cheviots; from 7th to 11th c. it was part of Northumbria.

Lōti' (-tē), Pierre. Pen-name of Louis Marie Julien Viaud (1850–1923), French naval officer and romantic novelist.

lō'tion *n.* Liquid preparation used externally for healing wounds, beautifying skin, etc.

lŏtt'ery *n.* Arrangement for distributing prizes by chance among purchasers of tickets; (fig.) thing that defies calculation.

lŏtt'ō[1] *n.* Game of chance played with boards or cards divided into numbered sections, which are covered as numbers are drawn from a bag; when one player has covered all numbers on one row of his card he wins the money staked.

Lŏtt'ō[2], Lorenzo (*c* 1480–1556). Italian painter of the Venetian school.

lō't'us *n.* 1. Plant represented in ancient Greek legend as inducing luxurious dreaminess and distaste for active life. 2. Water-lilies of Egypt and Asia, *Nymphae* and *Nelumbium* species; (archit.) ornament representing Egyptian water-lily.

Lŏtz'ė, Rudolf Hermann (1817–81). German philosopher.

loud *adj.* Strongly audible, sonorous; clamorous, noisy; (of colour etc.) obtrusive, conspicuous, flashy; ~-*speaker*, instrument (esp. as part of wireless receiving apparatus) for converting electrical impulses into sounds loud enough to be heard at a distance. **loud'ly** *adv.* **loud'nėss** *n.* **loud** *adv.* Loudly.

lough (lŏχ) *n.* (Anglo-Ir.) Lake or arm of the sea.

Louis[1] (lōō'ē). Name of many French kings: *Louis I* (778–840), 'the Pious', 'le Débonnaire'; 3rd son of Charlemagne; co-emperor with his father, 813; sole emperor, 814; *Louis II* (846–79), 'le Bègue' or 'the Stammerer'; son of Charles the Bald; king of the West Franks 877–9; *Louis III* (*c* 863–82), joint-king of France with his brother Carloman, 879–82; *Louis IV* (921–54), king of France 936–54; called 'd'Outremer' because his mother, sister of king Athelstan, fled with him to England when his father, Charles III, was imprisoned; *Louis V* (967–87), 'le Fainéant'; last Carolingian king of France 986–7; *Louis VI* (1081–1137), 'the Fat'; king 1108–37; soldier and popular hero; constantly opposed the English in Normandy; *Louis VII* (*c* 1121–1180), king of France 1137–80; proclaimed and led the disastrous second CRUSADE, 1146–9; *Louis VIII* (1187–1226), king of France 1223–6; leader of crusade against the Albigenses; *Louis IX* (1214–70), (St. Louis); king of France 1226–70; went on crusade 1248, was captured 1250 and passed 4 years in Syria; returned to

France 1254; adjusted with the English king Henry III England's claims in France; sailed for Tunis 1270 on a second crusade, and died there of the plague; canonized 1297; *Louis X* (1287–1316), 'the Quarrelsome', king of France 1314–16; *Louis XI* (1423–83), king of France 1461–83; ruled as absolute monarch, broke the power of the feudal nobles, and greatly increased the royal domain; *Louis XII* (1462–1515), king of France 1499–1515; *Louis XIII* (1601–43), king of France 1610–43; *Louis XIV* (1638–1715), king of France 1643–1715; during his minority power was in the hands of his mother, Anne of Austria, and her minister Mazarin; his own rule was a time of absolute monarchy, constant ruinous wars, and great extravagance at court; *Louis XV* (1710–74), great-grandson and successor of Louis XIV; king of France 1715–74; his reign saw the Seven Years War and the loss to France of India and Canada; *Louis XVI* (1754–93), grandson and successor of Louis XV; king of France from 1774 to 1792, when the Convention declared royalty abolished; he was guillotined on 21st Jan. 1793; *Louis XVII* (1785–1795?), titular king of France second son of Louis XVI; he was reported to have died in prison, but many legends of his escape were current; *Louis XVIII* (1755–1824), younger brother of Louis XVI; fled from France 1791; proclaimed himself king after death of Louis XVII (1795); was restored to the throne by the allies in 1814.

Louis[2] (lōō′ē). Name of several Holy Roman Emperors: *Louis I*: see LOUIS[1]; *Louis II* (825–75), eldest son of Lothair I; king of Italy 844–; emperor 855; *Louis III* (*c* 880–928), 'the Blind'; son of Boso, king of Provence, and of Irmengarde, daughter of Louis II; emperor in succession to Arnulf, 900–; *Louis IV* (*c* 1287–1347), 'the Bavarian'; duke of Upper Bavaria, German king 1314–, emperor 1328–; involved in disputes with popes which led to declaration that election by the electors conferred rule over the Empire without confirmation by the pope.

Louis[3] **I, II, III,** kings of Bavaria: see LUDWIG.

louis-d'or (lōō′ĭ dôr′) *n.* French gold coin worth about 17*s.*, first issued by Louis XIII in 1640 and superseded in 1795; gold 20-franc piece.

louis heel (lōō′ē) *n.* High curved heel of woman's shoe, French heel. [f. name of the French kings]

Louisiana (lōōēzĭăn′*a*). West South Central State of U.S., on N. coast of Gulf of Mexico; capital, Baton Rouge. The territory was claimed by France in 1682 and named in honour of Louis XIV; transferred to Spain 1762 and back to France 1800; finally sold by the French republic to the U.S. in 1803; ~ *Purchase*, the territory sold by France to the U.S. in 1803.

Louis Philippe′ (lōō′ē, -ēp) (1773–1850). Duke of Orleans, son of Philippe Egalité; spent many years in exile in England and America; was appointed king of France by the French Chamber after the 'July revolution' of 1830; in 1848 he was forced to abdicate; he died in exile in England.

Louis Quatorze (lōō′ē, kătôrz′). (Of style in furniture, architecture, etc.) of the reign of Louis XIV of France, 1643–1715. Similarly **Louis Quinze** (kănz), Louis XV, 1715–74; **Louis Seize** (sĕz), Louis XVI, 1774–92; **Louis Treize** (trĕz), Louis XIII, 1610–43.

lounge (-j) *v.* Go lazily, saunter; loll, recline; idle. ~ *n.* Spell of lounging, saunter, stroll; place where one can lounge, esp. entrance-hall or gallery furnished for the purpose, but now freq. = sitting-room; sofa or deep chair; ~*-lizard*, (slang) one who spends his time idling in fashionable society; ~*-suit*, man's ordinary dress as contrasted with sports or formal clothes. **loun′ger** *n.* **loun′gingly** *adv.*

loupe (lōōp) *n.* Magnifying instrument consisting of a system of lenses mounted on a frame (in *binocular* ~ a modified spectacle-frame).

loup′ing ill (lōō-) *n.* Disease of sheep, a form of encephalitis, caused by a virus which occas. attacks other mammals including man.

lour, lower (lowr) *v.i.* Frown, scowl, look sullen; (of clouds etc.) look dark and threatening. ~ *n.* Scowl; gloominess of sky etc. **lour′ingly** *adv.* **lour′y** *adj.*

Lourdes (loord). Town of SW. France at foot of Pyrenees, site of a cave where the Virgin Mary is said to have appeared in 1858 to a peasant girl, Bernadette Soubirous (d. 1878, canonized 1933); now a centre of pilgrimage where many miraculous cures have been reported.

louse *n.* (pl. *lice*). (zool.) One of various wingless blood-sucking insects of order *Anoplura*, parasitic on mammals; esp., the best-known species of these, *Pediculus humanus*, which infests man and is agent in

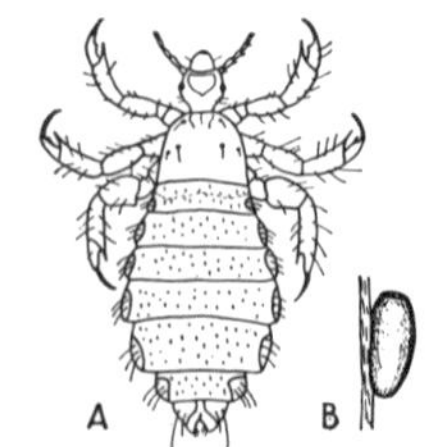

LOUSE: A. ADULT. B. NIT ATTACHED TO HUMAN HAIR, ×15

transmission of many diseases, e.g. typhus. **lous′y** (-z-) *adj.* Infested with lice; (slang) disgusting; (slang) 'swarming' *with*; abundantly supplied *with* money etc. **lous′inėss** *n.*

lout *n.* Awkward fellow, bumpkin, clown. **lout′ish** *adj.* **lout′ishly** *adv.* **lout′ishnėss** *n.*

Louth. Maritime county of Leinster, Eire.

lou′ver, louvre[1] (lōōv′*er*) *n.* Domed turret-like erection on medieval hall-roof etc., with side openings to let smoke out or air in; (pl., also ~*-boards*) arrangement of overlapping boards or strips of glass to admit air but exclude rain.

Louvre[2] (lōōvr). Ancient palace of the kings of France, on N. bank of Seine in Paris; rebuilt in the reign of Philip II and enlarged by François I and his successors down to Napoleon III; now the principal art museum of France.

lov′able (lŭ-) *adj.* Deserving love, amiable. **lov′ablenėss** *n.* **lov′ably** *adv.*

lov′age (lŭ-) *n.* Various plants, esp. the S. European umbelliferous herb *Levisticum officinale*, grown in old gardens and used as domestic remedy.

love (lŭv) *n.* 1. Warm affection, attachment, liking, or fondness; paternal benevolence; affectionate devotion. 2. Sexual affection, passion, or desire; affection between sweethearts, this feeling as literary subject, personified influence, or a god; representation of Cupid or of naked winged child symbolizing love; *labour of* ~, task one delights in or does for love of someone; *in* ~ *with*, enamoured of, fond of; *fall in* ~, become enamoured; *make* ~, pay amorous attentions *to*. 3. Beloved one, sweetheart; (colloq.) delightful person, pretty thing. 4. (tennis, rackets, etc.) No score, nothing, nil; ~ *all*, state of game when neither side has yet scored; ~ *game*, one in which loser has not scored. 5. ~*-affair*, temporary relationship between two people who have fallen in love; ~*-apple*, (old name for) tomato; ~*-bird*, one of several species of parakeet, esp. the W. Afr. *Agapornis pullarius*, remarkable for the affection it shows its mate; ~*-child*, illegitimate child; ~*-feast*, meal in token of brotherly love among early Christians; religious service among Methodists etc., imitating this; ~*-in-a-mist*, *Nigella damascena*, with blue flowers surrounded by green thread-like bracts; S. Amer. passion-flower, *Passiflora foetida*, with similar bracts; ~*-in-idleness*, hearts-ease, *Viola tricolor*; ~*-knot*, intricate knot of ribbon etc. with double bow; ~*-letter*, letter between sweethearts, expressing love; ~*-lies-bleeding*, garden-plant *Amaranthus caudatus*, with long drooping spikes of purplish-red bloom; *love′lock*, tress or curl worn on temple or forehead; ~*-lorn*, pining with love, deserted by one's love; ~*-match*, marriage for the sake of love, not for money or convenience; ~*-sick*, languishing with love; ~*-song*, song about or expressing love; ~*-story*, novel etc. of which main theme is love; story of a wooing etc.; ~*-token*, thing given in sign of love. ~ *v.* Hold dear, bear love to; be in love (with); be fond of; cling to, delight in, enjoy having, be addicted to, admire or be glad of the existence of; be (habitually) inclined *to*; (colloq.) like, be delighted.

Love'lace[1] (lŭvl-). A character in Richardson's novel 'Clarissa Harlowe'; hence, libertine, accomplished rake.

Love'lace[2] (lŭvl-), Richard (1618–58). English lyric poet.

love'lėss (lŭvl-) *adj.* Unloving; unloved. **love'lėssly** *adv.* **love'lėssnėss** *n.*

lovely (lŭv'lĭ) *adj.* Attractively or admirably beautiful; (colloq.) delightful, very pleasing, intensely amusing. **love'lily** *adv.* (rare). **love'linėss** *n.* **love'ly** *n.* Glamorous woman or girl, esp. in an entertainment.

lov'er (lŭ-) *n.* Woman's sweetheart or suitor; (pl.) pair in love; paramour, gallant; admirer, devotee, *of* thing, etc.; ~*s' knot*, love-knot. **lov'erlėss, lov'erlīke** *adjs.*

lov'ing (lŭ-) *adj.* That loves, affectionate; manifesting or proceeding from love; ~*-cup*, large drinking vessel, usu. of silver with two or more handles, passed round at banquet; ~*-kindness*, tender regard.

low[1] (lō) *v.* Utter cry (as) of cow, moo; say, utter *forth*, with lowing sound. ~ *n.* Cow's cry.

low[2] (lō) *adj.* 1. Not reaching far up, not high or tall (not used of persons); not elevated in geographical etc. position. 2. Of small amount as measured by a scale or degrees; (of liquid, receptacle, supply of anything) nearly exhausted or empty; *at lowest*, to mention the least possible amount, etc. 3. Of or in humble rank or position; not exalted or sublime, commonplace, undignified, little civilized, not highly organized; abject, mean, degraded, coarse, vulgar; *high and* ~, everyone. 4. Ill-nourished, not nourishing, indicative of ill nutrition; wanting in vigour, depressed, not intense. 5. (Of sounds) not shrill or high, produced by slow vibrations; not loud. 6. (Of church etc.) giving low place to authority of bishops and priests, inherent grace of sacraments, ecclesiastical organization, and ritual; not sacerdotal; approximating to protestant non-conformity; *L~ Church, Church'man*, (member of) party in Church of England thus minded. 7. *Bring* ~, depress, reduce, in health, wealth, or position; *lay* ~, overthrow; *lie* ~, crouch; be prostrate, dead, or abased; (slang) keep quiet or out of the way, say nothing; bide one's time. 8. ~*-brow*, (person) not highly or not pretentiously intellectual; ~*-browed*, (esp. of rocks) beetling, (of building etc.) with low entrance, gloomy; ~ *comedian*, actor in ~ *comedy*, in which subject and treatment border on farce; *L~ Countries*, NETHERLANDS; ~*-down*, abject, mean, dishonourable; *low'-down*, (slang, orig. U.S.) true facts, correct information; ~ *dress, neck*, (dress with) neckline leaving part of shoulders and breast exposed; *lower case*: see CASE; *lower deck*, that immediately above hold; *the* petty officers and men of the Navy or of a ship; *Lower House*, lower branch of legislative assembly (e.g. House of Commons); *lower school*, (in public schools etc.) usu. forms below the fifth; *lower world*, the earth; (also) hell; ~ *frequency*: see FREQUENCY; *L~ German*: see GERMAN; *low'land*: see separate entry; *L~ Latin*: see LATIN; ~ *latitudes*, those near equator; ~ *life*, that of the lower classes; *L~ Mass*: see MASS[1]; ~ *pitch*, low key or tone; slight angular elevation of a roof; ~ *relief*, bas-relief, shallow carving or modelling on background, less than half the true depth; *L~ Sunday, Week*, Sunday, week, after Easter Day and week; ~ *tide, water*, level of ebbed sea, time of extreme ebb; *in* ~ *water*, out of funds etc.; ~*-wing*, (of monoplane) with wings set low in fuselage. ~ *adv.* In or to low or mean position; on poor diet; for small stakes; in low tone, on or to low note; ~*-born*, of humble birth; ~*-bred*, of vulgar manners; ~ *down*, far down; in mean or ungenerous way. **low'ermost, low'ish** *adjs.* **low'nėss** *n.* **low** *n.* What is low; low level or figure (chiefly U.S.); area of low atmospheric pressure, centre of a depression.

Low'ell[1] (lō-), Amy (1874–1925). American poet and literary critic.

Low'ell[2] (lō-), James Russell (1819–91). American essayist and poet.

Low'ell[3] (lō-), Percival (1855–1916). American astronomer; founder of the ~ *Observatory* at Flagstaff, Arizona.

low'er[1] (lō-) *v.* Let or haul down; (naut.) let down boat, haul down sail etc.; diminish height of; sink, descend, slope downwards; diminish (price etc.); (of price etc.) come down; diminish in intensity or pitch; degrade, disgrace; reduce bodily condition of.

lower[2] *v.*: see LOUR.

Lowes'tŏft (lōs-). Town in Suffolk, England, a seaport and centre of fishing industry; ~ (*china*), kind of soft-paste porcelain made there in second half of 18th c.

low'land (lō-) *n.* (usu. pl.) Less mountainous part of a country, esp. (*L~s*) that part of Scotland S. and E. of the Highlands. **low'land** *adj.* **low'lander** *n.* Inhabitant of lowlands, esp. (*L~*) those of Scotland.

low'ly (lō-) *adj.* Humble in feeling, behaviour, or condition; modest, unpretending. ~ *adv.* In lowly manner. **low'lily** *adv.* **low'linėss** *n.*

lŏxodrŏm'ĭc *adj.* Of oblique sailing or navigating by the RHUMB. ~ *n.* Rhumb line or table. **lŏxodrŏm'ĭcs** *n.pl.*

loy'al *adj.* True, faithful, to duty, love, or obligation (*to*); faithful in allegiance to sovereign, government, or mother country; enthusiastically devoted to sovereign's person and family; exhibiting loyalty. **loy'ally** *adv.* **loy'alism, loy'alist** *ns.* **loy'al** *n.* Person who remains loyal in time of disaffection.

loy'alty *n.* Loyal temper or conduct.

Loyola: see IGNATIUS LOYOLA.

lŏz'ėnge (-j) *n.* 1. Rhomb, diamond figure, esp. as bearing in heraldry (ill. HERALDRY); lozenge-shaped shield for spinster's or widow's arms; lozenge-shaped facet of cut gem; lozenge-shaped pane in casement etc. 2. Small tablet, orig. lozenge-shaped, usu. of flavoured or medicated sugar, to be dissolved in mouth.

l.p. *abbrev.* Large paper; long playing (record; also **L.P.**); long primer; low pressure.

L.P.T.B. *abbrev.* London Passenger Transport Board.

L.R.A.M. *abbrev.* Licentiate of the Royal Academy of Music.

L.R.C. *abbrev.* Leander Rowing Club; London Rowing Club.

L.R.C.P., L.R.C.S. *abbrevs.* Licentiate of the Royal College of Physicians, Surgeons.

l.s. *abbrev. Locus sigilli* (= the place of the seal, on documents).

£.s.d. (ĕl' ĕs' dē') *n.* Pounds, shillings, and pence; (colloq.) money, riches. [L *librae, solidi, denarii*]

L.S.O. *abbrev.* London Symphony Orchestra.

Lt *abbrev.* Lieutenant.

l.t. *abbrev.* Low tension.

L.T.A. *abbrev.* Lawn Tennis Association; London Teachers' Association.

Lt-Col., Lt-Com(m). *abbrevs.* Lieutenant-Colonel, -Commander.

Ltd *abbrev.* Limited (liability company); see LIABILITY.

Lt-Gen., Lt-Gov. *abbrevs.* Lieutenant-General, -Governor.

lŭbb'er *n.* Big clumsy stupid fellow, lout; clumsy seaman, unseamanlike fellow; ~*s line, mark*, vertical line inside a compass case, indicating the direction of the ship's head. **lŭbb'erlīke, lŭbb'erly** *adjs.*

Lüb'eck. City of N. Germany, a Baltic seaport, formerly head of the HANSEATIC League.

lub'rĭcāte (lo͞o, lū-) *v.t.* Make slippery or smooth by applying fluid or unguent; minimize friction of (machinery) with grease etc. **lub'rĭcant** *adj.* & *n.* **lub'rĭcā'tion** *n.*

lubrĭ'cĭty (lo͞o, lū-) *n.* Slipperiness, smoothness, oiliness; lewdness, wantonness.

Luc'an[1] (lo͞o-) *adj.* Of St. Luke.

Luc'an[2] (lo͞o-) (A.D. 39–65). Marcus Annaeus Lucanus, Roman poet; his chief work is 'Pharsalia', an heroic poem describing the struggle between Caesar and Pompey.

Lucc'a (lo͝o-, lū-). City and province of N. Italy; ~ *oil*, superior quality of olive oil. **Lucchese** (lo͝okāz'ĭ) *adj.*

luce (lo͞os, lūs) *n.* Pike, esp. when full-grown.

lu'cent (lo͞o-, lū-) *adj.* Shining, luminous, translucent. **lu'cency** *n.*

lucẽrn(e)'[1] (lo͞o, lū-) *n.* Leguminous plant (*Medicago sativa*) with trifoliate leaves and bluish-purple clover-like flowers, used for fodder.

Lucẽrne'[2] (lo͞o, lū-). Canton and city of central Switzerland; *Lake of* ~, English name for the *Lac des Quatre Cantons* or *Vierwaldstättersee*, the principal lake of central Switzerland, on which stands the city.

Lucian (lo͞o'sĭan, -shĭan) (*c* A.D. 120–190). Greek rhetorician, sophist, and author of satiric dialogues, prose romances, etc., born at Samosata on the Euphrates. **Luciăn'ic** *adj.*

lu'cid (lo͞o-, lū-) *adj.* Bright (poet.); clear, pellucid; (entom., bot.) with smooth shining surface; ~ *interval*, period of sanity between attacks of madness. **lu'cidly** *adv.* **lucĭd'ĭty** *n.*

Lu'cifer (lo͞o-). 1. The planet Venus when it appears in the sky before sunrise; the morning star. 2. By misunderstanding of Isa. xiv. 12 (where the Hebrew epithet 'shining one', translated as *Lucifer* in the Vulgate, is applied to the king of Babylon), Satan, the rebel archangel, before his fall; now chiefly in phr. *as proud as Lucifer.* [L, = 'light-bringer']

Lucīn'a (lo͞o, lū-). Roman goddess who presided over birth; chiefly as epithet of Juno or occas. of Diana.

lŭck *n.* (Chance as bestower of) good or ill fortune; fortuitous event affecting one's interests; person's apparent tendency to be (un)fortunate; supposed tendency of chance to bring a succession of (un)favourable events; good fortune, success due to chance; *as ~ would have it*, fortunately or unfortunately; *down on* one's *luck*, dispirited by misfortune, temporarily unfortunate; *try one's ~*, make venture at gaming-table etc.; *worse ~*, more's the pity; *for ~*, to bring good luck; *~-penny*, piece of money kept for luck; sum returned by seller to buyer, esp. in livestock sale. **lŭck'lėss** *adj.* **lŭck'lėssnėss** *n.*

lŭck'ĭly *adv.* By luck (rare); fortunately.

Lŭck'now (-nō). Capital city of Uttar Pradesh, India, formerly capital of Oudh; during the Indian Mutiny of 1857 the English in Lahore were besieged in the Residency at Lucknow, and reinforcements under Havelock and Outram arriving after several months were unable to fight their way out again; the garrison was relieved in March 1858 by troops under Sir Colin Campbell.

lŭck'y[1] *adj.* Constantly attended by good luck, enjoying it on a particular occasion; (of guess etc.) right by luck, of the nature of a fluke; occurring by chance and bringing happy results; presaging, bringing, worn etc. for, good luck, well-omened; *~-bag, -dip, -tub*, receptacle at bazaars etc. containing articles of more or less value for one of which payer of small sum may dip.

lŭck'y[2] *n.* (slang) *Cut one's ~*, make off.

lu'crative (lo͞o, lū-) *adj.* Yielding gain, profitable. **lu'cratively** *adv.* **lu'crativenėss** *n.*

lucre (lo͞o'ker, lū-) *n.* (derog.) Gain, pecuniary profit as motive; FILTHY ~, money.

Lucrē'tia (lo͞o-, lū-, -shĭă), **Lucrēce'.** A Roman lady, wife of Lucius Tarquinius Collatinus; acc. to Roman legend she was raped by Sextus, son of Tarquinius Superbus, and took her own life; this led to the expulsion of the Tarquins from Rome and the establishment of the republic.

Lucrē'tius (lo͞o-, lū-, -shus). Titus Lucretius Carus (*c* 99–55 B.C.), Latin poet; author of a philosophical poem 'De Rerum Natura', in which he tried to show that the course of the world can be explained without resorting to divine intervention.

luc'ūbrāte (lo͞o-, lū-) *v.i.* Express one's meditations in writing; produce lucubrations. **lucūbrā'tion** *n.* Nocturnal study or meditation; literary work esp. of pedantic or elaborate character. [L *lucubrare*, work by lamplight (*lux*, light)]

luc'ūlent (lo͞o-, lū-) *adj.* (rare) Clear, convincing, lucid. **luc'ūlently** *adv.*

Lucŭll'us (lo͞o-, lū-), Lucius Lucinius (*c* 110–56 B.C.). Roman general; consul 74 B.C.; famous for magnificence and luxury esp. in his banquets. **Lucŭll'an, Lucŭll'ian** *adjs.*

Lu'cy (lo͞o-), St. (3rd c. A.D.). Sicilian virgin and martyr, commemorated 13th Dec.; patron saint of the blind.

lŭd[1]. Minced form of *lord*, esp. in representation of affected or hurried pronunciation of lawyers addressing judge.

Lŭd[2]. Mythical king of Britain, legendary builder of the walls round the city subsequently known as London.

Lŭdd'īte *adj.* & *n.* (Member) of organized bands of English artisans who in the period 1811–16 destroyed newly introduced machinery in the Midlands and N. of England on the ground that it took away their livelihood. [said to be f. Ned *Ludd*, a feeble-minded person who broke up some machinery in a fit of insane rage]

Lud'endōrff (lo͞o-), Erich von (1865–1937). German general; shared with Hindenburg the credit of the victories of Tannenberg and the Masurian Lakes in the war of 1914–18; was responsible for the German offensive of 1918; was associated with Hitler in the 'Beer-Hall Putsch' at Munich, 1923.

Lŭd'gate. One of the ancient gates of London W. of St. Paul's Cathedral, traditionally associated with King LUD[2]; destroyed 1760; the gatehouse was a debtors' prison.

lud'icrous (lo͞o-, lū-) *adj.* Absurd, ridiculous; exciting or deserving derision. **lud'icrously** *adv.* **lud'icrousnėss** *n.*

lud'ō (lo͞o-, lū-) *n.* Game played on a chequered board with counters which are moved according to throw of dice, the object being to get all the counters round the board. [L *ludo* = 'I play']

Lud'wĭg (lo͞odv-). Name of 3 kings of Bavaria: *Ludwig I* (1786–1868), king 1825–48; patron of the arts; was popular until he allowed most of the power of government to fall into the hands of his mistress, LOLA MONTEZ; abdicated 1848 in favour of his son Maximilian II; *Ludwig II* (1845–86), son of Maximilian II, king 1864–86; patron of the arts, esp. music, and friend of Wagner; was declared insane and committed suicide 1886; *Ludwig III* (1845–1921), crowned king of Bavaria 1913, abdicated 1918.

lues (lo͞o'ēz) *n.* Plague, contagious disease, contagion; ~ (*venerea*), syphilis. **luĕt'ic** *adj.*

lŭff *n.* Side of fore-and-aft sail next mast or stay (ill. SAIL[1]); broadest part of ship's bow where sides begin to curve in. ~ *v.* Bring ship's head, bring head of (ship), nearer wind, turn (helm) so as to secure this; (yacht-racing) get windward side of.

Luftwaffe (lo͝oft'văffe) *n.* The German Air Force.

lŭg[1] *n.* (also *~-worm*) large marine worm (*Arenicola marina*) burrowing in sand, and used for bait.

lŭg[2] *n.* LUGSAIL.

lŭg[3] *v.* Drag or tug (heavy object) with effort or violence; pull hard *at*; bring (subject etc.) irrelevantly *in*(*to*); force (person) along. ~ *n.* Hard or rough pull.

lŭg[4] *n.* Ear (Sc. and north.); one of two projections or handles on vase etc.; projection from a casting etc. by which it may be fixed in place.

Lugano, Lake of (lo͞ogah'nō). Lake of N. Italy and Switzerland, in foothills of the Alps between L. Maggiore and L. Como.

lūge (-zh) *n.* Small raised toboggan for one person (ill. SLEDGE).

lŭgg'age (-ĭj) *n.* Traveller's

baggage, portmanteaux or other receptacles for it.

lŭgg'er *n.* Small ship with four-cornered sails set fore-and-aft.

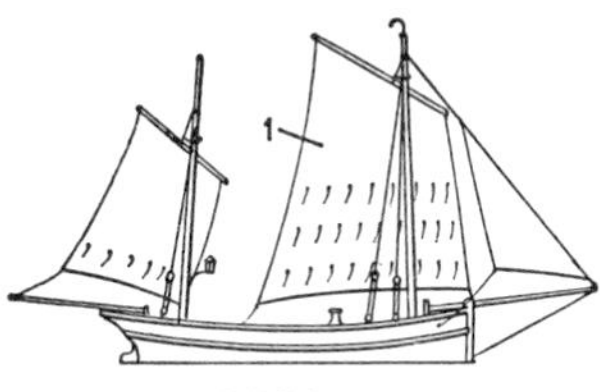

LUGGER
1. Lugsail

lŭg'sail (-sl) *n.* Four-cornered sail bent on yard slung at a third or quarter of its length from one end (ill. LUGGER).

lugū̆b'rious (lōō-, lū-) *adj.* Doleful, dismal, mournful. **lugū̆b'riously** *adv.* **lugū̆b'riousnĕss** *n.*

lug-worm *n.* = LUG[1].

Lui'ni (lōōēn'ē), Bernardino (*c* 1475–*c* 1532). Italian painter of the Lombard school.

Luke (lōōk, lūk), St. A physician, possibly the son of a Greek freedman of Rome, closely associated with St. Paul, and traditional author of the 3rd Gospel and the Acts of the Apostles; commemorated 18th Oct.; *St. ~'s summer*, period of fine weather expected about 18th Oct.

luke'warm (lōō-, lū-) *adj.* Moderately warm, tepid; not zealous, indifferent. **luke'warmly** *adv.* **luke'warmnĕss** *n.*

lŭll *v.* Soothe or send to sleep by sounds or caresses; quiet (suspicion etc.); (usu. pass.) quiet (sea, storm); (of storm etc.) lessen, fall quiet. ~ *n.* Intermission in storm, interval of quiet.

lŭll'abȳ *n.* Soothing refrain or song to put child to sleep. ~ *v.t.* Sing to sleep.

Lully (lūlē'), Jean-Baptiste (1639–87), French musical composer of Italian birth, founder of French grand opera.

lŭmbā'gō *n.* Painful affection, usu. inflammatory, of the muscles of the loins. **lŭmbā'gĭnous** *adj.*

lŭm'bar *adj.* & *n.* (Artery, vein, nerve, or vertebra) of or in loin (ill. SPINE).

lŭm'ber[1] *v.i.* Move in clumsy blundering noisy way. **lŭm'bering** *adj.* **lŭm'beringly** *adv.* **lŭm'bersome** *adj.*

lŭm'ber[2] *n.* 1. Disused articles of furniture etc. taking up room inconveniently; useless or cumbrous material; *~-room*, room for lumber. 2. (N. Amer.) Roughly prepared timber; *lumberjack*, lumberman; *~-mill*, sawmill for cutting up lumber; *lum'berman*, feller, dresser, or conveyer of lumber. ~ *v.* Fill up inconveniently, obstruct; heap together, treat, as lumber; cut and prepare forest timber. **lŭm'berer** *n.*

lŭm'brĭcal *adj.* & *n.* ~ (*muscle*), one of the muscles flexing fingers or toes.

lum'ĕn[1] (lōō-, lū-) *n.* Unit of light energy or luminous flux, the light energy emitted in a unit solid angle by a uniform point source of one candle; *~-hour*, the unit of luminous energy, equal to the emission of one lumen for one hour.

lum'ĕn[2] (lōō-, lū-) *n.* (physiol.) Interior or 'bore' of a tubular structure, e.g. a vein.

lum'inal (lōō-, lū-) *n.* Trade-name of a preparation of phenobarbitone ($C_{12}H_{12}O_3N_2$), used medicinally as a sedative.

lum'inary (lōō-, lū-) *n.* Natural light-giving body, esp. sun or moon; person of intellectual, moral, or spiritual eminence.

luminĕs'cent (lōō-, lū-) *adj.* Emitting light from some cause other than high temperature. **luminĕs'cence** *n.*

luminif'erous (lōō-, lū-) *adj.* Producing or transmitting light.

lum'inous (lōō-, lū-) *adj.* Emitting or full of light, bright, shining; *~ paint*, phosphorescent kind making thing conspicuous at night. **lum'inously** *adv.* **lum'inousnĕss, luminŏs'ity** *ns.*

lŭmm'ė *int.* (vulg.) Of surprise or emphasis. [= '(Lord) love me']

lŭmp[1] *n.* Compact shapeless or unshapely mass; great quantity, lot, heap; mass of clay or dough ready for moulding or baking; protuberance, excrescence, swelling, bruise; heavy dull person; *~ in throat*, feeling of pressure caused by emotion; *in the ~*, taking things as a whole, in gross, wholesale; *~ sugar*, loaf sugar broken or cut into lumps or cubes; *~ sum*, sum covering or including a number of items; sum paid down at once (opp. *instalments*). ~ *v.* Put together in one lump; mass *together*, treat as all alike, disregard differences between or among; rise or collect into lumps; go heavily *along*, sit heavily *down*.

lŭmp[2] *n.* (also *~-fish*, *~-sucker*) Clumsy spiny-finned leaden-blue fish (*Cyclopterus lumpus*) with sucking-disc on belly.

lŭmp[3] *v.t.* Be displeased at, put up with ungraciously (now only in *if you don't like it you may ~ it* etc.).

lŭm'per *n.* Labourer employed in (un)loading cargoes; small contractor taking work in the lump and giving it out in the piece.

lŭm'ping *adj.* (colloq.) Big, plentiful.

lŭm'pish *adj.* Heavy and clumsy; stupid, lethargic. **lŭm'pishly** *adv.* **lŭm'pishnĕss** *n.*

lŭm'py *adj.* Full of or covered with lumps; (of water) cut up by wind into small waves. **lŭm'pily** *adv.* **lŭm'pinĕss** *n.*

lun'acy (lōō-, lū-) *n.* Being a lunatic, insanity (formerly of the intermittent kind attributed to moon's changes); (law) such mental unsoundness as interferes with civil rights or transactions; great folly; *Commission of ~*, authorization of inquiry into person's sanity; *Commissioner in ~*, member of board appointed by Lord Chancellor to inspect asylums etc.; *Master in ~*, legal officer investigating cases of alleged lunacy.

lun'ar (lōō-, lū-) *adj.* Of, in, as of, the moon; (of light, glory, etc.) pale, feeble; crescent-shaped, lunate; of or containing silver (from alchemists' use of *luna* moon for silver); *~ bone*, half-moon-shaped bone in wrist; *~ caustic*, nitrate of silver fused; *~ distance*, distance of moon from sun, planet, or star, used in finding longitude at sea; *~ month*, interval between new moons: about 29½ days; (pop.) period of 4 weeks; *~ rainbow*, one made by moon's rays.

lunār'ian (lōō-, lū-) *n.* Inhabitant of moon; astronomer or navigator with special knowledge of the moon.

lun'āte (lōō-, lū-) *adj.* Crescent-shaped.

lun'atic (lōō-, lū-) *adj.* & *n.* Insane, mad (person); (of action etc.) outrageously foolish, frantic, mad; eccentric, foolish; *~ asylum*, hospital for reception and treatment of lunatics. [L *luna* moon, because insanity was thought to be caused by the moon's changes]

lunā'tion (lōō-, lū-) *n.* Time from one new moon to next.

lŭnch *n.* (Now the more usual wd, exc. in formal use, for) luncheon; (U.S.) light meal, snack. ~ *v.* Take lunch; (colloq.) provide lunch for.

lŭn'cheon (-shon) *n.* Orig., slight repast between two ordinary meal-times, esp. between breakfast and midday dinner; now (esp. among those who dine in the evening) the midday meal, usu. less substantial and less ceremonious than dinner; (U.S.) similar meal at any time.

Lŭn'dy Island. Small rocky island at entrance to Bristol Channel, off N. coast of Devonshire, England.

lune (lōōn, lūn) *n.* (geom.) Figure formed on sphere or plane by two arcs of circles enclosing a space (ill. CIRCLE).

lunĕtte' (lōō-, lū-) *n.* Arched aperture in concave ceiling to admit light (ill. DOME); crescent-shaped or semicircular space in dome or ceiling decorated with painting etc.; watch-glass of flattened shape; hole for neck in guillotine; (fortif.) work larger than redan, with two faces forming salient angle, and two flanks.

lŭng *n.* Either of the pair of saccular respiratory organs in man and other vertebrates, placed within cavity of thorax on either side of heart and communicating with trachea or windpipe; (pl.) open space(s) in or near a city; *~-fish*, one having lungs as well as gills; *~-power*, power of voice; *lung'wort*, plant (*Pulmonaria officinalis*, order *Boraginaceae*) having leaves with white spots supposed to resemble those of diseased lung; various plants of allied Amer. genus *Mertensia*; (also ~ *of oak*), a lichen (*Sticta pulmonacea*) supposed to be remedy for lung-disease.

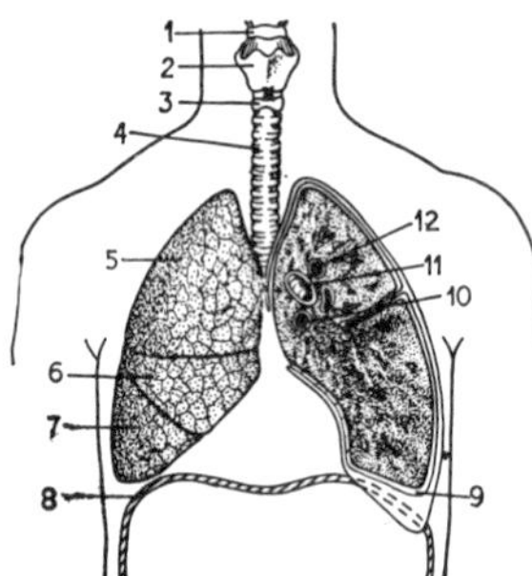

RESPIRATORY SYSTEM: DIAGRAM OF LUNGS WITH LEFT SIDE IN SECTION

1. Hyoid bone. 2. Thyroid cartilage. 3. Cricoid cartilage. 4. Trachea. 5. Upper lobe of lung. 6. Middle lobe of lung. 7. Lower lobe of lung. 8. Diaphragm. 9. Pleura. 10. Pulmonary veins. 11. Bronchus. 12. Pulmonary artery

lŭnge[1] (-j), **longe** (lŭnj) *n.* Long rope with which horse-trainer holds horse while he makes it canter in circle; circular exercise-ground for training horses. ~ *v.t.* Exercise (horse) with or in lunge.

lŭnge[2] (-j) *n.* Thrust with sword etc., esp. in fencing; sudden forward movement, plunge, rush; (gymnastics) forward movement, in which one foot is advanced, the knee being bent and directly over the instep, while the other foot remains stationary. ~ *v.* Make lunge in fencing or gymnastics, deliver blow from shoulder in boxing; drive (weapon, sting, etc.) violently in some direction; rush, make sudden start in some direction.

lunisōl'ar (lōō-, lū-) *adj.* Of mutual relations or combined action of sun and moon; ~ *period*, cycle of 532 years between agreements of solar and lunar cycles (which are of 28 and 19 years); ~ *year*, year with divisions regulated by changes of moon and average total length made to agree with revolution of sun.

lŭnk'ah (-*a*) *n.* Kind of strong Indian cheroot. [Hindi *lanka* islands (of Godavery delta in which tobacco is grown)]

luny: see LOONY.

Lup'ercal (lōō-, lū-). Cave on Palatine hill in ancient Rome, sacred to *Lupercus*, or Faunus in the guise of a wolf-deity, connected with the story of Romulus and Remus. **Lupercāl'ia.** Very ancient Roman festival held on 15th Feb., in which two youths ran a course purificatory round the Palatine with strips of goat's-hide (*februa*) in their hands; a blow from one of these thongs was believed to produce fertility in women.

lup'in(e) (lōō-, lū-) *n.* Plant of genus *Lupinus*; esp. *L. albus*, cultivated in warmer districts of Europe for fodder, and the Amer. species cultivated in gardens, with long tapering spikes of blue, rosy-purple, white, or yellow flowers; (usu. pl.) seed of these.

lup'ine (lōō-, lū-) *adj.* Of wolf or wolves, wolf-like.

lup'us (lōō-, lū-) *n.* Ulcerous disease of skin; ~ *vulgaris*, tuberculosis of the skin.

lûrch[1] *n.* *Leave in the* ~, desert (friend, ally) in difficulties. [formerly = state of score in some games in which one player was far ahead of the other, f. Fr. *lourche* game like backgammon, also bad defeat in this]

lûrch[2] *n.* Sudden lean to one side, stagger. ~ *v.i.* Make lurch(es), stagger.

lûrch'er *n.* 1. Petty thief, swindler; spy. 2. Cross-bred dog between collie or sheep-dog and greyhound, used esp. by poachers.

lûre *n.* 1. Falconer's apparatus for recalling hawk, usu. a bunch of feathers (within which hawk finds food during training) attached to cord (ill. FALCON). 2. Something used to entice; enticing quality *of*. ~ *v.t.* Recall (hawk) with lure; entice (*away*, *into*, etc.).

Lur'ia (loor-), Isaac ben Solomon (1534–72). Jewish mystic; founder of a school which strongly influenced Judaism.

lûr'id *adj.* Wan and sallow, ghastly; shining with a red glare or glow amid darkness; terrible, ominous, sensational; (bot. etc.) dingy yellowish-brown. **lûr'idly** *adv.* **lûridnėss** *n.*

lûrk *v.i.* Be hidden *in*, *under*, etc., prowl; escape notice, exist unobserved, be latent.

Lusā'tia (lōō-, lū-, -shĭ*a*). Ancient name for district of central Germany between Elbe and Oder, home of a Slavonic people, the WENDS. **Lusā'tian** *adj.* & *n.* Of Lusatia or its people or their language, Wend(ish), Sorbian.

lŭ'scious (-sh*u*s) *adj.* Richly sweet in taste or smell; sickly sweet, cloying; (of style etc.) over-rich in sound, imagery, or voluptuous suggestion. **lŭ'sciously** *adv.* **lŭ'sciousnėss** *n.*

lŭsh *adj.* Luxuriant and succulent (of plants, esp. grass).

Lusitān'ia (lōō-, lū-). 1. Ancient province of Hispania, almost identical with modern Portugal. 2. A Cunard liner which was sunk in the Atlantic by a German submarine in May 1915 with loss of over 1,000 lives.

lŭst *n.* Sensuous appetite regarded as sinful (bibl., theol.); animal desire for sexual indulgence, lascivious passion; passionate enjoyment or desire *of*. ~ *v.i.* Have strong or excessive desire (*after*, *for*). **lŭst'ful** *adj.* **lŭst'fully** *adv.* **lŭst'fulnėss** *n.*

lŭst'ral *adj.* Of, used in, ceremonial purification.

lŭstrāte' *v.t.* Purify by expiatory sacrifice, ceremonial washing, or other rite. **lŭstrā'tion** *n.* [see LUSTRUM]

lŭs'tre[1] (-*ter*) *n.* 1. Quality of shining by reflected light, often with effect of changing colour; sheen, gloss; luminous splendour, radiant beauty; splendour, glory, distinction. 2. (Prismatic glass pendant of) chandelier. 3. Thin dress-material with cotton warp, woollen weft, and lustrous surface; kind of wool with lustrous surface. 4. Iridescent glaze applied to pottery and porcelain; ware glazed with this. ~ *v.t.* Put lustre on. **lŭs'treless, lŭs'trous** *adjs.* **lŭs'trously** *adv.*

lŭs'tre[2] *n.* = LUSTRUM.

lŭs'trine *n.* (formerly) Glossy silk fabric; (now) cotton fabric rendered smooth by lead glazing and polishing, used for linings.

lŭs'trum *n.* (pl. -*a*, -*ums*). Period of 5 years. [L, orig. purificatory sacrifice made every 5 years after census had been taken]

lŭs'ty *adj.* Healthy and strong; vigorous, lively. **lŭs'tily** *adv.* **lŭs'tinėss** *n.*

lu'sus natūr'ae (lōō-, lū-) *n.* Freak of nature, strikingly abnormal natural production, sport.

lut'anist (lōō-, lū-) *n.* One who plays (and sings to) the lute; composer for the lute.

lute[1] (lōōt, lūt) *n.* Musical instrument, much used in 14th–17th centuries, resembling guitar in shape, with strings struck with fingers of right hand and stopped on frets with those of left. [Arab. *al'ud* the lute (*'ud* orig. wood)]

LUTE

lute[2] (lōōt, lūt) *n.* Tenacious clay or cement used to stop hole, make joint airtight, coat crucible, protect graft, etc. ~ *v.t.* Apply lute to.

lutē'cium (lōō-, lū-, -shĭ*u*m) *n.* Metallic element of rare-earth group, resembling ytterbium in properties; symbol Lu, at. no. 71, at. wt 174·97. [L *Lutetia* Paris]

lut'ėous (lōō-, lū-) *adj.* (nat. hist.) Of deep orange yellow.

lute'string (lōōts-, lū-) *n.* (archaic) Glossy silk fabric; dress or ribbon of this. [app. alteration of *lustring* lustrine]

Lutē'tia (Parisiorum) (lōō-, lū-, -shĭ*a*). Roman name of the capital on the Seine of the Parisii, a Gallic tribe; Paris.

Lu'ther (lōō-), Martin (1483–1546). Leader of the Protestant Reformation in Germany; translator (1522–34) of the Bible into German and author of many hymns. **Lu'theran** *adj.* Of Luther, his opinions and followers, or the Lutheran Church; ~ *Church*, those Churches, esp. in Germany and Scandinavia, which accept the doctrines of the Augsburg Confession (1530) and whose cardinal doctrine is that of justification by faith alone.

lŭx *n.* The international unit of illumination, the illumination of a surface at a uniform distance of one metre from a symmetrical point source of one candle, equal to one LUMEN[1] per square metre.

lŭx'āte *v.t.* Dislocate (joint etc.). **lŭxā'tion** *n.*

luxe (lŭks, lo͝oks) *n.* Luxuriousness, sumptuous elegance (in *edition, train*, etc., *de* ~).

Luxembourg (lŭksahṅboor'), Palais du. Palace S. of the Seine in Paris, built 1615–20 for Marie de Médicis and now the meeting-place of the Senate, with gardens open to the public.

Lŭx'embûrg[1], -bourg. 1. (sp. *-burg*) Independent grand duchy S. of Belgium between France and Germany; its capital city. 2. (sp. *-bourg*) Province of SE. Belgium.

Lux'emburg[2] (lo͝oks'emboorg), Rosa (1870–1919). German socialist revolutionary, born in Russian Poland; a leader of the SPARTACIST party, she was murdered with Karl Liebknecht in Berlin in 1919.

Lŭx'ôr. Town of Upper Egypt on right bank of Nile, containing, along with Karnak, the ruins of ancient THEBES.

lŭxūr'ĭant *adj.* Prolific; profuse of growth, exuberant, rank; florid, richly ornamented. **lŭxūr'ĭantly** *adv.* **lŭxūr'ĭance** *n.*

lŭxūr'ĭāte *v.i.* Revel, enjoy oneself; take one's ease, be luxurious.

lŭxūr'ĭous *adj.* Given, contributing, to luxury, self-indulgent, voluptuous, very comfortable. **lŭxūr'ĭously** *adv.* **lŭxūr'ĭousnėss** *n.*

lŭx'ury (-ksherĭ) *n.* (Habitual use of) choice or costly food, dress, furniture, etc.; refined and intense enjoyment; thing conducing to comfort or enjoyment in addition to what are considered necessaries, thing desirable but not essential.

L.W.M. *abbrev.* Low-water mark.

LXX *abbrev.* Septuagint.

Lyautey (lyōtā'), Louis Hubert Gonzalve (1854–1934). French soldier and colonial administrator (in Algeria and Morocco); marshal of France.

lўcăn'thropy *n.* 1. Witchcraft consisting in assumption by human beings of form and nature of wolves. 2. Form of insanity in which patient imagines himself a beast and exhibits depraved appetites etc. **lўc'anthrōpe** *n.* 1. Werewolf. 2. Person afflicted by lycanthropy.

Lўcā'on. (Gk legend) King of Arcadia who, as the host of Zeus, offered him human flesh to eat, in order to try his divinity; he was killed by lightning or turned into a wolf.

lycée (lē'sā) *n.* State secondary school in France (dist. from *collège*, municipal secondary school). [Fr., f. LYCEUM]

Lўcē'um. 1. Grove and gymnasium near Athens, sacred to Apollo Lyceus, where Aristotle taught; hence, Aristotle's philosophy or followers. 2. (U.S.) Institution providing literary or scientific lectures, concerts, etc. 3. ~ (*Theatre*), London theatre built in 1794, rebuilt after a fire in 1834; Sir Henry Irving was lessee and manager for many years from 1878; the last theatrical performance was in 1939.

lych: see LICH.

lўch'nĭs (-k-) *n.* Genus of *Caryophyllaceae* including campion and ragged robin.

lўc'opŏd *n.* (bot.) Club-moss.

lўcopō'dĭum *n.* (Plant of) genus of cryptogamous plants, club-moss; fine highly inflammable powder from spores of species of this, used in surgery as absorbent, and in making stage-lightning, fireworks, etc.

Lўcûrg'us. (Gk hist.) Reputed founder of constitution of Sparta, prob. of about end of 9th c. B.C.

lўdd'īte *n.* High explosive chiefly of picric acid, formerly used in shells. [*Lydd* in Kent, where first tested in England]

Lўd'gate, John (*c* 1370–*c* 1451). English poet; author of devotional, philosophical, and historical poems and of allegories and moral romances.

Lўd'ĭa. Ancient kingdom and (7th to 6th c. B.C.) empire of W. Asia Minor. **Lўd'ĭan** *adj.* 1. Of ancient Lydia, its people, or their language. 2. ~ *mode*, (mus.) ancient Greek mode, reputedly effeminate in character; 5th of eccles. modes with F as final and C as dominant (ill. MODE). 3. Soft or effeminate; voluptuous.

lye (lī) *n.* Water made alkaline by lixiviation of vegetable ashes; any strong alkaline solution esp. for washing, any detergent.

Lў'ell, Sir Charles (1797–1875). English geologist; completely revolutionized the prevailing ideas of the age of the earth, and substituted for the old conception of 'catastrophic' change the gradual process of natural laws.

lў'ĭng[1] *adj.* Part. of LIE[1]; (esp.) Deceitful, false. **lў'ĭngly** *adv.*

lў'ĭng[2] *n.* Part. of LIE[2]; (esp.) *~-in*, being in childbed (also attrib., as *~-in hospital*).

lўke'-wāke *n.* Watch kept at night over dead body.

Lўl'y, John (*c* 1554–1606). English author of plays, pamphlets and a prose romance, 'Euphues, or the Anatomy of Wit'.

lўmph *n.* 1. (poet.) Pure water. 2. (physiol.) Colourless slightly alkaline fluid which is derived from the blood by permeation through the walls of the capillaries and drains into the lymphatic vessels; exudation from sore etc.; (*vaccine* ~), matter taken from cowpox vesicles and used in vaccination; other matter used for similar purpose; ~ *glands* (*nodes*), small masses of specialized tissue at intervals in lymphatic system, filtering off foreign particles from lymph. **lўm'phoid** *adj.*

lўmphăt'ĭc *adj.* 1. Of, secreting, conveying, lymph; ~ *system*, system of fine vessels in which lymph circulates and which communicates with the venous system (ill. GLAND). 2. Flabby-muscled, pale-skinned, sluggish (qualities formerly attributed to excess of lymph). ~ *n.* Vein-like vessel conveying lymph.

lўm'phocўte *n.* Form of white blood-cell (ill. BLOOD).

lўncē'an *adj.* Lynx-eyed, keen-sighted.

lўnch *n.* ~ (or *L*~) *law*, infliction of summary punishment on offender by self-constituted court with no legal authority; summary execution of one charged with some offence. ~ *v.* Condemn and punish by lynch law. [after Capt. W. *Lynch* (1742–1820) of Pittsylvania, Virginia]

lўnn *n.* U.S. var. of LINN.

lўnx *n.* Various members of the cat family found only in N. hemisphere, with tufted ear-tips, short tail, spotted fur, and rather long legs; lynx-fur; *~-eyed*, sharp-sighted.

Lў'on (King of Arms). Title (from the lion on the royal shield) of chief herald in Scotland.

Lўon(n)ĕsse'. In Arthurian legend, country off S. coast of Cornwall, between Land's End and Scilly Isles, now supposed to be submerged.

Lў'ons. Engl. name of *Lyon*, city of E. France at confluence of Saône and Rhône, famous esp. for manufacture of silk.

Lўr'a. 'The Harp', a northern constellation containing Vega, the 4th brightest star in the heavens.

Lўr'aĭd, Lўr'ĭd *n.* (usu. pl.) Meteor(s) radiating from Lyra about 20th April.

lўr'ate *adj.* (biol.) Lyre-shaped.

lўre *n.* Obsolete instrument of harp kind, chiefly used for accompanying voice, with strings supported by two symmetrically curved horns; the strings were stopped with the left hand and struck with a plectrum in the right (*illustration, p.* 494); *~-bird, Menura superba*, Australian pheasant-like bird with beautiful lyre-shaped tail. **lўr'ĭst** *n.*

lў'rĭc *adj.* Of or for the lyre, meant to be sung; of the nature of, expressed or fit to be expressed in,

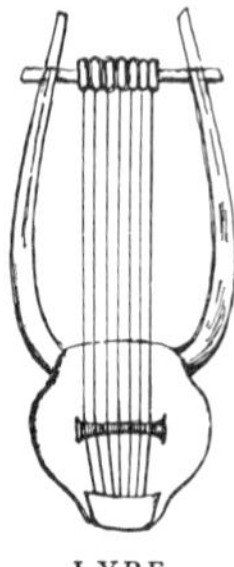

LYRE

song; (of poem) short, usu. divided into stanzas or strophes, and directly expressing poet's own thoughts and sentiments rather than a description of events; (of poet) writing in this manner. ~ *n.* Lyric poem; (in mod. trivial use) words of song.

lў'rĭcal *adj.* 1. Lyric (now rare). 2. Resembling, couched in, or using language appropriate to, lyric poetry. **lў'rĭcally** *adv.*

lў'rĭcism *n.* Lyric character or expression; high-flown sentiments.

Lўsăn'der (d. 395 B.C.). Spartan naval commander in latter part of Peloponnesian War.

Lўsĭm'achus (-k-) (*c* 355–281 B.C.). Macedonian general who served under Alexander the Great and became king of Thrace.

Lўsĭpp'us (4th c. B.C.). Greek sculptor of Sicyon who was famous for his statues of Zeus and portraits of Alexander the Great.

lўs'ĭs *n.* 1. (physiol.) Disintegration of bacterial or other cells. 2. (med., obs.) Gradual reduction of body temperature in certain fevers.

lўs'ŏl *n.* Proprietary name for a mixture of cresols and soft soap, used as an antiseptic and disinfectant.

Lўtt'on, Edward George Earle Lytton Bulwer-, first Baron Lytton (1803–73). English novelist and politician; author of 'Eugene Aram', 'Rienzi', 'The Last Days of Pompeii', etc.

M

M, m. 13th letter of the modern English and 12th of the ancient Roman alphabet, representing a bilabial nasal (usu. voiced) consonant; the form of the letter is derived from Phoenician 𐤌 (early Gk & L M, M, M). As a Roman numeral, M = 1000.

m. *abbrev.* Maiden (over); male; mark(s) (coin); married; masculine; metre(s); mile(s); million(s); minute(s).

M. *abbrev.* Monsieur.

ma (mah) *n.* (vulg.) = MAMMA[1].

M.A. *abbrev.* Master of Arts; Military Academy.

ma'am (mahm, măm, m'm) *n.* Madam (esp. used at Court in addressing Queen or royal princesses, pronounced mahm, or officers in the women's services, pronounced măm, or by servants, pronounced m'm).

Maas: see MEUSE.

Măbĭnō'ğion. A collection of ancient Welsh prose tales (*Mabinogi* pr. -ŏgĭ, = 'instruction for young bards') dealing with Celtic legends and mythology; four of them are contained in the 'Red Book of Hergest' which was compiled in the 14th and 15th centuries.

Mabūse', Jan Gossaert (d. *c* 1535). Flemish painter, active also in Holland; painted in an Italian style.

măc *n.* Colloq. abbrev. of MACINTOSH.

maca'bre (-ahbr) *adj.* Grim, gruesome; *danse* ~, dance of death.

maca'co[1] (-ahkō) *n.* = MACAQUE. [Port., = 'monkey']

maca'co[2] (-ahkō) *n.* Any of several lemurs, esp. the black lemur, *Lemur macaco.*

macăd'am *n.* & *adj.* (Of roads) made with successive layers of small broken stones rolled in with some binding material; material for such roads. **macăd'amīze** *v.t.* **macădamīzā'tion** *n.* [John Loudon *McAdam*, Scottish engineer (1756–1836)]

macaque' (-kahk) *n.* A monkey of genus *Macacus*, of Asia and N. Africa (ill. MONKEY).

măcarōn'ĭ *n.* Wheaten paste formed into long tubes, used as food esp. in Italy; (hist.) 18th-c. dandy affecting continental manners and fashions.

măcarŏn'ic(s) *adj.* & *n.pl.* (Verses) of burlesque form containing Latin or other foreign words and vernacular words with Latin etc. terminations.

măcarōōn' *n.* Small cake or biscuit of ground almonds, white of egg, sugar, etc.

Macăss'ar. Port of Celebes (Indonesia); ~ (*oil*), kind of hair-oil, said to consist of ingredients obtained from Macassar; also applied commercially to other oils imported from the East.

Macaul'ay, Thomas Babington, first Baron Macaulay (1800–59). English historian and essayist.

macaw' *n.* Kinds of large, long-tailed, brightly coloured parrot, mostly native to S. and Central America.

Măcbĕth' (d. 1057). King of Scotland; seized the throne (to which he perhaps had some claim through his wife Gruach) after slaying the king, Duncan, in 1040; hero of a tragedy by Shakespeare.

Macc. *abbrev.* Maccabees (Apocr.).

Măcc'abees (-z). A family of Jews, consisting of Mattathias and his 5 sons, Jochanan, Simon, Judas, Eleazar, and Jonathan; they led a revolt against the oppression of the Syrian king Antiochus Epiphanes (175–64 B.C.), and established a dynasty of priest-kings which ruled until the time of Herod (40 B.C.); (*Books of*) ~, several books of the O.T. Apocrypha dealing chiefly with Jewish history in the 2nd and 1st centuries B.C. **Măccabē'an** *adj.*

Macdŏn'ald[1], Flora (1722–90). Jacobite heroine, daughter of a farmer in the Hebrides; she helped Prince Charles Edward, the Young Pretender, to escape to Skye after his defeat at Culloden, 1746; for this she was imprisoned in the Tower of London, but released 1747.

Macdŏn'ald[2], James Ramsay (1866–1937). Scottish Labour politician; prime minister in Labour govt 1924 and 1929–31, and of 'National' govt 1931–5.

Măcdŭff', thane of Fife. A partly or wholly mythical personage who helped Duncan's son, Malcolm Canmore, against MACBETH.

māce[1] *n.* 1. (hist.) Heavy, usu. metal-headed and spiked club. 2. Staff of office resembling this (*illustration, p.* 495); *the M~*, the symbol of the Speaker's authority in the House of Commons, placed on the table when he is in the chair. 3. Flat-headed stick used in bagatelle.

māce[2] *n.* Dried outer covering of nutmeg, as spice.

mă'cédoine (-ĕdwahn) *n.* Mixed fruit or vegetables, esp. cut up small. [Fr. *Macedoine* Macedonia]

Măcėdōn'ĭa (in ancient history also **Mă'cėdon**). Mountainous Balkan country, N. of Greece, now divided between Greece and Yugoslavia. In the 4th c. B.C., under

Philip II and his son Alexander III (the Great), the kingdom of Macedonia dominated Greece; in 146 B.C. it became a Roman province, and when the Roman Empire was divided it was assigned to the eastern half; in the 5th c. A.D. Slavs began to invade and colonize it and it became in turn an independent kingdom, a part of the Bulgarian and then of the Serbian Empire; from the end of the 14th c. until the Balkan war of 1912 it was under Turkish rule. **Măcėdōn'ian** *adj.* & *n.*

mă'cerāte *v.* Make or become soft by soaking; become emaciated by fasting. **măcerā'tion** *n.*

McGill University (m*a*gĭl'). Canadian university at Montreal; founded 1821 from bequests by James McGill (1744–1813).

Mach (mahχ, mahk). ~ *number*, ratio of the velocity of a body passing through a fluid medium to the velocity of sound in that medium. [E. *Mach*, Austrian physicist]

machair' (-χ-) *n.* (geog.) Flat or low-lying strip of calcareous natural grassland usu. overlying shell sand.

machete (-āt'ā) *n.* Broad heavy knife used in Central America and W. Indies as implement and weapon.

Măchĭavĕll'ĭ (-k-), Niccolo di Bernardo dei (1469–1527). Florentine political philosopher, author of a famous and influential treatise on statecraft, 'The Prince' (*Il Principe*, 1513), advocating the principle that any political means, however unscrupulous, are justifiable if they strengthen the power of a State; hence, ~, an unscrupulous schemer, one who practises duplicity in statecraft. **Măchĭavĕll'ian** *adj.* & *n.* **Măchĭavĕll'ism** *n.*

machĭc'olāte (-tsh-) *v.t.* Furnish (parapet etc.) with openings between supporting corbels for dropping stones etc. on assailants. **machĭcolā'tion** *n.* (ill. CASTLE).

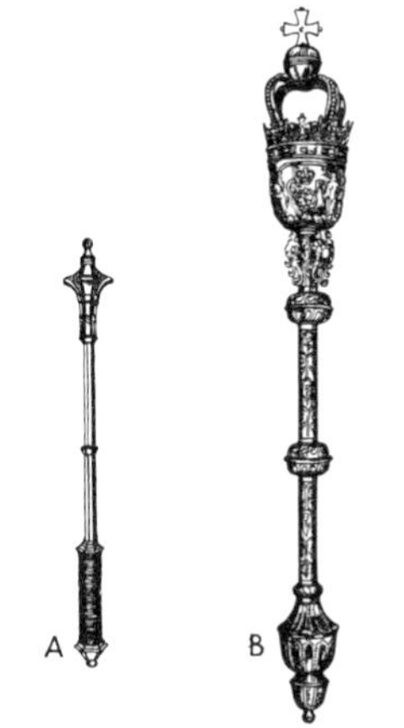

A. WAR MACE, *c* 1480. B. CEREMONIAL MACE CARRIED BY THE SERGEANTS AT ARMS AT CORONATIONS, LATE 16TH C.

măch'ĭnāte (-k-) *v.i.* Lay plots, intrigue. **măch'ĭnā'tion, mach'ĭnātor** *ns.*

machine' (-shēn) *n.* Apparatus for applying mechanical power, having several parts each with definite function (the kind often being specified as *sewing-*, *printing-* ~); bicycle, tricycle; aeroplane; person who acts mechanically and without intelligence or with unfailing regularity; (mech.) instrument directing application of, or transmitting, force; organized system for carrying out specific functions, as the *political*, *party* ~; ~-*gun*, belt-fed, water-cooled, single-barrelled gun, firing solid bullets from a fixed mounting, designed to utilize part of the energy of one explosion to extract the spent cartridge-case and load and fire the next round; it is capable of very high speeds of firing (over 1,000 rounds a minute) for hours on end; ~-*tool*, cutting or shaping tool, worked by machinery, not by hand. ~ *v.t.* Make, operate on, print, sew, etc., with a machine.

machin'ery (-shēn-) *n.* Machines; mechanism; organization.

machin'ĭst (-shēn-) *n.* Maker of machinery; worker who operates a machine.

machŏm'ėter (-k-) *n.* Instrument recording air speed in terms of the local speed of sound in air. [f. Ger. surname *Mach*, on analogy of barometer, thermometer, etc.]

măc'ĭntŏsh *n.* Waterproof material of cloth and rubber; coat or cloak of this or of plastic or nylon material; waterproof sheet. [Charles *Macintosh* (1766–1843), inventor]

Mackĕn'zĭe, Henry (1745–1831). Scottish novelist; author of 'The Man of Feeling' (1771); sometimes referred to as 'the Addison of the North'.

măck'erel *n.* Edible sea-fish, genus *Scomber*, of N. Atlantic, having a silvery belly and greenish back with dark-blue stripes; ~ *sky*, one covered with clouds resembling the patterns on a mackerel's back (cirrocumulus).

McKĭn'ley (m*a*kĭn-), William (1843–1901). 25th president of U.S., 1897–1901; assassinated by an anarchist.

mackintosh: see MACINTOSH.

Maclise (-ēz), Daniel (1806–70). Irish-born historical painter and illustrator.

Măc-Măhōn', Marie Edmé Patrice Maurice de, Duke of Magenta (1808–93). French marshal and president of the Republic 1873–9.

Macmĭll'an, Rt. Hon. Harold (1894–). Prime minister of Gt Britain 1957–63.

Mâcon (mahkawṅ'). City on the river Saône in central France; the wine made in this neighbourhood.

Macphĕr'son, James (1736–96). Scottish poet; he claimed to have translated from the Gaelic two ancient epics by a poet called Ossian; after his death an investigating committee reported that he had used traditional Gaelic poems but edited them freely and added inventions of his own.

macramé (-ahm'ĭ). A fringe or trimming of knotted thread or cord.

Macready (-rēd'ĭ), William Charles (1793–1873). English actor, famous for Shakespearian tragic parts.

măcrocėphăl'ĭc *adj.* Long- or large-headed.

măc'rocŏsm *n.* The great world, the universe (contrasted with *microcosm*); any great whole.

măcromŏl'ėcūle *n.* Very large molecule like those in proteins, synthetic plastics, etc.

măc'ron *n.* A straight horizontal line (¯) over a vowel to indicate that it is 'long'.

măcroscŏp'ĭc *adj.* Visible to the naked eye (opp. *microscopic*).

măc'ūla *n.* (pl. *-ae*). Dark spot on sun or moon (ill. SUN); spot in mineral due to presence of particles of another mineral; spot, blemish, on the skin; ~ (*lūt'ėa*), (anat.) region of greatest visual acuity in the retina (ill. EYE). **măc'ūlar** *adj.* **măcūlā'tion** *n.*

măd *adj.* Of disordered mind, insane; (of animals) rabid; wildly foolish, (colloq.) annoyed; *mad'cap*, wildly impulsive person; *mad'house*, lunatic asylum; *mad'man*, *mad'woman*. **măd'ly** *adv.* **măd'nėss** *n.*

Mădagăs'car. Large island in Indian Ocean, off SE. coast of Africa; a republic within the French Community; capital Tananarive.

măd'am *n.* Polite formal address to woman. [OF *ma dame* my lady]

măd'ame (-ahm; *or* madahm') *n.* French form of *madam*, as title or form of address.

mădapŏll'am *n.* Kind of cotton cloth orig. made in India and later in England. [*Madapollam*, suburb of Narsapur, Madras]

mădd'en *v.* Make, become, mad; irritate.

mădd'er *n.* Herbaceous climbing plant (*Rubia tinctorum*) with yellowish flowers; red dye obtained from its root.

māde *adj.* (past part. of MAKE) Special uses: ~ *dish*, food prepared from several ingredients; ~ *man*, one who has attained success in life.

Madeir'a (-ēr*a*). Island in Atlantic Ocean, off W. coast of Africa, in Portuguese possession; the fortified wine produced there, amber-coloured or brownish, varying in sweetness, and resembling sherry; ~ *cake*, kind of sponge-cake.

mademoiselle (mădamazĕl') *n.* Unmarried Frenchwoman; French governess; title prefixed like *Miss* to French name or used as form of address.

Măd'ĭson[1], James (1751–1836). 4th president of U.S., 1809–17.

Măd'ĭson[2]. Capital city of Wisconsin, U.S.

madŏnn'a *n.* (Picture, statue, of) Virgin Mary; ~ *lily,* tall white lily (*Lilium candidum*), as often depicted in pictures of the Annunciation.

Mădrăs'. State (formerly presidency) of S. India; its capital city, a large seaport on the E. coast.

măd'rĕpōre *n.* Genus (*Madrepora*) of perforate corals; animal producing these. [It. *madre* mother +*poro* coral-like but porous substance]

Madrĭd' (m*a*-). Capital city of Spain.

măd'rĭgal *n.* Short amatory poem; part-song for several voices in elaborate contrapuntal style, usu. without accompaniment.

Maeăn'der. Ancient name of a river of Phrygia, Asia Minor (now R. *Menderes,* Turkey) remarkable for its winding course.

Maecēn'ăs (mī-), Gaius Cilnius (*c* 70–8 B.C.). Roman knight; patron of Virgil and Horace and friend and adviser of Augustus; celebrated for his patronage of learning and letters; hence, a generous patron of literature or art.

mael'strom (māl-) *n.* Great whirlpool (also fig.). [f. *Maelström,* the whirlpool S. of the Lofoten Is. off W. coast of Norway]

maen'ad *n.* Bacchante or priestess of Bacchus; wild fury or shrew. **maenăd'ĭc** *adj.*

maĕs'tro (mah-) *n.* (pl. *-ri* pr. -rē). Eminent musical composer, teacher, or conductor.

Maet'erlĭnck (mah-), Maurice (1862–1949). Belgian poet and dramatist; awarded the Nobel Prize for literature in 1911.

Mae Wĕst (mā) *n.* (R.A.F. slang) Airman's inflatable life-jacket. [f. professional name of a film actress]

Măf'ėkĭng. Town in Cape Province, S. Africa; during the 2nd Boer War a small British force under Baden-Powell withstood a siege there for 7 months; its relief, in May 1900, caused riotous rejoicing (*mafficking*) in London.

măff'ĭck *v.i.* Celebrate with riotous rejoicings. [back formation from MAFEKING, treated as gerund]

mafia (mah'fĭ*a*) *n.* In Sicily, the spirit of hostility to the law and its ministers prevailing among a part of the population; also, those who share in this spirit; not, as often supposed, an organized secret society.

măgazine' (-ēn) *n.* 1. Store for explosives, arms, or military provisions; receptacle for number of rounds loaded at one time in rifle and various types of automatic guns (ill. GUN); reservoir or supply-chamber in a machine, store, battery, etc. 2. Periodical publication containing articles on various subjects by different writers. [Arab. *makhasin* storehouses]

Măg'dalen, Măgdalē'nė. The appellation (= 'woman of Magdala') of a disciple of Christ named Mary 'out of whom went seven devils' (Luke viii. 2); she has commonly been identified with the 'sinner' of Luke vii. 37 and therefore appears in Western hagiology as a harlot restored to purity and sanctified by repentance and faith.

Magdalen Cŏll'ege (mawd'lĭn). College of the University of Oxford founded in 1458 by William Waynflete, bishop of Winchester.

Magdalene Cŏll'ege (mawd'lĭn). College of the University of Cambridge founded in 1542 by Baron Audley of Walden.

Măgdalēn'ĭan *adj.* Applied to the palaeolithic culture which followed the Aurignacian and is characterized by weapons and tools of horn and bone. [f. rock-shelter of La *Madeleine,* Dordogne, France]

Magĕll'an (-g-). Fernão de Magalhães (*c* 1470–1521), Portuguese navigator; the first European to pass through the strait that bears his name, between Tierra del Fuego and the S. American mainland; he undertook the first expedition round the world, but perished in the Philippines (only one of his ships completed the voyage).

Magĕn'ta (-j-). Town in Lombardy near which the Austrians were defeated in 1859 by the French under Napoleon III and Mac-Mahon. **magĕn'ta** *n.* A brilliant crimson aniline dye (fuchsin), discovered in the year of the battle; the colour of this.

Ma'gersfontein' (mah-, ān). In Orange Free State; scene of an action (1899) in the Boer War, in which the Boers under Cronje repulsed the British with great loss.

măgg'ot *n.* Grub or larva, esp. of blue-bottle or cheese-fly; fad, crotchet; **măgg'otў** *adj.*

Mā'gī (-j- *or* -g-) *n.pl.* (with sing. *Mā'gus*). The ancient Persian priestly caste; hence, those skilled in Oriental magic and astrology; *The Magi,* the (traditionally three) 'wise men' who came from the East bearing gifts to the infant Christ (Matt. ii. 1). **Mā'gĭan** *n.* (One) of the Magi; magician. **Mā'gĭanĭsm** *n.* Doctrines, philosophy, of the Persian Magi.

mă'gĭc *adj.* & *n.* (Of) the pretended art of influencing events by occult control of nature or of spirits, witchcraft; mysterious agency or power; ~ *lantern,* optical instrument for projecting magnified and illuminated images of glass slide etc. on to a white screen; ~ *square,* square divided into smaller squares each containing a number, so arranged that the sums of the rows, vertical, horizontal, or diagonal, are the same; ~ *wand,* small staff used by magicians and conjurors. **mă'gĭcal** *adj.* **mă'gĭcally** *adv.*

magĭ'cian (-shn) *n.* One skilled in magic, wizard.

Maginot line (măzh'ĭnō). A line of fortifications extending along the eastern borders of France from Montmédy to Belfort; crossed by German forces in 1940. [André *Maginot,* French war minister]

măgĭstēr'ĭal *adj.* Of a magistrate; dictatorial. **măgĭstēr'ĭally** *adv.*

mă'gĭstracy *n.* Magistrates; magisterial office.

mă'gĭstrate *n.* Civil officer administering law; in England, person appointed to try minor offences and small civil cases, either an unpaid layman (Justice of the Peace) or, in London and some other large towns, a paid judicial officer (*stipendiary* ~). **mă'gĭstrateshĭp, mă'gĭstrature** *ns.*

măg'ma *n.* (geol.) The mixture of molten and crystalline materials which on cooling forms igneous rocks.

Măg'na C(h)ar'ta. The Great Charter of the liberties of England, granted by King John, under pressure from his barons, at Runnymede in 1215; among its chief provisions was that no freeman should be imprisoned or banished except by the law of the land and that supplies should not be exacted without the consent of the Common Council of the realm.

măgnāl'ĭum *n.* Alloy of magnesium and aluminium combining lightness with rigidity.

măgnăn'ĭmous *adj.* High-souled, above petty feelings. **măgnăn'ĭmously** *adv.* **măgnanĭm'ĭty** *n.*

măg'nāte *n.* Man of high position, wealth, authority, power, etc., often with reference to class or occupation, as *financial* ~.

măgnē'sia (-sh*a*) *n.* (chem.) Magnesium oxide (MgO); *cream, milk of* ~, a suspension of magnesium hydroxide in water, used medicinally. **măgnē'sian** *adj.* [Gk *Magnes -ētos* (*lithos*) stone from Magnesia (in Thessaly), loadstone]

măgnēs'ĭum (-zĭum *or* -shĭum) *n.* (chem.) A silvery-white metallic element, symbol Mg, at. no. 12, at. wt 24·312, burning with a bright white light; magnesium powder, mixed with powdered potassium chlorate, burns explosively when ignited with the emission of intense light and is used in photography and in star shells; ~ *ribbon, wire,* a thin strip or wire of magnesium, prepared for burning to produce a magnesium light.

măg'nėt *n.* 1. Piece of naturally magnetic iron ore (Fe_3O_4) having the power of attracting iron or steel; = LOADSTONE. 2. Piece of iron or steel or nickel to which the characteristic properties of loadstone have been imparted by contact, by induction, or by means of an electric current; when a magnetized bar or needle is suspended freely it aligns its axis so as to point approx. north and south, and on account of this property it is used as the directional part of a compass; *horseshoe* ~, magnetized bar of steel shaped like a horseshoe. 3. ELECTRO-magnet. 4. (fig.) Something which attracts.

măgnĕt'ĭc *adj.* Of or like or acting as magnet; (fig.) very attractive; ~ *declination, deviation*: see ~ *pole*; ~ *equator*, imaginary line round the earth, at all points along which the magnetic inclination is zero; ~ *field*, a region associated with a magnet or an electric current in which there are observable magnetic effects; ~ *inclination*, the vertical angle between the horizontal and the direction of the earth's magnetic field at any point; ~ *mine*, sea-mine designed to be detonated by the magnetic field of a steel ship passing near it; ~ *movement*, the turning movement exerted by a magnetic field on any magnetized object within it; ~ *needle*: see MAGNET, sense 2; ~ *pole*, either of the poles of a magnet; specif., either of the two points on the earth's surface towards which the compass needle points and at which it dips vertically (ill. EARTH); the ~ *north* is some 6 degrees W. of true N. and the ~ *south* some 6 degrees E. of true S., the angular difference between the true and magnetic meridians being the ~ *declination* or *deviation*; ~ *pole unit*, pole which exerts a force of 1 dyne upon an equal pole 1 cm. long; ~ *storm*, erratic disturbance of earth's magnetism, probably due to solar electric activity. **măgnĕt'ĭcally** *adv.* **măgnĕt'ĭcs** *n.pl.* That branch of physics which deals with magnetic phenomena.

măg'nėtĭsm *n.* 1. Magnetic phenomena; science of these; *terrestrial* ~, magnetic properties of the earth as a whole. 2. *animal* ~: see MESMERISM. 3. (fig.) Attraction, personal charm.

măg'nėtīte *n.* Magnetic iron oxide (Fe_3O_4); loadstone.

măg'nėtīze *v.t.* Make into a magnet; attract as a magnet does; mesmerize. **măgnėtīzā'tion** *n.*

măgnĕt'ō *n.* Magneto-electric machine, esp. an alternating-current generator with permanent magnets used to generate the electric ignition spark in an internal combustion engine.

măgnĕt'ō-chĕm'ĭstry *n.* That branch of science which treats of the relation of magnetic to chemical phenomena. **măgnĕt'ō-chĕm'ĭcal** *adj.*

măgnĕt'ō-ĕlėctrĭ'cĭty *n.* Electricity generated by relative movement of electric conductors and magnets. **măgnĕt'ō-ėlĕc'trĭc** *adj.*

măgnėtŏm'ėter *n.* Instrument for the measurement of magnetic forces, esp. terrestrial magnetism.

măgnētomōt'ive *adj.* ~ *force*, (abbrev. m.m.f.) the sum of the magnetizing forces in a magnetic circuit (the magnetic analogy of electromotive force).

măgnē'tŏn *n.* A unit of magnetic moment, used in atomic physics to describe the magnetic fields of atoms.

măgnētostăt'ĭcs *n.* The science of the properties of non-varying magnetic fields.

măg'nėtrŏn *n.* 1. Kind of thermionic vacuum tube in which the motion of the ions is controlled by an externally applied magnetic field. 2. Electronic device utilizing an axial magnetic field for generating electro-magnetic radiations of very short wave-length. [f. *magnet* and *electron*]

măgnĭf'ĭcăt *n.* The hymn of the Virgin Mary in Luke i. 46–55, in the Vulgate beginning *Magnificat anima mea Dominum* ('My soul doth magnify the Lord').

măgnĭf'ĭcent *adj.* Splendid, sumptuous; imposing, stately; fine, excellent. **măgnĭf'ĭcently** *adv.* **măgnĭf'ĭcence** *n.*

măg'nĭfȳ *v.t.* Increase apparent size of, as with lens, microscope, or concave mirror; exaggerate; (archaic) extol. **măgnĭfĭcā'tion** *n.*; *angular* ~, (optics) ratio of the angle subtended by the object.

măgnĭl'oquent *adj.* Lofty in expression; boastful. **măgnĭl'oquently** *adv.* **măgnĭl'oquence** *n.*

măg'nĭtūde *n.* Largeness; size; importance; one of the classes into which the fixed stars have been arranged acc. to their brilliancy; (fig.) *of the first* ~, of great importance.

măgnōl'ĭa *n.* Genus of trees with conspicuous wax-like flowers and dark-green foliage, native in America and Asia; *M~ State*, pop. name of Mississippi. [Pierre *Magnol*, Fr. botanist (1638–1715)]

măg'num *n.* (Bottle containing) two quarts (of wine etc.).

măg'pīe *n.* European bird (*Pica pica*) with long pointed tail and black-and-white plumage; idle chatterer; (shot hitting) circle on target between inner and outer circles.

Magus: sing. of MAGI; see also SIMON MAGUS.

Magyar *adj.* & *n.* 1. (măg'- *or* mŏd'-) (Member) of a Mongoloid race now forming the predominant section of the population of Hungary; (of) their language. 2. (măg'-) ~ *blouse* etc., one with sleeves and bodice cut in one piece (ill. SLEEVE).

Mahabharata (mah-hahbah'-*rata*). One of the two great epics (the other being the Ramayana) of the Hindus, supposed to have been composed *c* 500 B.C.

maharaja(h) (mah-h*a*rah'j*a*) *n.* Title of some Indian princes. **maharanee** (-ah'nĭ) *n.* Maharajah's wife. [Hind. *maha* great, *raja* king, *rani* queen]

Măharăsh'tra. State of W. India bordering on Arabian Sea, formed 1960 from SE. part of former Bombay State; capital, Bombay.

mahăt'ma (m*a*-h-). In Buddhism one of a class of persons with preternatural powers supposed to exist in India and Tibet; in theosophy, a sage or 'adept', reputed to have superior knowledge and powers. [Sansk. *mahātman* great-souled]

Mahd'i (-ē *or* -ĭ). A spiritual and temporal leader expected by the Mohammedans. The title has been claimed by various insurrectionary leaders in the Sudan, but is usu. applied to Mohammed Ahmed (1843–85), who besieged General Gordon in Khartoum and overthrew the Egyptian power in the Sudan. **Mahd'ĭsm** *n.* [Arab. *mahdiy* he who is guided right, past part. of *hada* guide]

mah-jŏngg' *n.* A Chinese game for 4 players played with 144 decorated pieces called tiles; by discarding and drawing tiles each player attempts to obtain 4 sets of 3 tiles each together with one pair.

Mahl'er, Gustav (1860–1911). Austrian musician; composer of 9 symphonies for very large orchestra.

mahl'stick: see MAULSTICK.

mahŏg'any (m*a*-h-) *n.* Reddish-brown wood esp. of a tropical Amer. tree (*Swietenia mahogani*), used for furniture etc. and taking high polish; the tree; colour of this wood.

Mahŏm'ėt(an) (m*a*-h-): see MOHAMMED(AN).

mahout (m*a*howt') *n.* Elephant-driver.

Mahrătt'a (m*a*-), **Maratha** (m*a*raht'*a*) *n.* One of a warlike Hindu race inhabiting the central and SW. parts of India. [perh. f. Sansk. *mahâ râshtra* great country]

Maia (mī'*a*). 1. In Gk myth., the daughter of Atlas and mother of Hermes (Mercury). 2. In Rom. myth., a goddess associated with the fire-god Vulcan, and also (by confusion with 1 above) with Mercury. [Gk, = 'mother', 'nurse']

maid *n.* Girl; young unmarried woman; spinster; female servant; ~ *of honour*, unmarried lady attending queen or princess; (also) kind of cheesecake; *old* ~, elderly spinster; round game of cards; *the M~*, JOAN OF ARC.

maid'en *n.* 1. Girl; spinster. 2. One of two supports for bobbin in spinning wheel (ill. SPINNING). ~ *adj.* Unmarried; untried; with blank record; (of horse) that has never won a race; ~-*name*, woman's surname before marriage; ~ *over*, (cricket) one in which no runs are scored; ~ *speech*, one made in Parliament by a member speaking for the first time; *maid'enhair* (*fern*), kind of fern, genus *Adiantum*, with hair-like stalks and delicate fronds; *maidenhair tree*, GINKGO; *maid'enhead*, virginity; the hymen. **maid'enhŏŏd** *n.* **maid'enly** *adv.*

Maid Marian. In the legend of Robin Hood, the companion of the outlaw.

maieut'ĭc (māū-) *adj.* (Of Socratic mode of inquiry) serving to bring out person's latent ideas into clear consciousness. [Gk *maieuomai* act as midwife]

mail[1] *n.* Armour of rings or chainwork, or of metal plates (ill. ARMOUR). ~ *v.t.* Clothe (as) with mail; *the mailed fist*, physical force.

mail[2] *n.* Bag of letters for conveyance by post; the post (esp. for foreign letters); *~-cart*, cart for carrying mail; light vehicle, pushed by hand, for carrying children; *~-coach*, (hist.) stage-coach carrying mail; ~ *order*, an order for goods to be sent by post; *~-train*, train conveying mail, usu. with sorting van attached. ~ *v.t.* Send (letters etc.) by post.

maim *v.t.* Cripple, mutilate.

Maimŏn'idēs (mī-, -z), Moses (1135–1204). Spanish-Jewish philosopher and Rabbinic scholar, much influenced by Greek, esp. Aristotelian, philosophy.

main[1] *adj.* Chief, principal; exerted to the full; *main brace*, (naut.) brace of main yard (ill. SHIP); *splice the main brace*, serve out extra rum ration on special occasion, celebrate such occasion by drinking (said to be because splicing so thick a rope would justify a special reward); *main'land*, country or continent without its adjacent islands; *main'mast*, principal mast of a ship (ill. SHIP); *main'sail* (-sl), (in square-rigged vessel) lowest sail of mainmast (ill. SHIP); (in fore-and-aft rig) sail set on after part of mainmast; *main'-spring*, chief spring of watch or clock (ill. CLOCK) (also fig.); *main'-stay*, stay running from top of mainmast to foot of foremast; (fig.) chief support; *~-top*, platform at top of lower mainmast. **main'ly** *adv.*

main[2] *n.* Physical force (only in *with might and* ~); (poet.) high sea; principal channel, duct, conductor, etc., for water, sewage, electricity, etc.; *Spanish M*~: see SPANISH.

main[3] *n.* Number (from 5 to 9) called before dice are thrown, in hazard; match between fighting-cocks.

Maine. North-eastern State of U.S., on the Atlantic coast; admitted to the Union in 1820; capital, Augusta.

maintain' *v.t.* Carry on, keep up; support; assert as true.

main'tėnance *n.* 1. Maintaining; enough to support life. 2. (law) Offence of aiding a party in litigation without lawful cause.

Maintenon (măṅtenawṅ'), Françoise d'Aubigné, Marquise de (1635–1719). Mistress and 2nd wife of Louis XIV of France.

maison(n)ĕtte' (mĕz-) *n.* Small house; part of house let or used separately but not all on the same floor.

maize *n.* Amer. cereal plant (*Zea mays*); edible seed of this plant, Indian corn.

Maj. *abbrev.* Major; **Maj.-Gen.,** Major-General.

majĕs'tĭc *adj.* Characterized by majesty, imposing, stately. **majĕs'tĭcally** *adv.*

măj'ėsty *n.* 1. Impressive stateliness; sovereign power; *Your, His, Her, M*~, title used in speaking to or of sovereign. 2. Representation of God (the Father or Son) enthroned within an aureole.

Măj'lĭs *n.* The Persian parliament.

majŏl'ĭca *n.* Italian earthenware coated with an opaque white enamel ornamented with metallic colours; modern imitation of this. [It., f. former name of *Majorca*, ships of which brought Spanish wares to Italy]

māj'or[1] *n.* Army officer next in rank below lieutenant-colonel and above captain. [Fr., short for *sergent-major*]

māj'or[2] *adj.* Greater of two things, classes, etc.; senior; (mus.) of intervals, greater by a chromatic semitone than those called minor; normal or perfect; (of keys) in which the scale has a major third (ill. SCALE); ~ *premiss*, (logic) the first of a syllogism, containing a statement of the general rule; ~ *suit*, (bridge) spades or hearts; ~ *term*, (logic) the predicate of the conclusion of a syllogism. ~ *n.* Person of full age; major premiss; (in U.S. universities) subject to which special attention is given in a course of study, whence ~ (*v.i.*) take, or qualify *in*, such subject; ~ *-dō'mo*, chief official of Italian or Spanish princely household; house-steward; *~-general*, Army officer ranking next above a brigadier and below a lieutenant-general.

Majŏr'ca. (Span. *Mallorca*) Largest of the BALEARIC Islands in W. Mediterranean.

majŏ'rĭty *n.* 1. Greater number or part (*of*); *absolute* ~, more than half number of electors or actual voters. 2. Number by which votes cast on one side exceed those on the other. 3. Full age. 4. Office of major in army.

majŭs'cūle *adj.* & *n.* Capital (letter); formal script, orig. based on Roman monumental lettering, used in manuscripts until the development of the MINUSCULE from cursive writing (ill. SCRIPT). **majŭs'cūlar** *adj.*

māke[1] *v.* (past t. and past part. *māde*). Create, manufacture; cause to exist, bring about; amount to, constitute; bring total up to; represent as being or doing; acquire by effort, earn; win (trick at cards); score (runs at cricket etc.); produce by cookery; perform, execute; utter or record (remark etc.); ~ *believe*, pretend, whence *~-believe* (*n.*) pretence; ~ *do*, manage *with* what is available or inferior substitute; ~ *for*, take direction of; ~ *good*, fulfil (promise etc.), prove (statement); pay for, repair (damage etc.); succeed in an undertaking; ~ *out*, draw up or write out (list etc.); prove; represent as; understand; ~ *shift with*, use as temporary expedient or device, whence *makeshift* (*n.* & *adj.*) substitute, temporary; ~ *up*, supply deficiency, complete; arrange; concoct; adapt (face etc. of actor) for his part; paint (face); *~-up* (*n*). way actor etc. is made up; way type is made up into pages; materials for making up, cosmetics; *one's ~-up*, fundamental qualities of one's nature; *~-weight*, small quantity added to make up required weight; unimportant argument etc. to supply deficiency.

māke[2] *n.* Way thing is made; figure, shape; brand, sort; *on the* ~, (slang) intent on gain.

māk'er *n.* One who makes; esp. *M*~, the Creator.

māk'ĭng *n.* Creating, manufacturing, etc.; (pl.) what one earns; essential characteristics, necessary qualities, as *he has the ~s of a general.*

Mal. *abbrev.* Malachi (O.T.).

mal- *prefix.* 1. Bad(ly), as *maltreat.* 2. un-, as *maladroit.*

Măl'abar̂. Coastal district of SW. India, in Madras State.

Malăcc'a. Town and district on W. coast of Malay peninsula; ~ *cane*, rich-brown walking-cane made of the stem of a palm-tree (*Calamus Scipionum*).

Măl'achī (-k-). A prophetic book of the O.T., belonging to a period immediately before Ezra and Nehemiah; Malachi is prob. not a personal name. [Heb., = 'my messenger']

măl'achīte (-k-) *n.* Hydrated copper carbonate, a bright-green mineral taking a high polish and used as decorative stone.

măladjŭst'ment *n.* Faulty adjustment; person's psychological inability to adjust himself, his wishes, etc., to his environment; so **măladjŭst'ėd** *adj.*

măladmĭnĭstrā'tion *n.* Faulty administration.

măl'adroit *adj.* Bungling; tactless. **măl'adroitly** *adv.* **măl'-adroitnėss** *n.*

măl'adȳ *n.* Ailment, disease.

Măl'aga. Province of S. Spain, part of the ancient kingdom of Granada; its capital, a Mediterranean seaport; the dark sweet fortified wine made in the neighbourhood of the city.

Mălagăs'ȳ *adj.* & *n.* (A native, the language) of Madagascar.

măl'aise (-z) *n.* Feeling of uneasiness or discomfort.

malanders: see MALLENDERS.

Măl'aprŏp, Mrs. In Sheridan's play 'The Rivals' (1775), a lady who ludicrously misuses long words, as *illiterate him from your memory.* **măl'aprŏpĭsm** *n.* Misapplication of a (long) word.

mălăpropos' (-pō) *adv.* & *adj.* (Done, said, etc.) inopportunely. ~ *n.* Inopportune remark etc.

măl'ar *adj.* & *n.* (Bone) of the cheek.

malār'ia *n.* Kinds of intermittent and remittent fever, caused by a micro-organism (*Plasmodium*) which is transmitted by the bite of certain mosquitoes of the genus *Anopheles*. **malār'ial, malār'ious** *adjs.* [It. *mal' aria* bad air (because formerly attributed to unwholesome exhalations of marshes)]

Malay' *adj.* & *n.* (Member) of a light-brown race of mixed Caucasian and Mongolian stock, predominating in the Malay Peninsula and Archipelago; (of) the language spoken by these, written in a modified Arabic script; ~ *Archipelago*, a very large group of islands, including Sumatra, Java, Borneo, the Philippines, and New Guinea, lying SE. of Asia and N. and NE. of Australia; ~ *Peninsula*, the most southerly projection of the mainland of Asia, running southward from Siam; ~ *States*: see below. **Malay'a.** The *Federation of Malaya*, from 1957 to 1963 an independent country within Br. Commonwealth, consisting of 9 native States (formerly called the *Malay States*) and the former British settlements of Penang and Malacca.

Mălaya'lăm (-yah-). A Dravidian dialect, closely related to Tamil, spoken on the W. coast of S. India.

Malay'sĭa (-z-). *The Federation of* ~, an independent State within the Br. Commonwealth, formed in 1963 out of MALAYA and the former Br. colonial territories of Singapore, N. Borneo, and Sarawak; capital, Kuala Lumpur.

măl'contĕnt *n.* Discontented person, one inclined to rebellion.

mal de mer (mār) *n.* Seasickness.

Măl'dīve Islands. Chain of coral islands in the Indian Ocean, SE. of India.

māle *adj.* Of the sex in human beings, other animals, and plants, which begets young by fecundating the female; (of parts of machinery, e.g. screws) designed to enter or fill the corresponding female part; ~ *fern*, fern (*Dryopteris filix-mas*), producing an oleo-resin used for expelling tape-worms. ~ *n.* Male person, animal, or plant.

Malebranche' (mălbrahṅsh), Nicolas (1638–1715). French philosopher, a follower of Descartes and of St. Augustine.

mălėdĭc'tion *n.* Curse. **mălėdĭc'tory** *adj.*

măl'ėfăctor *n.* Criminal, evildoer. **măl'ėfăction** *n.*

malĕf'ĭc *adj.* Harmful, baneful. **malĕf'ĭcent** *adj.* Hurtful; criminal. **malĕf'ĭcence** *n.*

malĕv'olent *adj.* Wishing ill to others. **malĕv'olently** *adv.* **malĕv'olence** *n.*

mălfea'sance (-ēz-) *n.* Official misconduct.

mălformā'tion *n.* Faulty formation. **mălfōrmed'** (-md) *adj.*

Malherbe (mălārb'), François de (1555–1628). French poet, prose writer, and critic.

māl'ĭc *adj.* ~ *acid*, $C_4H_6O_5$, present in many acid fruits such as apples, grapes, and esp. mountain ash berries.

măl'ice *n.* Ill will; desire to do harm. **malĭ'cious** (-shus) *adj.* **malĭ'ciously** *adv.*

malign' (-īn) *adj.* Maleficent; (of diseases) = MALIGNANT. **malign'ly** *adv.* **malign'** *v.t.* Speak ill of, slander.

malĭg'nant *adj.* 1. Feeling or showing intense ill will. 2. (path., of disease) Of the form which kills, as dist. from milder forms. 3. (path., of tumour) Cancerous, growing into surrounding tissue and destroying it (as dist. from *benign* tumour which merely displaces it) and giving rise to secondary growths in other parts. **malĭg'nantly** *adv.* **malĭg'nancy** *n.* **Malĭg'nant** *n.* (hist.) Supporter of Charles I against Parliament.

malĭg'nĭty *n.* Malignant character or feeling.

malĭng'er (-ngg-) *v.i.* Pretend illness to escape duty (esp. of soldiers, sailors, or airmen). **malĭng'erer** *n.*

măl'ĭsm *n.* Doctrine that evil predominates over good in the world.

Măll, The. Avenue along the N. side of St. James's Park, London, originally a 'mall' or alley where the game of 'pall-mall' was played.

măll'ard *n.* Wild duck (*Anas boscas*).

Măllarmé (-mā'), Etienne (Stéphane) (1842–98). French symbolist poet; author of 'L'Après-midi d'un Faune'.

măll'ėable *adj.* (of metal etc.) That can be hammered, beaten, or rolled into a different form without a tendency to return to its original form or to fracture; adaptable, pliable. **măllėabĭl'ĭty** *n.*

măll'enders, măl'an- *n.pl.* Dry eruption inside horse's knee (cf. SALLENDERS).

măllėōl'us *n.* (pl. -*ī*). Bone of hammer-head shape, esp. ankle-bone (ill. FOOT).

măll'ėt *n.* Hammer (usu. wooden); implement for striking croquet or polo ball.

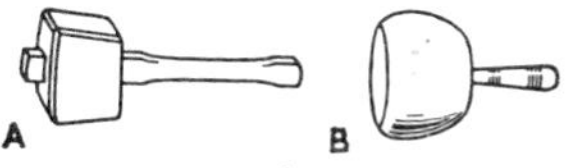

A. CARPENTER'S MALLET. B. MASON'S MALLET

măll'ėus *n.* Small bone of middle ear transmitting vibrations of tympanum to incus (ill. EAR). [L, = 'hammer']

Mallorca: see MAJORCA.

măll'ow (-ō) *n.* Wild plant of genus *Malva*.

malm (mahm) *n.* Soft chalky rock; loamy soil from disintegration of this.

mălmais'on (-āzn) *n.* A variety of carnation. [name of palace of Empress Josephine]

malmsey (mah'mzĭ) *n.* Strong sweet wine made formerly in Greece, now also in Spain, Madeira, and the Azores. [Gk *Monembasia*, place in the Peloponnese]

mălnūtrĭ'tion *n.* Underfeeding; diet that does not include what is needful for health.

mălōd'orous *adj.* Evil-smelling.

Măl'ory, Sir Thomas (fl. 1470). English (or Welsh) author of the 'Morte d'Arthur', a collection of the stories concerned with King Arthur; nothing certain is known of his life except that he compiled his book in prison.

Mălpighi (-ēg'ē), Marcello (1628–94). Italian physician and anatomist. **Mălpigh'ian** *adj.* (anat.) Of certain structures (esp. in the substance of the kidneys) discovered by Malpighi.

Mălplaquet (-kā'). Village near Mons, France; scene of a victory (1709) of the allied British and Austrian troops under Marlborough and Prince Eugene over the French.

mălprăc'tice *n.* Wrong-doing; (law) improper treatment of patient by medical attendant; illegal action for one's own benefit while in position of trust.

malt (mawlt) *n.* Barley or other grain for brewing, steeped in water, allowed to germinate and then dried slowly in a kiln; ~ *liquor*, made from fermented malt (e.g. beer), not by distillation. ~ *v.t.* Convert grain into malt.

Mal'ta (-awl-). Island in the Mediterranean; occupied successively by Arabs (870), Sicily (1090), the Order of St. John (1530), France (1788), and Britain (1814); independent 1964; site of a British naval station; capital, Valletta; the island was awarded the George Cross for the gallantry of its population under air attack during the war of 1939–45; *Knights of* ~, the Order of St. John (see HOSPITALLER). **Maltēse'** (-z) *adj.* Of Malta; ~ *cross*, the cross of the Order of St. John, with 4 equal limbs broadened at the ends and indented (ill. CROSS). ~ *n.* Native of Malta; its language, a dialect of Arabic, written in Roman characters.

Măl'thus, Thomas Robert (1766–1835). English clergyman, author of an essay (1798) arguing that population increases faster than the means of subsistence and urging that its increase should be checked, mainly by moral restraint. **Mălthūs'ian** (-z-) *adj.* & *n.* **Mălthūs'ianĭsm** *n.*

mal'tōse (mawl-) *n.* (chem.) Sugar obtained by hydrolysis of starch by enzymes present in malt.

mătreat' *v.t.* Ill-treat. **măltreat'ment** *n.*

malt'ster (mawl-) *n.* One who makes malt.

mălvā'ceous (-shus) *adj.* Of the genus *Malva* (mallow).

mălversā'tion *n.* Corrupt handling of public or trust funds.

măm'ba *n.* Any of the venomous African tree snakes of the genus *Dendraspis.*

măm'elon *n.* Small rounded hillock.

Măm'ėluke, Măm'luk (-ōō-) *adj.* & *n.* (Member) of a body of Turkoman warriors who were brought to Egypt as slaves to act as bodyguard for the caliphs and sultans, and became powerful; in 1250 they set up one of themselves as sultan, and Mameluke sultans reigned in Cairo until 1517 when the Ottoman Turks conquered Egypt; afterwards they ruled locally as 'beys' under a Turkish viceroy; Napoleon defeated them in the battle of the Pyramids, 1798, and the surviving Mamelukes were massacred by Mohammed Ali, pasha of Egypt, in 1811. [Arab. *mamluk* slave]

mamĭll'a *n.* Nipple of female breast; nipple-shaped organ. **măm'ĭllary, măm'ĭllate, mamĭll'ĭform** *adjs.*

mam(m)a'[1] (-ah) *n.* (Child's name for) mother.

mămm'a[2] *n.* (pl. *-ae*). Milk-secreting organ of female in mammals; corresponding rudimentary structure in males. **mămm'ary, mammĭf'erous, mămm'ifōrm** *adjs.*

mămm'al *n.* Member of *Mammā'lia,* class of animals having mammae or milk-secreting organs for nourishment of young. **mammāl'ian** *adj.*

mammăl'ogĭst, mammăl'ogy *ns.* Student, study, of mammals.

mămm'ary *adj.* Of the mammae or breasts.

mămm'ato- *prefix.* (meteorol.) Descriptive of clouds resembling rounded festoons, as *~-cirrus, ~-cumulus.*

Mămm'on. The Aramaic word for 'riches' used in Matt. vi. 24 and Luke xvi. 9–13; taken by medieval writers as the proper name of the devil of covetousness; this use was revived by Milton in 'Paradise Lost'.

mămm'oth *n.* Large extinct elephant with long hairy coat and curved tusks whose fossilized remains are found in N. America, Northern Europe, and Asia. *~ adj.* Huge.

mămm'ȳ *n.* Child's word for mother; (U.S.) coloured nurse of white children.

măn[1] *n.* (pl. *men*). Human being, individual of the genus *Homo,* distinguished from other animals by his superior mental development, his power of articulate speech, and his upright posture, etc.; person; the human race; adult male; husband; manservant; workman; (pl.) soldiers, the rank and file, as dist. from officers; piece in chess, draughts, etc.; *~-at-arms',*(archaic) mounted, fully armed soldier; *~-eater,* cannibal; man-eating shark or tiger; *man'hole,* opening in floor, sewer, etc., for man to pass through; *~-hour,* one hour's work by one man, as measure of output in industry etc.; *~-of-war,* warship; *manpower,* amount of men available for military or other service; *~-trap,* trap formerly set to catch trespassers, consisting of two iron half-hoops, hinged together, which closed when a spring was released. *~ v.t.* Furnish with men for service or defence; place men at (part of ship); fill (post); fortify spirits or courage of (esp. one*self*).

Măn[2], Isle of. Island in the Irish Sea, a British crown possession enjoying 'home rule'; it has its own parliament (the Council and the House of Keys), a Court (the Tynwald) which controls the revenue, and its own judicial system.

Man., Manit. *abbrevs.* Manitoba.

măn'acle *n.* (usu. pl.) & *v.t.* Fetter, handcuff.

măn'age[1] *n.* (archaic) Training, management, of a horse; riding-school; now usu. MANEGE.

măn'age[2] *v.* Handle, wield (tool etc.); conduct working of (business etc.); have effective control of (household, institution, etc.); subject (animal, person, etc.) to one's control; gain one's ends with (person etc.) by flattery etc.; contrive (*to* do), succeed in one's aim; cope with.

măn'ageable (-ja-) *adj.* **mănageabĭl'ity, măn'ageablenėss** *ns.* **măn'ageably** *adv.*

măn'agement (-ĭjm-) *n.* Act of managing; state of being managed; body of persons managing a business etc.; administration of business concerns or public undertaking.

măn'ager (-nĭj-) *n.* Person conducting a business, institution, etc. **măn'agerėss** *n.* **mănagēr'ial** *adj.*

măn'akĭn *n.* One of the small gaily-coloured birds of the passerine family *Pipridae,* inhabiting Central and S. America.

Manăss'eh (-i). The first-born son of Joseph: see Gen. xlviii. 19; one of the tribes of Israel, traditionally descended from him.

mănatee' *n.* Large aquatic herbivorous mammal of W. African and American coasts, sea-cow.

Măn'chėster. City in S. Lancashire, the chief centre of cotton manufacture in England; *~ School,* a name first applied by Disraeli to Cobden and Bright and their followers, who, before the repeal of the Corn Laws, held their meetings at Manchester and advocated free trade and *laissez-faire.*

Mănchu' (-ōō) *adj.* & *n.* (Member) of a Tatar people who conquered China and founded the Ch'ing dynasty (1644–1912); (of) their language, written in a modified Mongolian script, at one time an official language of China, but now spoken only in parts of N. Manchuria.

Mănchūkuo (-kwō'): see MANCHURIA.

Mănchūr'ia. Country forming the NE. portion of China; in 1932 declared an independent State by Japan and renamed *Manchukuo*; restored to China in 1945.

măn'cĭple *n.* Official who buys provisions for college etc.

Mancun. *abbrev.* (Bishop) of Manchester (replacing surname in his signature).

Măncūn'ĭan *adj.* & *n.* (Inhabitant) of Manchester; (member) of Manchester Grammar School. [*Mancunium,* name of the Roman settlement]

Măndae'an *adj.* & *n.* (Member) of body of Pagan gnostics of whom a small community survives in Iraq. They revere John the Baptist, but are hostile to Christianity, worshipping a 'Light King'.

Măndalay'. Chief city of Upper Burma, on the Irrawaddy river.

măndām'us *n.* Judicial writ issued from King's Bench Division as command to inferior court. [L, = 'we command']

măn'darĭn[1] *n.* Chinese official in any of the 9 grades; (transf.) pedantic official bureaucrat; nodding toy figure in Chinese costume; form of the Chinese language spoken by officials and educated persons and used in official documents. [Sansk. *mantrin* counsellor]

măn'darin[2] *n.* 1. Small flattened deep-coloured Chinese orange, also cultivated in N. Africa. 2. Deep-orange dye obtained from coal-tar. [prob. f. MANDARIN[1], from the yellow silk robes of mandarins]

măn'datary *n.* One to whom a MANDATE is given.

măn'date *n.* Authoritative command from superior; commission to act for another, esp. one given by League of Nations to a State (the *mandatary*) to administer certain colonies of the defeated enemy powers in the war of 1914–18 for the benefit of the inhabitants; political instructions inferred from votes of electorate. *~ v.t.* Commit (State etc.) *to* mandatary.

măn'datory *adj.* Of, conveying, a command. *~ n.* = MANDATARY.

Măn'dėvĭlle, Sir John. The ostensible author of a 14th-c. book of travels and travellers' tales, written in French and much translated (actually compiled by an unknown hand from the works of several writers).

măn'dĭble *n.* Lower jaw-bone (ill. HEAD); either part of bird's beak; either half of crushing organ in mouth parts of many arthropods (ill. INSECT). **măndĭb'ūlar(y)** *adjs.*

măndōl'a *n.* Large kind of mandolin.

măn'dolĭn(e) *n.* Musical instrument of lute kind with paired metal strings stretched on deeply rounded body, played tremolo with a plectrum.

MANDOLIN

măndōr'a *n.* = MANDOLA.

măndōrl'a *n.* Almond-shaped oval around figure in medieval sculpture and painting; vesica.

măndrăg'ora, măn'drāke *n.* Poisonous plant with emetic and narcotic properties, with root formerly thought to resemble human form and to shriek when plucked up from the ground.

măn'drel, -ĭl *n.* Axis on which material revolves in lathe; rod round which metal etc. is forged or shaped.

măn'drill *n.* Large and ferocious baboon (*Cynocephalus maimon*) of W. Africa with highly coloured patches and callosities on face and hindquarters

măn'dūcāte *v.t.* Chew. **măndūcā'tion** *n.* **măn'dūcatory** *adj.*

māne *n.* Long hair on neck of horse, lion, etc. (also fig. of person's hair).

manège, -ege (manāzh') *n.* Riding-school; movements of trained horse; horsemanship.

mān'ēs[1] (-z) *n.pl.* Deified souls of departed ancestors (Rom. myth.); shade of dead person as object of reverence.

Mān'ēs[2] (-z): see MANICHEE.

Măn'et (-nā), Edouard (1832–83). French Impressionist painter.

măn'ful *adj.* Brave, resolute. **măn'fully** *adv.* **măn'fulnėss** *n.*

măn'gabey (-bā) *n.* Genus, *Cercocebus*, of small long-tailed W. African monkeys. [name of a region in Madagascar]

măn'ganēse (-ngg-, -z) *n.* (chem.) Grey brittle metallic element, used in making alloys of steel, symbol Mn, at. no. 25, at. wt 54·938; ~ *dioxide* (MnO_2), a black mineral used in glass-making, electric batteries, etc. [Fr. *manganèse*, corrupt. of MAGNESIA]

mānge (-j) *n.* Skin-disease caused by a parasite which destroys hairy coat of animals, occas. communicated to man.

măng'el-wūrz'el, măn'gold (-wūrz'el) (-ngg-) *n.* Large kind of beet used as cattle-food. [Ger. *mangold* beet, *wurzel* root]

mān'ger (-j-) *n.* Box or trough in stable etc. for horses or cattle to eat from.

mangle[1] (măng'gl) *n.* Machine of two or more cylinders between which washed clothes are rolled to press out the water. ~ *v.t.* Press (clothes) in mangle.

mangle[2] (măng'gl) *v.t.* Hack, lacerate, mutilate; spoil, garble (text, pronunciation, etc.).

măng'o (-nggō) *n.* Fleshy fruit, eaten ripe or used green for pickles etc., of the Indian tree *Mangifera indica*; this tree; ~*-fish*: see THREAD-fish; ~*-trick*, Indian juggling trick in which a mango-tree appears to grow from a seed and bear fruit in a few hours.

mangold: see MANGEL-WURZEL.

măng'ōsteen (-ngg-) *n.* (E. Indian tree, *Garcinia mangostana*, bearing) fruit with thick red rind and white juicy pulp.

măng'rōve (-ngg-) *n.* Tropical tree or shrub growing in mud at sea-shore with aerating roots above ground.

mān'gy (-jĭ) *adj.* Having the mange; squalid, shabby. **mān'gily** *adv.* **mān'ginėss** *n.*

mănhăn'dle *v.t.* Move by man's strength without mechanical aid; treat roughly, pull or hustle about.

Mănhătt'an. Island at mouth of Hudson River, now part of New York city. **mănhătt'an** *n.* Cocktail made of vermouth and whisky with a dash of bitters.

măn'hood *n.* State of being a man; manliness, courage; the men of a country.

Mani (mahn'ē): see MANICHEE.

mān'ia *n.* 1. Mental derangement marked by excitement, hallucination, and violence. 2. Excessive enthusiasm.

mān'ĭăc *n.* Person afflicted with mania. **manī'acal** *adj.* **manī'acally** *adv.*

Mănichee' (*or* măn'-; -k-) *n.* Adherent of a dualistic ascetic religious system, regarding existence as a conflict between the powers of light and the demons of darkness, which was widely accepted from the 3rd to the 5th c. It was founded by Mani (or Manes or Manichaeus), who lived in Persia in the 3rd c. A.D. **Mănich(a)e'an** *adj.* & *n.* **Măn'ich(a)eĭsm** *n.*

măn'icūre *n.* (One who undertakes as a profession) treatment of hands and finger-nails. ~ *v.t.* Apply manicure treatment to (hands, person). **măn'icūrist** *n.*

măn'ifĕst[1] *n.* List of ship's cargo for use of customs officials.

măn'ifĕst[2] *adj.* Clear to sight or mind. **măn'ifestly** *adv.* **măn'ifĕst** *v.* Show plainly to eye or mind; be evidence of, prove; display, evince (quality, feeling) by one's acts; (of thing) reveal *itself*; (of ghost) appear. **mănifĕstā'tion** *n.* **mănifĕs'tative** *adj.*

mănifĕs'tō *n.* Public declaration by sovereign, State, or body of individuals, of principles and future policy.

măn'ifōld *adj.* Having various forms, applications, functions, etc.; many and various. ~ *v.t.* Multiply copies of (letter etc.). ~ *n.* (mech.) Pipe or chamber with several openings. **măn'ifōldly** *adv.* **măn'ifōldnėss** *n.*

măn'ikin *n.* Little man, dwarf; artist's lay figure; anatomical model of the body.

mănill'a[1] *n.* Metal bracelet worn as ornament by W. African tribes and used as money.

Manil(l)'a[2]. City on island of Luzon, capital of the Philippine Islands; ~ (*cheroot*), one made from special tobacco leaf of the Philippines; ~ (*hemp*), a fibrous material, obtained from the leaves of *Musa textilis*, a tree native to the Philippines, and used for ropes, matting, textiles, etc.; ~ *paper*, stout brown wrapping-paper made from Manilla hemp.

manille' (-ĭl) *n.* Second highest trump or honour in quadrille and ombre.

măn'ĭŏc *n.* Sweet CASSAVA, *Manihot aipi*; farinaceous substance obtained from tuberous roots of this plant. [native Brazilian *mandioca*]

măn'iple *n.* 1. (Rom. antiq.) subdivision of a legion, containing 120 or 60 men. 2. One of the Eucharistic vestments, orig. a napkin, consisting now of a strip of stuff 2–4 ft in length, worn hanging from left arm (ill. VESTMENT).

manĭp'ūlāte *v.t.* Handle; deal skilfully with; manage craftily. **manĭpūlā'tion** *n.* **manĭp'ūlātor** *n.*

Mănitōb'a. Province of central Canada, with coast-line on Hudson Bay; capital, Winnipeg.

măn'itou (-ōō) *n.* (Amer. Ind.) Good or evil spirit, thing having supernatural power.

mankind *n.* 1. (mănkīnd') The human species. 2. (măn'kīnd) Male sex, males.

măn'līke *adj.* Like a man; (of woman) mannish.

măn'ly *adj.* Having the qualities or bearing of a man; befitting a man. **măn'linėss** *n.*

Mănn, Thomas (1875–1955). German novelist; author of 'Buddenbrooks', which describes the decline of a Lübeck merchant family.

mănn'a *n.* Substance miraculously supplied as food to Israelites in wilderness (Exod. xvi); sweet juice from bark of ~*-ash* (*Fraxinus Ornus*) and other plants, used as gentle laxative.

mănn'ėquin (*or* -kin) *n.* Person employed by dressmakers etc. to wear and show off costumes before possible purchasers; lay-figure of wax etc. used to exhibit clothes in shop window etc.

mănn'er *n.* Way a thing is done or happens; outward bearing; (pl.) behaviour in social intercourse, habits indicating good breeding. **mănn'ered** (-*erd*) *adj.* Showing mannerisms, affected; *ill-*, *well-*, ~, having good, bad, manners. **mănn'erlėss** *adj.* Ill-mannered, rude.

Mănn'erheim (-hīm) **line.** A Finnish defensive system across the Karelian isthmus. [C. E. E.

Mannerheim (1867–1951), Finnish marshal and statesman]

măn'erism *n.* 1. Trick of speech, gesture, or style; excessive addiction to a distinctive manner in art or literature. 2. Style of art which originated in Italy *c* 1530 and preceded the Baroque, characterized by contorted figures, startling light effects, etc. **mănn'erist** *adj.* & *n.* (Exponent) of mannerism in art etc.

mănn'erly *adj.* Well-mannered, polite. **mănn'erliness** *n.*

Mănn'ing, Henry Edward (1808–92). English churchman; joined R.C. Church 1851, and became cardinal 1875.

mănn'ish *adj.* (Of woman) masculine; characteristic of a man as opp. to woman. **mănn'ishness** *n.*

manœuvre (-ōō'ver) *n.* Strategical or tactical movement; skilful plan. ~ *v.* Perform, make (troops, ships, or aircraft) perform, manœuvre(s); force, drive *into, out,* etc., by contrivance. **manœuv'rable** *adj.* Capable of being (easily) manœuvred, esp. of aircraft. **manœuvrabil'ity** *n.*

manŏm'eter *n.* Instrument for measuring the pressure of gases and vapours by the difference in level which they produce in a liquid in a U-tube, one side of which may be open to the atmosphere or evacuated and sealed off.

măn'or *n.* English territorial unit, orig. feudal, the lord's demesne and lands from whose holders he could exact certain fees etc.; ~*-house,* house of *lord of the* ~. **manōr'ial** *adj.*

măn'sard *n.* Form of roof (usu. ~ *roof*) in which each face has two slopes, the lower one steeper than the upper, usu. broken by projecting windows (ill. ROOF). [François *Mansart*(1598–1666), Fr. architect]

mănse *n.* Ecclesiastical residence, esp. that of Scottish Presbyterian minister.

măn'sion (-shn) *n.* Large residence (in the pl. often of large buildings divided into flats); ~*-house,* mansion, manor-house; *the M~- house,* official residence of Lord Mayor of London

măn'slaughter (-slawt-) *n.* Slaughter of human beings; (law) unlawful killing of a human being without malice aforethought.

măn'suetūde (-swĭ-) *n.* Gentleness, meekness.

Măntegna (-tăn'ya), Andrea (1431–1506). Italian painter and engraver.

măn'tel *n.* Structure of wood, marble, etc., above and around fire-place (ill. FIRE); *mantelpiece,* mantel; ~*-shelf,* shelf projecting above fire-place; ~*-tree,* beam across opening of fire-place.

măn'tic *adj.* Of divination.

măntill'a *n.* Lace veil worn by Spanish women over the head and shoulders.

măn'tis *n.* Orthopterous insect, esp. the *praying* ~, *Mantis religiosa,* which holds its forelegs in a position suggesting hands folded in prayer. [Gk, = 'prophet']

măntiss'a *n.* Decimal part of a logarithm. [L, = 'makeweight']

măn'tle *n.* Loose sleeveless cloak; fragile hood consisting usu. of oxides of thorium and cerium, fixed round gas-jet to give incandescent light; (zool.) covering or envelope, as that enclosing body of mollusc; (geol.) region lying between crust and core of earth; (fig.) covering. ~ *v.* Envelop, cover (as) with mantle; (of liquids) form a scum; (of blood) suffuse cheeks; blush.

mănt'lėt *n.* Short mantle; bullet-proof screen for gunners.

mănt'ling *n.* (her.) Ornamental drapery or scrollwork behind and around an achievement (ill. HERALDRY).

Măn'tūa. City of Lombardy, birthplace of Virgil. **Măn'tūan** *adj.* & *n.*; *the* ~, Virgil.

măn'ūal *adj.* Of or done with the hands. **măn'ually** *adv.* **măn'ual** *n.* 1. Handbook, textbook, primer. 2. Keyboard of organ (ill. ORGAN).

mănūfăc'ture *n.* Making of articles by physical labour or machinery, esp. on large scale; branch of such an industry; anything manufactured from raw products. ~ *v.t.* Produce by labour, esp. on large scale; invent, fabricate. **mănūfăc'turer** *n.* **mănūfăc'tory** *n.* Factory.

mănūmit' *v.t.* Give freedom to (slave). **mănūmi'ssion** (-shn) *n.*

manūre' *n.* Dung or compost, artificial or chemical fertilizer, used for fertilizing soil. ~ *v.t.* Apply manure to.

măn'us *n.* (zool.) That part of the forelimb of any tetrapod which corresponds to the human hand, esp. the bones within it.

măn'ūscript *adj.* & *n.* (Book, document) written by hand, not printed. (abbrev. MS., pl. MSS.).

Mănx *adj.* & *n.* Of the Isle of MAN[2]; (of) the Celtic language spoken there; ~ *cat,* cat of tailless breed originating there.

many (mĕn'ĭ) *adj.* & *n.* Numerous (people, things); *the* ~, the multitude; ~*-sided,* having many sides; having a variety of interests, accomplishments; ~*-sidedness* (*n*).

Maori (mowr'ĭ) *adj.* & *n.* (Member of) aboriginal race of New Zealand, of Polynesian stock; (of) the language of this race.

Mao Tse-tung (mow tsĭ-tŏŏng') (1893–). Chinese revolutionary leader; became head of the Communist republic in Kiangsi province (SE. China), 1931; after defeat by Kuomintang forces, led his followers on the 'long march' of 1934–5 to Shensi province (N. China) where they established a new State; since 1936 chairman of central committee of Chinese Communist party.

măp *n.* Representation on paper etc. of earth's surface or part of it, showing physical and political features etc.; similar representation of heavens showing position of stars

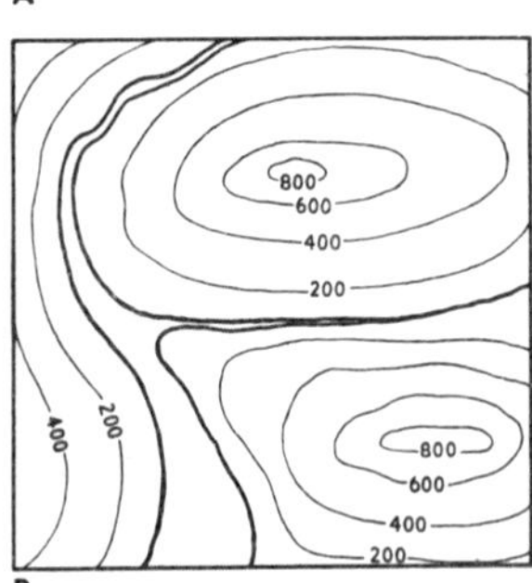

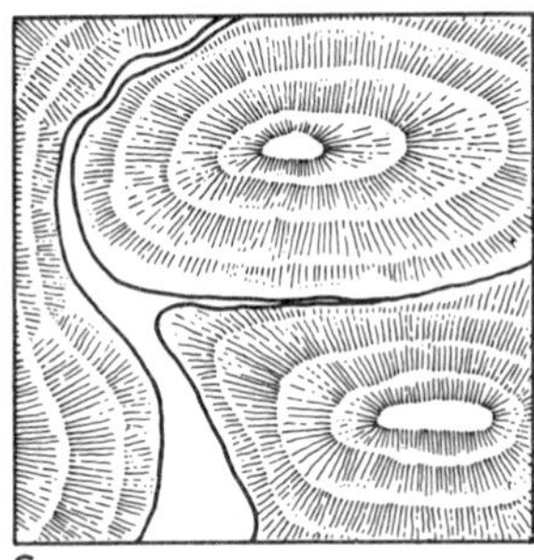

A. OBLIQUE AIR VIEW. B. MAP WITH CONTOURS. C. MAP WITH HACHURES

etc.; *put on the* ~, establish position or vogue of. ~ *v.t.* Make map of; ~ *out,* plan out, arrange in detail.

mā'ple *n.* Genus, *Acer,* of trees and shrubs grown for shade, ornament, wood, or sugar; ~*-leaf,* emblem of Canada; ~*-sugar,* sugar got by evaporation of sap of a kind of maple.

maquette (makĕt') *n.* Small preliminary model for a statue.

maquis (măk'ē, mahk'ē) *n.* Dense scrubby forest of various dwarf trees and shrubs in Corsica etc.; secret army of patriots in France during the German occupation (1940–5), so named from their being conceived as hiding in the undergrowth. **măquisard'** (-kēzahr) *n.* Member of this army.

[Fr., f. Corsican It. *macchia* thicket]

mar *v.t.* Impair fatally, ruin.

Mar. *abbrev.* March.

măr'abou (-ōō) *n.* Large W. African stork (*Leptoptilus crumenifer*); tuft of down from its wings or tail as trimming for hat etc.

măr'about (-ōōt) *n.* Mohammedan hermit or saint, esp. in N. Africa; shrine marking marabout's burial-place.

măraschi'nō (-skē-) *n.* Strong sweet liqueur made from the *marasca*, a small black cherry grown in Dalmatia.

maras'mus (-ăz-) *n.* (path.) Wasting away of the body. **marăs'mic** *adj.*

Mărat (-rah'), Jean Paul (1743–93). French revolutionary leader, philosopher, and scientist; stabbed to death by Charlotte Corday.

Mara'thi (-ahtī) *n.* Language of the *Marathas*, a warlike Hindu race of central and SW. India.

Mă'rathon. Plain on E. coast of Attica, Greece, where the invading Persian army was defeated by the Athenians and Plataeans under Miltiades (490 B.C.); the Athenian courier Pheidippides ran to Sparta to bring the news of the Persian landing and ask for help, and is said to have completed the distance (150 miles) in 2 days; hence, ~ (*race*), long-distance road race, esp. the 26-mile race which is a principal event of the modern Olympic Games (also attrib. of any lengthy feat of great endurance).

maraud' *v.i.* Make raid, pillage. **maraud'er** *n.*

mar'ble *n.* Limestone (calcium carbonate, $CaCO_3$) in crystalline or granular state and capable of taking polish, used in sculpture etc.; (pl.) collection of sculptures; small ball of marble, glass, clay, etc., used as toy; *M~ Arch*, arch with 3 gateways erected (1827) in front of Buckingham Palace, London, and moved (1851) to present site at NE. corner of Hyde Park. ~ *v.t.* Stain, colour, to look like variegated marble.

Mar'burg. University town of central western Germany; scene of conference (1529) between Luther and Zwingli, and other divines, on the doctrine of transubstantiation.

marc *n.* Mass left after juice has been pressed from fruit.

marc'asīte *n.* Pyrites, esp. crystalline; white iron pyrites; used for ornaments etc.

marcĕl' wāve *n.* Kind of deep-grooved artificial wave in hair, made by a special curling-iron. ~ *v.t.* Produce this wave in. [f. name of Paris hairdresser]

March[1]. 3rd month of year in modern western calendar, containing 31 days; *Ides of* ~, (in the Roman calendar) the 15th of March, the day on which Julius Caesar was assassinated. [L *Martius* (*mensis*) month of Mars]

march[2] *v.* (Cause to) walk in military manner or with regular paces; progress steadily. ~ *n.* Marching of troops; progress; distance covered in marching or walking; uniform step of troops etc.; piece of music meant to accompany march, usu. in $\frac{4}{4}$ or $\frac{2}{4}$ time; musical composition, or part of one, of similar character.

march[3] *n.* (hist.) Boundary, limit, frontier, (often pl., esp. of borderland between England and Wales); tract of (often debatable) land between two countries. ~ *v.i.* Have common boundary *with*.

mar'chionėss (-sho-) *n.* Wife, widow of a marquis; lady holding in her own right rank equal to that of marquis.

march'pāne *n.* = MARZIPAN.

Marcōn'i, Guglielmo (1874–1937). Italian electrical engineer; inventor of methods of communication by wireless telegraphy etc.; awarded the Nobel Prize for physics in 1909. **marcōn'igrăm** *n.* Wireless telegram. **marcōn'i-graph** (-ahf) *n.* The apparatus used for transmitting marconigrams; also as verb.

Marco Polo: see POLO.

Marc'us Aurēl'ius Antonīn'us (121–180). Roman emperor, 161–180, and Stoic philosopher; author of 12 books of 'Meditations' in Greek.

mare *n.* Female of horse or other equine animal; *~'s-nest*, illusory discovery; *~'s-tail*, tall slender plant (*Hippuris vulgaris*) growing in marshy ground; long straight streaks of cirrus cloud.

Marengo (-ĕng'gō). Village in N. Italy, scene of defeat of Austrians by Napoleon, 1800.

Marg'aret, Queen (d. 1093). Scottish saint and queen of Scotland.

Marg'aret of Anjou (1430–82). Queen consort of Henry VI of England; a determined leader of her faction in Wars of the Roses.

marg'arine (-g-, -j-; -ēn') *n.* Edible fat made by the catalytic reduction of unsaturated acids in animal and vegetable oils and fats and freq. coloured to resemble butter.

marg'ay *n.* Small S. Amer. tiger-cat (*Felis tigrina*) related to the ocelot.

marge[1] *n.* (poet.) MARGIN.

marge[2] *n.* (colloq.) MARGARINE.

mar'gin *n.* Border; strip near edge of anything; plain space round printed page, picture, etc.; extra amount over what is necessary; sum deposited with stockbroker to cover risk of loss on transaction.

mar'ginal *adj.* Of, written in, the margin; of, at, the edge; close to the limit (freq. fig.).

marginăl'ia *n.pl.* Marginal notes.

mar'grāve *n.* (hist.) German title, orig. of ruler of a border province; later, hereditary title of some princes of the Holy Roman Empire. **mar'gravine** *n.* Margrave's wife.

marguerite' (-gerēt) *n.* Ox-eye daisy, *Chrysanthemum leucanthemum.* [Gk *margaritēs* pearl]

Mar'ian *adj.* Of the Virgin Mary; of Mary, Queen of England or Mary, Queen of Scots. ~ *n.* Adherent of the last.

Maria'na (-ahna), Juan de (1536–1624). Spanish Jesuit priest and historian; remembered for a work defining the circumstances in which it was legitimate to get rid of a tyrannical prince.

Măria'na (Mărianne') Islands. Group of islands in the S. Pacific, administered by U.S. Navy under trusteeship of U.N.

Mariănne'. Sobriquet of the French Republic, from name of a secret society (perhaps called after Juan de MARIANA) formed *c* 1852 with the object of establishing the Republic.

Mari'a There'sa (mărē'a terāza) (1717–1780). Queen of Hungary and Bohemia and archduchess of Austria; succeeded her father Charles VI as Empress of Germany in 1740. Her right to the throne was contested and gave rise to the War of the Austrian Succession (1740–8); during her reign Austria was attacked by Frederick the Great and defeated in the Seven Years War (1756–63).

Marie Antoinette (mărē' ahn-twahnĕt') (1755–93). Daughter of MARIA THERESA and queen of Louis XVI of France; guillotined on 16th Oct. 1793.

Marie de Médicis (mărē', mă'dēsēs) (1573–1642). Wife of Henry IV of France; regent of France 1610–17.

mă'rigōld *n.* 1. Kinds of plant, of genera *Calendula* and *Tagetes*, with bright-yellow or golden composite flowers; *fig-~*, a species of MESEMBRIANTHEMUM. 2. = MARSH marigold. [f. *Mary* (prob. the Virgin)+*gold*]

mărijua'na (-hwah'na) *n.* Dried leaves of common hemp, smoked as a narcotic in Mexico and U.S.; the plant itself.

marim'ba *n.* Primitive African xylophone; modern orchestral instrument evolved from this.

mărināde' *n.* Pickle of wine or vinegar with herbs and spices, in which fish or meat is steeped before cooking. ~ *v.t.* Steep in marinade.

marine' (-ēn) *adj.* Of, from, beside, the sea; for use at sea; of shipping; ~ *stores*, old ships' materials as merchandise; shop selling them. ~ *n.* Country's fleet of ships, naval or mercantile; soldier serving in the navy.

mă'riner *n.* Sailor; *master* ~, captain of a merchant ship.

Mărinĕtt'i, Filippo Tommaso (1876–1944). Italian author; initiator of FUTURISM.

Mărin'i (-ēnī), Giovanni Battista (1569–1625). Neapolitan poet, noted for the flamboyance of his style. **Marin'ism** *n.* Artificial affected style of writing. **Marin'ist** *n.*

Măriŏl'atrў̆ *n.* Idolatrous worship of the Virgin Mary.

mărionĕtte' *n.* Puppet worked with strings.

Marischal, Earl (mar'shal). Title of former Scottish officer of state; ~ *College*, a college of the University of Aberdeen, founded (1593) by an Earl Marischal, George Keith.

mă'rĭtal (*or* marī'-) *adj.* Of a husband; of or between husband and wife. **măr'itally** *adv.*

mă'rĭtime *adj.* Of or connected with the sea or seafaring; situated near the sea.

Mar'ius, Gaius (155–86 B.C.). Roman general and consul; conqueror of Jugurtha in Africa and the Cimbri and Teutones; rival of Sulla, who outlawed him in 88 B.C.

Mărivaux (-ēvō'), Pierre Carlet de Chamblain de (1688–1763). French author of comedies and romances marked by elaborate analysis of sentiment.

marj'oram *n.* Genus, *Origanum*, including *sweet* ~, aromatic culinary herb.

mark[1] *n.* 1. Principal monetary unit of Germany, = 100 pfennig (official name now *Deutsche M~*, abbrev. D.M.). 2. (hist.) English money of account = 13*s.* 4*d.*

mark[2] *n.* 1. Target, thing aimed at; *beside, wide of, the* ~, not hitting it, (fig.) not to the point. 2. Trace left by something; stain, scar, spot, dent. 3. Sign, indication, (*of* quality, character, etc.). 4. Affixed or impressed sign, seal, etc.; written symbol; cross etc. made by person who cannot write his name. 5. Unit in appraising merit of schoolchild's work in class, candidate's in examination, etc. 6. Line serving to indicate position, e.g. starting-point in race. 7. (boxing) Pit of stomach. 8. (Rugby football) Heelmark on ground made by player who has obtained fair catch. 9. (hist.) Tract of land held by Teutonic village community, frontier district. 10. (mil.) *M~ I, M~ II*, etc., designation of weapon or piece of equipment indicating first, second, etc., design, whence *M~ I*, (colloq.) primitive, antiquated. ~ *v.* Make a mark on; distinguish with a mark, characterize; serve as a mark of; assign marks of merit to; notice, observe, watch; record as score or act as scorer in games; ~*down*, note and remember (place etc.); (also) reduce price of; ~ *off*, separate by boundary, ~ *out*, trace out (boundary etc.); ~ *time*, move feet as in marching, but without advancing (often fig.); ~ *up*, raise price of.

Mark[3], King. In the Arthurian legend, king of Cornwall and husband of Iseult (Isolde).

Mark[4], St. Evangelist, a disciple and companion of Peter and Paul; traditional author of the 2nd gospel (the earliest in date); commemorated 25th April; his 'emblem' is a winged lion.

marked (-kt) *adj.* (esp.) Noticeable, conspicuous. **mark'ĕdly** *adv.*

mark'er *n.* 1. Scorer at billiards. 2. Thing used to mark place (in book etc). 3. Flare used above cloud (*sky*~) or bomb (*ground*~) dropped to mark out the pattern of an air-raid; ~ *bomb*, bomb emitting coloured light, dropped in raid to serve as point of direction.

mark'ĕt *n.* Gathering of people for sale of provisions, livestock, etc.; time of this, space or building used for it; demand *for*; seat of trade; *buyer's* ~, state of purchasing favourable to buyer; so *seller's* ~; ~*-cross*, cross erected in ~-place; ~*-day*, day on which market is held; ~ *garden*, garden in which vegetables are grown for market; ~*-place*, square, open place, where market is held; ~*-price*, prevailing price in ordinary conditions; ~*-town*, town where market is held on fixed days; ~ *value*, saleable value. ~ *v.* Buy or sell in market. **mark'ĕtable** *adj.* Fit for sale; sellable.

mark'ing *n.* (esp.) Colouring of feathers, skin, etc.; ~*-ink*, indelible ink for marking linen.

markk'a *n.* Principal monetary unit of Finland, = 100 penni.

marks'man *n.* (pl. *-men*). One skilled at aiming at mark, esp. rifleman of certain standard of proficiency. **marks'manship** *n.*

marl *n.* Rock, freq. soft but sometimes hard, of mud and lime; soil consisting of this in broken or powdered state, used as fertilizer. ~ *v.t.* Apply marl to. **marl'y** *adj.*

Mar'lăg *n.* German prison camp for sailors. [Ger., abbrev. of *mar*ine navy, *lag*er camp]

Marlborough (mawl'boro), John Churchill, 1st Duke of (1650–1722). English soldier; in the War of the Spanish Succession he defeated the French and their allies at BLENHEIM, RAMILLIES, OUDENARDE and MALPLAQUET; married Sarah Jennings, favourite of Queen Anne; both later fell out of favour.

Marlborough (mawl'boro) **College.** English public school in Wiltshire, founded 1843.

Marlborough (mawl'boro) **House.** House in Pall Mall, London, designed *c* 1710 by Sir Christopher Wren for the 1st Duke of Marlborough; f. 1863–1959 a royal residence; now a Commonwealth centre.

mar'līne *n.* (naut.) Small line of 2 strands used for binding shrouds etc.; ~*-spike*, pointed tool for separating strands of rope in splicing.

MARLINE-SPIKE

marl'īte *n.* Variety of marl which does not become pulverized by the action of air.

Mar'lowe (-lō), Christopher (1564–93). English poet and playwright; author of 'Tamburlaine', 'The Jew of Malta', 'Edward II', and 'The Tragedy of Dr Faustus'; became involved in political intrigues; was killed in obscure circumstances after a brawl in a Deptford tavern.

marm'alāde *n.* Preserve of oranges or other citrous fruit, cut up and boiled with the peel and sugar. [Port. *marmelada* f. *marmelo* quince]

marm'īte *n.* Proprietary term for an extract made from fresh brewers' yeast. [Fr., = 'stock-pot']

Marm'ora, Sea of. Small inland sea lying between the Black Sea and the Aegean.

marmor'ĕal *adj.* Of or like marble.

marm'osĕt (-z-) *n.* Small tropical Amer. monkey with bushy tail, of several genera in family *Hapalidae* (ill. MONKEY).

marm'ot *n.* Genus, *Arctomys*, of burrowing hibernating rodents of squirrel family. [Fr. *marmotte* prob. ult. f. L *murem montis* mountain mouse (*mus* mouse)]

Marne. River of N. France; *battle of the* ~, Sept. 1914, one of the decisive battles of the war of 1914–18, when the German advance towards Paris was checked; *2nd battle of the* ~, successful counter-offensive by the allies, July–Aug. 1918.

mă'rocain *n.* Dress-fabric with wavy texture, of silk etc. [Fr., = 'Moroccan']

Mar'onīte *n.* One of a sect of Syrian Christians living in Lebanon, named after their founder Maron, who lived probably in the 4th c.

maroon'[1] *n.* & *adj.* 1. (Of) brownish-crimson colour. 2. Firework exploding with loud report. [Fr. *marron* chestnut]

maroon'[2] *n.* One of a class of Negroes, orig. fugitive slaves, living in mountains of W. Indies; marooned person.

maroon'[3] *v.t.* Put (person) ashore and leave on desolate island or coast as punishment; leave without means of getting away. [Fr. *marron*, perh. f. Span. *cimarron* wild]

Marot (mărō'), Clément (1497–1544). French Protestant poet and translator of the Psalms.

Marprĕl'ate, Martin. Pseudonym of author of several satirical pamphlets issued from a secret press in 1588–9, abusing the bishops and defending the Presbyterian system of discipline.

marque (-k) *n.* (hist.) *Letters of* ~, licence given to private person to fit out armed vessel and employ it in capture of enemy's merchant shipping.

marquee' (-kē) *n.* Large tent, esp. one used at fêtes, shows, etc.

Marque'sas Islands (-kā-).

Group of islands in the Pacific, in French possession.

mar͡q'uetry, -terie (-kĭ-) *n.* Decoration of flat surface, as of furniture, by glueing together shaped pieces of wood, ivory, or other substance(s) so as to cover the whole surface; also, inlay; furniture etc. so decorated.

mar͡q'uis, mar͡q'uėss *n.* Noble ranking below duke and above earl or count. **mar͡q'uisate** *n.* **mar͡-quise'** (-kēz) *n.* 1. (Of foreign nobility) marchioness. 2. Finger-ring set with large oval stone or cluster. 3. (archaic) Tent. [It. *marchese* ruler of MARCH[3]]

mar͡'quois (-kwoiz) *n.* ~ *scale*, apparatus for drawing equidistant parallel lines.

mă'rram *n.* Coarse, tough, binding grass (*Ammophila arenaria*) growing on dunes near sea-shore.

mă'rriage (-rĭj) *n.* Act, ceremony, or state of being married; wedlock, wedding; (fig.) intimate union; *civil* ~, one performed by an officer of state, without religious ceremonies; *communal* ~, (anthrop.) system by which within a small community all the men are regarded as married to all the women; *companionate* ~, (U.S.) probationary union of man and woman; *religious* ~, one performed with religious rites; ~ *articles*, agreement concerning rights of property, succession, etc., made before marriage; ~ *licence*, official permit for two persons to marry; ~ *lines*, certificate of marriage. **mă'rriageable** (-ja-) *adj.*

mă'rrŏn glacé (glah'sā) *n.* Chestnut preserved in sugar as sweetmeat.

mă'rrow (-rō) *n.* 1. Soft fatty substance in cavities of bones (ill. BONE); essential or best part of anything, essence; ~*-bone*, bone containing edible marrow; (pl. facet.) knees; *ma'rrowfat* (*pea*), kind of large rich pea; ~ *scoop*, narrow spoon-like utensil for extracting marrow. 2. (*vegetable*) ~, kind of edible gourd, the fruit of *Curcubita peps.* **mă'rrowy** (-ōĭ) *adj.*

mă'rrȳ *v.* Unite, give, or take in wedlock; take a wife or husband; (fig.) unite intimately.

Mă'rrȳat, Captain Frederick (1792–1848). English naval captain; author of 'Peter Simple', 'Mr Midshipman Easy', 'Masterman Ready', and other novels and stories, mostly of sea life.

Mar͡s (-z). 1. The Roman god of war, identified with the Greek ARES. 2. The 4th planet in the order of distance from the sun, with an orbit lying between that of the earth and Jupiter (ill. PLANET); the surface of the planet shows long straight dark streaks popularly called 'canals'. **Mar͡'tian** (-shĭan) *n.* A supposed inhabitant of Mars.

Mar͡sa'la (-sah-). Town on W. coast of Sicily; the fortified wine made there, orig. as imitation of sherry for English consumption.

Mar͡seillaise' (-selāz), **The.** The French national anthem, composed by a young engineer officer, Rouget de Lisle, at Strasbourg in 1792, on the declaration of war against Austria, and first sung in Paris by Marseilles 'patriots'.

Mar͡seilles' (-āls). French seaport, on the Mediterranean coast, on site of an ancient Greek colony, Massilia.

mar͡sh *n.* Low-lying land, more or less permanently waterlogged; bog, morass; ~*-gas*, light inflammable gas (CH_4) formed by the decay of vegetable matter in marshy places and in coal-mines; methane; ~*-mallow*, (sweetmeat made from root of) shrubby herb (*Athaea officinalis*) growing near salt-marshes; ~*-marigold*, genus of plants of *Ranunculus* family with bright golden flowers, growing in moist meadows. **mar͡sh'ȳ** *adj.* **mar͡'shinėss** *n.*

mar͡sh'al *n.* 1. Official of a royal household or court directing ceremonies, in England the *Earl M*~; (hist.) *knight* ~, officer of royal household with judicial functions. 2. Military officer of highest rank in some foreign armies, in the British Army, a *Field M*~. 3. Part of title of officers of high rank in the R.A.F., as *Air* (*Chief*, *Vice*-) *M*~. ~ *v.t.* Arrange in due order (persons at banquet etc., soldiers, facts, etc.); lead, conduct, with ceremony; (her.) put in due order quarterings etc. on an escutcheon (ill. HERALDRY); *marshalling yard*, railway yard in which trains are assembled and distributed.

Mar͡sh'all, George Catlett (1880–1959). U.S. general; chief of staff of U.S. army in war of 1939–45; secretary of state 1947–9; devised ~ *Plan*, scheme authorized by Congress in April 1948 to provide financial aid (~ *Aid*) to certain European countries as part of the European Recovery Programme.

Mar͡sh'alsea. A debtors' prison in Southwark, under the control of the knight marshal, dating from the 14th c.; abolished 1842. [orig. *marshalcy*]

Mar͡s'ton Moor. Battle (1644) fought 7 miles W. of York between Royalist army under Prince Rupert and Parliamentary army; a decisive Parliamentary victory.

mar͡sūp'ĭal *adj.* & *n.* (Animal) of the class of mammals which are born in a very immature condition, as e.g. the kangaroo, wombat, and are carried in a pouch until able to fend for themselves.

Mar͡s'ȳas. (Gk myth.) A satyr, who took to flute-playing; he challenged Apollo to a musical contest and was flayed alive when he lost.

mar͡t *n.* (poet.) Market-place; auction room; trade centre.

Martĕll'ō tower. A small circular fort with massive walls; many of these towers were erected on the S. and E. coasts of England to guard against invasion in the Napoleonic wars. [corrupt. of Cape *Mortella* in Corsica, where a tower of this kind was captured by the English fleet in 1794]

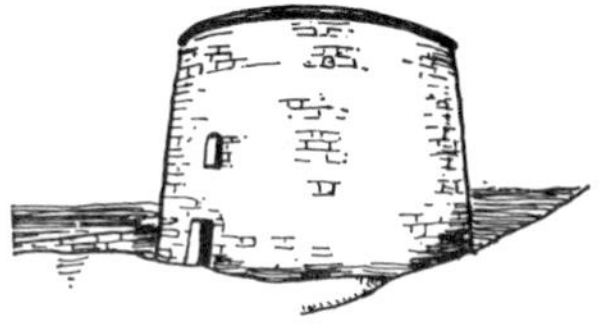

MARTELLO TOWER

mar͡t'ėn *n.* Any of various carnivorous mammals of the genus *Martes*, resembling large weasels, with valuable fur.

Mar͡th'a. Sister of Lazarus and Mary and friend of Jesus (Luke x. 40); in Christian allegory she symbolizes the active life and her sister the contemplative life.

mar͡'tial[1] (-shl) *adj.* Of, suitable for, appropriate to, warfare; militant, ready, eager, to fight; ~ *law*, military government, during which ordinary law is suspended. **mar͡'tially** *adv.* **mar͡'tialīze** *v.t.* Make suitable, prepare, for war; impart martial spirit to.

Mar͡'tial[2] (-shl). Marcus Valerius Martialis (43–*c* 102), Roman satiric poet and epigrammatist.

mar͡t'ĭn[1] *n.* Name given to several birds of swallow family, esp. the house-martin (*Chelidon urbica*), which builds a mud nest under eaves etc., and the sand-martin (*Cotile riparia*).

HOUSE-MARTIN
Length 5 in.

Mar͡t'ĭn[2], St. Bishop of Tours *c* 371; legend represents him as a Roman soldier who cut his cloak in two and gave half to a beggar; patron saint of tavern-keepers; commemorated 11th Nov. (MARTINMAS); *St.* ~*'s Summer*, a period of fine mild weather often occurring about this date.

Mar͡t'ĭneau (-nō), Harriet (1802–76). English Unitarian and writer of works on political economy and social reform. ~, James (1805–1900). Her brother; Unitarian divine and philosopher.

mar͡tĭnĕt' *n.* Strict (esp. military) disciplinarian. **mar͡tĭnĕt't'ĭsh** *adj.* **mar͡tĭnĕtt'ĭsm** *n.* [name of French drillmaster in reign of Louis XIV]

mar͡t'ĭngāle (-ngg-) *n.* 1. Strap fastened to bridle and girth of horse to prevent rearing etc. (ill.

SADDLE). 2. Gambling system of doubling stakes at each venture.

mar̄ti'ni[1] (-ēnĭ) *n.* Cocktail of gin, vermouth, orange bitters, etc. [name of inventor]

Mar̄ti'ni[2] (-ēnĭ), Frederic (1832–97). Swiss inventor, whose name, together with that of A. *Henry* (–1894), Scottish gunmaker, was given to the ~*–Henry rifle*, which combines Henry's 7-grooved barrel with Martini's block-action breech mechanism.

Mar̄tĭnique' (-ēk). French W. Indian island, one of the Lesser Antilles; capital, Fort de France; the former capital, St. Pierre, was completely destroyed by an eruption of Mont Pelé in 1902.

Mar̄'tĭnmas, Mar̄t'lemas. The feast of St. Martin, 11th Nov.; formerly the usual time in England for hiring servants and for slaughtering cattle to be salted for the winter; one of the Scottish term days.

mar̄t'lėt *n.* Swift; martin; (her.) footless bird.

mar̄t'yr (-*er*) *n.* Person who undergoes death or suffering for any great cause, specif. one who suffers death on account of his adherence to the Christian faith; ~ *to*, constant sufferer from (ailment etc.). ~ *v.t.* Put to death as martyr, torment. [Gk *martus* witness].

mar̄t'yrdom (-*ter*-) *n.* Sufferings and death of martyr, torment.

mar̄t'yrīze *v.t.* Make martyr of.

mar̄tyrŏl'ogy *n.* List, history, of (esp. Christian) martyrs. **mar̄tyrolŏ'gical** *adj.* **mar̄tyrŏl'ogist** *n.*

mar̄t'yry *n.* Shrine, church, erected in honour of martyr.

mar̄v'el *n.* Wonderful thing; wonderful example *of* (quality). ~ *v.i.* Be surprised (*at, that*); wonder (*how, why*, etc.).

Mar̄v'ell, Andrew (1621–78). English poet and political writer of Parliamentarian sympathies.

mar̄v'ellous *adj.* Astonishing; extravagantly improbable. **mar̄v'ellously** *adv.* **mar̄v'ellousnėss** *n.*

Mar̄x, Karl (1818–83). German revolutionary writer; settled in England after 1849; wrote 'Das Kapital' (1867), criticizing the capitalistic system as permitting a diminishing number of capitalists to appropriate the benefits of improved industrial methods, while the labouring class were left in increasing dependency and misery. The remedy Marx found in the total abolition of private property, to be effected by the class-war; when the community owned all means of production and all property, it would provide every individual with work and the means of subsistence. **Mar̄x'ĭst, Mar̄x'ian** *adjs.* & *ns.* **Mar̄x'ism** *n.*

Mār'y[1] **(the Virgin).** Mary of Nazareth, the mother of Jesus.

Mār'y[2]. Name of two reigning queens of England: *Mary I* or Mary Tudor (1516–58), daughter of Henry VIII and Catherine of Aragon; reigned 1553–8; married Philip II of Spain, 1554; fervently Catholic; known as 'Bloody Mary' because of the religious persecutions of her reign; *Mary II* (1662–94), eldest child of James II; married William of Orange, 1677; was invited, with him, to take the throne of England and Scotland after the deposition of her father, and reigned 1689–94.

Mār'y Cėlĕste'. An American brig found in the N. Atlantic by a British barque on 5th Dec. 1872, in perfect condition but abandoned and without her boats; the fate of the crew was never discovered.

Marylănd (-ĕr'ĭ-). South Atlantic State of U.S., one of the 13 original States; capital, Annapolis. [named after Henrietta *Maria*, queen of Charles I]

Marylebone (mă'rĭlebon, mă'rĭbon). District of London N. of Oxford Street; ~ *Cricket Club* (the M.C.C.), a cricket club founded towards the end of the 18th c., and now the legislative authority on the game. [orig. called TYBURN; altered to *Maryborne* f. church dedicated to St. Mary, and later to *Marylebone* as if = 'Mary the Good']

Mary Magdalene: see MAGDALEN.

Mār'y, Queen of Scots (1542–87). Mary Stuart, daughter of James V of Scotland and granddaughter of Henry VII; married the dauphin (François II) of France; claimed English throne on Mary I's death, and returned to Scotland, 1560; married, 1565, her cousin the Earl of Darnley, by whom she had a son (James I); soon after Darnley's mysterious death she married the Earl of Bothwell, 1567; was imprisoned by Elizabeth I, 1567; was tried for conspiracy, 1586, and beheaded.

mar̄zĭpăn' *n.* Paste of pounded almonds, sugar, and white of egg, eaten as sweetmeat and in cakes.

Masaccio (-ăch'ō), Tommaso di Giovanni (1401–28), Italian painter of the early Renaissance.

Masai (m*a*sī'). Warlike pastoral race of mixed Hamitic stock, inhabiting S. Kenya and N. Tanganyika.

Mas'arўk (-z-), Thomas Garrigue (1850–1937). Czech statesman and philosopher; first president of Czechoslovakia, 1918–37.

Mascagni (-kăn'yĭ), Piero (1863–1945). Italian composer of operas, famous for his 'Cavalleria Rusticana'.

măscar̄'a *n.* Preparation for darkening eyelashes, eyebrows, etc., in make-up. [name of a town in Oran, Algiers]

măs'cle *n.* (her.) Charge in form of lozenge with lozenge-shaped opening (ill. HERALDRY).

măs'cot *n.* Person, animal, thing, supposed to bring luck; talisman.

măs'cūline (*or* mah-) *adj.* (gram.) Of the gender to which names of male beings belong; male; manly, vigorous; mannish; ~ *rhyme*, (in French verse) one between words ending in stressed syllables, not *e* mute; ~ *ending*, (of verse-line) one rhyming in this way. ~ *n.* Masculine gender; masculine noun, pronoun, etc. **măs'cūlinenėss** (-n-n-), **măscūlĭn'ĭtў** *ns.*

Māse'field, John (1878–1967). English poet and novelist; poet laureate 1930– .

măsh[1] *n.* Malt mixed with water for brewing; boiled grain, bran, etc., given warm to horses etc.; soft pulp made by crushing, mixing with water, etc.; (slang) mashed potatoes. ~ *v.t.* Make into mash; crush, pound, to pulp.

măsh[2] *v.t.* (obs. slang) Excite sentimental admiration in (one of opposite sex). **măsh'er** *n.* (slang) Lady-killer, coxcomb, fop.

măsh'ie, măsh'ў *n.* Golf-club having iron head with straight sole and face slightly more lofted than the iron, used for medium distances (ill. GOLF).

Mashōn'alănd. District of S. Rhodesia.

mas'jĭd (mŭ-) *n.* Mosque.

mask (mah-) *n.* Covering, usu. of velvet or silk, for concealing face at balls etc.; masked person; sterile gauze covering for nose and mouth, used by doctors and nurses; covering of wire gauze stretched on framework, worn to protect face in fencing; grotesque representation of a face worn on festive and other occasions to produce a humorous or terrifying effect; hollow figure of human head esp. as worn by Greek and Roman actors; clay or wax likeness of person's face, esp. one made by taking mould from face during life or after death (*life-~, death-~*); face, head, of fox; (fig.) disguise. ~ *v.t.* Cover with mask; disguise or hide as with mask; *masked ball*, one at which masks are worn. **ma'sker** *n.* One who takes part in masque or masquerade.

măs'ochism (-z-, -k-) *n.* A form of sexual perversion in which one finds pleasure in abuse and cruelty from his or her associate, opp. to SADISM. **măs'ochĭst** *n.* **măsochĭs'tĭc** *adj.* [L. von Sacher-*Masoch* (1835–95), Austrian novelist who described it]

mās'on *n.* 1. Worker in stone. 2. Freemason (see FREE). **masŏn'ĭc** *adj.* Of freemasons. **mās'onry** *n.* 1. Stonework. (*Illustration, p.* 507.) 2. Freemasonry.

Mason and Dixon Line. Line marking the boundary between Maryland and Pennsylvania, established 1763–7 by two English astronomers, Charles Mason and Jeremiah Dixon; later, the line was of importance as separating the slave States from the free. See also DIXIE.

masque (mahsk) *n.* Amateur histrionic and musical performance, orig. in dumb-show, later with metrical dialogue etc.; dramatic composition for this. **mas′quer** *n.* Masker.

masquerāde′ (mahske-) *n.* Masked ball; false show, pretence. ~ *v.i.* Appear in disguise; ~ *as*, pretend to be.

Măss[1] *n.* Celebration (now usu. R.C.) of the Eucharist; liturgy, musical setting of liturgy, used in this; *High* ~, with incense, music and assistance of deacon and subdeacon; *Low* ~, without music and with minimum of ceremony. [Low L *messa*, possibly f. words of dismissal at end of service: *ite, missa est*]

măss[2] *n.* Coherent body of matter of indefinite shape; dense aggregation, large number, *of*; unbroken expanse *of* (light etc.); (physics) quantity of matter a body contains, as determined by comparing the changes in the velocities that result when the body and a standard body impinge; *the masses*, the lower classes of society; ~*-energy*: see ENERGY; ~*-meeting*, large assembly of people; ~ *observation*, study and record of the social habits of the masses of the people; ~ *production*, production in large quantities of standardized article(s) by standardized mechanical means; hence, ~*-produce(d)*. ~ *v.* Gather into mass; (mil.) concentrate (troops). **măss′ȳ** *adj.* Solid, bulky.

Mass. *abbrev.* Massachusetts.

Măssachus′ĕtts (-ōō-). New England State of U.S., one of the 13 original States; capital, Boston.

măss′acre (-ker) *n.* General slaughter, carnage. ~ *v.t.* Make a massacre of.

măssage′ (-ahzh; *or* măs′ahzh) *n.* Kneading and rubbing of muscles, joints, etc., with hands, to stimulate their action. ~ *v.t.* Treat thus. [Fr., f. L *massa* lump]

massé (măsā′) *n.* (billiards) Stroke made with cue held perpendicularly.

Măssenet′ (-enā), Jules Émile Frédéric (1842–1912). French composer of operas and other music.

măssē′ter *n.* Masticatory muscle (ill. HEAD).

măsseur′ (-ẽr), (fem.) **măsseuse′** (-ẽrz) *ns.* One who practises massage.

măss′ĭf *n.* Mountain heights forming compact group; *M~ Central* (măsēf′sahṅtrahl′), plateau in central France occupying about a fifth of the country and including the Cévennes, Auvergne, and Limousin mountains.

Măss′ĭnger (-jer), Philip (1583–1640). English poet and playwright.

măss′ĭve *adj.* Large and heavy or solid; (fig.) solid, substantial; (psychol., of sensation etc.) having large volume or magnitude. **măs′sĭvely** (-vl-) *adv.* **măss′ĭvenėss** *n.*

Măs(s)ōr′a(h). The critical notes and traditions relating to the text of the Hebrew Bible, compiled by Jewish scholars in the 10th and preceding centuries.

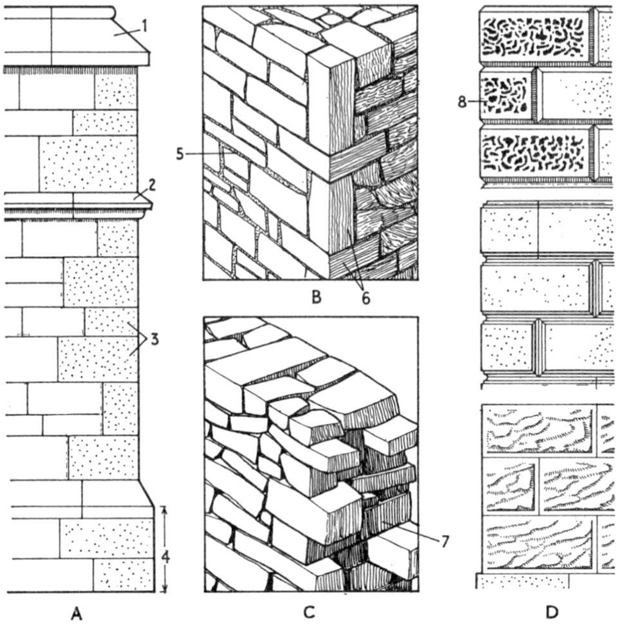

Mă(s)s′orētes *n.pl.* These scholars. **Măs(s)orĕt′ĭc** *adj.*

mast[1] (-ah-) *n.* Fruit of beech and other forest trees, esp. as food for swine.

mast[2] (-ah-) *n.* Long pole of timber etc. set upright in ship to support sails etc. (ill. SHIP); long pole supporting flag, wireless aerial, etc.; *before the* ~, as an ordinary seaman, so described because sailors are quartered in the forecastle; *half-*~: see HALF; ~*-head*, highest part of mast, esp. lower mast, as place of observation or punishment; (*v.t.*) send (sailor) to this as punishment (now an obs. practice); raise (sail) to its position. ~ *v.t.* Furnish with masts.

măs′taba *n.* 1. Among Moslems, outdoor stone platform attached to a dwelling. 2. Ancient Egyptian tomb with sloping sides and flat roof.

ma′ster (-ah-) *n.* Person having control; captain of merchant-vessel; employer; owner of dog etc.; male head of household; teacher in school; title given to heads of certain colleges at Oxford and Cambridge, as ~ *of Balliol*; title given to eldest son and heir of some ancient Scottish baronies, as ~ *of Lovat*; form of address employed esp. by servants to young gentlemen; skilled workman; great artist, esp. *old* ~; ~ *at arms*, police officer on warship or liner; *M~ of Arts* (M.A.), *Science* (M.Sc.), etc., holder of university degree ranking above bachelor, and orig. qualifying to teach in university; ~ *of ceremonies*, person presiding over arrangements at social gathering etc.; ~ *of foxhounds* (M.F.H.), person having control of a pack; ~*-key*, one made to open many locks, each also opened by separate key; *ma′sterpiece*, consummate piece of workmanship, best work; *ma′stersinger*: see MEISTERSINGER. ~ *v.t.* Overcome; reduce to subjection; acquire complete knowledge of or facility in.

ma′sterful (mah-) *adj.* Self-willed, imperious. **ma′sterfully** *adv.* **ma′sterfulnėss** *n.*

ma′sterly (mah-) *adj.* Worthy of a master, very skilful.

ma′stery (mah-) *n.* Sway; masterly skill, use or knowledge; upper hand.

măs′tĭc *n.* Gum or resin exuding from certain trees, growing esp. in the Levant, used in making varnish; trees yielding this; mastic colour, pale yellow; kind of cement made of mastic.

măs′tĭcāte *v.t.* Grind (food) with teeth, chew. **măstĭcā′tion, măs′tĭcātor** *ns.* **măs′tĭcatory** *adj.*

măs′tĭff (*or* mah-) *n.* Large strong dog with drooping ears and pendulous lips, valuable as a watch-dog (ill. DOG).

măstī′tis *n.* Inflammation of the breast.

Măs′todŏn *n.* Extinct genus of large mammals like elephants,

MASONRY: A. ASHLAR. B. RANDOM RUBBLE WALLING. C. DRY WALLING. D. RUSTICATED ASHLAR

1. Coping. 2. String-course. 3. Quoins. 4. Plinth. 5. Pointing. 6. Long-and-short work. 7. Binder or parpen. 8. Vermiculated rustication

having nipple-shaped tubercles on crowns of molar teeth.

măs'toid *adj.* (anat.) Shaped like female breast; ~ *process*, conical prominence in temporal bone to which muscles are attached (ill. HEAD). ~ *n.* Mastoid process. **măstoidī'tis** *n.* Inflammation of mastoid process.

măs'turbāte (-ter-) *v.i.* Practise self-abuse. **măsturbā'tion** *n.*

Masur'ian Lakes (-zoor-). Large group of lakes in E. Prussia, scene of two battles (Tannenberg, Aug. 1914, and the 'winter battle', Jan. 1915) in which the Russians were driven out of Germany.

măt[1] *n.* Coarse fabric of plaited rushes, straw, etc.; piece of this for wiping shoes upon; small piece of cork, linen, etc., laid on table to prevent damage to polish. ~ *v.* Entangle, become entangled, in thick mass.

măt(t)[2] *adj.* Dull, without lustre. ~ *v.t.* Make dull; frost (glass); ~ *n.* Dull-gold border round framed picture; dull, lustreless appearance (of metal etc.); roughened or frosted groundwork. [Fr. *mat* dull]

Mătabĕl'ê. A S. African people, one of the main branches of the Zulu group of tribes; now settled, after various migrations, in the W. part of S. Rhodesia (*Mătabĕl'êlănd*).

măt'adŏr *n.* 1. Man appointed to kill bull in bull-fight. 2. One of three chief cards in ombre and quadrille.

mătch[1] *n.* Person equal in some particular, person or thing exactly corresponding, to another; contest in which persons or teams are matched against each other; matrimonial alliance; person viewed in light of eligibility for marriage; ~-*board*, one with tongue cut along one edge and groove along another, so as to fit into similar boards; ~-*maker*, person fond of trying to arrange marriages; ~ *point*, state of game when one side needs only one point to win the match; the point itself. ~ *v.* Find or be a match for; place (person etc.) in competition *with*, in conflict *against*, another; be equal, correspond in colour, shape etc.

mătch[2] *n.* Short strip of wood (~-*stick*) etc. with tip (~-*head*) covered with some combustible substance which ignites when rubbed on rough or (*safety* ~) specially prepared surface; fuse for firing cannon etc.; ~-*box*, box for holding matches; ~-*lock*, (hist.) (gun with) lock in which match was placed for igniting powder (ill. MUSKET); *match'wood*, wood of suitable size for making matches; (wood reduced to) minute splinters.

mătch'lêss *adj.* Without an equal, peerless. **mătch'lêssly** *adv.*

māte[1] *n.* & *v.t.* (chess) = CHECKMATE; *fool's* ~, in which first player is mated at opponent's second move.

māte[2] *n.* 1. Companion, fellow worker (also as a general form of address). 2. Fitting partner in marriage; one of a pair, esp. of birds. 3. (naut.) Officer on merchant ship who sees to execution of master's commands and deputizes for him. 4. Assistant to some specialist, as *gunner's* ~, *plumber's* ~. ~ *v.* Join in marriage, marry; pair. **māt'(e)y** *adj.* (colloq.) Companionable, sociable. **māt'(e)yness** *n.*

maté (mă'tā) *n.* Paraguay tea, infusion of leaves of S. Amer. shrub *Ilex paraguayensis*; vessel for this.

matelot (măt'lō) *n.* (naut. slang) Sailor.

măt'êlote (-ot) *n.* Dish of fish stewed with wine, onions, etc.

māt'er *n.* (school slang) Mother; DURA MATER, PIA MATER: see entries.

matēr'ial *adj.* Concerned with or composed of matter; unspiritual; concerned with bodily comfort, riches, etc.; important, essential. **matēr'ially** *adv.* **matēr'ial** *n.* Matter from which thing is made; elements; stuff, fabric; *writing*-~*s*, requisites for writing.

matēr'ialism *n.* Opinion that nothing exists but matter and its movements and modifications and that consciousness and will are wholly due to material agency; (art) tendency to lay stress on material aspect of objects; desire for material rather than spiritual prosperity etc. **matēr'ialist** *n.* & *adj.* **matērialis'tic** *adj.* **matērialis'tically** *adv.*

matēr'ialize *v.* Make, represent as, material; appear, cause (spirit) to appear, in bodily form; make materialistic; become actual fact. **matērializā'tion** *n.*

matēr'iă mĕd'ica *n.* Remedial substances used in practice of medicine; branch of science dealing with their origin and properties.

matériel (matārīĕl') *n.* Stock of materials, equipment, etc., used in any complex operation (opp. *personnel*).

matērn'al *adj.* Of mothers; motherly; related on mother's side, as ~ *uncle*, mother's brother. **matērn'ally** *adv.*

matērn'ity *n.* Motherhood; motherliness; ~ *home*, *hospital*, institution for care of women during (or immediately after) childbirth; ~ *nurse*, nurse for women at childbirth.

măthêmăt'ics *n.pl.* (usu. treated as sing.) Abstract science of space and number (also *pure* ~); this applied to branches of physics etc. (also *applied* ~). **măthêmăt'ical** *adj.* Of mathematics; (of proof etc.) rigorously precise. **măthêmăt'ically** *adv.* **măthêmatĭ'cian** *n.* **măths,** (U.S.) **măth** *abbrevs.* Mathematics.

Matil'da (1102–67). Daughter and heir of Henry I of England; married Henry V of Germany and was crowned empress, 1114; on her father's death in 1135 her cousin Stephen was chosen as king; she returned to England 1139, captured Stephen, and was acknowledged in 1141 as 'Lady of England and Normandy', but was eventually forced to withdraw to the Continent; her son became Henry II.

matinée (măt'ĭnā) *n.* Afternoon theatrical or musical performance, afternoon cinema show; ~ *coat*, baby's woollen coat.

măt'ins *n.* One of the canonical hours of the breviary, a midnight office, but also recited at daybreak; morning prayer in Church of England (also *mattins*).

Matisse' (-ēs), Henri (1869–1954). French Post-Impressionist painter.

măt'rass *n.* Long-necked glass vessel with round or oval body, used in distilling etc.

māt'riarch (-k) *n.* Woman corresponding in status to patriarch (usu. joc.).

māt'riarchy (-k-) *n.* Social organization in which the mother is head of the family and descent and relationship are reckoned through mothers. **māt'riarchal** *adj.*

matric' *n.* (colloq. abbrev. of) MATRICULATION.

māt'ricīde *n.* Killing of one's own mother; person guilty of this. **māt'ricīdal** *adj.*

matric'ūlate *v.* Admit, be admitted, to privileges of university. **matricūlā'tion** *n.* Matriculating; examination qualifying for this.

măt'rimony *n.* 1. Rite of marriage, state of being married. 2. Declaration of king and queen of trumps in some card-games. **mătrimōn'ial** *adj.* **mătrimōn'ially** *adv.*

māt'rix *n.* (pl. *-ices* pr. ĭsēz, *-ixes*). Womb; place in which thing is developed; mass of rock etc. enclosing gems etc.; mould in which type etc. is cast or shaped; (physiol.) formative part of animal organ; (biol.) substance between cells.

māt'ron *n.* Married woman; woman managing domestic affairs of schools etc.; woman in charge of nursing in hospital. **māt'ronage, māt'ronhood, māt'ronship** *ns.* **māt'ronal** *adj.* **māt'ronly** *adj.* Resembling a married woman in appearance and bearing; staid; portly.

Matt. *abbrev.* Matthew.

matt: see MAT[2].

mătt'er *n.* 1. Substance(s) of which a physical thing is made; *grey* ~, parts of central nervous system which appear grey owing to presence of massed groups of nerve-cells (also, joc., brain, intellectual power), as dist. from *white* ~, parts consisting mainly of nerve-fibre tracts. 2. Physical substance in general as dist. from spirit, mind, etc. 3. Purulent discharge. 4. Content as dist. from form; material for thought or expression; substance of book, speech, etc.

5. Thing(s); material, as *printed* ~. 6. Affair, concern; ~ *of fact*, what pertains to the sphere of fact (opp. to *opinion* etc.); *as a* ~ *of fact*, (law) part of a judicial inquiry concerned with truth of alleged facts (opp. to ~ *of law*); ~-*of-fact'* (*adj.*) unimaginative, prosaic. ~ *v.i.* 1. Be of importance, signify. 2. Secrete or discharge pus.

Mătt'erhŏrn. Alpine peak on Italian-Swiss frontier, first climbed in 1865.

Matthew (măth'ū), St. One of the 12 apostles; traditionally, but erroneously, supposed to be the author of the 1st gospel, which was written after A.D. 70, and based largely on St. Mark.

Matthew Paris: see PARIS[3].

mătt'ĭng *n.* Fabric of hemp, bast, etc., as covering etc.

mătt'ock *n.* Tool shaped like pick, with adze and chisel edge as ends of head.

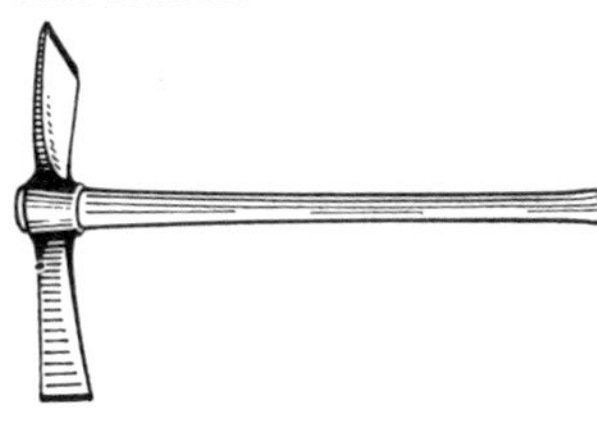

MATTOCK

mătt'rĕss *n.* Case of canvas or other strong material stuffed with hair, straw, wool, etc., as bed; (usu. *spring* ~) series of wire springs stretched in frame as support for bed; series of wires (*wire* ~) stretched on frame to support mattress of hair etc. [It. *materasso* prob. f. Arab. *almaṭrah* place, cushion (*ṭaraḥa* throw)]

măt'ūrāte *v.i.* (med.) Attain full development, ripen. **mătūrā'tion** *n.* Final series of changes in the growth and formation of germ cells. **matūr'ative** *adj.* Causing maturation.

matūre' *adj.* Fully developed; ripe; adult. **matūre'ly** *adv.* **matūre'nĕss, matūr'ity** *ns.* **matūre'** *v.* Bring to or reach mature state.

Măt'ūrin, Charles Robert (1782–1826). Irish playwright and author of novels of 'terror'.

mătūtīn'al *adj.* Of, in, the morning, early.

maud *n.* Scotch shepherd's grey striped woollen plaid; travelling-rug like this.

maud'lin *adj.* Mawkishly sentimental, esp. of tearful and effusively affectionate stage of drunkenness. ~ *n.* Mawkish sentiment. [f. MAGDALEN]

maul *n.* Heavy hammer, usu. of wood (ill. BEETLE[1]). ~ *v.t.* Beat and bruise; handle or paw roughly; lacerate; damage by criticism.

maul'stick, mahl- *n.* Long thin stick held by painter in left hand as support for right, with padded ball at one end. [Du. *maalstok* (*malen* paint, *stok* stick)]

maun'der *v.i.* Talk ramblingly; wander about vaguely and listlessly.

Maun'dy̆ *n.* The ceremony of washing the feet of the poor, performed by royal or other eminent persons on the Thursday before Easter (~ *Thursday*) in commemoration of Christ's washing of the apostles' feet, and commonly followed by almsgiving; it survives in England in the distribution of ~ *money* (silver coins minted for this), usu. at Westminster Abbey. [L *mandatum* commandment]

Maupassant (mōpăsahṅ'), Guy de (1850–93). French novelist, famous as a writer of short stories.

Mauresque: MORESQUE.

Maurĕtān'ia. 1. An ancient country of N. Africa; this as a Roman province, roughly equals N. Morocco and Algeria. 2. Name of a passenger liner on the N. Atlantic route. [L, = 'country of the Moors' (*Mauri*)]

Mau'rĭsts (mō-). A congregation of French Benedictine monks, established in 1618 in order to reform the order; famous for scholarship and literary zeal; named after St. MAURUS.

Maurĭtān'ia. Republic of the French Community, in W. Africa; capital, Nouakchott.

Mauritius (morĭsh'*us*). Island in Indian Ocean E. of Madagascar, British colony from 1810 to 1968; independent State of British Commonwealth; capital, Port Louis.

Maur'us (mō-), St. (d. 565). Legendary founder of the Benedictine order in France.

Mauser (mowz-) *n.* Repeating rifle with interlocking bolt-head and box magazine; ~ *pistol*, self-loading pistol. [Peter Paul *Mauser* (1838–1917), German inventor]

mausolē'um *n.* Large, magnificent tomb, orig. that at Halicarnassus, ordered for himself by *Mausōl'us*, king of Caria (d. 353 B.C.), and erected by his queen Artemisia (d. 351).

mauve (mōv) *adj.* & *n.* Pale purple; delicate purple dye from coal-tar aniline. [L *malva* mallow]

māv'ĭs *n.* (poet.) Song-thrush.

maw *n.* Stomach (of animal); last of ruminant's four stomachs, abomasum (ill. RUMINANT).

mawk'ĭsh *adj.* Of faint sickly flavour; feebly sentimental. **mawk'ĭshly** *adv.* **mawk'ĭshnĕss** *n.* [obs. *mawk* maggot]

maw'seed *n.* Seed of opium poppy.

măxĭll'a *n.* Upper jaw in most vertebrates (ill. HEAD); component of mouth parts of many arthropods. **măxĭll'ary, măxĭll'ifŏrm** *adjs.*

măxĭll'ipĕd *n.* Crustacean's fore-limb modified so as to assist in mastication (ill. LOBSTER).

măx'ĭm[1] *n.* A general truth drawn from science or experience; principle, rule of conduct.

Măx'ĭm[2]. ~ (*automatic*) *gun*, a single-barrelled, rapid-firing, water-cooled machine-gun. [Sir H. S. *Maxim* (1840–1916), American-born inventor]

măx'ĭmalĭst *n.* Person who holds out for maximum of his demands and rejects compromises (esp. member of section of Russian Socialist Revolutionary Party, distinguished for terrorist activities *c* 1905–7).

Măxĭmĭl'ian[1] (-ly*a*n). Name of 2 Holy Roman Emperors: *Maximilian I* (1459–1519), reigned 1493–1519; *Maximilian II* (1527–76), reigned 1564–76.

Măxĭmĭl'ian[2] (-ly*a*n) (1832–67). Emperor of Mexico; brother of Austrian Emperor Francis Joseph; was offered throne of Mexico 1863; French troops supported him, but after their withdrawal he was defeated by republican forces, captured, and shot.

măx'ĭmīze *v.t.* Increase, magnify, to the utmost; interpret (doctrine etc.) vigorously. **măxĭmīzā'tion** *n.*

măx'ĭmum *n.* (pl. *-ima*). Highest possible or highest recorded magnitude or quantity (freq. attrib.).

măx'ĭmus *adj.* (In schools) Eldest of the name.

Măx'well[1], James Clerk: see CLERK-MAXWELL. ~ *demon*, (physics) a hypothetical intelligent being imagined by J. C. Maxwell to illustrate limitations of the second law of thermodynamics.

măx'well[2] *n.* The practical c.g.s. electromagnetic unit of magnetic flux, equal to the flux of magnetic induction per square centimetre in a magnetic field whose intensity is one gauss. [f. J. CLERK-MAXWELL]

may[1] *v. auxil.* (3rd sing. *may*, past t. *might* pr. mīt). Expressing possibility, permission, request, wish. **may'bē** *adv.* Perhaps.

May[2]. 5th month of the modern calendar; (fig.) bloom, prime; hawthorn blossom; (Camb. Univ., pl.) examinations held in May; boat races held during ~-*week*, late in May or early in June; ~-*day*, the first of May, traditionally celebrated with dancing round a maypole, gathering garlands of flowers, and the choice of a May queen; since 1889, the international Labour holiday; *may'flower*, flower that blooms in May, used locally for cowslip, lady's smock, etc.; the

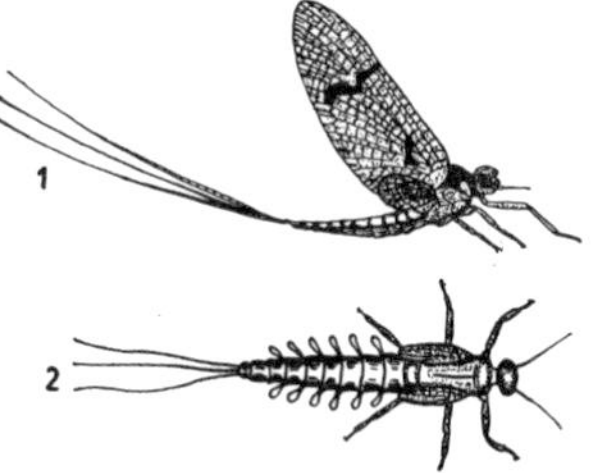

MAY-FLY (*EPHEMERA*)
1. Adult. 2. Nymph

Mayflower, the ship in which the PILGRIM FATHERS sailed to America from Southampton in 1620; *may'-fly*, an insect of the family *Ephemeridae*; imitation of this used by anglers; *may'pole*, gaily coloured pole decorated with flowers and ribbons, which is danced round on May-day; ~ *queen*, a girl chosen to be queen of the May and crowned with flowers. [L *Maius*, perh. f. the Roman goddess *Maia*]

ma'ya[1] (mah-) *n.* (Hind. philos.) Illusion, esp. the material world regarded as deceptive and unreal.

Ma'ya[2] (mah-). An Amer. Indian people, remarkable for their art and knowledge of astronomy, who lived from *c* 300 in Guatemala (the 'Old Empire') in city states, and migrated in 9th c. to Yucatan in E. Mexico ('New Empire'); here their culture partially merged with that of the Toltecs, but disintegrated in mid-15th c. owing to civil wars, and was found in decay by the invading Spaniards in 1511. **Ma'yan** *adj.* & *n.*

May'fair. District N. of Piccadilly, London, very fashionable in 19th c. [so called from annual fair held there in May from Stuart times until end of 18th c.]

Mayo (mā'ō). Western maritime county of Connaught, Eire.

mayonnaise' (-z) *n.* Sauce of yolk of eggs, oil, and vinegar used as dressing for salads, fish, etc.

mayor (mār̄) *n.* Head of municipal corporation of city or borough. **may'oral** *adj.* **mayoralty** (mār̄'-) *n.* Mayor's (period of) office. **mayoress** (mār̄'ĭs) *n.* Mayor's wife; lady who fulfils duties of mayor's wife.

măz'ard *n.* 1. (archaic) Head, skull. 2. Small black cherry.

Măzarin' (-ăṅ), Jules (1606–61). Italian papal legate in Paris, 1634; became cardinal, 1641, and succeeded Richelieu, 1642, as prime minister of France; ~ *Bible*, the earliest printed bible (printed prob. by Gutenberg before 1456), so called because the first known copy was in the library (*Bibliothèque Mazarine*) which Mazarin founded in Paris.

măzarine' (-ēn) *n.* & *adj.* Deep rich blue.

Măz'daism *n.* ZOROASTRIANISM. [Avestic *mazda* good principle in Persian theology (see AHURAMAZDA)]

māze *n.* Confusing and baffling network of winding and inter-

MAZE

communicating paths with hedges on either side, designed as a puzzle for those who try to find their way in it; labyrinth; (fig.) confusion, bewilderment. ~ *v.t.* Confuse, bewilder. **māz'y** *adj.* **māz'ĭly** *adv.* **māz'ĭnėss** *n.*

māz'er *n.* (hist.) Hardwood drinking bowl, usu. silver-mounted.

MAZER

Maple wood with silver rim and base

mazŭrk'a *n.* Lively Polish dance; music for this, in triple time. [Polish, = 'woman of province of Mazovia']

Mazzini (mădzēn'ĭ), Giuseppe (*c* 1805–72). Italian patriot and republican; agitated for the liberation of Italy, and spent many years in exile.

M.B. *abbrev. Medicinae baccalaureus* (= Bachelor of Medicine).

M.B.E. *abbrev.* Member (of the Order) of the British Empire.

m/c., Mc *abbrev.* Megacycle.

M.C. *abbrev.* Master of Ceremonies; Member of Congress (*or* Council); Military Cross.

M.C.C. *abbrev.* Marylebone Cricket Club.

M.Ch. *abbrev. Magister chirurgiae* (= Master of Surgery).

Md *abbrev.* Maryland.

M.D. *abbrev. Medicinae doctor* (= Doctor of Medicine); mentally deficient.

me[1] (mē, mĭ) *pron.*, obj. case of *I*.

me[2], **mi** (mē) *n.* 3rd note of hexachord and of major scale in 'movable-doh' systems; note E in 'fixed-doh' system. [see UT]

Me *abbrev.* Maine; *Maître* (French advocate's title).

mead[1] *n.* Alcoholic liquor of fermented honey and water.

mead[2] *n.* (poet.) = MEADOW.

meadow (mĕd'ō) *n.* Piece of grassland, esp. one used for hay; low-lying ground, esp. near river; ~-*sweet*, rosaceous plant, *Filipendula Ulmaria*, common in meadows, growing to a height of about 2 feet, with dense heads of creamy-white and very fragrant flowers.

mea'gre (-ger) *adj.* Lean, scanty. **mea'grely** *adv.* **mea'greness** *n.*

meal[1] *n.* Edible part of any grain or pulse (usu. exc. wheat) rather coarsely ground; (Sc.) = OATmeal; (U.S.) = INDIAN corn. **meal'y** *adj.* Of, like, meal; (of boiled potatoes) dry and powdery; ~-(*mouthed*), apt to mince matters, soft-spoken. **meal'ĭnėss** *n.*

meal[2] *n.* Customary, or any, occasion of taking food; food so taken; ~-*time*, usual time of eating.

meal'ie *n.* (usu. pl.) (S. Afr.) Maize; cob of Indian corn.

mean[1] *n.* 1. Condition, quality, amount, equally removed from two opposite extremes. 2. (pl.) That by which a result is brought about; pecuniary resources; wealth; ~*s test*, official inquiry into applicant's private resources, determining or limiting grant or allowance from public funds. ~ *adj.* Equally far from two extremes; (math.) intermediate in value, position, etc., between two other quantities, points, etc.; average. **mean'tīme, mean'-while** *advs.* (also *in the meantime*) In the intervening time.

mean[2] *adj.* Inferior, poor; shabby; ignoble, small-minded; stingy. **mean'ly** *adv.* **mean'nėss** *n.*

mean[3] *v.* (past. t. & part. *meant* pr. mĕnt) Purpose; design, destine; intend to convey or indicate; signify, import. **mean'ĭng** *n.* What is meant. **mean'ĭnglėss** *adj.* **mean'ĭnglėssnėss** *n.* **mean'-ĭng** *adj.* Expressive, significant. **mean'ĭngly** *adv.*

mėăn'der *v.i.* Wind about; wander at random. **mėăn'derĭng** *n.* **mė'ănder** *n.* (pl.) Sinuous windings, circuitous journey, winding paths, etc.; (sing., geog.) twisting course of river in its flood plain; (sing.) fret pattern (see FRET and ill.) [f. MAEANDER]

meas'les (-zlz) 1. *n.pl.* Acute infectious disease of man (*Rubeola*), caused by a virus, and characterized by fever, skin rash, and inflammation of the conjunctival membranes and air passages; *German* ~: see GERMAN[2]. 2. Disease in swine, caused by tapeworm. **meas'ly** *adj.* Of, affected with, measles; (slang) contemptible, worthless.

measure (mĕzh'*er*) *n.* Size or quantity found by measuring; vessel of standard capacity for measuring liquids; rod, tape, etc., for measuring; system of measuring; degree, extent, amount; quantity contained in another an exact number of times; *greatest common* ~, largest quantity exactly dividing each of two or more given quantities; prescribed extent or quantity; metre; time of piece of music; (archaic) dance; suitable action; legislative enactment. ~ *v.t.* Ascertain extent or quantity of by comparison with fixed standard or thing of known size; mark off; be of specified length etc.; deal *out*; bring into competition *with*. **meas'urable** *adj.* **meas'urably** *adv.* **meas'urement** *n.* **meas'-ured** *adj.* Rhythmical, regular in movement; carefully weighed.

meat *n.* Animal flesh as food, usu. excluding fish and poultry; ~-*fly*, bluebottle fly; (archaic) food; meal. **meat'y** *adj.*

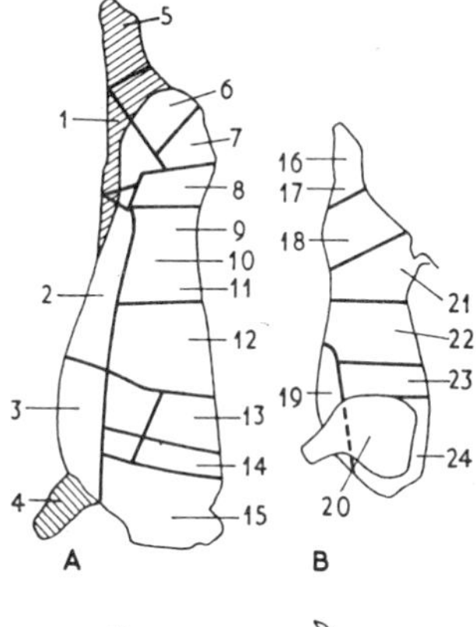

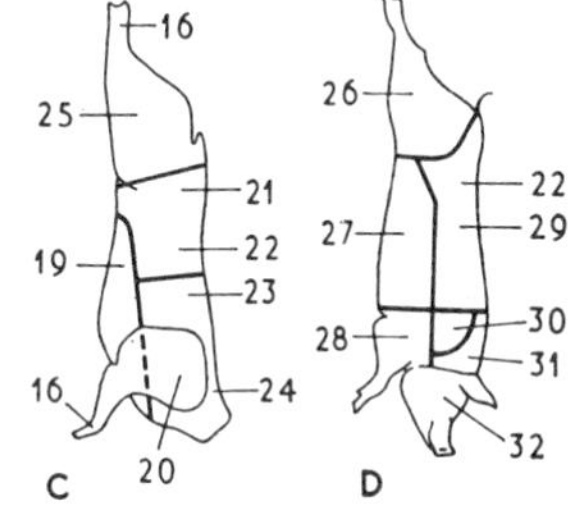

CUTS OF MEAT: A. BEEF (LONDON CUTTING). B. VEAL. C. MUTTON. D. PORK

A. 1. Thick flank or top rump. 2. Thin flank. 3. Brisket. 4. Shin. 5. Leg. 6. Topside and silverside. 7. Aitch-bone. 8. Rump steak. 9. Sirloin. 10. Undercut or fillet. 11. Wing rib. 12. Fore rib. 13. Middle rib. 14. Chuck. 15. Clod and sticking. B. 16. Shank. 17. Knuckle. 18. Fillet. 19. Breast. 20. Shoulder. 21. Chump-chops. 22. Loin. 23. Best end of neck. 24. Middle neck. C. 25. Leg. D. 26. Leg or gammon. 27. Belly. 28. Hand or forehock. 29. Tenderloin. 30. Blade bone. 31. Spare ribs or chine. 32. Head

Full of meat; (fig.) full of substance; of or like meat.

Meath (-dh). North-eastern maritime county of Leinster, Eire.

mėāt'us *n.* (pl. *-ūs, -uses*). (anat.) External opening of channel, duct, passage, in the body, as *auditory* ~, channel of the ear (ill. EAR).

Mĕcc'a. City in Arabia, the birthplace of Mohammed and the chief place of Moslem pilgrimage.

mėchăn'ic (-k-) *n.* Skilled workman, esp. one who makes or uses machinery. **mėchăn'ĭcs** *n.* Branch of applied mathematics treating of motion; science of machinery.

mėchăn'ĭcal (-k-) *adj.* Of machines or mechanism; like machines, automatic; working, produced, by machines; belonging to the science of mechanics; ~ *advantage*, ratio of load to effort; *the* ~ *powers*, the lever, wheel and axle, pulley, inclined plane, wedge, and screw. **mėchăn'ĭcally** *adv.* **mėchăn'ĭcalnėss** *n.*

mĕch'anĭsm (-k-) *n.* 1. Way a machine works; structure, parts, of a machine; (fig.) framework, structure, technique; (physiol.) system of mutually adapted parts working together. 2. (philos.) Theory that organic life admits of a mechanico-chemical explanation (opp. to VITALISM). **mĕch'anĭst** *n.* 1. Expert in mechanics. 2. (philos.) Adherent of mechanism. **mĕchanĭs'tĭc** *adj.*

mĕch'anīze (-k-) *v.t.* Make mechanical; substitute mechanical power for man- or horse-power in (army etc.). **mĕch'anīzā'tion** *n.*

Mĕch'lĭn (-k-). ~ (*lace*), the lace produced at Malines, a town in Belgium. [Flemish *Mechelen* Malines]

Mĕck'lenbûrg. Province of E. Germany, on Baltic coast; capital, Schwerin.

mĕd'al *n.* Piece of metal, usu. in form of coin, struck or cast with inscription and device to commemorate event etc., or awarded as distinction to soldier, scholar, etc., for services rendered (*illustration below*); ~ *play*, (golf) scored by strokes, not holes as in a match.

mėdăll'ion (-yon) *n.* Large medal; medal-shaped picture, panel, etc.

mĕd'allĭst *n.* 1. Winner of prize-medal. 2. Engraver, designer, of medals.

mĕdd'le *v.i.* Busy oneself unduly *with*; interfere *in*. **mĕdd'lesome** *adj.* Given to meddling. **mĕdd'lesomenėss** *n.*

Mēde *n.* One of the earliest Iranian inhabitants of Persia; *the law of the* ~*s and Persians*, an immutable law (see Dan. vi. 8). **Mēd'ĭan, Mēd'ĭsh** *adjs.*

Mėdē'a. (Gk legend) Sorceress, daughter of Aeetes king of Colchis; helped JASON to obtain the Golden Fleece; married him but was deserted by him in Corinth and avenged herself by killing their two children.

mēd'ĭa *n.* (pl. *-ae*). 1. (phonet.) Voiced stop consonant (*b, d, g*), as dist. f. TENUIS. 2. (anat.) Middle membrane of artery or vessel.

mediaeval: see MEDIEVAL.

mēd'ĭal *adj.* Situated in the middle; of average size. **mēd'ĭally** *adv.*

Mēd'ĭan[1]: see MEDE.

mēd'ĭan[2] *adj.* Situated in the middle. ~ *n.* 1. (anat.) Median artery, vein, nerve, etc. 2. (math.) Each of 3 lines drawn from the angles of a triangle to the middle points of the opposite sides and meeting in a point within it (ill. TRIANGLE).

mēd'ĭant *n.* (mus.) 3rd note of any scale (ill. SCALE).

mēd'ĭate *adj.* Involving an intermediary. **mēd'ĭately** (-tl-) *adv.* **mēd'ĭāte** *v.* Form connecting link; intervene (between two persons etc.) for purpose of reconciling them; be the medium for bringing about (result). **mēdĭā'tion, mēd'ĭātor** *ns.* **mēdĭatōr'ĭal, mēd'ĭatory** *adjs.*

mĕd'ĭcable *adj.* Admitting of remedial treatment.

mĕd'ĭcal *adj.* Of medicine; requiring, supplying, medical not surgical treatment; ~ *man*, doctor. ~ *n.* (colloq.) Student of medicine; (colloq.) medical examination for fitness.

mėdĭc'ament (*or* mĕd'-) *n.* Substance used in curative or palliative treatment.

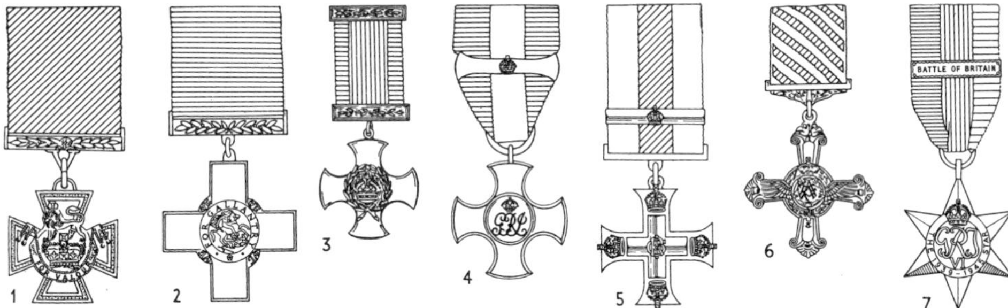

MEDALS AND DECORATIONS

1. Victoria Cross. 2. George Cross. 3. Distinguished Service Order. 4. Distinguished Service Cross. 5. Military Cross and Bar. 6. Distinguished Flying Cross. 7. 1939–45 Star, with clasp for Battle of Britain

mĕd'ĭcāte *v.t.* Treat medically; impregnate with medicinal substance. **mĕdĭcā'tion** *n.*

Mĕd'ĭci (-chĭ). The ruling family of Florence from 1434; orig. merchants and bankers; grand dukes of Tuscany 1569–1737; patrons of art and letters, esp. Cosimo dei (or de') ~ (1389–1464), his son Piero (1416–69), Piero's son Lorenzo 'the Magnificent' (1449–92), and Lorenzo's son Giovanni (1475–1521), who became Pope Leo X; Giulio (1478–1534) became Pope Clement VII; Catarina (CATHERINE DE MÉDICIS) married Henri II; Maria (MARIE DE MÉDICIS) married Henri IV. **Mĕdĭcē'an** *adj.*

medĭ'cĭnal *adj.* Of medicine; curative.

mĕdicine (mĕd'sn) *n.* 1. Art of restoring and preserving health, esp. by means of remedial substances and regulation of diet etc., as opp. to surgery. 2. Substance taken internally to cure disease; (among savages) spell, charm, fetish; hence, *~-man*, magician, witch-doctor. ~ *v.t.* Give medicine to, cure with medicine.

mĕd'ĭcō *n.* (joc.) Doctor.

mĕdiēv'al, mĕdiaev'al *adj.* Of the Middle Ages. **mĕdĭēv'alĭst, mĕdĭēv'alĭsm** *ns.*

Mĕdin'a (-ē-). City in Arabia, to which Mohammed fled from Mecca and where he died and was buried.

mēd'ĭōcre (-k*er*) *adj.* Of middling quality, indifferent. **mēdĭŏc'rĭty** *n.* Mediocre quality; mediocre person.

mĕd'ĭtāte *v.* Plan mentally; exercise the mind in contemplation *on*. **mĕdĭtā'tion** *n.* **mĕd'ĭtātive** *adj.* **mĕd'ĭtātively** (-vl-) *adv.*

mĕdĭterrān'ėan *adj.* (Of land) remote from coast; (of water surfaces) land-locked; (of peoples) living near the *M~* (*Sea*), inland sea lying between S. Europe and N. Africa, communicating with the Atlantic by the Strait of Gibraltar and with the Persian Gulf by the Suez Canal.

mēd'ĭum *n.* (pl. *-s*, *-ia*). 1. Middle quality, degree, etc. 2. Means, agency. 3. (art) Method by which work of art is produced, branch of art (e.g. painting, sculpture); (also) liquid substance in which pigments are ground in preparation of paint, substance which makes pigment adhere to ground (e.g. oil, gum). 4. (spiritualism) Person claiming to be the vehicle for spirits' communication with human beings (*mental* ~) or to have the power of moving objects at a distance (*physical* ~). ~ *adj.* Intermediate between two degrees etc.; average, moderate; ~ *wave*, electromagnetic wave having a length between 100 and 800 metres (in broadcasting, between 200 and 550 metres).

mēd'ĭumĭsm *n.* Profession or occupation of a spiritualistic medium. **mēdĭumĭs'tĭc** *adj.*

mĕd'lar *n.* (Tree, *Mespilus germanica*, with) fruit like small brown apple, eaten when decayed.

mĕd'ley *n.* Heterogeneous mixture.

Médoc (mādŏk'). A wine-growing district in the Bordeaux region; the wine made there.

mėdŭll'a *n.* 1. Marrow of bones; spinal marrow. 2. Central parts of some organs, esp. kidney (ill. KIDNEY). 3. Cellular inner part of animal hair. 4. Soft internal tissue of plants (ill. STEM). 5. ~ (*oblongata*), brain-stem, prolonged hindmost segment of brain (ill. BRAIN). **mėdŭll'ary** (*or* mĕd'-) *adj.*

Mėdūs'a. (Gk legend) One of the three Gorgons: see GORGON; she was the only mortal one of the three and was slain by PERSEUS. **mėdūs'a** *n.* (pl. *-sae*). (zool.) Jellyfish, pelagic sexual stage in life-cycle of hydrozoan coelenterate.

meed *n.* (poet.) Reward; merited portion (*of* praise etc.).

meek *adj.* Piously humble and submissive; tamely submissive. **meek'ly** *adv.* **meek'nėss** *n.*

meer'kat: see SURICATE.

meer'schaum (-shm) *n.* Hydrated magnesium silicate, occurring in soft white masses, used for tobacco-pipe bowls; pipe with bowl made of this. [Ger., = 'sea-foam']

meet[1] *adj.* (archaic) Suitable, fit. **meet'ly** *adv.* **meet'nėss** *n.*

meet[2] *v.* (past t. and past part. *mĕt*). Come into contact or company (with); assemble; become perceptible to; satisfy (demand); experience. ~ *n.* Assembly for hunting etc.

meet'ĭng *n.* (esp.) Assembly of people for entertainment, worship, etc.; duel; race-meeting; *~-house*, Friends' place of worship.

M.E.F. *abbrev.* Middle East Forces.

mĕga- *prefix.* Great; also prefixed to names of units of measurement, force, etc., with sense 'a million times', as in *megacycle*, *megadyne*, *megavolt*, *megawatt*, etc.

mĕgacėphăl'ĭc *adj.* Large-headed.

mĕg'acȳcle *n.* 1,000,000 cycles, as unit in measuring frequency of electromagnetic waves (abbrev. m/c.).

Mėgaer'a (-gēr*a*). One of the Furies: see FURY.

mĕg'alĭth *n.* Large stone used in construction or as a monument. **mĕgalĭth'ĭc** *adj.*

mĕgalomān'ĭa *n.* Insanity of self-exaltation; passion for big things. **mĕgalomān'ĭăc** *n.*

Mĕgalosaur'us *n.* Extinct genus of huge carnivorous reptiles.

mĕg'aphōne *n.* Large speaking-trumpet, used for making the voice travel to a distance.

mĕg'apŏd, -pōde *n.* Member of family of birds, almost all in Australian region, whose eggs are left to hatch without incubation.

Mĕg'ara. Ancient Greek city on the Saronic Gulf. **Megār'ian, Megār'ĭc** *adjs.* ~ *School*, a school of philosophy established at Megara by Eucleides, a pupil of Socrates, noted for its study of dialectics and its invention of logical fallacies or puzzles.

mĕg'ascōpe *n.* Kind of camera obscura or magic lantern for throwing a magnified image on to a screen. **mĕgascŏp'ĭc** *adj.* 1. Pertaining to a megascope. 2. MACROSCOPIC.

mĕg'ăss *n.* Fibrous residue after expression of sugar from cane.

Mĕgathēr'ĭum *n.* Extinct genus of large herbivorous sloth-like mammals.

mĕg'aton (-tŭn) *n.* Explosive force equal to 1,000,000 tons of TNT.

mĕg'awatt (-ŏt) *n.* 1,000,000 watts (abbrev. mW., MW.).

mĕgilp' (-g-) *n.* Any of various preparations of varnish, oil, etc., which artists mix with paint to facilitate handling or hasten drying.

mē'grĭm *n.* Severe headache, usu. on one side only, migraine; whim; (pl.) low spirits, vapours; (pl.) staggers in horses and cattle. [Fr. *migraine*) f. Gk *hemi-* half, *kranion* skull)]

meiōs'ĭs (mī-) *n.* (pl. *-ōsēs*). 1. Understatement, freq. ironical or jocular. 2. (biol.) Splitting of cell or nucleus without increase in number of chromosomes, so that each of the resulting two cells or nuclei has only half the chromosomes of the original one (cf. MITOSIS). 3. var. of. MIOSIS. **meiŏt'ĭc** *adj.*

Meissen (mīs'n). German town (near Dresden, Saxony) where the earliest European porcelain factory was founded, 1710, and still exists; *~ china*, porcelain made there (freq. called *Dresden china*).

Meissonier (mĕsŏnyā'), Jean Louis Ernest (1811–91). French painter of military and historical subjects.

meis'tersĭnger (mī-, -z-) *n.pl.* German lyric poets and musicians of 14th–17th centuries, organized in guilds and using elaborate technique; (sing.) member of such guild. [Ger., = 'mastersingers']

Mĕkh'ĭtar (-χ-). Armenian monk; founder (1701) of the **Mekhitār'ĭst** (R.C.) congregation of Armenian monks established in the island of San Lazzaro, S. of Venice.

mĕlanchōl'ĭa (-k-) *n.* Mental illness characterized by depression (obsolesc. as psychol. term). [Gk *melas* black, *khole* bile]

mĕlanchŏl'ĭc (-k-) *adj.* (Of person) melancholy; liable to melancholy.

mĕl'ancholy (-k-) *n.* 1. (Habitual tendency to) sadness and depression; pensive sadness. 2. (hist.) One of the four HUMOURS. ~ *adj.* Sad, saddening.

Mĕlănch'thŏn (-ngkth-). Graecized name of Philip Schwartzerd (1497–1560), German humanist, who was professor of Greek at Wittenberg and a supporter of Luther and the Reformation. [Gk *melas* black, *hkthon* earth]

Mĕlanē'sĭa (-z-). General term for islands of W. Pacific including New Hebrides, New Caledonia, Fiji, etc. **Melanēs'ian** *adj.* & *n.* [Gk *melas* black (from the colour of the predominant native race, the Papuans), *nēsos* island]

mélange(mālahṅzh') *n.* Mixture, medley.

mĕl'anĭsm *n.* Darkness of colour resulting from abnormal development of black pigment in epidermis, hair, etc.

mĕlanŏch'rōī(-k-) *n.pl.* Smooth-haired class of mankind with dark hair and pale complexion. **mĕlanŏch'roid** *adj.*

mĕlanōs'ĭs *n.* Morbid deposit, abnormal development, of black pigment in tissue.

Mĕl'ba, Dame Nellie. Helen Porter Mitchell (1859–1931), Australian soprano singer, born near Melbourne, from which she took her professional name.

Mĕl'bourne[1]. City of Australia, capital of Victoria.

Mĕl'bourne[2], William Lamb, Viscount Melbourne (1779–1848). English statesman; prime minister 1835–41.

Mĕl'chĭŏr (-k-). Traditional name of one of the MAGI, a king of Nubia.

Mĕlchĭz'ĕdĕk (-lk-). In Gen. xiv. 18, king of Salem and the priest of the most high God, to whom Abraham paid tithes; he is sometimes quoted as the type of self-originating power, with reference to Heb. vii. 3–4.

mĕld *n.* In the game of canasta, 3 or more cards of the same value.

Mĕlĕāg'er[1] (-g-). (Gk myth.) A hero, at whose birth the Fates declared that he would die when a brand then on the fire was consumed; his mother Althaea seized the brand and kept it; when Meleager grew up he slew a boar which was ravaging the country, but his fellow huntsmen, Althaea's brothers, quarrelled with him for giving away its head to the huntress Atalanta, and he killed them; whereupon Althaea threw the brand into the fire.

Mĕlĕāg'er[2](-g-)(*c* 140–*c* 70 B.C.). Greek poet; lived at Tyre and Cos; author of short poems on love and death, and of many epigrams in the Greek Anthology.

mêlée (mĕl'ā) *n.* Mixed fight, skirmish.

mĕl'īne *adj.* (zool.) Of the subfamily *Melinae*, the badgers and skunks.

mĕl'iorāte *v.* Improve. **mĕliorā'tion** *n.*

mĕl'iorĭsm *n.* Doctrine that the world may be made better by human effort (opp. to PESSIMISM).

mĕl'iorĭst *n.*

mĕllĭf'erous *adj.* Yielding, producing, honey.

mĕllĭf'luous (-lōō-) *adj.* (Of voice, words, music) sweet-sounding. **mĕllĭf'luence** *n.* **mĕllĭf'luent** *adj.*

mĕll'ow (-ō) *adj.* Soft and rich in flavour, colour, or sound; softened by age or experience; genial, jovial; partly intoxicated. **mĕll'owly** *adv.* **mĕll'owness** *n.* **mĕll'ow** *v.* Make or become mellow; ripen.

mĕlŏd'ĕon, -dĭon, -dĭum *n.* Wind-instrument with keyboard and bellows worked by pedals; kind of accordion.

mĕlŏd'ĭc *adj.* Of melody; ~ *minor*, minor scale in which 6th and 7th are sharpened when ascending and flattened when descending (so called as more suitable for melody than HARMONIC minor; ill. SCALE).

mĕlōd'ious *adj.* Of, producing, melody; sweet-sounding. **mĕlōd'iously** *adv.* **mĕlōd'iousnĕss** *n.*

mĕl'odĭst *n.* Singer; composer of melodies.

mĕl'odrama (-rah-) *n.* Sensational dramatic piece with violent appeals to emotions and happy ending; language, behaviour, suggestive of this; (formerly) play, or passage in play, using spoken voice against musical background. **mĕlodramăt'ĭc** *adj.* **mĕlodramăt'ĭcally** *adv.* **mĕlodrăm'atĭst** *n.* **mĕlodrăm'atīze** *v.t.*

mĕl'odȳ *n.* Sweet music; arrangement of single notes in musically expressive succession; principal part in harmonized music.

mĕl'on *n.* Kinds of gourd bearing sweet fruit, esp. the *musk-~*, *Cucumis melo*, and *water-~*, *Citrullus vulgaris*.

Mĕl'ŏs. Ancient name of the island now called Milo, in the Aegean Sea.

Mĕlpŏm'ĕnē. (Gk myth.) The muse of tragedy.

mĕlt *v.* (past part. *mĕl'tĕd*, *mōlten*). (Cause to) become liquefied by heat; soften, be softened; dissolve; pass imperceptibly *into*; ~ *away*, dissolve, disappear; ~ *down*, reduce (metal articles etc.) to molten metal for use as raw material. ~ *n.* Molten metal.

mĕl'ton *n.* Kind of cloth with very close-cut nap, used for overcoats etc.; *M~ Mowbray* (mōb-) *pie*, kind of pork pasty. [*Melton Mowbray*, town in Leicestershire]

Mĕl'vĭlle, Herman (1819–91). American sailor, author of 'Moby Dick' and other adventure stories.

mem. *abbrev. Memento* (= remember).

mĕm'ber *n.* 1. Limb or other bodily organ, constituent portion of complex structure. 2. Person belonging to a society etc.; *M ~ of Parliament*, (abbrev. M.P.) person formally elected to the House of Commons. **mĕm'bershĭp** *n.*

mĕm'brāne *n.* Fine layer of connective tissue enveloping an organ, lining a cavity, or separating adjacent parts in a living organism; (palaeog.) skin of parchment; *cell ~*, surface layer of living cell limiting the diffusion of its contents. **mĕmbrān'ĕous, mĕm'branous** *adjs.*

mĕmĕn'tō *n.* Object serving as reminder or warning, or kept as memorial; ~ *mori* (= remember you must die), warning or reminder of death, e.g. skull.

Mĕm'nŏn. (Gk legend) An Ethiopian prince slain at Troy; a colossal statue at Thebes (in reality that of Amenhotep), which gave forth a musical note when struck by the rays of the rising sun, was supposed to represent him.

mĕmo. *abbrev.* Memorandum.

mĕm'oir (-wâr) *n.* Record, history, written from personal knowledge or special sources of information; (auto-)biography; essay on learned subject by expert.

mĕm'orabĭl'ĭa *n.pl.* Memorable things.

mĕm'orable *adj.* Likely or worthy to be remembered. **mĕmorabĭl'ĭty** *n.* **mĕm'orably** *adv.*

mĕmorăn'dum *n.* (pl. *-da*). Note to help the memory, record for future use; informal letter without signature etc.

mĕmôr'ial *adj.* Commemorative, of memory. ~ *n.* Memorial object, custom, etc.; (usu. pl.) chronicle; statement of facts as basis of petition etc. **mĕmôr'ialīze** *v.t.* Commemorate; address memorial to.

mĕm'orīze *v.t.* Put on record; commit to memory.

mĕm'orȳ *n.* 1. Faculty by which things are recalled to or kept in the mind; recollection; posthumous repute; length of time over which memory extends. 2. Part of computer in which information is stored during its operation.

Mĕm'phĭs. Early capital of ancient Egypt, on W. bank of Nile S. of Cairo.

mĕm'-sah'ĭb *n.* (In India) European married lady.

mĕn'ace *n.* Threat. ~ *v.t.* Threaten. **mĕn'acĭngly** *adv.*

ménage (mĕnahzh') *n.* Household; household management.

menă'gerie (-jerĭ) *n.* Collection of wild animals kept in captivity for exhibition etc.

Mĕn'ai (-nī) **Strait.** Channel separating Anglesey from NW. Wales.

Mĕnăn'der (342–291 B.C.). Greek poet and writer of comedies.

mĕnd *v.* Restore to sound condition, repair; improve; rectify; regain health. ~ *n.* Repaired place; *on the ~*, improving.

mĕndā'cious(-shus) *adj.* Lying. **mĕndā'ciously** *adv.* **mĕndă'cĭty** *n.*

Mĕn'del, Gregor Johann (1822–84). Abbot of Brünn, Moravia; his experiments in the cross-fertilization of sweet peas led to the formulation of ~*'s law* of heredity. Mendel showed that certain characteristics, as height, colour, etc., depend on the presence of hereditary determining factors (later called *genes*) which may be either *dominant* or *recessive*. **Mendēl'ian** *adj.* **Měn'dělism** *n.*

Mĕndeleev (-lā'ĕf), Dmitri Ivanovich (1834–1907). Russian chemist; discovered the PERIODIC law.

mĕndelēv'ium *n.* A TRANSURANIC element, symbol Mv, at. no. 101.

Mĕn'delssohn-Bartholdy (-sn *or* -sōn), Felix (1809–47). German-Jewish musical composer of oratorios, concert-overtures, etc.

mĕn'dicant *n.* & *adj.* Beggar; begging; (member of religious order) living entirely on alms. **mĕn'dicancy, mĕndi'city** *ns.*

Mĕnėlā'us. (Gk legend) King of Sparta; brother of Agamemnon, and husband of Helen, who was stolen from him by Paris and restored after the fall of Troy.

mĕnhād'en *n.* Kind of large herring (*Brevoortia menhaden*) found on E. coast of N. America, used for manure and yielding a valuable oil. [Amer. Ind.]

mĕn'hir (-ēr) *n.* Tall upright monumental stone. [Breton, = 'long stone']

mēn'ial *adj.* & *n.* Domestic (servant); servile, degrading; sordid. **mēn'ially** *adv.*

Mĕn'in Gate. Eastern exit from the town of Ypres; now the site of a memorial to British soldiers of the war of 1914–18 who have no known graves.

mĕningit'is (-j-) *n.* Inflammation of the meninges.

mėning'ocēle (-ngg-) *n.* Tumour on the meninges.

mēn'inx *n.* (pl. *mėnin'gēs* pr. -z). Any of 3 membranes (*dura mater, arachnoid, pia mater*) enveloping brain and spinal cord (ill. SPINE). **mėnin'geal** (-j-) *adj.*

mėnis'cus *n.* (pl. *-cī*). Lens convex on one side and concave on the other (ill. LENS); convex or concave upper surface of a column of liquid; (math.) figure of crescent form.

Mĕnn'onite *adj.* & *n.* (Member) of a Christian sect which arose in Friesland in the 16th c., maintaining principles similar to those of the Anabaptists; they baptize only after confession of faith and will not take oaths or fight or undertake State service; German Mennonites settled in Russia under Catherine the Great, but when rendered liable to conscription in the 19th c. many emigrated to U.S. and Brazil; most are farmers. [f. *Menno* Simons (1492–1559), their early leader]

mĕnŏl'ogy *n.* Calendar, esp. that of Greek Church, with biographies of saints and martyrs.

mĕn'opause (-z) *n.* Period of life, generally between 40 and 50, in women, at which menstruation ceases.

mĕnorrhā'gia *n.* Excessive menstruation.

mĕn'sēs (-z) *n.pl.* Discharge of blood and tissue debris from uterus of primates, normally at monthly intervals. [L, = 'months']

Mĕn'shėvik *n.* Member of the moderate Socialist party in Russia, which was in the minority at the Socialist conference in 1903; at the Revolution of 1917, after being in power for a brief period, the Mensheviks were overthrown by Lenin and the BOLSHEVIKS. [Russ. *menshe* smaller]

mĕn'strual (-ōō-) *adj.* 1. (astrol.) Monthly. 2. (physiol.) Of the menses. **mĕn'struāte** *v.i.* Discharge the menses. **mĕn'struā'tion** *n.*

mĕn'struum (-ōōŭ-) *n.* (pl.- *a*). Solvent (lit. and fig.).

mĕn'sūrable *adj.* Measurable; (mus.) having fixed time or rhythm.

mĕn'sūral *adj.* Of measure; (mus.) measurable.

mĕnsūrā'tion *n.* Measuring; (math.) branch of mathematics concerned with measurement of lengths, areas, and volumes.

mĕn'tal *adj.* Of, relating to, the mind; (slang) feeble-minded; ~ *age*, age at which normal children reach a certain stage of mental development, used as standard for assessing the feeble-minded or precocious (e.g. a subnormal boy of 17 who has the mental development of a normal 10-year-old has a mental age of 10); ~ *arithmetic*, calculations performed without the use of written figures; ~ *deficiency*, congenital feeble-mindedness, condition of person who is not an idiot or insane but is unequal to the conduct of ordinary affairs; ~ *home, hospital*, institutions for care of persons suffering from mental disorder or defect; ~ *patient*, one under care for disordered mind. **mĕn'tally** *adv.*

mĕntăl'ity *n.* Mental quality; mode of thinking; (degree of) intellectual power; (loosely) mind, disposition, character.

mĕn'thŏl *n.* Crystalline camphor-like substance obtained from mint-oils.

mĕn'tion *v.t.* Refer to; state incidentally. ~ *n.* Mentioning.

Mĕn'tŏr. (Gk legend) Friend of Odysseus and guide and adviser of the young Telemachus. **mĕn'tŏr** *n.* Experienced and trusted counsellor.

mĕn'ū *n.* Bill of fare. [Fr., = 'detailed list', f. *adj.* = 'small']

Mĕphĭstŏph'ėlēs (-z). In the legend of FAUST, the demon to whom Faust sold his soul. **Mĕphistophēl'ėan, -līan** *adj.*

mĕphit'is *n.* Noxious emanation, esp. from the earth; noisome stench. **mĕphit'ic** *adj.*

mêr'cantīle *adj.* Trading; of merchants or trade; mercenary, fond of bargaining; ~ *marine*, shipping employed in commerce; ~ *system*, that based on the old economic theory that money is the only form of wealth and that the object of trade is to export goods at the highest prices. **mêr'cantīlism, mêr'cantīlist** *ns.*

Mêrcāt'or, Gerardus. Latinized name of *Gerhard Kremer* (1512–94), Flemish geographer; inventor of a system of projecting maps (~*'s projection*) in which the globe is projected on to a cylinder and the meridians of longitude are at right angles to the parallels of latitude (ill. PROJECTION).

mêr'cėnary *adj.* Working merely for money or other reward; having love of money as motive; hired (now only of soldiers serving in a foreign army). ~ *n.* Hired soldier. **mêr'cenarinėss** *n.*

mêr'cer *n.* Dealer in textile fabrics, esp. silks etc. **mêr'cery** *n.* [L *merx* merchandise]

mêr'cerīze *v.t.* Prepare (cotton) for dyeing by treating with solution of caustic potash etc. which produces a silky lustre. [John *Mercer* (1791–1866), inventor]

mêrch'andīse (-z) *n.* Mercantile commodities; goods for sale.

mêrch'ant *n.* Wholesale trader, esp. one trading with foreign countries; (slang, esp. in compounds) person, individual (chiefly in disparagement, as *speed-*~); *merchantman*, merchant ship; ~ *service*, mercantile marine. **mêrch'antable** *adj.* Saleable, marketable.

Mêr'cia. An Anglian kingdom founded in the 6th c. by the *Mercians* (= men of the border) between Wessex, Northumbria, and Wales; under Canute and his successors until the Norman Conquest Mercia was an earldom.

mêr'ciful *adj.* Disposed to mercy; compassionate. **mêr'cifully** *adv.* **mêr'cifulnėss** *n.*

mêr'cilėss *adj.* Showing no mercy; pitiless, unrelenting. **mêr'cilėssly** *adv.* **mêr'cilėssnėss** *n.*

mercūr'ial *adj.* Born under the planet Mercury; of or like mercury or quicksilver; sprightly, ready-witted, and volatile (from supposed influence of the planet). **mercūr'ially** *adv.* **mercūriăl'ity** *n.*

mercūr'ialism *n.* Mercurial poisoning.

mercūr'ialīze *v.t.* Affect with mercury.

mercūr'ic *adj.* (chem.) Of compounds in which mercury has a valency of two; ~ *chloride* ($HgCl_2$), corrosive sublimate, formerly used in dilute aqueous solution as an antiseptic for wounds and for sterilizing non-metallic surgical instruments.

mercūr'ous *adj.* (chem.) Of compounds in which mercury has a valency of one; ~ *chloride* ($HgCl$), calomel.

Mêr'cūry[1]. 1. Roman god of eloquence, skill, trading, and thieving, and messenger of the gods, early identified with HERMES; represented as a young man with winged sandals and hat and bearing the caduceus. 2. The planet nearest to the sun, the smallest planet of the solar system (ill. PLANET). [L *Mercurius*, f. *merx* merchandise]

mĕr'cūry[2] *n.* Silvery-white metallic element of high density, symbol Hg, at. no. 80, at. wt 200·59, pop. called *quicksilver*; its high density, its property of not wetting glass, and the wide range of temperature at which it is liquid make it valuable for scientific instruments esp. thermometers and barometers; it dissolves many metals, forming amalgams, and its compounds are used in medicine as purgatives and stimulants.

mĕr'cy *n.* Forbearance and compassion to one who has no claim to kindness; disposition to forgive; an act of mercy, a gift of God, a blessing; *~-killer*, one who kills another with the intention of preventing needless suffering; *~-seat*, golden covering of Ark of Covenant; hence, throne of God.

mēre[1] *n.* Lake.

mēre[2] *adj.* Pure, unmixed; barely or only what it is said to be, nothing more than. **mēre'ly** *adv.*

Mĕ'rėdith, George (1828–1909). English novelist and poet; author of 'Diana of the Crossways', 'The Ordeal of Richard Feverel', 'The Egoist', etc.

mĕrėtrĭ'cious (-sh*us*) *adj.* Showily attractive, flashy. **mĕrėtrĭ'ciously** *adv.* **mĕrėtrĭ'ciousnėss** *n.* [L *meretrix* harlot]

mergăn'ser *n.* Various fish-eating ducks of great diving powers, with long narrow serrated bill hooked at the tip, inhabiting northern parts of Old World and N. America. [L *mergus* diver, *anser* goose]

mĕrge *v.* Lose, cause (thing) to lose, character or identity in something else; join or blend gradually (*into, with*). **mĕrg'er** *n.* Absorption of estate etc. in another; consolidation of one trading company or firm with another.

mėrĭd'ian *n.* Great circle passing through celestial poles and zenith of any place on earth's surface (ill. CELESTIAL) or passing through the poles and any place on the earth (ill. EARTH); point at which star or sun attains its highest altitude; prime, full splendour. *~ adj.* Of noon; (fig.) of the period of greatest splendour, vigour, etc.

mėrĭd'ional *adj.* Of the south (of France, or of Europe); southern. *~ n.* Inhabitant of a southern country, esp. of France or S. Europe.

Mérimée (mārēmā'), Prosper (1803–70). French novelist and playwright.

meringue' (-răng) *n.* Confection made of sugar and beaten white of egg, baked till crisp; thin case of meringue filled with whipped cream.

meri'nō (-rē-) *n.* Variety of sheep with fine silky wool, orig. bred in Spain; fine yarn or soft fabric of this wool; fine woollen yarn.

Mĕrĭŏn'ėthshire. County of N. Wales.

mĕ'rĭstĕm *n.* (bot.) Cell or region where growth is initiated.

mĕ'rĭt *n.* Quality of deserving well or being entitled to reward or gratitude; goodness; (pl.) good works, deserts; intrinsic rights and wrongs (of case etc., esp. law); *Order of M ~* (abbrev. O.M.), British order, limited in membership, for high and distinguished civil or military service, founded in 1902. *~ v.t.* Deserve (reward, punishment).

mĕrĭtŏr'ious *adj.* Deserving praise, reward, etc. (often as term of limited praise, = well-meant, well-meaning). **mĕrĭtŏr'iously** *adv.* **mĕrĭtŏr'iousnėss** *n.*

mĕrle *n.* (archaic) Blackbird.

mĕr'lĭn[1] *n.* Small European falcon, *Falco aesalon*.

Mĕr'lĭn[2]. In the Arthurian legend, a magician and bard who aided and supported King Arthur and made the Round Table.

mĕrl'on *n.* Solid part of embattled parapet between two embrasures (ill. CASTLE).

mĕr'maid, mĕr'man *ns.* Fabled being inhabiting the sea, with head and trunk of a woman (or man) and tail of a fish. [f. MERE[1]]

MERMAID

Mĕr'maid Tavern. A tavern in Bread Street, near Cheapside, London (with an entrance in Friday Street); meeting-place of the Friday Street Club, founded by Sir Walter Ralegh and frequented by Shakespeare, Ben Jonson, and other wits and men of letters; it was destroyed in the Great Fire in 1666.

mĕ'roblăst *n.* (physiol.) Ovum of two parts, one of which is germinal and the other nutritive.

mĕrohĕd'ral *adj.* (of crystal) Having less than the full number of faces of the type of symmetry to which it belongs.

Mĕrŏvĭn'gian (-j-) *adj.* & *n.* (Member) of the line of Frankish kings founded by Clovis (481–511) and reigning in Gaul and Germany until 752.

mĕrr'y *adj.* Mirthful, hilarious; full of animated enjoyment; slightly tipsy; *make ~*, be festive; *~-andrew*, mountebank's assistant; clown, buffoon, (also fig.); *~-go-round*, revolving machine carrying wooden horses or cars, on or in which people ride; a roundabout; *~-making*, festivity; *~ monarch*, Charles II of England; *~-thought*, forked bone between neck and breast of bird; wish-bone. **mĕ'rrĭly** *adv.* **mĕ'rrĭment, mĕ'rrĭnėss** *ns.*

Mĕrs'ey (-zĭ). English river rising in the Peak district and flowing into the Irish Sea between Cheshire and Lancashire.

Mĕrt'on Cŏll'ege. An Oxford college founded in 1264 by Walter de Merton (d. 1277), bishop of Rochester and chancellor of England.

me'sa (mā-) *n.* High rocky tableland with precipitous sides.

mésalliance (mĕzăl'ĭahṅs) *n.* Marriage with a social inferior.

mĕscăl' *n.* Strong intoxicant distilled in Mexico etc. from the fermented juice (*pulque*) of the American aloe; the plant itself; *~ buttons*, button-shaped tops of the plant, dried and used as intoxicant.

mĕs'calĭne *n.* Alkaloid obtained from mescal buttons, occas. used in medicine, and capable of producing hallucinations.

mĕsĕmbrĭăn'thėmum, -brȳ- *n.* Genus of S. African herbs and shrubs with bright pink or white flowers, which open around midday; fig-marigolds. [Gk *mesēmbria* noon, *anthemon* flower]

mĕs'entery *n.* Fold of peritoneum attaching intestinal canal to posterior wall of abdomen. **mĕsentĕ'rĭc** *adj.* **mĕsĕnterĭt'ĭs** *n.* Inflammation of the mesentery.

mĕsh *n.* One of the spaces between the threads of a net; (pl.) net. *~ v.* Catch in a net; (of gear-wheels etc.) engage, interlock.

mesĭal (mēz'-, mĕs'-) *adj.* Of, in, directed towards, middle line of a body. **mes'ĭally** *adv.*

Mĕs'mer (-z-), Friedrich Anton (1733–1805). Austrian doctor, popularizer of hypnotism, called **mĕs'merism** after him. **mĕsmĕ'rĭc** *adj.* **mĕs'merĭst** *n.* **mĕs'merīze** *v.t.*

mesne (mēn) *adj.* (law) Intermediate; *~ lord*, one who is himself a tenant of a superior lord but has tenants holding from him; *~ profits*, those received from an estate by an occupier in unlawful possession, as e.g. after the expiry of a lease.

mĕs'ocărp *n.* (bot.) Middle layer of pericarp (ill. FRUIT).

mĕs'odĕrm *n.* (physiol.) Middle of 3 layers of cells formed by embryo at early stage, layer from which skeletal muscles, heart muscle, and blood are developed.

mĕsogăs'ter *n.* Membrane attaching stomach to dorsal walls of abdomen **mĕsogăs'tric** *adj.*

mĕsolĭth'ĭc *adj.* (archaeol.) Of the Stone Age between palaeolithic and neolithic.

mĕs'ŏn *n.* Fundamental particle intermediate in mass between proton and electron, found in cosmic rays and atomic nuclei.

mĕs'opause *n.* Top of the mesosphere.

mĕs'ophȳll *n.* (bot.) Inner tissue of leaf (ill. LEAF).

Mĕsopotām'ĭa. The larger part of modern Iraq, between the rivers Tigris and Euphrates; centre of the ancient civilizations of SUMER, ASSYRIA, and BABYLON; scene (1915–16) of a disastrous British campaign against the Turks, ending with the surrender of Kut. **Mĕsopotām'ĭan** *adj.* [Gk, = '(country) between the rivers' (*mesos* middle, *potamos* river)]

mĕs'osphēre *n.* Part of atmosphere above stratosphere, in which temperature generally falls with increasing height.

mĕsothŏr'ĭum *n.* (chem.) A radio-active element, a member of the thorium decay series, symbol MsTh, at. no. 88, at. wt 228.

mĕs'otrŏn *n.* = MESON.

mĕsozō'ĭc *adj.* (geol.) Of the series of rock-formations above the Palaeozoic, comprising the triassic, jurassic, and cretaceous systems; of the era to which these belong. **Mĕsozō'ĭc** *n.* These formations; this era (ill. GEOLOGY).

Mĕs'pŏt. Slang abbrev. of MESOPOTAMIA.

mĕs'quit(e) (-kēt) *n.* N. American shrub of mimosa family, the seed-pods of which are used as cattle-fodder. [Mexican *misquitl*]

mĕss *n.* 1. Portion of food; concoction, medley. 2. Dirty or untidy state. 3. Company of persons who take meals together, esp. in armed forces; taking of such a meal, place where it is eaten. ~ *v.* 1. Make dirty or untidy; potter *about.* 2. Take meals, esp. as member of a mess. **mĕss'y** *adj.* Untidy, dirty. **mĕss'ĭly** *adv.* **mĕss'ĭness** *n.*

mĕss'age *n.* Communication sent from one person to another; divinely inspired communication of a prophet; mission, errand. ~ *v.t.* Send as message; transmit (plan etc.) by signalling.

Mĕssalĭ'na (-lē-) (d. 48 A.D.). 3rd wife of Emperor CLAUDIUS, proverbial for her profligacy.

mĕss'enger *n.* Bearer of message.

Mĕss'erschmĭtt (-sh-). German military aircraft (esp. fighter) used in war of 1939–45. [named after the designer, *W. Messerschmitt*]

Mĕssī'ah (-*a*). In O.T. prophetic writings, the promised deliverer of the Jews; hence applied to Jesus of Nazareth; *The* ~, an oratorio by Handel, based on O.T. prophecies. **Mĕssĭăn'ĭc** *adj.* Of or relating to the or a Messiah. [Heb. *mashiah* anointed]

mĕssieurs' (-yẽr) *n.pl.* Plural of Fr. MONSIEUR or (in abbrev. form *Messrs*, pron. mĕs'*erz*) of Mr, and esp. as prefix to name of a firm, or introducing a list of gentlemen.

Mĕssina (-ēn'*a*). City and harbour of NE. Sicily; *Strait of* ~, that separating Sicily from Italy.

Mĕssines' Ridge (-ēn). Ridge of high ground in Flanders, extensively mined and subsequently blown up and captured (1917) by British troops under General Plumer as a preliminary measure in the battle of PASSCHENDAELE.

Messrs: see MESSIEURS.

mĕss'uage (-w*a*j) *n.* Dwelling-house with its outbuildings and land.

mĕs'tizō (-tē-) *n.* Spanish or Portuguese half-caste, esp. child of Spaniard and Amer. Indian. [Span., f. L *miscere* mix]

met. *abbrev.* Meteorology etc.

mĕtabŏl'ĭc *adj.* Of metabolism; *basal* ~ *rate*, (abbrev. B.M.R.) measure of the energy used up by the body while maintaining itself in a condition of complete rest.

mėtăb'olĭsm *n.* Process in a cell or organism by which nutritive material is built up into living matter (*constructive* ~, *anabolism*) or by which protoplasm is broken down to perform special functions (*destructive* ~, *katabolism*). **mėtăb'olīze** *v.t.*

mėtăb'olīte *n.* Substance undergoing change during METABOLISM.

mĕtacar̃p'us *n.* The 5 bones of the palm of the hand in humans (ill. HAND); corresponding part in other species. **mĕtacar̃p'al** *adj.*

mĕt'age (-ĭj) *n.* Official measuring of coal etc.; duty paid for this.

mĕtagĕn'ėsĭs *n.* (biol.) Reproduction of new generations by processes alternately sexual and asexual. **mĕtagėnĕt'ĭc** *adj.*

mĕt'al *n.* 1. One of a class of elements of which gold, silver, copper, iron, lead, and tin are examples; or a mixture of these (alloy); they have a characteristic lustrous appearance and are good conductors of heat and electricity; other properties such as high specific gravity, fusibility, and malleability, formerly viewed as characteristic of a metal, are possessed by some but not all metals. 2. Material for making glass, in molten state. 3. Broken stone (*road*-~) for macadam roads or railway ballast. 4. (pl.) Rails of a railway line. ~ *v.t.* Furnish or supply with metal; mend (road) with metal.

mėtăll'ĭc *adj.* Of or like metal; yielding metal.

mĕtallĭf'erous *adj.* Bearing, producing metals.

mĕt'allīze *v.t.* Render metallic; vulcanize (rubber). **mĕtallīzā'tion** *n.*

mĕtallŏg'raphy *n.* Study, description of alloys and metals, their structure and properties.

mĕt'alloid *adj.* Having form or appearance of metal. ~ *n.* Element having physical properties of a metal and chemical properties of a non-metal, e.g. tellurium.

mĕt'allur̃gy (*or* metăl'*er*jĭ) *n.* Science of the extraction, working, and properties of metals and their alloys. **mĕtallur̃'gĭc(al)** *adjs.* **mĕt'allur̃gĭst** (*or* metăl'*er*-) *n.*

mĕt'amēre *n.* (zool.) One of a series of more or less similar segments of an animal body, as of a worm. **mĕtamĕ'rĭc** *adj.* (zool.) Of metameres; (chem.) having same percentage composition and molecular weight, but different chemical properties. **mėtăm'erĭsm** *n.* (chem. and zool.).

mĕtamor̃ph'ĭc *adj.* (geol., of rocks) Altered after formation by heat or pressure or both. **mĕtamor̃ph'ĭsm** *n.* This process.

mĕtamor̃ph'ōse (-z) *v.t.* Change in form, change nature of.

mĕtamor̃ph'osĭs *n.* (pl. *-osēs*). Change of form, esp. magic transformation as of person into beast or plant etc.; changed form; change of character, circumstance, etc.; (zool.) change, usually rapid, between immature form and adult.

mĕt'aphor *n.* Figure of speech in which name or descriptive term is transferred to an object to which it is not properly applicable (e.g. *a glaring error*); instance of this; *mixed* ~, combination of inconsistent metaphors. **mĕtaphŏ'rĭc(al)** *adjs.* **mĕtaphŏ'rĭcally** *adv.*

mĕt'aphrāse (-z) *n.* Translation, esp. word-for-word rendering, as dist. from *paraphrase*. ~ *v.t.* Translate thus. **mĕtaphrăs'tĭc** *adj.*

mĕtaphȳs'ĭcs (-z-) *n.pl.* Branch of philosophy dealing with first principles of things, including such concepts as being, substance, space, time, identity, etc. **mĕtaphȳs'ĭcal** *adj.* Of metaphysics; ~ *poets*, a term used to designate certain 17th-c. English poets addicted to 'witty conceits' and far-fetched imagery; they include Donne, Cowley, Herbert, and Vaughan. **mĕtaphȳs'ĭcally** *adv.* **mĕtaphȳsĭ'cian** (-shn) *n.* [Gk *ta meta ta phusika* the works (of Aristotle) placed after the 'Physics']

mĕta'plăsm *n.* (biol.) That part of PROTOPLASM that contains formative matter; the non-living constituents.

mĕtapŏl'ĭtĭcs *n.pl.* Abstract political science (often contempt.). **mĕtapolĭt'ĭcal** *adj.* **mĕtapŏlĭtĭ'cian** (-shn) *n.*

Metastasio (mātăstah'syō) (Pietro Bonaventure Trapassi, 1698–1782). Italian poet and librettist for Gluck, Handel, Haydn, Mozart, etc.

mĕtastās'ĭs *n.* (pl. *-es*). (path.) Transference of disease from a primary focus to one in another part of the body by agents transported in the blood or lymph. **mĕtastăt'ĭc** *adj.*

mĕtatar̃s'us *n.* The 5 long bones between tarsus and toes (ill. FOOT). **mĕtatar̃s'al** *adj.*

mėtăth'ėsis *n.* (pl. *-esēs*). 1. (gram.) Transposition of letters or sounds. 2. (chem.) Substitution of one radical or atom for another in a molecule. **mĕtathĕt'ĭcal** *adj.*

Mĕtazō'a *n.pl.* (zool.) Sub-kingdom comprising multicellular animals with differentiated tissues, a nervous system, and co-ordination between the various cells.

mēte *v.t.* (literary) Measure; portion *out*, allot (punishment, reward).

mĕtĕmpsȳchō'sĭs (-k-) *n.* (pl. *-osēs* pr. -z). Supposed migration of soul at death into another body.

mēt'ėor *n.* One of the small solid bodies in the solar system which become luminous when passing into earth's atmosphere; shooting star; (fig.) any bright, dazzling, but transient object. **mētėŏ'rĭc** *adj.* Of the atmosphere; dependent on atmospheric conditions; of meteors; (fig.) dazzling, rapid.

mēt'ėorīte *n.* Fallen meteor, fragment of rock or nickel iron which has fallen from space on to earth's surface.

mēt'ėoroid *n.* Body moving through space, of same nature as those which by passing into earth's atmosphere become visible as meteors. **mētėoroid'al** *adj.*

mētėorŏl'ogy *n.* Study of, science treating of, atmospheric phenomena, esp. for forecasting weather. **mētėorolŏ'gĭcal** *adj.* **mētėorolŏ'gĭcally** *adv.* **mētėorŏl'ogĭst** *n.*

mēt'er *n.* Apparatus for measuring, esp. automatically, and recording quantity of gas, water, electricity, etc., passing through it. ~ *v.t.*

mē'thāne *n.* Marsh-gas, CH_4, a colourless hydrocarbon gas emanating from stagnant pools etc. and coal-seams, and forming fire-damp when mixed with air.

mėthinks' *v.impers.* (archaic) It seems to me.

mĕth'od *n.* Procedure; way of doing anything, esp. according to a regular plan; systematic or orderly arrangement; orderliness and regularity. **mėthŏd'ĭc(al)** *adjs.* **mėthŏd'ĭcally** *adv.*

Mĕth'odism *n.* Religious movement, founded in the 1730's by John WESLEY, his brother Charles, and George WHITEFIELD, in reaction against apathy in the Church of England, and developed by missionary tours in Georgia, U.S., and in Great Britain; the meetings, often in the open air, were characterized (as now) by lay preaching and hymn-singing. The movement later gave rise to various sects, but the principal groups (United Methodist Church, Primitive Methodists, and Wesleyan Methodists) united in 1932. **Mĕth'odĭst** *adj.* & *n.* [*The Methodist*, sobriquet given to Charles Wesley when in 1729 he assembled a group of fellow-students at Oxford (the 'Holy Club') to follow a specified 'method' of devotional study]

Mėthus'elah (-ōōzela). One of the patriarchs, said (Gen. v. 27) to have lived 969 years, hence regarded as type of longevity.

mĕth'ȳl (*or* mē-) *n.* (chem.) A univalent organic radical, CH_3; ~ *alcohol*, colourless volatile liquid distilled from wood and also made synthetically; wood-spirit. **mĕth'ȳlāte** *v.t.* Mix (alcohol etc.) with wood-spirit, usu. to render it unfit for drinking and therefore exempt from duty, as *methylated spirit*.

mėtĭc'ūlous *adj.* Over-attentive to minute details. **mėtĭc'ūlously** *adv.*

métier (mā'tyā) *n.* Trade or profession; a person's 'line'.

Mĕtŏn'ic cycle. A period of 19 solar years, after the lapse of which the new and full moons return to the same day of the year. It was the basis of the Greek calendar and is still used for fixing movable feast days, such as Easter. [after *Meton*, an Athenian astronomer of the 5th c. B.C.]

mėtŏn'ȳmȳ *n.* Substitution of name of an attribute or adjunct for that of the thing meant (e.g. *the turf* for *horse-racing*). **mĕtonȳm'ĭcally** *adv.*

mĕt'ope (-opĭ, -ōp) *n.* (archit.) Square space between triglyphs in Doric frieze (ill. ORDER); carving etc. on this.

mē'tre[1] (*-er*) *n.* Any form of poetic rhythm, determined by character and number of feet; group of metrical feet.

mē'tre[2] (*-er*) *n.* Unit of length in the METRIC system, = approx. 39·37 in.

mĕt'rĭc *adj.* Of the metre; ~ *system*, decimal measuring system orig. devised in 1791 by the French Academy of Sciences, who based their unit of length on a quadrant of the earth (i.e. quarter of circle round the earth through N. and S. poles); one ten-millionth of this distance as it was then measured was called a *metre*; multiples of the metre were designated by the Greek prefixes *deca-* (10 times), *hecto-* (100 times), *kilo-* (1,000 times, and fractions by the Latin prefixes *deci-* (here used to mean one tenth), *centi-* (one hundredth), *milli-* (one thousandth). The standard for capacity is the LITRE; that for weight is now the KILOGRAM (orig., the *gram*); for metric measures and their equivalents in British measures see Appendix X.

mĕt'rĭcal *adj.* Of, composed in, metre; of, involving, measurement, as ~ *geometry*. **mĕt'rĭcally** *adv.*

Mĕt'rō (-ĕ-) *n.* (colloq.) The Metropolitan (underground) Railway of Paris.

mėtrŏl'ogy *n.* Science, system, of weights and measures. **mĕtrolŏ'gĭcal** *adj.*

mĕt'ronōme *n.* Musician's instrument for marking time by means of a graduated inverted pendulum with a sliding weight. **mĕtronŏm'ĭc** *adj.*

mėtrŏp'olĭs *n.* Chief city, capital; see of metropolitan bishop. [Gk *mētropolis* parent State *mētēr* mother, *polis* city]

mĕtropŏl'ĭtan *adj.* Of a metropolis; of, forming (part of) State as dist. from its colonies or dependencies; ~ *bishop*, *archbishop*, one who has authority over the bishops of a province; ~ *borough*: see BOROUGH. *n.* Metropolitan bishop or archbishop; inhabitant of a metropolis. **mĕtropŏl'ĭtanate** *n.* Office, jurisdiction, of a metropolitan bishop.

Mĕtt'ernĭch (-χ). Prince Clemens Wenzel Lothar Metternich-Winneburg (1773–1859), Austrian statesman; led the Congress of Vienna in devising the settlement of Europe after the Napoleonic Wars.

mĕtt'le *n.* Quality of disposition; natural vigour and ardour, spirit, esp. of a horse. **mĕtt'lesome** (-ls-) *adj.* High-spirited.

Mĕtz. Fortified town of E. France, on the R. Moselle.

Meuse (mẽrz) or **Maas** (mahs). River of NE. France, Belgium, and Holland.

mew[1] *n.* Gull, esp. the common gull, *Larus canus*; sea-mew.

mew[2] *v.* (Of hawk) moult; shut up (hawk) in mew; shut *up*, confine. ~ *n.* Cage for hawks.

mew[3] *v.i.* Cry like cat. ~ *n.* Cat's cry.

mewl, mūle *v.i.* Cry feebly, whimper; mew like a cat.

mews (-z) *n.* Series of private stables built round a yard or on both sides of a lane, as in towns when there is no room for stables adjoining houses. [f. MEW[2], orig. of royal stables on site of hawks' mews]

Mĕx'ĭcō. Independent federal republic of southern N. America and Central America; orig. inhabited by various Amer. Indian peoples, esp. MAYA, AZTECS; was a Spanish colony ('New Spain'), *c* 1519–1821; since then it has been a republic except for the years 1864–7 when MAXIMILIAN[2], Archduke of Austria, was emperor; the long presidency of Diaz (1877–80 and 1884–1911) was followed by a period of revolution. The question of the possession of Texas led to war between the United States and Mexico in 1846–8, Texas having applied for admission to the American Union as early as 1836. *Gulf of* ~, a large area of sea, part of the Atlantic Ocean, almost surrounded by the southern coast of N. America, the coast of Mexico, and the island of Cuba. **Mĕx'ĭcan** *adj.* & *n.*

Meyer (mī'*er*), Conrad Ferdinand (1825–96). Swiss poet and historical novelist.

Meyerbeer (mī′erbār), Giacomo (Jakob) (1791–1864). German-Jewish composer of operas.

mĕzz′anine (-ēn) *adj.* & *n.* (Low storey) between two higher storeys, esp. between ground and 1st floors.

mezzo (mĕt′sō) *adv.* (mus.) Moderately; ~ *fŏr′tė*, moderately loud; ~*-soprano*, (person with, part for) voice between contralto and soprano.

mezzotint (mĕt′so-) *n.* Method of engraving on copper or steel in which the plate is roughened uniformly, lights and half-lights being produced by scraping away the roughness, deep shadows by leaving it; print produced in this way. ~ *v.t.* Engrave in mezzotint.

mf. *abbrev.* MEZZO *forte*.

M.F.H. *abbrev.* Master of Foxhounds.

mg. *abbrev.* Milligram (s).

m.g. *abbrev.* Machine-gun.

M.G.B. *abbrev.* Motor gunboat.

Mgr *abbrev.* Monseigneur; Monsignor (pl. **Mgri**).

mho (mō) *n.* The unit of electrical conductance, the reciprocal of the ohm; thus, a conductor having a resistance of 4 ohms has a conductance of 0·25 mho.

mi (mē) *n.* (mus.) = ME².

M.I. *abbrev.* Military Intelligence; Mounted Infantry.

M.I.5. Section of Military Intelligence which deals with matters of State security.

miaow (mīow′) *n.* & *v.i.* (Make) cat's cry, mew.

miăs′ma (-z-) *n.* Noxious exhalation from marshes, putrid matter, etc. **miăs′mĭc** *adj.*

Mic. *abbrev.* Micah (O.T.).

mī′ca *n.* One of a group of minerals composed of aluminium silicate combined with other silicates, occurring as small glittering scales in granite etc., or as larger crystals separable into thin transparent plates, used as a dielectric and insulator in electrical equipment etc. **mĭcā′ceous** (-shus) *adj.* [L, = 'crumb']

Micah (mīk′a). One of the minor prophets of the Old Testament, a contemporary of Isaiah; the O.T. book of his prophecies.

Mĭcawb′er, Mr. In Dickens's 'David Copperfield', a sanguine idler trusting that something good will turn up. Hence, **mĭcawb′erĭsm** *n.*

M.I.C.E. *abbrev.* = M.INST.C.E.

mīcĕll(e)′, mīcĕll′a *ns.* (pl. *-s*, *-ae*). (biol.) One of the minute elongate particles with regular molecular structure of which many fibres (e.g. wool, cotton) are composed.

Mich. *abbrev.* Michaelmas; Michigan.

Michael (mīk′el), St. One of the archangels, usu. represented slaying a dragon (see Rev. xii. 7).

Michaelmas (mĭk′elmas). The feast of St. Michael, 29th Sept., a quarter-day; ~ *daisy*, herbaceous perennial of genus *Aster*, native in N. America, flowering at Michaelmas; ~ *goose*, goose traditionally eaten at Michaelmas; ~ *Term*, in universities etc., the autumn term beginning in late Sept. or early Oct.

Michelangelo Buonarrōt′ĭ (mīkelăn′jėlō bwō-) (1475–1564). Italian sculptor, painter, and poet; one of the greatest artists of the Renaissance; famous esp. for his frescoes in the Sistine Chapel at Rome.

Michelet (mēshelā′), Jules (1798–1874). French historian.

Michelozzo (mīkėlŏt′sō) di Bartolommeo (1396–1472). Italian architect; designed the Riccardi Palace in Florence.

Mich′ėlson (mīk-), Albert Abraham (1852–1931). Amer. physicist; devised with E. W. Morley the ~*-Morley experiment*, which attempted to discover the effect of the velocity of the earth on the velocity of light, as a means of measuring the velocity of the earth through the 'ether'; the failure to discover any such effect was the starting-point for the theory of RELATIVITY.

Mich′ĭgan (mĭsh-). East North Central State of U.S., with its northern boundary formed by Lakes Huron and Superior; admitted to the Union in 1837; capital, Lansing; *Lake* ~, one of the chain of great lakes in N. America.

Mĭck′ey Mouse *n.* (R.A.F. slang) Electrical distributor which releases bombs from aircraft. [f. name of mouse-like character in Walt Disney's cartoons]

mīcro- *prefix.* Used chiefly in scientific terminology, meaning 'small', 'minute', contrasted with *macro-*; also (abbrev. μ) as a prefix to names of electrical units, to denote 'the millionth part of', as in *micro-ampere*, *microfarad*.

mī′crōbe *n.* MICRO-ORGANISM, esp. one of the bacteria causing diseases and fermentation. **mīcrōb′ial, mīcrŏb′ĭc** *adjs.*

mīcrobiŏl′ogy *n.* Study of micro-organisms. **mīcrobiŏl′ogist** *n.*

mīcrocėphăl′ĭc *adj.* Small-headed.

mī′crocŏsm *n.* Man as an epitome of the universe; any community viewed as epitome of the world; miniature representation (*of*). **mīcrocŏs′mĭc** *adj.*

mī′crofĭlm *n.* (Photographic reproduction of MS. etc. on) very small film, projected on screen for purposes of reading etc. ~ *v.t.* Make such a reproduction.

mīcrŏm′ėter *n.* Precision instrument, variously designed, for measuring minute distances.

mī′cron *n.* Millionth of a metre or thousandth of a millimetre (symbol μ).

Mīcronē′sĭa (-z-). Division of Oceania comprising the small NW. Pacific islands including the Mariana, Caroline, Marshall, and Gilbert Islands.

mīcrō-ŏr′ganĭsm *n.* Any of the organisms not visible to the unaided eye, as bacteria, protozoa, unicellular algae and fungi, and viruses.

mī′crophōne *n.* Instrument producing electrical impulses corresponding to the vibrations of sound waves falling on it and thus performing an essential part in telephonic and radio transmission. **mīcrophŏn′ĭc** *adj.*

mī′croscōpe *n.* Lens or combination of lenses magnifying objects so that details invisible to the naked eye are revealed. **mīcroscŏp′ĭc** *adj.* Of a microscope; with the functions of a microscope; so minute as only to be seen clearly with a microscope. **mīcroscŏp′ĭcal** *adj.* Pertaining to a microscope. **mīcroscŏp′ically** *adv.* **mīcrŏs′copy, mīcrŏs′copist** *ns.*

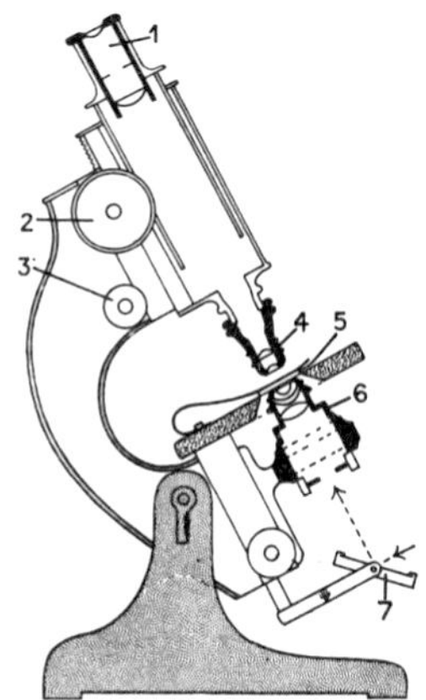

MICROSCOPE

1. Eyepiece. 2. Coarse adjustment head. 3. Fine adjustment head. 4. Objective. 5. Slide. 6. Condenser. 7. Mirror for directing light into condenser

mī′crosōme *n.* (biol.) Small particle in a cell, not visible with an ordinary microscope.

mī′crostrŭcture *n.* (metallurgy) Arrangement of crystals observable under a microscope. **mīcrostrŭc′tural** (-cher-) *adj.*

mī′crotōme *n.* Instrument for cutting very thin sections of organic tissue for examination under the microscope. **mīcrŏt′omy** *n.*

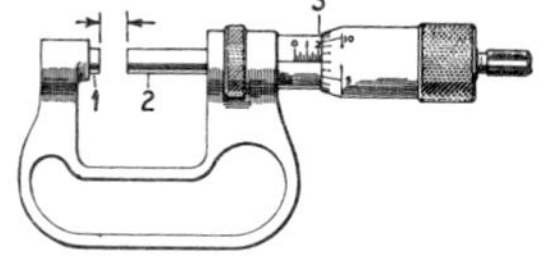

MICROMETER

1. Anvil. 2. Plunger. 3. Scale

mī′crō-wāves *n.pl.* Radio waves of wave-length less than 20 cm.

mī′crŭrgy *n.* Art or science of

dissection and injection under a microscope. **micrŭr′gĭcal** *adj.*

mictūri′tion *n.* Morbid desire to urinate; (erron.) urination.

mĭd *adj.* The middle of; (phonetics) with the tongue or part of it in a middle position between high and low; *mid-off, -on,* (cricket) fielders on off, on, sides, in front of batsman and near bowler (ill. CRICKET); *mid′rib,* main vein of a leaf (ill. LEAF).

Mī′das. (Gk legend) King of Phrygia; he was granted a request by Silenus, the tutor of Bacchus, in return for hospitality, and chose that everything he touched should be turned to gold. The wish was interpreted literally; Midas, unable to eat or drink, prayed to be relieved of the gift, and was instructed to wash in the river Pactolus, whose sands turned to gold at his touch. Another time, when Midas declared Pan a better flute-player than Apollo, Apollo turned his ears into an ass's, and Midas tried to hide them, but a servant whispered the secret to some reeds, which repeated it whenever the wind rustled them.

mĭd′day *n.* Noon (often attrib.).

mĭdd′en *n.* Dung-hill, refuse-heap.

mĭdd′le *adj.* Equidistant from extremities; intermediate in rank, quality, etc.; (gram.) of a special form of the verb, the ~ *voice,* as in Greek, expressing reflexive action of the verb on the subject or intransitive action; (of languages) in a stage of development between the old and modern forms, as *M~* ENGLISH; ~ *age,* period between youth and old age; *M~ Ages,* period of history intermediate between ancient and modern times, variously calculated, but commonly applied to period from the fall of the Roman Empire in the West (5th c.) to the beginning of the Renaissance (middle of 15th c.); ~ *article,* brief essay of literary kind in weekly or other journal, usu. placed between political articles and reviews; *M~ Atlantic States,* a geographical division of the U.S., made by the U.S. Census Bureau, comprising New York, New Jersey, and Pennsylvania; ~ *class,* class of society between 'upper' and 'lower', including professional, business or shop-keeping classes (often attrib.); ~ *distance,* that part of a picture which lies between the foreground and the background; *M~ East,* States lying between the Near and Far East, including those countries between Egypt and Iran; *M~ Kingdom*: see KINGDOM; *midd′le-man,* trader intermediate between producer and consumer; ~ *term,* (logic) term in a syllogism common to both premisses; ~ *watch,* (naut.) the watch between midnight and 4 a.m.; *~-weight,* boxer of not more than 11 st. 6 lb.; *M~ West,* that part of U.S. occupying the N. half of the Mississippi River basin, including the States of Ohio, Indiana, Illinois, Michigan, Wisconsin, Iowa, and Minnesota; *M~ Western(er).* ~ *n.* A middle, central part or point in position or time; middle part of the body, waist. ~ *v.t.* Place in the middle; kick (football) into mid field.

Mĭdd′lesĕx. English county on Thames, including in its geographical area the greater part of London.

Mĭdd′leton, Thomas (1570–1627). English writer of satirical comedies of contemporary manners and of romantic comedies.

mĭdd′lĭng *adj.* & *adv.* (commerc.) Of goods of middle size or quality; moderately good; second-rate; (colloq.) fairly well (in health).

mĭdd′lĭngs *n.pl.* Grades of commodities, such as flour, of second quality or fineness.

mĭdd′y *n.* Colloq. abbrev. of MIDSHIPMAN.

Mĭd′gard. (Scand. myth.) The region, surrounded by the sea, in which men live; ~ *Serpent,* a monstrous serpent, the offspring of Loki, thrown by Odin into the sea, where, with its tail in its mouth, it encircled the earth.

mĭdge *n.* Gnat, small insect.

mĭdg′ĕt *n.* Extremely small person; dwarf.

Mĭd′ĭanīte *adj.* & *n.* (One) of a nomadic people of N. Arabia often mentioned in the O.T., supposed to be descended from Abraham; they became proverbial for leading Israel astray.

mĭdĭnĕtte′ *n.* Parisian shop-girl or seamstress.

mĭd′land *adj.* & *n.* (Part of a country) remote from the sea or borders; *the Midlands,* the counties of England S. of the Humber and Mersey and N. of the Thames, except Norfolk, Suffolk, Essex, Middlesex, Hertfordshire, Gloucestershire, and the counties bordering on Wales.

Mĭdlō̆th′ĭan (-dh-). Eastern Scottish county on S. coast of Firth of Forth.

mĭd′night (-nīt) *n.* The middle of the night, 12 o'clock (often attrib.).

Mĭd′răsh *n.* (pl. *-im,* pr. -ăsh′ēm). Ancient Jewish commentary on part of the Hebrew scriptures.

mĭd′rĭff *n.* The diaphragm.

mĭd′shĭp *n.* Middle part of ship or boat; *midshipman,* (hist., in British Navy) junior officer ranking between cadet and sub-lieutenant.

mĭd′shĭps *adv.* AMIDSHIPS.

mĭdst *n.* Middle. ~ *adv.* Amidst.

mĭd′sŭmmer *n.* Period of summer solstice, about 21st June; *M~ Day,* 24th June, an English quarter-day; ~ *madness,* extreme folly, supposed to be due to midsummer moon and heat.

mĭd′wīfe *n.* Woman who assists others in childbirth. **mĭd′wĭfery** (-frĭ) *n.*

mien (mēn) *n.* (literary) Bearing or look.

might[1] (mīt) *v.* Past t. of MAY.[1]

might[2] (mīt) *n.* Great (bodily or mental) strength; power to enforce one's will.

mighty (mīt′ĭ) *adj.* Powerful, strong in body or mind. ~ *adv.* (colloq.) Very, extremely. **might′-ĭly** *adv.* **might′ĭnĕss** *n.*

mignonĕtte′ (mĭny-) *n.* 1. Plant with fragrant greyish-green blossoms (*Reseda odorata*). 2. Fine, open-work French pillow-lace.

migraine′ (mē-) *n.* Recurrent paroxysmal headache, often accompanied by nausea, visual disturbances, and other severe symptoms. [Fr., f. Gk *hemi* half, *kranion* skull]

mī′grant *adj.* That migrates. ~ *n.* Migrant bird etc.

mīgrāte′ *v.i.* Move from one place of abode, or esp. one country, to another; (of birds and fishes) go from one habitat to another, esp. come and go regularly with the seasons. **mīgrā′tion** *n.* **mī′-gratory** *adj.*

Mĭka′dō (-kah-) *n.* Popular title, as used by foreigners, of the Emperor of Japan. [Jap. *mi* august, *kado* door]

mīke *n.* Slang abbrev. of MICROPHONE.

Mĭl′an (*or* mĭlăn′). (It. *Milano*) Chief city of Lombardy, N. Italy.

Mĭl′anēse (-z) *adj.* Of Milan; ~ (*silk*), finely woven material of silk or artificial silk.

mĭlch *adj.* Giving, kept for, milk; *~-cow,* cow kept for milk; (fig.) source of regular (and easy) profit.

mīld *adj.* Gentle; not severe or harsh or drastic; not bitter; ~ *steel,* malleable and tough steel, having a low percentage of carbon. **mīld′-ly** *adv.* **mīld′nĕss** *n.*

mĭl′dew *n.* Growth of minute fungi on plants or on leather etc. exposed to damp. ~ *v.* Taint, be tainted, with mildew. **mĭl′dewy** *adj.*

mīle *n.* (*Statute*) ~, British unit of linear measure of 1,760 yards; race extending over one mile; *geographical* ~, one minute of longitude (1/60°) measured on the equator, 6,087·2 ft; *nautical, sea,* ~, length of one minute of latitude, standardized at 6,080 ft but actually varying with latitude (6,046–6,108 ft); *mile′stone,* stone set up on road to indicate the miles to and from a given place; (fig.) stage, event, in life. [L *mille* thousand (the Roman mile being 1,000 paces)]

mīl′eage (-lĭj), **mīl′age** *n.* Distance in miles; travelling allowance at fixed rate per mile.

mīl′er *n.* (colloq.) Man, horse, trained specially to run a mile; also in comb. as *two-~.*

Mīlē′sian[1] (-shn) *adj.* & *n.* (Inhabitant) of Miletus, ancient Greek city of Asia Minor.

Mīlē′sian[2] (-shn) *adj.* & *n.* Irish-(man). [f. *Milesius,* a legendary Spanish king whose sons are said to have conquered Ireland *c* 1300 B.C.]

mĭl′foil *n.* Common yarrow (*Achillea millefolium*), which has many finely divided leaves.

mĭl'ĭary *adj.* (path.) Like millet-seed in size or form, as ~ *fever*, a disease of the sweat-glands, marked by an eruption of small red pustules, resembling millet-seeds; ~ *tuberculosis*, form of tuberculosis, usu. acute, in which small tubercular nodules are distributed throughout the body.

mĭl'ĭtant *adj.* & *n.* (Person) engaged in warfare; warlike, combative; *Church* ~, the Christian Church considered as at war on earth with the powers of evil, contrasted with the heavenly *Church triumphant*; ~ *suffragette*, one who adopted violent measures to secure suffrage for women. **mĭl'ĭtancy** *n.* **mĭl'ĭtantly** *adv.*

mĭl'ĭtărism *n.* Spirit, tendencies, of the professional soldier; undue reliance on, and exaltation of, military force and methods; **mĭl'ĭtarist** *n.*

mĭl'ĭtarīze *v.t.* Make military or warlike; instil principles of militarism into. **mĭlĭtarīzā'tion** *n.*

mĭl'ĭtary *adj.* Of, done by, befitting, soldiers, or the army, contrasted with *civil*; ~ *age*, the age at which, under compulsory service, a person is liable for service, or, under a voluntary system, may enlist, in the armed forces; *M~ Cross* (abbrev. M.C.), a decoration awarded to British army officers for bravery in battle, instituted 1914 (ill. MEDAL); *M~ Medal* (abbrev. M.M.), a similar decoration awarded to warrant and non-commissioned officers and men; ~ *police*, body of soldiers doing police duty in the army. ~ *n.* Soldiery. **mĭl'ĭtarĭly** *adv.*

mĭl'ĭtāte *v.i.* Take part in warfare (obs. or rare); (of facts, evidence, etc.) have force, tell (*against* conclusion or result).

mĭlĭ'tia (-sh*a*) *n.* Military force, esp. citizen army; branch of British military service, forming part of 'auxiliary forces' as dist. from regular army; (U.S.) all men liable to military service; *mili'tiaman*, member of the militia.

mĭlk *n.* Opaque white fluid secreted by female mammals for nourishment of their young; cow's milk as article of food; milk-like fluid of certain plants, as the juice of the coconut, the latex of the caoutchouc, etc.; preparation of drugs, herbs, etc., resembling milk in appearance, as ~ *of almonds*; ~ *and water*, feeble or mawkish discourse or sentiment; ~ *fever*, fever to which women are liable after child-birth during lactation; ~*-leg*, inflammatory condition of leg, in women after child-birth, accompanied by white swellings; *milk'maid*, woman who milks or is employed in dairy; *milk'man*, man who sells or delivers milk; ~ *pudding*, baked pudding made of rice, sago, tapioca, etc., and sweetened milk; ~*-punch*, drink made of spirits and milk; ~ *shake*, (orig. U.S.) glass of milk or milk and egg flavoured and shaken up; *milk'sop*, effeminate or spiritless fellow; ~*-sugar*, lactose; ~*-tooth*, one of the first, temporary set of teeth in young mammals; *milk'wort*, any plant of genus *Polygala*, growing in meadows, formerly supposed to increase milk in cows eating it. ~ *v.t.* Draw milk from (cow, ewe, goat, etc.); get money out of, exploit (person); extract juice, virus, etc., from (snake etc.).

mĭl'ky *adj.* Of, like, mixed with, milk; (of liquid) cloudy, not clear; effeminate, weakly amiable; *M~ Way*, the GALAXY. **mĭl'kinėss** *n.*

mĭll[1] *n.* Building or apparatus for grinding corn; machine for grinding any solid substance to powder; any machine, or building fitted with machinery, for manufacturing processes etc., as *saw-*, *cotton-~*; *put through*, *go through the* ~, subject to, undergo, training or experience; be severely disciplined; *mill'board*, stout pasteboard for bookbinding; ~*-dam*, dam across a stream to make water available for mill; ~*-hand*, factory worker; ~*-pond*. one formed by a mill-dam; *like a mill-pond*, said of very calm sea; ~*-race*, current of water that drives mill-wheel; *mill'-stone*, one of pair of circular stones used in grinding corn; (fig.) heavy burden, crushing weight; *Millstone Grit*, hard siliceous rock of carboniferous system, found immediately below Coal Measures; ~*-wheel*, one that turns the machinery of a water-mill; *mill'wright*, one who constructs mills. ~ *v.* Grind or treat in mill; produce grooves etc. in (metal) by rotary cutter; produce regular markings on edge of (coin, esp. in past part.); thicken (cloth) by fulling; beat (chocolate) to a froth; beat, strike, fight (person); (of cattle etc.) move round and round in a mass; *milling machine*, rotary cutter for metal.

mĭll[2] *n.* (U.S.) One-thousandth part of a dollar, as a money of account.

Mĭll[3], John Stuart (1806–73). English political economist; author of 'On Liberty' (1859) and 'Utilitarianism' (1861).

Mĭll'ais (-ā), Sir John Everett (1829–96). English painter; founder, with W. Holman Hunt and D. G. Rossetti, of the PRE-RAPHAELITE Brotherhood.

mĭllėnār'ĭan *adj.* Of, expecting, the millennium. ~ *n.* Believer in the millennium.

mĭll'ėnary *adj.* Consisting of a thousand (esp. years).

mĭllĕnn'ĭum *n.* Period of a thousand years; period of one thousand years foretold in Rev. xx. 1–5 in which Christ will reign on earth; period of happiness and prosperity. **mĭllĕnn'ĭal** *adj.*

mĭll'ėpēde, mĭlli- *n.* Any of certain myriapods with numerous legs characteristically placed on each of the segments in double pairs (ill. MYRIAPOD).

mĭll'er[1] *n.* One who works or owns a flour or corn mill; (entom.) popular name for some varieties of white or white-powdered insects; cockchafer; ~*'s-thumb*, pop. name of a small freshwater fish, *Coltus gotio*, also called the bull-head.

Mĭll'er[2], Joe (1684–1738). English actor; *Joe ~'s Jests, or Wits' Vade Mecum*, a collection of coarse witticisms, many of them old, published after his death; hence, *a Joe* ~, a stale joke, a 'chestnut'.

mĭllĕs'ĭmal *adj.* Thousandth.

mĭll'ėt *n.* Cereal plants, esp. *Panicum miliaceum*, native of India, growing three or four feet high and bearing a large crop of minute nutritious seeds; the seed itself; ~*-grass*, a tall N. Amer. woodland grass, *Milium effusum*.

mĭll'i- *prefix.* One-thousandth of a — (esp. metric system).

mĭll'iard (-y*a*rd) *n.* A thousand millions.

mĭll'ĭbār *n.* (meteor.) Thousandth part of a BAR[2], as a unit of atmospheric pressure.

mĭll'ĭgram *n.* Thousandth of a gram, = 0·0154 English grains (abbrev. mg.)

mĭll'ĭlitre (-lēt*er*) *n.* Measure of capacity, thousandth of a LITRE, = 0·061 cu. in. (abbrev. ml.).

mĭll'ĭmētre (-t*er*) *n.* Measure of length, thousandth of a METRE, = 0·03937 in. (abbrev. mm.).

mĭll'ĭner *n.* Maker or seller of women's hats, ribbons, etc. **mĭll'ĭnery** *n.* [f. MILAN; orig. = vendor of Milan goods]

mĭll'ion (-y*o*n) *n.* One thousand thousand, 1,000,000, abbrev. m.; an enormous number; *the* ~, the bulk of the population; the masses.

millionaire' (-yon-) *n.* Person who possesses a million pounds, dollars, etc.; person of great wealth.

mĭll'ĭsĕcond *n.* Thousandth of a second (abbrev. m.sec.).

Mills bomb *n.* An oval-shaped hand grenade. [invented by Sir William *Mills* (1856–1932)]

Mĭl'ō[1] (6th c. B.C.). A Greek athlete of Crotona, Italy, famous for his strength; a pupil of Pythagoras, whose life he is said to have saved by holding up the roof of the school when a pillar gave way.

Mĭl'ō[2] = MELOS.

mĭl'reis (-āīs) *n.* 1. Portuguese gold coin superseded in 1911 by the escudo. 2. Brazilian money of account, 1,000 reis, replaced in 1942 by the cruzeiro.

Mĭltĭ'adēs (-z) (d. *c* 488 B.C.). Athenian statesman and general, victor at MARATHON.

mĭlt *n.* Spleen of mammals; roe of male fish. **mĭl'ter** *n.* Male fish in the breeding season.

Mĭl'ton, John (1608–74). English Puritan poet; author of the epics 'Paradise Lost' and 'Paradise Regained' and many other poems. **Mĭltōn'ĭan, Mĭltŏn'ĭc** *adjs.*

mīme *n.* 1. (Gk & Rom. antiq.) Kind of simple farcical drama, characterized by mimicry and dialogue for this. 2. Similar modern performance, play with mimic gestures and action usu. without words. 3. Actor in a mime; buffoon, jester. ~ *v.i.*

M.I.M.E., M.I.Mech.E. *abbrevs.* Member of the Institution of Mining, Mechanical, Engineers.

mim'ėograph (-ahf) *n.* Apparatus in which stencils are placed for making copies of MSS. ~ *v.t.* Make copies with a mimeograph.

mīmēs'ĭs *n.* (zool.) = CRYPTIC coloration.

mīmĕt'ĭc *adj.* Of, addicted to, imitation, mimicry, or mimesis.

mĭm'ĭc *adj.* Feigned, esp. to amuse; sham; imitative. ~ *n.* Person who mimics. ~ *v.t.* Copy speech or gestures of, esp. to amuse others, imitate closely. **mĭm'ĭcry** *n.* Mimicking; thing that mimics another; (zool.) cryptic coloration, mimesis.

mĭmō'sa (-z-) *n.* (bot.) Any plant of genus *Mimosa* of leguminous plants, including the common Sensitive Plant (*M. pudica*) bearing clusters of small flowers and leaves which curl up when touched.

clined; (colloq.) alive to importance of, keenly interested in, as *air-*, *politically* ~.

mīnd'ful. Taking thought or care (of). **mīnd'fully** *adv.* **mīnd'fulnėss** *n.*

mīne[1] *pron.* & *adj.* (The one(s)) belonging to me; also used (archaic & poet.) before noun beginning with vowel or *h*.

mīne[2] *n.* 1. Excavation from which minerals are extracted; (fig.) abundant source (*of* information etc.). 2. (mil.) Subterranean gallery in which explosive is placed to destroy enemy's fortifications etc.; (nav.) water-tight metal case containing a charge of high explosive, detonated acoustically, electrically, or on contact, placed in sea to protect harbours etc. or destroy enemy's shipping; (mil.) similar receptacle placed or dropped in or on ground (*land-*~) as an engine of war; *minefield*, a sea or land area sown with mines; ~*-layer*, vessel for laying sea-mines; ~*-sweeper*, vessel for sweeping and destroying sea-mines. ~ *v.* Dig for minerals; burrow or make subterranean passage

China 1368–1644; (porcelain etc. of) this period.

mĭng'le (-nggl) *v.* (Cause to) mix; blend; unite *with*.

mĭn'gy (-jĭ) *adj.* (colloq.) Stingy, mean.

mĭn'ĭāte *v.t.* Paint with vermilion; illuminate (manuscript). [L *minium* red lead]

mĭn'iature *n.* 1. Picture in illuminated manuscript. 2. Painted portrait on small scale and with minute finish; reduced image or representation. ~ *adj.* Represented on a small scale. **mĭn'iatūrist** *n.* Painter of miniatures. [L, as prec.]

mĭn'ĭkĭn *n.* Size of type (approx. 3–3½ point) smaller than brilliant.

mĭn'ĭm *n.* 1. Musical note (𝅗 or 𝅗𝅥) half as long as semibreve. 2. Smallest fluid measure, $\frac{1}{60}$ drachm. 3. Object of smallest size or importance.

mĭn'ĭmal *adj.* Very minute, the least possible.

mĭn'ĭmalĭst *n.* Person willing to accept minimum of his demands as compromise (opp. MAXIMALIST).

mĭn'ĭmīze *v.t.* Reduce to, estimate at, smallest possible amount or degree. **mĭnĭmīzā'tion** *n.*

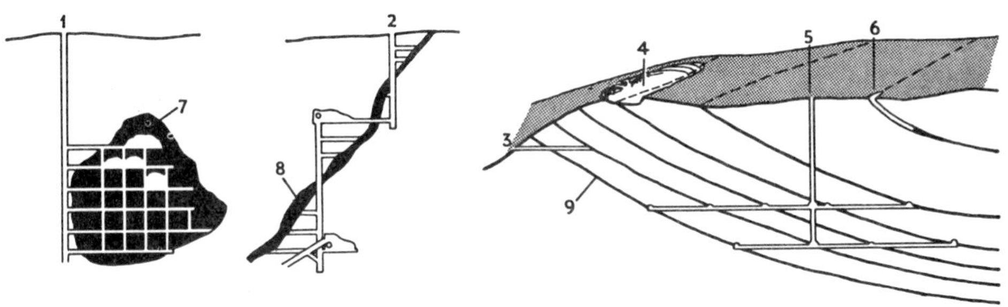

TYPES OF MINE (FOR COAL-MINE SEE p. 522)

1, 2. Deep level. 3. Adit. 4. Opencast. 5. Horizontal. 6. Drift. 7. Body of ore. 8. Lode or vein. 9. Seam

mīn'a, mȳn'a, mīn'or *ns.* Bird of starling family, of SE. Asia, esp. common starling of India (*Gracula religiosa*); grackle.

mĭnā'ceous (-shus) *adj.* Threatening. **mĭnā'ceously** *adv.*

mĭn'arĕt *n.* Tall slender tower or turret of mosque, with projecting balcony, from which muezzin summons the faithful to prayer. [Arab. *manarat* tower of mosque]

mĭn'atory *adj.* Threatening.

mĭnce *v.* Cut (meat etc.) very small; walk, speak, with affected delicacy; (usu. with negative) ~ *matters*, express oneself politely in condemnation. ~ *n.* Minced meat; *mince'meat*, mixture of raisins, currants, apples, suet, spices, etc.; ~*-pie*, small patty filled with mincemeat.

mīnd *n.* The seat of consciousness, thought, volition, and emotion; intellectual powers; memory; opinion. ~ *v.* Bear in mind; heed; take charge of; (chiefly in neg. sentences or questions) have any objection.

mīnd'ėd *adj.* Disposed, in-

in; lay, sow, mines under or in.

min'enwerfer (mē-, -vār-) *n.* Mine-thrower. [Ger.]

mīn'er *n.* 1. Worker in mine. 2. Soldier who lays mines.

mĭn'eral *n.* 1. Substance got by mining. 2. (chem.) Any element or compound occurring naturally as a product of inorganic processes. 3. (pop.) Any substance which is neither animal nor vegetable. ~ *adj.* Of, belonging to, minerals; belonging to any of the species into which inorganic substances are divided; ~ *water*, water naturally impregnated with mineral(s), esp. those of a medicinal character; an aerated drink, as lemonade, ginger-beer, etc.

mĭnerăl'ogy *n.* Scientific study of minerals. **mĭneralŏg'ĭcal** *adj.* **mĭneralŏg'ĭcally** *adv.* **mĭnerăl'ogist** *n.*

Minĕr'va. Roman goddess of wisdom, identified with Greek Athene (which led to her being regarded also as the goddess of war).

mĭn'ėver *n.*: see MINIVER.

Mĭng. Dynasty which ruled in

mĭn'ĭmum *n.* (pl. *-ma*). Least amount attainable, usual, etc. (opp. MAXIMUM); ~ *thermometer*, one registering lowest temperature within a period; ~ *wage*, lowest wage that may be legally offered.

mĭn'ĭmus *adj.* (In schools) youngest of the name, as *Jones* ~; (hort.) very small variety.

mĭn'ion (-yon) *n.* Spoilt darling, favourite; (contempt.) servile agent; (print.) size of type (7 point), between nonpareil and brevier.

mĭn'ĭster *n.* 1. Executive agent; person in charge of a department of State. 2. Diplomatic representative ranking below ambassador. 3. Clergyman (esp. Nonconformist). ~ *v.i.* Be serviceable or contributory; officiate as minister of religion.

mĭnĭstēr'ial *adj.* Of a minister or his office; of the government. **mĭnĭstēr'ialist** *n.* Supporter of the government.

mĭnĭstrā'tion *n.* Ministering, esp. in religious matters. **mĭn'ĭstrant** *adj.* & *n.*

mĭn'ĭstry *n.* 1. Priestly office;

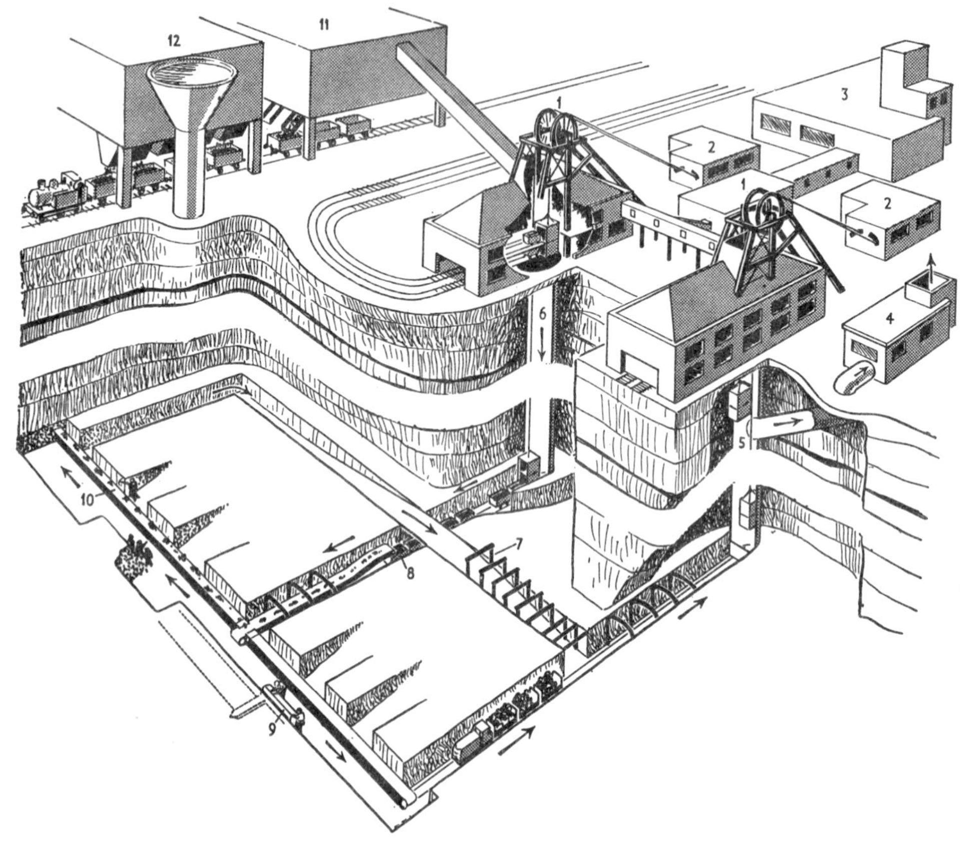

DIAGRAM OF A COAL-MINE

1. Head-gear. 2. Winding engine house. 3. Pit-head baths and canteen. 4. Fan house. 5. Upcast air-shaft. 6. Downcast air-shaft. 7. Pit props. 8. Mine-cars ready to be loaded into cage. 9. Cutting machine at coal face. 10. Conveyor. 11. Screens. 12. Washery

ministers of a church. 2. Office of minister of State; ministerial department of government, the building belonging to it; ministers forming a government.

mĭn'ĭver, minė- *n.* The plain white fur used in ceremonial costume, esp. that of peers; ~ *pure,* (Fr. *puré*) powdered, i.e. spotted, miniver. [Fr. *menu vair* (*menu* small, *vair* kind of fur)]

mĭnk *n.* Small semi-aquatic stoat-like animal of the genus *Putorius,* valued for its thick brown fur; this fur.

Minn. *abbrev.* Minnesota.

mĭnn'ėsinger (-z-) *n.* German lyrical poet and song-writer of the 12th to 14th centuries (also sing.). [OHG *minna* love]

Mĭnnėsōt'a. West North Central State of U.S.; on Canadian border; admitted to the Union in 1858; capital, St. Paul.

mĭnn'ow (-ō) *n.* Small fresh-water fish (*Leuciscus*) of carp family, common in streams, ponds, etc.

Mĭnō'an *adj.* Of the Bronze Age civilization (lasting from *c* 2400 to 1400 B.C.) revealed by excavations made in the palace of Minos at Knossos in Crete.

mīn'or[1] *adj.* 1. Lesser (not followed by *than*); comparatively unimportant, as ~ *poet, prophet*; (in schools) the younger of the name, as *Jones* ~; ~ *canon,* clergyman attached to a cathedral but not a member of the chapter; ~ *suit,* (bridge) diamonds or clubs; ~ *term,* (logic) subject of conclusion of categorical syllogism, contained in the ~ *premiss.* 2. (mus.) Of intervals less by a semitone than the corresponding major intervals; ~ *key, mode,* one having a scale containing a minor 3rd (and a minor 6th and 7th; ill. SCALE); *in a* ~ *key,* (fig.) doleful. ~ *n.* 1. Person under age. 2. Minor interval, key, chord, etc. 3. Minor term or premiss. 4. MINORITE.

minor[2]: see MINA.

Minŏrc'a. Second largest of the Balearic Islands, in W. Mediterranean; ~ (*fowl*), black domestic fowl introduced from Spain.

Mīn'orīte *n.* Franciscan friar, so called because the Franciscans regarded themselves as of humbler rank than members of the other orders.

mīnŏ'rĭty *n.* Being a minor; period of this; smaller number or part, esp. smaller party voting against majority; number of votes cast for this.

Mīn'os. Legendary king of Crete; in Attic tradition a cruel tyrant who every year exacted a tribute of Athenian youths and maidens, to be devoured by the **Mīn'otaur,** a bull-like monster confined in a labyrinth made by Daedalus until it was slain by THESEUS; *Palace of Minos,* name given to the remains of the Bronze Age palace at Knossos.

M.Inst.C.E. *abbrev.* Member of the Institution of Civil Engineers.

mĭn'ster *n.* Church of a monastery; any large church.

mĭn'strel *n.* Medieval singer or musician; poet; (*nigger*) ~*s*, band of entertainers with blackened faces, singing Negro songs etc. **mĭn'strelsy** *n.* Minstrels' art, poetry; body of minstrels.

mĭnt[1] *n.* Aromatic culinary herb of genus *Mentha*, esp. *M. viridis*, garden mint or SPEARMINT; PEPPERMINT; ~ *sauce*, sauce made of finely chopped mint, vinegar, and sugar, used esp. with roast lamb.

mĭnt[2] *n.* Place, usu. under State control, where money is coined; (fig.) source of invention; vast sum *of money*. ~ *v.t.* Coin (money); invent. **mĭn'tage** *n.* Coinage, money, esp. that issued from a particular mint at a specified time.

mĭnūĕt' *n.* Slow stately dance; music for this, in triple time; piece of music in this rhythm and style, often as movement of suite or sonata.

mī'nus *adj.* & *prep.* Less, with the deduction of (symbol —); (colloq.) deprived of. ~ *n.* Minus sign or quantity.

mĭnŭs'cūle *adj.* (Of kind of cursive script developed in 7th c.) small. ~ *n.* Small letter in this script (ill. SCRIPT), as dist. from MAJUSCULE or uncial; (mod. typ.) lower-case letter.

mĭn'ute[1] (-ĭt) *n.* 1. Sixtieth part of an hour or of a degree (symbol ′); short time. 2. Memorandum, brief summary, (pl.) official record of proceedings at a meeting. 3. ~-*gun*, gun fired at intervals of a minute as a signal of distress by a ship at sea; ~-*hand*, that indicating minutes on watch or clock. ~ *v.t.* Draft; make a minute of.

mīnūte'[2] *adj.* Very small; precise, going into details. **mīnūte'ly** (-tl-) *adv.* **mīnūte'nėss** *n.*

mĭnū'tia (-sha; usu. in pl., -*tiae*) *n.* Trivial point; small detail.

mĭnx *n.* Pert girl, hussy.

mī'ocēne *adj.* (geol.) Of the 3rd series of rocks in the Tertiary, above the Oligocene and below the Pliocene. ~ *n.* (*The M*~), the miocene series or epoch (ill. GEOLOGY).

mīō̆s'is (less usu. **mei-, my-**) *n.* Constriction of the pupil of the eye.

Mirabeau (mērabō'), Honoré Gabriel de Riqueti, Comte de (1749–91). French statesman and author; an important figure in the first National Assembly.

mĭ'racle *n.* Event due to supernatural agency; remarkable event or object; ~ *plays*, medieval dramas based on bible stories or legends of saints. **mĭrăc'ūlous** *adj.* **mĭrăc'ūlously** *adv.* **mĭrăc'ūlousnėss** *n.*

mĭrage' (-ahzh) *n.* Optical illusion, common in sandy deserts, caused by refraction of nearly horizontal light-rays by the hotter, and therefore less dense, layers of air near the surface, by which a distant object, directly invisible, appears to be near at hand, as though reflected in a sheet of water (also fig.).

Mirandola: see PICO DELLA MIRANDOLA.

mīre *n.* Swampy ground, boggy place; mud. ~ *v.* Sink in, bespatter with, mud. **mīr'y** *adj.*

mĭ'rror *n.* Polished or very smooth surface which reflects images; looking-glass; (fig.) pattern, example. ~ *v.t.* Reflect as in a mirror (lit. and fig.).

mīrth *n.* Rejoicing, merriment. **mīrth'ful** *adj.* **mīrth'fully** *adv.* **mīrth'fulnėss** *n.* **mīrth'lėss** *adj.*

mis- *prefix.* Amiss, bad(ly), wrong(ly), unfavourably, or intensifying unfavourable meaning contained in verb, as *misdoubt*.

mĭsadvĕn'ture *n.* Ill luck, bad fortune; (law) accidental homicide committed in doing a lawful act.

mĭsallī'ance *n.* Unsuitable marriage.

mĭs'anthrōpe *n.* Hater of mankind; one who avoids human society. **mĭsanthrŏp'ic(al)** *adjs.* **mĭsăn'thropy̆** *n.* **mĭsăn'thropist** *n.*

mĭsapplȳ' *v.t.* Apply wrongly. **mĭsăpplĭcā'tion** *n.*

mĭsăpprėhĕnd' *v.t.* Misunderstand. **mĭsăpprėhĕn'sion** *n.*

mĭsapprōp'rĭāte *v.t.* Apply dishonestly to one's own use. **mĭsapprōprĭā'tion** *n.*

mĭsbėcome' (-ŭm) *v.t.* Suit ill.

mĭsbėgŏtt'en *adj.* Illegitimate (often as vague term of opprobrium).

mĭsbėhāve' *v.refl.* & *i.* Behave improperly. **mĭsbehāv'iour** (-yer) *n.*

misc. *abbrev.* Miscellaneous; miscellany.

mĭscăl'cūlāte *v.* Calculate wrongly. **mĭscălcūlā'tion** *n.*

mĭscall' (-awl) *v.t.* Call by wrong name.

mĭscă'rriage (-rĭj) *n.* Miscarrying. **mĭscă'rry** *v.i.* 1. Fail of success; go astray. 2. Be delivered prematurely of a child (strictly, of foetus which is not viable).

mĭscėgėnā'tion *n.* Interbreeding between races, esp. sexual union of whites with Negroes.

mĭscellān'ėa *n.pl.* Miscellany; odds and ends.

mĭscellān'ėous *adj.* Of mixed character, of various kinds.

mĭscĕll'any (*or* mĭs'-) *n.* Medley; miscellaneous writings etc. collected together.

mĭschance' (-ah-) *n.* (Piece of) ill luck, ill success.

mĭs'chief (-chĭf) *n.* Harm, evil, wrought by person or particular cause; worker of mischief; vexatious or annoying conduct, esp. of children; playful malice. **mĭs'chievous** (-ĭv-) *adj.* **mĭs'chievously** *adv.* **mĭs'chievousnėss** *n.*

mĭs'cible (-sĭ-) *adj.* Capable of being mixed, esp. (of liquids) to form a homogeneous substance. **mĭscĭbĭl'ĭty** *n.*

mĭsconceive' (-sēv) *v.* Have wrong idea of, misunderstand. **mĭsconcĕp'tion** *n.*

mĭscŏn'duct *n.* Bad management; improper conduct, esp. adultery. **mĭscondŭct'** *v.t.* & *refl.*

mĭsconstrue' (-ōō; *or* -cŏn'-) *v.t.* Put wrong construction on (word, action). **mĭsconstrŭc'tion** *n.*

mĭscount' *v.t.* Count wrongly. **mĭs'count** *n.* Wrong count, esp. of votes.

mĭs'crėant *n* Vile wretch, villain.

mĭs-cue' (-ū) *v.i.* (billiards) Fail to strike the ball properly. ~ *n.* Such a stroke.

mĭsdāte' *v.t.* Put wrong date on.

mĭsdeal' *v.* Make mistake in dealing (cards). ~ *n.* Wrong deal.

mĭsdeed' *n.* Evil deed.

mĭsdėmean'ant *n.* Person convicted of misdemeanour.

mĭsdėmean'our (-nor) *n.* Misdeed; (law) any indictable offence less than felony, such as perjury, obtaining money by false pretences, etc.

mĭsdīrĕct' *v.t.* Direct wrongly; put wrong name, address, etc., on letter, etc.; give wrong instructions to, specif. (of a judge) give wrong instructions to a jury; aim badly or without precision. **mĭsdirĕc'tion** *n.*

mĭsdo'ĭng (-ōō-) *n.* Misdeed.

mĭsdoubt' (-dowt) *v.t.* Have misgivings or suspicions about; doubt.

mise-en-scène (mēz ahṅ sān') *n.* Scenery and properties of an acted play; (fig.) setting of an event or action.

mī'ser (-z-) *n.* One who lives miserably in order to hoard wealth. **mī'serly** *adj.* **mī'serlinėss** *n.*

mĭs'erable (-z-) *adj.* Wretchedly unhappy, uncomfortable, or poor; causing wretchedness; pitiable, mean. **mĭs'erably** *adv.*

misère (mēzār') *n.* Call in solo-whist by which declarer undertakes not to take a single trick.

mĭserēr'ė (-z-) *n.* 1. One of the Penitential Psalms (Ps. li), beginning *Miserere mei Deus* ('Have mercy upon me O God'); cry for mercy. 2. (erron.) MISERICORD, sense 2.

mĭsĕ'rĭcōrd (-z-) *n.* 1. Room set apart in a monastery, where monks might take special food as an indulgence. 2. Projection on under-side of hinged seat in choir stall, serving when seat is turned up to support person standing (ill. STALL). 3. (hist.) Thin pointed dagger used in medieval warfare for giving *coup de grâce* to a fallen knight.

mĭs'ery (-z-) *n.* 1. Wretched state of mind or circumstances. 2. = MISÈRE.

mĭsfeas'ance (-z-) *n.* Wrongful exercise of lawful authority, as dist. from MALFEASANCE.

mĭsfīre' *v.i.* (Of gun) fail to go off; (of internal combustion engine) fail to ignite (also transf.). ~ *n.* Failure to explode or ignite.

misfit' *n.* Garment etc. that does not fit; (fig.) person ill adapted to his work or surroundings.

misfŏrt'ūne *n.* Calamity, bad luck.

misgive' *v.t.* (Of heart, mind, etc.) suggest misgivings to. **misgiv'ing** *n.* Apprehension, uneasy doubt.

mishănd'le (-s-h-) *v.t.* Handle (person, thing) roughly, rudely, or improperly.

mishăp' (-s-h-) *n.* Unlucky accident.

mishear' (-s-h-) *v.t.* Hear amiss or imperfectly.

mishit' (-s-h-) *v.t.* Hit wrongly or inaccurately, esp. at games. ~ *n.* Faulty hit.

Mish'nah (-n*a*). The collection of binding precepts which forms the basis of the Talmud and embodies the contents of the oral law of the Jews. [post-bibl. Heb., = 'repetition', 'instruction']

mislay' *v.t.* Put (thing) by accident where it cannot readily be found; hence, (euphemism for) lose.

mislead' (-lĕd) *v.t.* Lead astray, give wrong impression to.

mismăn'age *v.t.* Manage badly or wrongly. **mismăn'agement** *n.*

misnāme' *v.t.* Call by wrong name.

misnōm'er *n.* Wrongly applied name.

misŏg'amy *n.* Hatred of marriage. **misŏg'amist** *n.*

misŏg'ўny (-j-, -g-) *n.* Hatred of women. **misŏg'ўnist** *n.*

misplāce' *v.t.* Put in wrong place; bestow (affection etc.) on ill-chosen object. **misplāce'ment** *n.*

misprint' *n.* Error in printing. ~ *v.t.*

mispris'ion (-zhn) *n.* (law) Wrong action or omission, esp. on part of public official; ~ *of treason*, concealment of one's knowledge of treasonable designs etc.

misprize' *v.t.* Despise, fail to appreciate.

mispronounce' *v.t.* Pronounce wrongly. **mispronŭnciā'tion** *n.*

misquōte' *v.t.* Quote wrongly. **misquotā'tion** *n.*

misread' *v.t.* Read or interpret wrongly.

misrĕpresĕnt' *v.t.* Represent wrongly, give false account of. **misrĕpresĕntā'tion** *n.*

misrule' (-ōōl) *v.t.* Rule badly. ~ *n.* Bad government; *Lord* (also *Abbot, Master*, etc.) *of M~*, in the late 15th and early 16th centuries, person appointed at court, in nobleman's house, or in a college or Inn of Court, to superintend Christmas revels.

miss[1] *v.* Fail to hit, reach, meet, find, catch, or perceive; pass over; regret absence of; fail. ~ *n.* Failure; (colloq.) *give* (a thing) *a* ~, pass by, leave alone.

miss[2] *n.* (Title of) unmarried woman or girl; (usu. contempt.) girl, esp. schoolgirl. [abbrev. of MISTRESS]

Miss. *abbrev.* Mississippi.

miss'al *n.* (R.C. Ch.) Book containing the service of the Mass for whole year; (loosely) book of hours, prayers, esp. one that is illuminated.

miss'el, ~-thrŭsh *ns.* Large thrush (*Turdus viscivorus*) which feeds partly on mistletoe-berries. [OE *mistel* basil, mistletoe]

mis-shāp'en *adj.* Deformed.

miss'ïle *n.* Object or weapon capable of being thrown.

miss'ing *adj.* Not present, not found; ~ *link*, pop. name of hypothetical intermediate type of animal between anthropoid apes and man.

miss'ion (-shn) *n.* 1. Body of persons sent to foreign country to conduct negotiations etc. 2. Body sent by religious community to convert heathen; field of missionary activity; missionary post; organization in a district for conversion of the people; course of religious services etc. for this purpose. 3. Errand of political or other mission. 4. (U.S.) Dispatch of aircraft on operational sortie. 5. Person's vocation or divinely appointed work in life.

miss'ionary (-sh*o*-) *adj.* Of religious missions. ~ *n.* Person doing missionary work; *police-court* ~, person employed to attend police-court and work for spiritual and moral benefit of those brought to it.

miss'ioner (-sh*o*-) *n.* Missionary; person in charge of parochial mission.

miss'is, miss'us (-iz) *n.* (As used by servants) the mistress; (vulg., facet.) *the* ~, one's own or another's wife.

Mississipp'i. 1. The greatest river of N. America, rising in Minnesota and flowing south to the Gulf of Mexico. 2. East South Central State of U.S. on E. bank of the lower Mississippi River, admitted to the Union 1817; capital, Jackson.

miss'ive *n.* Letter, esp. official letter from superior.

Missour'i (-oor-). 1. One of the main tributaries of the Mississippi, flowing into it from the W. above St. Louis, and rising in the Rocky Mountains. 2. West North Central State of U.S., lying W. of the Mississippi River, admitted to the Union in 1821; capital, Jefferson City.

miss'y *n.* (Affectionate, playful, or contempt.) = MISS[2] (not followed by name).

mist *n.* Water-vapour precipitated in droplets smaller and more densely aggregated than those of rain; (meteor.) atmosphere in which visibility is between 1,100 yds and 1¼ miles, i.e. better than in FOG; dimness or blurred effect caused by tears in the eyes etc. ~ *v.* Cover, be covered, as with a mist. **mis'ty** *adj.* **mis'tily** *adv.* **mis'tinĕss** *n.*

mistāke' *v.* (past t. -*tŏŏk*, past part. -*tāk'en*). Misunderstand, take in wrong sense; be in error; take (one thing) erroneously *for* another; err in choice of. ~ *n.* Error, blunder; mistaken opinion or act. **mistāk'enly** *adv.* **mistāk'ennĕss** *n.* **mistāk'able** *adj.*

mis'ter *n.* Title prefixed to surname of man (always written *Mr*); (vulg.) as form of address without any name following; untitled person.

mistīme' *v.t.* Time wrongly, do or perform at wrong time.

mis'tletoe (-zltō, -sltō) *n.* Parasitic plant (*Viscum album*) with whitish sticky berries, growing on apple-trees etc.; associated in England with Christmas, and anciently venerated by Druids when found growing on the oak.

mis'tral *n.* Violent cold northerly or north-westerly wind in Mediterranean provinces of France etc., blowing esp. down Rhône valley. [L *magistralis* masterful]

mis'trĕss *n.* 1. Woman in authority over servants; female head of household. 2. Woman who has power to control or dispose *of*, as *you are* ~ *of the situation, you are your own* ~ (also fig.). 3. Woman who has thorough knowledge (*of* subject). 4. Woman loved and courted by a man; woman illicitly occupying place of wife. 5. Female teacher in school or of special subject, as *music*-~. 6. *M~ of the Robes*, lady charged with care of Queen's wardrobe; *wardrobe* ~, woman in charge of costumes in theatre.

mistrŭst' *v.t.* Not trust; have uneasy doubts or suspicions about. ~ *n.* **mistrŭst'ful** *adj.* **mistrŭst'fully** *adv.* **mistrŭst'fulnĕss** *n.*

misŭnderstănd' *v.* Not understand rightly, misinterpret. **misŭnderstănd'ing** *n.*

misūse'(-z) *v.t.* Use wrongly, ill-use. **misūse'** (-s) *n.*

mīte[1] *n.* (orig.) Flemish copper coin of small value; (pop.) half-farthing (as in Mark xii. 43); modest contribution; small object, esp. a child.

mīte[2] *n.* A small arachnid of many kinds, found as parasite or in food, esp. *cheese-mite*.

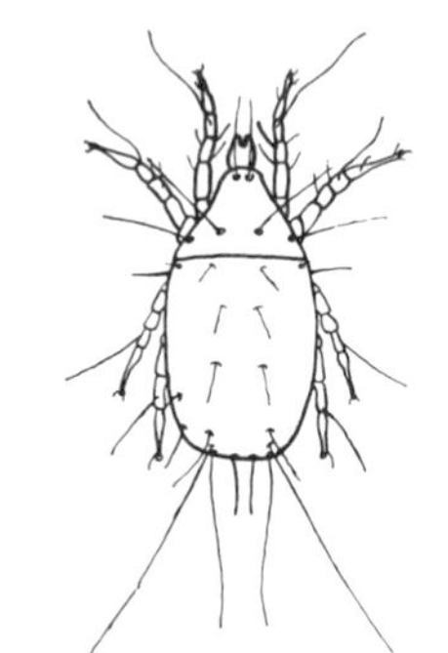

CHEESE-MITE (approx. × 100)

Mĭth′răs. One of the chief gods of the ancient Persians, in later times often identified with the sun. **Mĭth′rāism** *n.* The religion of the worshippers of Mithras, which was introduced among the Romans under the Empire and spread over most of N. and W. Europe during the first three centuries A.D., becoming the principal rival at that time of Christianity.

Mĭthrĭdāt′ēs (-z). Name of 3 kings of Parthia and of several kings of Pontus; *Mithridates VI Eupator* (131–63 B.C.), of Pontus, called 'the Great', tried to drive the Romans out of Asia Minor, but was defeated by Sulla, and finally in 66 B.C. by Pompey; he was said to have rendered himself proof against poisons by taking them constantly in small quantities; hence, **mĭth′rĭdāte** *n.* Ancient name for an antidote against poison. **mithrĭd′ātize** *v.t.* Render proof against poison by gradually increasing doses of it.

mĭt′ĭgāte *v.t.* Appease, alleviate, reduce severity of. **mitigā′tion** *n.* **mĭt′ĭgātory** *adj.*

mitochŏn′dria *n.pl.* (embryol.) Minute thread-like or rounded bodies within a cell, providing sites for the release of energy (ill. CELL).

mĭtō′sĭs *n.* (pl. *-oses* pr. -ōs′ēz). (biol.) Splitting of cell or nucleus accompanied by doubling of number of chromosomes, so that each of the resulting two cells or nuclei has the same number as the original one (cf. MEIOSIS). **mĭtŏt′ĭc** *adj.*

mitrailleuse′ (-trahyẽrz) *n.* Many-barrelled breech-loading machine-gun designed to fire bullets in rapid succession or simultaneously.

mĭt′ral *adj.* (anat.) Of the ~ *valve*, two-cusped valve (so called from fancied resemblance to bishop's mitre) between left atrium and ventricle of human heart, preventing reflux of blood into atrium when ventricle contracts (ill. HEART).

mī′tre[1] (-ter) *n.* Bishop's tall pointed head-dress, deeply cleft at the top (ill. VESTMENT); episcopal office or dignity. ~ *v.t.* (rare) Bestow mitre on (bishop). **mī′tred** (-terd) *adj.* Wearing mitre.

mī′tre[2] (-ter) *n.* (carpentry) Joint in which line of junction bisects the angle (usu. a right angle) between the two pieces, as in picture-frame. ~ *v.* Join thus; shape to make mitred corner.

mĭtt *n.* Mitten; (slang, pl.) boxing-gloves.

mĭtt′en *n.* Glove leaving fingers and thumb-tip bare; glove having no separate partitions for fingers, but only for thumb.

Mitylene: see MYTILENE.

mĭx *v.* Mingle, blend, into one mass; compound; have intercourse *with*; ~ *in, it,* (colloq.) join in fighting; ~ *up*, confuse; ~*-up* (*n.*) confused fight, mêlée. ~ *n.* Mixture of materials (e.g. concrete, plastics) ready for a process.

mixed (-kst) *adj.* Of diverse qualities or elements; (of company) not select, containing persons of doubtful status; comprising both sexes; for persons of both sexes, as ~ *bathing*; (colloq.) confused, muddled.

mĭx′er *n.* (esp.) 1. In sound films etc., apparatus that controls contributions of various microphones. 2. Apparatus, usu. electrical, for mixing or pulping food in cookery. 3. *good, bad,* ~, (colloq.) person who gets on well, badly, with others.

Mĭxolȳd′ian *adj.* ~ *mode*, Ancient Greek MODE; also, 7th of the eccles. modes with G as final and D as dominant (ill. MODE).

mĭx′ture *n.* Mixing; what is mixed, esp. medicinal preparation; mechanical mixing of two or more substances, involving no change in their character, opp. to *chemical combination*; (in internal combustion engines) the gas or vaporized fuel mixed with air to form the explosive charges.

mĭz(z)′en *n.* (naut.) Fore-and-aft sail on after side of *mizen-mast*, the aftermost mast of a three-masted ship (ill. SHIP).

mĭzz′le[1] *v.impers.* Drizzle.

mĭzz′le[2] *v.i.* (slang) Run away, decamp.

mk *abbrev.* Mark (coin).

ml. *abbrev.* Millilitre(s).

M.L.A. *abbrev.* Member of the Legislative Assembly; Modern Languages Association.

Mlle *abbrev.* Mademoiselle (pl. **Mlles**).

M.L.N.S. *abbrev.* Ministry of Labour and National Service.

mm. *abbrev.* Millimetre(s).

MM. *abbrev.* Messieurs.

M.M. *abbrev.* Military Medal.

Mme *abbrev.* Madame (pl. **Mmes**).

m.m.f. *abbrev.* Magnetomotive force.

M.Mus. *abbrev.* Master of Music.

M.N. *abbrev.* Merchant Navy.

mnėmŏn′ĭc (n-) *adj.* Of, intended to aid, the memory. **mnėmŏn′ĭcs** *n.pl.* Mnemonic art or system; mnemonic rhyme.

Mnēmŏs′ȳnē (n-; -z-). Mother of the MUSES. [Gk, = 'memory']

M.N.I. *abbrev.* Ministry of National Insurance.

Mo. *abbrev.* Missouri.

M.O. *abbrev.* Mass observation; Medical Officer; money order.

mō′a *n.* Various large extinct flightless birds of New Zealand, resembling ostrich (many species in family *Dinornithidae*). [Maori name]

Mō′ăb. An ancient Palestinian people of a district E. of the Jordan and the Dead Sea and N. of Edom, frequently mentioned in the O.T. **Mō′abīte** *adj.* & *n.* ~ *Stone*, a monument erected by Mesha, king of Moab, *c* 850 B.C., which describes the campaign between Moab and Israel of 2 Kings iii and furnishes the earliest known inscription in the Phoenician alphabet; now in the Louvre, Paris.

moan *n.* Low inarticulate sound expressing pain or grief. ~ *v.* Utter moan; lament.

moat *n.* Deep, wide, usu. water-filled, ditch round castle, town, etc. (ill. CASTLE). ~ *v.t.* Surround (as) with moat. **moat′ėd** *adj.*

mŏb *n.* Riotous or tumultuous crowd; rabble; promiscuous gathering. **mŏbb′ĭsh** *adj.* **mŏb** *v.t.* Attack in a mob; crowd round and molest.

mŏb′-căp′ *n.* Woman's round indoor cap covering whole head, worn in 18th and early 19th centuries.

mō′bīle *adj.* Movable; characterized by freedom of movement; (of troops etc.) that may be easily moved from place to place; of changing expression, volatile. **mōbĭl′ĭty** *n.* **mō′bīle** *n.* (In modern art) piece of sculpture with light loosely attached parts which may be agitated by currents of air.

mō′bĭlīze *v.* Render movable, bring into circulation; place (army etc.) on a war footing. **mō′bĭlīzable** *adj.* **mōbĭlīzā′tion** *n.*

mŏcc′asĭn *n.* 1. Amer. Indian soft shoe of deerskin etc. 2. Venomous snake of southern U.S.

mō′cha (-ka) *n.* Coffee of fine quality produced in the Yemen. [formerly exported from *Mocha*, Arabian port on Red Sea]

mŏck *v.* Hold up to ridicule, ridicule by imitation, counterfeit; set at nought; jeer, scoff; befool, tantalize; *mock′ing-bird*, Amer. passerine song-bird, *Mimus polyglottus*, that imitates other birds' notes. ~ *n.* Mockery; object of derision. ~ *attrib. adj.* Sham, counterfeit, pretended; ~*-heroic*, burlesque imitation of, burlesquely imitating, the heroic style; ~*-moon* = PARASELENE; ~ *orange*, common syringa; ~*-sun* = PARHELION; ~*-turtle* (*soup*), made of calf's head to imitate real turtle soup; ~*-up*, stage of design preceding the model that is adopted for production.

mŏck′ery *n.* Derision; laughing-stock; impudent simulation; ludicrously or insultingly futile action.

mŏd *n.* Gaelic congress for music and poetry, initiated 1891 in Scotland as equivalent of Welsh eisteddfod.

mōd′al *adj.* Of mode or form as opp. to substance; (mus.) of mode; (logic) involving affirmation of possibility, necessity, or contingency; (gram.) of the mood of a verb, (of particle) denoting manner. **modăl′ĭty** *n.* **mōd′ally** *adv.*

mōde *n.* 1. Way, manner, in which thing is done; prevailing fashion or conventional usage. 2. (mus.) Ancient Greek scale system (as AEOLIAN, DORIAN, IONIAN, LYDIAN, MIXOLYDIAN, PHRYGIAN); any of the scale-systems similarly named in medieval eccles. music (see also AUTHENTIC, PLAGAL); in more modern music the two (MAJOR and MINOR) chief scale-systems. 3. (statistics) That value of a character or graded quality at which the instances are most numerous.

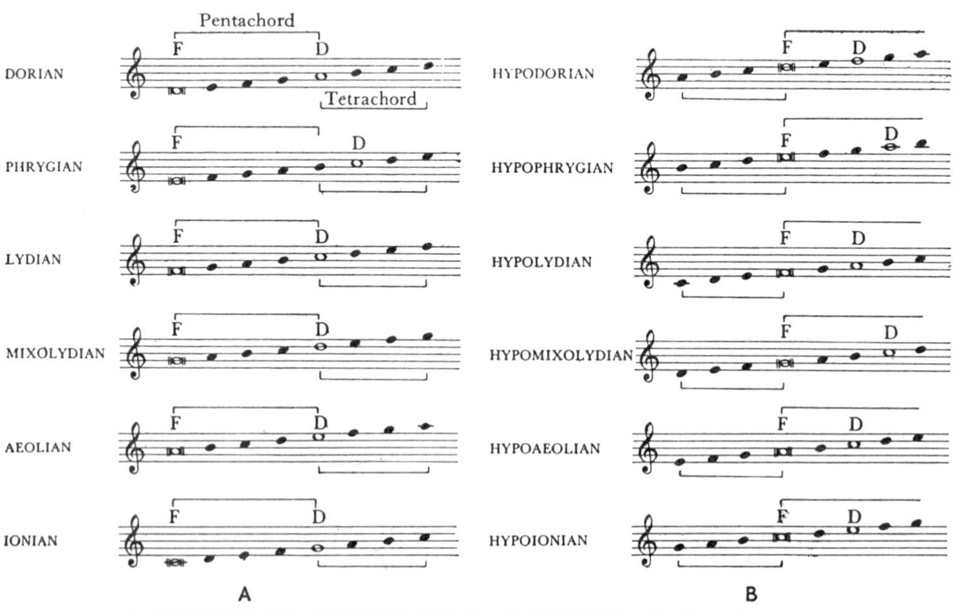

A. INTERVALS OF AUTHENTIC MODES. B. INTERVALS OF PLAGAL MODES
F = Final. D = Dominant

mŏd′el *n.* Representation in three dimensions of projected or existing structure or material object; design, pattern; object of imitation; mannequin; (freq. *Paris* ~) woman's dress, hat, etc., designed to be used as model for others. ~ *adj.* That is a model; exemplary, excellent of its kind. ~ *v.* 1. Mould, fashion; produce in clay, wax, etc. 2. Wear for display (as mannequin); pose as artist's model. **mŏd′elling** *n.* Making models, manipulating clay etc.; representation of form in sculpture or of material relief and solidity in painting.

mŏd′erate *adj.* Avoiding extremes, temperate; tolerable, mediocre; not excessive. **mŏd′erately** *adv.* **mŏd′erateness** *n.* **mŏd′erate** *n.* Person, esp. politician, of moderate views. **mŏd′erāte** *v.* Make or become less violent or excessive; act as moderator.

mŏderā′tion *n.* 1. Moderating, moderateness. 2. *M~s* (pl., Oxford Univ.) 1st public examination for Degree of B.A., pop. abbrev. *Mods.*

mŏd′erātor *n.* 1. Mediator; Presbyterian minister presiding over presbytery, synod, or general assembly. 2. (nuclear physics) Material used to dilute fissile material so as to control nuclear reaction. **mŏd′erātorship** *n.*

mŏd′ern *adj.* Of the present and recent times; new-fashioned, not antiquated; of school subjects, not concerned with the classics. **modĕrn′ity, mŏd′ernness** *ns.*

mŏd′ernism *n.* Modern usage, expression, etc.; modern fashion in art; mode of theological inquiry in which the traditions and doctrines of Christianity are examined in the light of modern thought. **mŏd′ernist** *n.* One who favours modernism in theology. **mŏdernis′tic** *adj.* (Of art, architecture, etc.) stridently imitating new fashions, superficially 'advanced'.

mŏd′ernize *v.t.* Make modern. **mŏdernizā′tion** *n.*

mŏd′est *adj.* Not overestimating one's own merits; not excessive; unpretentious; retiring, bashful; (of women) decorous in manner and conduct. **mŏd′estly** *adv.* **mŏd′esty** *n.*

mŏd′icŭm *n.* Small quantity or portion.

mŏd′ifȳ *v.t.* Tone down; alter without radical transformation; (gram.) qualify sense of (word etc.); change vowel by mutation. **mŏdifī′able** *adj.* **mŏdificā′tion** *n.* Act of modifying, state of being modified; change made in vowel by mutation, graphic representation of this (¨).

mŏdill′ion (-yon) *n.* (archit.) Projecting bracket under corona of cornice in Corinthian and other orders (ill. ORDER).

mōd′ish *adj.* Fashionable. **mōd′ishly** *adv.* **mōd′ishness** *n.*

mŏdiste′ (-ēst) *n.* Milliner, dressmaker.

Mŏd′red, Mordred. In Arthurian legend, Arthur's nephew, who treacherously seized the kingdom during Arthur's absence and was killed by him in the last battle in Cornwall.

Mods *abbrev.* MODERATIONS (Oxf. Univ.).

mŏd′ūlar *adj.* ~ *design* (archit.) Design based on a module or unit which is repeated throughout the building.

mŏd′ūlāte *v.* 1. Adjust, tone down; attune to a certain pitch or key, vary in tone. 2. (mus.) Pass from one key to another. 3. (physics) Modify (a wave) so that some property of that wave (the *modulated* or *carrier wave*) varies as a function of the instantaneous value of some other wave (the *modulating wave*). **mŏdūlā′tion** *n.*; *amplitude* ~ (abbrev. A.M.), transmission of signals by modulating the amplitude of the transmitted radio wave but keeping its frequency constant; *frequency* ~ (abbrev. F.M.), transmission of signals by modulating the frequency of the radio wave but keeping its amplitude constant.

mŏd′ūlātor *n.* 1. (mus.) Chart used in tonic sol-fa system for exercise in sight-singing. 2. (radio) Apparatus used for modulating a carrier wave.

mŏd'ūle *n.* Unit or standard of measurement, as for flow of water; (archit.) unit of measurement for determining the proportions of a building, in classical architecture usu. half the diameter of a column at the base (ill. ORDER); independent unit forming section of spacecraft.

mŏd'ūlus *n.* (math.) Constant multiplier or coefficient, esp. for converting Napierian into common logarithms.

mōd'us *n.* Method, manner, mode; ~ *ŏperăn'dī*, method, system, of working; plan of operations; ~ *vīvĕn'dī*, mode of living, esp. arrangement between disputants pending settlement.

Mogul Empire (mogŭl' *or* mō'gul). The Mohammedan Mongol empire in India, founded in 1526 by Babur, a descendant of Tamburlane; it reached its zenith under Akbar and Aurengzebe, was broken up after the death of the latter, and finally disappeared in 1857; *The Great* ~, the Mogul emperor. [Pers. *Mughal*, mispronunciation of *Mongol*]

M.O.H. *abbrev.* Medical Officer of Health; Ministry of Health.

mō'hair *n.* (Yarn or fabric made from) hair of Angora goat; imitation of this made of a mixture of wool and cotton.

Mohămm'ĕd or **Mahŏm'ĕt** (*c* 570–632). The Prophet of ISLAM, whose utterances are preserved in the KORAN; born at Mecca and buried at Medina; declared himself the Prophet, *c* 611, and sought to turn his fellow-Arabs from the local gods whom they then worshipped to the ancient religion of Abraham and other O.T. patriarchs and prophets; meeting with opposition in Mecca, fled to Medina in 622; this flight (the HEGIRA) is regarded as beginning the Moslem era. **Mohămm'ĕdan** *adj.* & *n.*

Mohămm'ĕd Ali (ahl'ī) (1769–1849). Viceroy of Egypt; founder of royal house of Egypt.

Mō'hawk. 1. A tribe of N. Amer. Indians belonging to the Iroquois. 2. The language of this tribe. 3. (skating) Stroke from an edge on one foot to the same edge on the other foot in an opposite direction.

Mohican (mōhē'c*an*). A warlike tribe of N. Amer. Indians, of Algonkin stock, formerly occupying W. parts of Connecticut and Massachusetts.

Mō'hŏck *n.* (hist.) One of a class of aristocratic ruffians who infested the London streets at night in the early years of the 18th c. [f. MOHAWK]

Mohs (mōs), Friedrich (1773–1839), German mineralogist, inventor of *Mohs' scale*: see HARDNESS, 2.

M.o.I. *abbrev.* Ministry of Information.

moi'dōre *n.* Former Portuguese gold coin worth about 27*s.* 6*d.*, current in England in early 18th c. [Port. *moeda d'ouro* money of gold]

moi'ĕty *n.* Half, esp. in legal use; (loosely) either of two parts into which thing is divided.

moil *v.i.* Drudge.

moire (mwahr) *n.* Watered silk fabric. [Fr., perh. f. Engl. *mohair*]

moiré (mwah'rā) *adj.* (Of silk) watered; (of metals) having clouded appearance like watered silk. ~ *n.* Appearance like that of watered silk. [Fr., f. *moirer* water (silk)]

Moissan (mwăsahn'), Henri (1852–1907). French chemist; first isolated fluorine; awarded the Nobel Prize for chemistry in 1906.

moist *adj.* Slightly wet, damp; rainy. **moist'nĕss** *n.*

mois'ten (-sn) *v.* Make or become moist.

mois'ture *n.* Liquid diffused through air or solid, or condensed on a surface.

mōke *n.* (slang) Donkey.

mōl'ar[1] *adj.* & *n.* Grinding (tooth), back tooth of mammals; in man there are three in each half of each jaw (ill. TOOTH). [L *mola* millstone]

mōl'ar[2] *adj.* (physics) Of, acting on or by, masses (often opp. to MOLECULAR); ~ *solution*, (chem.) solution containing one gram molecule of a specified substance per litre.

molăss'ĕs (-z) *n.* Thick viscid syrup, resembling treacle, drained from raw sugar during manufacture. [Port. *melaço*, f. LL *mellaceus* like honey]

Mŏldāv'ia. 1. (hist.) Danubian principality, from which, together with Wallachia, the kingdom of Rumania was formed in 1859. 2. A constituent republic of the Soviet Union, formed from territory in Rumania ceded to Russia in 1940; capital, Kishinev.

mōle[1] *n.* Abnormal pigmented prominence on skin.

mōle[2] *n.* Small animal, genus *Talpa*, with velvety, usu. blackish-grey, fur, very small eyes, and very short strong fore-limbs for burrowing; ~*-hill*, mound of earth thrown up by mole; *mole'skin*, mole's fur; strong, soft, fine-piled cotton fustian with surface shaved before dyeing, used for trousers etc.

mōle[3] *n.* Massive structure, esp. stone, serving as pier or breakwater.

mōle[4], **mōl** *n.* A weight of an element or compound numerically equal to its molecular weight in grams.

mŏl'ĕcūle (*or* mō-) *n.* 1. (chem. and physics) One of the minute groups of atoms of which material substances consist; the smallest particle to which a compound can be reduced by subdivision without losing its chemical identity. 2. (loosely) Small particle. **molĕc'ūlar** *adj.* Of molecules; ~ *weight*, weight of a molecule of a substance relative to weight of hydrogen atom.

molĕst' *v.t.* Meddle with injuriously or with hostile intent. **mŏlĕstā'tion** *n.*

Molière (mŏl'ïār). Stage-name of Jean Baptiste Poquelin (1622–73), French author of comedies satirizing contemporary manners.

Mŏl'inism *n.* 1. Religious doctrine taught by the Spanish Jesuit Luis Molina (1535–1600), that the efficacy of grace depends simply on the will that freely accepts it. 2. Doctrine of religious quietism taught by the Spanish mystic Miguel de Molinos (1640–96) **Mŏl'inist** *n.*

mŏll'ifȳ *v.t.* Soften, appease. **mŏllificā'tion** *n.*

mŏll'usc *n.* Any animal of the phylum *Mollusca* which comprises soft-bodied unsegmented invertebrates (usu. having a hard protective shell) and includes limpets, snails, cuttlefish, oysters, etc. (ill. MUSSEL). **mollŭs'can, mollŭs'coid, mollŭs'cous** *adjs.*

mŏll'y-coddle *n.* Milksop. ~ *v.t.* coddle, pamper, pet; f. **mŏll'y** *n.* Effeminate man or boy, milksop. [pet form of *Mary*]

Mōl'ŏch (-k). A Canaanite god to whose image children were sacrificed as burnt-offerings: see Lev. xviii. 21, 2 Kings xxiii. 10; (fig.) power or influence to which everything is sacrificed. **mōl'ŏch** *n.* The Australian thorn-lizard or thorn-devil, *Molochus horridus.*

mōl'ten *adj.* (past part. of *melt*) Liquefied by great heat.

Mŏlt'kė, Helmuth von, Count (1800–91). Prussian field marshal; reorganized the Prussian army before the Franco-German War of 1870–1.

mŏl'tō *adv.* (mus.) Very (preceding mus. direction, as ~ *espressivo*).

Molŭcc'as. Islands of Indonesia, SE. of Philippines.

mōl'y *n.* Fabulous plant with white flower and black root, given by Hermes to Odysseus as a charm against the sorceries of Circe.

molȳb'dėnite *n.* Molybdenum disulphide (MoS_2), a soft flaky black mineral resembling graphite.

molȳb'dėnum *n.* Greyish-white metallic element resembling tungsten and having a very high melting-point, a constituent of special steel alloys; symbol Mo, at. no. 42, at. wt 95·94. [Gk *molubdos* lead]

mōm'ent *n.* Point of time, instant; importance, weight; (mech.) measure of power of a force to cause rotation round an axis.

mōm'entary *adj.* Lasting but for a moment. **mōm'entarily** *adv.* **mōm'entarinĕss** *n.*

mōm'ently *adv.* Every moment.

momĕn'tous *adj.* Important; weighty. **momĕn'tously** *adv.* **momĕn'tousnĕss** *n.*

momĕn'tŭm *n.* (mech.) 'Quantity of motion' of a moving body, product of mass multiplied by velocity; (pop.) impetus gained by movement.

Mŏmm'sen, Theodor (1817–1903). German historian and archaeologist; author of a 'History of Rome'.

Mŏm'us. (Gk myth.) The god of mockery; expelled from heaven for his criticisms and ridicule of the gods; hence, a fault-finder.

Mon. *abbrev.* Monday; Monmouthshire.

Mōn'a. An island, anciently inhabited by Druids, lying between England and Ireland; supposed to be the Isle of Man or Anglesey.

mŏn'achal (-k-) *adj.* Monastic. **mŏn'achism** *n.*

Mŏna'cō (-ah-). Independent principality, under French protection since 1861, on French Riviera, including Monte Carlo within its borders.

mŏn'ad *n.* 1. (hist.) The number one, unit. 2. (philos.) Ultimate unit of being (e.g. a soul, an atom, a person, God), esp. in philosophy of LEIBNIZ. 3. (biol.) Primary individual organism assumed as first term in a genealogy. **monăd'ic** *adj.* **mŏn'adism** *n.* Theory of monadic nature of matter or of substance generally, applied esp. to philosophy of Leibniz.

mŏnadĕl'phous *adj.* (bot.) (Of stamens) having filaments united into one bundle.

Mŏn'aghan (-*a*-han). Inland county of Ulster, Eire.

Mŏn'a Lisa (lēz'*a*). Portrait, now in the Louvre, of a lady traditionally identified as the wife of Francesco del Gioconda, painted by Leonardo da Vinci and famous for its strange smile.

mŏn'arch (-k) *n.* 1. Sovereign with title of king, queen, emperor, or equivalent; supreme ruler (often fig.). 2. Large orange-and-black butterfly (*Danaus plexippus*). **monarch'al, monarch'ic(al)** *adjs.*

mŏn'archism (-k-) *n.* Principles of, attachment to, monarchy. **mŏn'archist** *n.*

mŏn'archy (-kĭ) *n.* (State under) monarchical government.

mŏn'astery *n.* Residence of community of monks.

monăs'tic *adj.* Of monks or monasteries; secluded, austere. **monăs'tically** *adv.* **monăs'ticism** *n.*

mŏn'azite *n.* Phosphate mineral, containing thorium and rare-earth elements, found in alluvial sands in India and Brazil.

Monday (mŭn'dā, -dĭ). 2nd day of the week; *Black*~, (school slang) first day of term. [OE *Monan dæg* (= moon's day), rendering of LL *lunae dies*]

monde (mawnd) *n.* The fashionable world, society; the set in which one moves.

Mŏnet' (-nā), Claude (1840–1926). French Impressionist painter.

mon'ĕtary (mŭ-, mŏ-) *adj.* Of coinage or money.

mon'ĕtize (mŭ-, mŏ-) *v.t.* Put in circulation as money; give standard value to (metal) in coinage of a country; **monĕtizā'tion** *n.*

money (mŭn'ĭ) *n.* (pl. -*s*). 1. Current coin; coin and promissory documents representing it, esp. (*paper* ~) government and bank-notes; (econ.) anything generally accepted in settlement of debts. 2. (with pl.) Particular coin. 3. (pl., archaic or legal) Sums of money. 4. ~ *of account*, term of value or price, as the Engl. *pound* and *guinea*; ~ *bill*, a bill, originating in the House of Commons, involving expenditure or raising of money for public purposes; *-changer*, one whose business it is to change money at a fixed rate; ~*-grubber*, one bent on accumulating money; avaricious person; ~*-lender*, one who lends money at interest; ~*-market*, sphere of operations of dealers in loans, stocks and shares; ~*-order*, order for payment of money, issued by a post-office; ~*-spinner*, pop. name of a small red garden spider supposed to bring good luck in money matters; ~*-wort*, creeping herb (*Lysimachia nummularia*) with round leaves and single yellow flower; creeping-jenny. **mon'eyed** (-ĭd) *adj.* Wealthy.

mong'er (mŭngg-) *n.* Dealer, trader (chiefly in combination, as *fishmonger*, *ironmonger*, and fig. *scandal-monger*).

Mŏng'ol, Mongōl'ian (-ngg-) *adj.* & *n.* 1. (One) of an Asiatic race now chiefly inhabiting **Mongō'lia,** a country between China proper and Siberia. 2. More widely, one belonging to the yellow-skinned straight-haired type of mankind, a Mongoloid. 3. Also applied to a type of mental defectives resembling Mongolians in appearance, i.e. in having high cheek-bones, flat noses, and slanting 'almond'-shaped eyes. **Mŏng'olism** *n.* This type of mental deficiency.

Mŏng'oloid (-ngg-) *adj.* & *n.* 1. (Member) of that one of the five principal races of mankind which prevails over the region lying E. of a line drawn from Lapland to Siam. 2. (Defective) of the Mongolian type.

mŏng'ōōse (-ngg-) *n.* (pl. -*gooses*). 1. Small carnivorous mammal of Old World tropics (genus *Herpestes*), esp. the Indian mongoose (*H. griseus*). 2. Species of lemur found in Madagascar (*Lemur mongoz*).

mong'rel (mŭngg-) *n.* & *adj.* (Dog, animal, etc.) of no definable breed, resulting from various crossings; (person etc.) not of pure race. **mong'relism** *n.* **mong'relize** *v.t.*

Mŏn'ica, St. (332–87). Mother of St. AUGUSTINE[1] of Hippo.

mŏn'ism *n.* (philos.) Any theory denying the duality of matter and mind, as dist. from DUALISM and PLURALISM. **mŏn'ist** *n.* **mŏnis'tic** *adj.*

moni'tion *n.* Warning; official or legal (esp. ecclesiastical) notice (admonishing a person to refrain from a specified offence).

mŏn'itor *n.* 1. One who admonishes (archaic). 2. Senior pupil in school with disciplinary functions. 3. One who is appointed to listen to and report on foreign broadcasts, telephone conversations, etc. 4. Detector for induced radio-activity, esp. in atomic plant workers. 5. Kind of Old World tropical lizard of genus *Varanus*, supposed to give warning of the vicinity of crocodiles (ill. LIZARD). 6. Ironclad with low freeboard and revolving gun-turrets, for coast

MONASTERY

1. Gatehouse. 2. Church. 3. Abbot's lodging. 4. Store-rooms. 5. Cloister. 6. Garth. 7. Chapter-house. 8. Kitchen. 9. Refectory or frater. 10. Dorter or dormitory. 11. Infirmary. 12. Bakehouse. 13. Mill

defence, so called from name of first vessel of this type, designed by Capt. Ericsson, in the Amer. Civil War, 1862. ~ *v.t.* Regulate volume and intensity of (sound records); listen to and report on (foreign broadcasts, telephone conversations, etc.) **mŏnĭtôr'ĭal** *adj.* Admonishing; connected with, pertaining to, school monitors.

monk[1] (mŭ-) *n.* Member of community of men living apart from the world under religious vows and according to a rule; *monk's-hood*, aconite. **monk'dom** *n.* **monk'ĭsh** *adj.*

Monk[2], **Monck** (mŭ-), George (1608–70). English general and admiral; supporter and trusted adviser of Cromwell; instrumental in restoring the monarchy (1660); created first Duke of Albemarle.

monk'ey (mŭ-) *n.* 1. One of a group of mammals allied to and resembling man and ranging from anthropoid apes to marmosets; any animal of order *Primates* except

MONKEYS
1. Marmoset. 2. Macaque

man, the tarsiers, and the lemurs, usu. restricted to the small, long-tailed members, as dist. from the large, short-tailed apes. 2. Mischievous, playful young person. 3. Machine hammer for pile-driving. 4. (slang) £500. 5. *his ~ is up*, he is angry or enraged; *~-bread*, fruit of the baobab tree; *~ engine*, engine which lifts the head of a pile-driver; *~-jacket*, sailor's short close-fitting jacket; *~-nut*, PEA-nut; *~ puzzle*, the Chile pine, *Araucaria imbricata*, with broad prickly spines growing at intervals down the branches; *~-wrench*, wrench or spanner with adjustable jaws. ~ *v.i.* Fool *about*, play mischievous tricks (*with*).

Monmouth[1] (mŭn'm*u*th), James Scott, Duke of (1649–85). Illegitimate son of Charles II and Lucy Walters; collected an army in the W. of England and led it against James II; was defeated at Sedgemoor, captured, and beheaded.

Monmouth[2] (mŭn'm*u*th). County town of **Mon'mouthshire**, English county on Welsh border N. of Severn estuary.

mŏno- (before vowels **mon-**) *prefix.* Alone, sole, single.

mŏnobās'ĭc *adj.* (chem., of an acid) Having only one acidic hydrogen atom in its molecule.

mŏnocârp'ĭc, mŏnocârp'ous *adjs.* (bot.) Bearing fruit once and then dying.

mŏnochlamȳd'ėous (-k-) *adj.* (bot.) Having only one floral envelope; having a single perianth.

mŏn'ochôrd (-k-) *n.* Musical instrument with single string, used for mathematical determination of musical intervals.

mŏn'ochrōme (-k-) *n.* & *adj.* (Picture etc.) having only one colour, or executed in different shades of one colour. **mŏnochromăt'ĭc** *adj.*

mŏn'ocle *n.* Single eye-glass.

mŏnoclĭn'ĭc *adj.* (Of a crystal) having one of the axial sections oblique (ill. CRYSTAL).

mŏnocŏtȳlēd'on *n.* Plant having a single cotyledon or seed-leaf (ill. SEEDLING). **mŏnocŏtȳlēd'onous** *adj.*

monŏc'ūlar *adj.* Of, adapted for, one eye, as ~ *microscope.*

mŏn'ocȳte *n.* One of the several forms of leucocytes or white blood-cells (ill. BLOOD).

mŏn'odrama (-drah-) *n.* Dramatic piece for performance by a single person.

mŏn'ody *n.* (Gk literature) Lyric ode sung by a single voice; dirge, elegy. **monŏd'ĭc** *adj.* **mŏn'odĭst** *n.*

monoe'cious (-nē'sh*u*s) *adj.* (bot.) Having reproductive organs of both sexes on same plant (but, if a flowering plant, in different flowers; ill. FLOWER).

monŏg'amy *n.* Condition, rule, or custom of being married to only one person at a time, as dist. from *polygamy*. **monŏg'amĭst** *n.* **monŏg'amous** *adj.*

mŏn'ogrăm *n.* Character composed of two or more interwoven letters. **mŏnogrammăt'ĭc** *adj.*

mŏn'ograph (-ahf) *n.* Treatise on single object or class of objects. **monŏg'rapher, monŏg'raphĭst** *ns.* **mŏnogrăph'ĭc** *adj.* **mŏnogrăph'ĭcally** *adv.*

mŏn'olĭth *n.* 1. Single block of stone as pillar or monument. 2. (building) Mass of concrete, masonry, etc., forming a solid element in a structure. 3. Political or social structure presenting an indivisible or unbroken unity. **mŏnolĭt'hĭc** *adj.* Of, like, a monolith; unified and homogeneous; not exhibiting deviation or minority interests.

mŏn'olŏgue (-g) *n.* Soliloquy; dramatic composition for a single performer. **mŏnolŏ'gĭcal** (-j-) *adj.* **monŏl'ogĭst** (-j-) *n.* **monŏl'ogīze** (-j-) *v.i.*

mŏnomān'ĭa *n.* Form of insanity, obsession of the mind by a single idea or interest. **mŏnomān'ĭăc** *n.*

mŏn'omârk *n.* One of a system of registered marks (letters and figures) identifying articles, goods, addresses, etc.

mŏn'omêr *n.* (chem.) 1. One of the units forming a polymer molecule (see POLYMER). 2. A compound which can undergo polymerization.

mŏnomĕt'alĭsm *n.* Use of standard of currency based on one metal.

monōm'ĭal *adj.* & *n.* (alg.) (Expression) consisting of a single term.

mŏn'ophthŏng *n.* A single vowel sound, as dist. from *diphthong*. **mŏn'ophthŏngīze** (-ngg-) *v.t.* Reduce (diphthong) to a monophthong.

Monŏph'ȳsīte. One who holds there is only one nature in the person of Christ.

mŏn'oplāne *n.* Aeroplane with one plane, as dist. from *biplane* (ill. AEROPLANE).

monŏp'olĭst *n.* Holder or supporter of monopoly.

monŏp'olīze *v.t.* Secure monopoly of. **monŏpolīzā'tion** *n.*

monŏp'olȳ *n.* Exclusive possession or control; exclusive trading privilege.

mŏn'orail *n.* A railway in which the track consists of a single rail.

mŏnosȳll'able *n.* Word of one syllable. **mŏnosȳllăb'ĭc** *adj.*

mŏn'othēĭsm *n.* Doctrine that there is only one God. **mŏn'othēĭst** *n.* **mŏnothėĭs'tĭc** *adj.*

mŏn'otōne *n.* Sound continuing or repeated on one note, or without change of tone. **mŏnotŏn'ĭc** *adj.* 1. (mus.) In monotone. 2. (math., of a sequence) Such that all members of it either do not increase or do not decrease.

monŏt'onous *adj.* Having no variation in tone or cadence; lacking in variety, always the same. **monŏt'onously** *adv.* **monŏt'onousnėss, monŏt'ony** *ns.*

mŏn'otrēme *n.* (zool.) Mammal of sub-class *Monotremata*, primitive egg-laying forms of Australasia including duck-billed platypus and spiny ant-eaters.

mŏn'otȳpe *n.* 1. Print taken from a freshly painted card, plate, or block. 2. '*M~*', proprietary name of printing apparatus which casts and sets up type in single letters by means of a perforated roll which has been previously produced on another part of the apparatus.

mŏnovāl'ent (*or* monŏv'a-) *adj.* (chem.) Having a VALENCY of 1, univalent.

mŏnŏx'īde *n.* (chem.) An oxide with one oxygen atom in the molecule.

Monroe (m*u*nrō'), James (1758–1831). Amer. politician; 5th president of U.S., 1817–25; formulator (1823) of the ~ *Doctrine* that interference by any European State in the Spanish-American republics would be regarded as an act unfriendly to the U.S., and that the

American continents were no longer open to European colonial settlement.

Mŏns. Town in Hainaut, Belgium, near the French frontier, where the British Expeditionary Force fought its first battle (1914) in the war of 1914–18, followed by the great retreat to the Marne.

monseigneur (mŏnsānyẽr′) *n.* French title given to dignitaries, esp. princes, cardinals, and bishops (abbrev. Mgr).

monsieur (mosyẽr′) *n.* French title prefixed to man's name, surname, or nobiliary or other title; sir, Mr; Frenchman; (hist.) second son or younger brother of king of France.

monsignor (-sēn′yōr) *n.* Honorific title granted by pope to high officials of the papal household.

mŏnsōōn′ *n.* Seasonal wind prevailing in southern Asia, from south-west (*wet* ~) in summer and north-east (*dry* ~) in winter; rainy season accompanying SW. monsoon. [prob. f. Arab. *mausim*, lit. season]

mŏn′ster *n.* 1. Imaginary animal compounded of elements from various creatures. 2. Person or thing of portentous appearance or size. 3. Inhumanly cruel or wicked person. 4. (path.) Grossly malformed product of human conception.

mŏn′strance *n.* (R.C. Ch.) Receptacle in which the consecrated Host is exposed for veneration, consisting usu. of a glass or crystal case set in a gold or silver frame (ill. CIBORIUM).

mŏnstrŏs′ĭty *n.* Monstrousness; misshapen or outrageous thing.

mŏn′strous *adj.* Like a monster; huge; outrageous. **mŏn′strously** *adv.* **mŏn′strousnėss** *n.*

Mont. *abbrev.* Montana; Montgomeryshire.

mŏn′tage (-ahzh) *n.* 1. Selection and fitting together of cinematographic shots in making film. 2. Arrangement of cut-out illustrations, or fragments of them, as artist's technique of making pictures.

Montagna (mŏntahn′ya), Bartolomeo (d. 1523). Italian painter.

Mŏn′tagū, Lady Mary Wortley (1689–1762). English letter-writer and traveller.

Mŏntaigne′ (-ān), Michel Eyquem de (1533–92). French writer; author of 'Essais' which reveal a sagacious and tolerant philosophy of life, stressing the fallibility of the human reason and the relativity of human science.

Mŏntăn′a. Mountain State of U.S., on the Canadian border E. of the Rocky Mountains; admitted to the Union in 1889; capital, Helena.

mŏn′tāne *adj.* Of, inhabiting, mountainous country.

Mŏntăn′us (2nd c.). Founder in Phrygia of **Mŏn′tanism,** the belief of a heretical Christian sect, who reacted against the growing secularism of the Church, desired a stricter adhesion to the principles of primitive Christianity, and prepared for the earthly kingdom of Christ. **Mŏn′tanist** *adj.* & *n.*

Mont Blanc (mawn̄ blahn̄). Mountain in France on Italian border; highest in Europe (15,782 ft).

mŏntbrē′tia (-sh*a*) *n.* English name of a commonly cultivated and extensively naturalized hybrid plant of two species of the genus *Crocosmia.* [A. F. E. Coquebert de *Montbret* (1780–1801), French botanist]

Montcalm (mŏnkahm′), Louis-Joseph de Montcalm-Gozon, Marquis de (1712–59). French soldier; defended Quebec against Wolfe and was mortally wounded in the battle which followed the scaling of the Heights of Abraham.

mŏn′tė *n.* A Spanish-American game of chance, played with 45 cards.

Mŏn′tė Cārl′ō. One of the 3 communes of Monaco; famous as a gambling resort.

Mŏn′tė Cassino (-ēn′ō). Hill midway between Rome and Naples, site of the principal monastery of the Benedictine Order, founded by St. Benedict *c* 529. The monastery, previously demolished and rebuilt several times, was almost totally destroyed in a battle between German and Allied forces in 1944, but has since been restored.

Mŏntėnēg′rō. Former monarchy of SE. Europe, on the Adriatic; since 1919 a part of Yugoslavia. **Mŏntėnēg′rĭn** *adj.* & *n.* (Native) of Montenegro.

Mŏntėspan′ (-ăn̄), Françoise-Athénaïs de Pardaillar, Marquise de (1641–1707). Mistress of Louis XIV, to whom she bore 7 children.

Montesquieu (mawn̄teskyẽr′), Charles Louis de Secondat de (1689–1755). French political philosopher; author of 'L'Esprit des Lois' (1748), in which he analysed the types of political constitution and denounced the abuses of the French monarchy.

Mŏntėssōr′ĭ, Maria (1870–1952). Italian educationalist; originator of a system of training small children by the use of apparatus teaching manual dexterity, the matching of colours or shapes, etc., under less rigid discipline than was formerly common.

Mŏntėverd′ĭ (-vār-), Claudio (1567–1643). Italian composer of instrumental music, madrigals, and operas.

Mŏntėzūm′a II (1466–1520). Aztec emperor of Mexico at the time of the Spanish conquest; was seized and held as a hostage by Cortez, and mortally wounded when his people attempted to rescue him.

Mŏnt′fort, Simon de, (1208 ?–65). Norman-English earl of Leicester; married Eleanor, sister of Henry III of England; led the barons in a revolt against the king, 1263, and captured him at Lewes, 1264; summoned, 1265, a parliament which included, besides the barons, knights, and ecclesiastics, two citizens from every borough in England.

Montgolfier (mawn̄gŏl′fyā), Joseph Michel (1740–1810), and Jacques Étienne (1745–99), brothers. French inventors of a balloon raised by heated air.

Montgo′mery[1] (-gŭ-), Bernard Law, Viscount ~ of Alamein (1887–). British field marshal; commander of 8th Army from 1943 during the N. African campaign; C.-in-C. of British group of armies in France and Germany, 1944–6.

Montgŏm′ery[2]**.** Capital of Alabama, U.S.

Montgo′meryshire (-gŭ-). Welsh inland county on the English border.

month (mŭ-) *n.* Period of moon's revolution (*lunar* ~); one of 12 portions into which conventional year is divided (*calendar* ~); (loosely) period of 4 weeks.

month′ly *adj.* Done, recurring, payable, etc., once a month; ~ *rose*, semi-single pink China rose, which flowers for several months. ~ *n.* Magazine etc. published each month; (pl.) menses. ~ *adv.*

Montmārtre′ (mawn̄-, -tr) District in the N. of Paris; during the 19th c. the 'artistic quarter' and the site of many famous cafés and cabarets.

Montrachet (mawn̄răshā′). District of the Côte d'Or, S. France; the white wine made there.

Mŏntrėal′ (-awl). Canadian city and port on the St. Lawrence River.

Montreux Convention (mawn̄trẽr′). Agreement between Turkey and the Allies of the war of 1914–18, signed at Montreux, Switzerland, in 1936, restoring to Turkey the right of re-militarizing the Dardanelles and Bosporus.

Montrōse′ (-z), James Graham, Marquis of (1612–50). Scottish soldier; played a large part in Scottish history in the reign of Charles I; he was first a Covenanter but fought for Charles in Scotland during the Civil War.

Mont St. Michel (mawn̄, mē-sh′ĕl). Islet off the coast of Normandy, a rocky peak crowned by a medieval Benedictine abbey-fortress.

mŏn′ūment *n.* Anything that by its survival commemorates person, action, or event, esp. erection intended to do this; outstanding survival of an early literature; *The M~*, a Doric column 202 ft high in the City of London, built by Wren (1671–7) to commemorate the Great Fire of 1666, which broke out in Pudding Lane near by.

mŏnūmĕn′tal *adj.* Like, of, serving as, a monument; colossal, stupendous; ~ *mason*, tombstone-maker. **mŏnūmĕn'tally** *adv.* **mŏnūmĕntăl'ity** *n.*

mŏnūmĕn'talīze *v.t.* Record, commemorate, as by monument.

mōō *v.i.* (Of cow or ox) low, make the sound *moo*; hence, **mōō** *n.*

mōōch *v.i.* (slang) Loaf *about*; slouch *along*.

mōōd[1] *n.* Frame of mind or state of feelings. **mōōd'y** *adj.* Subject to changes of mood; depressed, sullen. **mōōd'ily** *adv.* **mōōd'inėss** *n.*

mōōd[2] *n.* 1. (gram.) Group of forms in conjugation of verb serving to indicate function in which it is used, as INDICATIVE, IMPERATIVE, SUBJUNCTIVE ~. 2. (logic) Any of the classes into which each of the figures of a valid categorical syllogism is divided.

Mōōd'y and Sănk'ey. Dwight Lyman Moody (1837–99) and Ira David Sankey (1840–1908), American religious revivalists and hymn-writers.

mōōn *n.* Earth's satellite; secondary planet reflecting light from sun to earth during night, and revolving round the earth in one lunar month; aspect of this at any one time, as *full* ~, *new* ~, etc.; (poet.) month; *moon'calf*, misshapen birth, f. supposed influence of the moon; stupid person; *moon'flower*, the ox-eye daisy; *moon'light*, light of moon (often attrib.); *moonlight flitting*, removal of household goods by night to avoid paying rent; *moon'lighting*, in Ireland, perpetration by night of outrages on tenants who incurred the hostility of the Land League; hence, *moon'lighter*; modified street lighting; *moon'lit*, lit up by moon; *moon'shine*, moonlight; (fig.) visionary talk or ideas; illicitly distilled or smuggled spirits, esp. whisky; hence, *moon'shiner*, (U.S.) illicit distiller, smuggler of spirits; *moon'stone*, variety of felspar having a pearly lustre, used as a gem; *moon'struck* (*adj.*) lunatic, distracted or dazed, a condition formerly supposed to be due to the moon's influence. ~ *v.i.* Go *about* dreamily or listlessly. **mōōn'y** *adj.* Of, like, the moon; listless, stupidly dreamy.

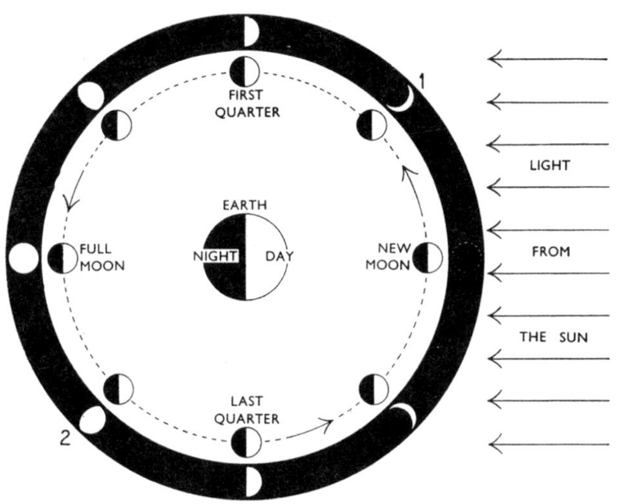

PHASES OF THE MOON

The diagram shows how the light from the sun falls on the moon, giving the appearance as in the black ring. 1. Crescent. 2. Gibbous

moor[1] *n.* Tract of unenclosed, often heather-covered, waste land, or of similar land preserved for shooting (also *moor'land*); ~*-cock*, male red grouse; ~*-hen*, water-hen. **moor'ish, moor'y** *adjs.*

moor[2] *v.t.* Attach (boat etc.) by rope to shore or something fixed. **moor'age** *n.* Place, charge, for mooring. **moor'ings** *n.pl.* Place where vessel can be moored.

Moor[3] *n.* One of a Mohammedan people of mixed Berber and Arab race, inhabiting NW. Africa, who in the 8th c. conquered Spain (see also MOROCCO[1]). **Moor'ish** *adj.*

Moore[1], Francis (1656–1715). Astrologer and quack physician; advertised his pills by publishing an almanac forecasting weather etc., 1699; *Old* ~*'s Almanac*, any of various imitations of this.

Moore[2], George (1852–1933). Irish novelist; author of 'Esther Waters', 'The Brook Kerith', 'Héloïse and Abélard', etc.

Moore[3], Sir John (1761–1809). English soldier; C.-in-C. in the Peninsular War, 1808; was mortally wounded at Coruña during the retreat, and buried there in 1809.

mōōse (-s) *n.* (pl. same). N. Amer. elk (*Alces machlis*), largest of the deer; ~*-horn*, instrument used by hunters for imitating its call.

mōōt *n.* (hist.) (Legislative or judicial) meeting. ~ *adj.* That can be argued, debatable. ~ *v.t.* Raise (question etc.) for discussion.

mŏp *n.* Bundle of yarn etc. fixed to stick for use in cleaning, polishing, etc.; *Mrs M*~, joc. name for charwoman. ~ *v.t.* Clean or wipe with or as with mop; wipe tears, sweat, etc., from (brow etc.); ~ *up*, wipe up (as) with mop; (slang) absorb (profits etc.), dispatch, finish off, make an end of; (mil.) complete occupation of (place) by capturing or killing remaining enemy troops.

mōpe *v.i.* Be dull, dejected, and spiritless. ~ *n.* Person who mopes; (chiefly pl.) gloomy state of mind. **mōp'ish** *adj.* **mōp'ishnėss** *n.*

mŏquĕtte' (-k-) *n.* Fabric with velvety pile, made of wool on basis of cotton or jute, used in upholstery etc.

môr *n.* Humus formed under acid conditions (opp. MULL[4]).

moraine' *n.* Debris of sand, clay, and boulders deposited by melting glacier (ill. MOUNTAIN).

mŏ'ral *adj.* Concerned with character or disposition, or with the distinction between right and wrong; morally good, virtuous, righteous; ~ *certainty*, probability so great as to admit of no reasonable doubt; ~ *courage*, courage to encounter odium, contempt, etc., rather than abandon right course; ~ *philosophy*, ethics; *M*~ *Re-Armament* (abbrev. M.R.A.) name of the ideological campaign launched by Dr Buchman in 1938 as an extension of the OXFORD Group; ~ *victory*, defeat, indecisive result, that eventually produces the moral effects of victory. **mŏ'rally** *adv.* **mŏ'ral** *n.* Moral teaching (of fable, story, etc.); (pl.) habits or conduct from point of view of morality.

morale' (-ahl) *n.* Mental state or condition, esp. (of troops) as regards discipline and confidence.

mŏ'ralism *n.* Natural system of morality; principles of conduct based on distinction between right and wrong, not on religion.

mŏ'ralist *n.* One who practises or teaches morality; adherent of moralism. **mŏralĭs'tic** *adj.*

morăl'ity *n.* 1. Moral principles or rules; moral conduct. 2. Kind of drama (popular in 16th c.) inculcating moral or spiritual lesson.

mŏ'ralīze *v.* Indulge in moral reflection; interpret morally or symbolically. **mŏralīzā'tion** *n.*

morăss' *n.* Wet swampy tract, bog.

mŏratôr'ium *n.* Legal authorization to debtor to postpone payment.

Morāv'ĭa. Province of Czechoslovakia. **Morāv'ĭan** *adj.* & *n.* 1. (Inhabitant) of Moravia. 2. (One) of a Hussite Protestant sect, the

'Unity of Moravian brethren' founded in Saxony in the early 18th c. by emigrants from Moravia; the sect obtained many adherents in England and the American colonies.

Morayshire (mŭ'rĭ-). County of NE. Scotland S. of the Moray Firth; formerly called Elgin.

mŏrb'id *adj.* (Of mind, ideas, etc.) unwholesome, sickly; (med.) of the nature, or indicative, of disease. **mŏrb'idly** *adv.* **mŏrb'idness** *n.* **mŏrbid'ity** *n.* Morbidness; prevalence of disease (in a district).

mŏrbif'ic *adj.* Causing disease, pathogenic.

mŏrd'ant *adj.* (Of sarcasm etc.) caustic, biting; pungent, smarting; (of acids) corrosive. ~ *n.* Substance used for fixing textile dyes; acid used in etching. **mŏrdā'cious** (-shus) *adj.* **mŏrdă'city, mŏrd'ancy** *ns.*

mŏrd'ent *n.* (mus.) Grace consisting of two 'timeless' notes rapidly inserted before principal note, in *upper* ~, consisting of principal note, note above, and back to principal note, in *lower* ~, of principal note, note below, and back to principal note.

mōre[1] *adj.* Greater; (something) in greater quantity, amount, or degree; greater number of, further. ~ *adv.* To a greater extent, in a greater degree, additionally.

Mōre[2], Henry (1614–87). English Platonist and philosophical poet.

Mōre[3], Sir Thomas (1478–1535). English statesman, author of 'Utopia' (1516), a description, in Latin, of an imaginary perfect State; he succeeded Wolsey as Lord Chancellor, 1529, but resigned in 1532, refusing to take any oath that would impugn the pope's authority or assume the justice of Henry VIII's divorce from Catherine of Aragon; he was therefore indicted of high treason, found guilty, and beheaded; canonized (as St. Thomas ~), 1935.

moreen' *n.* Woollen or woollen and cotton fabric with a rib or twill in it, used esp. for curtains.

morĕll'ō *n.* Dark-coloured bitter cherry.

moreov'er (mōrōv-) *adv.* Besides, further.

Morĕsque' (-k) *adj.* Moorish in style or design.

Mŏrg'an, John Pierpont (1837–1913). American banker who amassed a large fortune.

mŏrganăt'ic *adj.* (Of a marriage) between man of exalted rank and woman of lower rank in which it is provided that the wife and her children shall not share the rank or inherit the possessions of the husband. [OHG *morgangeba* gift from husband to wife the morning after consummation of marriage]

Mŏrg'an le Fay. 'Morgan the Fairy', a magician, sister of King Arthur; see also FATA MORGANA.

mŏrgue (-g) *n.* Building (esp. one formerly in Paris) in which bodies of persons found dead are exposed for identification; (journalism) repository of material for obituary notices.

mŏ'ribŭnd *adj.* In a dying state.

Moris'cō *n.* Descendant of the Moors in Spain.

Mŏrl'and, George (1763–1804). English painter of animals, genre, and landscape.

Mŏrl'ey, John, first viscount Morley of Blackburn (1838–1923). English liberal politician and author, famous esp. for his 'Life of Gladstone' (1903).

Mŏrm'on *n.* Member of the 'Church of Jesus Christ of Latter-day Saints', founded in New York, 1830, by Joseph Smith of Vermont; he claimed that a 'parallel volume' to the Bible, the 'Book of Mormon', had been revealed to him, and that its author, the prophet Mormon, had been one of a race which had colonized America from Palestine in ancient times; the sect grew rapidly but met with hostility esp. for advocating polygamy (which they did until 1890); eventually, led by Brigham YOUNG, they migrated to Utah and there founded Salt Lake City in 1847. **Mŏrm'onism** *n.*

mŏrn *n.* (poet.) Morning; dawn.

mŏrn'ing *n.* Early part of daytime, ending at noon or at time of midday meal; *good* ~, form of greeting; *~-coat*, man's tail-coat with front sloped away; *~-dress*, dress other than evening dress; *~-glory*, Amer. plant of genus *Ipomaea*, with showy flowers; *~-room*, sitting-room, other than dining- or drawing-room; ~ *sickness*, nausea commonly experienced in morning in early months of pregnancy; ~ *star*, Venus (or other planet or bright star) seen to the east before sunrise; *~-watch*, (naut.) the watch at sea from 4 a.m. to 8 a.m.

Morŏcc'ō[1]. Country of NW. Africa, bounded on N. and W. by the Mediterranean Sea and Atlantic Ocean and on S. and E. by Algeria; inhabited by people descended from Berbers, Arabs, and Moors; formerly a French Protectorate, with a Spanish 'sphere of influence'; since 1956 an independent kingdom ruled by a Sultan, with the exception of the international zone of TANGIER; capital, Rabat. **Morŏcc'an** *adj.*

morŏcc'ō[2] *n.* Fine flexible leather made orig. in Morocco, now also elsewhere, from goatskins tanned with sumac; imitation of this made from calf- or sheepskins, grained to resemble true morocco; *Levant* ~, high-grade, large-grained morocco, used for book-binding.

morŏccōĕtte' *n.* Textile material for bookbinding, imitating morocco.

mōr'on *n.* Adult whose mental development corresponds to that of a normal average child between the ages of 8 and 12. **mōrŏn'ic** *adj.*

morōse' *adj.* Sour-tempered, sullen, and unsocial. **morōse'ly** (-sl-) *adv.* **morōse'nĕss** *n.*

mŏrph'ēme *n.* (philol.) A morphological element considered in respect of its functional relations to a linguistic system.

Mŏrph'eus (-fūs). (Rom. myth.) Son of Somnus, god of sleep, and himself the god of dreams.

mŏrph'ia *n.* Morphine.

mŏrph'ine (-ēn) *n.* Alkaloid narcotic principle of opium, used to alleviate pain. **mŏrph'inism** *n.* Effect of morphine; excessive use of morphine.

mŏrphŏl'ogy *n.* 1. Study of the form of animals and plants. 2. Study of the form of words, branch of philology dealing with inflexion and word-formation. 3. *Social* ~, study of the structure of society, i.e. of social groups and institutions. **mŏrpholŏ'gical** *adj.* **mŏrpholŏ'gically** *adv.* **mŏrphŏl'ogist** *n.*

Mŏ'rris, William (1834–96). English designer, printer, poet, and prose writer; advocated the revival of medieval hand-craftsmanship and inspired the 'arts and crafts' movement; founded, with Burne-Jones and other PRE-RAPHAELITES, a firm of decorators (1861), also the Kelmscott Press (1890); was active as a socialist.

mŏ'rris (dance) *n.* Grotesque dance by persons in fancy costume, usu. representing characters from Robin Hood legend. [*morys*, var. of MOORISH]

mŏ'rris tube *n.* Small-bore rifle barrel inserted in rifle for practice on miniature range, now superseded by miniature rifle. [R. *Morris*, inventor]

Mŏ'rrison shelter *n.* Portable indoor steel table-shaped air-raid shelter. [Herbert S. *Morrison*, Home Secretary 1940–5]

mŏ'rrow (-rō) *n.* (literary) The next day.

mŏrse[1] *n.* = WALRUS.

mŏrse[2] *n.* The fastening or clasp (often jewelled) of a cope (ill. VESTMENT).

Mŏrse[3], Samuel Finley Breese (1791–1872). American inventor of recording telegraph, deviser of the ~ *code*, a telegraphic alphabet in which letters are represented by combinations of long and short electrical contacts, sounds, flashes, etc. ('dots and dashes').

mŏrs'el *n.* Mouthful; small piece, fragment.

mŏrt *n.* Note sounded on horn announcing killing of deer.

mŏrt'al *adj.* Subject to or causing death, fatal; (of enemy) implacable; (of sin) deadly, entailing spiritual death (opp. to VENIAL); accompanying death, as ~ *agony*; (slang) long and tedious. **mŏrt'ally** *adv.* **mŏrt'al** *n.* One who is subject to death; (facet.) person.

mŏrtăl'ĭty *n.* Mortal nature; loss of life on large scale; death-rate.

mŏrt'ar *n.* 1. Hard vessel in which ingredients are pounded with a pestle. 2. Short gun with large bore for throwing shells at high angles. 3. Mixture of lime, sand, and water used to make joints between stones and bricks in building; ~*-board*, board for holding builders' mortar; college cap, with stiff, flat, square, top, resembling a mason's mortar-board. ~ *v.t.* Bind, join (bricks or stones) together with mortar; fire upon with mortars.

mortgage (mŏrg'ĭj) *n.* Conveyance of property as security for money-debt, with provision for reconveyance on repayment of the sum secured; deed effecting this. ~ *v.t.* Make over by mortgage; pledge in advance. **mortgagee'** (-jē) *n.* Holder of mortgage. **mortgagor'** (-jŏr) *n.* Person who pledges property etc. in mortgage. [OF *mort gage* dead pledge]

mŏrtĭ'cian (-shn) *n.* (U.S.) Undertaker.

mŏrt'ĭfȳ *v.* 1. Chasten (the body, passions, etc.) by self-denial. 2. Cause (person) to feel humiliated, wound (feelings). 3. (Of flesh) become gangrenous. **mŏrtĭfĭcā'tion** *n.*

mŏrt'ĭse, mŏrt'ĭce *n.* Hole or cavity into which end of some other part of framework or structure is fitted (ill. JOINT). ~ *v.t.* Cut mortise in, fasten with mortise.

mŏrt'main *n.* Condition of lands etc. held inalienably by corporation; *in* ~, (fig.) inalienable. [OF f. med. L *mortua manus* dead hand]

Mŏrt'on's fork. The argument used by John Morton (1420 ?–1500), lord chancellor to Henry VII, when demanding gifts for the royal treasury; if a man lived handsomely, Morton argued that he was obviously rich; if simply, that economy must have made him so.

A	·—	S	···
B	—···	T	—
C	—·—·	U	··—
D	—··	V	···—
E	·	W	·——
F	··—·	X	—··—
G	——·	Y	—·——
H	····	Z	——··
I	··	1	·————
J	·———	2	··———
K	—·—	3	···——
L	·—··	4	····—
M	——	5	·····
N	—·	6	—····
O	———	7	——···
P	·——·	8	———··
Q	——·—	9	————·
R	·—·	0	—————

MORSE CODE

mŏrt'ūary *adj.* Of or for burial or death. ~ *n.* Place for temporary reception of corpses.

mosā'ĭc[1] (-z-) *n.* (Production of) picture or pattern of small cubes of coloured stone, glass, etc., cemented together (also fig. of any diversified whole). ~ *adj.* Of or like such work. ~ *v.t.* Decorate with mosaics; combine (as) into mosaic. **mosā'ĭcist** *n.* [med. L *mosaicus*, f. Gk *mousaikos* of the Muses]

Mosā'ĭc[2] *adj.* Of MOSES; ~ *law*, the ancient Hebrew law contained in the Pentateuch.

mŏschatĕl' (-sk-) *n.* Small plant (*Adoxa moschatellina*), having pale-green flowers with a musky smell.

Mŏs'covīte *adj.* & *n.* = MUSCOVITE.

Mŏs'cow (-kō) (Russ. *Moskva*). Province and city of W. Russia, capital of Russia from 1240 to 1703 (when the capital was transferred to St. Petersburg) and since 1918.

Mose'ley (mōz-), Henry Gwyn-Jeffreys (1887–1915). English physical chemist; first produced experimental evidence (from X-ray spectra) for the allocation of atomic numbers to elements; ~ *number*, (occas. used for) atomic number.

Mosĕlle' (-z-). River rising in Vosges Mountains and flowing into Rhine at Coblenz; dry white wine from the vineyards in the valley of this river.

Mō'ses (-zĭz). Jewish patriarch, the great law-giver of the Jews; led them from Egypt after the captivity there; was inspired by God on Mount Sinai to write down the Ten Commandments on tablets of stone (Exod. xx); died before the 'Promised Land' was reached (Joshua i. 34).

Mŏs'lĕm, Mŭs'lĭm (-z-) *n.* One who professes Islam. ~ *adj.* Of or pertaining to the Moslems.

mŏsque (-sk) *n.* Moslem place of worship. [Fr. *mosquée*, f. Arab. *masgid*]

mŏsqui'tō (-kē-) *n.* Two-winged fly of the family *Culicidae*, gnat; esp., various species of *Culex* and *Anopheles*, females of which have a long blood-sucking proboscis; ~*-curtain*, *-net*, fine-meshed net for keeping mosquitoes from room, bed, etc.; ~ *craft*, collective name for small naval vessels, as motor torpedo-boats etc.

mŏss *n.* Peat-bog; kinds of small herbaceous cryptogamous plants growing in bogs, or in crowded masses on ground, wood, stone, etc.; ~*-rose*, cabbage-rose (*Rosa centifolia*), with moss-like growth on calyx and stalk; ~*-trooper*, 17th-c. freebooter on Scottish border. **mŏss'y** *adj.* Of or like moss; overgrown with moss. **mŏss'inėss** *n.*

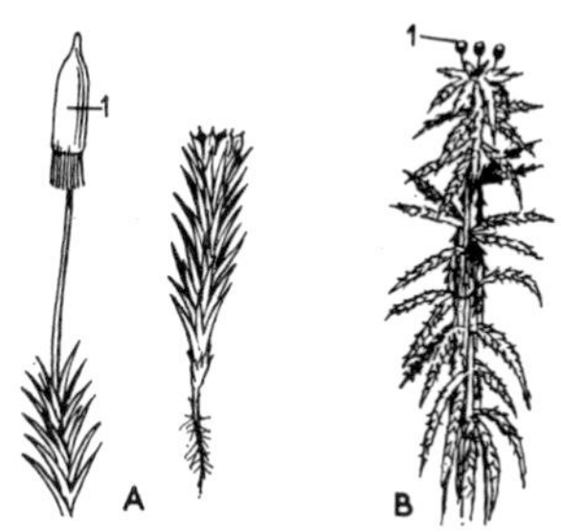

MOSS: A. *POLYTRICHUM* FEMALE (LEFT) AND MALE. B. SPHAGNUM

1. Capsule or theca

mōst *adj.* & *n.* The greatest number, quantity, or degree (of). ~ *adv.* In a great or the greatest degree. **mōst'ly** *adv.* For the most part.

Mōsul' (-sōōl). Vilayet of Mesopotamia (Iraq), roughly corresponding to ancient Assyria; town on right bank of Tigris, opposite site of Nineveh.

mot (mō) *n.* (pl. *mots* pr. mōz). Witty saying; ~ *juste*, the expression that conveys a desired shade of meaning with more precision than any other.

mōte[1] *n.* Particle of dust, esp. speck seen floating in sunbeam.

mote[2]: see MOTTE.

motĕt' *n.* (mus.) Anthem in R.C. or Lutheran Church, generally unaccompanied; non-eccles. work on similar lines. [Fr., dim. of *mot* word]

mŏth *n.* Popular name for the majority of insects belonging to the order *Lepidoptera*, those not *butterflies*, distinguished from them by not having clubbed antennae and by being mostly nocturnal in habit; clothes-moth, *Tinea*, or any other insect whose larvae feed on silk and woollen fabrics, fur, etc.; (fig.) person hovering round temptation, as a moth flutters about light; ~*-ball*, small ball of naphthalene used to keep moths away from fabrics etc.;

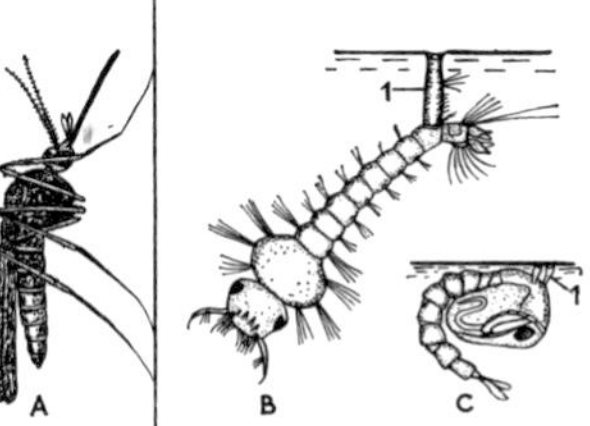

MOSQUITO: A. ADULT FEMALE. B. LARVA. C. PUPA

1. Spiracles at surface of water

(also) airtight plastic cover sprayed on and enclosing working parts of gun-mountings, machinery, etc.

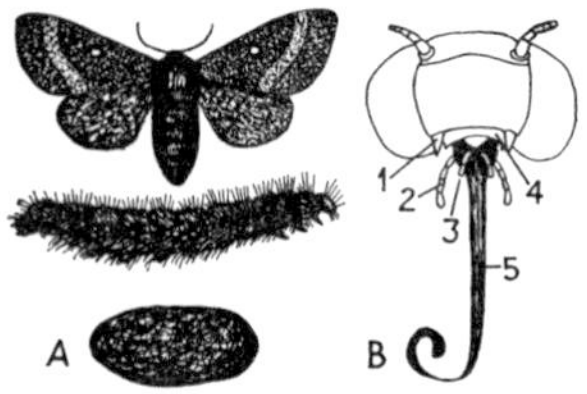

MOTH. A. IMAGO, CATERPILLAR, AND COCOON. B. HEAD

1. Mandible. 2. Labial palp. 3. Maxillary palp. 4. Labrum. 5. Proboscis

of ship; ~*-eaten*, injured by moths; (fig.) antiquated, time-worn. **mŏth'y** *adj.* Infested by moths.

mo'ther (mŭdh-) *n.* Female parent; head of female religious community (often ~ *superior*); term of address for elderly woman of lower class; incubator, artificial apparatus for rearing chickens; ~ *country*, country in relation to its colonies; native land; ~*-craft*, skill in rearing children; ~ *earth*, earth as mother of its inhabitants; (facet.) the ground; *M~ Hubbard*, person in nursery rhyme, kind of cloak; ~*-in-law*, one's wife's or husband's mother; ~*-of-all*, part of spinning-wheel supporting the maidens (ill. SPINNING); ~ *of pearl*, pearly iridescent lining of certain shells, as of oysters, mussels, etc., used in making buttons etc.; ~ *of vinegar*, mucilaginous substance produced in vinegar during fermentation by bacteria (usually of the *Acetobacter* family); ~ *ship*, ship acting as base for submarines, aeroplanes, etc.; ~ *tongue*, one's native language; ~ *wit*, native wit, common sense. **mo'therhood** *n.* **mo'therlėss** *adj.* **mo'ther** *v.* Take care of as a mother; *mo'thering*, custom of visiting parents and giving or receiving presents on mid-Lent Sunday (*Mothering Sunday*).

mo'therly (mŭdh-) *adj.* Befitting or resembling a mother. **mo'therlinėss** *n.*

motif' (-ēf) *n.* Distinctive feature or dominant idea of a design or composition; (mus.) FIGURE.

mō'tīle *adj.* (zool., bot.). Capable of motion.

mō'tion *n.* 1. Moving, movement; gait; gesture. 2. Proposition formally made in deliberative assembly; (law) application to judge or court for some rule or order of court. 3. Evacuation of bowels. 4. ~*picture*, cinematograph, moving picture. **mō'tionlėss** *adj.* **mō'tion** *v.* Make motion to direct or guide (person).

mō'tive *adj.* Tending to initiate motion; ~ *power*, esp. form of mechanical energy used to drive machinery. ~ *n.* 1. That which induces a person to act, e.g. desire, fear, circumstance. 2. = MOTIF. **mō'tive, mō'tivāte** *vbs.t.* Supply a motive to, be the motive of. **mōtivā'tion** *n.*

mŏt'ley[1] *adj.* Parti-coloured; heterogeneous. ~ *n.* Fool's motley garb.

Mŏt'ley[2], John Lothrop (1814–77). American historian of the Netherlands.

mō'tor *n.* Motive agent or force; motor muscle or nerve; apparatus or engine supplying motive power for vehicle or machinery, esp. internal combustion engine; motor-car. ~ *adj.* Giving, imparting, or producing motion; ~ *area*, that part of frontal lobe of mammal's brain from which muscular activity of opposite side of body is most easily evoked; ~*-bicycle, -boat, -car*, bicycle etc. propelled by internal combustion engine (ill. *motor-car*, *p.* 535); ~ *nerve*, any nerve consisting of fibres which carry impulses from spinal cord or brain to induce contractions of muscle. ~ *v.* Go, convey, by motor-car. **mō'torist** *n.* Driver of motor-car.

mō'torīze *v.t.* Transform (esp. military units) by substituting motor for horse transport. **mōtorīzā'tion** *n.*

mŏtte, mōte *n.* Mound, hillock, as site of castle, camp, etc. (ill. CASTLE).

mŏtt'le *v.t.* Mark or cover with spots or blotches.

mŏtt'ō *n.* Inscription (esp. heraldic) or saying expressing appropriate sentiment or aspiration; maxim adopted as rule of conduct; short quotation prefixed to book or chapter, suggestive of the contents.

mouff'lon (mōō-) *n.* Various wild sheep of S. Europe, esp. *Ovis musimon*, native of Corsica.

moujik, muzhik (mōō'zhĭk) *n.* Russian peasant.

mould[1] (mōld) *n.* Loose or broken earth, surface soil; the earth of the grave; soil rich in organic matter; ~*-board*, curved iron plate at back of plough-share that turns over furrow-slice (ill. PLOUGH).

mould[2] (mōld) *n.* Woolly or furry fungous growth forming on surfaces in moist warm air.

mould[3] (mōld) *n.* Matrix, vessel, in which fluid or plastic material is cast or shaped; pudding etc. shaped in mould; form, shape, distinctive nature. ~ *v.t.* Shape in or as in a mould; shape (bread) into loaves; model.

moul'der (mōl-) *v.i.* Turn to dust by natural decay, crumble away.

moul'dĭng (mōl-) *n.* Moulded object; ornamental contour given to stone-, wood-, or metal-work; material, esp. long strip of wood, prepared for this. (*Illustration, p.* 535.)

moul'dy (mōl-) *adj.* Covered with MOULD[2]; mouldering; (slang) dull, tiresome, 'rotten'. **moul'dinėss** *n.* **moul'dy** *n.* (naval slang) Torpedo.

Moulin Rouge (mōōlăṅ' rōōzh). A famous cabaret or *café chantant* in Montmartre, Paris, frequented in the late 19th and early 20th centuries by painters, poets, and other artists.

moult (-ō-) *v.* (Of birds) shed (feathers), in changing plumage. ~ *n.* Moulting.

mound[1] *n.* Embankment; heap, bank, hillock, of earth etc.

mound[2] *n.* Ball of gold etc. representing earth, surmounting crown etc.; (her.) figure of this as a bearing.

mount[1] *n.* Mountain, hill (abbrev. Mt, preceding name, as *Mt Everest*); (palmistry) fleshy prominence on palm of hand.

mount[2] *v.* Ascend; climb on to; increase in amount; amount *to*; set on horseback, furnish (person) with saddle-horse; put in position for use or exhibition; put (picture) in a MOUNT[3]; fit (gems etc.) in gold etc.; fix (object) on microscope slide; display specimen (e.g. butterfly); put (play) on stage; (mil.) organize (an offensive).

mount[3] *n.* Margin surrounding picture, card on which drawing is mounted; ornamental metal parts of thing; horse for person to ride.

moun'tain (-tĭn) *n.* Natural elevation of earth's surface of impressive height; large heap or pile; *the M~*, extreme party led by Danton and Robespierre in French Revolution, so called from occupying highest position in chamber of assembly; ~ *ash*, ROWAN-tree; ~ *dew*, Scotch whisky; ~ *sickness*, the difficult breathing, muscular weakness, mental lethargy, etc., caused by rarefied air at high altitudes; *M~ States*, a geographical division of the U.S., made by the U.S. Census Bureau, comprising Montana, Idaho, Wyoming, Colorado, New Mexico, Arizona, Utah, and Nevada. (*Illustration, p.* 536.)

mountaineer' (-tĭn-) *n.* Mountain-climber. ~ *v.i.* Climb mountains.

MOUNTAINEERS ROPED TOGETHER

The rope is knotted behind the first man, at the side of the middle man, and in front of the third man

moun'tainous (-tĭn-) *adj.* Abounding in mountains; huge, enormous.

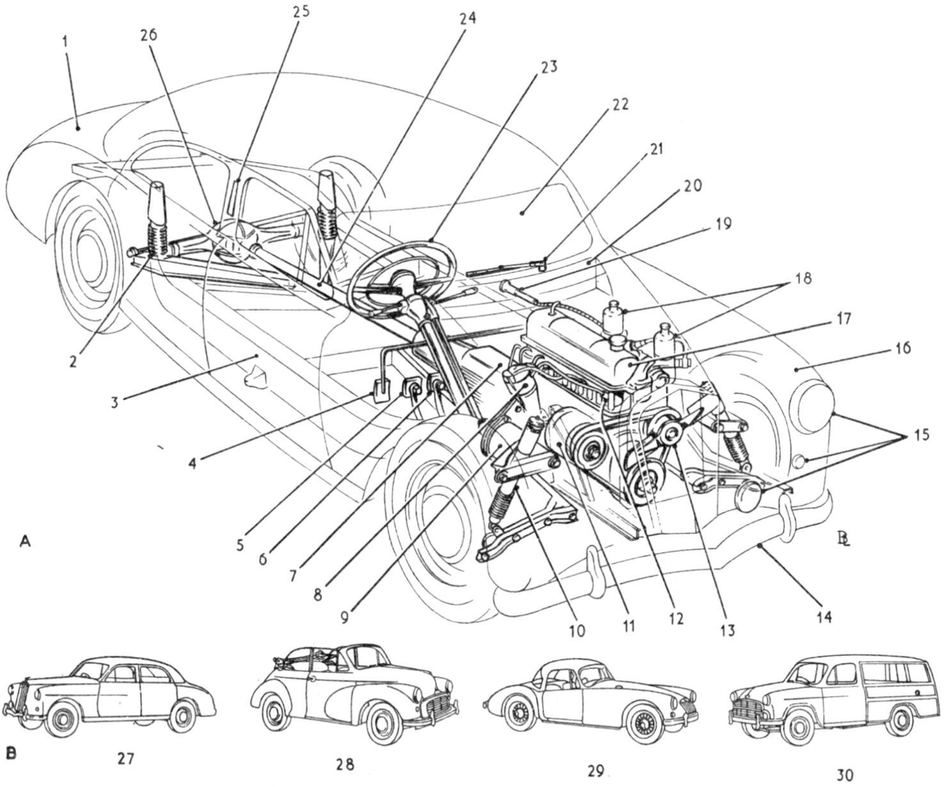

A. PARTS OF A MOTOR-CAR. B. CAR BODIES

A. 1. Boot. 2. Rear spring. 3. Chassis. 4. Accelerator pedal. 5. Brake pedal. 6. Clutch pedal. 7. Gear-box. 8. Distributor. 9. Starting motor. 10. Shock-absorber. 11. Dynamo. 12. Sparking-plug. 13. Fan. 14. Bumper. 15. Lights. 16. Wing. 17. Cylinder head. 18. Carburettors. 19. Choke handle. 20. Dashboard. 21. Windscreen wiper. 22. Windscreen. 23. Steering-wheel. 24. Propeller shaft. 25. Trafficator. 26. Rear axle. B. 27. Saloon. 28. Convertible. 29. Coupé. 30. Estate car

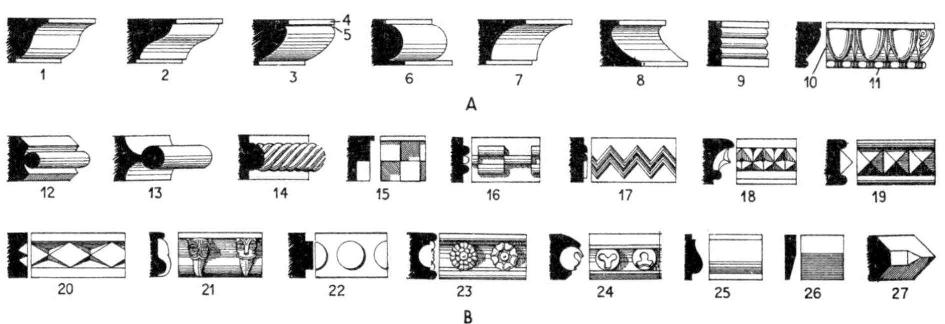

MOULDINGS WITH PROFILES: A. CLASSIC. B. MEDIEVAL

1. Cyma recta. 2. Ogee or cyma reversa. 3. Ovolo. 4. Fillet. 5. Quirk. 6. Torus. 7. Cavetto. 8. Scotia. 9. Reed. 10. Egg-and-tongue. 11. Bead-and-reel. 12. Bowtel. 13. Roll. 14. Cable. 15. Square billet. 16. Roll billet. 17. Chevron. 18. Dog-tooth. 19. Nail-head. 20. Lozenge. 21. Beakhead. 22. Pellet. 23. Rosette. 24. Ball-flower. 25. Bolection. 26. Bevel. 27. Chamfer with stopped end

MOUNTAIN AND GLACIER

1. Pass. 2. Peak. 3. Cwm or Corrie. 4. Saddle. 5. Shoulder. 6. Col. 7. *Arête*. 8. *Couloir*. 9. Chimney. 10. Névé. 11. Lateral moraine. 12. Medial moraine. 13. Crevasses. 14. Séracs. 15. Terminal moraine

moun'tėbănk *n.* Itinerant quack (archaic); impudent charlatan. [It. *montambanco* = *monta in banco* mount on bench]

Moun'ty *n.* (colloq.) Member of the Royal Canadian Mounted Police.

mourn (mōrn) *v.* Sorrow, grieve, lament, esp. lament death of; put on mourning. **mourn'er** *n.* One who mourns; person attending funeral.

mourn'ful (mōr-) *adj.* Exhibiting, expressing, or feeling, mourning or deep sorrow. **mourn'fully** *adv.* **mourn'fulnėss** *n.*

mourn'ing (mōr-) *n.* (esp.) Feeling or expression of sorrow; (wearing of) black clothes as sign of bereavement; *~-band*, band of black crape or other material worn round arm as sign of mourning; *~-card*, black-edged card giving name and date of death of deceased person; *~-paper*, black-edged notepaper.

mouse (-s) *n.* (pl. *mīce*). Small rodent of genus *Mus.*; timid or shy person; *~ -ear*, hawkweed; *~-trap*, trap for catching mice. **mous'y** *adj.* **mouse** (-z) *v.i.* Hunt for or catch mice; search *about* for something. **mous'er** *n.* Animal that catches mice, esp. cat.

mousse (-ōōs) *n.* Sweet of frozen whipped cream, or of cream mixed with beaten egg-white and flavoured with fruit etc. [Fr., = 'froth']

moustache' (mustahsh) *n.* Hair growing on upper lip, esp. of a man; similar hair round mouths of some animals, as cats etc.; *~-cup*, drinking-cup with partial cover to prevent the moustache from becoming wet.

Moustēr'ian (mōō-). Name applied to a form of Middle Palaeolithic culture, characterized by flints worked usu. on one side only, and associated with Neanderthal Man; found in many localities in W. Asia, Europe, and N. Africa. [Le *Moustier*, a rock-shelter in Dordogne, France]

mouth *n.* (pl. pr. -dhz) External orifice in head, with cavity behind it containing apparatus for mastication and organs of vocal utterance; person viewed only as consumer of food; opening or entrance of anything; outfall of river; *~-organ*, thin rectangular box containing series of metal reeds, tuned to a particular key and fitted in separate compartments so as to be capable of separate sounding by either blowing or sucking; *~-piece*, part of some portable wind-instruments placed before or between lips; similar part of tobacco-pipe; part of telephone spoken into; one who speaks on behalf of others. ~ (-dh) *v.* Utter or speak pompously, declaim; take (food) in, touch with, mouth; train (horse) to answer to bit and reins; grimace. **mouth'ful** *n.*

mouth'y (-dh-) *adj.* Ranting, bombastic; prolix.

mo'vable (-ōōv-) *adj.* That can be moved; (of property) that can be removed, personal as opp. to *real*. **movabĭl'ĭty, mo'vablenėss** *ns.*

move (mōōv) *v.* Change position (of); change abode; stir, rouse; cause (bowels) to act; affect with emotion; propose as resolution; *moving picture*, cinematograph film; *moving staircase*, escalator. ~ *n.* Moving of piece at chess etc.; way in which piece is allowed to move; act of moving from rest; change of abode or premises; device, trick, action to some end.

move'ment (mōōvm-) *n.* Moving; moving mechanism of watch etc.; principal division of (usu. instrumental) musical work; combined action or endeavour of body of persons for some special end.

mo'ver (mōō-) *n.* (esp.) One who moves a proposal; *prime ~*, initial source (natural or mechanical) of motive power; author of fruitful idea.

movie (mōō'vĭ) *n.* (colloq.) Moving picture.

mow[1] (mō) *n.* Stack of hay, corn, etc.

mow[2] (mō) *v.* (past part. *mown*). Cut down grass, corn, etc., with scythe or machine; (fig.) cut, sweep down, like grass; *mowing-machine*, machine for cutting grass etc., pushed by hand or drawn by a horse or mechanically driven, with a cutting mechanism consisting of a reciprocating knife (or knives) operating through slotted fingers. **mow'er** *n.* Person who mows grass etc.: mowing-machine, lawn-mower.

mow[3] (mō *or* mow) *n.* & *v.i.* (Make) a grimace.

mŏx'a *n.* Down from dried leaves of *Artemisia moxa*, prepared for burning on skin as a counter-irritant for gout etc. (Jap. *mokusa* (*moe kusa* burning herb)]

Mōzambique' (-bēk). A Portuguese colony in E. Africa.

Mōză'rabic *adj.* Of those Christians in Moorish Spain who were allowed the exercise of their own religion on condition of owning allegiance to the Moorish king and conforming to certain Moorish customs.

Mō'zart (-ts-), Wolfgang Amadeus (1756–91). Austrian composer of symphonies, chamber-music, and operas, as 'Figaro', 'Don Giovanni', 'The Magic Flute'.

mp *abbrev. Mezzo piano* (= half soft).

m.p. *abbrev.* Melting-point.

M.P. *abbrev.* Member of Parliament; military police.

m.p.g., m.p.h. *abbrevs.* Miles per gallon, per hour.

M.P.S. *abbrev.* Member of the Pharmaceutical (*or* Philological *or* Physical) Society.

M.R. *abbrev.* Master of the Rolls; municipal reform(er).

Mr (mĭs'ter), **Mrs** (mĭs'ĭz) *ns.* Titles prefixed to name of man, married woman, with no superior titles: see MISTER, MISTRESS.

M.R.A. *abbrev.* MORAL Re-Armament.

M.R.C.P.(E., I.) *abbrevs.* Member of the Royal College of Physicians (of Edinburgh, of Ireland).

M.R.C.S.(E., I.) *abbrevs.* Member of the Royal College of Surgeons (of Edinburgh, of Ireland).

M.R.C.V.S. *abbrev.* Member of the Royal College of Veterinary Surgeons.

M.R.G.S. *abbrev.* Member of the Royal Geographical Society.

MS. *abbrev.* (pl. MSS.) Manuscript.

M.Sc. *abbrev.* Master of Science.

M.S.E. *abbrev.* Member of the Society of Engineers.

m.sec. *abbrev.* Millisecond.

M.S.L. *abbrev.* Mean sea-level.

M.S.M. *abbrev.* Meritorious Service Medal.

M.T. *abbrev.* Mechanical (*or* Motor) Transport.

Mt *abbrev.* Mount.

M.T.B. *abbrev.* Motor torpedo-boat.

M.T.(C.) *abbrev.* Mechanical Transport (Corps).

mū *n.* Greek letter m (M, μ); (physics etc., μ) symbol for micron, millionth part of metre; (elect., μ) placed before symbol for electrical unit to denote millionth part of that unit, as μF, microfarad; (radio, μ or *mu*) symbol for amplification factor of a valve.

mŭch *adj.* & *n.* A great quantity or amount (of). ~ *adv.* In a great degree; pretty nearly; for a large part of one's time. **mŭch'nėss** *n.* *much of a* ~, very much alike.

mū'cilage *n.* Viscous substance obtained from plants by maceration; adhesive substance. **mūcilă'ginous** *adj.*

mŭck *n.* Farmyard manure; (colloq.) dirt, filth. ~ *v.* Manure; ~ *out*, clean out (stable etc.); (slang) bungle; ~ *about*, (slang) loaf; go about aimlessly. **mŭck'y** *adj.*

mŭck'er *n.* (slang) Heavy fall; *come a* ~, come to grief.

mū'cous *adj.* Secreting or covered by mucus; ~ *membrane*, inner surface-lining of hollow organs of the body. **mūcŏs'ity** *n.*

mū'crō *n.* (bot., zool.) Pointed part of an organ. **mū'cronate** *adj.*

mū'cus *n.* Sticky secretion of mucous glands usu. forming a protective covering for mucous membrane.

mŭd *n.* Wet soft soil or earthy matter, mire; ~ *bath*, bath in mud impregnated with salts, as a remedy for rheumatism etc.; *mud'guard*, guard over wheel of cycle or other vehicle as protection against mud; *mud'lark*, street arab; ~*-pack*, preparation used for cleansing the pores and beautifying the skin of the face; ~*-pie*, mud formed by children in the shape of a pie.

mŭdd'le *v.* Bewilder, confuse; bungle; act in confused, unmethodical and ineffective manner. ~ *n.* Muddled condition.

mŭdd'y *adj.* Like mud; covered with, abounding in, mud; thick, turbid; not clear, mentally confused. **mŭdd'ily** *adv.* **mŭdd'inėss** *n.* **mŭdd'y** *v.* Make or become muddy.

muĕzzin' (mo͞o-) *n.* Official of Moslem mosque who proclaims hour of prayer from minaret. [Arab. *mu'adhdhin* (*adhdhana* proclaim)]

mŭff[1] *n.* Covering (usu. of fur and cylindrical) into which hands are thrust from opposite ends to keep them warm (ill. COAT); *foot*-~, contrivance serving same purpose for feet.

mŭff[2] *n.* (colloq.) Duffer, bungler; failure. ~ *v.t.* Bungle, make muddle of; miss (catch at cricket).

mŭff'in *n.* Light flat circular spongy cake eaten toasted and buttered; ~ *bell*, bell rung by ~ *man*, who sold muffins in the street. **mŭff'ineer** *n.* Covered dish for keeping toasted muffins hot.

mŭff'le *n.* (obs.) Mitten; chamber or covering in furnace or kiln which protects contents from direct contact with fire. ~ *v.t.* Wrap, cover *up* for warmth; wrap up (oars, bell, drum, etc.) to deaden sound; wrap up (head of person) to prevent his speaking; repress, deaden, sound of (curse etc., usu. in past part.).

mŭff'ler *n.* Wrap or scarf worn round neck for warmth; silencer for motor-car or motor-cycle; felt pad between hammer and strings of a piano.

mŭf'ti *n.* 1. Mohammedan priest or expounder of law. 2. Plain clothes worn by anyone who has the right to wear a uniform. [Arab. *afta* decide point of law]

mŭg *n.* Drinking-vessel, usu. cylindrical and with handle; (slang) face, mouth; (slang) stupid person, dupe. ~ *v.* (slang) Study hard (*at* subject); ~ *up*, (slang) get up (subject).

mŭgg'er *n.* Broad-snouted Indian crocodile (*Crocodilus palustris*) venerated by many Hindus.

mŭgg'ins *n.* Simpleton; children's game of cards; game of dominoes in which the object is to make the sum of the two ends of the line a multiple of five.

Mŭggletōn'ian *adj.* & *n.* (Member) of an English religious sect founded by Lodswick Muggleton (1609–98) and his cousin John Reeve (d. 1658), who claimed to be the two 'witnesses' of Rev. xi. 3–6.

mŭgg'y *adj.* (Of weather etc.) damp, warm, and oppressive. **mŭgg'inėss** *n.*

mŭg'wŭmp *n.* (U.S.) Great man, 'chief'; political independent, (specif.) Republican who refused to support party's nominee in presidential election of 1884. [N. Amer. Ind. word]

mūlătt'ō *n.* (pl. ~*s*). Offspring of white and Negro. ~ *adj.* Of brownish-yellow colour, as mulattos. [Span. *mulato* young mule]

mŭl'berry *n.* 1. A tree, genus *Morus*, with dark-purple or white edible berries; the dark-green leaves are used for feeding silkworms; fruit of this; dark-purple colour. 2. (Cover-name for) prefabricated harbour(s) towed across the English Channel and erected off the Normandy beaches during the invasion of Europe, June 1944.

mŭlch *n.* Half-rotten straw, with leaves, loose earth, etc., spread on the ground to protect roots of newly planted trees etc. ~ *v.t.* Cover or spread with mulch.

mŭlct *v.t.* Punish (person) by a fine; deprive (person *of*). ~ *n.* Fine imposed for offence.

mūle[1] *n.* 1. Offspring of he-ass and mare; hence, stupid or obstinate person. 2. Kind of spinning jenny invented by S. Crompton.

mūle[2] *n.* Kind of slipper (ill. SHOE).

mūlėteer' *n.* Mule-driver.

mūl'ish *adj.* Obstinate as a mule, intractable. **mūl'ishly** *adv.* **mūl'ishnėss** *n.*

mŭll[1] *n.* Thin soft kind of plain muslin. [shortened f. *mulmull*, f. Hind. *malmal*]

mŭll[2] *v.t.* Make a mess or muddle of. ~ *n.* Mess, muddle.

mŭll[3] *v.t.* Make (wine, beer) into hot drink with sugar, spices, yolk of egg, etc.

mŭll[4] *n.* Humus formed under non-acid conditions (opp. MOR).

mŭll'ah *n.* Mohammedan learned in theology and sacred law; expounder of the Koran. [Arab. *maula*]

mŭll'ein (-ĭn) *n.* Kinds of herbaceous plant of genus *Verbascum*, with woolly leaves and erect woolly spike of yellow flowers.

mŭll'er *n.* Stone or piece of thick glass used for powdering drugs, pigments, etc., on a slab; apparatus for grinding ores.

mŭll'ĕt *n.* 1. An edible sea-fish; *red* ~, member of family *Mullidae*, esp. *Mullus*, some species of which are bright red; *grey* ~, member of family *Mugilidae*, esp. *Mugil*, greenish-grey. 2. (her.) Figure like rowel of spur or 5-pointed star (ill. HERALDRY).

mŭlligatawn'y *n.* Highly flavoured E. Indian soup, made with curry-powder and hot seasonings; ~ *paste*, curry paste used for this. [Tamil *milagutannir* pepper-water]

mŭll'ion (-yon) *n.* Vertical shaft, usu. of stone, dividing lights in a window (ill. WINDOW).

mŭlt(i)- *prefix.* Much, many.

mŭltifar'ious *adj.* Having great variety. **mŭltifar'iously** *adv.* **mŭltifar'iousnĕss** *n.*

mŭl'tifŏrm *adj.* Having many forms; manifold. **mŭltifŏrm'ity** *n.* Variety, diversity (opp. to *uniformity*).

mŭltilăt'eral *adj.* Having many sides; (of agreement, treaty, etc.) in which more than two sides or States participate; ~ *trade*, trade carried on between several countries without the necessity of balancing trade or payments between them.

mŭltimillionaire' (-lyon-) *n.* Person with a fortune of several millions (of pounds, dollars, etc.).

mŭltinōm'ial *adj.* & *n.* (alg.) (Expression) of more than two terms connected by + or −.

mŭltip'ăra *n.* (med.) Pregnant woman who has borne one child or more.

mŭltip'arous *adj.* Producing more than one at birth.

mŭltipart'īte *adj.* Divided into many parts.

mŭl'tiple *adj.* Of many parts, elements or individual components; (math.) repeated, occurring more than once; (elect.) of a circuit with a number of parallel conductors; ~ *shop*, retail business with branches in many places. ~ *n.* (math.) Number or quantity containing another an exact number of times; *lowest* (*least*) *common* ~ (abbrev. L.C.M.), least quantity that contains two or more given quantities exactly, as 12 is the L.C.M. of 3 and 4.

mŭl'tiplĕx *adj.* Manifold, of many elements.

mŭl'tipliable, mŭl'tiplicable *adjs.* Capable of being multiplied.

mŭl'tiplicănd' *n.* (math.) A number which is to be multiplied by another, the MULTIPLIER.

mŭltiplicā'tion *n.* Multiplying; (math.) finding the quantity produced by taking a given quantity (MULTIPLICAND) as many times as there are units in another given quantity (MULTIPLIER); ~ *table*, a table of a set of numbers, usu. 1 to 12, with the products of multiplication by the same numbers successively. **mŭl'tiplicative** *adj.*

mŭltiplic'ity *n.* Manifold variety; great number *of*.

mŭl'tiplier *n.* That which multiplies; (math.) a number by which another number, the MULTIPLICAND, is multiplied; (elect.) device for multiplying intensity of force, currect, etc., to bring it to a desired strength; (econ.) the proportion of an increment of a consumer's income to the consequent increment of saving.

mŭl'tiplȳ *v.* Produce large number of (instances etc.); breed (animals), propagate (plants); (math.) perform process of MULTIPLICATION (symbol ×).

mŭl'titūde *n.* Great number; throng; *the* ~, the many, the common people. **mŭltitūd'inous** *adj.* **mŭltitūd'inously** *adv.* **mŭltitūd'inousnĕss** *n.*

mŭm *int.* Hush!, silence! ~ *adj.* Strictly silent or secret. ~ *v.i.* Act in dumb show.

mŭm'ble *v.* Speak or utter indistinctly or with lips partly closed. ~ *n.*

Mŭm'bō-jŭm'bō. A grotesque idol said to have been worshipped by certain tribes of Negroes; hence, (any object of) senseless veneration.

mŭmm'er *n.* Actor in traditional popular performance in dumb-show. **mŭmm'ery** *n.* Mummer's performance; 'play-acting', buffoonery.

mŭmm'ifȳ *v.t.* Make into a mummy. **mŭmmificā'tion** *n.*

mŭmm'y[1] *n.* Dead body preserved from decay by embalming, esp. one so preserved by the ancient Egyptians; dried-up body; rich brown pigment obtained from bitumen; pulpy substance or mass, esp. *beat* (thing) *to a* ~; ~-*case*, case of wood, modelled to shape of human body, in which Egyptian mummies were placed for burial. [Arab. *mumiya* (*mum* wax)]

mŭmm'y[2] *n.* Mother. [nursery form of MAMMA[1]]

mŭmps *n.* Virus infection which causes acute inflammation of parotid gland and consequent swelling of neck and face; (colloq.) fit of the sulks.

mŭnch *v.* Eat with noticeable action of the jaws.

Mŭnchausen (-owz'n), Baron. Hero of a book of fantastic traveller's tales (1785) written in English by a German, Rudolph Erich Raspe; the original Freiherr von Münchhausen is said to have served in the Russian army against the Turks and to have related extravagant tales of his prowess.

mŭn'dāne *adj.* Worldly. **mŭndāne'ly** *adv.* **mŭndāne'nĕss** (-n-n-) *n.*

mŭng'o[1] (-nggō) *n.* Cloth made from rags of heavily felted woollen cloth, like SHODDY but inferior.

Mungo[2]: see KENTIGERN.

Mūn'ich (-k) (Ger. *München*). Capital of Bavaria, Germany; ~ *pact*, an agreement between England, France, Germany, and Italy, signed at Munich on 29th Sept. 1938, under which a part of Czechoslovakia was ceded to Germany.

mūni'cipal *adj.* Of the local self-government or corporate government of city or town; ~ *borough*: see BOROUGH. **mūni'cipally** *adv.* **muni'cipalism, mūni'cipalist** *ns.*

mūnicipăl'ity *n.* Town, district, having local self-government; governing body of this.

mūni'cipalize *v.t.* Take over (private industries) and administer under municipal government. **mūnicipalizā'tion** *n.*

mūnif'icent *adj.* Splendidly generous. **mūnif'icently** *adv.* **mūnif'icence** *n.*

mūn'iments *n.pl.* Title-deeds etc. preserved as evidence of rights or privileges.

mūni'tion *n.* (pl. exc. in combination). Military weapons, ammunition, equipment, and stores. ~ *v.* Provide, furnish with munitions.

Mŭn'ster. An ancient province or kingdom of SW. Ireland, including the counties of Cork, Waterford, Tipperary, Limerick, Clare, and Kerry.

mŭnt'jăk *n.* Small horned deer (*Cervulus*) of E. Indies and SE. Asia.

mŭntz *n.* Alloy (~ *metal*) of copper and zinc used esp. for sheathing the bottoms of ships. [G. F. *Muntz* of Birmingham, inventor]

mūr'al *adj.* Of, on, a wall; ~ *crown*, (Rom. antiq.) garland given to soldiers who first scaled walls of a besieged town. ~ *n.* Mural painting.

Murat (mūră'), Joachim (1767–1815). French marshal; brother-in-law of Napoleon, by whom he was made king of Naples, 1808.

mûrd'er *n.* Unlawful killing of human being with malice aforethought, dist. f. (*accidental* or *justifiable*) *homicide* and *manslaughter*. ~ *v.t.* Kill unlawfully and with malice aforethought; massacre, butcher; (fig.) spoil by bad execution, representation, etc. **mûrd'erer, -ess** *ns.* **mûrd'erous** *adj.* **mûrd'erously** *adv.*

mūre *v.t.* (archaic or literary) Confine as in prison; shut *up*.

mūr'ĕx *n.* (pl. -*icēs*, -*exes*). Genus of molluscs allied to whelks, yielding purple dye.

Mūrill'ō, Bartolomé Esteban (1617–82). Spanish painter of genre and religious pictures.

mûrk *adj.* (archaic, poet.) Dark, gloomy; misty, dense. **mûrk'y** *adj.* Dark, gloomy; (of darkness) thick. **mûrk'ily** *adv.* **mûrk'inĕss** *n.*

mûrm'ur *n.* Subdued continuous sound; (med.) sound of this kind heard in auscultation; muttered grumbling or repining; subdued or nearly inarticulate speech. **mûrm'urous** *adj.* **mûrm'urously** *adv.* **mûrm'ur** *v.* Produce murmur; speak or say in murmur.

mûrph'y *n.* (slang) Potato. [Irish surname]

mŭ'rrain (-ĭn) *n.* Infectious disease in cattle.

Murray[1] (mŭ'rĭ), Sir James Augustus Henry (1837–1915). Scottish philologist, editor of the 'Oxford English Dictionary'.

Murray[2] (mŭ'rĭ), John (1745–93). Founder of the famous publishing house, whose son John (1778–1843) started the 'Quarterly Review' and was Byron's publisher.

murrhine (mûr'ĭn) *adj.* ~ *glass*, Modern delicate glassware from the East, with small particles of coloured metal embedded in it. [L *murra* substance of which precious vases were made]

Mus.B(ac). *abbrev. Musicae baccalaureus* (Bachelor of Music).

mŭs'cadĭne, mŭs'cat *ns.* Kinds of grape with flavour or odour of musk.

mŭs'carĭne *n.* Drug, obtained from fungus *Amanita muscaria*, which stimulates parasympathetic nerves, reduces rate of heart-beat, etc.; various other drugs with similar effects.

mŭscatĕl', mŭscadĕl' *ns.* Muscadine; strong sweet white wine made from muscadines; raisin prepared from muscadine, Malaga raisin.

mŭ'scle (-sl) *n.* Contractile fibrous band or bundle producing motion in animal body; muscular strength; ~*-bound*, having the muscles stiff and enlarged owing to excessive exercise. [L *musculus* little mouse, f. fancied resemblance to a mouse]

Mŭs'covy. (hist.) The principality of Moscow; Russia in the period (16th and 17th centuries) when that principality was dominant; ~ *duck*: see MUSK. **Mŭs'covīte** *adj.* & *n.* (Native) of Muscovy or of Moscow. [*Muscovia*, latinized form of Russ. *Moskva* Moscow]

mŭs'cūlar *adj.* Of, in, the muscles; having well-developed muscles; ~ *Christianity*, Christian life of cheerful, physical activity, as described in the writings of Charles Kingsley. **mŭscūlăr'ĭty** *n.*

mŭs'cūlature *n.* System, arrangement, of muscles in the animal body.

mŭs'cūlo- *prefix.* Pertaining to muscle and . . .

Mus.D(oc). *abbrev. Musicae doctor* (Doctor of Music).

mūse[1] (-z) *v.i.* Ponder, reflect (*on*, *upon*); gaze meditatively (*on* scene etc.).

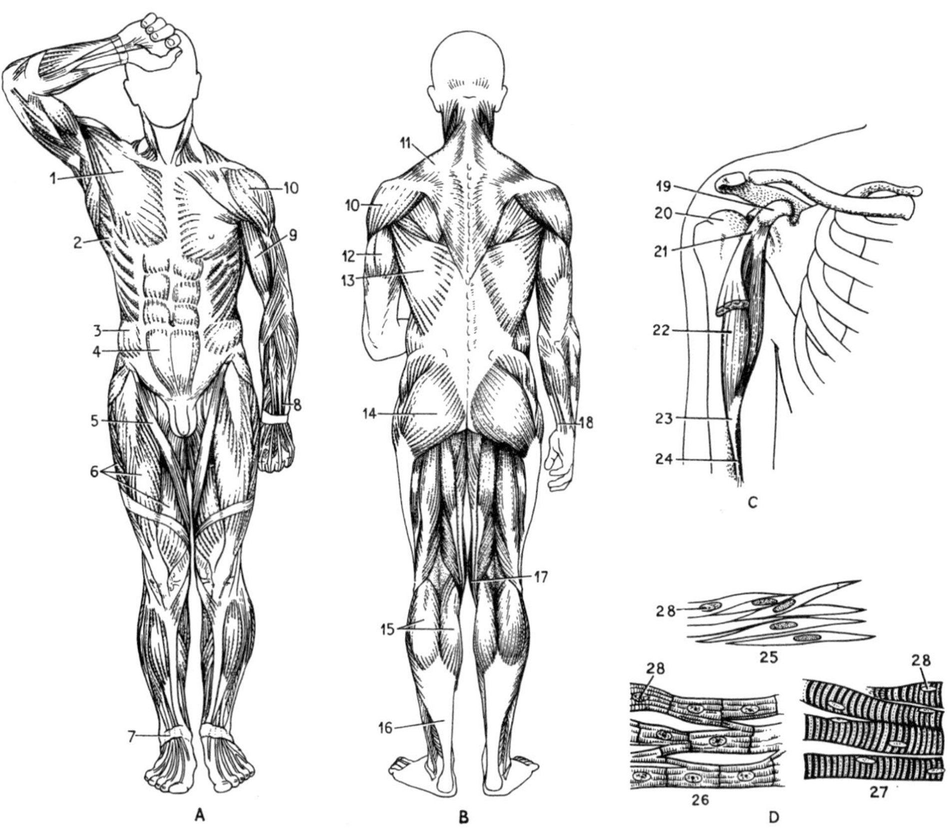

MUSCLES OF THE BODY: A. FRONT. B. BACK. C. PARTS OF A MUSCLE. D. MUSCLE-CELLS

A. 1. Pectoral muscle. 2. *Serratus anterior*. 3. External oblique muscle. 4. *Rectus abdominis*. 5. Sartorius. 6. *Quadriceps*. 7. Fascial band. 8. Extensor tendons of hand and fingers. 9. Biceps. 10. Deltoid. B. 11. Trapezius. 12. Triceps. 13. *Latissimus dorsi*. 14. Gluteal muscles. 15. *Gastrocnemius*. 16. Achilles tendon. 17. Hamstrings. 18. Flexor tendons of hand and fingers. C. 19. Coracoid process of scapula. 20. Head of humerus. 21. Origin of muscle. 22. Body of muscle. 23. Tendon. 24. Insertion of muscle. D. 25. Plain (visceral) muscle. 26. Cardiac muscle. 27. Striated (somatic) muscle. 28. Nucleus

Mūse[2] (-z) *n.* (Gk myth.) One of the 9 goddesses who presided over the arts and sciences (Calliope, epic poetry; Clio, history; Erato, lyric poetry; Euterpe, erotic poetry; Melpomene, tragedy; Polyhymnia, sacred song; Terpsichore, dancing; Thalia, comedy; Urania, astronomy); they were daughters of Zeus and Mnemosyne, born at the foot of Mt Olympus; Mt Helicon was sacred to them, and Mt Parnassus was one of their chief seats. Hence, **mūse,** poet's inspiring goddess, poet's genius.

mūsĕtte′ (-z-) *n.* Small soft-toned French bagpipe; dance for this, pastoral; reed stop on organ.

mūsē′um (-z-) *n.* Building for storing and exhibiting objects illustrative of antiquities, natural history, the arts, etc.; *~-piece,* object fit for a museum; (also in derogatory sense) person or thing regarded merely as a survival or curiosity. [Gk *mouseion* seat of the Muses]

mŭsh *n.* Soft pulp; (U.S.) porridge made from maize flour. **mŭsh′y** *adj.* Soft, pulpy; (fig.) weakly sentimental, rubbishy. **mŭsh′inėss** *n.*

mŭsh′rōōm *n.* Popular name of any edible fungus, esp. *Agaricus campestris,* the common field-mushroom, proverbial for its rapid growth (ill. FUNGUS); (fig., attrib.) growing suddenly, as *~ growth, suburb,* etc.; (fig.) upstart, parvenu; (colloq.) lady's straw hat with down-curved brim. *~ v.i.* Gather mushrooms; (of rifle-bullet) expand and flatten on striking an object.

mū′sĭc (-z-) *n.* Art of combining sounds for reproduction by the voice or various kinds of musical instruments in rhythmic, melodic, and harmonic form so as to express thought or feeling and affect the emotions; sounds so produced; pleasant sound, e.g. song of a bird, murmur of a stream, cry of hounds; written or printed score of musical composition; *face the ~,* face one's critics; *~ drama,* Wagnerian form of opera in which music and the other elements are combined on equal terms and made subservient to dramatic expression; *~-hall,* theatre for variety entertainments; *~-stool,* backless stool with adjustable seat for piano-player. [Gk *mousikē* (*tekhnē*) (art) of the Muses (*Mousa* Muse)]

mū′sĭcal (-z-) *adj.* Of, resembling, fond of or skilled in, music; melodious, harmonious; set to, accompanied by, music; *~-box,* mechanical musical instrument containing a revolving cylinder furnished with small pegs which strike on strips of metal, graduated to produce different notes; *~ chairs,* drawing-room game in which a number of players move round a row of chairs, less by one in number than the players, until piano ceases, when the one who finds no seat is eliminated, and a chair is removed before the next round; *~ comedy,* light dramatic entertainment of songs, dialogue, and dancing connected by a slender plot; *~ glasses,* set of glasses, graduated in tone, struck by small sticks; similar instrument with glass bells or tubes; *~ instrument,* any of a variety of instruments with which music is produced, usu. classified as *stringed, wind,* and *percussion.* **mū′sĭcally** *adv.* **mū′sĭcalnėss** *n.*

cus, common throughout N. America, also called musquash; *~-rose,* variety of climbing rose with fragrant white flowers; *~-tree, -wood,* any of a variety of trees having a musky smell. **mŭs′ky** *adj.*

mŭs′kĕg *n.* Level swampy or boggy area in some regions of Canada.

mŭs′kėt *n.* (hist.) Hand-gun, esp. unrifled, carried by infantry soldier. [It. *moschetto* sparrow-hawk]

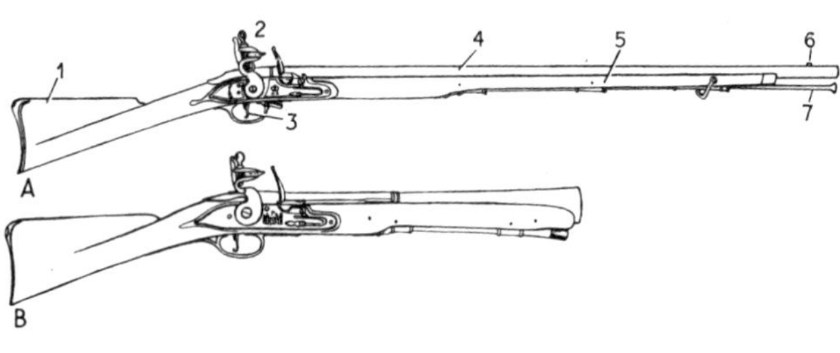

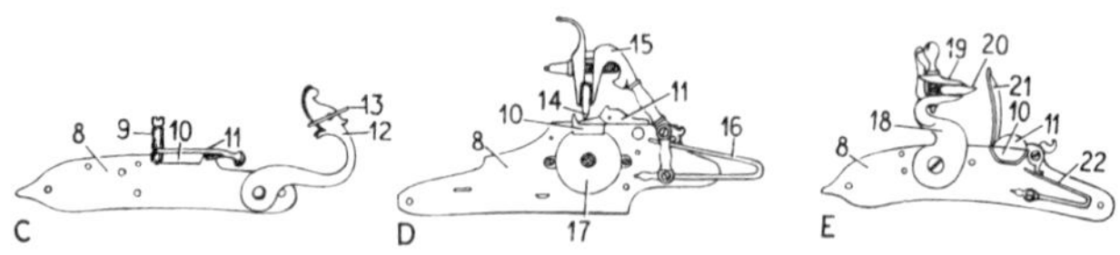

A. FLINT-LOCK MUSKET, *c* 1800. B. BLUNDERBUSS, *c* 1750. C. MATCH-LOCK, *c* 1650. D. WHEEL-LOCK, *c* 1650. E. FLINT-LOCK *c* 1740

A. 1. Butt. 2. Flint-lock. 3. Trigger. 4. Barrel. 5. Stock. 6. Bayonet stud. 7. Ramrod. C. 8. Lockplate. 9. Pan cover screw and flash-guard support. 10. Pan. 11. Pan cover. 12. 'Serpent'. 13. Screw for tightening 'serpent' jaws on match. D. 14. Iron pyrites. 15. Dog. 16. Dog spring. 17. Wheel enclosed in wheel case. E. 18. Cock. 19. Upper jaw. 20. Flint. 21. Steel. 22. Pan cover spring

mū′sĭcal *n.* Film or theatrical piece (not opera or operetta) of which music is essential element.

mūsĭ′cian (-zĭshn) *n.* Person skilled in art or practice of music. **mūsĭ′cianshĭp** *n.* Skill, insight, in interpreting and performing music.

mūsĭcŏl′ogy (-z-) *n.* All study of music except that directed to proficiency in performance or composition. **mūsĭcŏlo′gist** *n.* **mūsĭcolŏg′ical** *adj.*

mŭsk *n.* Odoriferous reddish-brown substance secreted in a gland or sac by male musk-deer, used as a basis of perfumes; kinds of plant with musky smell (but the plant commonly called 'musk', *Mimulus moschatus,* has now no scent); *~-deer,* small hornless deer (*Moschus*) of Central Asia; *~-duck,* tropical Amer. duck, *Cairina moschata,* so called from its slightly musky smell, erron. called the *Muscovy* and *Barbary duck*; also, an Australian duck, *Biziura lobata,* so called from the musky smell of the male; *~ melon,* common melon; *~-ox, Ovibos moschatus,* allied to sheep and bovines, with curved horns and shaggy pelt, now found only in Arctic America; *~-rat,* large aquatic rodent, *Fibes zibethi-*

mŭskėteer′ *n.* (hist.) Soldier armed with musket.

mŭs′kėtry *n.* (mil.) Instruction, practice, in rifle-shooting.

Muslim: see MOSLEM.

mŭs′lĭn (-z-) *n.* Fine delicately woven cotton fabric for ladies' dresses, curtains, etc. **mŭslĭnĕt′** *n.* Thick kind of muslin. [*Mosul,* town in Iraq where muslin was orig. made]

Mus.M. *abbrev. Musicae magister* (Master of Music).

mŭs′quash (-ŏsh) *n.* (Fur of) MUSK-rat. [Algonkin *muskwessu*]

mŭss′el *n.* Any of several genera of marine or freshwater bivalve molluscs, esp. *Mytilus,* the common edible sea-mussel, and *Unio,* the freshwater pearl-forming mussel. (*Illustration, p.* 541.)

Musset (mūsā′), Alfred de (1810–57). French romantic poet.

Mussolĭ′nĭ (mōō-, -lēn-), Benito (1883–1945). Italian FASCIST politician; originally a socialist and revolutionary; seized the government and became dictator in 1922; resigned in 1943 following the Allied invasion of Italy and was put to death in 1945.

Mussŏrg′skĭ (mōō-), Modest Petrovich (1839–81). Russian

musician; composer of the opera 'Boris Godunov' (1874).

Mŭss'ulman *adj.* & *n.* (pl. *-s*). Moslem.

mŭst[1] *n* New wine; unfermented or incompletely fermented grape-juice.

mŭst[2] *adj.* & *n.* (Male elephant or camel) in state of dangerous frenzy. [Pers. *mast* intoxicated]

mŭst[3] *v.* (followed by inf. without *to*) Be obliged to; be certain to. ~ *n.* (colloq.) Something imperative.

mŭs'tăng *n.* 1. Wild or half-wild horse of Mexico, California, etc. 2. Small red Texas grape.

Mustapha Kemal: see ATATÜRK.

mŭs'tard *n.* A plant, genus *Sinapis*, with yellow flowers and black or white seeds contained in pods; hot pungent powder made from the crushed seeds of this plant, mixed to a paste with water (*English* ~) or with vinegar, spices, etc. (*French* ~) and used as a condiment with meat or applied to the skin as a poultice or plaster; *grain of* ~ *seed*, small thing capable of vast development (Matt. xiii. 31); ~ *and cress*, salad made of cress and young shoots or leaves of white mustard plant; ~ *gas*, dichlorodiethyl sulphide, a colourless oily liquid with faint garlic odour, the vapour of which is one of the vesicant (blister) gases used in chemical warfare; ~*-pot*, vessel for holding mustard at table.

mŭs'ter *n.* Assembling of men for inspection, instruction, etc.; *pass* ~, undergo muster without censure; bear examination or inspection; come up to standard; ~*-roll*, official list of officers and men in army or ship's company (also fig.). ~ *v.* Collect or assemble for inspection etc.; collect, bring or come together; summon (courage, strength, etc., *up*).

mŭs'ty *adj.* Spoiled with damp; moist and fetid; mouldy; (fig.) stale, antiquated. **mŭs'tinėss** *n.*

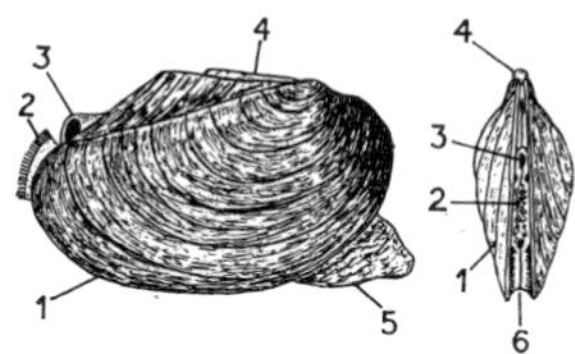

MUSSEL, A BIVALVE MOLLUSC

1. Shell or valve. 2. Inhalant siphon. 3. Exhalant siphon. 4. Ligament joining valves. 5. Foot. 6. Mantle

mūt'able *adj.* Liable to change, fickle. **mūtabĭl'ity** *n.*

mūt'ant *adj.* & *n.* (biol.) (Individual) differing from its parents as a result of mutation.

mūtā'tion *n.* 1. Change, alteration. 2. (biol.) Inception of a heritable variation, i.e. change in gene structure of a reproductive cell resulting in phenotypic difference in offspring. 3. (gram.) Change in vowel sound through influence of another vowel in following syllable.

mūtāt'ĭs mūtăn'dĭs. With the necessary alterations or changes.

mŭtch *n.* (Sc.) Woman's or child's close-fitting linen cap.

mūte[1] *adj.* Silent; not capable of speech, dumb; (of hounds) not giving tongue; not expressed in speech, as ~ *appeal*; (law, of prisoner) refusing to plead; (of consonants) stopped; produced with a closing at some point in throat or mouth, as *b*, *p*, *t*, etc.; (of letters) not pronounced, although written, as *e* in *mute*. **mūte'ly** (-tl-) *adv.* **mūte'nėss** *n.* **mūte** *n.* 1. Dumb person; actor without speaking part in a play; hired mourner at funeral. 2. (mus.) Clip for deadening resonance of strings of violin etc.; pad for deadening sound of wind instrument. 3. Mute consonant. ~ *v.t.* (mus.) Deaden, soften, sound of an instrument with a mute.

mūte[2] *v.* (Of birds) void the faeces, discharge thus.

mūt'ĭlāte *v.t.* Injure, make imperfect, by depriving of part. **mūtĭlā'tion** *n.*

mūtineer' *n.* One who mutinies.

mūt'ĭnous *adj.* Guilty of mutiny, rebellious. **mūt'ĭnously** *adv.*

mūt'ĭny *n.* Open revolt against constituted authority, esp. refusal of 5 or more members of armed forces to obey orders of a superior officer. ~ *v.i.* Be guilty of mutiny.

mūt'ĭsm *n.* Muteness, silence; dumbness.

mŭtt'er *v.* Speak, utter, in low and barely audible tones, with mouth nearly closed. ~ *n.* Muttering.

mŭtt'on *n.* Flesh of sheep as food; *dead as* ~, quite dead; ~*-chop*, piece of rib or loin of mutton, usu. served fried or grilled; ~*-chop whiskers*, short bushy whiskers shaped like a mutton-chop.

mūt'ūal *adj.* (Of feelings, actions, etc.) felt, done, by each to(wards) the other, as ~ *affection, benefit*; performed by joint action, done in common; (improp.) common to two or more persons, as *our* ~ *friend*; (insurance) referring to a system by which insured persons are shareholders of a company and share in its profits. **mūt'ūally** *adv.* **mūtūăl'ity** *n.* Reciprocity, interdependence.

mūt'ūalĭsm *n.* (ethics) Doctrine that mutual dependence is necessary to social well-being; **mūt'ūalĭst** *n.*

mūt'ūle *n.* (Gk antiq.) Block projecting under Doric cornice (ill. ORDER).

mŭz'zle *n.* 1. Projecting part of animal's head including nose and mouth; snout. 2. Arrangement of straps or wires over animal's mouth to prevent its biting, eating, etc. 3. End of fire-arm from which the projectile is discharged (ill. CANNON); ~*-loader*, fire-arm loaded at muzzle, dist. f. *breech-loader*; ~ *velocity*, velocity of projectile at its discharge from muzzle of a gun. ~ *v.t.* Put muzzle on (animal, and fig. a person); impose silence on, restrict freedom of speech of.

mŭzz'y *adj.* Mentally hazy; stupid with drink. **mŭzz'ĭly** *adv.* **mŭzz'ĭnėss** *n.*

M.V. *abbrev.* Motor vessel; (also (m.v.) muzzle velocity.

M.V.D. The Ministry of Internal Affairs of Soviet Russia (freq. in ref. to its secret police); formerly known as N.K.V.D. [initials of Russ. *M*inisterstvo ministry, *V*nutrennikh *D*el internal affairs; *N*arodny *K*ommissariat, people's commissariat]

M.V.O. *abbrev.* Member of the (Royal) Victorian Order.

MW *abbrev.* Mega-watt(s).

Mx *abbrev.* Middlesex.

my (mī, mĭ) *poss. adj.* Of, belonging to, affecting, me; prefixed to some terms of address, as ~ *lord*; as int., ~ *goodness!*, *oh* ~*!*

M.Y. *abbrev.* Motor Yacht.

mȳăl'gia (-j*a*) *n.* Pain in the muscles; muscular rheumatism.

mȳ'alism *n.* Kind of sorcery practised esp. in W. Indies.

mȳ'all (-awl) *n.* Australian acacia with hard sweet-scented wood used for pipes. [native *maial*]

mȳcēl'ium *n.* (bot.) Vegetative part of a fungus, consisting of microscopic hyphae or threads (ill. FUNGUS).

Mȳcēn'ae. City of ancient Greece in the plain of Argos; first inhabited *c* 3000 B.C. by peoples akin to the Minoans of Crete; in Middle and Late Bronze Age (*c* 2100–1150 B.C.) occupied by Greeks, who built the Lion Gate and beehive tombs which still survive. In Homer, Agamemnon is king of Mycenae. **Mȳcėnae'an, Mȳcēn'ian** *adjs.*

mȳcŏl'ogy *n.* Study of fungi. **mȳcŏl'ogist** *n.*

mycorrhiz'a (mīkorī-) *n.* (bot.) Association between fungi and the absorbing organs of other plants (excluding algae) which occurs in normally healthy plants under natural conditions; the organ so formed.

mȳcŏt'rophy *n.* State of a plant living in symbiosis with a fungus.

mȳelīt'ĭs *n.* Inflammation of the spinal cord.

myna: see MINA.

mȳocar̃d'ĭum *n.* Muscular substance of the heart. **mȳocar̃d'ĭal** *adj.*

mȳogĕn'ic *adj.* Produced by, arising in, the muscles.

mȳŏl'ogy *n.* Study of muscles. **mȳolŏ'gical** *adj.* **mȳŏl'ogist** *n.*

mȳŏp'athy *n.* Any affection of the muscles.

mȳ'ōpe *n.* Short-sighted person. **mȳŏp'ĭc** *adj.* Short-sighted.

myōp'ia *n.* Short-sightedness, a condition of the eye in which the rays from distant objects are brought to a focus before they reach the retina and so form a blurred image.

myosis: see MIOSIS.

myosōt'is *n.* (bot.) Genus of small plants with blue, pink, or white flowers, of which the forget-me-not (*Myosotis palustris*) is a species.

mȳ'otōme *n.* One of the serially repeated muscle blocks in a developing metamerically segmented animal (ill. LANCELET).

mȳ'riad *adj.* & *n.* Ten thousand; (of) indefinitely great number.

mȳ'riapŏd *adj.* & *n.* (zool.) (Animal) with many legs, of the class of arthropods which includes the centipedes and millepedes.

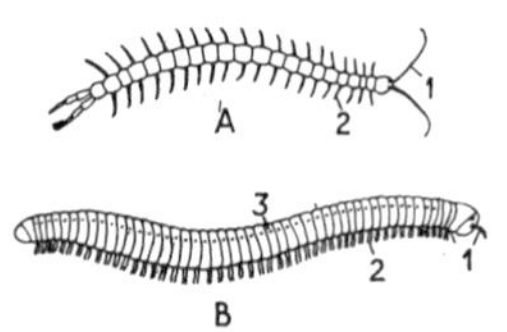

MYRIAPODS: A. CENTIPEDE. B. MILLEPEDE

1. Antenna. 2. Legs. 3. Pores for the escape of products of stink glands

mȳrioram'a (-rah- *or* -rā-) *n.* Entertainment consisting of a large number of pictures and views.

Myrm'idon (mēr-) *n.* In Gk legend, one of a warlike people on the S. borders of Thessaly who followed Achilles to the siege of Troy. **myrm'idon** *n.* Faithful follower; unscrupulously faithful attendant, hired ruffian.

mȳrŏb'alan *n.* Dried astringent plum-like fruit of certain E. Indian trees, containing tannin and used in dyeing, tanning, etc.

myrrh (mēr) *n.* Gum-resin, obtained from various species, esp. *Commiphora molmol*, used in perfumes and incense, and in medicine as astringent and antiseptic mouthwash.

myrt'le (mēr-) *n.* (bot.) Any shrub of genus *Myrtus*, esp. *M. communis*, the European myrtle with dark glossy evergreen leaves and white fragrant flowers.

mȳsĕlf' *pron.* Used as reflexive and emphatic form of *me* (or *I*).

Mȳsōre'. State of S. India.

mȳs'tagŏgue (-g) *n.* Teacher of mystical doctrines. **mȳstagŏ'gic(al)** *adjs.*

mȳstēr'ious *adj.* Full of, wrapt in, mystery; (of persons) delighting in, affecting, mystery. **mȳstēr'iously** *adv.* **mȳstēr'iousness** *n.*

mȳs'tery *n.* Hidden or inexplicable matter; secrecy, obscurity; religious truth known only by divine revelation; religious rite, esp. (pl.) Eucharist; (pl.) secret religious rites of Greeks, Romans, etc.; miracle-play.

mȳs'tic *adj.* Spiritually symbolic; occult, esoteric; enigmatical. ~ *n.* One who seeks by contemplation and self-surrender to attain union with the Deity, or who believes in the spiritual apprehension of truths beyond the understanding. **mȳs'tical** *adj.* Of mystics or mysticism; spiritually significant, connected with God in some way transcending understanding. **mȳs'tically** *adv.* **mȳs'ticism** *n.*

mȳs'tifȳ *v.t.* Bewilder; hoax, humbug. **mȳstificā'tion** *n.*

mȳstique (-tēk') *n.* Atmosphere of mystery and veneration investing some doctrines, arts, professions, etc., or personages; any professional skill or technique which mystifies and impresses the layman.

mȳth *n.* Fictitious (primitive) tale, usu. involving supernatural persons, embodying some popular idea concerning natural or historical phenomena; fictitious person or object. **mȳth'ic(al)** *adjs.* **mȳth'ically** *adv.*

mȳth'icīze *v.t.* Treat (story etc.) as myth, interpret mythically. **mȳth'icism** *n.*

mȳthŏg'raphy *n.* Representation of myths in painting or sculpture.

mȳthŏl'ogy *n.* Body of myths, esp. as relating to particular person or subject or current in a particular country; study of myths; picture etc. illustrating a myth. **mȳthŏl'oger, mȳthŏl'ogist** *ns.* Student of myths. **mȳtholŏ'gical** *adj.* **mȳthŏlŏ'gically** *adv.* **mȳthŏl'ogīze** *v.t.* Treat of myths and mythology; invent myths.

Mȳtilēn'ē, Mītȳlēn'ē. Ancient (and modern) capital of Lesbos (*Mitilini*).

mȳxoedēm'a (-ed-) *n.* Disorder due to deficient secretion of the thyroid gland.

mȳx'omatōs'is *n.* Contagious fatal disease of rabbits, caused by a virus.

mȳxomȳ'cēte *n.* (bot.) Slime fungus, member of a group of organisms which pass part of their life-cycle in an amoeboid state and later reproduce by spores.

N

N, n (ĕn). 14th letter of modern English, and 13th of ancient Roman alphabet, representing historically Gk *nū* and Semitic *nun*; earlier Greek forms were ꓠ and ꓥ, corresponding to Phoenician ꓥ. Usu. denotes a voiced nasal consonant with front closure (point of tongue touching teeth or teeth-ridge), but sometimes also sonant or vowel, and before *g*, *k*, a nasal with back tongue-closure. 1. *n* (also *en*), unit of measurement in printing, half the width of an EM. 2. (math.) indefinite number; *to the nth (power)*, to any required power; (fig.) to any extent, to the utmost.

n. *abbrev.* Neuter; nominative; noon; noun.

N. *abbrev.* Nationalist; Navigator; New; North.

N.A.A.F.I., Naafi (năf'ĭ) *abbrev.* Navy, Army, and Air Force Institutes.

Nā'aman. Syrian captain cured of leprosy by Elisha, who told him to bathe in Jordan (2 Kings v).

năb *v.t.* (slang) Apprehend, arrest; catch in wrong-doing.

Năbatae'an. One of an Arabic people of ancient Arabia, with kingdom to E. and SE. of Palestine destroyed by the Romans A.D. 105; the Aramaic language of these people.

nāb'ŏb *n.* 1. = NAWAB. 2. (hist.) Retired servant of East India Company, esp. between battle of Plassey, 1757, and appointment of Warren Hastings, 1772, returning to England with large fortune and orientalized ways. 3. Any ostentatiously wealthy person.

Nāb'ŏth. (O.T.) A Jezreelite who was stoned to death because he would not give up his vineyard to Ahab (1 Kings xxi); *~'s vineyard*, possession that one will stick at nothing to secure.

nacĕlle' *n.* 1. Outer casing of aircraft's engine 2. Car of airship.

nā'cre (-ker) *n.* (Shell-fish yielding) mother-of-pearl. **nāc'rėous, nāc'rous** *adjs.*

nād'ir *n.* Point of heavens diametrically opposite zenith or directly under observer (ill. CELESTIAL); (transf.) lowest point, place or time of great depression. [Arab. *naḍīr* (*es-semt*) opposite to (zenith)]

Naev'ĭus, Gnaeus (*c* 270–*c* 199 B.C.). Early Roman poet and dramatist.

naev'us *n.* (path.) Congenital lesion of skin, birth-mark, a network of hypertrophied blood-vessels causing sharply defined red patch level with skin surface; (also) pigmented mole.

Năff'y. (colloq.) Canteen of the Navy, Army, and Air Force Institutes (abbrev. N.A.A.F.I.).

năg[1] *n.* Small riding-horse or pony; horse (colloq.).

năg[2] *v.* Find fault or scold persistently (*at* person); annoy thus. **năgg'ĭng** *adj.* (esp. of pain) Gnawing, persistent.

Na'ga (nah-). 1. (Hindu myth.) One of a race of semi-human serpents, genii of rain, rivers, etc. 2. Group of primitive tribes inhabiting parts of Assam and Burma.

nagana (-ahn'a) *n.* Disease carried by certain species of tsetse fly affecting domestic animals and some wild ones. [Zulu *nakane*]

năg'ôr *n.* Reedbuck, African antelope (*Redunca arundinum* and *R. redunca*) with short forward-curving horns in the male. [named by BUFFON]

Nah. *abbrev.* Nahum.

Nā'hum. Hebrew prophet; Old Testament book (7th of the minor prophets) containing his prophecy against Nineveh (beginning of 7th c. B.C.).

nai'ad (nī-) *n.* (Gk etc. myth.) Nymph living in river or spring as its tutelary spirit.

naif (nah-ēf') *adj.* (rare) = NAÏVE.

nail *n.* 1. Horny oval-shaped protective covering of modified epidermis on upper surface of tip of finger or toe; claw, talon. 2. Hard excrescence on upper mandible of some soft-billed birds. 3. Small metal spike, usu. with point and broadened head, driven in with hammer to hold things together or as peg or ornament;

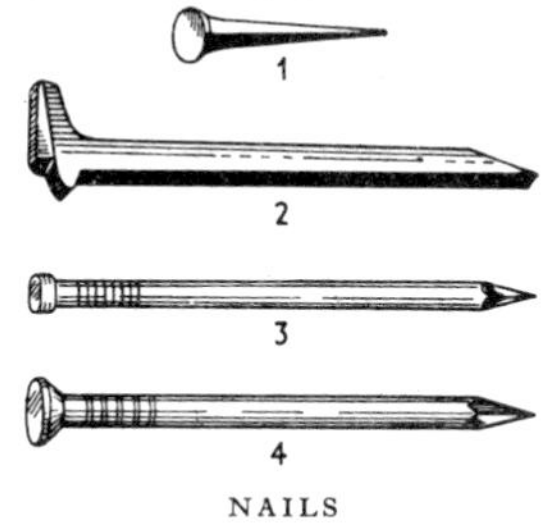

NAILS

1. Cut tack. 2. Steel rail dog 3. Lost head oval wire brad. 4. Round wire nail

hit (*right*) ~ *on the head*, give true explanation, propose or do right thing, hit the mark; *on the* ~, (chiefly of payment) without delay. 4. ~-*brush*, small brush for cleaning finger-nails; ~-*head*, architectural ornament shaped like head of nail (ill. MOULDING); ~-*file*, ~-*scissors*, instruments for paring finger-nails. ~ *v.t.* Fasten with nails; fix or keep fixed (person, attention, etc.); secure, catch, engage, succeed in getting hold of; ~ *to the counter*, expose as false or spurious (in allusion to shopkeepers' practice of dealing thus with bad coins). **nail'er** *n.* Nail-maker.

nain'sŏŏk *n.* Fine soft plain-woven cotton fabric with high gloss on one side. [Hind. f. *nain* eye, *sukh* pleasure]

Nairn'shire. County of NE. Scotland, S. of Moray Firth.

Nairōb'ĭ (nīr-). Capital of Republic of Kenya, E. Africa.

naïve (nah-ēv'), **naive** (nāv) *adj.* Artless, innocent, unsophisticated; amusingly simple. **naïve'ly** (-vl-) *adv.* **naïveté** (-vtā), **naïv'ėty** *ns.*

nāk'ėd *adj.* Unclothed, nude; defenceless; unsheathed; plain, undisguised, exposed for examination; devoid *of*; treeless, leafless, barren; (of rock) exposed; without ornament; (of light, flame, etc.) not placed within case or receptacle; (bot., zool.) without pericarp, leaves, hairs, scales, etc.; without addition, comment, support, etc.; ~ *boys, ladies*, meadow saffron, autumn crocus; ~ *eye*, eye unassisted by telescope, microscope, etc.; ~ *truth*, strict truth, without concealment or addition. **nāk'ėdly** *adv.* **nāk'ėdnėss** *n.*

N.A.L.G.O. *abbrev.* National and Local Government Officers' Association.

năm'by-păm'by *adj.* & *n.* Sentimental, pretty, trifling (work of art); (person) lacking in vigour. [formed on name of *Ambrose* Philips (d. 1749), author of pastorals]

nāme *n.* Word by which individual person, animal, place or thing is spoken of or to; person as known, famed, or spoken of; family, clan; reputation; merely nominal existence, practically non-existent thing; *call* ~*s*, describe by uncomplimentary names; *by the* ~ *of*, called; *put* one's ~ *down for*, apply as candidate etc.; *keep* one's ~ *on*, *take* one's ~ *off*, *the books*, remain, cease to be, member of college, club, etc.; *in the* ~ *of*, invoking, acting as deputy for or in the interest of; ~-*day*, day of saint after whom person is named; ~-*part*, that after which play is named, title-role; (one's) *name'-sake*, person or thing with same name as oneself. ~ *v.t.* Give name to, call by right name, appoint (to office etc.); specify; (of Speaker) mention (M.P.) as disobedient to Chair.

nāme'lėss (-ml-) *adj.* Obscure, left unnamed; unknown; bearing no name or inscription; indefinable; too bad to be named.

nāme'ly (-ml-) *adv.* That is to say, viz.

Na'na Sah'ĭb (nah-). Name by which Dandu Panth (b. *c* 1821), a Mahratta, became known as leader of INDIAN Mutiny.

năn'cy *n.* Effeminate man or boy; homosexual (also used attrib.). [pet form of the female name *Ann*]

nănkeen' *n.* Chinese cloth of natural buff-yellow cotton; cloth of dyed cotton resembling this; pale buff-yellow colour; (pl.) trousers of nankeen. [f. NANKING]

Nănkĭng'. City of China, on Yangtze, capital of China during two first reigns of Ming dynasty, and capital of Nationalist government from 1929 until the Japanese invasion of China in 1937. [Chin., = 'southern capital']

nănn'y *n.* Child's nurse (also *nannie*); ~-*goat*, she-goat (cf. BILLY). [pet form of female name *Ann*]

Năn'sen, Fridtjof (1861–1930). Norwegian Arctic explorer, scientist, and statesman; League of Nations high commissioner for refugees after war of 1914–18; ~ *passport*, League of Nations passport for stateless refugees.

Nantes (nahn̈t). City of W. France, on River Loire; *Edict of* ~, edict of Henry IV of France (1598) granting toleration to Protestants, revoked by Louis XIV (1685).

Nanteuil (nahn̈tėr'ē), Robert (1623–78). French engraver of portraits, famous for his portraits of Louis XIV, Mazarin, Colbert, etc.

Năntŭck'ėt. Island in Atlantic S. of Cape Cod, Massachusetts, U.S.

Nā'omĭ. Mother-in-law of RUTH (Ruth i).

nā'ŏs *n.* (Gk antiq.) Inner sanctuary of temple, cella (ill. TEMPLE).

năp[1] *v.i.* Sleep lightly or briefly; *catch napping*, find asleep; take unawares or off one's guard. ~ *n.* Short sleep, doze, esp. by day.

năp[2] *n.* Surface given to cloth by raising the fibres; soft or downy surface. ~ *v.t.* Raise nap on (cloth). **năp'lėss** *adj.*

năp[3] *n.* 1. Card-game in which each player is given 5 cards and calls the number of tricks he expects to win; *go* ~, call 5 tricks; stake all one can; ~ *hand*, hand suitable for going nap. 2. Tip that horse etc. is certain to win. ~ *v.t.* Tip (horse etc.) as certain winner. [abbrev. of *Napoleon*]

năp(p)'a *n.* Leather prepared from sheep- or goat-skin by special tawing process. [county and town in California, U.S.]

nāp'alm (-ahm) *n.* Mixture of aluminium salts of naphthenic acid from crude petroleum with palmitic and stearic acids obtained from coconut oil, for jellying petrol for incendiary use in war (whence ~ *bomb*). [*na*(phthenic) + *palm*(itic)]

nāpe *n.* Back of neck.

nāp'ery *n.* Household, esp. table, linen.

Năph'talī. Son of Jacob and ancestor of one of the tribes of Israel.

năph'tha *n.* Orig., inflammable volatile liquid (a constituent of asphalt and bitumen) issuing from earth in some places; now, kinds of inflammable oil got by dry distillation of organic substances, esp. coal, shale, and petroleum.

năph'thacēne *n.* Orange-yellow crystalline aromatic hydrocarbon.

năph'thalēne *n.* White crystalline aromatic hydrocarbon, $C_{10}H_8$, with peculiar smell and pungent taste, obtained from coal-tar etc. and used in the manufacture of dyes and chemicals and for soil fumigation; ~ *ball*, small ball of compressed naphthalene used to protect clothes against moth.

năph'thēne *n.* One of a series of hydrocarbons occurring in petroleum, shale-tar, etc.

năph'thŏl *n.* Either of two white crystalline hydroxyl derivatives of naphthalene, distinguished as α-*naphthol* and β-*naphthol*, used as disinfectants, in manufacture of dyes, etc.

Nāp'ier (Neper), John (1550–1617). Scottish mathematician; inventor of logarithms and of the modern notation of decimal numbers; ~*'s bones (rods)*, graduated slips of bone, wood, etc., for performing multiplications and divisions. **Nāpier'ian** (-ēr-) *adj.*

năp'kin *n.* Square of linen or cotton used for wiping lips or fingers at meals, or in serving certain dishes (*table-*~); piece of towelling or tissue worn by baby to absorb excreta; ~*-ring*, ring for holding rolled-up table-napkin.

Nāp'les (-lz). (It. *Napoli*) City and seaport of SW. Italy. [L *Neapolis* f. Gk *nea polis* new city]

napŏl'ėon[1] *n.* 1. French gold coin issued by Napoleon I, of value of 20 francs. 2. Kind of long boot. 3. = NAP[3] *n.*

Napŏl'ėon[2] **I.** Napoléon Bonaparte (1769–1821), French soldier of Corsican family; became First Consul of France, 1799, and Emperor of the French, 1804; conquered large parts of Europe; after various defeats, abdicated and withdrew to Elba, 1814; returned to Paris, 1815; was defeated at Waterloo 3 months later and again abdicated; was exiled to St. Helena, where he died.

Napŏl'ėon[3] **II.** Napoléon François Joseph Charles, Duke of Reichstadt (1811–32). Son of Napoleon I and Marie Louise; king of Rome; known as Napoleon II (although he never ruled France) because Napoleon I abdicated in his favour in 1814.

Napŏl'ėon[4] **III.** Charles Louis Napoléon Bonaparte (1808–73), nephew of Napoleon I; elected president of the French Republic 1848; proclaimed emperor 1852; captured by the Germans at SEDAN 1870, and deposed.

Napōlėŏn ĭc *adj.* Of NAPOLEON[2] I; ~ *Wars*, series of campaigns (1799–1815), of French armies under Napoleon against Austria, Russia, Gt Britain, Portugal, Prussia, and other powers.

napōō' (nah-) *int.* & *adj.* (now obs. army slang) Finished, gone, done for, useless. [Fr. dial. *n'a pu* (= *il n'y en a plus* there isn't any more)]

nappa: see NAPA.

năppe *n.* 1. Sheet of water falling over weir etc. 2. (geol.) Recumbent fold or anticline (ill. ROCK).

năpp'y[1] *adj.* (archaic) (Of ale etc.) foaming, heady, strong.

năpp'y[2] *n.* (nursery colloq.) Baby's napkin.

napu (nah'pōō) *n.* Any of various species of chevrotain, small deer-like ruminant mammals, esp. *Tragulus napu* of Sumatra and *T. javanicus* of Java. [Malay wd]

nar'cėine *n.* Bitter crystalline narcotic alkaloid present in opium.

narciss'ism *n.* (psychol.) Excessive or erotic interest in one's own body or personality. **narcissĭs'tic** *adj.* [f. NARCISSUS[2]]

narciss'us[1] *n.* Genus of bulbous plants including the daffodils; esp. *N. poeticus*, bearing in spring heavily-scented single white flower with undivided corona with a red crisped edge.

Narciss'us[2]. (Gk myth.) A beautiful youth who, falling in love with his reflection in a spring, committed suicide (or pined away), and was changed into the flower that bears his name.

narc'olĕpsy *n.* Disease characterized by irresistible attacks of true sleep, usually of brief duration. **narcolĕp'tic** *adj.*

narcōs'is *n.* Operation or effects of narcotics; state of insensibility.

narcŏt'ic *adj.* Inducing drowsiness, sleep, stupor, or insensibility (also fig.). ~ *n.* Narcotic drug used in medicine; any of several such drugs taken habitually by addicts.

nard *n.* (Plant, prob. *Nardostachys jatamansi*, yielding) aromatic balsam of ancients, usu. called *spikenard*.

narg'hile (-gĭlĕ) *n.* Oriental tobacco-pipe in which smoke is drawn through water before reaching mouth, a hookah. [Pers. *nargi* coconut]

nark *n.* (slang) Police spy or informer; person informing on others. ~ *v.* Act as nark. [Romany *nak* nose]

Narragăn'sėtt. ~ *Bay*, inlet of Atlantic Ocean running northward from S. shore of Rhode Island; ~ *Indians*, Amer. Indian tribe of Algonkin linguistic stock, formerly inhabiting parts of Rhode Island.

narrāte' *v.t.* Relate, recount, give continuous account of. **narrā'tion, narrāt'or** *ns.*

nă'rrative *n.* Tale, story, recital of facts; kind of composition or talk that confines itself to these. ~ *adj.* In the form of, concerned with, narration.

nă'rrow (-ō) *adj.* Of small width in proportion to length, confining; restricted; with little margin; illiberal, prejudiced, exclusive, whence ~*-minded*, ~*-mindedly*, ~*-mindedness*; searching, precise; (phonet.) tense; ~ *boat*, canal and river boat of not more than 7 ft in the beam; ~ *cloth*, cloth under 52 in. wide; ~ *goods*, braids, ribbons, etc.; ~ *gauge*, (on railway) gauge of less than 4 ft 8½ in. (but formerly ~ *gauge* meant 4 ft 8½ in., the British standard gauge); ~ *seas* English Channel and Irish Sea. **nă'rrowly** *adv.* **nă'rrowness** *n.* **nă'rrow** *n.* (usu. pl.) Narrow part of sound, strait, river, pass, etc. ~ *v.* Make or become narrower, diminish, lessen, contract.

narth'ĕx *n.* Porch or vestibule in early Christian church, extending across width of nave at opposite end from main altar, and used by those not in full communion (ill. BASILICA).

nar'whal (-wal) *n.* Arctic delphinoid cetacean (*Monodon monoceros*), the male having a very long spirally twisted straight tusk developed from one, or sometimes both, of its two teeth (ill. WHALE).

nar'y *adj.* (U.S. and dial.) Not a, no. [var. of *ne'er a*]

nās'al (-z-) *adj.* Of the nose; (of sounds) produced with nose passages open (as *n*, *m*, *ng*); (of voice etc.) characterized by unusual or disagreeable number of sounds produced by means of nose. **nās'ally** *adv.* **nasăl'ĭty** *n.* **nās'alīze** *v.* **nāsalīzā'tion** *n.* **nās'al** *n.* Nasal letter or sound.

năs'cent (-snt) *adj.* In the act of being born; just beginning to be, not yet mature; ~ *state*, (chem.) highly active condition of certain elements, esp. hydrogen, at the moment of liberation from a compound. **năs'cency** *n.*

Nāse'by (-zbĭ). Village of Northamptonshire, scene of battle (1645) in which Puritan army under Fairfax and Cromwell won decisive victory over Royalists under Charles I and Prince Rupert.

Năsh[1], John (1752–1835). English architect; designer of the terraces near Regent's Park, London; also of Regent St (buildings since replaced) and other parts of London.

Năsh[2], Richard (1674–1762). 'Beau Nash', English man of fashion, master of ceremonies at Bath.

Năsh(e), Thomas (1567–1601). English poet, dramatist, and pamphleteer.

Năsh'ville. Capital of Tennessee, U.S.

Nās'mўth[1], Alexander (1758–1840). Scottish landscape and portrait painter.

Nās'mўth[2], James (1808–90). Scottish engineer, inventor of the steam-hammer.

Nās′ō. Cognomen of OVID.

nāso- (-z-) *prefix.* Nose, as in ~-*frontal*, of nose and forehead.

Năss′au[1] (-ow). Territory of central Germany on E. bank of the Rhine; formerly an independent grand duchy; incorporated 1866 with kingdom of Prussia.

Năss′au[2] (-aw). Capital city of Bahama Islands, on N. shore of New Providence.

nastŭr′tium (-shm) *n.* 1. (bot.) Genus of cruciferous pungent-tasting plants including watercress. 2. (pop.) Unrelated group of garden plants of genus *Tropaeolum*, mostly climbers, having spurred flowers in shades of red and yellow; *T. majus*, Indian cress, is used in salads, and its fruits are pickled.

na′sty (-ah-) *adj.* Unpleasant to taste or smell; disgusting; obscene; spiteful; extremely disagreeable. **na′stĭly** *adv.* **na′stĭnėss** *n.*

Nat. *abbrev.* Nathaniel; National(ist).

nāt′al[1] *adj.* Of, from, birth. **natăl′ĭty** *n.* (rare) Birth-rate.

Natăl′[2]. Eastern coastal province of Republic of South Africa; first settled by a few British traders in 1823, then by Boers in 1838, becoming a Boer Republic; annexed by British, 1845; representative government, 1856; responsible government, 1893; province of South Africa, 1910; capital, Pietermaritzburg. [named *Terra Natalis* by Vasco da Gama because he sighted the entrance to what is now Durban harbour on Christmas Day, 1497]

natā′tion *n.* Swimming.

nātatŏr′ial, nāt′atory *adjs.* Swimming, of swimming.

Nătch′ėz. Amer. Indian tribe, of lower Mississippi River; conquered and scattered by French, 1730.

nāt′ēs (-z) *n.pl.* (anat.) 1. Buttocks. 2. Anterior pair of optic lobes of brain.

Nāth′an. (O.T.) Hebrew prophet of time of David and Solomon (2 Sam. vii, xii; 1 Kings i; 1 Chron. xxix; 2 Chron. ix).

Nathăn′āĕl. (N.T.) Disciple mentioned in first and last chapters of Gospel of St. John; freq. identified with BARTHOLOMEW.

nā′tion *n.* 1. Society united under one government in a political State; considerable group of people having common descent, history, or language. 2. (In medieval and some Sc. universities) body of students from particular country or district.

nă′tional (-shon-) *adj.* Of a (or the) nation; common to the whole nation, concerned with its interests as dist. from those of a faction or region; ~ *anthem*, song adopted by a nation as an expression of patriotism, and played or sung on formal and ceremonial occasions; in Britain, poem and air 'God save the King' (or Queen) of unknown origin, first printed 1744; *N~ Assembly*, (esp.) first revolutionary assembly of France 1789–91; ~ *bank*, (U.S.) any of numerous commercial banks chartered under the federal government in accordance with the banking acts of 1863–4, empowered to receive, lend, and transmit money, and to issue currency notes; *N~ Coal Board*, British public corporation, which in 1946 took over the assets and responsibilities of the coal industry; *N~ Committee*, (U.S.) the 'permanent' committee at the head of a political party, chosen at each national convention for a period of four years; *N~ Convention*, (hist.) elected assembly which governed France 1792–5, abolished royalty, and established republic; (U.S. politics) convention of major political party which nominates candidate for presidency etc.; *N~ Debt*: see DEBT; *N~ Gallery*, gallery for permanent exhibition of pictures belonging to a nation, esp. that in Trafalgar Square, London; *N~ Health Service*, British system, initiated 1946, providing a medical service financed chiefly by taxation; *N~ Insurance Act*, that of 1911 (requiring wage-earners to make weekly payments supplemented by their employers, in return for which they were entitled to State assistance in sickness, unemployment, etc.) or that of 1946 (by which all citizens in receipt of a personal income became compulsorily insured); *N~ Library of Scotland*, the Advocates' Library, Edinburgh, presented to the nation and endowed in 1924; ~ *park*, (orig. U.S.) extensive area set aside by government action for the preservation of historic or prehistoric sites and of flora and fauna, and for the benefit of the public; *N~ Portrait Gallery*, public collection in London, initiated 1856, of portraits of 'eminent persons in British history'; *N~ Society*, founded 1811 to promote education of the poor, hence *N~ School*; *N~ Socialist Party*, party with ultra-nationalistic, anti-Semitic, and totalitarian programme which acquired dictatorial power in Germany under HITLER in 1933; *N~ Socialism*; *N~ Trust*, privately subscribed trust (incorporated 1907) for preservation of places of historic interest or natural beauty in Great Britain; *Grand N~* (*Steeplechase*), chief steeplechase of year in England, run at Aintree near Liverpool in March. **nă′tionally** *adv.* **nă′tional** *n.* Person legally considered a member of a specified State.

nă′tionalism (-shon-) *n.* Patriotic feeling, principle, or efforts; policy of national independence. **nă′tionalist** *n.* **nătionalis′tic** *adj.*

nătionăl′ity (-shon-) *n.* National quality; nation, existence as a nation; ethnic group; fact of belonging to a particular nation or ethnic group; cohesion due to common history etc.; person's status as member of a nation, alterable by legal process.

nă′tionalize (-shon-) *v.t.* Make national; make into a nation; naturalize (foreigner); transfer (land, mines, railways, etc.) from private ownership and control to that of the State. **nătionalizā′tion** *n.*

nāt′ive *n.* 1. One born, or whose parents are domiciled, in a particular place or country; (Austral.) white born in Australia; original or usual inhabitant of country as dist. from strangers or foreigners, esp. one of non-European race. 2. Indigenous animal or plant. 3. Oyster reared wholly or partly in British waters, esp. in artificial beds. ~ *adj.* 1. Belonging to a person or thing by nature, innate, natural *to*; of one's birth; where one was born; belonging to one by right of birth. 2. (Of metals etc.) occurring naturally in pure state; occurring in nature, not produced artificially. 3. Born in a place (esp. of non-Europeans), indigenous, not exotic; of the natives of a place; *N~ State*, territory ruled by an Indian prince.

nāt′ivism *n.* 1. (philos.) Doctrine of innate ideas. 2. (U.S.) Prejudice in favour of natives against strangers, esp. immigrants. **nāt′ivist** *n.*

nativ′ity *n.* Birth, esp. of Christ; picture of Christ's nativity; festival of birth of Christ (Christmas) or of Virgin (8th Sept.) or St. John Baptist (24th June); (astrol.) horoscope.

N.A.T.O., Nātō. North Atlantic Treaty Organization, international organization with headquarters at Paris, set up to carry out provisions of North Atlantic Treaty signed 1949.

nătt′er *v.i.* Scold, fret; 'rattle on' in talk; chat cosily.

nătt′erjăck *n.* Species of small toad (*Bufo calamita*) found in Britain and NW. Europe, with yellow stripe down back and running, not hopping, gait.

Nattier (nătyā′), Jean-Marc (1685–1766). French portrait painter; ~ *blue*, soft shade of blue much used by him.

nătt′y *adj.* Spruce, trim, deft. **nătt′ily** *adv.* **nătt′inėss** *n.*

nă′tural (-cher-) *adj.* 1. Based on the innate moral sense, instinctive, as ~ *law*, ~ *justice*. 2. Constituted by nature; ~ *day*: see DAY; ~ *selection*, (biol.) process of differential survival whereby in general those organisms most suited to their environment leave most offspring. 3. Normal, conformable to the ordinary course of nature, not exceptional or miraculous; ~ *death*, by age or disease, not by violence. 4. Not enlightened, unregenerate, as ~ *man*; not communicated by revelation, as ~ *religion*, ~ *theology*.

5. Physically existing, not spiritual or intellectual or fictitious, as *the ~ world*; one's *~ life*, duration of one's life on earth. 6. Existing in or by nature, not artificial; innate, inherent; self-sown, uncultivated. 7. Lifelike; unaffected, easy-mannered; not disfigured or disguised. 8. Not surprising; to be expected. 9. Consonant or easy *to* (person etc.). 10. Destined to be such by nature, as *~ enemies*. 11. So related by nature only, illegitimate, as *~ child, son*. 12. dealing with nature as a study; *~ classification*, the classification of species into *~ orders* (abbrev. N.O.), esp. Jussieu's arrangement of plant species acc. to likeness as opp. to Linnaeus's sexual system; *~ history*, orig. = systematic study of all natural objects, animal, vegetable, and mineral; now usu. = study of animal life, freq. implying popular rather than scientific treatment; aggregate of facts about the natural objects or characteristics of a place or class; *~ historian*; *~ philosophy*, physics; *~ philosopher*, physicist; *~ science*, the physical or natural sciences collectively. 13. (mus.) Not sharp or flat; (of scale or key) having no sharps or flats; *~ scale*, C major. **nă'turalnėss** *n.*

nă'tural *n.* 1. Person half-witted from birth. 2. Note in natural scale; white key on piano; sign ♮ used to cancel preceding sharp or flat. 3. (cards, in vingt-et-un) Hand making 21 as first dealt. 4. (colloq., orig. U.S.) One who is naturally endowed for or 'born to' something, as *a ~ for television*.

năt'uralĭsm (-cher-) *n.* 1. Moral or religious system on purely natural basis; philosophy excluding supernatural or spiritual. 2. Faithful representation of nature or reality in literature, art, etc.

nă'turalĭst *n.* 1. One who believes in or studies naturalism. 2. Student of animals or plants.

năturalĭs'tĭc *adj.* Of, according to, naturalism in philosophy, literature, etc.; of natural history. **năturalĭs'tĭcally** *adv.*

nă'turalīze (-cher-) *v.* Admit (alien) to citizenship; adopt (foreign word, custom, etc.); introduce (animal, plant) into new environment. **năturalīzā'tion** *n.*

nă'turally (-cher-) *adv.* (esp.) As might be expected, of course.

nā'ture *n.* 1. Thing's essential qualities, person's innate character; general characteristics and feelings of mankind; specified element of human character; person of specified character; kind, sort, class; *by ~*, innately. 2. Inherent impulses determining character or action; vital force, functions, or needs; resin or sap in wood; *against ~*, unnatural, immoral; *light of ~*: see LIGHT[1]. 3. Creative and regulative physical power conceived of as immediate cause of phenomena of material world; these phenomena as a whole; these personified; naturalness in art etc.; *in the course of ~*, in the ordinary course; *in ~*, in real fact; *state of ~*, unregenerate condition (opp. *state of grace*); condition of man before society is organized; uncultivated or undomesticated state of plants or animals; bodily nakedness.

naught (nawt) *n.* Nothing, nought; (arith.) cipher, nought. *~ pred. adj.* Worthless, useless.

naughty (nawt'ĭ) *adj.* (Now used almost exclusively of, to, or by children.) Wayward, disobedient, badly behaved; (archaic) wicked, blameworthy, indecent. **naught'ĭly** *adv.* **naught'ĭnėss** *n.*

naus'ėa *n.* Feeling of sickness; sea-sickness; loathing. **naus'ėāte** *v.t.* Affect with nausea.

naus'ėous *adj.* Causing nausea; offensive to taste or smell, nasty; disgusting, loathsome. **naus'ėously** *adv.* **naus'ėousnėss** *n.*

Nausĭcā'a. In the 'Odyssey', daughter of Alcinous. king of Phaeacia; she found the shipwrecked Odysseus on the shore and took him to her father's palace.

nautch *n.* E. Indian exhibition of professional dancing-girls; *~-girl*, one of these.

naut'ĭcal *adj.* Of sailors or navigation, naval, maritime; *~ mile*: see MILE, and Appendix X. **naut'ĭcally** *adv.*

naut'ĭlus *n.* 1. (*Paper*) *~*, small two-gilled cephalopod mollusc of warm seas (genus *Argonauta*), related to octopus; the female secretes in two of its arms a translucent single-chambered false shell. 2. (*Pearly*) *~*, four-gilled cephalopod of Indian and Pacific Oceans (genus *Nautilus*), having, in both sexes, a many-chambered true shell.

Năv'ajo (-hō), **Nav'aho.** Amer. Indian people of N. Arizona and New Mexico; *~ blanket*, bright-coloured woollen blanket with geometrical pattern, made by Navajo women.

nāv'al *adj.* Of ships, esp. ships of war; of the (or a) navy; *~ officer*, officer in navy; (U.S., also) customs official; *~ stores*, supplies for warships. **nāv'ally** *adv.*

Năvarin'ō (-rē-). Seaport and bay of S. Greece; scene of naval battle (1827) in which allied Russians, French, and British defeated Turks and Egyptians.

Navârre' (Span. *Navarra*). Province of N. Spain; (hist.) a medieval kingdom which included also parts of SW. France.

nāve[1] *n.* Central block of wheel holding axle and spokes, hub (ill. WHEEL).

nāve[2] *n.* Body of church from inner door to chancel or choir, usu. separated by pillars from aisles (ill. CHURCH).

nāv'el *n.* Depression in front of belly left by severance of umbilical cord; central point of anything; *~ orange*, large orange with navel-like formation at top; *~-string*, structure connecting foetus and placenta, umbilical cord; *~-wort*, various plants, esp. pennywort, *Cotyledon umbilicus*.

năv'icêrt *n.* A consular certificate granted to a neutral ship testifying that her cargo is correctly described according to the manifest and does not contravene contraband regulations, first put into operation 16th Mar. 1916. *~ v.t.* Authorize with a navicert. [L *navis* ship+*cert*(ificate)]

navĭc'ūlar *adj.* Boat-shaped; *~ bone*, tarsal bone; see ill. FOOT; *~ disease*, disease in feet of horses. *~ n.* Navicular bone or disease.

năv'ĭgable *adj.* Affording passage for ships; seaworthy; (of balloon) dirigible. **năvĭgabĭl'ĭty** *n.*

năv'ĭgāte *v.* Voyage, sail ship; sail over, up, down (sea, river); manage, direct course of (ship, aeroplane, etc.) with the aid of instruments.

năvĭgā'tion *n.* Navigating; methods of determining position and course of ship, aeroplane, etc., by geometry and nautical astronomy; voyage; *inland ~*, communication by canals and rivers.

năv'ĭgator *n.* 1. One charged with or skilled in navigation; sea explorer. 2. (now rare) Navvy.

năvv'y *n.* Labourer employed in excavating etc. for canals, railways, roads, etc.; (*steam-*), mechanical excavator. [abbrev. of *navigator*]

nāv'y *n.* Whole of State's ships of war with their crews and all the organization for their maintenance; *~ bill*, bill issued by Admiralty in lieu of cash payment; *~(-)blue*, (of) the dark blue used in British naval uniform; *~-cut*, cake tobacco finely sliced; *N~ Department*, U.S. department of State controlling the navy; *~ League*, association founded to arouse civilian interest in navy; *~ list*, official publication containing list of officers of navy etc.; *~-yard*, (now U.S.) government dockyard.

nawab' (-wawb) *n.* Indian nobleman; (hist.) Mohammedan governor of one of the lesser of the 15 provinces of the Mogul Empire; (rare) rich retired Anglo-Indian, nabob. [Arab. *nā'ib* deputy]

Năx'ŏs. Greek island, largest of the Cyclades; in ancient times a centre of the worship of Dionysus.

nay *adv.* No (archaic); or rather, and even, and more than that. *~ n.* The word *nay*; *yea and ~*, shilly-shally; *say ~*, utter denial or (usu.) refusal, refuse.

Năzarēne' *adj.* & *n.* 1. (Native, inhabitant) of Nazareth; *the ~*, Jesus Christ. 2. Follower of Jesus, Christian (so called esp. by Jews and Mohammedans). 3. Member of an obscure early Jewish-Christian sect allied to Ebionites. 4. Member of a group of German romantic painters in early 19th c. with aims resembling those of PRE-RAPHAELITES.

Năz'arèth. Town of Lower Galilee, Palestine, now in Israel; home of Joseph and Mary, parents of Jesus, who spent his youth there.

Năz'arīte[1] = NAZARENE 1.

Năz'arīte[2]. (O.T.) One of a Hebrew sect who abstained from all products of the vine, from cutting the hair, etc. (Num. vi). [Heb. *nāzar* separate or consecrate oneself]

nāze *n.* Promontory, headland, ness.

Nazi (nah'tsĭ) *n.* & *adj.* (Member, adherent) of the German NATIONAL Socialist party. **Na'zĭdom, Na'z(ĭ)ism** *ns.* **na'zĭfȳ** *v.t.* **nazĭfĭcā'tion** *n.* [abbrev. f. Ger. *Nationalsozialist* National Socialist]

n.b. *abbrev.* No ball.

N.B. *abbrev.* New Brunswick; North Britain; *nota bene* (= note well).

N.B.G., n.b.g. colloq. *abbrev.* No bloody good.

N. by E., N by E *abbrevs.* North by East.

N. by W., N by W *abbrevs.* North by West.

N.C. *abbrev.* North Carolina.

N.C.B. *abbrev.* National Coal Board.

N.C.O. *abbrev.* Non-commissioned officer.

n.d. *abbrev.* No date; not dated.

N. Dak. *abbrev.* North Dakota.

NE., NE *abbrevs.* North-east(ern).

Neagh (nā), Lough. Lake of NE. Ireland, largest in the British Isles.

Nèăn'derthal (-tahl). Valley in Rhineland, Germany; ~ *man*, type of man (ill. PRIMATE) widely distributed in palaeolithic Europe in the early stages of the last glaciation, with long low wide skull, retreating forehead, and massive brow-ridges (so called because parts of skeleton were discovered in a cave in this valley, 1857).

neap *adj.* & *n.* ~(-*tide*), tide soon after moon's 1st and 3rd quarters in which high-water level is at lowest. ~ *v.* (Of tides) tend towards neap; reach highest point of neap-tide; (pass., of ship) be prevented from getting off by neaping of tides.

Nēapŏl'ĭtan (nēa-) *adj.* & *n.* (Native, inhabitant) of Naples; ~ *ice*, ice-cream in layers of various colours and flavours; ~ *violet*, sweet-scented double variety of cultivated violet. [see NAPLES]

near *adv.* To, at, a short distance, in(to) proximity in space or time; almost, nearly; (with *not*) anything like; closely; parsimoniously; ~ *at hand*, within easy reach; not far in the future; ~ *by*, not far off; *go, come* ~ (*to* do, do*ing*), nearly do. ~ *prep.* Near in space, time, condition, or resemblance, to. ~ *adj.* 1. Closely related, intimate. 2. (Of horse, part of vehicle etc.), left (i.e. on the side where one mounts). 3. Close at hand, close to, in place or time; (of road or way) direct; ~ *distance*, part of scene between background and foreground. 4. (Of guess, translation, escape, etc.) close, narrow. 5. (Of persons) niggardly. 6. *N~ East*, SE. parts of Europe; Balkan States together with Asia Minor; ~ *miss*, (of shell, bomb, etc.) not a hit, but falling close enough to damage the target; ~-*sighted*, short-sighted. ~ *v.* Draw near (to), approach.

near'ly *adv.* Closely, almost; *not* ~, nothing like.

neat[1] *n.* Any animal of ox kind; (collect.) cattle; ~-*herd*, cowherd; ~'*s foot, tongue*, foot, tongue, of ox as food; ~'*s leather*, ox-hide.

neat[2] *adj.* 1. (Of liquor, esp. alcoholic) undiluted. 2. Nicely made or proportioned; pleasantly simple or compact; deft, dextrous, cleverly done; tidy, methodical; (of language, style, etc.) brief, clear, and pointed, cleverly phrased, epigrammatic. **neat'ly** *adv.* **neat'nèss** *n.*

neath *prep.* (poet.) Beneath.

nĕb *n.* 1. (Sc.) Beak; nose; snout; tip, spout, point. 2. Handle of scythe.

Neb(r). *abbrev.* Nebraska.

Nèbrăsk'a. West North Central State of U.S., admitted to the Union in 1867; capital, Lincoln.

Nĕbūchadnĕzz'ar (-kad-), **-drezzar, Nabūchodonŏs'or** (-z-). King of Babylon 605–562 B.C.; built the great walls of the city; after the rebellion of Jehoiakim of Judah he besieged and took Jerusalem 597; when ZEDEKIAH revolted, he took it again and destroyed it, 588.

nĕb'ūla *n.* (pl. -*ae*) 1. Clouded speck on cornea causing defective sight. 2. (astron.) Cloud of dust or gas within the galactic system illuminated by neighbouring stars. 3. (astron.) A luminous mass believed to consist of an enormous number of stars, usu. not separately discernible, situated outside the galactic system. **nĕb'ūlar** *adj.* Of nebula(e); ~ *hypothesis*, theory that solar and stellar systems developed from nebulae.

nèbūl'ium *n.* Element formerly assumed to exist in gaseous nebulae as cause of bright lines in green part of spectrum (the lines are now believed to be due to known terrestrial elements under conditions of exceptionally intense excitation).

nĕb'ūlous *adj.* 1. Of, like, nebula(e). 2. Cloud-like; hazy, vague, indistinct, formless; clouded, turbid. **nĕbūlŏs'ĭty** *n.*

nĕb'ūly, -lé *adj.* (her.) Wavy, serpentine (ill. HERALDRY).

NE. by E., NE by E, NE. by N., NE by N *abbrevs.* North-east by East, by North.

nĕcèssār'ĭan *n.* & *adj.* = NECESSITARIAN.

nĕ'cèssarĭly *adv.* As a necessary result, inevitably.

nĕ'cèssary *adj.* Indispensable, requisite; requiring to, that must, be done; determined by predestination or natural laws, not by free will; happening or existing by necessity; (of concept etc.) inevitably resulting from nature of things or the mind, inevitably produced by previous state of things; (of agent) having no independent volition. ~ *n.* Thing without which life cannot be maintained; (loosely) desirable thing not generally regarded as a luxury; *the* ~, (slang) money or action needed for a purpose.

nècĕssitār'ĭan *n.* & *adj.* (Person) denying free will and maintaining that all action is determined by antecedent causes. **nècĕssitār'ĭanism** *n.*

nècĕss'ĭtāte *v.t.* Force, compel, *to* do (now rare); render necessary; involve as condition, accompaniment, or result.

nècĕss'ĭtous *adj.* Poor, needy.

nècĕss'ĭty *n.* 1. Constraint or compulsion regarded as a law prevailing through the material universe and governing all human action; constraining power of circumstances, state of things compelling to certain course; *of* ~, unavoidably. 2. Imperative need (*for*); indispensability; indispensable thing, necessary. 3. Want, poverty, hardship, pressing need.

nĕck *n.* 1. Part of body that connects head with shoulders; flesh of animal's neck as food; part of garment covering or lying next to neck; *break one's* ~, dislocate cervical vertebrae, be killed so; *save one's* ~, escape hanging; ~ *and crop*, headlong, bodily; *get it in the* ~, (slang) suffer fatal or severe blow; ~ *or nothing*, desperate(ly), staking all on success; ~ *and* ~, running even in race. 2. Narrow part *of* vessel, esp. of bottle near mouth, or *of* passage, pass, or channel; pass, narrow channel, isthmus; narrow connecting part between two parts of thing; (archit.) lower part of capital. 3. (geol.) Conical hill consisting of igneous rock which has accumulated in throat of volcano and been exposed later when the mountain itself weathered away. 4. ~-*band*, part of garment round neck; *neck'cloth*, cravat; *neck'erchief* (-chĭf), kerchief worn round neck; *neck'lace*, ornament of precious stones, beads, etc., worn round neck; ~-*tie*, narrow band of woven or knitted material placed round neck and tied in front (a usu. part of modern men's costume); ~-*verse*, (hist.) Latin verse printed in black-letter (usu. beginning of 51st psalm) by reading which person claiming benefit of clergy might save his neck. ~ *v.i.* (slang, orig. U.S.) Hug, exchange amorous caresses.

Nĕck'ar. River of S. Germany, flowing into the Rhine from E.

Nĕcker' (-ār), Jacques (1732–1804). French financier and statesman; finance minister to Louis XVI.

nĕck'ing *n.* (archit.) Part of column between shaft and capital (ill. ORDER).

nĕck'lėt *n.* Ornament, small fur, etc., worn round neck.

nĕc'romăncy *n.* Act of predicting by means of communication with the dead; magic, enchantment. **nĕc'romăncer** *n.* **nĕcromăn'tic** *adj.*

nėcrŏph'agous *adj.* Feeding on carrion.

nėcrŏph'ily *n.* Morbid preoccupation with corpses, death, etc.

nėcrŏp'olis *n.* Cemetery.

nĕc'rŏpsy, nėcrŏs'copy *ns.* Post-mortem examination, autopsy.

nėcrō'sis *n.* (path.) Death of circumscribed piece of tissue, esp. mortification of bones. **nėcrŏt'ic** *adj.* **nĕc'rotize** *v.i.*

nĕc'tar *n.* 1. (Gk myth.) Drink of the gods; any delicious drink. 2. Sweet fluid or honey produced by plants. **nĕctār'ėan, nĕctār'ėous, nĕctarĭf'erous** *adjs.*

nĕc'tarine (*or* -ēn) *n.* Kind of peach with thin downless skin and firm flesh.

nĕc'tary *n.* (bot.) Glandular organ or tissue secreting nectar, occurring mainly in flowers, occasionally in leaves and stems (ill. FLOWER).

N.E.D. *abbrev.* New English Dictionary (= O.E.D.).

nĕdd'y *n.* Donkey. [dim. of *Edward*]

née (nā) *adj.* (Before married woman's maiden name) born, as *Mrs Smith, née Jones.*

need *n.* 1. Necessity arising from circumstances of case; imperative demand for presence or possession *of*; *have ~ of*, require, want. 2. Emergency, crisis, time of difficulty; destitution, lack of necessaries, poverty. 3. Thing wanted, respect in which want is felt, requirement. ~ *v.* Be necessary (archaic); stand in need of, require; be needy; be under necessity or obligation to or *to* do. **need'ful** *adj.* Requisite, necessary, indispensable; *the ~*, what is necessary, esp. (slang) the money required. **need'fulnėss** *n.*

nee'dle *n.* 1. Instrument used in sewing, usu. small slender piece of polished steel with fine point at one end and hole or eye for thread at other; knitting-pin; one of parallel wires forming part of stocking-frame or Jacquard loom. 2. Piece of magnetized steel used as indicator in compass or magnetic or electrical apparatus; strip of gold or silver of standard fineness used with touchstone in testing purity of these metals. 3. Pointed etching or engraving instrument; long slender pointed instrument used in surgery; pointed end of hypodermic or other syringe; steel pin exploding cartridge of breech-loader; (in gramophones etc.) small pointed piece of wood, steel, etc., transmitting vibrations from record to sound-box; stylus used in recording. 4. Obelisk; sharp rock, peak; beam of wood, esp. used as temporary support in under-pinning; sharp slender leaf of fir or pine; (chem. etc.) needle-shaped crystal. 5. (slang) *the ~*, fit of nervousness. 6. *~-bath*, shower-bath with fine strong spray; *~-fish*, various fishes, esp. garfish; *needleful*, length of thread etc. put into needle; *~ game, match*, one closely contested and arousing personal feeling or animosity; *~-gun*, (hist.) early type of breech-loader using percussion cap; *~-point*, fine sharp point; *needlepoint* (*lace*), lace made with needle (see LACE and ill.); *needlewoman*, woman who sews, seamstress; *needlework*, sewing, embroidery, etc. ~ *v.* Sew, pierce, operate on, with needle; probe, question (person) persistently (colloq.); thread (one's way) between or through things; underpin with needle beams; form needle-shaped crystals.

need'lėss *adj.* Unnecessary, uncalled for. **need'lėssly** *adv.* **need'lėssnėss** *n.*

needs *adv.* Of necessity (now only after or before *must*).

need'y *adj.* Poor, indigent, necessitous. **need'ily** *adv.* **need'inėss** *n.*

ne'er (nār) *adv.* (poet.) Never; *~-do-well, -weel*, good-for-nothing (person).

nėfār'ious *adj.* Wicked, iniquitous. **nėfār'iously** *adv.* **nėfār'iousnėss** *n.*

nėgāte' *v.t.* Nullify; deny existence of, imply or involve non-existence of; be the negation of.

nėgā'tion *n.* Denying; negative statement or doctrine; refusal, contradiction, denial *of*; (logic) affirmation of difference or exclusion; absence or opposite of something actual or positive; negative or unreal thing, nonentity. **nĕg'atory** *adj.*

nĕg'ative *adj.* 1. Expressing or implying denial, prohibition, or refusal; wanting, consisting in the want of, positive attributes; of opposite nature to thing regarded as possible. 2. (math., physics, etc.) Denoting quantities to be subtracted from others; less than zero; in the opposite direction from that which (arbitrarily or by convention) is regarded as positive; (elect.) having a negative charge; *~ charge*, one of the two kinds of electric charge, the charge of an electron (cf. POSITIVE, 6); *~ pole*, region of excess of electrons, cathode; also (magnetism) applied to the south-seeking pole of a magnet and the corresponding (north) pole of the earth. 3. (phot.) Applied to image in which lights appear dark and shadows light (see ~ *n.* 3 below). **nĕg'atively** (-vl) *adv.* **nĕg'ativenėss, nĕgativ'ity** *ns.* **nĕg'ative** *n.* 1. Negative statement, reply, or word; right of veto; *in the ~*, negative(ly), no. 2. Negative quality, want of something; (math.) negative or minus quantity. 3. (phot.) Print in which lights and shadows of nature are reversed, made by direct action of light on an emulsion deposited on glass or other transparent substance, and used for producing a positive print. ~ *v.t.* Veto, reject, refuse to accept or countenance; disprove (inference, hypothesis); contradict (statement); neutralize (effect).

nĕg'ativism *n.* Doctrine characterized by denial of accepted beliefs etc. **nĕg'ativist** *n.*

nėglĕct' *v.t.* Disregard, slight; leave uncared-for; omit *to* do. ~ *n.* Neglecting, being neglected; negligence. **nėglĕct'ful** *adj.* **nėglĕct'fully** *adv.* **nėglĕct'fulnėss** *n.*

négligé (nā'glēzhā) *n.* Free-and-easy or unceremonious attire, esp. woman's loose garment worn on informal occasions.

nĕg'ligence *n.* Want of proper care or attention, (piece of) carelessness; *contributory ~*, negligence on a person's part that has helped to bring about the injury that he has suffered. **nĕg'ligent** *adj.* **nĕg'ligently** *adv.*

nĕg'ligible *adj.* That need not be regarded, that may be neglected.

nėgō'tiāte (-shĭ-) *v.* 1. Confer (*with* another) with view to compromise or agreement; arrange (affair), bring about (desired object) by negotiating. 2. Transfer (bill) to another for a consideration; convert into cash or notes, get or give value for (bill, cheque) in money. 3. Clear, get over, dispose of (fence, obstacle, difficulty). **nėgō'tiable** *adj.* **nėgō'tiant, nėgōtiā'tion, nėgō'tiātor** *ns.*

Nĕg'rĕss *n.* Female Negro.

nėgrill'ō *n.* Small Negro; one of dwarf negro race of Central and S. Africa.

nėgrit'ō (-rē-) *r.* One of small negroid race in Malaya–Polynesian region.

Nēg'rō *n.* (pl. *-es*) Member, esp. male, of black-skinned woolly-haired flat-nosed thick-lipped African race; *negro-head*, strong black-plug tobacco. **nēg'rō** *adj.* Of this race, black-skinned; occupied by, connected with, Negroes; black or dark. **nēg'roid** *adj.* & *n.* (Member of a race) displaying negro characteristics.

nēg'us[1] *n.* Mixture of sweetened and flavoured wine (esp. port or sherry) and hot water. [Col. F. *Negus*, d. 1732, inventor]

Nēg'us[2]. Supreme ruler of Ethiopia.

Neh. *abbrev.* Nehemiah.

Nēhėmī'ah (4th c. B.C.). Jewish

governor of Judaea under Artaxerxes; rebuilder of walls of Jerusalem; *Book of* ~ (in Vulgate, 2 Esdras), book of Old Testament forming concluding part of the historical compilation Chronicles, Ezra, Nehemiah, and giving account of rebuilding of walls of Jerusalem and of various reforms.

Nehru (nā'rōō), Pandit Jawaharlal (1889–1964). Indian Congress leader; 1st prime minister of India 1947–64.

neigh (nā) *v.i.* & *n.* (Utter) cry (as) of horse.

neighbour (nāb'*er*) *n.* Dweller next door, near, in same street, village, or district, or in adjacent country, esp. regarded as one who should be friendly or as having claim on others' friendliness; person or thing next or near another; (*attrib.*) neighbouring. ~ *v.* Adjoin, border upon, border *upon*. **neigh'bourless** *adj.* **neigh'bourship** *n.*

neighbourhood (nāb'er-) *n.* Neighbourly feeling or conduct; nearness, vicinity *of*; neighbours, people of a district, district (in U.S., freq. *attrib.*, as in ~ *school* etc.); (town planning) part of large city planned as a unit with own shopping centre etc.

neighbourly (nāb'*er*-) *adj.* Like a good neighbour, friendly, helpful. **neigh'bourliness** *n.*

neith'er (nīdh-, nēdh-) *adv.* (Introducing mention of alternatives or different things, about each of which a negative statement is made) not either; nor, nor yet; (strengthening preceding negative) either. ~ *adj.* Not the one or the other; (loosely) not any one.

Nĕjd. Region of Arabia on Persian Gulf, forming with Hejaz and Asir the kingdom of Saudi Arabia.

nĕk *n.* (S. Afr.) = COL.

nĕll'y *n.* Large sea-bird (*Ossifraga gigantea*), the giant petrel. [prob. the feminine name]

nĕl'son[1] *n.* (wrestling) Class of holds (*double, full, half, quarter* ~) in which arm is passed under opponent's from behind and the hand applied to his neck.

Nĕl'son[2], Horatio, Viscount Nelson, Duke of Bronte (1758–1805). British admiral and naval hero, killed in the battle of TRAFALGAR.

nĕm'atocȳst *n.* Cell in jellyfish, sea-anemones, etc., containing coiled thread that can be projected as sting (ill. JELLY).

nĕm'atoid, nĕm'atōde *adjs.* & *ns.* (Worm) of slender unsegmented cylindrical shape; of the phylum *Nematoda.*

nem. con., nem. dis(s). *abbrevs. Nemine contradicente, dissentiente* (= with no dissentients).

nėmēs'ia (-zhĭ*a*) *n.* S. Afr. genus of flowering plants, many cultivated as hardy annuals, with variously coloured irregular, slightly spurred flowers. [Gk *nemesis* snapdragon]

Nĕm'ėsĭs. (Gk and L myth.) Daughter of Night and goddess of vengeance; regarded as personification of the gods' resentment at, and punishment of, insolence towards them. Hence, **nĕm'ėsis** *n.* Retributive justice.

nėmŏph'ĭla *n.* N. Amer. genus of ornamental herbaceous annuals, often cultivated.

Nĕnn'ĭus (active 796). Welsh historian; compiler or reviser of 'Historia Britonum', giving oldest legends of King ARTHUR.

nĕn'ūphar *n.* Water-lily, esp. the common yellow species.

nē'o- *prefix.* New; used as prefix to adjs. and ns. and adding the notions *new, modern, later, lately found* or *invented.*

nēodȳm'ium *n.* (chem.) Metallic element of rare-earth group; symbol Nd, at. no. 60, at. wt 144·24. [NEO- + DIDYMIUM]

Nē'ogēne *n.* (geol.) The upper part of the tertiary rocks including the miocene and pliocene series.

nēo-Hĕll'enism *n.* Revival of ancient Greek ideals in modern life or art.

nēolĭth'ic *adj.* Of the later stone age, characterized by the use of ground or polished stone implements (as dist. from the chipped implements of the palaeolithic age) and by great advances in food production and simple skills.

nēolō'gian *adj.* Of, inclined to, marked by, neologism in theology. ~ *n.* Neologist in theology.

nėŏl'ogism, nėŏl'ogy *ns.* Coining or using of new words, new-coined word; tendency to, adoption of, novel or rationalistic religious views. **nėŏl'ogist** *n.*

nē'ŏn *n.* 1. (chem.) Colourless, odourless, inert, gaseous element present in minute quantities in the atmosphere; symbol Ne, at. no. 10, at. wt 20·183; ~ *light*, bright orange-red light obtained by passing an electrical discharge through a tube or bulb containing neon at low pressure, extensively used for illuminated signs in advertising etc.; also light of blue, green, etc., obtained by mixing other inert gases with neon.

nē'ophrŏn *n.* The Egyptian vulture (*Neophron perchopterus*) of India and Africa; bird of same genus. [name of man turned into vulture in *Metamorphoses* of Antoninus Liberalis]

nē'ophȳte *n.* New convert, esp. among primitive Christians or Roman Catholics; newly ordained R.C. priest, novice of religious order; beginner, novice, tyro.

nē'oplăsm *n.* (path.) Autonomous new growth in some part of the body, tumour.

Nēoplăt'onism *n.* A philosophical and religious system, chiefly consisting of a mixture of Platonic ideas with Oriental mysticism, which originated at Alexandria in the 3rd c. and is represented in the works of Plotinus, Porphyry, and Proclus. **Nēoplatŏn'ic** *adj.* **Nēoplăt'onist** *n.*

Nėŏptŏl'ėmus. (Gk legend) Son of ACHILLES; in the Trojan War he killed PRIAM, and ANDROMACHE fell to his lot when the Trojan captives were distributed.

nēotĕ'ric *adj.* Recent, new-fangled, modern.

nēozō'ic *adj.* (geol.) Of the later period of geological history, after the palaeozoic.

NEP (ĕn-ē-pē, nĕp). Programme initiated in the Soviet Union 1921 for revival of the wage system and private ownership of industry. [*N*ew *E*conomic *P*olicy]

Nėpal' (-awl). Independent kingdom NE. of India, on frontier of Tibet; capital, Katmandu. **Nĕpalēse'** (-z) *adj.* & *n.*

nėpĕn'thė(s) *n.* 1. Egyptian drug mentioned in the 'Odyssey' as banishing grief; (poet.) any drug having this power. 2. (*Nepenthes*) genus of plants with pitcher-shaped leaves, pitcher-plant.

nĕph'ew (-vū, -fū) *n.* Brother's or sister's son.

nėphŏl'ogy *n.* Study of clouds.

nĕph'rīte *n.* = JADE, sense 1. [Gk *nephros* kidney, from its supposed value in kidney-disease]

nėphrĭt'ic *adj.* Of or in the kidneys, renal.

nėphrī'tis *n.* Inflammation of the kidneys.

nē plŭs ŭl'tra. Prohibition of further advance; impassable obstacle; farthest or highest point attained or attainable. [L, = 'not more beyond' (supposed inscription on Pillars of Hercules)]

Nēp'ŏs, Cornelius (*c* 100–*c* 25 B.C.). Roman historian, friend of Cicero, Atticus, and Catullus.

nĕp'otism *n.* Favouritism shown to relatives esp. in conferring offices; (hist.) practice on the part of some medieval and renaissance popes of showing special favour to their natural children, who were known euphemistically as their 'nephews'. **nĕp'otist** *n.*

Nĕp'tūne. 1. (Roman myth.) God of the sea, identified with the Greek POSEIDON. 2. (astron.) Third largest of the planets (ill. PLANET), with one known satellite; discovered 1846 as a result of mathematical computations of J. C. Adams in England and Leverrier in France; symbol ♆. **Nĕptūn'ian** *adj.* & *n.* 1. Of the planet Neptune. 2. (geol.) Formed by the agency of water.

Nĕp'tūnist *n.* (geol.) Adherent of the view that the action of water has played a principal part in the formation of rocks (opp. VULCANIST).

nĕptūn'ium *n.* A TRANSURANIC element, not found in nature, occurring as a temporary stage in the formation of plutonium from uranium 238; symbol Np, at. no. 93, principal isotope 237.

Nēr'ėid. 1. (Gk myth.) One of the sea-nymphs, daughters of

Nereus. 2. (zool.) Marine polychaete worm.

NEREID

Nēr'eus (-rūs). (Gk myth.) A sea-deity having the power, like Proteus, of assuming various forms.

Nēr'ĭ, Philip, St. (1515–95), Italian churchman; founder of the Congregation of the Oratory, an order of secular priests.

Nēr'ō. Nero Claudius Caesar Augustus Germanicus (A.D. 37–68), Roman emperor 54–68; proverbial for tyranny and brutality.

nēr'olĭ *n.* Essential oil from flowers of bitter orange, used in perfumery. [f. name of Italian princess supposed to have invented it]

Nēr'va, Marcus Cocceius (*c* A.D. 35–98). Roman emperor 96–98.

nērv'āte *adj.* (bot.) (Of leaves) having ribs. **nērvā'tion** *n.*

nērve *n.* 1. Sinew, tendon (now only poet. exc. in *strain every* ~, make all possible effort); vigour, energy, well-strung state. 2. (bot.) Rib, esp. mid-rib, of leaf. 3. (anat.) Fibre or bundle of fibres connecting and conveying impulses of

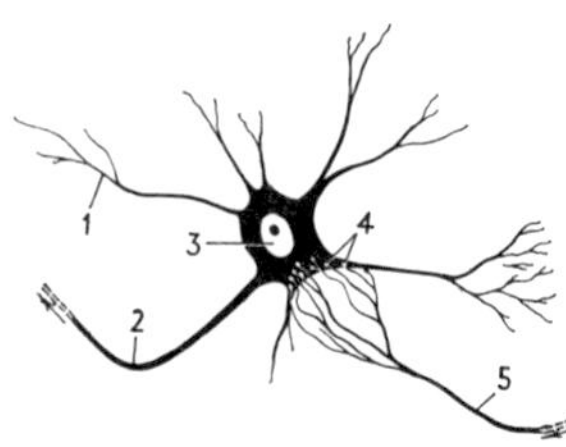

NERVE-CELL OR NEURON

1. Dendrite. 2. Beginning of axon. 3. Nucleus. 4. Synapse. 5. End of axon of another cell

sensation and motion between brain or spinal cord or ganglionic organ and some part of body; nervous fibre; (pl.) bodily state in regard to physical sensitiveness and interaction between brain and other parts, disordered state in these respects, exaggerated sensitiveness, nervousness; *get on one's* ~*s*, affect one with irritation, impatience, fear, etc.; *war of* ~*s*, campaign against an enemy consisting of intimidation, propaganda intended to undermine morale; ~*-centre*, ganglion, group of closely connected nerve-cells associated in performing some function. 4. Coolness in danger; boldness; assurance; *lose one's* ~, become timid or irresolute. ~ *v.t.* Give strength, vigour, or courage, to; collect *oneself* to face danger or suffering.

nērve'lėss (-vl-) *adj.* Inert, wanting in vigour or spirit, listless; (of style) flabby, diffuse; (bot., entom.) without nervures; (anat., zool.) without nerves. **nērve'lėssly** *adv.* **nērve'lėssnėss** *n.*

nērv'ous *adj.* 1. Of the nerves; ~ *system*, system of specialized conducting tissue which enables an organism to co-ordinate its activity in relation to its environment; in mammals highly complex and divided anatomically into the *central, peripheral,* and *autonomic* nervous systems. 2. Sinewy, muscular; (of style) vigorous, terse. 3. Having disordered or delicate nerves; excitable, highly strung, easily agitated, timid. **nērv'ously** *adj.* **nērv'ousnėss** *n.*

nērv'ure (-*yer*) *n.* 1. One of the tubes strengthening an insect's wing (ill. INSECT). 2. Principal vein of leaf (ill. LEAF).

nērv'y *adj.* Sinewy, strong (poet.); jerky, nervous; (slang) cool, confident, impudent; (slang) trying to the nerves.

nĕs'cience (-shĭ, -sĭ-) *n.* Not knowing, absence of knowledge *of*. **nĕs'cĭėnt** *adj.* & *n.* Ignorant (*of*); agnostic.

nĕss[1] *n.* Promontory, headland, cape.

Nĕss[2], Loch. Lake in Inverness-shire, Scotland, forming part of Caledonian Canal.

Nĕss'us. (Gk myth.) Centaur shot by Heracles (Hercules) for trying to carry off his wife Deianira; Nessus's blood-stained tunic, given to Deianira as a charm to reclaim an unfaithful husband, eventually caused Heracles' death.

nĕst *n.* Structure or place made or chosen by bird for laying eggs and sheltering young; animal's or insect's abode or spawning or breeding place; snug or secluded retreat, lodging, shelter, bed, receptacle; haunt *of* robbers etc.; fostering-place *of* vice etc.; brood, swarm; collection, series of similar objects; small chest *of drawers*, set *of* (small) *tables* fitting together; ~*-egg*, real or imitation egg left in nest to induce hen to go on laying there; sum of money kept as reserve or nucleus. ~ *v.* Make or have nest in specified place; take to nest-building; take birds' nests. **nĕs'ter** *n.* (esp. U.S.) Squatter on cattle-range.

nĕ'stle (-sl) *v.* Make nest (now rare); settle oneself, be settled, comfortably *down, in, among,* etc., leaves, wraps, chair, etc.; press oneself affectionately (*close*) *to* person; lie half-hidden or embedded; push (head, shoulder, etc.) affectionately or snugly *in*; hold embraced (usu. in past part.).

nĕs'tlĭng (-sl-) *n.* Bird too young to leave nest.

Nĕs'tōr[1]. (Gk legend) King of Pylos; in old age led his subjects to the Trojan War, where his wisdom, justice, and eloquence were proverbial; hence, a wise old man.

Nĕs'tōr[2] (*c* 1056–*c* 1114). Russian monk; reputed author of earliest Russian chronicle.

Nĕstōr'ius (d. *c* 451). Syrian ecclesiastic; disciple of St. Chrysostom and patriarch of Constantinople (428–31); held that Christ had distinct human and divine persons and hence that the Virgin Mary should not be called 'Mother of God'; was condemned by the Councils of Ephesus (431) and Chalcedon (451). **Nĕstōr'ian** *adj.* & *n.* ~ *Church*, Ancient Persian Christian community (now with few adherents, in Persia, Kurdistan, and Malabar) having liturgy in Syriac and customs resembling those of Greek Church.

nĕt[1] *n.* Meshed fabric of twine, cord, hair, etc.; piece of this used for catching fish etc. or for covering, confining, protecting, carrying, etc.; moral or mental snare; reticulation, network; *netball*, game between teams of seven players, the object being to throw a large ball

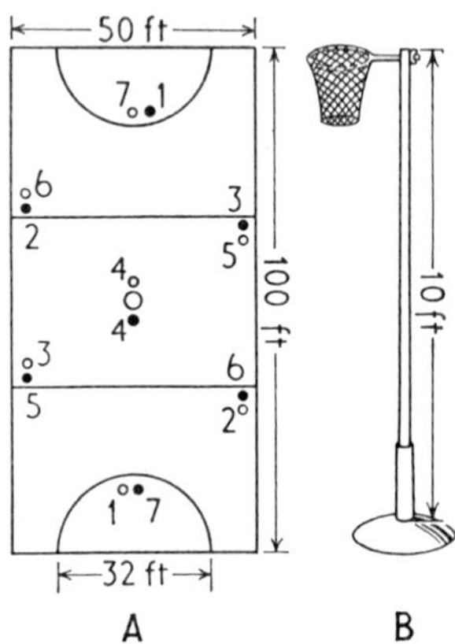

A. NETBALL PITCH WITH POSITIONS OF PLAYERS. B. NET

1. Goal shooter. 2. Goal attack. 3. Wing attack. 4. Centre. 5. Wing defence. 6. Goal defence. 7. Goalkeeper

like a football so that it falls through a net suspended from a ring on the top of a post; ~*-cord*, cord supporting top of a tennis net; ~ (*stroke*), stroke in which ball hits this; *net'work*, arrangement with intersecting lines and interstices resembling those of net; complex system *of* railways, rivers, canals, etc., ramification; broadcasting system of several stations linked together. ~ *v.* Cover, confine, catch, with net(s); fish (river etc.) with nets, set nets in (river); make netting; make (purse, hammock, etc.) by netting.

nĕt[2] (also **nett**) *adj.* Free from deduction, remaining after necessary deductions; ~ *price*, real price off which discount is not allowed; ~ *profit*, true profit, actual gain after working expenses have been paid. ~ *v.t.* Gain or yield (sum) as net profit.

nĕth'er (-dh-) *adj.* (archaic or joc.) Lower. **nĕth'ermōst** *adj.*

Nĕth'erlands (-dh-)(Du. *Nederland*). 1. Small kingdom in N. Europe, in English freq. called Holland; capital, Amsterdam, seat of govt., The Hague; principal language, Dutch. 2. (hist.) The 'Low Countries', the whole area of the Rhine, Meuse, and Scheldt deltas, that now occupied by Holland, Belgium, Luxembourg, and small parts of France and Germany. During the Middle Ages it was divided between numerous countships and dukedoms; by the mid-16th c. these were united under the Habsburg emperor Charles V, but in the wars of religion the N. (Dutch) part revolted (1555–88) and became an independent Protestant Republic (*United Provinces of the* ~, or States General); meanwhile the S. part passed to the Spanish Habsburgs (*Spanish* ~) and later, in 1713, to the Austrian Habsburgs (*Austrian* ~). In 1815 both N. and S. were united under a monarchy (*Kingdom of the* ~), but the S. revolted in 1830 and became an independent kingdom, BELGIUM. **Nĕth'erlander** *n.* **Nĕth'erlandish** *adj.*

nĕt'suke (-sōōkā) *n.* Carved or otherwise ornamented piece of ivory etc. worn by Japanese as bob or button on cord by which articles are suspended from girdle.

nĕtt'ing *n.* (esp.) Netted string, wire, or thread; piece of this.

nĕt'tle *n.* Plant of genus *Urtica*, with two common species (*U. dioica* and *U. urens*) growing profusely on waste land and noted for stinging properties of leaf-hairs; other plants resembling these, esp. *dead-nettle*; *~-rash*, skin eruption in patches like those produced by nettle-stings, urticaria. ~ *v.t.* 1. Beat or sting with nettles; get one*self* stung with nettles. 2. Irritate, provoke, annoy.

neum'a, neum(e) (nū-) *n.* (mus.) Sign in plainsong indicating

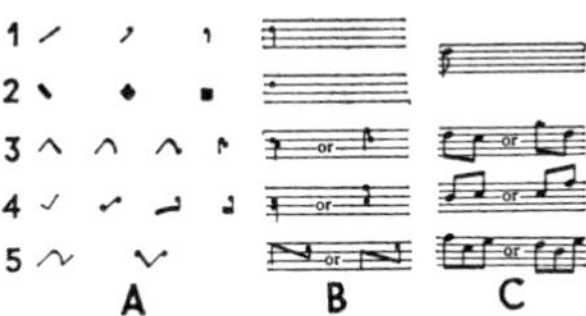

NEUMS: A. EARLY NEUMS. B. NEUMS USED NOW. C. MODERN EQUIVALENT

Accents: 1. Acute 2. Grave. 3. Circumflex. 4. Grave+acute. 5. Acute+grave+acute

note or group of notes to be sung to a single syllable.

neur'al (nūr-) *adj.* Of the nerves; of the nervous system.

neurăl'gia (nūr-) *n.* Affection of nerves (usu. of head or face) causing intense intermittent pain. **neurăl'gic** *adj.*

neurăsthēn'ia (nūr-) *n.* Functional nervous weakness, nervous debility. **neurăsthĕn'ic** *adj.*

neurā'tion (nūr-) *n.* Distribution of nervures.

neurīt'is (nūr-) *n.* Inflammation of nerve(s). **neurĭt'ic** *adj.*

neuroglī'a (nūr-) *n.* Non-nervous tissue present in nervous system.

neurŏl'ogy (nūr-) *n.* Scientific study of the anatomy, functions, and diseases of the nervous system. **neurolŏ'gical** *adj.* **neurŏl'ogist** *n.*

neurōm'a (nūr-) *n.* Tumour on a nerve or in nerve-tissue.

neur'ŏn, -ōne (nūr-) *n.* Nerve-cell with its appendages, the basic structural unit of the nervous system (ill. NERVE).

neur'opăth (nūr-) *n.* Person of abnormal nervous sensibility; person affected by nervous disease. **neuropăth'ic** *adj.* **neurŏp'athy** *n.*

neurŏp'terous (nūr-) *adj.* Of the *Neuroptera*, order of insects having 4 naked membranous transparent wings with reticulate neuration.

neurōs'is (nūr-) *n.* (pl. *-ōsēs*). (path., psychol.) Derangement of normal function due to disorders of nervous system, esp. such as are unaccompanied by demonstrable organic change. **neurŏt'ic** *adj.* & *n.* (Person) affected with neurosis. **neurŏt'icism** *n.*

neut'er *adj.* 1. (gram.) Neither masculine nor feminine; (of verb) intransitive. 2. Neutral (now rare). 3. Neither male nor female, epicene; (bot.) having neither pistils nor stamens; (entom.) sexually undeveloped, sterile. ~ *n.* 1. Neuter noun, adjective, verb, or gender. 2. Neutral (rare). 3. Sexually undeveloped female insect, esp. bee or ant; castrated animal; epicene person.

neut'ral *adj.* 1. Not assisting either of two belligerent States, belonging to a State remaining inactive during hostilities, exempted or excluded from warlike operations; taking neither side in dispute or difference of opinion, indifferent, impartial. 2. Not distinctly marked or coloured, indefinite, vague, indeterminate; (of colour) greyish or brownish; (of sound) indistinct, obscure. 3. (chem.) Neither acid nor alkaline; (elect.) neither positive nor negative. 4. Neuter, asexual. **neut'rally** *adv.* **neutrăl'ity** *n.* **neut'ral** *n.* 1. Neutral State or person; subject of neutral State. 2. (mech.) Position of gear mechanism in which the propelling mechanism may revolve freely without transmitting power to the parts to be driven.

neut'ralīze *v.t.* Counterbalance, render ineffective by opposite force or effect; exempt or exclude (place) from sphere of hostilities. **neutralizā'tion** *n.*

neut'ron *n.* Electrically neutral particle consisting of electron and proton in close association.

Neuve Chăpĕlle' (nērv sh-). Village W. of Lille, France, scene of an attack (1915) by British on German positions, in which artillery barrage was used for first time.

Nev. *abbrev.* Nevada.

Nēv'a. River of N. Russia, draining Lakes Ladoga, Onega, and Ilmen into Gulf of Finland, and running through Leningrad.

Nėvad'a (-vah-). Mountain State of western U.S., admitted to the Union in 1864; capital, Carson City.

névé (nĕv'ā) *n.* Expanse of granular snow not yet compressed into ice at head of glacier (ill. MOUNTAIN).

nĕv'er *adv.* At no time, on no occasion, not ever; not at all; (colloq., expressing surprise or incredulity) surely not; ~ *mind*, do not be troubled; ~ *a*, not a, no — at all; ~ *a one*, none; ~ *so*, (in conditional clauses) to unlimited extent, ever so; ~ *the*, (with comparative) none the; *nevermore'*, at no future time; *N~-Never* (*Land*), North Queensland; *the ~-never*, (colloq.) hire-purchase; *nevertheless*, notwithstanding, but for all that.

Nĕv'is. Island of Leeward Islands, British West Indies.

new *adj.* Not existing before, now first made, brought into existence, invested, introduced, known or heard of, experienced, or discovered; unfamiliar *to*; renewed, fresh, further, additional; later, modern, new-fangled; of recent growth, origin, arrival, or manufacture, now first used, not worn or exhausted; not yet accustomed *to*, fresh *from*; (of family or person) lately risen in position; *~-comer*, person lately arrived; *N~ Deal*: see DEAL[3]; *~-fangled*, different from the good old fashion, having no merit but novelty; *~-laid*, (of eggs) recently laid; ~ *learning*, study of the Bible and the Greek classics in their original language at the time of the Reformation and Renaissance in England; ~ *moon*, moon when first visible as a crescent after conjunction with sun, time of such appearance; *N~ Model Army*, army organized by English Parliament, 1645, with Sir Thomas Fairfax as general; *N~ Order*, (f. Ger. *die neue Ordnung*) (esp.) Hitler's plan for the reconstitution of the States of Europe on the basis of a National-Socialist régime; ~ *poor*, *rich*, classes recently impoverished, enriched; *new'speak*, (joc. in derogatory sense) reformed version of a language; *N~ Style*, (abbrev. N.S.) the rearrangement of the calendar introduced by Pope Gregory XIII in 1582 and adopted in England in

1752 (see GREGORIAN); *N~ Testament*, 2nd part of Bible, dealing with life and teaching of Christ and with his followers and the early Christian Church; ~ *woman* (at end of 19th and beginning of 20th c.) woman aspiring to freedom and independence and rejecting convention; *N~ World*, the Americas; *N~ Year*, coming or lately begun year, first few days of year; *N~ Year's Day*, (U.S. freq. *N~ Year's*), 1st Jan. *N~ Year honours*, titles of honour conferred annually by the English Sovereign and announced on New Year's Day. **new'ish** *adv.* **new'ness** *n.* **new** *adv.* Newly, recently, just; anew.

New Brit'ain. Island of Bismarck Archipelago; formerly part of German New Guinea, now under trusteeship to Commonwealth of Australia.

New Bruns'wick (-z-). SE. maritime province of Canada; capital, Fredericton.

New'castle (upon Tyne) (-kahsl, -kăsl). City and port of Northumberland, England, with important coal-shipping and ship-building industries; *carry coals to* ~, perform superfluous action.

New Coll'ege. College of University of Oxford; founded 1379 by William of Wykeham.

New'digate. *The* ~, annual prize for English verse open to undergraduates of University of Oxford, founded by Sir Roger *Newdigate* (1719–1806), English antiquary.

new'el *n.* (archit.) Centre pillar or (*open* or *hollow* ~) well of winding stair; post supporting stair-handrail at top or bottom (ill. STAIR).

New Eng'land (ingg-). Part of U.S. comprising NE. States of Maine, New Hampshire, Vermont, Massachusetts, Rhode Island, and Connecticut. **New Eng'lander** *n.* Native, inhabitant, of New England.

New Fŏ'rest. Ancient royal hunting-ground in Hampshire, England.

New'foundland (-fund-; *or* nūfown'd-). Large island, with famous fisheries, at mouth of St. Lawrence River; discovered and claimed for England 1497 by John Cabot; formerly a Dominion of the British Empire; united with Canada as one of its provinces, 1949; capital, St. John's. ~ *dog*, large dog of a breed native to N. America, with thick coarse coat, noted for sagacity, good temper, strength, and swimming powers (ill. DOG). **New'foundlănder** *n.*

New'gate. Prison, orig. the W. gatehouse of City of London, used for this purpose from 12th c.; burnt down 1780 by Gordon rioters and rebuilt; demolished 1902 and replaced by present Central Criminal Court; ~ *Calendar*, (hist.) publication, first issued 1773, giving accounts of the prisoners and their crimes; ~ *fringe*, fringe of hair worn under chin.

New Guinea (gĭn'ĭ). Large island and numerous small ones in N. Pacific, inhabited by Papuans, Malays, and Polynesians; divided into (1) *Netherlands* ~, (2) *Papua*, formerly British New Guinea, a territory of Australia, (3) *Territory of* ~, formerly German New Guinea, now under Australian trusteeship.

New Hămp'shire. A NE. State of U.S., one of the New England States; capital, Concord.

New Hĕb'rĭdēs (-z). Group of islands in W. Pacific, under joint French and British administration.

New Hŏll'and. Former name of Australia.

New Ire'land (īrl-). Island of Bismarck archipelago, in W. Pacific, E. of New Guinea.

New Jer's'ey (-zĭ). Middle Atlantic State of U.S.; capital, Trenton.

new'ly *adv.* Recently, just; in new manner; *newlywed(s)* (*adj.* & *n.pl.*) recently married (couple).

New'man, John Henry (1801–90). English theologian and author; as an Anglican clergyman, was one of the founders of the Oxford or TRACTARIAN movement; was received into R.C. Church 1845; published his 'Apologia pro Vita sua' 1864; was created cardinal 1879.

New'markĕt. 1. Market-town in Cambridgeshire, England, near which is a heath used for horse-racing since early 17th c. 2. Close-fitting coat (~ *coat*) for men or women, orig. worn for riding. 3. Card-game, in which the object is to play the same cards as certain duplicates which are exhibited and on which stakes are laid.

New Mĕx'ĭcō. Mountain State of south-west U.S.; admitted to Union 1912; capital, Santa Fé.

Newn'ham Cŏll'ege (-nam). College for women at Cambridge, England, opened 1876.

New Prŏv'ĭdence. Island of BAHAMAS.

news (-z) *n.pl.* (usu. with sing. v.) Tidings, new information, fresh event reported; wireless or television report of this; ~-*agent*, dealer in newspapers etc.; ~-*boy*, -*man*, one selling newspapers in streets; *news'cast*, wireless broadcast of news; ~-*letter*, (orig.) letter sent out periodically with the news to country towns etc.; now, periodical sent by post to subscribers; *news'monger*, gossip; *news'paper*, printed, now usu. daily or weekly, publication containing news, advertisements, and literary matter; *news'print*, paper for printing newspapers on; ~-*reel*, talking-film giving items of recent news; ~-*stand*, stall for sale of newspapers; *news'vendor*, newspaper-seller.

New South Wāles (-lz). SE. State of Commonwealth of Australia; capital, Sydney.

news'y (-zĭ) *adj.* (colloq.) Full of (sensational) news.

newt *n.* Small tailed amphibian (*Triturus*) allied to salamander.

New'ton, Sir Isaac (1642–1727). English natural philosopher; formulator of laws of motion and law of gravitation. **Newtōn'ian** *adj.* Of Newton or his theory of the universe; devised etc. by Newton. ~ *n.* Follower of Newton.

New York. 1. Middle Atlantic State of U.S.; capital, Albany. 2. Largest city of U.S., in New York State at mouth of Hudson River. **New York'er** *n.* Native, inhabitant, of New York City.

New Zeal'and (abbrev. N.Z.). State, a member of the British Commonwealth of Nations, occupying two large and many smaller islands in S. Pacific *c* 1,000 miles SE. of Australia; capital, Wellington; the islands were discovered by Tasman 1642 and visited by Cook 1769; became an English colony; acquired self-government 1852 and dominion status 1907. **New Zeal'ander** *n.* Native, inhabitant, of New Zealand. [f. ZEELAND]

nĕxt *adj.* Lying, living, being, nearest, nearest *to*, or nearest to; nearest in relationship or kinship; soonest come to, first ensuing, immediately following, coming nearest in order etc., *to*, immediately *before*; ~ *door*, (door of the) nearest or adjoining house; (also freq. fig.); ~-*door to*, almost. ~ *prep.* In or into the next place, on the next occasion, in the next degree, to. ~ *n.* (or ellipt. use of adj.) Next person or thing; ~ *of kin*, person nearest of kin (*to*).

nĕx'us *n.* Bond, link, connexion.

Ney (nā), Michel (1769–1815). French soldier, marshal of France; one of Napoleon's marshals; supported the Bourbons when Napoleon abdicated, but joined forces with him when he returned from Elba; commanded the Old Guard at Waterloo; was shot for treason.

N.F. *abbrev.* Newfoundland; Norman French.

N.F.S. *abbrev.* National Fire Service.

N.F.U. *abbrev.* National Farmers' Union.

N.H. *abbrev.* New Hampshire.

N.H.I. *abbrev.* National Health Insurance.

n.h.p. *abbrev.* Nominal horse-power.

N.H.S. *abbrev.* National Health Service.

Niăg'ara. N. Amer. river flowing from Lake Erie into Lake Ontario and forming part of boundary between Canada and U.S.A.; famous for its waterfalls over 150 ft high.

nĭb *n.* Point of quill pen; metal or quill pen-point for insertion in penholder; point of tool etc.; (pl.) fragments of crushed cocoa-beans. ~ *v.t.* Make, mend, insert nib of (pen).

nĭb'ble *v.* Take small bites at; bite gently or cautiously or playfully. ~ *n.* Act of nibbling, esp. of fish at bait.

Nib'ėlung (nē-, -o͝ong). (Germanic legend) king of a race of dwarfs in Norway; (pl. *-s, -en*) these dwarfs. **Nib'ėlungenlied** (-lēd). 13th-c. German poem (embodying a story found in the EDDA) which tells how SIEGFRIED, having obtained the hoarded gold of the Nibelungs, woos Kriemhild, a Burgundian princess, and by a trick obtains for her brother Gunther the hand of Brunhild, queen of Issland. Brunhild, learning of the trick, contrives Siegfried's death with the help of Hagen, the retainer of Kriemhild's brothers, who then sink the treasure in the Rhine. The rest of the poem deals with Kriemhild's revenge on her brothers and Hagen, who never reveal where the treasure lies.

nĭb'lĭck *n.* Golf-club with round heavy iron head, considerably lofted, used esp. for playing out of bunkers (ill. GOLF).

nibs *n.* (slang) *His* ~, burlesque title (after *his Grace* etc.).

Nīcae'a. Ancient city of Bithynia, Asia Minor, scene of first oecumenical council (see NICENE).

Nĭcarăg'ūa. Central American republic, between Honduras and Costa Rica; an independent republic since 1821; capital, Managna.

nīce *adj.* 1. Fastidious; punctilious; requiring precision or discrimination; minute, subtle. 2. (colloq.) Agreeable, delightful; satisfactory; kind, friendly, considerate; generally commendable. **nīce'ly** *adv.* **nīce'nėss** *n.*

Nīcēne' (*or* nī'-) *adj.* Of NICAEA; ~ *Council*, either of two ecclesiastical councils held there: one, in 325, convened by CONSTANTINE, to deal with the ARIAN controversy, the other, in 787, to consider the question of images; ~ *Creed*, formal statement of Christian belief based on decisions of first Council of Nicaea; official creed of Orthodox, Roman Catholic, and some Protestant Churches.

nī'cėty *n.* Punctiliousness; precision, accuracy; minute distinction, subtle or unimportant detail, (pl.) minutiae; *to a* ~, as closely or precisely as possible.

nĭche (-ch) *n.* Shallow recess in wall to contain statue, vase, etc.; (fig.) place or position adapted to the character, or suited to the merits, of a person or thing. ~ *v.t.* Place in niche; ensconce, settle, in some hollow or corner.

Nĭch'olas[1] (-k-). (Russ. *Nikolai*) Name of two emperors of Russia: *Nicholas I* (1796–1855), emperor 1825–55; his accession, after the death of his brother Alexander I and the abdication of his brother Constantine, was marked by the DECEMBRIST revolution, which he subdued and punished mercilessly; *Nicholas II* (1868–1918), emperor of Russia 1894–1917; forced to abdicate, March 1917; killed with his family, 1918.

Nĭch'olas[2] (-k-), St. (d. 326). Bishop of Myra in Asia Minor; patron of scholars, esp. schoolboys, and patron saint of Russia; festival, 6th Dec.

Nī'ciăs (d. 413 B.C.). Athenian statesman and general in Peloponnesian War; negotiated a peace (421 B.C.) which was only temporary.

nĭck[1] *n.* Notch, groove, serving as catch, guide, mark, etc.; *in the* ~ (*of time*), just at the right moment, only just in time. ~ *v.* Make nick(s) in, indent; make incision at root of (horse's tail) to make him carry it higher; (slang) catch, nab; (in hunting, racing, etc.) cut *in*.

Nĭck[2]. *Old* ~, the Devil.

nĭck'el *n.* 1. Hard silvery-white lustrous malleable ductile metallic element much used esp. in alloys; symbol Ni, at. no. 28, at. wt 58·71. 2. (U.S.) Five-cent piece (of copper and nickel alloy). 3. ~ *brass*, alloy of 79% copper, 1% nickel, and 20% zinc, used for British three-penny piece; ~ *silver*, alloy of nickel, zinc, and copper, formerly used for cutlery and now for taps, ornamental castings, etc.; ~ *steel*, alloy of iron with nickel. ~ *v.t.* Coat with nickel. [abbrev. of Ger. *kupfernickel* copper-coloured ore from which nickel was first got (*kupfer* copper, *nickel* demon, w. ref. to disappointing nature of ore, which yielded no copper); cf. COBALT]

nĭck'-năck *n.* = KNICK-KNACK.

nĭck'nāme *n.* Name added to or substituted for proper name of person, place, or thing. ~ *v.t.* Call (person etc. by a nickname), give nickname to.

Nĭcobar' Islands. Group of islands in Bay of Bengal, with inhabitants of mixed Malay and Indonesian origin; administered by Republic of India.

Nĭcodē'mus. (N.T.) A member of the Sanhedrin who helped Joseph of Arimathea to bury Jesus (John iii, vii, xix).

NICHE OR TABERNACLE

nĭcō'tian (-shĭ-) *adj.* Of tobacco. ~ *n.* Smoker. **nĭcōtiā'na** (-shĭ-) *n.* (bot.) Tobacco-plant. [Jacques *Nicot*, who introduced tobacco into France in 1560]

nĭc'otine (-ēn) *n.* Poisonous alkaloid contained in tobacco, from which it is obtained as a pungent oily liquid soluble in water.

nĭcotĭn'ĭc *adj.* ~ *acid, pyridine carboxylic acid*, a member of the vitamin B group.

nĭc'otinĭsm (-ēn-) *n.* Morbid state produced by excessive use of tobacco.

nĭc'tāte, nĭc'tĭtāte *vbs.i.* Close and open the eyes, wink; chiefly in *nict(it)ating membrane*, third or inner eyelid of many animals vestigial in man (ill. EYE). **nĭctā'tion, nĭctĭtā'tion** *ns.*

nīdamĕn'tal *adj.* (zool.) Secreting shell-covering material.

nīde *n.* Brood of pheasants.

nĭd'ĭfĭcāte, nĭd'ĭfȳ *vbs.i.* Build nest(s). **nĭdĭfĭcā'tion** *n.*

nīd'us *n.* Place in which insects etc. deposit eggs; place in which spores or seeds develop; place of origin or development of disease etc.; place in which something is deposited or lodged.

Niebuhr (nē'boor), Barthold Georg (1776–1831). German historian of ancient Rome.

niece (nēs) *n.* Brother's or sister's daughter.

nĭĕll'ō *n.* Black metallic amalgam of sulphur added to copper, silver, lead, etc., for filling engraved lines in silver or other metal, as decoration; (specimen of) such ornamental work; ~ *print*, print taken from engraved plate which is to be filled with niello.

Nier'steiner (nērstī-). A white Rhine wine. [*Nierstein*, German village in Hesse, on left bank of Rhine]

Nietzsche (nēch'*e*), Friedrich Wilhelm (1844–1900). German philosopher; originator of idea of 'superman' and of doctrine of perfectibility of man through forcible self-assertion and superiority to ordinary morality. **Nie'tzschėan** *adj.*

nĭf'ty *adj.* (U.S. slang) Attractively smart or spruce.

Nīg'er (-g-). River of W. Africa, flowing in a curve from NE. frontier of Sierra Leone to Gulf of Guinea; *Republic of* ~, W. central African State within the French Community. [L, = 'black']

Nīgēr'ĭa (-j-). *The Federation of* ~, republic of W. Africa, occupying basin of lower Niger, with coastline on Gulf of Guinea; capital, Lagos. Former British Protectorate, in 1960 it became an independent sovereign State within the British Commonwealth and republic in 1963.

nĭgg'ard *n.* Stingy person, grudging giver *of*. ~ *adj.* Niggardly (rhet. and poet.).

nĭgg'ardly *adj.* Parsimonious, stingy, sparing, scanty; giving or given grudgingly or in small amounts. **nigg'ardliness** *n.*

nigg'er *n.* Negro (usu. contempt.); (loosely) member of any dark-skinned race; dark shade of brown; *work like a ~*, work very hard; *~ minstrels*: see MINSTREL.

nigg'le *v.i.* Spend time, be over-elaborate, on petty details. **nigg'-ling** *adj.* Trifling, petty; lacking in breadth, largeness, or boldness of effect; (of handwriting) cramped.

nigh (nī) *adv., prep.,* & *adj.* Near (archaic, poet., or dial.).

night (nīt) *n.* Dark period after twilight and before dawn, time from sunset to sunrise, darkness then prevailing, the dark; end of daylight; (law, in distinguishing burglary from housebreaking) period from one hour after sunset until an hour before sunrise; weather, experiences, or occupation of a night; *make a ~ of it*, spend night in festivity; *~ out*, festive evening; evening on which servant is allowed out; *night-*, (attrib.) by, like, during, appropriate to, employed for, active in, the night; *~-bird*, esp. owl or nightingale; person esp. of disreputable character who goes about by night; *~-blindness*: see NYCTALOPIA; *~-cap*, covering for the head, worn in bed; drink, usu. alcoholic, taken before going to bed; *~-clothes*, clothes worn in bed; *~-club*, club open at night for dancing, supper, etc.; *~-dress*, *-gown*, long loose robe worn by women or children in bed; *~-glass*, short refracting telescope for use at night; *night'jar*: see GOATSUCKER; *~-light*, short thick candle or other dimly burning light for use at night, esp. in sick-rooms; *~-line*, line left with baited hooks to catch fish by night; *night'mare*, female monster sitting upon and seeming to suffocate sleeper, incubus; oppressive, terrifying, or fantastically horrible dream; haunting fear, thing vaguely dreaded; *~ office*, (liturgy) matins and lauds; *~-piece*, (painting of) night scene or landscape; *~-school*, school, class, held in evening for those at work during day; *~-soil*, contents of cesspools etc., removed at night; *~-stick*, (U.S.) stick carried by policemen at night; *~-watch*, (person or party keeping) watch by night; Hebrew or Roman division (one of 3 or 4) of the night.

night'ingāle[1] (nītingg-) *n.* Small reddish-brown migratory bird (*Daulias luscinia*) of Europe, Asia, and N. Africa, celebrated for the melodious song of the male, often heard at night during the breeding season.

Night'ingāle[2] (nītingg-), Florence (1820–1910). English reformer; founder of modern nursing profession; organized hospital unit for Crimean War and established new type of war hospital in Crimea.

night'ly (nīt-) *adj.* Happening, done, existing, etc., in the night; happening every night. *~ adv.* Every night.

night'shāde (nīt-) *n.* Various poisonous plants, esp. *Solanum nigrum* (*black ~*), herbaceous plant with ovate bluntly-toothed leaves, white flowers, and black poisonous berries, or *S. dulcamara* (*woody ~*), a climber with purple flowers and clusters of bright-red berries; *deadly ~*, *Atropa belladonna*, with solitary wine-coloured flowers and large shiny black berries; *enchanter's ~*, *Circaea lutetiana*.

night'y (nīti) *n.* (colloq.). Night-dress.

nigrĕs'cent *adj.* Blackish. **nigrĕs'cence** *n.* Becoming black; blackness.

nig'ritūde *n.* Blackness.

nihilism (nī'il-, nī'hil-) *n.* 1. Negative doctrines, total rejection of current beliefs, in religion or morals; (philos.) scepticism that denies all existence. 2. Doctrines of extreme revolutionary party in 19th- and 20th-c. Russia (orig. used of a small group in the 1860's who repudiated the established order and its standards). **nī'hilist** *n.* **nīhilis'tic** *adj.* [L *nihil* nothing]

Nik'on (nē-). Nikita Minin (1605–81), Russian churchman; patriarch of Moscow 1652–66; reformed Church discipline and ritual.

nil *n.* Nothing (esp. in scoring at games etc.); *~ admirari*, nonchalance, attitude of being surprised at, or admiring, nothing.

Nile. Longest river of Africa, flowing from E. Central Africa 4,000 miles northwards to Mediterranean; *Battle of the ~*, naval battle fought in Aboukir Bay, near Alexandria, 1798, between English fleet under Nelson and French fleet which had carried Napoleon to Egypt; Nelson's overwhelming victory restored British prestige in the Mediterranean and enabled England to recapture Malta and Minorca. *~ green* = EAU de Nil.

nil'gai (-gī) *n.* Large short-horned Indian antelope (*Boselaphus tragocamelus*), male of which is bluish or iron-grey; Indian Blue Bull. [Pers. *nīl* blue, *gāw* ox]

Nilŏt'ic *adj.* Of the river Nile, the Nile region, or its inhabitants.

nim'ble *adj.* Quick in movement, agile, swift; (of mind etc.) versatile, clever, quick to apprehend. **nim'bleness** (-ln-) *n.* **nim'bly** *adv.*

nimbostrāt'us *n.* (meteor.) Type of low cloud, dark grey and sometimes trailing (ill. CLOUD).

nim'bus *n.* 1. Bright cloud or halo investing deity, person, or thing; bright disc, aureole, round or over head of saint etc. in picture. 2. (meteor.) Rain-cloud.

nim'iny-pim'iny *adj.* Mincing, prim.

Nim'rŏd *n.* Great hunter or sportsman (f. the ruler mentioned in Gen. x. 8–9 as 'a mighty one in the earth' and 'the mighty hunter before the Lord').

ninc'ompoop *n.* Simpleton, ninny.

nine *adj.* One more than eight (9, ix, or IX); *the N~*, the Muses; *~ days' wonder*, novelty that attracts much attention but is soon forgotten; *nine'pins*, game of knocking down nine wooden 'pins' by throwing a ball or bowl at them. *~ n.* The number nine; card of nine pips; (U.S.) baseball team; *to the ~s*, to perfection (esp. in *dressed up to the ~s*). **nine'fōld** *adj.* & *adv.*

nīne'teen' (-nt-) *adj.* & *n.* One more than eighteen (19, xix, or XIX). **nīneteenth'** *adj.* *The ~ hole*, bar-room in golf club-house.

nīne'ty (-ntĭ) *adj.* & *n.* Nine times ten (90, xc, or XC); the number ninety.

Nin'ėveh (-vĭ). Ancient capital of Assyrian Empire, on right bank of Tigris.

Nin'ian, St. (d. *c* 432). Briton trained in Rome and sent to convert pagans in N. Britain; he was consecrated bishop and his see was established in Galloway.

ninn'y *n.* Person of weak character or mind.

ninon (nēn'awṅ) *n.* Light silk dress-fabric.

ninth *adj.* Next after eighth. *~ n.* Ninth part; (mus.) interval of octave and second. **ninth'ly** *adv.* In the ninth place.

Nī'obė. (Gk legend) Daughter of Tantalus; Apollo and Artemis, enraged because she boasted herself superior to their mother Latona, slew her six sons and five of her six daughters; Niobe herself was turned into a rock, and her tears into streams that trickled from it. **Nī'obids** *n.pl.* The children of Niobe.

nīōb'ium *n.* (chem.) Rare metallic element very similar to tantalum and usu. found associated with it (also known as *columbium*, esp. in U.S.); symbol Nb, at. no. 41, at. wt 92·906. [named after NIOBE, daughter of Tantalus]

nip[1] *v.* Pinch, squeeze sharply, bite; pinch *off*; check growth of; (of cold) affect injuriously, pain; (slang) move rapidly or nimbly. *~ n.* Pinch, sharp squeeze, bite; (check to vegetation caused by) coldness of air; *~ and tuck*, (U.S.) neck and neck.

nip[2] *n.* Small quantity of spirits etc. *~ v.* Take nips (of).

Nip[3] slang *abbrev.* NIPPON.

nī'pa (nē-, nī-) *n.* Kind of E. Indian palm (*N. fruticans*), with creeping trunk, large feathery leaves, and large round bunches of fruit; alcoholic drink made from the sap of this tree.

nipp'er *n.* (esp.) 1. (slang) Boy, lad, esp. costermonger's assistant or street arab. 2. (pl.) Implement with jaws for gripping or cutting; forceps, pinchers, pliers; (usu. pl.) crustacean's great claw.

nipp'le *n.* 1. Small projection in which mammary ducts terminate in mammal of either sex; teat, esp. on woman's breast; teat of nursing-bottle. 2. Nipple-like protuberance on skin, glass, metal, etc.; small rounded elevation on mountain; (hist.) perforated projection of musket-lock on which percussion-cap is placed.

Nĭpp'on. Japanese name for JAPAN. [Jap. *ni-pun* sunrise (*ni* sun, *pun* origin)]

nĭpp'y *adj.* Cold; (colloq.) nimble.

nīrva'na (-vah-) *n.* In Buddhist theology, extinction of individual existence and absorption into supreme spirit, or extinction of all passions and desires and attainment of perfect beatitude. [Sansk. *nirvāna* blowing out, extinction]

nīs'ī *conj.* (legal) Unless; *decree, order*, etc., ~, decree etc. valid unless cause is shown for rescinding it before appointed time at which it is 'made absolute'; ~ *prius*, hearing of civil causes by judges of assize, court-business of this kind (from L words of writ, 'unless before', directing sheriff to provide jury on certain day unless the judges come sooner).

Niss'en hut *n.* Tunnel-shaped hut made of corrugated iron with a cement floor. [Lt-Col. P. N. *Nissen*, inventor (1871–1930)]

nĭt *n.* Egg of louse or other parasitic insect (ill. LOUSE).

nī'tŏn *n.* Orig. name of RADON. [L *nitere* shine]

nī'trate *n.* Salt of nitric acid; potassium or sodium nitrate used as fertilizer. **nītrāte'** *v.t.* Treat, impregnate, or cause to interact, with nitric acid. **nītrā'tion** *n.*

nī'tre (-ter) *n.* Saltpetre, potassium nitrate, KNO_3.

nī'tric *adj.* Of nitre; ~ *acid*, clear, colourless, pungent, highly corrosive liquid, HNO_3; ~ *oxide*, a colourless gas (NO), obtained by the action of nitric acid on copper turnings or by the combination of nitrogen and oxygen at high temperatures.

nī'trifȳ *v.* Turn into nitre, make or become nitrous. **nītrificā'tion** *n.*

nītrobĕn'zēne *n.* Poisonous yellow liquid ($C_6H_5NO_2$) used in the preparation of aniline etc.

nītrocĕll'ūlōse *n.* = CELLULOSE nitrate.

nī'tro-chalk *n.* Fertilizer consisting of a mixture of calcium carbonate and ammonium nitrate.

nī'tro-cŏm'pound *n.* Organic substance containing the group $-NO_2$.

nī'trogėn *n.* Colourless tasteless odourless gaseous element forming about four-fifths of the atmosphere and occurring also in nature as nitrates, and as proteins in animal and vegetable tissues, used commercially in the large-scale synthesis of ammonia; symbol N, at. no. 7, at. wt 14·006; ~ *fixation*, (chem.) process by which atmospheric nitrogen is combined with other elements (oxygen, hydrogen, calcium, etc.) in the manufacture of commercially important nitrogen compounds, as nitric acid, ammonia, etc. **nītrŏ'gėnous** *adj.* Of, belonging to, containing, nitrogen.

nī'tro-glȳ'cerine *n.* Glyceryl trinitrate, a yellowish oily violently explosive liquid formed by action of a mixture of nitric and sulphuric acid on glycerine; a constituent of dynamite, gelignite, and cordite.

nī'trous *adj.* Of, like, impregnated with, nitre; (chem.) of, containing, nitrogen, esp. of compounds in which nitrogen has a lower valency than *nitric* compounds; ~ *acid*, acid (HNO_2) containing less oxygen than nitric acid; ~ *oxide*, colourless sweet-smelling gas (N_2O), used as a mild anaesthetic, laughing-gas.

nĭt'-wĭt *n.* (slang) Person of little intelligence.

nĭx[1] *n.* (slang) Nothing.

nĭx[2] *n.* Water-elf. **nĭx'ie** *n.* Female water-elf.

Nizam (nĭzahm'). Title of former ruler of Hyderabad.

Nizh'ni Nŏv'gorod. Former name of *Gor'ki*, river port at confluence of Volga and Oka, central Russia; scene of an annual fair. [Russ., = 'lower Novgorod']

N.K.V.D.: see M.V.D.

N.J. *abbrev.* New Jersey.

N.L. *abbrev.* National Liberal; north latitude (also **N. lat.**).

N.L.C., N.L.F. *abbrevs.* National Liberal Club, Federation.

N. Mex. *abbrev.* New Mexico.

NNE., NNE *abbrevs.* North-north-east.

NNW., NNW *abbrevs.* North-north-west.

nō *adj.* Not any; not a, quite other than a; hardly any; ~ *ball*, (umpire's announcement of) unlawfully delivered ball in cricket; *no-ball* (*v.*) pronounce (bowler) to have bowled no ball; *no'body*, no person; person of no importance; ~ *man*, no person; ~ *man's land*, piece of waste, unowned or debatable ground, esp. (mil.) the space between opposed lines; ~ *one*, no person; (as adj.) no single; ~ *side*, (Rugby footb.) (announcement of) end of game; ~ *trumps*, (cards), (bid calling for) hand played without trump suit; *no'ways* (archaic), *no'wise*, in no manner, not at all; ~ *whit*, (archaic or joc.) not at all. ~ *adv.* 1. (as alternative after *or*) Not. 2. (with comparatives) By no amount, not at all; ~ *more*, nothing further; not any more; no longer, never again, to no greater extent; just as little, neither. 3. Used to express negative reply to request, question, etc. ~ *n.* The word *no*, a denial or refusal; (pl., *noes*) voters against a motion.

n.o. *abbrev.* Not out.

N.O. *abbrev.* Natural order.

N°, No. *abbrevs.* (*pl.* N°ˢ, Nos.) *Numero* (= in number); number.

Nōā'chĭan (-k-) *adj.* Of Noah or his times.

Nō'ah. (O.T.) Patriarch, represented as 10th in descent from Adam; at God's command he made the ARK which saved his family and specimens of every animal from the flood sent by God to destroy the world; his sons Shem, Ham, and Japheth were regarded as ancestors of all the races of mankind; see Gen. v–x; ~*'s ark*, child's toy model of the ark with figures of Noah, his family, and the animals.

nŏb[1] *n.* (slang) Head; (cribbage) knave of same suit as turn-up card, counting one to holder.

nŏb[2] *n.* (slang) Member of upper classes. **nŏbb'y** *adj.* (slang) Suitable for a nob, smart, elegant.

nŏbb'le *v.t.* (slang) Tamper with (race-horse) to prevent its winning; secure partiality of by underhand means; get hold of (money etc.) dishonestly; catch (criminal).

Nōb'ĕl, Alfred Bernhard (1833–96). Swedish chemist and engineer; inventor of dynamite and other high explosives; founder, by his will, of the five ~ *Prizes*, which are awarded annually to the persons adjudged by Swedish learned societies to have done the most significant work during the year in physics, chemistry, medicine, and literature, and to the person who is adjudged by the Norwegian parliament to have rendered the greatest service to the cause of peace.

nobĕl'ium *n.* A TRANSURANIC element, symbol No, at. no. 102.

nobĭl'iary (-lya-) *adj.* Of (the) nobility; ~ *particle*, preposition (as French *de*, German *von*) prefixed to title.

nobĭl'ĭty *n.* 1. Noble character, mind, birth, or rank. 2. Persons of noble rank as a class; (in England) the peerage.

nō'ble *adj.* 1. Illustrious by rank, title, or birth, belonging to the nobility. 2. Of lofty character or ideals; showing greatness of character, magnanimous; splendid, magnificent, stately; impressive in appearance; excellent, admirable; (of metals such as gold, silver, sometimes platinum) resisting chemical action; *no'bleman*, peer; *no'blewoman*, woman of noble birth or rank. **nō'bleness** *n.* **nō'bly** *adv.*

nō'ble *n.* 1. Nobleman. 2. (hist.) English gold coin, orig. minted by Edward III, usu. worth 6*s.* 8*d.*

noblesse' (-ĕs) *n.* The class of nobles (esp. of a foreign country); ~ *oblige* (-ēzh), privilege entails responsibility.

nŏck *n.* Notch at ends of bow for holding string; notched horn tip of arrow for receiving bowstring. ~ *v.t.* Set (arrow) on string.

nŏc'tūle *n.* The Great Bat (*Nyctalus noctula*), European species of brown bat, the largest found in Britain.

nŏctûrn'al *adj.* Of, in, done by, active in, the night.

nŏc'tūrne *n.* Pensive, melancholy musical composition; (paint.) night-piece.

nŏd *v.* Incline head slightly and quickly in salutation, assent, or command; let head fall forward in drowsiness, be drowsy, make mistake from inattention; *nodding acquaintance*, very slight one (*with*); ~ *n.* Nodding of the head; this as sign of absolute power; *land of N~*, (with pun on Gen. iv. 16), sleep.

N.O.D. *abbrev.* Naval Ordnance Department.

nŏd'al: see NODE.

nŏdd'le *n.* (colloq.) Head, pate.

nŏdd'y *n.* 1. Simpleton, noodle. 2. Soot-coloured tropical sea-bird (*Anocus stolidus*), resembling tern but with shorter wings and tail less forked.

nōde *n.* 1. (bot.) Point at which leaves spring (ill. LEAF). 2. (path.) Hard tumour esp. on gouty or rheumatic joint. 3. (astron.) Intersecting point of planet's orbit and ecliptic or of two great circles of celestial sphere (ill. CELESTIAL). 4. (physics) Point or line of rest in vibrating body. 5. Central point in system. 6. (math.) Point at which curve crosses itself. **nōd'al** *adj.*

nŏd'ūle *n.* Small rounded lump of anything, small node in plant; small knotty tumour, ganglion. **nŏd'ūlar, nŏd'ūlātėd, nŏd'ūlōse, nŏd'ūlous** *adjs.* **nŏdūlā'tion** *n.*

nōd'us *n.* Knotty point, difficulty, complication in plot of story etc.

Nōĕl', Nōwĕl'. Word shouted or sung as expression of joy, to commemorate birth of Christ (now only in Christmas carols). [OF, f. L *natalis* natal]

nōĕt'ic *adj.* Of the intellect; purely intellectual or abstract; given to intellectual speculation. **nōĕt'ics** *n.* Science of the intellect.

nŏg¹ *n.* Pin, peg, small block, of wood; wood block built into wall in place of a brick so that interior woodwork may be nailed to it; snag or stump on tree. ~ *v.t.* Secure with nogs; build in form of *nogging*, brickwork between wooden quarters of framing (ill. HALF-timber).

nŏg² *n.* Kind of strong beer brewed in E. Anglia; EGG-nog.

nŏgg'in *n.* Small mug; small measure, usu. ¼ pint, of liquor.

Nō(h) drama. Traditional Japanese drama evolved from the rites of Shinto worship and practically unchanged since 15th c.; the oldest form of drama in Japan.

N.O.I.C. *abbrev.* Naval Officer in Charge.

noil(s) *n.* Short fibres combed from yarn during preparation.

noise (-z) *n.* Sound, esp. loud or harsh one; din, clamour. *~s off*, in a play, sounds, usu. loud or confused, produced off the stage. **noise'lėss** (-zl-) *adj.* **noise'lėssly** *adv.* **noise'lėssnėss** *n.* ~ *v.* Make public, spread *abroad.*

nois'ome (-sum) *adj.* Harmful, noxious; ill-smelling; objectionable, offensive. **nois'omenėss** *n.*

nois'y (-zĭ) *adj.* Clamorous, turbulent; full of, making much, noise; loud. **nois'ily** *adv.* **noisinėss** *n.*

nōl'ēns vōl'ēns (-z) *adv.* Willy-nilly, perforce. [L, = 'unwilling, willing']

nōl'ī mē tăn'gerė (-j-) *n.* 1. Picture of Christ as he appeared to Mary Magdalene at sepulchre (John xx. 17). 2. (path.) Lupus. 3. (bot.) Kind of balsam of N. of England, forcibly expelling ripe seeds when touched. [L, = 'touch me not']

nŏll'ė prŏs'ėquī *n.* (Entry on court record of) abandonment of part or all of suit by plaintiff or prosecutor. [L, = 'refuse to pursue'] ***nŏl(l'ė) prŏs(sė)*** *v.t.* (U.S.) Abandon (case etc.) thus.

nom. *abbrev.* Nominal; nominative.

nōm'ăd *n.* & *adj.* (Member of tribe) roaming from place to place for pasture; wanderer, wandering. **nomăd'ic** *adj.* **nōm'adism** *n.*

nŏm'bril *n.* (her.) Point on an escutcheon midway between the true centre (fesse point) and the base point (ill. HERALDRY).

nom de guerre (nŏm de gār) *n.* Pseudonym, sobriquet, assumed name under which person fights, plays, writes, etc. [Fr., = 'war name']

nom de plume (nŏm de plōōm) *n.* Writer's pseudonym, pen-name. [English formation on Fr. words *nom* name, *de* of, *plume* pen]

nōm'ėnclātor *n.* 1. (hist.) Slave or client in ancient Rome charged with supplying his master, when canvassing for office, with names of persons met; usher assigning places at banquet. 2. Giver or inventor of names, esp. classifier of natural objects.

nōm'ėnclāture (*or* nomĕn'-) *n.* System of names for things; terminology of a science etc.; systematic naming. **nōm'ėnclative** *adj.*

nŏm'inal *adj.* Of, as, like, a noun; of, in, names; existing in name only; not real or substantial; ~ *fee, rent*, etc., virtually nothing; consisting of, giving, the names. **nŏm'inally** *adv.*

nŏm'inalism *n.* (philos.) Doctrine of the scholastics that universal or abstract concepts are mere names, without any corresponding reality (opp. REALISM). **nŏm'inalist** *n.* **nŏminalis'tic** *adj.*

nŏm'ināte *v.t.* Name or appoint (date, place); appoint, propose for election, to office. **nŏminā'tion** *n.* (esp.) Right of nominating for appointment. **nŏm'inātor, nŏminee'** *ns.*

nŏm'inative *n.* Case used as or in agreement with subject of verb; word in this case, (loosely) subject (*of* verb); ~ *absolute*, construction like Latin ablative absolute, as *this being so, I did nothing.* ~ *adj.* 1. (Of case) used as or in agreement with subject of verb; of this case. 2. Of, appointed by, nomination. **nŏminatīv'al** *adj.* Of the nominative case.

non- *prefix.* Not; now freely prefixed to nouns, adjectives, etc.

nŏn-ăc'cĕss (-ăks-) *n.* (law) Impossibility of access for sexual intercourse.

nŏn'age *n.* Being under age, minority; immaturity, early stage.

nŏnagėnār'ian *adj.* & *n.* (Person) aged 90 years or more but less than 100.

nŏn-appear'ance *n.* Failure to appear, esp. in court of law.

nōn'ary *adj.* (arith., of scale of notation) Having nine as basis.

nŏn-bellĭ'gerent *adj.* & *n.* (State) not taking active or open part in war. **nŏn-bellĭ'gerency** *n.*

nŏnce *n.* Time being, present occasion (only in *for the* ~); *~-word*, word coined for a special occasion and used only for a short time.

nŏn'chalant (-shal-) *adj.* Unexcited, unmoved, cool, indifferent. **nŏn'chalantly** *adv.* **nŏn'chalance** *n.*

nŏn-collē'giate *adj.* Of the students (in certain universities) not attached to any particular college or hall; not having a collegiate system.

nŏn-cŏm *n.* (colloq.) Non-commissioned officer.

nŏn-cŏm'batant *adj.* Not fighting. ~ *n.* Civilian in time of war; member of army etc. whose duties do not include fighting.

nŏn-commĭ'ssioned (-shond) *adj.* Not holding commission (esp. of army officers such as *sergeant, corporal*).

nŏn-committ'al *adj.* Refusing to commit oneself to particular view or course of action.

nŏn-commūn'icant *adj.* & *n.* (Person) who does not attend communion service, esp. (one) who is not member of the Church of England.

nŏn cŏm'pŏs mĕn'tĭs. 'Not master of one's mind', insane.

nŏn-condŭc'ting *adj.* That does not conduct heat or electricity. **nŏn-condŭc'tor** *n.*

nŏnconfôrm'ist *n.* One who does not conform to doctrine or discipline of an established Church, esp. member of Church dissenting from Anglican Church (usu. not including Roman Catholics); Protestant dissenter. **nŏnconfôrm'ity** *n.* Principles, practice, the body, of nonconformists, Protestant dissent; failure to conform (*to*); want of correspondence between things.

nŏn-cō-ŏperā'tion *n.* The Indian movement, led by Mahatma Gandhi, of non-violent civil disobedience to British rule, SATYAGRAHA; similar refusal or failure to co-operate with authority elsewhere.

nŏn'dėscrĭpt *adj.* & *n.* (Person, thing) not easily classified, neither one thing nor another, hybrid.

none (nŭn) *pron.* Not any *of*; no person, no one (now rare); no persons. ~ *adj.* (usu. ellipt.) No, not any; not to be counted in specified class. ~ *adv.* By no amount, not at all; ~ *the less*, nevertheless.

nŏn-ĕg'ō *n.* All that is not the ego or conscious self.

nonĕn'tĭty *n.* Non-existence, non-existent thing, figment; person or thing of no importance, cipher.

nōnes (-nz) *n.pl.* 1. (Rom. antiq.) 9th day (by inclusive reckoning) before IDES; 7th of March, May, July, Oct., and 5th of other months. 2. (eccles.) Daily office orig. said at 9th hour (about 3 p.m.), but now at midday.

nŏn-ėssĕn'tial *adj.* & *n.* (Thing) that is not essential.

nonesuch: see NONSUCH.

nōnĕt' *n.* (mus.) Composition for nine instruments or voices.

nŏn-Euclidē'an *adj.* (of geometry) Not in accordance with principles of Euclid.

nŏn-exĭs'tent *adj.* Not existing. **nŏn-exĭs'tence** *n.*

nŏn-flăm *adj.* (of cinema-film etc.) Not inflammable.

nonĭll'ion (-lyon) *n.* 9th power of million, 1 with 54 ciphers; (U.S.) 10th power of a thousand, 1 with 30 ciphers.

nŏn-intervĕn'tion *n.* Absence of intervention; esp., in international politics, systematic refusal to interfere in affairs of another nation.

Nōn'ius. Pedro Nuñez (1492–1577), Portuguese mathematician. **nōn'ius** *n.* Contrivance invented by Nuñez for graduating mathematical instruments, of which the VERNIER is an improved form.

nŏn-jur'or (joor'*er*) *n.* (hist.) Beneficed clergyman who refused to take oath of allegiance to William and Mary in 1689. **nŏn-jur'ĭng** *adj.*

nŏn nōb'ĭs (first words of Ps. cxiii in Vulgate). Expression of humble gratitude for mercies vouchsafed. [L, = 'not unto us']

nŏnpareil' (-rĕl) *adj.* Unequalled, peerless. ~ *n.* Person or thing without equal, something unique; size of type (6 point) intermediate between emerald and ruby (in America between minion and agate); kinds of comfit, apple, finch, etc.

nŏn-pàrt'y *adj.* That may be dealt with irrespective of political partisanship.

nŏnplŭs' *n.* State of perplexity, standstill. ~ *v.t.* (past t. *-ssed*) Reduce to hopeless perplexity. [L *non plus* not more]

nŏn pŏss'ūmus. Statement of inability, refusal to act or move. [L, = 'we cannot']

nŏn-rĕs'ĭdent (-z-) *adj.* Sojourning in place only for short time or residing elsewhere; not residing at one's place of work; (of post) not requiring holder to reside. ~ *n.* Non-resident person; clergyman not residing where his duties require him, absentee.

nŏn-rėsĭs'tance (-zĭs-) *n.* (Principle of) not resisting authority even when it is unjustly exercised.

nŏn'sense *n.* Absurd or meaningless words or ideas, foolish or extravagant conduct, worthless things, rubbish; *no* ~, no foolish or extravagant conduct, no foolery or humbug; ~ *verse(s)*, verse(s) having no sense or an absurd one. ~ *int.* Absurd! rubbish! **nŏnsĕn'sĭcal** *adj.* **nŏnsĕn'sĭcally** *adv.*

nŏn sĕq'uĭtur. Illogical inference, paradoxical result. [L, = 'it does not follow']

nŏn-skĭd *adj.* (Of tyres) designed so as not to skid.

nŏn-smōk'er *n.* Person who does not smoke; railway-compartment in which smoking is not permitted.

nŏn-stŏp *n.* & *adj.* (Train etc.) travelling between two places without stopping at intermediate ones. ~ *adv.* Without a stop.

non'sŭch, none'sŭch (nŭns-) *n.* 1. Person or thing that is unrivalled, paragon. 2. Kind of lucerne.

nŏn'suit (-ūt) *n.* (law) Stoppage of suit by judge when plaintiff fails to make out legal case or bring sufficient evidence. ~ *v.t.* Subject to nonsuit.

nŏn-ūn'ion *adj.* Not belonging to a trade union; not made by union labour.

nŏn-ūs'er (-z-) *n.* (law) Neglect to use a right, by which it may become void.

nōō'dle[1] *n.* Simpleton.

nōō'dle[2] *n.* Strip or ball of dough made with flour and eggs and served esp. in soup. [Ger. *Nudel*]

nŏŏk *n.* Out-of-the-way corner, recess, secluded place.

nōōn *n.* 12 o'clock in the day, midday; *noon'day, noon'tide*, midday. [L *nona* (*hora*) ninth hour; orig., 3 p.m.]

nōōse *n.* Loop with running knot, tightening as string is pulled, halter; (fig.) the marriage tie; snare or bond. ~ *v.t.* Capture with noose, ensnare; make noose on (cord); arrange (cord) in noose *round* neck etc.

nōp'al *n.* Amer. cactus, *Nopalea cochinellifera*, cultivated for support of cochineal-insect.

nor (nôr, n*o*r) *conj.* Neither (archaic); and not, and no more, neither, and not either.

nor'. *abbrev.* of NORTH.

Nôrd'ic *adj.* Of, belonging to, the racial type of the Germanic peoples of N. Europe, esp. the Scandinavians, with tall stature, long narrow head, bony frame, and light colouring of hair, eyes, and skin; in transf. use, applied to an alleged race of Germanic type, having distinctive qualities that are held to give it superiority over all others, often identified with *Germanic* or *Aryan*. ~ *n.* Person of Nordic type or race.

Nōre. Sandbank at mouth of Thames off Sheerness; *Mutiny of the* ~, mutiny which broke out, 1797, in fleet stationed there, occasioned by bad food and inadequate pay.

Nôrf'olk (-*o*k). Eastern maritime county of England; ~ *jacket*, man's loose-fitting single-breasted belted jacket with box-pleats back and front (ill. COAT).

nôrm *n.* Standard, type; (U.S.S.R) standard unit of work prescribed.

nôrm'al *adj.* 1. Rectangular (rare); standing at right angles, perpendicular. 2. Conforming to standard, regular, usual, typical; ~ *school* (after Fr. *école normale*) training school for teachers. **nôrm'ally** *adv.* **nôrmăl'ĭty, nôrm'alcy** *ns.* **nôrm'al** *n.* (geom.) Normal line (ill. EVOLUTE); (physics) average or mean of observed quantities; usual state, level, etc.; normal temperature (98·4° F.) of human body.

nôrm'alīze *v.t.* Make normal. **nôrmalīzā'tion** *n.*

Nôrm'an. Native or inhabitant of NORMANDY, belonging to or descended from mixed Scandinavian and Frankish race inhabiting that part of France; orig. one of the Northmen or Scandinavians who conquered Normandy in 10th c. ~ *adj.* Of the Normans or Normandy; ~ *architecture*, style of round-arched Romanesque architecture developed by Normans and employed in England after Norman Conquest, with characteristic geometrical ornament; ~ *Conquest*, conquest of England by Normans under William I, 1066; ~ *French*, form of medieval French spoken by Normans; later form of this in English legal use, law French.

Nôrm'andy. Old province of NW. France with coastline on English Channel; given by Charles the Simple to Rollo, first Duke of Normandy, 912; united to England from Norman Conquest until 1204.

Nôrn *n.* *The* ~*s*, (Scand. myth.) the Three Fates who sit under the tree Yggdrasil and spin or weave the destiny of man.

Nŏr'roy. (heraldry) ~ *King of Arms*, the herald whose jurisdiction is N. of river Trent. [AF *nor* north + *rey, roy* king]

Nôrse *adj.* Of ancient Scandinavia, esp. Norway; of the language of its inhabitants. ~ *n.*: see OLD Norse.

nôrth[1] *adv.* (abbrev. N.) Towards or in the region lying to right of observer on equator at equinox who faces setting sun. ~ *n.* Cardinal point lying north; northern part of any country (in England, part beyond Humber; in

U.S., States lying N. of Maryland, the Ohio River, and Missouri); north wind. ~ *adj.* Situated, dwelling, in or more towards the north; *N~ Atlantic Treaty Organization*: see N.A.T.O.; *N~ Britain*, Scotland; ~ *country* (from, characteristic of) north of England or Great Britain; *~-countryman*, native of northern England; *North'man*, inhabitant or native of Norway or of Scandinavia; ~ *star*, pole-star; *N~ Star State*, pop. name of Minnesota, U.S. **nŏrth'ward** *adv.*, *adj.*, & *n.* **nŏrth'wardly** *adv.* & *adj.* **nŏrth'wards** *adv.*

Nŏrth[2], Christopher, pseudonym of John WILSON[1].

Nŏrth[3], Frederick, Earl of Guilford (1732–92; better known as Lord North). English statesman; supporter of George III.

Nŏrth Amĕ'rica. Northern part of continent of America, including Mexico, U.S., and Canada.

Nŏrthămp'ton. County town of **Nŏrthămp'tonshire,** east midland county of England.

Northants. *abbrev.* Northamptonshire.

Nŏrth Carolī'na. South Atlantic State of U.S.; admitted to Union in 1789; capital, Raleigh.

Nŏrth'cliffe, Alfred Charles William Harmsworth, Viscount (1865–1922). British newspaper owner, founder of the 'Daily Mail' and chief proprietor of 'The Times' from 1908 until his death.

Nŏrth Dakō'ta. West North Central State of U.S.; admitted to the Union in 1889; capital, Bismarck.

nŏrth-east, -west *advs.*, *ns.*, & *adjs.* (Regions) midway between north and east or north and west; *north-east passage*, passage for ships along northern coasts of Europe and Asia, formerly thought of as possible route to Far East; similarly *north-west passage*, presumed route along northern coast of America from Atlantic to Pacific; *north-eas'ter*, *north-wes'ter*, wind from north-east, north-west; *northeas'terly*, *-wes'terly* (*adjs.* & *advs.*) coming from these directions; *north-east'ern*, *-west'ern*, *-east'ward*, *-west'ward*, *-east'wardly*, *-west'wardly* (*adjs.* & *advs.*) in or towards these directions.

nŏrth'er (-th-) *n.* (U.S.) Strong cold north wind blowing in autumn and winter over Texas, Florida, and Gulf of Mexico.

nŏrth'erly (-dh-) *adj.* & *adv.* Towards the north; (of wind) blowing from the north or thereabouts.

nŏrth'ern (-dh-) *adj.* Living or situated in, coming from, the north, esp. of England or Europe, or (U.S.) of the United States; characteristic of the north; ~ *lights*, aurora borealis; ~ *n.* northerner. **nŏr'therner** *n.* One belonging to or coming from the north.

Nŏrth'ern Ireland (-dh-). Autonomous unit of United Kingdom, that part of province of Ulster which refused to enter Irish Free State; comprises six counties, Armagh, Down, Londonderry, Antrim, Tyrone, and Fermanagh; capital, Belfast.

nŏrth'ing (-th-) *n.* Northward progress or deviation in sailing etc.

Nŏrth Sea. Part of Atlantic lying between mainland of Europe and E. coast of Gt Britain.

Northumb. *abbrev.* Northumberland.

Nŏrthŭm'berland. Extreme NE. county of England.

Nŏrthŭm'bria. Ancient Anglo-Saxon kingdom, extending from Humber to Forth. **Nŏrthŭm'brian** *adj.* & *n.* (esp.) Anglo-Saxon dialect spoken in Northumbria.

Nŏrth-Wĕst Frontier Province. Formerly a province of British India, lying N. of Baluchistan, between river Indus and Afghanistan; ceded to Pakistan in 1947.

Norvic. *abbrev.* (Bishop) of Norwich (replacing surname in his signature).

Nŏr'way. Kingdom of N. Europe occupying W. part of Scandinavian peninsula, founded 872; united with Denmark 1397–1814, and thereafter with Sweden under a personal union of the crowns which was dissolved in 1905; capital, Oslo.

Nŏrwē'gian *adj.* Of Norway, its inhabitants or its language. ~ *n.* 1. Native, inhabitant of Norway. 2. Language of Norway, in its literary form almost identical with Danish.

nŏr-wĕst'er *n.* 1. Wind from NW. 2. Glass of strong liquor. 3. Oilskin hat or coat, sou'-wester.

nose (nōz) *n.* 1. Member of face or head above mouth, containing nostrils and serving as organ of smell; sense of smell; *as plain as the ~ on your face*, easily seen; *follow one's ~*, go straight forward, be guided by instinct; *poke, thrust, one's ~*, pry or intrude *into*; *turn up one's ~ at*, show disdain for; *put person's ~ out of joint*, supplant, disconcert, or frustrate him; *bite* or *snap person's ~ off*, answer him snappishly; *pay through the ~*, be charged exorbitant prices; *speak through the ~*, speak with nasal twang; *under person's ~*, right in front of him. 2. Open end or nozzle of pipe, tube, bellows, etc.; prow; projecting part. 3. *~-ape*, proboscis monkey; *~-bag*, bag suspended from horse's head so that he may eat the fodder contained in it; *~-band*, lower band of bridle passing over nose and attached to cheek-straps; *~-dive*, aeroplane's downward plunge, with nose first; (*v.i.*) perform nose-dive; *~-flute*, musical instrument blown with nose, among Siamese, Fijians, etc.; *nose'gay*, bunch of (esp. sweet-scented) flowers; *~-monkey*, proboscis monkey; *~-rag*, (slang) pocket-handkerchief; *~-ring*, ring fixed in nose of bull etc. for leading, or worn in nose as ornament by savages. ~ *v.* Perceive smell of, discover by smell; detect, smell *out* (fig.); rub with the nose, thrust nose against or into; sniff (*at* etc.), pry or search (*after, for*); push one's way, push (one's *way*), with the nose (esp. of ship); ~ *over*, (of aircraft) fall nose forward.

nōs'er (-z-) *n.* Strong head wind.

nōs'ey (-zĭ) *adj.* (esp., slang) Inquisitive, curious; *N~ Parker*, (slang) inquisitive person.

nōs'ing (-z-) *n.* Rounded edge of step, moulding, etc., or metal or rubber shield for it.

nŏsŏl'ogy *n.* (Branch of medical science dealing with) classification of diseases.

nŏstăl'gia *n.* 1. Severe homesickness. 2. Sorrowful longing *for* conditions of a past age; regretful or wistful memory of earlier time. **nŏstăl'gic** *adj.*

nŏs'toc *n.* Genus of unicellular algae with cells arranged in intertwining rows which form gelatinous mass. [name invented by Paracelsus]

Nŏstradām'us. Michel de Notredame (1503–66), Provençal astrologer of Jewish origin; favourite of Catherine de Médicis and physician to Charles IX of France.

nŏs'tril *n.* Either opening in nose admitting air to lungs and smells to olfactory nerves.

nŏs'trum *n.* Medicine prepared by person recommending it, quack remedy, patent medicine; pet scheme for political or social reform etc. [L, neut. of *noster* our]

nos'y *adj.* = NOSEY.

nŏt *adv.* Expressing negation; now archaic following verbs other than auxiliaries and the verb *be* (freq. as *n't* joined to verb); *~-being*, non-existence; ~ *half*, (slang) very, very much.

nōt'a bēn'ē. (abbrev. N.B.) Mark well, observe particularly.

nōtabĭl'ity *n.* Prominent person; being notable.

nōt'able *adj.* Worthy of note, remarkable, striking, eminent. ~ *n.* Eminent person; (pl., French hist.) assembly of members of the privileged classes summoned by the king in an emergency.

nōt'ary *n.* Person publicly authorized to draw up or attest contracts etc., protest bills of exchange etc., and perform other formal duties (chiefly used about foreign countries, exc. in ~ *public*). **notār'ial** *adj.* **notār'ially** *adv.*

notā'tion *n.* Representing of numbers, quantities, etc., by symbols; any set of symbols used for this, esp. in arithmetic, algebra, and music.

nŏtch *n.* V-shaped indentation

or incision on edge or across surface; nick on stick etc., by way of keeping count; (U.S.) deep narrow pass. ~ *v.t.* Make notches in; score, mark, record, by notches; make (number of runs) at cricket; fix or insert by means of notches.

nōte *n.* 1. Written sign representing pitch and duration of a musical sound; key of pianoforte etc.; single tone of definite pitch made by musical instrument, voice, etc.; (single tone in) bird's song or call; *change one's* ~, alter one's way of speaking or thinking. 2. Sign, token, characteristic, distinguishing feature; stigma, mark of censure; mark *of exclamation* or *interrogation*; (theol.) sign or proof of genuine origin, authority, and practice. 3. Brief record of facts etc. to assist memory or serve as basis for fuller statement or as help in speaking (usu. pl.); annotation appended to passage in book etc. 4. Short or informal letter; formal diplomatic communication; (usu. ~ *of hand*) written promise to pay sum by certain time; BANK-note. 5. Distinction, eminence; notice, attention. 6. *~-book,* book for taking notes or containing notes and memoranda; *~-paper,* paper of size or quality used for correspondence. ~ *v.t.* Observe, notice, give attention to; set down, set *down*, as thing to be remembered or observed; annotate; *noted*, celebrated, well known *for*. **nōte'worthy** (-twẽrdhĭ) *adj.* Worthy of note or attention, remarkable.

noth'ĭng (nŭ-) *n.* No thing; not anything, nought; trifle, very inferior thing; (arith.) no amount, nought; non-existence, what does not exist; (with pl.) trifling thing, event, remark, person; *make* ~ *of doing*, do without hesitation or as ordinary matter; *come to* ~, turn out useless, fail, not amount to anything. ~ *adv.* Not at all, in no way.

noth'ĭngness (nŭ-) *n.* Non-existence, the non-existent; worthlessness, triviality, unimportance.

nōt'ĭce *n.* 1. Intimation, warning; placard etc. conveying information or directions; formal intimation of something or instructions *to* do something, announcement by party to agreement that it is to terminate at specified time (esp. between landlord and tenant or employer and employed). 2. Heed, attention, cognizance, observation; *take* ~, give heed. 3. Short comment, review, etc., in newspaper or journal etc. ~ *v.t.* Remark upon, speak of; perceive, take notice of; treat with attention, favour, or politeness. **nōt'ĭceable** (-s*a*-) *adj.* **nōt'ĭceably** *adv.*

nōt'ĭfiable *adj.* (of diseases) That must be notified to public health authorities.

nōt'ĭfȳ *v.t.* Make known, announce, report; inform, give notice to. **nōtĭficā'tion** *n.*

nō'tion *n.* General concept under which particular thing may be classed; idea, conception; view, opinion, theory; inclination, disposition, desire; (U.S., pl.) haberdashery, small wares, esp. cheap useful articles of some ingenuity; (pl.) traditional special vocabulary of Winchester College.

nō'tional (-sh*o*n-) *adj.* (of knowledge etc.) Speculative, not based on experiment or demonstration; (of things etc.) existing only in thought, imaginary; (of persons) fanciful. **nō'tionally** *adv.*

nōt'ochŏrd (-k-) *n.* In CHORDATE animals, rudimentary spinal cord, rod of tissue lying along back below nerve cord (ill. LANCELET); in vertebrates, elongated cord of embryonic tissue from which vertebral column develops.

notŏr'ious *adj.* Well or commonly known; undisguised, talked of, generally known to deserve the name; unfavourably known (*for*). **notŏr'iously** *adv.* **nōtorī'ėty** *n.*

Notre-Dame (nŏtr*e*-dahm). Church dedicated to the Virgin Mary, esp. cathedral church of Paris. [Fr., = 'Our Lady']

Nŏtt'ĭnghamshire (-ng-*a*m-). Midland county of England.

Notts. *abbrev.* Nottinghamshire.

nōt'um *n.* (pl. *-ta*). (zool.) Dorsal part of thorax in insects.

nŏtwĭthstănd'ĭng *prep.* In spite of, not the less for. ~ *adv.* Nevertheless, all the same. ~ *conj.* (archaic) Although, in spite of the fact *that*.

nougat (nōōg'ah) *n.* Sweetmeat of sugar, honey, almonds or other nuts, and egg-white.

nought (nawt) *n.* Nothing (literary, exc. in arith.); figure 0, cipher; *come, bring, to* ~, be ruined, fail; ruin, baffle; *set at* ~, disregard, ridicule; *~s and crosses,* game in which each of two players tries to mark 3 noughts or crosses in line on a grid of 9 spaces.

noum'ėnŏn *n.* (pl. *-mėna*). Object of purely intellectual intuition, devoid of all phenomenal attributes. **noum'ėnal** *adj.* **noum'ėnally** *adv.* [Gk, = '(thing) apprehended' (*noeō* apprehend); taken by Kant as antithesis to *phenomenon*]

noun *n.* (gram.) Word used as name of person or thing, substantive; (formerly) substantive or adjective.

nou'rish (nŭ-) *v.t.* Sustain with food; foster, cherish, nurse, (feeling, hope, etc.) in one's heart. **nou'rĭshĭng** *adj.* **nou'rĭshment** *n.* Sustenance, food; nourishing.

nous *n.* (Gk philos.) Mind, intellect; (colloq.) common sense, gumption.

nouveau riche (nōōv'ō rēsh) (pl. *-x*, *-s*) Newly enriched person, parvenu.

Nov. *abbrev.* November.

nōv'a *n.* (pl. *-vae*). New star or nebula; properly, star which suddenly and greatly increases its light and energy and then sinks gradually to former state.

Nōval'ĭs (-vah-). Pseudonym of F. L. von HARDENBERG.

Nōv'a Scō'tia (-sh*a*). Province of SE. Canada, comprising peninsula projecting into Atlantic and the adjoining Cape Breton Island; capital, Halifax. **Nōv'a Scō'tian** *adj.* & *n.*

Nōv'a(ya) Zĕm'lya. Arctic territory comprising two large islands off NE. coast of European Russia. [Russ., = 'new land']

nŏv'el[1] *n.* 1. Fictitious prose narrative of sufficient length to fill one or more volumes; *the* ~, this type of literature. 2. (Rom. law) New decree supplementary to Codex, esp. one of those made by Justinian.

nŏv'el[2] *adj.* Of new kind or nature, strange, hitherto unknown.

nŏvelĕtte' *n.* 1. Short novel, story of moderate length, romantic novel without literary merit. 2. (mus.) Composition of free form with several themes.

nŏv'elĭst *n.* Novel-writer. **nŏvelĭs'tĭc** *adj.*

nŏv'elīze *v.t.* Convert into a novel. **nŏvelīzā'tion** *n.*

nŏv'elty *n.* New or unusual thing or occurrence; novel character *of* something.

Novĕm'ber. 9th month of old Roman year, 11th of modern year, with 30 days. [L *novem* nine]

novē'na *n.* (R.C. Ch.) Special prayers or services on 9 successive days.

nŏv'ĭce *n.* Person received in religious house on probation before taking the vows; new convert; inexperienced person, beginner, tyro.

novi'ciate, novi'tiate (-shĭ*a*t) *n.* Novice's probationary period, initiation, or apprenticeship; novice; quarters assigned to novices.

nōv'ocaine (-kān) *n.* Proprietary name of a synthetic drug used as a local anaesthetic.

now *adv.* 1. At the present time; by this time; immediately; in the immediate past; then, next, by that time; (*every*) ~ *and then,* ~ *and again*, from time to time, intermittently. 2. In sentences expressing command, request, reproof, etc., with purely temporal sense weakened or effaced. ~ *conj.* Consequently upon or simultaneously with the fact that. ~ *n.* This time, the present (chiefly after prepositions). **now'adays** (-z) *adv.* & *n.* (At) the present day.

Nowĕl': see NOEL.

nō'where (-(h)wār) *adv.* In, at, to, no place.

nŏ'xious (-ksh*us*) *adj.* Harmful, unwholesome; **nŏ'xiously** *adv.* **nŏ'xiousnėss** *n.*

noyade (nwahyahd') *n.* Execution by drowning, esp. as practised at Nantes during the Reign of Terror, 1794.

noyau (nwahyō') *n.* Liqueur of brandy flavoured with fruit-kernels.

nŏzz'le *n.* The projecting vent of anything, small spout, mouthpiece, end fitted to hose-pipe, etc.

n.p. *abbrev.* Net personalty; new paragraph.

N.P. *abbrev.* Notary Public.

nr *abbrev.* Near.

N.R. *abbrev.* North Riding (of Yorkshire).

N.R.A. *abbrev.* (U.S.) National Recovery Administration; National Rifle Association.

n.s. Not sufficient (funds to meet cheque).

N.S. *abbrev.* New style; Nova Scotia.

N.S.P.C.C. *abbrev.* National Society for the Prevention of Cruelty to Children.

N.S.W. *abbrev.* New South Wales.

N.T. *abbrev.* New Testament; Northern Territory (Australia).

N.T.P. *abbrev.* Normal temperature and pressure.

nū'ance (*or* nūahṅs') *n.* Delicate difference in or shade of meaning, feeling, opinion, colour, etc.

nŭb, nŭbb'le *ns.* Small knob or lump, esp. of coal. **nŭbb'ly** *adj.*

Nū'bĭa. Region of NE. Africa in Nile valley S. of Egypt; politically part of Sudan. **Nū'bĭan** *adj.* & *n.* (esp.) Native of Nubia; monosyllabic language of Nubians.

nū'bĭle *adj.* Marriageable (esp. of women). **nūbĭl'ĭty** *n.*

nū'chal (-kl) *adj.* Of the nape of the neck.

nū'cĭfōrm *adj.* Nut-shaped.

nūc'lėar *adj.* Having the character or position of a nucleus; pertaining to or constituting a nucleus; esp. in physics and chem., as ~ *charge, physics, structure,* etc.; ~ *bomb,* ATOMIC bomb; ~ *fission,* splitting of certain large atomic nuclei into several parts, during which process part of the nuclear mass disappears and is converted into a large quantity of energy; ~ *fuel,* any substance from which atomic energy can be readily obtained.

nūc'lėāse *n.* (chem.) Enzyme which induces hydrolysis of nucleic acid.

nūc'lėĭc *adj.* (chem.) ~ *acid,* an acid composed of the non-protein portion of nucleoproteins (the group of proteins which are constituents of the nuclei of cells).

nūclėŏl'us *n.* (pl. *-lī*). Spherical body observable in nucleus of living resting cells but disappearing during mitosis (ill. CELL).

nūc'lėŏn *n.* (physics) Proton or neutron of an atomic nucleus. **nūclėŏn'ĭcs** *n.* Branch of physics which treats of nucleons or the nucleus.

nūc'lėus *n.* (pl. *-lėī*). Central part or thing round which others are collected; kernel of aggregate or mass; central part of ovule, seed, plant-cell, animal cell, etc. (ill. CELL); group of nerve-cells in the central nervous system concerned with a particular function; (physics, chem.) the internal core of an atom, surrounded by electrons and containing the positive charge of the electrically neutral atom; (astron.) bright dense part forming head of comet.

nūde *adj.* Naked, bare, unclothed, undraped; ~ *contract,* (law) one lacking a consideration and therefore void unless under seal. ~ *n.* Nude figure, in painting, etc.; *the* ~, (representation of) the undraped human figure; condition of being naked. **nūd'ĭty** *n.*

nŭdge *v.t.* Push slightly with elbow to draw attention privately; draw attention of. ~ *n.* Such a push.

nūd'ĭst *n.* One who advocates or practises going unclothed. ~ *adj.* Of nudists. **nūd'ĭsm** *n.*

Nŭff'ield College. A college of the University of Oxford, founded 1937 by William Morris, 1st Viscount Nuffield, for research in social studies.

nūg'atory *adj.* Trifling, worthless, futile; inoperative, not valid.

nŭgg'ėt *n.* Rough lump of native gold or platinum.

nuis'ance (nūs-) *n.* Anything injurious or obnoxious to the community or a member of it for which legal remedy may be had; obnoxious person, offensive object, annoying action; anything disagreeable.

N.U.J. *abbrev.* National Union of Journalists.

nŭll *adj.* Not binding, invalid; without character or expression; (rare) non-existent, amounting to nothing.

nŭll'ah (-*a*) *n.* (Anglo-Ind.) Stream, watercourse, ravine. [Hind. *nālā* brook]

nŭll'ĭfȳ *v.t.* Cancel, neutralize. **nŭllĭfĭcā'tion** *n.*

nŭll'ipōre *n.* Form of marine vegetation having power of secreting lime like coral polyp.

nŭll'ĭty *n.* Being null, invalidity; act, document, etc., that is null; nothingness; a mere nothing.

Num. *abbrev.* Numbers (O.T.).

N.U.M. *abbrev.* National Union of Mineworkers.

Nŭm'a Pŏmpĭl'ĭus. Legendary 2nd king of Rome, successor to Romulus; revered by ancient Romans as founder of nearly all their religious institutions.

nŭmb (-m) *adj.* Deprived of feeling or power of motion. **nŭmb'ly** *adv.* **nŭmb'nėss** *n.* **nŭmb** *v.t.* Make numb; stupefy, paralyse.

nŭm'ber *n.* Count, sum, company, or aggregate, of persons, things, or abstract units; symbol or figure representing such aggregate; person or thing (esp. single issue of periodical) whose place in series is indicated by such figure; numerical reckoning (sing. or pl.) large (or *large, small,* etc.) collection or company (*of*); (pl.) numerical preponderance; (gram.) property in words of denoting that one, two, or more persons or things are spoken of, form of word expressing this; (pl.) groups of musical notes, metrical feet, verses; *Numbers,* 4th book in O.T., earlier part of which contains census of Israelites; ~ *one,* oneself; (nav. slang) first lieutenant; *golden* ~: see GOLDEN; ~ *10,* (used for) 10 Downing Street, Prime Minister's official residence (when he is also First Lord of the Treasury); *his* ~ *is up,* he is doomed or 'done for', his hour is come; *back* ~, earlier issue of magazine etc.; (fig.) anything out of date; *without* ~, innumerable. **nŭm'berlėss** *adj.* **nŭm'ber** *v.t.* Count, ascertain number of; include, regard as, *among, in,* or *with* some class; assign a number to, distinguish with a number; have lived, live (so many years); have, comprise (so many); equal, amount to; (pass.) be restricted or few in number.

nūm'erable *adj.* That can be numbered.

nūm'eral *adj.* & *n.* (Word, figure, group of figures) denoting a number; of number.

nūmerā'tion *n.* Method or process of numbering or computing; calculation; assigning of numbers; (arith.) expression in words of number written in figures.

nūm'erātor *n.* Number above line in vulgar fraction, showing how many of the parts indicated by the denominator are taken; person who numbers.

nūmĕ'rĭcal *adj.* Of, in, denoting, etc., number. **nūmĕ'rĭcally** *adv.*

nūm'erous *adj.* Comprising many units; coming from many individuals; (of verse or prose) rhythmic, harmonious. **nūm'erously** *adv.*

Nūmĭd'ĭa. Ancient name of a kingdom and Roman province of N. Africa, comprising approximately modern ALGERIA.

nūm'ĭnous *n.* *The* ~, the combined feeling of attraction and awe characteristic of man's sense of communion with God and religion. [L *numen* divine will, divinity]

nūmĭsmăt'ĭc (-z-) *adj.* Of coins or coinage. **nūmĭsmăt'ĭcally** *adv.* **nūmĭsmăt'ĭcs, nūmĭs'matĭst, nūmĭsmatŏl'ogy** *ns.*

nŭmm'ary, nŭmm'ūlary *adjs.* Of, in, coin.

nŭmm'ūlīte *n.* Disc-shaped fossil protozoan of order *Foraminifera* (many species, some very large).

nŭm'skŭll *n.* Dolt or his head.

nŭn *n.* Woman living in convent, usu. under vow of poverty, chastity, and obedience; votaress of pagan deity; ~*'s thread,* fine white sewing cotton; ~*'s veiling,* thin woollen dress-stuff. **nŭn'līke, nŭnn'ĭsh** *adjs.*

nŭn'-buoy (-boi) *n.* (naut.) Buoy consisting of two cones placed base to base.

nŭnc dĭmĭtt'ĭs *n.* First words of Song of Simeon (Luke ii. 29);

canticle beginning with these words ('Lord, now lettest thou thy servant depart'); hence, *sing one's* ~, be willing to depart from life etc.

nŭn'cĭo (-shĭō) *n.* Diplomatic representative of the pope at foreign court. **nŭn'ciature** (-sha-) *n.* (Tenure of) office of nuncio.

nŭn'cūpāte *v.t.* Declare (will etc.) orally, not in writing. **nŭncūpā'tion** *n.* **nŭn'cūpative** *adj.*

Nuñez, Pedro: see NONIUS.

nŭnnā'tion *n.* Addition of final *n* in declension of (orig. Arabic) nouns.

nŭnn'ery *n.* House, community, of nuns.

nŭp'tial (-shl) *adj.* Of marriage or wedding. ~ *n.* (usu. pl.) Wedding.

N.U.R. *abbrev.* National Union of Railwaymen.

Nūr'embĕrg (Ger. *Nürnberg*). City of Bavaria, Germany; ~ *laws*, series of laws, enacted under the Nazi régime, depriving Jews in Germany of certain civil rights and prohibiting intermarriage between Germans and Jews; ~ *trials*, trials of war criminals conducted at Nuremberg after war of 1939–45.

nûrse[1] *n.* 1. Woman employed to suckle and take charge of infant (usu. *wet-*~), or having charge of young children; *nurse'maid*, girl having charge of child. 2. (fig.) Something which nourishes or fosters some quality etc. 3. Person, usu. woman, charged with or trained for care of the sick or decrepit. 4. (entom.) Sexually imperfect bee, ant, etc., caring for the young brood, worker; (zool.) individual in asexual stage of metagenesis. ~ *v.* 1. Suckle (child), give suck, act as wet-nurse; act as nursemaid to, have charge of; foster, tend, promote development of; manage (plants, estate) with solicitude; cherish (grievance etc.); (pass.) be brought up. 2. Wait upon (sick person); try to cure (sickness); be sick-nurse; *nursing home*, house (freq. under private management) receiving surgical cases, invalids, etc. 3. Clasp or hold carefully or caressingly; sit close over (fire); keep in touch with (constituency) in order to obtain votes; (billiards) keep balls together for series of cannons.

nûrse[2] *n.* Kinds of dog-fish or shark.

nûrs'ery *n.* 1. Room assigned to children and their nurses; *day* ~, institution taking charge of young children during day. 2. Practice, institution, sphere, place, by or in which qualities or classes of people are fostered or bred. 3. Plot of ground in which young plants are reared for transplantation, esp. one in which trees or plants are reared for sale; fish-rearing pond; place where animal life is developed. 4. ~*-garden*, see sense 3; ~ *governess*, person combining duties of nurse and governess; *nurs'eryman*, owner of nursery-garden; ~ *rhyme*, verses often embodying traditional tales sung to, and by, young children; ~*-school*, school for young children, esp. for children between 2 and 5 years of age.

nûrs(e)'lĭng (-sl-) *n.* Infant, esp. in relation to its nurse.

nûr'ture *n.* Bringing up, training, fostering care; nourishment. ~ *v.t.* Nourish, rear, foster, train, educate.

N.U.S. *abbrev.* National Union of Students.

nŭt[1] *n.* 1. Fruit consisting of hard or leathery indehiscent shell enclosing edible kernel (ill. FRUIT); kernel of this; (slang) head; (*dead*) ~*s on*, (slang) devoted to, fond of; *off one's* ~, out of one's mind. 2. Small toothed projection on spindle engaging with cog-wheel, small spur-wheel; small block of metal etc. pierced with female screw for adjusting or tightening bolt (ill. SCREW); holder for tightening or relaxing horsehair of fiddle-bow. 3. (pl.) Small lumps of coal. 4. ~*-brown*, coloured like ripe hazel-nut; ~*-butter*, butter-substitute made from nut-oil; *nut'-cracker*, (usu. pl.) instrument for cracking nuts; prominent chin and nose with points near each other; brown corvine bird (*Nucifraga caryocatactes*) rare in Britain; ~*-gall*, gall found on dyer's oak, used for dyes; *nut'hatch*, small creeping bird (*Sitta europaea*) feeding on nuts; ~*-oil*, oil from nut-kernels; *nut'shell*, hard exterior covering of nut; something extremely small; *in a nutshell*, briefest possible way of expressing something; ~*-tree*, tree bearing nuts, esp. hazel. ~ *v.i.* Seek or gather nuts.

nŭt[2] *n.* (obs. slang) Showy young man of affected elegance.

·N.U.T. *abbrev.* National Union of Teachers.

nū'tāte *v.i.* Nod, droop. **nū'tant** *adj.*

nūtā'tion *n.* Nodding; (astron.) oscillation of earth's axis making motion of pole of equator round pole of ecliptic wavy; oscillation of spinning top in its precession around an axis.

nŭt'mĕg *n.* Hard aromatic spheroidal seed from fruit of evergreen E. Ind. tree (*Myristica fragrans*), used as spice and in medicine; ~*-apple*, fruit of nutmeg-tree, containing mace and nutmeg; *N~ State*, pop. name of Connecticut, U.S.

nū'tria *n.* Fur of the coypu, a S. Amer. aquatic rodent.

nū'trient *adj.* Serving as or providing nourishment.

nū'triment *n.* Nourishing food.

nūtri'tion (-shn) *n.* (Supplying or receiving of) nourishment, food. **nūtri'tional** (-shon-) *adj.* Of, relating to, nutrition.

nūtri'tious (-shus) *adj.* Nourishing, efficient as food. **nūtri'tiously** *adv.* **nūtri'tiousnĕss** *n.*

nū'tritive *adj.* Serving as food; concerned in nutrition.

nŭts *adj.* (slang) Crazy.

nŭtt'y *adj.* Abounding in nuts; tasting like nuts, of rich mellow flavour.

nŭx vŏm'ĭca *n.* Seed of pulpy fruit of E. Ind. tree (*Strychnos nux-vomica*), yielding the poison strychnine.

nŭzz'le *v.* Nose; burrow, press, rub, sniff, with the nose; press nose or press (nose) *into*, *against*; nestle, lie snug.

N.W., NW *abbrevs.* North-west(ern).

NW. by N., NW by N *abbrevs.* North-west by North.

NW. by W., NW by W *abbrevs.* North-west by West.

N.W. Prov. *abbrev.* North-west Provinces (India).

N.W.T. *abbrev.* North-west Territories (Canada).

nyala: see INYALA.

Nyăn'za. In Central Africa, any large lake (esp. in place-names).

Nyăs'a. Third-largest of great Central African lakes, in SE. Central Africa. **Nyăs'alănd.** Former British protectorate; became independent State of Malawi, 1964.

nyctalōp'ia *n.* 1. Night-blindness, inability to see in a dim light. 2. (rare) Inability to see clearly except at night.

N.Y.(C.) *abbrev.* New York (City).

nȳl'ŏn *n.* Any of a group of long-chain synthetic polymeric amines of which the structural units or molecules can be oriented in one direction, and which are thus capable of being formed into filaments of great tensile strength; a textile fibre of this structure and character; (pl.) garments, esp. women's stockings, made of this.

nȳmph *n.* 1. One of class of mythological semi-divine maidens inhabiting sea, rivers, fountains, woods, or trees; (poet.) young and beautiful woman. 2. (zool.) Immature insect which from time of hatching has a general resemblance to the imago (ill. DRAGON-fly). 3. Edible frog.

nȳm'pha *n.* (pl. -ae). 1. Pupa. 2. (pl.) Labia minora of the vulva.

nȳmphae'a *n.* (Genus of aquatic plants including) common white water-lily.

nȳm'pholĕpsy *n.* Ecstasy or frenzy caused by desire of the unattainable. **nȳm'pholĕpt** *n.* Person inspired by violent enthusiasm, esp. for an ideal. **nȳmpholĕp'tic** *adj.*

nȳmphomān'ia *n.* (path.) Morbid and uncontrollable sexual desire in women. **nȳmphomān'iăc** *n.*

nȳstăg'mus *n.* Rapid involuntary oscillation of eyeball; *miner's* ~, form of this affecting persons who work in cramped quarters and poor light. **nȳstăg'mic** *adj.*

N.Z. *abbrev.* New Zealand.

O

O[1], **o** (ō). 15th letter of modern English and 14th of ancient Roman alphabet, representing a variety of mid-back-round vowels, and corresponding in form to ancient Greek O, derived from Phoenician and ancient Semitic ◯, ◇, ▽ (Heb. ע), which, however, represent not a vowel but a 'glottal stop'. **O** *n.* O-shaped mark, circle; a cipher or nought.

O[2], **oh** *int.* prefixed to vocative name or expressing various emotions.

o' *prep.* short for *of*, *on*, still in some phrases as (= *of*) *o'clock*, *will-o'-the-wisp*, *man-o'-war*, (= *on*) *cannot sleep o' nights*.

O. *abbrev.* Observer; Ohio.

oaf *n.* (pl. *-s*, *oaves*). Misbegotten, deformed, or idiot child; awkward lout. **oaf'ish** *adj.* [ON. *álfr* elf]

oak *n.* 1. Kinds of common forest tree, esp. *Quercus robur* (*common* ~) and *Q. petraea* (*durmast* ~), with hard timber, bearing fruit called acorn; any species of *Quercus*, including the *holm* ~, *turkey* ~, and *white* ~; various trees or plants in some way resembling oak; *poison* ~, species of sumach, esp. *Rhus toxicodendron*; (Austral.) various trees of genus *Casuarina*. 2. Wood of the oak; this as material for ships; (univ.) outer door of set of rooms. 3. Leaves of oak. 4. *The Oaks*, (f. name of estate near Epsom) race for 3-year-old fillies, founded 1779 and run at Epsom on Friday after the Derby; *~-apple*, globular oak-gall; *~-apple day*, anniversary of restoration of Charles II (29th May), when oak-apples or oak-leaves are worn in memory of his hiding in an oak-tree at Boscobel on 6th Sept. 1651; *~-fern*, smooth 3-branched polypody, *Thelypteris dryopteris*; *~-gall*, excrescence on various species of oak produced by punctures of gall-flies (ill. GALL); a gall-nut used in making ink; *~-tree*, oak. **oak'en** *adj.* Made of oak, chiefly poet.).

oak'um *n.* Loose fibre got by untwisting and picking old hemp ropes and used esp. in caulking; *pick* ~, make this, esp. as formerly common task of convicts and paupers.

oar (ōr) *n.* Long stout wooden shaft widened and flattened at one end into a blade, used to propel (row) a boat by leverage against a rowlock which serves as a fulcrum (ill. BOAT); esp. oar pulled by one rower with both hands, as dist. from a scull (one hand) and a sweep (two rowers); oarsman; *rest on one's ~s*, lean on handles of oars, raising blades out of water; (fig.) suspend one's efforts, take things easy; *put in one's* ~, interfere; *oar'lock*, rowlock; *oars'man*, rower; *oars'manship*. ~ *v.* Row.

O.A.S. *abbrev.* On active service.

ōā'sĭs *n.* (pl. *ōāsēs* pr. -z). Depression in desert where cultivation is possible owing to presence of water (also fig.).

oast *n.* Hop-drying kiln; *~-house*, building containing this.

oat *n.* (pl.) (Grain yielded by) hardy cereal, *Avena sativa*, grown in cool climates as food for man and horses; (sing., rare exc. in comb.) oat-plant, variety of oats; (sing., poet.) oat-stem used as musical pipe by shepherds etc., pastoral or bucolic poetry; *wild* ~, tall grass (*Avena fatua*) resembling oats, a frequent weed in cornfields; *sow one's wild ~s*, indulge in youthful follies or excesses (usu. implying subsequent reform); *oat'-cake*, thin unleavened cake of oatmeal; *oat'meal*, meal made from oats; oatmeal porridge. **oat'en** *adj.* Made of oats (chiefly poet.).

Oates (ōts), Titus (1649–1705). The fabricator of the POPISH Plot, 1678; was condemned and imprisoned for perjury, but subsequently released and granted a pension.

oath *n.* (pl. pr. ōdhz). 1. Solemn appeal to God (or to something sacred), in witness of truth of statement or binding character of promise. 2. Name of God, or of something sacred, used as expletive to give emphasis or express anger etc.; piece of profanity in speech.

Ob (ŏb), **Obi** (ŏb'ĭ). River of Asiatic Russia, flowing northwards into *Gulf of Ob*, an arm of the Arctic Ocean.

ob-, (before *c*) **oc-**, (before *f*) **of-**, (before *p*) **op-** *prefixes*, occurring chiefly in words already compounded in L with senses: 1. Exposure, openness. 2. Meeting. 3. Opposition or hostility. 4. Hindrance, blocking, veiling. 5. Finality or completeness. 6. In modern scientific words, inversely, in direction or manner contrary to the usual.

ob. *abbrev.* *Obiit* (= died).

Obad. *abbrev.* Obadiah.

Obadī'ah. (O.T.) One of the 'minor prophets', author of the short O.T. book bearing his name.

ŏbblĭga'tō (-ah-) *adj.* & *n.* (mus.) (Part, accompaniment) forming integral part of composition; often wrongly used for *ad libitum*, of which it is the opposite.

obdt. *abbrev.* Obedient.

ŏb'dūrate *adj.* Hardened, impenitent, stubborn. **ŏb'dūrately** *adv.* **ŏb'dūracy** *n.*

O.B.E. *abbrev.* Officer of the (Order of the) British Empire.

ōb'ėah, ōb'ĭ *ns.* Sorcery or witch-doctoring associated with the snake-god Obi whose worship was introduced by W. African negro slaves into W. Indies and U.S.

obēd'ience *n.* 1. Obeying as act, practice, or quality; submission to another's rule; compliance with law or command. 2. (eccles., esp. R.C.) (Sphere of) authority; district or body of persons subject to some rule.

obēd'ient *adj.* Submissive to, complying with, superior's will; dutiful. **obēd'iėntly** *adv.*

obēdiĕn'tiary (-sha-) *n.* Holder of any office under superior in monastery or convent.

obei'sance (-bā-) *n.* Gesture, esp. bow or curtsy, expressing submission, respect, or salutation.

ŏb'ėlĭsk *n.* 1. Tapering shaft of stone, square or rectangular in section with pyramidal apex; mountain, tree, etc., of similar shape. 2. (also *obelus*) mark (—, ÷), used in ancient MSS. to indicate that word or passage is spurious etc.; mark (†) of reference to note in margin etc.; *double* ~, ‡.

ŏb'ėlīze *v.t.* Mark with obelisk as spurious etc.

Oberămm'ergau (ō-, -gow). Village in Upper Bavaria, Germany, where the inhabitants vowed in 1633 that they would perform a Passion Play as an act of thanksgiving for deliverance from the plague; since 1680 the play has been performed every 10 years exc. for 1810, 1920, and 1940.

Ob'eron (ō-). In W. European tradition, king of the fairies.

obēse' (-s) *adj.* Corpulent. **obēs'ity** *n.*

obey' (-ā) *v.* Perform bidding of, be obedient (to); execute (command).

ŏb'fuscāte *v.t.* Darken, obscure; stupefy, bewilder. **ŏbfuscā'tion** *n.*

ō'bĭ[1] *n.* Japanese woman's bright-coloured sash.

obi[2]: see OBEAH.

Obi[3]: see OB.

ŏb'iit. Died (with date of death).

ŏb'it *n.* (archaic) Yearly (or other) memorial service, esp. to founder or benefactor.

ŏb'iter *adv.* By the way, in passing; ~ *dic'tum*, *dicta*, judge's expression(s) of opinion on matters of law, given in course of argument or judgment but not essential to decision and therefore without binding authority; incidental remark.

obit'ūary *n.* Notice of death, esp. in newspaper, brief biography of deceased person. ~ *adj.* Recording a death; concerning deceased person. **obit'uarist** *n.*

ŏb'jĕct[1] *n.* 1. Thing placed before eyes or presented to sense; material thing; thing observed with optical instrument or represented in picture. 2. Person or thing of pitiable or ridiculous aspect. 3. Person or thing to which action or feeling is directed, subject *of* or *for*; thing aimed at, end, purpose. 4. Thing thought of or apprehended as correlative to the thinking mind or subject; external thing; *the* non-ego. 5. (gram.) Substantive word, phrase, or clause governed by active transitive verb or by preposition; *direct, indirect*, ~, that primarily, secondarily, affected by action. 6. *no* ~, not to be taken into account, forming no obstacle; ~*-ball*, that at which player aims his ball in billiards etc.; ~*-glass, -lens*, lens in telescope etc. nearest the object; ~*-lesson*, instruction about material object that is present for inspection; (fig.) striking practical application of some principle.

objĕct'[2] *v.* Bring forward or state in opposition, urge as objection; state objection; express or feel disapproval. **objĕc'tor** *n.*

objĕc'tifȳ *v.t.* Present as object of sense; make objective; express in concrete form, embody.

objĕc'tion *n.* Objecting, thing objected; adverse reason or statement; expression or feeling of disapproval or dislike. **objĕc'tionable** (-shon-) *adj.* Open to objection; undesirable, unpleasant, offensive. **objĕc'tionably** *adv.*

objĕc'tive *adj.* 1. Belonging to what is presented to consciousness; that is the object of perception or thought, as dist. from perceiving or thinking subject; external to the mind, real. 2. Dealing with outward things and not with thoughts or feelings; exhibiting actual facts uncoloured by exhibitor's feelings or opinions. 3. (gram.) Constructed as, appropriate to, the object. 4. ~ *point*, point aimed at; (orig. mil.) point towards which advance of troops is directed. **objĕc'tively** *adv.* **objĕc'tiveness, ŏbjectiv'ity** *ns.* **objĕc'tive** *n.* 1. Object-glass (ill. MICROSCOPE). 2. (gram.) Objective case. 3. Object or purpose aimed at in an action; (mil.) position to the attainment or capture of which an operation is directed, objective point.

objĕc'tivism *n.* Tendency to lay stress on the objective; doctrine that knowledge of non-ego is prior in sequence and importance to that of ego.

ŏb'jurgāte *v.t.* Chide, scold. **ŏbjurgā'tion** *n.* **ŏb'jurgātory** *adj.*

ŏb'lāte[1] *n.* Person dedicated to monastic or religious life or work.

ŏb'lāte[2] (*or* oblăt') *adj.* (geom., of spheroid) Flattened at the poles (ill. CONE).

oblā'tion *n.* (Presenting of bread and wine to God in) Eucharist; thing offered to God, sacrifice, victim; donation for pious uses. **oblā'tional** (-shon-), **ŏb'latory** *adjs.*

ŏb'lĭgāte *v.t.* Bind (person, esp. legally) *to* do; (U.S.) oblige.

ŏblĭgā'tion *n.* 1. Binding agreement, esp. one enforceable under legal penalty, written contract, or bond; constraining power of a law, precept, duty, contract, etc.; one's bounden duty, a duty, burdensome task; *of* ~, obligatory. 2. (Indebtedness for) service or benefit.

ŏb'lĭgatory (*or* oblĭg'-) *adj.* Legally or morally binding; imperative, not merely permissive; constituting an obligation.

oblīge' *v.t.* Bind by oath, promise, contract, etc., *to* (archaic, legal); be binding on. 2. Make indebted by conferring favour, gratify *by, with*; (colloq.) make contribution to entertainment (*with*); (pass.) be bound (*to*) by gratitude. 3. Constrain, compel, *to* do.

ŏblĭgee' *n.* (law) Person to whom another is bound by contract or to whom bond is given.

oblī'ging *adj.* Courteous, accommodating, ready to do kindness, complaisant. **oblī'gingly** *adv.* **oblī'gingnėss** *n.*

ŏb'lĭgor *n.* (law) One who binds himself to another or gives bond.

oblique' (-ēk) adj. 1. Slanting; declining from vertical or horizontal; diverging from straight line or course; (geom.) (of line etc.) inclined at other than right angle, (of angle) acute or obtuse, (of cone etc.) with axis not perpendicular to plane of base; (anat.) neither parallel nor perpendicular to body's or limb's long axis; (bot., of leaf) with unequal sides. 2. Not going straight to the point, roundabout, indirect. 3. (gram.) ~ *case*, any case other than nominative or vocative (on occas. the accusative); ~ *narration, oration, speech*, indirect speech. **oblique'ly** (-ēklĭ) *adv.* **oblĭq'uĭtȳ** *n.*

oblĭt'erāte *v.t.* Blot out, efface, erase, destroy. **oblĭterā'tion** *n.*

oblĭv'ion *n.* Having or being forgotten; disregard, unregarded state.

oblĭv'ious *adj.* Forgetful, unmindful, (*of*); (poet.) of, inducing, oblivion. **oblĭv'iously** *adv.* **oblĭv'iousnėss** *n.*

ŏb'lŏng *adj.* Elongated in one direction (usu. as deviation from exact square or circular form); (geom.) rectangular with adjacent sides unequal. ~*n.* Oblong figure or object.

ŏb'loquy (-kwĭ) *n.* Abuse, detraction; being generally ill spoken of.

obnŏxious (-k'sh*us*) *adj.* 1. (now rare) Exposed, liable, *to* harm or evil. 2. Offensive, objectionable, disliked. **obnŏx'iously** *adv.* **obnŏx'iousnėss** *n.*

ō'boe (-ō) *n.* Musical instrument of wood-wind family (ill. WOOD), played vertically, with a double reed, having a range of nearly 3 octaves upwards from the B flat below middle C, and a plaintive incisive tone; organ reed-stop imitating this. **ō'bōist** *n.*

ŏb'ol *n.* Ancient Greek silver (later, bronze) coin; ⅙ of drachma (about 1½*d.*).

obscēne' *adj.* Repulsive, filthy, loathsome (archaic); indecent, lewd. **obscēne'ly** *adv.* **obscē'nĭty** *n.*

obscūr'ant *n.* Opponent of inquiry, enlightenment, and reform. **obscūr'antism** *n.* **obscūr'antist** *n.* & *adj.*

obscūre' *adj.* Dark, dim; (of colour) dingy, dull, indefinite; indistinct, not clear; hidden, remote from observation; unnoticed; unknown to fame, humble; unexplained, doubtful; not perspicuous or clearly expressed. **obscūre'ly** *adv.* **obscūr'ĭty** *n.* **obscūre'** *v.t.* Make obscure, dark, indistinct, or unintelligible; dim glory of, outshine; conceal from sight. **ŏbscūrā'tion** *n.*

ŏbsėcrā'tion *n.* Earnest entreaty.

ŏb'sėquies (-kwĭz) *n.pl.* Funeral rites, funeral. **obsēq'uĭal** *adj.*

obsēq'uĭous *adj.* Servile, fawning. **obsēq'uĭously** *adv.* **obsēq'uĭousnėss** *n.*

obsėrv'ance (-z-) *n.* Keeping or performance of law, duty, ritual, etc.; act of religious or ceremonial character, customary rite; the rule of a religious order. **obsėrv'ancy** *n.*

obsėrv'ant (-z-) *adj.* 1. Attentive in observance. 2. Acute or diligent in taking notice. ~ *n.* Member of branch of Franciscan order observing the strict rule. **obsėrv'antly** *adv.*

ŏbservā'tion (-z-) *n.* 1. Noticing or being noticed; perception, faculty of taking notice; (mil.) watching of fortress or hostile position or movements. 2. Observing scientifically, accurate watching and noting of phenomena as they occur in nature; taking of altitude of sun or other heavenly body to find latitude or longitude; reading or value of any observed quantity, esp. when noted down. 3. Remark, statement, esp. one of the nature of comment. **ŏbservā'tional** (-shon-) *adj.* **ŏbservā'tionally** *adv.*

obsėrv'atory (-z-) *n.* Building etc. whence natural, esp. astronomical, phenomena may be observed.

obsėrve' (-z-) *v.* 1. Keep, follow, adhere to, perform duly. 2. Perceive, watch, mark, take notice of, become conscious of; examine and note (phenomena) without aid of experiment. 3. Say, esp. by way of comment; make remark(s) *on*. **obsėrv'er** *n.* (esp.) Interested spectator; person carried in aeroplane to note enemy's position etc.; person trained to watch and identify aircraft.

obsĕss' *v.t.* (Of evil spirit,

delusion, fixed idea, etc.) haunt, preoccupy, fill mind of. **obsĕ'ssion** (-shn) *n.* **obsĕss'ĭve, obsĕ'ssional** (-sho-) *adjs.*

obsĭd'ĭan *n.* Dark vitreous volcanic rock with appearance like bottle-glass, used by primitive societies for knives etc. [f. personal name *Obsius*]

ŏbsolĕs'cent *adj.* Becoming obsolete; gradually disappearing. **ŏbsolĕs'cence** *n.*

ŏb'solēte *adj.* Disused, discarded, antiquated. **ŏb'solēteness** *n.*

ob.s.p. *abbrev.* *Obiit sine prole* (= died without issue).

ŏb'stacle *n.* Hindrance, impediment; ~ *race*, one in which artificial or natural obstacles have to be passed.

obstĕt'rĭc(al) *adjs.* Of midwifery; of childbirth and its antecedents and sequels, as branch of medicine and surgery. **obstĕt'rĭcs, ŏbstetrĭ'cian** (-shn) *ns.*

ŏb'stĭnate *adj.* Stubborn, inflexible, self-willed, refractory. **ŏb'stĭnately** *adv.* **ŏb'stĭnacy** *n.*

obstrĕp'erous *adj.* Noisy, vociferous; turbulent, unruly, noisily resisting control. **obstrĕp'erously** *adv.* **obstrĕp'erousness** *n.*

obstrŭct' *v.* Block up, fill with impediments, make impassable or difficult of passage; prevent or retard progress of, impede; practise (esp. Parliamentary) obstruction. **obstrŭc'tion** *n.* Blocking or being blocked, making or becoming more or less impassable; hindering, esp. of Parliamentary business by talking against time; obstacle. **obstrŭc'tionĭsm, obstrŭc'tionĭst** (-shon-) *ns.*

obstrŭc'tĭve *adj.* Causing, intended to produce, obstruction. **obstrŭc'tĭvely** *adv.* **obstrŭc'tĭveness** *n.*

obtain' *v.* 1. Acquire, secure, have granted one, get. 2. Be prevalent, established, or in vogue. **obtain'able** *adj.*

obtĕc'tėd *adj.* (entom.) (Of pupa) having limbs etc. indistinctly discernible through outer covering.

obtĕst' *v.* (archaic) Adjure, supplicate, call to witness; protest. **ŏbtĕstā'tion** *n.*

obtrude' (-ōōd) *v.t.* Thrust forward (*on, upon*) importunately. **obtru'sion** (-ōōzhn) *n.* **obtru'sĭve** *adj.* **obtrus'ĭvely** *adv.* **obtrus'ĭveness** *n.*

obtŭnd' *v.t.* (med.) Blunt, deaden (sense, faculty).

ŏb'tūrāte *v.t.* Stop up, close, seal. **ŏbtūrā'tion** *n.*

obtūse' (-s) *adj.* 1. Of blunt form, not sharp or pointed; (geom., of plane angle) greater than right angle (ill. ANGLE). 2. Dull, not acute; stupid, slow of perception. **obtūse'ly** (-sl-) *adv.* **obtūse'ness** *n.*

ŏb'vêrse *adj.* 1. Narrower at base or point of attachment than at apex. 2. Answering as counterpart to something else. **ŏb'vêrsely** *adv.* **ŏb'vêrse** *n.* Side of coin or medal bearing head or principal design (opp. to REVERSE; ill. COIN); face of anything meant to be presented, front; counterpart of a fact or truth.

obvêrt' *v.t.* (logic) Infer another proposition with contradictory predicate by changing quality of (proposition). **obvêr'sion** (-shn) *n.*

ŏb'vĭāte *v.t.* Clear away, get rid of, get round, neutralize (danger, inconvenience, etc.).

ŏb'vĭous *adj.* Open to eye or mind, clearly perceptible, palpable, indubitable. **ŏb'vĭously** *adv.* **ŏb'vĭousness** *n.*

O.C. *abbrev.* Officer Commanding.

ŏcari'na (-ē-) *n.* Egg-shaped terra-cotta or metal musical wind instrument of small compass with whistle-like mouthpiece and finger-holes. [It. *oca* goose]

Occ'am (ŏ-), William of (*c* 1300–*c* 1349). English scholastic philosopher; founded a speculative sect reviving the doctrines of Nominalism; ~*'s razor*, the principle that 'entities must not be unnecessarily multiplied'.

occā'sion (-zhn) *n.* Juncture suitable for doing something, opportunity; reason, ground, justification, need; subsidiary, incidental, or immediate cause; (particular time marked by) special occurrence; (pl.) affairs, business. ~ *v.t.* Be the occasion or cause of; bring about, esp. incidentally; cause.

occā'sional (-zhon-) *adj.* Arising out of, made or meant for, acting on, special occasion(s); happening irregularly as occasion presents itself; coming now and then, not regular or frequent. **occā'sionally** *adv.*

Occĭdent (ŏk's-) *n.* (chiefly poet. and rhet.) The West; western Europe; Europe; Europe and America; America; European as opp. to Oriental civilization. **ŏccĭdĕn'tal** *adj.* **ŏccĭdĕn'tally** *adv.* **ŏccĭden'talĭsm, ŏccĭdĕn'talist** *ns.*

occĭput (ŏk's-) *n.* Back of head. **occĭp'ĭtal** *adj.*: ~ *bone*, see ill. HEAD; ~ *lobe*: see ill. BRAIN.

occlude' (-ōōd) *v.t.* Stop up, close, obstruct; (chem.) absorb and retain (gases); *occluded front*, (meteor.) warm front forced upwards by cold front, when the cold air overtakes the warm and flows in underneath it (ill. WEATHER).

occlu'sion (-ōōzhn) *n.* Act or process of occluding; (phonet.) momentary closure of vocal passage as in formation of stop consonants; (chem.) absorption of gases by certain substances.

occlus'ĭve (-ōōs-) *adj.* Tending to occlude; (phonet., of a consonant) produced with occlusion.

occŭlt'[1] *adj.* Kept secret, esoteric; recondite, mysterious, beyond the range of ordinary knowledge; involving the supernatural, mystical, magical; *the* ~, the supernatural. **occŭlt'ly** *adv.* **occŭlt'ness** *n.*

occŭlt'[2] *v.* Conceal, cut off from view by passing in front (usu. astron.); *occulting light*, in lighthouse etc., one that is cut off at regular intervals.

ŏccultā'tion *n.* (astron.) Eclipse of one heavenly body by another, usu. larger, passing between it and the earth.

occŭlt'ĭsm *n.* Theory of, belief in, supernatural, occult forces and powers.

ŏcc'ūpant *n.* Person holding property, esp. land, in actual possession; one who occupies, resides in, or is in, a place; one who establishes title to ownerless thing by taking possession. **ŏcc'ūpancy** *n.*

ŏccūpā'tion *n.* 1. Occupying or being occupied; taking or holding possession, esp. of country or district by military force; tenure, occupancy; ~ *bridge, road*, private bridge, road, for occupier of land. 2. What occupies one, means of filling one's time; temporary or regular employment, business, calling, pursuit. **ŏccūpā'tional** (-shon-) *adj.* (esp. of disease etc.) Incidental to, caused by, one's occupation; ~ *therapy*, treatment of disease by means of purposeful occupation, as handicrafts, cultural activities, etc.

ŏcc'ūpȳ *v.t.* Take possession of (country etc.) by military force or settlement; hold (office); reside in, tenant; take up or fill (space, time); be in (place, position); busy, keep engaged. **ŏcc'ūpier** *n.* Person in (esp. temporary or subordinate) possession, esp. of land or house; holder, occupant.

occûr' *v.i.* Be met with, be found, exist, in some place or conditions; come into one's mind; take place, befall, happen.

occŭ'rrence *n.* Happening; incident, event.

ocean (ōsh'n) *n.* Great body of water surrounding the land of the globe; one of the main areas into which this is geographically divided (usu. reckoned as five, the *Atlantic, Pacific, Indian, Arctic, and Antarctic* (*Southern*) *Oceans*); *the* sea; immense expanse or quantity of anything.

Oceān'ĭa (ōshĭ-, ōsĭ-). The islands of the Pacific Ocean and adjacent seas, sometimes including Australasia and Malaysia. **Oceān'ĭan** *adj.* & *n.*

oceăn'ĭc (ōshĭ-, ōsĭ-) *adj.* Of the ocean; (*O*~) of Oceania.

Ocē'anĭd (ō-) *n.* (Gk myth.) One of the ocean nymphs, daughters of Oceanus and Tethys.

oceanŏg'raphy (ōsha-) *n.* Branch of science concerned with the study of the ocean, the composition and characteristics of the water, plant, and animal life, and the ocean floor. **oceanŏg'rapher** *n.*

Ocē'anus (ō-). (Gk myth.) Son of Uranus and Ge, and god of the 'great primeval water'.

ocĕll'us *n.* (pl. *-lī*). 1. One of the simple as dist. from the compound eyes of insects and some other arthropods etc. (ill. INSECT). 2. One facet of a compound eye. 3. Eye-like spot in insects, fishes, etc. **ŏ'cĕllate, -ātĕd** *adjs.*

ŏ'cĕlot *n.* One of the larger cats (*Felis pardalis*) of Central and S. America, with grey body marked with elongated fawn spots edged with black, and white or whitish underparts marked with black. [Fr., abbrev. by Buffon f. Mex. *tlal*(*ocelotl* jaguar) of the field, and applied to a different animal]

och (ŏχ) *int.* (In Ireland and Scotland) oh!, ah!

ŏchlŏc'racy (-kl-) *n.* Mob-rule. **ŏch'locrăt** *n.* **ŏchlocrăt'ic** *adj.*

ochre (ōk'*er*) *n.* Mineral or class of minerals consisting of hydrated ferric oxide mixed with varying proportions of clay, used as pigment, ranging in colour from light yellow to deep orange or brown. **ōch'rĕous, ōch'rous** *adjs.*

o'clock: see CLOCK.

O'Cŏnn'ell, Daniel (1775–1847). 'The Liberator', Irish Catholic political leader; advocated Catholic emancipation and repeal of the union of Gt Britain and Ireland.

oct. *abbrev.* Octavo.

Oct. *abbrev.* October.

oct(a)-, octo- *prefixes.* Eight.

ŏct'achŏrd (-k-) *n.* (mus.) Series of 8 notes, e.g. the diatonic scale; any 8-stringed musical instrument.

ŏc'tad *n.* Group of 8.

ŏc'tagon *n.* Plane figure with 8 angles and sides; object or building of such section. ~ *adj.* Octagonal. **ŏctăg'onal** *adj.* **ŏctăg'onally** *adv.*

ŏctahĕd'ron *n.* Solid figure contained by 8 plane faces, and usu. by 8 triangles; body, esp. crystal, of regular octahedral form; *regular* ~, figure contained by 8 equal and equilateral triangles (ill. SOLID). **ŏctahĕd'ral** *adj.*

ŏc'tāne *n.* (chem.) A hydrocarbon of the paraffin series (C_8H_{18}); ~ *number*, a measure of the anti-knock properties of a petrol; *high* ~, one having good anti-knock properties.

ŏc'tant *n.* Eighth part of circle; either arc of $\frac{1}{8}$ of circumference or $\frac{1}{8}$ of area contained between two radii at angle of 45°; one of 8 parts into which solid figure or body is divided by three planes intersecting (usu. at right angles) at central point; (astron.) point in planet's apparent course 45° from another planet, esp. point at which moon is 45° from conjunction or opposition with sun; alternative name for QUADRANT.

ŏc'tastȳle *adj.* & *n.* (Portico or building) with 8 columns at end or in front (ill. TEMPLE).

ŏc'tave *n.* 1. (eccles.) Eighth day after a festival (both days being counted); period of 8 days beginning with a festival. 2. Group or stanza of 8 lines, octet. 3. (mus.) Note 8 diatonic degrees above or below given note (both notes being counted), and produced by vibrations of twice or half the rate (ill. INTERVAL); interval between any note and its octave; series of notes etc. extending through this interval; two notes an octave apart played or sung together; organ-stop sounding an octave higher than ordinary pitch; ~ *coupler*, device connecting organ-keys an octave apart. 4. Eighth position in fencing, that of parrying or attacking in low outside line with sword-hand in supination (ill. FENCE).

Octāv'ia (ŏ-) (d. 11 B.C.). Roman lady, sister of Octavian (Augustus) and wife of Mark Antony.

Octāv'ian (ŏ-) (63 B.C.–A.D. 14). Gaius Octavius, named Gaius Julius Caesar Octavianus after his adoption by Caesar: = AUGUSTUS.

ŏctāv'ō *n.* (abbrev. 8vo, oct.). Book or page given by folding sheets three times or into 8 leaves; size of this, varying according to size of sheet (crown, demy, etc.).

ŏctĕnn'ial *adj.* Lasting, recurring every, 8 years.

ŏctĕt(te)' *n.* (Composition for) 8 singers or players; group of 8 lines, esp. the first 8 of a sonnet.

ŏctĭll'ion (-lyon) *n.* One million raised to the 8th power (1 followed by 48 ciphers); (U.S.) one thousand raised to the 9th power (1 followed by 27 ciphers).

octo- *prefix.* Eight.

Octōb'er (ŏ-). 1. Tenth (orig. 8th) month of the year; ~ *Revolution*, the Russian revolution of the 25th Oct. 1917 (7th Nov. by Western calendar) when the Bolsheviks under Lenin and Trotsky displaced the provisional government of Kerensky and established the soviets in power. 2. (archaic) Ale brewed in October.

Octōb'rist (ŏ-) *n.* Member of Russian moderate liberal political party, whose principles of constitutional government were proclaimed in the imperial Manifesto of Oct. 1905.

ŏctodĕ'cimō *n.* (abbrev. 18mo). (Size of) book or page given by folding sheets into 18 leaves.

ŏctogĕnār'ian *adj.* & *n.* (Person) aged 80 years or more but less than 90.

ŏc'tonary *adj.* Of 8; consisting of 8; proceeding by eights. ~ *n.* Group of 8; 8-line stanza.

ŏc'topus *n.* A cephalopod mollusc with 8 'arms', provided with suckers, surrounding mouth.

ŏctoroōn' *n.* Offspring of quadroon and white, person of one-eighth negro blood.

ŏctosȳllăb'ic *adj.* & *n.* Eight-syllable (verse). **ŏctosȳll'able** *adj.* & *n.* (Verse, word) of 8 syllables.

ŏc'troi (-rwah) *n.* Duty levied in some continental countries on goods entering town; place where, officials by whom, it is levied.

O.C.T.U., Oc'tū. *abbrevs.* Officer Cadets Training Unit.

ŏc'tūple *adj.* Eightfold. ~ *n.* Product (*of*) after multiplication by 8. ~ *v.t.* Multiply by 8.

ŏc'ūlar *adj.* Of, for, by, with, etc., the eye(s) or sight, visual. ~ *n.* Eye-piece of optical instrument.

ŏc'ūlarĭst *n.* Maker of artificial eyes.

ŏc'ūlĭst *n.* Medical practitioner who specializes in diseases of the eye.

ōd'alĭsque (-k) *n.* Eastern female slave or concubine, esp. in Turkish sultan's seraglio. [Fr., f. Turk. *ōdaliq*]

ŏdd *adj.* 1. Remaining over after division or distribution into pairs; (of number) not divisible by 2; numbered or known by such a number; (appended to number, sum, weight, etc.) with something over of lower denomination etc.; by which round number, given sum, etc., is exceeded; ~ *trick*, (whist) single trick by which one side wins when the score is 7–6. 2. Additional, casual, beside the reckoning, unconnected, unoccupied, incalculable; forming part of incomplete pair or set. 3. Extraordinary, strange, queer, remarkable, eccentric. 4. *Odd'fellow*, member of friendly society of Oddfellows (founded prob. in early part of 18th c.) with rites imitative of freemasonry; ~ *job*, casual disconnected piece of work. **ŏdd'ly** *adv.* **ŏdd'ness** *n.* **ŏdd** *n.* (golf) Handicap given by deduction of one stroke from the score at each hole; stroke by which one player is above his opponent at a particular hole.

ŏdd'ĭty *n.* Strangeness; peculiar trait; queer person; fantastic object, strange event.

ŏdd'ments *n.pl.* Odds and ends.

ŏdds *n.pl.* (freq. treated as sing.). Inequalities; difference; variance, strife; balance of advantage; equalizing allowance to weaken competitor; ratio between amounts staked by parties to bet, advantage conceded by one of the parties in proportion to assumed chances in his favour; chances or balance of probability in favour of some result; ~ *and ends*, remnants, stray articles.

ōde *n.* 1. (orig.) Poem meant to be sung; *choral* ~, song of chorus in Greek play etc. 2. Rhymed (or, rarely, unrhymed) lyric, often in form of address, usu. of exalted style and enthusiastic tone, often in varied or irregular metre, and usu. between 50 and 200 lines in length.

Od'er (ō-). European river rising in Carpathians and flowing NW. to Baltic.

Odĕss'a (*o*-). Ukrainian city and seaport on NW. coast of Black Sea.

Od'ĭn (ō-). (Scand. myth.)

Supreme god and creator, god of victory and the dead; represented as an old one-eyed man of great wisdom.

ōd'ious *adj.* Hateful, repulsive. **ōd'iously** *adv.* **ōd'iousness** *n.*

ōd'ium *n.* General or widespread dislike or reprobation incurred by person or attaching to action; ~ *theologicum*, bitterness proverbially characterizing theological discussions.

Odoā'cer (ō-) (*c* 434–93). First barbarian ruler of Italy, proclaimed king by the German soldiers; defeated several times and finally assassinated by Theodoric the Ostrogoth.

odŏntoglŏss'um *n.* Genus of orchids, with large beautifully coloured flowers.

ŏdontŏl'ogy *n.* Scientific study of the teeth. **ŏdontolŏ'gical** *adj.* **ŏdontŏl'ogist** *n.*

ōdorif'erous *adj.* Diffusing (usu. agreeable) scent, fragrant. **ōdorif'erously** *adv.*

ōd'orous *adj.* (chiefly poet.) Odoriferous. **ōd'orously** *adv.*

ōd'our (-*er*) *n.* Pleasant or unpleasant smell; fragrance; (archaic, usu. pl.) substance(s) emitting sweet scent, perfume(s); (fig.) savour, trace; ~ *of sanctity*, sweet or balsamic odour supposed to be exhaled by dying or exhumed saint; reputation for holiness. **ōd'ourless** *adj.*

Odўss'eus (*o*-, -sūs). (Gk legend) The hero called by the Romans Ulysses; king of the isle of Ithaca; renowned for cunning; he survived the Trojan War, but the sea-god Poseidon kept him from home 10 years while his wife Penelope waited in Ithaca pestered by suitors who wasted his property. **Od'ўssey** (ŏd-). Greek epic poem of Homer, in 24 books, describing the wanderings and return of Odysseus.

oecology: see ECOLOGY.

oecūmĕn'ical (ēk-) *adj.* (eccles.) Of or representing the whole Christian world or universal church, general, universal, catholic; world-wide.

O.E.D. *abbrev.* Oxford English Dictionary.

oedema (ėdēm'*a*) *n.* (path.) Abnormal accumulation of fluid in tissue, dropsy. **oedēmăt'ic, oedĕm'atous** *adjs.*

Oed'ipus (ēd-). (Gk legend) Son of Laius king of Thebes, and Jocasta, daughter of Creon king of Corinth; he unwittingly killed his father and married his own mother, and when the facts were discovered, went mad and put out his own eyes, while Jocasta hanged herself; ~ *complex*, in Freudian psychoanalysis, manifestation of infantile sexuality in relations of child to parents, with attraction towards parent of opposite sex and jealousy of other parent.

O.E.E.C. *abbrev.* Organization for European Economic Co-operation.

Oenōn'ė (ēn-). (Gk legend) Nymph of Mount Ida and lover of Paris, who deserted her for Helen.

oenothēr'a (ēn-) *n.* (bot.) Genus of (chiefly Amer.) plants with large handsome yellow, white, or purple flowers, freq. opening in evening; evening primrose.

o'er (ōr) *adv.* & *prep.* (poet.) = OVER.

Oerl'ikon (ōr-). Type of rapid-firing anti-aircraft gun using small explosive shell. [f. Swiss place-name]

oer'sted (ōr-) *n.* The practical c.g.s. electromagnetic unit of magnetic intensity; formerly, the practical c.g.s. electromagnetic unit of magnetic reluctance. [Hans Christian *Oersted* (1777–1851), Danish physicist]

oesŏph'agus (ēs-) *n.* Canal leading from mouth to stomach, gullet (ill. ALIMENTARY).

oes'trum, oes'trus (ēs-) *ns.* 1. Genus of dipterous insects of which larvae are parasitic in various animals; gad-fly, bot-fly. 2. Stimulus, vehement impulse, frenzy. 3. Period of sexual activity in female mammals.

of (ŏv, *ov*) *prep.* connecting noun with preceding noun, adj., adv., or verb, and indicating: 1. Removal, separation, point of departure, privation. 2. Origin, derivation, cause, agency, authorship; material, substance, closer definition, identity; concern, reference, direction, respect. 3. Objective relation. 4. Description, quality, condition; partition, classification, inclusion, selection. 5. Belonging, connexion, possession.

O.F.C. *abbrev.* Overseas Food Corporation.

ŏff (*or* awf) *adv.* 1. Away, at or to a distance; (so as to be) out of position, not on or touching or dependent or attached; loose, separate, gone; so as to break continuity or continuance, discontinued, stopped, not obtainable; to the end, entirely, so as to be clear. 2. *Take oneself, be, make*, ~, depart; *go, fall*, ~, deteriorate; *fall* ~, (of ship) become less close to wind; *well, badly, comfortably*, etc., ~, so circumstanced or supplied with money; ~ *and on*, intermittently, waveringly, now and again. ~ *prep.* From; away, down or up from; disengaged or distant from; (so as to be) no longer on; *take* ~ *person's hands*, relieve him of; ~ *the point*, irrelevant(ly); *off'hand*, extempore, without premeditation, curt, casual, unceremonious; *offhan'ded(ly)* (*adv.*); *offhan'dedness* (*n.*); ~ *shore*, a short way out to sea; ~-*shore wind*, one blowing seawards; *offside'*, (football or hockey) of a player in a position on the field where he may not kick, handle, or hit the ball because he is in front of the last player on his side who touched it (Rugby), or, being in front, has only a certain number of opponents, usu. two, between him and their goal (Association and hockey). ~ *adj.* 1. Farther, far; (of horses etc. or vehicles) on the right; (cricket) towards, in, coming from, that side of the field which the batsman faces when playing. 2. Subordinate, divergent; (of chance etc.) contingent, improbable; disengaged. 3. ~-*licence*, licence to sell beer etc. for consumption off the premises; ~-*print*, separate copy of article etc. that was originally part of larger publication. ~ *n.* (cricket) The off side.

Off'a[1] (ŏ-). King of Angel and hero of the early Angli.

Off'a[2] (ŏ-) (d. 796). King of Mercia 757–96; remote descendant of OFFA[1]; ~*'s Dyke*, entrenchment running from near mouth of Wye to near mouth of Dee, built or repaired by Offa of Mercia for defence against the Welsh.

ŏff'al *n.* Refuse, waste stuff, scraps, garbage; parts cut off in dressing carcass of animal killed for food, orig. entrails, now a trade term for edible organs such as liver, kidneys, etc.; carrion, putrid flesh; low-priced fish; bran or other by-product of grain (freq. pl.).

Off'aly (ŏ-). County of Leinster, Eire; formerly called King's County.

Off'enbach (ŏ-, -ahχ), Jacques (1819–80). French composer of burlesque opera (*opĕra bouffe*), of German-Jewish origin.

offĕnce' *n.* 1. (now rare) Stumbling-block, occasion of unbelief, etc. 2. Attacking, aggressive action, taking the offensive. 3. Wounding of the feelings; wounded feeling, annoyance, umbrage. 4. Transgression, misdemeanour, illegal act. **offĕnce'lėss** (-sl-) *adj.*

offĕnd' *v.* 1. Stumble morally, do amiss, transgress (*against*). 2. Wound feelings of, anger, cause resentment or disgust in, outrage. **offĕnd'ėdly** *adv.* **offĕnd'er** *n.*

offĕn'sive *adj.* 1. Aggressive, intended for or used in attack. 2. Meant to give offence, insulting. 3. Disgusting, nauseous, repulsive. **offĕn'sively** *adv.* **offĕn'sivenėss** *n.* **offĕn'sive** *n.* Attitude of assailant, aggressive action; attack, offensive campaign or stroke.

ŏff'er *v.* 1. Present to deity, revered person, etc., by way of sacrifice; give in worship or devotion. 2. Hold out in hand, or tender in words or otherwise, for acceptance or refusal; make proposal of marriage; show for sale; give opportunity to enemy for (battle); express readiness *to* do; essay, try to show (violence etc.); show an intention *to* do. 3. Present to sight or notice; present itself, occur. ~ *n.* Expression of readiness to give or do if desired, or to sell on terms; proposal, esp. of marriage; bid. **ŏff'ering** *n.* Thing offered.

ŏff'ertory *n.* Part of Mass or

Communion service at which offerings are made, offering of these, gifts offered; collection of money at religious service.

ŏff'ice *n.* 1. Piece of kindness, attention, service, (*ill* ~) disservice. 2. Duty attaching to one's position, task, function. 3. Position with duties attached to it; place of authority, trust, or service, esp. of public kind; tenure of official position, esp. that of minister of State. 4. Ceremonial duty; (eccles.) authorized form of worship, daily service of R.C. breviary, Anglican morning and evening prayer; (introit at beginning of) Mass or Communion service, any occasional service. 5. Place for transacting business; room etc. in which clerks of an establishment work, counting-house; (with qualification, as *booking*-~, *inquiry* ~) room etc. set apart for business of particular department of large concern, local branch of dispersed organization, or company for specified purpose; (U.S.) consulting-room of doctor etc. 6. (with capital) Quarters, staff, or collective authority of a Government department, as *Foreign O*~, *War O*~. 7. (pl.) Parts of house devoted to household work, storage, etc. 8. (slang) Hint, private intimation, signal (esp. in *give the* ~). 9. *Holy O*~, the Inquisition.

ŏff'icer *n.* 1. Holder of public, civil, or ecclesiastical office; king's servant or minister, appointed or elected functionary; president, treasurer, secretary, etc., of society; bailiff, catchpole, constable. 2. Person holding authority in armed forces or mercantile marine, esp. one with a commission in the armed forces as dist. from a *private* or from a *non-commissioned*, *petty*, or *warrant* ~. ~ *v.t.* Provide with officers; act as commander of.

offī'cial (-shl) *adj.* Of an office, the discharge of duties, or the tenure of an office; holding office, employed in public capacity; derived from or vouched for by person(s) in office, properly authorized; usual with persons in office; (med.) according to the pharmacopoeia, officinal. **offī'cially** *adv.* **offī'cialdom, offī'cialism** *ns.* **offī'cialize** *v.t.* **offī'cial** *n.* 1. Person holding public office or engaged in official duties. 2. Presiding officer or judge of archbishop's, bishop's, or esp. archdeacon's court.

offī'ciāte (-shĭ-) *v.i.* Discharge priestly office, perform divine service; act in some official capacity, esp. on particular occasion. **offī'ciant** *n.*

offī'cinal *adj.* (Of herb or drug) used in medicine or the arts; (of medical preparation) kept in readiness at druggists', made from recipe in pharmacopoeia (obs.). **offī'cinally** *adv.*

offī'cious (-shus) *adj.* 1. (Given to) offering service that is not wanted, doing or undertaking more than is required, intrusive, meddlesome. 2. (diplomacy, opp. to *official*) Informal, unofficially friendly or candid, not binding. **offī'ciously** *adv.* **offī'ciousnėss** *n.*

ŏff'ing (*or* aw-) *n.* Part of visible sea distant from shore or beyond anchoring ground; position at distance from shore; *in the* ~, (fig.) near by; ready or likely to appear.

ŏff'ish (*or* aw-) *adj.* (colloq.) Inclined to aloofness, distant or stiff in manner. **off'ishnėss** *n.*

off'scourings (ŏfskowr-, awf-) *n.pl.* Refuse, filth, dregs.

ŏff'sĕt (*or* aw-) *n.* 1. Short side-shoot from stem or root serving for propagation; offshoot, scion, mountain spur. 2. Compensation, set-off, consideration or amount diminishing or neutralizing effect of contrary one. 3. (surv.) Short distance measured perpendicularly from main line of measurement. 4. (archit.) Sloping ledge in wall etc. where thickness of part above is diminished (ill. BUTTRESS). 5. Bend made in pipe to carry it past obstacle. 6. (printing, engraving) Transfer of ink from a newly printed surface to another surface so that the final impression is in the same sense as the plate or type (~ *proof*, engraver's trial proof made thus as aid to working); ~ *lithography*, method of printing in which ink is transferred from a lithographic stone or plate to a rubber roller and thence, while still wet, to paper.

ŏff'shōōt (*or* aw-) *n.* Side-shoot or branch, derivative.

ŏff'spring (*or* aw-) *n.* Progeny, issue.

Of'lăg (ŏ-) *n.* German prison camp for officers. [Ger., abbrev. of *offizier* officer, *lag*er camp]

O.F.M. *abbrev.* Order of Friars Minor.

O.F.S. *abbrev.* Orange Free State.

ŏft (*or* aw-) *adv.* Often (archaic exc. in combination); ~-*times*, (archaic) often.

often (ŏf'n, aw'fn) *adv.* Frequently, many times, at short intervals; in many instances; ~-*times*, (archaic) often. ~ *adj.* (archaic) Frequent.

ō'gēē *n.* & *adj.* (Moulding) showing in section a double continuous curve, concave below passing into convex above; cyma reversa (ill. MOULDING); S-shaped (line); ~ *arch* etc., arch etc. with two ogee curves meeting at apex (ill. ARCH).

ŏg'(h)am *n.* Ancient British and Irish alphabet of characters formed by parallel strokes arranged along either side of, or crossing, continuous medial line, e.g. edge of stone; inscription in this; one of the characters.

ō'gīve *n.* Diagonal groin or rib of vault; pointed or Gothic arch. **ogīv'al** *adj.* 1. (archaic) Of, like, an ogive; having ogives. 2. (now usu.) Curved like an OGEE, S-shaped.

ō'gle *v.* Cast amorous glances, eye amorously. ~ *n.* Amorous glance.

Ogpu (ŏg'pōō), **O.G.P.U.**: see G.P.U.

ō'gre (-*er*) *n.* Man-eating giant. **ō'greish** (-ger-), **ō'grish** *adjs.* **ō'grėss** *n.*

Ogyges (ŏj'ĭjēz). (Gk myth.) Legendary first king of Thebes, in whose reign a destructive flood occurred. **Ogȳ'gian** *adj.* Of Ogyges; of obscure antiquity, of great age.

oh (ō), *int.*: see O[2] *int.*

Ohī'ō (*o*-). East North Central State of U.S., admitted to the Union in 1803; capital, Columbus; ~ *River*, chief eastern tributary of Mississippi.

Ohm[1] (ōm), Georg Simon (1787–1854). German physicist who determined mathematically the law of the flow of electricity.

ohm[2] (ōm) *n.* Unit of electrical resistance, resistance of a circuit in which potential difference of one volt produces current of one ampere. **ohm'ĭc** *adj.* [f. G. S. OHM[1]]

O.H.M.S. *abbrev.* On His (Her) Majesty's Service.

ohō' *int.* Expressing surprise or exultation.

oil *n.* 1. (One of) large group of liquid viscid substances with characteristic smooth and sticky unctuous) feel, lighter than water and insoluble in it, inflammable, and chemically neutral; there are 3 classes: (*a*) *fatty* or *fixed oils*, of animal or vegetable origin, chemically *triglycerides* of fatty acids, producing permanent greasy stains on paper etc.; subdivided into *drying oils*, which by exposure to air absorb oxygen and harden and thicken into varnishes, and *non-drying oils*, decomposing by exposure and used as lubricants, in making soap etc.; (*b*) *essential* or *volatile oils*, chiefly of vegetable origin, acrid and limpid, characteristic odoriferous substances found in plants, and chemically hydrocarbons or mixtures of hydrocarbons with resins etc.; used in medicine, the arts, and perfumery; (*c*) *mineral oils*, chemically mixtures of hydrocarbons, used as fuels, illuminants, etc. 2. Oil-colour (freq. pl.). 3. Oilskin (usu. pl.). 4. ~-*bomb*, incendiary bomb containing oil; ~-*cake*, mass of compressed linseed etc. left when oil

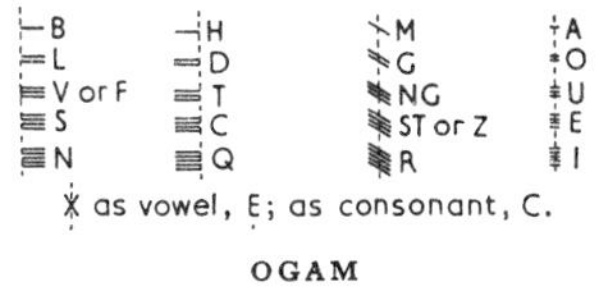

B H M A
L D G O
V or F T NG U
S C ST or Z E
N Q R I

X as vowel, E; as consonant, C.

OGAM

has been expressed, used as cattle-food or manure; ~-*can*, can for holding oil, esp. with long nozzle for oiling machinery; ~-*cloth*, fabric waterproofed with oil, oil-skin; canvas coated with preparation containing drying oil, used to cover tables etc.; ~-*colour*, paint made by grinding pigment in a drying oil; ~-*engine*, one driven by explosion of vaporized oil mixed with air; ~-*field*, tract of oil-bearing strata; *oil'man*, maker or seller of oils; ~-*meal*, ground oil-cake; ~-*paint*, oil-colour; ~-*painting*, art of painting, picture painted, in oil-colours; ~-*paper*, paper made transparent or waterproof by soaking in oil; ~-*shale*, rock from which petroleum can be produced by distillation; ~-*silk*, oiled silk; *oil'skin*, cloth waterproofed with a drying oil; garment or (pl.) coat and trousers of this; *oil'stone*, fine-grained stone used with oil as whetstone; ~-*well*, well yielding mineral oil. ~ *v.* 1. Apply oil to, lubricate. 2. Turn into oily liquid. 3. Impregnate or treat with oil; *oiled silk*, silk waterproofed with a drying oil. 4. *oiled*, (slang) slightly drunk.

oil'er *n.* Oil-can for oiling machinery; ship built for carrying oil.

oil'y *adj.* 1. Of, like, covered or soaked with, oil. 2. (Of manner etc.) fawning, insinuating, unctuous. **oil'ĭly** *adv.* **oil'inĕss** *n.*

oint'ment *n.* Unctuous preparation applied to skin to heal or beautify, unguent.

Oireachtas (ēr'*aχ*thăs). Legislature of Eire, consisting of the President and two houses, Dáil Eireann (Chamber of Deputies) and Seanad Eireann (Senate). [Ir., = 'assembly']

Oisin: see OSSIAN.

Ojib'wā(y). Large group of N. Amer. Indians of Algonkin linguistic stock, belonging to region of Great Lakes.

O.K. (ō kā) *adj.* (orig. U.S. slang) All right. ~ *n.* & *v.t.* (Mark with) the letters 'O.K.', esp. as denoting approval of contents of document etc.; sanction. [used as abbrev. for *oll korrect*, misspelling of *all correct*]

oka'pi (-ah-) *n.* Rare ungulate mammal, *Okapia johnstoni*, related to giraffes, found in dense forests of W. Africa.

ōkay' *adj.* & *v.t.* = O.K.

Okhŏtsk' (*oχ*-), Sea of. Arm of NW. Pacific Ocean, lying between Kamchatka peninsula and mainland of Siberia.

Okla. *abbrev.* Oklahoma.

Oklahōm'a (ō-). West South Central State of U.S., admitted to the Union in 1907; capital, Oklahoma City.

ŏk'ra, ŏk'rō *n.* Tall malvaceous African plant (*Hibiscus esculentus*, called also *gumbo*) cultivated in W. Indies, southern U.S., etc.; the young fruits are used as a vegetable and for thickening soups, the stem-fibres for ropes.

Ol. *abbrev.* Olympiad.

Ol'ăf I Tryggvason (ō-) (*c* 969–1000). King of Norway 995–1000; raided coast of France and British Isles until he became a Christian; began conversion of Norway to Christianity. **Olaf II** (995–1030). 'St. Olaf', 'Olaf the Fat'; patron saint of Norway; king of Norway 1015–28; active in diffusion of Christianity in his kingdom until his expulsion by CANUTE.

Olā'us Magnus (*o*-) (1490–1558). Swedish ecclesiastic; archbishop of Uppsala; author of a history of the northern peoples (1555).

Ol'bers (ŏ-), Heinrich Wilhelm Matthias (1758–1840). German astronomer; discoverer of several comets and some minor planets.

ōld *adj.* 1. Advanced in age, far on in natural period of existence, not young or near its beginning; having characteristics, experience, feebleness, etc., of age; worn, dilapidated, shabby. 2. (appended to period of time) Of age (as *10 years* ~); (ellipt.) person or animal, esp. race-horse, of specified age (as *three-year*-~). 3. Practised or inveterate *in* action or quality, or as agent etc. 4. Dating from far back; made long ago; long established, known, familiar, or dear; ancient, not new or recent, primeval; (of language) belonging to the earliest known period or stage; *of* ~ *standing*, long established. 5. Belonging only or chiefly to the past; obsolete, obsolescent, out of date, antiquated, antique; concerned with antiquity; not modern, bygone, former. 6. ~ *Adam*, original sin; *O*~ *Bailey*, English Central Criminal Court, on site of NEWGATE prison, situated in ancient bailey of London city wall between Lud Gate and New Gate; *O*~ *Believers*, Russian sect originating in 17th c. in protest against liturgical reforms of patriarch NIKON; *O*~ *Bulgarian* = OLD SLAVONIC; *O*~ *Catholics*, group of small national Churches which have separated at various times from Rome; now in full communion with C. of E.; ~-*clothes-man*, dealer in discarded clothes; *O*~ *Colony*, part of Massachusetts within original limits of Plymouth colony; *O*~ *Contemptibles*: see CONTEMPTIBLE; ~ *countries*, countries long inhabited or civilized; the ~ *country*, *home*, etc., (used by colonials etc. of) mother country; *O*~ *Dominion*, Virginia; *O*~ *English*, Anglo-Saxon; language spoken in England from *c* 5th c. to *c* 1100; ~ *English sheep-dog*, medium-sized breed of dog with very long, shaggy, whitish coat and short or no tail; ~ *face*, style of printing type as dist. from modern face (ill. TYPE); *O*~ *Faithful*, geyser in Yellowstone National Park, U.S. erupting regularly at intervals of a little over an hour; ~-*fashioned*, belonging to a fashion that has gone or is going out; *O*~ *French*, French from *c* 9th to *c* 13th (or sometimes 16th) centuries; *O*~ *Glory*, (U.S.) the Stars and Stripes; ~ *gold*, colour of tarnished gold; *O*~ *Guard*, French Imperial Guard created by Napoleon I in 1804; ~ *hand*, practised workman; person of experience in (*at*) something; *O*~ *Harry*, *O*~ *Nick*, the Devil; *O*~ *Hickory*, (U.S.) nickname of Andrew JACKSON, from his toughness of character; *O*~ *High German*, High German from *c* 750 to *c* 1100; *O*~ *Hundred(th)*, tune (first published 1551) set to 100th psalm in 'old' version of metrical psalms, and usually sung to doxology; *O*~ *Icelandic*, Old Norse; *O*~ *Lady of Threadneedle Street*, familiar name for Bank of England; *O*~ *Line State*, pop. name of Maryland, U.S.; ~ *maid*, elderly spinster; precise, tidy, and fidgety man; (cards) round game in which object is to avoid holding of unpaired card; ~-*maidish* (*adj.*); ~ *man*, southernwood; (naut. slang) ship's captain; (colloq.) husband; *the* ~ *man*, one's unregenerate self; ~ *man of the sea*, (from character in 'Arabian Nights' tale of Sindbad the Sailor) person who cannot be shaken off; ~ *man's beard*, kind of moss; traveller's joy and other species of *Clematis*; *O*~ *Moore*: see MOORE[1]; *O*~ *Norse*, ancestor of modern Scandinavian languages, best represented in Old Icelandic literature; *O*~ *Pretender*: see PRETENDER; *O*~ *Red Sandstone*, series of rocks of DEVONIAN period, chiefly sandstone of red colour, found esp. in Wales and Scotland, and other parts of NW. Europe; ~ *school tie*, necktie of characteristic pattern as worn by former members of a particular (public) school; used symbolically to denote extreme loyalty to a traditional mode of thought or behaviour; *O*~ *Slavonic* (~ *Bulgarian*, ~ *Church Slavonic*), earliest written Slavonic language, a Bulgarian dialect fixed in writing towards end of 9th c.; *O*~ *Stone Age*, the PALAEOLITHIC age; ~ *style* (abbrev. O.S.), the Julian calendar (so-called after the introduction of the GREGORIAN calendar), with 365 days in ordinary year, and 366 days in leap year (every 4th year); *O*~ *Testament*, the first of the two main divisions of the canonical books of the Bible; ~ *time*, of the ancient or olden time; ~-*timer*, (U.S.) one whose experience goes back to old times; one of long standing; old-fashioned person or thing; *O*~ *Vic*, theatre in Waterloo Road, London, opened 1818 as Coburg Theatre and renamed Victoria 1833, which was reopened 1880 by Emma Cons as a 'temperance music-hall' and under the management of Lilian Baylis (1912–37) became the headquarters of a company performing Shakespeare's plays and other classics; ~ *wives' tale*, foolish story such as is told by garrulous old women; ~ *woman*, (colloq.) wife; fussy or timid man; *O~ World*, the eastern hemisphere; *~-world*, of the old world, not American; (also) belonging to old times; *the ~ year*, the year just ended or about to end. **ōld'ish** *adj.* **ōld** *n.* Old time (only in *of old* (*adj.* & *adv.*) as *men of old, of old there were giants*).

Oldcastle (ōld'kahsl), Sir John (d. 1417). English soldier; a leader of the Lollards; was arrested, but escaped and lived as an outlaw; was recaptured and executed as a heretic; Shakespeare used his name in 'Henry IV' but changed it, after a protest, to Falstaff.

ōl'den *adj.* (archaic & literary) Old-time, of a former age.

Oldenbārn'ėvěldt (ŏ-, -felt), Johan van (1547–1619). Dutch statesman; supporter of William the Silent in struggle for independence of the Netherlands; his execution under Maurice of Nassau is regarded as a judicial murder.

ōld'ster *n.* One who is no longer a youngster.

ōlėā'ginous *adj.* Having properties of or producing oil; oily, fatty, greasy.

ōlėăn'der *n.* Evergreen poisonous Levantine shrub (*Nerium oleander*) with leathery lanceolate leaves and handsome red or white flowers.

ōl'ėfine *n.* (chem.) Name for series of hydrocarbons homologous with ethylene, $C_n H_{2n}$.

ōl'ėograph (-ahf) *n.* Picture printed in oil-colours.

ōlėo-mārg'arine *n.* Fatty substance extracted from clarified beef-fat and made into margarine with addition of butyrin, milk, etc.

ōl'ėo-rĕs'in (-z-). A natural product containing a volatile oil and a resin; e.g. the exudations from coniferous trees.

ōl'ėum *n.* (chem.) Fuming (or Nordhausen) sulphuric acid, $H_2SO_4xSO_3$, a solution of sulphur trioxide in sulphuric acid.

ŏlfăc'tion *n.* Smelling, sense of smell. **ŏlfăc'tive** *adj.* **ŏlfăc'tory** *adj.* Concerned with smelling.

olĭb'anum *n.* Aromatic gum resin obtained from trees of genus *Boswellia*, used as incense.

ŏl'ĭd *adj.* Rank-smelling, fetid.

ŏl'ĭgārch (-k) *n.* Member of oligarchy.

ŏl'ĭgārchy (-kĭ) *n.* Government, State governed, by a few persons; members of such a government. **ŏlĭgārch'ĭc(al)** *adjs.* **ŏlĭgārch'ĭcally** *adv.*

ŏlĭgocārp'ous *adj.* (bot.) Having few fruits.

ŏl'ĭgocēne *adj.* & *n.* (geol.) Of the 3rd series of rocks in the Tertiary, above the Eocene and below the Miocene; *the O~*, this series, epoch to which it belongs (ill. GEOLOGY).

ōl'iō *n.* Mixed dish, hotchpotch, stew of various meats and vegetables; medley, farrago, miscellany.

ŏlĭvā'ceous (-sh*us*) *adj.* Olive-green, of dusky yellowish green.

ŏl'ĭvary *adj.* (anat.) Olive-shaped, oval.

ŏl'ĭve *n.* 1. Evergreen tree (*Olea europaea*), esp. the cultivated variety, with narrow leaves green above and hoary below and axillary clusters of small whitish flowers, bearing small oval drupes, blackish when ripe, with bitter pulp abounding in oil, and hard stone, cultivated in Mediterranean countries etc. for its fruit and oil; the fruit of this tree; any tree of the genus *Olea*, various similar trees and shrubs. 2. Leaf, branch, or wreath of olive as emblem of peace. 3. Olive-shaped gasteropod mollusc (*Oliva*). 4. (pl.) Slices of beef or veal rolled up with onions and herbs and stewed in brown sauce. 5. Olive-colour. 6. *~-branch*, branch of olive-tree, esp. as emblem of peace (freq. fig.); (usu. pl.) children; *~-crown*, garland of olive as sign of victory; *~-oil*, clear, pale-yellow, non-drying oil obtained from pulp of olives, used in cookery, salads, as a medicine, as a lubricant, and in the manufacture of toilet soap, etc.; *Mount of Olives*, ridge facing Temple mount at Jerusalem on the east, with Garden of Gethsemane on western slope. ~ *adj.* Coloured like unripe olive, dull yellowish green; (of complexion etc.) brownish yellow; of colour of olive foliage, dull ashy green with silvery sheen.

ŏl'ĭver¹ *n.* Tilt-hammer attached to axle and worked by treadle, for shaping nails etc.

Ol'ĭver² (ŏ-). In the Charlemagne cycle of legends, one of Charlemagne's paladins and the close friend of ROLAND.

ŏl'ĭvĭne *n.* Yellowish-green mineral, a magnesium silicate, found in basalt and gabbro.

ŏll'a podri'da (-rē-) *n.* = OLIO. [Span., lit. 'rotten pot']

Olȳm'pia¹. Plain on N. bank of river Alpheus about 20 miles from W. coast of Peloponnese; in ancient Greece a great religious centre second only to Delphi, and site of the OLYMPIC Games.

Olȳm'pia². Capital of Washington State, U.S.

olȳm'pĭăd *n.* 1. Period of 4 years between celebrations of OLYMPIC Games, used by ancient Greeks in dating events, 776 B.C. being 1st year of 1st Olympiad. 2. Meeting of mod. OLYMPIC Games.

Olȳm'pĭan *adj.* Of Olympus, celestial; (of manners) magnificent, condescending, superior; aloof. ~ *n.* Dweller in Olympus, one of the greater ancient Greek gods; person of superhuman calmness and detachment.

Olȳm'pĭc *adj.* Of Olympia in Greece; of the Olympic Games; ~ *Games*, (1) athletic contests held by the ancient Greeks every 4th year at Olympia and including foot-races, boxing, wrestling, and chariot- and horse-races; (2) international amateur athletic contests begun in 1896 as revival of ancient Greek games and held every 4th year; organized by an international committee which decides where each festival is to be held; acc. to the Charter of the Olympic Games the competitions must include athletics, gymnastics, combative sports, swimming, equestrian sports, the pentathlon, and art.

Olȳm'pus. Lofty mountain in Greece at E. end of range dividing Thessaly from Macedonia; in Greek mythology the court of Zeus and home of the gods.

O.M. *abbrev.* Order of Merit.

Om (ŏm). In Hinduism etc., mystic and holy word regarded as summing up all truth.

Om'ār (ō-) (*c* 581–644). 2nd Mohammedan caliph, 634–44; reputed builder of *Mosque of ~*, on platform of Temple at Jerusalem, a much-altered Byzantine church, containing rock on which, acc. to Jewish legend, Abraham prepared to sacrifice Isaac, and from which, acc. to Mohammedans, Mohammed ascended to heaven.

Om'ār Khayyam (ō-, kī-yahm'). Ghiyāthuddīn Abulfath 'Omar bin Ibrāhīm al-Khayyāmī (*c* 1100), Persian mathematician and epigrammatist, many of whose quatrains were translated into English by Edward FITZGERALD.

omās'um *n.* PSALTERIUM.

ŏm'bre (-b*er*) *n.* Card-game for three, very popular in 17th–18th centuries, played with 40 cards (the eights, nines, and tens of ordinary pack being thrown out).

Om'durmăn (ŏ-). Town of Sudan on left bank of Nile opposite Khartoum; chosen by the MAHDI as his capital, 1884; scene of a battle, 1898, in which an Anglo-Egyptian army under KITCHENER defeated the dervishes.

ōm'ėga *n.* Last letter (Ω, ω) of Greek alphabet, long o; last of series; final development etc. [Gk, = 'great o']

ŏm'ėlĕt(te) (-ml-) *n.* Dish of eggs lightly beaten and fried usu. in butter, freq. containing herbs, cheese, chopped ham, etc. (*savoury ~*) or jam (*sweet ~*).

ōm'ĕn *n.* Event or object portending good or evil, prognostic, presage; prophetic signification.

omĕn'tum *n.* (anat.) Fold of peritoneum connecting stomach with other viscera, caul (ill. ABDOMEN). **omĕn'tal** *adj.*

omĭc'ron *n.* Greek letter (O, o), short o. [Gk, = 'small o']

ŏm'ĭnous *adj.* Giving, being, an omen (*of* good or evil), portentous (rare); of evil omen, inauspicious, threatening. **ŏm'ĭnously** *adv.*

omĭs'sion (-shn) *n.* Omitting, non-inclusion; non-performance, neglect, duty not done.

omĭt *v.t.* Leave out, not insert or include; leave undone, neglect do*ing*, fail *to* do.

ŏm'nĭbus *n.* (pl. *-es*). (usu. *bus*) Large public road vehicle with one or two decks plying on fixed route and taking up and setting down passengers at fixed, or at any, points in this; vehicle conveying guests between hotel and railway station; (*private, family,* ~) vehicle provided by railway company for conveying party and luggage to or from station. ~ *adj.* Serving several objects at once; comprising several items; ~ (*book*), volume containing several stories, plays, etc. (usu. by a single author) published at a popular price; ~ *box*, box on pit tier in theatre, appropriated to number of subscribers; ~ *train*, one stopping at all stations. [L, = 'for all', i.e. everyone]

ŏmnĭcŏm'pėtent *adj.* Having jurisdiction in all cases.

ŏmnĭfār'ious *adj.* Of all sorts.

ŏmnĭp'otence *n.* Infinite power; God; great influence. **ŏmnĭp'otent** *adj.* **ŏmnĭp'otently** *adv.*

ŏmnĭprĕs'ence (-z-) *n.* Ubiquity; being widespread or constantly met with. **ŏmnĭprĕs'ent** *adj.*

ŏmnĭ'science (*or* -shens) *n.* Infinite knowledge; God; wide information or the affectation of it. **ŏmnĭ'scient** *adj.* **ŏmnĭ'sciently** *adv.*

ŏm'nium găth'erum (-dh-) *n.* Miscellaneous assemblage of persons or things, queer mixture. [mock L]

ŏmnĭv'orous *adj.* Feeding on anything that offers (esp. fig. of reading). **ŏmnĭv'orously** *adv.* **ŏmnĭv'orousnėss** *n.*

Om'phalė (ŏ-). (Gk legend) Queen of Lydia whom Hercules served for three years as a slave, doing female tasks while she wore his lion's skin.

ŏm'phalŏs *n.* 1. (Gk antiq.) Boss on shield; conical stone at Delphi supposed to be central point of earth. 2. Centre, hub.

on (ŏn, *on*) *prep.* 1. (So as to be) supported by, attached to, covering, or enclosing; ~ *one*, about one's person. 2. With axis, pivot, basis, motive, standard, confirmation, or guarantee, consisting in. 3. (So as to be) close to, in the direction of, touching, arrived at, against, just at. 4. (Of time) during, exactly at, contemporaneously with, immediately after, as a result of; ~ *the instant*, immediately; ~ *time*, punctual(ly). 5. In manner specified by adj., or state or action specified by noun; concerning, about, while engaged with, so as to affect; *gone* ~, (sl.) enamoured of. 6. Added to. 7. (U.S.) Against (a person); (colloq., esp. of treat of any kind) to be paid for by; *have something* ~, have advantage over. ~ *adv.* 1. (So as to be) supported by, attached to, covering, enclosing, or touching, something. 2. In some direction, towards something; farther forward, towards point of contact, in advanced position or state; with continued movement or action, in operation or activity; *broadside, end, head,* etc., *on*, with that part forward; *send* ~, send in front of oneself, in advance; (of bowler) *go on*, begin bowling; *gas, water,* etc., *is on*, gas, water, etc., is turned on, running, or procurable by turning tap; *get, be,* ~, make, have made, bet. 3. *on to* (compound prep. corresponding to *on* as *into* to *in*, but usu. written as two words), to a position on. ~ *adj.* (cricket) Towards, from, or in that part of the field behind the batsman as he stands to play; ~ *licence*, licence for selling beer etc. to be drunk on the premises. ~ *n.* The on side in cricket.

on-, pref. used with attrib. participles, gerunds, verbal nouns, etc., and other derivations of verbs followed idiomatically by ON; *on'-coming*, approach(ing); *on'looker*, one who looks on; *on'rush*, onset.

ŏn'ager *n.* Wild ass, esp. the species *Equus onager* of Central Asia, with broad brown stripe along the back.

ōn'anism *n.* Uncompleted coition, masturbation. [f. prop. name. *Onan* (Gen. xxxviii. 9)]

once (wŭns) *adv.* 1. For one time or on one occasion only; multiplied by one, by one degree; ~ *or twice*, ~ *and again*, a few times; ~ *for all*, in final manner, definitively; ~ *in a way, while*, very rarely. 2. (in negative or conditional etc. clause) Ever, at all, even for one or the first time. 3. On a certain but unspecified past occasion; at some period in the past, former(ly). 4. *at* ~, immediately, without delay; at the same time; *for* (*this, that*) ~, on one occasion by way of exception; *once-over* (*n.*) (U.S. colloq.) single and rapid survey or examination. ~ *conj.* As soon as; if once; when once. ~ *n.* One time, performance, etc.

one (wŭn) *numeral adj.* 1. Lowest cardinal number, number of a single thing without any more; a. 2. *the* only; single; forming a unity, united; identical, the same, unchanging; a particular but undefined, to be contrasted with another; *made* ~, married; *become* ~, coalesce. ~ *n.* (freq. used as substitute for repetition of previously expressed or implied noun). 1. The number one, thing numbered with it, written symbol for it, 1, i, or I; a unit, unity; a single thing, person, or example; *number* ~, oneself, esp. as object of selfish care; *never a* ~, none; *ten* etc. *to* ~, long odds, high probability; *at* ~, reconciled; in agreement. 2. Single person or thing of the kind implied; ~ (i.e. hour) *o'clock*; ~ (i.e. shilling) *and sixpence*; *go* ~ *better*, bid, offer, risk, more by one point; ~ *too many for*, too hard etc. for . . . to deal with; *all* ~ *to*, the same thing, indifferent to; ~ *and all*, all jointly and severally; ~ *with another*, on the average; ~ *another*, formula of reciprocity with *one* orig. subjective and *another* objective or possessive. ~ *pron.* A particular but unspecified person (archaic); a person of specified kind; any person, esp. the speaker, spoken of as representing people in general; *the Evil O*~, the Devil.

one- (wŭn) in combination: ~-*eyed*, having only, blind of, one eye; ~-*horse*, drawn or worked by single horse; (fig.) petty, poorly equipped; ~-*man*, requiring, consisting of, done or managed by, one man; ~-*pair*, room, set of rooms, on first floor (above one pair or flight of stairs); *oneself'*, reflexive and emphatic appositional form of *one* as generalizing pronoun; ~-*sided*, having, occurring on, one side only; larger etc. on one side; partial, unfair, prejudiced; ~-*sidedly* (*adv.*), ~-*sidedness* (*n.*); ~-*step*, ballroom dance in quick time with steps resembling walk; ~-*track*, (of mind) that is fixed on one line of thought or action; ~-*way* (of thoroughfares) along which traffic is permitted in one direction only.

Onĕg'a. Second largest lake in Russia, in NW. of European Russia.

Oneida (ōnēd'*a*). Tribe of N. Amer. Indians of Iroquoian stock, formerly living round Oneida Lake in New York State; ~ *Community*, American religious and communistic community founded 1848 at Oneida Creek, New York State, by J. H. Noyes (1811–86); its members held the doctrine of 'perfectionism' and entered into free-love relationships; marriage was introduced in 1879 and a joint-stock system subsequently replaced the common ownership of property.

O'Neill' (nēl), Eugene Gladstone (1888–1953). American playwright, author of 'The Emperor Jones,' 'Mourning Becomes Electra', 'The Iceman Cometh', etc.

ŏneirŏl'ogy (-nīr-) *n.* Study, psychological interpretation, of dreams. **oneirolŏ'gĭcal** *adj.* **ŏneirŏl'ogist** *n.* **oneir'omăncy** (-nīr-) *n.* Divination by dreams.

one'nėss (wŭn-n-) *n.* Being one, singleness; singularity, uniqueness; wholeness, unity, union, agreement; identity, changelessness.

on'er (wŭ-) *n.* (slang) Remarkable or pre-eminent person or thing.

ŏn'erous *adj.* Burdensome, causing or requiring trouble. **ŏn'erously** *adv.* **ŏn'erousnėss** *n.*

onion (ŭn'yon) *n.* (Plant, *Allium cepa*, with) edible rounded bulb of close concentric leaves, with pungent smell and flavour, used as culinary vegetable; *flaming onions*: see FLAME; ~-*fly*, small fly (*Delia antiqua*) harmful to onion bulbs; ~ *shell*, various molluscan shells of rounded form; ~-*skin*, outermost or any outer coat of onion; very thin smooth translucent kind of paper. **on'iony** *adj.*

ŏn'ly *adj.* That is (or are) the one (or all the) specimen(s) of the class, sole. ~ *adv.* Solely, merely, exclusively; and no one or nothing more, besides, or else; and that is all. ~ *conj.* The only thing to be added being; with this restriction, drawback, or exception only; but then.

ŏnomatopoe'ia (-pē*a*, -pēy*a*) *n.* Formation of names or words from sounds resembling those associated with the object or action to be named, or seeming naturally suggestive of its qualities (e.g. *cuckoo, rustle*); word so formed. **ŏnomatopoe'ic, ŏnomatopōĕt'ic** *adjs.* **ŏnomatopoe'ically, ŏnomatopōĕt'ically** *advs.*

Onŏnda'ga (ŏ-, -dah-). Tribe of N. Amer. Indians of Iroquoian stock, living in New York State; one of the Six Nations, and guardians of the council-fire of the Iroquois.

ŏn'sĕt *n.* Attack, assault, impetuous beginning.

ŏn'slaught (-awt) *n.* Onset, fierce attack.

Ont. *abbrev.* Ontario.

Ontār'iō (ŏ-). Province of SE. Canada; capital, Toronto; *Lake* ~, smallest and most easterly of the Great Lakes, lying between the province and New York State.

ŏn'to *prep.*: see ON.

ŏntogĕn'ĕsis *n.* Origin and development of the individual being. **ŏntogėnĕt'ic** *adj.* **ŏntogėnĕt'ically** *adv.*

ŏntŏ'gėny *n.* 1. = ONTOGENESIS. 2. Science of the development of the individual being; embryology. **ŏntŏ'gėnist** *n.*

ŏntŏl'ogy *n.* Department of metaphysics concerned with the essence of things or being in the abstract. **ŏntolŏ'gical** *adj.* **ŏntolŏ'gically** *adv.*

ōn'us *n.* Burden, duty, responsibility.

ŏn'ward, ŏn'wards (-z) *advs.* Farther on; towards the front; with advancing motion. **ŏn'ward** *adj.* Directed onward.

ŏn'yx (*or* ō-) *n.* 1. Type of chalcedony with different colours in layers, a form of silica, regarded as semi-precious stone. 2. (path.) Opacity of lower part of cornea, resembling finger-nail, caused by infiltration of pus behind it or between its layers.

oo'dle *n.* (colloq.) (always in pl.) Superabundance (*of money* etc.).

oof *n.* (slang) Money. [for Yiddish *oof-tish* = Ger. *auf dem tische* on the table]

ōogĕn'ĕsis *n.* (biol.) Process leading to production of ripe ovum from germ-cell.

ō'olīte *n.* Rock, freq. a limestone, composed of minute spheres of carbonate, resembling fish-roe in appearance, found esp. in the jurassic strata. **ōolĭt'ic** *adj.*

ōŏl'ogy *n.* Study, collecting, of birds' eggs. **ōŏl'ogist** *n.*

oo'lŏng *n.* Dark-coloured kind of tea grown esp. in Formosa. [Chin. *wu* black, *lung* dragon]

oom *n.* (S. Afr.) Uncle; *Oom Paul*, President KRUGER.

oom'iăk *n.* Large Eskimo boat of skins drawn over wooden frame, propelled by paddles. [Eskimo]

oomph *n.* (slang) Sex appeal.

oont *n.* (Anglo-Ind. slang) Camel. [Hind.]

ooze *n.* 1. Wet mud, slime, esp. in river-bed or estuary or on ocean bottom. 2. Tanning liquor, infusion of oak-bark etc. 3. Exudation; sluggish flow; something that oozes. **ooz'y** *adj.* **ooz'ily** *adv.* **ooz'inėss** *n.* **ooze** *v.* (Of moisture) pass slowly through the pores of a body, exude, percolate; (of substance) exude moisture; emit (moisture, information, etc.); (fig.) leak *out* or *away*.

op. *abbrev.* (Military) operation; operator; opus.

o.p. *abbrev.* Out of print; over proof.

O.P. *abbrev.* Observation post; (also **o.p.**) opposite prompt (side, in theatre, i.e. actors' right); *Ordinis Praedicatorum* (= of the Order of Preachers, i.e. Dominicans).

opă'city *n.* Being opaque; quality of not allowing passage to or (rarely) not reflecting light; nontransparency, obscurity; obscurity of meaning, obtuseness of understanding.

ōp'al *n.* Amorphous quartz-like form of hydrated silica, some kinds of which are valued as gems and show changing colours (*common* ~, milk-white or bluish with green, yellow, and red reflections); (commerc.) semi-translucent white glass.

ōpalĕs'cence *n.* Changing of colour as in an opal. **ōpalĕs'cent** *adj.* Showing such changes, iridescent.

ōp'aline *adj.* Opal-like; opalescent. ~ *n.* Opal glass.

opāque' (-k) *adj.* Not reflecting (rare) or transmitting light; impenetrable to sight; not lucid, obscure; obtuse, dull-witted. **opāque'ly** (-kl-) *adv.* **opāque'nėss** *n.*

op. cit. *abbrev.* *Opere citato* (= in the work quoted).

ōpe *v.* (Poet. for) open.

ōp'en *adj.* 1. Not closed or blocked up; allowing of entrance, passage, or access; having gate, door, lid, or part of boundary withdrawn; unenclosed, unconfined, uncovered, bare, exposed, undisguised; public, manifest; not exclusive or limited. 2. (of vowel) Produced with wider opening of oral cavity than *close* vowel; (mus., of organ pipe) not closed at top; (mus., of string) not stopped by finger; (of note) produced by such pipe or string, or without aid of slide, key, or piston. 3. Expanded, unfolded, outspread; spread out, not close, without intervals; porous; communicative, frank. 4. ~ *air*, outdoors; *with* ~ *arms*, heartily; ~*-armed* (*adj.*); ~ *boat*, undecked boat; *opencast* (surface) *coal*: ill. MINE; ~ *champion*, winner of a competition which any candidate may enter (~ *competition*); ~ *country*, country unenclosed or affording wide views; *the* ~ *door*, principle of free commerce for all comers; *with* ~ *eyes*, not unconsciously or under misapprehension; in eager attention or surprise; ~*-eyed* (*adj.*); ~ *hand*, freedom in giving, generosity; ~*-handed* (*adj.*), ~*-handedly* (*adv.*), ~*-handedness* (*n.*); *keep* ~ *house*, entertain all comers; ~ *letter*, letter printed in newspaper etc. but addressing an individual; ~ *mind*, accessibility to new ideas; unprejudiced or undecided state; ~*-minded* (*adj.*), ~*-mindedly* (*adv.*), ~*-mindedness* (*n.*); ~ *mouth*, mouth opened in voracity etc., and esp. in gaping stupidity or surprise; ~*-mouthed* (*adj.*), ~ *order*, formation with wide spaces between men or ships; ~ *question*, matter on which differences of opinion are legitimate; ~ *weather, winter*, not frosty; ~*-work*, pattern with interstices in metal, lace, etc. **ōp'ennėss** *n.* **ōp'en** *n.* *The* ~, open space, country or air, public view. ~ *v.* 1. Make or become open or more open; start, establish, set going (business, campaign, etc.); ~ *case*, (of counsel in law court) make preliminary statement before calling witnesses; ~ *debate*, be first speaker; ~ *the door to*, give opportunity for; ~ one's *eyes*, show surprise; ~ *the eyes of*, undeceive, enlighten. 2. Commence speaking; make a start; begin to be sold; (of hounds) begin to give tongue. 3. (naut.) Get view of by change of position; come into full view. 4. ~ *out*, unfold, develop, expand; become communicative; open throttle of a motor engine, accelerate; ~ *up*, make accessible; bring to notice, reveal; begin firing *on*.

ōp'ening (-pn-) *adj.* (esp.) Initial, first. ~ *n.* (esp.) Gap, passage, aperture; commencement, initial part; counsel's preliminary statement of case; opportunity, favourable conjuncture *for*; (chess) recognized sequence of moves for beginning game.

ōp'enly *adv.* Without concealment, publicly, frankly.

ŏp'era *n.* Dramatic performance or composition of which music is an essential part; branch of art concerned with these; *grand* ~, opera without spoken dialogue; *comic* ~, opera of light character and usu. with spoken dialogue; *opéra bouffe, opera buffa*, French, Italian, types of comic opera (Ital. *buffa* comic); ~*-glass(es)* small binoculars for use at opera or theatre; ~*-hat*, man's collapsible tall hat; ~*-house*, theatre for performance of opera.

ŏp′erable *adj.* (med.) That admits of being operated upon.

ŏp′erāte *v.* 1. Be in action, produce an effect, exercise influence; play (*up*)*on*, try to act (*up*)*on*; have desired effect. 2. Perform surgical or other operation; carry on warlike operations; deal or speculate in stocks and shares. 3. Bring about, accomplish; (chiefly U.S.) manage, work, conduct. 4. Conduct, be in charge of (machine, apparatus). 5. *Operating-table*, table for use in surgery; *operating-theatre*, room reserved in hospital etc. for the performance of surgical operations. **ŏp′erātor** *n.*

ŏperăt′ic *adj.* Of, like, opera. **ŏperăt′ically** *adv.*

ŏperā′tion *n.* 1. Working, action, way thing works; efficacy, validity, scope. 2. Active process, activity, performance; discharge of function; financial transaction. 3. Act or series of acts performed with hand or instrument on some part of body to remedy deformity, injury, disease, pain, etc. 4. Strategic movement of troops, ships, etc. 5. (math.) Subjection of number or quantity to process affecting its value or form, e.g. multiplication. **ŏperā′tional** *adj.* (esp.) Engaged on, used for, warlike operations.

ŏp′erative *adj.* 1. Having effect, in operation, efficacious; practical, not theoretical or contemplative. 2. Of surgical operations. ~ *n.* Factory worker, mechanic, workman. **ŏp′eratively** *adv.*

opẽrc′ūlum *n.* Gill-cover of fish (ill. FISH); lid or valve closing aperture of shell when tenant is retracted; similar lid-like structure in plants etc. **opẽrc′ūlar, opẽrc′ūlate, -ātėd** *adjs.*

ŏperĕtt′a *n.* Short, usu. one-act, light opera.

ŏp′erōse *adj.* Requiring, showing, or taking great pains, laborious. **ŏp′erōsely** *adv.* **ŏp′erōseness** *n.*

Ophēl′ia. In Shakespeare's 'Hamlet', daughter of Polonius; because of HAMLET's treatment of her and his killing of her father she goes mad and drowns herself.

ŏph′icleide (-īd) *n.* Obsolete wind-instrument of powerful tone, development of the 'serpent', consisting of conical brass tube bent double, with (usu.) eleven keys, serving as bass or alto to key-bugle.

ophĭd′ian *adj.* & *n.* (Member) of the *Ophidia* or suborder of reptiles comprising snakes.

Ophir (ōf′*er*). In O.T. geography, unidentified region (perhaps in SE. Arabia) famous for its fine gold and precious stones.

ŏphthăl′mia *n.* Inflammation of the eye, esp. affecting the conjunctiva.

ŏphthăl′mĭc *adj.* Of, relating to, or situated near, the eye.

ŏphthălmŏl′ogy *n.* The study of the eye and its diseases. **ŏphthălmŏl′ogist** *n.*

ŏphthăl′moscōpe *n.* Instrument for inspecting the interior of the eye, esp. the retina.

ōp′iate *adj.* (archaic) Containing opium, narcotic, soporific. ~ *n.* Drug prepared from opium; sleep-inducing drug, narcotic.

Opie (ōp′ĭ), John (1761–1807). English painter of portraits and historical pieces.

opīne′ *v.t.* Express or hold the opinion (*that*).

opĭn′ion (-yon) *n.* Judgement or belief based on grounds short of proof, provisional conviction, view held as probable; views or sentiment, esp. on moral questions, prevalent among people in general; what one thinks on a particular question, a belief, conviction; formal statement by expert when consulted of what he holds to be the fact or the right course, professional advice; *have no ~ of*, think unfavourably of.

opĭn′ionātėd, opĭn′ionative (-nyo-) *adjs.* Obstinate in opinion, dogmatic; self-willed. **opĭn′ionātėdness** *n.*

ōp′ium *n.* Dried latex from unripe capsules of a poppy (*Papaver somniferum*), of reddish-brown colour, with heavy smell and bitter taste, smoked or eaten as stimulant, intoxicant, or narcotic, and used in medicine as sedative; *~-den*, haunt of opium-smokers.

opŏp′anăx *n.* Fetid gum-resin obtained from root of a yellow-flowered parsnip-like umbelliferous plant, *O. chironium*, formerly used in medicine; gum-resin obtained from *Balsamodendron katof*, used in perfumery.

Opôrt′ō. City and port of Portugal, from which PORT[5] is exported.

opŏss′um *n.* Any small marsupial of the Amer. family *Didelphoidea*, mostly arboreal, some aquatic, of nocturnal habits, with usu. prehensile tail; (Australia) phalanger.

AMERICAN OPOSSUM

opp. *abbrev.* Opposite.

ŏpp′ĭdan *adj.* & *n.* (Inhabitant) of a town (rare); at Eton, boy who lives in a boarding-house in the town (opp. *colleger*, foundation scholar who lives in the college).

ŏpp′ĭlāte *v.t.* (med.) Block up, obstruct. **ŏppĭlā′tion** *n.*

oppōn′ent *adj.* (now rare) Opposing, contrary, opposed. ~ *n.* Adversary, antagonist.

ŏpp′ortūne *adj.* (Of time) suitable, well-selected, favourable; (of action or event) well-timed, done or occurring at favourable conjuncture. **ŏpp′ortūnely** *adv.* **ŏpp′ortūneness** *n.*

ŏpportūn′ĭsm *n.* Policy of doing what is opportune or at the time expedient, in politics, as opp. to rigid adherence to principles; method or course of action adapted to the circumstances of the moment; time-serving. **ŏpportūn′ĭst** *n.*

ŏpportūn′ĭty *n.* Favourable juncture, good chance, opening.

oppōse′ (-z) *v.t.* 1. Place, produce, or cite as obstacle, antagonist, counterpoise, or contrast *to*; represent as antithetical. 2. Set oneself against, withstand, resist, obstruct; propose the rejection of; act as opponent or check. 3. *opposed*, contrary, opposite, contrasted; hostile, adverse. **oppōs′able** *adj.* (of digit, esp. thumb) Capable of being applied so as to meet another.

ŏpp′osite (-zĭt) *adj.* 1. Contrary in position (*to*), facing, front to front or back to back (with); *~ number*, person or thing similarly placed in another set etc. to the given one. 2. Of contrary kind, diametrically different *to* or *from*; *the* other of a contrasted pair. **ŏpp′ositely** *adv.* **ŏpp′ositeness** *n.* **ŏpp′osite** *n.* Opposite thing or term. ~ *adv.* & *prep.* In opposite place, position, or direction (to); *~ prompter* (abbrev. O.P.), in theatre, to actors' right; *play ~*, have (specified actor or actress) as one's leading man or lady.

ŏpposi′tion (-zĭshn) *n.* 1. Placing opposite; diametrically opposite position (esp. astron., of two heavenly bodies when their longitude differs by 180°; opp. CONJUNCTION). 2. Contrast, antithesis; (logic) relation between two propositions with same subject and predicate but differing in quantity or quality or both. 3. Antagonism, resistance, being hostile; any party opposed to some proposal; *the, Her Majesty's O~*, chief Parliamentary party opposed to that in office. **ŏpposi′tional** (-zĭsho-) *adj.* (psychol.) Apt to take an opposing point of view.

oppŏs′ĭtĭve (-z-) *adj.* (rare) Adversative, antithetic; fond of opposing.

opprĕss′ *v.t.* Overwhelm with superior weight or numbers, or irresistible power; lie heavy on, weigh down (spirits etc.); govern tyrannically, keep under by coercion, subject to continual cruelty or injustice. **opprĕ′ssion** (-shn), **opprĕss′or** *ns.* **opprĕss′ĭve** *adj.* **opprĕss′ĭvely** *adv.* **opprĕss′ĭveness** *n.*

opprōb′rious *adj.* Conveying reproach, abusive, vituperative. **opprōb′riously** *adv.*

oppröb'rium *n.* Disgrace attaching to some act or conduct, infamy, crying of shame.

oppugn' (-ūn) *v.t.* Controvert, call in question; (rare) attack, resist, be in conflict with.

ŏpsŏn'ĭc *adj.* Of, produced by, arising from, opsonins; ~ *index*, index of proportion of opsonins present in blood.

ŏp'sonin *n.* Heat-sensitive substance, present in serum, which promotes destruction of bacteria by white blood-corpuscles.

ŏpt *v.i.* Exercise an option, make choice.

ŏptāt'ive *adj.* (gram.) Expressing wish; ~ *mood*, set of verbal forms of this kind. **ŏptāt'ively** *adv.* **ŏptāt'ive** *n.* Optative mood, verbal form belonging to it.

ŏp'tic *adj.* Of the eye or sense of sight; ~ *disc*, the 'blind spot', circular patch on retina where optic nerve originates (ill. EYE); ~ *nerve*, 2nd cranial nerve, from eyeball to fore-brain, conducting the impulses responsible for visual sensations (ill. EYE); ~ *tract*, continuation of optic nerve within brain. ~ *n.* Eye (now usu. joc.). **ŏp'tics** *n.* Science of sight, branch of physics dealing with properties etc. of light.

ŏp'tical *adj.* Visual, ocular; of sight or light in relation to each other; belonging to optics; constructed to assist sight or on the principles of optics; ~ *activity*, (physics and chem.) the property possessed by certain transparent solids and liquids of rotating the plane of polarization of polarized light passing through them. **ŏp'tically** *adv.*

ŏpti'cian (-shn) *n.* Maker or seller of optical instruments.

ŏp'timė *n.* One placed in second (*senior* ~) or third (*junior* ~) division in mathematical tripos at Cambridge (see also WRANGLER). [L, = 'best', 'very well']

ŏp'timism *n.* Doctrine, esp. as set forth by Leibniz, that the actual world is the best of all possible worlds; view that good must ultimately prevail over evil in the universe; sanguine disposition, inclination to take bright views. **ŏp'timist** *n.* & *adj.* **ŏptimist'ic** *adj.* **ŏptimis'tically** *adv.*

ŏp'timum *n.* (biol.) That degree or amount of heat, light, food, moisture, etc. most favourable for growth or other vital processes; (also attrib.) best. [L, = 'best']

ŏp'tion *n.* Choice, choosing, thing that is or may be chosen; liberty of choosing, freedom of choice; purchased right to call for or make delivery within specified time of specified stocks etc. at specified rate; *local* ~: see LOCAL. **ŏp'tional** (-shon-) *adj.* Not obligatory.

ŏptŏm'ėter *n.* Instrument for testing refracting power and visual range of the eye. **ŏptŏm'ėtry** *n.* **ŏptŏm'ėtrist** *n.*

ŏp'ūlent *adj.* Rich, wealthy; abounding, abundant, well stored. **ŏp'ūlently** *adv.* **ŏp'ūlence** *n.*

ŏp'us *n.* (L pl. *opera*). Musical composition or set of compositions as numbered among works of composer in order of publication etc. (abbrev. op.); *magnum* ~, great literary undertaking, writer's or other artist's chief production. [L, = 'work']

opŭs'cūle, opŭs'cūlum (pl. -*la*) *ns.* Minor musical or literary composition.

ŏr[1] *n.* (her.) Gold or yellow (ill. HERALDRY).

ŏr[2] *prep.* & *conj.* (archaic) Before, ere.

or[3] (ŏr, *or*) *conj.*, introducing second of two alternatives (*white or black*), all but the first (*white or grey or black*) or only the last (*white, grey, or black*) of any number, the second of each of several pairs (*white or black, red or yellow*), or (poet.) each of two (*or in the heart or in the head*).

O.R. *abbrev.* Other ranks.

ŏ'rach (-ĭch) *n.* Plant of genus *Atriplex*, commonest by the seashore.

ŏ'racle *n.* Place at which ancient Greeks etc. were accustomed to consult the gods for advice or prophecy; response, freq. ambiguous or obscure, given at such place; holy of holies or mercy-seat in Jewish temple; (vehicle of) divine inspiration or revelation; infallible guide, test, or indicator; authoritative, profoundly wise, or mysterious judge, judgement, prophet, etc.; *work the* ~, secure desired answer from oracle by tampering with priests etc.; (fig.) bring secret influence to bear in one's favour.

orăc'ūlar *adj.* Of an oracle; obscure like an oracle. **orăc'ūlarly** *adv.*

ŏr'al *adj.* Spoken, verbal, by word of mouth; (anat.) of the mouth. **ŏr'ally** *adv.* **ŏr'al** *n.* Oral examination.

ŏ'range[1] (-ĭnj) *n.* 1. Evergreen tree, *Citrus aurantium* and allied species, native of the East, widely cultivated in S. Europe and other warm, temperate or subtropical regions, with fragrant white flowers and large globose many-celled berries with sub-acid juicy pulp and tough outer rind of bright reddish-yellow; the fruit of this; *bitter* ~, fruit of *Citrus aurantium* var. *bigaradia*; *Blenheim* ~, kind of apple (see BLENHEIM); *blood* ~, red-pulped variety of orange; *China* ~, former name of the sweet or common orange; *mandarin* ~: see MANDARIN; *mock* ~, shrub *Philadelphus*; *Seville* ~, bitter orange; *squeezed* ~, thing from which no more good can be got; *tangerine* ~: see TANGERINE; *oranges and lemons*, nursery game in which song beginning with these words is sung and players take sides acc. to which fruit they name in answer to question; ~-*blossom*, flowers of orange or mock orange, freq. worn or carried by brides at wedding; ~-*flower water*, fragrant aqueous solution of orange flowers; ~(-*wood*) *stick*, small stick of orange-wood used for manicuring nails. 2. Colour of orange-rind, reddish-yellow. ~ *adj.* Orange-coloured. [Arab. *nāranj*]

Orange[2] (ŏ'rĭnj, the town orahṅzh'). Small town (orig. a Roman colony) and principality on River Rhône, which passed in 16th c. to the house of Nassau, subsequently rulers of the Netherlands; hence, *House of* ~, the Dutch royal house; *William of* ~-*Nassau*: see WILLIAM THE SILENT; *William of* ~: see WILLIAM[1] III. [L *Arausio* name of the town]

Orange[3] (ŏ'rĭnj). Epithet applied to the ultra-Protestant party in Ireland, in ref. to the secret political *Association of Orangemen*, formed 1795 for defence of Protestantism and maintenance of Protestant ascendancy in Ireland, and prob. named from wearing of orange badges etc. as symbol of adherence to William III, prince of ORANGE[2], and the Protestant succession in Ulster. **O'rangism** *n.*

ŏrangeade' (-jād) *n.* Drink of orange-juice, sugar, etc.; synthetic substitute for this.

O'range Free State. Inland province of the Republic of S. Africa; first settled by Boers trekking from Cape Colony (1836–8); annexed by Britain 1848, but restored in 1854 to Boers who established the Orange Free State Republic; annexed by Britain as Orange River Colony in 1900; responsible government, 1907; province of the Union (1910) as Orange Free State. **O'range River.** Longest river of S. Africa, running westward into Atlantic across almost whole breadth of the continent. [f. Dutch House of ORANGE[2]]

ŏ'rangery *n.* Building, hothouse, for protection of orange-trees; esp., in 17th-c. mansions, (part of) building having solid N. wall and large freq. arched windows on S. side.

orăng'-ut'an (-ōō-), **-outăng'** (-ōō-) *n.* Large long-armed mainly arboreal anthropoid ape, *Pongo satyrus*, of Borneo, Sumatra, and formerly Java (ill. APE). [Malay *ŏ'rang-uton* man of the woods]

orāte' *v.i.* (joc.) Make speech, hold forth, play the orator.

orā'tion *n.* Formal address, harangue, or discourse, esp. of ceremonial kind; (gram.) *direct* ~, person's words as actually spoken (as *I will go*), opp. to *oblique* ~, in which persons, tenses, etc., are changed in reporting (as *he said he would go*).

ŏ'rator *n.* Maker of a speech; eloquent public speaker; *Public O*~, official at Oxford and Cambridge speaking for university on State occasions.

ŏratŏr′iō *n.* Semi-dramatic musical composition usu. on sacred theme performed by soloists, chorus, and orchestra, without action, scenery, or costume. [It., orig. of musical services at oratory of St. Philip Neri]

ŏ′ratory[1] *n.* (Art of making) speeches, rhetoric; highly coloured presentment of facts, eloquent or exaggerating language. **ŏratŏ′rical** *adj.* **ŏratŏ′rically** *adv.*

ŏ′ratory[2] *n.* Small chapel, place for private worship; Roman Catholic society of simple priests without vows, founded at Rome in 1564, for plain preaching and popular services; any branch or house of this.

ŏrb *n.* Circle, disc, ring (now rare); sphere, globe; heavenly body; eyeball, eye (poet.); globe surmounted by cross as part of regalia (ill. REGALIA), symbolizing domination of the world by Christ. ~ *v.* Enclose in, gather into, orb.

ŏrbĭc′ūlar *adj.* Circular, discoid, ring-shaped; spherical, globular, rounded; (fig.) forming complete whole. **ŏrbĭc′ūlarly** *adv.*

ŏrb′it *n.* 1. Eye-socket; border round eye of bird or insect. 2. Curved course esp. of planet, comet, satellite, or binary star; (fig.) range, sphere, of action. **ŏrb′ital** *adj.* Of an orbit. ~ *n.* (physics) That part of the region surrounding an atomic nucleus in which an associated electron is most likely to be found; mathematical equation describing this.

ŏrc, ŏrc′a *n.* Cetacean of genus *Orca*, esp. the killer whale, *O. gladiator*.

Orcād′ian (ŏr-) *adj.* & *n.* (Native or inhabitant) of Orkney. [L *Orcades* the Orkney Islands]

Orcagna (ŏrkahn′y*a*). Andrea di Cione (d. 1377), Florentine painter, sculptor, and architect.

ŏrch′ard *n.* Enclosure with fruit-trees.

ŏrchĕs′tic (-k-) *adj.* Of dancing.

ŏr′chĕstra (-k-) *n.* 1. Semicircular space in front of stage in ancient Greek theatre, where chorus danced and sang. 2. Part of modern theatre or concert-room assigned to band or chorus; body of instrumental performers, or combination of stringed, woodwind, brass, and percussion instruments, in theatre or concert room; ~ *pit*, pit for orchestra in front of stage (ill. THEATRE). **orchĕs′tral** *adj.*

ŏr′chĕstrāte *v.* Arrange, or score, for orchestral performance. **ŏrchĕstrā′tion** *n.*

ŏrchestri′na (-kĭstrē-), **ŏrchĕs′trion** (-k-) *ns.* Mechanical organ imitating orchestral effects.

ŏr′chĭd (-k-) *n.* Plant of orchis family (*Orchidaceae*), large and widely distributed order of monocotyledons with three sepals and three petals, of which one (the lip or labellum) is usu. much larger than the others and of special colour or shape (ill. FLOWER); esp. one of the exotic cultivated species, freq. brilliantly coloured or grotesquely shaped. **ŏrchĭdā′ceous** (-sh*u*s) *adj.*

ŏr′chĭl *n.* Red or violet dye from certain lichens, esp. *Roccella tinctoria*.

ŏr′chĭs (-k-) *n.* = ORCHID, esp. wild one.

ord. *abbrev.* Ordained; order; ordinary.

ŏrdain′ *v.t.* 1. Appoint ceremonially to Christian ministry; confer holy orders (esp. those of deacon or priest) on. 2. Destine, appoint; appoint authoritatively, decree, enact.

ordē′al (*or* ŏrd′ēl) *n.* Ancient Teutonic mode of deciding suspected person's guilt or innocence by subjecting him to physical test such as plunging of hand in boiling water, safe endurance of which was taken as divine acquittal; experience that tests character or endurance, severe trial.

ŏrd′er *n.* 1. Rank of community, social division, grade or stratum; definite rank in State; separate and homogeneous set of persons. 2. Kind, sort. 3. Any of the 9 grades of angels in medieval theology (seraphim, cherubim, thrones, dominations, principalities, powers, virtues, archangels, angels). 4. Grade of Christian ministry; (pl.) status of clergyman; *holy ~s*, in Anglican Church, those of bishop, priest, and deacon, in R.C. these and subdeacon; *minor ~s*, in R.C. Church, those of acolyte, exorcist, reader, and doorkeeper; *in ~s*, ordained; *take ~s*, be ordained. 5. Fraternity of monks or friars, or formerly of knights, bound by common rule of life; company, usu. instituted by sovereign, to which distinguished persons are admitted by way of honour or reward, insignia worn by members of this. 6. (archit.) Mode of treatment with established proportions between parts, esp. one of the *five* (*classical*) *~s* of column and entablature (Doric, Ionic, Corinthian, Tuscan, and Composite, the first three of Greek origin, the others Roman). 7. (archit.) Row of voussoirs (ill.

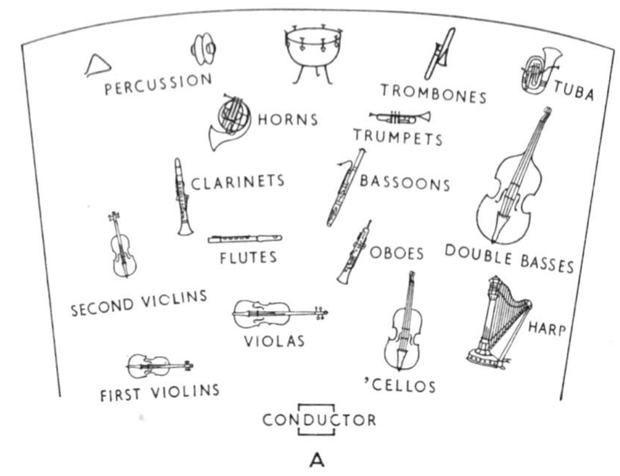

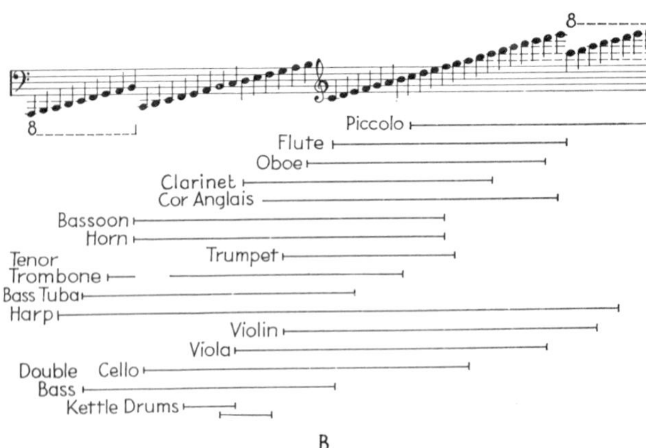

A. POSITION OF PLAYERS IN A MODERN ORCHESTRA.
B. RANGE OF ORCHESTRAL INSTRUMENTS

ARCH). 8. (math.) Degree of complexity. 9. (biol.) Classificatory group below *class* and above *family*; *natural* ~, (bot.) order of plants allied in general structure, not merely agreeing in single characteristic as in Linnaean system. 10. Sequence, succession, manner of following; regular array, condition in which every part or unit is in its right place; tidiness; normal, healthy, or efficient state; (mil.) equipment, uniform, etc., for some purpose; *out of* ~, not systematically arranged; not working rightly; *in (good)* ~, fit for use. 11. Constitution of the world, way things normally happen, collective manifestations of natural forces or laws. 12. Stated form of divine service; principles of decorum and rules of procedure accepted by legislative assembly or public meeting, or enforced by its president; ~, ~!, protest against infringement of this; *rise to (a point of)* ~, interrupt debate etc. with inquiry whether something being said or done is in or out of order; ~ *of the day*, programme, business set down for treatment; prevailing state of things. 13. Prevalence of constituted authority, law-abiding state. 14. Mandate, injunction, authoritative direction or instruction (freq. pl.); (banking etc.) instruction to pay money or deliver property signed by owner or responsible agent; direction to manufacturer, tradesman, etc., to supply something; pass admitting bearer gratis, cheap, or as privilege, to theatre, museum, etc.; *O~ in Council*, sovereign order on some administrative matter given by advice of Privy Council; *postal, money*, ~, kinds of Post Office cheque for remitting money; *made to* ~, made according to special directions, to suit individual measurements etc. (opp. to *ready-made*); *on* ~, ordered but not yet supplied; ~ *to view*, requisition from estate agent to occupier to allow client to inspect premises; *a large* ~, (colloq.) difficult job; *in* ~, suitable, fitting, appropriate; *in short* ~ (U.S.), without delay, immediately. 15. *in* ~ *to do*, with a view to, for the purpose of, doing; *in* ~ *that*, with the intention or to the end that. ~ *v.t.* 1. (archaic) Put in order, array, regulate. 2. Ordain; command, bid, prescribe; command or direct to go *to, away*, etc.; direct tradesman etc. to supply.

ōr'derly *adj.* Methodically arranged or inclined, regular, obedient to discipline, not unruly, well-behaved; (mil.) on duty, concerned with carrying out orders; ~ *book*, book kept in orderly room for entering orders etc.; ~ *officer*, officer on duty for the day; ~ *room*, one set apart in barracks etc. for administrative business. **ōr'derlinėss** *n.* **ōr'derly** *n.* Soldier in attendance on officer to execute orders etc.; attendant in (esp. military) hospital.

ōr'dĭnal *adj.* & *n.* 1. (Number) defining thing's position in a series (*first, tenth* are ~ *numbers*; see also CARDINAL). 2. Prescribed form of ceremony to be observed at consecration of bishops and ordination of priests and deacons; book containing words and directions for this ceremony.

ōr'dĭnance *n.* Authoritative

ORDERS OF ARCHITECTURE: A. GREEK DORIC. B. GREEK IONIC. C. GREEK CORINTHIAN. D. ROMAN CORINTHIAN. E. COMPOSITE. F. TUSCAN

A. 1. Acroterion. 2. Taenia. 3. Guttae. 4. Mutule. 5. Triglyph. 6. Metope. 7. Abacus. 8. Echinus. 9. Annulet. 10. Hypotrachelium. 11. Flute. 12. Arris. 13. Module. B. 14. Volute. 15. Stria. 16. Apophyge. 17. Plinth. C. 18. Acanthus. D. 19. Corona. 20. Modillion. 21. Dentil. 22. Fascia. F. 23. Necking. 24. Astragal

direction, decree; religious rite; (U.S.) by-law.

ŏr'dĭnary *adj.* 1. Regular, normal, customary, usual; not exceptional, not above the usual, commonplace; ~ *seaman* (abbrev. O.S.), lower rating than *able seaman*. 2. Having immediate or *ex officio* and not deputed jurisdiction. ~ *n.* 1. Ordinary authority; *the O~*, archbishop in province, bishop in diocese; (*Lord*) *O~*, in Scotland, one of five judges of Court of Session constituting Outer House. 2. Rule or book laying down order of divine service. 3. Public meal provided at fixed time and price in tavern etc.; (U.S.) in Virginia etc., any tavern or inn. 4. (her.) Charge of earliest, simplest, and commonest kind, esp. chief, pale, bend, fess, bar, chevron, cross, or saltire (ill. HERALDRY). 5. Ordinary condition, course, etc.; what is ordinary; *in ~*, (of officials etc.) by permanent appointment, not temporary or extraordinary; (of ships) laid up, not in commission. **ŏr'dĭnarily** *adv.* **ŏr'dĭnarĭnėss** *n.*

ŏr'dĭnate *n.* (geom.) Any of series of parallel chords of conic section in relation to bisecting diameter (esp. used of half the chord, from curve to diameter); straight line from any point drawn parallel to one co-ordinate axis and meeting the other (correlative to ABSCISSA; ill. GRAPH).

ŏrdĭnā'tion *n.* 1. Arrangement in ranks, classification. 2. Conferring of holy orders, admission to church ministry. 3. Decreeing, ordainment.

ŏrdĭnee' *n.* Newly ordained deacon.

ŏrd'nance *n.* Mounted guns, artillery; branch of public service dealing esp. with military stores and materials; ~ *survey*, official survey of Gt Britain (and formerly Ireland), orig. carried out under Master-General of the Ordnance, now by a civil department partially staffed by the R.E.; ~ *datum*, sea-level as defined for ordnance survey, mean sea-level at Newlyn, Cornwall, derived from the mean of hourly readings between 1915 and 1921.

Ŏrdovĭ'cian (-shĭ-) *adj.* (geol.) Of the 2nd system of rocks in the Palaeozoic, above the Cambrian and below the Silurian. ~ *n.* (*The O~*), this system or period (ill. GEOLOGY). [*Ordovices*, ancient tribe in N. Wales]

ŏrd'ūre (*or* -dy*er*) *n.* Excrement, dung.

ōre *n.* Solid naturally-occurring mineral aggregate of economic interest from which one or more valuable constituents may be recovered by treatment; (poet.) metal, esp. precious metal.

Ore(g). *abbrev.* Oregon.

ŏr'ėăd *n.* (Gk and L myth.) Mountain nymph.

orĕc'tĭc *adj.* Of desire or appetite, appetitive.

O'rėgon (ŏ-). Pacific State of U.S.; admitted to the Union in 1859; capital, Salem; ~ *pine*, name for Douglas fir, esp. in timber trade; ~ *Trail*, (U.S. hist.) route from Missouri across Oregon, used by emigrants esp. 1842–7.

Orĕs'tēs (-z). (Gk legend) Son of AGAMEMNON and Clytemnestra; killed his mother and her lover Aegisthus in revenge because they had murdered his father; was pursued by the Furies until he was pardoned by Artemis, having rescued her statue (and his sister Iphigenia) from the island of Tauris; became king of Argos, Sparta, and Mycenae, and married Hermione, daughter of Menelaus.

ŏrfe *n.* Fish, golden-yellow variety of the ide (*Leuciscus idus*).

ŏr'gan *n.* 1. Part of animal or vegetable body adapted for special vital function, as *~s of digestion, speech*, etc. 2. Person's voice with ref. to its power or quality. 3. Medium of communication, esp. newspaper or journal representing a party, cause, etc. 4. Musical instrument consisting essentially of pipes which are supplied with wind by a bellows (or an electric fan) and sounded by means of keys and pedals, each key or pedal controlling the mechanism (usu. a valve) which admits air to a particular pipe; the pipes are arranged in ranks (*stops*) each of which has a different quality of tone and is brought into action by drawing out a knob, and the keys are arranged in rows (*manuals*); each manual is linked with a group of stops. (*Illustration, p.* 577.) 5. Various keyboard instruments producing more or less similar effects by different means, as AMERICAN ~, ELECTRONIC ~. 6. *barrel-~*: see BARREL; *choir ~*: see CHOIR ORGAN; *great ~*, the principal manual of an organ, linked with the louder stops; *mouth-~*: see MOUTH; *pedal ~*, the foot-pedals of an organ which sound the deeper notes; *~-blower*, person or mechanism working organ bellows; *~-builder*, maker of organs; *~-grinder*, player on barrel-organ; *~-loft*, loft or gallery in which organ is placed, freq. above *~-screen*, ornamental screen between nave and choir in church; *~-stop*, set of pipes of similar tone-quality in organ; handle of mechanism that brings such a set into action; *swell ~*: see SWELL *n.*, sense 3.

ŏr'gandĭe *n.* Thin stiff translucent muslin.

ŏrgăn'ĭc *adj.* 1. Of the bodily organs, vital; (path., of disease) affecting structure of an organ (opp. *functional*). 2. Having organs or organized physical structure; of animals or plants; (chem., of compound substances) occurring naturally as constituent of organized bodies, formed from such compounds (all of which contain or are derived from hydrocarbon radicals); ~ *chemistry*, chemistry of organic compounds, chemistry of hydrocarbons and their derivatives. 3. Constitutional, inherent, fundamental, structural; organized, systematic, co-ordinated. **ŏrgăn'ĭcally** *adv.*

ŏr'ganĭsm *n.* Living animal or plant; anything capable of maintaining the processes characteristic of life, esp. reproduction; (material structure of) individual animal or plant; whole with interdependent parts compared to living being.

ŏr'ganĭst *n.* Player of organ.

ŏrganĭzā'tion *n.* (esp.) Organized body, system, or society.

ŏr'ganīze *v.* 1. Furnish with organs, make organic, make into living being or tissue (usu. in past part.); become organic. 2. Form into an organic whole; give orderly structure to, frame and put into working order; make arrangements for, get up (undertaking involving co-operation). **ŏr'ganīzer** *n.*

ŏr'ganŏn, ŏr'ganum *n.* Instrument of thought, system of a treatise on logic. [Gk *organon* tool, work; *Organon* was the title of Aristotle's logical writings, and *Novum* (new) *Organum* that of Bacon's]

ŏr'ganothĕ'rapy *n.* Treatment of disease with animal organs or extracts of these.

ŏr'ganzine (-ēn) *n.* Strongest kind of silk thread, in which main twist is in contrary direction to that of strands.

ŏr'găsm *n.* Paroxysm of excitement or rage; climax of venereal excitement in coition. **ŏrgăs'tĭc** *adj.*

ŏrgĭăs'tĭc *adj.* Of the nature of an orgy.

ŏr'gy (-j-) *n.* 1. (Gk and Rom. antiq., usu. pl.) Secret rites in worship of various gods, esp. festival in honour of Dionysus (Bacchus), celebrated with extravagant dancing, singing, drinking, etc. 2. Drunken or licentious revel; (pl.) revelry, debauchery.

ŏr'ĭėl *n.* Large windowed polygonal recess projecting usu. from upper storey and supported from ground or on corbels; window of oriel, projecting window of upper storey (ill. WINDOW).

Or'iel Coll'ege (ŏr-). College of University of Oxford founded 1326 by Adam de Brome; so called from a tenement (Seneschal Hall or La Oriole) granted to the college in 1327.

ŏr'ĭėnt[1] *n.* 1. *The* eastward part of sky or earth (poet.); *the* East or countries E. of Mediterranean and S. Europe. 2. Orient pearl; peculiar lustre of pearl of best quality. ~ *adj.* 1. (Of precious stones, esp. pearls, of finest kinds, as coming anciently from the East) lustrous, sparkling, precious. 2. (Of sun etc.) rising, nascent.

ŏr'ĭĕnt[2], **ŏr'ientāte** *vbs.t.* 1. Place (building etc.) so as to face east; build (church) with chancel end due E.; bury with feet east-

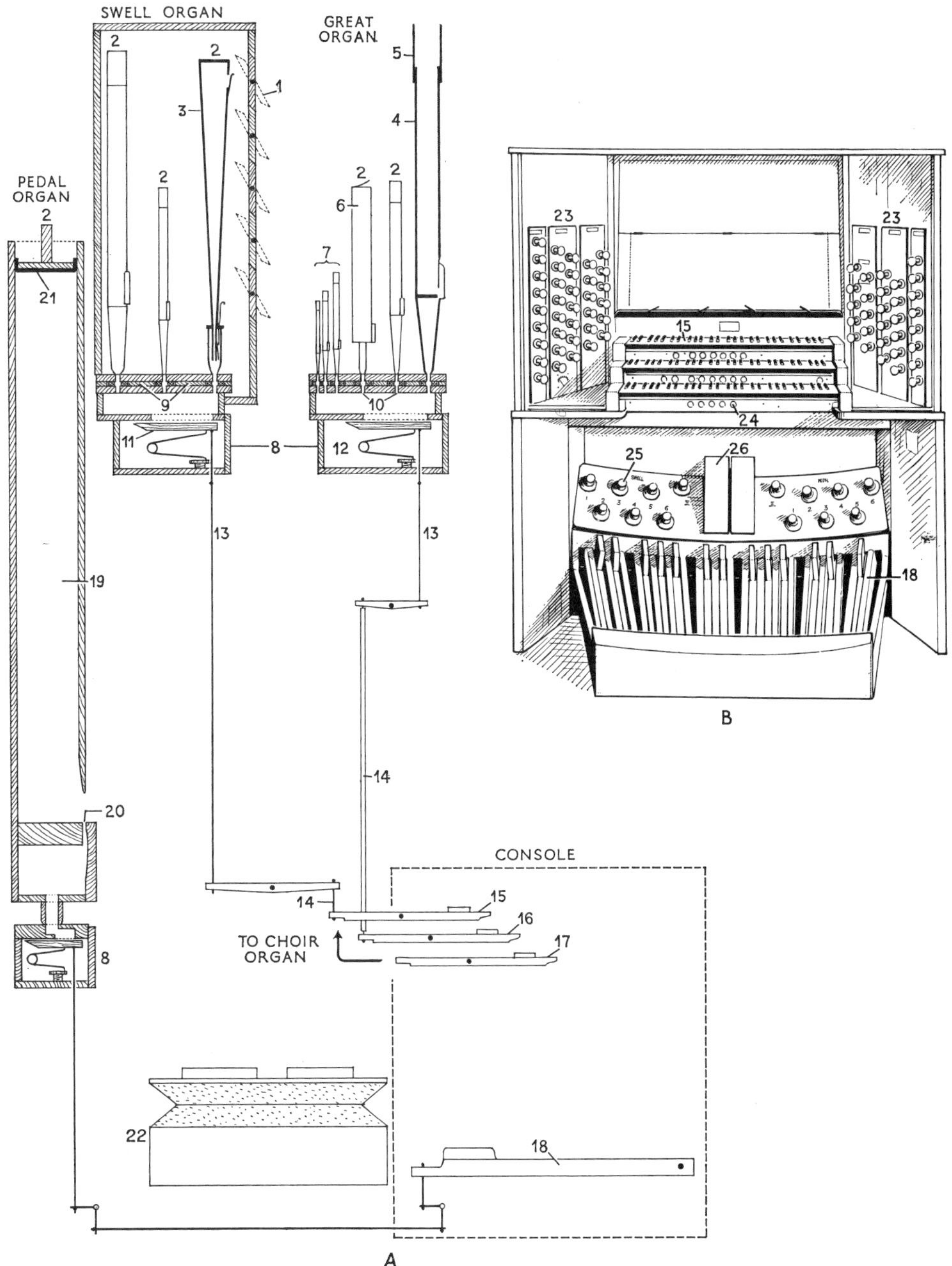

ORGAN WITH TRACKER ACTION: A. DIAGRAMMATIC SECTION. B. CONSOLE

1. Swell. 2. Rank of pipes or stop. 3. Reed-pipe (section). 4. Diapason: open metal flue-pipe (section). 5. Tuning slide to vary length of pipe when tuning. 6. Wooden open flue-pipe. 7. Mixture stop: 3 ranks of pipes on one slide, each note of keyboard thus playing 3 pipes of this stop simultaneously. 8. Wind-chest. 9. Stop slide. 10. Wind groove. 11. Pallet admitting wind into wind groove and thence to pipes. 12. Lower part of wind-chest supplied with wind from wind reservoir. 13. Tracker. 14. Sticker. 15. Swell organ manual. 16. Great organ manual. 17. Choir organ manual (mechanism, wind-chest, and pipes omitted). 18. Pedal organ keyboard or pedal-board. 19. Bourdon stopped wood pipe (section). 20. Flue of pipe. 21. Tampion or pipe stopper. 22. Bellows. 23. Stop knobs. 24. Thumb-pistons controlling manual stops. 25. Toe-pistons controlling pedal stops. 26. Swell pedals

ward. 2. Place or exactly determine position of with regard to points of compass, settle or find bearings of; (fig.) bring into clearly understood relations; ~ one*self*, determine how one stands. **orĭentā′tion** *n.*

orĭĕn′tal *adj.* Of the East or countries E. of Mediterranean and S. Europe, esp. Asiatic; occurring in, coming from, the East, characteristic of its civilization etc.; (of pearls) orient. **orĭĕn′tally** *adv.* **orĭĕn′tal** *n.* Inhabitant of the East. **orĭĕn′talism** *n.*

ŏ′rĭfĭce *n.* Aperture, mouth of cavity, perforation, vent.

ŏ′rĭflamme (-m) *n.* Sacred banner of St. Denis, a banderole of two or three points of (orange-)red silk attached to a lance, received by early French kings from abbot of St. Denis on starting for war; anything, material or ideal, serving as rallying-point in struggle; bright conspicuous object, blaze of colour, etc. [Fr., f. L *aurum* gold, *flamma* flame]

Orĭgen (ŏr′ĭjĕn) (*c* 185–253). Christian theologian and scholar of Alexandria.

ŏ′rĭgĭn *n.* Derivation, beginning or rising from something; extraction; source, starting-point.

orĭ′gĭnal *adj.* 1. Existent from the first; primitive, innate, initial, earliest; ~ *sin*, innate depravity common to all human beings in consequence of the Fall. 2. That has served as pattern, of which copy or translation has been made; not derivative or dependent, first-hand, not imitative; novel in character or style, inventive, creative; thinking or acting for oneself. **orĭ′gĭnally** *adv.* **orĭgĭnăl′ĭty** *n.* **orĭ′gĭnal** *n.* Derivation, descent, origin (rare); pattern, archetype, thing from which another is copied or imitated; eccentric person.

orĭ′gĭnāte *v.* Give origin to, initiate, cause to begin; have origin, take rise. **orĭgĭnā′tion, orĭ′gĭnātor** *ns.*

Orĭnō′cō (ŏ-). River of northern S. America, flowing N. and E. through Venezuela to Atlantic Ocean.

ŏr′ĭōle *n.* 1. Bird of genus *Oriolus*, esp. *O. galbula* (golden ~), a summer visitor to Europe, with rich yellow and black plumage. 2. Unrelated Amer. bird of family *Icteridae*, mostly with yellow or orange and black coloration.

Orī′on. 1. (Gk legend) Giant and hunter of Boeotia, changed at his death into a constellation. 2. A conspicuous constellation containing many bright stars; *Orion's belt*, three bright stars in short line across Orion. **Orī′onid** *n.* Any of a shower of meteors with radiant point in Orion.

ŏ′rĭson (-zn) *n.* (archaic) Prayer.

Orĭss′a. A State of the Republic of India, formerly a province of British India.

Ork′ney (ŏr-) **Islands.** County of Scotland formed by a group of islands off N. coast.

Orlăn′dō (ŏr-). Italian form of ROLAND.

ŏrle *n.* (her.) Narrow band following outline of shield but not extending to edge of it (ill. HERALDRY).

Orlē′anĭst (ŏr-). (Fr. hist.) Adherent of those princes of the house of Orleans who were descended from Louis XIV's younger brother Philippe and whose descendant Louis Philippe reigned as king of France 1830–48.

Orleans (ŏrlē′*a*nz). French city on River Loire; besieged by the English, 1428, and relieved by Joan of Arc. ~ *n.* 1. Variety of plum. 2. Fabric of cotton warp and worsted weft.

ŏrl′op *n.* Lowest deck of a ship which has three or more decks. [Du. *overloop* covering]

Orm′azd (ŏr-), **Ahura-Măz′da** (*a*hoor′a). In ZOROASTRIAN religion, the supreme deity, principle of goodness and light, in perpetual conflict with Ahriman, the spirit of evil.

ŏrm′er *n.* The sea-ear, kind of edible gasteropod mollusc, *Haliotis tuberculata.*

ŏrm′olu (-lōō) *n.* Gilded bronze used for the mounts of furniture and other decorative metalwork, esp. in 18th-c. France; various cheaper imitations of this, esp. gold-coloured alloy of copper, zinc, and tin; articles made of or decorated with these. [Fr. *or moulu* ground gold (for use in gilding)]

Ormuz, Hormuz (ŏrm′ōōz, hŏr-). Ancient city on island at mouth of Persian Gulf; an important centre of commerce in Middle Ages.

ŏrn′ament *n.* 1. (eccles., usu. pl.) Accessories of church or worship (e.g. altar, chalice, service-books, vestments, organ, bells, etc.). 2. Thing used or serving to adorn; quality or person whose existence or presence confers grace or honour. 3. (sing. only) Adorning, being adorned, embellishment; features or work added for decorative purposes. **ŏrnamĕn′tal** *adj.* **ŏrnamĕn′tally** *adv.* **ŏrn′amĕnt** *v.t.* Adorn, beautify. **ŏrnamĕntā′tion** *n.*

ŏrnāte′ *adj.* Elaborately adorned; embellished. **ŏrnāte′ly** *adv.* **ŏrnāte′nėss** *n.*

ŏrnĭthŏl′ogy *n.* Branch of zoology dealing with birds. **ŏrnĭthŏl′ogĭst** *n.* **ŏrnĭtholŏ′gĭcal** *adj.*

Ornĭthorhy̆n′chus (-k-) *n.* Duck-billed platypus, an Australian aquatic egg-laying mammal (monotreme) with glossy dark-brown fur, webbed feet, and bill like duck's.

Orohĭpp′us (ŏr-) *n.* Small fossil horse of N. Amer. Eocene deposits, with four toes on fore feet and three on hind feet, regarded as one of earliest known forms of horse. [Gk *oros* mountain, *hippos* horse]

Oropēs′a float (-*za*) *n.* (mine-sweeping) Cigar-shaped float for supporting sweep-wires. [f. name of the ship on which it was first used]

Orōs′ĭus, Paulus (5th c.). Spanish priest, historian, and theologian.

ŏr′otŭnd *adj.* (Of utterance etc.) swelling, mouth-filling, imposing, dignified, pompous, magniloquent, pretentious. [L *ore rotundo* with round mouth]

ŏrph′an *n.* & *adj.* (Child) bereaved of parent(s). ~ *v.t.* Bereave of parent(s). **ŏrph′anage** *n.* Institution for education etc. of orphans.

Orph′eus (ŏrf′ūs). (Gk legend) Legendary Thracian pre-Homeric poet; son of Calliope or another Muse; played so marvellously on the lyre (given to him by Apollo) that wild beasts were spellbound by his music; visited Hades and charmed Pluto into releasing his wife Eurydice from the dead, but lost her because he failed to obey the condition that he must not look back at her until they had reached the world of the living.

Orph′ĭc (ŏr-) *adj.* & *n.* Of Orpheus; (adherent) of Orphism. **Orph′ĭsm, Orph′ĭcĭsm** *ns.* A mystic religion of ancient Greece, originating in 7th or 6th c. B.C. and based in poems (now lost) attributed to Orpheus; its doctrines emphasized the mixture of good (or divine) and evil in human nature and the necessity that the individual should rid himself of the evil part by ritual and moral purification throughout a series of reincarnations.

ŏrph′rey, ŏrf′ray *n.* One of the bands or panels, freq. embroidered, with which an ecclesiastical vestment is decorated (ill. VESTMENT); the cross-shaped piece on the back of a chasuble.

ŏrp′ĭment *n.* A bright-yellow mineral, *arsenious trisulphide* (As_2S_3), used as a pigment.

ŏrp′ĭn(e) *n.* Succulent herbaceous plant (*Sedum telephium*) with smooth fleshy leaves and corymbs of purple flowers.

Orp′ĭngton (ŏr-). Breed of large hardy dual-purpose poultry, usu. buff, with white legs. [town in Kent, England]

ŏ′rrery *n.* Clockwork model of the planetary system. [named after Charles Boyle, 4th Earl of Orrery, *c* 1700]

ŏ′rrĭs[1] *n.* Kind of iris, flower-de-luce (now rare); ~*-root*, violet-scented root of three species of iris used in perfumery etc.

ŏ′rrĭs[2] *n.* Lace of gold and silver thread; embroidery made of gold lace.

Orsini(ŏrsēn′ĭ), Felice(1819–58). Italian patriot and revolutionary; was convicted of an attempt in 1858 on the life of Napoleon III, and executed.

ŏrt *n.* (dial. & archaic; usu. pl.) Refuse scrap(s), leavings.

Ortĕl'ius (ŏr-), Abraham (1527–98). Flemish geographer and map-maker of Antwerp.

ŏrthochromăt'ic *adj.* (phot.) Reproducing colours in their correct relative intensities.

ŏrth'oclāse *n.* Common felspar, a silicate of aluminium and potassium occurring in crystals or masses with two cleavages at right angles.

ŏrthodŏn'tics *n.* Study of the normal formation of the teeth and the correction of malformations. **ŏrthodŏn'tic** *adj.*

ŏrth'odŏx *adj.* Holding correct or currently accepted opinions esp. on religious doctrine; not heretical, original, or independent in mind; generally accepted as right or true, esp. in theology; in harmony with what is authoritatively established; approved, conventional; *O~ Church*, the Eastern or Greek Church, recognizing patriarch of Constantinople as head; national Churches of Russia, Bulgaria, Rumania, etc., in communion with this. **ŏrth'odŏxy** *n.* Being orthodox.

ŏrthō'epy *n.* Science of correct pronunciation. **ŏrthōĕp'ic** *adj.* **ŏrthō'epist** *n.*

ŏrthogĕn'ĕsis *n.* View of evolution according to which variations follow a defined direction and are not merely sporadic and fortuitous.

ŏrthŏg'raphy *n.* 1. Correct or conventional spelling; spelling with ref. to its correctness. 2. Orthographic projection. **ŏrthogrăph'ic** *adj.* (Of perspective projection in maps, elevations, etc.) in which point of sight is supposed to be at infinite distance, so that rays are parallel (ill. DRAWING). **ŏrthogrăph'ical** *adj.* Of orthography. **ŏrthogrăph'ically** *adv.*

ŏrthopaed'ic (-pē-) *adj.* Curing deformity. **ŏrthopaed'ics** *n.* Orthopaedic surgery. **ŏrthopaed'ist** *n.*

ŏrthŏp'terous *adj.* Of the order *Orthoptera* of insects with straight narrow fore wings, broad longitudinally folded hind wings, and incomplete metamorphosis.

ŏrthŏp'tic *adj.* Of, concerning, the right or normal use of the eyes. **ŏrthŏp'tics** *n.* Correction of defective vision by means of exercises of the eye-muscles. **ŏrthŏp'tist** *n.* Expert in orthoptic training.

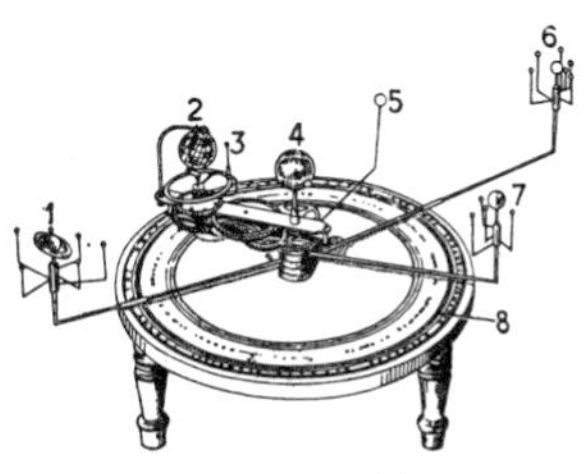

ORRERY, *c* 1800

1. Saturn and its satellites. 2. Earth. 3. Moon. 4. Sun. 5. Mars. 6. Uranus and its satellites. 7. Jupiter and its satellites. 8. Zodaic calendar scale

ŏrthorhŏm'bic (-rŏm-) *adj.* (cryst.) Having the three axes mutually at right angles and unequal (ill. CRYSTAL).

ŏrthoscŏp'ic *adj.* Having, producing, correct vision; free from, constructed to correct, optical distortion.

ŏrt'olan *n.* One of the buntings (*Emberiza hortulana*), a small bird of Europe, N. Africa, and W. Asia, esteemed as table delicacy.

ŏ'rўx *n.* Large antelope (genus *Oryx*) of Africa and Arabia, with long straight-pointed horns.

O.S. *abbrev.* Old style; ordinary seaman; Ordnance Survey; outsize.

O.S.A. *abbrev.* Of the Order of St. Augustine.

Osage (ōs'āj). Tribe of N. Amer. Indians of Siouan linguistic stock, formerly occupying territory in Missouri and Arkansas; ~ *orange*, N. Amer. thorny tree of mulberry family with large yellow fruit and hard flexible yellow wood used by Osage and other Indians for bows and clubs.

O.S.B. *abbrev.* Of the Order of St. Benedict.

Os'borne (ŏz-). Former English royal residence in Isle of Wight; purchased by Queen Victoria, 1845; presented to the nation by Edward VII, 1902; used as a Naval College, 1903–21.

Os'can (ŏ-) *adj.* & *n.* (Of) the ancient Italic (Indo-European) language spoken in Campania and farther S., and surviving only in inscriptions in an alphabet derived from Etruscan.

Os'car (ŏ-) *n.* Gold-plated statuette awarded annually by the Academy of Motion Picture Arts and Sciences, of Hollywood, U.S.A., for highest achievement in film production; (loosely) similar awards. [arbitrary use of Christian name]

os'cillāte (ŏsĭ-) *v.* 1. Swing like pendulum, move to and fro between two points; vacillate, vary between extremes of opinion, action, etc. 2. (Of wireless receiver) radiate electro-magnetic waves owing to faulty operation or construction. **ŏscillā'tion** *n.* **ŏs'cillatory** *adj.*

oscitā'tion (ŏsĭ-) *n.* (rare) Yawning, inattention, negligence.

Os'co-Um'brian (ŏ-, ŭ-) *adj.* & *n.* (Of) the group of Italic languages comprising Oscan, Umbrian, and Volscian.

ŏs'cūlar *adj.* Of the mouth; of kissing; (math.) that osculates.

ŏs'cūlāte *v.* 1. Kiss (usu. joc.). 2. (biol., of species etc.) Have contact through intermediate species etc.; have common characters *with*. 3. (math., of curve or surface) Have contact of higher order with, coincide in three or more points. **ŏs'cūlant, ŏs'cūlatory** *adjs.* **ŏscūlā'tion** *n.*

ŏs'cūlum *n.* (pl. *-la*). Mouth-like aperture; mouth or 'flue' of sponge (ill. SPONGE).

O.S.F. *abbrev.* Of the Order of St. Francis.

osier (ō'zh*er*) *n.* (Shoot of) species of willow, esp. *Salix viminalis*, with tough pliant branches used in basket-work; attrib., of osiers.

Osīr'ĭs. Great deity of ancient Egyptians, husband of Isis and god of the underworld; sometimes identified with sun.

Os'lō (ŏ-). Capital city of Norway, on SE. coast; formerly (1624–1925) called Kristiania in honour of King Christian IV, who re-founded it.

Os'man I (ŏz-), **Oth'man** (1259–1326). Turkish sultan and conqueror; founder of Ottoman or Osmanli dynasty; declared himself sultan on collapse of Seljuk Empire.

Osmăn'lĭ (ŏz-) *adj.* & *n.* (Turk) of Ottoman Empire; member of western branch of Turkish peoples. [f. OSMAN]

ŏs'mĭum (-z-) *n.* (chem.) Metallic element of the platinum group, hard, brittle, bluish-white, and of high density; symbol Os, at. no. 76, at. wt 190·2. [Gk *osmē* smell]

ŏsmōs'ĭs (-zm-) *n.* The tendency of a solvent, when separated from a solution by a suitable membrane (often animal or vegetable), to pass through the membrane so as to dilute the solution. **ŏsmŏt'ic** *adj.* ~ *pressure*, the pressure produced by the solvent in osmosis.

ŏs'prey (-ā, -ĭ) *n.* 1. Large diurnal bird of prey, *Pandion haliaetus*, found on rocky sea-shores etc. and preying on fish; sea-eagle, fish-hawk. 2. Egret-plume worn as ornament on hat etc.

Oss'a (ŏ-). Lofty mountain in Thessaly, Greece, S. of Olympus; in Gk legend, the giants were said to have heaped it on PELION.

ŏss'ĕous *adj.* Consisting of bone, ossified; having bony skeleton; abounding in fossil bones.

Oss'ĭan (ŏ-), **Oisin** (ō'shēn). Legendary Gaelic 3rd-c. warrior and bard. **Ossiăn'ĭc** *adj.* Of Ossian; of the style or character of the rhythmic prose of MACPHERSON's supposed translation of the poems of Ossian; hence, bombastic, grandiloquent.

ŏss'ĭcle *n.* (anat.) Small bone, esp. one of three in the middle ear (ill. EAR); small piece of bony, chitinous, or calcareous substance in animal framework.

ŏss'ĭfȳ *v.* Turn into bone; harden; make or become rigid, callous, or unprogressive. **ŏssĭfĭcā'tion** *n.*

ŏss'ūary *n.* Receptacle for bones of dead, charnel-house, bone-urn; cave in which ancient bones are found.

Ostade (ŏstahd'*e*), Adriaen van

(1610–85). Dutch genre painter and etcher. ~, Isack van (1621–49). Dutch genre and landscape painter, brother and pupil of A. van Ostade.

ŏstĕn'sĭble *adj.* Professed, for show, put forward to conceal the real. **ŏstĕn'sĭbly** *adv.*

ŏstĕn'sory *n.* Receptacle for displaying the Host to congregation, monstrance.

ŏstentā'tion *n.* Pretentious display, esp. of wealth or luxury; showing off; attempt or intention to attract notice. **ŏstentā'tious** (-shus) *adj.* **ŏstentā'tiously** *adv.*

ŏstėŏl'ogy *n.* Branch of anatomy concerned with the study of the skeleton and the structure of bones.

ŏstėŏp'athy *n.* Theory of disease and method of cure based on assumption that deformation of part of skeleton, notably the spine, and consequent interference with nerves and blood-vessels, are the cause of most diseases. **ŏstėopăth'ĭc** *adj.* **ŏs'tėopăth** *n.* Practitioner of osteopathy.

Os'tia (ŏ-). Ancient city and harbour of Latium, Italy; said to be the first colony founded by Rome; it was buried, and its ruins were preserved, by the gradual silting up of the River Tiber.

ŏst'ler (-sl-) *n.* Stableman at inn.

ŏs'tracīze *v.t.* 1. (at ancient Athens) Banish (dangerously powerful or unpopular citizen) for 10 or 5 years by voting with potsherds or tiles on which name of person to be banished was written. 2. Exclude from society, favour, or common privileges, 'send to Coventry', etc. **ŏs'tracĭsm** *n.*

ŏs'trĭch *n.* Very large swift-running bird (*Struthio camelus*) of sandy plains of Africa and Arabia, with small wings useless for flight, and habit of swallowing hard substances to assist working of gizzard; proverbial for self-delusion owing to the (unfounded) belief that when pursued it buries its head in the sand imagining that it cannot then be seen; ~ *plume*, wing or tail feather of ostrich as ornament.

Os'trogŏth (ŏ-) *n.* Member of eastern branch of GOTHS, who towards end of 5th c. conquered Italy, and under their leader THEODORIC established a kingdom in Italy, Sicily, and Dalmatia which lasted until 555. **Ostrogŏth'ĭc** *adj.*

Os'wald¹ (ŏz-), St. (*c* 605–42). King of Northumbria; defeated and slew British king Ceadwalla, 634; classed by Bede as one of the 7 greatest Anglo-Saxon kings; commemorated 5th Aug.

Os'wald² (ŏz-), St. (d. 992). English churchman, archbishop of York; commemorated 28th Feb.

O.T. *abbrev.* Old Testament.

Otaheite (ō-, -hē'tĭ) = TAHITI.

ōt'ary *n.* Member of the *Otariidae*, a mainly Antarctic family of seals with small external ear, including fur seals and sea-lions; eared seal.

O.T.C. *abbrev.* Officers' Training Corps.

oth'er (ŭdh-) *adj.* Not the same as one or more or some already mentioned or implied; separate in identity, distinct in kind; alternative, further, or additional; *the* only remaining; *every* second; different *than* or *from*; ~ *things being equal*, with conditions alike in everything but the point in question; *on the* ~ *hand*, used to introduce fact or argument making against or contrasted with previous one; *the* ~ *day*, a few days ago; *someone or* ~, a person unknown; *the* ~ *world*, future life; ~-*world*, concerned with or thinking of this only; ~-*worldly* (*adj.*). ~ *n.* or *pron.* (orig. elliptic use of adj.) Other person, thing, specimen, etc. ~ *adv.* Otherwise.

oth'ernėss (ŭdh-) *n.* (rare) Being other, diversity, difference.

oth'erwīse (ŭdh-, -z) *adv.* In a different way; if circumstances are or were different, else, or; in other respects; in different state.

Oth'man (ŏ-) (*c* 574–656). 3rd Mohammedan caliph, son-in-law of Mohammed.

Otho, Othonian: see OTTO².

ōt'ĭc *adj.* Of the ear.

ō'tiōse (-shĭ-) *adj.* At leisure, lazy, unoccupied (rare); not required, serving no practical purpose, functionless. **ō'tiōsely** *adv.* **ō'tiōsenėss** *n.*

otī'tis *n.* Inflammation of the ear.

ōt'ō-rhīn'ō-lăryngŏl'ogy *n.* Branch of medicine dealing with diseases of ear, nose, and throat.

otta'va rima (-tah-, rē-) *n.* Italian stanza of eight 11-syllabled lines (10-syllabled in English), the first six lines rhyming alternately, the last two forming a couplet.

Ottawa (ŏt'*a*-wa). 1. City of Ontario and capital of Canada. 2. Tributary of St. Lawrence River, on which city of Ottawa is situated.

ŏtt'er *n.* 1. Aquatic fur-bearing carnivorous mammal (*Lutra vulgaris*) feeding chiefly on fish, with webbed feet and pointed tail somewhat flattened horizontally; fur of this; other related animals; ~-*hound*, dog of breed used for hunting otter. 2. Fishing-tackle of float with line and several hooks. 3. (mine-sweeping) Steel frame shaped like a box-kite for holding sweep-wires at required depth.

ŏtt'ō¹ *n.* ~ *of roses* = ATTAR.

Ott'ō² (ŏ-), **Oth'ō** (ō-). Name of several Holy Roman emperors and German kings: *Otto I* (912–73), 'the Great', German king 936–73; crowned emperor by pope, 962; *Otto II* (955–83), son of Otto I, crowned 967, sole emperor 973–83; *Otto III* (980–1002), son of Otto II crowned 996, emperor 983–1002; *Otto IV* (*c* 1182–1218), crowned 1209, emperor 1198–1212 (deposed). **Ottōn'ĭan, Othōn'ĭan** *adjs.* Of the dynasty of these emperors; of this age.

ŏtt'oman¹ *n.* Cushioned seat like sofa or chair without back or arms (freq. a box with cushioned top).

Ott'oman² *adj.* & *n.* = OSMANLI; ~ *Empire*, Turkish Empire founded *c* 1300 by OSMAN I and lasting until 1919.

Ot'way (ŏ-), Thomas (1652–85). English Restoration playwright, author of 'Venice Preserved' etc.

O.U. *abbrev.* Oxford University (esp. in names of clubs, as *O.U.B.C.*, Boat Club, *O.U.D.S.*, Dramatic Society); *O.U.P.*, Oxford University Press.

oubliĕtte' (o͞o-) *n.* Secret dungeon with entrance only by trapdoor above.

ouch *n.* (archaic) Clasp or buckle, freq. jewelled; setting of precious stone.

Oud'enārde (o͞o-) (Flem. *Oudenaarde*, Fr. *Audenarde*). Town of E. Flanders, Belgium; scene (1708) of victory of Marlborough and Prince Eugene over French forces under Vendôme.

Oudh (owd). Part of UNITED PROVINCES OF AGRA AND OUDH, India.

ought¹ (awt) *n.* (vulg.) Figure denoting nothing, nought.

ought² (awt) *v. aux.* expressing duty, rightness, shortcoming, advisability, or strong probability.

Ouida (wē'd*a*). Pen-name of Marie Louise de la Ramée (1839–1908), English novelist.

Ouija (wē'jah) *n.* Board with letters, signs, etc., used with planchette for obtaining messages in spiritualist séances. [trade name; Fr. *oui* yes; Ger. *ja* yes]

ounce¹ *n.* (abbrev. oz.). Unit of weight, $\frac{1}{16}$ lb. in avoirdupois, $\frac{1}{12}$ lb. in troy weight; *fluid* ~, 8 (fluid) drachms, $\frac{1}{20}$ of imperial pint; (U.S.) $\frac{1}{16}$ of pint; see Appendix X. [L *uncia* twelfth (of pound or foot)]

ounce² *n.* 1. (poet. etc.) Lynx or other vaguely identified feline beast. 2. (zool.) The snow leopard (*Felis uncia*) of highlands of central Asia, smaller and lighter in colour than leopard but with similar markings.

our (owr) *adj.* Of or belonging to us; that we are concerned with or speaking or thinking of.

ours (owrz) *pron.* The one(s) belonging to us; our regiment or corps. ~ *pred. adj.* Belonging to us.

oursĕlf' (owr-) *pron.*, **oursĕlves'** *pl. pron.* (emphat., usu. pl., exc. when *we* represents a sovereign etc.) We or us in person, in particular, in our normal condition, and not others; (refl.) the person(s) previously described as *we*.

Ouse (o͞oz). Name of several English rivers. 1. River of Yorkshire formed by junction of Swale and Ure, and forming, with Trent, the Humber estuary. 2. (*Great* ~), river of Midlands, flowing into the

Wash. 3. River of Sussex running into English Channel at Newhaven.

ousel: see OUZEL.

oust *v.t.* Put out of possession, eject, expel *from*, drive out; force oneself or be put into the place of.

out *adv.* 1. Away from or not in or at a place, the right or normal state, the fashion, etc.; not at home; (of batsman or side) having finished innings; (boxing) unable to put up a defence, e.g. *~ for the count* (i.e. the counting of seconds from one to ten); not at work, on strike; (of fire etc.) not burning. 2. In(to) the open, publicity, hearing, sight, notice, etc.; *~ for*, *~ to* do, (colloq.) engaged in seeking; *all ~*, (slang) showing one's utmost pace or effort; *~ and about*, able to leave bed or house. 3. To or at an end, completely; *~ and away*, by far; *~ and ~*, thorough(ly), surpassing(ly). 4. *~ of*, from within; not within; from among; beyond range of; (so as to be) without; from, owing to, by use of (material); at specified distance from; beyond; transgressing rules of; *~ of doors*, in, into, the open air; *~ of wedlock*, without marriage; (*times*) *~ of number*, beyond counting; *~ of it*, not included, forlorn, at a loss. *~ prep.* Out of (now only in *from ~*). *~ adj. An ~ match*, one played away from the home ground. **outs** *n.pl.* The party out of office; *ins and ~s*: see IN.

out- *prefix* in combination with vbs. and verbal derivatives (usu. with same senses as verb followed by *out* adv.), advs. and substantives. Chief meanings: 1. External. 2. Connected but separate; subordinate and detached; not at the centre, some way off. 3. Out of; beyond. 4. To excess; successfully; surpassingly, so as to surpass, defeat, or excel.

outbĭd′ *v.t.* Outdo in bidding, offer more than.

out′board (-ōrd) *adj.* On, towards, nearer to, outside of ship or aircraft; (of motor-boat) with engine and driving apparatus attached outside boat at stern. *~ adv.* To, towards, outside of ship or aircraft.

outbrāve′ *v.t.* Defy, stand against bravely; outdo in bravery, finery, splendour, etc.

out′break (-brāk) *n.* Breaking out of emotion (esp. anger), hostilities, disease, fire, volcanic energy, etc.; outcrop; insurrection.

out′building (-bĭ-) *n.* Outhouse.

out′bûrst *n.* Explosion of feeling, esp. expressed by vehement words, volcanic eruption.

out′cast (-kahst) *adj.* & *n.* (Person) cast out from home and friends; homeless and friendless (vagabond).

out′caste (-kahst) *n.* & *adj.* (Person) who has lost or been expelled from his caste, or who does not belong to a caste.

outclass′ (-ahs) *v.t.* Belong to higher class than, completely beat or surpass.

out′come (-kŭm) *n.* Issue, result.

out′crŏp *n.* Emergence of stratum, vein, or rock, at surface (ill. ROCK).

out′crȳ *n.* Clamour, uproar.

outdĭs′tance *v.t.* Get far ahead of.

outdo′ (-ōō) *v.t.* Surpass, excel.

out′door (-dōr) *adj.* Done, existing, or used outdoors; *~ relief*, that given to persons not resident in workhouse or institution. **outdoors′** (-z) *adv.* Out of doors, in the open air.

out′er *adj.* Farther from centre or inside, relatively far out; external, of the outside; objective, physical, not subjective or psychical; *~ man*, personal appearance, dress; *~ world*, people outside one's own circle. *~ n.* (Hit on) outermost of three circles round bull's eye on target (opp. *inner*). **out′ermōst** *adj.*

outfāce′ *v.t.* Look out of countenance, stare down; confront fearlessly or impudently, brave, defy.

out′field *n.* Outlying land of farm; outlying region of thought etc.; (cricket) part of field remote from wickets.

out′fĭt *n.* Complete equipment; (U.S.) party travelling or in charge of herds of cattle etc.; (slang) organized group of persons. *~ v.t.* Provide with outfit; supply *with*. **out′fĭtter** *n.* Supplier of equipment; retailer of men's ready-made clothes.

outflănk′ *v.t.* Get beyond flank of (opposing army), outmanœuvre by flanking movement.

out′flow (-ō) *n.* What flows out, amount flowing out.

outgĕn′eral *v.t.* Defeat by superior generalship.

out′gō *n.*, **outgō′ĭngs** *n.pl.* Expenditure, outlay. **outgō′** *v.t.* Go faster than; surpass.

outgrow′ (-ō) *v.t.* Grow faster, get taller, than; get too big for (clothes); get rid of (childish habit, ailment, taste) with advancing age.

out′growth (-ōth) *n.* Offshoot; excrescence.

out-hĕ′rod *v.t.* *~ Herod*, be more violent or hectoring than Herod (represented in old mystery plays as a blustering tyrant); outdo, surpass.

out′house *n.* House, building, shed, belonging to and near or built against main house.

out′ĭng *n.* Pleasure-trip, holiday away from home.

out-jŏck′ey *v.t.* Overreach.

out′lander *n.* (Before S. Afr. war of 1899–1902) alien settled or sojourning in S. African Republic. [Du. *uitlander* alien]

outlănd′ĭsh *adj.* Foreign looking or sounding; unfamiliar, bizarre, uncouth. **outlănd′ĭshly** *adv.* **outlănd′ĭshnėss** *n.*

outlast′ (-ahst) *v.t.* Last longer than.

out′law *n.* Person deprived of protection of the law, banished or exiled person. *~ v.t.* Proscribe, declare outlaw. **out′lawry** *n.* Condition of, condemnation as, outlaw.

out′lay *n.* What one spends, expenses.

out′lĕt *n.* Means of exit or escape, vent, way out.

out′līer *n.* Outlying or detached part of something; (geol.) part of stratum or formation at some distance from main body to which it belongs, the intervening part having been removed by denudation.

out′līne *n.* Line(s) enclosing the apparently plane figure presented by any object to sight, contour, external boundary; sketch containing only contour lines and no shading; rough draft, verbal description of essential parts only, summary; (pl.) main features, general principles. *~ v.t.* Draw or describe in outline; mark outline of.

outlĭve′ *v.t.* Live beyond; come safely through, get over effect of; live longer than.

out′lŏŏk *n.* What one sees on looking out, view, prospect; person's general view of life; what seems likely to happen.

out′lȳĭng *adj.* Situated far from a centre, remote.

outmanœu′vre (-ōōver) *v.t.* Get the better of by superior strategy.

outmătch′ *v.t.* Be more than a match for.

outmōd′ėd *adj.* Out of date, old-fashioned.

out′mōst *adj.* Outermost.

outnŭm′ber *v.t.* Exceed in number.

out′pātient (-shnt) *n.* One receiving treatment at hospital etc. without being lodged in it.

outpoint′ *v.t.* (yachting) Sail closer to the wind than.

out′pōst *n.* Detachment on guard at some distance from army to prevent surprise.

out′pouring (-pōr-) *n.* Effusion; verbal or literary expression of emotion.

out′put (-ŏŏt) *n.* Amount produced by manufacture, mining, labour, etc.

out′rāge *n.* Forcible violation of others' rights, sentiments, etc.; deed of violence, gross or wanton offence or indignity. *~ v.t.* Do violence to, subject to outrage, injure, insult, violate, ravish; infringe (law, morality, etc.) flagrantly. **outrā′geous** (-jus) *adj.* Immoderate, extravagant, extraordinary; violent, furious; grossly cruel, immoral, offensive, or abusive. **outrā′geously** *adv.* **outrā′geousnėss** *n.*

Out′ram (ōō-), Sir James (1803–63). English general and hero of the Indian Mutiny, one of the relievers of Lucknow.

outrānge′ *v.t.* (Of guns etc.) have longer range than.

outré (ōōt′rā) *adj.* Outside the bounds of propriety, eccentric, outraging decorum.

out′-relief′ *n.* Outdoor relief.

out'rīder *n.* Mounted attendant riding before, behind, or with carriage.

out'rigged (-ĭgd) *adj.* (Of boat) having outriggers.

out'rigger *n.* 1. Beam, spar, framework, rigged out and projecting from or over ship's side for various purposes; iron bracket supporting rowlock beyond boat's side to enable a long oar to be conveniently used in a narrow boat; boat with such outriggers; ~ *canoe*, canoe having a long float parallel to its side, attached by beams (ill. CANOE). 2. Projecting beam etc. in building. 3. Extension of splinter-bar enabling extra horse to be harnessed outside shafts; such horse

out'right' (-rīt) *adv.* Altogether, entirely, once for all, not by degrees or instalments or half-and-half; without reservation, openly. ~ *adj.* Downright, direct, thorough. **out'rightness** *n.*

outriv'al *v.t.* Outdo as a rival.

outrŭn' *v.t.* Outstrip in running; pass the limit of; ~ *the constable*, run into debt.

out'sĕt *n.* Start, commencement.

outshīne' *v.t.* Surpass in brightness, splendour, or excellence.

out'sīde' *n.* External surface, outer parts; external appearance, outward aspect; all that is without; position without; highest computation; outside passenger on coach etc.; (pl.) outer sheets of ream of paper. ~ *adj.* Of, on, nearer, the outside, outer; not belonging to some circle or institution; greatest existent or possible; ~ *edge*, (skating) progression on outer edge of one skate; ~ *porter*, one conveying luggage from station; ~ *broker*, one not member of Stock Exchange. **outsīde'** *adv.* On or to the outside, the open air, open sea, etc.; not within, enclosed, or included. ~ *prep.* External to, not included in, beyond the limits of; not in; to the outside of; at or to the exterior of.

outsīd'er *n.* Non-member of some circle, party, profession, etc., uninitiated person, layman; person without special knowledge, breeding, etc., or not fit to mix with good society; horse or person not thought to have a chance in race or competition.

out'size *n.* Person or thing larger than the normal, esp. ready-made article of dress larger than the standard size; also attrib.

out'skirts *n.pl.* Outer border, fringe, of city, district, etc.

out'spăn *v.* (S. Afr.) Unyoke, unharness. ~ *n.* Act, time, or place of outspanning.

out'spōk'en *adj.* Frank, unreserved. **out'spōk'enly** *adv.* **out'spōk'enness** *n.*

out'spread (-ĕd) *adj.* Spread out.

out'stănd'ing *adj.* Prominent; still unsettled.

outstay' *v.t.* Stay beyond limits of, exhaust by staying; stay longer than.

outstrip' *v.t.* Pass in running etc.; surpass in competition or relative progress or ability.

out'thrŭst *n.* Outward thrust or thrusting pressure in any structure.

outvīe' *v.t.* Excel in competition, rivalry, or emulation.

outvōte' *v.t.* Outnumber in voting.

out'ward *adj.* Outer (archaic); directed towards the outside; bodily, external, material, visible, apparent, superficial; ~ *form*, appearance; *to ~ seeming*, apparently. ~ *adv.* Outwards; ~*-bound*, (of ship or passenger) going away from home. ~ *n.* Outward appearance; (pl.) outward things, externals. **out'wardly** *adv.*

out'wardness *n.* External existence, objectivity; interest or belief in outward things, objectiveness.

out'wards *adv.* In an outward direction, towards what is outside.

outweigh' (-wā) *v.t.* Exceed in weight, value, importance, or influence.

outwit' *v.t.* Prove too clever for, overreach, take in.

out'work (-wẽrk) *n.* Part of fortifications lying outside parapet; detached or advanced part of fortification.

outwōrn' *adj.* Worn out; exhausted, spent.

ouzel, ousel (o͞o'zl) *n.* (Old name for) blackbird, *Turdus merula*; *ring ~*, *T. torquatus*, bird related to blackbird and somewhat resembling it but with white patch on throat; *water ~*, the dipper, *Cinclus aquaticus*, unrelated to these.

ōv'al *adj.* Egg-shaped, ellipsoidal; having the outline of an egg, elliptical. ~ *n.* Closed curve with one axis longer than the other, like ellipse or outline of egg; thing with oval outline; *the O~*, the Surrey County cricket ground, Kennington Oval, in London.

ōv'ary *n.* Organ of female reproductive system, that in which ova or eggs are produced (ill. PELVIS); in plants, lowest part of pistil, ultimately becoming fruit or seed-vessel (ill. FLOWER). **ovār'ian** *adj.*

ōv'āte *adj.* (biol.) Egg-shaped, oval.

ovā'tion *n.* 1. (Rom. antiq.) Lesser triumph. 2. Enthusiastic reception, spontaneous applause.

oven (ŭ'vn) *n.* Brick, stone, or iron receptacle for baking bread or cooking food by heat radiated from walls, roof, or floor; small furnace or kiln used in chemistry, metallurgy, etc.; *Dutch ~*: see DUTCH.

ōv'er, (poet.) **o'er** (ōr) *adv.* 1. Outward and downward from brink (as *push ~ the edge*) or from erect position (*lean ~*). 2. So as to cover or touch whole surface (*paint it ~*). 3. With motion above something so as to pass across something (*climb ~*). 4. So as to produce fold or reverse position (*bend it ~*; *turn ~*, turn other side of leaf up). 5. Across street or other space or distance; (cricket, as umpire's direction) change ends for bowling etc.; ~ *against*, in opposite situation to, in contrast with. 6. With transference or change from one hand, party, etc., to another. 7. Too, in excess; in addition, besides; more; apart; ~ *and above*, moreover, into the bargain. 8. From beginning to end, with repetition, with detailed consideration (*read ~*, *talk* (*matter*) ~). 9. At an end, done with (*the war is ~*). ~ *n.* Number of balls (usu. 6 or 8) bowled from either end of wicket before change is made to other end; play during this time. ~ *adj.* (usu. written as one word with n.) Upper; outer; superior; excessive. ~ *prep.* 1. Above, on, at all or various points upon; to and fro upon, all through, round about; concerning, engaged with; ~ *all*, from end to end; ~ *our heads*, beyond our comprehension; without consulting us; ~ *head and ears*, completely immersed. 2. With or so as to get or give superiority to; beyond, more than; ~ *and above*, besides, not to mention. 3. Out and down from, down from edge of; so as to clear; across, on or to the other side of; throughout, through duration of, till end of; *stumble ~*, be tripped up by.

ōv'er- *prefix* = OVER *adj.*, *prep.*, *adv.*

ōver-ăct' *v.* Act (part, emotion, etc.), act part, with exaggeration.

ōv'erall (-awl) *n.* Garment worn over others as protection against wet, dirt, etc.; (pl.) outer trousers, leggings, or combination suit for dirty work; (mil., pl.) officer's full-dress tight trousers. ~ *adj.* Taking into account all features or aspects; inclusive of everybody or everything.

ōv'er-arm = OVERHAND.

ōverawe' *v.t.* Restrain, control, or repress by awe.

ōverbăl'ance *v.* (Cause to) lose balance and fall; outweigh.

ōverbear' (-bār) *v.t.* Bear down or upset by weight or force; put down, repress, by power or authority; surpass in importance etc., outweigh. **ōverbear'ing** *adj.* Domineering, masterful. **ōverbear'ingly** *adv.* **ōverbear'ingness** *n.*

ōverblown' (-ōn) *adj.* (Of flower) too fully open, past its prime.

ōv'erboard (-ōrd) *adv.* From within ship into water; *throw ~*, (fig.) abandon, discard.

ōverbûrd'en *v.t.* Burden too much, overload, overcharge.

O'verbury (ō-), Sir Thomas (1581–1613). English poet and writer of 'characters'; slowly poisoned in the Tower by agents of the divorced Countess of Essex, for his opposition to her marriage with his friend Robert Carr, later Earl of Somerset.

ōvercall′ (-awl) *v.t.* (bridge) Bid more on (hand) than it is worth; bid higher than (opponent, previous bid, one's partner when opponent has not done so). **ōv′ercall** *n.* Bid made over partner's bid.

ōvercăp′italīze *v.t.* Fix or estimate capital of (company etc.) too high.

ōvercast′ (-ahst) *v.t.* 1. Cover (sky etc.) with clouds or darkness (usu. in past part. *overcast*). 2. Sew over raw edges of (material, esp. with blanket or buttonhole stitches) to prevent unravelling.

ōvercharge′ *v.t.* 1. Charge too highly with explosive, electricity, etc. 2. Put exaggerated details or too much detail into (description etc.). 3. Charge too high a price for (thing) or to (person); charge (specified sum) beyond right price. **ōv′ercharge** *n.* Excessive charge.

ōv′ercoat *n.* Large coat worn over ordinary clothing, esp. in cold weather.

ōvercome′ (-kŭm) *v.* Prevail over, master, get the better of; be victorious; (past part.) *overcome*, exhausted, made helpless, deprived of self-possession.

ōvercrowd′ *v.* Crowd to excess; esp., crowd more people into a space than there is proper accommodation for.

ōverdėtėrm′ine *v.* Fix, define, determine. with more data than necessary. **ōverdėtėrm′ined** (-nd) *adj.* (esp., psycho-anal.) Expressing two or more different desires or tendencies at once.

ōverdo′ (-ōō) *v.t.* Carry to excess, go too far in; cook too long (esp. in past part.); overtax strength of (esp. in past part.).

ōv′erdōse *n.* Excessive dose.

ōv′erdraft (-ahft) *n.* Overdrawing of bank account; amount by which draft exceeds balance.

ōverdraw′ *v.* 1. Draw cheque in excess of (one's account) or in excess of one's account. 2. Exaggerate in describing.

ōv′erdrĕss[1] *n.* Outer part of woman's gown worn over a skirt of a different material and colour and showing parts of it.

ōverdrĕss′[2] *v.* Dress with too much display and ornament.

ōverdrive′ *v.t.* Drive too hard, drive or work to exhaustion.

ōverdūe′ *adj.* More than due; late, in arrear.

ōvereat′ *v.* Eat to excess; ~ *oneself*, overeat.

ōverĕs′timāte *v.t.* Estimate too highly. ~ *n.* Too high an estimate.

ōv′erfall (-awl) *n.* Turbulent stretch of sea etc. caused by set of tide or current over submarine ledge or meeting of currents.

ōv′erflow (-ō) *n.* What overflows or is superfluous; ~ *meeting*, meeting elsewhere of those who have not found room at demonstration etc. **ōverflow′** *v.* Flow over (brim etc.), flood (surface); extend beyond limits of; (of receptacle) be so full that contents overflow; (of kindness, harvest, etc.) be very abundant. **ōverflow′ing** *n.* & *adj.* **ōverflow′ingly** *adv*

ōv′er-fulfil′ment *n.* Completion of a Soviet 5-year plan before the appointed time.

ōv′erglāze *n.* Second glaze applied to pottery over first glaze. ~ *adj.* (Of painting etc.) done on glazed surface.

ōvergrow′ (-ō) *v.* Grow over, cover with growth; grow too large; grow too big etc. for.

ōv′erhănd′ *adv.* & *adj.* With hand above object held; with hand above shoulder in bowling etc.; with hand or arm out of water in swimming.

ōverhăng′ *v.* Jut out over, jut; (fig.) impend (over). **ōv′erhăng** *n.* Fact or amount of overhanging.

ōverhaul′ *v.t.* Pull to pieces for purpose of examining, examine condition of; (esp. naut.) catch up, come up with.

ōverhead′ (-hĕd) *adv.* On high; in the sky; in the storey above. **ōv′erhead** *adj.* Placed overhead; ~ *charges* etc., those due to office expenses, management, interest on capital, and other general needs of a business. **ōv′erheads** *n.pl.* Overhead charges.

ōverhear′ *v.t.* Hear as eavesdropper or unperceived or unintended listener.

ōverjoyed′ (-joid) *adj.* Transported with joy (*at*).

ōverlăd′en *adj.* Overloaded, overburdened.

ōverlănd′ *adv.* By land and not sea. **ōv′erland** *adj.* Entirely or partly by land.

ōverlăp′ *v.* Partly cover; cover and extend beyond; partly coincide.

ōverlay′ *v.t.* Cover surface of *with* coating etc. **ōv′erlay** *n.* Thing laid over something, coverlet, small tablecloth, etc.

ōverleaf′ *adv.* On other side of leaf (of book etc.).

ōverleap′ *v.t.* Leap over, surmount; omit, ignore.

ōverlie′ *v.t.* Lie on top of, smother (child) thus.

ōverload′ *v.t.* Load to excess. **ōv′erload** *n.* Excessive load or charge, as of electric current.

ōverlo͝ok′ *v.t.* 1. Have prospect of or over from above; be higher than. 2. Fail to observe, take no notice of, condone. 3. Superintend, oversee. 4. Bewitch with evil eye.

ōv′erlord *n.* Supreme lord, suzerain. **ōv′erlordship** *n.*

ōv′erly *adv.* (dial. & U.S.) Over, excessively.

ōv′ermăntel *n.* Ornamental carving, mirror, etc., over mantelpiece (ill. FIRE).

ōverma′ster (-mah-) *v.t.* Master completely, get victory over, overcome.

ōvermŭch′ *adj.*, *n.*, & *adv.* Too much.

ōver-nīce′ *adj.* Too fastidious. **ōver-nīce′nėss, ōver-nī′cėty** *ns.*

ōvernight′ (-nīt) *adv.* On the preceding evening (in relation to following day); through the night (till the following morning). **ōv′ernight** *adj.* Done etc. overnight.

ōverpersuāde′ (-sw-) *v.t.* Persuade in spite of reluctance.

ōverpĭtch′ *v.t.* Bowl (cricket-ball) so that it pitches too near wicket.

ōv′erplŭs *n.* Surplus, superabundance.

ōverpow′er *v.t.* Reduce to submission, subdue, master; be too intense or violent for, overwhelm. **ōverpow′ering** *adj.* **ōverpow′eringly** *adv.*

ōverprint′ *v.t.* Print (photographic print) darker than intended; print (additional matter or another colour) on already printed surface, esp. of postage-stamp.

ōverprodūce′ *v.t.* Produce in excess of demand or of defined amount. **ōverprodŭc′tion** *n.*

ōv′erpro͞of *adj.* Containing more alcohol than proof spirit.

ōverrāte′ *v.t.* Have too high an opinion of; assess too high for rating purposes.

ōverreach′ *v.* 1. (refl.) Strain one*self* by reaching too far; (of horse) injure fore foot by striking it with hind hoof. 2. Circumvent, outwit, get the better of by cunning or artifice.

ōverrīde′ *v.t.* 1. Exhaust (horse) by riding. 2. Ride over (enemy's country) with armed force; trample (person) under one's horse's hoofs; (fig.) trample under foot, set aside, refuse to comply with, have or claim superior authority to. 3. Slip or lie over, be superimposed on; (surg., of fractured bone) overlap.

ōverrule′ (-ro͞ol) *v.t.* Set aside (decision, argument, etc.) by superior authority; annul decision or reject proposal of (person).

ōverrŭn′ *v.t.* Flood, harry and spoil (enemy's country); swarm or spread over; exceed (limit).

ōv′ersea(s) *adv.* & *adj.* Across or beyond sea.

ōversee′ *v.t.* Superintend, look after (workmen, execution of work, etc.). **ōv′erseer** (-sēr) *n.*

ōv′ersew (-sō) *v.t.* Sew together (two pieces of stuff) so that every stitch passes in the same direction through both and the thread between the stitches lies over the edges (ill. STITCH).

ōvershăd′ow (-ō) *v.t.* Cast a shadow over; (fig.) be more conspicuous than, outshine.

ōv′ershoe (-ōō) *n.* Shoe of rubber, felt, etc., worn outside another.

ōversho͞ot′ *v.t.* Send missile, go, beyond (mark etc.); ~ *the mark*, go too far, exaggerate, overdo something.

ōv′ershŏt *adj.* (Of wheel) turned by water flowing above it (ill. WATER).

ōv′ersight (-sīt) *n.* 1. (rare)

Supervision. 2. Omission to notice, mistake of inadvertence.

ŏv′erslaugh (-aw) *n.* (mil.) Passing over of turn of duty in consideration of another duty that takes precedence of it.

ōversleep′ *v.refl.* & *i.* Miss intended hour of rising by sleeping too long.

ōv′erstāte′ *v.t.* State too strongly, exaggerate. **ōv′erstāte′ment** (-tm-) *n.*

ōverstĕp′ *v.t.* Pass over (boundary).

ōverstrain′ *v.t.* Damage by exertion; make too much of (argument etc.). **ōv′erstrain** *n.* Overstraining, being overstrained.

ōverstrŭng′ *adj.* 1. (Of piano) with strings arranged in sets crossing each other obliquely. 2. (Of person, nerves, etc.) intensely strained.

ōversŭbscrībe′ *v.t.* (usu. in past part.) Subscribe more than amount of (loan etc.).

ōvĕrt′ *adj.* Openly done, unconcealed, patent. **ōvĕrt′ly** *adv.*

ōvertāke′ *v.t.* Come up with, catch up; (of storm, misfortune, etc.) come suddenly upon.

ōvertăx′ *v.t.* Make excessive demand on (person's strength etc.); burden with excessive taxes.

ōverthrow′ (-ō) *v.t.* Upset, knock down; cast out from power; vanquish, subvert; put an end to. **ōv′erthrow** *n.* 1. Defeat, subversion. 2. (cricket) Fielder's return not stopped near wicket and so allowing further run(s).

ōv′ertīme *adv.* Beyond regular hours of work. ~ *n.* Time during which workman etc. works beyond regular hours; payment for this.

ōv′ertōne *n.* (mus.) Harmonic.

ōv′erture *n.* 1. Opening of negotiations with another (usu. pl.); formal proposal or offer. 2. (mus.) Orchestral piece beginning opera, oratorio, etc.; *concert* ~, one-movement composition in same style.

ōvertŭrn′ *v.* Upset; (cause to) fall down or over; overthrow, subvert; abolish. **ōv′ertŭrn** *n.* Upsetting, revolution.

ōverween′ing *adj.* Arrogant, presumptuous, conceited, self-confident.

ōv′erweight (-wāt) *n.* Preponderance; excessive weight. ~ *adj.* Beyond weight allowed or desirable. **overweight′** *v.t.* Impose too great weight or burden on.

ōverwhĕlm′ *v.t.* Bury beneath superincumbent mass, submerge utterly; crush, bring to sudden ruin; overpower with emotion etc.; deluge *with*. **ōverwhĕlm′ing** *adj.* Irresistible by numbers, amount, etc. **ōverwhĕlm′ingly** *adv.*

ōverwīnd′ *v.t.* Wind (watch etc.) too far.

ōverwork′ (-wĕrk) *v.* (Cause to) work too hard; weary or exhaust with work. **ōv′erwork′** *n.* Excessive work.

ōverwrought′ (-rawt) *adj.* 1. Over-excited; suffering reaction from excitement. 2. Too elaborate.

ōvibōv′īne *adj.* & *n.* (Animal) having character intermediate between sheep and ox; musk-ox.

Ov′ĭd (ŏ-). Publius Ovidius Naso (43 B.C.–*c* A.D. 18), Roman poet; author of 'Ars Amatoria', 'Metamorphoses', 'Fasti', etc. **Ovĭd′ian** *adj.*

ōv′ĭdŭct *n.* (physiol.) In mammals, one of pair of tubes which conduct egg from ovary to uterus.

ōv′ifŏrm *adj.* Egg-shaped.

ōv′īne *adj.* Of, like, sheep.

ōvĭp′arous *adj.* (zool.) Producing young by means of eggs expelled from body before being hatched.

ōvipŏs′ĭtor (-z-) *n.* (zool.) Organ with which female insect deposits eggs; similar organ in some fish.

ōv′oid *adj.* Solidly or superficially egg-shaped, oval with one end more pointed. ~ *n.* Ovoid body.

ōv′olō *n.* Convex moulding of quarter-circle or quarter-ellipse section, receding downwards (ill. MOULDING). [It. *uovolo* little egg]

ōvo-tĕs′tĭs *n.* (zool.) Organ in certain vertebrates producing both ova and spermatozoa; hermaphrodite gland.

ōvovīvĭp′arous *adj.* (zool.) Producing young by means of eggs which hatch before reaching exterior (cf. OVIPAROUS).

Ov′ra (ŏ-), **O.V.R.A.** (hist.) Secret police of the Fascist régime in Italy. [f. initials of *O*pera di *V*igilanza e di *R*epressione dell' *A*ntifascismo, security organization for repression of anti-fascism]

ōv′ūle *n.* (bot.) Female germ-cell of seed-plant (ill. FLOWER). **ōv′ūlar** *adj.*

ōv′um *n.* (pl. *-a*). (biol.) Female germ-cell capable of developing into new individual when fertilized by male sperm; egg esp. of mammals, fish, or insects. [L, = 'egg']

owe (ō) *v.* Be under obligation to pay, repay, or render; be in debt (*for*); be indebted for *to*.

Ow′en (ō-), Robert (1771–1858). English philanthropist and socialist; had great influence on the co-operative movement.

ow′ing (ō-) *pred. adj.* Yet to be paid, owed, due; ~ *to* (also used adverbially), attributed to, caused by.

owl *n.* Bird of prey of mainly nocturnal group, with large head, raptorial beak, large eyes directed forwards, and soft plumage enabling it to fly noiselessly, feeding on mice, small birds, etc.; the common British species are the *barn*, *long-eared* or *horned*, *little*, and *tawny* ~*s*; any bird of suborder *Striges*; solemn person, wise-looking dullard; ~*-car*, *train*, (U.S.) tram-car, train, running late at night. **owl′ish** *adj* **owl′ishly** *adv.* **owl′ishnèss** *n.*

owl′ĕt *n.* Owl, young owl.

own[1] (ōn) *adj.* 1. (appended to poss. adj. or case) In full ownership, proper, peculiar, individual, and not another's; (abs.) private property, kindred, etc.; *of one's* ~, belonging to one; *hold one's* ~, maintain position, not be defeated; *on one's* ~, (slang) independently, on one's own account, responsibility or resources; *get one's* ~ *back*, be revenged (*on*). 2. (without possessive): ~ *brother*, *sister*, etc., with both parents the same; ~ *cousin*, first cousin.

own[2] (ōn) *v.* 1. Have as property, possess. 2. Acknowledge authorship, paternity, or possession, of; admit as existent, valid, true, etc.; submit to (person's sway etc.) without protest; ~ *up*, (colloq.) make frank confession. **own′er, own′ership** *ns.* **own′erlèss** *adj.*

ŏx *n.* (pl. *oxen*). Large domestic bovine animal, esp. male castrated and used as draught animal or reared for food; any bovine animal; ~*-eye*, various plants, esp. the British wild plants *Chrysanthemum segetum* or corn-marigold (*yellow* ~*-eye*), *C. leucanthemum*, the moon-daisy or ox-eye daisy, and the Amer. composite *Heliopsis laevis*, with large yellow flowers; *ox′herd*, cowherd; *ox′lip*, kind of primula; (pop.) hybrid of primrose and cowslip; *ox′tail*, tail of ox, much used for soup-making.

ŏxăl′ic *adj.* (chem.) ~ *acid*, highly poisonous and intensely sour acid $(COOH)_2$ found in wood-sorrel etc., used in calico-printing and in the manufacture of inks and polishes. [Gk *oxalis* wood-sorrel]

Oxf. *abbrev.* Oxford.

Ox′ford (ŏ-). City on River Thames, England, seat of *University of* ~, organized as a *studium generale* soon after 1167, the first of its colleges, University College, being founded in 1249; ~ *accent*, style of pronouncing English pop. supposed to be characteristic of members of Oxford University; ~ *blue*, blue of very low brilliance; ~ *frame*, picture-frame the sides of which cross each other and project at the corners; ~ *Group*, name of international religious movement founded by Dr Frank N. D. Buchman in Oxford in 1921: see MORAL Re-Armament; ~ *mixture*, a very dark grey woollen cloth; ~ *movement*: see TRACTARIAN; ~ *shoe*, *oxfords*, kind of low walking-shoe laced over instep (ill. SHOE); ~ *unit*, (biochem.) unit of penicillin. [*oxen*+*ford*]

Ox′ford and As′quith, Herbert Henry Asquith, 1st Earl of: see ASQUITH.

Oxfŏrd′ĭăn (ŏ-) *adj.* & *n.* 1. Pertaining to Oxford; (geol.) of the lower division of the Oxford oolite. 2. Pertaining to, adherent of, the view that the works attributed to Shakespeare were written by Edward de Vere, 17th Earl of Oxford.

Ox′fordshire (ŏ-). South-east midland county of England.

ŏx′ĭdāse *n.* (physiol., bot.) One

of a group of enzymes concerned with the uptake of oxygen by living cells (respiration).

ŏxĭdā′tion: see OXIDIZE.

ŏx′īde *n.* Compound of oxygen with another element or with a radical.

ŏx′idīze *v.* Cause to combine with oxygen; cover (metal) with coating of oxide, make rusty; take up or enter into combination with oxygen, rust; *oxidized silver*, silver with dark coating of silver sulphide. **ŏxĭdā′tion** *n.*

Oxon. *abbrev.* (Bishop) of Oxford (replacing surname in his signature); Oxfordshire; Oxford University.

Oxōn′ian (ŏ-) *adj.* & *n.* (Member) of University of Oxford; (citizen) of Oxford. [*Oxonia* latinized name of Oxford]

ŏx′ter *n.* (Sc. etc.) Armpit.

Ox′us (ŏ-). Former name of the Amu-Darya, great river of Central Asia, rising in Pamirs and flowing into Sea of Aral.

ŏxȳ-acĕt′ȳlēne *adj.* Using mixture of oxygen and acetylene (esp. of flame produced in this way for cutting and welding metals).

ŏx′ȳgėn *n.* Colourless, tasteless, odourless, gaseous element, essential to life and to combustion, comprising about one-fifth of the air, and present in combination in water and most minerals and organic substances; symbol O, at. no. 8, at. wt 15·999.

ŏx′ȳgėnate (*or* ŏksĭ′-) *v.t.* Supply, treat, or mix with oxygen, oxidize; charge (blood) with oxygen by respiration. **ŏxȳgėnā′tion** *n.*

ŏx′ȳgėnīze (*or* ŏksĭ′-) *v.t.* Oxygenate.

ŏxȳhȳd′rogėn *adj.* Of a mixture of oxygen and hydrogen.

ŏx′ȳmĕl *n.* Syrup of honey and vinegar.

ŏxȳmōr′on *n.* (rhet.) Figure of speech with pointed conjunction of seeming contradictories (e.g. *faith unfaithful kept him falsely true*).

ŏxȳōp′ia *n.* Abnormal keenness of vision.

ŏx′ȳtōne *adj.* & *n.* (Gk. gram.) (Word) with acute accent on last syllable.

oy′er *n.* Criminal trial under writ of ~ *and terminer* or commission to judges on circuit to hold courts.

ōyĕz′!, ōyĕs′! *int.* Uttered, usu. thrice, by public crier or court officer to bespeak silence and attention. [OF *oyez*, imper. pl. of *oir* hear]

oys′ter *n.* Edible bivalve mollusc of family *Ostreidae*, usu. eaten alive, esp. the common European *Ostrea edulis* and the Amer. *O. virginica* and *O. lurida* (Californian ~); oyster-shaped morsel of meat in fowl's back; ~*-bank*, *-bed*, part of sea-bottom where oysters breed or are bred; ~*-bar*, tavern where oysters are served; ~*-catcher*, maritime wading-bird (*Haematopus*) with black-and-white or black plumage and brilliant red feet and beak; ~*-farm*, sea-bottom used for breeding oysters; ~*-knife*, knife of shape adapted for opening oysters.

oz. *abbrev.* Ounce(s).

Oz′ark Mountains (ō-). Group of highlands between Arkansas and Missouri rivers, in States of Missouri, Arkansas, Oklahoma, Kansas, and Illinois, U.S.

ozō′cerīte, ozŏk′erĭt *n.* Wax-like brownish-yellow aromatic fossil resin occurring in bituminous shales etc. and used for candles, insulators, etc.

ōz′ōne *n.* 1. Allotropic form of oxygen with three atoms to the molecule (O_3), a pale-blue gas with a peculiarly pungent smell; formed by action of electric discharge or ultra-violet light; used for sterilizing water and purifying air. 2. (pop.) Invigorating, bracing air, esp. that of the seaside. **ozŏn′ĭc** *adj.*

P

P, p. 16th letter of modern English and 15th in the ancient Roman alphabet, corresponding to Gk *pi* (Π, π) and Semitic ℸ, ℸ, and representing a voiceless labial stop; *mind one's P's and Q's*, be careful not to do or say the wrong thing.

P. *abbrev.* (Car) park; pawn (chess); pedestrian (crossing).

p. *abbrev.* Page; participle; past; perch.

p. *abbrev. Piano.*

pa[1] (pah) *n.* (colloq.) Papa.

pa[2] (pah) *n.* Native fort in New Zealand. [Maori wd]

P.A. *abbrev.* Press Association.

p.a. *abbrev.* Per annum.

Pa *abbrev.* Pennsylvania.

păb′ulum *n.* Food, sustenance.

păc′a *n.* Genus (*Coelogenys*) of large spotted nocturnal rodents of S. America; spotted cavy.

pāce[1] *n.* 1. Single step in walking or running; space traversed in this, as vague measure of distance (about 30 in.); space between successive stationary positions of same foot in walking (about 5 ft). 2. Mode of walking or running, gait; any of various gaits of (esp. trained) horse, etc.; amble; *put (person) through his ~s*, test his qualities in action, etc. 3. Speed in walking or running; rate of progression; *keep* ~, advance at equal rate *with*; *go the* ~, go at great speed; (fig.) indulge in dissipation; ~*-maker*, rider, runner, etc., who sets pace for another in race, etc. ~ *v.* Walk with slow or regular pace; traverse thus; measure (distance) by pacing; (of horse) amble; set pace for (rider, runner, etc.). **pā′cer** *n.* (esp.) Horse that paces.

pā′cė[2] *prep.* By leave of, with all deference to. [L, abl. of *pax* peace]

păch′ydėrm (-k-) *n.* Large thick-skinned mammal esp. elephant or rhinoceros. **păchydėrm′atous** *adj.*

pacĭf′ĭc *adj.* Tending to peace, of peaceful disposition. **pacĭf′ically** *adv.*

păcĭfĭcā′tion *n.* Pacifying; treaty of peace. **pacĭf′icatory** *adj.*

Pacĭ′fic Ocean. Largest body of water on earth's surface, bounded by N. and S. America and Asia and Australia. [so named by Magellan, its first European navigator, because he experienced calm weather there]

Pacĭf′ĭc States. A geographical division of the U.S., made by the U.S. Census Bureau, comprising Washington, Oregon, and California.

pă′cifĭsm, pacĭf′ĭcĭsm (rare) *ns.* (Support of) policy of avoiding or abolishing war by use of arbitration in settling international disputes. **pă′cifĭst, pacĭ′fĭcist** (now rare) *ns.*

pă′cifȳ *v.t.* Appease; reduce (country etc.) to state of peace.

păck *n.* 1. Bundle of things wrapped up or tied together for carrying; parcel, esp. pedlar's bundle or soldier's knapsack; lot, set; (commerc.) method of packing for the market. 2. Number of hounds kept together for hunting, or of beasts (esp. wolves) or birds (esp. grouse) naturally associating; organized group of U-boats. 3. (Rugby footb.) Forwards of team. 4. Set of playing-cards. 5. Large area of large pieces of floating ice (~*-ice*) driven or packed together into nearly continuous mass. 6. Swathing of body or part of it in wet sheet, blanket, etc.; sheet etc. so used; *mud-* (*face-*) ~: see MUD-pack. 7. Quantity of fish, fruit, etc., packed in a season etc. 8. ~*-drill*, military punishment of marching up and down in full marching order; ~-*horse*, horse for carrying packs; *pack'man*, pedlar; ~-*saddle*, one adapted for supporting packs; *pack'thread*, stout thread for sewing or tying up packs. ~ *v.* 1. Put (things) together into bundle, box, bag, etc., for transport or storing (freq. ~ *up*, esp. abs.); (of things) admit of being packed *well*, *easily*, etc. 2. Prepare and put up (meat, fruit, etc.) in tins etc. for preservation. 3. Put closely together; form (hounds) into pack; place (cards) together in pack; crowd together; form into pack. 4. Cover (thing) with something pressed or wedged tightly round; (med.) wrap (body etc.) tightly in wet cloth. 5. Fill (bag, box, etc.) with clothes etc.; cram (space etc. *with*); load (beast) with pack. 6. Take oneself off with one's belongings; *send* (person) *packing*, dismiss him summarily; ~ (person) *off*, send him away; ~ *up*, (slang) retire from fight, contest, etc., cease to function. 7. [prob. different wd] Select (jury etc.) so as to secure partial decision. 8. *pack'ing-case*, case or framework for packing goods; *packing-needle*, large needle for sewing up packages in stout cloth.

păck'age *n.* Bundle of things packed, parcel; box etc. in which goods are packed. ~ *v.t.* (commerc.) Make up into, enclose in, a package.

păck'er *n.* (esp.) One who packs meat, fruit, etc., for market; machine for packing.

păck'ėt *n.* 1. Small package; (colloq.) considerable sum of money (esp. lost or won); *catch, get, stop a* ~, (colloq.) be (mortally) hit by bullet etc. 2. ~-*(boat)*, mail-boat.

păct *n.* Agreement, covenant.

păd[1] *n.* 1. (slang) Road. 2. Easy-paced horse. ~ *v.* Tramp along (road etc.) on foot; travel on foot; ~ *the hoof*, (slang) go on foot.

păd[2] *n.* Soft stuffed saddle without tree; part of double harness to which girths are attached; cushion, stuffing, used to diminish jarring, fill out hollows, etc.; guard for parts of body in cricket etc.; number of sheets of blotting-, writing-, or drawing-paper fastened together at edge; fleshy cushion forming sole of foot in some quadrupeds; paw of fox, hare, etc.; socket of brace, tool-handle; *launching-*~: see LAUNCH[1]. ~ *v.t.* Furnish with a pad, stuff; fill out (sentence etc.) with superfluous words; *padded cell*, room in lunatic asylum with padded walls. **păd'ding** *n.* Substance of pad, e.g. felt, hair, kapok, etc.; superfluous words in sentence etc.

păd[3] *n.* Open pannier used as measure of fruit etc.

păd'dle *n.* 1. Small spade-like implement with a long handle. 2. Short oar with blade at one or both ends used without rowlock; one of the boards fitted round circumference of paddle-wheel; paddle-shaped instrument; action or spell of paddling; (zool.) fin or flipper; ~-*wheel*, wheel for propelling ship, with boards round and at right angles to the circumference so as to press backward against the water. ~ *v.* Move on water, propel canoe, by means of paddles; row gently; walk with bare feet in shallow water; toy with the fingers (*in, on, about*).

pădd'ock[1] *n.* Small field, esp. as part of stud farm; turf enclosure near race-course, where horses are assembled before race; (Austral. and N.Z.) field (of any size).

pădd'ock[2] *n.* (archaic, dial.) Frog or toad.

pădd'y[1] *n.* Rice in the straw or in the husk. [Malay *padi*]

pădd'y[2], **pădd'ȳwhăck** *ns.* (colloq.) Rage, fit of temper. [f. PADDY[3]]

Pădd'y[3]. (Nickname for) Irishman. [pet-form of *Padraig* Patrick]

Păderew'skĭ (-rěf-), Ignacy Jan (1860–1941). Polish pianist and statesman; prime minister of Poland 1919–21 and 1940–1.

păd'lŏck *n.* Detachable lock hanging by hinged or pivoted hoop on object fastened. ~ *v.t.* Secure with this.

pa'dre (pah'drā) *n.* (nav., mil., and air force slang). Chaplain. [Port. etc., = 'father', 'priest']

padrōn'ĕ *n.* Master of Mediterranean trading-vessel; Italian employer of street musicians, begging-children, etc.; proprietor of Italian inn.

Păd'ūa (It. *Padova*). City of NE. Italy. **Păd'ūan** *adj.* & *n.*

păd'ūasoy *n.* Strong corded silk fabric much worn in 18th c.

pae'an *n.* Song of praise or thanksgiving; shout or song of triumph, joy, or exultation. [Gk *paian* hymn to Apollo under name of Paian]

pae'derasty, pĕd- *n.* SODOMY.

paedĭăt'rĭc *adj.* Of diseases of children. **paedĭăt'rĭcs** *n.* Study of these diseases.

paedobăp'tĭsm *n.* Infant baptism. **paedobăp'tĭst** *n.*

pae'on *n.* Metrical foot of 3 short syllables and one long, the latter occurring in any position in the group. **paeŏn'ĭc** *adj.*

pāg'an *n.* & *adj.* Heathen; unenlightened (person). **pāg'anĭsm** *n.* **pāg'anīze** *v.*

Păgani'ni (-nēnĭ), Niccolo (1782–1840). Italian violin virtuoso.

pāge[1] *n.* Boy, usu. in livery, employed (esp. in hotels) to attend to door, go on errands, etc.; also ~-*boy*; boy employed as personal attendant of person of rank; small boy attending bride at wedding; (hist.) boy in training for knighthood and attached to knight's service; ~ *of honour, of the presence,* etc., officers of royal household. ~ *v.t.* (orig. U.S.) Communicate with by means of page; have name of (person) called out by page.

pāge[2] *n.* One side of leaf of book etc. ~ *v.t.* Put consecutive numbers on pages of (book etc.).

pă'geant (-jnt) *n.* Brilliant spectacle, esp. procession, arranged for effect; spectacular representation of past history of place etc.; (hist.) tableau, allegorical device, etc., on fixed stage or moving car; (fig.) empty or specious show. **pă'geantry** *n.* Splendid display; empty show.

pă'ginal *adj.* Of pages; page for page. **pă'ginary** *adj.*

pă'ginate *v.t.* Page (book etc.). **pāginā'tion** *n.*

pagōd'a *n.* Temple or sacred building in India, China, etc., esp. tower, usu. of pyramidal form, built over relics of Buddha or a saint; ornamental imitation of

CHINESE PAGODA

this; gold coin (about 7*s.*) formerly current in southern India; ~-*tree*, one of several kinds of Chinese, Japanese, and Indian trees, whose habit of growth produces a pagoda form.

pagūr'ian *adj.* & *n.* (Crustacean) of the genus *Pagurus* or hermit-crabs.

pah *int.* expr. disgust.

Pahl'avĭ, Pehl'evĭ (pāl-). An Iranian language, the ancestor of modern Persian, used in Persia from *c* 3rd c. onwards; distinguished from other dialects of Middle Persian chiefly by its script, which has some Aramaic characters. [Pers. *Pahlav* Parthia]

paid (past part. of PAY[1]). Remunerated with money; given, as money, in discharge of an obligation; discharged, as a debt; for which money has been given, as a bill; *put* ~ *to*, (colloq.) settle the affairs of, finish off; ~-*up capital*, that part of the subscribed capital of an undertaking which has actually been paid.

Pai'fōrce (pī-). The Persia-Iraq command in the war of 1939–45. [f. initials of *P*ersia *a*nd *I*raq+*force*]

pail *n.* Vessel, usu. round, of

wood or metal for carrying liquids etc.; amount contained in this; (U.S.) tin vessel in which workman's mid-day meal etc. is carried.

paillasse, palliasse, (pălyăs', păl'yas) *n.* Straw mattress.

paillette (pălyĕt') *n.* Piece of bright metal used in enamel painting; spangle.

pain *n.* 1. Sensation experienced when the body is injured, or afflicted by certain diseases; suffering, distress, of body or mind; (pl.) throes of childbirth. 2. (pl.) Trouble taken; *pains'taking*, careful, industrious. 3. Punishment (now only in *~s and penalties, on* or *under ~ of*). ~ *v.t.* Inflict pain upon. **pain'ful** *adj.* **pain'fully** *adv.* **pain'fulnĕss** *n.* **pain'lĕss** *adj.* **pain'lĕssly** *adv.* **pain'lĕssnĕss** *n.*

Paine, Thomas (1737–1809). English political theorist; advocated independence of Amer. colonies in his 'Common Sense' (1776) and other works; wrote 'The Rights of Man' (1791); associated himself with the French Revolutionists and was made a member of the National Convention.

paint *n.* Solid colouring-matter, suspended in a liquid vehicle used to impart colour to a surface; something, esp. medicament, put on like paint with brush; colouring-matter applied to face etc. for adornment. ~ *v.t.* 1. Portray, represent, in colours; adorn (wall etc.) with painting; (fig.) represent in words vividly as by painting. 2. Cover surface of with paint, apply paint of specified colour to; *~ the town red*, cause commotion by riotous spree etc. 3. Apply rouge etc. to (face); use rouge etc. 4. *Painted lady*, orange-red butterfly with black and white spots. **paint'ing** *n.*

paint'er[1] *n.* 1. One who paints pictures. 2. Workman who colours woodwork etc. with paint; *~'s colic*, form of colic to which painters who work with lead paints are liable. **paint'erly** *adj.* (transl. of Ger. *malerisch*) (Of work of art) executed with attention to light and shade, mass, tone, etc., rather than line (opp. LINEAR).

paint'er[2] *n.* Rope attached to bow of boat for making it fast to ship, stake, etc. (ill. BOAT).

pair *n.* 1. Set of two, couple (esp. of things that usu. exist or are used in couples); article consisting of two corresponding parts not used separately; second member of a pair; *~ royal*, set of 3 cards of same denomination or of 3 dice turning up same number. 2. Engaged or married couple; mated couple of animals; ~ (*of horses*), two horses harnessed together. 3. (parl.) Two voters on opposite sides absenting themselves from division by mutual agreement; person willing to act thus. 4. Flight (*of stairs, steps*). ~ *v.* Arrange, be arranged, in couples; unite in love or marriage; mate; unite (*with* one of opposite sex); ~ *off*, put two by two; go off in pairs; (parl.) make a pair; (colloq.) marry (*with*).

Pais'ley (-zlĭ). Town of Renfrewshire, Scotland, near Glasgow; ~ *shawl*, shawl in soft bright colours resembling a cashmere shawl, orig. made at Paisley; ~ *pattern*, characteristic pattern of such shawl.

pajamas: see PYJAMAS.

Pakĭstan' (pah-, -ahn). Moslem autonomy; proposed separate Moslem State (established as a separate Dominion in 1947); since 1956 an independent Republic, consisting of East and West Pakistan, in N. part of Indo-Pakistan subcontinent; a member of the British Commonwealth; interim capital, Rawalpindi (former capital, Karachi). **Pakĭsta'nĭ** (-ahnĭ) *adj.* & *n.* [earlier *Pakstan*, f. initials of *P*unjab, *A*fghan Frontier, *K*ashmir, *S*ind, and last 3 letters of Baluchi*stan*, names of regions where Moslems predominate]

păl *n.* (slang) Comrade, mate. ~ *v.i.* (usu. ~ *up*) Associate, make friends (*with*). [Engl. Gipsy *pal* brother, mate]

păl'ace *n.* Official residence of sovereign, archbishop, or bishop; stately mansion; spacious building for entertainment, refreshment, etc. [L *Palatium* PALATINE HILL, Augustus's house built on it]

păl'adĭn *n.* Any of the Twelve Peers of Charlemagne's court, of whom the Count Palatine was the chief; knight errant.

păl'aeocēne *adj.* (geol.) Of the lowest series of rocks in the Tertiary. ~ *n. The P~*, this series or epoch (ill. GEOLOGY).

Păl'aeogēne *n.* Lower part of tertiary rocks (including palaeocene, eocene, and oligocene series).

pălaeŏg'raphy *n.* Study of ancient writing and inscriptions. **pălaeŏg'rapher** *n.* **păleogrăph'ic** *adj.*

pălaeolĭth'ĭc *adj.* Of the earlier Stone Age (as contrasted with NEOLITHIC), characterized by the use of chipped stone implements and weapons.

pălaeŏntŏl'ogy *n.* Study of extinct animals and plants. **pălaeŏntŏl'ogĭst** *n.*

pălaeozō'ĭc *adj.* Of, containing, ancient forms of life; of the era to which belong the geological systems from Cambrian to Permian; *the P~*, this era (ill. GEOLOGY).

palaes'tra, palĕs'tra *n.* Wrestling-school, gymnasium.

pălankeen', pălanquin' (-kēn) *n.* Covered litter for one, in India etc., carried usu. by 4 or 6 men. [Malay *palangki*]

păl'atable *adj.* Pleasant to the taste; (fig.) agreeable to the mind. **păl'atably** *adv.*

păl'atal *adj.* Of the palate; (of sound) produced by placing tongue against or near the palate, usu. hard palate. ~ *n.* Palatal sound. **păl'atalize** *v.t.* Make palatal, modify into palatal sound.

păl'ate *n.* 1. Roof of the mouth in vertebrates, partly bony and partly fleshy structure separating cavity of mouth from that of nose (ill. HEAD); *bony* or *hard ~*, front part of this; *soft ~*, back part of this, pendulous fold of musculo-membranous tissue separating mouth-cavity from pharynx. 2. Sense of taste; mental taste, liking.

palā'tial (-shl) *adj.* Like a palace; splendid.

palăt'inate *n.* Territory under a palatine; *the* (*Rhine*) *P~* (Ger. *Pfalz*), State of old German Empire under rule of the Count Palatine (*Pfalzgraf*) of the Rhine, orig. including district immediately dependent on Aachen, later comprising two districts higher up Rhine; now part of the province Rhineland Palatinate.

păl'atīne[1] *adj.* Of the imperial palace of the Caesars in Rome (see PALATINE HILL); of the palace or court of the German emperors; possessing royal privileges, having jurisdiction (within the territory) such as elsewhere belongs to the sovereign alone; of or belonging to a count or earl palatine; *count ~*, orig. in the later Roman Empire a count (*comes*) attached to the imperial palace and having supreme judicial authority in certain causes; under the German emperors, a count having supreme jurisdiction in his fief; in Engl. hist., an *earl ~*, the proprietor of a county palatine, now applied to the earldom of Chester and duchy of Lancaster, dignities which are attached to the Crown; *county ~*, in England, county of which the earl had orig. royal privileges, with exclusive jurisdiction (now Cheshire and Lancashire, formerly also Durham, Pembroke, Ely, etc.); *earl~*; see above. ~ *n.* Office of imperial palace; lord having sovereign power over province or dependency of empire or realm; (in England and Ireland) earl palatine.

păl'atīne[2] *adj.* Of the palate. **păl'atīnes** *n.pl.* Two bones forming hard palate.

Păl'atīne Hill. One of the 7 hills of Rome, that on which the first Roman settlement was made; later, site of imperial palaces.

pala'ver (-lah-) *n.* Conference, discussion, esp. between primitive natives and traders etc.; profuse or idle talk. ~ *v.i.* Talk profusely.

pāle[1] *n.* 1. Pointed piece of wood for fence etc., stake; 2. Boundary; enclosed place; *the P~*, (hist.) part of Ireland under English jurisdiction. 3. (her.) Vertical stripe (usu. ⅓ of breadth) in middle of shield (ill. HERALDRY); (*party*) *per ~*, (of shield) divided by vertical line through the middle.

pāle[2] *adj.* (Of person or complexion) of whitish or ashen appearance; (of colours) faint; faintly coloured; of faint lustre, dim; *~-face*, supposed N. Amer. Ind. name for white man. **pāle'ly** *adv.* **pāle'nėss** *n.* **pāle** *v.* Grow or make pale; (fig.) become pale in comparison (usu. *before* or *beside*).

păl'ėa *n.* (pl. *-eae*). 1. (bot.) Chaff-like bract or scale, esp. one of the inner bracts enclosing the stamens and pistil in the flower of grasses (ill. GRASS). 2. (ornith.) Wattle, dewlap.

Păl'ėstīne. Country of Asia at E. end of Mediterranean; the ancient home of the Jews and the Holy Land of Christendom; it was conquered by the Romans, 65 B.C., and by Arabs, A.D. 634; thenceforward, except when ruled by Crusaders (1098–1187) it remained under Moslem dominion until the defeat of Turkish and German forces by the British at Megiddo, 1917; under British mandate, 1923–48; invaded by Arab forces, 1948–9; the parts in the E. occupied by these are now incorporated in JORDAN and the rest is an independent republic, ISRAEL. **Pălėstĭn'ian** *adj.*

palestra: see PALAESTRA.

Pălėstri'na (-trē-), Giovanni Pierluigi da (1525–94). Italian composer of contrapuntal music for unaccompanied choir, esp. church music.

păl'etot (-etō) *n.* Loose outer garment for man or woman (ill. COAT).

păl'ėtte *n.* Artist's flat tablet for mixing colours on; colours used by particular artist or on particular occasion; *~-knife*, flexible steel blade with handle for mixing colours, also used for applying them to canvas.

Pāl'ey, William (1743–1805). English archdeacon and theologian; author of 'Evidences of Christianity' (1794) and 'Natural Theology' (1802), in which he finds proof of the existence of God in the design apparent in natural phenomena and particularly in the human body.

pal'frey (pawl-) *n.* (archaic, poet.) Saddle-horse for ordinary riding, esp. for ladies.

Pa'li (pah-). An Indo-Aryan language spoken in N. India in the 5th–2nd centuries B.C.; as the language of a large part of the Buddhist scriptures it was brought to Ceylon and Burma, and, though not spoken there, became the vehicle of a large literature of commentaries and chronicles. [for *pali-bhasa* (*pali* canon, *bhasa* language)]

păl'ĭkar *n.* Member of the band of a Greek or Albanian military chief, esp. during war of Independence.

păl'ĭmpsĕst *n.* Parchment or other material used for a second time after the original writing has been erased.

păl'ĭndrōme *n.* & *adj.* (Word, verse, etc.) that reads the same backwards as forwards (e.g. *madam*). **pălĭndrŏm'ic** *adj.*

pāl'ing *n.* (Fence of) pales.

pălĭngĕn'ėsĭs *n.* Regeneration; revival.

păl'ĭnōde *n.* Poem in which author retracts thing said in former poem; recantation.

pălĭsāde' *n.* 1. Fence of pales or of iron railings; (mil.) strong pointed wooden stake, of which number are fixed deeply in ground in close row as defence. 2. (bot.) Internal tissue of a leaf in which the cells are elongated and arranged in rows resembling a stockade (ill. LEAF). ~ *v.t.* Furnish, enclose, with palisade.

pāl'ish *adj.* Slightly pale.

pall[1] (pawl) *n.* 1. Cloth, usu. of black, purple, or white velvet, spread over coffin, hearse, or tomb; *~-bearer*, person holding up corner of pall at funeral. 2. Woollen vestment (now a narrow band passing over shoulders, with short lappets) worn by pope and some metropolitans or archbishops; (fig.) mantle, cloak.

pall[2] (pawl) *v.* Become insipid (now only fig.); satiate, clog.

Pallăd'ian *adj.* 1. Of Pallas ATHENE. 2. Of PALLADIO or his style; *~ window*: see ill. WINDOW.

Pallăd'ianism *n.* Style, opinions, of the followers of Palladio.

Palladiō (-lah'-). Andrea di Pietro (1508–80), Italian architect of Vicenza, who revived classical Roman styles and had great influence through his 'Four Books of Architecture' (1570), esp. in England on Inigo Jones and others. [It., = 'man of Pallas (Athene)']

pallăd'ium[1] *n.* Image of the goddess Pallas in the citadel of Troy, on which the safety of the city was held to depend, reputed to have been brought thence to Rome; safeguard.

pallăd'ium[2] *n.* Hard silvery-white metallic element of platinum group; symbol Pd, at. no. 46, at. wt 106·4. [f. the asteroid *Pallas*]

Păll'ăs. Title (of unknown meaning) of the Greek goddess ATHENE.

păll'ėt[1] *n.* Straw bed; mattress.

păll'ėt[2] *n.* 1. Flat wooden blade with handle, used by potters etc. 2. Projection on part of a machine, engaging with teeth of wheel and converting reciprocating into rotatory movement, or vice versa (ill. CLOCK). 3. Valve in upper part of wind-chest in organ, admitting wind to groove beneath set of pipes when corresponding key of keyboard is depressed (ill. ORGAN).

păll'ėt[3] *n.* (her.) Ordinary like PALE but half as long.

palliasse: see PAILLASSE.

păll'ĭāte *v.t.* Alleviate (disease) without curing; extenuate, excuse. **păllĭā'tion** *n.*

păll'ĭatĭve *adj.* & *n.* (Thing) serving to palliate.

păll'ĭd *adj.* Wan, pale. **păll'ĭdly** *adv.* **păll'ĭdnėss** *n.*

păll'ĭum *n.* 1. Man's large rectangular cloak, esp. among Greeks. 2. Archbishop's PALL[1]. 3. Integumental fold or mantle of mollusc.

pall-mall (pĕl'-mĕl', păl'-măl') *n.* 16th- and 17th-c. game in which a boxwood ball was driven with a mallet through an iron ring suspended at the end of a long alley; *Pall Mall*, street in London on site of such an alley, noted for its clubs. [It. *palla* ball, *maglio* mallet]

păll'or *n.* Paleness.

palm[1] (pahm) *n.* 1. Tree or shrub of an order of monocotyledons widely distributed in warm climates, with stem usu. upright and unbranched, head or crown of very large pinnate or fan-shaped leaves, and fruit of various forms; leaf of palm-tree as symbol of excellence; supreme excellence, prize for this. 2. Branch of various trees substituted for palm in northern countries, esp. in celebrating Palm Sunday. 3. *~-oil*, oil obtained from various palms; (with pun on PALM[2]) bribe-money; *P~ Sunday*, Sunday before Easter, on which Christ's entry into Jerusalem is celebrated, freq. with processions in which branches of palm are carried. **palmā'ceous** (-shus) *adj.*

palm[2] (pahm) *n.* Part of hand between wrist and fingers, esp. its inner surface; part of glove that covers this; *grease person's ~*, bribe him. ~ *v.t.* Impose fraudulently, pass *off* (thing *on* person); conceal (cards, dice, etc.) in hand in sleight-of-hand etc.; bribe.

păl'mar *adj.* Of, in, the palm of the hand.

păl'mary *adj.* Bearing the palm, pre-eminent.

păl'mate, -āted *adjs.* Shaped like open palm or hand.

Palm Beach (pahm). Winter resort in Florida, U.S.; *~ suit*, trade-name for man's suit of lightweight fabric of cotton and wool or mohair.

palm'er (pahm-) *n.* 1. Pilgrim who had returned from Holy Land with palm branch or leaf; itinerant monk under vow of poverty. 2. *~(-worm)* one of various kinds of destructive hairy caterpillars of migratory or wandering habits; hairy artificial fly.

Palm'erston (pahm-), Henry John Temple, 3rd Viscount (1784–1865). English statesman; foreign minister for many years; prime minister 1855–8, 1859–65.

pălmĕtte' *n.* Ornament somewhat like palm-leaf. (*Illustration, p.* 589.)

pălmĕtt'ō *n.* Various small species of palms, esp. dwarf fan-palm (*Chamaerops humilis*) of S. Europe and N. Africa, and cabbage palmetto (*Sabal palmetto*) of south-eastern U.S.; *~ flag*, flag of S. Carolina, bearing figure of cabbage-palmetto leaf; *P~ State*, pop. name of S. Carolina.

păl'mĭpĕd, -pēde *n.* & *adj.* Web-footed (bird).

palm'ĭstry (pahm-) *n.* Art or practice of telling character or fortunes from the lines etc. in palm of hand. **palm'ist** *n.*

palmy (pahm'ĭ) *adj.* Of, like, abounding in, palms; triumphant, flourishing (esp. in ~ *days*).

pălmy̆r'a[1] *n.* Species of palm (*Borassus flabellifer*) grown in India and Ceylon, with fan-shaped leaves used for matting etc.

Pălmy̆r'a[2]. (Aramaic *Tadmor*) Ancient city at an oasis in the Syrian Desert on the caravan route from Damascus to the Euphrates; prosperous under the Roman Empire but destroyed in 3rd c. A.D. **Pălmy̆r'ēne** *adj.* & *n.*

pălp, păl'pus (pl. *-pī*) *ns.* Jointed sense-organ in insects etc., feeler (ill. INSECT). **păl'pal** *adj.*

păl'pable *adj.* That can be touched or felt; readily perceived by senses or mind. **pălpabil'ity** *n.* **păl'pably** *adv.*

păl'pāte *v.t.* Examine by touch, handle, esp. in medical examination. **pălpā'tion** *n.*

păl'pėbral *adj.* Of the eyelids.

păl'pĭtāte *v.i.* Pulsate, throb; tremble. **pălpĭtā'tion** *n.* Throbbing; increased activity of heart due to exertion, agitation, or disease.

pa'lsgrāve (pawl-) *n.* Count PALATINE.

pa'lstāve (pawl-) *n.* (archaeol.) Metal celt shaped to fit into split handle (instead of having socket into which handle fits; ill. CELT).

palsy (pawl'zĭ) *n.* Paralysis (also fig.); *cerebral ~*, condition of weakness, imperfect control of movement, and spasticity, following damage to brain at birth. ~ *v.t.* Paralyse.

pa'lter (pawl-) *v.i.* Shuffle, equivocate; haggle; trifle.

pa'ltry (pawl-) *adj.* Worthless, petty, contemptible. **pa'ltrinėss** *n.*

palūd'al (*or* păl'-) *adj.* Of a marsh; malarial.

păl'ūdrīne *n.* Drug used in treatment of malaria, now known by official name *proguanil.*

palŭs'tral, palŭs'trīne *adjs.* Of, inhabiting, marshes.

păm *n.* Knave of clubs, esp. in 5-card loo.

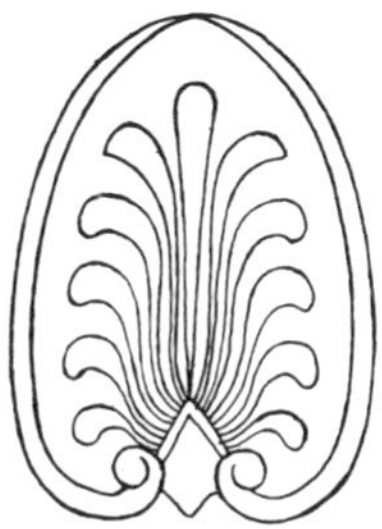

PALMETTE

Pamir' (-ēr), **Pamirs'.** Mountain system of central Asia.

păm'pas *n.pl.* Vast treeless grassy plains of S. America south of the Amazon, esp. great plain of Argentina stretching from Atlantic coast to Andes, and from Rio Colorado to Gran Chaco; *~-grass*, gigantic grass (*Cortarderia argentea*) with silvery-coloured silky panicles on stalks sometimes 12 or 14 ft high, introduced into European gardens from S. America. [Peruv. *bamba* steppe]

păm'per *v.t.* Over-indulge.

pămph'lėt *n.* Small unbound treatise, esp. on subject of current interest. **pămphlėteer'** *n.* Writer of pamphlets. ~ *v.i.* write pamphlets. [prob. f. *Pamphilet, Panflet*, familiar name of 12th-c. Latin amatory poem or comedy 'Pamphilus, seu de Amore']

păn[1] *n.* 1. Metal or earthenware vessel, usu. shallow and freq. open, for domestic purposes; pan-like vessel in which substances are heated etc.; contents of pan, panful. 2. Pan-shaped depression or concavity of any vessel or structure; part of lock that held priming in obsolete types of gun (ill. MUSKET). 3. Hollow in ground, esp. salt-pan. 4. Hard substratum of soil, more or less impervious to moisture. 5. *pan'cake*, thin flat batter-cake fried in pan; *flat as a pancake*, quite flat; (slang, of aeroplane) landing made without use of undercarriage; (*v.i.*) make such a landing; *Pancake day, Tuesday*, Shrove Tuesday, from the custom of eating pancakes on that day. ~ *v.* ~ *off, out*, wash (gold-bearing gravel) in pan; ~ *out*, yield gold, (fig.) succeed, work (*well* etc.).

pan[2] (pahn) *n.* Betel-leaf; combination of this with areca-nut etc. for chewing. [Hind. *pān*]

Păn[3]. Greek god of flocks and shepherds; orig. and chiefly an Arcadian deity, represented with the horns, ears, and legs of a goat; he invented the musical pipe (panpipe) of 7 reeds, and was reputed to cause sudden groundless fear such as that felt by travellers in remote and desolate places.

pănacē'a *n.* Universal remedy.

panache' (-ahsh, -ăsh) *n.* Tuft, plume, of feathers, esp. as headdress or on helmet; (fig.) display, swagger.

pana'da (-nah-) *n.* 1. Dish of bread boiled to pulp and flavoured with cinnamon, sugar, etc. 2. Thick mixture of flour cooked with butter and milk, used esp. for binding together other ingredients.

pan-Af'rĭcan *adj.* Of, for, all Africans.

Pănama' (-mah). Republic of Central and S. America, lying between Costa Rica and Colombia; its capital city, at Pacific end of Panama Canal; ~ *Canal*, canal connecting Atlantic and Pacific Oceans through narrow isthmus of Panama, built between 1882 and 1914, and under the control of the U.S. **panama** *n.* ~ (*hat*), fine soft plaited hat made from undeveloped leaves of stemless screw-pine (*Corludovica palmata*) of tropical S. America, or an imitation of this.

păn-Amĕ'rĭcan *adj.* Of all States of N. and S. America, of all Americans.

Pănchĕn Lama: see LAMA[1].

pănchromăt'ĭc (-k-) *adj.* (phot.) Equally sensitive to all colours of spectrum, representing all colours in proper intensities.

păncrăt'ĭc *adj.* 1. Of the pancratium. 2. (Of eyepiece) capable of adjustment to many degrees of power. **păncrā̆t'ĭum** *n.* (Gk antiq.) Athletic contest combining wrestling and boxing.

pănc'rėăs *n.* Gland near stomach discharging a digestive secretion (*pancreatic juice*) through ducts into duodenum, and also producing INSULIN which it passes directly into the blood-stream (ill. ABDOMEN); sweetbread. **păncrėăt'ĭc** *adj.*

păn'da *n.* Raccoon-like animal (*Aelurus fulgens*) of SE. Himalayas, with reddish-brown fur and long bushy ring-marked tail; *giant ~*, large rare bear-like black-and-white mammal (*Ailuropoda melanoleuca*) of Tibet.

Păn'darus. In Gk legend, a leader of the Trojans; in the medieval legend of Troilus and Cressida, Cressida's uncle, who acted as go-between for the lovers.

păn'dĕct *n.* (usu. pl.) Compendium in 50 books of Roman civil law made by order of Justinian in 6th c.; complete body of laws.

păndĕm'ĭc *adj.* & *n.* (Disease, usu. infectious) of world-wide distribution.

păndėmōn'ĭum *n.* Abode of all demons; place of lawless violence or uproar; utter confusion. [wd formed by Milton]

păn'der *n.* Go-between in clandestine amours, procurer; one who ministers to evil designs. ~ *v.* Minister (*to* base passions, evil designs) (also fig.); act as pander to. [f. PANDARUS]

P. & O. *abbrev.* Peninsular & Oriental (Steamship Co.).

păndōr'a[1], **pandōre'** *n.* Wire-stringed musical instrument of cithern type.

Păndōr'a[2]. (Gk myth.) The first woman, made by Hephaestus the fire-god at the order of Zeus to punish the human race because PROMETHEUS had stolen fire from heaven for their use; Pandora became wife of Epimetheus, brother of Prometheus, and from a box (*~'s box*) given her by Zeus she let loose all the evils that afflict mankind, hope alone remaining in the bottom of the box.

păn'dour (-oor), **pan'door** *n.* (pl.) Force of rapacious and brutal soldiers raised by Austria against the Turks in 18th c.

pāne[1] *n.* Single sheet of glass in compartment of window (ill. WINDOW); rectangular division of chequered pattern etc. **pāne'lėss** *adj.*

pāne[2] *n.* Pointed, edged, or ball-shaped end of hammer opposite face (ill. HAMMER).

păněgў'rĭc (-j-) *n.* Laudatory discourse (*upon*). ~ *adj.* Laudatory. **păn'ėgўrīze** *v.t.* Speak, write, in praise of, eulogize. **pănėgў'rĭst** *n.*

păn'el *n.* 1. Stuffed lining of saddle; kind of saddle, usu. a pad without framework. 2. Slip of parchment, esp. that on which sheriff entered names of jurors; list of jurymen, jury; (Sc. law) person(s) indicted, accused; *on the* ~, on his trial. 3. (hist.) List of doctors registered in a district as accepting patients under National Health Insurance Act (1913); *on the* ~, (of doctors) so registered; (of patients) under the care of such doctors. 4. Group of people gathered for special purpose, as ~ of experts. 5. Distinct compartment of surface, esp. of wainscot, door, etc., often sunk below or raised above general level (ill. WAINSCOT); piece of stuff of different kind or colour inserted in woman's dress etc. ~ *v.t.* Saddle (beast) with panel; fit (wall, door, etc.) with panels; ornament (dress etc.) with panels. **păn'ellĭng** *n.*

păng *n.* Shooting pain; sudden sharp mental pain.

păngōl'ĭn (-ngg-) *n.* Scaly ant-eater, large mammal (*Manis*), with body covered with horny scales, of tropical Asia and Africa (ill. ANT-eater). [Malay *peng-goling* roller]

păn'hăndle *n.* Handle of pan; (U.S.) narrow prolongation of State or territory extending between two others; *P~ State*, pop. name of W. Virginia. ~ *v.* (U.S. slang) Beg. **păn'hăndler** *n.* (U.S. slang) Beggar.

păn-Hĕll'ėnĭsm *n.* Political union of all Greeks. **păn-Hellĕn'ĭc** *adj.*

păn'ĭc[1] *n.* ~(*-grass*), genus of grasses (*Panicum*), including Italian millet, many of which are cultivated as cereal grains.

păn'ĭc[2] *adj.* (Of terror) unreasoning, excessive. ~ *n.* Infectious fright; sudden general alarm leading to hasty measures. ~ *v.* Affect, be affected, with panic. **păn'ĭcky** *adj.* [Gk *panikos* of the god Pan, reputed to cause panic]

păn'ĭcle *n.* (bot.) Compound inflorescence in which some pedicels branch again or repeatedly, forming loose irregular cluster, as in oats (ill. INFLORESCENCE).

pănĭfĭcā'tion *n.* Making into bread.

păn-Is'lam *n.* Union of Mohammedan world. **păn-Islăm'ĭc** *adj.* **păn-Is'lamĭsm** *n.*

pănjăn'drum *n.* Mock title of exalted personage; pompous official or pretender. [app. invented by S. Foote, 1720–77, in a piece of nonsense verse]

Pănk'hûrst, Mrs Emmeline (1858–1928). English leader of militant suffragism.

pănn'age *n.* (Right of, payment for) pasturage of swine; acorns, beech-mast, etc., as food for swine.

pănne *n.* Soft long-napped dress-material resembling velvet.

pănn'ier *n.* 1. Basket, esp. one of those carried, usu. in pairs, by beast of burden or on the shoulders. 2. Frame distending woman's skirt at the hips, part of skirt looped up round hips.

PANNIER: A. *c* 1693. B. *c* 1780

1. Steenkirk. 2. Stomacher. 3. Pannier. 4. Calash

pănn'ĭkin *n.* Small metal drinking-vessel; its contents.

păn'oply *n.* Complete suit of armour (now usu. fig.). **păn'oplied** (-lĭd) *adj.*

pănŏp'tĭcon *n.* Bentham's proposed circular prison with cells built round a central 'well', whence the warders could at all times see the prisoners; (U.S.) circular prison of this type.

pănora'ma (-rah-, -ră-) *n.* Picture of landscape etc. arranged on inside of cylindrical surface or successively rolled out before spectator; continuous passing scene; unbroken view of surrounding region. **pănorăm'ĭc** *adj.* **pănorăm'ĭcally** *adv.*

păn'-pīpe(s) *n.* Musical instrument of graduated series of reeds forming scale, with open ends level. [f. PAN[3]]

păn-Slav'ĭsm (slahv-) *n.* Movement for political union of all Slavs. **păn-Slavŏn'ĭc** *adj.*

păn'sy (-zĭ) *n.* 1. Wild or cultivated plant, *Viola tricolor*, with variously coloured flowers; heartsease. 2. (colloq.) An effeminate youth, homosexual; also used attrib. of such persons or things characteristic of them.

pănt *v.* Gasp for breath; yearn (*for, after, to*); throb violently; utter gaspingly. ~ *n.* Gasp, throb.

Păntăg'ruĕl (-rōō-). One of the characters of RABELAIS, giant son of Gargantua, represented as a great eater and drinker and an extravagant and satirical humorist. **Păntagruĕl'ĭan** *adj.*

păntalĕttes' *n.pl.* Long loose frilled drawers worn by young girls *c* 1825–53.

păntalōōn' *n.* 1. *P~*, character in Italian comedy represented as foolish old man wearing spectacles, pantaloons, and slippers; clown's butt and abettor in harlequinade or pantomime. 2. (hist.) Garment of breeches and stockings in one piece; tight-fitting trousers fastened with ribbons or buttons below calf, or strap passing under boots (ill. COAT); (chiefly U.S., archaic) trousers. [It. *Pantalone* Venetian character in Italian comedy; perh. f. San Pantaleone, favourite Venetian saint]

păntĕch'nĭcon (-k-) *n.* Furniture warehouse (orig. name of a bazaar in London where all kinds of artistic work were sold); ~ (*van*), furniture-removing van.

păn'thėĭsm *n.* Doctrine that God is everything and everything is God; heathen worship of all the gods. **păn'thėĭst** *n.* **pănthėĭs'tĭc(al)** *adjs.*

păn'thėon (*or* -ē'on) *n.* 1. Temple dedicated to all the gods, esp. the circular one still standing in Rome, erected in early 2nd c. A.D. prob. on site of an earlier one built by Agrippa. 2. Building (esp. former church of St. Geneviève in Paris) in which illustrious dead are buried or have memorials. 3. Deities of a people collectively.

păn'ther *n.* 1. = LEOPARD, esp. male one (now chiefly *black* ~, black form of leopard common in S. India). 2. (U.S.) Puma, COUGAR.

păn'ties (-z) *n.pl.* (colloq.) Pants worn by children; close-fitting knickers worn by women.

păn'tīle *n.* Roof tile transversely curved to ogee shape, one curve being much larger than the other (ill. ROOF).

păntĭsŏc'racy *n.* Community in which all are equal and all rule.

păn'tograph (-ahf) *n.* Instrument of four rods jointed together in parallelogram form, with tracing-points on one free end and one terminal joint, for copying plans etc. on any scale. **păntogrăph'ĭc** *adj.*

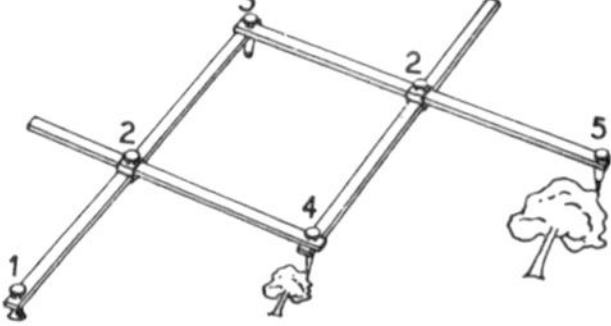

PANTOGRAPH

1. Fixed pivot. 2. Adjustable pivots. 3. Sliding pivot with ball foot. 4. Ivory point. 5. Pencil point

păn'tomīme *n.* 1. (hist.) Roman actor performing in dumb show, mimic actor. 2. (In Gt Britain and Br. Commonwealth) a dramatic entertainment now usu. produced at Christmas time and based on a traditional fairy-tale, with singing, dancing, acrobatics, clowning, topical jokes, a transformation scene, and certain stock roles, esp. the 'principal boy' (i.e. hero) acted by a woman and the 'dame' acted by a man. 3. Dumb show. **păntomĭm'ĭc** *adj.*

păn'trȳ *n.* Room in which bread and other provisions, or (*butler's, housemaid's*, ~) plate, table-linen, etc., are kept; *pan'tryman*, butler or his assistant.

pănts *n.pl.* 1. Drawers. 2. (U.S.) Trousers.

păn'zer (-tser) *n.* Armour; freq. used attrib. as ~ *division, grenadiers.* [Ger.]

Paolo Veronese: see VERONESE.

păp¹ *n.* (archaic) Nipple of woman's breast; corresponding part of man; (pl.) conical hilltops side by side.

păp² *n.* Soft or semi-liquid food for infants or invalids; mash, pulp.

păp³ *n.* (U.S.) Papa.

papa' (-ah; U.S. pah'-) *n.* Father (in England used chiefly by children).

pā'pacy *n.* Pope's (tenure of) office; papal system.

pā'pal *adj.* Of the pope or his office; ~ *cross*, cross with three transoms (ill. CROSS); *P~ State*, district of central Italy until 1870 subject to the Apostolic See. **pā'pally** *adv.* **pā'palĭsm, pā'palĭst** *ns.*

papāverā'ceous (-shus) *adj.* Of the poppy family.

papāv'erous *adj.* Of, like, allied to, the poppy.

papaw' *n.* 1. Palm-like tree (*Carica papaya*) of S. America; fruit of this, usu. oblong, of dull orange colour, with thick fleshy rind and numerous black seeds embedded in pulp, used as food. 2. (U.S., also *paw'paw*) Small N. Amer. tree (*Asimina triloba*) with purple flowers and oblong edible fruit with bean-like seeds embedded in sweet pulp.

pā'per *n.* 1. Substance composed of fibres interlaced into a compact web, made from linen and cotton rags, straw, wood, certain grasses, etc., which are macerated into a pulp, dried and pressed into a thin flexible sheet, used for writing, printing, drawing, wrapping up parcels, covering the interior of walls, etc.; substances of similar texture, as that made by wasps for their nests; substances made from paper-pulp, as papier mâché, etc. 2. Negotiable documents, e.g. bills of exchange; bank-notes etc. used as currency (opp. to *coin*). 3. (slang) (Persons admitted by) free passes to theatre &c. 4. (pl.) Documents proving person's or ship's identity, standing, etc.; *send in one's ~s*, resign. 5. Set of questions in examination; essay, dissertation, esp. one read to learned society. 6. Newspaper. 7. Paper used as wrapper or receptacle; small paper parcel; sheet of paper with pins or needles stuck in it. 8. *on ~*, hypothetically, to judge from statistics, etc.; *~-chase*, cross-country run in which trail of torn-up paper is laid by one or more runners to set a course for the rest; *~-hangings*, paper for covering walls of room etc.; *~-hanger*, one who covers walls with these; *~-knife*, knife of ivory, wood, etc., for cutting open leaves of book etc.; *~-mill*, one in which paper is made; *~-weight*, small heavy object laid on loose papers to prevent their being scattered. **pā'pery** *adj.* **pā'per** *v.t.* Enclose in paper; decorate (wall etc.) with wall-paper; furnish with paper; (slang) fill (theatre etc.) by means of free passes.

Pāph'ŏs. Ancient city on W. coast of Cyprus, sanctuary of a goddess identified by Greeks with Aphrodite. **Pāph'ĭan** *adj.* & *n.* (esp.) Of (illicit) love, of wantonness; prostitute.

papier mâché (păp'yā mah'shā) *n.* Moulded paper pulp used for boxes, trays, etc. [Fr., = 'chewed paper']

papĭlionā'ceous (-yonāshus) *adj.* (bot.) With corolla like a butterfly (i.e. having a large upper petal, two lateral petals, and two narrow lower petals between these).

papĭll'a *n.* Small nipple-like protuberance in a part or organ of the body; (bot.) small fleshy projection on plant. **păp'ĭllary, păp'ĭllate, păp'ĭllōse** *adjs.*

papĭ'llon (-lyon) *n.* Breed of toy dog with ears suggesting form of butterfly.

pā'pĭst *n.* Advocate of papal supremacy; Roman Catholic (usu. in hostile sense). **papĭs'tĭc(al)** *adjs.* **papĭs'tĭcally** *adv.* **pā'pĭstry** *n.*

papoose' *n.* N. Amer. Indian young child.

păpp'us *n.* (bot.) Downy appendage on seeds of thistles, dandelions, etc. (ill. FRUIT). **păppōse'** *adj.*

păp'rika (-rē-) *n.* Ripe fruit of 2 kinds of pepper (*Capsicum annuum* var. *longum*, and *C. tetragonum*); red condiment made from this. [Hungarian]

Păp'ūa. Part of the island of New Guinea; formerly called British New Guinea; became a territory of Australia, 1905. **Păp'ūan** *adj.* & *n.* (Native, language) of New Guinea and other islands of Melanesia; (member) of long-headed dark-skinned race with woolly hair and broad nose.

păp'ūla, păp'ūle *ns.* Pimple; small fleshy projection on plant. **păp'ūlar, păpūlōse', păp'ūlous** *adjs.*

păpȳrā'ceous (-shus) *adj.* (bot.) Of the nature of, thin as, paper.

papȳr'us *n.* (pl. *-ri*). Aquatic plant of sedge family (*Cyperus papyrus*), with creeping rootstock sending up long stems which bear spikelets of flowers in large clusters; writing material prepared by ancient Egyptians etc. by soaking, pressing, and drying strips of papyrus stem, laying them side by side, and placing similar layers over these at right angles; MS. written on this.

par¹ *n.* Equality, equal footing; average or normal amount, degree, or condition; (golf) number of strokes which scratch player should require for hole or course, allowing two putts for each green; *~ of exchange*, recognized value of one country's currency in terms of another's; *at ~*, (of stocks etc.) at face value; *above ~*, at a premium; *below ~*, at a discount; below the average degree, quality, etc.; not in one's usual health. [L, = 'equal(ity)']

par² *n.* (colloq.) Paragraph.

Par'a¹. State in N. Brazil; its capital city (officially Belem), on S. estuary of Amazon; ~ *rubber*, native rubber obtained from *Hevea brasiliensis* (and other species), tree growing on banks of Amazon.

par'a² *n.* 1. $\frac{1}{40}$ of a Turkish piastre. 2. $\frac{1}{100}$ of a Yugoslav dinar.

para- *prefix.* Beside; beyond; wrong; irregular

parăb'asis *n.* Part sung by chorus in Greek comedy, addressed to audience in the poet's name.

părabīōs'ĭs *n.* (zool.) Phenomenon in which individuals are conjoined by common tissues, as in Siamese twins. **părabīŏt'ĭc** *adj.*

pă'rable *n.* Fictitious narrative used to point a moral or illustrate some spiritual relation or condition; short allegory.

parăb'ola *n.* Plane curve formed by intersection of cone with plane parallel to its side (ill. CONE).

părabŏl'ĭc(al) *adjs.* 1. Of, expressed in, a parable. 2. Of, like, a parabola. **părabŏl'ĭcally** *adv.*

parăb'oloid *n.* Solid some of whose plane sections are parabolas, esp. that generated by revolution of parabola about its axis (~ *of revolution*; ill. CONE).

Păracĕl'sus, Philippus Aureolus. Name taken by Theophrastus Bombastus von Hohenheim (1493–1541), German-Swiss physician, alchemist, and astrologer.

parăch'ronĭsm (-k-) *n.* Error in chronology.

pă'rachute (-shoot) *n.* Umbrella-shaped apparatus of silk or other material attached by ropes to person or heavy object falling or being dropped from a height, esp. from aircraft, and designed to be expanded by the air it is falling through (or other means) and by its resulting drag to reduce the speed of falling to some desired limit, usu. one consistent with safety; ~ *flare*, flare dropped, esp. to illuminate bombers' target area, and having its time of falling prolonged by a parachute; ~ *mine*, mine dropped from aircraft and having a parachute attached;

PARACHUTE

1. Canopy. 2. Rigging lines

~ *troops*, invading troops landing from aircraft by parachute. ~ *v.* Convey, descend, by parachute. **pă'rachutĭst** *n.*

pă'raclēte *n.* Occasional variant of A.V.'s 'Comforter' to translate Gk *paraklētos* in John xiv. 16, 26 etc.

parāde' *n.* 1. Display, ostentation; serial display or recital of events etc. (e.g. *programme* ~ of the B.B.C.). 2. Muster of troops etc. for inspection, esp. one held regularly at set hours; ground used for this. 3. Public square or promenade. ~ *v.* 1. Assemble (troops etc.) for review or other purpose; march through (streets etc.) with display; march in procession with display. 2. Display ostentatiously.

pă'radĭgm (-ĭm) *n.* Example, pattern, esp. of inflexion of noun, verb, etc. **părădĭgmăt'ĭc** (-ig-) *adj.*

pă'radīse *n.* Garden of Eden (also *earthly* ~); heaven; region, state, of supreme bliss; *bird of* ~: see BIRD. **părădĭsā'ĭcal, părădīs'al, părădĭs'iac(al)** *adjs.* [O. Pers. *pairidaeza* park]

pă'radŏs *n.* Elevation of earth behind fortified place to secure it from rear attack or fire, esp. mound along back of trench.

pă'radŏx *n.* Statement contrary to received opinion; seemingly absurd though perhaps really well-founded statement; self-contradictory, essentially absurd or false, statement; person, thing, conflicting with preconceived notions of what is reasonable or possible. **părădŏx'ĭcal** *adj.* **părădŏx'ĭcally** *adv.*

pă'raffĭn *n.* 1. (usu. ~ *wax*) White tasteless odourless waxy substance, chemically a mixture of higher hydrocarbons, solid at ordinary temperatures and obtained by distillation of petroleum etc., used for making candles, rendering paper waterproof ('waxed paper') etc. 2. (chem.) Any of a series of saturated hydrocarbons of which methane is the simplest member; paraffin oil; ~ *oil*, mixture of hydrocarbons obtained by distillation of petroleum, used as fuel, illuminant, solvent, etc.; kerosene. [L *parum* little, *affinis* having affinity, referring to the relative unreactivity of the paraffins]

părăgō'ge (-jĭ) *n.* (gram.) Addition of letter or syllable to a word. **părăgŏ'gĭc** *adj.*

pă'ragon *n.* 1. Model of excellence, supremely excellent person or thing, model (*of* virtue etc.). 2. Perfect diamond, 100 carats or more. 3. Large size of type, between great primer and double pica (two-line long primer, 20 point).

pă'ragraph (-ahf, -ăf) *n.* Distinct passage or section in book etc., marked by indentation of first line; symbol (usu. ¶) formerly used to mark new paragraph, now as reference mark; detached short item of news etc. in newspaper. ~ *v.t.* Write paragraph about; arrange (article etc.) in paragraphs. **pă'ragrapher, pă'ragraphĭst** *ns.* **părăgrăph'ĭc** *adj.*

Pă'raguay (-gwā, -gwī). Inland republic of S. America; capital, Asuncion.

pă'r(r)akeet, pă'roquet (-kĕt) *n.* Small, esp. long-tailed, kinds of parrot. [OF, f. It. *parrochetto* dim. of *parroco* parson, or *parrucchetto* dim. of *parrucca* peruke]

părălĭp'sĭs, -leipsĭs (-lī-) *n.* Trick of securing emphasis by professing to omit all mention of subject, e.g. *I say nothing of his antecedents, how from youth upwards etc.*

pă'rallăx *n.* Apparent displacement of object, caused by actual change of point of observation; angular amount of this displacement. **părallăc'tĭc** *adj.*

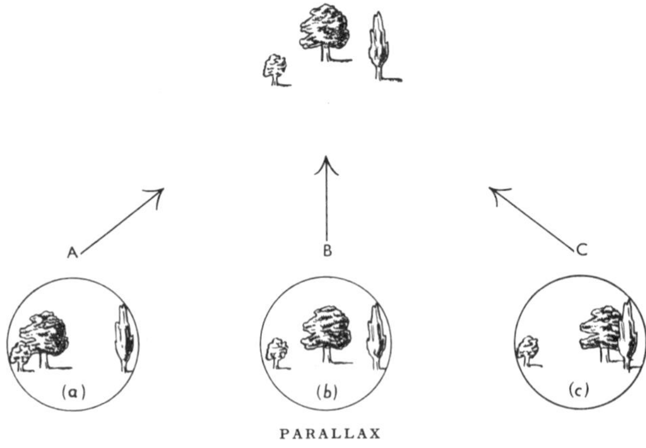

PARALLAX

a, b, c show the appearance of the trees to spectators at *A, B,* and *C* respectively

pă'rallel *adj.* (Of lines etc.) continuously equidistant, (of line) having this relation to; precisely similar, analogous, or corresponding; ~ *bars*, pair of horizontal parallel bars supported on posts for gymnastic exercises; ~ *circuit*, (elect.) circuit connecting the same two points as are connected by another circuit (ill. CIRCUIT); ~ *ruler*, two rulers connected by pivoted cross-pieces or single ruler fitted with rollers, for drawing parallel lines. ~ *n.* 1. ~ (*of latitude*) each of the parallel circles marking degrees of latitude on earth's surface on globe; lines on map corresponding to these. 2. Person, thing, precisely analogous to another; comparison. 3. Parallel position. 4. Two parallel lines (||) as reference mark. ~ *v.t.* Represent as similar, compare (*with, to*); find, mention, something parallel or corresponding to; be parallel, correspond, to.

părallelĕp'ĭpĕd (*or* -epīp'ĭd) *n.* Solid contained by parallelograms (ill. PRISM).

pă'rallelĭsm *n.* Being parallel; comparison or correspondence of successive passages, esp. in Hebrew poetry.

părallĕl'ogrăm *n.* Four-sided rectilineal figure whose opposite sides are parallel (ill. QUADRILATERAL); ~ *of forces*, (parallelogram illustrating) theorem that if two forces acting at a point be represented in magnitude and direction by two sides of a parallelogram, their resultant is represented by a diagonal drawn from that point.

parăl'ogĭsm *n.* Illogical reasoning, esp. of which reasoner is unconscious; fallacy.

pă'ralȳse (-z) *v.t.* Affect with paralysis; render powerless, cripple.

parăl'ȳsĭs *n.* Affection marked by impairment or loss of motor or sensory function of nerves; (fig.) state of utter powerlessness.

părałȳt'ĭc *adj.* & *n.* (Person) affected with paralysis. **păralȳt'ically** *adv.*

păramăgnĕt'ĭc *adj.* (Of substance, as tungsten, aluminium, manganese, and chromium) tending to become magnetized in the presence of a magnetic field and lie with its long axis parallel to the field (cf. DIAMAGNETIC). **paramăg'nėtĭsm** *n.*

păramătt'a *n.* Light dress fabric of merino wool and silk or cotton. [town in New South Wales]

parăm'ėter *n.* (math.) Quantity constant in case considered, but varying in different cases.

păramil'ĭtary *adj.* Having a function or status ancillary to that of military forces.

pă'ramō *n.* High treeless plateau in tropical S. America.

pă'ramount *adj.* Supreme; pre-eminent; superior (*to*). **pă'ramountly** *adj.* **pă'ramountcy** *n.*

pă'ramour (-oor) *n.* (archaic, rhet.) Illicit partner of married man or woman.

par'ăng (pah-) *n.* Large heavy Malay sheath-knife.

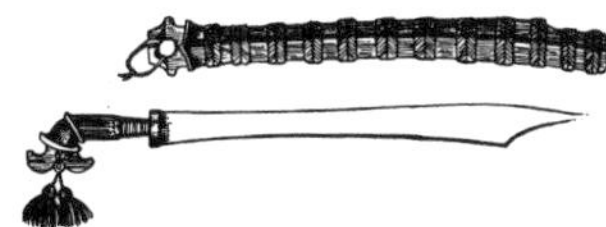

PARANG WITH SCABBARD

păranoi'a, păranoe'a (-nē'*a*) *n.* Form of mental illness characterized by systematic delusions. **păranoi'ăc** *adj.* & *n.*

pă'ranoid *adj.* Resembling, characterized by, paranoia.

pă'rapėt *n.* Low wall at edge of balcony, roof, etc., or along sides of bridge etc.; (mil.) defence of earth, stone, etc., to conceal and protect troops, esp. mound along front of trench.

pă'răph *n.* Flourish after a signature, orig. as precaution against forgery.

păraphernăl'ĭa *n.pl.* Personal belongings; mechanical accessories, odds and ends of equipment; (formerly) articles of personal property that law allowed married woman to keep and treat as her own.

pă'raphrāse (-z) *n.* Free rendering or amplification of a passage, expression of its sense in other words; any of a collection of metrical paraphrases of passages of Scripture (esp. psalms) used in Church of Scotland etc. ~ *v.t.* Express meaning of (passage) in other words. **păraphrăs'tĭc** *adj.* **păraphrăs'tically** *adv.*

păraphrēn'ĭa *n.* Variety of schizophrenic mental illness (esp. paranoid form), occurring in later life.

păraplē'gia (-j-) *n.* Paralysis confined to the lower limbs. **păraplē'gĭc** *adj.* & *n.* Of paraplegia; (person) affected by it.

pă'rasăng *n.* Ancient Persian measure of length (about 3¼ miles).

părasėlēn'ė *n.* Bright spot on lunar halo, mock-moon.

pă'rasīte *n.* 1. Interested hanger-on, toady. 2. Animal, plant, living in or upon another and deriving nutriment from it to the detriment of the host; (loosely) plant that climbs about another plant, walls, etc. **părasĭt'ĭc(al)** *adjs.* **pă'rasītĭsm** *n.* **pă'rasītīze** *v.t.* Infest as a parasite.

părasŏl' (*or* pă'-) *n.* Sunshade; ~ *pine*: see UMBRELLA pine.

părasȳmpathĕ'tĭc *adj.* Of the ~ *nervous system*, one of the two divisions of the AUTONOMIC nervous system, consisting of fibres which connect with nerve cells grouped within or near the viscera; so called because its peripheral nerves often run alongside those of the sympathetic system.

părasyn'thėsĭs *n.* (philol.). Derivation from a compound. **părasȳnthĕt'ĭc** *adj.*

păratăx'ĭs *n.* (gram.) Placing of clauses etc. one after another, without words to indicate co-ordination or subordination. **părată̆c'tĭc** *adj.* **parată̆c'tically** *adv.*

părathȳr'oid *adj.* ~ *glands*, 4 small bodies adjacent to thyroid gland, producing a secretion which maintains the balance between the calcium in the blood and that in the bones.

pă'ratroops *n.pl.* Airborne troops landing by parachute. **pă'ratrooper** *n.*

părатȳph'oid *n.* Form of enteric fever milder than true typhoid, and bacteriologically distinguishable from it.

pă'ravāne *n.* Apparatus towed from bows of a ship at a depth regulated by its vanes, with saw-edged jaws for cutting the moorings of submerged mines.

părazō'a *n.pl.* A division of the animal kingdom comprising aquatic animals (sponges), with 2 layers of cells but little co-ordination between the cells and no nervous system.

pa̅r̅b'oil *v.t.* Boil partially; (fig.) overheat.

pa̅r̅b'ŭckle *n.* Method of using a rope to raise or lower casks and cylindrical objects, the middle being secured at the upper level and both ends passed under and round the object and then hauled or let slowly out. ~ *v.t.*

pa̅r̅'cel *n.* 1. (archaic) Part (esp. in *part and* ~); piece of land, esp. as part of estate. 2. Goods etc. wrapped up in single package; ~ *post*, branch of postal service concerned with parcels. 3. (commerc.) Quantity dealt with in one transaction. ~ *adv.* (archaic) Partly; ~ *gilt*, partly gilded, esp. (of cup etc.) with inner surface gilt. ~ *v.t.* 1. Divide (usu. *out*) into portions; make (*up*) into parcel(s). 2. (naut.) Cover (caulked seam) with canvas strips and pitch; wrap (rope) with canvas strips. **pa̅r̅'celling** *n.* (esp., naut.) Strip of canvas, usu. tarred, for binding round rope.

pa̅r̅'cenary *n.* Joint heirship. **pa̅r̅'cener** *n.* Coheir.

pa̅r̅ch *v.* Roast slightly; make or become hot and dry.

pa̅r̅ch'ment *n.* Skin (strictly, inner part of split skin of sheep) dressed and prepared for writing, painting, etc.; parchment-like skin, esp. husk of coffee-bean; ~ *paper*, a thick, strong, specially toughened paper. [LL *pergamena* of *Pergamum*, city in Asia Minor]

pa̅r̅d[1] *n.* (archaic) Leopard.

pa̅r̅d[2], **pa̅r̅d'ner** *ns.* (slang, esp. U.S.) Partner.

pa̅r̅d'on *n.* Forgiveness; (law) remission of legal consequences of crime; courteous forbearance (esp. in *I beg your* ~, apology for thing done, for dissent or contradiction, or for not hearing or understanding what was said); (eccles.) indulgence, festival at which this is granted, esp. (in Brittany) festival of patron saint. ~ *v.t.* Forgive; make allowance for, excuse. **pa̅r̅d'onable** *adj.* **pa̅r̅d'onably** *adv.*

pa̅r̅d'oner *n.* (hist.) Person licensed to sell pardons or indulgences.

pa̅r̅e *v.t.* Trim (thing) by cutting away irregular parts etc.; cut away skin, rind, etc., of (fruit etc.); shave, cut *off*, *away* (edges etc.); (fig.) diminish little by little. **pa̅r̅'er, pa̅r̅'ĭng** *ns.*

părėgŏ'rĭc *adj.* & *n.* ~ (*elixir*), camphorated tincture of opium flavoured with aniseed and benzoic acid.

parĕn'chȳma (-k-) *n.* 1. (anat.) Proper tissue of gland, organ, etc., as dist. from flesh and connective tissue. 2. (bot.) Tissue of cells of about equal length and breadth placed side by side, usu. soft and succulent, found esp. in softer

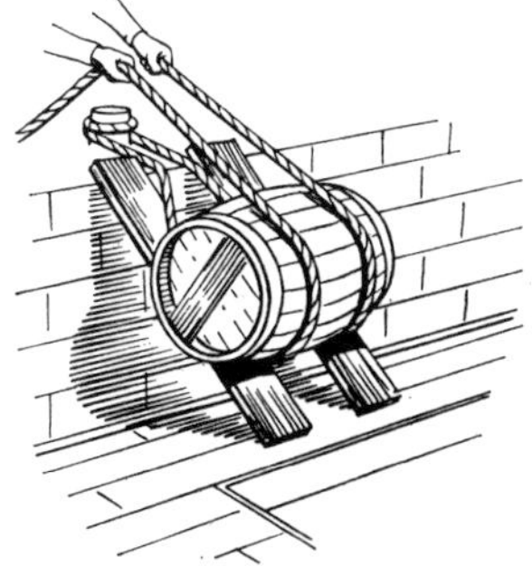

PARBUCKLING

parts of leaves, pulp of fruits, etc. (ill. LEAF). **parĕn′chȳmal, părĕnchȳm′atous** *adjs.*

pār′ent *n.* Father or mother; forefather; animal, plant, from which others are derived; (fig.) source, origin. **parĕnt′al** *adj.* **parĕn′tally** *adv.*

pār′entage *n.* Descent from parents, lineage.

parĕn′thĕsis *n.* (pl. *-theses*) Word, clause, sentence, inserted into a passage to which it is not grammatically essential, and usu. marked off by brackets, dashes, or commas; (sing. or pl.) round brackets () used for this. **parĕn′thĕsīze** *v.t.* Insert as parenthesis; put between marks of parenthesis; **părĕnthĕt′ĭc** *adj.* Of, inserted as a, parenthesis; (fig.) interposed. **părenthĕt′ĭcally** *adv.*

parĕr′gon *n.* Ornamental accessory or addition; subordinate or secondary work or business. **parĕr′gĭc** *adj.*

pă′rĕsĭs *n.* Partial paralysis or weakening of muscular power. **parĕt′ĭc** *adj.*

par ĕx′cellence (-lahns) *adv.* By virtue of special excellence, above all others that may be so called.

par′gĕt (-j-) *n.* Plaster spread upon wall, ceiling, etc., roughcast; (also *pargeting*) ornamental relief work in plaster. ~ *v.t.* Cover with parget or plaster; adorn with pargeting.

parhēl′ion (-lyon) *n.* Spot on solar halo at which light is intensified, mock sun. **parhēlī′acal, parhēl′ĭc** *adjs.*

pă′riah (*or* par-, pār-) *n.* Member of very extensive low caste in S. India; member of low or no caste; (fig.) social outcast; *~-dog*, yellow vagabond dog of low breed in India etc. [Tamil *paṟaiyar* (hereditary) drummers]

Pār′ĭan *adj.* & *n.* (Native) of PAROS; ~ *Chronicle*, chronicle of Greek history from reign of Cecrops, 1450 B.C., to archonship of Diotimus, 354 B.C., engraved on marble; found in 1627 in Paros, now among Arundel Marbles at Oxford; ~ *marble*, fine-textured white marble obtained from Paros, famous since 6th c. B.C. and much used by sculptors.

parī′ĕtal *adj.* 1. Of the wall of the body or of any of its cavities; ~ *bones*, pair forming part of sides and top of skull (ill. HEAD). 2. (bot.) Of or on the walls of a hollow structure etc.

pă′ri mūtūĕl′ (-rē) *n.* System of betting, carried on by a mechanical apparatus, in which the winners divide the losers' stakes less a percentage for managerial expenses (see TOTALIZATOR).

par′ī păss′ū *adv.* With equal pace; simultaneously and equally.

Pă′rĭs[1]. Capital city of France, on river Seine; *plaster of* ~: see PLASTER. [*Parisii*, L name of Gallic tribe which settled there]

Pă′rĭs[2]. (Gk myth.) Son of Priam, king of Troy, and Hecuba; as a baby he was left to die because of a prophecy that he would bring destruction upon Troy, but shepherds found him and brought him up; he carried off Helen, wife of Menelaus, thus bringing about the Trojan War in which he was killed and Troy sacked. *Judgement of* ~: the goddesses Hera, Athene, and Aphrodite quarrelled over a golden apple inscribed 'for the fairest': Paris was asked to arbitrate; all three tried to bribe him, and he chose Aphrodite, who had offered him the fairest woman in the world.

Pă′rĭs[3], Matthew (d. 1259). English chronicler and illuminator of manuscripts; a monk of St. Albans.

pă′rĭsh *n.* 1. Subdivision of diocese, having its own church and clergyman; inhabitants of this. 2. District (freq. identical with original parish) constituted for various purposes of civil government, esp. administration of poor law. 3. ~ *clerk*, official performing various church duties, and formerly leading the congregation in responses; ~ *council*, local administrative body in rural civil parish; ~ *register*, book recording christenings, marriages, and burials, at parish church. **parĭsh′ioner** (-sh*o*ner) *n.* Inhabitant of parish.

Parĭs′ĭan (-z-) *adj.* & *n.* (Native, inhabitant) of PARIS[1].

părĭsȳllăb′ĭc *adj.* (Of Greek and Latin nouns) having same number of syllables in nominative as in oblique cases of singular.

pă′rĭty *n.* Equality; parallelism, analogy; equivalence in another currency, being at par.

park[1] *n.* 1. Large enclosed piece of ground, usu. with woodland and pasture, attached to country house etc.; enclosure in town ornamentally laid out for public recreation; large tract of land kept in natural state for public benefit; *the P~*, (now) HYDE PARK; (formerly) St. James's Park. 2. (Space occupied by) artillery, stores, etc., in encampment; area, usu. in the open air, where motor-cars, cycles, aeroplanes, or other vehicles are left temporarily or until required. 3. Enclosed area for oyster-breeding, overflowed by sea at high tide. ~ *v.t.* Enclose (ground) in or as park; arrange (artillery etc.) compactly in a park; place and arrange (vehicles, aeroplanes, etc.) in a space usu. reserved for this purpose; (transf.) leave in suitable place until required.

Park[2], Mungo (1771–1806). Scottish surgeon; explored river Niger, 1795–7; published his 'Travels in the Interior of Africa', 1799; returned to the Niger, 1805, and perished there.

Park′hurst. Convict prison in Isle of Wight, built 1830, orig. for boys.

park′ĭn *n.* (north.) Gingerbread made with oatmeal and treacle.

Park′ĭnson's disease. *Paralysis agitans* or 'shaking palsy', a chronic progressive disease of the nervous system characterized by tremor, muscular rigidity, defective gait, and emaciation. [James *Parkinson*, British physician (1755–1824)]

park′y *adj.* (slang) Chilly.

parl′ance *n.* Way of speaking.

parl′ey *n.* Conference for debating of points in dispute, esp. (mil.) discussion of terms. ~ *v.* Discuss terms (*with*); speak (esp. foreign languages).

parleyvoo′ *n.* (joc.) French; Frenchman. ~ *v.i.* Speak French. [Fr. *parlez-vous* (*français*)? 'do you speak (French)?']

parl′iament (-l*a*m-) *n.* 1. Council forming with the sovereign the supreme legislature of United Kingdom, consisting of the House of Lords (Spiritual and Temporal) and the House of Commons (representatives of counties, cities, etc.) (*illustration, p.* 595); corresponding legislative assembly in other countries; *Long P~*, that which met in 1640, commenced the Civil War, was dispersed by Cromwell in 1653 and twice restored in 1659, being finally dissolved in 1660, after restoring Charles II; *Rump P~*, remnant of Long Parliament, in its later history; *Short P~*, that which sat from 13th April to 5th May 1640. 2. (Also ~ *cake*) thin crisp cake of gingerbread.

parliamentār′ĭan (-l*a*m-) *n.* Skilled debater in parliament; adherent of Parliament in Civil War of 17th c. ~ *adj.* Parliamentary.

parliamĕn′tary (-l*a*m-) *adj.* Of a parliament; enacted, established, by parliament; (of language) admissible in Parliament, (colloq.) civil; ~ *train*, (hist.) train carrying passengers at rate not above 1*d.* a mile, which every railway company was obliged by Act of Parliament (7 & 8 Vict., c. 85) to run daily each way over its system.

parl′our (-l*e*r) *n.* 1. Apartment in convent for conversation with outsiders etc. 2. In mansion, town-hall, etc., smaller room apart from great hall, for private conversation etc. 3. (now rarely used) Ordinary sitting-room of family in private house. 4. Room in inn more private than tap-room. 5. (U.S.) luxuriously fitted railway carriage; *~-maid*, maid who waits at table.

parl′ous *adj.* (archaic, joc.) Perilous; hard to deal with.

Parm′a. City and province (formerly a duchy) of N. Italy; ~ *violet*, sweet-scented cultivated violet.

Parmĕn′ĭdēs (-z). (6th c. B.C.) Greek philosopher of Elea (Italy); founder of the Eleatic school which believed in unity and continuity

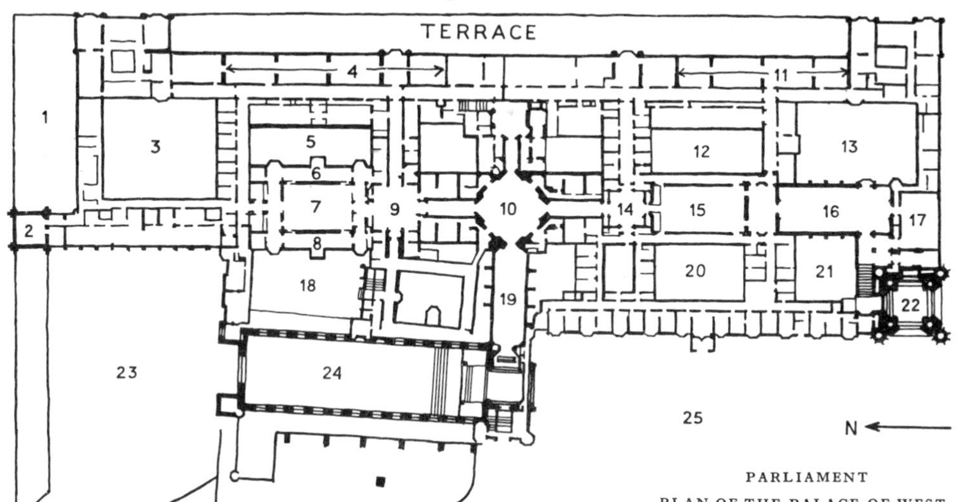

PARLIAMENT

PLAN OF THE PALACE OF WESTMINSTER (PRINCIPAL FLOOR)

1. Speaker's Green. 2. Big Ben. 3. Speaker's Court. 4. Commons Library. 5. Commons Court. 6. 'No' Division Lobby. 7. House of Commons. 8. 'Aye' Division Lobby. 9. Commons Lobby. 10. Central Lobby. 11. Peers' Library. 12. Peers' Court. 13. Royal Court. 14. Peers' Lobby. 15. House of Lords. 16. Royal Gallery. 17. Queen's Robing Room. 18. Star Chamber Court. 19. St. Stephen's Hall. 20. State Officers' Court. 21. Chancellor's Court. 22. Victoria Tower. 23. New Palace Yard. 24. Westminster Hall. 25. Old Palace Yard

HOUSE OF LORDS

1. Throne. 2. Woolsack on which the Lord Chancellor sits. 3. Woolsack on which judges sit at the opening of Parliament. 4. Table of the House. 5. Cross Benches where independent peers sit. 6. Bar of the House. 7. Bishops' seats. 8. Government peers' seats. 9. Opposition peers' seats. 10. Public Gallery above

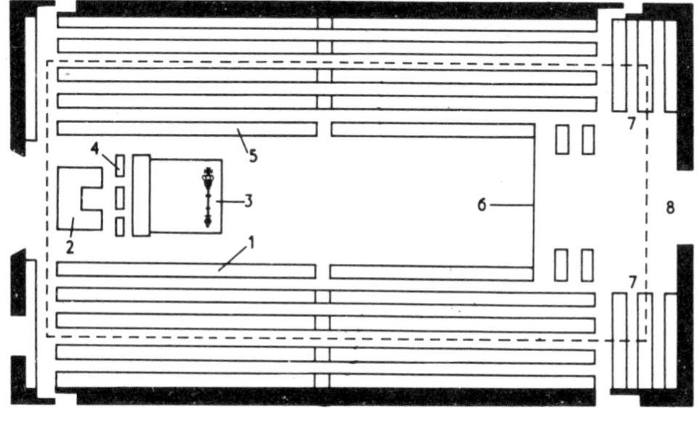

HOUSE OF COMMONS

1. Government Front Bench. 2. Speaker's chair. 3. Table of the House. 4. Clerks' chairs. 5. Opposition Front Bench 6. Bar of the House. 7. Cross Benches. 8. Public Gallery above

of being and unreality of change or motion.

Pârmèsăn′ (-z-) *adj.* Of Parma; esp. applied to hard easily grated kind of cheese made there and in other parts of N. Italy.

Pârnăss′ĭan *adj.* Of PARNASSUS; ~ *School*, founded by Leconte de Lisle, group of 19th-c. French poets, who insisted on importance of form and the *mot juste* and distrusted romantic sensibility and emotion as subjects of poetry. [f. title, 'Le Parnasse Contemporain', of three series of collections of their poetry, published 1866–76]

Pârnăss′us. Lofty mountain of Greece, N. of Delphi; associated in classical Greece with worship of Apollo and the Muses.

Pârnĕll′, Charles Stewart (1846–91). Irish nationalist political leader, who succeeded in converting Gladstone to his home-rule scheme.

parōch′ĭal (-k-) *adj.* Of a parish; (fig.) confined to narrow area; narrow, provincial. **parō-ch′ĭally** *adv.* **parōch′ĭalĭsm** *n.*

pă′rody *n.* Composition in which an author's characteristics are ridiculed by imitation; feeble imitation, travesty. ~ *v.t.* Make ridiculous by imitation. **pă′rodĭst** *n.*

parōle′ *n.* Word of honour, esp. (mil.) prisoner's promise that he will not attempt escape, or will return to custody if liberated, or will refrain from taking up arms against captors for stated period; (mil.) password used only by officers or inspectors of guard (as dist. f. COUNTERSIGN); *on* ~, (liberated) on parole. ~ *v.t.* Put (prisoner) on parole.

păronomās′ĭa (-z-, -s-) *n.* Word-play, pun.

paroquet: see PAR(R)AKEET.

Par′ŏs. Island in Aegean Sea, famous for its marble (see PARIAN).

părŏt′ĭd *adj.* Situated near the ear, esp. ~ *gland*, (in man, largest of three salivary glands) situated in front of ear (ill. GLAND). ~ *n.* Parotid gland. **părotīt′ĭs** *n.* (path.) Inflammation of parotid gland, mumps.

pă′roxȳsm *n.* Fit of disease; fit (*of* rage, laughter, etc.). **părox-ȳs′mal** (-zm-) *adj.* [Gk *oxunō* goad, render acute]

parŏx′ȳtone *adj.* & *n.* (Gk gram.) (Word) with acute accent on last syllable but one.

pâr′p′en *n.* Stone passing through wall from side to side (ill. MASONRY).

pâr′q′uet (-kĭ, -kā) *n.* Wooden flooring of pieces of wood, freq. of different kinds, arranged in pattern. ~ *v.t.* Floor (room) thus. **pâr′q′uetry** (-kĭtrĭ) *n.*

pâr(r) *n.* Young salmon; ~ *marks*, bright cross-bands on this.

pă′rrĭcīde *n.* 1. One who murders his father. 2. Murder of father, parent, near relative, or one whose person is considered sacred. **părrĭcīd′al** *adj.*

pă′rrot *n.* Bird of large mainly tropical group (order *Psittaciformes*) with short hooked bill, and freq. brilliant plumage, many species of which can be taught to repeat words and sentences; person who repeats another's words or imitates his actions unintelligently; ~ *disease*, PSITTACOSIS; ~-*fish*, various fishes with brilliant colouring or strong hard mouth like parrot's bill. ~ *v.t.* Repeat (words etc.) mechanically.

pă′rry[1] *v.t.* Ward off, avert (weapon, blow, etc.). ~ *n.* Warding off. [L *parare* prepare]

Pă′rry[2], Sir Charles Hubert Hastings (1848–1918). English musical composer.

Pă′rry[3], Sir William Edward (1790–1855). English rear-admiral and Arctic explorer; author of four narratives of voyages to the Polar Sea.

pârse (-z) *v.t.* Describe (word) grammatically, stating inflexion, relation to sentence, etc.; resolve (sentence) into component parts of speech and describe them grammatically.

pâr′sĕc *n.* (astron.) Unit in measuring stellar distances, distance at which a star would have an annual PARALLAX of one second of an arc. [*par*(*allax*)+*sec*(*ond*)]

Pârsee′ *adj.* & *n.* 1. (One) of the followers of ZOROASTER, descendants of those Persians who fled to India in 7th and 8th centuries to escape Mohammedan persecution. 2. (Of) the Iranian dialect of the Parsee religious literature.

Pârs′ĭfal. Hero of Wagner's music-drama of the same name, character based on that of Sir PERCEVAL in the Arthurian cycle.

pârs′ĭmony *n.* Carefulness in employment of money, etc.; stinginess. **pârsĭmōn′ĭous** *adj.* **pârsĭmōn′iously** *adv.* **pârsĭ-mōn′iousnèss** *n.*

pârs′ley *n.* Biennial umbelliferous plant (*Petroselinum sativum*) with white flowers and aromatic leaves, finely divided and curled in commonly cultivated variety, used for seasoning and garnishing dishes; *cow, fool's, hedge*, ~, umbelliferous plants with finely divided leaves.

pârs′nĭp *n.* Biennial umbelliferous plant (*Pastinaca sativa*) with pinnate leaves, yellow flowers, and (in cultivated variety) large, pale yellow, sweet, fleshy, and nutritious root used as culinary vegetable; the root itself.

pârs′on *n.* Rector; vicar or any beneficed clergyman; (colloq.) any clergyman; ~*'s nose*, rump of cooked table bird. **pârsŏn′ĭc(al)** *adjs.*

pâr′sonage *n.* Rector's or other incumbent's house.

pârt[1] *n.* 1. Some but not all of a thing or number of things; division or section of book etc., esp. as much as is issued at one time; part of animal body, esp. (pl., euphem.) = privy parts; each of several equal portions of a whole; ~ *of*, a part of, some of. 2. Portion allotted, share; interest, concern; person's share in action, his function, business, duty. 3. Character assigned to actor on stage; words spoken by actor on stage; copy of these; (fig.) character sustained by anyone. 4. Melody assigned to particular voice or instrument in concerted music. 5. (archaic, pl.) Abilities, capacities. 6. (pl.) Region. 7. Side in dispute. 8. ~ *and parcel*, (emphatic) constituent, element; essential portion; ~ *of speech*, each of the grammatical categories of words (noun, adjective, pronoun, verb, adverb, preposition, conjunction, interjection); *the most* ~, the greatest part, most; *for the most* ~, in most cases, mostly; *take* ~, assist (*in*); *take the* ~ *of*, support, back up; *for my* ~, as far as I am concerned; *in* ~, partly; *take in good* ~, not be offended at; *on the* ~ *of*, proceeding from; done etc. by; ~-*song*, song for three or more voice-parts, usu. without accompaniment and in simple harmony. ~ *adv.* In part, partly; ~-*owner* etc., owner etc. in common with another or others; ~-*payment*, payment in part; ~-*time* (*adj.*) employed for, taking up, only part of the working-day; ~-*timer* (*n.*).

pârt[2] *v.* Divide into parts, suffer division; separate (hair), as with comb, on each side of dividing line or *parting*; (naut.) break, suffer breaking of (rope), (of rope) break; separate (combatants, friends, etc.); quit one another's company; (colloq.) part with one's money, pay; (archaic) distribute (thing) in shares; ~ *company*, dissolve companionship (*with*); ~ *from, with*, say good-bye to; ~ *with*, give up, surrender (property etc.).

pârt′ing *n.* (esp.) Leave-taking; dividing line of combed hair; ~ *of the ways*, point at which road divides into two or more.

pârtāke′ *v.* (past t. -*tŏŏk*, past part. -*tāk′en*). Take a share in; take a share (*in, of, with*); take, esp. eat or drink some or (colloq.) all *of*; have some (*of* quality etc.).

pârterre′ (-târ) *n.* 1. Level space in garden occupied by flower-beds. 2. Part of ground-floor of auditorium of theatre, behind orchestra (ill. THEATRE).

pârthènogĕn′èsis *n.* (biol.) Reproduction without sexual union.

Pârth′ènon. Temple of Athene Parthenos ('the maiden') on the Acropolis at Athens, erected 447–438 B.C. under Pericles' administration and decorated with sculptures by Phidias or his school.

Pârth′ĭa. Ancient country of Asia, SE. of Caspian Sea. **Pârth′-ĭan** *adj.* & *n.* (Native) of Parthia; its people were celebrated as mounted archers, esp. for their trick of shooting their arrows while in real or pretended flight; hence, ~ *shot*, a parting shot.

pârti′ (-ē) *n.* Person regarded as eligible etc. in the marriage market; ~ *pris* (prē), preconceived view, bias.

pâr′tial (-shl) *adj.* 1. Biased, unfair; ~ *to*, having a liking for. 2. Forming only a part; not complete or total. **pâr′tially** *adv.* **pârtiăl′ĭty** (-shĭ-) *n.* Bias, favouritism; fondness (*for*).

pârt′ĭble *adj.* That can or must be divided (*among*; esp. of heritable property).

pârti′cĭpāte *v.* Have share in; have share (*in*); have something *of*. **pârti′cipant, pârticĭpā′tion** *ns.*

pârt′ĭciple *n.* Verbal adjective qualifying noun but retaining some properties of verb, e.g. tense and government of object. **pârtĭcĭp′ial** *adj.*

pârt′ĭcle *n.* Minute portion of matter; smallest possible amount; minor part of speech, esp. short indeclinable one; prefix or suffix having distinct meaning.

pârt′ĭcoloured (-ŭlerd) *adj.* Partly of one colour, partly of another.

partĭc′ūlar *adj.* 1. Relating to one as distinguished from others, special; one considered apart from others, individual; *P~ Baptists*, body of Baptists holding Calvinistic doctrines of ~ *election* and ~ *redemption*, i.e. divine election and redemption of only some of the human race. 2. Worth notice, special. 3. Detailed, minute; scrupulously exact; fastidious (*about*); *in* ~, especially. **partĭcūlă′rĭty** *n.* **partĭc′ūlarly** *adv.* **partĭc′ūlar** *n.* Detail, item; (pl.) detailed account.

partĭc′ūlarĭsm *n.* Doctrine of PARTICULAR election or redemption; exclusive devotion to a party, sect, etc.; principle of leaving political independence to each State in an empire etc. **partĭc′ūlarĭst** *n.*

partĭc′ūlarīze *v.t.* Name specially or one by one, specify. **partĭcūlarīzā′tion** *n.*

pârtĭc′ūlate *adj.* Of the nature of a particle; composed of particles.

pârtĭsăn′[1] (-z-; *or* pârt′-) *n.* Adherent of party, cause, etc., esp. unreasoning one; (hist.) member of light irregular troops employed in special enterprises; (in war of 1939–45) a guerrilla (applied orig. to Russians resisting in parts of their country occupied by the enemy). **pârtĭsăn′ship** *n.*

pârt′isan[2] (-zn), **-zan** *ns.* (hist.) Long-handled spear like halberd (ill. SPEAR).

pârt′īte *adj.* (bot., entom.) Divided (nearly) to the base.

pârti′tion *n.* 1. Division into parts; such part; structure separating two such parts, esp. slight wall. 2. (law) Division of real property between joint tenants etc. by which co-tenancy is abolished and individual interests are separated. ~ *v.t.* Divide into parts; ~ *off*, separate (part of room etc.) by a partition.

pârt′ĭtive *adj.* & *n.* (Word) denoting part of a collective whole; ~ *genitive*, that used to indicate that only a part of a collective whole is considered or spoken of, expressed in English by *of*, e.g. *one of many*, *pick of the bunch.* **pârt′ĭtively** *adv.*

Pârt′lėt. (archaic) Used as proper name for a hen, esp. *Dame* ~. [OF *Pertelote*, female proper name]

pârt′ly *adv.* With respect to a part; in some degree.

pârt′ner *n.* 1. Sharer; person associated with others in business of which he shares risks and profits; wife, husband; companion in dance; player associated with another in whist, tennis, etc. 2. (naut., pl.) Timber framework round hole in deck through which mast, pump, etc., passes. ~ *v.t.* Associate as partners; be partner of. **pârt′nershĭp** *n.*

pârt′rĭdge *n.* Kinds of game-bird, esp. British and Central European *common* or *grey* ~ (*Perdix perdix*); (U.S.) various birds of grouse or pheasant family; *~-wood*, W. Indian hard red wood with darker parallel stripes, used for cabinet work.

pârtūr′ĭent *adj.* About to bring forth young. **pârtūrĭ′tion** *n.* Act of bringing forth young.

pârt′y[1] *n.* 1. Those on one side in a contest etc., esp. considered collectively; persons united in maintaining cause, policy, etc., in opposition to others; system of taking sides on public questions, system of parties. 2. Body of persons travelling or engaged together. 3. Social gathering, esp. of invited guests at private house. 4. Each of the two or more persons making the two sides in legal action, contract, marriage, etc.; *third* ~, a person or persons other than these, esp. in insurance matters. 5. Participator, accessory (*to* action). 6. (now vulg. or joc.) person. 7. ~ *line*, telephone line shared by number of subscribers; (also) set policy of political party; ~ *wall*, wall shared by each of the occupiers of the two buildings etc. that it separates.

pâr′ty[2] *adj.* (her.) Divided into parts of different tinctures.

pârv′enū *n.* Person of obscure origin who has gained wealth or position, upstart.

pârv′ĭs *n.* Enclosed area in front of cathedral, church, etc. [OF *pare(v)is*, f. LL *paradisus* PARADISE, court in front of St. Peter's, Rome]

pas (pah) *n.* 1. Precedence. 2. Step in dancing.

P.A.S. Abbrev. of para-aminosalicylic acid, a drug used in treatment of pulmonary tuberculosis.

Pascal′ (-kahl), Blaise (1623–62). French mathmatician, phyiscist, and religious philosopher; author of 'Lettres à un Provincial' and 'Pensées'.

păs′chal (-k-) *adj.* Of the Jewish Passover; of Easter.

pasha, pacha (pah′sha, pă-) *n.* Turkish or Egyptian officer of high rank, e.g. military commander, governor of province, etc. (used as title after name). **pash′alĭc** *n.* Jurisdiction of pasha.

Pashtu (pŭsh′to͞o), **Pŭsh′tu** *adj.* & *n.* (Of) the language of the Afghans, belonging to the Eastern Iranian group of the Indo-European family.

Pashtunistan (pŭshto͞onĭstahn′) Name given by Afghan government to the part of Pakistan inhabited by Pathans, who speak Pashtu.

păsque′-flower (-sk-) *n.* Anemone (*A. pulsatilla*) with bell-shaped purple flowers. [Fr. *passe-fleur* surpassing flower, with assim. to *Pasque* Easter]

păsquināde′ (-kw-) *n.* Lampoon, satire, orig. one affixed to public place. [*Pasquino*, statue at Rome on which Latin verses were annually posted]

pass[1] (-ah-) *v.* (past part. *passed* or as adj. *past*). 1. Move onward, proceed; circulate, be current; be transported from place to place; change; die; go by; come to an end; ~ *for*, be accepted as; ~ *by the name of*, be currently known by the name of. 2. Get through, effect a passage; go uncensured, be accepted as adequate; (of Bill in Parliament, proposal, etc.) be sanctioned; (of candidate) satisfy examiner. 3. Adjudicate (*upon*); (of judgement) be given (*for* plaintiff etc.). 4. (cards etc.) Decline, declare inability, to play, bid, make trump, etc.; throw up one's hand. 5. Leave on one side or behind as one goes; go across (sea, frontier, mountain range). 6. (Of Bill) be examined and approved by (House of Commons etc.); reach standard required by (examiner, examination); ~ *muster*: see MUSTER. 7. Outstrip; surpass; be beyond compass or range of, transcend (any faculty or expression). 8. Transport (usu. with prep. or adv.); move, cause to go; cause to go by; hand round, transfer; give currency to; pledge (word etc.). 9. Cause, allow, (measure in Parliament, candidate for examination, etc.) to proceed after scrutiny. 10. Spend (*time* etc.); utter (criticism, judicial sentence, *upon*). 11. ~ *away*, die, come to an end; ~ *by*, omit, disregard; walk etc. past; ~ *off*, (of sensations etc.) fade away; (of proceedings) be carried through; palm off (thing *for* or *as* what it is not); distract attention from (awkward situation etc.); ~ *out*, (colloq.) die; become unconscious (from drinking etc.); ~ *over*, omit; make no remark upon; ~ *the time of day*: see TIME; ~ *through*, experience; ~ *water*, void urine. ~ *n.* 1. Passing, esp. of examination; (university) attainment of standard that satisfies examiners but does not entitle to honours. 2. Critical position, juncture, predicament. 3. Written permission to pass into or out of a place, be absent from quarters etc.; ticket authorizing holder to travel free on railway etc. 4. Thrust in fencing; juggling trick; passing of hands over anything, esp. in mesmerism; (football etc.) transference of ball to another player on same side. 5. ~*-book*, book supplied by bank to person having current or deposit account, showing all sums deposited and drawn; ~*-key*, private key to gate etc. for special purposes; master-key; *pass'man*, one who takes pass degree at university; *pass'word*, selected word or phrase distinguishing friend from enemy.

pass[2] (-ah-) *n.* Narrow passage through mountains; (mil.) such passage viewed as key to a country; navigable channel, esp. at river's mouth; passage for fish over weir; *sell the* ~, (fig.) betray a cause.

pass'able (pah-) *adj.* (esp.) That can pass muster, fairly good. **pass'ably** *adv.*

păssaca'glia (-ahlya) *n.* (mus.) Instrumental composition in 3/4 time, based on an unvarying ground (not necessarily in the bass as in CHACONNE); orig. a Spanish or Italian dance-tune. [It., perh. f. Span. *pasar* pass, *calle* street, because freq. played in street]

păss'age[1] (-ĭj) *n.* 1. Passing, transit; transition from one state to another; liberty, right, to pass through; voyage, crossing from port to port; right of conveyance as passenger by sea; *bird of* ~, see BIRD. 2. Passing of a measure into law. 3. Way by which person or thing passes; corridor etc. giving communication between different rooms in house. 4. (pl.) What passes between two persons mutually, interchange of confidences, etc. 5. ~ (*of* or *at arms*) fight (freq. fig.). 6. Part of speech or literary work taken for quotation etc.

păss'age[2] *v.* (Of horse or rider) move sideways, by pressure of rein on horse's neck and of rider's leg on opposite side; make (horse) do this.

păss'ant *adj.* (her.) (Of beast) walking and looking to dexter side, with three paws on ground and dexter fore-paw raised (ill. HERALDRY).

Passchendaele (păsh'endāl). Ridge and village in Flanders E. of Ypres, captured by Canadians 6 Nov. 1917 at end of 3rd battle of Ypres, and recaptured by Germans in 1918; ~ *offensive, battle of* ~, names freq. given to the whole British offensive (July–Nov. 1917) known officially as the 3rd battle of Ypres.

passé (pă'sā) *adj.* (fem. *passée*). Past the prime; behind the times.

passementerie (pahs'mahntrē) *n.* Trimming of gold or silver lace, braid, beads, etc.

păss'ènger (-j-) *n.* Traveller in (public) conveyance by land, air, or water; traveller in motor-car who is not driving; ineffective member of team, crew, etc.; *foot-*~, traveller on foot; ~ *pigeon*, N. Amer. wild pigeon (*Ectopistes migratorius*) capable of long sustained flight (now extinct).

păsse-partout' (-tōō) *n.* 1. Master-key. 2. Adhesive tape fastening edges of glass to mount of photograph or small picture as substitute for frame. [Fr., = 'pass everywhere']

pass'er (-ah-) *n.* One who passes; ~*-bӯ*, one who passes, esp. casually.

păss'erīne *adj.* & *n.* (Bird) of the order *Passeriformes* or Perchers.

păss'ĭble *adj.* (theol.) Capable of feeling or suffering. **păssĭbĭl'ĭty** *n.*

păss'ĭm *adv.* (Of allusions, phrases, etc., to be found in specified author or book) here and there, throughout, in all parts.

pass'ing (-ah-) *n.* ~*-bell*, one rung at moment of person's death; ~*-note*, (mus.) note not belonging to harmony, interposed for purpose of passing smoothly from one to the other of two notes essential to it. ~ *adj.* (esp.) Transient, fleeting, cursory, incidental. ~ *adv.* (archaic) Very.

pă'ssion (-shn) *n.* 1. Strong emotion; outburst of anger; sexual love; strong enthusiasm (*for*). 2. *The P*~, sufferings of Christ on the cross; (musical setting of) narrative of this from Gospels; ~ *flower*, genus, *Passiflora*, of (chiefly climbing) plants with parts supposed to suggest instruments of Christ's Passion, the corona representing the crown of thorns, etc.; ~*-fruit*, fruit of *Passiflora quadrangularis*, granadilla, native in tropical America; ~*-play*, mystery-play representing Christ's passion; *P*~ *Sunday*, 2nd Sunday before Easter; *Passiontide*, fortnight before Easter; *P*~ *Week*, week following Passion Sunday (but in Anglican usage freq. = week before Easter, Holy Week). ~ *v.i.* (poet.) Feel or express passion. **pă'ssionlèss** *adj.* **pă'ssionlèssnèss** *n.*

păss'ional (-shon-) *adj.* Of, marked by, passion. ~ *n.* Book of the sufferings of saints and martyrs.

păss'ionate (-shon-) *adj.* Easily moved to anger; dominated by, easily moved to, strong feeling; due to, showing, passion. **păss'ionately** *adv.* **păss'ionatenèss** *n.*

Păss'ionist (-shon-) *n.* Member of order (Congregation of the Discalced Clerks of the most Holy Cross and Passion of our Lord Jesus Christ), founded in Italy, 1720, pledged to do their utmost to keep alive the memory of Christ's Passion.

păss'ĭve *adj.* 1. Suffering action, acted upon; (gram.) ~ *voice*, those forms in which action of verb is treated as attribute of thing towards which action is directed (see also ACTIVE). 2. Offering no opposition, submissive; ~ *resistance*: see RESISTANCE. 3. Not active, inert; ~ *debt*, one on which no interest is paid. **păss'ĭvely** *adv.* **păss'ĭvenèss, passĭv'ĭty** *ns.* **păss'ĭve** *n.* Passive voice or form of verb.

Pass'ōver (-ah-). Jewish spring feast, held on evening of the 14th Nisan and the 7 following days (Nisan approx. = April); it commemorates the 'passing over' (i.e. sparing) of the houses of the Israelites whose doorposts were marked with the blood of the lamb, when the Egyptians were smitten with the death of their first-born (see Exodus xii); ~ *bread, cake*, kind of thin dry unleavened biscuit-like bread eaten during Passover.

pass'pŏrt (-ah-) *n.* Document issued by competent authority permitting person specified in it to travel in foreign country and entitling him to protection; (fig.) thing that ensures admission.

past[1] (-ah-) *adj.* (past part. of *pass* v.), (esp.) Gone by in time; just gone by; (gram.) expressing past action or state; ~ *master*, one who has been master in guild, freemasons' lodge, etc.; thorough master (*in*, *of*, subject). ~ *n.* Past time; what has happened in past time; person's past life or career, esp. one that will not bear inquiry.

past[2] (-ah-) *prep.* Beyond in time or place; beyond the range or compass of. ~ *adv.* So as to pass by, as *hastens* ~; ~*-pointing*, (path.) method of diagnosing certain brain diseases, sufferers from which will point past an object instead of at it.

pāste *n.* Flour moistened and kneaded, with lard, butter, suet, etc., as cooking material; various sweet doughy confections; relish of pounded fish, meat, etc.; mixture of flour and water used as cement for sticking paper etc.; any soft plastic mixture; hard vitreous composition used in making imitation gems; *paste'board*, stiff substance made by pasting together sheets of paper; (slang) visiting-card, railway-ticket; (attrib., fig.) unsubstantial, flimsy. ~ *v.t.* Fasten with paste; stick *up* on wall etc. with paste; cover (as) by pasting on or over; (slang) beat, thrash, 'plaster' with aerial bombs; ~*-down*, (in book) that part of the end-paper which is pasted to the inside of the cover.

păs'tel *n.* Drawing instrument consisting of a stick of powdered pigment bound with gum, usu. covered with paper; drawing made with pastels (usu. in several colours). **păs'tellist** *n.*

păs'tern *n.* Part of horse's foot between fetlock and hoof (ill. HORSE); corresponding part in other animals.

Păsteur' (-têr), Louis (1822–95). French chemist and biologist; founder of bacteriology and inventor of method of inoculation for hydrophobia.

păs'teurize (-ter-) *v.t.* Partially sterilize by Pasteur's method, prevent or arrest fermentation in (milk etc.) by keeping for some time at a temperature (131°–158° F.) which does not greatly affect chemical composition. **păsteurīzā'tion** *n.*

păsticc'io (-ĭtshō), **păstiche'** (-ēsh) *ns.* Medley, esp. musical composition, picture, made up from various sources; (usu. *-iche*) literary or other work of art composed in the style of a known author.

păs'tĭl, păstille' (-tēl) *n.* 1. Small roll of aromatic paste burnt as fumigator etc. 2. Small sweetmeat, freq. medicated, lozenge.

pas'tīme (-ah-) *n.* Recreation; game, sport.

Păs'ton letters. A collection of private correspondence (1440–86) of a well-to-do Norfolk family named Paston; of great historical value and interest.

pa'stor (-ah-) *n.* Minister in charge of (esp. continental Protestant) church or congregation; person exercising spiritual guidance. [Anglo-Fr., f. L. *pastorem* shepherd]

pa'storal (-ah-) *adj.* 1. Of shepherds; (of land) used for pasture; (of poems etc.) portraying country life. 2. Of a pastor; ~ *epistles*, those of Paul to Timothy and Titus, dealing with pastor's work. **pa'storally** *adv.* **pa'storal** *n.* 1. Pastoral play, poem, poetry, or picture. 2. Letter from pastor, esp. bishop, to clergy or people. **pa'storalism** *n.* Convention of pastoral poetry etc.

pastoralė (pahstorah'-) *n.* (pl. *-ali* pr. -lē, or *-ales*). Musical composition dealing with pastoral subject.

pa'storate (-ah-) *n.* Pastor's (tenure of) office; body of pastors.

pās'try *n.* Paste of flour, fat, water, etc., rolled and baked; articles of food (pies, tarts, etc.) made wholly or partly of this; *~-cook*, one who makes pastry, esp. for public sale.

pas'turage (-ahscher-) *n.* Pasturing; herbage for cattle etc.; pasture-land.

pas'ture (-ah-) *n.* Herbage for cattle; (piece of) land covered with this. ~ *v.* Lead, put, (cattle) to pasture; (of sheep etc.) eat down (grass-land); put sheep etc. on (land) to graze; graze. **pas'turable** (-ahscher-) *adj.*

pă'sty¹ (*or* -ah-) *n.* Pie of meat etc. seasoned and enclosed in crust of pastry and baked without dish.

pās'ty² *adj.* Of, like, paste; of pale complexion.

păt¹ *n.* Stroke, tap, esp. with hand as caress etc.; small mass (esp. of butter) formed (as) by patting; sound made by striking lightly with something flat. ~ *v.* Strike (thing) gently with flat surface; flatten thus; strike gently with inner surface of fingers, esp. to mark sympathy, approbation, etc.; beat lightly *upon*; ~ *on the back*, express approbation of; *~-ball*, (contempt.) poor or feeble lawn tennis.

păt² *adv.* & *adj.* Apposite(ly), opportune(ly); ready for any occasion.

Păt³. (Nickname for) Irishman.

Pătagōn'ĭa. Southern region of S. America, in Argentina between Andes and Atlantic. **Pătagōn'ĭan** *adj.* & *n.* [f. obs. *Patagon*, one of the S. Amer. Indians, of great stature, inhabiting this region]

pătch *n.* 1. Piece of cloth, metal, etc., put on to mend hole or rent or strengthen weak place; piece of court-plaster etc. put over wound; pad worn to protect injured eye; *not a ~ on*, not comparable to, nothing to. 2. Small piece of black silk or court-plaster worn esp. in 17th and 18th centuries to show off complexion. 3. Large or irregular spot on surface; piece of ground; number of plants growing on this; ~ *pocket*, pocket sewn on like patch; *strike a bad ~*, have a run of bad luck. ~ *v.t.* Put patch(es) on; serve as patch to; piece (things) together; appear as patches on (surface); ~ *up*, repair with patches; put together hastily; (fig.) repair, set to right (matter, quarrel, etc.); *patch'work*, work made up of fragments of different colours sewn together (freq. fig.). **pătch'y** *adj.* **pătch'ĭly** *adv.* **pătch'ĭness** *n.*

pătch'ouli (-o͞olĭ) *n.* Odoriferous plant (*Pogostemon patchouli*) of Silhat, Penang, and Malaysia; penetrating and lasting perfume prepared from this.

pāte *n.* (now colloq.) Head, often as seat of intellect.

pâté (păt'ā) *n.* Pie, patty; ~ *de foie gras* (fwah grah), paste of liver of fatted geese.

patĕll'a *n.* Knee-cap (ill. SKELETON). **patĕll'ar, patĕll'ate** *adjs.*

păt'en *n.* Shallow dish used for bread at Eucharist (ill. CHALICE); thin circular plate of metal.

păt'ent (in England pă- in *letters ~*, *~ office*, pā- usu. in all other senses; in U.S. pă- in sense 2, pă- usu. in all other senses), *adj.* 1. *Letters ~*, open document under seal, esp. royal, granting right, title, etc., esp. sole right for a term to make, use, or sell some invention; (of rights etc.) conferred, protected, by this; (fig.) to which one has proprietary claim; (colloq.) such as might be patented, ingenious, well-contrived. 2. (of door etc.) Open; (fig.) plain, obvious. 3. ~ *leather*: see LEATHER; ~ *medicine*, proprietary medicine, esp. one of which formula is not disclosed on container (but in U.K. disclosure is now obligatory). **pāt'ently** *adv.* **pāt'ency** *n.* **păt'ent** *n.* Letters patent; government grant of exclusive privilege of making or selling new invention; invention, process, so protected; (fig.) sign that one is entitled to something, possesses a quality, etc.; *P~ Office*, office from which patents are issued; ~ *-roll*, roll of patents issued in Great Britain in a year. ~ *v.t.* Obtain patent for (invention).

pătentee' *n.* Taker-out or holder of a patent, person for the time being entitled to the benefit of a patent.

pāt'er¹ *n.* (slang) Father.

Pāt'er², Walter Horatio (1839–94). English essayist, critic, and humanist; author of 'Studies in the History of the Renaissance' (1873) and 'Marius the Epicurean' (1885).

păt'erfamĭl'ĭăs *n.* (Rom. law and joc.) Head of family.

patêrn'al *adj.* Of a father; fatherly; related through the father, on the father's side. **patêrn'ally** *adv.*

patêrn'ĭty *n.* Fatherhood; one's paternal origin; (fig.) authorship, source.

păt'ernŏs'ter *n.* 1. Lord's Prayer, esp. in Latin; bead in rosary indicating that paternoster is to be said. 2. ~ (*line*), weighted fishing-line with hooks and sinkers at intervals. [*pater noster* our father].

path (-ah-) *n.* Footway, esp. one merely beaten by feet, not specially constructed; track laid for foot or cycle racing; line along which person or thing moves; *path'-finder*, (esp.) aircraft (or its pilot) sent ahead of main force to locate and mark out bombing targets. **path'lėss** *adj.*

Pathan (-tahn') *adj.* & *n.* (Member) of a Pashtu-speaking people inhabiting E. Afghanistan, NW. Pakistan, and other parts of the Indian peninsula.

pathĕt'ĭc *adj.* Exciting pity or sadness; of the emotions; ~ *fallacy*, ascription of human emotion to inanimate nature. **pathĕt'ĭcally** *adv.*

păthogĕn'ėsĭs *n.* Mode of development of a disease.

păthogĕn'ĭc *adj.* Capable of producing disease.

pathŏl'ogy *n.* Systematic study of bodily diseases, their causes, symptoms, and treatment. **pathŏl'ogist** *n.* **păthołŏ'gical** *adj.*

pāth'ŏs (*or* pă-) *n.* Quality in

speech, events, etc., that excites pity or sadness. [Gk, = 'suffering']

Pătiăl'a. Formerly chief native State of Punjab, India.

pā'tience (-shns) *n.* 1. Calm endurance of pain or any provocation; forbearance; quiet and self-possessed waiting for something; perseverance; *have no ~ with,* (colloq.) be unable to bear patiently; *out of ~,* provoked so as no longer to have patience. 2. (cards) Game, usu. for one person, in which object is to arrange cards in some systematic order.

pā'tient (-shnt) *adj.* Having, showing, patience. **pā'tiently** *adv.* **pā'tient** *n.* Person under medical treatment, esp. with reference to his doctor.

păt'ina *n.* Incrustation, usu. green, on surface of old bronze, esteemed as ornament; (also by extension) gloss on woodwork etc., produced by long use. **păt'ināted** *adj.* **pătinā'tion** *n.*

păt'iō *n.* Inner court open to sky in Spanish or Span. Amer. house.

Păt'mōre, Coventry Kersey Dighton (1823–96). English poet.

Păt'mŏs. Island of Sporades group in Aegean Sea, where, acc. to legend, St John lived in exile and saw the visions of the apocalypse.

păt'ois (-wah) *n.* Dialect of common people in particular district.

pāt'riarch (-k) *n.* 1. Father and ruler of family or tribe; (pl.) sons of Jacob; (pl.) Abraham, Isaac, Jacob, and their forefathers. 2. (in early and Eastern Churches) Bishop, esp. of Antioch, Alexandria, Constantinople, Jerusalem, or Rome; (in R.C. Church) bishop ranking next above primates and metropolitans. 3. Founder of an order, science, etc.; venerable old man; *the* oldest living representative (*of*). **pātriarch'al** *adj.*

pāt'riarchate (-k-) *n.* Office, see, residence, of ecclesiastical patriarch; rank of tribal patriarch.

pāt'riarchy (-k-) *n.* Government by father or eldest male of tribe or family; community so organized.

patri'cian (-shn) *n.* 1. Ancient Roman noble (contrasted with PLEBEIAN), one belonging to one of the original citizen families from whom, in first ages of Republic, senators, consuls and pontifices were exclusively chosen; member of noble order in later Roman Empire; officer representing Roman emperor in provinces of Italy and Africa. 2. Nobleman, esp. (hist.) in some medieval Italian republics. ~ *adj.* Noble, aristocratic; of the ancient Roman nobility.

patri'ciate (-shyat) *n.* Patrician order, aristocracy; rank of patrician.

păt'ricide *n.* Parricide. **pătricid'al** *adj.*

Păt'rick, St. (*c* 380–*c* 463). Patron saint of Ireland; prob. of mixed Roman and British parentage; missionary to Ireland, from which, according to legend, he drove all snakes; commemorated 17th Mar.

păt'rimony *n.* Property inherited from one's father or ancestors, heritage; endowment of church etc.

păt'riot *n.* One who defends or is zealous for his country's freedom or rights. **pătriŏt'ic** *adj.* **pătriŏt'ically** *adv.* **păt'riotism** *n.*

patris'tic *adj.* Of (the study of the writings of) the Fathers of the Church.

Patrŏc'lus. (Gk legend) Grecian warrior at siege of Troy, friend of Achilles; slain by Hector.

patrōl' *n.* Going the rounds of garrison, camp, etc.; perambulation of town etc. by police; detachment of guard, police constable(s), told off for this; ships, aircraft, guarding sea-route, etc.; routine operational flight of aircraft; detachment of troops sent out to reconnoitre; unit of Boy Scouts (six under *~-leader*); *patrol'man,* (U.S.) constable attached to particular beat or district; *~-wagon,* (U.S.) police van for prisoners. ~ *v.* Act as patrol; go round (camp, town, etc.) as patrol. [Fr. *patrouiller*, orig. = 'paddle in mud']

păt'ron *n.* 1. One who countenances, protects, or gives influential support to; (shop) regular customer; tutelary saint of person, place, craft, etc. 2. (Rom. antiq.) Former owner of manumitted slave; protector of CLIENT in return for certain services. 3. One who has right of presentation to benefice.

păt'ronage *n.* 1. Support, encouragement, given by patron; customer's support. 2. Right of presentation to benefice or office. 3. Patronizing airs.

păt'ronal *adj.* Of a patron saint.

pătr'onize *v.t.* 1. Act as patron towards, support, encourage. 2. Treat condescendingly.

pătronўm'ic *adj.* & *n.* (Name) derived from that of a father or ancestor.

patrōōn' *n.* (U.S. hist.) Possession of landed estate with manorial privileges (abolished *c* 1850) granted under old Dutch governments of New York and New Jersey to members of the (Dutch) West India Company.

pătt'en *n.* Wooden sole with leather loop passing over instep, mounted on oval iron ring, for raising wearer's shoes out of mud etc. (ill. SHOE).

pătt'er[1] *n.* Thieves' or beggars' cant; peculiar lingo of any profession or class; oratory, speechifying, of cheapjack, mountebank, conjurer, etc.; rapid speech introduced into (comic) song. ~ *v.* Repeat (prayers etc.) in rapid mechanical way; talk glibly. [f. PATERNOSTER]

pătt'er[2] *v.* Make rapid succession of taps, as rain on window-pane; run with short quick steps; cause (water etc.) to patter. ~ *n.* Succession of taps.

pătt'ern *n.* 1. Excellent example; (attrib.) perfect, ideal, model. 2. Model from which thing is to be made; (founding) wooden or metal figure from which mould is made for casting. 3. Sample (of tailor's cloth etc.). 4. Decorative design as executed on carpet, wall-paper, cloth, etc.; marks made by shot from gun on target; number of depth-charges or bombs dropped according to a particular arrangement; *~-welding,* welding of alternate strips of twisted or plaited iron and steel, producing a pattern. 5. (fig.) Form, order followed in action or procedure, as *~ of behaviour, life,* etc. ~ *v.t.* Model (thing *after*, upon design, etc.); decorate with pattern.

Pătt'i, Adelina (1843–1919). Italian operatic soprano.

pătt'y *n.* Little pie or pasty; *pattypan,* small tin pan or shape for baking patties.

paty, -t(t)ée (pah'ti) *adj.* (her.) Of cross, having nearly triangular arms, very narrow where they meet and widening towards extremities (ill. HERALDRY). [Fr. (*croix*) *pattée* (cross) in which extremities are widened like an open paw (*patte* paw)]

pau'city *n.* Smallness of number or quantity.

Paul[1], St. (d. *c* A.D. 67). A Jew, also called Saul, of Tarsus in Asia Minor, with the status of a Roman citizen; was converted to Christianity soon after martyrdom of Stephen; became 'Apostle of the Gentiles' and the first great Christian missionary and theologian; martyred at Rome; his missionary journeys are described in the Acts of the Apostles, and his letters (Epistles) to the Churches form a large part of the N.T.

Paul[2]. Name of 6 popes: *Paul III* (Alessandro Farnese, 1468–1549), pope 1534–49, patron of art, established the constitution of the Jesuits (1540); *Paul VI* (Giovanni Battista Montini, 1897–), pope 1963– .

Paul[3] (1754–1801). Emperor of Russia 1796–1801; son of Peter III and Catherine the Great; murdered when he refused to abdicate.

paul'dron *n.* (hist.) Piece of armour covering shoulder (ill. ARMOUR).

Paul'ine *adj.* Of St. Paul, his writings or his doctrines; ~ *epistles,* those in New Testament attributed to St. Paul. ~ *n.* 1. Pupil of ST. PAUL'S SCHOOL. 2. Member of one of many orders dedicated to St. Paul.

Paul Jones. Ballroom dance

during which dancers change partners at intervals indicated by change of music.

paulo-post-fū'ture *n.* (Gk gram.) Tense expressing state resulting from future act, future perfect. [mod. L, = 'future a little after']

Paul Prȳ. Inquisitive person. [character in comedy by J. Poole, 1825]

paunch *n.* Belly, stomach; ruminant's first stomach. ~ *v.t.* Disembowel.

paup'er *n.* Person without means of livelihood, beggar; recipient of poor-law relief; (law) person allowed to sue or defend *in forma pauperis*. **paup'erism, pauperizā'tion** *ns.* **paup'erize** *v.t.*

Pausān'ĭăs[1] (5th c. B.C.). Spartan general; regent of Sparta 479 B.C.–; commanded Greek forces which defeated Persians in battle of Plataea.

Pausān'ĭăs[2] (2nd c. A.D.). Greek traveller and geographer.

pause (-z) *n.* Interval of inaction or silence, esp. from hesitation; break made in speaking or reading; (mus.) mark (𝄐 or 𝄑) placed over or under note or rest as sign that it is to be lengthened; *give ~ to*, cause to pause or hesitate. ~ *v.i.* Make a pause, wait; linger *upon* (word etc.).

pāv'age *n.* Paving; tax, toll, towards paving of streets.

păv'an, pavane' (-ahn) *n.* Stately dance of 16th and 17th centuries in which dancers were elaborately dressed; music for this, in slow duple time.

pāve *v.t.* Cover (street, floor, etc.) with or as with pavement; (fig.) prepare (*the way for*). **pāv'iour** *n.*

păv'é (-ā) *n.* Pavement; setting of jewels placed close together.

pāve'ment (-vm-) *n.* Covering of street, floor, etc., made of stones, tiles, wooden blocks, asphalt, etc., esp. paved footway at side of road; (zool.) pavement-like formation of close-set teeth etc.; *crazy ~*, pavement of irregular flat stones for garden path etc.; *~ artist*, one who draws in chalks on pavement to get money from passers-by.

Pavi'a (-vē*a*). Town of Lombardy, Italy, old capital of Lombard kingdom, where François I of France was defeated and captured in 1525 by the army of the Emperor Charles V.

pavĭl'ion (-yon) *n.* 1. Tent, esp. large peaked one; light ornamental building, esp. one attached to cricket or other ground for spectators and players; projecting (usu. highly decorated) subdivision of building. 2. Part of brilliant-cut gem-stone below girdle (ill GEM). ~ *v.t.* Enclose (as) in, furnish with, pavilion. [L *papilionem* butterfly, in LL, tent]

Păv'lov (-f), Ivan Petrovich 1849–1916). Russian physiologist; Nobel Prize-winner, 1904; noted for research on conditioned reflexes.

Păv'lova, Anna Matveevna (1885–1931). Russian ballerina.

păv'onine *adj.* Of, like, a peacock.

paw *n.* Foot of beast having claws or nails; fur from lower part of animal's leg; (colloq.) hand. ~ *v.* Strike with paw; (of horse) strike (ground), strike ground, with hoofs; (colloq.) handle awkwardly or rudely.

pawk'y *adj.* (Sc., dial.) Sly, cunning, shrewd; dryly humorous. **pawk'ĭly** *adv.* **pawk'ĭness** *n.*

pawl *n.* Short pivoted catch engaging with toothed wheel to prevent recoil (ill. WINDLASS; (naut.) short bar used to prevent capstan, windlass, etc., from recoiling. ~ *v.t.* Secure (capstan etc.) with pawl.

pawn[1] *n.* One of the pieces of smallest size and value in chess (ill. CHESS); (fig.) unimportant person used by another as a mere tool. [AF *poun*, f. med. L *pedonem* foot-soldier]

pawn[2] *n.* Thing, person, left in another's keeping as security, pledge; state of being pledged; *pawn'broker*, one who lends money upon interest on security of personal property pawned; *pawn'-broking*, his occupation; *pawn'shop*, pawnbroker's place of business. ~ *v.t.* Deposit (thing) as security for payment of money or performance of action; (fig.) pledge.

pawnee'[1] *n.* Person with whom pawn is deposited.

Paw'nee[2] *n.* Indian of a N. Amer. confederacy, formerly living in Nebraska, now in Oklahoma.

păx *n.* 1. Tablet with representation of Crucifixion etc., kissed at Mass by priests and congregation; kiss of peace as liturgical form at High Mass. 2. ~ *vobis!* (as salutation), peace to you. 3. (school slang, as int.) Peace!, truce! 4. ~ *Britannica*, peace imposed by British rule; ~ *Romana*, peace between nationalities within Roman Empire.

pay[1] *v.* (past t. and past part. *paid*). 1. Give (person) what is due in discharge of debt or *for* services done or goods received; recompense (work); hand over (money owed); hand over amount of (debt, wages, etc.); (fig.) reward, recompense; *~ for*, hand over the price of, bear the cost of; (fig.) be punished for; *~ in*, pay to banking account; *~ off*, pay in full and discharge or be quit of (ship's crew, creditor, etc.); ~ (person) *out*, punish him; *~ up*, pay full amount of (arrears; or abs.); ~ one's *way*, not get into debt. 2. Render, bestow (attention, court, compliment, etc., *to*). 3. (Of business etc.) yield adequate return to (person); yield adequate return. 4. (naut.) ~ *off* (of ship) fall off to leeward when helm is put up; ~ *out, away*, let out (rope) by slackening it. 5. *~-as-you-earn*, (abbrev. P.A.Y.E.) method of collecting income tax by current deduction from earnings; *~-off*, (orig. U.S.) time of reckoning. ~ *n.* Amount paid; wages, hire, salary; (attrib., mining) containing precious metal or other mineral in sufficient quantity to be profitably worked; *in the ~ of*, employed by; *~-bed*, hospital bed for the use of which payment is made; *~-day*, day on which payment (esp. of wages) is (to be) made; (Stock Exch.) day on which transfer of stock has to be paid for; *pay'master*, officer, official, who pays troops, workmen, etc.; *Paymaster-General*, officer at head of the department of Treasury through which payments are made; *~ packet*, packet containing employee's wages; *~-roll*, list of employees receiving regular pay.

pay[2] *v.t.* (naut.) Smear with pitch, tar, etc., to render waterproof.

pay'able *adj.* That must be paid, due; that may be paid; (of mine etc.) profitable.

P.A.Y.E. *abbrev.* PAY[1]-as-you earn.

payee' *n.* Person to whom payment is made.

pay'ment *n.* Paying; amount paid; (fig.) recompense.

Paym.(-Gen.) *abbrev.* Paymaster(-General).

payn'ĭm *n.* (archaic) Pagan, esp. Mohammedan.

P.B. *abbrev.* Prayer Book.

P.B.I. *abbrev.* (colloq.) Poor bloody infantry.

p.c. *abbrev.* Per cent; postcard.

P.C. *abbrev.* Police constable; Privy Council(lor).

pd *abbrev.* Paid.

pdr *abbrev.* Pounder (of fish, gun, etc.).

p.e. *abbrev.* Personal estate.

pea *n.* Hardy climbing leguminous plant (*Pisum sativum*), with large papilionaceous flowers and long pods each containing a row of round seeds; various related leguminous plants; seed of this as food; *green peas*, peas gathered for food while still green, soft, and unripe; *everlasting ~*, plant (*Lathyrus latifolius*) cultivated for its variously-coloured flowers; *sweet ~*: see SWEET; *peanut*, (fruit of) *Arachis hypogaea* of W. Africa and W. Indies, with pod ripening underground, containing two seeds like peas, valued as food and for their oil; *peanut butter*, paste of ground peanuts; *~-shooter*, toy weapon, tube from which dried peas are shot by blowing; *~ soup*, soup made from (esp. dried) peas; (attrib., esp. of fog) suggestive of this in its dull-yellow colour or thick consistency; *~-souper*, (colloq.) thick yellow fog.

peace *n.* 1. Freedom from, cessation of, war; ratification or treaty of peace between powers previously at war. 2. Freedom from civil disorder; *the* (*king's*, *queen's*) ~, general peace of the realm as secured by law; so *breach*, *commission*, *justice*, *officer*, *of the* ~. 3. Quiet, tranquillity; mental calm. 4. *at* ~, in state of friendliness, not at strife (*with*); *hold* one's ~, keep silence; *keep the* ~, prevent, refrain from, strife; *make* (person's, one's) ~, bring person, oneself, back into friendly relations (*with*). 5. *peace'maker*, one who brings about peace; ~-*offering*, propitiatory gift; (bibl.) offering presented as thanksgiving to God; ~-*pipe*, tobacco-pipe smoked as token of peace among N. Amer. Indians.

peace'able (-s*a*-) *adj.* Disposed, tending, to peace; free from disturbance, peaceful. **peace'ableness** *n.* **peace'ably** *adv.*

peace'ful (-sf-) *adj.* Characterized by, belonging to a state of, peace; not violating or infringing peace. **peace'fully** *adv.* **peace'fulness** *n.*

peach[1] *n.* Large roundish fruit with downy white or yellow skin flushed with red, highly flavoured sweet pulp, and rough furrowed stone; tree (*Amygdalus persica*) bearing this, a native of Asia very early introduced into Europe; peach-colour; (slang) person or thing of superlative merit, attractive young woman; ~-*blow*, (glaze on some Oriental porcelain of) delicate purplish or pink; ~-*brandy*, spirituous liquor made from peach juice; ~-*colour(ed)*, (of) colour of ripe peach, a soft yellowish-pink, or of peach-blossom, a delicate purplish pink. **peach'y** *adj.* Like a peach, esp. in colour and softness. [L *persicum* (*malum*) Persian (apple)]

peach[2] *v.i.* (now slang) Turn informer; inform (*against*, *upon*).

pea'cŏck[1] *n.* 1. Male bird of any species of *Pavo*, esp. of *P. cristatus*, native of India, with striking plumage and tail marked with iridescent ocelli ('eyes'), able to expand its tail erect like fan (freq. as type of ostentatious display). 2. European butterfly (*Vanessa io*) with ocellated wings. 3. ~ *blue*, lustrous blue of peacock's neck; ~-*coal*, irridescent coal; ~-*fish*, European fish (*Cranilabrus pavo*) with brilliant green, blue, red, and white colouring, blue-striped wrasse; ~-*throne*, former throne of kings of Delhi, adorned with representation of fully expanded peacock's tail composed of precious stones. ~ *v.* Plume one*self*, make display; strut about ostentatiously. **pea'cŏckery** *n.* **pea'cŏckish** *adj.*

Pea'cŏck[2], Thomas Love (1785–1866). English satirical novelist.

pea'fowl *n.* Peacock or peahen.

pea'hĕn *n.* Female of the peacock.

pea'-jăckėt *n.* Sailor's short square-cut double-breasted overcoat of coarse woollen cloth.

peak[1] *n.* 1. Projecting part of brim of cap; (naut.) narrow part of ship's hold, esp. (*forepeak*) at bow; upper outer corner of sail extended by gaff (ill. SAIL[1]). 2. Pointed top, esp. of mountain; point, e.g. of beard; highest point in curve or record of fluctuations (whence ~-*load*, greatest frequency or maximum of electric power, traffic, etc.; ~-*hour*, time of day when this occurs). **peak'y**[1] *adj.*

peak[2] *v.i.* Waste away; *peaked*, sharp-featured, pinched. **peak'y**[2] *adj.* Sickly, puny.

peak[3] *v.* (naut.) Tilt (yard) vertically; raise (oar blades) almost vertically.

Peak[4]. *The* ~, hilly district in NW. Derbyshire, England.

peal *n.* Loud ringing of bell(s), esp. series of changes on set of bells; set of bells; loud volley of sound, esp. of thunder or laughter. ~ *v.* Sound forth in a peal; ring (bells) in peals; utter sonorously.

pear (pār̄) *n.* (Fleshy fruit, tapering towards stalk, of) the tree *Pyrus communis*, or other species with similar fruit; *alligator*, *avocado*, *prickly*, ~: see these words.

pearl (pẽrl) *n.* 1. Concretion, usu. white or bluish-grey, formed round foreign body within shell of ~-*oyster* (*Margaritifera*) and (loosely) genera of bivalve molluscs, having beautiful lustre and highly prized as gem; precious thing, finest example (*of* its kind); pearl-like thing, e.g. dewdrop, tear, tooth; *mother-of-*~: see MOTHER[1]. 2. Size of type (approx. 5 point) between ruby and diamond. 3. Small fragment of various substances. 4. ~-*ash*, the potassium carbonate of commerce; ~-*barley*, barley reduced by attrition to small rounded grains; ~ *button*, button made of mother-of-pearl or imitation of it; ~-*diver*, one who dives for pearl-oysters; ~-*fisher*, one who fishes for pearls; ~-*powder*, -*white*, cosmetic used to whiten skin; ~-*shell*, mother-of-pearl as naturally found. ~ *v.* Sprinkle with pearly drops; make pearly in colour etc.; reduce (barley, etc.) to small pearls; form pearl-like drops; fish for pearls. **pearl'y** *adj.*

pearl'ies (pẽrl'ĭz) *n.pl.* Costermonger's dress adorned with many pearl buttons; also, the costermongers themselves.

pearl'īte (pẽr-) *n.* Microstructural constituent of iron, a conglomerate of cementite and ferrite.

pear'main (pār̄-; *or* -mān') *n.* Kind of apple. [prob. f. L *parmanus* of Parma]

Pear'y (pẽr-), Robert Edwin (1856–1920). American Arctic explorer; reached N. Pole on 6th April 1909.

peas'ant (pĕz-) *n.* Countryman, rustic, esp. one working on land as small farmer or labourer. **peas'antry** *n.* (Body of) peasants.

pease (-z) *n.* Peas, esp. in ~ *pudding*; (archaic) *peasecod*, peapod.

peat *n.* Vegetable matter, varying in colour from light brown to black, decomposed by water and partly carbonized, freq. forming bogs or 'mosses'; cut piece of this, used as fuel; ~-*bog*, broken ground whence peats have been cut; ~-*reek*, smoke of, whisky distilled over, peat-fire. **peat'y** *adj.*

peau-de-soie (pō-d*e*-swah) *n.* Rich thick silk material with dull satin surface on both sides. [Fr., = 'silk skin']

pĕbb'le *n.* 1. Small stone worn and rounded by natural action; ~-*dash*, mortar with small pebbles in it as coating for wall. 2. Colourless transparent rock-crystal used for spectacles, lens of this; agate or other gem found as pebble in streams, esp. in Scotland (*Scotch* ~), various kinds of agate. **pĕbb'ly** *adj.*

pĕcăn' *n.* Species of hickory (*Carya olivaeformis*) common in Ohio and Mississippi valleys; olive-shaped finely flavoured nut of this.

pĕcc'able *adj.* Liable to sin. **pĕccabĭl'ity** *n.*

pĕccadĭll'ō *n.* Trifling offence.

pĕcc'ant *adj.* Sinning; (med.) morbid, inducing disease. **pĕcc'ancy** *n.*

pĕcc'ary *n.* Small gregarious pig (*Dicotyles*) of S. and Central America.

pĕccāv'ī. 'I have sinned' (in phr. *cry* ~). ~ *n.* Confession of guilt.

pêche mĕl'ba (pāsh) *n.* Confection of ice-cream and peaches. [Fr., after name of Dame Nellie MELBA, Australian prima donna]

pĕck[1] *n.* Measure of capacity for dry goods, 2 gallons, ¼ bushel; vessel used as peck measure.

pĕck[2] *v.* 1. Strike (thing) with beak; pluck *out* thus; make (hole) thus; aim *at* with beak; (colloq.) eat in nibbling fashion. 2. Strike with pick or other pointed tool. ~ *n.* Stroke with beak; mark made with this; (joc.) kiss like bird's peck; (slang) victuals.

pĕck'er *n.* Bird that pecks; kind of hoe; (slang) courage, resolution (in *keep* one's ~ *up*, perh. orig. = beak).

pĕck'ĭsh *adj.* (colloq.) Somewhat hungry.

Pĕck'sniff, Mr. Unctuously hypocritical character in Dickens's novel 'Martin Chuzzlewit'; hence, a canting hypocrite. **Pĕcksniff'ian** *adj.*

pĕc'tĕn *n.* (pl. -*ĭnes* pr. -ēz). (zool.) 1. Comb-like structure of various kinds (in animals), e.g. stiff hairs on legs of bees. 2. Genus of bivalve (lamellibranch) molluscs with radiating ribs suggesting comb on rounded shell, scallop. **pĕc'tĭnate, -āted**, *adjs.*

pĕc'tĭn *n.* (chem.) White gelatinous substance soluble in water, closely related to the carbohydrates, formed in the ripening of fruits, and constituting the gelatinizing agent in vegetable juices. **pĕc'tĭc** *adj.*

pĕc'toral *adj.* Of the breast or chest (~ *muscles*: see ill. MUSCLE); remedying diseases of the chest; worn on the breast; ~ *cross*, cross of precious metal worn on the breast by bishops, cardinals, and abbots. ~ *n.* Ornamental breastplate, esp. that of Jewish high priest.

pĕc'tōse *n.* (chem.) Insoluble substance related to cellulose and occurring with it in vegetable tissues, esp. in unripe fruits and fleshy roots, converted by the action of acids into PECTIN.

pĕc'ūlāte *v.* Embezzle. **pĕcūlā'tion, pĕc'ūlātor** *ns.*

pėcūl'iar *adj.* Belonging exclusively *to*; belonging to the individual; particular, special; singular, strange, odd; *P~ People*, the Jews as God's chosen people; (also) sect founded in London, 1838, without creed or church organization, relying on prayer and anointing for the cure of disease. ~ *n.* 1. Peculiar property, privilege, etc. 2. (hist.) Parish, church, exempt from jurisdiction of diocese in which it lies. 3. *P~*, one of the Peculiar People.

pėcūliă'rity *n.* Being peculiar; characteristic; oddity.

pėcūl'iarly *adv.* As regards oneself alone, individually; especially, more than usually; oddly.

pėcūn'iary *adj.* (Consisting) of money; (of offence) having pecuniary penalty. **pėcūn'iarily** *adv.*

pĕd'agogue (-ŏg) *n.* Schoolmaster, teacher (usu. contempt.) **pedagŏg'ic(al)** (-g-, -j-) *adjs.* **pĕdagŏg'ically** *adv.*

pĕd'agogy, pĕdagŏg'ics (-gĭ, -jĭ) *ns.* Science of teaching.

pĕd'al¹ *n.* 1. Lever worked by the foot to transmit power in machine, e.g. bicycle. 2. Foot-lever in various musical instruments; in organ, each of (wooden) keys played upon by feet (ill. ORGAN), (also) foot-lever for drawing out several stops at once, opening swell-box, etc.; in piano, foot-lever for raising dampers from strings, thus sustaining tone and making it fuller (*loud* ~), or for softening tone (*soft* ~) by shifting hammers so as to strike only one or two strings instead of three, by diminishing length of blow, or by interposing strip of cloth between hammers and strings. 3. (mus.) Note sustained or reiterated in one part (usu. bass) through a series of harmonies. 4. *~-board*, the row of pedals in an organ or pedal piano; ~ *notes*, the notes sounded by the pedals of an organ; (also) in brass instruments, the fundamental notes which are below their normal compass; ~ *organ*, that part of an organ controlled by the pedals; ~ *piano*, piano constructed with a pedal board. ~ *v.* Work pedals of bicycle etc.; work (bicycle etc.) thus; play on organ pedals.

pĕd'al² *adj.* (zool.) Of the feet or foot, esp. of mollusc.

pĕd'al³ *adj.* ~ *straw*, lower and thicker part of Italian straw grown for plaiting.

pĕd'ant *n.* One who overrates or parades book-learning or technical knowledge, or insists on strict adherence to formal rules. **pėdăn'tic** *adj.* **pėdăn'tically** *adv.* **pĕd'antry** *n.*

pĕd'ate *adj.* (zool.) Footed.

pĕdd'le *v.* Follow occupation of pedlar; trade or deal in as pedlar; trifle, dally.

pĕd'ėstal *n.* Base supporting column in construction; base of statue etc.; each of two supports of knee-hole writing-table; foundation; *~-table*, one with massive central support. ~ *v.t.* Set, support, on pedestal.

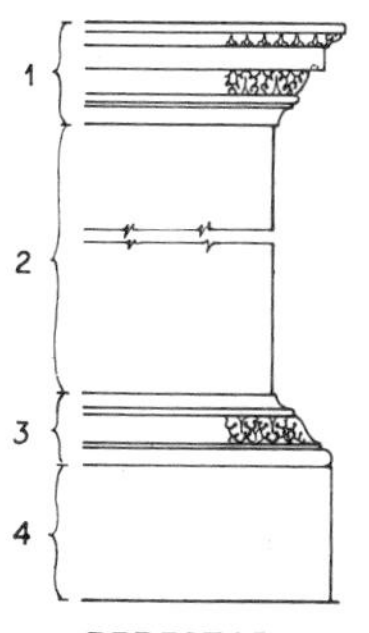

PEDESTAL

1. Cornice. 2. Dado. 3. Base. 4. Socle

pėdĕs'trian *adj.* Going, performed, on foot; of walking; for those who walk; prosaic, dull, uninspired. ~ *n.* One who walks or goes on foot. **pėdĕs'trianism** *n.*

pĕd'icel, pĕd'icle *ns.* (bot., zool.) Small, esp. subordinate, stalk-like structure in plant or animal (ill. INFLORESCENCE). **pėdic'ūlate** *adj.*

pėdic'ūlar, pėdic'ūlous *adjs.* Lousy. **pĕdicūlōs'is** *n.* Infestation with lice.

pĕd'icūre *n.* 1. Chiropody. 2. Chiropodist. ~ *v.t.* Cure or treat (feet) by removing corns etc.

pĕd'igree *n.* Genealogical table; ancestral line (of man or animal); derivation (of word); ancient descent; (attrib.) having known line of descent. **pĕd'igreed** *adj.* [OF *pie de grue* crane's foot, mark ⅄ denoting succession in pedigrees]

pĕd'iment *n.* Triangular low-pitched gable crowning front of building in Greek style, esp. over portico (ill. TEMPLE); similarly placed member of same or other form in Roman and Renaissance styles; *broken* ~, one without an apex. **pĕdimĕn'tal, pĕd'imentėd** *adjs.*

pĕd'lar *n.* Travelling vendor of small wares, usu. carried in pack; (fig.) retailer (*of* gossip etc.); *~'s French*, thieves' cant.

pėdŏl'ŏgy *n.* Science of soils.

pėdŏm'ėter *n.* Instrument for estimating distance travelled on foot by recording number of steps taken.

pėdŭnc'le *n.* (bot.) Stalk of flower, fruit, or cluster, esp. main stalk bearing solitary flower or subordinate stalks (ill. INFLORESCENCE); (zool.) stalk-like process in animal body. **pėdŭnc'ūlar, pėdŭnc'ūlate** *adjs.*

Pee'blesshire. Inland county of S. Scotland, also called Tweeddale.

peek *v.i.* Peep, peer; *~-a-boo*, (now U.S.) peep-bo. ~ *n.* Peep, glance (*take a ~ at*).

peel¹ *n.* (hist.) Small square tower built in 16th c. in border counties of England and Scotland.

peel² *n.* Shovel, esp. baker's shovel, pole with broad flat disc at end for thrusting loaves etc. into oven.

peel³ *v.* Strip peel, rind, bark, etc., from (fruit, vegetable, tree, etc.); take *off* (skin, peel, etc.); become bare of bark, skin, etc.; (of bark, surface, etc.) come off or *off* like peel; (now slang, of person) strip for exercise etc.; (U.S. colloq.) *keep* (*one's*) *eyes peeled*, keep them open, be on the alert. ~ *n.* Rind, outer coating, of fruit; *candied ~*, candied rind of various species of *Citrus*, used in cookery and confectionery. **peel'er¹** *n.* **peel'ings** *n.pl.* What is peeled off.

Peel⁴, John (1776–1854). Huntsman of Cumberland, England; hero of famous hunting-song 'D'ye ken John Peel?'.

Peel⁵, Sir Robert (1788–1850). English statesman; premier 1834–5; formed ministry (1841–6) which repealed corn laws; founded conservative party and police force.

peel'er² *n.* (colloq.) Policeman;

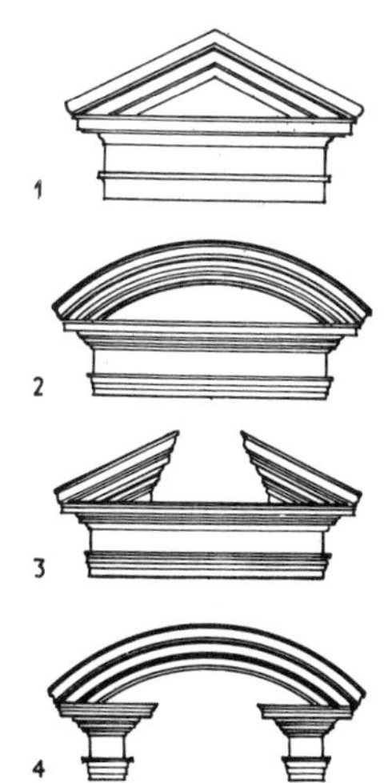

PEDIMENTS

1. Triangular. 2. Segmental. 3. Broken. 4. Open

(hist.) member of Irish constabulary, founded under secretaryship of Sir Robert PEEL[5].

peep[1] *v.i.* & *n.* (Make) feeble shrill sound of young birds, mice, etc.; chirp, squeak.

peep[2] *v.i.* Look through narrow aperture; look furtively; come cautiously or partly into view, emerge; (fig.) show itself unconsciously; *peeping Tom*, (in tale of GODIVA), type of prurient curiosity. ~ *n.* Furtive or peering glance; first appearance, esp. *of dawn, of day*; *~-of-day boys*, Protestant organization in Ireland (1784-93), searching opponents' houses at daybreak for arms; *~-hole*, small hole to peep through; *~-show*, small exhibition of pictures etc. viewed through lens in small orifice; *~-toe(d) sandal, shoe*, one which allows toes to be seen.

peep'-bō *n.* Game of hiding and suddenly appearing to child.

peep'er *n.* One who peeps; (slang) eye.

peep'ul, pi'pal (pē-) *n.* Indian species of fig-tree (*Ficus religiosa*) regarded as sacred.

peer[1] *n.* 1. An equal in civil standing or rank; equal in any respect. 2. Member of one of the degrees (duke, marquis, earl, viscount, baron) of nobility in United Kingdom; noble (of any country); ~ *of the realm*, one of the peers of the United Kingdom, all of whom when of age may sit in the House of Lords; *life ~*, (since 1958) one whose title is not hereditary. ~ *v.* Rank with, equal; rank as equal *with*; make (man) a peer.

peer[2] *v.i.* Look narrowly; appear, peep out; come in sight.

peer'age (-ĭj) *n.* Peers; nobility, aristocracy; rank of peer; book containing list of peers with genealogy etc.

peer'ėss *n.* Wife of peer; ~ *in her own right*, woman having rank of peer by creation or descent; *life ~*: see PEER[1].

peer'lėss *adj.* Having no equal, unrivalled. **peer'lėssly** *adv.* **peer'lėssnėss** *n.* [f. PEER[1]]

peeved (-vd) *adj.* (slang) Irritated.

peev'ĭsh *adj.* Querulous, irritable. **peev'ĭshly** *adv.* **peev'ĭshnėss** *n.*

peewit: see PEWIT.

pĕg *n.* 1. Pin, bolt, of wood, metal, etc., usu. round and slightly tapering, for holding together parts of framework etc., stopping up vent of cask, hanging hats etc. on, holding ropes of tent, tightening or loosening strings of violin etc. (ill. STRING), marking cribbage-score etc.; clothes-peg; (fig.) occasion, pretext, theme (*to hang* discourse etc. *on*); *take* (person) *down a ~ or two*, humble him. *~ leg*, wooden leg; *~-top*, pear-shaped spinning-top with metal peg; *~-top trousers*, trousers wide at hips, narrow at ankles; *off the ~*, (of garment) bought ready-made. 2. A drink, esp. of brandy and soda-water. ~ *v.* Fix with peg; (Stock Exch.) prevent price of (stock etc.) from falling or rising by freely buying or selling at given price; mark score with pegs on cribbage-board; mark *out* boundaries of (mining-claim etc.); strike, pierce, aim *at*, with peg; (slang) throw (stone), throw stones etc. (*at*); drive pegs into (cricket-bat); ~ (*away*), work persistently (*at*); ~ *down*, restrict (*to* rules etc.); ~ *out*, (croquet) hit peg with ball as final stroke in game; (slang) die, be ruined.

Pĕg'asus. 1. (Gk myth.) A winged horse, favourite of the Muses, sprung from blood of MEDUSA; a blow of its hoof gave rise to the fountain Hippocrene on Mt Helicon. 2. A northern constellation, figured as a winged horse, containing three stars of the 2nd magnitude forming with one star of Andromeda a large square (*square of ~*).

Peh'levi: see PAHLAVI.

peignoir (pān'wahr) *n.* Woman's loose dressing-gown worn during the toilet.

peine forte et dure (pān fôrt ā dūr) *n.* (hist.) Pressing to death, form of punishment inflicted on persons arraigned for felony who refused to plead. [Fr., = 'severe and hard punishment']

Peiping (pā-): see PEKING.

pėj'oratĭve *adj.* & *n.* Depreciatory (word).

pēke *n.* Pekinese dog.

Pēk'ĭn(g)'. Ancient city of N. China, capital of China; ~ *man*, extinct species of man, *Sinanthropus pekinensis*, represented by at least a dozen skulls and other remains found near Peking from 1929 onwards. [Chin., = 'northern capital']

Pēkin(g)ēse' (-z) *adj.* & *n.* 1. (Inhabitant) of Pekin(g). 2. Small breed of dog of the pug type, with long silky coat, flat face, and prominent eyes, orig. brought to Europe from Summer Palace at Peking in 1860.

pĕk'oe (-ō) *n.* Superior kind of black tea. [Chin. *pek-ho* white down (leaves being picked young with down on them)]

pėlā'gĭan[1], **pėlā'gĭc** *adjs.* Of, inhabiting, the open sea. **pelā'gĭan** *n.* Pelagic animal.

Pelā'gĭan[2] *adj.* & *n.* (Follower) of Morgan (*c* 360-*c* 420), a British monk and theologian, known as Pelagius; he denied the Catholic doctrine of original sin and maintained that the human will is capable of good without the help of divine grace; his doctrines were condemned by Pope Zosimus in 418.

pėlargōn'ĭum *n.* (bot.) Genus of plant with showy flowers and fragrant leaves (pop. called *geranium*). [Gk *pelargos* stork]

Pėlăs'gĭan (-zg- *or* -zj-) *n.* One of the pre-Greek inhabitants of Greece and the islands and coasts of the E. Mediterranean. **Pėlăs'gĭc** *adj.* Of Pelasgians.

pĕl'erĭne (*or* -ēn) *n.* (hist.) Woman's long narrow cape or tippet (ill. CLOAK).

Pēl'eus (-lūs). (Gk legend) King of Thessaly and father, by the nereid Thetis, of Achilles.

pĕlf *n.* Money, wealth (usu. contempt.).

Pĕl'ĭăs. (Gk legend) King who stole kingdom of Iolcos from his brother Aeson and sent Aeson's son JASON in quest of the Golden Fleece.

pĕl'ican *n.* Genus (*Pelecanus*) of large gregarious fish-eating birds, with large membranous pouch between lower mandibles of long hooked bill, used for storing fish (the fable, of Egyptian origin, that the pelican feeds or revives its young with its own blood app. referred originally to another bird); *P~ State*, (U.S.) pop. name of Louisiana (from device on its seal).

PELICAN

Pēl'ĭon. Wooded mountain near coast of SE. Thessaly, Greece; in Gk myth., home of centaurs; the giants were said to have piled Olympus on Mt Ossa and Ossa on Pelion in their attempt to reach heaven and destroy the gods.

pėlisse' (-ēs) *n.* (hist.) Woman's

PELISSE: A. AS CLOAK, *c* 1786. B. AS COAT, *c* 1806
1. Boa. 2. Reticule

mantle with armholes or sleeves, reaching to ankles; child's outdoor garment worn over other clothes; cape or cloak worn as part of military uniforms (ill. CAVALRY).

pėllăg'ra *n.* Deficiency disease, endemic in countries whose populations live chiefly on cereals with low protein content (as maize); characterized by disorders of the skin, digestion, and nervous system. [It., perh. orig. *pelle agra* rough skin]

pĕll'ėt *n.* Small ball of paper, bread, etc.; pill; small shot; circular boss in coins etc.; (her.) a roundel sable (ill. HERALDRY).

pĕll'ĭcle *n.* Thin skin; membrane; film. **pėllĭc'ūlar** *adj.*

pĕll'ĭtory *n.* 1. (~ *of Spain*) Composite plant (*Anacyclus pyrethrum*), native of Barbary, with pungent root used as local irritant etc. 2. (~ *of the wall*), low bushy plant (*Parietaria officinalis*) with small ovate leaves and greenish flowers, growing on or at foot of walls.

pĕll'-mĕll' *adv.* In disorder, promiscuously; headlong, recklessly. ~ *adj.* Confused; tumultuous. ~ *n.* Confusion, medley, mêlée.

pėllū'cĭd *adj.* Transparent, clear; clear in style or expression; mentally clear. **pėllū'cidly** *adv.* **pĕllūcĭd'ĭty** *n.*

pĕl'mėt *n.* Valance or narrow pendent border concealing curtain-rods above window or door (ill. WINDOW). [prob. f. Fr. *palmette*, conventional palm-leaf design on cornice]

Pĕl'oponnēse, Pĕloponnēs'us. That part of Greece S. of Isthmus of Corinth; = Morea. **Pĕloponnē'sian** (-shn) *adj.* ~ *War* (431–404 B.C.), war waged by Sparta and her allies upon Athens and Athenian Empire; it ended in surrender of Athens and transfer, for a brief period, of leadership of Greece to Sparta.

Pĕl'ŏps. (Gk myth.) Son of TANTALUS, brother of NIOBE, and father of ATREUS.

pėlōt'a *n.* Basque ball-game resembling tennis or rackets, played in large walled court with curved wickerwork racket attached to leather glove. [Span., = 'ball' (f. L *pila*)]

pĕlt[1] *n.* Skin of sheep or goat with short wool on; skin of fur-bearing animal, esp. undressed; raw skin of sheep etc. stripped of wool or fur. **pĕl'try** *n.* Pelts collectively.

pĕlt[2] *v.* Assail with missiles; (of rain etc.) beat with violence; strike *at* repeatedly with missiles; go on throwing (missiles). ~ *n.* Pelting.

pĕl'ta *n.* Small light shield of ancient Greeks, Romans, etc. (ill. SHIELD); (bot.) shield-like structure. **pĕl'tate** *adj.*

pĕl'vĭs *n.* 1. Basin-shaped cavity formed in most vertebrates by haunch-bones with sacrum and other vertebrae. 2. Funnel-shaped origin of ureter, having a wide end which lies within the kidney (ill. KIDNEY). **pĕl'vĭc** *adj.*

~, FOUNTAIN-~: see these words; ~-*and-ink*, (attrib., of drawing etc.) done, made, with pen and ink; ~-*and-wash* (attrib.) using both

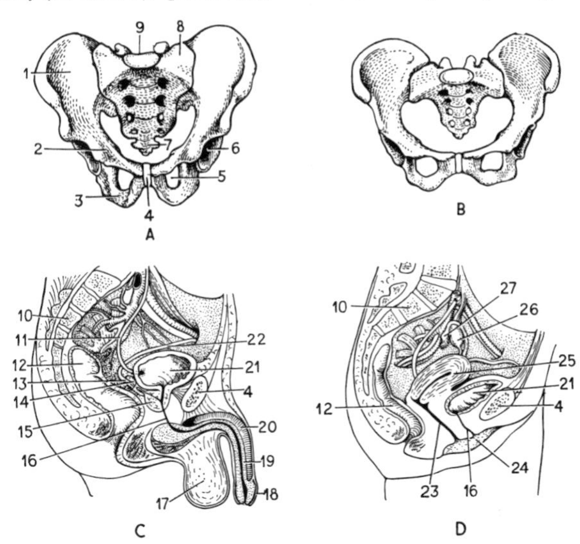

PELVIS AND PERINEUM: A, C. MALE. B, D. FEMALE

A. 1. Ilium. 2. Pubis. 3. Ischium. 4. Symphysis pubis. 5. *Obdurator foramen.* 6. Articular surface of head of femur. 7. Coccyx. 8. Sacrum. 9. Articular surface of 5th lumbar vertebra. C. 10. Spine. 11. Ureter. 12. Rectum. 13. Vas deferens. 14. Seminal vesicle. 15. Prostate gland. 16. Urethra. 17. Scrotum enclosing testicles. 18. Foreskin or prepuce. 19. Penis. 20. Erectile tissue. 21. Bladder. 22. Spermatic duct. D. 23. Vagina. 24. Labium. 25. Uterus or womb. 26. Ovary. 27. Fallopian tube

Pĕm'broke. Town in S. Wales; ~ (*table*), table on 4 fixed legs with hinged flaps that can be spread out and supported on brackets (ill. TABLE).

Pĕm'broke Cŏll'ege. 1. College of University of Cambridge, founded 1347 by Mary, Countess of Pembroke. 2. College of University of Oxford, founded 1624 when the Earl of Pembroke was chancellor of the university.

Pĕm'brokeshire. County of SW. Wales.

pĕmm'ĭcan *n.* N. Amer. Indian food of lean meat dried, pounded, mixed into paste with melted fat and pressed into cakes; beef similarly treated and freq. flavoured with currants etc. for Arctic and other travellers.

pĕn[1] *n.* Small enclosure for cows, sheep, poultry, etc.; enclosure resembling this, as *submarine-*~; (W. Ind.) farm, plantation. ~ *v.t.* Enclose, shut *up*, shut *in*; shut up (cattle etc.) in pen.

pĕn[2] *n.* Quill feather with quill pointed and split into two sections, for writing with ink; small instrument of gold, steel, etc., similarly pointed and split, fitted into rod of wood etc. (~-*holder*), pen and pen-holder together; any contrivance for writing with fluid ink; writing, style of this; BALL[1]-*point* pen and brush; ~-*feather*, quill-feather of bird's wing; *penknife*, small knife usu. carried in pocket, orig. for making or mending quill pens; *pen'man*, one who writes a (*good*, *bad*, etc.) hand; author; *pen'manship*, skill in writing, style of handwriting; action or style of literary composition; ~-*name*, literary pseudonym; ~ *wiper*, appliance usu. of small pieces of cloth for wiping pen after use. ~ *v.t.* Write, compose and write (letter etc.).

pĕn[3] *n.* Female swan.

pĕn[4] *n.* (U.S. slang) Prison. [abbrev. of *penitentiary*]

P.E.N. *abbrev.* (International Association of) Poets, Playwrights, Editors, Essayists, and Novelists.

pen(in). *abbrevs.* Peninsula.

pē'nal *adj.* Of punishment, concerned with inflicting this; (of offence) punishable, esp. by law; inflicted as punishment; used as place of punishment; ~ *servitude*, imprisonment for three years or longer with hard labour. **pē'nally** *adv.*

pē'nalīze *v.t.* Make, declare, penal; (sport.) subject competitor to penalty or comparative disadvantage (also freq. fig.).

pĕn'alty *n.* Punishment, esp. (payment of) sum of money, for breach of law, rule, or contract; (sport. etc.) disadvantage imposed on competitor for breaking rule or winning previous contest; (bridge) points added to opponents' score when declarer fails to make his contract; ~ *area*, (Assoc. football) area in front of goal within which breach of certain rules involves award of penalty kick (ill. ASSOCIATION); ~ *kick*, (Rugby football) free kick allowed because of some violation of rules by the opponents; (Assoc. football) free kick made from a mark 12 yards in front of the centre of the goal with all players except the one taking the kick and the opposing goalkeeper barred from the penalty area, allowed for certain infringements of the rules within this area.

pĕn'ance *n.* (Rom. and Gk Churches) sacrament including contrition, confession, satisfaction, and absolution for sin; act of self-mortification as expression of penitence, esp. one imposed by priest; *do* ~, perform such act.

Pėnāt'ēs (-z). (Rom. myth.) Gods of the store-room, regarded, with LARES, as protectors of the house.

pĕnce collect. pl. of PENNY.

penchant (pahṅ'shahṅ) *n.* Inclination, liking, (*for*).

pĕn'cil *n.* 1. Artist's paint-brush (archaic); (fig.) painter's art or style. 2. Instrument for drawing or writing, esp. (*lead* ~) of graphite enclosed in wooden cylinder or in metal case with tapering end; pencil-shaped object; ~-*case*, holder for pencil or pencil-lead. 3. (optics) Set of rays meeting at a point. 4. (geom.) Figure formed by set of straight lines meeting at a point. ~ *v.t.* Tint or mark (as) with lead pencil; jot down with pencil; (esp. in past part.) mark delicately with thin concentric lines of colour or shading.

Pĕn'da (577–*c* 655). King of Mercia; champion of heathenism against Christianity.

pĕn'dant (rarely **-ent**) *n.* 1. Hanging ornament, esp. one attached to necklace, bracelet, etc. 2. (naut., pr. pĕn'ant, also spelt *pennant*) Short rope hanging from head of mast etc. with eye at lower end for receiving hooks of tackles; tapering flag, esp. that flown at mast-head of vessel in commission (ill. FLAG); *broad* ~, short swallow-tailed pendant distinguishing commodore's ship in squadron. 3. Shank and ring of watch by which it is suspended. 4. Match, parallel, companion, complement (*to*).

pĕn'dent (rarely **-ant**) *adj.* Hanging; overhanging; undecided, pending; (gram.) of which the construction is incomplete. **pĕn'dency** *n.*

pĕndĕn'tė lĭt'ė *adv.* Pending the suit.

pĕndĕn'tive *n.* (archit.) Each of the spherical triangles formed by the intersection of a dome by two pairs of opposite arches springing from the 4 supporting columns (ill. DOME).

pĕnd'ing *adj.* Undecided, awaiting decision or settlement. ~ *prep.* During; until.

pĕndrăg'on *n.* Ancient British or Welsh prince; *Uther P~*: see UTHER. [Welsh, = 'chief leader', f. *pen* head, *dragon* dragon standard, f. L *draco* dragon, standard of cohort]

pĕn'dūlāte *v.i.* Swing like a pendulum.

pĕn'dūline *adj.* (Of nest) suspended; (of bird) building such nest.

pĕn'dūlous *adj.* Suspended, hanging down; oscillating. **pĕn'dūlously** *adv.*

pĕn'dūlum *n.* Body suspended so as to be free to swing, esp. rod with weighted end regulating movement of clock's works (ill. CLOCK); person, thing, that oscillates; *swing of the* ~, alternation of power between political parties etc.; (billiards) ~ *cannon*, ~ *stroke*, succession of cannons off two balls jammed in pocket-mouth.

Pėnĕl'opė. (In Odyssey) wife of Odysseus; when her husband did not return after fall of Troy, she told her importunate suitors that she would marry one of them when she had finished the piece of weaving on which she was engaged, but every night she undid the work that she had done during the day.

pĕnėtrāl'ia *n.pl.* Innermost shrine or recesses.

pĕn'ėtrāte *v.* Find access into or through, pass through; make a way (*with, through, to*); (of sight) pierce through; permeate; imbue (*with*); (fig.) see into, find out, discern (design, the truth, etc.); *penetrating*, gifted with or suggestive of insight; (of voice etc.) easily heard through or above other sounds. **pĕnėtrabĭl'ity, pĕnėtrā'tion** *ns.* **pĕn'ėtrable, pĕn'ėtrative** *adjs.*

pĕng'ö (-ngg-) *n.* Hungarian monetary unit, current 1925–46; replaced by FORINT.

pĕng'uin (-nggw-) *n.* Any bird of the family *Spheniscidae*, including several genera of sea-birds of the southern hemisphere, with wings reduced to scaly 'flippers' with which they swim under water.

pē'nial *adj.* Of the penis.

pĕn'icillate *adj.* (biol.) Furnished with, forming, small tuft(s); marked with streaks as of pencil or brush.

pĕnicĭll'in *n.* Substance obtained from the mould *Penicillium notatum*, effective against many micro-organisms of disease; the first ANTIBIOTIC to be used therapeutically (during war of 1939–45). [L *penicillus* painter's brush, f. brush-like sporangia of the mould]

pėnin'sūla *n.* Piece of land almost surrounded by water, or projecting far into the sea; *the P~*, Spain and Portugal; in war of 1914–18, Gallipoli.

pėnin'sular *adj.* Of (the nature of) a peninsula; of the Peninsula; *P~ War*, that carried on in the Peninsula (1808–14) between French under Napoleon and English, Spanish, and Portuguese under Wellington; *P~ State*, pop. name of Florida, U.S. ~ *n.* Inhabitant of a peninsula.

pėnin'sūlāte *v.t.* Make (land) into a peninsula.

pē'nis *n.* Intromittent copulatory organ of male animal (ill. PELVIS).

pĕn'itent *adj.* That repents, contrite. ~ *n.* Repentant sinner; person doing penance under direction of confessor; (pl.) various R.C. congregations or orders associated for mutual discipline, giving religious aid to criminals etc. **pĕn'itently** *adv.* **pĕn'itence** *n.*

pĕnitĕn'tial (-shl) *adj.* Of penitence or penance; ~ *psalms*, Ps. vi, xxxii, xxxviii, li, cii, cxxx, cxliii. **pĕnitĕn'tially** *adv.*

pĕnitĕn'tiary (-sha-) *n.* 1. Office in papal court deciding questions of penance, dispensations, etc.; *Grand P~*, cardinal presiding over this. 2. Asylum for penitent prostitutes; reformatory prison; (U.S.) state prison. ~ *adj.* Of penance; of reformatory treatment of criminals.

Pĕnn, William (1644–1718). English Quaker, founder of Pennsylvania, 1681.

Penn., Penna *abbrevs.* Pennsylvania.

pĕnn'ant *n.* = PENDANT, sense 2; PENNON; (U.S.) flag awarded as distinction.

pĕnn'ifōrm *adj.* (biol.) Having the form or appearance of a feather.

pĕnn'ilėss *adj.* Having no money; poor, destitute.

Pĕnn'ine Chain. System of hills in N. England, running northwards from the PEAK to the Lake District.

pĕnn'on *n.* Long narrow flag, triangular or swallow-tailed (ill. FLAG), esp. as military ensign of lancer regiments; long pointed streamer of ship; flag.

Pĕnnsy̆lvān'ia. Middle Atlantic State of U.S.; one of the original 13 colonies; capital, Harrisburg. [named 1681 in honour of Admiral Sir William *Penn*, father of William PENN, founder of the colony]

pĕnn'y *n.* (pl. *pence* of amounts, *pennies* of individual coins as such). Bronze coin worth $\frac{1}{12}$ of shilling or $\frac{1}{240}$ of POUND[1]; after numeral written *d.* (= DENARIUS); (bibl.) denarius; *a pretty* ~, a good sum of money; *turn an honest* ~, make something by an odd job; ~-*a-line*, (of writing) cheap, superficial; ~-*a-liner*, hack writer; ~-*bank*, savings bank at which sums as low as 1*d.* may be deposited; ~-*farthing*, early kind of bicycle with large front wheel and small rear one; ~-*in-the-slot*, (of mechanical devices esp. for the automatic supply of commodities) actuated by the fall of a penny inserted through a slot; ~ *post*, post for conveyance of letters at ordinary charge of 1*d*., esp. that established in the United Kingdom on 10th Jan. 1840 on the initiative of Rowland Hill; *penn'yweight*, (abbrev. *dwt*), measure of weight, 24 grains, $\frac{1}{20}$ of an ounce troy; ~ *wise*, (over-) careful in small expenditures; *penn'ywort* (-wert), plant (*Cotyledon Umbilicus*, wall pennywort) with rounded concave leaves, growing in crevices of rocks and walls; small umbelliferous herb (*Hydrocotyle vulgaris*, marsh or water pennywort) with rounded leaves, growing in marshy places; *penn'yworth*, *penn'orth* (-nerth), as much as can be bought for a penny.

pĕnnўroy'al *n*. Kind of mint (*Mentha pulegium*) with small leaves and prostrate habit, formerly cultivated for its supposed medicinal virtues.

pēnŏl'ogy *n*. Study of punishment and of prison management. **pēnolŏ'gical** *adj*. **pēnŏl'ogist** *n*.

pĕn'sile *adj*. Hanging down, pendulous; (of bird etc.) that constructs pensile nest.

pĕn'sion (-shn) *n*. 1. Periodical (usu. annual) payment made esp. by government, company, or employer, in consideration of past services, relinquishment of rights, disablement, widowhood, etc.; periodical payment to person who is not professed servant or employee for goodwill, secret service, etc., or to artists, scientists, etc., to enable them to carry on work of public interest; *Old-Age P~*, weekly payment by government to various classes of people, under the National Insurance Act. 2. Consultative assembly of members of Gray's Inn. 3. (pahṅ'syawṅ) Boarding-house where a fixed rate for board and lodging is charged. ~ *v.t.* Grant pension to; buy over with pension; ~ *off*, dismiss with pension. **pĕn'sionable** (-shon-) *adj*. Entitled, entitling person, to pension.

pĕn'sionary (-shon-) *n*. Recipient of a pension; creature, hireling; (hist.) chief municipal magistrate of Dutch city; *Grand P~*, first minister of Holland and Zealand (1619–1794). ~ *adj*. Of a pension.

pĕn'sioner (-shon-) *n*. Recipient of pension; hireling, creature; (Camb. Univ.) undergraduate who is not a scholar on the foundation of a college, or a sizar, but pays for his own commons etc.

pĕn'sive *adj*. Plunged in thought; melancholy. **pĕn'sively** *adv*. **pĕn'sivenėss** *n*.

pĕn'stŏck *n*. Sluice, flood-gate (ill. HYDRO-ELECTRIC).

pĕnt *adj*. Closely confined, shut *in* or *up*.

pent(a)- *prefix*. Five.

pĕn'tachord (-k-) *n*. Musical instrument with 5 strings; system or series of 5 notes (ill. MODE).

pĕn'tacle *n*. Figure used as symbol, esp. in magic; prop. = pentagram.

pĕn'tăd *n*. Number, group, of 5.

pĕn'tagon *n*. Five-sided (usu. plane rectilineal) figure; *The P~*, the U.S. Department of Defence at Washington, from the shape of its building. **pĕntăg'onal** *adj*.

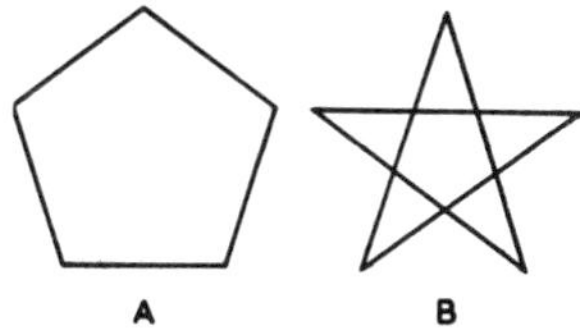

A. PENTAGON. B. PENTAGRAM

pĕn'tagrăm *n*. Five-pointed star formed by producing sides of pentagon both ways till they intersect, formerly used as mystic symbol.

pĕntahĕd'ron *n*. Solid figure of 5 faces; **pĕntahĕd'ral** *adj*.

pĕntăm'erous *adj*. (bot.) Having parts of flower-whorl 5 in number; (zool.) consisting of 5 joints.

pĕntăm'eter *n*. 1. In Greek and Latin prosody, verse composed of two equal parts each having 2½ dactylic feet, thus:

–⏖ | –⏖ | –‖ –⏑⏑ | –⏑⏑ | ⏓

(spondees may be substituted for dactyls in the first half); used alternately with hexameter to form elegiac couplet. 2. In English prosody, line of verse of 5 feet, e.g. 'heroic' or iambic verse of 10 syllables, thus:

⏑/ | ⏑/ | ⏑/ |

pĕn'tāne *n*. Any of a group of paraffin hydrocarbons containing 5 carbon atoms, including several colourless volatile liquids occurring in petroleum.

pĕn'tateuch (-tūk) *n*. First 5 books of O.T. (Genesis, Exodus, Leviticus, Numbers, Deuteronomy) traditionally ascribed to Moses. **pĕn'tateuchal** *adj*.

pĕntăth'lŏn *n*. 1. In ancient Greece, athletic contest of 5 events in each of which the same competitors took part (foot race, long jump, javelin-throwing, discus-throwing, wrestling). 2. Similar contest in modern Olympic Games (races of 200 and 1500 metres, long jump, javelin, discus).

pĕntatŏm'ic *adj*. (chem.) Containing 5 atoms in the molecule.

pĕntatŏn'ic *adj*. (mus.) Consisting of 5 notes or sounds; ~ *scale*, scale without semitones (ill. SCALE).

pĕntăv'alent *adj*. (chem.) Having a VALENCY of 5; quinquivalent.

Pĕn'tėcŏst. 1. Jewish harvest festival observed on 50th day after the 2nd day of Passover (Lev. xxiii. 15, 16). 2. Festival of Christian Church on 7th Sunday after Easter (Whit Sunday), commemorating descent of Holy Spirit upon disciples on day of Pentecost (Acts ii). **pĕntėcŏs'tal** *adj*. [Gk *pentēkostē* (*hēmera*) fiftieth (day)]

Pĕntĕl'icus, Mt. Mountain NE. of Athenian plain, famous for its marble, milky-white but weathering to golden-brown, used for many of chief buildings and sculptures of ancient Athens.

Pĕnthĕsilē'a. (Gk legend) Queen of Amazons; came to help of Troy after death of Hector and was slain by Achilles.

pĕnt'house (-t-h-) *n*. Sloping roof, esp. as subsidiary structure attached to wall of main building; awning, canopy, or the like; (U.S.) separate flat, house, or other structure on roof of block of flats or other building.

Pĕnt'land Fīrth. Channel separating Orkney Islands from mainland of Scotland.

Pĕnt'land Hills. Range of rounded hills in Midlothian, Lanark, and Peeblesshire, Scotland.

pĕn'tōde *n*. Electronic amplifying valve with 5 main electrodes.

Pĕn'tonville. Prison in Islington, London.

pĕntstēm'on (*or* pĕnt'-) *n*. Genus of Amer. herbaceous plants allied to foxglove with showy flowers, usu. tubular and two-lipped.

pėnŭlt'(ĭmate) *adjs*. Last but one. ~ *ns*. Last syllable but one.

pėnŭm'bra *n*. Partly shaded region around shadow of opaque body, esp. round total shadow of moon or earth in eclipse (ill. ECLIPSE); lighter outer part of sunspot; partial shadow. **pėnŭm'bral** *adj*.

pėnūr'ious *adj*. Poor, scanty; stingy, grudging. **pėnūr'iously** *adv*. **pėnūr'iousnėss** *n*.

pĕn'ūry *n*. Destitution, poverty; lack, scarcity, (*of*).

peon (pūn, pē'on) *n*. 1. In India, office-messenger, attendant, orderly. 2. In Span. Amer., day-labourer; in Mexico etc., debtor held in servitude by creditor until debts are worked off. **pē'onage** *n*. Employment, service, of peons.

pē'ony *n*. (Flower of) plant of genus *Paeonia* with large, handsome, crimson, pink, or white, globular, flowers, in cultivation freq. double.

people (pē'pl) *n*. Persons composing community, race, or nation; the persons belonging to a place or forming a company or class etc.; subjects of king etc.; congregation of parish priest etc.; one's parents or other relatives; *the* commonalty; *the* body of enfranchised or qualified citizens; persons in general; *People's Charter*: see CHARTER; *People's Palace*, East London institution with library, entertainments, educational classes, etc., for the use of the working classes; the *People's Palace Technical Schools*, after several changes, are now a school of the Univ. of Lond., called *Queen Mary College.* ~ *v.t.* Fill with people, populate, fill (place *with*); inhabit, occupy, fill (esp. in past part.).

pĕp *n.* (orig. U.S. slang) Vigour, go, spirit. ~ *v.t.* Fill *up* or inspire with energy and vigour. [abbrev. of *pepper*]

P.E.P. *abbrev.* Political and Economic Planning.

Pĕp'ĭn, Pĭppĭn. Name of several members of the Carolingian family. *Pepin I* (of Landen) (d. 639), Frankish mayor of the palace; *Pepin II* (of Héristal) (d. 714), Frankish ruler, father of Charles Martel; *Pepin III* 'the Short' (714–68), Frankish king, younger son of Charles Martel and father of Charlemagne.

pĕpp'er *n.* Pungent aromatic condiment got from dried berries of plants of genus *Piper*, used whole (*peppercorns*) or ground into powder; climbing shrub (*P. nigrum*, black ~) of East Indies, cultivated also in W. Indies, from which this is chiefly got; (fruit of) various species of *Capsicum*; (fig.) anything pungent; *black* ~, most usual form of the condiment, prepared from slightly unripe berries; *white* ~, milder form prepared from ripe berries, or from black by removing outer husk; *red* ~, CAYENNE pepper; (large red or yellow edible fruit of) *Capsicum annuum*; ~*-and-salt*, (cloth) of dark and light wools woven together, showing small dots of dark and light intermingled; ~*-box*, small usu. round box with perforated lid for sprinkling pepper; irregular buttress in Eton fives-court; ~*-castor, -caster*, pepper-box; *pepp'ercorn*, dried berry of black pepper, esp. as nominal rent; ~*-pot*, pepper-castor. ~ *v.t.* Sprinkle, treat, with pepper; besprinkle as with pepper; pelt with missiles; punish severely.

pĕpp'ermĭnt *n.* (Kind of mint, *Mentha piperita*, cultivated for its) essential oil, with characteristic pungent aromatic flavour leaving after-sensation of coolness; sweet flavoured with this.

pĕpp'ery *adj.* Of, like, abounding in, pepper; (fig.) pungent, stinging, hot-tempered.

pĕp'sĭn *n.* Enzyme contained in gastric juice, converting proteins into peptones in presence of dilute acid.

pĕp'tĭc *adj.* Digestive; ~ *glands*, those secreting gastric juice; ~ *ulcer*, any ulcer of the digestive system.

pĕp'tōne *n.* Any of a class of easily soluble albuminoid substances into which proteins are converted by action of pepsin etc. **pĕp'tonīze** *v.t.* (esp.) Subject (food) to artificial process of partial digestion, as aid to weak digestion.

Pepys (pēps), Samuel (1633–1703). English diarist; secretary of Admiralty 1673–9, 1684–8.

pėr *prep.* 1. Through, by means of (esp. in L phrases, for which see entries); ~ *post*, by post; *as* ~ *usual*, (joc.) as usual. 2. For each; — ~ *cent*, (symbol %) (so much) in every hundred; ~ *head*, for each person; ~ *hour*, in each hour (of speed); ~ *second per second*, (abbrev. per sec./sec.) per second every second (of rate of acceleration).

per- *prefix.* Completely, very; to destruction, to the bad; (in chem. compounds) denoting maximum of some element in combination.

pĕradvĕn'ture *adv.* (archaic) Perhaps. ~ *n.* Uncertainty, chance, conjecture; *beyond, without*, (*all*) ~, without doubt.

perai (-rī'), **pĭranha** (-ahn'ya), **pĭraya** (-rah'ya) *ns.* Tropical Amer. voracious freshwater fish (*Serrasalmo piraya*) with serrated belly and strong lancet-shaped teeth.

perăm'būlāte *v.t.* Walk through, over, or about; travel through and inspect (territory); formally establish boundaries of (parish etc.) by walking round them. **perămbūlā'tion** *n.* **perăm'būlatory** *adj.*

perăm'būlātor *n.* Hand carriage for one or two children, usu. with four wheels, pushed from behind.

pėr ănn'um. (So much) by the year.

percāle' *n.* Plain-woven cotton fabric resembling calico, but finer and wider.

perceive' (-sēv) *v.t.* Apprehend with the mind, observe, understand; apprehend through one of the senses, esp. sight.

percĕn'tage *n.* Rate, proportion, per cent; (loosely) proportion.

pėr'cept *n.* (philos.) Object of perception; mental product, as opp. to action, of perceiving. **percĕp'tūal** *adj.*

percĕp'tĭble *adj.* That can be perceived by senses or intellect. **percĕptĭbĭl'ĭty** *n.* **percĕp'tĭbly** *adv.*

percĕp'tion *n.* 1. Act, faculty, of perceiving; intuitive recognition (*of*); (philos.) action by which the mind refers its sensations to external object as cause. 2. (law) Collection (of rents etc.). **percĕp'tional** (-shon-) *adj.* **percĕp'tive** *adj.* **percĕp'tĭvely** *adv.* **percĕp'tĭvenėss** *n.* **pėrcĕptĭv'ĭty** *n.*

Pėr'cėval, Sir. Hero of a group of folk-tales later associated with the Arthurian cycle; in later versions, one of the knights successful in the quest for the HOLY GRAIL.

pėrch[1] *n.* Common European spiny-finned freshwater fish (*Perca fluviatilis*) used as food; N. Amer. species, *P. americana* (yellow ~).

pėrch[2] *n.* 1. Horizontal bar for bird to rest upon; anything serving for this; (fig.) elevated or secure position. 2. Centre pole of some four-wheeled vehicles; horizontal bar used in softening leather. 3. (also *pole, rod*) Measure of length, esp. for land, 5½ yds; (*square*) ~, 30¼ sq. yds; see Appendix X. ~ *v.* Alight, rest, as bird (*upon* bough etc.) settle, alight (*upon*); place (as) upon perch. **pėrch'er** *n.* Passerine bird with feet adapted for perching.

perchance' (-ahns) *adv.* By chance (archaic); possibly, maybe.

percheron (pār'sherawn) *n.* Strong swift horse of breed originating in le Perche, district in department of Orne, N. France.

percĭp'ĭent *adj.* Perceiving, conscious. ~ *n.* One who perceives, esp. (telepathy etc.) something outside range of senses. **percĭp'ĭence** *n.*

pėr'colāte *v.* Filter, ooze, through (freq. fig.); permeate; strain (liquid etc.) through pores etc. **pėrcolā'tion** *n.*

pėr'colātor *n.* (esp.) Apparatus for making coffee by allowing water to filter repeatedly through ground coffee.

pėr cŏn'tra. (On) the opposite side (of an account etc.).

percŭss' *v.t.* (med.) Tap gently with finger or instrument for purposes of diagnosis etc.

percŭ'ssion (-shn) *n.* Forcible striking of one (usu. solid) body against another; (med.) percussing; ~ *instruments*, (mus.) those played by percussion, esp. those struck with a stick or the hand (drum, triangle, tambourine) or struck together in pairs (cymbals); ~ *cap*, small copper cap or cylinder in fire-arm, containing fulminating powder and exploded by percussion of a hammer. **percŭss'ĭve** *adj.*

Pėr'cy[1], Sir Henry (1366–1403), called Hotspur. Eldest son of 1st Earl of Northumberland; helped to place Henry IV on throne; revolted, 1403, and was killed at battle of Shrewsbury.

Pėr'cy[2], Thomas (1768–1808). English antiquary; editor of 'Reliques of Ancient English Poetry', a collection of ballads, metrical romances, and historical songs.

pėr dĭ'ĕm. (So much) by the day.

perdĭ'tion *n.* Eternal death, damnation.

perdū(e)' *adj.* Hidden; (mil.) placed as an outpost in hiding (esp. in *lie* ~).

perdūr'able *adj.* Permanent; eternal; durable. **perdūrabĭl'ĭty** *n.* **perdūr'ably** *adv.*

pĕ'rėgrĭn(e) *adj.* & *n.* Foreign, outlandish (archaic); ~ (*falcon*), species of falcon (*Falco peregrinus*) esteemed for hawking (so called because the young were not taken from the nests but caught on their passages from their breeding-places).

pĕ'rėgrĭnāte *v.i.* (now joc.) Travel, journey. **pĕrėgrĭnā'tion** *n.*

Père Lachaise: see LACHAISE.

pĕ'remptory (*or* perĕmp'-) *adj.* 1. Decisive, final; esp. (law) ~

mandamus, in which the command is absolute, ~ *writ*, enforcing defendant's appearance without option. 2. (Of statement or command) admitting no denial or refusal; absolutely fixed, essential; (of person etc.) dogmatic, imperious, dictatorial. **pĕ'remptorĭly** *adv.* **pĕ'remptorĭnėss** *n.*

perĕnn'ĭal *adj.* Lasting through the year; (of stream) flowing through all seasons of the year; lasting long or for ever; (of plant) living several years (cf. ANNUAL). ~ *n.* Perennial plant. **perĕnn'ĭally** *adv.*

pẽr'fėct *adj.* 1. Complete, not deficient; faultless; (of lesson) thoroughly learned; thoroughly trained or skilled (*in*); exact, precise; entire, unqualified. 2. (gram., of tense) Denoting completed event or action viewed in relation to the present; *future* ~, expressing action completed at the time indicated. 3. (bot.) Having all four whorls of the flower; (mus., of interval) not augmented or diminished, in normal form (ill. INTERVAL); ~ *cadence*, one consisting of direct chord of tonic preceded by dominant or subdominant chord. **pẽr'fėctly** *adv.* **pẽr'fėctnėss** *n.* **pẽr'fėct** *n.* Perfect tense. **perfĕct'** *v.t.* Complete, carry through; make perfect; improve. **perfĕctibĭl'ĭty** *n.*

perfĕc'tion *n.* Completion; making perfect; full development; faultlessness; perfect person or thing; highest pitch, extreme, perfect specimen or manifestation (*of*); (with pl.) accomplishment.

perfĕc'tionist (-shon-) *n.* One who holds that perfection may be attained in religion, morals, politics, etc.; one who insists upon perfection; *P*~, member of communistic community established at ONEIDA Creek, N.Y. (1848–79). **perfĕc'tionism** *n.*

perfĕc'tō *n.* (U.S.) Large thick cigar tapering to point at both ends.

perfẽrv'ĭd *adj.* Very fervid.

pẽr'fĭdy *n.* Breach of faith, treachery. **perfĭd'ĭous** *adj.* **perfĭd'ĭously** *adv.* **perfĭd'ĭousnėss** *n.*

perfŏl'iate *adj.* (bot.) Having the stalk apparently passing through the leaf (ill. LEAF).

pẽr'forāte *v.* Make hole(s) through, pierce; esp. make rows of holes in (sheet) to separate stamps, coupons, etc.; make an opening into; pass, extend, through; penetrate (*into*, *through*, etc.). **pẽrforā'tion** *n.*

perfôrce' *adv.* Of necessity.

perfôrm' *v.* Carry into effect (command, promise, task, etc.); go through, execute (public function, play, piece of music, etc.); act in play, sing, etc.; (of trained animals) execute feats or tricks, esp. at public show. **perfôrm'er** *n.* **perfôrm'ing** *adj.*

perfôrm'ance *n.* Execution (*of* command etc.); carrying out, doing; notable feat; performing of play, public exhibition.

pẽr'fūme *n.* Odorous fumes of burning substance; sweet smell; smell; fluid containing essence of flowers etc., scent. **pẽr'fūmelėss** *adj.* **perfūme'** (*or* pẽrf'-) *v.t.* Impart sweet scent to, impregnate with sweet smell (esp. in past part.).

perfūm'er *n.* Maker, seller, of perfumes. **perfūm'ery** *n.*

perfŭnc'tory *adj.* Done merely for sake of getting through a duty, acting thus, superficial, mechanical. **perfŭnc'torĭly** *adv.* **perfŭnc'torĭnėss** *n.*

perfūse' (-z) *v.t.* Besprinkle (*with*); cover, suffuse; pour (water etc.) through or over. **perfū'sion** (-zhn) *n.* **perfūs'ĭve** *adj.*

Pẽrg'amēne *adj.* & *n.* (Native, inhabitant) of Pergamum.

Pẽrg'amum. (mod. *Bergama*) Ancient city of NW. Asia Minor, the capital of the Attalid kings (3rd–2nd c. B.C.), under whom it became a centre of art and learning, and manufactured parchment for the books of its famous library.

pẽrg'ola *n.* Arbour, covered walk, formed of growing plants trained over trellis-work.

Pergoles'e (-lāz'ĕ), Giovanni Battista (1710–36). Italian composer of cantatas, operas, and much sacred music, of which his 'Stabat Mater' is best known.

pergŭnn'ah, pergan'a (-gŭ-) *ns.* Division of territory in India, group of villages.

perhăps' (*colloq.* prăps) *adv.* It may be, possibly.

pẽr'ĭ *n.* (Pers. myth.) Fairy, good (orig. evil) genius, beautiful being.

pĕri- *prefix.* Round, about.

pĕ'rĭanth *n.* Outer part or envelope of flower, enclosing stamens and pistils (ill. FLOWER); corolla and calyx, or either of these.

pĕ'rĭăpt *n.* Thing worn about the person as charm, amulet.

pĕricârd'ium *n.* Membranous sac enclosing heart. **pĕricârd'ĭăc, pĕricârd'ĭal** *adjs.*

pĕ'rĭcârp *n.* Wall of ripened ovary of plant (ill. SEED).

pĕrĭchŏn'drĭum (-k-) *n.* Membrane enveloping cartilages (except at joints).

pĕ'rĭclāse *n.* Mineral consisting of magnesia with small admixture of iron protoxide, found in greenish crystals or grains in ejected masses of crystalline limestone at Vesuvius etc.

Pĕ'rĭclēs (-z) (*c* 492–429 B.C.). Athenian statesman and military commander, under whose administration (460–429 B.C.) Athens reached the summit of her power. **Pĕrĭclē'an** *adj.*

pĕrĭclīn'al *adj.* (geol.) Dome-like.

perĭc'opė *n.* Short passage, paragraph; portion of Scripture read in public worship.

pĕrĭcrān'ium *n.* Membrane enveloping skull; (joc.) skull, brain; intellect.

perĭd'ium *n.* (bot.) Outer envelope, enclosing spores, of some fungi.

pĕ'rĭdŏt *n.* (Jewellers' name for) olivine, kind of chrysolite.

pĕ'rĭgee (-jē) *n.* That point in planet's (esp. moon's) orbit at which it is nearest to earth (opp. to *apogee*). **pĕrĭgē'an** *adj.*

Périgord (-ĭgôr'). District (ancient province) in SW. France; ~ *pie*, meat pie flavoured with truffles.

perĭ'gy̆nous (-j-) *adj.* (of stamens) Situated around pistil or ovary; (of flower) having such stamens (ill. FLOWER).

pĕrĭhēl'ion (-yon) *n.* That point in planet's orbit at which it is nearest to sun (opp. to *aphelion*).

pĕ'rĭl *n.* Danger, risk. **pĕ'rĭlous** *adj.* **pĕ'rĭlously** *adv.* **pĕ'rĭlousnėss** *n.*

perĭm'ėter *n.* 1. Circumference, outline, of closed figure; length of this; ~ *track*, concrete runway round an airfield. 2. Instrument for measuring the field of vision. **perĭm'etry** *n.* Such measurement.

pĕrĭnē'um *n.* (anat.) Lower end of trunk with its contents, extending from coccyx or tail-bone to pubic symphysis (ill. PELVIS). **pĕrĭnē'al** *adj.*

pẽr'iod *n.* 1. Round of time marked by recurrence of astronomical coincidences; time of planet's revolution; time during which disease runs its course; (pl.) menses. 2. Indefinite portion of history, life, etc.; any portion of time; (attrib., esp. of furniture, architecture, etc.) of, characteristic of, a particular (past) period. 3. Complete sentence, esp. one of several clauses; (pl.) rhetorical language; full pause at end of sentence, full stop (.) marking this; set of figures marked (by comma etc.) in large number, as in numeration, recurring decimals, etc.; *put a* ~ *to*, bring to an end.

pẽrĭŏd'ic *adj.* 1. Of revolution of heavenly body (~ *motion*); recurring at (regular) intervals. 2. Expressed in (rhetorical) periods. 3. (chem.) ~ *law*, statement of fact that properties of chemical elements are periodic functions of their atomic weights, i.e. that when they are arranged in order of those weights, elements having similar chemical and physical properties occur at regular intervals; ~ *table*, table of chemical elements illustrating this law. **pẽrĭodĭ'cĭty** *n.*

pẽrĭŏd'ĭcal *adj.* = Periodic 1; (of magazine, miscellany, etc.) published at regular intervals, e.g. monthly. ~ *n.* Periodical magazine etc.

pĕrĭŏs'tėum *n.* Dense fibrovascular membrane enveloping bones (except where they are covered by cartilage), from inner layer of which bone-substance is produced (ill. BONE). **pĕrĭŏs′tėal** *adj.*

pĕrĭpatĕt′ĭc *adj.* 1. Of the school of Aristotle, Aristotelian (from Aristotle's custom of teaching while walking in the Lyceum at Athens). 2. Walking from place to place on one's business, itinerant. **pĕrĭpatĕt′ĭcally** *adv.* **pĕrĭpatĕt′ĭc** *n.* Aristotelian, (chiefly joc.) itinerant dealer.

pĕrĭpėtei′a (-ĭa, -ēa), **-tī′a** *n.* Sudden change of fortune in drama or life.

perĭph′ery *n.* Bounding line esp. of closed curvilinear figure; external boundary or surface. **perĭph′eral** *adj.* **perĭph′erally** *adv.*

perĭph′rasĭs *n.* (pl. *-es* pr. -ēz). Roundabout way of speaking, circumlocution; roundabout phrase. **pĕrĭphrăs′tĭc** *adj.* **pĕrĭphrăs′tĭcally** *adv.*

perĭp′teral *adj.* (archit.) Surrounded by a single row of columns (ill. TEMPLE).

perique′ (-ēk) *n.* Kind of dark strong-flavoured Louisiana tobacco.

pĕ′rĭscōpe *n.* Apparatus of tube and mirrors giving view of things above surface to observer

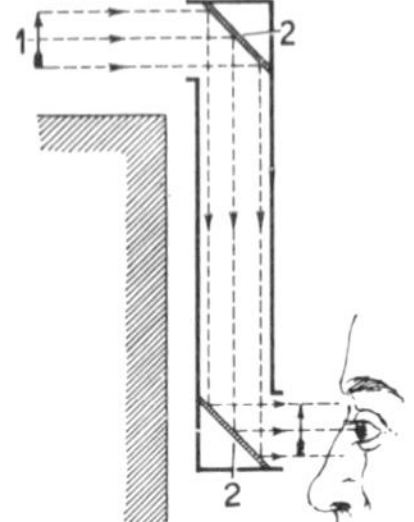

DIAGRAM OF A PERISCOPE

1. Object. 2. Mirrors reflecting at 90° rays of light from object

in submarine or trench, or enabling person to see over the heads of others in a crowd. **pĕrĭscŏp′ĭc** *adj.* Enabling one to see distinctly for some distance round axis of vision.

pĕ′rĭsh *v.* Suffer destruction, lose life, come to untimely end; (of cold or exposure) reduce to distress or inefficiency (usu. in pass.). **pĕ′rĭshĭng** *adj.* (of cold etc.). **pĕ′rĭshĭngly** *adv.*

pĕ′rĭshable *adj.* Liable to perish; subject to speedy decay. **pĕ′rĭshables** *n.pl.* Things, esp. foodstuffs in transit, of this nature.

pĕ′rĭspẽrm *n.* (bot.) Nutritive tissue outside embryo-sac in some seeds.

pĕ′rĭspōme, pĕrĭspōm′ėnon (pl. *-ena*) *adjs.* & *ns.* (Gk gram.) (Word) with circumflex accent on last syllable.

perĭs′talĭth *n.* (archaeol.) Ring of standing stones round burial-mound etc.

perĭstăl′sĭs *n.* (physiol.) Automatic muscular movement consisting of successive waves of contraction and relaxation, by which contents of alimentary canal etc. are propelled along it. **pĕrĭstăl′tĭc** *adj.* **pĕrĭstăl′tĭcally** *adv.*

pĕrĭsterŏn′ĭc *adj.* Of pigeons.

pĕ′rĭstōme *n.* 1. (bot.) Fringe of small teeth round mouth of capsule in mosses. 2. (zool.) Part round mouth in various invertebrates (ill. PROTOZOA).

pĕ′rĭstȳle *n.* Row of columns surrounding temple, court, cloister, etc. (ill. TEMPLE); space so surrounded.

pĕrĭthē′cium *n.* (pl. *-cia*). (bot.) Cup-shaped or flask-shaped receptacle enclosing fructification in certain fungi.

pĕrĭtonē′um *n.* (anat.) Double serous membrane lining cavity of abdomen, of complex form, with numerous folds investing and supporting abdominal viscera (ill. ABDOMEN). **pĕrĭtonē′al** *adj.* **pĕrĭtonīt′ĭs** *n.* Inflammation of (part of) peritoneum.

pĕ′rĭwĭg *n.* Wig (ill. WIG). [Fr. *perruque* peruke]

pĕ′rĭwĭnkle[1] *n.* Genus of plants (*Vinca*), esp. the European *lesser* and *greater* ~, (*V. minor*, *V. major*), evergreen trailing shrubs with light-blue starry flowers; ~ (*blue*), colour of these flowers.

pĕ′rĭwĭnkle[2] *n.* Gastropod mollusc (*Littorina*) esp. common European coast species (*L. littorea*), with dark-coloured turbinate shell, much used for food.

pẽrj′ure (-*jer*) *v.refl.* Forswear one*self*; *perjured*, guilty of perjury. **pẽrj′urer** (-*jerer*) *n.*

pẽrj′ury (-erĭ) *n.* Swearing to statement known to be false; wilful utterance of false evidence while on oath; breach of oath.

pẽrk[1] *n.* (Slang abbrev. of) PERQUISITE.

pẽrk[2] *v.* Lift (*up*) one's head, carry oneself smartly or briskly; smarten *up*; hold *up* (head, tail) self-assertively. **pẽrk′y** *adj.* Self-assertive, saucy, pert. **pẽrk′ily** *adv.* **pẽrk′ĭnėss** *n.*

Pẽrk′ĭn, Sir William Henry (1838–1907). English chemist, discoverer of aniline dyes.

pẽrl′īte *n.* Obsidian or other vitreous rock in form of enamel-like globules.

pẽrm *n.* (colloq.) Abbrev. of PERMANENT wave.

pẽrm′alloy *n.* Nickel steel alloy, containing about 78% nickel, characterized by a very high permeability in low magnetic fields, extensively used in submarine cables where this quality is valuable. [f. *perm(eable) alloy*]

pẽrm′anent *adj.* Lasting, intended to last, indefinitely; ~ *magnet*, one whose property continues after the magnetizing agent has been removed; ~ *wave*, artificial wave in hair which lasts until hair grows out; ~ *way*, finished road-bed of railway. **pẽrm′anence** *n.* Being permanent. **pẽrm′anency** *n.* Being permanent; permanent thing or arrangement.

permăn′ganate (-ngg-) *n.* (chem.) A salt of *permanganic acid* ($HMnO_4$); freq. = ~ *of potash* ($KMnO_4$), a crystalline substance, dark purple when dissolved, used as a disinfectant, stain, etc.

pẽrm′ėāte *v.* Penetrate, pervade, saturate; diffuse itself *through*, *among*, etc. **pẽrm′ėable** *adj.* **pẽrmėabĭl′ĭty** *n.*

pẽr mĕns′ĕm. (So much) by the month.

Pẽrm′ĭan *adj.* & *n.* (geol.) (Of) the geological system at the top of the Palaeozoic, i.e. above the carboniferous system and below the Triassic (ill. GEOLOGY). [f. *Perm*, former province of E. Russia]

permĭss′ĭble *adj.* Allowable. **permĭssĭbĭl′ĭty** *n.*

permĭ′ssion (-shn) *n.* Leave, licence (*to* do).

permĭss′ĭve *adj.* Giving permission; ~ *legislation*, legislation giving powers, but not enjoining their use. **permĭss′ĭvely** *adv.* **permĭss′ĭvenėss** *n.*

permĭt′ *v.* Allow; admit *of*; ~ *hours*, those during which sale of intoxicating liquor is legal.

pẽrm′ĭt *n.* Written order giving permission, esp. for landing or removal of dutiable goods, entry into a place etc.

pẽrmūtā′tion *n.* (math.) Variation of order of a set of things lineally arranged; each of different arrangement of which such a set is capable; (rare) change, alteration.

permūte′ *v.t.* Put in different order, change sequence of (things etc.).

pẽrn *n.* Bird of genus *Pernis*, honey-buzzard.

pernĭ′cious (-sh*us*) *adj.* Destructive, ruinous, fatal; ~ *anaemia*, progressive and, unless checked, fatal form of anaemia. **pernĭ′ciously** *adv.* **pernĭ′ciousnėss** *n.*

pernĭck′ėty *adj.* (colloq.) Fastidious; ticklish, requiring careful handling.

pẽrnŏctā′tion *n.* Passing the night; (eccles.) all-night vigil.

Per′on (pārŏn′), Juan Domingo (1895–). Argentinian general; seized government and became dictator 1943; twice elected president; exiled, after a revolution, 1955. **Peronĭs′ta** *adj.* & *n.* Supporting, supporter of, Peron.

pĕ′rorāte *v.i.* Sum up and conclude speech; speak at length. **pĕrorā′tion** *n.*

perŏx′īde *n.* (chem.) Compound of oxygen with another element containing greatest possible proportion of oxygen; esp. = ~ *of hydrogen* (H_2O_2), colourless liquid, used in aqueous solution as oxidizing and bleaching agent and antiseptic, in pure state a concentrated source of oxygen used in high-altitude rockets, submarine propulsion, etc.

perpĕnd′ *v.t.* (archaic) Ponder, consider.

pĕrpendĭc′ūlar *adj.* 1. At right angles to plane of horizon; (loosely) very steep; erect, upright; (joc.) in standing position. 2. (geom.) At right angles (*to* given line, plane, or surface). 3. (archit., *P∼*) Of the style of English Gothic architecture prevailing from the middle of the 14th c. to the middle of the 16th c., characterized by the vertical lines of its tracery (ill. WINDOW).

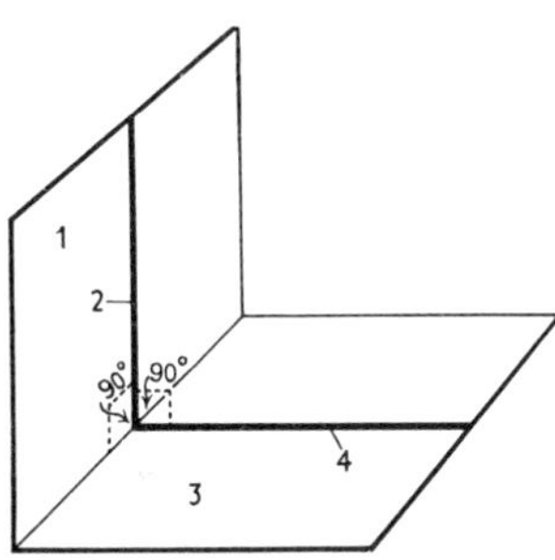

PERPENDICULAR LINES AND PLANES

1. Vertical plane. 2. Vertical line. 3. Horizontal plane. 4. Horizontal line. *1* and *2* are perpendicular to *3* and *4*

pĕrpendĭc′ūlarly *adv.* **pĕrpendĭcūlă′rĭty** *n.* **pĕrpendĭc′ūlar** *n.* Plumb-rule or other instrument for showing perpendicular line; perpendicular line; *the ∼*, perpendicular line or direction.

pĕrp′ėtrāte *v.t.* Perform, commit (crime, blunder, etc.). **pĕrpėtrā′tion, pĕrp′ėtrātor** *ns.*

perpĕt′ūal *adj.* Eternal; permanent during life; applicable, valid, for ever or for indefinite time; continuous; (colloq.) frequent, repeated; *∼ curate*: see CURATE; *∼ motion*, that of hypothetical machine that once set in motion should go on for ever unless stopped by external force or worn out. **perpĕt′ūally** *adv.*

perpĕt′ūāte *v.t.* Make perpetual; preserve from oblivion. **perpĕtūā′tion** *n.*

pĕrpėtū′ĭty *n.* Quality of being perpetual; perpetual possession or position; perpetual annuity; *in, to, for, ∼*, for ever.

perplĕx′ *v.t.* Bewilder, puzzle; complicate, confuse (matter); entangle, intertwine. **perplĕx′ėdly, perplĕx′ĭngly** *advs.*

perplĕx′ĭty *n.* Bewilderment; cause of this; entangled state.

pĕr prŏcūrātĭōn′ĕm (abbrev. *per pro(c).*, *p.p.*). By proxy, by the action of (person signing document).

pĕrq′uĭsĭte (-z-) *n.* Casual profit, esp. (law) that coming to lord of manor beyond regular revenue; thing that has served its primary use and to which subordinate or servant has then a customary right; customary gratuity.

Perrault (pĕrō′), Charles (1628–1703). French poet, critic, and author of fairy-tales.

pĕ′rry *n.* Cider-like drink from expressed fermented juice of pears.

pĕr sē. By or in itself, intrinsically.

pĕrs′ėcūte *v.t.* Pursue with enmity and injury (esp. holder of opinion held to be heretical); harass, worry; importune (*with* questions etc.). **pĕrsėcū′tion** *n.* *∼ mania*, insane delusion that one is persecuted. **pĕrs′ėcūtor** *n.*

Pĕrs′ėĭd. One of a group of shooting stars appearing yearly near beginning of August and having their radiant near the constellation Perseus.

Persĕph′onė. (Gk myth.) Daughter of Zeus and DEMETER; called by the Romans Proserpina; goddess of spring; while gathering flowers she was carried off by Hades (Pluto) and made queen of Hell; Demeter persuaded Zeus to let her return to earth for 6 (or 8) months of each year.

Persĕp′olĭs. Ruined city of S. Persia NE. of Shiraz; ancient capital of Persian Empire, under the Achaemenid kings.

Pĕrs′eus (-sūs). 1. (Gk myth.) A hero, son of Zeus and DANAE; with the help of the gods he cut off the head of the gorgon MEDUSA, and gave it to Athene; he saved ANDROMEDA from a sea-monster, married her, and founded the city of Mycenae. 2. Northern constellation between Cassiopeia and Taurus.

pĕrsėvēr′ance *n.* Steadfast pursuit of an aim, constant persistence; (theol.) continuance in state of grace.

pĕrsėvēre′ *v.i.* Continue steadfastly, persist (*in, with*). **pĕrsėvēr′ĭngly** *adv.*

Pĕr′sia (-sha). Kingdom of W. Asia, also called *Iran*, lying between Caspian Sea and Russia on N. and Persian Gulf on S.; capital, Tehran. **Pĕr′sian** (-shn) *adj.* & *n.* (Native, inhabitant) of Persia; (of) its language; the most important member of the Iranian branch of the Indo-European family; *∼ blinds*, PERSIENNES; *∼ carpet, rug*, carpet or rug made in Persia, usu. oblong, of very fine skilful weave, of silk or wool pile and traditional, freq. geometrical patterns; *∼ Empire*, great empire of ancient times formed (6th c. B.C.) by conquests of Media, Lydia, and Babylonia under Cyrus, including at its greatest all western Asia, Egypt, and parts of eastern Europe, and overthrown by Alexander the Great, 331 B.C.; *∼ Gulf*, landlocked sea extending in south-easterly direction from confluence of Euphrates and Tigris and communicating with Arabian Sea through Strait of Hormuz and Gulf of Oman; *∼ lamb*, young of Persian sheep, which furnish karakul or astrakhan; esp., the finest grade of astrakhan, with silky tightly curled fur; *∼ Wars*, wars in which the Persian emperors Darius and Xerxes vainly attempted to conquer Greece (499–449 B.C., but the defeat of Xerxes at SALAMIS, 479, decided the issue).

pĕrsiĕnnes′ (-nz) *n.pl.* Outside window-blinds of light horizontal laths.

pĕrs′iflage (-flahzh) *n.* Light raillery, banter.

persimm′on *n.* Yellowish-orange plum-like astringent fruit, becoming sweet when softened by frost, of the Amer. tree *Diospyros virginiana*; large red fruit of Chinese and Japanese species, *D. Kaki.*

persĭst′ *v.i.* Continue firmly or obstinately (*in* opinion, course, etc.) esp. against remonstrance etc. **persĭs′tence, persĭs′tency** *ns.* **persĭs′tent** *adj.* (esp., of horns, hair, leaves, etc.) Remaining after such parts normally wither or fall off. **persĭs′tently** *adv.*

Pĕrs′ius. Aulus Persius Flaccus (A.D. 34–62), Roman poet and satirist.

pĕrs′on *n.* 1. Individual human being; living body of human being; (zool.) individual of a compound or colonial organism; *young ∼*, young man or (usu.) woman (and esp. when speaker does not wish to specify her social position); *in ∼*, personally, oneself. 2. (law) Human being *natural ∼*) or body corporate (*artificial ∼*) with recognized rights and duties. 3. Character in play or story. 4. (theol.) Each of three distinctions, or modes of divine being, in the Godhead, God the Father, Son, Holy Ghost. 5. (gram.) Each of three classes of personal pronouns, and corresponding distinctions in verbs, indicating the person(s) speaking (*first ∼*), spoken to (*second ∼*), and spoken of (*third ∼*).

persōn′a *n.* (pl. *-nae*). (Jungian psychol.) Outer aspect of personality as revealed to other persons.

pĕrs′onable *adj.* Handsome, comely.

pĕrs′onage *n.* Person of rank or importance; person; character in play etc.

persōn′a grāt′a. Acceptable person.

pĕrs′onal *adj.* 1. One's own, individual, private; done, made, etc., in person; *∼ equation*; see EQUATION. 2. Directed, referring (esp. hostilely) to an individual; making, given to making, personal remarks. 3. (law) *∼ property, estate*, etc., chattels or chattel interests in land, all property except land and those interests in land that pass to one's heir. 4. (gram.) Of, denoting, one of the three persons (esp. in ~ *pronoun*). **pers'onally** *adv.* In person, in one's own person; for one's own part.

personăl'ity *n.* 1. Being a person; personal existence or identity; distinctive personal character; person; *multiple* ~, (psych.) apparent existence of two or more distinct and alternating personalities in a single individual. 2. (Of remarks) fact of being personal; (usu. pl.) personal remarks.

pers'onalize *v.t.* Personify. **personalizā'tion** *n.*

pers'onalty *n.* Personal estate.

pers'onate[1] *adj.* (bot. Of two-lipped corolla) having the opening of the lips closed by upward projection of the lower (as in snapdragon).

pers'onāte[2] *v.t.* Play the part of; pretend to be (person), esp. for fraudulent purpose. **personā'tion, pers'onātor** *ns.*

persŏnificā'tion *n.* Personifying; person, thing, viewed as striking example or embodiment *of*.

persŏn'ify *v.t.* Attribute personal nature to (abstraction); symbolize (quality) by figure in human form; embody (quality) in one's own person, exemplify typically (esp. in past part.).

personnĕl' *n.* Body of persons employed in an organization, as distinct from the equipment.

perspĕc'tive *n.* The art of delineating solid objects on a plane surface so as to give the same impression of relative positions, magnitudes, etc., as the actual objects do when viewed from a particular point (ill. DRAWING); picture so drawn; apparent relation between visible objects as to position, distance, etc.; (fig.) relation in which parts of subject are viewed by the mind; view, prospect (lit. and fig.); *in* ~, drawn according to rules of perspective; foreshortened. ~ *adj.* Of, in, perspective. **perspĕc'tively** *adv.*

pers'pĕx *n.* Trade-name of a plastic material, much lighter than glass, used esp. for wind-screens and transparent parts of aircraft. [irreg. f. L *perspicere* look through]

perspicā'cious (-sh*us*) *adj.* Having mental penetration or discernment. **perspicā'ciously** *adv.* **perspică'city** *n.*

perspic'ūous *adj.* Easily understood, clearly expressed; (of person) clear in expression. **perspic'ūously** *adv.* **perspicū'ity, perspic'ūousnėss** *ns.*

perspir'able *adj.* Allowing the passage of perspiration; that can be thrown off in perspiration.

perspirā'tion *n.* Sweating; sweat. **perspir'atory** *adj.*

perspire' *v.* Sweat; give off through pores in form of vapour or moisture.

persuade' (-swād) *v.t.* Convince (person, one*self*, *of*, *that*); induce (*to* do, *into* action); *persuaded*, convinced (*of*, *that*). **persuād'able, persuās'ible** *adjs.* **persuāsibil'ity** *n.*

persuā'sion (-swāzhn) *n.* Persuading; persuasiveness; conviction; religious belief, sect holding this.

persuās'ive (-swā-) *adj.* Able to persuade, winning. **persuās'ively** *adv.* **persuās'ivenėss** *n.*

pert *adj.* Forward, saucy, in speech or conduct; (U.S. and dial.) lively, sprightly, cheerful. **pert'ly** *adv.* **pert'nėss** *n.*

pertain' *v.i.* Belong as part, appendage, or accessory, *to*; be appropriate *to*; have reference, relate, *to*.

Perth. County town of **Perth'shire,** inland county of central Scotland.

pertinā'cious (-sh*us*) *adj.* Stubborn, persistent, obstinate. **pertinā'ciously** *adv.* **pertinā'ciousnėss, pertinā'city** *ns.*

pert'inent *adj.* Pertaining, relevant, apposite, (*to* matter in hand etc.); to the point. **pert'inently** *adv.* **pert'inence, pert'inency** *ns.*

perturb' *v.t.* Throw into (physical) confusion; disturb mentally, agitate. **perturbā'tion** *n.*

Peru (perōō'). Republic of Pacific coast of S. America; inhabited during the Middle Ages by the INCAS, whose empire was conquered by Spaniards 1527–35; won independence of Spain 1821; capital, Lima.

Perugino (pĕrōōjēn'ō). Pietro Vannucci (*c* 1450–1523), Italian painter of Umbrian school, one of the masters of Raphael. [*Perugia*, Italian city]

peruke' (-ōōk) *n.* Wig (ill. WIG).

peruse' (-ōōz) *v.t.* Read thoroughly or carefully; read; examine carefully. **perus'al** *n.*

Peru'vian (-rōō-) *adj.* & *n.* Native, inhabitant) of Peru; ~ *bark*, bark of CINCHONA tree. [*Peruvia*, latinized name of PERU]

pervāde' *v.t.* Spread through, permeate, saturate. **pervā'sion** (-zhn) *n.* **pervās'ive** *adj.* **pervās'ively** *adv.* **pervās'ivenėss** *n.*

perverse' *adj.* Persistent in error; different from what is reasonable or required; wayward; peevish; perverted, wicked; (of verdict) against weight of evidence or judge's direction. **perverse'ly** *adv.* **perverse'nėss, perver'sity** *ns.*

pervert' *v.t.* Turn aside (thing) from its proper use; misconstrue, misapply (words etc.); lead astray (person, mind) from right opinion or conduct, or esp. religious belief. **perver'sion** (-shn) *n.* **pervers'ive** *adj.* **perv'ert** *n.* Perverted person; apostate; homosexual.

perv'ious *adj.* Affording passage (*to*); permeable; (fig.) accessible (*to* reason etc.). **perv'iousnėss** *n.*

pĕse'ta (-sā-) *n.* Principal monetary unit of Spain, = 100 centimos.

peshwa (pāsh'wah) *n.* (hist.) Hereditary sovereign (earlier, chief minister) of the Mahratta State. [Pers., = 'chief']

pĕs'ky *adj.* (U.S. slang). Troublesome, confounded, annoying, plaguy.

peso (pās'ō) *n.* (pl. *-s*). Principal monetary unit in Argentina, Chile, Colombia, Cuba, Dominican Republic, Mexico, Philippines, and Uruguay, = 100 centavos.

pĕss'ary *n.* Instrument, medicated plug, inserted into or worn in vagina to prevent uterine displacements etc.

pĕss'imism *n.* Tendency to look at the worst aspect of things; doctrine that this world is the worst possible, or that all things tend to evil. **pĕss'imist** *n.* **pĕssimist'ic** *adj.* **pĕssimis'tically** *adv.*

pĕss'imum *n.* Worst or most unfavourable condition, amount, or degree.

pĕst *n.* Troublesome or destructive person, animal, or thing; (now rare) pestilence.

Pĕstalŏzz'i (-tsi), Jean Henri (1746–1827). Swiss reformer of elementary education; believed the faculties should be developed in natural order, beginning with sense perception; made much use of object-lessons.

pĕs'ter *v.t.* Trouble, plague.

pĕs'ticide *n.* Substance for destroying pests, esp. insects.

pĕstif'erous *adj.* Noxious, pestilential; (fig.) having moral contagion, pernicious.

pĕs'tilence *n.* Any fatal epidemic disease, esp. bubonic plague. **pĕs'tilent** *adj.* Destructive to life, deadly; (fig.) injurious to morals etc.; (colloq.) troublesome, plaguy. **pĕs'tilently** *adv.* **pĕstilĕn'tial** (-shl) *adj.*

pĕs'tle (-sl) *n.* Club-shaped instrument for pounding substances in a mortar; various mechanical appliances for pounding, stamping, etc. ~ *v.* Pound (as) with pestle; use pestle.

pĕstŏl'ogy *n.* Study of pests (esp. harmful insects) and the methods of dealing with them.

pĕt[1] *n.* Animal tamed and kept as favourite or treated with fondness; darling, favourite (often attrib.); ~ *aversion*, what one specially dislikes; ~*-cock*, small stop-cock for draining, letting out steam, etc.; ~ *name*, one expressing fondness or familiarity. ~ *v.* Treat as a pet, fondle, caress; (U.S.) indulge in hugging, kissing, and fondling.

pĕt[2] *n.* Offence at being slighted, ill-humour.

Pet. *abbrev.* Peter (N.T.).

Pétain (pātăn), Henri Philippe Benoni Omer Joseph (1856–1951), marshal of France. Defender of Verdun, 1916; 'head of state' in VICHY France 1940–5.

pĕt′al *n.* Each of the divisions of the corolla of a flower, esp. when separate (ill. FLOWER). **pĕt′-aloid** *adj.*

pĕt′alon *n.* Gold plate worn on linen mitre of Jewish high priest.

pėtard′ *n.* Small engine of war, orig. of metal, later wooden box charged with powder, formerly used to blow in door etc.; kind of firework, cracker; *hoist with his own* ~: see HOIST[2].

pĕt′asus *n.* Ancient Greek low-crowned broad-brimmed hat, esp. as worn by Hermes; winged hat of Hermes.

pēt′er[1] *v.i.* (orig. U.S. mining colloq.) ~ *out*, give out, come to an an end.

Pēt′er[2], St. (d. *c* 67). 'Simon called Peter', one of the apostles, most prominent of the disciples during the ministry of Jesus and in the early Church; martyred, probably in Rome; in R.C. tradition, founder and first bishop of Church of Rome, and in popular belief keeper of the door of heaven; *Epistles of St.* ~, two N.T. epistles ascribed to him; ~*'s pence*, in England, annual tribute of a penny from every householder having land of a certain value, paid to the papal see at Rome from Anglo-Saxon times until discontinued by statute in 1534; also, voluntary contributions of Roman Catholics to papal treasury since 1860; *rob* ~ *to pay Paul*, take away from one person, cause, etc., to pay, give, etc., to another. [Gk *petros* rock]

Pēt′er[3], **pēt′er** *n.* 1. = BLUE peter. 2. (whist) The signal or call for trumps.

Pēt′er[4]. Name of 3 tsars of Russia: *Peter I* (1672–1725), 'the Great', reigned 1682–1725; founded St. Petersburg (Leningrad); created the Russian navy; introduced many elements of Western civilization into Russia; *Peter II* (1715–30), grandson of Peter I, reigned 1727–30; *Peter III* (1728–62) maternal grandson of Peter I, reigned 1761–2; murdered prob. by orders of his wife, CATHERINE[2] the Great.

Pēt′erhouse. College of University of Cambridge, founded first of Cambridge colleges (1284).

Pēt′er Lŏm′bard (*c* 1100–60). Bishop of Paris; author of 'Sententiae', a collection of opinions of the Fathers, dealing with God, incarnation, redemption, and the nature of the sacraments; called 'magister sententiarum'.

Pēt′erloo′. The 'Marches to Massacre' (1819), when a large and peaceable meeting in St. Peter's Fields, Manchester, assembled to petition for repeal of the Corn Laws, was violently dispersed by yeomanry and hussars, with over 600 casualties.

Pēt′er Păn. 'The boy who wouldn't grow up', hero of play (1904) of same name by J. M. Barrie.

pēt′ersham *n.* Thick ribbed stiffened cotton ribbon used for waist-bands of skirts; corded ribbon with silk or rayon warp used for hat-bands. [Viscount *Petersham*, *c* 1812]

Pēt′er the Hermit (*c* 1050–1115). French priest; preacher of First CRUSADE.

pĕt′iōle *n.* (bot.) Leaf-stalk (ill. LEAF). **pĕt′iolar, pĕt′iolate** *adjs.*

petite (petēt′) *adj. fem.* (Of woman) of small dainty build.

petit four (petē′ foor) *n.* Very small fancy cake.

pėti′tion *n.* Asking, supplication, request; formal written supplication, request; formal written supplication from one or more persons to sovereign etc.; (law) kinds of formal written application to a court; *P~ and Advice*, (hist.) remonstrance presented to Cromwell by Parliament, 1657; *P~ of Right*, (hist.) parliamentary declaration of rights and liberties of the people assented to by Charles I in 1628. ~ *v.* Make petition to (sovereign etc. *for*, *to*); ask humbly (*for*, *to*). **pėti′tionary** (-shon-) *adj.* **pėti′tioner** *n.* (esp.) Plaintiff in divorce suit.

pėti′tio prĭncĭp′iī (-shiō) *n.* Begging the question.

petit măl (petē′) *n.* Mild form of epilepsy, as dist. from *grand mal*, severe form.

petit point (petē′ pwan) *n.* Kind of embroidery stitch, tent-stitch (as dist. from *gros point* cross-stitch; ill. STITCH).

Pēt′rarch (-k). Francesco Petrarca (1304–74), Italian poet and humanist; famous for his odes and sonnets to 'Laura'. **Pėtrar′chan** *adj.* ~ *sonnet*: see SONNET.

pĕt′rel *n.* Various sea-birds of the order *Procellariiformes* (which includes also the shearwaters and

STORM PETREL
Length 6 in.

albatrosses); *storm* ~, *stormy* ~, small bird (*Hydrobates pelagicus*) with black-and-white plumage.

Pēt′riburg *abbrev.* (Bishop) of Peterborough (replacing surname in his signature).

pĕtrifăc′tion *n.* Petrifying; petrified substance or mass.

pĕt′rifȳ *v.* Convert into stone or stony substance, be so converted (esp. of dead organism becoming fossilized); (fig.) paralyse, stupefy, with astonishment, terror, etc.; deprive (mind etc.) of vitality, stiffen.

Pēt′rīne *adj.* Of St. PETER[2]; ~ *liturgy*, the Roman liturgy traditionally ascribed to St. Peter.

pĕtro- *prefix.* Rock.

pĕt′roglȳph *n.* Rock-carving (usu. prehistoric).

Pĕt′rograd (-ahd). Name of St. Petersburg from 1917 to 1924, when it was renamed LENINGRAD.

pėtrŏg′raphy *n.* Scientific description of formation and composition of rocks. **pėtrŏg′rapher** *n.* **pĕtrogrăph′ic(al)** *adjs.*

pĕt′rol *n.* (in Engl. usage, not U.S.) Low-boiling fraction of crude petroleum consisting almost entirely of a mixture of various hydrocarbons and used as a fuel in internal combustion engines; gasolene.

pėtrōl′ėum *n.* Crude oil; inflammable mineral oil, varying from light yellow to dark brown or black, found in many places in the upper strata of the earth, containing large numbers of different hydrocarbons and used esp. as source of oils for illumination and mechanical power. [L & Gk *petra* rock, L *oleum* oil]

pėtrŏl′ic *adj.* Of petrol or petroleum.

pėtrŏl′ogy *n.* Study of origin, structure, etc., of rocks. **pĕtrolŏ′gic(al)** *adjs.* **pĕtrolŏ′gically** *adv.* **pėtrŏl′ogist** *n.*

pĕt′ronel *n.* (hist.) Large pistol or carbine used esp. by horse-soldiers in 16th–17th centuries (ill. PISTOL). [Fr. *poitrine* chest (because butt-end rested against chest in firing)]

Pėtrōn′ius Ar′biter, Gaius (d. A.D. 66). Roman satirist; intimate of Nero, chosen by him as his arbiter of taste (*arbiter elegantiae*); committed suicide to avoid being killed by Nero.

pĕt′rous *adj.* Of, like, rock; esp. (anat.) applied to dense hard part of temporal bone forming protective case for internal ear.

pĕtt′icoat *n.* Woman's (under-) garment fastened round waist or suspended from shoulders and hanging loose usu. inside a skirt; woman, girl; (pl.) female sex; (attrib.) feminine; ~ *government*, predominance of woman in the home or in politics.

pĕtt′ifŏg *v.i.* Practise legal chicanery; quibble, wrangle, about petty points. **pĕtt′ifŏgger** *n.* Inferior legal practitioner; rascally attorney; petty practitioner in any department. **pĕtt′ifŏggery** *n.* **pĕtt′ifŏgging** *adj.*

pĕtt′ish *adj.* Peevish, petulant, easily put out. **pĕtt′ishly** *adv.* **pĕtt′ishnėss** *n.*

pĕtt′itoes (-ōz) *n.pl.* Pig's trotters.

pĕtt′ō *n.* *In* ~, in one's own breast, in secret.

pĕtt′y *adj.* Unimportant, trivial; little-minded; minor, inferior, on a small scale; ~ *cash*, small cash items of receipt or expenditure; ~ *officer*, officer in navy corresponding in rank to N.C.O.; ~ LARCENY, SESSION: see these words. **pĕtti′ly** *adv.* **pĕtt′inėss** *n.*

pĕt'ūlant *adj.* Peevishly impatient or irritable. **pĕt'ūlantly** *adv.* **pĕt'ūlance** *n.*

pėtūn'ia *n.* Genus, nearly allied to tobacco, of S. Amer. herbaceous plants with white, purple, or violet flowers of funnel shape; dark violet or purple colour.

pėtun'tsė (-o͝on-, -ŭn-) *n.* White earth, made by pulverizing a partially decomposed granite, used in China with kaolin for making porcelain. [Chin. *pai* white, *tun* stone, with suffix *-tze*]

pew *n.* Place (often enclosed and raised) in church appropriated to a family (*family* ~) or others; fixed bench with back in church. ~ *v.t.* Furnish with pews, enclose in pew.

pewit, peewit (pē'wĭt, pū'ĭt) *n.* Lapwing; its cry; (U.S.) various species of tyrant-flycatchers (*Sayornis*). [imit.]

pewt'er *n.* Grey alloy of tin and lead or other metal, resembling lead in appearance when dull, but capable of receiving a high polish; utensils of this; pewter pot.

pf. *abbrev. Piano forte* (= soft, then loud); pianoforte (the instrument).

P.F. *abbrev.* Procurator Fiscal.

p.f.c. *abbrev.* (U.S.) Private first class.

pfĕnn'ĭg *n.* Small German coin, $\frac{1}{100}$ of a mark.

P.F.F. *abbrev.* Pathfinder Force.

P.G. *abbrev.* Paying Guest.

P.G.A. *abbrev.* Professional Golfers' Association.

pH. ~ *scale*, scale on which the acidity or alkalinity of a solution is measured, pH 7·0 representing neutrality, lower values acidity, and higher ones alkalinity.

Phaed'ra. (Gk legend) Daughter of Minos and wife of Theseus; became enamoured of Hippolytus, son of Theseus and the Amazon Hippolyta, and caused his death when he rejected her advances.

Phaed'rus (1st c. A.D.). A Macedonian slave; author of fables about animals, based on those of Aesop and others, in Latin verse.

Phā'ėthon. (Gk myth.) Son of the sun-god Helios; drove his father's chariot too near the earth and was killed by Zeus with a thunderbolt to save the earth from destruction.

HIGH PERCH PHAETON

phā'ėton (*or* fāt-) *n.* Light 4-wheeled open carriage usu. drawn by pair of horses. [f. PHAETHON]

phage (fahzh) *n.* (bacteriology) Destroyer of bacteria.

phăgėdaen'a (-j-, -g-) *n.* Spreading ulcer. **phăgėdaen'ĭc** *adj.*

phăg'ocȳte *n.* Type of colourless blood-cell (leucocyte) capable of ingesting and destroying dead or foreign material.

phăl'ănge (-j) *n.* = PHALANX 3.

phalăn'gėal *adj.* (anat.) Of a phalanx.

phalăn'ger (-j-) *n.* Any of the Australian opossums, small marsupials (of several genera) allied to the kangaroo, of arboreal habits, with thick woolly fur and freq. prehensile tail; *flying* ~, one of those which have a flying membrane, flying opossum. [mod. L, invented by Buffon f. Gk *phalanggion* spider's web, from webbed toes of hind feet]

phăl'anstery *n.* (Buildings of) socialistic PHALANX.

phăl'anx *n.* (pl. *-xes* or *-ges* pr. -jēz). 1. (Gk antiq.) Line of battle, esp. body of Macedonian infantry drawn up in close order. 2. Set of persons banded together for common purpose (cf. FALANGE); community of about 1800 persons, as proposed by Fourier, living together as one family, and holding property in common. 3. (anat.) Each bone of finger or toe (ill. HAND, FOOT).

phăl'arōpe *n.* Several related species of small wading and swimming bird allied to snipe.

phăll'us *n.* Image of penis, venerated in some religious systems as symbolizing generative power in nature. **phăll'ĭc** *adj.* **phăll(ĭc)ĭsm** *ns.*

phanăr'ĭot *n.* Resident of Phanar, chief Greek quarter in Constantinople after Turkish conquest; member of Greek official class under Turks.

phăn'erogăm *n.* (bot.) Plant that has stamens and pistils, flowering plant. **phănerogăm'ĭc, phănerŏg'amous** *adjs.*

phăn'tăsm *n.* Illusion, phantom; illusive likeness (*of*); supposed vision of absent (living or dead) person. **phăntăs'mal, phăntăs'mĭc** *adjs.*

phăntăsmagŏr'ĭa *n.* Exhibition of optical illusions produced chiefly by means of magic lantern first given in London in 1802; shifting scene of real or imagined figures. **phăntăsmagŏ'rĭc** *adj.*

phantasy: see FANTASY.

phăn'tom *n.* Apparition, spectre; image (*of*); vain show, form without substance or reality; mental illusion; (attrib.) apparent, illusive, imaginary.

Phār'aoh (-rō). Hebraized vertion of title of ruler of ancient Egypt; ~*'s serpent*, chemical toy made of mercury thiocyanate in shape of a small cone which on being ignited forms a long serpent-like coil. [f. Egyptian word meaning 'great house']

Phă'rĭsee. Member of an ancient Jewish sect distinguished by their strict observance of the traditional and written law and their pretensions to superior sanctity; hence, self-righteous person: formalist; hypocrite. **phărĭsā'ĭc(al)** *adjs.* **Phă'rĭsāĭsm, Phă'rĭseeĭsm** *ns.* [Heb. *parush* separated]

phārmaceut'ĭcal (-sū-) *adj.* Of, engaged in, pharmacy; of the use or sale of medicinal drugs. **phārmaceut'ĭcally** *adv.* **phārmaceut'ĭcs** *n.*

phārmacŏl'ogy *n.* The science concerned with the nature and action of drugs. **phārmacŏl'ogĭst** *n.*

phārmacopoe'ia (-pē'a) *n.* Book (esp. one officially published) containing list of drugs with directions for use; stock of drugs. **phārmacopoe'ial** *adj.*

phārm'acy *n.* Preparation and (esp. medicinal) dispensing of drugs; drug-store, dispensary.

Phār'ŏs[1]. Island off Alexandria on which stood a tower lighthouse built by Ptolemy Philadelphus; the lighthouse itself.

phār'ŏs[2] *n.* Lighthouse or beacon to guide mariners. [f. PHAROS[1]]

Phārsăl'ĭa. Territory of the town of Pharsalus in Thessaly, where Pompey was decisively defeated by Julius Caesar 48 B.C.

pharȳn'gal (-ngg-), **pharȳn'gėal** (-j-) *adjs.* Of the pharynx.

phărȳngĭt'ĭs *n.* Inflammation of the membranes of the pharynx.

pharȳng'ocēle (-ngg-) *n.* Abnormal enlargement at base of pharynx.

pharȳng'oscōpe (-ngg-) *n.* Instrument for inspecting pharynx.

phă'rȳnx *n.* Cavity, with enclosing muscles and mucous membrane, behind and communicating with nose, mouth, and larynx (ill. HEAD).

phāse (-z) *n.* 1. Stage of change or development. 2. (astron.) Aspect of moon or planet acc. to amount of illumination (esp. applied to new moon, first quarter, full moon, last quarter). 3. (physics) A particular stage or point in a recurring sequence of movements or changes, e.g. a vibration or undulation; time (measured from an arbitrary zero) at which a vibration attains a particular state; *three-*~ (of alternating currents), supplied in 3 parts differing in phase by one-third of a period or 120°; also of electric apparatus, producing or using such currents. 4. (phys. chem.) Each of three different physical states, usu. solid, liquid, and gas, in which a substance can exist. **phās'ĭc** *adj.*

Ph.B., Ph.D. *abbrevs. Philosophiae baccalaureus, doctor* (= Bachelor, Doctor, of Philosophy).

pheas'ant (fĕz-) *n* Long-tailed bright-plumaged gallinaceous game-bird (*Phasianus*), long naturalized in Europe; various birds of other families, as (U.S.) ruffed grouse (*Bonasa umbellus*); *~-eyed*, (of certain flowers) with rings of colour like pheasant's eye; *~'s eye*, various flowers, esp. *Adonis autumnalis*, and common white narcissus (*Narcissus poeticus*). [Gk *Phasianos* (bird) of the river Phasis]

Pheidias: see PHIDIAS.

Pheid'ippidēs (-z). (Gk hist.) The Athenian runner dispatched to solicit help from Sparta upon the news of the Persian landing at MARATHON, 490 B.C.

phėnă'cėtĭn *n.* White crystalline substance (ethyl ether of acetanilide), used in medicine as antipyretic.

phenix: see PHOENIX.

phen(o)- *prefix.* (chem.) Denoting certain substances derived from coal-tar (orig. in manufacture of illuminating gas).

phēnobar̄b'ĭtōne *n.* Hypnotic and sedative drug ($C_{12}H_{12}O_3N_2$).

phēn'ŏl *n.* 1. Hydroxy-benzene (C_6H_5OH), commonly called CARBOLIC acid. 2. Any of the hydroxy compounds of benzene and its homologues with the hydroxyl groups attached to the nucleus, e.g. cresol, thymol, pyrogallol.

phėnŏm'ėnal *adj.* Of the nature of a phenomenon; cognizable by, evidenced only by, the senses; concerned with phenomena; remarkable, prodigious. **phėnŏm'enally** *adv.*

phėnŏmėn(al)ĭsm *ns.* Doctrine that phenomena are the only objects of knowledge. **phėnŏm'ėn(al)ĭst** *ns.* **phėnŏmen(al)ĭs'tĭc** *adjs.*

phėnŏm'ėnon *n.* (pl. *-ena*). Thing that appears or is perceived, esp. thing the cause of which is in question; (philos.) that of which a sense or the mind directly takes note, immediate object of perception; remarkable person, thing, occurrence, etc.

phēn'otȳpe *n.* (biol.) Organism as it appears, as dist. from its genetic constitution (*genotype*). **phēnotўp'ĭc** *adj.* Appearing in an organism as a result of its genetic potentialities in a given environment.

phēn'ȳl *n.* The monovalent organic radical C_6H_5.

phew *int.* Expressing impatience or disgust.

phī *n.* Greek letter (Φ, φ), = ph.

phī'al *n.* Small glass bottle, esp. for medicine.

Phī Bēt'a Kăpp'a. Honour society in some U.S. universities and colleges; election for membership is based on high academic qualifications in one of three groups: undergraduates studying the liberal arts, graduates, and distinguished alumni and faculty members; founded in 1776 at the College of William and Mary, Williamsburg, Virginia. [f. the initial letters Φ, Β, Κ, of Gk *philosophia biou kubernītes* philosophy the guide to life]

Phĭd'ĭăs, Pheid'ĭăs (fī-) (5th c. B.C.). Greek sculptor; famous in antiquity for colossal statues of gold and ivory which have not survived; the sculptures of the Parthenon were prob. made under his supervision.

Phil. *abbrev.* Philippians (N.T.).

Phĭladĕl'phĭa. Chief city of PENNSYLVANIA, founded by William Penn and other Quakers. [Gk, = 'brotherly love']

Phĭladĕl'phĭan *adj.* & *n.* 1. (Member) of short-lived mystical religious sect established in England in 2nd half of 17th c. 2. (Inhabitant) of Philadelphia.

phĭlăn'der *v.i.* Make love esp. in trifling manner, dangle after women. **phĭlăn'derer** *n.*

phĭl'anthrōpe *n.* Philanthropist.

phĭlanthrŏp'ĭc *adj.* Loving one's fellow men, benevolent, humane. **phĭlanthrŏp'ĭcally** *adv.*

phĭlăn'thropĭst *n.* Lover of mankind; one who exerts himself for the well-being of his fellow men. **phĭlăn'thropĭsm** *n.*

phĭlăn'thropīze *v.* Practise philanthropy; make (persons) objects of this; make philanthropic.

phĭlăn'thropy *n.* Love, practical benevolence, towards mankind.

phĭlăt'ėly *n.* Stamp-collecting. **phĭlatĕl'ĭc** *adj.* **phĭlăt'ėlĭst** *n.* [Gk *philos* lover of, *ateleia* exemption from payment]

Phĭlēm'on. *Epistle to ~*, one of the books of the N.T., a letter from St. Paul to a well-to-do Christian living prob. at Colossae.

phĭlhar̄mŏn'ĭc *adj.* & *n.* (Person) fond of music (freq. used in names of musical societies, orchestras, etc.).

phĭl'hellēne (-lel-) *adj.* & *n.* (Person) loving or friendly to the Greeks or (hist.) supporting the cause of Greek independence. **phĭlhellēn'ĭc** *adj.* **phĭlhĕll'ėnĭsm, phĭlhĕll'ėnĭst** *ns.*

Phĭl'ĭp[1], St. (N.T.). 1. One of the 12 apostles, commemorated with St. James the Less, 1st May. 2. 'The evangelist', one of 7 deacons appointed to superintend the secular business of the Church at Jerusalem (Acts vi. 6).

Phĭl'ĭp[2]. Name of several kings of France: *Philip I* (1052–1108), reigned 1060–1108; *Philip II* (1165–1223), 'Philip Augustus', reigned 1180–1223; reconquered Normandy from English; *Philip III* (1245–85), 'the Bold', reigned 1270–85; *Philip IV* (1268–1314), 'le Bel', reigned 1285–1314; in his reign the papacy was established at Avignon; *Philip V* (*c* 1294–1322), reigned 1316–22; *Philip VI* (1293–1350), reigned 1328–50; his reign saw beginning of Hundred Years War.

Phĭl'ĭp[3]. Name of several kings of Spain: *Philip II* (1527–98), reigned 1556–98; married Mary I of England; *Philip III* (1578–1621), reigned 1598–1621; *Philip IV* (1605–65), reigned 1621–65; *Philip V* (1683–1746), reigned 1700–46; founder of Bourbon dynasty in Spain.

Phĭl'ĭp of Mă'cėdon (382–336 B.C.). Philip II, king of Macedonia 359–336; reorganized Macedonian army and conquered Greece; father of Alexander the Great.

Phĭl'ĭppa of Hainault (*c* 1314–69). Queen of Edward III of England.

Phĭl'ĭppī (*or* fĭlĭp'ī). Ancient city of Macedonia, fortified by Philip of Macedon and named after him; scene of battle (42 B.C.) in which Octavian (Augustus) and Mark Antony defeated Brutus and Cassius. **Phĭlĭpp'ĭan** *n.*

Phĭlĭpp'ĭans. *Epistle to the ~*, book of N.T., letter of St. Paul to the Church at Philippi.

phĭlĭpp'ĭc *n.* (pl.) *The Philippics*, three speeches of Demosthenes against Philip of Macedon; (also) Cicero's speeches against Antony; hence (sing.) bitter invective.

Phĭl'ĭppīne Islands (*or* -ēn). Archipelago in E. Pacific lying between SE. coast of China and Borneo, formerly a colony of U.S., since 1946 an independent republic; capital, Manila. [f. PHILIP II of Spain]

Phĭl'ĭstīne. 1. One of the warlike inhabitants of ancient Philistia, a district comprising the fertile Mediterranean coastal plain from Jaffa to Egypt, who in early times constantly harassed the Israelites. 2. Person regarded as one's natural enemy. 3. Illiberal person, one whose interests are material and commonplace. **phĭl'ĭstīne** *adj.* Uncultured, commonplace, materialistic. **phĭl'ĭstĭnĭsm** *n.* [Assyr. *Palaistu, Palistu*; sense 3 taken f. Ger. *philister*, used by univ. students of townsmen, allegedly since 1693 when a student was killed at Jena in a 'town-and-gown' brawl and the sermon at his funeral was based on the text 'The Philistines be upon thee!']

phĭlŏl'oġy *n.* Science of language; (now rare) love of learning and literature. **phĭlŏl'oġĭst** *n.* **phĭlolŏ'ġĭcal** *adj.* **phĭlolŏ'ġĭcally** *adv.* **phĭlŏl'oġīze** *v.i.*

phĭl'omăth *n.* Lover of learning, esp. mathematics.

Phĭl'omĕl, Phĭlomē'la. (Gk myth.) Daughter of Pandion, a legendary king of Athens; was turned into a swallow and her sister Procne into a nightingale (or, in Latin versions, into a nightingale, and Procne into a swallow).

phĭloproġĕn'ĭtĭve *adj.* Prolific; (phrenology) loving one's offspring. **phĭloproġĕn'ĭtĭvenėss** *n.*

phĭlŏs'opher *n.* Lover of wisdom; student of philosophy; one who regulates his life by the light of philosophy; one who shows philosophic calmness in trying circumstances; ~*s' stone*, supreme object of alchemy, substance supposed to change other metals into gold or silver.

phĭlosŏph'ĭc(al) *adjs.* Of, consonant with, philosophy; skilled in, devoted to, philosophy (freq. in titles of societies); wise; calm; temperate. **phĭlosŏph'ĭcally** *adv.*

phĭlŏs'ophism *n.* Philosophizing system (usu. contempt., esp. of the French Encyclopaedists).

phĭlŏs'ophīze *v.* Play the philosopher; speculate, theorize; moralize; render philosophic.

phĭlŏs'ophy *n.* 1. Love, study, or pursuit, of wisdom or knowledge, esp. that which deals with ultimate reality, or with the most general causes and principles of things; philosophical system; system for conduct of life; *natural* ~, study of natural objects and phenomena; *moral* ~, study of principles of human action or conduct. 2. Serenity, resignation.

phĭl'tre (-t*er*), **phĭl'ter** *n.* Love-potion.

phĭz[1] *n.* (colloq.) (Expression of) face. [abbrev. of PHYSIOGNOMY]

Phĭz[2]. Pseudonym of Hablot Knight Browne (1815–82), illustrator of 'The Pickwick Papers' and other novels by Dickens.

phlėbī't'ĭs *n.* Inflammation of walls of a vein. **phlėbĭt'ĭc** *adj.*

phlėbŏt'omy *n.* Cutting into a vein, blood-letting, an early and now obsolete form of medical treatment.

Phlĕg'ėthon. (Gk & L myth.) A river of fire, one of the 5 rivers of Hades.

phlegm (-ĕm) *n.* 1. Thick slimy substance secreted by mucous membrane of respiratory passages (formerly regarded as one of the 4 HUMOURS). 2. Coolness, sluggishness, apathy (supposed to result from predominance of phlegm in constitution). **phlĕgmăt'ĭc** (-gm-) *adj.* **phlĕgmăt'ĭcally** *adv.*

phlō'ĕm *n.* (bot.) Softer portion of the fibro-vascular tissue, as dist. from the xylem or woody portion; soft bast (ill. STEM).

phlogĭs'tĭc (-j-, -g-) *adj.* Of phlogiston; (med.) inflammatory.

phlogĭs'ton (-j-, -g-) *n.* 'Principle' of inflammability formerly supposed to exist in combustible bodies.

phlŏx *n.* N. Amer. genus of chiefly herbaceous plants with clusters of usu. showy salver-shaped flowers. [Gk, = 'flame']

phōb'ĭa *n.* Fear, horror, or aversion, esp. morbid.

Phoeb'ė, Phoeb'us (fē-). (Gk myth.) Artemis and Apollo as goddess of moon and god of sun; moon and sun personified. [Gk, = 'bright', 'radiant']

Phoenĭ'cia (fēnĭsh'ĭa). Ancient country of E. Mediterranean, a narrow strip along the coast of the modern Lebanon, including Tyre and Sidon. **Phoenĭ'cian** (-shn) *adj.* & *n.* (One) of the Semitic people who inhabited this area from *c* 2000 B.C., famous as pioneers of navigation and trade (Carthage was their colony) and as craftsmen; regarded by the Greeks as inventors of letters, since the Greek alphabet was based on the Phoenician.

phoen'ĭx (fē-), **phēn'ĭx** *n.* Mythical bird, the only one of its kind, that after living 5 or 6 centuries in the Arabian desert burnt itself on a funeral pile and rose from the ashes with renewed youth to live through another cycle; paragon.

Phoen'ĭx Park (fē-). Park in Dublin, Ireland; ~ *Murders*, assassination by the Irish Invincibles, of Lord Frederick Cavendish, Secretary for Ireland, and Thomas Burke, the Under-secretary.

phŏn *n.* (physics) A unit used in measuring noise.

phōne[1] *n.* Elementary sound of spoken language.

phōne[2] *n.* (colloq.) Telephone; ear-phone, head-phones. ~ *v.* Telephone.

phōn'ēme *n.* (phonet.) Group of variants regarded as essentially the same vocal sound.

phonĕt'ĭc *adj.* Representing vocal sounds, esp. (of systems of spelling) using always same symbol for same sound; of the sounds of spoken language. **phonĕt'ĭcally** *adv.* **phōnėtĭ'cian** (-shn) *n.* **phonĕt'ics** *n.pl.* (Study of) phonetic phenomena of a language.

phōn'ėtĭst *n.* One versed in phonetics, advocate of phonetic spelling.

phōn'(e)y *adj.* (slang) Sham, false, counterfeit.

phŏn'ĭc *adj.* Of sound, acoustic; of vocal sounds.

phōn'ogrăm *n.* 1. Symbol representing spoken sound (ill. HIEROGLYPH). 2. Sound-record made by phonograph.

phōn'ograph (-ahf) *n.* Early form of gramophone, using cylinders, not discs; (U.S.) gramophone. ~ *v.t.* Record, reproduce, by phonograph. **phonogrăph'ĭc** *adj.* **phonogrăph'ĭcally** *adv.* **phonŏg'raphy** *n.*

phonŏl'ogy *n.* Science of vocal sounds; system of sounds in a language. **phŏnolŏ'gĭc(al)** *adjs.* **phŏnolŏ'gĭcally** *adv.* **phonŏl'ogist** *n.*

phŏs'gēne (-z-) *n.* Carbonyl chloride, $COCl_2$, colourless gas, used as a poison gas, with a characteristic suffocating smell.

phŏs'phate *n.* (chem.) Salt of phosphoric acid; (geol. etc.) deposit containing phosphate of lime usu. derived from droppings of birds or reptiles. **phŏsphăt'ĭc** *adj.*

phŏs'phīde *n.* (chem.) Compound of phosphorus with other element or radical.

phŏs'phīte *n.* Salt of phosphorous acid.

phŏs'phor *n.* 1. Phosphorus; esp. in ~*-bronze, -copper*, etc., alloys of phosphorus with metals named. 2. Fluorescent material, esp. that used to form screen of cathode-ray tube.

phŏsphorĕsce' *v.i.* Emit luminosity without combustion, or by slow combustion without sensible heat. **phŏsphorĕs'cence** *n.* **phŏsphorĕs'cent** *adj.*

phŏsphŏ'rĭc *adj.* Containing phosphorus in its higher valency.

phŏs'phorīte *n.* (min.) A variety of apatite (calcium phosphate).

phŏs'phorous *adj.* Containing phosphorus in its lower (trivalent) valency.

phŏs'phorus *n.* A non-metallic chemical element found in all animal and vegetable organisms and in some minerals (symbol P, at. no. 15, at. wt 30·973) and occurring in several allotropic forms; *yellow* ~, a white or cream-coloured wax-like highly inflammable solid, not found in free state, oxidizes rapidly in air, appearing luminous, and is transformed esp. in sunlight into *red* ~, a stable dark-red micro-crystalline powder, non-poisonous and less readily inflammable, used in safety matches; ~ *necrosis*, gangrene of jawbone due to white phosphorus, formerly prevalent in match industry. [L *phosphorus* morning star (Gk *phōs* light, *phorus* bringing)]

phŏs'phūrĕttėd *adj.* Combined chemically with phosphorus (now disused).

phŏss'y *adj.* (colloq.) ~ *jaw*, PHOSPHORUS necrosis.

phōt *n.* A unit of illumination equal to one LUMEN per sq. cm.

phōt'ō *n.* & *v.t.* (colloq.) Photograph.

phōtō-ėlĕc'trĭc *adj.* Marked by or utilizing emission of electrons from solid, liquid, or gaseous, bodies, when exposed to light of suitable wave-lengths; ~ *cell*, cell or vacuum-tube that uses the photo-electric effect to produce an electric current. **phōtō-ĕlĕctrĭ'city** *n.*

phōtō-fĭn'ĭsh *n.* Close finish of race in which winner is identified by photography.

phōtogĕn'ĭc *adj.* 1. Producing or emitting light. 2. Suitable for photography; photographing well (of person as good subject for photography).

phōto-grămm'ėtry *n.* Process of making surveys or geodetic measurements by photography.

phōt'ograph (-ahf) *n.* Picture, likeness, taken by means of chemical action of light on sensitive film superimposed on glass, paper, celluloid, metal, etc. ~ *v.* Take photograph of; 'come out' (well, badly) on photograph. **photŏg'rapher, photŏg'raphy** *ns.* **phōtogrăph'ĭc** *adj.* **phōtogrăph'ĭcally** *adv.*

phōtogravūre' *n.* Printing process in which the subject-matter is photographically etched into a polished copper cylinder; suitable for reproducing photographs in black and white or colour; this process (ill. PRINT). ~ *v.t.* Reproduce thus.

phōtolithŏg'raphy *n.* Lithographic process in which printing plates are made photographically.

phōtō-mėchăn'ĭcal (-k-) *adj.* Pertaining to the production of pictures by mechanical printing from a photographic plate.

photŏm'ėter *n.* Instrument for measuring intensity of light. **phōtomĕt'rĭc** *adj.* **photŏm etry** *n.*

phōt'on *n.* Quantum unit of light energy equal to the product of Planck's constant *h* and the frequency *v*. On the Quantum Theory basis, light is regarded as a stream of particles (quanta or photons) each of energy *hv*.

phōtŏp'ĭc *adj.* ~ *vision*, vision of normal persons in bright daylight, with perception of detail and accurate recognition of colour (cf. SCOTOPIC).

phōt'osphēre *n.* Luminous envelope of sun or star from which its light and heat radiate (ill. SUN).

phōt'ostăt *n.* Trade name of apparatus for making photographic copies of documents etc.; copy made by this. **phōtostăt'ĭc** *adj.*

phōtosȳn'thėsis *n.* (bot.) Process by which carbon dioxide is converted into carbohydrates by chlorophyll under influence of light. **phōtosȳnthĕt'ĭc** *adj.* **phōtosȳnthĕt'ĭcally** *adv.*

phōtothĕ'rapy *n.* Treatment of skin affections etc. by action of light.

phrāse (-z) *n.* 1. Mode of expression, diction; an idiomatic expression; small group of words, usu. without predicate, esp. preposition with the word(s) it governs, equivalent to adjective, adverb, or noun; short pithy expression; (pl.) mere words; ~-*monger*, person addicted to fine-sounding phrases. 2. (mus.) Short and more or less independent passage forming part of longer passage or of whole piece. **phrās'al** (-z-) *adj.* ~ *verb*, (gram.) idiomatic phrase consisting of verb and adverb, often followed by a preposition, as *put up with*. **phrāse** *v.t.* Express in words.

phrās'ėogrăm (-z-) *n.* Written symbol representing a phrase, esp. in shorthand. **phrās'ėograph** (-ahf) *n.* Word for which there is a phraseogram.

phrāsėŏl'ogy (-z-) *n.* Choice or arrangement of words; mode of expression. **phrāsėolŏ'gĭcal** *adj.* **phrāsėolŏ'gĭcally** *adv.*

phrāt'ry *n.* (Gk hist.) Politico-religious division of people, arising orig. from kinship; in Athens, each of three subdivisions of the phyle or tribe; (transf.) tribal division among primitive races.

phrėăt'ĭc *adj.* (geol.) Applied to gases of atmospheric or oceanic origin which, coming into contact with ascending magma, may set off volcanic eruptions.

phrenĕt'ĭc *adj.* Frantic; fanatic.

phrĕn'ĭc *adj.* (anat.) Of the diaphragm.

phrėnŏl'ogy *n.* Study of external contours of cranium as index to development and position of organs supposedly belonging to the different mental faculties. **phrĕnolŏ'gĭcal** *adj.* **phrĕnolŏ'gĭcally** *adv.* **phrėnŏl'ogist** *n.*

phrŏn'tĭstery *n.* (joc.) Place for thinking in, thinking-shop.

Phrȳ'gĭa. Ancient country of central and N. Asia Minor. **Phrȳ'gĭan** *adj.* & *n.* ~ *bonnet, cap*, conical cap with peak bent over in front, cap of liberty; ~ *mode*, the ancient Greek MODE, reputedly warlike in character; third of the eccles. modes, with E as final and C as dominant (ill. MODE).

Phrȳn'ė (4th c. B.C.). Greek courtesan.

phthăl'ĭc *adj.* (chem.) Of or derived from ~ *acid*, $C_6H_4(COOH)_2$.

phthĭs'ĭs (fth-, th-) *n.* Pulmonary tuberculosis; (formerly) any progressive wasting disease. **phthĭs'ĭcal** (tĭz-) *adj.* Of, having, phthisis.

phŭt *adv.* *Go* ~, come to grief, collapse. [Hind. *phaṭnā* burst]

phȳlăc'tery *n.* 1. Small leathern box containing Hebrew texts (Deut. vi. 4–9, xi. 13–21; Ex. xiii. 1–10, 11–16) on vellum, worn by Jews during morning prayer as reminder of obligation to keep the law; (usu. ostentatious) religious observance. 2. Amulet, charm.

phȳ'lē *n.* Ancient Greek clan or tribe; in Attica, political, administrative, and military unit, based on geographical division.

phȳlĕt'ĭc *adj.* (biol.) Of a phylum or line of descent.

phȳll'īte *n.* Slate which glitters owing to presence of minute scales of mica.

phȳll'ōde *n.* (bot.) Flattened petiole resembling a leaf (ill. LEAF).

phȳll'otăxy, -tăxĭs *ns.* Arrangement of leaves on a stem.

phȳlloxēr'a *n.* Genus of plant-lice, esp. species very destructive to grape-vine.

phȳlogĕn'ėsĭs *n.* (biol.) Racial evolution of animal or plant life.

phȳl'um *n.* (pl. *-la*). (biol.) One of the major classificatory divisions of the plant and animal kingdoms, comprising organisms of the same general form (the further main subdivisions, in descending order, being class, order, family, genus, and species).

phȳs'ĭc (-z-) *n.* Art of healing; medical profession; (colloq.) medicine. ~ *v.t.* Dose with physic.

phȳs'ĭcs *n.* Science of the properties and nature of matter in general (excluding chemistry), the various forms of energy, and the mutual interaction of energy and matter.

phȳs'ĭcal (-z-) *adj.* 1. Of matter, material; of the body; of, according to the laws of, natural philosophy; ~ *geography*, that dealing with natural features. 2. Of the science of physics. **phȳs'ĭcally** *adv.*

phȳsĭ'cian (-zĭshn) *n.* One who practises the healing art including medicine and surgery; one legally qualified in medicine as well as in surgery; (fig.) healer.

phȳs'ĭcist (-z-) *n.* 1. Person learned in physics. 2. Believer in the material origin of vital phenomena.

phȳs'ĭcky (-z-) *adj.* Suggestive of physic.

phȳsĭŏc'racy (-z-) *n.* Government according to natural order, esp. that advocated by political economists (followers of Francis Quesnay) in 18th-c. France, who held that the soil is the sole source of wealth and only proper object of taxation and that security of property and freedom of industry and exchange are essential. **phȳs'ĭocrăt** (-z-) *n.*

phȳsiogn'omy (-zĭŏn'-) *n.* Art of judging character from features of face or form of body; cast of features, type of face; (vulg.) face; external features of country etc.; characteristic (moral or other) aspect. **phȳsĭognŏm'ĭc(al)** *adjs.* **phȳsĭognŏm'ĭcally** *adv.* **phȳsĭŏgn'omist** *n.*

phȳsĭŏg'raphy (-z-) *n.* Description of nature, of natural phenomena, or of a class of objects; physical geography. **phȳsĭŏg'rapher** *n.* **phȳsĭogrăph'ĭcal** *adj.*

phȳsĭŏl'ogy (-z-) *n.* Science dealing with the functioning of living organisms as systems of mutually adapted and interacting parts. **phȳsĭolŏ'gĭcal** *adj.* **phȳsĭolŏ'gĭcally** *adv.*

phȳsĭothĕ'rapy (-z-) *n.* Treatment of disease by exercise, massage, heat, light, electricity, or other physical agencies, not by drugs. **phȳsĭothĕ'rapist** *n.*

phȳsique' (-zēk) *n.* Bodily structure, organization, and development.

pī[1] *n.* Greek letter p (Π, π); esp. (math.) as symbol of ratio of circumference of circle to diameter (3·14159).

pī[2] *adj.* (school slang) Pious; ~ *jaw*, sermonizing, moral lecture.

pĭăc'ular *adj.* Expiatory.

pĭăffe' *v.i.* (Of horse etc.) move as in trot, but slower. **pĭăff'er** *n.* This movement.

pī'a māt'er *n.* (anat.) The innermost meninx, a delicate fibrous membrane, consisting of a network of blood-vessels, covering the brain and spinal cord (ill. SPINE). [med. L transl. of Arab. *umm raqiqah* tender mother]

pĭanĭss'ĭmō *adv.* & *n.* (mus.) (Passage to be played) very softly. [It., f. PIANO]

pi'anist (pē-) *n.* Player on piano.

pianis'tic *adj.* Of, adapted for playing on a piano.

***pia'nō*[1]** (pyah-) *adv.* & *n.* (Passage to be played) softly. [It.]

pĭă'nō[2], pĭănofŏrt'ė *ns.* Large musical instrument played by means of keys which cause hammers to strike on metal strings (the

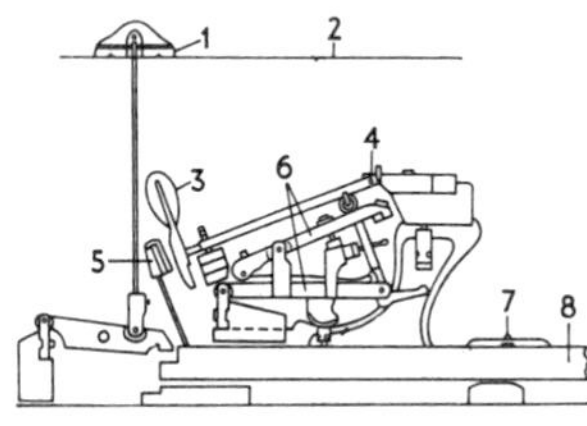

GRAND PIANO ACTION

1. Damper or sordine. 2. String. 3. Hammer. 4. Pivot of hammer. 5. Check. 6. Levers lifting hammer. 7. Pivot of key. 8. Key

vibrations being stopped by dampers); *grand* ~, large wing-shaped piano on legs, with strings arranged horizontally; *upright* ~, piano with strings in vertical position; *cottage* ~, small upright piano; *player* ~, mechanical piano, pianola; ~ *organ*, mechanical piano constructed like barrel-organ. [It., earlier *piano e forte* soft and strong, i.e. loud]

pĭănōl'a *n.* (orig.) Device, attachable to piano, by means of which music can be reproduced mechanically; (now usu.) piano incorporating such a mechanism; the hammers are made to strike the strings by means of air pressure and the passage of air to particular hammers is regulated by the perforations in a revolving roll (~ *roll*).

pĭăs'tre (-ter), **-ter** *n.* 1. Principal monetary unit of Turkey and Cyprus, = 40 paras. 2. 1/100 of an Egyptian, Lebanese, Libyan, or Syrian pound.

pi'ăt (pē-) *n.* Anti-tank rocket-projector, the British equivalent of the BAZOOKA. [initials of *P*rojector *I*nfantry *A*nti-*t*ank]

pĭăzz'a (-tsa) *n.* Public square or market-place, esp. in Italian town; (U.S.) verandah of house. [It., ult. f. Gk *plateia* (*hodos*) broad (street)]

pibroch (pē'broχ) *n.* Series of variations for bagpipe, chiefly martial. [Gael. *piobaireachd*, f. *piobair* piper]

pĭc'a *n.* Size of type (12 point), of about 6 lines to the inch; *small* ~ (11 point), size between long primer and pica; *double* ~ (prop. *double small* ~), size equal to 2 lines of small pica.

pĭcadŏr' *n.* Mounted man with lance in bull-fight.

Pĭc'ardy. (*Picardie*) Old province of N. France between Normandy and Flanders, comprising the modern department of Somme and parts of Pas-de-Calais, Aisne, and Oise.

pĭcarĕsque' (-k) *adj.* (Of a style of fiction) dealing with adventures of rogues.

pĭcarōōn' *n.* Rogue; thief; pirate; pirate ship.

Pĭcăss'ō, Pablo (1881–). Spanish painter, one of the original exponents of CUBISM.

pĭcayune' (-yōōn) *n.* (U.S.) (Formerly, in Louisiana, Florida, etc.) Spanish half-real (about 3*d.*); now, U.S. 5-cent piece or other small coin; small, mean, or insignificant person or thing. ~ *adj.* Mean, contemptible, paltry.

Pĭcc'adĭll'ȳ. Street in West End of London. [f. *Pickadilly Hall*, a tailor's house so nicknamed f. *pickadill* scallop at edge of doublet]

pĭcc'alĭllĭ *n.* Pickle of chopped vegetables, mustard, and hot spices.

pĭcc'anĭnny *n.* Child, esp. of Negroes or S. Afr. or Australian natives.

pĭcc'olō *n.* Small flute, an octave higher than the ordinary flute. [It., = 'small']

pīce *n.* Former Indian and Pakistani coin, ¼ of an anna.

pĭchĭcĭăg'ō *n.* Small pink burrowing armadillo (genus *Chlamydophorus*) of Bolivia and Argentina. [perh. f. native *pichey* little armadillo, Span. *ciego* blind]

pĭck[1] *n.* Tool consisting of an iron bar, usu. curved with a point at one end and a point or chisel-edge at the other, with a wooden

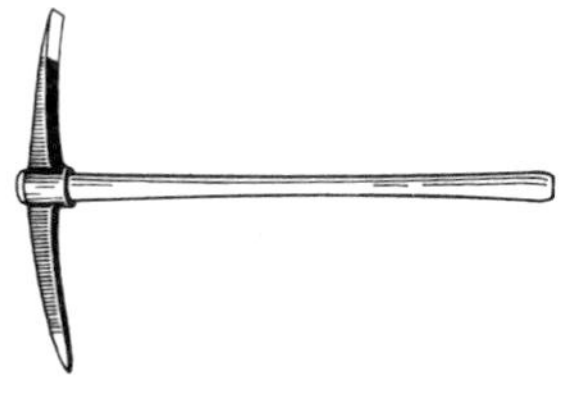

PICK

handle passing through the middle perpendicularly, used for breaking up hard ground etc.; instrument for picking, toothpick.

pĭck[2] *v.* 1. Break surface of (ground etc.) with or as with pick; make (hole etc.) thus. 2. Probe (teeth etc.) with pointed instrument to remove extraneous matter; clear (bone, carcass) of adherent flesh. 3. Pluck, gather (flower, fruit, etc.) from stalk, etc. 4. (Of birds) take up (grains etc.) in bill; (of persons) eat in small bits; (colloq.) eat. 5. Select carefully; ~ *and choose*, select fastidiously. 6. Pull asunder (esp. ~ *oakum*); ~ *to pieces*, pull asunder; (fig.) criticize hostilely. 7. ~ *a quarrel*, contrive to quarrel *with*; ~ *pocket*, steal its contents; ~ *and steal*, pilfer; ~ *a lock*, open it (esp. with intent to rob) with pointed instrument, skeleton key, etc.; ~ *off*, pluck off; shoot deliberately one by one; ~ *out*, select; distinguish from surrounding objects; relieve (ground colour *with* another); make out (meaning of passages etc.), play (tune) by ear; ~ *up*, break up (ground etc.) with pick; lay hold of and take up; raise oneself from a fall etc.; gain, acquire (livelihood, profit, tricks, information); take (person, or thing) along with one; regain; recover health; make acquaintance with casually (or *with*); (games) select (sides) by alternate choosing; succeed in receiving by wireless, seeing with searchlight, etc.; *picklock*, person who picks locks; instrument used for this; ~-*me-up*, stimulating drink; *pick'pocket*, one who steals from pockets; ~-*up*, picking up (of ball in cricket, etc.); game between sides chosen by picking up; (colloq.) man or girl 'picked up', e.g. in the street; power (of motor, etc.) to accelerate; mechanism (replacing sound-box of gramophone) which converts impulses imparted to needle by record into electrical impulses which can then be amplified. ~ *n.* 1. Picking; selection; *the* best part *of*. 2. (weaving) Thread, group of threads, of weft.

pĭck'-a-băck *adv.* On shoulders or back like a bundle.

pĭck'ăxe *n.* Pick. ~ *v.* Break (ground etc.) with pickaxe; work with pickaxe.

pĭck'er *n.* One who picks, gathers, or collects; kinds of instrument for picking.

pĭck'erel *n.* Young pike.

pĭck'ėt *n.* 1. Pointed stake or peg driven into ground to form palisade, tether horse, etc.; (hist.) (stake with pointed top on which person stood as) form of military punishment. 2. (mil., also *pi*(*c*)-*quet*) Small body of troops sent out to watch for enemy or held ready in quarters; party of sentinels, outpost; (now, chiefly) camp-guard doing police duty in garrison town etc. 3. (usu. pl.) Man or body of men stationed by trade-union to dissuade men from work during strike etc. ~ *v.* Secure (place) with stakes; tether; post (men) as picket; beset (workmen) with pickets; act as picket.

pĭck'ĭng *n.* (esp., pl.) Gleanings, remaining scraps; pilferings.

pĭck'le *n.* Brine, vinegar, or similar liquor in which flesh, vegetables, etc., are preserved; food, esp. (pl.) vegetables preserved in pickle and eaten as relish; acid solution for cleaning purposes etc.; (fig.) plight, predicament; mischievous child. ~ *v.t.* Preserve in pickle; treat (wood etc.) with acid solution. **pĭck'led** (-ld) *adj.* (slang) Drunk.

Pĭck'wĭck, Mr. Samuel. Hero of Dickens's novel 'The Pickwick Papers'. **Pĭckwĭck'ĭan** *adj.* Of Mr. Pickwick or the Pickwick Club; *used in its ~ sense,* applied to uncomplimentary language which should not be interpreted literally ('Pickwick Papers', ch. i).

pĭc'nĭc *n.* Pleasure party including meal out of doors. ~ *v.i.* Take part in this. **pĭc'nĭcker** *n.*

Pic'ō (pē-) **dĕlla Mĭrăn'dola,** Giovanni (1463–94). Italian humanist and neo-Platonic philosopher; pioneer in the study of Hebrew philosophy and the Cabbala.

picot (pēk'ō) *n.* Small loop of twisted thread, one of series forming edging to lace, ribbon, etc. (ill. LACE).

pĭcotee' *n.* Carnation, tulip, etc., of which flowers have light ground with darker edging to petals.

picquet[1]**:** see PIQUET[1].

picquet[2]**:** see PICKET, sense 2.

pĭc'rĭc *adj.* ~ *acid,* trinitrophenol, intensely bitter yellow crystalline substance used, in aqueous solution, as a treatment for burns etc., and formerly as a high explosive (lyddite).

Pĭct *n.* One of an ancient, prob. pre-Celtic, race formerly inhabiting parts of N. Britain and Ireland, later (9th c.) united with SCOTS. **Pĭct'ĭsh** *adj.*

pĭc'tograph (-ahf) *n.* Pictorial symbol which stands for the thing depicted, e.g. representation of an eye standing for 'eye' (ill. HIEROGLYPH); primitive writing or record consisting of these. **pĭctogrăph'ĭc** *adj.* **pĭctŏg'raphy** *n.*

pĭctōr'ĭal *adj.* Of, expressed in, pictures; illustrated; picturesque. **pĭctōr'ĭally** *adv.* **pĭctōr'ĭal** *n.* Journal of which pictures are main feature.

pĭctūr'a *n.* (ornith.) Pattern of coloration of a particular part, e.g. feather.

pĭc'ture *n.* 1. Painting, drawing, of objects esp. as work of art; portrait; beautiful object; (fig.) symbol, type, figure. 2. Scene, total visual impression produced; mental image; (*be*) *in the ~,* have all the relevant information; *out of the ~,* irrelevant; *clinical ~,* total idea of diseased condition formed by physician. 3. Cinematograph picture or film; (pl.) exhibition of these, place where they are exhibited. 4. *~-card,* court-card; *~-gallery,* (hall etc. containing) collection of pictures; *~ hat,* lady's wide-brimmed hat resembling those in pictures of Reynolds and Gainsborough; *~ palace,* cinema; *~ postcard,* postcard with picture on back; *~-writing,* mode of recording events etc. by pictures, as in early hieroglyphs etc. ~ *v.t.* Represent in picture; describe graphically; imagine.

pĭcturesque' (-kcherĕsk) *adj.* Like, fit to be the subject of, a striking picture; (of language etc.) strikingly graphic, vivid. **pĭcturĕsque'ly** *adv.* **pĭcturĕsque'nĕss** *n.*

pĭdd'le *v.i.* (archaic) Work, act, in trifling way; (colloq. or childish) make water.

pĭdg'ĭn, pĭ'geon *n.* (colloq.) Person's business or job. ~ *adj.* ~ *English,* jargon chiefly of English words used esp. between Chinese and Europeans. [Chin. corrupt. of *business*]

pīe[1] *n.* Magpie.

pīe[2] *n.* Dish of meat, fruit, etc., encased in or covered with or surrounded by paste and baked; various other baked dishes of meat, fish, etc.; *have a finger in the ~,* be (esp. officiously) concerned in the matter; *bran ~,* tub of bran with toys etc., hidden in it to be drawn at random at Christmas festivities etc.; *pie'crust,* baked paste of pie; *pie'man,* vendor of pies; *~ in the sky,* (slang) heavenly or paradisiacal state.

pīe[3] *n.* (print.) Confused mass of type such as results from breaking down of a forme; (fig.) chaos. ~ *v.t.* Make (type) into pie.

pīe[4] *n.* Formerly the smallest Indian and Pakistani coin, $\frac{1}{12}$ of an anna.

pie'bald (pībawld) *adj.* Of two colours irregularly arranged, esp. black and white; (fig.) motley, mongrel. [f. PIE[1] (magpie)]

piece (pēs) *n.* 1. One of the distinct portions of which thing is composed; *in pieces,* broken; *break to pieces,* break into fragments. 2. Enclosed portion *of* (land); detached portion (*of* a substance); definite quantity in which thing is made up (e.g. 12 yds of wallpaper); cask (*of* wine etc.) varying in capacity; *a ~ of one's mind,* one's candid opinion, rebuke. 3. Example, specimen; *~ of work,* product of work; task. 4. Cannon, gun, pistol; man at chess, draughts, etc.; coin; *~ of eight,* Spanish dollar (which was marked with figure 8), of value of eight reals. 5. Picture; literary or musical composition, usu. short; drama. 6. *by the ~,* (payment etc.) according to amount done (not time taken); *of a ~,* uniform, consistent, in keeping (*with*); *~-goods,* textile fabrics (esp. Lancashire cotton goods) woven in recognized lengths; *~-work,* work paid for by the piece. ~ *v.t.* Put together, form into a whole; join threads in spinning; fit *on* (thing *to* another); eke *out*; make *out* (story, theory, etc.) by combination of parts; join *together*; patch *up*.

pièce de résistance (pyĕs de rāzē'stahṅs) *n.* Most substantial dish at meal (also fig.).

piece'meal (pēs-) *adv.* Piece by piece, part at a time. ~ *adj.* Done etc. piecemeal.

pied (pīd) *adj.* Particoloured.

Pied'mŏnt (pēd-, pyā-). (It. *Piemonte*) District of NW. Italy, united with Italy 1859. **Piedmŏntēse'** (-z) *adj.* & *n.*

pier (pēr) *n.* Breakwater, mole; structure of iron or wood, open below, running out into sea and used as promenade and landing-stage; support of spans of bridge; pillar (ill. ARCADE); solid masonry between windows etc.; *~-glass,* large tall mirror, orig. used to fill up this; *~-table,* table for standing against pier between windows.

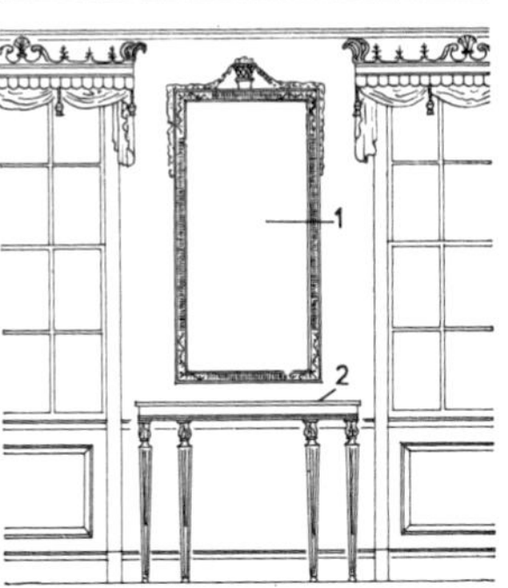

PIER, LATE 18TH C.

1. Pier-glass. 2. Pier-table

pierce[1] (pērs) *v.* Penetrate; prick (*with* pin etc.); make hole in; force one's way through or into; penetrate *through, into,* etc. **pier'cĭngly** *adv.*

Pierce[2] (pērs), Franklin (1804–69). 14th president of U.S. 1853–7.

Piēr'ĭa. District on N. slopes of Mt OLYMPUS, whence the cult of the Muses was prob. carried to Helicon. **Piēr'ĭan** *adj.* Of Pieria; of the Muses.

pierrot (pēr'ō, pyĕ'rō) *n.* (fem. *pierrette*) French pantomime character with whitened face and loose white dress; itinerant entertainer (esp. member of troupe) similarly dressed. [Fr., dim. of *Pierre* Peter]

pietà (pyāt'ah) *n.* Picture, sculpture, of Virgin Mary holding dead body of Christ on her lap. [L *pietas* piety]

pī'ĕtĭsm *n.* Movement for revival of piety in the Lutheran Church begun by P. J. Spener about 1670; pious sentiment, exaggeration or affectation of this. **pī'ĕtĭst** *n.* **piĕtĭs'tĭc(al)** *adjs.*

pī'ĕty *n.* Quality of being pious.

pīĕzŏm'ĕter *n.* Kinds of instrument for measuring (something connected with) pressure.

Pĭff'er *n.* Member of the *P*unjab *I*rregular *F*rontier *F*orce.

pĭf'fle *v.i.* Talk or act feebly, trifle. ~ *n.* Twaddle. **pĭff'lĭng** *adj.* Trivial, worthless.

pĭg *n.* 1. Swine, hog; *buy a ~ in a poke,* buy something without seeing it or knowing its value; flesh of (usu. young or sucking) pig as meat; (colloq.) greedy, dirty, sulky, obstinate, or annoying person. 2. Oblong mass of metal (usu. cast-iron) cooled in a mould into which it is run from smelting-furnace. 3.

~*-headed*, obstinate, stupid; ~*-iron*: see 2 above, and IRON; ~ *jump*, (of horse) jump sportively from all four legs not brought together as in buck-jumping; *pig'nut*, earth-nut, tuber of *Bunium flexuosum*; *pig'skin*, (leather made of) pig's skin; (slang) saddle; *pig'sticking*, hunting of wild boar with spear; *pig'sty*, sty for pigs; (fig.) dirty hovel; *pig's wash*, *pig'wash*, swill of brewery or kitchen given to pigs; *pig'tail*, tobacco twisted into thin rope or roll; plait of hair hanging from back of head, esp. as worn by Chinese under the Manchus, by young girls, and formerly by soldiers and sailors; *pig'weed*, kinds of herb eaten by pigs. ~ *v.* Bring forth (pigs), bring forth pigs; herd together like pigs, live in disorderly or untidy fashion.

pigeon (pĭj'n) *n.* 1. Bird of the family *Columbidae*, dove, esp. (*rock-*~) the rock-dove, *Columba libia*, which haunts rocks and large buildings and is also domesticated in many varieties produced by fancy breeding; *carrier*, *homing*, ~, domesticated rock-pigeon trained to fly home over long distances with message attached to its neck or leg; *clay* ~, clay saucer thrown into air from trap as mark for shooting; *wood-*~, the ring-dove, *Columba palumbus*, a wild bird eaten as game; ~ *breast*, deformed human breast laterally constricted; ~ *English*: see PIDGIN; ~*-hole*, small recess for pigeon to nest in; one of a set of compartments in cabinet etc. for papers, etc.; (*v.t.*) deposit (document) in this, put aside (matter) for future consideration; assign (thing) to definite place in memory; ~ *pair*, boy and girl twins, or boy and girl as sole children; ~*'s milk*, partly-digested food with which pigeons feed their young; imaginary article for which children are sent on fool's errand; ~*-toed*, having toes arranged on a level, as in pigeons; (of persons or horses) turning toes or feet inwards. 2. Simpleton, 'gull'. ~ *v.t.* Cheat (person *of* thing).

pĭgg'ery *n.* Pig-breeding establishment; pigsty; dirty place; piggishness.

pĭgg'ish *adj.* Like a pig, esp. greedy or dirty. **pĭgg'ishly** *adv.* **pĭgg'ishnėss** *n.*

pĭgg'y *n.* Little pig; game of tip-cat. ~ *adj.* (nursery) Piggish.

pĭg'lėt, pĭg'lĭng *ns.* Young pig.

pĭg'ment *n.* The colouring-matter in a paint or dye; natural colouring-matter of a tissue. **pĭgmĕn'tal, pĭg'mentary, pĭg'mentėd** (*or* -mĕn'-) *adjs.*

pigmy: see PYGMY.

pīke[1] *n.* 1. Long wooden shaft with steel or iron head, infantry weapon superseded by bayonet (ill. SPEAR); (dial.) pickaxe, spike. 2. Peaked top of hill. 3. Large voracious freshwater fish (*Esox lucius*) of northern temperate zone, with long slender snout (prob. abbrev. of *pike fish*, from its pointed snout). ~ *v.t.* Thrust through, kill with pike.

pīke[2] *n.* Toll-bar; toll; turnpike road.

pīke[3] *v.i.* (dial. and U.S.) Depart, go *off*.

pīke'lėt (-kl-) *n.* Crumpet or (in some districts) muffin. [Welsh (*bara*) *pyglyd* pitchy (bread)]

pīk'er *n.* (U.S.) Cautious gambler; mean-spirited person.

pīke'staff (-kstahf) *n.* Wooden shaft of pike; *plain as a* ~ (orig. *packstaff*, smooth staff used by pedlar), quite plain.

pĭlăff', pĭlau' (-ow), **pĭlaw'** *ns.* Oriental dish of rice with meat, spices, etc.

pĭlăs'ter *n.* Column of rectangular section projecting from a wall (ill. DOOR).

Pĭl'ate, Pontius. Roman governor of Judaea A.D. 26–36; presided at trial of Jesus.

pĭlch *n.* Infant's woollen or towelling wrapper worn over napkin.

pĭl'chard *n.* Small sea-fish (*Clupea pilchardus*) allied to herring but smaller and rounder, found esp. off the coasts of Cornwall, Devon, and W. France.

pĭl'cōrn *n.* Variety of cultivated oat in which husk does not adhere to grain.

pīle[1] *n.* 1. Pointed stake or post; heavy beam or column of wood, concrete, steel, etc., driven or bored into the ground as support for heavy structure; ~*-driver*, machine for driving piles. 2. (her.) Charge in form of wedge, usu. point downwards (ill. HERALDRY). ~ *v.t.* Furnish with piles; drive piles into.

pīle[2] *n.* 1. Heap of things laid more or less regularly upon one another; lofty mass of buildings. 2. Series of plates of dissimilar metals, such as copper and zinc, laid one upon another alternately, with cloth or paper moistened with an acid solution placed between each pair, for producing electric current; any similar arrangement for producing electric current. 3. (also *atomic* ~) Nuclear reactor, apparatus containing fissile material and a moderating agent used in the study or utilization of atomic energy. 4. (colloq.) Heap of money, fortune. 5. (*funeral*) ~, heap of combustibles on which corpse is burnt. ~ *v.t.* Heap up (freq. with *up*, *on*); load (table, etc., *with*); ~ *arms*, place (usu. three) rifles with butts on ground and muzzles interlocked; ~ *up*, (naut.) run (ship) on rocks or aground.

pīle[3] *n.* (archaic) Reverse of coin; *cross or* ~, heads or tails.

pīle[4] *n.* 1. Soft hair, down, wool of sheep. 2. Soft surface of some woven fabrics, produced by weaving in extra yarns and cutting them short (as in ~ *velvet*) or by knotting them on to warp threads (as in ~ *carpet*) (ill. WEAVE).

pīle[5] *n.* Haemorrhoid, cluster of varicose veins of lower rectum, protruding from skin around anus (*external* ~) or within anal canal (*internal* ~); (pl.) this complaint; *pile'wort*, lesser celandine (from reputed efficacy against piles).

pĭl'ėus *n.* (pl. *-lĕī*). (bot.) Caplike part of mushroom or other fungus (ill. FUNGUS).

pĭl'fer *v.* Steal, esp. in small quantities. **pĭl'ferer** *n.*

pĭl'grĭm *n.* One who journeys to sacred place as act of religious devotion; person regarded as journeying to a future life; traveller; *P*~ *Fathers*, earliest English Puritan settlers of colony of Plymouth, Massachusetts, and esp. those who left Delft Haven and Plymouth, England, in the *Mayflower* in 1620; *P*~ *Trust*, trust founded 1930 by Stephen Harkness, Amer. millionaire, to meet some of Gt Britain's 'most urgent needs', and used for social welfare and for preservation of historic buildings etc. ~ *v.i.* Wander like a pilgrim.

pĭl'grĭmage *n.* Pilgrim's journey; (fig.) mortal life viewed as a journey; *P*~ *of Grace*, rising in Yorkshire in 1536 to protest against dissolution of the monasteries. ~ *v.i.* Go on a pilgrimage.

pĭlĭf'erous *adj.* (chiefly bot.) Having hair.

pĭl'ĭfōrm *adj.* (chiefly bot.) Hair-shaped.

pill *n.* Small ball of medicinal substances, frequently coated with sugar, for swallowing whole; (fig.) something that has to be done, a humiliation etc.; (slang or joc.) ball; (pl.) billiards; ~*-box*, shallow cylindrical box for holding pills; cap shaped like this; (mil.) small round concrete emplacement; *pill'-wort*, plant of genus *Pilularia*, with small globular involucres. ~ *v.t.* (slang) Blackball, defeat.

pĭll'age *n.* Plunder, esp. as practised in war. ~ *v.t.* Sack, plunder. **pĭll'ager** *n.*

pĭll'ar *n.* Vertical structure of stone, wood, metal, etc., slender in proportion to height, used as support or ornament; post, pedestal; upright mass of air, water, etc.; (mining) solid mass of coal etc. left to support roof of the working; (fig.) person who is a main supporter (*of*); (*drive*) *from* ~ *to post*, to and fro, from one resource to another; ~*-box*, hollow pillar about 5 ft high in which letters may be posted; *P*~*s of Hercules*, two promontories, Calpe (Gibraltar) in Europe and Abyla (Ceuta) in Africa, at E. end of Strait of Gibraltar, anciently supposed to have been parted by the arm of Hercules and regarded as the western limits of the inhabited world. ~ *v.t.* Support (as) with pillars.

pĭll'ion (-yon) *n.* (hist.) Woman's light saddle; cushion attached to hinder part of saddle for second rider, usu. woman; (mod.) seat for passenger behind saddle of motor-cycle or scooter; *ride* ~, travel on this seat.

pĭll'ĭwĭnks *n.* (hist.) Instrument of torture for squeezing fingers.

pĭll'orў *n.* Wooden framework with holes for head and hands of offender exposed to public ridicule etc. ~ *v.t.* Put in the pillory; (fig.) expose to ridicule.

PILLORY

pĭll'ow (-ō) *n.* Cushion of linen etc. stuffed with feathers etc. as support for head in reclining, esp. in bed; (techn.) pillow-shaped block or support; ~*-case*, washable case of linen etc. for pillow; ~*-fight*, mock fight with pillows in bedroom; ~ *lace*, lace plaited with bobbins on a pillow (see LACE and ill.). ~ *v.* Rest, prop up, (as) on pillow.

pīl'ōse, pīl'ous *adjs.* Covered with hair. **pīlŏs'ĭty** *n.*

pī'lot *n.* Person qualified to take charge of ships entering or leaving a harbour, or wherever navigation requires local knowledge; steersman (archaic); one who operates flying controls of an aircraft, one duly qualified to do so; automatic device for maintaining an aeroplane in flight; (fig.) guide, esp. in hunting-field; (attrib.) small-scale, experimental; ~*-cloth*, thick blue woollen cloth for greatcoats, etc.; ~*-engine*, locomotive engine going on ahead of a train to make sure that the way is clear; ~*-fish*, small silvery-blue dark-barred fish of warm seas (*Naucrates ductor*), said to act for shark as pilot or guide to food; ~ *officer*, lowest commissioned rank in R.A.F.; ~ *v.t.* Conduct as pilot; act as pilot on. **pī'lotage** *n.* **pī'lotlėss** *adj.* ~ *plane*, explosive-carrying reaction-propelled crewless aeroplane.

Pĭl'sen. German name of Plzen, town of Czechoslovakia, famous for lager-beer (*Pilsener*).

Pĭlsud'ski (-sōōt-), Joseph (1867–1935). Polish soldier and statesman; first marshal of Poland; chief of state 1918–23; premier and virtual dictator 1926–8, 1930–5.

Pĭlt'down. Down near Lewes, Sussex, where prehistoric remains of a human skull and ape-like lower jaw and of worked flints and bone implements were discovered (1912); they were claimed as belonging to the early pleistocene period, but scientific tests (1953) proved them to be forgeries.

pĭl'ūle, pĭll'ūle *n.* Pill; small pill. **pĭl'ūlar** *adj.*

pĭmĕn'tō *n.* 1. (Dried aromatic berry of) West Indian evergreen tree, *Pimenta officinalis*; allspice. 2. Any of various peppers.

Pĭm'lĭcō. District of SW. London, on left bank of Thames.

pĭmp *n.* & *v.i.* Pander.

pĭm'pernĕl *n.* Small annual (*Anagallis arvensis*) found in corn-fields and waste ground, with scarlet (also blue or white) flowers closing in cloudy or rainy weather.

pĭm'pĭng *adj.* Small, mean; sickly.

pĭm'ple *n.* Small solid round tumour of the skin, usu. inflammatory. **pĭm'pled, pĭm'ply** *adjs.*

pĭn *n.* Thin piece of (usu. tinned brass or iron) wire with sharp point and round flattened head for fastening together parts of dress, papers, etc.; peg of wood or metal for various purposes; each of pegs round which strings of musical instrument are fastened (ill. STRING); skittle; (pl. colloq.) legs; DRAWING-~ HAIRpin, SAFETY-~: see these words; *split* ~, metal cotter to be passed through hole and held there by the gaping of its split end; *pins and needles*, tingling sensation in limb recovering from numbness; *pin'cushion*, small cushion for sticking pins in to keep them ready for use; ~*-feather*, ungrown feather; ~*-head*, (fig.) minute thing; ~*-hole*, hole made by pin or into which peg fits; ~*-money*, allowance to woman for dress expenses etc.; allowance settled on wife for private expenditure; ~*-point*, point of a pin; (attrib. of targets) small and requiring very accurate and precise bombing and shelling; (*v.t.*) locate or bomb (such target) with the accuracy and precision required (also fig.); ~*-prick*, (fig.) trifling irritation; ~*-spot*, small round spot or part of pattern on fabric; ~*-stripe*, very narrow stripe in textile fabric; *pin'tail*, kinds of duck and grouse with pointed tail; ~*-tuck*, narrow ornamental tuck; ~*-wheel*, small catherine-wheel. ~ *v.t.* Fasten (*to, together, up*) with pin(s); transfix with pin, lance, etc.; seize and hold fast; bind (person *down*) *to* (promise, arrangement); ~ *up*, (archit.) underpin; fasten (on wall etc.) by means of a pin; ~*-up* (*n.*) picture (of glamorous girl or celebrity) pinned up on a wall, etc.; *pin-up girl*, (colloq.) glamorous girl.

pĭn'afōre *n.* Washable sleeveless covering worn over dress etc. to protect from dirt.

pince-nez (păṅs'nā) *n.* Pair of eyeglasses with spring to clip nose. [Fr., = 'pinch-nose']

pĭn'cers *n. pl.* (*Pair of*) ~ gripping tool made of two limbs pivoted together forming pair of jaws with

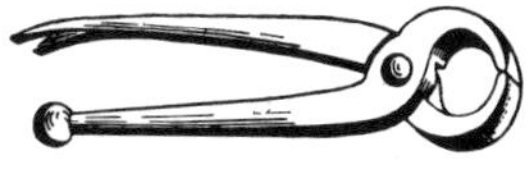

PINCERS

manipulating handles; similar organ in crustaceans, etc.; ~ *movement*, (mil.) operation involving the convergence of two forces on enemy position like the jaws of a pair of pincers.

pĭnch *n.* Nip, squeeze; as much as can be taken up with tips of finger and thumb; (fig.) stress (of poverty etc.); *at a* ~, in a strait or exigency. ~ *v.* Nip, squeeze, esp. between tips of finger and thumb; (of cold, hunger, etc.) nip, shrivel; stint; be niggardly; sail (vessel) close-hauled; (slang) steal, arrest, take into custody.

pĭnch'bĕck *n.* Gold-like alloy of copper and zinc used in cheap jewellery etc. ~ *adj.* Made of pinchbeck; counterfeit, sham. [Christopher *Pinchbeck*, London watch- and toy-maker (*c* 1730)]

Pĭn'dar (*c* 520–443 B.C.). Greek lyric poet. **Pĭndă'rĭc** *adj.* Of Pindar; resembling the style, diction, etc., of Pindar; ~ *ode*, (English prosody), ode with irregular number of feet in lines and arbitrary disposition of rhymes.

pīne[1] *n.* Genus (*Pinus*) of trees with evergreen needle-shaped leaves growing in sheathed clusters of two or more, many species of which afford timber, tar, and turpentine; ~*-cone*, characteristic organ of the pine, containing its seeds; ~*-kernel*, edible seed of some pine-trees; *Pine-tree State*, (U.S.) pop. name of Maine.

pīne[2] *v.i.* Languish, waste away, from grief, disease, etc.; long eagerly (*for, after, to*).

pĭn'ėal *adj.* (anat.) Shaped like a pine-cone; ~ *gland*, small conical gland of unknown function behind third ventricle of brain (ill. BRAIN).

pīne'ăpple *n.* Juicy edible collective fruit of *Ananas*, surmounted by crown of small leaves (so called from resemblance to pine-cone); (slang) hand-grenade, bomb.

Pĭnĕr'ō (*or* -nār̄ō), Sir Arthur Wing (1855–1934). English playwright.

pīn'ery *n.* Place in which pineapples are grown; plantation of pines.

pĭn'fōld *n.* Pound for stray cattle etc. ~ *v.t.* Confine in this.

pĭng *n.* Abrupt ringing sound as of rifle bullet flying through air. ~ *v.i.* Make, fly with, this. [imit.]

pĭng'-pŏng *n.* Game like lawn tennis played on table with celluloid balls and bats of wood, parchment, etc.; table-tennis. [imit.]

pĭng'uĭd (-nggw-) *adj.* (usu. joc.) Fat, oily, greasy.

pĭn'ion[1] (-nyon) *n.* Terminal segment of bird's wing; any flight-feather of wing; (in carving) part of wing corresponding to forearm; (poet.) wing. ~ *v.t.* Cut off pinion of (wing, bird) to prevent flight; bind the arms of (person), bind (arms); bind (person etc.) fast *to*.

pĭn'ion[2] (-nyon) *n.* Small cog-wheel engaging with larger one; cogged spindle engaging with wheel (ill. GEAR).

pĭnk[1] *n.* 1. Species of *Dianthus*, esp. *D. plumarius*, garden plant, native of E. Europe, with white, crimson, pink, or variegated sweet-smelling flowers; various other allied or similar plants; *sea-pink*, thrift, *Armeria maritima*; *the* ~, 'flower' or finest example of excellence; *in the*~, (slang) quite well. 2. Pale red slightly inclining to purple. 3. Fox-hunter's red coat; cloth of this; fox-hunter. ~ *adj.* Of pale red colour of various kinds, as *rose*, *salmon*, ~; ~ *disease*, *erythroedema*, disease of children characterized by extreme weakness and wasting and pink rash on skin; ~*-eye*, contagious fever of horses; contagious ophthalmia in man, marked by redness of the eyeball.

pĭnk[2] *n.* Yellowish pigment made by combining vegetable colouring matter with some white base.

pĭnk[3] *n.* (hist.) Sailing-vessel esp. with narrow stern (orig. small and flat-bottomed).

pĭnk[4] *n.* Young salmon; (dial.) minnow.

pĭnk[5] *v.t.* Pierce with sword etc.; ornament (leather etc.) with perforations or with scalloped or zigzag edge; adorn, deck (freq. ~ *out*).

pĭnk[6] *v.i.* (Of petrol engine) knock, emit dull metallic sound from detonation of (part of) charge, due to poor quality of fuel. [app. imit.]

Pĭnk'erton, Allan (1819–84). American detective, of Scottish origin, whose work led to establishment of U.S. federal secret service; forestalled an attempt on life of Abraham Lincoln, 1861; wrote his reminiscences. ~ *n.* (U.S., usu. pl.) Member of a Pinkerton detective agency, a private detective or law-enforcement officer.

pĭnk'ster *n.* (U.S.) Whitsuntide. [Du., = 'PENTECOST']

pĭnn'a *n.* (pl. *-ae*). 1. Broad upper part of external ear (ill. EAR). 2. Primary division of pinnate leaf (ill. LEAF). 3. Fin, fin-like structure.

pĭnn'ace *n.* Man-of-war's double-banked (usu. eight-oared) boat; also applied to other ships' boats, now usu. driven by motor; (hist.) small, usu. two-masted, vessel.

pĭnn'acle *n.* Small ornamental turret usu. ending in pyramid or cone, crowning a buttress, roof, etc.; natural peak; (fig.) culmination, climax. ~ *v.t.* Set (as) on pinnacle; form the pinnacle of; furnish with pinnacles.

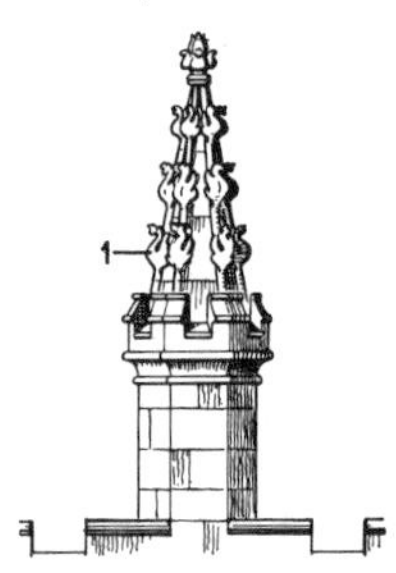

MEDIEVAL PINNACLE
1. Crocket

pĭnn'ate *adj.* 1. (bot., of compound leaf) With series of leaflets on each side of common stalk (ill. LEAF). 2. (zool.) With branches, tentacles, etc., on each side of an axis. **pĭnn'ately** *adv.*

pĭnn'er *n.* (esp.) Coif with two long side-flaps pinned on.

pĭnn'otherē *n.* Genus of small crabs (*Pinnotheres*) inhabiting shells of oysters, mussels, etc., and sharing their food.

pĭnn'ūle *n.* (bot.) Secondary division of pinnate leaf (ill. FERN); (zool.) part, organ, like small wing or fin; sight at end of index of astrolabe etc. **pĭnn'ūlar** *adj.*

pĭnn'y *n.* Childish abbrev. of PINAFORE.

pĭn'oc(h)le (-ŏkl; *or* pē-) *n.* (U.S.) Card-game like bezique; occurrence of queen of spades and knave of diamonds together at this game.

pĭnōl'ė *n.* Meal made from parched cornflour mixed with sweet flour of mesquit-beans, sugar, spice, etc. [Aztec *pinolli*]

pīnt *n.* Measure of capacity, ⅛ gallon, 20 fluid ounces in U.K., 16 in U.S. (see Appendix X).

pĭn'tle *n.* Kinds of pin or bolt, esp. one on which some other part turns (ill. BOAT).

pĭn'tō *adj.* & *n.* (south-western U.S.) Piebald (horse). [Span., = 'painted']

pinx. *abbrev. Pinxit.*

pĭnx'ĭt, pĭnxēr'unt. (So-and-so) painted it (in signature to picture, inscription on engraving etc.).

pīn'y *adj.* Of, like, abounding in, pines.

pioneer' *n.* 1. Orig. one of a body of foot-soldiers marching in advance with spades etc. to prepare road for main body; now, member of a military unit equipped for road-making, bridging, demolitions, etc. 2. Beginner of enterprise; original explorer. ~ *v.* Act as pioneer; open up (road etc.) as pioneer; act as pioneer to, conduct.

piou-piou (pū-pū) *n.* The typical French private soldier.

pī'ous *adj.* Devout, religious; (archaic) dutiful; ~ *fraud*: see FRAUD. **pī'ously** *adv.*

pĭp[1] *n.* Disease of poultry, hawks, etc., marked by thick mucus in throat and often by white scale on tip of tongue; (slang) *give* (person) *the* ~, make (him) feel unwell, disgust.

pĭp[2] *n.* Each spot on playing-cards, dice, or dominoes, or star on army officer's shoulder; single blossom of clustered inflorescence; rhomboidal segment of surface of pineapple.

pĭp[3] *n.* Seed of apple, pear, orange, etc.

pĭp[4] *n.* Signaller's name for letter P.

pĭp[5] *n.* High-pitched momentary sound, usu. produced mechanically, as in a wireless time-signal. [imit.]

pĭp[6] *v.* (colloq.) Blackball; defeat; fail in examination; hit with shot; do for.

pipal: see PEEPUL.

pīpe *n.* 1. Tube of wood, metal, etc., esp. for conveying water, gas, etc. 2. Musical wind-instrument consisting of single tube blown by mouth; each of tubes by which sounds are produced in organ (ill. ORGAN); boatswain's whistle, sounding of this; (pl.) bagpipes. 3. Voice, esp. in singing; song, note, of bird. 4. Tubular organ, vessel, etc., in animal body; cylindrical vein of ore; channel of decoy for wild fowl. 5. Narrow tube of clay, wood, etc., with bowl at one end, for drawing in smoke of tobacco; quantity of tobacco held by this; *King's*, *Queen's*, ~, furnace at London Docks used formerly for burning contraband tobacco; ~ *of peace*, calumet; *put that in your* ~ *and smoke it*, digest that fact etc. if you can. 6. Cask for wine, esp. as measure usu. = 105 gal. 7. ~*-clay*, fine white clay used for tobacco-pipes and (esp. by soldiers) for cleaning white breeches, belts, etc.; (*v.t.*) whiten with pipe-clay; ~*-dream*, (orig. U.S.) kind of extravagant fancy induced by smoking opium; hence, notion unlikely to be realized; ~ *major*, N.C.O. commanding regimental pipers; ~*-rack*, rack for tobacco-pipes; ~*-line*, line of pipes for conveying petroleum, gas, or water across country; ~*-stone*, hard red clay used by Amer. Indians for tobacco-pipes, catlinite. ~ *v.* 1. Play (tune etc.) on pipe; ~ *down*, be quiet, be less insistent or confident; lead, bring, (person etc.) by sound of pipe; summon (crew) by sounding whistle; whistle; utter in shrill voice; ~ one's *eyes*, weep. 2. Propagate (pinks etc.) by cuttings taken off at joint of stem. 3. Trim (dress), ornament (cake etc.) with piping (see below). 4. Furnish with pipes.

pīp'er *n.* One who plays on pipe, esp. strolling musician; bagpipe-player; *pay the* ~, defray cost, bear expense or loss, of proceeding etc.

pĭpĕtte' *n.* Glass tube having a definite volume when filled (usu. by suction) up to an etched mark and used esp. in chemistry for measuring and transferring small quantities of liquid.

pīp'ing *n.* (esp.) Ornamentation of dress etc. by means of cord enclosed in pipe-like fold along seam etc.; ornamental cord-like line of sugar on cake. ~ *adj.* (esp.) *The* ~ *times of peace*, those characterized by pastoral piping as opp. to more martial music; (*quasi-adv.*) ~ *hot*, so hot as to make piping or hissing sound.

pĭpistrĕl(le)' *n.* Small species of bat, *Vesperugo pipistrellus*, common in British Isles.

pĭp'it *n.* Bird of a group superficially resembling larks but allied to the wagtails; *meadow* ~, *Anthus pratensis*. [prob. imit.]

pĭp'kin *n.* Small earthenware pot or pan.

pĭpp'in[1] *n.* Kinds of apple raised from seed.

Pĭpp'in[2]: see PEPIN.

pĭp'-squeak *n.* (slang) Insignificant person, petty object; (army slang) small high-velocity shell making characteristic sound in flight.

piquant (pēk'ant) *adj.* Agreeably pungent, sharp, appetizing; (fig.) pleasantly stimulating or disturbing to the mind. **pi'quantly** *adv.* **pi'quancy** *n.*

pique[1] (pēk) *v.t.* Irritate, wound the pride of; arouse (interest, curiosity); plume *oneself on*. ~ *n.* Ill-feeling, enmity, resentment.

pique[2] (pēk) *n.* Winning of 30 points at piquet before opponent begins to count. ~ *v.* Score a pique (against).

piqué (pēk'ā) *n.* Stiff fabric, usu. cotton, with lengthwise ribs.

piquet'[1] (-kĕt) *n.* Card-game for two players with pack of 32 cards, points being scored on various groups or combinations of cards.

piquet[2] (pĭk'et) *n.*: see PICKET.

Pīrae'us. Chief port of Athens.

pĭră'gua (-gwa) *n.* 1. Long narrow canoe made from a single tree-trunk. 2. Two-masted sailing-barge. [Carib, = 'dug-out']

Pĭrandĕll'ō, Luigi (1867–1936). Italian playwright and novelist.

pĭranha, piraya: see PERAI.

pīr'ate *n.* (Ship used by) sea-robber; marauder; one who infringes another's copyright; bus etc., that encroaches on recognized routes. ~ *v.* Plunder; reproduce (book etc.) without leave for one's own profit; play the pirate. **pīr'acy** *n.* **pīrăt'ical** *adj.* **pīrăt'ically** *adv.*

pĭrogue' (-ōg) *n.* see PIRAGUA.

pĭrouette' (-ŏŏĕt) *n.* Ballet-dancer's spin round on one foot or on point of toe. ~ *v.i.* Dance thus. [Fr., = 'top']

Pisa (pēz'*a*). City of Tuscany, N. Italy; *Leaning Tower of* ~, campanile of cathedral, built 1174–1350, about 180 ft high and leaning some 16 ft from the perpendicular.

pis aller (pēz ăl'ā) *n.* Course etc. taken for want of a better. [Fr. *pis* worse, *aller* go]

pĭs'cary *n.* *Common of* ~, right of fishing in another's water in common with owner (and others).

pĭsta'chĭo (-āshĭō, -ăshō, -ăchō) *n.* Tree, *Pistachia vera*, of W. Asia, cultivated in S. Europe; nut of this, with greenish edible kernel; colour of the kernel.

pĭs'tĭl *n.* Organ of flower bearing ovules, comprising ovary, style, and stigma (ill. FLOWER). **pĭs'tĭllate** *adj.*

pĭs'tol (-tl) *n.* Small fire-arm, usu. with curved butt, held and fired by one hand. ~ *v.t.* Shoot with this.

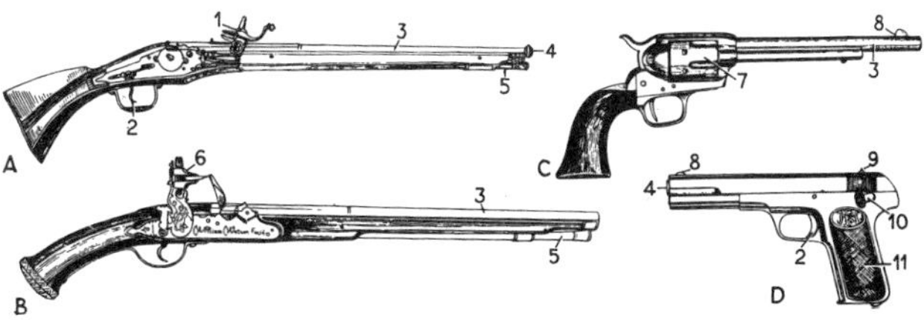

PISTOLS: A. GERMAN WHEEL-LOCK PETRONEL, *c* 1600. B. ENGLISH FLINT-LOCK PISTOL, *c* 1650. C. COLT 45 SINGLE-ACTION 6-CHAMBERED REVOLVER, 1873. D. BROWNING 9 MM. SHORT AUTOMATIC PISTOL

1. Wheel-lock. 2. Trigger. 3. Barrel. 4. Muzzle. 5. Ramrod. 6. Flint-lock. 7. Chambers. 8. Foresight. 9. Backsight. 10. Safety-catch. 11. Magazine holding eight rounds

pĭs'catory *adj.* Of fishers or fishing; addicted to fishing. **piscatōr'ial** *adj.*

Pisces (pĭs'ēz). A constellation, the Fishes; 12th sign (♓) of zodiac, which sun enters about 22nd Feb.

pĭs'cĭcŭlture (-sĭ-) *n.* Artificial rearing of fish. **pĭscĭcŭl'tural** *adj.*

piscī'na (-sē-; -sī-) *n.* 1. Fish-pond; ancient Roman bathing-pond. 2. (eccles.) Perforated stone basin for carrying away water used in rinsing chalice etc. (ill. FENESTELLA).

pĭs'cīne[1] (*or* -ēn) *n.* Bathing-pool.

pĭs'cīne[2] *adj.* Of fish.

piscĭv'orous *adj.* Fish-eating.

pisé (pēz'ā) *n.* Stiff clay or earth (and gravel) rammed between boards (removed as it hardens) as building-material. [Fr., = 'pounded']

Pĭs'gah (-zg*a*). Mountain of Transjordan, NE. of Dead Sea, from which Moses viewed the 'promised land' before his death.

pĭsh *int.* expressing contempt, impatience, or disgust. ~ *v.i.* Say 'pish!'

pĭshogue' (-ōg) *n.* (Ir.) Sorcery; charm, spell.

pĭs'ĭfōrm (*or* pĭz-) *adj.* Pea-shaped; ~ *bone*, small bone of upper row of carpus (ill HAND).

Pĭsĭs'tratus, Peis- (*c* 605–527 B.C.). Athenian statesman and soldier; became tyrant of Athens in 560 B.C.; was twice expelled, but returned to power.

pĭs'mīre *n.* Ant. [f. *piss* (from smell of ant-hill), and obs. *mire* ant, f. Du. *mier*.]

piss *v.* (Not now in polite use.) Make water; discharge with the urine; wet with urine. ~ *n.* Urine.

pĭstōle' *n.* (hist.) Foreign gold coin, esp. Spanish, worth about 18*s*.

pĭs'ton *n.* Disc or short cylinder of wood, metal, etc., fitting closely within cylindrical vessel in which it moves to and fro, used in steam-engine, pump, etc., to impart or receive motion by means of ~*-rod* (ill. COMBUSTION); sliding valve in cornet etc. (ill BRASS); ~*-ring*, elastic cast-iron packing-ring fitted on piston.

pĭt *n.* 1. Natural hole in ground; hole made in digging for mineral etc. or for industrial purposes; (shaft of) coal-mine; depression in floor of workshop enabling persons to reach underside of motor vehicles for inspection or repair; covered hole as trap for wild beasts or (esp. bibl.) for enemies. 2. *the* ~, hell. 3. COCKPIT. 4. Hollow in animal or plant body or on any surface; depressed scar, as after smallpox; (bot.) hollow between plant cells on either side of lamella (~ *membrane*); ~ *of the stomach*, depression between cartilages of false ribs. 5. That part of auditorium of theatre etc. which is on floor of house; now usu. the part of this behind stalls (ill. THEATRE); people occupying this. 6. (U.S.) Part of floor of exchange appropriated for special branch of business. 7. *pit'fall*, covered pit as trap for animals etc.; (fig.) unsuspected snare or danger; ~*-head*, top of shaft of coal-mine, or ground immediately around it; *pit'man*, collier; (U.S.) connecting rod. ~ *v.* Put into a pit (esp. vegetables etc. for storage); set (cock etc.) to fight in pit (*against* another), (fig.) match (*against*); make pits, esp. scars, in (esp. in past part.); (path., of flesh etc.) retain impression of finger etc. when touched.

pit-(a-)păt *adv.* With the sound pit-(a-)pat, palpitatingly, falteringly. ~ *n.* This sound.

Pĭt'cairn Island. Small island in S. Pacific (British since 1839), inhabited by descendants of mutineers of the *Bounty*.

pitch[1] *n.* Black or dark-brown tenacious resinous substance, the residue from distillation of tar or turpentine, hard when cold but becoming viscid and semi-liquid when heated; used for caulking seams of ships, protecting wood from moisture, road-making, etc.; ~ *black*, ~ *darkness*, with no light at all; *pitch'blende*, mineral containing uranium oxide, one of the chief sources of radium and uranium; ~*-pine*, specially resinous kinds of pine; ~*-stone*, obsidian or other vitreous rock looking like pitch. ~ *v.t.* Smear, cover, coat, with pitch. **pitch'y** *adj.* Of, like, dark as, pitch.

pitch[2] *v.* 1. Fix and erect (tent, camp); encamp; fix, plant, (thing) in definite position; pave (road) with set stones; (cricket) ~ *wickets*, fix stumps in ground and place bails; *pitched battle*, battle of set kind, not casual. 2. (mus.) Set at particular pitch; (fig.) express in particular style. 3. Throw, fling; (in games) throw (flat object) towards a mark; throw (ball) to batter in baseball etc.; (of ball etc.) land, fall (in specified manner or position); fall heavily. 4. (slang) Tell (tale, yarn). 5. (Of ship) plunge in longitudinal direction. 6. Incline, dip (of stratum, roof, etc.). 7. ~ *in*, (colloq.) set to work vigorously; ~ *into*, (colloq.) assail forcibly with blows, words, etc.; make vigorous attack on; ~ *upon*, happen to select; ~*-and-toss*, game of skill and chance in which coins are pitched at a mark, and afterwards tossed up by players in turn, each keeping those that turn up 'heads'; ~*-farthing*, chuck-farthing. ~ *n.* 1. Pitching; mode of delivering ball in cricket, baseball, etc. 2. Place at which one (e.g. street performer or vendor) is stationed; (cricket) place between and about wickets. 3. Height to which falcon etc. soars before swooping on prey; height, degree, intensity (*of* quality etc.); (mus.) quality of musical sound depending on comparative rapidity of vibrations producing it, degree of acuteness; ~*-pipe*, small pipe blown by mouth to set pitch for singing or tuning. 4. Degree of slope; steepness of roof's slope. 5. (mech.) Distance between successive points or lines, e.g. between successive teeth of cog-wheel; ~*-wheel*, toothed wheel engaging with another.

pitch'er[1] *n.* (esp.) Player who delivers ball, esp. in baseball; stone used for paving.

pitch'er[2] *n.* Large usu. earthenware vessel with handle or two ears and usu. a lip, for holding liquids; (bot.) modified leaf in pitcher-form; ~*-plant*, various plants with such leaves, freq. containing liquid secretion by which insects are caught and digested. **pitch'erful** *n.*

pitch'fōrk *n.* Long-handled fork with two sharp prongs for pitching hay etc.; tuning-fork. ~ *v.t.* Cast (as) with pitchfork; (fig.) thrust (person) forcibly (*into* office, position, etc.).

pĭt'ėous *adj.* Calling for pity, deplorable. **pĭt'ėously** *adv.* **pĭt'ėousnėss** *n.*

pith *n.* 1. Spongy cellular tissue in stem and branches of dicotyledonous plants (ill. STEM); similar tissue lining rind of orange etc.; spinal cord; (fig.) essential part, quintessence. 2. Physical strength, vigour; force, energy. **pith'lėss** *adj.* **pith** *v.t.* Slaughter (animal) by severing spinal cord.

pĭthėcăn'thrōpe, pĭthėcănthrōp'us *ns.* Ape-man, link between ape and man (also called Java man; ill. PRIMATE).

pĭthē'coid *adj.* & *n.* Ape-like (animal).

pith'y *adj.* Of, like, full of, pith; condensed and forcible, terse. **pith'ĭly** *adv.* **pith'ĭnėss** *n.*

pĭt'ĭable *adj.* Calling for pity or contempt. **pĭt'ĭablenėss** *n.* **pĭt'ĭably** *adv.*

pĭt'ĭful *adj.* Compassionate; calling for pity; contemptible. **pĭt'ĭfully** *adv.* **pĭt'ĭfulnėss** *n.*

pĭt'ĭlėss *adj.* Showing no pity. **pĭt'ĭlėssly** *adv.* **pĭt'ĭlėssnėss** *n.*

Pĭt'man, Sir Isaac (1813–97). English inventor of a system of shorthand based on sounds instead of letters.

Pitot (pētō'), Henri (1695–1771). French physicist, inventor of ~ *tube*, right-angled tube open at both ends, used in anemometers and for determining velocity of fluids (ill. ANEMOMETER).

pĭt'păn *n.* Central American dug-out boat.

Pitt, William (1708–78), 1st Earl of Chatham. English Whig statesman; prime minister 1766–8. ~, William (1759–1806), his second son, prime minister 1783–1801, 1804–6.

pitt'ance *n.* 1. (hist.) Pious bequest to religious house for extra food etc. 2. Allowance, remuneration, esp. scanty one; small number or amount.

pitt'ite *n.* Person occupying seat in theatre-pit.

pĭtū'ĭtary *adj.* Of or secreting phlegm, mucous; ~ *body*, *gland*, (*the*~), small bilobed ductless gland at base of brain producing hormones which regulate many important bodily functions and co-ordinate the working of other endocrine organs (ill. BRAIN). **pĭtū'ĭtous** *adj.* **pĭtū'ĭtrĭn** *n.* Hormone produced by pituitary body; solution of this used medicinally.

pĭt'y *n.* 1. Feeling of tenderness aroused by distress or suffering; *take* ~ *on*, feel or act compassionately towards. 2. Regrettable fact, ground for regret; *more's the* ~, so much the worse. ~ *v.t.* Feel pity for. **pĭt'ўingly** *adv.*

Pī'us. Name of 12 popes: *Pius II* (Enea Silvio de Piccolomini, 1405–64); pope 1458–64; author and patron of letters; *Pius IV* (Giovanni Angelo Medici, 1499–1565); pope 1559–65, reconvened Council of Trent in 1562; *Pius IX* (Giovanni Maria Mastai-Jenetti, 1792–1878); pope 1846–78; during this pontificate the temporal power of the papacy was lost and the doctrine of papal infallibility proclaimed; *Pius XI* (Achille Ratti, 1857–1939); pope 1922–39; the breach between Church and State was healed in this pontificate and the Vatican City State founded; *Pius XII* (Eugenio Pacelli, 1876–1958); pope 1939–58.

pĭv'ot *n.* Short shaft or pin on which something turns or oscillates; (mil.) man on whom body of troops wheels; (fig.) cardinal or central point. ~ *v.i.* Turn as on pivot, hinge (*upon*). **pĭv'otal** *adj.*

pĭx'y, pĭx'ie *n.* Supernatural being akin to fairy. **pĭx'ĭlātėd** *adj.* (U.S.) Slightly crazy.

Pizărr'ō, Francisco (*c* 1471–1541). Spanish discoverer and conqueror of Peru.

pizz. *abbrev.* *Pizzicato.*

pizzica'to (pĭtsĭkah'tō) *adv.* & *adj.* (mus.) (Played) by plucking string of violin etc. with finger instead of using bow. ~ *n.* Passage, note, so played.

pĭzz'le *n.* (now vulg.) Penis of animal, esp. that of bull, formerly used as flogging instrument.

pl. *abbrev.* Place; plate; plural.

P.L.A. *abbrev.* Port of London Authority.

plăc'able *adj.* Easily appeased, mild, forgiving. **plăcabĭl'ĭty** *n.* **plăc'ably** *adv.*

plăc'ard *n.* Document printed on one side of single sheet for posting up, poster. ~ *v.t.* Set up placards on (wall etc.); advertise (wares etc.) by placards; display (poster etc.) as placard.

placāte' (pl*a*-; U.S. plăk'āt) Pacify, conciliate. **placā'tion** *n.* **placāt'ory** *adj.*

plāce *n.* 1. Particular part of space; part of space occupied by person or thing. 2. City, town, village, etc.; group of houses in town etc., usu. one not forming a street; residence, dwelling; country-house with surroundings; building, spot, devoted to specified purpose; *another* ~, (in House of Commons use) House of Lords. 3. Particular spot on surface etc.; particular point or passage in book etc. 4. Rank, station; (racing) position among placed competitors; position of figure in series as indicating its value in decimal or similar notation; step in progression of argument, statement, etc. 5. Proper or natural position; space, seat, accommodation, for person etc. at table, in conveyance, etc.; *in ~ of*, instead of; *take the ~ of*, be substituted for. 6. Office, employment, esp. government appointment; duties of office etc. 7. *in, out of*, ~, (un)suitable, (in)appropriate; *give ~ to*, make room for; be succeeded by; *take ~*, happen; *~ brick*, brick imperfectly burnt from being on windward side of kiln; *~-hunter, -seeker*, one persistently seeking place in public service, esp. by undue influence or from interested motives; *~-(kick)*, (football) kick made when ball is previously placed by another player for that purpose on ground. ~ *v.t.* 1. Put in particular place; arrange in their proper places. 2. Appoint (person) to post; find situation etc. for. 3. Invest (money); dispose of (goods) to customer; put (order for goods etc.) into hands of firm etc. 4. Repose (confidence etc. *in, on*). 5. Assign rank to; locate; state position of (usu. any of first three horses or runners) in race; identify fully, determine who (or what) a particular person (or thing) is, assign to a class; *be placed*, be among first three. 6. Get (goal) by place-kick.

placēb'ō *n.* (pl. *-s, -es*). 1. Medicine given to humour patient (now used in experiments to test the effect of drugs, the drug being given to one group and the placebo to those who act as 'controls'). 2. (eccles.) Opening antiphon of the vespers for the dead. [L, = 'I shall be acceptable', first wd of Ps. cxvi. 9 in Vulgate]

placĕn'ta *n.* (pl. *-ae*). 1. Spongy vascular structure (in some mammals and some other vertebrates) formed by the interlocking of foetal and maternal tissue, through which the foetus is supplied with nutriment and rid of waste products (ill. EMBRYO); it is usu. expelled, attached to the umbilical cord, after the foetus at parturition. 2. (bot.) Part of carpel to which ovules are attached. **placĕn'tal** *adj.*

plā'cer *n.* Deposit of sand, gravel, etc., in bed of stream etc., containing valuable minerals in particles.

plā'cĕt. (In old universities, in voting for or against measure), ~, *non ~*, it pleases me (not). ~ *n.* Such vote.

plă'cĭd *adj.* Mild; peaceful; serene. **plă'cĭdly** *adv.* **placĭd'ĭty** *n.*

plăck'ĕt *n.* Pocket, esp. in woman's skirt; opening or slit at top of skirt for convenience in putting on or off.

plăc'oid *adj.* (Of scales) plate-shaped; (of fish) with placoid scales.

plāg'al *adj.* (mus., of eccles. modes) Having their sounds comprised between the dominant and its octave, with final near middle of the compass (ill. MODE; cf. AUTHENTIC); ~ *cadence*, one in which chord of subdominant immediately precedes that of tonic.

plā'giarize *v.t.* Take and use another person's (thoughts, writings, inventions) as one's own. **plā'giarism, plā'giarist** *ns.*

plā'giary *n.* Plagiarism; plagiarist.

plăgiocĕphăl'ĭc *adj.* Having anterior part of skull more developed on one side, posterior on the other.

plă'gioclāse *n.* (Mineral of) the soda-lime felspar group (so called because they cleave obliquely). **plăgioclăs'tĭc** *adj.* Having oblique cleavage.

plā'giostōme *n.* Fish with mouth placed transversely beneath snout, as shark, ray.

plāgue (-g) *n.* 1. Affliction, esp. as divine punishment; (colloq.) nuisance, trouble. 2. Pestilence, esp. *the* oriental or bubonic ~; *Great P~*, the bubonic plague that visited London in 1665; *~-spot*, spot on skin characteristic of plague; locality infected with plague; (fig.) source or symptom of moral corruption. ~ *v.t.* Afflict with plague; (colloq.) annoy, bother.

plā'guy (-gĭ) *adj.* & *adv.* Annoying(ly); exceeding(ly).

plaice *n.* European marine flat-fish, *Pleuronectes platessa*, much used as food; allied American species.

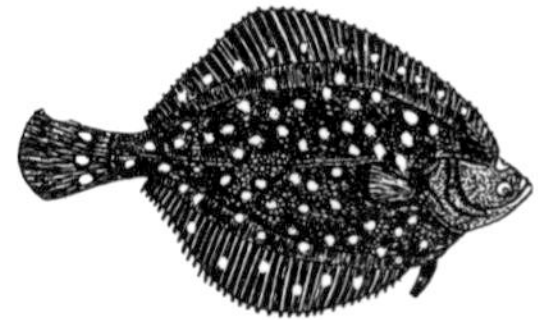

PLAICE

plaid (plăd, Sc. plād) *n.* Long piece of twilled woollen cloth, usu. with chequered or tartan pattern, outer article of Highland costume; cloth used for this, other fabric with tartan pattern.

PLAID

1. Glengarry bonnet. 2. Sporran. 3. Plaid. 4. Kilt. 5. Claymore. 6. Balmoral bonnet. 7. Tam-o'-shanter. 8. Trews. 9. Brogues

plain[1] *adj.* 1. Clear, evident; simple, readily understood; not elaborate or intricate. 2. Unembellished, (of drawings etc.) not coloured; (of food) not rich or highly seasoned; not luxurious. 3. Outspoken, straightforward. 4. Unsophisticated, ordinary, simple; of homely manners, dress, or appearance; not beautiful, ill-favoured, ugly. 5. *~-chant*, plainsong; ~ *clŏthes*, ordinary civil or citizen dress, not uniform or fancy dress; ~ *dealing*, candour, straightforwardness; ~ *sailing*, sailing in a plain course, with no difficulty or obstruction; (fig.) simple course of action; *plain'song*, traditional church music sung in unison in medieval modes and in free rhythm depending on accentuation of the words; *~-spoken*, outspoken. ~ *adv.* Clearly. ~ *n.* 1. Level tract of country; *plains'-man*, inhabitant of a plain. 2. ~ (*knitting*), stitch in which needle is inserted through loop from left to right, and yarn is looped over needle from the back (ill. KNIT). **plain'ly** *adv.* **plain'nĕss** *n.*

plain[2] *v.i.* (archaic, poet.) Mourn; complain; emit plaintive sound.

plaint *n.* 1. (law) Accusation, charge. 2. (poet.) Lamentation, complaint.

plain'tĭff *n.* Party who brings suit into court of law, prosecutor.

plain'tĭve *adj.* Expressive of sorrow; mournful. **plain'tĭvely** *adv.* **plain'tĭvenĕss** *n.*

plait (-ăt) *n.* 1. Interlacing of three or more strands of hair, ribbon, straw, etc. 2. Fold, crease (now usu. PLEAT). ~ *v.t.* Form (hair, straw, etc.) into plait.

plăn *n.* Drawing, diagram, made by projection on flat surface, esp. one showing relative position of parts of (one floor of) a building; large-scale detailed map of town or district; table indicating times, places, etc., of intended proceedings, etc.; scheme of arrangement; project, design; way of proceeding; (perspective) any of the imaginary planes, perpendicular to line of vision, passing through objects shown in picture. ~ *v.t.* Make a plan of (ground, existing building); design (building to be constructed etc.); scheme, arrange beforehand. **plăn'lĕss** *adj.*

plănch (-sh) *n.* Slab of metal, stone, etc.; esp. of baked fire-clay used in an enamelling oven.

plăn'chĕt (-sh-) *n.* Plain disc of metal of which coin is made.

plănchette' (-shĕt) *n.* Small usu. heart-shaped board supported by two castors and a pencil, which when one or more persons rest their fingers lightly on the board is supposed to write without conscious direction.

Planck (-ŭnk), Max 1858–1947). German physicist, Nobel Prize-winner (1918); originator of of the QUANTUM theory; *Planck's constant*, (physics) the constant in the expression for the quantum of energy, symbol *h*, numerical value $6{\cdot}61 \times 10^{-27}$.

plāne[1] *n.* Genus (*Platanus*) of tall spreading trees with broad angular palmately-lobed leaves, and bark which scales off in irregular patches; ~*-tree*, tree of this genus.

plāne[2] *n.* Tool for smoothing surface of woodwork by paring shavings from it, consisting of wooden or metal stock from smooth bottom of which projects a steel blade; similar tool for smoothing metal; *smoothing* ~, one used to finish surface; *moulding* ~, one for making mouldings. ~ *v.t.* Smooth (wood, metal) with plane; pare *away* or *down* (irregularities) with plane; (archaic) level.

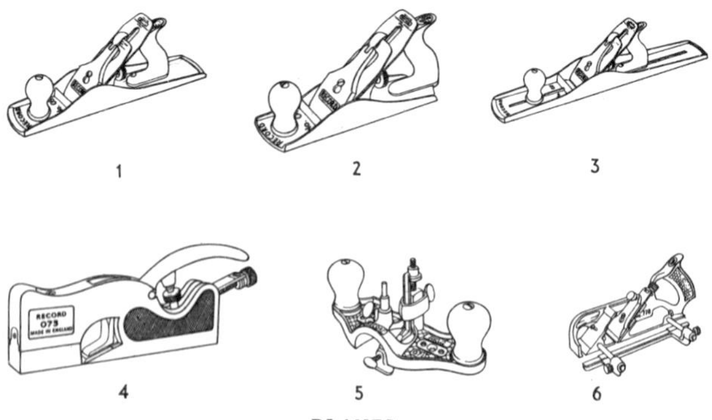

PLANES

1. Jack plane. 2. Smoothing plane. 3. Trying plane. 4. Rabbet plane. 5. Router plane. 6. Fillister plane

plāne[3] *n.* 1. Surface such that the straight line joining any two points in it lies wholly in it; imaginary surface of this kind in which points or lines in material bodies lie; level surface. 2. Flat thin object, esp. one used in aerostatical experiments; (one of) the principal supporting surface(s) in an aeroplane; aeroplane; each of natural faces of a crystal. 3. Main road in mine. 4. (fig.) Level (*of* thought, knowledge, etc.). 5. ~ *sailing*, art of determining ship's place on the theory that she is moving on a plane; (fig., now usu. *plain sailing*) simple course. ~ *v.i.* Travel, glide (*down* etc.) in aeroplane. ~ *adj.* Perfectly level, forming a plane; (of angle, figure, etc.) lying in a plane; ~ *chart*, one on which meridians and parallels of latitude are represented by equidistant straight lines, used in plane sailing; ~*-table*, surveying instrument used for measuring angles in mapping, consisting of a circular drawing-table mounted on a tripod and a ruler for pointing at the object observed; (*v.t.*) survey (area) with this.

plăn'ėt[1] *n.* 1. (hist.) Heavenly body distinguished from fixed stars by having apparent motion of its own, esp. (astrol.) with reference to its supposed influence on persons and events. 2. Each of the heavenly bodies revolving in approximately circular orbits round sun (*primary* ~*s*), or of those revolving round these (*secondary* ~*s* or *satellites*); *major* ~*s*, (in order of distance from sun) Mercury, Venus, Earth, Mars, Jupiter, Saturn, Uranus, Neptune, Pluto; *minor* ~*s*, the asteroids (with orbits between those of Mars and Jupiter); ~*-gear(ing)*, gearing in which planet-wheels are used (ill. GEAR); ~*-wheel*, one of two or more gear-wheels in mesh with a central sun-wheel and an outer annulus which may be free to revolve (giving direct drive) or prevented from revolving (when drive from sun-wheel to planet-wheels effects a reduction in speed).

plăn'ėt[2] *n.* Chasuble.

plănėtār'ium *n.* Model or structure representing planetary system, orrery.

plăn'ėtary *adj.* Of planets; terrestrial, mundane; wandering, erratic.

plăn'gent (-j-) *adj.* (Of sound) thrilling, vibrating, moaning, insistent. **plăn'gency** *n.*

planĭm'ėter *n.* Instrument for mechanically measuring area of irregular plane figure. **planĭm'ėtry** *n.* Measurement of plane surfaces.

plăn'ĭsh *v.t.* Flatten (sheet metal etc.) with smooth-faced hammer; flatten out (coining-metal) between rollers.

plăn'ĭsphēre *n.* Device for showing the part of the heavens visible at a given time and place. **plănĭsphĕ'ric** *adj.*

plănk *n.* Long flat piece of smoothed timber, 2 to 6 in. thick, 9 or more in. wide; item of political or other 'platform' or programme; *walk the* ~, walk blindfold into sea along plank laid over side of ship, esp. as pirates' method of disposing of victims; ~*-bed*, bed of boards, without mattress, used as prison discipline etc. ~ *v.t.* Furnish, cover, floor, with planks; (U.S.) cook (fish) by splitting open and fixing to board; (slang) put *down* (esp. money on the spot).

plănk'ton *n.* (biol.) Collective name for all the forms of drifting or floating organic life found at various depths in the ocean or in fresh water.

plāno- *prefix.* Flatly, in a flattened manner; comb. of plane with another surface.

plāno-cŏnc'āve, -cŏn'vĕx *adjs.* (of lens etc.) with one surface plane and the other concave, convex (ill. LENS).

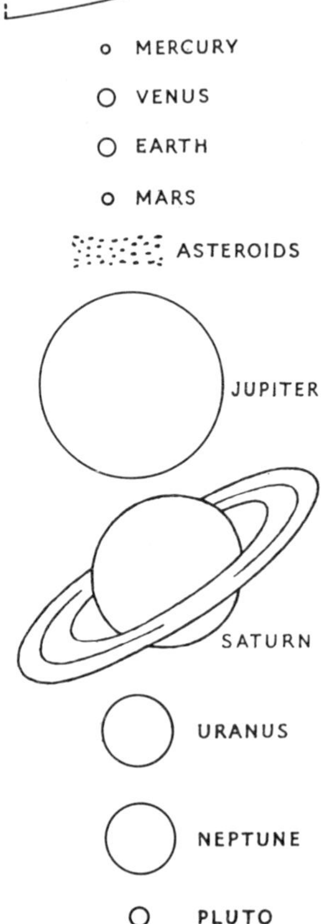

SIZES AND POSITIONS OF THE PLANETS IN RELATION TO THE SUN

plant (-ah-) *n.* 1. Living organism generally capable of living wholly on inorganic substances and having neither power of locomotion nor special organs of sensation or digestion, member of the vegetable kingdom (freq. restricted to the smaller plants, excluding trees and shrubs); ~-*louse*, kinds of insect that infest plants, esp. aphis. 2. Mode of planting oneself, pose. 3. Fixtures, implements, machinery, etc., used in industrial process. 4. (slang) Planned swindle or burglary; hoax. ~ *v.t.* 1. Place (tree, shoot, seed, etc.) in ground that it may take root and grow; naturalize (animals, fish, etc.); cause (idea etc.) to take root *in* (mind); ~ *out*, transfer (plant) from pot or frame to open ground; set out (seedlings) at intervals. 2. Fix firmly (*in*, *on*, ground, etc.); station (person), esp. as spy; ~ *oneself*, take up a position. 3. Establish, found (community, city, church); settle (person) in place as colonist etc. 4. Furnish (land *with* plants, district *with* settlers, etc.). 5. Deliver (blow, thrust) with definite aim. 6. (slang) Conceal (stolen goods etc. on innocent person's premises to incriminate him); bury; place (gold-dust, ore) in mining claim to encourage prospective buyer; devise (fraudulent scheme).

Plăntă'ġėnėt. Orig., nickname of Geoffrey, Count of Anjou, father of Henry II of England; adopted as surname (*c* 1460) by Richard, Duke of York; applied to the whole royal house which occupied English throne 1154–1399 (Henry II to Richard II). [L *planta* sprig, *genista* broom, w. ref. to Geoffrey's habit of wearing on his helmet a sprig of the common broom of Anjou]

plăn'tain[1] (-tĭn) *n.* Genus (*Plantago*) of plants, esp. *greater* ~ (*P. major*), low herb with broad flat leaves spread out close to ground and dense cylindrical spikes of seeds much used for cage-birds.

plăn'tain[2] (-tĭn) *n.* Tree-like tropical herbaceous plant (*Musa paradisiaca*) allied to banana, with immense undivided oblong leaves, cultivated for its fruit borne in long densely clustered spikes; the long pod-shaped somewhat fleshy fruit of this.

plăn'tar *adj.* (anat.) Of the sole of the foot.

plăntā'tion *n.* 1. Assemblage of planted growing plants, esp. trees. 2. Estate on which cotton, tobacco, etc., are cultivated (formerly by servile labour). 3. (hist.) Colonization; colony.

pla'nter (-ah-) *n.* 1. Cultivator of soil; (in Ireland) English settler on forfeited lands in 17th c., (19th c.) person settled in evicted tenant's holding. 2. Occupier of plantation, esp. in (sub-) tropical countries. 3. Machine for planting.

plănt'ĭgrāde *adj.* & *n.* (Animal) that walks on its soles (cf. DIGITIGRADE, on toes); (of human being) placing whole sole on ground at once in walking, flat-footed.

plănx'ty *n.* (Ir. mus.) Animated harp-tune, slower than jig, moving in triplets.

plaque (-ahk) *n.* Ornamental tablet of metal, porcelain, etc., plain or decorated; small tablet as badge of rank in honorary order.

plăsh[1] *n.* Marshy pool; puddle. **plăsh'y**[1] *adj.*

plăsh[2] *v.* Strike surface of (water) so as to break it up; splash. ~ *n.* Splash, plunge. **plăsh'y**[2] *adj.*

plăsh[3] *v.t.* Bend down (branches, twigs) and interweave them to form hedge; make, renew (hedge) thus.

plasm *n.* = PLASMA, sense 2.

plăs'ma (-z-) *n.* 1. Green variety of quartz. 2. (physiol.) Coagulable solution of salts and protein in which blood-cells (corpuscles) are suspended. 3. (physics) Region, e.g. between electrodes, in which many gaseous ions are present, the numbers of positive and negative charges being equal. **plăsmăt'ĭc, plăs'mĭc** *adjs.*

plăsmōd'ium (-z-) *n.* (biol.) Mass of naked protoplasm formed by fusion or aggregation of amoeboid bodies (ill. PROTOZOA).

plăsmŏl'ўsis *n.* Contraction of protoplasm of vegetable cell due to loss of water to solution with which it is in contact.

Plăss'ey. Village of Bengal, scene of victory (1757) of CLIVE over forces of Nawab Suraj ud Daula, through which Bengal passed into British hands.

pla'ster (-ah-) *n.* 1. Curative application consisting of some substance spread upon muslin etc. and capable of adhering at temperature of the body. 2. Soft plastic mixture, esp. of lime, sand, and hair, spread on walls etc. to form smooth surface. 3. Sulphate of lime, gypsum; ~ *of Paris*, fine white plaster of calcined gypsum used for making moulds, as cement etc. (orig. prepared from gypsums of Montmartre, Paris). ~ *v.t.* 1. Cover (wall etc.) with plaster or the like; coat, bedaub; (slang) bomb heavily. 2. Apply medical plaster to; stick, fix, like plaster upon surface. 3. Treat (wine) with gypsum etc. to neutralize acidity. **pla'sterer** *n.* **pla'stery** *adj.*

plăs'tĭc (*or* -ah-) *adj.* 1. Moulding, giving form to clay, wax, etc.; produced by moulding; capable of being (easily) moulded; (fig.) pliant, supple; ~ *arts*, those concerned with modelling, e.g. sculpture, ceramics; ~ *clay*, (geol.) middle group of eocene beds; ~ *surgery*, that concerned with remedying deficiency of structure. 2. Causing growth of natural forms, formative; (biol.) capable of forming living tissue, accompanied by this process. ~ *n.* Any of a group of substances, natural or synthetic, chiefly polymers of high molecular weight, that can be moulded into any form by heat or pressure or both, as bakelite, cellulose acetate, nylon, etc. **plăs'tĭcally** *adv.* **plăstĭ'cĭty** *n.*

plăs'tĭcine (-ēn) *n.* Proprietary composition of specially treated clay, used in schools etc. as a substitute for modelling clay.

plăs'tĭd *n.* 1. (biol.) Individual mass or unit of protoplasm, as cell or unicellular organism. 2. (bot.) Differentiated corpuscle or granule occurring in protoplasm of vegetable cell (ill. CELL).

plăs'tron *n.* 1. Fencer's leather-covered breast-plate; ornamental front to woman's bodice; breast-covering of cloth worn by lancers; (hist.) steel breast-plate (ill. ARMOUR). 2. Ventral part of shell of tortoise or turtle (ill. TORTOISE); analogous part in other animals.

plăt *n.* Patch, plot, of ground.

Plata, Rio de la (rē'ō, plah'*ta*). (also *River Plate*) Long funnel-shaped estuary on E. side of S. America, between Argentina and Uruguay; scene (1939) of naval battle between German 'pocket battleship' *Admiral Graf Spee*, subsequently scuttled, and 3 British cruisers, *Ajax*, *Achilles*, and *Exeter*. [Span., = 'river of silver', with ref. to export of silver from the region]

plāte[1] *n.* 1. Flat thin usu. rigid sheet of metal etc. of even surface and more or less uniform thickness; this as part of mechanism etc., esp. one of the sheets of which a ship's armour and steam-boilers are composed; (anat., zool., & bot.) thin flat organic structure or formation. 2. The portion of a denture which fits to the mouth and holds the teeth. 3. Smooth piece of metal etc. for engraving; impression from this, esp. as illustration of book; full-page illustration of book; book-plate. 4. Piece of metal with name or inscription for affixing to something; (baseball) (flat piece of metal or stone, marking) home base. 5. Stereotype or electrotype cast of page of composed movable types, from which sheets are printed. 6. Thin sheet of metal, glass, etc., coated with sensitive emulsion, for taking photographs; *whole* ~, one of these measuring $8\frac{1}{2} \times 6\frac{1}{2}$ in.; *half*-~, $6\frac{1}{2} \times 4\frac{3}{4}$ in.; (U.S.) $5\frac{1}{2} \times 4\frac{1}{4}$ in.; *quarter*-~, $4\frac{1}{4} \times 3\frac{1}{4}$ in. 7. Horizontal timber laid along top of wall to support ends of joists or rafters, or at top or bottom of a framing (ill. ROOF). 8. (collect. sing.) Table and domestic utensils of silver, gold, or other metals; silver or gold cup as prize for (orig. horse-) race, such race; *selling* ~, horse-race, winner of which must be sold at fixed price. 9. Shallow usu. circular vessel, now usu. of earthenware or china, from which food is eaten; contents of this; similar vessel used for collection in churches etc. 10. ~-*basket*, basket for spoons, forks, etc.; ~ *glass*, thick glass of fine quality rolled out in plates for shop windows etc.; ~-*layer*, man employed in laying and repairing railway lines; ~-*mark*: = HALL-mark; (also) impression left on margin of engraving by edge of plate; imitation of this on mount of photograph; whence ~-*marked* (*adj.*); ~-*powder*, powder for cleaning silver etc.; ~-*rack*, rack in which domestic plates are kept or placed to drain after washing; ~-*rail*, early form of railroad, flat strip of iron etc. with projecting flange, on which colliery trams are run; ~-*tracery*: see ill. WINDOW. **plāte'ful** *n.* **plāte** *v.t.* Cover (esp. ship) with plates of metal for protection, ornament, etc.; cover (other metal) with thin coat of silver, gold, tin, etc.; make a plate of (type) for printing.

Plate[2], River: see PLATA.

plăt'eau (-tō; *or* plătō') *n.* Elevated tract of comparatively flat or level land, table-land.

plāte'lĕt (-tl-) *n.* (*blood*) ~, ovoid or circular body suspended in the plasma, important in blood-clotting (ill. BLOOD).

plăt(t)'en *n.* Iron plate in printing-press by which paper is pressed against inked type; corresponding part in typewriter etc.

plāt'er *n.* One who plates with silver etc.; one who makes or applies plates in ship-building; inferior race-horse, competing chiefly for plates.

plăt'fōrm *n.* 1. Raised level surface, natural or artificial terrace; raised surface of planks, stone, etc., along side of line at railway station, from which passengers enter the carriages, and upon which they alight on leaving the train. 2. Raised flooring in hall or open air from which speaker addresses audience; (fig.) political basis of party etc. programme, esp. (U.S.) declaration issued by representatives of party assembled to nominate candidates for election.

plāt'ing *n.* (esp.) Coating of gold, silver, etc.; plate-racing.

plăt'inīze *v.t.* Coat with platinum.

plăt'inoid *n.* Alloy of nickel, zinc, copper, etc.; kinds of metal found associated with platinum.

plăt'inotȳpe *n.* (Print produced by) a process of photographic printing depending on the use of platinum salts.

plăt'inum *n.* A somewhat rare metallic element, white, of high density, ductile and malleable, unaffected by simple acids and fusible only at very high temperatures; symbol Pt, at. no. 78, at. wt 195·09; ~ *black*, platinum in form of finely divided black powder; ~ *blonde*, woman with flaxen or nearly white hair; ~ *metals*, name given to certain elements, found with and resembling platinum, as iridium, osmium, palladium, etc.

plăt'itūde *n.* Commonplaceness; commonplace remark, esp. one solemnly delivered. **plătitūd'inous** *adj.* **plătitūd'inously** *adv.*

Plāt'ō (*c* 427–348 B.C.). Greek philosopher, pupil of SOCRATES and author of Dialogues based on the teaching of Socrates and the doctrines of Pythagoras; the principal dialogues were 'Protagoras', 'Gorgias', 'Phaedo', 'Symposium', 'Republic', 'Phaedrus', 'Parmenides', 'Theaetetus', 'Sophist', 'Philebus', 'Timaeus', 'Laws', and the 'Apology'.

Platŏn'ic *adj.* Of Plato or his doctrines; esp. applied to love or affection for one of the opposite sex entirely free from sensual desire (orig. used without reference to women).

Plāt'onism. Philosophical system of Plato, of which central conception is existence of a world of ideas, divine types, or forms of material objects, which ideas are alone real and permanent, while individual material things are but their ephemeral and imperfect imitations. **Plāt'onist** *n.* Follower of Plato; *Cambridge Platonists*, group of 17th-c. philosophers (Ralph Cudworth, Henry More, John Smith, Nathanael Culverwel, and others) with headquarters in University of Cambridge.

platōōn' *n.* (hist.) Small infantry detachment, esp. a unit for volley-firing etc.; volley fired by it; (now, in British Army) subdivision of a company, a tactical unit commanded by a lieutenant and divided into three sections.

plătt'er *n.* (chiefly archaic) Flat dish or plate, freq. of wood.

plătȳhĕl'minth *n.* One of the phylum *Platyhelminthes*, including tape-worms and flukes; a flat-worm.

plăt'ȳpus *n.* (also *duck-billed* ~) Primitive aquatic and burrowing mammal (*Ornithorhynchus anatinus*) of Tasmania and SE. Australia, which has a bony duck-like beak and flattened tail, and lays shelled eggs. [Gk *platus* broad, *pous* foot]

DUCK-BILLED PLATYPUS

plăt'yrrhine (-tīrīn) *adj.* & *n.* (Monkey) with nostrils wide apart, and thumbs nearly or quite non-opposable (i.e. any New World monkey).

plaud'it *n.* (usu. pl.) Round of applause; emphatic expression of approval. [shortened f. L *plaudite* applaud, imper. of *plaudere*, customary appeal for applause by Roman actors at end of play]

plaus'ible (-z-) *adj.* (Of arguments etc.) specious, seeming reasonable or probable; (of persons) fair-spoken (usu. implying deceit). **plausibil'ity** *n.* **plaus'ibly** *adv.*

Plaut'us, Titus Maccius (*c* 254–184 B.C.). Roman comic dramatist.

play *v.* 1. Move about in lively or capricious manner, frisk, flit, flutter, pass gently; strike lightly; alternate rapidly; (of part of mechanism etc.) have free movement. 2. Allow (fish) to exhaust itself by pulling against line; direct (light *on*, *over*, etc.); (of light) pass (*over*, *along*, etc.). 3. Perform, execute (trick, prank, etc.). 4. Amuse oneself, sport, frolic; employ oneself in the game of; pretend for fun; (of ground etc.) be in good etc. condition for play; contend against (person) in game; employ (person) to play in game, include in team; (dial., esp. of workmen on strike) abstain from work; ~ *at*, engage in (game); (fig.) engage in (work etc.) in trivial or half-hearted way; ~ *fair*, *foul*, play or (fig.) act (un)fairly; ~ *the game*, observe the rules of the game, play fair (freq. fig.); ~ *into the hands of*, act so as to give advantage to (opponent or partner); ~ *up*, put all one's energy into the game etc.; ~ *upon words*, pun; ~ *with*, amuse oneself with, trifle with, treat lightly; *played out*, exhausted of energy, vitality, or usefulness; 5. Move (piece in chess etc.); take (playing-card) from one's hand and lay it face upwards on table in one's turn; strike (ball) in specified, esp. defensive, manner; ~ one's *cards well*, (fig.) make good use of opportunities; ~ *on*, (cricket) play the ball on to one's own wicket and so put oneself out; ~ *off*, oppose (person *against* another) esp. for one's own advantage; cause (person) to exhibit himself disadvantageously; pass off as something else. 6. Perform on (musical instrument), perform (*on* instrument); perform (music *on* instrument); ~ (congregation etc.) *in*, *out*, play on organ etc., as they come in, go out; ~ (*up*)*on*, make use of (person's fears, credulity, etc.). 7. Perform (drama) on stage; act (*in* drama); act (part) in drama; (fig.) act in real life the part of (*the deuce*, *the man*, *truant*, etc.); ~ *up to*, act in drama so as to support (another actor); (fig.) back up; flatter, toady. ~ *n.* 1. Brisk, light, or fitful movement; activity, operation; freedom of movement, space for this, scope for activity; *make* ~, act effectively, esp. (racing, hunting) exercise pursuers or followers. 2. Amusement; playing of game; manner, style, of this; cessation of work (of workmen on strike etc.); *at* ~, engaged in playing; *in ~*, not seriously; (of ball) being used in ordinary course of play; *out of ~*, (of ball) temporarily removed from play according to rules; *~ on words*, pun. 3. Dramatic piece, drama. 4. Gaming, gambling. 5. *~-acting*, playing a part, posing; *~-actor*, actor (usu. contempt.); *~-bill*, bill, placard, announcing theatrical play; *playboy*, man fond of pleasure and gaiety; *~-day*, school holiday, weekday on which miners etc. do not work; *play'fellow*, companion in (usu. children's) play; *play'goer*, frequenter of theatre; *play'ground*, piece of ground used for play, esp. at school; *play'house*, theatre; *play'mate*, playfellow; *~ pen*, portable wooden enclosure for keeping young child out of harm's way; *play'thing*, toy; (fig.) person, etc., treated as mere toy; *play'wright*, dramatist.

play'er *n.* (esp.) Person engaged at the time, person skilful, in a game; professional player at cricket etc.; actor, performer on musical instrument; *~-piano*, piano with apparatus for playing it mechanically.

play'ful *adj.* Frolicsome, sportive; humorous, jocular. **play'fully** *adv.* **play'fulnėss** *n.*

play'ing *n.* (esp.) *~-cards*, set or pack of cards used in games.

plea *n.* Pleading, argument, excuse; (law) formal statement by or on behalf of defendant; (hist.) action at law; *Court of Common P~s*: see COMMON; *special ~*, defendant's plea alleging new fact.

pleach *v.t.* Entwine, interlace; esp. = PLASH[3] *v.*

plead *v.* 1. Address court as advocate on behalf of either party; maintain (cause) in court; allege formally as plea; (fig.) allege as excuse etc.; *~ guilty*, confess liability or guilt, *~ not guilty*, deny it. 2. *~ with*, make earnest appeal to (person). **plead'ingly** *adv.* **plead'er** *n.*

plead'ing *n.* (esp.) Formal (now usu. written) statement of cause of action or defence; *special ~*, see SPECIAL.

pleasance (plĕz'ans) *n.* (archaic) Pleasure, enjoyment; pleasure-ground, esp. one attached to mansion.

pleasant (plĕz'nt) *adj.* Agreeable to mind, feelings, or senses; (archaic) jocular, facetious. **pleas'antly** *adv.* **pleas'antnėss** *n.*

pleas'antry (plĕz-) *n.* Jocularity; humorous speech, jest.

please (-z) *v.* 1. Be agreeable (to); *~ oneself*, do as one likes, take one's own way; *be pleased with*, derive pleasure from. 2. Be pleased, like; have the will or desire, think proper; (*if you*) *~*, (as courteous qualification to request etc.) if it please you, if you like, if it is your will or pleasure. **pleased** (-zd), **pleas'ing** *adjs.* **pleas'ingly** *adv.*

pleas'urable (plĕzher-) *adj.* Affording pleasure. **pleas'urablenėss** *n.* **pleas'urably** *adv.*

pleasure (plĕzh'er) *n.* 1. Enjoyment, delight; sensuous enjoyment as chief object of life. 2. Will, desire.

pleat *n.* 1. Fold, crease; esp., flattened fold in cloth made by doubling it upon itself; *box, knife, inverted, ~*: see illustration. *~ v.t.* Fold (cloth etc.) in pleats.

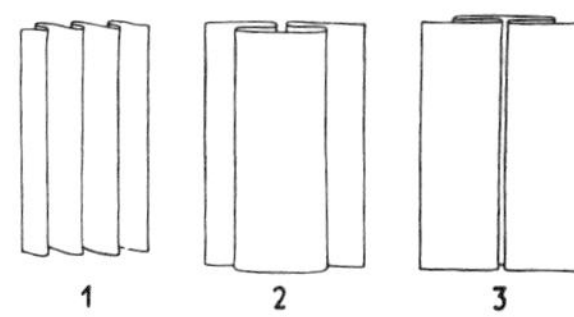

PLEATS
1. Knife. 2. Box. 3. Inverted

plėbei'an (-bēan) *n.* Commoner in ancient Rome; commoner. *~ adj.* Of low birth; of the common people; coarse, base, ignoble. **plėbei'annėss** *n.*

plĕb'iscite (-sĭt) *n.* 1. (Rom. hist.) Law enacted by the commons (plebeians) voting by tribes. 2. Direct vote of all electors of State on important public question; public expression of community's opinion, with or without binding force.

plĕc'trum *n.* (pl. *-ra*). Small spike of ivory, quill, metal, etc., sometimes attached to a ring fitting on the finger, for plucking strings of zither etc.; part of keyboard instrument with same function (ill. HARPSICHORD).

plĕdge *n.* 1. Thing handed over to person as security for fulfilment of contract, payment of debt, etc., and liable to forfeiture in case of failure; thing put in pawn; (fig.) child. 2. Thing given as token of favour etc. or of something to come; drinking of a health, toast. 3. Vow, promise; *the ~*, solemn engagement to abstain from intoxicants. 4. State of being pledged. *~ v.t.* Deposit as security, pawn; (fig.) plight (one's honour, word, etc.); drink to the health of.

plĕdg'ėt *n.* Small wad of lint etc.

Plei'ad (plī-, plē-). 1. Name given by critics of Alexandria to the 7 most eminent Greek tragic poets of reign of Ptolemy II. 2. (*la Pléiade*) Group of French poets, including Ronsard and du Bellay, of latter part of 16th c., animated by a common veneration for writers of antiquity and a desire to improve the quality of French verse.

Pleiades (plī'adēz). 1. (Gk myth.) 7 daughters of Atlas, turned on their deaths into a constellation. 2. Conspicuous constellation or cluster of stars in Taurus.

plein air (plĕnnār) *attrib.* Of the Impressionist style of painting (originated in France *c* 1870) concerned with representing effects of atmosphere and light that cannot be observed in studio. **plein-air'ist(e)** *n.* [f. Fr. *en plein air* in the open air]

pleis'tocēne (plī-, plē-) *adj.* (geol.) Of the series of rocks immediately above the Pliocene, associated with glacial deposits in N. Europe and N. America. *~ n.* (*The P~*), this series or epoch (ill. GEOLOGY). [Gk *pleistos* most, *kainos* new]

plēn'ary *adj.* Entire, absolute, unqualified; (of assembly) fully attended; *~ inspiration*: see INSPIRATION. **plēn'arĭly** *adj.*

plĕnĭpotĕn'tiary (-sha-) *adj.* & *n.* (Person) invested with full power, esp. as ambassador deputed to act at discretion; (of power) absolute.

plĕn'itūde *n.* Fullness, completeness; abundance.

plĕn'tėous *adj.* (chiefly poet.) Plentiful. **plĕn'tėously** *adv.* **plen'tėousnėss** *n.*

plĕn'tĭful *adj.* Abundant, copious. **plĕn'tĭfully** *adv.* **plen'tĭfulnėss** *n.*

plĕn'ty *n.* Abundance, as much as one could desire; *horn of ~*, cornucopia. *~ adv.* (colloq.; with adj. followed by *enough*) Quite.

plĕn'um *n.* Space filled with matter; full assembly.

plē'onăsm *n.* (gram.) Redundancy of expression. **plēonăs'tĭc** *adj.* **plēonăs'tĭcally** *adv.*

plēsĭosaur'us *n.* (pl. *-rī*, *-ruses*). Member of a genus (*P~*) of extinct marine reptiles with long neck, small head, short tail, and four large paddles. [Gk *plesios* near, *sauros* lizard]

plĕth'ora (*or* plĕthōr'a) *n.* (path., obs.) Morbid condition marked by excess of red corpuscles in blood; (fig.) unhealthy repletion. **plĕthŏ'rĭc** *adj.* **plĕthŏ'rĭcally** *adv.*

pleura (-oora) *n.* 1. Either of two serous membranes lining thorax and enveloping lungs in mammals (ill. LUNG). 2. Either of the two side plates of the exoskeleton in arthropods. **pleur'al** *adj.*

pleur'ĭsy (-oor-) *n.* Inflammation of the pleura, marked by pain in chest or side, fever, etc. **pleurĭt'ĭc** *adj.*

pleurodȳn'ĭa (ploor-) *n.* Pain from the chest.

pleuro-pneumōn'ĭa (plo- o-nū-) *n.* Pneumonia complicated with pleurisy, esp. as contagious disease of horned cattle.

plĕxĭm'ėter *n.* (med.) Thin plate of ivory etc. placed on body and struck with plexor in medical percussion.

plĕx'or *n.* (med.) Small hammer used with pleximeter.

plĕx'us *n.* Network of nerve fibres or minute blood-vessels in animal body; network, complication.

plī'able, plī'ant *adjs.* Bending, supple; (fig.) yielding, compliant. **pliabĭl'ity, plī'ancy** *ns.* **plī'ably, plī'antly** *advs.*

plĭc'a *n.* (pl. *-ae*). Fold, as of skin or membrane; (path.) ~ (*polon'ica*), matted condition of hair due to filth and neglect.

plĭc'ate *adj.* (bot., zool., geol.) Folded. **plĭcāt'ĕd** *adj.* **plĭcā'tion** *n.* Folding; fold; folded condition.

plī'ers *n.pl.* Pincers having long jaws, usu. with parallel surfaces, sometimes toothed, for bending wire, holding small objects, etc.

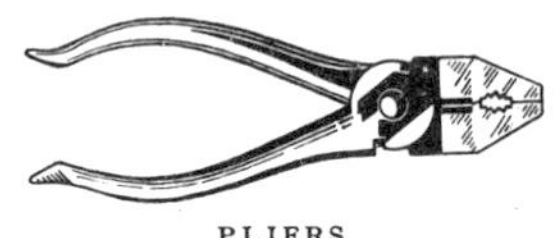

PLIERS

plight' (plīt) *v.t.* (archaic) Pledge (troth, faith, etc., esp. in past part.); engage one*self* (*to* person).

plight² (plīt) *n.* Condition, state (usu. unhappy).

plĭm'sŏll mark. Name sometimes given to load lines on merchant-ship's side indicating limit to which it may be legally loaded. [Samuel *Plimsoll* (1824–98), Engl.

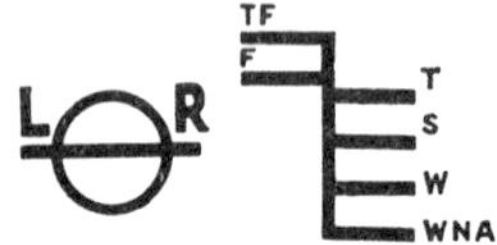

PLIMSOLL MARK AND LOAD LINES

L R, Lloyd's Register. Horizontal lines on right show variations of loading depths allowed in water of differing densities. TF, tropical fresh water. F, fresh water. Sea water: T, tropics. S summer. W, winter. WNA, winter North Atlantic

radical M.P., largely instrumental in passing Merchant Shipping Act, 1876]

plĭm'sŏlls *n.pl.* Kind of cheap rubber-soled canvas shoes.

plĭnth *n.* Lower square member of base of column (ill. ORDER); projecting part of wall (or piece of furniture) immediately above ground.

plĭnth'īte *n.* (min.) Kind of brick-red clay found among trap rocks of Antrim and the Hebrides.

Plĭn'y. ~ *the Elder* (Gaius Plinius Secundus, *c* A.D. 23–79), Roman author of a 'Natural History', who perished in the eruption of Vesuvius; ~ *the Younger*, his nephew (Gaius Plinius Caecilius Secundus, *c* A.D. 61–*c* 113), famous for his published 'Letters'.

plī'ocēne *adj.* (geol.) Of the series of rocks at the top of the Tertiary. ~ *n.* (*The P~*), this series or epoch (ill. GEOLOGY). [Gk *pleion* more, *kainos* new]

plŏd *v.* Walk laboriously, trudge; drudge, slave (*at*); make (one's way) laboriously. ~ *n.* Laborious walk or work. **plŏdd'er** *n.* **plŏdd'ing** *adj.* Slow and painstaking. **plŏdd'ingly** *adv.*

plōs'ive *adj.* & *n.* (phonet.) Explosive (consonant).

plŏt *n.* 1. Piece of ground, usu. small. 2. Plan, story, of play, poem, novel, etc. 3. Conspiracy; sly plan. ~ *v.t.* Make plan or map of (existing object, place or thing to be laid out, constructed, etc.); mark the position of values of a variable on a graph or the like; plan, contrive (evil object, or abs.). **plŏtt'er** *n.*

Plotīn'us (*c* A D. 205–62). Egyptian-born founder of NEOPLATONISM.

plough (-ow) *n.* 1. Implement for cutting furrows in soil and turning it up, consisting essentially of a vertical coulter which cuts the furrow from the unploughed ground, a *plough'share* which cuts the furrow horizontally underneath, and a mould-board which turns it over, drawn by horses etc. (or now, by tractor), and guided by *plough'man*; ploughed land; kinds of instrument resembling plough, for cutting up blocks of ice, clearing away snow, etc.; *the P~*, CHARLES'S WAIN; *~-beam*, central beam of plough; *~-boy*, boy who leads plough-horses etc.; *~-land*, (hist.) as much land as could be ploughed by one team of 8 oxen in a year, unit of assessment in northern and eastern counties of England after Norman Conquest; arable land; *P~ Monday*, first after Epiphany on which beginning of ploughing season was celebrated; *~-tail*, rear of plough. 2. (slang) Rejection of candidate in examination. ~ *v.* 1. Turn up (earth, or abs.) with plough, esp. before sowing; rout *out*, cast *up*, thrust *down* (roots, weeds) with plough; furrow, scratch (surface) as with plough; produce (furrow, line) thus; produce wrinkles in (brow etc.); ~ *back*, plough (grass, clover, etc.) into soil to enrich it; (fig.) reinvest (profits) in business etc. 2. Advance laboriously (*through* snow, book, etc.); (of ship etc.) cleave (surface of water, its way, etc.). 3. (slang) Reject (candidate) in examination.

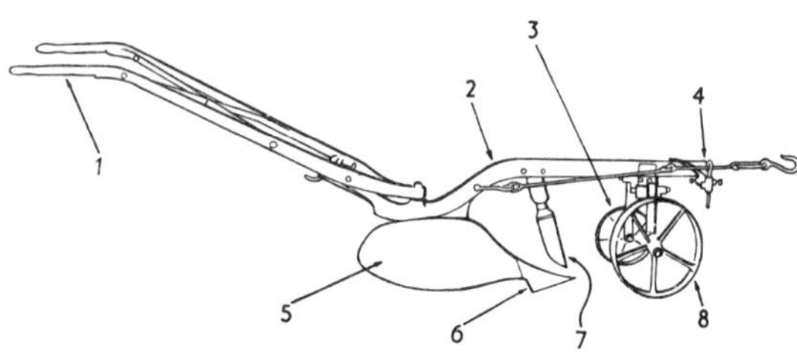

PLOUGH

1. Handle. 2. Beam. 3. Land wheel. 4. Head. 5. Mould-board. 6. Share. 7. Coulter 8. Furrow wheel

plov'er (plŭ-) *n.* Several kinds of gregarious birds, esp. of genera *Charadrius* (e.g. ringed plover) and *Squatarola* (grey plover); also (pop.) lapwing, eggs of which were formerly sold as 'plovers' eggs'.

ploy *n.* (north.) Expedition, undertaking, occupation, job.

plŭck *n.* 1. Plucking, twitch. 2. Rejection, failure, in examination. 3. Heart, liver, and lungs, of beast as food. 4. Courage, spirit. ~ *v.* 1. Pull off, pick (flower, feather, hair); pull at, twitch; tug, snatch, *at*; strip (bird) of feathers; (archaic) pull, drag, snatch (*away*, *off*, etc.). 2. Plunder, swindle. 3. Reject (candidate) in examination. 4. ~ *up heart, spirits, courage*, take courage. **plŭck'y** *adj.* Having pluck or courage, brave, spirited; (photog., of print or negative) bold, with well-marked contrasts. **plŭck'ily** *adv.* **plŭck'inĕss** *n.*

plŭg *n.* 1. Piece of wood etc. fitting tightly into hole, used to fill gap or act as wedge etc.; freq. in technical use, e.g. pin etc. for making electrical contacts, SPARKING plug; natural or morbid concretion acting thus; kinds of stopper for vessel or pipe; fire-plug. 2 Tobacco pressed into cake or stick; piece of this cut off for chewing ~ *v.* Stop (*up*) with plug; (slang) shoot; (slang) strike with fist; (colloq.) plod (*away at* work etc.); (slang) popularize (song etc.) by frequent repetition.

plŭm *n.* 1. Roundish fleshy fruit of *Prunus domestica*, drupe with sweet pulp and flattish pointed stone; tree bearing this. 2. Dried grape or raisin as used for puddings, cakes, etc.; sugar-plum; *French ~*, fine kind of prune. 3. (fig.) Good thing; best of a collection; prize in life; (slang, now rare) £100,000. 4. ~ *cake*, one containing raisins, currants, etc.; *~-duff*, plain flour and suet pudding with raisins or currants; ~ *pudding*, boiled pudding of flour, suet, bread-crumbs, raisins, currants, eggs, spices, etc., eaten at Christmas.

plum'age (-ōō-) *n.* Bird's feathers.

plŭmb (-m) *n.* Ball of lead, esp. that attached to mason's *~-line*, string for testing perpendicularity of wall, etc.; sounding-lead, plummet; *out of* ~, not vertical; ~-*rule*, mason's plumb-line attached to board. ~ *adj.* Vertical; (fig.) (cricket, of wicket) level, true; downright, sheer. ~ *adv.* Vertically; (fig.) exactly; (U.S., slang) quite, utterly. ~ *v.* 1. Sound (sea), measure (depth), with plummet; make vertical. 2. Work as plumber.

plŭmbāg'ō *n.* 1. Graphite, 'black lead', allotropic form of carbon used for pencils etc. 2. Genus of herbaceous plants with spikes of tubular white, blue, or purplish flowers, leadwort.

plŭm'bėous *adj.* Of, like, lead; lead-glazed.

plŭmb'er (-m*er*) *n.* Artisan who fits and repairs pipes, cisterns, tanks, etc., with lead, zinc, iron, or tin.

plŭmb'ing (-ming) *n.* System of water and drainage pipes in a building etc.

plŭm'bism *n.* Poisoning caused by absorption of lead into the system.

plume (-ōō-) *n.* Feather, esp. large one used for ornament; ornamental feather or bunch of feathers or horsehair, esp. as attached to helmet or hat, or worn in hair; (zool.) feather-like part or formation. ~ *v.t.* Furnish with plume(s); pride one*self* (*on* esp. something trivial or to which one has no claim); (of bird) preen (feathers).

plŭmm'ėt *n.* (Weight attached to) plumb-line; sounding-lead; weight attached to fishing-line to keep float upright. ~ *v.i.* Plunge.

plŭmm'y *adj.* Of, abounding in, plums; (colloq., of voice) speaking as if with a plum in the mouth; (colloq., now rare) rich, good, desirable.

plumōse' (-ōō-) *adj.* Feathered; featherlike.

plŭmp[1] *adj.* (esp. of persons or parts of body) Full, rounded, fleshy, filled out. ~ *v.* Make or become plump, fatten *up*, swell *out*. **plŭmp'ly** *adv.* **plŭmp'nėss** *n.*

plŭmp[2] *v.* Drop or plunge with abrupt descent; vote *for* (one candidate alone, when one might vote for two); ~ *for*, vote for, choose (something). ~ *n.* Abrupt plunge, heavy fall. ~ *adv.* With sudden or heavy fall; flatly, bluntly. ~ *adj.* Direct, unqualified.

plŭm'per *n.* Ball, disc, formerly carried in mouth to fill out hollow cheeks.

plu'mūle (-ōō-) *n.* Rudimentary stem of embryo plant (ill. SEED); little feather of down. **plum'ūlar, plumūlā'ceous** (-sh*us*) *adjs.*

plum'y (-ōō-) *adj.* Plume-like; feathery; adorned with plumes.

plŭn'der *v.t.* Rob (place, person) forcibly of goods, esp. as in war; rob systematically; steal, embezzle. ~ *n.* Violent or dishonest acquisition of property; property so acquired; (slang) profit, gain. **plŭn'derer** *n.*

plŭn'derage *n.* Plundering, esp. embezzling of goods on shipboard; spoil thus obtained.

plŭnge (-j) *v.* Thrust violently (*into* liquid, cavity, etc.); throw oneself, dive, (*into*); enter impetuously; (of horse) throw itself violently forward; (of ship) pitch; (slang) gamble deeply, run into debt. ~ *n.* Plunging, dive; (fig.) critical step; ~-*bath*, one large enough to dive into.

plŭn'ger (-j-) *n.* (esp.) 1. Part of mechanism that works with plunging motion. 2. (slang) Gambler, speculator.

plu'pĕrf'ėct (-ōō-) *adj.* & *n.* (Tense) expressing action completed prior to some past point of time specified or implied (as *I had done*). [L *plus quam perfectum* more than perfect]

plur'al (-oor-) *adj.* & *n.* (Form of noun, verb, etc.) denoting more than one (or, in languages with dual form, more than two); more than one in number; ~ *vote*, vote of one person in more than one constituency. **plur'ally** *adv.*

plur'alism (-oor-) *n.* 1. Holding of more than one office, esp. benefice, at a time. 2. (philos.) System that recognizes more than one ultimate principle. **plur'alist** *n.* **pluralis'tic** *adj.*

plurăl'ity (-oor-) *n.* State of being plural; large number, multitude; holding of two or more benefices or offices; benefice, office, held with another; majority (*of* votes etc.).

plur'alize (-oor-) *v.* Make plural, express in the plural; hold more than one benefice.

pluriprĕs'ence (-oor-, -z-) *n.* Presence in more than one place at same time.

plŭs *prep.* (As oral rendering of symbol +) with the addition of (cf. MINUS); (after number etc.) or more, but not less. ~ *adj.* Additional, extra; having plus sign (+) prefixed, positive; (elect.) positive, having a positive charge; ~- *fours*, long wide knickerbockers, suit with these, freq. associated with golf, so named because, to produce the overhang, the length was orig. increased by 4 in. (ill. COAT). ~ *n.* The symbol +; additional quantity; positive quantity. [L, = 'more']

plŭsh *n.* Cloth of silk, cotton, etc., resembling velvet but with longer and softer pile; (pl.) footman's plush breeches. **plŭsh'y** *adj.*

Plut'ârch (-ōō-, -k) (*c* A.D. 46–120). Greek biographer and moral philosopher, author of 'Parallel Lives' of eminent Greeks and Romans.

plut'ârchy (-ōō-, -kĭ) *n.* Plutocracy.

Plut'ō[1] (-ōō-). 1. (Gk & L myth.) God of the infernal regions, brother of Jupiter and Neptune. 2. Planet, remoter than Neptune, discovered in 1930; symbol ♇ (ill. PLANET).

Plut'ō[2] (-ōō-). The pipe-line laid for conveying fuel stores under English Channel in invasion of France, 1944. [f. initials of *P*ipe-*l*ine *u*nder *t*he *o*cean]

plutŏc'racy (-ōō-) *n.* Rule of the wealthy; ruling class of wealthy persons. **plut'ocrăt** *n.* **plutocrăt'ic** *adj.*

plutŏl'atry (-ōō-) *n.* Worship of wealth.

plu'ton (-ōō-) *n.* (geol.) Any body of rock that has crystallized deep in the earth's crust and has been exposed later by erosion. **plutŏn'ic** *adj.* [f. PLUTO[1]]

Plutōn'ian (-ōō-) *adj.* Of Pluto or his kingdom; infernal.

plutōn'ium *n.* A transuranic element, not found in nature, formed from uranium in a nuclear reactor (pile), a fissile material used in atomic bombs; symbol Pu, at. no. 94, principal isotope 239. [named after planet PLUTO[1]]

pluv'ial (-ōō-) *adj.* Of rain, rainy; (geol.) caused by rain. ~ *n.* (eccles. hist.) Long cloak as ceremonial vestment.

pluviŏm'ėter (-ōō-) *n.* Rain-gauge. **pluviomĕt'rical** *adj.*

plȳ[1] *n.* Fold, thickness, layer, of cloth, etc.; strand of rope, etc.; *two-*, *three-*, etc. ~, having two etc. thicknesses or strands; *ply'wood*, strong thin board made by gluing or cementing layers of wood together with grains crosswise.

plȳ[2] *v.* 1. Use, wield vigorously (tool, weapon); work at (business, task); supply (person etc.) persistently *with* (food etc.); assail vigorously (*with* questions, arguments). 2. Work to windward (naut.); (of vessel, its master, coach, etc.) go to and fro *between* (places); (of porter, cabman, etc.) attend regularly for custom (*at* place).

Plȳm'outh[1] (-m*u*th). City of Devonshire, seaport and naval base; ~ *Brethren*, Calvinistic religious sect founded at Plymouth *c* 1830, with no formal creed or official order of ministers.

Plȳm'outh[2]. Town of Massachusetts, landing-place of PILGRIM FATHERS; ~ *Rock*, (1) granite boulder at Plymouth on which Pilgrim Fathers are supposed to have stepped from *Mayflower*; (2) American breed of domestic fowl, of medium size and usu. with grey plumage barred with blackish stripes and yellow beak, legs, and feet.

p.m. *abbrev. Post meridiem*; *post mortem*.

P.M. *abbrev.* Police Magistrate; Prime Minister; Provost Marshal.

P.M.G. *abbrev.* Paymaster-General; Postmaster-General.

p.m.h. *abbrev.* Production per man-hour.

P.M.O. *abbrev.* Principal Medical Officer.

P.N.E.U. *abbrev.* Parents' National Educational Union.

pneumăt'ĭc (nū-) *adj.* Of, acting by means of, wind or air; containing, connected with, air-cavities, esp. in bones of birds; ~ *dispatch*, conveyance of parcels etc. along tubes by compression or exhaustion of air; ~ *trough*, trough for collecting gases in jars over surface of water or mercury; ~ *tyre*, one inflated with air. **pneumăt'ĭcally** *adv.* **pneumăt'ĭc** *n.* 1. Pneumatic tyre; bicycle with such tyres. 2. (pl.) Science of mechanical properties of air or other elastic gases or fluids.

pneum'atocȳst (nū-) *n.* Air-sac (in body of bird etc.).

pneumocŏcc'us (nū-) *n.* (pl. *-cī*). Infective micro-organism in pneumonia.

pneumocŏniō̆s'ĭs (nū-) *n.* (pl. *-sēs*). Any of a group of chronic lung diseases (e.g. silicosis) caused by inhaling abrasive dust.

pneumogăs'trĭc (nū-) *adj.* Of lungs and stomach; ~ *nerves*, 10th pair of cerebral nerves.

pneumonĕc'tomy (nū-) *n.* Surgical removal of a lung.

pneumōn'ĭa (nū-) *n.* Acute inflammation of the lungs, converting their normally spongy tissue into a solid mass; produced by many causes esp. infection with the micro-organism *Diplococcus pneumoniae* (pneumococcus). **pneumŏn'ĭc** *adj.*

pneumothôr'ax (nū-) *n.* Presence of air or gas in the pleural cavity, whether accidental or effected deliberately, e.g. to collapse a lung in treatment of pulmonary tuberculosis.

pnxt *abbrev. Pinxit.*

P.O. *abbrev.* Petty Officer; Pilot Officer; postal order; Post Office.

pō'ă *n.* Large genus of grasses widely distributed in temperate and cold regions, meadow-grass.

poach[1] *v.t.* Cook (egg) without its shell by boiling in water or steaming; cook (fish) by simmering in water, milk, etc.

poach[2] *v.* 1. Trample, cut *up* (turf etc.) with hoofs; (of land) become sodden by being trampled. 2. Encroach, trespass (*on* person's *preserves* (freq. fig.), lands, etc.), esp. in order to steal fish or game; trespass on (land etc.); capture (game, fish) by illicit or unsportsmanlike methods; (in various games) enter on partner's portion of field or court, depriving him of some of his share in the game. **poach'er** *n.*

Pōcahŏn'tăs (1595–1617). Daughter of Powhattan, an Amer. Indian chief in Virginia; according to the story of an English colonist, Capt. John Smith, she rescued him from death at the hands of her father, who had imprisoned him; she was seized as a hostage, 1612, and married a colonist, John Rolfe; was taken to England, 1616, and died there.

pŏch'ard (*or* -k-) *n.* A diving-duck or sea-duck (*Fuligula ferina*) of Europe, N. Asia, and N. America, male of which has bright reddish-brown head and neck; esp. male pochard (female being known as *dunbird*).

pŏchette' (-shĕt) *n.* Woman's envelope-shaped hand-bag.

pŏck *n.* Eruptive spot esp. in smallpox.

pŏck'ėt *n.* 1. Bag, sack, esp. as measure of hops (168 lb.) or wool (= half sack). 2. Small bag inserted in garment for carrying small articles, as money, etc.; (fig.) pecuniary resources; *put* one's *pride in* one's ~, submit to doing something that mortifies it; *in* ~, having money available; having (so much) as profit; *out of* ~, a loser (by some transaction); *out-of-~ expenses*, actual outlay incurred. 3. Pouch at each corner and on each side of billiard-table into which balls are driven (ill. BILLIARDS); cavity in earth filled with gold or other ore; cavity in rock esp. (geol.) filled with foreign matter; AIR-pocket; isolated area occupied by the enemy, forces occupying this. 4. (attrib.) Of suitable size or shape for carrying in pocket; small-sized, diminutive; ~ *battleship*, (esp. German) ship armoured and equipped like, but smaller than, a battleship; ~*-book*, notebook, book-like case for papers, currency notes, etc., carried in pocket; (U.S.) handbag; ~ *borough*: see BOROUGH; ~ *handkerchief*, one carried in pocket; ~ *money*, money for occasional expenses, esp. that allowed to children. ~ *v.t.* Put into one's pocket; confine as in pocket; hem in (competitor) in race; appropriate, usu. dishonestly; submit to (affront, injury); conceal, suppress (feelings); (billiards) drive (ball) into pocket. **pŏck'ėtful** *n.*

pōcocūrăn'tė (*or* -koorahntā), *adj.* & *n.* Indifferent (person). [It., = 'caring little']

pŏd[1] *n.* Socket of brace and bit (ill. DRILL).

pŏd[2] *n.* Long seed-vessel, esp. of leguminous plants (ill. FRUIT); cocoon of silkworm; case of locust's eggs; narrow-necked eel-net. ~ *v.* Bear pods; shell (peas etc.).

pŏd[3] *n.* Small herd of seals or whales. ~ *v.t.* Drive (seals etc.) into pod or bunch for purpose of clubbing them.

pŏd'ăgra (*or* podăg'-) *n.* (med.) Gout, esp. in feet. **pŏd'agral, podăg'rĭc, pŏd'agrous** *adjs.*

pŏdĕsta' (-ah) *n.* (hist.) Governor appointed by Frederick Barbarossa over one or more Lombard cities; chief magistrate in medieval Italian towns and republics.

pŏdg'y *adj.* Short, thick, and fat.

pōd'ĭum *n.* Continuous projecting base or pedestal; raised platform round arena of amphitheatre (ill. AMPHITHEATRE); continuous bench round room.

pŏdophȳll'ĭn *n.* (chem.) Yellow bitter resin of cathartic properties from root of *Podophyllum peltatum*, plant of eastern N. America, with long thick creeping rhizomes, large long-stalked palmate leaves, and solitary white flower.

pŏd'sŏl *n.* Stratified soil in which various materials have been leached from the upper layers and redeposited in a well-defined lower stratum.

Pōe, Edgar Allan (1809–49). American poet and critic; author of tales of mystery and imagination.

pō'ėm *n.* A metrical composition, esp. of elevated character; elevated composition in prose or verse; (fig.) something (other than a composition of words) akin or compared to a poem.

pō'ėsy *n.* (archaic) Art, composition, of poetry; poems collectively.

pō'ėt *n.* Writer of poems; writer in verse, esp. one possessing high powers of imagination, expression, etc.; ~ *laureate*: see LAUREATE; *Poets' Corner*, part of south transept of Westminster Abbey containing graves or monuments of several great poets. **pō'ėtĕss** *n.*

pōėtăs'ter *n.* Inferior poet.

pōĕt'ĭc *adj.* Of, proper to, poets or poetry; having the good qualities of poetry; ~ *justice, licence*: see JUSTICE, LICENCE. **pōĕt'ĭcal,** *adj.* Of, proper to, poets or poetry; written in verse. **pōĕt'ĭcally** *adv.* **pōĕt'ĭcs** *n.* Part of literary criticism dealing with poetry; treatise on poetry, esp. that of Aristotle.

pōĕt'ĭcīze *v.t.* Make (theme) poetic.

pō'ėtīze *v.* Play the poet, compose poetry; treat poetically; celebrate in poetry.

pō'ėtry *n.* Art, work, of the poet; expression of beautiful or elevated thought, imagination, or feeling in appropriate language and usu. in metrical form; poems, quality (in anything) that calls for poetical expression; *prose* ~, prose having all the qualities of poetry except metre.

pogrŏm' *n.* Organized massacre in Russia of any body or class; in English, chiefly applied to those directed against Jews. [Russ., = 'destruction' (*grom* thunder)]

poign'ant (poin- *or* poinyant) *adj.* Sharp, pungent, in taste or smell; painfully sharp; pleasantly piquant. **poig'nantly** *adv.* **poign'ancy** *n.*

poilu (pwă'-) *n.* (colloq.) French private soldier. [Fr., = 'hairy']

Poincaré (pwăṅkărā'), Raymond (1860–1934). French statesman, president during war of 1914–18.

poinsĕtt'ĭa *n.* Mexican species of *Euphorbia*, *E. pulcherrima*, with large scarlet leaves surrounding small yellowish flowers. [f. J. R. *Poinsett*, Amer. minister to Mexico, who discovered it]

point *n.* 1. Small dot on a surface. 2. Stop or punctuation-mark; dot, small stroke, used in Semitic languages to indicate vowels or distinguish consonants; dot separating integral from fractional parts in decimals, as *two ~ five* (2·5). 3. Single item, detail, particular; thing under discussion; *to the ~*, relevant(ly); *make a ~*, establish proposition, prove contention; *make a ~ of*, treat as essential. 4. Distinctive trait, characteristic, as *good, bad, ~*; *strong ~*, thing one is good at. 5. Salient feature of story, joke, etc.; pungency, effectiveness. 6. Unit in appraising qualities of exhibit in show or achievements of competitor in contest; unit (of varying value) in quoting price of stocks etc.; unit of value in rationing (*on ~s*, of commodity, rationed on basis of such units); *give ~s to*, allow (opponent) to count so many points at starting, (fig.) be superior to; *win on ~s*, (boxing) win by securing more points in a number of rounds, not by knock-out. 7. (print.) Unit of measurement for type bodies, in Britain and U.S. 0·0138 in. ($\frac{1}{72}$ in., $\frac{1}{12}$ of a pica). 8. (geom.) That which has position but not magnitude, e.g. *~ of intersection of two lines*. 9. Precise place or spot, as *~ of contact*. 10. (hunting) Spot to which straight run is made, such run; *~-to-~ race*, race over course defined only by certain landmarks. 11. (her.) Any of 9 particular spots on shield used for determining position (ill. HERALDRY). 12. Stage, degree, in progress or increase, esp. of temperature, as *boiling-, freezing-, ~*. 13. Precise moment for action etc.; exact moment (of death etc.). 14. (mus.) Important phrase or subject, esp. in contrapuntal music; (archaic) snatch of melody, esp. *~ of war*, short phrase sounded on instrument as signal. 15. Sharp end of tool, weapon, pin, pen, etc.; sharp-pointed tool, e.g. etching needle; *~ (lace)*, lace made wholly with needle. 16. Tip; promontory, esp. in names, as *Start P~*; *the ~*, (boxing) point of the jaw, tip of chin as spot for knock-out blow. 17. Tine of deer's horn. 18. Tapering movable rail by which train is directed from one line to another (ill. RAIL[1]). 19. Tapered division on backgammon board. 20. (hist.) Tagged lace for lacing bodice, attaching hose to doublet, etc. (ill. DOUBLET). 21. (naut.) Short piece of cord at lower edge of sail for tying up a reef. 22. *~s of the compass*, 32 equidistant points on circumference of mariner's compass indicated by rays drawn from centre (ill. COMPASS); angular interval (11° 15′) between two successive points; any (corresponding) point of horizon, direction. 23. (cricket) (Position of) fieldsman placed more or less in line with popping-crease a short distance on off side of batsman (ill. CRICKET). 24. (Of dog) act of pointing. 25. *at all ~s*, in every part; *in ~*, apposite; *in ~ of fact*, as a matter of fact; *(up)on the ~ of*, on the very verge of (action, doing); *~ of honour*, matter regarded as vitally affecting one's honour; *~ of view*, position from which thing is viewed or seen; *~-duty*, that of constable stationed at particular point to regulate traffic etc.; *points'man*, man in charge of railway points; constable on point-duty. *~ v.* 1. Sharpen (pencil etc.); furnish with point; give point to (words, actions). 2. Punctuate (now rare); mark (Psalms etc.) for chanting, by means of points; mark in the vowels in Hebrew script. 3. Fill in joints of (brickwork etc.) with mortar or cement smoothed with trowel; prick *in* (manure), turn *over* (soil), with point of spade. 4. Direct attention *to, at*, by or as by extending finger; (of dog) indicate presence of (game) by standing rigidly, looking towards it; direct (finger, weapon, etc., *at*); direct attention of (person *to*); aim *at*, tend *towards*; *~ out*, indicate, show.

point'-blănk' *adj.* (Of shot) fired horizontally, level; (of range) within which gun may be fired horizontally. *~ adv.* With direct aim, horizontally, in direct line; (fig.) directly, flatly. [prob. f. *blank* white spot in centre of target]

point d'appui (pwăn dăpwē′) *n.* (mil.) Point of support, rallying-place.

point-dėvīce' *adj.* (archaic) Perfectly correct, extremely neat or precise. *~ adv.* In point-device manner. [app. f. Fr. *à point devis* to the point arranged, or arranged to the proper point]

point'ėd *adj.* Having, sharpened to, a point; (of remark etc.) having point, penetrating, cutting; emphasized, made evident; (of Hebrew script) having the vowels marked. **point'ėdly** *adv.* **point'ėdnėss** *n.*

point'er *n.* (esp.) 1. Index hand of clock, balance, etc. 2. Rod used for pointing to words etc. on blackboard, map, etc. 3. Dog that on scenting game stands rigidly, with muzzle stretched towards it and usu. one foot raised. 4. (pl.) Two stars in Great Bear, straight line through which points nearly to pole-star. 5. (colloq.) Hint.

pointillé (pwăn'tīlā) *adj.* 1. (Of bookbinding) decorated with gilt dots. 2. (Of picture) painted with numerous small spots of two or more pure colours which at a distance produce the effect of a mixed colour, whence **point'illism** *n.* **point'illist** *n.* Painter using this technique.

point'ing *n.* (esp.) 1. Punctuation. 2. Filling up joints of brickwork etc. with cement, facing thus given to the joints (ill. MASONRY).

point'lėss *adj.* Without a point, blunt; without point, meaningless; not having scored a point. **point'lėssly** *adv.* **point'lėssnėss** *n.*

poise (-z) *v.* Balance; hold suspended or supported; carry (one's head etc.) in specified way; be balanced; hover in air etc. *~ n.* Balance, equilibrium; state of indecision, suspense; carriage (of head etc.); (orig. U.S.) ease of manner, grace, assurance.

pois'on (-zn) *n.* Substance that when introduced into or absorbed by a living organism destroys life or injures health, esp. (pop.) one that destroys life by rapid action and when taken in small quantity; (fig.) baneful principle, doctrine, etc.; *slow ~*, one of which repeated doses are injurious; *~ gas*: see GAS; *~-ivy*, N. Amer. trailing or climbing sumac, *Rhus toxicodendron*, with trifoliate leaves, producing poisonous effects when touched; *~ oak*, low-growing variety of poison-ivy, allied plant (*R. diversiloba*) of Pacific N. America; *~ pen*, anonymous writer of libellous or scurrilous letters to a private individual; *~-tree, -wood*, various trees with poisonous properties, esp. species of *Rhus*. *~ v.t.* Administer poison to; kill, injure, thus; produce morbid effects in (blood etc.); infect (air, water, etc.), smear (weapon) with poison; corrupt, pervert (person, mind); destroy, spoil (pleasure etc.); render (land etc.) foul and unfit for its purpose by noxious applications, etc. **pois'oner, pois'oning** *ns.* **pois'onous** *adj.* **pois'onously** *adv.*

Poitiers (pwătyā′). Town of W. France, where armies of England under Edward the BLACK PRINCE defeated those of France under King John (1356).

pōke[1] *n.* Bag, sack (now dial. exc. in *buy a pig in a ~*: see PIG).

pōke[2] *v.* 1. Thrust, push (thing *in, up, down*, etc.) with hand, arm, point of stick, etc.; stir (fire) with poker; produce (hole etc. *in*) by poking; make thrusts with stick, etc. (*at* etc.); thrust forward, esp. obtrusively; pry (*into*); *~ fun at*, assail with ridicule; *~ one's head*, carry head thrust forward, stoop. 2. (colloq.) Shut (*oneself* etc.) *up* in poky place. *~ n.* 1. Poking; thrust, nudge. 2. Device fastened on cattle etc., to prevent their breaking through fences. 3. Projecting brim or front of woman's bonnet; *~ bonnet*, bonnet with this.

pōk'er[1] *n.* Stiff metal rod with handle, for poking fire; kinds of instrument used in poker-work; *red-hot ~*, species of *Tritoma* (*Kniphofia*), S. Afr. liliaceous plants with tall spikes of red or yellow flowers; *~-work*, burning of designs on white wood etc. with heated implement.

pŏk'er[2] *n.* Card-game for two or more players each of whom receives 5 cards (of which he may change any number); the value of the hand depends on the combinations of cards in it; the players may bet on their hands, and the winner is the one who holds the strongest hand or who succeeds in bluffing the others into throwing in their hands, i.e. ceasing to bet; *~-face*, one appropriate to poker-player, one in which person's thoughts or feelings are not revealed.

pŏk'y *adj.* (Of place, room, etc.) confined, mean, shabby.

pola'cre (-ahk*er*), **polăcc'a** *n.* Three-masted Mediterranean merchant vessel. [Fr. *polacre*, *polaque* Polish, Pole]

Pōl'and. Country of NE. Europe, formerly a kingdom, which was divided by three partitions of 1772, 1793, and 1795 between Prussia, Russia and Austria; reconstituted by Napoleon under the title of the Duchy of Warsaw, but re-partitioned at the Congress of Vienna (1815); recognized as an independent republic by treaties of Versailles (1919) and Riga (1921); invaded and overrun by German and later by Russian armies, 1939, and again recognized as an independent republic in 1945; capital, Warsaw.

pōl'ar *adj.* 1. Of, near, either pole of the earth or of the celestial sphere; *~ bear*, the white bear, *Ursus maritimus*; *~ circles*, circles, parallel to equator at distance of 23° 28′ from the poles (Arctic and Antarctic Circles: ill. EARTH); *~ distance*, angular distance of point on sphere from nearer pole. 2. Having polarity, having associated positive and negative poles (either electrical or magnetic); (of forces) acting in two opposite directions; (of molecules) symmetrically arranged in definite directions. 3. (geom.) Relating to a pole. 4. (zool.) Of poles of nerve-cell, ovum, etc. 5. (fig.) Analogous to pole of the earth or to pole-star; directly opposite in character. *~ n.* (geom.) Curve related in particular way to given curve and fixed point called pole; in conic sections, straight line joining points at which tangents from fixed point touch curve.

polă'riscōpe *n.* Instrument for showing polarization of light or viewing objects in polarized light. **polărıscŏp'ic** *adj.*

polă'rity *n.* Tendency of magnetized bar etc. to point with its extremities to magnetic poles of earth; tendency of a body to place its mathematical axis in particular direction; possession of two poles having contrary qualities; electrical condition of body as positive or negative; (fig.) direction (of thought, feeling, etc.) towards a single point.

pōl'arīze *v.* 1. Modify electromagnetic vibrations (e.g. light, radio waves) so that the electric and magnetic vibrations are confined to definite directions. 2. (magnetism, elect.) Give polarity to (bar, coil). **pōlarīzā'tion, pōl'arīzer** *n.*

pōl'der *n.* Piece of low-lying land reclaimed from sea or river in Netherlands.

pōle[1] *n.* 1. Long slender rounded tapering piece of wood or metal, esp. as support for tent, telegraph wires, etc.; wooden shaft fitted to fore-carriage of vehicle and attached to yokes or collars of horses etc.; *under bare ~s*, (naut.) with no sail set; *up the ~*, (slang) in a fix; crazed or tipsy; *~-jump, -jumping, -vault*, jump etc. with help of pole held in hands. 2. (as measure) Rod, perch, 5½ yds; (*square*) *~*, 30¼ square yds; see Appendix X. *~ v.t.* Furnish with poles; push, move, with pole.

pōle[2] *n.* Two points (*north* and *south ~*) in celestial sphere about which the stars appear to revolve; N. and S. extremities of earth's axis (ill. EARTH); (geom.) each of two points *of a circle of the sphere* in which axis of that circle cuts surface of sphere; (geom.) fixed point to which others are referred; each of two opposite points on surface of magnet at which magnetic forces are manifested; each of two terminal points (POSITIVE and NEGATIVE) of electric cell, battery, etc.; (biol.) extremity of main axis of any spherical or oval organ; (fig.) each of two opposed principles etc., hence *~s apart*; *~-star*, star of Ursa Minor, now about 1¼° distant from N. pole of heavens; (fig.) thing serving as guide, lodestar, centre of attraction.

Pōle[3]. Native or inhabitant of Poland.

pōle'-ăxe *n.* Battle-axe; axe formerly used in naval warfare as weapon and for cutting ropes etc. (ill. BATTLE-axe); halbert; butcher's axe with hammer at back. *~ v.t.* Slaughter (beast etc.) with pole-axe.

pōle'căt *n.* Small dark-brown fetid carnivorous European mammal of weasel family, *Putorius foetidus*; certain other species of this genus.

pŏl'ėmârch (-k) *n.* (Gk hist.) Military commander-in-chief, with varying civil functions; in Athens, 3rd archon, who orig. had military functions.

polĕm'ic *adj.* Controversial, disputatious. *~ n.* Controversial discussion; (pl.) practice of this, esp. in theology; (sing.) controversialist. **polĕm'ical** *adj.* **polĕm'ically** *adv.*

polĕn'ta *n.* Italian porridge made of maize, barley, chestnut meal, etc.

police' (-ēs) *n.* Civil administration, public order; department of government concerned with this; civil force responsible for maintaining public order; (as pl.) members of this; any body officially employed to keep order, enforce regulations, etc.; *~-court*, court of summary jurisdiction, dealing with charges preferred by the police; *~-dog*, dog employed by police to track criminals, etc.; *~-magistrate*, magistrate presiding in police-court; *police'man*, *police'woman*, member of police force; *~-office*, headquarters of police in city or town; *~-officer*, policeman; *~ state*, State regulated by means of a national police having secret supervision and control of the citizens' activities; *~-station*, office of local police force. *~ v.t.* Control (country etc.) by means of police; furnish with police; (fig.) administer, control.

pŏl'icy[1] *n.* 1. Political sagacity; statecraft; prudent conduct, sagacity; craftiness; course of action adopted by government, party, etc. 2. (Sc., usu. pl.) Park round country seat etc.

pŏl'icy[2] *n.* (*~ of assurance, insurance ~*) Document containing contract of assurance or insurance.

pōl'iō *n.* Abbrev. of POLIOMYELITIS.

pŏl'iomȳėlīt'is *n.* (Used for) *acute anterior ~*, pop. called infantile paralysis, an infectious disease of the central nervous system; it is caused by a virus, is of epidemic tendency, attacks adults as well as children, and is characterized esp. by temporary (or less freq. permanent) paralysis. [Gk *polios* grey, *muelos* marrow]

pŏl'ish[1] *v.* Make, become, smooth and glossy by friction; (fig.) make elegant or cultured, refine; smarten *up*; *~ off*, finish off quickly. *~ n.* Smoothness, glossiness, produced by friction; such friction; substance used to produce polished surface; (fig.) refinement. **pŏl'isher** *n.*

Pōl'ish[2] *adj.* Of Poland or the Poles; *~ Corridor*: see CORRIDOR. *~ n.* Language of Poland, belonging to Western branch of Slavonic languages.

polīte' *adj.* Of refined manners, courteous; cultivated, cultured; well-bred; (of literature etc.) refined, elegant. **polīte'ly** *adv.* **polīte'nėss** *n.*

pŏl'ĭtic *adj.* 1. (Of person) sagacious, prudent; (of action etc.) judicious, expedient; scheming, crafty. 2. *body ~*: see BODY. **pŏl'iticly** *adv.* **pŏl'itics** *n.pl.* Science and art of government; political affairs or life; political principles.

polit'ical *adj.* 1. Of the State or its government; of public affairs; of politics; (of person) engaged in civil administration; *~ agent, resident*, (hist., in India) British government official advising ruler of native State. 2. Having an organized polity. 3. Belonging to, taking, a side in politics. ~ *economy*: see ECONOMY; ~ *geography*, that dealing with boundaries, divisions, and possessions of States; ~ *prisoner*, one imprisoned for a political offence. **polĭt'ĭcally** *adv.*

pŏlĭtĭ'cian (-shn) *n.* One skilled in politics, statesman; one interested or engaged in politics, esp. as profession; (U.S.) one who makes a trade of politics.

polĭt'ĭcō *n.* Political agent, officer, or resident.

pŏl'ĭty *n.* Condition of civil order; form, process, of civil government; organized society, State.

Pŏlk, James Knox (1795–1849). American Democratic statesman; 11th president of U.S., 1845–9.

pŏl'ka (*or* pō-) *n.* Lively dance of Czech origin, with music in duple time; music for this; ~-*dot(s)*, pattern of dots of uniform size and arrangement.

pōll[1] *n.* 1. Human head (now dial. or joc.); part of head on which hair grows; ~-*tax*, one levied on every person. 2. Counting of voters esp. at parliamentary or other election; voting at election; number of votes recorded. 3. Questioning of a sample of the population in order to estimate trend of public opinion, whence (colloq.) **pōll'ster** *n.* **pōll** *v.* 1. Crop the hair of (archaic); cut off top of (tree, plant), esp. make a pollard of; cut off horns of (cattle, esp. in past part.). 2. Take the votes of; (of candidate) receive (so many votes); give (vote); give one's vote. ~ *adj.* (Of legal writing or deed) polled or cut even at edge, executed by single party and therefore not indented.

pŏll[2] *n.* *P*~, conventional name of parrot; ~ *parrot*, parrot; user of conventional phrases and arguments.

pŏll[3] *n.* (Camb. Univ. slang) *The* ~, the passmen; (attrib.) ~ *degree.*

pŏll'ack, pŏll'ock *n.* Sea-fish (*Gadus pollachius*) allied to cod but with lower jaw protruding, used as food.

pŏll'an *n.* Freshwater fish (*Coregonus pollan*) allied to trout of Irish inland loughs.

pŏll'ard *n.* 1. Animal that has cast or lost its horns; ox, sheep, goat, of hornless variety. 2. Tree polled so as to produce close rounded head of young branches. 3. Bran sifted from flour; fine bran containing some flour. ~ *v.t.* Make a pollard of (tree).

pŏll'ĕn *n.* Fine powdery substance discharged from anther of flower, male element that fertilizes ovules. ~ *v.t.* Convey pollen to, cover with pollen. **pollĭn'ic, pollinĭf'erous** *adjs.*

pollĭcĭtā'tion *n.* (civil law) Promise not yet formally accepted, and therefore revocable.

pŏll'ĭnāte *v.t.* Besprinkle with pollen, shed pollen upon. **pollĭnā'tion** *n.*

pŏllĭn'ĭum *n.* Pollen grains united into a mass.

pollūte' (*or* -ōōt) *v.t.* Destroy the purity or sanctity of; make (water etc.) foul or filthy. **pollū'tion** *n.*

Pŏll'ux: see CASTOR.

pōl'ō[1] *n.* Game of Eastern origin resembling hockey, played on horseback by teams of usu. four players, with long-handled mallets (~-*sticks*) and wooden ball; *water* ~, handball game played by swimmers with ball like football.

Pōl'ō[2], Marco (1254–1324). Venetian traveller; reached the court of Kublai Khan in China; spent 17 years in China and wrote an account of his experiences.

pŏlonaise' (-āz) *n.* 1. (hist.) Woman's dress consisting of bodice with skirt open from waist

POLONAISE *c* 1778

1. Petticoat

downwards. 2. (Music for) slow dance in triple rhythm of Polish origin, with intricate march or procession of dancers in couples. [Fr., fem. of *polonais* Polish]

polōn'ĭum *n.* Radio-active metallic element discovered by P. and M. Curie in pitchblende; symbol Po, at. no. 84, principal isotope 210. [med. L *Polonia* Poland]

polōn'y *n.* Sausage, usu. with bright-red skin, of partly cooked pork. [app. f. *Bologna*]

pŏl'tergeist (-gīst) *n.* Noisy ghost or hobgoblin; in spiritualism, the name given to the supposed agent of certain manifestations, such as the overturning of furniture, breaking of crockery, etc. [Ger.]

pŏltrōōn' *n.* Spiritless coward. **pŏltrōōn'ery** *n.*

pŏly- *prefix.* Many.

pŏlyăn'drous *adj.* 1. Of, practising, polandry. 2. (bot.) With numerous stamens. **pŏlyăn'dry** *n.* Plurality of husbands.

pŏlyăn'thus *n.* Kinds of cultivated primula, with yellow, brown, crimson, etc., flowers in umbel on common peduncle.

Polўb'ĭus (*c* 204–122 B.C.). Greek historian.

Pŏl'ўcărp (*c* 69–*c* 155), St. Bishop of Smyrna, martyr, and Father of the Church; commemorated 26th Jan.

pŏl'ўchaete (-kēt) *adj.* & *n.* (Animal) of the *Polychaeta*, a class of the *Annelida* comprising worms, mostly marine, with bristles on the foot-stumps.

pŏlўchromăt'ĭc (-kr-) *adj.* Many-coloured.

pŏl'ўchrōme (-kr-) *adj.* Painted, printed, decorated, in many colours. ~ *n.* Work of art in several colours, esp. coloured statue. **pŏlўchrōm'ic, pŏl'ўchrōmous** *adjs.* **pŏl'ўchrōmy** *n.* Art of painting in several colours, esp. as applied to ancient pottery or sculpture.

pŏlўclĭn'ĭc *n.* Clinic devoted to various diseases; general hospital.

Pŏlўclīt'us, Pŏlўcleit'ŏs (5th c. B.C.). Greek sculptor; his statue of the Doryphoros or Spear-bearer was known as 'The Canon' or rule, as being an ideal representation of human proportions.

polўg'amous *adj.* 1. Having more than one wife or (less usu.) husband at once. 2. (zool.) Having more than one mate at one time. 3. (bot.) Bearing some flowers with stamens only, some with pistils only, some with both, on same or different plants. **pŏlўgăm'ĭc** *adj.* **polўg'amist, polўg'amy** *ns.*

pŏl'ўglŏt *adj.* & *n.* Of many languages; (person) speaking or writing several languages; (book, esp. Bible) written in several languages. **pŏlўglŏtt'al, pŏlўglŏtt'ĭc** *adjs.*

pŏl'ўgon *n.* Figure (usu. plane rectilinear) with many (usu. more than 4) angles or sides; ~ *of forces*, polygon illustrating theorem relating to number of forces acting at a point, each represented in magnitude and direction by one side of the figure. **polўg'onal** *adj.* **polўg'onally** *adv.*

polўg'onum *n.* Large and widely distributed genus of plants (including knotgrass, snakeweed, etc.) with swollen stem-joints sheathed by stipules, and small flowers.

polўg'ўnous (-g-) *adj.* 1. Of, practising, polygyny. 2. (bot.) With many pistils, styles, or stigmas. **polўg'ўny** *n.* Plurality of wives.

pŏlўhĕd'ron *n.* Many- (usu. more than 6-) sided solid. **pŏlўhĕd'ral, pŏlўhĕd'rĭc** *adjs.*

pŏlўhis'tor *n.* = POLYMATH.

pŏl'ўmăth *n.* Man of varied learning, great scholar. **polўm'athy** *n.*

pŏl'ўmer *n.* (chem.) Compound formed by the combination of a (usu. very large) number of identical molecules of a simpler substance. **pŏlўmĕ'rĭc** *adj.* (Of compounds) composed of the same elements in the same proportions but differing in molecular weight.

polўm'erīze *v.* (chem., of a number of identical molecules) Combine together to form a polymer. **pŏlўmerīzā'tion** *n.*

polўm'erous *adj.* (biol.) Composed of many parts, members, or segments.

pŏl'ўmorph *n.* (Short for) polymorphonuclear leucocyte, white blood-cell of a class in which the nuclei occur in various forms.

pŏlўmorph'ic, -morph'ous *adjs.* Multiform; esp. (biol., of a species) of which more than one form exists in a population.

pŏlўmorph'ism *n.* The diversity occurring within biological populations, determined genetically or by environment.

Pŏlўnē'sia (-shĭa, -zhĭa). General name for all islands in central and W. Pacific or (more usu.) for the easternmost of the 3 great groups of these islands, including New Zealand, Hawaii, the Marquesas, and Samoa. **Pŏlўnē'sian** *adj.* & *n.* (Member) of a black-haired brown-skinned race inhabiting Polynesia.

pŏlўneurīt'ĭs *n.* (path.) Multiple neuritis, condition in which many peripheral nerves are inflamed simultaneously.

pŏl'ўp *n.* (zool.) Single individual of a coelenterate or other colony (i.e. of a compound animal of plant-like appearance, as sea-fern); similar individual of a non-colonial form, e.g. sea-anemone (ill. HYDRA). **pŏl'ўpoid, pŏl'ўpous** *adjs.*

Pŏlўphēm'us. (Gk legend) A giant or CYCLOPS from whom Odysseus and some of his companions escaped by putting out his one eye while he slept.

pŏl'ўphōne *n.* Written character having more than one phonetic value.

pŏlўphŏn'ic *adj.* 1. (mus.) Of polyphony, contrapuntal. 2. (Of written character) having more than one phonetic value. 3. Producing many sounds.

polўph'ony *n.* (mus.) Simultaneous combination of number of parts each forming an individual melody; style of composition in which parts are so combined; counterpoint.

pŏl'yploid *adj.* & *n.* (biol.) (Organism) having a chromosome number which is a multiple greater than 2 of the basic group number.

pŏl'ўpŏd *adj.* & *n.* (Animal) with many feet.

pŏl'ўpŏdў *n.* Large and widely distributed genus (*Polypodium*) of ferns, esp. *P. vulgare*, growing on moist rocks, old walls, and trees.

pŏl'ўpōre *n.* Fungus of the family *Polyporaceae* whose members have large fruiting bodies in which the spores are produced in tubes.

pŏl'ўpus *n.* (pl. *-pī*). (path.) Kinds of tumour with ramifications like tentacles, occurring usu. in nose, uterus, or bladder.

pŏlўsўllăb'ic *adj.* (Of word) having many syllables; marked by polysyllables. **pŏlўsўllăb'ically** *adv.* **pŏlўsўll'able** *n.* Polysyllabic word.

pŏlўsўnthĕt'ic *adj.* (Of language) combining several words of a sentence into one.

pŏlўtĕch'nic (-kn-) *adj.* & *n.* Dealing with, devoted to, various arts; *P~* (*Institution*), technical school, esp. one in London orig. opened 1838.

pŏl'ўthėism *n.* Belief in, worship of, many gods or more than one god. **pŏl'ўthėist** *n.* **pŏlўthėĭs'tic** *adj.*

pŏlўzō'a *n.pl.* (zool.) Phylum of compound or colonial (usu. marine) animals of small size (now usu. considered as two phyla, *Ectoprocta* and *Endoprocta*).

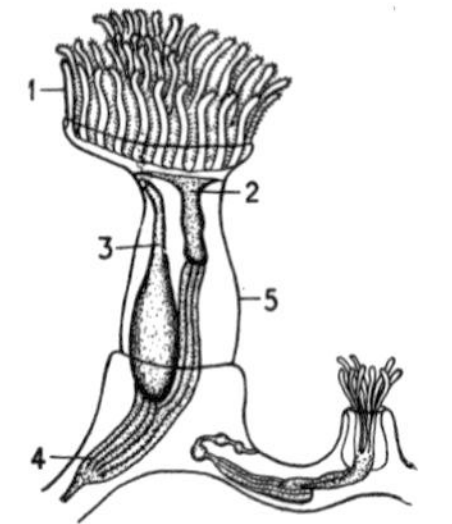

POLYZOA (*PLUMATELLA*)
1. Tentacles. 2. Mouth. 3. Intestine. 4. Stomach. 5. Cuticle

pŏm *n.* (colloq.) Pomeranian dog.

pomace (pŭm'ĭs) *n.* Mass of crushed apples in cider-making before or after juice is pressed out; any pulp; refuse of fish, etc., after oil has been extracted, used as fertilizer.

pomade' (-ahd) *n.* Scented ointment (perh. orig. from apples) for hair and skin of head. ~ *v.t.* Anoint with pomade.

pomăn'der (*or* pŏm'an-) *n.* (hist.) Ball of mixed aromatic substances carried in box, bag, etc., as preservative against infection; spherical box of gold, silver, etc., in which this was carried. [OF. *pomme d'ambre* apple of amber]

pom(m)ard' *n.* A red Burgundy wine. [village in Côte d'Or, France]

pomāt'um *n.* & *v.t.* Pomade.

pōme *n.* 1. (bot.) Succulent inferior fruit with firm fleshy body enclosing carpels forming core, e.g. apple, pear, quince (ill. FRUIT); (poet.) apple. 2. Ball or globe, esp. of metal; the royal globe or ball of dominion. **pomĭf'erous** *adj.* Bearing pomes.

pŏme'grănate (-mg-; *also* pŭm-) *n.* Fruit of tree (*Punica granatum*) native to N. Africa and W. Asia, large roundish many-celled berry about size of orange with tough golden or orange rind and acid reddish pulp enveloping the many seeds; the tree.

pŏm'ėlō *n.* Shaddock, grapefruit.

Pŏmerān'ia. Province of Poland with sea-coast on Baltic, formerly part of Prussia (Ger. *Pommern*). **Pŏmerān'ian** *adj.* & *n.* (Native) of Pomerania; ~ (*dog*), dog of small breed with long thick silky hair, usu. black or white, pointed muzzle, pricked ears, and prominent eyes.

pom'frėt-cake (pŭ-, pŏ-) *n.* Sweetmeat made at Pontefract, (earlier *Pomfret*), Yorkshire, small round flat cake of liquorice.

pōm'ĭcŭlture *n.* Fruit-growing.

pomm'el (pŭ-) *n.* 1. Rounded knob esp. at end of sword-hilt (ill. SWORD). 2. Upward projecting front part of saddle (ill. SADDLE). ~ *v.t.* Strike or beat (as) with pommel of sword; beat with fists.

pŏmm'y *n.* (Austral. and N.Z.) Immigrant from Britain.

pomŏl'ogy *n.* Science of fruit-growing. **pōmolŏ'gĭcal** *adj.* **pomŏl'ogĭst** *n.*

Pomōn'a[1]. Roman goddess of fruit-trees.

Pomōn'a[2]. Largest island of Orkneys, now usu. called *Mainland.*

pŏmp *n.* Splendid display, splendour.

Pŏm'padour (-oor), Marquise de (1721–64). Jeanne Antoinette Poisson le Normant d'Étioles, mistress of Louis XV of France.

pŏm'padour *n.* Style of hair-dressing with hair turned back from forehead in high roll.

Pŏmpei'i (-ēī, -āē). Ancient town of Campania, Italy, buried by eruption of Mt Vesuvius in A.D. 79 and since 1755 gradually laid bare by excavation.

Pŏm'pey[1]. Gnaeus Pompeius Magnus (106–48 B.C.), Roman general and consul; member, with Julius Caesar and Crassus, of the 1st triumvirate; later he opposed Caesar and was defeated by him at Pharsalia, 48 B.C.

Pŏm'pey[2]. Naval slang name for PORTSMOUTH.

pŏm'-pŏm[1] *n.* Automatic quick-firing gun. [imit.]

pŏm'pŏm[2], **pŏm'pŏn** *ns.* Ornamental tuft or bunch of silk threads, ribbon, etc., on hat, shoe, dress, etc.; varieties of chrysanthemum and dahlia with small globular flowers.

pŏmp'ous *n.* Magnificent, splendid; self-important, consequential; (of language) inflated. **pŏmp'ously** *adv.* **pŏmp'ousnėss, pŏmpŏs'ity** *ns.*

Ponce de Leon (pŏn'sě, lāŏn'), Juan (*c* 1460–1521). Spanish conqueror of Puerto Rico and discoverer of Florida.

pŏn'chō (*or* -shō) *n.* (pl. *-s*). S. Amer. cloak, oblong piece of cloth with slit in middle for head.

pŏnd *n.* Small body of still water artificially formed by hollowing or embanking; natural pool or small lake; (joc.) the sea, esp. the Atlantic Ocean; *~-lily*, water-lily; *~-skater*, bug of family *Gerridae* etc. which moves rapidly on surface of fresh water; *pond'-weed*, kinds of aquatic herb (esp. *Potamogeton*) growing in still waters. ~ *v.* Hold *back*, dam *up*, (stream); form a pool or pond.

pŏnd'age *n.* Capacity of pond; storage of water.

pŏn'der *v.* Weigh mentally, think over; think *on*, muse *over*. **pŏn'deringly** *adv.*

pŏn'derable *adj.* Having appreciable weight. **pŏnderabĭl'ity** *n.*

pŏnderā'tion *n.* Weighing, balancing.

pŏn'derous *adj.* Heavy; unwieldy; laborious; laboured. **pŏn'derously** *adv.* **pŏn'derousnėss, pŏnderŏs'ĭty** *ns.*

pōn'ė[1] *n.* In some card-games, player who leads, or his partner.

pōne[2] *n.* Orig., N. Amer. Ind. bread, thin cakes of maize flour cooked in hot ashes; now, in southern U.S., any maize bread; also, very fine light bread made with eggs, milk, etc., and baked in flat cakes.

pŏngee' (*or* pŭ-; -jē) *n.* Soft, freq. unbleached fabric of Chinese or Japanese silk, made from cocoons of a wild silkworm feeding on oak-leaves; imitation of this in cotton etc. [perh. f. Chin. *pun-chi* own loom]

pŏn'iard (-yard) *n.* Dagger (ill. DAGGER). ~ *v.t.* Stab with poniard.

pŏns *n.* 1. ~ *asinorum*, 'bridge of asses', 5th proposition of 1st book of Euclid; anything found difficult by beginners. 2. ~ (*Varolii*), 'bridge of Varoli' (Italian 16th-c. anatomist), band of nerve fibres in brain connecting two hemispheres of cerebellum, and medulla with cerebrum (ill. BRAIN). [L, = 'bridge']

pŏn'tĭfĕx *n.* (pl. *-ĭf'ĭces* pr. -ēz) (Rom. antiq.) Member of principal college of priests in Rome; ~ *maximus*, head of this; the pope.

pŏn'tĭff *n.* The pope; bishop; chief priest.

pŏntĭf'ĭcal *adj.* Of, befitting, a pontiff; solemnly dogmatic; ~ *Mass*, Mass celebrated by bishop while wearing full vestments. **pŏntĭf'ĭcally** *adv.* **pŏntĭf'ĭcal** *n.* Office-book of Western Church containing forms for rites to be performed by bishops; (pl.) vestments and insignia of bishop.

pŏntĭf'ĭcate *n.* Office of pontifex, bishop, or pope; period of this. **pŏntĭf'ĭcāte** *v.i.* Officiate as bishop, esp. at Mass; assume airs of pontiff, act pompously or dogmatically.

pŏn'tĭl *n.* Iron rod for handling and rapidly twirling soft glass, esp. crown glass, in process of manufacture.

pŏn'tīne *adj.* Of the PONS (*Varolii*).

pŏntōōn'[1] *n.* Flat-bottomed boat used as ferry-boat etc.; one of several boats, hollow metal cylinders, etc., used to support temporary bridge (ill. BRIDGE); caisson.

pŏntōōn'[2] *n.* Corruption (orig. soldiers') of the name of the card-game VINGT-ET-UN.

pŏn'ty *n.* PONTIL.

pō'ny *n.* 1. Horse of any small breed, esp. not more than 13 or (pop.) 14 hands high. 2. (slang) £25. 3. (U.S. slang) School crib.

pōōd *n.* Obsolete Russian weight, about 36 lb. avoirdupois.

pōō'dle *n.* Kinds of pet dog with long curling hair, usu. black or white, often clipped and shaved fantastically (ill. DOG). [Ger. *pudel(hund)*, f. *pudeln* splash]

pōō'dle-fāk'er *n.* (slang) Youth too much given to tea-parties and ladies' society generally.

pooh (pōō, pŏŏh) *int.* Expressing impatience or contempt.

pooh-pooh' *v.t.* Express contempt for, make light of.

Pooh-Bah' (pōōb-) *n.* Holder of many offices at once. [name of character in Gilbert and Sullivan's 'The Mikado']

pōō'kōō, pu'ku *n.* Red waterbuck or antelope (*Kobus vardoni*) of S. Central Africa.

pōōl[1] *n.* Small body of still water, usu. of natural formation; puddle of any liquid; deep still place in river; *the P~* (*of London*), part of Thames immediately below London Bridge. ~ *v.t.* Make (hole) for insertion of wedge in quarrying; undermine (coal).

pōōl[2] *n.* 1. (In some card-games) collective amount of players' stakes and fines; receptacle for these. 2. Game on billiard-table in which each player has ball of different colour with which he tries to pocket the others in fixed order, winner taking the whole stakes; similar game in U.S. with balls numbered from 1 to 15, number of ball pocketed being added to player's score. 3. Collective stakes in betting etc.; arrangement between competing parties by which prices are fixed and business divided to do away with competition; common fund, e.g. of profit of separate firms; common supply of commodities, persons, etc. (also attrib, as ~ *petrol*). ~ *v.t.* Place in common fund; merge (supplies from several sources); (of competing companies etc.) share (traffic, profits).

pōōp *n.* Stern of ship; aftermost and highest deck (ill. SHIP). ~ *v.t.* (Of wave) break over stern of (ship); (of ship) receive (wave) over stern.

poor *adj.* 1. Wanting means to procure comforts or necessaries of life, needy, indigent; ill supplied, deficient (*in* possession or quality); (of soil) unproductive; *the* ~, poor people as a class. 2. Scanty, inadequate, less than is expected; paltry, sorry; spiritless, despicable; humble, insignificant. 3. (expr. pity or sympathy) Unfortunate, hapless. 4. *~-box*, money-box esp. in church for relief of the poor; *~-house*, (hist.) institution where paupers were maintained; *P~ Law*, law relating to support of paupers; *~-rate*, rate, assessment, for relief or support of the poor; *~-spirited*, timid, cowardly.

poor'ly *adv.* Scantily, defectively; with no great success. ~ *pred. adj.* Unwell.

poor'nėss *n.* Defectiveness; lack of some good quality or constituent.

pŏp[1] *v.* 1. Make small quick explosive sound as of cork when drawn; let off (fire-arm etc.); fire gun (*at*); *~-gun*, child's toy gun shooting pellets by compression of air with piston. 2. Put (*in*, *out*, *down*, etc.) quickly or suddenly; move, come, go (*in* etc.) thus; put (question) abruptly; (colloq.) ~ *the question*, propose marriage. 3. (slang) Pawn; *~-shop*, pawnbroker's shop. 4. (U.S.) Parch (maize) till it bursts open; *~-corn*, maize so parched. ~ *n.* Abrupt, not very loud, explosive sound; (colloq.) effervescing drink, esp. ginger-beer or champagne; (slang) pawning; *in* ~, in pawn. ~ *adv.* & *int.* With (the action or sound of) a pop. [imit.]

pŏp[2] *n.* (colloq.) Popular concert.

Pŏp[3]. Social and debating club at Eton. [L *popina* cookshop (orig. meeting-place)]

pop[4]: see POPPA.

pop. *abbrev.* Population.

pōpe[1] *n.* 1. The Bishop of Rome as head of the Roman Catholic Church. 2. (fig.) Person assuming or credited with infallibility. 3. *P~ Joan*, fabulous female pope placed by some chroniclers *c* 855, under name of John; card-game played with pack from which eight of diamonds is removed, and a tray with 8 compartments holding stakes to be won by players playing certain cards; *~'s eye*, lymphatic gland surrounded with fat in middle of leg of mutton; *~'s nose*, PARSON's nose. **pōpe'dom** *n.*

pōpe[2] *n.* Parish priest of Greek Church in Russia etc. [Russ. *pop*]

Pōpe[3], Alexander (1688–1744). English poet, satirist, and translator of Homer.

pō'pery *n.* (in hostile use) The papal system, Roman Catholicism.

pŏp'ĭnjay *n.* 1. (archaic) Parrot; (hist.) figure of parrot on pole as mark to shoot at. 2. Fop, coxcomb.

pō'pĭsh *adj.* Of popery, papistical; *P~ Plot*, supposed plot to murder Charles II and suppress Protestantism, deposed to by Titus

OATES and largely fabricated by him (1678). **pŏp'ishly** *adv.*

pŏp'lar *n.* Genus (*Populus*) of large trees of rapid growth, freq. with tremulous leaves (aspen) and producing soft light loose-textured timber.

Pŏp'larism *n.* Policy of giving generous or (allegedly) extravagant relief, as practised by the Board of Guardians of Poplar, London, in 1919 and later.

pŏp'lin *n.* Closely woven fabric with corded surface, orig. of silk warp and worsted weft, now freq. of cotton. [It. *papalina* papal (because made in the papal town Avignon)]

poplit'ėal *adj.* Of the ham, or the hollow at back of knee.

Pŏp'ocătėpĕt'l. Volcanic mountain, dormant since 1802, in Mexico.

pŏp (pa) *n.* (U.S.) Papa.

pŏpp'ėt *n.* 1. (dial. or colloq.) Small person, esp. as term of endearment. 2. (also *~-head*) Lathe-head. 3. (mining) Frame at top of shaft supporting pulleys for ropes used in hoisting. 4. (naut.) Short piece of wood for various purposes, e.g. forming rowlocks of boat, supporting ship in launching (ill. LAUNCH). 5. *~-valve,* mushroom-shaped valve operated by cams etc., used in engines to ensure quick action.

pŏpp'ing *n.* (esp., cricket) *~-crease,* line 4 ft in front of and parallel to wicket within which batsman must stand (ill. CRICKET).

pŏp'ple *v.i.* (Of water) tumble about, toss to and fro, ripple. *~ n.* Rolling, tossing; ripple. **pŏp'ply** *adj.*

pŏpp'y *n.* Plant or flower of genus *Papaver*, herbs of temperate and subtropical regions having milky juice with narcotic properties, showy flowers of scarlet or other colour, and roundish capsules containing numerous small seeds; *Californian ~* = ESCHSCHOLTZIA; *Flanders ~,* (esp.) artificial poppy made for and worn on Poppy Day; *horn(ed) ~,* any plant of genus *Glaucium*, distinguished by its long horn-like capsules; *Iceland ~*: see ICELAND; *Opium ~,* species (*P. somniferum*) with white or light-purple flowers, from whose unripe capsules opium is obtained; *prickly ~,* any plant of genus *Argemone*, esp. *A. mexicana*, with yellow or white flowers and prickly leaves and capsules; *Shirley ~,* a variety of field poppy with flowers of many different colours; *P~ Day*, Armistice Day (11th Nov. 1918), now commemorated on REMEMBRANCE Day by wearing of artificial poppies (because poppies were very conspicuous on the Flanders battlefields) in memory of those killed in the wars of 1914–18 and 1939–45; *~-head,* capsule of poppy; (archit.) carved finial crowning end of seat in church (ill. STALL).

pŏpp'ycŏck *n.* (orig. U.S. slang) Nonsense, rubbish.

pŏp'ūlace *n.* The common people; the rabble.

pŏp'ūlar *adj.* 1. Of, carried on by, the people; adapted to the understanding, taste, or means of the people; prevalent among the people; *~ front,* political group representing 'left' elements. 2. Liked, admired, by the people or by people generally or a specified class. **pŏp'ūlarly** *adv.* **pŏpūlă'rity** *n.*

pŏp'ūlarīze *v.t.* Make popular, cause to be generally known or liked; extend to the common people; present in popular form. **pŏpūlarīzā'tion** *n.*

pŏp'ūlāte *v.t.* Inhabit, form the population of, (county, town, etc.); supply with inhabitants. **pŏpūlā'tion** *n.* Degree in which place is populated; total number of inhabitants; the people of a country etc.; *the* inhabitants of a place.

pŏp'ūlist *n.* 1. Adherent of a Russian political movement (*c* 1870–80) advocating collectivism. 2. Adherent of a U.S. party aiming at public control of railways, graduated income-tax, etc., formed 1892.

pŏp'ūlous *adj.* Thickly inhabited. **pŏp'ūlousnėss** *n.*

pôrb'eagle *n.* Certain sharks of genus *Lamna*, esp. *L. cornubica*, up to 10 ft long and with pointed snout; mackerel-shark.

pôrce'lain (-slĭn), *n.* The finest and hardest kind of earthenware, consisting largely of china-clay (kaolin) or felspathic clay, baked at a high temperature and usu. covered with a coloured or transparent glaze; article or vessel of this; (attrib.) of porcelain, (fig.) delicate, fragile; *~-clay,* china-clay, kaolin; *~-shell,* cowrie. **pôrcĕll'ainous, pôrcėllān'ėous, pôrcėllăn'ic, pôrcĕll'anous** *adjs.* [It. *porcellana* Venus shell (*porcella* dim. of *porco* hog, f. resemblance of the shell to hog's back)]

pôrc'elainize (-slĭn-) *v.t.* Convert (clay, shale, etc.) into porcelain or similar substance.

pôrch *n.* Covered approach to entrance of building; (U.S.) veranda; *the P~,* public ambulatory in market-place of ancient Athens to which Zeno and his disciples resorted; Stoic school or philosophy.

pôr'cīne *adj.* Of or like swine.

pôrc'ūpīne *n.* 1. Rodent (*Hystix*) with body and tail covered with long erectile spines; other genera of same family. 2. Kinds of machine with many spikes or teeth, e.g. for heckling flax etc.

pōre[1] *n.* Minute opening in skin of animal body (ill. SKIN) or membrane of plants, for transpiration, absorption, etc.

pōre[2] *v.* *~ over,* be absorbed in studying (book etc.); (fig.) meditate, think intently upon (subject).

pôrg'ȳ (-g-) *n.* (U.S.) Various sea-fishes of family *Sparidae* related to the bass, of wide distribution.

pŏr'ism (*or* pŏ'r-) *n.* (math.) Proposition affirming possibility of finding condition that will make a given problem capable of innumerable solutions. **pŏrĭsmăt'ic pŏris'tic** *adjs.*

pôrk *n.* Flesh of swine as food; *~-barrel,* (U.S. fig.) Federal treasury viewed as source of grants for local purposes; *~-butcher,* one who slaughters pigs for sale; *~-pie,* cylindrical pie of chopped pork; (attrib., of hat) with flat crown and no brim, or brim turned up all round.

pôrk'er *n.* Pig raised for food; young fattened hog.

pôrnŏc'racy *n.* Dominant influence of harlots, esp. in government of Rome in 10th c.

pôrnŏg'raphy *n.* Description of manners etc. of harlots; treatment of obscene subjects in literature; such literature. **pôrnŏg'rapher** *n.* **pôrnogrăph'ic** *adj.*

pōroplăst'ic *adj.* Both porous and plastic; *~ felt,* (surg.) a porous readily moulded felt used in preparation of splints and jackets.

pōr'ous *adj.* Full of pores; not watertight. **pōr'ousnėss, pōrŏs'ĭty** *ns.*

pôrph'ȳrīte *n.* Rock resembling porphyry but with slightly different composition of crystals.

pôrph'yrȳ[1] *n.* Volcanic purplish-red rock composed of large crystals set in a fine-grained ground mass, anciently quarried in Egypt as material for statues etc.

Pôrph'yrȳ[2]. Porphyrius (A.D. 233–*c* 305), scholar and philosopher; orig. called Malchus; by birth prob. a Syrian; became a disciple of Plotinus at Rome; left numerous works in Greek.

PORPOISE

pôrp'oise (-pus) *n.* Small whale of genus *Phocaena*, esp. *P. communis* which is about 5 ft long, blackish above and paler beneath, and has a blunt rounded snout.

PORCUPINE

pŏrrā'ceous (-shus) *adj.* Leek-green.

porrĕct′ *v.t.* 1. (biol.) Stretch out, extend (part of body). 2. (eccles. law) Tender, submit (document).

pŏ′rridge *n.* Soft food made by stirring oatmeal or other meal or cereal in boiling water or milk.

pŏrrĭg′ō *n.* (obs.) Scaly eruption of scalp. **porrĭ′ginous** *adj.*

pŏ′rringer (-j-) *n.* Small basin from which soup etc. is eaten.

PORRINGER

Pŏrs′ĕn(n)a, Lars (*Lars* = 'lord'). (Rom. hist.) A prince of Clusium in Etruria; acc. to tradition, when the Romans expelled the Tarquin kings and formed a republic (*c* 510 B.C.), he led an Etruscan army against Rome to restore the Tarquins, but was repulsed.

pōrt[1] *n.* Harbour; town, place, possessing harbour, esp. one where customs officers are stationed; *free* ~, one open for merchants of all nations to load and unload in; *cinque* ~*s*: see CINQUE PORTS.

pōrt[2] *n.* 1. (chiefly Sc.) Gate, gateway, esp. of walled town. 2. (naut.) Opening in side of ship for entrance, loading, etc.; port-hole; (mech.) aperture for passage of steam, water, etc.; curved mouthpiece of some bridle-bits; ~-*hole*, aperture in ship's side for admission of light and air (ill. SHIP) or (formerly) for pointing cannon through; aperture in wall etc. for firing through.

pōrt[3] *n.* External deportment, carriage, bearing. ~ *v.t.* (mil.) Carry (rifle, sword) diagonally across and close to the body, with barrel or blade opposite middle of left shoulder.

pōrt[4] *n.* Left-hand side of ship looking forward (formerly called larboard) (ill. BEARING); corresponding side of aircraft. ~ *v.* Turn (helm) to left side of ship; (of ship or aircraft) turn to port side.

pōrt[5] *n.* Heavy sweet fortified wine, dark red or (less freq.) white, made in the Douro valley of Portugal; wine of similar type made in other countries (but by various Anglo-Portuguese treaties only Douro wines may be sold in U.K. under the name of 'port'). [*Oporto*, seaport where the wine is shipped]

pōr′table *adj.* Movable, convenient for carrying. **pōrtabĭl′ity** *n.*

pōrt′age *n.* Carrying, carriage; cost of this; carrying of boats or goods across land between two navigable waters, place at which this is necessary. ~ *v.t.* Convey (boat, goods) over a portage.

pōrt′al[1] *n.* Door(way), gate(way), esp. elaborate one.

pōrt′al[2] *adj.* Of the *porta* or transverse fissure of the liver; ~ *vein*, the *vena portae*, great vein formed by union of veins from stomach, intestine, and spleen, conveying blood to the liver (ill. BLOOD).

pōrtamĕn′tō *n.* (mus.) Gliding continuously from one pitch to another, in singing, violin-playing, etc.

Pōrt Arth′ur (ar-). Harbour in S. Manchuria, leased to Russia 1898; besieged and taken by Japanese, 1904, in Russo-Japanese war; restored to Russia in 1945.

pōrt′ative *adj.* (chiefly hist.) Portable, esp. applied to kind of small organ.

pōrtcŭll′is *n.* Strong heavy grating blocking gateway of fortress, made to slide up and down in vertical grooves (ill. CASTLE). **pōrtcŭll′ised** (-st) *adj.*

Pōrte. *The* (*Sublime* or *Ottoman*) ~, (hist.) Ottoman court at Constantinople, Turkish Government until 1923. [Fr. *la Sublime Porte*, transl. of Turkish *bab-i-ali* high gate, title of central office of Turkish Government]

pōrte-cochère (pōrtkoshar′) *n.* Gateway and passage for vehicles through house into courtyard.

pōrtĕnd′ *v.t.* Foreshow, foreshadow, as an omen; give warning of.

pōr′tĕnt *n.* Omen, significant sign; prodigy, marvellous thing. **pōrtĕn′tous** *adj.* **pōrtĕn′tously** *adv.*

pōrt′er[1] *n.* Gate-keeper, doorkeeper, esp. of large building, public institution, etc.

pōrt′er[2] *n.* 1. Person employed to carry burdens, esp. servant of railway company who handles luggage; (U.S.) attendant in Pullman coaches etc.; ~'*s knot*, pad resting on shoulders and secured to forehead used by porters in carrying loads. **pōrt′erage** *n.* Work of porters; charge for this.

pōrt′er[3] *n.* Dark-brown bitter beer, like stout but weaker, brewed from charred or browned malt (now chiefly in Ireland); ~-*house*, (U.S.) house at which porter, etc., was retailed; place where steaks, chops, etc., were served, chop-house; ~-*house steak*, choice cut of beef between sirloin and tenderloin. [short for *porter's ale* etc., app. because orig. brewed for porters and other labourers]

pōrtfŏl′iō *n.* Case, usu. like large book-cover, for keeping loose sheets of paper, drawings, etc.; such receptacle containing official documents of State department, (fig.) office of minister of State; *minister without* ~, one not in charge of any department of State.

pōrt′icō *n.* Colonnade, roof supported by columns at regular intervals, usu. attached as porch to a building (ill. TEMPLE).

portière (pōrtyar′) *n.* Curtain hung over door(way).

pōr′tion *n.* Part, share; dowry; one's destiny, one's lot; *a* ~, amount of a dish served to a person in a restaurant, etc.; some (*of*) anything. ~ *v.t.* Divide (thing) into shares, distribute *out*; assign (*to* person) as share; give dowry to.

Pōrt′land, Isle of. Peninsula on coast of Dorsetshire, England, site of a convict prison converted (1921) into a Borstal institution; ~ *cement*, kind of cement hardening in water and resembling Portland stone when set; ~ *stone*, yellowish-white limestone from Isle of Portland, extensively used for building.

Pōrt′land Club. London card-playing club, the recognized authority on the games of whist and bridge.

Pōrt′land Vase. Roman vase (*c* 1st c. A.D.) of dark-blue transparent glass with engraved figure decoration in white opaque glass; acquired in 18th c. by Duchess of Portland from Barberini Palace, Rome; now in British Museum, where it was damaged by a madman in 1845.

pōrt′ly *adj.* Bulky, corpulent; of stately appearance. **pōrt′liness** *n.*

pōrtmăn′teau (-tō) *n.* (pl. -*s*, -*x*, pr. -z). Oblong case for carrying clothing etc., opening like book with hinges in middle of back; (fig.) word like those invented by Lewis Carroll, blending the sounds and combining the meanings of two others (e.g. *slithy* = lithe and slimy).

pōrtola′nō (-lah-) *n.* (hist.) Book of sailing directions with description of harbours etc., illustrated with charts.

Porto Rico: see PUERTO RICO.

pōrt′rait (-rĭt) *n.* Likeness of person or animal made by drawing, painting, photography, etc.; verbal picture, graphic description; (fig.) type, similitude. **pōrt′raitist** *n.* Maker of portraits.

pōrt′raiture (-rĭcher) *n.* Portraying; portrait; graphic description.

pōrtray′ *v.t.* Make likeness of; describe graphically. **pōrtray′al** *n.*

pōrt′reeve *n.* (hist.) Chief officer of town or borough; (now) officer inferior to mayor in some towns.

pōrt′rĕss *n.* Female porter.

Port-Royal (des Champs) (pōr, rwāyahl′). Cistercian convent near Versailles which from 1636 onwards became the home of the community of Jansenists (see JANSENISM) and the centre of their educational work; the institution was persecuted by the Jesuits and closed by Louis XIV in 1710.

Pŏrt Said (sād, sīd). Egyptian seaport at N. end of Suez Canal.

Pŏrt'smouth (-m*u*th). City and seaport of Hampshire; chief naval station of Gt Britain.

Pŏrt'ūgal. Republic (kingdom until 1910) occupying W. part of Iberian peninsula; capital, Lisbon. **Pŏrtūguese'** (-gēz) *adj.* & *n.* (Native, inhabitant) of Portugal; (of) the Romance language of Portugal, spoken also in Brazil; ~ *man-of-war*, marine hydrozoan of genus *Physalia.*

pōse[1] (-z) *n.* Attitude of body or mind, esp. one assumed for effect; (dominoes) posing, right to pose. ~ *v.* Lay down (assertion, claim, etc.); propound (question); place (artist's model etc.) in certain attitude; assume an attitude, esp. for artistic purposes; set up, give oneself out, *as*; dominoes) place first domino on table.

pōse[2] (-z) *v.t.* Puzzle (person) with question or problem. **pō'ser** *n.* (esp.) Puzzling question or problem.

Poseid'on (-sī-). (Gk myth.) God of the sea, brother of Zeus and Pluto; identified by Romans with Neptune.

pōseur (-zer̃) *n.* Affected person.

pŏsh *adj.* (slang) Smart, stylish; first-rate, high-class.

Pŏsīdōn'ius (*c* 135–51 B.C.). Syrian-Greek Stoic philosopher.

pŏs'ĭt (-z-) *v.t.* Assume as fact, postulate; put in position, place.

posĭ'tion (-zishn) *n.* 1. (chiefly logic and philos.) Proposition; laying down of this. 2. Bodily posture, attitude. 3. Mental attitude, way of looking at question. 4. Place occupied by a thing, site, situation; *in* (*out of*) ~, in (out of) its proper place; (mil.) place where troops are posted esp. for strategical reasons. 5. Situation in regard to other persons or things; condition. 6. Rank, social status; official employment. 7. Situation of vowel in syllable, esp. (Gk and L prosody) of short vowel before two consonants, making syllable metrically long. ~ *v.t.* Place in position; determine position of. **posĭ'tional** (-shon-) *adj.*

pŏ'sĭtĭve (-z-) *adj.* 1. Explicitly laid down; definite; admitting no question. 2. Absolute, not relative; (gram., of degree of adjective or adverb) expressing simple quality, without qualification or comparison; (colloq.) downright, out-and-out. 3. (of person) Confident, assured; opinionated; (also) given to constructive action. 4. Dealing only with matters of fact, practical. 5. Marked by presence, not absence, of qualities; tending in the direction regarded as that of increase or progress. 6. (math., physics, etc.) Greater than zero; in the direction which for purposes of calculation is to be regarded as upwards from zero; (elect.) having a positive charge; ~ *charge*, one of the two kinds of electric charge, that of the atomic nucleus as dist. from the negative charge of the electrons (the terms *positive* and *negative* were applied to electricity before the discovery of electrons and their meaning is now purely conventional); ~ *pole*, region of deficiency of electrons, anode; also (magnetism) applied to the north-seeking pole of a magnet and the corresponding (south) pole of the earth; ~ *sign*, the sign +, plus sign. 7. (photog.) Showing the lights and shades as seen in nature. 8. ~ *organ*, small (orig. portable) organ occas. used to supplement large one in church. **pŏs'ĭtĭvely** *adv.* **pŏs'ĭtĭvenėss, pŏsĭtĭv'ĭty** *ns.* **pŏs'ĭtĭve** *n.* Positive degree, adjective, quantity, photograph, etc.

pŏs'ĭtĭvism (-z-) *n.* Philosophical system of Auguste Comte, recognizing only positive facts and observable phenomena and abandoning all inquiry into causes or ultimate origins; religious system founded upon this. **pŏs'ĭtĭvist** *n.* **pŏsĭtĭvĭs'tic** *adj.*

pŏs'ĭtrŏn (-z-) *n.* A positive particle, prob. one of the fundamental constituents of matter, having a mass equal to that of the electron and electrically its counterpart. [*posit*(*ive elect*)*ron*]

pŏss'ė *n.* 1. Body (*of* constables); strong force or company; ~ (*cŏmĭtā'tus*), body of men in a county whom sheriff may summon to suppress riot etc. 2. *in* ~, in possibility, in potentiality (opp. to *in esse*). [L, = 'to be able'; in med. L, 'power']

possĕss' (-zĕs) *v.t.* Hold as property, own; have (faculty, quality, etc.); maintain (*in* patience etc.); (of demon or spirit) occupy, dominate (person etc.); ~ *oneself of*, take, get for one's own; *be possessed of*, own, have. **possĕss'or** *n.* **possĕss'ory** *adj.*

posse'ssion (-zĕshn) *n.* 1. Possessing; actual holding or occupancy; (law) visible power of exercising such control as attaches to (but may exist apart from) lawful ownership; *in* ~, (of thing) possessed; (of person) possessing; *man in* ~, one placed in charge of chattels on which there is a warrant for distress; *in* ~ *of*, having in one's possession; *in the* ~ *of*, possessed or held by; ~ *is nine points*, or *tenths*, *of the law*, possession or occupancy gives every advantage short of actual lawful ownership. 2. Thing possessed; subject territory, esp. foreign dominion(s); (pl.) property, wealth.

possĕss'ĭve *adj.* Of possession; indicating possession; desirous of keeping as one's own. ~ *n.* Possessive case or word. **possĕss'ĭvely** *adv.* **possĕss'ĭvenėss** *n.*

pŏss'ėt *n.* (archaic) Drink made of hot milk curdled with ale, wine,

POSSET POT

etc., and freq. flavoured with spices, formerly much used as remedy for colds etc.

pŏssĭbĭl'ĭty *n.* State, fact, of being possible; thing that may exist or happen.

pŏss'ĭble *adj.* That can exist, be done, or happen; that may be or become; tolerable to deal with, reasonable, intelligible. ~ *n.* Highest possible score, esp. in rifle practice; possible candidate, member of team, etc. **pŏss'ĭbly** *adv.* In accordance with possibility; perhaps, maybe, for all one knows to the contrary.

pŏss'um *n.* (colloq.) Opossum; *play* ~, feign illness, death, etc.

pōst[1] *n.* 1. Stout piece of timber usu. cylindrical or square and of considerable length placed vertically as support in building; stake, stout pole, for various purposes; *starting-*, *winning-*, ~, post that marks starting, finishing, point in race. 2. Vertical mass of coal left as support in mine; thick compact stratum of sandstone etc. ~ *v.t.* Stick (paper etc., usu. *up*) to post or in prominent place; advertise (fact, thing, person) by placard; (in colleges) place in list that is posted up the names of (unsuccessful students); publish name of (ship) as overdue or missing; placard (wall etc.) with bills.

pōst[2] *n.* 1. (hist.) One of series of men stationed with horses along roads at intervals, the duty of each being to ride forward with letters to next stage; (hist.) courier, letter-carrier; mail-cart. 2. A single dispatch of letters, letters so dispatched; letters taken from post-office or pillar-box on one occasion; letters delivered at one house on one occasion. 3. Official conveyance of letters, parcels, etc.; post office or postal letter box; *by return of* ~, (hist.) by same courier who brought the dispatch; (now) by next mail in opposite direction. 4. Size of writing-paper (about 20 × 16 in.), half-sheet of which when folded forms ordinary quarto letter-paper. 5. ~*-bag*, mail-bag; ~*-boy*, letter-carrier; postilion of stage-coach etc.; *post'-card*, card of regulation size for conveyance by post; *~-chaise* (-sh-), (hist.) travelling carriage hired from stage to stage or drawn by horses so hired; *~-free*, carried free of charge by post or with postage prepaid; *~-haste*, with great expedition; *~-horn*, horn of kind formerly used by postman or guard of mail-coach to announce arrival; *~-horse*, one of those formerly kept at inns etc. for use of posts or travellers; *post'man*, one who delivers or collects letters; *post'mark*, official mark stamped on letters etc., esp. one giving place, date, and hour, of dispatch or arrival, and serving to deface stamp; hence *post'mark* (*v.t.*); *post'master*[1], official in charge of a post-office; *Post'master General*, administrative head of postal service; *post'mistress*, woman in charge of a post-office; *~-office*, public department for conveyance of letters etc. by post; house or shop where postal business is carried on; *~-paid*, on which postage has been paid. ~ *adv.* (archaic) With post-horses; express, with haste. ~ *v.* 1. (hist.) Travel with relays of horses; travel with haste, hurry. 2. Put (letter etc.) into post-office or letter-box for transmission. 3. (book-keeping) Carry (entry) from auxiliary book to more formal one, esp. from day-book or journal to ledger; (also ~ *up*) complete (ledger etc.) thus; (fig.) supply (person) with full information.

pōst[3] *n.* 1. Place where soldier is stationed, (fig.) place of duty; position taken by body of soldiers, force occupying this; fort; (also *trading-~*) place occupied for purposes of trade esp. in uncivilized country. 2. Situation, employment; (naval, hist.) commission as officer in command of vessel of 20 guns or more; ~ *captain*, holder of such commission. 3. (mil.) *first, last, ~*, bugle-call giving notice of hour of retiring for night (*last ~* is also blown at military funerals etc.). ~ *v.t.* Direct (soldiers etc.) to go to a specified station etc.; (mil., naval) commission (person) as captain.

pōst- *prefix.* After, behind.

pŏs'tage *n.* Amount charged for carriage of letters etc. by post, now usu. prepaid by ~ *stamp*, adhesive label to be affixed (or stamp embossed or impressed) on envelope etc., having specified value, or by franking.

pŏs'tal *adj.* Of the POST[2] *n.*; ~ *order*: see ORDER *n.*; (*International*) *P~ Union*, union of governments of various countries for regulation of international postage.

pōst-clăss'ĭcal *adj.* Occurring later than the classical period of (esp. Greek and Latin) language, literature, or art.

pōstdāte' *v.t.* Affix, assign, to (document, event, etc.) a date later than the actual one. ~ *n.* Such date.

pōstdĭluv'ĭan (-ōō-) *adj.* & *n.* (Person) existing, occurring after the Flood.

pōst-ĕn'try *n.* Late or subsequent entry (for race, in book-keeping, etc.).

pōs'ter *n.* 1. (also *bill-~*), One who posts bills. 2. Placard displayed in public place.

pōste rĕs'tante (-tahnt) *n.* Department in post-office in which letters are kept till applied for.

pŏstēr'ĭor *adj.* 1. Later, coming after in series, order, or time. 2. Hinder; as viewed from behind. ~ *n.* (sing. or pl.) The buttocks. **pŏstērĭŏ'rĭty** *n.* **pŏstēr'iorly** *adv.*

pŏstĕ'rĭty *n.* The descendants of any person; all succeeding generations.

pŏs'tern *n.* Back door; side way or entrance.

pōst-ĕxĭl'ĭan, -ĕxĭl'ĭc *adjs.* Subsequent to the Babylonian exile of the Jews.

pōst-fĭx' *v.t.* Append (letters) at end of word. **pōst'fix** *n.* Suffix.

pōst-glā'cial *adj.* Subsequent to the glacial period.

pōstgrăd'ūate *adj.* (Of course of study) carried on after graduation. ~ *n.* Student taking such course.

pōst hŏc ĕr'gō prŏp'ter hŏc. L phr. ('after this, therefore on account of this') ridiculing the tendency to confuse sequence with consequence.

pŏst'humous (-tū-) *adj.* Occurring after death; (of child) born after death of its father; (of book etc.) published after author's death.

pŏstīc'ous *adj.* (bot.) Posterior, hinder.

pŏs'tĭl *n.* (hist.) Marginal note, comment, esp. on text of Scripture; commentary.

postĭl(l)'ion (-yon) *n.* One who rides the near horse of the leaders when 4 or more are used in a carriage, or near horse when one pair only is used and there is no driver on box.

Pōst-Imprĕ'ssionĭsm (-shon-) *n.* Comprehensive term for various developments in painting (Neo-Impressionism, Expressionism, Cubism, etc.) which followed IMPRESSIONISM in late 19th and early 20th centuries. **Pōst-Imprĕs'sionĭst** *n.* One of the painters responsible for these (as Cézanne, Gauguin, Van Gogh, Picasso). **pōst-ĭmprĕssionĭs'tĭc** *adj.*

pōstlĭm'ĭny *n.* (Rom. law) Right of banished person to resume civic privileges on return; (international law) restoration to their former state of persons and things taken in war, when they come again into the power of the nation they belonged to.

pōst'lūde *n.* (mus.) Concluding piece or movement played at end of oratorio.

pōst'master[1] (-mah-) *n.* See POST[2] *n.*

pōst master[2] (-mah-) *n.* Scholar of Merton College, Oxford. **pōst'mastership** *n.*

pōst merĭd'ĭēm *adv.* (usu. abbrev. p.m., pronounced pē ĕm). After midday. **pōst-merĭd'ĭan** *adj.*

pōst mōrt'ĕm *adv.* After death. **pōst-mōrt'ĕm** *adj.* & *n.* (Examination) made after death to determine its cause; discussion of game of bridge etc. after it is finished.

pōst-nāt'al *adj.* Occurring after birth.

pōst-nŭp'tial (-shl) *adj.* Subsequent to marriage.

pōst-ŏb'ĭt *adj.* Taking effect after death. ~ *n.* Bond securing to lender a sum to be paid on death of a specified person from whom borrower has expectations.

pōst-ōr'al *adj.* Situated behind the mouth.

pōstpōne' (*or* po-) *v.* Put off, defer; (path., of ague etc.) be later in coming on. **postpōne'ment** *n.*

pōst-posi'tion (-zĭshn) *n.* Particle etc. (as Engl. *-wards*) which is placed after the word whose sense it modifies. **pōst-pŏs'itive** (-z-) *adj.*

pōst-prăn'dĭal *adj.* (chiefly joc.). Done etc. after dinner.

pōst'scrĭpt *n.* (abbrev. P.S.) Additional paragraph esp. at end of letter after signature.

pŏs'tūlant *n.* Candidate esp. for admission into religious order.

pŏs'tūlate *n.* Thing claimed or assumed as basis of reasoning, fundamental condition; prerequisite; (geom.) claim to take for granted possibility of simple operation, e.g. of drawing straight line between any two points. **pŏs'tūlāte** *v.* Demand, require, claim, take for granted; stipulate *for*; (eccles. law) nominate or elect to ecclesiastical dignity, subject to sanction of superior authority. **pŏstūlā'tion** *n.*

pŏs'ture *n.* Carriage, attitude of body or mind; condition, state (*of* affairs, etc.). ~ *v.* Dispose the limbs of (person) in particular way; assume posture.

pōst-war' (wōr) *adj.* Of the period after a war, esp. the world war of 1914–18 or that of 1939–45.

pŏs'y (-zĭ) *n.* (archaic) Short motto, line of verse, etc., inscribed within ring; nosegay.

pŏt[1] *n.* 1. Rounded vessel of earthenware, metal, glass etc., for holding liquids or solids; (nursery abbrev.) chamber-pot; ink-pot, flower-pot, tea-pot, coffee-pot, etc.; such vessel for cooking; drinking vessel of pewter etc.; contents of pot; vessel, usu. of silver, as prize in athletic sports, (slang) any prize in these; *make the ~ boil, keep the ~ boiling*, make a living; *go to ~*, (colloq.) be ruined or destroyed. 2. Fish-pot, lobster-pot; chimney-pot. 3. Large sum; (racing slang) large sum staked or betted; (*big*) ~, important person.

4. *pot(t) (paper)*, writing- or printing-paper, normally 15½×12½ in., named from original water-mark of a pot. 5. *~-belly*, (person with) protuberant belly; *~-boiler*, work of literature etc. done merely to make a living; writer or artist who produces this; *~-bound*, (of plant) with roots filling flower-pot and wanting room to expand; *~-boy, pot'man*, publican's assistant; *~-cheese*, (U.S.) cheese of coagulated milk from which water is separated by heating in a pot; *pot'herb*, herb grown in kitchen-garden; *~-hook*, hook over fire-place for hanging pot etc. on, or for lifting hot pot (ill. FIRE); curved stroke in handwriting, esp. as made in learning to write; *~-house*, ale-house; *~-hunter*, sportsman who shoots anything he comes across; person who takes part in contest merely for sake of prize; *~ lead*, black-lead esp. as used for hull of racing yacht; *~ luck*, whatever is to be had for a meal; *~-metal*, stained glass coloured in melting-pot so that the colour pervades the whole; *~-shot*, shot taken at game merely to provide a meal; shot aimed at animal etc. within easy reach (also fig.); *~-still*, kind of still in which heat is applied directly and not by steam-jacket; *~-valiant*, valiant because drunk; *~-wall(op)er*; householder voter (before 1832). **pŏt'ful** *n.* **pŏt** *v.* Place (butter, fish, minced meat, etc., usu. salted or seasoned) in pot or other vessel to preserve it; plant (plant) in pot; (billiards) pocket; bag (game), kill (animal) by pot-shot; shoot (*at*); seize, secure.

pŏt² *n.* (chiefly dial.) Deep hole or pit in river-bed or in ground, as in limestone districts.

pō'table *adj.* Drinkable. **pō'tables** *n.pl.* (usu. joc.) Drinkables.

potăm'ĭc *adj.* Of rivers.

pŏt'ăsh *n.* An alkaline substance, crude potassium carbonate; (*caustic*) ~, potassium hydroxide, KOH, white brittle substance, soluble in water and deliquescent in air, with powerful caustic and alkaline properties. [Du. *pot-asschen*, because orig. got by lixiviating vegetable ashes and evaporating the solution]

potăss'ium *n.* (chem.) A light metallic element, one of the alkali metals, which is soft at ordinary temperatures, oxidizes immediately on exposure to air, and instantly decomposes water on contact with it, liberating and igniting hydrogen which burns with a characteristic violet flame; symbol K (f. *kalium*), at. no. 19, at. wt 39·102. [latinized form of POTASH]

potā'tion *n.* Drinking; (usu. pl.) tippling; draught. **pō'tatory** *adj.*

potā'tō *n.* (pl. *-es*) 1. Batata or sweet potato. 2. Plant (*Solanum tuberosum*), native of Pacific slopes of S. America, introduced into Europe late in 16th c., with roundish or oval starch-containing tubers used for food; tuber of this; *~ beetle*, the COLORADO beetle; *~-ring*, (usu. silver) ring used as stand for a bowl in which potatoes were brought to table in Ireland. [Haitian *batata*]

pot(h)een' *n.* Irish whiskey from illicit still.

Potem'kin (-tyŏm-), Grigory Aleksandrovich, Prince (1739–91). Russian soldier and statesman, favourite of Catherine the Great.

pō'tent¹ *adj.* Powerful, mighty (chiefly poet. or rhet.); having sexual power; (of reasons etc.) cogent; (of drugs etc.) strong. **pō'tently** *adv.* **pō'tency** *n.*

pō'tent² *adj.* (her., of line parting a field) Resembling a series of crutchheads (ill. HERALDRY); (of cross) having limbs terminating in crutchheads.

pō'tentāte *n.* Monarch, ruler.

potĕn'tial (-shl) *adj.* Capable of coming into being or action, latent; (gram.) expressing potentiality or possibility; (physics) *~ energy*, energy existing in potential form, not as motion; *~ function*, mathematical function by differentiation of which the force at any point in space arising from any system of bodies etc. can be expressed. **potĕn'tially** *adv.* **potĕn'tial** *n.* 1. Potential mood. 2. (Amount of energy or quantity of work denoted by) potential function; possibility, potentiality; resources that can be employed for an undertaking. **potĕntiăl'ity** (-shĭăl-) *n.* Inherent, latent, capacity to exert power; possibility, promise, of development.

potĕn'tialīze (-sha-) *v.t.* Make potential; convert (energy) into potential condition.

potĕn'tiāte (-shĭ-) *v.t.* Endow with power; make possible.

potĕntiŏm'ēter (-shĭ-) *n.* Instrument for measuring differences of electrical potential.

pŏth'er (-dh-) *n.* Choking smoke or cloud of dust; noise, din; verbal commotion or fuss.

pŏt-hōle *n.* (geol.) Deep hole of more or less cylindrical shape; esp. one formed by wearing away of rock by rotation of a stone, or gravel, in an eddy of running water, or in glacier bed; POT²; depression or hollow in road-surface caused by traffic etc. **pŏt-hōler, pŏt-hōling** *ns.* Explorer, exploring of pot-holes.

pō'tion *n.* Dose, draught, of liquid medicine or of poison.

Pŏt'ĭphar. (O.T.) An Egyptian, captain of Pharaoh's guard; he bought Joseph and made him his chief servant, but when Potiphar's wife falsely accused Joseph of an attempt on her virtue, Potiphar imprisoned him (Gen. xxxix).

Potō'măc. River of U.S. flowing into Chesapeake Bay and forming part of N. boundary of Virginia.

pot-pourri (pōpo͝o'rĭ) *n.* Mixture of dried petals and spices kept in jar for its perfume; musical or literary medley. [Fr., lit. rotten pot]

pŏt'shērd *n.* (archaic) Broken piece of earthenware.

pott *n.*: see POT¹ *n.* sense 4.

pŏtt'age (-ij) *n.* (archaic) Soup, stew.

pŏtt'er¹ *n.* Maker of earthenware vessels; *~'s lathe*, machine rotating the *~'s wheel*, on which, as it spins rapidly round, the potter moulds the clay. **pŏtt'ery** *n.* Earthenware (sometimes distinguished from PORCELAIN); potter's work or workshop; *the Potteries*, district in N. Staffordshire, chief centre of English pottery industry.

pŏtt'er² *v.* Work in feeble or desultory manner (*at, in*); dawdle, loiter (*about* etc.); trifle *away* (time etc.).

pŏtt'le *n.* (archaic) Measure for liquids, half gallon; pot etc. containing this; small wicker or chip basket for strawberries etc.

pŏtt'ō *n.* Reddish-grey loris of genus *Perodicticus*, a slow-moving arboreal mammal of W. Africa.

Pŏtt's fracture. Fracture of lower end of fibula, usu. accompanied by dislocation of ankle (ill. BONE).

pŏtt'y *adj.* (slang). 1. Insignificant, trivial. 2. Foolish, crazy.

pouch *n.* Small bag or detachable outside pocket for carrying e.g. tobacco; purse (archaic); soldier's leathern ammunition bag; mail-bag; bag-like receptacle in which marsupials carry their undeveloped young; cheek-pouch or other bag-like natural receptacle; (bot.) bag-like cavity in plant, esp. purse-like seed-vessel. ~ *v.* Put into pouch; take possession of, pocket; make (part of dress) hang like pouch, hang thus.

pouffe (po͞of) *n.* 1. Low stuffed seat or cushion. 2. Woman's high roll or pad of hair. 3. Part of dress gathered up in bunch.

poulp(e) (po͞o-) *n.* Octopus or other cephalopod.

poult (pōlt) *n.* Young of domestic fowl, turkey, pheasant, etc.

poult-de-soie (po͞odeswah') *n.* Fine corded silk.

poul'terer (pōl-) *n.* Dealer in poultry.

poul'tice (pōl-) *n.* Paste of starch, linseed, etc., usu. made with boiling water and spread on muslin etc., applied to sore or inflamed part. ~ *v.t.* Apply poultice to.

poul'try (pōl-) *n.* Domestic fowls, as barn-door fowls, geese, turkeys.

pounce¹ *n.* Claw, talon, of bird of prey; pouncing, sudden swoop. ~ *v.* Swoop down upon and seize; make sudden attack *upon*, seize eagerly *upon*.

pounce² *n.* Fine powder used to prevent ink from spreading on unsized paper etc.; powdered charcoal etc. dusted over perforated pattern to transfer design to object beneath. ~ *v.t.* Smooth (paper etc.) with pumice or pounce; transfer (design) by use of pounce, dust (pattern with pounce).

poun'cĕt-bŏx *n.* (archaic) Small box with perforated lid for perfumes.

pound[1] *n.* 1. (abbrev. lb. = L *libra*). Measure of weight, 16 oz. avoirdupois, 12 oz. troy. 2. (also ~ *sterling*; written £ before figure) Principal monetary unit of the United Kingdom, = 20 shillings or 240 pence. 3. Principal monetary unit of various other countries, as *Australian, Egyptian, Libyan*, etc. ~ (written £A, £E, £L, etc.). 4. ~*-cake*, rich cake containing 1 lb. (or equal weight) of each of chief ingredients; ~*-day*, day on which a charity etc. receives contributions from all comers of a pound of anything; ~ *note*, bank- or treasury-note for £1; ~ *Scots*, (hist.) 1*s.* 8*d.* ~ *v.t.* (coining) Test weight of (coins) by weighing the number that ought to weigh 1 lb.

pound[2] *n.* Enclosure for detention of stray cattle or of distrained cattle or goods till redeemed; enclosure for animals; (fig.) place of confinement; (hunting) difficult position; ~ *lock*, lock with two gates. ~ *v.t.* Shut (cattle etc.) in pound; *pounded*, (of rider in hunt) in enclosed place from which he cannot get out to follow the chase.

pound[3] *v.* Crush, bruise, as with pestle; thump, pummel, with fists etc.; knock, beat (*to pieces, into a jelly*, etc.); deliver heavy blows, fire heavy shot (*at* etc.); walk, run, ride, make one's way, heavily.

poun'dage (-ij) *n.* Commission, fee, of so much per pound sterling; percentage of total earnings of a business, paid as wages; payment of so much per pound weight; charge on postal order etc.

poun'dal *n.* (physics). A unit of force which acting on a mass of 1 lb. will impart to it an acceleration of 1 ft per sec. per sec., corresponding to the DYNE except that pound and foot replace gram and centimetre.

poun'der[1] *n.* Thing that, gun firing shot that, weighs a pound or specified number of pounds; thing worth, person possessing, specified number of pounds sterling.

poun'der[2] *n.* (esp.) Instrument for pounding with or in, pestle, mortar.

pour (pōr) *v.* Cause (liquid, granular substance, light, etc.) to flow, discharge copiously; discharge (missiles, crowd from building, etc.) copiously or in rapid succession; send *forth, out* (words, music, etc.); flow (*forth, out, down*) in stream; (of rain) descend heavily; (fig.) come (*in, out*) abundantly. ~ *n.* Heavy fall of rain, downpour; (founding) amount of molten metal etc. poured at a time. **pour'ing** *adj.*

pourparler (poorpârl'ā) *n.* (usu. in pl.) Informal discussion preliminary to negotiation.

pour'point (poor-), **pûr'point** *ns.* (hist.) Padded and quilted doublet

poussĕtte' (pōō-) *n.* Country-dance figure in which two couples, each with hands joined, dance round one another.

Poussin (pōōsăň), Nicolas (1594–1665). French painter in the classical tradition.

pout[1] *n.* The bib, a sea-fish (*Gadus luscus*) allied to cod, used as food.

pout[2] *v.* Protrude (lips), protrude lips, (of lips) protrude, esp. as sign of displeasure. ~ *n.* Such protrusion.

pout'er *n.* Person, animal, that pouts; esp., domestic variety of rock-pigeon with great power of inflating crop.

pŏv'erty *n.* Indigence, want; scarcity, deficiency (*of*); deficiency *in* (a property); inferiority, poorness, meanness; ~*-stricken*, poor.

P.O.W. *abbrev.* Prisoner of war.

powd'er *n.* Mass of dry particles or granules, dust; medicine in the form of powder; cosmetic powder applied to face, skin, or hair; gunpowder; ~*-blue*, powdered smalt, esp. for use in laundry; (of) deep blue colour of this; ~*-flask*, case for carrying gunpowder; ~*-horn*, powder-flask orig. and esp. of horn; ~*-magazine*, place where gunpowder is stored; ~ *metallurgy*, moulding of finely ground (esp. metal) powders into intricate shapes to which solidity is restored afterwards by special treatment; ~*-monkey*, boy formerly employed on board ship to carry powder to guns; ~*-puff*, soft pad of swansdown, etc., for applying powder to skin. ~ *v.t.* Sprinkle powder upon, cover (with powder etc.); apply powder to (hair, face, etc.); decorate (surface) with spots or small figures; reduce to powder. **powd'ery** *adj.*

pow'er *n.* 1. Ability to do or act; vigour, energy; particular faculty of body or mind. 2. Active property, as *heating* ~. 3. Government, influence, authority (*over*); personal ascendancy (*over*); political ascendancy. 4. Authorization, delegated authority; ~ *of attorney*: see ATTORNEY. 5. Influential person, body, or thing; State having international influence; *the* ~*s that be*, (w. ref. to Rom. xiii. 1) constituted authorities. 6. Deity; (pl.) 6th order of angels. 7. Mechanical energy as opp. to hand-labour (freq. attrib., as ~*-lathe*, ~*-loom*); capacity for exerting mechanical force, esp. HORSE-~; electrical power distributed to consumer; ~ *factor*, ratio between actual power delivered and apparent power suggested by voltage and current. 8. (math., of a number) The product of a specified number of factors, each of which is the number itself, the specified number of factors being the *index*; similarly of algebraic quantities etc. 9. Magnifying power of lens. 10. (vulg.) Large number or amount. 11. ~ *dive*, (of aircraft), dive made without shutting off the motor power; ~ *egg*, engine with its auxiliaries compacted into one removable unit; ~ *politics*, diplomacy backed by (threat of) force; ~ *station*, station in which electric power is generated for distribution. **pow'ered** (-erd) *adj.* Equipped with mechanical power.

pow'erful *adj.* Having great power or influence. **pow'erfully** *adv.*

pow'erlĕss *adj.* Without power; wholly unable (*to* help etc.). **pow'erlĕssly** *adv.* **pow'erlĕssnĕss** *n.*

pow'wow *n.* N. Amer. Indian medicine-man or sorcerer; magic ceremonial, conference, of N. Amer. Indians; (U.S.) political or other meeting or conference; (slang) conference of officers during army manœuvres etc. ~ *v.* Hold powwow, confer *about* something; doctor, treat with magic.

pŏx *n.* Syphilis.

pozz(u)olana (pŏtsolah'na, -tswo-) *n.* Volcanic ash found at Pozzuoli, near Naples, much used for hydraulic cement.

pp. *abbrev.* Pages.

pp. *abbrev.* *Pianissimo.*

p.p. *abbrev.* Past participle; *per procurationem.*

P.P. *abbrev.* Parcel post; Parish Priest.

P.P.C. *abbrev.* *Pour prendre congé* (= to take leave).

P-plane *abbrev.* PILOTLESS plane.

P.P.S. *abbrev.* Parliamentary Private Secretary; *post postscriptum* (= further postscript).

pr *abbrev* Pair; -pounder.

P.R. *abbrev.* Proportional representation.

P.R.A. *abbrev.* President of the Royal Academy.

praam: see PRAM[1].

prăc'ticable *adj.* That can be done, feasible; that can be used, (of road etc.) that can be traversed; (theatr., of door, window, etc.) real, that can be used as such. **prăcticabil'ity, prăc'ticablenĕss** *ns.* **prăc'ticably** *adv.*

prăc'tical *adj.* 1. Of, concerned with, shown in, practice; available, useful, in practice; engaged in practice, practising. 2. Inclined to action rather than speculation. 3. That is such in effect though not nominally, virtual. **prăc'ticalnĕss, prăcticăl'ity** *ns.* **prăc'tically** *adv.* In a practical manner; virtually, almost.

prăc'tice *n.* 1. Habitual action or carrying on; method of legal procedure; habit, custom; repeated exercise in an art, handicraft, etc.; spell of this. 2. Professional work, business, or connexion, of lawyer or doctor. 3. (archaic) Scheming, (usu. underhand) contrivance, artifice (esp. pl.); *sharp* ~: see SHARP. 4. (arith.) Mode of finding value of given number of articles or quantity of commodity at given price, when quantity or price or both are in several denominations. 5. *in* ~, in the realm of action; actually; lately practised in skill or ability; *put in(to)* ~, carry out.

prăctĭ'cian (-shn) *n.* Worker, practitioner.

prăc'tĭse *v.* Perform habitually, carry out in action; exercise, pursue (profession); exercise oneself in or on (art, instrument, or abs.); exercise (*in* action or subject); (archaic) scheme, contrive; ~ *(up)on*, impose upon, take advantage of. **prăc'tĭsed** (-st) *adj.* Experienced, expert.

prăctĭ'tioner (-sho-) *n.* Professional or practical worker, esp. in medicine; *general* ~ (abbrev. G.P.), doctor qualified to practise medicine and surgery.

Pra'dō (prah-). Spanish national museum of painting and sculpture, at Madrid, containing part of the royal collections. [Span., = 'meadow', f. the adjoining park]

prae- *prefix.* L form of PRE-, kept only in a few words.

praemūnīr'ė *n.* (law) Writ charging sheriff to summon person accused of prosecuting in a foreign court a suit which is cognizable in England, or (later) of asserting or maintaining papal jurisdiction in England; *Statute of P*~, statute of 16 Richard II, on which writ is based. [L; so called because the words *praemunire facias* warn (so-and-so to appear) occur in the writ]

praepŏs'tor *n.* (public school) Prefect, monitor.

praet'or *n.* (orig.) Roman consul as leader of army; (later) annually elected magistrate performing some duties of consul. **praetōr'ĭal** *adj.*

praetōr'ian, prėtōr'ian *adj.* Of a praetor; ~ *guard*, bodyguard of a Roman general or emperor. ~ *n.* Man of praetorian rank, soldier of praetorian guard.

prăgmăt'ic(al) *adjs.* 1. Meddlesome; dogmatic. 2. Of philosophical pragmatism. 3. (*-ic*) Treating facts of history with reference to their practical lessons. 4. (*-ic*, hist.) Of the affairs of a State; ~ *sanction*, imperial or royal ordinance issued as fundamental law, esp. that of the Emperor Charles VI in 1724 settling Austrian succession. **prăgmăt'ĭcally** *adv.* **prăg'matism** *n.* 1. Officiousness; pedantry. 2. Matter-of-fact treatment of things. 3. Philosophical doctrine that estimates any assertion solely by its practical bearing upon human interests. **prăg'matist** *n.*

prăg'matīze *v.t.* Represent as real; rationalize (myth.).

Prague (-ahg) (Czech *Praha*). City of central Europe, capital of Czechoslovakia.

prair'ĭe *n.* Large treeless tract of level or undulating grassland, esp. in N. America; ~ *chicken*, a N. Amer. grouse (*Pedioecetes phasianellus*); ~*-dog*, N. Amer. burrowing rodent (*Cynomys*) of squirrel family; ~ *hen*, a N. Amer. grouse (*Tympanuchus americanus*); ~ *oyster*, raw egg seasoned and swallowed in spirits; ~ *schooner*, large covered wagon of kind used by emigrants in crossing N. Amer. plains; *P*~ *State*, (U.S.) popular name of Illinois.

praise (-z) *v.t.* Express warm approbation of, commend the merits of; glorify, extol the attributes of. ~ *n.* Praising, commendation.

praise worthy (prāz'wĕrdhi) *adj.* Worthy of praise, commendable. **praise'worthĭly** *adv.* **praise'worthĭnėss** *n.*

Pra'krĭt (prah-). Any of the vernacular Indo-European dialects of India, as dist. from Sanskrit; all these collectively.

pra'lĭne (-ah-) *n.* Sweetmeat made by browning nuts in boiling sugar.

***pram*[1], *praam*,** (prahm) *ns.* Flat-bottomed boat used in Baltic etc. for shipping cargo etc.; flat-bottomed boat mounted with guns; Scandinavian ship's boat corresp. to dinghy.

prăm[2] *n.* (colloq.) Perambulator; milkman's hand-cart.

prance (-ah-) *v.* (Of horse) rise by springing from hind legs; cause (horse) to do this; (fig.) walk, behave, in elated or arrogant manner. ~ *n.* Prancing, prancing movement.

prăn'dĭal *adj.* (joc.) Of dinner.

prăng *v.t.* (R.A.F. slang) Bomb (target) hard from air; crash (aircraft). ~ *n.*

prănk[1] *n.* Mad frolic, practical joke. **prănk'ful, prănk'ĭsh** *adjs.*

prănk[2] *v.* Dress, deck (*out*); adorn, spangle (*with*); show oneself off.

prāsėōdy̆m'ĭum (-z-) *n.* Metallic element of rare-earth group forming leek-green salts; symbol Pr, at. no. 59, at. wt 140·907. [Gk *prasios* leek-green, (DI)DYMIUM].

prāte *v.* Chatter; talk too much, blab; tell, say, in prating manner. ~ *n.* Prating, idle talk. **prāt'er** *n.* **prāt'ing** *adj.*

prăt'ĭque (-k; *or* pratēk') *n.* Licence to hold intercourse with a port, granted to a ship after quarantine or on showing clean bill of health.

prătt'le *v.* Talk or say in childish or artless fashion. ~ *n.* Childish chatter, small talk. **prătt'ler** *n.* **prătt'lĭng** *adj.*

prawn *n.* Various small lobster-like marine decapod crustacea (e.g. *Palaemon*) larger than shrimp. ~ *v.i.* Fish for prawns.

prăx'ĭs *n.* Accepted practice, custom; (gram.) set of examples for practice.

Prăxĭt'ėlēs (-z) (4th c. B.C.). Greek sculptor, creator of 'Apollo Slaying a Lizard' and 'Hermes with the Infant Dionysus'.

pray *v.* Make devout supplication to (God, object of worship); beseech earnestly (*for, to, that*); ask earnestly for; engage in prayer, make entreaty; ~ (contr. of *I pray you*), used parenthetically for emphasis, e.g. *what,* ~, *is the use of that?*

prayer (prār) *n.* Solemn request to God or object of worship; formula used in praying; form of divine service consisting largely of prayers; action, practice, of praying; entreaty to a person; thing prayed for; ~*-book*, book of forms of prayer, esp. *Book of Common Prayer*, public liturgy of Church of England; ~*-meeting*, religious meeting at which several persons offer prayer; ~*-wheel*, revolving cylindrical box inscribed with or containing prayers, used esp. by Buddhists of Tibet. **prayer'ful** *adj.* **prayer'fully** *adv.* **prayer'fulnėss** *n.* **prayer'lėss** *adj.* **prayer'lėssly** *adv.* **prayer'lėssnėss** *n.*

P.R.B. *abbrev.* Pre-Raphaelite Brotherhood.

pre- *prefix.* Before.

preach *v.* Deliver sermon or religious address, deliver (sermon); give moral advice in obtrusive way; proclaim, expound (the Gospel, Christ, etc.) in public discourses; advocate, inculcate (quality, conduct, etc.) thus. **preach'er** *n.* **preach'ment** *n.* (usu. contempt.).

preach'ĭfy̆ *v.i.* Preach, moralize, hold forth, tediously.

preach'y *adj.* (colloq.) Fond of preaching or holding forth.

Prē-ăd'amīte *adj.* & *n.* (One of supposed race) existing before time of Adam. **prē-adăm'ic** *adj.*

prēăm'ble *n.* Preliminary statement in speech or writing; introductory part of statute, deed, etc. ~ *v.i.* Make preamble.

Preb. *abbrev.* Prebendary.

prĕb'end *n.* Part of revenue of cathedral or collegiate church granted to canon or member of chapter as stipend; portion of land or tithe from which this stipend is drawn; prebendary. **prĕb'endal** (*or* prėbĕn'-) *adj.*

prĕb'endary *n.* Holder of prebend.

Prē-Căm'brĭan *adj.* Of the rocks which lie below the Cambrian; of the period to which these belong (ill. GEOLOGY).

prėcār'ious *adj.* Held during the pleasure of another; question-begging; doubtful, uncertain; dependent on chance; perilous. **prėcār'iously** *adv.* **prėcār'iousnėss** *n.*

prē-cast' (-ah-) *adj.* (Of concrete) cast in blocks before use in construction.

prĕc'atory *adj.* Of, expressing, entreaty; ~ *words*, (in will) words requesting that a thing be done;

~ *trust*, precatory words that are held to be binding.

prėcau'tion *n.* Prudent foresight; measure taken beforehand to ward off evil or ensure good result. **prėcau'tionary** (-shon-) *adj.*

prėcēde' *v.* Go before in rank or importance; come before in order; walk in front of; come before in time; cause to be preceded *by*.

prĕ'cėdence (*or* prĭsē'-) *n.* Priority in time or succession; superiority, higher position; (usu. prĭsē'-) right of preceding others in ceremonies and social formalities. **prĕc'ėdency** *n.* (rare).

prĕ'cėdent *n.* Previous case taken as example for subsequent cases or as justification; (law) decision, procedure, etc., serving as rule or pattern. **prėcēd'ent** (*or* prĕs'ĭ-) *adj.* (now rare) Preceding in time, order, rank, etc. **prėcēd'ently** *adv.* **prĕc'ėdĕntėd** *adj.* Having a precedent; supported by precedent.

prėcĕn'tor *n.* (In some Presbyterian churches etc.) one who leads singing of congregation; (in English cathedrals) member of clergy in general control of musical arrangements, in 'old foundations' ranking next to dean and having succentor as his deputy, and in 'new foundations' being a minor canon. **prėcĕn'torshĭp, prėcĕn'trĭx** *ns.*

prē'cĕpt *n.* Command, maxim; moral instruction; divine command; writ, warrant; written order to arrange for and hold election; order for collection or payment of money under a rate. **prėcĕp'tĭve** *adj.*

prėcĕp'tor *n.* Teacher, instructor. **prēcĕptôr'ial** *adj.* **prėcĕp'trėss** *n.*

prėcĕp'tory *n.* (hist.) Subordinate community of Knights Templars; estate, buildings, of this.

prėcĕss' *v.i.* (Of rapidly revolving globe, spinning top, etc.) sway in such a way that its axis describes a circle.

prėcĕ'ssion (-shn) *n.* ~ *of the equinoxes*, the earlier occurrence of the equinoxes in each successive sidereal year; the effect is produced by a slow change in the direction of the earth's axis, which moves (like the axis of a spinning top) so that the pole of the equator describes an approximate circle round the pole of the ecliptic once in about 25,800 years.

prē-Chris'tian *adj.* Before Christ, before Christianity.

prē'cĭnct *n.* 1. Space enclosed by walls or other boundaries of a place or building, esp. of place of worship; boundary; (pl.) *the* environs *of*. 2. (town planning) Area from which main-road traffic is excluded. 3. Subdivision of county or city or ward for election and police purposes.

prėcĭŏs'ĭty (-shĭŏs-) *n.* Affectation of refinement or distinction.

prĕ'cious (-shus) *adj.* 1. Of great price, costly; of great non-material worth; ~ *metals*, gold, silver, (sometimes) platinum; ~ *stone*, gem. 2. Affectedly refined in language, workmanship, etc. 3. (colloq., as intensive) Out-and-out (*made a ~ mess of it*); (as adv.) extremely, very. 4. (*my*) ~, term of endearment. **prĕ'ciously** *adv.* **prĕ'ciousnėss** *n.*

prĕ'cĭpĭce *n.* Vertical or steep face of rock, cliff, mountain, etc.

prėcĭp'ĭtāte[1] *v.t.* 1. Throw down headlong, hurl, fling; hurry, urge on; hasten the occurrence of. 2. (chem.) Cause (a solid substance) to be deposited from a solution by the addition of another solution; condense (vapour) into drops and so deposit. **prėcĭpĭtā'tion** *n.* (esp., meteor.) Fall of rain, sleet, snow, or hail. **prėcĭp'ĭtate** (-*a*t) *n.* (chem.) Substance precipitated from solution; moisture condensed from vapour by cooling and deposited.

prėcĭp'ĭtate[2] *adj.* Headlong, violently hurried; hasty, rash, inconsiderate. **prėcĭp'ĭtately** *adv.* **prėcĭp'ĭtatenėss, prėcĭp'ĭtance, prėcĭp'ĭtancy** *ns.*

prėcĭp'ĭtous *adj.* Of, like, a precipice; steep. **prėcĭp'ĭtously** *adv.* **prėcĭp'ĭtousnėss** *n.*

précis (prā'sē, prĕ-) *n.* Summary, abstract.

prėcīse' *adj.* Accurately expressed, definite, exact; punctilious, scrupulous in observance of rules etc. **prėcīse'ly** *adv.* In precise manner; (in emphatic or formal assent) quite so. **prėcīse'nėss** *n.*

prėcĭ'sian (-zhn) *n.* One who is rigidly precise or punctilious, esp. in religious observance. **prėcĭ'sianĭsm** (-zh*a*-) *n.*

prėcĭ'sion (-zhn) *n.* Accuracy; (attrib., of apparatus) designed for exact or precise work.

prē-clăss'ĭcal *adj.* Before the classical age (usu. of Greek and Roman literature).

prėclude' (-ōōd) *v.t.* Exclude, prevent, make impracticable. **prėclus'ĭve** (-lōō-) *adj.*

prėcō'cious (-sh*u*s) *adj.* (Of plant) flowering or fruiting early; (of person) prematurely developed in some faculty; (of actions etc.) indicating such development. **prėcō'ciously** *adv.* **prėcō'ciousnėss, prėcŏ'cĭty** *ns.*

prēcŏgnĭ'tion *n.* 1. Antecedent knowledge. 2. (Sc. law) Preliminary examination of witnesses etc., esp. in order to know whether there is ground for trial. **prēcŏg'nĭtĭve** *adj.*

prēconceive' (-sēv) *v.t.* Conceive beforehand, anticipate in thought. **prēconcĕp'tion** *n.* (esp.) Prejudice.

prē-condĭ'tion (-shn) *n.* Prior condition, one that must be fulfilled beforehand.

prēc'onīze *v.t.* Proclaim publicly; summon by name; (of pope) approve publicly the appointment of (bishop). **prēconīzā'tion** *n.*

prē-Cŏnq'uĕst *adj.* Before the Norman Conquest.

prē-cŏns'cious (-sh*u*sh) *adj.* Antecedent to consciousness; ~ *n.* (in Freudian psycho-analysis) = FORECONSCIOUS.

prėcûrs'or *n.* Forerunner, harbinger; one who precedes in office etc. **prėcûrs'ory** *adj.* Preliminary, introductory, serving as harbinger (*of*). **prėcûrs'ĭve** *adj.*

prėdā'cious (-sh*u*s) *adj.* (Of animals) naturally preying on others, predatory; of such animals. **prėdă'cĭty** *n.*

prĕd'ator *n.* Animal that preys upon others.

prĕd'atory *adj.* Of, addicted to, plunder or robbery; (of animal) preying upon others.

prēdėcease' *v.t.* Die before (another). ~ *n.* Death before another's.

prēd'ėcĕssor *n.* Former holder of any office or position; thing to which another thing has succeeded; forefather.

prėdĕll'a *n.* (Painting on vertical face of) altar-step; (painting, sculpture, on) raised shelf at back of altar (ill. ALTAR); small painting(s) done as pendant to altarpiece. [It., = 'stool']

prėdĕstĭnār'ĭan *adj.* & *n.* (Holder of the doctrine) of predestination.

prėdĕs'tĭnāte *v.t.* (Of God) foreordain (person) to salvation or *to* (any fate), *to* (do); determine beforehand. **prėdĕs'tĭnate** (-*a*t) *adj.*

prėdĕstĭnā'tion *n.* God's appointment from eternity of some of mankind to salvation and eternal life; God's foreordaining of all that comes to pass; fate, destiny.

prėdĕs'tĭne *v.t.* Determine beforehand; appoint as if by fate; (theol.) predestinate.

prēdėtêrm'ĭne *v.t.* Decree beforehand; predestine; (of motive, etc.) impel (person) beforehand. **prēdėtêrm'ĭnate** *adj.* **prēdėtêrmĭnā'tion** *n.*

prēd'ĭal *adj.* Of land or farms; rural, agrarian; (of slaves) attached to the land.

prĕd'ĭcable *adj.* That may be predicated or affirmed. **prĕdĭcabĭl'ĭty** *n.* **prĕd'ĭcable** *n.* Predicable thing, esp. (pl.) Aristotle's classes of predicates viewed relatively to their subjects (viz. genus, definition, property, accident).

prėdĭc'ament *n.* 1. Thing predicated, esp. (pl.) ten categories of predications formed by Aristotle. 2. Unpleasant, trying, or dangerous situation.

prĕd'ĭcant *adj.* (Of religious order, esp. Dominicans) engaged in preaching.

prĕd'ĭcate *n.* (logic) What is predicated; what is affirmed or denied of the subject by means of the copula (e.g. *a fool* in *he is a fool*); (gram.) what is said of the subject, including the copula (e.g. *is a fool* in preceding example); quality, attribute. **prĕd'icāte** *v.t.* Assert, affirm, as true or existent; (logic) assert (thing) about subject. **prĕdicā'tion** *n.*

prėdĭc'atĭve *adj.* Making a predication; (gram., of adj. or n., opp. *attributive*) forming part or the whole of the predicate. **prėdĭc'atĭvely** *adv.*

prėdĭct' *v.t.* Foretell, prophesy. **prėdĭct'able, prėdĭct'ĭve** *adjs.* **prėdĭct'ion** *n.*

prėdĭc'tor *n.* (esp.) Instrument for determining height, direction, speed, and range of aircraft and the fuse-setting etc. required in engaging hostile aircraft with anti-aircraft fire.

prē-dĭgĕst' *v.t.* Render (food) easily digestible before introduction into stomach. **prē-dĭgĕs'tion** (-schon) *n.*

prĕdĭkant' (-ahnt) *n.* Minister of Dutch Protestant Church, esp. in S. Africa.

prēdĭlĕc'tion *n.* Mental preference, partiality, (*for*).

prēdĭspōse' (-z) *v.t.* Render liable, subject, or inclined (*to*). **prēdĭsposĭ'tion** (-z-) *n.* State of mind or body favourable *to*.

prėdŏm'ĭnāte *v.i.* Have or exert control (*over*), be superior; be the stronger or main element, preponderate. **prėdŏm'ĭnance** *n.* **prėdŏm'ĭnant** *adj.* **prėdŏm'ĭnantly** *adv.*

prē-ĕm'ĭnent *adj.* Excelling others; distinguished beyond others in some quality. **prē-ĕm'ĭnently** *adv.* **prē-ĕm'ĭnence** *n.*

prē-ĕmpt' *v.t.* Obtain by pre-emption; (U.S.) occupy (public land) so as to have right of pre-emption; (fig.) appropriate beforehand.

prē-ĕmp'tion *n.* Purchase by one person etc. before opportunity is offered to others; right of actual occupant to purchase public land thus at nominal price, on condition of his improving it. **prē-ĕmp'tĭve** *adj.* (esp., in bridge, of bid) Higher than necessary, so as to prevent opponents from exchanging information by bidding.

preen *v.t.* Trim (feathers) with beak; trim one*self*, smooth and adorn one*self* (also fig.).

pref. *abbrev.* Preference etc.; prefix.

Pref. *abbrev.* Preface.

prēfăb' *n.* Colloq. abbrev. of *prefabricated house*.

prēfăb'rĭcāte *v.t.* Manufacture component parts of (a building or other structure) in preparation for their assembly on a site. **prēfăbrĭcā'tion** *n.*

prĕf'ace *n.* Introduction to book stating subject, scope, etc.; preliminary part of a speech; introduction to central part of Eucharistic service. ~ *v.* Furnish (book etc.) with preface, introduce (*with*); lead up to (event etc.); make preliminary remarks. **prĕfatōr'ial, prĕf'atory** *adjs.*

prĕf'ĕct *n.* Various civil and military officers in ancient Rome, e.g. civil governor of province, colony, etc.; chief administrative officer of French department; (in some schools) senior pupil authorized to maintain discipline; ~ *of Police*, head of police administration of Paris and the department of the Seine. **prėfĕct'oral, prēfĕctōr'ial** *adjs.*

prĕf'ĕcture *n.* (Period of) office, official residence, district under government, of a prefect. **prēfĕc'tural** (-cher-) *adj.*

prėfėr' *v.t.* 1. Promote (person *to* office). 2. Bring forward, submit (statement, information, etc., *to* person in authority etc. *against* offender etc.). 3. Choose rather, like better; *preferred stock*, PREFERENCE stock. **prĕf'erable** *adj.* **prĕf'erably** *adv.*

prĕf'erence *n.* Liking of one thing better than another; thing one prefers; prior right esp. to payment of debts; favouring of one person or country before others in business relations, esp. favouring of country by admitting its products at lower import duty; ~ *stock, share*, one on which dividend is paid before any is paid on ordinary stock.

prĕferĕn'tial (-shl) *adj.* Of, giving, receiving, preference; (of duties etc.) favouring particular countries, esp. favouring trade between Gt Britain and her colonies etc. **prĕferĕn'tially** *adv.*

prėfėr'ment *n.* Advancement, promotion; appointment, esp. ecclesiastical, giving social or pecuniary advancement.

prēfĭg'ure (-ger) *v.t.* Represent beforehand by figure or type, picture to oneself beforehand. **prēfĭgurā'tion, prēfĭg'urement** (-germ-) *ns.* **prēfĭg'urative** *adj.*

prĕf'ĭx *n.* Verbal element placed at beginning of word to qualify meaning or (in some languages) as inflexional formative; title placed before name. **prėfĭx'** *v.t.* Add (*to* book etc.) as introduction; join as prefix (*to* word).

prēfôrm' *v.t.* Form beforehand. **prēfôrmā'tion** *n.* Previous formation.

prēfôrm'atĭve *adj.* & *n.* Forming beforehand; (syllable, letter) prefixed as formative element, esp. in Semitic languages.

prĕg'nable *adj.* Capable of being captured.

prĕg'nant *adj.* (Of woman or female animal) with child, gravid; teeming with ideas, imaginative, inventive; fruitful in results, big *with* (consequences etc.); (of words or acts) having a hidden meaning, significant, suggestive; ~ *construction*, (gram.) one in which more is implied than the words express. **prĕg'nantly** *adv.* **prĕg'nancy** *n.*

prėhĕn'sĭle *adj.* (zool., of tail or limb) Capable of grasping.

prėhĕn'sion (-shn) *n.* Grasping, seizing; mental apprehension.

prēhĭstŏr'ĭc *adj.* Of the period antecedent to history. **prēhĭstŏr'ĭcally** *adv.*

prēhĭs'tory *n.* Prehistoric matters or times.

prē-ĭgnĭ'tion *n.* Too-early ignition in internal combustion engine.

prējŭdge' *v.t.* Pass judgement on before trial or proper inquiry; form premature judgement upon. **prējŭdge'ment, prējudĭcā'tion** (-jōō-) *ns.*

prĕj'udĭce (-jōō-) *n.* Preconceived opinion, bias; injury that results or may result from some action or judgement; *without* ~, without detriment to existing right or claim. ~ *v.t.* Impair the validity of (right, claim, etc.); cause (person) to have a prejudice (*against, in favour of*).

prĕjudĭ'cial (-jōōdĭsh'*a*l) *adj.* Causing prejudice, detrimental (*to*). **prĕjudĭ'cially** *adv.*

prĕl'acy *n.* Office, rank, see, of a prelate; prelates collectively; church government by prelates.

prĕl'ate *n.* High ecclesiastical dignitary, e.g. (arch)bishop, metropolitan, patriarch; (hist.) abbot or prior. **prėlăt'ĭc(al)** *adjs.* **prelăt'ĭcally** *adv.*

prĕl'ature *n.* Prelacy.

prėlĕct' *v.i.* Discourse, lecture (esp. in university). **prėlĕc'tion, prėlĕc'tor** *ns.*

prėlĭm'ĭnary *adj.* Introductory, preparatory. ~ *n.* Preliminary arrangement.

prĕl'ūde *n.* Performance, action, event, condition, serving as introduction (*to* another); (mus.) introductory movement, esp. one preceding fugue or forming first part of suite. ~ *v.* Serve as prelude to, introduce, foreshadow; introduce with a prelude; be, give, a prelude *to*; (mus.) play a prelude. **prėlū'sion** (-zhn) *n.* **prėlū'sĭve** *adj.*

prĕmatūre' (*or* prĕm'-) *adj.* Occurring, done, before the usual or proper time, too early, hasty. **prĕmatūre'ly** *adv.* **prĕmatūre'nėss, prĕmatūr'ĭty** *ns.*

prēmĕdĭcā'tion *n.* Administration of sedative or hypnotic drug to patient before giving general anaesthetic.

prēmĕd'ĭtāte *v.t.* Think out, design, beforehand. **prēmĕd'ĭtātėdly** *adv.* **prēmĕdĭtā'tion** *n.*

prĕm'ĭėr (*or* prē-) *adj.* (now chiefly slang and journalese) First in position, importance, order, or time. ~ *n.* Prime minister; (U.S.) the Secretary of State. **prĕm'ĭėrshĭp** *n.*

première (premyār') *n.* First performance of play etc.

prĕm'ise (-s), **prĕm'ĭss** *n.* 1. (logic, freq. spelt *premiss*) Previous statement from which another is inferred; esp. (pl.) the two propositions (*major* and *minor* ~) from which the conclusion is derived in a syllogism. 2. (pl.) The aforesaid, the foregoing, esp. (law) the aforesaid houses, lands, or tenements. 3. (pl.) House, building, with grounds and appurtenances. **prėmīse′** (-z) *v.t.* Say, write, by way of introduction.

prēm′ium *n.* 1. Reward, prize (now chiefly in *put a ~ on*, provide or act as incentive to). 2. Amount to be paid in consideration of contract of insurance. 3. Sum additional to interest, wages, etc., bonus; fee for instruction in profession etc.; charge for changing one currency into another of greater value; *at a ~*, at more than nominal value; (fig.) in high esteem.

prēmōl′ar *adj.* & *n.* (Tooth) developed between canines and molars, (in man) bicuspid (ill. TOOTH).

prēmonī′tion *n.* Forewarning; presentiment. **prėmŏn′itor** *n.* **prėmŏn′itory** *adj.*

Prēmŏnstratĕn′sian (-shn) *adj.* & *n.* (Member) of R.C. order of regular canons founded (12th c.) by St. Norbert at Prémontré, France.

prē-nāt′al *adj.* Existing, occurring, before birth.

prĕn′tice *n.* & *v.t.* Apprentice (archaic; now chiefly in *~ hand*, inexpert hand).

prėŏccūpā′tion *n.* Prepossession, prejudice; occupation of a place beforehand; occupation, business, that takes precedence of all others; mental absorption.

prėŏcc′ūpȳ *v.t.* Engage beforehand, engross (mind etc.); appropriate beforehand; *preoccupied*, distrait, with thoughts elsewhere.

prē-ôrdain′ *v.t.* Appoint beforehand; foreordain.

prĕp *adj.* & *n.* (colloq. or slang) Preparatory; preparation, homework.

prĕp. *abbrev.* Preparation; preposition.

prĕparā′tion *n.* 1. Preparing; (usu. pl.) thing(s) done to make ready (*for*); (abbrev. *prep*) preparation of lessons as part of school routine; (mus.) preparing of a discord. 2. Substance, e.g. food or medicine, specially prepared.

prėpă′rative *adj.* & *n.* Preparatory (act). **prėpă′ratively** *adv.*

prėpă′ratory *adj.* & *n.* Serving to prepare, introductory (*to*); *~ (school)*, school where pupils are prepared for higher, esp. public, school. **prėpă′ratorily** *adv.*

prėpâre′ *v.* Make ready (*for*); make (food, meal) ready for eating; make mentally ready or fit (*for* news, *to* hear, etc.); get (lesson, speech, etc.) ready by previous study, get (person) ready by teaching (*for* college, examination, etc.); make preparations (*for*, *to* do, etc.); make (chemical product etc.) by regular process; (mus.) lead up to (discord) by sounding the dissonant note in it as consonant note in preceding chord; *be prepared*, be ready or willing (*to* do).

prēpay′ *v.t.* (past t. & past part. *-paid*) Pay (charge) beforehand; pay (postage), pay postage of (parcel etc.) beforehand, e.g. by affixing stamp. **prēpay′ment** *n.*

prėpĕnse′ *adj.* Deliberate, intentional (chiefly in *malice ~*, intention to injure).

prėpŏn′derāte *v.i.* Weigh more, be heavier; be of greater moral or intellectual weight; be the chief element, predominate; *~ over*, exceed in number, quantity, etc. **prėpŏn′derance** *n.* **prėpŏn′derant** *adj.* **prėpŏn′derantly** *adv.*

prĕposi′tion (-z-) *n.* Indeclinable word serving to mark relation between the noun or pronoun it governs and another word (e.g. the italic words in: found him *at* home, wait *in* the hall, what did you do it *for*?, the bed that he slept *in*, won *by* waiting, came *through* the roof, that is what I was thinking *of*). **prĕposi′tional** (-sho-) *adj.* **prĕposi′tionally** *adv.*

prēpossĕss′ (-zĕs) *v.t.* Imbue, inspire (*with*); (of idea etc.) take possession of (person); prejudice, usu. favourably. **prēpossĕss′ing** *adj.* **prēpossĕss′ingly** *adv.* **prēpossĕss′ingness, prēpose′ssion** (-zĕshn) *ns.*

prėpŏs′terous *adj.* Contrary to nature, reason, or common sense; perverse, foolish; absurd. **prėpŏs′terously** *adv.* **prėpŏs′terousness** *n.*

prėpŏt′ent *adj.* Very powerful; more powerful than others. **prėpōt′ence, prėpōt′ency** *ns.*

prēp′ūce *n.* Foreskin, loose integument covering end of penis (ill. PELVIS). **prėpū′tial** (-shl) *adj.*

Prē-Răph′ăėlīte *adj.* & *n.* (Member, follower) of the *~ Brotherhood*, a group of young English artists and men of letters formed *c* 1848 to resist existing conventions in art and literature by a return to standards which they supposed to have existed in European art before the time of Raphael; the group was composed of Holman Hunt, Millais, D. G. Rossetti, W. M. Rossetti, and others. **Prē-Răph′ăėl(īt)ism** *n.*

prē-rėlease′ *adj.* & *n.* (Film) exhibited before date fixed for release.

prērĕq′uisite (-z-) *adj.* & *n.* (Thing) required as previous condition.

prėrŏg′ative *n.* 1. (*Royal ~*), right of the sovereign, theoretically subject to no restriction. 2. Peculiar right or privilege; natural, or divinely given advantage, privilege, faculty. 3. (hist.) *~ court*, archbishop's court for probate of wills etc. *~ adj.* Privileged, enjoyed by privilege; (Rom. hist.) having the right to vote first.

Pres. *abbrev.* President.

prĕs′age *n.* Omen, portent; presentiment, foreboding. **prėsāge′ful** (-jf-) *adj.* **prėsāge′** *v.t.* Portend, foreshadow; give warning of (event etc.) by natural means; (of person) predict; have presentiment of.

prĕsbȳōp′ia (-s-, -z-) *n.* Form of long-sightedness incident to old age, caused by loss of power of accommodation. **prĕsbȳŏp′ic** *adj.*

prĕs′bȳter (-s-, -z-) *n.* (In early Christian Church) one of several officers managing affairs of local church; (in Episcopal Church) minister of second order, priest; (in Presbyterian Church) elder. **prĕsbȳt′eral, prĕsbȳtēr′ial** *adjs.* **prĕsbȳt′erate, prĕs′bȳtership** *ns.*

Prĕsbȳtēr′ian (-s-, -z-) *adj.* & *n.* (Member) of the *~ Church*, the national church of Scotland, whose system of church government recognizes no higher office than that of presbyter or elder; all elders are ecclesiastically of equal rank, and every church is governed by its session of elders, themselves subordinate to provincial Presbyteries, and these to the General Assembly; the doctrines of the Church are Protestant with a strong element of Calvinism. **Prĕsbȳtēr′ianism** *n.*

prĕs′bȳtery (-s-, -z-) *n.* 1. Eastern part of chancel beyond choir, sanctuary (ill. CHURCH). 2. Body of presbyters, esp. court above kirk-session; district represented by this. 3. (R.C. Ch.). Priest's house.

prĕ′scient (-shĭ-) *adj.* Having foreknowledge or foresight. **prĕ′sciently** *adv.* **prĕ′science** *n.*

prėscĭnd′ (-s-) *v.* Cut off (part *from* whole), esp. prematurely or abruptly; *~ from*, leave out of consideration.

Prĕs′cott, William Hickling (1796–1859). American historian, author of 'The History and Conquest of Mexico' and 'The History and Conquest of Peru'.

prėscrībe′ *v.* 1. Lay down or impose authoritatively; (med.) advise use of (medicine etc.). 2. Assert prescriptive right or claim (*to*, *for*).

prēs′cript *n.* Ordinance, law, command.

prėscrĭp′tion *n.* 1. Prescribing; physician's (usu. written) direction for composition and use of medicine. 2. (law) (*positive*) *~*, uninterrupted use or possession from time immemorial, or for period fixed by law as giving title or right; such title or right; *negative ~*, limitation of the time within which action or claim can be raised; (fig.) ancient custom viewed as authoritative, claim founded on long use.

prėscrĭp′tive *adj.* Prescribing; based on prescription, as *~ right* (see PRESCRIPTION, 2); prescribed by custom. **prėscrĭp′tively** *adv.*

prē-sėlĕc′tive *adj.* (Of motor-car gears) provided with mechanism for automatic engagement of any desired gear which is set in advance with a small lever on a selector dial on the steering column.

prĕs′ence (-z-) *n.* 1. Being present; place where person is; *the* ~, ceremonial attendance on person of high esp. royal rank; ~-*chamber*, one in which great personage receives guests etc. 2. Carriage, bearing. 3. ~ *of mind*, calmness and self-command in sudden emergencies.

prĕs′ent[1] (-z-) *adj.* 1. Being in the place in question (chiefly pred.); being dealt with, discussed, etc. 2. (archaic) Ready at hand; ready with assistance. 3. Existing, occurring, being such, now; (gram., of tense) denoting action etc. now going on. ~ *n. The* present time, the time now passing; present tense; *at* ~, now; *for the* ~, just now, as far as the present is concerned; *by these* ~*s*, by this document (now legal or joc.).

prĕs′ent[2] (-z-) *n.* Gift.

prèsĕnt′[3] (-z-) *v.* 1. Introduce (*to*); introduce (person) to sovereign at court; (of theatr. manager) cause (actor) to take part in play, produce (play); recommend (clergyman) to bishop for institution (*to* benefice); ~ one*self*, appear esp. as candidate for examination etc. 2. Exhibit (*to*); show (quality etc.); (of idea etc.) offer, suggest it*self*; (physiol., of part of unborn child) be foremost at outlet of womb; (law) bring formally under notice, submit (complaint, offence, *to* authority); aim (weapon *at*), hold out (weapon) in position for aiming; (mil.) hold (fire-arm) in position for taking aim; ~ (*arms*), hold fire-arm etc. in deferential position in saluting. 3. Offer, give, as present; offer (compliments, regards, *to*); deliver (bill etc.) for acceptance etc.; ~ (person) *with* (thing), present it to him. ~ *n.* Act of aiming weapon, esp. fire-arm; position of weapon when aimed; position of 'present arms' in salute.

prèsĕn′table (-z-) *adj.* Of decent appearance, fit to be introduced or go into company; suitable for presentation as a gift etc. **prèsĕntabĭl′ĭty** *n.* **presĕnt′ably** *adv.*

prĕsentā′tion (-z-) *n.* 1. Presenting, esp. formal; gift, present; exhibition, theatrical representation, etc.; formal introduction, esp. at court. 2. (metaphys.) All the modification of consciousness directly involved in the knowing or being aware of an object in a single moment of thought. **prĕsentā′tional** (-sho-) *adj.*

prĕsentā′tionĭsm (-z-, -sho-) *n.* (metaphysics) Doctrine that in perception the mind has immediate cognition of the object.

prèsĕn′tative (-z-) *adj.* (Of benefice) to which patron has right of presentation; serving to present an idea to the mind; (metaphysics) of (the nature of) presentation.

prĕsentee (-z-) *n.* Clergyman presented to benefice; person recommended for office; person presented at court; recipient of present.

prèsĕn′tient (-shĭ-) *adj.* Having a presentiment (*of*).

prèsĕn′tĭment (-z- *or* -s-) *n.* Vague expectation, foreboding.

prèsĕn′tĭve (-z-) *adj.* (Of word) presenting an object or conception directly to the mind (opp. SYMBOLIC).

prĕs′ently (-z-) *adv.* Soon, after a short time.

prèsĕnt′ment (-z-) *n.* Theatrical representation; delineation, portrait; statement, description (*of*); act, mode, of presenting to the mind; (law) statement on oath by jury of fact within their knowledge; formal complaint of offence made by parish authorities to bishop or archdeacon at his visitation.

prĕservā′tion (-z-) *n.* Preserving, being preserved, from injury or destruction; state of being well or ill preserved.

prèsêrv′ative (-z-) *adj.* & *n.* (Drug, measure, etc.) tending to preserve; chemical substance for preserving perishable foodstuffs etc.

prèsêrve′ (-z-) *v.t.* Keep safe (*from* harm etc.); keep alive; maintain (state of things); retain (quality, condition); prepare (fruit, meat, etc.) by boiling with sugar, pickling, etc., to prevent decomposition or fermentation; keep from decomposition by chemical treatment etc.; keep (game, river, etc.) undisturbed for private use; *well-preserved* (of elderly person) showing little sign of age. ~ *n.* Jam; ground set apart for protection of game (freq. fig.); piece of water for fish. **prèsêrv′er** *n.*

prèsīde′ (-z-) *v.i.* Occupy chair of authority at meeting of society or company; sit at head of table; exercise control, sit or reign supreme; *presiding officer*, person in charge of polling-station at election.

prĕs′idency (-z-) *n.* Office of president; period of this; district administered by president, esp. (formerly) division of E. India Company's territory.

prĕs′ident (-z-) *n.* Head of temporary or permanent body of persons, presiding over their meetings and proceedings; head of some colleges; person presiding over meetings of academy, literary or scientific society, etc.; (U.S.) person presiding over proceedings of bank or company; head of advisory council, board, etc.; elected head of government in U.S. and other modern republics; (hist.) governor of province, colony, etc.; *Lord P*~ *of the Council*, English crown officer presiding at meetings of Privy Council. **prĕsidĕn′tial** (-shl) *adj.* **prĕsidĕn′tially** *adv.*

prèsĭd′iary (-s-) *adj.* Of, having, serving as, a garrison.

prèsĭd′ium (-s-) *n.* Presiding body or standing committee (esp. in communist organization).

prĕss[1] *v.* 1. Exert steady force against (thing in contact); move by pressing; exert pressure, bear with weight or force; squeeze (juice etc. *from* etc.); compress, squeeze, (thing) to flatten or shape or smooth it, or to extract juice etc. 2. Bear heavily on in attack etc.; weigh down, oppress; produce strong mental or moral impression, esp. weigh heavily (*up*)*on* (mind, person); *be pressed for*, have barely enough (time etc.); ~ *the button*, set electric machinery in motion (freq. fig.); ~-*stud*, fastener of which the two parts engage by pressure. 3. Be urgent, demand immediate action; urge, entreat; urge (course etc. *upon* person). 4. Insist on strict interpretation of (words etc.). 5. Force (offer, gift, etc. *upon*). 6. (golf) Attempt to hit harder than can be done with accuracy. 7. Crowd, throng; hasten, urge one's way, *on*, *forward*, etc. ~ *n.* 1. Crowding; crowd (*of* people etc.); throng, crush, in battle. 2. Pressure, hurry, of affairs; pressing; (naut.) ~ *of sail*, *canvas*, as much sail as wind etc. will allow. 3. Kinds of instrument for compressing, flattening, or shaping, or for extracting juice, etc. 4. Machine for printing; printing-house or establishment; *the* art, practice, of printing; *the* newspapers generally; *in the* ~, being printed; *freedom of the* ~, right to print and publish anything without censorship; ~-*agent*, person employed by theatre, actor, etc., to attend to advertising and other publicity; ~-*box*, shelter for newspaper reporter at cricket-match etc.; ~ *cutting*: see CUTTING; ~-*gallery*, gallery for reporters esp. in House of Commons; *press′-man*, journalist; operator of printing-press. 5. Large usu. shelved cupboard for clothes, books, etc., esp. in recess in wall; ~-*mark*, mark, number, in book or catalogue showing press or shelf in a library where it belongs.

prĕss[2] *v.t.* Force to serve in army or navy (hist.); take (horses, boats, etc.) for royal or public use. ~ *n.* (hist.) Compulsory enlistment in navy or (less usu.) army; ~-*gang* (hist.) body of men employed to press men.

prĕss′ĭng *adj.* (esp.) Urgent; importunate; persistent. **prĕss′ingly** *adv.*

prĕ′ssure (-sher) *n.* 1. Exertion of continuous force, force so exerted upon or against a body by another body, or by a liquid or gas, in contact with it; amount of this, expressed by the weight upon a unit area; *high*, *low*, (*atmospheric*) ~: see ATMOSPHERIC; *blood*-~: see BLOOD; *high*-~, (of compound engines or turbines) used esp. of those in which steam is used at different pressures in different parts of the machine; *~-casting*, metal casting obtained by injecting fluid metal under pressure into a rigid mould; *~-cooker*, strong sealed metal vessel for cooking in steam at high pressure; ~ *mine*, mine detonated by pressure. 2. Affliction, oppression; trouble, embarrassment; constraining influence; ~ *group*, body of people exerting pressure upon legislature etc. by concerted agitation.

prĕ'ssurīzed (-sher-) *adj.* (Of aircraft cabins, breathing apparatus, etc.) designed so that normal air-pressure can be artificially maintained at high altitudes.

Prĕs'ter John. Fabulous Christian priest and king believed in the Middle Ages to rule over an empire in Asia; in 15th c. identified with the king of Abyssinia (Ethiopia).

prĕstidĭ'gĭtātor *n.* Conjurer. **prĕstidĭgĭtā'tion** *n.*

prĕstige' (-ēzh) *n.* Influence, reputation, derived from past achievements, associations, etc.

prĕstĭss'ĭmō *adj.*, *adv.*, & *n.* (mus.) Very quick (piece, movement).

prĕs'tō[1] *adj.*, *adv.*, & *n.* (mus.) Quick (piece, movement).

prĕs'tō[2] *adv.* (In conjurer's formula, esp. *hey ~!*), quickly. ~ *adj.* Rapid, juggling.

Prĕs'tonpăns. Village of East Lothian, Scotland, near which the Young PRETENDER gained victory (1745) over English royal forces under Sir John Cope.

prėsūme' (-z-) *v.* Take the liberty, venture (*to* do); assume, take for granted; be presumptuous, take liberties; ~ (*up*)*on*, take advantage of, make unscrupulous use of. **prėsūm'able** *adj.* **prėsūm'ably, prėsūm'ĭngly** *advs.*

prėsŭmp'tion (-z-) *n.* Arrogance, assurance; taking for granted, thing taken for granted; ground for presuming; (law) ~ *of fact*, inference of fact from known facts; ~ *of law*, assumption of truth of thing until contrary is proved; inference established by law as universally applicable to certain circumstances.

prėsŭmp'tive (-z-) *adj.* Giving ground for presumption; *heir* ~, one whose right of inheritance is liable to be defeated by birth of nearer heir.

prėsŭmp'tūous (-z-) *adj.* Unduly confident, arrogant, forward. **prėsŭmp'tūously** *adv.* **prėsŭmp'tūousnėss** *n.*

prēsuppōse' (-z) *v.t.* Assume beforehand; involve, imply. **prēsŭpposĭ'tion** (-zi-) *n.* Presupposing; thing assumed beforehand as basis of argument etc.

prėtĕnce' *n.* 1. Claim (*to* merit etc.). 2. Ostentation, display; false profession of purpose, pretext; pretending, make-believe.

prėtĕnd' *v.* 1. Feign, give oneself out (*to* be or do); make-believe in play; profess falsely to have; allege falsely. 2. Venture, aspire, presume (*to* do); lay claim *to* (right, title, etc.); ~ *to*, try to win (person, person's hand) in marriage; profess to have (quality etc.).

prėtĕn'der *n.* One who makes baseless pretensions (*to* title etc.); *Old P~*, James Francis Edward Stuart (1688–1766), James II's son, called by Jacobites James III; took part in the unsuccessful Scottish rising of 1715; *Young P~*, Charles Edward Stuart (1720–88), son of the Old Pretender; led the rebellion of 1745.

prėtĕn'sion (-shn) *n.* Assertion of a claim; justifiable claim; pretentiousness.

prėtĕn'tious (-sh*us*) *adj.* Making claim to great merit or importance, esp. when unwarranted; ostentatious. **prėtĕn'tiously** *adv.* **prėtĕn'tiousnėss** *n.*

prēter- *prefix.* Past, beyond.

prēterhū'man *adj.* Beyond what is human, superhuman.

prĕt'erite *adj.* & *n.* (gram.) ~ (*tense*), one expressing past action or state; *~-present* (*tense*, *v.*), one orig. preterite but now used as present (e.g. *can*, *dare*, *may*).

prēterĭ'tion *n.* Omission, disregard (*of*); (theol.) passing over of the non-elect.

prētermĭt' *v.t.* Omit to mention, do, or perform, neglect; leave off (custom, continuous action) for a time; (improp.) leave off. **prētermĭ'ssion** (-shn) *n.*

prēternă'tural (-cher-) *adj.* Outside the ordinary course of nature; supernatural. **prēternă'turally** *adv.*

prēt'ĕxt *n.* Ostensible reason, excuse. **prėtĕxt'** *v.t.* Allege as pretext.

prētŏn'ĭc *adj.* Coming immediately before stressed syllable.

Prėtôr'ĭa. Capital city of Transvaal and administrative capital of Republic of South Africa. [Andries Wilhelmus Jacobus *Pretorius* (1799–1853), S. African Boer leader, one of founders of Transvaal]

prett'ĭfȳ (prĭ-) *v.t.* Make pretty; represent with finicking prettiness.

prett'ĭly (prĭ-) *adv.* In a way that pleases the eye, ear, or aesthetic sense.

prett'ĭnėss (prĭ-) *n.* Beauty of a dainty or childish kind; pretty thing, ornament, etc.; affected or trivial beauty of style in literature or art.

prett'y (prĭ-) *adj.* 1. Beautiful in dainty or diminutive way; attractive to eye, ear, or aesthetic sense. 2. Fine, good of its kind; (archaic) fine, stout (freq. iron.); (archaic) considerable in amount or extent; *a ~ penny*, a good deal of money. 3. (abs. as n.) Pretty one, pretty thing; *the ~*, (golf) the fairway. 4. *pretty-pretty*, overdoing the pretty, aiming too much at prettiness; *pretty-pretties*, ornaments, knick-knacks, pretty things. **prett'ÿish** *adj.* **prett'y** *adv.* Fairly, moderately, as ~ *good*, ~ *well*.

prĕt'zel *n.* Crisp salted biscuit, freq. baked in form of a knot.

preux chevalier (prêr shĕvăl'yā) *n.* Gallant knight.

prėvail' *v.i.* Gain the mastery, be victorious (*against*, *over*); be the more usual or prominent, predominate; exist, occur, in general use or experience, be current; ~ (*up*)*on*, persuade. **prėvail'ĭng, prĕv'alent** *adjs.* **prĕv'alently** *adv.* **prĕv'alence** *n.*

prėvă'rĭcāte *v.i.* Speak, act, evasively; quibble, equivocate. **prėvărĭcā'tion, prėvă'rĭcātor** *ns.*

prėvēn'ient *adj.* Preceding, previous; having in view the prevention (*of*); ~ *grace*, (theol.) grace preceding repentance and predisposing the heart to seek God.

prėvĕnt' *v.t.* 1. Hinder, stop. 2. (archaic) Meet, deal with (wish, question, etc.) before it is expressed; (theol., of God) go before, guide. **prėvĕn'table, prėvĕn'tĭble, prėvĕn'tative** *adjs.* **prėvĕn'tion** (-shn) *n.*

prėvĕn'ter *n.* (esp., naut.) Rope, chain, bolt, etc., used to supplement another.

prėvĕn'tive *adj.* Serving to prevent, esp. (med.) to keep off disease; of the department of Customs concerned with prevention of smuggling. **prėvĕn'tively** *adv.* **prėvĕn'tive** *n.* Preventive agent, measure, drug, etc.

prēv'iew (-vū) *n.* View of a picture, film, etc., arranged before it is open to public view.

prē'vious *adj.* Coming before in time or order; prior *to*; (slang) done or acting hastily; ~ *question*, (parl.) question whether vote shall be taken on main question (put to avoid putting of main question); *P~ Examination*, little-go. **prē'viously** *adv.* **prē'viousnėss** *n.* **prē'vious** *adv.* Previously (usu. ~ *to*, before, prior to).

prėvīse' (-z) *v.t.* Foresee, forecast. **prėvĭ'sion** (-zhn) *n.* **prėvĭ'sional** *adj.* **prėvĭ'sionally** *adv.*

Prévost d'Exiles (prāvō' dĕgzēl'), Antoine François (1697–1763), 'l'Abbé Prévost'. French novelist and miscellaneous writer; author of 'Manon Lescaut'.

prē-war' (-wôr) *adj.* Before the war (esp. of 1914–18 or of 1939–45).

prey (prā) *n.* Animal hunted or killed by carnivorous animal for food; person, thing, that falls a victim (*to* sickness, fear, etc.); *bird, beast, of ~*, kinds that kill and devour other animals. ~ *v.i.* ~ (*up*)*on*, seek, take, as prey, plunder; exert baneful or wasteful influence upon.

Prī'ăm. (Gk legend) Last king of Troy, father of 50 sons and many daughters; slain by Neoptolemus, son of Achilles, after the fall of Troy.

prī′apism *n.* Licentiousness; (path.) persistent erection of penis. [f. PRIAPUS]

Priāp′us. Ancient god of fertility whose cult spread from Asia Minor to Greece and Italy; he became the god of gardens and herds and is represented as small, grotesque, and misshapen.

price *n.* Money for which thing is bought or sold; (betting) odds; (fig.) what must be given, done, sacrificed, etc., to obtain a thing; *above, beyond, without,* ~, so valuable that no price can be stated; *a* ~ *on* person's *head*, reward offered for his death or capture; *at any* ~, whatever it may cost; (with neg.) on any terms, for any consideration; *at a* ~, at a relatively high cost; *what* ~ . . .*?*, (slang) taunting allusion to worthlessness or failure of something; ~*-ring*, association of traders formed to maintain price of product or commodity. ~ *v.t.* Fix, inquire, the price of (thing for sale); estimate the value of. **prīced** (-st) *adj.* To which a price is assigned.

prīce′lėss (-sl-) *adj.* Invaluable; (slang) incredibly or extremely amusing, absurd, etc. **prīce′lėssnėss** *n.*

prĭck *n.* Pricking, puncture; mark made by pricking; (archaic) goad for oxen, esp. in *kick against the* ~*s*, (fig.) hurt oneself by useless resistance (see Acts ix. 5); ~*-ears*, erect pointed ears of some dogs etc.; conspicuous ears of person, esp. Roundhead. ~ *v.* Pierce slightly, make minute hole in; cause sharp pain to; make a thrust (*at, into*, etc.); disable (bird) by shooting; mark off (name etc. in list) with a prick, select (sheriff) thus; mark (pattern *off, out*) with dots; (archaic) spur, urge on, (horse); advance on horseback; ~ *in, out, off*, plant (seedlings etc.) in small holes pricked in earth; ~ *up* one's *ears*, (of dog) erect the ears when on the alert; (fig.) become suddenly attentive.

prĭck′er *n.* (esp.) Pricking instrument, e.g. awl.

prĭck′ėt *n.* 1. Buck in second year, with straight unbranched horns. 2. Spike to stick candle on.

prĭc′kle *n.* Thorn-like process developed from epidermis of plant and capable of being peeled off with it; (pop.) small thorn; hard-pointed spine of hedgehog etc. ~ *v.* Affect, be affected, with sensation as of prick.

prĭck′ly *adj.* Armed with prickles; tingling; ~ *heat*, inflammation of sweat glands with eruption of vesicles and prickly sensation, common in hot countries; ~ *pear*, (various species of cactaceous genus *Opuntia*, with) pear-shaped fleshy edible fruit. **prĭck′lĭnėss** *n.*

prīde *n.* 1. Overweening opinion of one's own qualities, merits, etc., considered the first of the 'seven deadly sins'; arrogant bearing or conduct; ~ *of place*, exalted position, consciousness of this, arrogance. 2. (Also *proper* ~) sense of what befits one's position, preventing one from doing unworthy thing; *false* ~, mistaken feeling of this kind. 3. Feeling of elation and pleasure; object of this feeling, esp. in names of plants, as *London* ~; best condition; *take* ~ *in*, be proud of; ~ *of the morning*, mist or shower at sunrise; *peacock in his* ~, (her.) peacock with tail expanded and wings drooping. 4. Company (of lions). ~ *v.refl.* ~ *oneself* (*up*)*on*, be proud of. **prīde′ful** (-df-) *adj.* (chiefly Sc.). **prīde′fully** *adv.* **prīde′less** *adj.*

Prīde's Purge. The exclusion of Charles I's supporters from the Long Parliament; carried out by Col. Thomas Pride and a body of troops who arrested members at the door of the House of Commons (1648); about 130 Presbyterians and Royalists were thus excluded or deterred.

prie-dieu (prēdyẽr′) *n.* Kneeling-desk; chair with tall sloping back for use in praying.

priest *n.* 1. Clergyman, esp. one above deacon and below bishop with authority to administer sacraments and pronounce absolution (now usu. *clergyman*, exc. in official and R.C. use); minister of the altar, esp. officiant at Eucharist; official minister of non-Christian religion; *high* ~: see HIGH; *priest′craft*, ambitious or worldly policy of priests; ~*'s hole*, secret chamber in house where R.C. priests hid during times of persecution; ~*-ridden*, held in subjection by priest(s); ~*-vicar*, minor canon in some cathedrals. 2. Mallet used to kill fish when spent (chiefly in Ireland); kind of artificial fly. ~ *v.t.* Make (person) a priest. **priest′ėss, priest′hŏŏd, priest′lĭng** *ns.* **priest′lėss, priest′lĭke** *adjs.*

Priest′ley, Joseph (1733–1804). English chemist, man of science, and theologian; 'discoverer' of oxygen and inventor of the 'pneumatic trough'.

priest′ly *adj.* Of, like, befitting, a priest; (O.T. criticism) ~ *code*, one of the constituent elements of the hexateuch, constituting framework of whole in its existing form.

prĭg *n.* Precisian in speech or manners; conceited or didactic person; (slang) thief. ~ *v.t.* (slang) Steal. **prĭgg′ery, prĭgg′ism** *ns.* **prĭgg′ish** *adj.* **prĭgg′ishly** *adv.* **prĭgg′ishnėss** *n.*

prĭm *adj.* Consciously or affectedly precise; formal, demure. ~ *v.* Assume prim air; form (face, lips, etc.) into prim expression. **prĭm′ly** *adv.* **prĭm′nėss** *n.*

prīm′acy *n.* Office of a primate; pre-eminence.

pri′ma dŏnn′a (prē-). Principal female singer in opera. [It., = 'first lady']

prī′ma fā′cie (-shĭē) *adv.* & *adj.* (Arising) at first sight, (based) on the first impression.

prīm′age[1] *n.* Percentage addition to freight, paid to owners or freighters of vessels.

prīm′age[2] *n.* Amount of water carried off suspended in steam from boiler.

prīm′al *adj.* Primitive, primeval; chief, fundamental.

prīm′ary *adj.* Earliest, original; of the first rank in a series, not derived; of the first importance, chief; (geol.) of the lowest series of strata, palaeozoic; (biol.) belonging to first stage of development; ~ *amputation*, one performed before inflammation supervenes; ~ *assembly, meeting*, meeting for selection of candidates for election; ~ *colour*: see COLOUR; ~ *education*, that which begins with the rudiments of knowledge, esp. that provided for children liable to compulsory attendance; so ~ *school, scholar*; ~ *feather*, one of large flight feathers of bird's wing, growing directly from manus (ill. BIRD); ~ *planets*, those revolving directly round sun as centre. ~ *n.* Primary planet, meeting, feather, etc.

prīm′ate *n.* 1. Archbishop; ~ *of England*, archbishop of York; ~ *of all England*, archbishop of Canterbury. 2. (zool.) Member of the **prīmāt′ēs** (-z), highest order of mammals, including man, apes, monkeys, tarsiers, and lemurs.

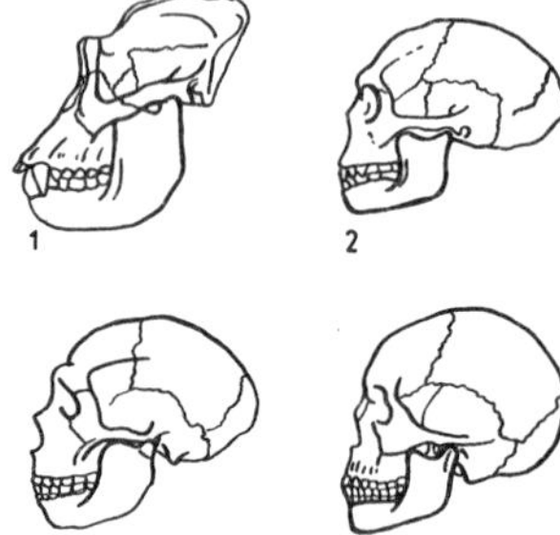

SKULLS OF PRIMATES

1. Gorilla. 2. Pithecanthrope. 3. Neanderthal man. 4. Man (*Homo sapiens*)

prīme[1] *n.* 1. State of highest perfection; *the* best part (*of* thing). 2. Beginning, first age, of anything; a canonical hour of the divine office, appointed for first hour of day (i.e. 6 a.m. or sunrise), (archaic) this time. 3. Prime number. 4. (mus.) Fundamental note or tone; lower of any two notes forming an interval. 5. Position in fencing, first of the 8 parries or guards in sword-play, used to protect the head (ill. FENCE); a thrust in such position. ~ *adj.* 1. Chief, most important; ~ *minister*, principal minister of any sovereign or State (now official title of first minister of State in Gt Britain). 2. First-rate (esp. of cattle and provisions), excellent. 3. Primary, fundamental; (arith., of number) having no integral factors except itself and unity (e.g. 2, 3, 5, 7, 11). 4. ~ *cost*: see COST; ~ *mover*: see MOVER; ~ *vertical* (*circle*), great circle of the heavens passing through E and W. points of horizon and through zenith, where it cuts meridian at right angles.

prīme[2] *v.* Supply (fire-arm, or abs.) with gunpowder for firing charge (hist.); wet (pump) to make it start working; equip (person *with* information etc.); inject petrol into (carburetter or cylinder of internal combustion engine); fill (person *with* liquor); cover (wood, canvas, etc.) with glue, gesso, oil, etc., to prevent paint from being absorbed; (of engine-boiler) let water pass with steam into cylinder in form of spray.

prīm'er[1] *n.* (esp.) Cap, cylinder, etc., used to ignite powder of cartridge etc. (ill CARTRIDGE).

prĭm'er[2] *n.* 1. Elementary school-book for teaching children to read; small introductory book; (hist.) prayer-book for use of laity esp. before Reformation. 2. *great* ~, size of type between paragon and English, of 51 ems to a foot (18 point); *long* ~, size between small pica and bourgeois, of 89 ems to a foot (10 point); *two-line long* ~, PARAGON.

prĭmēr'ō *n.* Gambling card-game fashionable *c* 1530–1640, in which 4 cards were dealt to each player and each card had three times its ordinary value.

prīmēv'al, prīmaev'al *adj.* Of the first age of the world; ancient, primitive. **prīmēv'ally** *adv.*

prīm'ing[1] *n.* (esp.) 1. Gunpowder placed in pan of fire-arm. 2. Train of powder connecting fuse with charge in blasting etc. 3. Mixture used by painters for preparatory coat. 4. Preparation of sugar added to beer. 5. Hasty imparting of knowledge, cramming.

prīm'ing[2] *n.* Acceleration of the tide taking place from neap to spring tides, opp. to LAG[1].

prīmĭp'arous *adj.* Bearing child for the first time. **prīmĭpă'ra** *n.*

prĭm'ĭtive *adj.* Early, ancient; old-fashioned, simple, rude; original, primary; (gram., of words) radical, not derivative; (math., of line, figure, etc.) from which another is derived, from which some construction begins, etc.; (geol.) of the earliest period; (biol., of animal or plant) appearing in earliest or very early stage of evolution; (also) having more in common with its supposed ancestors than its contemporary relatives have; *P~ Methodist Connexion*, society of Methodists founded 1810 by Hugh Bourne by secession from main body; *P~ Methodist, Methodism*, member, principles, of this. **prĭm'ĭtively** *adv.* **prĭm'ĭtivenėss** *ns.* **prĭm'ĭtive** *n.* (Picture by) painter of period before Renaissance; (picture by) untutored painter who ignores rules of perspective etc. (chiefly U.S.); primitive word, line, etc.; Primitive Methodist.

prim'ō (-ē-) *n.* Upper part in duet etc.

Primō de River'a (prē-, -vār'*a*), Miguel, Marquis de Estella (1870–1930). Spanish general, premier and dictator (1923–30).

prīmogĕn'ĭtor *n.* Earliest ancestor; (loosely) ancestor.

prīmogĕn'ĭture *n.* Fact of being the first-born of the children of the same parents; (*right of*) ~, right of succession belonging to first-born, esp. feudal rule by which the whole real estate of an intestate passes to the eldest son.

prīmŏrd'ial *adj.* Existing at or from the beginning, primeval; original, fundamental. **prīmŏrd'ially** *adv.* **prīmŏrdiăl'ity** *n.*

prĭm'rose (-z) *n.* Plant (*Primula veris*) bearing pale-yellowish flowers in early spring, growing wild in woods and hedges and on banks, and with many cultivated varieties; flower of this; (attrib.) of the colour of this flower; *evening* ~, the genus *oenothera*, with large pale-yellow flowers opening in evening; *P~ Day*, anniversary of death of DISRAELI (who died 19th April 1881); *P~ League*, political association formed 1883 in memory of Disraeli and in support of his principles of conservatism; ~ *path*, pursuit of pleasure (w. ref. to 'Hamlet', I. iii. 50).

prĭm'ūla *n.* Genus of herbaceous perennials, of low growing habit with yellow, white, pink, or purple flowers mostly borne in umbels. **prĭmūlāceous** (-sh*us*) *adj.*

prī'mum mō'bĭlė *n.* Outermost sphere added in Middle Ages to Ptolemaic system of astronomy, supposed to revolve round earth from E. to W. in 24 hours, carrying with it the (8 or 9) contained spheres; (fig.) prime source of motion or action. [med. L, lit. 'first moving thing']

prīm'us *adj.* (In boys' school) eldest (or of longest standing) of the name. ~ *n.* 1. Presiding bishop in Scottish Episcopal Church. 2. *P~* (*stove*), trade name of stove burning vaporized paraffin oil. [L, = 'first']

prĭnce *n.* 1. Sovereign ruler (now rhet.); ruler of small State, actually or nominally feudatory to king or emperor; *P~ of Peace*, Christ; ~ *of darkness*, Satan. 2. Male member of royal family, esp. (in Gt Britain) son or grandson of king or queen; *P~ of Wales*, title (since 1301) conferred upon eldest son and heir apparent of English sovereign; ~ *of Wales's feathers*, triple ostrich plume. 3. (As English rendering of foreign titles) noble usu. ranking next below duke; (as courtesy title in some connexions) duke, marquis, earl; (fig.) chief, greatest (*of*); ~ *of the* (*Holy Roman*) *Church*, title of cardinal. 4. ~ *bishop*, bishop who is also a prince; *P~ Consort*, husband of reigning female sovereign being himself a prince; esp., Albert, Prince of Saxe-Coburg, as husband of Queen Victoria; *P~ Regent*, prince who acts as regent; esp., George Prince of Wales (afterwards George IV) during mental incapacity of George III (1811–20); ~*'s* (or *P~ Rupert's*) *metal*, gold-coloured alloy of about three parts of copper and one of zinc. **prĭnce'dom** (-sd-), **prĭnce'lĭng** (-sl-) *ns.*

PRINCE OF WALES'S FEATHERS

Prĭnce Ed'ward Island. Smallest province of Canada, a large island in the Gulf of St. Lawrence; capital, Charlottetown.

Prĭnce Impēr'ial. Napoleon Eugène Louis Jean Joseph (1856–79), son of Napoleon III, killed with British forces in Zulu War of 1879.

prĭnce'ly (-insl-) *adj.* (Worthy) of a prince; sumptuous, splendid. **prĭnce'linėss** *n.*

Prĭnce Rup'ert (rōō-): see RUPERT; ~*'s drops*, pear-shaped drops of glass with long tail, made by dropping melted glass into water, and remarkable for the property, due to internal strain, of disintegrating explosively into powder when the tail is broken off or the surface scratched; ~*'s metal*: see PRINCE's metal.

Princes in the Tower. Edward V and his brother Richard, Duke of York, sons of Edward IV, lodged in Tower of London and murdered there 1483 by order of their uncle Richard III.

prĭn'cĕss (*or* -ĕs' *exc. when followed by name*) *n.* Queen (archaic); wife of prince; daughter, grand-daughter, of sovereign; ~ *royal*, (title conferrable on) sovereign's eldest daughter; ~ *dress, petticoat*, etc., dress etc. made without a seam at the waist.

Prĭnce'ton University (-st-). American university for men at Princeton, New Jersey; orig. a college founded 1747.

prĭn'cĭpal *adj.* First in rank or importance, chief; main, leading; (of money) constituting the original sum invested or lent; ~ *clause, sentence,* (gram.) one to which another is subordinate; ~ *parts* (of verb), those from which the others can be derived. ~ *n.* 1. Head, ruler, superior; head of some colleges. 2. Person for whom another acts as agent etc.; person directly responsible for crime, either as actual perpetrator (~ *in the first degree*) or as aiding (~ *in the second degree*); person for whom another is surety; combatant in duel. 3. Any of the main rafters on which rest the purlins that support the common rafters (ill. ROOF). 4. Capital sum as distinguished from interest, sum lent or invested on which interest is paid. 5. Organ-stop of same quality as open diapason, but an octave higher in pitch. **prĭn'cĭpalshĭp** *n.*

prĭncĭpăl'ity *n.* Government of a prince; State ruled by a prince; (pl.) one of the nine orders of angels; *the P~*, Wales.

prĭn'cĭpally *adv.* For the most part, chiefly.

prĭn'cĭpate (-*a*t) *n.* 1. (Rom. hist.) Rule of early emperors while some republican forms were retained. 2. State ruled by a prince.

prĭn'cĭple *n.* 1. Fundamental source, primary element; fundamental truth as basis of reasoning etc.; law of nature seen in working of machine etc.; (physics etc.) general or inclusive law exemplified in numerous cases; general law as guide to action. 2. (pl. and collect. sing.) Personal code of right conduct; *on* ~, from settled moral motive. 3. (chem., obsolesc.) Constituent of a naturally occurring substance, esp. one giving rise to some quality etc.

prĭnk *v.* Make (one*self* etc.) spruce; dress one*self up*; titivate, esp. in front of a mirror.

prĭnt *n.* 1. Indentation in surface preserving the form left by pressure of some body; mark, spot, stain. 2. Language embodied in printed form, printed lettering; handwritten letters imitating this. 3. State of being printed; *book is in* ~, (i) in printed form, (ii) on sale, not *out of* ~ (sold out). 4. (chiefly U.S.) Printed publication, esp. newspaper. 5. Printed cotton fabric. 6. Picture, design, printed from block or plate; (photog.) picture produced from negative; ~*-seller*, dealer in engravings etc. ~ *v.t.* 1. Impress, stamp, (surface *with* seal, die, etc.; mark or figure *on, in*, surface); (fig.) impress (*on* mind, memory). 2. Produce (book, picture, etc., or abs.) by applying inked types, blocks, or plates to paper, vellum, etc.; cause (book, MS.) to be so printed; express, publish, in print; write (words etc.) in imitation of typography. 3. Mark (textile fabric) with decorative design in colours; transfer (coloured design) from paper etc. to unglazed surface of pottery; (photog.) produce (picture) by transmission of light through negative. **prĭnt'able** *adj.*

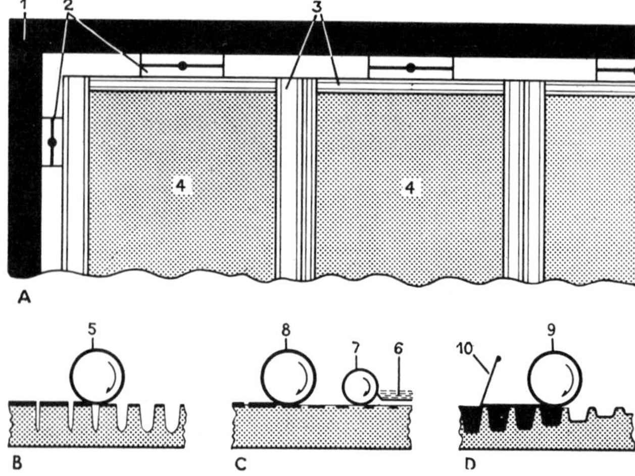

A. PART OF A FORME READY FOR PRINTING. B. C, D. METHODS OF PRINTING: B. LETTERPRESS (SURFACE). C. LITHOGRAPHY (PLANOGRAPHIC). D. PHOTOGRAVURE OR GRAVURE (INTAGLIO)

1. Chase. 2. Quoins which, when expanded, lock forme up tight, i.e. make it rigid. 3. Metal spacing material. 4. Pages of imposed type. 5. Ink roller inking surface. 6. Water. 7. Water roller wetting non-greasy section of surface to repel ink. 8. Ink roller inking greasy section of surface. 9. Ink roller filling depressions. 10. Doctor blade cleaning ink off surface

prĭn'ter *n.* (esp.) One who prints books; owner of printing business; printing instrument; *P~s' Bible*, the Bible which contains the misreading *Printers* for *Princes* in Ps. cxix. 161; *printer's devil, ink, pie*: see DEVIL, INK, PIE[3].

prī'or[1] *n.* Superior officer of religious house or order; (in abbey) officer next under abbot; (hist.) chief magistrate in some Italian republics. **prī'orĕss** *n.* **prī'orshĭp** *n.*

prī'or[2] *adj.* Earlier; antecedent in time, order, or importance. ~ *adv.*: ~ *to*, before. **priŏ'rity** *n.* Condition or quality of being earlier in time, or *of* preceding something else; precedence in order, rank, or dignity; an interest having prior claim to consideration, often with qualification, as *first, top* ~.

Prī'or[3], Matthew (1664–1721). English poet and diplomatist.

prī'ory *n.* Monastery, nunnery, governed by prior or prioress.

Priscian (prĭsh'*a*n), (6th c. A.D.). Latin grammarian of Constantinople; *break* ~*'s head*, violate the rules of grammar.

prise: see PRIZE[3].

prism (-zm) *n.* Solid figure whose two ends are similar, equal, and parallel rectilineal figures and whose sides are parallelograms; transparent body of this form, usu. of triangular section, which splits light into a rainbow-like spectrum. **pris'mal** (-z-) *adj.*

prĭsmăt'ic (-z-) *adj.* Of like, a prism; (of colours) distributed by transparent prism, (also) brilliant; ~ *astrolabe*: see ASTROLABE; ~ *binoculars, glasses*, type of binocular field-glass, each telescope of which contains two right-angled prisms so placed as to secure a better stereoscopic effect with a shorter tube than an ordinary binocular (ill. BINOCULAR); ~ *colours*, the seven colours (violet, indigo, blue, green, yellow, orange, and red) into which a ray of white light is separated by a prism; ~ *compass*, hand compass furnished with a prism enabling the compass to be read while taking a bearing or sight; ~ *powder*, gunpowder of which grains are hexagonal prisms. **prĭsmăt'ically** *adv.*

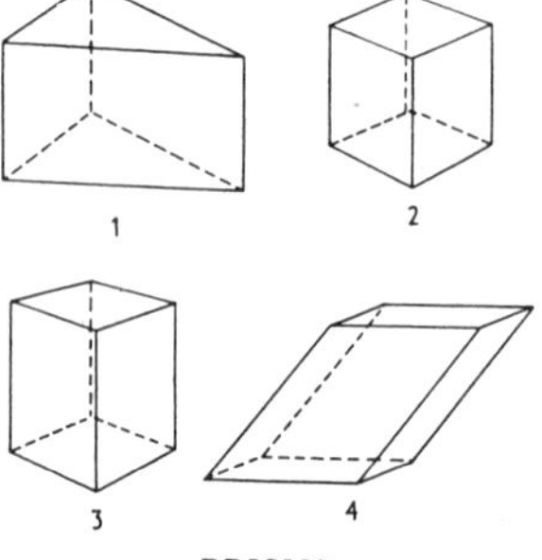

PRISMS

1. Wedge. 2. Cube. 3. Box. 4. Parallelepiped

prĭs′moid (-z-) *n.* Body, figure, resembling a prism, with similar but unequal parallel polygonal ends. **prĭsmoid′al** *adj.*

prĭs′on (-zn) *n.* Place in which person is kept in captivity, esp. building to which person is legally committed while awaiting trial or for punishment; custody, confinement. ~ *v.t.* (poet., rhet.) Imprison.

prĭs′oner (-z-) *n.* Person kept in prison; (also ~ *of war*), member of the enemy's armed forces captured in war; ~ *of State, State* ~, one confined for political reasons; *take* (person) ~, seize and hold as prisoner; *prisoners' bars, base*, game played by two parties of boys etc., each occupying distinct base or home, aim of each side being to make prisoner by touching any player who leaves his base.

prĭs′tīne (*or* -ēn) *adj.* Ancient, primitive, unspoilt.

prĭth′ee (-dhĭ) *int.* (archaic) Pray, please. [= (I) pray thee]

prīv′acy *n.* Being withdrawn from society or public interest; avoidance of publicity.

privat-docent (prēvaht′ dōtsĕnt′) *n.* (In German universities) private teacher or lecturer recognized by university but not on salaried staff.

prīv′ate *adj.* 1. Not holding public office or official position; ~ *member* (of House of Commons), one not member of Ministry; ~ *soldier*, ordinary soldier not holding commissioned or non-commissioned rank. 2. Kept, removed, from public knowledge; not open to the public; ~ *house*, dwelling-house of private person (opp. to shop or office, public-house or public building); ~ *parts*, genitals; ~ *school*, school owned and managed by private individual, not vested in a public body; ~ *view*, view of exhibition of pictures etc., esp. before it is opened to the public. 3. One's own; individual, personal, not affecting the community; confidential. 4. (Of place) retired, secluded; (of person, archaic) given to retirement. **prīv′ately** *adv.* **prīv′ate** *n.* 1. Private soldier. 2. *in* ~, privately; in private life. 3. (pl.) Private parts.

prīvateer′ *n.* (hist.) Armed vessel owned and officered by private persons holding commission from government (*letters of marque*) and authorized to use it against hostile nation, esp. in capture of merchant shipping; commander, (pl.) crew, of this.

prīvā′tion *n.* Loss, absence (*of* quality), as *cold is the* ~ *of heat*; want of the comforts or necessaries of life.

prĭv′ative *adj.* Consisting in, marked by, the loss, removal, or absence of some quality or attribute, as *cold is merely* ~ (cf. prec.); denoting privation or absence of quality etc.; (gram.) expressing privation. **prĭv′atively** *adv.*

prĭv′ĕt *n.* European bushy evergreen shrub (*Ligustrum vulgare*) with smooth dark-green leaves, clusters of small white flowers, and small shining black berries, much used for hedges; other species of *Ligustrum* or similar (usu. evergreen) shrubs.

prĭv′ilège (-j) *n.* Right, advantage, immunity, belonging to person, class, or office; special advantage or benefit; monopoly, patent, granted to individual, corporation, etc.; *parliamentary* ~, any or all of numerous privileges which belong to the Houses of Parliament or to their individual members in virtue of their office (freq. used of M.P.'s immunity in discussing matters which if discussed by others might become subject of legal action); *bill of* ~, petition of peer demanding to be tried by his peers; *writ of* ~, writ to deliver privileged person from custody when arrested in civil suit. ~ *v.t.* Invest with privilege; allow (*to* do) as privilege; exempt (*from* burden etc.). **prĭv′ileged** (-ĭjd) *adj.*

prĭv′ity *n.* 1. Being privy (*to*). 2. (law) Any relation between two parties that is recognized by law, e.g. that of blood, lease, service.

prĭv′y *adj.* Hidden, secluded; secret; ~ *to*, in the secret of (person's designs, etc.); *P~ Council*, sovereign's private counsellors; (in Gt Britain) body of advisers chosen by sovereign (now chiefly as personal dignity), together with princes of the blood, archbishops, etc.; ~ *parts*, external organs of sex; ~ *purse*, allowance from public revenue for monarch's private expenses; keeper of this; ~ *seal*, seal affixed to documents that are afterwards to pass, or that do not require, the Great Seal. **prĭv′ily** *adv.* **prĭv′y** *n.* 1. Private place for the evacuation of bowels and urination. 2. (law) Person having a part or interest in any action, matter, or thing.

Prix de Rome (prē), **(Grand).** French government prize (founded 1666 by Louis XIV) awarded after competitive examination to students of art or music, entitling them to 4 years' study at French Academy of Art in Rome.

prīze[1] *n.* Reward given as symbol of victory or superiority, to student in school or college who excels in attainments, to competitor in athletic contest, to exhibitor of best specimen of manufactured products, works of art, etc., in exhibition; (fig.) anything striven for or worth striving for; money or money's worth offered for competition by chance, in lottery, etc.; ~*-fight*, boxing-match for money, whence ~*-fighter*; *prize′man*, winner of prize; ~*-ring*, enclosed area (now usu. square), for prize-fighting. ~ *v.t.* Value highly.

prīze[2] *n.* Ship, property, captured at sea in virtue of rights of war; (fig.) find or windfall; ~*-court*, department of admiralty court concerned with prizes; ~*-money*, money realized by sale of prize. ~ *v.t.* Make prize of.

prīze[3], **prīse** (-z) *v.t.* Force (lid etc. *up, out*, box etc. *open*) by leverage. ~ *n.* Leverage, purchase.

prō *n.* Colloq. abbrev. of PROFESSIONAL.

pro- *prefix.* 1. In front of, for, on behalf of, on account of. 2. (Person) favouring or siding with.

P.R.O. *abbrev.* Public Records Office; Public Relations Officer.

prō′a *n.* Malay boat, esp. fast sailing-boat of type used in Malay archipelago, about 30 ft long, with sharp stem and stern and one side flat and straight (instead of curved) to reduce leeway; a small canoe or the like is rigged parallel to the proa like an outrigger.

prō and cŏn *adv.* (Of arguments or reasons) for and against, on both sides. **prōs and cŏns** *n.pl.* Reasons for and against. [L *pro et contra*]

prŏbabĭl′iorism *n.* (R.C. casuistry) Doctrine that the side on which evidence preponderates ought to be followed. **prŏbabĭl′iorist** *n.*

prŏb′abilism *n.* Doctrine that where authorities differ any course may be followed for which a recognized doctor of the Church can be cited; theory that there is no certain knowledge, but may be grounds of belief sufficient for practical life. **prŏb′abilist** *n.*

prŏbabĭl′ity *n.* Quality of being probable; (most) probable event; (math.) likelihood of an event, measured by the ratio of the favourable cases to the whole number of cases possible; *in all* ~, most likely.

prŏb′able *adj.* That may be expected to happen or prove true, likely; (as *n.*) probable candidate, competitor, member of team, etc. **prŏb′ably** *adv.*

prōb′ate *n.* Official proving of will; verified copy of will with certificate as handed to executors; ~ *duty*, tax on personal property of deceased testator, now merged in estate duty.

probā′tion *n.* Testing of conduct or character of person, esp. of candidate for membership in religious body; moral trial or discipline; system of releasing criminals, esp. first offenders, by placing them under the supervision of a person (~ *officer*) acting as friend and adviser. **probā′tionary** (-sho-) *adj.* Of, serving for, done in the way of, probation; undergoing probation.

probā′tioner (-sho-) *n.* Person on probation, esp. novice in religious house, nurse in training, offender under probation.

prōb′ative *adj.* Affording proof, evidential.

prōbe *n.* Blunt-ended surgical instrument for exploring wound etc.; act of probing. ~ *v.t.* Explore (wound, part of body) with probe; penetrate (thing) with sharp instrument; (fig.) examine closely, sound.

prŏb'ity *n.* Uprightness, honesty.

prŏb'lėm *n.* Doubtful or difficult question; thing hard to understand; (geom.) proposition in which something has to be done; (log.) the question (usu. only implied) involved in a syllogism; (physics, math.) inquiry starting from given conditions to investigate a fact, result, or law; (chess) arrangement of pieces on board in which player is challenged to accomplish specified result, often under prescribed conditions; ~ *picture, play, novel,* one in which social or other problem is treated.

prŏblėmăt'ĭc(al) *adjs.* Doubtful, questionable; (log.) enunciating or supporting what is possible but not necessarily true. **prŏblėmăt'ĭcally** *adv.*

prŏb'lėm(at)ĭst *n.* One who studies or composes (esp. chess) problems.

probŏs'cĭs *n.* Elephant's trunk; long flexible snout of tapir etc.; elongated part of mouth in some insects (ill. MOTH); sucking organ in some worms; (joc.) human nose; *~-monkey,* large, long-tailed, Bornean ape (*Nasalis larvatus*) with nose projecting far beyond mouth. **probŏscĭd'ėan, -ĭan** *adjs.* & *ns.* Having a proboscis; of, like, a proboscis; (mammal) of the order *Proboscidae,* containing the elephants and extinct allies, and characterized by long flexible proboscis and incisors developed into long tusks.

prō-cathē'dral *adj.* & *n.* (Church) used as substitute for a cathedral.

procēd'ure (-dyer) *n.* Proceeding; mode of conducting business (esp. in parliament) or legal action. **procēd'ūral** *adj.*

proceed' *v.i.* Go on, make one's way, (*to*); go on (*with, in,* action etc., *to* do, *to* another course etc.); adopt course of action; go on to say; (of action) be carried on, take place; come forth, issue, originate; take legal proceedings *against.* **proceed'ĭng** *n.* (esp.) Action, piece of conduct; (pl.) record of account of doings of a society; *legal ~s,* (steps taken in) legal action.

prō'ceeds *n.pl.* Produce, outcome, profit.

prō'cĕss[1] (*or* -ŏ-) *n.* 1. Progress, course; *in ~ of time,* as time goes on; natural or involuntary operation, series of changes; course of action, proceeding, esp. method of operation in manufacture, printing, photography, etc. 2. (Print from block produced by) method (e.g. chemical or photographic) other than simple engraving by hand; *~-block,* block for printing from produced by such method. 3. Action at law; formal commencement of this; summons or writ; *~-server,* sheriff's officer who serves processes or summonses. 4. (anat., zool., bot.) Outgrowth, protuberance. ~ *v.t.* 1. Institute legal process against (person). 2. Treat (material), preserve (food), reproduce (drawing etc.) by a process.

procĕss'[2] *v.i.* (colloq.) Walk in procession.

procĕ'ssion (-shn) *n.* 1. Proceeding of body of persons (or of boats etc.) in orderly succession, esp. as religious ceremony or on festive occasion; body of persons doing this; (fig.) ill-contested race. 2. (theol.) Emanation of the Holy Ghost. ~ *v.* Go in procession; walk along (street) in procession. **procĕ'ssional** (-sho-) *adj.* Of processions; used, carried, sung, in processions. ~ *n.* Processional hymn, (eccles.) office-book of processional hymns etc.

procĕ'ssionary (-sho-) *adj.* Going in procession (esp. of caterpillars of the moth *Cnethocampa processionea*).

procès-verbal (prŏsĕvārbahl') *n.* Written report of proceedings, minutes; (Fr. law) written statement of facts in support of charge.

prō'chronĭsm (-k-) *n.* Referring of event etc. to an earlier than the true date, as *races held in June and called by a ~ the Mays.*

proclaim' *v.t.* Announce publicly and officially; declare (war, peace); announce officially the accession of (sovereign); declare (person, thing) officially to be (traitor etc.); declare publicly or openly (thing, *that*); place (district etc.) under legal restrictions, prohibit (meeting etc.), by declaration. **prŏclamā'tion** *n.* **proclăm'atory** *adj.*

proclĭt'ĭc *adj.* & *n.* (Gk gram.) (Monosyllable) closely attached in pronunciation to following word and having itself no accent.

proclĭv'ĭty *n.* Tendency (*to, towards* action or habit, esp. bad one).

Prŏc'lus (*c* A.D. 410–85). Neoplatonic philosopher.

Prŏc'nė, Prŏg'nė: see PHILOMELA.

prōcŏn'sul *n.* 1. (Rom. hist.) Governor of Roman province, in later republic usu. an ex-consul; (under empire) governor of senatorial province. 2. (rhet.) Governor of modern colony etc.; (*pro-consul*) deputy consul. **prōcŏn'sūlar** *adj.* **prōcŏn'sūlate, prōcŏn'sulshĭp** *ns.*

procrăs'tĭnāte *v.* Defer action, be dilatory; (rare) postpone (action). **procrăstĭnā'tion** *n.* **procrăs'tĭnatĭve, procrăs'tinatory** *adjs.*

prō'crėāte *v.t.* Beget, generate (offspring). **prōcrėā'tion** *n.* **prō'crėātĭve** *adj.*

Procrŭs'tēs (-z). (Gk legend) Robber who laid travellers on a bed and made them fit it by cutting off their limbs or stretching them; he was killed by Theseus. **Procrŭs'tėan** *adj.* Compelling conformity by violent means.

prŏc'tor *n.* 1. Each of 2 officers (*senior, junior,* ~) in university, appointed annually and charged with various functions, esp. discipline of undergraduates. 2. (law) Person managing causes in court (now chiefly eccles.) that administers civil or canon law; *King's, Queen's, P~,* official who may intervene in probate, divorce, and nullity cases when collusion or suppression of facts is alleged. **prŏctŏr'ĭal** *adj.*

prŏc'torīze *v.t.* Exercise proctor's authority on (undergraduate etc.). **prŏctorīzā'tion** *n.*

procŭm'bent *adj.* Lying on the face, prostrate; (bot.) growing along the ground.

prōcūrā'tion *n.* 1. Procuring, obtaining; bringing about; (fee for) negotiation of loan. 2. Function, authorized action, of attorney or agent; (rare) letter or power of attorney. 3. (eccles.) Provision of entertainment for bishop or other visitor by incumbent etc., now commuted to money payment. 4. Procurer's trade or offence.

prŏc'ūrator *n.* 1. (Rom. hist.) Treasury officer in imperial province. 2. Agent, proxy, esp. one who has power of attorney. 3. Magistrate in some Italian cities. 4. *~ fiscal,* in Scotland, public prosecutor of a district. **prŏc'ūratŏr'ĭal** *adj.* **prŏc'ūrātorshĭp** *n.*

prŏc'ūratory *n.* Authorization to act for another.

prŏc'ūrātrĭx *n.* Inmate of nunnery managing its temporal concerns.

procūre' *v.* Obtain by care or effort, acquire; act as procurer or procuress; (archaic) bring about. **procūr'able** *adj.* **procūr'ance, procūre'ment** *ns.*

procūr'er *n.* (esp.) Man or woman who procures women for gratification of another's lust. **procūr'ėss** *n.*

prŏd *v.t.* Poke with pointed instrument, end of stick, etc.; goad, irritate. ~ *n.* Poke, thrust; pointed instrument.

prŏd'ĭgal *adj.* & *n.* Recklessly wasteful (person); (one) lavish *of*; ~ (*son*): see Luke xv. 11–32; **prŏd'ĭgally** *adv.* **prŏdĭgăl'ĭty** *n.*

prŏd'ĭgalīze *v.t.* Spend lavishly.

prodĭ'gious (-jus) *adj.* Marvellous, amazing; enormous; abnormal. **prodĭ'giously** *adv.* **prodĭ'giousnėss** *n.*

prŏd'ĭgy̆ *n.* Marvellous thing, esp. one out of the course of nature; wonderful example *of* (some quality); person endowed with surprising qualities, esp. precocious child.

prŏd'rome (-om) *n.* Preliminary book or treatise (*to* another); (med.) premonitory symptom. **prŏd'romal, prodrŏm'ĭc** *adjs.*

prodūce′ *v.t.* 1. Bring forward for inspection or consideration; bring (play, performer, book, etc.) before the public. 2. (geom.) Extend, continue (line *to* a point). 3. Manufacture (goods) from raw materials etc. 4. Bring about, cause (sensation etc.). 5. (Of land etc.) yield (produce); (of animal, plant) bear, yield (offspring, fruit). **prodū′cĭble** *adj.* **prŏd′ūce** *n.* Amount produced, yield, esp. in assay of ore; agricultural and natural products collectively; result (*of* labour, efforts, etc.).

prodū′cer *n.* 1. (pol. econ.) One who produces articles of consumption, opp. to *consumer*; person who 'produces' a play, etc., person financing a film and controlling its production (cf. DIRECTOR). 2. (*gas*) ~, special form of furnace for making ~ *gas*, an inflammable gas containing carbon monoxide together with nitrogen, made by passing air through red-hot coke and used for gas-engines etc.

prŏd′uct *n.* Thing produced by natural process or manufacture; result; (math.) quantity obtained by multiplying quantities together; (chem.) compound formed during chemical reaction.

prodŭc′tion *n.* Producing; thing(s) produced; literary or artistic work.

prodŭc′tĭve *adj.* Producing, tending to produce; producing abundantly; (econ.) producing commodities of exchangeable value. **prodŭc′tĭvely** *adv.* **prodŭc′tĭveness** *n.* **prŏductĭv′ĭty** *n.* (esp.) Efficiency in industrial production.

prō′ėm *n.* Preface, preamble, to book or speech; beginning, prelude. **prōēm′ĭal** *adj.*

Prof. *abbrev.* Professor.

profāne′¹ *adj.* Not belonging to what is sacred or biblical; not initiated into religious rites or any esoteric knowledge; (of rites etc.) heathen; irreverent, blasphemous. **profāne′ly** *adv.* **profāne′nėss** *n.* **profăn′ĭty** *n.* (esp.) Profane words or acts.

profāne′² *v.t.* Treat (sacred thing) with irreverence or disregard; violate, pollute (what is entitled to respect). **prŏfanā′tion** *n.*

profĕss′ *v.* 1. Lay claim to (quality, feeling); pretend (*to* be or do); openly declare; take vows of religious order; receive into religious order. 2. Make (law, medicine, etc.) one's profession or business. 3. Teach (subject) as professor; perform duties of a professor.

profĕssed′ (-st) *adj.* Self-acknowledged; alleged, ostensible; claiming to be duly qualified; that has taken the vows of a religious order. **profĕss′ėdly** *adv.*

profĕ′ssion (-shn) *n.* 1. Declaration, avowal; declaration of belief in a religion; vow made on entering, fact of being in, a religious order. 2. Vocation, calling, esp. one that involves some branch of learning or science; *the* body of persons engaged in this, esp. (theatr. slang) actors; *the learned* ~*s*, divinity, law, medicine.

profĕ′ssional (-shon-) *adj.* Of, belonging to, connected with, a profession; following occupation (esp. one usu. engaged in as pastime or by amateurs) as means of livelihood; making a trade of something usu. or properly pursued from higher motives; maintaining a proper standard, businesslike, not amateurish. ~ *n.* Professional man, esp. (abbrev. pro) one who plays football, golf, etc., for money, as dist. from AMATEUR. **profĕ′ssionally**.

profĕ′ssionalism (-shon-) *n.* Qualities, stamp, of a profession; practice of employing professionals in sport etc. **profĕ′ssionalīze** *v.t.*

profĕss′or *n.* 1. One who makes profession (*of* a religion). 2. Public teacher of high rank, esp. holder of a chair in university (prefixed as title, abbrev. Prof.). 3. (as grandiose title) *P~ Smith's Boxing Dormice* etc.; (slang) professional. **profĕss′orate, profĕss′orshĭp** *ns.* Position, period of activity, of university professor. **prŏfėssôr′ĭal** *adj.* **prŏfėssôr′ĭally** *adv.*

prŏff′er *v.t.* & *n.* (literary) Offer.

profĭ′cient (-shnt) *adj.* & *n.* Adept, expert (*in*, *at*). **profĭ′ciently** *adv.* **profĭ′ciency** *n.*

prō′file (-ēl, -īl) *n.* Drawing, silhouette, or other representation, of side view esp. of human face; side outline esp. of human face; flat outline piece of scenery on stage; (fort.) transverse vertical section of fort; comparative thickness of earthwork etc.; (journalism) biographical sketch of a subject, usu. accompanied by a portrait. ~ *v.t.* Represent in profile; give a profile to.

prŏf′ĭt *n.* Advantage, benefit; pecuniary gain, excess of returns over outlay (usu. pl.); ~ *and loss account*, (book-keeping) account in which gains are credited and losses debited so as to show net profit or loss at any time; ~-*sharing*, sharing of profits esp. between employer and employed. **prŏf′ĭtlėss** *adj.* **prŏf′ĭtlėssly** *adv.* **prŏf′ĭtlėssnėss** *n.* **prŏf′ĭt** *v.* Be of advantage to; be of advantage; be benefited or assisted.

prŏf′ĭtable *adj.* Beneficial, useful; yielding profit, lucrative. **prŏf′ĭtablenėss** *n.* **prŏf′ĭtably** *adv.*

prŏfĭteer′ *v.i.* Make inordinate profits on sale of necessary supplies or goods, esp. in time of war. ~ *n.* Profiteering person.

prŏf′lĭgate (-*a*t) *adj.* & *n.* Licentious, dissolute, or recklessly extravagant (person). **prŏflĭg′ately** *adv.* **prŏf′lĭgacy** *n.*

prō fôrm′a. Done for form's sake, as a matter of form; ~ *invoice*, invoice sent to purchaser in advance of goods to show him how much will be payable.

profound′ *adj.* 1. Having, showing, great knowledge or insight; demanding deep study or thought. 2. (Of state or quality) deep, intense, unqualified. 3. Having, coming from, extending to, a great depth. **profound′ly** *adv.* **profound′nėss, profŭn′dĭty** *ns.* **profound′** *n.* (poet.) *The* vast depth (*of*).

profūse′ (-s) *adj.* Lavish, extravagant (*in*, *of*); exuberantly plentiful. **profūse′ly** *adv.* **profūse′nėss, profū′sion** (-zhn) *ns.*

prŏg¹ *n.* (slang) Food, esp. for journey or excursion.

prŏg² *n.* (slang) Proctor at Oxford or Cambridge. ~ *v.t.* Proctorize.

progĕn′ĭtĭve *adj.* Capable of, connected with, the production of offspring.

progĕn′ĭtor *n.* Ancestor; (fig.) political or intellectual predecessor, original of a copy. **progĕnĭtôr′ĭal** *adj.* **progĕn′ĭtrėss** *n.*

progĕn′ĭture *n.* (Begetting of) offspring.

prŏ′gėny *n.* Offspring; descendants; (fig.) issue, outcome.

proglŏtt′ĭs *n.* (pl. -*idēs*). Propagative segment of tapeworm.

prŏg′nathous *adj.* With projecting jaws; (of jaws) projecting. **prognăth′ĭc** *adj.* **prŏg′nathĭsm** *n.*

prŏgnōs′ĭs *n.* (pl. -*osēs*). Prognostication, esp. (med.) forecast of course of disease.

prŏgnŏs′tĭc *n.* Pre-indication, omen (*of*); prediction, forecast. ~ *adj.* Foretelling, predictive (*of*).

prŏgnŏs′tĭcāte *v.t.* Foretell; betoken. **prŏgnŏsticā′tion** *n.* **prŏgnŏs′tĭcatĭve, prŏgnŏs′tĭcatory** *adjs.*

prō′grăm(me) *n.* Descriptive notice of series of events, e.g. of course of study, concert, etc.; definite plan of intended proceedings; ~-*music*, music intended to suggest series of scenes or events; ~ *picture*, cinematographic film forming part, but not the main feature, of a programme.

prŏg′rėss *n.* 1. Forward or onward movement in space; advance, development. 2. (archaic) State journey, official tour. **progrĕss′** *v.i.* Move forward or onward; be carried on: advance, develop.

progrĕ′ssion (-shn) *n.* 1. Progress. 2. (mus.) Passing from one note or chord to another. 3. (math.) Succession of series of quantities, between every two successive terms of which there is some constant relation; *arithmetical* ~, a series in which each number increases or decreases by the same quantity, as 2, 4, 6, etc.; *geometrical* ~, series in which the increase or decrease is by a common ratio, as 3, 9, 27. 4. (astron.) Movement of planet in order of signs of zodiac, i.e. from west to east. **progrĕ'ssional** *adj.*

progrĕ'ssionist (-sho-) *n.* Advocate of or believer in progress, e.g. in political or social matters.

progrĕss'ive *adj.* 1. Moving forward; proceeding step by step, successive; ~ *whist* etc., whist etc. played by several sets of players at different tables, certain players passing after each round to next table. 2. Advancing in social conditions, character, efficiency, etc.; favouring progress or reform; (of disease) continuously increasing. **progrĕss'ively** *adv.* **progrĕss'iveness** *n.* **progrĕss'ive** *n.* Advocate of progressive policy.

prohĭb'it *v.t.* Forbid, debar.

prōhĭbi'tion *n.* 1. Forbidding; edict, order, that forbids. 2. Forbidding by law of sale of intoxicants for common consumption. 3. (law) Writ from High Court of Justice forbidding inferior court to proceed in suit as being beyond its cognizance. **prōhĭbi'tionist** (-sho-) *n.* Advocate of prohibition (esp. of sale etc. of intoxicants).

prohĭb'itive *adj.* Prohibiting; (of tax etc.) serving to prevent the use or abuse of something; (of price) so high that it precludes purchase. **prohĭb'itively** *adv.* **prohĭb'itiveness** *n.* **prohĭb'itory** *adj.*

projĕct' *v.* 1. Plan, contrive; form a project of. 2. Cast, throw, impel; cause (light, shadow) to fall on surface; (fig.) cause (idea etc.) to take shape. 3. Jut out, protrude. 4. (geom.) Draw straight lines from a centre through every point of (given figure) to produce corresponding figure on a surface by intersecting it; draw (such lines), produce (such corresponding figure); make projection of (earth, sky, etc.). **prŏj'ĕct** *n.* Plan, scheme; (in schools) scheme of study lasting for a limited period (e.g. one term) during which the pupils make their own inquiries and collectively record their findings.

projĕc'tile *adj.* 1. Impelling, as ~ *force.* 2. Capable of being projected by force, esp. from gun. ~ *n.* Projectile missile, shell, bullet.

projĕc'tion *n.* 1. Throwing, casting. 2. Protruding; protruding thing; thrusting forward. 3. Planning; realization of plan or idea; mental image viewed as objective reality. 4. (geom.) Projecting of a figure (see PROJECT *v.* 4); ~ *of a point*, point in derived figure corresponding to point in original figure. 5. (geog.) Any orderly system of representing the meridians and parallels of the earth (or celestial sphere) by lines on a plane surface, e.g. by first projecting the meridians on to a cone (*conical* ~) or a cylinder (*cylindrical* ~). 6. Display of film in cinema by throwing image on screen (and producing corresponding sound). 7. (alchemy) Transmutation of metals by casting *powder of* ~ (powder of philosophers' stone) into crucible containing them.

projĕc'tionist *n.* Person who projects cinema film.

projĕc'tive *adj.* Mentally projecting or projected; (geom.) of, derived by, projection; ~ *property* (of a figure), property unchanged after projection. **projĕc'tively** *adv.*

projĕc'tor *n.* 1. One who forms a project; promoter of bubble companies. 2. Apparatus for projecting rays of light, as from a lighthouse lantern; apparatus for throwing a picture on to a screen,

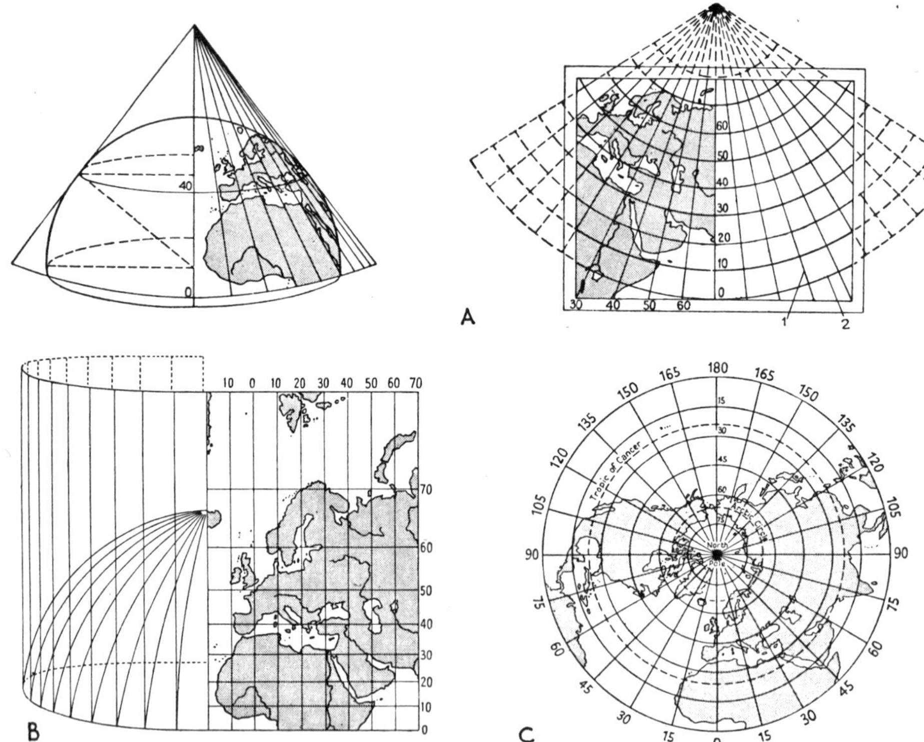

MAP PROJECTIONS. A. CONICAL. B. CYLINDRICAL OR MERCATOR. C. ZENITHAL

1. Line of longitude. 2. Line of latitude. In A the meridians are projected on to a cone which touches the earth along a parallel, in this case 40° N. In B the meridians are projected on to a cylinder touching the earth, in this case at the equator. In C the surface of projection is a plane tangential to a point on the earth's surface, in this case the North Pole

as a cinematograph (*sound ~*, one for sound film, producing corresponding sound at same time).

Prol. *abbrev.* Prologue.

prolăpse′ *v.i.* (path.) Slip forward or down out of place. **prō′lăpse, prolăp′sus** *ns.* (path.) Slipping forward or down of part or organ, esp. of uterus or rectum.

prōl′āte *adj.* Growing, extending, in width; (fig.) widely spread; (gram.) prolative; (geom., of spheroid) lengthened in direction of polar diameter (ill. CONE). **prōl′ātely** *adv.*

prolāt′ive *adj.* (gram.) Serving to extend or complete predication; in 'you can go' *go* is a prolative infinitive.

prōlĕgŏm′ĕnon *n.* (usu. in pl. *-ena*). Preliminary discourse or matter prefixed to book etc. **prōlegŏm′ĕnary, prōlĕgŏm′ĕnous** *adjs.*

prolĕp′sis *n.* (pl. *-psēs*). Anticipation; (gram.) anticipatory use of adjectives, as in *So those two brothers and their* murdered *man Rode past fair Florence.* **prolĕp′tic** *adj.* **prolĕp′tically** *adv.*

prōlĕtār′ian *adj.* & *n.* (Member) of the proletariat. **prōlĕtār′ianism** *n.*

prōlĕtār′iat(e) *n.* 1. (Rom. hist.) Lowest class of community in ancient Rome, regarded as contributing nothing to the State but offspring. 2. (freq. contempt.) Lowest class of community; (econ.) class which is dependent on daily labour for subsistence, and has no reserve of capital; sometimes, all wage-earners, working men; *dictatorship of the ~*, Communist ideal of domination by the proletariat after the suppression of capitalism and the *bourgeoisie*.

prolĭf′erāte *v.* Reproduce itself, grow, by multiplication of elementary parts; produce (cells etc.) thus; (of human beings etc.) multiply. **prolĭferā′tion** *n.* **prolĭf′erative** *adj.*

prolĭf′erous *adj.* (bot.) Producing leaf or flower buds from leaf or flower; producing new individuals from buds; (zool.) multiplying by budding etc.; (path.) spreading by proliferation.

prolĭf′ic *adj.* Producing (much) offspring; abundantly productive *of*, abounding *in*. **prolĭf′ically** *adv.* **prolĭf′icacy, prolĭfĭ′city, prolĭf′icness** *ns.*

prōl′ix (*or* prolix′) *adj.* Lengthy, wordy, tedious. **prōl′ixly** *adv.* **prolĭx′ity** *n.*

prŏl′ocūtor (*or* prolŏc′-) *n.* Chairman esp. of lower house of convocation of either province of Church of England.

prŏl′ogīze (-j-), **prŏl′oguize** (-gīz) *vs.* Write, speak, a prologue.

prŏl′ŏgue (-g) *n.* Preliminary discourse, poem, etc., esp. introducing play; act, event, serving as introduction (*to*). *~ v.t.* Introduce, furnish, with prologue.

prolŏng′ *v.t.* Extend in duration; extend in spatial length; lengthen pronunciation of. **prōlŏngā′tion** (-ngg-) *n.*

prŏm *n.* Abbrev. of PROMENADE *concert.*

prŏmėnade′ (-ahd, -ād) *n.* Walk, ride, drive, taken for exercise, amusement, or display, or as social ceremony; place, esp. paved public walk for this; (U.S.) school or college ball or dance; *~ concert*, one at which (part of) audience is not provided with seats and can move about; *~ deck*, an upper deck on a liner, where passengers may walk about. *~ v.* Make a promenade through (place); lead (person) about a place esp. for display.

Promēth′eus (-thūs). (Gk myth.) Son of the Titan Iapetus; he made mankind out of clay, taught them many arts, and stole fire for them from heaven; to punish him, Zeus chained him to a rock in the Caucasus, where a vulture fed each day on his liver, which was restored in the night. **Promēth′ėan** *adj.* Of, like, Prometheus in his skill or punishment.

promēth′ium *n.* (chem.) A radio-active element (symbol Pm, at. no. 61, principal isotope 147) not found in nature but formed by the fission of uranium in a pile.

prŏm′inent *adj.* Jutting out, projecting; conspicuous; distinguished. **prŏm′inently** *adv.* **prŏm′inence** *n.* Being prominent; thing that projects; *solar ~*, cloud of incandescent hydrogen projecting from sun (ill. SUN).

promĭs′cūous *adj.* Of mixed and disorderly composition; of various kinds mixed together; indiscriminate, undiscriminating. **promĭs′cūously** *adv.* **promĭs′cūousnėss, prŏmiscū′ity** *ns.*

prŏm′ise *n.* Assurance given to a person that one will do or not do something or will give or procure him something; thing promised; (fig.) ground of expectation of future achievements or good results. *~ v.* Make (person) a promise to give or procure him (thing); make (person) a promise (*to, that*); make promise; (fig.) afford expectation of, seem likely (*to*); hold out good etc. prospect; *~ oneself*, look forward to; *promised land*, Canaan, as promised to Abraham and his posterity (Gen. xii. 7, xiii. 15, etc.); heaven, any place of expected felicity.

prŏmisee′ *n.* (law) Person to whom promise is made.

prŏm′ising *adj.* Likely to turn out well, hopeful, full of promise. **prŏm′isingly** *adv.*

prŏm′issory *adj.* Conveying or implying a promise; *~ note*, signed document containing written promise to pay stated sum to specified person or to bearer at specified date or on demand.

prŏm′ontory *n.* Point of high land jutting out into sea etc., headland; (anat.) various protuberances in body.

promōte′ *v.t.* 1. Advance, prefer (person *to* position, higher office); (chess) raise (pawn) to rank of queen etc. 2. Help forward, encourage (process, result); support actively the passing of (law), take necessary steps for passing of (local or private act of parliament). 3. (eccles. law) Set in motion (office of ordinary or judge) in criminal suit in ecclesiastical court, institute (such suit).

promō′ter *n.* (esp.) One who promotes formation of joint-stock company (freq. with implication of fraud or sharp practice). **promō′tion** *n.* Promoting; *sales ~*, (commerc.) information or instruction given to dealer by manufacturer or agent to enable him to sell a product. **promōt′ive** *adj.*

prŏmpt[1] *adj.* Ready in action, acting with alacrity; made, done, etc., readily or at once; (commerc., of goods) for immediate delivery and payment. *~ n.* Time-limit for payment of account, stated on *~-note.*

prŏmpt[2] *v.t.* 1. Incite, move (person etc. *to*); inspire, give rise to (feeling, thought, action). 2. Supply (actor, reciter) with the words that come next; assist (hesitating speaker) with suggestion. *~ n.* Thing said to help memory esp. of actor; *~-book*, copy of play for prompter's use; *~-box*, prompter's box on stage; *~-side*, side of stage to actor's left.

prŏmp′ter *n.* One who prompts, esp. (theatr.) person stationed out of sight of audience to assist actor's memory.

prŏm′ulgāte *v.t.* Make known to the public, disseminate, proclaim. **prŏmulgā′tion, prŏm′ulgātor** *ns.*

pronā′ŏs *n.* (Gk antiq.) Space in front of body of temple, enclosed by portico and projecting side walls (ill. TEMPLE).

prōn′āte *v.t.* (physiol.) Put (hand, fore-limb) into prone position. **prōnā′tion** *n.*

prōnāt′or *n.* (anat.) Muscle that effects or helps pronation.

prōne *adj.* 1. Having the front or ventral part downwards, lying face downwards; (loosely) lying flat, prostrate. 2. (Of ground) having downward aspect or direction; (loosely) steep, headlong. 3. Disposed, liable (*to*). **prōne′nėss** (-n-n-) *n.*

prŏng *n.* Forked instrument, e.g. hay-fork; each pointed member of fork; *~-buck, ~-horn(ed antelope)*, N. Amer. deer-like ruminant, (*Antilocapra americana*), male of which has deciduous horns with short prong in front. *~ v.t.* Pierce, stab, turn up (soil etc.) with prong.

pronŏm′inal *adj.* Of (the nature of) a pronoun. **pronŏm′inally** *adv.*

prōn′oun *n.* Word used instead of (proper or other) noun to designate person or thing already mentioned, known from context, or forming subject of inquiry; *personal ~s*, I, we, thou, you, he, she, it, they; *interrogative ~s*, who?, what?, which?; *relative ~s*, who, that, which; *demonstrative ~s*, this, that, these, those; *indefinite ~s*, any, some, etc.; *distributive ~s*, each, every, either, etc.; *possessive ~s*, adjectives representing possessive case of personal pronouns (my, our, etc.) with absolute forms (mine, ours, etc.).

pronounce′ *v.* 1. Utter, deliver (judgement, curse, etc.) formally or solemnly; state, declare, as one's opinion; pass judgement, give one's opinion. 2. Utter, articulate, esp. with reference to different modes of pronunciation; *pronouncing dictionary*, one in which pronunciation is indicated. **pronoun′cable** (-sabl) *adj.*

pronounced′ (-st) *adj.* (esp.) Strongly marked, decided.

pronŭnciamĕn′tō *n.* Proclamation, manifesto, esp. (in Spanish-speaking countries) one issued by insurrectionists.

pronŭnciā′tion *n.* Mode in which a word is pronounced; a person's way of pronouncing words.

proof *n.* 1. Evidence sufficing or helping to establish a fact; spoken or written legal evidence; proving, demonstration; (Sc. law) evidence given before judge, upon record or issue in pleading, trial before judge instead of by jury. 2. Test, trial; (place for) testing of fire-arms or explosives; (archaic) proved impenetrability; *~ stress*, (eng.) load slightly greater than that which a mechanism etc. will normally have to bear. 3. Standard of strength of distilled alcoholic liquors; *~ spirit*, a standard mixture of pure alcohol and water (containing 57·3% alcohol by volume) in terms of which the alcoholic strengths of liquors are computed for excise purposes; e.g. if 100 volumes of a liquor contain enough alcohol to make 70 volumes of proof spirit the liquor is defined as '70% proof' or '30% under proof'. 4. Trial impression taken from type, in which corrections etc. may be made; each of limited number of careful impressions made from engraved plate before printing of ordinary issue and usu. (also *~ before letters*) before inscription is added; *artist's, engraver's, ~*, one taken for examination or alteration by him; *signed ~*, early proof signed by artist; *~-reader*, person employed in reading and correcting printers' proofs. 5. Rough uncut edges of shorter or narrower leaves of book, left to show it has not been cut down in binding. *~ adj.* (Of armour) of tried strength; impenetrable (esp. as second element of compound, as *bombproof, windproof*). *~ v.t.* Make (thing) proof; make (fabric etc.) waterproof; submit (mechanism etc.) to proof stress.

prŏp *n.* Rigid support, esp. one not forming structural part of thing supported; (fig.) person etc. who upholds institution etc. *~ v.t.* Support (as) by prop, hold *up* thus.

prop. *abbrev.* Proposition.

prŏpagăn′da *n.* 1. (*Congregation, College, of*) *the ~*, committee of cardinals of R.C. Ch. in charge of foreign missions. 2. Association, organized scheme, for propagation of a doctrine or practice; doctrines, information, etc., thus propagated (freq. with implication of bias or falsity, esp. in politics); efforts, schemes, principles, of propagation. **prŏpagăn′dist** *adj.* & *n.* **prŏpagăn′dize** *v.*

prŏp′agāte *v.* 1. Multiply specimens of (plant, animal, disease, etc.) by natural process from parent stock; (of plant etc.) reproduce (*itself*), reproduce itself. 2. Hand down (quality etc.) from one generation to another. 3. Disseminate, diffuse (statement, belief, practice). 4. Extend the action or operation of, transmit, convey in some direction or through some medium. **prŏpagā′tion, prŏp′agātor** *ns.*

prōp′āne *n.* (chem.) Colourless inflammable hydrocarbon gas (C_3H_8), one of the paraffin series, occurring in natural gases.

prōparŏx′ȳtone *adj.* & *n.* (Gk gram.) (Word) with acute accent on last syllable but one.

propĕl′ *v.t.* Drive forward, give onward motion to. **propĕll′ant, -ent** *adj.* & *n.* Propelling (agent); (explosive) that propels projectile from fire-arm.

propĕll′er *n.* (esp.) Revolving shaft with blades usu. set at an angle and twisted like thread of screw, for propelling ship; similar device on an aircraft producing the thrust which drives it forward.

propĕn′sity *n.* Inclination, tendency (*to, for*).

prŏp′er *adj.* 1. (archaic) Own; (astron.) *~ motion*, that part of apparent motion of fixed star etc. supposed to be due to its actual movement in space. 2. Belonging, relating, exclusively or distinctively (*to*); (her.) represented in natural colouring; *~ name, noun*, name used to designate an individual person, animal, town, ship, etc. 3. Accurate, correct; (usu. following its noun) strictly so called, real, genuine; thorough, complete (colloq.); handsome (archaic); *~ fraction*, one whose value is less than unity. 4. Suitable, right; in conformity with demands of society, decent, respectable. **prŏp′erly** *adv.* Fittingly, suitably; rightly, duly; with good manners; (colloq.) thoroughly.

Propĕr′tius (-sh*u*s), Sextus (*c* 51–*c* 15 B.C.) Roman elegiac poet.

prŏp′erty *n.* 1. Owning, being owned; thing owned; landed estate; *~ qualification*, one based on possession of property; *~ tax*, one levied directly on property. 2. (theatr.) Portable thing, as article of costume, furniture, etc., used on stage; *~-man, -master*, (colloq. *props*), man in charge of stage properties. 3. Attribute, quality; (logic) quality common to a whole class but not necessary to distinguish it from others.

prŏph′ėcy *n.* Faculty of a prophet; prophetic utterance; foretelling of future events.

prŏph′ėsȳ *v.* Speak as a prophet, foretell future events; foretell; (archaic) expound the Scriptures.

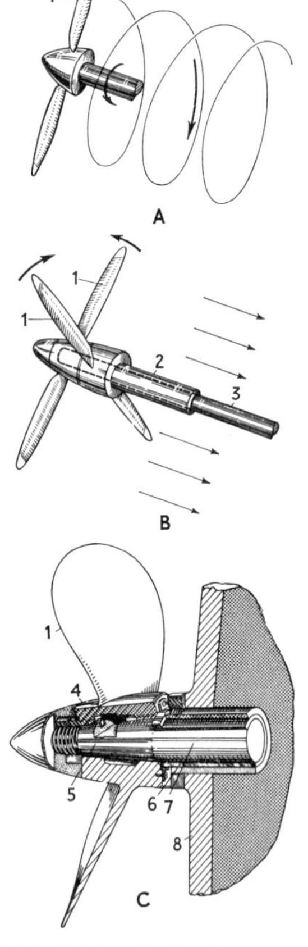

PROPELLERS. A. SINGLE ROTATION AIRCRAFT PROPELLER. B. CONTRAPROP. C. MARINE PROPELLER OR SCREW

1. Blade. 2. Back shaft. 3. Front shaft. 4. Boss. 5. Tail-end shaft. 6. Stern tube. 7. Shaft. 8. Hull. The arrows behind the propellers in *A* and *B* show the direction of the slipstreams

prŏph'ėt *n.* Inspired teacher, revealer or interpreter of God's will; spokesman, advocate (*of*); one who foretells events; (slang) tipster; *the prophets*, the prophetical writers of the O.T., the first 4 (Isaiah, Jeremiah, Ezekiel, Daniel) being called the *major prophets*, and the last 12 (from Hosea to Malachi), the *minor prophets*; *the P~*, Mohammed; (also) Joseph Smith, founder of Mormonism. **prŏph'ėtėss** *n.*

prophĕt'ĭc *adj.* Of a prophet; predicting, containing a prediction *of*. **prophĕt'ĭcal** *adj.* **prophĕt'ĭcally** *adv.*

prŏphylăc'tĭc *adj.* & *n.* (Medicine, measure) tending to prevent disease. **prŏphylăx'ĭs** *n.* Preventive treatment of disease.

propinq'uĭty *n.* Nearness in place; close kinship; similarity.

prōpiŏn'ĭc *adj.* ~ *acid*, (chem.) colourless liquid with odour resembling that of acetic acid, present in products of the distillation of wood.

propĭ'tiāte (-shĭ-) *v.t.* Appease (offended person etc.); make propitious. **propitiā'tion** *n.* Appeasement; atonement; (archaic) gift etc. meant to propitiate.

propĭ'tiatory (-sha-) *adj.* Serving, meant, to propitiate.

propĭ'tious (-shus) *adj.* Well-disposed, favourable; suitable *for*, favourable *to*. **propĭ'tiously** *adv.*

propŏr'tion *n.* Comparative part, share; comparative relation, ratio; due relation of one thing to another or between parts of a thing; (pl.) dimensions; (math.) equality of ratios between two pairs of quantities, set of such quantities; (arith.) method by which, three quantities being given, a fourth may be found which is in same ratio to third as second is to first. ~ *v.t.* Make proportionate *to*.

propŏr'tional (-sho-) *adj.* In due proportion, corresponding in degree or amount; ~ *representation*, a method of parliamentary representation designed to allow the various political parties to be represented in proportion to their size and characterized by the use of the transferable vote, i.e. the filling up of seats, where a quota is not secured by first choices, by the transference of votes from second choices, and so on. **propŏr'tionăl'ĭty** *n.* **propŏr'tionally** *adv.* **propŏr'tionate** *adj.* **propŏr'tionately** *adv.*

propō'sal (-z-) *n.* Act of proposing something; offer of marriage; scheme of action etc. proposed.

propōse' (-z) *v.* Put forward for consideration, propound; set up as an aim; nominate (person) as member of society etc.; offer (person, person's health, etc.) as toast; make offer of marriage (*to*); put forward as a plan; intend, purpose.

prŏposĭ'tion (-z-) *n.* 1. Statement, assertion, esp. (logic) form of words consisting of predicate and subject connected by copula; (math., abbrev. *prop.*) formal statement of theorem or problem, freq. including the demonstration. 2. Proposal, scheme proposed; (U.S.) task, project, enterprise, problem for solution. **prŏposĭ'tional** (-sho-) *adj.*

propound' *v.t.* Offer for consideration, propose (question, problem, scheme, etc.); produce (will) before proper authority in order to establish its legality.

prōpraet'or *n.* (Rom. hist.) Ex-praetor with authority of praetor in province not under military control.

proprī'ėtary *adj.* Of a proprietor; holding property; held in private ownership (esp. of medicines etc. of which manufacture or sale is restricted by patent or otherwise to particular person(s)). ~ *n.* Proprietorship; body of proprietors.

proprī'ėtor *n.* Owner. **proprīėtŏr'ial** *adj.* **proprīėtŏr'ially** *adv.* **proprī'ėtorshĭp, proprī'ėtrėss** *ns.*

proprī'ėty *n.* Fitness, rightness; correctness of behaviour or morals; (pl.) details of correct conduct.

prō-prŏc'tor *n.* Assistant or deputy proctor in university.

prŏps *n.pl.* (slang) Abbrev. of (stage) PROPERTIES, property-man.

propŭl'sion (-shn) *n.* Driving or pushing forward; means of this; (fig.) impelling influence. **propŭl'sĭve** *adj.*

prōp'ȳl *n.* (chem.) The hydrocarbon radical C_3H_7; ~ *alcohol*, colourless liquid (C_3H_7OH), occurring in fusel-oil and separated by distillation, used as a solvent.

prōp'ȳlēne *n.* Colourless hydrocarbon gas (C_3H_6), occurring esp. in the gases from the cracking of petroleum.

prŏpȳlae'um *n.* (pl. *-aea*). Entrance to temple; *the Propylaea*, entrance to the Acropolis at Athens.

prō rāt'a *adv.* & *adj.* Proportional(ly).

prorōgue' (-g) *v.* Discontinue meeting of (British Parliament etc.) without dissolving it; be prorogued. **prōrogā'tion** *n.*

prōsā'ĭc (-z-; *or* pro-) *adj.* Like prose, lacking poetic beauty; unromantic, commonplace, dull. **prōsā'ĭcally** *adv.*

proscēn'ium *n.* (In ancient theatre) the stage; (in modern theatre) space between curtain or drop-scene and orchestra, esp. with the enclosing arch (ill. THEATRE).

proscrībe' *v.t.* Put (person) out of protection of law; banish, exile; reject, denounce (practice etc.) as dangerous etc. **proscrĭp'tion** *n.* **proscrĭp'tĭve** *adj.*

prōse (-z) *n.* Ordinary non-metrical form of written or spoken language; (eccles.) piece of rhythmical prose or rhymed accentual verse sung or said between epistle and gospel at certain Masses; prosy discourse. ~ *v.i.* Talk prosily; turn (poem etc.) into prose.

prŏs'ėcūte *v.t.* 1. Follow up, pursue (inquiry, studies); carry on (trade, pursuit). 2. Institute legal proceedings against.

prŏsėcū'tion *n.* Prosecuting; carrying on of legal proceedings against person; prosecuting party; (law) exhibition of criminal charge before court.

prŏs'ėcūtor *n.* One who prosecutes, esp. in criminal court; *public* ~, law officer conducting criminal proceedings in public interest. **prŏsėcū'trĭx** *n.*

prŏs'ėlȳte *n.* Convert from one opinion, creed, or party, to another; Gentile convert to Jewish faith. ~ *v.t.* Make proselyte of. **prŏs'ėlȳtism, prŏs'ėlȳtīzer** *ns.* **prŏs'ėlȳtīze** *v.t.*

prosĕn'chȳma (-ngk-) *n.* (bot.) Tissue of elongated cells placed with their ends interpenetrating, esp. fibro-vascular tissue. **prŏsĕnchȳm'atous** *adj.*

Prosĕr'p'ina. Latin name of PERSEPHONE.

prŏs'ĭfȳ (-z-) *v.* Turn into prose, make prosaic; write prose.

prŏs'ody *n.* Science of versification. **prosŏd'ĭc** *adj.* **prŏs'odĭst** *n.*

prŏsōpopoe'ia (-pēĭa) *n.* (rhet.) Introduction of pretended speaker; personification of abstract thing.

prŏs'pĕct *n.* 1. Extensive view of landscape etc.; mental scene. 2. Expectation; what one expects. 3. (colloq.) Possible or likely purchaser, subscriber, etc. 4. (mining) Spot giving prospects of mineral deposit; sample of ore for testing, resulting yield. **prospĕct'** *v.* Explore region (*for* gold etc.); explore (region) for gold etc., work (mine) experimentally; (of mine) promise (well, ill; specified yield). **prospĕc'tor** *n.*

prospĕc'tĭve *adj.* Concerned with, applying to, the future; expected, future, some day to be. **prospĕc'tĭvely** *adv.*

prospĕc'tus *n.* Circular describing chief features of school, commercial enterprise, forthcoming book, etc.

prŏs'per *v.* Succeed, thrive; make successful. **prŏspĕ'rĭty** *n.*

prŏs'perous *adj.* Flourishing, successful, thriving; auspicious. **prŏs'perously** *adv.*

prŏs'tāte *n.* Large gland, accessory to male generative organs and surrounding neck of bladder and commencement of urethra (ill. PELVIS). **prŏstăt'ĭc** *adj.*

prŏs'thėsĭs *n.* 1. (surg.) Making up of deficiencies (with artificial teeth, limb, etc.); this as branch of surgery. 2. (gram.) Addition of letter or syllable at beginning of word. **prŏsthĕt'ĭc** *adj.* Of prosthesis; (biochem.) of a group or radical of a different kind added or substituted in a compound.

prŏs′titūte *n.* Woman who offers her body to indiscriminate sexual intercourse, esp. for hire. ~ *v.t.* Make a prostitute of; (fig.) sell for base gain, put (abilities etc.) to infamous use. **prŏstitū′tion** *n.*

prŏs′trāte (*or* -at) *adj.* Lying with face to ground, esp. as token of submission or humility; lying in horizontal position; overcome, overthrown; physically exhausted; (bot.) lying flat on ground. **prostrāte′** (*or* prŏs′-) *v.t.* Lay flat on ground; cast one*self* down prostrate; (fig.) overcome, make submissive; (of fatigue etc.) reduce to extreme physical weakness. **prŏstrā′tion** *n.*

prō′stȳle *n.* Portico of not more than 4 columns in front of Greek temple (ill. TEMPLE). ~ *adj.* Having a prostyle.

prōs′y (-zĭ) *adj.* Commonplace, tedious, dull. **prōs′ĭly** *adv.* **prōs′ĭnėss** *n.*

prōtăctĭn′ium *n.* (chem.) A radio-active element of the actinium series, which by disintegration yields actinium; symbol Pa, at. no. 91, principal isotope 231.

prōtăg′onist *n.* Chief person in drama or plot of story; leading person in contest, champion of cause, etc.

Prōtăg′orăs of Abdera (5th c. B.C.). Greek philosopher, a sophist; portrayed in Plato's dialogue of that name.

prōt′amīne *n.* (chem.) One of the simple basic proteins, present only in the nuclear material of fish, containing a higher percentage of nitrogen than most proteins.

prōtăn′drous *adj.* Having stamens ripening before the stigmas.

prō tăn′tō. So far, to such an extent.

prŏt′asis *n.* (pl. *-asēs*). (gram., rhet.) Introductory clause, esp. clause expressing condition, opp. to APODOSIS. **protăt′ic** *adj.*

prōt′ėan *adj.* Variable, versatile; of or like Proteus.

protĕct′ *v.t.* Keep safe, defend, guard (*from, against*); (econ.) guard (home industry) against competition, by imposing tariffs on foreign goods; (commerc.) provide funds to meet (bill, draft); provide (machinery etc.) with appliances to prevent injury from it.

protĕc′tion *n.* Protecting, defence; patronage; protecting person or thing; safe-conduct; system or policy of protecting home industries by tariffs etc.; (U.S.) certificate of American citizenship issued to seamen. **protĕc′tionism** (-sho-), **protĕc′tionist** *ns.*

protĕc′tive *adj.* Serving to protect; ~ *custody*, detention of person by State in order to protect him from harm. **protĕc′tively** *adv.* **protĕc′tivenėss** *n.*

protĕc′tor *n.* Person who protects; thing, device, that protects; regent in charge of kingdom during minority, absence, etc., of sovereign; *Lord P~ of the Commonwealth*, title of Oliver Cromwell 1653–8 and Richard Cromwell 1658–9. **protĕc′toral** *adj.*

protĕc′torate *n.* 1. Office of protector of kingdom or State; period of this, esp. of the protectorate of Oliver and Richard Cromwell. 2. Protectorship of weak State by stronger one, esp. of territory inhabited by native tribes; such territory.

protĕc′tory *n.* (R.C. Ch.) Institution for care of destitute or vicious children.

protégé (prŏt′āzhā) *n.* (fem. *-ée*). Person under protection or patronage of another.

prōt′ėifôrm *adj.* Multiform, extremely changeable.

prōt′ėin (*or* -tēn) *n.* Any of a class of organic compounds (of carbon, hydrogen, oxygen, nitrogen, and often sulphur) forming an important part of all living organisms and the essential nitrogenous constituents of the food of animals.

prō tĕm′porė. (abbrev. *pro tem.*) For the time, temporary, temporarily.

prōt′ĕst *n.* Formal statement of dissent or disapproval, remonstrance; written statement of dissent from motion carried in House of Lords signed by any peer of minority; written declaration, usu. by notary public, that bill has been duly presented and payment or acceptance refused; solemn declaration. **protĕst′** *v.* Affirm solemnly; write a protest in regard to (bill); make (freq. written) protest *against* (action, proposal). **protĕst′er, protĕst′or** *ns.* **protĕst′ingly** *adv.*

prŏt′ėstant *n.* 1. (*P~*) Member, adherent, of any of the Christian Churches or bodies that repudiated papal authority and were separated from Roman communion in the Reformation (16th c.), or of any Church or body descended from them; (hist., usu. pl.) those German princes and free cities who dissented from the decision of the Diet of Spires (1529), which reaffirmed the edict of the Diet of Worms against the Reformation; German adherents of Reformed doctrines and worship. 2. (*also* protĕs′-) One who protests. ~ *adj.* Of Protestants or Protestantism; *P~ Episcopal Church*, official style of Church in U.S. descended from and in communion with Church of England. **Prŏt′ėstantĭsm** *n.*

prŏtėstā′tion *n.* Solemn affirmation; protest.

Prōt′eus (-tūs). 1. (Gk legend) An 'ancient one of the sea', who herds seals, knows all things, and has the power of assuming different shapes to avoid being questioned. 2. (zool.) A blind white urodele (*Proteus anguinus*) living in caves in Yugoslavia.

prŏth′ėsĭs *n.* 1. (eccles.) The placing of the elements etc. in readiness for use in the Eucharistic office; credence-table, part of the church where this stands. 2. (gram.) = PROSTHESIS. **prothĕt′ic** *adj.*

proto- *prefix.* 1. First, primary, primitive. 2. In chem. terms indicates: (*a*) a substance held to be the parent of the substance to the name of which it is prefixed, as *protoactinium* (= PROTACTINIUM); (*b*) (now obs.) a substance which is the first or lowest of a series or which has the smallest relative amount of the element or radical to the name of which it is prefixed.

prōt′ocŏl *n.* Original draft of diplomatic document, esp. of terms of treaty agreed to in conference and signed by the parties; formal statement of transaction; (in France) etiquette department of Ministry of Foreign Affairs; rigid prescription or observance of precedence and deference to rank as in diplomatic and military services; official formula at beginning and end of charter, papal bull, etc. ~ *v.* Draw up protocols; record in protocol. [Gk *protokollon* flyleaf glued to case of book (*kolla* glue)]

prōtogȳn′ous (-g-) *adj.* Having stigmas ripening before the stamens.

prōt′omârt′yr *n.* First person martyred for a cause (esp. applied to first Christian martyr, St. Stephen).

prōt′ŏn *n.* Fundamental atomic particle of nature, the nucleus of the hydrogen atom, having a single positive electric charge equal and opposite to that of the electron ($4{\cdot}80 \times 10^{-10}$ e.s.u.) and a mass of $1{\cdot}660 \times 10^{-24}$ g.; a constituent of the nucleus of all atoms.

prōtonōt′ary *n.* Chief clerk in some law courts, esp. (hist.) Chancery, Common Pleas, and King's Bench, (orig. in Byzantine court); *Protonotaries Apostolic(al)*, (R.C. Ch.) 12 prelates who register papal acts, direct canonization of saints, etc.

Protŏph′ȳta *n.pl.* (bot.) A primary division of the vegetable kingdom, comprising the most simply organized plants, each consisting of a single cell. **prōt′ophȳte** *n.* Such a plant.

prōt′oplăsm *n.* Viscous translucent substance, the essential matter of living organisms, the substance of which cells principally consist, capable of being irritated, of moving spontaneously, contracting itself, assimilating other matter, and reproducing itself; differentiated (in most organisms) into the *nucleus*, or reproductive part, and the *cytoplasm*, a viscous fluid forming the general body of the cell. **prōtoplăs′mic** *adj.*

prōt′oplăst *n.* Mass of cytoplasm which is visibly distinct from the rest. **prōtoplăs′tic** *adj.*

Prōtothēr′ĭa *n.pl.* (zool.) = Monotremata (see MONOTREME).

prōt′otȳpe *n.* An original thing or person in relation to any copy, imitation, representation, later specimen, improved form, etc. **prōt′otȳpal, prōtotȳp′ical** *adjs.*

Prōtozō′a *n.pl.* A division of the animal kingdom comprising animals of the simplest type each

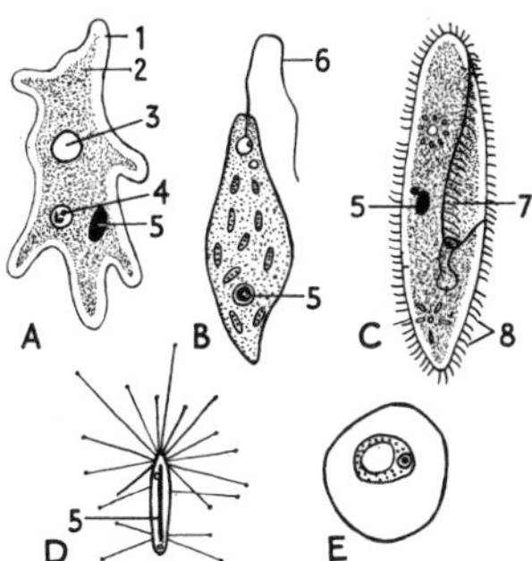

PROTOZOA: A. AMOEBA. B. FLAGELLATE (*EUGLENA*). C. CILIATA (*PARAMECIUM*). D. SUCTORIA (*PODOPHRYA*). E. PLASMODIUM IN RED CORPUSCLES (ANNULAR STAGE)

1. Ectoplasm. 2. Endoplasm. 3. Contractile vacuole. 4. Gastric vacuole. 5. Nucleus. 6. Flagellum. 7. Peristome. 8. Cilia

essentially consisting of a simple cell, usu. of microscopic size. **prōtozō′on** *n.* Such an animal.

prōtozō′ic *adj.* (geol., of strata) Containing earliest traces of living beings.

protrăct′ *v.t.* 1. Prolong, lengthen out; extend. 2. Draw (plan of ground etc.) to scale.

protrăc′tīle *adj.* (zool.) (Of organ etc.) that can be extended.

protrăc′tion *n.* 1. Protracting; action of protractor muscle. 2. Drawing to scale.

protrăc′tor *n.* 1. Instrument for setting off and measuring angles, usu. in form of graduated semicircle. 2. Muscle serving to extend limb etc.

protrude′ (-ōōd) *v.* Thrust forth, cause to project; stick out, project; obtrude. **protru′sion** (-zhn) *n.* **protrus′ible, -īve** *adjs.*

protūbe′rant *adj.* Bulging out, prominent. **protūb′erance** *n.*

proud *adj.* 1. Valuing oneself highly or too highly, esp. on the ground *of* (qualities, rank, etc.); haughty, arrogant; feeling oneself greatly honoured; feeling or showing a proper pride; (of actions etc.) showing pride; of which one is or may be justly proud. 2. (Of things) imposing, splendid; (of waters) swollen, in flood; ~ *flesh*, overgrown flesh round healing wound. **proud′ly** *adv.*

Proud′hon (prōōdawṅ), Pierre Joseph (1809–65). French socialist and writer on politics and economics.

Proust (-ōōst), Marcel (1871–1922). French novelist; author of the series of volumes grouped under the title 'A la Recherche du Temps perdu', remarkable for their conception of the unreality and reversibility of time and for their minute psychological analysis.

Prov. *abbrev.* Proverbs (O.T.).

prove (-ōōv) *v.* 1. Test qualities of, try (archaic exc. in technical uses); subject (manufactured article etc.) to testing process; (arith.) test correctness of (calculation); take proof impression of (composed type, stereotype plate, etc.). 2. Establish as true, demonstrate truth of by evidence or argument; establish genuineness and validity of, obtain probate of (will). 3. Show itself, turn out, to be (or *to* be or do).

prŏv′ėnance *n.* (Place of) origin.

Prŏvençal (-vahṅsahl′) *adj.* & *n.* (pl. *-çaux*). (Inhabitant) of Provence; (of) the Romance language spoken in S. France, esp. in the old province of Provence.

Provence′ (-vahṅs). District, former province, of SE. France east of the lower Rhône; orig. a Roman province, the first to be established outside Italy. [L *provincia* (*romana*) (the Roman) province]

prŏv′ėnder *n.* Food, provisions, esp. for horses.

prŏv′ērb *n.* Short pithy saying in general use, adage, saw; byword, thing that is proverbial or matter of common talk; (*Book of*) *P~s*, didactic poetical O.T. book consisting of maxims ascribed to Solomon and others.

provērb′ial *adj.* Of, expressed in, proverbs; that has become a proverb or byword, notorious. **provērb′ially** *adv.* **provērbiăl′ity** *n.*

provīde′ *v.* 1. Make due preparation (*for, against*); stipulate (*that*); supply, furnish (*with, for, to*); equip with necessaries; make provision, esp. secure maintenance (*for*). 2. (hist.) Appoint (incumbent *to* benefice); (of pope) appoint (successor *to* benefice not yet vacant).

provīd′ėd *adj.* (esp., hist.) ~ *school*, public elementary school provided by local authority. **provīd′ėd, provīd′ing** *conjs.* On the condition or understanding (*that*).

prŏv′ĭdence *n.* 1. Foresight, timely care; thrift. 2. Beneficent care of God or nature; *special* ~, particular instance of this. 3. *P~*, God.

prŏv′ĭdent *adj.* Having or showing foresight, thrifty. **prŏv′ĭdently** *adv.*

prŏvĭdĕn′tial (-shl) *adj.* Of, by, divine foresight or interposition; opportune, lucky. **prŏvĭdĕn′tially** *adv.*

prŏv′ince *n.* 1. (Rom. hist.) Territory outside Italy under Roman governor. 2. Administrative (esp. principal) division of country or State, esp. one that has been historically, linguistically, etc., distinct; (eccles.) district under archbishop or metropolitan; *the provinces*, all parts of country outside the capital. 3. Sphere of action, business; branch of learning etc.

provĭn′cial (-shl) *adj.* Of a province; of the provinces; having the manners, speech, narrow views or interests, etc., associated with or attributed to inhabitants of provinces. **provĭn′cially** *adv.* **provĭnciăl′ity** (-shĭal′-) *n.* **provĭn′cialize** *v.t.* **provĭn′cial** *n.* 1. Inhabitant of a province or the provinces; countrified person. 2. (eccles.) Head of, chief of religious order in, a province.

provĭn′cialism (-sh*a*l-) *n.* Provincial manner, mode of thought, etc.; word, phrase, peculiar to province(s); attachment to one's province rather than country.

provĭ′sion (-zhn) *n.* 1. Providing (*for, against*); provided amount *of* something; (pl.) supply of food, eatables and drinkables. 2. Legal or formal statement providing for something; clause of this; (Engl. hist., pl.) certain early statutes or ordinances; *P~s of Oxford*, ordinances for checking king's misrule etc. drawn up (1258, in Henry III's reign) by barons under Simon de Montfort. 3. (hist.) Appointment to benefice not yet vacant. ~ *v.t.* Supply with provisions. **provĭ′sionment** *n.*

provĭ′sional (-zh*o*-) *adj.* For the time being, temporary, subject to revision. **provĭ′sionally** *adv.* **provĭsionăl′ity, provĭ′sionalnėss** *ns.*

provīs′ō (-z-) *n.* Stipulation; clause of stipulation or limitation in document.

provīs′or (-z-) *n.* 1. (hist.) Holder of provision or grant (esp. from pope) of right of next presentation to benefice not yet vacant; *Statute of P~s*, act of 25 Edw. III (1350–1) to prevent pope from granting such provisions. 2. (R.C. Ch.) Ecclesiastic assisting archbishop or bishop and acting in his stead; vicar-general; deputy-inquisitor.

provīs′ory (-z-) *adj.* Conditional; making provision.

prŏvocā′tion *n.* Incitement, instigation, irritation.

provŏc′ative *adj.* & *n.* (Thing) tending to provocation (*of* curiosity etc.); intentionally irritating.

provōke′ *v.t.* Rouse, incite (*to*); irritate; instigate, tempt, allure; call forth (anger, inquiry, etc.); cause. **provōk′ing** *adj.* **provōk′ingly** *adv.*

prŏv′ost *n.* 1. Head of some

colleges at Oxford, Cambridge, etc.; (hist.) head of chapter or religious community; Protestant clergyman in charge of principal church of town etc. in Germany etc. 2. Head of Scottish municipal corporation or burgh, corresponding to *mayor* in England. 3. (mil., *usu.* provō′) Officer of military police in garrison, camp, etc.; ~-*marshal*, head of military police in camp or on active service; master-at-arms of ship on which court martial is to be held; chief police official in some colonies; ~-*sergeant*, sergeant of military police. **prŏv′ostship** *n.*

prow *n.* Fore-part immediately about stem of boat or ship; (zool., also *prora*) prow-like projection in front.

prow′ėss *n.* Valour, gallantry.

prowl *v.* Go about in search of plunder or prey; traverse (streets, place) thus. ~ *n.* Prowling. **prowl′er** *n.*

prox. *abbrev. proximo.*

prox. acc. *abbrev. proxime accessit.*

prŏx′ĭmal *adj.* (anat.) Situated towards centre of body or point of attachment. **prŏx′ĭmally** *adv.*

prŏx′ĭmate *adj.* Nearest, next before or after; approximate. **prŏx′ĭmately** *adv.*

prŏx′ĭmė (accĕss′ĭt) (aks-) *n.* & *phr.* (Person, position of person, who) is nearly equal (to actual winner of prize, scholarship, etc.).

prŏxĭm′ĭty *n.* Nearness in space, time, etc.; ~ *of blood*, kinship.

prŏx′ĭmō *adj.* (abbrev. *prox.*) Of next month.

prŏx′y *n.* Agency of substitute or deputy; person authorized to act for another; writing authorizing person to vote on behalf of another, vote so given; (attrib.) done, given, made, by proxy.

prude (-ōō-) *n.* Woman of extreme (esp. affected) propriety in conduct or speech. **prud′ery** *n.* **prud′ĭsh** *adj.* **prud′ĭshly** *adv.* **prud′ĭshness** *n.*

prud′ent (-ōō-) *adj.* Sagacious, discreet, worldly-wise. **prud′ently** *adv.* **prud′ence** *n.*

prudĕn′tial (-ōō-, -shl) *adj.* Of, involving, marked by, prudence. **prudĕn′tially** *adv.*

prune[1] (-ōō-) *n.* Dried plum; colour of its juice, dark reddish purple; *prunes and prisms*, prim and mincing manner of speaking etc.

prune[2] (-ōō-) *v.t.* Trim (tree etc.) by cutting away superfluous branches etc.; lop *off*, *away* (branches etc.); (fig.) remove (superfluities), clear *of* what is superfluous; *pruning-hook*, curved knife used for pruning.

prunĕll′a (-ōō-) *n.* Strong silk or worsted stuff used formerly for barristers' gowns etc. and later for uppers of women's shoes.

prunĕll′ō (-ōō-) *n.* (archaic) Finest kind of prune, made esp. from greengages.

prŭnt *n.* Piece of ornamental glass laid on to vase etc.; tool for applying this.

prur′ĭent (-oor-) *adj.* Given to the indulgence of lewd ideas. **prur′iently** *adv.* **prur′ĭence, prur′ĭency** *ns.*

prurĭg′ō (-oor-) *n.* Disease of skin marked by violent itching.

prurī′tus (-oor-) *n.* (med.) Itching of skin.

Prussia (-ŭsh′*a*). (Ger. *Preussen*) The greater part of N. Germany; a kingdom, 1701–1871; the dominant federal State of Germany, 1871–1918; a republic, 1918–46. **Pruss′ian** *adj.* & *n.* (Native, language) of Prussia; *Old* ~, language belonging to Baltic group of Balto-Slavonic (Indo-European) languages, which became extinct in 17th c.; ~ *blue* [so-called from its discovery in Berlin, 1704], deep greenish-blue pigment of great covering power, consisting chiefly of ferric ferro-cyanide.

prŭss′ĭc *adj.* Of, got from, Prussian blue; ~ *acid*, hydrocyanic acid (HCN).

prȳ[1] *v.i.* Look, peer, inquisitively; inquire impertinently *into*. **prȳ′ĭng** *adj.* **prȳ′ĭngly** *adv.*

prȳ[2] *v.t.* (U.S.) Variant of PRIZE[2].

prȳtanē′um *n.* (Gk antiq.) Public hall, esp. one in Athens for entertainment of ambassadors, presidents of senate, and specially honoured citizens.

Ps. *abbrev.* Psalms (O.T.).

P.S. *abbrev.* Police sergeant; postscript; (also p.s.) prompt side.

psalm (sahm) *n.* Sacred song, hymn; (*Book of*) *P~s*, (pop.) *P~s of David*, O.T. book. **psalm′ĭst** *n.* Author of a psalm; *the P~*, David.

Psalmanăz′ar (săl-), George (*c* 1679–1763). Assumed name of a Frenchman who represented himself as a pagan from Formosa and invented a language ('Formosan') and a religious system; he later repented of the imposture, which is described in his Memoirs, and became a serious scholar; he was a friend of Dr Johnson.

psalm′ody (sahm- *or* săl-) *n.* Practice, art, of singing psalms, hymns, anthems, etc., esp. in public worship; arrangement of psalms for singing, psalms so arranged. **psalmŏd′ĭc** *adj.* **psalm′odĭst** *n.*

psal′ter (sawl-) *n.* The Book of Psalms; version of this; copy of the Psalms esp. for liturgical use.

psaltēr′ĭum (sawl-) *n.* Ruminant's third stomach, omasum (ill. RUMINANT).

psal′tery (sawl-) *n.* Ancient and medieval triangular stringed instrument, like dulcimer, but played by plucking with fingers or plectrum.

psephŏl′ogy (sēf-) *n.* Statistical analysis of votes cast in elections. **psephŏl′ogĭst** *n.*

pseud(o)- (*or* s-) *prefix.* False(ly), seeming(ly), professed(ly) but not real(ly).

pseud′ō-archā′ĭc (sū-; -k-) *adj.* Artificially archaic in style etc.

pseud′ograph (sū-; -ahf) *n.* Literary work purporting to be by a person other than the real author.

pseud′omorph (sū-) *n.* False form, esp. (min.) crystal etc. consisting of one compound but having the form proper to another. **pseudomorph′ĭc, -morph′ous** *adjs.*

pseud′onȳm (sū-) *n.* Fictitious name, esp. one assumed by author. **pseudŏn′ȳmous** *adj.* Writing, written, under a false name. **pseudonȳm′ĭty** *n.*

pshaw (psh-, sh-) *int.* Expressing contempt or impatience. ~ *n.* This exclamation. ~ *v.* Say 'pshaw!' (*at*); show contempt for thus.

psī *n.* Greek letter (Ψ, ψ) = ps; ~ *phenomena*, psychical phenomena supposedly independent of bodily processes, e.g. telepathy, clairvoyance.

psĭtt′acīne (sĭ-) *adj.* Of parrots, parrot-like.

psĭtt′acoid (sĭ-) *adj.* Like, akin, to the *Psittacidae* or parrots.

psittacōs′ĭs (sĭ-) *n.* Contagious disease of birds, esp. parrots, characterized by diarrhoea and wasting, and causing bronchial pneumonia when communicated to human beings.

psorī′asĭs (s-) *n.* Non-contagious skin disease marked by red scaly patches.

Psyche[1] (psīk′ĭ, s-). (Gk myth.) Soul personified as beloved of Eros (Cupid) and represented in art with butterfly wings, or as butterfly.

psyche[2] (sīk′ĭ) *n.* 1. Soul, spirit, mind. 2. Genus of day-flying moths.

psychī′atrĭst (sīk-) *n.* One who treats mental disease. **psȳchĭăt′rĭc(al)** *adjs.* **psȳchī′atry** *n.*

psy′chĭc (sīk-) *adj.* & *n.* Psychical; (person) susceptible to psychic influences, medium(istic). **psȳch′ĭcal** *adj.* 1. Of the soul or mind. 2. Of phenomena and conditions apparently outside domain of physical law and therefore attributed by some to spiritual or hyperphysical agency. **psȳch′ĭcally** *adv.* **psȳch′ĭcs** *n.pl.* Science of psychical or mental phenomena; psychology.

psych′ō-anăl′ȳsĭs (sīk-) *n.* Therapeutic method, devised by FREUD, of dealing with certain mental disorders by bringing to light complexes or repressed affects persisting in the unconscious mind; branch of psychology dealing with unconscious mind. **psȳch′ō-ăn′alȳse** (-z) *v.t.* **psȳch′ō-ănalȳt′ĭc(al)** *adjs.* **psȳch′ō-ăn′alȳst** *n.*

psychokīnēs′ĭs (sīk-) *n.* Supposed interference with physical causation by psychical intentions.

psycholŏ′gĭcal (sīk-) *adj.* Of psychology; ~ *moment*, [f. Fr.

mistranslation of Ger. *moment* (neut.) potent element, momentum, as *moment* (masc.) moment of time], the psychologically appropriate moment; (esp. joc.) the nick of time. **psȳchŏlŏ'gically** *adv.*

psychŏl'ogy (sīk-) *n.* Science of the nature, functions, and phenomena of human mind and conduct; treatise on, system of, this; *analytical* ~, introspective analysis of mental processes; (also) method of psychological inquiry akin to psycho-analysis, psychological system elaborated by C. G. JUNG.

psychŏm'ėtry (sīk-) *n.* Alleged faculty of divining from physical contact or proximity the qualities of an object or of persons etc. that have been in contact with it.

psychōmōt'or (sīk-) *adj.* Inducing movement by psychic action.

psychōneurōs'is (sīk-) *n.* (pl. *-ōsēs*). Functional disorder of the nervous system characterized by anxiety, depression, or obsessional states, without any ascertainable organic disease. **psȳchōneurŏt'ic** *adj.* & *n.* Of psychoneurosis; (person) afflicted with it.

psych'ōpăth (sīk-) *n.* Mentally deranged person. **psȳchōpăth'ic** *adj.*

psychōpathŏl'ogy (sīk-) *n.* Pathology of the mind.

psychŏp'athy (sīk-) *n.* Mental disease or disorder, esp. one affecting character or moral sense.

psychōs'is (sīk-) *n.* (pl. *-ōsēs*). Severe form of mental illness involving the entire personality. **psychŏt'ic** *adj.*

psychōsōmăt'ic (sīk-) *adj.* (Of illness) involving both mind and body; exhibiting physical symptoms but instigated by mental processes.

psychōthě'rapy (sīk-) *n.* Treatment of disease by action on the mind only, by hypnotism, suggestion etc. **psȳchōthěrapeut'ic** *adj.*

psychrŏm'ėter (sīk-) *n.* Wet-and-dry-bulb thermometer, used for measuring the relative humidity of the atmosphere.

pt *abbrev.* Part; pint; point; port.

P.T. *abbrev.* Physical training.

ptar'migan (t-) *n.* Various birds of grouse family (*Lagopus*), with black or grey plumage in summer and white in winter, inhabiting high altitudes in Scotland and northern Europe, the Alps and Pyrenees. [Gaelic *tàrmachan*]

Pte *abbrev.* Private (soldier).

ptěrodăc'tȳl (t-) *n.* Extinct winged reptile, one of the pterosaurs.

RECONSTRUCTION OF A PTERODACTYL

ptě'ropus (t-) *n.* Member of genus (*P*~) of large tropical and sub-tropical bats, flying-fox.

ptě'rosaur (t-) *n.* One of the *Pterosauria*, extinct order of mesozoic flying reptiles, with one digit of each forefoot prolonged to great length and supporting flying-membrane.

P.T.O. *abbrev.* Please turn over.

Ptŏlėmā'ic (t-) *adj.* 1. Of the PTOLEMIES. 2. Of the astronomer PTOLEMY; ~ *system*, astronomical system elaborated by Ptolemy, in which the relative motions of the sun, moon, and planets are explained as taking place round a stationary earth.

Ptŏl'ėmies (t-, -z). Dynasty of kings named Ptolemy, of Macedonian origin, that ruled over Egypt from death of Alexander the Great until Roman conquest in the reign of Cleopatra.

Ptŏl'ėmy (t-). Claudius Ptolemaeus (2nd c. A.D.), Greek astronomer, mathematician, and geographer of Alexandria.

ptomaine (tōm'ān, tomān') *n.* Formerly general name for products formed in the decay of animal organisms believed to cause food-poisoning; now applied to a particular group of organic amine compounds. [Gk *ptoma* corpse]

ptōs'is (tō-) *n.* (pl. *-sēs*). (path.) Drooping of one or both upper eyelids; downward displacement of any organ.

pŭb *n.* (colloq.) Public house; ~ *crawl*, calling at several pubs and drinking at each.

pū'berty *n.* Being functionally capable of procreation; *age of* ~, age at which puberty begins (in England, legally, 14 in boys, 12 in girls).

pū'bēs *n.* Hypogastric region, covered with hair in the adult.

pūbĕs'cence *n.* 1. Arrival at puberty. 2. (bot.) Soft down on leaves and stems of plants; downiness; (zool.) soft down on parts of animals, esp. insects. **pūbĕs'cent** *adj.*

pū'bic *adj.* Of pubes or pubis.

pū'bis *n.* Part of innominate bone forming anterior wall of pelvis (ill. PELVIS).

pŭb'lic *adj.* 1. Of, concerning, the people as a whole. 2. Done by or for, representing, the people. 3. Open to, shared by, the people; provided by, managed or controlled by, the community as a whole. 4. (universities) Of, for, acting for, the whole university (as dist. from colleges, etc.). 5. ~ *house*, inn, tavern, providing food and lodging, esp. alcoholic liquors to be consumed on premises; *P*~ *Orator*: see ORATOR; ~ *relations officer* (abbrev. P.R.O.), person who gives out information to the public in connexion with some department etc.; ~ *school*, secondary school, esp. (in England) endowed grammar- (usu. boarding-) school administered by a board of governors, preparing pupils chiefly for universities or public services, and of which the headmaster is a member of the Headmasters' Conference; (in Scotland, America, etc.) school provided at public expense and managed by public authority as part of system of public (and usu. free) education; ~ *utilities*, services or supplies commonly available in large towns, as buses, drainage, water, gas, electricity, etc. 6. Open to general observation, done or existing in public; of, engaged in, the affairs or service of the people; ~-*spirited*, animated or prompted by zeal for the common good. **pŭb'licly** *adv.* **pŭb'lic** *n.* 1. The (members of the) community in general; section of the community; *in* ~, publicly, openly. 2. (colloq.) Public house.

pŭb'lican *n.* 1. (Rom. hist.) One who farmed public taxes; tax-gatherer. 2. Keeper of public house.

pŭblicā'tion *n.* Making publicly known; issuing of book, engraving, music, etc., to the public; book etc. so issued.

pŭb'licist *n.* 1. Writer on, person skilled in, international law. 2. Writer on current public topics, esp. journalist. 3. Publicity agent.

pŭbli'city *n.* Being or making public; esp. (business of) advertising or making things or persons publicly known; ~ *agent*, person employed for this purpose.

pŭb'licize *v.t.* Bring to public notice, advertise.

pŭb'lish *v.t.* Make generally known, noise abroad; announce formally, promulgate (edict etc.); ask, read (banns of marriage); issue copies of (book etc.) for sale to the public. **pŭb'lisher** *n.* (esp.) One whose business is producing copies of books etc., and distributing them to booksellers etc. or to the public.

Puccini (po͝ochēn'ĭ), Giacomo (1858–1924). Italian operatic composer, famous for his 'La Bohème', 'Tosca', and 'Madame Butterfly'.

pūce *adj.* & *n.* Flea-colour, purple-brown.

pŭck[1] *n.* Rubber disc used in ice hockey.

Pŭck[2]. A merry mischievous sprite or goblin believed, esp. in 16th and 17th centuries, to haunt the English countryside; also called Robin Goodfellow or Hobgoblin; in earlier superstition, an evil demon. **pŭck** *n.* Mischievous child. **pŭck'ish** *adj.*

pucka: see PUKKA.

pŭck'er *v.* Contract, gather (*up*), into wrinkles, folds, or bulges, intentionally or as fault e.g. in sewing. ~ *n.* Such wrinkle etc.

pudd'ing (po͝o-) *n.* Soft or stiffish mixture of animal or vegetable ingredients, esp. mixed or enclosed in flour or other farinaceous food, cooked by boiling, steaming, or baking (*plum* ~, steamed mixture of dried fruits, flour, fat, etc.); intestine of pig etc. stuffed with minced meat, suet, oatmeal, etc.; sweet course of meal; (naut.) pad, tow binding, to prevent chafing, etc.; *~-cloth*, cloth in which some puddings are tied up for boiling; ~ *face*, large fat face; *~-stone*, conglomerate rock of rounded dark pebbles set in a brown matrix, resembling plum pudding in appearance.

pŭdd'le *n.* 1. Small dirty pool, esp. of rain on road etc. 2. Clay (and sand) mixed with water as watertight covering for embankments etc. ~ *v.* 1. Dabble, wallow (*about*) in mud or shallow water; busy oneself in untidy way; make (water) muddy. 2. Knead (clay and sand) into, make, line (canal etc.) with, puddle. 3. Stir about (a mixture of molten cast iron and iron ore) in a reverberatory furnace so as to expel the carbon and convert it into malleable iron. **pŭdd'ler** *n.* **pŭdd'ly** *adj.*

pūd'ency *n.* Modesty.

pūdĕn'dum *n.* (usu. in pl. *-da*). Privy parts, external genital organs. **pūdĕn'dal** *adj.* [L *pudere* be ashamed]

pŭdge *n.* (colloq.) Short thick or fat person, animal, or thing. **pŭdg'y** *adj.*

pueb'lo(pwĕ-) *n.* (pl. *-s*). Spanish (-American) town or village, esp. communal village or settlement of Indians in Arizona, New Mexico, and adjacent parts of Mexico and Texas; *P~ Indians*, short, dark-skinned agricultural Indians, of several linguistic stocks, dwelling in pueblos in semi-desert areas in SW. of N. America.

pū'erīle *adj.* Boyish, childish; trivial. **pū'erīlely** *adv.* **pūerĭl'ĭty** *n.*

pūĕrp'eral *adj.* Of, due to, childbirth.

Puert'ō Ric'o (pwẽr-, rē-), **Pōrt'ō Rico.** Easternmost island of Greater Antilles, taken by U.S. in Spanish-American war (1898); capital, San Juan.

pŭff *n.* 1. Short quick blast of breath or wind; sound (as) of this; small quantity of vapour, smoke, etc., emitted at one puff. 2. Round soft protuberant mass of material in dress, of hair of head, etc.; (*powder-~*) small pad of down or the like for applying powder to skin. 3. Piece, cake, etc., of light pastry, esp. of ~ *paste*, light flaky paste. 4. Unduly or extravagantly laudatory review of book, advertisement of tradesman's goods, etc., esp. in newspaper. 5. *~-adder*, large very venomous African viper (*Bitis arietans*) which inflates upper part of body when excited; *~-ball*, fungus (*Lycoperdon*) with ball-shaped spore-case, emitting spores in cloud of fine powder when broken; *~-sleeve*, short very full sleeve gathered into band, etc., at bottom. ~ *v.* 1. Emit puff of air or breath; come *out*, *up*, in puffs; breathe hard, pant; put out of breath; utter pantingly; emit puffs, move with puffs; blow (dust, smoke, light object, *away*, *out*, etc.) with puff; smoke (pipe) in puffs. 2. Blow *out*, *up*, inflate; become inflated, swell *up*, *out*; ~ *up*, elate, make proud (esp. in past part.). 3. Advertise (goods etc.) with exaggerated or false praise.

pŭff'in *n.* N.-Atlantic sea-bird (*Fratercula arctica*) with very large furrowed particoloured bill; other birds of this genus.

pŭff'y *adj.* Gusty; short-winded; puffed out; corpulent. **pŭff'inėss** *n.*

pŭg[1] *n.* 1. Dwarf squat-faced breed of dog like miniature bulldog; *~-nose*, short squat or snub nose. 2. Small locomotive for shunting etc.

pŭg[2] *n.* Loam or clay mixed and prepared for brickmaking etc. ~ *v.t.* Prepare (clay) for brickmaking by kneading and working it into soft and plastic condition; pack (space, esp. that under floor, to deaden sound) with pug, cement, etc.

pŭg[3] *n.* (Anglo-Ind.) Footprint of a beast. ~ *v.t.* Track by pugs. [Hindi *pag* footprint]

pŭg[4] *n.* (slang) Abbrev. of PUGILIST.

pŭgg'aree (-rĭ) *n.* (Anglo-Ind.) Indian's light turban; thin scarf of muslin etc. worn round hat and sometimes falling down behind to keep off sun.

pū'gilist *n.* Boxer, fighter. **pū'gilism** *n.* **pūgilis'tic** *adj.* **pūgilis'tically** *adv.*

Pū'gin, Augustus Welby Northmore (1812–52). English architect; one of the leaders of the Gothic revival; designer of the decorative detail of the Houses of Parliament.

pŭgnā'cious (-shus) *adj.* Disposed to fight, quarrelsome. **pŭgnā'ciously** *adv.* **pŭgnă'city** *n.*

puisne (pūn'ĭ) *adj.* & *n.* (law) Later, of subsequent date; ~ (*judge*), inferior or junior judge in superior courts of common law.

pū'issant (*or* pwĭs-) *adj.* (archaic) Having great power or influence, mighty. **pū'issantly** *adv.* **pū'issance** *n.*

pūke *v.* Vomit.

pŭkk'a (less usu. **pucka**) *adj.* (Anglo-Ind.) Real, genuine, true; permanent, solidly built; ~ *sahib*, (freq. derisive) real gentleman. [Hindi *pakkā* cooked, ripe; thorough, permanent]

puku: see POOKOO.

pŭl'chritūde (-k-) *n.* Beauty.

pūle *v.i.* Cry querulously or weakly, whine. **pūl'ingly** *adv.*

Pul'itzer (pŏŏ-), Joseph (1847–1911). American newspaper-owner and editor, of Hungarian origin, one of the founders of American sensational journalism; ~ *Prizes*, money prizes established under his will and offered annually to American citizens for work in music, journalism, American history and biography, poetry, drama, and fiction.

pull (pŏŏl) *v.* 1. Exert upon (thing) force tending to draw it to oneself; draw (thing etc.) towards oneself or in direction so regarded; exert pulling force; pluck (plant, freq. *up*) by root; proceed with effort (*up* hill etc.); (of horse) strain against bit; (U.S.) draw or fire (gun etc.); ~ *to pieces*, forcibly separate parts of; (fig.) criticize unfavourably; ~ *person's leg*: see LEG. 2. Draw, suck, *at* (pipe, tankard, etc.); tear, pluck, *at*. 3. Print upon (sheet), print (copy, proof), orig. in old hand-press by pulling bar towards one. 4. Move (boat), move boat, by pulling oar; (of boat) be rowed, be rowed by (so many oars); ~ one's *weight*, row with effect in proportion to one's weight; perform one's due share of work etc. 5. (slang) Arrest; make raid on (gambling-house etc.). 6. Check (horse), esp. so as to make him lose race. 7. (cricket) Strike (ball, or abs.), strike ball bowled by (bowler), from off to leg; (golf) hit (ball, or abs.) widely to the left, or (of left-handed player) to the right. 8. ~ *a face*, distort features into grimace; ~ *about*, pull from side to side; treat roughly; ~ *down*, demolish (building etc.); lower in health, spirits, price, etc.; ~ *off*, win (prize, contest); ~ *out*, row out; draw out of (a position); (of train) move out of station; *~-out* (*n.*) page or plate in book that folds out from front edge of leaves to facilitate reference; *pull'over*, knitted or woven garment for upper part of body, pulled on over head; ~ *through*, get (person), get oneself, safely through (danger, illness, etc.); *~-through* (*n.*) cord with which cleaning-rag is drawn through rifle; ~ *together*, work in harmony; ~ one*self together*, rally, recover oneself; ~ *up*, cause (person, horse, vehicle) to stop; reprimand; check oneself; advance one's relative position in race etc. ~ *n.* 1. Act of pulling, wrench, tug; force thus exerted; (fig.) means of exerting influence, interest with the powerful; *have the* ~ *on*, *of*, *over*, etc., have (esp. unfair) advantage over. 2. (print.) Rough proof. 3. Spell of rowing; pulling at bridle to check horse; (cricket, golf) pulled stroke; deep draught of liquor; draw at pipe. 4. Handle etc. by which pull is applied.

pull'ėt (pŏŏ-) *n.* Young fowl, esp. hen from time she begins to lay till first moult.

pull'ey (pŏŏ-) *n.* One of the simple mechanical powers, consisting of grooved wheel(s) for cord etc. to pass over, mounted in block and used for lifting a weight or changing direction of power; wheel, drum, fixed on shaft and turned by belt, used esp. to increase speed or power. ~ *v.t.* Hoist, furnish, work, with pulley.

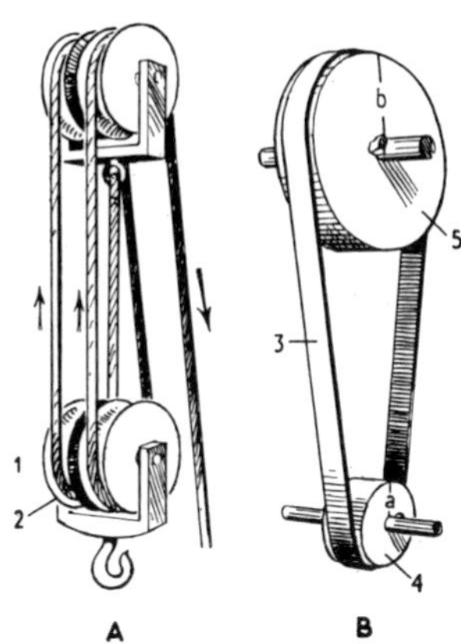

A. PULLEY, HOIST, OR TACKLE. B. BELT DRIVE

A. 1. Block. 2. Pulley or sheave. The theoretical mechanical advantage is 4:1. B. 3. Belt. 4. Driving pulley. 5. Driven pulley. The theoretical mechanical advantage is in the ratio of *b* to *a*

Pull'man (pŏŏl-) *adj.* & *n.* ~ (*coach*), railway-coach constructed and arranged as comfortable saloon, dining-car, or sleeping-car. [George M. *Pullman*, designer]

pŭll'ūlāte *v.i.* (Of shoot, bud) sprout out, bud; (of seed) sprout; (fig.) develop, spring up. **pŭll'ūlant** *adj.* **pŭllūlā'tion** *n.*

pŭl'monary *adj.* Of, in, connected with, the lungs; having lungs or lung-like organs; affected with, subject to, lung-disease. **pŭl'monate, pŭlmŏn'ĭc** *adjs.*

pŭl'mōtor *n.* (U.S.) Apparatus used to sustain artificial respiration by mechanical means.

pŭlp *n.* Fleshy part of fruit; any fleshy or soft part of animal body, e.g. nervous substance in interior cavity of tooth; soft formless mass, esp. that of linen, wood, etc., from which paper is made; ore pulverized and mixed with water. ~ *v.* Reduce to pulp; remove pulp from (coffee-beans); become pulpy. **pŭlp'y̆** *adj.*

pul'pĭt (pŏŏ-) *n.* Raised enclosed platform usu. with desk and seat from which preacher in church or chapel delivers sermon; *the* profession of preaching, preachers; (R.A.F. slang) cockpit of aeroplane.

pulque (pŏŏl'kē) *n.* Mexican fermented drink from sap of agave etc.

pŭlsāte' (*or* pŭl'-) *v.* Expand and contract rhythmically, beat, throb; vibrate, quiver, thrill; agitate (diamonds) with machine called *pulsator* to separate them from earth in which they are found. **pŭlsā'tion** *n.* **pŭl'satory** *adj.*

pŭl'satĭle *adj.* Of, having the property of, pulsation; (of musical instrument) played by percussion.

pŭlsatĭll'a *n.* Pasque-flower, kind of anemone; its extract used in pharmacy.

pŭlse[1] *n.* Rhythmical throbbing of arteries as blood is pumped into them from the heart, used, as felt in wrists, temples, etc., to measure the heart rate; each successive beat of arteries or heart; (fig.) throb, thrill, of life or emotion; rhythmical recurrence of strokes, e.g. of oars; single beat or vibration of sound, light, etc.; (mus.) beat. ~ *v.* Pulsate; send *out*, *in*, etc., by rhythmic beats. **pŭlse'lėss** (-sl-) *adj.* **pŭlse'lėssnėss** *n.*

pŭlse[2] *n.* Edible seeds of leguminous plants, e.g. peas, beans, lentils; (with pl.) any kind of these.

pŭl'verīze *v.* Reduce to powder or dust, crumble into dust; divide (liquid) into spray; (fig.) demolish, crush, smash. **pŭlverīzā'tion** *n.*

pŭlvĕ'rŭlent *adj.* Powdery, of dust; covered with powder; (of rock etc.) of slight cohesion, apt to crumble.

pūm'a *n.* = COUGAR.

pŭm'ĭce *n.* (also ~*-stone*) Very light porous stone formed by the solidified froth on the surface of glassy lava, used, freq. powdered, for polishing and abrading; piece of this for removing stains from hands.

pŭmm'el *v.t.* Strike repeatedly, esp. with fist.

pŭmp[1] *n.* Machine for moving fluid from one place to another, e.g. raising water, or for compressing or rarefying gas, or for similar purpose, e.g. inflating tyres, formerly always with rod and piston, now freq. rotary in action; action of working a pump; stroke of pump; (fig.) attempt at extracting information from person; ~*-handle* (*v.*) (colloq.) shake (person's hand) effusively; ~*-room*, room where pump is worked, esp. at spa where medicinal water is dispensed. ~ *v.* 1. Work a pump; remove, raise, (water etc.) thus; make *dry* by pumping; inflate (pneumatic tyre), inflate tyres of (bicycle etc.). 2. Bring out, pour forth, (*upon*) as by pumping; elicit information from (person) by artful or persistent questions. 3. (Of exertion) put completely out of breath. 4. (Of mercury in barometer) rise and fall instantaneously.

PULPIT

1. Sounding board

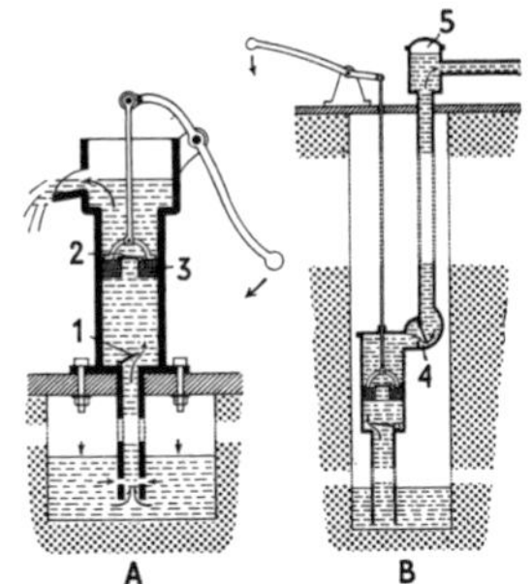

A. SUCTION-PUMP. B. FORCE PUMP

1. Flap valve or clack. 2. Piston valve. 3. Piston. 4. Delivery valve. 5. Air bottle to give even flow

pŭmp[2] *n.* (usu. pl.) Light shoe, usu. of patent leather and without fastening, worn with evening dress and for dancing.

pu'mpernĭckel (pŏŏ-) *n.* German wholemeal rye bread, dark brown and freq. sweetened and spiced.

pŭmp'kĭn *n.* Trailing plant, *Cucurbita pepo*, with heart-shaped five-lobed leaves; large egg-shaped or globular fruit of this, with edible layer next to rind, used in cookery and for cattle.

pŭn[1] *n.* Humorous use of word to suggest different meanings, or of words of same sound with different meanings, play on words. ~ *v.i.* Make puns (*upon*).

pŭn[2] *v.t.* Consolidate (earth, rubble) by pounding or ramming; work *up* to proper consistency with punner.

pu'na (pŏŏ-) *n.* High bleak plateau in Peruvian Andes; mountain sickness.

pŭnch[1] *n.* Instrument or machine for cutting holes in leather, metal, paper, etc., or for driving a bolt etc. out of a hole (*starting* ~) or forcing a nail beneath a surface (*driving* ~); tool of machine for impressing design or stamping die on material; *bell-*~, conductor's ticket-punch with bell to announce punching of ticket.

pŭnch[2] *v.* 1. Strike, esp. with closed fist; prod with stick etc., esp. (U.S.) drive (cattle) thus; *punch*(*ing*)*-ball*, inflated ball held by elastic bands etc., and punched as form of exercise. 2. Pierce (metal, leather, railway ticket, etc.) as or with punch; pierce (hole) thus; drive (nail etc. *in*, *out*) with punch. ~ *n.* Blow with fist;

(slang) vigour, momentum, effective force; *pull* one's *punches*, refrain from using one's full force; *~-drunk* (*adj.*) stupefied through being severely punched; *~-drunkenness* (*n.*) morbid condition in pugilists, marked by muscular failure and mental confusion, and resulting from repeated head concussions caused by punches.

pŭnch[3] *n.* Drink usu. of wine or spirits mixed with hot water or milk, sugar, lemons, spice, etc.;

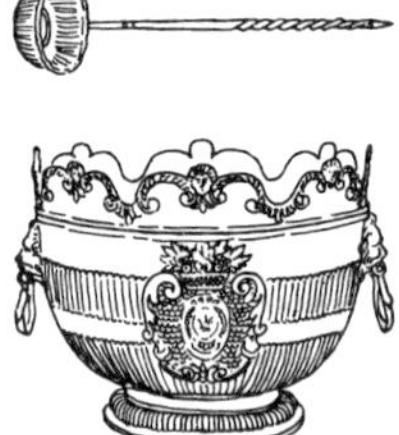

PUNCH-BOWL AND LADLE

similar mixture taken cold; bowl of punch; *~-bowl*, bowl in which punch is mixed; round deep hollow in hill(s).

pŭnch[4] *n.* (*Suffolk*) *P~*, short-legged thick-set draught horse.

Pŭnch[5]. Hook-nosed hump-backed buffoon, English variant of a stock character derived from Italian popular comedy who appeared in Italy as Pulcinella, in France as Polichinelle, in England as Punchinello or Punch; now preserved chiefly as title of an English humorous weekly periodical (founded 1841) and in *~ and Judy*, open-air puppet-show performed at fairs etc. [Neapolitan dial. *policenella*, dim. of *policena* turkey-cock, prob. with ref. to its hooked beak]

pŭn'cheon[1] (-shn) *n.* Short post, esp. one supporting roof in coal-mine.

pŭn'cheon[2] (-shn) *n.* (hist.) Large cask for liquid etc. holding from 72 to 120 gals. (ill. CASK).

Pŭnchinĕll'o: see PUNCH[5].

pŭnc'tāte *adj.* (biol., path.) Marked or studded with points, dots, or holes. **pŭnctā'tion** *n.*

pŭnctĭl'io *n.* (pl. *-s*). Nice point of ceremony or honour; petty formality. [It. *puntiglio* little point]

pŭnctĭl'ious (-lyus) *adj.* Attentive to punctilios; very careful about detail. **pŭnctĭl'iously** *adv.* **pŭnctĭl'iousnėss** *n.*

pŭnc'tūal *adj.* Observant of appointed time; in good time, not late; (archaic) punctilious. **pŭnc'tūally** *adv.* **pŭnctūăl'ity** *n.*

pŭnc'tūāte *v.t.* Insert stops, commas, etc., in (writing), mark or divide with stops, commas, etc.; (fig.) interrupt (speech etc.) *with* exclamations etc. **pŭnctūā'tion** *n.* Practice, art, of punctuating; insertion of vowel and other points in Hebrew etc.

pŭnc'tum (pl. *-a*), **pŭnc'tūle** *ns.* (biol., path.) Speck, dot, spot of colour or elevation or depression on surface. **pŭnc'tūlate** *adj.* **pŭnctūlā'tion** *n.*

pŭnc'ture *n.* Pricking, prick, esp. accidental pricking of pneumatic tyre; hole thus made. *~ v.* Prick, pierce; experience a puncture.

pŭn'dĭt *n.* Hindu learned in Sanskrit and in philosophy, religion, and jurisprudence of India; (joc.) learned expert or teacher.

pŭn'gent (-j-) *adj.* 1. Sharp-pointed (nat. hist.); (of reproof, etc.) biting, caustic; mentally stimulating, piquant. 2. Affecting organs of smell or taste, or skin etc., with pricking sensation. **pŭn'gently** *adv.* **pŭn'gency** *n.*

Pū'nĭc *adj.* Of Carthage, Carthaginian; of the character attributed by the Romans to the Carthaginians, treacherous, perfidious; *~ Wars*, 3 wars between Romans and Carthaginians (264–241, 218–201, 149–146 B.C.); in the 1st, Rome captured Sicily, her first province, from the Carthaginians under HAMILCAR; in the 2nd, the Carthaginians under HANNIBAL invaded Italy and the Romans after long resistance drove them out and destroyed the position of Carthage as a great Mediterranean power; in the 3rd, Carthage itself was besieged and destroyed.

pŭn'ĭsh *v.t.* Cause (offender) to suffer for offence; chastise; inflict penalty on (offender); inflict penalty for (offence); (colloq.) inflict severe blows on (opponent in boxing), tax severely the powers of (competitor in race etc.), take full advantage of (weak bowling, stroke at tennis, etc.), make heavy inroad on (food etc.). **pŭn'ĭshable, pŭn'ĭshĭng** *adjs.* **pŭn'ĭshment** *n.*

pū'nĭtĭve *adj.* Inflicting punishment, retributive. **pū'nĭtory** *adj.*

Pŭnja(u)b' (-jahb, -jawb). Formerly a NW. province of British India; partitioned in 1947 between the republics of India and Pakistan.

pŭnk[1] *n.* (archaic) Prostitute.

pŭnk[2] *n.* (chiefly U.S.) Rotten wood, fungus growing on wood, used as tinder; anything worthless.

pŭnk'a(h) (-ka) *n.* (E. Ind.) Portable fan usu. of leaf of palmyra; large swinging cloth fan on frame worked by cord.

pŭnn'er *n.* Tool for ramming earth about post etc.

pŭnn'ėt *n.* Small chip basket for fruit or vegetables.

pŭn'ster *n.* Maker of puns.

pŭnt[1] *n.* Flat-bottomed shallow boat, broad and square at both ends, propelled by long pole thrust against bottom of river etc. *~ v.* Propel (punt, boat, or abs.) thus; convey in a punt. **pŭnt'er**[1] *n.*

pŭnt[2] *v.t.* Kick (football) after it has dropped from the hands and before it reaches ground. *~ n.* Such kick; *~-about*, kicking about of football for practice, ball so used.

pŭnt[3] *v.i.* (At faro and other card-games) lay stake against bank; (colloq.) bet on horse etc. *~ n.* Player who punts; point in faro. **pŭnt'er**[2] *n.*

pŭnt'y̆ *n.* = PONTIL.

pū'ny *adj.* Undersized; weak, feeble; petty. **pū'nĭnėss** *n.*

pŭp *n.* Young dog, puppy; (usu. contempt.) boy, young man; *in ~*, (of bitch) pregnant; *sell person a ~*, swindle him esp. by selling thing on prospective value. *~ v.* Bring forth (pups, or abs.).

pū'pa *n.* (pl. *-ae*). Insect in its inactive pre-adult form, after larva but before imago (ill. MOSQUITO); in Lepidoptera = chrysalis. **pū'pal** *adj.*

pū'pāte *v.i.* Become a pupa. **pūpā'tion** *n.*

pū'pĭl *n.* 1. One who is taught by another, scholar; (law) person below age of puberty and under care of guardian; *~-teacher*, (hist.) boy, girl, teaching in elementary school under head teacher and concurrently receiving general education from him or elsewhere. 2. Opening (circular, in man) in centre of iris of eye regulating passage of light to the retina (ill. EYE).

pū'pĭl(l)age *n.* Nonage, minority; being a pupil. **pū'pĭl(l)ar, pū'pĭl(l)ary** *adjs.* **pūpĭl(l)ă'rity** *n.* (law).

pŭpp'ėt *n.* Figure, usu. small, representing human being etc., esp. one with jointed limbs moved by strings etc., or (*glove-~*) one made to fit over the operator's hand so that its head and arms may be manipulated by his fingers; person whose acts are controlled by another; *~-play, -show*, one with puppets as characters; *~ State, country*, one professing to be independent but actually under the control of some greater power. **pŭpp'ėtry** *n.* [Fr. *poupette* doll]

pŭpp'y̆ *n.* Young dog: vain empty-headed young man, coxcomb. **pŭpp'y̆dom, pŭpp'y̆hŏŏd, pŭpp'y̆ism** *ns.* **pŭpp'y̆ish** *adj.*

pura'na (poorah-) *n.* Any of a class of Sanskrit sacred poems, containing mythology of Hindus. **pura'nĭc** (poorah-) *adj.* [Sansk. *purana'* of former times]

Pûr'bĕck, Isle of. Peninsula on coast of Dorsetshire, England; *~ marble*, name for the finer qualities of a hard limestone quarried there for building and paving.

pûr'blĭnd *adj.* Partly blind, dim-sighted; (fig.) obtuse, dull. *~ v.t.* Make purblind.

Pûr'cell, Henry (*c* 1658–95). English musical composer, best known for his opera 'Dido and Aeneas'.

pûrch'ase *n.* 1. Buying; (law) acquisition of property by one's personal action, not by inheritance; thing bought; annual return from land; (hist.) practice of buying commissions in army; *~-money*, price (to be) paid; *~ tax*, tax levied on goods sold by retailer. 2. Mechanical advantage, leverage, fulcrum; appliance for gaining this, esp. (naut.) rope, windlass, pulley. ~ *v.t.* Buy; acquire (*with* toil, blood, etc.); (naut.) haul up (anchor etc.) by means of pulley, lever, etc. **pûrch'aser** *n.*

pûrd'ah (-da) *n.* (E. Ind.) Curtain, esp. one serving to screen women from sight of strangers; striped material for curtains; (fig.) Indian system of secluding women of rank.

pūre *adj.* Unmixed, unadulterated; (of sounds) not discordant, esp. (mus.) perfectly in tune; of unmixed descent, pure-blooded; mere, simple, nothing but, sheer; not corrupt; morally undefiled, guiltless, sincere; sexually undefiled; (Gk gram. etc.), (of vowel) preceded by another vowel, (of stem) ending in vowel, (of consonant) not accompanied by another; *~ mathematics*, theoretical mathematics, not including practical applications. **pure'ly** (-ūrl-) *adv.* **pūre'nĕss** *n.*

purée (pūr'ā) *n.* Vegetables, fruit, etc. (boiled to pulp and) passed through sieve.

pûr'fle *n.* (archaic) Border, esp. embroidered edge of garment. ~ *v.t.* Adorn (robe) with purfle: ornament (edge of building *with* crockets etc.); beautify. **pûr'fling** *n.* (esp.) Inlaid bordering on back and belly of fiddles.

pûrgā'tion *n.* Purification, purging; purging of bowels; spiritual cleansing, esp. (R.C. Ch.) of soul in purgatory; (hist.) clearing of oneself from accusation or suspicion by oath or ordeal.

pûrg'ative *adj.* Aperient; serving to purify. ~ *n.* Purgative medicine.

pûrg'atory *n.* Condition, place, of spiritual purging, esp. (R.C. Ch.) of souls departing this life in grace of God but requiring to be cleansed from venial sins etc.; place of temporary suffering or expiation. ~ *adj.* Purifying. **pûrgatôr'ial** *adj.*

pûrge *v.t.* Make physically or spiritually clean; rid (political party, army, etc.) of objectionable, alien, or extraneous elements or members; remove by cleansing process; (of medicine) relieve (bowels, or abs.) by evacuation; clear (*of* charge, suspicion); (law) atone for, wipe out, (offence, sentence) by expiation and submission. ~ *n.* 1. Aperient medicine. 2. Purging; ridding of objectionable or hostile elements; PRIDE's ~: see entry.

pūrificā'tion *n.* Purifying; ritual cleansing, esp. that of woman after child-birth enjoined by Jewish law; *the P~ (of the Blessed Virgin Mary)*, festival (in Western Church, 2nd Feb.) of presentation of Christ in the Temple or completion of 'days of her purification' (Luke ii. 22). **pūr'ificātory** *adj.*

pūr'ificātor *n.* (eccles.) Cloth used at communion for wiping chalice and paten, and fingers and lips of celebrant.

pūr'ifȳ *v.t.* Make pure, cleanse (*of, from,* impurities, sin, etc.); make ceremonially clean; clear of foreign elements.

Pūr'im. Jewish festival on 14th and 15th of month Adar (Feb.–March), commemorating defeat of Haman's plot (Esther ix).

pūr'ist *n.* Stickler for, affecter of, scrupulous purity esp. in language. **pūr'ism** *n.* **pūris'tic(al)** *adjs.*

Pūr'itan. 1. Member of that party of English Protestants who regarded the Reformation under Elizabeth as incomplete and demanded further 'purification' of the Church from forms and ceremonies still retained; any of those who later separated from the Established Church on points of ritual, polity, or doctrine, held by them to be at variance with 'pure' New Testament principles. 2. One who is, is thought or affects to be, extremely strict, precise, or scrupulous in religion or morals. **Pūrităn'ic(al)** *adjs.* **Pūr'itanism** *n.*

pūr'ity *n.* Pureness, cleanness, freedom from physical or moral pollution.

pûrl[1] *n.* 1. Cord of twisted gold or silver wire for bordering; chain of minute loops, each loop of this, ornamenting edges of lace, ribbon, etc. 2. (knitting) Stitch in which needle is inserted through loop from right to left, and yarn is looped over needle from the front (ill. KNIT). ~ *v.* Border with purl; invert (stitches or abs.), invert stitches of, in knitting.

pûrl[2] *v.i.* (Of brook etc.) flow with whirling motion and babbling sound. ~ *n.* Such motion or sound.

pûrl[3] *n.* (hist.) Ale or beer with wormwood infused; hot beer mixed with gin as morning draught, dog's-nose.

pûrl[4] *v.* (colloq.) Turn upside down, upset. ~ *n.* Cropper, heavy fall. **pûrl'er** *n.* (colloq.) Headlong fall.

pûrl'ieu (-lū) *n.* Tract on border of forest, esp. one earlier included in it and still partly subject to forest laws; one's bounds, limits; (pl.) outskirts, outlying region. [prob. f. AF *puralé* perambulation to settle boundaries]

pûrl'in *n.* Horizontal beam running along length of roof, resting on principals and supporting common rafters or boards (ill. ROOF).

purloin' (per-) *v.t.* Steal, pilfer.

pûr'ple *n.* & *adj.* 1. (Of) a colour mixed of red and blue in varying proportions. 2. (hist., also *Tyrian* ~) (Of) the colour got from the molluscs *Purpura* and *Murex*, and associated with the dress and rank or office of emperors, consuls, kings, etc.; crimson; *the ~*, imperial, royal, or consular rank, power, or office; scarlet official dress of cardinal's rank or office. ~ *v.* Make, become, purple. **pûr'plish, pûr'plȳ** *adjs.*

purpoint: see POURPOINT.

pûrp'ort *n.* Meaning, sense, tenor, of document or speech. **purpôrt'** (per-) *v.t.* (Of document or speech) have as its meaning, convey, state; profess, be intended to seem (*to* do).

pûrp'ose (-us) *n.* Object, thing intended; fact, faculty, of resolving on something; *on ~*, in order (*to, that*); designedly, not by accident; *to the ~*, relevant, useful for one's purpose; *to good, little, no,* etc., *~*, with good, little, etc., effect or result. ~ *v.t.* Design, intend. **pûrp'osely** *adv.* **pûrp'oseful** (-sf-) *adj.* **pûrp'osefully** *adv.* **pûrp'osefulnĕss** *n.* **pûrp'oselĕss** *adj.* **pûrp'oselĕssly** *adv.* **pûrp'oselĕssnĕss** *n.*

pûrp'osive *adj.* Having, serving, done with, a purpose; having purpose and resolution.

pûrp'ūra *n.* 1. Disease, due to morbid state of the blood or blood-vessels, characterized by purple or livid spots on skin. 2. (Mollusc of) gastropod genus including some from which ancient purple dye was derived. **purpūr'ic** (per-) *adj.*

pûrp'ure *n.* (her.) Purple (ill. HERALDRY).

pûrp'ūrin *n.* Red dye orig. got from madder.

pûrr *v.* (Of cat or other feline animal, fig. of person) make low continuous vibratory sound expressing pleasure; utter, express (words, contentment) thus. ~ *n.* This sound. [imit.]

pûrse *n.* Small pouch of leather etc. for carrying money on the person, orig. closed by drawing strings together; (fig.) money, funds; sum collected, subscribed, or given, as present or as prize for contest; bag-like natural or other receptacle, pouch, cyst, etc.; *public ~*, national treasury; *~-bearer*, one who has charge of another's or a company's money; official carrying Great Seal before Lord Chancellor in purse; *~-net*, bag-shaped net for catching rabbits etc., mouth of which can be drawn close with cords; *~-proud*, puffed up by wealth; *~-strings*, strings for closing mouth of purse; *hold the ~-strings*, have control of expenditure. ~ *v.* Contract (lips etc., freq. *up*) in wrinkles; become wrinkled.

pûrs'er *n.* Officer on ship who keeps accounts and usu. has charge of provisions; in modern passenger ship, head of stewards' department, superintending comfort and requirements of passengers.

pûrs′lane (-ĭn) *n.* Low succulent herb, *Portulaca oleracea* var. *sativa*, used in salads and pickled.

pursū′ance (per-) *n.* Carrying out, pursuing, esp. in *in* ~ *of* (plan etc.).

pursū′ant (per-) *adj.* Pursuing. ~ *adv.* Conformably *to*.

pursūe′ (per-) *v.* Follow with intent to capture or kill; persistently attend, stick to; seek after, aim at; proceed in compliance with (plan etc.); proceed along, continue, follow (road, inquiry, studies, etc.); go in pursuit. **pursū′er** *n.* (esp. civil and Sc. law) Prosecutor.

pursuit (persūt′) *n.* Pursuing; profession, employment, recreation, that one follows.

pûrs′uivant (-sw-) *n.* Officer of College of Arms below herald; (poet.) follower, attendant.

pûrs′y *adj.* Short-winded, puffy; corpulent.

pûrt′enance *n.* (archaic) Inwards, pluck, of animal.

pūr′ulent (-rōō-) *adj.* Of, full of, discharging, pus. **pūr′ulently** *adv.* **pūr′ulence** *n.*

purvey (pervā′) *v.* Provide, supply (articles of food) as one's business; make provision, act as purveyor.

purvey′ance (pervā′ans) *n.* Purveying; (hist.) right of crown to provisions etc. at price fixed by *purveyor*, and to use of horses etc.

purvey′or (pervā′er) *n.* One whose business it is to supply (esp.) articles of food, dinners etc., on large scale; (hist.) officer making purveyance for sovereign.

pûrv′iew (-vū) *n.* Enacting clauses of statute; scope, intention, range (*of* act, document, etc.); range of physical or mental vision.

pŭs *n.* (path.) Yellowish viscid fluid formed by the liquefaction of dead tissues, usu. containing leucocytes, cell debris, and bacteria.

Pusey (pūz′ĭ), Edward Bouverie (1800–82). English churchman, one of the leaders of the Oxford or TRACTARIAN movement. **Pus′eyism** (-zĭĭ-), **Pus′eyite** *ns.*

push (pōō-) *v.* 1. Exert upon (body) force tending to move it away; move thus; exert such pressure; (billiards) make push-stroke; (cause to) project, thrust *out*, *forward*, etc.; make one's way forcibly or persistently, force (one's *way*) thus; ~ *off*, (of person in boat) push against bank etc. with oar to get boat out into stream etc.; (colloq. or slang) leave, go away. 2. Exert oneself, esp. to surpass others or succeed in one's business etc.; urge, impel; follow up (claim etc.); carry (action, matter, etc.) to further point, or to farthest limit; press the adoption, use, sale, etc., of (goods, etc.) esp. by advertisement; press (person) hard, esp. in passive. **push′er** *n.* **push′ing** *adj.* **push′ingly** *adv.* **push** *n.* 1. Act of pushing, shove, thrust; (billiards) stroke in which ball is pushed, not struck; thrust of weapon, beast's horn, etc.; *give, get the* ~, (slang) dismiss, be dismissed. 2. Vigorous effort; exertion of influence; (mil.) attack in force; pressure of affairs, crisis, pinch. 3. Enterprise, determination to get on, self-assertion. 4. (slang) Gang or band; 'set'. 5. Contrivance etc. pushed or pressed to operate mechanism; ~*-ball*, game in which very large ball is pushed, not kicked, towards opponents' goal; ~*-bike*, (slang), *-cycle*, bicycle worked by pedalling; ~*-chair*, light chair on wheels for pushing; ~*-stroke*, push (in billiards etc.). **push′ful** *adj.*

Pu′shkin (pōō-), Alexander Sergevevich (1799–1837). Russian poet and prose-writer, the first national poet of Russia.

Pushtu: see PASHTU.

pūsillăn′imous (-z-) *adj.* Fainthearted, mean-spirited. **pūsillăn′imously** *adv.* **pūsillanim′ity** *n.*

puss (pōōs) *n.* Cat (esp. as conventional proper name); (quasi-proper name for) hare; (colloq.) girl; ~ *in the corner*, children's game in which player standing in centre tries to capture one of the 'bases' as the others change places; ~ *moth*, large downy-looking European moth (*Cerura vinula*), with whitish or light-grey forewings marked with darker colour.

puss′y (pōō-) *n.* Cat (esp. in nursery use); ~ *willow*, the goat willow (*Salix caprea*) and allied species, with silky catkins; (U.S.) the glaucous willow (*S. discolor*).

puss′yfōōt (pōō-) *n.* (U.S.) One who advocates or supports the prohibition of alcoholic liquor. ~ *v.* (U.S.) Tread softly or lightly; proceed warily. [nickname of Amer. prohibition lecturer, W. E. Johnson (1862–1945), given on account of his stealthy methods when a magistrate]

pŭs′tūlāte *v.* Form into pustules.

pŭs′tūle *n.* Pimple; *malignant* ~, anthrax. **pŭs′tūlar, pŭs′tūlous** *adjs.*

put[1] (pōōt) *v.* (past t. and past part. *put*). 1. Propel, hurl (*the weight, stone*) from hand placed close to shoulder, as athletic exercise; (naut.) proceed, take one's course (*back, in, off, out*, etc.). 2. Move (thing etc.) so as to place it in some situation; convey (person) across river etc.; harness (horse etc.) *to* vehicle. 3. Bring into some relation, state, or condition; translate *into* another language, turn (*into* speech or writing, words); apply *to* use or purpose; submit *to* vote etc.; subject *to* (suffering); ~ *an end, stop*, etc., bring to an end, stop; ~ *upon*, oppress, victimize; ~ (horse) *at*, urge him towards (obstacle etc.). 4. ~ *about*, lay (sailing vessel) on opposite tack; cause to turn round; (of vessel) go about; (chiefly north. and Sc.) trouble, put to inconvenience; ~ *away*, (archaic) divorce; lay by (money etc.) for future use; (slang) consume (food, drink); ~ *back*, check the advance of, retard; move back the hands of (clock); restore to former place; ~ *by*, lay aside esp. for future use; ~ *down*, suppress by force or authority; take down, snub, put to silence; (of domestic animals) put to death, have destroyed; cease to maintain (expensive thing); account, reckon; ~ *forth*, exert (strength, effort, etc.); (of plant) send out (buds, leaves, etc.); ~ *forward*, thrust into prominence; advance, set forth (theory etc.); ~ *in*, install in office etc.; present formally (evidence, plea, etc.) as in law-court; interpose; throw in (additional thing); (colloq.) pass, spend (time); make (*an appearance*); ~ *off*, postpone; postpone engagement with (person); evade (person, demand, freq. *with* excuse, etc.); hinder, dissuade *from*; foist (thing *upon* person); remove, take off (clothes); (of boat etc.) leave shore; ~ *on*, clothe oneself or another with; assume, take on (character, appearance); develop additional (flesh, weight); add (*to*); stake (*on* horse etc.); advance the hands of (clock); bring into action, exert (force, speed, steam, etc.); appoint, arrange for, (person) to bowl etc., (train) to run etc.; ~ *out*, dislocate (joint); (cricket) cause (batsman) to be out; extinguish; disconcert, confuse; annoy, irritate; put to inconvenience; exert (strength etc.); lend (money) at interest, invest; give (work) to be done off the premises; ~ *through*, carry out (task); place (person) in telephonic connexion with another through exchange(s); ~ *together*, form (whole) by combination of parts; ~ *up*, employ as jockey; cause (game bird) to rise from cover; raise (price); offer (prayer), present (petition); propose for election; publish banns; offer for sale by auction or for competition; pack in parcel, place in receptacle for safe keeping; sheathe (sword); lodge and entertain; construct, build; ~ (person's) *back up*, enrage him; ~ (person) *up to*, inform him of, instruct him in, instigate him; ~ *up with*, submit to, tolerate; ~*-up* (*adj.*) fraudulently concocted. ~ *n.* Throw, cast, of the weight or stone.

pŭt[2] *v.* Now less usual form of PUTT.

pūt′ative *adj.* Reputed, supposed. **pūt′atively** *adv.*

pŭt′lŏg *n.* One of the short horizontal timbers on which scaffold-boards rest (ill. SCAFFOLDING).

pūt′rėfȳ *v.i.* Become putrid, rot, go bad; fester, suppurate. **pūtrėfăc′tion** *n.* **pūt′rėfăctive** *adj.*

pūtrĕs′cent *adj.* In process of rotting; of, accompanying, this process. **pūtrĕs′cence** *n.*

pūt'rĭd *adj.* Decomposed, rotten; foul, noxious; (fig.) corrupt; (slang) of poor or bad quality, unpleasant. **pūt'rĭdly** *adv.* **pūt'rĭdnėss, pūtrĭd'ĭty** *ns.*

putsch (-ŏŏ-) *n.* A revolutionary attempt, *coup d'état.* [Swiss Ger., = 'thrust', 'blow']

pŭtt *v.* Strike golf-ball, strike (golf-ball) gently and carefully with the putter so as to make it roll along the putting-green with the object of getting it into the hole; *putt'ing-green,* smooth piece of turf round each hole on golf-course on which the ball is putted; similar piece of ground usu. with 9 or 18 holes for putting. ~ *n.* Putting stroke.

pŭtt'ee *n.* Long strip of cloth wound spirally round leg from ankle to knee for protection and support. [Hind. *paṭṭī* bandage]

pŭtt'er *n.* Straight-faced club used in putting (ill. GOLF).

pŭtt'y *n.* 1. (*jewellers'* ~) Powder of calcined tin (and lead) for polishing glass or metal. 2. (*plasterers'* ~) Fine mortar of lime and water without sand. 3. (*glaziers'* ~) Cement of whiting, raw linseed oil, etc., for fixing panes of glass, filling up holes in woodwork, etc. ~ *v.t.* Cover, fix, join, fill *up,* with putty.

pŭzz'le *n.* Bewilderment, perplexity; perplexing question, enigma; problem, toy, contrived to exercise ingenuity and patience. ~ *v.* Perplex; be perplexed; make *out* by exercising ingenuity and patience. **pŭzz'lement** *n.* **pŭzz'lingly** *adv.*

P.W.D. *abbrev.* Public Works Department.

pxt *abbrev. Pinxit.*

pȳaem'ĭa *n.* Severe infection of the blood by virulent bacteria accompanied by acute fever and formation of abscesses in liver, lungs, kidneys, etc.

Pȳgmāl'ion (-yon). (Gk legend) A king of Cyprus who made a statue of a woman and fell in love with it; he prayed Aphrodite for a wife like it, and she endowed the statue with life.

pў̆g'my, pĭ- *n.* One of a diminutive race of men stated in ancient history and tradition to have inhabited parts of Ethiopia or India; member of dwarf races of equatorial Africa, Negrillo; dwarf; elf, pixy. ~ *adj.* Of the pygmies; dwarf. [Gk *pugmē* length from elbow to knuckle]

pў̆jamas (-ahm'*az*), **paj-** (U.S.) *n.pl.* Loose silk or cotton trousers tied round waist, worn by both sexes among Mohammedans and adopted esp. for night wear by Europeans; sleeping suit of loose trousers and jacket. [Pers. *pae jamah* leg clothing]

pȳl'on *n.* 1. Gateway, esp. of Egyptian temple, with two truncated pyramidal towers connected by lower architectural member containing the gate. 2. Structure used to mark out aeroplane course; tall (metal) structure for supporting power cables.

pȳlōr'us *n.* (anat.) Opening from stomach into duodenum; part of stomach where this is (ill. ALIMENTARY canal). **pȳlŏ'rĭc** *adj.* [Gk *pulōros* gate-keeping]

Pў̆m, John (1584–1643). English statesman and Parliamentary leader; one of the 5 members whom Charles I attempted to seize before the outbreak of the Civil War.

pyorrhoea (pīorē'*a*) *n.* Disease of the tooth-sockets, accompanied by a discharge of pus and slight local haemorrhage.

pȳr'acănth, pȳracăn'thus *ns.* Evergreen thorny shrub (of genus *Pyracantha*) with white flowers and scarlet berries.

pў̆'ramid *n.* Monumental (esp. ancient Egyptian) structure of stone etc. with polygonal or (usu.) square base and sloping sides meeting at apex; solid of this shape

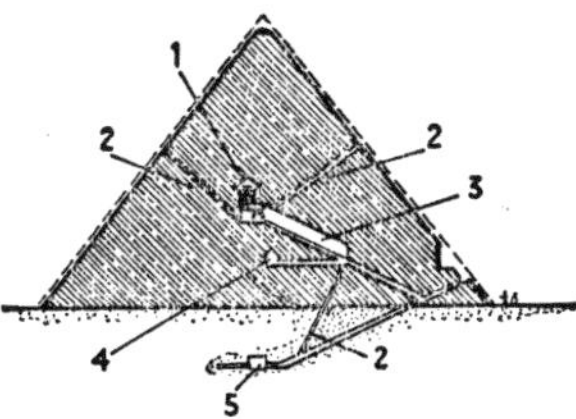

SECTION OF THE GREAT PYRAMID OF CHEOPS

1. King's chamber. 2. Air vent. 3. Grand gallery. 4. Queen's chamber. 5. Underground chamber

with base of three or more sides; pyramid-shaped thing or pile of things; fruit-tree trained in pyramid shape (ill. FRUIT); (pl., billiards) game played (usu.) with 15 coloured balls arranged in triangle and one cue-ball. **pў̆răm'ĭdal** *adj.*; ~ *tract,* great tract of motor nerve fibres running down spine, concerned in voluntary movement. **pў̆răm'ĭdally** *adv.*

Pў̆'ramus and Thĭs'bė (-z-). Lovers in a legend told by Ovid; forbidden to marry by their parents, who were neighbours in Babylon, they exchanged vows through a chink in the wall, and agreed to meet at a tomb outside the city; here Thisbe was frightened away by a lioness, and Pyramus, finding her bloodstained cloak and supposing her dead, stabbed himself; Thisbe, returning, threw herself upon his sword.

pȳre *n.* Heap of combustible material, esp. funeral pile for burning corpse.

pȳr'ēne *n.* (chem.) Solid aromatic hydrocarbon obtained from dry distillation of coal etc.

Pў̆rėnēēs' (-z). Range of mountains in SW. Europe separating Spain from France. **Pў̆rėnē'an** *adj.*

pȳrēth'rum *n.* Genus of composite plants; feverfew; ~ *powder,* insecticide made of powdered heads of some species of *Pyrethrum* or from *Chrysanthemum cinerariifolium.*

pȳr'ĭdĭne (*or* pĭ-) *n.* (chem.) Colourless volatile liquid base with offensive odour, present in bone-oil and coal-tar, whence it is obtained by distillation.

pȳrīt'ēs (-z; *or* pĭ-) *n.* (*Iron* ~), iron sulphide, FeS_2, occurring as a mineral; (*copper* ~) double sulphide of copper and iron ($Cu_2S.Fe_2S_3$). **pȳrĭt'ĭc** *adj.*

pȳr'ō: see PYROGALLIC ACID.

pȳro-ėlĕc'trĭc *adj.* Becoming electrically polar when heated.

pȳrŏgăll'ĭc ă'cĭd, pȳrogăll'ŏl (colloq. abbrev. *pyro*) *ns.* White crystalline substance, tri-hydroxybenzene, very soluble in water, used as a developer in photography etc.

pȳrogĕn'ĭc *adj.* Fever-producing.

pȳrŏl'atry *n.* Fire-worship.

pȳr'omăncy *n.* Divination by fire.

pȳromān'ĭa *n.* Incendiary mania. **pȳromān'ĭăc** *n.*

pȳrŏm'ėter *n.* Instrument for measuring high temperatures.

pȳrotĕch'nĭc(al) (-tĕk-) *adjs.* Of (the nature of) fireworks; (fig., of wit etc.) brilliant, sensational. **pȳrotĕch'nĭcally** *adv.* **pȳrotĕch'nĭcs** *n.pl.* Art of making, display of, fireworks. **pȳrotĕch'nĭst, pȳr'otĕchny** *ns.*

pȳr'ŏxēne *n.* A black, crystalline mineral common in igneous rocks.

pȳrŏx'ȳlĭn *n.* Any of a class of highly inflammable compounds (nitrates of cellulose), less highly nitrated than gun-cotton, produced by treating vegetable fibres with a mixture of nitric and sulphuric acids. **pȳroxȳl'ĭc** *adj.*

Pyrrhic[1] (pĭ'rĭk) *adj.* ~ *Dance,* a war-dance of the ancient Greeks, performed in armour, with mimicry of actual warfare.

Pyrrhic[2] (pĭ'rĭk) *n.* Ancient Greek and Latin metrical foot of two short syllables, ᴗ ᴗ. ~ *adj.* Consisting of such feet.

Pyrrhic[3] (pĭ'rĭk) *adj.* Of PYRRHUS; ~ *victory,* victory achieved at too great a cost (from saying attributed to Pyrrhus after battle of Asculum, where he routed the Romans but lost the flower of his army: 'One more such victory and we are lost').

Pyrrho (pĭ'rō) of Elis (*c* 360–270 B.C.). Greek Sceptic philosopher, founder of *Pyrrhōn'ian* school, holding that nothing can be certainly known and that suspension of judgement is true wisdom and the source of happiness.

Pyrrhus (pĭ'rus) (*c* 319–272 B.C.). King of Epirus, military adventurer who fought a series of campaigns against Rome in Italy and Sicily (280–275); see also PYRRHIC[3].

Pȳr'us *n.* Genus of rosaceous

trees and shrubs including pear and apple.

Pȳthăg'orăs (6th c. B.C.). Greek philosopher and mathematician of Samos; his philosophical teaching included the doctrine of the immortality and transmigration of the soul, and he evolved the idea that the explanation of the universe is to be sought in numbers and their relations; *theorem of* ~, geometrical proposition, of which Pythagoras is credited with discovering the proof, that the square on the hypotenuse of a right-angled triangle is equal to the sum of the squares on the other two sides. **Pȳthăgorē'an** *adj.* & *n.*

Pȳth'ĭa. The priestess of Apollo at Delphi, who delivered the oracles. **Pȳth'ĭan** *adj.* & *n.* (Native) of Delphi; Delphic (priestess); ~ *Apollo*, Apollo as giver of oracles at Delphi; ~ *games*, one of 4 national festivals of ancient Greece, held near Delphi and said to have been founded by Apollo when he slew the Python.

Pȳth'ĭăs, Knights of. American benevolent and fraternal secret society, founded 1864.

pȳth'on *n.* 1. (Gk myth.) Huge serpent or monster slain near Delphi by Apollo. 2. Member of genus (*P*~) of large non-venomous snakes inhabiting the tropical regions of the Old World, which kill their prey by constriction; other related snakes. **pȳthŏn'ĭc** *adj.*

Pȳth'onĕss *n.* = PYTHIAN priestess.

pȳx *n.* 1. (eccles.) Vessel, often of precious metal, in which host is reserved. 2. Box at Royal Mint in which specimen gold and silver coins are deposited to be tested at annual *trial of the* ~ by jury of Goldsmiths' Company.

PYX

pȳxĭd'ĭum *n.* (bot.) Seed-capsule of which the top comes off like lid of box (ill. FRUIT).

Q

Q, q (kū). 17th letter of modern English and 16th of ancient Roman alphabet, derived from Phoenician ϙ, Ϙ, ϙ (representing guttural *k* sound). The letter, followed by *v*, was used in Latin to represent kw-, and *qu-* is used in English to represent this sound in many native English words as well as in those derived from Latin, even when these have now the pronunciation *k-* (as in words derived through French).

q. *abbrev.* Query.

Q. *abbrev.* Queen.

Q.A.R.A.N.C. *abbrev.* Queen Alexandra's Royal Army Nursing Corps, formerly Q.A.I.M.N.S. (Imperial Military Nursing Service).

Q.B., Q.C. *abbrev.* Queen's Bench, Counsel.

Q.E.D. *abbrev. Quod erat demonstrandum*

Q.F. *abbrev.* Quick-firing (gun).

Q fē'ver *n.* Disease allied to typhus but milder, caused by a different variety of *Rickettsia.* [f. Queensland, Australia, where first observed]

Q.H.C., Q.H.P., Q.H.S. *abbrevs.* Honorary Chaplain, Physician, Surgeon, to the Queen.

qĭntar *n.* $\frac{1}{100}$ of a lek.

q.l. *abbrev. Quantum libet* (= as much as is desired).

Q.M. *abbrev.* Quartermaster.

Q.M.G., Q.M.S. *abbrevs.* Quartermaster-General, -Sergeant.

q.p. *abbrev. Quantum placet* (= as much as is desired).

qr *abbrev.* Quarter.

q.s. *abbrev. Quantum sufficit* (= as much as suffices).

Q.S. *abbrev.* Quarter Sessions.

qt *abbrev.* Quart(s).

q.t. *abbrev.* (slang) Quiet (*on the strict q.t.*, privately, avoiding notice).

qu. *abbrev.* Quasi; query.

quā *conj.* As, in the capacity of.

quăck[1] *v.i.* (Of duck) utter characteristic note. ~ *n.* Harsh cry characteristic of duck.

quăck[2] *n.* Ignorant pretender to skill esp. in medicine and surgery; one who offers wonderful remedies or devices; charlatan. **quăck'ery** *n.*

quăck'sălver *n.* (now rare) = QUACK[2].

quad (-ŏd) *abbrev.* Quadrangle; quadrat; (colloq.) quadruplet.

Quadragĕs'ĭma (-ŏd-) *n.* First Sunday in Lent. **quadragĕs'ĭmal** *adj.* Lasting 40 days (of fast, esp. Lent); Lenten. [L, = 'fortieth (day)']

quadrangle (kwŏd'rănggl) *n.* Four-sided figure, esp. square or rectangle; four-sided court (partly) enclosed by parts of large building, such court with buildings round it. **quadrăng'ūlar** *adj.* **quadrăng'ūlarly** *adv.*

quad'rant (-ŏd-) *n.* Quarter of circumference of circle; plane figure enclosed by two radii of circle at right angles and arc cut off by them (ill. CIRCLE); quarter of sphere; thing, esp. graduated strip or plate of metal, shaped like quarter circle; (obs.) instrument, so shaped and graduated for measuring angles and altitudes in astronomy, navigation, surveying, etc., or for use as a sundial.

quad'rat (-ŏd-) *n.* Small metal block used by printers in spacing (*em* ~, larger size, thus □; *en* ~, smaller size, ▯).

quad'rate (-ŏd-) *adj.* Square, rectangular (rare exc. anat. in names of squarish parts of body); ~ *bone*, bone in heads of birds, amphibia, reptiles, and fish, by which lower jaw is articulated to skull. ~ *n.* Quadrate bone, muscle, etc.

quadrăt'ĭc *adj.* (math.) Involving the second and no higher power of an unknown quantity or variable (esp. ~ *equation*). ~ *n.* Quadratic equation; (pl.) branch of algebra dealing with these.

quad'rature (-ŏd-) *n.* (math.) Expression of area bounded by curve, esp. circle, by means of equivalent square; (astron.) either of two points in space or time at which moon is 90° distant from sun; position of heavenly body in relation to another 90° away.

quadrĕnn'ĭal *adj.* Occurring every, lasting, 4 years.

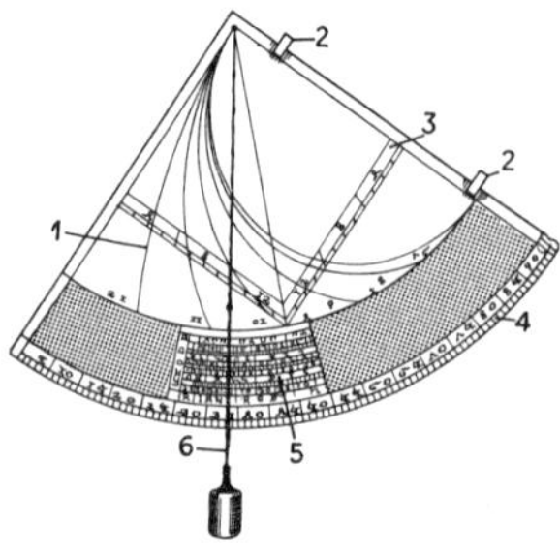

MEDIEVAL QUADRANT FOR TIME TELLING AND SURVEYING

1. Unequal (planetary) hour line. 2. Sight. 3. Shadow square. 4. Scale of 90°. 5. Cursor (half missing) to enable instrument to be used in any latitude. 6. Plumb-line and bob

quadri- *prefix.* Four.
quad'ric (-ŏd-) *adj.* & *n.* (solid geom.) Of the 2nd degree; surface whose equation is in the 2nd degree.
quadrĭg'a *n.* (pl. *-ae*). Ancient chariot with 4 horses abreast.
quadrĭlăt'eral (-ŏd-) *adj.* & *n.* (Figure) bounded by 4 straight lines; (space, area) having 4 sides.

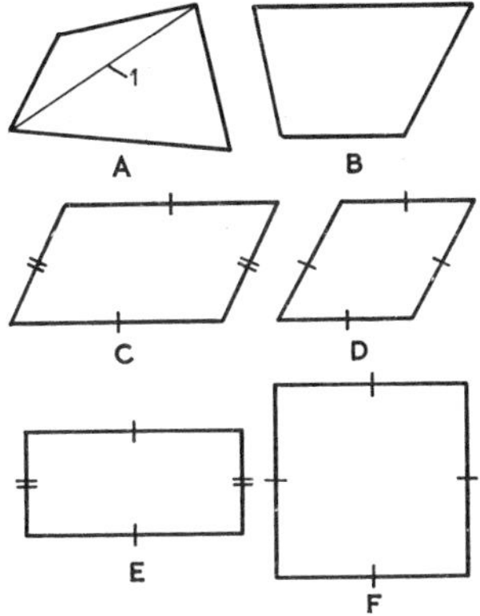

QUADRILATERALS: A. TRAPEZOID. B. TRAPEZIUM. C. PARALLELOGRAM OR RHOMBOID. D. RHOMB OR RHOMBUS. E. RECTANGLE. F. SQUARE
1. Diagonal

quadrille[1] (k*a*drĭl', kw*a*-) *n.* Card-game fashionable in 18th c., played by 4 persons with 40 cards (i.e. an ordinary pack without the 8s, 9s, and 10s).
quadrille[2] (k*a*drĭl', kw*a*-) *n.* Square dance for 4 couples, containing 5 figures; music for this. [Fr., f. Span. *cuadrilla* squadron (*cuadra* square)]
quadrĭll'ion (kw*a*drĭl'yon) *n.* 4th power of a million (1 followed by 24 ciphers); (U.S.) 5th power of a thousand (1 followed by 15 ciphers).
quadrĭnōm'ial (-ŏd-) *adj.* Consisting of 4 algebraic terms.
quadripãrt'īte (-ŏd-) *adj.* Consisting of 4 parts; shared by or involving 4 parties.
quad'rĭrēme (-ŏd-) *n.* Ancient galley with 4 banks of oars.
quadrĭsy̆llăb'ic (-ŏd-) *adj.* Four-syllabled. **quadrĭsy̆ll'able** *n.* Word of 4 syllables.
quadrĭvāl'ent (-ŏd-; *or* -drĭv'*a*-) *adj.* Having a VALENCY of 4.
quadrĭv'ium *n.* In Middle Ages, the higher division of the 7 liberal arts, comprising arithmetic, geometry, astronomy, and music.
quadrōōn' *n.* Offspring of white and mulatto, person of quarter-negro blood. [Span. *cuarteron* (*cūartō* 4th)]
quadrum'anous (-rōō-) *adj.* (zool.) Four-handed (obs.).
quad'rupĕd (-ŏdrŏŏ-) *n.* Four-footed animal, esp. four-footed mammal. ~ *adj.* Four-footed. **quadru'pedal** (-rōō-) *adj.*
quad'ruple (-ŏdrōō-) *adj.* Fourfold, consisting of 4 parts or involving 4 parties; amounting to 4 times the number or amount *of*, equivalent to fourfold the amount of, superior by 4 times in amount or number *to*; ~ *rhythm* or *time*, (mus.) with 4 beats to a measure. **quad'ruply** *adv.* **quad'ruple** *n.* Number or amount 4 times greater than another. ~ *v.* Multiply by 4.
quad'ruplĕt (-ŏdrŏŏ-) *n.* One of 4 children born at a birth.
quadrup'lĭcate (-ŏdrōō-) *adj.* Fourfold, 4 times repeated or copied. ~ *n.* *In* ~, in 4 exactly similar examples or copies; (pl.) 4 such copies. **quadrup'lĭcāte** *v.t.* Multiply by 4; make in quadruplicate. **quadruplĭcā'tion** *n.*
quadruplĭ'cĭty (-ŏdrŏŏ-) *n.* Fourfold nature, being fourfold.
quaere (kwēr'ĭ) *v.* Ask, inquire (imper.); hence, 'one may ask', 'it is a question'. ~ *n.* Question, query.
quaes'tor *n.* Ancient-Roman official, state-treasurer, paymaster, etc. **quaestōr'ial** *adj.* **quaes'torshĭp** *n.*
quaff (-ah-) *v.* Drink, drain (cup etc.), in long or copious draughts.
quăg *n.* Marshy or boggy spot, quaking bog. **quăgg'y** *adj.*
quăgg'a *n.* Species of zebra (*Equus quagga*) of S. Africa, now extinct; (also, erron.) Burchell's zebra (*Equus burchelli*).
quăg'mīre *n.* Quaking bog, fen, marsh, slough.
Quai d'Orsay' (kā). Quay on left bank of Seine at Paris, on which stands French Ministry of Foreign Affairs; hence, French foreign policy.
quail[1] *n.* Migratory bird of Old World and Australia allied to partridge, esp. European species (*Coturnix coturnix*) esteemed as food; any of various Amer. birds resembling this; ~*-call*, *-pipe*, whistle with note like quail's used for luring the birds into net.
quail[2] *v.* Flinch, be cowed, give way *before* or *to*; (rare) cow, daunt.
quaint *adj.* Attractive or piquant in virtue of unfamiliar, esp. old-fashioned, appearance, ornamentation, manners, etc.; daintily odd. **quaint'ly** *adv.* **quaint'nĕss** *n.*
quāke *v.i.* Shake, tremble, rock to and fro; *quaking-grass*, kinds of grass (*Briza*) with slender foot-stalks trembling in wind. ~ *n.* Act of quaking; earthquake. **quāk'ĭngly** *adv.* **quāk'y** *adj.*
Quāk'er *n.* Member of the religious society (Society of Friends) founded by George Fox in 1648–50, distinguished by peaceful principles and plainness of dress and manners; *Quakers' meeting*, religious meeting of the Friends, silent except when some member is moved by the spirit to speak; hence, silent meeting, company in which conversation flags. **Quāk'erĭsm** *n.* **Quāk'erish** *adj.* [nickname of early members of the society, who were said to 'tremble at the Word of the Lord']
qualĭfĭcā'tion (-ŏl-) *n.* 1. Modification, restriction, limitation; restricting or limiting circumstance. 2. Quality, accomplishment, etc., fitting person or thing (*for* post etc.). 3. Condition that must be fulfilled before right can be acquired or office held; document attesting such fulfilment. 4. Attribution of quality. **qual'ĭfĭcātory** *adj.*
qual'ĭfȳ (-ŏl-) *v.* 1. Attribute quality to, describe *as*; (gram., of adj.) express some quality of noun. 2. Invest or provide with the necessary qualities, make competent, fit, or legally entitled (*for*, *to*); make oneself competent (*for*) or capable of holding some office, exercising some function, etc. 3. Modify (statement etc.), make less absolute or sweeping, subject to reservation or limitation; moderate, mitigate, esp. make less violent, severe, or unpleasant.
qual'ĭtatĭve (-ŏl-) *adj.* Concerned with, depending on, quality.
qual'ĭty (-ŏl-) *n.* 1. Degree of excellence, relative nature or kind or character (opp. of QUANTITY); class or grade of thing as determined by this; general excellence. 2. Faculty, skill, accomplishment, characteristic trait, mental or moral attribute. 3. (archaic) High rank or social standing. 4. (logic, of proposition) Being affirmative or negative. 5. (Of sound, voice, etc.) distinctive character apart from pitch or loudness, timbre.
qualm (kwahm, -awm) *n.* Momentary faint or sick feeling, queasiness: misgiving, sinking of heart; scruple of conscience.
qua'ndary (-ŏn-; *or* kwŏndār'ĭ) *n.* State of perplexity, difficult situation, practical dilemma.
quant (-ŏn-) *n.* Punting-pole used by E.-coast bargemen etc., with prong to prevent its sinking in mud. ~ *v.* Propel (boat), propel boat, with quant.
qua'ntĭc (-ŏn-) *n.* (math.) Rational integral homogeneous function of two or more variables.
qua'ntĭfȳ (-ŏn-) *v.t.* (logic) Determine application of (term, proposition) by use of *all*, *some*, etc.; determine quantity of, measure, express as quantity. **quantifī'able** *adj.* **quantĭfĭcā'tion** *n.*
qua'ntĭtatĭve (-ŏn-) *adj.* Measured or measurable by, concerned with, quantity; of, based on, the quantity of vowels. **qua'ntĭtatĭvely** *adv.*
qua'ntĭty (-ŏn-) *n.* 1. Property of things that is regarded as determinable by measurement of some kind; amount, sum; (pros. etc.) length or shortness of sounds or

syllables; (mus.) length or duration of notes; (logic) degree of extension given by proposition to term forming its subject. 2. Specified or considerable portion, number, or amount of something; *the* amount of something present; (pl.) large amounts or numbers, abundance. 3. (math.) Thing having quantity, figure or symbol representing this; *unknown* ~, (transf.) person or thing whose action cannot be foreseen; *negligible* ~, (transf.) person etc. that need not be reckoned with; ~ *surveyor*, one who measures up and prices builders' work.

quant. suff. *abbrev. Quantum sufficit.*

qua'ntum (-ŏn-) *n.* (pl. *-ta*). Sum, amount; share, portion; (physics) discrete unit quantity of energy, proportional to frequency of radiation, emitted from or absorbed by atom; ~ *dynamics, mechanics*, etc., dynamics, etc., taking account of quanta; ~ *theory*, theory originated by M. Planck (1910) and extended by N. Bohr, which accounts for certain atomic phenomena by assuming that radiant energy (heat, light, etc.) is emitted from atoms only in discrete packets or quanta and not continuously.

quăn'tum sŭff'ĭcĭt. (abbrev. *quant. suff.* or *q.s.*) As much as suffices (in prescriptions); sufficient quantity; to sufficient extent.

qua'rantine (-ŏr-, -ēn) *n.* (Period, orig. 40 days, of) isolation imposed on infected ship, or on persons (esp. travellers) who might spread contagious or infectious diseases; (period of) isolation for animals (esp. dogs and cats) after landing from abroad. ~ *v.t.* Impose such isolation on, put in quarantine. [prob. f. It. *quarantina* 40 days]

quār'ē ĭm'pĕdĭt. (law) Writ issued against objector in cases of disputed presentation to benefice. [L, = 'why does he hinder?']

qua'renden, -der (kwŏ-) *n.* Early deep-red apple common in Somerset and Devon.

qua'rrel[1] (kwŏ-) *n.* Short heavy arrow or bolt used in crossbow or arbalest (ill. BOW).

qua'rrel[2] (kwŏ-) *n.* Occasion of complaint against person or his actions; violent contention or altercation *between* persons, rupture of friendly relations; *pick a* ~, invent or eagerly avail oneself of occasion of quarrel. ~ *v.i.* Take exception, find fault *with*; contend violently (*with* person), fall out, have dispute, break off friendly relations. **qua'rrelsome** *adj.* **qua'rrelsomely** *adv.* **qua'rrelsomeness** *n.*

qua'rry[1] (kwŏ-) *n.* Object of pursuit by bird of prey, hounds, hunters, etc.; intended victim or prey. [OF *curée* (*cuir* skin); orig. sense, parts of deer placed on hide and given to hounds]

qua'rry[2] (kwŏ-) *n.* 1. Excavation made by taking stone for building etc. from its bed; place whence stone, or (fig.) information etc., may be extracted. ~ *v.* Extract (stone) from quarry; form quarry in (hill, etc.); cut or dig (as) in quarry; (fig.) extract (information etc.), search documents, etc., laboriously.

qua'rry[3] (kwŏ-) *n.* Diamond-shaped pane of glass (ill. WINDOW); square floor-tile. [earlier *quarrel*, f. It. *quadrello*, dim. of *quadro* square]

quart[1] (-ōrt) *n.* Measure of capacity, quarter of gallon, 2 pints; pot or bottle containing this amount.

quart[2] (kârt) *n.* 1. (also carte) Fourth of the 8 positions in fencing (ill. FENCE). 2. Sequence of 4 cards in piquet etc. ~ *v.* (fencing) Use the position 'quart'; draw back (head etc.) in this.

quart'an (-ōr-) *adj.* & *n.* (Ague or fever) with paroxysm every third (by inclusive reckoning fourth) day, former name for malaria.

quarte *n.* Var. of QUART[2].

quar'ter (-ōr-) *n.* 1. Fourth part; one of 4 equal or corresponding parts; fourth part of; *bad* ~ *of an hour*, short unpleasant experience. 2. Quarter of dollar, 25 cents, as amount or coin (U.S. & Canada). 3. One of 4 parts, each including a limb, into which beast's or bird's carcass is divided; (pl.) similar parts of traitor quartered after execution; (freq. pl.) haunch(es) of living animal or man. 4. Either side of ship abaft the beam (ill. BEARING). 5. (her.) One of 4 divisions of quartered shield, charge occupying quarter placed in chief. 6. Dry measure of 8 bushels. 7. Fourth part of cwt., 28 lb. (in U.S. 25 lb.). 8. Fourth part of fathom. 9. Quarter-mile race or running-distance. 10. Fourth part of year for which payments become due on quarter-day. 11. Fourth part of lunar period, moon's position between 1st and 2nd or 3rd and 4th of these. 12. Point of time 15 minutes before or after any hour o'clock. 13. (Region lying about) point of compass; direction; district, locality; portion or member of community, some thing or things, without reference to actual locality. 14. Division of town, esp. one appropriated to or occupied by special class. 15. (pl.) Lodgings, abode, esp. place where troops are lodged or stationed; assigned or appropriate places, station; *winter* ~*s*, place occupied, esp. by troops, for winter; (naut.) *beat to* ~*s*, summon crew to appointed stations as for action. 16. Exemption from death offered or granted to enemy in battle who will surrender. 17. ~ *binding*, (of book) with narrow strip of leather at back and none elsewhere (ill. BOOK); ~*-butt*, (billiards) cue of short length; ~*-day*, day on which quarterly payments are due, tenancies begin and end, etc. (in England and Ireland, Lady Day 25th Mar., Midsummer Day 24th June, Michaelmas 29th Sept., Christmas 25th Dec.; in Scotland, Candlemas 2nd Feb., Whitsunday 15th May, Lammas 1st Aug., Martinmas 11th Nov.); ~*-deck*, part of upper deck between stern and after-mast; *the* officers of ship or navy; ~*-ill*, disease in cattle and sheep causing putrefaction in one or more of the quarters; *quar'termaster*, (naut.) petty officer in charge of steering, signals, hold-stowing, etc.; (mil., abbrev. Q.M.) regimental officer with duties of assigning quarters, laying out camp, and looking after rations, clothing, equipment, etc.; *Q*~*-master-General*, (abbrev. Q.M.G.) staff officer at head of department controlling quartering, equipment, etc.; ~*-master-sergeant*, non-commissioned officer assisting quartermaster and ranking as staff-sergeant; ~*-note*, (U.S.) crotchet; ~*-plate*, photographic plate or film $3\frac{1}{4} \times 4\frac{1}{4}$ in., photograph produced from it; ~*-section*, (U.S. & Canada) quarter of square mile of land, 160 acres; ~ *sessions*, court of limited civil and criminal jurisdiction and of appeal held quarterly by justices of peace in counties and by recorder in boroughs; *quarter-staff*, stout iron-tipped pole 6–8 ft long formerly used by English peasantry as weapon; ~*-tone*, (mus.) half a semitone. ~ *v.t.* 1. Divide into 4 equal parts; divide (traitor's body) into quarters. 2. (her.) Place, bear (charges, coats of arms) quarterly on shield; add (another's coat) to one's hereditary arms; place in alternate quarters *with*; divide (shield) into quarters or into divisions formed by vertical and horizontal lines. 3. Put (esp. soldiers) into quarters; station or lodge in specified place. 4. (Of dogs) range or traverse (ground) in every direction.

quar'terage (-ōr-) *n.* Quarterly payment; a quarter's wages, allowance, pension, etc.

quar'tering (-ōr-) *n.* (esp., her., pl.) Coats marshalled on shield to denote alliances of family with heiresses of others (ill. HERALDRY).

quar'terly (-ōr-) *adj.* Occurring every quarter of a year. ~ *n.* Quarterly review or magazine. ~ *adv.* Once every quarter of a year; in the four, or in two diagonally opposite, quarters of a shield.

quar'tern (-ōr-) *n.* Quarter of a pint; ~ (*-loaf*), 4-pound loaf.

quartĕt(te') (-ōr-) *n.* Musical composition for 4 voices or instruments; players or singers rendering this; set of four; *piano* ~, three stringed instruments with piano; *string* ~, two violins, viola, and cello.

quar'tō (-ôr-) *n.* (Also 4to, 4°). Size given by folding sheet of paper twice; book consisting of sheets so folded; ~ *paper*, paper folded so as to form 4 leaves out of original sheet; paper of size or shape of quarter-sheet.

quartz (-ôr-) *n.* Kinds of mineral, massive or crystallizing in hexagonal prisms, consisting of silica (silicon dioxide); *fused* ~, type of glass made by melting quartz, capable of withstanding very high temperature and used for scientific apparatus, ultra-violet lamps, etc.

quar'tzite (-ôr-) *n.* Hard sand-stone rock of quartz grains cemented together by silica.

quash (-ŏ-) *v.t.* Annul, make void, reject as not valid, put an end to (esp. by legal procedure or authority).

quās'ī *conj.* That is to say, as if it were.

quāsi- *prefix.* Seeming(ly), not real(ly); practical(ly); half-, almost.

Quăs'ĭmō'dō Sunday. First Sunday after Easter. [f. first two words of introit of Mass of the day]

quăss'ia (*or* -ŏsh'*a*) *n.* S. Amer. tree (*Quassia amara*), found esp. in Surinam; wood, bark, or root of this and other trees (now esp. *Picraena excelsa*, bitter wood tree, of W. Indies etc., yielding bitter medicinal tonic and also much used horticulturally for destroying aphids). [S. Amer. tree named by Linnaeus after *Graman Quassi*, Surinam Negro, who discovered its virtues in 1730]

quăt'er-cĕntĕn'ary *n.* 400th anniversary.

quatērn'ary *adj.* 1. Having 4 parts; (chem.) compounded of 4 elements or radicals. 2. (geol.) Belonging to the period subsequent to the Tertiary, i.e. that of recent and present-day formations, that yielding fossils of shells, bones, and plants all of which represent species still living. ~ *n.* 1. Set of 4 things; the number 4. 2. (*The Q*~), the quaternary period in geology (ill. GEOLOGY).

quatērn'ion *n.* Set of 4; quire of 4 sheets folded in two; (math.) quotient of two vectors or operator that changes one vector into another (so named as depending on 4 geometrical elements); (pl.) form of calculus of vectors in which this operator is used.

quatorzain (kăt'*er*zān) *n.* 14-line poem, irregular sonnet.

quat'rain (kwŏt'rĭn) *n.* Stanza of 4 lines, usu. with alternate rhymes.

quatre (kătr, kāt'*er*) *n.* Four in dice.

Quatrebras (kătr*e*brah'). Small village near Brussels, Belgium, scene of battle (1815) between French under Marshal Ney and English, two days before WATERLOO.

quat'refoil (kătr*e*-) *n.* 4-cusped figure, esp. as opening in architectural tracery, resembling symmetrical 4-lobed leaf or flower (ill. WINDOW).

quattrocĕn'tō (-ahtrōch-) *n.* 15th century as period of Italian art and literature. [It., lit. 400, but used = 1400]

quā'ver *v.* Vibrate, shake, tremble (esp. of voice or musical sound); use trills in singing; sing with trills; say in trembling tones. ~ *n.* 1. Trill in singing; tremulousness in speech. 2. (mus.) Note equal in length to half crotchet or one-eighth of semibreve (symbol ♪). **quā'verĭngly** *adv.* **quā'very** *adj.*

quay (kē) *n.* Solid stationary artificial landing-place usu. of stone or iron, lying alongside or projecting into water, for (un)-loading ships. **quay'age** *n.* Quay-room; due levied on ships using quay or goods (un)loaded there.

Que. *abbrev.* Quebec.

quean *n.* (archaic) Impudent or ill-behaved girl, jade, hussy.

queas'y (-zĭ) *adj.* (Of food) unsettling the stomach, causing or tending to sickness (rare); (of person, stomach) easily upset, inclined to sickness or nausea; (of conscience etc.) tender, scrupulous. **queas'inėss** *n.*

Quėbĕc'. Province of E. Canada; its capital, on the St. Lawrence River, orig. settled by the French, and captured from them by a British force under Wolfe, 1759.

queen *n.* 1. King's wife (also ~ *consort* for distinction from next sense; ~ *dowager*, wife of late king; ~ *mother*, queen dowager who is mother of sovereign); also prefixed to personal name as title. 2. Female sovereign ruler, usu. hereditary; *Q*~ *Empress*, title assumed by Queen Victoria as Queen of England and Empress of India. 3. Adored female (*Q*~ *of grace*, *Q*~ *of heaven*, the Virgin Mary); ancient goddess (*Q*~ *of heaven*, Juno, *of love*, Venus, *of night*, Diana, etc.); person's sweetheart or wife or mistress; majestic woman; belle, mock sovereign, on some occasion (as *Q*~ *of the May* at May festival); personified best example of anything regarded as feminine. 4. Person, country, etc. regarded as ruling over some sphere (~ *of the Adriatic*, Venice). 5. Perfect female of bee (ill. BEE), wasp, ant, or termite. 6. (chess) Piece with greatest freedom of movement, placed next to king at beginning of game (ill. CHESS). 7. One of court-cards in each suit, bearing figure of a queen. 8. ~-*bee*, fully developed female bee; ~-*cake*, small soft rich currant-cake, freq. heart-shaped; ~-*post*, one of two upright timbers between tie-beam and principal rafters of roof-truss (ill. ROOF); Q~'s BENCH, COUNSEL, ENGLISH, EVIDENCE, PROCTOR, SHILLING: see these words. **queen'-like** *adj.* **queen** *v.* 1. Make (woman) queen; ~ *it*, play the queen. 2. (chess) Advance (pawn) to opponent's end of board, where it is replaced by a queen or other piece; (of pawn) reach this position.

Queen Anne, Queen Anne's Bounty: see ANNE[1].

queen'ing *n.* Kind of apple.

queen'ly *adj.* Fit for, appropriate to, a queen; majestic, queen-like. **queen'linėss** *n.*

Queens'berry Rules (-z-). Standard rules for boxing in Gt Britain, drawn up 1867 under supervision of 8th Marquess of Queensberry.

Queen's Cŏll'ege. College of the University of Oxford, founded 1340 and named in honour of Philippa, consort of Edward III.

Queens' Cŏll'ege. 'The Queen's College of St. Margaret and St. Bernard', a college of the University of Cambridge, founded 1448 by Margaret of Anjou, consort of Henry VI, and refounded 1465 by Elizabeth, consort of Edward IV.

Queen's Coun'ty. Former name of LEIX.

Queens'land (-z-). State of NE. Australia; capital, Brisbane.

queer *adj.* Strange, odd, eccentric; of questionable character, shady, suspect; out of sorts, giddy, faint; *in Q*~ *Street*, (slang) in a difficulty, in debt, trouble, or disrepute. **queer'ly** *adv.* **queer'nėss** *n.* **queer** *n.* (slang) Homosexual. ~ *v.t.* (slang) Spoil, put out of order; esp. ~ *the pitch*, spoil chances of success *for* another, esp. by unfair means.

quĕll *v.t.* (poet. & rhet.) Suppress, forcibly put an end to, crush, overcome, reduce to submission.

quĕnch *v.t.* Extinguish (chiefly poet. or rhet.); cool, esp. with water (heat, heated thing); stifle, suppress (desire, speed, etc.); slake (thirst). **quĕnch'lėss** *adj.*

quenĕlle' (ke-) *n.* (cookery) Seasoned ball of fish or meat pounded to paste.

quēr'ist *n.* One who asks questions.

quērn *n.* Hand-mill for grinding corn; small hand-mill for pepper etc.

quĕ'rulous (-rōō-) *adj.* Complaining, peevish. **quĕ'rulously** *adv.* **quĕ'rulousnėss** *n.*

quēr'y̆ *n.* 1. (Introducing a question) QUAERE. 2. A question; mark of interrogation (?), or word *query* or *qu.*, used to indicate doubt of correctness of statement in writing. ~ *v.* Ask, inquire; put a question; call in question, question accuracy of.

Quesnay (kĕnā), François (1694–1774). French economist, founder of physiocratic school.

quĕst *n.* Official inquiry, jury, etc., making it (now only in vulg. *crowner's* ~, coroner's inquest); seeking by inquiry or search;

thing sought, esp. object of medieval knight's pursuit; *in ~ of*, seeking. ~ *v.* Go *about* in search of something; (of dogs etc.) search (*about*) for game; (poet.) search for, seek *out*.

quĕs'tion (-chon) *n.* 1. Interrogative statement of some point to be investigated or discussed; problem; subject for discussion in meeting etc., esp. in Parliament; subject of discussion, debate, or strife; *the ~*, the precise matter receiving or requiring discussion or deliberation; *in ~*, under consideration; *out of, past, without*, etc., ~, certainly, undoubtedly; *it is a ~ of*, what is required or involved is; *out of the ~*, foreign to the subject; not to be considered or thought of; *beg the ~*: see BEG. 2. Sentence in interrogative form, meant to elicit information, interrogation, inquiry; *~-mark*, mark of interrogation (?). 3. Action of questioning; (archaic) application of torture as part of judicial examination. **quĕs'tionlėss** *adj.* **quĕs'tion** *v.t.* Ask questions of, interrogate, subject (person) to examination; seek information from study of (phenomena, facts); call in question, throw doubt upon, raise objections to. **quĕs'tioningly** *adv.*

quĕs'tionable (-chon-) *adj.* (esp.) Doubtfully true; not clearly consistent with honesty, honour, or wisdom. **quĕs'tionably** *adv.*

questionnaire' (kĕstiŏn-, kwĕs-tyon-) *n.* Series of questions usu. for obtaining information on special points esp. in statistical investigations.

quet'zal (kĕts-) *n.* 1. Extremely beautiful Central Amer. bird (*Pharomacrus mocinno*), cock of which has very long golden-green tail-coverts. 2. Principal monetary unit of Guatemala, = 100 centavos. [Aztec *quetzalli* tail-feather of this bird]

Quetzalcōat'l (kĕt-, -ahtl). One of the chief gods of the Aztecs (also a hero whose connexion with the god is obscure); worshipped as bestower of arts of civilization on mankind, and having as symbol a plumed serpent (snake with quetzal feathers instead of scales).

queue (kū) *n.* 1. Hanging plaited tail of hair or wig, pigtail (ill. WIG). 2. Line of persons, vehicles, etc., awaiting their turn to be attended to or proceed. ~ *v.i.* Form *up* in, take one's place in, queue.

quĭbb'le *n.* Play on words, pun; equivocation, evasion; unsubstantial or purely verbal argument etc., esp. one depending on ambiguity of word. ~ *v.i.* Use quibbles. **quĭbb'ler** *n.* **quĭbb'ling** *adj.*

Quichua, Quechua (kĕch'wa). S. Amer. Indian tribe and linguistic stock; official language of Inca Empire.

quĭck *adj.* 1. (archaic or dial.) Living, alive; (of hedge etc.) composed of living plants, esp. hawthorn; ~ *with child*, at stage of pregnancy when motion has been felt. 2. Vigorous, lively, active; prompt to act, perceive, be affected, etc.; (of fire) burning strongly, (of oven) heated by quick fire, hot. 3. Moving rapidly, rapid, swift; done in short time or with little interval; *~-change*, (of actor etc.) quickly changing costume or appearance to play another part; *quick'lime*, lime which has been burned and not yet slaked with water, calcium oxide (CaO); ~ *march*, (mil.) march in quick time (esp. as word of command); ~ *one*, quick drink; *quick'sand*, (bed of) loose wet sand readily swallowing up any heavy object resting on it; *quick'set*, (of hedge) formed of living plants; (*n.*) live slips of plants, esp. hawthorn, set in ground to grow; quickset hedge; *quick'silver*, mercury; (*v.t.*) coat back of (mirror-glass) with amalgam of tin; ~ *step*, step used in quick time; (mus.) march in military quick time; fast foxtrot; ~ *time*, rate of marching now (in British army) reckoned as 128 paces of 33 in. to the minute, or four miles an hour; ~ *trick*, (bridge) card that should take trick in first or second round of suit, ace or king. **quĭck'ly** *adv.* **quĭck** *n.* Tender or sensitive flesh below skin or esp. nails; tender part of wound or sore where healthy tissue begins; seat of feeling or emotion. ~ *adv.* Quickly, at rapid rate, in comparatively short time; (imper.) make haste; *~-firer, -firing gun*, gun in which the propellant is contained in a metal cartridge case (opp. BREECH-loading).

quĭck'en *v.* 1. Give or restore natural or spiritual life or vigour to; animate, stimulate, rouse, inspire, kindle; receive, come to, life; (of human female) reach stage of pregnancy at which embryo makes clearly perceptible movements. 2. Accelerate; make or become quicker.

quĭck'ie *n.* Thing hastily done or made; film so produced.

quĭck'nėss *n.* Readiness or acuteness of perception or apprehension; speed, rapidity, suddenness; hastiness (*of temper*).

quĭd[1] *n.* (slang; pl. same) A sovereign, a pound.

quĭd[2] *n.* Lump of tobacco etc. for chewing.

quĭdd'ity *n.* 1. Essence of a thing, what makes a thing what it is. 2. Quibble, captious subtlety.

quĭd'nŭnc *n.* Newsmonger, person given to gossip. [L *quid* what, *nunc* now]

quĭd prō quō *n.* Compensation, return made, consideration. [L, = 'something for something']

quīĕs'cent *adj.* Motionless, inert, silent, dormant. **quīĕs'cently** *adv.* **quīĕs'cence** *n.*

quī'et *n.* Peaceful condition of affairs in social or political life; silence, stillness; freedom from disturbance, agitation, etc., rest, repose, peace of mind; unruffled deportment, calm. ~ *adj.* 1. Making no stir, commotion, or noise; not active; free from excess, not going to extremes; avoiding or escaping notice, secret, private; *on the ~*, (slang) *on the q.t.*, secretly, covertly. 2. Free from disturbance, interference, or annoyance; calm, unruffled, silent, still. **quī'etly** *adv.* **quī'etnėss, quī'ėtūde** *ns.* **quī'et** *v.* Reduce to quietness, soothe, calm; become quiet. **quī'eten** *v.* Quiet.

quī'etism *n.* 1. Form of religious mysticism (originated *c* 1675 by a Spanish priest, Molinos) consisting in passive devotional contemplation with extinction of will and withdrawal from all things of the senses. 2. State of calmness and passivity. **quī'etist** *n.* **quīetĭs'tic** *adj.*

quīē'tus *n.* Acquittance, receipt, given on payment of account etc. (now rare); release from life, extinction, final riddance. [med. L *quietus* (*est*) (he is) quit, used as receipt form]

quĭff *n.* Curl plastered down on forehead, formerly affected by men; also, lock of (man's) hair brushed upwards in front.

quĭll *n.* Hollow stem of feather (ill. FEATHER); whole large feather of wing or tail; pen, plectrum, fishing-float, or toothpick, made of this; spine of porcupine; bobbin of hollow reed, any bobbin; musical pipe made of hollow stem; curled-up piece of cinnamon or cinchona bark; *~-coverts*, feathers covering base of quill-feathers; *~-driver*, clerk, journalist, author; *~-feather*, stiff, comparatively large, feather of edge of bird's wing, similar feather of tail.

quĭlt *n.* Bed-coverlet made of padding enclosed between two layers of linen etc. and kept in place by lines of stitching; any coverlet or counterpane. ~ *v.t.* Cover, line, etc., with padded material; make or join together after the manner of a quilt. **quĭlt'ing** *n.*

quĭn *n.* Colloq. abbrev. of QUINTUPLET.

quī'nary *adj.* Of the number 5; consisting of 5 things.

quĭnce *n.* Hard acid yellowish pear-shaped fruit used as preserve or as flavouring; small tree (*Cydonia oblonga*) bearing this; *Japanese ~*, fruit of garden japonica (*Chaenomeles speciosa*). [ult. f. L *Cydonium* of Cydonia in Crete]

quĭncĕntē'nary *n.* 500th anniversary.

Quincey, Thomas De: see DE QUINCEY.

quĭnc'ŭnx *n.* (Arrangement of) 5 objects set so that 4 are at corners of square or rectangle and the other at its centre; esp. as basis of arrangement in planting trees.

quĭnine' (-ēn) *n.* Alkaloid found in CINCHONA bark and used in treatment of malaria and as febrifuge and tonic; (pop.) quinine sulphate, usual form in which it is taken. [Peruv. *kina* bark]

quĭn'ōne (*or* -ōn') *n.* 1. Crystalline compound ($C_6H_4O_2$) obtained by oxidizing aniline. 2. General name for a benzene derivative in which 2 oxygen atoms replace 2 hydrogen.

quĭnquagėnār'ĭan *adj.* & *n.* (Person) aged 50 or more but less than 60.

Quĭnquagĕs'ĭma (Sunday). Sunday before Lent. [med. L *quinqagesima* (*dies*) 50th day, so called as the 50th day before Easter by inclusive reckoning or loosely as the Sunday before Quadragesima Sunday]

quĭnqu(e)- *prefix.* Five.

quĭnquĕnn'ĭum *n.* 5-year period. **quĭnquĕnn'ĭal** *adj.* 5-year-long, 5-yearly.

quĭnquėpart'īte *adj.* Divided into, consisting of, 5 parts.

quĭn'quėrēme *n.* Ancient galley with 5 banks of oars.

quinquina (kĭnkēn'*a*, kwĭnkwī'-) *n.* (obs.) Bark of several species of CINCHONA. [Peruv. *kina* bark]

quĭnquivāl'ent *adj.* (chem.) Having a VALENCY of 5.

quĭn'sy (-zĭ) *n.* Abscess forming round the tonsil usu. as a complication of tonsillitis. [Gk *kunaghkē* (*kuōn kun-* dog, *aghkōm* throttle)]

quint *n.* 1. (kwĭnt) Musical interval of a 5th; organ-stop giving tone a 5th higher than normal. 2. (kĭnt, kw-) Sequence of 5 of same suit in piquet.

quĭn'tain (-tĭn) *n.* (hist.) (Medieval military exercise of tilting at) post set up as mark and often provided with sandbag to swing round and strike unskilful tilter.

quĭn'tal *n.* Weight of 100 lb.; hundredweight, 112 lb.; 100 kilograms. [Arab. *qinṭar*]

quĭn'tan *adj.* & *n.* (Ague or fever) with paroxysm every 4th (by inclusive reckoning 5th) day.

quinte (kănt) *n.* Fifth thrust or parry of the 8 positions in fencing (ill. FENCE).

quĭntĕss'ence *n.* 1. (ancient and medieval philos.) 5th substance, apart from the four elements, composing the heavenly bodies entirely and latent in all things, extraction of which was one of the aims of alchemy. 2. Most essential part of any substance, refined extract; purest and most perfect form, manifestation, or embodiment, *of* some quality or class. **quĭntėssĕn'tial** (-shl) *adj.* [*quinta essentia* 5th essence]

quĭntĕt(te)' *n.* (mus.) (Performers of) piece for 5 voices or instruments; set of 5.

Quĭntĭl'ian (-yan). Marcus Fabius Quintĭlianus (*c* A.D. 35–*c* 95), Roman rhetorician, author of 'De Institutione Oratoria', the 10th book of which contains judgements on Greek and Roman writers.

quĭntĭll'ion (-yon) *n.* 5th power of a million (1 with 30 ciphers); (U.S.) cube of a million (1 with 18 ciphers).

quĭn'tūple *adj.* Fivefold; consisting of 5 things or parts. ~ *v.* Multiply, increase, fivefold.

quĭn'tūplėt *n.* 1. Set of 5 things; (mus.) group of 5 notes played in the time of 4. 2. One of 5 children born at a birth.

quĭntūp'lĭcate *adj.* Quintuple.

quĭp *n.* Sarcastic remark, clever hit, smart saying, verbal conceit; quibble.

quipu (kēp'o͞o, kwĭ-) *n.* Ancient-Peruvian device for sending messages, keeping accounts, etc., by variously knotting threads of various colours. [Peruv., = 'knot']

quīre[1] *n.* 4 sheets of paper etc. folded to form 8 leaves as in medieval MSS.; any collection of leaves one within another in MS. or book; 24 sheets of writing paper; *in* ~*s*, (of book) in folded sheets, unbound.

quīre[2] *n.* & *v.* See CHOIR.

Quĭ'rĭnal. One of the hills on which ancient Rome was built; site of Italian royal residence 1870–1947, now of official residence of president of the republic.

quĭrk *n.* 1. Quibble, quip; trick of action or behaviour; twist or flourish in drawing or writing. 2. (archit.) Acute hollow between convex part of moulding and soffit or fillet (ill. MOULDING).

quĭrt *n.* (U.S.) Short-handled riding whip with braided leather lash used in western U.S. and Span. America. ~ *v.t.* Lash with this.

quĭs'lĭng (-z-) *n.* Collaborationist, traitor to one's country. **quĭs'lĭngīte** *adj.* & *n.* [Major Vidkun *Quisling*, a Norwegian who collaborated with the Germans when they invaded Norway 1940]

quĭt[1] *pred. adj.* Free, clear, absolved (archaic); rid of; *quit'-claim*, renunciation of right; (*v.t.*) renounce claim to, give up (thing) *to*; ~*-rent*, (usu. small) rent paid by freeholder or copyholder in lieu of service.

quĭt[2] *v.t.* 1. (archaic) Rid one-*self of*; behave, acquit, conduct oneself *well*, etc. 2. Give up, let go, abandon; depart from, leave; (abs., of tenant) leave occupied premises. **quĭtt'er** *n.* (U.S.) Shirker, one who abandons project etc.

quĭtch *n.* ~ (*grass*), COUCH[2]-grass.

quīte *adv.* 1. Completely, wholly, entirely, altogether, to the utmost extent, in the fullest sense, positively, absolutely. 2. Rather, to some extent, as ~ *a long time*; ~ *a few*, a fair number.

quĭts *pred. adj.* On even terms by retaliation or repayment.

quĭtt'ance *n.* (archaic, poet.) Release *from*; acknowledgement of payment, receipt.

quĭv'er[1] *n.* Case for holding arrows; ~ *full* (*of children*), large family (see Ps. cxxvii. 5).

quĭv'er[2] *v.* Tremble or vibrate with slight rapid motion; (of bird) make (wings) quiver. ~ *n.* Quivering motion or sound.

qui vive (kē vēv). *On the* ~, on the alert. [Fr., = '(long) live who?', i.e. 'on whose side are you?', as sentinel's challenge]

Quĭx'ote. *Don* ~, hero of romance (1605–15) by CERVANTES, written to ridicule the books of chivalry; hence, enthusiastic visionary, pursuer of lofty but impracticable ideals. **quĭxŏt'ĭc** *adj.* **quĭx'otry** *n.*

quĭz *n.* Odd or eccentric person, in character or appearance (now rare); one who quizzes; hoax, banter, ridicule (now rare); (orig. U.S.) informal oral examination of class or pupil, now, general knowledge test, esp. one organized as an entertainment or competition. ~ *v.t.* Make report of (person, his ways); regard with mocking air; look curiously at, observe the ways or oddities of, survey through an eye-glass; (orig. U.S.) put series of questions to (person). **quĭzz'ĭcal** *adj.* **quĭzz'ĭcally** *adv.*

quŏd *n.* (slang) Prison. ~ *v.t.* (slang) Imprison.

quŏd ĕ'răt dĕmŏnstrăn'dum. (abbrev. Q.E.D.) Which was to be proved (formula concluding geometrical demonstration etc.).

quŏd vĭ'dė. (abbrev. q.v.) Which see (in cross-references etc.).

quoin (koin) *n.* 1. External angle of building; stone or brick forming angle, corner-stone (ill. MASONRY); internal corner of room. 2. Wedge for locking type in form (ill. PRINT), raising level of gun, keeping barrel from rolling, etc. ~ *v.t.* Raise or secure with quoins.

quoit (k(w)oit) *n.* Heavy, flattish ring of iron or (in *deck-quoits*) rope, thrown to encircle iron peg or to stick in ground near it in game of *quoits*.

quŏn'dam *adj.* Sometime, former. [L, = 'formerly']

Quorn. A celebrated pack of fox-hounds, hunting in Leicestershire, named after Quorndon Hall where the kennels now are.

quōr'um *n.* Fixed number of members that must be present to make proceedings of assembly, society, board, etc., valid. [L, = 'of whom']

quot. *abbrev.* Quotation etc.

quōt'a *n.* Part or share which is, or ought to be, contributed by one to a total sum or amount; part or share of a total which belongs, is given, or is due, to one. [L *quota* (*pars*) how great (a part), f. *quot* how many]

quotā'tion *n.* 1. (print.) Large quadrat used for filling up blanks (orig. between marginal references). 2. Quoting, passage quoted; amount stated as current price of stocks or commodities; *~-marks,* inverted commas and apostrophes, single (' ') or double (" "), used to mark beginning and end of quoted passage.

quōte *v.t.* Cite or appeal to (author, book, etc.) in comfirmation of some view, repeat or copy out passage(s) from; repeat or copy out (borrowed passage) usu. with indication that it is borrowed; (abs.) make quotations (*from*); adduce or cite *as*; state price of (usu. *at* figure). ~ *n.* (colloq.) Passage quoted; (usu. pl.) quotation-mark(s).

quōth *v.t.*, 1st & 3rd pers. past indic. (archaic) Said.

quotĭd'ian *adj.* Daily, of every day; commonplace, trivial; ~ *fever, ague,* with paroxysms recurring every day. ~ *n.* Quotidian fever or ague.

quō'tient (-shnt) *n.* Result given by dividing one quantity by another.

Qur'ān: see KORAN.

q.v. *abbrev. Quantum vis* (= as much as you wish); *quod vide* (= which see).

qy *abbrev.* Query.

R

R, r (ar). 18th letter of modern English and 17th of ancient Roman alphabet, derived through early Gk Ʀ, P from Phoenician ᑫ. In modern standard English this letter represents, before a vowel, an open voiced consonant, with almost no 'trill', in formation of which the point of the tongue approaches the palate a little way behind the teeth; in other positions, an obscure vowel sound, disappearing altogether after some vowels.

r. *abbrev.* Railway; right; röntgen(s); run(s).

R, ₨ *abbrevs.* Rupee.

R. *abbrev.* Réaumur; *Regina*; *retarder* (on timepiece regulator, = to retard); *Rex*; River.

℞ *abbrev.* (in med. prescriptions) *Recipe*: = take.

Ra (rah). Sun-god of ancient Egypt, freq. represented with head of falcon.

R.A. *abbrev.* Royal Academy (*or* Academician); Royal Artillery.

R.A.A.F. *abbrev.* Royal Australian Air Force; Royal Auxiliary Air Force.

răbb'ėt *n.* 1. Step-shaped reduction cut along edge, face, or projecting angle of wood, etc., usu. to receive edge or tongue of another piece (ill. JOINT); ~ *plane,* tool for making groove along an edge (ill. PLANE). 2. Elastic beam fixed so as to give rebound to large fixed hammer. ~ *v.t.* Join, fix, with rabbet; make rabbet in.

răbb'ī *n.* Jewish doctor of the law, esp. one authorized by ordination to deal with law and ritual and perform certain functions; *Chief R~*, ecclesiastical head of United Synagogue in Gt Britain. **răbb'ĭn** *n.* Rabbi. **răbb'ĭnate, răbb'ĭnism, răbb'ĭnist** *ns.* **rabbĭn'ĭcal** *adj.* **rabbĭn'ĭcally** *adv.*

răbb'ĭt *n.* Burrowing rodent-like gregarious mammal (*Oryctolagus cuniculus*), native to W. Europe, allied to the hare but with shorter legs and smaller ears, brownish-grey in natural state, also black, white, or pied in domestication; (slang) poor performer at any game, esp. cricket, golf, or lawn tennis; *~-punch,* (boxing) punch on back of neck. ~ *v.i.* Hunt rabbits.

răb'ble[1] *n.* Disorderly crowd, mob; contemptible or inferior set of people; *the* lowest classes of the populace. **răb'blement** (-lm-) *n.* (now rare) (Tumult as of) a rabble.

răb'ble[2] *n.* Iron bar with bent end for stirring molten metal in puddling.

Răb'ėlais (-lā), François (*c* 1495–1553). French physician, humanist, and satirical writer; author of 'Pantagruel' and 'GARGANTUA'. **Răbėlais'ĭan** (-lāz-) *adj.* Of or like Rabelais; having the extravagance and grossness of humour, or the exuberance of imagination and language, characteristic of Rabelais.

răb'ĭd *adj.* Furious, violent, raging, unreasoning; (esp. of dog) affected with rabies; of rabies. **răb'ĭdly** *adv.* **răb'ĭdnėss, rabĭd'ĭty** *ns.*

rāb'ies (-ēz, -ĭēz) *n.* Canine madness, a contagious disease principally of the dog but occas. affecting other domestic animals and also man (in which case it is usu. known as *hydrophobia*).

R.A.C. *abbrev.* Royal Armoured Corps; Royal Automobile Club.

rac(c)ōōn' *n.* Amer. nocturnal carnivore (*Procyon*), esp. common N. Amer. greyish-brown kind (*P. lotor*) with bushy tail and pointed snout.

rāce[1] *n.* 1. Onward sweep or movement, esp. strong current in sea or river; course of sun or moon, course of life. 2. Channel of stream; track or channel in which something moves or slides, as that of a shuttle crossing the web or the balls in a ball-bearing (ill. BEARING). 3. Contest of speed between runners, ships, horses, etc., or persons doing anything; (pl.) series of these for horses at fixed time on regular course; *~-card,* programme of races; *race'-course,* ground for horse-racing; *race'horse,* horse bred or kept for racing; *~-meeting,* horse-racing fixture. ~ *v.* Compete in speed *with*; have race with, try to surpass in speed; cause (horse etc.) to race; indulge in horse-racing; make (person, thing) move at full speed; go at full speed; (of machinery) move, revolve with uncontrolled speed, when resistance is diminished, as when the propeller of a ship is raised out of the water.

rāce[2] *n.* Group of persons, animals, or plants connected by common descent; posterity *of* (person); house, family, tribe, or nation regarded as of common stock; distinct ethnical stock; any great division of living creatures; descent, kindred; class of persons etc. with some common feature; (biol.) subdivision of a species; variety.

racēme' *n.* (bot.) Inflorescence opening from below upwards with flowers on short lateral stalks springing from a central stem, as in hyacinth, lily of the valley, etc. (ill. INFLORESCENCE).

racĕm'ic *adj.* (chem.) Derived from grapes or grape-juice; ~ *acid,* colourless crystalline acid, an optically inactive variety of tartaric acid, found in the juice of grapes.

ră'cėmōse *adj.* (bot.) Arranged in, having form of, a raceme; (anat.) arranged in, having form of, a cluster, as e.g. the pancreas.

rā'cer *n.* (esp.) Horse, yacht, motor-car, etc., used for racing.

rā'chĭs (-k-) *n.* (pl. *-ides* pr. -ĭdēz). 1. (bot.) Axis of inflorescence with flower-stalks at short intervals, as in grasses; axis of pinnately compound leaf or frond (ill. LEAF). 2. (anat.) Vertebral column or cord from which it develops. 3. (ornith.) Feather-shaft, esp. part bearing barbs (ill. FEATHER).

rachĭt'ic (-k-) *adj.* Of, affected with, RICKETS (**rachī'tĭs**).

Rachmăn'ĭnŏv (raχ-, -f), Sergei Vassilievich (1873–1943). Russian pianist and composer.

rā'cial (-shl) *adj.* Of, belonging to, characteristic of, race. **rā'cially** *adv.*

rā'cialism (-sha-) *n.* (Encouragement of) antagonism between races of men.

Racine (răsēn'), Jean (1639–99). French tragic poet and dramatist; author of 'Phèdre', 'Andromaque', 'Athalie', etc.

rā'cism *n.* Theory that fundamental characteristics of race are preserved by an unchanging tradition.

răck[1] *n.* 1. Driving clouds. 2. Destruction (usu. ~ *and ruin*). ~ *v.i.* (Of clouds) drive before wind.

răck[2] *n.* 1. Fixed or movable frame of wooden or metal bars for holding fodder; framework with rails, bars, pegs, or shelves, for keeping articles on or in. 2. Cogged or indented bar or rail gearing with wheel, pinion, or worm, or serving with pegs etc. to adjust position of something (ill. GEAR); *~-railway*, railway with cogged rail between bearing-rails; *~-wheel*, cog-wheel. ~ *v.* Fill *up* stable-rack with hay or straw for the night; fasten (horse) *up* to rack; place in or on rack.

răck[3] *v.t.* 1. Stretch joints of (person) by pulling esp. with instruments of torture made for the purpose; (of disease etc.) inflict tortures on; shake violently, injure by straining, task severely. 2. Exact utmost possible amount of (rent); oppress (tenants) with excessive rent; exhaust (land) with excessive use; *~-rent* (*n.*) extortionate rent equal or nearly equal to full value of land; (*v.t.*) extort this from (tenant) or for (land); *~-renter*, tenant paying, landlord exacting, rack-rent. ~ *n.* Instrument of torture, frame with roller at each end to which victim's wrists and ankles were tied so that his joints were stretched when rollers were turned; *on the* ~, (fig.) in state of acute mental or physical suffering, in keen anxiety or suspense.

răck[4] *n.* Arrack.

răck[5] *n.* Horse's gait between trot and canter, both legs of one side being lifted almost at once, and all four feet being off ground together at moments. ~ *v.i.* Progress thus.

răck[6] *v.t.* Draw off (wine etc.) from the lees.

răck'ėt[1], **răc'quet** (-kĭt) *n.* Bat used in tennis, rackets, etc., network of cord, catgut, nylon, etc., stretched across elliptical frame with handle attached (ill. LAWN); (pl.) ball-game for 2 or 4 persons played with rackets in a closed four-walled court, each player striking the ball in turn and trying to keep it rebounding from the end wall of the court; *~-ball*, small hard kid-covered ball of cork and string; *~-press*, press for keeping racket taut and in shape.

răck'ėt[2] *n.* 1. Disturbance, uproar, din; social excitement, gaiety, dissipation; trying experience (esp. in *stand the* ~, come successfully through test, face consequences of action). 2. (slang) Dodge, game, line of business; scheme, procedure, for obtaining money etc. by dubious or illegal means, esp. as form of organized crime. ~ *v.i.* Live gay life; move about noisily. **răck'ėty** *adj.* Noisy, uproarious, dissipated.

răckėteer' *n.* Member of (orig. U.S.) criminal gang practising extortion, intimidation, violence, etc., esp. on large scale. **răckėteer'ing** *n.* Systematic extortion of money by threats, violence, or other illegal methods.

răcŏnteur' (-têr) *n.* (fem. *-euse* pr. -êrz). Teller of anecdotes.

racq'uet: see RACKET[1].

rā'cy *adj.* Of distinctive quality or vigour, not smoothed into sameness or commonness; lively, spirited, piquant. **rā'cily** *adv.* **rā'cinėss** *n.*

rad. *abbrev.* Radical.

R.A.D.A. *abbrev.* Royal Academy of Dramatic Art.

rād'âr *n.* System for ascertaining direction and range of aircraft, ships, coasts, and other objects by sending out electromagnetic radiations of short wave-length and interpreting the reflections of these produced by certain types of surface; apparatus used for this. [f. *ra*dio *d*etection *a*nd *r*anging]

R.A.D.C., R.A.E.C. *abbrevs.* Royal Army Dental, Educational, Corps.

Răd'cliffe, Mrs Ann (1764–1823). English author of romances of 'mystery and terror'.

rădd'le *n.* Red ochre. ~ *v.t.* Paint with raddle; plaster with rouge.

rād'ĭal *adj.* 1. Arranged like rays or radii, having position or direction of a radius; having spokes or radiating lines; acting or moving along lines that diverge from a centre; ~ *axle*, axle (of railway-carriage etc.) assuming position of radius to curve of track; ~ *engine*, internal combustion engine with cylinders arranged like spokes of wheel; ~ *velocity*: see VELOCITY. 2. Of the radius of the forearm. **rād'ially** *adv.* **rād'ĭal** *n.* Radial nerve or artery.

rād'ĭan *n.* Angle at centre of circle subtending arc whose length is equal to the radius.

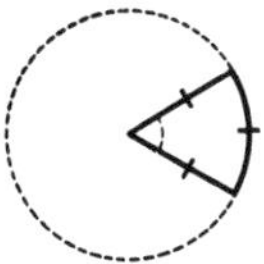

RADIAN

rād'ĭant *adj.* Emitting rays of light; beaming with joy, hope, etc.; issuing in rays, bright, shining, splendid; extending or operating radially; (her.) having wavy points; ~ *heat*, electromagnetic radiation emitted by hot bodies, having a wave-length greater than that of visible light and capable of crossing a vacuum; ~ *heat therapy*, treatment, esp. of injured muscles and joints, by such radiation; ~ *point*, point from which rays or radii proceed; (astron.) apparent focal point of meteoric shower. **rād'ĭantly** *adv.* **rād'ĭance** *n.* **rād'ĭant** *n.* Point or object from which light or heat radiates; (astron.) radiant point.

rād'ĭate[1] *adj.* Having divergent rays or parts radially arranged. **rād'iately** *adv.*

rād'ĭāte[2] *v.* Emit rays of light, heat, etc.; issue in rays; diverge or spread from central point; emit (light, heat, etc.) from centre; transmit by wireless.

rādĭā'tion *n.* The manner in which the energy of a vibrating body is transmitted in all directions by a surrounding medium; emission and diffusion of heat-rays; emission of Röntgen or X-rays, or the rays and particles characteristic of radio-active substances; ~ *sickness*, effects of exposure to radio-activity (e.g. after an atomic bomb explosion) including nausea and, later, disorders of the blood; temporary symptoms of patient who has been treated by a radio-active substance, relieved when treatment is stopped.

rād'ĭātor *n.* (esp.) Small chamber or arrangement of pipes heated with hot air, steam, etc., and radiating warmth into room; that part of the engine-cooling system of most automobiles and certain types of aeroplane engine in which the circulating fluid is air-cooled; (U.S.) electric fan.

răd'ĭcal *adj.* 1. Of the root(s); naturally inherent, essential, fundamental; forming the basis, primary. 2. Affecting the foundation, going to the root; (of politicians) desiring or advocating fundamental or drastic reforms; (hist.) of, belonging to, extreme section of Liberal party or opinion. 3. (philol.) Of the roots of words. 4. (mus.) Of the root of a chord. 5. (bot.) Of, springing direct from, the root, or the main stem close to it. 6. (math.) Of the root of a number or quantity; ~ *sign*, the sign $\sqrt{}$ ($\sqrt[3]{}$, $\sqrt[4]{}$, etc.) used to indicate that the square (cube, fourth, etc.) root of the number to which it is prefixed is to be extracted. **răd'ĭcally** *adv.* **răd'ĭcal** *n.* 1. Fundamental thing or principle. 2. (politics) Person holding radical opinions. 3. (philol.) Root. 4. (math.) Quantity forming or expressed as root of another; radical sign. 5. (chem.) Element or atom, or group of these, forming base of compound and remaining unchanged during ordinary chemical reactions to which this is liable.

răd'ĭcle *n.* 1. Part of plant embryo that develops into primary root (ill. SEED); rootlet (ill. SEEDLING). 2. (anat.) Root-like subdivision of nerve or vein. 3. (chem.) Radical. **radĭc'ūlar** *adj.*

rā'dĭō *n.* Transmission and reception of messages etc. by means of electromagnetic waves of frequency between *c* 15 kilocycles and *c* 30,000 megacycles (~ *frequency*), either as acoustic signals (RADIOTELEPHONY) or as morse-code signals (RADIOTELEGRAPHY); wireless, broadcasting; (attrib.) of radiotelephony or radiotelegraphy; concerned with phenomena occurring at radio frequency; ~ (*receiver*), apparatus which detects signals transmitted by radio-frequency waves and reproduces them as audible sounds; ~ *telescope*: see TELESCOPE; ~ *transmitter*, apparatus which gives out signals by producing power at radio frequencies, delivering it to an aerial and radiating it.

rā'dĭō-ăc'tĭve *adj.* Of, exhibiting, radio-activity. **rād'ĭō-ăctĭv'ĭty** *n.* (physics & chem.) The property possessed by certain elements of high atomic weight (radium, thorium, uranium, etc.) of spontaneously emitting alpha, beta, or gamma rays by the disintegration of the nuclei of the atoms; these rays are capable of penetrating opaque bodies and affecting a photographic plate even when separated by thin sheets of metal; radio-activity may be induced in certain elements which are not normally radio-active by exposure to the action of bombarding particles as protons, deuterons, or neutrons, and a new species of radio-active atom, usually of short life, is thus formed.

rādĭō-astrŏn'omy *n.* Study of celestial objects by their emission or reflection of radio-frequency radiation, using radio and radar techniques.

rādĭocarb'on *n.* A radio-active isotope of carbon existing in organic matter and having its origin in the radio-active carbon dioxide produced by the interaction of cosmic ray neutrons and atmospheric nitrogen at high altitudes; ~ *dating*, method of dating organic materials from ancient deposits, esp. archaeological remains of the period 30,000 B.C. to A.D. 1000, made possible by the discovery that after the death of plants and animals the radiocarbon content decays at a regular rate (by half in every period of *c* 5600 years); also called *carbon-14 dating*.

rādĭogŏnĭŏm'ėter *n.* Apparatus for discovering direction from which electromagnetic impulses are coming.

rād'ĭogrăm *n.* 1. Image produced on photographic plate by X-rays. 2. Message sent by radiotelegraphy. 3. Radio receiver combined with gramophone.

rād'ĭograph (-ahf) *n.* 1. Instrument for measuring and recording the duration and intensity of sunshine. 2. = RADIOGRAM (sense 1). **rādĭogrăph'ĭc** *adj.*

rādĭŏg'raphy *n.* Photography by means of X-rays. **rādĭŏg'rapher** *n.*

rādĭolocā'tion *n.* Determination by means of radio devices of the position or course of ships, aircraft, etc.; RADAR.

rādĭŏl'ogy *n.* Scientific study of X-rays, radio-activity, and other radiations, and (esp.) the use of these in medicine. **rādĭŏl'ogist** *n.*

rādĭŏm'ėter *n.* Instrument showing conversion of radiant energy into mechanical force.

rād'ĭōphāre *n.* Radio transmitting station sending out signals to enable ships, aircraft, etc., to determine their position.

rādĭŏs'copy *n.* Examination of the internal structure etc. of opaque bodies by means of X- or other rays.

rādĭotėlĕg'raphy *n.* Transmission and reception of morse code signals by electromagnetic waves of radio-frequency. **rādĭotĕl'ėgrăm** *n.* Message transmitted by radiotelegraphy.

rādĭotėlĕph'ony *n.* Transmission and reception of acoustic signals (e.g. voices) by electromagnetic waves of radio-frequency. **rādĭotĕl'ėphōne** *n.* Apparatus for communicating by radiotelephony.

rādĭōthĕrapeut'ĭcs, rādĭōthĕ'rapy *ns.* Treatment of disease by X-rays, radium, or other forms of radiation.

răd'ĭsh *n.* Cruciferous plant, *Raphanus sativum*; fleshy slightly pungent root of this, often eaten raw as relish or in salads.

rād'ĭum *n.* Rare radio-active metallic element, isolated from pitchblende in 1898 by P. and M. Curie; symbol Ra, at. no. 88, at. wt 226·05; (pop.) various salts of this element, used in radiotherapy etc.; ~ *emanation*, RADON; ~ *needle*, needle with hollow tip enclosing radio-active material, used in radiotherapy for treating underlying tissue.

rād'ĭus *n.* (pl. *-ĭī*). 1. Thicker and shorter bone of forearm in man (ill. SKELETON); corresponding bone in beast's foreleg or bird's wing. 2. (math.) Straight line from centre to circumference of circle or sphere (ill. CIRCLE); radial line from focus to any point of curve; ~ *vector*, variable line drawn to curve from fixed point, esp. (astron.) from sun or planet to path of satellite. 3. Any of set of lines diverging from a point like radii of circle, object of this kind (e.g. spoke). 4. Circular area as measured by its radius; the *four-mile* ~, that of which Charing Cross is the centre. 5. (bot.) Outer rim of composite flower-head (e.g. daisy); radiating branch of umbel.

rād'ĭx *n.* (pl. *-ices* pr. -ĭsēz). Number or symbol used as basis of numeration scale; source or origin *of*. [L, = 'root']

Răd'nor(shire). Inland county of S. Wales.

rād'ŏn *n.* Chemically inert heavy gaseous radio-active element, the first disintegration product of radium (also called *radium emanation*); symbol Rn, at. no. 86, principal isotope 222. [f. *radium* and the termination of *argon*, *neon*, etc.]

răd'ūla *n.* File-like structure in molluscs used to scrape off particles of food and draw them into the mouth.

Raeburn (rāb'*ern*), Sir Henry (1756–1823). Scottish portrait-painter.

R.A.F.(V.R.) *abbrevs.* Royal Air Force (Volunteer Reserve).

răff *n.* Riff-raff.

Raffaello Sanzio: see RAPHAEL[2].

răff'ĭa *n.* Palm of genus *Raphia*; soft fibre from leaves of *R. ruffia* and *R. taedigera*, used for tying up plants and making hats, baskets, mats, etc.

răff'ĭsh *adj.* Disreputable, dissipated, esp. in appearance. **răff'ĭshly** *adv.* **răff'ĭshnėss** *n.*

răff'le[1] *n.* Lottery in which article is assigned by lot to one person of a number who have each paid a certain part of its value. ~ *v.* Take part in raffle *for* (thing); sell (thing) by raffle.

răff'le[2] *n.* Rubbish, refuse, lumber, debris.

raft (-ah-) *n.* Collection of logs, casks, etc., fastened together in the water for transportation; flat floating structure of timber, etc., for conveying persons or things, esp. as substitute for boat in emergencies; floating accumulation of trees, ice, etc. ~ *v.* Transport (as) on raft; form into a raft; cross (water) on raft(s); work raft.

raft'er[1] (-ah-) *n.* Man who rafts timber.

raft'er[2] (-ah-) *n.* One of the sloping beams forming framework on which slates etc. of roof are upheld (ill. ROOF). ~ *v.t.* Furnish with rafters; plough (land) so that earth from furrow is turned over on same breadth of unploughed ground next it.

răg[1] *n.* Torn or frayed piece of woven material; one of the irregular scraps to which cloth etc. is reduced by wear and tear; (usu. with neg.) smallest scrap of cloth or sail; remnant, odd scrap, irregular piece; (contempt.) flag, handkerchief, newspaper, etc.; (pl.) tattered clothes; (collect.) rags used as material for paper, stuffing, etc.; ~*-baby*, doll made of rags; ~*-bag*, bag in which scraps of linen etc. are kept for use; ~*-bolt*, bolt with barbs to keep it tight when driven in; (*v.t.*) join together with these; ~*-book*, children's book with pages of untearable cloth; ~ *fair*, old-clothes sale held in Houndsditch; ~ *paper*, good-quality paper made from rags; ~ *tag* (*and bobtail*), the riff-raff; ragged, low, or disreputable people; ~-*time*, popular music of U.S. Negro origin, with much syncopation; ~-*wheel*, wheel with projections catching in links of chain that passes over it, sprocket-wheel; *rag'wort*, common yellow-flowered ragged-leaved plant (*Senecio Jacobaea*) and other species of *Senecio*.

răg[2] *n.* Large coarse roofing-slate; kinds of hard coarse stone breaking up in thick slabs.

răg[3] *n.* Act of ragging, noisy disorderly conduct; (in some universities) annual parade of students in fancy dress to collect money for charity. ~ *v.* Annoy, tease, torment; esp., (univ. slang) play rough jokes upon, throw into wild disorder (person's room etc.) by way of practical joke; act in this way.

răg'amŭffĭn *n.* Ragged dirty fellow.

R.A.G.C. *abbrev.* Royal & Ancient Golf Club, St. Andrews; also **R. & A.**

rāge *n.* (Fit of) violent anger; violent operation of some natural force or some sentiment; poetic, prophetic, or martial ardour; vehement desire or passion *for*; object of widespread temporary enthusiasm or fashion. ~ *v.i.* Rave, storm, speak madly or furiously, be full of anger; (of wind, sea, passion, battle, etc.) be violent, be at the height, operate unchecked, prevail. **rā'gingly** *adv.*

răgg'ĕd (-g-) *adj.* Rough, shaggy, hanging in tufts; of broken jagged outline or surface, full of rough or sharp projections; faulty, wanting finish, smoothness, or uniformity; rent, torn, frayed, in ragged clothes; ~ *robin*, common English crimson-flowered wild plant (*Lychnis floscuculi*); ~ *school*, (hist.) free school for poor children. **răgg'ĕdly** *adv.* **răgg'ĕdnĕss** *n.*

răg'lan *n.* Overcoat without shoulder-seams, top of sleeve being carried up to neck; ~ *sleeve*, sleeve of this kind (ill. SLEEVE). [f. Lord *Raglan*, British commander in Crimean War]

Ragnarök (răg'narĕrk'). (Scand. myth.) Day of great battle between the gods and the powers of evil, when both are destroyed and the old order disappears, to be replaced by a new and happier scheme of things when Balder returns from the nether world.

răgout' (-ōō) *n.* Meat in small pieces stewed with vegetables and highly seasoned. ~ *v.t.* Cook thus.

răg'ūly *adj.* (her.) Like a row of sawn-off branches (ill. HERALDRY).

ra'hăt lakoum' (rah-h-, -ōōm) *n.* Kinds of Turkish sweetmeat, esp. TURKISH delight.

raht *n.* Principal monetary unit of Siam, = 100 satang.

raid *n.* Sudden incursion of military force into or upon a country for the purposes of plunder or attack; (international law) hostile invasion by military forces of territory of a State at peace unauthorized by the government of the country from which the raiding forces come; AIR-raid; sudden descent of police etc. upon suspected premises or illicit goods. ~ *v.* Make raid *into* etc.; make raid on. **raid'er** *n.*

Raikes (rāks), Robert (1735–1811). English promoter of Sunday schools.

rail[1] *n.* 1. Horizontal or inclined bar or continuous series of bars of wood or metal used to hang things on, as top of banisters, as part of fence, as protection against contact or falling over, or for similar purpose; any horizontal piece in frame of wooden panelling (ill. WAINSCOT). 2. Iron bar or continuous line of bars laid on ground as one side or half of railway track; *by* ~, by railway; ~-*chair*, metal clamp, attached to sleeper, in which railway line rests and is secured; *rail'head*, farthest point reached by railway under construction; (mil.) point on railway at which road transport begins; *rail'road*, (esp. in U.S.) railway; (*v.*) transport, travel, by rail; accomplish (action) with great speed, rush *into*, through, etc.; *rail'way*, track or set of tracks of iron or steel rails for passage of trains of cars drawn by locomotive

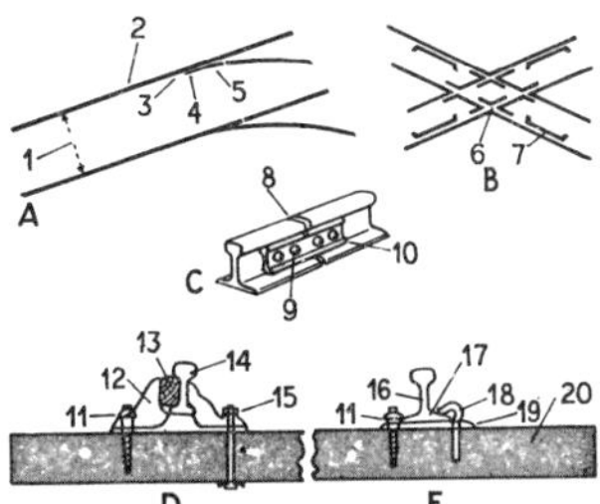

RAILWAY TRACK: A. POINTS. B. CROSSING. C. METHOD OF JOINING RAIL. D. BULL-HEADED RAIL. E. FLAT-BOTTOMED RAIL

1. Gauge. 2. Stock rail. 3. Throw of point. 4. Point. 5. Tongue. 6. Frog. 7. Check rail. 8. Gap. 9. Fish bolt. 10. Fish-plate. 11. Screw. 12. Chair. 13. Key. 14. Head. 15. Bolt. 16. Web. 17. Base. 18. Spike. 19. Base plate. 20. Sleeper

engine and conveying passengers and goods; the tracks of this kind worked by a single company, the whole of the organization and persons required for their working; (hist.) road laid with rails for heavy horse-carts. ~ *v.* Furnish or enclose with rail (often ~ *in*, *off*); provide with rail; lay (railway route) with rails; convey (goods), travel, by rail.

rail[2] *n.* Any of various kinds of small birds of the family *Hallidae*, of which the *land*-~ or corncrake (*Crex crex*), and the *water*-~ (*Rallus aquaticus*) are members.

rail[3] *v.i.* Use abusive language (*at*, *against*).

rail'age *n.* Charges for freight etc. made by railway.

rail'ing *n.* (esp.) Fence or barrier of rails etc.

raill'ery *n.* (Piece of) good-humoured ridicule, rallying.

raim'ent *n.* (poet., rhet.) Clothing, dress, apparel.

rain *n.* Condensed moisture of atmosphere falling visibly in separate drops; fall of such drops; (rain-like descent of) falling liquid or solid particles or bodies; (pl.) showers of rain; *the* ~*s*, rainy season in tropical countries; ~-*coat*, coat which keeps out rain, waterproof; ~-*day*, day when recorded rainfall is 0·01 inch or more; *rain'drop*, single drop of rain; *rain'fall*, shower; quantity of rain falling within given area in given time; ~-*gauge*, instrument measuring rainfall; *rain'proof*, impervious to rain; (*n.*) rainproof coat; ~-*spell*, period of 15 or more *rain-days* (see above); *rain'-water*, water which has fallen from clouds as rain (not got from wells). **rain'lĕss** *adj.* **rain** *v.* 1. *It rains*, rain falls; there is a shower of (something falling etc.); *it* ~*s cats and dogs*, it rains violently; *it* ~*s in*, rain penetrates house etc. 2. Send down rain; fall or send down in showers or like rain.

rain'bow (-ō) *n.* Arch showing prismatic colours in their order formed in sky (or across cataract etc.) opposite sun by reflection, double refraction, and dispersion, of sun's rays in falling drops of rain, spray, etc.; (attrib.) many-coloured; *lunar* ~, (rarely seen) rainbow formed by moon's rays; ~ *fish*, various bright-coloured Amer. and New Zealand fishes; ~ *trout*, Californian species of trout (*Salmo irideus*).

rain'y *adj.* In or on which rain is falling or much rain usu. falls; (of clouds, wind, etc.) laden with, bringing, rain; ~ *day*, (fig.) time of esp. pecuniary need.

Rais (rās), (*or* **Retz**), Gilles de (1404–40). Marshal of France; supporter of Joan of Arc; tried and hanged for murder (the number of his victims was said to be 140); his name is associated with legend of BLUEBEARD.

raise (-z) *v.t.* 1. Set upright, make stand up, restore to or towards vertical position; rouse; ~ *from the dead*, restore to life; ~ *the country*, etc., rouse inhabitants in some emergency; ~ *the wind*, (fig.) procure money for some purpose; *raised pie*, *pastry*, etc., pie etc. standing without support of dish at sides. 2. Build up, construct; create, produce, breed; (chiefly U.S.) rear, bring up (person); utter, make audible; start; give occasion for, elicit; set up, advance; ~ *one's voice*, speak; ~ *a laugh*, cause others to laugh. 3. Elevate, put or take into higher position; extract from earth; direct upwards; promote to higher rank; make higher or nobler; cause to ascend; make (voice) louder or shriller; increase amount of, heighten level of; (naut.) come in sight of (land, ship); ~ one's *hat*, take it off in greeting; ~ one's *eyebrows*, look supercilious or shocked; ~ *Cain, hell*, etc., make a disturbance; ~ *bread* etc., cause it to rise with yeast etc. 4. Levy, collect, bring together, procure, manage to get. 5. Relinquish, cause enemy to relinquish (siege, blockade). ~ *n.* Increase in amount, esp. of stakes at poker, bid at bridge, etc., (U.S.) rise (in salary etc.).

rais'in (-zn) *n.* Partially dried grape.

raison d'être (rā'zawṅ dā'tr) *n.* What accounts for or justifies or has caused a thing's existence.

raj (rahj) *n.* (Anglo-Ind.) Sovereignty, rule.

raja(h) (rahj'*a*) *n.* Indian king or prince (also as title of petty dignitary or noble in India, or of Malay or Javanese chief). **ra'jahship** *n.* [Hind. *rājā*, f. *rāj* to reign]

Rajasthan (rahj'astahn). State in NW. India; capital, Jaipur.

Rajput (rahj'pŏŏt). Member of Hindu land-owning warrior caste of NW. India. **Rajputa'na** (-tah-). The country of the Rajputs; formerly a group of States including Jodhpur, Bikaner, Jaipur, Udaipur, etc.; now, RAJASTHAN.

rāke[1] *n.* Implement consisting of pole with cross-bar toothed like comb at end for drawing together hay etc., or smoothing loose soil or gravel; wheeled implement drawn by horse for same purpose; kinds of implement resembling rake used for other purposes, e.g. by croupier drawing in money at gaming-table. ~ *v.* Collect, draw *together*, gather *up*, pull *out*, clear *off*, (as) with rake; clean or smooth with rake; search (as) with rake, ransack; make *level, clean*, etc., with rake; use rake, search as with rake; sweep with shot, enfilade, send shot along (ship) from stem to stern; sweep with the eyes; (of window etc.) have commanding view of; *rake'-off*, (slang, orig. U.S.) profit or commission made, often illegitimately, by one or more persons concerned in a transaction.

rāke[2] *n.* Dissipated or immoral man of fashion. [f. earlier *rake-hell* (RAKE[1] *v.*)]

rāke[3] *v.* (Of ship, its bow or stern) project at upper part of bow or stern beyond keel; (of masts or funnels) incline from perpendicular towards stern; give backward inclination to. ~ *n.* Amount to which thing rakes; raking position or build.

rāk'ish[1] *adj.* (As) of, like, a RAKE[2].

rāk'ish[2] *adj.* (Of ship) smart and fast-looking, seeming built for speed (freq. with implication of suspicious or piratical character). [perh. same wd as prec., with extra association of raking masts]

râle (rahl) *n.* (path.) Sound additional to that of respiration heard in auscultation of unhealthy lungs.

Rale(i)gh (raw'lĭ, rah-, rǎ-), Sir Walter (*c* 1552–1618). English military and naval commander, explorer, and poet; explored the eastern seaboard of America; and wrote accounts of his adventures; fell out of favour with Elizabeth I; was convicted of conspiring against James I, 1603, reprieved, but eventually executed.

rall. *abbrev. Rallentando.*

răllentăn'dō (as mus. direction). Gradually slower; (*n.*) passage played thus, manner of playing such passage.

răll'īne *adj.* Belonging to the group of birds which contains the rails, i.e. the various species of *Rallus*.

răll'y[1] *v.* Reassemble, get together again, after rout or dispersion, (cause to) renew conflict; bring, come, together as support or for concentrated action; revive (faculty etc.) by effort of will, pull oneself together, assume or rouse to fresh energy. ~ *n.* 1. Act of rallying, reunion for fresh effort; recovery of energy; mass-meeting. 2. (tennis etc.) Series of strokes made between service and failure to return the ball.

răll'y[2] *v.t.* Banter, chaff.

răm[1] *n.* 1. Uncastrated male sheep. 2. *R*~, zodiacal sign Aries. 3. (hist.) Swinging beam for breaching walls, battering-ram; (warship with) projecting beak at bow for charging side of other ships. 4. Falling weight of pile-driving machine; rammer; hydraulic water-raising or lifting machine; piston of hydrostatic press; plunger of force pump; ~*-jet*, jet engine for aircraft in which the motion through the air provides compression. ~ *v.t.* 1. Beat down (soil etc.) into solidity with wooden block etc.; make (post, plant, etc.) firm by ramming soil round it; drive (pile etc.) *down, in*, etc., by heavy blows; force (charge) home, pack (gun) tight, with ramrod; squeeze or force into place by pressure; (abs.) use rammer; *ram'rod*, (hist.) rod for ramming home charge of muzzle-loader (ill. PISTOL). 2. (Of ship) strike with ram; dash or violently impel *against, at*, etc. **rămm'er** *n.*

răm[2] *n.* (naut.) Boat's length over all.

R.A.M. *abbrev.* Royal Academy of Music.

Rămadan' (-ahn). 9th month of Moslem year, rigidly observed as 30 days' fast during hours of daylight.

Rām'an, Sir Chandrasekhara Venkata (1888–), Indian physicist. ~ *effect*, the appearance of additional lines (~ *lines*) in the spectrum of light when scattered by the molecules of a substance; ~ *spectrum*, the spectrum so obtained.

Rama'yana (r*a*mah'-). Ancient Sanskrit epic poem (500–300 B.C.).

răm'ble *v.i.* Walk for pleasure and without definite route; wander in discourse, talk or write disconnectedly. ~ *n.* Rambling walk.

răm'bler *n.* (esp.) Kinds of freely climbing rose, esp. the *crimson* ~.

răm'blĭng *adj.* Peripatetic, wandering; disconnected, desultory, incoherent; (of plants) straggling, climbing; (of house, street, etc.) irregularly planned. **răm'blingly** *adv.*

Rambouillet (rahṅbwēyā'), Cathérine de Vivonne-Pisani, Marquise de (1588–1655). Founder of first French 'salon', in which most distinguished persons of her day met and conversed.

R.A.M.C. *abbrev.* Royal Army Medical Corps.

Rameau (rahmō'), Jean Philippe (1683–1764). French composer of operas and harpsichord music.

Ramée[1], Marie Louise de la: see OUIDA.

Ramée[2], Pierre de la: see RAMUS.

răm'ėkĭn, răm'ėquĭn (-kĭn) *n.* Small quantity of cheese baked with bread-crumbs, eggs, etc.; ~ (*case*), small mould in which this is baked.

ramĕn'tum *n.* (chiefly in pl. *-ta*). (bot.) Thin membranous scale formed on surface of leaves and stalks.

Răm'ėsēs, Ramses (-z). Name of several Egyptian kings of 19th and 20th dynasties; *Rameses II* (? 1292–1225 B.C.), is supposed to have been the Pharaoh who oppressed the Jews.

rămĭfĭcā'tion *n.* Ramifying, (arrangement of) tree's branches; subdivision of complex structure comparable to tree's branches.

răm'ĭfȳ *v.* Form branches, subdivisions, or offshoots; branch out; (usu. pass.) cause to branch out, arrange in branching manner.

Răm'ĭllies (-lĭz). Belgian village near Louvain, scene (1706) of Marlborough's victory over French; ~ (*wig*), wig with long plait behind tied with bow at top and bottom (ill. WIG).

rămm'ĭsh *adj.* Rank-smelling.

rāmōse' *adj.* Branched, branching.

rămp[1] *n.* Slope, inclined plane joining two levels of ground, esp. in fortification, or of wall-coping; difference in level between opposite abutments of rampant arch; upward bend in stair-rail.

~ *v.* 1. (Chiefly of lion) stand on hind-legs with fore-paws in air, assume or be in threatening posture; (now usu. joc.) storm, rage, rush about. 2. Furnish or build with ramp; (of wall) ascend or descend to different level.

rămp[2] *n.* (slang) Swindle; levying of exorbitant prices.

rămpāge′ *v.i.* Behave violently, storm, rage, rush about. ~ *n.* Violent behaviour. **rămpā′geous** (-j*us*) *adj.* **rămpā′geously** *adv.* **rămpā′geousnėss** *n.*

rămp′ant *adj.* Ramping (chiefly of lion, esp. in her.; ill. HERALDRY); violent or extravagant in action or opinion, arrant, aggressive, unchecked, prevailing; rank, luxuriant; (of arch etc.) having one abutment higher than the other, climbing. **rămp′antly** *adv.* **rămp′ancy** *n.*

rămp′art *n.* Broad-topped and usu. stone-parapeted defensive mound of earth; (fig.) defence, protection. ~ *v.t.* Fortify or protect (as) with rampart.

rămp′ion *n.* Kind of bell-flower (*Campanula rapunculus*), with white tuberous roots occas. used as salad.

Răm′say[1] (-zĭ), Allan (1686–1758). Scottish poet. ~, Allan (1713–84), his son, portrait-painter.

Răm′say[2] (-zĭ), Sir William (1852–1916). British chemist; discoverer of helium, argon (with Rayleigh), and neon in the atmosphere.

răm′shăckle *adj.* Tumble-down, crazy, rickety.

răm′sons (-z) *n.pl.* Broad-leaved garlic, *Allium ursinum*; bulbous root of this, eaten as relish.

Rām′us. Pierre de la Ramée (1515–72), French philosopher; a victim of the massacre of St. Bartholomew.

răn[1] *n.* A certain length of twine.

ran[2]: see RUN[1].

R.A.N. *abbrev.* Royal Australian Navy.

ranch (-ah-) *n.* Cattle-breeding establishment in U.S., Canada, etc. ~ *v.i.* Conduct ranch. [Span. *rancho* mess, persons feeding together]

răn′cĭd *adj.* Smelling or tasting like rank stale fat. **răn′cĭdnėss** *n.* **răncĭd′ity** *n.*

rănc′our (-k*er*) *n.* Inveterate bitterness, malignant hate, spitefulness. **rănc′orous** *adj.* **rănc′orously** *adv.*

rănd *n.* 1. Strip of leather placed under quarters of shoe to level it before heel-lifts are attached. 2. (S. Afr.) Highlands on either side of river valley; *the R~*, gold-mining district near Johannesburg in the Transvaal.

răndăn′[1] *n.* Style of rowing in which middle one of three rowers pulls a pair of sculls, stroke and bow an oar each; boat for this.

răndăn′[2] *n.* Spree. [var. of *random*]

răn′dom *n.* *At* ~, at haphazard; without aim, purpose, or principle; heedlessly. ~ *adj.* Made, done, etc., at random. [OF *randon* great speed (*randir* gallop)]

răn′dy *adj.* Loud-tongued, boisterous, lusty (Sc.); (of cattle etc., dial.) wild, restive; lustful, in lustful mood. **răn′dĭnėss** *n.*

ranee: see RANI.

Răn′elagh (-*ela*). Former place of public amusement in Chelsea, London, opened 1742, closed 1803; now part of grounds of Royal Hospital, Chelsea, and scene of the Royal Horticultural Society's show (Chelsea Flower Show). [named after Earl of *Ranelagh*, an earlier owner]

rānge (-j) *n.* 1. Row, line, tier, or series, of things, esp. of buildings or mountains; (U.S.) series of townships lying between two successive meridian lines six miles apart. 2. Liberty to range; area over which ranging takes place or is possible, (U.S.) stretch of grazing or hunting ground; piece of ground with targets for shooting; area over which plant etc. is distributed, area included in or concerned with something, scope, compass, register; limits of variation, limited scale or series; distance attainable by gun or projectile, distance between gun, etc., and objective; *~-finder*, instrument for estimating this distance. 3. Cooking fire-place, usu. with oven(s), boiler(s), and iron top plate with openings for saucepans, etc. ~ *v.* 1. Place or arrange in a row or ranks or in specified situation, order, or company; run in a line, reach, lie spread out, extend; be found or occur over specified district; vary between limits; be level (*with*), rank or find right place *with* or *among*. 2. Rove, wander; go all about (place), sail along or about (coast, sea). 3. (Of gun) throw projectile over, (of projectile) traverse, (distance).

rān′ger (-j-) *n.* (esp.) Keeper of royal or other park; (pl.) body of mounted troops; (U.S.) member of commando unit; senior member of Girl Guides (over 16).

Răngōōn′ (-ngg-). Capital city and seaport of Burma, on Rangoon river, one of the mouths of the Irrawaddy.

rān′gy (-j-) *adj.* (chiefly U.S.) Adapted for ranging, of long slender form.

ra′ni, -nee (rahnĭ) *n.* Hindu queen or princess. [Hind. *rani* fem. of RAJAH]

rănk[1] *n.* 1. Row, line (now chiefly of taxis standing); (mil.) number of soldiers drawn up in single line abreast; *the ~s*, *~ and file*, common soldiers; (transf.) lower classes or ordinary undistinguished people. 2. Distinct social class, grade of dignity, station; high station; *persons of ~*, members of nobility; *~ and fashion*, high society; *all ~s*, men of every grade or rank in army etc. 3. Place in a scale. ~ *v.* Arrange (esp. soldiers) in rank; classify, give certain grade to; have rank or place. **rănk′er** *n.* (Commissioned officer who has been) a soldier in the ranks.

rănk[2] *adj.* Too luxuriant, gross, coarse, over-productive, choked with or apt to produce weeds; foul-smelling, offensive, rancid; loathsome, corrupt; flagrant, virulent, gross. **rănk′ly** *adv.* **rănk′nėss** *n.*

Ranke (rahng′k*e*), Leopold von (1795–1886). German historian; author of 'The Popes of Rome' etc.

rănk′le *v.i.* (Of wound etc.) fester (archaic); (of envy etc.) be bitter, give intermittent or constant pain. [OF (*d*)*rancle* festering sore, f. LL *dracunculus*, dim. of *draco* serpent]

răn′săck *v.t.* Thoroughly search; pillage, plunder.

răn′som *n.* (Liberation of prisoner of war or other captive in consideration of) sum of money or value paid for release; *king's ~*, large sum. ~ *v.t.* Redeem, buy freedom or restoration of; set free on payment of ransom, demand ransom from or for.

rănt *v.* Use bombastic language; declaim, recite theatrically; preach noisily. ~ *n.* Piece of ranting, tirade; empty turgid talk. **rănt′er** *n.* (esp.) Primitive Methodist preacher.

ranŭn′cūlus *n.* Genus of plants including buttercups, crowfoot; plant of this genus, esp. the cultivated *R. asiaticus*. **ranŭncūlā′ceous** (-sh*us*) *adj.*

R.A.O.C., R.A.P.C. *abbrevs.* Royal Army Ordnance, Pay, Corps.

răp[1] *n.* Smart slight blow; sound made by knocker on door etc.; sound as of striking wooden surface supposed to be produced by spirit at seance. ~ *v.* Strike (esp. person's knuckles) smartly; make the sound called a rap; *~ out*, utter abruptly; (of supposed spirit) express (message etc.) by raps.

răp[2] *n.* Counterfeit coin passing current for halfpenny in Ireland in 18th c.; an atom, the least bit (esp. in *not care a ~*).

răp[3] *n.* Skein of 120 yds of yarn.

rapā′cious (-sh*us*) *adj.* Grasping, extortionate, predatory. **rapā′ciously** *adv.* **rapă′city** *n.*

rāpe[1] *v.t.* Take by force (poet.); ravish, force, violate (woman). ~ *n.* Carrying off by force (poet.); ravishing or violation of a woman; (law) unlawful sexual intercourse with a woman without her consent.

rāpe[2] *n.* Any of 6 administrative districts of Sussex.

rāpe[3] *n.* Plant (*Brassica napus*, esp. var. *arvensis*) grown as food for sheep, and for its seed from which colza-oil is made, coleseed; *~-cake*, rape-seed pressed into flat cake after extraction of oil and used as food for livestock; ~-*oil*, oil made from rape-seed and used as lubricant etc.

rāpe[4] *n.* Refuse of grapes after wine-making, used in making vinegar.

Răph'āėl[1]. An archangel; in apocryphal book of Tobit, the companion and helper of Tobias.

Răph'āėl[2]. Raffaello Sanzio *or* Santi (1483–1520), great painter of Italian Renaissance. **Răphāėlĕsque'** (-k) *adj.* In the style of Raphael.

răp'ĭd *adj.* Speedy, quick, swift; (of slope) descending steeply. **răp'ĭdly** *adv.* **rapĭd'ĭty** *n.* **răp'ĭd** *n.* Steep descent in river-bed, with swift current.

rāp'ĭer *n.* Light slender sword for thrusting only (ill. SWORD).

răp'īne *n.* (rhet.) Plundering, robbery.

răpparee' *n.* (hist.) 17th-c. Irish irregular soldier or free-booter.

răppee' *n.* Coarse kind of snuff made from dark rank leaves. [Fr. (*tabac*) *râpé* rasped (tobacco)]

rappôrt' (*or* rapôr') *n.* Communication, relationship, connexion, esp. in spiritualistic terminology of the communication through a medium with alleged spirits.

răpprŏche'ment (-shmahṅ) *n.* Re-establishment or recommencement of harmonious relations, esp. between States.

răpscăll'ion (-yon) *n.* Rascal, scamp, rogue.

răpt *adj.* (orig. past part. of RAPE[1]) Snatched away bodily or carried away in spirit from earth, consciousness, or ordinary thoughts and perceptions; absorbed, enraptured, intent.

răptôr'ial *adj.* & *n.* Predatory, (as) of predatory birds or animals; (zool.) (member) of the *Raptores*, an order of birds of prey, including eagles, hawks, buzzards, etc.

răp'ture *n.* Mental transport, ecstatic delight. **răp'turous** (-tyer-) *adj.* **răp'turously** *adv.*

rār'a ăv'ĭs *n.* Rarity, kind of person or thing rarely encountered. [L, = 'rare bird']

rāre[1] *adj.* 1. (Of air or gases) not dense; with constituent particles not closely packed together. 2. Uncommon, unusual, seldom found or occurring; of uncommon excellence, remarkably good; very amusing. 3. ~ *earths*, the basic oxides of the elements from lanthanum to lutecium inclusive in the PERIODIC system (the ~-*earth elements*) together with those of scandium and yttrium; ~ *gases*, the 6 gases, helium, neon, argon, krypton, xenon and radon, the first 5 of which occur in small amounts in the atmosphere, also known as the inert gases. **rāre'ly** (-ārl-) *adv.* **rāre'nėss** *n.*

rāre[2] *adj.* (Now dial. and U.S.) (Of meat) underdone.

rarebit: see WELSH rabbit.

rār'ee-show *n.* Show carried about in a box, peep-show; any show or spectacle.

rār'ėfȳ *v.* Lessen density or solidity of (esp. air); purify, refine; make subtle; become less dense. **rārėfăc'tion** *n.* **rār'ėfăctive** *adj.*

rār'ĭty *n.* Rareness; uncommon thing, thing valued as being rare.

R.A.S.C. *abbrev.* Royal Army Service Corps.

ra'scal (rah-) *n.* Rogue, knave, scamp (freq. used playfully to child etc.) **rascăl'ĭty** *n.* **ra'scally** *adj.*

rase: see RAZE.

răsh[1] *n.* Eruption of the skin in spots or patches.

răsh[2] *adj.* Hasty, impetuous, overbold, reckless; acting or done without due consideration. **răsh'ly** *adv.* **răsh'nėss** *n.*

răsh'er *n.* Thin slice of bacon or ham.

Ra'smussen (rahsmōō-), Knud Johan Victor (1879–1933). Danish Arctic explorer and ethnologist.

rasp (-ah-) *n.* Coarse kind of file with separate teeth raised by means of pointed punch (ill. FILE). ~ *v.* Scrape with rasp; scrape roughly; grate upon, irritate; make grating sound.

ra'spatory (rah-) *n.* Rasp used in surgery.

ra'spberry (rahzb-) *n.* (Plant, *Rubus idaeus*, bearing) white, yellow, or usu. red subacid fruit of many small juicy drupelets arranged on conical receptacle; (slang) sound or gesture expressing derision or dislike; ~-*cane*, raspberry plant.

Răsput'in (-pōō-), Grigori Efimovich (1871–1916). Russian monk, an illiterate peasant who acquired great influence over the household of Nicholas II; he was assassinated as result of a conspiracy among a small group of nobles.

răt *n.* 1. Various rodents of the genus *Rattus*, esp. the *black* or

A. BROWN RAT. B. BLACK RAT

house-~ (*R. rattus*), found esp. on shipboard, and the larger *brown* or *grey* ~ (*R. norvegicus*) which is now the commoner, both regarded as pests, infesting sewers, warehouses, docks, etc., and acting as carriers of several diseases. 2. (pol.) Person who deserts his party when in difficulties as rats are said to leave doomed house or ship. 3. Workman who refuses to join strike or takes striker's place or accepts less than trade-union wages. 4. *musk*-~, *water*-~: see MUSK, WATER; *smell a* ~, have suspicions; ~*s!* (slang) nonsense!; ~-*catcher*, person whose business is to catch rats; (slang) unconventional hunting dress; *rats'bane*, rat-poison (now rare); ~'*s-tail*, thing shaped like rat's tail, e.g. kind of file; ~-*tail*, hairless horse's tail; ~-*tailed*, (of spoon) with tail-like prolongation of handle along back of bowl (ill. SPOON); ~-*trap*, trap for rats; (cycle pedal) having two parallel steel plates with teeth on edges to prevent the foot slipping. ~ *v.i.* Hunt or kill rats; play the rat in politics etc.; betray one's friends. **rătt'er** *n.*

rāt(e)'able *adj.* Liable to payment of local rates. **rāt(e)abĭl'ĭty** *n.* **rāt(e)'ably** *adv.*

rătafī'a (-ēa) *n.* Liqueur flavoured with almonds or kernels of peach, apricot, or cherry; kind of biscuit similarly flavoured.

rătăplăn' *n.* Drumming sound. ~ *v.* Play (as) on drum; make rataplan. [Fr., imit.]

rătch, rătch'ėt *ns.* Set of angular or saw-like teeth on edge of bar or wheel, into which a cog, click, or pawl may catch, usu. for the purpose of preventing reversed motion (ill. WINDLASS); ~ (-*wheel*), wheel with rim so toothed. ~ *vbs.t.* Provide with ratchet, give ratchet form to.

rāte[1] *n.* 1. Estimated value or worth; price, sum paid or asked for single thing. 2. Amount or number of one thing corresponding or having some relation to certain amount or number of another thing; value as applicable to each piece or equal quantity of something; basis of exchange; amount (*of* charge or payment), esp. in relation to some other amount or basis of calculation; assessment on property levied by local authorities for local purposes, hence, *rate'payer*; degree of speed, relative speed; relative amount of variation, increase, etc. 3. Standard in respect of quality or condition; class, kind, sort; class of (esp. war-) vessels; degree of action, feeling, etc. 4. *at any* ~, at all events, at least; *at this* (*that*) ~, things being so, under these circumstances. ~ *v.* Estimate worth or value of; assign fixed value to in relation to monetary standard; consider, regard as; (naut.) class under certain rating; rank or be rated *as*; (usu. pass.) subject to payment of local rate, value for purpose of assessing rates on.

rāte[2] *v.* Scold angrily.

ra'tel (rah-) *n.* S. Afr. and Indian carnivorous mammal (*Mellivora capensis*) allied to weasel, 'honey-badger'.

rāt'er *n.* Vessel etc. of specified rate.

rāthe (-dh) *adj.* (poet.) Coming, blooming, etc., early in the year or day.

Rathenau (raht'enow), Walther (1867–1922). German industrialist and statesman, of Jewish origin; assassinated 1922.

ra'ther (rahdh-) *adv.* 1. More truly or correctly, more properly speaking; *the* more readily, all the more. 2. More (so) than not; to some extent, somewhat, slightly. 3. By preference, for choice, sooner (*than*); more properly. 4. (colloq., in answer to question) Most emphatically, yes without doubt.

răt'ifȳ *v.t.* Confirm or make valid (esp. what has been done or arranged for by another) by giving consent, approval, or formal sanction. **rătificā'tion** *n.*

rătine' (-ēn) *n.* Dress-fabric of rough open texture resembling sponge cloth.

rāt'ing *n.* (esp.) 1. Amount fixed as local rate. 2. (naut.) Person's position or class in warship's crew; member of ship's company who is not a commissioned officer. 3. Any of the classes into which racing yachts are distributed by tonnage.

rā'tiō (-shĭ-) *n.* Quantitative relation between two similar magnitudes determined by number of times one contains the other integrally or fractionally (*27 and 18 are in the ~ of three to two* or *3 : 2*; *the ~s 1 : 5 and 20 : 100 are the same*).

rătiŏ'cināte (*or* -shĭ-) *v.i.* Reason, carry on process of reasoning. **rătiŏcinā'tion** *n.* **rătiŏ'cinative** *adj.*

ră'tion *n.* Fixed allowance or individual share of provisions, esp. daily allowance for man or animal in armed forces; (pl.) provisions. ~ *v.t.* Put on fixed allowance of provisions etc.; share (food etc.) in fixed quantities.

ră'tional (-sho-) *adj.* Endowed with reason, reasoning; sensible, sane; based on, derived from, reason or reasoning; not foolish, absurd, or extravagant; (math., of ratio or quantity) expressible without radical signs. **ră'tionally** *adv.* **rătionăl'ity** *n.*

rătiona'lė (-shonahlĭ) *n.* Reasoned exposition of principles; logical or rational basis *of*.

ră'tionalism (-sho-) *n.* Practice of explaining the supernatural in religion in a way consonant with reason, or of treating reason as the ultimate authority in religion as elsewhere; theory that reason is foundation of certainty in knowledge. **ră'tionalist** *n.* & *adj.* **rătionalist'ic** *adj.* **rătionalis'tically** *adv.*

ră'tionalīze (-sho-) *v.* 1. Explain, explain *away*, by rationalism; bring into conformity with reason; be or act as a rationalist. 2. (math.) Clear from irrational quantities. 3. Reorganize (industry etc.) on scientific lines, with elimination of waste of labour, time, and materials, and reduction of other costs. **rătionalīzā'tion** *n.*

Răt'isbŏn (Ger. *Regensburg*). Town of Bavaria; scene of victory of Napoleon over the Austrians, 1809.

răt'līne, răt'ling *ns.* (usu. pl.) (One of) small lines fastened across ship's shrouds like ladder-rungs (ill. SAIL[1]).

ratōōn' *n.* New shoot springing from root of plant, esp. sugar-cane, after cropping. ~ *v.* Send up ratoons; cut down (plant) to induce ratooning.

rat(t)ăn' *n.* One of several species of *Calamus*, climbing palms with long thin pliable jointed stems, growing chiefly in E. Indies; piece of rattan stem used as cane or for other purposes; rattans used as material in building etc.

răt-tăt', rătatăt', răt'-tăt-tăt' *ns.* Rapping sound, esp. of knocker. [imit.]

rătt'le *v.* 1. Give out rapid succession of short sharp hard sounds, cause such sounds by shaking something; move or fall with rattling noise; drive, run, ride, briskly; make rattle. 2. Say or recite rapidly; talk in lively thoughtless way. 3. (slang) Excite, agitate, fluster, make nervous, frighten. ~ *n.* 1. Instrument or plaything made to rattle, esp. in order to give alarm or to amuse babies; end of rattlesnake's tail (see below); kinds of plant with seeds that rattle in their cases when ripe, esp. *yellow* ~, cock's-comb (*Rhinanthus Crista-galli*). 2. Rattling sound; uproar, noisy gaiety, stir; rattling sound in throat caused by partial obstruction; noisy flow of words; empty or trivial talk; lively incessant talker. 3. *~-brain, -head, -pate*, (person with) empty head; *ratt'lesnake*, various venomous Amer. snakes of genus *Crotalus* with horny rings at end of tail making rattling noise when vibrated; *~-trap*, rickety, shaky (vehicle etc.).

rătt'ler *n.* (esp.) Rattlesnake.

rătt'ling *adj.* (slang) Remarkably good, fast, etc. ~ *adv.* Remarkably, extremely.

rătt'y *adj.* Rat-like, esp. (slang) snappish, irritable.

rauc'ous *adj.* Hoarse, harsh-sounding. **rauc'ously** *adv.*

răv'age *v.* Devastate, plunder; make havoc. ~ *n.* Devastation, damage, (esp., pl.) destructive effects *of*.

rāve[1] *n.* Rail of cart; (pl.) permanent or removable framework added to sides of cart to increase capacity.

rāve[2] *v.* Talk wildly or furiously (as) in delirium; (of sea, wind, etc.) howl, roar; utter with ravings; speak with rapturous admiration *about* or *of*, go into raptures.

răv'el[1] *v.* 1. Entangle or become entangled, confuse, complicate. 2. Disentangle, unravel. ~ *n.* Entanglement, knot, complication; frayed or loose end.

Răvĕl'[2], Maurice (1875–1937). French musical composer.

răv'elin (-vl-) *n.* (fort.) Outwork of two faces forming salient angle outside main ditch before the curtain.

rāv'en[1] *n.* Large black hoarse-voiced bird (*Corvus corax*), feeding chiefly on carrion or other flesh; related species. ~ *adj.* Of glossy black.

răv'ėn[2] *v.* Plunder, go plundering *about*, seek *after* prey or booty, prowl for prey; eat voraciously; have ravenous appetite for.

Ravĕnn'a. City of Emilia in NE. Italy, founded before Roman era; became the western capital of the Empire after the fall of Rome, and was the seat of THEODORIC's court; was added to the papal States, 1509; passed to Italy, 1860.

răv'enous *adj.* Rapacious (now rare); voracious; famished, very hungry. **răv'enously** *adv.*

ravine' (-ēn) *n.* Deep narrow gorge, mountain cleft.

răv'ish *v.t.* 1. Carry off (person, thing) by force (now rare); commit rape upon, violate (woman). 2. Enrapture, charm, entrance, fill with delight. **răv'ishing** *adj.* **răv'ishingly** *adv.* **răv'ishment** *n.*

raw *adj.* 1. Uncooked; in natural or unwrought state, not yet dressed or manufactured; ~ *edge*, (of cloth) edge without hem or selvage; ~ *grain*, unmalted grain; ~ *hide*, untanned leather; rope or whip of this; ~ *material*, that out of which any process of manufacture makes the articles it produces; ~ *silk*, silk as reeled from cocoons; ~ *spirit*, undiluted spirit. 2. Crude, not brought to perfect composition or finish; uncultivated, uncivilized, brutal; ~ *deal*, (colloq.) the worst of a transaction, bad or harsh treatment. 3. (Of persons, esp. soldiers) inexperienced, untrained, unskilled. 4. Stripped of skin, excoriated; sensitive to touch from being so exposed; *~-boned*, with projecting bones hardly covered with flesh, gaunt. 5. (Of weather etc.) damp and chilly, bleak. ~ *n.* Raw place on esp. horse's skin; *touch on the* ~, wound feelings etc. of person on points on which he is sensitive. **raw'nėss** *n.*

ray[1] *n.* 1. Single line or narrow beam of light; straight line in which radiant energy capable of producing sensation of light is propagated to or from given point; analogous propagation-line of heat or other non-luminous physical energy; (fig.) remnant or beginning of enlightening or cheering influence; BECQUEREL, RÖNTGEN, *rays*, X-RAYS: see these words. 2. Radius of circle (rare); any of the lines forming a pencil or set of straight lines passing through one point; any of a set of radiating lines, parts, or things; (bot.) marginal part of composite flower, as daisy; (zool.) radial division of starfish or other echinoderm. ~ *v.* Issue, come *forth, off, out,* in rays; radiate (poet.) **rayed** (rād), **ray'less** *adjs.*

ray[2] *n.* Several species of fish of genus *Raia*, closely allied to skate.

RAY

ray[3], **re** (rā) *ns.* (mus.) Second note of hexachord and of major scale in 'movable-doh' systems; note D in 'fixed-doh' system. [see UT]

Ray[4], John (1628–1705). English naturalist.

Ray'leigh (-lĭ), John William Strutt, 3rd Baron (1842–1919). English mathematician and physicist; discoverer (with Ramsay) of argon.

ray'on *n.* Artificial silk made from cellulose; also used loosely of other artificial yarns or fibres. [trade-name, f. *ray*[1]]

ray'ony, -onn'é *adj.* (her., of a division between parts of the field) Having flame-like indentations (ill. HERALDRY).

rāze, rāse (-z) *v.t.* Erase (rare); completely destroy, level with the ground.

razee' *n.* Ship reduced in rating by removal of upper deck(s). ~ *v.t.* Reduce rating of (ship) thus.

rāz'or *n.* Sharp-edged instrument used in shaving hair from skin; *safety* ~, razor with guard to lessen risk of cuts; ~*-back*, back sharp as razor's edge; kind of whale, rorqual; ~*-bill*, any of various birds with a bill shaped like a razor, esp. *Alca torda*, a species of auk; ~*-edge*, keen edge; sharp mountain ridge; critical situation; sharp line of division; ~*-fish*, bivalve mollusc (*Solen*) with long narrow shell like razor-blade; ~*-shell*, (shell of) razor-fish. [f. OF *rasor*, f. *raser*]

răzz'le *n.* Spree (usu. in *go on the* ~).

R.B. *abbrev.* Rifle Brigade.

R.B.A. *abbrev.* Royal (Society of) British Artists.

R-boat *n.* German motor minesweeper. [Ger. *R-boot*, f. *Räumboot*]

R.C. *abbrev.* Red Cross; right centre (of stage); Roman Catholic.

R.C.A.F. *abbrev.* Royal Canadian Air Force.

R.C.M. *abbrev.* Royal College of Music.

R.C.M.P. *abbrev.* Royal Canadian Mounted Police.

R.C.N. *abbrev.* Royal Canadian Navy; Royal College of Nursing.

R.C.O., R.C.P. *abbrevs.* Royal College of Organists, of Physicians.

R.C.S. *abbrev.* Royal College of Surgeons; Royal Corps of Signals.

rd *abbrev.* Road.

R.D. *abbrev.* Refer to drawer (in banking); Royal (Naval Reserve) Decoration.

R.D.C. *abbrev.* Rural District Council.

re[1] (rā) *n.* (mus.) see RAY[3].

rē[2] *prep.* In the matter of (chiefly in legal and business use as first word of headline stating matter to be dealt with). [L, ablative of *res* thing]

re- *prefix.* Forming part of large numbers of already compounded words borrowed from Latin or Romance languages; it may also be prefixed to any verb or verbal derivative with the meanings: (i) once more, again, anew, afresh, repeated; (ii) back, with return to previous state. Only a few of these compounds of *re-* with English words are given here.

're. Colloq. abbrev. of *are* appended to *we, you,* and *they*.

R.E. *abbrev.* Royal Engineers.

reach *v.* Stretch out, extend; stretch out the hand etc., make reaching motion or effort (lit. & fig.); succeed in touching or grasping with hand or anything held in it, etc., extend to; come to, arrive at; hand, pass or take with outstretched hand; (naut.) sail with the wind abeam (ill. SAIL[2]); ~*-me-down*, (slang) ready-made (garment). ~ *n.* 1. Act of reaching out; extent to which hand, etc., can be reached out; scope, range, compass. 2. Continuous extent, esp. part of river etc. lying between two bends, or of canal between two locks. 3. (naut.) Tack.

rèăct' *v.i.* Act in return (*upon* agent or influence); act, display energy, in response to stimulus; act in opposition to some force; move or tend in reverse direction; undergo change (esp. chemical change) under some influence.

rèăc'tance *n.* (elect.) That part of the impedance of an alternating-current circuit which is due to capacitance or induction or both.

rèăc'tion *n.* 1. Responsive or reciprocal action; return of previous condition after interval of opposite (e.g. depression after excitement); (loosely) opinion, impression; (physiol.) response of organ etc. to external stimulus; (chem.) interaction of two or more substances resulting in chemical change; (wireless) feedback. 2. Retrograde tendency esp. in politics. **rèăc'tionary** *adj.* & *n.* (Person) inclined or favourable to reaction.

rèăc'tive *adj.* Tending to react.

rèăc'tor *n.* 1. (nuclear physics) Atomic pile, large-scale assembly in which nuclear reactions in fissile material are controlled by the introduction of non-fissile materials (moderators). 2. (med.) Animal, patient, reacting positively to a foreign substance.

read (rēd) *v.* (past t. & past part. *read* pr. rĕd). 1. Discover or expound significance of (dream, riddle, etc.); foresee, foretell (esp. *the future*, one's *fortune*). 2. (Be able to) convert into the intended words or meaning (written, printed, or other symbols, or things expressed by their means); reproduce mentally or vocally, while following their symbols with eyes or fingers, the words of (author, book, letter, etc.); study by reading; find (thing) stated, find statement, in print, etc.; convey when read, run; (of recording instrument) present (figure, etc.) to one reading it; ~ *proofs*, read printer's proofs and mark for correction; *well read, deeply read,* etc. (rĕd; past part. in active sense), versed *in* subject by reading, acquainted with literature. 3. Interpret (statement, action) in certain sense; assume as intended in or deducible from writer's words, find implications; (of editor etc.) give as the word(s) probably used or intended by author; sound or affect reader *well, ill,* etc., when read; ~ *between the lines*, search for or discover hidden meanings. 4. Bring into specified state by reading; ~ *oneself in*, (of incumbent) enter upon office by public reading of 39 Articles etc. ~ *n.* Time spent in reading.

read'able *adj.* Interestingly written; (rare) legible. **read'ableness, read'abil'ity** *ns.* **read'ably** *adv.*

rēaddrĕss' *v.t.* Change address of (letter).

Reade, Charles (1814–84). English novelist, author of 'The Cloister and the Hearth' etc.

read'er *n.* (esp.) 1. Person employed by publisher to read and report on proffered MSS.; printer's proof-corrector. 2. Person appointed to read aloud, esp. (*lay*-~) parts of service in church; senior lecturer at a university. 3. Book containing passages for exercise in reading, instruction in foreign language, etc. **read'ership** *n.* Office of university reader.

read'ily (rĕd-) *adv.* Without showing reluctance, willingly; without difficulty.

read'iness (rĕd-) *n.* Prompt compliance, willingness; facility, prompt resourcefulness, quickness in argument or action; ready or prepared state.

read'ing *n.* (esp.) 1. Literary knowledge, scholarship. 2. One of successive occasions on which Bill must have been presented to each House of Parliament before it is ready for royal assent; *first* ~, that permitting introduction of Bill; *second* ~, that accepting general principles; *third* ~, that accepting details as amended in committee. 3. Entertainment at which something is read to audience. 4. Word(s) read or given by an editor etc. or found in MS. in text of a passage; interpretation, view taken, rendering. 5. Figure etc. shown by graduated instrument. 6. (Specified quality of) matter to be read. 7. ~*-desk*, desk for supporting book, etc., lectern; ~*-room*, room in club, library, etc., for persons wishing to read.

ready (rĕd'ĭ) *adj.* With preparations complete; in fit state; with resolution nerved, willing; apt, inclined; about *to*; prompt, quick, facile; provided beforehand; within reach, easily secured; unreluctant; easy; fit for immediate use; *make* ~, prepare; ~ *money*, (slang) *the* ~, cash, actual coin; payment on the spot; ~ *reckoner*, (collection of) table(s) showing results of arithmetical calculations commonly required in business etc. ~ *adv.* Beforehand, so as not to require doing when the time comes; ~*-made*, (of clothes) made in standard shapes and sizes, not to customer's individual measure. ~ *n.* Position in which rifle is held before the present; (slang) ready money. ~ *v.t.* Prepare.

reā'gent *n.* Chemical substance used to produce a chemical reaction.

rē'al[1] (*or* rā-) *n.* Former silver coin and money of account used in Spain and some Spanish-speaking countries. [Span., f. L *regalis* regal]

rē'al[2] *adj.* 1. Actually existing as a thing or occurring in fact, objective; genuine, rightly so called; natural, not artificial or depicted; actually present or involved, not merely apparent; *the* ~ *thing*, the thing itself, not an imitation or inferior article; *the* ~ *presence*, actual presence of Christ's body and blood in the Eucharist. 2. (law, of actions, etc.) Relating to things, esp. real property; (of estate, property) consisting of immovable property, as lands and houses; (philos. etc.) relating to, concerned with, things. ~ *adv.* (usu. with adjs.) Really; (chiefly Sc. & U.S.) very, extremely. ~ *n.* A real thing; *the* ~, what actually exists, esp. opp. the ideal.

reăl'gar *n.* Arsenic disulphide (As_2S_2), red orpiment, red arsenic, used as pigment and in fireworks. [Arab. *rehj alghār* powder of the cave]

rē'alism *n.* 1. Scholastic doctrine that universal or general ideas have objective existence; belief that matter as object of perception has real existence. 2. Practice of regarding things in their true nature and dealing with them as they are; fidelity of representation, rendering precise details of real thing or scene. **rē'alist** *n.* **rēalis'tic** *adj.* **rēalis'tically** *adv.*

reăl'ity *n.* Property of being real; resemblance to original; real existence, what is real, what underlies appearances; existent thing; real nature *of*.

rē'alize, -ise (-z) *v.t.* 1. Convert (hope, plan, etc.) into fact; give apparent reality to, make realistic, present as reality. 2. Conceive as real; apprehend clearly or in detail. 3. Convert (securities, property) into money (freq. abs.); amass (fortune, specified profit), fetch as price. **rēalizā'tion** *n.*

really (rĭ'alĭ) *adv.* In fact, in reality; positively, indeed; ~*?*, is that so?

realm (rĕlm) *n.* Kingdom; sphere, province, domain.

realpolitik (rāahl' pŏlĭtēk') *n.* Policy of placing the material greatness and success of one's own country before all other considerations. [Ger., = 'real politics']

rē'ăltor *n.* (U.S.) Real-estate agent or broker (prop. one who is a member or affiliated member of the National Association of Real Estate Boards).

rē'alty *n.* Real estate.

ream[1] *n.* Twenty quires or 480 sheets of paper (often 500, to allow for waste); (freq. pl.) large quantity of paper; *printers'* ~, 516 sheets. [Arab. *rizmah* bundle]

ream[2] *v.t.* Widen (hole in metal) with borer or **ream'er** (ill. DRILL); turn over edge of (cartridge-case etc.); (naut.) open (seam) for caulking.

reap *v.* Cut (grain or similar crop), cut grain, etc., with sickle etc. in harvest; gather in thus, or fig. as harvest; harvest crop of (field etc.); *reaping-hook*, sickle.

reap'er *n.* One who reaps; (fig.) death; ~ (*-and-binder*), mechanical device for reaping crops (and binding sheaves) without manual labour.

rear[1] *n.* 1. Hindermost part of army or fleet; back of, space behind, position at back of, army or camp or person; back part of anything; (colloq.) water-closet, latrine; *bring up the* ~, come last. 2. Attrib., hinder, back-; ~*-admiral*, flag-officer in navy, next below vice-admiral; (U.S.) highest rank in navy (except in special circumstances); ~*-guard*, body of troops detached to protect rear, esp. in retreats; ~*-guard action*, engagement between rear-guard and enemy; ~*-lamp*, *-light*, red lamp or light at back of vehicle.

rear[2] *v.* 1. Raise, set upright, build; uplift, hold upwards. 2. Raise, bring up, breed, foster, nourish; educate; cultivate, grow. 3. (of horse etc.) Rise on hind feet.

rear-arch, rēre- *n.* (archit.) Inner arch of window or door opening when of different size or form from outer (ill. WINDOW).

rēarm' *v.* Arm again, esp. with more modern weapons or after disarming. **rēarm'ament** *n.*

rear-vault *n.* Vaulted space connecting arched window or door head with arch in inner face of wall (ill. WINDOW).

reas'on (-ēz-) *n.* 1. (Fact adduced or serving as) argument, motive, cause, or justification; (logic) one of premisses of syllogism, esp. minor premiss when given after conclusion; ~ *of State*, political justification, esp. for immoral proceeding. 2. The intellectual faculty characteristic esp. of human beings by which conclusions are drawn from premisses; intellect personified; (tr. Kant's *Vernunft*) faculty transcending the understanding and providing *a priori* principles, intuition. 3. Sanity; sense; sensible conduct; what is right, practical, or practicable; moderation; *it stands to* ~, it cannot reasonably be denied; *hear, listen to,* ~, allow oneself to be persuaded. **reas'onless** *adj.* **reas'on** *v.* 1. Use argument *with* person by way of persuasion; persuade by argument *out of, into*. 2. Form or try to reach conclusions by connected thought; discuss *what, whether*, etc.; conclude, assume as step in argument, say by way of argument, (*that*); express in logical or argumentative form; think *out*; *reasoned amendment*, one in which reasons are embodied with a view to directing course of debate. **reas'oning** *adj.* & *n.*

reas'onable (-ēz-) *adj.* 1. Endowed with reason, reasoning (rare). 2. Of sound judgement, sensible, moderate, not expecting too much, ready to listen to reason. 3. Agreeable to reason, not absurd, within the limits of reason; not greatly less or more than might be expected; inexpensive, not extortionate; tolerable, fair. **reas'onableness** *n.* **reas'onably** *adv.*

rēassure' (-shoor) *v.* Restore (person etc.) to confidence; confirm again in opinion or impression; reinsure. **rēassur'ance** *n.*

Réaumur (rā'ō-), René Antoine Ferchault de (1683–1757). French scientist, inventor of ~ *thermometer*, with scale on which the freezing-point of water is 0° and the boiling-point 80°.

reave, reive *v.* (past t. & past part. *reft*). (archaic, poet.) Commit ravages (usu. *reive*); forcibly deprive *of* (usu. in past part.); take by force, carry off. **reiv'er** *n.* Marauder, raider.

rēb'āte[1] *n.* Deduction from sum to be paid, discount, drawback. **rėbāte'** *v.t.* (archaic) Diminish, reduce force or effect of; blunt, dull.

rebate[2] (răb'ĭt, rĭbāt') *n.* & *v.t.* RABBET.

Rėbĕcc'a. (O.T.) Wife of Isaac and mother of Jacob and Esau.

rĕb'ĕc(k) *n.* Medieval three-stringed instrument, early form of fiddle. [Arab. *rebab*]

rĕb'el *n.* Person who rises in

arms against, resists, or refuses allegiance to, the established government; person or thing that resists authority or control; (attrib.) rebellious, of rebels, in rebellion. **rėbĕl′** *v.i.* Act as rebel (*against*); feel or manifest repugnance to some custom etc. (*against*).

rėbĕll′ion (-yon) *n.* Organized armed resistance, esp. (Sc. hist.) the risings of 1715 and 1745, to established government; open resistance to any authority; *the Great R~*, (Engl. hist.) Royalist name for the Civil War of 1642–52.

rėbĕll′ious (-lyus) *adj.* In rebellion; disposed to rebel, insubordinate, defying lawful authority; (of diseases, things) difficult to treat, unmanageable, refractory. **rėbĕll′iously** *adv.* **rėbĕll′iousnėss** *n.*

rēb′ōant *adj.* (poet.) Re-echoing loudly.

rėbound′ *v.i.* Spring back after impact; have reactive effect, recoil upon agent. ~ *n.* (also rē′bound) Act of rebounding, recoil; reaction after emotion.

rėbŭff′ *n.* Check given to one who makes advances, proffers help or sympathy, shows interest or curiosity, makes request, etc.; snub. ~ *v.t.* Give rebuff to.

rėbūke′ *v.t.* Reprove, reprimand, censure authoritatively. ~ *n.* Rebuking, being rebuked; a reproof.

rēb′us *n.* Enigmatic representation of name, word, etc., by pictures etc. suggesting its syllables.

rėbŭt′ *v.t.* Force or turn back, give check to; refute, disprove (evidence, charge). **rėbŭtt′al, rėbŭt′ment** *ns.*

rėbŭtt′er *n.* (esp., law) Defendant's answer to plaintiff's surrejoinder.

rėcăl′cĭtrant *adj.* & *n.* Obstinately disobedient or refractory (person). **rėcăl′cĭtrance** *n.*

rėcăl′cĭtrāte *v.i.* (rare) Be refractory; kick out *against* or *at*.

rėcall′ (-awl) *v.t.* Summon back from or to a place, from different occupation, inattention, digression, etc.; bring back *to* memory, cause to remember; recollect, remember; revive, resuscitate; revoke, annul (decision etc.), take back (gift). ~ *n.* Summons to return to or from a place; signal to return; possibility of recalling, revoking, or annulling.

rėcănt′ *v.* Withdraw and renounce (opinion, statement, etc.) as erroneous or heretical; disavow former opinion, esp. with public confession of error. **rēcăntā′tion** *n.*

rē′căp *v.* & *n.* (colloq.) Recapitulate, -ation.

rēcapĭt′ūlāte *v.t.* Give heads or substance of (what has already been said); summarize, restate briefly. **rēcapĭtūlā′tion** *n.*

rēcast′ (-ah-) *v.t.* (esp.) Refashion, remodel, reconstruct; give new form or character to.

rĕcc′ė, rĕcc′ō *n.* (service slang) Reconnaissance.

recd *abbrev.* Received.

rėcēde′ *v.i.* Go back or farther off; become more distant; slope backwards; withdraw (*from* opinion etc.); decline in character or value.

rėceipt′ (-sēt) *n.* 1. Recipe. 2. Amount of money received; fact or action of receiving or being received into person's hands or possession; written acknowledgement of such receipt, esp. of payment of sum due. 3. (archaic) Place where money is officially received; esp. ~ *of custom*, customhouse. ~ *v.t.* Write or print receipt on (bill).

rėceive′ (-sēv) *v.t.* Take into one's hands or possession; accept (something proffered); accept or buy (stolen goods) from thief; take (bread and wine of Eucharist); admit, consent or prove able to hold, provide accommodation for; submit to, endure; admit (impression etc.) by yielding or adaptation of surface. 2. Entertain as guest; greet, welcome; give specified reception to; admit to membership of society etc.; give credit to, accept as true; (abs.) receive company, hold reception. 3. Acquire, get, come by; be given or provided with; have sent to or conferred or inflicted on one.

rėceiv′er (-sēv-) *n.* (esp.) 1. Person appointed by *receiving-order* of court to administer property of bankrupt or property under litigation. 2. Person who receives stolen goods, fence. 3. Receptacle etc. for receiving something in machine or instrument, esp. earpiece of telephone; apparatus for transforming wireless waves into audible sound, wireless *receiving set*.

rėcĕn′sion (-shn) *n.* Revision of, revised, text.

rē′cent *adj.* Not long past, that happened or existed lately, late; not long established, lately begun, modern. **rē′cently** *adv.* **rē′centnėss, rē′cency** *ns.*

rėcĕp′tacle *n.* 1. Containing vessel, place, or space. 2. (bot.) Common base of floral organs, axis of cluster (ill. FLOWER).

rėcĕp′tion *n.* 1. Receiving, being received; receiving esp. of person, being received, into a place or company; formal or ceremonious welcome; occasion of receiving guests, assembly held for this purpose; *~-room*, room available or suitable for receiving guests (esp. opp. *bedroom*). 2. Receiving of ideas or impressions into the mind. 3. Welcome or greeting of specified kind; demonstration of feeling towards person or project; *warm ~*, vigorous resistance or enthusiastic welcome. 4. Receiving of wireless signals or the efficiency with which they are received.

rėcĕp′tionĭst (-sho-) *n.* Person employed by doctor, photographer, etc., to receive clients, or in hotel etc. to receive guests.

rėcĕp′tĭve *adj.* Able or quick to receive impressions or ideas; (rare) concerned with receiving. **rėcĕp′tĭvely** *adv.* **rėcĕp′tĭvenėss, rĕcėptĭv′ity** *ns.*

rėcĕp′tor *n.* 1. Receiving apparatus, receiver. 2. (physiol.) Minute organ at peripheral end of sensory nerve, capable of specially sensitive response to a particular form of energy, as light or heat; (also) specialized region of cell.

rėcĕss′ *n.* 1. Temporary cessation from work, vacation, esp. of Parliament. 2. Retired or secret place; receding part of mountain chain etc., niche or alcove of wall; (anat.) fold or indentation in organ. ~ *v.t.* Place in a recess; set back; provide with recess(es).

rėcĕ′ssion (-sĕshn) *n.* 1. Receding, withdrawal, from a place or point; receding part of object etc.; illusion of distance in picture. 2. (orig. U.S.) Temporary decline or set-back in industrial or economic activity or prosperity.

rėcĕ′ssional (-sho-) *adj.* Of the parliamentary recess; ~ *hymn*, hymn sung while clergy and choir withdraw after service. ~ *n.* Recessional hymn.

rėcĕss′ĭve *adj.* 1. Tending to recede. 2. (biol., of an inherited character) Not manifest in the organism which inherits it, though liable to be manifest in the next generation; having its effect obscured by a DOMINANT character.

Rĕch′abīte (-k-). 1. (O.T.) One of a Jewish family, descended from Jonadab son of Rechab, who refused to drink wine or live in houses (Jer. xxxv. 2–19). 2. One who abstains from intoxicating liquors, esp. member of the Independent Order of Rechabites, a benefit society founded 1835.

réchauffé (rĕshōf′ā) *n.* Warmed-up dish; rehash.

recherché (reshārsh′ā) *adj.* Devised or got with care or difficulty; choice, far-fetched, thought out.

rėcĭd′ĭvĭst *n.* One who relapses into crime. **recĭd′ĭvĭsm** *n.*

rĕ′cĭpė *n.* Statement of ingredients and procedure for preparing dish etc.; medical prescription or remedy prepared from it (archaic); expedient, nostrum, device for effecting something. [2nd pers. sing. of L *recepere* receive (i.e. take) as used in prescriptions]

rėcĭp′ient *adj.* Receptive. **recĭp′iency** *n.* **rėcĭp′ient** *n.* Person who receives something.

rėcĭp′rocal *adj.* Given, felt, shown, etc., in return; felt or shared by both parties, mutual; inversely correspondent, complementary, esp. (math.) based on inverse relationship; (gram.) reflexive, expressing mutual action or relationship (‘*each other*’ *is a ~ pronoun*). **rėcĭp′rocally** *adv.* **rėcĭp′rocal** *n.* Equivalent, counterpart, complement; (math.) function or expression so related to another that their product is unity (⅕ *is the ~ of* 5).

rĕcip′rocāte *v.* 1. (mech.) Go with alternate backward and forward motion; give such motion to. 2. Give and receive mutually, interchange; return, requite (affection etc.); make a return (*with*). **rĕciprocā′tion** *n.*

rĕciprŏ′city *n.* Reciprocal condition, mutual action; principle or practice of give-and-take, esp. interchange of privileges between States as basis of commercial relations.

rĕcīt′al *n.* 1. Detailed account *of* a number of connected things or facts, relation *of* the facts of an incident etc., a narrative; part of document stating facts. 2. Act of reciting; musical performance by, or of works of, one person.

rĕcitā′tion *n.* (esp.) Reciting as entertainment, poem or passage recited; (U.S.) repetition of prepared lesson or exercise, examination on something previously learned or explained.

rĕcitative′ (-ēv) *n.* Musical declamation, between song and ordinary speech, of kind usual in narrative and dialogue parts of opera and oratorio; words, part, given in recitative.

rĕcīte′ *v.* 1. Repeat aloud or declaim (poem, passage) from memory, esp. before audience; give recitation. 2. Rehearse (facts) in document; mention in order, enumerate.

rĕcīt′er *n.* Person who recites; book of passages for recitation.

rĕck *v.* (rhet., poet.; in neg. and interrog. sentences only). Care, be troubled, concern oneself; ~ *of*, pay heed to, take account of, care about.

rĕck′lĕss *adj.* Devoid of caution, regardless of consequences, rash; heedless *of* danger etc. **rĕck′lĕssly** *adv.* **rĕck′lĕssnĕss** *n.*

rĕck′on *v.* 1. Ascertain (number, amount), ascertain number or amount of, by counting or usu. by calculation, compute; start *from*, go on *to*, in counting; count *up*, sum *up* character of; arrive at as total; include in computation; make calculations, cast up account or sum; settle accounts *with*. 2. Count *in*, place in class *among*, *with*, *in*; take *for*, regard *as*, consider (*to be*); conclude after calculation, be of the confident opinion (*that*); rely, count, base plans, *upon*.

rĕck′oner *n.* (esp.) Aid to reckoning; *ready* ~: see READY.

rĕck′oning *n.* (esp.) Tavern bill; *day of* ~, time when something must be atoned for or avenged; *out in* one's ~, mistaken in a calculation or expectation; *dead* ~: see DEAD.

rĕclaim′ *v.* 1. Win back, recall, from wrong course, error, etc.; reform, tame, civilize; bring back (land) into cultivation from a waste state or from the sea. 2. (rare) Make protest, say in protest. ~ *n.* Reclaiming, reclamation.

rĕclamā′tion *n.* Reclaiming, being reclaimed.

réclame (rāklahm′) *n.* Art or practice by which publicity is secured.

rĕc′lināte *adj.* (bot. etc.) Bending downwards.

rĕclīne′ *v.* Lay (esp. one's head, body, limbs) in more or less horizontal or recumbent position; assume or be in recumbent position, lie, lean, sit with back or side supported at considerable inclination; (fig.) rely confidently *upon*.

rĕcluse′ (-lo͞os) *adj.* & *n.* (Person) given to or living in seclusion, retirement, or isolation, esp. as religious discipline.

rĕcognĭ′tion *n.* Recognizing, being recognized.

rĕcŏg′nĭzance (*or* -kŏn′-) *n.* Bond by which person engages before court or magistrate to observe some condition, e.g. to keep the peace, pay a debt, or appear when summoned; sum pledged as surety for such observance.

rĕcŏg′nĭzant (*or* -kŏn′-) *adj.* Showing recognition (*of* favour etc.).

rĕc′ognīze *v.t.* 1. Acknowledge validity, genuineness, character, claims, or existence of; accord notice or consideration to; discover or realize nature of; treat *as*, acknowledge *for*; realize or admit *that*. 2. Know again, identify as known before. **rĕc′ognīzable** *adj.* **rĕcognīzabĭl′ity** *n.* **rĕc′ognīzably** *adv.*

rĕcoil′ *v.i.* Retreat before enemy etc.; start or spring back, shrink mentally, in fear, horror, or disgust; rebound after impact; spring back to original position or starting-point; (of fire-arms) be driven backwards by discharge, kick. ~ *n.* Act, fact, sensation, of recoiling. **rĕcoil′lĕss** *adj.* (chiefly of guns).

rĕcollĕct′ *v.t.* Succeed in remembering, recall to mind, remember. **rĕcollĕc′tion** *n.* Act, power, of recollecting; thing recollected, reminiscence; person's memory, time over which it extends. **rĕcollĕct′ive** *adj.*

rĕcommĕnd′ *v.t.* 1. Give (oneself or another, one's spirit, etc.) in charge *to* God, a person, his care, etc. 2. Speak or write of, suggest, as fit for employment or favour or trial; make acceptable, serve as recommendation of. 3. Counsel, advise. **rĕcommĕn′dable, rĕcommĕn′datory** *adjs.* **rĕcommĕndā′tion** *n.*

rĕc′ompĕnse *v.t.* Requite, reward or punish; make amends to (person) or for (another's loss, injury, etc.). ~ *n.* Reward, requital; atonement or satisfaction for injury; retribution.

rĕc′oncīle *v.t.* 1. Make friendly after estrangement. 2. (eccles.) Purify (church etc.) by special service after profanation. 3. Bring into state of acquiescence or submission (*to*). 4. Adjust, settle (quarrel etc.); make (facts, statements, etc.) consistent or accordant; make compatible or consistent, regard or show as consistent (*with*). **rĕc′oncīlable** *adj.* **rĕc′oncīlement, rĕconcĭliā′tion** *ns.*

rĕc′ondīte (*or* rĭkŏn′-) *adj.* Abstruse, out of the way, little known; dealing in recondite knowledge or allusion, obscure. **rĕc′ondītely** *adv.* **rĕc′ondītenĕss** *n.*

rēcondĭ′tion *v.t.* Restore to proper, habitable, or usable condition, overhaul, repair.

rĕcŏnn′aissance (-ĭsans) *n.* Reconnoitring survey or party.

rĕconnoi′tre (-ter) *v.* Approach and try to learn position and condition or strategic features of (enemy, district), make reconnaissance.

rĕcord′ *v.t.* 1. Register, set down for remembrance or reference, put in writing or other legible shape; represent in some permanent form, esp. on gramophone record or otherwise for reproduction; *recording angel*, one supposed to register men's good and bad actions. 2. (of bird) Practise or sing tune in undertone.

rĕc′ord *n.* 1. State of being recorded or preserved in writing, esp. as authentic legal evidence; official report of proceedings and judgement in cause before court of record, copy of pleading etc. constituting case to be decided by court; piece of recorded evidence or information, account of fact preserved in permanent form, document or monument preserving it; object serving as memorial of something; *off the* ~, (orig. U.S.) unofficial; *on* ~, legally or otherwise recorded; *matter of* ~, something established as fact by being recorded; *court of* ~, court whose proceedings are recorded and valid as evidence of fact; (*Public*) *R~ Office*, building in London in which State papers and other public documents are kept. 2. Trace made by marker in groove of revolving disc or cylinder, from which sounds can afterwards be reproduced by means of a gramophone or other device; similar trace made on tape or wire by mechanical, magnetic, photographic, or other means; grooved disc, cylinder, etc., bearing such trace; *~-player*, apparatus for reproducing sound of record as oscillating electrical current (which is amplified electronically). 3. Facts known about person's past. 4. Best performance or most remarkable event of its kind on record; *break, beat, the* ~, outdo all predecessors; ~, (attrib.) best hitherto recorded.

rècŏrd'er *n.* (esp.) 1. City or borough magistrate with criminal and civil jurisdiction and holding court of quarter sessions. 2. Recording-apparatus in instruments. 3. Wood-wind instrument resembling flageolet, played vertically, and varying in range.

rècŏrd'ing *n.* (esp.) Process of registering wave-form by mechanical, photographic, electrical, or magnetic means for subsequent reproduction on gramophone, cinematograph, wireless, or television; disc, film, or tape on which the wave-form has been registered; sound or television programme so reproduced.

rècount'[1] *v.t.* Narrate, tell in detail.

rē-count'[2] *v.t.* Count afresh. **rē'-count** *n.*

rècoup' (-ōōp) *v.* Compensate for (loss), compensate (*for*); (law) deduct, keep back (part of sum due), make such deduction; ~ one*self*, recover what one has expended or lost. **rècoup'ment** *n.*

rècourse' (-ŏrs) *n.* Resorting or betaking of oneself *to* possible source of help; thing resorted to; *have ~ to*, adopt as adviser, helper, or expedient; *without ~*, formula used by the indorser of a bill of exchange to indicate that he declines responsibility for non-payment.

rècov'er (-kŭ-) *v.* 1. Regain possession, use, or control of; acquire or find (out) again; reclaim; ~ one*self*, regain consciousness, calmness, or control of limbs or senses. 2. Secure restitution or compensation, secure (damages) by legal process. 3. Bring or come back to life, consciousness, health, or normal state or position; ~ *sword*, bring it back after thrust etc.; (mil.) hold it upright with hilt opposite mouth. 4. Retrieve, make up for; get over, cease to feel effects of. ~ *n.* Position to which sword etc. is brought back in fencing or drill; act of coming to this.

rècov'ery (-kŭ-) *n.* Act or process of recovering or being recovered; (law) obtaining of a thing, right, damages, etc., by verdict or judgement of a court of law; *common ~*, (hist.) the process, based on a legal fiction, by which entailed estate was commonly transferred from one party to another.

rĕc'rèant *adj.* & *n.* Craven, coward(ly), apostate. **rĕc'rèantly** *adv.* **rĕc'rèancy** *n.*

rĕc'rèāte[1] *v.* (Of pastime, holiday, employment, etc.) refresh, entertain, agreeably occupy; amuse oneself, indulge in recreation. **rĕcrèā'tion** *n.* (esp.) Means of recreating oneself, pleasurable exercise or employment; ~ *ground*, public playground. **rĕc'rèative** *adj.*

rē-crèāte'[2] *v.t.* Create anew.

rĕc'rèment *n.* (rare) Refuse, dross; waste product, esp. (physiol.) fluid separated from blood and again absorbed into it, as saliva, bile.

rècrĭm'ĭnāte *v.i.* Retort accusation, indulge in mutual or counter charges. **rècrĭmĭnā'tion** *n.* **rècrĭm'ĭnative, rècrĭm'ĭnātory** *adjs.*

rĕcrudĕsce' (-ōōd-) *v.i.* (Of sore, disease, etc., or fig.) break out again. **rĕcrudĕs'cence** *n.* **rĕcrudĕs'cent** *adj.*

rècruit' (-ōōt) *n.* Newly enlisted and not yet trained soldier; person who joins society etc.; tyro. ~ *v.* 1. Enlist recruits for (army, society, etc.); enlist (person) as recruit; get or seek recruits. 2. Replenish, fill up deficiencies or compensate wear and tear in, refresh, reinvigorate; (seek to) recover health etc. **rècruit'ment** *n.*

rĕc'tal *adj.* Of or by the rectum.

rĕc'tangle (-nggl) *n.* Plane rectilinear 4-sided figure with 4 right angles, esp. one with adjacent sides unequal (ill. QUADRILATERAL).

rĕctăng'ūlar (-ngg-) *adj.* Shaped, having base or sides or section shaped, like rectangle; placed, having parts or lines placed, at right angles. **rĕctăng'ūlarly** *adv.*

rĕc'tĭfȳ *v.t.* 1. Put right, correct, amend, reform, adjust (method, calculation, statement, etc.); abolish, get rid of, exchange for what is right (error, abuse, omission, etc.). 2. (chem.) Purify or refine esp. by renewed distillation. 3. (geom.) Find straight line equal to (curve). 4. (elect.) Change (current) from alternating to direct. **rĕctĭfĭcā'tion, rĕct'ĭfier** *ns.*

rĕctĭlĭn'èar, -èal *adjs.* In or forming a straight line; bounded or characterized by straight lines. **rĕctĭlĭn'èarly** *adv.* **rĕctĭlĭnèă'rity** *n.*

rĕc'tĭtūde *n.* Moral uprightness, righteousness.

rĕc'tō *n.* Right-hand page of open book; front of leaf (opp. VERSO).

rĕc'tor *n.* 1. (In England) Parson of parish who receives full amount of tithe rent charge (cf. VICAR); (U.S. and Scotland) Episcopal clergyman having charge of congregation; (R.C. Ch.) head parish priest. 2. Head of university, college, school, or religious institution, esp. Jesuit college or seminary (esp. abroad; in England only of heads of Lincoln and Exeter Colleges, Oxford; in Scotland of headmaster of secondary schools etc.); *Lord R~*, president of a Scottish university elected by the students. **rĕc'torate, rĕc'torship** *ns.* **rĕctŏr'ĭal** *adj.*

rĕc'tory *n.* Rector's benefice; rector's house.

rĕc'trĭcēs (-z) *n.pl.* Strong feathers of bird's tail, directing flight (ill. BIRD).

rĕc'tum *n.* Final section of the large intestine terminating at the anus (ill. ALIMENTARY). [L *rectum* (*intestinum*) straight (intestine)]

rècŭm'bent *adj.* Lying down, reclining; ~ *fold*: see ill. ROCK. **rècŭm'bently** *adv.* **rècŭm'bency** *n.*

rècū'perāte *v.* Restore, be restored or recover, from exhaustion, illness, loss, etc. **rècūperā'tion** *n.* **rècū'perative** *adj.*

rècŭr' *v.i.* Go back in thought or speed *to*; (of idea etc.) come back *to* one's mind etc., return to mind; (of problem etc.) come up again; occur again, be repeated; *recurring curve*, one that returns upon itself, e.g. circle; *recurring decimals*, figures in decimal fraction that recur in same order again and again (indicated by dots above figures, as $0{\cdot}\dot{1}4285\dot{7}$). **rècŭ'rrence** *n.*

rècŭ'rrent *adj.* Occurring again, often, or periodically; (of nerve, vein, etc.) turning back so as to reverse direction. ~ *n.* Recurrent artery or nerve, esp. one of the two recurrent laryngeal nerves. **rècŭ'rrently** *adv.*

rècŭrve' *v.* Bend backwards. **rècŭrv'ate** *adj.* **rècŭrv'ature** *n.*

rĕc'ūsant (-z-; *or* rèkū'-) *n.* & *adj.* (Person) who refused to attend Church of England services (hist.); (person) refusing submission to authority or compliance with regulation. **rĕc'ūsance, rĕc'ūsancy** *ns.*

rècūse' (-z) *v.t.* (now rare) Reject (person, his authority); object to (judge) as prejudiced.

rĕd *adj.* 1. Of or approaching the colour seen at lower or least refracted end of visible spectrum, of shades varying from crimson to bright brown and orange, esp. those seen in blood, sunset clouds, rubies, glowing coals, human lips, and fox's hair; stained or covered with blood; (of eyes) bloodshot, or with lids sore from weeping; (of persons or animals) having red or tawny hair; (of certain peoples, esp. N. Amer. Indians) having reddish skin; (of places etc.) coloured red on maps to indicate British possession or control. 2. Marked or characterized by blood, fire, or violence; anarchistic or communistic. 3. Soviet-Russian. 4. In combinations: ~ *admiral*: see ADMIRAL; *R~ Army*, the Soviet-Russian army; ~ *arsenic*, REALGAR; ~ *bark*, superior kind of cinchona; ~ *biddy*, intoxicating drink of cheap red wine and methylated spirits; ~*-bird*, various small red-plumaged Amer. birds; ~ *blooded*, full of vigour and zest; ~ *book*, book bound in red; *R~ Book of the Exchequer*, volume of charters, statutes, surveys, etc., compiled in 13th c.; *R~ Book of Hergest*, Welsh 14–15th-c. MS. containing Mabinogion, etc.; *red'breast*, robin; *red'brick*, applied attrib. to modern Engl. universities, as built of red brick, in distinction from Oxford and Cambridge; ~*-cap*, military policeman; ~ *cent*, (U.S.) smallest coin, orig. of copper (in *don't care a ~ cent* etc.); *red'coat*, British soldier, so called from the scarlet uniform formerly worn by most regiments of the army; *R~ Cross*, a red cross on a white ground, St. George's Cross, the national emblem of England; similar emblem adopted at the Geneva Convention of 1864 for the international societies organized for the treatment of sick and wounded in war and borne by ambulances, hospitals, etc., attached to such service; ~ *currant*, (fruit of) *Ribes rubrum*; ~ *deer*, reddish-brown species of deer (*Cervus elaphus*) of Europe, W. Asia, and N. Africa; common deer of N. Amer., Virginia deer (*Odocoileus virginianus*); Caspian or Persian deer (*Cervus maral*); ~ *ensign*, red flag with union flag in its canton, used by British merchant ships; ~*-eye*, a European fish, the rudd; various Amer. fishes; ~ *fish*, male salmon in spawning season; red gurnard; various Amer. fishes; ~ *flag*, symbol of revolution or socialism (the *R~ Flag*, revolutionary song); danger signal on railways, shooting-ranges, etc.; ~ *gold*, gold alloyed with copper; (also, archaic and poet.) real gold, money; ~ *gum*, teething-rash in children; (kinds of eucalyptus yielding) reddish resin; ~*-handed*, in the act of crime; ~ *hat*, cardinal's hat; (slang) British staff-officer; ~ *heat*, being red-hot; temperature of red-hot thing; ~ *herring*, herring reddened by being cured in smoke; irrelevant question introduced to turn attention from the real one (as *draw a ~ herring across the track*, with ref. to use of herring in exercising hounds); ~*-hot*, heated to redness; highly excited, enthusiastic, furious; ~*-hot poker*, flame-flower (*Tritoma*), with tall spike of red flowers; ~ *lamp*, night-sign of doctor or chemist; ~ *lane* (colloq.) throat; ~ *lead*, red oxide of lead, much used as pigment; ~*-letter*, (of day) marked with red letter(s) in calendar as saint's-day or festival; memorable as date of joyful occurrence; ~ *light*, red lamp as danger signal; rear light on vehicle; ~ *man*, N. Amer. Indian; ~ *meat*, beef, mutton, etc., as dist. from veal, pork, or chicken; ~ *pepper*, Cayenne pepper; ~*-poll*, kinds of red-coated passerine bird, esp. *Carduelis flammea*; (pl.) red-haired polled cattle; ~ *rag*, thing that excites person's rage as red object is supposed to enrage bull; ~ *sanders*, red sandalwood, wood of the E. Indian *Pterocarpus santalinus*, used in dyeing etc.; *red'shank*, red-legged wading bird (*Tringa totanus*); ~*-short*, (of iron) brittle while red-hot; *red'skin*, N. Amer. Indian; ~ *spider*, small red spider-like mite, of family *Tetranychidae*, infesting plants; *red'start*, red-tailed European song-bird (*Phoenicurus phoenicurus*); ~*-streak*, red-streaked apple formerly esteemed for cider making; ~ *tape*, pink tape used for tying legal documents etc.; excessive use of or adherence to formalities esp. in public business; *red'wing*, red-winged thrush (*Turdus musicus*); N. Amer. red-winged blackbird (*Agelaeus phoeniceus*); S. Afr. red-winged francolin; *red'wood*, red wood obtained from many tropical trees, used in dyeing etc.; tall Californian timber-tree (*Sequoia sempervirens*); ~ *worm*, kind of earthworm used as fishing bait. **rĕdd'en** *v.* **rĕdd'ish** *adj.* **rĕd'ly** *adv.* **rĕd'nėss** *n.* **rĕd** *n.* Red colour; *a* shade of red; the red colour in roulette and rouge-et-noir; *the* red ball at billiards; *the* debtor side of an account, shown in red figures; red cloth or clothes; one of former three squadrons or divisions (the ~, *white*, *blue*) of British fleet; radical, republican, anarchist, or (esp.) communist; *see* ~, become so angry as to lose self-control.

rėdăn' *n.* (mil.) Fieldwork with two faces forming salient angle.

rĕdd *v.t.* (Sc.) Clear up, arrange, tidy, put right, settle.

rĕdd'le *n.* = RUDDLE.

rēde *n.* (archaic) Counsel, advice; narrative. ~ *v.t.* (archaic) Advise; read (riddle, dream).

rėdeem' *v.t.* Buy back, recover by expenditure of effort or by stipulated payment; compound for, buy off, (charge or obligation) by payment; perform (promise); purchase the freedom of, save (one's life), by ransom; save, rescue, reclaim; (of God or Christ) deliver from sin and damnation; make amends for, counterbalance (fault, defect); save *from* a defect. **rėdeem'able** *adj.* **rėdeem'er** *n.* (esp. of Christ).

rėdĕmp'tion *n.* Redeeming or being redeemed, esp. the deliverance from sin and damnation wrought by Christ's atonement; thing that redeems; purchase. **rėdĕmp'tive** *adj.*

rēdėploy'ment *n.* Improved organization and arrangement of factories as a means of increasing output.

rėdĭf' *n.* (Soldier of) Turkish military reserve.

rĕd'ĭngōte (-ngg-) *n.* Woman's long double-breasted outer coat with skirt sometimes cut away in front (ill. COAT). [Fr., f. Engl. *riding-coat*]

rėdĭn'tėgrāte *v.t.* Restore to wholeness or unity; renew or re-establish in united or perfect state. **rėdĭntėgrā'tion** *n.*

Rĕd'mond, John Edward (1856–1916). Irish political leader; leader of Parnellites after Parnell's death.

rĕd'olent *adj.* Fragrant (now rare); having a strong smell; strongly suggestive or reminiscent *of*. **rĕd'olence** *n.*

rėdoub'le[1] (-dŭ-) *v.* Intensify, increase; make or grow greater or more intense or numerous.

rēdoub'le[2] (-dŭ-) *v.t.* (bridge) Double again (bid already doubled by opponent). ~ *n.* Instance of redoubling.

rėdoubt' (-owt) *n.* (fort.) Outwork or fieldwork, usu. square or polygonal and without flanking defences.

rėdoubt'able (-owt-) *adj.* Formiddable. **rėdoubt'ėd** *adj.* (archaic) Redoubtable.

rėdound' *v.i.* Result in, have effect of, contributing or turning *to* some advantage or disadvantage; turn *to* credit etc.; (of advantage, honour, disgrace, etc.) result, attach, *to* (person), recoil or come back *upon*.

rėdrĕss' *v.t.* Readjust, set straight again; set right, remedy, make up for, rectify (distress, wrong, damage, etc.). ~ *n.* Reparation for wrong, redressing of grievances, etc.

Rĕd Sea. Long narrow strip of water between Asia and Africa, connected with Mediterranean by Suez Canal and with Arabian Sea by Gulf of Aden.

rėdūce' *v.* 1. Bring *to* certain order or arrangement, *to* a certain form or character; convert (*in*)*to* different physical state or form, esp. crush *to* powder etc. 2. Compel *to* do (rare); bring by force or necessity *to* some state or action, subdue, bring back to obedience. 3. Bring down, lower; weaken, impoverish; diminish, contract; ~ *to the ranks*, degrade (non-commissioned officer) to rank of private; *reduced circumstances*, poverty after prosperity. 4. (surg.) Restore (dislocated, fractured, or ruptured part) to proper position. 5. (chem.) Remove from (a compound) oxygen or other electro-negative atom or group; add to (compound) hydrogen or other electro-positive atom or group. 6. (arith.) Change (number, quantity) (*in*)*to* another denomination or different form. 7. (logic) Bring syllogism into different form. 8. (intrans.) Lessen one's weight. **rėdū'cer** *n.* (esp., photog.) Agent for reducing the density of negatives. **rėdū'cible** *adj.*

rėdŭc'tion *n.* Reducing or being reduced; reduced copy of picture, map, etc.

rėduit' (-dwē) *n.* (fort.) Keep for garrison to retire to and hold when outworks are taken.

rėdŭn'dant *adj.* Superfluous, excessive, pleonastic; copious, luxuriant, full; (of employee or his post) liable to be dispensed with because no longer necessary. **rėdŭn'dantly** *adv.* **rėdŭn'dance, rėdŭn'dancy** *ns.*

rėdŭp'licāte *v.t.* Make double,

repeat; (gram.) repeat (letter, syllable), form (tense) by reduplication.

rėdūplicā′tion *n.* Doubling, repetition; counterpart; (gram.) repetition of syllable or letter in word-formation, part so repeated.

rē-ĕch′ō (-k-) *v.* Echo; echo again and again, resound.

reed *n.* 1. (Tall straight stalk of) kinds of firm-stemmed water or marsh plant of genus *Phragmites*; (collect.) reeds, growth or bed of reeds; reeds or wheat-straw for thatching, used as lath for plastering etc.; *broken* ~, unreliable person or thing. 2. Musical pipe of reed or straw, (fig.) pastoral poetry; one of two vibrating concave wedge-shaped pieces of reed or cane fixed face to face on metal tube as part of mouthpiece of oboe or bassoon (ill. WOOD); small metal tube with opening closed by vibrating metal tongue in lower end of organ-pipe; metal tongue, slip of cane, producing sound by vibration, in organ-pipe, clarinet, etc.; (pl.) reed instrument(s). 3. Weaver's instrument of metal wires (formerly thin strips of reed or cane) fixed into parallel bars of wood, for separating threads of warp and beating up weft (ill. LOOM). 4. (archit.) One of a set of small semi-cylindrical mouldings (ill. MOULDING). 5. ~-*babbler*, -*bird*, -*warbler*, -*wren*, bird (the common British *Acrocephalus scirpaceus*, or various other birds) frequenting reed-beds; ~-*bunting*, -*sparrow*, common British bird (*Emberiza schoeniclus*) frequenting reedy places; ~-*mace*, large persistent fruiting head of the water-plant *Typha*; the plant itself; ~ *pen*, reed sharpened for use in (esp. large) writing; ~-*pipe*, musical pipe made of reed; reeded organ-pipe; ~-*stop*, organ-stop consisting of reed-pipes. ~ *v.t.* Thatch with reed; make (straw) into reed; fit (musical instrument, organ-pipe) with reed.

reed′lĭng *n.* Bearded titmouse (*Panurus biarmicus*).

reed′y *adj.* 1. Abounding with reeds; made of reed (chiefly poet.); like a reed in weakness, slenderness, etc. 2. (Of voice) like reed-instrument in tone, scratchy, not round and clear. **reed′ĭnėss** *n.*

reef[1] *n.* One of three or four strips across top of square or bottom of fore-and-aft sail that can be taken in or rolled up to reduce sail's surface; ~-*knot*, knot consisting of two bights each enclosing the other's parallel-laid shanks, ordinary double-knot made symmetrically (ill. KNOT); ~-*point*, one of a set of short ropes to secure the sail when reefed (ill. SAIL[1]). ~ *v.* Take in reef(s) of sail; shorten (topmast, bowsprit, etc.).

reef[2] *n.* Ridge of rock, shingle, or sand, at or just above or below surface of water; (gold-mining) lode of auriferous quartz, bedrock.

reef′er[1] *n.* 1. One who reefs; (slang) midshipman. 2. Reef-knot. 3. Close double-breasted stout jacket.

reef′er[2] *n.* Marijuana cigarette.

reek *n.* 1. (Sc. & literary) Smoke; vapour, visible exhalation. 2. Foul or stale odour; fetid atmosphere. ~ *v.i.* Emit smoke (chiefly of houses after conflagration or object burnt in open air); emit vapour, steam; smell unpleasantly (usu. *of*). **reek′y** *adj.* (chiefly Sc. & literary); *Auld Reekie*, Edinburgh.

reel[1] *n.* Kinds of rotatory apparatus on which thread, silk, yarn, paper, wire, etc., are wound at some stage of manufacture; apparatus capable of easy revolution for winding and unwinding cord, line, etc.; small cylinder, with rim at each end, on which sewing-cotton etc. is wound for convenience; cylinder on which length of cinematographic film is wound; quantity of such a film wound on a reel (the standard length of one reel is 1,000 ft); revolving part in various machines; (*straight*) *off the* ~, without stopping, uninterruptedly. ~ *v.* Wind on reel; take (cocoon silk etc.) *off*, draw (fish, log-line, etc.) *in* or *up*, by use of reel; rattle (story, list, etc.) *off* without pause or apparent effort.

reel[2] *v.i.* Be in a whirl, be dizzy, swim; sway, stagger; stand, walk, or run unsteadily; rock from side to side, swing violently, be shaken physically or mentally; seem to shake. ~ *n.* Reeling motion.

reel[3] *n.* Lively, esp. Sc., dance, usu. of 2 (foursome ~) or 4 (eightsome ~) couples in line, forming a chain figure.

rē-ĕn′trant *adj.* & *n.* (Angle) that points inward (opp. SALIENT).

rē-ĕn′try *n.* 1. (law) Act of re-entering upon possession of lands, tenements, etc., previously granted or let to another. 2. *card of* ~, (bridge and whist), high card that can be relied on to give holder the lead again by winning a trick.

reeve[1] *n.* (hist.) Chief magistrate of town or district; (Canada) president of village or town council.

reeve[2] *n.* Female of RUFF[2].

reeve[3] *v.t.* (naut.) Thread (rope etc.) *through* ring or other aperture; thread (aperture, block, etc.) with rope; fasten (rope, block, etc.) *in*, *on*, *to*, something by reeving.

rėfĕc′tion *n.* Refreshment by food or drink; slight meal, repast.

rėfĕc′tory (*or in monastic use* rĕf′ĭ-) *n.* Room used for meals in monasteries etc. (ill. MONASTERY); ~ *table*, long narrow table.

rėfêr′ *v.* 1. Trace or ascribe *to* person or thing as cause or source; assign *to* certain date, place, or class. 2. Commit, hand over, *to* person etc.; send on or direct (person), make appeal or have recourse, *to* some authority or source of information; cite authority or passage. 3. (Of statement etc.) have relation, be directed, (of hearer) interpret as directed, *to*; make allusion, direct attention, *to*. 4. *referred pain*, pain felt at a point in a sensory system remote from the part actually affected. **rĕf′erable** *adj.*

rĕferee′ *n.* Arbitrator, person to whom dispute is to be or is referred for decision; umpire, esp. in football. ~ *v.* Act as referee, esp. in football.

rĕf′erence *n.* 1. Referring of matter for decision, settlement, or consideration, to some authority; scope given to such authority. 2. Relation, respect, correspondence, *to*; *in*, *with*, ~ *to*, regarding, as regards, about; *without* ~ *to*, irrespective of. 3. Allusion *to*. 4. Direction *to* book, passage etc. where information may be found; mark used to refer reader of text to note etc.; act of looking up passage etc. or of referring another or applying to person, for information; *cross* ~, reference to another passage in same book; *book of* ~, book to be used not for continuous reading but to consult on occasion; ~ *library*, library where books may be consulted without being taken away. 5. Person named by one applying for post or offering goods etc. as willing to vouch for him or them; (loosely) testimonial. ~ *v.t.* Provide (book) with references to authorities etc. **rĕferĕn′tial** (-shl) *adj.*

rĕferĕn′dum *n.* Referring of question at issue to electorate for direct decision by a general vote.

rēfĭll′ *v.t.* Fill again. **rē′fĭll** *n.* What serves to refill pencil-case, notebook, etc.

rėfīne′ *v.* 1. Free from dross, impurities, or defects; purify, clarify; become pure. 2. Polish, improve, make or become more elegant or cultured; use or affect subtlety of thought or language; improve (*up*)*on* by introducing refinements.

rėfīne′ment (-nm-) *n.* Refining or being refined; fineness of feeling or taste, polished manners, etc.; subtle or ingenious manifestation *of* (luxury etc.), piece of elaborate arrangement; piece of subtle reasoning, fine distinction.

rėfīn′er *n.* (esp.) Person whose business is to refine metal, sugar, etc. **rėfīn′ery** *n.* Place where raw material (e.g. sugar, petroleum) is refined.

rēfĭt′ *v.* Restore (ship) to serviceable condition; (of ship) undergo renewals and repairs. **rēfĭt′**, **rēfĭt′ment** *ns.*

rėflā′tion *n.* Inflation of currency after deflation to restore the system to its previous condition.

rėflĕct′ *v.* 1. (Of surface or body) throw (heat, light, sound, etc.) back, cause to rebound; (of mirror etc.) show image of, reproduce to eye or mind, exactly correspond in appearance or effect to; (of action etc.) bring back or cause to redound (credit, discredit, etc.), bring discredit, (*up*)*on* person etc. 2. Go back in thought, meditate, or consult with oneself (*on*). 3. Make disparaging remarks (*up*)*on*.

rėflĕc'tion, -ĕ'xion (-kshn) *n.* 1. Reflecting or being reflected; reflected light, heat, colour, or image; *angle of* ~, that made by reflected ray with perpendicular to the surface. 2. (Piece of) censure, animadversion; thing bringing discredit (*up*)*on*. 3. Reconsideration, meditation; mental faculty dealing with products of sensation and perception; idea arising in the mind; thought expressed in words.

rėflĕc'tĭve *adj.* 1. Giving back reflection or image; (rare) reflected. 2. Concerned in reflection or thought; thoughtful, given to meditation. **rėflĕc'tĭvely** *adv.* **rėflĕc'tĭvenėss** *n.*

rėflĕc'tor *n.* Body or surface reflecting rays, esp. piece of glass, metal, etc., usu. concave, for reflecting in required direction; apparatus for reflecting images; (telescope etc. provided with) concave mirror for bringing parallel light to a focus.

rē'flĕx *n.* 1. Reflected light, colour, or glory; (painting etc.) light reflected from a surface in light to one in shade; reflection, image. 2. Reflex action; *conditioned* ~: see CONDITION *v.t.* ~ *adj.* Recurved; reflected; (of thought etc.) turned back upon the mind itself or its operations; coming by way of return or reflection; ~ *action*, involuntary action of muscle, nerve, etc., excited as automatic response to stimulus of sensory nerve (e.g. sneezing); ~ *angle*, angle larger than 180° (ill. ANGLE); ~ *camera*, hand camera in which, by means of a pivoted mirror, the reflected image can be seen and focused up to the point of exposure (ill. CAMERA). ~ *v.t.* Bend back, recurve (only in past part.; chiefly bot. and her.).

rėflĕx'ĭve *adj.* & *n.* (gram.) (Word, form) implying agent's action upon himself; (verb) indicating identity of subject and object; (personal pronoun or possessive adjective) referring to subject. **rėflĕx'ĭvely** *adv.*

rĕf'luent (-lōō-) *adj.* Flowing back. **rĕf'luence** *n.*

rėfôrm' *v.* Make or become better by removal or abandonment of imperfections, faults, or errors; abolish, cure (abuse, malpractice); *reformed churches, religion*: see REFORMATION. ~ *n.* Removal of abuse(s) esp. in politics; improvement made or suggested; *R~ Bill*, (in U.K.) any of several Bills to reform the representation of the people in Parliament: 1st, that of William Pitt, 1785, defeated; 2nd, that of Lord John Russell, 1831, defeated in House of Lords; 3rd (1st *R~ Act*), that of Earl Grey, passed 1832; *R~ Club*, London club founded 1832 as rival to Carlton Club; ~ *school*, REFORMATORY. **rėfôrm'atĭve** *adj.*

rĕformā'tion *n.* Reforming or being reformed, esp. radical change for the better in political, religious, or social affairs; *the R~*, 16th-c. religious movement directed to reform of doctrines and practices of Church of Rome and ending in establishment of Reformed or Protestant Churches of central and NW. Europe.

rėfôrm'atory *adj.* Tending or intended to produce reform. ~ *n.* Institution to which juvenile offenders are sent for reform purposes (in U.K. now known as Approved School).

rėfôrm er *n.* One who reforms; leader in the 16th-c. REFORMATION of religion; advocate or supporter of parliamentary reform, esp. of the reform movement of 1831–2.

rėfôrm'ĭsm *n.* Policy of reforming existing institutions rather than abolishing or revolutionizing them.

rėfrăct' *v.t.* Deflect (light) at certain angle at point of passage from one medium into another of different density; *refracting telescope*, one in which rays of light are converged to focus by object-glass. **rėfrăc'tion** *n.* **rėfrăc'tĭve** *adj.*

rėfrăc'tor *n.* Refracting medium, lens, or telescope.

rėfrăc'tory *adj.* Stubborn, unmanageable, rebellious; (of wounds etc.) not yielding *to* treatment; (of substances) hard to fuse or work. **rėfrăc'torĭly** *adv.* **rėfrăc'torĭnėss** *n.* **rėfrăc'tory** *n.* Substance, as fireclay, graphite, silica, specially resistant to the action of heat and suitable for lining furnaces etc. where high temperatures must be withstood.

rėfrain'[1] *n.* Recurring phrase or line, esp. at end of stanzas.

rėfrain'[2] *v.* Put restraint upon, curb (one*self* etc.; archaic); abstain from doing something, abstain *from*.

rėfrăn'gĭble (-j-) *adj.* That can be refracted. **rėfrăngĭbĭl'ĭty** *n.*

rėfrĕsh' *v.* Cool, make fresh, with water etc. (rare); (of food, rest, etc.) impart fresh vigour to, reanimate, reinvigorate; freshen up (memory); restore (fire etc.) with fresh supply; refresh oneself, take refreshment.

rėfrĕsh'er *n.* (esp.) Extra fee paid to counsel in prolonged or frequently adjourned cases; attrib. (of course of instruction etc.) serving to refresh memory or make up-to-date.

rėfrĕsh'ment *n.* Refreshing or being refreshed in mind or body; thing, esp. (usu. in pl.) food or drink, that refreshes.

rėfrĭ'gerāte *v.* Make, become, cool or cold; expose (food) to low temperature in order to preserve it. **rėfrĭ'gerant** *adj.* & *n.* (Medium etc.) that refrigerates. **rėfrĭgerā'tion** *n.*

rėfrĭ'gerātor *n.* (esp.) Cupboard or room in which ice can be made and food etc. kept cold by the mechanical production of low temperature.

rėfrĭ'geratory *n.* Cold-water vessel through which worm of still passes, for condensing alcoholic and other vapours. ~ *adj.* That refrigerates.

rĕf'ūge *n.* (Place of) shelter from pursuit, danger, or trouble; person, thing, course, that gives shelter or is resorted to in difficulties; (*street-*) ~, part of roadway marked off on busy crossings etc. for pedestrians.

rĕfūgēē' *n.* Person escaped, esp. to foreign country, from religious or political persecution, war, etc.

rėfŭl'gent *adj.* Shining, gloriously bright. **rėfŭl'gently** *adv.* **rėfŭl'gence** *n.*

rėfŭnd' *v.* Pay back (money received or taken, expenses incurred by another); reimburse; make repayment. ~ *n.* Repayment.

rėfūs'al (-z-) *n.* (esp.) Right or privilege of deciding to take or leave a thing before it is offered to others.

rėfūse'[1] (-z) *v.* Say or convey by action that one will not accept, submit to, give, grant, gratify, consent; deny (*to* person etc.), refuse request of; make refusal; (of horse) stop short at (fence etc.), fail to take jump.

rĕf'ūse[2] *n.* & *adj.* (What is) rejected as worthless or left over after use.

rėfūte' *v.t.* Prove falsity or error of (statement, argument, etc.), rebut or repel by argument. **rėfūt'al, rĕfūtā'tion** *ns.*

rėgain' *v.t.* Recover possession of; reach (place) again; recover (*feet, footing*, etc.).

rē'gal *adj.* Of or by kings; fit for a king, magnificent. **rē'gally** *adv.*

rėgāle'[1] *n.* (rare) Choice repast, feast; a dainty.

rėgāle'[2] *v.* Entertain choicely with food, *with* food, etc. (freq. iron.); give delight to; feast (*on*). **rėgāle'ment** (-lm-) *n.*

rėgāl'ĭa[1] *n.pl.* Insignia of royalty used at coronations; decorations or insignia of an order. (*Illustration, p.* 692.)

rėgāl'ĭa[2] *n.* Large cigar of special quality.

rē'galĭsm *n.* Doctrine of sovereign's ecclesiastical supremacy.

rėgăl'ĭty *n.* Attribute of kingly power, being king; royal privilege.

rėgârd' *v.* 1. Gaze upon; bestow attention or notice on, show interest in. 2. Give heed to; take into account in regulating actions or conduct; show consideration for; pay attention, give heed.

3. Look on *as* being something; look on *with* some feeling; consider. 4. Concern, have relation to; *as* ~*s*, so far as relates to; *regarding*, concerning, relating to. ~ *n.* 1. Look, gaze; observant attention or heed; consideration; care or concern *for*. 2. Thing or circumstance looked to or taken into account, respect; *in* ~ *of* or *to*, in respect of, with respect or reference to. 3. Esteem, kindly feeling or respectful opinion (*for*); (pl.) as expression of friendliness in letter etc. **rėgârd'ful** *adj.* **rėgârd'fully** *adv.* **rėgârd'fulnėss** *n.* (rare). **rėgârd'lėss** *adj.* (freq. slang as ellipt. adv., = 'regardless of expense'). **rėgârd'lėssly** *adv.* **rėgârd'lėssnėss** *n.*

rėgâr'dant *adj.* (her.) Looking backward (ill. HERALDRY).

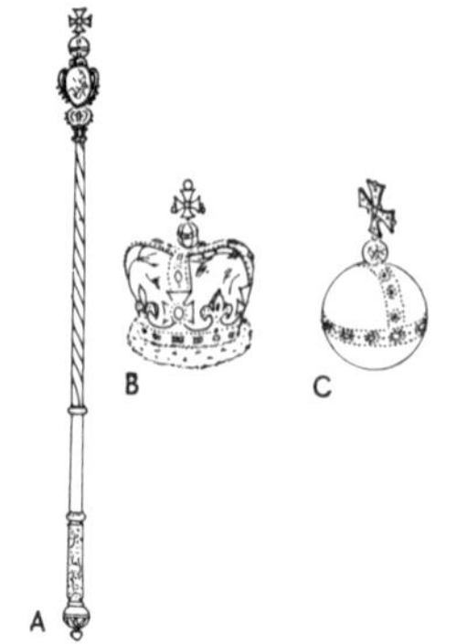

ROYAL REGALIA: A. SCEPTRE. B. CROWN. C. ORB

rėgătt'a *n.* Meeting for boat or yacht races.

rēgėlāte' *v.i.* Freeze again; esp., of pieces of ice with moist surfaces, fuse at temperature above freezing-point. **rēgėlā'tion** *n.*

rē'gency *n.* 1. Rule, control (now rare). 2. Office of regent; commission as regent; period of office of regent or regency-commission; *the R~*, (Engl. hist.) period (1810–20) in which George, Prince of Wales acted as regent; (as adj.) of the style of architecture, dress, etc., of this period.

rėgĕn'erāte *v.* 1. Invest with new and higher spiritual nature; improve moral condition of; breathe new, more vigorous, and higher life into. 2. Generate again; bring or come into renewed existence. **rėgĕn'erate** (-*a*t), **rėgĕn'eratīve** *adjs.* **rėgĕnerā'tion** *n.*

rē'gent *n.* 1. (rare) Ruler; ruling principle. 2. Person appointed to administer kingdom during minority, absence, or incapacity of monarch. 3. (U.S.) Member of governing board of State University; (hist.) at Oxford and Cambridge, Master of Arts presiding over disputations in schools, Master of not more than five years' standing; (hist.) in Scottish universities, one of several instructors acting as tutors. ~ *adj.* (placed after n.) Acting as, having position of, regent; *Prince R~*, (Engl. hist.), George, Prince of Wales (later George IV), who was regent 1810–20 during incapacity of George III; *Regent's Park*, London, park laid out 1814 by John Nash and later containing Zoological Gardens.

rĕ'gĭcīde *n.* 1. Killer or participator in killing of a king; (Engl. hist.) one of those concerned in trying and executing Charles I. 2. Killing of a king. **rĕ'gĭcīdal** *adj.*

régie (rāzhē') *n.* State monopoly or control of tobacco, salt, etc.

régime, regime (rāzhēm') *n.* Method of government; prevailing system of things; *ancien* (ahṅsyăṅ) ~, system of government in France before the Revolution; any now abolished or past system.

rĕ'gĭmen *n.* 1. (now rare) Rule, system of government, régime. 2. (med.) Prescribed course of exercise, way of life, and esp. diet. 3. (gram.) Relation of syntactic dependence between words, government.

rĕ'gĭment *n.* 1. (now rare) Rule, government. 2. Army recruiting and training unit with permanent depot and often local name, consisting of a varying number of battalions, grouped for operational purposes into brigades; (freq. pl.) large array or number, legion. ~ *v.t.* Form (men) into regiment or regiments; organize (workers, labour) in groups or according to a system.

rĕgĭmĕn'tal *adj.* Of a regiment; military, maintaining or demanding strict discipline. **rĕgĭmĕn'tals** *n.pl.* Dress worn by regiment; military uniform.

rĕgĭmĕntā'tion *n.* Regimenting, organizing.

Rėgīn'a *n.* (abbrev. R.) Reigning queen (esp. in signatures to proclamations, as *E.R.*, Elizabeth Regina, and in titles of crown lawsuits, as ~ *v. Jones*, the Queen versus Jones).

rē'gion (-jn) *n.* Tract of country, place, space, of more or less definitely marked boundaries or characteristics; separate part of world or universe; sphere or realm *of*; part of the body round or near some organ etc. **rē'gional** (-jo-) *adj.*

rĕ'gĭster *n.* 1. Book in which entries are made of details to be recorded for reference; official or authoritative list kept e.g. of births, marriages, and burials or deaths, shipping, qualified voters in constituency, etc.; ~ *office*, registry. 2. (Set of pipes controlled by) slides in an organ; compass of voice or instrument (*upper, lower*, etc., ~, part of this). 3. Adjustable plate for widening or narrowing an opening and regulating draught, esp. in fire-grate. 4. Recording indicator of speed, force, etc. 5. (print.) Exact correspondence of printed matter on two sides of leaf or of impressions of colour-blocks in colour-print; (photog.) correspondence of focusing screen with plate or film. 6. ~ *ton*, cubic measure, 100 cubic feet. ~ *v.* 1. Set down (name etc.) formally, record in writing; enter or cause to be entered in particular register; (U.S.) enter name in register of hotel or lodging-house; (fig.) make mental note of; *registered letter*, letter, the acceptance of which is registered at the post office and a receipt given to the sender. 2. (of instrument) Record automatically, indicate; (of person) express or show (emotion etc.) in face, or in any manner. 3. (print. etc.) Correspond, make correspond, exactly. **rĕgĭstrā'tion** *n.*

rĕgĭstrâr' *n.* Official recorder, person charged with keeping register. **rĕ'gĭstrary** *n.* Registrar of Cambridge University.

rĕ'gĭstry *n.* 1. Registration. 2. Place, office, where registers are kept; ~ *office*, (esp.) place where registers of births, marriages, etc., are kept, and where marriages may be performed without religious ceremony; (*servants'*) ~ *office*, agency where lists of vacant situations and servants seeking them are kept.

Rē'gius professorships. Certain professorships at the Universities of Cambridge (divinity, civil law, physic, Hebrew, and Greek) and Oxford (divinity, medicine, civil law, Hebrew, and Greek), founded 1540 by Henry VIII at Cambridge and 1546 at Oxford; professorships of modern history at Cambridge and of modern history, ecclesiastical history, and moral and pastoral theology at Oxford, more recently founded; certain professorships at Scottish universities, to which appointments are made by the Crown.

rĕg'nal *adj.* Of a reign; ~ *year*, year of sovereign's reign, dated from moment of accession; ~ *day*, anniversary of sovereign's accession.

rĕg'nant *adj.* Reigning (*Queen R~*, queen who rules in her own right and not as consort); predominant, prevalent.

rēgôrge' *v.* Disgorge; gush or flow back again.

rėgrāte' *v.t.* (hist.) Buy up (goods, esp. victuals) with view to retailing at profit (a practice formerly prohibited).

rē'grĕss *n.* Going back; declension, backward tendency. **rėgrĕss'** *v.i.* Move backwards.

rėgrĕ'ssion (-shn) *n.* Backward movement, retreat; return of curve; relapse, reversion. **rėgrĕss'-**

ĭve *adj.* **rėgrĕss'ĭvely** *adv.* **rėgrĕss'ĭvenėss** *n.*

rėgrĕt' *v.* Remember (something lost) with distress or longing, feel sorrow for loss of; grieve at, feel mental distress on account of; feel regret. ~ *n.* Sorrow for loss; repentance or sorrow for something done or left undone; (intimation of) sorrow or disappointment at inability to do something, esp. accept invitation. **rėgrĕt'ful** *adj.* **rėgrĕt'fully** *adv.* **rėgrĕtt'able** *adj.* **rėgrĕtt'ably** *adv.*

regt *abbrev.* Regiment.

rĕg'ūlar *adj.* 1. (eccles.) Bound by religious rule; belonging to religious or monastic order. 2. Following or exhibiting a principle; harmonious, consistent, systematic; symmetrical; *the five ~ solids*, tetrahedron or triangular pyramid bounded by 4 triangles, hexahedron or cube by 6 squares, octahedron by 8 triangles, dodecahedron by 12 pentagons, and icosahedron by 20 triangles. 3. Acting, done, recurring, uniformly or calculably in time or manner; habitual, constant, not capricious or casual; orderly; *keep ~ hours*, do same thing at same time daily. 4. Conforming to a standard, in order; properly constituted or qualified, not defective or amateur, devoted exclusively or primarily to its nominal function. 5. (gram., of verbs, nouns, etc.) Following a normal type of inflexion. 6. (colloq.) Complete, thorough, indubitable. 7. ~ *army*, army of ~ *soldiers*, professional soldiers as opp. to volunteers, militia, or temporary levies. **rĕg'ūlarly** *adv.* **rĕg'ūlar** *n.* One of the regular clergy; regular soldier; (colloq.) regular customer, contributor, etc. **rĕgūlă'rity** *n.* **rĕg'ūlarīze** *v.t.* **rĕgūlarīzā'tion** *n.*

rĕg'ūlāte *v.t.* Control by rule, subject to restrictions; moderate, adapt to requirements; adjust (machine, clock) so that it may work accurately. **rĕg'ūlative** *adj.*

rĕgūlā'tion *n.* 1. Regulating, being regulated. 2. Prescribed rule, authoritative direction; (attrib.) fulfilling what is laid down by regulations, ordinary, usual, formal.

rĕg'ūlātor *n.* (esp.) Device for regulating passage of steam, air, etc.; device for regulating speed of watch etc. by adjusting balance.

rĕg'ūlus[1] *n.* 1. (chem.) Metallic content of mineral, liberated by reduction and sinking to bottom in crucible; impure metallic product of smelting various ores. 2. Golden-crested wren, *R. cristatus.* [L, dim. of *rex* king]

Rĕg'ūlus[2], Marcus Atilius. Roman consul in 267 and 256 B.C.; captured in the Punic War, he was sent to Rome to negotiate peace, but refused to do so, returned to Carthage and was put to death with torture.

rėgûr'gitāte *v.* Gush back; (of stomach or receptacle) pour or cast out again. **rėgûrgitā'tion** *n.*

rēhabĭl'itāte *v.t.* Restore to rights, privileges, reputation, etc., reinstate; restore to previous condition; enable (disabled person) to earn his living or attain some degree of independence. **rēhabĭlitā'tion** *n.*

rēhăsh' *n.* (colloq., of books etc.) New presentation of material in different form.

rėhears'al (-hêr-) *n.* Rehearsing; practising of play etc. before performing it in public; *in* ~, in process of being rehearsed.

rėhearse' (-hêrs) *v.t.* Recite, say over, repeat from beginning to end; give list of, recount, enumerate; have rehearsal of (play, part, etc.); practise for later public performance.

Rēhobō'am. (O.T.) Son of Solomon; succeeded him as king of Israel; the northern tribes broke away from his rule and set up a new kingdom under Jeroboam. **rēhobō'am** *n.* Wine-bottle of largest size, holding equivalent of 8 standard bottles.

Reich (rīχ) *n.* The German State or commonwealth; *the First* ~, the Holy Roman Empire, A.D. 962–1806; *the Second* ~, 1871–1918; the *Third* ~, the Nazi régime, 1933–45.

Reichstadt (rīχ'shtăt), Duke of. Title of NAPOLEON[3] II.

Reichstag (rīχs'tahχ). Supreme legislature of the former German Empire and of the Republic; building in Berlin in which this met, burnt down on Nazi accession to power (1933).

Reichswehr (rīχs'vār). German armed forces, 1919–45.

reign (rān) *n.* Sovereignty, rule, sway; period during which sovereign reigns; *R~ of Terror*, period of violence and bloodshed under rule of revolutionaries or reactionaries, esp. that (1793–4) during the French Revolution. ~ *v.i.* Hold royal office, be king or queen; exercise authority, hold sway, rule; be acknowledged as supreme.

rēimbûrse' *v.t.* Repay (person who has expended money, out-of-pocket expenses). **rēimbûrse'ment** (-sm-) *n.*

Reims: see RHEIMS.

rein (rān) *n.* Long narrow strap with each end attached to bit, used to guide or check horse etc. in riding or driving (freq. pl. in same sense) (ill. HARNESS); (fig.) means of control; *draw* ~, stop one's horse, pull up; *give ~ to*, let have free scope. ~ *v.t.* Check or manage with reins; pull *up* or *back*, hold *in* with reins; (fig.) govern, restrain, control.

rein'deer (rān-) *n.* Caribou, sub-arctic deer (*Rangifer tarandus*) with large branching or palmated antlers in both sexes, used for drawing sledges and kept in herds for its milk, flesh, and hide.

rēinfôrce' *v.t.* Strengthen or support by additional men or material or by increase of numbers, quantity, size, thickness, etc.; *reinforced concrete*, concrete with steel bars or wire netting embedded in it to increase its tensile strength. ~ *n.* Thicker part of gun next breech (ill. CANNON); strengthening part, band, etc., added to object.

rēinfôrce'ment (-sm-) *n.* Reinforcing, being reinforced; anything that reinforces; (freq. pl.) additional men, ships, aircraft, etc., for military, naval, or air force.

reins (rānz) *n.pl.* (archaic) The kidneys; the loins.

rēinstāte' *v.t.* Restore to, replace *in*, lost position, privileges, etc.; restore to health or proper order. **rēinstāte'ment** (-tm-) *n.*

rēinsure' (-shoor) *v.t.* Insure again, esp. (of insurer or underwriter) against risk one has undertaken.

reis (rās) *n.pl.* Former Portuguese and Brazilian money of account of very small value.

rēit'erāte *v.t.* Repeat, do over again or several times.

reive(r): see REAVE *v.*

rėjĕct' *v.t.* 1. Put aside as not to be accepted, practised, believed, chosen, used, etc. 2. Cast up again, vomit, evacuate. **rėjĕc'tion** *n.* **rē'jĕct** *n.* Thing rejected.

rėjoice' *v.* Cause joy to, make glad; feel great joy; be glad (*to, that, in, at*); make merry, celebrate some event. **rėjoi'cings** *n.pl.*

rėjoin' *v.* 1. Reply to charge or pleading, esp. to plaintiff's replication (law); say in answer, retort. 2. Join again.

rėjoin'der *n.* What is rejoined or said in reply, retort.

rėjuv'enāte (-jōō-) *v.* Make or become young again. **rėjuvenā'tion** *n.*

rėlăpse' *v.i.* Fall back, sink again, into wrong-doing, error, heresy, weakness, or illness, etc. *n.* Act or fact of relapsing, esp. deterioration in patient's condition after partial recovery.

rėlāte' *v.* 1. Narrate, recount. 2. Bring into relation, establish relation between; have reference *to*, stand in some relation *to*; *related*, (past part.) connected, allied, akin by blood or marriage.

rėlā'tion *n.* 1. Narration; a narrative; (law) laying of information before Attorney-General for him to take action upon. 2. Way in which one thing is thought of in connexion with another; any connexion, correspondence, or association between things or persons. 3. Kinsman, kinswoman, relative. **rėlā'tionshĭp** *n.* Being related; kinship.

rĕl'ative *adj.* 1. (gram.) Referring, and attaching a subordinate clause, to an expressed or implied antecedent; (of clause) attached to antecedent by relative word. 2. Comparative; in relation to something else; proportioned to something else; involving or implying comparison or relation; having application or reference *to*, with reference *to*; ~ *humidity*: see HUMIDITY. **rĕl'atively** *adv.* **rĕl'ative** *n.* 1. (gram.) Relative word, esp. pronoun, as *who, which, that, what.* 2. (philos.) Relative thing or term. 3. Kinsman, kinswoman; one related by blood or marriage.

rĕl'ativism *n.* Doctrine that knowledge is of relations only.

rĕlativ'ity *n.* 1. Relativeness. 2. Branch of physics concerned with correlation of descriptions of phenomena by observers using frames of reference in relative motion with respect to each other; (*special*) *theory of* ~, theory, mainly due to Einstein, based on principle of constant velocity of light and showing that all motion is relative, treating space and time as four related dimensions and invalidating previous conceptions of geometry; (*general*) *theory of* ~, that developed by Einstein in 1915 extending the special theory to include cases of acceleration and the phenomena of gravity.

rėlăx' *v.* Cause or allow to become loose, slack, or limp; enfeeble, enervate, mitigate, abate; grow less tense, rigid, stern, etc. **rĕlaxā'tion** (*or* rēlăks-) *n.* Partial remission *of* penalty, duty, etc.; cessation from work, recreation, amusement; diminution of tension, severity, precision, etc.

rėlay' (*or* rēl'ā) *n.* Set of fresh horses substituted for tired ones; gang of men, supply of materials, etc., similarly used; switch or other device by which one electric current is made to control another; instrument used in long-distance telegraphy to reinforce weak current with local battery; ~*-race*, one between teams of which each person does part of the distance, the 2nd etc. members starting when the 1st etc. end. ~ *v.* Arrange in, provide with, replace by, get, relays; pass on or re-broadcast (wireless signal, programme, etc., originating at, and received from, another station).

rėlease' *v.t.* 1. (law) Remit (debt), surrender (right), make over (property) to another. 2. Set free, liberate, deliver, unfasten (*from*). 3. (cinemat.) Exhibit (film etc.) for first time, or generally. 4. Make (information) public. ~ *n.* 1. Deliverance, liberation, from trouble, life, duty, confinement, etc. 2. Written discharge, receipt; legal conveyance of right or estate to another, document effecting this. 3. Handle, catch, etc., that releases part of machine etc. 4. Public exhibition of cinema film etc. for first time or generally; film etc. so shown.

rĕl'ėgāte *v.t.* Banish *to* some place of exile; consign or dismiss *to* some usu. inferior position, sphere, etc.; transfer (matter) for decision or execution, refer (person) for information etc. *to.* **rĕlėgā'tion** *n.*

rėlĕnt' *v.i.* Relax severity, become less stern; abandon harsh intention, yield to compassion. **rėlĕnt'lėss** *adj.* **rėlĕnt'lėssly** *adv.* **rėlĕnt'lėssnėss** *n.*

rĕl'ėvant *adj.* Bearing upon, pertinent *to*, the matter in hand. **rĕl'ėvantly** *adv.* **rĕl'ėvance, rĕl'ėvancy** *ns.*

rėlī'able *adj.* That may be relied upon; of sound and consistent character or quality. **rėlīabĭl'ĭty, rėlī'ablenėss** *ns.* **rėlī'ably** *adv.*

rėlī'ance *n.* Trust, confidence; thing depended upon. **rėlī'ant** *adj.*

rĕl'ĭc *n.* 1. Part of holy person's body or belongings kept after his death as object of reverence; memento, souvenir; (pl.) dead body, remains, of person. 2. (pl.) What has survived destruction or wasting, remnant, residue, scraps; (sing.) surviving trace or memorial *of* custom, period, people, etc.; object interesting for its age or associations.

rĕl'ĭct *n.* Widow.

rėlief'[1] *n.* 1. Alleviation of or deliverance from pain, distress, anxiety, etc.; redress of hardship or grievance. 2. Feature etc. that diversifies monotony or relaxes tension. 3. Assistance given to the poor esp. formerly under the Poor Law or to persons in special danger or difficulty; ~ *work*, organized effort to help victims of earthquake or other calamity; ~ *works*, building etc. operations started to give work to unemployed. 3. Reinforcement and esp. raising of siege *of* besieged town. 4. (Replacing of person or persons on duty by) person(s) appointed to take turn of duty.

rėlief'[2] *n.* Method of moulding, carving, or stamping in which design stands out from plane or curved surface with projections proportioned and more or less closely approximating to those of objects imitated (*low* ~ or *bas-*~, that in which projection is very slight, opp. to *high* ~); piece of sculpture etc. in relief; appearance of being done in relief given by arrangement of line or colour or shading; distinctness of outline, vividness; ~ *map*, map in which the conformation of an area of the earth's surface is shown by (exaggerated) elevations and depressions or by suitable colouring.

rėlieve' *v.t.* 1. Bring, give, be, relief to; ease, free, from pain, discomfort, etc.; make less burdensome, monotonous, etc.; release from watch or other duty by becoming or providing a substitute; raise siege of; *relieving arch*, arch built into wall to relieve pressure or weight upon wall (ill. ARCH); *relieving officer*, parish or union or borough official charged with care of poor. 2. Bring into relief, make stand out.

rėliev'ō *n.* (pl. -*s*) = RELIEF[2].

rėlĭ'gion (-jn) *n.* 1. Human recognition of superhuman controlling power and esp. of a personal God or gods entitled to obedience and worship, effect of such recognition on conduct or mental attitude; particular system of faith and worship, as *Christian, Mohammedan, Buddhist*, ~. 2. Monastic condition, being monk or nun (*enter into, be in*, ~, enter or be member of a monastic order). 3. (rare) Practice of sacred rites. 4. *make a* ~ *of*, make a point of (esp. doing some habitual action).

rėlĭ'giōse *adj.* Morbidly or excessively religious. **rėligiŏs'ĭty** *n.* Being religious or religiose.

rėlĭ'gious (-jus) *adj.* 1. Imbued with religion, pious, god-fearing, devout. 2. Of, concerned with, religion; scrupulous, conscientious. 3. Of, belonging to, a monastic order. **rėlĭ'giously** *adv.* **rėlĭ'giousnėss** *n.* **rėlĭ'gious** *n.* Person bound by monastic vows.

rėlĭn'quish *v.t.* Give up, abandon, resign, surrender; let go (something held). **rėlĭn'quishment** *n.*

rĕl'iquary *n.* Receptacle for relic(s).

rėlĭq'uĭae *n.pl.* Remains; (geol.) remains of early animals or plants.

rĕl'ĭsh *n.* 1. Flavour, distinctive taste *of*; slight dash or tinge *of*; appetizing flavour, attractive quality; thing eaten with plainer food to add flavour. 2. Enjoyment of food or other things; zest; liking *for*. ~ *v.* Serve as relish to, make piquant etc.; get pleasure out of, like, be pleased with; taste, savour, smack, suggest presence *of*; effect taste *well, badly*, etc.

rėlŭc'tant *adj.* Struggling, offering resistance, hard to work, get, or manage (esp. poet.); unwilling, disinclined (*to*). **rėlŭc'tantly** *adv.* **rėlŭc'tance** *n.*

rėlūme' (*or* -o͞om) *v.t.* (poet.) Rekindle; make bright again; light up again.

rėlȳ' *v.i.* Put one's trust, depend with confidence, (*up*)*on.*

rėmain' *v.i.* 1. Be left over after removal of some part or quantity, or after rest has been done or dealt with in some way. 2. Abide, stay in same place or condition; continue to exist, be extant; be left behind; continue to be (something specified). ~ *n.* (usu. pl.) What remains over, surviving members, parts, or amount; (usu. pl.) relic(s) of obsolete custom or of antiquity; (pl.) works, esp. those not before published, left by author; (pl.) dead body, corpse.

rėmain'der *n.* 1. (law) Residual interest in estate devised to another simultaneously with creation of estate; right of succession to title or position on holder's decease. 2. Residue, remaining persons or things; (arith.) number left after subtraction; copies of book etc. left unsold when demand has ceased and often offered at reduced price. ~ *v.t.* Treat or dispose of (edition) as remainder.

rėmand′ (-ah-) *v.t.* Send back (prisoner) into custody to allow of further inquiry. ~ *n.* Recommittal to custody.

rĕm′anĕt *n.* Remaining part, residue; postponed lawsuit or parliamentary Bill. [L, = 'it remains']

rėmark′ *v.* Take notice of, perceive, regard with attention, observe; say by way of comment; make comment (*up*)*on*. ~ *n.* Noticing, observing, commenting; written or spoken comment, anything said.

rėmark′able *adj.* Worth notice, exceptional, striking, conspicuous. **rėmarkabĭl′ity, rėmark′ableness** *ns.* **rėmark′ably** *adv.*

Rĕm′brandt (-ant) **Harmensz van Rijn** (rīn) (1606–69). Greatest painter of the Dutch school, and also a great etcher; has been called the 'King of Shadows', from his practice of painting pictures illuminated by a clear but limited light, emerging in the midst of masses of shadow.

R.E.M.E. *abbrev.* Royal Electrical and Mechanical Engineers.

rĕm′ėdy *n.* Cure for disease, healing medicine or treatment; means of removing, counteracting, or relieving any evil; redress, legal or other reparation; the small margin within which coins as minted are allowed to vary from the standard fineness and weight (also called the *tolerance*). ~ *v.t.* Cure medically (now rare); rectify, make good. **rėmēd′iable, rėmēd′ial, rĕm′ėdilėss** *adjs.*

rėmĕm′ber *v.t.* 1. Retain in, recall to, the memory, recollect, not forget (freq. abs.). 2. Fee, reward, tip; mention in one's prayers; convey greetings from (person) *to* another.

rėmĕm′brance *n.* Remembering, being remembered, memory, recollection; keepsake, souvenir, memorial; (pl.) greetings conveyed through third person; *R~ Day*, Sunday nearest 11th Nov., as day of remembrance of those who lost their lives in the wars of 1914–18 and 1939–45.

rėmĕm′brancer *n.* One who reminds another; reminder, souvenir; *King's, Queen's, R~*, officer (now of Supreme Court) collecting debts due to sovereign; *City R~*, officer representing Corporation of City of London before parliamentary committees etc.

rĕm′ĕx *n.* (pl. *rĕmi′gēs*) One of principal feathers of bird's wing. [L, = 'rower'].

rėmīnd′ *v.t.* Put (person) in mind *of*, *to* do, etc.

rėmīn′der *n.* Thing that reminds or is meant to remind.

rėmīnd′ful *adj.* Acting as reminder, reviving the memory, *of*.

rĕmĭnĭsce *v.i.* (colloq.) Indulge in reminiscence(s).

rĕmĭnĭs′cence *n.* Remembering; act of recovering knowledge by mental effort; expression, fact, etc., recalling something else; remembered fact or incident; (pl.) collection in literary form of person's memories etc.

rĕmĭnĭs′cent *adj.* Recalling past things; given to or concerned with retrospection, mindful or having memories *of*; reminding or suggestive of. **rĕmĭnĭs′cently** *adv.*

rėmise′[1] (-ēz) *n.* 1. (archaic) Coach-house; carriage hired from livery-stable. 2. (fencing) Second thrust made for recovery from first. ~ *v.i.* Make remise in fencing.

rėmise′[2] (-īz) *v.t.* (law) Surrender, make over (right, property).

rėmĭss′ *adj.* Careless of duty, lax, negligent; lacking force or energy. **rėmiss′ly** *adv.* **rėmiss′nėss** *n.*

rėmĭss′ĭble *adj.* That may be remitted.

rėmĭ′ssion (-shn) *n.* Forgiveness *of* sins etc., forgiveness of sins; remittance of debt, penalty, etc.; diminution of force, effect, degree, violence, etc. **rėmiss′ĭve** *adj.*

rėmĭt′ *v.* 1. Pardon (sins etc.); refrain from exacting, inflicting, or executing (debt, punishment, sentence). 2. Abate, slacken, mitigate; partly or entirely cease from or cease. 3. Refer (matter for decision etc.) *to* some authority; send back (case) to lower court; send or put back (*in*)*to* previous state; postpone, defer, *to* or *till*. 4. Transmit, get conveyed by post etc. (money etc.).

rėmĭtt′ance *n.* Money sent to person; sending of money; *~-man*, emigrant subsisting on remittances from home.

rėmĭtt′ent *adj.* & *n.* (Fever) that abates at intervals.

rėmĭtt′er *n.* (law) Substitution, in favour of holder of two titles to estate, of the more valid for the other by which he entered on possession; remitting of case to other court.

rĕm′nant *n.* *The* small remaining part, quantity, or number; a small remaining quantity, part, or piece, esp. end of piece of cloth etc. left over after rest has been used or sold.

rēmŏn′ėtīze (*or* -mŭ-) *v.t.* Restore (metal etc.) to former position as legal tender. **rēmŏnėtīzā′tion** *n.*

rėmŏn′strance *n.* 1. (hist.) Formal statement of public grievances; *Grand R~*, that presented by House of Commons to Crown in 1641; (eccles. hist.) document presented (1610) by Dutch Arminians to States of Holland, on differences between themselves and strict Calvinists. 2. Remonstrating, expostulation; a protest.

rėmŏn′strant *adj.* & *n.* (esp.) Of, member of, Arminian party in Dutch Reformed Church.

rėmŏn′strāte (*or* rĕm′on-) *v.* Make protest, expostulate; urge in remonstrance. **rėmŏn′strative** *adj.*

rĕm′ora *n.* 1. Fish (genera *Echeneis* and *Remora*) which attaches itself to sharks, turtles, ships, etc., by means of adhesive organ on top of head, sucking-fish. 2. Obstruction, impediment (because the fish was formerly supposed to stay the course of the ship to which it adhered).

rėmorse′ *n.* Bitter repentance for wrong committed; compunction, compassionate reluctance to inflict pain or be cruel. **rėmorse′ful(ly)** (-sf-), **rėmorse′lėss(ly)** *adjs.* & *advs.* **rėmorse′lėssnėss** *n.*

rėmōte′ *adj.* Far apart; far away or off in place or time; not closely related; distant, widely different, *from*; out-of-the-way, secluded; (chiefly superl., of idea etc.) slight(est), faint(est); ~ *control*, control from a distance. **rėmōte′ly** (-tl-) *adv.* **rėmōte′nėss** *n.*

rēmount′ *v.* 1. Mount (hill, horse, etc.) again; go up again, get on horseback again; provide (cavalry) with fresh horses. 2. Go back *to* specified date, period, source. ~ *n.* (mil.) Horse to replace another which is worn out or killed.

rėmo′vable (-ōō-) *adj.* (esp., of magistrate or official) Subject to removal from office, holding office during pleasure of Crown or other authority. **rėmovabĭl′ity** *n.*

rėmo′val (-ōō-) *n.* Removing; being removed.

rėmove′ (-ōōv) *v.* 1. Take off or away from place occupied, convey to another place; change situation of; get rid of, dismiss; convey (furniture etc.) to another place for persons changing house; (pass., of course at table) be succeeded *by*. 2. Change one's residence; go away *from*. 3. (past part.) Distant or remote *from*; (of cousins) *once, twice*, etc., *removed*, with difference of one, two, etc., generations. ~ *n.* 1. Dish that succeeds another at table. 2. Promotion to higher form at school; (at some schools) a certain form or division. 3. (rare) Change of residence, departure, removal. 4. Distance (rare); stage in gradation, degree, esp. in consanguinity.

rėmūn′erāte *v.t.* Reward, pay for services rendered; serve as or provide recompense for (toil etc.) or to (person). **rėmūnerā′tion** *n.* **rėmūn′erative** *adj.* **rėmūn′eratively** *adv.* **rėmūn′erativenėss** *n.*

Rēm′us. (Rom. legend) Twin brother of ROMULUS.

Rėnaiss′ance (-ans *or* -ahńs) *n.* Great revival of art and letters, under influence of classical models, beginning in Italy in 14th c. and continued during 15th and 16th; style of art or architecture characteristic of this period (freq. attrib.); any similar revival.

rē′nal *adj.* Of the kidneys.

Renan (renahṅ), Ernest (1823–92). French scholar, philosopher, and historian; author of 'Origines du Christianisme', in which he applied the method of the historian to the biblical narrative.

rėnăs′cence *n.* Rebirth, renewal; RENAISSANCE. **rėnăs′cent** *adj.* Springing up anew, being reborn.

rĕncoun′ter (rare), **rĕncŏn′tre** (-*ter*; *or* rahṅkawṅtr′) *n.* Encounter, battle, skirmish, duel; casual meeting.

rĕnd *v.* (past t. and past part. *rĕnt*) Tear, wrench (*off*, *away*, *apart*, etc.); split or divide in two, in pieces, or (usu.) into factions.

rĕn′der *v.t.* 1. Give in return; give back, restore (archaic); hand over, deliver, give *up*, surrender (chiefly archaic); pay (tribute etc.), show (obedience etc.), do (service etc.); submit, produce for inspection or payment. 2. Reproduce, portray; give representation or performance of, execute; translate. 3. Make, cause to be, convert into. 4. Melt (fat) *down*, extract by melting; cover (stone, brick) with first coat of plaster; *~-set*, plaster (wall etc.) with two coats; (plastering) of two coats. ~ *n.* (law) Return in money, kind, or service, made by tenant to superior.

rendezvous (rahṅ′dāvōō) *n.* Place appointed for assembling of troops or ships or aircraft; place of common resort; meeting-place agreed on, meeting by agreement. ~ *v.i.* Meet at rendezvous.

rĕndi′tion *n.* 1. (now rare) Surrender of place or person. 2. (orig. U.S.) Rendering, performance, of dramatic role, musical piece, etc.; translation.

rĕn′ėgāde *n.* Apostate, esp. from Christianity to Mohammedanism; deserter of party or principles, turncoat. ~ *v.i.* Turn renegade.

rėnew′ *v.* 1. Restore to original state, make (as good as) new; resuscitate, revivify, regenerate; patch, fill up, reinforce, replace. 2. Get, begin, make, say, or give, anew; continue after intermission; (rare) become new again; ~ *lease*, *bill*, grant or be granted continuation of it. **rėnew′al** *n.*

Rĕn′frewshire (-rōō-). County of SW. Scotland, S. of River Clyde and Firth of Clyde.

rĕn′ifôrm *adj.* Kidney-shaped.

rĕnn′ėt[1] *n.* Curdled milk found in stomach of unweaned calf, used in curdling milk for making cheese, junket, etc.; preparation of inner membrane of calf's stomach, or of kinds of plant, used for this and other purposes.

rĕnn′ėt[2] *n.* Kinds of smallish, firm-fleshed dessert apple, good for keeping.

Rĕnn′ie, John (1761–1821). Scottish civil engineer; designed London bridge, Southwark bridge, and (the original) Waterloo bridge.

Renoir (renwâr′), Pierre Auguste (1841–1919). French Impressionist painter.

rėnounce′ *v.* Resign, surrender, esp. completely and formally; cast off, repudiate, decline to recognize, observe, etc.; abandon, discontinue, give up, esp. openly; (law) refuse or resign right or position, esp. as heir or trustee; (cards) follow with card of another suit for want of right one. **rėnounce′ment** *n.*

rĕn′ovāte *v.t.* Make new again, repair, (house, garment, etc.); restore to good condition or vigour. **rĕnovā′tion, rĕn′ovātor** *ns.*

rėnown′ *n.* Celebrity, fame, high distinction. **rėnowned′** *adj.* Famous, celebrated.

rĕnt[1] *n.* Tear in garment etc.; opening in clouds etc. resembling tear; cleft, fissure, gorge.

rĕnt[2] *n.* Tenant's periodical payment to owner or landlord for use of land, house, or room; payment for hire of machinery etc.; *~-charge*, periodical charge on land etc. reserved to one who is not the owner; *~-free*, exempt from rent; *~-roll*, register of person's lands etc. with rents due from them; sum of person's income from rents; *~-service*, (tenure by) personal service in lieu of or addition to rent. ~ *v.* Take, occupy, use, at a rent; let or hire for rent; be let *at* specified rent; impose rent on (tenant).

rĕn′tal *n.* Income from rents; amount paid or received as rent.

rĕn′ter *n.* One who holds land etc. by payment of rent; distributor of cinematographic films to exhibitors.

rentier (rahṅtyā′) *n.* One who derives his income from property, investments, etc.

rėnŭncia′tion (-sĭā-) *n.* Renouncing, document expressing this; self-denial, giving up of things. **rėnŭn′ciative** (-sha-), **rėnŭn′ciatory** (-sha-) *adjs.*

rĕp[1]**, rĕpp, rĕps** *ns.* Textile fabric with corded surface, resembling poplin but heavier, used for curtains, upholstery, etc.

rĕp[2] *n.* (school slang) Verse etc. learnt by heart. [abbrev. of *repetition*]

rĕp[3] *n.* (slang) Person of loose character. [perh. f. *reprobate* (*n.*)]

rĕp[4] *n.* (colloq.) Repertory (theatre).

rēpaint′ *v.t* Paint again. **rēp′aint** *n.* Repainted golf-ball.

rėpair′[1] *v.i.* Resort, have recourse, go often or in numbers, *to*. ~ *n.* (archaic) Place to which one repairs, haunt.

rėpair′[2] *v.t.* Restore to good condition, renovate, mend, by replacing or refixing parts or compensating loss or exhaustion; remedy, set right again, make amends for (loss, wrong, error). ~ *n.* Restoring to sound condition; good condition, relative condition, for working or using.

rėpănd′ *adj.* (bot., zool.) Having an undulating margin, wavy.

rĕp′arable *adj.* (Of loss etc.) that can be repaired.

rĕparā′tion *n.* Repairing or being repaired, repair; making of amends, compensation (esp., pl., that paid to victorious country by defeated one for damage done in war). **repă′rative** *adj.*

rĕpârtee′ *n.* Witty retort; (making of) witty retorts.

rėpast′ (-ah-) *n.* (Food supplied for or eaten at) meal.

rēpăt′rïāte *v.* Restore or return to native land. ~ *n.* Person who has been repatriated. **rēpătrïā′tion.**

rėpay′ *v.* (past t. & past part. *-paid*). Pay back (money); return, retaliate (blow, service, visit, etc.); give in recompense *for*; make repayment to (person); make return for, requite (action); make repayment. **rėpay′ment** *n.*

rėpeal′ *v.t.* Revoke, rescind, annul (law etc.). ~ *n.* Abrogation, repealing; cancelling of Union between Great Britain and Ireland, esp. as demanded by O'CONNELL in 1830 and 1841–6.

rėpeat′ *v.* Say or do over again; recite, report, reproduce; recur, appear again or repeatedly; (of watch etc.) strike last quarter etc. over again when required; (of fire-arm) fire several shots without reloading; (refl.) recur in same form, say or do same thing over again. ~ *n.* Repeating, esp. of item in programme in response to encore; (mus.) passage intended to be repeated, mark indicating this; pattern repeated in cloth, paper, etc.; (commerc.) fresh consignment similar to previous one, order given for this. **rėpeat′able** *adj.* **rėpeat′ėdly** *adv.*

rėpeat′er *n.* (esp.) 1. Watch, fire-arm, etc., that repeats. 2. One who repeats an indictable offence.

rėpĕl′ *v.t.* 1. Drive back, repulse, ward off; refuse admission, acceptance, or approach, to. 2. Be repulsive or distasteful to. **rėpĕll′ent** *adj.* **rėpĕll′ently** *adv.*

rĕp′ent[1] *adj.* (chiefly bot.) Creeping, esp. growing along or ust under surface of ground.

rėpĕnt′[2] *v.* Feel contrition, compunction, sorrow, or regret for what one has done or left undone; think with contrition or regret *of*. **rėpĕn′tance** *n.* **rėpĕn′tant** *adj.* **rėpĕn′tantly** *adv.*

rēpercŭ′ssion (-shn) *n.* Repulse or recoil after impact; return or reverberation of sound, echo; indirect effect or reaction *of* event or act. **rēpercŭss′ive** *adj.*

rĕp′ertoire (-twâr) *n.* Stock of dramatic or musical pieces etc. which company or player is accustomed or prepared to perform.

rĕp′ertory *n.* 1. Storehouse, magazine, or repository, where something may be found. 2. Repertoire; ~ *company*, theatrical company which keeps a stock of plays ready for performance, or (now usu.) one which presents a different play each week etc. (whence ~ *system*).

rĕpėtĭ′tion *n.* Repeating or being repeated; recitation of something learnt by heart, piece set to be learnt and recited; copy, replica; comparative ability of musical instrument to repeat same note in quick succession. **rĕpėtĭ′tious** (-sh*u*s), **rėpĕt′ĭtive** *adjs.*

rėpīne′ *v.i.* Fret, be discontented (*at*).

rėpique′ (-ēk) *n.* (piquet) Winning of 30 points on cards alone before beginning to play (and before adversary begins to count), entitling player to begin his score at 90. ~ *v.* Score repique against; win repique.

rēplāce′ *v.t.* Put back in place; take place of, succeed, be substituted for; fill up place of (*with, by*), find or provide substitute for; (pass.) be succeeded, have one's or its place filled *by*, be succeeded. **rēplāce′able** (-s*a*-) *adj.* **rēplāce′ment** (-sm-) *n.*

rėplĕn′ĭsh *v.t.* Fill up again (*with*); (past part.) filled, fully stored, full (*with*). **rėplĕn′ĭshment** *n.*

rėplēte′ *adj.* Filled, stuffed, fully imbued, well stocked, *with*; gorged, sated (*with*). **rėplē′tion** *n.*

rėplĕv′ĭn *n.* Restoration or recovery of distrained goods on security given for submission to trial and judgement; writ granting, action arising out of, replevin. ~, **rėplĕv′y** *vbs.t.* Recover by replevin.

rĕp′lĭca *n.* Duplicate made by original artist of his picture etc.; facsimile, exact copy.

rėplȳ′ *v.* Make answer, respond, in word or action (*to, that*). ~ *n.* Act of replying; what is replied, response; (law) pleading by plaintiff after delivery of defence, final speech of counsel in trial; ~-*paid*, (of telegram) with cost of reply paid by sender.

rėpôrt′ *v.* Relate, give an account of; convey, repeat (something said or heard); take down (law-case, speech, etc.) in writing, esp. with view to publication in newspaper; give formal account or statement of; make report; relate or state as result of observation or investigation; name (person) to superior authority as having offended in some way; (refl. & intrans.) make known to some authority that one has arrived or is present; ~ *progress*, state what has been done so far; *move to* ~ *progress*, in House of Commons, propose that debate be discontinued, freq. for obstructive purposes. ~ *n.* 1. Common talk, rumour; way person or thing is spoken of, repute. 2. Account given or opinion formally expressed after investigation or consideration, (esp.) account by teacher of pupil's conduct and progress; description, epitome, or reproduction of scene, speech, law-case, etc., esp. for newspaper publication; ~ *stage*, that reached by Bill in House of Commons when chairman of committee announces conclusion of committee's dealings with it between second and third readings. 3. Sound of explosion; resounding noise.

rėpôrt′age (*or* -ahzh) *n.* (Style of) reporting events for the press.

rėpôrt′er *n.* (esp.) One employed to report events for newspaper.

rėpōse′[1] (-z) *v.t.* Place (trust etc.) *in.*

rėpōse′[2] (-z) *v.* Rest; lay (one's *head* etc.) to rest; give rest to, refresh with rest; lie, be lying or laid, esp. in sleep or death; be supported or based *on.* ~ *n.* Rest, cessation of activity or excitement, respite from toil; sleep; peaceful or quiescent state, stillness, tranquillity; restful effect; composure or ease of manner. **rėpōse′ful** (-zf-) *adj.* **rėpōse′fully** *adv.*

rėpŏs′ĭtory (-z-) *n.* Receptacle; place where things are stored or may be found, museum, warehouse, shop, etc.; burial-place; recipient of confidences or secrets.

rėpoussé (-ōōs′ā) *adj.* & *n.* (Ornamental metal work) hammered into relief from reverse side.

repp: see REP[1].

repr. *abbrev.* Represent etc.; reprinted.

rĕprėhĕnd′ *v.t.* Rebuke, blame, find fault with. **rĕprėhĕn′sĭble** *adj.* **rĕprėhĕn′sĭbly** *adv.* **rĕprėhĕn′sion** (-shn) *n.*

rĕpresĕnt′ (-z-) *v.t.* 1. Bring clearly before the mind, esp. by description or imagination; point out explicitly or seriously, freq. in expostulation etc.; describe as having specific character or quality. 2. Display to the eye, make visible; (esp.) exhibit by means of painting, sculpture, etc.; reproduce in action or show, play, perform, act the part of. 3. Symbolize, serve as embodiment of; serve as specimen or example of; stand for or in place of, denote *by* a substitute; take or fill the place of, be substitute for in some capacity; (esp.) be accredited deputy for (number of persons) in deliberative or legislative assembly. **rĕprėsĕntā′tion** *n. proportional* ~: see PROPORTIONAL.

rĕpresĕn′tative (-z-) *adj.* Serving to represent; esp. typical of a class; holding place of, acting for, larger body of persons (esp. the whole people) in government or legislation; of, based upon, system by which people is thus represented. **rĕprėsĕn′tatively** *adv.* **rĕprėsĕn′tativenėss** *n.* **rĕprėsĕn′tative** *n.* 1. Sample, specimen; typical embodiment *of.* 2. Agent, delegate, substitute; person appointed to represent sovereign or nation in foreign court or country; one representing section of community as member of legislative body; *House of Representatives*, lower house of U.S. Congress or of a State legislature.

rėprĕss′ *v.t.* Check, restrain, put down, keep under; reduce to subjection, subdue, suppress, quell; (psychol.) actively exclude (distressing idea or memory) from the field of conscious awareness. **rėprĕ′ssion** (-shn) *n.* **reprĕss′ĭve** *adj.* **reprĕss′ĭvely** *adv.*

rėprieve′ *v.t.* Suspend or delay execution of (condemned person); give respite to. ~ *n.* Reprieving, being reprieved; (warrant for) remission or commutation of capital sentence; respite.

rĕp′rĭmand (-ah-) *n.* Official rebuke. ~ *v.t.* Rebuke officially (*for* fault).

rėprĭnt′ (*or* rē-) *v.t.* Print again, esp. in new edition. **rē′prĭnt** *n.* Reproduction in print of matter previously printed; new impression of work without alteration of the matter.

rėprīs′al (-z-) *n.* Act of retaliation (freq. pl.); (hist.) forcible seizure of foreign subjects' persons or property in retaliation.

rėprīse′ (-z) *n.* (law) Rent-charge or other payment to be made yearly out of estate.

rėproach′ *v.t.* Upbraid, scold (freq. *with* offence); rebuke (offence); (of look etc.) convey protest or censure to. ~ *n.* Thing that brings disgrace or discredit (*to*); opprobrium, disgraced or discredited state; upbraiding, rebuke, censure. **rėproach′ful** *adj.* **rėproach′fully** *adv.* **rėproach′fulnėss** *n.*

rĕp′robāte *v.t.* Express or feel disapproval of, censure; (of God) cast off, exclude from salvation. **rĕprobā′tion** *n.* **rĕp′robate** (-*a*t *or* -āt) *adj.* & *n.* (Person) cast off by God, hardened in sin, of abandoned character, immoral.

rēprodūce′ *v.* (esp.) Produce copy or representation of; multiply by generation. **rēprodŭc′tion** *n.* **rēprodŭc′tĭve** *adj.* **rēprodŭc′tĭvely** *adv.* **rēprodŭc′tĭvenėss** *n.*

rėprōōf′[1] *n.* Blame; rebuke, expression of blame.

rē-prōōf′[2] *v.t.* Render (coat etc.) waterproof again.

rėprove′ (-ōōv) *v.t.* Rebuke, chide.

reps: see REP[1].

rĕp′tant *adj.* (biol.) Creeping, crawling.

rĕp′tīle *n.* Crawling animal; (biol.) member of *Reptĭl′ia*, a class of cold-blooded, lung-breathing vertebrates which includes snakes, lizards, crocodiles, turtles, and tortoises; mean grovelling person. ~ *adj.* Creeping (of animals); mean and grovelling. **rĕptĭl′ian** (-ly*a*n) *adj.*

Rĕp'ton. English public school in Derbyshire, founded 1556.

rėpŭb'lĭc *n.* State in which supreme power rests in the people and their elected representatives and officers, as opp. to one governed by king etc.; any community or society with equality between members; *1st, 2nd, 3rd, 4th, 5th R~*: see FRANCE[1]; *~ of letters*, (all those engaged in) literature.

rėpŭb'lĭcan *adj.* 1. Of, constituted as, characterizing, republic(s); advocating or supporting republican government. 2. (*R~*) Of the Republican party in U.S.; *R~ party*, the political party which opposes the DEMOCRATIC party in U.S.; it was formed in 1854 and its first leader to achieve the presidency was Abraham LINCOLN; (also, hist.) the first party which supported Jefferson. 3. (Of birds) social, living in large communities. *~ n.* Person supporting or advocating republican government; (*R~*) member, supporter, of U.S. Republican party. **rėpŭb'lĭcanĭsm** *n.*

rėpūd'ĭāte *v.t.* Divorce (wife); cast off, disown (person, thing); refuse to accept or entertain, or to have dealings with; refuse to recognize or obey (authority) or discharge (obligation, debt). **rėpūdiā'tion** *n.*

rėpugn' (-ūn) *v.* (rare) Offer opposition, strive *against*; strive against; be repugnant to.

rėpŭg'nance *n.* Contradiction, incompatibility, of ideas, statements, tempers, etc.; antipathy, dislike, aversion (*to, against*).

rėpŭg'nant *adj.* Contradictory (*to*), incompatible (*with*); distasteful, objectionable, *to*.

rėpŭlse' *v.t.* Drive back (attack, attacking enemy) by force of arms; rebuff (friendly advances etc.); refuse (request, offer, etc.). *~ n.* Repulsing or being repulsed; rebuff.

rėpŭl'sion (-shn) *n.* 1. (physics) Tendency of bodies to repel each other or increase their mutual distance; *capillary ~*: see CAPILLARY. 2. Dislike, aversion, repugnance.

rėpŭl'sĭve *adj.* 1. (physics) Exercising repulsion. 2. (archaic) Repelling by denial, coldness of manner, etc. 3. Exciting aversion or loathing, disgusting. **rėpŭl'sĭvely** *adv.* **rėpŭl'sĭvenėss** *n.*

rĕp'ūtable *adj.* Of good repute. **rĕp'ūtably** *adv.*

rĕpūtā'tion *n.* What is generally said or believed about the character of a person or thing; state of being well reported of, credit, respectability, good fame; *the* credit or distinction *of*.

rėpūte' *v.t.* (usu. pass.) Be generally considered, reckoned, spoken, or reported of; (past part.) supposed, accounted, reckoned; *reputed pint*, bottle of beer etc., sold as pint but not guaranteed as imperial pint. **rėpūt'ėdly** *adv.* **rėpūte'** *n.* Reputation.

rėquĕst' *n.* 1. Act of asking for something, petition; thing asked for; *by ~*, in response to expressed wish. 2. State of being sought after, demand. *~ v.t.* Seek permission *to* do; ask to be given, allowed, or favoured with; ask (person) *to* do; ask *that*.

rĕ'quĭem *n.* Mass for repose of souls of the dead; musical setting for this; dirge. [L (accus.), = 'rest', first word of Introit in Mass for the Dead]

rĕquĭĕs'căt *n.* Wish for repose of the dead. [L *requiescat in pace* 'may he rest in peace']

rėquīre' *v.* 1. Demand of (person) *to* do; demand or ask in words, esp. as of right; lay down as imperative. 2. Need, call for, depend for success, etc., on. **rėquire'ment** (-īrm-) *n.*

rĕ'quĭsĭte (-z-) *adj.* Required by circumstances, necessary. *~ n.* Requirement; what is required or necessary.

rĕquĭsĭ'tion (-z-) *n.* Requiring, demand made, esp. formal and usu. written demand that some duty should be performed; order given to town etc. to furnish specified military supplies; being called or put into service. *~ v.t.* Demand use or supply of for military purposes or public services; demand such supplies etc. from (town, individual, etc.); press into service, call in for some purpose.

rėquīte' *v.t.* Make return for, reward or revenge (*with*); make return to, repay with good or evil; give in return. **rėquīt'al** *n.*

rere'dōs (rērd-) *n.* Ornamental screen covering wall at back of altar (ill. ALTAR).

rėscĭnd' *v.t.* Abrogate, revoke, annul, cancel. **rėscĭ'ssion** (-zhn) *n.*

rēs'crĭpt *n.* 1. Roman emperor's written reply to appeal for guidance esp. from magistrate on legal point; pope's decretal epistle in reply to question, any papal decision; official edict or announcement of ruler or government. 2. Rewriting; thing rewritten.

rĕs'cūe *v.t.* Deliver from or *from* attack, custody, danger, or harm; (law) unlawfully liberate (person), forcibly recover (property). *~ n.* Rescuing, being rescued; succour; deliverance; illegal liberation, forcible recovery. **rĕs'cūer** *n.*

rėsearch' (-sėr-) *n.* Careful search or inquiry *after, for*; (freq. pl.) endeavour to discover facts by scientific study of a subject, course of critical investigation. *~ v.i.* Make researches.

rėsĕct' *v.t.* (surg.) Cut out or pare down (bone, cartilage, nerve, etc.). **rėsĕc'tion** *n.*

rėsēd'a *n.* 1. Genus of herbaceous plants including mignonette and dyer's weed. 2. (pr. rĕs'ėd*a*) Pale greyish-green colour as of mignonette.

rėsĕm'ble (-z-) *v.t.* Be like, have similarity to or some feature or property in common with. **rėsĕm'blance** *n.*

rėsĕnt' (-z-) *v.t.* Show or feel indignation at, feel injured or insulted by.

rėsĕnt'ful (-z-) *adj.* Feeling or showing resentment. **rėsĕnt'fully** *adv.*

rėsĕnt'ment (-z-) *n.* Strong feeling of ill will or anger against author(s) of a wrong or affront.

rĕservā'tion (-z-) *n.* (esp.) 1. (eccles.) Right reserved to pope of nomination to vacant benefice; power of absolution reserved to superior in certain cases; practice of retaining for some purpose a portion of the Eucharistic elements (esp. the bread) after celebration. 2. (law) Right or interest retained in estate being conveyed; clause reserving this. 3. (orig. U.S.) Tract of land reserved for special purpose, esp. for exclusive occupation by native tribe. 4. Express or tacit limitation or exception made about something; *mental ~*, qualification tacitly added in making statement, taking oath, etc. 5. (orig. U.S.) Engaging of seats, rooms, etc., in advance; seat etc. so engaged.

rėsėrve' (-z-) *v.t.* 1. Keep for future use, enjoyment, or treatment, keep back for later occasion, hold over; keep one*self* in reserve *for*. 2. Retain possession or control of, esp. by legal or formal stipulation; set apart, destine, *for* some use or fate; (pass.) be left by fate *for*, fall first or only *to*; *reserved seats*, at entertainment etc., seats that may be engaged beforehand; *reserved list*, list of naval officers removed from active service but liable to be called out. **rėsėrved'** (past. part. as adj.) Reticent, slow to reveal emotions or opinions, uncommunicative. **rėsėrv'ėdly** *adv.* **rėsėrve'** *n.* 1. Something reserved for future use, extra stock or amount; *in ~*, unused but available. 2. (banking) That part of the assets held in the form of cash; (in central banks) that part of the assets held in the form of gold or foreign exchange. 3. (in joint-stock companies) That part of the profit which is not distributed to shareholders but added to capital; *hidden ~*, part of the profit concealed in the balance-sheet by the device of assessing the value of assets below its true level. 4. (mil., sing. or pl.) Troops withheld from action to reinforce or to cover retreat; forces outside regular army and navy liable to be called out in emergencies, member of such forces; (in games) extra player chosen in case substitute should be needed. 5. Place reserved for some special use, esp. tract of land occupied exclusively by native tribe; = RESERVATION 3;

nature ~, one where wild life is left undisturbed by man. 6. (at exhibitions etc.) Distinction conveying that exhibit will have prize if another is disqualified. 7. Limitation, exception, restriction, or qualification, attached to something; *without* ~, fully; (of auction sale) not subject to a fixed price's being reached; ~ *price*, stipulated price, less than which will not be accepted. 8. Self-restraint; avoidance of exaggerated or ill-proportioned effects in art etc.; reticence; want of cordiality or friendliness; intentional suppression of truth.

rėsẽrv'ĭst (-z-) *n.* Member of military or naval reserve.

rĕs'ervoir (-zervwâr) *n.* Receptacle constructed of earthwork, masonry, etc., in which large quantity of water is stored; any natural or artificial receptacle esp. for or of fluid; place where fluid etc. collects; part of machine, organ of body, holding fluid; reserve supply or collection *of* knowledge, facts, etc. ~ *v.t.* Store in reservoir.

rēsĕt'[1] *v.* (Sc.) Receive (stolen goods); receive stolen goods. ~ *n.* Receiving of stolen goods. **rēsĕtt'er** *n.*

rēsĕt'[2] *v.t.* Set again (gem, book or its type, etc.).

rėsīde' (-z-) *v.i.* Have one's home, dwell permanently; (of officials) be in residence; (of power, rights, etc.) rest or be vested *in* person, etc.; (of qualities) be present or inherent *in*.

rĕs'ĭdence (-z-) *n.* Residing; *in* ~, living or staying regularly at or in some place for the discharge of special duties, or to comply with some regulation; place where one resides, abode *of*; house esp. of considerable pretension, mansion.

rĕs'ĭdency (-z-) *n.* (hist.) Official residence of Governor-General's representative at Indian native court; (hist.) an administrative area in certain protected States in the East Indies.

rĕs'ĭdent (-z-) *adj.* Residing; (of birds etc.) staying all the year round, not migrating; staying at or in some place in fulfilment of duty or compliance with regulation. ~ *n.* 1. Permanent inhabitant (opp. *visitor*). 2. (hist.) Indian Governor-General's political agent residing at native court; representative of the British Crown in certain protected States; senior Government official in certain overseas Administrations.

rĕsĭdĕn'tial (-z-, -shl) *adj.* Suitable for or occupied by private houses; connected with residence; (of post) requiring holder to live at place of work.

rĕsĭdĕn'tiary (-z-, -sha-) *n.* Ecclesiastic bound to residence. ~ *adj.* Bound to, requiring, of or for, official residence.

rėsĭd'ūal (-z-) *adj.* Remaining, left over, left as residuum; (of error etc.) left unexplained or uncorrected; (math.) resulting from subtraction. ~ *n.* Residual quantity; remainder; substance of the nature of a residuum.

rėsĭd'ūary (-z-) *adj.* Of the residue of an estate; of, being, a residuum, residual, still remaining.

rĕs'ĭdūe (-z-) *n.* Remainder, rest, what is left or remains over; what remains of estate after payment of charges, debts, and bequests; (chem. etc.) residuum.

rėsĭd'ūum (-z-) *n.* What remains, esp. (chem. etc.) substance left after combustion or evaporation.

rėsīgn' (-zīn) *v.* Relinquish, surrender, give up, hand over (office, right, property, charge, hope, etc.); reconcile one*self*, one's *mind*, etc. (*to*); give up office, retire. **rėsīgned'** (-zīnd) *adj.* Submissive, acquiescent, having resigned oneself to sorrow etc. **rėsīgn'ėdly** *adv.*

rĕsĭgnā'tion (-zĭg-) *n.* (esp.) 1. Resigning of an office, document conveying this. 2. Being resigned, uncomplaining endurance of sorrow or other evil.

rėsĭl'ience (-zĭlyens) *n.* Rebound, recoil; elasticity, power of resuming original shape or position after compression, bending, etc. **rėsĭl'iency** *n.* Resilience; buoyancy, power of recovery. **rėsĭl'ient** *adj.* **rėsĭl'iently** *adv.*

rĕs'ĭn (-z-) *n.* Adhesive, highly inflammable substance, hardening on exposure to air, formed by secretion in trees and plants and exuding naturally from many of them (as fir and pine) or obtained by incision, and used in making varnishes etc. and in pharmacy. ~ *v.t.* Rub or treat with resin. **rĕsĭnā'ceous** (-sh*u*s), **rĕsĭnĭf'erous** *adjs.* Yielding, containing resin.

rĕs'ĭnous (-z-) *adj.* Of, containing, resin; produced by burning resin.

rėsĭp'ĭscence *n.* Recognition of error, returning to good sense.

rėsĭst' (-z-) *v.* Stop course of, withstand action or effect of; strive against, oppose; offer resistance. **rėsĭs'tant, rėsĭs'tent, rėsĭs'tĭble, rėsĭs'tĭve** *adjs.* **rėsĭst'** *n.* Composition applied to surfaces for protection from some agent employed on them, esp. in textile printing to parts that are not to take dye.

rėsĭs'tance (-z-) *n.* 1. Power of resisting; *passive* ~, resistance without resort to violence or active opposition, non-co-operation; ~ (*movement*), any (esp. underground) organization resisting German authority in occupied countries during the war of 1939–45. 2. Hindrance, impeding or stopping effect, exercised by material thing upon another; (elect., magn., heat) non-conductivity; (elect.) measure of capacity in a conducting body to resist flow of a current (the resistance of a circuit is given by OHM's law as the ratio of the applied voltage (electromotive force) to the current which flows); part of apparatus used to offer definite resistance to current; *line of* ~, direction in which resistance acts; *line of least* ~, (fig.) easiest method or course.

rėsĭst'lėss (-z-) *adj.* 1. That cannot be resisted. 2. Unresisting. **rėsĭst'lėssly** *adv.*

rĕs'oluble (-z-) *adj.* That can be resolved; analysable *into*.

rĕs'olute (-zoloot, -ūt) *adj.* Determined, decided, bold, not vacillating, unshrinking, firm of purpose. **rĕs'olutely** *adv.*

rĕsolu'tion (-zoloo-, -lū-) *n.* 1. Separation into components, decomposition, analysis; conversion *into* another form; (med.) disappearance of inflammation, return of diseased tissue to normal state; (pros.) substitution of two short syllables for one long; (mus.) process by which discord is made to pass into concord; (mech.) replacing of single force by two or more which are jointly equivalent; (optics) quality of optical instruments whereby definition of fine detail is obtained. 2. Solving *of* doubt, problem, question, etc. 3. Formal expression of opinion by legislative body or public meeting; form proposed for this. 4. Resolve, thing resolved on; determined temper or character, boldness and firmness of purpose.

rėsŏlve' (-z-) *v.* 1. Dissolve, disintegrate, analyse, break up into parts, dissipate, convert or be converted *into*; reduce by mental analysis *into*; (mus.) convert (discord), be converted, into concord. 2. Solve, explain, clear up, settle. 3. Decide upon, make up one's mind *upon* action or *to* do; form mentally or (of legislative body or public meeting) pass by vote the resolution *that*; (of circumstances etc.) bring (person) to resolution *to* do, *upon* action. 4. *resolved*, resolute. ~ *n.* Determination or resolution come to in the mind; (poet.) resolution, steadfastness.

rėsŏl'vent (-z-) *adj.* & *n.* (chiefly med. & chem.) (Drug, application, substance) effecting resolution of tumour etc. or division into component parts.

rĕs'onant (-z-) *adj.* (Of sound) re-echoing, resounding, continuing to sound or ring; (of bodies) causing reinforcement or prolongation of sound, esp. by vibration; (of places) echoing, resounding, *with*. **rĕs'onantly** *adv.* **rĕs'onance** *n.*

rĕs'onātor (-z-) *n.* Instrument responding to single note and used for detecting it in combinations; appliance for giving resonance to sounds.

rėsõrb' *v.t.* Absorb again. **rėsõrb'ence** *n.* **rėsõrb'ent** *adj.*

rėsõr'cĭnōl (-z-) *n.* Metadihydroxy-benzene, a synthetic substance used in the production of various dyestuffs and drugs.

rėsõrp'tion *n.* Resorbing, being resorbed; (path.) disappearance of tissue by absorption into body fluids.

rĕsŏrt' (-z-) *v.i.* 1. Turn for aid *to*. 2. Go in numbers or often *to*. ~ *n.* 1. Thing to which recourse is had, what is turned to for aid, expedient; recourse; *in the last* ~, as a last expedient. 2. Frequenting, being frequented. 3. Place frequented, usu. for specified purpose or quality (as *health*, *holiday*, *seaside* ~).

rĕsound' (-z-) *v.* 1. (Of place) ring or echo (*with*); (of voice, sound, etc.) produce echoes, go on sounding, fill place with sound; be much mentioned or repeated, be celebrated. 2. Repeat loudly (praises etc.); re-echo, give back (sound). **rĕsound'ingly** *adv.*

rĕsource' (-sŏrs) *n.* 1. (usu. pl.) Means of supplying a want, stock that can be drawn on; (pl.) country's collective means for support and defence. 2. Possibility of aid (now rare); expedient, device, shift; means of relaxation or amusement; skill in devising expedients, ingenuity. **rĕsource'ful** (-sf-) *adj.* **rĕsource'fully** *adv.* **rĕsource'fulnĕss** *n.* **rĕsource'lĕss** *adj.* **rĕsource'lĕssnĕss** *n.*

rĕspĕct' *n.* 1. Reference, relation. 2. Heed or regard *to*, *of*, attention *to*; ~ *of persons*, partiality or favour shown esp. to the powerful. 3. Particular, detail, point, aspect. 4. Deferential esteem felt or shown towards person or quality; state of being esteemed or honoured; (pl.) polite messages or attentions. ~ *v.t.* 1. Be directed, refer or relate, to. 2. Treat or regard with deference, esteem, or honour; treat with consideration, spare. 3. (her., of charges) Look at, face.

rĕspĕc'table *adj.* 1. Deserving respect. 2. Considerable in number, size, quantity, etc.; fairly good, tolerable. 3. Of good or fair social standing, honest, decent, worthy; befitting respectable persons. **rĕspĕctabĭl'ĭty** *n.* **rĕspĕc'tably** *adv.*

rĕspĕct'ful *adj.* Showing deference. **rĕspĕct'fully** *adv.* **rĕspĕct'fulnĕss** *n.*

rĕspĕc'tĭve *adj.* Pertaining to, connected with, each individual, group, etc., of those in question; separate, several, particular. **rĕspĕc'tĭvely** *adv.*

Respighi (rĕspēg'ē), Ottorino (1879–1936). Italian musical composer.

rĕs'pĭrable *adj.* That can be breathed, fit for breathing.

rĕspĭrā'tion *n.* Breathing; single inspiration and expiration; (biol.) process by which an organism utilizes oxygen from its environment and gives out carbon dioxide; *artificial* ~, manual or mechanical procedure designed to restore the natural function of breathing when this has been suspended; ~ *pump*, apparatus for administering artificial respiration continuously (e.g. the 'iron lung').

rĕs'pĭrātor *n.* Apparatus worn over mouth and nose to warm or filter inhaled air or prevent inhalation of poisonous gases etc., gas-mask; device for maintaining respiration artificially.

rĕspīre' *v.* Inhale and exhale air; breathe; breathe again, take breath, recover hope or spirit, get rest or respite. **rĕs'pĭrātory** *adj.*

rĕs'pīte *n.* Delay permitted in the discharge of an obligation or suffering of a penalty; interval of rest or relief. ~ *v.t.* Grant respite to; postpone execution or exaction of (sentence, obligation).

rĕsplĕn'dent *adj.* Brilliant, dazzlingly or gloriously bright. **rĕsplĕn'dently** *adv.* **rĕsplĕn'dence, rĕsplĕn'dency** *ns.*

rĕspŏnd' *v.i.* Make answer; act in response (*to*). ~ *n.* 1. (eccles.) Responsory; response to versicle. 2. (archit.) Half-pillar or half-pier attached to wall to support arch, freq. as termination of arcade (ill. ARCADE).

rĕspŏn'dent *adj.* Making answer; responsive *to*; in position of defendant. ~ *n.* One who answers, esp. one who defends thesis; defendant in divorce case.

rĕspŏnse' *n.* Answer; (eccles.) responsory; any part of liturgy said or sung by congregation in answer to priest; (mus.) repetition by one part of a theme given by another part.

rĕspŏnsĭbĭl'ĭty *n.* Being responsible; charge for which one is responsible.

rĕspŏn'sĭble *adj.* Liable to be called to account, answerable; morally accountable for actions, capable of rational conduct; of good credit and repute, reliable, trustworthy; involving responsibility. **rĕspŏn'sĭbly** *adv.*

rĕspŏn'sions (-shnz) *n.pl.* First examination (from which candidates are freq. exempted by other qualifications) for Oxford B.A. degree.

rĕspŏn'sĭve *adj.* Answering; by way of answer; responding readily to or *to* some influence, impressionable, sympathetic; (of liturgy etc.) using responses. **rĕspŏn'sĭvely** *adv.* **rĕspŏn'sĭvenĕss** *n.*

rĕspŏn'sory *n.* (eccles.) Anthem said or sung by soloist and choir after lesson.

rĕssaldâr' *n.* Native captain in Indian cavalry regiment.

rĕst[1] *v.* 1. Take repose by lying down, esp. in sleep; lie in death or the grave; cease, abstain or be relieved from exertion, action, movement, or employment; be at ease or in peace, stay, remain; give rest or repose to, lay to rest; allow to rest or remain inactive or quiescent; (theatr. slang) be temporarily unemployed. 2. Have place or position, place, set, lay, (*upon*); (of eyes) be directed (*on*, *upon*); lie or lean, lay, *on*, *upon* for repose or support; rely, depend, be based, base, found, allow to depend *on*, *upon*. 3. *resting-place*, place provided or used for resting; *last resting-place*, the grave. ~ *n.* 1. Repose or sleep, esp. in bed at night; intermission of, freedom from, labour, exertion, or activity; freedom from distress, trouble, etc.; quiet or tranquillity of mind; repose of the grave; *day of* ~, the sabbath; *at* ~, tranquil, quiet, inert; settled; *set at* ~, satisfy, assure; settle; *lay to* ~, bury. 2. Place of resting or abiding; lodging-place or shelter provided for sailors, cabmen, or other class. 3. Prop, support; what something rests on. 4. (mus.) Interval of silence, pause, indicated by various signs according to duration, as *breve* ~ 𝄺, *semibreve* ~ 𝄻, *minim* ~ 𝄼 or 𝄼, *crotchet* ~ 𝄽, *quaver* ~ 𝄾, *semiquaver* ~ 𝄿, etc.; pause in elocution, caesura in verse. 5. ~-*cure*, rest in bed as medical treatment; ~-*day*, day spent in rest; ~-*house*, (in India) dak-bungalow; boarding-house or inn.

rĕst[2] *v.i.* Remain over (now rare); remain in specified state; ~ *with*, be left in the hands or charge of. ~ *n.* *The* remainder or remaining parts or individuals (*of*); (banking) reserve fund; (tennis etc.) rally, spell of sending ball etc. backwards and forwards without intermission; *for the* ~, as regards anything beyond what has been specially mentioned.

rĕst[3] *n.* (hist.) Contrivance fixed to cuirass to receive butt-end of lance when couched for the charge.

rĕs'taurant (-orahṅ) *n.* Place where meals or refreshments may be had.

rĕstaurateur' (-orahtẽr) *n.* Restaurant-keeper.

rĕst'ful *adj.* Favourable to repose, free from disturbing influences, soothing. **rĕst'fully** *adv.* **rĕst'fulness** *n.*

rĕst'-hărrow (-ō) *n.* Field-shrub (*Ononis*) with tough roots.

rĕstĭtū'tion *n.* Restoring of or *of* thing to proper owner; reparation for injury; restoring of thing to its original state; resumption of original shape or position by elasticity; ~ *of conjugal rights*, resumption of cohabitation demanded in matrimonial suit.

rĕs'tĭve *adj.* (Of horse) refusing to go forward, obstinately moving backwards or sideways when being driven or ridden, intractable, resisting control; (of person) unmanageable, rejecting control, fidgety. **rĕs'tĭvely** (-vl-) *adv.* **rĕs'tĭvenĕss** *n.*

rĕst'lĕss *adj.* Finding or affording no rest; uneasy, agitated, unpausing, fidgeting. **rĕst'lĕssly** *adv.* **rĕst'lĕssnĕss** *n.*

rĕstorā'tion *n.* (esp.) 1. *The R*~, (period of) re-establishment of monarchy in England with return of Charles II in 1660. 2. Representation of original form of ruined building, extinct animal, etc.; action or process of restoring to original form or perfect condition.

rėstŏ'rative *adj.* Tending to restore health or strength. ~ *n.* Restorative food, medicine, or agency.

rėstōre' *v.t.* 1. Give back, make restitution of. 2. Repair, alter, (building, painting, etc.) so as to bring back as nearly as possible to original form, state, etc.; reproduce or represent in original form; reinstate, bring back *to* dignity or right; bring back to or *to* health, cure. 3. Re-establish, renew, bring back into use; replace or insert (words etc. in text, missing parts of thing etc.); replace, put back, bring *to* former place or condition. **rėstōr'er** *n.*

rėstrain' *v.t.* Check or hold in *from*, keep in check or under control or within bounds, repress, keep down; confine, imprison. **rėstrain'ėdly** *adv.* With restraint.

rėstraint' *n.* 1. Restraining, being restrained; check; controlling agency or influence; confinement, esp. in asylum; *without* ~, freely, copiously. 2. Constraint, reserve.

rėstrict' *v.t.* Confine, bound, limit (*to, within*). **rėstrict'ėdly** *adv.* **restric'tion** *n.* **rėstric'tive** *adj.* ~ *practices*, arrangements in industry and trade which restrict or control competition between firms; arrangements by groups of workers to control output or restrict the entry of new workers. **rėstric'tively** *adv.*

rėsŭlt' (-z-) *v.i.* Arise as consequence, effect, or conclusion *from*; end *in* specified way. ~ *n.* Consequence, issue, outcome; quantity, formula, etc., obtained by calculation.

rėsŭl'tant (-z-) *adj.* Resulting. ~ *n.* Product, outcome; force which is equivalent of two or more forces acting from different directions at one point; composite or final effect of any two or more forces.

rėsūme' (-z-) *v.* 1. Get or take again or back; recover; reoccupy. 2. Begin again; go on (with) after interruption; recommence. 3. Make résumé of.

résumé (rāz'ūmā) *n.* Summary, epitome, abstract.

rėsŭmp'tion (-z-) *n.* Resuming. **rėsŭmp'tive** *adj.* **rėsŭmp'tively** *adv.*

rėsūp'inate *adj.* (bot., of leaf etc.) Inverted, upside-down.

rėsûrge' *v.i.* (now rare) Rise again.

rėsûr'gent *adj.* That rises or tends to rise again. **rėsûr'gence** *n.*

rĕsurrĕct' (-z-) *v.t.* (colloq.) Raise from the dead (rare); revive practice or memory of; take from grave, exhume.

rĕsurrĕc'tion (-z-) *n.* 1. *R~*, (festival in memory of) rising of Christ from the grave; rising again of men at the last day. 2. Exhumation; revival from disuse, inactivity, or decay; restoration to vogue or memory; *~-man*, body-snatcher. **rĕsurrĕc'tional** (-sho-) *adj.* **rĕsurrĕc'tionist** *n.* (esp.) Body-snatcher.

rėsŭs'citāte *v.* Revive, return or restore to life, consciousness, vogue, vigour, etc. **rėsŭscitā'tion, rėsŭs'citātor** *ns.* **rėsŭs'citative** *adj.*

Reszke (rĕs'kĕ), Jean de (1850–1925). Polish tenor singer.

rĕt *v.t.* Soften (flax, hemp) by soaking in water or exposing to moisture.

rėtā'ble (*or* rĕt'*a*bl) *n.* Frame enclosing decorated panels on or above back of altar, altarpiece (ill. ALTAR); shelf above back of altar.

rē'tail *n.* Sale of goods in small quantities (freq. attrib. and in adverbial expressions; opp. WHOLESALE). **rėtail'** (*or* rē-) *v.* 1. Sell (goods) by retail; (of goods) be retailed. 2. Recount, relate details of. **rėtail'er** (*or* rē-) *n.*

rėtain' *v.t.* 1. Keep in place, hold fixed; *retaining wall*, one supporting and confining mass of earth or water. 2. Secure services of (esp. barrister) by engagement and preliminary payment; *retaining-fee*, retainer. 3. Keep possession of, continue to have; continue to practise or recognize, allow to remain or prevail, keep unchanged; bear in mind, remember.

rėtain'er *n.* 1. Retaining, being retained; fee paid to barrister to secure his services; sum paid to secure special services; (U.S.) authorization to lawyer to act in case. 2. One who retains. 3. (hist.) Dependent or follower of person of rank or position; (joc.) servant.

rėtăl'iāte *v.* Repay (esp. injury, insult, etc.) in kind; retort (accusation) *upon* person; make return or requital (esp. of injury). **rėtăliā'tion** *n.* **rėtăl'iative, rėtăl'iatory** *adjs.*

rėtard' *v.* Make slow or late, delay progress, arrival, accomplishment, or happening of; (esp. of physical phenomena, e.g. motion of tides, or celestial bodies) happen, arrive, behind normal or calculated time; *retarded child*, one whose mental or physical development is behind what is normal at his age. **rētardā'tion** *n.* **rėtard'ative, rėtard'atory** *adjs.* **rėtard'** *n.* Retardation; *in* ~, delayed; ~ *of tide* or *high water*, interval between full moon and following high water.

rētard'er *n.* Substance used to delay chemical action.

rĕtch *v.i.* Make motion of vomiting, esp. ineffectually and involuntarily. ~ *n.* Such motion, sound of it.

rėtĕn'tion *n.* Retaining; esp. (med.) retaining in body of secretion (esp. urine) usually evacuated.

rėtĕn'tive *adj.* 1. (Of memory) tenacious, not forgetful. 2. Tending, inclined, apt, to retain. 3. (surg. etc.) Serving to keep dressing etc. in place. **rėtĕn'tively** *adv.* **rėtĕn'tivenėss** *n.*

R. et I. *abbrev. Regina et Imperatrix* (= Queen and Empress); *Rex et Imperator* (= King and Emperor).

rĕt'icence *n.* Reserve in speech, avoidance of saying too much or of speaking freely. **rĕt'icent** *adj.* **rĕt'icently** *adv.*

rĕt'icle *n.* Network of fine threads or lines in object-glass of telescope to help accurate observation.

rėtic'ūlar *adj.* Net-like.

rėtic'ūlāte *v.* Divide, be divided or marked, into a network; arrange, be arranged, in small squares or with intersecting lines. **rėtic'ūlate** (-*a*t) *adj.* **rėtic'ūlately** *adv.* **rėticūlā'tion** *n.*

rĕt'icūle *n.* 1. Reticle. 2. (archaic) Lady's bag of woven or other material carried or worn to serve purpose of pocket.

rėtic'ūlum *n.* (pl. -*la*). 1. Second stomach of ruminant (ill. RUMINANT). 2. Net-like structure, reticulated membrane, etc.

rĕt'ifôrm *adj.* Net-like, reticulated.

rĕt'ina *n.* (pl. -*as*, -*ae*). Innermost layer or coating, sensitive to light, at back of eyeball, in which optic nerve terminates (ill. EYE). **rĕt'inal** *adj.*

rĕt'inūe *n.* Suite or train of persons in attendance upon someone.

rėtīre' *v.* 1. Withdraw, go away, seek seclusion or shelter; withdraw *to* usual place or occupation, *to* bed, etc.; retreat, move back or away, recede; vanish *from* sight; *retired*, withdrawn from society or observation, secluded; *retiring*, reserved, shy. 2. Cease *from* or give up office or profession or employment or business, esp. after having made a competence or earned a pension; compel (officer, employee) to retire; give up candidature; (cricket) voluntarily terminate one's innings; *retired list*, list of retired officers. 3. (mil.) Lead back (troops etc.), move back. 4. (finance) Withdraw (bill, note) from operation or currency. ~ *n.* Signal to troops to retire.

rėtīre'ment (-īrm-) *n.* (esp.) Seclusion, privacy; secluded place; condition of having retired from work.

rėtôrt'[1] *v.* 1. Repay (esp. injury) in kind; cast back (*up*)*on* offending party, use (argument etc.) *against* its author. 2. Make, say by way of, repartee, countercharge, or counter-argument. ~ *n.* Incisive reply, repartee; turning of argument or charge against its author; piece of retaliation. **rėtôrt'ėd** *adj.* Recurved, twisted or bent backwards.

rėtŏrt′[2] *n.* Vessel usu. of glass with long downward-bent neck used in distilling liquids (now obsolescent); vessel for purifying

RETORT

mercury by distillation; clay or iron cylinder in which coal is heated to produce gas; furnace in which iron is heated with carbon to produce steel. ~ *v.t.* Purify (mercury) by distilling from retort.

rėtŏr′tion *n.* 1. Bending back. 2. Retaliation, esp. by one State on subject of another.

rētouch′ (-tŭch) *v.t.* Amend or improve by fresh touches, touch up (esp. photographic negative or print).

rėtrāce′ *v.t.* Trace back to source or beginning; look over again; trace again in memory; go back over (one's steps, way, etc.).

rėtrăct′ *v.* 1. Draw (esp. part of one's body or of machine) back or in; (of such part etc.) shrink back or in, be capable of being retracted; (phonet.) pronounce with tongue retracted. 2. Withdraw, revoke, cancel; acknowledge falsity or error of; disavow; retract opinion or statement. **rėtrăc′table, rėtrăc′tīle** *adjs.* **rētrăctā′tion, rėtrăc′tion** *ns.*

rėtreat′ *v.* Go back, retire, relinquish a position (esp. of army etc.); recede; (chiefly in chess) move (piece) back from forward or threatened position. ~ *n.* 1. Act of, (mil.) signal for, retreating; (mil.) bugle-call at sunset; *beat a* ~, retreat, abandon undertaking; *make good one's* ~, get safely away. 2. Withdrawing into privacy or security; (place of) seclusion; (eccles.) temporary retirement for religious exercises; asylum for inebriates, lunatics, or pensioners; lurking-place; place of shelter.

rėtrĕnch′ *v.* 1. Cut down, reduce amount of (esp. expenses etc.); economize, reduce expenses; cut off, remove, cut out. 2. (fort.) Furnish with inner line of defence, usu. consisting of trench and parapet. **rėtrĕnch′ment** *n.*

rētrī′al *n.* Retrying of a case in a court of law.

rĕtrĭbū′tion *n.* Recompense, usu. for evil, vengeance, requital. **rėtrĭb′ūtive** *adj.* **rėtrĭb′ūtively** *adv.*

rėtrieve′ *v.* 1. (Of dogs) find and bring in (killed or wounded game). 2. Recover by investigation or effort of memory, restore to knowledge or recall to mind; regain possession of. 3. Rescue *from* bad state etc.; restore to flourishing state, revive (esp. fortunes etc.); make good, repair, set right (loss, disaster, error). ~ *n.* Possibility of recovery.

rėtriev′er *n.* Dog of breed specially adapted for retrieving game (ill. DOG).

retro- *prefix.* Backwards, back.

rĕtrōăct′ *v.i.* React; operate in backward direction; have retrospective effect. **rĕtrōăc′tion** *n.* **rĕtrōăc′tĭve** *adj.* **rĕtrōăc′tĭvely** *adv.*

rĕt′rocēde[1] *v.i.* 1. Move back, recede. 2. (Of gout) strike inward. **rĕtrocēd′ent** *adj.*

rĕt′rocēde[2] *v.t.* Cede (territory) back again.

rĕtrocĕ′ssion *n.* **rĕtrocĕss′ive** *adj.* In verbal senses of RETROCEDE[1] and [2].

rĕt′rochoir (-kwīr) *n.* Part of cathedral or large church behind high altar (ill. CHURCH).

rĕt′roflĕx *adj.* Turned backwards.

rĕtrogradā′tion *n.* 1. (astron.) Apparent backward motion of planet in zodiac; motion of heavenly body from east to west; backward movement of lunar nodes on ecliptic. 2. Retrogression.

rĕt′rogrāde *adj.* 1. (astron.) In or showing retrogradation. 2. Directed backwards, retreating; reverting, esp. to inferior state, declining; inverse, reversed. **rĕt′rogrādely** *adv.* **rĕt′rogrāde** *v.i.* Show retrogradation, move backwards, recede, retire, decline, revert.

rĕtrogrĕss′ *v.i.* Go back, move backwards, deteriorate. **rĕtrogrĕss′ĭve** *adj.* **rĕtrogrĕss′ĭvely** *adv.*

rĕtrogrĕ′ssion (-shn) *n.* Backward or reversed movement; return to less advanced state, decline, deterioration; (astron.) retrogradation.

rĕt′rospĕct *n.* Regard or reference *to* precedent, authority, or previous conditions; view or survey of past time or events.

rĕtrospĕc′tion *n.* Action of looking back, esp. into the past, indulgence or engagement in retrospect. **rĕtrospĕc′tĭve** *adj.* Of, in, proceeding by, retrospection; (of statutes etc.) operative with regard to past time, not restricted to the future, retroactive. **rĕtrospĕc′tĭvely** *adv.*

retroussé (-ōōs′ā) *adj.* (Of nose) turned up.

rĕt′rovĕrtėd *adj.* Turned backwards (esp. path., of womb).

rėtûrn′ *v.* 1. Come or go back; revert. 2. Bring, convey, give, send, put, or pay, back or in return or requital; (in games) respond to (play of one's partner or opponent, esp. partner's lead); give, render (thanks); *returned empties*, packing-cases etc. sent back. 3. (archit.) Continue (moulding etc.) round angle of structure. 4. Say in reply, retort. 5. Report in answer to official demand for information, state by way of report or verdict; (of sheriff) report as having been appointed to serve on jury or sit in Parliament; (of constituency) elect as member of Parliament; *returning officer*, official conducting election and announcing name of person elected. ~ *n.* 1. Coming back; coming round again; return ticket; (*many*) *happy* ~*s* (*of the day*), birthday or festival greeting; ~ *ticket*, ticket for journey to place and back again to point of departure. 2. Side or part falling away, usu. at right angles, from front or direct line of any work or structure. 3. (Coming in of) proceeds or profit of undertaking. 4. Giving, sending, putting, or paying back; thing so given, sent, etc., esp. report of sheriff etc. in answer to writ or official demand for information; (returning officer's announcement of) candidate's election as member of Parliament; ~ (*match, game*), match, game, between same sides as before. 5. (pl.) Refuse tobacco (obs.); mild, light-coloured tobacco for smoking.

rėtūse′ *adj.* (Of leaf, part of insect, etc.) having a broad or rounded end with depression in centre.

Retz, Gilles de: see RAIS.

Reub′en (rōō-). (O.T.) Eldest son of Jacob and Leah, and ancestor of one of the 12 tribes.

rēū′nion (-yon) *n.* Reuniting, being reunited; social gathering, esp. of intimates or persons with common interests.

rēūnīte′ *v.* Bring or come together again, join after separation.

Reu′ter (roi-), Paul Julius, Baron von (1816–99). German-born British founder of a telegraphic news agency (*Reuters*), now owned and directed by various newspaper associations of Gt Britain and the Commonwealth.

rĕv *n.* (mech.) Abbrev. of REVOLUTION. ~ *v.* Cause (internal combustion engine) to run quickly, esp. before bringing it into use, speed *up*; (of engine) revolve, be speeded *up*.

Rev. *abbrev.* Revelation (N.T.); Reverend.

Reval: see TALLINN.

rēvălorīzā′tion *n.* Action or process of establishing fresh value for something, esp. a currency. **rēvăl′ōrīze** *v.t.*

Revd *abbrev.* Reverend.

rėveal′[1] *v.t.* Disclose, make known, in supernatural manner (esp. of God); disclose, divulge, make known; display, show, let appear.

rėveal′[2] *n.* Internal side surface of opening or recess, esp. of doorway or window-aperture (ill. WINDOW).

rėveille (-vĕl′ĭ, -văl′ĭ) *n.* Military waking-signal sounded in morning on bugle or drums. [Fr. *réveillez*, imper. pl. of *réveiller* awaken, f. L *vigilare* keep watch]

rĕv′el *v.i.* Make merry, be riotously festive, feast; take keen delight *in.* ~ *n.* Revelling; (occasion of indulgence in) merry-making (freq. pl.). **rĕv'eller, rĕv'elry** *ns.*

rĕvėlā'tion *n.* 1. Disclosing of knowledge, knowledge disclosed, to man by divine or supernatural agency; *The R~*, (pop.) *R~s*, last book of N.T., the Apocalypse. 2. Striking disclosure; revealing of some fact.

rĕvėlā'tionist (-sho-) *n.* 1. Author of the Apocalypse. 2. One who believes in divine revelation.

rėvĕnge' (-j) *v.* Avenge one*self* (*on* or *upon* a person); inflict punishment, exact retribution, for (injury, harm, etc.); avenge (person). ~ *n.* Revenging, act done in revenging; desire to revenge, vindictive feeling; (in games) opportunity given for reversing former result by return game. **rėvĕnge'ful** (-jf-) *adj.* **rėvĕnge'fully** *adv.* **rėvĕnge'fulnėss** *n.*

rĕv'ėnūe (*in parl. and legal usage freq.* rėvĕn'ū) *n.* Income, esp. of large amount, from any source; (pl.) collective items or amounts constituting this; (sing.) annual income of Government or State, from which public expenses are met; department of civil service collecting this; *inland* ~: see INLAND; ~ *cutter, officer*, etc., one employed to prevent smuggling.

rėvėrb'erāte *v.* Return, reflect, re-echo (sound, light, etc.); be reflected or re-echoed; (of flame, heat etc.) be forced back *into, over, upon* (furnace, substance, etc.); subject to action of reverberatory furnace. **rėvėrberā'tion** *n.* **rėvėrb'erant, rėvėrb'erative** *adjs.*

rėvėrb'erātor *n.* Reflector, reflecting lamp.

rėvėrb'eratory *adj.* Reverberating; ~ *furnace*, furnace with a shallow hearth and low arched roof from which the heat contained in the products of combustion is reflected or 'reverberated' on to the charge.

rėvēre'[1] *v.t.* Regard as sacred or exalted, hold in deep and usu. affectionate or religious respect, venerate.

Rėvēre'[2], Paul (1735–1818). American patriot, famous for his midnight ride from Charlestown to Lexington (1775) to give warning that British troops were advancing from Boston.

rĕv'erence *n.* Revering; capacity for this; gesture indicating respect, bow or curtsy (archaic); being respected or venerated; *your, his,* ~, (archaic, joc., or vulg., esp. in Ireland) titles used to, of, clergyman. **rĕverĕn'tial** (-shl) *adj.* **rĕverĕn'tially** *adv.* **rĕv'erence** *v.t.* Regard with reverence, venerate.

rĕv'erend *adj.* Deserving reverence by age, character, or associations; esp. as respectful epithet applied to members of the clergy, freq. prefixed to name and designation of clergyman, and abbrev. *Rev.*; of, connected with, the clergy; *Very R~*, (in C. of E.) title of dean, *Right R~* of bishop, *Most R~* of archbishop.

rĕv'erent *adj.* Feeling or showing reverence. **rĕv'erently** *adv.*

rĕv'erie *n.* (Fit of) musing, day-dream(ing); (mus.) instrumental composition suggesting dreamy or musing state.

revers' (revēr) *n.* Turned back edge of coat etc. displaying under surface; material covering this edge.

rėvėrse' *adj.* Opposite or contrary (*to*) in character or order, back or backwards, upside-down; ~ *gear*, one permitting vehicle to be driven backwards. **rėvėrse'ly** *adv.* **rėvėrse'** *n.* 1. *The* contrary (*of*); *in* ~, with the position reversed, the other way round; (of vehicle) in reverse gear. 2. (Device on) side of coin, medal, etc., which does not bear main device or inscription; verso (of leaf in book etc.); back. 3. Piece of misfortune, disaster, esp. defeat in battle. ~ *v.* Turn the other way round or up, or inside-out; invert; transpose; convert to opposite character or effect; cause (engine etc.) to work in contrary direction; revoke, annul (decree, act, etc.); (dancing, esp. in waltz) move or turn in opposite direction. **rėvėrs'al** *n.* **rėvėrs'ible** *adj.*

rėvėrs'ĭ (*or* -ē) *n.* Obsolete card-game in which object was to avoid winning tricks; also, game played on draught-board with counters coloured differently above and below.

rėvėr'sion (-shn) *n.* 1. (Return to grantor or his heirs, right of ultimate succession to) estate granted till specified date or event, esp. death of original grantee; sum payable on person's death, esp. by way of life-insurance; thing to which one has a right or expects to succeed when relinquished by another. 2. Return to a previous state, habit, etc., esp. (biol.) to ancestral type. **rėvėr'sional** (-sho-) *adj.* **rėvėr'sionally** *adv.* **rėvėr'sionary** *adj.*

rėvėr'sioner *n.* One who has the reversion of an estate, office, etc.

rėvėrt' *v.* 1. (Of property, office, etc.) fall in by reversion. 2. Return *to* former condition, primitive state, etc.; fall back into wild state. 3. Recur *to* subject in talk or thought. **rėvėrt'ible** *adj.* (Of property) subject to reversion.

rėvĕt' *v.t.* Face (rampart, wall, etc.) with masonry etc., esp. in fortification. **rėvĕt'ment** *n.* Retaining-wall or facing (ill. CASTLE).

rėview' (-vū) *n.* 1. Revision, esp. legal. 2. Display and formal inspection of troops, fleet, etc.; *pass in* ~, (fig.) examine, be examined. 3. General survey or reconsideration of subject or thing. 4. Published account or criticism of literary work, play, cinema film, etc. (esp. a new or recent one). 5. Periodical publication with articles on current events, new books, art, etc. 6. Second view. ~ *v.* View again; subject to esp. legal revision; survey, glance over, look back on; hold review of (troops etc.); write review of (book etc.), write reviews, whence **rėview'er** (-vūer) *n.*

rėvīle' *v.* Call by ill names, abuse, rail at; talk abusively, rail. **rėvīl'er** *n.* **rėvīl'ing** *adj.* **rėvīl'ingly** *adv.*

rėvīse' (-z) *v.t.* Read carefully over, examine, go over again, in order to correct, improve, or amend (literary matter, printer's proofs, law, etc.); *Revised Version*, (abbrev. R.V.), revision (1870–84) of Authorized or 1611 Version of Bible. **rėvīs'al, rėvĭ'sion** (-zhn) *ns.* **rėvĭ'sional, rėvīs'ory** *adjs.* **rėvīse'** *n.* Revision, revising (rare); revised form (rare); (print.) proof-sheet embodying corrections made in earlier proof.

rėvīv'al *n.* 1. Bringing or coming back into vogue, use, etc.; restoring of old play, etc., to stage, etc.; ~ *of learning, letters*, the Renaissance in its literary aspect. 2. Reawakening of religious fervour; campaign with meetings etc. to promote this. 3. Restoration to bodily or mental vigour or to life or consciousness. **rėvīv'alism** *n.* State or kind of religion characterized by revivals. **rėvīv'alist** *n.*

rėvīve' *v.* Come or bring back to life, consciousness, existence, vigour, notice, activity, validity, or vogue; (chem.) convert or restore (metal, esp. mercury) to natural form.

rėvīv'er *n.* (esp.) Stimulating drink (slang); preparation for restoring faded colour etc.

rėvĭv'ĭfȳ *v.t.* Restore to animation, activity, vigour, or life. **rėvĭvĭfĭcā'tion** *n.*

rėvīv'or *n.* (law) Proceeding for revival of suit after death of party etc.

rėvōke' *v.* 1. Repeal, annul, withdraw, rescind, cancel (decree, consent, promise, permission). 2. (whist etc.) Make a revoke. ~ *n.* Card-player's failure to follow suit when he holds a card of that suit. **rĕv'ocable, rĕv'ocātory** *adjs.* **rĕvocā'tion** *n.*

rėvōlt' *v.* 1. Cast off allegiance; make rising or rebellion; fall away *from* or rise *against* ruler; go over *to* rival power. 2. Feel revulsion or disgust *at*, rise in repugnance *against*, turn in loathing *from*; affect with strong disgust, nauseate. **rėvōlt'ing** *adj.* **rėvōlt'ingly** *adv.* **rėvōlt'** *n.* 1. Act of revolting, state of having revolted; rising, insurrection. 2. Sense of loathing; rebellious or protesting mood.

rĕv'olute (-ōōt, -ūt) *adj.* (bot.) Rolled backwards, downwards, or outwards.

rěvolu'tion (-lōō-, -lū-) *n.* 1. Revolving; motion in orbit or circular course, or round axis or centre; rotation; single completion of orbit or rotation, time it takes. 2. Complete change, turning upside-down, great reversal of conditions, fundamental reconstruction; esp. forcible substitution by subjects of new ruler or polity for the old; (Engl. hist.) expulsion (1688) of Stuart dynasty under James II and transfer of sovereignty to William and Mary; (Amer. hist.) overthrow of British supremacy by War of Independence, 1775–81; (Fr. hist.) overthrow of monarchy and establishment of republic, 1789–95; *Russian R~*; see RUSSIAN. **rěvolu'tionīze** *v.t.* **rěvolu'tionary** (-lōōsho-, lū-) *adj.* Of revolution; involving great and usu. violent changes; (rare) of rotation or revolving. ~ *n.* Instigator of revolution.

rėvŏlve' *v.* Turn round or round and round; rotate; go in circular orbit; roll along.

rėvŏl'ver *n.* (esp.) Pistol with mechanism by which set of cartridge-chambers is revolved and presented in succession before hammer, so that several shots may be fired without reloading (ill. PISTOL).

rėvūe' *n.* Theatrical entertainment purporting to give a review (often satirical) of current fashions, events, etc.; often, an elaborate entertainment consisting of numerous unrelated scenes or episodes.

rėvŭl'sion (-shn) *n.* 1. Sudden violent change of feeling, sudden reaction in taste, fortune, etc. 2. (rare) Drawing or being drawn away. 3. (med.) Counter-irritation, treatment of one disordered organ etc. by acting upon another. **rėvŭl'sĭve** *adj.* (chiefly med.) Of, producing, revulsion. ~ *n.* Counter-irritant application.

rėward' (-ôrd) *n.* Return or recompense for service or merit, requital for good or evil; sum offered for detection of criminal, restoration of lost property, etc. ~ *v.t.* Repay, requite, recompense.

Rĕx *n.* (abbrev. R.) Reigning king (in use as REGINA).

rĕx'ine (-ēn) *n.* Trade name for a kind of artificial leather used in upholstery etc.

rĕx'ĭst *n.* Member of a Belgian political party of Fascist tendencies. [(*Christus*) *Rex* (Christ) the King]

Rey'kjavĭk (rākya-). Capital city of Iceland.

Rey'nard (rĕn-, rān-). (Proper name for) the fox, esp. as hero of cycle of medieval folk-stories.

Rey'nolds (rĕn-), Sir Joshua, (1723–92). English portrait-painter; first president of Royal Academy, where he delivered his 'Discourses'.

R.F. *abbrev.* Royal Fusiliers.

R.F.C. *abbrev.* Reconstruction Finance Corporation (U.S.); Rugby Football Club.

R.G.S. *abbrev.* Royal Geographical Society.

Rh: see RHESUS.

R.H. *abbrev.* Royal Highlanders; Royal Highness.

R.H.A. *abbrev.* Royal Horse Artillery.

rhăb'domăncy *n.* Divination by means of a rod, as in water-divining.

Rhădamăn'thus. (Gk myth.) Son of Zeus and Europa, and one of the judges in the lower world; hence, stern and incorruptible judge.

Rhaetia (rēsh'ĭa). Ancient (Latin) name of a district in the Alps, a Roman province. **Rhaetian** (rēshn) *adj.* ~ *Alps*, chain in central part of Alpine mountain system, in E. Switzerland.

Rhaet'ĭc (rē-) *adj.* (geol.) Of the topmost division of the Triassic in Europe. ~ *n.* (also **Rhaeto-Romăn'ic, -Romănce'**) Group of Romance dialects spoken in some parts of the Alps, esp. SE. Switzerland and N. Italy; = Ladin.

rhăp'sōde *n.* Ancient-Greek reciter of epic, esp. Homeric, poems.

rhăp'sody *n.* 1. (Gk. antiq.) Epic poem or part of one suitable for recitation at one time. 2. Enthusiastic extravagant high-flown utterance or composition; emotional musical composition of indefinite form. **rhăpsŏd'ĭc(al)** *adjs.* **rhăpsŏd'ĭcally** *adv.* **rhăp'sodīze** *v.* Recite as rhapsode; talk or write rhapsodies (*about*, *on*, etc.). **rhăp'sodĭst** *n.*

rhea[1] (rē'a) *n.* S. Amer. 3-toed ostrich-like bird of several species (*Rhea*).

Rhea[2] (rē'a). (Gk & Rom. myth.) One of the Titans, wife of Cronus and mother of Zeus, Demeter, Poseidon, and Hades.

Rheims (rēmz). Usu. English spelling of *Reims*, ancient cathedral city of N. France, centre of champagne trade.

Rhēm'ish *adj.* Of Rheims; ~ *Testament*, English translation (1582) of N.T. made at English college at Rheims.

Rhĕn'ish *adj.* Of the Rhine or neighbouring regions.

rhēn'ĭum *n.* Rare, very hard, very heavy metallic element resembling manganese in properties, found in ores of tantalum and platinum; symbol Re, at. no. 75, at. wt 186·2. [L *Rhenus* Rhine]

rhēŏl'ogy *n.* Science dealing with the flow and deformation of matter.

rhē'ostăt *n.* Device for varying the resistance of an electric current.

rhēs'us *n.* Small catarrhine monkey (*Macaea mulatta*) common in N. India; ~ *factor* (abbrev. Rh), a specific complex substance (or antigen) normally present in human red blood cells (so called because first observed in rhesus monkeys). Its presence (Rh-positive) or absence (Rh-negative) is an inherited characteristic. Individuals lacking it are most numerous in the European races (about 15%). If Rh-positive blood cells enter the circulation of Rh-negative individuals from an Rh-positive foetus during pregnancy, antibodies may develop and subsequent Rh-positive offspring may suffer from a form of haemolytic anaemia. If they enter the circulation of Rh-negative individuals by transfusion, antibodies may develop with possibly serious reactions. [arbitrary use of Gk *Rhesus*, mythical king of Thrace]

rhĕt'or *n.* Ancient Greek or Roman teacher or professor of rhetoric; (mere) orator (rare).

rhĕt'orĭc *n.* (Treatise on) the art of persuasive or impressive speaking or writing; language designed to persuade or impress (freq. with implication of insincerity, exaggeration, etc.).

rhėtŏ'rĭcal *adj.* Expressed with a view to persuasive or impressive effect; artificial or extravagant in language; of the nature of rhetoric; of the art of rhetoric; given to rhetoric, oratorical; ~ *question*, question asked not for information but to produce effect. **rhėtŏ'rĭcally** *adv.*

rhĕtorĭ'cian (-shn) *n.* Rhetor; rhetorical speaker or writer.

rheum[1] (rōōm) *n.* (archaic) Watery secretion or discharge of mucous membrane etc.; catarrh; (pl.) rheumatic pains.

Rhē'um[2]**:** see RHUBARB.

rheumăt'ĭc (rōōm-) *adj.* Of, suffering from, rheumatism; subject to, producing, produced by, this; ~ *fever*, acute non-infectious febrile disease with inflammation and pain of joints. ~ *n.* Rheumatic patient; (pl., colloq.) rheumatism. **rheumăt'ĭcally** *adv.* **rheumăt'ĭcky** *adj.* (colloq.).

rheum'atĭsm (rōōm-) *n.* Disease marked by inflammation and pain in joints; esp. (pop.) rheumatoid arthritis; *acute* ~, rheumatic fever; *muscular* ~, myalgia.

rheum'atoid (rōōm-) *adj.* Having the characters of rheumatism; ~ *arthritis*, chronic progressive general disease of uncertain origin, leading to inflammatory changes in the tissues, esp. joints.

rheum'y (rōōm-) *adj.* (archaic) Consisting of, flowing with, rheum; (of air) damp, raw.

R.H.G. *abbrev.* Royal Horse Guards.

rhīn'al *adj.* (anat. etc.) Of nostril or nose.

Rhīne. (Ger. *Rhein*) Great European river, rising in Switzerland and flowing northwards through W. Germany and Holland to North Sea; ~ *wine*, wine produced in valley of Rhine, usu. white, light, and dry. **Rhine′land** (-nl-). Valley of the Rhine; ~-*Palatinate*, province of the Federal Republic of Germany (capital, Mainz).

rhīne′stōne *n.* 1. Kind of rock-crystal. 2. Artificial gem of colourless paste cut like diamond. [f. RHINE]

rhīn′ō[1] *n.* (slang) Money.

rhīn′ō[2] *n.* (slang, pl. *-s*). Short for RHINOCEROS.

rhīnŏ′ceros *n.* Large mammal of Africa and S. Asia, usu. with a horn on nose (or, in some species, two) and very thick freq. folded skin. **rhīnŏcerŏt′ic** *adj.*

rhīnŏl′ogy *n.* Branch of medicine dealing with diseases of the nose.

rhīnoplăs′tic *adj.* Of plastic surgery of the nose.

rhīnŏs′copy *n.* Examination of nasal cavity.

rhīz′oid *adj.* (bot.) Resembling a root. ~ *n.* Root-hair or filament (ill. LIVERWORT).

rhīz′ōme *n.* Prostrate or subterranean root-like stem emitting roots from the lower side and sending up leafy shoots from the upper surface.

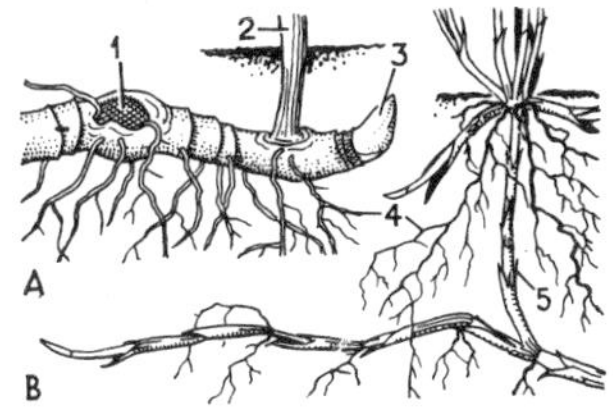

RHIZOME: A. SOLOMON'S SEAL. B. COUCH GRASS

1. Last year's scar. 2. Present year's shoot. 3. Next year's bud. 4. Adventitious roots. 5. Scale leaf

Rhōde Is′land (īl-). Atlantic State of north-eastern U.S., admitted to the Union 1790; capital, Providence; ~ *Red*, Amer. breed of domestic fowls with brownish-red plumage.

Rhodes[1] (rōdz). (Gk *Rhodos*) Most easterly island of Aegean Sea, largest of the Dodecanese, acquired by Italy 1912 and restored to Greece 1946; its principal city and harbour; *Knights of* ~, Knights HOSPITALLERS.

Rhodes[2] (rōdz), Cecil John (1853–1902), English imperialist, largely instrumental in extending British territory in S. Africa and in development of Rhodesia; ~ *scholarships*, scholarships endowed at Oxford University under will of Cecil Rhodes, for students from the principal British colonies and dominions and from every State and Territory of the U.S.

Rhōdē′sia (-zĭa, -sĭa, -zha, -sha). Territory of Central Africa, colonized chiefly by British settlers, between Transvaal and Bechuanaland on S. and Tanganyika and Republic of the Congo on N.; in 1953 Northern Rhodesia (N. of Zambezi River) and the self-governing Southern Rhodesia were united with Nyasaland into the *Federation of* ~ *and Nyasaland* or Central African Federation. which was dissolved in 1963. **Rhōdē′sian** *adj.* & *n.* [named after Cecil RHODES[2]]

Rhōd′ĭan *adj.* & *n.* (Native) of Rhodes.

rhōd′ĭum *n.* Hard white metallic element of the platinum group, used as a protective coating for silver articles, and in some special alloys for scientific purposes; symbol Rh, at. no. 45, at. wt 102·905. [Gk *rhodon* rose, from the colour of some of its salts]

rhōdodĕn′dron *n.* Genus of showy evergreen shrubs or low trees with large flowers, including azaleas. [Gk *rhodon* rose, *dendron* tree]

rhŏmb (-m) *n.* Plane equilateral figure with opposite angles equal, two being acute and two obtuse (ill. QUADRILATERAL); lozenge- or diamond-shaped object, marking, formation, etc.; (cryst.) rhombohedron. **rhŏm′bĭc** *adj.*

rhŏmbohĕd′ron *n.* (Crystal in shape of) solid bounded by six equal rhombs. **rhŏmbohĕd′ral** *adj.*

rhŏm′boid *adj.* Of or near the shape of a rhomb; ~ *muscle* (or *rhomboid′eus*), either of two muscles connecting spinous process of last cervical and first dorsal vertebrae with scapula. ~ *n.* 1. Quadrilateral figure having its opposite sides and angles equal (ill. QUADRILATERAL). 2. Rhomboid muscle. **rhŏmboid′al** *adj.* Rhomboid; having shape of a rhomboid. **rhŏmboid′ally** *adv.*

rhŏm′bus *n.* 1. Rhomb. 2. (*R*~) (Flat-fish of) genus comprising turbot and brill.

Rhondda (rŏn′da). District in Glamorganshire, Wales, on River Rhondda, esp. coal-mining area in lower part of valley.

Rhône (rōn). 1. Great river rising in Switzerland and flowing eastward through Lake of Geneva into France and southward to Mediterranean. 2. A department of France on the right bank of the river.

rhōt′acĭsm *n.* Excessive use or peculiar pronunciation of *r*; (philol.) conversion of another sound (esp. *s*) into *r*. **rhōt′acīze** *v.i.*

R.H.S. *abbrev.* Royal Horticultural Society; Royal Humane Society.

rhub′ârb (rōō-) *n.* 1. (Purgative made from) root of Chinese and Tibetan species of *Rheum*; orig. imported into Europe through Russia and the Levant; now usu. called *Turkey, East Indian,* or *Chinese* ~. 2. Plant of the genus *Rheum*, esp. (*garden* ~) any species having heart-shaped smooth deep-green leaves, growing on thick fleshy stalks which are cooked and eaten as fruit. [L *rhabarbarum* foreign rha or rhubarb (*rha* Gk, perh. f. ancient name *Rha* of River Volga)]

rhŭmb (-m) *n.* Any one of the 32 points of the compass; angular distance (11° 15′) between two successive points of the compass; ~ (*-line*), (naut.) line on the surface of a sphere which makes equal oblique angles with all meridians, indicating the course of an object moving always in the same direction (hist.).

rhȳme, rīme *n.* Agreement in terminal sounds of two or more words or metrical lines, such that (in English prosody) the last stressed vowel and any sounds following it are the same, while the preceding sounds are different (examples: *which, rich*; *peace, increase*; *descended, extended*); verse marked by rhymes; a poem with rhymes; the employment of rhyme; word providing a rhyme (*to* another); *feminine, masculine* ~: see FEMININE, MASCULINE; ~ *royal*, stanzas of seven ten-syllable lines, rhyming *a b a b b c c*; *nursery* ~: see NURSERY; *neither* ~ *nor reason*, nothing reasonable. ~ *v.* Write rhymes, versify; put or make (story etc.) into rhyme; (of words or lines) terminate in sounds that form a rhyme, form a rhyme *to* or *with*; use (words) as rhymes; *rhyming dictionary*, book in which words are arranged in groups according to the sound of their last syllable or syllables; *rhyming slang* (also called 'Cockney slang'), vocabulary, dating from early 19th c., of rhyming substitutions for certain words, e.g. *apples and pears* = stairs.

rhȳthm (-dhm) *n.* Metrical movement determined by relation of long and short, or stressed and unstressed, syllables in foot or line, measured flow of words and phrases in verse or prose; (mus.) systematic grouping of notes according to duration, structure determined by arrangement of such groups; (art etc.) harmonious correlation of parts, movement with regulated succession of strong and weak elements or of opposite or different conditions. **rhȳth′mĭc(al)** *adjs.* **rhȳth′mĭcally** *adv.*

R.I. *abbrev.* *Regina Imperatrix* (= Queen Empress); *Rex Imperator* (= King Emperor); Rhode Island; Royal Institute (of Painters in Water-colours); Royal Institution.

R.I.A. *abbrev.* Royal Irish Academy.

ria (rē′*a*) *n.* River mouth formed by the submergence of a valley or valleys.

ri′al (rē-) *n.* Principal monetary unit of Persia, = 100 dinars.

Riăl′tō. Single-span 16th-c. marble bridge over Grand Canal,

Venice, in centre of the old mercantile quarter.

rĭa'ta (-ah-) *n.* = LARIAT.

rĭb *n.* 1. One of the curved bones articulated in pairs to spine and enclosing and protecting thoracic cavity and its organs (ill. SKELETON); one of these bones from animal carcass, with the meat adhering to it, as food; (joc., with ref. to Gen. ii. 21) wife, woman; *sternal, true,* ~*s,* those attached to sternum or breast-bone; *false, floating, asternal,* ~*s,* those not so attached. 2. Denser, firmer, or stronger part extending along or through organ or structure; spur of mountain, vein of ore, ridge between furrows, wave-mark on sand; central vein of leaf, shaft or quill of feather, nervure of insect's wing; one of ship's curved timbers to which planks are nailed, or corresponding ironwork; arch supporting vault, groin, raised moulding on groin or across ceiling etc. (ill. VAULT); wooden or iron beam helping to carry bridge; hinged rod of umbrella frame; ~, *ribbing,* (knitting) combination of plain and purl stitches, producing a rib-like fabric with a certain elasticity (ill. KNIT). ~ *v.t.* Provide with ribs, act as ribs of; mark with ridges; plough with ribs between furrows, rafter.

R.I.B.A. *abbrev.* Royal Institute of British Architects.

rĭb'ald *n.* Irreverent jester, user of scurrilous, blasphemous, or indecent language. ~ *adj.* Scurrilous, obscene, irreverent. **rĭb'aldry** *n.*

rĭb'and *n.* (archaic) Ribbon.

rĭbb'and *n.* Wale, strip, scantling, or light spar, of wood, used esp. in shipbuilding to hold ribs in position; in launching, square timber on outer side of bilge-ways to prevent cradle from slipping outwards.

rĭbb'on *n.* (Piece or length of) silk, satin, or other fine material woven into narrow band, esp. for adorning costume; ribbon of special colour etc. worn to indicate membership of knightly order, possession of medal, order, or other distinction, membership of club, college, etc.; long narrow strip of anything, ribbon-like object or mark; (pl.) driving-reins; *blue* ~: see BLUE; ~ *building, development,* building of houses etc. in narrow strips along main roads; ~-*fish,* one with very long slender flattened body; ~-*grass,* grass with long slender leaves, esp. variegated variety of *Phalaris*; *R*~ *Society,* Roman Catholic secret society, associated with agrarian disorders, in 19th c. in Ireland.

rī'bēs (-z) *n.* (bot.) Genus of plants comprising currant and gooseberry.

Rĭb'ston pĭpp'ĭn. Choice variety of dessert apple, introduced into England from Normandy *c* 1707. [*Ribston* Park, Yorkshire]

R.I.C. *abbrev.* Royal Institute of Chemistry; (hist.) Royal Irish Constabulary.

Rĭcār'dō, David (1772–1823). English political economist of the free-trade school, author of 'Principles of Political Economy and Taxation', which deals with the causes determining the distribution of wealth. **Rĭcār'dĭan** *adj.*

Riccio: see RIZZIO.

rīce *n.* Pearl-white seeds, used as staple food in many Eastern countries, and elsewhere in puddings, savoury dishes, etc., of an annual cereal grass (*Oryza sativa*) cultivated in marshy or easily flooded ground in warm climates; this plant; ~-*bird, -bunting,* Java sparrow; bobolink; ~-*paper,* thin paper made from rice-straw; Chinese painting-paper (so named in error) made from pith of Formosan tree (*Tetrapanax papyriferum*); ~-*pudding,* baked pudding of sweetened milk and rice.

rĭch *adj.* Wealthy, having riches; abounding in or *in* natural resources or some valuable possession or production, fertile; valuable; splendid, costly, elaborate; (of food etc.) containing or involving large proportion of fat, oil, butter, eggs, sugar, etc.; (of colours, sounds, etc.) mellow, deep, full, not thin; abundant, ample; (of incidents) highly amusing, full of entertainment. **rĭch'nèss** *n.*

Rĭch'ard. Name of 3 kings of England: *Richard I* (1157–99), 'Cœur de Lion', reigned 1189–99, 3rd son of Henry II; a leader in the Third Crusade, on his return from which he was captured and held to ransom by Leopold of Austria; *Richard II* (1367–1400), reigned 1377–99, son of the Black Prince, deposed and imprisoned by Henry IV; *Richard III* (1452–85), reigned 1483–5, last king of House of York; younger brother of Edward IV; he usurped the throne from his nephew Edward V and probably caused the death in the Tower of the young king and his brother; he was defeated and killed at BOSWORTH FIELD.

Rĭch'ardson, Samuel (1689–1761). English novelist; author of 'Pamela', 'Clarissa Harlowe', and 'Sir Charles Grandison'.

Richelieu (rēshelyēr'), Armand Jean du Plessis, Duc de (1585–1642). French cardinal and statesman; prime minister of Louis XIII 1624–42; founder of French Academy.

rĭch'ès *n.* (usu. as pl.) Abundant means, wealth, valuable possessions; being rich.

rĭch'ly *adv.* In rich manner; amply, fully, thoroughly.

Rĭch'mond. Capital city of Virginia, U.S.

Rĭch'ter (rĭχ-), Johann Paul Friedrich (1763–1825). German romantic novelist, who wrote under name of 'Jean Paul'.

rĭck[1] *n.* Stack of hay, corn, peas, etc., esp. one regularly built and thatched; ~-*cloth,* canvas cover for unfinished rick; ~-*yard,* enclosure for ricks. ~ *v.t.* Form into rick(s).

rĭck[2] *n.* & *v.t.* Wrench, sprain.

rĭck'ėts *n.* Disease of children marked by softening of the bones and consequent distortion (bow-legs, curvature of spine, etc.), usu. associated with a deficiency of vitamin D resulting from malnutrition or lack of sunlight.

Rĭckĕtt'sĭae *n.pl.* Group of micro-organisms or very minute particulate bodies apparently intermediate between bacteria and viruses; *Rickettsia prowazekii,* cause of typhus fever. [H. T. *Ricketts,* Amer. pathologist]

rĭck'ėty *adj.* Of (the nature of), suffering from, rickets; shaky, tottering, insecure, fragile. **rĭck'ėtinėss** *n.*

rĭck'sha(w) *n.* Abbrev. of JINRICKSHA.

rĭc'ochet (-shā, -shĕt) *n.* Rebounding of projectile or other object from an object which it strikes, hit made after this; (mus.) effect produced by letting fiddle-bow bounce on strings. ~ *v.i.* (of projectile) Glance or skip with rebound(s).

rĭc'tus *n.* (anat., zool.) Gape of mouth or beak.

rĭd *v.t.* (past t. and past part. *rid* or less usu. *ridded*). Make free, disencumber, *of* (usu. in past part. with *be* or *get,* as *get* ~ *of him*); (archaic) abolish, clear away.

rĭdd'ance *n.* (esp. in *good* ~*!* as exclamation of joy).

rĭdd'el *n.* Curtain at side of altar (ill. ALTAR).

rĭdd'le[1] *n.* Question, statement, or description, designed or serving to test ingenuity of hearers in divining its answer, meaning, or reference; conundrum, enigma; puzzling or mysterious fact, thing, or person. ~ *v.* Speak in, propound, riddles; solve (riddle).

rĭdd'le[2] *n.* Coarse sieve for corn, gravel, cinders, etc.; board or metal plate set with pins, for straightening wire. ~ *v.t.* 1. Pass (corn etc.) through riddle, sift; (fig.) test (evidence, truth). 2. Fill (ship, person, etc.) with holes esp. of gunshot; (fig.) subject to searching criticism, refute (person, theory) with facts.

rīde *v.* (past t. *rōde,* past part. *rĭdd'en*). 1. Sit on and be carried by horse etc.; go on horseback etc. or on bicycle etc. or in train or other vehicle; sit, go, be *on* something as on horse, esp. astride; sit on and manage horse; (of boat etc.) lie at anchor; float buoyantly; (of sun etc.) seem to float; (of things normally level or even) project or overlap: ~ *to hounds,* hunt; ~ *for a fall,* ride, (fig.) act, recklessly; ~ one *down,* put one's horse at him; ~ *out the storm,* (of ship, and fig.) come safely through it.

2. Traverse on horseback etc., ride over or through. 3. Ride on; sit heavily on; oppress, haunt, dominate, tyrannize over. 4. Give ride to, cause to ride. ~ *n.* Journey in vehicle; spell of riding on horse, bicycle, person's back, etc.; road esp. through woods for riding on; *take for a* ~, (U.S. slang) take (person) away in a motor-car in order to murder him.

rīd'er *n.* (esp.) 1. (naut., pl.) Additional set of timbers or iron plates strengthening ship's frame; (sing.) overlying rope or rope-turn. 2. Additional clause amending or supplementing document, esp. parliamentary Bill at third reading; corollary, naturally arising supplement; expression of opinion, recommendation, etc., added to verdict. 3. Piece in machine etc. that surmounts or bridges or works over others.

ridge *n.* Line of junction in which two sloping surfaces meet; long narrow hill-top, mountain range, watershed; (agriculture) one of a set of raised strips separated by furrows; (gardening) raised hotbed for melons etc.; any narrow elevation across surface; *~-piece*, beam along ridge of roof (ill. ROOF); *~-pole*, horizontal pole of long tent; ~ *rib*: see ill. VAULT; *~-tile*, tile used for ridge of roof; *ridge'way*, road along ridge. ~ *v.* Break up (land) into ridges; mark with ridges; plant (cucumbers etc.) in ridges; gather (esp. of sea) into ridges.

rĭd'icūle *n.* Ridiculous thing, ridiculousness (archaic); holding or being held up as laughing-stock, derision, mockery. ~ *v.t.* Make fun of, subject to ridicule, laugh at.

rĭdĭc'ūlous *adj.* Deserving to be laughed at, absurd, unreasonable. **rĭdĭc'ūlously** *adv.* **rĭdĭc'ūlousnėss** *n.*

rīd'ĭng[1] *n.* (esp.) Road for riders; green track through or beside wood; *~-habit*: see HABIT; *~-lamp*, *-light*, light shown by ship riding at anchor.

rĭd'ĭng[2] *n.* One of 3 administrative districts (*East*, *West*, and *North*) into which Yorkshire is divided; (hist.) similar division of other county in U.K. or its colonies. [for *thriding*, f. THIRD]

Rĭd'ley, Nicholas (*c* 1500–55). English bishop and Protestant martyr; burnt as heretic at Oxford with Latimer.

Rie'mann (rēm-), Georg Friedrich Bernhard (1826–66). German mathematician, originator of a non-Euclidean system of geometry; *~'s surface*, (math.) a surface imagined by Riemann for the uniform representation of a function defined by an algebraic equation; if the algebraic function has *n* branches, the corresponding Riemann's surface consists of *n* planes superimposed on one another and infinitely close together.

Riĕn'zi (-ntsĭ), Nicholas (or Cola) di (*c* 1313–54). Tribune of the people at Rome; led rebellion against nobles and established a republic (1347), but was excommunicated and exiled; he returned to Rome 7 years later and was assassinated.

Rievaulx (rĭv'*erz*) Village in N. Riding of Yorkshire, England, with ruins of Cistercian abbey.

rīfe *pred. adj.* Of common occurrence, met with in numbers or quantities, prevailing, current, numerous; well provided *with*.

Rif(f). 1. (usu. *Rif*) Mountain system of Mediterranean coast of Morocco. 2. (usu. *Riff*) One of the fierce and warlike Berbers inhabiting this.

rĭff'-răff *n.* *The* rabble, disreputable persons.

rīfl'e *v.* 1. Search and rob, esp. of all that can be found in various pockets or storing-places; carry off as booty. 2. Make spiral grooves in (gun or its barrel or bore) to produce rotatory motion in projectile; *rifled*, having such grooves or (of projectile) projecting studs or ribs to fit them. 3. Shoot with rifle. ~ *n.* 1. One of the grooves made in rifling a gun. 2. Portable fire-arm, esp. musket or carbine, with rifled bore; (pl.) troops armed with rifles; *ri'fleman*, soldier armed with rifle, esp. member of certain specially raised regiments or companies; *~-range*, distance rifle carries; place for rifle-practice.

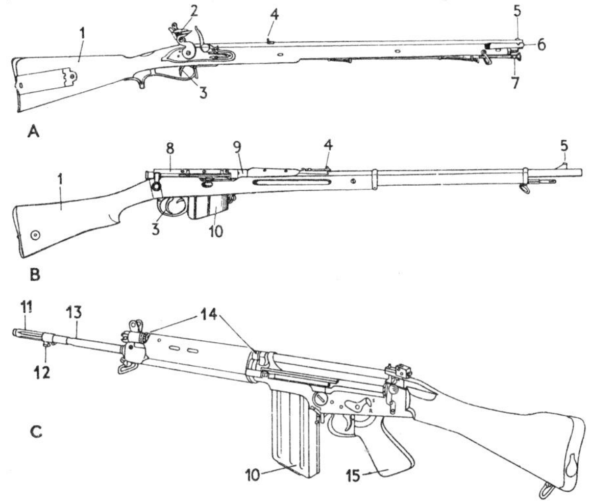

A. FLINT-LOCK, MUZZLE-LOADING 'BAKER' RIFLE, *c* 1800. B. 'LEE-METFORD', BREECH-LOADING MAGAZINE RIFLE, *c* 1889. C. MODERN AUTOMATIC RIFLE

1. Butt. 2. Flint-lock. 3. Trigger. 4. Backsight. 5. Foresight. 6. Muzzle. 7. Ramrod. 8. Bolt. 9. Breech. 10. Magazine. 11. Flash eliminator. 12. Bayonet lug. 13. Barrel. 14. Gas cylinder. 15. Pistol grip

rĭft *n.* Cleft, fissure, chasm, in earth or rock (freq. fig.); rent, crack, split, in an object, opening in cloud, etc.; *~-valley*, valley with steep parallel walls, formed by subsidence of earth's crust (ill. ROCK[1]).

rĭg[1] *v.* Provide (ship), (of ship) be provided, with necessary spars, ropes, etc.; prepare for sea in this respect; fit (*out*, *up*) with or *with* clothes or other equipment; set *up* (structure) hastily or as makeshift or by utilizing odd materials. ~ *n.* Way ship's masts, sails, etc., are arranged; (transf.) person's or thing's look as determined by clothes etc.; outfit, costume, also *~-out*.

rĭg[2] *n.* Trick, dodge, way of swindling; (commerc.) corner. ~ *v.t.* Manage or conduct fraudulently; ~ *the market*, cause artificial rise or fall in prices.

rĭg[3] *n.* Imperfectly developed or partially castrated male animal.

Rīg'a (*or* rē-). Seaport and capital city of Latvia; *Gulf of* ~, inlet of Baltic Sea between Latvia and Estonia.

rĭgadōōn' *n.* (hist.) Lively and complicated dance for two persons; music for this, in $\frac{4}{4}$ or $\frac{2}{4}$ time.

Rīg'el (-gl). Very bright star of first magnitude in foot of constellation Orion.

rĭgg'er *n.* (esp.) One who attends to the rigging of an aircraft.

rĭgg'ĭng *n.* (esp.) 1. Ropes etc. used to support masts (*standing* ~) and work or set yards, sails, etc. (*running* ~) (ill. SHIP). 2. The operation of adjusting and aligning the various components of an aircraft.

right (rīt) *adj.* 1. Straight (archaic; now only in ~ *line*, *~-lined*); (of angle) neither acute nor obtuse, of 90°, made by lines meeting perpendicularly (ill. ANGLE); involving right angles, not oblique; *at ~ angles*, turning or placed with right angle; *~ cone, cylinder, prism*, etc., cone, etc., with ends or base perpendicular to axis; *~ sailing*, sailing due N., S., E., or W. 2. Just, morally good, required by equity or duty, proper; (freq. in comb., as *~-minded, ~-principled*). 3. Correct, true; *the* preferable or most suitable; *the* less wrong or not wrong; in good or normal condition, sound, sane, satisfactory, well-advised, not mistaken; *~ side* (of fabric etc.) that meant for use or show; *in one's ~ mind*, not mad, sane; *put, set, ~*, restore to order, health, etc.; correct mistaken ideas of; justify one*self* usu. *with* person; *get ~*, bring or come into right state; *~*, *~ you are, all ~*, (slang) *right oh!*, forms of approval or of assent to order or proposal. 4. (archaic) Rightful, real, veritable, properly so called; *~ whale*: see WHALE[1]. 5. (Of position) having the relation to front and back that equinoctial sunrise has to north and south; on or towards that side of human body of which the hand is normally more used; on or towards that part of an object which is analogous to person's right side or (with opposite sense) which is nearer to spectator's right hand; *~ bank* (of river etc.) that on right side of one looking downstream. 6. Phrases, etc.: *~ about*, (turn) so far to right as to face opposite way; *send*, etc., *to the ~ about*, dismiss summarily; *~ and left*, to or on both sides, on all hands; with, of, to both hands or sides; pugilist's two blows in quick succession with different hands; *~ arm*, (fig.) most reliable helper; *~ hand*, hand on right side; this as the better hand; region or direction on this side of person; chief or indispensable assistant; *~-hand*, placed on the right hand; *~-hand man*, chief or indispensable assistant; *~-hand screw*, screw with thread turning to right; *~-handed*, using right hand more than left; (of blow etc.) struck, made, with right hand; *~ turn*, turn right into a position at right angles with original one; *~ wing*, (esp.) the extreme right in politics (see *~ n.*, sense 5). **right'nėss** *n.* **right** *v.* 1. Restore to proper, straight, or vertical position; *~ oneself*, recover balance, (of ship) recover vertical position. 2. Make reparation for or to, avenge (wrong, wronged person); vindicate, justify, rehabilitate; correct (mistakes etc.), correct mistakes in, set in order. *~ n.* 1. What is just; fair treatment; *be in the ~*, have justice or truth on one's side; *by ~(s)*, if right were done; *the ~*, what is right, the cause of truth or justice. 2. Justification; fair claim; being entitled to privilege or immunity; thing one is entitled to; *divine ~*: see DIVINE; *~ of way*, right established by usage to pass over another's ground; path subject to such right; *assert, stand on, one's ~s*, refuse to relinquish them; *Declaration* or *Bill of R~s*, Bill declaring rights and liberties of England, and succession to the Crown, passed in 1689. 3. (pl.) Right condition, true state; *set* or *put to ~s*, arrange properly. 4. Right-hand part, region, or direction. 5. Conservative members of continental legislature, those who sit on right of chamber; hence, more traditional part of any political group. **right'lėss** *adj.* **right** *adv.* 1. Straight; all the way *to, round*, etc.; completely *off, out*, etc.; (U.S.) straight away, immediately. 2. Exactly, quite; very, to the full; *~-down*, thorough(ly). 3. Justly, properly, correctly, aright, truly, satisfactorily; *it serves him ~*, it is no worse than he deserves. 4. To right hand. **right'ward** *adj.* & *adv.*

right'eous (rīch'*us*) *adj.* Just, upright, virtuous, law-abiding. **righ'teously** *adv.* **right'eousnėss** *n.*

right'ful (rīt-) *adj.* Equitable, fair; legitimately entitled to position etc.; that one is entitled to. **right'fully** *adv.* **right'fulnėss** *n.*

right'ly (rīt-) *adv.* Justly, fairly; properly, correctly, accurately; justifiably.

ri'gid *adj.* Not flexible, stiff, unyielding; inflexible, harsh, strict, precise. **ri'gidly** *adv.* **rigid'ity** *n.*

rig'marōle *n.* Rambling or meaningless talk or tale. [app. f. obs. *ragman roll* list, catalogue]

rig'or *n.* (path.) Sudden chill with shivering; *~ (mortis)*, stiffening of body after death.

rig'our (-ger) *n.* Severity, strictness, harshness; (pl.) harsh measures;(sing.) strict enforcement *of* rules etc.; extremity or excess *of* weather, hardship, famine, etc., great distress; austerity of life, Puritanic strictness of observance or doctrine; logical accuracy, exactitude. **rig'orous** *adj.* **rig'orously** *adv.*

Rigs'dăg (-z-). Parliament of Denmark.

Rig-ve'da (-vā-). Chief of the VEDAS. [Sansk., f. *ṛic* praise]

R.I.I.A. *abbrev.* Royal Institute of International Affairs.

Riks'dăg. Parliament of Sweden.

rīle *v.t.* (slang, orig. U.S.) Raise anger in, irritate.

Ril'ke (-ke), Rainer Maria (1875–1926). Austrian lyric poet and writer of lyrical prose.

rill *n.* Small stream, runnel, rivulet. **rill'ėt** *n.*

rille *n.* (astron.) Long narrow trench or valley on moon's surface.

rillėtt(e)s' *n.pl.* Preparation of minced meat cooked very slowly in fat for storing, potted meat.

rim *n.* Outer ring of wheel (not including tyre), connected with nave or boss by spokes etc. (ill. WHEEL); outer frame of sieve etc.; edge, margin, border, esp. a raised one, etc., of more or less circular object; *~-brake*, one acting on rim of wheel. *~ v.t.* Furnish with rim, serve as rim to, edge, border. **rim'lėss** *adj.*

Rimbaud (rănbō'), Arthur (1854–91). French symbolist poet.

rīme[1] *n.* & *v.* = RHYME.

rīme[2] *n.* 1. (meteor.) Water-droplets from cloud or fog which freeze on hill-tops, high branches, etc., esp. in windy weather. 2. (chiefly poet.) Hoar-frost. *~ v.t.* Cover with rime. **rīm'y** *adj.*

Rimm'on. (O.T.) Deity worshipped at Damascus (2 Kings v. 18).

Rim'sky-Kors'akov (-f), Nicolas Andreyevich (1844–1908). Russian musical composer.

rīnd *n.* Bark of tree or plant; peel of fruit or vegetable; harder enclosing surface of cheese or other substance; skin of bacon etc.; external aspect, surface. *~ v.t.* Strip bark from.

rin'derpėst *n.* Virulent infectious disease of ruminant animals, with fever, dysentery, and inflammation of mucous membranes.

ring[1] *n.* 1. Circlet, usu. of precious metal and often set with gem(s), worn round finger as ornament or token (esp. of betrothal or marriage) or signet, or (usu. with defining word) hung to or encircling other part of body. 2. Circular object or appliance of any material and any (but esp. of no great) size. 3. Raised, sunk, or otherwise distinguishable line or band round cylindrical or circular object, rim; circular fold, coil, bend, structure, part, or mark; excision of bark round branch or trunk of tree; one of the expanding circular ripples caused by something falling or being thrown into water; *(annual) ~*, one of the concentric circular bands of wood constituting yearly growth of a tree (ill. STEM). 4. Persons, trees, etc., disposed in a circle, such disposition. 5. Combination of traders etc. to monopolize and control a particular trade, market, or policy, or (*price-~*) to stabilize or keep up price of goods. 6. Circular enclosure for some sport, performance, or exhibition (esp. in circus); space marked off (usu. rectangular) for prize-fight or wrestling-match, enclosed space for bookmakers etc., or for displaying livestock etc.; *the ~*, pugilism; bookmakers. 7. Circular or spiral course; *make ~s round*, excel or surpass easily. 8. *~-bark* (*v.t.*) cut ring in bark of (tree) to kill it or to check its growth and bring it into bearing; *~-bolt*, bolt with ring attached for fastening rope to, etc.; *~-bone*, (horse-disease with) deposit of bony matter on pastern-bones;

~-*cartilage*, cricoid; ~-*dove*, wood-pigeon (*Colomba palumbus*); ~-*fence*, one completely enclosing estate etc.; ~-*finger*, third finger esp. of left hand; *ring'leader*, (one of) chief instigator(s) in mutiny, riot, etc.; ~-*master*, manager of circus performance; ~-*neck*, ring-necked plover or duck; ~-*necked*, with band(s) of colour round neck; ~-*net*, kind of salmon-net; ~-*ouzel*, bird (*Turdus torquatus*) allied to blackbird, with white ring or bar on breast; ~ *road*, circular road passing round a town; ~-*snake*, common European grass-snake; ~-*stand*, stand (usu. branched) for keeping finger-rings on; ~-*straked*, (bibl.) marked with rings of colour round body; ~-*tail*, female of hen-harrier; golden eagle till its third year; ring-tailed opossum or phalanger; ~-*tailed*, with tail ringed in alternate colours; (of phalanger) with tail curled at end; ~-*velvet*, velvet fine enough to be drawn through a ring; *ring'worm*, contagious skin-disease, tinea, characterized by ring-shaped eruptions, usu. on the scalp, caused by a fungoid parasite. **rĭnged'** (-ngd), **rĭng'lėss** *adjs.* **rĭng** *v.* 1. (Of hawk etc.) rise in spirals; (of hunted fox) take circular course. 2. Encompass (*round*, *about*, *in*); hem in (game, cattle) by riding or beating in circle round them. 3. Put ring upon; put ring in nose of (pig, bull). 4. Ring-bark. 5. Cut (onions etc.) into rings.

rĭng[2] *v.* (past t. *rang* or rarely *rŭng*; past part. *rŭng*). 1. Give out clear resonant sound (as) of vibrating metal; (of bell) convey summons by ringing; (of place) resound, re-echo (*with*); (of utterance or other sound) linger *in* one's ears, memory, etc.; (of ears) be filled with sensation as of bell-ringing or *with* sound; ~ *true*, *false*, (of coin tested by throwing on counter, and fig. of sentiments, etc.). 2. Make (bell) ring; throw (coin) on counter to test it; ring bell as summons; sound (peal, knell, etc.) on bell(s); announce (hour etc.) by sound of bell(s); summon *up* etc., esp. on telephone, by ringing bell; usher *in*, *out*, with bell-ringing; ~ *the knell of*, announce or herald end, abolition, etc., of; ~ *off*, terminate telephone conversation; ~ *the bell*, (colloq.) achieve complete success; strike a sympathetic or responsive note; ~ *the curtain up* or *down* in theatre, direct it by bell to be raised or lowered; ~ *the changes*: see CHANGE. ~ *n.* Set *of* (church) bells; ringing sound; ringing tone in voice etc.; resonance of coin or vessel; act of ringing bell, sound so produced; a call on the telephone.

rĭng'er (-g-) *n.* 1. Quoit that falls round pin. 2. Fox that runs in ring when hunted. 3. Bell-ringer; device for ringing bell.

rĭng'lėt *n.* Curly lock of hair, curl; (rare) small ring, fairy ring on grass, ring-shaped mark, etc. **rĭng'lėtėd, rĭng'lėty** *adjs.*

rĭnk *n.* Stretch of ice used for game of curling; sheet of natural or artificial ice for skating, building containing this; floor for roller-skating; bowling-green.

rĭnk'hăls *n.* S. African hooded snake (*Sepidon haemachates*) with light band round neck. [Du., f. *hals* neck]

rĭnse *v.t.* Wash out or *out* (vessel, mouth) by filling with water etc. and shaking and emptying; pour liquid over or wash lightly; put (clothes etc.) through clean water to remove soap; clear (soap, impurities) *out* or *away* by rinsing; wash (food) *down* with liquor. ~ *n.* Rinsing.

Rio (de Janeir'ō) (rē'ō). Seaport and former capital of Brazil.

Rio Grande[1] (rē'ō grahn'dā, rī'ō grănd). N. Amer. river rising in S. Colorado and flowing south and east through New Mexico and along N. boundary of Mexico to Gulf of Mexico.

Ri'o Gran'de[2] (do Sul) (rē'ō grahn'dā). Southern state, city, and seaport of Brazil.

rī'ot *n.* 1. Loose living, debauchery (rare); loud revelry, revel; unrestrained indulgence in or display or enjoyment of something. 2. (hunting) Following of any scent indiscriminately; *run* ~ (orig. of hounds, now usu. fig.) act without restraint or control, disregard all limitations. 3. Disorder, tumult, disturbance of the peace, outbreak of lawlessness, on part of a crowd; *R~ Act*, act (1715) providing that if twelve or more persons unlawfully or riotously assembled refuse to disperse within an hour after specified part has been read by a competent authority they shall be considered as felons; *read the R~ Act*, announce that some course of action or conduct must cease. **rī'otous** *adj.* **rī'otously** *adv.* **rī'otousnėss** *n.* **rī'ot** *v.* Live wantonly, revel (rare); throw *away* (time, money), wear *out* (life), in dissipation; make or engage in political riot or offence against the Riot Act. **rī'oter** *n.*

rĭp[1] *n.* Worthless horse, screw; dissolute person, rake.

rĭp[2] *v.* 1. Cut or tear (thing) quickly or forcibly away from something; make long cut or tear in, cut or tear vigorously apart; split (wood, rock), saw (wood) with the grain; strip (roof) of tiles or slates and laths; make (fissure, passage) by ripping; open *up* (wound etc.) again; come violently asunder, split; ~-*saw*, saw for ripping wood. 2. Rush along; *let her* ~, do not check speed or interfere. ~ *n.* Rent made by ripping, tear.

rĭp[3] *n.* Stretch of broken water in sea or river, overfall.

R.I.P. *abbrev.* *Requiesca(n)t in pace* (= may he or she, they, rest in peace).

rīpār'ian *adj.* Of, on, river-bank. ~ *n.* Riparian proprietor.

rīpe *adj.* Ready to be reaped, gathered, eaten, drunk, used, or dealt with; fully developed, mellow, mature; prepared or able *to* undergo something, in fit state *for*. **rīpe'ly** (-pl-) *adv.* **rīpe'nėss** *n.* **rīp'en** *v.*

rĭpōste' *n.* Quick return thrust in fencing; counter-stroke; retort. ~ *v.i.* Deliver riposte.

rĭpp'er *n.* One who rips; tool for ripping roof; rip-saw.

rĭpp'le[1] *n.* Toothed implement used to clear away seeds from flax. ~ *v.t.* Treat with ripple.

rĭpp'le[2] *n.* Ruffling of water's surface, small wave(s); wavy or crinkled appearance in hair, ribbons, etc.; gentle lively sound that rises and falls; method of firing torpedoes in succession; ~-*mark*, ridge, ridged surface, left on sand, mud, or rock, by water or wind. **rĭpp'ly** *adj.* **rĭpp'le** *v.* Form, flow in, show, agitate or mark with, sound like, ripples.

rĭp'-roar'ĭng *adj.* (U.S.) Uproarious, boisterous, full of vigour, spirit, or excellence.

Rĭpūār'ian *adj.* Of the ancient Franks living on Rhine between Moselle and Meuse; ~ *law*, code observed by them.

Rĭp văn Wĭnk'le. Hero of a story (1820) by Washington Irving; he fell asleep in the Catskill Mountains and awoke after 20 years to find the world completely changed; hence, person of antiquated ideas and information.

rīse (-z) *v.* (past t. *rose* pr. rōz, past part. *risen* pr. rĭz'n). 1. Get up from lying, sitting, or kneeling position; get out of bed; (of meeting etc.) cease to sit for business; recover standing or upright position, become erect; leave ground; come to life again (freq. *from the dead*). 2. Cease to be quiet; abandon submission, make revolt; *gorge*, *stomach*, ~*s*, indignation or disgust is felt. 3. Come or go up; grow upwards; ascend, mount, soar; project or swell upwards; become higher, reach higher position, level, price, pitch, or amount; increase; incline upwards; come to surface; (of fish) come to surface of water to take fly, bait, etc.; become or be visible above or *above* surroundings; develop greater energy or intensity; be progressive; (of dough etc.) swell with yeast or other agent; (of spirits) become more cheerful; *the rising generation*, the young; ~ *in the world*, attain higher social position; *rising ground*, ground sloping upwards; *rising 5, 14*, getting on for that age. 4. Develop powers equal *to* (an *occasion* etc.). 5. Have origin) begin to be, flow, *from*, *in*, *at*, etc. 6. Make or see (fish, bird, etc.. rise; (naut.) ~ *ship*, *land*, etc., see it appear above horizon. ~ *n.* 1. Ascent, upward slope; knoll, hill. 2. Social advancement; upward progress; increase in power, rank, value, price, amount, height, pitch, wages, etc. 3. Movement of fish to surface; *have, get, take, a ~ out of,* (fig.) draw (person) into display of temper or other foible. 4. Vertical height of step, arch, incline, etc.; riser of staircase. 5. Origin, start.

rīs'er (-z-) *n.* (esp.) Vertical piece connecting two treads of stair (ill. STAIR).

rĭs'ĭble (-z-) *adj.* Inclined to laugh; of laughter; laughable, ludicrous. **rĭsĭbĭl'ĭty** *n.* **rĭs'ĭbly** *adv.*

rīs'ĭng (-z-) *n.* (esp.) 1. Insurrection, revolt. 2. (naut.) Narrow strake of board fastened inside frame of boat to support thwarts (ill. BOAT).

rĭsk *n.* Hazard; chance of or *of* bad consequences, loss, etc.; exposure to mischance; *run ~s, run a* or *the ~,* expose oneself, be exposed, to loss etc. ~ *v.t.* Expose to chance of injury or loss; venture on, take the chances of.

rĭs'ky *adj.* 1. Hazardous, full of risk. 2. [after Fr. *risqué*] Involving suggestion of indecency, offending against propriety. **rĭs'kily** *adv.* **rĭs'kĭnėss** *n.*

Rĭsŏrgĭmĕn'tō. Movement of middle 19th c. for union and liberation of Italy, associated with names of Cavour, Mazzini, and Garibaldi. [It., = 'resurrection']

rĭsŏtt'ō *n* Italian dish of rice stewed with butter, onions, chicken, etc.

risqué (rĭs'kā) *adj.* = RISKY, 2.

rĭss'ōle *n.* Fried ball or cake of minced meat or fish coated with breadcrumbs etc.

rĭtardăn'dō (as mus. direction). Slower.

rīte *n.* Religious or solemn ceremony or observance; form of procedure, action required or usual, in this.

rĭtornĕll'ō *n.* (mus.) Instrumental refrain, interlude, or prelude in a vocal work. [It., dim. of *ritorno* return]

rĭt'ūal *adj.* Of, with, consisting in, involving, religious rites. **rĭt'ūally** *adv.* **rĭt'ūal** *n.* Prescribed order of performing religious service; book containing this; performance of ritual acts.

rĭt'ūalĭsm *n.* (Excessive) practice of ritual. **rĭt'ūalĭst** *n.* **rĭtūalĭs'tĭc** *adj.* **rĭtūalĭs'tĭcally** *adv.*

rīv'al *n.* Person's competitor for some prize (esp. woman's or man's love) or in some pursuit or quality (also of things). ~ *attrib. adj.* That is a rival or are rivals. ~ *v.* Vie with, be comparable to, seem or claim to be as good etc. as; (rare) be in rivalry. **rīv'alry** *n.* [L *rivalis,* orig. = 'on same stream', f. *rivus* stream]

rīve *v.* (past t. *rīved,* past part. *rĭv'en*). Tear apart, rend, lacerate, tear *off, away,* etc.; split (esp. wood, stone); rend (heart etc.), be rent, with painful thoughts or feelings; cleave, split, crack; admit of splitting. **rĭv'en** *adj.*

rĭv'er *n.* Copious stream of water flowing in channel to sea, lake, marsh, or another river; copious flow or stream *of*; (freq. attrib., prefixed to many names of animals, plants, and things living in, situated or used on, rivers); *~-bottom,* (U.S.) low-lying alluvial land along banks of river; *~-god,* tutelary deity supposed to dwell in and preside over river; *~-horse,* hippopotamus. **rĭv'ered** (*-erd*), **rĭv'erlėss** *adjs.*

rĭv'erain *adj.* Of river or its neighbourhood; situated, dwelling, by river. ~ *n.* Person dwelling by river.

rĭv'erīne *adj.* Of, on, river or its banks, riparian.

rĭv'ėt *n.* Nail or bolt for holding together metal plates etc., its headless end being beaten out or pressed down after insertion. ~ *v.t.* Clinch (bolt); join or fasten with rivets; fix, make immovable; concentrate, direct intently (eyes etc. *upon*); engross (attention), engross attention of. **rĭv'ėter** *n.*

Rĭvĭer'a (-āra). Strip of coast of N. Italy and S. France, between mountains and Mediterranean, famous for its beauty, fertility, and mild climate; hence, extended to other coasts (as *Cornish ~*) regarded as similar in some respects.

rĭv'ière (-vyār) *n.* Necklace of diamonds or other gems, esp. of more than one string.

rĭv'ūlėt *n.* Small stream.

rĭx'-dŏllar *n.* Silver coin and money of account, of value varying from about 4*s.* 6*d.* to 2*s.* 3*d.*, current in various European countries from 16th to 19th centuries. [Du. *rijcksdaler,* (*rijk* kingdom, *daler* dollar)]

riyal (rē'ahl) *n.* Principal monetary unit of Saudi Arabia.

Rĭzz'īō (rĭts-) or **Rĭcc'io** (-chō), David (*c* 1533–66). Italian secretary to MARY, QUEEN OF SCOTS, murdered by Darnley.

R.M. *abbrev.* Resident Magistrate; Royal Mail; Royal Marines.

R.M.A. *abbrev.* Royal Military Academy (Sandhurst; formerly Woolwich).

R.M.C. *abbrev.* Royal Military College (Sandhurst; now R.M.A.).

R.M.S. *abbrev.* Royal Mail Steamer.

R.M.S.P. *abbrev.* Royal Mail Steam Packet (Company).

R.N. *abbrev.* Royal Navy.

R.N.C., R.N.D. *abbrevs.* Royal Naval College, Division.

R.N.L.I. *abbrev.* Royal National Lifeboat Institution.

R.N.(V.)R. *abbrev.* Royal Naval (Volunteer) Reserve.

R.N.Z.A.F., R.N.Z.N. *abbrevs.* Royal New Zealand Air Force, Navy.

roach[1] *n.* Small freshwater fish (*Rutilus rutilus*) of the carp family of N. European rivers; (U.S.) various small fishes resembling this.

roach[2] *n.* (naut.) Upward curve in foot of square sail.

road[1] *n.* 1. (Usu. pl.; also *road'stead*) piece of water near shore in which ships can ride at anchor. 2. Line of communication between places for use of foot-passengers, riders, and vehicles; way of getting *to*; one's way or route; *on the ~,* travelling; *take the ~,* set out; *the ~,* the highway; *take to the ~,* (archaic) become highwayman, (now) tramp; *rule of the ~,* custom regulating side to be taken by vehicles, riders, or ships, meeting or passing each other; *royal ~,* smooth or easy way (*to* success etc.). 3. Underground passage or way in mine; (U.S.) railroad, railway. 4. *~-book,* book describing roads of country etc., itinerary; *~ fund,* fund established by Roads Act 1920 (10 & 11 Geo. V, c. 72) for maintenance of roads etc.; *~-hog,* reckless, dangerous, or bad-mannered driver of motor vehicle etc.; *~-house,* inn on main road in country district; *road'man,* man employed in repairing roads; *~-metal,* broken stone for road-making; *~-sense,* capacity for intelligent handling of vehicles on road; *~-side,* border of road (esp. attrib.); *road'stead*: see sense 1; *road'way,* road; central part of road, esp. part used by vehicular traffic; *road'worthy,* (of vehicle) fit to be used on the road. **road'lėss** *adj.*

road[2] *v.t.* (Of dog) follow up (game-bird) by foot-scent.

road'ster *n.* Ship at anchor in roadstead; horse, bicycle, etc., for use on the road; two- or three-seater motor-car with open body.

roam *v.* Ramble, wander; walk or travel unsystematically over, through, or about (country, seas, etc.). **roam'er** *n.* **roam** *n.* Ramble, rambling walk.

roan[1] *adj.* (Of animal) with coat in which the prevailing colour is thickly interspersed with another, esp. bay, sorrel, or chestnut mixed with white or grey. ~ *n.* Roan horse, cow.

roan[2] *n.* Soft sheepskin leather used in bookbinding as substitute for morocco. [perh. f. *Rouen*]

roar (rōr) *n.* Loud deep hoarse sound (as) of lion, person or company in pain or rage or loud laughter, the sea, cannon, thunder, furnace, etc. ~ *v.* Utter, send forth, roar; (of horse) make loud noise in breathing due to disease; (of place) be full of din, re-echo; say, sing, utter (words etc.) in loud tone; make *deaf, hoarse,* etc., put *down,* by roaring. **roar'er** *n.* (esp.) Roaring horse.

roar'ĭng (rōr-) *adj.* (esp.) Riotous, noisy, boisterous, brisk; stormy; *the ~ forties*: see FORTY.

roast *v.* Cook (esp. meat) by

exposure to open fire or (improperly for *bake*) in oven; heat or calcine (ore) in furnace; heat (coffee-beans) in preparation for grinding; expose to fire or great heat; ridicule, banter, chaff; undergo roasting; *roasting* (pres. part.), very hot; *roasting-jack*, appliance keeping meat in motion while roasting. ~ *n.* Roast meat or a dish of it; operation of roasting; *rule the* ~, be master.

roast'er *n.* (esp.) Kind of oven for roasting; utensil for baking meat etc. in; ore-roasting furnace; coffee-roasting apparatus; fowl etc. fit for roasting or baking.

rŏb *v.t.* Despoil (person etc.) of or *of* property by violence; feloniously plunder; deprive *of* what is due; (abs.) commit robbery. **rŏbb'er, rŏbb'ery** *ns.*

Rŏbb'ĭa, della. Florentine family of sculptors in glazed terracotta: Luca ~ (1400–82); Andrea, his nephew (1435–1525); Giovanni, son of Andrea (1469–1529).

rōbe *n.* 1. Long loose outer garment, esp. one worn as indication of wearer's rank, office, profession, etc., gown, vestment; dressing-gown, bath-wrap; *the long* ~, (dress of) legal or clerical profession. 2. (U.S., Canada) Dressed skin of animal used as garment or rug. ~ *v.* Invest (person) in robe; dress; assume one's robes or vestments.

Rŏb'ert[1]. Name of 2 kings of France: *Robert I* (*c* 865–923), king of the Franks (922–3), grandfather of Hugh Capet; *Robert II* (*c* 970–1031), king of France, son of Hugh Capet.

Rŏb'ert[2]. Name of 3 kings of Scotland: *Robert I*, 'the Bruce' (1274–1329): see BRUCE; *Robert II*, 'the Steward' (1316–90), son-in-law of Robert I; reigned 1371–90; *Robert III* (*c* 1340–1406), illegitimate son of Robert II, reigned 1390–1406.

Robert Guiscard (rŏbār' gēskār'), (*c* 1015–85). Norman adventurer, one of Norman conquerors of S. Italy and Sicily.

Rŏb'ert 'the Devil' (or 'the Magnificent'), (d. 1035). Duke of Normandy and father of William the Conqueror; figures in many legends in consequence of his violence and cruelty.

Rŏb'erts, Frederick Sleigh, 1st Earl Roberts of Kandahar (1832–1914). English field marshal; defeated Afghans near Kabul, and led famous march from Kabul to Kandahar; commander-in-chief in S. Africa 1899–1900.

Robespierre (rŏbz'pyār), Maximilian François Marie Isidore de (1758–94). French revolutionist; leader of extreme party and chief promoter of 'Reign of Terror'; overthrown and guillotined 1794.

rŏb'in *n.* (Also ~ *redbreast*) small brown red-breasted European bird (*Erithacus rubecula*); (U.S.) red-breasted thrush (*Turdus migratorius*); various birds of Australia, New Zealand, India, etc.; ~*'s eye*, herb Robert. [OF, dim. of *Robert*]

Robin Good'fellow: see PUCK[2].

Rŏb'in Hŏŏd. A legendary outlaw, hero of many ballads and plays, who robbed the rich and helped the poor; associated esp. with Sherwood Forest in Nottinghamshire; said to have lived in 12th–13th centuries.

robin'ia *n.* Genus of N. Amer. trees and shrubs of bean family, including the locust tree. [*Robin*, royal gardener in Paris, who introduced these trees to Europe (1635)]

Rŏb'inson Crusoe (krōō'sō). Hero of a novel (1719) by DEFOE, based on adventure of Alexander Selkirk, who lived alone on the uninhabited Pacific island of Juan Fernandez for 5 years (1704–9).

rŏb'orant *adj.* & *n.* (med.) Strengthening (drug).

rō'bŏt *n.* Apparently human automaton; machine-like person, soulless automaton; automatic traffic-signal; ~ *bomb*, flying bomb. [term in play 'R.U.R.' by Karel Čapek for mechanical apparatus doing work of a man; f. Czech *robota* compulsory labour, *robotnik* serf]

Rŏb Roy[1]. Robert Macgregor or Campbell (1671–1734), Scottish Highland freebooter and cattle-lifter.

Rob Roy[2]. Pseudonym of John Macgregor (1825–92), Scottish traveller, inventor of ~ *canoe*, a decked-over canoe with double-bladed paddle.

Robt *abbrev.* Robert.

robŭst' *adj.* Of strong health and physique; not slender, delicate, or weakly; strong, vigorous, healthy; (of exercise etc.) tending to or requiring strength, invigorating, vigorous. **robŭst'ly** *adv.* **robŭst'nĕss** *n.*

robŭst'ious *adj.* Boisterous, self-assertive, noisy.

rŏc *n.* Gigantic bird of Eastern legend.

R.O.C. *abbrev.* Royal Observer Corps.

rŏc'ambōle *n.* N. European species of leek (*Allium scorodoprasum*), Spanish garlic.

Rŏch'ĕster, John Wilmot, Earl of (1648–80). English poet, wit, and libertine; favourite of Charles II.

rŏch'ĕt *n.* Surplice-like vestment used chiefly by bishops and abbots (ill. VESTMENT).

rŏck[1] *n.* 1. Large rugged mass of stone forming cliff, crag, or prominence; large detached stone, boulder; (U.S.) stone of any size; (fig.) source of danger or destruction; sure foundation or support, shelter or protection; (U.S. slang, pl.) money; *on the rocks*, in financial straits; *the R*~, Gibraltar; *R*~ *of ages*, Christ. 2. Hard and massive stone; (geol.) any formation of natural origin in the earth's crust, whether composed of a single mineral or an aggregate of many. 3. Hard confection of candied sugar, esp. flavoured with peppermint. 4. (usu. *blue* ~) rock pigeon. 5. ~*-bed*, base of rock; ~*-bottom* (slang, of prices etc.) very lowest; ~*-cake*, bun with rugged surface; ~ *cod*, various Amer. and Australian fishes; ~*-crystal*, crystallized quartz; ~*-dove*,

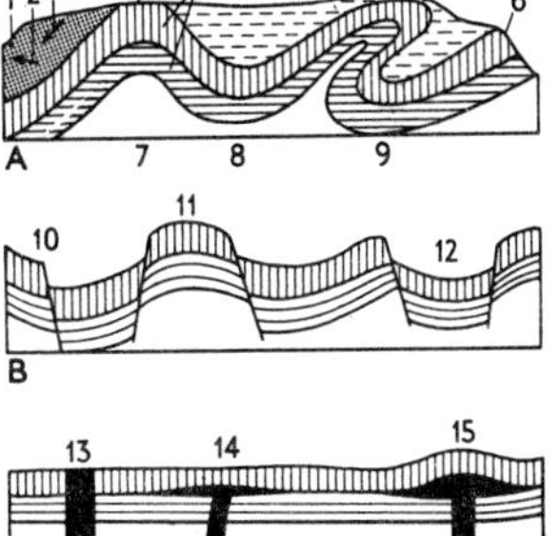

ROCK FORMATIONS: A. FOLDS. B. FAULTS. C. INTRUSIONS

A. 1. Bedding plane (at right angle to 5). 2. Strike. 3. Dip. 4. Outcrop. 5. Strata. 6. Escarpment. 7. Anticline. 8. Syncline. 9. Recumbent fold or nappe. B. 10. Fault 11. Horst. 12. Rift-valley. C. 13. Dike. 14. Sill. 15. Laccolith

rock-pigeon; ~*-drill*, rock-boring tool or machine; ~*-fish*, kinds of fish frequenting rocks or rocky bottoms; ~*-garden*, rockery; ~*-oil*, native naphtha; ~*-pigeon*, species of dove (*Columba livia*) inhabiting rocks and buildings, species from which domestic pigeons are bred; ~*-plant*, plant growing among rocks or suitable for rockeries; ~*-rose*, kinds of *Cistus* with yellow, pink, or salmon flowers; ~*-salmon*, fishmongers' name for dogfish; ~*-salt*, common salt occurring as a massive bed or deposit in the earth's crust; ~*-tar*, petroleum; ~*-work*, rough stone-work resembling or imitating rocks; rockery.

rŏck[2] *v.* Move gently to and fro (as) in cradle; set or keep (cradle etc.), be, in such motion; (gold-mining) work (cradle), work cradle; shake in cradle, sway, cause to sway, from side to side; shake, oscillate, reel; ~*-shaft*, one that oscillates about axis without making complete revolutions; ~*-staff*, part of apparatus working smith's bellows. ~ *n.* Rocking motion, spell of rocking.

rŏck[3] *n.* (hist.) Distaff.

Rŏck'efĕller (-ke-), John Davison (1839–1937). American financier, who made a large fortune from petroleum; ~ *Foundation*, fund established 1913 'to promote the well-being of mankind throughout the world'; ~ *Institute for Medical Research*, founded 1901 in New York.

rŏck'er *n.* (esp.) One of the curved bars upon which cradle, chair, etc., rocks; rocking-chair; gold-miner's cradle; mezzotint engraver's cradle for roughening surface of plate (ill. ENGRAVE); skate with highly curved blade; rocking turn.

rŏck'ery *n.* Artificial heap of rough stones and rock for growing rock-plants.

rŏck'ėt[1] *n.* Cruciferous plant of genus *Hesperis*, esp. *H. matronalis*, sweet-scented after dark; *blue* ~, kinds of wolf's-bane (*Aconitum*) or larkspur (*Delphinium*). [It. *ruchetta* f. L *eruca*, because formerly applied to the salad-plant *Eruca sativa*]

rŏck'ėt[2] *n.* Cylindrical paper or metal case that can be projected to a height or distance by the reaction of the gases discharged from the rear when its (highly combustible) contents are ignited, used as fireworks, for signalling, to carry line to ship in distress etc.; shell or bomb projected by rocket propulsion; projectile containing scientific instruments, etc., for exploration of earth's upper atmosphere and interplanetary space; ~-*(firing) plane*, aeroplane fitted with rocket apparatus for firing shells; ~ *propulsion*, propulsion by means of the reaction of gases expelled backward from the rocket at high velocity. ~ *v.t.* Bound upwards like rocket; (of game-bird) fly straight upwards, fly fast and high; (of prices) rise rapidly. **rŏck'ėtry** *n.* Science, practice, of rocket propulsion.

Rŏck'ies (-ĭz), **Rŏck'y Mountains.** Great mountain-range of western N. America, extending from the Mexican frontier to the Arctic regions.

rŏck'ing *adj.* That rocks; swaying, oscillating; ~-*chair*, chair mounted on rockers; ~-*horse*, child's wooden horse on rockers; ~-*stone*, large stone or boulder so poised that it rocks easily; ~-*turn*, turn in skating from any edge to same in opposite direction with body revolving away from convex of first curve.

rŏck'y[1] *adj.* Of rock, full of or abounding in rocks; like rock in ruggedness, firmness, solidity, etc.

rŏck'y[2] *adj.* Unsteady, tottering.

rocŏc'ō *adj.* Of the style of decoration, originating in France and Italy in the late 17th c. and prevalent in Europe until *c* 1770, characterized esp. by scroll-work, shell motifs, asymmetrical effects, and lightness of colouring; (erron.) of the style of the 18th c. in general; (loosely) airily fantastic, frivolous, sophisticated, merely ornamental. ~ *n.* The rococo style. [Fr., perh. f. *rocaille* rock-work (in ref. to encrusting grottoes with shells)]

rŏd *n.* Slender straight round stick growing as shoot on tree or cut from it or made from wood, switch, wand (freq. as symbol of office etc.), such stick, or bundle of twigs, for use in caning or flogging; fishing-rod; (as measure) = PERCH[2]; slender metal bar, connecting bar, shaft; rod-shaped structure; *kiss the* ~, take punishment meekly or gladly; *a* ~ *in pickle*, a punishment in store.

rō'dent *adj.* & *n.* (Mammal) of the order *Rodentia* which have only one pair of strong incisors in each jaw and no canine teeth (including rats, voles, beavers, mice, etc.); ~ *ulcer*, (path.) slow-growing form of cancer causing extensive destruction of tissue.

rōde'o (-dāō) *n.* Round-up of cattle for branding etc.; exhibition of cowboys' skill.

Rō'din (-dăṅ), Auguste (1840–1917). French sculptor.

Rŏd'ney, George Brydges, Baron (1718–92). English admiral; victor over Spanish fleet off Cape St. Vincent (1780) and over a French fleet off Dominica (1782).

rŏdomontāde' *n.* & *adj.* Boastful, bragging (saying or talk). ~ *v.i.* Brag, talk big. [It. *Rodomonte*, character in Ariosto's 'Orlando Furioso']

Rŏdrig'uez (-rēgĕz). British island in Indian Ocean, dependency of Mauritius, nearly 400 miles to westward.

rōe[1] *n.* (also ~-*deer*) Small European and W. Asiatic species of deer (*Capreolus capraea*); ~-*buck*, male roe.

rōe[2] *n.* Mass of eggs (*hard* ~) in fish's ovarian membrane; *soft* ~, male fish's milt; ~-*stone*, kind of limestone, oolite.

Roentgen: see RÖNTGEN.

Roffen. *abbrev.* (Bishop) of Rochester (replacing surname in his signature).

rogā'tion *n.* 1. (usu. pl.) Solemn supplication consisting of litany of the saints chanted on the three days before Ascension Day; *R*~ *days*, Monday, Tuesday, and Wednesday preceding Ascension Day; *R*~ *Sunday*, Sunday before Ascension Day. 2. (Rom. antiq.) Law proposed before the people by consul or tribune.

Rŏg'er. Masculine proper name; *Jolly* ~, pirates' black flag; (*Sir*) ~ *de Coverley*, English country dance, with dancers facing each other in two rows; the music of this.

rōgue (-g) *n.* Idle vagrant (archaic); knave, rascal, swindler (freq. playfully of mischievous child etc.); inferior plant among seedlings; wild beast, esp. elephant, driven or living apart from the herd and of savage temper; horse that shirks work on racecourse or in hunting-field. **rōg'uery** (-ge-) *n.* **rōg'uish** (-gĭ-) *adj.* **rōg'uishly** *adv.* **rōg'uishnėss** *n.*

rois'ter *v.i.* Revel noisily, be uproarious (esp. in part. *roistering* as adj.). **rois'terer, rois'tering** *ns.*

Rōl'and. Hero of medieval (esp. French and Italian) legend, one of the paladins of Charlemagne; becomes friend of Oliver, another paladin, after single-handed combat in which neither wins; killed in a rear-guard action at Roncevaux (Roncesvalles) in the Pyrenees; *a* ~ *for an Oliver*, tit for tat.

rōle, rôle (rōl) *n.* Actor's part; one's task or function.

rōll[1] *n.* 1. Cylinder formed by turning flexible fabric such as paper over and over upon itself without folding; quantity of textile fabric rolled thus (esp. as definite measure of cloth); (U.S.) quantity of notes or bills rolled together, person's money; (archit.) volute of Ionic capital. 2. Document, esp. official record, in this form; *Master of the R*~*s*, one of four *ex officio* judges of Court of Appeal, with charge of rolls, patents, and grants that pass the great seal, and of Chancery records; *the R*~*s*, former building in Chancery Lane, London (now represented by Public Record Office) where these documents were kept. 3. List of names (freq. fig., as in ~ *of fame*, ~ *of saints*); official list of those qualified to act as solicitors; *strike off the* ~*s*, debar from practising as solicitor; ~-*call*, calling over of list (as in school or army) so that each person present answers to his name and absentees are detected; ~ *of honour*, esp. list of those who have died for their country in war. 4. More or less (semi-) cylindrical straight or curved mass of anything however formed; ~ (*of bread*), small loaf for one person; (archit., also ~-*moulding*) moulding of convex section; *roll'mop*, salted spiced herring rolled up and skewered. 5. Cylinder, roller. 6. Bookbinder's revolving patterned tool for marking cover.

rōll[2] *v.* 1. Move, send, go, in some direction by turning over and over on axis; (cause to) go, convey, with smooth rolling or sweeping motion (freq. fig.); undulate; make revolve between two surfaces; wrap (*up in*) by rolling motion; (of eyes) change direction (of) with rotatory motion. 2. Wallow, turn about in fluid or loose medium; (of animal) lie on back and kick about; sway or rock, walk with swaying gait as of sailor, reel. 3. (Of sound) utter, be uttered, sound, with vibratory, undulating, or trilling effect. 4. Flatten by passing roller over or by passing between rollers; shape (metal) by passing between or beneath rolls. 5. Turn over and over upon itself into more or less cylindrical shape. 6. Form in(to) cylindrical or spherical shape or accumulate into mass, by rolling. 7. *rolled gold*, thin coating of gold applied by rolling; *rolling mill*, mill which rolls steel into thin sheets or strips; *rolling-pin*, wooden etc. roller for pastry, bread, etc.; *rolling-press*, copper-plate-printer's press with revolving cylinder; press with rollers for various purposes; *rolling-stock*, railway company's wagons and trucks; *roll-top desk*, desk with flexible cover sliding in curved grooves. ~ *n.* 1. Rolling motion; spell of rolling; rolling gait; turn of aircraft about its longitudinal axis through 360° (used on return to airfield as sign of victory; ill. AEROBATICS). 2. In steel mill, grooved cylinder, usu. one of a set revolving simultaneously, beneath which or between which white-hot ingots are passed to shape them. 3. Quick continuous beating of drum; long peal of thunder or shout; rhythmic flow of words.

Rolland (rŏlahṅ'), Romain (1866–1944). French novelist, essayist, and man of letters.

rōll'er *n.* (esp.) 1. Cylinder of wood, stone, metal, etc., used alone or as rotating part of machine for lessening friction, smoothing ground, pressing, stamping, crushing, flattening, spreading printer's ink, rolling up cloth on, etc.; (~ *bandage*) long surgical bandage rolled up for convenience of applying. 2. Long swelling wave. 3. Breed of tumbler-pigeon. 4. Brilliant-plumaged crow-like bird (esp. *Coracias garrulus*); breed of canary with trilling or rolling song. 5. ~*-skate*, skate mounted on small wheels or rollers, for skating on smooth flooring etc.; ~*-towel*, towel with ends joined, running on roller.

rŏll'ick *v.i.* Be jovial, indulge in high spirits, enjoy life boisterously, revel (chiefly in part. *rollicking* as adj.). ~ *n.* Exuberant gaiety; frolic, spree, escapade.

Rŏll'ō (d. *c* 932). Leader of Normans who settled at mouth of River Seine, and first Duke of Normandy.

rōl'y-pōl'y *n.* Pudding made of sheet of paste covered with jam etc. formed into roll and boiled or baked. ~ *adj.* (usu. of children) Podgy, plump.

rom. *abbrev.* Roman (type).

Rom. *abbrev.* Romans (N.T.).

Romā'ĭc *adj.* & *n.* (Of) the vernacular language of modern Greece.

Romains (rŏmăṅ'), Jules. Pseudonym of Louis Farigoule (1885–), French novelist, poet, and playwright.

Rōm'an *adj.* & *n.* 1. (Native, inhabitant, citizen) of ancient or modern Rome or the Roman Empire. 2. (Member) of the ROMAN CATHOLIC Church. 3. (Of nose) having prominent upper part or bridge like those seen in portraits of ancient Romans. 4. (Of letters, type) of the modern kind which most directly represents that used in ancient Roman inscriptions, of the kind now in ordinary use in W. Europe and the New World; upright, as dist. from *italic*; (of numerals) expressed in letters of the Roman alphabet, thus: I = 1, V = 5, X = 10, L = 50, C = 100, D = 500, M = 1000; the letters composing a number are ranged in order of value and the number meant is found by addition, e.g. MDCLXVI = 1666; if a letter or set of letters is placed before a letter of higher value, it is to be subtracted from it before the addition is done, e.g. IIC = 98, MCM = 1900. 5. ~ *candle*, tube discharging coloured balls in fireworks; ~ *Empire*, that established by Augustus 27 B.C. and divided by Theodosius A.D. 395 into *western* or *Latin* and *eastern* or *Greek* empires, of which the eastern lasted until the fall of Constantinople (1453), and the western, after lapsing in 476, was revived in 800 by Charlemagne and continued as the *Holy Roman Empire* till 1806; ~ *law*, the system of law of ancient Rome, esp. as codified under the Emperor JUSTINIAN; the code, modified or derived from the Justinian code, in force in many parts of Europe in modern times; ~ *road*, road surviving from the period of Roman rule.

Rōm'an Căth'olĭc *adj.* & *n.* (Member) of that part of the Western or Latin Christian Church which owes allegiance to the Bishop of Rome (the Pope). **Rōm'an Cathŏl'ĭcism** *n.*

Romănce' *adj.* & *n.* (Of) the vernacular language of France, descended from Latin; (of) the whole group of languages descended from Latin, including French, Spanish, Portuguese, Italian, Rumanian, etc.; derived or descended from Latin; composed in a Romance language. **romănce'** *n.* 1. Medieval tale, usu. in verse, of some hero of chivalry (orig. because written in Romance, i.e. not in Latin). 2. Prose or rarely verse tale (esp. of the class prevalent in 16th and 17th centuries) with scene and incidents remote from everyday life; class of literature consisting of such tales; set of facts, episode, love affair, etc., suggesting such tale by its strangeness or moving nature; romantic or imaginative character or quality; (an) exaggeration, (a) picturesque falsehood. 3. (mus.) Short composition of simple or informal character. ~ *v.i.* Exaggerate, draw the long bow.

romăn'cer *n.* Writer of romances; fantastic liar.

Rōmanĕsque' (-sk). (Art, architecture) of the style prevalent in W. Europe between the end of the classical period and the rise of Gothic style; (in mod. usage esp.) the style prevalent *c* 950–1150, characterized by the use of massive stone vaulting and the round-headed arch, often with richly carved columns and capitals, and sculptured figures; the style known in ref. to English buildings as 'Norman'.

Romăn'ĭc. (Of languages) = ROMANCE.

Rōm'anīze *v.t.* Render Roman in character; bring under the influence or rule of Rome.

Romanov (romahn'of). Surname of the imperial dynasty ruling in Russia from the accession of Michael Romanov (elected tsar 1613) to 1917.

Rōm'ans, Epistle to the. 6th book of N.T., an epistle addressed by St. Paul from Corinth to the Church of Rome.

Romănsh'. *adj.* & *n.* (Of) the Rhaeto-Romanic dialect spoken in the Grisons, E. Switzerland.

romăn'tĭc *adj.* Characterized by, suggestive of, given to, romance; imaginative, remote from experience, visionary; (of projects etc.) fantastic, unpractical, quixotic, dreamy; (of music, literary or artistic method, etc.; opp. CLASSIC) preferring grandeur, picturesqueness, passion, or irregular beauty to finish and proportion, subordinating whole to parts or form to matter; *R~ Movement*, *Revival*, movement of European literature and art of late 18th and early 19th centuries. **romăn'tĭcally** *adv.* **romăn'tĭcism, romăn'tĭcist** *ns.* **romăn'tĭc** *n.* Romantic person; (*R~*) participant in Romantic Movement; (pl.) romantic ideas or talk.

Rŏm'any *adj.* & *n.* (Of) a gipsy or the gipsies; (of) the language of the gipsies, an Indo-European language related to Hindi.

romaunt' *n.* (archaic) Romance or tale of chivalry etc.

Rōme. 1. City on River Tiber, about 20 miles from sea near centre of W. coast of Italy, founded 753 B.C.; a republic from *c* 500 B.C. until the reign of Augustus (*c* 31 B.C.), and conqueror and chief city of most of the known world; in modern times, capital city of Italy (*King of* ~, title given to NAPOLEON[3] II at his birth). 2. Rome as see of the Pope and original capital of Western Christendom; hence, the ROMAN CATHOLIC Church.

Rōm'ėō. Hero of Shakespeare's romantic tragedy 'Romeo and Juliet'; hence, a romantic young lover.

Rŏm'ney[1]. Town and former port, one of the CINQUE PORTS, in Kent, England.

Rŏm'ney[2] (*or* rŭ-), George (1734–1802). English portrait painter.

rŏmp *v.i.* (Of children etc.) play about together, chase each other, wrestle, etc.; (racing slang) get *along*, *past*, etc., without effort, come *in* or *home* as easy winner. ~ *n.* Child or woman fond of romping, tomboy; spell of romping, boisterous play. **rŏmp'er** *n.* (sing. or pl.) Garment, usu. covering trunk only, for young child to play in.

Rŏm'ūlus. Legendary founder of Rome, one of the twin sons of Mars by the vestal Rhea Silvia, exposed at birth with his brother Remus and found and suckled by a she-wolf.

Roncevaux, Roncesvalles (rawṅsevō', -văl). Village in Navarre, N. Spain, in W. Pyrenees, site of legendary defeat of rear-guard of Charlemagne's army and death of ROLAND.

rŏn'deau (-ō) *n.* Poem of 10 or 13 lines having only two rhymes throughout and with opening words used twice as refrain.

rŏn'del *n.* Poem of 13 or 14 lines, with two rhymes only, and with the first two lines recurring after the sixth, and the first two or the first only at the end.

rŏn'dō *n.* Piece of music (freq. as last movement of sonata) in which principal theme recurs twice or oftener in same key, after introduction of contrasting themes.

rŏn'dure *n.* (poet.) Round outline or object.

Rōn'ēō *n.* Proprietary name of a type of duplicating machine. ~ *v.t.* Reproduce by means of a Roneo.

Ronsard (rawṅsar'), Pierre de (1524–85). French lyric poet, chief figure in the PLEIAD.

Rönt'gen[1] (rerntyen), Wilhelm Konrad von (1845–1923). German physicist, discoverer of X-RAYS, hence freq. called *~-rays*; *~ therapy*, treatment of disease by X-rays.

rönt'gen[2] (rerntyen) *n.* (abbrev. r.) Quantity of X or gamma radiation used as unit of radioactivity. [f. RÖNTGEN[1]]

rōōd *n.* 1. The cross of Christ (archaic); crucifix, esp. one raised on middle of *~-screen*, wooden or stone carved screen separating

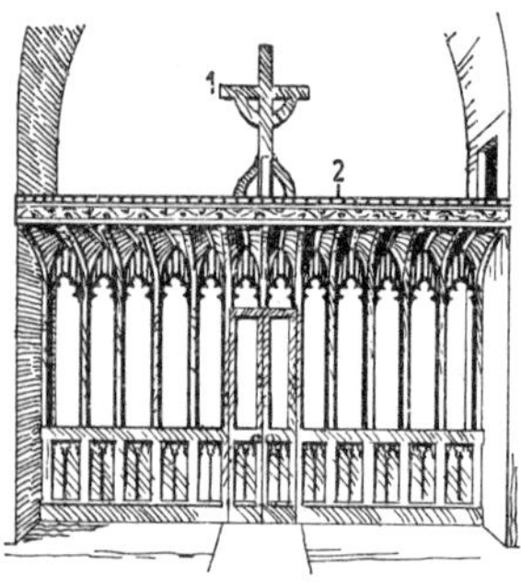

ROOD-SCREEN

1. Rood. 2. Rood-loft

nave and choir; *~-arch*, arch between nave and choir; *~-loft*, gallery above rood-screen. 2. Measure of land, properly 40 sq. poles or a quarter acre but varying locally; esp. as loose term for small piece of land.

rōōf *n.* Upper covering of house or building, usu. supported by its walls (*illustration, p.* 715); top of covered vehicle, esp. when used for outside passengers; *~ of the mouth*, palate; *~ of the world*, high mountain range; *~-spotter*, observer on top of a building to spot hostile aircraft; *~-tree*, ridge-pole of roof. **rōōf'age, rōōf'ing** *ns.* **rōōf'lėss** *adj.* **rōōf** *v.t.* Cover with roof; be roof of.

rōōf'er *n.* (colloq.) Letter of thanks for entertainment sent by departed visitor (f. stock phrase *under your hospitable roof*).

roo'inĕk (rō-) *n.* Englishman, esp. new-comer, in S. Africa. [S.-Afr. Du., = 'red-neck' (*rood* red)]

rōōk[1] *n.* Common black raucous-voiced European and Asiatic bird (*Corvus frugilegus*) of crow family, nesting in colonies; cheat, swindler, esp. at dice or cards; *~-pie*, pie of young rooks; *~-rifle*, rifle of small bore for rook-shooting. ~ *v.t.* Defraud by cheating at dice, cards, etc.; charge (customer) extortionately.

rōōk[2] *n.* (chess) Castle, one of 4 pieces which at beginning of game are set in corner squares, and have power of moving in a straight line forwards, backwards, or laterally over any number of unoccupied squares (ill. CHESS). [Pers. *rukh* chariot]

rōōk'ery *n.* (Clump of trees with) colony of rooks; colony of penguins etc. or seals; crowded cluster of mean houses or tenements.

rōōk'ie, rōōk'y *n.* (army slang) Recruit.

rōōm *n.* 1. Space that is or might be occupied by something; capaciousness, ability to accommodate contents; *make ~*, vacate standing-ground etc., or post etc., *for* another, withdraw, retire; clear a space *for* by removal of others; *in the ~ of*, instead of, in succession to, as substitute for. 2. Opportunity, scope, *to* do or *for*. 3. Part of house or other building enclosed by walls or partitions; (pl.) set of these occupied by person or family, apartments or lodgings; (transf., sing.) the company in a room. **rōōm'ful** *n.* **rōōm** *v.i.* (U.S.) Have room(s), lodge, board; *rooming house*, lodging-house. **rōōm'er** *n.* (U.S.) Lodger.

rōōm'y *adj.* Capacious, large, of ample dimensions.

Roosevĕlt (rōz'e-), Theodore (1858–1919). 26th president of U.S., 1901–9. ~, Franklin Delano (dĕl'*a*-) (1882–1945), 32nd president of U.S., 1933–45.

rōōst[1] *n.* Tumultuous tidal race off various parts of Orkneys and Shetlands.

rōōst[2] *n.* Bird's perching- or resting-place, esp. hen-house or part of it in which fowls sleep; *come home to ~*, come back upon originator. ~ *v.* (Of birds etc.) settle for sleep, be perched or lodged for night; provide with sleeping-place. **rōōst'er** *n.* (esp. U.S.) Domestic cock.

rōōt[1] *n.* 1. Part of plant normally below earth's surface and serving to attach it to earth and convey nourishment to it from soil; (pl.)

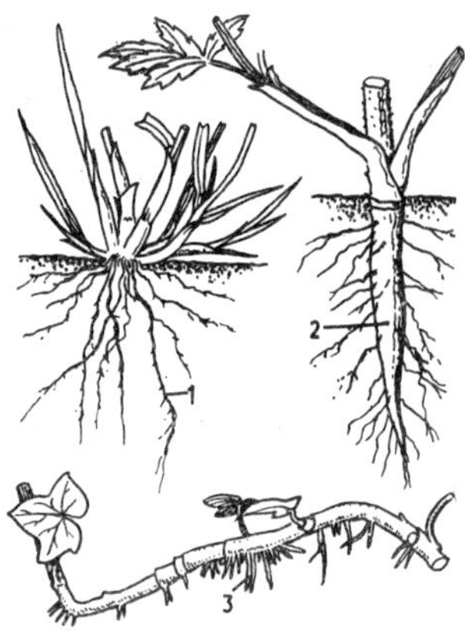

ROOTS

1. Fibrous root (grass). 2. Tap-root (wild carrot). 3. Adventitious root (ivy)

such part divided into branches or fibres; (sing.) corresponding organ of epiphyte, rootlet attaching ivy to its support; permanent underground stock of plant; (hort.) small plant with root for transplanting; (bibl.) scion, offshoot; *pull up by the ~s*, uproot; *take, strike, ~*, begin to draw nourishment from soil; get established; *~-stock*, primary form whence offshoots have arisen. 2. (Plant, such as turnip, carrot, etc., with) root used for food or in medicine. 3. Imbedded part of some bodily organ or structure, as hair, tooth, nail; part of thing attaching it to greater or more fundamental whole. 4. Source or origin (*of*); basis, dependence, means of continuance, or growth; bottom, essential substance or nature. 5. (math.) Number, quantity or dimension which when multiplied by itself a requisite number of times produces a given expression (symbol √). 6. (philol.) Ultimate unanalysable element of language, forming basis of vocabulary. 7. (mus.) Fundamental note of chord. **rōōt'let** *n.* **rōōt** *v.* (Cause to) take root; fix firmly to the spot; establish.

rōōt[2], **rout** *vbs.* 1. (Of swine etc.) turn up ground with snout, beak, etc., in search of food; turn *up* (ground) thus. 2. Search *out*, hunt *up*, rummage *among*, *in*. **rōōt'le** *v.* Root.

rōpe *n.* 1. (Piece of) stout cordage (technically, over 1 in. in circumference) made by twisting strands of hemp, flax, hide, or wire into one; *the ~*, halter for hanging person; *the ~s*, those enclosing boxing-ring or other arena; *know the ~s*, be familiar with the conditions in some sphere of action; *give one* (*enough*) *~* (*to hang himself*), *plenty of ~*, etc., not check him, trust to his bringing about his own discomfiture; *~ of pearls* etc., pearls etc. strung together. 2. Viscid or gelatinous stringy formation in beer or other liquid. 3. *~-dancer*, *-dancing*, performer, performance, on tight-rope; *~-ladder*, two long ropes connected by cross-ropes as ladder; *~'s-end*, short piece of rope used to flog (esp. sailor) with; *~-walk*, long piece of ground used for twisting rope; *~-yarn*, (piece of the) material (esp. when unpicked) of which rope-strands consist. **rōp'y** *adj.* **rōp'inėss, rōp'ing** *ns.* **rōpe** *v.* 1. Fasten or secure with rope; catch with rope; (mountaineering) connect (party) with rope, attach (person) to rope, put on rope; use ropes in towing etc.; enclose, close *in*, shut *off*, (space) with rope; *~ in*, draw into some enterprise. 2. Become ropy or viscid.

Roquefort (rŏk'fōr). Town of S. France; a 'blue' cheese, of type orig. made there, usu. of ewes' milk and ripened in limestone caves, with strong characteristic flavour.

rōq'uelaure (-kelōr) *n.* (hist.) Man's cloak (18th and early 19th centuries) reaching to knees. [Fr., f. Duke of *Roquelaure* (1656–1738)]

rōq'uet (-kĭ) *n.* In croquet, hitting another player's ball with one's own. *~ v.* Cause one's ball to strike, (of ball) strike, another.

rōrq'ual *n.* Whale (*Balaenoptera*) with dorsal fin; *Sibbald's ~* or *Blue whale*, hunted for oil (ill. WHALE). [Norw. *raud* red, *hval* whale]

Rōs'a (-z-), Salvator (1615–73). Italian painter and etcher.

rōs'āce (-z-) *n.* Rose-window; rose-shaped ornament or design.

rosa'ceous (-zāshus) *adj.* Of the order *Rosaceae*, of which the rose is the type.

rōsăn'ĭlĭne (-z-; *or* -ēn) *n.* Magenta or fuchsine, a purple-red dye-stuff obtained by the oxidation of a mixture of aniline and toluidines (crude aniline).

rosār'ĭan (-z-) *n.* 1. Rose-fancier. 2. (R.C. Ch.) Member of a Confraternity of the Rosary.

rōs'ary (-z-) *n.* 1. Rose-garden, rose-bed. 2. (R.C. Ch.) Form of prayer in which 15 decades of Aves are repeated, each decade preceded by Paternoster and followed by Gloria; book containing this; string of 165 beads for keeping count in this.

Roscius (rŏsh'*us*). Quintus

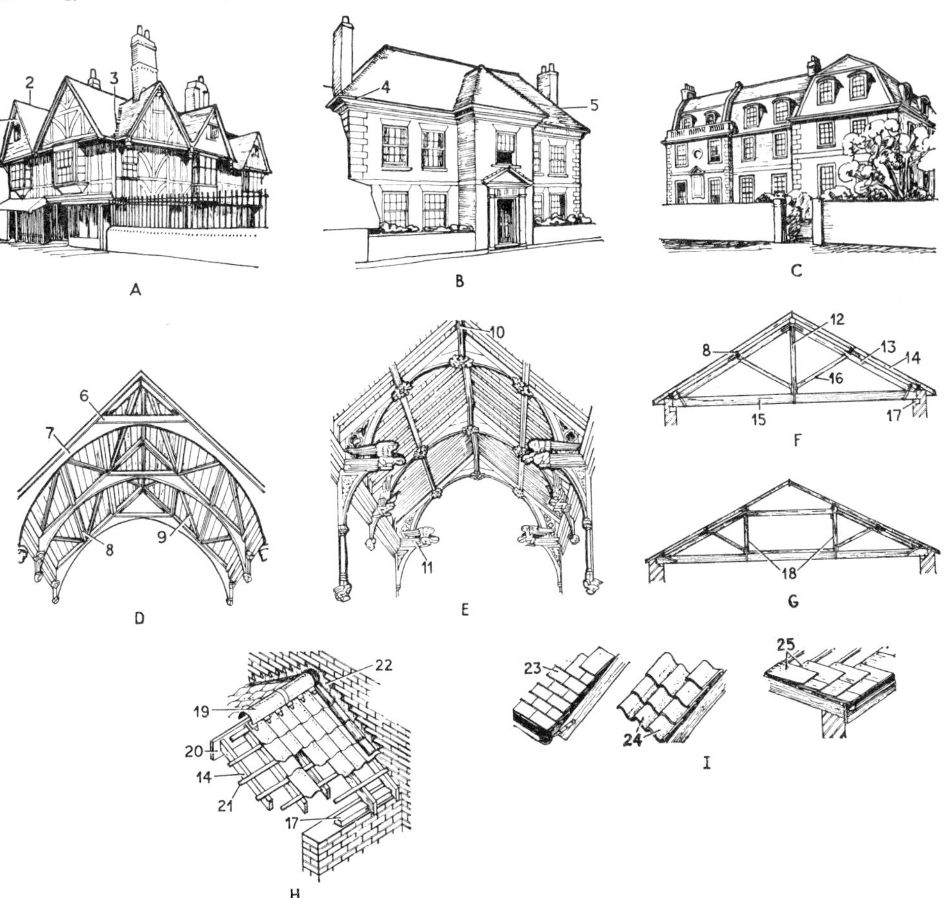

ROOFS: A. GABLED. B. HIPPED. C. MANSARD. ROOF-TRUSSES: D. ARCH-BRACED COLLAR-BEAM. E. HAMMER-BEAM. F. KING-POST. G. QUEEN-POST. H. ROOF CONSTRUCTION. I. TILES AND SLATES

1. Gable. 2. Ridge. 3. Valley. 4. Eaves. 5. Hip. 6. Collar-beam. 7. Arched brace. 8. Purlin. 9. Wind brace. 10. Ridge pole. 11. Hammer-beam. 12. King-post. 13. Principal rafter. 14. Common rafter. 15. Tie-beam. 16. Strut. 17. Wall-plate. 18. Queen-posts. 19. Ridge tile. 20. Ridgepiece. 21. Batten. 22. Flashing. 23. Tiles. 24. Pantiles. 25. Slates

Roscius Gallus (d. 62 B.C.), Roman comic actor.

Rŏscŏmm'on. Inland county of province of Connaught, Eire.

rōse (-z) *n.* 1. (Prickly bush or shrub bearing) a beautiful and usu. fragrant flower (*Rosa*) usu. of red, yellow, or white colour; (with defining word) various other flowering plants; ~ *of Sharon*, unidentified Eastern plant; cistus; *path strewn with ~s*, life of delight; *bed of ~s*, perfect conditions, pleasant easy post or condition; *under the ~*, in secret. 2. Representation of the flower in heraldry or decoration, esp. as emblem of England (see Wars of the ROSES); rose-shaped design; rosette worn on shoe or clerical hat; protuberance round base of animal's horn or eye of some birds; sprinkling-nozzle of watering-pot or hose; rose diamond; rose-window; *Golden ~*, ornament blessed by pope on 4th Sunday in Lent and sent as compliment to R.C. sovereign, city, etc. 3. Light-crimson colour, pink; (usu. pl.) rosy complexion. 4. *~-apple*, (edible sweet-scented fruit of) small tropical tree (*Eugenia*) with beautiful foliage; *~-bay*, oleander; rhododendron, azalea; willow-herb; *~-bud*, bud of rose; pretty girl; (U.S.) debutante; *~-bush*, rose plant; *~-chafer*, beetle of genus *Cetonia*, frequenting roses; very destructive in grub-state; *~-colour*, rosy red, pink; (fig.) pleasant state of things or outlook; *~-coloured*, rosy; (fig.) optimistic, sanguine, cheerful; *~-cut*, cut as a ~ *diamond*, hemispherical with upper surface cut into many triangular facets (ill. GEM); *~-gall*, excrescence on dog-rose etc. made by insect (ill. GALL); *~-leaf*, leaf, usu. petal, of rose; *crumpled ~-leaf*, slight vexation alloying general felicity; *~-nail*, nail with head shaped like rose diamond; *~-noble*, (hist.) 15th–16th-c. gold coin of varying value stamped with rose; *~-pink*, rose-colour(ed); *~-red*, red as (of) a rose; *~-water*, perfume distilled from roses; *~-window*, round window, usu. filled with tracery suggesting rose-shape or divided by spoke-like mullions (ill. WINDOW); *rose'wood*, several kinds of valuable close-grained fragrant cabinet wood. ~ *adj.* Coloured like a pale-red rose, of warm pink.

rōs'ėate (-z-) *adj.* Rose-coloured. **rōs'ėately** *adv.*

Rōse'bery (-zb-), Archibald Philip Primrose, 5th Earl of (1847–1929). English Liberal statesman, foreign secretary in Gladstone's governments of 1886 and 1892, and prime minister 1894–5.

rōse'mary (-zm-) *n.* Evergreen fragrant shrub (*Rosmarinus officinalis*), native of S. Europe, with leaves used in perfumery etc., and taken as emblem of remembrance. [L *ros* dew, *marinus* marine]

rōsē'ola (-z-) *n.* (path.) Any reddish rash. **rōsē'olar, rōsē'olous** *adjs.*

Roses, Wars of the. Series of civil wars in England during reigns of Henry VI, Edward IV, and Richard III (15th c.), between followers of house of York (with white rose as badge) and of house of Lancaster (red rose); the accession in 1485 of the Lancastrian Henry Tudor, Earl of Richmond (Henry VII), who united the two houses by marrying Elizabeth, daughter of Edward IV, brought the wars to an end, except for the rebellion of Lambert Simnel.

Rosĕtt'a stone (-z-). Stone found near Rosetta on the W. mouth of the Nile by Napoleon's soldiers in 1799; its inscription, in Egyptian hieroglyphics, demotic characters, and Greek, made it possible to decipher hieroglyphics.

rōsĕtte' (-z-) *n.* Rose-shaped ornament for dress or harness made of ribbons, leather strips, etc.; rose diamond; rose-like object or arrangement of leaves, parts, etc.; (archit.) carved or moulded conventional rose on wall etc.; rose-window.

Rōsicru'cian (-zĭkrōōshn). Member of supposed society (reputed to have been founded 1484 by a Christian Rosenkreuz, but first mentioned 1614), which was said to claim secret and magic knowledge of transmutation of metals, prolongation of life, power over elements and elemental spirits, etc. **Rōsicru'cianism** (-sha-) *n.* [L *rosa crux* rose cross, as transl. of Ger. *Rosenkreuz*]

rŏs'in (-z-) *n.* Resin (esp. of solid residue after distillation of oil of turpentine from crude turpentine). ~ *v.t.* Smear, seal up, rub (e.g. fiddle-bow or -string, acrobat's shoes), with rosin.

Rŏsinăn'tė (-z-). Don QUIXOTE's horse; hence, poor worn-out horse, hack, jade.

rosōl'iō (-z-) *n.* S. European cordial of spirits, raisins, sugar, etc. [It., f. L *ros* dew, *solis* of the sun, the cordial being orig. made from the plant sundew]

Rŏss[1], Sir James Clark (1800–62). English admiral and polar explorer; commander of the Antarctic expedition of *Erebus* and *Terror* (1839–43).

Rŏss[2], Sir John (1777–1856). Arctic explorer, author of two narratives of voyages (1818 and 1829–33) in search of the North-west passage.

Rŏss[3], Sir Ronald (1857–1932). English physician and bacteriologist; demonstrated transmission of malaria by mosquito-bites.

Rŏss and Crŏm'arty. County of N. Scotland, extending from N. Sea to Atlantic, and including the Isle of Lewis.

Rossetti (rozĕt'ĭ). English family of Italian origin: Dante Gabriel ~ (1828–82), poet and painter, and his brother William Michael ~ (1829–1919), critic, both members of the PRE-RAPHAELITE Brotherhood; Christina Georgina ~ (1830–94), their sister, poet.

Rŏssi'ni (-ēnĭ), Gioachino Antonio (1792–1868). Italian composer of 'The Barber of Seville', 'William Tell', and other operas.

Rŏss-shire; see ROSS AND CROMARTY.

Rŏstand (-tahṅ'), Edmond (1868–1918). French poet and dramatist, author of 'Cyrano de Bergerac'.

rŏstĕll'um *n.* (pl. *-la*). 1. (bot.) Short beak-shaped process on stigma of many violets and orchids. 2. (zool.) Protruding fore-part of head of tapeworm (ill. TAPEWORM).

rŏs'ter *n.* List or plan showing turns of duty or leave for individuals or companies esp. of a military force. [Du. *rooster* list, orig. gridiron (*rooster* roast) w. ref. to parallel lines]

rŏs'tral *adj.* (Of column etc.) adorned with actual or sculptured etc. beaks of ancient war-galleys; (zool. etc.) of, on, the rostrum.

rostrā'ted *adj.* (Of column etc.) rostral; (zool. etc.) having, ending in, a rostrum.

rŏs'trum *n.* (pl. *-ra*, *-rums*). 1. Platform for public speaking (orig. that in Roman forum adorned with beaks of captured galleys); pulpit; office etc. that enables one to gain the public ear. 2. (Rom. antiq.) beak of war-galley. 3. (zool., entom., bot.) Beak, stiff snout, beak-like part. **rŏs'trate, rŏs'trĭfōrm** *adjs.* Beak-like.

rōs'y (-zĭ) *adj.* Coloured like a red rose (esp. of complexion as indicating health, of blush, wine, sky, etc.); (fig.) rose-coloured, promising, hopeful; ~ *cross*, supposed emblem of Rosicrucians. **rōs'ily** *adv.* **rōs'inėss** *n.*

Rosȳth'. British naval base on N. shore of Firth of Forth, Scotland.

rŏt *n.* 1. Decay, putrefaction, rottenness (esp. in timber); virulent liver-disease of sheep; (slang) sudden series of unaccountable failures. 2. (slang; freq. as int. of incredulity or ridicule) Nonsense; absurd statement, argument, or proposal; foolish course; undesirable state of things. ~ *v.* Undergo natural decomposition, decay, putrefy; cause to rot, make rotten; (fig.) gradually perish from want of vigour or use, pine away; (slang) spoil or disconcert; (slang) chaff, banter, tease; *~-gut*, (liquor) injurious to stomach.

rōt'a *n.* 1. List of persons acting, or duties to be done, in rotation; roster. 2. (R.C. Ch.) Supreme ecclesiastical and secular court. [L, = 'wheel']

Rōtār'ian *adj.* & *n.* (Member) of a ROTARY[2] Club.

rōt'ary[1] *adj* Acting by rotation. ~ *n.* Rotary machine, esp. type of engine, as the turbine, in which the necessary rotary motion is obtained directly, instead of being converted, as in the *reciprocating engine*.

Rō'tary[2] *adj.* ~ *Club*, Local organization of business men, first founded 1905 by Paul Harris in Chicago and imitated in Gt Britain 1911; it includes one representative of each business, profession, or institution in the community and aims at furthering business service and social relations and promoting international understanding and goodwill; ~ *International*, international organization of Rotary Clubs. ~ *n.* Rotary movement or organization.

rōt'ate[1] *adj.* (bot.) Wheel-shaped.

rotāte'[2] *v.* Move round axis or centre, revolve; arrange (esp. crops) or take in rotation. **rōt'atory, rōt'ative** *adjs.*

rotā'tion *n.* Rotating; recurrence, recurrent series or period, regular succession in office etc.; ~ *of crops*, growing of different crops in regular order to avoid exhausting soil. **rotā'tional** (-sho-) *adj.*

rotāt'or *n.* Revolving apparatus or part; (anat.) muscle that rotates a limb etc.

rōte *n.* Mere habituation, knowledge got by repetition, unintelligent memory (only in *by* ~).

Rŏth'schild. Name of a Jewish family of financiers, founders at Frankfort-on-Main, towards end of 18th c., of famous banking-house, with branches at Paris, Vienna, London, and Naples.

rōt'ifer *n.* Member of the phylum *Rotifera* of minute (usu. microscopic) metazoan animals

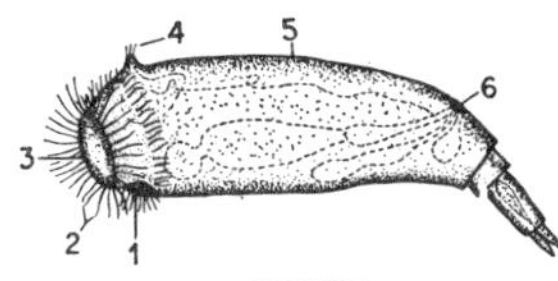

ROTIFER

1. Mouth. 2. Cilia. 3. Trochal disc. 4. Dorsal feeler. 5. Cuticle. 6. Anus

with (usu.) ring(s) of beating cilia giving the impression of revolving wheels; wheel-animalcule.

rōt'ograph (-ahf) *n.* Photographic print (esp. of page of book or MS.) made by exposing the object through lens and prism, so that negative image is thrown upon roll of sensitive paper. ~ *v.t.* Photograph by this method.

rōtogravūre' (*or* -grāv'yer) *n.* Photogravure printed on rotary machine.

rōt'or *n.* Rotary part of machine; rotating system of a helicopter (ill. HELICOPTER).

rŏtt'en *adj.* 1. Decomposed or decomposing, putrid, perishing of decay; falling to pieces, friable, easily breakable or tearable, from age or use. 2. (Of sheep) affected with the rot. 3. Morally, socially, or politically corrupt. 4. (slang) Disagreeable, regrettable, beastly, ill-advised. 5. ~ *borough*: see BOROUGH; ~*-stone*, decomposed siliceous limestone used as polishing powder. **rŏtt'enly** *adv.* **rŏtt'enness** *n.*

Rŏtt'en Row (rō). Wide track in Hyde Park, London, for horse-riders.

rŏtt'er *n.* (slang) Person objectionable on moral or other grounds.

Rŏtt'erdăm. City and principal port of Holland, on river Maas (Meuse).

rotŭnd' *adj.* Round, circular (rare); (of mouth) rounded in speaking etc.; (of speech etc.) as from rotund mouth, sonorous, sounding, grandiloquent; (of persons) plump, podgy. **rotŭnd'ly** *adv.* **rotŭn'dity** *n.*

rotŭn'da *n.* Building of circular ground-plan, esp. one with dome; circular hall or room.

rou'ble (rōō-) *n.* Principal monetary unit of Russia, = 100 copecks.

roué (rōō'ā) *n.* Debauchee, rake. [Fr., past part. of *rouer* break on wheel, = one deserving this]

Rouen (rōō'-ahṅ). City of N. France, on river Seine; ancient capital of Normandy.

rouge[1] (rōōzh) *n.* Fine red powder made (originally) from safflower and used for colouring cheeks and lips; any cosmetic used thus; red plate powder of oxide of iron; the red in ~ *et noir* (ā nwahr'), card-game played on table with two red and two black diamond-shaped marks upon which stakes are placed. ~ *adj.* Red (only in *R~ Croix*, ~ *Dragon*, two pursuivants of English College of Arms, so called from their badges). ~ *v.* Colour, adorn oneself, with rouge.

rouge[2] (rōōj) *n.* In Eton football, scrummage, touch-down counting as point to opponents.

rough (rŭf) *adj.* 1. Of uneven or irregular surface; not smooth, level, or polished; diversified or broken by prominences; hairy, shaggy, coarse in texture, rugged. 2. Not mild, quiet, or gentle; unrestrained, violent, stormy, boisterous, disorderly, riotous; inconsiderate, harsh, unfeeling, drastic, severe; grating, astringent. 3. Deficient in finish, elaboration, or delicacy; incomplete, rudimentary; entirely or partly unwrought; merely passable; inexact, approximate, preliminary. 4. ~ *and ready*, not elaborate, just good enough; not over-particular; roughly efficient or effective; ~*-and-tumble*, irregular, scrambling, disorderly, regardless of procedure rules; (*n.*) haphazard fight, scuffle; ~*-cast*, (of wall etc.) coated with mixture of lime and gravel; (*n.*) plaster of lime and gravel for walls; (*v.*) coat (wall) with rough-cast; ~ *coat*, first coat of plaster laid on; ~ *coating*, rough-cast; ~ *diamond*: see DIAMOND; ~*-dry*, dry (clothes) without ironing; ~*-grind*, give preliminary grinding to (edged tool etc.); ~*-hew*, shape out roughly, give crude form to; ~*-house*, (orig. U.S.) disturbance, row; ~ (*luck*) *on* person, what bears hardly on him; ~*-neck*, (U.S.) rowdy fellow; ~ *passage*, crossing over rough sea (also fig.); ~*-rider*, horsebreaker, man who can ride unbroken horses; irregular cavalryman; ~*-shod*, (of horse) having shoes with the nail-heads projecting; *ride* ~*-shod*, domineer *over*. **rough'en** *v.* **rough'ish** *adj.* **rough'ly** *adv.* **rough'ness** *n.* **rough** *adv.* In rough manner. ~ *n.* 1. Rough ground; (golf) *the* rough uncut ground bordering the fairway or between the tee and the green. 2. One of the spikes inserted in roughing horse. 3. Hard part of life, piece of hardship. 4. Rowdy, hooligan, man or boy of lower classes ready for lawless violence. 5. *The* unfinished or *the* natural state. ~ *v.t.* 1. Turn *up* (feathers, hair, etc.) by rubbing against the grain. 2. Secure horse, its shoes) against slipping by insertion of spikes or projecting nails in shoes. 3. Shape or plan *out*, sketch *in*, roughly; give first shaping to. 4. ~ *it*, do without ordinary conveniences of life.

rough'age (rŭf-) *n.* Less useful or refuse part of crops (U.S.); indigestible fibrous matter or cellulose in foodstuffs.

roulade (rōōlahd') *n.* Florid passage of runs, etc., in solo vocal music, usu. sung to one syllable.

rouleau (rōōlō') *n.* Number of gold or other coins made up into cylindrical packet; coil or roll, esp. as trimming.

roulĕtte' (rōō-) *n.* 1. Gambling game played on table with revolving centre, on which ball is set in motion, and finally drops into

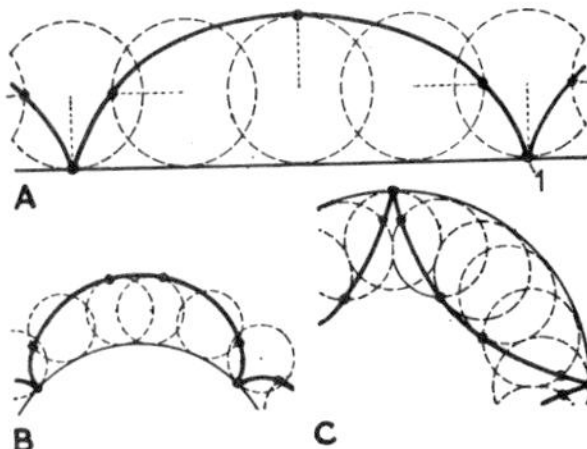

ROULETTES: A. CYCLOID (TROCHOID). B. EPICYCLOID. C. HYPOCYCLOID

1. Cusp

one of set of numbered compartments. 2. (math.) Curve traced by point on curve rolling over another fixed curve. 3. Revolving toothed wheel for making dotted lines in engraving (ill. ENGRAVE); similar wheel for perforating postage stamps.

Roumania: see RUMANIA.

Roumelia: see RUMELIA.

round[1] *adj.* 1. Spherical, circular, or cylindrical, or approaching these forms; presenting convex outline or surface; done with or involving circular motion. 2. Entire, continuous, all together, not broken or defective or scanty, sound, smooth; plain, genuine, candid, outspoken; (of voice etc.) full and mellow; *be ~ with*, (archaic) speak home-truths to; *~ arch*, semicircular arch characteristic of Romanesque architecture; *~-arm*, (of bowling) with arm swung horizontally; *~ cheeks*, plump, not hollow, cheeks; *~ dance*, one in which dancers form a ring; waltz; *~ game*, one in which each player plays on his own account; *~ hand*, writing with bold curves; *Round'head*, member of Parliamentary party in civil war of 17th c. (from custom of wearing hair close-cut); *~ house*, (hist.) lock-up or place of detention; (naut.) cabin or set of cabins on after-part of quarterdeck, chiefly in old sailing-ships; *~ jacket*, one cut level below, without skirts; *~ numbers*, tens, hundreds, etc., with neglect of minor denominations; roughly correct figures; *~ robin*, written petition with signatures radiating from centre of circle to conceal order in which they were written; *~ shot*, spherical ball for smooth-bore cannon; *~ shoulders*, shoulders so bent forward that back is convex; *~ sum*, considerable sum of money; *R~ Table, Table R~*, that round which King Arthur and his knights are supposed to have sat, so that none might have precedence; *~-table conference*, conference at which parties present are all on equal footing; *~-top*, platform about masthead, formerly circular; *~ towel*, roller towel; *~ trip, voyage*, circular tour or trip, outward and return journey; *round'worm*, nematode worm, often parasitic, e.g. species infesting human intestines. **round'en** *v.* **round'ish** *adj.* **round'ness** *n.*

round[2] *n.* 1. Round object; rung of ladder; large round piece *of* beef, cut from haunch; slice of toast etc.; *the ~*, form of sculpture in which figure stands clear of any ground, as dist. from *relief*; a rounded or convex form. 2. Circumference, bounds, extent, *of*. 3. Revolving motion; circular, circuitous, or recurring. course; circuit, cycle, series; (mil., pl.) watch that goes round inspecting sentries, circuit it makes; (golf) playing of all holes in course once; *the daily ~*, ordinary occupations of the day; *make, go, one's ~s*, take customary walk, esp. of inspection; *rounds'man*, tradesman's employee going round for orders and with goods. 4. (mus.) Kind of canon for three or more voices singing the same melody, the first voice completing a phrase before the second enters, and so on. 5. Allowance of something distributed or measured out; one of set or series; one bout or spell; one stage in competition; (archery) fixed number of arrows discharged at fixed distance. *~ adv.* 1. With more or less circular motion, with return to starting-point after such motion, with rotation, with change to opposite position; by circuitous way; through, throughout. 2. To, at, affecting, all or many points of a circumference or area or members of a company etc.; in every direction from a centre or within a radius; *show ~*, take to all points of interest; *an all-~ man*, one of varied talents; *~ about*, in a ring (about), all round; on all sides (of); with change to opposite position; circuitously; about, approximately; *round'about* (*n.*) circuitous way; piece of circumlocution; merry-go-round; place, as road junction, where all traffic must follow circular course; (*adj.*) circuitous; circumlocutory; plump or stout. *~ prep.* So as to encircle or enclose; with successive visits to, at or to points on the circumference of; in various directions from or with regard to; having as axis of revolution or central point; so as to double or pass in curved course, having thus passed, in the position that would result from thus passing; *~ the clock*, continuing throughout the 24 hours of the day. *~ v.* 1. Invest with, assume, round shape; round the lips in pronouncing (vowel); bring to complete, symmetrical, or well-ordered state (freq. *~ off*). 2. Gather *up* (cattle) by riding round (freq. transf.), whence *~-up* (*n.*) this action. 3. (naut.) Sail round, double (headland etc.). 4. Turn round (rare, chiefly naut.). 5. *~ on*, make unexpected retort to, turn on; (of informer) peach upon.

roun'del *n.* 1. Small disc, esp. decorative medallion etc. 2. Rondeau; rondel.

roun'dĕlay *n.* Short simple song with refrain.

roun'ders *n.pl.* Game with bat and ball between two sides, the unit of scoring being the round (or complete run of player through all the bases arranged in a circle).

round'ly *adv.* 1. In thoroughgoing manner; bluntly, with plain speech; without qualification, severely. 2. In circular way.

roup[1] (ro͞op) *n.* Kinds of highly infectious poultry-disease characterized by an acute fever generally ending in death. **roup'y** *adj.*

roup[2] (rowp) *v.t.* (Sc. & north.) Sell by auction. *~ n.* Auction.

rouse[1] (-z) *n.* (archaic) Draught of liquor, bumper; toast; revel, drinking-bout.

rouse[2] (-z) *v.* 1. Startle (game) from lair or cover; wake, stir up, or startle (person etc.) from sleep, inactivity, complacency, or carelessness; provoke temper of, inflame with passion; evoke (feelings). 2. Stir (fire, liquid, esp. beer while brewing); (naut.) haul vigorously *in, out, up*. 3. Cease to sleep; become active. **rous'ing** *adj.* (esp., of fire) Blazing strongly; (of trade) brisk, lively.

Rousseau[1] (ro͞osō'), Henri (1844–1910). French painter; a customs officer, hence called 'le douanier').

Rousseau[2] (ro͞osō'), Jean Jacques (1712–78). French philosopher, advocate of return to natural state, in which man is both good and happy; the 'Contrat Social' (1762), expounding the view that society is founded on a contract and that the head of a State is not the people's master but their mandatory, had profound influence on French thought and prepared the way for the revolution.

Rousseau[3] (ro͞osō'), Pierre Étienne Théodore (1812–67). French landscape painter of BARBIZON school.

rout[1] *n.* 1. Assemblage or company esp. of revellers or rioters; (law) assemblage of three or more persons engaged in unlawful act; riot, tumult, disturbance, clamour, fuss. 2. (archaic) Large evening party or reception. 3. Disorderly retreat of defeated army or troops; *put to ~*, utterly defeat. *~ v.t.* Put to rout.

rout[2] *v.* = ROOT[2]; (also) force or fetch *out* (of bed or from house etc.). **rout'er** *n.* (esp.) Kind of plane used in moulding (ill. PLANE).

route (ro͞ot, *mil.* rowt) *n.* Way taken in getting from starting-point to destination; (mil.) marching orders; *column of ~*, formation of troops on the march; *~-march*, training march of soldiers etc.; *en ~* (ahn ro͞ot), on the way. *~ v.t.* Plan route of (goods etc., esp. by rail). **rout(e)ing** *n.* Direction according to a prescribed route.

routine (ro͞otēn') *n.* Regular course of procedure, unvarying performance of certain acts; set form, fixed arrangement (e.g. of steps in dancer's performance); (attrib.) performed by rule or habitually. **routin'ism, routin'ist** *ns.*

roux (ro͞o) *n.* (cookery) Flour cooked in melted fat, used to thicken sauces etc. [Fr. = 'red', 'browned']

rōve[1] *v.* Wander without fixed destination, roam, ramble; (of eyes) look in various directions; wander over or through; (angling) troll with live bait; *roving commission*, authority granted by the Admiralty to the officer in command of a vessel to cruise wherever he may think fit; (transf.) authority given to pursue an inquiry or investigation in whatever quarters it may be considered necessary. *~ n.* Act of roving. [orig. term used in archery, = 'shoot at casual mark with range not determined']

rōve[2] *n.* Sliver of cotton, wool, etc., drawn out and slightly twisted. ~ *v.t.* Form into roves. **rōv′er**[1] *n.*

rōve[3] *n.* Small metal plate or ring for rivet to pass through and be clinched over.

rōv′er[2] *n.* 1. (archery) Mark chosen at undetermined range; mark for long-distance shooting. 2. Wanderer; member of senior branch of Boy Scouts. 3. (croquet) (Player of) ball that has passed all hoops but not pegged out.

rōv′er[3] *n.* Sea-robber, pirate.

row[1] (rō) *n.* Number of persons or things in a more or less straight line; row of houses, street with this on one or each side (freq. in street names); line of seats in theatre etc.; row of plants in garden etc.; *the R~*, ROTTEN Row; *a hard ~ to hoe*, (U.S.) a difficult task.

row[2] (rō) *v.* Propel boat, propel (boat), convey (passenger) in boat, with oars or sweeps; row race with; be oarsman of specified number in boat; (of boat) be fitted with (so many *oars*); ~ *down*, overtake in rowing, esp. bumping, race; *~-boat*, (U.S.) rowing-boat; *rowed out*, (of crew) exhausted by rowing. ~ *n.* Spell of rowing, boat-excursion. **row′er** *n.*

row[3] *n.* (colloq.) Disturbance, commotion, noise, dispute; shindy, free fight; being reprimanded; *make, kick up, a ~*, raise noise; make protest. ~ *v.t.* Reprimand.

row′an (rō-, row-) *n.* (Berry of) *~-tree*, *Pyrus Aucuparia*, characterized by pinnate leaves and scarlet berries, mountain ash.

rowd′y *adj.* & *n.* Rough, disorderly, and noisy (person). **rowd′inėss, rowd′yism** *ns.*

Rowe (-ō), Nicholas (1674–1718). English playwright and poet; author of 'Tamerlane', 'The Fair Penitent', etc.

row′el *n.* Spiked revolving disc at end of spur (ill. SPUR); (now rare) circular piece of leather etc. with hole in centre, inserted between horse's skin and flesh to discharge exudate; ~ *v.t.* Urge with rowel.

Row′landson (rō-), Thomas (1756–1827). English caricaturist and illustrator.

rowlock (rŭl′ok) *n.* Pair of thole-pins or other contrivance on boat's gunwale serving as point of support for oar (ill. BOAT).

Rowt′on, Montague William Lowry-Corry, Baron (1838–1903). English originator of scheme of ~ *Houses*, model lodging-houses for poor men at prices similar to those of common lodging-houses.

Rŏx′burghshire (-bro-). Inland border county of S. Scotland.

roy′al *adj.* 1. Of, from, suited to, worthy of, belonging to family of, in service or under patronage of, a king or queen; ~ *blue*, deep vivid blue; ~ *borough, burgh*, one holding charter from crown; ~ *evil*, KING's evil; ~ *oak*, oak in which Charles II hid after battle of Worcester (1651); sprig of oak worn to commemorate Restoration of Charles II (1660); ~ *oak day*, 29th May; ~ *standard*, banner with royal arms (ill. FLAG). 2. Kingly, majestic, stately, splendid; first-rate; on great scale; of exceptional size etc.; *battle ~*, free fight; ~ *fern, Osmunda regalis*, flowering fern; ~ *paper*, size of paper, 24 × 19 in. for writing and 25 × 20 in. for printing (~ *octavo* etc., octavo etc. folded from this); ~ *stag*, one with head of 12 or more points; ~ *sail, mast*, above topgallant sail and mast (ill. SHIP). **roy′ally** *adv.* **roy′al** *n.* Royal stag; royal sail or mast.

Royal Academy (of Arts). Institution, founded in London 1768 under patronage of George III, for annual exhibition of works of contemporary artists and establishment of school of art; housed in Burlington House, Piccadilly, since 1869.

Royal Courts of Justice. Building in Strand, London, in which superior courts of law and appeal are held.

Royal Exchange. Building in Cornhill, London, for dealings between merchants, orig. founded by Sir T. Gresham, 1566; the building was twice destroyed by fire, and in its present form was opened 1844.

Royal George. English naval vessel which sank at Spithead 1782 while at anchor undergoing repairs, with Admiral Kempenfelt and about 800 visitors and crew.

Royal Institution. Society founded 1799 in London for diffusion of scientific knowledge.

roy′alist *n.* Monarchist, supporter of monarchy as institution or of the royal side in civil war etc.; (U.S.) die-hard. **roy′alism** *n.* **royalist′ic** *adj.*

Royal Society (of London for the Advancement of Science). Scientific society, founded 1660 in London from nucleus of Philosophical Society (founded 1645), to promote scientific discussion esp. in the physical sciences.

roy′alty *n.* 1. Office, dignity, or power of king or queen; sovereignty. 2. Royal persons; member of royal family. 3. Prerogative or privilege of sovereign (usu. pl.); royal right (now esp. over minerals) granted by sovereign to individual or corporation, lessee's payment to land-owner for privilege of working mine. 4. Sum paid to patentee for use of patent or to author, composer, etc., for each copy of his book, piece of music, etc., sold, or for the presentation of a play.

Roys′ton crow *n.* Hooded or grey crow (*Corvus c. cornix*). [f. *Royston* on borders of Hertfordshire and Cambridgeshire]

R.P. *abbrev.* Rocket projectile.

R.P.S. *abbrev.* Royal Photographic Society.

R.Q.M.S. *abbrev.* Regimental Quartermaster-Sergeant.

R.R.C. *abbrev.* (Lady of the) Royal Red Cross.

Rs, ~~Rs~~ *abbrevs.* Rupees.

R.S. *abbrev.* Royal Scots; Royal Society.

R.S.A. *abbrev.* Royal Scottish Academy; Royal Society of Arts.

R.S.F. *abbrev.* Royal Scots Fusiliers.

R.S.F.S.R. *abbrev.* RUSSIAN SOVIET FEDERAL SOCIALIST REPUBLIC.

R.S.M. *abbrev.* Regimental Sergeant-Major.

R.S.O. *abbrev.* Railway sub-office.

R.S.P.C.A. *abbrev.* Royal Society for the Prevention of Cruelty to Animals.

R.S.V.P. *abbrev.* *Répondez s'il vous plaît* [= 'answer, if you please']

R.S.W. *abbrev.* Royal Scottish Society of Painters in Water-colours.

R.T., R/T *abbrevs.* Radio-telegraphy; radio-telephony.

Rt Hon. *abbrev.* Right Honourable.

R.T.O. *abbrev.* Railway Transport Officer.

R.T.R. *abbrev.* Royal Tank Regiment.

Rt Rev. *abbrev.* Right Reverend.

R.U. *abbrev.* Rugby Union.

rŭb *v.* 1. Subject to friction, slide one's hand or an object along over or up and down the surface of; polish, clean, abrade, chafe, make *dry, bare, sore*, etc., by rubbing; slide (hands, object) *against, on* or *over* something, (objects) *together*, with friction; bring *away, off*, or *out*, force *in, into, through*, reduce *to* powder, etc., bring size or level of *down*, spread *over*, groom *down*, freshen or brush *up*, mix *up* into paste, by rubbing (lit. & fig.); ~ *one's hands (together)*, rub each with the other, usu. in sign of keen satisfaction; ~ *noses*, (of some savages) greet each other; ~ *shoulders*, come into contact *with* other people; ~ *(up) the wrong way*, stroke against the grain, irritate or repel as by stroking cat upwards. 2. Reproduce design of (sepulchral brass or stone) by rubbing paper laid on it with coloured chalk etc. 3. Come into or be in sliding contact, exercise friction, *against* or *on*; (of bowl) be retarded or diverted by unevenness of ground; (fig., of person etc.) go *on, along, through*, with more or less restraint or difficulty; (of cloth, skin, etc.) get frayed, worn, sore, or bare with friction. ~ *n.* Spell of rubbing; (bowls) inequality of ground impeding or diverting bowl, being diverted etc. by this; (transf.) impediment or difficulty; (golf) ~ *of the green*, accidental interference with course or position of ball.

rŭb′-a-dŭb *n.* & *v.i.* (Make) rolling sound of drum. [imit.]

rubato (rōōbaht'ō) *adj.* & *n.* (mus.) (*Tempo*) ~, time occasionally slackened or hastened for the purposes of expression. [It., = 'robbed']

rŭbb'er[1] *n.* 1. Person who rubs, as Turkish-bath attendant who rubs bathers. 2. Implement used for rubbing; part of machine operating by rubbing. 3. (from its use in erasing pencil-marks; also *india-~*) Elastic solid made from the milky juice (latex) of certain plants and trees (esp. *Hevia brasiliensis*) of S. America, Africa, the E. Indies, etc., and used for many purposes in industry, e.g. for making pneumatic tyres, waterproofing cloth; piece of this or other substance for erasing pencil-marks; (pl.) galoshes, rubber boots, rubber-soled shoes; *rubb'erneck*, (U.S. slang) sight-seeing tourist, inquisitive person; (*v.*) act as rubberneck; ~ *stamp*, stamp for quickly endorsing papers with signature, date, etc., whence ~-*stamp* (*v.*) give (unconsidered) endorsement to others' decision. **rŭbb'ery** *adj.* **rŭbb'er** *v.* 1. Coat or cover with rubber. 2. (U.S. slang) Turn head to look at something.

rŭbb'er[2] *n.* Three successive games (or two games won by same side) between sides or persons at bridge, whist, cribbage, backgammon, etc.

rŭbb'ish *n.* Waste material, debris, refuse, litter; worthless material or articles, trash; absurd ideas or suggestions, nonsense (freq. as exclam. of contempt). **rŭbb'ishy** *adj.*

rŭb'ble *n.* Waste fragments of stone, brick, etc., esp. from old or demolished buildings; pieces of undressed stone used, esp. as filling-in, for walls (ill. MASONRY); (geol.) loose angular stones etc. forming upper covering of some rocks; water-worn stones. **rŭbb'ly** *adj.*

rubefacient (rōōbĭfăsh'ent) *n.* & *adj.* (med.) (Counter-irritant etc.) producing redness or slight inflammation. **rubėfăc'tion** *n.*

Rub'ens (rōō-), Sir Peter Paul (1577–1640). Flemish painter and diplomatist, active at Antwerp and in Italy, France, Spain, and England.

rub'icĕlle (rōō-) *n.* Orange-red or yellow variety of spinel.

Rub'icon (rōō-). Ancient name of a small stream flowing into Adriatic, forming part of boundary of Cisalpine Gaul; by taking his army across it, i.e. outside his own province, Julius Caesar committed himself to war against the Senate and Pompey; hence, *cross, pass, the* ~, take decisive step, esp. at outset of enterprise; ~ *bezique*, card-game, kind of bezique in which four packs are used, 9 cards being dealt by three to each player.

rub'icŭnd (rōō-) *adj.* (Of face etc.) reddish, ruddy, high-coloured. **rubicŭn'dity** *n.*

rubĭd'ium (rōō-) *n.* Rare soft silvery metallic element, one of the alkali metals: symbol Rb, at. no. 37, at. wt 85·478. [L *rubidus* red, from two red lines in its spectrum]

rubĭ'ginous (rōō-) *adj.* Rusty, rust-coloured.

Rub'instein (rōō-, -īn), Anton Grigorevich (1829–94). Russian-Jewish pianist and musical composer.

rub'rĭc (rōō-) *n.* Heading of chapter, section, etc., also special passage or sentence, written or printed in red or in special lettering; direction for conduct of divine service (prop. in red) inserted in liturgical book; (red-letter entry in) calendar of saints (now rare). **rub'rĭcal** *adj.* **rub'rĭcally** *adv.* **rubri'cian, rub'rĭcist** *ns.*

rub'rĭcāte *v.t.* Mark with, print or write in, red; furnish with rubrics. **rub'rĭcā'tion, rub'rĭcātor** *ns.*

rub'y (rōō-) *n.* 1. Rare and valuable precious stone (*true* or *Oriental* ~), a species of corundum, of colour varying from deep crimson to pale rose-red; a less valuable stone (*spinel* ~), an aluminate of magnesium, or a rose-pink variety of this (*balas* ~); ~ *wedding*, 40th anniversary of wedding. 2. Colour of ruby, a rich glowing purple-tinged red; red wine; (boxing slang) blood. 3. Size of type (5½ point) intermediate between nonpareil and pearl (= U.S. *agate*). ~ *adj.* Of ruby colour.

ruche (rōōsh) *n.* Frill or gathering of lace etc. as trimming, esp. one with both edges sewn to garment; parallel rows of gathering. ~ *v.t.* Ornament, gather, thus.

rŭck[1] *n.* Main body of competitors left out of the running, undistinguished crowd or general run of persons or things.

rŭck[2], **rŭck'le** *ns.* & *vbs.* Crease, wrinkle.

rŭck'săck (*or* rōō-) *n.* Bag for carrying walker's necessaries, slung by straps from both shoulders and resting on back.

rŭck'us (U.S.), **rŭc'tion** *ns.* (slang, usu. pl.) Disturbance, tumult, row.

Rŭdbĕck'ia *n.* Genus of plants of the aster family, native to N. America, much grown in gardens. [Olaus *Rudbeck* (1630–1702), Swedish botanist]

rŭdd *n.* Freshwater fish (*Leuciscus erythrophthalmus*) of the carp family resembling roach, red-eye.

rŭdd'er *n.* Broad flat wooden or metal piece hinged to vessel's stern-post for steering with (ill. BOAT); similar device on an aircraft; (fig.) guiding principle, etc.; (brewing) paddle for stirring malt in mash-tub. **rŭdd'erlėss** *adj.*

rŭd'dle *n.* Red ochre, esp. of kind used for marking sheep. ~ *v.t.* Mark or colour (as) with ruddle.

rŭdd'ock *n.* Robin redbreast.

rŭdd'y *adj.* 1. Freshly or healthily red, rosy; reddish. 2. (slang) 'Bloody', damnable. **rŭdd'ily** *adv.* **rŭdd'inėss** *n.*

rude (rōōd) *adj.* 1. Primitive, simple, unsophisticated; in natural state; rugged, unimproved, uncivilized, uneducated; roughly made, contrived, or executed; coarse, artless, wanting subtlety or accuracy. 2. Violent, not gentle; unrestrained, startling, abrupt. 3. Vigorous, hearty, (chiefly in ~ *health*). 4. Insolent, impertinent, offensive. **rude'ly** *adv.* **rude'nėss, rud'ery** (slang) *ns.*

ru'dĭment (rōō-) *n.* (pl.) Elements or first principles of or *of* knowledge or some subject; (pl.) imperfect beginning *of* something that will develop or might have developed; (sing.) part or organ imperfectly developed as having no function. **rudĭmĕn'tary** *adj.*

rue[1] (rōō) *v.t.* (pres. part. *rueing*). Repent of, bitterly feel the consequences of, wish undone or unbefallen. ~ *n.* (archaic) Repentance, dejection at some occurrence. **rue'ful** *adj.* Doleful, dismal; *Knight of the* ~ *countenance*, Don QUIXOTE. **rue'fully** *adv.* **rue'fulnėss** *n.*

rue[2] (rōō) *n.* Perennial evergreen shrub (*Ruta graveolens*) with bitter strong-scented leaves.

rŭff[1] *n.* Deep projecting starched frill of several separately goffered folds of linen or muslin worn round neck, esp. in 16th c. (ill. DOUBLET); projecting or conspicuously coloured ring of feathers or hair round bird's or beast's neck; kind of domestic pigeon resembling jacobin.

rŭff[2] *n.* (fem. *reeve*). Bird of sandpiper kind (*Tringa* or *Machetes pugnax*) of which male has ruff and ear-tufts in breeding-season.

rŭff[3] *n.* Small olive-brown freshwater fish of perch family (*Acerina cernera*), with rough prickly scales and brown and black spots.

rŭff[4] *n.* & *v.* Trump(ing) at whist, bridge, etc.

rŭff'ian *n.* Brutal violent lawless person, desperado, bully, rough. **rŭff'ianism** *n.* **rŭff'ianly** *adj.*

rŭf'fle *v.* Disturb smoothness or tranquillity of; suffer ruffling, lose smoothness or calmness (rare); swagger about, behave arrogantly or quarrelsomely. ~ *n.* 1. Perturbation, bustle (rare); rippling effect on water. 2. Ornamental gathered or goffered frill of lace etc. worn at opening of garment, esp. about wrist, breast, or neck; ruff of bird etc.

ru'fous (rōō-) *adj.* (chiefly nat. hist.) Reddish brown.

rŭg *n.* 1. Large wrap or coverlet of thick woollen etc. stuff. 2. Floor-mat of shaggy material or thick pile, esp. (freq. *hearth-*~) laid down before fire-place.

Rŭgbeian (-bē´an) *adj.* & *n.* (Member) of Rugby School.

Rŭg´by. Town in Warwickshire, England, site of famous public school founded 1567; ~ *football*, one of the two main types of football (the other being ASSOCIATION football); ~ *Union*

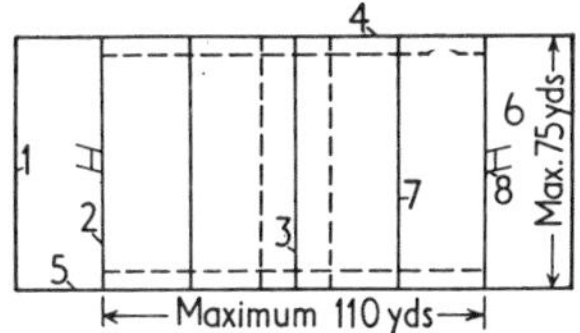

RUGBY UNION FOOTBALL GROUND

1. Dead-ball line. 2. Goal line. 3. Half-way line. 4. Touch line. 5. Touch-in-goal. 6. In-goal. 7. 25-yard line. 8. Goal

football is played by 15 players a side, a full-back, 4 three-quarter backs, 2 half-backs, and 8 forwards who form the 'scrummage'; the ball is oval in shape and is punted, dropped, or passed from hand to hand, the object being to 'touch down' behind the opponents' line (a *try*), and to kick the ball over the crossbar and between the side-posts of the goal; ~ *League football*, a later version, is played mainly in N. Engl., with 13 a side.

rŭgg´ėd (-g-) *adj.* Of rough uneven surface; unsoftened, unpolished; lacking gentleness or refinement; harsh in sound; austere, unbending; involving hardship. **rŭgg´ėdly** *adv.* **rŭgg´ėdnėss** *n.*

rŭgg´er *n.* (colloq.) Rugby football.

rugōse´ (rōō-) *adj.* (chiefly nat. hist.) Wrinkled, corrugated. **rugōse´ly** *adv.* **rugŏs´ĭty** *n.*

Rühm´kŏrff, Heinrich Daniel (1805–77). German physicist, inventor of induction-coil named after him.

Ruhr (roor). River of W. Germany, flowing into Rhine on right bank at Ruhrort; coal-mining district, with iron and steel and other heavy industries, along this river.

ru´ĭn (rōō-) *n.* Downfall, fallen or wrecked state (lit. or fig.); (freq. pl.) what remains of building, town, structure, etc., that has suffered ruin; (sing.) what causes ruin, destroying agency, havoc. ~ *v.t.* Reduce (place) to ruins; bring to ruin. **ruinā´tion** *n.*

ru´ĭnous (rōō-) *adj.* In ruins, dilapidated; bringing ruin, disastrous. **ru´ĭnously** *adv.* **ru´ĭnousnėss** *n.*

rule (rōōl) *n.* 1. Principle to which action or procedure conforms or is bound or intended to conform; dominant custom, canon, test, standard, normal state of things; *standing* ~, one made by corporation to govern its procedure; ~ *of thumb*, method or procedure based on experience or practice, not theory; ~ *of three*, method of finding fourth number from 3 given numbers, of which first is in same proportion to second as third is to unknown fourth; *by* ~, in regulation manner, mechanically; *hard and fast* ~, rigid formula; *exception proves the* ~: see EXCEPTION; *as a* ~, usually, more often than not; *work to* ~, (of workers) work according to rules laid down by their trade union. 2. Sway, government, dominion; *bear* ~, hold sway. 3. (eccles.) Code of discipline observed by religious order; (law) order made by judge or court with reference to particular case only; (hist.) *the* ~, limited area outside Fleet and King's Bench prisons in which prisoners, esp. debtors, were allowed to live on certain terms. 4. Graduated, freq. jointed, strip of metal or wood used for measuring, esp. by carpenters etc.; (print.) thin slip of metal for separating headings, columns, etc., short (*en* ~) or long (*em* ~) dash in punctuation etc. ~ *v.* 1. Exercise sway or decisive influence over; keep under control, curb; (pass.) consent to follow advice, be guided *by*; *ruling passion*, motive that habitually directs one's actions. 2. Be the ruler(s), have the sovereign control of or *over*, bear rule. 3. (Of prices etc.) have specified general level, be for the most part. 4. Give judicial or authoritative decision; ~ *out*, exclude, pronounce irrelevant or ineligible. 5. Make parallel lines across (paper); make (straight line) with ruler or mechanical help.

rul´er (rōō-) *n.* 1. Person or thing bearing (esp. sovereign) rule. 2. Straight strip or cylinder (usu. of wood) used in ruling paper or lines. **rul´ership** *n.*

rul´ĭng (rōō-) *n.* (esp.) Authoritative pronouncement, judicial decision.

rŭll´ey *n.* Flat four-wheeled dray, lorry.

rŭm[1] *n.* 1. Spirit distilled from products of sugar-cane chiefly in W. Indies and Guiana. 2. (U.S.) Any intoxicating liquor; ~-*runner*, (U.S.) smuggler of alcoholic liquor.

rŭm[2] *adj.* (slang) Odd, strange, queer; ~ *start*, surprising occurrence. **rŭm´ly** *adv.* **rŭm´nėss** *n.*

Rumān´ĭa (rōō-), **Rom-, Roum-.** Country of SE. Europe, on the Black Sea, formed by union in 1861 of Moldavia and Wallachia; a monarchy from 1881 to 1947, when it was declared a republic. **Rumān´ĭan** *adj.* & *n.* 1. (Native, inhabitant) of Rumania. 2. Language of Rumania, a ROMANCE language much influenced by Slavonic.

rŭm´ba *n.* Cuban negro dance; ballroom dance imitative of this.

rŭm´ble[1] *v.* Make sound (as) of thunder, earthquake, heavy cart, wind in the bowels, etc.; go *along*, *by*, etc., making or in vehicle making such sound; utter, say, give *out*, *forth*, with such sound. ~ *n.* 1. Rumbling sound. 2. Hind part of carriage or (U.S.) motor-car arranged as extra seat or for luggage; ~-*seat*, (U.S.) dickey-seat.

rŭm´ble[2] *v.t.* (slang) Grasp, detect, see through, understand.

rŭmbŭs´tious *adj.* (colloq.) Boisterous, uproarious.

Rumēl´ĭa (rōō-). Orig., Turkish name for Turkish possessions in Balkans; later esp. central Albania and W. Macedonia.

ru´mĕn (rōō-) *n.* Ruminant's first stomach (ill. RUMINANT).

ru´mĭnant (rōō-) *n.* Animal

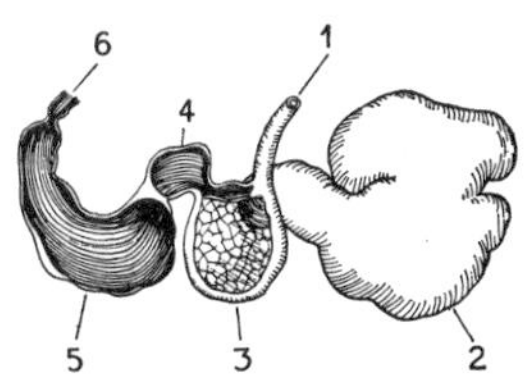

STOMACH OF A RUMINANT

1. Gullet. 2. Paunch or rumen. 3. Reticulum or honeycomb. 4. Psalterium. 5. Maw or abomasum. 6. Intestine

that chews cud. ~ *adj.* 1. Belonging to the ruminants. 2. Given to, engaged in, rumination.

ru´mĭnāte (rōō-) *v.* 1. Chew the cud. 2. Meditate, ponder. **ruminā´tion** *n.* **ru´mĭnative** *adj.* **ru´mĭnatively** *adv.*

rŭmm´age *v.* Ransack, make search in or *in*, make search; fish *out* or *up* from among other things; disarrange, throw *about*, in search. ~ *n.* Things got by rummaging, miscellaneous accumulation; rummaging search; ~-*sale*, clearance sale of unclaimed articles at docks etc.; sale of odds and ends to raise money for charity.

rŭmm´er *n.* Large drinking-glass. [f. W.Fl. *rummer*, Ger. *römer*, or Du. *romer*, perh. = 'Roman glass']

rŭmm´y[1] *adj.* (slang) = RUM[2].

rŭmm´y[2] *n.* Card-game played by 3 or more players with 2 packs of cards, the object being to get rid of cards by forming sequences or sets and 'declaring' them.

rumour (rōōm´er) *n.* General talk, report, or hearsay, of doubtful accuracy; *a* or *the* current but unverified statement or assertion. ~ *v.t.* (chiefly pass.) Report by way of rumour.

rŭmp *n.* 1. Tail-end, posterior, buttocks, of beast or bird, or rarely of person; ~ *steak*, steak cut from ox's rump (ill. MEAT). 2. Small or contemptible remnant of a parliament or similar body, esp. (hist.) that of the Long Parliament, either from its Restoration (1659) to its final dissolution (1660), or from PRIDE'S PURGE (1648) to its first dissolution (1653).

rŭmp'le *v.t.* Wrinkle, crease, tousle, disorder (fabric, leaves, hair, etc.).

rŭm'pus *n.* (slang) Disturbance, brawl, row, uproar.

rŭm'-tŭm *n.* Light racing-boat for one sculler, with outriggers and sliding seat, used on lower Thames.

rŭn *v.* (past t. *răn*, past part. *rŭn*). 1. (Of human beings) move legs quickly (one foot being lifted before the other is set down) so as to go at faster pace than walking; (of animals) go at quick pace, amble, trot, gallop, etc.; (start to) cross cricket-pitch to score run; flee, abscond; go or travel hurriedly, precipitately, etc.; *running jump*, one in which jumper runs to the take-off; *running fight*, (naut.) one kept up by retreating ship or fleet with pursuer; *run over, down, up*, pay flying visit (*to*). 2. Compete in or *in* race; seek election etc. (*for* parliament, president, etc.). 3. Go straight and fast (of fish, ship, etc.); advance (as) by rolling or on wheels, spin round or along, revolve (as) on axle; go with sliding, smooth, continuous, or easy motion; be in action; work freely; be current or operative; (of play) be performed; (of fire, news, etc.) spread rapidly from point to point; *running fire*, successive shots from different points; *running hand*, writing in which pen, etc., is not lifted after each letter; *running knot*, knot that slips along rope so as to enlarge or diminish loop; ~ *in the family*, be found in all members of it; ~ *in the head*, (of tune etc.) seem to be heard over and over again. 4. (Of colour in fabric, ink on paper, etc.) spread from marked or dyed to other parts. 5. (Of thought, eye, etc.) pass in transitory or cursory way; *running commentary*, continuous written commentary accompanying text; oral description of events that are taking place. 6. (Of liquid, sand, etc., vessel etc.) flow, be wet, drip, flow with; (of nose, eyes, etc.) drop mucus or tears; (of candle) gutter; (of sore) suppurate; *person's blood* ~*s cold*, he is horrified; *the sands are running out*, time of grace etc. is nearly up; *feeling* ~*s high*, excitement, partisanship, etc., is prevalent, etc.; ~ *dry*, cease to flow, be exhausted; ~ *low, short*, become scanty. 7. Extend, be continuous; have a certain course or order, progress, proceed; have a tendency, common characteristic, or average price or level; *runn'ing* (part., placed after noun), in succession, following each other without interval; *running head* (*-line*), *title*, repeated or varying heading of page. 8. (with cognate object) Pursue, follow, traverse, cover; make way swiftly through or over; wander about in; perform; essay, be exposed or submit to; ~ *the blockade*: see BLOCKADE; ~ *errands, messages*, be a messenger; ~*s a chance of being*, may be; ~ *the gauntlet*: see GAUNTLET[2]; ~ *rapids*, shoot them; ~ *risk*: see RISK. 9. Sew loosely or hastily or with *running-stitches*, small straight stitches made by passing needle in and out in straight line through materials (ill. STITCH). 10. Chase, hunt; have running race with; ~ *to earth*, chase to its lair; (fig.) discover after long search; ~ *hard* or *close*, press severely in race, competition, or comparative merit. 11. Make run or go; smuggle (contraband goods) by evading coast-guard etc.; keep (coach, steamer, business, person, etc.) going, manage, conduct operations of; ~ *the show*, (slang) dominate in an undertaking etc.; ~ (thing) *fine*, leave very little margin of time or amount concerning it. 12. *run'about* (*adj.*) roving; (*n.*) light motor-car, aeroplane, etc.; *run'away*, fugitive, bolting (horse); (of marriage) after elopement; *run'way*, track or gangway; specially prepared surface on airfield for taking off and landing; groove in which thing slides; place for fowls to run in. 13. (with preps.) ~ *across*, fall in with; ~ *after*, pursue with attentions; seek society of; give much time to; ~ *against*, fall in with; ~ *at*, assail by charging or rushing; ~ *into*, incur (debt); fall into (practice etc.); be continuous or coalesce with; have collision with; reach or attain; ~ *on*, be concerned with; ~ *over*, review, glance over, peruse, recapitulate; touch (notes of piano etc.) in quick succession; (of vehicle) pass over (person etc.); ~ *through*, examine cursorily; peruse; deal successively with; consume (estate etc.) by reckless or quick spending; pervade; ~ *to*, reach (amount, number, etc.); have money or ability, (of money) be enough, for; fall into (ruin); (of plants) tend to develop chiefly (seed); indulge inclination towards; ~ *upon*, (of thoughts etc.) be engrossed by, dwell on; encounter suddenly. 14. (with advs.) ~ *about*, bustle, hurry from one person etc. to another; play or wander without restraint; ~ *away*, flee, abscond, elope; (of horse) bolt; get clear away *from* competitors in race; ~ *away with*, carry off; accept (notion) hastily; consume (money etc.); (of horse etc.) bolt with; ~ *down*, (of clock etc.) stop for want of winding; (of health etc.) become enfeebled from overwork, poor feeding, etc.; knock down or collide with; overtake in pursuit; discover after search; disparage; ~ *in*, (of combatant) rush to close quarters; (Rugby footb.) carry ball over opponents' goal-line and touch it down; pay short visit *to*; (colloq.) arrest and take to prison; bring (new machinery) to proper condition by careful working; ~ *off*, flee; flow away; digress suddenly; write or recite fluently; produce on machine; drain (liquid) off; decide (race) after tie or trial heats; ~ *on*, be joined together (of written characters); continue in operation; elapse; speak volubly, talk incessantly; (print.) begin in same line as what precedes; ~ *out*, come to an end; exhaust one's stock *of*; escape from containing vessel; advance from block to hit ball in cricket; (of rope) pass or be paid out; jut out; come out of contest in specified position etc., complete required score etc.; complete (race); advance so as to project; put down wicket of (batsman, while running); exhaust one*self* by running; ~ *over*, overflow; recapitulate; review, glance over; ~ *through*, pierce with sword etc.; draw line through (written words); ~ *up*, grow quickly; rise in price; amount *to*; be runner-up; accumulate (number, sum, debt) quickly; force (rival bidder) to bid higher; force up (price etc.); erect (wall etc.) to great height or in unsubstantial or hurried way; add up (column of figures); (of aircraft) approach (target) preparatory to dropping bombs. ~ *n.* 1. Act or spell of running; short excursion or visit; (cricket) traversing of pitch by both batsmen without either's being put out, point scored thus or otherwise; *a* ~ *for one's money*, some enjoyment etc. in return for expenditure or effort; *on the* ~, fleeing; bustling about; *at a* ~, running; *with a* ~, rapidly, with a rapid fall. 2. Rhythmical motion; way things tend to move; direction. 3. (mus.) Rapid scale-wise passage. 4. Continuous stretch, spell, or course; distance travelled by a ship in a specific time; long series or succession; general demand; *in the long* ~: see LONG[1]; *a* ~ *on the bank*, sudden demand from many customers for immediate payment. 5. Common, general, average, or ordinary type or class; class or line of goods; batch or drove of animals born or reared together; shoal of fish in motion. 6. Regular track of some animals; enclosure for fowls etc.; range of pasture; trough for water to run in. 7. (chiefly U.S.) Small stream or water-course. 8. Part of ship's bottom narrowing towards stern. 9. (chiefly U.S.) Ladder in stocking etc. 10. Licence to make free use of; *the* ~ *of one's teeth*, free board. 11. ~*-back*, additional space at either end of tennis-court; ~*-down*, progressive reduction, esp. in the numbers of armed forces; ~*-in*, act of running in at football; ~*-off*, deciding race after dead heat; ~*-up*, race between greyhounds up to hare's first turn; (golf) low approach shot; flight (of aircraft) on even course preparatory to the dropping of bombs on the target.

rŭn'agāte *n.* Vagabond. [alteration of RENEGADE]

rŭn'cĭble *adj.* (Orig.) nonsense word used by Edward Lear; ~ *spoon,* (now) three-pronged pickle fork, curved like spoon, with one sharp edge.

rune (rōōn) *n.* 1. Letter or character of earliest Teutonic alphabet (most extensively used by Scandinavians and Anglo-Saxons),

F U Th O R C G W H N I J/A I/H P

[X] S T B E Ng D L M Œ A Æ Y Ea

RUNES WITH ROMAN EQUIVALENTS

dating from at least 2nd or 3rd c. A.D. and based on Roman or Greek letters modified to make them suitable for cutting on wood or stone; similar character of mysterious or magic significance; ~-*staff,* magic wand inscribed with runes; runic. 2. (Division of) Finnish poem, esp. one of the separate songs of the Kalevala.

rŭng *n.* Short stick attached at each end as rail, spoke, or cross-bar in chair etc., or esp. in ladder.

ru'nic (rōō-) *adj.* Of, in, marked with, runes; (of poetry etc.) such as might be written in runes, esp. ancient Scandinavian or Icelandic. ~ *n.* (print.) Display lettering with thick face and condensed form.

rŭn'lĕt[1] *n.* (archaic) Cask of varying size for wine etc.

rŭn'lĕt[2] *n.* Small stream.

rŭnn'able *adj.* Proper for the chase.

rŭnn'el *n.* Brook, rill; gutter.

rŭnn'er *n.* (esp.) 1. Messenger, scout, collector, or agent for bank etc.; tout; (hist., esp. *Bow-Street* ~) police officer. 2. Water-rail (*Rallus aquaticus*). 3. Revolving millstone. 4. (naut.) Rope rove through single block, with one end passed round tackle-block and other attached to hook. 5. Naked creeping stem thrown out from base of main stem of strawberry or

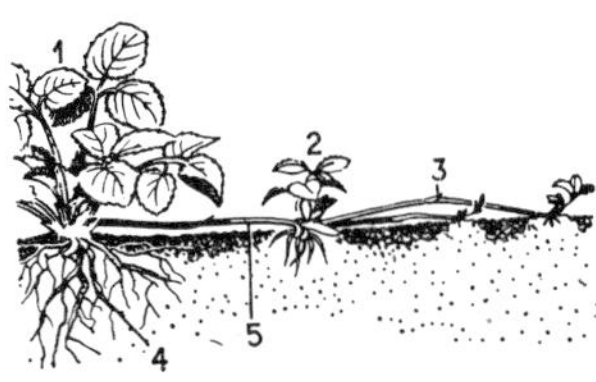

STRAWBERRY RUNNERS

1. Parent plant. 2. Young plant. 3. Scale leaf. 4. Roots 5. Runner

other plant, and itself taking root; any of various kinds of cultivated bean (esp. SCARLET ~) which twine round stakes for support. 6. Ring etc. that slides on rod, strap, etc. 7. Long piece of wood or metal, curved at end(s), supporting body of sledge etc.; blade of skate, skate with blade curving up at toe. 8. Groove or rod for thing to slide along; roller for moving heavy article. 9. Long narrow strip of (embroidered) cloth etc., placed along or across table etc. as ornament; long narrow rug or strip of carpet. 10. ~-*up,* competitor or team taking second place.

rŭnn'ĭng *n.* (esp.) *Make, take up, the* ~, take the lead, set the pace; *in, out of, the* ~, with good, no, chance of winning; ~-*board,* narrow gangway on either side of keel-boat (U.S.); footboard extending along either side of locomotive, motor-car, etc.; ~ *powers,* right granted by railway to another to run trains over its lines.

Rŭnn'ymēde. Meadow at Egham on S. bank of Thames near Windsor, famous for its association with Magna Carta, which was signed by King John on the meadow or on the island near by.

rŭnt *n.* 1. Ox or cow of small, esp. Scottish or Highland or Welsh breed. 2. Smallest animal of a litter; dwarfed or undersized person. 3. Large breed of domestic pigeon.

rupee' (rōō-) *n.* Monetary unit of India and Pakistan (= 100 paise) and of Ceylon (= 100 cents); *Burma* ~, KYAT. [Hind. *rupiyah,* f. Sansk. *rupya* wrought silver]

Ru'pert (rōō-), Prince, Count Palatine of the Rhine and Duke of Bavaria (1619–82). Son of Frederick V of Bohemia and Elizabeth, daughter of James I of England; general of the horse in army of Charles I in English Civil War; admiral in fleet of Charles II after Restoration.

rupiah (rōōpē'*a*) *n.* Principal monetary unit of Indonesia, = 100 sen. [see RUPEE]

rŭp'ture *n.* 1. Breach of harmonious relations, disagreement and parting. 2. (path.) Abdominal HERNIA. 3. Breaking, breach. ~ *v.* Burst, break (cell, vessel, membrane); sever (connexion etc.); affect with hernia; suffer rupture.

R.U.R. *abbrev.* Royal Ulster Rifles; 'Rossum's Universal Robots' (title of play by K. ČAPEK).

rur'al (roor-) *adj.* In, of, suggesting, the country; pastoral or agricultural. **rur'ally** *adv.* **rurăl'ity, ruralīzā'tion** *ns.* **rur'alīze** *v.*

rurĭdēcān'al (roor-) *adj.* Of rural dean (see DEAN) or deanery.

Rur'ĭk (rōōr-), (d. 879). Reputed founder of Russian empire, leader of a band of Scandinavians (VARANGIANS) who settled in Novgorod in 862.

Rurĭtān'ĭa (roor-). Imaginary kingdom in central Europe, scene of two novels by Anthony Hope, 'The Prisoner of Zenda' and 'Rupert of Hentzau'; hence, scene of romantic adventure and court intrigue in modern European setting. **Rurĭtān'ĭan** *adj.* & *n.*

ruse (rōōz) *n.* Stratagem, feint, trick.

rŭsh[1] *n.* Marsh or water-side plant of order *Juncaceae,* with naked slender tapering pith-filled stems (prop. leaves) formerly used for strewing floors and still for making chair bottoms and plaiting baskets etc.; *a* stem of this; (collect.) rushes as a material; *a* thing of no value; ~-*bearing,* annual northern-English festival on occasion of carrying rushes and garlands to strew floor and decorate walls of church; ~ *candle,* one made by dipping pith of a rush in tallow; *rush'light,* rush candle; feeble light or glimmer; ~ *ring,* ring made of rush(es) formerly used in (esp. mock) weddings. ~ *v.t.* Supply (chair-bottom), strew (floor) with rushes.

rŭsh[2] *v.* 1. Impel, drag, force, carry along, violently and rapidly; (mil.) take by sudden vehement assault; pass (obstacle etc.) with a rapid dash; swarm upon and take possession of (goldfield, platform at meeting, etc.); charge (customer) exorbitant price (colloq.). 2. Run precipitately, violently, or with great speed; go or resort without proper consideration; flow, fall, spread, roll, impetuously or fast; ~ *at,* charge. ~ *n.* Act of rushing, violent or tumultuous advance, spurt, charge, onslaught; (football) combined dash of several players with the ball; sudden migration of large numbers, esp. to new goldfield; strong run *on* or *for* some commodity; (pl., cinema) preliminary showings of film before cutting; ~-*hour,* that at which traffic is busiest.

rŭsk *n.* Piece of bread pulled or cut from loaf and rebaked.

Rŭs'kĭn, John (1819–1900). English writer on art and social subjects; ~ *ware,* kind of pottery with leadless glaze produced at Birmingham.

Rŭs'kĭn College. Residential college at Oxford for adult education, founded 1899 by Walter Vrooman, an American, orig. for men, later opened to women; named after John Ruskin.

Rŭss'ell[1], George William (1867–1935). Irish poet and painter, widely known under his pseudonym 'A.E.'.

Rŭss'ell[2], Lord John, first Earl Russell (1792–1878). English Whig statesman; introducer (1832) of Reform Bill into Parliament; prime minister 1846–52 and 1865–6.

Rŭss'ell[3], Sir William Howard (1821–1907). English war correspondent, special correspondent of 'The Times' in Crimean War.

rŭss'ĕt *n.* 1. (hist.) Coarse home-spun reddish-brown or grey cloth worn by peasants. 2. Reddish-brown. 3. Rough-skinned russet-coloured apple. ~ *adj.* 1. Reddish-brown. 2. (archaic) Rustic, homely, simple.

Rŭ′ssia (-sh*a*). Vast territory of E. Europe and N. Asia, until 1917 an empire under the autocratic rule of the tsars, since 1917 a federation of socialist republics (see SOVIET UNION); ~ *leather*, fine leather tanned with birch-, willow-, or oak-bark and rubbed with birch-oil (which imparts characteristic smell) as protection against insects. **Rŭ′ssian** *adj.* & *n.* (Native) of Russia, esp. of the Slavonic-speaking European Russia; (of) the three principal languages or dialects (*Great* ~, *Little* ~ or Ukrainian, and *White* ~), forming the eastern group of Slavonic languages; usu., Great Russian; ~ *ballet*, form of ballet developed at the beginning of the 20th c. at the Imperial School of Ballet at St. Petersburg from older Italian ballet; ~ *crash* = CRASH²; ~ *Revolution*, series of revolutionary movements in Russia in 1917, beginning with a revolt of workers, peasants, and soldiers in February (*February revolution*) and formation of a provisional government, and culminating in the Bolshevik revolution (*October revolution*), which led to the establishment of the Soviet Union; ~ *wolfhound*, = BORZOI.

Russian Soviet Federal Socialist Republic (abbrev. R.S.F.S.R.). The largest and most important of the constituent republics of the Soviet Union; it occupies more than three-quarters of the total area of the Union, contains more than half its population, and consists of 12 'autonomous' republics and numerous provinces; capital, Moscow.

Rŭss′o-Jăpanēse′ War. War between Russia and Japan, 1904–5, in which Russia was decisively defeated at sea and on land.

rŭst *n.* 1. Yellowish-brown coating formed on iron or steel by oxidation, esp. as effect of moisture, and gradually corroding the metal; similar coating on other metals; colour of this; (fig.) impaired state due to disuse or inactivity, inaction as deteriorating influence. 2. (Plant-disease with rust-coloured spots caused by) kinds of fungus; blight, brand. ~ *v.* Contract rust, undergo oxidation or blight; (of bracken etc.) become rust-coloured; lose quality or efficiency by disuse or inactivity; affect with rust, corrode. **rŭst′lĕss** *adj.*

rŭs′tĭc *adj.* Rural; having the appearance or manners of country-people, characteristic of peasants, unsophisticated, unpolished, uncouth, clownish; of rude or country workmanship; of untrimmed branches or rough timber; (archit.) with rough-hewn or roughened surface or with chamfered joints; ~ *capitals*: see ill. SCRIPT. **rŭs′tĭcally** *adv.* **rŭstĭ′cĭty** *n.*

rŭs′tĭcāte *v.* 1. Retire to, sojourn in, the country, lead a rural life; countrify. 2. Send down temporarily from university as punishment. 3. Mark (masonry) with sunk joints or roughened surface (ill. MASONRY). **rŭstĭcā′tion** *n.*

rŭs′tle (-sl) *v.* 1. Make sound (as) of dry leaves blown, rain pattering, or silk garments in motion; go with rustle; cause to rustle. 2. (U.S.) Get, acquire, pick up, by one's own exertions (also ~ *up*); steal (cattle or horses). ~ *n.* Sound of rustling. **rŭs′tler** *n.* (esp., U.S.) Cattle or horse thief.

rŭs′ty¹ *adj.* Rusted, affected with rust; of antiquated appearance; (of voice) croaking, creaking; stiff with age or disuse; antiquated, behind the times; impaired by neglect, in need of furbishing; rust-coloured; (of black clothes) discoloured by age. **rŭs′tĭly** *adv.* **rŭs′tĭness** *n.*

rŭs′ty² *adj.* Rancid (esp. of bacon). [obs. *resty*, f. OF *reste* left over, stale]

rŭt¹ *n.* Track sunk by passage of wheels; established mode of procedure, beaten track, groove. **rŭtt′y** *adj.* **rŭt** *v.t.* Mark with ruts (usu. in past part.).

rŭt² *n.* Periodic sexual excitement of male deer (also of goat, ram, etc.), heat. **rŭtt′ish** *adj.* **rŭt** *v.i.* Be affected with rut.

ruth¹ (rōōth) *n.* (archaic) Pity, compassion.

Ruth² (rōōth). (O.T.) A Moabite woman, heroine of the Book of Ruth; her widowed mother-in-law Naomi, a Jewess, returned to her own country, and Ruth being also a widow went with her; in Bethlehem Ruth gleaned corn in the fields of Boaz, who proved to be her husband's kinsman and married her.

Ruthēn′ĭa (rōō-). Province of central Europe, lying largely in the Carpathian Mountains, formerly easternmost province of Czechoslovakia, now incorporated in the Soviet Union. **Ruthēn′ĭan** *adj.* Of Ruthenia or the Ruthenians. ~ *n.* Little Russian or Ukrainian of former Austrian Galicia and other parts of Austria-Hungary, or modern Ruthenia; Ukrainian or Little Russian language of these people.

ruthēn′ĭum (rōō-) *n.* Rare metallic element of the platinum group, a hard, greyish-white metal; symbol Ru, at. no. 44, at. wt 101·07. [med. L *Ruthenia* Russia (from its discovery in the Urals)]

ruth′lĕss (rōō-) *adj.* Without pity. **ruth′lĕssly** *adv.* **ruthlĕssnĕss** *n.*

Rŭt′land. Midland county, the smallest county in England.

Ruy Lōp′ĕz (rōō′ĭ). Conventional opening in game of chess. [f. name of Spanish author of book on chess (1561)]

Ruysdael (rois′dahl), Jacob van (*c* 1628–82). Dutch landscape-painter and etcher.

R.V. *abbrev.* Revised Version (of Bible).

R.W.S. *abbrev.* Royal Society of Painters in Water-colours.

Rx, ~~Rx~~ *abbrevs.* Tens of rupees.

Ry *abbrev.* Railway.

rȳe¹ *n.* (Grain of) a cereal, *Secale cereale*, widely grown in N. Europe as food-crop, in England chiefly as fodder; (U.S.) rye-whisky; ~*-grass*, kinds of fodder grass (*Lolium*, esp. *L. perenne*, common rye, and *L. italicum*, Italian rye); ~*-whisky*, whisky made from rye.

Rȳe². Town and former harbour of Sussex, England, one of the CINQUE PORTS.

Rȳe House Plot. Plot (1683) to assassinate Charles II and his brother James, Duke of York, for alleged complicity in which Lord William Russell and Algernon Sidney were executed. [f. name of a house in Hertfordshire]

rȳ′ot *n.* Indian peasant.

R.Y.S. *abbrev.* Royal Yacht Squadron.

S

S, s (ĕs). 19th letter of modern English and 18th of ancient Roman alphabet, derived in form (through early Latin and Greek ϟ, Σ, Ƹ), from Phoenician W (Hebrew ש), representing *s* or *sh* in Semitic languages. In modern English the letter represents chiefly a voiceless sibilant (*s*) initially or when doubled in combination with a voiceless consonant, and the corresponding voiced sound (*z*) finally and medially between vowels. But there are many exceptions to this rule, and *s* frequently represents also the phonetic combinations (sy), (zy), as in *sure, vision* (in this dictionary written sh, zh).

s. *abbrev.* Second; shilling; singular; solidus; son.

S. *abbrev.* Saint; Signor; soprano; South(ern); Submarines.

S.A. *abbrev.* Salvation Army; sex appeal; South Africa; *Sturm Abteilung* (= storm detachment; Nazi party army).

S.A.A. *abbrev.* Small arms ammunition.

Saar (zar̄, s-). River of France and W. Germany, right-bank tributary of Moselle; Saarland. **Saar'lănd.** Mining and industrial district surrounding the Saar river, since 1957 a 'Land' of the Federal German Republic; capital, Saarbrücken.

Sāb'a. Ancient name (the biblical *Sheba*) of Yemen, S. Arabia. **Sab(a)e'an** (-bē-) *adj.* & *n.* (Language, native) of Saba.

Sāb'aism *n.* Star-worship. [Heb. *çaba* host]

Săb'āoth. *The Lord of Sabaoth* (in English N.T.), 'the Lord of Hosts'.

săbbatar̄'ian *n.* Sabbath-keeping Jew; Christian who regards Lord's Day as Sabbath, or whose opinion and practice with regard to observance of Sunday are strict. ~ *adj.* Of sabbatarian tenets. **săbbatar̄'ianism** *n.*

săbb'ath *n.* 1. (Also ~ *day*) 7th day of week (Saturday) as day of religious rest enjoined on Israelites; also, the Christian Sunday (Lord's Day), esp. as day of obligatory abstinence from work and play. 2. Period of rest. 3. *Witches'* ~: see WITCH[1]. [Heb. *shabbāth*, f. *shābath* to rest]

sabbăt'ical *adj.* Of, appropriate to, the sabbath; ~ *year*, 7th year in which Israelites were to cease tilling and release debtors and Israelite slaves; year of absence from duty for purposes of study and travel, granted to teachers in (esp. Amer.) universities etc. at certain intervals. **sabbăt'ically** *adv.*

săbb'atīze *v.* Keep the, have a, sabbath; make (day) into, keep as, a sabbath.

Sabĕll'ĭan[1] *adj.* & *n.* (Rom. hist.) (Member) of a group of tribes in ancient Italy including Sabines, Samnites, Campanians, etc.

Sabĕll'ĭan[2] *adj.* & *n.* (Holder) of doctrine of **Sabĕll'ius** (3rd c.), African heresiarch, that the Father, Son, and Holy Spirit are merely aspects of one Divine person.

Sāb'ian *adj.* & *n.* 1. (Member) of a sect classed in Koran with Moslems, Jews, and Christians, as believers in the true God. 2. (erron.) (Adherent) of SABAISM. [Arab. *çabi*, perh. f. Aramaic vb. = 'baptize']

Săb'īne *adj.* & *n.* (Member) of a tribe in ancient Italy, whose lands were in the neighbourhood of Rome, celebrated in legend as having taken up arms against the Romans to avenge the carrying off of their women by the Romans at a spectacle to which they had been invited.

sā'ble[1] *n.* Small dark-brown-furred arctic and subarctic carnivorous mammal allied to martens (*Martes zibellina*, European species; *M. americana*, American); its skin or fur.

sā'ble[2] *n.* 1. Black, as heraldic colour (ill. HERALDRY); (poet., rhet.) the colour black; (poet., rhet.; pl.) mourning garments. 2. ~ *antelope*, large stout-horned antelope of S. and E. Africa (*Hippotragus niger*), male of which is dark glossy brown with white belly. ~ *adj.* (poet., rhet.) Black, dusky; gloomy, dread; *his* ~ *Majesty*, the devil.

săb'ot (-ō) *n.* 1. Shoe hollowed out from one piece of wood, worn by French peasants etc.; wooden-soled shoe. 2. (mil.) Wooden disc riveted to spherical projectile to keep it in place in bore of piece; metal cup strapped to conical projectile to cause it to 'take' rifling of gun; (mech.) shoe or armature of pile, boring-rod, etc.

săb'otage (-ahzh, -ĭj) *n.* Deliberate destruction of machinery, damaging of plant, manufacture of faulty product, etc., by dissatisfied or disaffected workmen, or by enemy agents in war-time. ~ *v.t.* Commit sabotage on; (fig.) destroy, render useless. **săboteur** (-er̄') *n.* One who commits sabotage.

sā'bre (-ber) *n.* Cavalry sword with curved blade (ill. SWORD); implement for removing scum from molten glass; ~*-toothed lion, tiger*, large extinct feline mammal of several genera (e.g. *Smilodon*) with long sabre-shaped upper canines. ~ *v.t.* Cut down or wound with sabre.

să'bretache (-ertăsh) *n.* Flat leather bag worn suspended by long straps from the sword-belt as part of the full uniform of cavalry and artillery officers (ill. CAVALRY).

săc *n.* Bag-like membrane enclosing cavity in animal or vegetable organism; membranous envelope of hernia, cyst, tumour, etc.

săcc'adĭc *adj.* Jerky, twitching; ~ *movement*, (psychol.) sudden movement of eyes from one point of fixation to another, as in reading.

săcc'ate *adj.* Dilated into form of sac (bot.); encysted.

săcch'arāte (-k-) *n.* Salt of saccharic acid.

săcchă'rĭc (-k-) *adj.* (chem.) ~ *acid*, dibasic acid formed by oxidation of dextrose.

săccharĭf'erous (-k-) *adj.* Sugar-bearing.

săccharĭm'ėter (-k-) *n.* Instrument for determining the amount of sugar in a solution by polarized light.

săcch'arin(e) (-k-, -ēn) *n.* White, intensely sweet, crystalline substance got from toluene and used as a substitute for sugar, esp. in cases of diabetes. **săcch'arīne** *adj.* Sugary (also fig.); of, containing, like, sugar.

săcch'aroid (-k-) *adj.* (geol.) Granular like sugar. ~ *n.* Sugar-like substance.

săcch'arōse (-k-) *n.* Any one of a group of sugars having formula $C_{12}H_{22}O_{11}$.

săc'cĭfōrm (-ks-) *adj.* Sac-shaped.

săcc'ūle *n.* Small sac or cyst. **săcc'ūlar, săcc'ūlate, -ātėd** *adjs.* **săccūlā'tion** *n.*

săcerdōt'al *adj.* Of priest(s) or priesthood, priestly; (of doctrines etc.) ascribing sacrificial functions and supernatural power to ordained priests, claiming excessive authority for the priesthood. **săcerdōt'ally** *adv.* **săcerdōt'alĭsm, săcerdōt'alist** *ns.*

sā'chem (-tsh-) *n.* 1. Supreme chief of some American Indian tribes. 2. (U.S.) One of 12 high officials in Tammany Society.

săch'et (-shā) *n.* Small perfumed bag; (packet of) dry perfume for laying among clothes etc.

Săchs (-ks), Hans (1494–1576). German shoemaker of Nuremberg, one of the master singers (MEISTERSINGER); author of several plays.

săck[1] *n.* 1. Large, usu. oblong, bag of coarse flax, hemp, etc., usu. open at one end, and used for storing and conveying goods; sack with contents; amount (of corn, coal, flour, wool, etc.) usu. put in sack as unit of measure or weight; *give, get, the* ~, dismiss, be dismissed, from service (perh. f. Fr. phrase referring to giving of passport). 2. Woman's short loose dress of sack-like appearance; woman's loose-fitting straight coat; (also *sac, sacque*) woman's loose gown; voluminous train hanging loosely from shoulders of gown. 3. *sack'cloth*, coarse fabric of

SACK DRESS, *c* 1760

1. Flounce. 2. Petticoat. 3. Furbelow or falbala. 4. Turban

flax or hemp, sacking; (fig.) mourning or penitential garb (esp. in *sackcloth and ashes*); ~*-race*, race between competitors with lower part of body in sacks. **săck'ful** *n.* **săck** *v.t.* Put into sack(s); (colloq.) give the sack to, dismiss from service. **săck'ing** *n.* Closely woven material of hemp, jute, flax, etc., for sacks etc.

săck[2] *v.t.* (Of victorious army etc.) plunder, give over to plunder (city etc.). ~ *n.* Sacking of captured place.

săck[3] *n.* (hist.) Kinds of white wine formerly imported from Spain and the Canaries. [Fr. *vin sec* dry wine]

săck'but *n.* (mus.) Obsolete bass trumpet, precursor of the trombone, with slide like trombone's for altering pitch (in Dan. iii a mistranslation of Aramaic *sabbekā*, a stringed instrument).

sacque: see SACK[1] *n.*

sā'cral *adj.* (anat.) Of the sacrum.

săc'rament *n.* Religious ceremony or act regarded as 'outward and visible sign of inward and spiritual grace' (applied by the Eastern, pre-Reformation Western, and R.C. Churches to the 7 rites of baptism, confirmation, the Eucharist, penance, extreme unction, orders, and matrimony; by many Protestants restricted to baptism and the Eucharist); thing of mysterious and sacred significance, sacred influence, symbol, etc.; oath or solemn engagement taken; *the* (*Blessed* or *Holy*) ~, *the* ~ *of the altar*, the Eucharist; the consecrated elements, esp. the bread or Host.

săcramĕn'tal *adj.* Of (the nature of) a or the sacrament; attaching great importance to the sacraments. ~ *n.* Observance analogous to but not reckoned among the sacraments, e.g. use of holy water or sign of the cross. **săcramĕn'tally** *adv.* **săcramĕn'talism, săcramĕn'talist** *ns.*

săcramentār'ian *n.* 1. (hist.) Name given in 16th c. and afterwards to Zwinglians and Calvinists who repudiated the Lutheran doctrine of Consubstantiation and the doctrine of Transubstantiation and denied the Real Presence, holding that the bread and wine were only symbols of the body and blood of Christ. 2. One who holds definite views on the efficacy of the sacraments. ~ *adj.* Pertaining to a sacrament or the sacraments; pertaining to sacramentarians. **săcramentār'ianism** *n.*

Săcramĕn'tō. Capital of California, U.S.

sacrār'ium *n.* 1. (Rom. antiq.) Shrine; adytum of temple; place in house where Penates were kept. 2. Sanctuary, part of church within altar-rails. 3. (R.C. Ch.) Piscina.

sā'crėd *adj.* Consecrated, esteemed dear, *to* a deity; dedicated, reserved, appropriated, *to* some person or purpose; made holy by religious association, hallowed; safeguarded or required by religion, reverence, or tradition; indefeasible, inviolable, sacrosanct; ~ *poetry*, *music*, poetry, music, on religious themes; ~ *concert*, concert of sacred music. **sā'crėdly** *adv.* **sā'crėdnėss** *n.*

săc'rifice *n.* 1. Slaughter of animal or person, surrender of possession, as offering to a deity, (fig.) act of prayer, thanksgiving, or penitence as propitiation; what is thus slaughtered, surrendered, or done, victim, offering; (eccles.) the Crucifixion, the Eucharist as either a propitiatory offering of the body and blood of Christ or an act of thanksgiving. 2. Giving up of thing for the sake of another that is higher or more urgent; *make the supreme* ~, die for one's country; thing thus given up, loss thus entailed. ~ *v.* Offer (as) sacrifice (*to*); give up, treat as secondary or of inferior importance, devote *to*; resign oneself to parting with. **săcrifi'cial** (-shl) *adj.* **săcrifi'cially** *adv.*

săc'rilège *n.* Robbery or profanation of sacred building, outrage on consecrated person or thing, violation of what is sacred. **săcrilē'gious** (-jus; *or* -ĭj'us) *adj.* **săcrilē'giously** *adv.* [L *sacrilegus* one who steals sacred things (*sacer* holy, *legere* gather)]

sā'cring *n.* (archaic) Consecration of elements in the Mass; ordination and consecration of bishop, sovereign, etc.; ~*-bell*, bell rung at elevation of Host.

sā'crist *n.* Official keeping sacred vessels etc. of religious house or church.

săc'ristan *n.* Sexton of parish church; SACRIST.

săc'risty *n.* Repository for vestments, vessels, etc., of a church.

săc'rosănct *adj.* Secured by religious sanction against outrage, inviolable. **săcrosănc'tity** *n.*

sā'crum *n.* Composite triangular bone of ankylosed vertebrae forming back of pelvis (ill. PELVIS). **sā'cral** *adj.* [L *os sacrum* sacred bone (from sacrificial use)]

săd *adj.* 1. Sorrowful, mournful; showing or causing sorrow. 2. (contempt., usu. joc.) Shocking; deplorably bad; incorrigible. 3. (Of pastry, bread, etc.) heavy, doughy; (of colour) dull, neutral-tinted. **sădd'en** *v.* **sădd'ish** *adj.* **săd'ly** *adv.* **săd'nėss** *n.*

sădd'le *n.* 1. (*Illustration, p.* 727) Rider's seat placed on back of horse etc. (usu. concave-shaped, of leather, with side-flaps and girths and stirrups), or forming part of bicycle etc., or of some agricultural machines; part of shaft-horse's harness that bears shafts (ill. HARNESS); *in the* ~, mounted; (fig.) in office or control. 2. Saddle-shaped thing, e.g. ridge between two summits, support for cable or wire on top of suspension-bridge pier or telegraph-pole; joint *of* mutton or venison consisting of the two loins. 3. *sadd'leback*, (archit.) tower-roof with two opposite gables; saddle-backed hill; various birds and fishes (esp. grey or hooded crow); (*adj.*) saddle-backed; ~*-backed*, with upper outline concave, (archit.) having saddleback; ~*-bag*, one of pair of bags laid across horse, etc., behind saddle; kind of carpeting (in imitation of Eastern saddle-bags of camels) used in upholstering chairs etc.; ~*-bow*, arched front of saddle; ~*-cloth*, cloth laid on horse's back under saddle; ~*-horse*, horse for riding; ~*-tree*, frame of saddle; N. Amer. tulip-tree (*Liriodendron tulipifera*). ~ *v.t.* Put saddle on (horse etc.); burden (person) *with* task, responsibility, etc.; put (burden) (*up*)*on* person.

sădd'ler *n.* Maker of or dealer in saddles and other equipment for horses; (mil.) man in charge of saddlery of cavalry regiment. **sădd'lery** *n.* (*Illustration, p.* 727.)

Sădd'ūcee *n.* Member of one of the 3 sects (the others being the Pharisees and the Essenes) into which the Jews were divided in the time of Christ; acc. to the N.T. they denied the resurrection of the dead and the existence of angels and rejected the traditions of the elders. [Heb. *Çadduqi* prob. = descendant of Zadok]

Sade (sahd), Donatien Alphonse, Count (generally known as Marquis) de (1740–1814). French author, whose licentious writings have given his name to SADISM.

sadhu (sahd'ōō) *n.* Hindu holy man, sage, or ascetic. [Sansk. *sādhú* good]

săd'ism (*or* sah'-) *n.* The deriving of perverse sexual pleasure from the infliction of cruelty upon others. **săd'ist** *n.* **sadis'tic** *adj.* [f. Count D. A. de SADE]

Sadō'wa (-va). Village in Bohemia, scene of a battle (also called Königgrätz) in which the Austrians were defeated by the Prussians in 1866.

safar'i *n.* Hunting or other expedition, esp. on foot, in E. Africa etc. [Swahili, f. Arab. *safar* journey]

sāfe[1] *n.* Ventilated cupboard for provisions (also *meat-*~); fireproof and burglar-proof receptacle for valuables; ~*-deposit*, building containing a number of separate safes or strong-rooms, which can be hired for the deposit of valuables etc.

sāfe[2] *adj.* 1. Uninjured (pred. after *come*, *bring*, *keep*, etc.); secure, out of or not exposed to danger. 2. Affording security or not involving danger; *on the* ~ *side*, with margin of security against risks. 3. Debarred from escaping or doing harm. 4. Cautious and unenterprising; consistently moderate; that can be reckoned on, unfailing, certain *to* do or be; sure to become; ~ *cŏn'duct*, (document conveying) privilege granted by sovereign, commander, etc., of being protected from arrest or harm on particular occasion or in district; *safe'guard*, safe conduct; (usu.) proviso, stipulation, quality, or circumstance that tends to prevent some evil or protect; (*v.t.*) guard, protect (esp. rights, etc.) by precaution or stipulation; *safe'guarding*, protection of native products and manufactures against foreign imports; ~ *keeping*, custody. **sāfe'ly** (-flĭ) *adv.*

sāfe'ty (-ftĭ) *n.* Being safe, freedom from danger or risks; safeness, being sure or likely to bring no danger; (also *~-bolt, catch*), contrivance for locking gun-trigger, gun with this; (now rare; also *~-bicycle*) bicycle of usual low-saddled modern form with two wheels equal in size; *play for ~*, avoid risks in game etc.; ~ *belt*, strap securing occupant to seat esp. in aeroplane; ~ *curtain*, fireproof curtain in theatre cutting off auditorium from stage; ~ *film*, slow-burning film specially prepared for cinematographic work; *~-fuse*, fuse that can be ignited at a safe distance from the charge; *~-glass*, glass so made as to prevent splintering; *~-lamp*, miner's lamp so constructed as to prevent the flame from coming into direct contact with fire-damp and causing an explosion; ~ *man*, man engaged to guard a temporarily disused pit in readiness for the resumption of work; *~-match*, one igniting only on specially prepared surface; *~-pin*, pin bent back on itself so as to form a spring, with guard or sheath to cover point; *~-razor*, razor with guard to prevent blade from cutting deeply; *~-valve*, valve in steam-boiler opening automatically to relieve excessive pressure; (fig.) means of giving harmless vent to excitement etc.

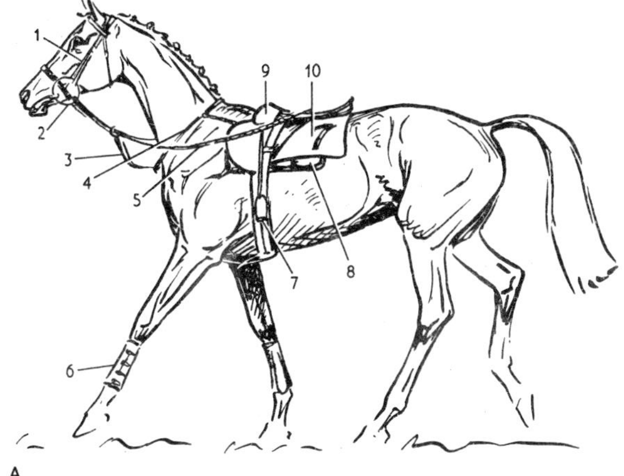

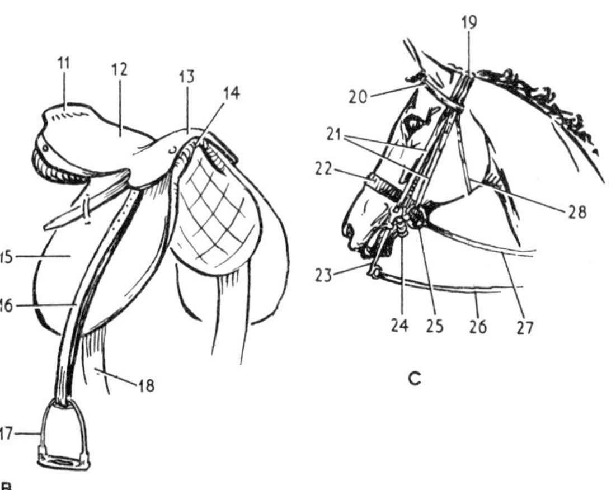

SADDLERY: A. RACING SADDLERY. B. HUNTING SADDLE (FACING RIGHT). C. DOUBLE BRIDLE

A. 1. Racing bridle. 2. Big ring snaffle. 3. Running martingale. 4. Neck strap. 5. Rein. 6. Gaiter. 7. Stirrup. 8. Weight cloth. 9. Racing saddle. 10. Saddle-cloth. B. 11. Cantle. 12. Seat. 13. Pommel. 14. Saddle-tree. 15. Flap. 16. Stirrup-leather. 17. Stirrup-iron. 18. Girth. C. 19. Head-stall. 20. Brow band. 21. Cheek-straps. 22. Nose band. 23. Curb. 24. Curb chain. 25. Snaffle. 26. Curb rein. 27. Snaffle rein. 28. Throat lash

săff'lower *n.* Thistle-like plant (*Carthamus tinctorius*) yielding red dye used in rouge etc.; dried petals of this; dye made from them.

săff'ron *n.* Orange-coloured stigmas of *Crocus sativus* (saffron crocus) used for colouring and flavouring confectionery, liquors, etc.; the plant itself; orange-yellow colour of saffron; *bastard ~*, the plant safflower; *~-cake*, cake flavoured with saffron; tablet of pressed saffron. ~ *adj.* Of saffron colour. ~ *v.t.* Colour with or like saffron.

săf'ranĭn *n.* (chem.) Yellow colouring-matter of saffron; synthetic orange-red dye-stuff.

săg *v.* Sink or subside under weight or pressure; hang sideways, be lopsided; have downward bulge or curve in middle, cause to curve thus; (commerc.) decline in price; (of ship) drift from course. ~ *n.* Amount that rope etc. sags, distance from middle of its curve to straight line between supports; sinking, subsidence; decline in price; (naut.) tendency to leeward.

sa'ga (sah-) *n.* Medieval Icelandic or Norwegian prose narrative, esp. one embodying history of Icelandic family or Norwegian king; (transf.) story of heroic achievement or adventure, long family chronicle. [ON, = 'narrative']

sagā'cious (-sh*us*) *adj.* Mentally penetrating, gifted with discernment, practically wise, acute-minded, shrewd; (of speech etc.) showing sagacity; (of animals) exceptionally intelligent, seeming to reason or deliberate. **sagā'ciously** *adv.* **sagă'cĭty** *n.*

săg'amōre *n.* = SACHEM (sense 1).

sāge[1] *n.* Aromatic herb (*Salvia officinalis*) with dull greyish-green leaves; its leaves used in cookery etc.; any plant of the genus *Salvia*; *~-brush*, various N. Amer. hoary-leaved shrubs (*Artemisia*), freq. covering large flat tracts in Western States; *Sagebrush State*, popular name of Nevada, U.S.; ~ *cheese*, cheese flavoured and mottled by addition of sage-infusion to the curd; *~-green*, greyish-green colour of sage leaves.

sāge² *adj.* Wise, discreet, judicious, having the wisdom of experience, of or indicating profound wisdom (freq. iron.); wise-looking, solemn-faced. **sāge'ly** (-jl-) *adv.* **sāge'nėss** *n.* **sāge** *n.* Profoundly wise man (freq. iron.), esp. any of the ancients traditionally reputed wisest of their time; *the seven* ~*s*: see SEVEN.

săgg'ar *n.* 1. Case of baked fireproof clay enclosing pottery while it is baked. 2. Case in which cast iron can be decarbonized and made malleable.

Sagĭtt'a. A northern constellation, the Arrow.

sagĭtt'al *adj.* (anat.) In the same plane as the sagittal suture (suture between parietal bones of skull; ill. HEAD), i.e. longitudinal and from front to back. **sagĭtt'ally** *adv.*

Săgĭttār'ĭus. A southern constellation, the Archer; the 9th sign of the zodiac (♐), which sun enters about 22nd Nov.

să'gĭttāte *adj.* (bot., zool.) Shaped like arrow-head.

sāg'ō *n.* Kinds of palm and cycad, esp. *Metroxylon*; kind of starch used in cookery for puddings etc., obtained from pith of these plants.

Sahār'a. The great desert of N. Africa; hence, any great arid tract (also fig.). **Sahār'an, Sahār'ĭc** *adjs.*

Sah'ĭb *n.* (fem. *mĕm'sahib*). 1. (India) European as spoken of or to by Indians; an honorific affix (as *Jones* ~, *Raja* ~). 2. (colloq.; *s*~) Gentleman.

saig'a (*or* sī-) *n.* Kind of antelope (*Saiga tartarica*) of Russian steppes.

sail¹ *n.* 1. Piece of canvas or other textile material extended on rigging to catch wind and propel vessel; (collect.) some or all of ship's sails; *take in* ~, (fig.) moderate one's ambitions; *full* ~, with all sail spread (lit. & fig.); *under* ~, with sails set. 2. (collect.) Ships; ship (esp. in *S*~ *ho!*, cry announcing that ship is in sight). 3. Wind-catching apparatus, now usu. set of boards, attached to arm of windmill; sail-fish's dorsal fin, tentacle of nautilus, float of Portuguese man-of-war; (also *wind-*~) funnel-shaped bag on ship's deck giving ventilation; ~*-arm*, arm of windmill; ~*-cloth*, canvas for sails; kind of coarse linen dress material; ~*-fish*, kinds with large dorsal fin, esp. basking shark. **sail'less** *adj.*

sail² *v.* (Of vessel or person on board) travel on water by use of sails or engine-power; start on voyage; (of bird etc.) glide in air;

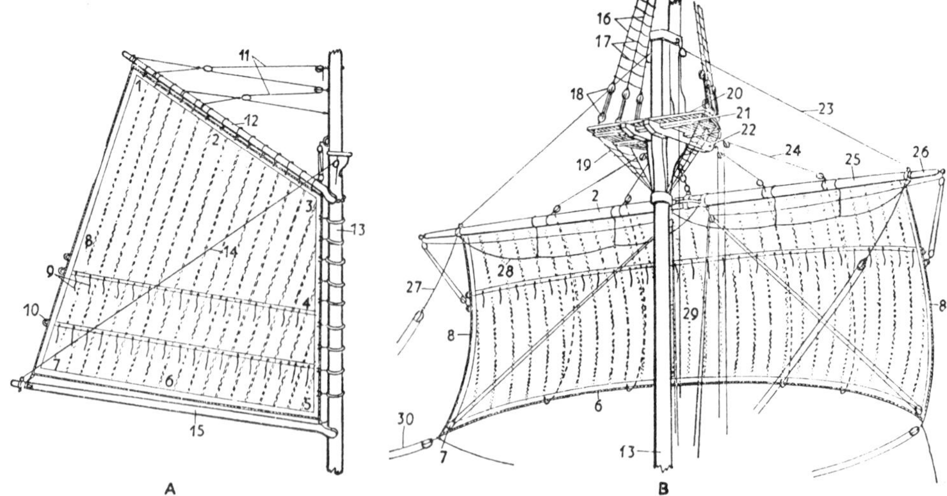

PARTS OF SAILS, SPARS, AND RIGGING. A. FORE-AND-AFT. B. SQUARE

A. 1. Peak. 2. Head. 3. Throat. 4. Luff. 5. Tack. 6. Foot. 7. Clew. 8. Leech. 9. Reef points. 10. Cringle. 11. Halyards. 12. Gaff. 13. Mast. 14. Topping lift. 15. Boom. B. 16. Topmast shrouds. 17. Ratlines. 18. Deadeyes. 19. Futtock shrouds. 20. Top. 21. Cross-trees. 22. Trestle-trees. 23. Lift. 24. Bunt-line. 25. Yard. 26. Yard-arm. 27. Brace. 28. Foot-rope. 29. Bunt. 30. Sheet

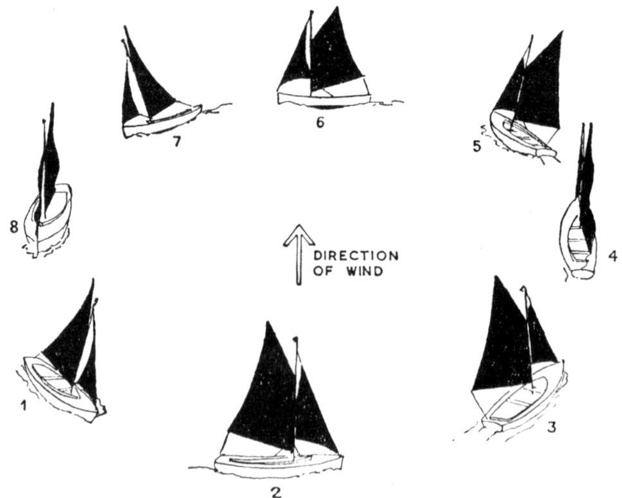

SAILING TERMS

1. Close-hauled on the starboard tack. 2. Reaching on the starboard tack. 3. Running on the starboard gybe. 4. Gybing for wearing. 5. Running on the port gybe. 6. Reaching on the port tack. 7. Close-hauled on the port tack. 8. Coming about

walk in stately manner; travel over or along, navigate, glide through (sea, sky, etc.); control navigation of (ship), set (toy boat) afloat; ~ *close to* or *near the wind*, sail nearly against it; (fig.) come near transgressing a law or moral principle; ~ *into*, (slang) inveigh against, rate, attack; *sailing orders*, instructions to captain of ship for departure, destination, etc.; *sailing-master*, officer navigating yacht; *sailing-ship*, *-vessel*, vessel propelled by sails, not engines. ~ *n.* Voyage or excursion in sailing-vessel; voyage of specified duration; *sailplane*, high performance glider.

sail'er *n.* Ship of specified sailing-power.

sail'or *n.* Seaman, mariner (esp. one below rank of officer); *good*, *bad*, ~, person not, very, liable to sea-sickness; ~ (*hat*), straw hat with flat usu. narrow brim and flat top, or with turned-up brim; ~*-man*, (vulg. and joc. for) sailor; ~*s' home*, institution for lodging sailors cheaply ashore; ~*'s knot*, knot used by sailors; kind of knot used in tying neck-tie, so that both ends hang down. **sail'orly** *adj.*

sain *v.t.* (archaic) Make sign of the cross on, bless, protect by divine power or enchantment.

sain'foin *n.* Low-growing perennial herb (*Onobrychis viciifolia*) with pinnate leaves and pink flowers, cultivated as fodder. [Fr. *sain* wholesome, *foin* hay]

saint (snt or sent when unstressed; abbrev. St., S., in pl. Sts., SS.) *adj.* Holy; canonized or officially recognized by the Church as having won by exceptional holiness a high place in heaven and veneration on earth (usu. as prefix to name of person or archangel as *St. Paul*, *St. Michael*; hence in names of churches and of towns called after their churches, and in Christian and family names, as *St. John*, pr. Sinjn, taken from patron saint etc.). ~ *n.* One of the blessed dead or other member of the company of heaven; canonized person; (bibl., archaic, and in some modern sects) one of God's chosen people, member of Christian Church or of some (esp. puritanical) branch of it; Mormon; person of great real or affected holiness; *patron* ~, saint selected as heavenly protector of person or place, esp. church, often named after him; ~*'s day*, Church festival in memory of a saint, freq. observed as holiday. **saint'ly** *adj.* **saint'liness** *n.* **saint** *v.t.* Canonize, admit to the calendar of saints; call or regard as a saint; *sainted*, worthy to be so regarded, of saintly life; hallowed, sacred.

St. An'drews (-ōōz). University town on E. coast of Scotland; seat of the Royal and Ancient Golf Club, the governing body of the game of golf.

St. Andrew's cross: see ANDREW.

St. Anne's Cŏll'ege. Women's college of the University of Oxford since 1952; founded 1879 as the *Society of Oxford Home Students*.

St. Anthony's cross, fire: see ANTHONY[1].

St. An'tony's Cŏll'ege. A college of the University of Oxford, founded 1948 with special provision for the admission of Frenchmen; endowed by Antonin Besse of Aden. [named after St. ANTHONY[1] of Egypt]

St. Bernard dog: see BERNARD[2].

St. Căth'arine's Cŏll'ege. College of the University of Cambridge, founded 1473.

St. Căth'erine's Cŏll'ege. A college of the University of Oxford since 1962; orig. *St. Catherine's Society*, est. 1868 for non-collegiate students.

Saint-Cyr (săṅ-sēr'). College for French army cadets, established 1806 near Versailles in the buildings of a former convent school founded by Louis XIV for young ladies of the nobility; the buildings were destroyed in the war of 1939–45 and the college is now at Coëtquidan in Brittany.

St. Dŭn'stan's. Organization for the care of British soldiers, sailors, and airmen blinded in war, founded 1915 by Sir Arthur Pearson.

Sainte-Beuve (săṅt bẽrv'), Charles Augustin (1804–69). French literary critic.

St. Edm. & Ipswich. *abbrev.* (Bishop) of St. Edmundsbury and Ipswich (replacing surname in his signature).

St. Ed'mund Hall. College of the University of Oxford, founded 1269 and named after St. Edmund (Rich), archbishop of Canterbury 1234–40.

St. El'mō's fire: see ELMO

St. George's cross, day: see GEORGE[1].

St. Helē'na. Island in the S. Atlantic, in British possession, the place of Napoleon's exile (1815–21).

St. Hil'da's Cŏll'ege. Women's college of the University of Oxford, founded 1893 and named after St. Hilda, 7th-c. abbess of Whitby.

St. Hugh's Cŏll'ege (hūz). Women's college of the University of Oxford, founded 1886.

St. James's (jām'zĭz). Old Tudor palace of the kings of England in London, built by Henry VIII; *Court of St. James's*, official title of the British court, to which ambassadors from foreign countries are accredited.

St. Jŏhn's Cŏll'ege. 1. A college of the University of Cambridge, founded 1511 in honour of St. John the Evangelist by the Lady Margaret, Countess of Richmond and Derby, mother of Henry VII. 2. *St. John Baptist College*, a college of the University of Oxford, founded 1555 by Sir Thomas White, a London alderman.

St. John's wort: see JOHN[1].

Saint-Just (săṅ zhūst'), Louis Antoine Léon (1767–94). French revolutionary.

St. Kil'da. Island of the Outer Hebrides, Scotland.

St. Kitts. One of the Leeward Islands, W. Indies.

St. Lawrence (lŏ'rens). River of N. America, flowing from Lake Ontario to the Atlantic.

St. Leger (lĕj'-). The annual horse-race for 3-year-old colts and fillies, held in September at Doncaster; instituted by Lt-Gen. St. Leger in 1776.

St. Louis. Louis IX of France: see LOUIS[2].

St. Lucia (lūsh'*a*). Largest of the Windward Islands.

St. Luke's summer: see LUKE.

St. Martin's summer: see MARTIN[2].

St. Paul. Capital of Minnesota, U.S.

St. Paul's. Cathedral church of the bishop of London, in the City; designed by Sir Christopher Wren and built 1675–1710 on the site of a medieval church (*Old* ~) destroyed in the Great Fire.

St. Pēt'er's. The basilica of St. Peter adjoining the Vatican palace in Rome, built during the years 1506–1626 from plans drawn by Bramante and adapted by Michelangelo.

St. Pēt'ersbûrg (-z-). Former name of LENINGRAD.

St. Pēt'er's Cŏll'ege. College of the University of Oxford, founded 1929 as *St. Peter's Hall*.

Saint-Pierre (săṅ-pyār'), Jacques Henri Bernardin de (1737–1814). French author of the romantic novel 'Paul et Virginie'.

Saint-Saëns (săṅ-sahṅ), Charles Camille (1835–1921). French musical composer, famous for his symphonic poems and the opera 'Samson and Delilah'.

Saint-Simon[1] (săṅ-sēmawṅ'), Claude Henri, Comte de (1760–1825). French socialist; advocated the State control of property and division of profits among the workers according to the value of their work. **Saint-Sim'onism** *n.*

Saint-Simon[2] (săṅ-sēmawṅ'), Louis, Duc de (1675–1755). French writer of memoirs of the reign of Louis XIV.

St. Sophī'a. Principal church of Constantinople; built by Emperor Justinian (532–7); converted into a mosque after the capture of Constantinople by the Turks (1453).

St. Stephen's (-ēv'nz). The House of Commons; so called from the ancient chapel of St. Stephen, Westminster, in which the House used to sit.

St. Swithin's day: see SWITHIN.

St. Valentine's day: see VALENTINE[2].

St. Vĭn'cent. One of the Windward Islands.

St. Vitus's dance: see VITUS.

Sais (sā'ĭs). Ancient capital of Lower Egypt, in the Nile delta. **Sāĭt'ĭc** *adj.* Of Sais; ~ *dynasties*, 26th–30th of the Egyptian kings.

saithe (-ādh) *n.* = COAL-fish.

sāke *n.* *For the ~ of, for* (one's, a thing's) ~, out of consideration for, in the interest of; because of, owing to; in order to please, honour, get, or keep; *for goodness'*, *heaven's*, ~, form of entreaty or exclamation; *for old sake's, time's*, ~, in memory of old days.

sakê (săk'ā) *n.* Japanese fermented liquor made from rice.

sāk'er *n.* 1. Large falcon (*Falco sacer*) used in hawking, esp. the female, which is larger than the male. 2. (hist.) Old form of cannon.

Sakyamūn'ĭ (sah-). 'Sage of the Sakyas', a name of the BUDDHA.

sal (sahl), **saul** *ns.* Indian timber-tree (*Shorea robusta*), yielding resin.

salaam' (-ahm) *n.* Oriental salutation 'Peace'; Indian obeisance accompanying this, low bow of head and body with right palm on forehead. ~ *v.* Make salaam (to). [Arab. *salam*]

săl'able, săl'eable (-labl) *adj.* Fit for sale; finding purchasers. **săl(e)abĭl'ĭty** *n.*

salā'cious (-shus) *adj.* Lustful, lecherous; (of literature) dealing with or suggestive of lewdness. **salā'ciously** *adv.* **salā'ciousnėss, sală'cĭty** *ns.*

săl'ad *n.* Cold dish of vegetables, raw or cooked, usu. served with or including hard-boiled egg, fish, meat, etc.; vegetable (e.g. lettuce, endive) suitable for eating raw in salads; *~-days*, inexperienced youth; *~-dressing*, mixture of oil, vinegar, etc., used for seasoning salad; *~-oil*, olive or other vegetable oil used for dressing salads.

Săl'adĭn (1137–1193). Sultan of Egypt, who invaded Palestine and captured Jerusalem.

Sălamănc'a. Province of W. Spain; capital of this province, scene of a battle (1812) in which the French were defeated by Wellington.

săl'amănder *n.* 1. Lizard-like animal supposed to live in fire; figure of this used as emblem; person who can endure great heat; a spirit supposed to live in fire. 2. (zool.) Tailed urodele amphibian,

SALAMANDER

related to newts, of family *Salamandridae*. 3. (hist.) Red-hot iron or poker used for firing gunpowder etc. 4. Hot iron plate used for browning top of pudding etc.

sălamăn'drĭan, sălamăn'drĭne *adjs.* **sălamăn'droid** *adj.* & *n.*

sala'mė, -ĭ (-lah-) *n.* Italian highly seasoned sausage, freq. flavoured with garlic.

Săl'amĭs. Island off SW. coast of Attica, near the Piraeus, scene of a naval battle in 480 B.C. in which the Persian fleet under Xerxes was defeated by the Greeks.

săl-ammōn'ĭăc *n.* Ammonium chloride (NH_4Cl), a white crystalline solid with characteristic saline taste, used medicinally and in primary electric cells.

salăr'ĭat *n.* Salaried class.

săl'ary *n.* Fixed periodical payment made to person doing other than manual or mechanical work, which is remunerated by *wages*. ~ *v.t.* (chiefly in past part.) Pay salary to. [L *salarium*, orig. soldier's salt-money, f. *sal* salt]

sāle *n.* Exchange of a commodity for money or other valuable consideration, selling; amount sold; public auction; rapid disposal at reduced prices of (part of) shop's stock at end of season etc.; charity bazaar; *on, for*, ~, offered for purchase; *~-ring*, ring of buyers at auction; *sales'man, sales'woman*, person engaged in selling goods in shop, etc., or as middleman between producer and retailer; *salesmanship*, skill in selling; *sales resistance*, (orig. U.S.) opposition or apathy of the prospective customer regarded as requiring to be overcome by salesmanship.

Săl'ĕm. A place mentioned in Gen. xiv. 18 as the seat of the kingdom of Melchizedek, doubtfully identified with Jerusalem; hence, a Nonconformist chapel.

săl'ėp *n.* Nutritive meal, starch, or jelly, from dried tubers of orchidaceous plants, esp. of genus *Orchis*. [Arab. *tha'leb*]

Sales (sālz, sahlz), St. Francis de (1567–1622). French R.C. bishop of Geneva. **Sălē'sian** (-zhn) *adj.* & *n.* (Member) of an order named after St. Francis de Sales.

Săl'ĭan[1] *adj.* (Rom. religion) of the Salii or priests of Mars.

Săl'ĭan[2] *adj.* & *n.* (Member) of Frankish tribe on the lower Rhine from which the Merovingians were descended.

Săl'ĭc, Sălique' (-ēk) *adjs.* Of, pertaining to, the Salian Franks; *Salic Law*, code of law of the Salian Franks which contains a passage to the effect that a woman can have no portion of the inheritance of the 'Salian land'; the alleged fundamental law of the French monarchy excluding females from dynastic succession.

săl'ĭcėt *n.* Organ-stop one octave higher than SALICIONAL.

săl'ĭcĭn *n.* Bitter crystalline substance got from willow-bark etc. and used medicinally.

salĭ'cional (-shon-) *n.* Organ-stop of soft reedy tone like willow-pipe.

săl'ĭcȳl *n.* (chem.) Radical of salicylic acid. **sălĭcȳl'ĭc** *adj.* ~ *acid*, hydroxy-benzoic acid, colourless crystalline substance orig. obtained from salicin but now made synthetically, used as antiseptic and in treatment of rheumatism etc.; its acetyl derivative is aspirin. **salĭ'cȳlate** *n.* Salt of salicylic acid.

săl'ĭent *adj.* 1. Leaping or dancing (pedantic, joc.); (of water etc., poet.) jetting forth. 2. (Of angle, esp. in fortification) pointing outwards. 3. Jutting out; prominent, conspicuous, most noticeable. **săl'ĭently** *adv.* **săl'ĭence, săl'ĭency** *ns.* **săl'ĭent** *n.* Salient angle or part in fortification; projecting section of line of offence or defence.

Salieri (sălyăr'ĭ), Antonio (1750–1825). Italian musical composer.

salĭf'erous *adj.* (geol.) (Of stratum) containing much salt.

săl'ĭne *adj.* (Of natural waters, springs, etc.) impregnated with salt or salts; (of taste) salt; of chemical salts, of the nature of a salt; (of medicines) containing salt(s) of alkaline metals or magnesium. ~ *n.* Salt lake, spring, marsh, etc.; salt-pan, salt-works; saline substance; saline purge; *physiological* ~, solution of sodium chloride approx. equivalent to salt concentration of body fluids in mammals. **salĭn'ĭty** *n.*

Salique: see SALIC.

Salisbury[1] (sawlz'berĭ). Cathedral city of Wiltshire, England.

Salisbury[2] (sawlz'berĭ), Robert Arthur Talbot Gascoyne Cecil, 3rd Marquis of (1830–1903). English Conservative statesman; prime minister 1885–6, 1886–92, 1895–1902.

Salisbury[3] (sawlz'berĭ). Capital of Southern Rhodesia and federal capital of the Federation of Rhodesia and Nyasaland.

salīv'a *n.* Colourless, normally alkaline, liquid, the mixed secretion of salivary glands and mucous glands of the mouth, which mixes with food in mastication; spittle. **săl'ĭvary** *adj.* Secreting or conveying, of, existing in, saliva; ~ *gland*: see ill. GLAND.

săl'ĭvāte *v.* Produce unusual secretion of saliva in (person), usu. with mercury; secrete or discharge saliva, esp. in excess. **sălĭvā'tion** *n.*

săl'enders *n.pl.* Dry eruption inside hock of horse's leg (cf. MALLENDERS, of knee).

săll'ėt *n.* In medieval armour, light globular head-piece without crest and with lower part curving outwards behind (ill. ARMOUR).

săll'ow[1] (-ō) *n.* Willow-tree, esp. of low-growing or shrubby kinds; a shoot, the wood, of this. **săll'owy** (-ōĭ) *adj.*

săll'ow[2] (-ō) *adj.* (Of skin or complexion) of sickly yellow or yellowish-brown colour; having such skin. ~ *n.* Sallow hue. ~ *v.*

Make, grow, sallow. **săll'owish** (-ōĭ-) *adj.* **săll'owness** *n.*

Săll'ust. Gaius Sallustius Crispus (86–34 B.C.), Roman historian; accompanied Caesar in his African war and became governor of Numidia.

săll'y[1] *n.* 1. Rush (*out*) from besieged place upon enemy, sortie; a going forth, excursion; *~-port*, opening in fortified place for making sallies from. 2. Sudden start into activity, outburst; escapade (rare); outburst, flash (esp. *of* wit); witticism, piece of banter, lively remark. 3. Projection, prominence (archit., carpentry, etc.). ~ *v.i.* Make sally (usu. *out*); go *forth* or *out* on journey, for a walk, etc.; issue, come out, suddenly (rare).

săll'y[2] *n.* First movement of bell when set for ringing, bell's position when set; part of bell-rope prepared with inwoven wool for holding.

Săll'y[3]**.** Familiar for *Sarah*; *Aunt ~*: see AUNT; ~ *Lunn*, kind of sweet light tea-cake served hot (perhaps f. name of a girl hawking them at Bath *c* 1800).

sălmagŭn'dĭ *n.* Dish of chopped meat, eggs, anchovies, onions, etc., with oil and condiments; general mixture, miscellaneous collection. [Fr. *salmigondis*]

săl'mĭ *n.* Ragout, esp. of game-birds, partly roasted and then stewed with wine or sauce. [Fr., prob. short for prec.]

salm'on (săm-) *n.* Large silver-scaled pink-fleshed fish (*Salmo*, esp. *S. salar*) which ascends rivers to spawn, much prized for food and sport; various other fishes (esp. *Oncorhynchus*) of same family, or resembling salmon in some way; *~-ladder, -leap, -pass, -stair*, series of steps or other arrangement for allowing salmon to pass dam and ascend stream; *~-pink*, (of) the orange-pink colour of salmon-flesh; ~ *trout*, sea-trout (*Salmo trutta* of northern European rivers); various other N. Amer. or Australian fishes. ~ *adj.* Salmon-pink.

Sălmonĕll'a *n.* Large group of micro-organisms, members of which are responsible for many forms of enteritis (e.g. food-poisoning, typhoid and paratyphoid fevers) and hog cholera. [D. E. *Salmon* (1850–1914), Amer. pathologist]

săl'monĭd *adj.* & *n.* (zool.) (Fish) of the family *Salmonidae* (salmon, trout, etc.).

Salōm'ē. (N.T.) Stepdaughter of Herod Antipas; she danced before him, and at the bidding of her mother, Herodias, she asked for the head of John the Baptist in a charger (i.e. a dish) as a reward; see Matt. xiv.

Sălomŏn'ĭc, Sălomōn'ĭan *adjs.* Of, as of, Solomon.

salon (săl'awn) *n.* Reception-room in continental, esp. French, great house; (reunion of notabilities in) reception-room of (esp. Parisian) lady of fashion; *the S~*, annual exhibition of living artists' pictures in Paris; ~ *music*, light music for drawing-room.

Salŏn'ĭka (*or* sălonēk'*a*, -ēk'*a*). *Thessaloniki* (the ancient THESSALONICA), a seaport in NE. Greece, capital of Macedonia; ~ *campaign*, in war of 1914–18, campaign by French and British in support of Serbia, during which they occupied Salonika (Oct. 1915); they maintained a huge fortified camp there until the end of the war.

salōōn' *n.* 1. Hall or large room, esp. in hotel or place of public resort, fit for assemblies, exhibitions, etc. 2. Large cabin for first-class or for all passengers on ship; cabin for passengers in large aircraft. 3. (also *~-car, ~-carriage*) luxurious railway carriage without compartments furnished as drawing-room etc. (also *sleeping-, dining-~*). 4. Public room(s) or gallery for specified purpose (*billiard-, dancing-, shaving-, shooting-~*, etc.). 5. (U.S.) Drinking-bar. 6. ~ *bar*, first-class bar in English public-house; ~ *car*, motor-car with closed body and no partition behind driver (ill. MOTOR); ~ *deck*, deck reserved for saloon passengers; *~-keeper*, keeper of saloon bar; ~ *pistol, rifle*, one adapted for short-range practice in shooting-saloon.

salōōp' *n.* = SALEP; hot drink of salep or sassafras formerly sold as substitute for coffee at London street-stalls.

Săl'op. Shropshire. **Salōp'ĭan** *adj.* & *n.* 1. (Native) of Shropshire. 2. (Member) of Shrewsbury School. [AF *Sloppesberie* Shrewsbury]

sălpĭglŏss'ĭs *n.* Showy-flowered herbaceous garden-plant allied to petunia, orig. from Chile. [Gk *salpigx* trumpet, *glōssa* tongue]

săl'sĭfy *n.* European biennial composite plant (*Tragopogon porrifolius*) with long cylindrical fleshy roots eaten as vegetable, purple goat's-beard.

salt (sŏlt, sawlt) *n.* 1. (also *common ~*) Sodium chloride, NaCl, a substance with characteristic taste, very abundant in nature (in the sea, and in crystalline form); used as a condiment, as a preservative of food, and in many industrial processes; *rock-~*, impure brownish salt found in salt-mines; *white ~*, this refined for household use; *table ~*, finely powdered salt for table use; *eat* person's **~,** be his guest or dependant; *take ~ with*, be guest of; *take with a grain of ~*, accept (statement etc.) with reserve; *worth one's ~*, efficient, useful; *the ~ of the earth*, people for whose existence the world is better, moral *élite* (see Matt. v. 13). 2. Vessel for table salt, salt-cellar (now chiefly in trade use; and hist. in *above the ~*, seated with family and their equals, and *below the ~*, among servants and dependants). 3. Sting, piquancy, pungency, wit. 4. (chem.) Substance formed from an acid when all or part of its hydrogen is replaced by a metal or metallic radical. 5. (old chem.) A solid soluble non-inflammable substance (obs. exc. in some compound

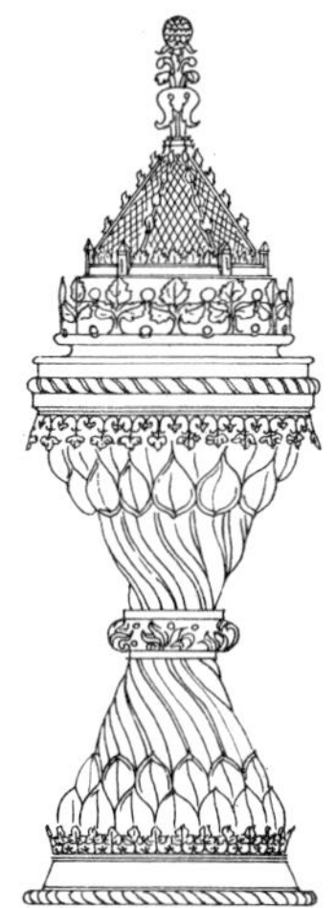

CEREMONIAL SALT

names as *~s of lemon, Glauber's ~*, etc.). 6. (also ~ *bottom, ~-marsh, salting*) Marsh overflowed by sea, freq. used as pasture or for collecting water for salt-making. 7. (pl.) Exceptional rush of sea-water up river. 8. Experienced sailor (esp. *old ~*). 9. *salt'bush*, various plants of genus *Atriplex*; *~-cat*, mass of salt mixed with gravel, cummin-seed, urine, etc., to attract pigeons and keep them at home; *~-cellar*, vessel holding salt for table use; (colloq.) one of hollows at base of neck; *~-glaze*, glaze made by throwing salt on to stoneware while in furnace; *~-grass*, (U.S.) grass growing in salt meadows; pasture-grass of arid plains of western States; *~-lick*, place where animals collect to lick earth impregnated with salt; *~-marsh*, see 6 above; ~ *meadow*, (chiefly U.S.) meadow liable to be flooded with salt water; *~-mine*, mine yielding rock-salt; *~-pan*, depression near sea, vessel, used for getting salt by evaporation; *~-spoon*, spoon usu. with short handle and roundish deep bowl for helping salt; *salt'wort*, kinds of maritime and salt-marsh plants (esp. *Salsola Kali*, prickly saltwort, and other species of *Salsola*). ~ *adj.* Impregnated with, containing, tasting of, cured or preserved or seasoned with, salt; (of plants) growing in sea or salt-marshes; (of tears, grief, etc.)

bitter, afflicting; (of wit etc.) pungent (rare); ~ *horse*, (naut. slang) salt beef; ~ *water*, sea-water; tears; ~*-water*, of, living in, the sea. **sal'ty** *adj.* **salt'iness, salt'ness** *ns.* **salt** *v.t.* 1. Cure or preserve with salt or brine; sprinkle with salt; make salt, season; ~ *away*, *down*, put by, store away (money etc.). 2. (usu. in past part.) Render immune to disease etc. by inoculation or habituation. 3. Make (mine etc.) appear to be paying one by fraudulently introducing rich ore etc.

sălta'tion *n.* Leaping, dancing, a jump; sudden transition or movement.

salt'er (sŏl-, sawl-) *n.* Manufacturer of, dealer in, salt; DRY-salter; workman at salt-works; person who salts fish etc.

salt'ern (sŏl-, sawl-) *n.* Salt-works; set of pools for natural evaporation of sea-water.

săl'tigrāde *adj.* (zool.) Moving by jumping.

săltĭmbăncō *n.* Mountebank, quack.

salting *n.* See SALT *n.* 6.

săl'tire *n.* (her.) Ordinary in form of St. Andrew's cross (X), dividing shield etc. into 4 compartments (ill. HERALDRY).

Salt Lake (City) (sŏlt). Capital of Utah, U.S.; orig. a Mormon settlement (1847).

saltpetre (sŏltpēt'er, sawl-) *n.* Nitre, potassium nitrate, KNO_3, white crystalline salty substance used as constituent of gunpowder, in preserving meat etc.; *Chili* or *cubic* ~, sodium nitrate, $NaNO_3$. [prob. f. L *sal petrae* salt of stone, because it occurs as an incrustation on stones]

salub'rious (-ōō- *or* -ū-) *adj.* Healthy (chiefly of air, climate, etc.). **salub'riously** *adv.* **salub'rity** *n.*

saluk'i (-ōō-) *n.* Arabian gazelle-hound.

săl'ūtary *adj.* Producing good effect, beneficial.

sălūtā'tion *n.* (Use of) words spoken or written to convey interest in another's health etc., pleasure at sight of or communication with him, or courteous recognition of his arrival or departure; greeting.

salute' (-ōōt, -ūt) *v.* Make salutation to, greet; greet with gesture conventionally expressive of respect or courteous recognition; (rare) hail, greet, as (king etc.); (mil., nav., etc.) pay respect to superior by prescribed movement of body, (esp. of hand to forehead); honour by discharge of artillery, lowering of flags, etc.; (archaic) kiss, greet with kiss; become perceptible to (eye, ear, etc.). ~ *n.* Gesture expressing respect, homage, or courteous recognition; (mil., nav., etc.) prescribed movement or position of body or weapons, use of flag(s), discharge of gun(s) in sign of respect; (fencing) formal performance of certain guards, etc., by fencers before engaging; kiss, prop. as greeting.

Sălvădōr'. Republic of Central America, on the Pacific coast; capital, San Salvador.

săl'vage (-ij) *n.* (Payment made or due for) saving of a ship or its cargo from loss by wreck or capture; rescue of property from fire etc.; saving and utilization of waste material of all kinds; property salvaged. ~ *v.t.* Make salvage of, save from wreck, fire, etc.

săl'varsăn *n.* Organic compound of arsenic (also called 606) used in treatment of syphilis; superseded by *neo-*~ (called 914).

sălvā'tion *n.* 1. Saving of the soul; deliverance from sin and its consequences, and admission to heaven, brought about by the merits of Christ's death. 2. Preservation from loss, calamity, etc.; thing that preserves from these.

Sălvā'tion Arm'y. Religious missionary body founded by the Rev. William (afterwards known as 'General') Booth in 1878 and organized on a quasi-military basis; the organization engages in evangelical and charitable work among the destitute throughout the world.

sălvā'tionism (-sho-) *n.* Doctrines, principles, of the SALVATION ARMY. **sălvā'tionist** *n.*

Săłva'tor Rōs'a (-vah-, -za) (1615–73). Italian landscape painter and etcher.

sălve[1] (*or* sahv) *n.* Healing ointment for sores or wounds; mixture of tar and grease for smearing sheep; something that soothes wounded feelings or uneasy conscience. ~ *v.t.* Anoint (wound etc.); smear (sheep); soothe (pride, self-love, conscience, etc.).

sălve[2] *v.t.* Save (ship, cargo) from loss at sea or (property) from fire etc.

săl'vē[3] *n.* (Also ~ *regina*) R.C. antiphon beginning with *Salve*, recited after Divine Office from Trinity Sunday to Advent; music for this. [L, = 'hail']

săl'ver *n.* Tray of precious or other metal for handing refreshments or presenting letters, visiting-cards, etc. [f. Fr. *salve* tray for presenting certain things to king, f. Span. *salva* assaying of food (*salvo* safe)]

SILVER SALVER

săl'via *n.* (bot.) (Genus of) plants of the sage family, of which *S. officinalis* is the common garden sage; flower of sage family cultivated for its bright-blue or scarlet colour.

săl'vō[1] *n.* (pl. *-s*). Saving clause, reservation; tacit reservation, quibbling evasion, bad excuse; expedient for saving (reputation) or soothing (pride, conscience).

săl'vō[2] *n.* (pl. *-es*, *-s*). Simultaneous discharge of cannon or other fire-arms esp. as salute, or in sea-fight; number of bombs or parachutists released from an aircraft at one time (as opp. to STICK *n.* 3); round or volley of applause.

săl volăt'ilė *n.* Alcoholic solution of ammonium carbonate flavoured with the oils of lemon and nutmeg and used as a restorative in faintness etc. [mod. L, = 'volatile salt']

săl'vor *n.* Person, ship, making or assisting in salvage.

Sălz'bŭrg (-lts-). Town in Austria where a summer festival of music and drama has been held annually, except in war-time, since 1920.

Săm. Familiar for *Samuel*; *stand* ~ (slang) pay for everyone present, esp. for drinks; *Uncle* ~: see UNCLE.

Sam. *abbrev.* Samuel (O.T.).

samār'a *n.* Winged one-seeded indehiscent fruit, single (as in ash) or double (as in sycamore) (ill. FRUIT).

Sămarcănd', -k(h)and. City of Uzbekistan, U.S.S.R.; TAMBURLAINE's capital.

Samār'ia. District of Palestine between the Jordan and the Mediterranean; its capital, former holy city of the Samaritans.

Samă'ritan *adj.* & *n.* (Inhabitant, language) of ancient Samaria; *a good* ~, person always ready to help the unfortunate (with ref. to Luke x. 33 etc.). **Samă'ritanism** *n.* Charitableness, charity.

samār'ium *n.* Element of rare-earth group, symbol Sm, at. no. 62, at. wt 150·35.

săm'ba *n.* Brazilian native dance; ballroom dance imitative of this.

săm'bō *n.* 1. Half-breed, esp. of negro and Indian or European blood. 2. *Sambo*, (nickname for) Negro.

Săm Browne. Leather belt with a supporting strap passing over the right shoulder, worn by officers in the British Army. [f. name of Gen. Sir *Sam*uel J. *Browne*, 1824–1901]

săm'bŭr, -bār *n.* Indian elk (*Cervus unicolor*), distributed over SE. Asia.

sāme *adj.* 1. Identical; not different; unchanged; indifferent; identical *with*; (freq. as emphatic substitute for) the, that, those, the very. 2. Monotonous, uniform, unvarying. 3. Aforesaid, previously alluded to or thought of. 4. (*abs.* and as *pron.*) *the* ~, the same person; the same thing; (archaic, legal, commercial) the aforesaid thing or person. 5. *the* ~ (*adv.*) in the same manner; *all the* ~, nevertheless, notwithstanding, even under different circumstances; *just the* ~, in spite of changed conditions. **sāme'nėss** (-mn-) *n.*

săm'el *adj.* (Of brick, tile) imperfectly baked.

Sām'ian *adj.* & *n.* (Native) of Samos; ~ *ware*, orig., pottery made of Samian earth; extended to a fine kind of pottery found extensively on Roman sites.

săm'ite *n.* (hist.) Rich medieval dress-fabric of silk sometimes interwoven with gold. [late Gk *hexamitum* (*hex* six, *mitos* thread), perh. = fabric in which weft-threads are caught only at every 6th warp-thread]

săm'lėt *n.* Young salmon.

Săm'nīte. Member of an ancient tribe of S. Central Italy, inhabiting the district of Samnium.

Samō'a. Group of Polynesian islands. *Western* ~, independent Republic since 1962; capital, Apia; *E.* (*American*) ~, U.S. territory. **Samō'an** *adj.* & *n.* (Native, language) of Samoa.

Sām'ŏs. A large island in the Aegean, the birthplace of Pythagoras.

Săm'othrāce. Island in the Aegean; *Victory* or *Nike of* ~, the 'Winged Victory', a large female statue of *c* 200 B.C. found in Samothrace and now in the Louvre, representing Victory alighting on the prow of a warship.

săm'ovar *n.* Russian tea-urn. [Russ., = 'self-boiler']

SAMOVAR

1. Lid of water container. 2. Lid of charcoal container. 3. Tap

Săm'oyĕd (-mo-) *n.* Name of Mongolian race inhabiting Siberia; white Arctic breed of dog. **Sămoyĕd'ic** *adj.* & *n.*

săm'păn *n.* Small boat used in river and coastal traffic of China, Japan, and neighbouring islands, rowed with a scull from the stern and usu. having a sail of matting and an awning. [Chin. *san-pan* boat (*san* three, *pan* board)]

săm'phīre *n.* Cliff-plant (*Crithmum maritimum*) with aromatic saline fleshy leaves used in pickles. [Fr. (*herbe de*) *St. Pierre* St. Peter's (herb)]

sa'mple (sah-) *n.* Small separated part of something illustrating qualities of the mass etc. it is taken from, specimen, pattern. ~ *v.t.* Take or give samples, try the qualities, get representative experience, of. **sa'mpler**[1] *n.*

sa'mpler[2] (sah-) *n.* 1. Piece of embroidery worked by girl as specimen of proficiency, usu. containing alphabet and various decorative motifs. 2. (forestry) Young tree left standing when others are cut down.

Săm'son. 1. Name of an Israelite hero of mighty strength (Judges xiii–xvi); he confided to a woman, Delilah, that his strength lay in his hair, and she betrayed him to the Philistines, who cut off his hair while he slept and captured and blinded him; but when his hair grew again his strength returned and he pulled down the pillars of the house of Gaza, destroying himself and a large concourse of Philistines. 2. Man of abnormal strength; ~ (*'s*) *post*, (naut.) strong supporting pillar or post in a ship usu. resting on the keelson and supporting a deck beam; post in a whaler to which harpoon-rope is attached.

Săm'ūėl. A Hebrew prophet who rallied the Israelites after their defeat by the Philistines and became their ruler; either of the two O.T. books of Samuel covering the history of Israel from Samuel's birth to the end of the reign of David.

săm'urai (-ŏŏrī) (pl. same). In Japanese feudal system, military retainer of the daimios; any member of military caste; (now) Japanese army officer.

săn'ative, săn'atory *adjs.* Healing, of or tending to physical or moral health, curative.

sănatōr'ium *n.* (pl. *-ia*). Establishment for treatment of invalids, esp. convalescents and consumptives; room or building in school or college for the sick.

sănbėni'tō (-nē-) *n.* Penitential scapular-shaped yellow garment with red St. Andrew's cross before and behind worn by confessed and penitent heretic under Spanish Inquisition; similar black garment painted with flames and devils worn by impenitent heretic at auto-da-fé. [Span. *sambenito* f. *San Benito* St. Benedict, because shaped like scapular introduced by him]

Sănch'o Păn'za (-kō). The squire of Don QUIXOTE, who accompanies him on his adventures; he is an ignorant and credulous peasant, but has a store of proverbial wisdom and is thus a foil to his master.

sănc'tĭfȳ *v.t.* Consecrate, set apart or observe as holy; purify or free from sin; impart sanctity to, make legitimate or binding by religious sanction; give colour of innocence to, justify, sanction; make productive of or conducive to holiness. **sănctĭfĭcā'tion** *n.*

sănctĭmōn'ious *adj.* Making a show of sanctity or piety. **sănctĭmōn'iously** *adv.* **sănctĭmōn'iousnėss, sănc'tĭmony** (archaic) *ns.*

sănc'tion *n.* 1. (hist.) Law or (esp. eccles.) decree; *pragmatic* ~: see PRAGMATIC. 2. Penalty or reward for (dis)obedience attached to a law, clause containing this, (now esp.) penalty imposed for non-compliance with international agreement; consideration operating to enforce obedience to any rule of conduct. 3. Confirmation or ratification of law etc. by supreme authority; express authoritative permission; countenance or encouragement given to action etc. by custom etc. ~ *v.t.* Ratify, invest with authority, make binding; authorize; countenance (action etc.); attach penalty or reward to (law etc.).

sănc'tĭtūde *n.* (now rare) Saintliness.

sănc'tĭty *n.* Holiness of life, saintliness; sacredness, being hallowed, right to reverence, inviolability; (pl.) sacred obligations, feelings, etc.

sănc'tūary *n.* 1. Place recognized as holy, church, temple, tabernacle, holy place; inmost recess of place of worship; part of church within altar-rails (ill. CHURCH). 2. Sacred place by retiring to which fugitive from law or debtor was secured by medieval Church law against arrest or violence, place in which similar immunity was established by custom or law, asylum, place of refuge; (right of affording) such immunity. 3. (hunting etc.) Close time or place for bird, beast, or fish.

sănc'tum *n.* Holy place in Jewish etc. tabernacle or temple; person's private room, study, den; ~ *sanctorum*, Holy of holies.

sănc'tus *n.* The 'angelic hymn' (from Isa. vi. 3) beginning 'Holy, holy, holy', forming conclusion of Eucharistic preface; music for this; ~ *bell*, bell in turret at junction of nave and chancel, or handbell, rung at the sanctus.

sănd[1] *n.* Minute fragments resulting from wearing down of esp. siliceous rocks and found covering parts of the sea-shore, river-beds, deserts, etc.; (also pl.) shoal or submarine bank of sand; (usu. in pl.) grain of sand; (pl.) expanse or tracts of sand; (fig.) pluck, 'grit'; ~*-bag*, bag filled with sand, used for making trenches, for protecting buildings etc. against blast and splinters, as ballast, as weapon leaving no mark on victim, as draught-excluder, etc.; *sand'bag* (*v.t.*) protect with sand-bags; fell with blow from sand-bag; *~-bank*, shoal in sea or river; *~-bar*, sand-bank at mouth of harbour or river; *~-bath*, vessel of heated sand as equable heater in chemical processes; *~-blast*, jet of sand impelled by compressed air or steam for giving rough surface to glass etc.; *~-box*, (hist.) castor for sprinkling sand over wet ink; mould of sand used in founding; box of sand on locomotive for sprinkling slippery rails; (golf) receptacle for sand used in teeing; *~-casting*, metal casting obtained from sand mould; process of making such castings; *~-devil*, (S. African) small whirlwind; *~-fly*, small fly or midge (*Simulium*); kind of fishing-fly; *~-glass*, device for measuring intervals of time,

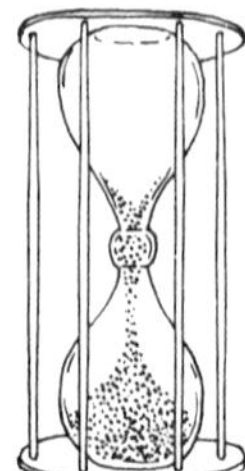

SANDGLASS OR HOUR-GLASS

consisting of wasp-waisted reversible glass with two bulbs containing sand which takes a definite time in passing from upper to lower bulb, now practically obsolete except for measuring the time required to boil an egg; *~-hill*, dune; *~-hopper*, small jumping crustacean of family *Talitridae*, most species of which burrow in sand of sea-shore; *~-man*, (nursery name for) personification of sleep or sleepiness; *~-martin*, kind of martin (*Hirundo riparia*) nesting in side of sand-pit or sandy bank; *~-paper*, paper with layer of sand stuck on for smoothing or polishing wood etc.; *sand'paper* (*v.t.*) polish with sand-paper; *~-piper*, bird (esp. *Tringordes lypoleucus* or the N. Amer. *Actitis macularia*) haunting open wet sandy places; *~-shoes*, shoes for use on sands, usu. of canvas with rubber or hemp soles; *sand'stone*, sedimentary rock composed of small grains usu. of quartz cemented together; *Old, New, Red Sandstone*, two series of British rocks lying below, above, Carboniferous; *~-storm*, desert storm of wind with clouds of sand. ~ *v.t.* Sprinkle with sand; overlay with, bury under, sand; adulterate (sugar, wool, etc.) with sand; polish with sand.

Sand[2] (sahṅ), George. Pen-name of Armandine Lucile Amore Dupin-Dudevant (1804–76), French novelist, friend of Alfred de Musset and Chopin, author of 'Indiana', 'Lélia', 'Consuelo', etc.

săn'dal[1] *n.* Sole without uppers, attached to foot by thongs passing over instep and round ankle; various modifications of this, worn by ancient Greeks and Romans, by some orientals, as modern revival, etc. ~ *v.t.* Put sandals on (foot, person; esp. in past part.).

săn'dal[2], **săn'dalwōōd** *ns.* Kinds of scented wood, true sandalwood being obtained from species of *Santalum*; inodorous dye-wood, red sanders (*Pterocarpus santalinus*).

săn'darăc(h) (-k) *n.* 1. REALGAR. 2. (also *gum* ~) Resin exuding from NW. African tree *Tetraclinis articulata*, used in making spirit varnish and pounce.

sănd'-blīnd *adj.* (archaic & dial.) Dim-sighted, purblind. [prob. for *samblind*, f. OE *sam*-half-]

săn'derlĭng *n.* Common small wading bird of sea-shores (*Calidris arenaria*).

Sănd'hûrst. Training college, now at Camberley, Surrey, for officers of the British Regular Army, officially known as 'The Royal Military Academy, Sandhurst', being an amalgamation of the Royal Military College at Sandhurst in Berkshire (founded 1799) and the Royal Military Academy at Woolwich, London (founded 1741).

S. & M. *abbrev.* (Bishop) of Sodor and Man (replacing surname in his signature).

Săn'down. Race-course near Esher, Surrey.

Săn'drĭngham (-ng-*a*m). A country seat of the sovereign of England, in Norfolk, near the Wash, on an estate purchased by Edward VII when Prince of Wales.

sănd'wĭch *n.* Two or more thin slices of bread or toast with meat or other relish between; *~-board*, board carried by sandwich-man (see below); *~-boat*, (in bumping race) boat rowing last in higher and first in lower division on same day; ~ *course, training*, course of study, training, in which periods of theoretical and practical work alternate; *~-man*, man walking street with two advertisement-boards hung one before and one behind. ~ *v.t.* Insert (thing, statement etc.) between two of another character. [perh. f. name of 4th Earl of *Sandwich* (1718–92), said to have eaten slices of cold beef between slices of toast, while gaming for 24 hours]

Sănd'wĭch Islands. Group of volcanic and coral islands in the N. Pacific, in U.S. possession.

sănd'y[1] *adj.* Covered with sand; sand-coloured, (of hair) yellowish-red; having such hair. **sănd'ĭnėss** *n.*

Sănd'y[2]. Familiar for *Alexander*; (nickname for) Scotchman.

sāne *adj.* Of sound mind, not mad; sensible, rational. **sāne'ly** (-nl-) *adv.* **sāne'nėss** *n.*

Săn Francĭs'cō. City and seaport of California, U.S.

săngaree' (-ngg-) *n.* Cold drink of wine diluted and spiced. [Span. *sangria* 'bleeding', a drink of red wine and lemon-water]

sang-de-bœuf (sahṅ de bẽrf) *n.* & *adj.* (Of) deep-red colour of some old Chinese porcelain. [Fr., = 'ox's blood']

sang-froid (sahṅfrwah') *n.* Composure, coolness, in danger or under agitating circumstances. [Fr., = 'cold blood']

sangrail, sangreal: see GRAIL[2] *n.*

săng'uĭnary (-nggw-) *adj.* Attended by, delighting in, bloodshed or slaughter, bloody, bloodthirsty; (of laws) prescribing death for slight offences. **săng'uĭnarĭly** *adv.* **săng'uĭnarĭnėss** *n.*

săng'uĭne (-nggwĭn) *adj.* 1. Blood-red. 2. (hist.) Belonging to that one of the four HUMOURS supposed to be characterized by predominance of blood over other humours, and indicated by ruddy face and courageous, hopeful, and amorous disposition; (mod., of complexion) ruddy, florid. 3. Habitually hopeful, confident; expecting things to go well. **săng'uinely** *adv.* **săng'uĭnenėss** *n.* **săng'uĭne** *n.* Crayon coloured brownish-red with iron oxide; drawing made with this.

sănguĭn'ėous (-nggwĭ-) *adj.* Of blood; blood-coloured; full-blooded, plethoric.

sanhedrĭn, -ĭm (săn'ĭ-) *ns.* Highest court of justice and supreme council, of 71 members, in ancient Jerusalem. [late Heb., f. Gk *sunedrion* (*sun* together, *hedra* seat)]

săn'ĭcle *n.* Umbelliferous plant (*Sanicula europaea*).

sănĭtār'ium *n.* (pl. *-ia*). = SANATORIUM.

săn'ĭtary *adj.* Of the conditions that affect health, esp. with regard to dirt and infection; free from or designed to obviate influences deleterious to health; ~ *towel*, kind used in menstruation. **săn'ĭtarĭly** *adv.* **săn'ĭtarĭnėss** *n.*

sănĭtā'tion *n.* Measures conducing to the preservation of public health, esp. efficient drainage and disposal of sewage, ventilation, pure water supply; (specif.) drainage and disposal of sewage in houses and towns generally.

săn'ĭty *n.* Being sane, mental health; tendency to avoid extreme views.

săn'jăk *n.* One of the administrative districts of a Turkish vilayet. [Turk. *sanjāq* banner]

Săn Marī'no (-ēnō). A small republic near Rimini, Italy, on the Adriatic; its capital.

săns[1] (-z) *prep.* (archaic.) Without.

săns[2] (-z) *n.* SANSERIF.

sans cérémonie (sahṅ sārāmonē′). Without the usual ceremony or polite forms.

sanscūlŏtte′ (sănz- *or* sahṅ-) *n.* Republican of Parisian lower classes in French Revolution; any extreme republican or revolutionary. [Fr., lit. 'breechless']

sans doute (sahṅ dōōt). Doubtless.

sănsĕ′rĭf *n.* & *adj.* (Form of type) without serifs, thus.

sans façon (sahṅ făs′awṅ). Outspokenly, unceremoniously.

sans-gêne (sahṅ-zhĕn) *n.* Disregard of ordinary forms of civility and politeness.

Săns′krĭt *adj.* & *n.* (Of) the ancient, classical, and sacred language of the Hindus in India, in which the Vedic hymns were composed; the oldest known member of the Indo-European family of languages.

sans peur et sans reproche (sahṅ pēr ā sahṅ reprŏsh′). Of chivalrous character.

sans-souci (sahṅ-sōōsē′) *n.* Carelessness, unconcern; *Sans-Souci*, palace at Potsdam built 1745–7 for Frederick the Great.

Săn′ta Claus (-z). St. Nicholas, who is supposed to come, on the night before Christmas Day, to fill children's stockings with presents. [U.S., f. Du. *Sint Klaus* St. Nicholas]

Săn′ta Fé (fā). Capital city of N. Mexico.

Săntănder′ (-ār). Province of N. Spain; its capital.

Saorstat Eireann (s*a*yŏr′st*a*th ār′*a*n). The Irish Free State, Eire.

săp[1] *n.* Juice in plants; (also *~-wood*), soft layers of wood growing between the bark of trees and the heart-wood, alburnum (ill. STEM); *~-green*, pigment made from buckthorn berries, (of) colour of this. **săp′less, săpp′y** *adjs.* **săp** *v.t.* Drain or dry (wood) of sap; remove sap-wood from (log); (fig.) exhaust vigour of.

săp[2] *n.* Making of trenches or tunnels to cover assailant's approach to besieged place or enemy's trenches; covered siege-trench; (fig.) insidious or slow undermining of belief, resolution, etc.; *~-head*, front end of sap. *~ v.* Dig sap, approach by sap; undermine, make insecure by removing foundations; (fig.) destroy insidiously.

săp[3] *v.i.* (school slang) Be studious, work hard at books or lessons. *~ n.* Studious or hard-working person; tiresome task, trouble, grind.

săp[4] *n.* (slang) Simpleton, fool.

săp′ajou (-jōō) *n.* Small monkey (*Cebus*) of Central and S. America, capuchin-monkey.

săp′ĭd *adj.* Having (esp. agreeable) flavour, savoury, palatable, not insipid. **sapĭd′ĭty** *n.*

sāp′ĭent *adj.* Wise (now rare); would-be wise, of fancied sagacity, aping wisdom. **sāp′iently** *adv.* **sāp′ience** *n.*

săpiĕn′tial (-shl) *adj.* Of wisdom; *~ books*, (in O.T. and Apocrypha) Proverbs, Ecclesiastes, Canticles, Wisdom, Ecclesiasticus.

săp′lĭng *n.* Young tree; (fig.) a youth; greyhound in first year.

săpodĭll′a *n.* Large evergreen tropical Amer. tree (*Achras sapota*), with durable wood and edible fruit; fruit of this.

săponā′ceous (-sh*u*s) *adj.* Of, like, containing, soap; soapy.

sapŏn′ĭfȳ *v.* (chem.) Convert (fat or oil) into soap by boiling with alkali: convert (an ester) into its constituent acid and alcohol; be converted thus. **sapŏnĭfĭcā′tion** *n.* *~ value*, in the analysis of oils and fats, the number of milligrams of potassium hydroxide neutralized in the saponification of one gram of the substance.

sāp′ŏr *n.* Quality perceptible by taste; distinctive taste; sensation of taste.

săp(p)′an-wood *n.* Red or yellow wood yielding dye, obtained from trees (*Caesalpinia*) native to tropical Asia and Indian Archipelago.

săpp′er *n.* (esp.) Private of Royal Engineers.

Sapphic (săf′ĭk) *adj.* Of SAPPHO; *~ verse, stanza*, metre used by Sappho and imitated in Latin by Horace, consisting of

—◡—⏑—◡◡—◡—⏑

thrice repeated and followed by —◡◡—⏑. **Sapph′ics** *n.* Sapphic verse.

sapphire (săf′īr) *n.* Transparent blue precious stone, variety of alumina akin to ruby; (min.) any precious transparent native crystalline alumina, including sapphire and ruby; bright blue of sapphire, azure. *~ adj.* Of sapphire blue.

Sappho (săf′ō). Greek lyric poetess of Lesbos (flourished 610 B.C.); according to legend, she threw herself into the sea in despair at her unrequited love for Phaon.

săprogĕn′ĭc *adj.* Causing or produced by putrefaction.

săp′rophīle *adj.* & *n.* (Bacterium) inhabiting putrid matter.

săp′rophȳte *n.* Vegetable organism living on decayed organic matter.

sār *n.* A fish, the sea bream (*Sargus*).

Sār′a. (O.T.) Wife of Abraham and mother of Isaac.

să′rabănd *n.* Slow Spanish dance in triple time; music for this or in rhythm of it (often with long note on second beat of bar).

Să′racen *n.* Among the later Greeks and Romans, a name for the nomadic peoples of the Syro-Arabian desert; hence, an Arab; by extension, a Moslem, esp. with reference to the crusades; *~ corn*, buckwheat; *~'s head*, head of a Saracen, Arab, or Turk, used as a charge in heraldry, as an inn-sign, etc. **Săracĕn′ĭc** *adj.* Of, connected with, the Saracens; of Mohammedan architecture.

să′rafăn *n.* Long sleeveless cloak or veil as part of Russian peasant woman's dress.

Sār′ah = SARA.

Sarajevo (să′r*a*yĕvō). City of Yugoslavia, formerly capital of Bosnia, where the Archduke Francis Ferdinand of Austria was assassinated on 28th June 1914.

Sărasa′te (-ah′tē), Pablo de (1844–1908). Spanish violinist and composer.

Săratŏg′a. Scene, near the Hudson River, U.S., of the decisive victory of the American army under Gates over the British under Burgoyne in 1777, in the American War of Independence, and of the surrender of Burgoyne and his army; *~ trunk*, (f. *Saratoga Springs*, fashionable watering-place in New York State) lady's travelling trunk.

Sarawak (-ah′w*a*k). State on NE. coast of Borneo, ruled over by descendants of Sir James BROOKE until 1946, when it was ceded to Gt Britain.

sārc′ăsm (-zm) *n.* Bitter or wounding remark, taunt, esp. one ironically worded; language consisting of, faculty of uttering, use of, such remarks. **sārcăs′tĭc** *adj.* **sārcăs′tĭcally** *adv.*

sār′cėlly *adj.* (her., of cross) Having the points split and curled back (ill. CROSS).

sarcenet: see SARSENET.

sārcŏl′ogy *n.* Anatomy of fleshy parts of body.

sārcōm′a *n.* (path.) Variety of malignant growth (cancer) differing from CARCINOMA in that it commonly attacks connective or non-epithelial tissue.

sārcŏph′agus *n.* (pl. *-gi* pr. -gī, -jī). Stone coffin, esp. one adorned with sculpture or bearing inscription etc. [L, f. Gk *sarkophagos*, orig. = flesh-consuming (stone) (*sar* flesh, *-phagos* eating]

sārc′oplăsm *n.* Component of muscular tissue, substance filling the spaces in between the fibres.

sārd *n.* Yellow or orange cornelian. [f. *Sardis* in Lydia]

Sārdanapāl′us (d. 626 B.C.). The last king of Assyria, notorious for his luxury and effeminacy. **Sārdanapāl′ĭan** *adj.*

sārd′īne[1] *n.* Precious stone mentioned in Rev. iv. 3, prob. = SARD.

sārdine′[2] (-ēn) *n.* Small fish of herring family (*Clupea pilchardus*) abundant off coasts of Sardinia and Brittany, or young pilchard of Cornish coast, cured and tinned in oil; *like ~s*, packed tight, very crowded.

Sārdĭn′ĭa. Large island W. of the Italian mainland, formerly a kingdom (including Savoy and Piedmont), which became by expansion part of the kingdom of Italy in 1861. **Sardin'ian** *adj.* & *n.*

sard'ius *n.* = SARD.

sardŏn'ic *adj.* (of laughter etc.) Bitter, scornful, mocking, sneering, cynical. **sardŏn'ically** *adv.* [Gk *sardonios* Sardinian, substituted for Homeric *sardanios* (epithet of bitter or scornful laughter) because of belief that convulsive laughter ending in death resulted from eating a Sardinian plant]

sard'onyx *n.* Variety of onyx with white layers alternating with sard.

sargăss'ō *n.* Kinds of seaweed (*Sarga sum*) with berry-like air-vessels, found floating in island-like masses in Gulf Stream.

Sargăss'ō Sea. Region in N. Atlantic, S. of the 35th parallel. [f. prevalence in it of SARGASSO]

Sar'gent, John Singer (1856–1925). American portrait and genre painter, chiefly active in England.

sa'ri (sah-) *n.* Length of material wrapped round the body, worn as main garment by Hindu women.

sariss'a *n.* (pl. *-ae*). (Gk antiq.) Long lance of ancient Macedonians.

sark[1] *n.* (Sc. and north.) Shirt or chemise.

Sark[2]. One of the Channel Islands.

Sarmā'tia (-sh*a*). Ancient name of a region N. of the Black Sea inhabited by ancestors of the Slavs, used occasionally by English poets to signify Poland. **Sarmā'tian** *adj.* & *n.*

sărŏng' *n.* Malay and Javanese garment, long piece of cloth worn as skirt, tucked round waist or under armpits.

sarsaparill'a *n.* Kinds of tropical Amer. smilax (esp. *S. ornata,* Jamaica smilax); dried roots of these, or extract of them, used as tonic etc.

sars'en *n.* One of the large boulders of sandstone found scattered on chalk downs, esp. in Wiltshire. [prob. f. SARACEN]

sars'enėt, sar'cenet (-sn-) *n.* Fine soft silk material now used chiefly for linings. [prob. f. *sarzin* Saracen]

Sart'ō, Andrea del (1486–1531). Florentine painter.

sartŏr'ial *adj.* Of tailors or tailoring; of men's clothes.

sartŏr'ius *n.* Long narrow muscle crossing thigh obliquely in front (ill. MUSCLE). [mod. L, so called as being concerned in producing tailor's cross-legged working position]

Sar'um. Ecclesiastical name of SALISBURY[1] and its diocese (*Sarum.*, used by bishop of Salisbury in his signature in place of surname); *Old* ~, hill 2 miles from Salisbury on which Norman castle and town were built, now deserted; ~ *use,* form of liturgy used in the diocese of Salisbury from the 11th c. to the Reformation. [med. L., supposed to be due to a misreading of an abbreviated form of L *Sarisburia* Salisbury]

săsh[1] *n.* Ornamental scarf worn over one shoulder or round waist by man, usu. as part of uniform or insignia, or by woman or child round waist. [Arab. *shāsh* muslin, band twisted round head as turban]

săsh[2] *n.* Frame, usu. of wood, fitted with pane(s) of glass forming (part of) window, esp. sliding frame or one of pair of frames made to slide up and down and forming ~*-window* (ill. WINDOW); glazed sliding light of glass-house or garden-frame; (now U.S.) casement; ~*-cord, -line,* strong cord used for attaching sash-weights to sash; ~ *cramp*: see ill. CRAMP; ~*-pocket,* space on each side of window-frame in which sash-weights run; ~*-pulley,* pulley over which sash-cord runs; ~*-weight,* weight attached to sash-cord at each side of sash to counterbalance it. [corrupt. of CHASSIS]

Sask. *abbrev.* Saskatchewan.

Săskătch'ėwan. River of Canada, flowing from the Rocky Mountains to Lake Winnipeg; province of central Canada (capital, Regina).

săss, săss'y. dial. (now chiefly U.S.) variant of SAUCE, SAUCY.

sassăb'y *n.* Large antelope (*Damaliscus lunatus*) of central and S. Africa, resembling hartebeest but with more regularly curved horns.

săss'afrăs *n.* Small N. Amer. tree (*Sassafras variifolium*) of laurel family, with green apetalous flowers and dimorphous leaves; dried bark of root of this used medicinally as sudorific etc.; various other trees of similar medicinal properties.

Săs(s)ān'ian, Săs(s)'anid *adjs.* & *ns.* (Member, esp. a king) of the family of Sas(s)an, rulers of the Persian Empire A.D. 211–651; of this period in Persia.

Săss'enach (-ahχ) *n.* (Sc. and Ir. for) Englishman. [Gaelic and Irish form of *Saxon*]

Sat. *abbrev.* Saturday.

Sāt'an. The Devil, Lucifer.

Satăn'ic *adj.* Of, like, or befitting Satan, diabolical; *his* ~ *majesty,* Satan; ~ *school,* Southey's designation for Byron, Shelley, and their imitators. **Satăn'ically** *adv.* [Heb. *ṣaṭan* enemy]

Sāt'anism *n.* Worship of the Devil with a travesty of Christian ceremonial and with celebration of the Black Mass; diabolical wickedness. **Sāt'anist** *n.*

Sātanŏl'ogy *n.* (History or collection of) beliefs concerning the Devil.

satar'a *n.* Heavy ribbed and lustred woollen cloth. [f. *Satara* in India]

S.A.T.B. *abbrev.* Soprano, alto, tenor, bass.

sătch'el *n.* Small bag, esp. for carrying school-books, freq. with straps to hang over shoulders.

sāte *v.t.* Gratify (desire, appetite, etc.) to the full; cloy, surfeit weary with over-abundance.

sateen' *n.* Cotton fabric, glossy on one side, woven like satin.

săt'ellīte *n.* 1. Follower, henchman, hanger-on; member of great man's retinue, underling. 2. Small or secondary planet revolving round larger one; (also) artificial body launched from the earth and encircling it or other celestial body. 3. ~ (*State*), nation nominally independent but dominated by powerful neighbour; ~ *town,* small town built near larger one to house excess population.

sā'tiate (-shy*a*t) *adj.* Sated, satiated. **sā'tiāte** *v.t.* Sate. **satiā'tion** (sāshĭ-) *n.*

satī'ėty *n.* State of being glutted or satiated; feeling of disgust or surfeit caused by excess.

săt'in *n.* 1. Fabric of silk or similar yarn with glossy surface on one side produced by twill weave in which weft-threads are almost concealed by warp, or vice versa (ill. WEAVE). 2. (*white*) ~, the plant honesty; a glossy white moth (*Stilpnotia salicis*); (slang) gin. 3. *attrib.* or as *adj.* Made of satin; like satin; ~ *beauté* (bōtā), soft fine silk material with dull crêpe back and brilliant satin surface; ~ *cloth,* woollen cloth woven like satin; ~*-flower,* honesty; greater stitchwort; Australian umbelliferous plant (*Actinotus helianthi*); various other plants; ~ *gypsum,* fibrous kind of gypsum with pearly lustre; ~*-stitch,* in embroidery, long straight stitches laid close together, producing smooth surface (ill. STITCH); ~*-wood,* (hard light-coloured wood with satiny surface, of) Indian tree (*Chloroxylon swietinia*) and various W. Indian, Australian, etc., trees. **săt'iny** *adj.*

săt'inĕt(te)' *n.* Satin-like material of silk, or silk and cotton; satin-surfaced material with cotton warp and woollen weft.

săt'īre *n.* Poetic medley (Rom. antiq.), esp. poem aimed at prevalent vices or follies; literary composition holding up vice or folly to ridicule or lampooning individual(s); this branch of literature; thing bringing ridicule on something; use in speech or writing of ridicule, irony, sarcasm, etc., in denouncing or exposing vice, folly, etc.

satĭ'ric *adj.* Of satires or satire; containing satire; writing satires.

satĭ'rical *adj.* Satiric; given to the use of, characterized by, satire; sarcastic. **satir'ically** *adv.*

săt'irist *n.* Writer of satires; satirical person.

săt'irīze *v.t.* Assail with satire, write satire(s) upon, describe satirically.

sătisfăc'tion *n.* 1. Payment of debt, fulfilment of obligation, atonement *for*; thing accepted by way of satisfaction; (eccles.) performance of penance; (theol.) atonement made by Christ for sins of men. 2. Opportunity of satisfying one's honour by duel, acceptance of challenge to duel. 3. Satisfying, being satisfied, in regard to desire or want or doubt; thing that satisfies desire or gratifies feeling.

sătisfăc'tory *adj.* 1. (theol.) Serving as atonement for sin. 2. Sufficient, adequate, (of argument) convincing; such as one may be content or pleased with. **sătisfăc'torily** *adv.* **sătisfăc'toriness** *n.*

săt'isfȳ *v.* 1. Pay (debt), fulfil (obligation), (now rare except in *law*); pay (creditor); make atonement or reparation. 2. Meet expectations or desires of, come up to (notion etc.), be accepted by (person etc.) as adequate, content; give satisfaction, leave nothing to be desired; fully supply needs of, put an end to (appetite etc.) by fully supplying it; furnish with adequate proof, convince; adequately meet (objection, doubt, etc.); (math.) be a solution e.g. of an equation; (pass.) be content or pleased (*with*), demand no more than, consider it enough *to* do; ~ *examiners*, (at English universities) pass examination without attaining honours. **săt'isfȳing** *adj.* **săt'isfȳingly** *adv.*

săt'răp *n.* Holder of provincial governorship (*sat'rapy*) in ancient-Persian Empire, viceroy; subordinate ruler, colonial governor, etc. (freq. with implication of luxury or tyranny). [Pers. *khsatrapava* province guardian]

Sătsūm'a (*or* săt'-). Group of islands and province of Japan; ~ (*ware*), kind of Japanese glazed pottery with a yellow ground.

săt'urāte (-cher-) *v.t.* 1. Soak thoroughly, imbue *with*. 2. (physics etc.) Cause to absorb or hold the maximum quantity of moisture, electrical charge, etc., that can be held under given conditions of temperature etc.; (chem.) cause (a substance) to combine with or dissolve the maximum quantity possible of another substance; *saturated*, (of a solution) containing the maximum quantity possible of the dissolved substance at a given temperature (cf. *unsaturated*, able to dissolve more than it contains); (also, of chemical compounds, esp. hydrocarbons) containing no double bonds and hence unable to undergo addition reactions (*unsaturated*, containing one or more double bonds and capable of such reactions). 3. Bomb (target) from the air so thoroughly that anti-aircraft defences are powerless. **săturā'tion** *n.*

Săt'urday (-*erdā or* -dĭ) *n.* The seventh day of the week; *Holy* ~: see HOLY. [OE, f. L, *Saturni dies* day of Saturn]

Săt'ûrn. 1. An ancient-Italian god of agriculture, later identified with the Greek Cronos, father of Zeus, ruler of the world in a golden age of innocence and plenty. 2. A major planet, next in size to Jupiter, distinguished by its 9 satellites or moons and its engirdling system of rings (ill. PLANET); (astrol.) the leaden planet supposed to produce a cold sluggish gloomy temperament in those born under its influence. 3. (alchemy) The metal lead.

Sătûrnāl'ia *n.pl.* (Rom. antiq.) The yearly festival of Saturn, held in December, observed as a time of unrestrained merrymaking with temporary release of slaves, predecessor of the modern Christmastide; (not cap.) scene or time of wild revelry or tumult. **Sătûrnāl'ian** *adj.*

Satûrn'ian *adj.* Of the god or the planet Saturn; ~ *age*, the supposed golden age when Saturn reigned; ~ *metre, verse*, metre used in early Latin poetry before the introduction of Greek metres, generally taken to have consisted of a line of three iambic feet and an extra syllable followed by one of three trochees. ~ *n.* Supposed inhabitant of Saturn; (pl.) Saturnian verses.

săt'urnīne (-*ter*-) *adj.* 1. Born under, influenced by, the planet Saturn (astrol.); sluggish, cold and gloomy in temperament, (of looks etc.) suggesting such temperament. 2. Of lead; of, affected by, lead-poisoning.

sătyagra'ha (-grah-). Passive resistance to government, non-violent disobedience, as policy of GANDHI and his followers in India, initiated *c* 1919. [Hind., = 'soul force']

săt'yr (-*er*) *n.* (Gk & Rom. myth.) One of a class of woodland gods supposed to be companions

SATYR

of Bacchus (represented in Gk art of pre-Roman period with ears and tail of horse, but by Roman artists given ears, tail, and legs of goat, and budding horns, like faun); (fig.) type of lustfulness.

sătyrī'asis *n.* Excessive sexual excitement in males.

satȳ'ric *adj.* Of satyrs; ~ *drama*, form of ancient-Greek drama burlesquing the legends of the gods and having a chorus dressed as satyrs.

sauce *n.* 1. Preparation, usu. liquid or soft, taken as relish with some article of food; (fig.) something that adds piquancy; (U.S.) vegetables or fruits as part of meal or as relish; (techn.) solution of salt and other ingredients used in some manufacturing processes; *hard* ~, sauce which is not liquid. 2. Sauciness; impertinent speech; cheek. 3. ~-*alone*, hedge-weed (*Alliaria petiolata*) formerly used to flavour salads and sauces; ~-*boat*, vessel in which sauce is served; ~-*box*, impudent person. ~ *v.t.* 1. Season with sauces or condiments (rare); (fig.) make piquant, add relish to. 2. (vulg.) Be impudent to, cheek.

sauce'pan *n.* Kitchen utensil of metal with a cover and long handle projecting from side, in which food is boiled.

sau'cer *n.* Shallow vessel for standing esp. tea- or coffee-cup on, to catch liquid that may be spilled from it; any small shallow vessel resembling this; round shallow depression in the ground; *flying* ~, disc-like phenomenon occas. reported as observed in the sky, variously explained.

sau'cy *adj.* Impudent to superiors, cheeky; (slang) sprightly; smart, stylish. **sau'cily** *adv.* **sau'ciness** *n.* [orig. = savoury, flavoured with sauce]

Sau'di Arāb'ia (saōōd'ĭ). Kingdom in Arabia formed in 1932 by the union of Nejd and the Hejaz; capitals, Riyadh and Mecca.

sauerkraut (sowr'krowt) *n.* German dish of cabbage cut fine and pickled in brine.

Saul[1]. 1. The first king of Israel. 2. Saul of Tarsus, afterwards St. PAUL the Apostle.

saul[2]: see SAL.

sa(u)nders *n.* Sandalwood.

saun'ter *v.i.* Walk in leisurely way, stroll. ~ *n.* Leisurely ramble or gait. **saun'teringly** *adv.*

saur'ian *adj.* & *n.* (Of or like) a lizard; (obs.) of the *Sauria* (an order of reptiles no longer used in classification).

sausage (sŏs'ĭj) *n.* Meat (esp. pork) minced, seasoned, and stuffed into long cylindrical cases made from intestine, bladder, or other animal tissue; *a* short length of this made by twisting or tying the containing case; (slang or colloq.) sausage-shaped observation balloon, wind-sleeve; ~-*meat*, meat minced and seasoned to be used in sausages or as stuffing etc.; ~ *roll*, sausage or sausage-meat enclosed in roll of pastry and baked.

sauté (sōt'ā) *adj.* & *n.* (cookery) (Dish of meat, vegetables, etc.)

quickly and lightly fried by being tossed in butter or other fat over heat. ~ *v.* Cook (food) thus.

Sauterne (sōtārn′). A light sweet white wine from the Bordeaux region. [*Sauternes*, name of a district of Gironde, France]

săv′age *adj.* 1. Uncultivated, wild (archaic); uncivilized, in primitive state; fierce, cruel, furious; (colloq.) angry, out of temper. 2. (her., of human figure) Naked. ~ *n.* Member of savage tribe, esp. one living by hunting or fishing; brutally cruel or barbarous person. ~ *v.t.* (Of animal, esp. horse) attack and bite (person etc.). **săv′agely** *adv.* **săv′ageness, săv′agery** (-ĭjrĭ) *ns.*

savănn′ah (-*a*) *n.* Wide treeless plain, great tract of meadow-like land, esp. in tropical America.

săv′ant (-ahn̄) *n.* Man of learning, scholar.

savate′ (-aht) *n.* Kind of French boxing in which blows are given with feet as well as hands.

sāve[1] *v.* 1. Rescue, preserve, deliver from danger, misfortune, harm, or discredit; bring about spiritual salvation of, preserve from damnation; prevent loss of (game etc.), (footb. etc.) prevent opponent from scoring; ~ *the situation*, find or provide way out of difficulty; ~ *one's face*, avoid being disgraced or humiliated. 2. Keep for future use, husband, reserve, put by; lay by money; live economically; ~ *up*, try to accumulate money by economy. 3. Relieve from need of expending (money, trouble, etc.) or from exposure to (annoyance etc.). ~ *n.* Act of preventing other side from scoring in football etc.; (bridge) action taken to avoid heavy loss.

sāve[2] *prep.* Except, but. ~ *conj.* (archaic) Unless, but.

săv′ěloy *n.* Highly seasoned dried sausage. [corrupt. of Fr. *cervelas* (It. (*cervello* brain), named as orig. made f. pig's brain)]

săv′in(e) *n.* European and W. Asiatic small bushy evergreen shrub (*Juniperus sabina*) with dark-green leaves and small bluish-purple berries; dried tops of this, used as drug; various similar shrubs, esp. (U.S.) red cedar (*J. virginiana* and *J. horizontalis*). [L (*herba*) *Sabina* Sabine herb]

sāv′ing *n.* (esp., usu. pl.) Sum of money saved and put by; *savings bank*, bank receiving small deposits at interest and devoting profits to the benefit of depositors. ~ *adj.* (esp.) Making a reservation, furnishing a proviso. ~ *prep.* & *conj.* = SAVE[2] *prep.* & *conj.*

sāv′iour (-vy*er*) *n.* Deliverer, redeemer; *the, our, S~*, Christ.

săv′oir faire′ (-vwâr) *n.* Quickness to see and do the right thing, tact, address.

Săvonarōl′a, Girolamo (1452–98). Dominican monk, whose sermons at Florence gave expression to the religious reaction against the artistic licence and social corruption of the Renaissance; he became the leader of the democratic party in Florence after the expulsion of the Medici, but aroused the hostility of Pope Alexander VI and was burnt at the stake as a heretic.

sāv′ory *n.* Herb of mint family (*Satureia*), used in cooking; esp. *S. hortensis* (summer ~), and *S. montana* (winter ~).

sāv′our (-v*er*) *n.* Characteristic taste, flavour; power of affecting sense of taste; essential virtue or property; tinge, hint, smack, *of*. ~ *v.* Appreciate or perceive taste of; give flavour to (rare); smack, offer suggestion, suggest presence, *of*. **sāv′ourless** *adj.*

sāv′oury *adj.* With appetizing taste or smell; free from bad smells, fragrant (now only with negative); (of dishes etc.) of stimulating or piquant flavour and not sweet. ~ *n.* Savoury dish, esp. one served at end of dinner.

Savoy′[1]**.** Former duchy in NW. Italy forming part of the kingdom of Sardinia; ceded to France in 1860.

Savoy′[2]**,** The. A precinct between the Strand, London, and the Thames, so called from having been given by Henry III in 1246 to Peter of Savoy, who built a palace there.

savoy′[3] *n.* Rough-leaved hardy cabbage grown for winter use. [f. SAVOY[1]]

Savoy′ard (-oi-) *n.* 1. Native of Savoy. 2. Member of the D'Oyly Carte Company which originally performed the SAVOY OPERAS.

Savoy′ Operas. The operas written by W. S. Gilbert and A. Sullivan, so called because they were produced at the Savoy Theatre, London.

săvv′y *v.* (slang) Know. ~ *n.* (slang) Knowingness, wits. [orig. negro- and pidgin-English, after Span. *sabe usted* you know]

saw[1] *n.* Tool, worked by hand or mechanically, for cutting wood, metal, stone, etc., consisting essentially of plate, band, or tube of steel, one edge of which (except in some stone-cutting saws) is

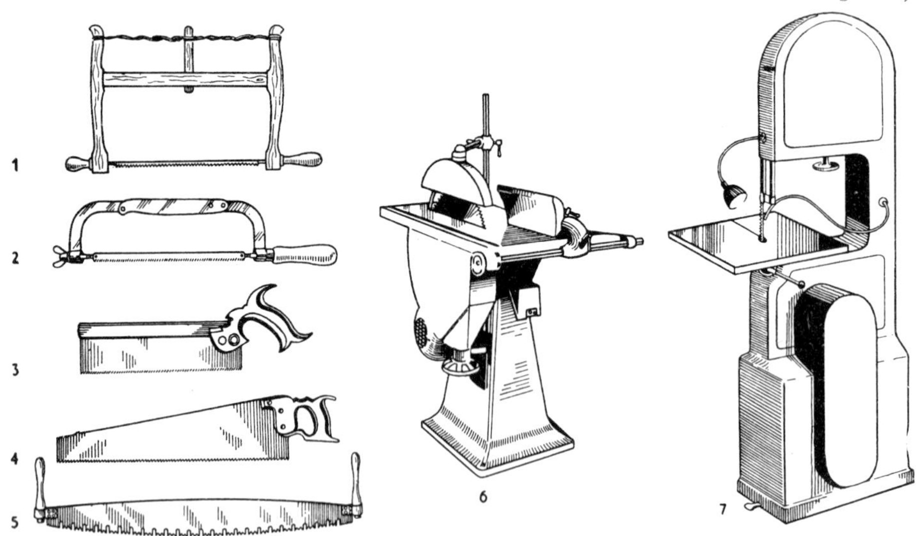

SAWS

1. Bow saw. 2. Hack saw. 3. Tenon saw. 4. Hand saw. 5. Cross-cut saw. 6. Circular saw in machine. 7. Bandsaw in machine

formed into continuous series of teeth; (zool.) part or organ with saw-like teeth; *saw'dust*, tiny fragments of wood produced in sawing, used for stuffing, packing, etc.; *~-edged*, with serrated edge; *~-fish*, sea-fish (*Pristis*) with snout ending in long flat projection with teeth on each edge; *~-fly*, insect of family *Tenthredinidae*, usu. very destructive to vegetation, with saw-like ovipositor; *~-horse*, frame or trestle for supporting wood being sawn; *saw'mill*, mill in which wood is sawn into planks or logs by machinery; *~-pit*, excavation with framework over mouth holding timber to be sawn with long two-handled saw by two men, one in pit and other on raised platform. ~ *v.* Cut (wood etc.) with, make (boards etc.) with, use, saw; move backward and forward, divide (the air etc.) with motion as of saw or person sawing; admit of being sawn *easily*, *badly*, etc.; (bookbinding) make incisions to receive binding-bands in (gathered sheets); *saw'bones*, (slang) surgeon.

saw[2] *n.* Proverbial saying, old maxim.

sawd'er *n.* *Soft ~*, flattery, blarney. [app. = SOLDER]

saw'yer *n.* 1. Man employed in sawing timber. 2. New Zealand longicorn beetle (*Monochamus*), boring in wood. 3. (U.S.) Uprooted tree held fast by one end in stream etc. with free end bobbing up and down with current.

săx[1] *n.* Chopping-tool for trimming slates.

săx[2] *n.* Short for SAXOPHONE.

săx'atile *adj.* Living or growing among rocks.

săxe (blue) *n.* Shade of bright slightly greenish blue. [Fr. *Saxe* Saxony]

Săxe'-Cōb'ŭrg. The name of the English royal house from the accession of Edward VII in 1901; changed to *Windsor* in 1917.

săx'hôrn *n.* Group of seven brass instruments of trumpet kind, with cup-shaped mouthpieces (ill. BRASS). [invented 1845 by Adolphe *Sax*, Belgian instrument-maker]

săx'ifrage *n.* Genus (*Saxifraga*) of Alpine or rock-plants with tufted foliage and panicles of white, yellow, or red flowers. [L *saxifraga* spleenwort, f. *saxum* rock, *frangere* break (prob. because growing in rock-clefts)]

Săx'ō Grammăt'icus (d. *c* 1210). Danish chronicler.

Săx'on *n.* Member, language, of a Germanic people which in the early centuries of the Christian era dwelt in a region near the mouth of the Elbe, and of which one portion, distinguished as the Anglo-Saxons, conquered and occupied part of Britain in the 5th and 6th centuries, while the other, the Old Saxons, remained in Germany; native of modern Saxony; Englishman as opp. to Irish and Welsh, Scottish Lowlander as opp. to Highlander; the Germanic elements in the English language; *plain ~*, homely direct speech. ~ *adj.* Connected with, pertaining to, the Saxons, their language or country; (of English words) of Germanic origin.

Săxōn'ian *adj.* (geol.) Designating a division of the European Permian, or second glacial epoch.

Săx'onism *n.* Word, idiom, surviving in English, derived from Anglo-Saxon (opp. LATINISM).

Săx'ony[1]. Former province of E. central Germany on the upper reaches of the Elbe, earlier part of the larger kingdom of Saxony; now divided between provinces of Saxony and Saxony-Anhalt in E. Germany (capitals, Dresden and Halle) and Lower Saxony in W. Germany (capital, Hanover).

săx'ony[2] *n.* Fine kind of wool; various kinds of cloth (~ *coating*, ~ *flannel*, ~ *cord*) made from it. [f. SAXONY[1]]

săx'ophōne *n.* Keyed wind instrument with conical tube, made of brass but regarded as belonging to wood wind group (ill. WOOD), its mouthpiece being equipped with a reed like a clarinet's. [invented *c* 1840 by Adolphe *Sax*, Belgian instrument-maker; cf. SAXHORN]

say *v.* Utter, recite, rehearse, in ordinary speaking voice; speak, talk (rare); put into words, express; adduce or allege in argument or excuse; form and give opinion or decision; select as example, assume, take as near enough. ~ *n.* (Opportunity of saying) what one has to say; share in decision. **say'ing** *n.* (esp.) Sententious remark, maxim, adage.

S. by E., S by E, S. by W., S by W *abbrevs.* South by East, by West.

sc. *abbrev.* *Scilicet*; *sculpsit*.

S.C. *abbrev.* South Carolina; Special Constable.

scăb *n.* 1. Dry rough incrustation formed over sore in healing, cicatrice. 2. Cutaneous disease in animals, resembling itch. 3. Parasitic disease of plants causing scab-like roughness. 4. (slang) Mean low fellow; (orig. U.S.) blackleg. ~ *v.* Form scab, heal over. **scăbb'y** *adj.*

scăbb'ard *n.* Sheath of sword, bayonet, etc. (ill. SWORD); ~ *fish*, long, silver-coloured, eel-like sea fish (*Lepidopus caudatus*), frost-fish.

scāb'ies (-ēz, -ĭēz) *n.* The itch, a contagious skin-disease due to a parasite, the mite *Sarcoptes scabiei*.

scāb'ious *n.* Genus of herbaceous plants (*Scabiosa*) with blue, pink, or white pincushion-shaped aggregate flowers. [med. L. *scabiosa* (*herba*), named as specific against itch, f. SCABIES]

scāb'rous *adj.* 1. (zool., bot., etc.) With rough surface, scurfy. 2. (literature; of subject, situation, etc.) Requiring tactful treatment, hard to handle with decency.

scăd *n.* Horse-mackerel, fish (*Trachurus*), abundant off British coasts, with enlarged plates on side of body.

scăff'old *n.* 1. Temporary raised platform for execution of criminals; *the ~*, death at executioner's hands. 2. (rare) SCAFFOLDING 1. **scăff'olding** *n.* 1. Temporary structure of wooden poles (or metal tubes) and planks

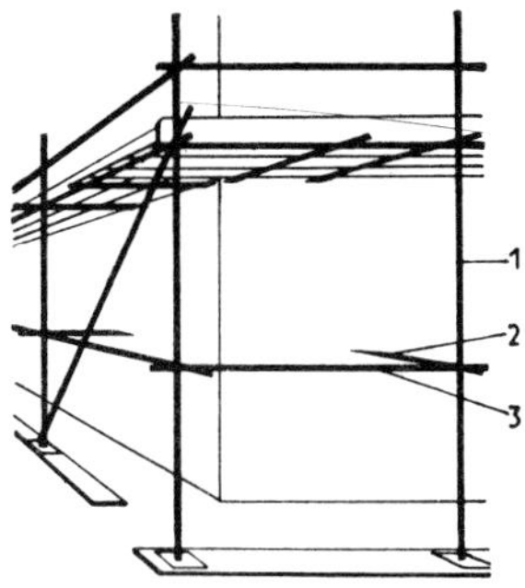

SCAFFOLDING

1. Standard. 2. Putlog fixed in wall. 3. Ledger

providing platform(s) for workmen to stand on while erecting or repairing building. 2. Materials for making such structure. 3. Temporary framework for other purposes (also fig.). **scăff'old** *v.t.* Attach scaffolding to (building).

scagliola (skălyōl'*a*) *n.* Kind of plaster-work (of gypsum and glue with surface of marble dust etc.) imitating stone. [It. *scagliuola*, dim. of *scaglia* chip of marble]

scald[1] (-aw-) *v.t.* Injure or pain with hot liquid or vapour; affect like boiling water; cleanse with boiling water; pour hot liquid over; heat (liquid, esp. milk) nearly to boiling-point. ~ *n.* Injury to skin by scalding.

scald[2] (-aw-), **skald** *n.* Ancient-Scandinavian composer and reciter of poems in honour of heroes and their deeds.

scāle[1] *n.* 1. One of the small thin membranous horny or bony outgrowths or modifications of skin in many fishes, reptiles, etc., freq. overlapping, and forming covering for (part of) the body (ill. FISH). 2. Flattened membranous plate of cellular tissue (usu. rudimentary or degenerate leaf) as covering of leaf-buds of deciduous trees etc. (ill. BULB). 3. Protective covering of many female insects (*~-insect*, *-bug*) of family *Coccidae* infesting and injuring various plants (ill. BUG). 4. Thin plate, lamina, or film of any kind; (fig., after Acts ix. 18) what causes physical or moral blindness; (usu. collect.) film of oxide forming on iron or other metal when heated and hammered or rolled; hard deposit or 'fur' in boilers etc.; incrustation of lime or dirt on bottom of salt-pan; tartar on teeth. 5. *~-armour*, armour of small overlapping plates of metal, horn, etc.; *~-board*, very thin board for hat-boxes, veneer, etc.; *~-insect*: see sense 3. ~ *v.* Take away scale(s) from; form, come off in, drop, scales; (of scales) come *off*. **scāl'y** *adj.* Covered with, having, scales.

scāle[2] *n.* Pan of balance; weighing instrument, esp. (*pair of ~s*) one consisting of beam pivoted at middle and with dish, pan, board, etc., suspended at either end (ill. BALANCE); *hold the ~s even*, judge impartially; *turn the ~*, exceed weight in other pan etc. of balance, outweigh other considerations, motives, etc. ~ *v.t.* Weigh (specified amount).

scāle[3] *n.* 1. (mus.) Definite series of sounds ascending or descending by fixed intervals; any of graduated series of sounds into

SCALES

1. Tonic. 2. Supertonic. 3. Mediant. 4. Subdominant. 5. Dominant. 6. Submediant. 7. Leading note. 8. Tonic (octave above 1). 1–2, 2–3, 4–5, 5–6, 6–7 are tones; 3–4, 7–8 are semitones

which octave may be divided; any of these series as subject of instruction or practice. 2. Series of degrees, graduated arrangement, system, or classification; standard of measurement, calculation, etc.; (arith.) system of numeration or numerical notations, in which the value of a figure depends on its place in the order (the usual or *denary* ~ is that in which successive places from right to left represent units, tens, hundreds, etc.); relative dimensions, proportion which representation of an object bears to the object itself. 3. Set of marks at measured distances on line for use in measuring or making proportional reductions or enlargements; rule determining intervals between these; piece of metal, wood, etc., apparatus, on which they are marked. ~ *v.* 1. Climb with ladder or by clambering; *scaling-ladder*, one used in escalades. 2. Represent in dimensions proportional to actual ones; reduce to common scale; ~ *up*, *down*, make larger, smaller, in due proportion. 3. (Of quantities etc.) have common scale, be commensurable.

scalēne' (*or* skāl'ēn) *adj.* ~ *triangle*, triangle with no two sides equal (ill. TRIANGLE); ~ *cone*, *cylinder*, one of which axis is not perpendicular to base; ~ *muscle*, scalenus.

scalēn'us *n.* (pl. *-nī*). (anat.) One of set of triangular muscles (three on each side of neck) extending from cervical vertebrae to first or second rib (ill. HEAD).

Scăl'iger, Joseph Justus (1540–1609). Renaissance scholar of Italian origin, known as 'the founder of historical criticism'.

scal(l)awag: see SCALLYWAG.

scăll'ion (-yon) *n.* Shallot; Welsh onion (kind of *Allium* intermediate in appearance between onion and leek); onion which fails to bulb but forms long neck and strong blade. [OF *eschaloigne*, see SHALLOT]

scall'op (skŏ- *or* skă-) *n.* 1. Bivalve mollusc (*Pecten*) with shell having ridges radiating from middle of hinge and edged with small rounded lobes; one valve of this as utensil in which various dishes (of fish, minced meat, etc., with bread-crumbs or sauce) are cooked and served; (hist.) pilgrim's cockle-shell worn as sign that he had visited shrine of St. James at Compostella. 2. One of series of convex rounded projections at edge of garment etc. ~ *v.t.* 1. Bake in scallop-shell or similar shallow pan or dish. 2. Ornament (edge, material) with scallops.

scăll'ywăg, scăl(l)'awăg *n.* (colloq., orig. U.S.) Rogue, rascal, disreputable person; (U.S. hist.) native white of southern State accepting Republican principles after Civil War; (U.S., pl.) undersized or ill-conditioned cattle.

scălp *n.* Top of head (now dial.); skin of upper part of head, with hair covering it, this cut or torn from man's head as battle trophy by Amer. Indians (freq. fig.). ~ *v.t.* Take scalp of (freq. fig.).

scăl'pel *n.* Surgeon's or anatomist's small straight knife.

scăl'per, scaup'er, scŏrp'er *ns.* Engraver's tool for hollowing out bottom of sunken designs (ill. ENGRAVE).

scămm'ony *n.* (Kind of convolvulus, *C. Scammonia*, of Syria and Asia Minor, with fleshy root yielding) gum-resin used as strong purgative.

scămp[1] *n.* Rascal, knave (freq. joc.).

scămp[2] *v.t.* Do (work etc.) in perfunctory or inadequate way.

scăm'per *v.i.* Run or caper about nimbly, rush hastily. ~ *n.* Hasty run, gallop; rapid tour.

scăn *v.* 1. Analyse, test metre of (verse) by examining number and quantity of feet and syllables; (of verse) be metrically correct. 2. Look intently at all parts successively of. 3. Read off a picture in terms of light and shade in a pre-arranged number and pattern of lines as a stage in televising. 4. (radar) (Cause particular region) to be traversed by a controlled beam.

scăn'dal *n.* (Thing that occasions) general feeling of outrage or indignation, esp. as expressed in common talk; malicious gossip, backbiting; (law) public affront, irrelevant abusive statement in court. **scăn'dalous** *adj.* **scăn'dalously** *adv.* **scăn'dalmonger** (-ŭngg-) *n.* One who invents or spreads scandals.

scăn'dalīze[1] *v.t.* Offend moral feelings, sense of propriety, etc.; shock.

scăn'dalīze[2] *v.t.* (naut.) Reduce area of (sail) by lowering peak and tricing up tack. [alteration of obs. *scantelize*, f. SCANTLE]

scăn'dalum măgnāt'um *n.* (hist.) Utterance or publication of malicious report against holder of position of dignity.

Scăndĭnāv'ĭa. Geographical term for Sweden, Norway, and Denmark, together with the adjacent islands and Iceland. **Scăndĭnāv'ĭan** *adj.* & *n.* (Native, family of languages) of Scandinavia.

scăn'dĭum *n.* Rare metallic element (discovered 1879 in Scandinavian mineral euxenite) usu. included in rare-earth group; symbol Sc, at. no. 21, at. wt 44·956. [L *Scandia* Scandinavia]

scănn'er *n.* (esp.) Instrument which scans television pictures.

scăn'sion (-shn) *n.* Metrical scanning; way verse scans.

scănsōr'ial *adj.* (Of feet of birds and animals) adapted for climbing; that is given to climbing.

scănt *adj.* Barely sufficient, deficient, with scanty supply *of*.

scănt'lĭng *n.* 1. Small beam or piece of wood, esp. one less than 5 in. × 8 in.; block or slice of stone of fixed size. 2. Size to which stone or timber is to be cut; set of standard dimensions for parts of structure, esp. in ship-building. 3. Trestle for cask.

scăn'ty *adj.* Of small extent or amount; barely sufficient. **scăn'tĭly** *adv.* **scăn'tĭness** *n.*

Scapa Flow (skahp'a flō). British naval base in the Orkney Islands.

scāpe[1] *n.* & *v.t.* (archaic) Escape.

scāpe[2] *n.* 1. (archit.) Shaft of column. 2. (bot.) Long flower-stalk rising directly from root or rhizome of plant having only radical leaves. 3. (entom.) First segment of antenna (ill. INSECT). 4. (ornith.) Shaft of feather.

scāpe'goat (-pg-) *n.* (In Mosaic ritual of Day of Atonement) goat allowed to escape into wilderness, the sins of the people having been symbolically laid upon it (see Lev. xvi); hence, person blamed or punished for sins of others.

scāpe'grāce (-pg-) *n.* Reckless or careless person, esp. young man or boy constantly in 'scrapes'. [= 'one who escapes the grace of God']

scăph'oid *adj.* Shaped like boat. ~ *n.* (also ~ *bone*) First proximal carpal bone in mammals (ill. HAND).

s. caps *abbrev.* Small capital letters.

scăp'ūla *n.* (pl. *-lae*). Shoulder-blade (ill. SKELETON).

scăp'ūlar *adj.* Of the scapula; ~ *arch*, shoulder girdle; ~ *feather*, one growing from scapular region (ill. BIRD). ~ *n.* 1. (eccles.) Monk's short cloak covering shoulders; badge of affiliation to religious order consisting of two strips of cloth hanging down breast and back and joined across shoulders, worn under clothing. 2. Bandage for shoulder-blade. 3. Scapular feather. **scăp'ūlary** *n.* = SCAPULAR *n.* 1, 3.

scar̄[1] *n.* Trace of healed wound, sore, or burn, cicatrix (freq. fig.); *leaf* ~, mark on plant left by fall of leaf etc., hilum. ~ *v.* Mark with scar or scars; heal over, form scar.

scar̄[2] *n.* Precipitous craggy part of mountain-side.

scă rab *n.* Dung-beetle (*Scarabaeus sacer*) revered by ancient Egyptians as symbol of resurrection and immortality; carnelian, obsidian, emerald, etc., in form of beetle, with intaglio design on flat under-side, worn in ring or as pendant round neck, esp. by ancient Egyptians, Etruscans, etc.

scărabae'id *adj.* & *n.* (Beetle) of lamellicorn family *Scarabaeidae*, including cockchafers, dung-beetles, stag-beetles, etc.

scărabae'us *n.* (pl. *-ae'ī*). Scarab; (*S*~) genus of beetles including scarab etc.

scă'ramouch *n.* (archaic) Boastful poltroon, braggart. [Fr., f. It. *Scaramuccia*, stock character in Italian farce]

scar̄ce *adj.* Insufficient, not plentiful, scanty; seldom met with, rare; *make oneself* ~, go away, keep away. ~ *adv.* (archaic, poet., rhet.) Scarcely. **scar̄ce'ly** (-sl-) *adv.* Hardly, barely, only just. **scar̄ce'nėss** *n.* **scar̄'city** *n.* (esp.) Dearth of food.

scar̄ce'ment (-sm-) *n.* Set-back in wall etc.; ledge resulting from this.

scār̄e *v.t.* Strike with sudden terror, frighten; frighten away, drive off; *scare'crow*, device for frightening birds away from crops, usu. figure of man in ragged clothes; bogy; badly dressed or grotesque person. ~ *n.* Sudden fright or alarm; esp. general public alarm caused by baseless or exaggerated rumours. **scare'-monger** (-ār̄mŭngg-) *n.* Alarmist.

scar̄f[1] *n.* Long narrow strip of material worn for ornament or warmth round neck, over shoulders, from one shoulder to opposite hip, or round waist; man's necktie with wide flowing ends; ~*-pin*, usu. ornamental pin for fastening scarf or neck-tie; ~*-ring*, ring for holding ends of neck-tie together; ~*-skin*, outer layer of skin, epidermis.

scar̄f[2] *v.t.* Join ends of (pieces of timber, metal, or leather) by bevelling or notching so that they overlap without increase of thickness and then bolting, brazing or sewing them together. ~ *n.* Joint made by scarfing (ill. JOINT); notch, groove.

scar̄'ifier (*or* skă-) *n.* Agricultural machine with prongs for loosening soil.

scar̄'ifȳ (*or* skă-) *v.t.* Make superficial incisions in (surg.); make sore, wound (now fig.); break up ground with scarifier. **scar̄ificā'tion** *n.*

scar̄'ious *adj.* (bot.) Thin, dry, and membranous (of bracts etc.).

scar̄lati'na (-tē-) *n.* Scarlet fever (pop. applied to what is supposed to be a milder form of the disease).

Scar̄lătt'ĭ, Alessandro (1658–1725). Italian musical composer, founder of the Neapolitan school of opera. ~, Domenico (1685–1757). Son of Alessandro; composer of many 'sonatas'.

scar̄l'ėt *n.* & *adj.* (Of) brilliant red colour inclining to orange; scarlet cloth or clothes; ~ *fever*, contagious fever, due to streptococcal infection, with scarlet eruptions of skin and mucous membrane of mouth and pharynx; ~ *hat*, cardinal's hat, esp. as symbol of the rank of cardinal; ~ *pimpernel*, red-flowered common pimpernel (*Anagallis arvensis*); ~ *runner*, red-flowered climbing bean (*Phaseolus multiflorus*); ~ *woman*, harlot; (also) abusive epithet applied to the Church of Rome (in allusion to Rev. xvii. 1–5). [perh. f. Pers. *sagalat* scarlet cloth]

scă'roid *adj.* & *n.* (Fish) of family *Scaridae* of fishes inhabiting warm seas and including scarus etc.

scar̄p *n.* Inner wall or slope of ditch in fortification (ill. CASTLE); any steep slope. ~ *v.t.* Give steep face to, slope steeply.

scar̄'us *n.* Mediterranean parrot-fish esteemed by Romans as food; (*S*~) genus of mostly bright-coloured fishes allied to wrasse family, with coalescent teeth giving beak-like appearance to jaws.

scāthe (-dh) *v.t.* Injure, esp. by fire, lightning, etc. (poet.); 'wither' with fierce invective or satire. **scāth'ing** *adj.*

scătŏl'ogy *n.* Study of coprolites or obscene literature.

scatŏph'agous *adj.* Feeding on, eating, dung.

scătt'er *v.* 1. Throw here and there, strew, sprinkle; (of gun, cartridge) distribute (shot); (physics) diffuse in various directions by reflection from molecules, atoms, electrons, or other particles, e.g. a ray of light is scattered by dust particles. 2. Separate and disperse in flight etc. 3. ~*-brain*, heedless person; ~*-brained*, heedless, desultory. **scătt'ered** (-*erd*) *adj.* (esp.) Not situated together, wide apart; sporadic. **scătt'er** *n.* Act of scattering; extent of distribution, esp. of shot.

scaup(-dŭck) *n.* Kinds of duck (*Fuligula*, esp. *F. marila*) of N. European, Asiatic, and American coasts, the head of the male being black glossed with green.

scauper: see SCALPER.

scăv'ėnger (-j-) *n.* Person employed to keep streets etc. clean by carrying away refuse; animal feeding on carrion, garbage, or any decaying organic matter. **scăv'ėnge** *v.* Be, act as, scavenger.

scăz'on *n.* (Gk and L prosody) Iambic trimeter ending with spondee or trochee instead of iambus, ⏓ – | ⏑ – | ⏑ – | ⏓ – | ⏑ – | – ⏓; choliamb. [Gk *skazōn*, f. *skazō* limp]

scena (shā'nah) *n.* (Words and music of) scene in Italian opera; long vocal solo with recitatives and arias, and with orchestral accompaniment.

scenario *n.* (pl. *-s*). 1. (shānar̄'ĭō). Skeleton libretto of play or opera. 2. (sĭnar̄'ĭō) Complete plot of film play, with all necessary directions for actors, details of scenes, etc. **scēn'arist** *n.* Composer of scenario, sense 2. [It., f. *scena* scene]

scēne *n.* 1. Stage of Greek or Roman theatre (hist.); stage (archaic); place where action of (part of) play, novel, etc., is supposed to take place; locality of event. 2. Portion of a play during which action is continuous, or (esp. of French plays) in which no intermediate entries or exits occur; subdivision (rarely, the whole) of an act; episode, situation, as subject of narrative or description; action, episode, situation, in real life. 3. Stormy encounter or interview; agitated colloquy, esp. with display of temper. 4. Any of the pieces of painted canvas, woodwork, etc., used to represent scene of action on stage; picture presented by these to audience; (transf.) landscape or view spread before spectator like scene in theatre; *behind the* ~*s*, amidst actors and stage-machinery; (fig.) acting upon information not accessible to the public; *change of* ~, variety of surroundings esp.

secured by travel; ~-*dock*, space near stage where scenes are stored (ill. THEATRE); ~-*painter*, painter of theatrical scenery; ~-*shifter*, person helping to change scenes in theatre.

scēn'ery *n.* 1. Accessories used in theatre to make stage resemble supposed scene of action. 2. General appearance of natural features etc. of place or district; picturesque features of landscape.

scēn'ĭc *adj.* Of, on, the stage; of the nature of a show, picturesque in grouping; having fine natural scenery, giving landscape views; ~ *railway*, miniature railway running through artificial scenery. **scēn'ĭcally** *adv.*

scĕnt *v.* 1. Discern by smell; perceive as if by smell, detect. 2. Impregnate with odour, perfume. ~ *n.* 1. Distinctive odour, esp. of agreeable kind; odour of man or animal as means of pursuit by hound, trail; (in paper-chase) paper strewn by 'hares' as trail for 'hounds'. 2. (of animals, esp. dogs) Power of detecting or distinguishing smells; (fig.) flair. 3. Liquid perfume made by distillation from flowers etc.

scĕp'sĭs (sk-) *n.* Philosophic doubt, sceptical philosophy.

scĕp'tĭc (sk-) *n.* One who doubts the possibility of real knowledge of any kind; one who doubts the truth of the Christian or of all religious doctrines; person of sceptical temper, or unconvinced of the truth of a particular fact or theory. **scĕp'tĭcal** (sk-) *adj.* Inclined to suspense of judgement, given to questioning truth of facts and soundness of inferences; critical, incredulous, hard to convince. **scĕp'tĭcally** *adv.* **scĕp'tĭcism** *n.*

scĕp'tre (-t*er*) *n.* Staff borne in hand as symbol of regal or imperial authority (ill. REGALIA); (fig.) royal or imperial dignity, sovereignty. **scĕp'tred** (-t*erd*) *adj.*

Sch. *abbrev.* Scholar; school.

schadenfreude (shahd'*e*nfroid*e*) *n.* Malicious enjoyment of others' misfortunes.

schăppe (sh-), **shăp** *ns.* Fabric or yarn made from waste silk.

schĕd'ūle (sh-; U.S. sk-) *n.* Tabulated statement of details, inventory, list, etc., esp. as appendix or annexe to principal document; (chiefly U.S.) timetable; *on* ~, at time provided for in time-table. ~ *v.t.* Make schedule of; enter in schedule; *scheduled territories*, countries in the STERLING area.

Scheldt (skĕlt). River flowing from the Aisne department, France, through Belgium and Holland to the North Sea.

Schĕll'ĭng (sh-), Friedrich Wilhelm Joseph von (1775–1854). German philosopher; regarded nature as a single living organism working towards self-consciousness, a faculty dormant in inanimate objects and fully awake only in man, whose being consists in 'intellectual intuition' of the world he creates.

schēm'a (sk-) *n.* Diagram, outline; (Kantian philos.) form (a product of the imagination) through which what is perceived is subsumed under a 'category'. **schēmăt'ĭc** *adj.* **schēmăt'ĭcally** *adv.*

schēme (sk-) *n.* 1. Systematic arrangement; table of classification or of appointed times; plan for doing something. 2. Artful or underhand design. ~ *v.i.* Make plans, plan esp. in secret or underhand way. **schēm'er** *n.* **schēm'ĭng** *adj.*

scherzăn'dŏ (skārts-) *adv.*, *adj.*, & *n.* (mus.) Playfully, sportively; playful, sportive (passage, movement).

scherzo (skārt'sō) *n.* (mus.) Vigorous (properly light and playful) composition, independent or as movement in work of sonata type. [It., f. Teut. (Ger. *scherz* jest)]

Schiedăm' (skĭ-). Town of Holland; kind of gin made there.

Schĭll'er (sh-), Johann Christoph Friedrich von (1759–1805). German dramatist, lyric poet and historian; author of the dramas 'Die Räuber', 'Don Carlos', 'Wallenstein', 'Maria Stuart', 'Die Jungfrau von Orleans', 'Die Braut von Messina', 'Wilhelm Tell', etc.

schĭll'ĭng (sh-), *n.* Principal monetary unit of Austria, = 100 groschen.

schĭpp'erkė (sk-, sh-) *n.* Kind of small black dog, tailless, smooth-haired and with prick ears, orig. bred in Holland and Flanders and used as a watch-dog on barges. [Du. dim. of *schipper* boatman]

schism (sĭzm) *n.* Breach of unity of a Church, separation into two Churches or secession of part of Church owing to difference of opinion on doctrine or discipline; offence of promoting schism.

schismăt'ĭc (sĭz-) *adj.* & *n.* (Person) tending to, guilty of, schism; (member) of seceded branch of a Church.

schĭst (sh-) *n.* Fine-grained metamorphic rock with component minerals arranged in more or less parallel layers, splitting in thin irregular plates. **schĭs'tōse**, **schĭs'tous** *adjs.*

schīzăn'thus (sk-) *n.* Genus of flowering annuals, natives of Chile, with finely divided leaves and showy variegated flowers, usu. white, violet, or crimson.

schiz'oid (skĭdz-) *adj.* & *n.* Of, resembling, schizophrenia; (person) having schizophrenic features of personality.

schīzomȳcēte' (sk-) *n.* Member of class *Schizomycetae* of minute, freq. single-celled, lowly organisms between algae and fungi, including bacilli, bacteria, etc. **schīzomȳcēt'ous** *adj.*

schizophrēn'ĭa (skĭdz-) *n.* Mental disease marked by disconnexion between thoughts, feelings, and actions. **schīzophrĕn'ĭc** *adj.* & *n.*

Schle'gel (shlāgl), August Wilhelm von (1767–1845). German Romantic critic, chiefly known in England for his translation into German, with the collaboration of others, of the plays of Shakespeare. ~, Friedrich von (1772–1829), his younger brother, Romantic critic and novelist.

Schleswig (shlās'vĭk). Former duchy of the Danish Crown, acquired by conquest by Prussia in 1864 and incorporated into the province of Schleswig-Holstein; the N. part of this territory was returned to Denmark in 1920 after a plebiscite held in accordance with the Treaty of Versailles; ~-*Holstein*, province of the Federal Republic of Germany (capital, Kiel).

Schliem'ann (shlē-), Heinrich (1822–90). German archaeologist, who excavated Troy, Tiryns, and Mycenae.

schmelz (shmĕlts) *n.* Kinds of coloured glass, esp. red kind used to flash white glass.

schnăpps (shn-) *n.* Strong hollands gin.

schnauzer (shnow'ts*er*) *n.* Wire-coated black, black-and-brown, or pepper-and-salt terrier of German breed.

schnĭtzel (shn-) *n.* Veal cutlet, esp. (*Wiener* ~) one fried in bread-crumbs in the Viennese style and garnished with lemon, anchovies, etc.

schnŏrk'el (shn-) *n.* 1. (also *snorkel*) Funnel providing German submarine with air, snort. 2. Breathing-tube used by divers who swim just below surface of water. [Ger. *schnorchel*]

schnŏr'rer (shn-) *n.* (Yiddish term for) beggar.

schŏl'ar (sk-) *n.* 1. Schoolboy, schoolgirl, esp. at elementary school; one who learns. 2. Holder of scholarship at school or university. 3. Learned person, person versed in literature. **schŏl'arly** *adj.*

schŏl'arship (sk-) *n.* 1. Attainments of a scholar; learning, erudition. 2. (Right to) emoluments paid, during a fixed period, from funds of school, college, university, etc., or State, for defraying cost of education or studies, usu. granted after competitive examination.

scholăs'tĭc (sk-) *adj.* 1. Of schools or other educational establishments; educational, academic; pedantic, formal. 2. (As) of the SCHOOL[1]men; dealing in logical subtleties. **scholăs'tĭcally** *adv.* **scholăs'tĭcism** *n.* **scholăs'tĭc** *n.* 1. Schoolman; modern theologian of scholastic tendencies. 2. Jesuit between novitiate and priesthood.

schŏl'ĭast (sk-) *n.* Writer of scholia (see foll.).

schŏl'ium (sk-) *n.* (pl. *scholia*). Marginal note, explanatory comment, esp. one by an ancient grammarian on a passage in a classical author.

schōōl[1] (sk-) *n.* 1. Institution for educating children or giving instruction, usu. of more elementary or more technical kind than that given at universities; buildings, pupils, of this; time given to teaching; being educated in a school; (fig.) circumstances or occupation serving to discipline or instruct. 2. Organized body of teachers and scholars in any of higher branches of study in Middle Ages, esp. as constituent part of medieval university; any of the branches of study with separate examinations at university; (or pl.) hall in which university examinations are held; (pl.) such examinations. 3. Disciples, imitators, followers, of philosopher, artist, etc.; band or succession of persons devoted to some cause, principle, etc. 4. *~-board*, (hist.) from 1870 to 1902, body of persons elected by ratepayers of a district to provide and maintain public elementary schools (hence called *board-schools*); *school'boy*, boy at school; *~-days*, time of being at school; *school'girl*, girl at school; *~-ma'am*, *-marm*, (colloq.) schoolmistress; *school'man*, teacher in medieval university; writer (9th–14th centuries) treating of logic, metaphysics, and theology as taught in medieval 'schools' or universities of Europe; *school'master*, *school'mistress*, head or assistant male, female, teacher in school; *school'room*, room used for lessons in school or private house; *~-teacher*, teacher esp. in elementary school. ~ *v.* Send to school, provide for education of (rare); discipline, bring under control, train or accustom *to*. **schōōl'ing** *n.*

schōōl[2] (sk-) *n.* Shoal of or *of* fish.

schōōn'er[1] (sk-) *n.* Small seagoing fore-and-aft rigged sailing vessel, orig. with only two masts, later with three or four, and usu. carrying one or more topsails.

SCHOONER

schōōn'er[2] (sk-) *n.* (U.S.) Large tall beer-glass.

Schŏp'enhauer (sh-, -how-), Arthur (1788–1860). German pessimistic philosopher, who taught that the absolute reality is a blind and restless will, that all existence is essentially evil, and that release can be attained only by overcoming the will to live.

schottische (shŏtēsh') *n.* Kind of dance like polka but slower; music for this. [Ger., = 'Scottish']

Schub'ert (shōō-), Franz Peter (1797–1828). Austrian musical composer, esp. famous for his songs.

Schum'ann (shōō-), Robert Alexander (1810–56). German Romantic musical composer, author of many songs and much piano and chamber music etc.

sciăt'ic (sī-) *adj.* Of the hip; of, affecting, the sciatic nerve; suffering from, liable to, sciatica; *~ nerve*, each of two divisions of the sacral plexus, esp. the *great ~ nerve*, largest nerve in human body, emerging from pelvis and passing down back of thigh to foot.

sciăt'ica (sī-) *n.* Neuritis or neuralgia of sciatic nerve, with paroxysms of pain along course of nerve and its branches.

science (sī'-) *n.* 1. Systematic and formulated knowledge; pursuit of this, principles regulating such pursuit. 2. Branch of knowledge, organized body of the knowledge that has been accumulated on a subject; *exact ~*, one admitting of quantitative treatment; *pure ~*, one depending on deductions from self-evident truths, (also) one pursued for its own sake, as opp. to *applied ~*, one studied for practical purposes; *natural ~*, *physical ~*, one dealing with material phenomena and based mainly on observation, experiment, and induction, as chemistry, biology. 3. The natural sciences collectively, the systematic study of the phenomena of the material universe and their laws. 4. (in sport, esp. boxing) Expert's skill as opp. to strength or natural ability.

sciĕn'tial (sī-, -shl) *adj.* Of knowledge. **sciĕn'tially** *adv.*

scientĭf'ic (sī-) *adj.* Of science, esp. the natural sciences; devised according to the rules of science for testing soundness of conclusions etc.; systematic, accurate; assisted by expert knowledge.

sci'entist (sī-) *n.* One who studies or professes the natural sciences.

sci'lĭcĕt (sī-) *adv.* (abbrev. *sc.*, *scil.*). That is to say, namely.

scĭll'a (s-) *n.* (Plant or flower of) genus of liliaceous bulbous plants, the squills, esp. the frequently cultivated blue-flowered *S. sibirica.*

Scĭll'y (sĭ-), **Isles of.** Group of small islands off W. extremity of Cornwall.

scĭm'ĭtar (sĭ-) *n.* Oriental short curved single-edged sword, usu. broadening towards point.

scĭntĭll'a (sĭ-) *n.* Spark, atom.

scĭn'tĭllāte (sĭ-) *v.i.* Sparkle, twinkle (freq. fig.); emit sparks. **scĭn'tillant** *adj.* **scĭntĭllā'tion** *n.*

sci'olĭst (sī-) *n.* Superficial pretender to knowledge, smatterer. **sci'olism** *n.* **sciolĭs'tic** *adj.*

sci'on (sī-) *n.* Shoot of plant, esp. one cut for grafting or planting (ill. GRAFT); descendant, young member of (esp. noble) family.

scirrhus (sĭ'rus, skĭ-) *n.* (path.) Hard carcinoma; organ which has hardened. **scĭ'rrhoid, scĭ'rrhous** *adjs.* **scĭrrhŏs'ĭty** *n.*

scission (sĭ'shn) *n.* Cutting, being cut; division, split.

scissors (sĭz'orz) *n.pl.* 1. Cutting instrument consisting of pair of handled blades so pivoted that the instrument can be opened to X-shape and then closed with the object to be cut between the edges of the blades. 2. (wrestling) Hold in which opponent's head or body is clasped with legs. **scissor** *v.t.* Cut with scissors.

sclēr'a *n.* = SCLEROTIC *n.*

ˌ**sclērĕnch'ȳma** (-ngk-) *n.* Hard tissue of coral; tissue of higher plants composed of cells with thickened and lignified walls, forming e.g. nut-shell or seed-coat.

sclēr'ogĕn *n.* Hard lignified matter deposited on inner surface of plant-cells.

sclerōs'is *n.* (pl. *-es* pr. -ēz). 1. (path.) Replacement of normal tissue, esp. of nervous system or arteries, by overgrowth of fibrous or supporting tissue, resulting in hardening and loss of function. 2. (bot.) Hardening of cell-wall by lignification.

sclerŏt'ic *adj.* Of, affected with, sclerosis; of the sclerotic. ~ *n.* Hard opaque white outer coat covering eyeball except over cornea and forming white of eye (ill. EYE).

S.C.M. *abbrev.* State Certified Midwife; Student Christian Movement.

scŏff *v.i.* Speak derisively, esp. of something deserving respect, mock, jeer (*at*). ~ *n.* Derisive jest; object of derision or scoffing. **scŏff'er** *n.*

scōld *v.* Find fault noisily, rail; rate, rebuke. ~ *n.* Railing or nagging woman. **scōl'ding** *n.*

scŏnce[1] *n.* Flat candlestick with handle; bracket candlestick to hang on wall (ill. CANDLE).

scŏnce[2] *n.* (Old joc. term for) head, crown of head.

scŏnce[3] *n.* Small fort or earthwork, usu. covering a ford, pass, etc.

scŏnce[4] *v.t.* (at Oxford Univ.) Inflict forfeit of beer upon, for offence against table etiquette. ~ *n.* Such forfeit.

scŏne[1] *n.* Soft flat cake of flour, freq. with currants etc., usu. round or quadrant-shaped, and orig. baked on a griddle.

Scone[2] (-ōōn). Village in Perthshire, ancient capital of the Scots where their kings were crowned; *stone of* ~: see CORONATION stone.

scōōp *n.* 1. Short-handled deep shovel for dipping up and carrying such materials as flour, grain,

MARROW SCOOP

coal; long-handled ladle; instrument with spoon- or gouge-shaped blade for cutting out piece from soft material or removing embedded substance, core, etc.; coal-scuttle. 2. Motion as of, act of, scooping; slurring of interval by singer or fiddler. 3. (orig. U.S. slang) Obtaining of news etc. by newspaper before, or to exclusion of, competitors, news so obtained; lucky stroke of business etc., large profit. ~ *v.t.* 1. Lift (*up*), hollow (*out*), (as) with scoop; slur (notes) in music. 2. (slang) Secure (large profit etc.) by sudden action or stroke of luck; get advantage over (rival) by obtaining newspaper scoop.

scōōt *v.i.* Run, dart, make off.

scōōt'er *n.* 1. Child's toy vehicle, consisting of a narrow foot-board mounted on two tandem wheels, the front one attached to a long steering-handle, propelled by a series of pushes given by one foot on the ground, the other foot resting on the foot-board; simple kind of motor bicycle. 2. (U.S.) Sail-boat with runners for use on either ice or water.

scōp'a *n.* (entom.) Small brush-like tuft of hairs esp. on bee's leg, by which pollen is gathered from hairs on body.

scōpe *n.* End aimed at, purpose (now rare); outlook, purview, sweep or reach of observation or action, range; opportunity, outlet; (naut.) length of cable out when ship rides at anchor.

scopŏl'amine (*or* -ēn) *n.* = HYOSCINE.

scorbūt'ic *adj.* & *n.* Of, like, (person) affected with, scurvy.

scorch *v.* 1. Burn surface of with flame or heat so as to discolour, injure, or pain; affect with sensation of burning; become discoloured, slightly burnt, etc., with heat; *scorched earth*, applied to a policy of destroying all means of sustenance and supply in a country that might be of use to an invading enemy. 2. (slang, of motorist etc.) Go at very high or excessive speed.

score *n.* 1. Notch cut, line cut, scratched, or drawn. 2. Running account kept by scores against customer's name, esp. for drink in old inns; reckoning, esp. for entertainment; *pay off old* ~*s*, (fig.) pay person out for past offence. 3. Number of points made by player or side in some games; register of items of this. 4. (mus.) Copy of composition on set of staves braced and barred together; *full* ~, with each part on separate staff. 5. (pl. same exc. in ~*s* = large numbers) Twenty; set of 20; weight of 20 (or 21) lb., used in weighing pigs or oxen. 6. Category, head. 7. (slang) Remark or act scoring off person; piece of good luck. ~ *v.* 1. Mark with notches, incisions, or lines, slash, furrow; make (line, notch, incision); mark *up* in inn-score; enter; (fig.) mentally record (offence *against* offender); record (score in cricket and other games), keep score; win and be credited with, make points in game, secure an advantage, have good luck; ~ *off*, (slang) worst in argument or repartee, inflict humiliation on. 2. (mus.) Orchestrate; arrange *for* an instrument; write out in score.

scor'ia *n.* (pl. *-iae, -ias*). Cellular lava, fragments of this; slag. **scorĭā'ceous** (-sh*us*) *adj.*

scor'ify *v.t.* Reduce to scoria or slag, esp. in assaying. **scorificā'tion** *n.*

scorn *v.t.* Hold in contempt, despise, consider unworthy or beneath notice. ~ *n.* Disdain, contempt, derision; object of contempt. **scorn'ful** *adj.* **scorn'fully** *adv.* **scorn'fulnĕss** *n.*

scorper: see SCALPER.

Scorp'iō. Zodiacal constellation; 8th sign of zodiac (♏), between Libra and Sagittarius, entered by sun about 23rd Oct.

scorp'ion *n.* 1. Arachnid with lobster-like claws and jointed tail that can be bent over to inflict poisoned sting on prey held in claws. 2. (O.T.) Kind of whip, prob. armed with metal points. 3. The constellation Scorpio. 4. ~*-shell*, kind of marine snail with long spines fringing outer lip of aperture.

scorzonēr'a *n.* Genus of narrow-leaved yellow-flowered herbs, esp. *S. hispanica*, black salsify, with parsnip-like root used as vegetable.

Scŏt[1]. 1. Native of Scotland. 2. (hist.) One of an ancient Gaelic-speaking people who migrated from Ireland to Scotland in 6th c.

scŏt[2] *n.* (hist.) Payment corresponding to modern tax, rate, or other assessed contribution; ~*-ree*, unharmed, unpunished, safe, esp. in *go, get off*, ~*-free*.

Scŏtch[1] *adj.* Of Scotland or its inhabitants; in the dialect(s) of English spoken in the Lowlands of Scotland; (the modern inhabitants of Scotland usu. prefer the form *Scottish* except in expressions like *Scotch whisky, tweeds*); ~ *barley*, pot barley with the husk ground off; ~ *broth*, mutton broth thickened with pearl barley and vegetables; ~ *cap*, kind worn with Highland costume, GLENGARRY; ~ *collops*, collops of beef cut small and stewed; ~ *fir*, the common N. European pine, *Pinus sylvestris*; *Scotchman, Scotchwoman* (Sc. *Scots-*), natives of Scotland; ~ *mist*, thick wet mist; ~ *pebble*, variety of crystalline quartz, as agate, chalcedony, cairngorm, etc., cut and polished and used as an ornamental stone in brooches, etc.; ~ *terrier*, breed of short-legged terrier with a rough, wiry, greyish coat and short erect tail (ill. DOG); ~ *whisky*, whisky, often having a smoky flavour of peat, as distilled in Scotland; ~ *woodcock*, scrambled eggs served on toast with anchovy paste. ~ *n.* The Scotch dialect of English (Sc. *Scots*); (colloq.) Scotch whisky.

scŏtch[2] *v.t.* Make incisions in, score; wound without killing; crush, stamp out. ~ *n.* Slash; mark on ground for HOPscotch.

scŏt'er *n.* Large sea-duck (genus *Oidemia*) of northern coasts.

scō'tia (-sh*a*) *n.* Concave moulding esp. in base of column (ill. MOULDING).

Scŏt'ism *n.* The scholastic philosophy of DUNS SCOTUS and his followers. **Scŏt'ist** *n.*

Scŏt'land. The northern part of Great Britain, formerly a separate kingdom; the crowns of England and Scotland were united by the accession of James VI of Scotland (James I of England) to the English throne in 1603; the two parliaments were united by the Act of Union in 1707, when Scotland became a part of the United Kingdom.

Scŏt'land Yard. Headquarters of London metropolitan police, formerly in Great Scotland Yard, a short street off Whitehall, and in 1890 moved to New Scotland Yard on Thames Embankment; allusively, the Criminal Investigation Department (C.I.D.) of the Metropolitan Police Force.

scotŏp'ic *adj.* ~ *vision*, vision of normal persons in twilight, with some perception of form but poor recognition of colour (cf. PHOTOPIC).

Scŏts *adj.* Scottish, esp. in phrases as ~ *language*, the form of English spoken in the Lowlands of Scotland, ~ *law, Fusiliers, Guards*, etc. ~ *n.* The Scots language.

Scŏtt[1], Sir George Gilbert (1811–78). English architect, restorer of Gothic churches and designer of the Albert Memorial, London. His son, George Gilbert ~ (1839–97), and grandson, Sir Giles Gilbert ~ (1880–1960), were also architects.

Scŏtt[2], Robert Falcon (1868–1912), captain R.N. Explorer, leader of two Antarctic expeditions, in the second of which the S. Pole was reached on 18th Jan. 1912, but Scott and the rest of the Pole party perished storm-bound in a blizzard on the return journey.

Scŏtt[3], Sir Walter (1771–1832). Scottish writer of historical novels and verse romances, author of 'Waverley', 'Guy Mannering',

'Rob Roy', 'Heart of Midlothian', 'Kenilworth', 'Ivanhoe', etc.

Scŏtt'ice (-ĭsē) *adv.* In the Scots language.

Scŏtt'icism *n.* A Scots phrase, idiom, word, pronunciation, etc.

Scŏtt'icize *v.* Imitate the Scots in idiom or habits; imbue with, model on, Scottish ways.

Scŏtt'ish *adj.* Connected with, pertaining to, Scotland, its people, language, etc.

Scŏtt'y *n.* (colloq.). Scotch terrier.

Scotus, John Duns: see DUNS SCOTUS.

scoun'drel *n.* Unscrupulous person, villain, rogue. **scoun'drelly** *adj.*

scour[1] (-owr) *v.t.* Cleanse or brighten by friction; clean out by flushing with water, or (of water) by flowing through or over; purge drastically; purge (worms) by placing in damp moss etc. to fit them for bait; clear (rust, stain) *away, off,* by rubbing etc. ~ *n.* Act, action, of scouring; artificial current or flow for clearing channel etc.; kind of diarrhoea in cattle.

scour[2] (-owr) *v.* Rove, range, go along hastily; hasten over or along, search rapidly.

scourge (skẽrj) *n.* Whip for chastising persons; person or thing regarded as instrument of divine or other vengeance or punishment. ~ *v.t.* Use scourge on; chastise, afflict, oppress. [LL *excoriare* strip off the hide]

scout[1] *n.* 1. Man sent out to reconnoitre position and movements of enemy (mil.); official of motorists' organization employed to assist motorists on road; ship designed for reconnoitring; aircraft used for reconnoitring, esp. small fast single-seat aeroplane. 2. Male college servant at Oxford (formerly also at Yale and Harvard). 3. Act of seeking (esp. military) information. 4. = *Boy S~* (see BOY); *~-master,* officer in charge of scouts or Boy Scouts. ~ *v.i.* Act as scout.

scout[2] *v.t.* Reject with scorn or ridicule.

scow *n.* (esp. U.S.) Kind of large flat-bottomed square-ended boat used esp. as lighter.

scowl *v.i.* Wear sullen look, frown ill-temperedly. ~ *n.* Scowling aspect, angry frown.

S.C.R *abbrev.* Senior Common (or Combination) Room.

scrăbb'le *v.i.* Scratch or grope (*about*) to find or collect something.

scrăg *n.* Lean skinny person, animal, etc.; bony part of animal's carcass, esp. of neck of mutton, as food; (slang) person's neck. **scrăgg'y** *adj.* **scrăgg'ily** *adv.* **scrăgg'iness** *n.* **scrăg** *v.t.* Hang (on gallows), wring neck of, garotte.

scrăm *int.* (slang) Be off!

scrăm'ble *v.* 1. Make way over steep or rough ground by clambering, crawling, etc.; struggle to secure as much as possible of something from competitors; deal with in a hasty manner. 2. Cook (eggs) by stirring slightly in pan with butter, milk, etc., and heating; mix together indiscriminately or confusedly; alter frequency of the voice in telephoning or radio-telephony by means of automatic mechanical or electrical devices fitted to the transmitter so as to make the message unintelligible except to a person using a receiver fitted with a similar device. ~ *n.* Eager struggle or competition (*for*); climb or walk over rough ground.

scrăm'bler *n.* (esp.) Telephone or wireless transmitter fitted with a device for scrambling speech.

scrănn'el *adj.* (archaic) (Of sound) weak, reedy, feeble.

scrăp[1] *n.* Small detached piece of something, fragment; picture, paragraph, etc., cut from book or newspaper for keeping in collection; (pl.) odds and ends; (collect.) rubbish, waste material, clippings, etc., of metal collected for re-working; metal wasted in production; residuum of melted fat; *~-book,* book for collection of newspaper cuttings etc.; *~-heap,* collection of waste material (freq. fig.); *~-iron, -metal,* scrap. ~ *v.t.* Consign to scrap-heap; condemn as past use; discard. **scrăpp'y̆** *adj.* Fragmentary, disconnected.

scrăp[2] *n.* Fight, scrimmage, quarrel. ~ *v.i.* Engage in a scrap.

scrāpe *v.* 1. Clean, clear of projections, abrade, smooth, polish, etc., by drawing sharp or angular edge breadthwise over, or by causing to pass over such edge; take (projection, stain, etc.) *off, out, away,* by scraping. 2. Draw along with scraping sound, produce such sound from, emit such sound. 3. Pass along something so as to graze or be grazed by it or just avoid doing so; ~ *through,* get through with a squeeze or narrow shave (freq. fig.). 4. Amass by scraping, with difficulty, by parsimony, etc.; contrive to gain; practise economy. ~ *n.* 1. Act or sound of scraping; scraping of foot in bowing. 2. Awkward predicament, difficult position, esp. as result of escapade etc.

scrāp'er *n.* (esp.) Scraping instrument in various technical operations; (archaeol.) primitive wedge-shaped flint implement; appliance fixed outside door of house, with horizontal blade for scraping mud etc. from shoes.

scrătch[1] *v.* 1. Score surface of, make long narrow superficial wounds in, with nail, claw, or something pointed; get (part of body) scratched; form, excavate, by scratching; scrape without marking, esp. with finger-nails to relieve itching; scratch oneself; make scratch; scrape *together* or *up.* 2. Score (something written) *out,* strike *off* with pencil etc.; erase (horse's name in list of entries for race, competitor's name); withdraw from competition. ~ *n.* 1. Mark or sound made by scratching; sound made by friction of needle in sound-recording apparatus and heard in playing of record etc.; spell of scratching oneself; slight wound. 2. Line from which competitors in race, or those receiving no start in handicap, start; zero, par, in games or contests in which handicaps are allowed; *come up to* ~, be ready to start race, match, etc., at the proper time; (fig.) be ready to embark on an enterprise, to fulfil one's obligations; *start from* ~, have no handicap (also fig.). ~ *adj.* Collected by haphazard, scratched together, heterogeneous.

Scrătch[2]. Old ~, the Devil.

scrătch'y *adj.* (Of drawing etc.) Done in scratches, careless, unskilful; (of pen) making scratching sound or given to catching in paper; (of action etc.) uneven, 'ragged'. **scrătch'ily** *adv.* **scrătch'iness** *n.*

scrawl *v.* Write, draw, in hurried, sprawling, untidy way; cover with scrawls. ~ *n.* Something scrawled; hasty or illegible writing.

scrawn'y *adj.* (U.S.) Lean, raw-boned, scraggy.

scream *v.* Utter piercing cry, normally expressive of terror, pain, sudden or uncontrollable mirth, etc.; make noise like this; utter in screaming tone. **scream'ing** *adj.* **scream'ingly** *adv.* (freq. in *screamingly funny* etc.). **scream** *n.* Screaming cry or sound; (slang) irresistibly comical affair or object.

scream'er *n.* (esp.) Kinds of bird, e.g. swift; (slang) something that raises screams of laughter; (slang) exclamation mark.

scree *n.* (freq. pl.) (Mountain slope covered with) loose stones that slide when trodden on.

screech *v.* Scream with fright, pain, or anger, or in harsh or uncanny tones. ~ *n.* Loud shrill cry; *~-owl,* the barn owl, from its discordant cry, supposed to be of ill omen; Amer. genus (*Otus*) of small owls with harsh cry.

screed *n.* 1. Long and tedious harangue, letter, etc. 2. (plastering etc.) Strip of accurately levelled plaster on wall, ceiling, etc., as guide in running cornice, laying coat of plaster, etc.; board, strip of wood, used for levelling concrete etc.

screen *n.* 1. Partition of wood, stone, or ironwork, separating without completely cutting off part of church or room, esp. that between nave and choir of cathedral etc.; ornamental wall masking front of building. 2. Movable piece of furniture designed to shelter from excess of heat, light, draught, etc., or from observation;

any object utilized as shelter esp. from observation, measure adopted for concealment, protection afforded by these; SMOKE-screen; windscreen of motor-car; (cricket) movable erection of white canvas, wood, etc., placed so that batsman can see ball and bowler's arm more clearly. 3. Upright surface for display of objects for exhibition, reception of images from cinematograph projector, etc.; *the* ~, moving-pictures, films. 4. Body, part of optical, electrical, or other instrument, serving to intercept light, heat, electricity, etc.; (photog.) transparent plate ruled with fine cross-lines, through which picture etc. is photographed for half-tone reproduction; *~-grid valve*, (wireless) valve (tetrode, pentode, etc.) in which electrostatic capacity between anode and grid is much reduced. 5. Large sieve or riddle to separate coarser from finer parts of sand, grain, coal, etc. ~ *v.t.* 1. Afford shelter to; hide partly or completely; (mil.) employ a body of men to cover (an army's movement); (wireless) furnish (valve) with screen; prevent from causing electrical interference. 2. Show (esp. cinematograph film) on screen. 3. Clean, sift, grade (coal, gravel, etc.) by passing through a screen; grade, separate out (articles, persons, of the required kind).

screen'ings *n.pl.* Material which has been screened; refuse separated by screening.

screev'er *n.* (slang) Pavement artist. **screeve** *v.i.*

screw[1] (-o͞o) *n.* 1. Cylinder with spiral ridge (*thread*) running round it outside (*male* ~) or inside (*female* ~); metal male screw with slotted head and sharp point for fastening pieces of wood etc. together, or with blunt end to receive nut and bolt things together; wooden or metal screw as part of appliance or machine to erect pressure in various ways; *have a ~ loose*, be slightly mad; *put the ~ on, apply the ~ to*, (fig.) put moral pressure on, coerce. 2. Revolving shaft with spiral blades projecting from ship or airship at stern and propelling it by acting on screw principle upon water or air; AIRscrew of aeroplane. 3. One turn of a screw; oblique curling motion or tendency as of billiard-ball struck sideways and below centre. 4. Small twisted-up paper *of* tobacco etc. 5. Miser; stingy or extortionate person. 6. (slang) Salary, wages. 7. *screwdriver*, tool with thin wedge-shaped end or blade for turning screws by slot in head; *~-palm, -pine*, plant of tropical genus *Pandanus*, with slender palm-like stems and branches, with terminal crown of sword-like leaves; *~-press*, press worked by screw; *~-propeller* = SCREW 2. ~ *v.* 1. Fasten, tighten, etc., by use of screw or screws; turn (screw), twist round like screw; make tauter or more efficient; revolve like screw; take curling course, swerve. 2. Press hard on, oppress. 3. Be miserly; squeeze, extort *out* of. 4. Contort, distort, contract.

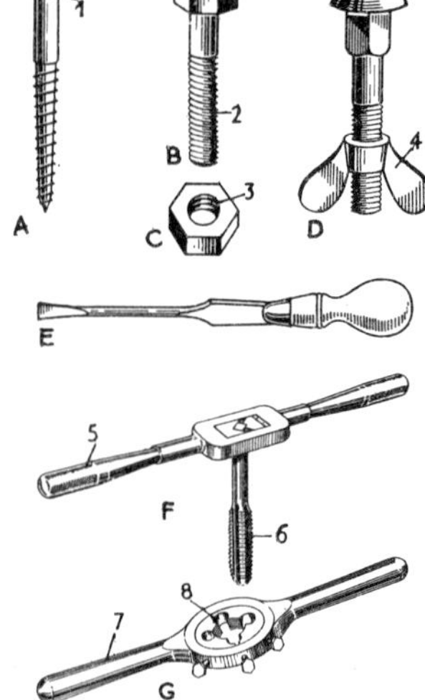

A. WOOD SCREW. B. BOLT. C. NUT. D. COACH BOLT. E. SCREWDRIVER. F. TAP WRENCH FOR CUTTING FEMALE SCREW THREADS. G. STOCK AND DIE FOR CUTTING MALE SCREW THREADS

1. Countersunk head. 2. Male thread. 3. Female thread. 4. Wing or butterfly nut. 5. Wrench. 6. Tap. 7. Stock. 8. Adjustable die

screw[2] (o͞o) *n.* Vicious, unsound, or worn-out horse.

screw'ball (-awl) *n.* & *adj.* (U.S. slang) Mad, crazy (person).

screw'y *adj.* (U.S. slang) Mad, crazy: suspicious, 'fishy'.

scrĭbb'le[1] *v.* Write hurriedly or carelessly; be author or writer. ~ *n.* Careless writing, thing carelessly written, scrawl. **scrĭbb'ler**[1] *n.*

scrĭbb'le[2] *v.t.* Card (wool, cotton) coarsely, pass through scribbling-machine or **scrĭbb'ler**[2] *n.*

scrībe *n.* 1. Person who writes or can write (rare); copyist, transcriber of manuscripts, calligrapher. 2. Ancient-Jewish maker and keeper of records etc.; member of class of professional interpreters of the Law after return from Captivity. 3. Tool for marking or scoring (wood, bricks, etc.) to indicate shape to be cut etc. ~ *v.t.* Mark with scribe.

scrĭm *n.* Kind of thin canvas used for embroidery, as lining in upholstery, etc.

scrĭmm'age *n.* Tussle, confused struggle, brawl, skirmish; (Rugby football, *rare*) scrum; (Amer. football) play when holder of ball places it flat on ground with long axis at right angles to goal-line, and puts it in play; *lines of* ~, imaginary lines parallel to goal-line passing through points of ball resting on ground before being put in play.

scrĭmp *v.* Skimp.

scrĭm'shănk *v.i.* (mil. slang) Shirk duty. **scrĭm'shănker** *n.*

scrĭp[1] *n.* (archaic) Beggar's, traveller's, or pilgrim's wallet, satchel.

scrĭp[2] *n.* Provisional document of allotment issued to holder of stocks or shares entitling him to formal certificate when the necessary payments have been completed, and to dividends etc.; (collect.) such documents. [abbrev. of (*sub*)*scrip*(*tion receipt*)]

scrĭpt *n.* 1. (law) Original document. 2. Handwriting, written characters; printed cursive characters, imitation of handwriting in type; style of handwriting in which characters resemble those of print and are not joined together (*illustration, p.* 747). 3. Manuscript, typescript, of play, film, etc.; text of broadcaster's announcement or talk; examinee's written answers.

scrĭptôr'ĭum *n.* (pl. *-ia*). Room set apart for writing, esp. in monastery.

scrĭp'ture *n.* Sacred book or writings; the Bible with or without the Apocrypha; (attrib.) taken from or relating to the Bible. **scrĭp'tural** *adj.*

scrĭv'ener *n.* (hist.) Writer, drafter of documents, notary, broker, moneylender.

scrŏf'ūla *n.* Name formerly given to a prob. tubercular condition affecting the lymphatic glands and bones, also called the 'king's evil' because reputed to be cured by the royal touch. **scrŏf'ūlous** *adj.*

scrōll *n.* 1. Roll of parchment or paper, esp. written on; book or volume of ancient roll form. 2. Ornamental design, esp. in architecture, made to imitate scroll of parchment more or less exactly; volute of Ionic capital or of chair etc., head of violin etc. (ill. STRING); flourish in writing; ribbon bearing heraldic motto etc.; any tracery of spiral or flowing lines. 3. ~ *gear, wheel*, (gear with) cogwheel in shape of disc with cogs in spiral line on one face; ~ *saw*, fretsaw, saw stretched in frame, for carving curved lines; *scroll'work*, ornament of spiral or curving lines, esp. as cut by scroll-saw. ~ *v.* Curl or roll up like paper; adorn with scrolls.

scro͞op *n.* Harsh grating noise; crisp rustle of silk. ~ *v.* Make scroop; treat (silk) with dilute mineral acids so that it will rustle crisply.

scrŏt'um *n.* (anat.) Pouch or

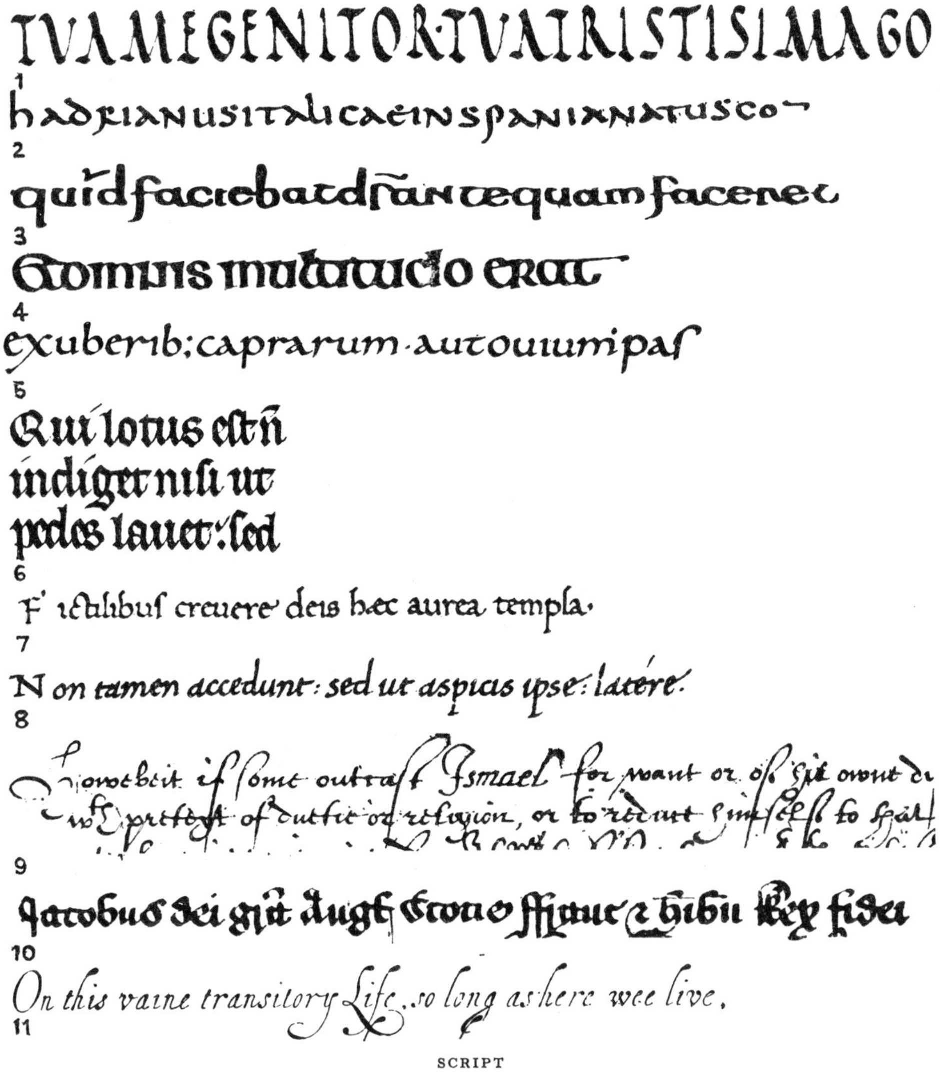

SCRIPT

1. Rustic capitals, 4th–5th c. 2. Uncial, mid-5th c. 3. Half-uncial, 6th c. 4. Insular (Anglo-Saxon) majuscule, early 8th c. 5. Carolingian minuscule, early 9th c. 6. Gothic, *c* 1250. 7. Humanist script, late 15th c. 8. Italic, late 15th c. 9. Secretary hand, 1593. 10. Court hand, 1611. 11. Copperplate, 1673

bag enclosing testicles (ill. PELVIS). **scrōt'al** *adj.*

scrounge (-nj) *v.* (colloq.) Appropriate without leave; cadge; search about. **scroun'ger** *n.*

scrŭb[1] *n.* (Ground covered with) plant community dominated by shrubs; stunted or insignificant person, animal, etc.; *~-oak, pine,* stunted oak, pine, of several Amer. species; ~ *typhus,* acute febrile disease, caused by bites of certain larval mites, esp. prevalent in Japan; Japanese river fever. **scrŭbb'y** *adj.*

scrŭb[2] *v.* 1. Rub hard to clean or brighten, esp. with soap and water applied with hard-bristled brush (*scrubbing-brush*); use such brush. 2. Pass (coal-gas) through a scrubber to extract certain components. ~ *n.* Scrubbing, being scrubbed.

scrŭbb'er *n.* (esp.) Any of various apparatuses for removing impurities etc. from coal-gas etc. as (1) a tower in which gas ascends through coke or other material down which water or a watery solution trickles; (2) a vessel in which gas is forced through a liquid, or a tank in which the gas is forced over blades or brushes that rotate in a liquid.

scrŭff *n.* Nape *of the neck.*

scrŭm *n.* Scrummage; (colloq.) dense crowd; *~-half,* half-back who puts ball into scrum.

scrŭmm'age *n.* (Rugby football) Formation in which two sets of forwards pack themselves together with heads down and try to obtain ball placed on the ground between them by pushing their opponents away from it.

scrŭm'ptious (-sh*u*s) *adj.* (slang) Delicious, delightful.

scrŭnch *n.* & *v.* CRUNCH.

scru'ple (-ōō-) *n.* 1. In apothecaries' weight, unit equivalent to 20 grains or ⅓ drachm; symbol ℈.

2. Doubt, uncertainty, or hesitation in regard to right and wrong, duty, etc. ~ *v.i.* Hesitate owing to scruples *to* do.

scrup'ūlous (-ōō-) *adj.* Conscientious even in small matters, not neglectful of details, punctilious; over-attentive to details, esp. to small points of conscience. **scrup'ūlously** *adv.* **scrup'ūlousnėss, scrupūlŏs'ĭty** *ns.*

scrutāt'or (-ōō-) *n.* One who examines, scrutineer.

scrutineer' (-ōō-) *n.* Person examining ballot-papers for irregularities.

scru'tĭnīze (-ōō-) *v.t.* Look closely at, examine in detail. **scru'tĭny** (-ōō-) *n.* Critical gaze; close investigation, examination into details; official examination of votes at election to eliminate irregularities or confirm numbers stated in return.

scrȳ *v.i.* Practise crystal-gazing.

scŭd *v.i.* Run, fly, straight and fast, esp. with smooth or easy motion; (naut.) run before the wind.

Scudéry (-dārē'), Madeleine de (1607–1701). French author of heroic romances.

scŭff *v.* Walk with dragging feet, shuffle; shuffle, drag along (feet); wear, rub, esp. with feet.

scŭff'le *v.i.* & *n.* (Engage in) confused struggle or scrambling fight.

sculduddery: see SKULDUGGERY.

scŭll *n.* Each of pair of short light oars used by single rower; oar used to propel boat by working it from side to side over stern, reversing blade at each turn. ~ *v.* Propel (boat), propel boat, with scull(s). **scŭll'er** *n.* User of sculls; boat intended for sculling.

scŭll'ery *n.* Back kitchen, small room attached to kitchen for washing dishes etc.

scŭll'ion (-yon) *n.* (archaic & rhet.) Menial servant, washer of dishes and pots.

scŭlp *v.* (colloq.) Sculpture.

scŭl'pĭn *n.* Kinds of small Amer. sea-fish with barbels on head, esp. of genus *Hemitripterus*.

scŭlp'sĭt. (abbrev. *sc.*, *sculps.*). (So-and-so) carved or sculptured or engraved (this work).

scŭlpt *v.* (usu. joc.) Sculpture.

scŭlp'tor *n.* One who practises sculpture.

scŭlp'ture *n.* 1. Art of forming representations of objects etc. in the round or in relief by chiselling stone, carving wood, modelling clay, casting metal, or similar processes; a work of sculpture. 2. (zool., bot.) Raised or sunk markings on shell etc. **scŭlp'tural** *adj.* **scŭlp'turally** *adv.* **scŭlp'ture** *v.* Form by, represent in, sculpture; adorn with sculpture; be sculptor, practise sculpture. **scŭlp'tured** *adj.* (esp., biol.) With markings etc. like those produced by sculpture.

scŭm *n.* Impurities that rise to surface of liquid; (fig.) worst part, refuse, offscouring. **scŭmm'y** *adj.* **scŭm** *v.* Take scum from, skim; be, form, scum on; (of liquid) develop scum.

scŭm'ble *v.t.* Soften, make less brilliant, blend (colours, hard outlines in painting etc.) by applying coat of opaque or semi-opaque colour with nearly dry brush, by rubbing pencil- or charcoal-marks lightly, etc. ~ *n.* Softened effect produced by scumbling.

scŭn'cheon (-tshn) *n.* Stones or arches across angles of square tower supporting alternate sides of octagonal spire (ill. SPIRE).

scŭpp'er[1] *n* Opening in ship's side level with deck to drain off water.

scŭpp'er[2] *v.t.* (slang) Sink (ship, crew), disable, throw into disorder.

scûrf *n.* Flakes on surface of skin cast off as fresh skin develops below, esp. those of head; any scaly matter on a surface. **scûrf'y** *adj.* **scûrf'inėss** *n.*

scŭ'rrĭlous *adj.* Grossly or obscenely abusive; given to, expressed with, low buffoonery. **scŭ'rrilously** *adv.* **scŭrrĭl'ĭty** *n.*

scŭ'rry *v.i.* Run hurriedly, scamper. ~ *n.* Act of scurrying, rush, bustle; flurry, fluttering assemblage (e.g. of snowflakes) moving or driven rapidly through the air.

scûrv'y[1] *adj.* Worthless, contemptible, paltry, low, mean. **scûrv'ĭly** *adv.*

scûrv'y[2] *n.* Disease resulting from deficiency of vitamin C, characterized by swollen gums, haemorrhage esp. into skin and mucous membrane, and great debility, formerly common among sailors and others who lived for long periods without fresh vegetables; *~-grass*, any of several cresses used against scurvy, esp. *Cochlearia officinalis*, found in Arctic regions.

scŭt *n.* Short tail, esp. of hare, rabbit, or deer.

scŭt'age *n.* (hist.) Money paid to the Crown by feudal landowner in lieu of personal service.

scŭtch *v.t.* Dress (fibrous material, esp. retted flax) by beating. ~ *n.* Scutcher; bricklayer's tool for cutting bricks etc.; refuse of scutched flax. **scŭtch'er** *n.* Hand tool for scutching flax; machine for scutching; part of threshing-machine for striking off the grain.

scŭtch'eon (-chon) *n.* ESCUTCHEON; pivoted cover of keyhole (ill. DOOR); plate for name or inscription.

scŭtĕll'um *n.* Small shield, plate, or scale, in plants; shield-like part of insect; one of the horny scales on bird's foot. **scŭt'ėllate, scŭtĕll'ar** *adjs.* **scŭtėllā'tion** *n.*

scŭtt'er *v.i.* Scurry.

scŭtt'le[1] *n.* 1. Shallow open basket for carrying corn, earth, etc. 2. Metal or other receptacle for carrying and holding small supply of coal (*coal-~*) for a fire in a room. 3. Part of motor-car connecting bonnet with body.

scŭtt'le[2] *n.* Lidded opening smaller than hatchway in ship's deck; similar opening in ship's side for ventilation, lighting, etc.; (U.S.) lidded opening in floor or roof of house. ~ *v.t.* Cut hole(s) in (ship, boat, etc.), sink thus.

scŭtt'le[3] *v.i.* Scurry, run away, make off. ~ *n.* Hurried gait, precipitate flight or departure.

scŭt'um *n.* (pl. *-ta*). (zool.) Bony, horny, etc., plate, esp. second of 3 parts forming upper surface of notum in insects; shield-like dermal plate in crocodile, turtle, etc. **scŭt'al** *adj.*

Scyll'a (sĭ-). (Gk myth.) A female sea-monster who devoured sailors when they tried to navigate the narrow channel between her cave and the whirlpool CHARYBDIS; later legend substituted a dangerous rock for the monster and located it on the Italian side of the Strait of Messina; hence, ~ *and Charybdis*, two dangers such that to avoid the one is to court the other.

Scyth (sĭth) *n.* Native of SCYTHIA.

scythe (sīdh) *n.* Agricultural implement for mowing and reaping, with long thin slightly curved blade fastened at an angle

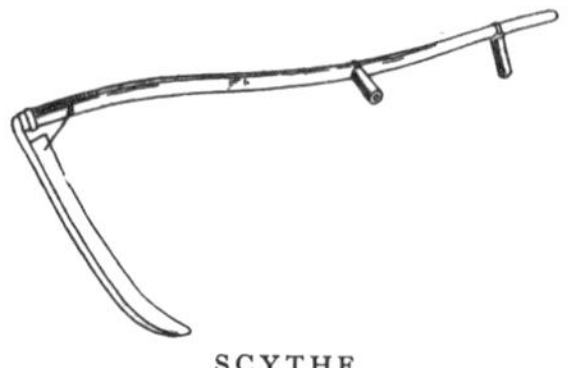

SCYTHE

with handle and wielded with long sweeping stroke. ~ *v.t.* Cut with scythe.

Scyth'ĭa (sĭ-). Ancient region of S. European and Asiatic Russia, between the Carpathians and the Don, inhabited by a savage nomadic people (*Scyths*) who overran W. Asia in 7th c. B.C. **Scyth'ĭan** *adj.* & *n.* (Language) of Scythia; Scyth.

s.d. *abbrev.* Several dates.

S. Dak. *abbrev.* South Dakota.

SE., SE *abbrevs.* South-east; south-eastern (London postal district).

sea *n.* 1. Continuous body of salt water covering most of earth's surface; part of this having certain land-limits or washing a particular coast and having a proper name; *at ~*, away from land, aboard ship; (fig.) perplexed, bewildered, at a loss; *the four ~s*, those bounding Gt Britain; *the high ~s*: see HIGH; *the seven ~s*, the Arctic, Antarctic, N. and S. Pacific, N.

and S. Atlantic, and Indian Oceans. 2. Local motion or state of the sea; swell, rough water. 3. Large quantity or level expanse *of*. 4. *~-anchor*, floating, expanding anchor, usu. of canvas, used to keep a boat's head into the wind in rough weather; drag-anchor; *~ anemone*, any of numerous usu. large and solitary polyps with

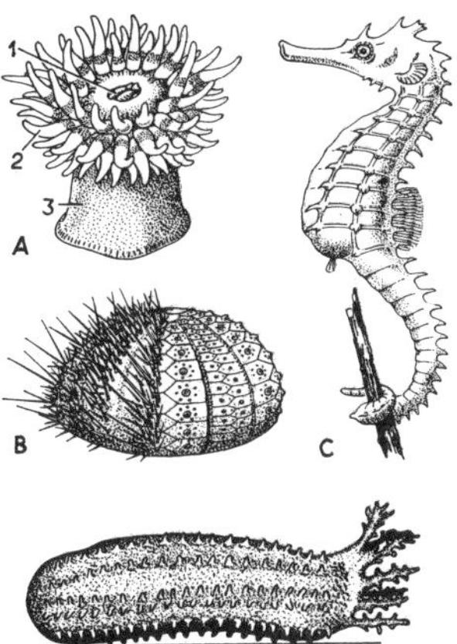

A. SEA ANEMONE. B. SEA URCHIN (HALF THE SPINES REMOVED). C. SEA-HORSE. D. SEA-CUCUMBER (HOLOTHURIAN)

1. Mouth. 2. Tentacles. 3. Column

bright colours and many petal-like tentacles surrounding mouth; *~-bird*, bird frequenting sea; *~-board*, coast bordering the sea; *~-borne*, conveyed by sea; *~-breeze*, cool breeze blowing landward from sea, usu. in daytime; *~-calf*, the common seal; *~ chest*, sailor's chest; *~ coal*, (archaic) coal (because formerly brought by sea from Newcastle to London etc.); coal mined from sea-coast veins; *~-coast*, land adjacent to the sea; *~-cock*, valve by which sea-water can be let into ship's interior; *~-colander*, brownish seaweed with fronds perforated like a colander; *~-cow*, manatee or other sirenian; *~-cucumber*, sea-slug, one of the holothurians, esp. the bêche-de-mer; *~-dog*, old sailor, privateer or pirate, esp. of Elizabethan days; luminous appearance near the horizon supposed to presage bad weather; *~-eagle*, any of the various eagles feeding largely on fish, esp. the white-tailed eagle; *~-elephant*, elephant seal, large seal of S. hemisphere with proboscis; *sea'farer*, traveller by sea, sailor; *seafaring* (*adj.* & *n.*); *~ food*, (U.S.) sea-fish, esp. shell-fish, as food; *~-front*, part of town etc. facing sea; *sea'going*, (of ship) designed for open sea, not rivers, etc.; seafaring; *~-green* (*adj.* & *n.*) (of) bluish green as of sea; *S~-green Incorruptible*, Carlyle's term for Robespierre; *sea'-gull*, gull; *~-hog*, porpoise; *~-horse*, (Gk and Rom. myth.) fabulous marine animal with fore-parts of horse and tail of fish, drawing sea-god's chariot; walrus; hippocampus, genus of small fishes covered with rough bony plates, with prehensile tail and forepart of body resembling horse's head and neck; *~-island cotton*, fine variety of long-stapled cotton, grown orig. and esp. on islands off coast of Georgia and S. Carolina; *sea'kale*, W. European cruciferous plant grown as culinary vegetable; *seakale beet*, CHARD; *~ lane*, course prescribed for ocean steamers; *~-lavender*, any maritime herb of genus *Limonium*, of plumbago family; *~-lawyer*, argumentative or captious sailor; (also) TIGER-shark; *~ legs*, ability to walk on deck of rolling ship; *~ level*, mean level of sea, mean level between high and low tides, used as a standard for measurements of heights and depths; *~-lion*, any of several large eared seals; *sea'man*, sailor; sailor below rank of officer; navigator; *sea'manship*, skill of good seaman; *~-mark*, conspicuous object serving to guide or warn sailors in navigation; *sea'-mew*, common gull; *~-mile*, nautical mile, one minute ($\frac{1}{60}$°) measured along a meridian; *~-mouse*, pop. name of a marine annelid worm, covered with minute iridescent setae, of the genus *Aphrodite*; *~-pie*, dish of meat, vegetables, etc., baked or boiled together in crust of paste or in layers between crusts; *~-pig*, porpoise; *~-pink*, the plant thrift; *sea'-plane*, aeroplane fitted with floats to enable it to alight on or take off from water; *sea'port*, (town with) harbour or port on sea-coast; *~-power*, naval strength, State having this; *~-room*, unobstructed space at sea for ship to manœuvre in; *~-rover*, pirate; *~-salt*, salt obtained by evaporation from sea-water; *sea-scape*, picture of a scene at sea; *~ serpent*, sea-monster of great length and more or less resembling a serpent freq. reported to have been seen at sea; *~-shell*, shell of any salt-water mollusc; *~-shore*, land close to sea, ground between high and low water-marks; *~-sick*, suffering from nausea and vomiting induced by motion of ship at sea; *~-sickness*; *sea'side*, edge of sea, sea-coast as health or pleasure resort; *~-slug* = sea-cucumber; *~-squirt* sessile marine animal of class *Urochorda* which squirts water when touched (ill. ASCIDIAN); *~-swallow*, tern; *~-trout*, salmon-trout; various other sea-fishes; *~-urchin*, marine animal of order *Echinoidea*, esp. one of nearly globular form covered with (freq. very sharp) movable spines; *~- wall*, wall or embankment made to check encroachment of sea or act as breakwater; *sea'weed*, plant growing in sea, esp. marine alga (ill. ALGA); *~-worthy*, (of ship) in fit state to put to sea.

S.E.A.C., Sē'ăc *abbrevs.* South-eastern Asia Command.

seal[1] *n.* Marine amphibious fish-eating mammal, of family *Phocidae*, with limbs developed into flippers and adapted for swimming, elongated body covered with thick fur or bristles, and short tail, hunted for its hides and oil; = *seal'skin*, skin or prepared fur of seals; coat, cape, etc., made of this. ~ *v.i.* Hunt seals. **seal'er** *n.* (esp.) Ship or man engaged in seal-hunting.

seal[2] *n.* 1. (Impressed device on) piece of wax or other plastic material attached to document as evidence of authenticity of signature etc., or on folded letter, envelope-flap, door, lid of box, etc., so that it cannot be opened without breaking seal; impression stamped on a wafer etc. stuck to document as symbol equivalent to wax seal; (fig.) mark of ownership; obligation to silence or secrecy. 2. Engraved stamp of metal or other hard material used to make impression on wax etc., used as seal; this as mark of office, esp. (pl.) as symbol of position of Lord Chancellor or Secretary of State; *Great S~*, seal used for authentication of important documents issued in name of highest executive authority; *~-ring*, finger-ring with seal. 3. Substance used to close aperture etc., esp. water standing in drain-pipe to prevent ascent of foul air. ~ *v.t.* 1. Place seal on (document), fasten (letter etc.), esp. with seal or sealing-wax; close tightly or hermetically; stop or shut *up*; (fig.) prove authenticity of (devotion etc.) *with* one's life etc.; set significant mark on; set apart, destine, devote; decide irrevocably; ~ *off*, cut off (an area) so that troops in it have no escape. 2. *sealed book*, MS. copy of Book of Common Prayer, annexed to official copy of Act of Uniformity (1662) preserved in House of Lords, and constituting final authority for the text; something obscure *to* a person, beyond his capacity to understand; *sealed orders*, written instructions for a commander of a ship, esp. in time of war, in a sealed envelope, only to be opened at a stated time or place; *sealed pattern*, regulation pattern of weapon, uniform, etc., accepted by War Office, Admiralty, etc.; *sealing-wax*, coloured mixture of shellac, rosin, and turpentine, which becomes soft when heated and hardens as it cools, thus easily receiving and preserving the impression of a seal, used for sealing letters, documents, etc.

Seal'yham (-lĭam) *n.* Wiry-haired, long-bodied, short-legged terrier, usu. white with brown or grey markings on head, noted for spirit and gameness. [f. name of estate in Pembrokeshire, Wales]

seam *n.* Line of junction between two edges, esp. those of two pieces of cloth etc. turned back

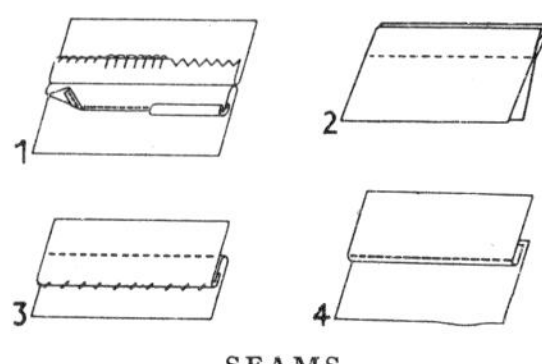

SEAMS

1. Flat seam, showing five different ways of finishing edges. 2. French seam. 3. Run-and-fell seam. 4. Lapped seam

and sewn together, or of boards fitted edge to edge; line, groove, furrow, formed by two abutting edges, mark resembling this; scar; line of purl stitches in knitting resembling sewn seam; thin layer or stratum, esp. of coal, between two wider strata (ill. MINE); *~-stitch*, (knitting) purl-stitch. ~ *v.* Join *together*, *up*, etc., with seam(s); (knitting) make seam-stitch; score or mark with seams, furrow, ridge.

seam'strĕss (sĕm-), **sĕmp'strĕss** *ns.* Sewing-woman.

seam'y *adj.* Showing seams; ~ *side*, wrong side of garment etc. where rough edges of seams are visible; (usu. fig.) of worst, roughest, or least presentable aspect, esp. of life.

Seanad Eireann (shăn'*a*dh ar'*a*n). Upper Chamber of the legislature of Eire, the Senate, with 60 members. [Ir., = 'Irish senate']

séance (sā'*a*ns, sā'ahns) *n.* Sitting of society or deliberative body; meeting for exhibition or investigation of spiritualistic phenomena.

sear *v.t.* Wither up, blast (rare); scorch surface of, esp. with hot iron, cauterize, brand; (fig.) render (conscience etc.) incapable of feeling. ~ *adj.* SERE.

search (sẽr-) *v.* Examine thoroughly (place, person, etc.) for what may be found or to find something of which presence is known or suspected; make search or investigation (*for*); ~ *me!* (slang, orig. U.S.) used to imply that the speaker has no knowledge of some fact or no idea what course to take. **sear'chĭng** *adj.* (Of examination etc.) thoroughgoing, leaving no loopholes. **sear'chĭngly** *adv.* **search** *n.* Act of searching, investigation, quest; *right of* ~, belligerent's right to stop neutral vessel and search it for contraband; *searchlight*, lamp designed to throw strong beam of light in any desired direction, used in warfare for discovering hostile aircraft, observing movements of troops, passing ships, etc.; light from this; *~-party*, party of persons going out to look for lost or concealed person or thing; *~-warrant*, legally issued warrant to enter premises to search for suspected persons, stolen property, or other things kept or concealed in violation of law.

seas'on (-zn) *n.* 1. Each of the periods into which year is divided by earth's changing position in regard to sun, with particular conditions of weather etc., esp. one of the four equal periods (spring, summer, autumn, winter) marked by passage of sun from equinox to solstice and from solstice to equinox; or each of two periods, rainy and dry, into which year is divided in tropical climates; time of year when a plant flourishes, blooms, etc., or when an animal pairs, breeds, is hunted, etc., or which is regularly devoted to a particular occupation etc., or when a particular place is most frequented (esp., in London, the time from May to July when fashionable society is assembled there). 2. Proper time, favourable opportunity; period of indefinite or various length; *~-ticket*, ticket issued at reduced rates permitting any number of journeys to be taken, performances attended, etc., within year, month, or other specified length of time. ~ *v.* 1. Bring into efficient or sound condition by habituation, exposure, special preparation, use, or lapse of time; inure, mature; become fit for use by being seasoned. 2. Make palatable or piquant by introduction of salt, condiments, wit, jests, etc.; give zest to, flavour; temper, moderate; *seasoning*, condiments.

seas'onable (-z-) *adj.* Suitable to, of the kind usual at, the season; opportune, meeting the needs of the occasion. **seas'onably** *adv.* **seas'onablenĕss** *n.*

seas'onal (-z-) *adj.* Occurring at a particular season; (of trades, workers, etc.) dependent on the seasons, employed only during a particular season. **seas'onally** *adv.*

seat *n.* 1. Manner of sitting, esp. on horse. 2. Place on which person sits; (right to) use of seat; right to sit as member esp. of Parliament etc.; authority or dignity symbolized by sitting on particular seat or throne; something made for sitting upon; part of chair etc. on which occupant sits; sitting part of body, buttocks; part of garment covering this. 3. Site, location, temporary or permanent scene; abiding-place; county mansion, esp. with park or large grounds. ~ *v.t.* 1. Cause to sit, place one*self* in sitting posture. 2. Fit or provide with seats; (of room etc.) have seats for (specified number). 3. Mend seat of (chair, trousers, etc.). 4. Establish position; fix in particular place.

-seat'er *n.* (in comb.) *single-~*, *two-~*, etc., motor-car, aeroplane, etc., with seat(s) for one, two, etc.

seat'ĭng *n.* (esp.) Seats; arrangement, provision, of seats.

S.E.A.T.O., SEATO *abbrev.* South East Asia Treaty Organization.

sėbā'ceous (-sh*u*s) *adj.* Of tallow or fat, fatty; ~ *gland*, *duct*, etc., organ secreting or conveying fatty matter which lubricates hair and skin (ill. SKIN).

Sėbăs'tian St. (3rd c.). Roman soldier and Christian martyr, usu. represented as youth pierced by many arrows.

Sebăs'topol. (Russ. *Sevastopol'*). Seaport of the Crimea, besieged and destroyed by the English and French during the Crimean War, 1854–5.

SE. by E., SE by E, SE. by S., SE by S *abbrevs.* South-east by East, by South.

sĕc[1] *n.* Short for SECOND[1] *n.* sense 5; SECANT.

sĕc[2] *adj.* (Of wine) dry.

Sec. *abbrev.* Secretary.

sē'cant *adj.* (math.) Cutting, intersecting. ~ *n.* 1. (trig.) Straight line drawn from centre of circle through one end of arc to tangent drawn from other end, ratio of this line to radius (reciprocal of the *cosine*; ill. TRIGONOMETRY). 2. (geom.) Line cutting another, esp. straight line cutting curve at two or more points.

sécateurs (sĕk'*a*tẽrz) *n.pl.* Kind of pruning shears with crossed blades.

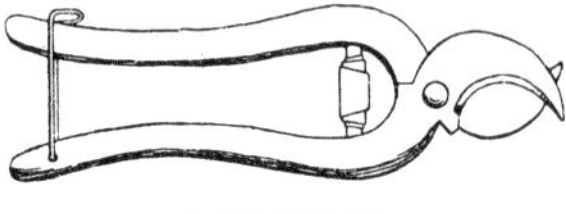

SECATEURS

Sĕcc'otine (-ēn) *n.* Proprietary name of a liquid composition serving as a strong adhesive.

sėcēde' *v.i.* Withdraw formally from membership esp. of Church or federation of States.

sėcĕ'ssion (-shn) *n.* Act of seceding, body of seceders; *War of* ~, the AMERICAN Civil War (1861–5), which arose from an attempt by 11 of the Southern States to secede from the U.S. **sėcĕ'ssional** (-sh*o*-) *adj.* **sėcĕ'ssionĭsm, sėcĕ'ssionĭst** *ns.*

sėclude' (-ōōd) *v.t.* Keep retired or away from company or resort.

sėclu'sion (-ōōzhn) *n.* Secluding, being secluded; retirement, privacy, avoidance of intercourse; secluded place.

sĕc'ond[1] *adj.* Coming next after first in order of time, position, quality, etc.; next in rank, quality, degree, etc., *to*; (mus., of part) next below highest in concerted music; that performs such a part; other, another; *S~ Advent*, return of Christ to earth expected by some Christians; *S~ Adventist*; *~ ballot*, electoral method by which, if the winner on the first ballot has not polled more than half of the votes cast, a second is taken in which only he and the next candidate are eligible; *~ best*, (what is) next in quality, inferior, to the first; *come off ~ best*, be worsted; *~ chamber*, the upper house in a legislature which consists of two chambers or houses; *~ class*, (place in examination etc.) of class next to first; (U.S., of postal matter) consisting of periodicals sent from publishing office; *~ class mail*, printed matter sent by air at reduced rate; *~-class* (*adj.* & *adv.*) inferior in quality, second-rate; *S~ Coming*, Second Advent; *~ cousin*, child of a first cousin of one's parent; *~ distance*, the portion of a picture between the foreground and background, middle distance; *S~ Empire*, French Empire of Napoleon III (1852–70); *~ fiddle*, (fig.) inferior or less important part; *~-hand*, not new, not original, previously worn, used, etc., by another; *~ lieutenant*, army officer of lowest commissioned rank; *~ nature*, acquired tendency or habit that has become instinctive; *~-rate*, of inferior quality, value, etc.; (of ship) rated in second class; *~-ra'ter*; *S~ Republic*, French Republic of 1848–52; *~ sight*, faculty, claimed by, or attributed to, some persons, of seeing, as in a vision, future events; *~ thoughts*, reconsideration, decision or opinion after reconsidering matter; *~ wind*, recovered breath after first exhaustion during exertion (freq. fig.). *~ n.* 1. Second person in race etc.; (person who takes) second class in examination. 2. (mus.) Next to highest part; interval of which the span involves six alphabetical names of notes; harmonic combination of the two notes thus separated. 3. (pl.) Goods (esp. flour, bricks) of quality inferior to best. 4. Supporter, helper, esp. person representing and supporting principal in duel. 5. Sixtieth part of minute of time or angular measurement; vaguely, a short time; *~ hand*, hand or pointer in some watches and clocks recording seconds. *~ v.t.* Supplement, support, back up; esp. support (motion, mover) in debate etc. as necessary preliminary to further discussion or adoption of motion. **sĕc'onder** *n.*

sėcŏnd'[2] *v.t.* (mil.) Remove (officer) temporarily from regiment etc., with a view to staff or other extra-regimental appointment; transfer (official) temporarily to another department. **sėcŏnd'ment** *n.*

sĕc'ondary *adj.* Not in the first class in dignity, importance, etc., of minor importance, subordinate; subsidiary, auxiliary; not original or primary, derivative, belonging to a second stage or period; (geol.) of the series of rock-formations between Primary and Tertiary, Mesozoic (ill. GEOLOGY); *~ colours*, (painting) those obtained by mixing two primary colours (see COLOUR); *~ education*, that between primary or elementary and higher or university education; *~ feather*, one growing from second joint of bird's wing (ill. BIRD); *~ planet*, planet's satellite; *~ school*, one giving secondary education. **sĕc'ondarĭly** *adv.* **sĕc'ondary** *n.* Secondary feather, planet, series of rocks.

seconde' (secawṅd) *n.* The second of the 8 parries in fencing (ill. FENCE).

sĕc'ondly *adv.* In the second place.

sē'crėcy *n.* Being secret.

sē'crėt *adj.* Hidden, concealed, not (to be) made known; known only to the initiated; not given to revealing secrets; *~ service*, services rendered to government, nature of which is not revealed, and which are paid for from special fund; (pop.) espionage. **sē'crėtly** *adv.* **sē'crėt** *n.* Thing (to be) kept secret; thing known only to initiated or to a limited number; mystery; *in ~*, secretly.

sĕcrėtaire' *n.* Piece of furniture for keeping private papers etc., with shelf for writing on (ill. DESK).

sĕcrėtār'ĭat(e) *n.* Body or department of secretaries; place where secretary does business, keeps records, etc.

sĕ'crėtary *n.* 1. Person employed by another to assist him in correspondence, literary work, and other confidential matters; official appointed by society, company, etc., to keep its records, conduct correspondence, etc. 2. Minister in charge of Government department. 3. Secretary-bird, long-legged, long-tailed raptorial African bird (*Serpentarius secretarius*), with crest of long feathers (thought to resemble pens stuck behind the ear). *~ adj.* Applied to style of handwriting used chiefly in legal documents of 16th and 17th centuries (ill. SCRIPT). **sĕcrėtār'ial** *adj.* **sĕ'crėtaryship** *n.*

sėcrēte' *v.t.* 1. Put into place of concealment. 2. Produce by secretion. **sėcrē'tory** *adj.*

sėcrē'tion *n.* 1. Concealing, concealment. 2. Action of gland etc. in extracting and elaborating certain substances from blood, sap, etc., to fulfil function within body or be excreted; any substance (as saliva, urine, resin) produced by such process.

sē'crėtive (*or* sĭkrē'-) *adj.* Given to making secrets, uncommunicative, needlessly reserved. **sē'crėtĭvely** *adv.* **sē'crėtĭveness** *n.*

sĕct *n.* Body of persons agreed upon religious doctrines usu. different from those of an established or orthodox Church; party or faction in a religious body; religious denomination; school of opinion in philosophy, politics, etc. **sĕctār'ĭan** *adj.* & *n.* **sĕctār'ĭanism** *n.*

sect. *abbrev.* Section.

sĕct'ary *n.* Member of a sect, esp. (hist.) of English Protestant Dissenters in 17th–18th centuries.

sĕc'tĭle *adj.* That can be cut (esp. of soft minerals).

sĕc'tion *n.* 1. Cutting (rare exc. in ref. to surgery etc.). 2. Part cut off from something; one of the parts into which something is divided; one of the minor subdivisions of a book etc. (usu. indicated by *~-mark*, §, as § 15); (mil.) subdivision of platoon; part of community having separate interests or characteristics; thin slice of something cut off for microscopic examination; (U.S.) area of one square mile into which public lands are divided; (U.S.) part of sleeping-car containing two berths. 3. Cutting of solid by plane, (area of) figure resulting from this; representation of internal structure of something supposed to be cut thus (ill. DRAWING); *conic ~s*, (math.) study of curves of intersection produced by allowing plane to cut cone at various angles (ill. CONE). 4. Section-mark (see sense 2) used as mark of reference or to indicate beginning of section. **sĕc'tional** (-sho-) *adj.* **sĕc'tionally** *adv.* **sĕc'tion** *v.t.* Arrange in, divide into, sections.

sĕc'tor *n.* 1. Plane figure contained by two radii and the arc of a circle, ellipse, etc. (ill. CIRCLE); anything having this shape; *~ of a sphere*, solid generated by revolution of plane sector about one of its radii. 2. Mathematical instrument, now consisting of two flat rules inscribed with various scales and stiffly hinged together, for mechanical solution of various problems; astronomical instrument, telescope turning about centre of graduated arc, for measuring angles. 3. (mil.) Subdivision of defensive position or system under one commander; territory for which one group, e.g. of air-raid wardens, is responsible.

sĕctōr'ĭal *adj.* & *n.* 1. Of, like, sector of a circle. 2. (Carnivore's tooth) adapted for cutting; premolar of upper jaw, one of first pair of molars of lower jaw.

sĕc'ūlar *adj.* 1. Occurring once in, lasting for, an age or a century; lasting or going on for ages or an indefinitely long time. 2. Concerned with the affairs of this world, worldly; not sacred; not monastic or ecclesiastical, temporal, profane, lay; sceptical of religious truth or opposed to religious education; *~ arm*, (hist.)

civil jurisdiction to which criminal was transferred by the Church for severer punishment; ~ *clergy, priests*, those not belonging to monastic orders (opp. *regular*). ~ *n.* Secular priest. **sĕc'ūlarĭsm** *n.* **sĕc'ūlarĭst** *n.* & *adj.* **sĕc'ūlarīze** *v.t.* **sĕcūlarīzā'tion, sĕcūlă'rĭty** *ns.* **sĕc'ūlarly** *adv.*

sėcūre' *adj.* 1. Untroubled by danger or apprehension; safe against attack, impregnable. 2. Reliable, certain not to fail or give way; (usu. pred.) in safe keeping, firmly fastened. 3. Having sure prospect *of*; safe *against, from.* **sėcūre'ly** *adv.* **sėcūre'** *v.t.* 1. Fortify. 2. Confine, enclose, fasten close, securely. 3. Guarantee, make safe against loss. 4. Succeed in getting, obtain.

sėcūr'ĭty *n.* (esp.) 1. Thing deposited or hypothecated as pledge for fulfilment of undertaking or payment of loan; document as evidence of loan; certificate of stock, bond, exchequer bill, etc. 2. Safety of State from foreign interference or espionage; ~ *officer, service*, person, organization, having responsibility for this. 3. *S~ Council*, Council of the General Assembly of the United Nations, consisting of 11 members of which 5 (U.S.A., Gt Britain, U.S.S.R., France, and China) are permanent and the remainder elected, charged with the duty of dealing with disputes between nations which threaten the peace of the world.

Sėdăn'[1]. Town of N. France, near Belgian border, scene (1870) of defeat of army of Napoleon III by Germans and of the French emperor's surrender.

sėdăn'[2] *n.* 1. ~(-*chair*), 17th–18th-c. portable covered-in chair

SEDAN CHAIR

for one person, usu. carried on poles by two men. 2. (U.S.) Motor-car with enclosed body for 4 to 7 persons including driver.

sėdāte' *adj.* Tranquil, equable, composed, settled; not impulsive or lively. **sėdāte'ly** (-tl-) *adv.* **sėdāte'nėss** *n.*

sėdā'tion (-shn) *n.* (med.) Treatment by sedatives.

sĕd'atĭve *adj.* & *n.* (Drug etc.) tending to soothe.

sĕd'entary *adj.* Sitting; (of occupation etc.) requiring continuance in sitting posture; (of persons) accustomed or addicted to sitting still, engaged in sedentary occupation; (zool.) permanently attached; (of spiders) lying in wait until prey is in web. **sĕd'entarĭly** *adv.* **sĕd'entarĭnėss** *n.*

sĕdge *n.* Grass-like plant of genus *Carex*, growing in marshes or by waterside; bed of such plants; ~-*warbler*, small brown migratory bird of Europe and Asia, (*Acrocephalus schoenobaenus*) with sweet loud song, breeding among sedges. **sĕdg'y** *adj.*

Sĕdge'moor. Plain in Somerset, scene of battle (1685) in which Monmouth, who had landed at Lyme Regis as champion of Protestant party, was defeated by Royal troops.

sėdĭl'ia *n.pl.* Series of usu. 3 freq. canopied seats set in the S. wall of the chancel of a church.

SEDILIA

sĕd'ĭment *n.* Matter that settles to bottom of liquid, lees, dregs; (geol.) the material carried by water or wind which settles and consolidates to make rocks. **sĕdĭmĕn'tary** *adj.* **sĕdĭmĕntā'tion** *n.*

sėdĭ'tion *n.* Conduct or language directed unlawfully against State authority; public commotion, riot, not amounting to insurrection or rebellion and therefore not treason. **sėdĭ'tious** (-shus) *adj.* **sėdĭ'tiously** *adv.* **sėdĭ'tiousnėss** *n.*

sėdūce' *v.t.* Lead astray, tempt into sin or crime, corrupt, induce (esp. woman) to surrender chastity. **sėdū'cer** *n.*

sėdŭc'tion *n.* Seducing, being seduced; thing that seduces.

sėdŭc'tĭve *adj.* (esp.) Alluring, enticing, winning. **sėdŭc'tĭvely** *adv.* **sėdŭc'tĭvenėss** *n.*

sĕd'ūlous *adj.* Diligent, persevering, assiduous, painstaking. **sĕd'ūlously** *adv.* **sĕd'ūlousnėss, sėdūl'ĭty** *ns.*

see[1] *v.* (past t. *saw*, past part. *seen*). Have the power of discerning objects with the eyes, exercise this power; perceive objects by sight; perceive mentally; learn by reading; look at, visit; admit as visitor; ascertain by inspection, experiment, consideration, etc.; supervise; escort *home, to the door*, etc.; consider, judge; know by observation, experience; imagine; ~ *about*, attend to; take into consideration; ~ *over*, go over and inspect; ~ *through*, (esp., fig.) penetrate, see real character of through disguise or false appearance; continue to watch or take care of until the end, or until difficulties are overcome; ~ *to*, attend to; take special care about.

see[2] *n.* Office, position, jurisdiction, of a bishop; *Apostolic, Holy, Papal*, or *Roman S~*, office, jurisdiction, authority, of pope.

seed *n.* 1. (One of) grains or ovules of plants, esp. as used for sowing; seed-like fruit, any other part of plant (as bulb) used for propagating new crop. 2. (bot.) Fertilized and ripened ovule of

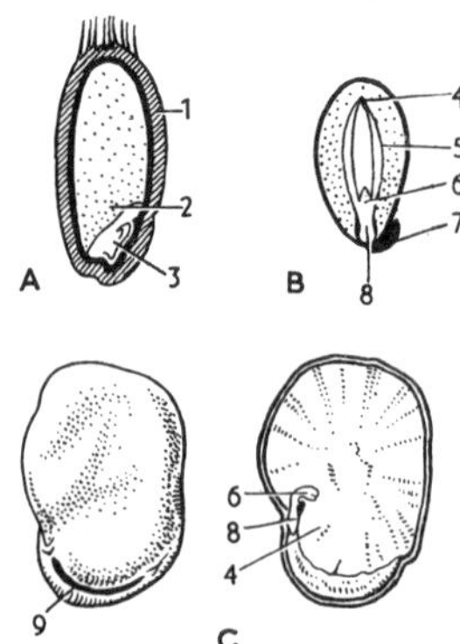

SEEDS: A. LONGITUDINAL SECTION OF WHEAT GRAIN (MONOCOTYLEDON). B. LONGITUDINAL SECTION OF CASTOR OIL SEED. C. EXTERIOR AND LONGITUDINAL SECTIONS OF BROAD BEAN (*B* AND *C* ARE DICOTYLEDONS)

1. Pericarp. 2. Albumen. 3. Embryo or germ. 4. Cotyledon. 5. Endosperm. 6. Plumule. 7. Aril. 8. Radicle. 9. Hilum

flowering plant, containing embryo capable of developing by germination. 3. Sperm, semen, milt; germ or latent beginning *of* (idea etc.). 4. (bibl.) Progeny, descendants; *go, run, to* ~, cease flowering as seed develops; (fig.) become shabby, worn-out, etc. 5. ~-*cake*, cake flavoured with caraway seeds; ~-*corn*, grain preserved to sow for new crop; ~-*pearl*, very small pearl; *seeds'man*, dealer in seeds; ~-*time*, sowing-season; ~-*vessel*, pericarp; ~-*wool*, raw cotton before being cleaned of its seeds. ~ *v.* Go to seed, produce or let fall seed; sprinkle (as) with seed; remove seeds from; disperse chemical material in (cloud) to make artificial rain; (sport, esp. lawn tennis) sort (competitors in competition or tournament) so that certain players do not meet in the early rounds; *seeded player*, one so dealt with.

seed'lĭng *n.* Young plant raised from seed.

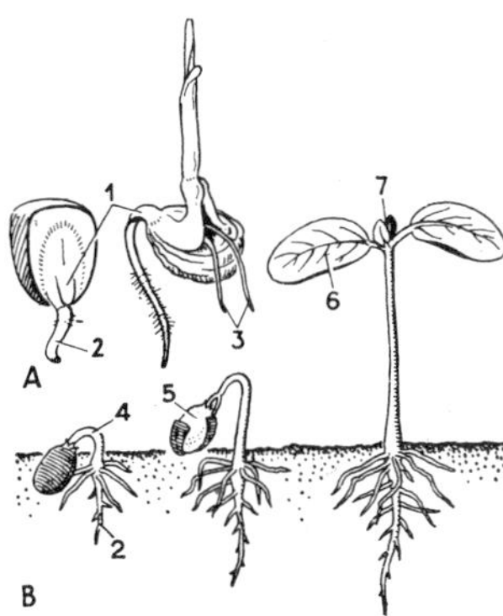

SEEDLINGS: STAGES IN GROWTH OF (A) MAIZE (MONOCOTYLEDON), (B) CASTOR OIL (DICOTYLEDON)

1. Root sheath. 2. Radicle. 3. Adventitious roots. 4. Hypocotyl. 5. Endosperm. 6. Cotyledon. 7. Epicotyl

seed'y *adj.* 1. Full of seed. 2. Shabby, ill-looking; unwell, out of sorts. **seed'ĭly** *adv.* **seed'ĭnėss** *n.*

see'ĭng *quasi-conj.* Considering the fact *that*; since, because.

seek *v.* (past t. & past part. *sought* pr. sawt). Go in search of, look for; try to obtain or bring about, *to* do; ask for, request; make search; *be yet to* ~, be lacking; *sought-after* (*adj.*) much in demand, generally desired or courted. **seek'er** *n.* (esp. *S*~), one of a small sect of English 17th-c. Independents who professed to be seeking further light on the true Church.

seem *v.i.* Have the appearance of, be apparently; appear *to be* or *do*; appear to exist; appear to be true or the fact. **seem'ĭng** *adj.* Apparent; apparent only. **seem'ingly** *adv.*

seem'ly *adj.* Decent, decorous, becoming. **seem'lĭnėss** *n.*

seep *v.i.* Ooze, percolate. **seep'age** *n.*

seer *n.* Visionary, prophet, one gifted with second sight.

seer'sŭcker *n.* Thin linen, cotton, or other fabric with puckered surface, freq. striped, orig. of Indian manufacture. [Pers. *shīr o shakkar* milk and sugar]

see'-saw *adj.* & *adv.* With backward-and-forward or up-and-down motion. ~ *n.* Game in which two persons sit one at each end of a long board balanced on a central support and move each other up and down alternately; board thus used (freq. fig.). ~ *v.i.* Play at see-saw; move up and down as in game of see-saw; vacillate.

seethe (-dh) *v.* Cook by boiling (archaic); (fig.) boil, bubble over, be agitated.

sĕg'ment *n.* 1. (geom.) Plane figure contained by chord and arc of circle (ill. CIRCLE); finite part of line between two points; ~ *of a sphere*, part cut off by plane; (physics) each of parts into which length of vibrating string etc. is divided by nodes. 2. Division, section, of something, esp. each of longitudinal divisions of body of some animals, somite, metamere. 3. Segmental arch. ~ *v.* Divide into segments; (of cell) undergo cleavage or divide into many cells.

sĕgmĕn'tal *adj.* (esp. of arch, pediment, etc.) Having form of segment of circle. **sĕg'mentary** *adj.* **sĕgmĕntā'tion** *n.*

sĕg'rėgāte *v.* Set apart, isolate; separate from general mass and collect together, as in crystallization or solidification; (biol., of Mendelian hybrids) separate into dominants, recessives, and hybrids, in conformity with numerical law. **sĕgrėgā'tion** *n.* **sĕg'rėgate** (-*a*t) *adj.* Isolated, set apart (rare); (zool., bot., etc.) separated from the parent or from one another, not aggregated. ~ *n.* (zool., bot.) Species separated from aggregate species; (biol.) segregated individual.

seiche (sāsh) *n.* Oscillation of lake waters due to variation of barometric pressure.

Seid'lĭtz pow'der (sĕd-) *n.* Aperient medicine of two powders, one of tartaric acid, the other of potassium tartrate and sodium bicarbonate, mixed separately with water and then poured together to produce effervescence. [name of village in Czechoslovakia with spring impregnated with magnesium sulphate and carbon dioxide]

seigneur (sānyẽr') *n.* Federal lord, lord of manor (formerly in France and Canada and still in Channel Islands). **seigneur'ĭal** *adj.*

seigneury (sān'yerĭ) *n.* Territory governed by seigneur; in Canada, landed estate held (until 1854) by feudal tenure.

seignior (sān'yor) *n.* (hist.) Feudal superior, lord of a manor; seigneur. **seignĭŏr'ĭal** *adj.*

seigniorage (sān'yorĭj) *n.* Something claimed by sovereign or feudal superior as prerogative, esp. Crown's right to percentage on bullion brought to mint for coining; profit made on coins issued at a rate above their intrinsic value.

seigniory (sān'yorĭ) *n.* Lordship, sovereign authority; domain of seignior.

seine[1] (sān, sēn) *n.* Fishing net hanging vertically in water, ends being drawn together to enclose fish; ~*-net*, seine. ~ *v.* Catch, catch fish, with seine; use seine in.

SEINE NET

Seine[2] (sān). River of France on which Paris stands, flowing into the English Channel.

seis'in, seiz'ĭn (sēz-) *ns.* (law) Possession of land by freehold; act of taking such possession; what is so held.

seis'mĭc (sīz-) *adj.* Of earthquakes; ~ *focus*, place below earth's surface where an earthquake originates.

seis'mograph (sīz-) *n.* Instrument for recording tremors of earthquakes. **seismŏg'raphy** *n.* **seismŏl'ogy** *n.* Scientific study of earthquakes. **seismolŏ'gical** *adj.* **seismŏl'ogist** *n.*

seize (sēz) *v.* 1. (law) Put in possession *of*; take possession of, confiscate, by warrant or legal right, impound, attach. 2. Lay hold of forcibly or suddenly, snatch; grasp with hand or mind, comprehend quickly or clearly; lay hold eagerly *upon*. 3. (naut.) Lash, fasten with several turns of cord. 4. (Of bearings or other moving part of machinery) become stuck, jam, from undue heat or friction. **sei'zure** (-zh*er*) *n.* (esp.) Sudden attack of apoplexy etc., stroke.

seizin: see SEISIN

sēj'ant *adj.* (her.) Sitting with forelegs upright (ill. HERALDRY).

Sekhet (sĕk'ĕt). Egyptian goddess, wife of Ptah, who destroys the souls of wicked in underworld.

sĕl'ah. Hebrew word of unknown meaning occurring freq. in psalms and supposed to be a musical direction.

sĕl'dom *adv.* Rarely, not often.

sėlĕct' *adj.* Chosen for excellence, choice, picked; (of society etc.) exclusive, cautious in admitting members; *select'man*, (U.S.) one of a board of annually elected officers managing various local concerns in New England towns. **sėlĕct'nėss** *n.* **sėlĕct'** *v.t.* Pick out as best or most suitable.

sėlĕc'tion *n.* Selecting, choice; what is selected; (biol.) the sorting out in various ways of the types of animal or plant better fitted to survive, regarded as a factor in evolution. **sėlĕc'tĭve** *adj.* (esp., of wireless receiver) Able to receive a desired signal (frequency) to the exclusion of others. **sėlĕc'tĭvely** *adv.* **sĕlĕctĭv'ĭty** *n.*

sĕl'ėnate *n.* Salt of selenic acid.

Sėlēn'ė. (Gk myth.) Goddess

of the moon, in later myths identified with Artemis.

sėlĕn′ĭc *adj.* ~ *acid*, an acid (H_2SeO_4), crystalline when pure, resembling sulphuric acid in many of its characteristics.

sėlēn′ious *adj.* ~ *acid*, colourless crystalline acid (H_2SeO_3).

sĕl′ėnīte *n.* 1. (min.) Calcium sulphate ($CaSO_42H_2O$), gypsum, in crystalline or foliated form; slip of this used to polarize light. 2. (chem.) Salt of selenious acid. **sĕlėnĭt′ĭc** *adj.*

sėlēn′ium *n.* Non-metallic element, chemically resembling sulphur and tellurium, and having the property that its conductivity of electricity increases with intensity of light falling on it; hence used in various photoelectric devices; symbol Se, at. no. 34, at. wt 78·96; ~ *cell*, piece of selenium to which electrical connexions are made, used as a photoelectric device etc. [Gk *selēnē* moon; named f. its association in nature with *tellurium*]

sėlēn′odŏnt *n.* & *adj.* (Mammal) with crescent-shaped ridges on crowns of teeth.

sĕlėnŏg′raphy *n.* Science dealing with the physical geography of the moon, mapping the moon's surface.

Sėleu′cĭd *adj.* & *n.* (One) of the dynasty founded by Seleucus Nicator, one of the generals of Alexander the Great, ruling over Syria and a great part of W. Asia, 312–65 B.C.

sĕlf *n.* (pl. *-ves*). Person's or thing's own individuality or essence, person or thing as object of introspection or reflexive action; one's own interests or pleasure, concentration on these; (commerc., vulg., joc.) = myself, yourself, himself, etc. ~ *adj.* (Of colour) uniform, the same throughout; (of material) the same; (of flower) self-coloured.

sĕlf- *prefix* expressing reflexive action, automatic or independent action, or sameness; *~-abuse*, (esp.) solitary sexual indulgence; *~-acting*, acting automatically; *~-assertion*, insistence on one's own rights, claims, individuality, etc.; *~-assertive* (*adj.*); *~-assurance*, self-confidence; *~-binder*, reaping-machine with apparatus for binding sheaves automatically; *~-centred*, centred in oneself, itself; engrossed in self, preoccupied with one's own personality or affairs; *~-colour(ed)*, (of) one uniform colour; *~-command*, self-control; *~-complacency*, complacency; *~-complacent* (*adj.*); *~-confidence*, confidence in oneself; arrogant reliance on oneself; *~-confident* (*adj.*); *~-conscious*, having consciousness of one's identity, actions, sensations, etc.; unduly or morbidly preoccupied with oneself; *~-consciously* (*adv.*), *~ consciousness* (*n.*); *~-contained*, (esp., of flat etc.) complete in itself, having a private entrance; *~-control*, control of oneself, one's desires, emotions, etc.; *~-defence*, (*in ~-defence*) not by way of aggression; (*noble*) *art of ~-defence*, boxing; *~-denying* (*adj.*) sacrificing one's personal desires; *~-denying ordinance*, (Engl. hist.) ordinance of Long Parliament (1645), forbidding members to accept any civil or military office; *~-denial* (*n.*); *~-determination*, (esp.) people's decision of its political status, as form of government, independence, etc.; *~-esteem*, favourable opinion of oneself; *~-evident*, not needing demonstration, axiomatic; *~-forgetful*, with no thought of or concern for oneself; *~-forgetfully* (*adv.*); *~-forgetfulness* (*n.*); *~-governing*, (esp., of colony, dominion) autonomous; *~-government* (*n.*); *~-heal*, any of various plants credited with great healing properties, esp. *Prunella vulgaris*, a blue-flowered mint of Europe and Asia; *~-help*, providing for oneself without assistance from others; *~-important*, having an exaggerated idea of one's own importance; *~-importantly* (*adv.*); *~-importance* (*n.*); *~-indulgent*, indulging one's own desires for ease, pleasure, etc.; *~-indulgently* (*adv.*); *~-indulgence* (*n.*); *~-interest*, what one conceives to be for one's own interests; *~-interested* (*adj.*); *~-love*, selfishness, self-centredness; regard for one's own well-being or happiness; *~-made*, made by one's own action or efforts; *~-made man*, one who has risen from obscurity or poverty by his own exertions; *~-opinionated*, obstinate in one's own opinion; *~-possessed*, cool, composed, in command of one's faculties or feelings; *~-possession* (*n.*); *~-preservation* (*n.*), (esp.) natural instinct impelling living creatures to go on living and avoid injury; *~-raising* (*adj.*), (of flour) not needing addition of baking-powder etc.; *~-reliance*, reliance on one's own powers etc.; *~-reliant* (*adj.*); *~-respect* (*n.*) proper regard for one's dignity, standard of conduct etc.; *~-righteous*, righteous in one's own esteem; *~-sacrifice*, postponing private interest and desires to those of others; *~-same* (*adj.*) (the) very same; *~-satisfaction*, conceit; *~-sealing*, having a device for filling up a hole in a structure caused by shot etc.; *~-service*, arrangement of shop, restaurant, etc., whereby customers help themselves and pay cashier afterwards (also *attrib.* of shop etc.); *~-starter*, device for starting internal combustion engine without use of crank-shaft or auxiliary starting engine; *~-sufficient*, requiring nothing from outside, independent; sufficient in one's own opinion, presumptuous; *~-sufficiency* (*n.*).

sĕl′fĭsh *adj.* Deficient in consideration for others, regarding chiefly personal profit or pleasure; actuated by, appealing to, self-interest. **sĕl′fĭshly** *adv.* **sĕl′fĭshnėss** *n.*

sĕlf′lėss *adj.* Oblivious of self, incapable of selfishness. **sĕlf′lėssnėss** *n.*

Sĕljuk′ (-ōōk). (Member) of certain Turkish dynasties ruling over large parts of Asia from 11th c. to 13th c., or of branch of Turkish people to which these belonged. [f. name of reputed ancestor]

Sĕl′kĭrk[1], Alexander (1676–1721). Scottish sailor; at his own request he was put ashore on the uninhabited island of Juan Fernandez, where he remained 1704–9; the original of 'Robinson Crusoe'.

Sĕl′kĭrk[2]. County town of **Sĕl′kĭrkshire,** county of S. Scotland.

sĕll *v.* (past t. and past part. *sōld*). 1. Make over, dispose of, in exchange for money; keep stock of for sale, be dealer in; prostitute for money or other consideration, make a matter of corrupt bargaining; find purchasers; ~ *off*, sell remainder of (goods), clear out stock, at reduced prices; ~ *out*, (hist.) leave army by selling commission; sell (one's shares in company, whole stock-in-trade, etc.); ~ *up*, sell goods of (debtor) by distress or legal process; *selling-plate, race*, etc., race in which winning horse must be sold to highest bidder. 2. (slang) Disappoint by not keeping engagement etc., by failing in some way, or (esp.) by trickery. ~ *n.* Something by which person is 'sold', hoax, take-in, swindle.

sĕl′tzer *n.* (also ~ *water*) Effervescent mineral water from Nieder-*Selters*, near Wiesbaden, Germany; similar artificial mineral water.

sĕl′vage, sĕl′vėdge *ns.* Edge of piece of material so woven that weft will not unravel (ill. WEAVE); edge-plate of lock with opening for bolt.

sĕlvagee′ *n.* Coil of rope-yarn bound together, used as sling etc.

Sĕl′wyn College. College of the University of Cambridge, founded 1882 in memory of George Augustus Selwyn, bishop of Lichfield and (earlier) of New Zealand.

sėmăn′tēme *n.* Element of a language that expresses or denotes an image or idea.

sėmăn′tĭc *adj.* Of meaning. **sėmăn′tĭcs** *n.pl.* Branch of philology concerned with meanings. **sėmăn′tĭcĭst** *n.*

sĕm′aphōre *n.* Signalling apparatus of post with one or more movable arms; signal(ling) by person holding flag in each hand. (*Illustration, p.* 755.) ~ *v.* Signal, send, by semaphore. **sĕmaphŏ′rĭc** *adj.* **sĕmaphŏ′rĭcally** *adv.*

sėmăsĭŏl′ogy *n.* Semantics.

sėmăt′ĭc *adj.* (biol.) (Of colour, markings in animals) serving to warn off enemies or attract attention.

sĕm'blance *n.* Outward appearance; likeness, image, *of*; resemblance.

semé(e) (sĕm'ā) *adj.* (her.) Sprinkled, strewn, covered, with small bearings of indefinite number (e.g. stars, fleurs-de-lis) arranged over field.

Sĕm'ėlė. (Gk myth.) Daughter of Cadmus and Harmonia and mother, by Zeus, of Dionysus; she entreated Zeus to come to her in his full majesty and was destroyed by his lightning.

sēm'ĕn *n.* Seed, esp. of flowering plants; viscous whitish fluid secreted by male animal, containing spermatozoa.

semi- *prefix.* Half-, partly-, to some extent; partial(ly), imperfect(ly).

sĕm'ĭ-ănn'ūal *adj.* & *n.* Half-yearly; (plant) lasting half a year (only).

sĕm'ĭbrēve *n.* (mus.) Longest note in general use (written 𝅝), with half length of BREVE; in U.S. called 'whole note'.

sĕm'ĭcĭrcle *n.* Half of circle divided by its diameter, or half its circumference (ill. CIRCLE); anything in this shape. **sĕmĭcĭr'cūlar** *adj.*; ~ *canals*, 3 curving fluid-filled channels, each in a different plane, opening into the cavity of the inner ear, jointly serving to inform the brain of changes in speed and direction during movements of the head (ill. EAR). **sĕmĭcĭr'cūlarly** *adv.*

sĕm'ĭ-cōke' *n.* Fuel obtained by carbonizing coal etc. at low temperature.

sĕmĭcōl'on *n.* Punctuation-mark (;), indicating a more marked separation than the comma, and less than a full stop or colon.

sĕmĭ-cȳl'ĭnder *n.* Half of cylinder cut longitudinally. **sĕmĭcȳlĭn'drĭcal** *adj.*

sĕm'ĭ-dėtăched' (-cht) *adj.* (Of house) joined to another by party wall on one side only.

sĕmĭfīn'al *adj.* & *n.* (Match, round) preceding final.

sĕm'ĭfluĭd (-ōō-) *adj.* & *n.* (Substance) of consistency halfway between fluid and solid.

sĕmĭlun'ar (-lōō-, -lū-) *adj.* Half-moon-shaped, crescent.

sĕm'ĭnal *adj.* Of seed, semen, or reproduction; germinal, reproductive, propagative; ~ *fluid*, semen. **sĕm'ĭnally** *adv.*

sĕm'ĭnar *n.* In German, and some British and American universities, group of advanced students pursuing special study and original research under professor.

sĕm'ĭnary *n.* Place of education (now rare exc. fig. or of R.C. and esp. Jesuit schools for training priests). **sĕm'ĭnarĭst** *n.* Student in seminary; (hist.) R.C. priest educated in foreign seminary in 16th and 17th centuries, esp. at Douai for English mission.

Sĕm'ĭnōle *adj.* & *n.* (Member) of tribe of N. Amer. Indians, allied to Creeks, formerly and still partly resident in Florida.

sĕm'ĭ-offĭ'cial (-shl) *adj.* Applied esp. to communications made to newspaper by official with stipulation that they shall not be formally attributed to him. **sĕm'ĭ-offĭ'cially** *adv.*

sĕm'ĭ-pōrce'lain (-sl-) *n.* Kind of porcelain of inferior finish, resembling earthenware; kind of earthenware resembling porcelain.

sĕm'ĭ-prĕ'cious (-sh*us*) *adj.* (Of gems) of less value than those called 'precious' (as amethyst, jade, garnet, etc.).

sĕm'ĭquāver *n.* (mus.) Note (𝅘𝅥𝅯) half length of quaver.

Sėmĭ'ramĭs. Mythical queen of Assyria of great beauty and wisdom, wife and successor of Ninus, reputed founder of Nineveh; she built many cities, including Babylon; ~ *of the North*, a term applied to (1) Margaret (1353–1412), daughter of Valdemar IV of Denmark and wife of Haakon VI of Norway, who became in 1381 regent of Norway and Denmark, and in 1388 ruler of Sweden; (2) Catherine II of Russia (1729–96), empress of Russia from 1762.

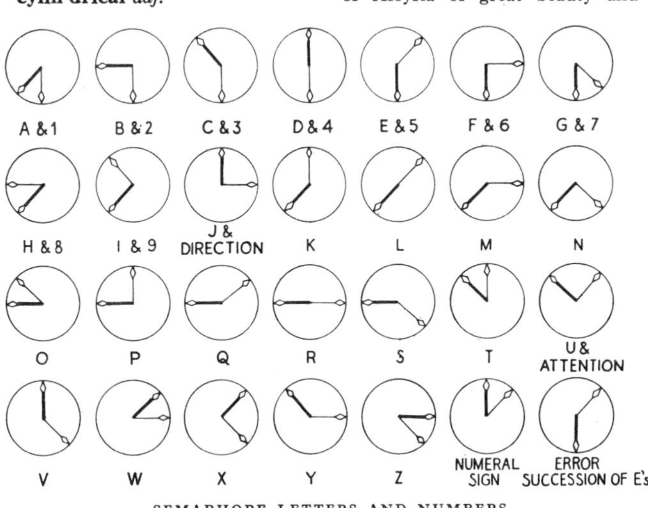

SEMAPHORE LETTERS AND NUMBERS

The thick lines represent the right arm and thin lines the left arm

sĕm'ĭ-sŏl'ĭd *adj.* & *n.* Extremely viscous, partially solid (substance).

Sĕm'īte. Member of any of the races supposed to be descended from SHEM (Gen. x), including Jews, Arabs, Assyrians, Phoenicians, and other peoples of SW. Asia. **Sėmĭt'ĭc** *adj.* & *n.* (Language) of the Semites; (of) the family of languages, now spoken chiefly in N. Africa and SW. Asia, including Hebrew, Aramaic, Arabic, ancient Assyrian, and Ethiopic. **Sĕm'ĭtĭsm** *n.*

sĕm'ĭtōne *n.* (mus.) Interval of (approximately) half a tone (ill. SCALE).

sĕm'ĭvowel *adj.* & *n.* Vocal sound partaking of nature of vowel and consonant, letter (e.g. *w*, *y*) representing this.

sĕmolĭ'na (-lē-) *n.* Hard portions of 'flinty' wheat which resist action of millstones and are collected in form of rounded grains and used in milk puddings, for making macaroni, etc.

sĕmpĭtĕrn'al *adj.* (rhet.) Everlasting, eternal.

sĕm'plice (-plēchā). (mus. direction). Simple in style of performance.

sĕm'pre (-ā). (mus. direction) Throughout, as in ~ *forte*, loudly throughout.

sempstress: see SEAMSTRESS.

sĕn *n.* (pl. same) $\frac{1}{100}$ of a YEN; $\frac{1}{100}$ of an Indonesian rupiah.

Sen. *abbrev.* Senate; Senator; Senior.

sėnār'ĭus *n.* Latin verse of 6 feet, esp. iambic trimeter.

sĕn'ary *adj.* Of the number 6; (of system of numeration) of which radix is 6.

sĕn'ate *n.* 1. Ancient Roman legislative and administrative body, orig. of representatives elected by patricians, later of appointed members and actual and former holders of various high offices. 2. Upper and less numerous branch of the legislature in various countries (in U.S. consisting of 2 members from each State of the Union). 3. Governing body of some British and Amer. universities; council in some Amer. colleges composed of members of faculty and elected students, and having control of discipline etc. 4. ~-*house*, place for meetings of senate.

sĕn'ator *n.* Member of senate. **sĕnatōr'ĭal** *adj.* **sĕn'atorship** *n.*

sĕnd *v.* (past t. and past part.

sĕnt). Cause to go, dispatch, secure conveyance of, to some destination, *to*, *into*, *away*, etc.; drive, cause to go, *into* some condition, *to sleep*, etc.; send message or letter; (of deity) grant, bestow, inflict, bring about, cause to be; ~ *down*, rusticate, expel, from university; ~ *for*, summon; esp., of head of State, summon politician in order to offer him premiership; ~ *off*, send away; witness departure of (person) as sign of respect, etc.; ~*-off* (*n.*). **sĕn'der** *n.*

sĕn'dal *n.* (hist.) (Garment of) thin rich silk material.

Sĕn'ėca[1], Lucius Annaeus (*c* 4 B.C. – A.D. 65). Roman Stoic philosopher and author of tragedies; tutor and adviser to Nero; ordered to take his own life on charge of complicity in Piso's conspiracy. **Sĕn'ėcan** *adj.*

Sĕn'ėca[2]. One of a numerous and warlike tribe of Iroquoian Indians, formerly occupying W. part of New York State.

Sĕnėgal' (-awl). River of W. Africa; republic of the French Community, lying to the S. of Senegal River; capital, Dakar.

sėnĕs'cent *adj.* Growing old. **sėnĕs'cence** *n.*

sĕn'ėschal (-shl) *n.* (hist.) Steward or major-domo in medieval great house.

sē'nīle *adj.* Belonging, incident, peculiar, to old age; having weakness of old age; ~ *dementia*, severe mental deterioration in old age. **sėnĭl'ĭty** *n.*

sē'nior *adj.* More advanced in age, older in standing; superior in age or standing *to*; of higher or highest degree; senior to another of the same name; of, belonging to, final year in American universities, schools, etc.; ~ *partner*, head of firm; *S~ Service*, Royal Navy; ~ *wrangler*: see WRANGLER. **sēniŏ'rity** *n.* **sē'nior** *n.* One superior or worthy of deference etc. by reason of age; person of comparatively long service, standing, etc.; one's elder or superior in length of service, membership, etc.; senior wrangler, student, etc.

sĕnn'a *n.* (Dried pods or leaflets, used as purgative, of) various species of *Cassia*.

Sĕnnăch'erĭb (-k-). King of Assyria 705–681 B.C.; invaded Palestine in reign of Hezekiah and was forced to retire on account of pestilence among his troops (2 Chron. xxxii).

sĕnn'ėt *n.* (hist.) Signal call on trumpet (in stage-directions of Elizabethan plays).

sĕnn'ight (-īt) *n.* (archaic) Week. [for *seven-night*]

sĕñōr' (-ny-), **sĕñōr'a, sĕñōrĭ'ta** (-rē-) *ns.* (Titles of respect for) Spanish man, lady, young or unmarried lady.

Sĕnou's(s)ĭ, Sĕnuss'ĭ (-ōō-). N. African Mohammedan religious sect, noted for fanatical and belligerent attitude, founded *c* 1835 by Sidi Mohammed Ben Ali es-Senousi.

sĕnsā'tion *n.* 1. Consciousness of perceiving or seeming to perceive some state or affection of one's body, its parts or senses, or of one's mind or its emotions; contents of such consciousness. 2. Excited or violent feeling, strong impression, as of horror, surprise, esp. among community; event, person, etc., arousing this. **sĕnsā'tional** (-sho-) *adj.* **sĕnsā'tionally** *adv.*

sĕnsā'tionalĭsm (-sho-) *n.* 1. (philos.) Theory that sensation is sole source of knowledge. 2. Pursuit of the sensational in literature, journalism, etc.

sĕnse *n.* 1. Any of those faculties, each dependent upon specialized groups of receptors connected with the brain, by which man and other animals are aware of their environment or recognize changes in their own bodily condition such as pain, movement of muscles and joints, or cold and warmth; *the five ~s*, those providing knowledge of the external world (sight, hearing, smell, taste, touch); *~-datum*, element of experience due to stimulation of a sense-organ; *~-organ*, part of body concerned in producing sensation. 2. (usu. pl.) The senses considered as channels for gratifying the desire for pleasure. 3. (pl.) Person's sanity regarded as attested by possession of the senses. 4. Ability to perceive or feel; consciousness *of*; quick or accurate appreciation *of*; instinct regarding, insight into, specified matter. 5. Practical wisdom, judgement, common sense, conformity to these. 6. Meaning, way in which word etc. is to be understood; intelligibility, coherence, possession of a meaning; *in a ~*, in a way, under limitations. 7. Prevailing sentiment among a number of people. ~ *v.t.* Perceive by sense; (esp.) be vaguely aware of.

sĕnse'lėss (-sl-) *adj.* 1. Deprived of sensation; unconscious; unfeeling. 2. Stupid, silly, foolish. 3. Unmeaning, meaningless, purposeless. **sĕnse'lėssly** *adv.* **sĕnse'lėssnėss** *n.*

sĕnsĭbĭl'ĭty *n.* 1. Capacity to feel. 2. Susceptibility, sensitiveness (*to*); delicacy of feeling; oversensitiveness.

sĕn'sĭble *adj.* 1. Perceptible by the senses; great enough to be perceived, appreciable. 2. Sensitive (*to*) (archaic); aware, not unmindful, *of*. 3. Of good sense, reasonable, judicious; moderate; practical. **sĕn'sĭblenėss** *n.* **sĕn'sĭbly** *adv.*

sĕn'sĭtive *adj.* Having sensibility *to*; very open *to* or acutely affected by external impressions, esp. those made by the moods or opinions of others in relation to oneself; (of instrument etc.) readily responding to or recording slight changes of condition; (chem.) readily affected by or responsive *to* appropriate agent; (photog., of paper, etc.) susceptible to influence of light; ~ *plant*, tropical Amer. plant (*Mimosa pudica*) with leaflets that fold together at slightest touch; other plants with similar quality. **sĕn'sĭtively** *adv.* **sĕn'sĭtivenėss, sĕnsĭtĭv'ĭty** *ns.*

sĕn'sĭtīze *v.t.* Make sensitive; render (photographic paper etc.) sensitive to light; render (organism, tissue) sensitive to substance normally inert, or highly reactive to drug etc.

sĕnsōr'ĭal *adj.* Of the sensorium, sensation or sensory impressions.

sĕnsōr'ĭum *n.* Brain as seat of sensation; whole sensory apparatus.

sĕn'sory *adj.* Of sensation or the senses; ~ *nerve*, any of those which consist of fibres conducting impulses from the peripheral sense-organs to the central nervous system.

sĕn'sūal (*or* -shōō-) *adj.* Of or dependent on the senses only, carnal, fleshly, voluptuous; given to the pursuit of sensual pleasures or gratification of the appetites; lewd, licentious. **sĕn'sūally** *adv.* **sĕn'sūalĭsm, sĕn'sūalist, sĕnsūăl'ĭty** *ns.* **sĕnsūalĭs'tĭc** *adj.*

sĕn'sum *n.* (philos.) SENSE-datum.

sĕn'sūous *adj.* Of, derived from, affecting, the senses. **sĕn'sūously** *adv.* **sĕn'sūousnėss** *n.*

sĕn'tence *n.* 1. Judgement or decision of court (now rare exc. of decisions of ecclesiastical and admiralty courts); (judicial declaration of) punishment allotted to person condemned in criminal trial (also transf.). 2. (archaic) Pithy or pointed saying, maxim. 3. Series of words in connected speech or writing, forming grammatically complete expression of single thought, and usu. containing subject and predicate, and conveying statement, question, command, or request; loosely, part of writing or speech between two full stops; (mus.) complete musical idea. ~ *v.t.* Pronounce judicial sentence on, condemn *to* a punishment.

sĕntĕn'tious (-sh*us*) *adj.* Aphoristic; full of, given to, pointed maxims; pompously moralizing. **sĕntĕn'tiously** *adv.* **sĕntĕn'tiousnėss** *n.*

sĕn'tient (-shĭ-) *adj.* Having the power of sense-perception, that feels or is capable of feeling. **sĕn'tience** *n.* **sĕn'tiently** *adv.*

sĕn'tĭment *n.* 1. Mental attitude; opinion, view. 2. Mental feeling, emotion, thought or reflection coloured by or proceeding from emotion; emotional thought expressed in literature, art, etc.; feeling or meaning (intended to be) conveyed by passage etc. 3. Refined and tender feeling; emotional weakness, mawkish tenderness, nursing of the emotions. **sĕntimĕn'tal** *adj.* **sĕntimĕn'tally** *adv.* **sĕntimĕn'talism, sĕntimĕn'talist, sĕntimĕntăl'ity** *ns.* **sĕntimĕn'talize** *v.*

sĕn'tinel *n.* Sentry; ~ *crab*, crab of Indian Ocean (*Podophthalmus vigil*) with very long eye-stalks.

sĕn'try *n.* Soldier etc. posted to keep guard; ~*-box*, hut for sentry to stand in; ~*-go*, duty of pacing up and down as sentry.

sĕp'al *n.* (bot.) One of leaves or divisions of calyx (ill. FLOWER).

sĕp'arate (-*at*) *adj.* Divided or withdrawn from others, detached, shut off; forming a unit that is or may be regarded as apart or by itself, distinct, individual, of individuals. **sĕp'arately** *adv.* **sĕp'arateness** *n.* **sĕp'arāte** *v.* Make separate, sever, disunite; keep from union or contact; part, secede *from*, go different ways; remove (substance) *from* another with which it is combined or mixed, as cream from milk, esp. by some technical process.

sĕparā'tion *n.* (esp.) Divorce from bed and board without dissolution of marriage tie, either by mutual consent or (*judicial* ~) imposed by judicial decree; ~ *allowance*, allowance made by soldier to his dependants, augmented by Government.

sĕp'aratist *n.* One who favours separation; (esp., hist.) one of the 17th-c. Independents separated from the Church of England; one who favoured Home Rule for Ireland or secession of southern States from U.S. **sĕp'aratism** *n.*

sĕp'arātor *n.* (esp.) Machine or appliance for separating, esp. cream from milk by centrifugal force.

Sėphar'dim *n.pl.* Jews of Spanish or Portuguese descent. [mod. Heb., f. *Sepharad*, a country mentioned once in O.T. and held in late-Jewish tradition to be Spain]

sēp'ia *n.* (Rich brown colour of) pigment made from inky secretion of cuttle-fish; a sepia drawing. ~ *adj.* Of colour of sepia; drawn in sepia.

sē'poy *n.* Native Indian soldier under European, esp. British, discipline; *S~ Mutiny*, Indian Mutiny. [Hind., f. Pers. *sipahi* soldier (*sipah* army)]

sĕp'sis *n.* State of poisoning of the tissues or blood-stream, caused by bacteria.

sĕpt *n.* Clan, esp. in Ireland.

sept-, septem-, septi- *prefixes.* Seven.

Sept. *abbrev.* September.

sĕp'tal *adj.* Of a septum or septa. **sĕp'tate** *adj.* Having a septum or septa. **sĕptā'tion** *n.*

sĕp'tăngle (-ngg-) *n.* = HEPTAGON. **sĕptăng'ūlar** *adj.*

Sĕptĕm'ber. 9th month of year. [L, f. *septem* 7, since it was 7th month of old Roman year]

Sĕptĕm'brist. (Fr. hist.) Supporter of or participator in massacre of political prisoners in Paris, 2nd–5th Sept. 1792.

sĕptēn'ary *adj.* Of or involving the number 7, on basis of 7, by 7s, septennial. ~ *n.* Set of 7.

sĕptĕnn'ial *adj.* Of, for, (recurring) every, 7 years. **sĕptĕnn'ially** *adv.*

sĕptĕt(te)' *n.* (Musical work for) 7 voices, instruments, etc., in combination; set of 7.

sĕp'tic *adj.* Putrefying; caused by or in a state of sepsis; ~ *tank*, tank in which organic matter in sewage is rapidly decomposed through agency of anaerobic bacteria. **sĕp'tically** *adv.*

sĕpticaem'ia (-sēm-) *n.* Disease caused by pathogenic bacteria in the blood, blood-poisoning.

sĕptilăt'eral *adj.* Seven-sided.

sĕptill ion (-yon) *n.* 7th power of a million (1 followed by 42 ciphers); in U.S. usage, 8th power of a thousand (1 followed by 24 ciphers).

sĕp'time (-tĭm) *n.* Seventh of the 8 parries in fencing (ill. FENCE).

sĕptūagėnār'ian *adj.* & *n.* (Person) aged 70 or more but less than 80.

Sĕptūagĕs'ima (Sunday). Third Sunday before Lent, Sunday before Sexagesima. [L, = '70th']

Sĕpt'ūagint (abbrev. LXX). Greek version of Old Testament, traditionally said to have been made by 72 Palestinian Jews in 3rd c. B.C. and completed by them in 72 days. [L *Septuaginta* 70]

sĕp'tum *n.* (pl. -*ta*). (anat., bot., zool.) Partition, dividing wall, membrane, layer, etc., e.g. that between the nostrils.

sĕp'tūple *adj.* & *n.* Sevenfold (amount). ~ *v.* Multiply by 7, increase sevenfold.

sėpŭl'chral (-k-) *adj.* Of sepulchre(s) or sepulture; suggestive of the tomb, funereal, gloomy, dismal.

sĕp'ulchre (-k*er*) *n.* Tomb, esp. cut in rock or built of stone or brick, burial vault or cave; *Holy S~*, cave in which Jesus Christ was buried outside walls of Jerusalem; *whited* ~, hypocrite.

sĕp'ulture *n.* Burying, burial.

seq. Abbrev. for *sequens*, *sequentes*, *sequentia*, the following, *sequente* in what follows, *sequentibus* in the following places, *sequitur* it follows.

sėquā'cious (-sh*us*) *adj.* Following, attendant; coherent; lacking independence or originality, servile. **sėquā'ciously** *adv.* **sėquă'city** *n.*

sēq'uel *n.* What follows after, continuation or resumption of a story, process, etc., after pause or provisional ending; after-effects, upshot.

sėquē'la *n.* (pl. -*ae*). (path.) Morbid condition or symptom following upon some disease.

sēq'uence *n.* 1. (Order of) succession. 2. Set of things belonging next each other on some principle of order, series without gaps. 3. (mus.) Phrase or melody repeated at higher or lower pitch. 4. (eccles.) Composition in metrical prose or accentual metre said or sung after Alleluia and before Gospel. 5. (cinema) Incident in film story recorded consecutively, corresponding to scene of play. 6. (gram.) ~ *of tenses*, rule or practice according to which tense of verb in subordinate clause depends on that of verb in main clause (e.g. *he said you* would *be ready now*). **sēq'uent** *adj.* Following; successive; consecutive. **sėquĕn'tial** (-shl) *adj.* **sėquĕn'tially** *adv.*

sėquĕs'ter *v.t.* 1. Seclude, isolate, set apart. 2. Confiscate, appropriate; seize temporary possession of (debtor's effects).

sėquĕs'trāte (*or* sēk'wĭs-) *v.t.* = SEQUESTER (sense 2), divert (income of estate or benefice) temporarily from owner into other hands. **sēquėstrā'tion** *n.*

sėquĕs'trum *n.* (path.) Portion of dead tissue, esp. bone, detached from surrounding parts. **sėquĕs'tral** *adj.*

sēq'uin *n.* 1. (hist.) Venetian gold coin worth about 9*s.* 2. Small coin-like metal ornament sewn to dress etc.

sėquoi'a *n.* Tree of genus (*S~*) of Californian coniferous trees of great height. [f. name (*Seqouiah*) of the Cherokee Indian who invented a syllabary for his language]

sérac (sĕrăk') *n.* One of the castellated masses into which a glacier is divided at steep points by the crossing of crevasses (ill. MOUNTAIN). [Swiss Fr., orig. name of a cheese]

sera'glio (-ahlyō) *n.* Walled palace, esp. (hist.) that of sultan at Constantinople; harem.

serai (serī') *n.* Building for accommodation of travellers in the East; CARAVANSERAI. [Pers., = 'palace']

sĕ'raph *n.* (pl. -*im*, -*s*). One of the *seraphim*, in bibl. use the living creatures with 3 pairs of wings, seen in Isaiah's vision as hovering above the throne of God; in Christian theology, a class of angels represented as the highest of the 9 orders of angels.

sėrăph'ic *adj.* Of, resembling, the seraphim; angelic; *S~ Doctor*, St. BONAVENTURA. **serăph'ically** *adv.*

Serāp'is. (Egypt. myth.) A god invented and introduced into Egypt by Ptolemy I to unite Greeks and Egyptians in common worship, combining the Egyptian Osiris with attributes of Zeus, Hades, and Aesculapius.

Sĕrb. 1. Member of Slav tribe settled at the invitation of the emperor Heraclius in the Roman province of Maesia, now inhabiting the former kingdom of Serbia and parts of Croatia, Bosnia, and Dalmatia. 2. The Serbian language.

Sẽrb'ia. Former Balkan kingdom, since 1919 part of Yugoslavia. **Sẽrb'ian** *adj.* & *n.* (Native, language) of Serbia.

Sẽrbō-Crōā'tian (-shĭan). A branch of the Slavonic languages spoken in Yugoslavia.

Sẽrbōn'ĭs. A boggy lake in the delta of the Nile, in which whole armies were said to have been swallowed up. **Sẽrbōn'ĭan** *adj.* ~ *bog*, this lake; (fig.) difficult position from which escape is impossible.

sēre, sear *adjs.* (now poet. or shet.) Dry, withered.

sĕrėnāde' *n.* Performance of music at night in open, esp. by lover under lady's window; piece of music suitable for such performance. ~ *v.* Entertain with, perform, a serenade.

sĕrėna'ta (-nah-) *n.* (mus.) Cantata, freq. pastoral, suitable for performance in open air; kind of suite usu. opening with march and including minuet.

Sĕrendib' (-ēb). One of the ancient names of Ceylon.

sĕrendĭp'ity *n.* Faculty of making happy discoveries by accident. [coined by Horace Walpole f. title of a fairy-tale, 'The Three Princes of Serendip']

sėrēne' *adj.* Clear and calm; unruffled; placid, tranquil, unperturbed. **serēne'ly** *adv.* **serĕn'ity** *n.*

sẽrf *n.* Villein, person whose service is attached to the soil and transferred with it (hist.); oppressed person, drudge. **sẽrf'age, sẽrf'dom, sẽrf'hŏŏd** *ns.*

sẽrge *n.* Kind of durable twilled worsted cloth. [L *serica* silk f. *Seres* the Chinese]

sergeant (sar̃j'ant) *n.* Non-commissioned officer above corporal; police officer ranking between inspector and constable; ~ *at arms*: see SERJEANT, sense 2. ~*-major*, non-commissioned officer of highest grade.

Sergt *abbrev.* Sergeant.

sēr'ĭal *adj.* Of, in, forming, a series; (of story etc.) issued in instalments. **sēr'ĭally** *adv.* **sēr'ĭal** *n.* Serial story. **sēr'ĭalīze** *v.t.*

sĕrĭāt'ĭm (*or* sēr-) *adv.* One after another, one by one in succession.

Sēr'ĭc *adj.* (rhet. etc.) Chinese.

sĕr'ĭcŭlture *n.* Silkworm-breeding, production of raw silk.

sēr'ies (-ēz, -ĭēz) *n.* (pl. same). Succession of similar or similarly related things, sequence, order, row, set; set of successive issues of periodical, of literary compositions, of books issued by one publisher in common form and with some similarity of subject or purpose etc.; (geol.) set of strata with common characteristic; (chem.) group of elements with common properties or of compounds related in composition and structure; (math.) set of terms constituting progression or having common relation between successive terms; (elect.) set of circuits so arranged (*in* ~) that same current traverses all circuits (ill. CIRCUIT); (zool.) number of connected genera, families, etc.

sĕ'rĭf *n.* Cross-line finishing off a stroke of a letter (This has serifs: This is SANSERIF, i.e. has none).

sēr'ĭgraph (-ahf) *n.* Print made by **sėrĭg'raphy**, process of stencil printing through a silk screen. **sėrĭg'rapher** *n.*

sĕ'rĭn *n.* Small greenish finch (*Serinus canarius*) of Mediterranean countries, related to canary.

sĕrĭnĕtte' *n.* Instrument for teaching cage-birds to sing, 'bird-organ'.

sērio-cŏm'ĭc *adj.* Partly serious and partly comic.

sēr'ious *adj.* Grave in appearance, manner, intention, purpose, etc., solemn, earnest, not frivolous, trifling, or playful; requiring earnest thought or application; important, not slight; earnest about things of religion, religious-minded. **sēr'iously** *adv.* **sēr'iousnėss** *n.*

serjeant (sar̃j'ant) *n.* (Usu. form for) 1. (hist., also ~*-at-law*) Member of superior order of barristers (abolished 1880) from which Common Law judges were chosen; *Common S*~, judicial officer appointed by Corporation of London as assistant to Recorder. 2. ~*-at-arms*, title of certain court, parliamentary, and city officials with ceremonial duties, esp., officer of each House of Parliament with duty of enforcing commands of the house, arresting offenders, etc.; officer with corresponding duties under other legislative assemblies; *Serjeants' Inn*, collegiate building of the now extinct order of serjeants-at-law, esp. that in Chancery Lane, London.

sẽrm'on *n.* Discourse delivered from pulpit and usu. based on text of Scripture, by way of religious exhortation or instruction; similar discourse on religious or moral subject delivered elsewhere or published; moral reflection(s), homily. *S*~ *on the Mount*, discourse of Christ recorded in Matt. v–vii. **sẽrm'onīze** *v.*

sēr'ous *adj.* Of, like, serum; whey-like; ~ *gland*, gland elaborating a watery, as opposed to a mucous, secretion; ~ *membrane*, delicate membrane lining closed cavities of the body.

sẽrp'ent *n.* 1. Snake, esp. large snake; treacherous person. 2. Kind of firework with serpentine motion in air or on ground; *Pharaoh's* ~, chemical toy, small cone or ovoid, containing mercury thiocyanate, which when ignited extrudes ash in long coiling serpent-like form. 3. (mus.) Obsolete bass wind instrument of long wooden tube with several U-shaped bends, with finger-holes and mouthpiece like that of trumpet.

sẽrp'entīne *adj.* Of or like a serpent; writhing, coiling, tortuous, sinuous; cunning, subtle, treacherous; ~ *verse*, line beginning and ending with same word. ~ *n.* 1. (hist.) Kind of cannon. 2. Dull-green (or occas. red or brown) soft rock or mineral, chiefly hydrated magnesium silicate, with markings resembling those of snakeskin. 3. Waving or sinuous thing or line; *the S*~, ornamental water in Hyde Park, London.

sẽrpĭ'ginous *adj.* (Of skin disease etc.) creeping from one part to another. **sẽrpĭg'ō** *n.* Any creeping or spreading skin disease.

sĕr'rāte, sĕrrā'tėd *adjs.* Having, forming, row of small projections like teeth of saw; notched like saw. **sĕrrā'tion** *n.*

sĕr'ried (-rĭd) *adj.* (Of ranks etc.) pressed close together, in close order, crowded, compact.

sēr'um *n.* 1. Amber-coloured liquid which separates from clot when blood coagulates. 2. Blood serum as antitoxin or therapeutic agent; ~ *eruption, sickness*, manifestations following serum injection, e.g. skin eruption, fever, swelling of joints. 3. Watery animal fluid.

sẽrv'al *n.* Long-legged African cat-like animal, *Felis serval*, with tawny black-spotted coat and large ears.

sẽrv'ant *n.* One who has undertaken, usu. in return for salary or wages, to carry out orders of individual or corporate employer, esp. one who waits on master or mistress or performs domestic duties in household; devoted follower, person willing to serve another; *public* ~, State official; *civil* ~, member of civil service; *your obedient* ~, epistolary form preceding signature (now only in letters of official type).

sẽrve *v.* 1. Be servant (to), render service, be useful (to); be employed (*in* army, navy, etc.); be soldier, sailor, etc. (*in* war, *against* enemy, etc.); ~ *at table*, act as waiter. 2. Meet needs (of), avail, suffice, satisfy; perform function, be suitable, do what is required for; ~ one's *apprenticeship*, go through training; ~ *sentence*, undergo it; ~ (one's) *time*, undergo imprisonment, serve a sentence; serve apprenticeship. 3. Dish *up*, set (food) on table; set out ready; distribute; supply (person *with*); make legal delivery of (writ etc.), deliver writ etc. to (person); set ball, set (ball) in play; (tennis etc.) start play by striking ball towards opponent, into opposite court, etc.; (of male animal) cover (the female). ~ *n.* (tennis etc.) Setting ball in play, turn for doing this. **sẽrv'er** *n.* (esp.) Celebrant's assistant who arranges altar and makes responses.

Sẽrv'ia. Usu. name in Britain until 1914 for SERBIA. **Sẽrv'ian**[1] *adj.* & *n.*

Sẽrv'ian[2] *adj.* Of, pertaining to, SERVIUS TULLIUS; ~ *Wall*, wall built around Rome by Servius Tullius.

sẽrv'ice *n.* 1. Being servant, serving a master; work or duty of a servant; duty which feudal tenant was bound to render to lord; person's disposal or behalf; use, assistance. 2. Department of royal or public employ or of work done to meet some general need; persons engaged, employment, in this, esp. army, navy, and air force; (attrib.) belonging, issued, etc., to navy, army, or air force. 3. Liturgical form or office appointed for use on some occasion; single meeting of congregation for worship; musical setting of (parts of) liturgical service; *divine* ~, meeting for worship. 4. Legal serving of or *of* writ etc.; act of serving ball in tennis etc., way of doing this, ball served. 5. Set of dishes, plates, etc., required for serving meal; set of trains, steamers, omnibuses, etc., plying at stated times; supply or laying-on of gas, water, etc., through pipes to private houses etc.; provision of what is necessary for the due maintenance of a thing, esp. maintenance and repair work carried out by vendor after sale. 6. ~ *area*, area surrounding broadcasting station within which reception is assured; ~ *dress*, ordinary uniform (opp. to *full dress*); ~ *flat*, one in which domestic service is provided by the management; ~ *hatch*, one through which dishes are passed to the dining-room; ~ *pipe*, one conveying water or gas from the main to a building; ~ *road*, road constructed and situated for convenient service of houses etc. lying off the main road. ~ *v.t.* Provide service for (car, aircraft, etc.).

sẽrv'ice(-tree) *n.* Eur. tree, *Sorbus domestica*, like mountain ash, with small round or pear-shaped fruit edible when overripe; (also *service-berry*), Amer. small tree or shrub (*Amelanchier*) with berry-like fruits, shad-bush.

sẽrv'iceable (-sabl) *adj.* Profitable, useful, capable of rendering service; durable, hard-wearing, for rough or ordinary use rather than ornament. **sẽrv'iceableness** *n.* **sẽrv'iceably** *adv.*

sẽrviĕtte' *n.* Table-napkin.

sẽrv'ĭle *adj.* Of, being, suitable to, a slave or slaves; slavish, cringing, fawning, mean-spirited. **sẽrv'ĭlely** *adv.* **sẽrvĭl'ĭty** *n.*

sẽrv'itor *n.* (archaic) Attendant, henchman, servant; (hist.) at University of Oxford, undergraduate assisted from college funds and performing menial duties in return. **sẽrv'itorship** *n.*

sẽrv'itūde *n.* Slavery, subjection, bondage.

Sẽrv'ius Tŭll'ius. Semi-legendary 6th king of Rome (6th c. B.C.).

sẽrv'ō-mĕch'anism (-k-) *n.* Power-assisted device usu. for controlling movement (e.g. a brake), freq. deriving its power from the source of energy over which it exercises control. So **sẽrv'ō-contrōl'** *n.* **sẽrv'ō-assis'tėd** *adj.*

sĕs'amė *n.* (Seeds of) E. Indian herbaceous plant yielding oil and used as food; *open* ~, password or charm at which doors or barriers fly open (see ALI BABA).

sĕs'amoid *adj.* Shaped like a sesame-seed, nodular (esp. of small independent bones developed in tendons passing over angular structure, as the knee-cap or the navicular bone). ~ *n.* Such bone.

sesqui-. Prefix denoting one and a half, the ratio 3 : 2, etc.

sĕsquicĕntĕnn'ial *adj.* & *n.* (Of) 150th anniversary.

sĕsquipėdāl'ian *adj.* (Of word) a foot and a half long; cumbrous, pedantic.

sĕs'sile *adj.* (bot., zool.) Immediately attached; without foot-stalk, peduncle, etc. (ill. INFLORESCENCE).

sĕ'ssion (-shn) *n.* Sitting, continuous series of sittings, term of such sittings, of court, legislative or administrative body, etc., for conference or transaction of business; *petty sessions*, meeting of two or more justices of the peace for summary trying of certain offences; period between opening and prorogation of English parliament; (Sc., U.S., and in some English universities, etc.) part of year during which instruction is given; *Court of S*~, supreme civil court of Scotland. **sĕ'ssional** (-sho-) *adj.*

sĕs'tẽrce *n.* Ancient Roman coin, ¼ of denarius. **sĕstẽr'tium** (-shm) *n.* A thousand sesterces.

sĕstĕt' *n.* Sextet; last 6 lines of sonnet.

sĕt[1] *v.* (past t. and past part. *sĕt*). 1. Put, lay, stand; apply (thing) to; station, place ready; place, turn, in right or specified position or direction; dispose suitably for use, action, or display; plant (seed etc.) in ground; ~ *sail*, hoist sail; begin voyage; ~ *table*, lay table for meal; ~ (*up*) *type*, arrange it for printing. 2. Join, attach, fasten, fix; determine, decide, appoint, settle, establish; put parts of (broken bone etc.) into right relative position after fracture or dislocation; insert (precious stone etc.) in gold etc. as frame or foil; (past part.) unmoving, fixed; (of speech) composed beforehand; (of batsman, at cricket) have become accustomed to the bowling; ~ *fair*, (of weather) fine without sign of breaking; ~ (*up*)*on*, determined to get, absorbed in; ~ *piece*, fireworks built up on scaffolding; *of* ~ *purpose*, intentionally, deliberately; ~ *scene*, stage-scene built up of more or less solid material. 3. Bring by placing, arranging, etc., into specified state; make sit down *to* task, cause *to work*, apply oneself *to work*; exhibit or arrange as pattern or as material to be dealt with; draw up (questions, paper) to be answered by examinees; make insertions in (surface) *with*; ~ (*to music*), provide (song, words) with music usu. composed for the purpose. 4. Put or come into a settled or rigid position or state; curdle, solidify, harden; take shape, develop into definiteness; fix (hair) when damped by *setting-lotion* so that it dries in waves. 5. (of sun, moon, etc.) Sink below horizon. 6. (of tide, current, etc.) Have motion, gather force, sweep along; show or feel tendency. 7. (of sporting dog) Take rigid attitude indicating presence of game; (of dancers) take position facing partners; (of garment) adapt itself to figure, sit *well*, *badly*, etc. 8. ~ *about*, begin, take steps towards; (colloq.) set on, attack; ~ *back*, impede or reverse progress of; (U.S. slang) cost (person) specified amount; ~-*back* (*n.*) reversal or arrest of progress; ~ *down*, put in writing; attribute *to*, explain or describe oneself *as*; allow (passenger) to alight; ~ *in*, arise, get vogue, become established; fit (part of garment) into the rest; ~ *off*, act as adornment or foil to, enhance, make more striking; start (person) laughing, talking, etc.; begin journey; ~-*off* (*n.*) thing set off against another, thing of which the amount or effect may be deducted from another by opposite tendency; counterpoise, counterclaim; embellishment, adornment *to* something; (archit.) sloping or horizontal member connecting lower and thicker part of wall etc. with upper receding part; ~ *on*, urge (dog etc.) to attack (person etc.); attack; ~ *out*, demonstrate, exhibit; declare; begin journey; ~ *to*, begin doing something, esp. fighting or arguing, vigorously; ~-*to* (*n.*) combat, esp. with fists; ~ *up*, start; occasion, cause; establish (person, oneself) in some capacity; place in view; raise, begin to utter (cry, protest, etc.); propound (theory); prepare (machine) for operation; ~ *up for*, make pretension to the character of; ~-*up* (*n.*) manner or position in which a thing is set up; (orig. U.S.) structure or arrangement of an organization, or the like.

sĕt[2] *n.* 1. Number of things or persons belonging together as essentially similar or complementary; group, clique, collection; (tennis etc.) group of games counting as unit to side winning more than half of them; wireless receiving apparatus. 2. Slip or shoot for planting; young fruit just set. 3. (poet.) Setting *of* sun or day. 4. Way current, wind, opinion, etc., sets; drift or tendency *of*; configuration, conformation, habitual posture; warp, bend, displacement, caused by continued pressure or position; (amount of) alternate deflexion of saw-teeth; fixing of damped hair in waves. 5. Last coat of plaster on wall; timber frame supporting gallery etc. in coal-mine; amount of margin in type causing letters to be close or wide set; clutch of eggs; badger's burrow; granite paving-block; setter's pointing in presence of game; *dead* ~, pointed attack, determined onslaught *at* or *against*. 6. Theatrical or cinema setting, stage furniture, etc.

Sĕt[3]. (Egypt. myth.) God of evil, brother (or son) of Osiris and his constant enemy; represented with head of beast with long pointed snout.

sē′ta *n.* (pl. *-ae*). (bot., zool.) Stiff hair, bristle (ill. EARTHworm). **sētā′ceous** (-sh*us*) *adj.* Having bristles, bristle-like.

Sĕth. (O.T.) One of the sons of Adam.

sē′ton *n.* (surg., now only in occas. veterinary use) Thread or skein of thread drawn through fold of skin to produce counter-irritation.

sĕt squāre *n.* Draughtsman's appliance for drawing lines at certain angles, consisting of plate of wood, metal, etc., in shape of right-angled triangle, with other angles of 60° and 30°, or of 45° (ill. SQUARE).

sĕtt *n.* Var. of SET[2], in various technical uses; esp., paving-block.

sĕttee′ *n.* Long seat with back and usu. arms for more than one person (ill. SOFA).

sĕtt′er *n.* 1. (also ~*-up*) Worker who prepares a machine for an operation, as dist. from the *machinist* who operates it. 2. One of several varieties of sporting dogs, with long silky coat, trained to stand rigid on scenting game; the *English* ~ is white with brownish and black markings, the *Gordon* ~ black with tan markings, and the *Irish* ~ dark red or chestnut colour.

sĕtt′ing *n.* (esp.) 1. Music to which words are set. 2. Frame in which jewel is set; surroundings or environment of anything; mounting of play, film, etc., scenery, stage furniture, etc.

sĕtt′le[1] *n.* Bench with high back and arms, and freq. with box or chest under seat (ill. SOFA).

sĕtt′le[2] *v.* 1. Establish, become established, in more or less permanent abode, place, or way of life; (cause to) sit down (or *down*) to stay for some time; cease from wandering, motion, change, disturbance, or turbidity; bring to, attain, fixity, composure, certainty, decision, etc., determine, decide, appoint. 2. Colonize, establish colonists in, settle as colonists in (country). 3. Subside, sink to bottom of liquid or into lower position. 4. Deal effectually with, dispose or get rid of, do for; pay (bill), pay bill; ~ *up* (*accounts*), draw up accounts and liquidate balance; *settling-day*, esp. fortnightly account day at Stock Exchange. 5. Bestow legally for life *on*.

sĕtt′lement (-lm-) *n.* (esp.) 1. (law) Conveyance of, creation of estate(s) in, property, esp. on marriage. 2. Company of social workers established in poor or crowded district to give educational, medical, recreational, etc., services. 3. Newly settled tract of country, colony. 4. *Act of S*~, Act (1701) by which succession to British Crown was settled upon the Electress Sophia of Hanover and her descendants.

sĕtt′ler *n.* (esp.) One who settles in new colony or newly developed country, early colonist.

sĕtt′lor *n.* (law) One who makes a settlement of property.

sĕv′en *adj.* One more than six (7, vii, or VII); ~ *deadly sins*, pride, lechery, envy, anger, covetousness, gluttony, sloth; *S*~ *Dials*, district of London, formerly of narrow and squalid streets, with open space from which 7 streets radiated, having a hexagonal (not seven-sided) column in centre with sun-dials at top; ~*-league boots*, (in fairy story of Hop-o'-my-Thumb) boots enabling wearer to go 7 leagues at each stride; ~ *sages of Greece*, Thales of Miletus, Solon of Athens, Bias of Priene, Chilo of Sparta, Cleobulus of Rhodes, Periander of Corinth, and Pittacus of Mitylene, to each of whom some wise maxim is attributed by ancient writers; ~ *seas*: see SEA; *S*~ *Sisters*, the PLEIADES; *S*~ *Sleepers*, in early Christian legend, 7 noble Christian youths of Ephesus who fell asleep in a cave while fleeing from the Decian persecution and woke 187 years later; *S*~ *Weeks War*, that of 1866 between Austria and Prussia, as result of which Prussia became the predominant German power; *S*~ *Wonders of the World*, the structures regarded as the most remarkable monuments of antiquity: the Pyramids, the Mausoleum at Halicarnassus, the Hanging Gardens of Babylon, the temple of Artemis at Ephesus, Pheidias's statue of Zeus at Olympia, the Colossus of Rhodes, and the Pharos at Alexandria; *S*~ *Years War*, that waged 1756–63 by France, Austria, and Russia against Frederick the Great of Prussia and Gt Britain, in which France lost to Britain her possessions in America and India. ~ *n.* The number seven, the symbol 7; set of 7 persons or things, esp. playing-card with 7 pips.

sĕv′enteen′ *adj.* & *n.* One more than sixteen, ten plus seven (17, xvii, or XVII). **sĕv′enteenth′** *adj.* & *n.*

sĕv′enth *adj.* Next after sixth; ~ *day*, Saturday (in Quaker speech and among sects keeping Saturday as sabbath); *S*~*-day Adventists*, millenarian and sabbatarian sect; ~ *heaven*, abode of supreme bliss, highest of 7 heavens in Mohammedan and some Jewish systems. **sĕv′enthly** *adv.* **sĕv′enth** *n.* Seventh part; (mus.) interval of which the span involves 7 alphabetical names of notes, harmonic combination of notes thus separated.

sĕv′enty *adj.* Seven times ten (70, lxx, or LXX); ~*-five* (*n.*) French quick-firing 75-mm. gun; ~*-four*, (hist.) warship with 74 guns. ~ *n.* Number seventy, symbol 70; *the seventies*, years between 69 and 80 in life or century. **sĕv′entieth** *adj.* & *n.*

sĕv′er *v.* Separate, divide, part, disunite; cut or break off, take away, (part) from whole. **sĕv′erance** *n.*

sĕv′eral *adj.* 1. Separate, distinct, individual, respective. 2. A few, more than two or three but not many; *abs.* a moderate number (*of*). **sĕv′erally** *adv.*

sĕv′eralty *n.* Individual or unshared tenure of estate etc.

sėvēre′ *adj.* Austere, strict, harsh, rigorous; violent, vehement, extreme; trying, making great demands on endurance, energy, skill, etc.; unadorned, without redundance, restrained. **sėvēre′ly** *adv.* **sėvĕ′rity** *n.*

Sévigné (sāvēnyā′), Marie de Rabutin-Chantal, Marquise de (1626–96). French letter-writer, whose letters to her daughter give a vivid picture of age of Louis XIV.

Sėville′ (*or* sĕv′-). (Span. *Sevilla*) City and province of Andalusia, Spain; ~ *orange*, the bitter orange, *Citrus aurantium* var. *bigaradia*.

Sèvres (sĕvr). Town near Paris, site of the French national porcelain factory, which was orig. a private undertaking at Vincennes, and was moved to Sèvres, under Louis XV's patronage, in 1756; porcelain from this factory.

sew (sō) *v.* (past t. *sewed* pr. sōd, past part. *sewn* pr. sōn, *sewed*). Fasten, join (pieces of material, leather, etc.) by passing thread through series of punctures made by needle carrying the thread or with an awl; make by sewing; fasten together sheets of (book) by passing thread or wire through back fold of each sheet; use needle and thread or sewing-machine; *sewing-machine*, machine for sewing or stitching.

sew′age (sū-) *n.* The spent water supply of a community, including wastes from domestic and trade premises etc. and ground water; ~ *farm*, agricultural land used for the treatment of sewage, portions being used in rotation for sewage disposal, cultivation, and crops; ~ *treatment works*, plant for purifying sewage by artificial methods, rendering it fit for discharge into a river, lake, or tidal waters. ~ *v.t.* Irrigate, fertilize, with sewage.

sew'er[1] (sū-) n. Pipe or conduit for conveying sewage; ~-*gas*, foul air of sewers. ~ *v.t.* Provide, drain, with sewers. **sew'erage** *n.*

sew'er[2] (sū-) *n.* (hist.) Attendant at meal who arranged table, seated guests, and superintended serving and tasting of dishes.

sĕx *n.* The sum of the physiological difference in structure and function which distinguish the male from the female in animals and plants; males or females collectively; (loosely) the sexual relationship; (attrib.) arising from sex; ~ *appeal*, qualities attracting members of the opposite sex; ~-*limited*, (of Mendelian character) expressed only in one sex although the controlling gene is not on a sex chromosome; ~-*linked*, (of Mendelian character) controlled by a gene which is carried on a sex chromosome. **sĕx'lĕss** *adj.*

sĕx(i)- *prefix.* Six.

sĕxagėnār'ian *adj.* & *n.* (Person) aged 60 years or more but less than 70.

sĕxagēn'ary *adj.* Of 60; composed of, proceeding by, sixties.

Sĕxagĕs'ima (Sunday). Second Sunday before Lent, Sunday before Quinquagesima. [L, = '60th']

sĕxagĕs'imal *adj.* Proceeding by sixties; of, based on, involving, division into 60 equal parts; ~ *fraction*, one whose denominator is 60 or a power of 60. **sĕxagĕs'imally** *adv.*

sĕxcĕntēn'ary *adj.* & *n.* (Of) 600 (esp. years); (of) 600th anniversary.

sĕxĕnn'ial *adj.* Lasting, (occurring) once in, 6 years.

sĕxill'ion *n.* 6th power of a million (1 followed by 36 ciphers); (U.S.) 7th power of a thousand (1 followed by 21 ciphers).

sĕxt *n.* (eccles.) Canonical hour orig. belonging to 6th hour of day (midday); office said at this time.

sĕx'tan *adj.* (Of fever) recurring every 5th (in old reckoning 6th) day.

sĕx'tant *n.* Instrument with mirrors and graduated arc of 6th part of circle, used by navigators for finding position by measuring altitudes of heavenly bodies or horizontal angles between terrestrial objects.

sĕxtĕt(te)' *n.* (Musical work for) 6 voices, instruments, etc.; set of 6.

sextillion = SEXILLION.

sĕxtōdĕ'cimō *n.* (abbrev. 16mo) Sheet of paper folded in 16 leaves; this way of folding; book of such sheets.

sĕx'ton *n.* Church officer having care of fabric and contents of church, and freq. with duties of bell-ringer and grave-digger.

sĕx'tūple *adj.* & *n.* Sixfold (amount). ~ *v.* Multiply by 6.

sĕx'ūal (*or* -kshōō-) *adj.* Of sex, a sex, or the sexes; (bot., of classification) based on distinction of sexes in plants. **sĕx'ūally** *adv.* **sĕx'ūalist, sĕxūăl'ity** *ns.*

sĕx'ūalize (*or* -kshōō-) *v.t.* Make sexual, attribute sex to. **sĕxūalizā'tion** *n.*

sĕx'y *adj.* (chiefly colloq.) Immoderately engrossed with sex.

Seychelles (sāshĕlz'). Group of islands in the Indian Ocean, since 1810 in British possession.

Seym (sām). The Polish parliament.

Seym'our (sēm'*er*), Jane (*c* 1509–37). 3rd queen of Henry VIII of England and mother of Edward VI.

sf. *abbrev. Sforzando*

s.f. *abbrev. Sub finem* (= towards the end (of the chapter etc. referred to)).

S.F.A. *abbrev.* Scottish Football Association.

sfŏrzăn'dō (-ts-) (mus. direction). With sudden emphasis.

sfuma'tō (-ōōmah-) *adj.* (painting) Having indistinct, blurred, outlines. [It., = 'smoked']

s.g. *abbrev.* Specific gravity.

s.g.d.g. *abbrev. Sans guarantie du gouvernement* (= without government guarantee).

Sgt *abbrev.* Sergeant.

sh *int.* = HUSH.

shăbb'y *adj.* Contemptible, paltry, dishonourable; dingy and faded from wear or exposure; worn, dilapidated; shabbily dressed; ~-*genteel*, attempting to look genteel or keep up appearances in spite of shabbiness. **shăbb'ily** *adv.* **shăbb'inėss** *n.*

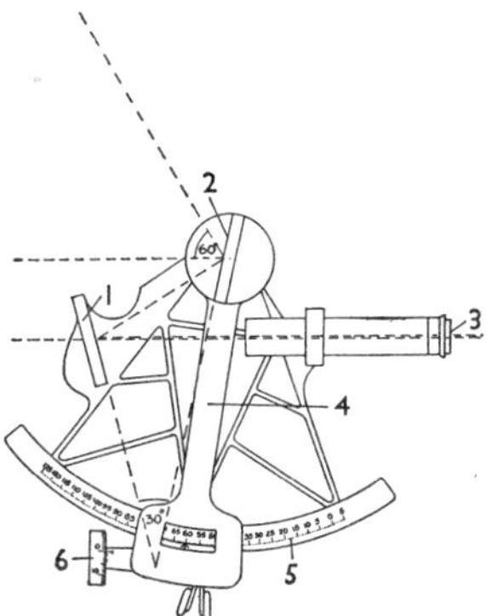

NAVIGATION SEXTANT

1. Horizon mirror. 2. Index mirror. 3. Eyepiece of telescope. 4. Index arm. 5. Graduated arc. 6. Decimal micrometer. The dotted lines indicate the direction of light from sun or star and horizon

shăck *n.* (orig. U.S. & Canada) Roughly built hut or shanty.

shăck'le *n.* Metal loop or staple, bow of padlock, link closed by bolt for connecting chains etc., coupling link; (pl.) fetters, impediments, restraints; ~-*bolt*, bolt for closing shackle; bolt with shackle on end. ~ *v.t.* Fetter, impede, trammel.

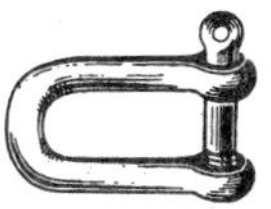

SHACKLE

Shăck'leton (-lt-), Sir Ernest Henry (1874–1922). Irish-born explorer, whose ship, the *Endurance*, was crushed in the ice when he tried to cross the Antarctic, 1914–16.

shăd *n.* Any of various deep-bodied herring-like fishes of genus *Clupea* much used as food; ~-*berry*, ~-*bush*, (U.S.) plant, berry, of genus *Amelanchier*, service-berry.

shădd'ock *n.* (Tree, *Citrus decumana* or *C. maxima*, bearing) largest citrous fruit, esp. large coarse pear-shaped varieties of this (the smaller and rounder being called grape-fruit). [Capt. *Shaddock*, who introduced the plants into Barbados (1696)]

shāde *n.* 1. Comparative or partial darkness, esp. caused by more or less opaque object intercepting rays of sun or other source of light; comparative obscurity; darker part of picture; (freq. pl.) place sheltered from sun, cool or sequestered retreat; (pl.) darkness *of* night or evening; *the ~s*, the abode of the dead, Hades. 2. Colour, esp. with regard to its depth or as distinguished from one nearly like it; gradation of colour; (painting) colour darkened by admixture of black. 3. Slight difference, small amount; unsubstantial or unreal thing. 4. Soul after death, ghost, disembodied spirit. 5. Screen excluding or moderating light, heat, etc.; eye-shield; glass cover for object. **shāde'lėss** (-dl-) *adj.* **shāde** *v.* Screen from excessive light; cover, keep off, or moderate power of (luminous object, light) with or as intervening object; make dark or gloomy; darken (parts of drawing etc.), esp. with parallel pencil lines, to give effects of light and shade or gradations of colour; (of colour, opinion, etc.) pass *off* by degrees into another colour or variety, make pass thus *into* another. **shăd'ėd** *adj.* **shăd'ing** *n.*

shăd'ow (-ō) *n.* 1. Shade; dark part of picture, room, etc.; patch of shade, dark figure projected by body intercepting rays of light, this regarded as appendage of person or thing; (fig.) inseparable attendant or companion. 2. Reflected image; delusive semblance or image; type, foreshadowing, adumbration; slightest trace; phantom, ghost. 3. Protection, shelter. 4. ~-*boxing*, boxing against imaginary opponent as form of training; ~ *cabinet*, a cabinet the prospective members of which are at present in the Opposition; ~ *factory*, factory erected (sometimes duplicating an existing one) as a provision for future production (esp. of war materials). **shăd'owlėss, shăd'owy** (-ōĭ) *adjs.* **shăd'ow** *v.t.* 1. Cast shadow over. 2. Indicate obscurely, set *forth* dimly or in slight outline, prefigure. 3. Follow (person) like shadow, dog the steps of.

Shād'răch (-k). (O.T.) One of 3 Jewish youths who came unharmed from a furnace into which they were thrown by Nebuchadnezzar (Dan. iii).

shād'y *adj.* 1. Affording shade; shaded; *on the* ~ *side of*, older than (specified age). 2. Not able to bear the light, disreputable, of doubtful honesty. **shād'ĭly** *adv.* **shād'inėss** *n.*

S.H.A.E.F., Shaef (-āf) *abbrev.* Supreme Headquarters Allied Expeditionary Force, set up 1943 to organize Allied invasion of Europe.

Shăf'iite (*or* shah-). Member of one of 4 sects of Sunnites or orthodox Mohammedans. [f. cognomen *ash-Shāfi'ī* of their founder Abu Abdallah Muhammed ibn Idris (767–819)]

shaft (-ah-) *n.* 1. Long slender rod forming body of spear, lance, or arrow; spear (archaic); arrow; ray *of* light, streak *of* lightning. 2. Stem; part of column between base and capital (ill. ORDER); upright part of cross; part of chimney above roof; rib of feather (ill. FEATHER); more or less long, narrow, and straight part supporting or connecting part(s) of greater thickness etc.; handle, haft, of tool, golf-club, etc. 3. (mech.) Long cylindrical rotating rod upon which are fixed parts for transmission of motive power in machine. 4. One of long bars between pair of which horse is harnessed to vehicle (ill. CART). 5. Vertical or inclined well-like excavation giving access to mine, tunnel, etc. (ill. MINE); any similar well-like excavation or passage, as that in which lift runs etc.

Shaftes'bury (-ahfts-), Anthony Ashley Cooper, 3rd Earl of (1671–1713). English moral philosopher. ~, Anthony Ashley Cooper, 7th Earl of (1801–85). Philanthropist, active in many movements for the protection of the working classes and the benefit of the poor.

shăg *n.* 1. Rough growth or mass of hair etc. 2. (archaic) Long-napped rough cloth. 3. Strong coarse kind of cut tobacco. 4. Sea-bird (*Phalacrocorax aristotelis*) resembling cormorant but smaller.

shăgg'y *adj.* Hairy, rough-haired; hirsute, villous; covered with rough tangled vegetation; (of hair) rough, coarse, tangled; ~ *dog story*, type of anecdote (orig. about a talking animal) with much detail and peculiar twist of humour at end. **shăgg'ĭly** *adv.* **shăgg'inėss** *n.*

shagreen' *n.* Kind of untanned leather with rough granular surface made from skin of horse, ass, shark, seal, etc., and freq. dyed green; imitation of this; hard rough skin of some sharks, rays, etc., covered with calcified papillae, used for polishing.

shah *n.* Title of the sovereign rulers of Persia. [Pers., = 'king']

shāke *v.* (past t. *shook*, past part. *shāk'en*). Move violently or quickly up and down or to and fro; (cause to) tremble, rock, or vibrate; jolt, jar; brandish; weaken, make less firm or stable; agitate, shock, disturb; ~ *hand(s)*, clasp right hands at meeting or parting, over concluded bargain, in congratulation, etc.; ~ *head*, move it from side to side in refusal, negation, disapproval, concern, etc.; ~ *down*, fetch or send down by shaking; *shake'down*, improvised bed of straw or bedding laid on floor; ~ *off*, get rid of by shaking; ~ *out*, empty of contents or dust, empty (contents or dust) from vessel, etc., by shaking; spread or open (sail, flag, etc.); ~ *up*, mix, loosen, by shaking; rouse with or as with shaking. ~ *n.* Shaking, being shaken; jolt, jerk, shock; crack in growing timber; (mus.) trill, rapid alternation of note with the note above; (orig. U.S.) glass of milk or milk and egg flavoured and shaken up (short for *milkshake*); *no great* ~*s*, not very good.

shāk'er *n.* (esp.) 1. Vessel in which ingredients of cocktails are shaken. 2. (*S*~) Member of Amer. religious celibate sect living in mixed communities, orig. founded (1747) in Manchester, England, by secession from the Quakers, and named from dancing movements which formed part of their worship.

Shākes'peare (-kspēr), William (1564–1616). England's greatest dramatist and poet. **Shakespe(a)r'ian** (-pēr-) *adj.*

shăk'ō *n.* Military cap, more or less cylindrical, with peak and upright plume or tuft (ill. CAVALRY). [Magyar *csákó*]

shāk'y *adj.* Unsteady, trembling, unsound, infirm, tottering; unreliable. **shāk'ĭly** *adv.* **shāk'inėss** *n.*

shāle *n.* Very fine-grained laminated sedimentary rock consisting of consolidated mud or clay; ~-*oil*, oil obtained from bituminous shale. **shāl'y** *adj.*

shăll (*unstressed* shal, shl) *v.aux.* (2nd pers. sing. *shălt*) Forming compound tenses or moods expressing: (1) (in 1st pers.) simple future action; (2) (in other persons) command; (3) (in all persons) obligation, intention, necessity, etc.

shalloon' *n.* Light twilled woollen fabric used chiefly for linings. [f. *Châlons*, France]

shăll'op *n.* Light open boat for shallow water.

shallŏt' *n.* Onion-like plant, *Allium ascalonicum*, native to Syria, with small clustered bulbs, resembling but milder than those of garlic, used for flavouring. [Fr. *eschalotte*, dim. of *eschaloigne*, f. L *ascalonia*, f. *Ascalon* in Palestine]

shăll'ow (-ō) *adj.* Of little depth (lit. & fig.), superficial, trivial. ~ *n.* Shallow place, shoal. ~ *v.* Become shallower; make shallow. **shăll'owly** *adv.* **shăll'ownėss** *n.*

shăm *n.* Imposture, pretence, humbug; person, thing, pretending or pretended to be something that he or it is not. ~ *adj.* Pretended, counterfeit, imitation. ~ *v.* Feign, simulate; pretend to be.

Sha'manism (shah-, shă-). Primitive religion of Ural-Altaic peoples of N. Asia in which gods, spirits, and demons influencing all human life are believed to be responsive to *shamans*, priests or witch-doctors; any similar religion, esp. among N. Amer. Indians.

shăm'ble *v.i.* Walk, run, in shuffling, awkward, or decrepit way. ~ *n.* Shambling gait.

shăm'bles (-blz) *n.pl.* (freq. with sing. construction). Butchers' slaughter-house; scene of carnage or chaotic confusion.

shāme *n.* Feeling of humiliation excited by consciousness of guilt or shortcoming, of appearing ridiculous, or of having offended against propriety, modesty, or decency; fear of this as restraint on behaviour; state of disgrace, ignominy, or discredit; person or thing that brings disgrace. ~ *v.t.* Bring shame on, be a shame to, make ashamed; put to shame by superior excellence; drive *into*, *out of*, through shame or fear of shame. **shāme'ful** (-mf-), **shāme'lėss** *adjs.* **shāme'fully, shāme'lėssly** *advs.* **shāme'fulnėss, shāme'lėssnėss** *ns.*

shāme'faced (-āst) *adj.* Bashful, shy; ashamed, abashed. **shāme'fācėdly** *adv.* **shāme'fācėdnėss** *n.*

shămm'y *n.* = CHAMOIS (leather).

shămpoo' *v.t.* Massage, esp. as part of Turkish bath (now rare); wash and rub (scalp, hair) with cleansing agent. ~ *n.* Shampooing; shampooing agent; *dry* ~, alcoholic saponaceous preparation for cleaning the hair, powder for similar use. [prob. f. Hind. *shāmpo*, imper. of *shāmpnā* to press]

shăm'rŏck *n.* Trifoliate plant, used, according to tradition, by St. Patrick to illustrate doctrine of Trinity, and hence adopted as national emblem of Ireland; now usu., the lesser yellow trefoil, *Trifolium minus.* [Ir. *seamróg,* dim. of *seamar* clover]

Shan (-ahn) *n.* & *adj.* (Member, language) of a Mongoloid race, related to the Thai or Siamese, found throughout Indo-China, and esp. in the ~ *States*, a group of semi-independent States in E. Burma.

shăn'drydăn *n.* Chaise with hood; rickety old-fashioned vehicle.

shăn'dy, shăn'dygăff *ns.* Drink made of mixture of beer and ginger beer or lemonade.

Shănghai' (-hī). Seaport of China. **shănghai'** *v.t.* Drug or otherwise render insensible and ship as a sailor while unconscious.

shănk *n.* 1. Leg, lower part of leg from knee to ankle; shin-bone, tibia; tarsus of bird, lower part of foreleg of horse. 2. Stem; straight part of nail, pin, fish-hook, etc.; stem of key, spoon, anchor, etc. (ill. ANCHOR); shaft of tool between head etc. and handle; narrow part of boot or shoe beneath instep; body of type (ill. TYPE).

Shănn'on. River of Ireland flowing from Cavan county to the Atlantic.

shăntŭng' *n.* Soft undressed Chinese silk, usu. undyed and sometimes mixed with cotton. [f. name of Chinese province]

shăn'ty[1] *n.* Hut, cabin; mean roughly constructed dwelling. [Canadian-Fr. *chantier* log hut, f. Fr. = 'workshop']

shăn'ty[2]: see CHANTY.

shāpe *n.* 1. External form, contour, configuration; visible appearance characteristic of person, thing, etc.; guise; concrete presentment, embodiment; phantom (now rare); dimly seen figure. 2. Kind, description, sort. 3. Definite or regular form, orderly arrangement. 4. Mould for jelly, blancmange, etc.; jelly, etc., moulded in this; body or frame of hat before trimming; portion of material etc. cut or moulded to have particular shape. ~ *v.* Create, form, construct; model, mould, bring into desired or definite figure or form; frame mentally, imagine; assume form, develop into shape, give signs of future shape. **shāpe'lėss** (-pl-) *adj.* **shāpe'lėssly** *adv.* **shāpe'lėssnėss** *n.*

S.H.A.P.E. *abbrev.* Supreme Headquarters of the Allied Powers in Europe.

shāpe'ly (-plĭ) *adj.* Well-formed or proportioned, of pleasing shape. **shāpe'linėss** *n.*

shärd, shẽrd *ns.* 1. = POTSHERD. 2. Hard wing-case of beetle, elytron (ill. BEETLE).

shāre[1] *n.* Portion detached for individual from common amount; part one is entitled to have or expected to contribute, equitable portion; part one gets or contributes; part-proprietorship of property held by joint owners, esp. one of the equal parts into which company's capital is divided; ~*-cropper*, (U.S.) tenant farmer paying rent with part of his crop; *share'holder*, owner of shares in joint-stock company; ~*-pusher*, one who peddles shares by circular or advertisement instead of selling them on the market. ~ *v.* Apportion, give share of; give away part of; get or have share of; possess, use, endure, jointly with others; have share(s), be sharer(s); (in the language of some religious groups) communicate to others one's spiritual experiences; ~ *out*, distribute; ~*'-out* (*n.*).

shāre[2] *n.* PLOUGHshare (ill. PLOUGH); blade of seeding-machine or cultivator.

shärk *n.* Any of various long-bodied cartilaginous fish, esp. large voracious kinds; rapacious person, swindler; ~*('s)-fin*, fin of shark, used as table delicacy by Chinese; ~*-skin*, skin of shark used as shagreen etc.

SHARK

shärp *adj.* 1. Having keen edge or point, not blunt; peaked, pointed, edged; well-defined; abrupt, angular. 2. Keen, pungent, acid, tart; shrill, piercing; biting, harsh, severe, intense, painful. 3. Acute, sensitive, keen-witted, vigilant, clever; quick to take advantage, artful, unscrupulous, dishonest; ~ *practice*, relentless pursuit of advantage; trickery. 4. Vigorous, speedy, impetuous. 5. (mus.) Above true pitch, too high; (following name of note, as *C sharp* etc.) a semitone higher than the note named; (of key) having sharps in the signature. **shärp'ly** *adv.* **shärp'nėss** *n.* **shärp** *n.* 1. Sewing-needle with sharp point. 2. (mus.) Note raised by a semitone above natural pitch; symbol (♯) indicating this raising. 3. (pl.) Finer parts of husk and coarser particles of flour of wheat and other cereals. ~ *adv.* Sharply; abruptly; punctually; (mus.) above true pitch; ~*-set*, hungry; *sharp'-shooter*, skilled shot, esp. one of division engaged in skirmishing and outpost work; shot attaining definite degree of skill in marksmanship. ~ *v.i.* Cheat, swindle, esp. at cards, whence **shärp'er** *n.* **shärp'en** *v.* Make, become, sharp.

shătt'er *v.* Break suddenly and violently in pieces; utterly destroy, wreck.

shāve *v.* (past part. *shāved* or *shāven*). 1. Remove (hair), free (chin etc.) of hair, relieve of hair on chin etc., with razor; shave oneself; *shaving-brush*, brush for applying lather before shaving. 2. Cut or pare away surface of (wood etc.) with spokeshave, plane, or other sharp tool. 3. Pass close to without touching; miss narrowly, nearly graze. ~ *n.* 1. Shaving, being shaved. 2. Close approach without contact; narrow miss, escape, or failure. 3. Knife-blade with handle at each end for shaving wood etc.

shāv'en *adj.* Shaved, tonsured; closely clipped.

shāv'er *n.* (esp.) 1. (colloq.) Lad, youngster. 2. Electrical appliance for shaving hair from face.

Shāv'ian *adj.* (In the manner) of G. B. SHAW[2].

shāv'ing *n.* (esp.) Thin slice taken from surface with sharp tool; thin slice of wood cut off with plane.

shaw[1] *n.* (archaic & poet.) Thicket, wood.

Shaw[2], George Bernard (1856–1950). Irish playwright, critic, and writer on social and political subjects; author of the plays 'Man and Superman', 'Back to Methuselah', 'Candida', 'Pygmalion', 'Saint Joan', etc.

shawl *n.* Oblong or square piece of material, freq. folded into triangle, worn over shoulders or head esp. by woman, and by Orientals as scarf, turban, or girdle. **shawled** (-ld) *adj.* Wearing shawl. [Pers. *shāl*]

shawm *n.* Obsolete musical instrument of oboe class, with double reed in globular mouthpiece.

shay *n.* (Archaic, joc., or vulg. for) CHAISE.

shē *pron.* Feminine pronoun of third person singular. ~ *n.* Female, woman. ~ *adj.* Female.

sheaf *n.* (pl. *-ves*). Large bundle of cereal plants bound together after reaping; cluster or bundle of things laid lengthwise together; bundle or quiverful of 24 arrows. ~ *v.t.* Bind into sheaf or sheaves.

shear *v.* (past t. *sheared*, past part. *shōrn*, *sheared*). 1. Cut with sharp instrument (poet. and archaic); clip, cut with scissors or shears; clip wool from (sheep); (fig.) fleece, strip bare. 2. Distort or break, be distorted or broken by, the strain called a shear. ~ *n.* 1. (pl.) Cutting-instrument with two meeting blades pivoted as in scissors or connected by spring and passing close over each other edge to edge. 2. (mech.) Kind of strain produced by pressure in structure of a substance, its successive layers being shifted laterally over each other (ill. STRESS). 3. (pl., also ~*-legs*) = SHEER[4]s. 4. ~ *steel*, blister steel improved in quality by heating and rolling or hammering, or both, used for cutting-tools.

shear′lĭng *n.* Sheep once shorn. **shear′water** (-waw-) *n.* Seabird of genus *Puffinus*, with long wings, skimming close to water in flight.

sheat′-fĭsh *n.* Largest European freshwater fish, a large catfish (*Silurus glanis*), common in Danube and other central European rivers.

sheath *n.* (pl. pr. -dhz). Close-fitting cover, esp. for blade of weapon or implement; (bot., anat., etc.) sheath-like covering, investing membrane, tissue, skin, horny case, etc.

sheathe (-dh) *v.t.* Put into sheath; encase, protect with casing or **sheath′ĭng,** protective layer of boards, metal plates, etc., on outside of bottom of wooden ship, on piece of machinery, roof, wall, etc.

sheave[1] *n.* Grooved wheel or pulley of pulley-block etc. (ill. PULLEY).

sheave[2] *v.t.* Gather (corn etc.) into sheaves.

Shēb′a. Biblical name of SABA; *Queen of* ~, Balkis, who visited Solomon (1 Kings x).

shėbăng′ *n.* (U.S. slang) House, store, saloon, business.

shėbeen′ *n.* (Chiefly in Ireland) Pot-house; unlicensed house selling drink.

shĕd[1] *n.* Slight structure for shelter, storage, etc., freq. built as lean-to, and sometimes with open front or sides; similar but large and strongly built structure on railway wharf, aerodrome, etc.

shĕd[2] *v.t.* (past t. and past part. *shĕd*). Part with, let fall (off), drop; cause (blood) to flow; disperse, diffuse, spread abroad.

sheen *n.* Splendour, radiance, lustre. **sheen′y**[1] *adj.*

sheen′y[2] *n.* (slang, derog.) Jew.

sheep *n.* (pl. same). Kinds of wild or domesticated timid, gregarious, woolly, often horned, ruminant mammal (*Ovis*) closely allied to goats, bred for flesh and wool; (usu. pl.) member(s) of minister's flock, parishioners, etc.; person as stupid, poor-spirited, unoriginal, or timid as a sheep; *~-fold*, enclosure for penning sheep; *~-dip*, preparation for cleansing sheep of vermin or preserving their wool; place for such cleansing; *~-dog*, collie; (*Old English ~-dog*), shaggy-coated bob-tailed breed of dog used for guarding and herding sheep (ill. DOG); *sheep′shank*, knot for temporarily shortening rope, made by doubling rope in three parts and taking hitch over bight at each end (ill. KNOT); *~'s-head*, (dish of) head of sheep; large food-fish of Atlantic coasts of U.S., with head supposed to resemble sheep's; *sheep′skin*, garment or rug of sheep's skin with wool on; leather of sheep's skin used in bookbinding, etc.; parchment of sheeps' skin, deed or diploma engrossed on this; *~-walk*, tract of land on which sheep are pastured; *~-wash*, sheep-dip.

sheep′ish *adj.* Embarrassed, shamefaced.

sheer[1] *adj.* Mere, unqualified, undiluted, absolute; (of textile fabric) thin, diaphanous; (of rock, fall, ascent, etc.) perpendicular, very steep and without a break. ~ *adv.* Plumb, perpendicularly, outright.

sheer[2] *v.i.* (naut.) Deviate from course; ~ *off*, part company, depart, esp. from person one dislikes.

sheer[3] *n.* Upward slope of ship's lines towards bow and stern; deviation of ship from course.

sheer[4] *n.* (pl.; also *~-legs* or *shear-legs*) Hoisting apparatus of two or more poles attached at or near top and separated at bottom for masting ships or putting in engines etc., used in dockyards or on *~-hulk*, dismasted ship used for the purpose. [var. of SHEAR; named from resemblance to pair of shears]

sheet *n.* 1. Rectangular piece of linen, cotton, etc., used as one of a pair of inner bed-clothes. 2. Broad more or less flat piece of some thin material, as paper; complete piece of paper of the size in which it was made; newspaper. 3. Wide expanse of water, snow, ice, flame, colour, etc. 4. Rope or chain at lower corner of sail, used to extend it or alter its direction (ill. SAIL[1]). 5. (pl.) Spaces of open boat forward of (*fore sheets*) and abaft (*stern sheets*) thwarts (ill. BOAT). 6. *in ~s*, (of book) printed but not bound; *three ~s in the wind*, rather or very drunk; ~ *bend* (ill. KNOT); ~ *glass*, kind made first as hollow cylinder which is cut open and flattened in furnace; ~ *iron, metal*, etc., spread by rolling, hammering, etc., into thin sheets; ~ *lightning*, lightning in diffused or sheet-like form due to reflection or diffusion by clouds (contrasted with *forked lightning*); ~ *music*, music published in sheets, not in book form. ~ *v.t.* Furnish with sheets; cover with sheet; secure (sail) with sheet.

sheet-ănch′or (-k-) *n.* Large, formerly always largest, anchor carried outside the waist of a ship, ready to be 'shot' or cast in an emergency; (fig.) one's best, surest, or only hope, refuge, or expedient.

Shĕff′ield. City and county borough of S. Yorkshire, famous for manufacture of cutlery and steel; ~ *plate*, copperware coated with silver by now disused process.

sheikh (-ēk, -āk) *n.* Chief, head, of Arab tribe, family, or village.

shĕk′el *n.* Ancient Babylonian, Phoenician, Hebrew, etc., weight; coin of this weight, esp. chief Jewish silver coin; (pl., colloq.) money, riches.

shĕl′drāke *n.* (fem. and pl. freq. **shĕl′dŭck** or **shĕld dŭck**). Bright-plumaged wild duck of genus *Tadorna*, frequenting sandy coasts in Europe, N. Africa, and Asia.

shĕlf *n.* (pl. *-ves*). Projecting slab of stone or board let into or hung on wall to support things; one of boards in cabinet, bookcase, etc., on which contents stand; ledge, horizontal step-like projection in cliff-face etc.; reef or sandbank under water; *on the* ~, (fig.) put aside, done with.

shĕll *n.* 1. Hard outer case enclosing kernel of nut, some kinds of seed or fruit, egg, some animals, as crustaceans and molluscs, or part of them; husk, crust, pod, carapace, scale, conch, pupa-case, etc. 2. Walls of unfinished or gutted building, ship, etc.; light narrow racing-boat; rough wooden coffin, inner thin coffin of lead, etc. 3. Hollow metal or paper case to contain explosives for fireworks, cartridges, etc.; cylindrical projectile of hardened steel with conical head fired from a gun, filled with a charge which is exploded either in flight by the action of a time-fuse, on impact with an object by a percussion fuse, or after penetrating the target or other body by a delayed-action fuse, the destructive effect being produced by the force of the explosion, by the fragmentation of the casing itself, or by the poison-gas or other substances which form its contents. 4. Apsidal end of schoolroom at Westminster School, form (intermediate between 5th and 6th) which orig. used this; in other English schools, an intermediate form. 5. *~-back*, (joc.) old sailor; *~-bark* (*hickory*), N. Amer. tree, *Carya ovata*, with rough shaggy bark of long narrow loosely adhering plates; *shellfish*, any aquatic animal with shell, esp. crustacean or mollusc; *~-jacket*, undress tight-fitting military jacket reaching only to waist behind, worn esp. as a mess-jacket by officers; *~-pink*, delicate shade of pale pink; *~-shock*, form of nervous breakdown provoked by exposure to battle conditions. **shĕlled** (-ld), **shĕll′-lėss, shĕll′y** *adjs.* **shĕll** *v.* 1. Take out of shell, remove shell or pod from; come away or *off* in thin pieces, scale *off*; ~ *out*, (slang) pay up, hand over (money); *~-out*, distribution of gains. 2. Bombard, fire at, with shells.

shĕllăc′ (*or* shĕl′-) *n.* Purified lac, esp. in thin plates, used in varnishes, insulating materials, gramophone records, on account of its high gloss, adhesiveness, and toughness. ~ *v.t.* Varnish, coat, with shellac.

Shĕll′ey, Percy Bysshe (1792–1822). English Romantic poet, author of 'Ode to the West Wind', 'To a Skylark', 'The Cloud', etc., and of the dramas 'The Cenci', 'Prometheus Unbound', etc. ~, Mary Wollstonecraft (1797–1851). His second wife, daughter of W. Godwin (1756–1836).

shĕll-out *n.* (billiards) Game of

pyramids played by three or more persons.

shĕl'ter *n.* Thing serving as shield or barrier against attack, danger, heat, wind, etc.; screen or cabin to keep off wind, rain, etc.; place of safety or immunity; sheltered or protected state (usu. *seek, take* ~). ~ *v.* Act or serve as shelter to; protect, conceal, harbour, defend *from* blame, screen, shield; take shelter; *sheltered industries*, those not exposed to foreign competition, e.g. building and inland transport.

shĕlve[1] *v.t.* Put on shelf; provide with shelves, esp. bookshelves; put aside (question etc.) from consideration; remove (person) from office, employment, etc. **shĕl'vịng** *n.* (esp.) Shelves, material for shelves.

shĕlve[2] *v.i.* Slope gently.

Shĕm. (O.T.) Eldest son of Noah.

shėmŏzz'le *n.* (orig. East End slang) A rough-and-tumble, uproar.

Shē'ol. Hebrew underworld, abode of the dead, represented as subterranean region of thick darkness whence return is impossible.

shĕp'herd (-perd) *n.* Man who guards, tends, and herds flock of sheep; pastor; *S~ Kings*: see HYKSOS; *~'s pie*, pie of chopped or minced meat with crust of mashed potatoes; *~'s plaid*, (woollen cloth with) small black-and-white check pattern; *~'s purse*, common cruciferous white-flowered weed, *Capsella bursa-pastoris*, with pouch-like pods. **shĕp'herdĕss** *n.* **shĕp'herd** *v.t.* Tend as shepherd; marshal, conduct, guide, like sheep.

Shĕ'raton, Thomas (1751–1806). English furniture designer, author of 'The Cabinet Maker's and Upholsterer's Drawing Book' (1791–4) and similar works illustrating the style then in vogue.

shẽrb'et *n.* Eastern cooling drink of sweetened and diluted fruit juice; effervescing drink or powder of flavoured sodium bicarbonate, tartaric acid, sugar, etc., from which it is made; water-ice. [Arab. *shariba* drink]

shẽrd: see SHARD.

Shĕ'rịdan, Richard Brinsley (1751–1816). Irish playwright and member of Parliament; author of the comedies 'The Rivals', 'The School for Scandal', etc.

sherif' (-eef), **shereef'** *ns.* Descendant of Mohammed through his daughter Fatima; title of certain Arab princes, esp. sovereign of Morocco; chief magistrate or local governor of Mecca. [Arab. *sharīf* noble, glorious]

shĕ'riff *n.* Chief executive officer of shire or county, charged with keeping of the peace, administration of justice under direction of the courts, execution of writs by deputy, presiding over elections, etc.; (Scotland) sheriff-depute; (U.S.) elective officer responsible for keeping the peace in his county; *~-depute*, (Scotland) a judicial officer of a county or stewartry having jurisdiction in minor civil and criminal cases.

Shẽrl'ŏck Holmes (hōmz). Amateur detective in series of stories by A. Conan DOYLE.

Shẽrp'a *n.* (fem. *Sherpa'ni* pr. -ahnĭ). Member of a people of Mongolian origin living on slopes of Himalayas and speaking a language allied to Tibetan.

shĕ'rry *n.* Still wine made near Jerez de la Frontera in Andalusia, Spain, varying in colour from pale gold to dark brown and usu. fortified, i.e. containing a proportion of brandy; similar wine made elsewhere, notably in S. Africa, Australia, California, and Cyprus; *~-glass*, small wine-glass. [Span. (*vino de*) *Xeres* (wine of) Jerez]

Shĕt'land Islands. Group of islands NNE. of Scottish mainland, constituting a county of Scotland; *Shetland pony*, pony of small hardy rough-coated breed orig. from Shetland Islands; *Shetland wool*, fine thin loosely twisted wool from Shetland sheep. **Shĕt'lander** *n.*

shew (shō) var. of SHOW *v.*; *shew'bread*, 12 loaves displayed in Jewish temple and renewed each sabbath.

Shiah (shē'*a*). Mohammedan sect (chiefly represented by Persians) holding that Mohammed's cousin and son-in-law Ali was the prophet's true successor and that the three first Sunnite caliphs were usurpers. [Arab., = 'sect']

shĭbb'olĕth *n.* Test word, principle, opinion, etc., the use of or inability to use which betrays one's party, nationality, etc. (see Judges xii. 6); catchword, (esp. outworn or empty) formula, etc., distinguishing a party or sect. [Heb.]

shield *n.* Article of defensive armour carried in hand or on arm as protection from weapons of enemy; protective plate or screen in machinery etc.; person or thing serving as protection or defence; shield-like part in animal or plant; (her.) escutcheon (ill. HERALDRY); (U.S.) policeman's shield-shaped badge. ~ *v.t.* Protect, screen, esp. from censure or punishment.

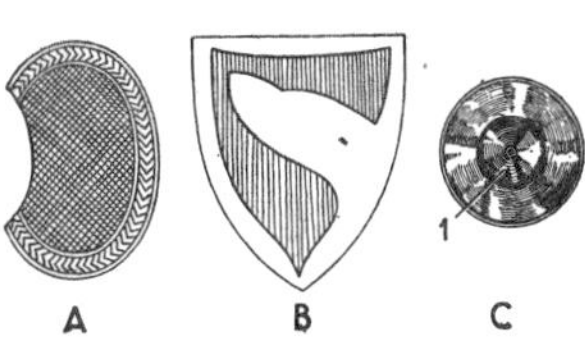

SHIELDS: A. GREEK PELTA, 5TH C. B.C. B. MEDIEVAL SHIELD. C. 16TH-C. FIST BUCKLER

1. Umbo or boss

shiel'ịng *n.* (Sc.) Small hut used by shepherds, fishermen, etc., during the summer.

shift *n.* 1. Change of place or character; substitution of one thing for another; vicissitude; rotation; *~-key*, key for adjusting typewriter when capitals etc. are to be used. 2. Expedient, device, stratagem, resource; dodge, trick, piece of evasion or equivocation. 3. (archaic) Chemise. 4. Relay or change of workmen; length of time during which such relay works. ~ *v.* 1. Change or move from one position to another, change form or character. 2. Use expedients, contrive; manage, get along; (rare) equivocate, practise evasion; ~ *for oneself*, depend on one's own efforts.

shĭft'lėss *adj.* Lacking in resource; lazy, inefficient. **shĭft'lėssly** *adv.* **shĭft'lėssnėss** *n.*

shĭf'ty *adj.* Not straightforward, evasive, deceitful. **shĭf'tĭly** *adv.* **shĭf'tĭnėss** *n.*

Shi'īte (shē-) *n.* Member of the SHIAH sect.

shĭkãr' *n.* Hunting. **shĭkãr'ee, shĭkãr'i** *ns.* Hunter, esp. native acting as guide for shooting party in India.

shĭllelagh (-lā'l*a*) *n.* Irish cudgel of blackthorn or oak. [name of village in County Wicklow]

shĭll'ịng *n.* (abbrev. *s.*) 12 pence, $\frac{1}{20}$ of a POUND[1]; silver or cupro-nickel coin worth this; *cut off* one's heir etc. *with a* ~, disinherit; *take the King's* (*Queen's*) ~, enlist in the army, from the now obs. custom of giving a recruit a shilling.

shĭll'y-shăll'y *n.* Vacillation, irresolution, indecision. ~ *v.i.* Vacillate, be irresolute or undecided. [orig. *shill I, shall I*]

shĭmm'er *v.i.* & *n.* (Shine with) tremulous or faint diffused light.

shĭmm'y *n.* (colloq., nursery, etc., for) CHEMISE; ~(*-shake*), (U.S.) kind of foxtrot accompanied by tremulous motion of the body.

shĭn *n.* Front of human leg below knee; lower part of leg of beef; *~-bone*, tibia; *~-guard*, guard worn at football or hockey to protect the shins. ~ *v.i.* Climb *up* by using arms and legs, without help of ladder, irons, etc.

shĭn'dy *n.* (colloq.) Brawl, disturbance, row, noise.

shīne *v.* (past t. and past part. *shŏne*). Emit or reflect light, be bright, glow; be brilliant, excel, in some respect or sphere; (colloq.) make bright, polish (boots etc.). ~ *n.* Light, brightness; sunshine; lustre, sheen.

shĭn'er *n.* (esp.) 1. Diamond; (pl., slang) money, coin. 2. (slang) Black eye. 3. (chiefly U.S.) Any of various small silvery fresh-water fishes.

shĭng'le[1] (-nggl) *n.* 1. Thin rectangular piece of wood thicker at one end, used like roof-tile.

2. Shingled hair. ~ *v.t.* 1. Cover, roof, with shingles. 2. Cut (woman's hair) short so that it tapers from back of head to nape of neck.

shĭng'le[2] (-nggl) *n.* Small rounded pebbles on seashore. **shĭng'ly** *adj.*

shĭng'les (-ngglz) *n.pl.* Virus infection of nerves, *Herpes zoster*, characterized by outbreaks of small blisters on skin and severe pain. [L *cingulum* girdle, because eruptions freq. appear round trunk]

Shĭn'tō *n.* Ancient, more or less pantheistic, religion of Japan, based on worship of ancestors and of nature, gradually absorbed and superseded by Buddhism from 6th c. onwards, but re-established as the State religion after 1868, when the cult of the emperor as a descendant of the sun became its principal feature. **Shĭn'tōĭsm** *n.* **Shĭn'tōĭst** *n.* & *adj.* [Chin. *shin* god, *tao* doctrine]

shĭn'ty *n.* Game similar to hockey, played chiefly in N. Britain and in America.

shī'ny *adj.* Glistening, shining, polished, rubbed bright. **shī'nĭness** *n.*

shĭp *n.* Any large sea-going cargo; *ship'mate*, fellow sailor; ~-*money*, (hist.) ancient tax levied on ports and maritime towns and counties of England in time of war to provide ships (revived by Charles I and abolished by statute in 1640); ~'*s articles*, terms on which seamen take service on her; ~'*s company*, crew of a ship, not including the officers; *ship'shape*, in good order, trim and neat; ~'*s papers*, documents carried on board ship establishing ownership, nationality, nature of cargo, etc.; ~-*way*, inclined track on which a ship is built and down which she is launched; *ship'wreck*, (cause, suffer) destruction of ship by storm, foundering, striking rock, etc.; (fig.) ruin; *shipwright*, shipbuilder, ship's carpenter; ~-*yard*, shipbuilding establishment. ~ *v.* 1. Put, take, send away, on board ship; take ship, embark; take service on ship; deliver (goods) to forwarding agent for conveyance by land or water. 2. Fix (mast, rudder, etc.) in its place; remove (oars) from rowlocks and lay them inside boat; ~ *a sea*, be flooded by wave.

shĭp'ment *n.* Putting of goods etc. on ship; amount shipped, consignment.

Shĩrl'ey pŏpp'y *n.* Cultivated variety of common corn poppy with single or double flowers of various delicate colours. [f. *Shirley* Rectory, Croydon, England, where first produced]

shĩrr *v.t.* (orig. U.S.) Gather (material) with several parallel threads. ~ *n.* Shirring, shirred trimming.

shĩrt *n.* Man's sleeved undergarment of linen, cotton, silk, etc., usu. worn beneath the waistcoat or coat, to the neckband of which a collar is attached, while the sleeves terminate in wristbands or cuffs; shirt-blouse; *in* ~-*sleeves*, without coat, or coat and waistcoat; ~-*blouse*, woman's blouse resembling a man's shirt; ~-*front*, breast of shirt, freq. stiffened or starched; dicky. **shĩrt'ĭng** *n.*

shĩrt'y *adj.* (slang) In a rage, annoyed.

Shĭva: see SIVA.

shĭv'er[1] *n.* Quivering or trembling, esp. of body under influence of cold, fear, etc. ~ *v.i.* Tremble, shake, quiver, esp. with cold or fear. **shĭv'erĭngly** *adv.*

shĭv'er[2] *n.* One of many small pieces into which thing is shattered by blow or fall. ~ *v.* Break into shivers.

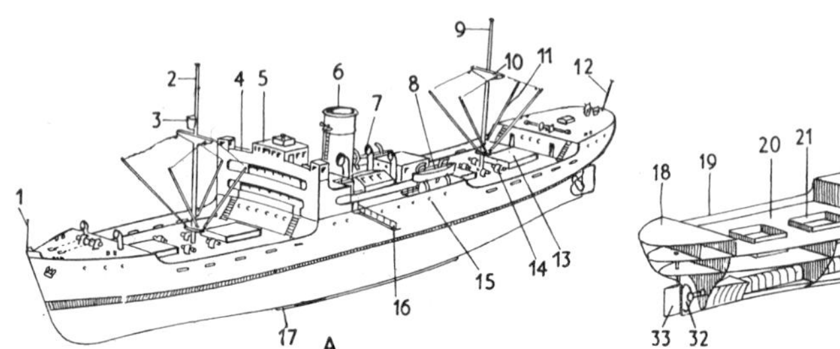

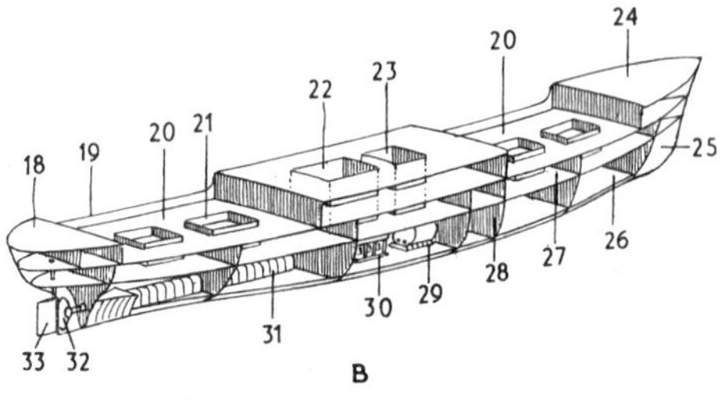

GENERAL CARGO SHIP: A. EXTERIOR (PORT SIDE).
B. DIAGRAM TO SHOW CONSTRUCTION (STARBOARD SIDE)

A. 1. Jackstaff. 2. Foremast. 3. Crow's-nest. 4. Navigating bridge. 5. Wheel-house. 6. Funnel. 7. Cowl ventilators. 8. Life-boat and davits. 9. Mainmast. 10. Cross-tree. 11. Derrick. 12. Ensign staff. 13. Cargo hatch. 14. Winch. 15. Port-hole. 16. Accommodation ladder. 17. Bilge keel. B. 18. Poop. 19. Bulwark. 20. Well-deck. 21. Hatch coaming. 22. Engine casing to skylight. 23. Boiler casing to funnel. 24. Forecastle. 25. Forepeak. 26. Cargo hold. 27. 'Tween-decks. 28. Watertight bulkhead. 29. Boiler-room or stokehold. 30. Engine-room. 31. Shaft tunnel. 32. Propeller or screw. 33. Rudder

vessel, propelled by sails, steam, or other mechanical means; (specif.) sailing-vessel with bowsprit and three square-rigged masts, each divided into lower, top, and topgallant mast; (esp. U.S. Air Force) aircraft; ~('*s*) *biscuit*, hard coarse kind of biscuit made for keeping, used on board ship; *on ship'board*, (adv. phrase) on board ship; ~-*broker*, agent of a shipping company, transacting business for their ships when in port; agent for marine insurance business; *ship'builder*, one whose business it is to build ships; *ship'-building*; ~-*canal*, canal large enough for sea-going vessels; ~('*s*) *chandler*, dealer supplying ships with stores; *ship'load*, quantity of something forming whole

shĭpp'er *n.* Merchant etc. who sends or receives goods by ship.

shĭpp'ĭng *n.* (esp.) Ships, esp. the ships of a country, port, etc.; ~-*agent*, person acting for (line of) ships at a port etc.; ~-*articles*, ship's articles; ~-*master*, official in whose presence ship's articles are signed, paying-off is done, etc.; ~-*office*, office of shipping-agent or -master.

shīre *n.* County; *the* ~*s*, (loosely) the foxhunting counties of Leicestershire, Rutland, and Northamptonshire; ~ *horse*, draught-horse of heavy powerful breed, chiefly bred in midland counties of England.

shĩrk *v.t.* Avoid meanly, evade, shrink selfishly from (duty, responsibility, etc.). **shĩrk'er** *n.*

shoal[1] *adj.* (Of water) shallow, not deep. ~ *n.* Shallow place in water, sand-bank or bar. ~ *v.i.* Grow shallow(er).

shoal[2] *n.* Multitude, crowd, great number, esp. of fish swimming in company. ~ *v.i.* Form shoals.

shŏck[1] *n.* Violent collision, concussion, or impact; one of the violent shakes or tremors of part of earth's surface constituting an earthquake; sudden and disturbing mental or physical impression; stimulation of nerve(s) with muscular contraction and feeling of concussion by passage of electric current through body; (path.) acute state of prostration accompanied by lowering of blood-volume and -pressure and weakening

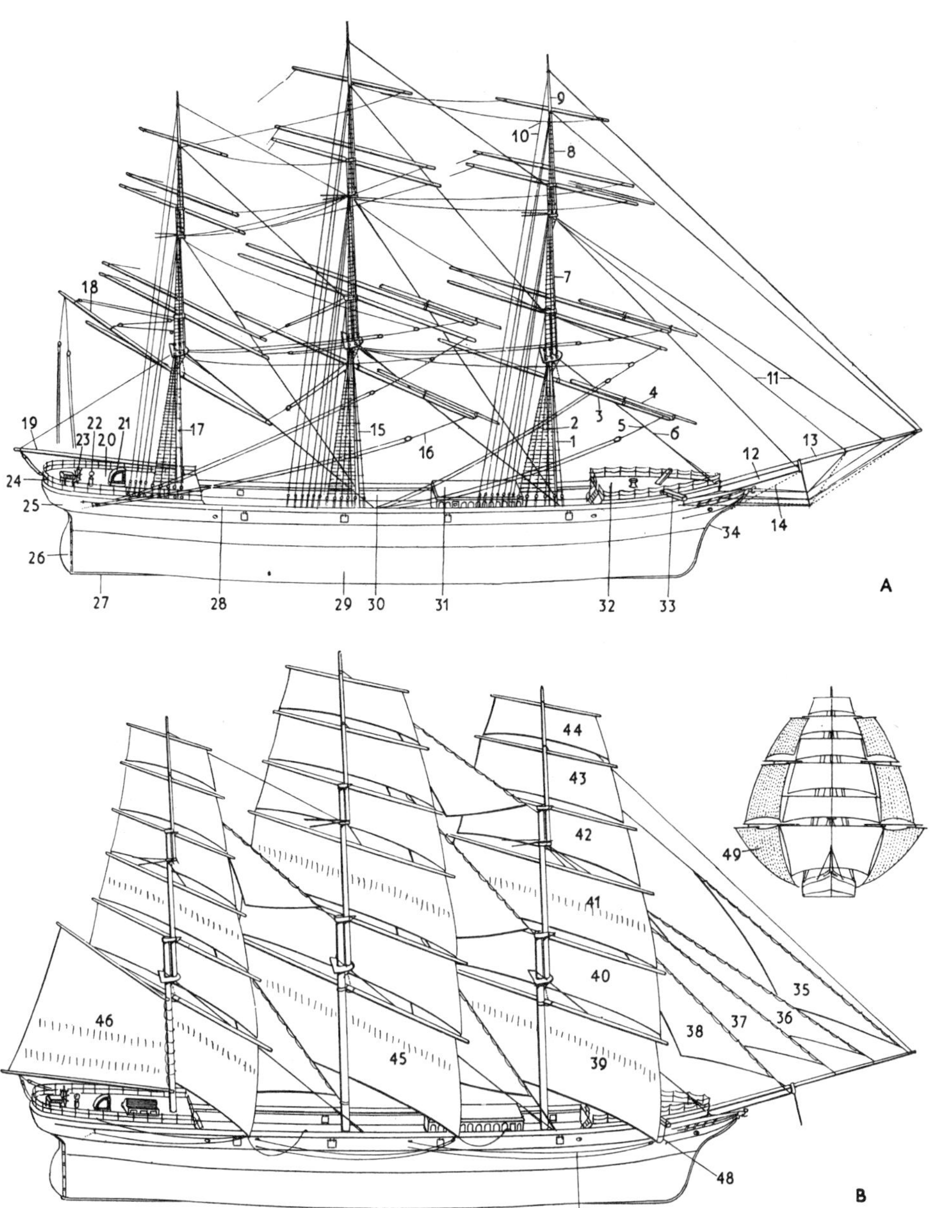

SHIP: A. RIGGING. B. SAILS (SQUARE-RIGGED)

A. Masts, spars, and rigging: 1. Foremast. 2. Fore shrouds. 3. Fore-lower yard. 4. Stunsail boom. 5. Fore brace. 6. Forestay. 7. Fore topmast. 8. Fore-topgallant mast. 9. Fore-royal mast. 10. Fore-royal backstay. 11. Jib-stays. 12. Bowsprit. 13. Jib-boom. 14. Bobstay. 15. Main-mast. 16. Mainbrace. 17. Mizzen-mast. 18. Gaff. 19. Boom. Decks and hull: 20. Poop. 21. Companionway. 22. Binnacle (holding compass). 23. Wheel or helm. 24. Taffrail. 25. Counter. 26. Rudder. 27. Keel. 28. Bulwarks. 29. Bilge. 30. Waist or amidships. 31. Deck-house (with galley). 32. Forecastle. 33. Cat-head. 34. Stem. B. Sails: 35. Flying jib. 36. Outer jib. 37. Inner jib. 38. Fore-topmast staysail. 39. Foresail or fore-course. 40. Fore-lower topsail. 41. Fore-upper topsail. 42. Fore-lower topgallant sail. 43. Fore-upper topgallant sail. 44. Fore-royal. 45. Mainsail. 46. Spanker. 47. Fore-tack. 48. Fore-sheet. 49. Fore-lower stunsail.

(The names of the upper masts, sails, yards, stays, and braces attached to the main- and mizzen-masts follow those given for the foremast)

of pulse and respiration, commonly following accidents, wounds, or burns; ~-*absorber*, device for absorbing vibration in mechanically propelled vehicles (ill. MOTOR); device on aircraft to lessen shock of landing; ~-*troops*, forces of picked men specially trained and armed for offensive operations (also transf. of workers etc.). ~ *v.* Affect with intense aversion, disgust, or strong disapproval, scandalize; outrage sentiments, prejudices, etc., of; cause to suffer shock; administer electric shock to. **shŏck'ĭng** *adj.* **shŏck'ĭngly** *adv.* **shŏck'ĭngnėss** *n.*

shŏck[2] *n.* Group of sheaves of corn etc. propped upright against each other in field to dry and ripen. ~ *v.t.* Arrange in shocks.

shŏck[3] *n.* Unkempt or shaggy mass of hair; ~ *head*, rough head of hair.

shŏck'er *n.* (esp., colloq.) 1. Very bad specimen of anything. 2. Sensational novel.

shŏd *adj.* Wearing shoes; tipped, edged, or sheathed with metal.

shŏdd'y *n.* (Cloth of) woollen yarn made from shreds of knitted or loosely woven woollen fabrics (cf. MUNGO); inferior cloth, anything of worse quality than it claims or seems to have. ~ *adj.* Counterfeit, pretentious, trashy.

shoe (-ōō) *n.* Outer covering for foot, of leather or other material, with more or less stiff sole and lighter upper part, esp. not reaching above ankle; plate of metal, usu. iron, nailed to underside of horse's hoof; thing like shoe in shape or use, e.g. ferrule or metal sheath for pole etc., wheel-drag, socket; (elect.) cast-iron block sliding over live rail to collect current therefrom; *shoe'-black*, boy or man who, for a small charge, cleans boots and shoes of passers-by; *shoe'horn*, curved piece of horn, metal, etc., for easing the heel into the back of a shoe; ~-*lace*, ~-*string*, lace, string, for tying up shoe. ~ *v.t.* (past t. and past part. *shŏd*, pres. part. *shoe'-ing*). Fit with shoe(s).

shō̆g'un (-ōōn) *n.* Japanese hereditary commander-in-chief and virtual ruler for some centuries until the office was abolished in 1868. [Jap., short for *sei-i-tai shōgun* barbarian-subduing great general]

shōō *int.* & *v.* (Utter) sound used to frighten birds away; drive *away* thus.

shōōt *v.* (past t. and past part. *shŏt*). 1. Come vigorously or swiftly (*out*, *forth*, *up*, etc.); dart, fly; sprout; pass quickly under (bridge), over (rapids), in boat. 2. Send out, discharge, emit, violently or swiftly; discharge (bullet etc.) from gun etc., cause (bow, gun, etc.) to discharge missile, discharge gun etc.; kill or wound with missile from gun etc.; hunt game etc. with gun, shoot the game *over* estate etc., shoot game on (estate etc.); (of gun etc.) go off, send missile; ~ *down*, bring down (aircraft) by gunfire; (footb.) take shot at goal; (of cricket ball) gain sudden increased speed after striking the ground. 3. Photograph with cine-camera. 4. (joinery) Plane edge of board accurately (*shot edges*). ~ *n.* 1. Young branch or sucker. 2. Shooting-party, expedition, practice, or land. **shōōt'ĭng** *n.* (esp.) Right of shooting over particular land; ~-*box*, sportsman's lodge for use in shooting season; ~-*brake*, vehicle used on shooting expeditions (now usu. motor-car with capacious box-like body made partly of wood); ~-*gallery*, place where shooting at targets with miniature rifles is practised; ~-*range*, ground with butts for rifle practice; ~-*stick*, walking-stick which may be adapted to form a seat.

shŏp *n.* Building, room, etc., for retail sale of some commodity; workshop of a joiner; engineering works or yard; (slang) institution, establishment; one's profession, trade, or business (esp. in *talk* ~); *the S*~, (army slang), Royal Military Academy, Woolwich; ~ *assistant*, salesman or saleswoman in retail shop; *shop'keeper*, owner and manager of shop; ~-*lifter*, pretended customer who steals goods in shop; *shop'man*, assistant in shop; ~-*soiled*, -*worn*, soiled or faded by being shown in shop; ~-*steward*, person elected by his fellow-workers in a factory workshop as their spokesman in disputes etc.; *shop'walker*, attendant in large shop who directs customers to the department they may require. ~ *v.* 1. Go to shop(s) to make purchases. 2. (slang) Imprison; (of informer etc.) cause to be imprisoned.

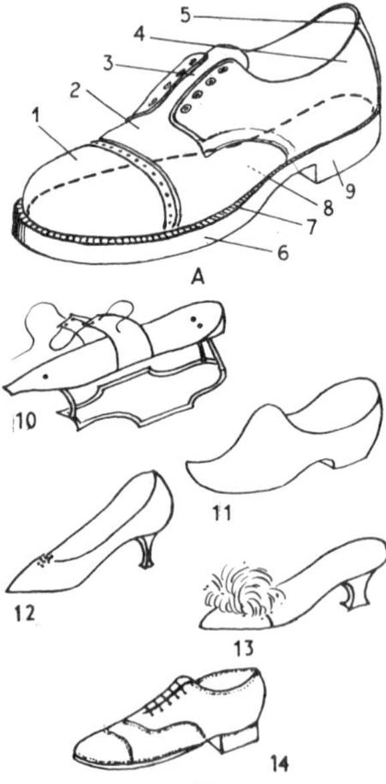

SHOE: A. PARTS OF A SHOE. B. KINDS OF SHOES

A. 1–5. Upper (1. Toecap. 2. Vamp. 3. Tongue. 4. Quarter. 5. Back strip). 6. Sole. 7. Welt. 8. Insole. 9. Heel. B. 10. Patten. 11. Clog. 12. Court shoe. 13. Mule. 14. Oxford shoe

shōre[1] *n.* Land that skirts sea or large body of water; (law) land between ordinary high- and low-water marks; *in* ~, on water near(er) to shore; ~-*based*, operating from a base on shore. **shōre'-lėss** *adj.* **shōre'ward** *adj.* & *adv.*

shōre[2] *n.* Prop, beam set obliquely against ship, wall, tree, etc., as support. ~ *v.t.* Support, prop *up*, with shores.

Shōre'ditch (-ŏrd-): Eastern borough of London, N. of the City. [= 'ditch leading to the shore' (of the Thames)]

shorn: see SHEAR.

shôrt *adj.* Measuring little from end to end in space or time, soon traversed or finished; of small stature, not tall; not far-reaching, acting near at hand; deficient, scanty, in want *of*, below the degree *of*; (of weight, change, etc.) less than it should be; concise, brief, curt; (of vowel or syllable) having the lesser of two recognized durations; (of pastry, clay, etc.) friable, crumbling; (of stocks, broker, crops, etc.) sold, selling, etc., when amount is not in hand, in reliance on getting the deficit in time for delivery; *short-bread*, *short'cake*, crisp dry cake made with flour and butter and sugar without liquid; ~ *circuit*, electric circuit through much smaller resistance than in the normal circuit, thus allowing a large current to flow through and causing overheating, fusing, etc.; ~-*circuit* (*v.t.*) cause short circuit in; shorten (process) by eliminating intermediate stages; *short'coming*, failure to come up to a standard, deficiency, defect; *short'hand*, stenography, system of graphic notation in which speech is recorded at great speed, economy of effort being obtained by use of symbols for combinations of sounds or letters and by contractions; ~-*handed*, undermanned, understaffed; ~ *headed*, (ethnol.) having a head which is broad in proportion to its length, brachycephalic; *short'horn*, one of a short-horned breed of cattle orig. from NE. counties of England; ~ *list*, list of selected candidates for a post from which it is intended to make the final selection; ~-*list* (*v.t.*) put on a short list; ~-*lĭved*, having a short life; brief, ephemeral; ~ *metre*, hymn stanza of four lines, of which the third has eight syllables and the others six; ~ *sight*, ability to see clearly what is comparatively near but not what is at a distance, myopia; ~-*sighted*, having short sight; (fig.) lacking imagination, deficient in foresight; ~-*sightedly*, ~-*sightedness*; ~ *story*, story with a fully worked-out motive but of smaller compass than a novel; ~ *tempered*, having a temper easily roused; ~ *time*, the condition of working fewer than the regular number of hours per day or days per week; ~-*wave*, wireless wave-length of from 10 to 100 metres; ~-*winded*, short of breath, becoming out of breath after slight exertion; ~-*windedly*, ~-*windedness*. **shôrt′nėss** *n*. **shôrt** *adv*. Abruptly; before the natural or expected time; in short manner. ~ *n*. Short syllable or vowel, mark indicating that a vowel is short; (colloq.) short circuit; short cinema film; (pl.) trousers reaching from waist to point above knee. ~ *v.t.* (colloq.) Short-circuit.

shôrt′age *n*. (Amount of) deficiency.

shôrt′en *v*. Become, make, actually or apparently short(er), curtail; reduce amount of (*sail*) spread.

shôrt′ly *adv*. Before long; a short time *before*, *after*; in few words, briefly; curtly.

shŏt[1] *n*. 1. Single missile for cannon or gun, non-explosive projectile; (pl. same) small lead pellets of which a quantity is used for single charge or cartridge, esp. in sporting guns; injection (of morphia etc.); (slang) dram of spirits. 2. Discharge of cannon or gun; attempt to hit with projectile or missile; (fig.) attempt to guess or do something; aim or stroke, esp. in a game, as tennis, golf, billiards; (football, hockey, etc.) attempt to drive a ball into the goal. 3. Possessor of specified skill with rifle, gun, pistol, etc. 4. Range, reach, distance to or at which thing will carry or act, as *rifle-*, *ear-*~. 5. Scene etc. photographed with cine-camera. 6. ~-*gun*, smooth-bore gun for firing small-shot; ~-*tower*, tower in which shot is made from molten lead poured through sieves at the top and falling into water at the bottom. ~ *v.t.* Load, weight, etc., with shot.

shŏt[2] *n*. Reckoning, (one's share of) tavern-bill.

shŏt[3] *adj*. (past part. of SHOOT). (esp., of textile) Woven with warp-threads of one colour and weft-threads of another, so that the fabric changes in tint when viewed from different points.

shoul′der (-ōl-) *n*. Part of body at which arm, foreleg, or wing is attached; either lateral projection below or behind neck; combination of end of upper arm with ends of collar-bone and shoulder-blade; (pl.) upper part of back; (pl.) body regarded as bearing burdens; part of mountain, bottle, tool, etc., projecting like human shoulder; ~-*belt*, band passing over one shoulder and under other arm; ~-*blade*, either of the pair of large flat bones of upper back, scapula; ~-*knot*, knot of ribbon or metal lace worn on shoulder of uniform or livery; ~-*strap*, band over shoulder connecting front and back of (esp. woman's) garment; band at shoulder of uniform keeping shoulder-belts in place and bearing name or number of regiment etc. ~ *v*. Push with shoulder, jostle, make one's *way* thus; take (burden) on one's shoulders (also fig.); ~ *arms*, (mil.) hold rifle vertically in front of shoulder with butt resting in palm of hand, the arm being fully extended downwards.

shout *n*. Loud cry expressing joy, grief, pain, defiance, etc., or to attract attention at a distance. ~ *v*. Utter shout; speak loudly; say loudly, call out.

shove (-ŭv) *n*. Push. ~ *v*. Push vigorously; move along by hand or rough pushing; make one's way by pushing; jostle (person); ~ *off*, start from shore in boat. ~-*halfpenny*, SHOVELBOARD.

shov′el (-ŭv-) *n*. Spade-like implement, freq. with slightly concave blade, for shifting coal, earth, grain, etc.; ~ *hat*, stiff broad-brimmed hat turned up at sides worn by some Church dignitaries. ~ *v.t.* Shift (coal, snow, etc.) with or as with shovel.

shov′elboard (-ŭvelbôrd), **shŭff′leboard** (-lb-) *ns*. Game in which coin or other disc is driven along highly polished board or table by blow with hand into a series of divisions; shipboard game in which wooden or iron discs are pushed along decks with cue called *shovel* into divisions marked by chalk etc.

shov′el(l)er (-ŭv-) *n*. The spoon-billed duck (*Spatula*), a brightly coloured river-duck with large very broad bill.

show (-ō) *v*. (past t. *showed* pr. shōd; past part. *shown* pr. shōn; also occas. spelt *shew*, *shewn*, *shewed*). 1. Allow or cause to be seen, expose to view, exhibit, reveal, point out; be visible or noticeable, come into sight; appear in public; have some appearance. 2. Demonstrate, prove, expound; point out; ~ *off*, display to advantage; act or talk for show, make ostentatious display of abilities etc.; ~ *up*, make, be, conspicuous or clearly visible; expose (fraud, impostor); ~-*case*, glazed case for exhibiting goods, curiosities, etc.; ~-*down*, (fig. from game of poker) final test, disclosure of achievements or possibilities; *S~ Me State*, pop. name of Missouri, U.S.; ~-*room*, room in which goods are exhibited for sale. ~ *n*. 1. Showing; display; spectacle, exhibition, entertainment; exhibit; ~-*boat*, passenger-boat, esp. on Mississippi, used as theatre; *show′man*, exhibitor or proprietor of show; *show′manship*, (esp.) capacity for exhibiting one's wares, capabilities, etc., to the best advantage. 2. Outward appearance, semblance; parade, ostentation, pomp, display. 3. (slang) Concern, undertaking, organization; action, deed; opportunity of acting etc.

show′er *n*. Brief fall of rain, *of* rain, hail, arrows, dust, etc.; ~ (-*bath*), bath in which water descends from above through perforated plate. **show′ery** *adj*. **show′eriness** *n*. **show′er** *v*. Discharge, descend, come, in a shower; bestow (gifts etc.) lavishly (*upon*).

show′y (-ōĭ) *adj*. Striking, making good display; brilliant, gaudy. **show′ily** *adv*. **show′inėss** *n*.

s.h.p. *abbrev*. Shaft horsepower.

shrăp′nel *n*. Hollow projectile containing bullets scattered in shower by small bursting charge; fragments of any shell, bomb, etc., scattered by explosion. [Gen. H. *Shrapnel* (1761–1842), inventor of the shell during Peninsular War]

shrĕd *n*. Scrap, fragment; small torn, broken, or cut piece; small remains; least amount. ~ *v.t.* Tear or cut into shreds.

shrew (-o͞o) *n*. 1. Small mouse-like insectivore of *Sorex* and other genera, with long pointed snout.

SHREW

2. Scolding woman. **shrew′ĭsh** (-o͞oĭ-) *adj*. Ill-tempered. **shrew′ĭshly** *adv*. **shrew′ĭshnėss** *n*.

shrewd (-o͞od) *adj*. 1. (Of blow etc.) severe, sharp, hard. 2. Sagacious, sensible, discriminating, astute. **shrewd′ly** *adv*. **shrewd′nėss** *n*.

Shrews′bury (-rōz-, -ro͞oz-). County town of Shropshire.

shriek (-ēk) *n*. & *v*. (Utter) loud shrill cry or sound of terror, pain, mirth, etc.; (make) high-pitched piercing sound.

shriev′alty *n*. (Tenure of) sheriff's office or jurisdiction.

shrĭft *n*. (archaic) Confession (and absolution); now only in *short* ~, little time between condemnation and execution or punishment.

shrīke *n*. Bird of genus *Lanius* or related genera, with strong hooked beak, preying usu. on insects, but also on mice and small birds; butcher-bird.

shrĭll *adj.* (Of sound) piercing and high-pitched; producing such sounds. ~ *v.* (poet. and rhet.) Sound, utter, shrilly. **shrĭll'y** *adv.* **shrĭll'nĕss** *n.*

shrĭmp *n.* Any of the small, marine decapod crustaceans of *Crangon* and allied genera, esp. the common shrimp, *C. vulgaris*, inhabiting sandy coasts, a common article of food; diminutive or puny person. ~ *v.i.* Go catching shrimps.

shrīne *n.* Casket, esp. one holding sacred relics; tomb, usu. sculptured or highly ornamented, of saint etc.; place where worship is offered or devotions paid to saint or deity; place hallowed by memory or associations.

Shrīn'er *n.* Member of *Ancient Arabic Order of Nobles of the Mystic Shrine*, established in U.S. in 1872, and open only to Knights Templar and Freemasons of 32nd degree.

shrĭnk *v.* (past t. *shrank*, past part. *shrunk* and rarely in vbl, commonly in adj., use *shrunken*). Become, make, smaller; (of textile fabric) contract when wetted, cause to do this; cower, huddle *together*, recoil, flinch *from*; be averse *from*. **shrĭnk'age** *n.*

shrīve *v.t.* (archaic; past t. *shrōve*, past part. *shriv'en*). Hear confession of, assign penance to, and absolve; ~ one*self*, make one's confession.

shrĭv'el *v.* Contract or wither into wrinkled, folded, contorted or dried-up state.

Shrŏp'shire. W. midland county of England.

shroud *n.* 1. Winding-sheet, garment for the dead; (fig.) concealing agency. 2. (pl.) Set of ropes forming part of standing rigging and supporting mast or topmast (ill. SHIP). 3. (elect.) Enlargement of conductor to reduce strain on insulating material. ~ *v.t.* Clothe (corpse) for burial; cover or disguise.

Shrōve Tuesday. Day before Ash Wednesday, forming with the two preceding days (*Shrove'tide*) period for confession before Lent. [f. SHRIVE]

shrŭb[1] *n.* Woody plant of less size than tree and usu. divided into separate stems from near the ground. **shrŭbb'y** *adj.*

shrŭb[2] *n.* Cordial of juice of acid fruit, sugar, and spirit (usu. rum). [Arab. *sharāb*]

shrŭbb'ery *n.* (Plantation of) shrubs.

shrŭg *n.* Raising and contraction of shoulders to express dislike, disdain, indifference, etc. ~ *v.* Raise (shoulders), raise shoulders, in shrug.

shrŭnk(en) *adj.*: see SHRINK.

shŭck *n.* (chiefly U.S.) Husk, pod; *shucks!* int. of contempt or indifference. ~ *v.t.* Remove shucks of, shell.

shŭdd'er *v.i.* & *n.* (Experience) sudden shivering due to fear, horror, repugnance, or cold.

shŭff'le *n.* 1. Shuffling movement; shuffling of cards; general change of relative positions. 2. Piece of equivocation or sharp practice. 3. Quick scraping movement of feet in dancing. ~ *v.* Move with scraping, sliding, dragging, or difficult motion; manipulate (cards in pack) so that their relative positions are changed; intermingle, confuse, push about or together in disorderly fashion; put *in*, *off*, *on*, etc., clumsily or fumblingly; put (responsibility etc.) *off*, *on to*, another etc., get *out of* shiftily or evasively; keep shifting position, fidget, vacillate; prevaricate, be evasive.

shuff'leboard: see SHOVELBOARD.

shŭn *v.t.* Avoid, keep clear of.

'shŭn! Abbrev. of *Attention!* as word of command.

shŭnt *v.* Divert (train, part of an electric current, etc.), diverge, on to a side track. ~ *n.* Turning, being turned, on to side track; conductor joining two points in an electric circuit so as to form a parallel circuit; such a circuit. **shŭnt'er** *n.* Railwayman shunting trains.

shŭt *v.* (past t. and past part. *shŭt*). Close (door, aperture, window, etc.), close door etc. of (room, box, etc.); become, admit of being, closed; keep *in*, *out*, etc., by shutting door etc.; ~ *in*, encircle, prevent free prospect or egress from or access to; ~ *off*, check flow of (water, gas, etc.) by shutting valve; separate *from*; ~ *up*, close doors and windows of (house), close securely, decisively, or permanently, put away in box etc.; imprison; reduce to silence, shut one's mouth, stop talking; ~ *up shop*, cease business.

shŭtt'er *n.* (esp.) Movable wooden or iron screen placed outside or inside window to shut off light or ensure privacy or safety (ill. WINDOW); device for opening and closing aperture of photographic lens (ill. PHOTOGRAPHY); (pl.) louver-boards of organ's swell-box, regulating volume of sound from swell-organs. ~ *v.t.* Provide with shutters, put up shutters of.

shŭtt'le *n.* Weft-carrier in a loom, a boat-shaped wooden implement with hollowed centre to hold the weft-thread, formerly thrown or 'shot' from hand to hand by the weaver, now moving by mechanical means backwards and forwards across and through the warp; thread-holder in sewing-machine carrying lower thread through the loop of the upper one; (attrib.) denoting an out-and-back course, as in ~ *train*, *service*, *bombing*; *shutt'lecock*, small piece of weighted cork or other light material with feathers projecting in a ring from one side, struck to and fro with a battledore in the old game of battledore and shuttlecock, and by a racket in badminton.

shȳ[1] *adj.* Easily startled, timid, avoiding observation, uneasy in company, bashful; avoiding company *of*, chary *of doing*; elusive; (as second element of compounds) frightened (of), averse (to), as *work-*, *gun-shy*. **shȳ'ly** *adv.* **shȳ'nĕss** *n.* **shȳ** *v.i.* Start suddenly aside in alarm (*at* object or noise, esp. of horse). ~ *n.* Act of shying.

shȳ[2] *v.* (colloq.) Fling, throw. ~ *n.* Act of shying.

Shȳ'lŏck. Jewish usurer in Shakespeare's 'Merchant of Venice'; hence, hard-hearted and grasping money-lender.

shȳ'ster *n.* (orig. U.S. slang) Tricky, unscrupulous lawyer (or other professional man).

si (sē) *n.* (mus.) 7th note of major scale (same as TE) in 'movable-doh' systems; note B in 'fixed-doh' system.

S.I. *abbrev.* (Order of the) Star of India.

sī'al *n.* (geol.) Lighter outer crust of earth's surface, composed mainly of solid or molten rocks rich in silica and alumina. [f. *si*lica and *al*umina]

Sīăm'. Independent kingdom of Indo-Chinese peninsula, officially known as Thailand; capital, Bangkok. **Sīamēse'** (-z) *adj.* & *n.* (Native) of Siam; its language, one of the Thai group of Siamese-Chinese languages; ~ *cat*, breed of domesticated cat, of a cream colour with chocolate markings; ~ *twins*, two male natives of Siam, Chang and Eng (1814–71), who were congenitally united by a thick fleshy ligament in the region of the waist; any pair of conjoined twins.

sĭb *adj.* (archaic & Sc.) Related, akin, (*to*). ~ *n.* (genetics) Brother or sister (disregarding sex). **sĭb'lĭng** *n.* (usu. pl.) One of two or more children having one or both parents in common. **sĭb'shĭp** *n.* (genetics) Group of children (disregarding sex) from the same two parents.

Sĭbelīus (-bā'-), Johan Julius (Jean), (1865–1957). Finnish musical composer of tone-poems, symphonies, etc.

Sībēr'ia. Russian territory of N. Asia, a vast tract stretching from the Ural Sea to Yakutsk and forming the larger part of the Russian Soviet Federal Socialist Republic; used by Russian governments as place of exile for offenders; capital of W. Siberia, Novosibirsk, of E. Siberia, Irkutsk. **Sībēr'ian** *adj.* Of Siberia; ~ *crab*: see CRAB[2]; ~ *dog*, breed of dog, resembling the Eskimo dog, used for drawing sledges; ~ *wallflower*: see WALLflower.

sĭb'ilant *adj.* Hissing, sounding like a hiss (of the consonants *s, z, sh*). **sĭb′ĭlance, sĭb′ĭlancy** *ns.* **sĭb′ĭlant** *n.* (phon.) Sibilant speech-sound.

sĭb′ȳl *n.* Any of the women who in ancient times acted in various places as mouthpiece of a god, uttering prophecies and oracles, the most famous of whom was the *Cumaean* sibyl; prophetess, fortune-teller, witch.

sĭbȳll′īne *adj.* Of a sibyl, oracular, mysteriously prophetic; *S~ Books*, collection of oracles kept in ancient Rome in temple of Jupiter Capitolinus and freq. consulted by magistrates for guidance; acc. to legend, 9 of these books were offered to Tarquin by a sibyl, who burnt 3 of them and then 3 more when they were refused because of their high price, and finally sold the last 3 at the same price as she had asked for them all.

sĭc. Latin adv., = so, used parenthetically in quotations to indicate that a word or expression is quoted exactly though its incorrectness or absurdity would suggest that it was not.

sicc′ative *adj.* & *n.* (Substance etc.) of drying properties.

Sī′cel, Sĭcŭl′ian *ns.* (ancient hist.) Native of Sicily as opp. to Greek immigrant (SICELIOT). ~ *adj.* Of the Sicels.

Sĭcĕl′iot *n.* Ancient-Greek settler in Sicily. ~ *adj.* Of the Siceliots.

Sĭcĭl′ian *adj.* & *n.* (Native) of Sicily; ~ *Vespers*, riot which broke out at a church near Palermo while the vesper-bell was ringing on Easter Monday 1282 and developed into a general massacre of the French in Sicily and the expulsion of the Angevins.

sĭcĭliĕnne′, sĭcĭliā′na (-ah-) *ns.* (mus.) Slowish dance (in $\frac{6}{8}$ or $\frac{12}{8}$ time), freq. in minor key, much used by 18th-c. composers as movement in suite or sonata etc. [Fr. & It. fem. adj., 'Sicilian']

Sĭ′cily. Large island in Mediterranean, separated from 'toe' of Italy by Strait of Messina; in Italian possession since 1860; in ancient times colonized by the Greeks.

sĭck *adj.* 1. Ill, unwell (now chiefly U.S. and literary); disposed to vomit, vomiting. 2. Disordered, perturbed; suffering effects *of*; disgusted; pining *for*; surfeited and tired *of*. 3. *~-bay*, part of (esp. naval) ship used as hospital; *~-bed*, invalid's bed; state of being invalid; ~ *headache*, headache caused by biliousness; *~-list*, list of sick esp. in regiment, ship, etc.; *S~ Man of Europe*, Turkey during latter part of 19th c.

sĭck′en *v.* Begin to be ill, show symptoms of illness; feel nausea or disgust (*at* etc.); affect with inclination to vomit, loathing, disgust, weariness, or despair. **sĭck′enĭng** *adj.* **sĭck′eningly** *adv.*

sĭck′le *n.* Reaping-hook, short-handled semicircular-bladed implement used for lopping, trimming, etc. (ill. HOOK); anything sickle-shaped, esp. crescent moon; *~-feather*, one of the long curved middle feathers of cock's tail.

sĭck′ly *adj.* Apt to be ill, chronically ailing; suggesting sickness, as of sick person, languid, pale; causing ill health or nausea; mawkish, weakly sentimental. **sĭck′lĭnĕss** *n.* **sĭck′ly** *v.t.* Cover *over, o'er*, with sickly hue (with ref. to 'Hamlet', III. i. 85).

sĭck′nĕss *n.* Being ill, disease; a disease; vomiting, inclination to vomit; *sleeping* ~, *sleepy* ~: see SLEEP, SLEEPY.

sīde *n.* 1. One of the flat(tish) surfaces bounding an object, esp. more or less vertical outer or inner surface; such surface as distinguished from top and bottom, front and back, or ends; either surface of thing regarded as having only two; (math.) bounding line of superficial figure. 2. Either of two lateral surfaces or parts of trunk in persons or animals, esp. extending from armpit to hip or from foreleg to hindleg; part of object in same direction as observer's right or left and not directly towards or away from him, or turned in specified direction; part or region near margin and remote from centre or axis of thing; subordinate, less essential, or more or less detached, part; (attrib.) subordinate; ~ *by* ~, standing close together, esp. for mutual support. 3. Region external but contiguous to, specified direction with relation to, person or thing; partial aspect of thing; (cause represented by, position in company with) one of two sets of opponents in war, politics, games, etc.; team. 4. Position nearer or farther than, right or left of, dividing line. 5. Line of descent through father or mother. 6. (billiards) Spinning motion given to ball by striking it on side. 7. (slang) Assumption of superiority, swagger. 8. *~-arms*, weapons worn at side, as swords, bayonets; *side′board*, piece of dining-room furniture, freq. with drawers and cupboards, for holding dishes, wine, plate, etc.; (pl., slang) side-whiskers (also *~-burns*); *~-car*, jaunting-car; car for passenger(s) attached to side of motor-cycle; kind of cocktail; *~-dish*, extra dish, freq. of elaborate kind, at dinner etc.; ~ *drum*, small double-headed (esp. mil.) drum; *~-light*, light at side of vehicle etc.; port or starboard light on ship under way; light coming from the side, (fig.) incidental light (*up*)*on* subject etc.; *~-saddle*, saddle for rider, usu. woman, with both feet on one (usu. left) side of horse; *~-show*, minor show attached to principal one (freq. fig.); *~-slip*, skid; (of aircraft) move, motion, sideways; *sides′man*, assistant churchwarden; *~-step*, step taken sideways; (*v.t.*) avoid, evade, (as) by stepping sideways; *~-stroke*, swimming-stroke made lying on the side; *~-track*, siding; (*v.t.*) turn into siding, shunt, postpone or evade treatment or consideration of ; *~-view*, view obtained sideways; profile; *~-walk*, (chiefly U.S.) path at side of road for foot-passengers; *~-whiskers*, hair left unshaven on cheeks. ~ *v.i.* Take part, be on same side, *with*.

sīde′lŏng (-dl-) *adv.* & *adj.* Inclining to one side, oblique(ly).

sīdēr′ĕal *adj.* Of the stars: (of time) measured by the stars; ~ *clock*, astronomical clock regulated to sidereal time; ~ *day*, interval between successive meridional transit of Aries, about 4 min. shorter than mean solar day (the 24 hours or day of civil time); ~ *year*, time in which earth makes one complete revolution round sun, about 20 min. longer than the *tropical year*.

sīd′erostăt *n.* (astron.) Instrument for keeping heavenly body in same part of telescope field.

sīde′wards (rare), **sīde′ways** (-dw-) *advs.* & *adjs.* Laterally, to or from a side.

sīd′ĭng *n.* Short track by side of railway line and connected with it by switches, for shunting etc.

sī′dle *v.i.* Walk obliquely, esp. in furtive or unobtrusive manner.

Sĭd′ney, Sir Philip (1554–86). English soldier, statesman, and poet; author of the prose romance 'Arcadia' and of a series of sonnets known as 'Astrophel and Stella'.

Sĭd′ney Sŭss′ex College. College of the University of Cambridge, founded in 1596 under the will of the Lady Frances Sidney, Dowager Countess of Sussex.

Sīd′on. Ancient seaport of the Phoenicians (mod. *Saida*); see TYRE[2].

siege (sēj) *n.* The surrounding or hemming in of a fortified place by a military force to compel its surrender or to take it by direct attack, period during which this lasts; besieging, being besieged.

Siegfried (sēg′frēd). Hero of first part of NIBELUNGENLIED, who forges the Nothung sword, slays Fafner, the dragon guarding the stolen Rhine gold, and helps Gunther to win Brunhild; at the instigation of Brunhild he was treacherously slain by Hagen; ~ *line*, German line of fortifications along the W. border of Germany from Cleves to Basle, constructed prior to the war of 1939–45.

Siĕn′a. City of Tuscany, Italy. **Sienēse** (-z) *adj.* & *n.* (Inhabitant) of Siena.

siĕnn′a *n.* Ferruginous earth used as pigment, brownish-yellow (*raw* ~) or reddish-brown (*burnt* ~). [It. (*terra*) *di Siena* (earth of) SIENA]

siĕ′rra *n.* In Spain and Spanish America, range of mountains with serrated outline. [Span., f. L *serra* saw]

Sĭĕr′ra Lēōne′. State on W. coast of Africa, between Liberia and Guinea; became independent 1961; member of the British Commonwealth; capital, Freetown.

sĭĕs′ta *n.* Midday nap or rest in hot countries. [Span., f. L *sexta* (*hora*) 6th (hour)]

sieve (sĭv) *n.* Utensil consisting of usu. circular frame with meshed or perforated bottom, for separating finer from coarser parts of loose material, or for straining liquids or pulping solids; coarsely-plaited basket for market produce, this as a measure. ~ *v.t.* Put through, sift with, sieve.

sĭff′leur (-ẽr) *n.*, fem. **siff′leuse** (-ẽrz). Whistling artiste.

sift *v.* Put through sieve; separate, get *out*, by use of sieve; use sieve; fall as from sieve; sprinkle (sugar etc.) with perforated spoon, castor, etc.; closely examine details of, analyse character of. **sĭf′ter** *n.*

sigh (sī) *n.* Prolonged deep audible respiration expressive of dejection, weariness, longing, relief, etc. ~ *v.* Give sigh or (of wind etc.) sound resembling sigh; utter or express with sighs; yearn, long, *for*.

sight (sīt) *n.* 1. Faculty of vision. 2. Seeing, being seen; way of looking at or considering thing; view, point or position commanding view, *of* something; range or field of vision; *at, on,* ~, as soon as person or thing has been seen; *~-reading, -singing,* reading music, singing, at sight. 3. Thing seen, visible, or worth seeing; display, show, spectacle; ridiculous, shocking, or repulsive sight; (colloq.) great quantity (*of*); *sight′seeing,* act of going to see places or objects of special interest, beauty, etc.; *sight′seer* (*n.*). 4. (Kinds of device for assisting) precise aim with gun, bomb, etc., or observation with optical instrument (ill. GUN). ~ *v.t.* Get sight of, esp. by coming near; take observation of (star etc.) with instrument; provide (gun etc.) with sights, adjust sights of; aim (gun etc.) with sights.

sight′lĕss (sīt-) *adj.* Blind.

sight′ly (sīt-) *adj.* Pleasing to the sight, not unsightly.

sĭg′ma *n.* The Greek ς (Σ, Є, ς, σ), occas. used (σ) as symbol for millisecond.

sĭg′moid *adj.* Crescent-shaped, like the uncial sigma C; having double curve like letter s; of the ~ *flexure,* curving portion of intestine between colon and rectum.

sign (sīn) *n.* 1. Significant gesture; mark or device with special meaning or used to distinguish thing on which it is put; written mark conventionally used for word, phrase, etc., symbol; token, indication, trace (*of* something); omen, portent; miracle as demonstration of divine power or authority; (path.) objective evidence or indication of disease etc. (sometimes distinguished from objective *symptom*). 2. Characteristic device, freq. painted on board, displayed by inn etc.; board bearing name or inscription in front of shop etc. 3. Any of twelve equal divisions of zodiac named from constellations formerly situated in them. 4. *~-board,* = sense 2; ~ *manual,* signature; *~-painter,* painter of sign-boards, shop-front inscriptions, etc.; *sign′-post,* post at cross-roads etc., with arm(s) indicating direction of place(s). ~ *v.* 1. Mark *with* sign of the CROSS; mark with sign; make sign, intimate with sign. 2. Attest or confirm by adding one's signature; write (name) as signature; affix one's signature; make *over,* give *away,* etc., by signing; ~ *off, on,* end, begin, occupation etc. esp. by signing one's name; ~ *off,* (bridge) indicate by a conventional bid that one is ending bidding.

sĭg′nal[1] *n.* Preconcerted or intelligible sign conveying information or direction, esp. to

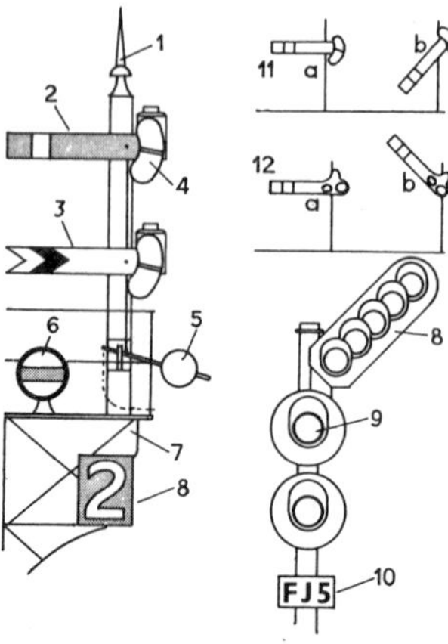

RAILWAY SIGNALS

1. Pinnacle. 2. Stop arm. 3. Distant arm. 4. Front 'spectacle'. 5. Balance weight. 6. 'Banner' signal. 7. Gantry. 8. Route indicator. 9. Colour-light signal. 10. Identification plate. 11. Lower quadrant system. 12. Upper quadrant system (*a* stop, *b* proceed)

person(s) at a distance; message made up of such signs; *~-book,* book containing code of signals, and esp. in army, air force, and navy; *~-box,* hut on railway from which signals are given or worked; *~-man,* signaller. ~ *v.* Make signal(s); make signal(s) to; transmit, announce, by signal, direct (person) *to* do) by signal. **sĭg′naller** *n.*

sĭg′nal[2] *adj.* Remarkable, conspicuous, striking. **sĭg′nally** *adv.*

sĭg′nalīze *v.t.* Distinguish, make conspicuous or remarkable.

sĭg′natory *adj.* & *n.* (Party, esp. State) whose signature is attached to document, esp. treaty.

sĭg′nature *n.* 1. Name, initials, or mark written with person's own hand as authentication of document or other writing; distinguishing mark; stamp, impression. 2. Letter(s) or figure(s) placed by printer at foot of first page (and freq. other pages) of each sheet of book as guide in making up and binding; a sheet as distinguished by its signature; (mus.) sign(s) placed at beginning of piece of music, movement, etc., to indicate key and time; ~ *tune,* special tune used in broadcasting etc. to announce a particular turn or performer.

sĭg′nėt *n.* Small seal, esp. one fixed in finger-ring; small seal orig. used by sovereigns of England and Scotland for private purposes and for certain official documents, in Scotland later serving as seal of Court of Session; *Writer to the S~*: see WRITER.

sĭgnĭf′icance *n.* Being significant, expressiveness; meaning, import; consequence, importance.

sĭgnĭf′ĭcant *adj.* Having, conveying, a meaning; full of meaning, highly expressive or suggestive; important, notable. **sĭgnĭf′ĭcantly** *adv.*

sĭgnĭfĭcā′tion *n.* (esp.) Exact meaning or sense.

sĭgnĭf′ĭcatĭve *adj.* Signifying; having a meaning; serving as sign or indication *of*.

sĭg′nĭfȳ *v.* Be sign or symbol of; represent, mean, denote; communicate, make known; be of importance, matter.

signor, signora, signorina (sēn′yôr, -ôr′*a*, -orēn′*a*) *ns.* (Titles of respect used in addressing or speaking of) Italian man, woman, young unmarried woman.

Sikh (sēk). Member of a monotheistic sect established in India (chiefly in Punjab) since 16th c.; esp., member of a martial community maintained by this sect; ~ *Wars,* wars between Sikhs and British, 1845 and 1848–9, culminating in the British annexation of the Punjab.

Sĭkk′ĭm. Small independent State of E. Himalayas; capital, Gangtok.

sĭl′age *n.* (also *ĕn′sĭlage*) Preservation of green fodder in silo or pit without drying; fodder thus preserved.

Sīl′as. (N.T.) Member of early Church at Jerusalem, companion of Paul on his second missionary journey.

sīl′ence *n.* Abstinence from speech or noise, taciturnity, reticence; absence of sound, stillness, noiselessness; neglect or omission to remark, notice, write, reply, etc. ~ *v.t.* Make silent, reduce to silence; put down, repress (expression of opinion etc.); compel (gun, ship, etc.) to cease firing.

sīl′encer *n.* (esp.) Device for rendering gun, internal combustion engine, etc., (comparatively) silent.

sīl′ent *adj.* Not speaking; not uttering, making, or accompanied by, any sound; (of letter) not pronounced; taciturn, speaking little; not mentioning or referring to, passing over, something. **sĭl'ently** *adv.*

Sīlēn'us. (Gk myth.) A demigod, foster-father of Bacchus and leader of satyrs, usu. represented as a fat, jolly, drunken old man.

Sīlē'sia (-sh*a*). Ancient duchy and district of E. Europe, partitioned at various times between States of Prussia, Austria-Hungary, Poland, and Czechoslovakia. **silē'sia** *n.* Thin, twilled cotton or linen cloth, used for dress-linings etc., orig. made in Silesia.

silhouette (sĭlo͞oĕt') *n.* Portrait of person in profile showing outline only, this being filled in with black, cut out in paper, etc.; dark outline, shadow in profile, thrown up against lighter background. ~ *v.t.* Represent, exhibit, in silhouette. [named after Étienne de *Silhouette*, Fr. author and politician, said to have made ridiculous petty economies when Controller-General in 1759, or, acc. to another account, to have made such portraits himself]

sĭl'ica *n.* Silicon dioxide (SiO_2), a hard, white or colourless, widely distributed mineral present in many precious and other stones, esp. quartz, and sand; ~ *bricks*, refractory bricks made of crushed silica rock with a small proportion of lime or clay, used esp. for furnaces.

sĭl'icate *n.* Salt of silicic acid.

sĭlĭ'ceous, sĭlĭ'cious (-sh*us*) *adjs.* Containing or consisting of silica.

sĭlĭ'cĭc *adj.* Of, formed from, silica.

sĭlĭ'cĭfȳ *v.* Convert, be converted, into silica.

sĭl'icon *n.* Non-metallic element occurring only in combination, manufactured commercially by reduction of sand and used in the manufacture of certain alloys; symbol Si, at. no. 14, at. wt 28·086; ~*-carbide* = CARBORUNDUM.

sĭlicōs'is *n.* (pl. *-sēs*). Chronic lung disease caused by inhalation of stone-dust and freq. affecting coal-miners, one of the group of diseases known as pneumoconioses.

sĭl'iqua *n.* (bot.) Long pod-like seed-vessel (ill. FRUIT).

silk *n.* Strong soft lustrous fibre produced, to form their cocoons, webs, etc., by certain insect larvae, spiders, etc., esp. by the caterpillars or so-called 'silkworms' of a moth, *Bombyx mori*; thread or textile fabric made from this; similar lustrous filament or fibre made by chemical processes from cellulose (*artificial* ~, now usu. *rayon*); silk gown of king's or queen's counsel (esp. in *take* ~, become K.C. or Q.C.); silky styles of female maize-flower; (attrib.) made of silk; ~*-hat*, tall stiff cylindrical hat covered with silk plush; ~ *screen printing*, serigraphy, stencil printing process in which ink is rolled through a screen of silk or similar material; *silk'worm*, mulberry-feeding caterpillar of moth (*Bombyx mori*), which spins cocoon of silk before changing into pupal state; caterpillar of other moths yielding silk cocoons of commercial value.

sĭl'ken *adj.* Made of silk; clad in silk; soft or lustrous as silk.

sĭl'ky *adj.* Like silk in smoothness, softness, fineness, or lustre. **sĭl'kinėss** *n.*

sĭll *n.* 1. Shelf or slab of stone or wood at base of doorway or esp. window (ill. WINDOW). 2. Timber across the bottom of the entrance to a lock on a canal or river against which the gates close (ill. DOCK). 3. Sheet of intrusive volcanic rock lying parallel to the bedding of other rocks (ill. ROCK).

sĭll'abŭb *n.* (archaic) Dish of cream or milk mixed with wine etc. into soft curd and sometimes whipped or solidified with gelatine.

Sĭll'ery *n.* Kinds of sparkling and esp. still champagne made at or near Sillery, a village in Champagne.

sĭll'y *adj.* Innocent, simple, helpless (archaic); foolish, weak-minded, unwise, imbecile; ~ *season*, late summer as time when newspapers print trivial articles or discussions for lack of important news; ~ *point*, *mid-on*, etc., (cricket) fielder placed close up to batsman (ill. CRICKET). **sĭll'ily** *adv.* **sĭll'inėss** *n.*

sĭl'ō *n.* Pit or airtight structure in which fodder is pressed to undergo fermentation for conversion into succulent winter feed. ~ *v.t.* Make silage of.

Sīlō'am. (N.T.) Spring and pool of water near Jerusalem, where the man born blind was bidden by Christ to wash (John ix. 7).

sĭlt *n.* Sediment deposited by water in channel, harbour, etc. ~ *v.* Choke, be choked, (*up*) with silt.

Sĭlūr'ēs (-z) *n.pl.* Short dark curly-haired people described by Tacitus as inhabiting SE. Wales; supposed pre-Celtic population of Britain. **Sĭlūr'ian** *adj.* & *n.* 1. (One) of the Silures. 2. (geol.) (Of) the third system of rocks in the Palaeozoic, above the Ordovician and below the Devonian; the period when this system was formed (ill. GEOLOGY).

Sĭlvān'us. (Rom. myth.) Spirit of woods, fields, flocks, etc.

sĭl'ver *n.* 1. White lustrous ductile malleable metallic element, one of the precious metals, used chiefly with alloy of harder metal for coin, plate, etc., and in form of salts as the light-sensitive materials in photography; symbol Ag, at. no. 47, at. wt 107·870. 2. Silver coins; the cupro-nickel coins now substituted for these in Britain; (chiefly Sc.) money in general; silverware, silver plate. 3. (attrib. as adj.) Of, producing, silver; (of lace etc.) containing threads of silver; resembling silver in lustre, colour, ringing sound, etc. 4. ~ *birch*, the common white birch, *Betula alba*, from the colour of the bark; ~ *fir*, kinds of fir with white or silvery colour on under-surface of leaves, esp. the central European and Asiatic *Abies alba*; ~*-fish*, various silvery fishes, esp. white variety of goldfish; small silvery wingless insect

SILVER-FISH
(*Lepisma saccharina*)

(*Lepisma saccharina*) found in damp places in houses; ~ *fox*, colour form of American red fox with highly prized black fur which appears silver-tipped because the long hairs are banded with white near tips; ~ *gilt*, silver gilded over; ~*-grey*, lustrous grey; ~ *paper*, fine white tissue-paper; tinfoil; ~ *plate*, domestic utensils etc. made of silver or of silver-plated metal; ~*-plate* (*v.t.*) plate with silver, electro-plate; ~ *sand*, fine white pure quartz sand used in glass-making for polishing and in gardening for assisting plant-growth; *sil'verside*, upper and choicer side of a round of beef; *sil'versmith*, worker in silver, maker of silverware; *sil'verware*, articles made of silver; *sil'verweed*, various plants with silvery leaves, esp. a common wayside plant (*Potentilla argentea*) with leaves silvery-white underneath and yellow flowers. ~ *v.* Coat or plate with silver; give silvery appearance to; turn (hair etc.), become, white or grey; provide (mirror-glass) with amalgam of tin and quicksilver.

sĭl'very *adj.* Resembling silver in lustre, whiteness, ringing sound, etc.

sīm'a *n.* (geol.) Part of earth's crust immediately below SIAL. [f. *si*licon and *ma*gnesium]

Sĭm'ėon Stȳlīt'ės (-z), St. (*c* 390–459). First of the stylites or pillar ascetics; he lived for 30 years on top of a pillar near Antioch.

sĭm'ian *adj.* & *n.* (Of) one of the apes, esp. the anthropoid apes; ape(-like), monkey(-like).

sĭm'ilar *adj.* Like, alike, having mutual resemblance or resemblance *to*, of the same kind; (geom.) having same shape. **sĭm'ilarly** *adv.* **sĭmĭlă'rĭty** *n.*

sĭm'ilė *n.* Writer's or speaker's introduction of an object or scene or action with which the one in hand is compared for the purpose of illustration or ornament (cf. METAPHOR, ALLEGORY, PARABLE); passage effecting this.

sĭmĭl'itūde *n.* Likeness, guise; simile, comparison; (rare) counterpart, facsimile.

sĭmm'er *v.* Be, keep, on the point of boiling, cook slowly in liquid at temperature just below boiling-point (freq. fig.). ~ *n.* Simmering state.

Sĭm'nel, Lambert (*c* 1475–1525). An English youth who impersonated the imprisoned Edward, Earl of Warwick (1475–99) immediately after the Wars of the Roses; he was crowned in Dublin as Edward VI, 1487, but defeated at Stoke-on-Trent by Henry VII, pardoned, and employed as a turnspit in the royal kitchen.

sĭm'nel-cāke *n.* Rich decorated fruit-cake made chiefly at mid-Lent and Easter.

Sī'mon. (N.T.) 1. The apostle, surnamed PETER. 2. A disciple of Jesus, called the Zealot. 3. A kinsman of Jesus.

Sī'mon (Mā'gus). (N.T.) A sorcerer of Samaria who was converted by Philip; he offered money to the Apostles if they would confer upon him the power to impart the Holy Ghost, and was rebuked by Peter (Acts viii. 9–19).

Sīmŏn'idēs (-z) (556–468 B.C.). Greek lyric poet.

sī'mony *n.* Buying or selling of ecclesiastical preferment. [f. SIMON MAGUS]

sĭmōōm', sĭmōōn' *ns.* Hot dry suffocating dust-laden wind of Arabian, Syrian, etc., deserts.

sĭm'per *n.* Affected and self-conscious smile, smirk. ~ *v.* Smile in silly affected manner, smirk; utter with simper.

sĭm'ple *adj.* 1. Not compound, complex, complicated, elaborate, involved, or composite; unmixed, consisting of one substance, ingredient, or element; presenting no difficulty; mere, pure, bare; ~ *equation,* one not involving second or any higher power of unknown quantity; ~ *interest*: see INTEREST; ~ *life,* life in more or less primitive conditions, without servants or luxuries; ~ *sentence,* one without subordinate clause. 2. Plain, unaffected, unsophisticated, natural, artless; foolish, ignorant, inexperienced; of low rank, humble, insignificant, trifling. ~ *n.* Herb used medicinally; medicine made from this. **sĭm'plenėss** (-ln-), **sĭmplĭ'cĭty** *ns.* **sĭm'ply** *adv.* In simple manner; without exception, absolutely.

sĭm'pleton (-lt-) *n.* Foolish, gullible, or half-witted person.

sĭm'plĭfȳ *v.t.* Make simple, make easy to do or understand. **sĭmplĭfĭcā'tion** *n.*

Simplon (săṅ'plawṅ). Alpine pass in SW. Switzerland; ~ *tunnel,* railway tunnel, about 12 miles long, driven through Monte Leone, NE. of the pass.

Sĭmp'son, Sir James Young (1811–70). Scottish surgeon; introduced the use of chloroform as an anaesthetic.

sĭmūlāc'rum *n.* (pl. *-ra*). Image of something; shadowy likeness, deceptive substitute, mere pretence.

sĭm'ūlāte *v.t.* Feign, counterfeit, put on; pretend to be, wear guise of, mimic. **sĭmūlā'tion** *n.*

sĭmultān'ėous *adj.* Existing, occurring, operating, at the same time (*with*); ~ *equations,* equations involving the same values of the unknown quantity or quantities and solved in conjunction with each other. **sĭmultān'ėously** *adv.* **sĭmultān'ėousnėss** *n.*

sĭn *n.* (A) transgression against divine law or principles of morality; offence *against* good taste, propriety, etc.; ORIGINAL, DEADLY, MORTAL ~: see these words; *seven deadly sins*: see SEVEN. **sĭn'ful, sĭn'lėss** *adjs.* **sĭn'fully, sĭn'lėssly** *advs.* **sĭn'fulnėss, sĭn'lėssnėss** *ns.* **sĭn** *v.i.* Commit sin; offend *against.* **sĭnn'er** *n.*

Sī'nāī. Peninsula at the N. end of the Red Sea; *Mount* ~, mountain in S. part of this peninsula, where (Exod. xix–xxxiv) the Ten Commandments and the Tables of the Law were given to Moses. **Sīnāĭt'ĭc** *adj.* Of Mount Sinai or the peninsula.

Sĭn'anthrŏp'us *n.* Ape-like man of the type represented by remains found at Peking, China, also called *Peking man.* [Gk *Sinai* the Chinese, *anthropos* man]

sĭn'apism *n.* Mustard plaster.

since *adv.* From that time till now; within the period between then and now, subsequently, later; ago, before now. ~ *prep.* From (specified time) till now; during the period between (specified past time) and now. ~ *conj.* 1. From the time that. 2. Seeing that, because, inasmuch as.

sincēre' *adj.*: Free from pretence or deceit, not assumed or put on, genuine, honest, frank. **sincēre'ly** *adv.*: *yours* ~, used before signature in letter (e.g. to acquaintance) which is neither formal nor intimate. **sincĕ'rĭty** *n.*

sĭn'cĭpŭt *n.* Front part of head or skull.

Sind. Province of W. Pakistan.

Sĭn(d)băd the Sailor. Hero of one of the tales in the 'Arabian Nights', who relates his fantastic adventures in a number of voyages.

sīne *n.* (trig.) (Of an angle) the ratio which the side of a right-angled triangle opposite to the angle concerned bears to the hypotenuse (abbrev. sin) (ill. TRIGONOMETRY); ~ *curve,* curve showing how this ratio varies with the angle (ill. VIBRATION).

sī'nėcūre *n.* Office of profit or honour without duties attached, esp. benefice without cure of souls.

sīn'ė dī'ē. (Adjourned) without any day for resumption of business etc. being specified; indefinitely. [L, = 'without day']

sīn'ė quā nŏn. Indispensable condition or qualification. [L, = 'without which not']

sĭn'ew *n.* (Piece of) tough fibrous tissue uniting muscle to bone, tendon; (pl., loosely) muscles, bodily strength, wiriness (freq. fig., esp. in ~*s of war,* money). **sĭn'ewy** (-ūĭ) *adj.*

sĭng *v.* (past t. *săng,* past part. *sŭng*). Utter words or sounds, utter (words, sounds), in tuneful succession, esp. in accordance with a set tune; produce vocal melody, utter (song, tune); make inarticulate melodious, humming, buzzing, or whistling sounds, (of ears) have sensation of being filled with humming sound; compose poetry, celebrate in verse; ~ *out,* (slang) call out loudly. **sĭng'er** *n.*

Sĭngapōre'. Republic consisting of the island of Singapore and a number of smaller islands, S. of Malay peninsula; former British colony; State of MALAYSIA 1963; independent State of British Commonwealth 1965.

sĭnge (-j) *n.* Superficial burn. ~ *v.t.* Burn superficially or lightly, burn ends or edges of.

Sĭngh (-ng). (Indian) Great warrior; title of warrior castes, as Rajputs and Sikhs.

sĭng'le (-nggl) *adj.* One only, not double or multiple, undivided, individual, separate; of, for, one person only; solitary, lonely, unaided; unmarried; (of flower) not double, having only one whorl or set of petals; (of game) with one person only on each side; (of journey, ticket for this) not return; ~ *bed,* one for use of one person only; ~*-breasted,* (of garments) having buttons on one edge, not double-breasted; ~ *court,* court for single game (lawn tennis etc.); ~ *entry,* simple method of book-keeping in which transactions are entered in the ledger under one account only (opp. *double* ENTRY); ~*file,* line of persons going one behind another, Indian file; ~*-handed,* (done etc.) without help from other persons; ~*-hearted,* sincere, honest; ~*-minded,* single-hearted; also, keeping one purpose in view; ~ *room,* room for use of one person only; ~*-stick,* (fighting or fencing with) basket-hilted stick. **sĭng'lenėss** *n.* **sĭng'ly** *adv.* **sĭng'le** *n.* Single ticket; (tennis etc.) single game (usu. pl.); hit for one in cricket; (pl.) twisted single threads of silk. ~ *v.t.* Choose *out* as example, to serve some purpose etc.

sĭng'lėt (-ngg-) *n.* Undershirt, vest; athlete's vest worn instead of shirt.

sĭng'leton (-nggl t-) *n.* (whist, bridge, etc.) Card which is the only one of its suit in the hand.

Sĭng Sĭng. New York State prison at Ossining, a suburb of New York city.

sĭng'sŏng *adj.* In, recited with, monotonous rhythm, rising and falling monotonously. ~ *n.* Monotonous rhythm or cadence; impromptu or informal vocal concert.

sĭng'ūlar (-ngg-) *adj.* 1. (gram.) Denoting, expressing, one person or thing. 2. Unusual, uncommon, extraordinary, surprising; strange, odd, peculiar. ~ *n.* Singular number; word in singular form. **sĭng'ūlarly** *adv.* **sĭngūlă'rity** *n.* (esp.) Eccentricity, oddness, strangeness.

Sĭnhalēse' (-z), **Singh-** *n.* 1. 1. (Member of) the majority community in Ceylon. 2. Indo-European language spoken in Ceylon, closely related to Pali, with many Dravidian words. ~ *adj.*

sĭn'ister *adj.* 1. Of evil omen; unfavourable, harmful; wicked, corrupt, evil; ill-looking, malignant, villainous. 2. (her.) On left side of shield etc. (from bearer's point of view) (ill. HERALDRY).

sĭn'istral *adj.* (Of spiral shells) with whorls going to left; (of flat fishes) having left side of body turned uppermost.

sĭnk[1] *n.* 1. Place in which foul liquid collects (now usu. fig.). 2. Large fixed basin for washing crockery etc., usu. rectangular, made of porcelain, stone, metal, etc., with pipe for escape of water to a drain, and usu. with supply of water connected with it.

sĭnk[2] *v.* (past t. *săṅk*, past part. *sŭnk*). 1. Become wholly or partly submerged in water, quicksand, snow, etc. (freq. fig.); fall slowly downwards, subside, descend, pass out of sight; pass, fall gently, lapse, degenerate, *into*; (of sun etc.) move downwards towards or pass below horizon; penetrate, make way *in(to)*. 2. Cause or allow to sink; send below surface of liquid or ground; lower level of; excavate, make by excavating; set aside, leave out of consideration; invest (money), lose by investment.

sĭnk'er *n.* (esp.) Weight used to sink fishing or sounding line.

sĭnk'ing *n.* (esp.) Internal bodily sensation caused by hunger or apprehension; *~-fund*, fund of money periodically set aside from revenue, usu. to reduce principal of national, municipal, or company's debt.

Sinn Fein (shĭn fān). Irish society, founded 1905 by Arthur Griffith, aiming at political independence and revival of Irish culture and language; policy of this; extreme Irish nationalist party. [Ir., = 'we ourselves']

Sĭn'ō-Jăpanēse' (-z) *adj.* Of China and Japan.

sĭnŏl'ogy *n.* Study of Chinese language, history, customs, etc. **sĭn'olŏgue** (-g), **sĭnŏl'ogist** *ns.* Person versed in this.

sĭn'ophil(e), **sĭn'ophōbe** *ns.* One who loves, hates, the Chinese.

sĭn'ter *n.* Siliceous deposit often found round hot springs. ~ *v.* Become or cause to become a solid mass.

sĭn'ūate *adj.* (esp. bot.) Wavy-edged. **sĭn'ūately** *adv.* **sĭnūā'tion** *n.*

sĭn'ūous *adj.* With many curves, tortuous, serpentine, undulating. **sĭn'ūously** *adv.* **sĭn'ūousnĕss** *n.* **sĭnūŏs'ity** *n.* Sinuousness; a curve or bend.

sīn'us *n.* 1. (anat., zool., etc.) Cavity of bone or tissue, esp. one of the cavities in the bone of the skull which communicate with the nostrils (ill. HEAD). 2. (path.) Passage communicating with deep-seated abscess, fistula. 3. (bot.) Curve between lobes of leaf.

sio'mīō (shō-) *n.* One of the inferior nobles of Japan who were vassals of the Shogun.

Sioux (sōō). (Member of) important group of N. Amer. Indian tribes, orig. of district W. and S. of Lake Superior, later of plains of Minnesota, N. and S. Dakota, and Nebraska.

sĭp *n.* Small mouthful of liquid; act of sipping. ~ *v.* Drink in very small quantities.

sīph'on *n.* Pipe or tube bent so that one leg is longer than the other and used for drawing off liquids by atmospheric pressure, which forces liquid up the shorter leg and over the bend in the pipe; aerated-water bottle from which liquid is forced out by pressure of gas through tube inserted in bottle; (zool.) tube-like organ, esp. in molluscs, serving as canal for passage of fluid etc.; siphuncle. **sīph'onal**, **sīphŏn'ic** *adjs.* **sīph'on** *v.* Conduct, flow, (as) through siphon.

sīph'onĕt *n.* (zool.) Honey-tube of aphis.

sīph'ŭncle *n.* (zool.) Small canal or tube connecting shell-chambers in some cephalopods.

sĭpp'ĕt *n.* Small piece of bread or esp. toast served in soup, with meat, etc.

sĭr *n.* 1. (*S~*) Title of honour placed before Christian name of knight or baronet. 2. Used (without name) in addressing master, superior in rank, age, etc., or an equal; sometimes with scornful, indignant, contemptuous, etc., force; (*Dear*) *S~(s)*, opening of formal letter. ~ *v.t.* Address as *sir*.

sĭrc'ar *n.* (Anglo-Ind.) The Government of India; head of government or household; house-steward; native accountant. [Hind., f. Pers. *sarkar* (*sar* head, *kār* work)]

sĭrd'ar *n.* (In India etc.) person in command, leader; (in Egypt) commander-in-chief of army, formerly a British officer. [Urdu, f. Pers. *sar* head, *dār* possessor]

sīre *n.* 1. Father, forefather (poet.); male parent of beast, esp. stallion. 2. (archaic) = 'your majesty'. ~ *v.t.* Beget (esp. of stallions).

sīr'ĕn *n.* 1. (Gk myth.) Any of several fabulous creatures, women or birds with women's heads, living on rocky isle to which they lured seafarers by their singing. 2. Sweet singer; dangerously fascinating woman, temptress; (attrib.) irresistibly tempting. 3. Apparatus producing loud sound by revolution of perforated disc over jet of compressed air or steam, used as ship's fog-signal, air-raid warning, etc.; ~ *suit*, one-piece suit of clothes, easily put on or off, for use during a night air-raid. 4. (*S~*) genus of eel-like tailed amphibians of southern U.S. with short fore-legs and no hind-legs; mud eel.

sīrēn'ian *adj.* & *n.* (Member) of order *Sirenia* of large aquatic herbivorous mammals, including manatee and dugong.

Sĭ'rius. The dog-star, a brilliant white star in the constellation Canis Major, the brightest star in the skies.

sĭrl'oin *n.* Upper and choicer part of loin of beef (ill. MEAT).

sĭrŏcc'ō *n.* (pl. *-s*). Hot and blighting oppressive wind blowing from N. coast of Africa over Mediterranean and parts of S. Europe, esp. Italy, Malta, and Sicily. [It. *s(c)irocco*, f. Arab. *sharq* east]

sĭ'rrah *n.* (archaic) = SIR used in contempt, reproach, reprimand, etc.

sirree' *n.* (U.S. colloq.) Sir.

sĭ'rup *n.* (U.S.) = SYRUP.

sīs'al *n.* *~-grass*, *~-hemp*, strong durable white fibre of a W. Indian agave (*A. sisalina*) and similar plants, used for cordage etc. [*Sisal*, former seaport of Yucatan]

Sĭs'era. (O.T.) Canaanite who led an army against the Israelites and was killed by JAEL (Judges iv, v).

sĭs'kin *n.* Small sharp-billed olive-green song-bird of Europe and Asia (*Carduelis spinus*), allied to goldfinch.

Sĭs'ley, Alfred (1840–99). French Impressionist landscape-painter.

sĭss'y *n.* (Little) sister, young girl (U.S. colloq.); effeminate boy or man.

sĭs'ter *n.* 1. Daughter of same parents as another person; one considered as or filling the place of a sister. 2. Member of a religious sisterhood, nun; head nurse of ward in hospital or infirmary; *S~ of Mercy*, member of one of various religious organizations devoted to educational and charitable work, esp. that founded 1827 in Dublin. **sĭs'terly** *adj.*

sĭs'terhŏŏd *n.* 1. Being a sister, relation between sisters. 2. Society of women bound by monastic vows or devoting themselves to religious or charitable work.

Sĭs'tīne *adj.* 1. Of, pertaining to, built by, one of the popes named Sixtus; ~ *chapel*, chapel in the Vatican, built by Sixtus IV, containing Michelangelo's famous painted ceiling and his fresco of the Last Judgement; ~ *Vulgate*, edition of the Vulgate issued under the papacy of Sixtus V. 2. ~ *Madonna*, painting by Raphael formerly in the Church of San Sisto, Piacenza, and later in Dresden.

sĭs'trum *n.* Jingling instrument of thin metal frame with transverse loose metal rods and handle by which it was shaken, used esp. in Egypt in worship of Isis.

Sĭs'ȳphus. (Gk myth.) Legendary king of Corinth, condemned for his misdeeds to Hades; his eternal task was to roll a large stone to the top of a hill from which it rolled back again to the plain. **Sĭsȳphē'an** *adj.* (As) of Sisyphus, everlastingly laborious.

sĭt *v.* (past t. and past part. *săt*). 1. Take, be in, position in which weight of body rests on buttocks; occupy seat as judge, with administrative function, as member of council or legislative assembly, etc.; (of assembly) hold a session, transact business; pose (*for* portrait etc. *to* painter etc.); take examination. 2. (of birds and some animals) Rest with legs bent and body close to ground or perch; remain on nest to hatch eggs. 3. (chiefly of inanimate things) Be in more or less permanent position. 4. Seat one*self* (usu. *down*); cause to sit (usu. *down*); sit on (horse); (of bird) sit on, hatch (eggs). 5. ~ *down*, seat oneself; (mil.) encamp *before* town etc. to besiege it; ~-*down strike*, one in which strikers refuse to leave the place where they are working; ~ *down under*, submit tamely to; ~ (*up*)*on*, hold session concerning; (slang) repress, squash, snub; ~ *out*, remain to end of; outstay; take no part in (dance etc.), sit out dance; ~ *up*, rise from lying to sitting posture; sit erect; (of animal) sit on hind-legs with forelegs straight or lifted in begging posture; remain out of bed. ~ *n.* (esp.) Set (of garment etc.).

sīte *n.* Ground on which town, building, etc., stood, stands, or is to stand; ground set apart for some purpose. ~ *v.t.* Locate, place, provide with site.

sĭt'rĕp *n.* (mil. abbrev.) Situation report.

sĭtt'er *n.* (esp.) 1. Person sitting for portrait etc.; ~-*in*, *baby*-~, person who looks after children when parents go out. 2. Easy catch, stroke, shot, etc.; something that can hardly be bungled.

sĭtt'ĭng *n.* (esp.) 1. Time during which one sits or remains seated; meeting of legislature or other body; single occasion of sitting for artist etc. 2. Clutch of eggs. 3. ~-*room*, space for sitting; room used for sitting in (opp. *bedroom*, *kitchen*, etc.).

sĭt'ūate (archaic), **sĭt'ūātėd** *adjs.* In specified situation.

sĭtuā'tion *n.* 1. Place, with its surroundings, occupied by something. 2. Set of circumstances, position in which one finds oneself; critical point or complication, position of affairs, in narrative, drama, etc. 3. Place or paid office, esp. of domestic servant.

sĭtz-bath *n.* Hip-bath. [Ger. *Sitzbad*, f. *sitzen* sit]

Si'va, Shiva (sē-, shē-). One of the supreme gods of Hinduism, third deity of the triad of which Brahma and Vishnu are the other members; he represents the principle of destruction and the regeneration which follows it; he has countless names and manifests himself in various shapes. **Siv'aĭsm, Shiv'aĭsm** *ns.* The worship of the god S(h)iva.

sĭx *adj.* One more than five (6, vi, or VI); ~-*foot*, measuring 6 feet; ~-*foot way*, (on railway) space between two parallel pairs of rails; *S*~ *Counties*, those of Northern Ireland (Antrim, Armagh, Down, Fermanagh, Londonderry, Tyrone); *S*~ *Nations*, confederation of N. Amer. Indians consisting of the FIVE nations and the Tuscaroras; *six'pence*, (6*d.*) six pence, silver or cupro-nickel coin worth this; *six'penny* (*adj.*) costing or worth 6*d.*; ~-*shooter*, revolver capable of firing 6 shots without reloading. ~ *n.* The number 6; card or die-face of 6 pips; (pl.) candles weighing six to the pound.

sĭx'fōld *adj.*

sĭx'er *n.* (colloq.) Hit for 6 runs in cricket.

sĭxte *n.* Sixth of the 8 positions in fencing (ill. FENCE).

sĭx'teen' *adj.* One more than fifteen (16, xvi, or XVI); *six'teen'mo*, 16mo, sexto-decimo. ~ *n.* The number 16. **sĭx'teenth'** *adj.* & *n.*

sĭxth *adj.* Next after fifth; ~ *day*, Friday (with the Society of Friends); ~ *sense*, supposed faculty by which a person perceives facts and regulates action without the direct use of any of the five senses. ~ *n.* Sixth part; sixth form in school; (mus.) interval of which the span involves 6 alphabetical names of notes; harmonic combination of the two notes thus separated. **sĭxth'ly** *adv.* In the sixth place.

Sĭx'tīne = SISTINE.

Sĭx'tus. Name of 5 popes, amongst them: *Sixtus IV*, pope 1471–84, patron of art and letters, builder of the SISTINE Chapel, refounded the Vatican library; *Sixtus V*, pope 1585–90, reorganized the papal finances and initiated (1589) the Sistine Vulgate.

sĭx'ty *adj.* Six times ten (60, lx, or LX). ~ *n.* The number 60; *the sixties*, years between 59 and 70 in life or century. **sĭx'tiėth** *adj.* & *n.*

sīz'(e)able (-zabl) *adj.* Of fairly large size.

sīz'ar *n.* In University of Cambridge and at Trinity College, Dublin, student receiving allowance from the college and formerly charged with certain menial offices. **sīz'arship** *n.* [f. SIZE[1], *n.* in obs. sense of 'portion']

sīze[1] *n.* Dimensions, magnitude; one of usu. numbered classes into which things, esp. garments, are divided in respect of size. ~ *v.t.* Group or sort in sizes or according to size; ~ *up*, estimate size of; (colloq.) form judgement of.

sīze[2] *n.* Glutinous substance, preparation of glue, shellac, etc., and water, used for glazing paper, stiffening textiles, mixing with colours, etc. ~ *v.t.* Treat with size.

sĭzz'le *v.i.* Make sputtering or hissing sound, esp. in frying, roasting, etc. ~ *n.* Sizzling noise.

S.J. *abbrev.* Society of Jesus.

S.J.A.A., S.J.A.B. *abbrevs.* St. John Ambulance Association, Brigade.

sjăm'bŏk (sh-) *n.* Rhinoceros-hide whip. ~ *v.t.* Flog with this. [S. Afr. Du., f. Malay *samboq*, f. Urdu *chābuk*]

S.J.C. *abbrev.* (U.S.) Supreme Judicial Court.

Skăg'errăk'. N. part of channel between S. Scandinavia and Denmark connecting North Sea with Baltic.

skald: see SCALD[2].

skăt *n.* Three-handed card-game played with 32 cards, the 2s, 3s, 4s, 5s, and 6s being left out; the four suits have a fixed relative value, clubs being highest and diamonds lowest, and spades being above hearts; the knaves take all other cards; the method of bidding and playing is similar to solo, but the method of scoring is by the cards in the tricks won, the 10 and the ace counting high; played in Germany and, in a different form, in America.

skāte[1] *n.* Cartilaginous fish of the genus *Raia*, esp. *R. batis*, large flat food-fish with very large pectoral fins giving fish a rhomboidal shape.

skāte[2] *n.* One of a pair of steel blades, each attached beneath boot-sole, enabling wearer to glide over ice; *roller*-~, similar contrivance with set of rollers instead of blade, for gliding on hard floor. ~ *v.i.* Move, glide, (as) on skates; *skating-rink*, prepared sheet of ice or hard floor for skating on, building containing this.

skean, skēne *ns.* Kind of knife or dagger formerly used in Ireland and Highlands of Scotland; ~-*dhu* (dōō) dagger stuck in stocking as part of Highland costume.

skėdădd'le *v.* (colloq.) Run away, retreat hastily. ~ *n.* Precipitate retreat or flight, scurry.

skein (-ān) *n.* 1. Quantity of yarn or thread coiled and usu. loosely twisted. 2. Flight of wild geese or other wild fowl.

skĕl'ėton *n.* Hard internal or

external framework of bones, cartilage, shell, woody fibre, etc., supporting or containing animal or vegetable body; dried bones of human being or other animal fastened together in same relative

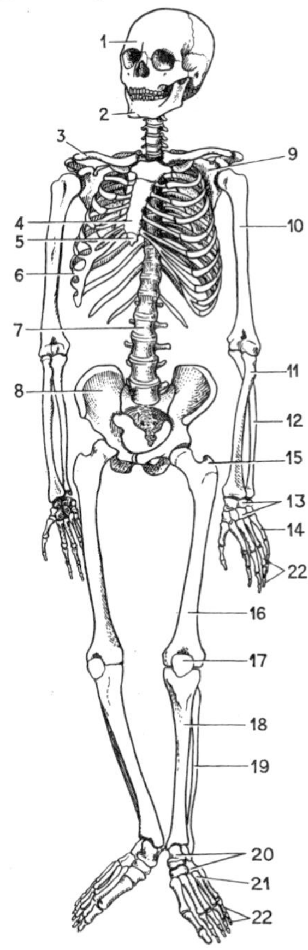

HUMAN SKELETON

1. Skull. 2. Mandible. 3. Clavicle or collar-bone. 4. Sternum or breastbone. 5. Xiphoid process. 6. Ribs. 7. Spine. 8. Pelvis. 9. Scapula or shoulder-blade. 10. Humerus. 11. Radius. 12. Ulna. 13. Carpal bones. 14. Metacarpal bones. 15. Trochanter. 16. Femur. 17. Patella or knee-cap. 18. Tibia. 19. Fibula. 20. Tarsal bones. 21. Metatarsal bones. 22. Phalanges

positions as in life; very thin or emaciated person, etc.; mere outlines, supporting framework, main features or most necessary elements, *of* something; *attrib.* (of staff, company, regiment, etc.) of the minimum size, forming a nucleus or cadre that can be added to as occasion arises; ~ *key*, key fitting many locks by having large part of bit filed away; ~ *leaf*, leaf of which parenchyma has been removed or rotted away, so that only network of veins remains. **skĕl'ėtal** *adj.*

skĕl'ėtonīze *v.t.* Reduce to a skeleton.

Skĕl'ton, John (*c* 1460–1529). English poet, author of satires, ballads, and allegories.

skene: see SKEAN.

skĕp *n.* (see also SKIP[5]). Wooden or wicker basket or hamper of kinds varying locally; amount contained in skep, formerly as measure of capacity; straw or wicker beehive; (north. dial.) coal-scuttle.

skĕtch *n.* Preliminary, rough, slight, merely outlined, or unfinished drawing or painting; brief account or narrative without detail, rough draft, general outline; short slight play, freq. of single scene; ~*-block*, *-book*, block or book of drawing-paper for making sketches on; ~*-map*, *-plan*, map, plan, with outlines but little detail. ~ *v.* Make or give sketch of; make sketches.

skĕtch'y *adj.* Giving only a slight or rough outline; resembling a sketch; light, flimsy, hurried, rough. **skĕtch'ĭly** *adv.* **skĕtch'ĭnėss** *n.*

skew *adj.* Oblique, slanting, squint, not symmetrical (now usu. archit., mech., etc.); ~ *arch*, arch springing from two points not level with each other; *skew'bald* (-awld), (esp. of horse) with irregular patches of white and some colour. ~ *n.* Sloping top of buttress; coping of gable; stone built into bottom of gable to support coping.

skew'er *n.* Pin of wood or metal for holding meat compactly together while cooking. ~ *v.t.* Fasten together, pierce, (as) with skewer.

ski (skē, shē) *n.* (pl. *-s*). 1. One of pair of long slender pieces of wood, usu. pointed and curved

SKI-ING TURNS

1. Stem turn. 2. Christiania. 3. Telemark

at front, fastened to boot and enabling wearer to glide over snow-covered surface. 2. Launching-ramp of a flying-bomb, the form of which suggests the lateral outline of a ski. ~ *v.i.* Travel on skis.

skĭd *n.* 1. Piece of frame or timber serving as buffer, support, inclined plane, for logs, etc. 2. Braking device, esp. wooden or metal shoe, fixed under the wheel of a cart etc. and so preventing its turning when descending a steep hill; runner on aircraft to facilitate landing, protect tail or wings on landing, etc. 3. Act of skidding. ~ *v.* 1. Support, move, protect, check, with skid(s). 2. (of wheel or vehicle) Slide without revolving, fail to grip ground, side-slip; (of car or aeroplane) slide sideways towards outside of curve when turning.

skĭff *n.* Small light boat, esp. for rowing or sculling; long narrow outrigged racing-boat for one oarsman, covered in fore and aft with canvas.

skĭl'ful *adj.* Having or showing skill, practised, adept, expert, ingenious. **skĭl'fully** *adv.*

skĭll *n.* Expertness, practised ability, dexterity, facility in doing something.

skĭlled (-ld) *adj.* (esp., of workman etc.) Properly trained or experienced; (of work) requiring skill and experience.

skĭll'ėt *n.* Metal cooking utensil, usu. with three or four feet and long handle; (U.S.) frying-pan.

SKILLET

skĭll'y *n.* Thin watery porridge, gruel, or soup, usu. of oatmeal and water, formerly served in prison, work-house, etc.

skĭm *v.* Take scum, cream, floating matter from surface of (liquid), remove (cream etc.) from surface of milk etc.; pass over (surface), pass *over*, *along*, rapidly and lightly with close approach or very slight contact; read superficially, look over cursorily. ~ *adj.* ~ *milk*, milk with the cream removed.

skĭmm'er *n.* (esp.) 1. Ladle, usu. perforated, or other utensil for skimming liquids. 2. Long-winged marine bird of N. Amer. genus *Rhynchops*, obtaining food by skimming along surface of water with knife-like lower mandible immersed; razor-bill or cut-water.

skĭmp *v.* Supply meagrely; be parsimonious. **skĭmp'y** *adj.* Meagre, inadequate.

Skĭm'pōle, Harold. In Dickens's 'Bleak House', a character (drawn partly from Leigh Hunt) who imposes on his friends' kindness by affecting a childlike innocence esp. in money matters.

skĭn *n.* 1. Tough flexible continuous integument of human or other animal body, consisting of two layers, the *epidermis* or outer layer, and the *dermis* or inner layer, with (in mammals) its sebaceous glands, hair follicles, etc.; one of the separate layers of which skin is composed; hide of flayed animal, esp. of smaller animals, as sheep, goat, etc., with or without the

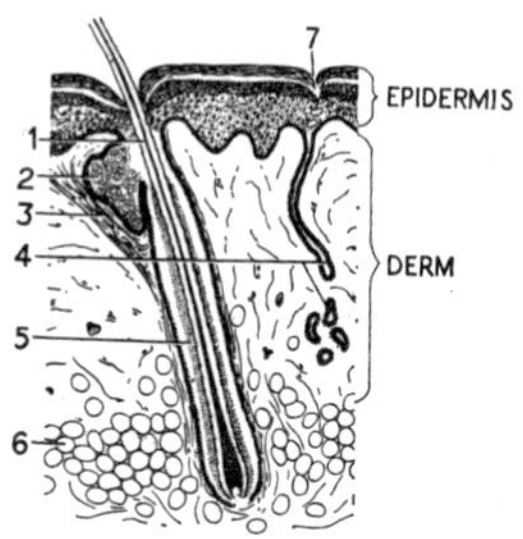

SECTION OF HUMAN SKIN

1. Hair in follicle. 2. Sebaceous gland. 3. *Erector pili* muscle. 4. Sweat glands. 5. Root sheath. 6. Fat and subcutaneous tissue. 7. Pore

hair or wool; vessel for wine or water made of animal's whole skin; *get under one's* ~, take a strong hold on, irritate. 2. Outer coating, peel, rind, of fruit, vegetable, etc.; thin film or pellicle; outer covering of ribs or frame of ship, boat, or aircraft. 3. *~-deep*, superficial, not deep or lasting; *~-dive* (*v.i.* & *n.*) dive without diving-suit (usu. in ref. to deep diving with aqualung); so *~-diver*; *skin'ful*, as much liquor as one can hold; ~ *game*, (U.S. slang) swindle; *~-tight*, (of garment) very close-fitting. ~ *v.* 1. Cover (usu. *over*), as with skin; form, become covered (usu. *over*) with, new skin. 2. Strip skin from, flay; remove skin of. 3. (slang) Swindle, fleece; *skin'flint*, niggard, miser.

skĭnk *n.* Any lizard of the family *Scincidae*, e.g. *Scincus officinalis* of N. Africa and Arabia.

skĭnn'er *n.* (esp., now chiefly in name of a City company) Dealer in skins, furrier.

skĭnn'y *adj.* (esp.) 1. Fleshless, lean, emaciated. 2. Mean, miserly, stingy.

skĭp[1] *v.* Jump about lightly, frisk, gambol, caper, move lightly from one foot to the other; spring or leap lightly and easily, esp. over rope revolved over head and under feet; shift quickly from one subject or occupation to another; omit, make omissions, in reading, dealing with a series, etc.; cause (bomb) to ricochet from a surface towards a target; hence, *skip-bombing*; *skipp'ing-rope*, rope used for skipping. ~ *n.* Skipping movement, esp. quick shift from one foot to the other.

skĭp[2] *n.* Captain of side at bowls, curling, etc. [abbrev. of SKIPPER]

skĭp[3] *n.* College servant, scout, esp. at Dublin. [prob. f. obs. *skip-kennel* lackey]

skĭp[4] *n.* Basket, cage, bucket, etc., in which men or materials are lowered and raised in mines and quarries.

skĭp[5], **skĕp** *ns.* Wooden box for freshly caught fish; amount of fish contained in skip.

skĭpp'er *n.* Captain or master of ship, esp. small trading or fishing vessel; captain of aircraft; captain of side in cricket and other games. [MDu. or MLG *schipper*, f. *schip* ship]

skîrl *n.* & *v.i.* (Make) shrill sound characteristic of bagpipes.

skîrm'ĭsh *n.* Irregular engagement between two small bodies of troops, esp. detached or outlying parties of opposing armies; any contest or encounter. ~ *v.i.* Engage in skirmish.

skĭ'rrėt *n.* Kind of water-parsnip, the perennial umbelliferous plant *Sium sisarum*, formerly much used as table vegetable.

skîrt *n.* Woman's outer garment covering body below waist; underskirt, petticoat; part of coat or shirt below waist; flap of a saddle; border, rim, outskirts, boundary of anything; diaphragm or midriff of animal (esp. of beef) used for food; *divided skirt*, woman's garment, loose trousers resembling skirt; *~-dancing*, dancing accompanied by manipulation of long full flowing skirts or drapery. ~ *v.* Go along, round, or past the edge of; be situated along, go *along*, coast, wall, etc.; *skirting(-board)*, narrow board round wall of room etc. close to floor (ill. WAINSCOT).

skĭt *n.* Light piece of satire, burlesque.

skĭtt'er *v.i.* Skip or skim along surface, esp., of wildfowl, along water in rising or settling; fish by drawing bait jerkily or skippingly over surface of water.

skĭtt'ĭsh *adj.* Frivolous, excessively lively, fickle, inconstant; spirited, lively; (of horse etc.) nervous, inclined to shy, excitable, fidgety. **skĭtt'ishly** *adv.* **skĭtt'-ishnėss** *n.*

skĭtt'le *n.* (pl.) Nine-pins, game played with nine wooden 'pins' set up at end of *~-alley* to be bowled down with as few throws as possible; one of the pins used in this game. ~ *v.* Play skittles; knock down (skittles); (cricket) get (batsmen, side) *out* easily and rapidly.

skīve *v.t.* Split, pare (hide, leather). **skīv'er** *n.* Thin soft kind of dressed leather split from grain-side of sheepskin and tanned in sumach; tool or machine for skiving leather.

skĭvv'y *n.* (colloq.) Female domestic servant (usu. derogatory).

skū'a *n.* Large rapacious predatory bird of genus *Stercorarius* or related genera, esp. the great skua (*S. skua*), largest European species, of N. Atlantic coasts.

skŭldŭgg'ery, scŭldŭdd'ery *n.* (orig. U.S.) Rascally conduct, underhand plotting.

skŭlk *v.i.* Lurk, conceal oneself, avoid observation, esp. with sinister motive or in cowardice.

skŭll *n.* Bony case of the brain, cranium; whole bony framework of head (ill. HEAD); ~ *and crossbones*, representation of human skull with two thigh-bones crossed below it, as emblem of death; *~-cap*, close-fitting brimless cap for top of head.

skŭnk *n.* N. Amer. animal of weasel family (*Mephitis*), with black coat, usu. striped with white, and bushy tail, able to emit, when attacked, powerful and offensive odour from two anal glands; fur of this; low contemptible person. [Amer. Indian *segongw*]

Skup'shtĭna (-ŏŏp-) *n.* Yugoslav parliament.

skȳ *n.* Apparent arch or vault of heaven; climate, clime; colour of blue sky, sky-blue; *~-blue*, colour of clear summer sky; *sky'lark*, common European lark, *Alauda arvensis*, soaring towards sky while singing; *Missouri skylark*, a N. American pipit, the prairie-lark (*Neocorys spraguii*); *sky'lark* (*v.i.*) frolic, play tricks or practical jokes, indulge in horse-play; *sky'light*, window in roof or ceiling; *~-line*, silhouette of anything against sky; visible horizon; *~-marker*, parachute flare dropped by raiding aircraft to mark the target area; ~ *pilot*, (slang) parson; *~-rocket*, rocket exploding high in air; (*v.i.*) ascend like sky-rocket, shoot up; *~-sail*, light sail above royal in square-rigged ship; *~-scraper*, very high building of many storeys; ~ *troops*, air-borne troops; *~-writing*, legible smoke-trails made by aircraft, esp. for advertising purposes. **skȳ'ey** *adj.* **skȳ'ward(s)** *advs.* & *adj.* **skȳ** *v.t.* Hit, throw, (ball) very high; hang (picture) on top line or near ceiling in exhibition, hang picture of (artist) thus.

Skȳe. Largest island of Inner Hebrides; ~ (*terrier*), small, long-bodied, short-legged, long-haired variety of Scotch terrier, of slate or fawn colour.

slăb[1] *n.* Flat, broad, comparatively thick piece of solid material, as stone, timber, etc.; large flat piece of cake, chocolate, etc.; (logging) rough outside piece cut from log or tree-trunk. ~ *v.t.* Cut slab(s) from (log, tree); cover, support, protect with slabs; roll steel ingots into slabs in *slabbing-mill*.

slăb[2] *adj.* (archaic, chiefly with ref. to 'Macbeth', IV. i. 32). Thick, viscous.

slăbb'er *n.* & *v.* = SLOBBER.

slăck[1] *adj.* Sluggish, remiss, relaxed, languid, loose, inactive, negligent; (of heat etc.) gentle, moderate; ~ *water*, water with no apparent motion, esp. tidal water about turn of tide. **slăck'ly** *adv.* **slăck'nĕss** *n.* **slăck** *n.* Slack part of rope; slack time in trade etc.; (pl.) trousers for informal or sports wear. ~ *v.* Slacken, make loose; take rest, be indolent, slow *up*; slake (lime); ~ *off*, abate vigour.

slăck² *n.* Very small or refuse coal, coal-dust.

slăck'en *v.* Make, become, loose or slack.

slăck'er *n.* Shirker, lazy person.

slăg *n.* Dross separated in fused vitreous state in smelting of ores; clinkers; volcanic scoria; ~ *wool*, mineral wool. ~ *v.i.* Form slag, cohere into slag-like mass.

slāke *v.t.* Quench, allay (thirst), cause (lime) to heat and crumble by action of water or moisture.

sla'lŏm (slah-) *n.* Ski-race downhill on zig-zag course between artificial obstacles, usu. flags.

slăm¹ *v.* Shut (door etc.) violently with loud bang; (of door etc.) shut thus; put *down* (object) with similar sound. ~ *n.* Sound (as) of slammed door.

slăm² *n.* Winning of all tricks (*grand* ~) or of all tricks but one (*little* ~) in whist, euchre, bridge, etc.

sla'nder (-ah-) *n.* False report maliciously uttered to person's injury; false oral defamation; defamation, calumny (compare LIBEL). ~ *v.t.* Utter slander about, defame falsely. **sla'nderous** *adj.* **sla'nderously** *adv.* **sla'nderousnĕss** *n.*

slăng *n.* Language in common colloquial use but considered to be outside standard educated speech and consisting either of new words or phrases or of current words used in new sense; cant, special language of some class or profession. ~ *adj.* Of, expressed in, slang. ~ *v.t.* Use abusive language to.

slăng'y (-ngĭ) *adj.* Of the character of, given to the use of, slang. **slăng'ily** *adv.* **slăngĭ'nĕss** *n.*

slant (-ah-) *n.* Slope, oblique position; (slang) opportunity; (slang) point of view, personal attitude or opinion. ~ *adj.* Sloping, inclined, oblique. ~ *v.* Slope, diverge from a line, have or take oblique direction or position.

slăp *n.* Smart blow esp. with palm of hand or something flat; smack. ~ *v.t.* Strike with such blow; ~-*bang*, violently, noisily; *slap'dash*, hasty, careless, happy-go-lucky; (*adv.*) in slapdash manner; *slap'stick*, (orig. U.S.) flexible lath used by harlequin in pantomime; (of) boisterous knockabout type of comedy; ~-*up*, (vulg.) first-rate, splendid, done regardless of expense. ~ *adv.* Suddenly, noisily, headlong.

slăsh *v.* Cut, cut at, with sweep of sharp weapon or instrument; make gashes (in); slit (garment) to show contrasting lining etc.; lash with whip, crack (whip); make drastic economies in (budget etc.). ~ *n.* (Wound or slit made by) slashing cut.

slăt *n.* Long narrow strip of wood or metal, lath, esp. one of a series forming a Venetian blind, one of the crosspieces of a bedstead on which the mattress rests. ~ *v.* Flap, strike, with noisy sound, esp. of sails, ropes, etc.

S. lat. *abbrev.* South latitude.

slāte¹ *n.* Very fine-grained grey metamorphic rock which cleaves perfectly in one direction, freq. at an angle to the bedding plane; thin usu. rectangular plate of this or other stone as roofing material (ill. ROOF); tablet of slate, usu. framed in wood, for writing on; ~-*coloured*, ~-*grey*, the dark, freq. bluish or greenish, grey of slate; ~-*pencil*, stick of soft slate used for writing on slate. **slāt'y** *adj.* **slāte** *v.t.* Cover, roof, with slates.

slāte² *v.t.* (colloq.) Criticize severely, scold, rate.

slătt'ern *n.* Sluttish woman. **slătt'ernly** *adj.*

slaught'er (-awt-) *n.* Slaying, esp. of many persons or animals at once, carnage, massacre; ~-*house*, place for killing cattle or sheep, shambles. ~ *v.t.* Kill in ruthless manner or on great scale; butcher, kill for food.

slaught'erous (-awt-) *adj.* Murderous.

Slav (-ahv) *n.* Member of any of the peoples belonging to the Slavonic linguistic group, inhabiting large parts of E. and central Europe, and including Russians, Poles, Czechs, Bulgarians, Serbo-Croats, Slovenes, etc. ~ *adj.* Of the Slavs, Slavonic, Slavonian.

slāve *n.* Person who is the legal property of another, servant completely divested of freedom and personal rights; human chattel; helpless victim *to*, *of*, some influence; submissive or devoted servant; drudge; ~ *bangle*, *bracelet*, wide bracelet freq. worn above elbow; ~-*driver*, superintendent of slaves at work; hard taskmaster; ~-*ship*, ship employed in slave-trade; ~ *States*, those southern States of N. America in which slave-holding was formerly legal; ~-*trade*, traffic in slaves, esp. former transportation of African Negroes to America. ~ *v.i.* Work like slave, drudge.

slāv'er¹ *n.* Ship or person engaged in slave trade.

slăv'er² *n.* Saliva flowing or falling from mouth. ~ *v.* Let saliva run from mouth; wet with saliva, slobber. **slăv'ery¹** *adj.*

slāv'ery² *n.* Condition of a slave; slave-holding; drudgery.

slāv'ey *n.* Hard-worked female domestic servant, maid of all work.

Slăv'ĭc *adj.* & *n.* (chiefly U.S.) Of the Slavs, SLAVONIC.

slāv'ĭsh *adj.* Of, like a slave, servile; showing no originality or independence.

Slavōn'ĭa. District of N. Yugoslavia bordering on Hungary, between the Sava, Drava, and Danube rivers. **Slavōn'ĭan** *adj.* & *n.* 1. (Language, native) of Slavonia. 2. (less freq.) Slav, Slavonic.

Slavŏn'ĭc *adj.* & *n.* (Language) of the Slavs; ~ *languages*, group of Indo-European languages spoken in E. and central Europe, including Russian, White Russian, Ukrainian, Polish, Czech, Bulgarian, Serbo-Croatian, and Slovene.

slaw *n.* Salad of sliced cabbage.

slay *v.t.* (past t. *slew* pr. -ōō, past part. *slain*). (chiefly poet. and rhet.) Kill.

S/Ld *abbrev.* Squadron Leader.

slĕd *n.* & *v.* (chiefly dial. and U.S.) = SLEDGE¹.

slĕdge¹ *n.* Vehicle mounted on runners instead of wheels for conveying loads or passengers, esp. over snow or ice. ~ *v.* Travel, go, convey, in sled or sledge.

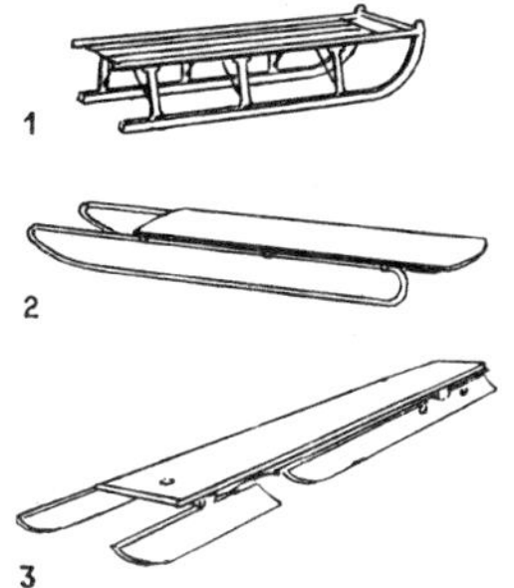

SLEDGES

1. Luge. 2. Steel skeleton toboggan. 3. Bob-sleigh

slĕdge² *n.* (also ~-*hammer*) Large heavy hammer usu. wielded with both hands, esp. that used by blacksmith (ill. HAMMER).

sleek *adj.* (Of hair, fur, surface, etc.) soft, smooth and glossy, polished. ~ *v.t.* Make sleek. **sleek'ly** *adv.* **sleek'nĕss** *n.*

sleep *n.* Bodily condition regularly and naturally assumed by man and other animals, in which the postural and other muscles are relaxed and consciousness is largely suppressed, though it may be re-established by a sensory disturbance; period or occasion of this; inert condition of some animals in hibernation; (fig.) death; rest, quiet, peace; ~-*walking*, somnambulism. ~ *v.* (past t. and past part. *slĕpt*). Be in state of sleep; fall, be, asleep; rest in death; spend in, affect by, sleeping; stay for the night *at*, *in*, etc.; provide sleeping accommodation for; be inactive or dormant; (of top) spin so steadily as to seem motionless; *sleeping-bag*, bag, usu. lined or padded, for sleeping in, esp. out-of-doors; *Sleeping Beauty*, heroine of fairy tale who slept for 100 years; *sleeping-car*, *-carriage*, railway carriage with berths or beds; *sleeping-draught*, drink inducing sleep, opiate; *sleeping partner*, partner taking no share in actual working of business; *sleeping sickness*, (1) freq. fatal disease characterized by extreme lethargy, prevalent in parts of W. and S. Africa and caused by a trypanosome (*Trypanosoma gambiense*) transmitted by the bite of an insect allied to the tsetse fly; (2) SLEEPY sickness; *sleeping-suit*, pyjamas.

sleep'er *n.* (esp.) Wooden beam etc. used as (usu. transverse) support for rails of railway etc. (ill. RAIL); (colloq.) sleeping-car; ~ *wall*, wall supporting beams of floor.

sleep'y *adj.* Drowsy, ready for sleep; inactive, indolent, without stir or bustle; (of fruit, esp. pears) beginning to rot; ~ *sickness*, pop. name of an epidemic disease, *Encephalitis lethargica*, a form of inflammation of the brain, usu. accompanied by extreme drowsiness and sometimes resulting in mental and nervous degeneration. **sleep'ily** *adv.* **sleep'iness** *n.*

sleet *n.* Hail or snow falling in a half-melted state. **sleet'y** *adj.*

sleeve *n.* Part of garment covering arm; tube or hollow shaft

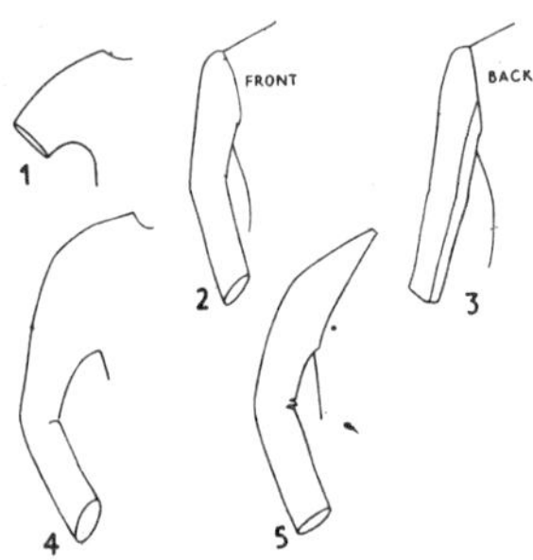

SLEEVE

1. Magyar. 2. Straight. 3. Tailored. 4. Dolman. 5. Raglan

fitting over rod, spindle, etc.; wind-sock, drogue; cover for gramophone record; ~*-board*, small ironing-board over which sleeves can be fitted for pressing; ~*-nut*, long nut with right- or left-hand screw-threads for connecting pipes or shafts conversely threaded; ~*-valve*, internal combustion engine's valve with sleeve(s) fitting interior of cylinder, sliding with piston, and so designed and controlled that inlet and exhaust ports are uncovered at proper stages in cycle. **sleeved** (-vd) *adj.*

sleeve'less (-vl-) *adj.* Without sleeves; (of errand, now rare) ending in, leading to, nothing, bootless.

sleigh (slā) *n.* Sledge, esp. as passenger-vehicle drawn by horse(s); ~*-bells*, small bells attached to sleigh or harness of sleigh-horse.

sleight (slīt) *n.* Dexterity, cunning, artifice (archaic exc. in) ~*-of-hand*, conjuring, legerdemain, trick(s) displaying great dexterity, esp. performed so quickly as to deceive the eye.

Sleip'nir (slāp-). (Norse myth.) Odin's 8-footed horse.

slĕn'der *adj.* Of small girth or breadth, slim, not stout; scanty, slight, meagre, relatively small. **slĕn'derly** *adv.* **slĕn'derness** *n.*

Slesvig = SCHLESWIG.

sleuth(-hound) (slōō-) *n.* Bloodhound; detective. ~ *v.* Track, trail; play the detective.

slew, slue (-ōō) *v.* Turn or swing round on its axis. ~ *n.* Slewing, sluing.

slīce *n.* Relatively thin flat broad piece or wedge cut from esp. meat, bread, or cake; share, portion; (golf) slicing stroke; kinds of implement with thin broad blade used in cookery etc., esp. (*fish-*~) for lifting or serving

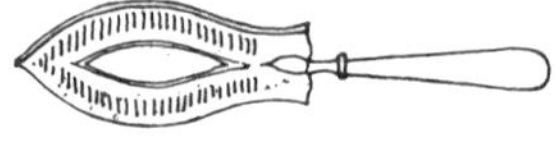

FISH SLICE

fish. ~ *v.* Cut into slices, cut (piece) *off*; cut cleanly or easily; (golf) strike (ball) so that it flies or curves to right (or, in the case of a left-handed player, to the left).

slĭck *adj.* Sleek; smooth, plausible; adroit, deft, quick, cunning. ~ *v.t.* Smooth, sleek. **slĭck'ly** *adv.* **slĭck'ness** *n.*

slĭck'er *n.* (U.S.) Long loose waterproof overcoat; (U.S. colloq.) well-dressed plausible rogue.

slīde *v.* (past t. and past part. *slĭd*). (Make) progress along smooth surface with continuous friction on same part of object progressing; glide over ice without skates in more or less erect posture; glide, go smoothly along, pass easily or gradually; *let* (something) take its own course; ~*-rule*, rule graduated along one edge according to the logarithms of the numbers from 1 to 100 and along the other according to the logarithms of the numbers from 1 to 10 (enabling squares and square roots to be read off directly), and having a similarly graduated sliding piece along its centre (enabling numbers to be multiplied or divided by adding or subtracting their logarithms); ~*-valve*, valve with sliding plate for opening and closing orifice, esp. in steam engine (ill. STEAM). ~ *n.* Act of sliding; track on ice made by sliding; slope prepared with snow or ice for tobogganing; inclined plane down which goods etc. slide to lower level; part(s) of machine on or between which sliding part works; part of machine or instrument that slides; *stop* ~, (organ) strip of wood perforated with holes under each rank of pipes, which stops off rank when moved sideways (ill. ORGAN); thing slid into place, esp. glass holding object for microscope or magic-lantern picture (ill. MICROSCOPE); kind of clasp for keeping hair tidy.

slīd'ing *adj.* That slides; ~ *door, lid, panel*, etc., door, lid, etc., drawn across aperture by sliding sideways instead of turning on hinges; ~ *rule*, slide-rule; ~ *scale*, scale (of payments, wages, etc.) rising or falling in proportion or conversely to, rise or fall of some other standard.

slight (-īt) *adj.* Slender, slim, thin; not good or substantial, rather flimsy or weak; small in amount, degree, etc., unimportant, trifling. **slight'ly** *adv.* **slight'ness** *n.* **slight** *n.* Instance of slighting or being slighted; contemptuous indifference or disregard. ~ *v.t.* Treat with indifference or disrespect, disregard, disdain, ignore.

Slĭg'ō. Maritime county in NW. Eire.

slĭm *adj.* Slender, (gracefully) thin; small, slight, meagre. **slĭm'ly** *adv.* **slĭm'ness** *n.* **slĭm** *v.* Make, become, slim, esp. by dieting, exercise, etc.

slīme *n.* Fine oozy mud; any substance of similar consistency. ~ *v.t.* Cover with slime.

slīm'y *adj.* Of the consistency of slime; covered or smeared with slime; vile, disgusting, repulsively meek or flattering. **slīm'ily** *adv.* **slīm'iness** *n.*

sling[1] *n.* 1. Weapon, consisting of strap attached to two cords or to staff, for hurling stones etc.; ballista. 2. Belt, rope, etc., formed into loop, with hooks and tackle, for securing bulky or heavy articles while being hoisted or lowered; strap, band, etc., supporting something suspended; bandage etc. formed into loop

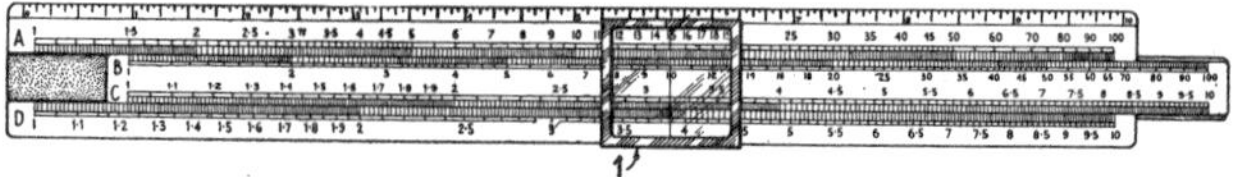

SLIDE-RULE

1. Cursor

round neck to support injured arm. ~ *v.* (past t. and past part. *slŭng*). 1. Throw, cast, hurl; hurl (stone etc.) from sling, use sling. 2. Suspend with sling; hoist or transfer with sling; hang up, suspend, esp. between two points.

slĭng[2] *n.* (U.S.) Spirit, esp. gin, with water, sugar, etc., drunk hot or iced.

slĭnk *v.i.* (past t. *slŭnk* or rarely *slănk*, past part. *slŭnk*). Move, go, in quiet, stealthy, or sneaking manner. **slĭnk'y** *adj.* (Of woman's garment) close-fitting.

slĭp[1] *n.* Finely ground clay, flint, etc., mixed with water to consistency of cream and used for making, cementing, decorating, etc., pottery, tiles, etc.; *~-ware*, pottery coated with slip.

slĭp[2] *n.* 1. Act of slipping; blunder, accidental piece of misconduct; slip-stream. 2. Kinds of loose covering or garment, e.g. pillow-case, petticoat, bathing-drawers. 3. Leash for slipping dogs; device for suddenly loosing clip or attachment. 4. Inclined plane on which ships are built or repaired. 5. Long narrow strip of thin wood, paper, etc.; printer's proof on such paper. 6. Cutting taken from a plant for grafting or planting; scion; young, esp. slender, person. 7. (cricket) Fielder stationed for balls glancing off bat to off side behind batsman (ill. CRICKET); (usu. pl.) this part of ground. ~ *v.* 1. Slide unintentionally for short distance; lose footing, balance, etc., by unintended sliding; go with sliding motion, move easily or unperceived, glide, steal; escape restraint or capture esp. by being slippery or hard to hold; make careless mistake (also, colloq., ~ *up*). 2. Let go (hounds etc.) from restraint of some kind; pull (garment etc.) hastily *on*, *off*; make pass or move stealthily, casually, or with gliding motion; escape from, give the slip to; (naut.) allow (anchor-cable) to run out when leaving anchorage hastily, drop (anchor) thus; (of animals) miscarry with, drop (young) prematurely. **slip-** in combination: *~-case*, close-fitting case in which a book is issued and from or into which it can be readily slipped; *~-carriage*, *coach*, etc., carriage that can be detached from railway train while running; *~-knot*, knot that can be undone by a pull; knot that slips up and down rope etc. and tightens or loosens loop; *~-stream*, current of air driven astern by propulsion unit of an aircraft producing the thrust which moves the aircraft forwards; *slip'way*, inclined way leading into water in a dock or shipbuilders' yard (ill. LAUNCH); runway for take-off of aircraft.

slĭpp'er *n.* Light loose comfortable indoor shoe; skid or shoe placed under wagon-wheel as drag; *~-bath*, partly covered slipper-shaped bath.

slĭpp'ery *adj.* With smooth, polished, oily, slimy, or greasy surface making foothold insecure, or making object etc. difficult to grasp or hold; (fig.) elusive, unreliable, shifty, unscrupulous; **slĭpp'erĭly** *adv.* **slĭpp'erĭnėss** *n.*

slĭpp'y *adj.* Slippery; *be*, *look*, ~, (slang) look sharp, make haste.

slĭp'shŏd *adj.* With shoes down at heel; slovenly, negligent, careless, unsystematic.

slĭt *n.* Long incision; long narrow opening comparable to cut. ~ *v.* Cut or tear lengthwise, make slit in, cut into strips; ~ *trench*, narrow trench made to accommodate a soldier or a weapon.

slĭth'er (-dh-) *v.i.* (colloq.) Slide unsteadily, go with irregular slipping motion.

slĭv'er *n.* Piece of wood torn from tree or timber, splinter; (fishing) side of small fish cut off as bait. ~ *v.* Break off as sliver, break up into slivers.

slivovice, -vitz (slēv'ovĭts) *n.* Alcoholic spirit distilled from plums esp. in Yugoslavia, plum brandy.

slŏbb'er *v.* & *n.* Slaver, drivel. **slŏbb'ery** *adj.*

slōe *n.* (Small ovate bluish- or purplish-black fruit of) blackthorn; ~ *gin*, gin flavoured with sloes and sweetened.

slŏg *v.* Hit hard and freq. wildly, esp. in boxing and cricket; work hard and doggedly, plod. ~ *n.* Heavy random hit. **slŏgg'er** *n.*

slōg'an *n.* Highland war-cry (Sc.); party-cry, watchword, motto; advertiser's phrase calculated to catch the eye. [Gael. *sluagh* host, *gairm* outcry]

slōōp *n.* Small one-masted fore-and-aft-rigged vessel; ~ (*of war*), small ship-of-war with guns on upper deck only.

slŏp[1] *n.* (pl.) Dirty water or liquid, waste contents of kitchen or bedroom vessels; (pl.) liquid or semi-liquid food of weak unappetizing kind; *~-basin*, *-bowl*, basin for receiving rinsings of cups at table; *~-pail*, pail for removing bedroom slops. ~ *v.* Spill, (allow to) flow over edge of vessel; spill or splash liquid upon.

slŏp[2] *n.* (pl.) Ready-made, esp. cheap or badly made clothes; (pl.) clothes and bedding supplied to sailors in navy; *~-room*, room from which slops are issued on man-of-war; *~-shop*, shop for cheap ready-made clothes.

slōpe *n.* Stretch of rising or falling ground; inclined surface or way; upward or downward inclination, deviation from horizontal or perpendicular. ~ *v.* Take, form, move in, be in, place or arrange in, a slope or inclined direction or position; (slang) make *off*, go away.

slŏpp'y *adj.* Wet, splashed, full of puddles; messy with liquid; watery and disagreeable; weak, feeble, slovenly, maudlin, weakly sentimental. **slŏpp'ĭly** *adv.* **slŏpp'ĭnėss** *n.*

slŏsh *v.t.* (slang) Beat, thrash. ~ *n.* 1. A heavy blow. 2. = SLUSH.

slŏt[1] *n.* Groove, channel, slit, long aperture, made in machine, fabric, etc., to admit some other part, esp. slit for coin that sets working *~-machine*, automatic retailer of small wares. ~ *v.t.* Provide with slot(s).

slŏt[2] *n.* Track of animal, esp. deer; trace, trail.

slōth *n.* 1. Laziness, indolence. 2. Kinds of long-haired slow-moving arboreal mammal of tropical Central and S. America, with two (*Choloepus*) or three (*Bradypus*) toes on each fore-foot; *~-bear*, common shaggy black-haired bear (*Melursus labiatus*), feeding on fruit, insects, and

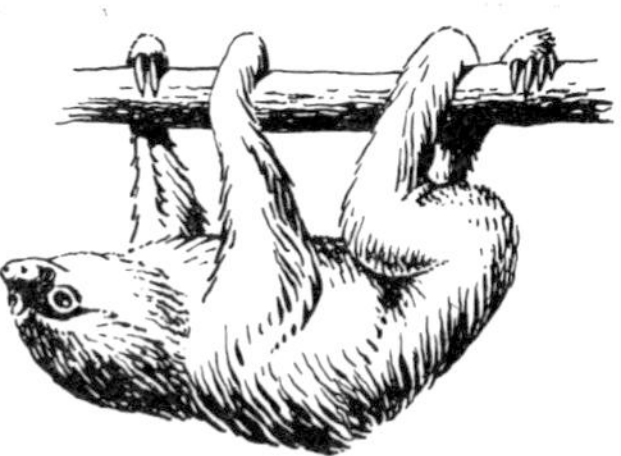

TWO-TOED SLOTH

honey, of India and Ceylon. **slōth'ful** *adj.* Lazy. **slōth'fully** *adv.* **slōth'fulnėss** *n.*

slouch *v.* Droop, hang down negligently; go, stand, etc., with loose ungainly stoop of head and shoulders; pull or bend down brim of hat, esp. over face. ~ *n.* Slouching gait or posture, stoop; downward bend of hat-brim; ~ *hat*, soft hat with wide flexible brim.

slough[1] (-ow) *n.* Quagmire, swamp, miry place; *S~ of Despond*, in Bunyan's 'Pilgrim's Progress', deep miry place between City of Destruction and wicket-gate at beginning of Christian's journey; state of hopeless depression.

slough[2] (-ŭf) *n.* Outer skin periodically cast by snake etc.; any part cast or moulted by an animal; dead tissue from surface of wound, ulcer, etc. ~ *v.* Drop off as slough; cast slough.

Slō'văk *adj.* & *n.* (Member) of a Slavonic people inhabiting chiefly Slovakia and S. Moravia; (of) their language. **Slova'kĭa** (-vah-). Territory forming the E. part of *Czechoslovakia*, formerly a part of Hungary.

slov'en (-ŭv-) *n.* Person who is careless, untidy, or dirty in personal appearance or slipshod and negligent in work etc. **slov'enly** *adj.* **slov'enliness** *n.*

Slōv'ēne *adj.* & *n.* (Member, language) of the Slavonic people inhabiting chiefly Slovenia and neighbouring parts of Yugoslavia. **Slōvēn'ia.** Territory forming a federal unit of NW. Yugoslavia, bordering on Austria and Italy. **Slovēn'ian** *adj.* & *n.* Slovene.

slow (-ō) *adj.* 1. Not quick, taking a long time to do a thing or traverse a distance; gradual; tardy, lingering; not hasty; (of clock etc.) behind correct time; (of surfaces) tending to cause slowness (*a ~ pitch, billiard-table*, etc.). 2. Dull-witted, stupid; deficient in liveliness or interest, dull, tedious. 3. *slow'coach*, slow, idle, or indolent person; *~ match*, slow-burning fuse or match for igniting explosives; *~-motion*, (of film etc.) exposed at high speed, so that all movements etc. appear slow when film is projected at normal speed. **slow'ly** *adv.* **slow'ness** *n.* **slow** *adv.* Slowly. *~ v.* Reduce one's speed, reduce speed of.

slow-worm (slō'-wĕrm) *n.* Small European legless lizard (*Anguis fragilis*), blindworm (ill. LIZARD).

slŭb *n.* Thick place or lump in yarn or thread; (attrib., of material etc.) with irregular effect produced by warp of uneven thickness.

slŭdge *n.* Thick greasy mud; sewage; muddy or slushy sediment or deposit; sea-ice newly formed in small pieces. **slŭdg'y** *adj.*

slue *n.* & *v.* = SLEW.

slŭg[1] *n.* 1. Kinds of slimy gastropod mollusc with rudimentary or no shell, many of which are very destructive to small plants. 2. Roughly or irregularly shaped bullet or other piece of metal; (printing) thick piece of metal used in spacing; line of type in linotype printing. 3. (eng., as measure in calculating acceleration) That mass to which a force of 1 lb. will impart an acceleration of 1 ft per second in every second.

slŭg[2] *n.* & *v.t.* (colloq., chiefly U.S.) (Strike with) hard heavy blow.

slŭg'-abĕd *n.* (archaic) One who lies late in bed.

slŭgg'ard *n.* Lazy sluggish person.

slŭgg'ĭsh *adj.* Inert, inactive, slow-moving, torpid. **slŭgg'ĭshly** *adv.* **slŭgg'ĭshness** *n.*

sluice (-ōōs) *n.* (Gate in) dam or embankment with sliding gate or other contrivance for controlling volume or flow of water (ill. LOCK); any device for regulating flow of water; artificial water-channel, esp. in gold-washing. *~ v.* Provide with sluice(s); flood with water from sluice; rinse, pour or throw water freely upon; (of water etc.) rush (as) from sluice.

slŭm[1] *n.* Dirty squalid overcrowded street, district etc. inhabited by the very poor. **slŭmm'y** *adj.* **slŭm** *v.i.* Go about in slums for philanthropic or charitable purposes, or out of curiosity.

slŭm[2] *n.* The non-lubricating part of crude oil; gummy residue formed in lubricating oil during use.

slum'ber *n.* & *v.i.* Sleep (chiefly poet. and rhet.). **slŭm'b(e)rous** *adj.* **slŭm'b(e)rously** *adv.*

slŭmp *n.* Heavy, sudden, or continued fall in prices, demand for commodity etc. (opp. BOOM[3]). *~ v.i.* Undergo slump, fall in price, fall through, fail; flop, sit, down heavily and slackly.

slŭng past t. and past part. of SLING.

slûr *v.* 1. Smudge, blur; pronounce indistinctly, with sounds running into one another; (mus.) sing, play, two or more notes smoothly and connectedly; mark with slur. 2. Pass lightly *over*, conceal, minimize. *~ n.* 1. Slight, discredit, blame. 2. Slurred sound or utterance; (mus.) curved line (⌒, ⌣,) over or under two or more notes to be sung or played without a break or as smoothly as possible.

slŭsh *n.* Watery mud or thawing snow; soft greasy mixture of oil etc. or other materials, used to lubricate or protect machinery etc.; (fig.) silly sentiment. **slŭsh'y** *adj.*

slŭt *n.* Slovenly woman, slattern. **slŭtt'ĭsh** *adj.* **slŭtt'ĭshly** *adv.* **slŭtt'ĭshness** *n.*

slȳ *adj.* 1. Cunning, wily, deceitful; practising concealment, working, moving, etc., in stealthy or underhand manner. 2. Knowing, arch, bantering, insinuating. **slȳ'ly** *adv.* **slȳ'ness** *n.*

slȳpe *n.* (archit.) Covered passage-way from transept or cloister of cathedral or monastic church to chapter-house or deanery (ill. CHURCH).

S.M. *abbrev.* Sergeant-Major; short metre.

smăck[1] *n.* Flavour, taste; trace, tinge, suggestion, *of* something. *~ v.i.* Have taste or savour *of*, suggest the presence *of*.

smăck[2] *n.* Sharp slight sound as of surface struck with palm, lips parted suddenly, etc.; blow with palm, slap; hard resounding hit with cricket-bat; loud kiss. *~ v.* Slap with palm; part (lips) noisily, (of lips) be parted, in eager anticipation or enjoyment of food etc.; crack (whip). *~ adv.* (colloq.) (As) with a smack, slap; outright, exactly.

smăck[3] *n.* Single-masted sailing-vessel, rigged like sloop or cutter, for coasting or fishing; (U.S.) fishing-vessel with well for keeping fish alive.

smăck'er *n.* (slang) Loud kiss; sounding blow; (U.S.) dollar.

small (-awl) *adj.* Not large, of comparatively little size, strength, power, or number; consisting of minute units; (of agent) not acting on large scale; poor, mean, humble; ungenerous, not much of; unimportant, trifling; petty, paltry; *~ arms*, portable fire-arms, esp. rifle, pistol, light machine-gun; *~ beer*, weak or poor beer; (fig.) trivial or unimportant matters, persons, etc.; *~-clothes*, (archaic) knee-breeches; *~-holding*, agricultural holding smaller than farm; also, piece of land (1 to 50 acres) let or sold by a county council to a *small-holder*; *~ hours*, the hours from 1 o'clock to 3 or 4, after midnight; *~-sword*, light tapering sword for thrusting only (ill. SWORD); *~ talk*, ordinary social conversation, chat. *~ n.* The small, slender, or narrow part of anything, esp. the back; (pl.) small kinds of bread etc.; (pl., formerly, at Oxford) responsions. *~ adv.* Into small pieces, on small scale, etc.; *sing ~*, adopt humble tone or manner.

small'pŏx (-awl-) *n.* Acute contagious febrile disease, often endemic in occurrence, characterized by pustular eruption, usu. leaving scars or pits on skin.

smalt (-awlt) *n.* Glass coloured deep blue with oxide of cobalt; this pulverized and used as pigment.

smarm, smalm (-ahm) *v.t.* (dial. & colloq.) Smooth, plaster *down*; flatter fulsomely. **smârm'y** *adj.* Fulsomely flattering or ingratiating.

smârt[1] *n.* Sharp pain, stinging sensation. *~ v.i.* Feel, cause, smart.

smârt[2] *adj.* 1. Severe, sharp; lively, vigorous, brisk. 2. Clever, quick, ingenious; quick at looking after one's own interests. 3. Alert, brisk; neat, trim; stylish, fashionable, elegant. **smârt'en** *v.* **smârt'ly** *adv.* **smârt'ness** *n.*

smăsh *n.* Breaking to pieces; violent fall, collision, or disaster; commercial failure, bankruptcy; violent and heavy blow; (lawn tennis) hard overhand stroke;

CUTTER-RIGGED SMACK

1. Gaff sail

~-*up*, complete smash. ~ *v.* Break utterly to pieces, shatter, bash *in*; utterly rout and disorganize; break, come to grief, go bankrupt; (of vehicle etc.) crash; (lawn tennis) hit (ball) in smash; ~-*and-grab*, (colloq.) (of robberies) in which shop-window etc. is broken and goods snatched from it. ~ *adv.* With a smash. **smăsh'ing** *adj.* (slang) Very fine, wonderful.

smătt'ering *n.* Slight superficial knowledge (*of*). **smătt'erer** *n.* One who possesses a smattering (*of*).

smear *v.* Daub with greasy or sticky substances or with something that stains, make greasy or sticky marks on; blot, obscure outlines of; (orig. U.S.) blacken character of, discredit publicly. **smear'y** *adj.* **smear** *n.* Mark, smudge, blotch, made by smearing.

smĕll *n.* 1. Sense by which odours are perceived, and of which nose is organ; act of smelling, sniff. 2. Property of things affecting sense of smell, odour; bad odour, stench. ~ *v.* 1. Perceive smell of, detect presence of by smell; use sense of smell, sniff *at*; hunt *out* by smell; (fig.) discover, find *out*, as if by smell; perceive smells, have sense of smell. 2. Emit smell; suggest or recall the smell *of*; stink, be rank. 3. *smelling-bottle*, small bottle of *smelling-salts*, preparation of ammonium carbonate and scent, to be sniffed as cure for faintness etc. **smĕll'y** *adj.* (colloq.) Evil-smelling, stinking.

smĕlt[1] *n.* Various small edible fishes, esp. of genus *Osmerus*, allied to salmon, with greenish backs, silvery sides and belly, and delicate tender rather oily flesh.

smĕlt[2] *v.t.* Fuse or melt (ore) to extract metal; obtain (metal) thus.

Smetana (smĕt'*ana*), Bedřich (1824–84). Czech musician, composer of 'The Bartered Bride', a humorous opera.

smew *n.* Small duck (*Mergus albellus*) of Europe and Asia, the smallest of the mergansers.

smĭl'ăx *n.* 1. Large genus of liliaceous climbing plants, freq. with prickly stems, some tropical species of which yield sarsaparilla from tuberous root-stocks. 2. S. African climbing asparagus (*Asparagus asparagoides*) much used in decoration.

smīle *v.* Express pleasure, amusement, affection, indulgent scorn, incredulity, etc., with slight more or less involuntary movement of features, upward curving of corners of mouth, parting of lips, etc.; look (*up*)*on*, *at*, with such expression; express by smiling; drive *away*, bring *into* or *out of* (mood), by smiling; be, appear, propitious; look pleasant, have bright aspect; ~ *on*, show favour to, approve of. ~ *n.* Act of smiling; smiling expression or aspect.

smĭrch *v.t.* & *n.* Stain, soil, smear, spot (also fig.).

smĭrk *v.* & *n.* (Put on) affected or silly smile; simper.

smīte *v.* (past t. *smōte*, past part. *smĭtt'en*). Strike (*upon*), hit, chastise, defeat (chiefly poet. and rhet.); (chiefly in past part. *smitten*) strike, seize, infect, possess, *with* disease, love, etc.

smĭth[1] *n.* Worker in metal, esp. iron, blacksmith.

Smĭth[2], Adam (1723–90). Scottish political economist, author of 'The Wealth of Nations' (1776) which established political economy as a separate science.

Smĭth[3], Joseph (1805–44). Founder of the sect of MORMONS.

Smĭth[4], Sydney (1771–1845). English churchman, essayist, and wit; author of the 'Letters of Peter Plymley' (1807) in defence of Catholic emancipation.

smĭthereens' (-dh-) *n.pl.* (colloq.) Small fragments.

Smĭth'field. Orig., open space outside the NW. walls of City of London, a market for cattle and horses; later the central meat-market; in 16th c., scene of burning of heretics.

Smĭthsōn'ian Institution. Establishment for increase and diffusion of knowledge founded 1846 in Washington under will of an English mineralogist and chemist, James Smithson (1765–1829; earlier known as James Lewis Macie); it comprises a national museum, mainly of zoology and ethnology, and an astrophysical observatory.

smĭth'y (-dhĭ) *n.* Blacksmith's workshop, forge.

S.M.O *abbrev.* Senior Medical Officer.

smŏck *n.* 1. Chemise (archaic). 2. Loose-fitting outer garment of shirt-like shape, usu. with closely gathered upper part, formerly worn by farm-labourers, now chiefly by small children. ~ *v.t.* Adorn with **smŏck'ing,** form of needlework with honeycomb ornamentation on basis of very close thick gathers.

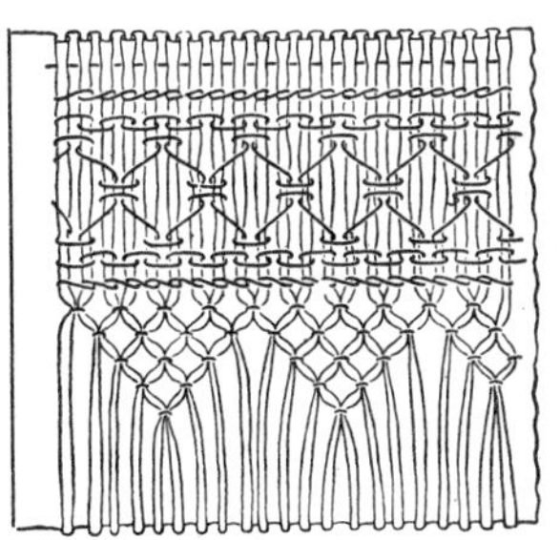

SMOCKING

smŏg *n.* Smoky fog.

smōke *n.* 1. Visible volatile product given off by burning or smouldering substances; *a* cloud or column of this esp. used as signal etc. 2. Cigar or cigarette; spell of smoking tobacco etc. 3. ~-*bomb*, bomb emitting dense clouds of smoke on bursting, for forming smoke-screen; ~-*box*, chamber in steam boiler between flues and chimney-stack; ~-*screen*, dense volume of smoke diffused by funnel of vessel, smoke-bomb, etc., to conceal naval or military operations etc.; ~-*stack*, chimney, chimney-pipe. ~ *v.* 1. Emit smoke or visible vapour, reek, steam; (of chimney, lamp, etc.) emit smoke, be smoky, as result of imperfect draught etc. 2. Colour, darken, obscure, with smoke; preserve or cure by exposure to smoke; fumigate; suffocate, stupefy, drive *out*, rid of insects, etc., with smoke. 3. Inhale and exhale smoke of (tobacco, opium, etc.); smoke tobacco; bring *into* specified state by smoking; *smoking-car*(*riage*), *compartment*, carriage, etc., for smokers on railway train; ~-*concert*, concert at which smoking and drinking are allowed; ~-*room*, room set apart for smoking in.

smōk'er *n.* (esp.) Person who habitually smokes tobacco; smoking-carriage on train.

smōk'y *adj.* Emitting, veiled or filled with, obscure (as) with, smoke; stained with, coloured like, smoke. **smōk'ĭly** *adv.* **smōk'inėss** *n.*

Smŏll'ėtt, Tobias George (1721–71). Scottish novelist, by profession a surgeon; author of 'Roderick Random', 'Peregrine Pickle', 'Humphrey Clinker', etc.

smōlt *n.* Young salmon at stage between parr and grilse, when it is covered with silvery scales and migrates to sea for first time.

smōōth (-dh) *adj.* With surface free from projections, wrinkles, lumps, or undulations; not rough, uneven, or hairy; (of ground etc.) not broken or obstructed, easily traversed; not harsh in sound, taste, etc.; pleasant, polite, unruffled; bland, insinuating, flattering; ~-*bore*, gun with unrifled barrel; ~-*faced*, hypocritically or plausibly bland, friendly, or polite; ~-*spoken*, -*tongued*, smooth, plausible, flattering, in speech; soft-spoken. **smōōth'ly** *adv.* **smōōth'nėss** *n.* **smōōth** *v.* Make or become smooth; free from impediments etc.; *smoothing-iron*, flat-iron. ~ *n.* Smoothing touch or stroke.

smo'ther (-ŭdh-) *n.* Dense or suffocating smoke, dust, fog, etc. ~ *v.* Suffocate, stifle, be suffocated or stifled, esp. with smoke; deaden or extinguish (fire) by excluding air with ashes etc.; suppress, conceal, cover (*up*); cover closely or thickly (*in*).

smoul'der (smōl-) *v.i.* Burn

and smoke without flame (freq. fig.).

s.m.p. *abbrev. Sine mascula prole* (= without male issue).

smŭdge[1] *n.* Dirty mark, smear, blur, blot. ~ *v.* Soil, stain, smirch, smear.

smŭdge[2] *n.* Outdoor fire with dense smoke to drive away insects.

smŭg *adj.* Self-satisfied, consciously respectable, complacent. **smŭg'ly** *adv.* **smŭg'nėss** *n.*

smŭgg'le *v.* Convey (goods), convey goods, clandestinely into or out of country to avoid payment of customs duties etc.; convey stealthily or secretly *in, out,* put *away* into concealment. **smŭgg'ler** *n.*

smŭt *n.* 1. Fungous disease of cereals and other plants, with (parts of) grain covered with blackish powdery spores; any fungus causing this. 2. (Black mark, smudge, made by) flake of soot. 3. Indecent or obscene language. **smŭtt'y** *adj.* **smŭtt'ĭly** *adv.* **smŭtt'inėss** *n.* **smŭt** *v.t.* Mark with smut(s); infect (grain etc.) with smut.

Smŭts, Jan Christiaan (1870–1950). South African general, philosopher, and statesman; prime minister of the Union of S. Africa 1918–24, 1939–48.

Smyr̄n'a. (Turk. *Izmir*). City and port of Asia Minor, at head of *Gulf of* ~, on W. coast of Anatolia. **Smyr̄n'ĭot(e)** *n.* Inhabitant of Smyrna.

snăck *n.* Slight, casual, or hurried meal; ~*-bar, -counter,* counter where sandwiches and other snacks may be obtained.

snăff'le *n.* Simple kind of bridle-bit. ~ *v.t.* Put snaffle on (horse); (slang) appropriate, seize, purloin.

snăg *n.* Jagged projecting point, as stump or branch left on tree after pruning or cutting, trunk or large branch of tree embedded in bottom of river etc., with end pointed upwards; (fig.) impediment, obstacle, unexpected drawback. ~ *v.t.* Run upon or damage by a snag.

snail *n.* Any aquatic or terrestrial gastropod mollusc with well-developed spiral or whorled shell capable of covering whole body; slow-moving or indolent person; ~(*-wheel*), spiral cam, esp. in striking mechanism of clock.

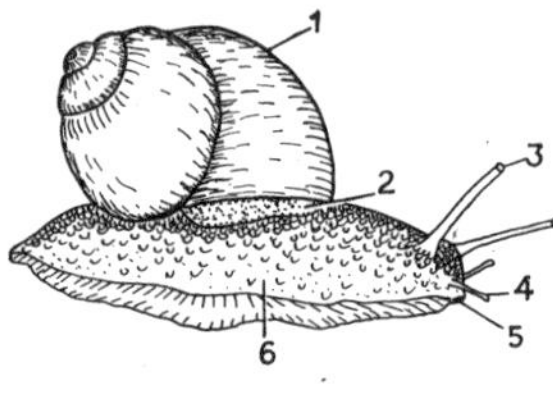

SNAIL

1. Shell. 2. Mantle. 3. Eye. 4. Tentacle. 5. Mouth. 6. Foot

snāke *n.* 1. Limbless reptile of sub-order *Ophidia,* serpent; pop., also snake-like limbless lizards and amphibians; treacherous or ungrateful person; ~ *in the grass,* lurking danger, secret enemy. 2. *S*~, Amer. Indian of various Shoshonee groups of western U.S. 3. ~*-fence,* (U.S.) zigzag fence of split rails or poles; ~*-root,* (root of) various Amer. plants, esp. *Aristolochia serpentia* and *Polygala senega,* reputed to be antidotes to snake-poison, and used in medicine; ~*'s head* (*lily*), common fritillary, *Fritillaria meleagris*; ~*-wood,* (wood, used as remedy for snake-poison, of) various E. Indian shrubs and trees of genus *Strychnos*; (hard heavy wood, with snake-like markings, of) S. Amer. timber-tree *Piratinera guianensis.* **snāk'y** *adj.* Infested with snakes; snake-like; (chiefly of hair of Furies) composed of snakes.

snăp *n.* 1. (Bite, cut, with) sudden quick closing of jaws or scissors; sudden break or fracture; sound of snapping, quick sharp sound. 2. Small crisp gingerbread cake or biscuit. 3. Spring-catch or one closing with snapping sound. 4. Card-game in which, when two cards of same value are turned up, the first player to call 'snap' has the right to take cards from other player(s). 5. Sudden, usu. brief, spell of frost or cold. 6. Alertness, vigour, energy; dash. 7. Snapshot. 8. *attrib.* (esp. of parliamentary and similar proceedings) Taken by surprise, brought on without notice, as ~ *debate* etc. 9. *snap'dragon,* various plants with pouched flowers that can be made to gape, esp. *Antirrhinum*; Christmas game of plucking raisins from burning brandy; ~*-fastener,* press-stud, fastener consisting of two parts which are pressed together; ~ *lock,* lock shutting automatically with spring when door etc. is closed; ~ *shot,* quick shot without deliberate aim; so ~*-shooter*; *snap'shot,* instantaneous photograph, esp. with hand-camera; (*v*). take such photograph (of). ~ *v.* 1. Make quick or sudden bite; speak irritably; say ill-tempered or spiteful things. 2. Pick *up* (esp. bargain) hastily. 3. Break sharply; produce sudden sharp sound from, emit sharp report or crack; close with snapping sound; ~ *fingers,* make audible fillip (*at*), esp. in contempt. 4. Take snapshot of. 5. *snapping turtle,* various large ferocious Amer. freshwater turtles seizing prey with snap of jaws. **snăpp'er** *n.* (esp.) Snap-fastener; snapping turtle; various carnivorous food-fishes (family *Lutianidae*) of warm seas.

snăpp'ĭsh *adj.* Peevish, testy, malicious, ill-natured. **snăpp'ĭshly** *adv.* **snăpp'ĭshnėss** *n.*

snăpp'y *adj.* 1. Snappish. 2. Quick, vigorous, lively, full of life or spring; *make it* ~, (colloq.) be quick about it.

snāre *n.* Device for catching birds or animals, esp. with running noose of cord, wire, etc. (freq. fig. of temptation etc.); (surg.) wire loop or similar device for removing morbid growths; gut or rawhide string stretched across lower head of side-drum; ~*-drum,* side-drum. *v.t.* Catch with snare.

snarl[1] *n.* (chiefly U.S.) Tangle, esp. of wool, hair, or the like; tangled condition.

snarl[2] *v.* (Of dog) make angry or quarrelsome sound with bared teeth; (of person) grumble viciously, use ill-tempered or surly language; express by snarling. ~ *n.* Act or sound of snarling.

snătch *v.* Make sudden snap or catch *at,* seize hurriedly or eagerly; rescue narrowly *from*; carry suddenly *away, from.* ~ *n.* Hasty catch or grasp, grab or snap *at*; brief period, short spell (*of*); small amount, fragment, short burst (*of* song, talk, etc.); brief view, glimpse. **snătch'y** *adj.* In short spells, disconnected. **snătch'ĭly** *adv.*

sneak *n.* Mean-spirited or underhand person; telltale; (cricket) ball bowled along ground; ~*-thief,* one who steals what is in reach without breaking into buildings. ~ *v.* 1. Slink, go furtively. 2. (slang) Make off with, steal. 3. (school slang) Peach, tell tales. 4. *sneaking,* furtive, not avowed.

sneak'ers *n.pl.* (slang) Soft-soled shoes or slippers.

sneer *v.* Smile derisively (*at*); express or suggest derision or disparagement in speech or writing; take *away* (person's reputation etc.) by sneering. ~ *n.* Sneering look or remark.

sneeze *v.i.* Perform sudden involuntary convulsive expiration through the nose as a result of irritation of the mucous membrane, from catarrh, effect of dust, etc.; ~ *at,* despise, disregard, underrate. ~ *n.* Act of sneezing; sound thus produced.

snĭb *n.* (chiefly Sc.) Bolt, fastening, catch, of door, window, etc. ~ *v.t.* Bolt, fasten.

snĭck *n.* 1. Slight notch or cut. 2. (*cricket*) Batsman's light glancing blow deflecting ball slightly. ~ *v.t.* Make snick in; (cricket) slightly deflect (ball) with bat.

snĭck'er *n.* & *v.i.* Whinny, neigh; snigger.

snĭckersnee' *n.* (joc.) Large knife. [f. earlier *snick-or-snee,* fight with knives, f. Du. *steken* thrust, *snijen,* cut]

snīde *adj.* & *n.* (slang) Counterfeit, bogus (jewellery, coin(s)).

snĭff *v.* Draw up air audibly through nose to stop it from running, in smelling *at* something, or as expression of contempt; draw (*up*) (air, liquid, scent), draw up scent of, into nose. ~ *n.* Act or sound of sniffing; amount sniffed up. [imit.]

snĭf'ter *n.* (slang) Small amount of spirits etc.

snĭft'ĭng-vălve *n.* Valve in steam-engine for blowing out air, steam, etc., or drawing in air (ill. LOCOMOTIVE).

snĭgg'er *v.i.* & *n.* (Utter) half-suppressed secretive laugh.

snĭp *v.* Cut with scissors etc., esp. in small quick strokes. ~ *n.* Act of snipping; piece snipped off; (sporting slang) something easily won or obtained, a certainty.

snīpe *n.* Various wading birds of genus *Gallinago*, related to woodcocks, frequenting marshy places and having characteristic

SNIPE
Length 10½ in.

long straight bill. ~ *v.* Shoot snipe; (mil.) shoot at (men) one at a time, usu. from cover and at long range; shoot, shoot *at*, thus. **snī'per** *n.*

snĭpp'ėt *n.* Small piece cut off, snipping; (fig.) scrap, fragment, (pl.) odds and ends. **snĭpp'ėty** *adj.*

snĭpp'ĭng *n.* (esp.) Clipping, cutting.

snĭtch *v.* (slang) 1. Inform, peach. 2. Steal, 'pinch'.

snĭv'el *v.i.* Run at the nose; make sniffing or snuffling sound; be in tearful state, show maudlin emotion. ~ *n.* Running mucus; slight sniff; hypocritical emotion.

S.N.O. *abbrev.* Senior Naval Officer.

snŏb *n.* 1. (chiefly dial.) Cobbler; cobbler's apprentice. 2. Person who meanly or vulgarly admires, imitates, or seeks to associate with, those of superior social position or wealth, and looks down on those he considers inferior; also *transf.* of intellectual and artistic levels etc. **snŏbb'ĭsh** *adj.* **snŏbb'ĭshly** *adv.* **snŏbb'ĭshnėss, snŏbb'ery** *ns.*

snoek (-ōō-) *n.* Large edible fish, *Thyrsites atun*, of S. Africa, allied to horse-mackerel.

snōōd *n.* 1. (Sc., archaic) Fillet worn round hair by young unmarried woman. 2. (sea-fishing) Any of the short lines attaching baited hook to main line.

snōōk (*or* -ōō-) *n.* (slang) Contemptuous gesture with thumb to nose and fingers spread out; *cock a* ~, make this gesture.

snōōk'er (pool) *n.* Variety of pool played with 15 red balls, having a value of one each, and 6 balls of other colours, having values of 2 to 7, which the striker may only play at after having pocketed a red ball. **snōōk'ered** (*-erd*) *adj.* With balls in such a position that direct play is impossible; (slang) defeated, baffled.

snōōp *v.i.* (slang, orig. U.S.) Pry inquisitively.

snōōt'y *adj.* (slang, orig. U.S.) Contemptuous, supercilious.

snōōze *v.* & *n.* (Take) short sleep, esp. in day-time; pass (time) thus.

snōre *n.* & *v.* (Make) harsh or noisy respiration through mouth, or mouth and nose, during sleep; pass (time) *away* in snoring.

snorkel: see SCHNORKEL.

Snŏ'rri Sturl'uson (stoor-) (1178–1244). Icelandic historian, author of the 'Heimskringla', a history of the kings of Norway, and of the Prose EDDA.

snōrt *n.* 1. Loud or harsh sound made by driving breath violently through nose, or noise resembling this. 2. Funnel providing submarine with air and enabling it to remain below surface for long periods. ~ *v.* Make sound of snort; express by snorting, utter with snorts.

snōrt'er *n.* (esp.) Stiff gale; anything remarkable for size, violence, etc.

snŏt *n.* (vulg.) Mucus of the nose. **snŏtt'y.** *adj.* (vulg.) Running or foul with snot. ~ *n.* (naval slang) Midshipman.

snout *n.* Projecting part of head of animal, including nose and mouth, (contempt.) person's nose; projecting part, structure, nozzle, etc., resembling snout.

snow (-ō) *n.* 1. Atmospheric vapour condensed and frozen into small, usu. hexagonal, crystals, and falling in clusters of these known as flakes; the fall of these, layer of them on ground; fall or accumulation of snow (usu. pl.). 2. Something resembling snow, esp. in whiteness; white hair; (cookery) creamy or snowy-looking dish; white blossom etc. 3. (slang) Cocaine. 4. *snow'ball*, snow pressed into ball, esp. as missile; anything growing or increasing rapidly, like snowball rolled along ground; guelder rose; *snow'ball* (*v.*) pelt with, throw, snowballs; increase rapidly; *snow'berry*, (fruit of) various plants or shrubs with white berries; *~-bird*, various small white or partly white birds, esp. *~-bunting*; *~-blind*, with vision affected by glare of sun on snow; *~-broth*, melted or melting snow; *~-bunting*, small finch, *Plectrophenax nivalis*, breeding in Arctic regions, and common in Europe and N. America in winter, with brown-and-white or black-and-white plumage; *~-drift*, snow piled up in heap by action of wind; *snow'drop*, (flower or plant of) small early-flowering bulbous plant, *Galanthus nivalis*, with white pendent flower; *snow'flake*, one of flakes or small crystalline masses in which snow falls; any (white flower or) plant of bulbous genus *Leucojum*, esp. spring-flowering *L. vernum*, resembling snowdrop; *~-goose*, white goose (*Anser hyperboreus*) of N. America and N. Asia, breeding in Arctic regions; *~-line*, level above which snow never completely disappears; *~-man*, mass of snow formed into figure of man; *~-plough*, device for clearing snow from railway track, road, etc.; *~-shoe*, one of pair of racket-shaped frames of light wood strung with rawhide, enabling wearer to walk on surface of snow; *~-storm*, storm with heavy fall of snow; an effect of electrical interference on a television screen; *~-white*, white as snow, pure white. **snow'y** (-ōĭ) *adj.* **snow** *v.* 1. *It is snowing*, snow falls. 2. Let fall as or like snow; strew, cover, (as) with snow; ~ *under*, bury in snow, (fig.) submerge, overwhelm; ~ *up*, block, imprison, with fallen snow.

Snowd'on (-ō-). Highest mountain (3,560 ft) of Wales.

snŭb[1] *v.t.* 1. Rebuff, reprove, humiliate, in sharp or cutting manner. 2. Check way of (ship) suddenly, esp. by rope wound round post. ~ *n.* Snubbing, rebuff.

snŭb[2] *adj.* (of nose) Short and turned up, whence *snub-nosed*.

snŭff[1] *n.* Charred part of candle-wick, esp. as black excrescence obscuring light. ~ *v.* Trim snuff from (candle, wick) with fingers, scissors, etc.; ~ *out*, extinguish thus; (slang) die. **snŭff'ers** *n.pl.* Scissors for snuffing candle, with box to catch snuff (ill. CANDLE).

snŭff[2] *n.* Powdered tobacco for sniffing up into nostrils; *~-box*, small box for holding this; *~-mill*, small mill for grinding snuff. **snŭff'y** *adj.* **snŭff** *v.* Sniff (*up*, *in*, *at*).

snŭff'le *v.* Sniff, esp. audibly or noisily; speak or say nasally, whiningly, or like one with a cold. ~ *n.* Sniff; snuffling sound or speech.

snŭg *adj.* Sheltered, comfortable, cosy; (of ship etc.) trim, neat, well protected from bad weather. **snŭg'ly** *adv.* **snŭg'nėss** *n.* **snŭg** *n.* (dial. or slang) Bar-parlour of inn.

snŭgg'ery *n.* Snug place, esp. private room or den; bar-parlour.

snŭg'gle *v.* Move, lie, close *up to* for warmth; hug, cuddle.

sō *adv.* & *conj.* To extent, in manner, with result, described or indicated; of the kind, in the condition, etc., already indicated, by that name or designation; on condition set forth or implied; for that reason, consequently, therefore, accordingly; indeed, in actual fact, also, as well; *so-and-so*, used as substitute for name or expression not exactly remembered or not needing to be specified; *so so*, indifferent(ly) only passable, only passably; *or so*, or thereabouts.

S.O. *abbrev.* Section Officer; Staff Officer; Stationery Office; sub-office.

soak *n.* Soaking; drinking-bout; hard drinker. ~ *v.* Place, lie, for some time in liquid, steep; make, be, saturated or wet through; take *up*, suck *in*, liquid; (of liquid) make way *in(to)*, *through*, by saturation; drink persistently, booze.

soap *n.* Cleansing agent, essentially sodium salts of fatty acids (palmitic, stearic) usu. forming lather when rubbed in water; *soft* ~, kind remaining semi-fluid, potassium salts of fatty acids; (fig.) flattery; ~*-bubble*, iridescent bubble made from thin film of soap and water; *soapflakes*, specially prepared flakes of soap for washing clothes etc.; ~*-stone*, steatite, a massive variety of talc with smooth greasy feel; ~*-suds*, water impregnated with dissolved soap; ~*-wort*, various herbaceous plants of genus *Saponaria*, yielding detergent substances, esp. *S. officinalis*. ~ *v.t.* Rub, smear, lather, treat, with soap; (slang) flatter.

soap'y *adj.* Like, smeared or impregnated with, suggestive of, soap; ingratiating, unctuous, flattering.

soar (sōr) *v.i.* Fly at, mount to, great height; hover or sail in air without flapping of wings or use of motor power.

sŏb *v.* Draw breath in convulsive gasps, usu. with weeping; utter with sobs; bring one*self into* state, *to sleep*, with sobbing. ~ *n.* Convulsive catching of breath, esp. in weeping.

sōb'er *adj.* Not drunk; temperate in regard to drink; moderate, well-balanced, sedate, temperate; (of colour) quiet, inconspicuous. **sōb'erly** *adv.* **sōb'er** *v.* Make, become, sober.

Sōbiĕs'kĭ, John (1624–96). King of Poland 1674–96; defender of his country against the Cossacks and Turks; relieved Vienna when it was besieged (1683) by the Turks.

Sōbra'nje, -ye (-ahnyĕ) *n.* Bulgarian elective national assembly.

sobrī'ėty *n.* Being sober.

sōb'rĭquet (-kā) *n.* Nickname.

Soc. *abbrev.* Socialist; Society.

sŏc'age *n.* (hist.) Feudal tenure of land by payment of rent or services other than military service.

sŏcc'er (-k-) *n.* (colloq. abbrev. for) ASSOCIATION football.

sō'ciable (-sh*a*-) *adj.* Fitted or inclined for company of others, not averse to society, ready to converse; of, characterized by, friendly or pleasant companionship. **sō'ciably** *adv.* **sōciabĭl'ĭty** *n.* **sō'ciable** *n.* 1. (obs.) Open four-wheeled carriage with seats facing each other, and box for driver; tricycle etc. with two seats side by side; Victorian S-shaped or circular couch. 2. (U.S.) Informal social gathering, esp. of church members.

sō'cial (-shl) *adj.* 1. Of, marked by, friendly intercourse; enjoyed, taken, in company with others; inclined to friendly intercourse, sociable. 2. Living in companies or more or less organized communities, gregarious. 3. Of, concerned with, interested in, society and its constitution, or the mutual relations of men or classes of men; ~ *contract*, contract assumed by Rousseau ('Contrat Social', 1762) and other writers by which true freedom was obtained by mutual agreement to substitute a state of law for a state of individualism; *S~ Credit*, an economic doctrine propounded chiefly by Major C. H. Douglas according to which the potential abundance which modern industry can produce belongs to the whole community and ought to be made available to all by certain changes in the monetary policy, esp. the issue of National Dividends of Consumer Credit; *S~ Democrat*, member of socialistic political party, esp. (i) that founded in Germany 1863 by Ferdinand Lassalle, and united with Marxists 1875; (ii) Russian Marxist socialist party; (iii) moderate state-socialist party in Germany after 1919; ~ *history*, history of social behaviour; *S~ Revolutionary*, member of former Russian non-Marxist socialist party; ~ *science*, the study of human society regarded as a science (freq. taken to include not only sociology but economics, political science, social anthropology, and social psychology); *S~ War*, (Gk hist.) war between Athenians and their allies, 357–355 B.C.; (Rom. hist.) war between Rome and her Italian allies, 90–89 B.C. **sō'cially** *adv.* **sō'cial** *n.* Social gathering, esp. one organized by club, association, etc.

sō'cialĭsm (-sh*a*-) *n.* Political and economic principle that community as a whole should have ownership and control of all means of production and distribution (opp. CAPITALISM and INDIVIDUALISM); policy aiming at this; state of society in which this principle is accepted. **sō'cialĭst** *n.* & *adj.*; *S~ International*, international organization with headquarters in London, formed 1923 at Hamburg chiefly from Second INTERNATIONAL. **sōcialĭs'tĭc** *adj.* **sōcialĭs'tĭcally** *adv.*

sō'cialīze (-sh*a*-) *v.t.* Make social or socialistic. **sōcialīzā'tion** *n.*

socī'ėty *n.* 1. State of living in association with other individuals; customs and organization of ordered community; any social community. 2. Leisured, well-to-do, or fashionable persons regarded as distinct part of community. 3. Association with others, companionship, company. 4. Association of persons with common interest, aim, principle, etc.; *S~ of Friends*: see FRIEND; *S~ of Jesus*: see JESUIT; *Royal S~*: see ROYAL SOCIETY.

Socī'ėty Islands. Group of islands in S. Pacific, named by Capt. Cook in honour of Royal Society; a French protectorate since 1844.

Socĭn'ĭan *adj.* & *n.* (Follower) of the doctrines of the Italian theologian *Socinus* (Lelio Sozzini, 1525–62) and his nephew Fausto Sozzini (1539–1604) who denied that Christ was divine. **Socĭn'ĭanĭsm** *n.*

sōcĭŏl'ogy (-sĭ- *or* -shĭ-) *n.* Study of human, esp. civilized, society; study of social problems, esp. with a view to solving them. **sōciolŏ'gĭcal** *adj.* **sōciolŏ'gĭcally** *adv.* **sōcĭŏl'ogĭst** *n.*

sŏck[1] *n.* 1. Short stocking not reaching knee. 2. Light shoe worn by comic actors on ancient Greek and Roman stage; comedy. 3. Removable inner sole for shoe, insole.

sŏck[2] *n.* (slang) Hard or violent blow. ~ *v.t.* Hit, strike hard; ~ (person) *one*, give him hard blow.

sŏck'ėt *n.* Hollow, usu. cylindrical, part or piece for thing to fit into, revolve in, etc.; hollow or cavity in which eye, tooth, bone, etc., is contained.

sŏck'eye (-kī) *n.* An Amer. fish, the blueback salmon, *Oncorhynchus nerka*. [Amer. Indian *sukai*]

sŏcl'e *n.* (archit.) Square block or plinth as support for pedestal, vase, statue, etc. (ill. PEDESTAL).

Socō'tra. Island E. of Gulf of Aden, in Aden Protectorate; capital, Tamarida.

Sŏc'ratēs (-z) (469–399 B.C.). Greek philosopher, who was tried at Athens on a charge of corrupting the young by his teaching, and sentenced to death (by drinking hemlock); he left no writings, but his method and doctrines are preserved in the Dialogues of PLATO. **Socrăt'ĭc** *adj.* Of, like, Socrates; ~ *irony*, pose of ignorance assumed in order to lead others into display of supposed knowledge; ~ *method*, method of inquiry and instruction by series of questions. **Socrăt'ĭcally** *adv.*

sŏd[1] *n.* Turf, (piece of) upper layer of grass-land, with grass growing on it. ~ *v.t.* Cover (ground) with sods.

sŏd[2] *n.* (vulg.) Sodomite.

sōd'a *n.* 1. (also *washing* ~) Sodium carbonate, Na_2CO_3, an alkaline substance occurring naturally in mineral state or in solution, used in manufacture of glass, soap, etc., and obtained orig. from ashes of marine plants; *baking-*~, sodium bicarbonate, $NaHCO_3$; *caustic* ~, sodium hydroxide, NaOH. 2.

Soda-water (see below). 3. ~ *biscuit*, ~ *bread*, ~ *cake*, ~-*scone*, biscuit, bread, etc., leavened with sodium bicarbonate; ~ *fountain*, apparatus for drawing soda-water kept under pressure; counter, shop, apparatus, for making and serving iced drinks, ice-cream, sundaes, etc.; ~-*water*, effervescent water charged under pressure with carbon dioxide and used alone or mixed with spirits, syrups, etc., as beverage.

sodăl'ity *n.* Confraternity, association, esp. Roman Catholic religious guild or brotherhood.

sŏdd'en *adj.* Saturated with liquid, soaked; heavy, doughy; stupid or dull with habitual drunkenness. [orig. past part. of SEETHE]

Sŏdd'y, Frederick (1877–1956). English chemist, researcher in radio-activity; awarded Nobel prize for chemistry, 1921.

sōd'ium *n.* Soft silver-white lustrous metallic element, oxidizing rapidly in air and reacting violently with water, closely resembling potassium in appearance and properties; symbol Na, at. no. 11, at. wt 22·989; ~ *bicarbonate*, $NaHCO_3$, used in baking (baking-soda) and medicinally as an antacid; ~ *carbonate*, Na_2CO_3, common washing soda; ~ *chloride*, NaCl, common salt; ~ *hydroxide*, NaOH, caustic soda. [named by Sir H. Davy, 1807, f. *soda*]

Sŏd'om. (O.T.) Ancient city near the Dead Sea, destroyed, along with Gomorrah, on account of its wickedness by fire from heaven (Gen. xviii–xix).

sŏd'omīte *n.* Person practising **sŏd'omy,** unnatural sexual intercourse, esp. between males.

Sōd'or. Medieval diocese comprising the Hebrides and the Isle of Man; now, as Sodor and Man, including only the Isle of Man.

S.O.E.D. *abbrev.* Shorter Oxford English Dictionary.

soĕv'er *adv.* & *suffix* used with generalizing or emphatic force after words or phrases preceded by *how*, *what*, *who*, etc.

sōf'a *n.* Long seat with raised back and end(s). [Arab. *ṣoffah*]

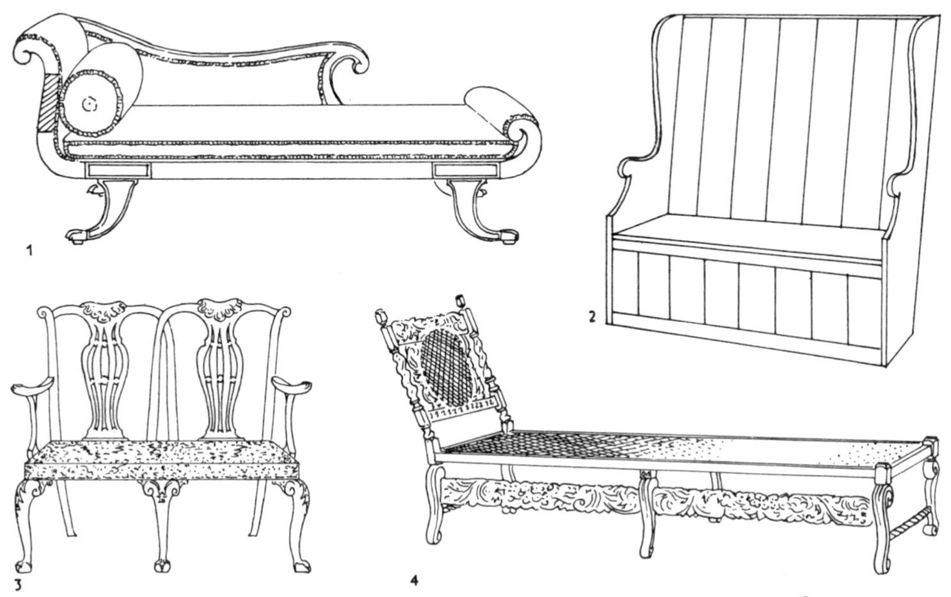

1. SOFA, EARLY 19TH C. 2. SETTLE, LATE 18TH C. 3. SETTEE, MID-18TH C. 4. DAY-BED, LATE 17TH C.

sŏff'ĭt *n.* (archit.) Under-surface of architrave, lintel, arch, etc. (ill. ARCH).

Sōf'i: see SUFI.

Sofī'a (-ē'*a*; *or* sŏf'ĭa). Capital city of Bulgaria.

soft (sŏ-, saw-) *adj.* 1. Not hard; yielding to pressure, malleable, plastic, easily cut; ~ *coal*, bituminous coal; ~ *currency*, currency of which other countries have earned more than they can willingly spend in the country whose currency it is and for which other economical outlets are not easily found (cf. HARD); ~ *goods*, textiles; ~ *palate*, membranous back part of the palate; ~ *roe*, roe of male fish; ~-*shell*(*ed*), having a soft or flexible shell; having shell not yet hardened owing to recency of moult; ~ *soap*: see SOAP. 2. Of smooth surface or fine texture, not rough or coarse; (of weather etc.) mellow, mild; rainy, moist. 3. (of water) Not containing calcium or other mineral salts which prevent formation of lather with soap. 4. Not astringent, sour, or bitter; not crude or brilliant; not sharply defined; not strident or loud; (phonet.) voiced; (of Russian consonants) palatalized, (of vowels) causing palatalization; (of the letters *c*, *g*) pronounced as spirants, not stops. 5. Gentle, quiet, conciliatory; sympathetic, compassionate; maudlin, feeble, flabby, weak; silly; (slang) easy; (colloq., orig. U.S., of drink) non-alcoholic. **soft'ly** *adv.* **soft'nėss** *n.* **soft** *adv.* Softly. ~ *int.* (archaic.) Wait a moment; hush!

soft'en (sŏfn, saw-) *v.* Become, make soft or softer; reduce strength of a defended position by bombing or bombardment (often with *up*); *softening of the brain*, morbid, esp. senile, degeneration of brain.

sŏgg'y *adj.* Sodden, saturated, heavy with moisture.

Sōhō' (*or* sō'hō). District of London S. of Oxford St and W. of Charing Cross Rd, with many French and Italian residents and foreign restaurants.

soigné (swahn'yā) *adj.* (Esp. of a woman's toilet) exquisite in detail, carefully arranged.

soil[1] *n.* The ground, upper layer of earth in which plants grow, consisting of disintegrated rock usu. with admixture of organic remains. **soil'lėss** *adj.*

soil[2] *v.* Make dirty, smear or

stain with dirt; tarnish, defile; admit of being soiled. ~ *n.* Dirty mark, smear, defilement; *~-pipe*, pipe conveying domestic sewage etc. to main sewer.

soil[3] *v.t.* Feed (cattle etc.) on fresh-cut green fodder.

soirée (swâr'ā) *n.* Evening party, social evening.

sojourn (sŭj'ern, sŏ-) *n.* & *v.i.* (Make) temporary stay in place.

sōke *n.* Right of local jurisdiction (hist.; now only in names of certain districts, as the *S~ of Peterborough*).

Sŏl[1] *n.* The sun personified.

sŏl[2] *n.* (mus.) 5th note of hexachord and of major scale in 'movable-doh' systems; note G in 'fixed-doh' system (see SOLMIZATION). [see UT]

sŏl[3] *n.* (physics, chem.) Liquid solution or suspension of colloid. [for *solution*]

sŏl[4] *n.* Principal monetary unit of Peru, = 100 centavos.

sōl'a *n.* Tall pithy-stemmed E. Indian swamp-plant; ~ *topee*, light-weight Indian sun-helmet of pith of this.

sŏl'ace *n.* Comfort, consolation. ~ *v.t.* Comfort, cheer, console.

sōl'an (goose) *n.* Gannet.

sŏlanā'ceous (-shus) *adj.* Belonging to the family (*Solanaceae*) which includes *Solanum*, *Capsicum*, *Atropa*, and other genera.

solān'um *n.* (Plant of) large genus (*S~*) of herbs, shrubs, and trees incl. nightshade, potato, etc.

sōl'ar *adj.* Of, concerned with, determined by, emanating from, the sun; ~ *month*, exact twelfth of the year; ~ *plexus*, (anat.) complex of nerves situated in abdomen behind stomach; ~ *system*, the sun with the 9 major planets and many minor planets, asteroids, comets, etc., held by its attraction and revolving round it; ~ *time*, time as shown on sun-dial. ~ *n.* = SOLARIUM; (in medieval house) upper chamber, esp. for private use of family (ill. HOUSE).

solar'ium *n.* (pl. *-ia*). Room, balcony, etc., enclosed in glass or open to air, for sun-bathing etc.

solā'tium (-shĭ-) *n.* Something given as compensation or consolation, esp. additional sum over and above actual damages.

sŏl'der (*or* sŏd-) *n.* Fusible metal or metallic alloy used for joining metal surfaces or parts. ~ *v.t.* Join with solder.

sōl'dier (-*jer*) *n.* Member of army, esp. private or non-commissioned officer; man of military skill and experience; ~ (*ant*), fighting ant or termite, larger and with larger head and jaws than workers (ill. TERMITE); ~ *crab*, hermit crab; ~ *of fortune*, one of adventurous character, willing to serve wherever his services are well paid. **sōl'dierlike, sōl'dierly** *adjs.* **sōl'dier** *v.* Serve as soldier; (naut. slang) shirk work. [OF *soude* pay f. L *solidus* gold coin]

sōl'diery (-jerĭ) *n.* *The* soldiers of a State, in a district, etc.

sōle[1] *n.* Lower surface of foot, that part of it which rests or is placed on ground in standing or walking; part of boot or shoe on which wearer treads (freq. excluding heel; ill. SHOE); bottom, foundation, or under-surface, of plough, wagon, golf-club head, etc. ~ *v.t.* Provide (boot etc.) with sole.

sōle[2] *n.* Common European flat-fish of genus *Solea*, highly esteemed as food; various other flat-fishes, esp. edible ones.

sōle[3] *adj.* One and only; exclusive; (archaic) alone, lonely; (law, of woman) unmarried. **sōle'ly** (-l-l-) *adv.*

sŏl'ėcism *n.* Offence against grammar or idiom, blunder in speech or writing; violation of good manners or etiquette. **sŏl'ėcist** *n.* **sŏlėcis'tic** *adj.*

sŏl'emn (-m) *adj.* Accompanied, performed, with religious rites or with ceremony; formal; ceremonious; impressive, awe-inspiring; serious, grave, earnest. **sŏl'emnly** (-mlĭ) *adv.* **sŏl'emnėss** *n.*

solĕm'nĭty *n.* Rite, celebration, festival, ceremony; solemn character, appearance, behaviour, etc.

sŏl'emnīze *v.t.* Celebrate, honour with ceremonies; duly perform (marriage ceremony); make solemn. **sŏlemnīzā'tion** *n.*

sōl'ėn *n.* Razor-shell (mollusc), (*S~*) genus to which this belongs.

solēn'oid (*or* sŏl'ė-) *n.* (elect.) Cylindrical coil of conducting wire which behaves as a bar magnet when a current is passed through it, and which can be used for producing magnets.

Sōl'ent. W. part of channel between Isle of Wight and mainland of England.

sŏl'-fa' (-ah) *n.* (mus.): see TONIC[2].

Sŏlferi'nō (-rē-). Village on Lake Garda, Italy, scene of defeat of Austrians by French and Sardinians, 1859.

Sol.-Gen. *abbrev.* Solicitor-General.

solĭ'cĭt *v.* Make appeals or requests to, importune; ask importunately or earnestly for; (of woman) accost and importune (man) for immoral purposes. **solĭcĭtā'tion** *n.*

solĭ'cĭtor *n.* 1. One who solicits or canvasses (chiefly U.S.). 2. (in English law) Member of legal profession qualified to advise clients and instruct barristers, but not to appear as advocate except in certain lower courts; *S~-General*, law-officer of Crown ranking next to Attorney-General or (in Scotland) Lord Advocate; in U.S., similar officer appointed by president to assist Attorney-General; in some States, chief law officer.

solĭ'cĭtous *adj.* Anxious, troubled, concerned; anxious, eager (*to* do). **solĭ'cĭtously** *adv.*

solĭ'cĭtūde *n.* Being solicitous, anxiety, concern.

sŏl'ĭd *adj.* Of stable shape, not liquid or fluid, rigid, hard and compact; of three dimensions; of solid substance throughout, not

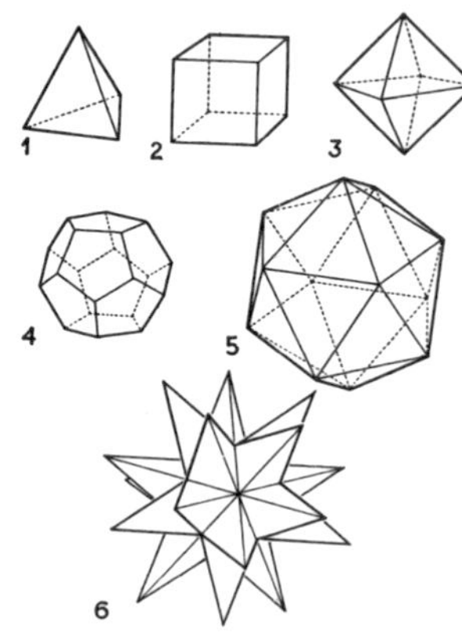

REGULAR SOLIDS

1. Tetrahedron. 2. Cube. 3. Octahedron. 4. Dodecahedron. 5. Icosahedron. 6. Stellated solid

hollow, without internal cavities or interstices, uninterrupted; homogeneous, alike all through; firm, substantial, well grounded, sober, real, genuine; concerned with solids. **sŏl'ĭdly** *adv.* **sŏl'ĭdnėss, solĭd'ĭty** *ns.* **solĭd'ĭfȳ** *v.* **sŏl'ĭd** *n.* (geom.) Body or magnitude of 3 dimensions; solid substance or body.

sŏlĭdă'rĭty *n.* Community of interests, sympathies, and action.

sŏlĭdŭng'ūlar, -ate (-ngg-) *adjs.* = SOLIPED.

sŏl'ĭdus *n.* (pl. *-dī*). Gold coin of the Roman Empire, orig. worth *c* 25 denarii; shilling(s) (only in abbrev. *s.*); shilling line as in 7/6.

solĭl'oquy (-kwĭ) *n.* Talking to oneself or without addressing any person; instance of this, esp. on part of character in play. **solĭl'oquīze** *v.i.*

sŏl'ĭpĕd *adj.* & *n.* Solid-hoofed (animal), as horse.

sŏl'ĭpsism *n.* (metaphys.) View that the self is the only object of real knowledge or the only really existent thing. **sŏl'ĭpsist** *n.*

sŏlĭtaire' *n.* 1. Precious stone, usu. diamond, set by itself. 2. Card-game for one person, patience (now chiefly U.S.); game for one player, played on a board with marbles or pegs which are removed by jumping as in draughts, the object being to clear the board.

sŏl'ĭtary *adj.* Alone, living alone, not gregarious, without companions; single, separate; secluded, lonely. **sŏl'ĭtarily** *adv.* **sŏl'ĭtarinėss** *n.* **sŏl'ĭtary** *n.* Recluse, hermit.

sŏl'ĭtūde *n.* Being solitary; lonely place.

sŏlmĭzā'tion *n.* Singing a

passage at sight to the sol-fa syllables by any of the systems in use ('fixed-doh', with C always as doh and other syllables accordingly; 'movable-doh', with keynote always as doh and other syllables accordingly).

sōl'ō *n.* 1. Piece of vocal or instrumental music, dance, performed by one person or instrument, with or without subordinate accompaniment. 2. Kinds of card-game in which one player plays or may play alone against the others. 3. Solo flight (see below). ~ *adj.* Alone, without companion or partners; ~ *flight*, aeroplane flight made without companion or instructor; ~ *whist*, form of whist in which person making highest bid (e.g. *solo*, 5 tricks; *misère*, no tricks; *abundance*, 9 tricks) plays alone against the other three; a player bidding abundance has the right to choose the trump suit.

sō'lōist *n.* Musician etc. who performs alone or takes principal part.

Sŏl'omon. (O.T.) King of Israel *c* 970–933 B.C.; son and successor of David; famed for his wisdom and magnificence; built the Temple at Jerusalem; *Judgement of* ~, his proposal to cut in two the baby that was claimed by two women at once (2 Kings iii. 16–28); *Song of* ~: see SONG; ~*'s seal*, herbaceous plant (*Polygonatum multiflorum*) with broad sessile leaves and drooping greenish-white flowers on arching stems; also, magic symbol formed by two interlaced triangles forming a six-pointed star. **Sŏlomŏn'ic** *adj.*

Sŏl'omon Islands. Group of islands in S. Pacific, E. of New Guinea, under British protection.

Sōl'on (*c* 638–558 B.C.). Early Athenian legislator and reformer of the constitution, renowned for his wisdom.

sŏl'stice *n.* Time when sun is farthest from equator and appears to stand still, occurring twice yearly, on 21st or 22nd June (*summer* ~) and 22nd or 23rd Dec. (*winter* ~), and corresponding with the longest and shortest days of the year; point in ecliptic reached by sun at solstice (ill. CELESTIAL). **sŏlstĭ'tial** (-shl) *adj.*

sŏl'ūble *adj.* That can be dissolved; that can be solved; ~ *glass* = WATER-glass. **sŏlūbĭl'ĭty** *n.* **sŏl'ūbilize** *v.*

solu'tion (-ōō-, -ū-) *n.* 1. Solving, being solved; instance or method of solving, explanation, answer. 2. Dissolving, being dissolved, conversion of solid or gas into liquid form by mixture with solvent; dissolved state; fluid substance produced by process of solution. 3. Breaking, breach (chiefly in ~ *of continuity*). **solu'tionist** (-sho-) *n.* (esp.) Solver of newspaper puzzles.

Solūt'rėan, Solūt'rian *adj.* Of the later Palaeolithic culture (immediately following the Aurignacian); named from remains found in a rock shelter at La Solutré, central France, with characteristic flint implements; worked by pressure-flaking (i.e. detaching flakes from the edges with a primitive form of hammer and punch).

sŏlve *v.t.* Explain, resolve, answer; (math.) find answer to (problem etc.). **sŏl'vable** *adj.* **sŏlvabĭl'ĭty** *n.*

sŏl'vency *n.* Being financially solvent.

sŏl'vent *adj.* 1. Able to pay all one's debts or liabilities. 2. That dissolves or can dissolve. ~ *n.* Substance (usu. liquid) capable of dissolving something; dissolving or disintegrating agent.

Sŏl'way Firth. Arm of Irish Sea forming estuary of River Esk and W. part of boundary between England and Scotland.

Som. *abbrev.* Somerset.

Soma'lĭ (-mah-) *adj.* & *n.* (Member) of a dark-skinned Mohammedan Hamitic race inhabiting Somalia; their language, belonging to the Ethiopian group of Hamitic languages. **Soma'lĭa.** *The Somali Republic* occupies part of the NE. horn of Africa, extending along Gulf of Aden to beyond Equator; it consists of the former *British Somaliland* protectorate and the former Italian colony of *Somalia*; independent since 1960; capital, Mogadishu. **Soma'lĭland.** Former name of *Somalia*; *French* ~, small territory NW. of Somalia, opposite Aden; member of French Community; capital, Djibouti.

sōmăt'ic *adj.* Of the body, corporeal, physical; of the framework of the body as dist. from the internal organs; ~ *cell*, one of the cells forming tissues, organs, etc., of the body (dist. from GERM-*cell*).

sōm'atōme *n.* One of the segments into which bodies of many animals are divided.

sŏm'bre (-*er*) *adj.* Dark, gloomy, dismal. **sŏm'brely** *adv.* **sŏm'breness** *n.*

sŏmbrer'o (-ārō) *n.* Broad-brimmed, usu. felt, hat, of kind common in Spain and Spanish America.

some (sŭm) *adj.* & *pron.* Particular but unknown or unspecified (person or thing); a certain quantity or number of (something); an appreciable or considerable quantity of; (emphat., orig. U.S. slang) such in the fullest sense, something like. ~ *adv.* (slang) In some degree.

some'body (sŭm-) *n.* & *pron.* Some person; person of some note or consequence.

some'how (sŭm-) *adv.* In some indefinite or unspecified manner, by some means or other.

someone (sŭm'wŭn) *pron.* Somebody.

so'mersault, (rare) **so'mersĕt** (sŭ-) *ns.* Leap, spring, in which person turns heels over head in the air and alights on feet. ~ *v.i.* Make or turn somersault.

So'mersėt (sŭ-). County of SW. England.

So'mersėt House (sŭ-). 18th-c. building in the Strand, London, on site of palace built by a 16th-c. Duke of Somerset; contains offices of Revenue Department, principal Probate Registry, and Registrar-General of births, marriages, and deaths.

So'merville College (sŭ-). Women's college of University of Oxford, founded in 1879, and named after Mrs Mary Somerville (1780–1872), scientific writer and mathematician.

so'mething (sŭm-) *n.* Some thing (esp. as vague substitute for a n., adj., etc.). ~ *adv.* (archaic, exc. in ~ *like*) In some degree.

so'metīme (sŭm-), *adv.* & *adj.* 1. (archaic) Former(ly). 2. At some time. **so'metīmes** *adv.* At some times.

so'mewhat (sŭm-) *adv.* In some degree. ~ *pron.* (archaic) A certain amount, part, etc., *of* something.

so'mewhere (sŭm'wār) *adv.* In, at, to, some place.

sōm'īte *n.* Segment of animal body, esp. of vertebrate or arthropod embryo, somatome (ill. LOBSTER). **somĭt'ic** *adj.*

Sŏmme. River of NE. France running into English Channel; scene of almost continuous heavy fighting from 1915 to 1917, esp. July–Nov. 1916 (*Battles of the Somme*).

sŏmnăm'būlism *n.* Walking or performing other action during sleep; state characterized by this. **sŏmnăm'būlist** *n.* **sŏmnămbūlĭs'tic** *adj.*

sŏmnĭf'erous *adj.* Inducing sleep, soporific.

sŏm'nolent *adj.* Sleepy, drowsy; inducing drowsiness. **sŏm'nolently** *adv.* **sŏm'nolence, sŏm'nolency** *ns.*

son (sŭn) *n.* 1. Male child in relation to parent; male descendant; offspring, product, native, follower; ~-*in-law*, daughter's husband; ~ *of the soil*, native of district; worker on the land; dweller in the country. 2. *The S*~, (theol.) 2nd person of Trinity; *S*~ *of God*, ~ *of Man*, Jesus Christ.

sōn'ant *adj.* & *n.* Voiced (sound, letter).

sona'ta (-nah-) *n.* (orig.) Musical composition for instruments (usu. strings and keyboard) as opp. voice ('cantata'), in several movements, in *chamber* ~ usu. in dance rhythms, in *church* ~ of more abstract form and usu. including fugue; later, composition for one or two instruments, in several (usu. four or three) movements contrasted and related in mood, key, etc.; ~ *form*, composition in which two themes (*subjects*) are successively set forth, developed, and restated.

sŏnati'na (-tē-) *n.* Shorter or simpler form of sonata.

sŏng *n.* Singing, vocal music; musical utterance of certain birds; short poem set to music or meant to be sung; short poem, esp. in rhymed stanzas; poetry, verse; *a(n old)* ~, a mere trifle; *~-bird*, bird with musical song; *S~ of Solomon, S~ of S~s*, poetic book of O.T., traditionally ascribed to Solomon; ~ *sparrow*, a common sparrow (*Melospiza melodia*) of eastern N. America, with sweet song; *~-thrush*, the common thrush (*Turdus philomelus*). **sŏng'lèss** *adj.*

Song of Sol. *abbrev.* SONG of Solomon.

sŏng'ster *n.* (poet.) Singer; song-bird. **sŏng'strèss** *n.*

sŏn'ic *adj.* Of, using, sound waves, esp. (of apparatus) determining depth of water by reflection of sound waves; (of a mine) set off by sound vibrations; ~ *barrier*, the excessive resistance which air offers to objects moving at speeds approaching or not greatly exceeding that of sound, and which has to be overcome before greater speed can be obtained.

sŏnn'èt *n.* Poem of 14 lines arranged according to any of various definite schemes, each line having normally 10 syllables in English verse (but in Italian verse 11, in French 12); the forms commonest in English are the *Petrarchan* or 'Italian' ~, divided into an *octave* of 8 lines rhyming *a b b a a b b a* and a *sestet* of 6 lines with three rhymes more freely arranged, and the *Shakespearian* or 'English' ~ which consists of three quatrains and a couplet.

sonn'y (sŭ-) *n.* Familiar form of address to boy.

sŏnorĕs'cent *adj.* Capable of converting light- or heat-radiations into sound. **sŏnorĕs'cence** *n.*

sonōr'ous (*or* sŏn'-) *adj.* Resonant, (capable of) giving out esp. loud or rich sound; high-sounding. **sonōr'ously** *adv.* **sonōr'ousnèss, sonōr'ity** *ns.*

sōōn *adv.* Not long after present time or time in question, in a short time; early; willingly; *as* (*so*) ~ *as*, the moment that, not later than, as early as; *sooner or later*, at some time or other; *Sooner State*, pop. name of Oklahoma, U.S.

sŏŏt *n.* Black carbonaceous substance or deposit in fine particles formed by combustion of coal, wood, oil, etc.; *a* flake of soot. ~ *v.t.* Smear, smudge, cover, choke (*up*), with soot; sprinkle or manure with soot. **sŏŏt'y** *adj.* **sŏŏt'ily** *adv.* **sŏŏt'inèss** *n.*

sōōth *n.* (archaic) Truth, fact.

sōōthe (-dh) *v.t.* Calm, tranquillize; reduce force or intensity of (passion, pain, etc.).

sōōth'sayer *n.* One who foretells future events, diviner.

sŏp *n.* Piece of bread etc. dipped or steeped in liquid before eating or cooking; ~ (*to* CERBERUS), something given to pacify or bribe. ~ *v.* Soak, steep (*in* liquid), take *up* (liquid) by absorption; be drenched. **sŏpp'y** *adj.* Soaked, wet; (colloq.) mawkish, foolishly sentimental.

sŏph'ism *n.* Specious but fallacious argument, esp. one intended to deceive or mislead.

sŏph'ist *n.* 1. Paid teacher of rhetoric and philosophy in ancient Greece. 2. Captious or fallacious reasoner, quibbler. **sophis'tic(al)** *adjs.* **sophis'tically** *adv.* **sŏph'istry** *n.*

sŏph'ister *n.* Student in 2nd or 3rd year at Cambridge (hist.), Harvard, etc., in 3rd or 4th year at Trinity College, Dublin, and some Amer. universities.

sophis'ticāte *v.* 1. Adulterate (now rare); falsify, tamper with (text etc.); corrupt, spoil, by admixture of baser principle or quality. 2. Make artificial, deprive of simplicity; make worldly wise. **sophisticā'tion** *n.*

Sŏph'oclēs (-z) (495–406 B.C.). Athenian tragic poet; author of 'Oedipus the King', 'Oedipus at Colonus', 'Antigone', 'Electra', 'Trachiniae', 'Ajax', and 'Philoctetes'.

sŏph'omōre *n.* (U.S.) 2nd-year student in Amer. universities and colleges. **sŏphomōr'ic** *adj.*

sŏporif'ic *adj.* & *n.* (Drug) tending to produce sleep.

sopra'nō (-rah-) *n.* (Music for) highest singing voice in women and boys (ill. VOICE); singer with soprano voice or singing soprano part; ~ *clef*, C clef on first line of treble stave. **sopra'nist** *n.* Male adult singer retaining boy's soprano voice.

Sorāb'ian *adj.* & *n.* = SORBIAN.

sōrb[1] *n.* (Fruit of) service-tree or rowan.

Sōrb[2]. One of a Slavonic people inhabiting parts of eastern Saxony and Brandenburg, Wend. **Sōrb'ian** *adj.* Of, pertaining to, the Sorbs or their language. ~ *n.* A Sorb; the Slavonic language of the Sorbs.

Sorbŏnne'. Orig. a theological college founded in Paris by Robert de Sorbon, chaplain and confessor to Louis IX, *c* 1257; later, faculty of theology in University of Paris, suppressed 1792; now, seat of faculties of science and letters of University of Paris.

sōr'cerer *n.* User of magic arts, wizard, magician. **sōr'cerèss, sōr'cery** *ns.*

sōrd'id *adj.* Dirty, foul, mean, squalid; ignoble, base; avaricious, mercenary. **sōrd'idly** *adv.* **sōrd'idnèss** *n.*

sōrd'ine (-ēn) *n.* (mus.) Mute for bowed or wind instruments etc.; damper of a piano string (ill. PIANO).

sōre *n.* Place where skin or flesh of animal body is diseased or injured so as to be painfully tender or raw. ~ *adj.* Painful, causing pain, distressing, irritating, grievous; suffering pain; irritable, sensitive; (colloq.) irritated, annoyed. **sōre'ly** *adv.* **sōre'nèss** *n.* **sōre** *adv.* (archaic) Grievously, severely.

sōr'ghum (-gum) *n.* (Plant of) genus of tropical grasses including the cereal Indian millet and the Chinese sugar-cane (*sweet* ~).

sorīt'ēs (-z) *n.* (logic) Series of propositions in which predicate of each is subject of next and conclusion is formed of first subject and last predicate. **sorit'ic(al)** *adjs.*

sorō'rity *n.* (U.S.) Women's college or university society.

sorō's'is *n.* (bot.) Fleshy or pulpy compound fruit, as pineapple, mulberry.

sŏ'rrel[1] *n.* Various small sour-tasting perennial plants of genera *Rumex* and *Oxalis*, freq. used in cookery or medicine.

sŏ'rrel[2] *adj.* & *n.* (Horse) of bright chestnut or reddish-brown colour; this colour.

sŏ'rrow (-ō) *n.* Grief, sadness; occasion or cause of this, misfortune, trouble. ~ *v.i.* Grieve, feel sorrow, mourn. **sŏ'rrowful** *adj.* **sŏ'rrowfully** *adv.* **sŏ'rrowfulnèss** *n.*

sŏ'rry *adj.* 1. Feeling regret, regretful (freq. in expressions of sympathy or apology). 2. Wretched, paltry, shabby, mean. **sŏ'rrily** *adv.* **sŏ'rrinèss** *n.*

sōrt *n.* Kind, species, variety (*of*); (print., usu. pl.) any particular letter or character in fount of type; *of ~s*, (colloq.) of a not very satisfactory kind; *out of ~s*, out of health, spirits, or temper; slightly unwell. ~ *v.* Separate into sorts; take *out* (certain sorts from others); (archaic) correspond, agree, *with*. **sōrt'er** *n.* (esp.) Letter-sorter at a post office.

sōrt'ēs (-z) *n.pl.* ~ *Virgilianae, Biblicae* or *Sacrae*, *Homericae*, divination by turning up at random a passage in Virgil, the Bible, or Homer. [L, pl. of *sors* lot, chance]

sōrt'ie (-tē, -tĭ) *n.* Sally, esp. of beleaguered garrison; operational flight by an aeroplane.

sōrt'ilège *n.* Divination by lots; enchantment, magic.

sōr'us *n.* Cluster of spore-cases or spores on under-surface of fern-leaves, in fungi, lichens, etc. (ill. FERN).

S O S (ĕs'ōĕs'). International code-signal (three dots, three dashes, three dots) of extreme distress, used esp. by ships at sea; hence (colloq.) any urgent appeal for help.

sō'-sō: see SO.

sŏstenu'tō (-nōō-) *adv.* (mus.) In sustained manner.

sŏt *n.* Person stupefied by habitual drunkenness. **sŏtt'ish** *adj.* **sŏtt'ishly** *adv.* **sŏtt'ishnèss** *n.*

Soth'èbȳ's (sŭdh-). Auction-rooms in New Bond St, London, a centre of book-sales.

Sōth'ĭc *adj.* Of the dog-star; ~ *cycle*, a period of 1460 Sothic years or 1461 solar years; ~ *year*, the Egyptian year of 365 days 6 hours, computed from one helical rising of the dog-star to the next. [Gk *Sōthis*, f. the Egyptian name of the dog-star]

sŏttō' vō'ce (-chĕ) *adv.* In an undertone, aside.

sou (sōō) *n.* French coin, orig. $\frac{1}{20}$ of livre; later, 5-centime piece, 5 centimes; (colloq.) a halfpenny.

soubrĕtte' (sōō-) *n.* Maid-servant or similar character (esp. with implication of pertness, coquetry, intrigue, etc.) in comedy, opera, etc.; actress playing such parts.

sou'chŏng' (sōōsh-) *n.* Fine variety of China tea, in *Lapsang* ~ with smoky or tarry flavour. [Chin. *siao-chung* small sort]

Soudan: see SUDAN.

souffle (sōō'fl) *n.* (path.) Low murmuring sound heard in auscultation.

soufflé (sōōf'lā) *n.* Light spongy savoury or sweet dish made by mixing a thick sauce or purée with the yolks and stiffly beaten whites of eggs and baking.

sough (sŭf, sow, sōōχ) *n.* & *v.i.* (Make) rushing, sighing, or rustling sound, as of wind in trees.

soul (sōl) *n.* 1. Spiritual or immaterial part of man; moral and emotional part of man; vital principle and mental powers of animals including man; animating er essential part, person viewed as this; personification or pattern *of*, embodiment of moral or intellectual qualities. 2. Departed spirit; disembodied spirit. 3. Person. **soul'lèss** *adj.* **soul'lèssly** *adv.* **soul'lèssnèss** *n.*

soul'ful (sōl-) *adj.* Having, expressing, appealing to, the (esp. higher) emotional or intellectual qualities; (colloq.) excessively emotional. **soul'fully** *adv.* **soul'fulnèss** *n.*

sound¹ *adj.* Healthy; not diseased, injured, or rotten; financially solid or safe; correct, logical, well-founded, valid; (of sleep) deep, unbroken; thorough, unqualified. **sound'ly** *adv.* **sound'nèss** *n.* **sound** *adv.* Deeply, profoundly (*asleep*).

sound² *n.* Sensation produced in organs of hearing when surrounding air etc. vibrates so as to affect these; what is or may be heard; vibrations causing this sensation; utterance, speech, or one of the separate articulations composing this; impression produced by sound, statement, etc.; *~-barrier*, = SONIC barrier; *~-board*, thin resonant board in musical instrument so placed as to reinforce tones; *~-bow*, thickest part of bell, against which clapper strikes (ill. BELL); *~-box*, (in gramophone) box carrying reproducing or recording stylus or needle; ~ *effects*, sounds, other than speech or music, broadcast as part of programme; *~-film*, cinema film with audible dialogue, music, etc., usu. recorded photographically on margin of film and reproduced by appropriate apparatus during the showing; *~-post*, small wooden peg beneath bridge of violin or similar instrument supporting belly and connecting it with back; *~-proof*, preventing passage of sound; (*v.t.*) make sound-proof; *~-track*, the area on a cinema sound-film which carries the photographic sound record; *~-wave*, one of a series of progressive longitudinal vibratory disturbances in air or other medium by which the auditory nerves are stimulated. **sound'lèss** *adj.* **sound** *v.* Give forth sound (freq. fig., with reference to impression created); cause to sound; utter, pronounce; give notice of by sound, cause to resound, declare, make known; examine (person etc.) by auscultation, examine medically.

sound³ *n.* Surgeon's probe for sounding or exploring cavities of body. ~ *v.* Investigate, test depth or quality of bottom of (water), with line and lead or other apparatus; measure (depth) thus; (of whale) dive deeply; inquire, esp. in cautious or indirect manner, into sentiments or inclination of (person); (surg.) examine with a sound.

sound⁴ *n.* 1. Narrow channel, esp. between island and mainland, or connecting two large bodies of water; arm of sea. 2. Swimming-bladder of cod, sturgeon, etc.

sound'ĭng¹ *adj.* Resonant, sonorous; high-sounding, imposing; *~-board* board or screen over or behind pulpit etc. to reflect speaker's voice towards the audience (ill. PULPIT); sound-board.

sound'ĭng² *n.* (esp. pl.) Measurement of depth of water at specific places; places where such measurements can or have been taken.

soup (sōōp) *n.* 1. Liquid food made by stewing vegetables, meat, etc.; *in the* ~, (slang) in difficulties; *~-kitchen*, public institution where soup etc. is supplied free to the poor in times of distress. 2. (U.S. slang) Nitro-glycerine, esp. when used to open safe. **soup'y** *adj.*

soupçon (sōōp'sawṅ) *n.* A dash or trace (*of* garlic, malice, etc.).

sour (sowr) *adj.* With tart or acid taste, esp. as result of unripeness or of fermentation; (of smell) suggesting fermentation; (of soil) cold and wet, dank; (of person etc.) harsh, peevish, morose; *~-dough*, (Amer.) prospector, one who lives in the open, esp. in Alaska or Canada (from keeping piece of sour dough for making bread); *~-sop*, (large, succulent, slightly acid fruit of) tropical American tree, *Anona muricata*. ~ *n.* Acid solution used in bleaching, tanning, etc.; (U.S.) acid drink, usu. of whisky or other spirit with lemon- or lime-juice. **sour'ĭsh** *adj.* **sour'ly** *adv.* **sour'nèss** *n.* **sour** *v.* Make become, sour.

source (sōrs) *n.* Spring, fountain-head, of stream or river; origin, chief or prime cause, *of*; document, work, etc., giving evidence, esp. original or primary, as to fact, event, etc.; literary works from which later writers have derived inspiration, plots, etc.

sourdine (soordēn') *n.* (mus.) = SORDINE; also, soft stop on harmonium.

Sousa (sōōz'a), John Philip (1854–1932). American bandmaster and composer of marches.

sous'aphōne (sōōz-) *n.* (mus.) Bass wind-instrument of tuba kind. [f. J. P. SOUSA]

souse (sows) *n.* 1. Pickle made with salt; food in pickle, esp. head, feet, and ears of swine. 2. Sousing. ~ *v.* Put in pickle; plunge (*into* water etc.), soak (*in* liquid), drench. ~ *adv.* With sudden plunge.

soused (-st) *adj.* (slang) Drunk, 'pickled'.

soutache (sōō'tahsh) *n.* Narrow flat ornamental braid.

soutane (sōōtahn') *n.* Cassock of R.C. priest.

souteneur (sōōtenêr') *n.* Man living on earnings of prostitute.

south *n.*, *adj.*, & *adv.* (abbrev. S.) (Towards, at, near) point of horizon directly opposite north; point of compass opposite north; southern part of England, Great Britain, Scotland, Ireland, Europe, southern States of U.S.; of, from, situated or dwelling in, looking towards, the south; *S~ Downs*, downs of Sussex and Hampshire; *south'down*, (one) of small hornless breed of sheep with short fine wool, yielding mutton of good quality, originating on South Downs; *~-east*, (of, in, to, from) direction or compass-point between south and east; *~-easter*, south-east wind; *~-easterly*, *-eastern*; *~-west*, (of, in, to, from) direction or compass-point between south and west; *~-wester*, south-west wind; waterproof hat with broad flap behind to protect neck; *~-westerly*, *-western*. **south'ward** *adv.*, *adj.*, & *n.* **south'wards** *adv.* **south** *v.i.* (Of moon etc.) cross the meridian of a place; turn, veer, move, towards south.

South Af'rĭca. Republic of ~ (formerly Union of ~) withdrew from British Commonwealth in 1961 and became independent republic. Constituted 1910, comprising 4 provinces (formerly self-governing colonies): Cape of Good Hope, Transvaal, Natal, Orange Free State; capitals, Pretoria (administrative), Cape Town (legislative); Appellate Division of the

Supreme Court, Bloemfontein.
South African *adj.* & *n.*

South Amě'rĭca. The S. part of the continent of America, joined to Central America by the isthmus of Panama.

Southămp'ton. Seaport and county borough in Hampshire, England.

South Atlăn'tĭc States. A geographic division of the U.S. made by the U.S. Census Bureau, comprising Delaware, Maryland, Virginia, W. Virginia, N. Carolina, S. Carolina, Georgia, and Florida.

South Austrāl'ia. A State of the Commonwealth of Australia; capital, Adelaide.

South Cărolīn'a. South Atlantic State of U.S., admitted to the Union in 1788; capital, Columbia.

South'cott, Joanna (1750–1814). English religious fanatic; announced herself as the woman mentioned in Rev. xii; left a sealed box which was to be opened in a time of national crisis; it was opened in 1927, but contained nothing of interest.

South Dakōt'a. West North Central State of U.S., admitted to the Union in 1889; capital, Pierre.

south'erly (sŭdh-) *adj.* & *adv.* Towards the south; blowing from the south.

south'ern (sŭdh-) *adj.* Of, in, the south; looking south; *S~ Cross*: see CROSS; *S~ States*, those States of U.S.A. lying south of MASON AND DIXON'S line, the Ohio river, and the States of Missouri and Kansas; *south'ernwood*, hardy shrubby southern-European wormwood (*Artemisia abrotanum*) with fragrant aromatic leaves.

south'erner (sŭdh-) *n.* Inhabitant of south, esp. of Southern States of U.S.

Southey (sowdh'ĭ), Robert (1774–1843). English poet, essayist, and historian.

south'ĭng (-th-) *n.* (esp.) Difference in latitude south from last point of reckoning.

South Island. Central and largest island of New Zealand.

South Sea. (hist.) The Pacific; *~ Company*, company formed in 1711 by Harley (later Earl of Oxford) to trade with Spanish America; in 1720 it assumed responsibility for the national debt in return for a guaranteed profit, a fever of speculation (*the ~ Bubble*) set in, and shortly afterwards the company failed.

Southwark (sŭdh'*er*k). A London borough, famous in literary history on account of its ancient inns and theatres. [orig. the 'south work' or bridgehead at the south end of London Bridge]

South West Af'rĭca. Former German colony between the Cape of Good Hope province and Angola, since 1919 a mandated territory of S. Africa.

souvenir (sōōv'enēr) *n.* Thing given, brought, kept, etc., for memento (*of* occasion, place, etc.). [Fr., = remember, f. L *subvenire* occur to the mind]

sou'wĕs'ter *n.* = SOUTH-wester.

sov., sovs *abbrevs.* Sovereign(s) (coin).

sovereign (sŏv'rĭn) *n.* 1. Supreme ruler, esp. monarch. 2. (hist.) English gold coin worth £1. *~ adj.* Supreme; possessing sovereign power; (of remedies etc.) very good or efficacious. **sŏv'ereignty** *n.*

sŏv'ĭĕt (*or* -yĕt) *n.* In Russia since 1917, council elected by workers, peasants, and soldiers of district as its governing body; all-Russia congress of delegates from these; *the* system of government by soviets; *the* RUSSIAN Government. [Russ. *sovet* council]

sŏv'ĭĕtīze (*or* -yĕt) *v.t.* Change or convert to a form of government by soviets.

Sŏv'ĭĕt (*or* -yĕt) **Union.** Soviet Russia, the Union of Soviet Socialist Republics (abbrev. U.S.S.R.) established after the RUSSIAN revolution of 1917; capital, Moscow; it comprises 16 constituent republics, namely the Russian Soviet Federal Socialist Republic (which is far the largest and itself contains 12 'autonomous' republics) and the Ukrainian, Belorussian, Armenian, Azerbaijan, Georgian, Turkmenian, Uzbek, Tadjik, Kazakh, Kirghiz, Kardo-Finnish, Moldavian, Estonian, Latvian, and Lithuanian Soviet Republics, the last 5 of these, and substantial parts of some of the others, being acquisitions made after the war of 1939–45.

sow[1] *n.* 1. Female of swine, adult female pig, esp. domestic one used for breeding. 2. Trough through which molten iron runs into side-channels to form pigs; large block of iron solidified in this; *~-bread*, wild cyclamen of central Europe, the fleshy tuberous root-stocks of which are eaten by swine; *~-thistle*, any plant of the genus *Sonchus*, common European weeds with sharply toothed thistle-like leaves and milky juice.

sow[2] (sō) *v.t.* Scatter (seed) on or in the earth; plant (ground *with* seed) by sowing; (fig.) cover thickly *with*. **sow'er** *n.*

soy *n.* Sauce for fish etc. made, chiefly in Japan, China, and India, from soya beans pickled in brine. [Jap., f. Chin. *shi-yu*, f. *shi* salted beans, *yu* oil]

soy'a (-bean, -pea) *ns.* (Seed of) a widely cultivated Asiatic bushy leguminous plant (*Soja hispida*), yielding valuable meal (*~-flour*), oil, fertilizer, forage, etc. [f. SOY]

sŏzz'led (-ld) *adj.* (slang) Very drunk.

s.p. *abbrev. Sine prole* (= without issue).

S.P. *abbrev.* Service Police; sparking plug; starting price (betting); stirrup pump.

spa (-ah) *n.* Watering-place, (place with) mineral spring. [f. *Spa*, watering-place in Belgium, fashionable in 18th c.]

spāce *n.* 1. Continuous extension viewed with or without reference to the existence of objects within it; the immeasurable expanse in which the solar and stellar systems, nebulae, etc., are situated; *spacecraft*, *~ ship*, vehicle designed to travel outside the earth's atmosphere; *~ time*, (philos.) a fusion of the concepts of space and time, regarded as a continuum in which the existent exists. 2. Interval between points or objects. 3. Interval of time. 4. (print.) Blank between words etc., piece of type-metal used to separate words etc. *~ v.* Set at intervals, put spaces between; make space between words on typewriter etc.

spā'cious (-sh*u*s) *adj.* Enclosing a large space, having ample space, roomy. **spā'ciously** *adv.* **spā'ciousnèss** *n.*

spāde[1] *n.* Tool for digging or cutting ground, turf, etc., usu. with flattish rectangular iron blade socketed on wooden handle, with grip or cross-piece at upper end, grasped with both hands while blade is pressed into ground with foot; anything resembling this in form or use; *~-guinea*, guinea coined 1789–99 with shield on reverse shaped like blade of pointed spade; *~-work*, (fig.) hard work, preliminary drudgery. *~ v.t.* Dig up with spade.

spāde[2] *n.* (Playing-card with) black figure(s) resembling pointed spade; (pl.) suit of these cards. [Span. *espada* sword]

spād'ĭx *n.* (bot.; pl. *-ices* pr. -īs'ēz). Inflorescence consisting of thick fleshy spike, usu. enclosed in spathe (ill. INFLORESCENCE).

spaghet'tĭ (-gĕ-) *n.* Wheaten paste formed into long rods, thinner than macaroni but thicker than vermicelli, for use as food.

spahi (spah'hē) *n.* 1. (hist.) Member of Turkish irregular cavalry disbanded *c* 1830. 2. Member of native Algerian cavalry in service of French Government and with French and Algerian officers.

Spain. A State in SW. Europe occupying the larger portion of the Iberian peninsula, formed in the last quarter of the 15th c. by the union of Aragon and Castile and ruled over until 1931, when a republic was proclaimed, by sovereigns of the Aragon, Habsburg, and Bourbon dynasties; renamed a kingdom by Generalissimo Franco in 1947; capital, Madrid.

spall (-awl) *n.* Splinter, chip. *~ v.* (mining) Prepare (ore) for sorting by breaking it up.

spăm *n.* Tinned ham manufactured in U.S. [proprietary term; f. *sp*iced *ham*]

spăn[1] *n.* Distance from tip of thumb to tip of little finger, occas. of forefinger, of fully extended hand; this as measure (9 in.); short distance or time; whole extent of a period of time; full extent or stretch between abutments of arch, piers of bridge, wing-tips of aircraft, etc.; arch of bridge. ~ *v.t.* Stretch from side to side of, extend across; bridge (river etc.), form arch across; measure, cover, extent of (thing) with one's grasp etc.

spăn[2] *n.* (naut.) Rope with both ends made fast to afford purchase in loop, rope connecting stays or other uprights; (U.S., Canada, etc.) pair of horses, mules, etc., (S. Africa) team of oxen. ~ *v.t.* (now esp. S. Afr.) Inspan, harness or yoke (oxen, horses, etc.); (naut.) fasten, attach, draw tight. [Du. *spannen* fasten]

spăn'drel *n.* Space between either shoulder of arch and surrounding rectangular moulding or framework, or between shoulders of adjoining arches and moulding above (ill. ARCADE).

spăngle (-ng'gl) *n.* Small round thin piece of glittering metal, esp. one of many sewn to dress etc. as ornament; any small sparkling object. ~ *v.t.* Cover (as) with spangles. **spăng'ly** *adj.*

Spăn'iard (-yard) *n.* Native of Spain.

spăn'iel (-yel) *n.* Dog of various small or medium-sized breeds, usu. with long silky hair, large drooping ears, keen scent, and docile and affectionate disposition, used as sporting dogs esp. for starting and retrieving game, or kept as pets (ill. DOG) [OF. *espaignol* Spanish (dog)]

Spăn'ish *adj.* & *n.* (Language, one of the Romance group) of Spain or the Spaniards; ~ *America*, those portions of America settled by Spaniards and now occupied by their descendants, including the greater part of S. America and some of the West Indian islands; ~ *American* (*adj.* & *n.*); ~ *Armada*: see ARMADA; ~ *black*, pigment obtained from charred cork; ~ *brown*, dark reddish-brown earth used as a pigment; ~ *chestnut*, the sweet chestnut (*Castanea sativa*); ~ *fly*, brilliant green beetle (*Lytta vesicatoria*) from which cantharides, used for raising blisters, is obtained; ~ *grass*, esparto grass; ~ *Main*, the mainland of America adjacent to the Caribbean Sea, esp. that portion from the Isthmus of Panama to the mouth of the Orinoco; in later use, the sea contiguous to this; ~ *Succession, War of*, that between France and Spain on the one side and England, Austria, and the United Provinces on the other, on the death of Charles II of Spain without issue (1701–14); ~ *windlass*, stick used as a lever for tightening cord or bandage.

spănk[1] *v.t.* & *n.* Slap or smack with open hand, esp. on buttocks.

spănk[2] *v.i.* Move or travel quickly or dashingly.

spănk'er *n.* (esp.) 1. Fast or spirited horse; (colloq.) person or thing of notable size or quality. 2. (naut.) A fore-and-aft sail set on aftermost mast of sailing vessel (ill. SHIP).

spănk'ing *adj.* (esp.) Very large or fine, striking, notable, excellent; (of horse etc.) fast-moving, dashing, showy.

spănn'er *n.* Tool, usu. steel bar with jaw, socket, or opening at end(s), for turning nut of screw, bolt, coupling, etc.

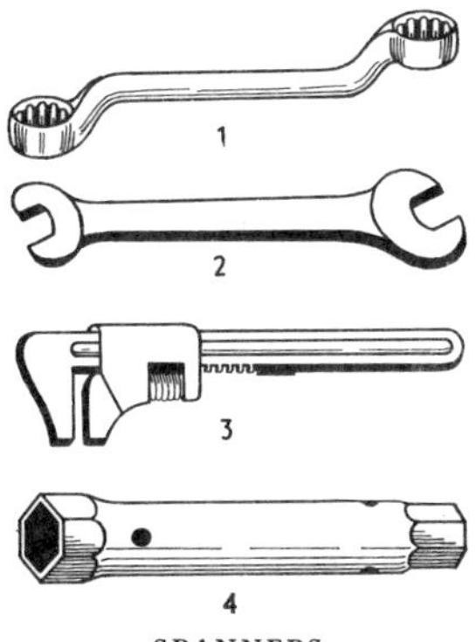

SPANNERS

1. Ring. 2. Open. 3. Adjustable spanner or wrench. 4. Box-spanner

spar[1] *n.* Stout pole, esp. such as is used for mast, yard, etc., of ship (ill. SHIP); either of main lateral members of wing of aircraft, carrying ribs (ill. AEROPLANE). ~ *v.t.* Furnish with spars.

spar[2] *n.* Various more or less lustrous crystalline easily cleavable minerals; see FLUOR-SPAR, ICELAND spar, etc.

spar[3] *v.i.* Make motions of attack and defence with fists, use hands (as) in boxing; (fig.) dispute, bandy words; (of cocks) strike with feet or spurs, fight. ~ *n.* Sparring; boxing-match; cock-fight.

spă'rable *n.* Small wedge-shaped headless nail for soles and heels of boots. [orig. *sparrow-bill*]

spāre *adj.* 1. Scanty, frugal; lean, thin. 2. That can be spared, not required for ordinary use; reserved for future, emergency, or extraordinary use; ~ *part*, duplicate of part of machine, esp. motor vehicle, kept in readiness to replace loss, breakage, etc. **spāre'ly** *adv.* **spāre'nėss** *n.* **spāre** *n.* Spare part. ~ *v.* 1. Be frugal or grudging of; be frugal. 2. Dispense with, do without. 3. Refrain from inflicting injury, affliction, or damage or punishment on, deal leniently or gently with; refrain from taking (life). **spār'ingly** *adv.* **spār'ingnėss** *n.*

spāre'-rib *n.* Part of closely trimmed ribs of meat, esp. pork (ill. MEAT).

spark[1] *n.* Fiery particle thrown off from burning substance, or still remaining in one almost extinguished, or produced by impact of one hard body on another; small bright object or point; (elect.) (brilliant flash of light accompanying) sudden disruptive discharge between two conductors separated by air etc.; electric spark for firing explosive mixture in internal combustion engine; (pl., colloq.) wireless operator on ship; (fig.) flash (of wit etc.); scintilla, particle (of fire, some quality, etc.); ~-*plug*, (U.S.) sparking-plug. ~ *v.i.* Emit spark(s) of fire or electricity; produce sparks at point where electric circuit is broken; *sparking-plug*, electrical device fitting into the cylinder-head of an internal combustion engine, consisting of two electrodes across the space between which the current from the ignition system passes and so produces the spark which fires the explosive mixture in the cylinders (ill. COMBUSTION.)

spark[2] *n.* Gay fellow; gallant. **spark'ish** *adj.* **spark** *v.i.* Play the gallant.

spark'le *n.* Sparkling; gleam, spark. ~ *v.i.* Emit sparks; glitter, glisten, scintillate. **spark'ler** *n.* (esp., colloq.) Diamond or other sparkling gem. **spark'ling** *adj.* (Of wines etc.) effervescing with small glittering bubbles of carbon dioxide.

spă'roid (*or* spār-) *adj.* Of the *Sparidae* or sea-bream family of fishes.

spă'rrow (-ō) *n.* Small brownish-grey bird of genus *Passer*, either the *house-*~ (*P. domesticus*), a native of Europe introduced into N. America, common about buildings and in towns, or the *tree-*~ (*P. montanus*) of Europe, not associated with buildings; *hedge-*~, (misleading name for) the dunnock or hedge accentor, *Prunella modularis occidentalis*; ~-*grass*, (vulg. corrupt. of) asparagus; ~-*hawk*, small hawk (*Accipiter nisus*) of N. Europe and Asia, preying on small birds; small N. Amer. falcon (*Falco sparverius*); various other small hawks and falcons.

sparse *adj.* Thinly dispersed or scattered, not crowded or dense, with wide distribution or intervals. **sparse'ly** (-sl-) *adv.* **sparse'nėss** *n.*

Spart'a. Capital of the ancient Doric State of Laconia in the Peleponnesus, the inhabitants of which were noted for the military organization of their State and for their rigorous discipline, simplicity, and courage. **Spart'an** *adj.* & *n.* (Native) of Sparta (esp. with allusion to the characteristics of the

Spartans); hence, austere, hardy; ~ *dog*, a kind of bloodhound.

Spa͡rt′acist *adj.* & *n.* (Member) of the extreme revolutionary Socialist party organized in Germany in 1918 under the leadership of Karl Liebknecht, who adopted the pen-name of SPARTACUS.

Spa͡rt′acus. Thracian leader of an army of slaves who rebelled against Rome in 73–71 B.C.

spasm (-zm) *n.* Involuntary sudden and violent muscular contraction; sudden convulsive movement, convulsion.

spăsmŏd′ĭc (-zm-) *adj.* Of, caused by, subject to, spasm(s); occurring, done, jerkily or by fits and starts. **spăsmŏd′ĭcally** *adv.*

spăs′tĭc *adj.* Showing spasticity, e.g. ~ *limb*; tightly contracted (muscle). ~ *n.* (colloq.) Person with cerebral PALSY.

spăstĭ′cĭty *n.* (med.) A state in which there is abnormal active pull or resistance of muscles to passive displacement of a limb, particularly in one direction of joint movement. It may be caused by damage to brain or spinal cord and is usu. associated with muscular weakness or paralysis.

spăt[1] *n.* Spawn of shell-fish, esp. oyster. ~ *v.* (Of oyster) spawn.

spăt[2] *n.* (usu. pl.) Short gaiter covering instep and reaching little above ankle (ill. COAT). [abbrev. of SPATTERDASH]

spăt[3] *n.* (U.S.) Tiff, quarrel.

spătch′cŏck *n.* Fowl hastily killed and dressed, split open and grilled. ~ *v.t.* Cook as, like, spatchcock; (colloq.) insert, interpolate (esp. incongruous matter).

spāte *n.* River-flood, esp. sudden; rush, outburst.

spāthe (-dh) *n.* (bot.) Large bract, freq. bright-coloured, enveloping inflorescence on same axis (spadix), as in arum etc. (ill. INFLORESCENCE).

spăth′ĭc *adj.* Of or like SPAR[2], foliated, lamellar.

spā′tial (-shl) *adj.* Of, relating to, occupying, occurring in, space. **spā′tially** *adv.*

spā′tialize (-shal-) *v.t.* Make spatial; localize in space.

spătt′er *v.* Scatter (liquid, mud, etc.) here and there in small drops, splash (*with* mud, slander, etc.) thus, (of liquid) fall thus or with sound suggesting heavy drops. ~ *n.* Spattering, splash; pattering.

spătt′erdăsh *n.* (chiefly pl.) Long gaiter or legging to protect stockings etc. from mud etc. (ill. INFANTRY).

spăt′ūla *n.* Flat broad-bladed knife-shaped implement used for spreading foods or ointments and for medical examination of certain organs etc. **spăt′ūlar** *adj.*

spăt′ūlate *adj.* With broadened rounded end like common form of spatula.

spăv′ĭn *n.* Disease of hock in horses, marked by hard bony tumour or excrescence and caused by strain etc. **spăv′ĭned** (-nd) *adj.*

spawn *n.* Minute eggs of frogs, fishes, etc., usu. extruded in large numbers and often forming coherent or gelatinous mass, fertilized by the MILT (ill. FROG); (contempt.) brood, (numerous) offspring; mycelium of fungi. ~ *v.* Cast spawn; produce or generate as spawn or in large numbers.

spay *v.t.* Remove ovaries of (female animal).

S.P.C.K. *abbrev.* Society for the Promotion of Christian Knowledge.

S.P.E. *abbrev.* Society for Pure English.

speak *v.* (past t. *spōke*, archaic *spāke*; past part. *spōk′en*). Utter words or articulate sound in ordinary (not singing) voice; hold conversation; make oral address, deliver speech; utter (words); make known (opinion, *the truth*, etc.) thus; use (specified language) in speaking; state in words; be evidence of, indicate; ~ *for*, act as spokesman of or for; ~ *of*, mention; ~ *out*, *up*, speak freely; speak loud(er) or so as to be distinctly heard; *~-easy*, (U.S. slang) illicit liquor shop.

speak′er *n.* 1. One who speaks, esp. one who makes a speech. 2. *S~*, member of House of Commons chosen by the House to preside over debates, preserve order, etc.; similar officer of U.S. House of Representatives and other legislative bodies. 3. LOUD-speaker.

speak′ĭng *n.* 1. (esp.) Speech-making; ~ *part*, part in play etc. containing words to be spoken; ~ *terms*, degree of acquaintanceship allowing exchange of conversation (*not on* ~ *terms*, (usu.) estranged); *~-trumpet*, trumpet-shaped instrument for magnifying sound of voice; *~-tube*, tube for conveying voice from one room or building to another, or from the inside to the outside of a closed carriage or motor-car, enabling the occupants to speak with the driver.

spear *n.* Thrusting or hurling weapon with long shaft and sharp-pointed head, usu. of iron or steel; sharp-pointed and barbed instrument for catching fish etc.; *~-grass*, various grasses with stiff pointed leaves; *~-head*, (fig.) person(s) leading, anything in forefront of, attack; *spear′mint*, common garden mint. ~ *v.t.* Pierce, strike, (as) with spear.

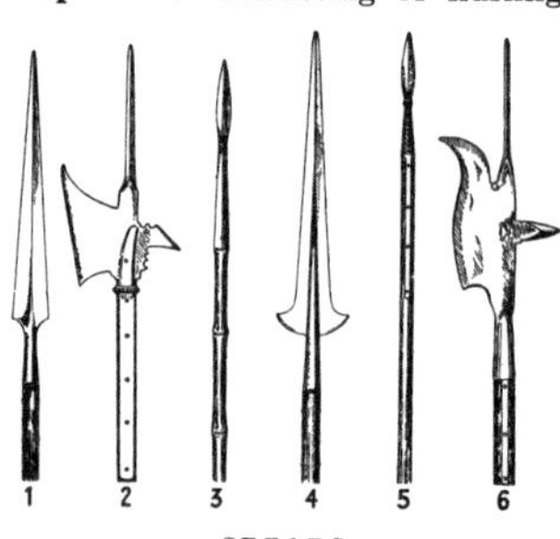

SPEARS

1. Long-bladed spear, *c* 1510. 2. Halberd, *c* 1500. 3. Cavalry lance, late 19th c. 4. Partisan, *c* 1510. 5. Pike, 16th–17th centuries. 6. English bill, *c* 1480

spĕc *n.* (colloq. abbrev. of) Speculation; *on ~*, experimentally, on the chance.

spĕ′cial (-shl) *adj.* Of a particular kind, peculiar, not general; for a particular purpose; exceptional in amount, degree, kind, etc.; ~ *area*, industrial area in a state of chronic depression; ~ *constable*, constable sworn in to assist police in time of war, civil disturbance, etc.; ~ *correspondent*, correspondent appointed by newspaper to report on special facts; ~ *licence*, licence allowing marriage to take place without usual publication of banns or at time or place other than those legally appointed; ~ *pleader*, counsel employed to give an opinion on special points submitted to him; ~ *pleading*, (law) allegation of special or new matter as opp. to denial of allegations of other side; (pop.) specious but unfair argument, statement of case designed to support point of view rather than discover truth; ~ *train*, additional train for special purpose. **spĕ′cially** *adv.* In special manner, to special degree or extent; of special purpose, expressly. **spĕ′cial** *n.* Special constable, train, edition of newspaper, etc.

spĕ′cialist (-shal-) *n.* One who devotes himself to particular branch of profession, science, etc., esp. medicine.

spĕciăl′ĭty (-shĭ-) *n.* Special feature or characteristic; special pursuit, product, operation, etc., thing to which person gives special attention.

spĕ′cialīze (-shal-) *v.* 1. Make specific or individual; modify, limit (idea, statement). 2. (biol.) Adapt (organ etc.) for particular purpose, differentiate; be differentiated, become individual in character. 3. Be, become, a specialist. **spĕcializā′tion** *n.*

spĕ′cialty (-shl-) *n.* 1. (law) Special contract under seal. 2. Speciality.

spē′cie (-shē, -shĭē) *n.* Coin, coined money. [L *in specie* in kind]

spē′cies (-shēz, -shĭēz) *n.* (pl. same) 1. (logic) Group subordinate to genus, containing individuals which have common attribute(s) and are called by a common name. 2. (biol.) Group of organisms which have certain characteristics not shared by other groups; usu. a group which is believed to be reproductively isolated, i.e. whose members will breed among themselves but not normally with members of other groups; the lowest group normally used in classification, the others being (in ascending order) genus, family, order, class, phylum. 3. (loosely) Kind, sort.

spėcĭf′ĭc *adj.* 1. Definite; distinctly formulated; precise, particular. 2. Of a species; possessing, concerned with, the properties characterizing a species. 3. (med., of remedies) Specially efficacious for a particular ailment etc.; (path.) characteristic. 4. ~ *gravity*, ratio of weight of any substance to weight of equal volume at same temperature of another substance (usu. water for solids and liquids, and hydrogen or air for gases) taken as standard; ~ *heat*, amount of heat required to raise temperature of one gram of substance one degree Centigrade; ratio of amount of heat required to raise temperature of body through one degree to that required to raise temperature of equal mass of water one degree. **spėcĭf′ĭcally** *adv.* **spėcĭf′ĭcnėss** *n.* **spėcĭf′ĭc** *n.* Specific remedy.

spĕcĭfĭcā′tion *n.* Specifying; specified detail, esp. detailed description of construction, workmanship, materials, etc., of work undertaken by engineer, architect, etc.; description by applicant for patent of nature, details, and use of invention.

spĕ′cĭfȳ *v.t.* Name expressly, mention definitely; include in specification.

spĕ′cĭmėn *n.* Individual or part taken as example of class or whole, esp. serving as example of class or thing in question for purposes of investigation or scientific study.

spē′cious (-sh*u*s) *adj.* Of good appearance; plausible; fair or right on the surface. **spē′ciously** *adv.* **spē′ciousnėss, spēciŏs′ĭty** (-shĭ-) *ns.*

spĕck *n.* Small spot, dot, stain; particle (*of* dirt etc.); spot of rottenness in fruit. ~ *v.t.* Mark with specks. **spĕck′lėss** *adj.*

spĕck′le *n.* Small speck, mark, or stain. ~ *v.t.* Mark with speckles.

spĕcs *n.pl.* (colloq. abbrev. for) Spectacles for the eyes.

spĕc′tacle *n.* 1. Public show, specially prepared or arranged display; object of public attention, curiosity, admiration, etc. 2. (*pair of*) ~*s*, pair of lenses to correct or assist defective sight set in frame supported on nose and usu. with side-pieces passing over ears. **spĕc′tacled** (-ld) *adj.* Wearing spectacles; (of animals etc.) marked in way that suggests spectacles.

spĕctăc′ūlar *adj.* Of, of the nature of, a spectacle or show, striking, imposing. **spĕctăc′ūlarly** *adv.*

spĕctāt′or[1] *n.* One who looks on, esp. at show, game, etc. **spĕctātōr′ĭal** *adj.*

Spĕctāt′or[2], The. A daily periodical conducted by STEELE and ADDISON 1711–12 and revived by Addison in 1714, containing articles on manners, morals, and literature.

spĕc′tral *adj.* 1. Ghostly, of ghosts. 2. Of spectra or the spectrum.

spĕc′tre (-t*er*) *n.* Ghost, apparition.

spĕc′troscōpe *n.* Optical instrument for producing and examining spectra. **spĕctroscŏp′ĭc** *adj.* **spĕctroscŏp′ĭcally** *adv.*

spĕc′trum *n.* (pl. *-ra*). Series of images formed when a beam of radiant energy is dispersed and then brought to focus, so that its component waves are arranged in order of wave-length; esp. coloured band into which beam of light is decomposed by prism etc.; after-image seen when eyes are turned away from bright-coloured object etc.; ~ *analysis*, analysis, esp. chemical analysis, by means of spectra.

spĕc′ūlar *adj.* Of (the nature of) a speculum or mirror; ~ *iron* (*ore*), haematite.

spĕc′ūlāte *v.i.* 1. Engage in thought or reflection, esp. of conjectural or theoretical kind (*on*, *upon*). 2. Buy or sell commodities etc. in expectation of rise or fall in their market value; engage in commercial operation, make investment, involving risk of loss. **spĕc′ūlatĭve** *adj.* **spĕc′ūlatĭvely** *adv.* **spĕc′ūlatĭvenėss, spĕc′ūlātor** *ns.*

spĕcūlā′tion *n.* 1. Meditation on, inquiry into, theory about, a subject. 2. Speculative investment or enterprise, practice of speculating, in business.

spĕc′ūlum *n.* 1. (surg.) Instrument for dilating cavities of human body for inspection. 2. Mirror, usu. of polished metal, esp. in optical instruments; ~ *metal*, alloy of copper and tin taking high polish used as a reflector in telescopes. 3. Lustrous coloured patch on wing of some birds.

speech *n.* Act, faculty, or manner of speaking; thing said, remark; public address; language, dialect; *King's*, *Queen's* ~, ~ *from the throne*, statement of foreign and domestic affairs and of chief measures to be considered by Parliament, read at opening of parliamentary session; ~*-day*, annual day for delivering prizes in schools, usu. marked by recitations etc.

speech′ĭfȳ *v.i.* (contempt.) Make speeches, hold forth.

speech′lėss *adj.* Dumb; temporarily deprived of speech by emotion etc. **speech′lėssly** *adv.* **speech′lėssnėss** *n.*

speed *n.* 1. Rapidity of movement, quickness; rate of progress, motion, or performance; (photog.) rapidity with which plate etc. is acted on by light. 2. (archaic) Success, prosperity. 3. ~*-boat*, motor-boat etc. capable of very high speed; ~*-cop*, (orig. U.S.) policeman with duty of checking excessive speed of motorists; ~*-limit*, maximum speed permitted on road, to vehicle etc.; *speed′way*, track for motor-racing, road intended only for fast motor vehicles; (U.S.) road for fast horse-driving. ~ *v.* 1. Go fast; travel at excessive or illegal speed; (archaic) send fast, send on the way. 2. (archaic) Be, make, prosperous; succeed, give success to. 3. Regulate speed of (engine etc.), cause to go at fixed speed; ~ *up*, increase speed of, increase rate of work, production; ~*-up* (*n.*).

speedŏm′ėter *n.* Instrument for registering speed at which vehicle, esp. motor-car, is moving.

speed′wĕll *n.* (Plant, flower) of genus *Veronica* of small herbaceous plants with leafy stems and small blue (occas. pink or white) flowers.

speed′y *adj.* Rapid, swift; prompt. **speed′ĭly** *adv.* **speed′ĭnėss** *n.*

spēl(a)eŏl′ogy *n.* Scientific study of caves. **spēl(a)eŏl′ogist** *n.*

spĕll[1] *n.* Words, formula, used as charm; incantation; attraction, fascination; ~*-binder*, (U.S.) political speaker who can hold audiences spell-bound; ~*-bound*, bound (as) by spell, fascinated, entranced.

spĕll[2] *v.* (past t. and past part. *spĕlt* or *spĕlled*, pr. -lt). Name or write in order letters of (word etc.); form words etc. thus; (of letters) make up, form (word); (fig.) signify, imply, involve; ~ *out*, make out (words etc.) laboriously letter by letter. **spĕll′ĭng** *n.*; ~*-bee*, competition in spelling.

spĕll[3] *n.* Turn of work, or *of* or *at* some occupation; short period. ~ *v.* (Allow to) rest for short period.

spĕlt *n.* Variety of wheat (*Triticum spelta*) grown in parts of S. Europe.

spĕl′ter *n.* Zinc (now commerc.); zinc solder.

Spĕn′cer[1], Herbert (1820–1903). English philosopher, who sought the unification of all knowledge on the basis of the single principle of evolution; the principle of his philosophy was laid down in his 'Programme of a System of Synthetic Philosophy' (1860), to the elaboration of which he devoted the rest of his life.

spĕn′cer[2] *n.* 1. Man's short double-breasted tailless coat worn at end of 18th and beginning of 19th centuries. 2. Woman's or child's close-fitting jacket or bodice (ill. COAT). [f. 2nd Earl *Spencer* (1758–1834)]

spĕnd (past t. and past part. *spĕnt*). Pay out (money) for a purchase etc., pay out money; use, use up, consume, exhaust, wear out; be consumed; live or stay through (period of time); *spend′-*

thrift, extravagant person, prodigal (freq. attrib. or as adj.); *spent fish*, fish exhausted by spawning.

Spĕn′ser, Edmund (*c* 1552–99). English poet, author of 'The Faerie Queene' etc. **Spĕnsēr′ian** *adj.*; ~ *stanza*, the stanza invented by Spenser, in which he wrote 'The Faerie Queene'; it consists of eight 5-foot iambic lines, followed by an iambic line of 6 feet, rhyming *a b a b b c b c c*.

spĕrm *n.* 1. Male generative fluid, semen; (biol.) spermatozoon. 2. (also ~ *whale*) The cachalot, a large whale (*Physeter macrocephalus*) found in warm oceans, with large head cavity containing spermaceti (ill. WHALE); ~ *oil*, spermaceti.

spĕrmacēt′ĭ *n.* White soft scaly solid, a mixture of fatty esters, separating from oil found in head of sperm whale and other cetaceans, and used for ointments, candles, etc. [med. L f. *sperma* seed, *cetus* whale (because it was thought to be whale-spawn)]

spĕrm′ary *n.* Male generative gland, testis.

spĕrmăt′ĭc *adj.* Of sperm or the spermary, seminal; ~ *cord*, structure connecting testicles with seminal vesicles.

spĕrmatogĕn′ĕsĭs *n.* Development of spermatozoa. **spĕrmatogenĕt′ĭc** *adj.*

spĕrm′atophōre *n.* (zool.) Capsule formed by some animals containing compact mass of spermatozoa.

spĕrmatozō′on *n.* (pl. -*zōa*). Minute active fertilizing cell of male organism.

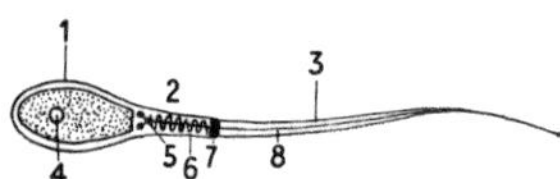

HUMAN SPERMATOZOON

1. Head. 2. Neck. 3. Tail. 4. Vacuole. 5. Centriole. 6. Mitochondria. 7. Annulus. 8. Axial filament

spew, spue *vbs.* Vomit.

S.P.G. *abbrev.* Society for the Propagation of the Gospel.

sp. gr. *abbrev.* Specific gravity.

sphăg′num *n.* Large genus of mosses growing in boggy and swampy places, used as packing, surgical dressings, etc.

sphēn′oid *adj.* ~ *bone*, compound bone at base of skull (ill. HEAD). ~ *n.* 1. (anat.) Sphenoid bone. 2. (cryst.) Wedge-shaped crystal with 4 equal and similar triangular faces. **sphenoi′dal** *adj.*

sphēre *n.* 1. Body or space bounded by surface every point of which is equidistant from a point within called the centre (ill. CONE); ball, globe; heavenly body; globe representing earth or apparent heavens. 2. Any of the (orig. 8, later 9 or 10) concentric transparent hollow globes formerly imagined as revolving with harmonious sound (*music of the* ~*s*) round earth and carrying with them moon, sun, planets, and fixed stars; sphere occupied by particular planet, star, etc.; field

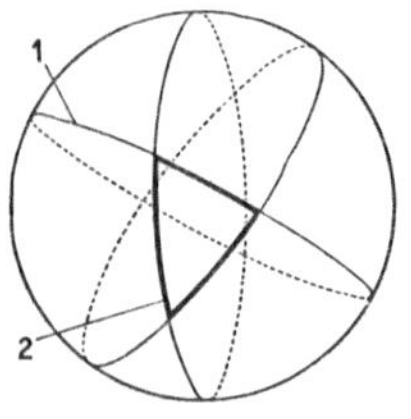

SPHERE

1. Great circle. 2. Spherical triangle

of action, influence, or existence, natural surroundings, place in society. ~ *v.t.* (rare, poet.) Enclose (as) in sphere; exalt among the spheres, set aloft.

sphĕ′ric *adj.* (poet.) Of the heavens, exalted; (rare) spherical. **sphĕ′rics** *n.pl.* Spherical geometry and trigonometry.

sphĕ′rical *adj.* 1. Sphere-shaped, globular. 2. Of spheres, concerned with properties of spheres; (of lines etc.) described in, on surface of, sphere. **sphĕ′rically** *adv.*

sphēr′oid *n.* Sphere-like but not perfectly spherical body, esp. one generated by revolution of ellipse about one of its axes (ill. CONE). **sphēroid′al** *adj.*

sphinc′ter *n.* Ring of muscle guarding or closing an orifice in the animal body, e.g. *anal, oral, pupillary* ~; *cardiac* ~, sphincter guarding upper orifice of stomach.

sphin′gĭd (-g-) *adj.* & *n.* (Member) of family *Sphingidae* or hawk-moths.

sphinx *n.* 1. (Gk myth.) Winged monster with woman's head and lion's body, which infested Thebes,

SPHINX
A. EGYPTIAN. B. GREEK

killing all who could not answer the riddle it propounded, until the riddle was solved by OEDIPUS; (loosely) enigmatic or mysterious person. 2. Ancient Egyptian figure of a recumbent lion with the head of a man, ram, or hawk, esp. (*the S*~) the colossal 4th-Dynasty stone one near the Pyramids at Gizeh; any similar figure. 3. (*S*~) Genus of hawk-moths.

sphўg′mograph (-ahf) *n.* = SPHYGMOMETER.

sphўgmŏm′ĕter *n.* Instrument recording graphically the movements of the pulse and variations in arterial pressure.

spĭc′a *n.* 1. First-magnitude star in constellation Virgo. 2. (surg.) Form of spiral bandage with reversed turns, suggesting ear of wheat.

spĭc′ate *adj.* (bot., zool.) Pointed, spiked, spike-shaped.

spice *n.* Various strong-flavoured or aromatic vegetable substances obtained from tropical plants, as ginger, cinnamon, nutmeg, allspice, used to season or preserve food etc.; spices collectively; slight touch, trace, dash, *of* some quality etc.; *spice′bush*, N. Amer. aromatic shrub, *Benzoin odoriferum*, with small yellow flowers and scarlet berries. ~ *v.t.* Flavour or season with spice(s).

spick and spăn *adj.* Smart and new; neat, trim. [extended f. ME *span-new* (ON *spánn* chip)]

spĭc′ūla *n.* (pl. -*ae*). Spicule; prickle.

spĭc′ūle *n.* Small, slender, pointed or needle-like process or formation; esp. (zool.) small hard calcareous or siliceous body stiffening tissues of various invertebrates, as sponges etc. (ill. SPONGE). **spĭc′ūlar, spĭc′ūlate** *adjs.*

spī′cy *adj.* Of, flavoured or fragrant with, spice; (fig.) pungent, sensational, scandalous, somewhat improper. **spī′cĭly** *adv.* **spī′cĭnĕss** *n.*

spīd′er *n.* 1. 8-legged animal of order *Araneida* of arachnids, many species of which spin webs esp. for capture of insects as food; (loosely) various other spider-like arachnids. 2. Kind of frying-pan with legs and long handle, (loosely, U.S.) frying-pan. 3. Kind of trap

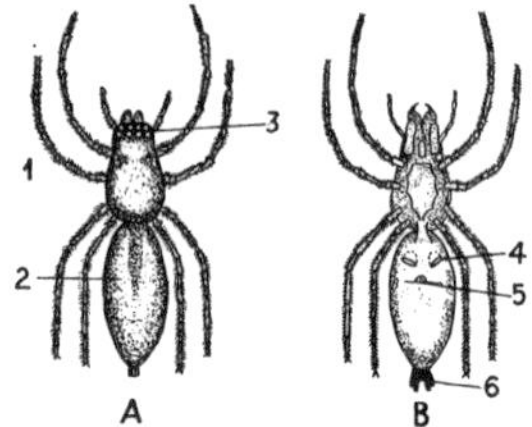

SPIDER: A. DORSAL VIEW. B. VENTRAL VIEW

1. Cephalothorax. 2. Abdomen. 3. Eyes. 4. Lung spiracle. 5. Genitals. 6. Spinnerets

or phaeton with very large light wheels. 4. Various parts of machinery with radiating arms. 5. ~-*catcher*, various birds which catch or eat spiders, esp. E. Indian sunbirds; ~-*crab*, various crabs of group *Oxyrhyncha* with long slender legs; ~ *monkey*, various S. and Central Amer. monkeys (*Ateles*) with long slender limbs and prehensile tail; *spid'erwort*, any plant of Amer. genus *Tradescantia*, with ephemeral white, pink, or violet flowers and slender hairy stamens. **spĭd'ery** *adj.* Spider-like, esp. long and slender like spider's legs; like cobweb.

spiegeleisen (spēg'elīzn) *n.* Kind of pig-iron containing much manganese, used in making steel by the Bessemer process. [Ger., = 'mirror-iron']

spiel (spēl) *n.* (U.S. slang) A talk, speech, story. ~ *v.* Speak. [Ger., = 'game']

spĭg'ot *n.* Small peg or plug esp. for insertion into vent-hole of cask; plain end of section of pipe fitting into socket of another.

spīke *n.* 1. Sharp point; pointed piece of metal, e.g. forming part of barrier, fixed in shoe-sole to prevent slipping etc.; large stout nail. 2. (bot.) Inflorescence of sessile flowers on elongated simple axis (ill. INFLORESCENCE). 3. French lavender (obs.); *oil of* ~, ~-*oil*, essential oil distilled from lavender. ~ *v.t.* Furnish with spike(s); fix on, pierce, with spike(s); plug vent of (cannon) with spike. **spīk'y** *adj.*

spīke'let (-kl-) *n.* (bot.) Small or secondary spike esp. as part of inflorescence of grasses etc. (ill. GRASS).

spīke'nard (-kn-) *n.* Ancient costly aromatic substance used in ointments etc. and obtained from the N. Indian plant *Nardostachys jatamansi*; this plant.

spile *n.* Wooden peg or plug, spigot; (U.S.) small spout for conducting sap from sugar-maple etc. ~ *v.t.* Provide (cask, tree, etc.) with spile.

spĭll[1] *n.* Thin strip of wood, folded or twisted piece of paper etc. for lighting candle, pipe, etc.

spĭll[2] *v.* (past t. and past part. *spĭlt* or *spĭlled*). Allow (liquid etc.) to fall or run out from vessel, esp. accidentally or wastefully, run out thus; shed (blood); empty (sail) of wind (naut.); cause to fall from horse or vehicle; *spill'way*, passage for overflow of surplus liquid (ill. DAM). ~ *n.* Throw or fall, esp. from horse or vehicle: tumble.

spĭll'er *n.* (dial. and U.S.) Long fishing-line with number of hooks; in mackerel-fishing, seine inserted into larger seine to take out fish, or used to hold part of catch.

spĭll'ikin, spĕll'ican *ns.* One of a heap of small rods or slips of wood, bone, etc., used in the game of *spillikins*, in which the object is to remove each rod with a hook without disturbing the rest.

spĭn *v.* (past t. *spăn* or *spŭn*, past part. *spŭn*). 1. Draw out and twist (wool, cotton, etc.) into threads, make (yarn) thus; be engaged in, follow, this occupation; (of insects) make (web, cocoon, etc.) by extrusion of fine viscous thread; ~ *out*, spend, consume (time etc.); prolong, extend; last out. 2. Revolve, turn (*round*), whirl; (aviation) make diving descent with continued rotation of aircraft; cause (minnow etc.) to revolve in water as bait for trout etc., fish thus. ~ *n.* Spinning motion, esp. in rifle bullet, in tennis ball, etc., struck aslant, or in aeroplane in diving descent; brisk or short run, spell of driving, etc.; ~ *drier*, machine which dries clothes etc. by rapid spinning in a rotating aerated drum.

spĭn'ach (-ĭj) *n.* Plant (*Spinacia oleracea*) with succulent leaves used as vegetable; ~ *beet*, kind of beet (*Beta cicla*) with large succulent leaves used like those of spinach.

spīn'al *adj.* Of the spine; ~ *canal*, channel formed by arches of vertebrae, containing spinal cord; ~ *column*, spine; ~ *cord*, rope-like mass of nerve-cells and nerve-fibres enclosed within and protected by spinal column, co-ordinating activities of limbs and trunk and transmitting impulses between the brain and the tissues of the body.

spĭn'dle *n.* 1. Slender rounded rod tapering at both ends, used to twist fibres of wool, flax, etc., into thread in spinning-frame (ill. SPINNING); steel rod by which thread is twisted and wound on bobbin; varying measure of length for yarn. 2. Pin, axis, that revolves or on which something revolves. 3. Anything spindle-shaped, esp. (biol.) spindle-shaped system of fibres formed during cell-division, to which the chromosomes become attached. 4. ~-*berry*, (bright-red fruit of) spindle-tree; ~-*shanked*, with long thin legs; ~-*shaped*, with circular cross-section and tapering towards each end; ~-*tree*, various species of *Euonymus*, esp. the ornamental European shrub, *E. europaeus*, with hard fine-grained yellowish wood formerly much used for spindles. ~ *v.i.* Have, grow into, long slender form. **spĭnd'ly** *adj.* Slender, attenuated.

spĭn'drift *n.* Spray blown along surface of sea.

spīne *n.* 1. In vertebrates, articulated series of vertebrae extending from skull to the hips (and in some animals continued to form the tail) and forming the supporting axis of the body, backbone. 2. (bot.) Stiff sharp-pointed woody or hardened process, usu. a shoot; (anat.) sharp-pointed slender process of various bones; (zool.) thorn-like process or appendage in certain fishes, insects, etc., prickle of hedgehog, quill of porcupine, etc. 3. Ridge, sharp projection, of rock, ground, etc.; resembling backbone. 4. The 'back' of a book (ill. BOOK).

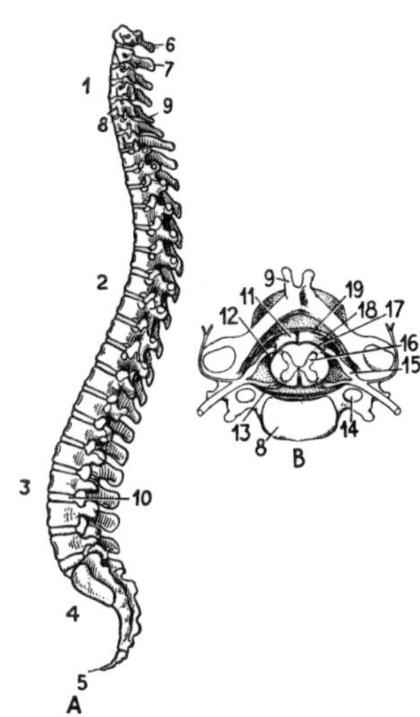

SPINE: A. VERTEBRAE. B. SECTION OF 5TH CERVICAL VERTEBRA

A. 1. Cervical vertebrae. 2. Thoracic vertebrae. 3. Lumbar vertebrae. 4. Sacrum. 5. Coccyx. 6. Atlas. 7. Axis. 8. Body of vertebra. 9. Spine of vertebra. 10. Intervertebral disc. B. 11. Spinal cord. 12. Posterior root of spinal nerve (sensory). 13. Anterior root (motor). 14. Foramen for vertebral artery. 15. Posterior root ganglion. 16. Grey matter. 17, 18, 19. Meninges (17. *Pia mater*, 18. *Arachnoid*, 19. *Dura mater*)

spĭn'el *n.* (min.) Hard crystalline (octohedral) mineral of various colours, essentially a compound of magnesium and alumina; esp. the deep-red variety (the gem ~ *ruby*).

spīne'less (-nl-) *adj.* Invertebrate; having no spines; (fig.) limp, weak.

spinĕt' (*or* spĭn'-) *n.* Small keyboard instrument (17th–18th c.) of harpsichord type but smaller, and with only one string to a note. [prob. f. name of Giovanni *Spinetti* of Venice (*c* 1500)]

spĭnn'aker *n.* Large 3-cornered sail carried on mainmast opposite mainsail of racing-yacht running before wind (ill. YACHT). [fanciful formation f. *Sphinx*, name of yacht first using it]

spĭnn'er *n.* (esp.) Spinning-machine; manufacturer engaged in (esp. cotton-) spinning; kinds of trout-fly, spinning bait.

spĭnn'eret *n.* 1. Organ in certain insects, esp. nipple-like process on spider's abdomen, tubule on lower lip of silkworm, for producing silk, gossamer, etc. (ill. SPIDER). 2. Contrivance of glass or metal with fine holes through which viscous solution is forced, to form filaments or threads, in making of artificial silk.

spĭnn'ey *n.* Small wood, thicket.

spĭnn'ĭng *n.* ~-*jenny*, spinning-machine with several spindles; ~-*wheel*, simple spinning-apparatus in which spindle is driven by wheel worked by hand or foot.

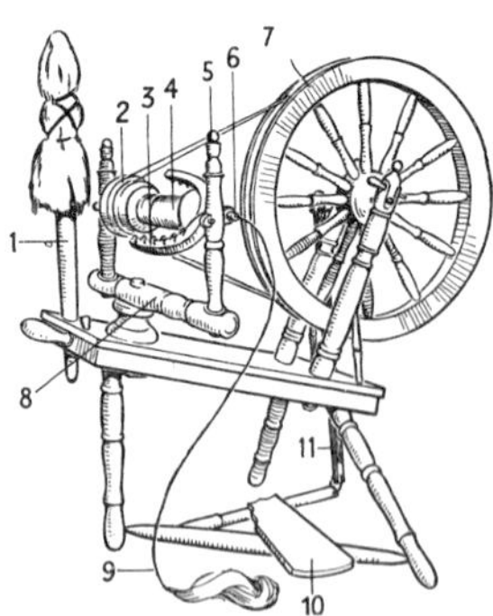

SPINNING WHEEL

1. Distaff. 2. Flier or spindle whorl. 3. Hackle. 4. Bobbin. 5. Maiden. 6. Spindle. 7. Wheel. 8. Mother-of-all. 9. Yarn. 10. Treadle. 11. Footman

spīn'ōse, spīn'ous *adjs.* Armed or furnished with spines; slender and sharp-pointed like a spine.

Spĭnōz'a, Benedict (Baurd) de (1632–77). Philosopher, a Dutch Jew of Portuguese origin; author of 'Ethics', in which he rejected the Cartesian dualism of spirit and matter and saw only 'one infinite substance, of which finite existences are modes or limitations'; God was for Spinoza the immanent cause of the universe, not a ruler outside it, and his system is thus in a sense pantheistic; he also denied personal immortality and the transcendent distinction between good and evil. **Spĭnōz'ĭsm, Spĭnōz'ĭst** *ns.*

spĭn'ster *n.* Unmarried woman, esp., in popular use, old maid. [orig. = 'woman who spins']

spĭnthă'rĭscōpe *n.* Instrument making radium emanations visible as tiny flashes or sparks on fluorescent screen.

spĭn'ūle *n.* (bot., zool.) Small spine. **spĭn'ūlōse, spĭn'ūlous** *adjs.*

spīn'y *adj.* Full of spines, prickly; (fig.) perplexing, troublesome, thorny.

spīr'acle *n.* (zool.) Special orifice or pore for respiration in insects etc. (ill. INSECT); reduced first gill-slit in fishes, blow-hole of cetacean.

spīrae'a *n.* Large genus of rosaceous plants or shrubs with simple leaves and small pink or white flowers in panicles, racemes, or corymbs.

spīr'al *adj.* Coiled in cylindrical or conical manner; curving continuously round fixed point in same place at a steadily increasing (or diminishing) distance from it. **spīr'ally** *adv.* **spīr'al** *n.* Anything of spiral form; (geom. etc.) continuous curve traced by point moving round fixed point in same

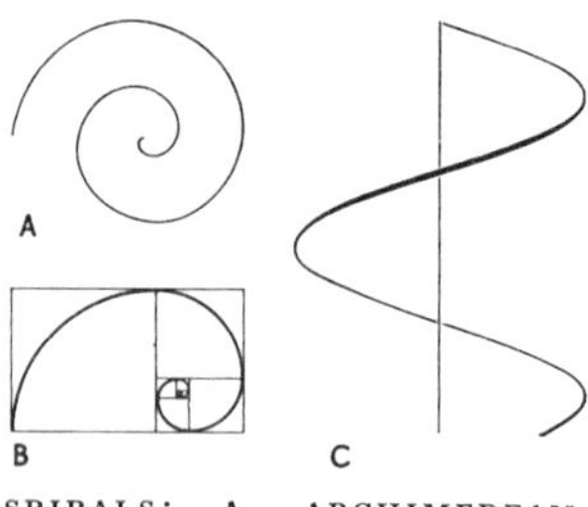

SPIRALS: A. ARCHIMEDEAN. B. VOLUTE. C. HELIX

The helix is three-dimensional

plane at steadily increasing or diminishing distance; curve traced by point simultaneously moving round and advancing along cylinder or cone; spiral nebula; flight in spiral path; progressive but gradual rise or fall, e.g. the vicious spiral of rising wages or prices; ~ *v.i.* Wind or move in spiral path, (of aeroplane, pilot) descend (or ascend) in spiral path.

spīr'ant *adj.* & *n.* (Consonantal sound) formed by a constriction, but not a total closure, of the air-passage, so that the air-stream passes continuously and the sound is capable of being prolonged (opp. STOP, sense 6).

spīre[1] *n.* Tapering structure in form of tall cone or pyramid rising

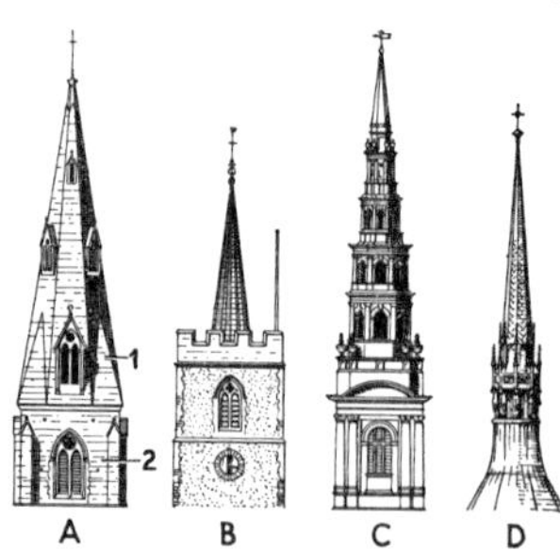

SPIRES: A. BROACH SPIRE. B. LEAD SPIRE ON PARAPETTED TOWER. C. ST. BRIDE'S LONDON (WREN). D. FLÈCHE

1. Scuncheon. 2. Belfry

above tower, esp. of church; tapering or pointed top of anything.

spīre[2] *n.* Spiral, coil; single fold or convolution of this.

spĭ'rĭt *n.* 1. Animating or vital principle, intelligent or immaterial part of man, soul; person viewed as possessing this, esp. with ref. to particular mental or moral qualities. 2. Rational or intelligent being not connected with material body; disembodied soul; incorporeal being, elf, fairy; ~-*rapping*, professed communication with spirits by means of raps thought to be made by them. 3. Person's mental or moral nature or qualities; essential character or qualities, prevailing tone, general meaning, *of* something; mental or moral condition or attribute, mood; mettle, vigour, courage, energy, dash. 4. Strong alcoholic liquor got by distillation (usu. pl.); distilled extract, alcoholic solution *of* some substance; ~(*s*) *of salt*(*s*), commerc. name of hydrochloric acid; ~(*s*) *of wine*, alcohol; ~ *lamp*, lamp, esp. for heating or boiling, fed by methylated or other spirits; ~ *level*, levelling instrument used for determining a horizontal line or surface, usu. consisting of a hermetically sealed glass tube filled with spirit and containing an air-bubble, which when the tube lies exactly horizontal occupies a position midway in its length. ~ *v.t.* Convey (*away*, *off*, etc.) rapidly and secretly (as) by agency of spirits.

spĭ'rĭtėd *adj.* 1. Full of spirit; animated, lively, brisk; courageous. 2. Having specified spirit(s). **spĭ'rĭtėdly** *adv.* **spĭ'rĭtėdnėss** *n.*

spĭ'rĭtĭsm *n.* = SPIRITUALISM. **spĭ'rĭtĭst** *adj.* & *n.* **spĭrĭtĭs'tĭc** *adj.*

spĭ'rĭtlėss *adj.* Wanting in ardour, animation, or courage. **spĭ'rĭtlėssly** *adv.* **spĭ'rĭtlėssnėss** *n.*

spĭ'rĭtūal *adj.* Of spirit as opp. to matter; of the soul esp. as acted upon by God; of, proceeding from, God, holy, divine, inspired; concerned with sacred or religious things; ecclesiastical; *Lords* ~, the bishops and archbishops in the House of Lords. **spĭ'rĭtūally** *adv.* **spĭ'rĭtūalnėss** *n.* **spĭ'rĭtūal** *n.* Characteristic religious song of Amer. Negroes.

spĭ'rĭtūalĭsm *n.* Belief that spirits of dead can communicate with the living, esp. through a 'medium'; system of doctrines or practices founded on this. **spĭ'rĭtūalĭst** *n.* **spĭrĭtūalĭs'tĭc** *adj.* **spĭrĭtualĭst'ĭcally** *adv.*

spĭrĭtūăl'ĭty *n.* 1. Spiritual quality. 2. (usu. pl.) What belongs or is due to the Church or to an ecclesiastic as such.

spĭ'rĭtūalīze *v.t.* Make spiritual.

spĭ'rĭtūous *adj.* Containing much alcohol; ~ *liquor*, one produced by distillation, not by fermentation alone.

spīr'ochaete (-kēt) *n.* Any of various slender flexible micro-organisms with spiral bodies, many of which cause diseases in man.

spîrt *v.* & *n.* = SPURT[2].

spĭt[1] *n.* 1. Slender pointed rod thrust into meat for roasting at fire (ill. FIRE). 2. Small low point of land running into water. ~ *v.t.* Pierce, transfix, (as) with spit.

spĭt[2] *v.* (past t. and past part. *spăt*). Eject saliva; eject (saliva, food, etc., *out*) from mouth; (fig.) utter vehemently; (of cat etc.) make noise as of spitting as sign of anger or hostility; (of rain etc.) fall thinly; (of pen etc.) sputter; *spit'fire*, fiery-tempered person; *Spit'fire* single-seater fighter aircraft of British design, used in war of 1939–45. ~ *n.* Spittle; act, instance, of spitting; *the very* ~ *of*, exact counterpart of.

spĭt[3] *n.* Depth of earth pierced by full length of spade-blade.

spĭtch'cŏck *n.* Eel split or cut up and boiled or fried. ~ *v.t.* Prepare (eel etc.) thus.

spīte *n.* Ill-will, malice; *in* ~ *of*, notwithstanding. **spīte'ful** (-tf-) *adj.* **spīte'fully** *adv.* **spīte'fulnėss** *n.* **spīte** *v.t.* Thwart, mortify, annoy.

Spĭts'bêrgen (-g-). Archipelago in the Arctic Ocean, N. of Norway, under Norwegian sovereignty.

spĭt'tle *n.* Saliva, spit.

spĭttōōn' *n.* Receptacle for spittle.

spĭv *n.* 'Contact man' who puts blackmarketeers in touch with their prospective customers, receiving a commission on sales for his services; hence, (flashily dressed) person living on his wits. **spĭv'ish** *adj.* **spĭvv'ery** *n.* Activity characteristic of a spiv. [prob. connected with Engl. colloq. and dial. *spiff*, flashily dressed person]

splăsh *v.* Bespatter (*with* water etc.); dash, spatter (liquid); (of liquid) fly about in drops or scattered portions; cause liquid to do this; step, fall, etc., *into* (water etc.) so as to cause it to splash; mark, mottle, with irregular patches of colour etc.; *splash'down*, landing of spacecraft in sea. **splăsh'y** *adj.* **splăsh** *n.* Act, result, or sound of splashing; quantity of fluid splashed; dash of soda-water in spirits; large irregular patch of colour etc.; (colloq.) striking or ostentatious display or effect; ~*-board*, guard in front of vehicle to keep mud off occupants; ~ *headline*, in newspaper, conspicuous one designed to attract attention.

splăt *n.* Flat piece of wood forming central part of chair-back, whence ~*-back*(*ed*) (*adj.*) (ill. CHAIR).

splay *n.* (archit.) Slope or bevel, esp. at sides of door- or window-opening (ill. WINDOW). ~ *adj.* Wide and flat, spread or turned out; ~(-)*foot*, (having) broad, flat clumsy foot turned outwards. ~ *v.* Bevel; construct (aperture) with divergent sides, be so constructed.

spleen *n.* Dark-red abdominal organ (in mammals situated beneath diaphragm on left side) which is concerned in the formation of antibodies and the destruction of red blood-cells (ill. ABDOMEN); this as the supposed seat of the passions; ill-nature, spite; lowness of spirits, melancholia (archaic); *spleenwort*, fern of genus *Asplenium*. **spleen'ful** *adj.* **spleen'fully** *adv.* **spleen'fulnėss** *n.*

splĕn'dent *adj.* Shining, bright, brilliant.

splĕn'dĭd *adj.* Magnificent, grand, sumptuous, brilliant, gorgeous; excellent, very good or fine. **splĕn'dĭdly** *adv.*

splĕndĭf'erous *adj.* (colloq.) Magnificent, splendid.

splĕn'dour *n.* Great brightness; magnificence, parade, pomp, brilliance.

splėnĕt'ĭc *adj.* & *n.* Ill-tempered, peevish, (person); of the spleen. **splėnĕt'ĭcally** *adv.*

splĕn'ĭc *adj.* Of, in, the spleen.

splīce *n.* Joining of two ends of rope etc. by untwisting and interweaving strands at point of junction; overlapping join of two

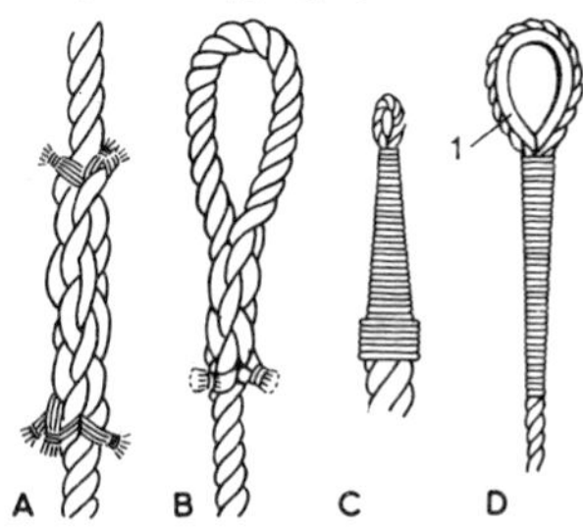

A. SHORT SPLICE. B. EYE SPLICE. C. BECKET. D. THIMBLE EYE

1. Thimble

pieces of wood etc.; part of cricket-bat handle inserted in blade. ~ *v.t.* Join by splice; (colloq.) join in marriage; ~ *the main brace*: see MAIN[1].

splĭnt *n.* Appliance to keep in position or protect injured part, esp. strip of more or less rigid material for holding fractured bone in position; bony excrescence in cannon-bone of leg of horse or mule, usu. on inner side; ~*-bone*, either of two small metacarpal or metatarsal bones in leg of horse etc. (ill. HORSE); ~ *coal*, hard bituminous laminated coal giving great heat. ~ *v.t.* Put into splints, secure with splint(s).

splĭn'ter *n.* Rough, sharp-edged, or thin piece of wood, bone, stone, etc., broken or split off. ~ *v.* Split into splinters. **splĭn'tery** *adj.* Like splinter(s); apt to splinter.

splĭt *v.* (past t. and past part. *splĭt*). Break forcibly, be broken, into parts, esp. with the grain or plane of cleavage; divide into parts, thicknesses, shares, etc.; divide into factions, groups, etc.; (slang) peach, inform (*on*). **splĭt** (past part.) *adj.* ~ *infinitive*, infinitive with adverb etc. inserted between *to* and verb, e.g. *seems to partly correspond*; ~ *personality*, alteration or dissociation of personality such as may occur in certain mental illnesses esp. schizophrenia and hysteria; ~ *pin*, pin with one end split so that it may be spread open to keep it in position; ~ *ring*, ring consisting of two turns of spiral or helix pressed flat together, on which keys etc. may be strung; ~ *second*, a very brief moment of time; ~ *stitch*: see ill. STITCH. ~ *n.* Act, result, of splitting; cleft, rent, fissure; rupture, breach; anything formed by splitting, as single thickness of split hide; half-bottle of mineral-water; split roll or bun; (pl.) in acrobatic dancing etc., movement in which body is lowered to floor between legs widely separated at right angles to trunk.

splŏdge, splŏtch *ns.* Large irregular spot or patch; blot, smear. **splŏtch** *v.t.* Cover or splash with splotches. **splŏtch'y** *adj.*

splŏsh *n.* (colloq.) Quantity of water suddenly dropped or thrown; (slang) money.

splûrge *n.* & *v.i.* (U.S.) (Make) noisy or ostentatious effort.

splŭtt'er *v.* Utter, talk, hastily and indistinctly or confusedly; scatter or fly in small splashes or pieces; make sputtering sound. ~ *n.* Noise or fuss; loud sputter or splash.

Spōde. Kind of fine pottery, named after the maker Josiah Spode (1754–1827) of Stoke on Trent, England.

spoil *v.* (past t. and past part. *spoilt* or *spoiled*). 1. (archaic) Plunder, deprive (*of* thing) by force or stealth. 2. Destroy or impair good, valuable, or effective qualities of; prevent full exercise or enjoyment of; ~*-sport*, one who spoils sport or enjoyment of others. 3. Injure character of (person) by over-indulgence; cosset. 4. Deteriorate, decay, go bad. ~ *n.* (usu. pl. or collect. sing.) Plunder, booty, taken from enemy in war or acquired by violence; (chiefly U.S. and pl.) public offices etc. distributed among supporters of successful political party; ~*s system*, practice of such distribution.

spōke *n.* Each of set of bars or rods radiating from hub to rim of wheel (ill. WHEEL); each radial handle of steering-wheel; rung of ladder; *spoke'shave*, tool with

SPOKESHAVE

blade or plane-bit between two handles used for planing curved surface, shaping spokes, etc. ~ *v.t.* Furnish with spokes.

spōkes'man (-ks-) *n.* One who speaks for others, representative.

spōliā'tion *n.* 1. Despoiling, plundering, pillaging. 2. (eccles.) Appropriation of fruits of benefice by one incumbent to detriment of another. 3. (law) Destruction of, tampering with, document to destroy its value as evidence.

spŏndā'ic *adj.* Composed of spondees; (of hexameter) with spondee as 5th foot.

spŏn'dee *n.* Metrical foot of two long syllables, — —.

sponge (-ŭnj) *n.* 1. Various aquatic (chiefly marine) animals of the group *Porifera*, with tough elastic skeleton of interlacing horny fibres. 2. Soft, light,

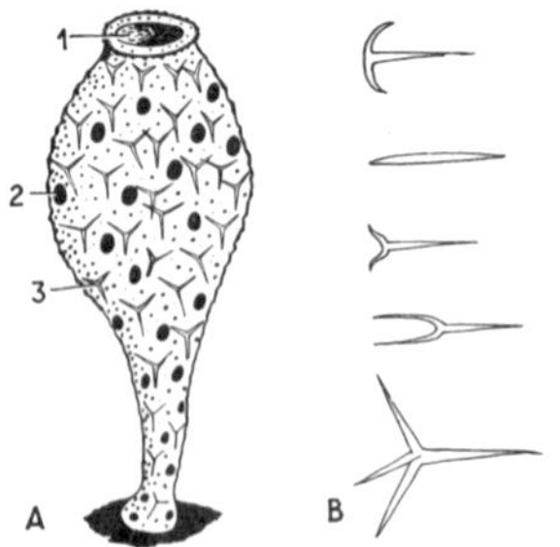

A. SPONGE. B. TYPES OF SPONGE SPICULES

1. Osculum. 2. Pore. 3. Spicule

porous, easily compressible, highly absorbent framework remaining after living matter has been removed from various *Porifera*, used in bathing, cleansing surfaces, etc.; porous rubber etc. used similarly. 3. Thing of sponge-like absorbency or consistence; sponge-cake; soft porous leavened dough in bread-making. 4. Immoderate drinker, soaker; person who contrives to live at others' expense. 5. Sponging; bath, swill, with sponge. 6. ~*-cake*, very light sweet cake of flour, beaten eggs, and sugar; ~*-cloth*, loose-textured cotton fabric with wrinkled surface. ~ *v.* 1. Wipe, cleanse, with sponge, wet *with* liquid applied with sponge; wipe out, efface, (as) with sponge; absorb, take *up* (liquid) with sponge. 2. Live on others as parasite, be meanly dependent *on* (esp. ~ *on* person *for* money etc.); *sponging-house*, (hist.) house kept by bailiff or sheriff's officer, used as place of preliminary confinement for debtors.

spon'ger (-ŭnj-) *n.* (esp.) One who sponges for money etc.

spon'giform (-ŭnj-) *adj.* (zool.) Formed like sponge.

spon'gin (-ŭnj-) *n.* Horny or fibrous substance forming skeleton of many sponges.

spŏngŏl'ogy (-ngg-) *n.* Study of sponges. **spŏngŏl'ogist** *n.*

spon'gy (-ŭnj-) *adj.* Sponge-like; esp. porous, compressible, absorbent, or soft, as sponge.

spŏn'sion (-shn) *n.* Being surety for another; (international law) engagement on behalf of State by agent not specially authorized.

spŏn'son *n.* Projection from ship's side, as gun-platform, triangular platform before or abaft paddle-box, etc. (ill. AIRCRAFT-carrier).

spŏn'sor *n.* Godfather or godmother; person making himself responsible for another; advertiser paying cost of broadcast programme into which advertisements of his wares are introduced. **spŏnsŏr'ial** *adj.* **spŏn'sorship** *n.* **spŏn'sor** *v.t.* Act as sponsor for; support, favour, advocate.

spŏntān'ėous *adj.* Acting, done, occurring, without external cause; voluntary; (of movements etc.) involuntary, not due to conscious volition; ~ *combustion*, combustion produced by chemical action within substance; ~ *generation*, abiogenesis, development of living organisms from non-living matter. **spŏntān'ėously** *adv.* **spŏntān'ėousnėss, spŏntanē'ity** *ns.*

spŏntōōn' *n.* (hist.) Kind of halberd used by some British infantry officers (ill. INFANTRY).

spōōf *n.* & *v.t.* Swindle, hoax, humbug. [orig. game invented by Engl. comedian A. Roberts (b. 1852)]

spōōk *n.* (colloq.) Ghost. **spōōk'ish, spōōk'y** *adjs.*

spōōl *n.* Reel for winding yarn, wire, photographic film, fishing-line, etc., on. ~ *v.t.* Wind on spool.

spōōn *n.* Utensil consisting of round or usu. oval bowl and a handle, used for conveying soft or liquid food to mouth, in cooking, etc.; spoon-shaped thing, esp. wooden golf-club with slightly concave face (ill. GOLF); kind of artificial bait used in spinning for fish; ~*-bill*, various wading-birds related to ibises, with long bill expanded and flattened at tip; ~*-bread*, (U.S.) kind of bread, usu. of corn-meal, so soft that it must be served with spoon; ~*-fed*, fed with spoon like child; (fig.) pampered, coddled. ~ *v.* 1. Take, lift, etc., with spoon. 2. Behave amorously, make love, esp. in sentimental fashion.

spōōn'erism *n.* Accidental transposition of initial or other sounds of two or more words (e.g. *blushing crow*, for *crushing blow*). [Rev. W. A. *Spooner* (1844–1930), Warden of New Coll., Oxford]

spōōn'y *adj.* Soft, silly; sentimentally amorous. **spōōn'ily** *adv.* **spōōn'inėss** *n.*

spoor *n.* Track, trail, of animal or person. ~ *v.t.* Trace by spoor.

sporăd'ic *adj.* Occurring in isolated instances or very small numbers; scattered, dispersed; occasional. **sporăd'ically** *adv.* **sporăd'icalnėss** *n.*

sporăn'gium (-j-) *n.* (pl. *-gia*). (bot.) Receptacle containing spores (ill. FERN).

spōre *n.* Minute reproductive body produced by plants and some protozoa and capable of development into new individual independently (ill. FERN); ~*-case*, sporangium.

spŏ'rran *n.* Pouch, usu. of skin with hair left on, worn with the kilt, slung round the waist and hanging down in front (ill. PLAID). [Gael. *sporan*]

spōrt *n.* 1. Amusement, diversion, fun; plaything, toy; pastime(s), game(s), esp. of athletic or open-air character; pastime afforded by taking or killing wild animals, game, or fish; (pl.) (meeting for competition in) athletic pastimes. 2. Animal, plant, etc., exhibiting abnormal variation from parent stock or type. 3. (slang) Good fellow; sportsman. 4. *sports car, model*, etc., car of open low-built fast type; *sports coat, suit*, etc., coat etc. suitable for outdoor sports or for informal wear; *sports'man, sports'woman*, person fond of sports, esp. hunting, shooting, etc.; good fellow; one displaying good qualities of sportsman, esp. desire for fair play, in ordinary life; *sports'manlike*, befitting, worthy of, a sportsman. ~ *v.* 1. Divert oneself; take part in pastime. 2. (bot. etc.) Become, produce, a sport. 3. Wear, exhibit, produce, esp. ostentatiously.

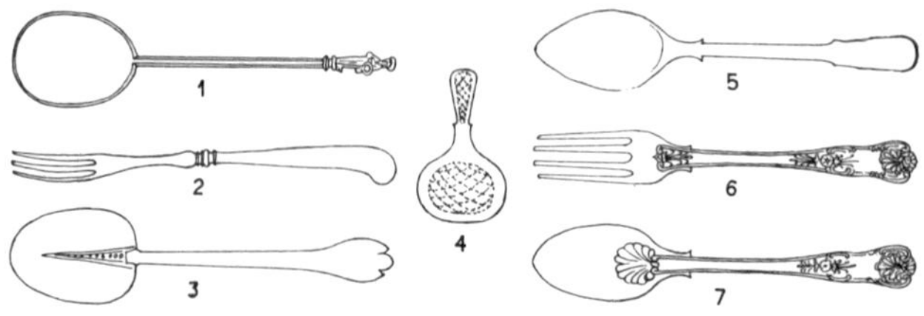

SPOONS AND FORKS

1. Apostle spoon. 2. Fork with pistol handle. 3. Rat-tailed spoon with trifid end to stem (back). 4. Caddy-spoon. 5. Fiddle pattern spoon. 6. King's pattern fork (back). 7. King's pattern spoon (back)

spŏrt′ing *adj.* Interested in sport; sportsmanlike; ~ *chance*, one involving risk, but offering possibility of success. **spŏrt′ingly** *adv.*

spŏrt′ive *adj.* Playful. **spŏrt′ively** *adv.* **spŏrt′ivenėss** *n.*

spŏrt′y *adj.* (slang) Sporting; characteristic of a sport, showy.

spŏ′rūle *n.* (Small) spore. **spŏ′rūlar** *adj.*

spŏt *n.* 1. Speck, stain, small discolouring or disfiguring mark; eruptive mark on skin, pimple; dark mark on sun etc.; small, usu. roundish mark on surface; moral blemish, stain; (billiards) marked place on table, esp. that on which red ball is placed (ill. BILLIARDS); (*be, put*) *in a* ~, in difficulties, in an awkward situation; *put on the* ~, (U.S. slang) determine assassination of. 2. Particular place, definite locality; *on the* ~, at once, straightway; at the very place; equal to situation, wide awake. 3. (colloq.) Small amount, particle, drop (*of*); a drink. 4. ~-*ball*, (billiards) ball marked with black spot; ~ *cash*, money paid, delivered, immediately on sale or other transaction; ~-*light*, (theatre) beam of light thrown on particular actor, projector used for this purpose; bright light on motor-car etc. which can be turned and focussed on particular object; (*v.t.*) illuminate with spot-light. **spŏtt′y, spŏt′lėss** *adjs.* **spŏtt′iness, spŏt′lėssnėss** *ns.* **spŏt** *v.* 1. Mark, stain, soil, with spots; (of textile etc.) be (liable to be) marked with spots. 2. (colloq.) Single out, detect, mark out, note; esp. single out (winner in race etc.) beforehand. 3. Act as spotter.

spŏtt′ėd *adj.* (past part. of SPOT). Marked with spots (freq. in names of animals etc.); ~ *dog*, Dalmatian dog; plum-duff, pudding spotted with currants; ~ *fever*, pop. name for cerebro-spinal meningitis; (also) typhus.

spŏtt′er *n.* (esp.) Watcher on roof, observer in aircraft, etc., noting approach or position of enemy forces, effect of gun-fire or bombing, etc.

spouse (-z) *n.* Husband or wife.

spout *n.* Projecting tube, pipe, or lip, through which rain-water is carried off from roof, liquid is poured from tea-pot, kettle, etc., or issues from fountain, pump, etc.; jet, column, of liquid, etc.; whale's spiracle; sloping trough down which thing may be shot into receptacle; *up the* ~, pawned, pledged; ~-*hole*, spiracle of whale etc.; natural hole in rocks through which sea spouts. ~ *v.* Discharge, issue, forcibly in a jet; utter in declamatory manner, speechify.

S.P.Q.R. *abbrev. Senatus Populusque Romanus* (= the senate and people of Rome); small profits and quick returns.

S.P.R. *abbrev.* Society for Psychical Research.

sprain *v.t.* Wrench (joint of body, esp. ankle or wrist) violently so as to cause pain and swelling. *n.* Such wrench; resulting inflammation and swelling.

sprăt *n.* Small European herring, *Clupea sprattus*, common on Atlantic coasts; any similar fish. *v.i.* Fish for sprats.

sprawl *v.* Spread oneself, spread (limbs) out in careless or ungainly way; straggle. ~ *n.* Sprawling movement or attitude; straggling group or mass.

spray[1] *n.* Slender shoot or twig, graceful branch with flowers etc., esp. used for decoration or ornament.

spray[2] *n.* Water or other liquid dispersed in small mist-like drops by wind, waves, atomizer, etc.; preparation intended for spraying; instrument or apparatus for applying spray. ~ *v.* Scatter, diffuse, as spray; sprinkle (as) with spray.

spread (-ĕd) *v.* (past t. and past part. *spread*). Extend surface of, stretch out, cause to cover larger surface, by unrolling, unfolding, smearing, flattening out, etc.; cover surface of; show extended or extensive surface; diffuse, be diffused. ~ (past part.) *adj.* ~ *eagle*, representation of eagle with legs and wings extended; something resembling this; *attrib.* (U.S., in allusion to figure of spread eagle on U.S. flags etc.) bombastic, noisily patriotic, jingoistic; ~-*eagle* (*v.t.*) extend, fix, in form of spread eagle; ~-*over*, arrangement by which fixed number of working-hours may be worked at any time within given period. ~ *n.* Spreading; being spread; extent or expanse, breadth, compass, span; feast, meal (colloq.); sweet or savoury paste for spreading on bread.

spree *n.* Lively frolic, bout of drinking, etc.

sprĭg *n.* 1. Small headless nail, usu. wedge-shaped; small projecting point. 2. Small branch, spray; ornament in form of sprig or spray. 3. (usu. contempt.) Youth, young man. ~ *v.t.* Ornament with sprigs.

spright′ly (-īt-) *adj.* Vivacious, lively, gay. **spright′linėss** *n.*

sprĭng *v.* (past t. *sprăng*, past part. *sprŭng*). 1. Leap, jump, move rapidly or suddenly, esp. from constrained position or by action of a spring; arise, take rise; originate; (of wood) warp, split, crack. 2. Rouse (game) from earth or cover; cause to spring, move suddenly, etc.; cause to work by a spring; produce, develop, suddenly or unexpectedly; explode (mine etc.); develop (leak). ~ *n.* 1. Leap; power of springing, elasticity, springiness; place from which vault or arch springs or rises. 2. Elastic contrivance possessing property of returning to normal shape after being compressed, bent, coiled, etc., used for lessening or preventing concussion, as motivating power in clockwork etc. (ill. CLOCK); moving or actuating agency, motive; source, origin. 3. Place where water, oil, etc., wells up from underground rocks; flow of water etc. rising from earth. 4. Season of year between winter and summer, season in which vegetation begins, popularly reckoned in N. hemisphere as comprising March, April, and May, but astronomically as lasting from vernal equinox (20th or 21st March) to summer solstice (21st or 22nd June). 5. ~-*balance*, balance measuring weight by elasticity of steel spring (ill. BALANCE); ~-*bed*, (bed with) spring mattress; *spring′-board*, elastic board, esp. stout projecting board from end of which person jumps or dives; ~-*clean*, clean house etc. thoroughly, esp. in spring; ~ *gun*, gun discharged by spring when trespasser or animal stumbles on it; ~-*halt*, convulsive movement of horse's hind leg in walking; ~ *lock*, lock with bolt closing by means of spring; ~ *mattress*, one containing or consisting of springs, esp. of small springs woven into mesh; *spring′tail*, various small insects leaping by means of long elastic caudal appendages; ~ *tide*, highest tide, occurring on days shortly after new and full moon; *spring′-tide, spring′time*, season of spring; ~-*water*, water from spring. **sprĭng′lėss, sprĭng′like, sprĭng′y** (-ngĭ) *adjs.* **sprĭng′inėss** (-ngĭ-) *n.*

sprĭng′bŏk *n.* S. African species of gazelle (*Antidorcas euchore*), springing lightly and suddenly in air when disturbed. [S. Afr. Du., f. *springen* spring, *bok* antelope]

sprĭnge (-j) *n.* Noose, snare, for catching small game.

sprĭng′er *n.* (esp.) 1. (archit.) Support from which arch springs (ill. ARCH). 2. Medium-sized gun-dog of spaniel sort, freq. black-and-white, used for flushing game.

sprĭnk′le (-ngkl) *v.* Scatter in small drops or particles; subject to sprinkling (*with* liquid etc.); (of liquid etc.) fall thus on. ~ *n.* Slight shower (*of* rain etc.). **sprĭnk′ler** *n.* Contrivance for sprinkling (water on soil etc.).

sprĭnt *v.i.* Run etc. at top speed, esp. for short distance. ~ *n.* Short spell of sprinting; short race run at full speed over whole distance.

sprĭt[1] *n.* Small spar reaching diagonally from mast to upper outer corner of sail (ill. BARGE); *sprit′sail* (-sāl, -sl), sail extended by sprit.

sprĭt[2] *n.* & *v.* (chiefly dial.) Shoot, sprout.

sprīte *n.* Elf, fairy, goblin.

sprŏck′ėt *n.* Projection or tooth on rim of wheel engaging with links of chain; ~-*wheel*, wheel with sprockets (ill. TRACTOR).

sprout *v.* Begin to grow, shoot forth, put forth shoots; spring up, grow to a height; produce by sprouting. ~ *n.* Shoot, new growth, from plant; (pl.) young and tender side-shoots of plants of cabbage kind, Brussels sprouts.

spruce[1] (-ōōs) *n.* Genus of fir (*Picea*) with dense foliage and soft light wood; wood of these; ~ *beer*, fermented drink made from leaves and small branches of spruce; ~ *fir*, spruce. [AF. *Pruce* Prussia]

spruce[2] (-ōōs) *adj.* Trim, neat, smart in appearance. **spruce'ly** (-sl-) *adv.* **spruce'nėss** *n.* **spruce** *v.t.* Smarten (*up*), make spruce.

sprue[1] (-ōō) *n.* Tropical disease with chronic inflammation of bowel and ulceration of mouth. [Du. *spr(o)uw* THRUSH[2]]

sprue[2] (-ōō) *n.* Hole through which metal is poured into mould; metal filling sprue.

sprue[3] (-ōō) *n.* Asparagus of inferior quality.

sprŭng *adj.* (esp.) 1. Furnished with springs. 2. (colloq.) Tipsy.

sprȳ *adj.* Active, nimble, lively. **sprȳ'ly** *adv.* **sprȳ'nėss** *n.*

s.p.s. *abbrev. Sine prole superstite* (= without surviving issue).

spŭd *n.* 1. Small sharp narrow spade, occas. with prongs instead of blade, for digging up big-rooted weeds etc. 2. (colloq.) Potato. ~ *v.t.* Dig (*up, out*) with spud.

spue: see SPEW.

spūme *n.* & *v.i.* Froth, foam. **spūm'ous, spūm'y** *adjs.*

spūmĕs'cence *n.* Foaminess.

spŭn *adj.* (past part. of SPIN). That has undergone spinning; (of butter, sugar, etc.) drawn out into threads for ornamenting cakes etc.; ~ *glass*, glass drawn into thread while liquid; ~ *gold, silver*, thread wound round with gold or silver ribbon or wire; ~ *silk*, thread or fabric made from floss or waste silk, freq. mixed with cotton.

spŭnk *n.* Spirit, mettle, pluck. **spŭnk'y** *adj.* [orig. 'spank']

spûr *n.* 1. Small spike or spiked wheel attached to rider's heel for urging horse etc. forward; (fig.)

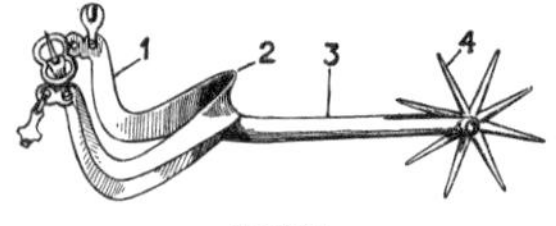

SPUR

1. Arm. 2. Crest. 3. Neck. 4. Rowel

incentive, stimulus; *on the ~ of the moment*, without premeditation; *win one's ~s*, (hist.) gain knighthood; gain distinction, make a name. 2. Spur-shaped thing; hard process or projection on cock's leg, steel point fastened to this in cockfight; range, ridge, mountain, etc., projecting from main system or mass; short branch or shoot, esp. one bearing fruit; (bot.) tubular projecting part, usu. nectary, of corolla or calyx (ill. FLOWER). ~ *v.* 1. Prick (horse) with spurs; incite, urge, prompt; provide with spur(s); ride hard, hasten.

spûrge *n.* Various plants of genus *Euphorbia*, with acrid milky juice with medicinal properties; ~ *flax, laurel*, shrubs of European and Asiatic genus *Daphne*.

Spûr'geon (-jn), Charles Haddon (1834–92). English popular Baptist preacher.

spûr'ious *adj.* Not genuine or authentic; not what it appears, claims, or pretends to be. **spûr'iously** *adv.* **spûr'iousnėss** *n.*

spûrn *v.* Repel, thrust back, with foot; reject with disdain, treat with contempt.

spŭ'rr(e)y *n.* Weed of chickweed family (*Spergula*), with slender stems and narrow leaves, esp. the white-flowered *corn* ~ (*S. arvensis*), occas. used as fodder.

spûrt[1] *v.i.* & *n.* (Make) short sudden violent effort, esp. in racing.

spûrt[2] *v.* (Cause to) gush out in a jet or stream. ~ *n.* Sudden gushing out, jet.

sput'nĭk (spŏŏ-) *n.* Russian earth SATELLITE. [Russ., = 'travelling companion']

spŭtt'er *v.* Emit with spitting sound; spit, splutter; speak, utter, rapidly or incoherently; speak in rapid or vehement fashion. ~ *n.* Sputtering; sputtering speech.

spūt'um *n.* (pl. *-ta*). Saliva, spittle; thick expectorated matter characteristic of some diseased states of lungs or throat.

spȳ *n.* Secret agent, one keeping secret watch on person, place, etc.; person employed by a government, esp. in time of war, to obtain information relating to defences, military and naval affairs, etc., of other countries. ~ *v.* 1. Act as spy (*on, upon*). 2. Discern, make out, esp. by careful observation; ~ *out*, explore secretly, discover thus; *~-glass*, small hand telescope, field-glass.

sq. *abbrev.* Square.

Sqn. Ldr *abbrev.* Squadron-Leader.

sq(q). *abbrev. Sequentes, sequentia* (= (and) the following lines, (and) what follows).

squab (-ŏb) *n.* Young, esp. unfledged, pigeon; short fat person; thickly stuffed loose cushion, esp. forming seat or back of seat of motor-car etc. ~ *adj.* Short and fat, squat.

squa'bble (-ŏbl) *v.i.* & *n.* (Engage in) petty or noisy quarrel.

squad (-ŏd) *n.* (mil.) Small number of men grouped or assembled for drill etc.; small party of persons; *flying* ~, small organized body, esp. of police, capable of rapid movement to any place.

squa'dron (-ŏd-) *n.* Division of cavalry regiment of between 100 and 200 men, 2 troops; division of fleet forming unit, esp. detachment employed on particular service; division of a military air-force, freq. of about 12 machines, with pilots, ground-staff, etc.; *~-leader*, officer of R.A.F. next above flight-lieutenant.

squa'lĭd (-ŏl-) *adj.* Dirty, foul, filthy, mean in appearance. **squa'lĭdly** *adv.* **squa'lĭdnėss, squa'lor** *ns.*

squall (-awl) *n.* 1. Sudden violent gust (*of* wind, rain, etc.). 2. Discordant cry, scream. ~ *v.* Scream loudly or discordantly; utter in harsh or screaming voice. **squa'lly** *adj.*

squāl'oid *adj.* & *n.* (Fish) of or resembling genus *Squalus* of sharks.

squām'a *n.* (pl. *-ae*). (zool., anat., bot., etc.) Scale; scale-like portion of bone etc. **squām'ōse, squām'ous** *adjs.*

squa'nder (-ŏn-) *v.t.* Spend wastefully, dissipate.

squāre *n.* 1. Plane rectilinear rectangular figure with 4 equal sides (ill. QUADRILATERAL); object (approximately) of this shape; quadrilateral area, open space, esp. enclosed by buildings or dwelling-houses, buildings surrounding this; (U.S.) block (of buildings), area, surrounded by streets; body of troops drawn up in square formation; *on the* ~, honest, genuine; *be on the* ~, be a freemason. 2. L-shaped or T-shaped

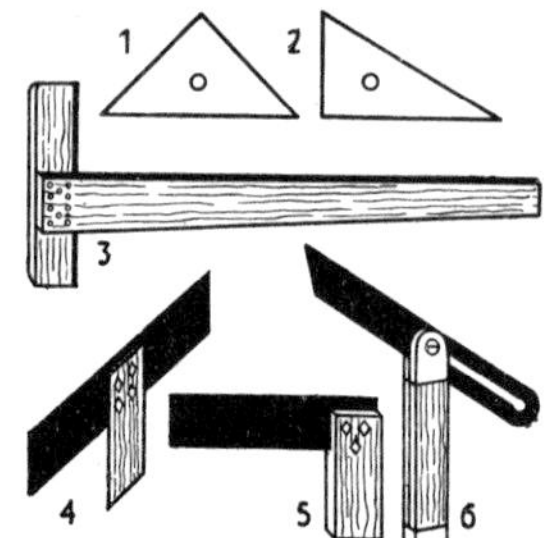

SQUARES

1, 2. Set squares (1. 45°, 2. 60°). 3. T-square. 4. Mitre-square. 5. Trying-square. 6. Bevel

instrument for measuring or obtaining right angles. 3. Product of number or quantity multiplied by itself. *~adj.* 1. Of the (approximate) shape of a square; rectangular; angular, not round; approximating to square section or outline, solid, sturdy; of stated length on each of 4 sides forming square; ~ *foot, metre*, etc. (area equal to that of) square whose side is a foot, metre, etc.; ~ *measure*, measure expressed in such units (see Appendix X); ~ *number*, square of an integer; ~ *root*, number or quantity which when multiplied by itself produces given number or quantity. 2. Properly arranged, in good order, on a proper footing; fair, honest; thorough, uncompromising; (of meal) solid, substantial. 3. ~ *dance*, one in which 4 couples face inwards from 4 sides; (loosely) country dance; *square'-head*, (U.S. colloq.) Scandinavian immigrant; German; ~ *leg*, in cricket, (position of) fielder on leg-side of batsman and nearly in line with wicket (ill. CRICKET); ~-*rigged*, having principal sails extended by horizontal yards slung to mast by middle; ~ *sail*, four-sided sail set from yards and slung at right angles to the mast (ill. SAIL[1]). **squāre'ly** (-ārl-) *adv.* **squāre'nėss** *n.* **squār'ish** *adj.* **squāre** *adv.* Squarely. ~ *v.* 1. Make square or rectangular; mark (*out*) in squares; multiply (number, quantity) by itself; ~ *the circle*, construct square equal in area to given circle (freq. fig. as type of impossibility). 2. Adjust, make or be consistent (*with*), reconcile; settle (accounts etc.), also (abs.) ~ *up*; conciliate or satisfy (person) esp. with bribe or compensation. 3. Assume boxing attitude, move *up to* (person) thus.

squă'rrōse *adj.* (Rough with scale-like processes) standing out widely.

squārs'on *n.* (joc.) Clergyman who is squire of his parish. [f. *squire* and *parson*]

squash[1] (-ŏ-) *v.* Crush, squeeze flat or into pulp; be so crushed or squeezed; pack tight, crowd; (fig.) silence (person) with crushing retort. **squash'y** *adj.* **squash'-inėss** *n.* **squash** *n.* 1. Squashing; something squashed or crushed; crush, crowd; drink made of juice of crushed fruit, freq. in compounds as *lemon-squash*. 2. ~ (-*rackets*), game resembling rackets but played in a smaller court, by two persons, with a soft ball.

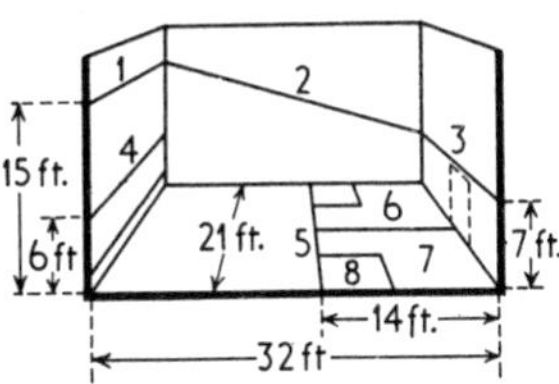

SQUASH RACKETS COURT

1. Front wall line. 2. Side wall line. 3. Back wall line. 4. Cut line. 5. Short line. 6. Forehand court. 7. Backhand court. 8. Service box

squash[2] (-ŏ-) *n.* (Gourd, used as vegetable etc., of) species of *Cucurbita*, trailing herbaceous annual plants. [Amer. Ind. *askutasquash*]

squat (-ŏt) *v.* 1. Sit with knees drawn up and heels close to or touching hams; crouch; put into this position; (colloq.) sit. 2. (orig. U.S.) Settle on uncultivated or unoccupied land without legal title or payment of rent; (Austral.) take up land as squatter. ~ *adj.* In squatting posture; short and thick, dumpy. ~ *n.* Squatting posture.

squa'tter (-ŏ-) *n.* Person who settles on common land or occupies a building, without right or permission; (Austral.) person acquiring title to pastoral land belonging to Government by settling on it; sheep-farmer, esp. on a large scale.

squaw *n.* N. American Indian woman or wife. [Amer. Ind. wd]

squawk *v.i.* & *n.* (Utter) harsh cry of pain or fear; (make) complaint.

squeak *v.* 1. Emit short, shrill, thin sound; utter in squeaking voice. 2. (slang) Turn informer, peach. ~ *n.* Short thin high-pitched sound; (*narrow*) ~, narrow escape, close shave.

squeal *v.* 1. Utter, emit, more or less prolonged loud shrill noise, esp. of pain or fright; utter with this sound. 2. (slang) Turn informer, squeak. ~ *n.* Sharp shrill sound.

squeam'ĭsh *adj.* Readily affected with nausea; prudish, sensitive, fastidious, over-nice. **squeam'-ĭshly** *adv.* **squeam'ĭshnėss** *n.*

squee'gee' *n.* Implement with rubber blade or roller for scraping, cleaning, squeezing away moisture, etc. ~ *v.t.* Treat with squeegee.

squeeze *v.* Press, compress hard, esp. so as to crush, drain liquid from, etc.; force by pressure, press out; force one's way; extort money etc. from, bring pressure to bear on, constrain; obtain (money etc.) *from*, *out of*, by extortion or pressure; take impression of (coin etc.), esp. with sheets of damp paper. ~ *n.* Application of pressure; crowd, crush; impression of coin etc.; sum appropriated as perquisite esp. by native servant making payments for employer, 'rake-off'.

squeez'er *n.* (esp.) Device for expressing juice from lemon and other fruits.

squĕlch *v.* Fall, stamp on (something soft), with crushing or squashing force; crush, squash; walk or tread heavily in water or wet ground, make sound (as) of this. ~ *n.* (Sound of) squelching. **squĕl'chy** *adj.*

squĭb *n.* 1. Firework, straight tube filled with mixture burning with hissing sound and usu. with small explosion at end. 2. Short satirical composition, lampoon.

squĭd *n.* Various 10-armed cephalopod molluscs, esp. of genus *Loligo*, some of which are used for bait.

squĭff'y *adj.* (slang) Drunk.

squĭgg'le *n.* Curly mark.

squĭll *n.* Sea-onion, bulbous-rooted sea-shore plant, *Scilla maritima*, with bulbs used dried as diuretic and stimulant; other species of *Scilla*.

squĭnch *n.* (archit.) Straight or arched support across interior angle to carry dome or other superstructure (ill. DOME).

squĭnt *n.* 1. Strabismus, abnormality of the eyes in which the visual axes do not coincide at the objective; stealthy or sidelong glance; (colloq.) glance, look. 2. (archit.) Oblique opening through wall of church etc., esp. affording view of altar from transept. ~ *adj.* Squinting, looking different ways. ~ *v.* Have the eyes turned in different directions, have strabismus; look obliquely at; give cast to (eye), cause to look asquint.

squīre *n.* 1. Attendant on knight (hist.); follower; man escorting or attending on lady. 2. Country gentleman, esp. chief landed proprietor in district. ~ *v.t.* Attend upon, escort (woman).

squīre'ârchy (-kĭ) *n.* Government by, influence of, landed proprietors, esp. in England before Reform Bill of 1832; class of landed proprietors. **squīre'ârch** (-k) *n.* **squīre'ârchal, squīr-âr'chical** *adjs.*

squīreen' *n.* Small landowner, esp. in Ireland.

squîrm *v.i.* Wriggle, writhe (freq. fig.). ~ *n.* Squirming movement.

squĭ'rrel *n.* Various rodents of the family *Sciuridae*, small and slender with long bushy tail, many being arboreal (*red* ~, *grey* ~, species found in Britain); *barking* ~, prairie-dog, allied to squirrel; ~-*grass*, ~-*tail grass*, various grasses (*Hordeum*) with bushy spikelets; ~ *monkey*, various S. Amer. small soft-haired long-tailed monkeys; marmoset.

squîrt *v.* Eject (liquid etc.) in jet as from syringe; be so ejected, spurt. ~ *n.* 1. Syringe; small jet or spray. 2. (colloq.) Insignificant person, whippersnapper.

squĭtch *n.* COUCH[2]-grass.

Sr *abbrev.* Senior.

S.R. *abbrev.* Scottish Rifles.

S.R.N. *abbrev.* State Registered Nurse.

S.R.O. *abbrev.* Statutory Rules and Orders.

S.R.U. *abbrev.* Scottish Rugby Union.

SS. *abbrev.* Saints.

S.S. *abbrev.* *Schutz Staffel* (= protection patrol; Nazi police force); (also **s.s.**) steamship.

S.S.A.F.A. *abbrev.* Soldiers', Sailors', and Airmen's Families Association.

S.S.C. *abbrev.* Solicitor to the Supreme Court (Scotland).

S.S.E., SSE *abbrevs.* South-south-east.

S.S.J.E. *abbrev.* Society of St. John the Evangelist.

S.S.W., SSW *abbrevs.* South-south-west.

st. *abbrev.* Stem; stone (weight); stumped.

St. *abbrev.* Saint; Strait; Street.

stăb *v.* Pierce, wound, with (usu. short) pointed weapon, needle, etc.; aim blow (*at*) with such weapon etc. ~ *n.* Act of stabbing, wound made thus; short stiff stroke with billiard-cue, bat, etc.; (colloq.) *have a ~ at*, make shot at, try; *~-culture*, in bacteriology, culture in which inoculation is by means of needle thrust deep into medium.

stăb'ilīze *v.t.* Make stable, bring into a state of stability. **stăbilīzā'tion** *n.* (esp.) Maintenance of purchasing power of a country's currency by fixing its value in terms of gold.

stăb'ilīzer *n.* (esp.) 1. One of a pair of retractable fins inserted into sides of ship's hull below waterline to prevent rolling. 2. (U.S.) Horizontal tail-plane of aircraft.

stā'ble[1] *n.* Building with stalls, loose-boxes, mangers, etc., for keeping horses; collection of horses from one stable; establishment for training race-horses. ~ *v.* Put, keep, (horse) in stable; be stabled. **stā'bling** *n.* (esp.) Accommodation for horses etc.

stā'ble[2] *adj.* Firmly fixed or established, not easily shaken, dislodged, decomposed, changed, destroyed, etc.; firm, resolute, steadfast. **stabil'ity, stā'bleness** *ns.* **stā'bly** *adv.*

stacca'tō (-aht-) *adj.* & *adv.* (mus.) (To be played) in detached disconnected manner, with breaks between successive notes.

stăck *n.* 1. Circular or rectangular pile of hay, straw, sheaves of grain, etc., usu. with sloping thatched top; pile, esp. one arranged in orderly way; (as measure of wood) 108 cu. ft; (colloq., pl.) large quantity, 'heaps'. 2. Group of chimneys etc. standing together (ill. CHIMNEY); chimney of house, factory, ship, locomotive, etc.; (building containing) compact arrangement of book-cases in library etc. ~ *v.t.* Pile in stack(s).

stădd'le *n.* 1. Young tree left standing when others are felled. 2. Platform of stone, wood, etc., supporting stack or rick; supporting framework.

stād'ium *n.* 1. Ancient Greek and Roman measure (about 600 ft). 2. Enclosed athletic ground with tiers of seats for spectators.

Staël (stah-ĕl'), Anne Louise Germaine, Madame de (1766–1817). French author, daughter of NECKER, wife of Swedish ambassador in Paris; hostess of a progressive and revolutionary salon.

staff (-ah-) *n.* (pl. *-s, stāves*). 1. stick used as aid in walking or climbing (now usu. literary); stick, rod, as sign of office or authority, as *pastoral ~*; shaft, pole, as support or handle, as *flagstaff*; rod used for measuring distances, heights, etc., in surveying etc. 2. (mus., pl. *staves*) = STAVE (now chiefly in ~ *notation*, musical notation on stave as dist. from sol-fa method). 3. Body of officers, not themselves in command, assisting a general or other commanding officer in the control of an army, brigade, etc., or in performing special duties; body of persons working under central direction, esp. in factory, educational institution, etc.; *general ~*, body of officers controlling an army from headquarters under the commander-in-chief; ~ *college*, (mil.) establishment for instruction and training of officers for staff appointments; ~ *sergeant*, non-commissioned officer serving on regimental staff. ~ *v.t.* Provide with staff of officers, teachers, servants, etc.

Stăff ordshire. County of central England.

Staffs. *abbrev.* Staffordshire.

stăg *n.* Male of (esp. red) deer; (Stock Exchange) person who applies for newly issued shares with a view to selling immediately on allotment at a profit; (attrib., orig. U.S.) for, of, males only, as *~-party*; *~-beetle*, various large beetles (family *Lucanidae*) of which males have long denticulated mandibles resembling stag's horns; *~-hound*, hound of large breed used for hunting stags etc.

stāge *n.* 1. Raised floor or platform, e.g. scaffold for workmen and their tools, platform used as gangway, landing-place, etc., surface on which object is placed for inspection through microscope, tier of shelves for plants, esp. in greenhouse. 2. Platform on which spectacles, plays, etc., are exhibited, esp. that in theatre, with scenery, etc. (ill. THEATRE); *the* theatre, *the* drama; *the* actor's profession; (fig.) scene of action. 3. Division of journey, process, development, etc.; point reached; regular stopping-place on stage-coach route where horses were changed; section of bus route for which a particular fare is charged; as much of journey as is performed without stopping for rest etc. 4. *~-coach*, (hist.) coach running regularly between two places for conveyance of passengers, parcels, etc.; ~ *direction*, instructions in written or printed play for appropriate action etc.; *~-door*, entrance for actors etc. to parts of theatre behind stage; ~ *fright*, nervousness at appearing before audience, esp. for first time; *~-hand*, one of persons handling scenery, lights, etc., during performance on stage; *~-manager*, person in charge of stage-hands etc. and having general control of stage during performance, rehearsals, etc.; *~-struck*, smitten with love for stage, esp. with desire to become actor; *~-wait*, hitch, pronounced delay, in theatrical performance; ~ *whisper*, whisper loud enough to be heard by audience or overheard by others than person addressed. ~ *v.* Put (play) on stage, organize (exhibition, pageant, etc.); put (plants) on stage, esp. for exhibition at show; (of play) lend itself to stage production.

stā'ger *n.* *Old ~*, experienced person, old hand.

stăgg'er *v.* 1. Walk or stand unsteadily or with swaying movement and irregular devious steps, totter, reel; cause to totter; (cause to) hesitate, waver in purpose, be unsettled or bewildered. 2. Arrange in zig-zag, slanting, or overlapping order; arrange (crossing) so that side roads are not exactly opposite one another; arrange (hours of work, holidays, etc.) so that those of various factories, individuals, etc., do not coincide. ~ *n.* Act, effect, amount, of staggering; (pl.) diseased condition in animals resulting in unsteady gait, sudden falling, etc.

stā'ging *n.* (esp.) Scaffolding, temporary platform or support; putting play on stage.

Stă'girīte. Native of ancient Macedonian city of Stagira, esp. Aristotle.

stăg'nant *adj.* Not flowing or running, without motion or current (freq. implying unwholesomeness); dull, sluggish, without activity or interest. **stăg'nantly** *adv.* **stăg'nancy** *n.*

stăgnāte' (*or* stăg'-) *v.i.* Be, become, stagnant. **stăgnā'tion** *n.*

stā'gy (-jĭ) *adj.* Theatrical, dramatically artificial or exaggerated.

staid *adj.* Steady, sober, sedate. **staid'ly** *adv.* **staid'ness** *n.*

stain *v.* 1. Discolour, soil; (fig.) sully, blemish. 2. Colour (textile fabrics, paper, wood, etc.) with pigment that penetrates instead of forming coating on surface; colour (tissues etc.) with pigment to render structure visible for examination with microscope etc.; colour (glass) with transparent colours. ~ *n.* Discoloration, spot or mark, esp. one caused by contact with foreign matter and not easily removable; dye etc. for staining; (fig.) blot, blemish. **stain'lėss** *adj.* (esp. of steel etc.) Alloyed with chromium so as not to be liable to rust or tarnish under ordinary conditions; made of such metal.

stair *n.* Each of succession of steps, esp. indoors; (pl.) set or flight of these; *below ~s*, in, to, basement, esp. as servants' part of house; *stair'case*, (part of building containing) flight, or series of flights, of stairs; *~-rod*, rod for securing stair-carpet in angle between two steps.

stāke *n.* 1. Stick or post sharpened at one end for driving into ground, used to mark boundary, to support plant, as part of fence, etc.; post to which person was bound to be burnt alive; *the* ~, death by burning. 2. What is staked or wagered on an event; (pl.) money etc. staked by entrants to be contended for, esp. in horse-race; (pl.) such race; (fig.)

interest involved, something to be gained or lost; *at* ~, at issue, in question, risked. 3. ~*-boat*, moored or anchored boat as starting-point or mark for racing boats. ~ *v.t.* 1. Fasten, secure, support, with stake(s); mark *off*, *out*, with stakes. 2. Wager, risk (*on* event etc.); (fig.) hazard, risk loss of; (U.S.) furnish with money, supplies, etc., esp. in order to share gains.

Stakha'novite (-χah-) *adj.* & *n.* (Member) of Soviet-Russian movement aiming at greater output in industry, initiated by Alexei Stakhanov, a Donetz miner, who in 1935 produced a phenomenal quantity of coal by a combination of new methods and great energy.

stăl'actite (*or* -lăk'-) *n.* Icicle-like formation of crystalline calcium carbonate formed by dripping of water through overlying limestone and depending from roof or wall of cavern etc. **stălactĭt'ic** *adj.*

Stăl'ăg *n.* German prison camp for non-commissioned officers and men. [abbrev. of *Stammlager* (*Stamm* main body, *Lager* camp)]

stăl'agmite (*or* -lăg'-) *n.* Deposit of calcium carbonate or other material on floor of cavern etc. resembling inverted stalactite and similarly formed. **stălagmĭt'ic** *adj.*

stāle *adj.* Not fresh; insipid, musty, or otherwise the worse for age; lacking novelty, trite; (of athlete) overtrained (similarly of other persons whose vigour is impaired by overwork); ~ *bread*, bread not of the day's baking; *stale'mate*, (chess) position in which player can make no move without bringing his king into check, (fig.) deadlock, drawn contest; (*v.t.*) place (player, his king) in position of stalemate. **stāle'ly** (-l-lĭ) *adv.* **stāle'nėss** (-ln-) *n.*

stāle *n.* Urine of horses and cattle. ~ *v.* 1. Make, become, stale or common. 2. (of horse etc.) Urinate.

Sta'lĭn (-ah-). Name adopted by Josef Vissarionovich Dzhugashvili (1879–1953), Soviet statesman; by birth a Georgian; worked as an 'underground' revolutionary from 1904 until the Bolshevik revolution of 1917; by *c* 1929 he was established as undisputed successor to Lenin and leader of the Communist party and administration, retaining that position until his death. **Sta'lĭnism** *n.* **Sta'lĭnist** *adj.* & *n.* [Russ., = 'man of steel']

Sta'lĭngrăd (stah-). Russian city (formerly *Tsaritsyn*, now *Volgograd*) on the lower Volga, where the German invasion of Russia was halted in Aug.–Nov. 1942.

stalk[1] (-awk) *n.* Main stem of herbaceous plant, bearing flowers and leaves; attachment or support of leaf, flower, fruit, animal organ, etc.; stem of wine-glass; cylindrical length of metal attached to carrier of depth-charge and fitting into barrel of thrower.

stalk[2] (-awk) *v.* 1. Pursue (game) stealthily; steal up to game under cover; *stalk'ing-horse*, horse, screen, behind which hunter approaches game; (fig.) pretext. 2. Walk with stiff measured steps; stride in stately or imposing manner. ~ *n.* Act of stalking game; stealthy pursuit.

stall[1] (-awl) *n.* 1. (Division for one animal in) stable, cattle-shed, cow-house. 2. Fixed seat enclosed wholly or partly at back and sides, and freq. canopied, in choir or chancel of church or in chapter-house, for clergyman, dignitary of church, knight of one of higher orders of chivalry, etc.; (fig.) office or dignity of canon etc.; each of set of seats in part of theatre nearest stage, usu. between pit and orchestra (ill. THEATRE). 3. Booth, table, stand, in market etc., compartment in building, for exposure and sale of goods. 4. (coal-mining) Compartment in which coal is worked. 5. Stalling, condition of

STALL, 15TH C.

1. Poppy-head. 2. Misericord on underside of upturned seat

aircraft whose speed is reduced beyond point at which machine answers normally to controls, a state which persists until it has recovered flying speed, usu. by diving and with a consequent loss of height. ~ *v.* 1. Place, keep, (cattle etc.) in stall, esp. for fattening; furnish with stalls. 2. (Cause to) stick fast in mud, snow, etc.; stop (internal combustion engine) undesignedly, (of engine) be accidentally stopped; (of aircraft) reduce flying-speed below the stalling speed; cause (aircraft) to do this; *stalling speed*, critical speed below which aircraft is in a stall.

stall[2] (-awl) *n.* Pickpocket's confederate distracting attention

STAIRS: A. SPIRAL STAIRS. B. STAIRCASE WITH HALF-LANDINGS. C. CURVED STAIR WITH WINDERS

1. Newel. 2. Half-landing. 3. Tread. 4. Riser. 5. Newel post. 6. String-board. 7. Hand-rail. 8. Banister or baluster. 9. Winder. 10. Open string. 11. Well

of victim during theft; (slang) act of stalling or stalling-off. ~ *v.* Act as stall for (pickpocket); (slang) stave *off* with trick, plausible tale etc., play for time thus, block, obstruct. [AF *estal* decoy-bird]

stall'age (-awl-) *n.* Space or rent for, right to erect, stall(s) in market etc.

stăll'ion (-yon) *n.* Uncastrated male horse, esp. one kept for breeding.

sta'lwart (-awl-) *adj.* (chiefly literary) Stout, strong, sturdy; valiant, courageous, resolute. ~ *n.* Resolute uncompromising partisan, esp. of political party. **sta'lwartly** *adv.* **sta'lwartnėss** *n.*

Stămboul' (-ōōl). Obsolescent anglicized spelling of *Istanbul* (= CONSTANTINOPLE).

stām'ĕn *n.* (bot.) Male fertilizing organ of flowering plants, with anther containing pollen supported on slender footstalk (filament) (ill. FLOWER).

stăm'ĭna *n.* Staying-power, power of endurance. [L, pl. of *stamen*]

stăm'ĭnal *adj.* Of stamina or stamens.

stăm'ĭnate *adj.* Having stamens, esp. without pistils.

stăm'ĭnōde *n.* (bot.) Infertile, aborted or reduced stamen.

stămm'er *v.* Falter or stumble in speech, esp. repeat involuntarily certain sounds in a word etc. several times in rapid succession through inability to complete the articulation; utter with stammer. ~ *n.* Stammering speech, tendency to stammer.

stămp *v.* 1. Bring down one's foot, bring down (foot), heavily on ground; ~ *out*, put an end to, crush, destroy; *stamping-ground*, (U.S.) animal's habitual place of resort. 2. Impress pattern, name, mark, upon with die or similar instrument of metal, wood, rubber, etc.; affix postage or other stamp to (document, envelope); assign a character to, characterize; impress *on* the memory. 3. Crush, pulverize (ores etc.). ~ *n.* 1. Act, sound, of stamping, esp. with foot. 2. Instrument for stamping pattern or mark, mark made by this; government's embossed or impressed mark, adhesive label with distinctive device, on deed or other document etc., to certify that duty, tax, etc., has been paid; postage stamp; mark impressed on, label etc. affixed to, commodity as evidence of quality etc.; (fig.) characteristic mark, impress (*of* some quality etc.); character, kind. 3. Heavy pestle operated by machinery for crushing ores; (pl.) stamp-mill. 4. *S~ Act*, Act for regulating stamp duties, esp. that of 1765 (repealed 1766) levying such duties on American colonies; *~-collector*, philatelist; *~-duty*, any duty collected by means of impressed or affixed stamps; *~-mill*, apparatus for crushing ores, with series of stamps; ~ *paper*, paper with government revenue stamp; gummed marginal paper of sheet of postage stamps.

stămpēde' *n.* Sudden rush and flight of number of frightened horses, cattle, etc.; sudden unreasoning rush or action of persons in a body or mass. ~ *v.* (Cause to) take part in stampede.

stănce *n.* (golf etc.) Player's position for making stroke; pose, attitude.

stanch, staunch (-ah-, -aw-) *v.t.* Check flow of (esp. blood); check flow from (esp. wound).

sta'nchion (-ahnshn) *n.* Upright bar, stay, or support (ill. GIRDER). ~ *v.t.* Provide, strengthen, support, with stanchion(s).

stănd *v.* (past t. and past part. *stŏŏd*). 1. Have, take, assume, erect attitude on one's feet; be set, remain, upright; be of specified height when standing; remain stationary, stop walking or moving on; be set, placed, or situated; remain firm, secure, valid, etc., or in specified condition; present a firm front; offer oneself as candidate, esp. for election to Parliament etc.; (naut.) sail, steer, in specified direction, to sea, etc. 2. Place, set, in upright or specified position. 3. Bear the brunt of, resist; endure, undergo (trial etc.); endure without succumbing or complaining. 4. Provide at one's expense. 5. ~ one's *chance*, take one's chance; ~ one's *ground*, maintain one's position; *all standing*, (naut.) without dismantling or unrigging; (transf.) without time for preparation; ~ *by*, uphold, support, side with; adhere to, abide by; stand near, be a bystander, stand and look on; stand ready, be on the alert; *~-by*, thing, person, that can be depended on; ~ *down*, step down from witness-box; retire, withdraw; go off duty; ~ *for*, represent, signify, imply; (colloq.) tolerate, acquiesce in; ~ *in*, cost (person) specified sum; (also) deputize; *~-in*, favourable position; (cinema) person employed to take place of actor until lights, cameras, etc., are ready; deputy, substitute; ~ *off*, move away, keep one's distance; *~-off half*, (Rugby footb.) half-back with position between scrum-half and three-quarters; *~-off'ish*, distant, reserved, not affable; *~-off'ishly* (*adv*).,*~-off'ishness* (*n.*); ~ *on*, insist on, observe scrupulously; ~ *out*, hold out, persist in opposition or endurance; be prominent or conspicuous; ~ *over*, be postponed; ~ *pat*, (in poker) play hand as dealt; oppose change, maintain one's position; *~-pipe*, vertical pipe for conveying water, gas, etc., or with spout or nozzle for hose, for attachment to water-main; *stand'point*, point of view; *stand'still*, halt, pause, cessation of movement or activity; ~ *to*, abide by, stick to, not desert; (mil.) take up position in preparation for an attack; ~ *to win, lose*, etc., be reasonably certain to win, lose, etc.; ~ *up*, rise to one's feet from sitting position etc.; maintain erect position; ~ *up for*, side with, maintain, support; *~-up*, (of collar) high, not turned down or folded over; (of fight) fair and square, in which opponents stand up to one another without flinching or evasion; (of meal etc.) taken standing. ~ *n.* 1. Cessation from motion or progress, stoppage; stationary condition, esp. for resistance (*against*); position taken up. 2. Table, set of shelves, rack, etc., on or in which things may be placed; stall in market etc.; standing-place for vehicles etc.; raised structure for persons to sit or stand on; (U.S.) witness-box. 3. Standing growth or crop.

stăn'dard *n.* 1. Distinctive flag, as *the* (*English*) *royal* ~ (banner with royal arms, ill. FLAG); flag of cavalry regiment (opp. to *colours* of infantry); (fig.) rallying principle; (bot.) vexillum, uppermost petal of sweet pea or other papilionaceous flower (ill. FLOWER). 2. Weight or measure to which others conform or by which the accuracy of others is judged (often attrib. as in ~ *pound, yard*, etc.); legal proportion of weight of fine metal and alloy in gold and silver coin (*monetary* ~) or in articles made of these metals; thing serving as basis of comparison. 3. Degree of excellence etc. required for a particular purpose; thing recognized as model for imitation etc. (attrib., of book) recognized as possessing merit or authority; (in primary schools) each of several degrees of proficiency, class studying to reach this. 4. Average quality. 5. Measure of timber (varying in different countries). 6. Upright support (ill. SCAFFOLDING); upright water or gas pipe; upright holder for lamp in street or room; tree, shrub, trained on erect stem (not as espalier or dwarfed); tree left standing when others are felled. 7. *~-bearer*, soldier etc. who bears standard; (fig.) prominent leader in cause; ~ *dialect, English, French*, etc., that variety of speech held to be best, as being spoken by cultured or educated classes; ~ *of living*, degree of material comfort enjoyed by community or class or person; ~ *lamp*, lamp set on tall holder standing on floor; ~ *time*, time established legally or by custom in country or region.

stăn'dardīze *v.t.* Make to conform to standard, make uniform. **stăndardīzā'tion** *n.*

stănd'ĭng *n.* (esp.) Estimation in which person is held, repute; duration; *~-room*, space to stand in. ~ *adj.* (esp.) Established; permanent, not made, formed, etc., for the occasion; ~ *orders*, series of instructions remaining in force until countermanded or repealed by a proper authority, esp. (mil.) orders not subject to change by an officer temporarily in command; (parliament) rules of procedure remaining in force through successive sessions (opp. *sessional orders*).

Stăn'ley, Sir Henry Morton (1841–1904). Engl. explorer; was sent in 1869 by Gordon Bennett, proprietor of the 'New York Herald', to find David Livingstone, who was believed to be lost in Central Africa.

stănn'ary *n.* Tin-mine; *the Stannaries*, tin-mining districts of Cornwall and Devon.

stănn'ate *n.* (chem.) Salt of stannic acid.

stănn'ic *adj.* Of tin; (chem.) containing tin as quadrivalent element.

stănn'ous *adj.* Containing tin as bivalent element.

stăn'za *n.* Group of (usu. rhymed) lines of verses forming division of song or poem.

stăp'ēs (-z) *n.* = STIRRUP-bone (ill. EAR).

stăph'ȳlocŏcc'us *n.* (pl. *-cī*). Any of numerous micro-organisms, globular and tending to grow in clusters, causing various morbid conditions such as boils, carbuncles, and abscesses (ill. BACTERIUM). **stăph'ȳlocŏcc'al** *adj.* [Gk *staphute* bunch of grapes, *kokkos* grain]

stā'ple[1] *n.* U-shaped bar or loop of metal with pointed ends to be driven into post, wall, etc., as hold for hook, bolt, etc.; various contrivances of similar shape or function, esp. bent wire used in bookbinding for wire-stitching. ~ *v.t.* Furnish, fasten, with staple; *sta'pling-machine*, bookbinder's wire-stitching machine.

stā'ple[2] *n.* 1. Important or principal product or article of commerce; raw material; (fig.) chief element or material. 2. Fibre of wool, cotton, etc., considered with respect to its length and fineness. ~ *adj.* Forming a staple; having important or principal place among exports, industries, etc. ~ *v.t.* Sort, classify (wool etc.), according to fibre. **stāp'ler** *n.*

stār *n.* 1. Celestial body appearing as luminous point; (also *fixed* ~) such body so far from earth as to appear motionless except for diurnal revolution of the heavens; *double* ~, 2 fixed stars appearing to naked eye as one; *multiple* ~, similar group of 3 to 6; *falling, shooting* ~, small meteor looking like rapidly moving star. 2. (astrol.) Heavenly body, esp. planet, considered as influencing human affairs or person's fortunes. 3. Thing suggesting star by its shape, esp. figure or object with radiating points; asterisk; white spot on forehead of horse etc. 4. Actor, singer, etc., of great celebrity; brilliant or prominent person; *stardom*, status of star; realm, sphere of stars. 5. (pool) Additional life bought by player whose lives are lost. 6. *S~ Chamber*, (hist.) room in royal palace at Westminster (said to have had gilt stars on the ceiling) where the Privy Council tried civil and criminal cases, esp. those affecting Crown interests, until in 1640 the court (*Court of S~ Chamber*) was abolished as too arbitrary in its judgements; *~-drift*, common proper motion of a number of fixed stars in same region; *star'fish*, echinoderm of the class *Asteroidea* with usu. five broad arms radiating

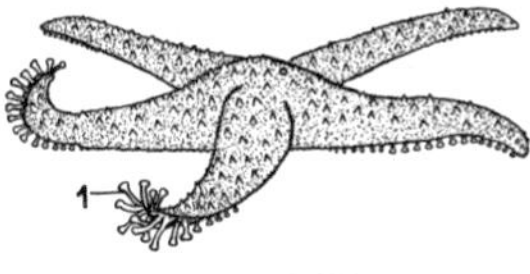

STARFISH

1. Tube-feet

from a central disc, esp. *Asterias rubens*, form commonest on European coasts; *~-gazer*, (contempt.) astrologer, astronomer; *star'light*, light of the stars; (*adj.*, also *star'lit*); *S~ of Bethlehem*, plant of genus *Ornithogalum*, esp. *O. umbellatum*, common in Palestine, with white stellate flowers; various other plants; ~ *sapphire*, cabochon sapphire, which shines like a cluster of stars; *S~-spangled Banner*, the U.S. national anthem, with ref. to the Stars and Stripes (see below); *~-stream*, either of two systematic drifts of stars (one of which comprises the nearer stars and moves towards Orion); ~ *turn*, principal item in an entertainment; *Stars and Stripes*, flag of the U.S.A. with 13 horizontal stripes, representing the 13 orig. States, and one star for each State in the Union (50 in 1961). **stār'let** *n.* Young star, sense 4. **stār'lėss, stārr'y** *adjs.* **stār** *v.* Set, adorn (as) with stars; mark with asterisk; appear, advertise or 'feature', as star actor.

stārb'oard (-berd) *n.* Right-hand side of boat or ship or aircraft looking forward (opp. PORT) (ill. BEARING). ~ *v.t.* Turn, put, (helm) to starboard. [OE *steor* rudder]

stārch *n.* White odourless tasteless carbohydrate occurring widely in plants, esp. cereals, potatoes, etc., and forming an important constituent of human food; gummy or pasty preparation of this with (usu. boiling) water used for stiffening linen etc. after washing, for sizing paper, etc.; (fig.) stiffness of manner or conduct, formality. **stārch'y** *adj.* **stārch'ily** *adv.* **stārch'inėss** *n.* **stārch** *v.t.* Stiffen with starch.

stāre *v.* Gaze fixedly with eyes wide open; open eyes in astonishment, be amazed; reduce (person) to specified condition by staring; be obtrusively conspicuous; ~ (person) *in the face*, (of thing) be glaringly obvious to. ~ *n.* Staring gaze.

stārk *adj.* Stiff, rigid; downright, sheer. ~ *adv.* Quite, completely (now chiefly in ~ *mad, naked*).

stārl'ing[1] *n.* Bird (*Sturnus vulgaris*) with dark light-speckled plumage having metallic lustre, of gregarious habits and often nesting near human habitations; any bird of the passerine family *Sturnidae* or (loosely) the unrelated Amer. family *Icteridae*.

stārl'ing[2] *n.* Outwork of piles protecting pier of bridge against force of stream, damage by floating objects, etc.

stārt *v.* 1. Make sudden movement from pain, surprise, etc., give start; move suddenly from one's place; rouse (game) from lair etc.; (of timbers etc.) spring from proper position, be displaced by pressure or shrinkage; cause, experience, starting of timbers etc. 2. Set out, begin journey, career, course of action, etc.; make a beginning (*on*); begin; originate, set going; cause to begin d*oing*, cause or enable to commence course of action etc.; give signal to (persons) to start in race etc.; ~ (*up*), cause (motor-engine) to begin to run; (of motor-engine) begin to operate. ~ *n.* 1. Sudden involuntary movement caused by surprise, fright, pain, etc.; (pl.) intermittent and sudden efforts or displays of energy. 2. Beginning of journey, action, race, career, etc.; starting-place of race; opportunity, or assistance for starting career, course of action, etc.; advantage gained by starting first in race, journey; position in advance of competitors.

stārt'er *n.* (esp.) 1. Person giving signal to start in race. 2. Horse, competitor, starting in race etc. 3. Apparatus for starting motor-engine, esp. *self-~*.

stārt'ing *n.* *~-gate*, movable barrier for securing fair start in horse-race; *~-post*, post from which competitors start in race; ~ *prices*, final odds on horse etc. at time of starting.

stārt'le *v.t.* Cause to start with surprise or fright; alarm; take by surprise.

stārve *v.* (Cause to) die of hunger; (cause to) suffer from lack of food; (colloq.) feel hungry; force *into* course of action, *out*, etc., by starvation; (fig.) (cause to) suffer mental or spiritual want. **stārvā'tion** *n.*

stārv'eling (-vl-) *n.* Starving or ill-fed person or animal.

stăs'is *n.* Stoppage of circulation of any body-fluids, esp. blood.

stāte[1] *n.* 1. Condition; manner or way of existence as determined by circumstances; (colloq.) excited or agitated condition of mind or feeling; (engraving etc.) stage of engraved or etched work, distinguishable variant of edition of book etc. 2. Rank, dignity; pomp; *in* ~, with all due ceremony; *lie in* ~, (of dead person) be ceremoniously exhibited in public place. 3. Organized political community under one government, commonwealth, nation; such community forming part of federation with sovereign government; civil government; *the States*, the UNITED STATES OF AMERICA; also, the legislative body in Jersey, Guernsey, and Alderney; *States General*, legislative assembly of clergy, nobles, and commons of whole realm in France before the Revolution, or in Netherlands from 15th c. to 1796. 4. *attrib.* or *adj.* Of, for, concerned with, the State (sense 3); reserved for, employed on, occasions of state or ceremony; ~ *capitalism*, system in which capital is owned or controlled by State; *S~ Department*, (U.S.) the Department of Foreign Affairs; *S~-house*, (U.S.) building in which legislature of a State holds its sessions; *S~ rights*, (U.S.) rights and powers not delegated to the Federal government but reserved to individual States; *~-room*, state apartment; sleeping apartment for one or two on ship, railway-train, etc.; ~ *socialism*, system of State control of industries, railways, etc.

stāte[2] *v.t.* Express, esp. fully or clearly, in speech or writing; specify (number etc.).

stāte'ly (-tlĭ) *adj.* Dignified, imposing, grand. **stāte'linėss** *n.*

stāte'ment (-tm-) *n.* Stating, expression in words; presentation of musical theme or subject; thing stated; formal account of facts, as of liabilities and assets; account presented periodically by tradesman to customer.

stāt'er *n.* Ancient Greek coin of gold or silver, of various values.

stātes'man (-tsm-) *n.* Person skilled or taking leading part in management of State affairs; *Elder Statesmen*, in Japan, body of retired statesmen and nobles who acted as emperor's advisers and controlled policy of Japan in late 19th and early 20th centuries.

stăt'ic *adj.* Of forces in equilibrium or bodies at rest (contrasted with *dynamic* or *kinetic*); acting by weight without motion; passive, not active or changing; (elect.) stationary, produced by friction; (wireless) atmospheric; (of a store of water in a tank) having no pressure of its own and requiring to be pumped; ~ *line*, length of cord in top half of a parachute bag which on becoming taut releases the parachute. ~ *n.* (U.S.) Atmospherics. **stăt'ical** *adj.* Of statics. **stăt'ics** *n.pl.* Branch of physical science concerned with bodies at rest and forces in equilibrium (contrasted with *dynamics*); (wireless) atmospherics.

stā'tion *n.* 1. Place in which person or thing stands or is placed, esp. habitually or for definite purpose or duties; in India, (hist.) place in which English officials etc. resided; in Australia, sheep- or cattle-run with its buildings. 2. Position in life, (high) rank, status. 3. Stopping-place on railway with buildings for accommodation of passengers and goods, or goods only; similar stopping-place for long-distance buses etc. 4. One of a series of holy places, esp. Roman churches, visited in turn for devotions; *Stations of the Cross*, series of 14 pictures or images of Christ's Passion (orig. crosses) in church or occas. in open air, before which devotions are performed. 5. *~-house*, police station; *~-master*, official in control of railway station; ~ *sergeant*, sergeant in charge of police-station. ~ *v.* Assign station or post to; post, place, in station.

stā'tionary (-sho-) *adj.* Remaining in one place, not moving; fixed, not movable; not changing in condition, quality, or quantity.

stā'tioner (-sho-) *n.* Tradesman selling writing-materials etc.; *Stationers' Company*, a livery company of the City of London, founded 1556, comprising stationers, booksellers, printers, bookbinders, etc.; *Stationers' Hall*, hall of this company, at which register of copyrights is kept. **stā'tionery** *n.* Articles sold by stationer, as paper, pens, ink, etc.

statĭs'tĭcs *n.pl.* Branch of study concerned with collection and classification of (esp.) numerical facts; facts so collected and classified. **statĭs'tĭcal** *adj.* **statĭs'tĭcally** *adv.* **stătĭstĭ'cian** (-shn) *n.*

Stā'tius (-shus), Publius Papinius (A.D. *c* 45–*c* 96). Roman poet, author of the THEBAID.

stāt'or *n.* Stationary part of electric generator (ill. DYNAMO).

stăt'ūary *n.* Sculptor; (art of making) statues. ~ *adj.* Of statues; sculptured; suitable for statues.

stăt'ūe *n.* Sculptural representation in the round of (esp.) deity, allegorical subject, or human being(s), usu. of life-size proportions.

stătūĕsque' (-k) *adj.* Resembling a statue, esp. in beauty or dignity.

stătūĕtte' *n.* Small statue.

stăt'ure (-yer) *n.* Height of (esp. human) body.

stāt'us *n.* 1. Social or legal position or condition, rank, standing. 2. (med.) ~ *lymphăt'icus*, bodily condition with excessive development of lymphatic tissue, in which sudden death may occur esp. in surgical anaesthesia. 3. ~ *(in) quo*, unchanged position, previous position, of affairs.

stăt'ūte *n.* Written law of a legislative body; ordinance of corporation etc. intended to be permanent; *S~ of Wales, Westminster*: see WALES, WESTMINSTER. **stăt'ūtable, stăt'ūtory** *adjs.* Enacted, required, imposed, by statute.

staunch *adj.* Trustworthy, loyal, firm; (of vessel etc.) watertight, airtight. **staunch'ly** *adv.* **staunch'nėss** *n.*

stāve *n.* 1. Each of the narrow shaped pieces of wood etc. placed together vertically to form sides of cask etc. (ill. CASK). 2. Stanza, verse, of poem, song, etc. 3. (mus.) Set of (now 5) parallel horizontal lines on and between which notes are placed so as to indicate pitch; *great* ~, stave of 11 lines combining treble and bass clefs. ~ *v.t.* (past t. and past part. *staved*, also (chiefly naut.) *stove*). 1. Break up (cask) into staves, break into, break hole *in* (boat, cask, etc.); crush, bash (*in*). 2. Furnish, fit (cask etc.) with staves. 3. ~ *off*, ward off, defer.

STAVE

1. Accolade. 2. Clef. 3. Key signature (A flat). 4. Time signature (Common or 4/4). 5. Crotchet to be played *staccato*. 6. Quaver with value increased by half. 7. Semiquaver. 8. Bar line. 9. Leger line. 10. Tie. 11. Accidental (natural). 12. Slur. 13. Stave or staff. 14. Names of notes

stay[1] *n.* Large rope supporting mast, leading from mast-head down to another mast or spar etc. (ill. SHIP); guy or rope supporting flagstaff etc.; tie-piece, cross-piece, holding parts together in aircraft etc.; *stay'-sail* (-sl), triangular sail carried on stay. ~ *v.t.* Support, steady, with stay(s).

stay[2] *v.* 1. Check, stop (now chiefly literary); postpone (judgement etc.). 2. Support, prop (*up*), as with buttress etc. 3. Remain; dwell temporarily; pause in movement, action, speech; ~ *put*, (orig. U.S.) remain in one's, or its, place. 4. Hold out, show powers of endurance; hold out for (specified distance, *the course*). 5. *~-at-home*, (person) remaining habitually at home; *~-down strike*, one in which miners remain underground; *~-in strike*, one in which workers do not leave place of employment; *staying-power*, endurance. ~ *n.* 1. Remaining, esp. dwelling temporarily, in a place; duration of this. 2. Suspension of judicial proceedings, esp. *of execu-*

tion of judgement delivered. 3. Prop, support; (pl.) corset; *~-lace*, tape for lacing stays or bodice.

stead (-ĕd) *n.* *Stand* (person) *in good ~*, be of advantage or service to; *in* person's *~*, instead of him, as his substitute.

stead'fast (-ĕd-) *adj.* Constant, firm, unwavering. **stead'fastly** *adv.* **stead'fastnėss** *n.*

stead'ing (-ĕd-) *n.* Farmstead, homestead.

stead'y (-ĕdĭ) *adj.* Firm, not tottering, faltering, rocking, or shaking; stable; unwavering, resolute; settled, unvarying; regular, maintained at even rate of action, change, etc., not erratic. **stead'ĭly** *adv.* **stead'ĭnėss** *n.* **stead'y** *adv.* Steadily (chiefly naut.); *~-going*, staid, sober. *~ v.* Make, become, steady.

steak (stāk) *n.* Thick slice or strip of meat (esp. beef) for grilling, frying, etc., esp. cut from hind-quarters of animal (ill. MEAT); thick slice of fish cut through backbone.

steal *v.* (past t. *stōle*, past part. *stōl'en*). 1. Take away dishonestly, and esp. secretly, what belongs to another; obtain surreptitiously or by surprise; win, get possession of, by insidious arts, attractions, etc. 2. Move secretly or silently. *~ n.* (chiefly U.S. colloq.) Stealing, theft; thing stolen.

stealth (-ĕl-) *n.* Secret, secret procedure; *by ~*, surreptitiously, clandestinely. **stealth'y** *adj.* **stealth'ĭly** *adv.* **stealth'ĭnėss** *n.*

steam *n.* Invisible vapour into which water is converted by heat; this used in specially contrived engines for generation of mechanical power; (pop.) steam mixed with air and with minute particles of water suspended in it, in form of white cloud or mist; (colloq.) energy, go; *steam'boat*, boat, esp. large river- or coasting-boat, driven by steam; *~-coal*, coal suitable for generating steam in boiler; *~-engine*, engine in which motive power is steam; freq., locomotive; *~-gauge*, gauge showing pressure of steam in boiler; *~ hammer*, hammer operated by steam; *~-heating*, central heating in which steam is circulated through radiators; *~-jacket*, casing round cylinder etc. that can be filled with steam; *~-navvy*, steam-operated machine for digging or excavating; *~-roller*, heavy locomotive engine with wide wheels and roller for crushing road-metal, levelling roads, etc.; *steam'ship*, ship driven by steam; *~-tug*, steamer for towing ships etc. *~ v.* 1. Emit, give off, steam or vapour, exhale (steam, vapour), cover, bedew, (surface), (of surface) become covered, with condensed vapour; generate steam. 2. Travel, move, by agency of steam. 3. Treat with steam, expose to action of steam; cook by steam. **steam'y** *adj.*

steam'er *n.* (esp.) 1. Vessel propelled by steam. 2. Vessel in which food is cooked by steam.

stē'arate *n.* Salt of stearic acid.

stėă'rĭc *adj.* Derived from, containing, stearin; *~ acid*, white crystalline fatty acid obtained from tallow etc.

stē'arĭn *n.* Any ester of glycerol and stearic acid, esp. white crystalline solid found in tallow and many other animal and vegetable fats; solid portion of any fixed oil or fat; (pop.) stearic acid used for making candles etc.

stē'atīte *n.* (min.) Greyish-green or brown massive variety of talc with soapy feel, soap-stone. **stēatĭt'ĭc** *adj.*

steed *n.* (poet., rhet., etc.) Horse, esp. war-horse.

steel *n.* Various hard, malleable, elastic alloys of purified iron with carbon (up to 1%) and metals such as nickel, manganese, or chromium, used as material for tools, weapons, etc.; this in form of weapons or cutting tools (ill. MUSKET); rod of steel, usu. tapering and roughened, for sharpening knives; strip of steel for stiffening corset etc.; *~ engraving*, engraving on, impression taken from, steel plate. *~ v.t.* Nerve, harden, fortify, (*against*).

Steele, Sir Richard (1672–1729). Irish essayist, playwright, and miscellaneous author; founder of the 'Tatler' and (with Addison) 'Spectator'.

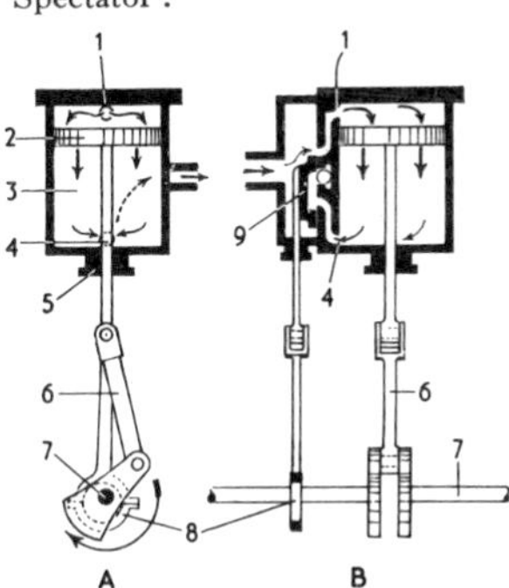

STEAM-ENGINE (DOWNWARD STROKE): A. END VIEW. B. SIDE VIEW

1. Inlet port. 2. Piston. 3. Cylinder. 4. Outlet port. 5. Gland. 6. Connecting rod. 7. Crank-shaft. 8. Eccentric. 9. Slide-valve. On upward stroke 1 is outlet port and 4 is inlet port

steel'y *adj.* Of, hard as, steel; inflexible, obdurate.

steel'yărd *n.* Lever with unequal arms used as balance, the article to be weighed being suspended from shorter arm while counterpoise is slid along longer, graduated arm until equilibrium is produced (ill. BALANCE).

steen'bŏck *n.* Small S. & E. African antelope (*Raphiceros campestris*).

steen'kĭrk, stein- (-ēn-) *n.* (hist.) Man's or woman's neckcloth with long lace ends hanging down or twisted and passed through ring (ill. COAT). [f. battle of *Steenkerke*, Belgium, 1692]

steep[1] *adj.* With precipitous face or slope, sloping sharply; (colloq., of price etc.) exorbitant, unreasonable; (of story etc.) exaggerated, incredible. **steep'ly** *adv.* **steep'nėss** *n.* **steep'en** *v.* **steep** *n.* Steep slope, precipice.

steep[2] *v.* Soak, be soaked, in liquid; (fig.) permeate, imbue, impregnate. *~ n.* Process of steeping; liquid in which thing is steeped.

stee'ple *n.* Lofty structure, esp. tower with spire, rising above roof of church (ill. CHURCH); spire; *steeplechase*, horse-race across country (orig. perhaps with steeple as goal) or on made course with hedges, water-jumps, and other obstacles; foot-race of similar kind; *steeplejack*, man who climbs steeples, tall chimneys, etc., to do repairs etc.

steer[1] *n.* Young, esp. castrated, male of ox kind; (U.S.) castrated male ox of any age.

steer[2] *v.* Guide (vessel), guide vessel, by rudder, helm, etc.; guide (motor-car, aircraft) by mechanical means; (of vessel etc.) be guided; direct one's course; *~ clear of*, avoid; *steering-wheel*, vertical wheel on ship, hand-wheel in motor-car etc. for steering; *steers'man*, one who steers ship, whence *steers'manship*. **steer'able** *adj.*

steer'age *n.* 1. Effect of helm on ship; *~ way*, amount of way or motion sufficient for ship to answer helm. 2. Part of ship allotted to passengers travelling at cheapest rate.

stein (-īn) *n.* (chiefly U.S.) Large earthenware mug, esp. for beer. [Ger., = 'stone']

stein'bŏck (-īn-) *n.* 1. The Alpine ibex (*Capra ibex*). 2. STEENBOCK.

steinkirk: see STEENKIRK.

stēl'ē *n.* (pl. *-ae*). 1. Upright slab with sculptured design or inscription, esp. as gravestone. 2. (bot.) Axial cylinder in stems and roots of vascular plants (ill. STEM).

stĕll'ar *adj.* Of stars; star-shaped.

stĕll'ate, -ātėd *adjs.* Star-shaped, radiating from centre like rays of star (ill. SOLID).

stĕm[1] *n.* 1. Main body above ground, ascending axis, of tree, shrub, or other plant; stalk supporting leaf, flower, or fruit; *~ stitch*, (needlework) kind of stitch used for stems and other slender lines in embroidery etc. (ill. STITCH). 2. Stem-shaped part or object, as slender upright support of cup, wineglass, etc., long slender part or tube of key, thermometer, tobacco-pipe, etc., pendant-shank of watch; *~-winder*, watch wound by turning head on end of stem, not by key. 3. Part of

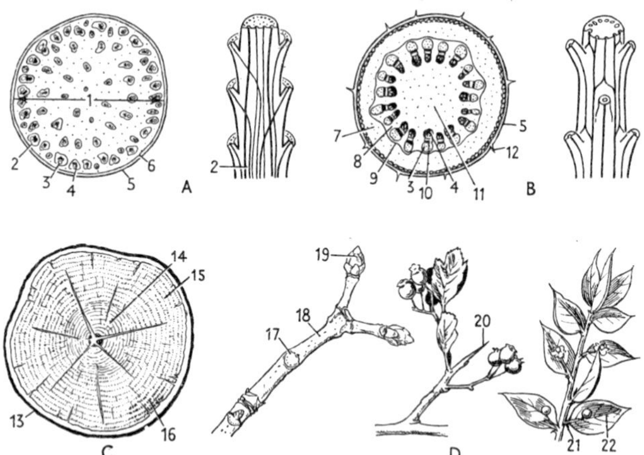

STEMS: TRANSVERSE AND LONGITUDINAL SECTIONS OF (A) MAIZE (MONOCOTYLEDON) AND (B) SUNFLOWER (DICOTYLEDON). C. TRANSVERSE SECTION OF TREE TRUNK. D. TWIGS OF HORSE-CHESTNUT, HAWTHORN, AND BUTCHER'S BROOM

A. 1. Stele. 2. Vascular bundle. 3. Phloem. 4. Xylem. 5. Epidermis. 6. Fibres. B. 7. Cortex. 8. Medulla. 9. Endodermis. 10. Cambium (forming fibre with phloem and xylem). 11. Pith. 12. Hair. C. 13. Bark. 14. Heart-wood. 15. Sapwood. 16. Annual ring. 17. Leaf-scar. 18. Lenticel. 19. Bud. 20. Thorn. 21. True leaf. 22. Cladode

word remaining essentially unchanged in inflexion, part to which flexional suffixes are added. 4. Line of ancestry; branch of family; stock, race. 5. (naut). Curved upright timber or metal piece at fore end of vessel, to which ship's sides are joined (ill. BOAT); bows or forepart of vessel. ~ *v.* 1. Remove stem of. 2. Make headway against (tide, current, etc.). 3. ~ *from*, originate in.

stĕm² *v.t.* Check, stop, dam up (stream etc.); (skiing) check (oneself), check progress, by forcing heel of ski(s) outwards from line of run (ill. SKI).

stĕmm′a *n.* (pl. *stĕmm′ata*). 1. Family tree; pedigree. 2. (zool.) Simple eye, facet of compound eye, in invertebrates (more usu. called *ocellus*). [L., f. Gk, = 'garland' (*stephō* crown)]

stĕnch *n.* Foul or offensive smell.

stĕn′cil *n.* Decoration, lettering, etc., produced by use of plate of metal, cardboard, etc. (~ or ~-*plate*), with holes cut in such a way that when a brush or roller charged with pigment is passed over it, desired design is produced on surface beneath. ~ *v.t.* Produce (pattern) on surface, ornament (surface) with pattern, by means of stencil(s).

Stendhal (stahṅdahl′). Pen-name of Henri Beyle (1783–1842), French novelist, author of 'Le Rouge et le Noir' and 'La Chartreuse de Parme'.

Stĕn gŭn *n.* Small mass-produced sub-machine-gun, usu. fired from the hip. [f. *S*, *T*, the initials of Shepherd and Turpin, the inventors, and *en*, as in BREN GUN]

stėnŏg′raphy *n.* Art of writing in shorthand. **stĕn′ograph** (-ahf) *n.* Writing, machine for writing, in shorthand. ~ *v.* Write in shorthand, act as stenographer. **stėnŏg′rapher** *n.* **stĕnogrăph′ic** *adj.* **stĕnogrăph′ically** *adv.*

Stĕn′tŏr. In the 'Iliad', a herald 'whose voice was as powerful as fifty voices of other men'; hence, person with very powerful voice. **stĕntŏr′ian** *adj.*

stĕp *v.* Lift and set down foot or alternate feet in walking etc.; go short distance, progress in some direction, by stepping; measure (distance) by stepping; (naut.) set up (mast) in step; ~ *down*, (elect.) lower voltage of (current) by means of a transformer; ~ *on the gas*, (colloq., orig. U.S.) accelerate motor-vehicle by means of the foot-operated throttle, speed up, hurry, hence ~ *on it*; ~ *out*, walk vigorously, stride; behave, live, in lively, gay, extravagant, or dissipated manner; ~ *up*, (elect.) increase voltage of (current) by means of a transformer; increase (efficiency, production) in rate, volume, etc., speed up; *stepp′ing-stone*, stone set in or projecting above water or muddy place as a help in crossing; (fig.) means of advancement or progress. ~ *n.* 1. Movement of stepping, distance gained by this; progress by stepping, course followed; manner of stepping; sound made by setting foot down; (fig.) action towards result, one of series of measures taken; *in* ~, stepping in time with other person(s) or music, stepping simultaneously and with corresponding legs with other person(s) or animal(s); *out of* ~, not in step. 2. Flat-topped structure, used singly or as one of series, to facilitate person's movement from one level to another; rung of ladder; foot-piece for entering, mounting, or alighting from vehicle; notch cut for foot in climbing; (pl.) step-ladder; (fig.) degree in an ascending scale, advance from one of these to another. 3. (naut.) Block or socket supporting mast etc. (ill. BOAT); (mech.) lower bearing on which vertical shaft revolves; step-like part or offset. 4. ~-*dance*, dance for display of special steps by (usu.) individual performer; ~-*ladder*, kind of portable short ladder with flat steps and prop hinged to back for steadying.

stĕp- *prefix* in terms of relationship expressing degrees resulting from remarriage of a parent; *step′-child* (-*daughter*, -*son*), child by previous marriage of one's wife or husband; *step′father*, (-*mother*, -*parent*), husband, wife, of one's mother, father, by subsequent marriage; ~-*brother*, -*sister*, child of step-parent.

stĕphanōt′is *n.* Genus of tropical woody climbing plants with fragrant white waxy flowers. [Gk, = 'fit for a wreath' (*stephanos*)]

Stephen¹ (stēv′en), St. First Christian martyr, stoned to death at Jerusalem (Acts vi, vii).

Stephen² (stēv′en), St. (*c* 977–1038). First king and patron saint of Hungary.

Stephen (stēv′en) **of Blois** (*c* 1097–1154). Grandson, through his mother, of William the Conqueror; king of England 1135–54.

Stephenson (stēv′en-), George (1781–1848). English engineer; built first railway (Stockton–Darlington, 1825) and greatly improved the locomotive engine.

stĕppe *n.* Vast plain, grassy and largely treeless, esp. in SE. Europe and Siberia.

stėrcorā′ceous (-shus), **stėrc′-oral** *adjs.* Of, produced by, dung or faeces.

stēr′ėō *n.* & *adj.* Stereotype(d); stereoscopic; stereophonic.

stĕ′rėobāte *n.* (archit.) Solid mass of masonry as foundation for wall, columns, etc.

stērėŏg′raphy (*or* stĕ′r-) *n.* Art of delineating forms of solid bodies on a plane. **stērėogrăph′ic** *adj.*

stērėŏm′ėtry (*or* stĕ′r-) *n.* Art of measuring solids; solid geometry. **stērėomĕt′ric(al)** *adjs.*

stērėophŏn′ic (*or* stĕ′r-) *adj.* Of a system of separate microphones or loud-speakers designed to enhance the actuality of sounds.

stēr′ėoscōpe (*or* stĕ′r-) *n.* Instrument for obtaining single image giving impression of solidity or relief from two pictures (usu. photographs) of object from slightly different points of view.

stēreoscŏp ĭc *adj.* Of the stereoscope or stereoscopy. **stēreŏs′copy** *n.* Vision of objects as solid or in three dimensions.

stēr′ēotȳpe (*or* stĕ′r-) *n.* Printing-plate cast from papier-mâché or other mould of forme of type; method or process of printing from this. ~ *v.t.* Make stereotype(s) of, print from stereotype(s); (fig.) fix or perpetuate in unchanging form, formalize.

stĕ′rīle *adj.* Barren; not producing, incapable of producing, fruit or offspring; free from living micro-organisms, as bacteria etc. **stĕ′rīlely** (-l-l-) *adv.* **sterĭl′ity** *n.*

stĕ′rĭlīze *v.t.* 1. Render (individual) incapable of producing offspring. 2. Render (object) free from contamination by micro-organisms by treating with heat, disinfectant, etc. **stĕrĭlīzā′tion** *n.*

stêrl′ĕt *n.* Small species of sturgeon (*Acipenser ruthenus*) found in and near Caspian Sea, and used for making finest caviare.

stêrl′ĭng *n.* English money. ~ *adj.* (Of coins and precious metals) genuine, of standard value or purity; of sterling; (fig.) solidly excellent, genuine, not showy or specious; ~ *area*, group of countries, mostly in the British Commonwealth, between which payment is freely made in sterling and for which certain institutions in the City of London act as bankers; ~ *silver*, silver of a fineness formerly fixed by law for British silver coinage (92½% silver and 7½% copper). [orig. as n. = the English silver penny]

stêrn[1] *n.* After or rear part of ship or boat, specif. that part of the hull abaft the sternpost (ill. BOAT); buttocks, rump; tail, esp. of fox-hound; ~*-chase*, pursuit of ship by another directly in its wake; *stern′post*, central upright timber or iron of stern, attached to keel and usu. bearing rudder; ~ *sheet(s)*, space in boat's stern, esp. aft of hindmost thwart (ill. BOAT); ~*-wheeler*, steamer with one large paddle-wheel at stern.

stêrn[2] *adj.* Severe, strict, not lenient, rigorous in principle, punishment, or condemnation; hard, grim, harsh, gloomy. **stêrn′ly** *adv.* **stêrn′nĕss** *n.*

Stêrne, Laurence (1713–68). Irish humorist and sentimentalist; author of 'Tristram Shandy' and 'A Sentimental Journey'.

Stêrnhōld and Hŏp′kins. The English metrical version of the Psalms by Thomas Sternhold (d. 1549) and John Hopkins (d. 1570), published in part in 1549, and complete, attached to the Prayer Book, in 1562.

stêrn′um *n.* Bone or series of bones running along middle line of front of trunk, usu. articulated with some of ribs (ill. SKELETON); breast-bone; ventral plate of body segment of arthropod.

stêrnūtā′tion *n.* Sneezing, sneeze. **sternūt′atĭve, sternūt′atory** *adjs.* & *ns.* (Substance, e.g. snuff) causing sneezing.

stêrn′ūtātor *n.* Poison gas that acts as a nose irritant.

stêr′ŏl *n.* (biochem.) One of a class of complex solid alcohols, as cholesterol, ergosterol, widely distributed in animals and plants.

stêrt′orous *adj.* (Of breathing etc.) producing snoring or rasping sound. **stêrt′orously** *adv.* **stêrt′orousnĕss** *n.*

stĕt. Direction to printer, written in margin of MS. or proof, to cancel a correction made in the text, the letters thus restored being indicated by dots beneath them. [L, = 'let it stand']

stĕth′oscōpe *n.* Instrument, consisting of ear tubes and a main tube to be applied to chest etc., for auscultation, esp. of heart or lungs. **stĕthoscŏp′ĭc** *adj.* **stĕthoscŏp′ĭcally** *adv.* **stĕthŏs′copy** *n.*

stĕt′son *n.* Man's slouch hat with very wide brim. [maker's name]

stēv′ēdōre *n.* Man employed in loading and stowing ships' cargoes; (north.) charge-hand supervising dockers.

Stēv′enson, Robert Louis (1850–94). Scottish essayist, novelist, and poet; author of 'Treasure Island', 'Dr Jekyll and Mr Hyde', 'Kidnapped', etc.

stew[1] *n.* (pl., archaic or hist.) Brothel.

stew[2] *v.* Cook by long simmering in closed vessel with liquid; (of tea) make bitter or strong with too long soaking; (fig.) be oppressed by close or moist warm atmosphere; (slang) study hard, 'swot'; ~ *in one's own juice*, be left to one's own devices, without help, etc. ~ *n.* Dish of stewed meat, usu. with vegetables; (fig.) state of great alarm or excitement; ~*-pan, -pot*, pan, covered pot, for stewing.

stew[3] *n.* Pond or tank for keeping live fish for table; artificial oyster-bed.

stew′ard *n.* 1. Person entrusted with management of another's property, esp. paid manager of great house or estate. 2. Purveyor of provisions etc. for college, club, ship, etc. 3. Attendant waiting on passengers in ship or aircraft. 4. Official managing race-meeting, ball, show, etc. 5. *Lord High S~ of England*, official managing coronation or presiding at trial of peer; *Lord S~ of the (King's, Queen's) Household*, high court officer, with nominal duty of controlling sovereign's household above stairs. **stew′ardĕss, stew′ardship** *ns.*

stew′artry *n.* Former territorial division of Scotland under jurisdiction of a steward.

St. Ex(ch). *abbrev.* Stock Exchange.

stg *abbrev.* Sterling.

stick *v.* (past t. and past part. *stŭck*). 1. Thrust point of (pin, weapon, etc.) *in(to), through*; insert pointed thing(s) into, stab; (of mounted sportsman) spear (wild pig); fix (*up*)*on* pointed thing, be fixed (as) by point *in(to)* or *on*; (colloq.) put in specified position. 2. ~ *out, up*, etc., protrude, (cause to) project; be, make, erect; ~ *up for*, maintain cause or character of, champion; ~ *up to*, offer resistance to, not humble oneself before; ~ *up*, rob with violence, hold up; *stuck-up*, conceited, insolently exclusive. 3. Fix, become or remain fixed (as) by adhesion of surfaces; (cause to) adhere or cleave; (slang) endure, bear; ~ *at* or *to it*, persist, not cease trying. 4. Lose or deprive of power of motion through friction, jamming, suction, difficulty, etc.; ~*-in-the-mud*, slow, unprogressive (person); *stick′ing-plaster*, adhesive plaster for wounds etc.; ~*-jaw*, toffee etc. tending to stick jaws together and difficult to chew; ~*-pin*, (U.S.) (ornamental) pin, esp. tie-pin, that is merely stuck in, as dist. from safety-pin; ~*-up*, (*adj.*) that sticks up or projects; (*n.*) hold-up. ~ *n.* 1. Short and relatively slender piece of wood; shoot or branch of tree cut to convenient length for use as walking-cane, bludgeon, staff, wand, support for climbing plant, etc.; ~ *of furniture*, (esp. in neg. or pl.) piece of furniture; fiddle-stick, drum-stick, composing-stick, etc.; twigs or small pieces of wood as fuel; (fig.) person of no liveliness or intelligence, poor actor. 2. Slender more or less cylindrical piece *of* sugar-candy, sealing-wax, shaving-soap, etc.; (pl.) thin pieces of ivory, bone, etc., as framework of fan. 3. Number of aerial bombs released in close succession, or of parachute troops from an aircraft. ~*-insect*, insect of family *Phasmidae*, usu. wingless, with long slender stick-like body resembling twigs of trees in which it lives; ~ *lac*, lac in natural state, incrusting the insects and small twigs.

stĭck′er *n.* (esp.) 1. Adhesive label or other paper gummed on back. 2. Dogged or persistent person. 3. Rod in mechanism of organ or pianoforte working under compression.

stĭck′ĭng *n.* Inferior meat at neck of beef (ill. MEAT).

stĭck′lebăck (-lb-) *n.* Any of small spiny-finned fishes (family *Gasterosteidae*) of N. hemisphere

stĭck′ler *n.* ~ *for*, one who insists on or pertinaciously supports or advocates. [obs. *stickle* be umpire]

stĭck′y *adj.* Tending to stick or adhere, glutinous, viscous; (of race-course, wicket) with yielding surface due to wet; (colloq.) unbending, 'difficult'; (slang) highly unpleasant and painful, as in *he'll come to a* ~ *end.* **stĭck′ĭly** *adv.* **stĭck′ĭnĕss** *n.*

stiff *adj.* 1. Rigid, not flexible;

unbending, unyielding, uncompromising, obstinate; lacking ease, grace, or freedom; formal, laboured, constrained, haughty; *~-necked*, stubborn. 2. Not working freely, sticking, offering resistance; (of joints, limbs, etc.) not supple, unable to move without pain; *~ neck*, affection in which head cannot be moved without pain. 3. Hard to cope with, trying, difficult. 4. (Of moist or semi-liquid substance) thick and viscous, not fluid. **stĭff'ly** *adv.* **stĭff'nėss** *n.* **stĭff'en** *v.* **stĭff'ener, stĭff'enĭng** *ns.* **stĭff** *n.* (slang) Corpse; rough clumsy person.

stī'fle *v.* Smother; (cause to) feel oppressed or unable to breathe. **stī'flĭng** *adj.* **stī'flĭngly** *adv.*

stī'fle(-joint) *n.* Joint between femur and tibia esp. in horses, corresponding to knee in man (ill. HORSE).

stĭg'ma *n.* (pl. *stigmas*, *stig'-mata*). Mark branded on slave, criminal, etc. (archaic); (fig.) mark of disgrace or infamy, stain on one's good name; (path.) definite characteristic of some disease, morbid red spot on skin, esp. one bleeding spontaneously; (anat., zool.) spot, pore, natural mark, esp. spot on surface of ovary where rupture of Graafian follicle will occur; (bot.) receptive surface of the floral gynaecium to which pollen grains adhere (ill. FLOWER); (pl.) marks resembling wounds on crucified body of Christ, said to have developed on bodies of some saints. **stĭgmăt'ĭc** *adj.*

stĭg'matīze *v.t.* Mark with stigmata, produce stigmata upon; (fig.) use opprobrious terms of, describe by disgraceful or reproachful name. **stĭgmatīzā'tion** *n.*

stīle[1] *n.* Arrangement of steps, rungs, etc., allowing passage to persons over or through fence or wall but excluding cattle etc.

stīle[2] *n.* (carpentry) Vertical bar of wainscot, sash, or other wooden framing (ill. WAINSCOT).

stĭlĕtt'ō *n.* (pl. *-s*, *-es*). Short dagger (ill. DAGGER); small pointed implement for making eyelet-holes etc.

stĭll[1] *adj.* Without or almost without motion or sound, silent, quiet, calm; (of wine etc.) not sparkling or effervescing; *~ birth*, delivery of dead child; so *~-born*; *~ life*, representation in painting etc. of inanimate things, as fruit, flowers, etc. **stĭll'nėss** *n.* **stĭll** *n.* 1. Deep silence. 2. Ordinary photograph, specif. single snapshot taken from a motion film and displayed for advertisement. *~ v.* Quiet, calm, appease, make still; (rare) grow still or calm. *~ adv.* 1. Without motion or change. 2. Now as formerly; then as before; now, in contrast with future; even then, even now; nevertheless; even, yet; always, even.

stĭll[2] *n.* Distilling apparatus, consisting essentially of a closed vessel for heating substance to be distilled, and spiral tube or worm for condensing the vapour so produced; *~-room*, orig., room for distilling perfumes, cordials, etc.; later, housekeeper's store-room in large house.

stĭll'age *n.* Stand or bench for keeping something, as a cask, from ground.

stĭll'y *adj.* (poet.) Still, quiet.

stĭlt *n.* 1. Each of pair of poles, usu. held by hands or under arms, with foot-rest some way from lower end, for enabling person to walk over marshy ground, stream, etc., with feet raised above ground; one of set of piles or posts supporting building, etc. 2. Marsh bird of the widely distributed genus *Himantopus*, with very long slender legs and sharp slender bill.

stĭl'tėd *adj.* (As) on stilts; (archit.) raised by a course of masonry, as *~ arch* (ill. ARCH); (of style, language, etc.) artificially lofty, formally pompous. **stĭl'tėdly** *adv.* **stĭl'tėdnėss** *n.*

Stĭl'ton. *~ cheese*, rich blue-veined cheese, orig. made in Leicestershire and formerly sold to travellers at a coaching inn at Stilton, Huntingdonshire, on the Great North Road from London.

stĭm'ūlant *n.* Agent producing temporary increase of activity in part of organism; esp., alcoholic drink.

stĭm'ūlāte *v.t.* Apply stimulus to, act as stimulus on; animate, spur on, make more vigorous or active. **stĭmūlā'tion** *n.* **stĭm'ūlātive** *adj.*

stĭm'ūlus *n.* (pl. *-lī*). Something that rouses to activity or energy; rousing effect; thing that rouses organ or tissue to specific activity or function, effect of this. [L, = 'goad']

stĭng *n.* 1. Sharp-pointed organ in some insects and other animals, freq. connected with poison gland, and capable of giving painful or dangerous wound; poison-fang of snake; (bot.) stiff sharp-pointed hair emitting irritating fluid when touched. 2. Stinging, being stung; wound made, pain or irritation produced, by sting; rankling or acute pain of body or mind; keenness, vigour; stimulus. 3. *~-ray*, ray of genus *Trygon* or related genera, with long tapering tail armed with flattened sharp-pointed serrated spine(s) capable of inflicting severe wounds. *~ v.* (past t. and past part. *stŭng*). 1. Wound with sting; (of some plants) produce kind of burning or itching rash or inflammation by contact with (skin); feel acute pain; be able to sting, have a sting; *sting'ing hair*, sting of plant; *sting'ing nettle*, common nettle *Urtica dioica*) and related plants, bearing stinging hairs. 2. (slang, chiefly *pass.*) Charge heavily, involve in expense, swindle.

stĭng'o (-nggō) *n.* (archaic) Strong beer.

stĭn'gy (-jĭ) *adj.* Meanly parsimonious, niggardly. **stĭn'gily** *adv.* **stĭn'ginėss** *n.*

stĭnk *v.* (past t. *stănk* or *stŭnk*, past part. *stŭnk*). Have, emit, strong offensive smell; drive *out* with stench or suffocating fumes; cause to stink. *~ n.* Such smell; (pl., slang) chemistry, natural science, as subject of study; *~-ball*, missile emitting suffocating vapour; *~-bomb*, small bomb giving off offensive smell on bursting; *~-horn*, various ill-smelling fungi, esp. *Ithyphallus impudicus*; *stink'wood*, various trees with unpleasant-smelling wood.

stĭnk'ard *n.* Stinking person or animal, esp. the teledu.

stĭnk'er *n.* Stinkard; (colloq.) anything particularly offensive or irritating.

stĭnk'ĭng *adj.* That stinks (freq. in names of plants etc.); (slang) objectionable in any way, that one dislikes.

stĭnt *n.* Limitation of supply or effort; fixed or allotted amount (of work etc.); (mining) area of coal-face to be worked in a shift. *~ v.* Keep on short allowance, supply or give in niggardly amount or grudgingly.

stīpe *n.* (bot.) Footstalk, esp. stem supporting pileus of fungus, leafstalk of fern etc. (ill. FUNGUS); (zool.) stipes.

stīp'ĕnd *n.* Fixed periodical money payment to teacher, public official, or esp. clergyman, for his services; salary.

stīpĕn'dĭary *adj.* & *n.* (Person) receiving stipend, not serving gratuitously; *~ (magistrate)*, in England, paid police-court magistrate appointed by Home Secretary.

stīp'ēs (-z) *n.* (zool.) Stalk-like part or organ, esp. second segment of maxilla of insect, eyestalk, etc.; (bot.) stipe.

stĭpp'le *n.* Method of painting, engraving, etc., by use of dots or small spots to produce gradations of shade or colour; layer of paint applied roughly over layer of another colour which shows through in places; effect, work, so produced. *~ v.* Engrave, paint, in stipple.

stĭp'ūlāte *v.* Require or insist upon as essential condition; make express demand *for* as condition of agreement. **stĭpūlā'tion** *n.*

stĭp'ūle *n.* One of pair of lateral appendages, freq. resembling small leaf or scale, at base of leaf in certain plants (ill. LEAF).

stĭr *n.* Commotion, bustle, disturbance, excitement; slight movement; act of stirring. *~ v.* Set, keep, (begin to) be, in (esp. slight) motion; agitate (soft or liquid or semi-liquid mass) with more or less circular motion, as with spoon, so as to mix ingredients, prevent burning in cooking, etc.; rouse (*up*), excite, animate, inspirit; *stir'about*, porridge made by stirring oatmeal or other meal into boiling water or milk. **stĭr'rĭng** *adj.* Exciting, stimulating. **stĭr'rĭngly** *adv.*

Stĭrl'ĭng. County town, on the river Forth, of **Stĭrl'ĭngshire,** county of S. Scotland.

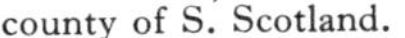

STOCKS

stĭ'rrup *n.* Support suspended by strap from side of saddle for rider's foot, now usu. iron loop with flattened base (ill. SADDLE); something resembling this, esp. U-shaped clamp or support; (naut.) rope with eye at end supporting foot-rope; ~ (*-bone*), (anat.) stirrup-shaped bone of middle ear, stapes (ill. EAR); *~-cup*, parting cup of wine etc. handed to rider on horseback; *~-iron*, iron part of rider's stirrup; *~-leather*, strap suspending stirrup from saddle; ~ *pump*, pump with stirrup-shaped foot-rest and a nozzle for producing a jet or spray of water, used for extinguishing small fires.

stĭtch *n.* 1. Sudden sharp pain, esp. in the side of the body. 2. Each movement of threaded needle in and out of fabric in sewing, or of awl in shoe-making; loop of thread etc. left in fabric by this movement; single complete movement of needle, hook, etc., in knitting, crochet, embroidery, etc., part of work produced by this; (surg.) movement of needle in sewing up wound, loop of catgut etc. left in skin or flesh by this; method of making stitch, kind of work produced. 3. *stitch'wort*, various chickweeds, esp. kind with erect stem and white starry flowers. ~ *v.* Sew, make stitches (in); fasten, make, ornament, with stitches.

stĭtch'ery *n.* Needlework.

stī'ver *n.* Thing of smallest value, (even) the smallest coin or amount.

stō'a *n.* (pl. *-ae*, *-as*). 1. Portico in ancient Greek architecture (ill. TEMPLE). 2. (cap.) Great hall at Athens, adorned with frescoes of battle of Marathon, in which Zeno of Citium lectured.

stoat *n.* European ermine of the weasel tribe, esp. in its brown summer coat.

stŏck *n.* 1. Trunk or stem of tree; stump, butt; plant into which graft is inserted; (bot.) rhizome; (geol.) cylindrical intrusive body of igneous rock (freq. granite) of moderate size. 2. Body-piece serving as the base or holder or handle for the working parts of an implement or machine, as whip, plough, gun, anchor, etc. (ill. ANCHOR). 3. (Source of) family or breed. 4. (hist., pl.) Instrument of punishment, wooden framework set up in public place with holes for offender's feet or feet and hands. 5. (pl.) Timbers on which ship rests while building; *on the ~s*, in construction (also fig.). 6. Cruciferous plant of genus *Matthiola*, with fragrant flowers; *Virginia ~*, small cruciferous plant, *Malcolmia maritima*, with flowers of various colours resembling those of *Matthiola*. 7. Hard solid brick pressed in mould. 8. Close-fitting wide band for neck, worn esp. as part of riding-kit; piece of black or purple silk etc. worn below clerical collar. 9. Swarm or hive of bees. 10. Livestock, animals on farm. 11. Liquor made by stewing meat, bones, vegetables, etc., and used as foundation for soup etc. 12. Raw material of manufacture. 13. Fund, store ready for drawing on, equipment for trade or pursuit. 14. Subscribed capital of trading company, or public debt of nation, municipal corporation, etc., regarded as transferable property held by subscribers or creditors and subject to fluctuations in market value. 15. (*attrib.* or as *adj.*) Kept regularly in stock for sale or use; commonly used, constantly recurring in discussion etc. 16. *take ~*, make inventory of merchandise etc. in hand; (fig.) make careful estimate of one's position, prospects, resources, etc.; *take ~ of*, reckon up, evaluate, scrutinize; *take ~ in*, invest money in; (fig.) concern oneself in; ~ *actor*, *company*, (member of) company regularly performing together at particular theatre; *stock'broker*, broker who buys and sells stocks for clients on commission; ~ *car*, old car painted in bright colours for use in *~-car racing*, rough racing with few or no rules; *~-dove*, the wild pigeon; ~ *exchange*, market, building, for buying and selling of stocks; association of brokers and jobbers doing business in particular place or market, esp. (building of) *the S~ Exchange* in City of London; *stock'fish*, cod, hake, etc., split open and dried in the air without salt; *~-gillyflower* = stock (sense 6); *stock'holder*, holder of stock in public funds etc., shareholder; *~-in-trade*, goods kept in stock, all requisites for a particular trade; *~-jobber*, member of Stock Exchange dealing in stocks on his own account; *stockman*, (chiefly Austral.) man employed to look after livestock; *~-market*, traffic in stocks and shares; ~ *piece*, *play*, play forming part of repertory; *stockpile*, (orig. U.S.) raw materials purchased and accumulated by country which cannot provide them in sufficient quantity from its own resources; *stockpiling*, this practice; *~-pot*, cooking-pot in which stock is made and kept; ~ *size*, size of ready-made garments regularly kept in stock; person able to wear these; *~-still*, quite motionless; *~-whip*, short-handled

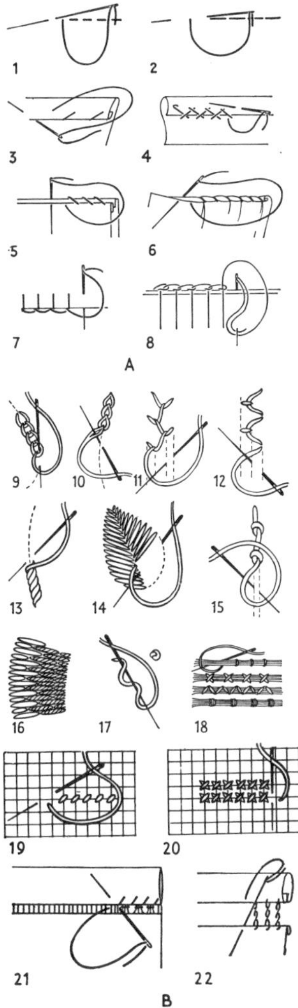

A. SEWING STITCHES. B. EMBROIDERY STITCHES

A. 1. Running. 2. Backstitch. 3. Hemming. 4. Herring-bone. 5. Oversewing. 6. Whipping. 7. Blanket stitch. 8. Tailor's buttonhole stitch. B. 9. Chain-stitch. 10. Split-stitch. 11. Feather-stitch. 12. Fly-stitch. 13. Stem stitch. 14. Satin-stitch. 15. Coral stitch. 16. Long-and-short stitch. 17. French knot. 18. Couching. 19. Tent-stitch (*petit point*). 20. Cross-stitch (*gros point*). 21. Hemstitching. 22. Faggotting

whip with very long lash for herding cattle; *stock'yard*, enclosure with pens etc. for sorting or temporary keeping of cattle. ~ *v.* 1. Fit (gun etc.) with stock. 2. Provide (shop, farm, etc.) with goods, livestock, or requisites. 3. Keep (goods) in stock.

stockāde' *n.* & *v.t.* (Fortify with) breastwork or enclosure of upright stakes.

Stŏck'holm (-hōm). Capital city and port of Sweden; ~ *tar*, kind of tar prepared from resinous pine-wood and used in shipbuilding and the manufacture of cordage, orig. exported from Stockholm.

stŏck'ĭnĕt (*or* -ĕt') *n.* Fine elastic machine-knitted textile material used for undergarments etc.

stŏck'ĭng *n.* Close-fitting, usu. knitted, covering for foot and leg up to or above knee; surgical appliance resembling this; leg of bird or animal, when of different colour from body; *~-frame, -loom, -machine*, knitting machine; ~ *stitch*, knitting-stitch resembling that commonly used in stockings, producing plain smooth surface (ill. KNITTING).

stŏck'ĭst *n.* One who stocks specified goods for sale.

stŏck'y *adj.* Thickset, short and strongly built. **stŏck'ĭly** *adv.* **stŏck'ĭnėss** *n.*

stŏdge *n.* 1. Thick semi-solid mass, esp. of food; full meal. 2. Greedy eater. ~ *v.i.* Eat greedily.

stŏdg'y *adj.* (Of food) heavy, filling, thick or semi-solid; (of person, book, etc.) dull, heavy, solid, uninspired. **stŏdg'ĭly** *adv.* **stŏdg'ĭnėss** *n.*

stoep (-o͞op) *n.* (S. Afr.) Verandah at front (and occas. sides) of house.

stō'gie, stō'gy (-gĭ) *n.* (U.S.) Kind of long slender cigar or cheroot.

stō'ĭc *n.* 1. (*S~.*) Philosopher of school founded *c* 315 B.C. by ZENO[1], who taught that virtue was the highest good, and inculcated repression of emotion, indifference to pleasure or pain, and patient endurance; later Stoic writers were Seneca, Epictetus, and Marcus Aurelius. 2. Person of great self-control, fortitude, or austerity. **stō'ĭcal** *adj.* **stō'ĭcally** *adv.* **stō'ĭcĭsm** *n.* [Gk *stoā* porch, hall where Zeno taught]

stōke *v.* Feed and tend (furnace), feed furnace of (engine etc.); act as stoker; ~ *up*, (fig., colloq.) feed, eat, esp. in hurried way; *stoke'hold*, apartment containing ship's boilers, where furnaces are tended; *~-hole*, space in front of furnace where stokers stand, opening through which furnace is tended, stokehold.

stōk'er *n.* One who feeds and tends furnace esp. of ship or steam-engine.

stōle *n.* 1. Long loose garment reaching to feet, esp. as outer dress of ancient-Roman matron. 2. Ecclesiastical vestment, narrow strip of silk or linen worn over shoulders and reaching to or below knees (ill. VESTMENT); woman's wrap of fur etc. of similar shape.

stŏl'ĭd *adj.* Not easily excited or moved, phlegmatic, dull and impassive. **stŏl'ĭdly** *adv.* **stolĭd'ĭty** *n.*

stōl'on *n.* 1. (bot.) Reclined or prostrate branch that strikes root and develops new plant (ill. GRASS). 2. (zool.) In hydrozoa etc., extension of body wall that develops buds, giving rise to new zooids.

stōm'a *n.* (pl. *-mata, -mas*). (anat., zool.) Small mouth-like opening, esp. in lower animals; (bot.) minute orifices in epidermis of plants, esp. of leaves, affording communication between outer air and intercellular spaces in interior tissue (ill. LEAF).

stom'ach (-ŭm*a*k) *n.* Internal pouch or cavity in human or other animal body in which food is digested; in man, a dilatation of alimentary canal at upper left of abdomen (ill. ALIMENTARY); in some animals, esp. ruminants, one of several digestive cavities; (loosely) belly, abdomen; (archaic) appetite *for* food; (fig.) relish, inclination, desire (*for* danger, conflict, an undertaking, etc.); *~-ache*, pain in belly, esp. bowels; *~-pump*, small pump or syringe for emptying stomach or introducing liquids into it. **stom'achal** *adj.* **stom'ach** *v.t.* Brook, endure, tolerate.

stom'acher (-ŭm*a*cher, -*ker*) *n.* (hist.) In female dress of 15th–17th centuries, ornamental piece, freq. embroidered or set with gems, covering breast and pit of stomach (ill. PANNIER).

stomăch'ĭc (-k-) *adj.* & *n.* Of the stomach; (drug etc.) promoting digestion or appetite.

stŏmatīt'ĭs *n.* Inflammation of the mouth.

stōne *n.* 1. Piece of rock, esp. of small or moderate size; hard compact material of which stones and rocks consist, particular kind of this; gem; piece of stone of definite form and size, for special purpose, as for building, paving, grinding, as a monument, etc. 2. Hard morbid concretion in body, esp. in kidney, urinary bladder, or gall-bladder, calculus; hard wood-like case of kernel in drupe or *~-fruit*; seed of grape etc.; testicle. 3. Unit of weight, usu. of 14 lb., but varying with different commodities from 8 to 24 lb. 4. *S~ Age*, stage of a culture marked by use of implements and weapons of stone, not metal; *~-blind*, quite blind; *stone'chat*, small European singing bird (*Saxicola torquata*), with plumage largely black and white; *~-cold*, quite cold; *stone'crop*, common creeping herb (*Sedum acre*) with bright yellow flowers and small cylindrical fleshy leaves, growing on rocks, old walls, etc.; other species of *Sedum* and allied genera; *~-dead*, quite dead; *~-deaf*, completely deaf; *~-fly*, insect of order *Plecoptera* with larvae often found under stones in streams, used by anglers as bait; *~-fruit*, drupe; *stone'hatch*, ring-plover; *~-horse*, (archaic) stallion; ~ *of Destiny*, stone of Scone: see CORONATION stone; *~-lily*, fossil crinoid; ~ *marten*: see BEECH marten; *~-mason*, mason; *~-pine*, species of pine (*Pinus pinea*) of S. Europe and Levant with wide-spreading branches and flat top; *~'s throw*, short or moderate distance; *stonewall'*, obstruct by stonewalling; *stonewalling*, (cricket) excessively cautious batting, (politics, esp. Austral.) parliamentary obstruction; *stone'ware*, hard dense kind of pottery made from very siliceous clay or mixture of clay with much flint or sand; *stone'work*, masonry. ~ *v.t.* Pelt with stones, esp. put to death thus; take stones out of (fruit); face, pave, etc., with stone.

Stōne'hĕnge' (-nj). Prehistoric stone monument on Salisbury Plain, Wiltshire, England, consisting of concentric circles of dressed stones erected mainly in the Bronze Age; some of the larger stones carry lintels and among the smaller are 'blue' stones which apparently come from Pembrokeshire.

Stonewall Jackson (stōn'-wawl). Nickname of Thomas Jonathan JACKSON[2].

stōn'y *adj.* Full of, covered with, having many, stones; hard, rigid, fixed, as stone, obdurate, unfeeling; *~(-broke)*, (slang) without any money, utterly 'broke'.

stooge *n.* (theatr. slang) Butt, foil, esp. for comedian; (orig. U.S. slang) person learning to fly; person deputed to do routine or spade-work for another. ~ *v.i.* (slang) Act as stooge (*for*); move, travel, esp. fly *about, around*, in an aircraft.

stoo͝k *n.* & *v.t.* (Make into) shock of corn.

stoōl *n.* 1. Seat for one person without arms or back, esp. wooden one on three or four legs; footstool. 2. (Place for) evacuation of bowels; faeces evacuated. 3. Stump of felled tree etc., esp. with new shoots. 4. (U.S.) Decoy-bird; *~(-pigeon)*, decoy (freq. fig., esp. = police-spy). ~ *v.* Throw up young shoots or stems; (U.S.) decoy; act as stool-pigeon.

stoōp[1] *v.* 1. Bring one's head nearer ground by bending shoulders, trunk, etc., forward; carry head and shoulders bowed forward; incline (head, shoulders, back, etc.) forward and down; (fig.) condescend, deign, *to* do; descend or lower oneself *to*. 2

(Of hawk or other bird of prey) swoop, descend steeply and swiftly, on quarry. ~ *n.* 1. Stooping carriage of back or shoulders; act of stooping. 2. Swoop of bird of prey on its quarry.

stōōp[2] *n.* (U.S. and Canada) Porch, platform, small verandah, before door of house.

stŏp *v.* 1. Close or almost close aperture or cavity by plugging, obstructing, etc., esp. block mouth(s) of (fox's earth), fill cavity in tooth with stopping, close (organ-pipe) at upper end with plug or cap; prevent or forbid passage through; make impervious or impassable. 2. Put an end to, arrest (motion etc.); check progress, motion or operation of; effectively hinder or prevent; suspend (payment etc.), give instructions to banker not to cash (cheque etc.). 3. (mus.) Press down (string of violin etc.) with finger to raise pitch of note, produce (note, sound) thus. 4. Cease, come to an end, cease from, discontinue; cease from motion, speaking, or action; make halt or pause; (colloq.) remain, stay, sojourn. 5. ~ *down*, reduce aperture of (lens); ~ *out*, (etching etc.) cover with varnish (parts of plate to be protected from action of acid); ~ *over*, (U.S.) halt (*at* place) and proceed by later conveyance. **stŏpp'age** *n.* **stŏp** *n.* 1. Stopping, being stopped; pause, check. 2. Punctuation-mark, esp. comma, semi-colon, colon, or period; *full* ~, period. 3. Batten, peg, block, etc., meant to stop motion of something at fixed point; something stopping aperture, plug. 4. (optics, photog.) Diaphragm. 5. (mus.) Graduated set of organ-pipes of like quality of tone, handle or knob (~-*knob*) by which such set is turned on or off (ill. ORGAN); closing of hole in tube of wind instrument to alter pitch of note, hole so closed, metal key closing it; pressing with finger on string of violin etc. to raise pitch of note, part of string where this pressure is applied. 6. (phonet.) Consonant in formation of which passage of breath is completely obstructed, mute. **stop-** in combination: *stop'cock*, tap or short pipe with externally operated valve to stop or regulate passage of liquid, gas, etc., key or handle for turning this; *stop'gap*, makeshift, temporary substitute; ~-*knob*: see STOP *n.*, sense 5; ~-*over*, (U.S.) act of stopping over; permission to passenger to break journey; ~-*press*, (news) inserted in paper after printing has begun; ~-*watch*, watch indicating fractions of a second by a hand that may be instantly stopped at will, used in timing races etc.

stōpe *n.* Working face of mine, area where ore is being extracted.

stŏpp'er *n.* (esp.) Plug for closing bottle etc., usu. of glass or of same material as vessel. ~ *v.t.* Close or secure with stopper.

stŏr'age *n.* Storing of goods, method of doing this; space for storing; cost of warehousing; *cold* ~, storing of provisions in refrigerating chambers; ~ *battery*, (elect.) apparatus for storing electrical energy in chemical form, accumulator.

stŏr'ăx *n.* (Trees yielding) fragrant gum-resin got from species of *Styrax*, esp. *S. officinalis*, or fragrant honey-like balsam got from *Liquidambar orientalis*.

stōre *n.* 1. Abundance, provision, stock of something ready to be drawn upon; *in* ~, in reserve, for future use; *in* ~ *for*, awaiting (person). 2. (Gt Britain) Large shop selling goods of many different kinds; (pl.) shop of a co-operative trading society; (U.S.) shop of any kind. 3. (pl.) Articles of particular kind or for special purpose accumulated for use; supply of things needed, stocks, reserves. 4. *attrib.* (Of animals) kept for breeding as part of farm stock or bought to be fattened; (U.S. etc.) of store or shop, bought at shop, (of clothes) ready-made; *store'house*, place where things are stored; store, treasury; *store'keeper*, person in charge of store(s); (U.S. etc.) shopkeeper; ~-*room*, room for storing goods or supplies, esp. of ship or household. ~ *v.t.* Furnish, stock (*with* something); lay *up* for future use, form stock of; deposit (goods, furniture, etc.) in warehouse for temporary keeping; have storage-accommodation for.

stŏr'ey, stŏr'y *ns.* (pl. -*eys*, -*ies*). Each stage or portion into which house or building is divided horizontally; anything compared to this.

stŏriā'tion *n.* Decoration with designs representing historical, legendary, etc., subjects.

stŏr'ied (-rĭd) *adj.* 1. Adorned with representations of historical or legendary scenes. 2. Celebrated in history or story.

stŏrk *n.* Large wading bird (of *Ciconia* and allied genera) with long legs and long stout bill, esp. the *common* or *white stork* (*Ciconia alba*), migratory European stork, often nesting on human habitations.

stŏrm *n.* Violent disturbance of atmosphere, with high winds and freq. thunder, heavy rain, hail, snow, etc.; wind of particular degree of violence, on Beaufort's scale, of force 11 and velocity of 64–75 m.p.h.; heavy discharge or shower (*of* blows etc.); violent disturbance of civil, political, domestic, etc., affairs; tumult, agitation, dispute, etc.; assault on fortified place, capture *of* place by such assault; *take by* ~, take by assault (freq. fig.); *S*~ *and Stress* [tr. Ger. *Sturm und Drang*], movement in German literature, *c* 1770–82, characterized by extravagant representation of violent passion and rejection of classical rules of composition; ~ *in a teacup*, commotion about a trivial matter; ~-*centre*, central, comparatively calm, area of cyclonic storm; (fig.) centre round which storm of controversy, trouble, etc., rages; ~-*cloud*, heavy rain-cloud; ~-*cock*, missel-thrush; ~-*cone*, cone of tarred canvas hoisted as a storm-signal; ~ *lantern*, one with flame protected from wind and rain; ~ *petrel*, various small petrels, esp. *Hydrobates pelagicus*, with black plumage marked with white on wing and tail, found in Mediterranean and Atlantic, and supposed to be active before a storm; ~-*signal*, any device for signalling approach of a storm; ~ *troops*, shock-troops, esp. a Nazi semi-military organization; ~-*trooper*, member of this. ~ *v.* 1. Take by storm, rush violently, esp. to attack. 2. (of wind etc.) Rage, be violent; bluster, fume; scold.

stŏrm'y *adj.* Characterized, marked by storm(s); associated or connected with storms; ~ *petrel*: see STORM. **stŏrm'ĭly** *adv.* **stŏrm'ĭnėss** *n.*

stŏr't(h)ĭng (-tĭ-) *n.* Norwegian parliament. [Norw. *stor* great, *ting* assembly]

stŏr'y[1] *n.* Past course of life of person, institution, etc.; account given of incident or series of events; narrative meant to entertain hearer or reader, tale in prose or verse of actual or fictitious events; legend, myth, anecdote, novel, romance; (amusing) anecdote; plot (of novel, play, etc.); (orig. U.S.) article in newspaper, material for this; (colloq.) lie.

story[2]: see STOREY.

stoup (-ōōp) *n.* Vessel for holy water, usu. stone basin in wall of church or near church porch; (archaic) flagon, tankard, beaker.

stout *adj.* 1. Valiant, brave, doughty, undaunted, staunch; strongly built. 2. Corpulent, bulky; not lean or slender. **stout'ish** *adj.* **stout'ly** *adv.* **stout'nėss** *n.* **stout** *n.* Heavy dark type of beer prepared with well-roasted barley or malt and sometimes caramelized sugar.

stōve[1] *n.* Portable or fixed closed apparatus to contain burning fuel or consume gas, electricity, etc., for use in warming rooms, cooking, etc.; ~-*pipe*, pipe to carry off smoke and gases from stove; (orig. U.S.) top hat, tall silk hat. ~ *v.t.* Dry, heat, in stove; fumigate, disinfect with sulphur or other fumes.

stōve[2]: see STAVE *v.*

stow (-ō) *v.* Pack (*away*) in proper receptacles or convenient places, esp. (naut.) place (cargo) in proper order in hold etc.; fill (receptacle) with articles compactly arranged; (slang) desist, refrain from; ~ *away*, conceal oneself on board ship; *stow'away*, person hiding in ship to avoid paying passage-money, to escape by stealth etc.

Stowe[1] (-ō). English public school founded 1923 at Stowe House in Buckinghamshire.

Stowe[2] (-ō), Mrs Harriet Elizabeth Beecher (1811–96). American author of 'Uncle Tom's Cabin', a novel describing the sufferings of negro slaves.

S.T.P. *abbrev. Sanctae theologiae professor* (= Professor of Sacred Theology).

str. *abbrev.* Stroke (oar).

strabĭs'mus (-z-) *n.* Squinting, a squint. **strabĭs'mal, strabĭs'mĭc** *adjs.*

Strāb'ō (*c* 64 B.C.–A.D. 19). A native of Pontus in Asia Minor who wrote, in Greek, a 'Geography' of the Roman Empire.

Strāch'ey (-chĭ), Giles Lytton (1880–1932). English literary critic and biographer.

Strad: see STRADIVARIUS.

strădd'le *v.* Spread legs wide apart in walking, standing, or sitting; (of legs) be wide apart; stand or sit across (thing) thus; part (legs) widely; drop shells beyond and short of a target in order to determine its range; drop bombs across (a target) beginning on one side and finishing on the opposite side. ~ *n.* 1. Action, position, of straddling. 2. (St. Exch.) Contract giving holder right of either calling for or delivering stock at fixed price.

Strădĭvār'ĭus. Antonio Stradivari (*c* 1644–1737), Italian maker of stringed instruments; a violin of his making (abbrev. *Strad*).

strafe (-ahf; in U.S. -āf) *v.t.* Bombard, worry with shells, bombs, sniping, etc.; reprimand sharply, abuse, thrash. ~ *n.* Strafing. [Ger., *Gott strafe England* God punish England, catchword in war of 1914–18]

Străff'ord, Sir Thomas Wentworth, 1st Earl of (1593–1641). English statesman, chief adviser to Charles I, whose authority he tried to restore; he was impeached in 1640, but when treason could not be proved the Commons (Long Parliament) brought in a Bill of Attainder and Strafford was executed.

străgg'le *v.i.* Stray from the main body, be dispersed or scattered, grow irregularly or loosely. **străgg'ler** *n.* **străgg'lĭng** *adj.* **străgg'lĭngly** *adv.* **străgg'ly** *adj.* **străgg'le** *n.* Body or group of scattered or straggling objects.

straight (-āt) *adj.* Not crooked, not curved, bent, or angular; (geom., of line) lying evenly between any two of its points; (of hair) not curly or waving; direct, undeviating, going direct to the mark; upright, honest, candid; in proper order or place; (orig. U.S.) unmixed, undiluted, (of spirits) neat; (poker, of cards) in sequences, without gap; *a ~ bat* (cricket) bat held upright, not inclining to either side (freq. fig.); *a ~ fight*, (politics) direct contest between two candidates; *~-edge*, strip of wood, steel, etc., with a perfectly straight edge, for testing accuracy of plane surface, drawing straight lines, etc. **straight'nėss** *n.* **straight** *n.* Straight condition; straight part of something, esp. concluding stretch of racecourse; sequence of cards in poker. ~ *adv.* In a straight line, direct, without deviation or circumlocution; in right direction, with good aim; ~ *away*, immediately, at once; ~ *off*, without hesitation, deliberation, etc.; ~ *out*, frankly, outspokenly; *~-cut*, (of tobacco) cut lengthwise into long silky fibres.

straight'en (-āt-) *v.* Make straight.

straightfŏr'ward (-āt-) *adj.* Honest, open, frank; (of task etc.) presenting no complications. **straightfŏr'wardly** *adv.*

straight'way (-āt-) *adv.* (archaic) At once, immediately.

strain[1] *n.* Breed, race, stock, line; inherited tendency or quality, moral tendency forming part of a character.

strain[2] *n.* 1. Straining, being strained, pull, tension, exertion; injury or damage due to excessive exertion, tension, or force; deformation or distortion in any body due to stress, molecular displacement. 2. Melody, tune; passage, snatch, of music, poetry, etc.; tone, mode, etc., adopted in talking or writing; tenor, drift, general tendency or character. ~ *v.* 1. Stretch lightly, make taut; stretch beyond normal degree, force to extreme effort, exert to utmost; wrest, distort, from true intention or meaning; hug (person) *to* oneself, one's breast, etc.; *strained* (past part.), produced under compulsion or by effort, artificial, forced, constrained. 2. Overtask; injure, try, imperil, by over-use, by making excessive demands on, etc.; *strained relations*, relations subjected to dangerous degree of tension, nearly at breaking-point. 3. Make intense effort; strive intensely *after*, try *at*. 4. Clear (liquid) of solid matter by passing through sieve etc.; filter (solids) *out* from liquid; (of liquid) percolate.

strain'er *n.* (esp.) Utensil for straining or filtering.

strait *adj.* Narrow, limited; confined, confining; (archaic exc. in) ~ *jacket*, ~ *waistcoat*, strong garment for upper part of body, admitting of being tightly laced and usu. confining arms, used to restrain violent lunatics or prisoners; *~-laced*, (now only fig.) severely virtuous, puritanical. ~ *n.* 1. Narrow passage of water connecting two seas or large bodies of water. 2. (usu. pl.) Difficult position; need, distress.

strait en *v.t.* (chiefly in past part.) Restrict in amount, scope, or range; reduce to straits; *straitened circumstances*, inadequate means of living, poverty.

Straits Settlements. Name of a former British colony now divided between SINGAPORE and the Federation of MALAYA.

strāke *n.* Section of iron rim of cart-wheel (ill. WHEEL); continuous line of planking or plates, of uniform breadth, from stem to stern of ship (ill. BOAT).

stramōn'ĭum *n.* Thorn-apple (*Datura*); dried leaves of this, used as drug in asthma etc.

strănd[1] *n.* Margin of sea, lake, or river, esp. part of shore between tide-marks; *the S~*, London street N. of Thames, orig. so called as occupying, with gardens of its houses, shore of Thames between cities of London and Westminster. ~ *v.* Run aground; *stranded*, in difficulties, esp. without adequate resources; left out of current of events.

strănd[2] *n.* Each of strings or wires twisted together to form rope, cord, cable, etc.; thread of woven material, string of beads, pearls, etc., tress of hair.

strānge (-j) *adj.* Foreign, alien, not one's own, not familiar or well known (*to*); novel, queer, peculiar, surprising, unexpected; fresh or unaccustomed *to*, unacquainted, bewildered. **strānge'ly** (-jlĭ) *adv.* **strānge'nėss** (-jn-) *n.*

strān'ger *n.* Foreigner; person in place, company, etc., to which he does not belong; person unknown to or *to* one; *I spy strangers*, formula in House of Commons demanding expulsion of all but members or officials before secret session.

străng'le (-nggl) *v.t.* Throttle, kill by external compression of throat; hinder growth of (plant) by overcrowding; (fig.) suppress; *stranglehold*, deadly grip (usu. fig.). **străng'les** *n.pl.* Infectious febrile disease, caused by a streptococcus, in equine animals.

străng'ūlāte (-ngg-) *v.t.* Strangle (rare); (path., surg.) constrict (organ, duct, etc.) so as to prevent circulation or passage of fluid. *strangulated hernia*, hernia so constricted as to arrest circulation in protruding part. **străngūlā'tion** *n.* Strangling, being strangled; strangulating.

străng'ūry (-ngg-) *n.* (Disease characterized by) slow and painful emission of urine.

străp *n.* Leather band; flat strip of leather etc. of uniform breadth with buckle or other fastening for holding things together etc.; strip of metal used to secure or connect, leaf of hinge, etc.; *strap'hanger*, passenger in bus, train, etc., who must stand and hold on by strap for want of sitting space; *strap'work*, ornamental work of narrow band or fillet folded, crossed, interlaced, etc. ~ *v.t.* Furnish, fasten, with strap; beat, flog, with strap; (surg.) close (wound), bind (part) up with adhesive plaster.

strappā'dō (*or* -ahdō) *n.* (pl. -*s*). (hist.) Form of punishment or torture in which victim was hoisted by rope, usu. by hands tied behind his back, and allowed to fall to length of rope. ~ *v.t.* Inflict strappado.

străpp'ing *adj.* (of persons). Strongly and stoutly built, big, sturdy.

străss[1] *n.* Vitreous composition used for making artificial gems, paste. [Ger., said to be f. name of inventor, Josef *Strasser*]

străss[2] *n.* 1. Silk refuse. 2. Silky-looking waxed straw used as trimming etc.

străt'agėm *n.* Artifice, trick, trickery; device(s) for deceiving enemy.

stratē'gic *adj.* Of, dictated by, serving the ends of, strategy; ~ *bombing*, bombing designed to disrupt the enemy's internal economy, destroy morale, etc. (opp. to TACTICAL *bombing*). **stratē'gical** *adj.* **stratē'gically** *adv.*

străt'ėgy *n.* Generalship, art of war; art of planning and directing larger military movements and operations of campaign or war (opp. to TACTICS). **străt'ėgist** *n*

Străt'ford on Avon (āv'*on*). Town in Warwickshire, England, birthplace of Shakespeare.

străthspey' (-ā) *n.* 1. Type of country-dance tune; dance to this. 2. First part of a Scotch reel. [Sc. place-name]

străt'ĭfȳ *v.t.* Arrange in strata. **strătĭfĭcā'tion** *n.*

stratĭg'raphy *n.* The study and description of stratified rocks; historical geology.

strătocŭm'ūlus *n.* (meteor.) Type of low cloud, a layer, usu. extensive, of globular masses (ill. CLOUD).

străt'osphēre *n.* Region of the atmosphere lying above the troposphere, in which the temperature does not decrease with increasing height (ill. ATMOSPHERE).

străt'opause (-z) *n.* The top boundary of the stratosphere.

strāt'um *n.* (pl. -*ta*). (geol.) Layer or bed of sedimentary rock (ill. ROCK); (biol.) layer of tissue; (archaeol.) layer of deposits in excavation etc. indicating distinct period or form of culture; (fig.) level or grade in social position, culture, etc.

strāt'us *n.* Continuous horizontal sheet of cloud (ill. CLOUD).

Strauss[1] (-ows), David Friedrich (1808–74). German theologian; author of a 'Life of Jesus', in which he attempted to prove that the biblical story of Jesus rested on a series of myths.

Strauss[2] (-ows). A Viennese family of composers, famous esp. for dance music; the best-known is Johann ~ (1825–99), composer of the 'Blue Danube' waltz and the opera 'Die Fledermaus'.

Strauss[3] (-ows), Richard Georg (1864–1949). German composer of 'Der Rosenkavalier' and other operas and of orchestral music.

Stravĭn'sky, Igor (1882–). Russian-born composer, famous esp. for ballet music.

straw[1] *n.* Dry cut stalks of various cereals used for bedding, thatching, litter for animals, plaited or woven as material for hats, beehives, etc.; stem of any cereal plant; single stalk or piece of straw; insignificant trifle; straw hat; *man of* ~, stuffed effigy; imaginary person put forward as adversary, surety, etc.; person of no substance, esp. one undertaking financial responsibility without means of discharging it; ~-*board*, coarse yellow cardboard made of straw pulp; ~-*colour(ed)*, (of) the pale light-yellow colour of straw; ~ *vote*, (U.S.) unofficial vote, esp. as sample or indication of public opinion. **straw'y** *adj.*

straw[2] *v.t.* (archaic) Strew.

straw'berry *n.* (Juicy edible pulpy, usu. red, fruit, dotted with small yellow seed-like achenes, and not properly a berry, of) plant of any species of *Fragaria*, stemless herbs with trifoliate leaves, white flowers, and slender trailing runners; colour of red strawberries; ~ *leaf*, leaf of strawberry, esp. as symbol of ducal rank (with ref. to strawberry leaves ornamenting duke's coronet); ~-*mark*, naevus birthmark, resembling strawberry; ~ *roan*, red roan; ~ *tree*, European evergreen tree, *Arbutus unedo*, with white flowers and strawberry-like fruit; (U.S.) spindle-tree.

stray *v.i.* Wander, go aimlessly; deviate from right way or (fig.) from virtue; lose one's way; get separated from flock, companions, home, or proper place. ~ *n.* Strayed domestic animal; homeless, friendless person, esp. child; (wireless, usu. pl.) atmospherics. ~ *adj.* Strayed; scattered, sporadic, occasional, casually met with.

streak[1] *n.* Thin irregular line of different colour or substance from material or surface in which it occurs; flash (*of* lightning); vein of mineral; trait, strain, element, of character, etc. ~ *v.t.* Mark with streak(s). **streak'y** *adj.* **streak'ĭly** *adv.* **streak'ĭnėss** *n.*

streak[2] *v.i.* Go quickly or at full speed.

stream *n.* Body of water flowing in bed, esp. rivulet or brook as dist. from river; current or flow of river, in sea, etc.; flow of any liquid, current of air, gas, etc.; continuous flow of persons etc. moving in one direction, or of words, events, influences, etc.; ~-*line*, path of particle of fluid in motion, current of air, etc.; form of body (esp. motor-car or aircraft) calculated to offer minimum of resistance to air, water, etc.; *stream'line*, give this shape to. **stream'lėt** *n.* **stream'y** *adj.*

stream *v.* Flow or move as a stream; run with liquid; emit stream of; float or wave in wind, current of water, etc.

stream'er *n.* Pennon; ribbon etc. attached at one end and floating or waving at the other; (pl.) Aurora Borealis.

street *n.* Road in town or village with houses on one side or both; this with its houses; *the S*~, (esp.) Fleet Street; (U.S.) Wall Street; *in the* ~, said of Stock Exchange business done after closing hours; *man in the* ~, ordinary man, as dist. from expert etc.; *on the* ~*s*, living by prostitution; ~-*arab*, homeless child living in streets; ~-*car*, (U.S.) tram-car; ~-*door*, main external door of house etc., opening on street; ~-*sweeper*, man employed, machine with revolving brush used, for cleaning streets; ~-*walker*, common prostitute.

strĕngth *n.* Being strong; degree in which person or thing is strong; what makes strong; number of men in army, regiment, etc., of ships in fleet etc., men enrolled; *on the* ~, (mil.) entered on rolls of regiment etc.; *on the* ~ *of*, encouraged by, relying on, arguing from. **strĕngth'lėss** *adj.*

strĕngth'en *v.* Make, become, stronger.

strĕn'ūous *adj.* Vigorous, energetic, persistently and ardently laborious (esp. of action or effort). **strĕn'ūously** *adv.* **strĕn'ūousnėss** *n.*

Strĕph'on. The shepherd whose lament for his lost Urania forms the opening of Sidney's 'Arcadia'; hence, a fond lover.

strĕptocŏcc'us *n.* (pl. -*cī*). (Micro-organism of) a genus of bacteria which form chains (ill. BACTERIUM); they are the infective agent in some diseases (e.g. scarlet fever, puerperal fever, endocarditis) and are a freq. cause of septicaemia. **strĕptocŏcc'al** *adj.*

strĕptomȳ'cĭn *n.* Antibiotic drug, produced from *Actinomyces griseus*, a mould-like micro-organism found in garden soil.

strĕss *n.* 1. Pressure, strain, *of* load, weight, some adverse force

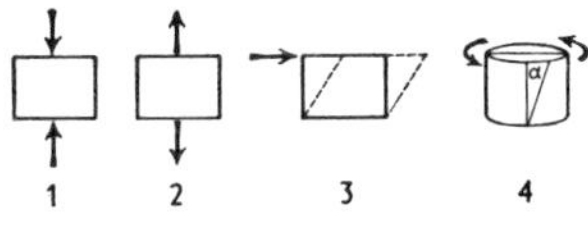

STRESSES

1. Compression. 2. Tension. 3. Shear. 4. Torsion. a = angle of torque

or influence etc.; condition of things demanding or marked by strained effort; (mech.) force exerted between contiguous bodies or parts of a body. 2. Emphasis; greater relative force of utterance given to one syllable of word, one part of syllable, word in sentence, etc. ~ *v.t.* Lay the stress on, accent, emphasize; subject to mechanical stress; *stressed-skin construction,* (aircraft fuselage, wing, etc.) construction in which some or most of the stresses are borne by the skin.

strĕtch *v.* 1. Make taut; tighten, straighten; place in tight-drawn or outspread state; lay (person) flat; ~ (one*self*) extend limbs to tighten muscles after sleeping etc.; ~ one's *legs,* straighten them by walking as relief from sitting etc.; ~ *out,* extend (hand, foot, etc.) by straightening arm or leg; reach out hand. 2. Strain; exert to utmost or beyond legitimate extent; do violence to; exaggerate. 3. Have specified length or extension; be continuous between points, to or from a point. 4. Draw, be drawn, admit of being drawn, out into greater length, extension, or size; (slang) hang (person). ~ *n.* Stretching, being stretched; continuous expanse, tract, or spell; (naut.) distance covered on one tack; (slang) term of imprisonment or penal servitude.

strĕtch'er *n.* (esp.) 1. Brick or stone laid with length in direction of wall (ill. BRICK); bar or rod used as tie or brace, e.g. between legs of chair (ill. CHAIR); board in boat against which rower presses feet (ill. BOAT). 2. Frame on which artist's canvas is spread and drawn tight by wedges etc. 3. Oblong frame, with handles at each end, for carrying sick or wounded persons on; *~-bearers,* persons who carry this.

strew (-ōō) *v.t.* Scatter (sand, flowers, small objects) over a surface; cover (surface, object) with small objects scattered.

strī a *n.* (pl. *striae*). (anat., zool., geol., etc.) Linear mark on surface; slight ridge, furrow, or score; (archit.) fillet between flutes of classical column (ill. ORDER). **strī'ate** *adj.* **strī'ately** *adv.* **strīāte'** *v.t.* **strīā'tion** *n.*

strĭck'en *adj.* (past part. of STRIKE). (Of deer etc.) wounded; (of person, mind, etc.) afflicted with disease, frenzy, trouble, grief, etc.; ~ *field,* pitched battle or place where it was fought; ~ *in years,* (archaic) of advanced age.

strĭck'le *n.* Rod for striking off grain etc. level with rim of measure.

strĭct *adj.* 1. Exact, precise, accurately determined or defined. 2. Rigorous, allowing no evasion, stringent; (of discipline etc.) admitting no relaxation or indulgence. **strĭct'ly** *adv.* **strĭct'nėss** *n.*

strĭc'ture *n.* 1. (usu. pl.) Adverse criticism, critical remark. 2. (path.) Morbid contraction of passage of the body, esp. urethra; contracted part.

strīde *v.* (past t. and past part. *strōde*). Walk with long steps; pass over or *over* (obstacle etc.) with one step; bestride. ~ *n.* Striding; long step; distance covered by this; striding gait; *take in one's* ~, (of horse or rider) clear (obstacle) without changing gait; (fig.) deal with incidentally, without interrupting course of action etc.

strīd'ent *adj.* Loud and harsh, grating. **strīd'ently** *adv.*

strĭd'ūlāte *v.i.* Make harsh grating shrill noise (esp., of grasshoppers etc.) by rubbing together hard parts of body. **strĭdūlā'tion** *n.*

strīfe *n.* Condition of antagonism or discord; contention, struggle, dispute.

strī'gĭl (-j-) *n.* (Gk & Rom. antiq.) Instrument with curved blade for scraping away sweat and dirt from skin at bath etc.

strīke *v.* (past t. *strŭck,* past part. *strŭck* or in some phrases *strĭck'en*). 1. Hit, hit upon or (*up*)*on,* deliver blow(s) or stroke(s); afflict (with infirmity or death); (of disease etc.) attack suddenly; (of lightning) descend upon and blast. 2. Produce or record or bring into specified state by strokes or striking; impress, stamp, print (*with* device etc.); coin (money); touch (string or key of instrument), produce (note) thus; (of clock) sound (hour etc.) with stroke(s) on bell etc.; (of hour) be sounded thus; produce (fire, spark) by percussion of flint and steel, friction of match, etc. 3. Arrest attention of; occur to mind of; produce mental impression on, impress *as.* 4. Lower or take down (sail, flag, tent); signify surrender by striking flag, remove tents of (camp etc.); (theatr.) remove (scene etc.). 5. (Of body of employees) cease work by agreement among themselves or by order of trade union etc. in order to obtain remedy for grievance, better working conditions, etc. 6. (Cause to) penetrate; pierce, stab (as) with sharp weapon. 7. Turn in new direction, go *across, down, over,* etc.; take specified direction. 8. Level (grain etc.) with rim of measure by passing strickle over it. 9. Assume (attitude) suddenly and dramatically. 10. ~ *home,* get blow well in; ~ *in,* intervene in conversation etc.; ~ *off,* cancel, erase, (as) by stroke of pen; print; *off the register, rolls,* remove (medical practitioner, solicitor) from official list for misconduct; ~ *out,* erase; open up (path, course) *for* oneself; lay about one with fists etc., begin to swim or skate; ~ *up,* begin to play or sing; start (acquaintance, conversation) esp. rapidly or casually. ~ *n.* 1. Concerted refusal to work by employees till some grievance is remedied; *on* ~, taking part in this; *general* ~, simultaneous strike by employees in all or most trades; *sit-down, stay-in,* ~, strike in which employees refuse to leave place of work; *~-breaker,* one who works for employer whose employees are on strike; *~-bound,* immobilized by a strike; ~ *pay,* trade union's allowance to workers on strike. 2. (U.S.) Sudden discovery of rich ore, oil, etc.; (fig.) sudden success or piece of good fortune. 3. (geol.) Horizontal course of stratum (ill. ROCK). 4. (baseball) Unsuccessful attempt to hit pitched ball.

strīk'er *n.* (esp.) 1. Employee taking part in industrial strike. 2. Blacksmith's assistant who wields heavy sledge-hammer.

strīk'ĭng *adj.* (esp.) Noticeable, arresting, impressive. **strīk'ĭngly** *adv.* **strīk'ĭngnėss** *n.*

strĭng *n.* 1. Twine or fine cord; piece of this or of leather, ribbon, or other material, used for tying up, lacing, drawing together, activating puppet, etc.; bowstring; *pull the ~s,* control course of affairs, exert (esp. hidden) influence; *have two ~s to one's bow,* have two alternative resources; *first, second,* etc., ~, person or thing that chief, alternative, etc., reliance is placed on. 2. Tendon, nerve, elongated muscle, etc., in animal body; tough piece connecting two halves of pod in beans etc. 3. Catgut, wire, etc., yielding musical tone(s) when stretched, in piano, harp, violin, and other instruments; (pl.) stringed instruments played with bow, players of these in orchestra etc. 4. Set of or *of* objects strung together; number of animals etc. in single file; set or stud of horses; number of things in row or line; continuous series or succession. 5. *~-bean,* (U.S.) French or kidney bean; *~-board,* board supporting ends of steps in staircase (ill. STAIR); *~-course,* raised horizontal band or course running round or along building (ill. MASONRY); *~-piece,* long piece of timber connecting and supporting parts of framework (ill. HALF-timber); ~ *quartet,* quartet of stringed instruments, esp. two violins, viola, and violoncello; music for this. ~ *v.* (past t. and past part. *strŭng*). Supply, fit, tie, with string(s); thread (beads etc.) on string; make (bow) ready for use by slipping loop of bow-string into its notch; remove strings of bean-pod; brace *up,* bring to specified condition of sensitiveness or tension; connect, put together in continuous series; arrange in row(s) or series; move in string or disconnected line (esp. ~ *out*).

strĭnged (-ngd) *adj.* (esp., of musical instruments) Having strings.

strĭn'gent (-j-) *adj.* (of regulations, obligations, etc.) Rigorous, strict, binding, requiring exact performance. **strĭn'gently** *adv.* **strĭn'gency** *n.*

strĭng'er *n.* Longitudinal stiffening member used in construction of ships (e.g. *deck* ~, *side* ~) and aircraft.

strĭng'y (-ngĭ) *adj.* Fibrous, like string; (of liquid) ropy.

strĭp[1] *n.* Long narrow piece or tract (of textile material, land, paper, etc.); narrow flat bar of iron or steel, iron or steel in this form; ~ *cartoon*; see CARTOON; ~ *lighting*, lighting of a room etc. by means of a number of lamps, usu. tubular, arranged in a line to give the effect of a continuous strip of light; ~*-mill*, place where steel slabs are rolled into strips for manufacture of tinplate.

strĭp[2] *v.* Denude, lay bare; deprive *of* covering, appurtenance, or property; undress; pull or tear off, *off* or *from* something; tear off (thread from screw, teeth from wheel); remove stalk and midrib from (tobacco-leaf); ~*-tease*, an entertainment in which a young woman divests herself of her garments one by one before an audience.

strĭp[3] *v.* Extract last milk from udder of (cow).

strīpe[1] *n.* (archaic; chiefly pl.) Stroke or lash with whip or scourge.

strīpe[2] *n.* Long narrow portion, usu. of uniform width, on surface, differing in colour or texture from adjacent parts; narrow strip of cloth, braid, etc., sewn on garment, esp. chevron indicating rank of non-commissioned officer. ~ *v.t.* Mark, ornament, with stripe(s). **strīped** (-pt), **strīp'y** *adjs.*

strĭp'lĭng *n.* Youth approaching manhood.

strīve *v.i.* (past t. *strōve*, past part. *strĭv'en*). Endeavour, try hard, struggle; contend, vie.

STRINGED INSTRUMENTS OF THE VIOLIN FAMILY WITH BOWS: A. VIOLIN. B. VIOLA. C. VIOLONCELLO OR CELLO. D. DOUBLE-BASS

1. Scroll. 2. Peg or pin. 3. Neck. 4. Finger-board. 5. Back. 6. Belly. 7. Bouts. 8. Bridge. 9. G string. 10. Tail-piece. 11. Chin-rest. 12. Sound hole or *f*-hole

strōb'ĭle *n.* (bot.) Cone of pine etc., inflorescence made up of imbricated scales (ill. CONIFER).

strōke[1] *n.* 1. Blow, shock given by blow; apoplectic or paralytic seizure; damaging or destructive discharge (of lightning). 2. Single effort put forth, one complete performance of recurrent action or movement; time or way in which such movements are performed; act or method of striking ball etc. in games; specially successful or skilful effort; ~ *of genius*, original or strikingly successful idea; ~ *of luck*, unforeseen opportune occurrence. 3. Mark made by movement in one direction of pen, pencil, paintbrush, etc.; detail, 'touch', in description etc. 4. Sound made by striking clock; *on the* ~ *of*, exactly at specified hour. 5. Oarsman rowing nearest stern and setting time of stroke. ~ *v.t.* Act as stroke to (boat, crew).

strōke[2] *v.t.* Pass hand etc. softly and usu. repeatedly in one direction over (hair, skin, etc.), as caress etc.; (needlework) arrange (gathers) neatly by drawing blunt point downwards from top of each; ~ *the wrong away*, irritate, ruffle; ~ *down*, soothe, mollify. ~ *n.* Act, spell, of stroking.

strōll *n.* Leisurely walk or ramble, saunter. ~ *v.i.* Walk in leisurely fashion. *stro'lling players, company*, etc., actors travelling about and giving performances in temporary buildings etc.

strōm'a *n.* 1. (anat.) Supporting framework of organ, usu. of connective tissue; spongy framework of red blood corpuscle etc. 2. (bot.) Fungous tissue in which perithecia or other organs of fructification are immersed. **stromăt'ĭc** *adj.*

Strōm'bolĭ. One of the Lipari islands in the Mediterranean; an active volcano on this island.

strŏng *adj.* 1. Physically powerful, vigorous, or robust; performed with muscular strength; having great muscular, moral, or mental power or strength; powerful in arms, numbers, equipment, authority, etc. 2. Difficult to capture, break into, invade, or escape from, capable of resisting force or strain, resistant, tough. 3. Energetic, effective, vigorous, decided. 4. Convincing, striking; powerfully affecting the senses, passions, mind, etc. 5. (Of tea, toddy, etc.) having large proportion of flavouring element, solid ingredient, alcohol, etc. 6. (gram., of verbs) Forming inflexions by vowel-change in root syllable, rather than by addition of suffixes. 7. ~*-box*, strongly made chest or safe for money, documents, etc.; ~ *drink*, alcoholic liquors; *strong'hold*, secure place of refuge or retreat, fortress, fastness, citadel; ~*-minded*, having strong, vigorous, or determined mind; ~*-point*, (mil.) a specially fortified position in a defence system; ~-*room*, fire- and burglar-proof room for valuables; ~ *waters*, spirits. **strŏng'ly** *adv.* **strŏng** *adv. Come it, go it* ~, act vigorously, boldly, recklessly, etc.; *be going* ~, be vigorous, thriving, or prosperous.

strŏn'tia (-sha) *n.* Alkaline earth, SrO, the monoxide of strontium.

strŏn'tianīte (-shn-) *n.* Native strontium carbonate; loosely, strontia; *strontian yellow*, (pigment of colour of) strontium chromate. [f. *Strontian* in Argyllshire]

strŏn'tium (-shm) *n.* Soft easily fusible metallic element (silver-white when pure); symbol Sr, at. no. 38, at. wt 87·62; ~ *90*, radio-active isotope of strontium which is present in fall-out of nuclear fission and if ingested concentrates in bone-marrow.

strŏp *n.* Strip of leather for sharpening razor, implement or machine serving same purpose. ~ *v.t.* Sharpen on or with strop.

strophăn'thĭn *n.* White crystalline bitter poisonous glucoside, used as a heart tonic, obtained from various species of *Strophanthus*, genus of plants of tropical Africa and Asia.

strō'phė *n.* (Lines recited during) movement made from right to left by chorus in ancient Greek choral dance; series of lines forming division of lyric poem. **strŏph'ĭc** *adj.*

strŭc'tural (-kcher-) *adj.* Of structure; ~ *engineering*, design and construction of large structures, as dams, bridges, etc; ~ *steel*, strong mild steel in shapes specially suitable for structural purposes. **strŭc'turally** *adv.*

strŭc'ture *n.* 1. Manner in which building or other complete whole is constructed; supporting framework or whole of essential parts of something; make, construction. 2. Thing constructed; complex whole; building.

strŭg'gle *v.i.* Throw one's limbs about in violent effort to escape grasp etc.; make violent or determined efforts under difficulties, strive hard; contend *with, against*; make one's way with difficulty *through, along*, etc. ~ *n.* Struggling; resolute contest, continued effort to resist force, free oneself from constraint etc.; determined effort or resistance; ~ *for existence, life*, competition between organic species, esp. as element in natural selection; continued effort to maintain life or obtain means of livelihood. **strŭg'glĭng** *adj.* (esp.) Experiencing difficulty in making a living, getting recognition, etc. **strŭg'glĭngly** *adv.*

Strŭld'brŭg *n.* In Swift's 'Gulliver's Travels', one of those cursed with immortality but not retaining or renewing youthful vigour.

strŭm *v.* Touch notes or twang strings of piano or other stringed instrument; play, esp. unskilfully, *on* (piano, guitar, etc.). ~ *n.* Sound made by strumming.

strum'a (-ōō-) *n.* 1. (med.) Goitre, or (formerly) scrofulous swelling. 2. (bot.) Cushion-like cellular dilatation of an organ. **strum'ōse, strum'ous** *adjs.*

strŭm'pėt *n.* (archaic) Prostitute.

strŭt[1] *n.* & *v.i.* (Walk with) pompous or affected stiff gait.

strŭt[2] *n.* Bar, rod, etc., of wood, iron, etc., inserted in framework to resist pressure or thrust in direction of its length; brace. ~ *v.t.* Brace with strut(s).

'struth (-ōō-) *int.* (vulgar colloq.) Short for *God's truth* as oath.

strȳch'nĭc (-k-) *adj.* Of strychnine; ~ *acid*, white crystalline substance obtained by heating strychnine with alkali.

strȳch'nine (-knēn *or* -ĭn) *n.* Highly poisonous vegetable alkaloid obtained from plants of genus *Strychnos*, esp. the nux vomica, used in medicine as stimulant and tonic.

S.T.S. *abbrev.* Scottish Text Society.

Sts. *abbrev.* Saints.

Stū'art. The royal house of Scotland from the accession (1371) of Robert II, one of the hereditary stewards of Scotland, and of England from the accession of James VI of Scotland to the English throne as James I (1603) to the death of Queen Anne (1714).

stŭb *n.* Stump of tree, tooth, etc., left projecting; short remnant *of* pencil, cigar, etc.; pen with short blunt point; counterfoil of cheque, ticket, receipt, etc. ~ *v.t.* Grub up (stubs, roots), clear (land) of stubs; hurt (toe) by striking it against something; extinguish (cigarette) by crushing lighted end against something hard.

stŭbb'le *n.* Lower ends of grain-stalks left in ground after harvest; short stubble-like growth of hair esp. on unshaven face.

stŭbb'orn *adj.* Obstinate, unyielding, obdurate, refractory, intractable. **stŭbb'ornly** *adv.* **stŭbb'ornnėss** *n.*

Stŭbbs[1], George (1724–1806). English painter and engraver of horses.

Stŭbbs[2], William (1825–1901). English constitutional historian; bishop of Oxford 1889–1901.

stŭcc'ō *n.* Fine plaster used to cover walls, ceilings, etc., and for making cornices, mouldings, etc.; coarse plaster or cement for covering exterior surfaces of walls in imitation of stone. ~ *v.t.* Coat or ornament with stucco.

stŭck *adj.* (past part. of STICK). (Of animal) that has been stabbed or had throat cut; ~-*up*, (colloq.) conceited, insolently exclusive.

stŭd[1] *n.* 1. Large-headed nail, boss, or knot, projecting from surface, esp. for ornament; rivet, cross-piece in each link of chain-cable; kind of two-headed button passed through one or more eyelet- or button-holes, esp. in shirt-front or to fasten collar to shirt. 2. Upright post in framing for lath-and-plaster partition walls (ill. HALF-timber); (chiefly U.S.) height of room as indicated by length of this. ~ *v.t.* Set with studs; be scattered over or about (surface); *studded*, thickly set or strewn *with*; *studd'ing*, woodwork of lath-and-plaster wall.

stŭd[2] *n.* Number of horses kept for breeding, hunting, racing, etc.; place where stud, esp. for breeding, is kept; ~-*book*, book giving pedigree of thoroughbred horses; ~-*farm*, place where horses are bred; ~-*horse*, stallion; ~-*poker*, (cards) kind of poker in which all but first round of cards are dealt face up.

stŭdd'ing-sail (*or* stun'sl) *n.* = STUNSAIL.

stū'dent *n.* 1. Person engaged in or addicted to study; person undergoing instruction at university or other place of higher education or technical training. 2. (At some colleges) one who receives emoluments from foundation to enable him to pursue studies, scholar or fellow. **stū'dentshĭp** *n.*

stū'dĭō *n.* (pl. -*s*). Work-room of sculptor, painter, photographer, etc.; room in which cinema-play is staged; (pl.) complete establishment of a film company; room in broadcasting station used for transmissions.

stū'dĭous *adj.* Given to study, devoted to learning; careful *to* do, anxiously desirous *of*; studied, deliberate, zealous, anxious, painstaking. **stū'dĭously** *adv.* **stū'dĭousnėss** *n.*

stŭd'y *n.* 1. Devotion of time and thought to acquisition of information esp. from books; (freq. pl.) pursuit of some branch of knowledge; careful examination or observation *of* (subject, question, object, etc.). 2. Thing to be secured by pains or attention; thing that is or deserves to be investigated. 3. Literary composition devoted to detailed consideration of a subject or problem or executed as exercise or experiment in style etc. 4. (painting etc.) Careful sketch made for practice in technique or as preliminary experiment for picture etc. or part of it; (mus.) composition designed to develop player's skill. 5. (theatr.) Learning of parts in play; *good, slow*, ~, person who learns part quickly, slowly. 6. Room used for literary occupation. ~ *v.* Make a study of, take pains to investigate or acquire knowledge of (subject) or to assure (desired result); examine carefully, read attentively, investigate (object); apply oneself to study; take pains *to* do; *stud'ied*, deliberate, intentional, affected.

stŭff *n.* 1. Material of which thing is made or which is or may be used for some purpose; articles of food or drink, produce of garden, farm, etc.; commodity dealt in or produced. 2. Textile material, esp. woollen fabric; ~ *gown*, (gown of) junior counsel. 3. Valueless matter; trash, nonsense; *do* one's ~, do what is required or what one is expected to do. ~ *v.* Pack, cram; stop *up*; fill, distend; fill out (skin of bird, beast, etc.) with material to restore original shape; fill (inside of bird, piece of meat, etc.) with forcemeat, seasoned bread-crumbs, herbs, etc., before cooking; cram food into, gorge (food); gorge oneself, eat greedily; ram or press into receptacle; gull, hoax, humbug. **stŭff'ing** *n.* (esp.) Ingredients for stuffing fowl etc. in cookery; *knock the ~ out of* (person), reduce to state of flabbiness or weakness.

stŭff'y *adj.* Lacking fresh air or ventilation, close, fusty; without freshness, interest, smartness, etc.; easily offended or shocked, strait-laced. **stŭff'ĭly** *adv.* **stŭff'ĭnėss** *n.*

stŭl'tĭfȳ *v.t.* Reduce to foolishness or absurdity; render worthless or useless; exhibit in ridiculous light.

stŭm *n.* Unfermented or partly fermented grape-juice, must. ~ *v.t.* Prevent from fermenting, secure (wine) against further fermentation in cask, by introduction of antiseptic.

stŭm'ble *v.* Lurch forward, have partial fall, from catching or striking foot or making false step; make blunder(s) in doing something; come accidentally (*up*)*on* or *across*; *stumbling-block*, obstacle; circumstance that causes difficulty, hesitation, or scruples. **stŭm'blĭngly** *adv.* **stŭm'ble** *n.* Act of stumbling.

stŭm'er *n.* (slang) Worthless cheque, counterfeit coin or note.

stŭmp *n.* Projecting remnant of cut or fallen tree; part remaining of broken branch or tooth, broken-off mast, amputated limb, etc.; fag-end, stub, of cigar, pencil, etc.; stalk of plant (esp. cabbage) with leaves removed; (pl., joc.) legs; stump of tree used by orator to address meeting from; cylinder of rolled paper etc. for softening pencil-marks and other uses in drawing; (cricket) one of three uprights of wicket (ill. CRICKET); ~ *speech*, open-air speech. ~ *v.* 1. Walk stiffly, clumsily, and noisily. 2. (cricket, of wicket-keeper) Put (batsman who is not in his ground) out by dislodging bail(s) while holding ball. 3. Nonplus, pose, cause to be at a loss. 4. Make stump speeches; traverse (district) doing this. 5. Use stump on (drawing etc.). 6. ~ (*up*), pay over money required, produce (sum).

stŭmp'er *n.* (cricket) Wicket-keeper.

stŭmp'y *adj.* Thickset, stocky; of small height or length in proportion to girth. **stŭmp'ĭly** *adv.* **stŭmp'ĭnėss** *n.*

stŭn *v.t.* (Of blow etc.) knock senseless, reduce to insensibility or stupor; daze, bewilder, with strong emotion, din, etc.; *stunn'ing*, (slang) splendid, delightful.

stŭn'sail, stŭn's'l *n.* Sail set on small extra yard and boom beyond leech of square sail in light winds (ill. SHIP).

stŭnt[1] *n.* (colloq.) Special effort, feat; showy performance, skilful trick or manœuvre, esp. with aeroplane; advertising device intended to attract public attention. ~ *v.i.* Perform stunt with aeroplane.

stŭnt[2] *v.t.* Check growth or development of, dwarf, cramp.

stūp'a *n.* Monument, usu. dome-like, erected over relics of Buddha or at place associated with him.

stūp'ėfȳ *v.t.* Make stupid or torpid, deprive of sensibility; stun with amazement, fear, etc. **stūpėfăc'tion** *n.*

stūpĕn'dous *adj.* Amazing, prodigious, astounding, esp. by size or degree. **stūpĕn'dously** *adv.* **stūpĕn'dousnėss** *n.*

stūp'ĭd *adj.* In a state of stupor or lethargy; dull by nature, slow-witted, obtuse, crass, characteristic of persons of this nature; uninteresting, dull. **stūp'ĭdly** *adv.* **stūpĭd'ĭty** *n.* **stūp'ĭd** *n.* Stupid person.

stūp'or *n.* Dazed state, torpidity; helpless amazement.

stûr'dy[1] *adj.* Robust, hardy, vigorous, strongly built. **stûr'dĭly** *adv.* **stûr'dĭnėss** *n.*

stûr'dy[2] *n.* Vertigo in sheep and cattle caused by tapeworm in brain.

stûr'geon (-jn) *n.* Various large fishes of rivers, lakes, and coastal waters of north temperate zone, with long almost cylindrical body and long tapering snout, esteemed as food and the source of caviare and isinglass; esp. *Acipenser sturio* of Atlantic coastal regions of Europe and N. America.

stŭtt'er *v.* Stammer; speak or say with continued involuntary repetition of parts of words, esp. initial consonants. ~ *n.* Act or habit of stuttering.

stȳ[1] *n.* Enclosure for keeping pig(s) in; mean or dirty hovel or room; place of debauchery. ~ *v.* Lodge in sty.

stȳ[2], **stȳe** *ns.* Inflamed swelling on edge of eyelid.

Stȳ'gian *adj.* (As) of the Styx or of Hades; murky, gloomy, black as the Styx.

stȳle *n.* 1. Ancient writing-implement, small rod with pointed end for scratching letters on wax-covered tablets, and flat broad end for erasing and smoothing tablet; (poet.) pen, pencil; style-like thing, as graver, blunt-pointed probe, gnomon of sundial; (bot.) narrowed prolongation of ovary supporting stigma (ill. FLOWER); (zool.) small slender pointed process or part; pointed sponge-spicule. 2. Manner of writing, speaking, or doing, esp. as opp. to the matter expressed or thing done; manner of execution of work of art etc.; manner characteristic of person, school, period, etc.; (esp. correct or pleasing) way of doing something; kind, sort, pattern, type; mode of behaviour, manner of life; fashion, distinction, noticeably superior quality or manner, esp. with regard to appearance. 3. Descriptive formula, designation of person or thing; full title. 4. Mode of expressing dates; *Old S~*, (abbrev. O.S.) according to the JULIAN calendar, used by all Christian nations until 1582; *New S~*, (abbrev. N.S.) according to the reformed or GREGORIAN calendar. ~ *v.t.* Call by specified name or style.

stȳl'ėt *n.* Stiletto; graving-tool, pointed marking instrument; (surg.) slender probe, wire run through catheter for stiffening or cleaning.

stȳl'ĭsh *adj.* Noticeably conforming to fashionable standard of elegance, showy, dashing; having good style. **stȳl'ĭshly** *adv.* **stȳl'ĭshnėss** *n.*

stȳl'ĭst *n.* Person having or aiming at good style in writing or doing something. **stȳlĭs'tĭc** *adj.* Of literary or artistic style. **stȳlĭs'tically** *adv.*

stȳl'īte, stȳlīt'ēs (-z) *ns.* Medieval ascetic living on top of a pillar; SIMEON STYLITES: see entry.

stȳl'īze *v.t.* Conform (work of art etc., or part of it) to the rules of a conventional style. **stȳlīzā'tion** *n.*

stȳl'ō *n.* Stylograph.

stȳl'obāte *n.* Continuous base supporting row(s) of columns (ill. ORDER).

stȳl'ograph (-ahf) *n.* Fountain-pen with ink flowing from reservoir through fine perforated writing-point. **stȳlogrăph'ĭc** *adj.*

stȳlohȳ'oid *adj.* & *n.* (Muscle) connecting styloid process and hyoid bone.

stȳl'oid *adj.* & *n.* ~ (*process*), slender pointed process projecting from base of temporal bone in man (ill. HEAD).

stȳlomăs'toid *adj.* Common to the styloid and mastoid processes.

stȳlopōd'ĭum *n.* (pl. *-dia*). Fleshy swelling at base of style in plants of carrot family.

stȳl'us *n.* Style, ancient writing-implement; tracing-point producing indented groove in gramophone record, or following such groove in reproducing sound.

stȳm'ie *n.* (formerly, in golf) Position on the putting-green in which the opponent's ball lies in a direct line between the player's ball and the hole. ~ *v.t.* Put into position of having to negotiate stymie (freq. fig.).

stўp'tĭc *adj.* & *n.* (Substance) that contracts organic tissue and checks bleeding.

stȳr'ăx *n.* Storax; (plant of) large genus of shrubs and trees, some of which yield valuable resins.

Stў'rĭa. Former duchy, later province, of S. Austria. **Stў'rĭan** *adj.* & *n.*

Stўx. (Gk myth.) River of Hades over which Charon ferried the shades of the dead.

suasion (swā'zhn) *n.* Persuasion; esp. in *moral* ~.

suave (swāv, swahv) *adj.* Bland, soothing, mollifying, polite. **suave'ly** *adv.* **suăv'ĭty** *n.*

sŭb *n.* Short for subaltern, submarine, subscription, substitute; money in advance on account of wages. ~ *v.* Pay or receive (part of wages in advance); sub-edit; act as substitute.

sub- *prefix.* Under, close to, up to, towards, etc.; occurs (freq. with last letter changed by assimilation) in many words borrowed or derived from Latin, and in English compounds with the following senses. 1. Situated under; below in degree. 2. Rather, more or less, roughly; not quite; approaching the specified character; on the borders of. 3. Under-, subordinate(ly); secondary; further. 4. (rare) Underlying.

sŭbă'cĭd *adj.* Moderately acid or tart; somewhat biting.

sŭbacūte' *adj.* (med.) Between acute and chronic.

sŭb-ā'gent *n.* Subordinate agent.

subahdār' (sōō-) *n.* (Anglo-Ind.) Chief native officer of company of sepoys. [Hind. (*subah* province, *dār* master)]

sŭbăl'pīne *adj.* Of higher slopes of mountains (about 4,000–5,500 ft), between the Alp line and the timber line.

sŭb'altern *adj.* 1. Of inferior rank; subordinate. 2. (logic, of a proposition) Particular, not universal. ~ *n.* (mil.) Junior officer below rank of captain.

sŭbăq'uėous *adj.* Existing, formed, performed or taking place, under water; adapted for use under water.

sŭbârc'tĭc *adj.* Of regions somewhat south of Arctic Circle or resembling these in climate etc.

sŭbatŏm'ĭc *adj.* Of, concerned with, phenomena occurring inside an atom.

sŭb'-bāse'ment (-sm-) *n.* Storey below basement in building.

sŭbclāv'ĭan *adj.* & *n.* (Artery, vein, muscle) lying or extending under clavicle; ~ *artery,* main trunk of arterial system of upper extremity (ill. BLOOD).

sŭbclĭn'ĭcal *adj.* (of disease) Not yet presenting definite symptoms.

sŭb'commĭttee *n.* Committee formed from main committee for special purpose.

sŭbcŏn'scious (-shus) *adj.* Of part of mind or mental field outside range of attention or imperfectly or partially conscious. ~ *n.* Subconscious part of mind.

sŭbcŏn'tĭnent *n.* Land-mass of great extent but smaller than those generally called continents.

sŭbcŏn'trăct *n.* Contract for carrying out (part of) previous contract. **sŭbcontrăct'** *v.* Make subcontract (for). **sŭbcontrăc'tor** *n.*

sŭbcôrt'ĭcal *adj.* Situated, formed, etc., below a cortex, esp. the cortex of the brain.

sŭbcŏs'tal *adj.* Below a rib.

sŭbcūtān'ėous *adj.* Lying, living, performed, etc., under the skin; hypodermic.

sŭbdeac'on *n.* (In some branches of Christian Church) minister of order next below deacon; cleric or lay clerk assisting next below deacon at solemn celebration of Eucharist, epistoler.

sŭbdīăc'onate *n.* Office of subdeacon.

sŭbdĭvīde' *v.* Divide again after first division. **sŭbdĭvĭ'sion** (-zhn) *n.* Subdividing; subordinate division; (mil.) half of division.

sŭbdŏm'ĭnant *n.* (mus.) 4th note of major or minor scale (ill. SCALE).

subdūe' *v.t.* Conquer, subjugate, overcome, prevail over; reduce intensity, force, or vividness of (sound, colour, light).

sŭb-ĕd'ĭt *v.t.* Act as assistant editor of (paper etc.), prepare (copy) for supervision of editor. **sŭb-ĕd'ĭtor** *n.*

sūbēr'ėous, sū'berōse, sū'berous *adjs.* (bot.) Of, like, cork, corky.

sūbĕ'rĭc *adj.* Of cork; (chem.) ~ *acid,* white crystalline dibasic acid obtained by action of nitric acid on cork etc.

sŭb'-făm'ĭly *n.* (zool.) Taxonomic category (with name ending in *-inae*) below family and above tribe or genus.

sŭb fĭn'ĕm. Towards the end (of chapter etc. referred to).

sŭbfŭsc' *adj.* Dusky, dull, or sombre in colour.

sŭb'-head, -heading (-ĕd-) *ns.* Subordinate division of subject etc.; subordinate heading or title in chapter, article, etc.

sŭb-hūm'an *adj.* Less than human; not quite human.

sŭb-ĭn'dĕx *n.* (math.) Inferior index written to right of symbol.

sŭbjā'cent *adj.* Underlying, situated below.

sŭb'jėct *n.* 1. Person owing allegiance to government or ruling power esp. sovereign; any member of a State except the Sovereign, any member of a subject State. 2. (logic, gram.) That member of a proposition or sentence about which something is predicated; the noun or noun-equivalent governing a verb. 3. (metaphys.) Thinking or feeling entity, the mind, the ego, the conscious self, as opp. to all that is external to the mind; the substance of anything as opp. to its attributes. 4. Theme of or *of* discussion or description or representation; matter (to be) treated of or dealt with; department of study. 5. (mus.) Principal phrase of a composition or movement; *first, second,* ~, first, second, to be introduced. 6. (chiefly med.) Person of specified usu. undesirable bodily or mental characteristics, as *hysterical, sensitive,* ~. 7. ~ *catalogue, index,* etc., catalogue, index, listing books, etc., according to subject; ~*-heading,* heading in index collecting references to a subject; ~*-matter,* matter treated of in book etc.; ~*-object,* immediate object of cognition presented to mind, as dist. from the real object. ~ *adj.* Under government, not independent, owing obedience *to*; liable, exposed, or prone *to*; ~ *to,* conditional(ly) upon, on the assumption of. **subjĕct'** *v.t.* Subdue, make subject, (*to* one's sway etc.); expose, make liable, treat, *to.* **subjĕc'tion** *n.*

subjĕc'tĭve *adj.* 1. Of, proceeding from, taking place within, the thinking subject, having its source in the mind; personal, individual; introspective; imaginary, illusory. 2. (gram.) Of the subject; ~ *case,* nominative. **subjĕc'tĭvely** *adv.* **subjĕc'tĭveness, sŭbjectĭv'ĭty** *ns.*

subjĕc'tĭvism *n.* Philosophical theory that all knowledge is merely subjective. **subjĕc'tĭvist** *adj.* & *n.*

subjoin' *v.t.* Add at the end, append.

sŭb ju'dĭcė (jōō-). (of case) Under judicial consideration, not yet decided.

sŭb'jugāte (-jōō-) *v.t.* Bring under the yoke or into subjection, subdue, vanquish. **sŭbjugā'tion** *n.*

subjŭnc'tĭve *adj.* & *n.* (gram.) ~ (*mood*), a verbal mood, so named as used in classical language chiefly in subordinate or subjoined clauses; obsolescent in English exc. in certain uses, e.g. to express wish (*I wish it* were *over*), imprecation (*manners* be *hanged!*), and contingent or hypothetical events (*if he* were *here now*). **subjŭnc'tĭvely** *adv.*

sŭb-lĕt' *v.t.* (past t. and past part. *-lĕt*). Let to subtenant.

sŭb-lieutĕn'ant (-left-, in navy -let-; U.S. -lōōt-, lŭt-) *n.* Officer ranking next below lieutenant.

sŭb'lĭmate *n.* (chem.) Solid produced when a substance is sublimed; *corrosive* ~, mercuric chloride, $HgCl_2$, a highly poisonous white crystalline salt. **sŭb'lĭmāte** *v.t.* 1. (chem., obs.) = SUBLIME[2]. 2. Transmute into something nobler, more sublime or refined;

(psycho-anal.) divert energy of (primitive impulse) into activity socially more useful or regarded as higher in cultural or moral scale. **sŭblimā′tion** *n.* Action, process, of subliming or sublimating.

sublīme′¹ *adj.* Of the most exalted kind, aloof from and raised far above the ordinary; inspiring awe, deep reverence, or lofty emotion by beauty, vastness, grandeur, etc.; *S~ Porte*: see PORTE. **sublīme′ly** *adv.* **sublĭm′ĭty** *n.* **sublīme′** *n.* What is sublime, sublimity.

sublīme′² *v.* 1. (chem.) Subject (substance) to action of heat so as to convert it to vapour which on cooling is deposited in solid form; purify (substance) by this means; (of substance) undergo this process; pass from solid to gaseous state without liquefaction. 2. (fig.) Purify or elevate, become pure, as by sublimation; make sublime.

sŭblĭm′ĭnal *adj.* (psychol.) Below threshold of consciousness, too faint or rapid to be recognized; *~ advertising*, advertising done e.g. by rapid flashes on cinema or television screen which though not consciously seen by observers may affect their subsequent behaviour.

sŭblĭng′ual (-ngg-) *adj.* Under the tongue.

sŭblun′ary (-lōō-) *adj.* Beneath the moon; between orbits of moon and earth; subject to moon's influence; of this world, earthly, terrestrial.

sŭb-machine′-gŭn *n.* Machine-gun of inferior calibre and weight (ill. GUN).

sŭb′-măn *n.* Markedly inferior, brutal or stupid, man.

sŭbmar′ginal *adj.* Situated near margin.

sŭb′marine (-ēn; *or* -ēn′) *adj.* Existing or lying under surface of sea; operating, operated, constructed, laid, intended for use, under surface of sea. *~ n.* Vessel, esp. warship, which can be submerged and navigated under water, used esp. for carrying and discharging torpedoes.

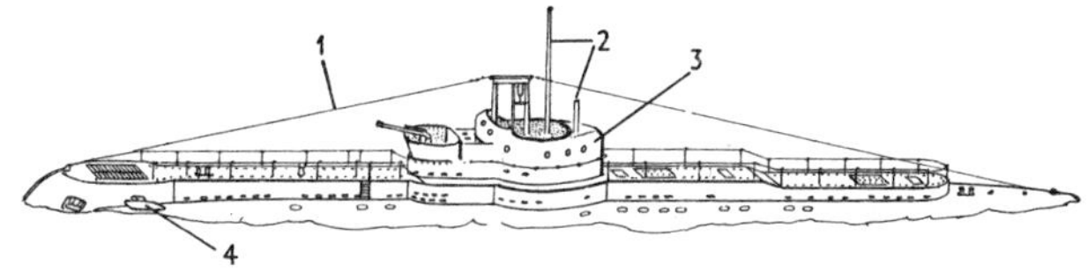

SUBMARINE

1. 'Jumping-wire' to prevent the submarine fouling obstructions. 2. Periscopes. 3. Conning-tower. 4. Hydroplane

sŭbmăx′illary *adj.* Beneath lower jaw.

sŭbmēd′iant *n.* (mus.) 6th note of major or minor scale (ill. SCALE).

submerge′ *v.* (Cause to) sink or plunge under water. **submer′gence, submer′sion** (-shn) *ns.*

submĭ′ssion (-shn) *n.* Submissive, yielding, or deferential attitude, condition, conduct, etc.; submitting, being submitted.

submĭss′ĭve *adj.* Inclined to submit, yielding to power or authority, humble, obedient. **submĭss′ĭvely** *adv.* **submĭss′ĭveness** *n.*

submĭt′ *v.* 1. Surrender oneself, become subject, yield (*to* person, his authority, etc., or *to* judgement, criticism, correction, or condition, etc.). 2. Bring under notice or consideration of person, refer *to* his decision or judgement; urge or represent deferentially (*that*).

sŭbnorm′al *adj.* Less than normal, below normal.

sŭb′order *n.* (zool., bot.) Subdivision of order, group, next below order in classification.

subord′inate *adj.* Of inferior importance or rank, secondary, subservient; (gram., of clause) dependent, containing subject and predicate but syntactically equivalent to noun, adjective, or adverb. *~ n.* Person under control or orders of superior. **subord′ināte** *v.t.* Make subordinate, treat or regard as of minor importance, bring or put into subservient relation (*to*). **subordinā′tion** *n.* **subord′inative** *adj.*

suborn′ *v.t.* Bribe, induce, or procure (person) by underhand or unlawful means to commit perjury or other unlawful act. **sŭbornā′tion** *n.*

sŭb′-plŏt *n.* Secondary plot in play etc.

subpoen′a (-pēn-) *n.* Writ commanding person's attendance in court of justice. *~ v.t.* Serve subpoena on. [L *sub poena*, = 'under penalty', first words of writ]

sŭbprī′or *n.* Prior's assistant and deputy.

sŭb rōs′a (-z-). In confidence, in secret. [L, = 'under the rose']

subscrībe′ *v.* 1. Write (one's name) at foot of document, sign one's name to (document etc.), signify assent or adhesion to by signing one's name; put one's signature *to* in token of assent, approval, etc.; express one's agreement, acquiescence, etc. 2. Enter one's name in list of contributors; make or promise a contribution, contribute (specified sum) to or *to* common fund, society, party, etc., or *for* common object, raise or guarantee raising of by subscribing thus; *~ to*, undertake to buy (periodical) regularly. **subscrĭp′tion** *n.*

sŭb′scrĭpt *adj.* Written below or underneath (math. etc., of index written below and to right of symbol, Gk gram., of *iota* written under ā, ē, or ō).

sŭb′sĕction *n.* Subordinate division of section.

sŭb′sequent *adj.* Following in order, time, or succession, esp. coming immediately after. **sŭb′sequently** *adv.* **sŭb′sequence** *n.*

subserve′ *v.t.* Be instrumental in furthering or promoting.

subserv′ient *adj.* 1. Serving as means to further end or purpose. 2. Subordinate, subject (*to*); cringing, truckling, obsequious. **subserv′iently** *adv.* **subserv′ience** *n.*

subsīde′ *v.i.* Sink down, sink to low(er) level (esp. of liquids or soil sinking to normal level); (of swelling etc.) go down; (of person, usu. joc.) sink *into*, *on to*, chair etc.; (of storm, strong feeling, clamour, etc.) abate, become less agitated, violent, or active; cease from activity or agitation. **sŭb′sĭdence** (*or* subsī′-) *n.*

subsĭd′iary *adj.* Serving to assist or supplement, auxiliary, supplementary; subordinate, secondary; *~ company*, one of which another company (the 'holding company') holds more than half issued share capital. *~ n.* Subsidiary person or thing; subsidiary company.

sŭb′sĭdīze *v.t.* Pay subsidy to.

sŭb′sĭdy *n.* 1. Money grant from one State to another in return for military or naval aid etc. 2. Financial aid given by government towards expenses of an undertaking or institution held to be of public utility; money paid by government to producers of a commodity so that it can be sold to consumers at a low price; *education*, *food*, *housing*, etc., *subsidies*, money from taxation or rates enabling these goods or services to be provided at low price to consumer. 3. (Engl. hist.) Pecuniary aid granted to sovereign by Parliament for special needs.

sŭb sĭlĕn′tĭō (*or* -shĭō). In silence, without remark; in hushed-up manner, privately.

subsĭst′ *v.* 1. Exist as a reality; continue to exist, remain in being. 2. Maintain, support, keep, provide food or funds for, provision; maintain or support oneself. **subsĭs′tence** *n.* Subsisting; means of supporting life, livelihood; *~ allowance*, allowance granted to employee for living expenses while travelling on employer's business; *~ diet*, minimum amount of food required to support life.

sŭb′soil *n.* Soil lying immediately under surface soil; *~ plough*, plough with no mould-board, used to loosen soil at some depth below surface in ploughed furrows.

sŭbsŏn'ĭc *adj.* (of aircraft etc.) Having speed less than that of sound (opp. SUPERSONIC).

sŭbspē'cies (-shēz, -shĭēz) *n.* Subdivision of species.

sŭb'stance *n.* 1. (philos.) What underlies phenomena, permanent substratum of things, that in which accidents or attributes inhere; essential nature; essence or most important part of anything, purport, real meaning. 2. Theme, subject-matter, material, esp. as opp. to form; reality, solidity, solid or real thing. 3. Possessions, goods, wealth (archaic). 4. Particular kind or species of matter.

substăn'tial (-shl) *adj.* 1. Having substance, actually existing, not illusory; of real importance or value, of considerable amount. 2. Of solid material or structure, not flimsy, stout; possessed of property, well-to-do, commercially sound. 3. That is such essentially, virtual, practical. **substăn'tially** *adv.* **substăntiality** (-shĭăl'-) *n.*

substăn'tialism (-shal-) *n.* (philos.) Doctrine that there are substantial realities underlying phenomena.

substăn'tialīze (-shal-) *v.* Invest with or acquire substance.

substăn'tiāte (-shĭ-) *v.t.* Give substantial form to; demonstrate or verify by proof or evidence. **substăntiā'tion** *n.*

sŭbstantīv'al *adj.* Of, consisting of, substantive(s). **sŭbstantīv'ally** *adv.*

sŭb'stantīve *adj.* 1. Having a separate and independent existence, not merely inferential or implicit or subservient. 2. (gram.) Expressing existence; denoting a substance; *noun* ~, (old name for) noun, part of speech used as name of person or thing, as dist. from *noun adjective* now called simply *adjective*; ~ *verb*, the verb *be*. 3. (law) Of, consisting of, rules of right administered by court as opp. to forms of procedure. 4. (mil.) Appointed to substantive rank; ~ *rank*, permanent rank in the holder's branch of the army (as opp. to brevet, honorary, or temporary rank). 5. (of dye) Not requiring the use of a mordant. **sŭb'stantively** *adv.* **sŭb'stantīve** *n.* (gram.) Noun substantive, noun in the now usual sense excluding adjectives.

sŭb'stitūte *n.* Person or thing acting or serving in place of another. ~ *v.t.* Put in place of another, cause to act as substitute *for*. **sŭbstitū'tion** *n.* (esp., chem.) Replacement of one atom or radical in molecule by another. **sŭbstitū'tional** (-sho-), **sŭb'stitūtive** *adjs.*

sŭbstrăt'osphēre *n.* Layer of atmosphere immediately below stratosphere.

sŭbstrāt'um *n.* (pl. *-ta*). What underlies or forms basis of anything.

subsūme' *v.t.* Bring (one idea, principle, etc.) *under* another, a rule, or a class. **subsŭmp'tion** *n.*

sŭbtĕn'ant *n.* One who holds or leases from a tenant.

subtĕnd' *v.t.* (geom.) (Of chord, side of figure, angle) be opposite to (angle, arc). **subtĕnse'** *n.* Subtending line.

sŭbter- *prefix.* Secretly; lower, less than (rare).

sŭb'terfūge *n.* Evasion, shift; artifice or device adopted to escape or avoid force of argument, condemnation, or censure, or to justify conduct.

sŭbterrān'ėan *adj.* Existing, lying, situated, formed, operating, taking place, performed, under surface of the earth; underground. **sŭbterrān'ėous** *adj.* Subterranean. **sŭbterrān'ėously** *adv.*

sŭb'tīle (*or* sŭt'l) *adj.* (archaic) Subtle.

subt'ilīze (sŭt-) *v.* Make subtle; elevate, sublime, refine; argue or reason subtly (upon).

sŭb'-tī'tle *n.* Subordinate or additional title of literary work etc.; caption of cinema film.

subtle (sŭt'l) *adj.* Tenuous, rarefied (archaic); pervasive or elusive by reason of tenuity; fine or delicate, esp. to such an extent as to elude observation or analysis; making fine distinctions, having delicate perceptions, acute; ingenious, elaborate, clever; crafty, cunning. **subt'ly** (sŭt-) *adv.* **subt'lety** (sŭt'ltĭ) *n.*

sŭbtŏn'ĭc *n.* (mus.) Note next below tonic, 7th note in ascending scale.

Sŭbtōp'ia *n.* (iron.) Suburban paradise, spread of small houses over countryside. [f. *sub*urb and UTOPIA]

subtrăct' *v.t.* Deduct (part, quantity, number) from or *from* whole or from quantity or number, esp. in arithmetic and algebra. **subtrăc'tion** *n.* **subtrăc'tīve** *adj.*

sŭb'trahĕnd' *n.* (math.) Quantity or number to be subtracted.

sŭbtrŏp'ĭcal *adj.* (Characteristic of regions) bordering on the tropics.

sŭb'ūlate, sŭb'ūlĭfōrm *adjs.* (biol.) Awl-shaped, slender and tapering.

sŭb'ûrb *n.* (One of) residential parts lying on or near outskirts of city. **subûrb'an** *adj.*

Subûrb'ia *n.* (iron.) The suburbs (esp. of London) and their inhabitants.

subvĕn'tion *n.* Grant from government etc., in support of enterprise of public importance, subsidy.

subvêr'sion (-shn) *n.* Overturning, ruin, overthrow from foundation.

subvêrs'īve *adj.* Tending to subvert or overthrow.

subvêrt' *v.t.* Overthrow, overturn, upset, effect destruction or ruin of (religion, morality, government).

sŭb vō'cė (abbrev. *s.v.*) Under the (specified) word.

sŭb'way *n.* Underground passage for water-pipes, telegraph lines, etc., or for pedestrians to cross below road(s) etc.; (U.S.) underground railway.

succėdān'ėum (sŭks-) *n.* (pl. *-nea*). Substitute, esp. (med.) remedy, freq. inferior, substituted for another. **succėdān'ėous** *adj.*

succeed' (-ks-) *v.* 1. Come next after and take the place of, follow in order, come next (to); be subsequent (to); come by inheritance or in due course to or *to* office, title, or property. 2. Have success, be successful; prosper; accomplish one's purpose; (of plan etc.) be brought to a successful issue.

succĕn'tor (-ks-) *n.* Deputy to precentor in cathedral choir.

succès d'ĕstime' (sōōksā, -ēm) *n.* Passably cordial reception given to performance or work out of the respect in which the performer or author is held rather than on account of the merits of the work itself.

succès fou (sōōksā fōō') *n.* Success marked by wild enthusiasm.

succĕss' (-ks-) *n.* Favourable issue; attainment of object, or of wealth, fame, or position; thing or person that succeeds or is successful; issue of undertaking (now rare exc. in *ill* ~). **succĕss'ful** *adj.* **succĕss'fully** *adv.*

succe'ssion (-ksĕshn) *n.* 1. A following in order, succeeding; series of things in succession; *in* ~, one after another in regular sequence. 2. (Right of) succeeding to the throne or any office or inheritance; set or order of persons having such right; *apostolic* ~, uninterrupted transmission of spiritual authority through bishops from the apostles downwards; ~ *duties*, taxes payable on succession to estate; *S~ States*, those resulting from dismemberment of Austria-Hungary after the war of 1914–18. **succĕ'ssional** (-sho-) *adj.*

succĕss'īve (-ks-) *adj.* Coming one after another in uninterrupted sequence. **succĕss'ively** *adv.*

succĕss'or (-ks-) *n.* Person or thing succeeding another.

succīnct' (-ks-) *adj.* Terse, brief, concise. **succīnct'ly** *adv.* **succīnct'nėss** *n.*

sŭcc'ory *n.* = CHICORY.

sŭcc'otăsh *n.* (U.S.) Dish of beans and green maize cooked together (sometimes with salt pork). [Amer. Ind. *msiquatash*]

sŭcc'our (-ker) *v.t.* Come to assistance of, give aid to in need or difficulty. ~ *n.* Aid given in time of need.

sŭcc'ūba, sŭcc'ūbus *ns.* (pl. *-bae, -bī*). Female demon supposed to have sexual intercourse with men in their sleep.

sŭcc'ūlent *adj.* Juicy; (bot.) having juicy or fleshy tissues, as the cactus. ~ *n.* Plant with fleshy foliage or stems or both. **sŭcc′ūlently** *adv.* **sŭcc′ūlence** *n.*

succŭmb′ (-m) *v.i.* Sink under pressure, give way to superior force, authority, etc.; (esp.) yield to effects of disease, wounds, etc., die.

sŭch *adj.* 1. Of the character, degree, or extent described, referred to, or implied; the previously described or specified; ~ *as*, of the kind or degree that, the kind of (person or thing) that; for example, e.g. 2. So great, so eminent, etc. (freq. emphatic and exclamatory); (preceding attrib. adj., with adverbial force) so. 3. Particular, but not specified; ~-*and*-~, a particular but unspecified. ~ *pron.* That, the action, etc., referred to; such people *as*, those *who* (chiefly archaic or rhet.); (vulg. or commerc.) the aforesaid thing(s); *as* ~, as what has been specified.

sŭck *v.* Draw (liquid, esp. milk from breast) into mouth by contracting muscles of lips, tongue, and cheeks so as to produce partial vacuum; (fig.) imbibe, absorb (knowledge etc.); apply lips to (breast etc.) to extract milk or obtain nourishment, apply lips and tongue, or analogous organs to (object, as sweetmeat) to absorb nourishment; perform action of sucking, use sucking action; (of pump etc.) make sucking or gurgling sound, draw in air instead of water; ~ *at*, take pull at (pipe etc.); ~ *down, in*, (of whirlpool, quicksand, etc.) engulf; ~ *dry*, exhaust of contents by sucking; ~ *in, up*, (of absorbent substance) absorb; ~ *up to*, (school slang) toady to, curry favour with. ~ *n.* Action, act, spell, of sucking (*give* ~, suckle); drawing action of whirlpool etc.; small draught of or *of* liquor.

sŭck′er *n.* 1. Person or thing that sucks, esp. sucking-pig or young whale-calf; organ adapted for sucking; kinds of esp. N. Amer. fish with mouths of form that suggests feeding by suction; piston of pump, syringe, etc. 2. Part or organ adapted for adhering to object by suction; fish with suctorial disc by which it adheres to foreign objects; toy consisting of round disc of leather or rubber which adheres to solid surface when wet and drawn up by string in centre, by reason of vacuum created. 3. Shoot thrown out by plant, esp. root under ground; axillary shoot in tobacco-plant. 4. (slang) Person easily victimized or gulled, greenhorn.

sŭck′ing *adj.* Not yet weaned; (fig.) budding, unpractised, immature; ~-*pig*, very young pig, esp. young milk-fed pig suitable for roasting whole.

sŭck′le *v.t.* Give suck to, feed at the breast. **sŭck′ling** *n.* Unweaned child or animal.

sucre (sōōk′rĕ) *n.* Principal monetary unit of Ecuador, = 100 centavos.

sūc′rōse *n.* The sugar ($C_{12}H_{22}O_{11}$) that comes from cane and from beet and is found widely in many plants.

sŭc′tion *n.* Action of sucking; production of complete or partial vacuum so that external atmospheric pressure forces fluid into vacant space or causes adhesion of surfaces; ~ *pipe*, pipe leading from bottom of pump barrel to reservoir from which fluid is to be drawn; ~-*pump*, pump drawing liquid through pipe into chamber exhausted by piston (ill. PUMP); ~ *stroke*, in internal combustion engine, stroke by which the gaseous mixture is drawn into the cylinder(s) (ill. COMBUSTION). **sŭc′tional** (-sho-) *adj.*

sŭctōr′ial *adj.* (of organ) Adapted for sucking; (of animal) having suctorial organs; of the group *Suctoria* of protozoa, with tubular suctorial tentacles (ill. PROTOZOA).

Sudăn′ (sōō-). Region of Africa, S. of Sahara and Libyan deserts, formerly consisting of *Anglo-Egyptian Sudan*, since 1956 independent republic of ~ (capital KHARTOUM), and the French colony of *Soudan*, now the republic of *Mali* within the French Community. **Sudanēse′** (-z) *adj.* & *n.* (Native) of the Sudan.

sūdār′ium *n.* (pl. -*ia*). Cloth for wiping face; esp. cloth with which St. Veronica wiped face of Christ on his way to Calvary, miraculously impressed with his features.

sūdatōr′ium *n.* (pl. -*ia*). (esp. in Roman baths) Room in which hot-air or steam-baths are taken to produce sweating.

sŭdd *n.* Impenetrable mass of floating vegetable matter impeding navigation on White Nile.

sŭdd′en *adj.* Happening, coming, performed, taking place, etc., without warning or unexpectedly, abrupt. ~ *adv.* (chiefly poet.) Suddenly. ~ *n.* (*All*) *of a* ~, suddenly. **sŭdd′enly** *adv.* **sŭdd′enness** *n.*

Sud′ermann (-ōō-) Hermann (1857–1928). German playwright and novelist.

Sude′ten (-dā-) *n.pl.* The Germans formerly living in the provinces of Bohemia and Moravia, Czechoslovakia, named after the *Sudetes*, a mountainous region on the boundary between Czechoslovakia and Silesia.

sūdorĭf′erous *adj.* Producing or secreting sweat. **sūdorĭf′ĭc** *adj.* & *n.* (Drug) promoting or causing sweating.

Sud′ra (sōō-). Lowest of the 4 great Hindu castes, the artisans and labourers.

sŭds *n.pl.* Water impregnated with soap; frothy mass on top of soapy water, lather.

sūe[1] *v.* Institute legal proceedings, bring civil action, against; (usu. ~ *out*) apply before court for grant of (writ, legal process); bring suit; plead, appeal, supplicate (*for*).

Sue[2] (sū), Eugène (1804–57). French novelist, author of 'Les Mystères de Paris' etc.

suède (swād) *n.* Kid or other skin with flesh-side rubbed into nap, as material for gloves, shoes, etc. [Fr. *Suède* Sweden]

sū′ĕt *n.* Hard fat round the kidneys and loins of cattle and sheep, used in cooking or rendered down to form tallow; ~ *pudding*, pudding made with suet and usu. boiled in cloth or steamed. **sū′ĕty** *adj.* Of or like suet; pale-complexioned.

Suetōn′ius (swē-). Gaius Suetonius Tranquillus (*c* A.D. 70–*c* 160). Roman historian and antiquary.

Su′ĕz (sōō-). District of Lower Egypt at N. end of the Red Sea; seaport at S. end of the ~ *Canal*, a ship-canal across the Isthmus of Suez to Port Said, cut (1859–69) by Ferdinand de LESSEPS.

sŭff′er *v.* 1. Undergo, experience, be subjected to (pain, loss, grief, defeat, punishment, etc.); undergo pain, grief, or damage. 2. Permit *to* do; allow, put up with, tolerate. **sŭff′erer, sŭff′ering** *ns.*

sŭff′erance *n.* 1. (archaic) Long-suffering, forbearance. 2. Sanction, or acquiescence, implied by absence of objection; tacit permission or toleration, esp. in *on* ~, under conditions of bare tolerance or tacit acquiescence.

suffīce′ *v.* Be enough, be adequate; satisfy, meet the needs of.

suffĭ′ciency (-shen-) *n.* Sufficient supply, adequate provision, a competence; sufficient number or quantity (*of*); (archaic) being sufficient, adequacy, ability.

suffĭ′cient (-shnt) *adj.* Sufficing; adequate, esp. in amount or number; enough; (archaic) competent, adequate in ability or resources. **suffĭ′ciently** *adv.* **suffĭ′cient** *n.* Enough, a sufficient quantity.

sŭff′ĭx *n.* 1. (gram.) Verbal element attached to end of word as inflexional formative or to form new word. 2. (math.) Sub-index. **suffĭx′** *v.t.* Add as suffix.

sŭff′ocāte *v.* Kill, stifle, choke, by stopping respiration; produce choking sensation in, smother, overwhelm; feel suffocated. **sŭffocā′tion** *n.*

Sŭff′olk (-ok). East Anglian county of England.

sŭff′ragan *adj.* & *n.* ~ (*bishop*), bishop appointed to assist diocesan bishop in particular part of his diocese; bishop in relation to his archbishop or metropolitan.

sŭff′rage *n.* 1. (eccles.) In Book of Common Prayer, intercessory petitions said by priest in litany, (pl.) set of versicles and responses; (archaic) intercessory prayer, esp. for souls of departed. 2. Vote;

approval or consent expressed by voting; right of voting as member of body, State, etc., franchise.

sŭffragĕtte′ *n.* (hist.) Woman advocating political enfranchisement of women, esp. militantly or violently.

sŭff′ragist *n.* Advocate of extension of political franchise, esp. to women.

suffūse (-z) *v.t.* Overspread as with a fluid, a colour, a gleam of light. **suffū′sion** (-zhn) *n.*

Suf′i (sōō-), **Sōf′i** *ns.* Moslem ascetic mystic of sect which originated in 8th c. and later, esp. in Persia, embraced pantheistic views. **Suf′ism, Sōf′ism** *ns.* [Arab. *çūfī* man of wool, f. *çūf* wool]

sug′ar (shŏŏ-) *n.* 1. Sweet crystalline substance, a *disaccharide* ($C_{12}H_{22}O_{11}$), white when pure, obtained by evaporation from plant juices, esp. those of sugar-cane and sugar-beet, and forming important article of human food, saccharose; (pl.) kinds of sugar. 2. Sweet words, flattery, anything serving purpose of sugar put round pill in reconciling person to what is unpalatable. 3. (chem.) Any of a group of carbohydrates, soluble in water and having a sweet taste, found esp. in plants and including glucose, lactose, saccharose, etc. 4. ~ *of milk*, lactose; *~-almonds*, sweetmeat of almond with hard sugar coating; *~-beet*, kind of white beet from which sugar is manufactured; *~-candy*: see CANDY[1], sense 1; *~-cane*, perennial tropical and sub-tropical grass, *Saccharum officinarum*, with tall stout jointed stems, cultivated as a source of sugar; *~-daddy*, (U.S. slang) elderly man who lavishes gifts on a young woman; *~-loaf*, conical moulded mass of hard refined sugar; thing, esp. hill, in shape of a sugar-loaf; *~-maple*, N. Amer. tree, *Acer saccharinum*, yielding maple sugar; *~-plum*, small round or oval sweetmeat of boiled sugar. **sug′arless** *adj.* **sug′ar** *v.t.* Sweeten, coat with sugar; make sweet or agreeable; form sugar, become crystalline or granulated like sugar; spread sugar mixed with gum etc. on (tree) to catch moths; ~ *off*, complete boiling down of maple syrup for sugar; (slang) make off, slip away; *sugared*, used as euphemistic imprecation.

sug′ary (shŏŏ-) *adj.* Like sugar; containing (much) sugar; (fig.) cloying, sentimental.

suggĕst′ (-j-) *v.t.* Cause (idea) to be present to mind, call up idea of; prompt execution of; put forward opinion or proposition (*that*), utter as a suggestion; give hint or inkling of, give impression of existence or presence of.

suggĕs′tĭble (-j-) *adj.* (esp.) Capable of being influenced by suggestion. **suggĕstĭbĭl′ity** *n.*

suggĕs′tĭō făl′sī *n.* Positive misrepresentation not involving direct lie but going beyond concealment of the truth (cf. SUPPRESSIO VERI).

sugges′tion (-jĕs′chon) *n.* Suggesting; idea, plan, or thought suggested, proposal; suggesting of prurient ideas; insinuation of belief or impulse into mind of subject by hypnosis or other means, such belief or impulse.

suggĕs′tĭve (-j-) *adj.* (esp.) Suggesting something indecent. **suggĕs′tĭvely** *adv.* **suggĕs′tĭveness** *n.*

sū′ĭcīde *n.* 1. Person who intentionally kills himself; (law) suicide of years of discretion and sane mind. 2. Intentional self-slaughter (in law, as in 1; *commit* ~, kill oneself); (fig.) action destructive to one's own interests etc. (*commit political* ~, ruin one's prospects as a politician; *race* ~, failure of a people to maintain its numbers). **sūĭcīd′al** *adj.* **sūĭcīd′ally** *adv.*

sū′ī gĕn′erĭs. Of its own kind, peculiar, unique.

suit (sūt) *n.* 1. Suing in court of law, legal prosecution; process instituted in court of justice, lawsuit. 2. Suing, supplication, petition; courting of a woman, courtship. 3. Set of man's or boy's outer garments (usu. coat, waistcoat, and trousers, breeches, or knickerbockers); woman's coat and skirt; *~-case*, case for carrying clothes, usu. box-shaped with flat hinged lid and one handle. 4. Any of the four sets (spades, clubs, hearts, diamonds) of playing-cards in pack; *follow* ~, play card of suit led; (fig.) follow another's example. ~ *v.* 1. Accommodate, adapt, make fitting or appropriate, *to*. 2. Be agreeable or convenient to; be fitted or adapted to; be good for, favourable to health of; go well with appearance or character of, be becoming to; be fitting or convenient.

suit′able (sūt-) *adj.* Suited *to* or *for*; well fitted for the purpose; appropriate to the occasion. **suit′ably** *adv.* **suitabĭl′ity, suit′ableness** *ns.*

suite (swēt) *n.* 1. Retinue, set of persons in attendance. 2. Set, series; number of rooms forming set used by particular person(s) or for particular purpose; set of furniture of same pattern. 3. (mus.) Old form of instrumental composition (*c* 1500–*c* 1750), later partly superseded by SONATA, and consisting of several (usu. four) movements based on dance tunes, in same or related keys; set of instrumental compositions related in theme etc. and freq. constituting music for ballet, incidental music for play, etc.

suit′or (sūt-) *n.* 1. Party to lawsuit; petitioner. 2. Wooer, one who seeks woman in marriage.

sŭl′cate *adj.* (anat., bot.) Furrowed, grooved. **sŭlcā′tion** *n.*

sŭl′cus *n.* Groove, furrow; esp. (anat.) fissure between two convolutions of brain (ill. BRAIN).

Sŭl′grāve Manor. Northamptonshire estate (1539–1610) of ancestors of George Washington, now maintained as memorial.

sŭlk *v.i.* Be sulky. ~ *n.* (usu. pl.) Sulky fit.

sŭl′ky *adj.* Sullen, morose; silent, inactive, or unsociable from resentment or ill-temper. **sŭl′kĭly** *adv.* **sŭl′kĭness** *n.* **sŭl′ky** *n.* Light two-wheeled carriage for single person, esp. one used for trials of speed between trotting-horses.

Sŭll′a, Lucius Cornelius (138–78 B.C.). Roman dictator and general; instituted reforms of the constitution designed to increase the power of the Senate and reduce that of the people and their tribunes.

sŭll′age *n.* Filth, refuse, sewage.

sŭll′en *adj.* Gloomy, ill-humoured, moody, morose, unsociable, dismal. **sŭll′enly** *adv.* **sŭll′ennĕss** *n.*

Sŭll′ĭvan, Sir Arthur Seymour (1842–1900). English musical composer, in collaboration with W. S. Gilbert, of comic operas.

sŭll′y *v.t.* Pollute, defile, soil, stain, tarnish (chiefly fig. or poet.).

sŭlph′amīde *n.* Amide of sulphuric acid, a colourless crystalline neutral compound, $SO_2(NH_2)_2$.

sŭlphanĭl′amīde *n.* Synthetic organic chemical compound (para-amino - benzene - sulphonamide), progenitor of the drugs known as sulphonamides.

sŭl′phate *n.* Salt of sulphuric acid. **sŭl′phāte** *v.* Treat, impregnate, with sulphuric acid or a sulphate; (elect.) form whitish scales of lead sulphate on plates of (storage battery); become sulphated. **sŭlphā′tion** *n.*

sŭl′phīde *n.* Compound of sulphur with another element or a radical.

sŭl′phīte *n.* Salt of sulphurous acid.

sŭl′phonal *n.* *Acetone diethyl sulphone*, a white crystalline substance used as an anaesthetic and hypnotic.

sŭlphŏn′amīde *n.* Any of a group of drugs derived from amides of sulphonic acids, capable of killing or preventing the multiplication of bacteria e.g. streptococci, used in the treatment of many different infections.

sŭl′phōne *n.* Any of a group of organic compounds containing the radical SO_2 united directly to two carbon atoms. **sulphŏn′ic** *adj.*

sŭlphŏx′īde *n.* Compound containing the *thionyl* group (SO) united directly to two carbon atoms.

sŭl′phur (-*er*) *n.* 1. Greenish-yellow non-metallic inflammable element, burning with blue flame, widely distributed free and in combination, and used in manufacture of matches, gunpowder, and sulphuric acid, for vulcanizing rubber, as a disinfectant (as sulphur dioxide), and in medicine as a laxative, a sudorific, and an ingredient of ointments; symbol S, at. no. 16, at. wt 32·064; *flowers of* ~, pure sulphur in form of yellow powder. 2. In popular belief, material of which hell-fire and lightning were held to consist; (alchemy) one of the supposed ultimate elements, the principle of combustion. 3. Various yellow (or orange) butterflies of family *Pieridae*. 4. ~ *candle*, candle used for disinfection, giving off sulphur dioxide; ~-*yellow*, (of) the bright pale-yellow colour of sulphur.

sŭlphūr'ėous *adj.* Of, like, suggesting, sulphur; with qualities associated with (burning) sulphur; full of 'sulphur' of hell; sulphur-yellow.

sŭlphurĕtt'ėd *adj.* Chemically combined with sulphur (now only in ~ *hydrogen*, hydrogen sulphide, H_2S, colourless gas with very offensive odour).

sŭlphūr'ĭc *adj.* Of, containing, sulphur; ~ *acid*, H_2SO_4, dense highly corrosive oily fluid, oil of vitriol; ~ *ether*, ether.

sŭl'phūrous (*chem.* sŭlfūr'-) *adj.* 1. Sulphureous. 2. (chem., of compounds) Containing sulphur of lower valency than sulphuric compounds; ~ *acid*, H_2SO_3, present in solutions of sulphur dioxide in water.

sŭl'tan *n.* 1. Sovereign of Mohammedan country, esp. (now hist.) of Turkey. 2. Small white domestic fowl with heavily-feathered legs and feet, orig. from Turkey. 3. (*sweet*) ~, either of two sweet-scented annuals, *Centaurea moschata* (purple or white sweet ~), and *C. suaveolens* (yellow ~). **sŭl'tanate** *n.* Rank, authority, of a sultan; jurisdiction, dominion, of a sultan. [Arab. *sulṭan* king]

sŭlta'na (-tah-) *n.* 1. Wife or concubine of sultan. 2. Bird of genus *Porphyrio* (*purple gallinule*), chiefly of W. Indies, southern U.S., and Australia. 3. Small light-coloured seedless raisin grown chiefly in region of Smyrna; pale-yellow grape from which sultanas are produced.

sŭl'tanĕss *n.* = SULTANA, sense 1.

sŭl'try *adj.* Oppressively hot, sweltering. **sŭl'trĭly** *adv.* **sŭl'trinėss** *n.*

sŭm *n.* 1. Total amount resulting from addition of two or more numbers, quantities, magnitudes, etc.; total number or amount *of*; ~ *total*, total amount, aggregate (*of*). 2. A quantity or amount of or *of* money. 3. (Working out of) arithmetical problem. ~ *v.* 1. Find sum of; reckon, count, or total *up*; collect (*up*) into small compass. 2. ~ *up*, summarize, epitomize; form estimate or judgement of; (of judge in trial, or counsel concluding his client's case) recapitulate (evidence or arguments), with any necessary exposition of points of law, before jury considers its verdict; so *summ'ing up* (*n.*).

sū'mac(h) (-k; *or* shōō-) *n.* Shrub or small tree of genus *Rhus*; dried leaves etc., rich in tannin, of various plants of this genus, esp. the S. European *R. coriaria*, used in tanning, dyeing, and staining leather black, and as astringent. [Arab. *summāq*]

Suma'tra (-mah- *or* sūm'*a*-). Large island of Indonesia, separated from the Malay Peninsula by the Malacca Strait.

Sūm'er (*or* sōō-). Ancient district of Babylonia. **Sūmēr'ĭan** *adj.* Pertaining to, characteristic of, the civilization of Sumer. ~ *n.* Inhabitant of Sumer; agglutinative language of the Sumerian inscriptions written in a cuneiform script.

sŭmm'arīze *v.t.* Make or constitute a summary of, sum up.

sŭmm'ary *adj.* Compendious and (usu.) brief; dispensing with needless detail, performed with dispatch; (law, of proceedings) carried out rapidly by omission of certain formalities required by common law; ~ *jurisdiction*, determination of minor cases before magistrate. **sŭmm'arĭly** *adj.* **sŭmm'ary** *n.* Summary account or statement, abridgement, epitome.

summā'tion *n.* Addition, summing (up); finding of total or sum. **summā'tional** (-sho-) *adj.*

sŭmm'er[1] *n.* 1. Warmest season of year, popularly reckoned in N. hemisphere as lasting from mid-May to middle or end of August, but astronomically as lasting from summer solstice (21st or 22nd June) to autumnal equinox (22nd or 23rd Sept.); summer weather; (pl.) year of life or age (chiefly poet., as in *boy of ten* ~*s*); INDIAN, St. LUKE's, St. MARTIN's, ~: see these words. 2. *attrib*, or as *adj.*: ~ *ermine*, brown fur of ermine in summer; ~-*fallow*, (land) lying fallow during summer; ~-*house*, (usu. simple and light) building in park or garden providing cool shady place in summer; ~ *lightning*, sheet lightning without noise of thunder; *S*~ *Palace*, ruined palace of Chinese emperors near Peking; ~ *school*, course of lectures etc. held during summer vacation, esp. at university; *summer's day*, a day in summer, a very long day; ~ *solstice*, time at which sun reaches summer tropic (in N. hemisphere tropic of Cancer, in S. hemisphere tropic of Capricorn); ~-*time*, season of summer; standard time, one hour in advance of ordinary time, adopted in some countries during summer to facilitate use of daylight (*double* ~-*time*, two hours in advance); ~-*weight*, (of clothes etc.) suitable in weight for use in summer. ~ *v.* Pass summer (*at* or *in* place); pasture (cattle) *at*, *in*.

sŭmm'er[2] *n.* Horizontal beam, esp. main beam supporting girders or joists of floor.

sŭmm'ĭt *n.* Highest point, top, apex; highest degree.

sŭmm'on *v.t.* Call together by authority for action or deliberation, require presence or attendance of, bid approach; call upon *to* do; call *up* (courage, resolution, etc.) to one's aid; cite by authority to appear before court or judge to answer charge or give evidence.

sŭmm'ons (-nz) *n.* Authoritative call or urgent invitation to attend on some occasion or to do something; citation to appear before judge or magistrate. ~ *v.t.* Take out summons against.

sŭmm'um bŏn'um *n.* The chief or supreme good.

sŭmp *n.* Pit or well for collecting water or other fluid, esp. in mine; oil-reservoir at bottom of crank-case of internal combustion engine (ill. COMBUSTION).

sŭmp'ter *n.* Pack-horse or its driver (archaic); ~-*horse*, -*mule*, etc., pack-animals.

sŭmp'tion *n.* (logic) Major premiss.

sŭmp'tūary *adj.* Regulating expenditure; ~ *law*, *edict*, one which limits private expenditure in the interest of the State.

sŭmp'tūous *adj.* Costly, splendid, magnificent in workmanship, decoration, appearance, etc. **sŭmp'tūously** *adv.* **sŭmp'tūousnėss** *n.*

sŭn *n.* Star forming centre of system of worlds or planets, esp. the central body of the solar system, round which the earth and other planets revolve, and which

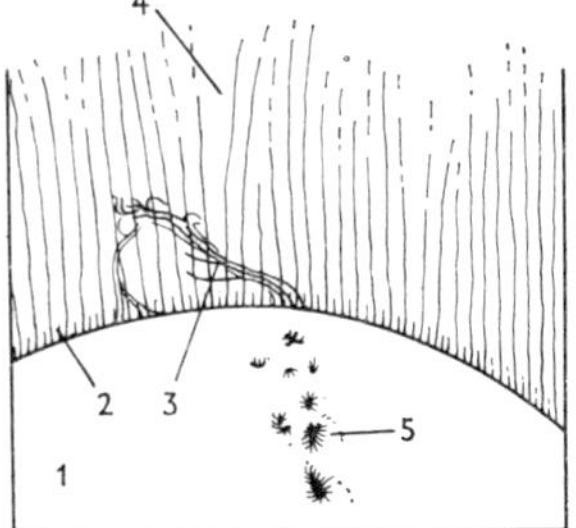

THE SUN'S ATMOSPHERE

1. Photosphere. 2. Chromosphere. 3. Prominence. 4. Corona. 5. Sun-spots or maculae

supplies them with light and warmth by its radiation; such light or warmth; (poet.) climate, clime; *a place in the* ~, position giving scope for development of individual or national life; *take the* ~, (naut.) make observation of meridian altitude of sun to determine latitude; ~-*and-planet gearing*, system of gearing in which axis of cogged wheel (*planet-wheel*) moves round that of central wheel (*sun-wheel*) to which it communicates motion (ill. GEAR); *~-bath*, exposure of skin to sun's rays; *~-bathe*, take sun-bath; *sun'beam*, beam of sunlight; *~-blind*, awning over window; *~-bonnet*, bonnet of cotton etc. shaped so as to shade eyes and neck from sun; *sun'burn*, tanning or superficial inflammation of skin caused by exposure to sun; brown colour produced thus; *sun'burnt* (*adj.*); *~-burst*, burst of sunlight; piece of jewellery representing sun surrounded by rays; *~-deck*, upper deck of ship; *sun'-dew*, plant of genus *Drosera* of small herbs growing in bogs, with leaves covered with glandular hairs secreting viscid drops; *sun'-dial*, contrivance for showing time

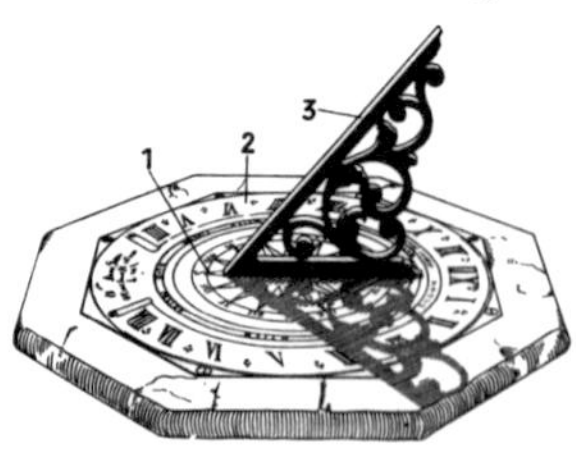

SUNDIAL (N. hemisphere)
1. South point of compass. 2. Hour-scale. 3. Gnomon

by shadow cast by sun on surface marked with hours; *~-dog*, parhelion, mock sun; *sun'down*, sunset; *sun'downer*, (Austral.) tramp arriving at station at sunset so as to obtain food and night's lodging; *sun'fish*, large fish (*Mola mola*) of warm seas, with round ungainly body and short fringe-like caudal fin; any of various small usu. brilliant-coloured Amer. freshwater fishes; *sun'flower*, (flower of) composite plants of genus *Helianthus*, chiefly natives of N. America, with conspicuous yellow flower-heads whose disc and rays suggest figure of sun; *Sunflower State*, pop. name of Kansas, U.S.; *~-glasses*, tinted spectacles for protecting eyes from sunlight or glare; *~-hat*, broad-brimmed hat worn to protect head from sun; *~-helmet*, hat with double crown for same purpose; *~ lamp*, large lamp with parabolic mirror reflector used in motion-picture photography; *sun'light*, light of sun; *~-parlour*, *-porch*, room, verandah, with walls largely of glass, designed to catch maximum amount of sunshine; *~-ray*, sunbeam; (pl.) ultra-violet rays used therapeutically as a substitute for sunlight; *sun'rise*, (time of) sun's apparent ascent above eastern horizon; *sun'set*, (time of) sun's apparent descent below western horizon at end of day; glow of light or display of colour in sky at this time; (fig.) decline, close (esp. of life); *Sunset State*, pop. name Arizona or Oregon, U.S.; *sun'-shade*, device providing protection from sun's rays, esp. parasol or awning over window; *sun'shine*, unimpeded sunlight, fair weather; (fig.) cheerfulness, bright influence; *Sunshine State*, pop. name of New Mexico or S. Dakota, U.S.; *~-spot*, one of the cavities in photosphere appearing as dark spots or patches on sun's surface, lasting from a few hours to several months, recurring in greatest numbers at intervals of a little over eleven years, and freq. accompanied by magnetic disturbances etc. on earth; *sun'stroke*, prostration or collapse caused by exposure to excessive heat of sun; *~-up*, (chiefly U.S.) sunrise; *~-wheel*, central wheel of *~-and-planet* gear. **sŭn'lėss** *adj.* **sŭn'-lėssnėss** *n.* **sŭn** *v.* Expose to the sun; *~ oneself*, bask in sun.

Sun. *abbrev.* Sunday.

sŭn'dae (-dā) *n.* (orig. U.S.) Confection of ice-cream with fruit, nuts, syrup, cream, etc.

Sŭn'day (*or* -dĭ) *n.* 1st day of week, observed by Christians as day of rest and worship; *a month of ~s*, a very long time; *~ best*, best clothes worn on Sunday; *~ school*, school held on Sunday, now only for religious instruction, and usu. attached to parish or church congregation.

sŭn'der *v.* (now poet. or rhet.) Separate, sever, keep apart.

sŭn'dry *adj.* Divers, several; *all and ~*, one and all. *~ n.* 1. (Austral.) An extra in cricket. 2. (pl.) Oddments, small items classed together without individual mention.

sŭnk, sŭnk'en *adjs.* (past parts. of SINK). That has sunk, lying below general surface; (of eyes, cheeks, etc.) hollow, fallen in.

Sŭnn'a(h) (-na). Traditional portion of Mohammedan law based on Mohammed's words or acts but not written by him, accepted as authoritative by the orthodox but rejected by the Shiites. **Sŭnn'i** (-nē), **Sŭnn'ite** *adjs.* & *ns.* (Mohammedan) accepting the Sunna as well as the Koran.

sŭnn'y *adj.* Bright with or as sunlight; exposed to, warm with, the sun; cheery, bright in disposition. **sŭnn'ĭly** *adv.* **sŭnn'ĭnėss** *n.*

Sŭn Yăt-sĕn (1866–1925). Leader of Chinese revolutionary movement, 1911–12; 1st president of the Chinese Republic, 1921–2.

sŭp *v.* Take (liquid food) by sips or spoonfuls; take supper; provide supper for. *~ n.* Mouthful of liquid, esp. soup; (*a*) *bite and* (*a*) *~*, a little food and drink.

sup. *abbrev.* Superlative; *supra* (= above).

sup'er (sōō-, sū-) *n.* 1. (colloq. or slang for) Supernumerary actor; superintendent. 2. Film-play designed for exhibition as the principal item in a cinema programme. *~ adj.* (shop) Superfine; (slang) excellent, unusually good.

sup'er- (sōō-, sū-) *prefix.* On the top (of); over; beyond, besides, in addition; exceeding, going beyond, more than, transcending; of higher kind; to a degree beyond the usual.

superabound' (sōō-, sū-) *v.i.* Be more abundant; abound excessively, be very or too abundant. **superabŭn'dant** *adj.* **superabŭn'dance** *n.*

superănn'ūāte (sōō-, sū-) *v.t.* Declare too old for work or use on account of age; dismiss or discharge as too old; discharge with pension; remove (pupil from school) because of backwardness in work. **sūperănnūā'tion** *n.*

supêrb' (sōō-, sū-) *adj.* Grand, majestic, splendid, magnificent. **supêrb'ly** *adv.*

sup'ercârgō (sōō-, sū-) *n.* Merchant ship's officer superintending cargo and commercial transactions of voyage.

sup'erchârger (sōō-, sū-) *n.* Device supplying internal combustion engine with air or explosive mixture at higher pressure than normal in order to increase its efficiency. **sup'erchârged** (-jd) *adj.*

supercĭl'ĭary (sōō-, sū-) *adj.* Of the eyebrow, over the eye.

supercĭl'ĭous (sōō-, sū-) *adj.* Haughtily contemptuous, disdainful, or superior. **supercĭl'ĭously** *adv.* **supercĭl'ĭousnėss** *n.*

superĕlėvā'tion (sōō-, sū-) *n.* Amount of elevation of outer above inner rail at curve on railway.

superĕrogā'tion (sōō-, sū-) *n.* Performance of more than duty or circumstances require; esp. (R.C. theol.) performance of good works beyond what God requires, which constitute a store of merit which the Church may dispense to make up others' deficiencies.

superfĭ'cial (sōō-, sū-; -shal) *adj.* Of, on, the surface; not going deep, without depth; (of measures) involving two dimensions, of extent of surface, square. **superfĭ'cially** *adv.* **superfĭcial'ĭty** (-shĭăl-) *n.*

superfĭ'cies (sōō-, sū-; -shĭēz) *n.* Surface.

sūp'erfīne *adj.* Extremely fine in quality, of the very best kind.

superflu'ĭty (sōō-, sū-; -lōō-) *n.* Superflous amount.

superfluous (sōōpêr'flŏŏ-; sū-) *adj.* More than enough, excessive, redundant; needless, uncalled-for. **supêr'fluously** *adv.* **supêr'fluousnėss** *n.*

superheat' (sōō-, sū-) *v.t.* Heat to very high temperature; esp. raise temperature of (steam) to increase its pressure.

superhĕt'erodȳne (sōō-, sū-) *adj.* & *n.* (abbrev. *superhet*). (Of) wireless reception or receiver in which, by means of a local oscillator, a beat-note is set up with the incoming signal and amplified at the resulting intermediate frequency.

superhūm′an (sōō-, sū-) *adj.* Beyond (normal) human capacity, strength, etc.; higher than (that of) man.

superimpōse′ (sōō-, sū-; -z) *v.t.* Impose or place, cause to follow, succeed, etc., *on* or on something else. **superimposi′tion** *n.*

superincŭm′bent (sōō-, sū-) *adj.* Lying or resting on something else.

superindūce′ (sōō-, sū-) *v.t.* Develop, bring in, introduce, induce, in addition.

superintĕnd′ (sōō-, sū-) *v.* Have or exercise charge or direction (of), oversee, supervise. **superintĕn′dence** *n.* **superintĕn′dent** *n.* Officer or official having control, oversight, or direction of business, institution, etc.; police officer above rank of inspector.

supēr′ior (sōō-, sū-) *adj.* 1. Upper, higher, situated above or farther up than something else; growing above another part or organ, that is higher than other(s) of the same kind; (of small letters, figures, etc.) printed or written above the line or near the top of other figures etc. 2. Higher in rank, dignity, degree, amount, quality, status, etc.; ~ *to*, above the influence or reach of, not affected or mastered by, higher in status or quality than. 3. Conscious, showing consciousness, of superior qualities; lofty, supercilious, dictatorial, etc. **supēr′iorly** *adv.* **supēriŏ′rity** *n.* **supēr′ior** *n.* 1. Person of higher rank, dignity, or authority, superior officer or official; person or thing of higher quality or value than another. 2. Head of religious community (freq. *Father*, *Mother*, etc., *S*~).

supêr′lative (sōō-, sū-) *adj.* Raised above or surpassing all others; of the highest degree; ~ *degree*, (gram.) inflexional form of adjective or adverb (or equivalent of this) expressing highest or very high degree of the quality or attributes denoted by the simple word. **supêr′latively** *adv.* **supêr′lative** *n.* Superlative degree or form; word in the superlative.

sup′ermăn (sōō-, sū-) *n.* Ideal superior man of the future, conceived by NIETZSCHE as evolved from normal human type; man of superhuman powers or achievement. [transl. Ger. *übermensch*]

sup′ermârket (sōō-, sū-) *n.* Self-service store selling food and household goods of all kinds.

supêrn′al (sōō-, sū-) *adj.* (poet., rhet.) Heavenly, divine; of the sky; lofty.

supernăt′ural (sōō-, sū-; -cher-) *adj.* Due to, manifesting, some agency above the forces of nature; outside the ordinary operation of cause and effect. **supernăt′urally** *adv.* **supernăt′uralnėss** *n.*

supernăt′uralism (sōō-, sū-) *n.* Belief in supernatural beings, powers, events, etc. **supernăt′uralist** *n.* **supernăturalis′tic** *adj.*

supernūm′erary (sōō-, sū-) *adj.* & *n.* (Person or thing) in excess of the normal number, esp. (extra person) not belonging to the regular body or staff but associated with it in some need or emergency; (theatr. and cinema) (actor) employed in addition to regular company, appearing on stage or in scene but not speaking.

superphŏs′phate (sōō-, sū-) *n.* Fertilizer made by treating phosphate-containing rock with sulphuric acid.

superpōse′ (sōō-, sū-; -z) *v.t.* Place above or on something else; bring into same position so as to coincide. **superposi′tion** *n.*

supersăt′ūrāte (sōō-, sū-) *v.t.* Add to (esp. solution) beyond saturation point.

sup′erscrībe (sōō-, sū-) *v.t.* Write upon, put inscription on or over; write (inscription) at top of or outside something. **superscrip′tion** *n.*

supersēde′ (sōō-, sū-) *v.* Set aside, cease to employ; adopt or appoint another person or thing in place of; take the place of, oust, supplant. **supersĕ′ssion** *n.*

sup′ersŏlid (sōō-, sū-) *n.* Solid of four or more dimensions.

supersŏn′ic (sōō-, sū-) *adj.* With a velocity greater than that of sound; (also, obs., of sound-waves) ULTRASONIC.

supersti′tion (sōō-, sū-) *n.* Irrational fear of unknown or mysterious, credulity regarding the supernatural; habit or belief based on such tendencies; irrational religious system, false or pagan religion. **supersti′tious** (-sh*us*) *adj.* **supersti′tiously** *adv.* **supersti′tiousnėss** *n.*

sup′erstrŭcture (sōō-, sū-) *n.* Building, upper part of building, any material or immaterial structure, resting upon something else or with some other part as a foundation; parts of warship or other vessel above main deck.

sup′ertăx (sōō-, sū-) *n.* Tax in addition to the normal tax; esp., tax levied on incomes above a certain amount in addition to ordinary income-tax (in Gt Britain replaced in 1929–30 by the *surtax*).

supertŏn′ic (sōō-, sū-) *n.* (mus.) Note next above tonic, 2nd note of ascending scale.

supervēne′ (sōō-, sū-) *v.i.* Occur as something additional or extraneous, follow closely upon some other occurrence or condition. **supervĕn′tion** *n.*

sup′ervīse (sōō-, sū-; -z; *or* -vīz′) *v.t.* Oversee, superintend execution or performance of (thing), movements or work of (person); **supervi′sion** (-zhn), **sup′ervīsor** *ns.* **supervīs′ory** *adj.*

sūp′ināte *v.t.* (physiol.) Turn (hand or fore-limb) so that back of it is downward or backward (opp. PRONATE). **sūpinā′tion** *n.*

sūp′īne[1] *adj.* 1. Lying face upward; supinated. 2. Disinclined for exertion, indolent, lethargic, inert. **sūp′inely** *adv.* **sūp′inenėss** (-n-n-) *n.*

sūp′īne[2] *n.* (gram.) Latin verbal noun with two cases, accus. sing. ending in *-tum*, *-sum*, used with verbs of motion to express purpose, and ablative sing. in *-tu*, *-su*, used with adjs.

sŭpp′er *n.* Meal taken at end of day, esp. evening meal less formal and substantial than dinner; evening meal when dinner is taken at midday. **sŭpp′erlėss** *adj.*

suppl. *abbrev.* Supplement.

supplant′ (-ah-) *v.t.* Dispossess and take the place of, oust, esp. by dishonourable or treacherous means.

sŭpp′le *adj.* Easily bent, pliant, flexible; (fig.) compliant, accommodating, artfully or servilely complaisant or submissive. **sŭpp′lenėss** *n.* **sŭpp′ly** *adv.*

sŭpp′lėment *n.* 1. Something added to supply a deficiency; part added to complete literary work etc., esp. special number or part of periodical dealing with particular item(s). 2. (math.) Amount by which arc is less than semicircle, or angle is less than 180°. **sŭpplėmĕnt′** *v.t.* Furnish supplement to. **sŭpplėmĕn′tal, sŭpplėmĕn′tary** *adjs.*

sŭpp′liant *n.* Humble petitioner. ~ *adj.* Supplicating; expressing supplication. **sŭpp′liantly** *adv.*

sŭpp′licāte *v.* Make humble petition to or *to* person, for or *for* thing. **sŭpplicā′tion** *n.* **sŭpp′licatory** *adj.*

supplī′er *n.* Person, firm, etc., that supplies.

supplȳ′[1] *v.t.* Furnish, provide (thing needed, or person, receptacle, etc. with or *with* thing needed); make up for (deficiency etc.). ~ *n.* Provision of what is needed; stock, store, quantity, of or *of* something provided or available; (pl.) food and other stores necessary for armed force; (pl. or collect. sing.) sum of money granted by legislature for cost of government; person, esp. minister or preacher, who supplies vacancy or acts as substitute for another; *Committee of S*~, House of Commons sitting to discuss estimates for public service; ~ *and demand*, (pol. econ.) chief factors determining price of commodities.

sŭpp′ly[2] *adv.*: see SUPPLE.

suppôrt′ *n.* Supporting, being supported; person or thing that supports. ~ *v.t.* 1. Carry (part of) weight of; hold up, keep from falling or sinking; keep from failing or giving way, give courage, confidence, or power of endurance to. 2. Endure, tolerate. 3. Supply with necessaries, provide for. 4.

Lend assistance or countenance to; back up, second, further; bear out, substantiate; second, speak in favour of (resolution etc.). **suppôrt'able** *adj.* **suppôrt'ably** *adv.*

suppôrt'er *n.* (esp., her.) One of pair of figures represented as holding up or standing one on each side of shield (ill. HERALDRY).

suppōse' (-z) *v.t.* 1. Assume as a hypothesis, as ~ *it were true*; in part. or imper. = if, as *supposing white were black you would be right*; also in imper. as formula of proposal, as ~ *we try again.* 2. (Of theory, result, etc.) involve or require as condition, as *design in creation supposes a creator.* 3. Assume in default of knowledge, be inclined to think, accept as probable. 4. *Be supposed,* have as a duty, as *he is supposed to clean the boots*; colloq., with neg., freq. = not be allowed, as *children are not supposed to go in.* **suppōsed'** (past. part.) *adj.* Believed to exist or to have specified character. **suppō'sėdly** *adv.* **suppō'sable** *adj.*

sŭpposĭ'tion (-z-) *n.* What is supposed or assumed. **sŭpposĭ'tional** (-zĭsho-) *adj.*

sŭppositious (-zĭsh'*us*) *adj.* Hypothetical, assumed.

sŭppositĭ'tious (-zĭtĭsh'*us*) *adj.* Substituted for the real; spurious, false. **sŭppositĭ'tiously** *adv.* **sŭppositĭ'tiousnėss** *n.*

suppŏs'ĭtory *n.* (med.) Cone or cylinder of medicated easily melted substance introduced into rectum, vagina, or urethra.

supprĕss' *v.t.* Put down, quell, put a stop to activity or existence of; withhold or withdraw from publication; keep secret or unexpressed, refrain from mentioning or showing. **supprĕ'ssion** (-shn) *n.*

supprĕss'iō vēr'ī *n.* Suppression of truth, misrepresentation by concealment of facts that ought to be made known.

sŭpp'ūrāte *v.i.* Form or secrete pus, fester. **sŭppūrā'tion** *n.* **sŭpp'ūrative** *adj.*

sūpra- *prefix.* Used with meanings of SUPER-, but more usual in scientific (esp. anat. and zool.) terms with sense: above, higher than; on, upon.

sūpraclavĭc'ūlar *adj.* Situated above the clavicle.

sūpralăpsār'ian *n.* (eccles. hist.) One of those Calvinists holding that predestination was antecedent to the creation and fall. ~ *adj.* Of the supralapsarians or their doctrine.

sūpra-ôrb'ĭtal *adj.* & *n.* (Artery, vein, bone, nerve) above the orbit of the eye.

sūprarēn'al *adj.* & *n.* (Gland) situated above the kidney, adrenal.

suprĕm'acy (sōō-, sū-) *n.* Being supreme, position of supreme authority or power; *Act of S~*, any Act of Parliament laying down position of sovereign as supreme head on earth of Church of England or supreme governor of England in spiritual and temporal matters, esp. that of 1534.

suprēme' (sōō-, sū-) *adj.* Highest in authority or rank; greatest, of the highest quality, degree, or amount; *S~ Court,* (esp.) highest judicial body in U.S. Government, consisting of 9 members appointed for life by President with Senate's approval. **suprēme'ly** *adv.*

Supt *abbrev.* Superintendent.

sûr'ah (*or* soor-) *n.* Soft twilled silk fabric used for scarves, linings, etc. [prob. f. *Surat,* town in Bombay State, India]

sûr'al *adj.* Of the calf of the leg.

surcease' (*ser-*) *n.* (archaic) Cessation, esp. temporary. ~ *v.i.* (archaic) Cease.

sûr'charge *n.* Additional or excessive pecuniary charge, or load or burden; extra charge on understamped letter etc.; additional mark printed on face of stamp, esp. to change its value. **surcharge'** (*ser-*) *v.t.* Charge (person) additional or excessive price or payment; exact (sum) as surcharge; overload, fill or saturate to excess; print surcharge on (postage-stamp).

sûr'cingle (-nggl) *n.* Band round horse's body, esp. to keep blanket, pack, etc., in place.

sûrc'oat *n.* (hist.) Rich outer garment, esp. (13th–14th centuries) loose coat worn over armour, with

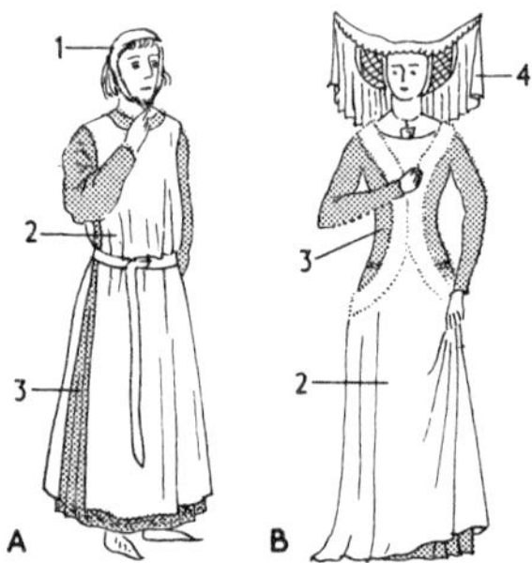

SURCOAT. A. 13TH-C. MALE. B. 15TH-C. FEMALE

1. Coif. 2. Surcoat. 3. Gown. 4. Veil

heraldic arms emblazoned on it (ill. ARMOUR).

sûrd *adj.* & *n.* 1. (math.) (Quantity, esp. root) that cannot be expressed in finite terms of ordinary numbers or quantities; irrational. 2. (phonet., now antiquated) (Sound) uttered without vibration of vocal cords; voiceless (speech sound).

sure (shoor) *adj.* 1. Certain, assured, confident, persuaded (*of*); having no doubt. 2. That may be relied on, trustworthy, unfailing, infallible; certainly true or truthful; safe; *~-footed,* treading securely or firmly. 3. Certain *to* do or be; ~ *of,* certain to get, keep, have, etc.; *make* ~, act so as to be certain *of.* **sure'nėss** *n.* **sure** *adv.* Assuredly, undoubtedly, certainly; *as* certainly *as.*

surely (shoor'lĭ) *adv.* 1. With certainty or safety (chiefly in *slowly but* ~). 2. Certainly, assuredly; (freq., expressing belief without absolute proof, or readiness to maintain a statement against possible denial) as may be confidently supposed, as must be the case.

sure'ty (shoor'tĭ) *n.* 1. Certainty (archaic; chiefly in *of a* ~, certainly); sureness (rare). 2. Formal engagement, pledge, guarantee, bond, security, for fulfilment of undertaking; person undertaking to be liable for default of another, or for his appearance in court, payment of debt, etc.

sûrf *n.* Swell and white foamy water of sea breaking on rock or (esp. shallow) shore; *~-board,* long narrow board for riding over heavy surf to shore; *~-duck, -scoter,* N. Amer. sea-duck (*Oidemia perspicillata*) with black plumage and white-marked head and neck; *~-riding,* sport of riding on surf-board.

sûrf'ace *n.* Outermost boundary of any material body, upper boundary on top of soil, water, etc.; superficial area; (fig.) outward aspect or appearance of anything immaterial, what is presented to casual view or consideration; (geom.) continuous extent with two dimensions only (length and breadth, without thickness); ~ *craft,* ship navigable on the surface of the sea (opp. *submarine*); *~-tension* (physics) tension of surface-film of liquid, due to attraction between its particles, which tends to bring it into form with smallest superficial area; *~-water,* water that collects on and runs off from surface of ground etc. ~ *v.* Put special surface on (paper etc.); raise (submarine etc.), (of submarine etc.) rise, to surface of water.

sûrf'eit (-fĭt) *n.* Excess, esp. in eating or drinking; oppression or satiety arising from excessive eating or drinking. ~ *v.* Overfeed; (cause to) take too much of something; cloy, satiate *with.*

surg. *abbrev.* Surgeon; surgery.

sûrge *v.i.* Rise and fall, toss, move to and fro (as) in waves or billows; (naut., of rope etc.) slip back or round with jerk. ~ *n.* Waves, a wave; surging motion.

sûr'geon (-jn) *n.* Medical practitioner treating wounds, fractures, deformities, and diseases by manual operation; person skilled in surgery; one who holds licence or diploma qualifying him to practise surgery; medical officer in army, navy, or military hospital; *~-fish,* fish of genus *Acanthurus* with sharp movable spine (like lancet) on each side of tail.

sŭr′gery *n.* 1. Manual treatment of injuries or disorders of body; correction of disorders etc. by manual or instrumental operations. 2. Room where medical practitioner, dentist, or veterinary surgeon sees patients for consultation or treatment.

sŭr′gical *adj.* Of surgeons or surgery. **sŭr′gically** *adv.*

sŭr′icāte *n.* Burrowing fourtoed mammal of S. Africa (*Suricata tetradactyla*), related to mongoose, and having grey blackstriped fur; meerkat.

Sūrĭnăm′. Dutch colony in northern S. America, Netherlands Guiana; capital, Paramaribo; ~ *toad*, large aquatic toad of Guiana and Brazil, the *pipa*.

sŭrl′y *adj.* Uncivil, churlishly ill-humoured, rude and cross. **sŭrl′ĭly** *adv.* **sŭrl′inėss** *n.*

surmise (sermīz′) *n.* Conjecture, idea formed without certainty and on slight evidence. ~ *v.* Infer doubtfully or conjecturally; conjecture, guess.

surmount (ser-) *v.t.* 1. Prevail over, overcome, get over (obstacle etc.). 2. Cap, be on the top of.

surmŭll′ėt (ser-) *n.* Red mullet.

sŭrn′āme *n.* Family name, name common to all members of family; (archaic) name or epithet added to person's name(s), esp. one derived from his birthplace or some quality or achievement. ~ *v.t.* Give surname to; give as surname.

surpass (serpahs′) *v.t.* Outdo, excel. **surpass′ing** *adj.* That greatly exceeds or excels others, of very high degree. **surpass′ingly** *adv.*

sŭrp′lice *n.* Loose full-sleeved white linen vestment worn, usu. over cassock, by clergy and choristers at divine service (ill. VESTMENT).

sŭrp′lus *n.* What remains over, excess; *attrib.* that is in excess of what is taken, used, or needed; ~ *value*, (econ.) difference between value of wages paid and labour expended or commodity produced. **sŭrp′lusage** *n.*

surprise (serprīz′) *n.* 1. Catching or taking of person(s) unprepared. 2. Emotion excited by the unexpected, astonishment. 3. Thing, event, that excites surprise. ~ *v.t.* 1. Assail, capture, by surprise; come upon unexpectedly, take unawares. 2. Affect with surprise, astonish; be a surprise to; lead unawares, betray, *into* doing something not intended. **surprīs′ing** *adj.* **surprīs′ingly** *adv.*

sŭrrē′alism *n.* A movement in art and literature, which originated in France (1924), purporting to express the subconscious activities of the mind by representing the phenomena of dreams and similar experiences; art, literature, produced in accordance with this theory. **sŭrrē′alist** *n.* & *adj.*

sŭrrėbŭt′ *v.i.* (In common-law pleading) reply by **sŭrrėbŭtt′er,** plaintiff's reply to defendant's rebutter. **sŭrrėbŭtt′al** *n.*

sŭrrėjoin′ *v.i.* Reply by **sŭrrėjoin′der,** plaintiff's answer to defendant's rejoinder.

surrĕn′der *v.* Yield up, give into another's power or control, relinquish possession of, esp. upon compulsion or demand; abandon claim under (insurance policy) in return for payment of consideration; abandon one*self*, give one*self* up *to* some influence, habit, emotion, etc.; (of army, fortress, etc.) yield to enemy or assailant; give oneself up, submit, cease from resistance; ~ *to* one's *bail*, appear in court at appointed time after being admitted to bail. ~ *n.* Surrendering, being surrendered; ~ *value*, amount to which insured is entitled if he surrenders insurance policy.

sŭrrėptĭ′tious (-shus) *adj.* Underhand, secret, clandestine, done by stealth. **sŭrrėptĭ′tiously** *adv.*

Sŭ′rrey[1]. County of SE. England.

sŭ′rrey[2] (-rĭ) *n.* (U.S.) Light 4-wheeled carriage with 2 seats facing forwards. [f. county of SURREY[1]]

sŭ′rrogate *n.* Deputy, esp. of bishop or his chancellor; in New York and other States of U.S., judge with jurisdiction over probate of wills and settlement of estates.

surround′ *v.t.* Come, lie, be, all round or on all sides; invest, enclose, encompass, environ, encircle. ~ *n.* Border or edging, as of linoleum, boards, round carpet.

surroun′dings *n.pl.* Things (collectively) surrounding person or thing, environs, environment.

sŭrs′um cŏrd′a. 'Lift up your hearts', versicle preceding Preface in Latin Mass; corresponding versicle in Anglican rite.

sŭrt′ăx *n.* & *v.t.* (Impose) additional tax (on); graduated tax on incomes above a certain level, in addition to ordinary incometax, since 1929–30 in Gt Britain replacing supertax.

Sŭrt′ees (-ēz), Robert Smith (1805–64). English author of humorous sporting novels, in some of which the principal character is a grocer named Jorrocks.

surveillance (servāl′ans, -l′yans) *n.* Supervision; close guard or watch, esp. over suspected person.

survey (servā′) *v.t.* Take general view of, let the eyes pass over, form general idea of arrangement and chief features of; examine condition of (building etc.); determine form, extent, etc., of (tract of ground etc.) by linear and angular measurements so as to settle boundaries or construct map, plan, or detailed description. **sŭrv′ey** *n.* General or comprehensive view of something; inspection, examination in detail, esp. for specific purpose; account given of result of this; department or persons engaged in, operations constituting, act of, surveying of land etc., map or plan setting forth results of such survey.

surveyor (servā′er) *n.* Official inspector *of* (weights and measures, highways, etc.); person professionally engaged in surveying. **survey′orship** *n.*

survīv′al (ser-) *n.* Surviving; person or thing remaining as relic of earlier time.

survīve′ (ser-) *v.* Outlive, continue to live or exist after death, cessation, or end of, or after the occurrence of (disaster, hardship, etc.); continue to live or exist, be still alive or existent. **survīv′or** *n.* **survīv′orship** *n.* (esp.) Right of person having some joint interest to take whole estate on death of other(s).

Susănn′a (sōōz-). In Apocryphal 'History of Susanna', the virtuous and beautiful wife of Joachim, accused of adultery by Jewish elders but proved innocent by Daniel.

suscĕp′tĭble *adj.* 1. (predic.) Admitting *of*; open, liable, accessible, sensitive, *to*. 2. Impressionable; sensitive; readily touched with emotion; touchy. **suscĕptĭbĭl′ĭty** *n* **suscĕp′tĭbly** *adv.*

suspĕct′ *v.t.* 1. Imagine something evil, wrong, or undesirable in, have suspicions or doubts about; imagine something, esp. something wrong, about. 2. Imagine to be possible or likely, have faint notion or inkling of; surmise. **sŭs′pĕct** *adj.* Regarded with suspicion or distrust; of suspected character. ~ *n.* Suspected person.

suspĕnd′ *v.t.* 1. Debar from exercise of function or enjoyment of privilege; deprive (temporarily) of office; put a (temporary) stop to, put in abeyance, annul for a time, abrogate temporarily; defer; refrain from forming (judgement, opinion); ~ *payment*, fail to meet financial engagements; become insolvent; *suspended animation*, state of temporary insensibility. 2. (mus.) Prolong (one note of chord) to following chord. 3. Hang up; hold, cause to be held, in suspension.

suspĕn′der *n.* (esp.) Device attached to top of sock or stocking to hold it up; (pl., chiefly U.S.) braces.

suspĕnse′ *n.* State of usu. anxious uncertainty, expectation, or waiting for information; doubtfulness, uncertainty; ~ *account*, (book-keeping) account in which items are temporarily entered until proper place is determined.

suspĕn′sion (-shn) *n.* Suspending, being suspended; condition of being diffused in form of particles through fluid medium;

(mus.) prolonging note of chord into following chord, discord so produced; ~ *bridge*, bridge in which roadway is suspended from ropes, chains, or wire cables extending between steel or masonry towers or other supports (ill. BRIDGE).

suspĕn'sory *adj.* That suspends or holds suspended or supported (esp. some part or organ). ~ *n.* Suspensory bandage.

sus. per coll. *abbrev. suspendatur per collum* (= let him be hanged by the neck), the entry recording that a person is to be hanged.

suspĭ'cion (-shon) *n.* Suspecting; feeling or state of mind of one who suspects; being suspected; slight belief or idea, faint notion, inkling; slight trace, very small amount *of*. ~ *v.t.* (chiefly U.S. and dial.) Suspect.

suspĭ'cious (-shus) *adj.* Prone to, feeling, indicating, open to, deserving of, exciting, suspicion. **suspĭ'ciously** *adv.* **suspĭ'ciousnėss** *n.*

suspīre' *v.i.* (now poet.) Sigh.

Sŭss'ėx. 1. Maritime county of SE. England. 2. English breed of domestic fowl with speckled or red plumage.

sustain' *v.t.* 1. Uphold or allow validity, rightfulness, truth, correctness, or justice of; be adequate as ground or basis for. 2. Keep from failing or giving way; keep in being, in a certain state or at the proper level or standard; keep up, keep going (sound, effort, etc.); keep up, represent (part, character) adequately. 3. Endure without failing or giving way; withstand; undergo, experience, suffer. 4. Hold up, bear weight of; be support of; bear, support (weight, pressure).

sŭs'tenance *n.* Livelihood; means of sustaining life, food.

sŭstentā'tion *n.* Support, upkeep, maintenance; support or maintenance of life; ~ *fund*, fund, esp. in Church of Scotland, to provide adequate support for ministers.

sūsŭrrā'tion *n.* Whispering, rustling.

Sŭth'erland (-dh-). County of N. Scotland.

sŭt'ler *n.* Camp-follower selling provisions etc. to soldiers.

Sut'ra (sōō-) *n.* Aphorism, set of aphorisms, in Sanskrit literature. [Sansk., = 'thread']

sŭttee' *n.* Hindu widow who immolates herself on husband's funeral pyre; such immolation. **sŭttee'ĭsm** *n.* [Sansk. *satī* virtuous wife]

sū'ture *n.* 1. (surg.) Joining of edges of wound etc. by stitch(es), stitch used for this. 2. (anat.) Seam-like line of junction of two bones, esp. of skull (ill. HEAD); (zool., bot.) line of junction of contiguous parts, as of valves in shell, plant's ovary, etc. **sū'tural** *adj.* **sū'ture** *v.t.* Stitch (wound).

sūz'erain *n.* Feudal overlord; sovereign or State having political control over another. **sūz'erainty** *n.*

s.v. *abbrev. sub voce* (= 'under that word').

svĕlte *adj.* Slim, slender, willowy.

SW., SW *abbrev.* South-west; South-western (London postal district); static water.

swab (-ŏb) *n.* Mop or other absorbent mass used for cleansing or mopping up; pad of cotton-wool or other absorbent material for applying medicament, cleaning wound, etc.; specimen of morbid secretion etc., taken with swab. ~ *v.t.* Clean or wipe (as) with swab, mop *up* (as) with swab.

Swāb'ia. Latinized form of *Schwaben*, former German duchy including Württemberg, Baden, and part of Bavaria. **Swāb'ĭan** *adj.* & *n.*

swadd'le (-ŏd-) *v.t.* Swathe in bandages, wrappings, etc.; bind (infant) in *swaddling-clothes*, narrow lengths of bandage wrapped round new-born infant to prevent free movement, infant's first garments (now chiefly fig.).

Swadeshi (swahdāsh'ĭ) *n.* (hist.) Movement in India, originating in Bengal, advocating the boycott of foreign, esp. British, goods. [Bengali, = 'native country']

swăg *n.* 1. Ornamental festoon of flowers, fruit, etc., fastened up

SWAG OR FESTOON

at both ends and hanging down in middle. 2. (slang) Thief's booty; dishonest gains. 3. (Austral.) Bundle of personal belongings carried by tramp, miner, or bush-traveller; *swag'man*, one travelling with a swag.

swāge *n.* Tool for bending cold metal, die or stamp for shaping

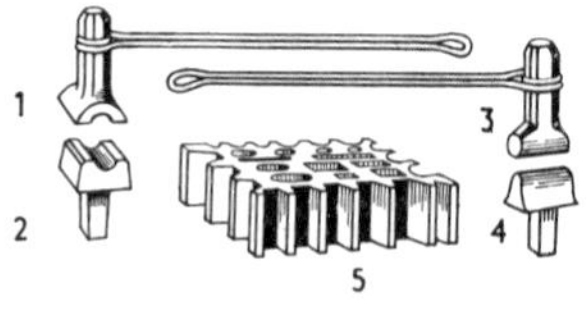

SWAGE AND FULLER

1. Top swage. 2. Bottom swage. 3. Top fuller. 4. Bottom fuller. 5. Swage-block

metal by striking with hammer or sledge; ~-*block*, smith's block of metal with perforations, grooves, etc., for this purpose. ~ *v.t.* Shape with swage.

swăgg'er (-g-) *v.i.* Walk, carry oneself, as if among inferiors, with superior, insolent, or blustering manner; talk boastfully or braggingly. ~ *n.* Swaggering gait or manner; ~-*cane*, -*stick*, short light cane carried by soldiers when walking out. ~ *adj.* (colloq.) Smart, fashionable.

Swahi'lĭ (-hē-). (One of) Bantu people of Zanzibar and adjacent coast; their language (also *Kiswahili*). [lit. 'of the coasts', f. Arab. *sawāḥil* pl. of *sāḥil* coast]

swain *n.* Countryman, young rustic, esp. shepherd (archaic); country gallant or lover; (joc.) suitor, lover.

swall'ow[1] (-ŏlō) *n.* Bird of genus *Hirundo* and related genera, esp. the migratory insect-eating *H. rustica*, with long pointed wings and forked tail, swift curving flight

SWALLOW

Length 7½ in.

and twittering cry, building mud-nests on buildings and associated (in N. Europe) with summer; (loosely) various other birds, esp. the unrelated swifts, resembling swallows in some respects; ~ *dive*, dive with head tilted backwards and arms spread sideways like swallow's wings; ~-*tail*, forked tail like swallow's; butterfly (*Papilio*, esp. *P. machaon*) in which border of each hind wing is prolonged into a tail-like process; cleft two-pointed end of flag or pennon, flag with this; swallow-tailed kite; (freq. pl.) swallow-tailed coat; ~-*tailed coat*, man's full-dress evening coat, with two long tapering tails; ~-*tailed kite*, white Amer. kite (*Elanoides furcatus*) with black wings and deeply forked tail.

swall'ow[2] (-ŏlō) *v.* Cause or allow (food etc.) to pass down one's throat; engulf, absorb, exhaust (usu. ~ *up*); accept (statement etc.) with ready credulity; put up with, stomach (affront); recant (words); keep down, repress (emotion). ~ *n.* 1. Gullet; act of swallowing; amount swallowed at once; capacity for swallowing. 2. ~(-*hole*), hole, esp. in limestone formations, through which stream disappears underground.

swa'mĭ (-wah-) *n.* Hindu religious teacher (esp. as form of address to Brahmin); Hindu idol; (U.S., colloq.) any person who wears a turban. [Sansk. *svāmin* master, prince]

swamp (-ŏ-) *n.* Piece of wet spongy ground, marsh; (esp., N. America) tract of rich soil with trees etc., too moist for cultivation; (*attrib.*, of many animals, birds, plants, etc.) growing, living, in swamps. **swamp'y** *adj.* **swamp** *v.* Submerge, inundate, soak, with water; (of boat) (cause to) fill with water and sink; overwhelm with numbers or quantity of anything.

swan[1] (-ŏ-) *n.* Large web-footed swimming bird usu. of genus *Cygnus*, with long gracefully curved neck, esp. the domestic, mute, or tame swan, *C. olor*, with pure white plumage in adult, black legs and feet and red bill with black knob, occurring wild in NE. Europe and W. Central Asia, and semi-domesticated all over Europe and America, formerly supposed to sing melodiously just before its death; (fig.) singer, poet (see *S~ of* AVON); (astron.) the northern constellation Cygnus; *~ dive*, (U.S.) swallow dive; *~-goose*, the largest goose (*Cygnopsis cygnoides*) of E. Asia; *~ knight*, Lohengrin or other legendary hero brought by swan to succour country; *~-neck*, something of curved cylindrical form more or less like swan's neck; *swans'down*, down or fine soft feathers of swan used for powder-puffs, trimmings, etc.; soft thick woollen cloth, thick cotton fabric with soft nap; *swan'skin*, thick soft kind of flannel or other fabric; *~-song*, legendary song of dying swan; last (esp. artistic) production of person etc.; *~-upping*, annual expedition on Thames for marking swans on beak as property of Crown or some City corporation. **swan'like** *adj.*

swan[2] (-ŏ-) *v.i.* (slang) Cruise, roam (esp. *around*).

swănk *n.* (slang) Ostentatious or pretentious behaviour, talk, etc., swagger, boastfulness, showing off. *~ v.i.* Show off, bounce, swagger. **swănk'y** *adj.*

swann'ery (-ŏ-) *n.* Place where swans are kept and reared.

swap (-ŏ-), **swŏp** *ns.* & *vbs.* (slang) Exchange by way of barter.

Swaraj' (-ahj) *n.* (hist.) Self-government of India, as the aim of Indian Nationalists. **Swaraj'ist** *n.* [Sansk., = 'self-ruling']

sward (-ôrd) *n.* (Stretch of) turf or greensward.

swarm[1] (-ôrm) *n.* Cluster of bees leaving hive or main body with queen bee to establish new hive; large or dense body, throng, multitude of persons, insects, or other small creatures, esp. flying or moving about. *~ v.i.* Move in a swarm; (of bees) gather in compact cluster round queen and leave hive in a body; congregate in number, be very numerous; (of places) be overrun or crowded.

swarm[2] (-ôrm) *v.* Climb *up* (rope, pole, tree) by clasping it with arms and legs alternately; climb up or *up* (any steep ascent) by clinging with hands and knees.

swart (-ôrt) *adj.* (archaic) Dark-hued, swarthy.

swar'thy (-ôrdhĭ) *adj.* Dark-complexioned, dark in colour. **swar'thily** *adv.* **swar'thiness** *n.*

swash[1] (-ŏsh) *v.* (Of water etc.) wash about, make sound of washing or rising and falling; (archaic) strike violently; *swash'buckler*, swaggering bravo or ruffian, bully.

swash[2] (-ŏ-) *adj.* (turning etc.) Inclined obliquely to axis of work; (printing, of italic capitals) having flourished strokes at top and bottom, as *T*, *N*; *~-plate*, rotating circular plate set at an oblique angle to its shaft, giving reciprocating motion to rod resting on it and parallel to its shaft.

swas'tika (-ŏs-, -ăs-) *n.* Primitive and ancient symbol or talisman in form of cross with equal arms, each arm having a limb of same length projecting from its end at right angles, all in same direction (usu. direction of sun's course, i.e. clockwise) (ill. CROSS); found in various parts of the world, esp. Mexico, Peru, and Tibet; used as emblem by the NAZI party and régime. [Sansk., f. *svasti* well-being]

swat (-ŏt) *v.t.* Hit hard, crush (fly etc.) with blow.

swath (-awth) *n.* (pl. pr. -dhs). Row or line of grass, corn, etc., as it falls when mown or reaped; space covered by mower's scythe, width of grass or corn so cut.

swāthe (-dh) *v.t.* Wrap up or round, envelop, like bandage or (as) with wrapping.

sway *v.* 1. Lean unsteadily to one side or in different directions by turns; have unsteady swinging motion; oscillate irregularly; waver, vacillate; give swaying motion to. 2. Govern the motion of; wield, control direction of; have influence over; govern, rule over. 3. *swayed*, *sway-back(ed)*, with back abnormally hollowed (esp. of horse). *~ n.* 1. Swaying motion or position. 2. Rule, government.

Swa'zilănd (swah-). Former British S. African Protectorate, between Mozambique, Transvaal, and Natal; independent kingdom since 1968; member of British Commonwealth; capital, Mbabane.

SW. by S., SW by S, SW. by W., SW by W *abbrevs.* South-west by South, by West.

swear (swār) *v.* (past t. *swōre*, past part. *sworn*). 1. State something, state (thing) on oath, take oath; promise or undertake something by oath; promise to observe or perform (something); take (oath); confirm by oath; affirm emphatically or confidently; *~ by*, (colloq.) profess or have great belief in; *~ off*, forswear. 2. Utter profane oath, use profane language, to express anger or as expletive(s); *~-word*, profane oath or word. 3. Cause to take oath, administer oath to; *~ (in)*, admit to office or function by administering oath.

sweat (-ĕt) *n.* 1. Salty fluid secreted by glands beneath the skin and exuded through the pores (i.e. mouths of ducts), perspiration; something resembling sweat, drops of moisture on a surface; condition or fit of sweating; (colloq.) state of impatience or anxiety; *~-band*, band of leather etc. as lining of hat or cap; *~-gland*, minute coiled tubular gland beneath skin secreting sweat; *~-shirt*, kind of sweater worn by athletes before or after exercise. 2. (chiefly colloq.) Drudgery, toil, laborious task; *old ~*, old soldier; *~-shop*, workroom in which workers are sweated (see below). **sweat'y** *adj.* **sweat'ily** *adv.* **sweat'iness** *n.* **sweat** *v.* 1. Exude sweat, perspire; emit or exude, ooze *out*, as or like sweat; cause (horse, athlete, etc.) to sweat by exercise etc.; exude or gather moisture in drops on surface; cause to exude moisture, force moisture out of; *sweating-pit*, (tanning) pit in which hides are sweated; *sweating-room*, room in Turkish bath etc. where persons are sweated; room in which cheeses are sweated or deprived of superfluous moisture; *sweating-sickness*, febrile disease, freq. rapidly fatal, with profuse sweating, epidemic in England in 15th and 16th centuries. 2. Work hard, toil, drudge; employ (workers) at starvation wages for long hours, exploit to the utmost; (of workers) work on such terms.

sweat'er (-ĕt-) *n.* (esp.) 1. Woollen jersey, esp. one worn during or after exercise. 2. Sweating employer.

Swēde[1] Native of Sweden.

swēde[2] *n.* Large variety of turnip with yellow edible root, first introduced into Scotland from Sweden in 18th c.

Swē'den. Kingdom of E. Scandinavia; capital, Stockholm.

Swē'denbôrg, Emanuel (1688–1772). Swedish religious mystic and philosopher; acc. to his theosophic system God, as Divine Man, is infinite love and infinite wisdom, and the end of creation is the approximation of man to God; he taught that there is a symbolic sense to the Scriptures, of which he was the appointed interpreter. **Swēdenbôr'gian** (-j-) *adj.* & *n.* (Follower) of Swedenborg, (member) of the New Jerusalem Church. **Swēdenbôr'gianism** *n.*

Swē'dish *adj.* & *n.* (Indo-European language, one of the Norse group) of Sweden; *~ drill*, system of muscular exercises as a form of hygienic or curative treatment; *~ nightingale*, Jenny Lind (1810–87), a famous Swedish singer; *~ turnip* = SWEDE[2].

sweep *v.* (past t. and past part.

swĕpt). 1. Glide swiftly, speed along with impetuous unchecked motion, go majestically; extend in continuous curve, line, or slope; *sweeping*, of wide range, regardless of limitations or exceptions. 2. Impart sweeping motion to; carry *along*, *down*, *away*, *off*, in impetuous course; clear *off*, *away*, *from*, etc. 3. Traverse or range swiftly, pass lightly across or along; pass eyes or hand quickly along or over; scan, scour, graze; (of artillery etc.) include in line of fire, cover, enfilade, rake. 4. Clear everything from; clear of dust, soot, litter, with broom; gather *up*, collect, (as) with broom; ~ *the board*, win all money on gaming-table; win all possible prizes etc. 5. ~*-net*, large fishing-net enclosing wide space; *sweep'stake(s)*, (prize won in) race or contest in which all competitors' stakes are taken by winner(s); form of gambling on horse-races etc. in which sum of participators' stakes goes to drawer(s) of winning or placed horse(s) etc. ~ *n.* 1. Sweeping, clearing up or away (now usu. *a clean* ~); moving in continuous curve (of an army, fleet, river, etc.); hostile reconnaissance by group of aircraft; sweeping motion or extension, curve in road, etc.; curved carriage drive leading to house. 2. Range or compass of something that has curving motion; extent, stretch, expanse, esp. such as can be taken in at one survey. 3. Long oar worked by rower(s) standing on barge etc.; long pole mounted as lever for raising bucket from well; gear for clearing submarine mines, usu. consisting of a long wire with a cutting device attached, streamed from a vessel (*mine-sweeper*) at the required depth. 4. Chimney-sweep; (slang) low fellow, blackguard. 5. (colloq.) Sweepstake.

sweet *adj.* 1. Tasting like sugar, honey, etc., corresponding to one of the primary sensations of taste; (of wine) opp. to DRY. 2. Pleasing to the sense of smell, fragrant, perfumed. 3. Fresh and sound, not salt(ed) or sour or bitter or putrid. 4. Agreeable, attractive, gratifying; inspiring affection, dear, amiable, gentle, easy; (colloq.) pretty, charming, delightful; ~ *(up)on*, (colloq.) very fond of, (inclined to be) in love with. 5. ~*-bay*, the bay laurel (*Laurus nobilis*); a N. Amer. magnolia (*Magnolia virginiana*); *sweet'bread*, pancreas or thymus gland of animal, esp. calf, used for food; ~*-brier*, eglantine (*Rosa rubiginosa*, and other species), with small hooked prickles, single flowers, and small aromatic leaves; ~ *chestnut*, the Spanish or edible chestnut; ~ *corn*, sweet-flavoured variety of maize or Indian corn; *sweet'heart*, darling; either of pair of lovers; ~ *herbs*, fragrant culinary herbs; ~ *marjoram*, aromatic cultivated herb (*Origanum marjorana*); *sweet'meat*, bonbon, sweet (see SWEET *n.* 1); ~ *(spirits of) nitre*, spirit of nitrous ether, a pale yellow sweet-tasting aromatic liquid used as diuretic, diaphoretic, etc.; ~ *oil*, any pleasant- or mild-tasting oil, esp. olive oil, rape oil; ~ *pea*, climbing leguminous annual (*Lathyrus odoratus*) cultivated for its many-coloured, sweet-scented flowers; ~ *potato*, (large sweet farinaceous tuberous root, eaten as vegetable, of) tropical climbing-plant (*Ipomoea batatas*) widely cultivated in warm regions; ~*-scented*, having a sweet scent (freq. in names of plants, flowers, etc.); ~*-shop*, sweetmeat shop; *sweet'sop*, (sweet pulpy fruit with thick green rind and black seeds of) tropical Amer. evergreen tree (*Annona squamosa*); ~*-spoken*, speaking pleasantly or sweetly; ~ *tooth*, a taste for sweet things; ~ *violet*, the common cultivated violet (*Viola odorata*); ~*-william*, cultivated species of pink (*Dianthus barbatus*), with closely clustered sweet-smelling freq. particoloured flowers. **sweet'ly** *adv.* **sweet'ness** *n.* **sweet** *n.* 1. Shaped morsel of sugar or chocolate confectionery; fruit preserved in sugar, bonbon, sugared nut, etc. 2. (freq. pl.) Sweet dish(es) such as puddings, tarts, jellies, forming a course at table. 3. Sweet part (chiefly fig.); (usu. pl.) fragrance; (pl.) delights, pleasures, gratifications; (chiefly in voc.) darling. **sweet'en** *v.* **sweet'ening** *n.*

sweet'ie *n.* (chiefly Sc.) Sweetmeat, bonbon; (U.S.) sweetheart.

sweet'ing *n.* Kind of sweet apple.

swĕll *v.* (past part. *swōll'en* or less usu. *swĕlled*). (Cause to) grow bigger or louder, dilate, expand; rise, raise, *up* from surrounding surface; bulge *out*; increase in volume, force, or intensity; (of emotion) arise and grow in mind with sense as of expansion; (of person, his heart, etc.) be affected with such emotion; *swelled head*, (colloq.) conceit; ~ *note* in music, sing it or play it with alternate *crescendo* and *diminuendo*. ~ *n.* 1. Being swollen; swollen part, protuberance, bulge. 2. Heaving of sea etc., with long rolling waves that do not break, as after storm; such waves collectively. 3. Gradual increase in loudness or force of sound; (mus.) *crescendo* followed by *diminuendo*, symbol denoting this (< >); mechanism in organ, harmonium, etc., for gradually varying force of tone, now usu. series of slats that can be opened or shut by means of pedal or lever worked by knee; ~*-box*, box, containing set of pipes or reeds, which is opened or closed by swell (ill. ORGAN); ~ *organ*, set of pipes enclosed in swell-box. 4. (colloq.) Fashionable or stylish person; person of distinction or ability; member of good society; ~ *mob(smen)*, well-dressed pick-pockets or swindlers. ~ *adj.* (colloq.) Distinguished, first-rate; stylishly dressed or equipped; of good social position.

swĕll'ing *n.* (esp.) Distension of injured or diseased part of body.

swĕl'ter *v.i.* Be oppressed or oppressive with heat; sweat profusely, languish, be faint, with excessive heat.

swerve *v.* Turn aside, (cause to) deviate from straight or direct course; (cricket etc.) cause (ball) to swerve in the air. ~ *n.* Swerving motion; divergence from course.

S.W.G., s.w.g. *abbrev.* Standard Wire Gauge.

swift[1] *adj.* Fleet, rapid, quick; soon coming or passing, not long delayed; prompt, quick *to* do. ~ *adv.* Swiftly (chiefly in combination, as ~*-footed*). **swift'ly** *adv.* **swift'ness** *n.* **swift** *n.* Various swift-flying insectivorous birds of the numerous and widely distributed family *Cypselidae* superficially resembling swallows, esp. *Apus apus*, the common swift, a summer visitant in Europe.

SWIFT

Length 6½ in.

Swift[2], Jonathan (1667–1745). Irish clergyman, Dean of St. Patrick's, Dublin; author of 'A Tale of a Tub', 'Gulliver's Travels' and other satires and political works.

swĭg *v.* (slang) Take draughts (of). ~ *n.* (Act of taking) a draught of liquor.

swill *v.* Wash or rinse (*out*), pour water over or through, flush; drink greedily. ~ *n.* 1. Liquid or partly liquid food, chiefly kitchen refuse, given to swine; pig-wash; inferior liquor. 2. Rinsing, swilling.

swim *v.* (past t. *swăm*, past part. *swŭm*). 1. Float on or at surface of liquid. 2. Progress at or below surface of water by working legs, arms, tail, webbed feet, fins, etc.; traverse (distance etc.) thus; compete in (race) thus; cause (horse, dog, etc.) to progress thus; (fig.) go with gliding motion. 3. Appear to undulate, reel, or whirl, have dizzy effect or sensation; be flooded or overflow with or *with* or *in* moisture. 4. ~*-bladder*, air-bladder of many fish (ill. FISH); *swimming-bath*, *-pool*, bath, pool, for swimming in; *swimming-bell*, bell-shaped swimming organ of jelly-fish etc. (ill. JELLY-fish). ~ *n.*

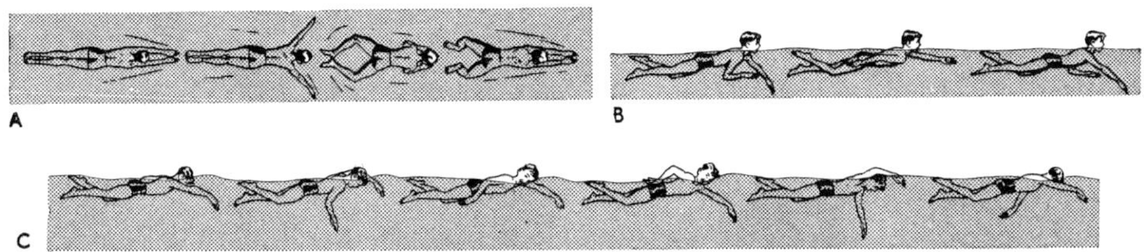

SWIMMING STROKES. A. BREAST-STROKE. B. DOG PADDLE. C. CRAWL

Spell of swimming; (fig.) main current of affairs (*in*, *out of*, *the* ~); ~*-suit*, bathing costume.

swĭmm′erĕt *n.* Abdominal appendage in some crustaceans (ill. LOBSTER).

swĭmm′ĭngly *adv.* (esp.) With easy and unobstructed progress.

Swĭn′burne, Algernon Charles (1837–1907). English poet, author of 'Songs before Sunrise', 'Atalanta in Calydon', etc.

swĭn′dle *v.* Cheat (person, *money out of* person, person *out of* money). **swĭn′dler** *n.* **swĭn′dle** *n.* Piece of swindling, fraudulent scheme, imposition; something represented as what it is not, fraud.

swīne *n.* (pl. same). Animal of family *Suidae* of non-ruminant hoofed mammals, with stout body, thick skin, longish snout with terminal nostrils, and small tail; pig; esp. the common species *Sus scrofa*, domesticated for its flesh and regarded as type of greediness and uncleanness; person of greedy or bestial habits (used esp. as strong term of abuse); ~*-fever*, infectious disease of swine caused by virus and chiefly affecting intestines, hog cholera; *swine′herd*, one who tends swine; ~*-plague*, infectious bacterial disease of swine resembling swine-fever but chiefly affecting lungs. **swīn′ĭsh** *adj.* **swīn′ĭshly** *adv.* **swīn′ĭshnĕss** *n.*

swĭng *v.* (past t. and past part. *swŭng*). 1. Move with the to-and-fro or curving motion of object having fixed point(s) or side but otherwise free; sway or so hang as to be free to sway like pendulum, door, etc.; oscillate, revolve, rock, wheel; ~ *the lead*, (slang) malinger, scrimshank. 2. Go with swinging gait; *swinging*, (of gait, melody, etc.) vigorously rhythmical. 3. (colloq.) Give (jazz music) character of 'swing'. ~ *n.* 1. Swinging, oscillation, swinging movement; swinging gait or rhythm; movement describing curve, as of arm or hand delivering blow etc.; ~ *of the pendulum*, (fig.) tendency to alternation. 2. Seat slung by ropes or chains for swinging in; swing-boat; spell of swinging in this. 3. (colloq.) Swing music. 4. ~*-back*, hinged or pivoted back of photographic camera, allowing plate to be kept vertical when camera is tilted etc.; ~*-boat*, boat-shaped swing at fairs etc.; ~ *bridge*, kind of bridge that can be swung aside on pivot(s) to let ships etc. pass (ill. BRIDGE). ~*-door*, *-gate*, door (esp. in two leaves hung separately and sprung), gate, that swings in either direction and closes of itself when released; ~ *glass*, looking-glass hung on pivots; ~ *music*, kind of jazz in which the time of the melody (usu. played by single instrument) is freely varied over simple harmonic accompaniment in strict time with strongly marked rhythm.

swĭnge (-j) *v.t.* Strike hard, beat (chiefly archaic); *swingeing*, huge, thumping.

swĭng′le (-nggl) *n.* Wooden sword-like instrument for beating flax and removing woody parts from it; striking or swinging part of flail; ~*-tree*, cross-bar pivoted in middle, to ends of which traces are fastened in cart, plough, etc. (ill. HARNESS). ~ *v.t.* Clean (flax) with swingle.

swĭnk *n.* & *v.i.* (archaic) Toil.

swīpe *v.* 1. Hit at or hit cricket-ball etc., hit (cricket-ball etc.) hard and recklessly, slog; (slang) steal by snatching. ~ *n.* 1. Reckless hard hit or attempt to hit. 2. (pl.) Washy or turbid or otherwise inferior beer.

swĭrl *n.* Eddy, whirlpool; eddying or whirling motion; twist, convolution, curl. ~ *v.* Eddy, carry (object), be carried, with eddying or whirling motion.

swĭsh[1] *n.* Sound of switch or similar object moved rapidly through air, of scythe cutting grass, or object moving rapidly through water. ~ *v.* Make, move with, swish; flog with birch or cane.

swĭsh[2] *adj.* (colloq.) Very smart.

Swĭss[1] *adj.* & *n.* (Native) of Switzerland; ~ *guards*, Swiss mercenary troops employed as bodyguards formerly by sovereigns of France etc. and still at Vatican; ~ *roll*, thin flat sponge cake spread with jam etc. and rolled up.

swĭss[2] *n.* (chiefly U.S.) Fine cotton fabric of plain weave freq. with dots or flecks formed by extra yarns (*dotted* ~).

swĭtch *n.* 1. Slender tapering whip; thin flexible shoot cut from tree, something resembling this. 2. Various devices for making and breaking contact or altering connexions in electric circuit; (on railway etc.) movable rail or pair of rails pivoted at one end at junction of tracks, used to deflect train etc. from one line to another. 3. Tress of dead or false hair, tied at one end, used in hairdressing. 4. ~*-back* (*railway*), form of railway used on steep slopes, with zigzag series of lines connected at ends by switches; railway used for amusement at fairs etc. with series of steep alternate ascents and descents, the momentum of each descent carrying the car or train (partly) up the following ascent; road with alternate ascents and descents; *switch′board*, board or frame with set of switches for varying connexion between a number of electric circuits, as of telephone, telegraph, etc.; *switch′man*, man who works switch(es), esp. on railway. ~ *v.* 1. Strike, whip, (as) with switch; flourish like a switch, whisk, lash, move with sudden jerk. 2. Turn (train etc.) on to another line by means of switch; turn (electric current, light, etc.) *on*, *off*, by means of switch, change (connexion) *over* with switch; (fig.) turn off, divert; (cards) change suit in bidding or leading; *switch-over*, diversion of effort, activity, or production.

swĭth′er (-dh-) *v.i.* (chiefly Sc.) Hesitate, be uncertain.

Swĭth′ĭn (-dh-), St. (d. 862). Bishop of Winchester, commemorated 15th July; acc. to legend, if it rains on this day there will be rain for the next 40 days.

Swĭt′zerland. Federal republic of central Europe, consisting of 22 cantons inhabited by German-, French-, Italian-, and Romansh-speaking people; an independent State since it broke away from the Holy Roman Empire in 1499; capital, Berne.

swĭv′el *n.* Simple joining or coupling device made so that object fastened can turn freely upon it, or so that each half of the swivel itself can turn independently; ring or staple turning on pin, or the like; ~ *bearing*, *chain*, *coupling*, *gun*, etc., one provided with or mounted on swivel; ~ *chair*, chair with seat turning horizontally on pivot; ~*-eye*(*d*), (with) squinting eye. ~ *v.* Turn (as) on swivel.

swĭzz′le *n.* 1. Various compounded drinks, esp. one of rum or other spirit and bitters; ~*-stick*, stick used to stir drink into a froth or to make gas escape from champagne. 2. (school slang) Disappointment, 'sell'.

swōll'en past part. of SWELL.

swōōn *n.* & *v.i.* (Have) fainting fit.

swōōp *v.* Come down or *down* with the rush of a bird of prey (often upon prey etc.); attack from a distance; (colloq.) snatch, seize, the whole of. ~ *n.* Act of swooping, esp. sudden pounce of bird of prey; *at one (fell)* ~, at a single blow or stroke.

swop: see SWAP.

sword (sōrd) *n.* Offensive weapon for cutting or thrusting, consisting of long straight or curved blade with handle or hilt and cross-guard, sharp point, and usu. one or two sharp edges; *draw, sheathe, the* ~, begin, cease from, war; *fire and* ~, destruction spread by invading army; *put to the* ~, kill, esp. after victory; ~*-arm*, right arm; ~*-bayonet*, bayonet that can be used as short sword; ~*-bearer*, person carrying sword for another, esp. municipal officer bearing sword before magistrate on ceremonial occasions; ~*-dance*, dance, esp. folk-dance, in which performers go through evolutions with swords, or one which is danced over naked swords laid on ground; ~*-fish*, large sea-fish used for food (*Xiphias gladius*), with upper jaw prolonged into sword-like point; ~*-grass*, various grasses with sharp-edged leaves; various plants with sword-shaped leaves, as the gladiolus; ~*-lily*, gladiolus; ~*-play*, fencing; ~*-stick*, hollow walking-stick containing a sword-blade; *swords'man*, one skilled in use of sword; *swords'manship*. **sword'līke** *adj.*

swōrn *adj.* Past part. of SWEAR; (esp.) bound by an oath; ~ *brother*, close friend; ~ *enemy, foe*, determined or irreconcilable enemy.

swŏt *n.* (school slang) Hard work or study; person who works hard, esp. at learning. ~ *v.* Work hard, esp. at books; study (subject) *up* hurriedly.

S.Y. *abbrev.* Steam yacht.

sўb'arīte *adj.* & *n.* 1. (*S*~) Inhabitant of ancient-Greek colony of Sybaris in S. Italy noted for luxury. 2. Luxurious and effeminate (person). **sўbarĭt'ĭc** *adj.*

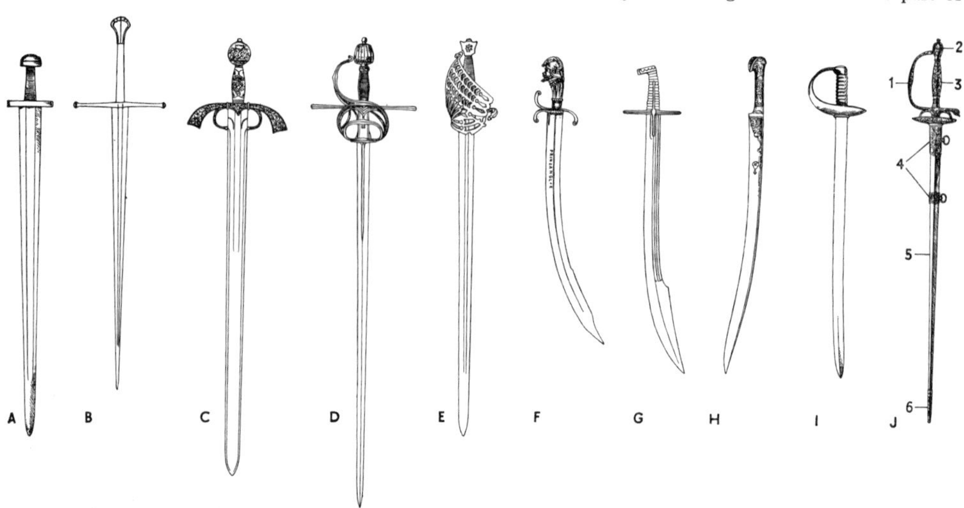

A. VIKING SWORD, 11TH C. B. HAND-AND-A-HALF SWORD, EARLY 15TH C. C. TWO-EDGED SWORD, *c* 1525. D. RAPIER, *c* 1620. E. VENETIAN BROADSWORD, *c* 1650. F. FALCHION, *c* 1600–20. G. HUNGARIAN SABRE, *c* 1650. H. TURKISH YATAGHAN, 19TH C. I. NAVAL CUTLASS, *c* 1790. J. SMALL-SWORD, *c* 1790

1, 2, 3. Hilt (1. Knuckle-bow, 2. Pommel, 3. Grip). 4. Lockets. 5. Scabbard. 6. Chape

sўc'amōre *n.* 1. Large Eurasian species of maple (*Acer pseudoplatanus*) grown as shady ornamental tree and for its wood. 2. (N. Amer.) Plane-tree (*Platanus*), esp. *P. occidentalis*, the 'buttonwood'. [f. SYCOMORE]

sȳce *n.* (Anglo-Ind.) Groom. [Hind., f. Arab. *sā'is*]

sўc'omōre *n.* Species of fig (*Ficus sycomorus*) common in Egypt and Syria. [Gk *sukon* fig, *moron* mulberry]

sўc'ophant *n.* Flatterer, toady, parasitic person. **sўc'ophancy** *n.* **sўcophăn'tĭc** *adj.* [Gk *sukophantes* informer, f. *sukon* fig, *phainō* show (reason for name unknown)]

sȳcōs'ĭs *n.* Skin-disease, esp. of bearded part of face, with inflammation of hair-follicles.

Sўd'ney. Seaport and capital of New South Wales, Australia.

sȳ'ènīte *n.* Crystalline rock allied to granite, mainly composed of felspar and hornblende. [L *Syenites* (*lapis*) (stone) of Syene, f. Gk *Suēnē* (mod. Aswan), town of Upper Egypt]

sўll'abary *n.* Collection, system, or table of syllables, esp. of written characters each representing a syllable.

sўllăb'ĭc *adj.* Of syllable(s); (of written symbols) denoting a syllable; consisting of such symbols; (pros.) based on number of syllables. **sўllăb'ĭcally** *adv.*

sўllăb'ĭcāte, sўllăb'ĭfȳ *vbs.t.* Divide into syllables. **sўllăbĭcā'tion, sўllăbĭfĭc'ātion** *ns.*

sўll'able *n.* Vocal sound(s), forming a whole word or part of a word, the utterance of which produces upon the hearer the impression of an uninterrupted unit, the essential condition of which is that the sonority shall be gradually reduced or gradually increased during the utterance, but not reduced and then increased; the least mention, hint, or trace (*of*). ~ *v.t.* Pronounce by syllables; articulate distinctly; (poet.) utter, speak.

syllabub: see SILLABUB.

sўll'abus *n.* (pl. *-bī, -buses*). 1. Concise statement of heads of discourse, contents of treatise, subjects of lectures, course of study, etc. 2. (R.C. Ch.) Summary statement of points decided, esp. catalogue of 80 heretical doctrines, practices, or institutions of rationalists, socialists, etc., appended to encyclical *Quanta cura* of Pope Pius IX (1864), or of 65 heretical propositions of Modernists issued by Pope Pius X (1907).

[mod. L, based on misreading in Ciceronian MS. of *sittybas* f. Gk *sittuba* parchment label or title-slip on book]

sўllĕp′sĭs *n.* (pl. *-sēs*). (gram.) Figure by which word is made to apply to two or more other words in same sentence while properly applying to or agreeing with only one of them (e.g. *neither you nor he knows*), or applying to them in different senses (e.g. *in a flood of tears and a sedan-chair*). **sўllĕp′tĭc** *adj.* **sўllĕp′tĭcally** *adv.*

sўll′ogĭsm *n.* Form of reasoning in which conclusion is deduced from two propositions called premisses (major and minor) containing a common or middle term which is absent from the conclusion; e.g. (major premiss) *All men are mortal*; (minor premiss) *Socrates is a man: therefore* (conclusion) *Socrates is mortal*; deductive as opp. to inductive reasoning. **sўllogĭs′tĭc** *adj.* **sўllogĭs′tĭcally** *adv.*

sўll′ogīze *v.* Use syllogisms; throw (facts, arguments) into syllogistic form.

sўlph *n.* In system of Paracelsus, mortal but soulless elemental spirit of the air; slender graceful woman; any of several S. Amer. humming-birds with long, brightly coloured tail. **sўlph′līke** *adj.* Slender and graceful.

sўl′van, sĭl′van *adjs.* Of wood(s); consisting of, abounding in, furnished with, woods or trees.

Sўl′vėster, St. A 4th-c. bishop of Rome, commemorated 31st Dec.

sym- *prefix.* With, together, alike.

sўmbīōs′ĭs *n.* (pl. *-sēs*). (biol.) Association of two different organisms living attached to one another or one as tenant of the other (used only of associations advantageous to both organisms, as dist. from PARASITISM; cf. ANTIBIOSIS). **sўmbīŏt′ĭc** *adj.* **sўmbīŏt′ĭcally** *adv.*

sўm′bol *n.* Thing standing for or representing something else, esp. material thing taken to represent immaterial or abstract thing, as an idea or quality; written character conventionally standing for some object, process, etc. **sўmbŏl′ĭc(al)** *adjs.* **sўmbŏl′ĭcally** *adv.*

sўm′bolĭsm *n.* System, use, meaning, of symbols; doctrine of the Symbolists. **sўm′bolĭst** *n.* & *adj.* One who uses symbols; (*S*~) (member) of a school of French poets etc. (*c* 1880–*c* 1900) who aimed at arousing emotions etc. by sounds and rhythms rather than direct expression and attached symbolic meaning to particular objects, words, etc.

sўm′bolīze *v.t.* Be symbol of; represent by symbol; treat as symbolic or emblematic.

sўmm′ėtry *n.* 1. (Beauty resulting from) right proportion between the parts of the body or any whole, balance, congruity, harmony. 2. Such structure as allows of an object's being divided by a point or line or plane or radiating lines or planes into two or more parts exactly similar in size and shape and in position relatively to the dividing point etc.; repetition of exactly similar parts in contrary or equally divergent directions; *axial* ~, symmetry about an axis; *bilateral* ~, about a plane; *radial* ~, about a point. 3. Approximation to such structure; possession by a whole of corresponding parts correspondingly placed. **sўmmĕt′rĭcal** *adj.*

sўm′pathīze *v.i.* Feel or express sympathy (*with*); suffer with or like another.

sўm′pathy *n.* Affinity or relation between things by virtue of which they are similarly or correspondingly affected by the same influence, or affect or influence each other; tendency to share, state of sharing, emotion, sensation, or condition of another person or thing; mental participation in another's trouble, compassion, commiseration; disposition to agree (*with*) or approve, favourable attitude of mind towards person, cause etc.

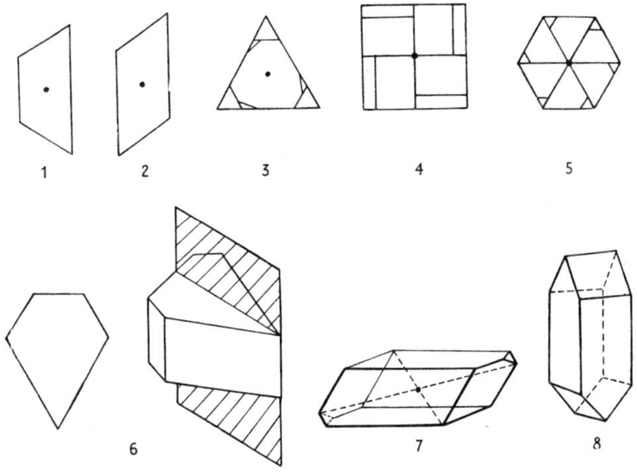

SYMMETRY IN CRYSTALS

1–5. Axes of symmetry. Each figure is brought into coincidence with itself by rotation round the axis perpendicular to the paper, through an angle of (1) 360°, (2) 180°, (3) 120°, (4) 90°, (5) 60°. 6. Plane of symmetry. This divides the figure into two parts which are mirror images of each other in that plane. 7. Centre of symmetry. A line drawn from the edge, corner, or plane through the centre, and produced an equal distance beyond it, reaches a corresponding part. 8. Inversion axis. The figure is brought into coincidence with itself on rotation through 90° round a vertical axis, accompanied by an inversion of every part through a centre of symmetry

sўmmĕt′rĭcally *adv.* **sўmm′ėtrīze** *v.t.*

sўmpathĕt′ĭc *adj.* 1. Of sympathy; full of, expressing, due to, effecting sympathy; (in literary criticism) capable of evoking sympathy, appealing *to* reader; ~ *strike*, strike of workers not to remedy their own grievances but to support other strikers. 2. (Of disorder, pain, etc.) induced in organ or part of body by a similar or corresponding one in another. 3. Of the ~ *nervous system*, one of the two divisions of the AUTONOMIC nervous system of vertebrates, consisting principally of a pair of ganglionated nerve trunks placed alongside the vertebral column and connected with nerve fibres which extend to the blood-vessels, viscera, sweat and salivary glands, and pupils. 4. ~ *ink*, liquid composition, writing with which remains invisible until colour is developed by heat or chemical reagent. **sўmpathĕt′ĭcally** *adv.*

sўmpĕt′alous *adj.* (bot.) Having petals united.

sўm′phony *n.* 1. Musical composition written in form of SONATA but for full orchestra and usu. comprising four movements; also (archaic) various other kinds of instrumental music occurring in vocal composition as introduction, overture, or conclusion; ~ *orchestra*, large orchestra including strings, wood wind, brass, and percussion instruments, playing chiefly symphonies or other works of serious artistic quality. 2. (archaic) Harmony of (esp. musical) sound, concord, consonance. **sўmphŏn′ĭc** *adj.* ~ *poem*, orchestral work, usu. of descriptive or rhapsodic character, freq. resembling first movement of symphony or sonata. **sўmphŏn′ĭcally** *adv.* **sўm′phonĭst** *n.*

sўm′phўsĭs *n.* (pl. *-sēs*). (anat., zool.) (Line of) union of two bones etc. originally separate, esp. union of two similar bones on opposite sides of body in median line, as of pubic bones or two halves of lower jaw-bone (ill. PELVIS). **sy̆mphy̆s'ĭal** *adj.*

sy̆mpōd'ĭum *n.* (pl. *-dia*). (bot.) Apparent main axis or stem made up of successive secondary axes, as in vine.

sy̆mpos'ĭum (-ōz- *or* -ŏz-) *n.* (pl. *-sia*). 1. Ancient-Greek drinking party, convivial meeting for drinking, conversation, and intellectual entertainment; account of such meeting and conversation at it (esp. as title of one of Plato's dialogues). 2. Meeting or conference for discussion of some subject; collection of opinions delivered or articles contributed by number of persons on special topic. **sy̆mpōs'ĭal** *adj.*

sy̆mp'tom *n.* Perceptible change in the body or its functions indicating presence of disease or injury, (*subjective* ~, one directly perceptible to the patient only, *objective* ~, to others); evidence or token of the existence of something. **sy̆mptomăt'ĭc** *adj.* **sy̆mptomăt'ĭcally** *adv.*

sy̆mp'tomatīze *v.t.* Be a symptom of.

sy̆n- *prefix.* With, together, alike.

sy̆naer'ėsis (-nēr- *or* -nĕr-) *n.* (pl. *-sēs*). (gram.) Contraction, esp. of two vowels into diphthong or single vowel.

sy̆naesthēs'ĭa (-z-) *n.* Sensation in one part of body produced by stimulus in another part; production of mental sense-impression of one kind by stimulus of a different sense. **sy̆naesthĕt'ĭc** *adj.*

sy̆n'agŏgue (-g) *n.* Regular assembly of Jews for religious instruction and worship, since the destruction of the Temple their sole form of public worship; building where this is held. **sy̆n'agōgal, sy̆nagŏ'gĭcal** (-gĭ-, -jĭ-) *adjs.*

sy̆năpse' *n.* (anat.). Locus where a nervous impulse passes from the axon of one neuron to the dendrites of another (ill. NERVE).

sy̆năp'sis *n.* (pl. *-sēs*). 1. (biol.) Fusion of pairs of chromosomes, the first process in meiotic division of germ-cells. 2. (anat.) = SYNAPSE. **sy̆năp'tĭc** *adj.*

sy̆nar̄thrōs'is *n.* (anat.) Articulation in which bones are immovably fixed, as in sutures of skull and sockets of teeth.

sy̆n'car̄p *n.* (bot.) Compound fruit, one arising from number of carpels in one flower (ill. FRUIT). **sy̆ncar̄p'ous** *adj.*

sy̆nchondrō'sis (-k-) *n.* (pl. *-sēs*). Nearly immovable articulation of two bones by layer of cartilage, as in spinal vertebrae.

sy̆nch'romĕsh (-k-) *n.* (Attrib., designating) a kind of automatic gear-changing box for motor-cars. [abbrev. f. *synchronized mesh*]

sy̆nch'ronīze (-ngk-) *v.* Occur at the same time, be contemporary or simultaneous (*with*); keep time (*with*); cause to go at same rate; add dialogue or other sound as synchronous accompaniment to (motion picture). **sy̆nchronīzā'tion** *n.*

sy̆nch'ronous (-ngk-) *adj.* Existing or happening at same time, contemporary, simultaneous, (*with*); keeping time, proceeding at same pace (*with*), having coincident periods. **sy̆nch'ronously** *adv.*

sy̆nch'rotron (-ngk-) *n.* An adaptation of the cyclotron designed for high acceleration of particles (electrons etc.) combined with a low-frequency magnetic field.

sy̆nclăs'tĭc *adj.* (Of curved surface) having same kind of curvature in all directions.

sy̆n'clīne *n.* (geol.) Rock-bed which forms a trough (opp. to ANTICLINE; ill. ROCK). **sy̆n'clīnal** *adj.*

sy̆n'copāte *v.t.* 1. (gram.) Shorten (word) by omitting syllable(s) or letter(s) in the middle. 2. (mus.) Affect, modify, by syncopation. **sy̆ncopā'tion** *n.* (esp., mus.) Displacement of accent, or beat, by beginning note on normally unaccented part of bar (and freq. prolonging it into normally accented part), putting strong accent on normally weakly accented part of bar etc.

sy̆nc'opė *n.* 1. (path.) Fainting, sudden temporary loss of consciousness due to cerebral anaemia associated with a severe disturbance of the circulation. 2. (gram.) Shortening of word by dropping of syllable(s) or letters in the middle. **sy̆nc'opal, sy̆ncŏp'ĭc** *adjs.*

sy̆n'crėtism *n.* (Attempted) reconciliation of diverse or opposite tenets or practices, esp. in philosophy or religion. **sy̆ncrĕt'ĭc, sy̆ncrėtĭs'tĭc** *adjs.* **sy̆n'crėtīze** *v.*

sy̆ndăct'y̆l *adj.* & *n.* (Animal) having (some of) fingers or toes wholly or partly united, as kangaroos, web-footed birds, etc.

sy̆n'dėsis *n.* (pl. *-sēs*). = SYNAPSIS.

sy̆n'dĭc *n.* Officer of government, with different powers in different countries, esp. each of four chief magistrates of Geneva; person representing and transacting affairs of a corporation; esp., in University of Cambridge, member of special committee of senate.

sy̆n'dĭcalĭsm *n.* Movement, orig. and esp. in France, for transfer of control and ownership of means of production and distribution to workers' unions. **sy̆n'dĭcalĭst** *adj.* & *n.* [Fr. *syndicalisme*, f. *syndicat* trade union]

sy̆n'dĭcate *n.* Body of syndics; combination of financiers etc. for promotion of financial or commercial undertaking; (journalism) combination of persons for syndicating articles etc. in newspapers.

sy̆n'dĭcāte *v.t.* Form into syndicate; publish simultaneously in a number of periodicals. **sy̆ndĭcā'tion** *n.*

sy̆n'drōme (*or* -omĭ) *n.* Concurrence of several symptoms in a disease, set of concurrent symptoms characterizing it.

sy̆nĕc'doche (-kĭ) *n.* (gram., rhet.). Figure of speech in which, when a part is named, the whole it belongs to is understood (e.g. *50 sail* for *50 ships*).

sy̆nergĕt'ĭc, sy̆nêr'gĭc *adjs.* Working together (of muscles which co-operate to produce some movement).

Synge (sĭng), John Millington (1871–1909). Irish playwright, author of 'Riders to the Sea', 'The Playboy of the Western World', etc.

sy̆n'od *n.* Assembly of clergy of church, diocese, nation, etc., for discussing and deciding ecclesiastical affairs; in Presbyterian churches, assembly of ministers and other elders constituting ecclesiastical court next above presbytery; any convention or council. **sy̆n'odal, sy̆nŏd'ĭcal** *adjs.* **sy̆nŏd'ĭcally** *adv.*

sy̆noe'cious (-ēsh*us*) *adj.* (bot.) Having male and female flowers in same flower-head, as many composites, or male and female organs in same receptacle, as some mosses (ill. FLOWER).

sy̆n'ony̆m *n.* Word having same meaning as another in same language; another name (*for*). **sy̆nŏn'y̆mous** *adj.* **sy̆nŏn'y̆mously** *adv.*

sy̆nony̆m'ĭc *adj.* Of or using synonyms.

sy̆nŏn'y̆my *n.* Being synonymous; use of synonyms, esp. for amplification or emphasis; subject or study of, a collection of, synonyms.

sy̆nŏp'sis *n.* (pl. *-sēs*). Summary, conspectus, brief or condensed statement of something.

sy̆nŏp'tĭc *adj.* Of, forming, furnishing, a synopsis; taking, affording, comprehensive mental view; ~ *gospels*, those of Matthew, Mark, and Luke, as giving an account of events under same general aspect or from same point of view. **sy̆nŏp'tĭcal** *adj.* **sy̆nŏp'tĭcally** *adv.* **sy̆nŏp'tĭst** *n.* Writer of a synoptic gospel.

sy̆nōv'ĭa *n.* (physiol.) Viscous fluid which is secreted by the inner lining membrane of the cavities of joints and the sheaths of tendons and lubricates them. **sy̆nōv'ĭal** *adj.* Of, containing, secreting, synovia; ~ *fluid*, synovia; ~ *membrane*, dense membrane of connective tissue secreting synovia (ill. BONE).

sy̆novīt'ĭs *n.* Inflammation of synovial membrane, freq. with swelling of joint.

sy̆n'tăx *n.* (gram.) Arrangement of words in sentence showing their connexion and relation; department of grammar dealing with usages of grammatical construction. **sy̆ntăc'tĭc** *adj.*

sy̆n'thėsis *n.* (pl. *-sēs*). Putting

together of parts or elements to make up a complex whole; (chem.) formation of a compound by combination of its elements or simpler compounds, esp. artificial production of organic compounds occurring naturally. **sȳn'thėsīze, sȳn'thėtīze** (rare) *vbs.t.*

sȳnthĕt'ĭc *adj.* Produced by synthesis, artificial. **sȳnthĕt'ĭcally** *adv.*

sȳph'ĭlĭs *n.* Venereal disease due to the micro-organism *Treponema pallidum*, usu. communicated by direct contact with an infected person, affecting first some local part (*primary* ~), secondly skin and mucous membrane (*secondary* ~), and thirdly bones, muscles, and brain (*tertiary* ~); *congenital* ~, condition in which the unborn child is infected through the maternal blood-stream. **sȳphĭlĭt'ĭc** *adj.* Of, affected with, syphilis. ~ *n.* Syphilitic person. [f. *Syphilus*, character in Latin poem on the subject (1530) by Girolano Fracastoro, Veronese physician]

sȳphĭlōm'a *n.* Syphilitic tumour.

Sȳr'acūse (-z). City in Sicily, scene of a battle (413 B.C.) in the Peloponnesian War, in which the Athenians under Demosthenes and Nicias were defeated in their attempt to take the city and their fleet was destroyed. **Sȳracūs'an** (-z-) *adj.* & *n.* (Native) of Syracuse.

Sȳ'rĭa. Ancient country at E. end of Mediterranean, covering modern Syria and Palestine; now, together with Lebanon, an independent republic lying to the N. of Palestine; until 1918 part of the Ottoman Empire and from 1918 to 1941 a French mandate; capital, Damascus. **Sȳ'rĭăc** *adj.* & *n.* (Of, in) the language of ancient Syria, a branch of Aramaic. **Sȳ'rĭacĭsm** *n.* **Sȳ'rĭan** *adj.* (Native) of Syria.

sȳrĭng'a (-ngga) *n.* Shrub of genus *Philadelphus*, esp. the mock-orange (*P. coronarius*) with creamy-white sweet-scented flowers. [Gk *surigx* pipe, w. ref. to use of stems cleared of pith as pipe-stems]

sȳ'rĭnge (-j) *n.* Cylindrical tube with nozzle and piston or rubber bulb for drawing in quantity of

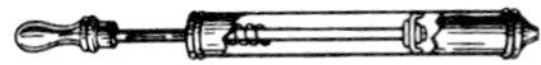

DIAGRAM OF GARDEN SYRINGE

liquid and ejecting it in stream or jet, for making injections, cleansing wounds, spraying plants, etc. ~ *v.t.* Sluice, spray, with syringe.

sȳ'rĭnx *n.* (pl. *-es* or *-ngēs*). 1. Pan-pipe. 2. (pl., archaeol.) Narrow channels or tunnels cut in rock in ancient-Egyptian tombs. 3. (anat.) Eustachian tube from throat to ear; (zool.), song-organ of birds, consisting of trachea and bronchi (ill. BIRD). **sȳrĭn'gėal** (-j-) *adj.*

Sȳr'o- *prefix.* Syrian, as in ~*-Arabian, -Phoenician.*

sȳ'rup *n.* Water (nearly) saturated with sugar, this combined with flavouring as beverage or with drug(s) as medicine; condensed sugar-cane juice, part of this remaining uncrystallized at various stages of refining, molasses, treacle; *golden* ~, trade-name for pale kind; *maple* ~, syrup obtained by evaporating maple sap or dissolving maple sugar. **sȳ'rupy** *adj.*

sȳstăl'tĭc *adj.* Contracting, esp. (physiol.) with alternate contraction (*systole*) and dilatation (*diastole*).

sȳs'tėm *n.* 1. Complex whole, set of connected things or parts, organized body of material or immaterial things; (physics) group of bodies moving about one another in space under some dynamic law, as that of gravitation, esp. (astron.) group of heavenly bodies moving in orbits about central body; (biol.) set of organs or parts in animal body of same or similar structure or subserving same function, *the* animal body as an organized whole. 2. Department of knowledge or belief considered as organized whole; comprehensive body of doctrines, beliefs, theories, practices, etc., forming particular philosophy, religion, form of government, etc.; scheme or method of classification, notation, etc.; (cryst.) any of 6 general methods or types in which substances crystallize. 3. Orderly arrangement or method.

sȳstėmăt'ĭc *adj.* Methodical; arranged, conducted, according to system or organized plan; of system(s). **sȳstėmăt'ĭcally** *adv.* **sȳstėmăt'ĭcs** *n.* Scientific study of classification of the plant and animal kingdoms, taxonomy. **sȳs'tėmatīze** *v.t.*

sȳstĕm'ĭc *adj.* (physiol.) Of, supplying, affecting, the system or body as a whole, or a particular system of bodily organs. **sȳstĕm'ĭcally** *adv.*

sȳs'tolė *n.* Contraction of heart, alternating with DIASTOLE. **sȳstŏl'ĭc** *adj.*

sȳz'ȳgȳ *n.* 1. (astron.) Point at which the heavenly bodies are in conjunction or opposition, esp. the moon with the sun. 2. (math.) Group of rational integral functions so related that if they are severally multiplied by other rational integral functions, the sum of the products vanishes identically.

T

T, t. 20th letter of modern English and 19th of ancient Roman alphabet, derived in form from Greek T (*tau*), from the Phoenician and ancient Semitic + ✗ X X, and representing a voiceless dental (or in English, rather alveolar) stop; in some combinations, as *-tion, -tial*, it has the sound usu. represented in English spelling by *sh*, and in southern English the sound represented by (*t*)*ch* in *-ture, -tual, -tue*, etc. The sounds represented by *th* are voiced and voiceless dental spirants, simple sounds for which the Roman alphabet has no single symbols. 1. The letter *t* or its sound; *cross the t's*, be minutely accurate; emphasize and particularize points in argument etc.; *to a T*, exactly, to a nicety. 2. (Object having) shape of the capital letter; (attrib.) shaped like the letter T; *T square*, T-shaped instrument for obtaining or testing right angles and parallel lines (ill. SQUARE).

t. *abbrev.* Taken (betting); ton(s).

T. *abbrev.* Tenor; Turkish (pounds).

ta (tah) *int.* (nursery, colloq.) Thank you.

T.A. *abbrev.* Territorial Army.

taal (tahl) *n.* Cape Dutch, Afrikaans. [Du., = 'language']

tăb *n.* Short broad strap, flat loop, strip, tag, attached by one end to object, or forming projecting tongue, by which thing can be taken hold of, hung up, fastened, identified, etc.; coloured tab, esp. red gorget patch worn by staff officer; (U.S. colloq.) account, check (esp. *keep* (*a*) *tab*(*s*) *on*).

tăb'ard *n.* (hist.) Short surcoat open at sides and with short sleeves worn by knight over armour and emblazoned with armorial bearings (ill. ARMOUR); short-sleeved or sleeveless jerkin emblazoned with royal arms forming official dress of herald or pursuivant.

tăb'arėt *n.* Upholstery fabric with alternate satin and watered-silk stripes.

Tabăs'cō *n.* Pungent pepper

made from fruit of *Capsicum annuum*; sauce made with this. [trade name]

tăbb'y *n.* 1. (often attrib.) Plain weave (ill. WEAVE); plain-woven fabric, as watered taffeta. 2. ~ (*cat*), brownish, tawny, or grey cat with darker stripes; (esp. female) cat; old maid, elderly gossiping woman. 3. Very hard concrete of mixture in equal proportions of lime and shells, gravel, or stones. ~ *v.t.* Water (fabric) by calendering; mark with dark stripes or streaks. [*'attābiy*, quarter of Baghdad where the fabric was woven]

tăb'ėfȳ *v.i.* (rare) Waste away, become emaciated. **tăbėfăc'tion** *n.*

tăb'erdar *n.* Scholar on foundation of Queen's College, Oxford. [*taberd* tabard, from the gown formerly worn]

tăb'ernăcle *n.* 1. Temporary or slightly built dwelling, hut, booth, tent; *Feast of Tabernacles*, Jewish festival, held in October, commemorating Israelites' sojourn in tents in the wilderness. 2. (Jewish hist.) Curtained tent containing Ark of the Covenant, which served as portable sanctuary of Jews during their wanderings in the wilderness. 3. Place of worship other than a church, esp. temporary structures used during rebuilding of churches after Fire of London; (freq. contempt.) nonconformist, esp. Baptist or Methodist, place of worship. 4. (eccles.) Canopied niche or recess in wall or pillar (ill. NICHE); ornamental receptacle for pyx or eucharistic elements. 5. Socket, step, or hinged post for a mast that has to be lowered frequently, for passing under bridges, etc. 6. ~ *roof*, roof sloping at ends as well as sides to central ridge shorter than sidewalls; ~-*work*, ornamental carved work or tracery over niches, stalls, pulpits, etc. **tăbernăc'ūlar** *adj.* **tăb'ernăcle** *v.* Provide with shelter or tabernacle; dwell temporarily.

tā'bēs (-z) *n.* (path.) Slow progressive emaciation; ~ *dorsāl'is*, locomotor ataxia.

tabĕt'ic *adj.* Of, affected with, tabes, esp. locomotor ataxia. ~ *n.* Tabetic patient.

tăb'inėt *n.* Watered poplin-like fabric of silk and wool made chiefly in Ireland.

tăb'lature *n.* 1. (mus.) Old form of musical notation indicating string, fret, hole, etc., to be touched or stopped with fingers. 2. (fig., archaic) Mental picture.

tā'ble *n.* 1. Article of furniture consisting of flat top of wood or other solid material supported on legs or central pillar, esp. one on which meals are laid out, articles of use or ornament kept, work done, or games played; each half of folding backgammon board; provision or supply of food for meals, fare; company of persons at a table; *at* ~, at a meal or meals; *lay, lie, on the* ~, (in Parliament etc.) postpone (measure, report), be postponed, indefinitely; *turn the* ~*s*, reverse relation between two persons or parties, cause a complete reversal of state of affairs. 2. Flat, usu. rectangular, horizontal or vertical surface in architecture etc.; flat part of machine tool on which work is put to be operated on; flat upper surface of table-cut diamond etc.; large flat plate or sheet of crown-glass; crystal of flattened or short prismatic form; flat elevated tract of land, plateau, flat mountain-top. 3. Slab of wood, stone, etc.; matter written on this; ~*s of the law* (*covenant*), the Ten Commandments, the stones on which they were written; *the Twelve* ~*s*, laws drawn up by decemviri in Rome, 451 and 450 B.C., embodying most important rules of Roman law. 4. Tabulated statement or arrangement; arrangement of numbers, words, etc., esp. in columns and lines occupying single sheet, so as to exhibit set of facts or relations distinctly and comprehensively for study, reference, or calculation; *T*~ *of Kindred and Affinity*, a list of the degrees of relationship by blood and by marriage within which marriage may not take place acc. to Church law; also, *T*~ *of Affinity, of Prohibited* or *Forbidden Degrees*. 5. ~-*cloth*, cloth spread on table for meals or at other times; ~-*cut*, (of diamond or other gem) cut with large flat upper surface surrounded by small facets (ill. GEM); ~ *diamond*, table-cut diamond; ~-*knife*, knife used at table, esp. of the size or shape used in cutting meat small; ~-*land*, extensive elevated region with level surface, plateau; ~-*linen*, table-cloths, napkins, etc.; ~-*rapping*, -*turning*, production of raps or knocking sounds on table, moving or turning a table, without apparent or apparently adequate physical means, as spiritualistic phenomena; ~-*spoon*, spoon, larger

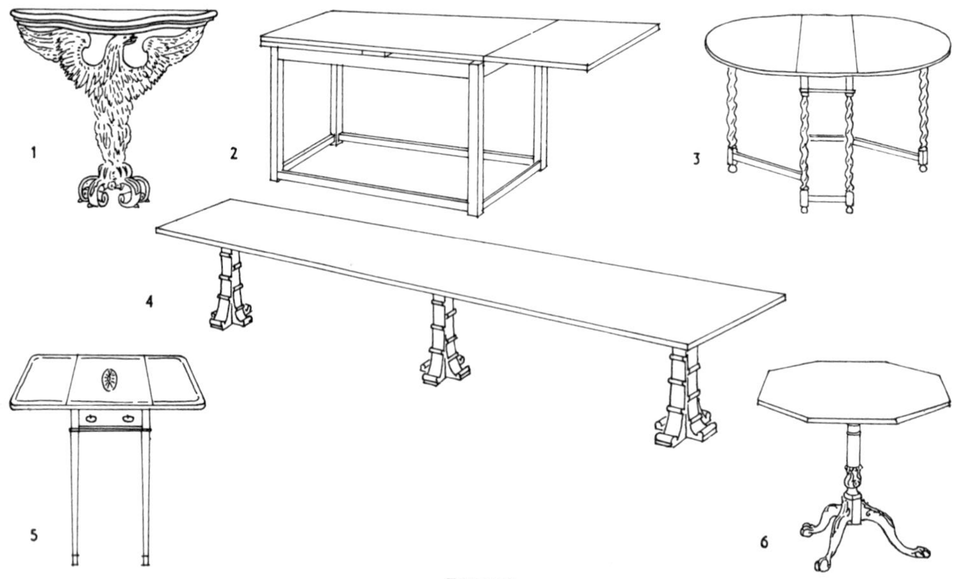

TABLES

1. Console-table. 2. Draw-table. 3. Gate-leg table. 4. Trestle table. 5. Pembroke table. 6. Tripod table

than dessert-spoon, used at table for taking soup, serving vegetables, etc.; ~-*talk*, informal conversation at table; ~ *tennis*, ping-pong, game resembling lawn tennis, played on table with net stretched across it. ~ *v.t.* Lay (measure, report, etc.) on table, esp. as way of postponing indefinitely; bring forward for discussion or consideration; join (timbers) together with projection in each fitting into groove in next; strengthen (sail) with wide hem.

tăb′leau (-lō) *n.* Presentation, esp. of group of persons etc., producing picturesque effect; striking or dramatic effect suddenly produced; ~ *curtains*, (theatr.) pair of curtains to draw across and meet in middle of stage; ~ *vivant* vēvahṅ), representation of painting, statue, scene, etc., by silent and motionless person or group. [Fr., = 'picture']

Tā′ble Bay. Harbour of Cape Town, S. Africa. **Tā′ble Mountain.** Flat-topped mountain on shore of Table Bay, with Cape Town at its foot.

table d'hôte (tahbl-dōt) *n.* Common table for guests at hotel etc.; public meal served at stated hour(s) and fixed price; ~ (*dinner, lunch*), dinner or lunch (of several courses) served at fixed price for whole, whatever may be actually consumed. [Fr., = 'host's table']

tăb′lėt *n.* Small thin flat piece of ivory, wood, etc., for writing on, esp. each of set fastened together; pad of sheets of notepaper fastened together at top; small slab, esp. with or for inscription; small flat or compressed piece of solid confection, drug, etc., flattened lozenge; flat cake of soap.

tăb′lier (-ā) *n.* (hist.) Apron-like part of woman's dress.

tăb′ling *n.* (esp.) Broad hem at edge of sail to strengthen it.

tăb′loid *n.* Trade-mark of certain small concentrated tablets of chemical substances used in medicine and pharmacy; anything in compressed or concentrated form; newspaper (usu. of sensational kind) giving news in concentrated and easily assimilable form.

taboo′, tabu′ (-ōō) *adj.* Set apart as sacred or prohibited. ~ *n.* Ban, prohibition. ~ *v.t.* Put under taboo. [Polynesian wd]

tā′bor *n.* (hist.) Small drum used to accompany pipe or fife.

tăb′o(u)rėt *n.* Low seat or stool, without back or arms, for one person; embroidery frame. [Fr., = 'small tabor']

tabu: see TABOO.

tăb′ūla *n.* (anat.) Hard, flat surface of bone etc.; ~ *rasa*, erased tablet; (fig.) human mind at birth viewed as having no innate ideas; complete obliteration, a blank. [L, = 'table']

tăb′ūlar *adj.* 1. Of, arranged in, computed, etc., by means of, tables. 2. Broad, flat, and (usu.) comparatively thin, like a table; formed of, tending to split into, pieces of this form; (of crystal etc.) of short prismatic form with flat base and top. **tăb′ūlarly** *adv.*

tăb′ūlāte *v.t.* Arrange, summarize, exhibit, in form of a table, scheme, or synopsis. **tăbūlā′tion** *n.* **tăb′ūlate** (-*at*) *adj.* Having flat surface, tabular.

tăb′ūlātor *n.* (esp.) Typewriter attachment for tabulating figures.

tăc′-au-tăc′ (-o-) *n.* (fencing) Parry followed immediately by riposte; rapid succession of attacks and parries.

tā′cĕt. In musical score, direction for voice or instrument to remain silent. [L, = 'is silent']

tăch(e)[1] (-sh) *n.* (bibl.) A clasp, link. [see TACK[1]]

tăche[2] (-sh) *n.* (sugar-boiling) Each of series of pans, esp. the last and smallest, in which sugar is evaporated.

tăcheŏm′ėter, tăchȳm′ėter (-k-) *n.* Surveying instrument for measuring distance by optical means. **tăcheŏm′ėtry** *n.*

tachŏm′ėter (-k-) *n.* Any instrument for measuring the velocity of machines or the rate of flow of liquids. **tachŏm′ėtry** *n.*

tăchycar̃d′ĭa (-kĭ-) *n.* (path.) Abnormally rapid action of heart.

tachȳg′raphy (-k-) *n.* Stenography, (esp. ancient Greek or Roman) shorthand; form of Greek or Latin written in Middle Ages with many abbreviations and compendia. **tăchygrăph′ic** *adj.*

tachȳm′ėter: see TACHEOMETER.

tă′cit *adj.* Implied, understood, inferred, but not openly expressed or stated; saying nothing, silent. **tă′citly** *adv.*

tă′citûrn *adj.* Reserved in speech, saying little, uncommunicative. **tăcitûrn′ity** *n.*

Tă′citus, Publius (?) Cornelius (*c* A.D. 55–117). Roman historian, son-in-law of Agricola; author of 'Agricola' (containing an account of Britain), 'Germania', 'Histories', and 'Annals'.

tăck[1] *n.* 1. Small sharp nail, usu. with large flat head, for fastening thin or light object to more solid one (ill. NAIL). 2. Fastening together, esp. in slight or temporary way; long slight stitch used in fastening together seams etc. before permanent sewing. 3. Rope used for securing lower corner of some sails; lower windward corner of sail, to which tack is attached (ill. SAIL[1]). 4. Tacking; ship's course in relation to direction of wind and position of sails; course obliquely opposed to direction of wind, one of consecutive series of such courses with wind alternately on port and starboard side; (fig.) course of action or policy. 5. (of varnish, printing-ink, etc.) Viscous condition. ~ *v.* 1. Attach with tacks, or in slight or temporary manner, esp. with long slight stitches; (fig.) annex, append (*to, on to*); (esp., English hist.) append (clause relating to extraneous matter) *to* money-bill, to ensure its passing House of Lords. 2. Change ship's course by shifting tacks and sails; make run or course obliquely against wind, proceed to windward by series of such courses; (fig.) change one's course, conduct, policy, etc.

tăck[2] *n.* Foodstuff (chiefly in *hard-~*, ship's biscuit, *soft-~*, bread, good fare).

tăck′le *n.* 1. Apparatus, utensils, instruments, appliances, esp. for fishing or other sport. 2. (naut. pr. *tā-*) Rope(s) and pulley-block(s) or other mechanism for hoisting weights etc. (ill. PULLEY); windlass with its ropes and hooks; running rigging of ship. 3. (football etc.) Tackling; (Amer. football) each of two players (*right* ~, *left* ~), with positions next to the ends in the forward line. ~ *v.* Grapple with, grasp, lay hold of, with endeavour to hold, manage, or overcome; (football etc.) seize and stop, obstruct, intercept (opponent in possession of ball).

tăck′y *adj.* (of gum, nearly dry varnish, etc.) Slightly sticky or adhesive. **tăck′inėss** *n.*

tăct *n.* Intuitive perception of what is fitting, esp. of the right thing to do or say; adroitness in dealing with persons or circumstances. **tăct′ful** *adj.* **tăct′fully** *adv.* **tăct′fulnėss** *n.* **tăct′lėss** *adj.* **tăct′lėssly** *adv.* **tăctlėssnėss** *n.*

tăc′tĭc *n.* (Piece of) tactics.

tăc′tĭcal *adj.* Of tactics; adroitly planning or planned; ~ *bombing*, aerial bombing carried out in immediate support of military or naval operations. **tăc′tĭcally** *adv.*

tăctĭ′cian (-shn) *n.* One versed or skilled in tactics.

tăc′tĭcs *n.* (as sing. or pl.) Art or science of deploying and manœuvring air, military, or naval forces, esp. when in contact with the enemy (contrasted with *strategy*); (pl.) procedure, device(s) for gaining some end.

tăc′tīle *adj.* Of, perceived by, connected with, sense of touch; (painting etc.) appealing to sense of touch, producing effect of solidity. **tăctĭl′ĭty** *n.*

tăc′tūal *adj.* Tactile. **tăc′tūally** *adv.*

tăd′pōle *n.* Larva of frog or toad, from time it leaves egg until it loses gills and tail, esp. early stage of this when it seems to consist simply of round head with a tail (ill. FROG); larva of similar appearance in other animals; ~-*fish*, European fish (*Raniceps raninus*) with broad flat head.

Tădzhĭkstan′ (-dj-, -ahn). Constituent Republic of the Soviet Union, in Central Asia; capital, Dushanbe.

tael (tāl) *n.* Chinese ounce (= $1\frac{1}{3}$ oz. avoirdupois), esp. of silver as former monetary unit. [Malay *tahil* weight]

taen′ĭa, tēn′ĭa *ns.* (pl. *-iae*). 1. (archit.) Band separating architrave from frieze in Doric order (ill. ORDER). 2. (anat.) Ribbon-like structure, esp. band of white nervous matter in brain and longitudinal muscles of colon. 3. (zool.) Tapeworm (ill. TAPEWORM); genus of cestode worms including tapeworm. **taen′ioid** *adj.*

T.A.F. *abbrev.* Tactical Air Force.

tăff′ėta *n.* Fine plain-woven usu. glossy fabric of silk or other material. [Pers. *tāftah* (*tāftan* twist)]

tăff′rail (-frĭl) *n.* Rail round ship's stern (ill. SHIP). [Du. *tafereel* panel, dim. of *tafel* table]

Tăff′y[1]. Colloq. nickname for Welshman. [supposed Welsh pronunciation of *Davy*, David]

tăff′y[2] *n.* (now Sc., northern Engl., and Amer.) Toffee.

tăf′ĭa *n.* Rum-like spirit distilled from molasses etc.

Tăft, William Howard (1857–1930). 27th President of U.S., 1909–13.

tăg[1] *n.* Metal point at end of lace; small pendent piece or part, as loop at back of boot for pulling it on, ragged lock of wool on sheep, address-label for tying on, any loose or ragged end; brief and usu. familiar, trite or much-used quotation; refrain or catch of song etc., last words of speech in play etc.; *tagrag* (*and bobtail*) the riffraff; all and sundry, esp. of the lower classes. ~ *v.* Furnish with a tag; join (*to, on to, together*); find rhymes for (verses), string (rhymes) together; follow closely, trail or drag behind.

tăg[2] *n.* Children's game in which one pursues the others until he touches one, who in turn becomes pursuer.

Taga′log (-gah-). (Member, language) of largest and most important Malayan people of Philippine Islands. [native name, f. *taga* native, *ilog* river]

Tagōre′, Sir Rabindranath (1861–1941). Indian poet and prose-writer.

Tā′gus. River of Spain and Portugal, flowing into Atlantic near Lisbon.

Tahi′tĭ (-hē-). One of the Society Islands in the S. Pacific, in Fr. possession. **Tahi′tĭan** *adj.* & *n.* (Polynesian native, language) of Tahiti.

Tai: see THAI.

taiga (tī′gah) *n.* Siberian pine-forest.

tail[1] *n.* Hindmost part of animal, esp. when prolonged beyond rest of body; thing, part, appendage, resembling this, as luminous train of comet, twisted or braided tress of hair, stem of musical note, train of woman's dress, pendent posterior part of man's coat, esp. dress-coat; appendage of string and paper at lower end of kite; outer corner of eye; rear-end of column, procession, etc.; weaker members of sports team; hinder part of cart, plough, or harrow; rear part of aircraft; tail-race of mill; reverse side of coin; (pl.) tail-coat; *turn* ~, turn one's back, run away; ~*-bandage*, one divided into strips at end; ~*-board*, usu. hinged or removable board at back of cart, lorry, etc. ~*-coat*, man's coat with long skirt divided at back and cut away in front (ill. COAT); ~*-end*, extreme end, concluding part; ~*-gate*, lower gate of canal-lock; ~*-lamp*, *-light*, light carried at back of train, cycle, car, etc.; ~*-piece*, piece forming tail; small decoration at end of book, chapter, etc.; ~*-plane*, horizontal stabilizing surface of tail of aircraft; ~*-race*, part of mill-race below wheel (ill. WATER); ~*-skid*, small skid or runner supporting tail of aircraft in contact with ground; ~*-spin*, (aviation) kind of spinning dive; ~ *stock*, one of two parts (~*-stock* and *head-stock*) which hold the work in a lathe (ill. LATHE); ~ *wind*, wind blowing in same direction as course of aircraft etc. ~ *v.* Furnish with tail; follow (person) inconspicuously to keep watch on him; cut or pull off what is regarded as tail, esp. of plant or fruit; ~ *away*, *off*, fall away in tail or straggling line; diminish and cease.

tail[2] *n.* (law) Limitation of freehold estate or fee to a person and (particular class of) the heirs of his body (freq. in phrase *in* ~). ~ *adj.* (Of estate) so limited.

tail′or *n.* Maker of men's outer garments, or of such women's garments as have similar character, e.g. coats, suits, riding-clothes; ~*-bird*, various Asiatic passerine singing-birds (esp. *Sutoria sutoria* of India, S. China, etc.) which stitch together edges of leaves to form cavity for nest; ~*-made*, made by tailor, usu. with little ornament and with special attention to exact fit; ~*'s dummy*, lay-figure for fitting or displaying clothes; (freq. contempt., of persons); ~*'s goose*, heavy pressing-iron used by tailors. **tail′orĕss** *n.* **tail′or** *v.* Do tailor's work; make (garments etc.) by tailor's methods; (of fabric) admit of being tailored; furnish with clothes, dress.

tain *n.* Thin tin plate; tin foil for backing mirror.

Taine (tĕn), Hippolyte Adolphe (1828–93). French literary critic and historian.

taint *n.* Spot, trace, of decay, corruption, or disease; corrupt condition, infection. ~ *v.* Introduce corruption or disease into, infect, be infected.

Tajikstan: see TADZHIKSTAN.

Taj Mahal (tahj mahahl′). Marble mausoleum of great splendour and beauty at Agra, India, built (1631–45) by the Mogul Emperor Shah-Jahan in memory of his favourite wife. [corrupt. of Pers. *Mumtāz-i-Mahall*, title of wife of Shah-Jahan, f. *mumtāz* distinguished, *mahall* abode]

tāke *v.* (past t. *tŏŏk*, past part. *tāk′en*). 1. Seize, grasp; capture; catch; (cards) win (trick); (of plant, seed, etc.) germinate, begin to grow; catch fancy or affection of; (of inoculation etc.) be successful or effective; *be taken ill*, fall ill. 2. Receive into body, as medicine, food, drink, etc.; bring or receive (person) into some relation to oneself; appropriate, enter into possession (of); secure, get, receive, by payment, esp. regularly, as a periodical; assume, charge oneself with, undertake; perform, discharge (function, service, etc.); range oneself on, ally oneself with, (side, in contest etc.); (gram.) have as proper construction; ~ *it*, (colloq.) endure punishment, affliction, etc., with fortitude. 3. Choose, adopt, take into use or employment; proceed or begin to deal with in some way; proceed to occupy; use (up), consume; need (specified size) *in* shoes, gloves, etc. 4. Obtain, derive, from some source or by some process; write (*down*) (notes, spoken words, etc.); obtain likeness, esp. by photography. 5. Receive, accept, enjoy (pleasure, money, wager, hint, etc.); exact (vengeance etc.); accept as true or correct, or in some specified way; face and attempt to get over, through, etc., negotiate; admit, absorb, contract, be affected by (moisture, infection, dye, a quality, etc.). 6. Grasp with mind, apprehend, understand; suppose, assume; regard, consider (*as*); feel, experience (emotion etc.). 7. Perform, do (action, movement, etc.); raise, make (objection, exception, etc.). 8. Carry, convey, cause to go with one; ~ *from*, *off*, carry away, remove, deprive or rid person or thing of; subtract, deduct; be capable of being taken *off*, *out*, etc. 9. ~ *aim*, aim (*at*); ~ *alarm*, become alarmed; ~ *charge*, make oneself responsible; ~ *fire*, become kindled or ignited, catch fire; ~ *care*, be careful; ~ *care of*, be careful of; be in charge of; (U.S.) deal with; ~ *hold* (*of*), grasp, seize, take under one's control; ~ *place*, happen; ~ *possession*, enter into possession (*of*). 10. ~ *after*, resemble (person, esp. parent) in character, feature, etc.; ~ *away*, remove, subtract, detract *from*; ~ *back*, retract (words); ~ *down*, write down; abuse, humiliate, humble; pull down (building), lower, carry or cut down; ~ *in*, admit, receive (lodgers etc.); undertake (work) to be done in one's own house; conduct into house, room, etc.; include, comprise; reduce (garment etc.) to smaller compass, furl (sail); understand, comprehend; deceive, cheat; believe (false statement); subscribe to (newspaper etc.). ~*-in* (*n.*) fraud, deception; ~ *off*, remove; conduct away; deduct (part of price); drink off; mimic; jump, spring; (of aircraft or pilot) leave ground at beginning of flight; ~-*off* (*n.*) caricature; spot from which jump etc. is made; aircraft's leaving of ground; ~ *on*, undertake (work, responsibility, etc.); play (person) *at* game; (colloq.) show violent emotion, be greatly agitated; ~ *out*, cause to come out; bring, convey, out; remove; accept payment or compensation *in* specified form; ~ *it out of*, exhaust, fatigue; exact satisfaction from; ~ *over*, succeed to possession or control of; ~ *to*, begin, begin to occupy oneself with; conceive a liking for; ~ *up*, lift up; absorb; occupy, engage; adopt as protégé; interrupt, correct (speaker); enter upon; pursue (occupation, subject, inquiry, etc.); secure, fasten; accept (challenge); subscribe for, subscribe amount of (shares, loan, etc.); ~ *up with*, begin to consort with. ~ *n.* Amount (of fish, game, etc.) taken or caught; takings; (cinemat.) scene or part of scene photographed at one time without stopping camera, photographing of this.

tāk'er *n.* (esp.) One who takes a bet.

tāk'ing *n.* (esp.) State of agitation (archaic); (pl.) money received in business. ~ *adj.* Attractive, captivating, charming. **tāk'ingly** *adv.*

tăl'apoin *n.* 1. Buddhist priest or monk in Burma, Siam, etc. 2. Small W. Afr. monkey (*Cercopithecus talapoin*).

talār'ia *n.pl.* Winged sandals as attribute in classical art of Hermes, Iris, and others.

tal'bot (tawl-) *n.* Kind of large whitish hound (now extinct) with long hanging ears and heavy jaws, formerly used for tracking and hunting and supposed to be ancestral stock of bloodhound; representation of this in heraldry, as inn-sign, etc. [perh. f. family name *Talbot*]

tal'botȳpe (tawl-) *n.* Photographic process invented by W. H. Fox Talbot in 1840, the basis of that now used.

tălc *n.* Soft, translucent, white, green, or grey mineral (a hydrated magnesium silicate) with greasy feel and shining lustre, freq. occurring in broad flat plates, and used in making soap, toilet powder, paper, lubricants, etc.; its varieties include *soapstone* and *french chalk*; (pop.) = MICA; ~ *powder*, talcum powder.

tăl'cum *n.* Talc; ~ *powder*, toilet powder of (usu. perfumed) powdered talc.

tāle *n.* 1. (archaic, rhet., poet.) Number, total. 2. Story, true or (usu.) fictitious narrative, esp. one imaginatively treated; idle or mischievous gossip, a malicious report (esp. in *tell ~s*); ~-*bearer*, one who reports maliciously what is meant to be secret; ~-*teller*, one who tells tales.

tăl'ent *n.* 1. Ancient weight and money of account, varying greatly with time, place, and people. 2. Special aptitude, faculty, gift [from the parable of the talents, Matt. xxv. 14–30 etc.]; high mental ability; ~-*money*, bonus to professional cricketer etc. for especially good performance. **tăl'entėd** *adj.*

tāl'ēs (-z) *n.* (law) Writ for summoning jurors, list of persons who may be so summoned, to supply deficiency; *tāl'ēsman* (*or* -lz-), person so summoned. [L *tales de circumstantibus* such of the bystanders, first words of the writ]

tăl'ipĕd *adj.* & *n.* Club-footed (person). **tăl'ipēs** (-z) *n.* Club-foot.

tăl'ipŏt, -pŭt *ns.* Fan-palm (*Corypha umbraculifera*) of Ceylon and Malabar, of great height, and with enormous fan-shaped leaves used as sunshades, fans, and as writing-material.

tăl'isman *n.* Charm, amulet, esp. stone, ring, etc., inscribed with astrological figures or characters and supposed to protect its wearer or bring him good fortune. **tălismăn'ic** *adj.* [Arab. *tilsam*, f. Gk *telesma* (*telesmos* consecration, ceremony)]

talk (tawk) *v.* Convey or exchange ideas, information, etc., by speech, esp. familiar speech of ordinary intercourse; express, utter, discuss, in words; exercise faculty of speech; utter words; use (language); gossip; bring into specified condition etc. by talking; ~ *down*, silence (person) by louder or more effective talking; ~ *down to*, address (person) in language suited to his supposed ignorance or stupidity; ~ *out*, get rid of (Bill, motion, in Parliament) by prolonging discussion till time of adjournment; ~ *to*, speak to, (colloq.) reprove. **talk'er** *n.* **talk** *n.* Conversation; short address or lecture in conversational style, esp. one broadcast by radio; theme of gossip.

talk'atĭve (tawk-) *adj.* Fond of talking, loquacious, garrulous. **talk'atĭvely** *adv.* **talk'atĭvenėss** *n.*

talky (tawk'ĭ) *n.* (slang) Cinema sound-film.

tall (tawl) *adj.* 1. (Of persons) of more than average height; (of things) high, lofty, higher than the average or than surrounding objects; of specified height; *tallboy*, tall chest of drawers, occas. in two sections, one standing above the other (ill. CHEST). 2. (Of talk etc.) high-flown; exaggerated, highly coloured; ~ *order*, unreasonable or excessive demand. **tall'ish** *adj.* **tall'nėss** *n.*

Tălleyrand (-Périgord) (-rahṅ, -ĭgŏr), Charles Maurice de, Prince de Bénévent (1754–1838). French statesman.

Tall'ĭnn (tah-). Seaport and capital city of Estonia, also called *Reval*.

tăll'ow (-ō) *n.* Fat of animals, esp. of sheep and ox kinds, separated by melting and clarifying and used for making candles, soap, etc.; ~-*chandler*, (obs.) maker, seller, of tallow candles; ~-*drop*, style of cutting precious stone with one or both sides convex (ill. GEM). **tăll'owy** (-ōĭ) *adj.*

tăll'ȳ *n.* 1. Piece of wood scored across with notches representing amount of debt or payment and

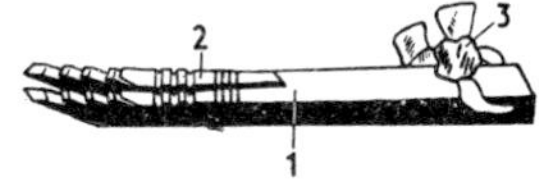

14TH-C. TALLY

1. Stock which is given to payer. 2. Foil which is kept by payee. 3. Seal. The notches represent the amount recorded, in this case £3. 13*s*. 4*d*. (3⅓£, 3*s*. 4*d*.)

split lengthwise across notches, each party keeping half; account so kept; score, reckoning. 2. Distinguishing mark, ticket, label, attached to thing for identification etc. 3. Corresponding thing, counterpart, duplicate. 4. ~-*card*, U.S.) score-card; *tall'yman*, one who sells goods which are paid for by instalments; ~-*shop*, shop where such goods are sold. ~ *v.* Record, reckon, by tally; agree, correspond (*with*).

tăll'ȳ-hō' *int.* & *n.* 1. Huntsman's cry to hounds, view-halloo. 2. (hist.) Fast passenger-coach, orig. one running between London and Birmingham (1823–); (U.S.) large four-in-hand coach. ~ *v.* Utter cry of 'tally-ho!'; incite (hounds) with this cry.

tăl'ma *n.* Woman's or man's long cape or cloak in first half of 19th c. [F. J. *Talma* (1763–1826), Fr. tragedian]

Tăl'mud. Body of Jewish civil and ceremonial law, comprising (1) the *Mishnah* (binding precepts of the elders, codified *c* A.D. 200) and (2) the later *Gemara* or commentary on these, known in two recensions, the Jerusalem or Palestinian (completed *c* A.D. 4th c.) and the Babylonian (A.D. 5th or 6th c.). **Talmŭd'ĭc(al)** *adjs.* **Tăl'mudĭst** *n.*

tăl'on *n.* Claw, esp. of bird of prey; (cards) remainder of pack after cards have been dealt; shoulder of bolt against which key presses in turning it; handle end of sword-blade; (archit.) ogee moulding.

tāl'us[1] (*or* tălū) *n.* Slope, esp. (fort.) sloping side of wall or earthwork; (geol.) the mass of rock debris gathering at the foot of a cliff.

tāl'us[2] *n.* (pl. -*lī*). (anat.) Ankle-bone (ill. FOOT); (path.) form of club-foot with toes drawn up and heel resting on ground.

tăm *n.* Shortened f. TAM-O'-SHANTER.

tama'l(ė) (-ahl) *n.* Mexican dish of crushed maize with pieces of meat or chicken, red pepper, etc., wrapped in corn-husks and baked or steamed.

tamăn'dūa (*or* tah'mandūah') *n.* Arboreal ant-eater (*Tamandua tetradactyla*) of Central and S. America; lesser ant-eater.

tăm'arack *n.* (Timber of) various Amer. larches, esp. *Larix americana* of northern N. America; ridge-pole pine (*Pinus murrayana* and *P. contorta*) of western U.S.

tăm'arĭnd *n.* Large tropical tree (*Tamarindus indica*) with hard heavy timber, dark-green pinnate leaves, and racemes of fragrant red-streaked yellow flowers; fruit of this, brown pods with seeds embedded in brown or reddish-black acid pulp, used in medicine, as relish, etc. [Arab. *tamr-hindi* date of India]

tăm'arĭsk *n.* Plant of genus *Tamarix*, esp. *T. gallica*, a graceful evergreen shrub or small tree with slender feathery branches and minute leaves, growing in sandy places.

tama'sha (-mah-) *n.* (Anglo-Ind.) Show, entertainment, public function. [f. Arab. *tamāshā*]

tăm'bour (-oor) *n.* 1. Drum, esp. bass drum. 2. Circular frame consisting of one hoop fitting closely within another, over which material is stretched for embroidering; embroidery worked on it; tambour-lace; ~*-lace*, kind in which pattern is embroidered or darned on machine-made net stretched in tambour. 3. (archit.) Cylindrical stone forming part of shaft of column; circular part of various structures; ceiled lobby with folding doors in church porch etc., to prevent draughts etc.; sloping buttress or projection in tennis-court etc. (ill. TENNIS). 4. (fort.) Small defensive work of palisades, earth, etc., defending entrance or passage. ~ *v.* Decorate, embroider, on tambour.

tăm'bourĭn (-bor-) *n.* Long narrow drum used in Provence; (music for) dance accompanied by this.

tămbourine' (-borēn) *n.* Musical instrument consisting of a wooden hoop with a skin stretched over one side and pairs of small cymbals in slots round the circumference, played by shaking, striking with knuckles, or drawing finger(s) across parchment; = timbrel.

Tăm'burlaine, Tăm'erlāne. *Timur Lenk* or *Lang* 'lame Timur' (*c* 1335–1405), Tatar conqueror of much of Asia and E. Europe; ancestor of the Mogul dynasty in India.

tāme *adj.* 1. (Of animals, birds, etc.) made tractable, domesticated, not wild; (colloq., of land or plant) cultivated. 2. Submissive, spiritless, insipid. **tāme'ly** *adv.* **tāme'nėss** *n.* **tāme** *v.t.* Make gentle and tractable, break in, domesticate (wild beast, bird, etc.); subdue, curb, humble, reduce to submission. **tām(e)'able** *adj.*

Tăm'ĭl. Member of people of SE. India and part of Ceylon; Dravidian language of this people.

Tămm'any. Central organization of Democratic party in New York City, founded in 1789 as a benevolent society (~ *Society*), located in ~ *Hall*, 14th Street, New York; freq. used as by-name for political and municipal corruption. [f. name of Indian chief (late 17th c.) noted for wisdom and friendliness towards whites, and regarded (*c* 1770–90) as 'patron saint' of Pennsylvania and other northern colonies]

Tammuz: see THAMMUZ, and JEWISH calendar.

tămm'y[1] *n.* Fine woollen or wool-and-cotton textile fabric, freq. with glazed finish.

tăm-o'-shăn'ter *n.* **tămm'y**[2] *n.* Round woollen or cloth cap with flat baggy top much wider than head band. [f. hero of Burns's poem 'Tam o' Shanter']

tămp *v.t.* Plug (blast-hole etc.) with clay above firing-charge; ram down.

tăm'per *v.i.* ~ *with*, meddle with; alter, corrupt, pervert.

tăm'pĭon *n.* Plug for top of organ-pipe (ill. ORGAN); plug or cover for muzzle of gun.

tăm'pon *n.* Plug inserted in wound, body cavity, or orifice, to stop haemorrhage or absorb secretions. ~ *v.t.* Plug with tampon.

tăm'ponage *n.*

tăn[1] *v.* 1. Convert (skin or hide) into leather by soaking in infusion of oak-bark or other substance rich in tannin, or by any other process. 2. Make, become, brown by exposure to sun or weather. 3. (slang) Beat, thrash. ~ *n.* 1. Crushed or bruised bark of oak or other trees, used for tanning; spent bark from tan-pits used for covering riding-track, circus ring, etc.; track etc. covered with this. 2. Brown colour of tan; bronzed colour of skin that has been exposed to sun or weather. 3. ~*-bark*, = sense 1; ~*-pit*, *-vat*, pit, cistern, tank, etc., in which hides are tanned. ~ *adj.* Of the colour of tan or tanned leather, yellowish or reddish brown.

tăn[2] *abbrev.* of TANGENT *n.*

Ta'na (tah-). Lake in Ethiopia, source of the Blue Nile.

tăn'ager (-j-) *n.* Amer. bird of family *Tanagnidae*, with numerous species, in which males are usu. bright-coloured.

Tana'gra (-ahg-). Ancient town of Boeotia, NE. Greece; ~ *figurine*, *statuette*, one of the terra-cotta figurines found near Tanagra in tombs mainly of 3rd and 4th centuries B.C.

Tăn'crėd (*c* 1078–1112). Norman leader in 1st crusade.

tăn'dem *adv.* (Of horses in harness) one behind the other; *drive* ~, drive horses so harnessed. ~ *n.* 1. (Carriage with) horses tandem. 2. ~ (*bicycle*), bicycle for two persons, one seated behind the other. [punning use of L *tandem* at length (of time)]

t. & o. *abbrev.* Taken and offered.

tăng[1] *n.* 1. Point, projection, esp. extension of knife, chisel, or other metal tool or instrument by which it is secured to its handle (ill. CHISEL). 2. Strong or penetrating taste or flavour; characteristic quality; trace, touch, suggestion, *of* something. ~ *v.t.* Furnish with tang.

tăng[2] *n.* Various large coarse seaweeds, esp. species of *Fucus*, tangle, sea-wrack.

T'ang, Tang[3] (tă-, tŭ-). Dynasty of Chinese emperors (A.D. 618–906); this period, noted for territorial conquest and great wealth, and regarded as golden age of Chinese poetry and art.

Tănganyi'ka (-ngg-, -yē-). Country of E. central Africa bordering on Indian Ocean; independent State and member of Brit. Commonwealth, 1961; republic, 1962; since 1964 ~ *and Zanzibar*, now **Tănzān'ia** (*or* -nē'*a*); capital, Dar es Salaam. *Lake* ~, large lake between Tanganyika and Congo.

tăn'gent (-j-) *adj.* (Of line or surface) touching a line or surface, but not intersecting it. ~ *n.* Straight line tangent to a curve (ill. CIRCLE); (trig.) one of the three fundamental trigonometrical functions (the others being SECANT and SINE[1]), orig. considered as functions of a circular arc, now usu. of an angle (viz. that subtended by such an arc at its centre) (ill. TRIGONOMETRY); orig. the length of a straight line perpendicular to the radius touching one end of the arc and terminated by the *secant* drawn from the centre through the other end; in mod. use, the ratio of this line to the radius or (equivalently, as the function of the angle) the ratio of the side of a right-angled triangle opposite the given angle (if acute) to that of the side opposite the other acute angle (abbrev. *tan*); *fly*, *go*, etc., *off at a* ~, diverge suddenly from previous course or direction, or from matter in hand. **tăn'gency** *n.* **tăngĕn'tial** (-shl) *adj.* **tăngĕn'tially** *adv.*

Tăngerine' (-jerēn) *adj.* & *n.* 1. (Native) of Tangier. 2. *t*~ (*orange*), small flattened deep-coloured sweet-scented variety of orange from Tangier.

tăn'gĭble (-j-) *adj.* That may be touched, perceptible by touch; real, objective, definite. **tăn'gĭbleness, tăngĭbĭl'ĭty** *ns.* **tăn'gĭbly** *adv.*

Tăngier(s)' (-jēr, -jērz). Seaport of Morocco at W. end of Strait of Gibraltar (Arab. *Tanja*); an International Zone.

tăng′le[1] (-nggl) *v.* Intertwine, become twisted or involved, in confused mass; entangle; complicate; *tang′lefoot* (U.S. slang) whisky or other intoxicant. ~ *n.* Tangled condition or mass. **tăng′ly** *adj.*

tăng′le[2] (-nggl) *n.* Either of two seaweeds (*Laminaria digitata* and *L. saccharina*) with long leathery fronds, occas. used as food; any large seaweed.

tăng′ō (-ngg-) *n.* Slow dance of Central African origin, brought by negro slaves to Central America and thence to Argentina where it was influenced by European rhythms, e.g. the Spanish *habanera*; fashionable in ballrooms since *c* 1910; music for this, in $\frac{2}{4}$ time.

tăng′ram (-ngg-) *n.* Chinese geometrical puzzle of square

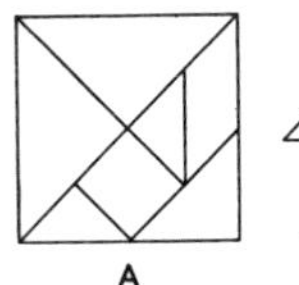

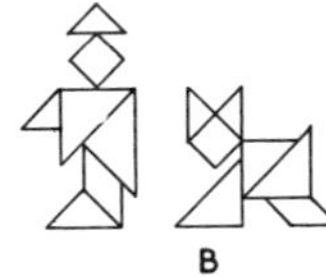

A. TANGRAM. B. TWO FIGURES WHICH CAN BE CONSTRUCTED WITH IT

divided into 7 pieces (5 triangles, a square, and a rhomboid), which can be fitted together to form many figures.

tănk *n.* 1. Large metal or wooden vessel for liquid, gas, etc.; part of locomotive tender containing water for boiler; ~-*car*, railway truck with large tank for carrying liquids; ~-*engine*, railway engine carrying its own fuel and water instead of drawing a tender (ill. LOCOMOTIVE). 2. In India, storage-pond or reservoir used for irrigation or as drinking-water. 3. (mil.) Armoured car carrying

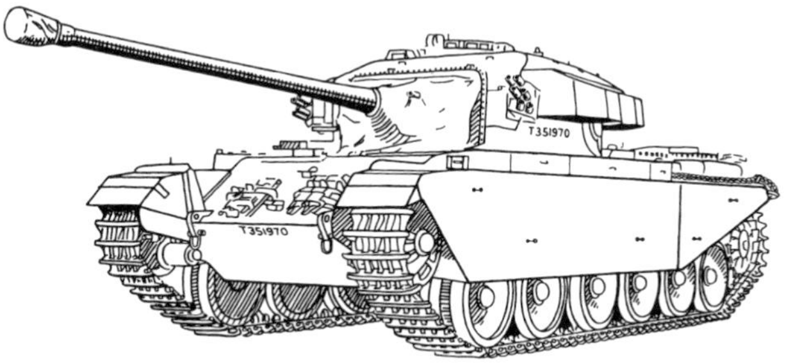

CENTURION MARK III TANK

guns and mounted on caterpillar tracks, capable of traversing rough ground; ~-*buster*, gun powerful enough to disable a tank.

tănk′age *n.* (Charge for) storage in tanks; cubic contents of tank(s).

tănk′ard *n.* Large one-handled drinking-vessel, esp. of pewter or silver, freq. with lid.

tănk′er *n.* Ship for carrying mineral oil etc. in bulk.

TANKER

tăn′nate *n.* Salt of tannic acid.

Tănn′enberg (-bârg). Village of E. Prussia (now in Poland); *Battle of* ~, (1) rout of Teutonic Knights by Poles and Lithuanians, 1410; (2) heavy defeat of Russians under Samsonov by Germans under Hindenburg, 1914.

tănn′er[1] *n.* One who tans hides.

tănn′er[2] *n.* (slang) A sixpence.

tănn′ery *n.* Place where hides are tanned.

Tănn′häuser (-hoiz-). Legendary 13th-c. German minnesinger.

tănn′ic *adj.* ~ *acid*, a complex glucoside found esp. in oak-galls, also in tea and many other plants.

tănn′in *n.* Any of a group of substances extracted from oak-galls and various barks and having the property of converting hides into leather; also used in medicine, dyeing, etc.

tăn′sy (-z-) *n.* Species (*Tanacetum*) of erect herbaceous plants, esp. the strongly aromatic bitter-tasting *T. vulgare*, with deeply divided leaves and corymbs of yellow button-like flowers. [Gk *athanasia* immortality]

tăn′talīte *n.* Rare heavy black mineral, the principal source of tantalum.

tăn′talīze *v.t.* Torment, tease, by sight or promise of something desired that is kept out of reach or withheld. **tăntalīzā′tion** *n.* [f. TANTALUS[1]]

tăn′talum *n.* Rare metallic element of vanadium group, a very hard ductile greyish-white metal, used commercially in the manufacture of alloys where hardness and resistance to heat and to the action of acids are of importance, and formerly for electric-lamp filaments; symbol Ta, at. no. 73, at. wt 180·948. **tăntăl′ic** *adj.* [f. TANTALUS[1], with ref. to incapacity of tantalum to 'absorb' acids]

Tăn′talus[1]. (Gk myth.) King of Phrygia, son of Zeus and the nymph Pluto; he served the flesh of his son Pelops to the gods (or committed some other crime variously described) and after his death was condemned to stand in Tartarus, in water that receded when he tried to drink and under branches of fruit that always eluded his grasp.

tăn′talus[2] *n.* 1. Spirit-stand containing decanters which can be seen but not withdrawn until bar holding them is unlocked. 2. Genus of storks including the Amer. wood ibis and similar birds in India and SE. Asia. [f. TANTALUS[1]]

tăn′tamount *adj.* Equivalent *to.*

tăn′tara (*or* -târ′a) *n.* Fanfare, flourish, of trumpets etc.

tăntĭv′y *int.* Expressing sound of galloping, esp. as hunting cry. ~ *n.* Swift movement, gallop, rush.

Tăn′tra *n.* 1. One of a class of Hindu writings, in Sanskrit, of a mystical and magical nature. 2. One of a group of Buddhist writings of somewhat similar character. **Tăn′trĭc** *adj.* Of the Tantras; ~ *Buddhism*, form of Buddhism, with emphasis on magic, practised esp. in Tibet; Lamaism. **Tăn′trism** *n.* [Sansk. *tantra* loom, groundwork, doctrine]

tăn′trum *n.* (colloq.) Outburst or display of bad temper or petulance.

Tao (tow), **Tao′ĭsm.** A Chinese religion, orig. a system of conduct based on writings attributed to the philosopher LAO-TSE (6th c. B.C.), later invested with magical beliefs and a large pantheon. [Chin., = 'way', 'doctrine']

tăp[1] *n.* 1. Cock, faucet, hollow or tubular plug with device for shutting off or controlling flow, through which liquid or gas may be drawn from pipe, cask, etc. (ill. COCK); liquor from a particular tap, particular quality or kind of drink; (colloq.) tap-room; *on* ~, on draught, ready for immediate use or consumption. 2. Tool in shape of male screw of hard steel, for cutting thread of internal screw (ill. SCREW). 3. ~-*room*, room in public-house etc. where liquors are kept on tap; ~-*root*, straight root growing vertically downwards, thick at top and tapering to a point (ill. ROOT); ~-*water*, water from a tap, esp. that supplied through system of pipes and taps to house etc. ~ *v.t.* 1. Furnish (cask etc.) with tap; pierce (cask, tree, etc.) so as to draw off liquid, draw liquid from (any reservoir); draw off (liquid); (slang) draw blood from (nose); (surg.) pierce body-wall of (person) to draw off accumulated liquid, drain (cavity) thus; (fig.) broach (subject). 2. Furnish (bolt, hole, etc.) with screw-thread. 3. Connect electric circuit to (another circuit), esp. as means of intercepting telegraph or telephone message, stealing current, etc.

tăp² *v.* 1. Strike lightly; cause (thing) to strike lightly (*against* etc.); strike gentle blow, rap; do tap-dancing. 2. Apply leather to (heel of shoe). ~ *n.* 1. Light blow, rap; sound of this; (pl., U.S. mil. and nav.) signal sounded on drum or bugle for lights out. 2. (U.S.) Piece of leather put on over worn sole in shoe-repairing. 3. ~-*dance*, kind of exhibition dance in which rhythm, esp. in elaborate syncopation, is tapped out with the feet; ~-*dancer*, -*dancing*; ~-*shoes*, shoes with metal plates.

tāpe *n.* Narrow woven strip of linen, cotton, etc., used as string for tying garments etc.; piece of tape stretched across race-course between winning-posts; piece of tape, flexible metal, etc., used as measuring-line etc.; paper strip on which messages are printed in receiving instrument of recording telegraph; ~-*machine*, receiving instrument of recording telegraph system; ~-*measure*, strip of tape or thin flexible metal marked for use as measure, and freq. coiled up in cylindrical case; ~-*recorder*, machine which records sounds on a tape and afterwards reproduces them; *tape'worm*, any of numerous cestode worms (*Taenia* and allied genera) parasitic in intestines of man and other vertebrates, and having long flat body of numerous

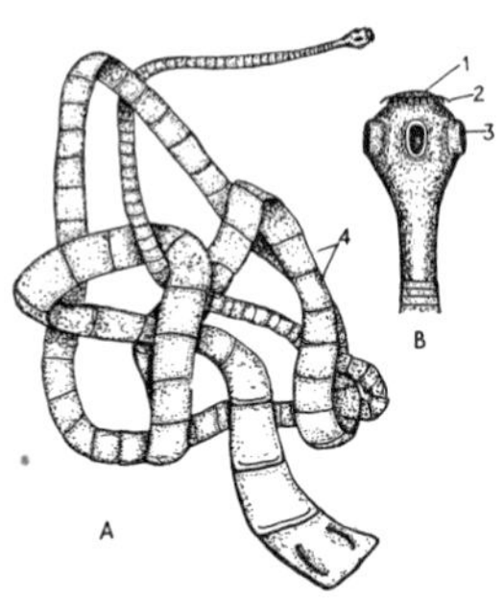

A. TAPEWORM. B. ENLARGEMENT OF HEAD

1. Rostellum. 2. Hooks. 3. Suckers. 4. Segments.

segments. ~ *v.t.* Furnish, measure, with tape(s); join sections of (book) with tape in bookbinding; (gunnery slang) get the range of; (fig.) *have* (person) *taped*, have summed him up.

tāp'er *n.* 1. Slender wax candle; long wick coated with wax for lighting lamp etc. 2. Tapering. ~ *adj.* (chiefly poet. and rhet.) Tapering; ~ *bearing*, roller bearing tapered at one end (ill. BEARING). ~ *v.* (freq. ~ *off*) Make, become, gradually smaller towards one end; (cause to) grow gradually less.

tăp'ĕstry *n.* Thick hand-woven fabric, usu. of wool, with a pictorial or ornamental design formed by the weft-threads, these being carried back and forth across the parts where their respective colours are needed and not from selvage to selvage (ill. WEAVE); wall-hanging of this; embroidered, painted, or machine-woven fabric imitating or resembling tapestry; ~ *carpet*, kind of carpet in which design is printed on warp before weaving; ~-*needle*, short comparatively thick needle; ~-*stitch*, Gobelin stitch, embroidery stitch like cross-stitch but with all threads parallel with warp on right side of fabric.

tapēt'um *n.* (pl. -*ta*). 1. (zool.) Irregular sector in eyes of certain animals (e.g. cat) which shines owing to absence of black pigment. 2. (bot.) Layer of nutritive tissue esp. in reproductive organs.

tăpĭōc'a *n.* Starchy granular foodstuff prepared from cassava and used in puddings etc. [Braz. *tipioca* juice of cassava (*tipi* dregs, *og*, *ók* squeeze out)]

tāp'ir (-*er*) *n.* Small pig-like mammal of tropical America and Malaya, with short flexible proboscis, related to rhinoceros.

TAPIR

tăp'is (-pē) *n.* *On the* ~, under discussion. [OF, = 'tapestry', perh. f. use of this for tablecloths]

tapōte'ment (-tm-) *n.* (med.) Percussion as part of massage treatment.

tăpp'ĕt *n.* Arm, collar, cam, etc., used in machinery to impart intermittent motion; ~ *loom*, loom in which hammers are worked by tappets; ~ *rod*, rod carrying tappet(s), used e.g. for opening and closing valves of internal combustion engine.

tăp'ster *n.* Person employed at bar to draw and serve liquor.

tar *n.* 1. Thick viscid inflammable black or dark-coloured liquid with heavy resinous or bituminous odour, obtained by distillation of wood, coal, or other organic substance, used for coating and preserving timber, cordage, etc., and as a preservative and antiseptic; source (by distillation) of a number of aromatic hydrocarbons and other substances which are starting materials for the manufacture of numerous chemicals and drugs; substances resembling this. 2. [perh. abbrev. f. TARPAULIN] Sailor. 3. ~-*brush*, brush used for applying tar; *a touch of the* ~-*brush*, a trace of negro or Indian blood; *tar'heel* (U.S., colloq.) nickname for inhabitant of pine-wood districts of N. Carolina; *Tarheel State*, N. Carolina; ~ *macăd'am*, (trademark) *tar'mac*, road-making material of crushed stone, slag, etc., mixed or covered with tar or other bituminous binder; ~-*water*, infusion of tar in cold water formerly used as medicine. ~ *v.t.* Cover, smear, with tar; ~ *and feather*, smear (person) with tar and cover him with feathers, as punishment or indignity.

tă'r(r)adiddle *n.* (colloq.) Fib, (petty or trifling) lie.

tărantĕll'a, tărantĕlle' *ns.* Rapid whirling dance of S. Italian peasants, formerly supposed to be the remedy for, or the effect of, tarantism; music for this; instrumental composition in rhythm of tarantella, now always in $\frac{6}{8}$ time, increasing in speed towards the end.

tă'rantism *n.* Obsolete term for a malady (prob. chorea) characterized by melancholy and overwhelming desire to dance, epidemic in S. Italy in 15th–17th centuries, and pop. supposed to be caused by bite of tarantula.

tarăn'tūla *n.* Various large black S. European spiders of genus *Lycosa*, with slightly poisonous bite formerly supposed to cause tarantism; various other large venomous spiders, esp. large hairy spiders of warm parts of America.

tarăn'tūlar *adj.* [f. *Taranto* in S. Italy]

Tarăx'acum *n.* Genus of weedy composite herbs, including dandelion, with bitter foliage and usu. yellow flowers; drug prepared from dried roots of dandelion (*T. officinale*) and used as tonic and laxative. [Pers. *talkh chakōk* bitter herb]

tarbōōsh' *n.* Fez, kind of (usu. red) brimless tasselled cloth or silk cap worn in some Mohammedan countries, alone or as part of turban.

tard'ĭgrāde *adj.* & *n.* Slow-moving (animal); (arthropod) of class *Tardigrada* of minute aquatic animals, water-bear (or *bear-animalcule*).

tard'ō *adj.* & *adv.* (mus.) Slow(ly).

tar̂d'y *adj.* Slow-moving, slow, sluggish; late, coming or done late. **tar̂d'ily** *adv.* **tar̂d'iness** *n.*

tar̂e[1] *n.* Kinds of vetch; vetch-seed; (bibl.) darnel.

tar̂e[2] *n.* (Allowance made for) weight of wrapping, box, conveyance, etc., in which goods are packed; (chem.) weight of vessel in which substance is weighed. ~ *v.t.* Ascertain, allow for, tare of.

tar̂ge *n.* (archaic and poet.) Shield, esp. light shield or buckler.

tar̂g'ĕt (-g-) *n.* Mark, esp. with concentric circles round central ring or spot, for shooting at; anything aimed at; (U.S.) disc-shaped railway signal indicating position of switch; *~-ship*, ship used as a target in naval gunnery practice.

Tar̂g'um. Any of various translations, interpretations, or paraphrases, in Aramaic, of parts of O.T., recorded in writing from *c* A.D. 100 onwards, but preserved from earlier times by oral transmission. **Tar̂g'umist** *n.* [Heb. *targūm* interpretation]

tă'rĭff *n.* 1. List of duties or customs to be paid on imports or exports; such duties collectively; law imposing these; duty on particular class of goods; *~-reform*, esp. (U.S.) movement favouring general reduction of tariffs; (in England at beginning of 20th c.) extension of tariffs on imports, as opp. 'free trade'. 2. List or scale of charges at hotel, on railway, etc. [Arab. *ta'rīf* notification (*'arafa* notify)]

tar̂l'atan *n.* Thin stiff muslin of very open weave, sometimes glazed.

tar̂m'ăc: see TAR.

tar̂n *n.* Small mountain lake.

tar̂n'ĭsh *v.* Dull or dim lustre of, discolour by oxidation etc.; lose lustre; (fig.) sully, taint, stain. ~ *n.* Tarnishing, being tarnished; stain, blemish, tarnished coating.

tar̂'ō *n.* Kinds of food-plant of arum family (*Colocasia antiquorum*) of Pacific islands, cultivated in tropics for its starchy root-stocks.

tă'rŏc, tă'rot (-ō) *ns.* One of a pack of 78 cards (*tarocchi*) first used in Italy in 14th c., and much used in fortune-telling, esp. any of the figured cards which constitute trumps; game played with these.

tar̂paul'ĭn *n.* Canvas made waterproof by coating or impregnating with tar and used as covering, esp. for ship's hatches, boats, etc.; other kinds of waterproof cloth; sailor's tarpaulin or oilskin hat.

Tar̂pei'an Rock (-pē'*an*). Cliff on Capitoline Hill in Rome, over which ancient-Roman criminals were hurled.

tar̂p'on *n.* Large silvery marine game-fish (*Megalops atlanticus*) found in warmer waters of W. Atlantic.

Tar̂q'uĭn. Name of two semi-legendary, perhaps Etruscan, kings of ancient Rome, Tarquinius Priscus and Tarquinius Superbus; when the latter was expelled (510 B.C.) the Republic was founded.

tă'rragon *n.* Plant of wormwood kind (*Artemisia dracunculus*), of S. Russia and E. Europe, with aromatic leaves used for flavouring salads etc.; ~ *vinegar*, vinegar flavoured with oil or leaves of tarragon. [Arab. *tarkhōn*, perh. f. Gk *drakōn* dragon]

tar̂'ry[1] *adj.* Of, like, smeared or impregnated with, tar.

tă'rry[2] *v.* Remain, stay, lodge; wait (*for*); delay, be late; (archaic) wait for.

tar̂s'al *adj.* Of the TARSUS[1].

tar̂s'ĭa *n.* Italian name for MARQUETRY.

tar̂s'ĭer *n.* Small nocturnal tree-climbing animal of E. Indies with soft fur and large prominent eyes (*Tarsius spectrum*), a primate related to the lemurs. [L *tarsus*, from formation of its foot]

TARSIER

tar̂s'us[1] *n.* (pl. *-sī*). 1. Ankle, collection of small bones (7 in man) between metatarsus and leg (ill. FOOT); shank of bird's leg; (entom.) terminal segment of limb (ill. INSECT). 2. Tarsal plate, plate of condensed connective tissue stiffening eyelid.

Tar̂s'us[2]. Ancient city in SW. corner of Asia Minor (now in Turkey), home of St. Paul.

tar̂t[1] *n.* 1. Pie containing fruit; piece of pastry spread on pie-plate etc. with jam, treacle, etc., on top. 2. (slang) Girl, woman, esp. of immoral character. **tar̂t'lĕt** *n.*

tar̂t[2] *adj.* Sharp-tasting, sour, acid; cutting, biting. **tar̂t'ly** *adv.* **tar̂t'nĕss** *n.*

tar̂t'an *n.* Woollen cloth with stripes of various colours crossing at right angles, esp. in the distinctive pattern of a Highland clan; such pattern; other fabric with similar pattern. ~ *adj.* Made of, chequered like, tartan.

tar̂t'ar[1] *n.* 1. Acid potassium tartrate deposited in form of crust in wine-casks etc. during fermentation of grape-juice; *cream of ~*, purified tartar in form of white crystals, used in cookery; *~ emetic*, poisonous white crystalline salt, potassium antimonyl tartrate, used in medicine, and in dyeing as mordant. 2. Hard deposit of calcium phosphate from saliva on teeth.

Tartar[2]: see TATAR.

tar̂tar̂e' sauce *n.* Sharp-flavoured sauce consisting of a mayonnaise dressing with chopped herbs, olives, and capers, served with fish etc.

tar̂tă'rĭc *adj.* Derived from tartar; ~ *acid*, organic acid present in numerous plants esp. unripe grapes, and used in calico printing and in manufacture of baking-powders and effervescent drinks.

Tar̂t'arus. (Gk myth.) Infernal regions, or lowest part of them, where the Titans were confined; place of punishment in Hades. **Tar̂tar̂'ĕan** *adj.*

Tar̂t'ary. Tatar regions of Asia and E. Europe, esp. high plateau of Asia and its NW. slopes.

tar̂t'rate *n.* Salt of tartaric acid.

Tă'shĭ La'ma (lah-). LAMA second in rank to Dalai Lama.

task (-ah-) *n.* Piece of work imposed or undertaken as a duty etc.; any piece of work that has to be done; *take to ~*, find fault with, rebuke (*for*); ~ *force*, (U.S.) an armed force organized for operations under a unified command; *task'master*, (now usu. fig.) one who sets a task, one who imposes heavy burden or labour. ~ *v.t.* Assign task to; occupy or engage fully, put strain upon.

Tăs'man (-z-), Abel Janszoon (*c* 1603–59). Dutch navigator and explorer, discoverer of TASMANIA, New Zealand, and Fiji Islands. *~('s) Sea*, part of Pacific Ocean lying between New Zealand and SE. Australia.

Tăsmān'ĭa (-z-). State of Commonwealth of Australia, consisting of one large and several smaller islands SE. of the continent; discovered 1642 by TASMAN; formerly called Van Diemen's Land; capital, Hobart. **Tăsmān'ĭan** *adj.* & *n.*; ~ *devil*, nocturnal carnivorous marsupial (*Sarcophilus ursinus*) of savage appearance, about size of badger, with coarse black hair with white patches.

Tăss. The telegraphic agency of the Soviet Union. [initials of Russ. *T*elegrafniy *A*gentstvo *SS*SR]

tăss'el *n.* 1. Tuft of loosely hanging threads or cords as ornament for cushion, cap, etc.; tassel-like head of some plants, esp. staminate inflorescence at top of stalk of Indian corn; ribbon sewn into book to be used as bookmark. 2. = TORSEL. ~ *v.t.* Furnish with tassel; remove tassels of (Indian corn) to strengthen plant. [OF., perh. f. L *taxillus* small die]

tăss'et *n.* (hist., usu. pl.) Overlapping plates hanging from corslet and protecting thighs (ill. ARMOUR).

tăss'ie *n.* Small cup.

Tăss'ō, Torquato (1544–95). Italian poet, author of 'Jerusalem Delivered' etc.

tāste *v.* Learn flavour of (food etc.) by taking it into the mouth; eat small portion of; experience, have experience *of*; (of food etc.) have a flavour *of*. ~ *n.* 1. Sensation excited in certain organs of mouth (~ *buds*) by contact of some soluble things, flavour. 2. Sense by which this is perceived. 3. (rare) Act of tasting. 4. Small portion (*of* food etc.) taken as sample. 5. Liking; predilection *for*. 6. Faculty of discerning and enjoying beauty or other excellence esp. in art and literature; sense of what is harmonious or fitting in art, language, or conduct (*in good* ~, manifesting this faculty; *in bad* ~, showing lack of it).

tāste'ful (-tf-) *adj.* Having, showing, done in, good taste (TASTE, sense 6). **tāste'fully** *adv.* **tāste'fulnėss** *n.*

tāste'lėss (-tl-) *adj.* 1. Flavourless, insipid. 2. Lacking physical sense of taste. 3. Lacking in good taste, or critical discernment and appreciation; not in good taste. **tāste'lėssly** *adv.* **tāste'lėssnėss** *n.*

tās'ter *n.* (esp.) Person employed to judge quality of tea, wine, etc., by taste; (hist.) person employed to taste food before it was touched by his employer, esp. to guard against poison; shallow cup for tasting wines etc.; instrument for taking small portion from interior of cheese; skewer for testing condition of hams.

tās'ty *adj.* (colloq.) Savoury, of pleasing flavour; (now vulg.) tasteful. **tās'tĭly** *adv.* **tās'tĭnėss** *n.*

tăt *v.* Do TATTING; make by tatting.

ta-ta' (-ah) *int.* (nursery or playful) Good-bye. ~ *n.* A walk.

Ta'tar (tah-), **Tar̄t'ar** *adjs.* & *ns.* (Member) of any of numerous, mostly Mohammedan and Turkic, tribes inhabiting various parts of European and Asiatic Russia, esp. parts of Siberia, Crimea, N. Caucasus, districts along Volga, etc.; one of the mingled horde of Mongols, Turks, Tatars, etc., who overran E. Europe under Genghis Khan; ~ *Republic*, autonomous republic of R.S.F.S.R. [Pers. *tātār*; altered to *tartar* by association with TARTARUS]

Tāte, Nahum (1652–1715). English playwright and poet laureate (from 1692); author, with Nicholas Brady, of a metrical version of the Psalms (1696).

Tate Gallery. The National Gallery of British Art and of modern foreign painting and sculpture; built at Millbank, London, at the expense of Sir Henry Tate (1819–99), sugar manufacturer, to house a collection presented by him and other works accumulated by various bequests since 1841; opened in 1897.

Tăt'ler. Periodical (consisting chiefly of short essays) published by Addison and Steele, 1709–11.

Ta'tra Mountains, High Tatra (tah-). Highest group of central Carpathians, partly in N. Slovakia, partly in Poland.

tătt'er *n.* Rag, irregularly torn piece, of cloth, paper, etc. **tătt'ered** (-erd) *adj.* Reduced to tatters.

tătterdemăl'ĭon *n.* Ragged fellow, ragamuffin.

Tătt'ersall's. Horse-dealing mart founded 1766 by Richard Tattersall in London, now at Newmarket; ~ *Committee*, unofficial organization concerned esp. with betting on horse-racing; ~ *Ring*, principal betting enclosure on any race-course.

tătt'ĭng *n.* Kind of knotted lace made from sewing-thread with small flat shuttle-shaped instrument.

TATTING

tătt'le *n.* Tattling, chatter, gossip, trivial talk. ~ *v.* Prattle, chatter, gossip; utter idly. **tătt'ler** *n.*

tattōō'[1] *n.* 1. (mil.) Signal by drum or bugle in evening summoning soldiers to quarters; elaboration of this as military entertainment, usu. by torch or other artificial light, with music, troop exercises, etc. 2. Drumming, rapping; drum-beat; *devil's* ~, idle drumming with fingers etc. ~ *v.* Rap quickly and repeatedly; beat devil's tattoo. [Du. *tap-toe*, lit. 'close the tap' (of the cask)]

tattōō'[2] *v.t.* Mark (skin) with permanent pattern or design by puncturing it and inserting pigment; make (design) thus. ~ *n.* Tattooing. [Tahitian *tatau*]

tătt'y[1] *n.* Cuscus-grass mat hung in doorway, window, etc., and kept wet to cool the air. [Hind. *ṭaṭṭī* wicker-frame]

tătt'y[2] *adj.* (colloq.) Tattered, shabby.

tau *n.* Letter T in Greek, Hebrew, and ancient Semitic alphabets; mark or cross (~ *cross*) in shape of this (ill. CROSS).

Tauch'nĭtz (towχ-). Family of German printers and publishers, founders of a firm at Leipzig which issued cheap reprints of British and American copyright works for circulation in the continent of Europe (~ *editions*).

taunt *v.t.* Reproach, upbraid, (*with*) insultingly or contemptuously. ~ *n.* Insulting or provoking gibe; scornful reproach.

taur'īne *adj.* Of, like, a bull, bovine; of the zodiacal sign Taurus.

Taur'ĭs. Name sometimes used for Crimea in ancient times, from *Tauri*, earliest known inhabitants of its S. coast.

taurŏm'achy (-kĭ) *n.* Bullfight(ing).

Taur'us. Bull, constellation including Pleiades and Hyades; 2nd sign (♉) of zodiac, into which sun enters about 21st April.

taut *adj.* (Of rope etc.) tightly drawn, stiff, tense, not slack; (of ship etc.) trim, neat. **taut'ly** *adv.* **taut'nėss** *n.* **taut'en** *v.*

tauto- *prefix.* The same.

taut'ochrōne (-k-) *n.* (math.) Curve upon which body sliding from state of rest under given force will reach lowest point in same time, from whatever point it starts. **tautŏch'ronism** *n.* **tautŏch'ronous** *adj.*

tautŏhēd'ral *adj.* (cryst.) Having the same face or side in common.

tautŏl'ogy *n.* Repetition of same word or phrase, or of same idea etc., in different words (e.g. *arrived one after the other in succession*). **tautolŏ'gical** *adj.* **tautolŏ'gically** *adv.* **tautŏl'ogous** *adj.*

tautŏm'erĭsm *n.* (chem.) Property possessed by some organic compounds of behaving in different reactions as if they possessed two or more different constitutions. **taut'omer̄** *n.* Compound having this property. **tautomĕ'rĭc** *adj.*

tautŏph'ony *n.* Repetition of same (vocal) sound.

tăv'ern *n.* Public house for supply of food and drink.

taw[1] *n.* Large, freq. streaked or variegated, marble with which player shoots; game played with these; line from which players shoot.

taw[2] *v.t.* Make (hides or skins) into leather by steeping in solution of alum and salt.

tawd'ry *adj.* Showy or gaudy without real value; having too much or ill-judged ornament. **tawd'rĭly** *adv.* **tawd'rĭnėss** *n.* [f. *tawdry lace* sold at *St. Audry's* Fair, i.e. St. Etheldreda's, in Isle of Ely]

tawn'y *adj.* & *n.* Brown (colour) with preponderance of yellow or orange; ~ *eagle*, brownish eagle (*Aquila rapax*) of Africa and Asia, with reddish back-feathers; ~ *owl*, common reddish-brown owl (*Strix aluco*) of Europe and N. Africa, with darker brown bars or markings. **tawn'ĭnėss** *n.*

taws(e) (-z) *n.* (Sc.) Leather strap with end slit into narrow strips, for chastising children.

tăx *n.* Contribution levied on person, property, business, or articles of commerce, for the support of the State (in U.S. including 'rates' levied by local bodies);

oppressive or burdensome charge etc.; strain, heavy demand (*up*)*on*; *~-collector*, (archaic) *~-gatherer*, collector of taxes; *~-free*, exempt from taxes, esp. from income-tax; (of dividends or interest) having the income-tax paid by the company and not deducted from the distributed dividend or interest; *~-payer*, one who pays taxes. ~ *v.* 1. Impose tax on, subject to taxation; make demands on, strain, burden. 2. (law) Assess (costs); examine and allow or disallow items of (costs of action etc.); *taxing-master*, official of law-court who taxes costs. 3. Accuse, charge (*with*); call to account, take to task. **tăx'able** *adj.* **tăxā'tion** *n.*

tăx'ĭ *n.* Motor-cab plying for hire and fitted with taximeter; aircraft plying for hire. ~ *v.* Go, convey, in taxi; (of aircraft) run along ground or over surface of water before taking off or after alighting.

tăx'ĭdẽrmy *n.* Art of preparing and mounting skins of animals in lifelike manner. **tăxĭdẽrm'al, tăxĭdẽrm'ĭc** *adjs.* **tăx'ĭdẽrmĭst** *n.*

tăxĭm'ėter *n.* Automatic device fitted to cab indicating fare due at any given moment.

tăx'ĭs *n.* 1. (biol.) Movement of organism in a particular direction in response to external stimulus (e.g. towards or away from light or heat). 2. (surg.) Manipulative operation to restore displaced part or reduce hernia etc. 3. (Gk antiq.) Division of Greek army, varying in size in different States. 4. (gram.) Order, arrangement.

tăxŏn'omy *n.* (biol.) (Laws and principles of) classification. **tăxŏn'omer, tăxŏn'omist** *ns.* **tăxonŏm'ic(al)** *adjs.* **tăxonŏm'ically** *adv.*

Tay. River of Scotland, flowing through *Loch ~*, large lake in Perthshire, and into North Sea by *Firth of ~*, between Angus and Fife; *~ Bridge*, railway bridge across Firth of Tay to Dundee; the first Tay Bridge, opened in 1877, was blown down in 1879 while a passenger-train was crossing it.

Tayl'or[1], John (1580–1653). The 'Water-Poet', English pamphleteer and Thames waterman.

Tayl'or[2], Zachary (1784–1850). American soldier; 12th president of U.S., 1849–50.

Tayl'or Institution. Institute for the teaching of modern languages at Oxford, named after Sir Robert Taylor (1714–88), sculptor and architect.

tazza (taht'sa) *n.* Shallow ornamental bowl or cup mounted on a base.

T.B. *abbrev.* Torpedo-boat; tubercle bacillus; tuberculosis.

T.B.D. *abbrev.* Torpedo-boat destroyer.

T.C. *abbrev.* Town Council(lor).

T.C.D. *abbrev.* Trinity College, Dublin.

Tchaikov'sky (chī-, -ŏf-). Commonest English spelling of name of Pyotr Ilyich Chaykovsky (1840–93), Russian composer.

Tchekhov: see CHEKHOV.

T.D. *abbrev.* *Teachta Dála* (= Deputy of Dáil); Territorial (Officer's) Decoration.

tē *n.* (mus.) 7th note of major scale in 'movable-doh' systems; note B in 'fixed-doh' system.

tea *n.* 1. Dried and prepared leaves of the tea-plant, classed acc. to their method of manufacture as *green*, *black*, and *oolong* (the leaves of green tea are rolled and fired immediately, those of black tea are fermented or oxidized before firing, and those of oolong tea are only partially oxidized before firing); drink made by infusion from tea-leaves, with slightly bitter and aromatic flavour and moderately stimulant action, widely used as a beverage; meal at which this is served, esp. light meal in the afternoon, or the evening meal (*high tea*) when dinner is eaten at midday. 2. Plant from which tea is obtained, shrub (*Thea*) with fragrant white flowers and evergreen lanceolate leaves, cultivated from ancient times in China and Japan and grown also in India, Ceylon, etc. 3. Infusion made in same way as tea from leaves, blossoms, etc., of other plants, beef extract, fruit preserves, etc., and freq. used medicinally; (with defining word) various plants used for tea, or the beverages prepared from them. 4. *~-cake*, light kind of flat sweet bun, freq. toasted, eaten at tea etc.; *~-chest*, lead-lined cubical chest in which tea is exported; *~-cloth*, cloth used for drying cups etc. after washing; cloth for tea-table or tea-tray; *~-cup*, cup from which tea is drunk; as measure, about 4 fluid ounces; *storm in a ~-cup*: see STORM; *~-garden*, garden in which tea etc. is served to public; *~-gown*, woman's usu. flowing dress worn at tea etc.; *~-leaf*, leaf of tea, esp. (pl.) leaves after infusion; *~-plant*: sense 2; *~-planter*, proprietor or cultivator of tea plantation; *~-pot*, vessel with spout in which tea is made; *~-room*, room in which tea and other refreshments are served to public; *~-rose*, delicate-scented half-hardy or tender varieties of cultivated rose derived from *Rosa odorata* of China; *~-set*, set of cups and saucers, plates, etc., for tea; *~-shop*, tea-room; *~-spoon*, small spoon used for stirring tea etc.; as measure, about $\frac{1}{3}$ tablespoon; *~-taster*, one whose business is to test quality of tea by tasting samples; *~-things*, articles used for serving tea at table. [Chinese (Amoy dialect) *tʻe*, Mandarin *ch'a*]

ENGRAVED SILVER-GILT TAZZA

teach *v.* Give (person) instruction or lessons in (a subject); show or make known to person (how to do something); give instruction to, educate; explain, state by way of instruction; be a teacher.

teach'able *adj.* Apt to learn, docile; (of subject etc.) that can be taught. **teachabĭl'ĭty, teach'ablenėss** *ns.*

teach'er *n.* (esp.) One who teaches in a school.

teach'ĭng *n.* (esp.) What is taught, doctrine.

teak *n.* (Yellowish-brown heavy durable oily wood of) large E. Indian tree (*Tectona grandis*) with large egg-shaped leaves and panicles of white flowers; (strong or durable timber of) various other trees.

teal *n.* Various small freshwater ducks of *Anas* and other genera, widely distributed in Europe, Asia, and America, esp. *A. crecca*.

team *n.* 1. Two or more draught animals harnessed together; two or more beasts, or a single beast, with the vehicle they draw. 2. Set of players forming side in football match or other game or sport; set of persons working together; *~-work*, combined effort, organized co-operation. ~ *v.* Harness in team; convey, transport, with team; (U.S.) drive team.

team'ster *n.* Driver of a team.

tear[1] (tēr) *n.* 1. Drop of limpid saline fluid secreted by lachrymal gland appearing in or flowing from eye, as result of emotion, esp. grief, or of physical irritation, nervous stimulus, etc.; (pl.) weeping, sorrow, grief. 2. Something resembling a tear, esp. various gums exuding from plants in tear-shaped or globular beads, defect in glass caused by particle of vitrified clay, Prince Rupert's drop, etc.; *~-duct*, lachrymal or nasal duct carrying off tears from eye to nose; lachrymal canal carrying tears to eyes; *~-gas*, lachrymatory 'gas' used to disable opponents; *~-gland*, lachrymal gland; *~-shell*, shell containing tear-gas. **tear'ful** *adj.* Shedding tears; mournful, sad. **tear'fully** *adv.* **tear'fulnėss** *n.* **tear'lėss** *adj.* **tear'lėssly** *adv.* **tear'lėssnėss** *n.*

tear[2] (tār) *v.* (past t. *tore*, past part. *torn*). 1. Pull apart, away, or asunder, by force; rend, lacerate; make a tear or rent; (of thing) lend itself to tearing. 2. Move violently or impetuously, rush. ~ *n.* Rent in cloth etc.

tear'ĭng (tār-) *adj.* (esp.) Violent, overwhelming.

tease (tēz) *v.t.* 1. Pull asunder fibres of, comb, card (wool, flax, etc.); comb surface of (cloth etc.) into nap with teasels etc. 2. Assail playfully or maliciously, vex, irritate, with jests, questions, or petty annoyances. ~ *n.* Person addicted to teasing.

teas'el (-z-), **teaz'le** *ns.* Plant of genus *Dipsacus,* herbs with prickly leaves and flower-heads, esp. *D. fullonum, fuller's* ~, heads of which have hooked prickles between flowers; dried prickly flower-head of fuller's teasel used for teasing cloth etc. so as to raise nap on surface; contrivance used as substitute for this. ~ *v.t.* Dress (cloth) with teasel(s).

teas'er (-z-) *n.* (esp., colloq.) Difficult question, problem, or task, thing hard to deal with.

teat *n.* Nipple, small protuberance at tip of breast in female mammalia, upon which ducts of mammary gland open and from which milk is sucked by young; artificial structure resembling this, esp. contrivance of rubber etc. through which milk is sucked from bottle.

teazle: see TEASEL.

tĕc *n.* (slang) Detective.

tĕchne'tium (-knēshm) *n.* (chem.) A radio-active metallic element not found in nature, the first otherwise unknown element to be produced artificially (1937); symbol Tc, at. no. 43, principal isotope 99. [Gk *tekhnētos* artificial]

tĕch'nĭc (-k-) *n.* Technical term or detail, technicality; (pl., rare) technique; (usu. pl.) technology. ~ *adj.* (rare) Technical.

tĕch'nĭcal (-k-) *adj.* Of or in a particular art, science, profession, handicraft, etc.; esp. of, for, in, the mechanical arts and applied science generally. **tĕch'nĭcally** *adv.* **tĕchnĭcăl'ity** *n.* Technical quality or character; technical point, detail, term, etc.

tĕchni'cian (-knĭshn) *n.* Person skilled in the technique of an art or subject; person expert in the practical application of science.

Technicolor (tĕk'nĭkŭl*er*) *n.* (cinematography) Proprietary name of a process of colour photography in which the colours are separately but simultaneously recorded and then transferred to a single positive print.

tĕchnique' (-knēk) *n.* Manner of execution or performance in painting, music, etc.; mechanical part of an art, craft, etc.; (loosely) method of achieving one's purpose.

tĕchnŏc'racy (-kn-) *n.* Government or control of society by technical experts. **tĕch'nocrăt** *n.* **tĕchnocrăt'ĭc** *adj.*

tĕchnŏl'ogy (-k-) *n.* Scientific study of practical or industrial arts; practical arts collectively; terminology of particular art or subject. **tĕchnolŏ'gĭcal** *adj.* **tĕchnŏl'ogist** *n.*

tĕch'y: see TETCHY.

tĕctŏn'ĭc *adj.* Of building or construction; ~ *geology,* that part of geology which deals with structure in the rocks and in the earth's crust. **tĕctŏn'ĭcs** *n.* Art of producing useful and beautiful buildings, furniture, vessels, etc.

tĕctōr'ial *adj.* Forming a covering, esp. ~ *membrane,* the covering part of the inner ear.

tĕctrī'cēs (-z) *n.pl.* (ornith.) Covering feathers of wings and tail; coverts.

tĕd *v.t.* Turn over and spread out (grass, hay) to dry. **tĕdd'er** *n.* Machine for drying hay.

Tĕdd'y bear (bār) *n.* Child's toy bear. [named after *Theodore* Roosevelt]

Tĕdd'y-boy *n.* Youth, esp. delinquent or criminal, affecting Edwardian style of dress.

Tē Dē'um. Ancient Latin hymn of praise beginning *Te Deum laudamus* 'We praise thee, O God', sung at matins in R.C. Ch. and Church of England, and as thanksgiving on special occasions; musical setting of this.

tē'dious *adj.* Tiresomely long, prolix, irksome. **tē'diously** *adv.* **tē'diousness** *n.*

tē'dium *n.* Weariness produced by tediousness, tedious circumstances.

tee[1] *n.* The letter T; any T-shaped thing; ~*-piece,* (eng.) T-shaped part.

tee[2] *n.* (golf) Small mound of sand on which golfer places the ball for driving off at the start and after each hole; small piece of wood, rubber, etc., for the same purpose; place from which the ball is played at the beginning of play for each hole; mark aimed at in quoits, curling, etc. ~ *v.* Place (ball) on tee; ~ *off,* play ball from tee.

tee[3] *n.* Umbrella-shaped usu. gilded ornament crowning tope or pagoda. [f. Burmese *h'ti* umbrella]

teem[1] *v.* (archaic) Bear (offspring); be prolific, be stocked to overflowing with, be abundant.

teem[2] *v.t.* (dial., tech.) Empty, discharge, pour out (vessel, cart, coal, molten metal, etc.).

teen *n.* (archaic) Grief, misfortune.

teens *n.pl.* (also *teen age*). Years of one's age from 13 to 19; *teen-age,* in the teens; *teen-ager* (*n.*).

teen'y *adj.* (nursery) Tiny.

Tees (tēz). English river flowing into North Sea, and forming boundary between Durham and Westmorland and Durham and Yorkshire.

teet'er *v.* Move like a see-saw; move unsteadily.

teeth: see TOOTH.

teethe (-dh) *v.i.* Grow or cut teeth. **teeth'ĭng** *n.*

teetōt'al *adj.* Of, advocating, total abstinence from intoxicants. **teetōt'alism** *n.* **teetōt'ally** *adv.* **teetōt'aller** *n.* Total abstainer. [reduplicated form of *total*]

teetōt'um *n.* Child's four-sided top with sides lettered to determine the spinner's luck; any top spun with the fingers. [f. T (the letter on one side) and L. *totum* the whole (stakes), for which it stood]

tĕg *n.* Sheep in its 2nd year.

t.e.g. *abbrev.* Top edge(s) gilt.

tĕg'ūlar *adj.* Of or like tiles.

tĕg'ūment *n.* Natural covering of (part of) animal body. **tĕgūmĕn'tal, tĕgūmĕn'tary** *adjs.*

Teh(e)ran (tārahn'). Capital city of Persia.

teind (tēnd) *n.* (Sc.) Tithe.

Teiresias: see TIRESIAS.

tĕknŏn'ўmy *n.* Practice of certain savage races of naming the parent from the child.

tĕlaesthēs'ia (-z-) *n.* (psychol.) Perception of distant occurrences or objects otherwise than by means of the recognized physical senses. **tĕlaesthĕt'ĭc** *adj.* [Gk TELE- and *aisthēsis* perception]

tĕl'amon *n.* (archit.) Male figure supporting an entablature (cf. CARYATID). [L, f. Gk *Telamōn* myth. person]

tĕlaut'ograph (-ahf) *n.* Device for transmitting pictures electrically over a distance.

tĕl'ė- *prefix.* Far; esp., in names of instruments, producing or recording results etc at a distance.

tĕlėar'chics (-k-) *n.pl.* Wireless control of aircraft from a distance.

tĕl'ėcast (-ahst) *n.* Programme or item broadcast by television.

tĕl'ėdu (-dōō) *n.* Stinking badger of Java and Sumatra (*Mydaus meliceps*).

tĕl'ėfĭlm *n.* Cinema film transmitted by television.

tĕlėgĕn'ĭc *adj.* Suitable for being televised.

tėlĕg'ony *n.* (biol.) Theory of supposed transmission of characteristics from a previous sire to offspring of the same mother by a later sire. **tĕlėgŏn'ĭc** *adj.*

tĕl'ėgrăm *n.* Message sent by telegraph.

tĕl'ėgraph (-ahf) *n.* Instantaneous conveyance of messages to any distance by means of two instruments so connected by electricity that the working of one excites movements in the other representing letters etc. acc. to some arranged code; apparatus needed for this; semaphore, signalling-apparatus; scoring-board with large figures, or other means of making facts known to a distant observer; ~*-key,* device for making and breaking the electric circuit of a telegraph; ~*-line,* telegraphic connexion; ~*-plant,* East Indian plant of the bean family whose leaves have spontaneous jerking motion; ~*-pole, -post,* pole, post, supporting telegraph wires; ~*-wire,* wire along which telegraphic messages may be transmitted. ~ *v.* Send (message *to* person, or abs.) by telegraph; make signals, convey by signals.

tĕlĕgraphēse′ (-z) *n.* The elliptical style used in telegrams.

tĕlĕgrăph′ĭc *adj.* Of, by, for, the telegraph; (of style) economically worded, with unessential words omitted; ~ *address*, abbreviated or other registered address used in telegrams. **tĕlĕgrăph′ĭcally** *adv.*

tėlĕg′raphĭst *n.* Operator of a telegraph.

tėlĕg′raphy *n.* Art of constructing, practice of communicating by, telegraph; *wireless* ~, transmission of signals through space by means of electro-magnetic waves.

tĕlėkĭn′ėma *n.* Picture-house for showing telefilms.

tĕlėkīnēs′ĭs *n.* Movement at a distance from the motive cause or agent without material connexion, esp. as a spiritualistic phenomenon.

Tėlĕm′achus (-k-). In the 'Odyssey', son of Odysseus and Penelope.

tĕl′ėmârk *n.* Swing turn in skiing used to change direction or to stop short (ill. SKI). [f. *Telemark*, district in Norway]

tĕlėmėchăn′ĭcs (-k-) *n.pl.* Art of transmitting power by radio and so controlling machinery from a distance.

tĕl′ėmēter *v.t.* Register (temperature, pressure, or other phenomena) at a distant meter, usu. by means of radio devices. ~ *n.*

tĕlėŏl′ogy *n.* Doctrine of final causes, view that developments are due to the purpose or design that is served by them. **tĕlėolŏ′gĭc(al)** *adjs.* **tĕlėolŏ′gĭcally** *adv.* **tĕlėŏl′ogĭsm, tĕlėŏl′ogĭst** *ns.*

tėlĕp′athy *n.* Communication of impressions from one mind to another without the aid of the senses. **tĕlėpăth′ĭc** *adj.* **tĕlėpăth′ĭcally** *adv.* **tėlĕp′athĭst** *n.* **tėlĕp′athīze** *v.*

tĕl′ėphōne *n.* Instrument for converting the vibrations caused by sound, esp. that of the voice, into an electric current which passes along a wire and is reconverted into sound at the other end; *the* ~, system of communication by a network of telephones; ~ *exchange*, office or central station of a local telephone system, where the various lines are brought to a central switchboard, and communication between subscribers is effected. **tĕlėphŏn′ĭc** *adj.* **tĕlėphŏn′ĭcally** *adv.* **tĕl′ėphōne** *v.* Send (message), speak (*to* person), by telephone.

tėlĕph′onĭst *n.* Telephone operator.

tėlĕph′ony *n.* Art or science of constructing telephones; the working of a telephone or telephones.

tĕlėphōte *n.* Apparatus for electrical reproduction of photographs at a distance.

tĕlėphōt′ō *adj.* Telephotographic; ~ *lens*, lens or combination of lenses for photographing distant objects.

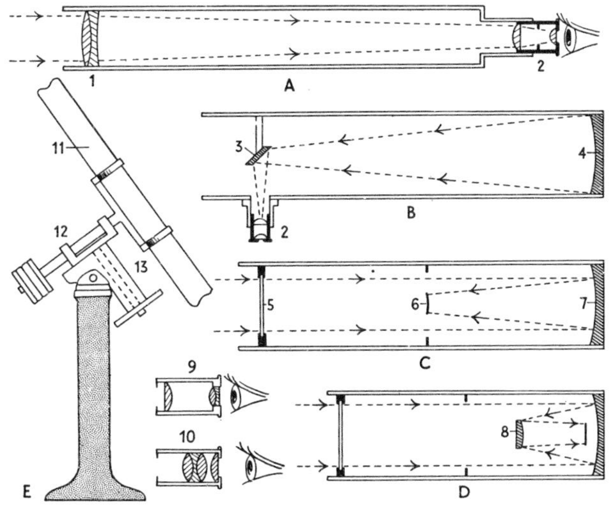

ASTRONOMICAL OPTICAL TELESCOPES: A. REFRACTING. B. NEWTONIAN REFLECTING. C. SCHMIDT PHOTOGRAPHIC. D. MODIFIED SCHMIDT GIVING FLAT FOCAL SURFACE. E. EQUATORIAL MOUNTING

1. Object glass. 2. Huyghenian eyepiece. 3. Flat mirror. 4. Parabolic concave mirror. 5. Glass correcting plate. 6. Curved focal surface. 7. Spherical mirror. 8. Convex mirror. 9. Achromatized Ramsden eyepiece. 10. Orthoscopic eyepiece. 11. Telescope tube. 12. Declination axis. 13. Polar axis

tĕlėphōt′ograph (-ahf) *n.* Photograph made with a telephoto lens; picture or image electrically reproduced at a distance. ~ *v.t.* Photograph with a telephoto lens or apparatus. **tĕlėphōtogrăph′ĭc** *adj.* **tĕlėphotŏg′raphy** *n.* Photography of objects at a distance by means of a camera with a telephoto lens; (rare, now usu. *phototelegraphy*) electric transmission of pictures or scenes to a distance.

tĕl′ėprĭnt *n.* Message sent by teleprinter. ~ *v.* Send (message etc.), communicate, by teleprinter.

tĕl′ėprĭnter *n.* Telegraphically operated kind of typewriter.

tĕl′ėprŏmpter *n.* Electronic device for prompting television speaker by slowly unrolling his text in large letters outside the audience's sight.

tĕl′ergy *n.* (psychol.) Force conceived as effecting telepathy. [f. *tel(epathic en)ergy*]

tĕl′ėscōpe *n.* Optical instrument for making distant objects appear nearer and larger, consisting of one or more tubes with an arrangement of lenses, or of one or more mirrors and lenses, by which the rays of light are collected and brought to a focus and the resulting image magnified. Telescopes are of 2 kinds: *refracting*, in which the image is reproduced by a lens (the object-glass), and *reflecting*, in which it is produced by a mirror; in each case the image is magnified by a lens or combination of lenses (the eyepiece); *radio* ~, a directional aerial system for collecting radio energy from different parts of the sky as an optical telescope collects light from different stars; it can be steerable, as the 250-ft Jodrell Bank instrument in Cheshire, or fixed and directed by the earth's rotation to successive points in the sky. ~ *v.* Force or drive one into another like the sliding-tubes of a hand-telescope; close, slide together, in this manner; be forced one into the other (esp. of colliding railway trains).

tĕlėscŏp′ĭc *adj.* Of, made with, a telescope; visible only through a telescope, as ~ *stars*; consisting of sections that telescope. **tĕlėscŏp′ĭcally** *adv.*

tėlĕs′copĭst *n.* User of telescope.

tėlĕs′copy *n.* Use and making of telescopes.

tĕl′ėsēme *n.* System of electrical signalling used in hotels etc.

tĕl′ėvīse (-z) *v.t.* Transmit (image of scene, object, etc.) by television.

tĕl′ėvĭsion (-zhn) *n.* Simultaneous visual reproduction of scenes, objects, performances, etc., at a distance; vision of distant objects obtained thus. The equipment consists of a camera which converts the image into electrical impulses; these are transmitted by radio to a receiver which converts the impulses by means of a CATHODE-ray tube into a corresponding image on a screen. **tĕl'ėvīsor** (-z-) *n.* Transmitting apparatus for television.

Tĕl'ford, Thomas (1757–1834). Scottish civil engineer, designer of numerous roads and bridges (notably the Menai Bridge) and the Caledonian Canal; called by Southey the 'Colossus of Roads'.

tĕll[1] *v.* (past t. and past part. *tōld*). Relate or narrate; make known, divulge, state, express in words; inform or give information *of, about, how,* etc.; betray secret, inform against (person); ascertain, decide about, distinguish; produce marked effect on, hence *tell'ing* (*adj.*), *tell'ingly* (*adv.*); count (votes, esp. in House of Commons); ~ one's *beads*, use rosary; ~ one's *fortune*, forecast his future by occult means; ~ *off*, number (party etc.), pick out (specified number of persons, person) *for* task or *to* do; (slang) tell (person) home truths, recite misdoings of; ~ *on*, inform against; ~ *that to the (horse-)marines* (formula of incredulity).

Tĕll[2], William. Legendary hero of the liberation in the 14th c. of Switzerland from Austrian oppression; the legend represents him as a skilled marksman who refused to do honour to the hat of Gessler, the Austrian bailiff, placed on a pole, and was in consequence required to shoot with an arrow an apple placed on the head of his son; this he successfully did and with a second arrow shot Gessler.

tĕll'er *n.* (esp.) Any of 4 persons appointed (2 for each side) to count votes in House of Commons; person appointed to receive or pay out money in bank etc.

tĕll'tāle *n.* Person who tells about another's private affairs; (fig.) thing, circumstance, that reveals person's thoughts, conduct, etc., esp. attrib., as ~ *blushes, stain*; kinds of automatic registering device; (naut.) index near wheel to show position of the tiller.

tĕllūr'ate *n.* Salt of telluric acid.

tĕllūr'ĭan *adj.* & *n.* (Inhabitant) of the earth.

tĕllūr'ĭc *adj.* Of, derived from, TELLURIUM; ~ *acid*, acid (H_2TeO_4), analogous to sulphuric acid, obtained by oxidizing tellurium.

tĕllūr'ĭum *n.* (chem.) Rare, brittle, lustrous, silver-coloured element, formerly classed among the metals, but chemically belonging to the same family as sulphur and selenium; symbol Te, at. no. 52, at. wt 127·60.

tĕll'ūrous *adj.* Of, containing, tellurium, esp. of compounds containing a greater proportion of tellurium than those called *telluric*; ~ *acid*, H_2TeO_3.

Tĕll'us. (Rom. myth.) Goddess of the earth; earth personified, the planet Earth.

tĕl'otȳpe *n.* Electric telegraph that automatically prints the messages received; telegram printed by this.

tĕl'pher *n* Travelling unit in telpherage; (attrib.) employing or worked by telpherage. **tĕl'pherage** *n.* Automatic electric transport of goods etc.

tĕl'son *n.* Posterior abdominal region of some crustaceans and other arthropods (ill. LOBSTER).

Tĕl'ugu (-ōōgōō). (Language, member) of Dravidian people in Coromandel coast region of India, N. of Madras.

tĕmerār'ĭous *adj.* (literary) Rash, reckless. **tĕmerār'ĭously** *adv.*

tėmĕ'rĭty *n.* Rashness, audacity.

tĕmp. abbrev. *tempore* (= 'in the time of'), as *temp. Henry I.*

Tĕm'pė. Ancient name of a beautiful valley in Thessaly, watered by R. Peneus, between Mts Olympus and Ossa.

tĕm'per *v.* Bring (clay etc.) to the desired consistency by moistening and kneading; toughen and harden (metal, esp. steel, glass) by heating, sudden cooling, and reheating; (of metal etc.) come to proper hardness and elasticity by this means; modify, mitigate (*justice* etc.) by blending *with* (*mercy* etc.). ~ *n.* 1. Consistency of clay etc. obtained by tempering; degree of hardness and elasticity in steel etc. produced by tempering. 2. Habitual or temporary disposition of mind; fit of anger; composure under provocation; *lose* one's ~, become angry.

tĕm'pera *n.* Painting with colours which have been mixed with a natural emulsion (e.g. egg-yolk) or an artificial emulsion (e.g. oil and gum), esp. the method used for movable pictures before the development of oil-painting.

tĕm'perament *n.* 1. Characteristic combination of physical, mental, and moral qualities which together constitute the character of an individual and affect his manner of acting, feeling, and thinking; (*artistic, musical*) ~, emotional character of artist or musician. 2. (mus.) Adjustment of the tones of the scale (in the tuning of instruments of fixed tone, e.g. piano) so as to adapt the scale for use in all keys; *equal* ~, that in which the 12 semitones are at equal intervals.

tĕmperamĕn'tal *adj.* Of, relating to, the temperament; liable to, marked by, variable or unaccountable moods. **tĕmperamĕn'tally** *adv.*

tĕm'perance *n.* Moderation, self-restraint, in speech, conduct, etc., esp. in eating and drinking; moderation in use of, total abstinence from, alcoholic liquors as beverages; (attrib.) non-alcoholic, aimed at the restriction or prohibition of alcoholic drinks, as in ~ *drinks, legislation, league*; ~ *hotel*, hotel not supplying alcoholic drinks.

tĕm'perate *adj.* Moderate, self-restrained; abstemious; (of climate) not exhibiting extremes of heat or cold, equable; ~ *zone*, the zone between either tropic and the corresponding polar circle. **tĕm'perately** *adv.* **tĕm'perateness** *n.*

tĕm'perature *n.* Degree or intensity of sensible heat of a body or of the atmosphere, esp. as shown by the thermometer; (med.) internal heat of the body (*normal* ~ in man, 98·4° F.); *take* one's ~, ascertain his internal heat with a clinical thermometer to detect any variation from the normal state of health; ~ *chart*, one showing a temperature curve; ~ *curve*, curve showing variations of temperature, esp. in clinical use.

tĕm'pėst *n.* Violent storm; (fig.) violent tumult or agitation.

tĕmpĕs'tūous *adj.* (Of weather, time, etc., and fig. of person or mood) stormy, violent. **tĕmpĕs'tūously** *adv.* **tĕmpĕs'tūousnėss** *n.*

Tĕm'plar *n.* 1. Member of a powerful and wealthy religious and military order of knights (*Knights* ~*s*), chaplains, and men-at-arms; it was founded *c* 1118 for the protection of the Holy Sepulchre and of Christian pilgrims to the Holy Land, and for some time occupied a building on or near the site of Solomon's Temple at Jerusalem; suppressed by Council of VIENNE, 1312. 2. Lawyer, student, with chambers in the Temple in London. 3. Member of an order of Freemasons (*Knights Templars*) or of a temperance society (*Good Templars*).

template: see TEMPLET.

tĕm'ple[1] *n.* Edifice dedicated to service of (esp. ancient Greek, Roman, Egyptian) god; any of the three successive religious edifices of the Jews in Jerusalem; place of Christian public worship, esp. Protestant church in France; (fig.) place in which God resides; *The T*~, the Inns of Court, Inner and Middle Temple, in London, the site of which formerly belonged to the Knights Templars; *T*~ *Bar*, gateway (removed 1879) that marked the westward limit of the City Corporation's jurisdiction, at junction of Fleet St. and the Strand in London.

tĕm'ple[2] *n.* Flat part of either side of the head between the forehead and the ear.

tĕm'ple[3] *n.* Device for keeping cloth taut on a loom.

tĕm'plėt, -āte *n.* Pattern, gauge, usu. thin board or metal plate, used as a guide in cutting or drilling metal, stone, wood, etc.; timber or plate used to distribute weight in a wall or under a beam etc.; wedge for building-block under ship's keel.

tĕm′pō *n.* (mus.) Speed at which a passage is (to be) played; (transf.) rate of movement, activity, or progress.

tĕm′poral *adj.* 1. Of, in, denoting, time; (gram.) pertaining to time or tense. 2. Of this life only, secular, lay (opp. *spiritual*); ~ *peers* or *lords* ~, members of the House of Lords other than the bishops; ~ *power*, the power of an ecclesiastic, esp. the pope, in temporal matters. 3. (anat.) Of the temples; ~ *bone*, a compound bone of the side of the human skull (ill. HEAD). **tĕm′porally** *adv.* **tĕm′poralnėss** *n.* **tĕm′poral** *n.* Temporal bone.

tĕmporăl′ity *n.* Secular possessions, esp. properties and revenues of a religious body or an ecclesiastic (usu. pl.); (law) temporariness.

tĕm′porary *adj.* Lasting only for a time, transient; held, occupied, during a limited time only, not permanent. **tĕm′porarily** *adv.* **tĕm′porarinėss** *n.*

tĕm′porize *v.i.* Pursue indecisive or time-serving policy; avoid committing oneself, act so as to gain time; comply temporarily with requirements of an occasion. **tĕmporizā′tion, tĕm′porizer** *ns.*

tĕm′poro- *prefix.* Of temples of head, as ~*-facial*, of temporal and facial regions.

tĕmpt *v.t.* (archaic, bibl.) Test, try, the resolution of; (archaic, bibl.) provoke, defy; entice, incite (*to do, to* action, esp. evil one); allure, attract.

tĕmptā′tion *n.* Tempting or being tempted; thing that attracts, attractive course.

tĕmp′ter *n.* One who tempts, esp. *the T*~, the Devil. **tĕmp′trėss** *n.* Woman who tempts (chiefly in bad sense).

tĕmp′ting *adj.* Alluring, attractive. **tĕmp′tingly** *adv.*

tĕn *adj.* & *n.* One more than nine (10, x, or X); *the upper* ~, for *ten thousand*, the aristocracy; ~*-pins*, (chiefly U.S.) game similar to NINE pins, played with 10 'pins'; ~*-pounder*, (hist.) person having a vote in parliamentary election by occupation of property of rental value of £10.

tĕn′able *adj.* Capable of being maintained or defended against attack or objection; (of office etc.) that can be held *for* a specified time, *by* person, etc. **tĕnabĭl′ity, tĕn′ablenėss** *ns.*

tĕn′ace (-ĭs) *n.* (whist) (Holding of) two cards, one next above, the other next below, the opponents' highest of the suit. [Span. *tenaza*, lit. 'pincers']

tėnā′cious (-sh*us*) *adj.* Holding fast; keeping firm hold (*of* property, rights, principles, etc.); (of memory) retentive; adhesive, sticky; strongly cohesive. **tėnā′ciously** *adv.* **tėnā′ciousnėss, tėnă′city** *ns.*

tėnăc′ūlum *n.* (pl. *-la*). Surgeon's sharp hook used for taking up arteries.

tėnail′, -aille′ (-āl) *n.* (fort.) Outwork in main ditch between two bastions.

tĕn′ancy *n.* Act of holding property as a tenant; period of such holding; property, land, etc., held by a tenant.

tĕn′ant *n.* (law) Person holding real property by private ownership; person who occupies land or tenement under a landlord; inhabitant, dweller. ~ *v.t.* Occupy as tenant (esp. in past part.).

tĕn′antable *adj.* Fit to be occupied by a tenant.

tĕn′antry *n.* Tenants.

tĕnch *n.* European freshwater fish (*Tinca vulgaris*) of the carp family.

tĕnd[1] *v.i.* Move, be directed, in a certain direction; be apt or inclined, serve, conduce (*to* action, quality, etc., *to* do).

tĕnd[2] *v.* Take care of, look after (flocks, invalid, machine, etc.); wait *upon*; (naut.) watch (ship at anchor) so as to keep turns out of her cable. **tĕn′dance** *n.* (archaic).

tĕn′dency *n.* Bent, leaning, inclination (*towards, to,* thing, *to* do).

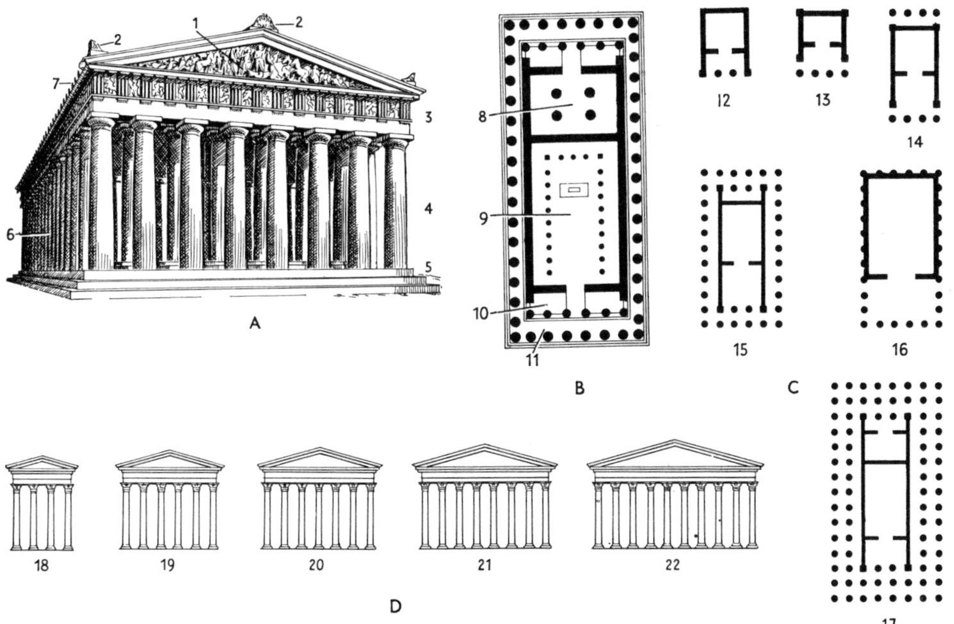

CLASSICAL TEMPLES: A, B. RECONSTRUCTION AND PLAN OF THE PARTHENON. C, D. PLANS AND ELEVATIONS OF TEMPLES

A. 1. Pediment. 2. Acroterion. 3. Entablature. 4. Column. 5. Stylobate. 6. Peristyle. 7. Antefix. B. 8. Inner cella. 9. Cella or naos. 10. Pronaos. 11. Portico or stoa. C. 12. Distyle in antis. 13. Prostyle. 14. Amphiprostyle. 15. Peripteral. 16. Pseudo-peripteral. 17. Dipteral. D. 18. Tetrastyle. 19. Hexastyle. 20. Heptastyle. 21. Octastyle. 22. Decastyle

tĕndĕn'tious (-sh*us*) *adj.* (Of writing etc.) having an underlying purpose, calculated to advance a cause.

tĕn'der[1] *n.* In verbal senses of TEND[2]; also: 1. Small ship in attendance upon a larger one to supply her with stores, convey orders, etc. 2. Truck attached to a locomotive and carrying fuel, water, etc. (ill. LOCOMOTIVE). 3. Small water reservoir fixed to mop etc.

tĕn'der[2] *v.* Offer, present, give in (one's *services, resignation,* etc.); offer (money etc.) as payment; make a tender (*for* supply of thing or execution of work). ~ *n.* Offer, esp. offer in writing to execute work or supply goods at a fixed price; *legal* ~, currency recognized by law as acceptable in payment of a debt.

tĕn'der[3] *adj.* Soft, not tough or hard; easily touched or wounded, susceptible to pain or grief; delicate, fragile, (lit., and fig. of reputation etc.); loving, affectionate, fond; solicitous, considerate; requiring careful handling, ticklish. *ten'derfoot,* (colonial and U.S. slang) new-comer in camp, settlement, etc., novice, greenhorn; (Boy Scouts) new recruit; ~-*hearted,* susceptible to, easily moved by, pity; kindly, compassionate; *ten'derloin,* (pork) middle part of loin; (U.S.) undercut of sirloin; amusements district of New York and other cities. **tĕn'derly** *adv.* **tĕn'derness** *n.*

tĕn'dĭnous *adj.* Of, connected with, resembling, a tendon.

tĕn'don *n.* Tough, fibrous tissue connecting a muscle to some other part (ill. MUSCLE); sinew; *Achilles* ~: see ACHILLES.

tĕn'drĭl *n.* Slender thread-like organ or appendage of a plant, often spiral in form, which stretches out and attaches itself to some other body so as to support the plant.

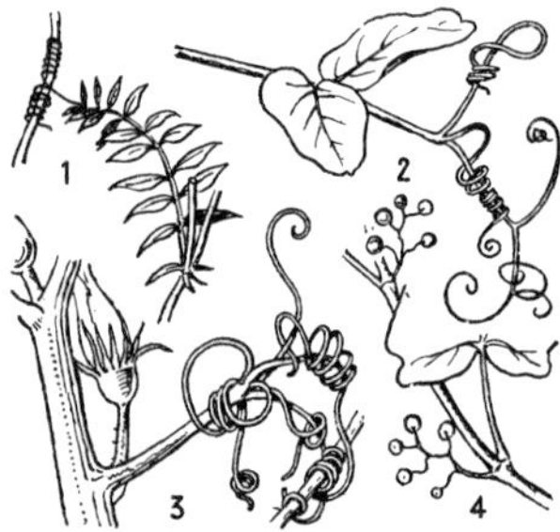

TENDRILS

1. Tendril formed from midrib of leaf (tare). 2. Tendril formed at end of leaf-bearing stem (pea). 3. Stem tendril (marrow). 4. Self-climbing tendril (Virginia creeper)

tĕn'ĕbrae *n.pl.* (R.C. Ch.) Matins and lauds for the last three days of Holy Week, at which the candles are successively extinguished. [L, = 'darkness']

tĕn'ement *n.* (law) Any kind of permanent property as lands, rents, held of a superior; dwelling-house; portion of a house, tenanted as a separate dwelling; ~-*house,* house containing tenements. **tĕnemĕn'tal** *adj.*

Tĕneriffe' (-rēf). Largest of the Canary Islands.

tĕn'ĕt *n.* Principle, dogma, doctrine, of a person or school. [L, = 'he holds']

tĕn'fōld *adj.* & *adv.* Ten times repeated; ten times as many.

tenia: see TAENIA.

Tĕn'iers (-ny*erz*), David. Name of two Flemish painters, father (1582–1649) and son (1610–90), the younger being the more famous.

Tenn. *abbrev.* Tennessee.

tĕnn'er *n.* (colloq.) A ten-pound note, ten pounds.

Tĕnn'ĕssēē. East South Central State of U.S., admitted to the Union in 1796; capital, Nashville.

Tĕnn'iel, Sir John (1820–1914). English painter and cartoonist; illustrator of the 'Alice' books of Lewis Carroll.

tĕnn'ĭs *n.* Game for two or four persons played by striking ball with racket (formerly with the palm of the hand) over a net stretched across a walled oblong court; similar game played on an open court, LAWN tennis; ~ *court,* court on which tennis or lawn tennis is played; ~ *elbow,* inflammatory condition of the elbow joint, caused by strain in playing tennis. [app. f. OF *tenez* 'take', 'receive', called by server to his opponent]

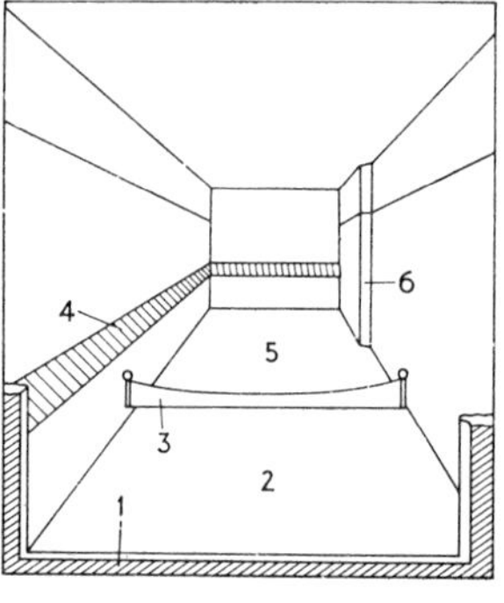

TENNIS COURT

1. Dedans. 2. Service side. 3. Net. 4. Penthouse. 5. Hazard side. 6. Tambour

Tĕnn'ÿson, Alfred, first Baron (1809–92). English poet; poet laureate from 1850; author of 'In Memoriam', 'Maud', 'Idylls of the King', 'Enoch Arden', etc. **Tĕnnysō'nian** *adj.*

tĕn'on *n.* Projection fashioned on the end or side of a piece of wood or other material, to fit into a corresponding cavity or mortice in another piece (ill. JOINT); ~-*saw,* fine saw for making tenons etc., having a thin blade, strong brass or steel back, and small teeth (ill. SAW). ~ *v.t.* Cut into a tenon; join by means of a tenon.

tĕn'or *n.* 1. Settled or prevailing course or direction (esp. fig. *of* one's *life, way,* etc.); general purport, drift (*of* speech, writing, etc.); (law) true intent, exact copy. 2. (mus.) (Music for, singer with) high adult male voice, usually ranging from the octave below middle C to the A above it; viola; instrument of any kind of which the range is approx. that of tenor voice; ~ *bell,* largest of a peal or set. [L *tenorem* holding on, (med. L) chief melody, formerly assigned to adult male voice]

tĕnŏt'omy *n.* Tendon-cutting, esp. as remedy for club-foot.

tĕnse[1] *n.* Any of the different forms or modifications in the conjugation of a verb which indicate the different times (*past, present,* or *future*) at which the action or state denoted by it is viewed as happening or existing, and also (by extension) the different nature of such action or state, as continuing (*imperfect*), completed (*perfect*), or indefinite (*aorist*).

tĕnse[2] *adj.* (Of cord, membrane, nerve, fig. of mind, emotion) stretched tight, strained to stiffness, highly strung; (phon., of vowel) uttered with the tongue in a tense condition (opp. *slack*). **tĕnse'ly** (-sl-) *adv.* **tĕnse'nĕss** *n.*

tĕn'sĭble *adj.* Capable of being stretched out or extended. **tĕnsĭbĭl'ity** *n.*

tĕn'sīle *adj.* Of tension; capable of being drawn out or stretched. **tĕnsĭl'ity** *n.*

tĕn'sion (-shn) *n.* Stretching, being stretched; tenseness; mental strain or excitement, strained (political, social, etc.) state; (physics) effect produced by forces pulling against each other; (elect.) the stress along lines of force in a dielectric, formerly used as a synonym for potential, electromotive force, and mechanical force exerted by electricity; still so applied, in industrial and commercial use, in *high* and *low* ~. **tĕn'sional** (-sho-) *adj.*

tĕn'son, tĕn'zon *n.* Contest of verse-making between troubadours.

tĕn'sor *n.* 1. (anat.) Muscle that tightens or stretches a part. 2. (math.) In quaternions, a quantity expressing the ratio in which the length of a vector is increased.

tĕnt[1] *n.* Portable shelter of canvas, cloth, etc., supported by pole(s) and stretched by cords secured to *tent-pegs* driven into the ground; *bell* ~, circular tent with one pole in the middle; ~-*bed,* bed with a tent-like canopy; bed for use in a tent, field-bed;

~-*fly*, piece of canvas pitched outside and over ridge of tent as extra protection from sun rain, etc. (also called *fly-sheet*); ~-*pegging*, cavalry exercise in which the rider tries at full gallop to carry off on point of his lance a tent-peg fixed in the ground; ~-*stitch*, series of parallel diagonal stitches (ill. STITCH). ~ *v.* Cover (as) with a tent; encamp in a tent.

tĕnt[2] *v.t.* Dilate (orifice of wound etc.) by inserting plug of lint etc. ~ *n.* Plug of lint, linen, etc., used for this purpose.

tĕnt[3] *n.* Sweet, dark-red, Spanish wine, chiefly used as sacramental wine. [Span. *tinto* deep-coloured]

tĕn'tacle *n.* Slender flexible process in animals, esp. invertebrates, serving as sensory or attachment organ (ill. JELLY); (bot.) sensitive hair or filament. **tĕn'tacled** (-kld), **tĕntăc'ūlar, tĕntăc'ūlate, -ātėd** *adjs.*

tĕn'tative *adj.* Done by way of trial, experimental. **tĕn'tatively** *adv.* **tĕn'tative** *n.* Tentative proposal or step.

tĕn'ter[1] *n.* Person in charge of something, esp. of machinery in a factory.

tĕn'ter[2] *n.* Machine or frame for stretching cloth to set or dry; *ten'terhooks*, hooks to which cloth is fastened on a tenter; *on tenterhooks*, (fig.) in a state of suspense, distracted by uncertainty.

tĕnth *adj.* & *n.* Next after the ninth; a tenth part, object in a series next after the ninth. **tĕnth'ly** *adv.*

tĕn'ūis *n.* (pl. *tenūēs*). (phonet.) Voiceless stop, as *p, t, k.*

tėnū'ity *n.* Slenderness; (of air, fluid) rarity, thinness; (of style) simplicity, lack of grandeur.

tĕn'ūous *adj.* (rare) Thin, slender, small; (of distinctions etc.) subtle, over-refined.

tĕn'ure (-yer) *n.* The holding *of* a piece of property or office; conditions or period of such holding.

tenu'tō (-ōō-) *adj.* (mus.) Sustained, given its full time value (contrasted with *staccato*).

tenzon: see TENSON.

tēocăll'ĭ *n.* (archaeol.) Temple of Aztec or other Mexican aborigines, usu. built on a truncated pyramidal mound. [wd used by Nahua-speaking Indians for a ruined temple, f. Mexican *teotl* god, *calli* house]

tēp'ee *n.* Conical tent, hut, or wigwam of the N. Amer. Indians.

tĕp'ėfȳ *v.* Make, become, tepid. **tĕpėfăc'tion** *n.*

tĕph'rīte *n.* Ash-coloured volcanic rock.

tĕp'ĭd *adj.* Slightly warm, lukewarm (lit. and fig.). **tėpid'ity, tĕp'idnėss** *ns.* **tĕp'idly** *adv.*

tĕpĭdār'ĭum *n.* (pl. -*ria*). Warm room in ancient Roman baths, situated between the *frigidarium* and the *caldarium.*

tėr *adv.* (mus.) Three times, indicating that a passage is to be played three times successively.

tĕr'aph *n.* (pl. *teraphim*, used as a sing. or collective sing.). Small image used in divination as a kind of domestic oracle among the ancient Hebrews.

tĕratŏl'ogy *n.* Tale or myth concerning prodigies, marvellous tale, collection of these; (biol.) study of monstrosities or abnormal formations, esp. in man. **tĕratolŏ'gical** *adj.*

tĕratōm'a *n.* Tumour made up of heterogeneous mixture of tissues.

tėrb'ium *n.* (chem.) Metallic element of rare-earth group found in combination in gadolinite and other minerals: symbol Tb, at. no. 65, at. wt 158·924. [f. *Ytterby* in Sweden]

tėrce *n.* Var. of TIERCE.

tėr'cel *n.* Male falcon. [L *tertius* 3rd, from belief that the 3rd egg of a hawk produced a small male bird]

tėrcentēn'ary (*or* -sĕn'tĭ-) *n.* 300th anniversary. ~ *adj.* Of 300 (esp. years). **tėrcentĕnn'ial** *n.* & *adj.* Tercentenary.

tĕ'rėbēne *n.* Mixture of terpenes obtained by action of sulphuric acid on oil of turpentine and used as antiseptic etc.

tĕ'rėbinth *n.* Small S. European tree, *Pistacia terebinthus*, yielding *Chian* turpentine. **tĕrėbinth'ine** *adj.* Of the terebinth; of turpentine.

terēd'ō *n.* The ship-worm (*Teredo navalis*), a mollusc which destroys submerged timbers in ships, piers, etc., by boring into the wood; genus including this.

Tĕ'rence. Publius Terentius Afer (*c* 190–*c* 159 B.C.). Roman author of comedies, born at Carthage.

Terēs'a (-*za*), St. (1515–82). Spanish mystic and religious reformer; born at Avila (as Teresa de Cepeda); became a Carmelite nun and founded the Discalced (barefooted) Carmelites, who follow a stricter rule; wrote 'The Way of Perfection' (1565) and other mystical works, and an autobiography.

tėrg'al *adj.* Of the back, dorsal.

tėr'giversāte (-j-, -g-) *v.i.* Turn one's coat, desert one's party or principles, apostatize. **tėrgiversā'tion** *n.*

tėrm *n.* 1. Boundary, limit, esp. of time (somewhat archaic); limited period; completion of period of pregnancy, (normal) time of childbirth; (law) estate or interest in land, etc., for fixed period; (esp. Sc.) quarter-day, each of days in year fixed for payment of rent, wages, etc. 2. Figure, post, stone, etc., marking boundary (see TERMINUS, sense 4). 3. Each period (usu. three or four in year) appointed for sitting of court of law, or for instruction and study in school, university, etc. 4. (math.) Each of two quantities composing a ratio or fraction; each of the quantities forming a series or progression; each of the quantities connected by signs of addition (+) or subtraction (−) in an algebraical expression or equation. 5. (logic) Word(s), notion, that may be subject or predicate of a proposition; hence, any word or group of words expressing a definite conception, esp. in particular branch of study etc.; (pl.) language employed, mode of expression; *terms of reference*, terms defining scope of inquiry, action, etc. 6. (pl.) Conditions, esp. charge, price; *terms of trade*, ratio between prices paid for imports and received for exports. 7. (pl.) Relation, footing. ~ *v.t.* Denominate, call.

tėrm'agant *n.* Brawling turbulent woman, shrew, scold. [imaginary deity supposed in medieval times to be worshipped by Mohammedans]

tėrm'inable *adj.* That may be terminated (esp. after definite period).

tėrm'inal *adj.* Of, forming, a limit or terminus; situated at, forming, the end or extremity of something; of, forming, a term, termly. **tėrm'inally** *adv.* **tėrm'inal** *n.* Terminating thing, extremity, esp. (structure or device forming) each of free ends of open electrical circuit, by connecting which circuit is closed; (physiol.) end of nerve fibre or neuron; ornament at end of something; (U.S.) end of railway line, terminus.

tėrm'ināte *v.* Bound, limit; bring, come, to an end, end (*at, in, with*). **tėrm'inative** *adj.* **tėrm'inatively** *adv.* **tėrm'inate** (-*at*) *adj.* Determinate, finite, esp. (math.) not recurring or infinite, expressible in finite number of terms.

tėrminā'tion *n.* (esp.) Final syllable or letter(s) of word, (inflexional or derivative) ending, suffix.

tėrm'inātor *n.* (esp., astron.) Line of separation between dark and light parts of moon or planet.

tėrminŏl'ogy *n.* System of terms belonging to a science or subject; technical terms collectively. **tėrminolŏ'gical** *adj.* **tėrminolŏ'gically** *adv.*

tėrm'inus *n.* (pl. -*uses*, -*ī*). 1. (now rare) Final point, goal. 2. (Station at) end of line of railway, tram-line, bus-route, etc. 3. Point to which motion or action tends; ~ *ad quem*, ~ *a quo*, terminating-, starting-, point (of argument, policy, period, etc.). 4. (Rom. antiq., also *term*) statue or bust of the god Terminus, who presided over landmarks and boundaries; figure of human bust supported on square pillar.

tėrm'itary, tėrmitār'ium *ns.* Termites' nest.

tėrm'īte *n.* Social insect of order *Isoptera*, chiefly tropical, and very destructive to timber, 'white ant' (not a true ant). **tĕrmĭt'ic** *adj.*

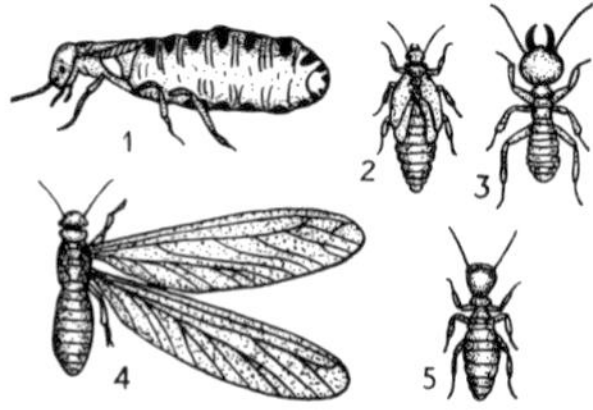

TERMITE

1. Queen. 2. Nymph. 3. Soldier. 4. Winged male. 5. Worker

tĕrn[1] *n.* Kinds of sea-bird of *Sterna* and allied genera, resembling gulls but usu. smaller and more slender-bodied, with long, pointed wing and forked tail; sea-swallow.

tĕrn[2] *n.* Set of three, esp. three lottery-numbers drawn together and winning large prize; such prize. ~ *adj.* = TERNATE.

tĕrn'ary *adj.* Of, in, set(s) of three; composed of three parts or elements; (mus.) ~ *form*, form of movement with independent subject or tune followed by another in a related key and then by a repetition of the first.

tĕrn'ate *adj.* Consisting of, arranged in, threes, esp. (bot.) composed of three leaflets, (of leaves) in whorls of three. **tĕrn'ately** *adv.*

tĕrne'(-plāte) *n.* Thin sheet-iron or steel coated with alloy of lead and tin, inferior tin-plate. [Fr. *terne* dull, tarnished]

tĕrp'ēne *n.* (chem.) Any of a large group of cyclic hydrocarbons which form the chief constituents of the volatile oils obtained by distilling plant material. [obs. *terpentin* TURPENTINE]

Tĕrpsĭch'orė (-k-). (Gk and Rom. myth.) Muse of dancing and choral song. **Tĕrpsĭchorē'an** *adj.* Of Terpsichore; of dancing.

tĕ'rra ăl'ba *n.* Pipe-clay; various other white mineral substances.

tĕ'rrace *n.* 1. Raised level place, natural or artificial, esp. raised walk in garden or level space in front of building on sloping ground; (geol.) horizontal shelf or beach bordering river, lake, or sea. 2. Row of houses on raised site or on face of rising ground; row of houses of uniform style built in one block. ~ *v.t.* Form into, furnish with, terrace(s).

tĕrracŏtt'a *n.* Hard unglazed pottery of fine quality used for decorative tiles, statuary, architectural decorations, etc.; statuette, figurine of this; the brownish-red colour of this pottery. ~ *adj.* Of, made of, of the colour of, terracotta. [It., = 'baked earth']

tĕ'rrae fĭl'ĭus. Son of the soil.

tĕ'rra fĭrm'a. Dry land, firm ground.

tĕrrain' *n.* Tract of country considered with regard to its natural features etc., esp. (mil.) its tactical advantages, fitness for manœuvring, etc.

tĕ'rra ĭncŏg'nĭta. Unknown or unexplored region.

tĕrramar'a, tĕrramare' (-mar) *n.* Kinds of earthy deposit used as a fertilizer, esp. that found in mounds on the site of later Bronze Age and early Iron Age settlements in the Po valley, Italy; the settlements themselves. [It., f. L *terra amara* bitter earth]

tĕrramȳ'cin *n.* Antibiotic substance used in medicine, obtained from the soil organism *Streptomyces rimosus.*

tĕrrāne' *n.* (geol.) Connected series, group, or system of rocks or formations, area over which a group of formations is prevalent.

tĕ'rrapin *n.* Various species of N. Amer. edible turtles of fresh or brackish water, esp. the diamond-backed terrapins (*Malaclemmys*) of salt marshes of coasts of Atlantic and Gulf of Mexico, famous for their delicate flesh.

tĕrrāq'uėous *adj.* Consisting of land and water; living in, extending over, land and water.

***terra verde*:** see TERRE-VERTE.

tĕrrēne' *adj.* Of earth, earthy; terrestrial.

terreplein (tār'plān) *n.* (fort.) Surface of rampart behind parapet, esp. level space on which guns are mounted; level base of battery in field fortifications.

terrĕs'trial *adj.* Of the earth, of this world, worldly; of land as opp. to water; ~ *globe*, globe with map of earth on its surface. **terrĕs'trially** *adv.*

tĕr'rėt *n.* Ring, esp. on swivel, to which chain, string, etc., is attached, esp. each of the loops or strings on harness-pad for driving-reins to pass through.

terre-verte (tārvārt) *n.* (also *terra verde* pr. vār'dā). Soft green earth, esp. *celadonite* or *glauconite*, used as pigment.

tĕ'rrible *adj.* Exciting, fitted to excite, terror; awful, dreadful, formidable; (colloq.) very great, excessive. **tĕ'rribly** *adv.*

tĕ'rrier[1] *n.* 1. Kinds of usu. small active hardy dog which pursues quarry (fox, badger, etc.) into burrow or earth (ill. DOG). 2. (colloq.) A Territorial.

tĕ'rrier[2] *n.* Register of landed property, with boundaries, acreage, etc.; rent-roll.

terrĭf'ic *adj.* Terrifying, dreadful, frightful; (colloq.) very great or severe, excessive. **terrĭf'ically** *adv.*

tĕ'rrĭfȳ *v.t.* Fill with terror, frighten.

tĕrrine' (-ēn) *n.* Earthenware vessel containing and sold with some table delicacy such as pâté de foie-gras.

tĕrrĭtŏr'ĭal *adj.* Of territory; of a particular territory or locality, local; *T~ Army*, British Army of Home Defence instituted on territorial or local basis in 1908 and consisting of men living at home and doing only occasional periods of drill and other training; similar force in other countries; ~ *waters*, that part of the high seas adjacent to its shores over which a State claims jurisdiction, esp. within a minimum of 3 miles from low-water mark. **tĕrrĭtŏr'ĭally** *adv.* **Tĕrrĭtŏr'ĭal** *n.* Member of Territorial Force or Army.

tĕrrĭtŏr'ĭalism *n.* System of Church government under which the civil rule has religious jurisdiction over the subjects of a State.

tĕ'rrĭtory *n.* Land under jurisdiction of sovereign, State, city, etc.; (large) tract of land, region; (in U.S., Canada, Australia, etc.) portion of country not yet admitted to full rights of a State or Province; area over which commercial traveller etc. operates; (games) half of field regarded as belonging to team whose goal etc. is in it; (fig.) sphere, realm, province.

tĕ'rror *n.* Extreme fear; person or thing causing this; (colloq.) exasperating or tiresome person, troublesome child; *king of ~s*, death personified; *reign of ~*, time in which community lives in dread of death or outrage, esp. (Fr. hist.) period during French Revolution (1793–4) during which rulers took remorseless measures against persons regarded as obnoxious and executed many.

tĕ'rrorist *n.* Person attempting to further his views or to rule by system of coercive intimidation. **tĕ'rrorism** *n.* **tĕrroris'tic** *adj.*

tĕ'rrorīze *v.* Fill with terror; rule or maintain power by terrorism. **tĕrrorīzā'tion** *n.*

tĕ'rry[1] *n.* & *adj.* (Pile-fabric) with loops forming pile left uncut (ill. WEAVE).

Tĕ'rry[2], Ellen Alicia (1848–1928). English actress.

tĕrse *adj.* (Of speech, style, writer) free from cumbrousness and superfluity, smooth and concise; curt. **tĕrse'ly** (-sl-) *adv.* **tĕrse'nėss** *n.*

tĕr'tian (-shn) *adj.* & *n.* 1. (Fever, ague) with paroxysm recurring every other day. 2. *T~* (*Father*), member of Society of Jesus undergoing **tĕr'tianship,** 3rd period of training or novitiate after ordination.

tĕr'tiary (-sha-) *adj.* 1. Of the third order, rank, class, etc. 2. (geol.) Of the 3rd great geological period, of the series of rock-formations above the Mesozoic, comprising the eocene and oligocene systems (*Lower T~*) and the miocene and pliocene (*Upper T~*); = Cainozoic. 3. (path.) Of the 3rd or last stage of syphilis. 4. (ornith., of wing-feathers) Borne on humerus. 5. ~ *colours*, (painting) the greyish hues obtained by mixing two secondary colours (e.g. purple with green). ~ *n.* Tertiary rock, colour, feather, etc.; (*T~*) member of 3rd order of monastic body; (*the T~*), the tertiary period (ill. GEOLOGY).

ter'tium quid (-shĭ-) *n.* Something (undefined) related in some way to two (definite or known) things but distinct from both. [L, = 'some third thing']

Tertŭll'ian (-lyan). Quintus Septimius Florens Tertullianus (*c* 155–*c* 222), Christian theological writer; a violent opponent of paganism and leader of the Montanist sect.

tervāl'ent (*or* terv'*a*-) *adj.* (chem.) Having a VALENCY of 3.

terza rima (tārt'sa rēm'*a*) *n.* Form of verse in sets of three 10 or 11-syllabled lines rhyming *aba*, *bcb*, etc., as in Dante's 'Divina Commedia'.

Tĕ'shu La'ma: see TASHI LAMA.

tĕss'ėllāte *v.t.* Make into mosaic, form (esp. pavement) by combining variously coloured blocks into pattern. **tĕss'ĕllātėd** *adj.* Composed of, ornamented with, small coloured blocks arranged in pattern; (zool., bot.) marked, coloured, in regularly arranged squares or patches, reticulated. **tĕssėllā'tion** *n.*

tĕss'era *n.* 1. (Gk and Rom. hist.) Small tablet of wood, bone, ivory, etc., used as token, tally, label, etc. 2. Each of small square pieces of marble, glass, tile, etc., of which mosaic pavement etc. is made up. 3. (math.) Curvilinear rectangle. **tĕss'eral** *adj.* (esp., math.) Of the tesserae of a spherical surface.

tĕst[1] *n.* 1. (orig.) Cupel used in treating gold or silver alloys or ore; now, cupel and iron frame containing it, forming movable hearth of reverberatory furnace. 2. Critical examination or trial of qualities of person or thing; means of so examining; standard for comparison or trial, circumstances suitable for this; (chem.) examination of substance under known conditions to determine its identity or that of one of its constituents, reagent used for this. 3. (colloq.) Test-match. 4. *T~ Act*, (esp.) act passed 1672 and repealed 1828, requiring holders of office under Crown to take oaths of supremacy and allegiance, receive Communion of Church of England, etc.; ~ *case*, (law) case in which decision is taken as settling a number of other cases involving same question of law; *~-match*, (esp., cricket) one of series of usu. 5 games played between sides representing England and Australia (or occas. other countries) as test of superiority; *~-meal*, meal of specified quantity and composition given to enable gastric secretions etc. to be examined; ~ *paper*, (chem.) paper impregnated with substance which changes colour under certain conditions, used to test presence of these conditions; *~-piece*, composition performed by all entrants in musical or other competition; *~-tube*, (chem.) tube of thin glass closed at one end, used to hold substance under test etc. ~ *v.t.* Put to the test, make trial of; try severely, tax (endurance etc.); subject to chemical test.

tĕst[2] *n.* External covering or shell of molluscs, crustaceans, and many other invertebrates.

tĕs'ta *n.* (bot.) Seed-coat.

tĕstā'ceous (-shus) *adj.* Having a shell, esp. a hard shell; of shells, shelly; (bot., zool.) of colour of tile or red brick, brownish-red.

tĕs'tacy *n.* Being testate.

tĕs'tament *n.* 1. (law) Will, esp. (formerly) disposition of personal as dist. from real property. 2. (bibl.) Covenant between God and man (archaic), hence, *Old*, *New*, *T~* (abbrev. O.T., N.T.), main divisions of Bible consisting respectively of books of old or Mosaic, and new or Christian, dispensation; *T~*, copy of New Testament. **tĕstamĕn'tary** *adj.* Of (nature of), relating to, a will.

tĕstām'ur *n.* Certificate from university examiners that candidate has satisfied them. [L, = 'we testify']

tĕs'tāte (*or* -at) *adj.* & *n.* (Person) that has left a valid will at death.

tĕstāt'or, tĕstāt'rĭx *ns.* Man, woman, who makes, or has died leaving, a will.

tĕs'ter[1] *n.* Canopy esp. over four-poster bed (ill. BED).

tĕs'ter[2] *n.* Shilling of Henry VIII, esp. as debased and depreciated; (colloq., archaic) sixpence.

tĕs'tĭcle *n.* Testis (usu. in ref. to man) (ill. PELVIS). **tĕstĭc'ūlar** *adj.*

tĕstĭc'ūlate *adj.* Having, shaped like, testicles; (bot., of some orchids) having two tubers of this shape.

tĕs'tĭfȳ *v.* Bear witness; (law) give evidence; affirm, declare, be evidence of, evince.

tĕstĭmōn'ial *n.* Certificate of character, conduct, or qualifications; gift presented, esp. in public, as mark of esteem, in acknowledgement of services, etc. **tĕstĭmōn'ialīze** *v.t.* Present with testimonial.

tĕs'tĭmony *n.* Evidence, esp. (law) statement made under oath or affirmation.

tĕs'tĭs *n.* (pl. *-tēs*). Male organ in which gametes are produced; in man, each of two glandular sperm-forming bodies enclosed in scrotum; testicle.

tĕstūd'ĭnate *adj.* Arched, vaulted, like tortoise-shell.

tĕstūd'ō *n.* (pl. *-dōs*, *-dĭnōs*). 1. (Rom. antiq.) Screen formed by body of troops in close array with overlapping shields; movable screen or roof under cover of which walls of besieged town could be attacked. 2. (*T~*) genus, comprising land tortoises, of family *Testudinidae* or turtles.

tĕs'ty *adj.* Irritable, touchy. **tĕs'tĭly** *adv.* **tĕs'tinėss** *n.*

tėtăn'ĭc *adj.* Of, like, producing, tetanus. ~ *n.* Remedy acting on spinal cord and tending to produce tetanic spasms.

tĕt'anus *n.* 1. (med.) Painful and often fatal disease caused by micro-organism, usu. introduced through wound, and characterized by tonic spasm and rigidity of voluntary muscles. 2. (physiol.) Prolonged contraction of muscle produced by rapidly repeated stimuli.

tĕt'any *n.* (med.) Condition characterized by spasms of the extremities, caused by disturbance in activity of parathyroid glands and consequent deficiency of calcium.

tĕ(t)ch'y *adj.* Peevish, irritable. **tĕ(t)ch'ĭly** *adv.* **tĕ(t)ch'ĭnėss** *n.*

tête-à-tête (tāt'*a*tāt') *n.* & *adj.* (Of) private conversation or interview between two persons. ~ *adv.* In private, without presence of third person.

tĕth'er (-dh-) *n.* Rope, chain, halter, by which grazing animal is confined; *the end of one's ~*, the extreme limit of one's resources. ~ *v.t.* Make fast, confine, with tether (freq. fig.).

tetra- *prefix.* Four.

Tĕth'ȳs. (Gk myth.) Sea deity, daughter of Uranus and Ge, and wife of Oceanus.

tĕtr'achord (-k-) *n.* Series of 4 notes with interval of perfect fourth between lowest and highest, as half of octave or unit of ancient Greek music (ill. MODE).

tĕt'răd *n.* The number four; set of 4; (biol.) group of 4 cells; group of 4 chromosomes formed by division of single chromosome.

tĕtradăc'tȳl *adj.* & *n.* (Animal) with 4 fingers or toes. **tĕtradăc'tȳlous** *adj.*

tĕtra-ĕth'ȳl *adj.* (chem.) Containing 4 ethyl groups; ~ *lead*, heavy colourless liquid used as anti-knock agent in internal combustion engine fuels.

tĕt'ragon *n.* Figure with 4 angles and 4 sides. **tėtrăg'onal** *adj.* ~ *crystal*: see ill. CRYSTAL.

tĕt'ragrăm *n.* 1. Word of 4 letters. 2. Quadrilateral.

tĕtragrămm'aton *n.* Word of 4 letters, esp. the Hebrew word of 4 consonants (YHWH or JHVH) representing the incommunicable name of God.

tĕtrahĕd'ron *n.* Solid figure bounded by 4 plane triangles; triangular pyramid (ill. SOLID); crystal of this form. **tĕtrahĕd'ral** *adj.*

tėtrăl'ogy *n.* Series of 4 connected operas, plays, etc., esp. (Gk antiq.) series of 3 tragedies and a satyric drama produced at Athens at festival of Dionysus.

tėtrăm erous *adj.* Having 4 parts; (bot.) having parts arranged in series of 4.

tėtrăm'ėter *n.* Verse of 4 feet.

tĕt'rapŏd *adj.* & *n.* (Vertebrate) having two pairs of limbs (zool.; now more usu. than *quadruped* and not necessarily implying walking on 4 feet).

tĕt'rarch (-k) *n.* One of 4 joint rulers; in Roman Empire, governor of a fourth part of a country or province, any subordinate ruler. **tĕt'rarchate, tĕt'rarchy** *ns.* **tėtrarch'ĭcal** *adj.*

tĕt'rastȳle *adj.* & *n.* (Portico) of 4 columns (ill. TEMPLE).

tĕtrasȳll'able *n.* Word of 4 syllables. **tĕtrasȳllăb'ĭc** *adj.*

tĕtravāl'ent (*or* tetrăv'*a*-) *adj.* Having a VALENCY of 4, quadrivalent.

tĕt'rōde *n.* Electronic amplifying valve with four main electrodes.

tĕtt'er *n.* (archaic, dial.) Any pustular skin-eruption, as eczema etc.

Teu'cer. (Gk myth.) 1. A legendary king in the region of Troy. 2. Son of Telamon and half-brother of Ajax, the greatest archer amongst the Greeks attacking Troy. **Teuc'rĭan** *adj.* & *n.* Ancient Trojan.

Teut'on. 1. One of the ancient *Teutones* or *Teutoni*, a N. European people first known to Romans as allies of Cimbri. 2. One of a N. European race of tall stature with long heads, blue eyes, and fair hair and skin, first appearing in Germany, Scandinavia, and the Netherlands. 3. A German.

Teutŏn'ĭc *adj.* Of the Teutons; of the GERMANIC group of Indo-European languages including German, English, Dutch, Frisian, Swedish, Danish, Norwegian, Icelandic, Gothic, etc.; ~ *Order*, ~ *Knights* (of St. Mary's Hospital at Jerusalem), a religious and military order founded at Acre (1190) by German Crusaders; it was invited early in 13th c. to undertake conquest of heathen Prussians and colonization of lands eastward of Germany, where it became a powerful governing aristocracy and administered large territories; the battle of TANNENBERG (1410) began the disintegration of its power and it was eventually suppressed in 1809; a semi-religious knighthood esp. devoted to ambulance service was resuscitated in Austria in 1840.

Tex. *abbrev.* Texas.

Tĕx'as. West South Central State of U.S., admitted to the Union in 1845; capital, Austin. **Tĕx'an** *adj.* & *n.*

tĕxt *n.* 1. Wording of anything written or printed, esp. the very words and sentences as orig. written, as opp. to translation, commentary, notes, etc. 2. Passage of Scripture quoted as authority or esp. chosen as subject of sermon etc.; subject, theme. 3. ~ (*-hand*), fine large kind of handwriting, esp. used for texts of MSS. 4. ~*-book*, manual of instruction in any branch of science or study, work recognized as an authority.

tĕx'tīle *adj.* Of weaving; woven, suitable for weaving. ~ *n.* Textile fabric or material.

tĕx'tūal *adj.* Of, in, the text. **tĕx'tūally** *adv.*

tĕx'tūalĭst *n.* One who adheres strictly to the letter of the text; one well acquainted with text, esp. of Bible. **tĕx'tūalĭsm** *n.*

tĕx'ture *n.* Character of textile fabric, resulting from way in which it is woven; arrangement of constituent parts, structure, constitution; representation of surface of objects in work of art, (also) character of surface of paint in picture etc. **tĕx'tural** (-cher-, -tūr-) *adj.* **tĕx'turally** *adv.*

T.F. *abbrev.* Territorial Force.

T.G.W.U. *abbrev.* Transport & General Workers' Union.

Thăck'eray, William Makepeace (1811–63). English novelist, author of 'Vanity Fair', 'Henry Esmond', 'The Virginians', 'The Newcomes', etc.

Thaddaeus: see JUDE.

Thai, Tai (tī). A people of Mongolian stock who migrated southwards from S. China (*c* 10th c.) and now form the larger part of the population of Siam; group of languages spoken by them. **Thai'land.** Official name of SIAM, chosen by its Government in 1939. [Siamese *thai* free]

Thā'ĭs. Athenian courtesan who accompanied Alexander the Great on his Asiatic campaign and later became wife of Ptolemy Lagus, king of Egypt; any cultured and intelligent courtesan.

thăl'amo-cŏrt'ĭcal *adj.* (physiol.) Involving the thalamus and cortex, two regions of the brain.

thăl'amus *n.* (pl. *-mī*). 1. (anat.) Interior region of brain where certain important sensory nerves, esp. the optic nerve, originate (hence sometimes called *optic* ~) (ill. BRAIN). 2. (bot.) Receptacle of flower.

thalăss'ĭc *adj.* Of sea(s), esp. of smaller or inland seas as dist. from oceans.

tha'ler (tah-) *n.* German silver coin: see DOLLAR.

Thāl'ēs (-z) of Miletus (end of 7th c. B.C.). Greek philosopher, one of the 'seven sages', believed to have founded the geometry of lines, discovered several theorems, and advanced the study of astronomy; he regarded water as the principle of all material things.

Thalī'a. (Gk myth.) Muse of comedy and idyllic poetry. **Thalī'an** (*or* thăl'ĭan) *adj.*

thăll'ĭum *n.* (chem.) Soft bluish-white leaden-lustred metallic element; symbol Tl, at. no. 81, at. wt 204·37. **thăll'ĭc, thăll'ous** *adjs.* [Gk *thallos* green shoot, from brilliant green line in its spectrum]

thăll'ophȳte *n.* Plant whose body is a thallus, e.g. seaweed, liverwort.

thăll'us *n.* (pl. *-ī*). The body of a primitive plant which is not divided into leaves, stem, and roots but consists of more or less uniform tissue (ill. ALGA). **thăll'oid** *adj.*

Thames (tĕmz). Chief river of England, on which London stands; rises in Gloucestershire and flows into North Sea.

Thămm'uz, Tam- (t-). 1. Syrian or Babylonian deity, god of agriculture and flocks, lover of Astarte, who brought him back from the lower world after his death. 2. 10th month of JEWISH calendar.

Thăm'ȳrĭs. Legendary Thracian or Delphian poet and musician.

than (dh*a*n, -ăn) *conj.* Introducing second member of comparison.

thāne *n.* (Engl. hist.) One holding land of king or other superior by virtue of military service, with rank between ordinary freemen and hereditary nobles; (Sc. hist.) one, ranking with earl's son, holding land of the king, chief of a clan.

thănk *v.t.* Express gratitude to (person *for* thing); ~ *you*, I thank you (as polite formula of gratitude etc.); ~*-you-ma'am*, (U.S. colloq.) ridge or hollow across road, causing heads of persons crossing it in vehicle to nod as if bowing. ~ *n.* (now only in pl.) (Expression of) gratitude; *thanks*, thank you; *thanks to*, owing to, as the result of; *thanks'giving*, expression of gratitude, esp. to God; form of words for this; *Thanksgiving* (*Day*), (U.S.) annual festival and legal holiday, on 4th Thursday of November, since 1863 annually fixed by President; first held (1621) by the Plymouth colony in thankfulness for their first harvest; *thank-offering*, offering made as expression of gratitude to God.

thănk'ful *adj.* Grateful; expressive of thanks. **thănk'fully** *adv.* **thănk'fulnėss** *n.*

thănk'lėss *adj.* Not feeling or expressing gratitude; of task etc.) not likely to win thanks, unprofitable. **thănk'lėssly** *adv.* **thănk'lėssnėss** *n.*

thăt (dh-) *demonstr. adj.* & *pron.* (pl. *thōse*). The (person, thing); the person or thing, referred to, already mentioned, pointed or drawn attention to, observed, understood, in question, etc.; (coupled or contrasted with *this*) esp., the farther, less immediate or obvious, etc., of two; ~ *is* (*to say*), introducing explanation of preceding word, phrase, etc.; *and all* ~, and so forth; *at* ~ (orig. U.S.), at that standard, (even) in that capacity; too, besides. ~ (dh*a*t), *rel. pron.* used to introduce defining clause (regarded as) essential to identification; now largely replaced by WHO, WHICH. ~ *conj.* Introducing dependent clause, esp. expressing result or consequence.

thătch *n.* Roof-covering of straw, reeds, etc. ~ *v.t.* Cover or roof (house, hay-stack, etc.) with, make (roof) of, thatch.

thaum'atrōpe *n.* A scientific toy illustrating the persistence of visual impressions, consisting of a card or disc with two different figures drawn upon the two sides, which are apparently combined into one when the disc is rotated rapidly.

thaum'atûrge *n.* Worker of miracles, wonder-worker. **thaumatûr'gic(al)** *adjs.* **thaum'atûrgy** *n.*

thaw *v.* Reduce (frozen substance) to liquid state by raising its temperature above freezing-point; unfreeze; become unfrozen, become liquid, flexible, or limp by rise of temperature; (fig.) free, be freed, from coldness or stiffness, (cause to) unbend or become genial. ~ *n.* Thawing, melting of ice and snow after frost; warmth of weather that thaws.

the (*before vowel* dhĭ, *before consonant* dhe, *emphatic* dhē) *demonstr. adj.* & *pron.* 'Definite article', applied esp. to person(s) or thing(s) already mentioned or under discussion, actually or potentially existent, unique, familiar, or otherwise sufficiently identified; to singular nouns as representing species, class, etc.; or with adjectives used abs., or rhet. viewed as part of definition; emphatically applied to person or thing best known or best entitled to the name. ~ *adv.* In that degree, by that amount, on that account; *the . . . the*, by how much . . . by so much; in what degree . . . in that degree.

thē'ârchy (-kĭ) *n.* Theocracy; a system or order of gods.

Thē'atīne. (R.C. Ch.) Member of an order of Clerks Regular founded 1524 in Italy to combat Lutheranism; member of the corresponding order of nuns, founded in early 17th c., now most numerous in U.S.

thē'atre (-*ter*) *n.* 1. (Gk & Rom. antiq.) Open-air edifice in form of segment of circle, with auditorium usu. excavated from hill-side, for viewing dramas or other spectacles, natural formation or place suggesting such structure. 2. Building for dramatic spectacles, playhouse; room, hall, for lectures etc., with seats in tiers; scene, field of operation; *operating-~*: see OPERATE, sense 5. 3. Dramatic literature or art.

thėăt'rĭcal *adj.* Of or suited to theatre; of acting or actors; calculated for effect, showy, affected, assumed, artificial. **thėăt'rĭcally** *adv.* **thėăt'rĭcalĭsm, thėătrĭcăl'ĭty** *ns.* **thėăt'rĭcals** *n.pl.* Theatrical performances, esp. by amateurs.

Thēbā'ĭd. Latin epic poem (*c* A.D. 92) by Statius, concerned with expedition against Thebes to recover throne for Polynices from his brother Eteocles.

Thēbes (-bz). 1. Ancient Greek city in Boeotia (now *Thivai*); its early history was subject of many legends including those of Cadmus, Oedipus, and Antigone; from the late 6th c. B.C. Thebes became the bitter enemy of Athens, and after the Peloponnesian War the rival of Sparta for the hegemony of Greece; it was razed to the ground in 335 B.C. but rebuilt, existed throughout Roman times, and was finally destroyed in 1311. 2. Greek name of ancient capital (from time of 12th dynasty) of Upper Egypt, on site of modern Luxor. **Thēb'an** *adj.*

thēc'a *n.* 1. (bot.) Part of plant serving as receptacle, as pollen-sac of anther, spore-case, capsule of moss, etc. (ill. MOSS). 2. (zool., anat.) Case or sheath enclosing some organ or part.

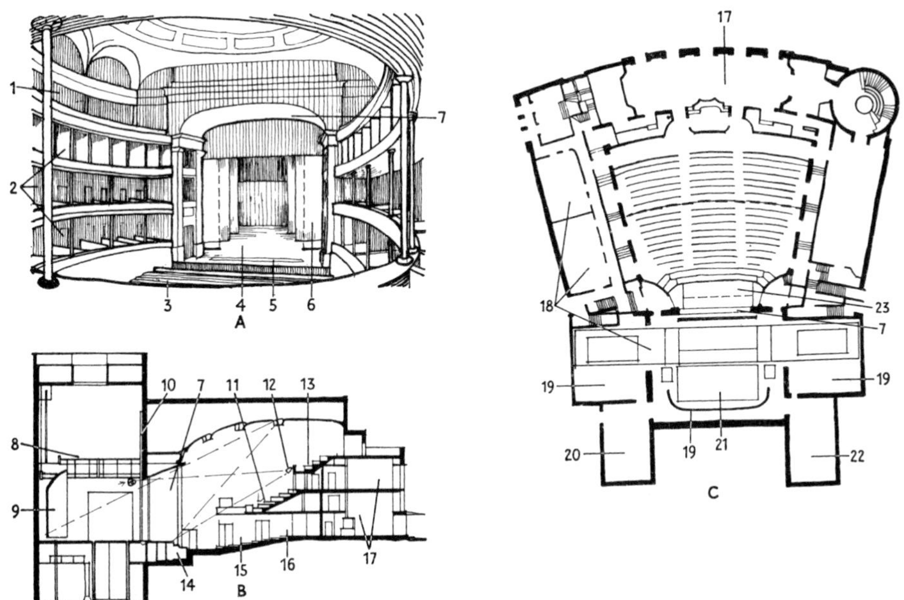

THEATRE: A. GENERAL VIEW OF AUDITORIUM AND STAGE. B. SECTION. C. PLAN

A. 1, 2, 3. Auditorium (1. Gallery, 2. Boxes, 3. Parterre). 4. Stage. 5. Footlights. 6. Wings or coulisses. 7. Proscenium opening. B. 8. Flies. 9. Back-cloth. 10. Safety curtain. 11. Dress circle. 12. Stage lights. 13. Balcony. 14. Orchestra pit. 15. Stalls. 16. Pit. 17. Foyers. C. 18. Green-room and dressing-rooms. 19. Scene-docks. 20 Stage carpenter's room. 21. Trap. 22. Property room. 23. Apron stage

thee (dh-) *pron.* Objective (accus., dat.) case of THOU; dial. and among Quakera occas. used for THOU.

thĕft *n.* Stealing, larceny.

their (dhār) *poss. pron.* Possessive case of THEY. **theirs** (dhārz) *poss. pron.* Form of THEIR used abs. or predic.

thē'ism *n.* Belief in gods or (esp.) a god, as opp. to ATHEISM, PANTHEISM, POLYTHEISM, esp. belief in one God as creator and supreme ruler of universe. **thē'ist** *n.* **thēis'tic(al)** *adjs.*

thĕm (dh-) *pron.* Objective case of THEY.

thėmăt'ic *adj.* Of, belonging to, constituting, a theme.

thēme *n.* Subject of discourse, conversation, composition, etc., topic; school composition, essay, exercise in translation; (mus.) subject, tune, or passage developed in musical composition, and recurring as a principal part of its material; tune on which variations are constructed; (gram.) inflexional base or stem of word, 'root' with modification or addition, to which inflexions are added; ~ *song*, a recurrent melody in a musical play or film.

Thĕm'is. (Gk myth.) Goddess of law and justice.

Themis'toclēs (-z) (*c* 524–459 B.C.). Athenian statesman and soldier, commander of the Athenian fleet at SALAMIS.

themsĕlves' (dh-, -vz) *pron.* Emphatic and reflexive form corresponding to THEY.

thĕn (dh-) *adv.* At that time; next, afterwards, after that; *now and* ~, at one time and another, from time to time. ~ *conj.* In that case; therefore; it follows that; accordingly. ~ *adj.* Existing etc. at that time. ~ *n.* That time; *every now and* ~, from time to time.

thĕn'ar *n.* (anat.) Ball of muscle at base of thumb; palm of hand; sole of foot.

thĕnce (dh-) *adv.* (archaic and literary) From that place, from there; from that source, for that reason. **thĕncefōrth', thĕncefōr'ward** *advs.* & *ns.* From (*from*) that time forward.

theo- *prefix.* God.

thēobrō'ma *n.* Genus of tropical Amer. trees including cocoa-tree (*T. cacao*). **thēobrō'mĭne** *n.* Bitter white crystalline alkaloid, related to caffeine, obtained from seeds of cocoa-tree.

thēocĕn'tric *adj.* Having God as its centre.

thėŏc'racy *n.* Government by God, directly or through a priestly class etc.; State so governed; *the T*~, the Jewish commonwealth from Moses to the monarchy.

thėŏc'rasy (*or* thē'okrăsĭ) *n.* Union of the soul with God through contemplation (among Neo-platonists, Buddhists, etc.).

thē'ocrăt *n.* Ruler in, subject under, a theocracy. **thēocrăt'ic** *adj.* **thėŏc'ratist** *n.* Believer in theocracy.

Thėŏc'rĭtus (3rd c. B.C.). Sicilian Greek poet; regarded as the originator of pastoral poetry.

thėŏd'ĭcy *n.* Vindication of the divine providence in view of the existence of evil.

thėŏd'olīte *n.* Surveying instrument for measuring horizontal and vertical angles, telescope rotating round a graduated circular plate and also free to swivel in vertical plane over a graduated arc. **thėŏdolĭt'ic** *adj.*

Thē'odore (Fe'odōr, Fy'odor). Name of 3 tsars of Russia: *Theodore I* (1557–98), succeeded his father Ivan the Terrible 1584; *Theodore II* (1589–1605), son of Boris Godunov, succeeded his father 1605 and was murdered in the same year; *Theodore III* (1661–82), succeeded his father Alexey 1679.

Thėŏd'orĭc (*c* 454–526). King of the Ostrogoths, invader (588–93) and conqueror of Italy, which he ruled from Ravenna; attempted to revive the Western Roman Empire.

Thēodō'sius (-shĭ-). Name of 3 Emperors of the Eastern Roman Empire; *Theodosius I* (*c* 346–95), 'the Great', Roman general, born in Spain, became emperor of the East 379; *Theodosius II* (401–50) succeeded his father Arcadius as emperor 408, promulgated (438) the *Theodosian Code* of all imperial legislation since time of Constantine; *Theodosius III* was proclaimed emperor 715 by the rebellious Byzantine army and deposed 717 by Leo III.

thėŏg'ony *n.* Genealogy of the gods; poem etc. dealing with this. **thēogŏn'ic** *adj.* **thėŏg'onist** *n.*

thēolō'gian *n.* Person skilled in, professor of, theology.

thėŏl'ogy *n.* Science of religion, study of God, His nature, attributes, and relations with man etc.; *dogmatic* ~, that dealing with the authoritative teaching of the Scriptures and the Church; *natural* ~, dealing with knowledge of God as gained from His works by the light of nature and reason; *positive, revealed*, ~, based on revelation; *speculative* ~, not confined to revelation but giving scope to human speculation; *systematic* ~, methodical arrangement of the truths of religion in their natural connexion. **thēolŏ'gical** *adj.* **thēolŏ'gically** *adv.*

thėŏm'achy (-kĭ), *n.* Strife among the gods.

thē'omăncy *n.* Divination by divinely inspired oracles.

thēomōrph'ic *adj.* Having the form or likeness of a god.

thėŏph'agous *adj.* God-eating. **thėŏph'agy** (-j-) *n.*

thėŏph'any *n.* Manifestation or appearance of God to man; Epiphany.

thėōrb'ō *n.* Large kind of lute with two necks and two sets of tuning-pegs, much used in 17th c.

thē'orĕm *n.* Universal or general proposition, not self-evident but demonstrable by chain of reasoning; algebraical or other rule, esp. expressed by symbols or formulae. **thēorėmăt'ic(al)** *adjs.*

thēorĕt'ic(al) *adjs.* Of, consisting in, relating to, conforming to, theory; existing only in theory, hypothetical; addicted to, constructing, dealing with, theories, speculative. **thēorĕt'ics** *n.pl.* Theory, theoretical parts of science etc.

thē'ory *n.* Scheme or system of ideas or statements held to explain group of facts or phenomena, statement of general laws, principles, or causes of something known or observed; systematic conception or statement of principles of something, abstract knowledge, formulation of this; department of art or technical subject concerned with knowledge of its principles or methods, as opp. to *practice*; systematic statement of general principles of some branch of mathematics; (a) mere hypothesis, conjecture, individual view or notion. **thē'orist** *n.* **thē'orīze** *v.*

thėŏs'ophy *n.* Philosophy professing to attain to knowledge of God by spiritual ecstasy, direct intuition, or special individual relations, esp. system of Jacob BOEHME; now usu., doctrines of *Theosophical Society*, founded 1875 in New York by Madame BLAVATSKY and others to form nucleus of universal brotherhood, study Aryan and other Eastern, esp. Brahmanistic and Buddhistic, literature, religions, and sciences, and investigate unfamiliar laws of nature and man's latent faculties. **thēosŏph'ic(al)** *adjs.* **thēosŏph'ically** *adv.* **thėŏs'opher, thėŏs'ophist** *ns.* **thėŏs'ophīze** *v.i.*

thĕrapeut'ic(al) *adjs.* Of the healing of disease, curative. **thĕrapeut'ics** *n.pl.* Branch of medicine concerned with remedial treatment of disease.

thĕ'rapy *n.* Curative medical treatment.

there (dhār, dher) *adv., n.,* & *int.* In or at that place; at that point in argument, situation, progress of affairs, etc.; to that place; used unemphatically to introduce sentence or clause in which verb comes before its subject; (*n.*) that place; (*int.*) expressing confirmation, triumph, dismay, etc.; *there'about(s)*, near that place; near that number, quantity, etc.; *thereaft'er*, (archaic) after that; *thereat'*, (archaic) there; thereupon, at that; *thereby'* (*or* dhār'bī), (archaic) by or through that; *thereby hangs a tale*, in that connexion there is something to be told; *therefor'*, (archaic) for that, for it; for that reason, on that account; *there'fore*, in consequence of that; for that reason, accordingly, consequently; *therein'*, (archaic) in that place; in that respect; *thereinaf'ter, thereinbefore'*, (archaic) later, earlier, in same document, etc.; *thereof'*, (archaic) of that, of it; *thereon'*, (archaic) on that, on it; *thereto'*, (archaic) to that, to it; in addition; *thereupon'*, in consequence of that; soon, immediately, after that; (archaic) upon that; *therewith'*, (archaic) with that; thereupon; *therewithal'* (archaic) in addition, besides.

thēr'ĭăc *n.* Antidote to poison, esp. to bite of venomous serpent.

thēriomŏrph'ĭc *adj.* Having form of a beast; of deity worshipped in form of a beast.

thĕrm *n.* 1. (physics) A British Thermal Unit (see THERMAL). 2. A unit of heat adopted in Britain as a basis of the charge for the use of coal-gas, = 100,000 British Thermal Units.

thĕrm'ae *n.pl.* (Gk and Rom. antiq.) Public baths.

thĕrm'al *adj.* Of heat; determined, measured, operated by heat; ~ *capacity*, (of a body) number of heat units required to raise its temperature by one degree; ~ *springs*, hot springs; ~ *unit*, unit of heat; *British T~ Unit*, (abbrevs. B.Th.U., B.T.U.) amount of heat required to raise the temperature of one pound of water at its maximum density by one degree Fahrenheit.

thĕrmăn'tĭdōte *n.* Apparatus used in hot countries for cooling the air.

Thĕrmĭdŏr' (*or* tārmēdŏr). 11th month of French revolutionary calendar, covering parts of July and August. **Thĕrmĭdŏr'ĭan** *n.* (Fr. hist.) One of those taking part in overthrow of Robespierre on 9th Thermidor (27 July 1794).

thĕrm'īon *n.* Electrically charged particle (electron or ion) emitted from a heated body. **thĕrmīŏn'ĭc** *adj.* Of, emitting, thermions; ~ *valve*, vacuum tube, in which electrons emitted by a heated filament carry electric current in one direction, used as a rectifier of an alternating current and in wireless receiving sets for the detection and amplification of wireless waves.

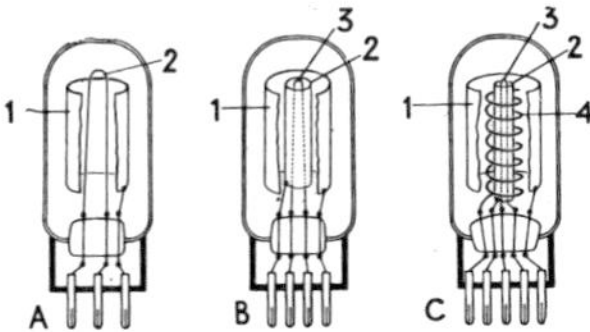

THERMIONIC VALVES: A, B. DIODES (A. DIRECT HEATING. B. INDIRECT HEATING). C. TRIODE

1. Anode. 2. Cathode. 3. Cathode heater. 4. Control grid

thĕrm'īte *n.* Mixture of finely divided aluminium and oxide of iron or oxide of other metal, producing very high temperature (*c* 3000° C.) on combustion, used in smelting, welding, and as filling for incendiary bombs.

thĕrmochĕm'ĭstry (-k-) *n.* Branch of chemistry dealing with the heat changes accompanying reactions. **thĕrmochĕm'ĭcal** *adj.* **thĕrmochĕm'ĭst** *n.*

thĕrmocoup'le (-kŭpl) *n.* Device consisting of two different metals joined at two places so that when a difference of temperature exists between the two joins an electromotive force is produced which can be used to measure that difference.

thĕrmodȳnăm'ĭcs *n.* The science dealing with the relationship between thermal energy (heat) and all other forms of energy (mechanical, electrical, etc.). **thĕrmodȳnăm'ĭc** *adj.* **thĕrmodȳnăm'ĭcally** *adv.*

thĕrmo-ēlĕctrĭ'cĭty *n.* Electricity developed by the action of heat at the junction of two different metals. **thĕrmo-ėlĕc'trĭc** *adj.*

thĕrmogĕn'ėsĭs *n.* Generation of heat in an animal body.

thĕrmolā'bĭle *adj.* (biochem.) Sensitive to heat.

thĕrmŏl'ȳsĭs *n.* (pl. *-sēs*). (chem.) Dissociation, decomposition, by action of heat.

thermŏm'ėter *n.* Instrument for measuring temperature, freq. a graduated glass tube with bulb containing a substance (as mercury, alcohol) whose expansion and contraction under the influence of temperature can be accurately measured. **thĕrmomĕt'rĭc(al)** *adjs.* **thĕrmomĕt'rĭcally** *adv.* **thermŏm'ėtry** *n.* Science dealing with the measurement of temperature.

thĕrm'ophĭl, -phĭle *adj.* & *n.* (Organism, as certain bacteria) requiring high temperature for development.

thĕrm'opīle *n.* Set of thermocouples arranged in series, used to detect radiant heat.

thĕrmoplăs'tĭc *adj.* Becoming plastic when heated.

Thermŏp'ȳlae (-lē). Pass in Greece from Locris into Thessaly, orig. narrow but now much widened by recession of sea; scene of the heroic defence (480 B.C.) against the Persian army of Xerxes by 6,000 Greeks including 300 Spartans under LEONIDAS.

thĕrm'ŏs *n.*, *also* ~ *flask, bottle, jug*, brand of VACUUM flask. [proprietary name]

thĕrm'ostăt *n.* Device which automatically maintains temperature at a constant value, or which gives notice of an undue change in temperature. **thĕrmostăt'ĭc** *adj.* **thĕrmostăt'ĭcally** *adv.*

thĕrmotăx'ĭs *n.* (physiol.) Regulation of bodily heat.

thĕrmŏt'ropĭsm *n.* (biol.) Property in plants etc. of turning towards (*positive* ~) or away from (*negative* ~) a source of heat. **thĕrmotrŏp'ĭc** *adj.*

thēr'oid *adj.* (esp. of idiot) Having beast-like propensities.

Thersīt'ēs (-z). (Gk legend) The most ill-favoured of the Greeks in the Trojan War, a scurrilous reviler of the leaders.

thēsaur'us *n.* 'Treasury' of knowledge, now esp. a collection of words, phrases, quotations, etc.

thēse (-z) *demonstr. pron.* & *adj.* Plural of THIS.

Thēs'eus (-sūs). Greek legendary hero, son of Aegeus, king of Athens (or of Poseidon); slayer of the Cretan Minotaur and hero of other famous exploits.

thēs'ĭs *n.* (pl. *-ses* pr. sēz). 1. Proposition laid down or stated, esp. as theme to be discussed and proved; dissertation to maintain and prove thesis, esp. submitted by candidate for university degree. 2. (*also* thĕ-) Unaccented syllable or part of foot in modern verse (orig. and properly the accented part of a metrical foot).

Thĕs'piae. Ancient Greek city of Boeotia from which 700 men accompanied Leonidas to THERMOPYLAE.

Thĕs'pĭan *adj.* 1. Of Thespis; of tragedy or the dramatic art. 2. Of Thespiae. ~ *n.* 1. Actor or actress. 2. Inhabitant of Thespiae.

Thĕs'pĭs (6th c. B.C.). Greek dramatic poet, regarded as father of Greek tragedy.

Thess. *abbrev.* Thessalonians (N.T.).

Thĕssalōn'ĭan *adj.* & *n.* (Inhabitant) of Thessalonica; *Epistles to the Thessalonians*, two books of N.T., earliest extant letters of St. Paul, written from Corinth to the new Church at Thessalonica.

Thĕssalonĭc'a. Ancient city in Macedonia, founded 316 B.C. by Cassander, a general of Alexander the Great; now *Thessaloniki* or SALONIKA.

Thĕss'aly. District of N. Greece.

thēt'a *n.* 8th letter of Greek alphabet, Θ, θ.

Thĕt'ĭs. (Gk myth.) A sea-nymph, mother of ACHILLES.

thē'ŭrgy *n.* Operation of divine or supernatural agency in human affairs; system of magic among Neoplatonists, supposed to procure communication with beneficent spirits and produce miraculous effects by their aid. **thėŭr'gĭc(al)** *adjs.* **thē'ŭrgĭst** *n.*

thews (-z) *n.pl.* Sinews, muscles; mental or moral vigour. **thew'lėss, thew'y** *adjs.*

they (dhā) *pers. pron.* Pronoun of 3rd person plural, nominative case; plural of HE, SHE, IT.

thī'amīde *n.* Any of a class of compounds resembling amides but with sulphur in place of oxygen.

thĭck *adj.* 1. Of great or specified depth between opposite surfaces; (of line etc.) broad, not fine. 2. Arranged closely, crowded together; numerous; abounding, packed, *with*; of great or considerable density, viscid, stiff; turbid, muddy, cloudy, not clear. 3.

Stupid, dull; (of voice) muffled, indistinct; (colloq.) intimate; (slang) excessive in some disagreeable quality, going beyond what is reasonable. 4. *thick'head*, blockhead; *~-headed*, stupid, slow-witted; *thick'set*, set or growing close together; heavily or solidly built; *thick'set* (*hedge*), close-grown hedge; *~-skinned*, (fig.) not sensitive to criticism, reproach, insult, etc. **thĭck'ĭsh** *adj.* **thĭck'ly** *adv.* **thĭck** *n.* Thick part of anything, esp. fight etc.; *through ~ and thin*, under all conditions, resolutely. *~ adv.* Thickly.

thĭck'en *v.* Make or become thick; make of stiffer consistence.

thĭck'ėt *n.* Dense growth of small trees, shrubs, underwood, etc.

thĭck'nėss *n.* Being thick; third dimension, dist. from *length* and *breadth*; what is thick; layer.

thief (-ēf) *n.* One who steals, esp. secretly and without violence.

thieve (-ēv) *v.* Be a thief, practise stealing; steal (thing). **thiev'ery** *n.* **thiev'ĭsh** *adj.* **thiev'ĭshly** *adv.* **thiev'ĭshnėss** *n.*

Thiers (tēar'), Louis Adolphe (1797–1877). French statesman and historian; negotiated peace with Germany 1870, suppressed the Commune, and became president of the republic 1871–3.

thigh (thī) *n.* Upper part of human leg, from hip to knee; corresponding part (or part pop. supposed to correspond) in other animals; *~-bone*, bone of the thigh, femur.

thĭll *n.* Pole or shaft of wagon, cart, etc., esp. one of pair of shafts between which draught-animal is placed (ill. CART).

thĭm'ble *n.* Bell-shaped sheath of metal etc. worn on end of finger to push needle in sewing; (mech. etc.) ring, tube, sleeve, ferrule, etc.; (naut.) metal ring with concave outer surface round which rope is spliced (ill. SPLICE); *thim'bleful*, small quantity (of spirits etc.) to drink; *thim'blerig*, swindling game with three thimble-shaped cups and pea, bystanders betting which cup covers pea; *thimblerigger, thimblerigging* (*ns.*).

thĭn *adj.* Having opposite surfaces close together; of small diameter; slender; lean, spare, not plump; not dense; not full or closely packed; of slight density or consistence; wanting body, fullness, volume, or substance; (of lines) narrow, fine; (fig.) shallow, transparent, flimsy; *a ~ time*, a wretched or uncomfortable period; *~-skinned*, (fig.) sensitive. **thĭn'ly** *adv.* **thĭn'nėss** *n.* **thĭnn'ĭsh** *adj.* **thĭn** *v.* Make or become thin; reduce in bulk or number; *~ out*, reduce number of (esp. seedlings, by pulling up the less promising). *~ adv.* Sparsely.

thīne (dh-) *poss. pron.* & *adj.* Belonging to thee; what is thine.

thĭng *n.* What is or may be an object of perception, knowledge, or thought; entity, being, esp. inanimate object; piece of property, possession, (pl.) clothes, garments, esp. outdoor garments; (pl.) implements, utensils; (pl.) affairs, concerns, matters; what is (to be) done, fact, deed, occurrence; what is said, expression, statement.

thĭng'amy, thĭng'umajĭg, thĭng'um(a)bŏb, thĭng'ummy *ns.* (colloq.) Person, thing, indicated vaguely because speaker cannot remember or does not wish to use correct name or word; 'what 's-his-name', 'what-d'you-call-it'.

thĭnk *v.* (past t. and past part. *thought*, pr. -awt). Consider, be of opinion; form conception of; exercise mind in active way, form connected ideas; consider a matter, reflect; conceive notion of doing something, contemplate, intend; *~ about*, consider; *~ of*, consider; imagine; intend, contemplate; entertain idea *of*; hit upon; *~ out*, consider carefully; devise (plan etc.); *~ over*, reflect upon. **thĭnk'er** *n.* (esp.) Person of skilled or powerful mind.

thī'o-ă'cĭd *n.* Acid in which oxygen is partly or wholly replaced by sulphur.

thīocyăn'ĭc *adj.* *~ acid*, colourless unstable liquid acid (HCNS) with penetrating odour. **thīocȳ'anate** *n.* Salt of this.

thīosŭlph'ate *n.* Salt of *thiosulphuric acid* ($H_2S_2O_3$), extremely unstable acid; used in photography, formerly called *hyposulphite* (see HYPO).

thĭrd *adj.* Ordinal numeral corresponding to cardinal three; next after second; *~-class*, (esp.) poor, inferior; *~ degree*, severe examination of prisoner to extort confession or information; (freemasonry) degree of master mason; *~ man*, (cricket) fielder placed between point and short slip but farther out (ill. CRICKET); *~ party*, (law) party in a case other than the two principals; *~-party insurance*, insurance against injury or damage sustained by person other than the insured; so *~-party risk*; *T~ Programme*, (in U.K.) radio service of more intellectual character than Home Service and Light Programme; hence, *~-programme*, (attrib.) intellectual, 'highbrow'; *~ rail*, (in some electric railways) rail through which current is conducted, lying alongside those on which train runs; *~-rate*, inferior, decidedly poor, in quality. *~ n.* Any of 3 equal divisions of a whole; third thing, person, place, class, etc.; sixtieth of a second of time or angular measurement; (pl.) goods of third degree of quality; (mus.) interval of which the span involves 3 alphabetical names of notes, harmonic combination of the two notes thus separated. **thĭrd'ly** *adv.*

Thĭrl'mēre. Lake in Cumberland, English Lake District.

thĭrst *n.* Uneasy or painful sensation caused by want of drink; desire for drink; (fig.) ardent desire, craving. *~ v.i.* Feel thirst. **thĭrst'y** *adj.* Feeling thirst; dry, parched, arid; (colloq.) causing thirst; (fig.) eager, greedy. **thĭrst'ĭly** *adv.* **thĭrst'ĭnėss** *n.*

thĭrteen' *adj.* & *n.* One more than twelve (13, xiii, or XIII). **thĭrteenth'** *adj.* & *n.* **thĭrteenth'ly** *adv.*

thĭrt'y *adj.* & *n.* Three times ten (30, xxx, or XXX); *Thirty-nine Articles*, articles of religion assented to by person taking orders in Church of England; *thirty-two-mo* (-tōō'mō), 32mo, book with sheets folded into thirty-two leaves; *Thirty Years War*, war (1618–48) originating between Catholics and Protestants of Germany and later involving most of Western Europe. **thĭrt'ĭėth** *adj.* & *n.* **thĭrt'ĭėthly** *adv.* **thĭrt'ȳfōld** *adj.* & *n.*

thĭs (dh-) *demonstr. pron.* & *adj.* (pl. *these*, pr. dhēz). The (person, thing), the person or thing present, near, just mentioned; this time; *~ much*, this amount.

thĭs'tle (-sl) *n.* Prickly composite herbaceous, often woody, plant of *Carduus* and related genera, with stems, leaves, and involucres thickly armed with prickles, usu. globular flower-heads and most freq. purple flowers; (figure of this as) heraldic emblem of Scotland, and part of insignia of distinctively Scottish order of knighthood, *Order of the T~*, instituted 1687 by James II and revived 1703 by Queen Anne; *~-down*, down or pappus crowning 'seeds' or achenes of thistle, by means of which they are carried along by wind (freq. as type of lightness or flimsiness). **thĭs'tly** *adj.*

thĭther (dhĭdh'er) *adv.* (archaic) To that place.

thōle *n.* *~* (*pin*), pin in gunwale of boat as fulcrum for oar; each of two such pins between which oar plays (ill. BOAT).

Thom'as (tŏ-), St. One of the 12 Apostles, who (John xx. 24–29) refused to believe that Christ had risen again unless he could see and touch his wounds; hence, *doubting ~*, sceptic.

Thomas à Kĕm'pĭs (tŏ-). Thomas Hämmerken (*c* 1380–1471); named from his birthplace, Kempen near Düsseldorf; Augustinian monk, author of 'De Imitatione Christi'.

Thomas Aquinas, St.: see AQUINAS.

Thōm'ĭsm (t-). System of theology and philosophy taught by St. Thomas AQUINAS. **Thōm'ĭst** *n.* **Thomĭs'tĭc(al)** *adjs.*

Thomp'son (tŏms-), Francis 1859–1907). English poet; author of 'Hound of Heaven', describing the poet's flight from God, the pursuit, and the overtaking.

Thom'son[1] (tŏ-), James (1700–

48). Scottish poet; author of 'The Seasons' etc.

Thom'son² (tŏ-) James (1834–82). Scottish poet; author of 'The City of Dreadful Night' etc.

thŏng *n.* Narrow strip of hide or leather used as lace, strap, whip-lash, etc. ~ *v.t.* Furnish with thong; lash, strike with thong.

Thŏr. (Scandinavian myth.) God of thunder, war, and agriculture, represented as armed with hammer.

thōrăx *n.* 1. (anat., zool.) Part of body of mammal between neck and abdomen, that enclosed by ribs, breast-bone, and vertebrae and containing chief organs of circulation and respiration. 2. (zool.) Middle section of body of insect etc. between head and abdomen (ill. INSECT). **thōră'cĭc** *adj.*

Thŏr'eau (-rō), Henry David (1817–62). American naturalist; author of 'Walden or Life in the Woods' (1854).

thŏr'ĭa *n.* Thorium oxide, ThO_2.

thŏr'ĭum *n.* A radio-active metallic element which (like uranium) will undergo fission when bombarded with neutrons and is therefore a potential source of atomic energy; symbol Th, at. no. 90, at. wt 232·038.

thŏrn *n.* 1. Stiff sharp-pointed process on stem or other part of plant; kinds of thorn-bearing bush or tree, esp. hawthorn, whitehorn, or other species of *Crataegus*. 2. Name of Old English and Icelandic runic letter þ (=th). 3. *~-apple*, poisonous plant of genus *Datura*, esp. *D. stramonium*, Jimson weed; *thorn'back*, common ray or skate, with rows of short sharp spines along back and tail; *~-bush*, any bush bearing thorns. **thŏrn'lėss** *adj.* **thŏrn'y** *adj.* (esp., fig.) Harassing, vexatious, difficult to handle, delicate, ticklish.

thorough (thŭ'ro) *adj.* Complete, unqualified, not superficial, out-and-out; ~ *bass*, figured bass, bass-part of piece of music written alone, with signs, esp. numerals, indicating chords or harmonies; *thoroughbred*, (animal, esp. horse) of pure breed; (person) with characteristics associated with a thoroughbred animal; *thoroughfare*, road, street, lane; any public way open at both ends, esp. main road; *~-going*, extreme, thorough, out-and-out; *~-paced*, (of horse, archaic) thoroughly trained in all paces; (fig.) complete, unqualified. **tho'roughly** *adv.* **tho'roughnėss** *n.* **tho'rough** *adv.* & *prep.* (archaic) Through.

thŏrp(e) *n.* (archaic and hist.) Village, hamlet.

Thos. *abbrev.* Thomas.

those (dhōz) *demonstr. pron.* & *adj.* Plural of THAT.

Thōth (*or* tōt). (Egyptian myth.) God of wisdom and magic, the scribe of the gods, identified with the Greek Hermes and represented in human form with head of an ibis.

thou (dhow) *pron.* Second singular nominative personal pronoun, now archaic or poet. ~ *v.t.* Use 'thou' to (person).

though (dhō), **tho'** *conj.* Notwithstanding that, in spite of the fact that; even if, granting that; and yet, but yet, nevertheless, however; *as ~*, as if.

thought¹ (-awt) *n.* Process, power, capacity, faculty, of thinking; what one thinks, what is or has been thought; idea, notion; consideration, heed; meditation; intention, purpose, design; *second ~s*, later and maturer consideration; *~-reader, -reading*, (person capable of) direct perception of what is passing in another's mind; *~-transference*, telepathy.

thought²: see THINK.

thought'ful (-awt-) *adj.* Engaged in, given to, meditation; showing thought or consideration; considerate (*of*), kindly. **thought'fully** *adv.* **thought'fulnėss** *n.*

thought'lėss (-awt-) *adj.* Unreflecting, unthinking, heedless, imprudent; inconsiderate. **thought'lėssly** *adv.* **thought'lėssnėss** *n.*

thous'and (-owz-) *n.* & *adj.* Ten hundred; 1000, m, or M; (loosely) many; *~-and-one*, myriad, numberless; *T~ and One Nights*, the 'ARABIAN NIGHTS'; *T~ Islands*, group of about 1,000 islands in St. Lawrence River. **thous'and-fōld** *adj.* & *adv.* **thous'andth** *adj.* & *n.*

Thrāce. District of eastern Balkan peninsula, in ancient times including Bulgaria and eastern Macedonia. **Thrā'cĭan** (*or* -shĭ-) *adj.* & *n.* (Inhabitant) of Thrace; its ancient Indo-European language, closely related to Illyrian, Phrygian, and Armenian.

thrall (-awl) *n.* Slave; bondage. **thral'dom** *n.*

thrăsh, thrĕsh *v.t.* 1. (usu. *thresh*) Beat out or separate grain from (corn etc.) on *threshing-floor* (prepared hard level for the purpose) or in *threshing-machine*; ~ *out* (fig.), discuss exhaustively, argue thoroughly. 2. Beat or strike (as) with flail. 3. (usu. *thrash*) Beat, esp. with stick or whip; conquer, surpass.

thrăsh'er, thrĕsh'er *ns.* 1. One who threshes; threshing-machine. 2. Kind of shark (*Alopias vulpes*), with very long upper division of tail, with which it lashes an enemy.

thrasŏn'ĭcal *adj.* Resembling *Thraso*, a braggart soldier in Terence's 'Eunuchus'; boastful, vainglorious. **thrasŏn'ĭcally** *adv.*

thread (-ĕd) *n.* 1. Fine cord of spun-out fibres or filaments of flax, cotton, wool, glass, etc., esp. of two or more twisted together; thread-shaped or thread-like thing, e.g. fine line or streak of colour or light, 'string' of any viscid substance; spiral ridge of screw, each complete turn of this (ill. SCREW). 2. (fig.) Something represented as like thread, esp. course of human life; that which connects successive points in narrative, train of thought, etc., or on which things hang; continuous or persistent feature running through pattern of anything. 3. *thread'bare*, with nap worn off and threads of warp and woof left bare; wearing such garments, shabby, seedy; (fig.) commonplace, trite, hackneyed; *~-fish*, fish (*Polynemus paradiseus*) with pectoral fin in long threads, inhabiting tropical seas between India and the Malay archipelago; = mango-fish; *thread'worm*, various thread-like worms, any nematode, esp. the *pin-worm*, parasitic in human rectum. **thread'y** *adj.* **thread** *v.t.* Pass thread through eye of (needle); string (beads etc.) on thread, make (chain etc.) thus; pick one's way through (street, crowded place, etc.), make one's *way* thus; form screw-thread on.

Thread'needle Street (-ĕd-). Street in City of London containing premises of Bank of England (the *Old Lady of ~*). [earlier *three-needle*, poss. f. a tavern with the arms of the Needlemakers]

threat (-ĕt) *n.* Declaration of intention to punish or hurt; (law) such menace of bodily hurt or injury to reputation or property as may restrain person's freedom of action; indication of coming evil.

threat'en (-ĕtn) *v.* Use threats (against); try to influence by threats; announce one's intention (*to* do) as punishment or in revenge etc.; be source of danger to; presage, portend. **threat'enĭngly** *adv.*

three *adj.* & *n.* One more than two (3, iii, or III); card, domino, etc., marked with three pips or spots; *the ~ R's*, reading, writing, arithmetic; *~-colour process*, printing-process in which coloured picture etc. is reproduced by superposition of the 3 primary colours or their complementaries; *~-cornered*, having 3 angles or corners; (of contest etc.) between 3 persons; *~-deck'er*, 3-decked ship, esp. (hist.) line-of-battle ship with guns on three decks; *~-halfpence* (-hāp'ens), penny and halfpenny, 1½*d.*; *~-handed*, (of games) played by 3 persons; *~-lane*, (of road) wide enough for three lines of traffic; *~-legged*, (of race) run by pairs with a right and a left leg tied together; *~-mast'er*, vessel with 3 masts; *~-mile limit*, limit of zone of territorial waters, extending 3 miles from coast; *three'pence* (thrĕp-, thrĭp-, thrŭp-), sum of three pence (3*d.*); *threepenny* (pr. as prec.) (*adj.*), *threepenny bit*, silver or nickel-brass coin worth 3*d.*; *~-ply*, having, woven with, three strands (of thread, yarn, etc.); (plywood) composed of three layers of wood; ~-*point landing*, landing of aircraft so that landing-wheels or floats and tail-skid or wheel touch ground etc. simultaneously; ~-*quart'er(s)*, (of portraits) showing figure down to hips or knees; (of coat) coming to point about half-way between waist and hem of coat of ordinary length; (Rugby football etc.) player with position between half-back and full-back; *three'some*, (game etc., esp. golf) in which 3 persons take part; ~-*toed sloth*, sloth of genus *Bradypus* with 3 long claws on each foot. **three'-fold** *adj.* & *adv.*

thrĕnĕt'ĭc(al) *adjs.* Mournful, like a dirge.

thrĕn'ōde, thrĕn'ody *ns.* Song of lamentation, esp. for death, dirge. **thrėnōd'ial, thrėnōd'ĭc** *adjs.* **thrĕn'odĭst** *n.*

thresh: see THRASH.

thrĕsh'ōld (*or* -sh-h-) *n.* Piece of stone, timber, etc., lying below bottom of door in dwelling-house, church, etc.; entrance; (fig.) border, limit, (physiol., psychol.) point at which effect begins to be produced, idea enters consciousness, etc.; limen.

thrīce *adv.* (archaic or literary) Three times.

thrĭft *n.* 1. Frugality, economical management. 2. Various species of *Statice*, esp. sea-pink (*S. Armeria*), sea-shore and alpine plant with pink, white, or purple flowers on naked stems rising from tuft of grass-like radical leaves. **thrĭft'lėss** *adj.* **thrĭft'lėssly** *adv.* **thrĭft'lėssnėss** *n.* **thrĭf'ty** *adj.* **thrĭf'tĭly** *adv.* **thrĭf'tĭnėss** *n.*

thrĭll *n.* Nervous tremor caused by intense emotion or sensation, wave of feeling or excitement; sensational quality (of story etc.). ~ *v.* Penetrate with wave of emotion or sensation, be thus penetrated or agitated; (of emotion etc.) pass *through*, *over*, etc.; quiver, throb, (as) with emotion. **thrĭll'er** *n.* (esp.) Sensational play or story. **thrĭll'ĭng** *adj.* **thrĭll'ĭngly** *adv.* **thrĭll'ĭngnėss** *n.*

thrĭps *n.* Any minute insect, with four hair-fringed wings, of order *Thysanoptera*, many of which injure plants by feeding on their juices.

THRIPS

thrīve *v.i.* (past t. *thrōve* or *thrīved*, past part. *thrĭv'en* or *thrīved*). Grow or develop well and vigorously, flourish; prosper; grow rich.

thro', thro: see THROUGH.

throat *n.* 1. Front of neck between chin and collar-bone region containing gullet and wind-pipe; narrow passage, esp. in or near entrance of something, narrow part in a passage; *sore* ~, inflammation of lining membrane of gullet etc. 2. Forward upper corner of fore-and-aft sail (ill. SAIL[1]). ~ *v.t.* Groove, channel.

throat'y *adj.* Guttural, uttered in the throat, hoarse. **throat'ĭly** *adv.* **throat'ĭnėss** *n.*

thrŏb *v.i.* (Of heart etc.) beat strongly, palpitate, pulsate, vibrate. ~ *n.* Throbbing, violent beat or pulsation.

thrōe *n.* (usu. pl.) Violent pang(s), esp. of childbirth; anguish.

thrŏmbōs'ĭs *n.* (pl. -*sēs*). Localized clotting of blood within the heart or blood-vessels. **thrŏmbŏt'ĭc** *adj.*

thrŏm'bus *n.* Blood-clot formed within vascular system which may impede circulation.

thrōne *n.* Chair of state for sovereign, bishop, etc., usu. decorated and raised on dais; sovereign power; seat for painter's model; (pl.) 3rd of 9 orders of angels. ~ *v.t.* Enthrone (lit. and fig.).

thrŏng *n.* Crowd, multitude (*of*) esp. in small space. ~ *v.* Come, go, press, in multitudes; fill with crowd or as crowd does.

thrŏstle (-sl) *n.* 1. (literary or dial.) Thrush, esp. song-thrush. 2. Machine for spinning wool, cotton, etc., in which the processes of drawing, twisting, and winding are continuous.

thrŏtt'le *n.* 1. Throat, gullet, wind-pipe (rare). 2. Valve controlling flow of steam in steam-engine or of fuel in internal combustion engine. ~ *v.t.* 1. Choke, strangle. 2. ~ (*down*), control, obstruct, flow of (steam, fuel, etc.) in engine, esp. with throttle; slow down (engine) thus.

through, thro', thro (-ōō) *prep.* & *adv.* From end to end or side to side (of), between the sides, walls, parts, etc., (of); from beginning to end (of); by reason of, by agency, means, or fault of. ~ *adj.* Going, concerned with going, through; (of railway or other travelling) going all the way without change of train, line, etc.

throughout' (-rōō-owt) *prep.* & *adv.* Right through, in every part (of), from end to end (of); in all respects.

throw (-ō) *v.* (past t. *threw* pr. -ōō, past part. *thrown* pr. -ōn). 1. Turn (wood etc.) in lathe, shape (pottery) on wheel (now dial. or tech.); prepare and twist (raw silk) into threads. 2. Project (thing) from hand or arm with force resembling jerk, esp. with sudden straightening of arm near shoulder-level, so that it passes through air or free space; fling, cast, hurl, project, shoot; (of wrestler, horse, etc.) bring (antagonist, rider) to the ground; put carelessly or hastily *on*, *off*, etc.; (of snake) cast (skin); (of animals) bring forth (young); make (specified cast) with dice; move (esp. part of body) quickly or suddenly; (slang) give (a party). 3. ~ *away*, (fig.) squander, waste; lose (chance etc.) by neglect; discard (card) when one cannot follow suit; ~-*away* (*n.*) printed paper, hand-bill, etc., not intended to be kept; ~ *back*, revert to ancestral type or character; ~-*back* (*n.*) such reversion, example of this; ~ *in*, add (thing) to bargain without extra charge; interpose (word, remark) in parenthesis or casually; ~ *in* one's *hand*, give up, withdraw from contest; ~ *in* one's *lot with*, decide to share fortunes of; ~-*in* (*n.*) (football) act of throwing in ball after it has gone out of play; ~ *off*, discard; get rid of; abandon (disguise); produce, deliver, in offhand manner; ~ one*self* (*up*)*on*, place one's reliance on; ~-*on*, (Rugby football) throwing ball forwards; ~ *out*, cast out; make (projecting or prominent addition to house etc.); suggest, insinuate; reject (Bill in Parliament); eject; disturb, distract (person) from train of thought etc.; (cricket) put (batsman) out by throwing ball so as to hit his wicket; ~ *over*, desert, abandon; ~ *up*, vomit; resign (office); raise (hands, eyes, etc.) quickly or suddenly; ~ *up the sponge*, give in, confess oneself beaten. ~ *n.* 1. Throwing, cast; cast of dice; cast of fishing-line; distance missile is or may be thrown; fall in wrestling; (geol., mining) (amount of vertical displacement caused by) fault in stratum. 2. (Extent of) action or motion of slide-valve, crank, cam, etc.; machine or instrument for imparting rotary motion.

throw'er (-ō'*er*) *n.* One who throws; apparatus for throwing a depth charge.

throw'ster (-rō-) *n.* One who throws silk.

thrŭm[1] *n.* Fringe of warp-threads remaining on loom when web has been cut off, single thread of this; any loose thread or tuft.

thrŭm[2] *v.* Strum; sound monotonously, hum. ~ *n.* (Sound of) thrumming.

thrŭsh[1] *n.* Small or medium-sized passerine bird of family *Turdidae*, esp. the European song-thrush, throstle, or mavis (*Turdus philomelus*) and the larger and less musical missel-thrush (*T. viscivorus*).

thrŭsh[2] *n.* 1. Disease, esp. of infants, characterized by whitish vesicular specks on inside of mouth and throat etc. and caused by a yeast (*Saccharomyces albicans*). 2. Inflammatory suppurative disease of foot in animals, esp. of frog of horse.

thrŭst *v.* (past t. and past part. *thrŭst*). Push, drive, exert force of impact on or against; pierce *through*; make sudden push *at* with pointed weapon; force oneself *through*, *past*, etc., make *way* thus. ~ *n.* Thrusting, lunge, stab; (mech. etc.) thrusting force of one part of structure etc. on contiguous part, esp. horizontal or diagonal pressure of part of building against abutment or support, driving force exerted by paddle, propeller-shaft, or jet-stream in ship or aircraft, (effect of) compressive strain in earth's crust.

thrŭst'er *n.* (esp.) One who pushes forward in hunting-field or rides too close to hounds; pusher.

Thūcȳd'idēs (-z) (5th c. B.C.). Athenian historian of the Peloponnesian War.

thŭd *n.* & *v.i.* (Make, fall with) low dull sound as of blow on soft thing.

thŭg *n.* Member of association (suppressed by British, 1830–40) of professional robbers and murderers, strangling their victims, in India; (transf.) cut-throat, ruffian, rough. **thŭgg'ee** (-gē) *n.* Practice of thugs. **thŭgg'ery** *n.*

Thūl'ē. Ancient Greek and Latin name of country 6 days' sail N. of Britain, supposed to be most northerly region in world; *ultima* ~, highest or uttermost point or degree.

thūl'ium *n.* A rare metallic element found in combination in some rare earths; symbol Tm, at. no. 69, at. wt 168·934. [f. THULE]

thŭmb (-m) *n.* Short thick inner digit, opposable to fingers, and with only two phalanges, of human hand; any inner digit opposable to and set apart from other digits; part of glove etc. covering thumb; *~s up!* exhortation to cheerfulness or expression of satisfaction; *rule of* ~: see RULE; *under* one's ~, under influence or domination of; *~-index*, reference-index consisting of grooves cut in, or tabs projecting from front edges of book, or margins so cut as to show initial letters or titles etc.; *~-mark*, mark made by thumb, esp. on page of book; *~-nail*, nail of thumb; *~-nail sketch*, small or hasty portrait, brief word-picture; *~-print*, impression of inner surface of top joint of thumb; *thumb'-screw*, screw with flattened or winged head that may be turned with thumb and fingers; instrument of torture for compressing thumb(s); *~-tack*, tack with broad head which may be pushed in with thumb, drawing-pin. ~ *v.t.* Soil, wear, with thumb; handle with thumb or awkwardly or clumsily; make a request for (a ride in a vehicle) by sticking out a thumb in the direction one wishes to go. **thŭmb'lėss** *adj.*

thummim: see URIM AND THUMMIM.

thŭmp *n.* Heavy blow, bang; sound of this. ~ *v.* Beat heavily, esp. with fist; deliver heavy blows (*at*, *on*, etc.). **thŭmp'er** *n.* (esp., colloq.) Large, striking, or impressive person or thing, esp. lie.

thŭn'der *n.* Loud noise accompanying lightning (but appearing to follow it because of difference in speeds of light and sound) and due to sudden violent disturbance of air by the electric discharge; any loud deep rumbling or resounding noise; terrifying, threatening, or impressive utterance(s); *thunderbolt*, imaginary bolt or dart formerly supposed to be the destructive agent when thing is 'struck' by lightning, esp. as attribute of Thor, Jupiter, etc.; conventional representation of this; something very startling, terrible, or destructive; *~-clap*, loud crash of thunder; *~-cloud*, storm-cloud charged with electricity and producing thunder and lightning; *~-head*, rounded cumulus cloud near horizon projecting above general body of cloud and portending thunder; *~-storm*, storm with thunder and lightning; *thunderstruck*, (fig.) amazed, terrified, confounded. **thŭn'derlėss, thŭn'derous, thŭn'dery** *adjs.* **thŭn'der** *v. It ~s*, there is thunder; sound with or like thunder; emit (threats etc.) in loud or impressive manner; fulminate. **thŭn'derer** *n.* (esp. as joc. epithet of) the London 'Times' newspaper. **thŭn'derĭng** *adj.* & *adv.* (esp., colloq.) Unusual(ly), decided(ly).

thūr'ible *n.* Censer.

Thūrĭn'gia (-j-). (Ger. *Thüringen*) State in central Germany formed in 1919 by union of the Thuringian duchies (Saxe-Coburg, Saxe-Gotha, Reuss, etc.); now a province of E. Germany; cap. Weimar. **Thūrĭn'gian** *adj.* Of Thuringia or the Thuringians. ~ *n.* Inhabitant of Thuringia; (hist.) one of an ancient tribe of central Germany conquered by Franks in 6th c.

Thurs. *abbrev.* Thursday.

Thūrs'day (-zdā *or* -zdĭ) *n.* 5th day of week; *Holy* ~: see HOLY. [OE *thur(e)sdæg* Thor's day, rendering LL *dies Jovis* day of Jupiter]

thŭs (dh-) *adv.* In this way, like this, as follows; accordingly, consequently, and so; to this extent, number, or degree. **thŭs'nėss** *n.* (colloq. and usu. joc.).

thū'ya, thū'ja *n.* (Tree or shrub of) coniferous genus including the N. Amer. and Chinese *Arbor Vitae* (*T. occidentalis* and *T. orientalis*).

thwăck *n.* & *v.t.* = WHACK.

thwart (-ôrt) *n.* Seat across boat, on which rower sits (ill. BOAT). ~ *adv.*, *prep.*, & *adj.* Athwart; *~-ship* (*adj.*), *-ships* (*adv.*), (lying) across ship. ~ *v.t.* Frustrate, cross.

T.H.W.M. *abbrev.* Trinity high-water mark.

thy (dhī) *poss. adj.* Of or belonging to thee.

thȳl'acīne *n.* The Tasmanian wolf (*Thylacinus*), a carnivorous marsupial, now extinct, which resembled a dog in appearance, greyish-brown with conspicuous black markings on the hinder half of the back.

thyme (tīm) *n.* Genus (*Thymus*) of shrubby herbs with fragrant aromatic leaves, chiefly of Mediterranean regions; plant of this genus, esp. *garden* ~ (*T. vulgaris*), native of Spain and Italy, cultivated as pot-herb, and *wild* ~ (*T. serpyllum*), occurring on dry banks etc. throughout Europe.

thym'ol (tī- *or* thī-) *n.* (chem.) White crystalline phenol obtained from oil of thyme, having pleasant aromatic smell and used as antiseptic.

thȳm'us *n.* (pl. *-mī*). (anat.) Ductless glandular body (of uncertain function) situated near base of neck in vertebrates, in man disappearing or diminishing after childhood.

thȳr'oid *adj.* (anat., orig.) Shield-shaped; (now chiefly) of, connected with, the ~ *gland*, large ductless gland lying near larynx and upper trachea in vertebrates and influencing growth and development; so called because of its proximity to the ~ *cartilage*, large cartilage of larynx consisting of two broad plates united in front at an angle, forming the 'Adam's apple'. ~ *n.* Thyroid gland (ill. GLAND); extract prepared from thyroid gland of some animals, used in treating goitre, cretinism, etc.

thȳrŏx'in *n.* (chem.) White crystalline active principle of thyroid gland.

thyrs'us (-ĕr-) *n.* (pl. *-sī*). 1. (Gk antiq.) Staff tipped with ornament like pine-cone, attribute of Dionysus. 2. (bot.) Kind of inflorescence in which primary axis is racemose and secondary etc. cymose, as in lilac and horse-chestnut.

thȳsĕlf' (dh-) *pron.* Reflexive and emphatic form of THEE, THOU.

ti (tē). Variant spelling of TE.

tiār'a (*or* tī-) *n.* Ancient-Persian form of head-dress; official head-dress of the pope, consisting of a high pointed cap encircled by three crowns, symbolic of the temporal, spiritual, and purgatorial sovereignty claimed by the papacy; papal office; jewelled coronet worn by women.

Tīb'er. River of central Italy flowing from Tuscan Apennines through Rome to Mediterranean Sea at Ostia.

Tībĕr'ĭăs. Ancient town (built by Herod Antipas *c* A.D. 21 and named after Tiberius) on W. shore of Sea of Galilee.

Tībēr'ius. Tiberius Claudius Nero (42 B.C.–A.D. 37), Roman emperor A.D. 14–37.

Tĭbĕt, Th-. Mountainous country of central Asia; capital, Lhasa. **Tibĕt'an, Th-** *adj.* & *n.* (Native) of Tibet; its language, allied to Burmese.

tĭb'ia *n.* (anat., zool.) Inner and usu. larger of two bones of lower leg, from knee to ankle, shinbone (ill. SKELETON); tibiotarsus of birds; (entom.) fourth segment of insect's leg, between femur and tarsus. **tĭb'ial** *adj.*

tĭbiotar's'us *n.* Tibia of birds, fused at lower end with some bones of tarsus.

Tĭbŭll'us, Albius (*c* 60–19 B.C.). Latin elegiac poet.

tic *n.* Habitual local spasmodic contraction of muscles, esp. of face; ~ (*douloureux* pr. dŏlerōō'), trigeminal neuralgia, severe facial neuralgia with twitching of facial muscles.

Tĭch'borne claimant. Arthur Orton (1834–98), a butcher, who came from Australia with claim to be Roger Charles Tichborne (1829–54), eldest son of 10th baronet, lost at sea; after a long trial (1871) Orton's ejectment action against the trustees of the Tichborne estates was lost, and he was found guilty of perjury.

tĭck[1] *n.* Any of several large blood-sucking mites of the order *Acarina* infesting hair or fur of various animals; similar parasitic dipterous insects (e.g. *Melophagus*) infesting birds, sheep, etc.

tĭck[2] *n.* Case or cover containing feathers, wool, hair, etc., and forming mattress or pillow; (also **tĭck'ĭng**) strong hard linen or cotton material for this.

tĭck[3] *n.* 1. Quick light dry recurring sound, distinct but not loud, esp. of alternate check and release of train in escapement of clock or watch; (colloq.) time between two ticks of clock, moment, instant. 2. Small mark (✓) set against items in list etc. in checking. ~ *v.* Mark (*off* item etc.) with tick; make ticking sound; wear *away*, *out*, etc., in ticking, (of tape-machine) throw *off*, *out* (message by ticking); ~ *off*, (slang) reprimand; ~ *over*, (of internal combustion engines) run slowly with gears disconnected (also fig.).

tĭck[4] *n.* (colloq.) Credit. [abbrev. of TICKET]

tĭck'er *n.* (esp., colloq.) Watch; telegraphic tape-machine; (joc.) heart.

tĭck'ėt *n.* Written notice for public information, esp. label, show-card; slip, usu. of paper or cardboard, bearing evidence of holder's title to some service or privilege, as railway journey, seat at entertainment, etc.; certificate of qualifications of pilot, ship's mate, or captain, etc.; pay-warrant, esp. discharge warrant of soldier etc.; ticket of leave; (U.S.) list of candidates of one party or group put forward for election; hence; (fig.) principles of a party; *the* ~, (slang) what is wanted, expected, etc.; ~*-card*, thick paper used for show-cards; ~*-collector*, railway official who takes or checks passengers' tickets; ~ *of leave*, licence giving convict his liberty, under certain restrictions, before sentence has expired; ~*-punch*, tool for punching holes in tickets to show that they have been used. ~ *v.t.* Put ticket on (article for sale etc.).

tĭck'le *n.* Act, sensation, of tickling. ~ *v.* Touch or stroke (person, part of his body) lightly with finger-tips, feather, etc., so as to excite nerves and usu. produce laughter; cause or feel peculiar uneasy sensation as of being tickled; excite agreeably, amuse, divert; catch (trout etc.) by stroking lightly with hand.

tĭck'ler *n.* (esp.) Puzzling or delicate question or matter.

tĭck'lĭsh *adj.* Easily tickled, sensitive to tickling; (of question etc.) difficult, critical, delicate, requiring careful handling. **tĭck'lĭshly** *adv.* **tĭck'lĭshnėss** *n.*

tĭck'-tăck' *n.*, *adv.*, *int.*, *adj.* Imitation of ticking sound, as of clock etc.; of, practising, system of signalling with arms etc. used by book-makers at race-meetings.

t.i.d. *abbrev.* *Ter in die* (three times a day, in medical prescriptions).

tīd'al *adj.* Of tides; (of motor traffic) running in opposite directions at different times of day; ~ *air*, (physiol.) volume of air breathed in and out of lungs during a normal respiration; ~ *river*, river affected by tides to some distance from mouth; ~ *stream*, horizontal water movement caused by tide-generating forces; ~ *wave*, wave caused by movement of tide; (pop.) exceptionally large ocean wave or very high water sometimes following earthquake or other local commotion; (fig.) widespread manifestation of feeling etc.

tidbit: see TITBIT.

tĭdd'lўwĭnks *n.* Game in which small counters are flipped across table into receptacle.

tīde *n.* 1. Time, season (archaic exc. in *Whitsuntide*, *Shrovetide*, etc.); period of time. 2. Flowing or swelling of sea, or its alternate rising (*flood-*~) and falling (*ebb* ~), twice in each lunar day, due to the attraction of moon (and sun); (fig.) something like a tide in ebbing and flowing, 'turning', etc.; flood-tide; *high*, *low* ~, completion of the flood, ebb, tide; *spring* ~, maximum tide, produced when the sun and moon are in conjunction or opposition, as at new moon and full; *neap* ~, minimum tide, produced when the moon is at first or third quarter and the sun's attraction in part counteracts the moon's; ~*-gate*, gate through which water passes into dock etc. at flood, and by which it is retained during ebb; ~*-lock*, double lock between tidal water and canal, basin, etc., beyond it; ~*-mark*, mark made by tide at high water; (colloq.) line between clean and dirty parts of body after partial wash; ~*-rip*, rough water caused by opposing tides; ~*-waiter*, (hist.) customs officer boarding ships to enforce customs regulations; *tide'-water*, water affected by ebb and flow of tides; (U.S.) district on coast of Virginia; ~*-way*, channel in which tidal current runs, tidal part of river. **tīde'lėss** *adj.* **tīde** *v.* 1. Drift with tide, esp. use tide to work in or out of harbour. 2. Get *over* (difficulty etc.).

tīd'ĭngs *n.pl.* (now chiefly literary) (Piece of) news.

tīd'y *adj.* Neatly arranged, neat, orderly; (colloq.) pretty large, considerable. ~ *n.* Ornamental loose covering for chair-back etc.; receptacle for odds and ends. ~ *v.t.* Make neat, put in good order. **tīd'ĭly** *adv.* **tīd'ĭnėss** *n.*

tīe *v.* 1. Attach, fasten, with cord or the like; secure (shoe, bonnet) by tightening and knotting its strings; arrange string, ribbon, etc., to form knot, bow, etc.; bind (rafters etc.) by crosspiece etc.; (mus.) unite (notes) by tie; restrict, bind (person etc.); ~ *up*, restrict, esp. annex conditions to (bequest etc.) to prevent its being sold or diverted from its purpose. 2. Make same score as (person) in game etc.; be equal in score *with*. 3. *tied house*, public-house bound to deal exclusively with one specified firm of brewers. ~ *n.* 1. Cord, chain, etc., used for fastening. 2. Neck-tie; fur necklet. 3. Rod, beam, holding parts of structure together; (U.S.) railway sleeper. 4. (mus.) Curved line placed over or under two notes to indicate that sound is to be sustained, not repeated. 5. (elect.) Circuit or land-line coupling two electrical systems, power stations, etc. 6. (fig.) Thing that connects or unites in some way, link, bond. 7. Equality of score between competitors or sides in match or contest, drawn match; deciding match played after draw, match between victors in previous matches or heats; match between any pair of several competing players or teams. 8. ~*-beam*, horizontal beam connecting rafters (ill. ROOF); ~*-pin*, ornamental pin worn in neck-tie; ~*-up*, obstructed situation, standstill, esp. (U.S.) obstruction of traffic on railway etc. caused by strike, breakdown, etc.; ~*-wig*, wig with hair tied in knot behind.

Tieck (tēk), Ludwig (1773–1853). German Romantic poet and novelist.

Tiepolo (tyāp'olō), Giovanni Ballista (1696–1770). Venetian painter.

tier (tēr), *n.* Row, rank, esp. one of several placed one above another as in theatre. ~ *v.t.* Arrange or pile in tiers.

tierce (tērs) *n.* 1. (eccles.) Third hour of canonical day, ending at 9 a.m. (hist.); office said at this hour. 2. Position in fencing, 3rd of 8 parries, or corresponding thrust, in sword-play (ill. FENCE). 3. (mus.) Interval of two octaves and a major third (= major 17th) above fundamental note; organ-stop giving tones at this interval. 4. Old measure of capacity, one-third of pipe; cask or vessel holding this quantity.

Tiĕ′rra del Fuego (fōōā′gō). (Main island of) archipelago at S. point of S. America, discovered 1520 by Magellan; divided between Chile and Argentina.

tiers état (tyārz′ātah′) *n.* Third estate, body of commons in French National Assembly before Revolution.

tiff *n.* (colloq.) Slight or petty quarrel. ~ *v.i.* Have a tiff.

tiff′any *n.* (archaic) Kind of thin transparent silk or muslin. [OF *tifanie* theophany, i.e. Epiphany (because orig. worn on Twelfth Night)]

tiff′in *n.* & *v.i.* (Anglo-Ind.) (Take) light meal, lunch. [app. f. obs. *tiff* drink, sip]

Tĭf′lĭs. (Georgian *Tbilisi.*) Capital of the Georgian Soviet Socialist Republic.

tĭg′er (-g-) *n.* 1. Large Asiatic carnivorous feline quadruped (*Felis tigris*), maneless, of tawny-yellow colour with blackish transverse stripes and white belly, proverbial for ferocity and cunning. 2. Various other feline animals, esp. (in America) the jaguar and puma, and (in S. Africa) the leopard. 3. Fierce, cruel, or rapacious person or animal; formidable opponent in a game (opp. *rabbit*). 4. (slang, archaic) Smartly liveried boy groom accompanying master in light vehicle. 5. (U.S. slang) Loud yell at end of burst of cheering. 6. *~-beetle*, active carnivorous voracious beetle of family *Cicindelidae*; *~-cat*, any of various moderate-sized feline beasts resembling tiger in markings etc.; (Australia) either of two carnivorous marsupials, *Dasyurus viverrinus* and *D. maculatus*; *~('s)-eye*, yellowish-brown quartz with brilliant lustre, used as gem; (U.S.) kind of crystalline pottery glaze resembling this; *~-lily*, tall garden lily (*Lilium tigrinum*) of Asiatic origin with orange flowers spotted with black; *~-moth*, moth of family *Arctiidae*, esp. *Arctia caja*, large scarlet-and-brown British species spotted and streaked with white; *~-shark*, various large voracious spotted or streaked sharks; *~-wood*, wood from a tree native to Guiana, used in cabinet-making. **tĭg′rĕss** *n.* Female tiger.

tĭg′erish (-g-) *adj.* Like, cruel as, a tiger. **tĭg′erĭshly** *adv.* **tĭg′erishnĕss** *n.*

tight (tīt) *adj.* 1. Close-textured, firmly constructed, so as to be impervious to fluid etc. 2. Closely held, drawn, fastened, fitting, etc.; tense, taut, stretched so as to leave no slack; neat, trim, compact. 3. Produced by, requiring, great exertion or pressure; (colloq., of person) close-fisted, (of money) difficult to obtain. 4. (slang) Drunk. 5. *~-fisted*, stingy, close-fisted; *~-rope*, tightly stretched rope, wire, etc., on which acrobats and rope-dancers perform; *~-wad*, (U.S. slang) tight-fisted person. ~ *adv.* Tightly; *~-laced*, having laces drawn tight, wearing tightly laced stays; (fig.) strict in observance of rules of morality or propriety, strait-laced. **tight′en** *v.* **tight′ly** *adv.* **tight′nĕss** *n.* **tights** *n.pl.* Thin tightly fitting garment worn by dancers etc. and covering legs and lower part of body or whole body.

Tĭg′rĭs. River of E. Mesopotamia, joining Euphrates to form Shatt al Arab, which flows into the Persian Gulf.

T.I.H. *abbrev.* Their Imperial Highnesses.

tiki (tēk′ē) *n.* (New Zealand) Maori large wooden or small ornamental greenstone image of creator of man or an ancestor.

tĭl′bury *n.* Light open two-wheeled carriage fashionable in first half of 19th c. [inventor's name]

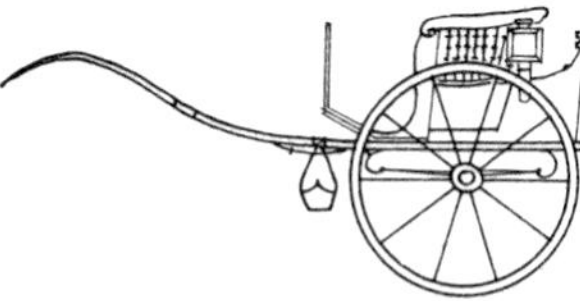

TILBURY

Tĭl′bury Docks. Large passenger and goods docks on N. shore of Thames 25 miles below London Bridge.

tĭl′de (-*e*) *n.* Diacritical mark (˜) placed in Spanish over *n* to indicate palatalized sound (ny) and in Portuguese over *a* and *o* to indicate nasal sound.

tīle *n.* Thin slab of baked clay for covering roof, paving floor, lining wall, fire-place, etc., or making drains etc.; material of this, burnt clay; tiles collectively; (slang) hat, esp. silk hat. ~ *v.t.* Cover, line, with tiles; (freemasonry, usu. *tyle*) protect (lodge, meeting) from intrusion or interruption. **tīl′er** *n.* Tile-layer; (freemasonry, usu. *tyler*) door-keeper at lodge or meeting.

tīle′-fĭsh *n.* Large deep-water yellow-spotted food-fish (*Lopholatilus chamaeleonticeps*), of coasts of New England etc.

tĭll[1] *n.* Money-drawer, box, etc., usu. under and behind counter of bank, shop, etc.

tĭll[2] *n.* Boulder-clay, stiff unstratified clay mixed with sand, gravel, and boulders.

tĭll[3] *v.t.* Labour upon (land) in order to produce crops. **tĭll′age** *n.* **tĭll′er**[1] *n.*

tĭll[4] *prep.* & *conj.* Up to, as late as; up to the time of; up to the time when.

tĭll′er[2] *n.* Shoot of plant springing from bottom of original stalk; sapling; sucker.

tĭll′er[3] *n.* Horizontal bar fixed to rudder head and acting as lever for steering (ill. BOAT).

tĭll′ite *n.* Old consolidated boulder-clay (TILL[2]) deposited in a pre-tertiary glacial period.

tĭlt[1] *n.* Covering or awning of canvas etc. esp. for cart (ill. WAGON). ~ *v.t.* Furnish with tilt.

tĭlt[2] *v.* 1. (Cause to) incline abruptly from vertical or horizontal, (cause to) assume sloping or slanting position, heel over; *tilted*, (geol., of strata) inclined abruptly upwards from horizontal. 2. Engage in tilt; strike, thrust, run, *at*, with weapon. 3. Forge, work, with tilt-hammer. ~ *n.* 1. Joust, combat between two armed men on horseback each trying to throw opponent from saddle with lance; *full* ~, at full speed, with full force or impetus; *~-yard*, enclosed place for tilting, tilting-ground. 2. Tilting, sloping position. 3. ~(*-hammer*), heavy forging hammer, fixed on pivot and alternately tilted up and dropped by action of cam-wheel or eccentric.

tĭlth *n.* Tillage, cultivation, husbandry; depth of soil dug or cultivated.

Tim. *abbrev.* Timothy (N.T.).

tĭm′bal, tў̆m′bal *n.* (archaic or hist.) Kettledrum. [Fr. *timbale*, earlier *attabale*, f. Arab. *al ṭabl* the drum]

timbale (tăṅbahl′) *n.* Dish of minced meat, fish, etc., cooked in drum-shaped mould of pastry etc.

tĭm′ber *n.* Wood prepared for building etc.; trees suitable for this; piece of wood, beam, esp. (naut.) any curved piece forming ribs of vessel (ill. BOAT); *standing* ~, trees, woods; *~-wolf*, large grey wolf of northern N. America. ~ *v.t.* Support (roof of mine or working, sides and roof of tunnel, etc.) with timber. **tĭm′bered** (-*erd*) *adj.* Made of timber or wood; wooded. **tĭm′berĭng** *n.*

timbre (tăṅbr) *n.* Distinctive quality of musical or vocal sound depending on voice or instrument producing it, tone colour. [Fr., = 'clock-bell', 'drum', f. L *tympanum*]

tĭm′brel *n.* (chiefly bibl.) Percussive musical instrument held in hand, tambourine or the like. [f. TIMBRE]

Tĭmbŭctōō′, -ŭktu (-tōō). Town of French Sudan, near Niger.

tīme *n.* 1. Indefinite continuous duration regarded as dimension in which sequence of events takes place (freq. personified, esp. as old man with scythe and hour-glass); finite duration as dist. from eternity; more or less definite portion of this associated with particular events or circumstances, historical or other period; (freq. pl.) conditions of life, prevailing circumstances, of a period; allotted or available portion of time, time at one's disposal; moment or definite portion of time destined or suitable for a purpose etc., esp. period of gestation, term of imprisonment, term of apprenticeship, length of round in boxing, part of football or other game, time to begin or end this; point of time; season; occasion; (payment for) amount of time worked; (amount of) time as reckoned by conventional standards; *standard* ~, local mean time of 24 regions of longitude, at intervals of 15°; *summer-*~: see SUMMER; *a good* ~, period of enjoyment. 2. (mus.) Rhythm or measure of musical composition, marked by division into bars and denoted by ~ *signature*, usu. fraction showing number of aliquot parts of semibreve in each bar; tempo. 3. (pl.) Preceded by numeral and followed by number or expression of quantity etc., expressing multiplication, comparison, etc. 4. *all the* ~, during the whole time referred to; (U.S.) at all times; *at the same* ~, simultaneously; all the same; *at* ~*s*, now and then; *from* ~ *to* ~, occasionally; *in* ~, not late; early enough; eventually, sooner or later; following the time of music etc.; *in no* ~, rapidly, in a moment; *on* ~, punctually; ~ *of day*, hour by the clock. 5. ~*-bomb*, bomb with time-fuse or other device so adjusted that it will explode after a predetermined interval, delayed-action bomb; ~*-card*, card with record of time worked; ~*-clock*, clock with device recording times, e.g. of arrival and departure of workmen etc.; ~*-constant*, mathematical expression giving indication of delay involved in heating, charging, moving, etc., when the process produces an opposing effect proportional to the temperature, charge, speed, etc.; ~*-exposure*, (photog.) exposure for regulated length of time, as dist. from instantaneous exposure; ~*-fuse*, fuse calculated to explode a charge after a predetermined time; ~*-honoured*, respected on account of its antiquity; ~*-keeper*, watch, clock, esp. in ref. to accuracy; one who records time, esp. of workmen; ~*-lag*, interval of time between cause etc. and result or consequence; *time'piece*, instrument for measuring time, chronometer; ~*-server*, one who on grounds of self-interest adapts himself to opinions of the times or of persons in power; ~*-serving*; ~*-sheet*, sheet of paper recording hours worked by employee(s) etc.; ~*-signal*, visible or audible signal, esp. wireless signal, announcing the time of day; ~ *signature*: see sense 2; ~*-table*, tabular list or schedule of times of classes in school etc., arrival and departure of trains, boats, buses, etc. ~ *v.* Choose the time for, do at chosen time; record time of event, duration of action, etc., keep time, harmonize (*with*).

tīme'lėss (-ml-) *adj.* Unending, eternal; not subject to time. **tīme'lėssly** *adv.* **tīme'lėssnėss** *n.*

tīme'ly (-ml-) *adj.* Seasonable, opportune. **tīme'linėss** *n.*

tim'(e)ous (-mus) *adj.* (chiefly Sc.) Timely.

tĭm'ĭd *adj.* Easily alarmed; shy. **tĭm'ĭdly** *adv.* **tĭm'ĭdnėss** *n.* **tĭmĭd'ĭty** *n.*

tīmŏ'cracy *n.* 1. In the Aristotelian sense: a polity with a property qualification for office. 2. In the Platonic sense: a polity (like that of Sparta) in which love of honour is said to be the dominant motive among the rulers. **tīmocrăt'ic(al)** *adjs.*

tīmŏl'ogy *n.* (philos.) The doctrine of values.

Tī'mon of Athens (5th c. B.C.). An Athenian who became a misanthrope owing to the ingratitude of his friends.

Tīm'ôr (*or* tēmôr'). Island of Lesser Sunda group, in southern Malay Archipelago; divided between Portugal and Indonesia. ~ *Sea*, part of Indian Ocean lying between Timor and NW. Australia.

tĭm'orous *adj.* Timid, easily alarmed. **tĭm'orously** *adv.* **tĭm'orousnėss** *n.*

Tĭm'othy. (N.T.) Convert and colleague of St. Paul, to whom two Epistles are addressed.

tĭm'othy (grass) *n.* (chiefly U.S.) Meadow grass (*Phleum pratense*), European grass with long cylindrical spikes, introduced into N. America from England for cultivation for hay in 18th c. [said to be f. *Timothy* Hanson, who introduced it into Carolina *c* 1720]

Timur (Lenk or **Lang):** see TAMBURLAINE.

tĭn *n.* 1. A metallic element nearly approaching silver in whiteness, highly malleable, and taking a high polish, used in the manufacture of alloys as bronze, pewter, etc., and, on account of its resistance to oxidation, for making tinplate and lining culinary and other iron vessels; symbol Sn (*stannum*), at. no. 50, at. wt 118·69. 2. Vessel made of tin, or more usu. tinned iron, esp. a vessel in which meat, fish, fruit, etc., is hermetically sealed for preservation; tin-plate, as the material of such vessels. 3. (slang) Money, cash. 4. ~*-foil*, tin hammered or rolled into a thin sheet; sheet of this rubbed with mercury, formerly used for backing mirrors and precious stones; similar sheet of an alloy of tin and lead used for wrapping and packing; (*v.t.*) cover, coat, with tin-foil; ~ *god*, (fig.) base or unworthy object of veneration; ~ *hat*, (mil. slang) steel helmet; ~ *Lizzie*; nickname for a Ford motor-car; ~*-opener*, instrument for opening hermetically sealed tins; *tinplate*, sheet-iron or sheet-steel coated with tin; ~*-pot*, pot made of tin or tin-plate; (attrib.) resembling or suggesting a tin-pot in quality or sound; hence contempt., of inferior quality, shabby, cheap; *tin'-smith*, worker in tin, maker of tin utensils; ~*-stone*, the most commonly occurring form of tin ore, cassiterite (SnO_2); ~*-tack*, short iron nail coated with tin. ~ *v.t.* Cover, coat, with tin; pack (meat, fruit, etc.) in tins for preservation.

tĭn'amou (-ōō) *n.* S. American bird of the family *Tinamidae*, resembling a quail.

tĭnc'al, tĭnk'al *n.* Crude borax, found in lake-deposits in parts of Asia.

tĭnctôr'ial *adj.* Of, used in, dyeing; yielding, using, dye or colouring matter.

tĭnc'ture *n.* 1. (her.) Colour or metal used in coat of arms etc. (ill. HERALDRY). 2. Solution, usu. in alcohol or alcohol and ether, of medicinal substance or principle. 3. Slight flavour, spice, smack; smattering; tinge. ~ *v.t.* Colour slightly; tinge, flavour; affect slightly.

tĭn'der *n.* Any dry inflammable substance readily taking fire from spark, esp. that formerly used in ~*-box* to catch spark from flint and steel for kindling fire etc. **tĭn'dery** *adj.*

tīne *n.* Prong, projecting sharp point of harrow, fork, etc. (ill. HARROW); pointed branch of deer's antler (ill. DEER).

tĭn'ėa *n.* (path.) Ringworm, fungus infection of skin usu. confined to scalp or face but also attacking other parts.

tĭng *n.* & *v.i.* (Make) tinkling sound.

tĭnge (-j) *v.t.* Colour slightly, modify tint or colour of; (fig.) qualify, modify, slightly alter tone of. ~ *n.* Tint, slight colouring; flavour, touch.

tĭng'le (-ngg-) *n.* & *v.* (Feel cause) slight pricking or stinging sensation.

tinkal: see TINCAL.

tĭnk'er *n.* Mender (esp. itinerant) of kettles, pans, etc.; (Scotland and N. Ireland) gipsy; clumsy mender or workman, botcher; (U.S.) jack-of-all-trades; act of tinkering. ~ *v.* Repair, patch (*up*), roughly; work amateurishly or clumsily *at*, esp. in attempt to repair or improve.

tĭnk'le *n.* & *v.* (Make, cause to make) succession of short light sharp ringing sounds, as of small bell.

tĭnn'er *n.* Tinsmith; one who tins meat, fruit, etc., canner.

tĭnnīt'us *n.* (med.) Noises

heard in the ear not due to external stimulation by sound-waves.

tinn'y *adj.* Consisting of, abounding in, yielding, tin; like or resembling tin, esp. of sounds; (slang) wealthy.

tin'sel *n.* Shining metallic gold- or silver-coloured material used in thin sheets, strips, or threads to give sparkling effect; fabric adorned with tinsel; (fig.) anything having or giving deceptively fine or glittering appearance, gaudy or showy but worthless thing. **tĭn'sėlly** *adj.* **tĭn'sel** *adj.* Showy, gaudy, cheaply splendid. ~ *v.t.* Adorn with tinsel. [L *scintilla* spark]

tint *n.* Colour, usu. slight or delicate, esp. one of several tones of the same colour; (in painting, esp.) lighter tone of a colour as dist. from *shade*, darker one; (engraving) effect produced by fine lines or dots set more or less closely together so as to produce an even tone. ~ *v.t.* Apply tint to, colour.

Tĭntă'gel (-jl). Village on coast of N. Cornwall, with ruins of castle; traditional birthplace of King Arthur.

Tĭn'tern Abbey. Ruins, on River Wye, Monmouthshire, of a Cistercian abbey founded 1131 and dissolved by Henry VIII.

tĭntĭnnăbūlā'tion *n.* Ringing or tinkling of bell(s).

Tĭntorĕtt'ō. Jacopo Robusti (1518–94), Venetian painter.

tĭn'y *adj.* Very small.

tip[1] *n.* Extremity, end, esp. of small or tapering thing; small piece or part attached to thing to form serviceable end, ferrule, etc.; thin flat brush used for gilding; light horse-shoe for front part of hoof; (*on*) *tip'toe*, on the tips of the toes, standing or walking with heels raised from ground; *tip'toe* (*v.i.*) walk on tiptoe; *tip'-top'*, highest point of excellence; first-rate. ~ *v.t.* Furnish with tip.

tĭp[2] *v.* 1. (Cause to) lean or slant, tilt, topple, esp. with slight effort; overturn, cause to overbalance; discharge (contents of jug, wagon, etc., *out* etc.) thus. 2. Strike or touch lightly; (ninepins etc.) knock down (pin) otherwise than by direct impact of bowl; (slang) hand, give, communicate, in informal manner; ~ (person) *the wink*, give private signal or warning to; (sport. slang) give secret information about (horse etc.) to; *~-and-run*, children's form of cricket in which batsman must run if he hits the ball; (attrib. of raid etc.) marked by hasty attack and immediate withdrawal from the scene; *~-cat*, small piece of wood tapering at both ends, which is struck with stick at one end so as to spring into air, and then knocked to a distance with same stick; game in which this is used; *~-car, -cart*, etc., one pivoted so that its contents can readily be tipped out; *~-up*, (of seat in theatre etc.) constructed so as to tip up to allow of passage between rows. 3. Give usu. small present of money to, esp. for service rendered or expected. ~ *n.* 1. Small present of money given esp. to servant or employee of another for service given or expected, or to schoolboy etc. 2. Piece of useful private or special information given by expert, esp. about horse-racing, money-market, etc.; special device, good dodge or 'wrinkle'. 3. Light touch or blow. 4. Place where refuse etc. is tipped.

Tĭpperār'y. County of Munster, Eire; song associated with the B.E.F. of 1914, the first words of which were *It 's a long way to ~*.

tĭpp'ėt *n.* 1. (hist.) Long narrow band of cloth attached to or forming part of dress, head-dress, or sleeve 2. Woman's small cape or collar of fur, silk, etc., usu. with two ends hanging in front (hist.); similar garment worn as part of official costume by judges, clergy, etc. (ill. VESTMENT).

tĭp'le *v.* Drink strong drink habitually; take (drink) constantly in small quantities. **tĭpp'ler** *n.* **tĭpp'le** *n.* Strong drink.

tip'staff (-ahf) *n.* (hist.) (Metal-tipped staff as badge of) sheriff's officer.

tip'ster *n.* One who gives tips about races etc.

tip'sy *adj.* (Partly) intoxicated; unsteady, staggering, from effects of drink; *~-cake*, cake soaked in wine or spirit and served with custard. **tĭp'sĭly** *adv.* **tĭp'sĭnėss** *n.*

tĭrāde' (*or* tīr-) *n.* Long vehement speech esp. of denunciation or abuse; long declamatory passage. [It. *tirada* volley]

Tĭra'na (-rah-). Capital city of Albania.

tīre[1] *v.* Make, grow, weary. **tired** (-īrd) *adj.* Weary (*of*); (slang) lazy. **tired'ly** *adv.* **tired'nėss** *n.* **tīre'lėss** *adj.* **tīre'lėssly** *adv.* **tīre'lėssnėss** *n.*

tire[2] *n.* & *v.*: see TYRE.

tīre[3] *n.* (archaic) Head-dress, attire. ~ *v.t.* Adorn, attire.

Tīrĕ'sĭas. A blind Theban prophet.

tire'some (-īrs-) *adj.* Tending to tire, fatiguing, tedious; annoying. **tīre'somely** *adv.* **tīre'somenėss** *n.*

Tír na nÓg (tẽrn'*a* nōg). Elysium of ancient Irish. [Irish, = 'land of the young']

tīr'ō *n.*: see TYRO.

Tirol: see TYROL.

Tirp'itz (tẽr-), Alfred von (1849–1930). German admiral.

Tī'ryns (-z). City of ancient Greece in the plain of Argos, near Mycenae, dating at least from Helladic times and having the best-preserved example of a Mycenaean palace and fortress (14th–13th c. B.C.).

'tis (tĭz), archaic or poet. or dial. abbrev. of *it is*.

tĭss'ue (-sū, -shū, -shōō) *n.* 1. Any (esp. rich or fine) woven stuff. 2. (biol.) Substance of animal or plant body, esp. of a particular part; organized mass of cells of similar kind, as *muscular ~*, *nervous ~*, etc. 3. (fig.) Interwoven series, set, collection (*of*). 4. ~ (*-paper*), thin soft gauze-like unsized paper for wrapping delicate articles, protecting illustrations in books, toilet use, etc.

tĭt[1] *n.* (also *titmouse*). Various small birds mostly of the common and widely distributed genus *Parus*, including the *blue ~* (*P. caeruleus*), *great ~* (*P. major*), and *coal ~* (*P. ater*).

tĭt[2] *n.* *~ for tat*, equivalent given in return, blow for blow, retaliation.

Tit. *abbrev.* Titus (N.T.).

Tī'tan. *n.* (Gk myth.) One of 12 gigantic children of Uranus and Ge (Oceanus, Coeus, Crius, Hyperion, Iapetus, Cronus, Theia, Rhea, Thamis, Mnemosyne, Phoebe, Tethys), from two of whom (Cronos and Rhea) Zeus and the Olympians descended; hence, a person of superhuman size, strength, etc.

tītăn'ĭc[1] *adj.* Of the Titans; gigantic, colossal.

tīt'anīte *n.* Monoclinic mineral, composed chiefly of *calcium titano-silicate* ($CaO.TiO_2.SiO_2$), occas. used as a gem.

tītān'ĭum *n.* Grey metallic element widely distributed in combination in many minerals and clays, used esp. in the manufacture of alloy steels, symbol Ti, at. no. 22, at. wt 47·90. **tītăn'ĭc**[2], **tīt'anous** *adjs.* [Gk *Titanes* Titans]

tĭt'bĭt, tĭd'bĭt *n.* Delicate bit, choice morsel.

tīthe (-dh) *n.* 1. Tenth of annual produce of agriculture etc. conceived as due to God and hence payable for support of priesthood, religious establishments, etc.(hist.); *~ barn*, barn built to hold tithes paid in kind; *~ rent charge*, money payment substituted for tithes in 1836, collected since 1936 by State on behalf of clergy. 2. (rhet.) Tenth part. ~ *v.t.* Subject to tithes.

Tīthōn'us. (Gk myth.) Brother of Priam, loved by the dawn goddess, Eos, who asked Zeus to make him immortal but omitted to ask for eternal youth for him.

Tĭt'ian (-shĭan). Tiziano Vecellio (1477–1576), Venetian painter; *~ red*, 'bright golden auburn' colour of the hair favoured by Titian in his pictures.

tĭt'ĭllāte *v.t.* Tickle, excite agreeably. **tĭtĭllā'tion** *n.*

tĭt'ĭvāte *v.* (colloq.) Adorn, smarten; adorn oneself; put finishing or improving touches to appearance (of).

tĭt'lârk *n.* Meadow-pipit (*Anthus pratensis*).

tī'tle *n.* 1. Descriptive heading of each section of law-book, formal heading of legal document; name of book, poem, etc., inscription at beginning of book indicating subject, contents, etc., name of author, publisher, etc., and place and (usu.) date of publication; title-page; distinctive name or style; personal appellation denoting or relating to rank, function, office, attainment, etc. 2. (law) Legal right to possession of (esp. real) property, title-deeds as evidence of this; just or recognized right or claim (*to*). 3. (eccles.) Any of principal or parish churches in Rome, of which incumbents are cardinal priests. 4. Fineness of gold expressed in carats. 5. *~-deed*, document constituting evidence of ownership; *~-part, -role*, part in play etc. from which title is taken; *~-page*, page at beginning of book bearing title.

tī'tled (-ld) *adj.* Having a title of nobility.

tī'tling *n.* (esp.) Impressing of name or title of book on cover.

tĭt'mouse *n.* (pl. *-mīce*). = TIT[1].

Ti'tō (tē-), Josip Broz, Marshal (1892–), prime minister of Yugoslavia 1945–53; president 1953– .

tĭt'rāte *v.t.* Determine volumetrically quantity of constituent in (solution) by adding reagent of known strength until a point is reached at which reaction occurs or ceases. **tĭtrā'tion** *n.*

tĭtt'er *n.* & *v.i.* (Produce) laugh of suppressed or covert kind, giggle.

tĭtt'le *n.* (archaic) Particle, whit. [late and med. L *titulus* stroke over letter, f. L *titulus* title]

tĭtt'lebăt *n.* Childish variant of STICKLEBACK.

tĭtt'le-tătt'le *n.* Petty gossip, trivial chatter. *~ v.i.* Gossip, chatter.

tĭtt'up *v.i.* Go, move, with up-and-down movement, mince, prance. **tĭtt'upy** *adj.* [perh. imit. of sound of hoof-beat]

tĭtūbā'tion *n.* Staggering, reeling, unsteadiness in gait or carriage (esp. path.).

tĭt'ūlar *adj.* & *n.* Held by virtue of a title; such, existing, only in name; *~ (bishop)*, (R.C. Ch.) bishop *in partibus infidelium*, one deriving his title from see lost to Roman pontificate; *~ (saint* etc.), (R.C. Ch.) sacred person or thing giving name to church. **tĭt'ūlarly** *adv.*

Tĭt'us[1]. (N.T.) Convert and helper of St. Paul, to whom an Epistle is addressed.

Tĭt'us[2]. Titus Flavius Sabinus Vespasianus (A.D. 40–81), Roman emperor 79–81; took Jerusalem (A.D. 70) after long siege.

tĭzz'y *n.* (slang) 1. Sixpence. 2. Dither.

tmēs'ĭs *n.* (gram.) Separation of parts of compound word by intervening word(s), e.g. *to* us *ward*.

T.N.T. *abbrev.* Trinitrotoluene.

to (tōō, tŏŏ, *te*) *prep.* 1. In the direction of; as far as, not short of. 2. After words expressing comparison, ratio, proportion, relative position, agreement, or adaptation, correspondence, reference, etc. 3. Introducing indirect object, supplying place of dative; indicating person or thing for whose benefit, use, disposal, etc., thing is done, etc. 4. As sign of infinitive; expressing purpose, consequence, etc.; limiting meaning or application of adjective; as sign of verbal noun etc.; as substitute for infinitive. *~ adv.* To the normal or required position or condition, esp. to a standstill; *~ and fro*, backwards and forwards, up and down, from place to place.

T.O. *abbrev.* Transport Officer; turn over.

toad *n.* Tailless leaping amphibian (*Bufo*), resembling a frog, but terrestrial in habits except at breeding season, more squat in shape and having a warty skin; *~ in a (the) hole*, sausage or other meat baked in batter; *~-eater*, sycophant, obsequious parasite; *~-fish*, various fishes with large heads or inflated bodies, esp. 'oyster-fish' (*Batrachus tau*) and 'puffer' (*Tetrodon turgidus*) of Amer. Atlantic coasts; *~-flax*, common European and Asiatic herb (*Linaria vulgaris*) with showy spurred orange-spotted yellow flowers; various related plants; *toad'stone*, various small stones formerly supposed to be found in head of toad and worn as jewel or amulet; *toad'-stool*, fungus with round disc-like top and slender stalk, mushroom, esp. of inedible or poisonous kind.

toad'y *n.* Toad-eater, sycophant. *~ v.i.* Fawn upon, behave servilely (*to* person). **toad'ўism** *n.*

toast *n.* 1. (Slice of) bread browned at fire or other heat; *~-rack*, rack for holding slices of dry toast. 2. Lady whose health was drunk by company, esp. reigning belle of season (hist.); any person or thing drunk to; *~-master*, one who proposes or announces toasts at public dinner etc. *~ v.t.* 1. Brown, cook (bread, cheese, etc.) by exposure to heat of fire etc.; warm (one's feet etc.) before fire; *toasting-fork*, long-handled fork for toasting bread etc. 2. Drink to health or in honour of.

tobăcc'ō *n.* Various species of *Nicotiana*, esp. *N. tabacum*, native of tropical America, tall annual plant with white or pink tubular flowers and large ovate leaves used, dried and variously prepared, for smoking or chewing or in form of snuff; these dried leaves, or cigars, cigarettes, etc., manufactured from them; various other plants resembling tobacco or used for same purposes; *~ heart*, affection of the heart due to excessive tobacco smoking.

tobăcc'onist *n.* Dealer in tobacco.

Tobī'as. In the Book of TOBIT, the son of Tobit.

Tōb'ĭt. *Book of ~*, a romance of the Jewish captivity, forming part of the Apocrypha.

tobŏgg'an *n.* Long light narrow sledge curved up at the forward end used esp. in sport of coasting down prepared slopes of snow or ice (ill. SLEDGE). *~ v.i.* Ride on toboggan.

Tobruk' (-ŏŏk). Harbour and small town in Cyrenaica, Libya; occupied (Jan. 1941) by British and allied forces, besieged by Germans April–Nov. 1941, besieged again and taken June 1942; evacuated by Germans Nov. 1942.

tōb'y *n.* 1. *~ (jug)*, mug or small jug for ale etc. in form of stout old man wearing long full-skirted coat and three-cornered hat. 2. Trained dog in Punch and Judy show, usu. wearing frill round neck. [dim. of TOBIAS]

tocca'ta (-kah-) *n.* (mus.) Composition for keyboard instrument, freq. as prelude to fugue etc., designed to exhibit touch and technique of performer. **tŏccatĕll'a, tŏccatī'na** (-tē-) *ns.* Short toccata.

Tŏc H. Society with many branches aiming at Christian fellowship and social service, founded 1915 by Rev. P. B. Clayton. [= *T.H.* (*toc* being signallers' name for T), initials of Talbot House, soldiers' club in Poperinghe in the Ypres Salient opened in memory of G. W. L. Talbot (killed 1915)]

Tochār'ian (-k-) *adj.* & *n.* (Member) of fairly highly cultured people living in first 1,000 years of Christian era in central Asia; (of) Indo-European language of these people, recovered (1904–8) from manuscripts and inscriptions found in ruined temples of northern Chinese Turkestan.

tŏc'sĭn *n.* (Bell rung as) alarm or signal. [Provençal *tocarsenh* (*tocar* touch, *senh* signal-bell, f. L *signum* sign)]

tŏd[1] *n.* (dial.) Fox.

tŏd[2] *n.* (archaic) 1. Bushy mass, esp. of ivy. 2. Old weight for wool, usu. 28 lb.

today', to-day' *adv.* & *n.* (On) this present day; (loosely) nowadays, in modern times.

tŏdd'le *n.* Toddling walk. *~ v.i.* Walk or run with short unsteady steps, as child learning to walk; take casual or leisurely walk. **tŏdd'ler** *n.* (esp.) Child just learning to walk.

tŏdd'y *n.* 1. Fresh or fermented sap of various species of palm, used as beverage. 2. Sweetened drink of spirits and hot water. [Hind. *tārī*, f. *tār* palm-tree (Sansk. *tâla* palmyra)]

to-do' (-dōō) *n.* Commotion, fuss, ado.

tōd'y *n.* Various small insectivorous W. Indian birds of genus *Todus*, allied to the kingfisher.

toe (tō) *n.* Each digit of foot, forepart of foot; part of stocking, shoe, etc., that covers toes; fore-part of hoof; something suggesting a toe by its position, shape, etc., esp. outer end of striking-surface of golf-club; *~-cap*, piece of leather covering toe of boot or shoe; *~-dance*, dance performed on extreme tips of toes; *~-dancer*, *-dancing*. ~ *v.t.* (pres. part. *toeing*). Furnish with toe, put new toe on (stocking etc.); touch or reach with toes; ~ *the line, mark*, etc., stand with tips of toes reaching line indicating starting-point in race etc.; (fig.) conform strictly to standard or requirement, esp. under pressure.

tŏff *n.* (slang) Distinguished or well-dressed person, swell. ~ *v.t.* Dress *up* like a toff (esp. reflex. and pass.).

tŏff'ee (-ĭ) *n.* Sweetmeat of sugar or treacle, butter, and other ingredients boiled together and allowed to cool and harden; ~ *apple*, apple coated with toffee and stuck on stick, as sweetmeat.

tŏg *n.* (pl., slang) Clothes. ~ *v.t.* Dress (*out, up*). **tŏgg'ery** *n.* Togs.

tōg'a *n.* Ancient Roman citizen's outer garment, flowing cloak or robe of single piece of stuff covering whole body except right

ROMAN COSTUME

1. Toga. 2. Tunic

arm, freq. with allusion to civil career or (~ *vĭrīl'ĭs*, manly toga) to its assumption at age of manhood; (transf.) gown or other garb associated with some profession; (U.S.) office, esp. senatorship.

togĕth'er (-dh-) *adv.* In(to) company or conjunction, so as to unite, in union; simultaneously; uninterruptedly, on end.

tŏgg'le *n.* (naut.) Short pin through eye or loop of rope, link of chain etc. to keep it in place etc.; any similar cross-piece on chain etc.; rod or screw with cross-piece or device enabling it to pass through hole in one position but not in other; movable pivoted cross-piece serving as barb in harpoon; *~-iron*, harpoon with toggle; ~(*-joint*), two plates or rods hinged together endwise, so that force applied at the elbow to straighten the joint is transmitted to the outer end of each plate or rod.

Tōg'ō. W. African republic between Ghana and Dahomey. Formerly part of German colony of *Togoland*; under French administration from 1914 to 1960.

toil[1] *v.i.* Work long or laboriously; move painfully or laboriously. ~ *n.* Labour, drudgery, hard and continuous work or exertion. **toil'er** *n.* **toil'some** *adj.* **toil'somely** *adv.* **toil'somenėss** *n.*

toil[2] *n.* (now only in pl.) Net, snare. [OF *toile* cloth, f. L *tela* web]

toil'ėt *n.* Articles required or used in dressing; toilet-table (now rare); process of dressing, arranging hair, etc.; style of dress; dress, costume; dressing-room; lavatory; *~-paper*, soft paper for use in lavatories; *~-powder*, dusting-powder used after bath, shaving, etc.; *~-roll*, roll of toilet-paper; *~-set*, set of utensils for toilet; *~-soap*, soap for use in toilet; ~ *vinegar*, aromatic vinegar used in washing [Fr. *toilette*, orig. = cloth thrown over shoulders in dressing]

toilette (twahlĕt') *n.* Dress, costume, esp. formal or fashionable dress.

Tokay'. Rich sweet aromatic wine made near Tokay in Hungary; similar wine made in California etc.

tōk'en *n.* Sign, symbol (*of*); characteristic mark; evidence; password, thing serving to authenticate person, message, etc.; keepsake; (hist.) piece of stamped metal used instead of coin, issued by tradesman, bank, large employer of labour, etc., without sanction of government; ~ *payment*, proportionately small payment made by debtor, esp. State, as indication that debt or obligation is not repudiated; ~ *strike*, strike of workers lasting a few hours only; ~ *vote* (*estimate*), (parl.) vote, estimate, of arbitrary (small) sum of money, proposed for purpose of enabling a public discussion to take place.

Tōk'yō. Capital city of Japan, at head of Tokyo Bay on SE. coast of main island. Largest city in the world.

tōl'bōōth *n.* (Sc.) Town hall or guildhall; town prison. [f. *toll*[1] (*n.*), *booth*]

Toled'o (-ēdō, -ādō). City of Spain, Spanish capital 1087–1560; long famous for manufacture of finely tempered sword-blades.

tŏl'erable *adj.* Endurable; fairly good, not bad. **tŏl'erablenėss** *n.* **tŏl'erably** *adv.*

tŏl'erance *n.* Willingness to tolerate, forbearance; capacity to tolerate (esp. med.); (eng.) permitted variation in dimension.

tŏl'erāte *v.t.* Endure, permit; allow to exist, be practised, etc., without interference or molestation; forbear to judge harshly; (med.) sustain use of (drug etc.) without harm. **tŏl'erant** *adj.* **tŏl'erantly** *adv.*

tŏlerā'tion *n.* Tolerating; esp. recognition of liberty to uphold one's religious opinions and forms of worship or to enjoy all social privileges etc. without regard to religious differences; *Act of T~*, (in U.K.) that of 1688 conditionally freeing dissenters from some restrictions on their forms of worship.

tōll[1] *n.* Tax, duty, charge, paid for selling goods or setting up stall in market, for passage along public road or over bridge or ferry, for transport of goods by railway or canal etc.; (charge for) short-distance telephone trunk call; *take* ~, (fig.) abstract a portion *of*; *~-bar, -gate*, bar or gate across road to prevent passage without paying toll; *~-bridge*, bridge at which toll is charged; *~-house*, house occupied by collector of tolls at toll-gate or toll-bridge. ~ *v.i.* Take, pay, toll.

tōll[2] *v.* Cause (bell) to ring, ring bell, with slow uniform strokes, esp. for death or funeral; (of bell or clock) give out (stroke, knell, hour of day), give out measured sounds. ~ *n.* Tolling, stroke, of bell.

Tŏl'pŭddle martyrs. Six farm labourers of village of Tolpuddle, Dorset, who attempted to form a union and were sentenced in 1834 to 7 years' transportation on a charge of administering unlawful oaths; their sentences were remitted, after public protest, in 1836.

Tŏlstoy', Lev (Leo) Nicolayovich, Count (1828–1910). Russian novelist and social reformer, author of 'War and Peace', 'Anna Karenina', etc. **Tŏlstoy'an** *n.* (Follower) of doctrines of Tolstoy, who advocated simple living and practice of manual labour and held that all property is sinful.

Tŏl'tĕc. (Member, language) of an Amer.-Indian people, remarkable esp. as architects, who flourished in Mexico from the 9th c. onwards, having their capital at Tula; they abandoned Tula in 1168, when some of them moved to Yucatan and lived in association with the MAYA.

tŏl'ū *n.* (*Balsam of*) ~, ~ *balsam*, fragrant brown balsam obtained by incision from tropical S. Amer. tree (*Myroxylon balsamum*) and used to flavour cough syrups and lozenges, as expectorant, and in perfumery. [f. (*Santiago de*) *Tolu* in Colombia]

tŏl'ūēne *n.* Colourless aromatic liquid hydrocarbon (*methyl benzene*) with smell like benzene and burning taste, orig. obtained from tolu balsam but now esp. from coal-tar, used in manufacture of explosives and other compounds. **tolū'ic** *adj.* ~ *acid*, any of four isomeric acids derived from toluene.

tŏl'ūŏl *n.* (Esp. crude commercial) toluene.

Tŏm. Abbrev. of *Thomas*; (*Great*) ~, large bell at Christ Church, Oxford; *Great ~ of Lincoln*, large bell in central tower of Lincoln Cathedral; *Long* ~, (naut.) long gun, esp. one carried amidships on swivel-carriage; *Old* ~, strong kind of gin; ~ *Collins*, drink of gin, sugar, lemon- or lime-juice and soda-water; ~, *Dick, and Harry*, persons taken at random, ordinary commonplace people; ~ *Fool*, type of witlessness (and see below); ~ *o' Bedlam*, (hist.) madman discharged from BEDLAM and licensed to beg; ~ *Quad*: see Tom Tower; ~ *Thumb*, dwarf in nursery tale, no bigger than his father's thumb; any diminutive person; dwarf variety of various plants; ~ *Tiddler's ground*, game in which children run over territory of player called Tom Tiddler, crying 'We're on Tom Tiddler's ground, picking up gold and silver', while he chases them; place where money can be had for the picking up; ~ *Tower*, tower, built by Wren, over entrance to W. quadrangle (~ *Quad*) of Christ Church, Oxford, containing the bell called Great Tom.

tŏm *n.* 1. Male animal, esp. cat (*tom'cat*). 2. *tom'boy*, wild romping girl, hoyden; *tom'cod*, various small Amer. fishes (*Micrógradus*) resembling cod; *tomfool'*, witless fellow; (*adj.*) stupid, senseless; (*v.i.*) play the fool; *tomfool'ery*, foolish trifling, foolish knick-knacks, etc.; *tomnodd'y*, blockhead, fool; (chiefly Sc.) puffin; *tom'tit'*, blue titmouse.

tŏm'ahawk *n.* Light axe of N. Amer. Indians, used as tool and as weapon of war; (Austral.) aboriginal stone hatchet, any hatchet. ~ *v.t.* Strike, kill, with tomahawk.

AMERICAN-INDIAN PIPE TOMAHAWK

tŏmăll'(e)y *n.* Fat or 'liver' of N. Amer. lobster, green when cooked.

toma'tō (-mah-; U.S. -mā-) *n.* (pl. *-oes*) (Glossy red or yellow fleshy edible fruit of) S. Amer. plant (*Lycopersicum esculentum*) with weak trailing or climbing stem, irregularly pinnate leaves, and yellow flowers, widely cultivated, usu. as annual. [Mex. *tomatl*]

tomb (tōōm) *n.* Excavation, chamber, vault, in earth or rock for reception of dead body; sepulchral monument; *the T~s*, New York city prison; *tombstone*, horizontal stone covering grave; any stone or monument over grave.

tŏm'băc *n.* Alloy of copper and zinc used as material for cheap jewellery. [Malay wd]

tŏm'bola (*or* tombōl'a) *n.* Kind of lottery resembling lotto.

tōme *n.* Volume, esp. large heavy one.

tomĕn'tum *n.* 1. (bot.) Pubescence of matted woolly hairs. 2. (anat.) Flocculent inner surface of pia mater. **tōm'entōse, tomĕn'tous** *adjs.*

tŏmm'y *n.* 1. *T~* (*Atkins*), private in British Army. 2. Short rod used as wrench or screwdriver. 3. Bread, goods or provisions, esp. as given to workmen in lieu of wages; truck system; food carried by workmen. 4. ~ *gun*, (f. name of the inventor J. T. *Thompson*, assim. to *tommy*) sub-machine-gun (orig. U.S.) (ill. GUN); ~ *rot*, nonsense. [familiar form of *Tom*]

tomŏ'rrow (-ō) *adv.* & *n.* (On) the day after today.

tŏm'tŏm *n.* Native E. Indian drum, usu. beaten with hands; any barbaric drum. [Hind. *tamtam*, imit.]

ton (tŭn) *n.* 1. (abbrev. t.) Measure of weight; *long* ~, used for coal, 2,240 lb. avoirdupois; *short* ~, used in U.S. and for metals, 2,000 lb. avoirdupois; *metric* ~, 2,204·6 lb. avoirdupois, 1,000 kilograms; see Appendix X. 2. Measure of capacity (often varying) for timber (40 cu. ft), stone (16 cu. ft), salt (42 bushels), lime (40 bushels), coke (28 bushels), wheat (20 bushels), wine (see TUN), etc. 3. Unit of internal capacity of ship (for purposes of registered TONNAGE, 100 cu. ft.; for purposes of freight, usu. 40 cu. ft). 4. (colloq.) Large number or amount. [var. of *tun*]

tōn'al *adj.* Of tone or tones; (of fugue) having *tonal* (opp. *real*) *answer*, in which intervals are modified instead of repeated exactly.

tōnăl'ĭty *n.* 1. (mus.) That relation between notes in a composition which constitutes the key; strict observation of key scheme or mode of musical composition. 2. (painting) Colouring in respect of its lightness and darkness, tones of a picture in relation to one another.

tŏn'dō *n.* Painting, carving in relief, within circular shape. [It., *rotondo* round]

tōne[1] *n.* 1. Sound, esp. with ref. to pitch, quality, and strength. 2. Particular quality, pitch, modulation, etc., of voice; intonation; pitch, inflexion, of spoken sound, expressing differences of meaning, esp. (in Chinese and similar languages) any of various inflexions or pitches distinguishing words which otherwise have the same sound. 3. (mus.) Sound of definite pitch and character produced by regular vibration of sounding body, musical note; each of the several tones (*fundamental* ~ and *overtones*) audible in sound of bell or similar instrument; (also) musical note without overtones. 4. (mus.) Interval of major second, e.g. C–D, E–F sharp (freq. *whole* ~, as opp. to *semitone*) (ill. SCALE). 5. (mus.) *Gregorian* ~*s*, traditional plainsong chants for psalms. 6. (med.) Degree of firmness or tension proper to strong and healthy organs or tissues of body. 7. Prevailing character of morals, sentiments, etc., in society or community; state of mind, mood. 8. Degree of lightness or darkness of colour(s); general effect of combination of light and shade, esp. in a picture or a scene in nature. 9. ~*-arm*, movable arm carrying sound-box of gramophone; ~*-colour*, (mus.) timbre; ~*-deaf(ness)*, insentive(ness) to differences in pitch between musical tones; ~*-language*, language in which similar sounds are distinguished by tones (see 2 above); ~ *poem*, symphonic poem, orchestral composition of indeterminate form and illustrative character, based on poetic or literary rather than purely musical ideas. ~ *v.* Give tone or quality (of sound or colour) to; alter tone or colour of (photographic print) in finishing it; harmonize; ~ *down*, lower tone, quality, or character of; make, become, less emphatic; become lower or softer in tone or quality; ~ *up*, improve tone of, give higher or stronger tone to.

Tōne[2], Theobald Wolfe (1763–98). Irish revolutionist; one of the founders of the society of 'United Irishmen'.

tōne'lėss (-nl-) *adj.* (esp.) Without distinctive quality of sound or colour, dull, lifeless, unexpressive. **tōne'lėssly** (-nl-) *adv.* **tōne'lėssnėss** *n.*

tŏng *n.* Chinese association, esp. secret society of Chinese in foreign country. [Chin. *t'ang* meeting-place]

tŏng'a[1] (-ngga) *n.* Light two-wheeled carriage in India.

Tŏng'a[2] (-ngga). Group of islands in S. Pacific E. of Fiji, also called the Friendly Islands; a monarchy under British protection. **Tŏng'an** *adj.* & *n.*

tŏngs *n.pl.* (*Pair of*) ~, implement consisting of two limbs connected by hinge, pivot, or spring bringing together lower ends so that objects may be grasped which it is impossible or inconvenient to lift with hand.

tongue (tŭng) *n.* 1. Organ in floor of mouth, usu. protrusible and freely movable; in man and many other vertebrates tapering, blunt-tipped, muscular, soft and fleshy, used in taking in and swallowing food, as principal organ of taste, and in man of articulate speech; animal's tongue as article of food. 2. Action of speaking, faculty of speech, words, talk, language; speech or language of a people or race, a language, a dialect; *give* ~, (of hound) bark, esp. on finding scent; *hold one's* ~, be silent; (*speak*) *with one's* ~ *in* *one's cheek*, (speak) insincerely; *gift of ~s*, power of speaking in unknown tongues, esp. as miraculously conferred on early Christians (Acts ii). 3. Thing like tongue in shape or function, as pin of buckle, narrow strip of land between two bodies of water, clapper of bell, pole of wagon or other vehicle, strip of leather closing gap in front of boot or shoe, movable tapered piece of steel in railway-switch, projecting tenon along edge of board, to be inserted into groove or mortise of another board etc. 4. *~-bit*, bit with plate to keep horse's tongue under mouthpiece; *~-fish*, sole; *~-grafting*, whip-grafting, in which wedge-shaped tongue of scion is inserted into cleft in stock; *~-tie(d)*, (condition of) having fraenum of tongue too short, so that distinct speech is difficult or impossible; speechless, dumb, from embarrassment, shyness, etc.; *~-twister*, sequence of words difficult to articulate quickly. ~ *v.* Utter, speak; furnish with tongue; interrupt stream of air with tongue in playing wind instrument.

tŏn'ĭc *adj.* 1. Producing tension, esp. of muscles; of, maintaining, restoring, tone or normal healthy condition of tissues or organs; strengthening, invigorating, bracing. 2. (mus.) Of, founded upon, tonic or key-note; ~ *major, minor*, major, minor scale or key, with same tonic as given major or minor; ~ *sol-fa*, system of sight-singing and notation in which tonic of all major keys is doh (and other notes correspondingly, as ray, me, fah, etc.) and tonic of all minor keys lah (and other notes correspondingly, as te, doh, etc.) with time-values shown by vertical lines, colons, etc. 3. Of tone or accent in speech. **tŏn'ĭcally** *adv.* **tŏn'ĭc** *n.* 1. Tonic medicine or agent; invigorating influence. 2. (mus.) Key-note.

tonĭ'cĭty *n.* Tonic quality or condition, tone.

tonight', to-night' (tonīt') *adv.* & *n.* (On) the present night, (on) the night of today.

tŏnk'a bean *n.* Black fragrant almond-shaped seed of large S. Amer. leguminous tree (*Dipteryx odorata* or *D. oppositifolia*), used for scenting tobacco, as ingredient in perfumes etc.; the tree itself.

Tŏn'kĭn', Tŏng'kĭng'. Northern province of Vietnam in Indo-China.

tonn'age (tŭ-) *n.* 1. (English hist., usu. ~ *and poundage*) customs duties on wine imported in tuns or casks (and on every pound's-worth of goods imported or exported), usu. granted by parliament to sovereign, and illegally imposed on his own authority by Charles I in 1629. 2. Carrying capacity of ship expressed in tons of 100 cu. ft; ships collectively, shipping; charge per ton on cargo or freight; *under-deck* ~, the cubic capacity of the space under the tonnage-deck; this with the addition of the capacity of all enclosed spaces above this deck gives the *gross* ~; the deduction from the latter of the space occupied by engines, crew's quarters, etc., gives the *register* or *net* ~, for which vessels are registered, and on which the assessment of dues and charges on shipping is based; *displacement* ~, the weight of water displaced by a ship when loaded up to her load-line, used in stating the tonnage of warships; *~-deck*, second deck from below in ships with more than one deck.

tŏnn'eau (-ō) *n.* Rear part, containing back seats, of a motor-car (orig. with the door at the back).

tonŏm'ėter *n.* Tuning-fork or other instrument for measuring the pitch of tones.

tŏn'sĭl *n.* Either of a pair of small organs on either side of the root of the tongue, composed of lymphatic tissue and instrumental in protecting the throat from infection, but themselves liable to become septic (ill. HEAD). **tŏn'sillar** *adj.* Of, affected by, the tonsils.

tŏnsĭllĕc'tomy *n.* Surgical removal of the tonsils.

tŏnsĭllī'tis *n.* Inflammation of the tonsils.

tŏnsōr'ial *adj.* (usu. joc.) Of a barber or his work.

tŏn'sure (-sher) *n.* Shaving of head (in Eastern Ch.) or part of it, esp. circular patch on crown (R.C. Ch.), as religious practice, esp. as preparation to entering priesthood or monastic order; part of head thus shaved. ~ *v.t.* Shave head of, give tonsure to.

tontine' (-tēn; *or* tŏn'tēn) *n.* Financial scheme by which subscribers to loan receive each an annuity for life, increasing as their number is diminished by death, until last survivor enjoys whole income; any arrangement, as form of insurance, in which benefits shared among members are increased on death or default of any of them, or in which they are distributed among all remaining members at end of fixed period. [Lorenzo *Tonti*, Neapolitan banker, who instituted scheme in France *c* 1653]

tōō *adv.* 1. In addition, moreover, besides, also. 2. In excess; more than is right or fitting, more than enough; (colloq.) extremely, very.

tōōl *n.* Implement for working upon something, usu. one held in and operated by hand, but also including simple machines, as lathe; (cutting-part of) machine-tool; anything used in performing some operation or in any occupation or pursuit; person used as mere instrument by another; (bookbinding etc.) small stamp or roller for impressing design on leather; large kind of chisel; house-painter's brush; *~-house, -shed*, shed, as in garden, where tools are kept; *~-post*, (in lathe) upright piece in *~-rest* holding or supporting tool (ill. LATHE); ~ *v.* Work with tool; smooth surface of building-stone with large chisel; ornament (leather) with tool; (slang) drive, ride, (*along*) esp. in casual or leisurely manner.

tōōl'ĭng *n.* (esp.) Dressing of stone with broad chisel; impressing of ornamental design with heated tools on leather, such design(s).

tōōt *n.* Note or short blast of horn, trumpet, or other wind instrument. ~ *v.* Sound (horn or other wind instrument); give out such sound.

tōōth *n.* (pl. *teeth*). 1. Each of the hard processes (in mammals usu. of dentine coated with cement round root and enamel in exposed part) attached, usu. in sockets, in a row to each jaw in most vertebrates except birds, with points, edges, or grinding surfaces, and used for biting, tearing, or chewing food, or as weapons of attack or defence; elephant's tusk; (fig.) sense of taste, taste, liking; *in the teeth of*, in spite of; in opposition to; in the face of (wind etc.); ~ *and nail*, (usu. fig.) vigorously, fiercely, with all one's might; *set one's teeth*, clench teeth firmly from indignation or fixed resolution (freq. fig.); *show one's teeth*, (usu. fig.) show hostility or malice, behave threateningly. 2. Projecting part or point resembling tooth, as pointed process on margin of leaf; projecting point of rock; prong or tine of comb, saw, file, harrow, rake, fork, etc.; one of series of projections on edge of wheel, pinion, etc., engaging with corresponding ones on another, cog; (sing. only) rough surface on paper, canvas, etc., to which pencil-marks, colours, etc., adhere;

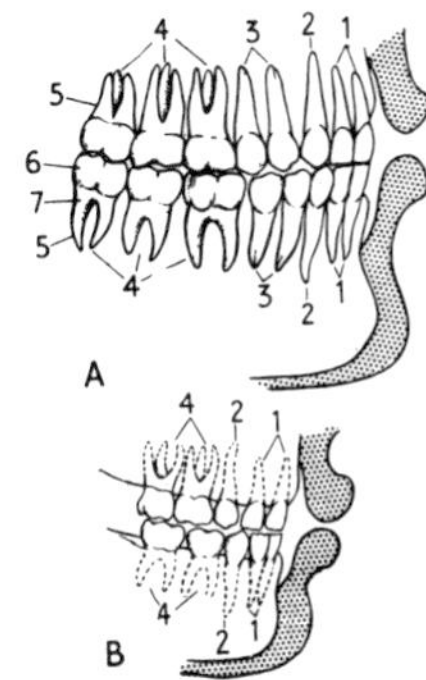

HUMAN TEETH: A. PERMANENT. B. MILK TEETH

1. Incisors. 2. Canine. 3. Premolars. 4. Molars. 5. Wisdom. 6. Crown. 7. Root

roughness made on surfaces to be glued together. 3. *tooth'ache*, ache in tooth or teeth; *~-brush*, small brush used for cleaning teeth; (*small-*) *~-comb*, comb with fine close-set teeth; *~-paste*, *-powder*, paste, powder, for cleaning teeth; *~-pick*, small pointed instrument of quill, wood, etc., used for removing matter lodged between teeth; (slang) very narrow pointed boat; (U.S. slang) bowie-knife (freq. *Arkansas ~-pick*); *~-shell*, (long tubular tusk-shaped shell of) mollusc of *Dentalium* or allied genus. ~ *v.* Furnish with tooth or teeth; give rough surface to; (of cog-wheels etc.) interlock; *toothing-plane*, plane with serrated iron used to score and roughen surface. **tōōth'lĕss** *adj.* **tōōth'-lĕssly** *adv.* **tōōth'lĕssnĕss** *n.*

tōōth'ful *n.* Small mouthful, esp. of spirit.

tōōth'some *adj.* Pleasant to eat. **tōōth'somely** *adv.* **tōōth'some-nĕss** *n.*

tōō'tle *v.i.* Toot gently or continuously, esp. on flute.

tōōt'sy(-wōōt'sy) *n.* (nursery or joc.) Foot.

tŏp[1] *n.* 1. Summit, highest part; apex; (usu. pl.) part of plant growing above ground, esp. of vegetable grown for the 'root'; end of anything conventionally regarded as the higher, e.g. end of billiard-table opposite balk; highest or chief position, highest pitch or degree, culminating point; *on ~*, (fig.) supreme, dominant; *from ~ to toe*, from head to foot, in every part. 2. Part or piece forming upper part or covering of something, e.g. platform near head of lower mast of ship (ill. SAIL[1]), in modern warship, armoured platform on a short mast; topsail; upper part of leg of high boot, esp. broad band of material round this; gauntlet part of glove; turned-down part of leg of sock or stocking; stopper of bottle; hood of carriage, motor-car, etc. ~ *adj.* Highest in position or degree, that is at or on top; *top'most*, uppermost, highest; *~-boot*, boot with high top, esp. with wide band of lighter colour or different material simulating turned-down top; *~-coat*, overcoat; ~ *drawer*, uppermost drawer of series; (fig.) high social position or origin; *~-dress*, apply material to surface of (land, road, etc.) without working it in; *~-dressing*, material, esp. manure, so applied; *topga'llant*, mast, sail, yard, rigging, immediately above topmast and topsail (ill. SHIP); ~ *gear*, gearing producing highest speed in proportion to that of the motor or other propelling force; ~ *hamper*, upper masts, sails, and rigging; weight or encumbrance aloft (freq. fig.); ~ *hat*, tall silk hat (ill. COAT); *~-heavy*, overweighted at top, so as to be unstable; *top'knot*, knot, bow of ribbon, tuft, crest, etc., worn or growing on top of head; *top'mast*, smaller mast on top of lower mast, esp. second section of mast above deck; *~-notch*, (colloq.) first-rate, excellent; ~ *note*, highest note of singer's compass; *top'sail* (-sl), in square-rigged vessel, sail next above lower sail, sometimes divided into *upper* and *lower topsails* (*double topsails*); *~-sawyer*, sawyer in upper position in saw-pit; (fig.) person in superior position; *~ sergeant*, (U.S. colloq.) chief or first sergeant of company, battery, etc.; *top'side*, upper part of ship's side, above water-line or main deck; outer side of round of beef, cut from haunch between leg and aitch bone (ill. MEAT). ~ *v.* 1. Provide with top or cap; remove top of (plant) to improve growth etc.; reach top of (hill etc.); be at top of, have highest position in; exceed in height, overtop; hit (golf-ball) above centre, make (stroke) thus; ~ *off*, put end or finishing touch to. 2. (naut.) Tip *up*, slant, raise (yard); (of yard) rise, tip up. **tŏpp'ĭng** *adj.* (colloq.) Tip-top, excellent.

tŏp[2] *n.* 1. Toy, usu. conical, spherical, or pear-shaped, rotating on point when set in motion by hand, spring, or string; *humming-top*, hollow, usu. metal top, with perforations, making humming noise in spinning; *sleep like a ~*, sleep soundly, (with ref. to apparent stillness of top spinning on vertical axis); ~ (*-shell*), marine snail of genus *Trochus* or family *Trochidae*, with short conical shell.

tōp'ăz *n.* A silicate of aluminium usu. in yellow, white, pale-blue, or pale-green transparent lustrous prismatic crystals, classed as semi-precious stone; *oriental ~*, a precious stone, the yellow sapphire; *false ~*, transparent pale-yellow variety of quartz; *pink ~*, rose-coloured kind produced by exposing yellow Brazilian topaz to great heat; ~ (*humming-bird*), either of two large brilliant-coloured S. Amer. humming-birds (*Topaza pella*, *T. pyra*).

tōp'azīne *adj.* Topaz-yellow.

tōp'azīte *n.* Rock consisting of quartz and topaz.

tōpe[1] *n.* Small European shark (*Galeus canis*); others of this genus.

tōpe[2] *n.* Buddhist monument, usu. a cylindrical tower surmounted by a cupola. [Sansk. *stupa* mound]

tōpe[3] *v.i.* (now chiefly literary) Drink to excess, esp. habitually. **tōp'er** *n.*

Tōph'ĕt. Orig., place near Gehenna, S. of Jerusalem, where Jews made human sacrifices to strange gods (see Jer. xix. 4); later used for deposit of refuse; hence, place of eternal fire, hell.

tōph'us *n.* 1. Tufa. 2. (path.) Mineral concretion in the body, esp. on the joints or on a bone, in gout. 3. Dental tartar.

tōp'ĭ, tōp'ee (-ĭ) *n.* Light pith hat or helmet, esp. *sola ~*. [Hind. *ṭopi* hat]

tōp'ĭary *adj.* & *n.* (Of) the art of clipping and trimming shrubs etc. into ornamental or fantastic shapes. **tōpĭār'ĭan** *adj.* **tōp'ĭarist** *n.* [L *topia* landscape gardening or painting, f. Gk *topos* place]

tŏp'ĭc *n.* Subject of discourse, argument, etc., theme; (rhet., logic) class of considerations from which arguments can be drawn.

tŏp'ĭcal *adj.* 1. Of topics; of topics of the day, containing local or temporary allusions. 2. (esp., med.) Local. **tŏp'ĭcally** *adv.*

topŏg'raphy *n.* Detailed delineation or description, physical features, of place; features of locality collectively; (study of) local distribution; (anat.) regional anatomy. **topŏg'rapher** *n.* **tŏpo-grăph'ĭc(al)** *adjs.* **tŏpogrăph'-ĭcally** *adv.*

topŏl'ogy *n.* Branch of mathematics dealing with the properties of spaces (sets of points) in respect of their being one connected piece and of forming a boundary, independently of shape and size.

topŏn'ȳmy *n.* Study of the place-names of a region.

tŏpp'er *n.* (esp., colloq.) Top hat.

tŏpp'le *v.* (Cause to) tumble or fall headlong, as if top-heavy.

tŏp'sy-tûrv'y *adv.* & *adj.* With the top where the bottom should be, upside down; in(to) utter confusion or disorder.

tōque (-k) *n.* 1. Small usu. brimless hat of folded or swathed material. 2. Monkey (*Macaca sinica*) of Ceylon, with tufted head.

tôr *n.* Craggy or rocky hill or peak, esp. in Devon and Cornwall.

tôr'ah *n.* Law, precept; divinely revealed law, esp. the Pentateuch. [Heb. *torāh* instruction]

torc: see TORQUE.

tôrch *n.* 1. Light for carrying in hand, consisting of piece of resinous wood or length of twisted hemp or flax soaked in resin, tallow, etc.; (fig.) source of conflagration, illumination, enlightenment, etc.; *carry ~ for*, (U.S. slang) have unrequited passion for; *hand on the ~*, pass on tradition. 2. (*electric*) ~, small portable electric lamp. 3. (U.S.) Blow-lamp or other portable device for producing hot flame. 4. Various flowers suggesting flaming torch in shape or colour, esp. (usu. pl.) mullein. 5. *~-bearer*, (esp.) one who guards or hands on light of truth, civilization, etc.; *~-fish*, deep-sea fish (*Linophryne lucifer*) with luminous stalked organ above eye; *~-lily*, plant of genus *Tritoma* with tall spikes of red flowers, 'red-hot poker'; *~-singer*, (chiefly U.S.) singer of *~-songs*, popular, esp. jazz, songs about unrequited love; *~-thistle*, any columnar cactus of genus *Cereus* with stems sometimes used for torches.

tor'chon (-shŏn, -shawṅ) *n.* ~ (*lace*), coarse strong linen bobbin-lace; similar machine-made linen or cotton lace; ~ *paper*, paper with rough surface used esp. for water-colours. [Fr., = 'duster' (*torcher* wipe)]

tore *n.* = TORUS, senses 1 and 3.

tŏ'rėadōr' *n.* (Term still current in English but not in mod. Spanish for) mounted bull-fighter. [Span. *toro* bull, f. L *taurus*]

torer'o (-ārō) *n.* (pl. -*s*). (Usu. Spanish name for) bull-fighter.

toreut'ic (-rōō-) *adj.* & *n.* (Of) the art of chasing, carving, and embossing, esp. metal.

tor'ment *n.* Severe bodily or mental suffering; cause of this. **torment'** *v.t.* Subject to torment. **tormĕn'tor** *n.*

tor'mentil *n.* Low-growing trailing yellow-flowered herb (*Potentilla erecta*) of Europe and Asia, common on heaths and dry pastures, with strongly astringent roots.

tor'mina *n.pl.* (med.) Griping pains in bowels, colic. **tor'minal** *adj.*

tornād'ō *n.* Violent storm, usu. with heavy rain, in which wind rotates or constantly changes direction, esp., in West Africa, Mississippi region of U.S., etc., destructive rotatory storm under funnel-shaped cloud like water-spout, advancing in narrow path for many miles; ~-*cellar*, -*pit*, underground shelter from tornadoes. [app. f. Span. *tronada* thunderstorm, assimilated to *tornar* turn]

tŏ'roid *n.* (geom.) Surface generated by the rotation of a plane closed curve about a line lying in its plane. **toroid(al)** *adjs.* Of, resembling, a tore or toroid.

Torŏn'tō. Capital city of province of Ontario, Canada.

torpēd'ō *n.* 1. Electric ray, flat fish with almost circular body and tapering tail, capable of emitting electric discharges to numb or kill its prey. 2. Self-propelled dirigible submarine missile, usu. cigar-shaped, carrying an explosive which is fired by impact with its objective, used for destroying or injuring ships at sea; similar missile discharged from aircraft (*aerial* ~); (U.S.) case containing explosive used for various military purposes, explosive cartridge for clearing obstructions etc. in oil-well, detonator placed on railway-line as fog-signal etc.; ~-*boat*, small fast lightly armoured vessel carrying torpedoes; ~-*boat destroyer* (now usu. *destroyer*), larger and more heavily armed torpedo-boat, orig. for attacking torpedo-boat (see also DESTROYER); ~-*net(ting)*, steel net round vessel or hung from a boom as a protection against torpedoes; ~-*tube*, steel tube through which torpedoes are discharged, usu. by compressed air. ~ *v.t.* Attack, damage, destroy, with a torpedo. [L, name of the fish (*torpere* be numb)]

torp'ėfy, torp'ify *v.t.* Make torpid, benumb.

torp'id *adj.* Benumbed; dormant; sluggish, inactive, dull. **torp'idly** *adv.* **torpid'ity, torp'idnėss, torp'or** *ns.* **Torp'id** *n.* (Oxford University) Clinker-built 8-oared boat (orig. second boat of college) used for *Torpids*, college boat-races in early spring.

torque (-k), **torc** *n.* 1. Necklace or collar, usu. of twisted metal, worn esp. by ancient Britons and

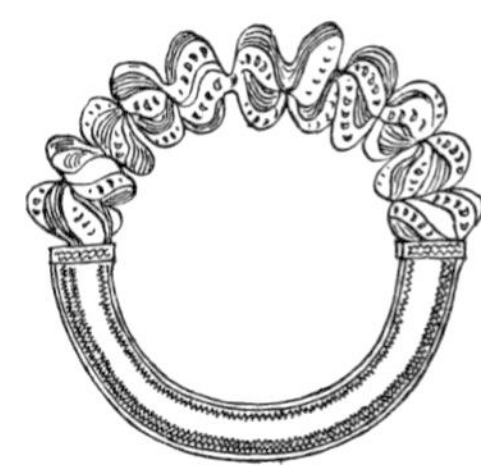

CELTIC GOLD TORQUE

Gauls. 2. (physics etc.) Twisting or rotary force in piece of mechanism, moment of system of forces producing rotation (ill. STRESS).

Torquėma'da (-mah-), Tomas de (1420–98). Spanish inquisitor-general.

tŏ'rrėfy *v.t.* Roast, scorch, or dry by heat; esp. dry (drugs etc.) on metallic plate by heat. **tŏrrėfăc'tion** *n.*

tŏ'rrent *n.* Swift violent rushing stream of water etc.; violent downpour of rain; (fig.) violent flow (of words etc.). **tŏrrĕn'tial** (-shl) *adj.* **tŏrrĕn'tially** *adv.*

Tŏ'rrės Strait. Strait between Australia and New Guinea.

Tŏrricell'i (-chĕ-), Evangelista (1608–47). Italian physicist and mathematician, deviser of experiment (1643) showing that height of mercury column in inverted closed tube corresponds to atmospheric pressure. **Tŏrricell'ian** (-chĕl-, -sĕl-) *adj.* ~ *tube*, early name for barometer; ~ *vacuum*, vacuum produced by filling closed tube with mercury and inverting it in cup of mercury.

tŏ'rrid *adj.* Scorched, parched, exposed to great heat; intensely hot, burning; ~ *zone*, region between the tropics of Cancer and Capricorn (ill. EARTH). **torrid'ity, tŏ'rridnėss** *ns.*

tors'el *n.* Block of stone, piece of iron or wood, in wall to support end of beam or joist (ill. FLOOR).

tor'sion (-shn) *n.* Twisting, twist; *angle of* ~, (geom.) infinitesimal angle between two consecutive osculating planes of tortuous curve; ~ *balance*, apparatus for measuring minute horizontal forces by means of wire or filament which is twisted by the application of the force. **tor'sional** (-sho-) *adj.* **tor'sionally** *adv.*

tors'ō *n.* (pl. -*s*). Statue lacking head and limbs; trunk of statue, or of human body; mutilated or unfinished work. [It., = 'stalk', 'stump', 'torso', f. L *thyrsus* (Gk *thursos* shaft, wand)]

tort *n.* (law) Breach of a duty imposed by law (but not breach of contract), making offender liable to action for damages. [med. L *tortum* wrong f. L *torquere tort* twist]

torticŏll'is *n.* (path.) Rheumatic or other affection of muscles causing twisting and stiffness of neck.

tortilla (-tē'ya) *n.* In Spanish America, thin flat cake of maize flour baked on flat plate of iron etc.

tor'tious (-shus) *adj.* Of, constituting, a tort.

tort'oise (-tus) *n.* Slow-moving four-footed reptile of order *Chelonia*, with body enclosed in heavy armour, and head and legs retractile; any of the land (and

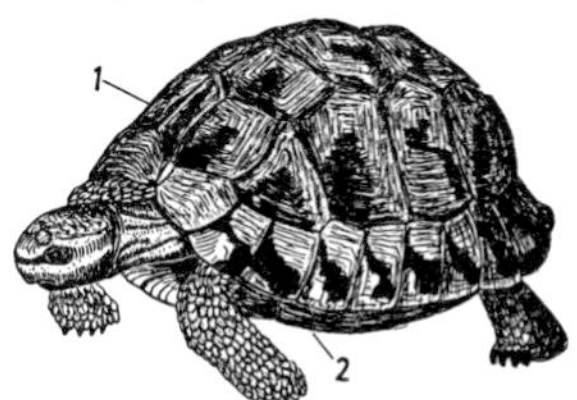

TORTOISE

1. Carapace. 2. Plastron

occas. freshwater) species; ~ (-*shell*), 'shell' of various turtles, esp. that of the hawksbill turtle (*Chelone imbricata*), semi-transparent, of rich yellowish-brown mottled colour, used for ornamental articles, in inlaying, etc.; ~-*shell* (*butterfly*), various butterflies with colouring resembling that of tortoise-shell; ~-*shell* (*cat*), cat of black, brown, and yellow mottled colouring.

tort'ūous *adj.* Full of twists or turns; (geom., of curve) of which no two successive portions are in same plane; (fig.) devious, circuitous, crooked, not straightforward. **tort'ūously** *adv.* **tort'ūousnėss, tortūŏs'ity** *ns.*

tor'ture (-cher) *n.* Infliction of severe bodily pain, e.g. as punishment or to force confession or extort information; severe physical or mental pain. ~ *v.t.* Subject to torture; (fig.) strain, wrench, distort, pervert.

tŏ'rūla *n.* (pl. -*lae*). Various non-spore-bearing yeasts which do not produce alcoholic fermentation.

tor'us *n.* (pl. -*ri*). 1. (archit.) Large convex moulding esp. at base of column (ill. MOULDING). 2. (bot.) Receptacle of flower, swollen summit of flower-stalk, supporting floral organs; (also) thickening of pit membrane, i.e. of membrane between plant cells.

3. (Solid enclosed by) surface described by a conic section, esp. circle, rotating about a straight line in its own plane. [L, = 'protuberance', 'bed']

Tōr'y *adj.* & *n.* (now chiefly in colloq. and hostile use) Conservative; (hist.) (member) of the parliamentary and political party in England that opposed the exclusion of the Duke of York (James II) from the succession, inclined to the House of Stuart after 1689, accepted George III and the established order in Church and State, opposed the Reform Bill of 1832, and has been known officially (since *c* 1830) as 'Conservative'; cf. WHIG. **Tōr'ȳism** *n.* [Ir. *tóraidhe* pursuer, applied orig. to 17th-c. Irish outlaws who robbed and killed English settlers and soldiers]

tŏsh *n.* (slang) Rubbish, twaddle.

tŏss *v.* Throw (*up, away, to,* person etc.), esp. lightly, carelessly, or easily; (of bull etc.) throw person up with horns; throw (coin), throw coin (*up*), into air to decide choice etc. by way it falls; settle question or dispute with (person *for* thing) thus; throw back *head*, esp. in contempt or impatience; throw about from side to side, throw oneself about thus in bed etc.; roll about restlessly; roll or swing with fitful to-and-fro motion; ~ *a pancake*, throw it up so that it returns to pan with other side up; ~ *off*, drink off at a draught; dispatch (work etc.) rapidly or without apparent effort; ~ *up*, toss coin. ~ *n.* Tossing; sudden jerk, esp. of head; tossing of coin; throw from horseback etc.; *full* ~, (cricket) ball which does not touch ground between wickets; ~*-up*, tossing of coin; doubtful question.

tŏt[1] *n.* Tiny child; small quantity (*of* drink, esp. spirits), dram.

tŏt[2] *v.* Add (*up*), mount *up* (*to*). [abbrev. of TOTAL or of L *totum* whole]

tōt'al *adj.* Complete, comprising or involving the whole; absolute, unqualified; ~ *abstinence*, complete abstention from alcoholic drink; ~ *eclipse*, one in which whole disc of sun or moon is obscured (opp. *partial*); ~ *war*, one in which all available resources are employed without reserve. **tōt'ally** *adv.* **tōtăl'ity** *n.* **tōt'al** *n.* Sum of all items, total amount. ~ *v.* Amount to, mount *up to*; reckon total of.

tōtălĭtār'ian *adj.* Of, pertaining to, régime which permits no rival loyalties or parties and arrogates to itself all rights including those normally belonging to individuals. **tōtălĭtār'ianism** *n.*

tōt'alīzātor *n.* Device for registering or finding total of something; esp. a machine for registering and indicating bets on each horse, dog, etc., in a race on the parimutuel system, in which the odds are calculated on the basis that the total amount of money staked, less a percentage for expenses, etc., is divided amongst the betters on the winners.

tōt'alīze *v.* Collect into a total, find the total of.

tōte[1] *n.* (orig. Australian colloq.) TOTALIZATOR.

tōte[2] *v.t.* (U.S.) Convey, transport, carry (supplies, timber, etc.).

tōt'em *n.* Natural, esp. animal, object assumed as emblem of family or clan; image of this; ~*-pole*, ~*-post*, post with carved and painted representation of totem, set up in front of N. Amer. Indian dwelling. **tōt'emism** *n.*

t'o'ther, to'ther (tŭdh-) *pron.* & *adj.* The other.

tŏtt'er *v.i.* Walk with unsteady steps, go shakily or feebly; rock or shake on its base, as if about to overbalance or collapse. **tŏtt'ering** *adj.* **tŏtt'eringly** *adv.* **tŏtt'er** *n.* Tottering gait. **tŏtt'ery** *adj.*

toucan (tōō'kn, tōōkahn') *n.* Tropical Amer. fruit-eating bird of *Rhamphastos* or allied genera, with huge light thin-walled beak and freq. brilliant colouring.

touch (tŭch) *v.* 1. Put hand or other part of body on or into contact with; bring (thing) into contact *with* another; be in, come into contact (with); (hist., of king) lay hand on (person), lay hand on persons, as cure for scrofula; (geom.) be tangent (to). 2. Affect in some way by contact; strike (strings, keys) of musical instrument so as to make it sound; mark, draw (*in*), modify, alter, by touching drawing etc. with pencil or brush; add touches to; mark, modify, slightly *with* colour, expression, etc.; (of ship etc.) call at (port); reach, (fig.) approach in excellence etc. 3. Affect mentally or morally; affect with tender feeling, soften; rouse painful or angry feeling in; concern. 4. Treat of (subject) lightly or in passing. 5. Affect slightly, produce slightest effect on; have to do with in the slightest degree, esp. hurt or harm in the least degree; (usu. with neg.) eat or drink the smallest quantity of. 6. ~ *at*, call at (port); ~ *down*, alight on ground from the air; (football) make touch-down (see *n.* 3); ~ *for*, (slang) get (money) from (person); ~ (*up*)*on*, treat (subject) briefly; ~ *off*, make (sketch) hastily, make hasty sketch of; discharge (explosive etc.); ~ *up*, give finishing, improving, or heightening touches to; jog (memory); strike (horse etc.) lightly with whip or spur. 7. ~*-me-not*, plant of European genus *Impatiens*, esp. yellow balsam (*I. noli-me-tangere*) with seed-capsules which split open when touched; ~ *wood*, touch (wooden object) to avert ill luck; *touch'-wood*, children's game in which touching wood gives immunity from pursuit. ~ *n.* 1. Act or fact of touching, contact; sense by which contact is perceived, general bodily sense diffused through all parts of skin; sensation conveyed by touching, 'feel'; light stroke with pencil, brush, etc., detail of any artistic work, slight act or effort in work of any kind; artistic skill, style of artistic work; manner of touching keys or strings of musical, esp. keyboard, instrument, manner or degree in which instrument responds to this. 2. Close relation of communication, agreement, sympathy, etc. (esp. *in, out of,* ~ *with*; *keep in, lose,* ~). 3. (football) Part of ground outside bounding lines of field of play (ill. RUGBY); ~*-down*, (Rugby) touching ball on ground behind opponents' goal-line; (Amer. footb.) scoring by being in possession of ball behind opponents' goal-line; ~*-judge*, umpire who marks where ball goes into touch; ~ *line*, boundary line on each side of field of play between goal-lines. 4. ~*-and-go*, of uncertain result, risky; risky business or situation; ~*-hole*, (hist.) small tubular hole in breech of cannon through which fire was applied to powder (ill. CANNON); ~*-needle*, slender rod of gold or silver of known fineness, used with touchstone to test fineness of gold or silver; ~*-paper*, paper impregnated with nitre so as to burn steadily without flame, formerly used for firing gunpowder etc.; *touch'stone*, smooth fine-grained black variety of quartz (also called *basanite*), used to test fineness of gold and silver alloys by colour of streak produced by rubbing them on it; (fig.) standard, criterion; ~ *typewriting, typing*, typewriting by touch, i.e. without looking at keys; *touch'wood*, wood or woody substance in such state as to catch fire readily, used as tinder; esp. soft white long-burning substance into which wood is converted by action of some fungi.

touch'ĭng (tŭ-) *prep.* (archaic or literary) Concerning, about. ~ *adj.* Affecting, pathetic. **touch'ĭngly** *adv.* **touch'ĭngnėss** *n.*

touch'y (tŭ-) *adj.* Easily taking offence, over-sensitive. **touch'ĭly** *adv.* **touch'ĭnėss** *n.*

tough (tŭf) *adj.* Of close tenacious substance or texture; hard to break or cut, not brittle; (of food) difficult to masticate; (of clay etc.) stiff, tenacious; hardy, able to endure hardship; unyielding, stubborn; difficult; (colloq., of luck etc.) hard, severe, unpleasant; (slang, chiefly U.S.) ruffianly, hardened in crime. **tough'ly** *adv.* **tough'nėss** *n.* **tough'en** *v.* **tough** *n.* Street ruffian, tough person.

Toulon (toolawṅ'). City, port, and naval base in S. France.

toupee' (tōō-) *n.* (hist.) Top-knot of hair esp. as crowning feature of wig (ill. WIG); wig with this; patch of false hair to cover bald spot. [OF *toup* tuft]

toupet (tōōp′ā) *n.* Front of false hair.

tour (toor) *n.* 1. Journey through (part of) a country from place to place; rambling excursion, short journey, walk, esp. for sake of observing what is noteworthy; *the Grand T~*, (hist.) journey through France, Germany, Switzerland, and Italy, fashionable esp. in 18th c. as finishing course in education of young man of rank; *on ~*, touring. 2. (esp. mil.) Spell of duty in service, time to be spent at station; (occas., chiefly U.S.) shift. ~ *v.* Make tour (of); (of actor, theatrical company, etc.) travel from town to town fulfilling engagements, travel about (country) thus, take (entertainment) about thus. **tour′er** *n.* Motor-car designed for touring, with accommodation for passengers and luggage, and usu. with open body. **tour′ing** *n.* & *adj.* *~-car*, tourer; *~ company*, theatrical company touring with play etc.

tour′acō (toor-) *n.* Various long-tailed, brilliant-plumaged, crested African birds of *Turacus* and allied genera, plantain-eater.

tour de force (toor de fŏrs) *n.* Feat of strength or (esp.) skill.

Tourgenieff: see TURGENEV.

tour′ist (toor-) *n.* Person who makes a tour; person who travels for pleasure; *~ camp*, (U.S.) place offering accommodation in tents or temporary buildings to tourists by car; *~ class*, class inferior to first on some ocean liners; *~ ticket*, railway ticket issued on special terms to tourists. **tour′ism** *n.* Organized touring; accommodation and entertainment of tourists as industry.

tour′maline (toor-, -ĭn *or* -ēn) *n.* Brittle pyro-electric mineral, freq. occurring as crystals, a complex silicate of boron and aluminium with vitreous lustre, usu. black or blackish and opaque (*schorl*), also blue (*indicolite*), red (*rubellite*), and other colours; used in polariscopes and other optical instruments; *precious ~*, rich transparent or semi-transparent shades used as gems. [Sinhalese *tòramalli* (orig. found in Ceylon)]

tour′nament (toor-, tẽr-) *n.* 1. Medieval martial sport in which a number of mounted combatants in armour fought with blunted weapons for prize of valour; later, meeting for knightly sports and exercises. 2. Any contest in which a number of competitors play a series of games or take part in athletic events.

tour′ney (tẽr-, toor-) *n.* & *v.i.* (hist.) (Take part in) tournament.

tourniquet (toor′nĭkĕt, -kā; *or* tẽr-) *n.* Bandage for arresting bleeding by compression, tightened by twisting a rigid bar put through it; surgical instrument usu. with pad and screw, for same purpose.

tournure (toornūr′) *n.* Curve, contour; pad etc. worn by women to give rounded outline to hips; back drapery of dress.

tousle (tow′zl) *v.t.* Pull about, handle roughly, make (esp. hair) untidy.

Toussaint Louverture (tōō-săṅ′ lōōvărtūr′), François Dominique (1743–1803). Negro who led a rising in Haiti in 1791; later became a general in French army, and governor of the island 1796–1802, but was arrested, and died a prisoner in France.

tout *v.i.* Solicit custom, pester possible customers with applications (*for* orders); spy out movements and condition of racehorses in training. ~ *n.* One who touts.

tow[1] (tō) *n.* Coarse and broken fibres of flax or hemp, separated by heckling and ready for spinning; *~-head(ed)*, (having) head of very light-coloured straight hair. **tow′y** *adj.*

tow[2] (tō) *v.t.* Pull (boat, barge, etc.) along in water by rope or chain; pull (person, thing) along behind one; *~(ing)-line, -rope*, line or rope by which something is towed; *~(ing)-net*, fine-meshed drag-net towed near surface of water for collecting natural specimens; *~(ing)-path*, path beside canal or navigable river for use in towing. **tow′age** *n.* **tow** *n.* Towing, being towed; *in ~*, being towed; *take in ~*, (fig.) take under one's guidance or patronage.

tō′ward[1] (-erd) *adj.* (archaic) Docile, apt. **tō′wardly** *adv.* **tō′wardness** *n.*

toward(s)[2] (tŏrdz, twŏrdz, to-wŏrdz) *prep.* In the direction of; as regards, in relation to; near, approaching (in time); (archaic, as *adv.*) coming on, at hand.

tow′ĕl *n.* Absorbent cloth, paper, etc., for drying or wiping oneself or thing after washing; *~-horse*, frame or stand on which towels are hung. ~ *v.t.* Wipe or dry with towel; (slang) beat, thrash. **tow′ĕlling** *n.* (esp.) Material for towels.

tow′er *n.* Tall, usu. square or circular structure, freq. forming part of church, castle, or other large building (ill. CHURCH); such structure (or whole fortress or stronghold of which it is part) used as stronghold or prison; (fig.) place of defence, protector (*~ of strength*, (of person) support); *the T~ (of London)*, large assemblage of buildings on north bank of Thames eastwards of City of London, orig. fortress and palace and later a State prison, now used as repository of ancient armour and weapons and other objects of public interest, and occas. as political prison; *~ Hill*, rising ground by Tower of London, formerly a place of execution. ~ *v.i.* Reach high (*above* surroundings); (of eagle etc.) soar, be poised, aloft; (of wounded bird) shoot straight up. **tow′ering** *adj.* High, lofty; (fig., of rage, passion) violent.

town *n.* Inhabited place usu. larger and more regularly built than *village* and with more complete and independent local government or (in England) dist. from village by having periodical market or fair; (without *the*) the business or shopping centre of a town or city; (without *the*) the chief town of district or neighbourhood, in England esp. London; (at Oxford, Cambridge, etc.) civic community as dist. from members of university (esp. in *~ and gown*); *man about ~*, fashionable idler, esp. in London; *woman of the ~*, woman belonging to shady or dissipated side of town life; *~-clerk*, secretary to civic corporation, with charge of records, correspondence, legal business, conduct of municipal elections, etc.; *~ council(lor)*, (member of) elective administrative body of town; *~-crier*, public crier; *~ hall*, building used for transaction of official business of town, often also used for public entertainments, court of justice, etc.; *~ house*, town (as dist. from country) residence; *~-meeting*, (U.S.) meeting of voters of town for transaction of public business, with certain powers of local government; *~-planning*, construction of plans for regulation of growth and extension of town, so as to secure best conditions of housing and traffic, situation of public buildings and open spaces, etc.; *towns′people*, people of a town; *~ talk*, common talk or gossip of people of town.

town′ship *n.* (hist.) Community inhabiting manor, parish, etc.; manor or parish as territorial division (chiefly hist.); small town or village forming part of large parish, or being one of parishes into which larger parish has been divided; (U.S. and Canada) division of county with some corporate powers of local administration, district 6 miles square whether settled or not; (Austral.) site laid out for town.

tŏxaem′ia *n.* Diseased condition due to presence of toxic substances in blood, usu. of bacterial origin.

tŏxăl′būmin *n.* (biochemistry) Any toxic protein.

tŏx′ic *adj.* Of, affected or caused by, a poison or toxin; poisonous. **tŏx′ically** *adv.* **tŏxĭ′city** *n.* [Gk *toxikon* poison for arrows (*toxa* arrows)]

tŏxicŏl′ogy *n.* Study of the nature and effects of poisons, their detection and treatment. **tŏxicolŏ′gical** *adj.* **tŏxicolŏ′gically** *adv.*

tŏxidẽrm′ic *adj.* Of skin disease produced by a toxin.

tŏx′in *n.* Poisonous substance of animal or vegetable origin; esp. (path.) one of the poisons produced in a human or animal body by micro-organisms of disease, provoking the formation of antitoxins.

tŏxŏph′ily *n.* Practice of, addiction to, archery. **tŏxŏph′ilite** *n.*

& *adj.* (Student, lover) of archery. **tŏxŏphĭlĭt'ĭc** *adj.*

toy *n.* Plaything, esp. for child; knick-knack, small or trifling thing, thing meant rather for amusement than for serious use; (attrib., of dogs etc.) of diminutive breed or variety. ~ *v.i.* Trifle, amuse oneself (*with*); deal *with* in trifling, fondling, or careless manner.

Toyn'bee Hall. Centre of social service in Whitechapel, London, the first SETTLEMENT, founded 1884 by Canon Samuel Barnett (1844–1913) and members of Oxford and Cambridge Universities. [named after Arnold *Toynbee* (1852–83), social reformer and economist]

trāce[1] *v.* 1. Delineate, mark out, sketch, write esp. laboriously. 2. Copy (drawing etc.) by following and marking its lines, using a transparent sheet placed over it or similar device. 3. Follow the track or path of (person, animal, footsteps, etc.); follow course or line of, decipher; follow course or history of; observe or find vestiges or signs of. **trāce'able** (-sa-) *adj.* **trāce** *n.* 1. Track left by person or animal walking or running, footprints or other visible signs of course pursued (usu. pl.); path of indicating spot in cathode-ray tube, shown as trace on a fluorescent screen. 2. Visible or other sign of what has existed or happened; minute quantity, esp. (chem.) too little to be measured; ~ *element*, substance which is essential, though only in minute amounts, to plant or animal life.

trāce[2] *n.* Each of pair of ropes, chains, or straps connecting collar of draught animal with swingletree etc. of vehicle (ill. HARNESS); *kick over the ~s*, (fig.) become insubordinate, act recklessly.

trā'cer *n.* (esp.) ~ (*bullet, shell*), bullet etc. emitting smoke or flame which makes its course visible; ~ (*element*), isotope which can be detected in minute quantities because of its radiations, so that the path of a molecule or radical containing it can be traced through a series of complex chemical reactions.

trā'cery *n.* Decorative stone open-work, esp. in head of Gothic window, or interlaced work of vault etc. (ill. WINDOW); anything resembling or suggesting this.

trăch'ėa (-k-; *or* trakē'a) *n.* (pl. *-eae*). 1. Musculo-membranous tube from larynx to bronchial tubes, conveying air to lungs in air-breathing vertebrates (ill. LUNG). 2. Each of tubes forming respiratory organ in insects etc. 3. (bot.) Duct, vessel. **trā'chėal, trā'chėate** *adjs.*

trăch'ėĭd (-k-; *or* trakē'ĭd) *n.* Water-conducting element in the wood of vascular plants.

trā'chėocēle (*or* trakē'-) *n.* Tumour in or on trachea; goitre.

trăchėŏt'omy (-k-) *n.* Incision of trachea; ~ *tube*, breathing-tube inserted into opening made by this.

trachōm'a (-k-) *n.* Contagious form of conjunctivitis with inflammatory granulation of inner surface of eyelids, freq. causing blindness. **trachŏm'atous** *adj.*

trăch'ȳte (-k-) *n.* Rough-surfaced, usu. light-coloured, volcanic rock consisting mainly of potash felspar. **trachȳt'ĭc** *adj.*

trā'cing *n.* (esp.) Copy made by tracing; record of self-registering instrument; ~*-paper*, tough semi-transparent paper for copying drawings etc.

trăck *n.* 1. Mark, series of marks, left by passage of anything, as wheel-rut, wake of ship, footprints; *in one's ~s*, on the spot, instantly; *on the ~ of*, in pursuit of, having a clue to; *cover (up) ~s*, conceal or screen actions etc. (of); *keep ~ of*, follow or grasp course, sequence, etc., of; *make ~s (for)*, make off, make for. 2. Path, esp. one beaten by use, rough unmade road; line of travel or motion, course; train, sequence; prepared course for racing etc. (esp. *cinder-~* for runners); continuous line of railway; (mech.) band of *tracked vehicle* (ill. TRACTOR). 3. The transverse distance between wheels of vehicle. ~ *v.* Follow track or footsteps (of); pursue, follow up; (of wheels) run in same track, be in alignment; ~ *down*, pursue until caught or found. **trăck'lėss** *adj.* **trăck'lėssnėss** *n.*

trăck'er *n.* (esp., organ-building) Strip of wood or rod exerting pulling action between key and pallet (ill. ORGAN).

trăct[1] *n.* Stretch, extent, region (*of*); region or area of natural structure, esp. bodily organ or system.

trăct[2] *n.* Short treatise or discourse, esp. on religious subject.

trăc'table *adj.* (usu. of persons or animals) Easily handled, manageable, pliant, docile. **trăctabĭl'ĭty, trăc'tablenėss** *ns.* **trăc'tably** *adv.*

Trăctār'ĭan. (Adherent, promoter) of **Trăctār'ĭanism,** 19th-c. English high-church movement (later called the *Oxford Movement*) intended to revive 'the true conception of the relation of the Church of England to the Catholic Church at large', and based on a series of 'Tracts for the Times' (1833–41) by Newman, Pusey, Keble, and others.

trăc'tāte *n.* Treatise.

trăc'tion *n.* Drawing, pulling (esp. as dist. from *pushing* or *pressure*); drawing of vehicles or loads along road or track, esp. in ref. to form of power used for this; ~*-engine*, steam or Diesel engine used for drawing loads on ordinary road, across fields, etc.; ~*-wheel*, driving-wheel of locomotive etc. **trăc'tional** (-sho-), **trăc'tĭve** *adjs.*

trăc'tor *n.* Traction-engine; motor-vehicle for drawing heavy loads etc., esp. one for farm-work.

TRACKED TRACTOR

1. Driving sprocket-wheel. 2. Track or caterpillar

trāde *n.* 1. Business, esp. mechanical or mercantile employment (opp. to PROFESSION), carried on as means of livelihood or profit; skilled handicraft. 2. Exchange of commodities for money or other commodities, commerce; *Board of T~*, department of British Government supervising commerce and industry. 3. Persons engaged in a trade; *the T~*, (colloq.) licensed victuallers. 3. (usu. pl.): = Trade-wind (see below). 4. ~ *board*, body now superseded by WAGES council; ~ *cycle*, recurring succession of trade conditions alternating between prosperity and depression; ~*-mark*, device, word(s), etc., used by manufacturer etc. to distinguish his goods, established by use and legally registered; ~ *name*, name of proprietary article; name by which a thing is called by the trade; name under which a person or firm conducts trade; ~ *price*, price at which an article is sold to retailers by manufacturers or wholesalers; *trades'man*, person engaged in trade, esp. shopkeeper; (esp. in armed services) craftsman, man skilled in one of a number of specified crafts or trades; ~(*s*) *union*, organized association of employees in a trade or allied trades to protect and further their common interests; *Trades Union Congress* (abbrev. T.U.C.), official representative body of trade unions in Gt Britain; ~ *unionism, unionist*; ~*-winds*, winds blowing constantly towards the equatorial region of calms from about the 30th parallel north and south, being deflected westward by the earth's rotation so that they blow from the north-east in the N. hemisphere and from the south-east in the S. hemisphere. ~ *v.* Buy and sell, engage in trade; have commercial transaction (*with*); carry merchandise (*to* place); exchange in commerce, barter (goods); ~ *in*, barter, buy and sell (influence, offices, etc.), esp. corruptly; hand over (e.g. used car) in (part) payment or exchange (*for* thing); ~ *on*, take (esp. unscrupulous) advantage of (person's credulity or good nature, one's knowledge of secret, etc.).

trād'er *n.* Person, ship, engaged in trading.

tradi'tion *n.* Transmission of statements, beliefs, customs, etc., esp. by word of mouth or by practice without writing; what is thus handed down from generation to generation; long-established and generally accepted custom, practice, etc., an immemorial usage; (theol.) doctrine etc. held to have divine authority but not orig. committed to writing, esp., among Christians, body of teachings transmitted orally from generation to generation from earliest times and by Roman Catholics held to derive from Christ and the apostles or to have authority of the Holy Spirit. **tradi'tional** (-sho-) *adj.* **tradi'tionally** *adv.* **tradi'tionalism, tradi'tionalist** *ns.* **traditionalis'tic** *adj.*

tradūce' *v.t.* Calumniate, misrepresent.

Trafăl'gar (orig. as in Span., trăfalgar'). Cape on S. coast of Spain near which British fleet under NELSON (who was killed in the action) achieved great victory over combined fleets of France and Spain (21st Oct. 1805); ~ *Square,* square adjoining upper end of Whitehall, London, laid out 1829–41, and containing Nelson monument and other statues; freq. used for popular demonstrations.

trăff'ic *n.* 1. Trade (*in* commodity); now esp. dealing or bargaining in something which should not be the subject of trade. 2. Transportation of goods, coming and going of persons, goods, or esp. vehicles or vessels, along road, railway, canal, etc.; amount of this; ~ *cop* (U.S.), *policeman,* policeman regulating road traffic; ~ *lights, signal,* mechanical signal for controlling road traffic, esp. at junctions or crossings, by means of coloured lights etc. ~ *v.* Trade (*in*), carry on commerce; barter.

tră'fficātor *n.* Device on side of motor vehicle whereby driver indicates his proposed course.

trăg'acănth *n.* Gum exuded from various species of *Astragalus,* usu. obtained in dried whitish flakes, and used as vehicle for drugs, in the arts, etc. [Gk *tragakantha* goat's-thorn (*tragos* he-goat, *akantha* thorn)]

tragēd'ian *n.* Writer of tragedies; actor in tragedies. **tragēdiĕnne'** *n.* Actress in tragedies.

tră'gėdy *n.* Literary composition, esp. play, of serious and usu. elevated character, with fatal or disastrous conclusion; branch of dramatic art dealing with sorrowful or terrible events in serious and dignified style; sad event, calamity, disaster. [Gk *tragōidia* app. goat-song (*tragos* goat, *ōidē* song)]

tră'gic *adj.* 1. Of, in the style of, tragedy; ~ *irony,* used in Gk tragedy of words having an inner esp. prophetic meaning for audience unsuspected by speaker. 2. Sad, calamitous, distressing. **tră'gical** *adj.* (now rare) Tragic. **tră'gically** *adv.*

tră'gicŏm'ėdy *n.* Drama of mixed tragic and comic elements. **trăgicŏm'ic(al)** *adjs.* **trăgicŏm'ically** *adv.*

trăg'opăn *n.* Various species of Asiatic pheasants (*Ceriornis*), with erectile fleshy horns on head of male, horned pheasant. [L f. Gk, reputed bird in Ethiopia (*tragos* goat + PAN[3])]

Trahērne', Thomas (*c* 1637–74). English metaphysical poet and writer of religious works.

trail *n.* Part drawn behind or in the wake of a thing, long (real or apparent) appendage; hinder end of stock of gun-carriage, resting on ground when piece is unlimbered (ill. GUN); track left by thing that has moved or been drawn over surface; track, scent; beaten path, esp. through wild region; *at the* ~, (mil.) being trailed. ~ *v.* Draw along behind one, esp. on ground, drag (one's limbs, oneself) along, walk wearily, lag, straggle; hang loosely; (of plant) grow decumbently and stragglingly to some length, esp. so as to touch or rest on the ground; (mil.) carry (rifle etc.) in horizontal or oblique position with arm extended downwards; track, follow the track or wake of, 'shadow'; *trailing edge,* rear edge of aircraft's wing.

trail'er *n.* (esp.) 1. Trailing plant. 2. Vehicle drawn along behind another, esp. caravan, luggage-carrier, small fire-pump, etc., designed to be drawn along behind a motor-car. 3. Short cinema film showing cast, parts of scenes, etc., of a longer film and exhibited in advance of it as an advertisement.

train *v.* Bring (person, child, animal) to desired state or standard of efficiency, obedience, etc., by instruction and practice; subject, be subjected to, course of instruction and discipline (*for* profession, art, etc.); teach and accustom (*to* do, *to* action); bring, bring oneself, to physical efficiency by exercise and diet, esp. in preparation for sport or contest; cause (plant) to grow in required shape; point, aim, (fire-arm, camera, *up(on)* object etc.). ~ *n.* 1. Trailing thing, esp. elongated part of skirt or robe trailing behind on ground, or sometimes carried on ceremonial occasions by page or attendant as *~-bearer*; long or conspicuous tail of bird. 2. Body of followers, retinue, suite; succession or series of persons or things; line of gunpowder or other combustible material to convey fire to explosive charge etc.; set of parts in mechanism actuating one another in series, esp. set of wheels and pinions actuating striking-part or turning hands of clock or watch. 3. Number of railway-carriages, vans, or trucks coupled together (usu. including locomotive drawing them); *~-ferry,* ferry conveying railway-trains across water; *~-sickness,* sickness or nausea caused by railway-travelling. **train'lėss** *adj.*

train-bănd *n.* (hist.) Company of citizen soldiers, organized in London and elsewhere in 16th, 17th, and 18th centuries. [abbrev. of *trained band*]

trainee' *n.* One who is being trained (for an occupation).

train'er *n.* (esp.) One who trains persons or animals for athletic performance, as race, boxing-match, etc.

train'ing *n.* (esp.) *In* ~, undergoing physical training, physically fit as a result of this; *~-college, -school,* college or school for training teachers; *~-ship,* ship on which boys are trained for naval service or merchant navy.

train-oil *n.* Thick kind of oil obtained from blubber of whale (esp. the RIGHT *whale*). [MDu. *traen,* app. meaning 'tear', 'drop']

traipse, trāpes (-ps) *v.* Walk in trailing or untidy way, walk about aimlessly or needlessly, trudge wearily; walk over (thus). ~ *n.*

trait (trā, trāt) *n.* Feature (of face or esp. of mind or character), distinguishing quality.

trait'or *n.* One who is false to his allegiance or acts disloyally (*to* his sovereign or country, his principles, religion, etc.). **trait'orous** *adj.* **trait'orously** *adv.* **trait'orousnėss** *n.*

Trāj'an. Marcus Ulpius Nerva Trajanus (*c* A.D. 52–117), Roman emperor 90–117, whose victories are commemorated on Trajan's Column in Rome.

trajĕc'tory (*or* trăj'ic-) *n.* Path of any body moving under action of given forces, esp. that of projectile in its flight through air; (geom.) curve or surface cutting all curves or surfaces of a given system at constant angle.

trăm[1] *n.* ~ (*silk*), silk thread of 2 or 3 loosely twisted strands used for weft of some velvets and silks. [L *trama* weft]

trăm[2] *n.* 1. (In some English colliery districts) small iron truck running on rails; undercarriage of this. 2. ~ (*-car*), passenger car running on rails on public road; *~-line,* track with rails flush with road surface on which tram-cars are run; (pl., colloq.) either pair of long parallel lines bounding a lawn tennis court; *tram'way* (now rare), road laid with rails for trams. ~ *v.* Convey in tram, perform (journey) in tram; travel by tram. [app. same wd as LG *traam* beam, barrow-shaft]

trămm'el *n.* 1. ~(*-net*), fishing-net consisting of fine net hung loosely between vertical 'walls' of coarser net, so that fish passing through carry some of the finer net through the coarser and are caught in the pocket thus formed.

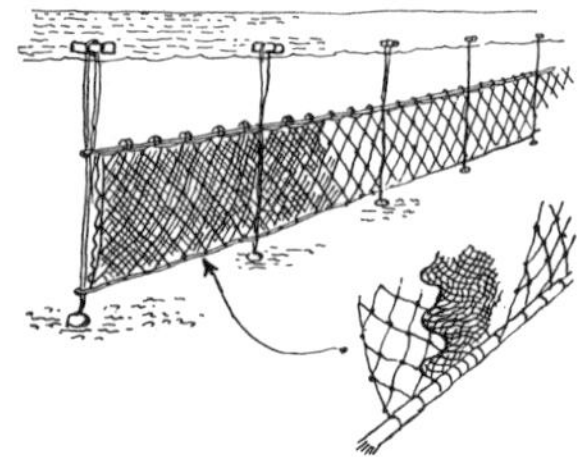

TRAMMEL NET WITH DETAIL TO SHOW INNER AND OUTER NETS

2. Shackle, esp. one used in teaching horse to amble; (fig., usu. pl.) impediment to free movement or action. 3. Instrument for drawing ellipses, esp. cross with grooves in which move pins carrying beam and pencil; kind of gauge for adjusting and aligning machine parts; (now chiefly U.S.) kind of hook for holding kettle etc. at adjustable heights in fire-place. 4. *~-wheel*, device for converting rotary into reciprocal motion, or vice versa, and consisting of wheel with crossing grooves in which slide blocks attached to connecting rod. ~ *v.t.* Confine, hamper, with trammels.

tramŏn'tāne *adj.* (Situated, living) on other side of the Alps; (fig., from It. point of view) foreign, barbarous; (of wind) blowing from beyond mountains, esp. Alps. ~ *n.* Tramontane person, wind.

trămp *v.* Walk heavily; walk, go on foot, perform (journey), traverse (country), on foot (usu. with implication of reluctance, weariness, etc.); be a tramp. ~ *n.* 1. Measured and continuous tread of body of persons or animals, sound of heavy footfalls. 2. Tramping, long or tiring walk or march; journey on foot, walking excursion. 3. Person who tramps roads in search of employment or as vagrant. 4. (*ocean*) ~, cargo-vessel not trading regularly between fixed ports, but taking cargoes wherever obtainable and for any port.

trămp'le *v.* Tread heavily and (esp.) injuriously (upon), crush or destroy thus (freq. fig.); put (fire) *out* by trampling. ~ *n.* Trampling.

trance *n.* (-ah-). Sleep-like state, with more or less inertness to stimulus and subsequent amnesia; hypnotic or cataleptic condition, similar state of spiritualistic 'medium'; mental abstraction from external things, absorption, exaltation, ecstasy.

trăng'ka *n.* Principal monetary unit of Tibet, approx. ⅛ of a rupee.

trăn'quil *adj.* Not agitated or disturbed, calm, placid, serene. **trăn'quilly** *adv.* **trănquill'ity** *n.* **trăn'quillize** *v.t.* **trăn'quillizer** *n.* (esp.) Sedative drug.

trans- *prefix.* Across, beyond, over, to or on farther side of.

trănsăct' (-z-, -s-) *v.t.* Perform, carry on, do (action, business, etc.). **trănsăc'tion** *n.* Transacting, being transacted; what is transacted, piece of business; (pl.) proceedings, dealings; (usu. pl.) learned society's, esp. published, records of its proceedings.

trănsăl'pīne (-z-) *adj.* & *n.* (Person living) beyond the Alps (usu. from Italian point of view).

trănsatlăn'tic (-z-) *adj.* & *n.* (Person living) across the Atlantic; esp., from European point of view, American; (of boat, aircraft, etc.) crossing the Atlantic.

Trănscaucās'ia (-nz-; -zha, -zia). That part of Russia which lies beyond (S. of) the Caucasus: Armenia, Azerbaijan, and Georgia.

transcĕnd' *v.t.* Go beyond, exceed, limits of; rise above, surpass, excel.

transcĕn'dent *adj.* That transcends ordinary limits, pre-eminent, supreme, extraordinary; (Kantian philos.) transcending, altogether outside, unrealizable in, experience. ~ *n.* Transcendent thing. **transcĕn'dently** *adv.* **transcĕn'dency** *n.*

trănscĕndĕn'tal *adj.* 1. (Kantian philos.) Not derived from experience, *a priori*; (of any philosophy) based on recognition of *a priori* element in experience; (pop., vaguely) abstract, metaphysical, obscure, visionary. 2. (math.) Not capable of being produced by a finite number of ordinary algebraical operations of multiplication, addition, involution, or the inverse operations. **trănscendĕn'tally** *adv.*

trănscĕndĕn'talism *n.* Transcendental philosophy, esp. idealism of Schelling, Fichte, and Hegel (which does not recognize Kantian distinction between *transcendent* and *transcendental*), and religio-philosophical doctrine of Emerson and his followers; extravagant, vague, or visionary quality, philosophy, language, etc. **trănscĕndĕn'talist** *n.* & *adj.*

trănscŏntinĕn'tal (-z-) *adj.* Extending or passing across a continent.

trănscrībe' *v.t.* Copy out (esp. in writing), make copy of; write out (shorthand) in ordinary characters; (mus.) adapt (composition) for voice or instrument other than that for which it was orig. written. **trăn'script** *n.* Written copy; (law) copy of legal record. **trănscrip'tion, trănscrip'tive** *adj.*

trănsdū'cer *n.* (physics) Device or apparatus conveying power from a system and supplying it to another.

trăn'sĕpt *n.* (Either arm of) transverse part of cruciform church (ill. CHURCH). **trănsĕp'tal** *adj.*

trănsfer' *v.* Convey, transmit, transport, hand over, from one person, place, etc., to another; (law) convey (title, property, etc.) by legal process; convey (design etc.) from one surface to another; change from one station, line, route, etc., to another to continue journey; transfer (esp. football-player, his services) to another club, group, etc. **trăns'fer** *n.* 1. Transferring, being transferred, esp. (law) conveyance of property, as shares, etc., from one person to another; means or place of transfer, esp. (U.S.) conveyance of passenger and luggage from one station or line to another, place where trains etc. are transferred to ferry for water transport etc.; ~ (*ticket*), ticket allowing journey to be continued on another line or route. 2. Transferred thing; design etc. (to be) conveyed from one surface to another, (freq. coloured) design or picture on prepared paper from which it can be transferred to another surface, as with water or hot iron. 3. ~ *company*, (U.S.) company conveying passengers and luggage between stations or from station; *~-fee, -money*, sum paid for transfer esp. of professional footballer to another club; *~-ink*, ink used for making designs for transfer, as on lithographic stone or *~-paper*, specially prepared paper for transferring designs; *~-machine*, machine which automatically carries a large component from one stage of a process to another.

trăns'ferable *adj.* Capable of being transferred; ~ *vote*, electoral method for securing that elected candidate shall represent a majority, each voter signifying on his ballot-paper to which candidate his vote shall be transferred if no candidate has an absolute majority of first preferences.

trăns'ference *n.* (esp., psycho-anal.) Transferring of emotions to new object.

trănsfigurā'tion *n.* Transfiguring, being transfigured; esp. change in appearance of Jesus on the mountain (Matt. xvii. 2; Mark ix. 2, 3), Church festival (6th Aug.) commemorating this, picture representing it.

trănsfig'ure (-ger) *v.t.* Alter form or appearance of, transform; esp. glorify, change so as to elevate or idealize.

trănsfix' *v.t.* Pierce with, impale on, sharp-pointed instrument; pierce through, render motionless (with fear, grief, horror, etc.). **trănsfix'ion** (-kshon) *n.*

trănsform' *v.t.* Change shape or form of, esp. considerably; change in character, condition, function, nature, etc.; (physics) change (one form of energy) into another, (elect.) change (current) in potential (as from high voltage to low) or type (as from alternating to continuous).

trănsformā'tion *n.* Transforming, being transformed; metamorphosis, as of insects; (math.) change of form without alteration of value, as substitution of one geometrical figure for another of equal magnitude, or of one algebraical expression for another of same value; change of form of substance, as from solid to liquid, or of potential or type of electric current etc.; woman's artificial head of hair; ~ (*-scene*), (theatr.) elaborate spectacular scene in pantomime, esp. one in which pantomime characters were changed into those of harlequinade.

trănsfôrm'er *n.* (esp., elect.) Apparatus for changing potential or type of electric current, consisting usually of a few turns of comparatively thick wire and a coil of fine wire wound on a laminated iron core.

trănsfūse' (-z) *v.t.* Cause (fluid, fig. quality etc.) to flow or pass from one vessel etc. to another; transfer (blood of one person or animal) into veins of another. **trănsfū'sion** (-zhn) *n.*

trănsgrĕss' (-z-, -s-) *v.t.* Violate, infringe (law, command, esp. of God); trespass, sin. **trănsgrĕss'ion** (-shn). **trănsgrĕss'or** *ns.*

trănshĭp *v.* = TRANS-SHIP.

trăns'ient (-z-) *adj.* Not durable or permanent, brief, momentary, fleeting; ~ *chord, note,* (mus.) unessential one, serving only to connect. **trăns'iently** *adv.* **trăns'ience, trăns'iency** *ns.*

trăn'sĭt (-s-, -z-) *n.* 1. Passing, passage, journey, conveyance, from one place to another. 2. (astrol.) Passage of planet across some region or point of zodiac; (astron.) passage of inferior planet across sun's disc, or of satellite or its shadow across planet's disc; passage of celestial body across meridian. 3. (colloq.) Transit-circle, -compass, or -instrument. 4. *~-circle,* astronomical instrument, consisting of *~-instrument* combined with meridian circle for determining right ascension and declination of star by observation of its transit; *~-compass,* kind of theodolite for measurement of horizontal angles; *~-duty,* duty on goods passing through a country; *~-instrument,* astronomical telescope mounted at right angles to fixed east-and-west axis, for determining time of transit of celestial body; *~-theodolite,* transit-compass; ~ *visa,* visa allowing passage through but not stay in a country. ~ *v.* (Of heavenly body) make transit (across).

trănsĭ'tion (-z-) *n.* Passage from one condition, action, style, subject, stage of development, etc., to another; period of this; modulation, esp. passing or brief, or into remote key. **trănsĭ'tional** *adj.* **trănsĭ'tionally** *adv.* **trănsĭ'tionary** *adj.*

trăns'itĭve *adj.* & *n.* (Verb) expressing action which passes over to an object, requiring direct object to complete the sense. **trăns'itĭvely** *adv.* **trăns'itĭveness** *n.*

trăns'itory *adj.* Not lasting; fleeting, momentary, brief. **trăns'itorĭly** *adv.* **trăns'itorĭness** *n.*

Trănsjôrd'an, Trănsjôrdān'ia (-z-). (hist.) District of Palestine E. of river Jordan; placed after war of 1914–18 under Arab administration and British mandate; in 1946 declared an independent kingdom, which now includes some parts W. of the river and is known as JORDAN.

trănslāte' (-s-, -z-) *v.* 1. Turn (word, sentence, book, etc.) from one language *into* another, express sense of it in another form of words. 2. Infer or declare the significance of, interpret (signs, movement, conduct, etc.). 3. Convey, introduce (idea, principle, design) *from* one art etc. *into* another. 4. Remove (bishop) to another see. 5. (bibl.) Convey to heaven without death. 6. (teleg.) Retransmit (message). 7. (mech.) Cause (body) to move so that all its parts follow same direction, impart motion without rotation to. **trănslā'tion** *n.* **trănslā'tional** (-sho-) *adj.*

trănslĭt'erāte (-z-) *v.t.* Replace (letters of one alphabet or language) by those of another. **trănsliterā'tion** *n.*

trănslocā'tion *n.* (bot.) Movement of dissolved substances inside plants.

trănslu'cent (-zlōō-) *adj.* Transparent (now rare); allowing passage of light but so diffusing it as to prevent bodies lying beyond from being clearly distinguished. **trănslu'cence, trănslu'cency** *ns.*

trănslun'ary (-zlōō-, -zlū-) *adj.* Lying beyond the moon; (fig.) insubstantial, visionary.

trănsmarine' (-z-, -ēn) *adj.* That is beyond the sea; crossing the sea.

trăns'mĭgrāte (*or* -īg'-) *v.i.* Migrate; (of soul) pass after death into another body, either human or animal. **trăns'mĭgrant** *n.* (esp.) Person passing as emigrant from one country through another in which he does not intend to settle. **trănsmĭgrā'tion** *n.* **trănsmī'gratory** *adj.*

trănsmi'ssion (-z-; -shn) *n.* (esp.) 1. Gear by which power is transmitted from engine to axle in motor-car etc. 2. Programme, series of programmes, transmitted by wireless or television from a particular transmitter.

trănsmĭt' (-z-) *v.t.* Send, convey, cause to pass or go, to another person, place, or thing; suffer to pass through, be medium for, serve to communicate (heat, light, sound, electricity, emotion, news). **trănsmiss'ĭble, trănsmiss'ĭve, trănsmitt'able** *adjs.*

trănsmĭtt'er (-z-) *n.* (esp.) Part of telegraphic or telephonic apparatus by means of which message etc. is transmitted; (part of) wireless set or station for transmitting or sending out wireless waves.

trănsmŏg'rĭfȳ (-z-) *v.t.* (joc.) Transform (esp. utterly, grotesquely, or strangely). **trănsmŏgrĭfĭcā'tion** *n.*

trănsmūtā'tion (-z-) *n.* Transmuting, being transmuted; (biol.) transformation of one species into another, evolution (esp. in Lamarckian theory).

trănsmūte' (-z-) *v.t.* Change form, nature, or substance of; convert (one element, substance, species, etc.) into another; esp. (alchemy) change (baser metal) into gold or silver.

trănsoceăn'ĭc (-zōshĭ-) *adj.* Situated, existing, beyond the ocean; crossing the ocean.

trăn'som *n.* Cross-beam, cross-piece, esp. one spanning an opening; horizontal bar across window (ill. WINDOW); cross-bar separating door from fan-light above it; (U.S.) window above transom, esp. of door.

trănspacĭf'ĭc (-z-) *adj.* Situated, being, beyond the Pacific Ocean; crossing the Pacific.

trănspār'ency *n.* Being transparent; transparent object or medium; esp. photograph or picture on glass or other transparent substance, to be viewed by transmitted light.

trănspār'ent *adj.* Transmitting light so that bodies lying beyond are completely visible; pervious to specified form of radiant energy, as heat-rays, X-rays; easily seen through, manifest, obvious, clear; candid, frank, open. **trănspār'ently** *adv.*

trănspierce' *v.t.* Pierce through.

trănspīre' *v.* Emit through excretory organs of skin or lungs, send off in vapour; be emitted thus; (bot., of plant or leaf) exhale watery vapour; (of gas or liquid) move through capillary tube under pressure; (of secret etc.) ooze out, come to be known; (misused for) occur, happen. **trănspirā'tion** *n.*

trănsplant' (-lah-) *v.* Remove (plant) from one place and plant it in another; remove and establish, esp. cause to live, in another place; (surg.) transfer (living tissue or organ) from one part of body, or one person or animal, to another; bear transplanting. **trăns'plant, trănsplantā'tion** *ns.*

trănspŏn'tīne *adj.* Of, on, the other side of the bridges in London, S. of the Thames; hence (from melodramas popular in the theatres there in 19th c.), cheaply or violently melodramatic.

trănspŏrt′ *v.t.* 1. Carry, convey, from one place to another. 2. Deport, convey (convict) to penal colony. 3. (usu. pass.) Carry away by strong emotion. **trăns′pŏrt** *n.* 1. Conveyance, carrying, of goods or passengers, from one place to another; means of conveyance, esp. vessel used in transporting troops or military stores, wagons or other vehicles carrying supplies of army etc. 2. Vehement (usu. pleasurable) emotion; (freq. pl.) fit of joy or rage.

trănsportā′tion *n.* Transport, conveyance (now somewhat rare); deportation, transfer to penal settlement; (U.S.) means of transport or conveyance.

trănspōse′ (-z) *v.t.* Alter order of (series of things) or position of (thing in series), interchange; esp. alter order of (letters) in word or (words) in sentence; (algebra) transfer (quantity) from one side of equation to the other; (mus.) put into different key, alter key of. **trănsposĭ′tion** (-zĭ-) *n.*

trănsrhēn′āne *adj.* Beyond the Rhine; German as opp. to Roman or French.

trăns-shĭp′, trănshĭp′ *v.* Transfer, change, from one ship, railway-train, etc., to another. **trăns-shĭp′ment, trănshĭp′ment** *n.*

trănsubstăn′tiāte (-shĭ-) *v.t.* Change from one substance into another.

trănsubstăntĭā′tion (-shĭ-) *n.* (esp., theol.) Doctrine that in the Eucharist a change is wrought in the elements at consecration, whereby the whole substance of the bread and wine is transmuted into the very Body and Blood of Christ, only the appearances (and other 'accidents') of bread and wine remaining.

trănsūde′ *v.i.* Exude through pores in body or anything permeable.

trănsūrăn′ĭc *adj.* (chem.) Belonging to a group of radio-active elements having atomic numbers and weights greater than those of uranium, not found in nature but produced artificially, e.g. in atomic pile.

Transvaal′ (trahnsvahl). Province of South Africa, formerly a republic, lying N. of Orange Free State and separated from it by River Vaal.

trănsvĕr′sal *adj.* (Of line) cutting a system of lines. ~ *n.* Transversal line.

trănsvĕrse′ (*or* trăns′-) *adj.* Situated, lying, across or athwart; ~ *magnet*, bar magnetized at right angles to its length, so that poles are at the sides, not at the ends. ~ *n.* Transverse muscle, piece, etc. **trănsvĕrse′ly** *adv.*

trănsvĕst′ *v.t.* Clothe in other garments, esp. those of opposite sex. **trănsvĕs′tĭsm** *n.*

Trănsy̆lvān′ĭa. Province of Rumania; before the war of 1914–18, part of Austria-Hungary. **Trănsy̆lvān′ĭan** *adj.*

trăn′ter *n.* (now dial.) Carrier; hawker.

trăp[1] *n.* 1. Device, as pitfall, snare, mechanical contrivance, for catching animals; device allowing pigeon to enter but not leave loft; police arrangement for timing motorists over measured distance to ensure that those exceeding speed-limit are caught; (fig.) something by which one is caught, led astray, etc. 2. Trap-door; movable covering of opening, falling when stepped upon; door flush with surface in floor, ceiling, roof of cab, etc. 3. Device for suddenly releasing bird etc. to be shot at; compartment from which greyhound is released at start of race; pivoted wooden instrument for throwing ball into air in trap-ball. 4. Light, esp. two-wheeled (horse-) carriage on springs. 5. Device, usu. U-shaped section of pipe with standing water, for preventing upward escape of noxious gases from pipe; contrivance for preventing passage of steam, water, silt, etc. 6. (slang) Mouth. 7. *~-ball*, game in which ball is thrown into air from 'heel' of shoe-shaped wooden device when other end is struck with bat, with which ball is then hit away; *~-door*, hinged or sliding door flush with surface of floor, roof, wall, etc.; *~-door spider*, large spider of *Ctenizα* and allied genera making tube-shaped nest with hinged lid like trap-door at top; *~-drummer*, performer on percussion instruments esp. of dance-band or theatre orchestra; *~-nest*, nest-box for hen, with hinged door by which she can enter but not leave; *~-shooting*, sport of shooting pigeons, balls, etc., released from spring trap. ~ *v.* Catch (as) in trap, snare, ensnare; set traps for game etc.; furnish with trap(s).

trăp[2] *n.* Various dark-coloured fine-grained igneous rocks, freq. columnar in structure, or in sheet-like masses rising like stairs.

trăp[3] *v.t.* (chiefly in past part.) Adorn with trappings, caparison. [OF *drap* cloth, covering]

trăp-cŭt *n.* Mode of cutting esp. coloured gems in straight facets arranged round centre of stone (ill. GEM).

trapes: see TRAIPSE.

trapēze′ *n.* Horizontal cross-bar suspended by ropes as apparatus for gymnastic exercises or acrobatics. **trapē′zĭst** *n.* Performer on trapeze.

trapēz′ium *n.* 1. Quadrilateral with two sides (thought of as base and opposite side) parallel (ill. QUADRILATERAL). 2. (U.S.) A trapezoid. 3. (anat.) Bone of carpus articulating with metacarpal bone of thumb (ill. HAND); band of nerve-fibres in *pons Variolii* of brain. 4. (astron.) *T~*, trapezium-shaped group of 4 stars in great nebula of Orion. [Gk *trapezion*, dim. of *trapeza* table]

trapēz′ĭus *n.* (anat.) Each of pair of large flat triangular muscles of back, extending over back of neck etc. (ill. MUSCLE).

trăpėzohē′dron *n.* Solid figure whose faces are trapeziums.

trăp′ėzoid *n.* 1. Quadrilateral with no sides parallel (ill. QUADRILATERAL). 2. (U.S.) A trapezium. 3. Second bone of distal row of carpus (ill. HAND). ~ *adj.* Of, in the form of, a trapezoid. **trăpėzoid′al** *adj.*

trăpp′ėan *adj.* (geol.) Of (the nature of) trap-rock.

trăpp′er *n.* (esp.) One engaged in trapping wild animals for their furs.

trăpp′ĭngs *n.pl.* Ornamental housing for horse; ornaments, embellishments, ornamental accessories.

Trăpp′ĭst *adj.* & *n.* (Monk) of reformed Cistercian order established 1664 at monastery of La Trappe in Normandy and observing extremely austere discipline and perpetual silence except with confessors and in choir. **Trăpp′ĭstīne** *adj.* & *n.* (Member) of order of nuns established 1796 and affiliated with Trappists.

trăps *n.pl.* (colloq.) Personal effects, portable belongings, baggage. [app. shortening of *trappings*]

trăsh *n.* Waste or worthless stuff, refuse, rubbish; stripped-off leaves and tops of sugar-canes (*field-~*) or refuse after juice has been extracted (*cane-~*); worthless or disreputable people; *white ~*, poor white population of southern States of U.S.; *~-ice*, broken ice mixed with water. **trăsh′y** *adj.* **trăsh′ĭly** *adv.* **trăsh′ĭnėss** *n.*

Trăsĭme′nō (-mā-). Lake near Perugia, Italy, where Hannibal fought and defeated the Romans (217 B.C.).

tràss *n.* Light-coloured volcanic tufa found esp. along lower Rhine and used for hydraulic cement.

traum′a *n.* (pl. *-ata*, *-as*). Injury, wound; condition resulting from this; (psychol.) unpleasant or disturbing experience in which neurosis etc. originates. **traumăt′ĭc** *adj.* **traumăt′ĭcally** *adv.* **traum′atism** *n.*

trăv′ail *n.* & *v.i.* (archaic) (Suffer) pangs of childbirth; (make) painful or laborious effort. [OF *travail*, app. f. LL *trepalium* instrument of torture (L *tres* three, *palus* stake)]

Trăvancōre′. Former native State on SW. coast of India, since 1956 part of the Indian State of Kerala.

trăv′el *v.* 1. Make journey, esp. of some length or to foreign countries; act as COMMERCIAL traveller; pass from one point or place to another, proceed; (of piece of mechanism) move, be capable of moving, along fixed course; (colloq.) bear transportation. 2. Journey through, pass over, traverse, cover (specified distance); cause (herds etc.) to journey. 3. *travelling-clock*, small clock or watch in leather case; *travelling crane*, crane that travels along esp. overhead support; *travelling fellowship*, *scholarship*, one enabling or requiring holder to travel for purposes of study or research. ~ *n.* 1. Travelling, esp. in foreign countries. 2. Single movement of part of mechanism; range, rate, mode of motion, of this.

trăv'eller *n.* (esp.) COMMERCIAL traveller; ~*'s joy*, shrub (*Clematis alba* and other climbing species of *Clematis*) trailing over wayside hedges; ~*'s tale*, incredible or mendacious story.

trăv'elogue (-ŏg) *n.* Illustrated narrative of travel.

trăv'erse *n.* 1. Movement or part of structure which crosses another; (each lap of) ascending zigzag road; (mountaineering) more or less horizontal motion across face of precipice from one practicable line of ascent or descent to another, place where this is necessary; (naut.) zigzag course taken owing to contrary winds or currents, each leg of this; (surveying) single line of survey across region, tract of country so surveyed; (geom.) TRANSVERSAL line; (mil.) earthwork in form of parapet protecting covered way etc., double or quadruple right angle in trench (˥˪, ˪˥˪˥); horizontal or lateral movement of gun; (eng.) platform for shifting engine etc. from one line of rails to another; sideways movement of part or machine; (archit.) gallery from side to side of church etc.; (hist.) curtain, partition across room etc., compartment so cut off; ~ *circle*, circular or segmental track on which gun-carriage is turned in traversing gun; ~ *sailing*, sailing on zigzag course; ~ *table*, table for computing (*working* or *solving*) nautical traverses. 2. (law) Formal denial of matter of fact alleged by other side. ~ *v.* 1. Travel or lie across; make a traverse in climbing; determine position of points, survey (road, river, etc.) by measuring lengths and azimuths of connected series of straight lines; turn (gun); (of needle of compass etc.) turn (as) on pivot; (of horse) walk crosswise; plane (wood) across grain; *traversing pulley*, one running over rope etc. that supports it. 2. (fig.) Consider, discuss, whole extent of (subject). 3. Deny, esp. (law) in pleading; thwart, frustrate (plan or opinion).

trăv'ertin(e) *n.* White or light-coloured crystalline concretionary limestone deposited from springs etc. and used for building. [L *tiburtinus*, f. *Tibur* Tivoli]

trăv'ėsty *v.t.* Make ridiculous by gross parody or imitation; be ridiculous imitation of. ~ *n.* Such treatment, such imitation.

trawl *n.* Large bag-net (~*-net*) with mouth held open by beam or otherwise, dragged along bottom of sea etc. by boat; (U.S.) long buoyed line, anchored at ends, and with numerous short baited lines attached, for sea-fishing. ~ *v.* Fish with trawl or in trawler; catch with trawl.

trawl'er *n.* One who trawls; vessel (now *steam-*~) used in fishing with trawl-net.

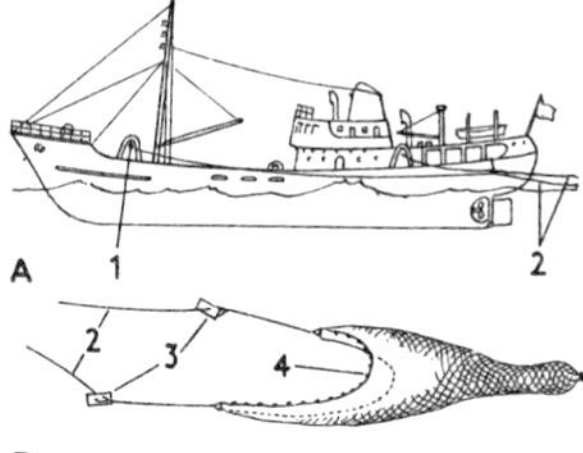

A. TRAWLER. B. TRAWL

1. Gallows through which warps are run. 2. Warps. 3. 'Otter boards' or trawl boards, which keep mouth of net open. 4. Floats to raise top of net

tray *n.* Flat shallow vessel usu. with raised rim for placing or carrying small articles on, steeping specimens in laboratory, holding correspondence on desk, etc.; shallow lidless box forming compartment of trunk.

T.R.C. *abbrev.* Thames Rowing Club.

treach'erous (-ĕch-) *adj.* Violating faith or betraying trust; perfidious; not to be relied on, deceptive. **treach'erously** *adv.* **treach'erousnėss, treach'ery** *ns.*

trea'cle *n.* Uncrystallized syrup produced in refining sugar; (loosely) molasses. **trea'cly** *adj.*

tread (-ĕd) *v.* (past t. *trŏd*, past part. *trŏdd'en*). Set down one's foot, (of foot) be set down; go through (dance) esp. in stately measure; press or crush with feet, trample (*on*); (of male bird) copulate (with); ~ *the boards*, be an actor, appear on stage; ~ *down*, press down with feet; trample on, destroy, oppress, crush; ~ *in*, press in or into earth etc. with feet; ~ *out*, stamp out; press out (wine, grain) with feet; ~ *under foot*, (fig.) trample on, destroy, treat contemptuously; ~ *water*, (in swimming) keep body erect and head above water while moving feet as in walking upstairs. ~ *n.* 1. Manner, sound, of walking. 2. (also ~*-board*) top surface of step or stair (ill. STAIR); each step of treadmill; rung of ladder. 3. Piece of metal, rubber, or other substance placed on step to lessen wear or sound. 4. Part of wheel that touches ground or rails; part of rails that wheels touch. 5. Part of stilt on which foot rests. 6. Part of boot-sole that rests on ground. 7. Distance between pedals of bicycle. 8. (Of male bird) copulation. 9. Round white spot on egg-yoke, *cicatricule* (formerly supposed to appear only in fecundated eggs). 10. *tread'mill*, appliance for producing motion by the stepping of man or horse etc. on steps fixed to revolving cylinder, esp. kind formerly used in prisons as punishment; (fig.) monotonous routine; ~*-wheel*, treadmill or similar appliance.

tread'le (-ĕd-) *n.* Lever moved by foot and imparting motion to machine, e.g. lathe, sewing-machine, bicycle. ~ *v.* Work treadle.

Treas. *abbrev.* Treasurer.

treas'on (-z-) *n.* 1. (also *high* ~) Violation by subject of his allegiance to sovereign or chief authority of State (e.g. compassing or intending sovereign's death, levying war against him, or adhering to his enemies); *constructive* ~, violation of allegiance not intended or realized as treason but held in law to be equivalent to it; *misprision of* ~: see MISPRISION; ~*-felony*, attempt to depose sovereign or levy war in order to compel change of measures, intimidate parliament, or stir up foreign invasion. 2. Breach of faith, disloyalty (*to* cause, friend, etc.). **treas'onous** *adj.*

treas'onable (-z-) *adj.* Involving, guilty of, treason. **treas'onablenėss** *n.* **treas'onably** *adv.*

trea'sure (-ĕzh*er*) *n.* Wealth or riches stored up, esp. in form of precious metals or gems; accumulated wealth; anything valued or preserved as precious; beloved person, esp. child; (colloq.) very efficient or satisfactory person, esp. servant; ~*-house*, place where treasure is kept, treasury; *T*~ *State*, pop. name of Montana, U.S.; ~*-trove*, gold or silver, money, etc., found hidden in ground or other place, owner of which is unknown. ~ *v.t.* Store (*up*) as valuable; cherish, prize; (fig.) store, lay up (e.g. in memory).

trea'surer (-ĕzh*e*-) *n.* (orig.) One charged with receipt and disbursement of revenues of king, noble, State, Church, etc.; now, one responsible for funds of public body or any corporation, society, or club; (U.S.) officer of Treasury Department who receives and keeps the moneys; (*Lord High*) *T*~ (*of England*), (hist.) third great officer of the Crown, controlling sovereign's revenues, with duties since reign of George I discharged by 5 Lords of the Treasury. **trea'surership** *n.*

trea'sury (-ĕzh*e*-) *n.* 1. Room, building, in which precious or valuable objects are preserved (freq. fig.). 2. Funds or revenue of State, corporation, etc.; (*T*~) in Gt Britain, department of State advising the Chancellor of the Exchequer, administering expenditure of public revenue, and co-ordinating the economic activities of other branches of government; building where business of this department is transacted; corresponding institution in other countries; *T~ bench*, front bench on Speaker's right in House of Commons, occupied by First Lord of the Treasury (usu. the Prime Minister), Chancellor of the Exchequer, and other members of the government; *~ bill*, security given by a government in exchange for a loan of short duration (freq. 91 days); *T~ Department*, finance department of U.S. Government, under Secretary of Treasury; *~ note*, (U.S.) demand note issued by Treasury Department, and legal tender for all debts; (in Engl. usage) currency note for £1 or 10*s*., issued by the Treasury 1914–28, now replaced by notes issued by the Bank of England. 3. (theatr. slang) Weekly payment of company of actors.

treat *v.* 1. Deal, negotiate (*with*), in order to settle terms. 2. Deal with (subject), deal with subject, in speech or writing; deal with in way of art, represent artistically; deal with to obtain particular result, esp. deal with disease etc. in order to relieve or cure. 3. Behave or act towards in specified way. 4. Entertain, esp. with food and drink, regale, feast. *~ n.* Entertainment, esp. one given gratuitously, pleasure party; treating, invitation to eat or esp. drink; a great pleasure, delight, or gratification.

treat'ĭse (-ĭz, -ĭs) *n.* Book or writing treating in formal or methodical manner of particular subject.

treat'ment *n.* (Mode of) dealing with or behaving towards person or thing; esp. treatment of patient or his disease.

treat'y *n.* (Document embodying) formal contract between States relating to peace, truce, alliance, commerce, etc.; *in ~*, negotiating, treating; *~-port*, port (esp. certain ports in Far East) opened to foreign commerce by treaty.

Trĕb'ĭzŏnd. City of Asia Minor on Black Sea (Turk. *Trabzon*), once capital of an empire (1204–1461) founded by Alexius Comnenus.

trĕb'le *n.* & *adj.* 1. Threefold, triple (sum, quantity); (crochet stitch) with 3 loops on hook together (ill. CROCHET). 2. Soprano (part, voice, singer, esp. boy); high-pitched, shrill (voice, sound, etc.); (string etc.) of treble pitch; *~ bob*: see BOB[2]; *~ clef*, the G clef, symbol 𝄞. *~ v.* Multiply, be multiplied, by 3.

trĕb'ŭchĕt (-sh-), **trĕb'ŭckĕt** *ns.* 1. (hist.) Medieval military engine, pivoted lever with sling at one end, used for throwing heavy missiles. 2. Small tilting balance or pair of scales.

trecĕn'tō (trăch-) *n.* The 14th century in Italian art and literature. [It., = 'three hundred', abbrev. of *mil trecento* 1300]

tree *n.* Perennial plant with self-supporting woody main stem (usu. developing woody branches at some distance from ground); erect bush or shrub with single stem; piece of wood shaped for some purpose (as BOOT-tree, SADDLE-tree); (archaic) gallows; (archaic and poet.) cross of Christ; genealogical chart like branching tree (*family ~*; cf. *~ ~ of* JESSE); *at the top of the ~*, in the highest position; *up a ~*, cornered, trapped, in a difficulty; *~ agate*, agate with tree-like markings; *~-calf*, (bookbinding) calf leather stained with acids in tree-like markings; *~-creeper*, various birds which creep on trunks and branches of trees, esp. the common European *Certhia familiaris* and Amer. variety of this; *tree'dozer*, bulldozer for felling trees; *~-fern*, fern with upright woody stem, growing to size of tree, found in tropics, Australia, and New Zealand; *~-frog*, toad-like or frog-like arboreal amphibian esp. of genus *Hyla*; *~-nail*, pin of hard wood for fastening ship's timbers together; *~ of knowledge of good and evil*: see Gen. iii; *~ onion*, variety of onion which produces bulbs on stems instead of flowers; *~ oyster*, oyster found on roots of mangrove, esp. *Ostrea glomerata*; *~-toad*, tree-frog. *~ v.t.* Cause to take refuge in tree, drive up a tree; stretch on boot-tree.

trĕf'oil *n.* 1. Clover, any plant of genus *Trifolium* with leaves of 3 leaflets. 2. Ornamental figure resembling clover-leaf; (archit.) opening divided by cusps suggesting three-lobed leaf (ill. ARCH).

Treitschke (trīch'ka), Heinrich von (1834–96). German historian and political writer.

trĕk *v.i.* (orig. S. Afr.) Travel, migrate, esp. by ox-wagon; make arduous journey or expedition. *~ n.* Such journey or stage of it; *Great T~*, migration northward (1835–7) of large numbers of Boers, discontented with British rule in the Cape, to the areas where they eventually founded the Transvaal Republic and the Orange Free State.

trĕll'ĭs *n.* Structure of light bars crossing each other with open square spaces between, used as screen, as support for climbing plants, etc.; *~-work*, trellis. *~ v.t.* Furnish, support, (as) with trellis. [L *trilix* three-ply (f. *licium* warp-thread)]

trĕm'ble *v.* Shake involuntarily as with fear or other emotion, cold, or weakness; (cause to) shake, quiver; (fig.) be affected with fear, agitation, suspense, etc. *~ n.* Trembling, quiver, tremor.

trĕm'bly *adj.* (colloq.)

trĕm'bler *n.* (esp.) Spring which makes electrical contact when shaken.

trĕm'blĭng *adj.* *~-bog*, bog-land formed over water or soft mud, shaking at every tread; *~ grass*, quaking grass (*Briza media*). **trĕm'blĭngly** *adv.*

trėmĕn'dous *adj.* Awful, fearful, terrible; (colloq.) extraordinarily great, immense. **trėmĕn'dously** *adv.* **trėmĕn'dousnėss** *n.*

trĕm'olō *adj.* & *n.* (mus.) (Having, producing) tremulous or vibrating effects in certain instruments or human voice; organ-stop producing this effect. [It., = 'trembling']

trĕm'or *n.* Tremulous or vibratory movement or sound, vibration, shaking, quaking; (instance, fit, of) involuntary agitation of body or limbs from physical weakness, fear, etc.

trĕm'ūlous *adj.* Trembling, quivering; shaky; timorous, timid; tremblingly sensitive or responsive. **trĕm'ūlously** *adv.* **trĕm'ūlousnėss** *n.*

trĕnch *n.* Long narrow usu. deep hollow cut out of ground, esp. with earth thrown up as parapet to protect soldiers under fire or from bombing; *~-coat*, thick, usu. lined, waterproof over-coat, orig. for wearing in trenches; *~-feet*, *-foot*, affection of feet resembling chilblains, sometimes with gangrene, due to exposure to extreme cold and wet and prevalent among soldiers serving in trenches; *~ fever*, low, intermittent, infectious fever carried by lice and common among men serving in trenches; *~-gun*, *-mortar*, small mortar for throwing bombs etc. into enemy trenches at short range; *~ warfare*, hostilities carried on from more or less permanent trenches. *~ v.* 1. Make trench(es) or ditch(es) in (ground); make series of trenches in digging or ploughing (ground) so as to bring lower soil to surface; dig trench(es); cut (groove), cut groove in (wood etc.). 2. Encroach (*up*)*on*; verge or border closely (*up*) *on*.

trĕnch'ant *adj.* (archaic and poet.) Keen, sharp; (zool., of tooth etc.) having cutting edge; (fig.) incisive, vigorous, decisive, energetic. **trĕnch'antly** *adv.* **trĕnch'ancy** *n.*

trĕnch'er *n.* Flat square or usu.

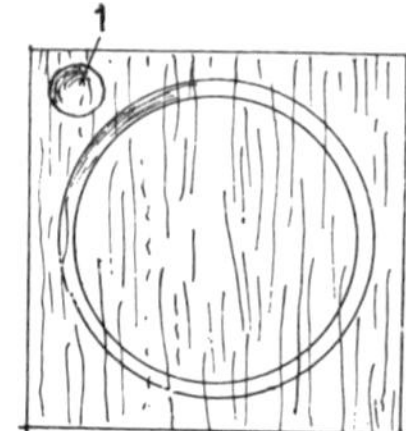

WOODEN TRENCHER

1. Depression for salt

circular piece of wood on which meat etc. was formerly cut; any flat round piece of wood; MORTAR-board; *trencherman*, feeder, eater, usu. qualified as *good, stout, valiant*.

trĕnd *n*. General direction, course, tendency. ~ *v.i.* Have specified direction, course, or general tendency.

Trĕnt[1]. River of English midlands, flowing into North Sea by Humber.

Trĕnt[2], **Council of.** An oecumenical council of the R.C. Ch. which met from time to time at Trent in the Tyrol (i.e. Trento in modern Italy), 1545–63; it settled the doctrines of the Church in opposition to those of the Reformation, reformed discipline, and strengthened the authority of the Papacy.

trĕn'tal *n*. Set of 30 requiem masses said daily or all on one day.

Trĕntin'ō (-tē-). Part of S. Tyrol with many Italian inhabitants, ceded by Austria to Italy after war of 1914–18; now called Tridentina.

trėpăn' *n*. 1. Surgeon's cylindrical saw (obs.; superseded by TREPHINE). 2. (mining etc.) Heavy boring instrument for sinking shafts. ~ *v.t.* Operate on with trepan.

trėpăng' *n*. Edible marine sea-cucumber, esp. of genera *Holothuria* and *Actinopyga*, esteemed as luxury by Chinese etc.; bêche-de-mer. [Malay *trīpang*]

trėphine' (-ēn, -īn) *n*. Surgeon's cylindrical saw with guiding centre-pin, for removing part of bone of skull. ~ *v*. Operate on with this. **trĕphĭnā'tion** *n*.

trĕpĭdā'tion *n*. Confused hurry or alarm, flurry, perturbation.

trĕs'pass *n*. Transgression, breach of law or duty; (law) actionable wrong committed against person or property of another, esp. wrongful entry upon another's lands with damage (however inconsiderable) to his real property. ~ *v.i.* Transgress, offend, sin; (law) commit trespass, esp. enter unlawfully on land of another or his property or right; (fig.) make unwarrantable claim or undesired intrusion *on*, encroach *on*, infringe. **trĕs'passer** *n*.

trĕss *n*. Lock, braid of (esp. woman's long) hair; *tresses*, woman's hair.

trĕss'ure (-sy*er*, -sh*er*) *n*. (her.) Small orle, narrow band one-quarter of width of bordure (ill. HERALDRY).

trĕ'stle (-sl) *n*. Supporting structure for table etc. consisting of horizontal beam with diverging legs, usu. two at each end, or of two frames hinged together or fixed at an angle; open braced framework of wood or metal for supporting bridge etc.; (naut.) ~*s*, ~*-trees*, two horizontal timbers on mast supporting cross-trees, top-mast, etc. (ill. SAIL[1]); ~*-bridge*, bridge supported on trestles; ~*-table*, table of board(s) laid across trestles or other supports (ill. TABLE).

trĕt *n*. Allowance of extra weight formerly made to purchasers of some goods for waste in transportation etc.

trews (-o͞oz) *n.pl.* Close-fitting trousers or breeches combined with stockings, formerly worn by Scottish highlanders and Irish; close-fitting usu. tartan trousers worn by some Scottish regiments (ill. PLAID).

trey (-ā) *n*. Three at dice or cards.

T.R.H. *abbrev*. Their Royal Highnesses.

tri- *prefix*. Three, thrice.

trī'ăd *n*. Group or set of 3; (Welsh literature) form of composition with subjects or statements arranged in groups of 3; (mus.) chord of 3 notes, esp. note with its third and fifth (e.g. common chord without octave) (ill. CHORD); (chem.) group of 3 chemical elements having similar properties, as iron, nickel, and cobalt. **trīăd'ĭc** *adj*.

trīadĕl'phous *adj*. (Having stamens) united by filaments into 3 bundles.

trī'al *n*. 1. Examination and determination of causes at law by judicial tribunal. 2. Testing or putting to proof of qualities of thing; test, probation; experimental treatment, investigation by means of experience; examination of person, esp. for Presbyterian ministry; (in some English public schools) terminal examination. 3. Being tried by suffering or temptation; painful test of endurance, patience, etc.; affliction, hardship, trouble. 4. Attempt, endeavour, effort. 5. Something serving as sample, proof, etc., trial-piece. 6. ~ *balance*, in double-entry book-keeping, addition of all entries on each side of ledger, when debits should balance credits; ~ *eight*, provisional crew of 8-oared boat, from among whom members of final eight may be chosen; (pl., also) race between such crews; ~*-piece*, anything made or taken as specimen; ~ *trip*, trip to test speed and other qualities of new vessel etc.

trī'ăngle (-nggl) *n*. Geometrical figure, esp. plane rectilineal figure, with 3 angles and 3 sides; any system of 3 points not in a straight line, with the 3 real or imaginary lines joining them; any 3-cornered body, object, or space, esp. musical percussion instrument consisting of steel rod bent into a triangle open at one corner and struck with a small steel rod, (naut.) kind of large tripod of 3 spars for hoisting weights etc.; (hist., usu. pl.) frame of 3 halberds joined at top to which soldier was bound for flogging; *the eternal* ~: see ETERNAL; ~ *of forces*, theorem that 3 forces in equilibrium acting at one point can be represented by a triangle with sides parallel to their directions and proportional in length to their magnitudes; the triangle representing such forces.

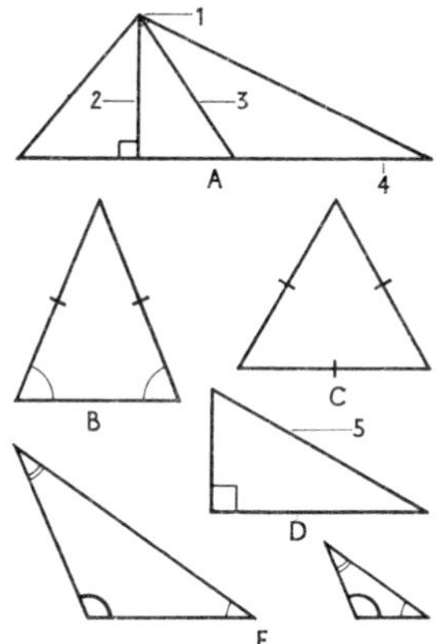

TRIANGLES: A. SCALENE. B. ISOSCELES. C. EQUILATERAL. D. RIGHT-ANGLED. E. TWO SIMILAR TRIANGLES

1. Vertex. 2. Altitude. 3. Median. 4. Base. 5. Hypotenuse

trīăng'ūlar (-ngg-) *adj*. Of the shape of a triangle, 3-cornered; 3-sided, between 3 persons or parties; ~ *numbers*, (math.) series of numbers (1, 3, 6, 10, 15, etc.) obtained by continued summation of the natural numbers 1, 2, 3, 4, etc. **trīăng'ūlarly** *adv*. **trīangūlă'rity** *n*.

trīăng'ūlate (-ngg-) *adj*. Consisting of, marked with, triangles. **trīăng'ūlately** *adv*. **trīăng'ūlāte** *v.t.* Divide or convert into triangles; (surveying etc.) measure, map out, by measurement of sides and angles of series of triangles on determined base-line(s). **trīăngūlā'tion** *n*.

Trianon (trē'*a*nawṅ). Either of two small palaces in great park at Versailles; the larger (*Grand* ~) was built by Louis XIV 1687; the smaller (*Petit* ~), built by Louis XV 1762–8, belonged first to Madame du Barry and afterwards to Marie Antoinette; *Treaty of* ~, that between the Allied Powers and Hungary, 1920.

Trī'ăs *n*. (geol.) = TRIASSIC.

Trīăss'ĭc *adj*. & *n*. (geol.) (Of) the system of rocks at the base of the Mesozoic; period of formation of these (ill. GEOLOGY). [Gk *trias* three, f. threefold sub-division of these rocks in Germany]

trīăt'ĭc *adj*. (naut.) ~ *stay*, rope, or two ropes joined by spar, attached at ends to foremast and mainmast and used for hoisting boats etc.; stay between mastheads of steamship.

trīatŏm'ic *adj.* Having 3 atoms in the molecule; having 3 replaceable atoms or groups.

trīb'al *adj.* Of tribe(s). **trīb'ally** *adv.*

trīb'alism *n.* Tribal system or organization.

trībās'ic *adj.* (chem.) Having 3 replaceable hydrogen atoms; containing 3 atoms of a univalent metal or 3 basic hydroxyl groups.

trībe *n.* 1. Group of primitive or barbarous clans under recognized chiefs. 2. (Rom. hist.) Each of the political divisions of the Romans (orig. 3, prob. representing clans, ultimately 35); (Gk hist.) = PHYLE. 3. Any similar division whether of natural or political origin; *Twelve Tribes*, divisions of people of Israel claiming descent from sons of Jacob; *Lost Tribes*, the 10 Israelite tribes (i.e. all but Judah and Benjamin) which revolted from the House of David and were deported by Shalmaneser, after which time their history is lost. 4. (biol.) Group ranking below sub-family and above genus (with name usu. ending in *-ini* for animals and *-eae* for plants). 5. Class, lot, set (usu. contempt.); (pl.) large numbers. **trībes'man** (-bz-) *n.* Man who is a member of a tribe.

trībōphȳs'ics (-z-) *n.* The physics of friction.

trĭb'răch (-k) *n.* Metrical foot of 3 short syllables.

trĭbūlā'tion *n.* Great affliction, oppression, or misery. [L *tribulare* press, oppress, f. *tribulum* threshing-sledge]

trībūn'al *n.* 1. Judgement-seat; court of justice, judicial assembly; (fig.) place of judgement, judicial authority. 2. Board or committee appointed to adjudicate on claims of a particular kind, e.g. for exemption from military service, or reduction of rent.

trĭb'ūne¹ *n.* (Rom. hist.) ~ *of the people*, one of 2 (later 5, then 10) officers protecting interests and rights of plebs from patricians; *military* ~, one of 6 officers of legion, each in command for 2 months of year; (fig.) protector of rights of people, popular leader, demagogue. **trĭb'ūnate, trĭb'ūneship** *ns.*

trĭb'ūne² *n.* Raised floor for magistrate's chair in apse of Roman basilica (ill. BASILICA); bishop's throne, apse containing this, in basilica; platform, stage, pulpit; raised and seated area or gallery.

trĭb'ūtary *adj.* 1. Paying or subject to tribute; furnishing subsidiary supplies or aid, auxiliary, contributory; (of stream or river) flowing into another. ~ *n.* Tributary person or State; stream contributing its flow to larger stream or lake.

trĭb'ūte *n.* Money or equivalent paid by one sovereign or State to another in acknowledgement of submission or for protection or peace; obligation of paying this; (fig.) contribution, offering or gift as mark of respect, affection, etc.; (mining) proportion of ore, or its equivalent, paid to miner for labour under ~ *system.*

trī'-căr *n.* 3-wheeled motorcar.

trīce¹ *n.* *In a* ~, in an instant.

trīce² *v.t.* (naut.) Hoist *up* and secure with rope or lashing, lash *up.*

trīcĕntēn'ary, trīcĕntĕnn'ial *adjs.* & *ns.* Tercentenary, tercentennial.

trī'cĕps *adj.* & *n.* (Muscle, esp. great extensor muscle of back of upper arm) with 3 heads or points of origin (ill. MUSCLE).

Trīcĕ'ratŏps *n.* Genus of gigantic dinosaurs found in parts of U.S., with two large horns above eyes and one on nose.

trĭch'ĭna (-k-; *or* -kīn'a) *n.* (pl. *-ae*). Minute nematode worm *Trichinella spiralis*) parasitic in muscles and intestines of man, pig, etc. **trĭchĭnōs'ĭs** (-k-) *n.* Disease caused by introduction of trichinae from infected pork into alimentary canal. **trĭch'ĭnous** (-k-) *adj.* Of trichinae or trichinosis.

Trĭchĭnŏp'oly. City and district in State of Madras, India; ~ (*cigar*), kind of Indian cheroot.

trĭchŏl'ogy (-k-) *n.* Study of structure, functions, and diseases of hair.

trĭch'ōme (-k-) *n.* Any outgrowth of epidermis or superficial tissue of plant, as prickles, hairs, etc.

trĭchopăth'ĭc (-k-) *adj.* Of diseases of hair.

trĭch'ophȳte (-k-) *n.* Member of genus (*Trichophyton*) of fungi parasitic on skin.

trĭchŏp'ter (-k-) *n.* Member of order *Trichoptera*, caddis flies, of insects with hairy wings. **trĭchŏp'terous** *adj.*

trĭchŏt'omy (-k-) *n.* Division into, classification or arrangement in, 3 (classes etc.); esp. division of human nature into body, soul, and spirit. **trĭchŏt'omous** *adj.*

trīchrō'ĭc *adj.* Having or showing 3 colours; esp. of crystal, presenting 3 different colours when viewed in 3 different directions. **trīch'rōĭsm** *n.*

trīchromăt'ic *adj.* Trichroic; esp. of or having 3 fundamental colour-sensations (red, green, violet) of normal vision; of (printing in) 3 colours. **trīchrōm'atism** *n.*

trĭck *n.* 1. Crafty or fraudulent device or stratagem, esp. of mean or base kind; prank, hoax, joke; capricious, foolish, or stupid act; clever device or contrivance, 'dodge', feat of skill or dexterity; knack (freq. in ~(*s*) *of the trade*). 2. Peculiar or characteristic practice; habit, mannerism. 3. (cards) Cards played and won in one round; such round, point(s) gained by winning it. 4. (naut.) Time, usu. two hours, of duty at helm. ~ *v.* 1. Deceive by trick, cheat; cheat *out of*, beguile *into*, by trickery; practise trickery. 2. Dress, deck, decorate (usu. *out, up*). **trĭck'ery** *n.* **trĭck'ish** *adj.*

trĭck'le *v.* (Cause to) flow in drops or in scanty halting stream; (of ball) run slowly over surface of ground, cause to do this. ~ *n.* Trickling, small fitful stream; ~ *charger*, (elect.) device for slow continuous charging of an accumulator. **trĭck'ly** *adj.*

trĭck'sy *adj.* Full of tricks or pranks, playful, sportive, frolicsome.

trĭck'y *adj.* Crafty, given to tricks, deceitful; skilful in clever tricks or dodges, adroit, resourceful; (colloq.) requiring cautious or adroit action or handling, ticklish. **trĭck'ĭly** *adv.* **trĭck'ĭness** *n.*

trīclĭn'ĭc *adj.* (cryst.) Having the 3 axes unequal and obliquely inclined (ill. CRYSTAL).

trĭc'olīne *n.* Fine cotton poplin resembling silk. [trade term]

trī'colour (-ŭler) *n.* & *adj.* (Flag, esp. that adopted as national flag of France at Revolution) having 3 colours.

trī'cŏrn *adj.* & *n.* 3-cornered (cocked hat).

trĭcot (trēk'ō, trĭk'ō) *n.* Fabric knitted by hand or machine; ~*-stitch*, plain simple crochet stitch producing straight pattern.

trīcŭs'pĭd *adj.* Having three cusps or points; ~ *valve*, (anat.) valve, consisting of three triangular segments, which guards the opening from the right atrium into the right ventricle of the heart (ill. HEART).

trī'cȳcle *n.* 3-wheeled pedal- or motor-cycle. ~ *v.i.* Ride tricycle.

trīd'ent *n.* 3-pronged instrument or weapon, esp. 3-pronged fish-spear or sceptre as attribute of Neptune or of Britannia; 3-pronged spear used by *retiarius* in Roman gladiatorial combats.

Trĭd'entīne (*or* trīdĕn'-). Of the Council of TRENT².

trĭd'ūum *n.* (R.C. Ch.) 3 days of prayer in preparation for feast or other solemn occasion.

trīĕnn'ial *adj.* Existing, lasting, for 3 years; occurring, done, every 3 years; ~ *n.* Triennial occasion, event, publication, etc.; esp. visitation of diocese by bishop every 3 years. **trīĕnn'ially** *adv.*

Trieste (trēĕst'). Seaport on the Adriatic, under Austrian control until 1918 when it passed to Italy; after the war of 1939–45 the port and surrounding country were claimed by both Italy and Yugoslavia until in 1954 the N. part (including the town) was assigned by treaty to Italy and the S. part to Yugoslavia.

trĭf′id *adj.* Split or divided into 3 by deep clefts or notches.

trī′fle *n.* 1. Thing, fact, circumstance, of slight value or importance; small amount, esp. of money; small article. 2. Sweet dish of sponge-cakes flavoured with wine, jam, etc., served with custard or whipped cream. ~ *v.i.* Toy, play, dally, fidget, *with*; act or speak idly or frivolously. **trī′fler** *n.* **trī′fling** *adj.* Unimportant, paltry, insignificant; foolish, frivolous, idle. **trī′flingly** *adv.*

trīfōl′iate *adj.* 3-leaved; consisting of 3 leaflets; having such leaves.

trifôr′ium *n.* (pl. *-ia*). Gallery or arcade in wall over arches at sides of nave and choir (and occas. transepts) in some large churches (ill. CHURCH).

trī′fôrm *adj.* Having a triple form, existing or appearing in 3 forms.

trĭg[1] *adj.* Trim, spruce, smart, neat.

trĭg[2] *n.* Colloq. abbrev. of TRIGONOMETRY.

trĭg′amy *n.* Having 3 wives or husbands at same time. **trĭg′amist** *n.* **trĭg′amous** *adj.*

trigĕm′ĭnal *adj.* Of the 5th and (in man) largest pair of cranial nerves, dividing into 3 main branches (ophthalmic, maxillary, and mandibular nerves).

trĭgg′er *n.* Movable catch or lever which is pulled or pressed to release a spring or otherwise set mechanism in motion, esp. small steel catch for releasing hammer of lock in fire-arm (ill. GUN); ~ *finger*, forefinger of right hand; ~*-fish*, fish of *Babistes* and related genera, so called because pressure on second spine of anterior dorsal fin depresses first.

trĭg′lȳph *n.* (archit.) Ornament of frieze in Doric order, consisting of block or tablet with two vertical grooves and a half-groove on each side, alternating with metopes (ill. ORDER).

trĭg′ŏn *n.* 1. Triangle. 2. (astrol.) Set of 3 signs of zodiac distant 120° from each other; each of 4 such groups (*airy*, *earthy*, *fiery*, *watery*) into which the 12 signs are divided; triplicity, trine. 3. (zool.) Cutting region of crown of upper molar. **trigŏn′ic** *adj.*

trĭg′onal *adj.* Triangular; having triangular cross-section (ill. CRYSTAL); of a trigon; (geom., cryst., of solid) having triangular faces, having 3 equal and equally inclined axes.

trĭgonocĕph′alous *adj.* Having triangular flat head.

trĭg′onoid *adj.* & *n.* (geom.) (Plane figure) contained by 3 arcs of equal radius meeting at angles.

trĭgonŏm′ètry *n.* Branch of mathematics dealing with measurement of sides and angles of triangles and with certain functions of their angles or of angles in general. **trĭgonomĕt′rĭc(al)** *adjs.* **trĭgonomĕt′rically** *adv.*

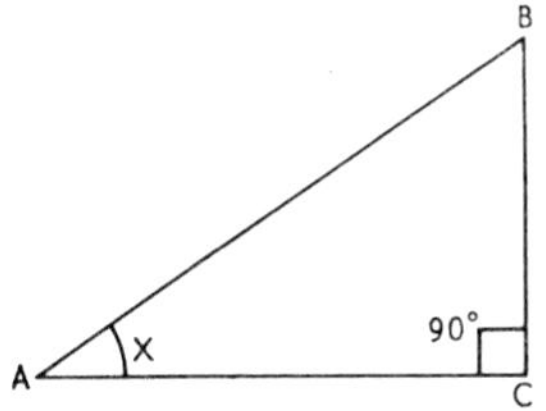

TRIGONOMETRICAL RATIOS

Sine $X = BC/AB$. Cosine $X = AC/AB$. Secant $X = AB/AC$. Cosecant $X = AB/BC$. Tangent $X = BC/AC$. Cotangent $X = AC/BC$

trī′grăm *n.* Inscription of 3 letters; figure of 3 lines or elements.

trī′graph (-ahf) *n.* Combination of 3 letters representing one sound.

trīhē′dron *n.* Figure formed by 3 surfaces meeting in point. **trīhē′dral** *adj.* & *n.*

trijugate (trī′jo͝o- *or* trijo͞o′-) *adj.* (bot.) With 3 pairs of pinnate leaves.

trīlăt′eral *adj.* & *n.* (Figure) having 3 sides; triangle, triangular.

Trĭl′by. Novel (1894) by George du Maurier describing life in Latin quarter of Paris in mid-19th c.; the heroine, Trilby O'Ferrall, is an artist's model; ~ (*hat*), soft felt hat with narrow brim and indented crown.

trīlĭn′ėar *adj.* (math.) Of, contained by, having some relation to, 3 lines.

trīlĭng′ual (-nggw-) *adj.* Speaking, using, expressed in, 3 languages.

trīlĭt′eral *adj.* Consisting of 3 letters, esp. (Semitic philol.) consisting of 3 consonants.

trĭl′ĭth, trĭl′ĭthon *ns.* Prehistoric structure of two upright stones with another resting on them as a lintel.

trĭll *n.* 1. (mus.) Rapid alternation of 2 notes a tone or semitone apart, shake. 2. (phonetics) Pronunciation of consonant, consonant pronounced, with vibration of tongue or other part of speech-organs. 3. Tremulous high-pitched sound or note(s), esp. in singing of birds. ~ *v.* Utter, sing, produce, with trill(s); make trill(s).

trĭll′ion (-yon) *n.* 1. (In Britain) 3rd power of a million, unit followed by 18 zeros. 2. (in France and U.S.) 4th power of a thousand, unit followed by 12 zeros.

trīlōb′ate (*or* trĭl′*o*-) *adj.* Having, consisting of, 3 lobes.

trīl′obīte *n.* Fossil crustacean with 3-lobed body found in lower palaeozoic rocks.

trĭl′ogy *n.* (Gk antiq.) Series of 3 tragedies performed at Athens at festival of Dionysus; any series or group of 3 related dramatic or other literary works.

trĭm *adj.* In good order; well arranged or equipped; neat, spruce. **trĭm′ly** *adv.* **trĭm′nėss** *n.* **trĭm** *v.* 1. Set in good order, make neat or tidy; remove irregular or superfluous or unsightly parts from; remove (such parts) by clipping, planing, etc. 2. Ornament (with ribbon, lace, etc.); dress (windows). 3. Adjust balance of (vessel, aircraft) by distribution of cargo, passengers, etc.; arrange (sails etc.) to suit wind; (fig.) hold middle course in politics or opinion, adjust oneself to prevailing opinion etc., be a time-server. ~ *n.* 1. (naut.) State of being trimmed and rigged ready for sailing, battle (*fighting* ~), etc.; state of ship, cargo, etc., in reference to fitness for sailing, esp. proper balance in water on fore-and-aft line; difference between draught forward and draught aft; (aeronautics) balance of aircraft in ref. to fore-and-aft horizontal plane. 2. State, degree, of adjustment, readiness, or fitness; good order. 3. Trimming, being trimmed; (U.S.) visible woodwork round openings of house etc.; (U.S.) window-dressing. 4. Trimming or cutting off; anything cut off or out, trimmings.

trĭm′ėter *adj.* & *n.* (Verse) of 3 measures (usu. 3 feet, but 6 feet in classical trochaics, iambics, and anapaestics, which have 2 feet per measure).

trĭmm′er (esp.) 1. One who trims between opposing parties in politics etc. or inclines to each of 2 opposite sides as interest dictates (orig. Lord Halifax or his followers, 1680–90). 2. One whose business is to stow coal or cargo in loading ship. 3. Short beam framed across an opening (as a stair-well or hearth) to carry the ends of those joists which cannot be extended across the opening (ill. FLOOR).

trĭmm′ing *n.* (esp.) Ornamental addition to dress, hat, etc.; (pl.) accessories, usual accompaniments; (pl.) pieces cut off in trimming something.

trīmôrph′ic, trīmôrph′ous *adjs.* (Of species etc.) having 3 distinct forms; (bot.) having 3 distinct forms of organs on individuals of same species; (cryst., of substance) crystallizing in 3 fundamentally distinct forms. **trī′môrph, trīmôrph′ĭsm** *ns.*

TRILOBITE

trīne *adj.* & *n.* Threefold, triple (group); (thing) made up of 3 parts; (astrol.) (aspect) of 2 heavenly bodies distant from each other by a third part of the zodiac (120°). **trīn′al, trīn′ary** *adjs.*

trĭng′le (-nggl) *n.* Curtain-rod, esp. for bed; (archit.) narrow straight, esp. square-sectioned, moulding.

Trĭn′idăd and Tobā′gō. W. Indian islands off coast of Venezuela; independent State and member of the British Commonwealth since 1962; capital, Port of Spain.

Trĭnitār′ian *adj.* & *n.* 1. (Member) of religious order of Holy Trinity, founded 1198 to redeem Christian captives from Mohammedans. 2. (Holder) of doctrine of Trinity of Godhead.

trīnī′trate *n.* (chem.) Compound formed from 3 molecules of nitric acid by the replacement of the 3 hydrogen atoms by a trivalent element or radical.

trīnītrotŏl′ūēne, -tŏl′ūŏl *ns.* Derivative of toluene with 3 nitro (NO_2) groups, high explosive used as shell filling and as ingredient of various explosives (abbrev. T.N.T.).

trĭn′ĭty *n.* Being 3; group of 3; *the T~*, 3 'persons' or modes of being of the Godhead as conceived in orthodox Christian belief; Father, Son, and Spirit as constituting one God; *T~ sittings*, session of English High Court of Justice beginning on Tuesday following Trinity Sunday; *T~ Sunday*, Sunday after Whit Sunday, observed as festival in honour of the Trinity; *T~ term*, former 4th session (22nd May–12th June) of English High Court of Justice; university term beginning after Easter.

Trĭn′ĭty College. 1. College of the University of Cambridge, founded 1546. 2. College of the University of Oxford, founded 1554. 3. The University of Dublin, founded 1591 (known as *Trinity College, Dublin*, abbrev. *T.C.D.*).

Trĭn′ĭty Hall. College of the University of Cambridge, founded 1350.

Trĭn′ĭty House (Corporation of). Guild or fraternity incorporated in reign of Henry VIII and having official regulation of British shipping, including erection and maintenance of lighthouses etc. and licensing of pilots.

trĭnk′ėt *n.* Small or trifling ornament or fancy article, esp. piece of jewellery.

trīnōm′ĭal *adj.* & *n.* (esp., math.) (Algebraical expression) consisting of 3 terms connected by + or −.

trī′o (-ēō) *n.* Group or set of 3, esp. (mus.) group of 3 performers; musical composition for 3 voices or instruments, or in 3 parts; middle division of minuet or scherzo (orig. in 3-part harmony), or of march.

trī′ōde *n.* Electronic amplifying valve with 3 main electrodes (anode, cathode, and grid) (ill. THERMIONIC)

trī′olėt (*or* trē-) *n.* Verse-form of 8 lines with 2 rhymes (*a b a a a b a b*), and with 1st line recurring as 4th and 7th, and 2nd as 8th.

trīŏx′īde *n.* (chem.) Compound of 3 atoms of oxygen with an element or radical.

trĭp *v.* 1. Walk, dance, skip, etc., with quick light tread, run lightly, move freely and quickly. 2. (freq. with *up*) Make false step, stumble; cause (person) to stumble by entangling or suddenly arresting his feet; make mistake, commit fault, inconsistency, or inaccuracy; detect in stumble, inconsistency, or inaccuracy. 3. Tilt, esp. (naut.) tilt or cant (yard or mast) in lowering it; (naut.) loose (anchor) from its bed and raise it clear of bottom; (mech.) release (catch, lever, etc.) by contact with projection, operate (mechanism) thus. ~ *n.* 1. Short voyage or journey, esp. each of series of such journeys over particular route; excursion for pleasure or health, esp. one at lower fare than usual. 2. Stumble; tripping or being tripped up. 3. Contrivance for tripping, projecting part of mechanism coming into contact with another part so as to cause or check movement; *~-hammer*, massive machine hammer operated by trip.

trīpar̃t′īte *adj.* Divided into, composed of, 3 parts or kinds; of, involving, such division; engaged in by, concluded between, 3 parties.

trīpe *n.* First or second stomach of ruminant, esp. ox, prepared as food; (pl., vulg.) entrails; (slang) worthless or trashy product or thing.

trīphĭb′ĭous *adj.* (Of military operations) on land, sea, and in the air.

trĭph′thŏng *n.* Combination of 3 vowel sounds in one syllable.

trī′plāne *n.* Aircraft with 3 superimposed main supporting surfaces.

trĭp′le *adj.* Threefold, 3 times as much or as many, of 3 parts; *T~ Alliance*, (1) alliance of England, Sweden, and Netherlands against France, 1668; (2) of France, Gt Britain, and Netherlands against Spain, 1717; (3) of Germany, Austria, and Italy against Russia and France, 1882–3; ~ *crown*, papal tiara; *T~ Entente*, friendly understanding based on treaty obligations between England, France, and Russia (*c* 1908–17); ~ *time*, (mus.) rhythm of 3 beats in the bar. ~ *v.* Increase threefold; be 3 times as great or as many as. **trĭp′ly** *adv.*

trĭp′lėt *n.* 1. Set of 3; esp. 3 successive lines of verse rhyming together; (mus.) group of 3 notes performed in the time of 2 of the same value; (microscope with) combination of 3 plano-convex lenses. 2. Each of 3 children born at a birth.

trĭp′lĕx *adj.* Triple, threefold; ~ *glass*, trade name of an unsplinterable glass used in motorcars, aircraft, etc., with a celluloid sheet cemented between 2 sheets of glass.

trĭp′lĭcate *adj.* Threefold, forming 3 exactly corresponding copies; ~ *ratio*, ratio of cubes of 3 quantities. ~ *n.* Each of set of 3 exactly corresponding copies or parts; *in* ~, in 3 exactly corresponding copies. **trĭp′lĭcāte** *v.t.* Triple, multiply by 3, make or provide in triplicate. **trĭplĭcā′tion** *n.*

trĭplĭ′cĭty *n.* State of being triple; trio, triplet; trinity; (astrol.) TRIGON.

trĭp′ŏd *n.* 3-legged support, table, seat, etc., esp. frame or stand with 3 diverging legs, usu. hinged at top, for supporting camera, theodolite, etc.; (Gk antiq.) altar at Delphi on which priestess sat to utter oracles; imitation of this as prize in Pythian Games etc.

trīpōl′ar *adj.* (biol.) Having 3 poles.

Trĭp′olĭ[1]. City and harbour of N. Africa, capital of Libya. **Trĭpŏl′ĭtan** *adj.*

trĭp′olĭ[2] *n.* Fine earth, freq. used as polishing powder, composed mainly of decomposed siliceous matter, esp. shells of diatoms. [f. TRIPOLI[1]]

Trĭpolĭtān′ia (Tripoli). Province of Libya; from 1911 until the war of 1939–45 an Italian colony; capital, Tripoli.

trĭp′ŏs *n.* (Cambridge Univ.) Final honours examination for Bachelor of Arts (orig. only in mathematics). [app. altered f. L *tripus*, after Gk *tripous* TRIPOD; orig. applied to 3-legged stool on which B.A. sat to dispute humorously with candidates for degrees]

trĭpp′er *n.* (esp.) Excursionist, one who goes on a pleasure trip.

trĭp′tȳch (-ĭk) *n.* Picture or carving, or set of 3, in 3 compartments side by side, with lateral panels usu. hinged so as to fold over central one, used esp. as altarpiece.

trīquĕt′ra *n.* (pl. *-ae*). Triangular ornament of 3 interlaced arcs or lobes.

TRIQUETRA

trīquĕt′rous *adj.* Triangular, having 3 salient edges or angles;

(bot., of stem) of triangular cross-section. **trīquĕt'rously** *adv.*

trīr'ēme *n.* Ancient-Greek or Roman warship with 3 banks of oars.

trīsĕct' *v.t.* Divide into 3, esp. (geom.) equal parts. **trīsĕc'tion** *n.*

Trismegistus: see HERMES Trismegistus.

trĭs'mus (-z-) *n.* (path.) Lockjaw.

Trĭs'tan da Cun'ha (dah kōōnya). Small volcanic island in S. Atlantic about half-way between Cape of Good Hope and S. America, in British possession.

Trĭs'tram, Trĭs'tan. Hero of medieval romance, lover of Iseult (Isolde) and hero of Wagner's opera 'Tristan and Isolde'.

trīsўll'able *n.* Word of 3 syllables. **trīsyllăb'ic** *adj.* **trīsyllăb'ically** *adv.*

trīte *adj.* Worn out by constant use or repetition, hackneyed, commonplace, stale. **trīte'ly** *adv.* **trīte'nėss** *n.*

trī'thēism *n.* Belief in 3 gods. esp. doctrine that 3 persons of Trinity are 3 distinct gods. **trī'thēist** *n.* **trīthēĭs'tic(al)** *adjs.*

trĭt'ium *n.* (chem.) An isotope of hydrogen (at. wt 3, symbol H^3 or T).

Trīt'on (Gk myth.). A merman, or one of several mermen, offspring of Poseidon and Amphitrite.

TRITON

trĭt'ūrāte *v.t.* Grind, rub, pound, etc., to powder or fine particles, pulverize. **trĭtūrā'tion** *n.*

trī'umph *n.* 1. (Rom. antiq.) Entrance of commander with army and spoils in solemn procession into Rome in celebration of victory. 2. Triumphing; victory, conquest, the glory of this; rejoicing in success, elation, exultation. ~ *v.i.* Celebrate a Roman triumph; be victorious, prevail; rejoice in victory, exult (*over*); rejoice, glory.

trīŭmph'al *adj.* Of, used in, celebrating, commemorating, a triumph or victory; ~ *arch*, arch erected, by Roman emperor or in modern times, in commemoration of victory etc.

trīŭm'phant *adj.* Victorious, successful; triumphing, exultant. **trīŭm'phantly** *adv.*

trīŭm'vir *n.* (pl. *-rs, -rī*). In ancient Rome, one of 3 public officers jointly charged with one department of administration; also, member of the 1st or the 2nd triumvirate (see below); hence, member of any group of 3 jointly exercising power. **trīŭm'virate** *n.* Office or function of triumvir; set of triumvirs; *1st* ~, coalition of Pompey, Julius Caesar, and Crassus (60 B.C.); *2nd* ~, administration of Mark Antony, Octavian (Augustus), and Lepidus (43 B.C.).

trī'ūne *adj.* 3 in one. **trīūn'ity** *n.*

trīvāl'ent (*or* trĭv'*a*-), (chem.) Having a VALENCY of 3, tervalent. **trīvāl'ence, trīvāl'ency** *ns.*

trĭv'ėt *n.* Stand for pot, kettle, etc., placed over fire, orig. and properly on 3 feet, now freq. with projection(s) by which it may be secured on top bar of grate; *right as a* ~, thoroughly or perfectly right.

trĭv'ial *adj.* Of small value or importance, trifling, slight, inconsiderable. **trĭv'ially** *adv.* **trĭv'ialnėss, trĭv'ialism, trĭviăl'ity** *ns.* [L *trivialis* commonplace f. *trivium* place where 3 ways meet (*via* way)]

trĭv'ium *n.* (In medieval schools) grammar, rhetoric, and logic, forming the lower division (the other being the QUADRIVIUM) of the 7 liberal arts. [see TRIVIAL]

trī-week'ly *adj.* & *adv.* (Occurring, appearing, etc.) every 3 weeks or 3 times a week.

trīzōm'al *adj.* (math.) Related to sum of 3 square roots.

trīzōn'al *adj.* Of or concerning the 3 zones of W. Germany occupied after the war of 1939–45 by Britain, France, and the U.S.A. **Trīzōn'ia** *n.*

Trō'ăd. Region of NW. Asia Minor of which ancient Troy was capital.

troat *n.* & *v.i.* (Make) cry of rutting buck. [imit.]

trōc'ar *n.* Surgical stylet with (usu.) triangular point enclosed in metal tube or cannula, for withdrawing fluid from cavity etc.

trōchā'ic (-k-) *adj.* Consisting of trochees, that is a trochee; ~*s* (*n.pl.*) trochaic verse.

trōch'al (-k-) *adj.* Wheel-shaped; ~ *disc*, (zool.) flattened end of rotifer (ill. ROTIFER).

trochăn'ter (-k-) *n.* (anat., zool.) Prominence or protuberance (usu., as in man, 2 in number) in upper part of thigh-bone, serving for attachment of certain muscles (ill. SKELETON); (entom.) second joint of insect's leg.

trōche (-k, -kī, -sh, -ch) *n.* Flat, usu. round, medicated tablet or lozenge.

trōch'ee (-k-) *n.* (pros.) Metrical foot (— ◡) of 2 syllables, the 1st long or accented and the 2nd short or unaccented. [Gk *trokhaios* (*pous*) running (foot) (*trekhō*, run)]

trŏch'ĭlus (-k-) *n.* 1. Small Egyptian bird said by ancients to pick teeth of crocodile; small bird, esp. humming-bird; genus of long-tailed American humming-birds. 2. (archit.) Concave moulding, scotia.

trŏch'lėa (-k-) *n.* (pl. *-ae*). (anat.) Pulley-like structure or arrangement of parts, as surface of inner condyle of humerus at elbow-joint, with which ulna articulates, fibrous ring through which superior oblique muscle of eye passes etc. **trŏch'lėar** *adj.* Of, connected with, a trochlea; ~ *muscle*, superior oblique muscle of eye; ~ *nerve*, each of 4th pair of cranial nerves, motor nerves for trochlear muscles.

trŏch'oid (-k-) *n.* (geom.) Curve traced by a point on a circle rolling on a straight line, or by a curve rolling upon another curve (ill. ROULETTE); (anat.) pivot-joint. ~ *adj.* (anat., of joint) In which one bone turns upon another with rotary motion. **trochoid'al** *adj.*

trochoid'ēs (-k-, -z) *n.* (anat.) Pivot-joint.

trŏdd'en *adj.* Past part. of TREAD; (of path) formed by treading, beaten.

trŏg'lodȳte *n.* Cave-dweller, cave-man; anthropoid ape. **trŏglodȳt'ic** *adj.*

troik'a *n.* (Russian vehicle drawn by) 3 horses abreast. [Russ.]

Trō'ĭlus. (Gk legend) A son of Priam and Hecuba, killed by Achilles; in medieval stories, forsaken lover of CRESSIDA.

Trōj'an *adj.* & *n.* (Inhabitant) of ancient TROY[1]; hence, person of great energy, endurance, or bravery; ~ *War*, (in Gk legend) siege of Troy by Greeks under Agamemnon, undertaken in order to recover his brother's wife, HELEN; it lasted 10 years and ended in the destruction of Troy after the stratagem of the ~ *horse*, a huge wooden figure of a horse concealing soldiers within it which the Greeks caused the Trojans to bring inside the city.

trōll[1] *n.* 1. Song sung in successive parts, catch. 2. Reel of fishing-rod; trolling-spoon. ~ *v.* 1. Sing out in carefree spirit. 2. Fish for, fish in (water), fish, with rod and line and dead bait or with spoon-bait (*trolling-spoon*) drawn along behind boat.

trōll[2] *n.* (Scand. myth.) One of race of supernatural beings formerly conceived as giants, now, in Denmark and Sweden, as dwarfs, inhabiting caves and subterranean dwellings.

trŏll'ey *n.* 1. Kind of truck that can be tilted; costermonger's cart pushed by hand or drawn by donkey; low truck worked by hand-lever along the rails for conveying railwaymen to work; (also ~*-table*) small table usu. on castors for use in serving food etc. 2. In tramcar etc., wheel running along overhead electric wire (~-*wire*), mounted usu. on a pole (~-*pole*) down which current is conveyed to vehicle; ~-*bus*, bus with motive power derived from trolley; ~-*car*, (U.S.) electric car running on tracks and driven by means of trolley.

trŏll'ey lace *n.* English bobbin lace with pattern outlined with thick thread.

trŏll'op *n.* Slatternly woman, slut.

Trŏll'ope, Anthony (1815–82). English novelist; author of 'BARCHESTER Towers', 'Doctor Thorne', 'The Last Chronicle of Barset', 'Phineas Finn', 'The Prime Minister', etc.

trŏm'ba *n.* (mus.) Trumpet; organ-stop like tuba.

trŏmbōne' (*or* trŏm'-) *n.* Large brass wind-instrument, usu. of tenor or bass range, having a tube which is adjusted in length for different notes (ill. BRASS); organ reed-stop of similar tone. **trŏmbōn'ist** *n.*

trōōp *n.* Body of soldiers; (pl.) armed forces; (mil.) subdivision of cavalry regiment commanded by a captain, artillery unit consisting in field artillery of 4 guns, formation of armoured vehicles of varying size; number of persons or things collected together, company, band, herd, swarm; company of not less than 3 patrols of Boy Scouts; ~-*carrier*, aircraft for transporting troops; ~-*ship*, -*train*, vessel, train, for conveyance of troops. ~ *v.* Flock, assemble, move along in or as a troop; come or go in great numbers; ~ *the colours*, (mil.) perform that part of ceremonial of mounting the guard in which the colours are received.

trōōp'er *n.* Cavalryman, horse-soldier; troop-ship; (Austral. and U.S.) mounted policeman.

trōpacocaine' *n.* (pharm.) A local anaesthetic (*benzoyl-pseudo-tropeine*).

trŏpae'olum *n.* (Plant of) genus (*T*~) of S. Amer. trailing or climbing herbs with roundish leaves and irregular spurred flowers, usu. deep orange or yellow, commonly called nasturtium. [Gk *tropaion* trophy, from resemblance of leaf to shield and of flower to helmet]

trōpe *n.* Figurative (e.g. metaphorical, ironical) use of a word; (eccles.) phrase or verse introduced as embellishment into some part of the Mass.

trŏph'ĭc *adj.* (biol.) Of nutrition; ~ *nerves*, nerves concerned with or regulating nutrition of tissues.

trŏph'oblast (-ahst) *n.* Layer of cells enclosing embryo, serving to nourish it and (in mammals) to attach it to the wall of the uterus (ill. EMBRYO). **trŏphoblăs'tĭc** *adj.*

trŏphoneurō̆s'ĭs *n.* Functional disorder due to derangement of trophic action of nerves.

trōph'y *n.* (Gk and Rom. antiq.) Arms or other spoils taken from enemy set up as memorial of victory, painted or carved figure

TROPHY

of such memorial; any (representation of) ornamental or symbolic group of objects; anything taken in war, hunting, etc., esp. if displayed as memorial; any token or evidence of victory, power, skill, etc., prize, memento.

trŏp'ĭc *n.* Each of 2 circles of celestial sphere (northern ~ *of Cancer*, and southern ~ *of Capricorn*) parallel to equator and 23° 28′ north and south of it, where sun reaches its greatest declination north or south; each of 2 corresponding parallels of latitude on earth's surface; (pl.) torrid zone, region lying between these parallels. ~ *adj.* Tropical; ~ *bird*, sea-bird of the chiefly tropical genus *Phaethon*, resembling terns, with webbed feet, rapid flight, and usu. white plumage marked with black.

trŏp'ĭcal[1] *adj.* Of, occurring in, inhabiting, peculiar to, suggestive of, the tropics; (fig.) very hot, ardent, or luxuriant; ~ *year*: see YEAR, sense 1. **trŏp'ĭcally** *adv.*

trŏp'ĭcal[2] *adj.* Metaphorical, figurative. **trŏp'ĭcally** *adv.*

trŏp'ĭsm *n.* (biol.) Turning of organism or part of one in particular direction in response to external stimulus or automatically.

tropŏl'ogy *n.* Figurative speech or writing; figurative interpretation, esp. of Scriptures. **trŏpolŏ'gĭcal** *adj.* **trŏpolŏ'gĭcally** *adv.*

trŏp'opause (-z) *n.* The boundary between the troposphere and the stratosphere (ill. ATMOSPHERE).

trŏp'osphēre *n.* Layer of atmospheric air extending from surface of earth to STRATOSPHERE, within which temperature falls with height (ill. ATMOSPHERE).

trŏpp'ō *adv.* (mus.) Too much.

Trŏss'achs (-χs). Picturesque narrow wooded glen in SE. Perthshire, Scotland.

trŏt *n.* Quadruped's gait between walk and gallop in which legs move in diagonal pairs almost together; similar gait between walking and running of man etc.; *on the* ~, on the go, continually moving. ~ *v.* (Make) go at a trot; cover (distance) by trotting; bring to specified condition by trotting; ~ *out*, lead out and show off paces of (horse); (fig.) exhibit, show off; *trotting-race*, race at trotting pace between horses drawing light vehicle (*sulky*).

trōth *n.* (archaic) Truth; faith, plighted word; *plight one's* ~, pledge one's faith, make solemn promise, esp. of marriage.

Trŏt'sky, Leon. Lev Davidovich Bronstein (1877–1940), Russian revolutionary leader; Soviet foreign commissar and minister of war and marine, 1918, organizer of Red Army, ordered to leave Russia 1929; advocate of world proletarian revolution and consistent opponent of Stalin; murdered in Mexico. **Trŏt'skyĭsm** *n.* **Trŏt'skyĭst** *adj.* & *n.*

trŏtt'er *n.* (esp.) Horse specially bred and trained for trotting; animal's foot, esp. used for food; (pl., joc.) human feet.

trou'badour (-ōō-, -oor) *n.* One of a class of 11th–13th-c. lyric poets living in S. France, E. Spain, and N. Italy and singing in Provençal, chiefly of chivalry and gallantry. [Fr., f. Provençal *trobador*, f. *trobar* find, invent, compose in verse]

troub'le (trŭb-) *n.* Affliction, grief, vexation, bother, inconvenience; pains, exertion; thing or person that gives trouble; *get into, be in,* ~ incur censure, punishment, etc.; (euphem., of unmarried woman) become, be, pregnant. ~ *v.* Disturb, agitate; distress, grieve; be disturbed or worried; subject, be subjected, to inconvenience or exertion.

troub'lesome (trŭbls-) *adj.* Causing trouble, vexatious; **troub'lesomely** *adv.* **troub'lesomenĕss** *n.*

troub'lous (trŭb-) *adj.* (archaic) Full of troubles, agitated, disturbed.

trough (-ŏf, -ŭf) *n.* Long narrow open box-like wooden or other receptacle for holding water or food for animals, kneading dough, washing ore, etc.; wooden or other channel for conveying liquid; hollow or valley resembling trough; (meteor.) elongated region of lower barometric pressure between 2 of higher; ~ *of the sea*, hollow between 2 waves.

trounce *v.t.* Beat severely, castigate; defeat heavily; scold, abuse.

troupe (-ōōp) *n.* Company, troop, esp. of actors, acrobats, etc.

troup'er *n.* (esp.) Actor.

trous'er (-z-) *n.* (pl.) Loose-fitting two-legged outer garment extending (usu.) from waist to ankles; ~-*clips*, clips used by cyclists to confine trouser-legs at ankles; ~-*press*, contrivance for pressing legs of trousers so as to produce lengthwise crease. **trous′ering** *n.* (shop-word) Material suitable for trousers.

trousseau (troo͞′sō) *n.* Bride's outfit of clothes etc.

trout *n.* Various small usu. speckled freshwater fish of genus *Salmo*, inhabiting rivers and lakes of temperate or colder parts of N. hemisphere, fished for sport and esteemed as food.

tro(u)vere (troo͞vār′) *n.* One of a school of chiefly epic or narrative poets which originated in N. France in the 11th c. [Fr., f. OF *trover* find, invent (cf. TROUBADOUR)]

trōve: see TREASURE-trove.

trōv′er *n.* (law) Finding and keeping of personal property; (*action of*) ~, common-law action to recover value of personal property illegally converted by another to his own use.

trow (-ō, -ow) *v.t.* (archaic) Think, believe.

trow′el *n.* Flat-bladed tool with short handle used for spreading mortar etc.; gardener's short-handled tool with hollow scoop-like blade. ~ *v.t.* Spread, smooth, lay on, etc., (as) with trowel.

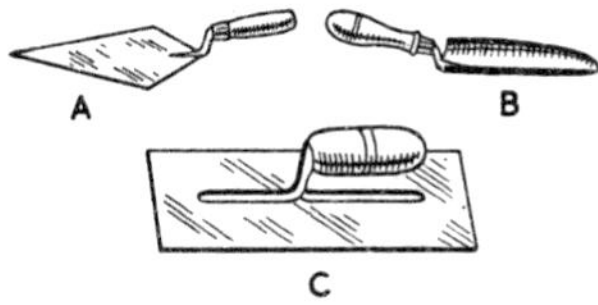

A. MASON'S TROWEL. B. GARDENER'S TROWEL. C. PLASTERER'S TROWEL OR FLOAT

Troy[1]. Ancient city on River Scamander in NW. Asia Minor, besieged by the Greeks in the TROJAN War; believed to be a figment of Greek legend until its remains were excavated (1873–81) by Heinrich Schliemann at Hissarlik.

troy[2] *n.* (also ~ *weight*) System of weights (1 lb. = 12 ounces = 240 pennyweights = 5760 grains) used for precious metals etc. [prob. f. city of *Troyes* in France]

trs. *abbrev.* Transpose.

tru′ant (-oo͞-) *n.* One who absents himself from duty or business, esp. child who stays away from school without leave; *play* ~, act thus. ~ *adj.* That plays truant or is a truant; shirking, idle, loitering, wandering. **tru′ancy** *n.*

truce (-oo͞-) *n.* (Agreement for) temporary cessation of hostilities; respite or intermission from something disagreeable or painful; ~ *of God*, (hist.) suspension of hostilities or private feuds ordered by Church during certain days and seasons in Middle Ages. **truce′lėss** *adj.*

trŭck[1] *n.* 1. Barter; (system of) payment of wages otherwise than in money; (fig.) dealings, intercourse. 2. Small miscellaneous articles, sundries; odds and ends, trash, rubbish; (U.S.) market-garden produce. ~ *v.* Exchange, trade, barter; bargain, trade (*in*); pay or deal with on truck system.

trŭck[2] *n.* 1. Strong usu. 4- or 6-wheeled vehicle for heavy goods, lorry; open railway-wagon; barrow for moving luggage on railway-platform etc.; hand-cart; set of wheels in framework for supporting whole or part of railway-carriage etc. 2. (naut.) Wooden disc at top of mast with holes for halyards. 3. (rare) Small wheel without tyres. ~ *v.t.* Carry, convey, on truck. **trŭck′age** *n.* (Cost of) conveyance by truck(s); supply of trucks.

trŭck′le *n.* (usu. ~-*bed*) Low bed on wheels that may be pushed under another, esp. as formerly used by servants. ~ *v.i.* Submit obsequiously, cringe (*to*). [*n.* f. L *trochlea* pulley f. Gk *trokhilia*; *v.* orig. in sense 'sleep in truckle-bed']

trŭc′ūlent (*or* troo͞-) *adj.* Showing ferocity or cruelty; aggressive, savage, harsh. **trŭc′ūlently** *adv.* **trŭc′ūlence, trŭc′ūlency** *ns.*

trŭdge *v.* Walk laboriously, wearily, or without spirit, but steadily; perform (distance) thus. ~ *n.* Trudging; laborious or wearisome walk.

trŭdg′en *n.* ~ (*stroke*), fast breast-stroke in swimming with double over-arm movement and vigorous leg-kicks. [f. proper name *Trudgen*]

true (-oo͞) *adj.* 1. Consistent with fact or reality, not false or erroneous; *come* ~, be verified in experience, be fulfilled. 2. Agreeing with reason, correct principles, or recognized standard; real, genuine, correct, proper; not spurious, counterfeit, hybrid, or merely apparent; (of voice etc.) in good tune; conformable to the type; accurately placed, fitted, or shaped; (of ground etc.) level, smooth; ~ *bill*, bill of indictment found by Grand Jury sufficiently well-supported to justify hearing of case. 3. Steadfast in adherence (*to*), constant, loyal, faithful, sincere. 4. ~-*blue*, (fig.) (person) of uncompromising loyalty or orthodoxy; ~-*born*, of genuine birth, truly such by birth; ~-*bred*, of true or pure breed, thoroughbred; ~-*love knot*, ~ *lover's knot*, (figure of) kind of knot symbolizing true love, usu. double-looped bow or knot formed of two loops intertwined. ~ *adv.* Truly. ~ *v.t.* Make (piece of mechanism etc.) true, adjust or shape accurately, make perfectly straight, smooth, level, etc.

trŭff′le (*or* troo͞-) *n.* Various edible central- and southern-European fungi of genus *Tuber*, esp. the French *T. melanospora*, usu. shaped like petals, with black warty exterior and rich flavour, esteemed as delicacy.

trŭg *n.* Shallow garden-basket made of wood strips, with handle from side to side.

tru′ism (-oo͞-) *n.* Self-evident truth, esp. of slight importance; hackneyed truth, platitude.

trŭll *n.* (archaic) Prostitute, strumpet.

tru′ly (-oo͞-) *adv.* Sincerely, genuinely; faithfully, loyally; accurately, truthfully.

Trum′an (troo͞-), Harry S. (1884–). 33rd president of U.S., 1945–52.

trumeau (troo͞mō′) *n.* (archit.; pl. -*x*). Piece of wall, pillar, between two openings, e.g. pillar dividing large doorway (ill. DOOR).

trŭmp[1] *n.* (archaic and poet.) (Sound of) trumpet.

trŭmp[2] *n.* Playing-card of suit ranking temporarily above other three; (colloq.) person of surpassing excellence, first-rate fellow, 'brick'; *turn up* ~*s*, (colloq.) turn out well or successfully; ~-*card*, card turned up to determine which suit shall be trumps; (fig.) valuable resource, important means of doing something, gaining one's point, etc. ~ *v.* Put trump on, take (trick, card) with trump; play trump, take trick with trump; ~ *up*, (colloq.) fabricate, invent.

trŭmp′ery *n.* Worthless stuff, trash, rubbish. ~ *adj.* Showy but worthless, delusive, shallow. [Fr. *tromper* deceive]

trŭmp′ėt *n.* Musical wind-instrument of bright ringing tone, consisting of narrow cylindrical, usu. metal, straight or curved tube with bell and cup-shaped mouth-piece and now usu. with valves (ill. BRASS); organ reed-stop with powerful trumpet-like tone; something shaped like trumpet, esp. ear-trumpet, speaking-trumpet, tubular corona of daffodil; sound (as) of trumpet, esp. elephant's loud cry; ~-*creeper*, N. Amer. creeper (*Campsis radicans*) with large scarlet trumpet-shaped flowers; ~-*flower*, various plants with trumpet-shaped flowers; ~-*lily*, white arum lily; various species of *Lilium*, esp. the Japanese *L. longiflorum*; ~-*major*, chief trumpeter of band or regiment; ~-*shell*, large marine univalve shell of *Triton* and allied genera; ~-*vine*, trumpet-creeper. ~ *v.* Proclaim (as) by sound of trumpet; celebrate, extol loudly; (of elephant) make loud sound as of trumpet.

trŭmp′ėter *n.* One who plays on or sounds trumpet, esp. cavalry-soldier giving signals with trumpet; various large S. Amer. birds of genus *Psophia*, allied to cranes, with loud trumpet-like note; various fishes making trumpeting noise when taken from water, esp. various Austral. and N. Zealand marine food-fishes of genus *Latris*; ~-*swan*, large N. Amer. wild swan, *Cygnus buccinator*, with loud sonorous note.

trŭnc′āte *adj.* Truncated. ~

v.t. Cut short, cut off top or end of. **trŭncāt'ed** *adj.* (esp.) (Of cone or pyramid) with vortex cut off by plane section, esp. parallel to base; (of edge or solid angle) cut off by plane face, esp. one equally inclined to adjacent faces; (of crystal, solid figure, etc.) having such angles; (biol.) looking as if tip or end were cut off. **trŭncā'tion** *n.*

trŭn'cheon (-shon) *n.* Short thick staff or club, esp. that carried by policeman. ~ *v.t.* Strike or beat with truncheon.

trŭnd'le *n.* 1. Small wheel; lantern-wheel, device of two discs connected by cylinder of parallel staves which engage with teeth of cog-wheel; roller with two arms for transmitting motion from stop knop of organ. 2. Trundling. ~ *v.* (Cause to) roll; draw, be drawn, along on wheel(s) or in wheeled vehicle.

trŭnk *n.* 1. Main stem of tree as dist. from roots and branches; shaft of column; human or animal body without head and limbs; main body or line of nerve, artery, etc., or of river, railway, telegraph, telephone, road, or canal system, as dist. from branches. 2. Box or chest with hinged lid for carrying clothes etc. while travelling; perforated floating box for keeping live fish; box-like passage, usu. of boards, used as shaft, conduit, shute, etc. 3. Elongated proboscis of elephant. 4. (pl.) Short full breeches worn with hose or tights, trunk-hose; short close-fitting breeches worn by swimmers, boxers, etc. 5. ~*-call*, telephone call to more or less distant exchange, involving use of trunk lines; ~*-fish*, fish of *Ostracion* and related genera, with body of angular cross-section and covered with bony hexagonal plates; ~*-hose*, full, freq. padded, breeches reaching about half-way down thigh, worn in 16th and early 17th centuries (ill. DOUBLET); ~ *line*, main line of railway, telephone system, etc.; ~ *road*, important main road. **trŭnk'ful** *n.* **trŭnk'lėss** *adj.*

trŭnn'ion (-nyon) *n.* Supporting cylindrical projection on each side of cannon or mortar (ill. CANNON); hollow gudgeon supporting cylinder in steam-engine and giving passage to steam.

Truron. *abbrev.* (Bishop) of Truro (replacing surname in his signature).

trŭss *n.* 1. Bundle of hay or straw (in England 60 lb. of new or 56 lb. of old hay, or 36 lb. of straw); compact cluster of flowers growing on one stalk. 2. Supporting structure or framework of bridge, roof, etc. (ill. ROOF); large corbel, projecting from face of wall and freq. supporting cornice etc.; (naut.) tackle for securing yard to mast, iron ring round mast with pivoted attachment to yard at centre. 3. Surgical appliance, now usu. pad with belt or spring, for support in cases of hernia etc. ~ *v.t.* 1. Tie (*up*), pack, in a bundle or parcel; tie, fasten (*up*) closely or securely; fasten limbs of (fowl etc. for cooking) to body with skewers etc.; (hist.) fasten (*up*) points or laces of (hose), tie up (points), tie up arms of (person). 2. Support or secure with truss(es).

trŭst *n.* 1. Confidence in, reliance on, some quality of person or thing, or truth of statement; confident expectation, hope; confidence in future payment for goods etc. supplied, credit; object of trust. 2. Condition of being trusted; obligation of one in whom confidence is placed or authority vested; (law) confidence reposed in person in whom legal ownership of property is vested to hold or use for benefit of another, property so committed, body of trustees; thing, person, duty, entrusted to one or committed to one's care; *in* ~, entrusted to person or body of persons, held as trust; ~ *company*, company formed or authorized to act as trustee or handle trusts; *investment* ~, joint-stock company whose profits are drawn from investments distributed among a number of other companies and from the sale of these investments. 3. Organized combination of producing or trading firms to reduce or defeat competition, control production and distribution, etc., esp. such a combination with central governing body holding majority or whole of stock of combining firms. ~ *v.* Have faith or confidence (in); place trust in, rely or depend on; hope; believe (statement), rely on truthfulness, etc., of (person); commit care or safety of (thing) *to* or *with* person; place or allow to be *in* place or condition, or *to do* something, without fear of the consequences; entrust to care, disposal, etc., of; give (person) credit *for*.

trŭstee' *n.* Person to whom property is entrusted for benefit of another; one of number of persons appointed to manage affairs of an institution; (U.S.) one in whose hands debtor's property is attached in ~ *process*, judicial process by which goods, effects, and credits of debtor may be attached while in hands of third person; ~ *stock*, stock in which trust-funds are or may legally be invested.

trŭstee'shĭp *n.* Position of a trustee; status of area for whose government another State is instructed by the United Nations to be responsible (corresponding to MANDATE of the League of Nations).

trŭst'ful *adj.* Full of trust, confiding. **trŭst'fully** *adv.* **trŭst'fulnėss** *n.*

trŭst'worthy (-wêrdhĭ) *adj.* Worthy of trust, reliable.

trŭs'ty *adj.* (chiefly archaic) Trustworthy. **trŭs'tĭly** *adv.* **trŭs'tĭnėss** *n.* **trŭs'ty** *n.* (U.S.) Trustworthy convict granted special privileges.

truth (-ōōth) *n.* Quality, state, of being true; loyalty, honesty, accuracy, integrity, etc.; what is true, true statement or account, true belief or doctrine, reality, fact.

truth'ful (-ōōth-) *adj.* Habitually speaking truth, not deceitful; true. **truth'fully** *adv.* **truth'fulnėss** *n.*

trȳ *v.* 1. Examine and determine (cause, question) judicially, determine guilt or innocence of (accused person) by consideration of evidence; test (quality), test qualities of (person, thing), by experiment; test effect or operation of, experiment with; attempt to ascertain by experiment or effort; subject to severe test or strain, strain endurance or patience of; ~ *on*, test fit or style of (garment) by putting it on; ~ *out*, put to the test, test thoroughly. 2. Attempt to do, perform, or accomplish; essay; make an effort, endeavour, attempt; ~ *one's hand*, make attempt *at* for first time; ~ *it on*, begin some doubtful action etc. experimentally to see how much will be tolerated; attempt an imposition; ~ *for*, attempt to attain (object, position, etc.) or to reach (place). 3. Dress (board etc.) to perfectly flat surface with trying-plane. 4. ~ (*out*), extract (oil) from blubber or fat by heat, extract oil from (fat etc.) thus, render. 5. *trying-plane*, long heavy plane used for accurate squaring of timber (ill. PLANE); ~*-on*, act or instance of trying it on (see 2 above); (colloq.) attempt to deceive; ~*-out*, experimental run, test of efficiency etc.; *try'sail* (*or* trī'sl), small strongly-made fore-and-aft sail used as substitute for normal sail in stormy weather; *try'(ing)-square*, carpenter's instrument of two straight edges fixed at right angles, for laying off short perpendiculars (ill. SQUARE); ~*-works*, apparatus for rendering blubber. ~ *n.* 1. Act of trying, attempt. 2. (Rugby football) Right of attempting to kick a goal, obtained by touching down ball on or behind opponents' goal-line, points (3) scored for this if goal is not successfully kicked; (Amer. football) ~ (*for point*), attempt to score additional point after touch-down by scoring goal, crossing opponents' line again, or completing forward pass in opponents' end zone.

trȳp'anosōme *n.* Parasite (*Trypanosoma* or allied genera of flagellate protozoa) infesting blood etc. of man and other animals and often causing disease. [Gk *trupanon* borer, *soma* body]

trȳp'sĭn *n.* Enzyme present in pancreatic juice, converting proteins into peptones.

trȳp'tĭc *adj.* Of, produced by, trypsin.

trўp'tophāne *n.* Crystalline amino-acid formed in tryptic digestion, the presence of which in the food of animals is necessary for proper growth.

trўst *n.* (archaic) Appointed meeting, appointment. **trўst'ing-place** *n.* Appointed place for meeting.

tsar *n.* (hist.) Emperor, title assumed *c* 1482 by Ivan Basilovich, Grand Duke of Muscovy, and used by emperors of Russia until 1917. [Russ. *tsar'* f. L CAESAR]

tsar'ėvĭch *n.* Son of tsar (in English usage, but erroneously, the eldest son and heir).

tsarĕv'na *n.* Daughter of a tsar.

tsari'na (-ēn*a*), **tsarĭts'a** *ns.* Empress of Russia.

tsar'ism *n.* (Devotion to, advocacy of) autocratic rule of tsars. **tsar'ist** *adj.* & *n.* **tsarĭs'tĭc** *adj.*

tsĕt'sė *n.* (also ~*-fly*) Fly of genus *Glossina*, abundant in parts of central and southern Africa and carrying disease to men and animals, esp. *G. palpalis*, carrier of the trypanosome causing sleeping sickness. [native wd]

T.S.H. *abbrev.* Their Serene Highnesses.

T.T. *abbrev.* Teetotaller; Tourist Trophy; tuberculin-tested.

t.t.d. *abbrev.* Three times daily.

T.U. *abbrev.* Trade Union.

tuan (tōōahn') *n.* Sir, master (used by Malayans as a respectful term of address).

tŭb *n.* Open cylindrical or slightly concave wooden vessel, usu. of staves and hoops, with flat bottom; (colloq.) bath-tub, bath (of any shape); measure of capacity for butter or other commodities; (mining) box or bucket for conveying coal etc. to surface; slow clumsy ship; short broad boat, esp. stout roomy boat for rowing practice; ~*-dress, -frock*, dress of washing material; ~*-thumper*, ranting preacher or orator. ~ *v.* Bathe or wash in tub; plant, pack, in tub; (slang) coach, practise, in tub.

tūb'a *n.* (mus.) Brass wind-instrument, the bass of the horn family, usu. with wide conical bore and cup-shaped mouthpiece (ill. BRASS); esp. the euphonium (*tenor* ~), bombardon, and the lower-pitched saxhorns and sousaphone; player of this; sonorous high-pressure reed-stop in organ.

tŭbb'y *adj.* Tub-shaped; short and fat, round, corpulent.

tūbe *n.* 1. Long hollow cylinder esp. for conveying or holding liquids, pipe. 2. Main body of wind instrument. 3. Short cylinder of flexible metal with screw cap for holding semi-liquid substance, e.g. toothpaste, artists' paint. 4. Inner tube containing air in pneumatic tyre. 5. Hollow cylindrical organ in animal body, as *bronchial* ~. 6. Cylindrical tunnel in which some London electric railways run; such railway. 7. (U.S.) Thermionic valve. ~ *v.* Furnish with, enclose in, tube(s); *tubed*, (esp., of race-horse) having metal tube inserted in air-passage.

tūb'er *n.* 1. Short, thick, more or less rounded, root or stem of plant, freq. bearing 'eyes' or buds from which new plants may grow,

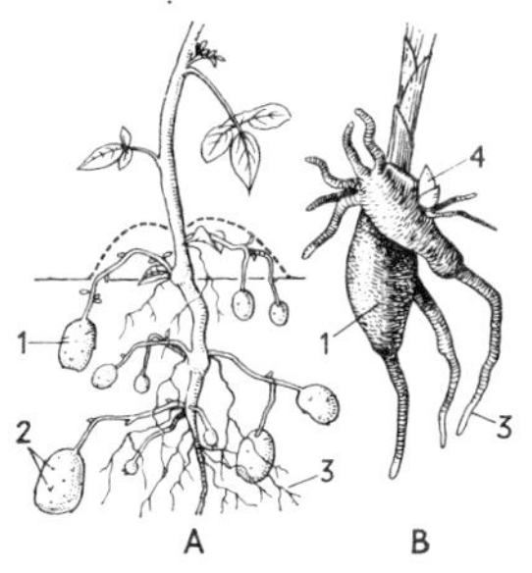

TUBERS

A. STEM TUBER (POTATO)
B. ROOT TUBER (ORCHID)

1. Tuber. 2. Eyes. 3. Roots. 4. Bud

as potato etc. 2. Genus of underground fungi, truffles. 3. (anat.) Rounded swelling or protuberant part.

tūb'ercle *n.* Small rounded projection or protuberance; esp. (path.) small rounded swelling on surface of body or in part or organ, esp. mass of granulation-cells characteristic of tuberculosis; tuberculosis; (bot.) small tuber, or root-growth resembling this, small wart-like excrescence; ~*-bacillus*, bacillus causing tuberculosis. **tūberc'ūlar** *adj.*

tūberc'ūlin *n.* Sterile liquid prepared from cultures of tubercle-bacillus and used for treatment and diagnosis of tuberculosis, esp. in children and cattle; ~ *test*, injection of tuberculin under skin, causing inflammation in tuberculous subjects; ~ *-tested*, (esp., of milk) from cows shown by tuberculin test to be free of tuberculosis.

tūbercūlōs'is *n.* Infectious disease in men and animals caused by tubercle-bacillus and characterized by formation of tubercles in bodily tissues, esp. lungs (*pulmonary* ~). **tūberc'ūlous** *adj.* (esp.) Affected with, of the nature of, tuberculosis.

tū'berōse (-s) *adj.* Tuberous. ~ *n.* (*pop.* tū'brōz). Tropical liliaceous plant (*Polianthes tuberosa*) with creamy-white funnel-shaped fragrant flowers and tuberous roots. **tūberŏs'ity** *n.* Tuberous formation or part; esp. (anat., zool.) large irregular projection of bone, usu. as attachment for muscle. [L *tuberosus* tuberous]

tūb'erous *adj.* Of the form or nature of a tuber; covered or affected with, bearing, tubers; ~ *root*, (esp.) root thickened so as to resemble tuber but bearing no buds. **tūb'erously** *adv.* **tū'berousnėss** *n.*

tūbĭc'olous *adj.* Living in a tube (of annelids and rotifers secreting tubular cases, spiders spinning tubular webs, etc.).

tūbĭlĭng'ual (-nggw-) *adj.* Having a tubular tongue, as honey-eaters.

tūb'ing *n.* (esp.) Tubes collectively; length or piece of tube; material for tubes.

tūb'ĭpōre *adj.* & *n.* (Member) of genus *Tubipora*, the 'organ-pipe' corals.

tūb'ūlar *adj.* Tube-shaped; cylindrical, hollow, and open at one or both ends; constructed with, consisting of, tubes. **tūb'ūlous** *adj.*

tūb'ūle *n.* Small tube, minute tubular structure in animal or plant.

T.U.C. *abbrev.* Trades Union Congress.

tŭck[1] *n.* 1. Flattened fold in garment etc., secured by stitching, for ornament or to shorten the article. 2. (naut.) Part of vessel where ends of bottom planks meet under stern. 3. (slang) Eatables, esp. sweets and pastry; ~*-in, -out*, hearty meal; ~*-shop*, (school slang) shop where tuck is sold. 4. Tucking in of ends or edges, anything so tucked in; ~*-in*, part to be tucked in; (*adj.*) (esp., of woman's blouse etc.) designed to be tucked into top of skirt etc. 5. ~ (*-net, -seine*), smaller net inside seine to gather and bring fish to surface. ~ *v.* 1. Put tuck(s) in, shorten or ornament with tuck(s); thrust or put (*away*) object into place where it is snugly held or concealed; thrust or turn (*in*) ends or edges of (anything pendent or loose, now esp. bed-coverings) so as to retain or confine them; be so disposed of; draw together into small compass. 2. ~ *in*, (slang) eat heartily.

tŭck[2] *n.* (archaic, chiefly Sc.) Blast, flourish (of trumpet); beat, tap (of drum).

tŭck'er[1] *n.* (esp.) Piece of lace, linen, etc., worn by women inside or round top of bodice in 17th–18th c. (now chiefly in *best bib and* ~).

tŭck'er[2] *v.t.* (U.S.) Tire (*out*), weary; *tuckered out*, exhausted, worn out.

tŭck'ėt *n.* (archaic) Flourish on trumpet.

Tūd'or. 1. (One) of the line of English sovereigns, from Henry VII to Elizabeth I, descended from Owen Tudor, who married Catherine, widowed queen of Henry V. 2. Of the architectural style (latest development of Perpendicular) prevailing in England during reigns of Tudors; of, resembling, imitating, the domestic architecture of this period, with much half-timbering, brickwork freq. in patterns, elaborate chimneys, many gables, rich oriel windows, much interior panelling and moulded plaster-work, etc.; ~ *arch*, flattened four-centred arch characteristic of the period; ~ *rose*, conventional 5-lobed decorative figure of rose, esp. combination of red and white roses of York and Lancaster adopted as badge by Henry VII. **Tūdorĕsque'** (-k) *adj.*

TUDOR ROSE

Tues. *abbrev.* Tuesday.

Tuesday (tūz'dā *or* -dĭ) *n.* 3rd day of week. [OE *Tīwesdæg* (rendering L *dies Martis*) f. *Tīw*, Germanic deity identified with MARS]

tūf'a *n.* (geol.) Porous deposit of calcium carbonate laid down round mineral springs. **tūfā'ceous** (-shus) *adj.*

tŭff *n.* (geol.) Rock formed from volcanic ashes. [Fr. *tuffe* TUFA]

tŭft *n.* Bunch, collection, of threads, grass, feathers, etc., held or growing together at the base; gold tassel on cap formerly worn by titled undergraduates at Oxford and Cambridge; ~*-hunter*, one who seeks society of titled persons, snob, sycophant. ~ *v.* Furnish with tuft(s); (upholstery) secure padding of (mattress, cushion, etc.) with thread drawn through tightly at regular intervals, producing depressions in surface usu. ornamented with tuft or button. **tŭft'ėd** *adj.* (esp., of birds) Having tuft of feathers on head, crested; (of plants etc.) growing in tuft(s), clustered, bearing flowers in tufts. **tŭft'y** *adj.*

tŭg *v.* Pull with great effort or violently; make vigorous pull *at*; tow (vessel) by means of tug-boat.

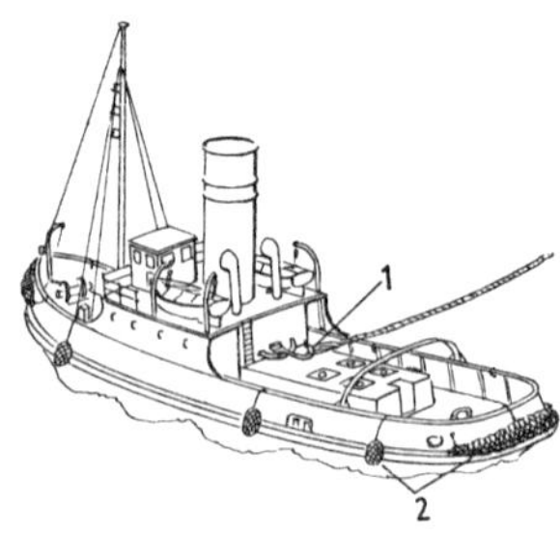

TUG-BOAT

1. Towing hook. 2. Rope fenders

~ *n.* 1. Tugging, violent pull; ~*-of-war*, decisive contest, struggle for supremacy; athletic contest between two teams hauling on rope, each team trying to pull other over line marked between them. 2. Trace, various other parts of harness; any chain, strap, or rope used for pulling. 3. ~ (*-boat*), small stoutly built steamer used to tow other vessels.

Tuileries (twēlerē). Royal palace on N. bank of Seine in Paris, begun 1564 by Catherine de Médicis and later joined by wings to Louvre; destroyed by fire 1871.

tūĭ'tion *n.* Teaching, instruction. **tūĭ'tional** (-sho-), **tūĭ'tionary** *adjs.*

tūl'ĭp *n.* (Flower of) bulbous spring-flowering plant of genus *Tulipa*, esp. any of the numerous cultivated varieties, with showy bell-shaped or cup-shaped flowers of various colours and markings; ~*-root*, disease of cereal and other plants caused by minute nematoid worm and marked by bulb-like swelling of lower stem; ~*-shell*, (large coloured shell of) various marine gastropods of family *Fasciolariadae*, esp. *Fasciolaria tulipa* of southern U.S.; ~*-tree*, large N. Amer. tree (*Liriodendron tulipifera*) with large greenish-yellow tulip-like flowers and soft white wood; various other trees with tulip-like flowers, as species of *Magnolia* etc.; ~*-wood*, light ornamental wood, used for cabinet-work etc., of tulip-tree; various coloured and striped woods, trees producing these. [Turk. *tul(i)-band* f. Pers. *dulband* turban]

tūlle (*or* tōōl) *n.* Thin soft fine silk net, used for dresses, veils, etc. [Fr., name of town]

Tŭll'y: see CICERO.

tŭl'wâr *n.* Curved sabre of N. India.

tŭm'ble *v.* 1. (Cause to) fall, esp. helplessly or violently; roll, toss, wallow; move in headlong or blundering fashion; overthrow, demolish; be overthrown, fall into ruin; handle roughly, disorder, rumple, disarrange by tossing; (fig.) stumble, blunder (*on, into*); ~ *to*, understand, grasp (esp. something hidden or not clearly expressed). 2. Perform leaps, somersaults, and other acrobatic feats; (of pigeon etc.) turn end over end in flight. 3. ~ (*home*), (of sides of ship) slope inwards above greatest breadth; ~*-bug*, (U.S.) dung-beetle, various scarabaeids rolling balls of dung in which they lay eggs; ~*-down*, falling or fallen into ruin, dilapidated, ruinous; ~*-home*, inward inclination of upper part of ship's sides; ~*-weed*, (U.S.) various plants which in late summer are broken off and blown along by wind in light globular rolling mass. ~ *n.* Fall; tumbled condition, confused or tangled heap.

tŭm'bler *n.* (esp.) 1. One who does somersaults, handsprings, etc., acrobat. 2. ~ (*-pigeon*) variety of domestic pigeon turning over and over backwards in flight. 3. Kind of tapering cylindrical or barrel-shaped drinking-cup or (now usu.) glass without handle or foot, orig. with rounded or pointed bottom so that it would not stand upright, now with flat usu. heavy bottom. 4. Pivoted plate through which mainspring acts on hammer of gun-lock; pivoted piece in lock which must be moved into proper position by key etc. before lock can be opened (ill. LOCK[2]); various mechanisms or parts, as projecting piece on revolving shaft for operating another piece, movable part of tumbling-gear, tumbling-box, revolving barrel for washing hides, etc. 5. ~*-bearing*, bearing falling out of position or knocked aside to make way for gear travelling on shaft which it supports; ~*-gear*, tumbling-gear; ~ *switch*, electric switch operated by pushing over small spring thumb-piece.

tŭm'blĭng *n.* & *adj.* ~ *barrel*, tumbling box; ~*-bay*, outfall from river, canal, or reservoir, pool into which this falls; ~*-bob*, weighted lever or arm in machinery falling when moved to certain point; ~*-box*, rotating drum in which small articles are cleaned and polished by attrition or small castings have cores broken out; ~ *gear*, gear with one or more idle wheels on swinging frame for producing reverse motion.

tŭm'brėl, -ĭl *n.* Cart with body tilting backwards to empty out load, esp. dung-cart (ill. CART); such cart or other conveyance used for carrying condemned persons to guillotine during French Revolution.

tūm'ėfȳ *v.* (Cause to) swell; make, become, tumid, turgid, or bombastic. **tūmėfăc'tion** *n.*

tūmĕs'cent (-sent) *adj.* Swelling up, becoming tumid. **tūmĕs'cence** *n.*

tūm'ĭd *adj.* Swollen, swelling, morbidly affected with swelling; inflated, turgid, bombastic. **tūm'ĭdly** *adv.* **tūmĭd'ĭty** *n.*

tŭm'(my) *n.* (Nursery or joc. form of) stomach.

tūm'our (-mer) *n.* Abnormal or morbid swelling, esp. (path.) permanent circumscribed morbid mass of new tissue without inflammation, or (*malignant* ~) non-circumscribed growth capable of giving rise to secondary ones, cancer. **tūm'orous** *adj.*

tūm'ŭlt *n.* Commotion of a multitude, esp. with confused cries and uproar, public disturbance, riot, insurrection; commotion, agitation, disorderly or noisy movement, confused and violent emotion. **tūmŭl'tūous** *adj.* **tūmŭl'tūously** *adv.* **tūmŭl'tūousnėss** *n.*

tūm'ūlus *n.* (pl. *-lī*). Ancient sepulchral mound, barrow.

tŭn *n.* Large cask or barrel for wine, beer, etc.; measure of capacity, usu. 2 pipes or 4 hogsheads.

tūn'a *n.* Tunny, esp. the game-fish *Thunnus thynnus*; *yellow-fin* ~, an albacore, *Neothunnus macropterus*.

tŭn'dra (*or* tōō-) *n.* Vast level treeless region of N. Russia, Siberia, and Alaska, with arctic climate and vegetation (chiefly mosses and lichens with dwarf shrubs etc.).

tūne *n.* Rhythmical succession of musical tones, air, melody (with or without harmony); being in proper pitch, correct intonation in singing or instrumental music; harmony or accordance in respect of vibrations other than those of sound; *in, out of*, ~, in or out of the proper pitch, in correct intonation; in or out of order or proper condition, (not) correctly adjusted; in or out of harmony (*with*); *to the* ~ *of*, to the (considerable or exorbitant) amount or sum of. ~ *v.* Adjust tones of (musical instrument) to standard of pitch, put in tune; attune, bring into accord or harmony; bring into proper or desirable condition; adjust (engine etc.) to run smoothly and efficiently, (wireless receiver) to desired wave-length etc.; ~ *in*, interpose in conversation etc.; adjust (wireless receiver) to receive transmission; ~ *out*, cut off (wireless signal etc.) by tuning receiver; ~ *up*, raise one's voice; bring (instrument) up to proper pitch, adjust instruments for playing together; bring (engine etc.) into most efficient working order by esp. fine adjustments. **tūn'able** *adj.* (archaic) Harmonious, melodious.

tūne'ful (-nf-) *adj.* Melodious, musical. **tūne'fully** *adv.* **tūne'fulnėss** *n.*

tūne'lėss *adj.* Untuneful, unmusical; not in tune; songless, silent. **tūne'lėssly** *adv.* **tūne'lėssnėss** *n.*

tūn'er *n.* (esp.) One whose occupation is to tune pianos or organs.

tŭng'sten *n.* Heavy steel-grey ductile metallic element, melting only at a very high temperature, occurring in combination in wolfram and other minerals, and used for electric-light filaments, electric contacts, sparking-plug points, hard steel alloys, etc.; symbol W (*wolfram*), at. no. 74, at. wt 183·85. **tŭng'stĭc** *adj.* [Swed. *tung* heavy, *sten* stone]

tūn'ĭc *n.* 1. Ancient Greek and Roman short-sleeved body garment reaching to about knees (ill. TOGA); in modern costume: (*a*) close-fitting short coat of police or military uniform; (*b*) garment worn by women, consisting of a bodice and upper skirt, belted or drawn in to the waist, worn over and displaying a longer skirt; belted frock worn by women and children at games. 2. (anat., zool.) Membranous sheath or lining of organ or part; (bot.) integument of seed etc.

tūn'ĭca *n.* (anat., zool.) Tunic.

tūn'ĭcate *n.* Member of *Urochorda* or *Tunicata*, a group of marine animals including sea-squirts etc. having body enclosed in a hard sheath and, at least in larval stage, a notochord; = ascidian. ~ *adj.* (zool.) Enclosed in a sheath; of the *Urochorda*; (bot.) consisting of a series of concentric layers, as a bulb.

tūn'ĭcle *n.* (eccles.) Short vestment like dalmatic worn at Eucharist by subdeacon over alb or by bishop between alb and dalmatic.

tūn'ing-fork *n.* Small 2-pronged steel instrument giving definite musical note of constant pitch when struck.

Tūn'ĭs. Capital city of **Tūnĭsia** (-z-), country of N. Africa, between Algeria on W. and Libya on SE.; former French protectorate, independent sovereign State since 1956. **Tūnĭs'ĭan** *adj.* & *n.* (Native) of Tunis or Tunisia.

tŭnn'el *n.* Subterranean passage under hill, river, roadway, etc., now esp. for railway; subterranean passage dug by burrowing animal; level or nearly level passage in mine etc.; tube, pipe, as that containing propeller-shaft in ship etc. ~ *v.* Make tunnel, make tunnel through.

tŭnn'y *n.* Large mackerel-like sea-fish of family *Thunnidae*, esteemed as food and as game-fish; esp. *Thunnus thynnus*, fished from ancient times in Mediterranean and Atlantic; tuna.

tŭp *n.* Male sheep, ram; various devices acting by impact, as striking-face of steam-hammer etc. ~ *v.t.* Copulate with (ewe).

tup'ėlō (tōō-) *n.* Various large N. Amer. trees of genus *Nyssa*, growing in swamps or on river banks in southern U.S.; wood of these.

tū quō'quė *n.* The retort *So are you* (or *So did you* etc.). [L, = 'you too']

tûrb'an *n.* Oriental men's head-dress of Moslem origin consisting of cap with long band or scarf of linen, cotton, or silk wound round it; woman's hat of scarf wound or twisted round; bright-coloured cotton cloth worn as head-dress by negro women in southern U.S. and West Indies; ~ *lily*, Siberian lily with deep-red spotted flowers. [Turk. *tulbant* f. Pers. *dulband*; cf. TULIP]

tûrb'ary *n.* Land where turf or peat may be dug for fuel; right to dig turf or peat on another's land.

tûrb'ĭd *adj.* Muddy, thick, not clear; (fig.) confused, disordered. **tûrb'ĭdly** *adv.* **tûrbĭd'ĭty, tûrb'ĭdnėss** *ns.*

tûrb'ĭnal *adj.* Turbinate. ~ *n.* Turbinate bone.

tûrb'ĭnate, -ātėd *adjs.* (Of shell) spiral with whorls decreasing rapidly in size; (bot.) inversely conical; *turbinate bone*, (anat.) one of scroll-like bones of the nose.

tûrb'ĭne *n.* Motor in which rotatory motion is produced by a fluid (water, steam, gas, etc.) impinging directly upon a series of vanes on the circumference of a revolving cylinder or disc, used to drive a ship, aircraft, generators for electric power, etc.

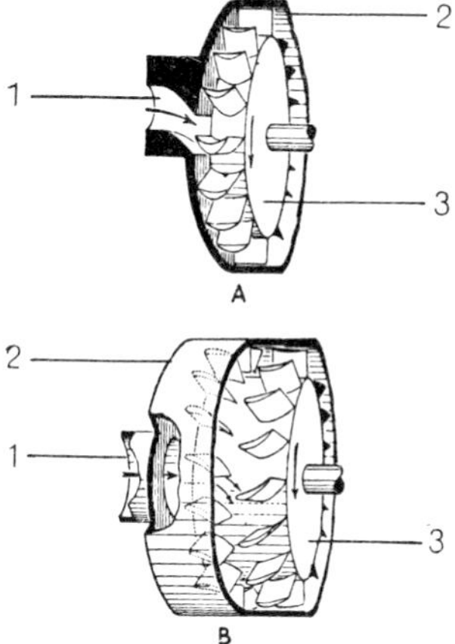

A. IMPULSE TURBINE. B. REACTION TURBINE.

1. Steam intake. 2. Stator. 3. Rotor

tûrb'ō- *prefix.* Turbine, in compounds forming the name of machines driven by a turbine, or which are themselves turbines, as ~*-dynamo, -generator*; ~*-jet*, power unit of a jet-propelled aircraft; jet produced by a gas-turbine.

tûrb'ot *n.* Large European flat fish (*Psetta maxima*) much esteemed as food; (loosely) various similar fish, as Californian diamond flounder.

tûrb'ūlent *adj.* Disturbed, in commotion, disorderly, troubled, stormy; tumultuous, unruly, violent. **tûrb'ūlently** *adv.* **tûrb'ūlence** *n.*

Turcoman: see TURKOMAN.

tûrd *n.* (not in polite use) (Lump or piece of) excrement.

tûrd'ĭne *adj.* Of the sub-family *Turdinae* of true thrushes.

tūrēēn' *n.* Deep covered dish from which soup is served.

Tūrĕnne', Henri de la Tour d'Auvergne, Vicomte de (1611–75. Marshal of France.

tûrf *n.* Covering of grass etc. with matted roots, forming surface of grass-land; sod; slab or block of peat dug for fuel; *the T*~, grassy course used for horse-racing; institution, action, or practice of horse-racing; ~ *accountant*, book-maker. ~ *v.t.* Cover (ground) with turf; (slang) throw (person or thing) *out*. **tûr'fy** *adj.*

Turgenev (toorgā'nyĕf), Ivan Sergeyevich (1818–83). Russian novelist; author of 'Fathers and Sons', 'Virgin Soil', etc.

tur'gid *adj.* Swollen, distended, puffed out; (fig., of language) pompous, bombastic. **tur'gidly** *adv.* **turgid'ity, turges'cence** *ns.* **turges'cent** *adj.*

turg'or *n.* (bot.) Rigidity due to uptake of water into living cells or tissues.

Turin'. (Ital. *Torino*) Capital city of province of same name, Piedmont, Italy.

tur'ion *n.* Scaly shoot produced from bud on underground stem.

TURION (ASPARAGUS)

Turk *n.* 1. Member of the Turkish race, specif. of the Osmanli or Ottoman branch. 2. Ferocious, wild, or unmanageable person; *~'s cap*, kind of lily (*Lilium martagon*); *~'s head*, long-handled broom with head of feathers, for dusting; knot resembling turban.

Turkestan', Turki- (-ahn). Region of Central Asia, divided between U.S.S.R. and China.

Turk'ey[1]**.** Country of Asia Minor and Europe, formerly part of the Ottoman Empire, declared a republic in 1923; *~ carpet*, one made of wool, with a thick pile and bold design in red, blue, and green; *~ red*, a scarlet pigment made from madder or synthetically; cotton cloth dyed with this; *~ rhubarb*, medicinal rhubarb.

turk'ey[2] *n.* Large gallinaceous bird of the Amer. genus *Meleagris*, with handsome plumage and naked wattled head, esp. *M. galloparo*, found domesticated in Mexico in 16th c. and highly esteemed as table fowl (in England associated esp. with Christmas festivities, in U.S. with those of Thanksgiving); *~-buzzard*, Amer. carrion vulture (*Carthartes aura*) with dark plumage and naked reddish head and neck; *~-cock*, male of turkey; *~-trot*, ragtime ballroom dance in vogue during war of 1914–18. [short for *turkey-cock, -hen*, orig. guinea-fowl, so-called f. being orig. imported through Turkey]

Turk'i (toor-) *adj.* & *n.* (Of, belonging to) a group of Ural-Altaic languages and races, including Turkish. **Tur'kic** *adj.*

Turk'ish *adj.* & *n.* (Language) of Turkey or the Turks, Turki; *~ bath*, hot-air or steam bath, inducing perspiration, after which body is washed, massaged, etc.; *~-delight*, sweet made of lumps of jelly flavoured with rosewater etc. and coated with icing-sugar; *~ towel*, rough towel with a long nap usu. of uncut loops.

Turk'men(istan)' (-ahn). Area between the Caspian Sea and Afghanistan, a constituent republic of the Soviet Union; capital, Ashkhabad. **Turk'men, Turkmen'ian** *adjs.* & *ns.*

Turk'oman, Turco-. Member of a group of tribes of E. Turkic stock, living in Turkestan, Afghanistan, Persia, and Russia; Ural-Altaic language of these tribes; *~ carpet, rug*, soft richly coloured carpet made by them. [Pers. *turkumān* Turk-like person]

Turku (toor'koo). (Swed. *Åbo*) Port of SW. Finland.

turm'eric *n.* East Indian herb (*Curcuma domestica*) of ginger family; pungent aromatic root-stock of this, used as condiment, esp. as chief ingredient in curry-powder, as yellow dye, and in *~-paper*, unsized paper tinged with turmeric solution and used as test for alkalis, which turn it from yellow to brown.

turm'oil *n.* Agitation, commotion, trouble.

turn *v.* 1. Move on or as on axis; give rotary motion to, receive such motion; execute (somersault etc.) with rotary motion; change from one side to another, invert, reverse; (fig.) revolve mentally. 2. Give new direction to, take new direction; adapt, be adapted. 3. Move to other side of, go round, flank; pass round (*flank* etc. of army) so as to attack from flank or rear; cause to go, send, put. 4. Change in nature, form, condition, etc.; esp. change for the worse; (cause to) become. 5. Shape (object, material) in lathe; (of material) lend itself to treatment in lathe; give (esp. elegant) form to. 6. *~ about*, turn so as to face in new direction; *~ against*, become hostile to; *~ down*, fold down; place upside down or face downwards; reduce flame of (gas, lamp, etc.) by turning tap etc.; (slang) reject (proposal, offer, etc.); *~ in*, fold inwards; incline inwards; (colloq.) go to bed; *~ off*, check flow of (water, electricity, etc.) by turning tap, switch, etc.; dismiss from employment; *~ on*, allow passage to (water, electricity, etc.) by turning tap etc.; depend upon; face hostilely, become hostile to; *~ out*, expel; (cause to) point or incline outwards; produce; clear (receptacle, room, etc.) of its contents, put (contents) out of room, pocket. etc.; extinguish (light) by turning tap, switch, etc.; (cause to) assemble for duty etc.; get out of bed; be found, prove to be so; *~ over*, reverse, invert; read (book) by turning over leaves; (cause to) fall over, upset; hand over, make over, transfer; do business to amount of; *~ round*, face about; change to opposite opinion, state of mind, etc.; (of ship) discharge cargo and be ready for new voyage: *~ to*, apply oneself to, set about; begin work; *~ up*, turn (playing-card) face upwards; disinter; appear; happen; look up, refer to; nauseate, cause to vomit. 7. *~-buckle*, coupling with internal screw-thread(s) for connecting metal rods, regulating their length, etc.; *~-button*, small pivoted bar engaging with catch, edge of door, etc.; *turn'coat*, one who changes his principles or party, renegade; *turn'cock*, person employed to turn on water from mains to supply-pipes etc.; *~-down*, turned-down part of anything; (*adj.*) made to wear with upper part turned down; *turn'key*, one in charge of keys of prison; *~-out*, (esp.) assemblage, muster; (style of) equipment, outfit, array; carriage with its horse(s) etc.; *~-over*, (esp.) article in last column of newspaper page and continued overleaf; kind of pie or tart in which filling is laid on one half of rolled-out pastry and other half is turned over it; amount of money turned over in business; *turn'pike*, (hist.) spiked barrier across road or passage, as defence against attack; (hist.) toll-gate; (hist. and U.S.) road with gates for collection of tolls; main road, highway; *~-round*, (of ship) process of entering port, discharging, reloading, and leaving port (also of motor transport); *turns'pit*, (hist., freq. contempt.) man or boy who turned spit upon which meat was cooked; short-legged breed of dog formerly used to turn a spit; *turn'stile*, post with four radiating arms revolving horizontally as person passes through, in gateway, door, etc., similar device with mechanism for registering number passing through; *turn'table*, revolving platform, table, stand, etc., esp. one for reversing railway or other wheeled vehicles; *~-up*, turned up part of anything, esp. of end of trouser-leg; turning up of card or die; (colloq.) commotion, tussle, fight. *~ n.* 1. Turning; rotation, esp. single revolution of wheel etc.; single) coil or twist. 2. (mus.) Ornament consisting of note above principal note, note itself, note below and note itself, performed instead of principal note or after it; *inverted ~*, similar figure begun on lower instead of higher note. 3. Change of direction or course, change of position by rotatory movement; curved or bent part of anything, bend, angle; turning back (esp. *~ of the tide*). 4. Change, alteration; change of colour, condition, etc.; (colloq.) momentary shock caused by sudden alarm etc.; *on the ~*, (of food etc.) turning sour. 5. Act of good or ill will, (*good, bad, ill*) service; attack of illness, faintness, etc.; *hand's ~*, stroke, piece of work. 6. Opportunity, occasion, privilege, obligation, etc., coming successively to each of several persons, etc.; public appearance on stage before or after others, (performer of) item in variety entertainment; *in* ~, in succession; ~ (*and* ~) *about*, in turn; *serve one's, its* ~, answer purpose or requirement. 7. Character, tendency, disposition, formation.

tûrn'er[1] *n.* (esp.) One who works with lathe. **tûrn'ery** *n.* Use of lathe; objects fashioned on lathe; turner's workshop.

Tûrn'er[2], Joseph Mallord William (1775–1851). English landscape-painter.

tûrn'ing *n.* (esp.) 1. Use of, art of using, lathe; (pl.) chips or shavings produced in process of turning. 2. Place where road, path, etc., turns or turns off from another; such road; ~*-point*, point at which decisive change takes place.

tûrn'ip *n.* Either of two biennial cruciferous plants (*Brassica rapa* and *B. napobrassica*) with fleshy globular or spheroidal root, toothed leaves, and yellow flowers; root of these, used as vegetable and for feeding cattle and sheep; (with defining word) various similar plants; (slang) large thick old-fashioned watch; ~*-tops*, young green shoots of turnips used as vegetable.

tûrp'entine *n.* Semifluid oleoresin (*Chian* ~) exuded by terebinth; (now usu.) yellowish viscous liquid oleo-resins, usu. solidifying on exposure, obtained from various coniferous trees (many varieties acc. to source, most having the same composition, $C_{10}H_{16}$); (*oil of* ~, pop. *turps*) colourless or yellowish volatile inflammable oil, of pungent smell and taste, distilled from turpentines and used in mixing paints and varnishes etc.; ~*-tree*, terebinth; any tree yielding turpentine.

Tûrp'in, Dick (1706–39). English highwayman.

tûrp'itūde *n.* Baseness, depravity, wickedness.

tûrps *n.* Colloq. abbrev. of TURPENTINE.

tûrq'uoise (-koiz, -kwoiz, -kwahz) *n.* Opaque or translucent sky-blue or blue-green hydrous aluminium phosphate found esp. in Persia and valued as gem; ~ (*-blue*), brilliant greenish-blue colour of turquoise. [OF (*pierre*) *turquoise* Turkish (stone)]

tŭ'rrėt *n.* Small or subordinate tower, esp. rounded addition to angle of building, freq. commencing at some height above ground; (mil., nav.) tower-like armoured usu. revolving structure in which guns are mounted in fort or tank or (usu.) warship (ill. BATTLEship); structure housing guns in aircraft; (mech.) rotating holder for various dies or cutting tools in lathe, drill, etc. ~ *v.t.* Furnish, equip, with turret(s) or turret-like structures; **tŭ'rrėted** *adj.*

tûr'tle[1] *n.* (now usu. ~*-dove*) Wild dove of species *Turtur*, esp. the common European *T. communis*, with cinnamon-brown plumage and white-tipped tail-feathers, noted for its soft cooing and affection for its mate.

tûr'tle[2] *n.* Reptile of any of the marine species of the order *Chelonia* (turtles and tortoises), resembling tortoise but with limbs compressed into flippers or paddles; flesh of certain turtles as food, much used for soup; *turn* ~, turn over, capsize; ~*-back, -deck*, arched structure over part of deck of vessel to protect it from heavy sea; ~*-neck*, high close-fitting neck of knitted garment.

Tŭs'can *adj.* & *n.* (Language, inhabitant) of Tuscany: ~ *order*, (archit.) simplest of the five classical orders (ill. ORDER); ~ *straw*, fine yellow wheat-straw used for hats etc. **Tŭs'cany.** Region of W. central Italy.

Tŭs'carora. Indian of tribe orig. of N. Carolina but since admission to Iroquois confederacy living mainly in New York.

tŭsh[1] *int.*, *n.*, & *v.i.* (archaic) (Make) exclamation of impatient contempt. **tŭsh'ery** *n.* Conventional style of romance characterized by frequent use of affected archaisms like 'tush!'.

tŭsh[2] *n.* Long pointed tooth, esp. horse's canine tooth; small or stunted tusk in some Indian elephants.

tŭsk *n.* Long pointed tooth projecting beyond mouth in certain animals, as elephant, wild boar, etc.; tusk-like thing, as long protruding tooth, kind of tenon, etc. ~ *v.t.* Dig (*up*), tear, wound, with tusk; furnish with tusks. **tŭsk'er** *n.* Elephant, wild boar, with developed tusks.

tŭss'ah, tŭss'er: see TUSSORE.

Tussaud's (tōōsōz'), **Madame.** Collection of wax models of eminent people (orig. victims of the French Revolution) exhibited by a Swiss, Madame Marie Tussaud, *née* Gresholtz (1760–1850) at various addresses in London from 1802 onwards; transferred 1885 to its present site in Marylebone, destroyed by fire 1925, and reopened 4 years later.

tŭss'le *n.* & *v.i.* Struggle, scuffle.

tŭss'ock *n.* Tuft, clump, small hillock, of grass, sedge, etc.; tuft of hair etc.; ~*-grass*, various grasses, esp. tall-growing stout grass (*Poa flabellata*) of Falkland Islands etc. introduced into Scotland as valuable fodder-grass; ~*-moth*, various moths with larva covered with long tufts of hair; ~*-sedge*, N. Amer. species of sedge (*Carex stricta*) growing in thick clumps. **tŭss'ocky** *adj.*

tŭss'ōre *n.* (Strong coarse brownish silk produced by) various undomesticated Asiatic silkworms, esp. *Antherae mylitta.* [Hindi *tasar* (Sansk. *tasara* shuttle)]

tŭt, tŭt-tŭt *int.*, *n.*, & *v.i.* (Make) exclamation of impatience, dissatisfaction, or rebuke.

Tutankha'mĕn (tōō-, -kah-) (14th c. B.C.). Egyptian king of XVIIIth dynasty who died at age of 18; successor and son-in-law of Akhnaton; his tomb at Karnak, containing remarkable treasures, was excavated in 1922.

tū'tėlage *n.* Guardianship, being under this; instruction, tuition.

tū'tėlary *adj.* Serving as protector, guardian, or patron, esp. of particular person, place, etc.; of a guardian, protective.

tū'tėnăg *n.* Zinc imported from China and E. Indies; white silver-like alloy of copper, nickel, and zinc, formerly used for domestic ware and fire-grates. (Marathi *tuttināg*]

tū'tor *n.* 1. Private teacher, esp. one having general charge of person's education; (in some British universities) graduate (usu. fellow of a college) directing studies of undergraduates assigned to him; (in some U.S. colleges) teacher ranking below instructor. 2. Instruction book in any subject. 3. (Rom. law) Guardian of a minor. ~ *v.* Act as tutor (to); exercise restraint over, subject to discipline. **tū'torage, tū'torship** *ns.* **tūtôr'ial** *adj.* & *n.* Period of individual instruction given to small group or single student. **tūtôr'ially** *adv.*

tutti (tōōt'ē) *n.* & mus. direction. (Passage rendered by) all performers together.

tutti-frutti (tōōt'ē-frōōt'ē) *n.* & *adj.* (Confection, esp. ice-cream) made of or flavoured with various fruits. [It., = 'all fruits']

tū'tū *n.* Dancer's short skirt made of layers of stiffened frills.

tu-whit' tu-whōō' (tōō-) Representation of owl's cry used as *int.*, *n.*, & *v.i.* (Make) cry of owl. [imit. of cry of tawny owl]

tŭxēd'ō (pl. *-s, -es*) *n.* (U.S.) Dinner-jacket. [name of fashionable country club at *Tuxedo* Park, N.Y.]

tuyère (twēyār', tōōyār', twēr) *n.* Nozzle through which blast is forced into furnace etc.

T.V. *abbrev.* Television; terminal velocity.

T.V.A. *abbrev.* Tennessee Valley Authority.

TWA *abbrev.* Trans-World Airways.

twadd'le (twŏ-) *n.* & *v.i.* (Indulge in) senseless, silly, or trifling talk or writing, nonsense.

twain[1] *adj.* & *n.* (archaic) Two.

Twain[2], Mark. Pseudonym of Samuel Langhorne Clemens (1835–1910), Amer. humorist, author of 'Tom Sawyer' (1876), 'Huckleberry Finn' (1884), 'A Connecticut Yankee at the Court of King Arthur' (1889), etc. [call of leadsmen taking soundings on Mississippi where Clemens served as a pilot; = 2nd mark on cable, i.e. 2 fathoms]

twăng *n.* Sharp ringing sound (as) of tense string of musical instrument or bow when plucked; nasal intonation; distinctive, esp. local, peculiarity of pronunciation. ~ *v.* (Cause to) make twanging sound; play on stringed instrument; utter, speak, with twang.

tweak *n.* Twitch, sharp pull, pinch. ~ *v.t.* Seize and pull sharply with twisting movement, pull at with jerk, twitch.

Tweed[1]. River of S. Scotland, flowing into North Sea at Berwick.

tweed[2] *n.* Twilled woollen (or woollen mixture) cloth of usu. rough surface, dyed, freq. in several colours, before weaving. **tweed'y** *adj.* [a trade-name originating in a misreading of *tweel*, Sc. form of TWILL, influenced by name of river TWEED]

tweedledŭm' and tweedledee'. Orig., the composers Handel and Bononcini (in a satire by John Byrom containing the lines 'Strange all this Difference should be Twixt Tweedle-dum and Tweedle-dee!'); hence, things differing only or chiefly in name. [imit.]

Tweedsmuir: see BUCHAN[2].

'tween *adv.* & *prep.* Between; *~-age*, the teens, adolescence; *~-decks*, (space) between decks.

tween'y *n.* (colloq.) Young servant girl who helps cook and housemaid (short for 'between-maid'); (U.S. colloq.) girl in her teens.

tweet(-tweet) *n.* & *v.i.* (Utter) note of small bird.

tweez'ers *n.pl.* Small pincer-like instrument for taking up small objects, plucking out hairs, etc. **tweez'er** *v.* Use tweezers.

twĕlfth *adj.* & *n.* (Thing) next in order after eleventh; (that is) one of 12 equal parts of anything; *the ~*, the 12th August, on which grouse-shooting legally begins; *T~-day*, *-night*, 12th day after Christmas, 6th Jan., feast of Epiphany, formerly last day of Christmas festivities and observed as time of merry-making. **twĕlfth'ly** *adv.*

twĕlve *adj.* & *n.* One more than eleven (12, xii, or XII); *twel'vemo*, *12mo*, duodecimo; *twelve'month*, year.

twĕn'tў *adj.* & *n.* Twice ten (20, xx, or XX); *~-five*, (Rugby footb., hockey, etc.) (space enclosed by) line drawn across ground 25 yards from each goal. **twĕn'tĭĕth** *adj.* & *n.* **twĕn'tўfōld** *adj.* & *adv.*

twẽrp *n.* (slang) Despicable fellow.

twice *adv.* Two times; on 2 occasions; doubly, in double degree or quantity.

twidd'le *n.* Slight twirl, quick twist; twirled mark or sign. ~ *v.* Trifle (with); twirl idly, play with idly or absently; ~ *one's fingers, thumbs*, keep turning them idly around each other (for lack of occupation). **twidd'ly** *adj.*

twĭg[1] *n.* Small shoot or branch of tree or plant; divining-rod; (anat.) small branch of artery etc.; *hop the ~*, (colloq.) die.

twĭg[2] *v.* (slang) Understand, catch meaning (of); perceive, observe.

twī'light (-līt) *n.* Light diffused by reflection of sun's rays between daybreak and sunrise or (usu.) sunset and dark; period of this; faint light; (fig.) condition of imperfect knowledge, understanding, etc.; ~ *of the gods*, (transl. Icel. *ragna rökkr*, orig. *ragna rök* judgement of the gods), in Scand. myth., destruction of the gods and the world in conflict with the giants; ~ *sleep*, partial narcosis for dulling pains of childbirth.

twī'lĭt *adj.* Dimly illuminated (as) by twilight.

twĭll *n.* (Textile fabric with) surface of parallel diagonal ribs produced by passing weft-threads over one and under two or more (not one as in plain weaving) warp-threads (ill. WEAVE). ~ *v.t.* Weave with twill (esp. in past part.). [Sc. & north. variant of obs. *twilly*, OE *twili*, f. OHG *zwîlîh*, after L *bilix* (*licium* thread)]

twĭn *adj.* Forming, being one of, a closely related pair, esp. of children born together; (bot.) growing in pairs; consisting of 2 closely connected and similar parts; *twin'flower*, (U.S.) either genus of *Linnaea* (*L. borealis* of northern Europe and Asia and *L. americana* of northern N. America), prostrate plants with fragrant flowers growing in pairs; *twin'screw*, (esp., of steamer) having 2 screw propellers on separate shafts and revolving in opposite directions. ~ *n.* One of 2 children or young carried simultaneously in uterus and born at short interval (FRATERNAL, IDENTICAL, *twins*: see these words); each of closely related pair; exact counterpart of person or thing; composite crystal consisting of 2 or more (usu. equal and similar) crystals in reversed position in respect to each other; *the Twins*, Castor and Pollux, a constellation and sign of the zodiac, Gemini. ~ *v.* Bear twins; join intimately together, couple, pair.

twīne *n.* Thread or string of 2 or more strands of hemp, cotton, etc., twisted together, used for sewing coarse materials, tying packages, making nets, etc.; twining or trailing stem, spray, etc.; coil, twist. ~ *v.* Twist (strands) together to form cord, make (thread) thus; form (garland etc.) by interlacing; wreathe, clasp, twist; coil, wind; (of plant) grow in twisting or spiral manner.

twĭnge (-nj) *n.* Sharp darting pain.

twĭnk'le *v.* Shine with rapidly intermittent light, sparkle, glitter; emit (light etc.) thus; wink, blink, quiver; move to and fro, in and out, etc., rapidly, flit, flicker; *in the twinkling of an eye, in a twinkling,* in an instant. ~ *n.* Wink, blink; twitch, quiver; intermittent or transient gleam.

twĩrl *v.* Revolve rapidly, spin, whirl; turn (one's *thumbs* etc.) round and round idly, twiddle; twist, coil, twine. ~ *n.* Whirling, twirling; anything that twirls, curved line, whorl of shell, etc.

twĭst *v.* Wind (strands etc.) one about another; form (rope etc.) thus; interweave; give spiral form to (rod, column, etc.) as by rotating ends in opposite directions; receive, grow in, spiral form; cause (ball, esp. in billiards) to rotate while following curved path; wrench out of natural shape, distort. **twĭs'ty** *adj.* **twĭst** *n.* 1. Thread, rope, etc., made by winding 2 or more strands etc. about one another; kinds of strong silk thread and of cotton yarn; roll of bread, tobacco, etc., in form of twist; paper packet with screwed-up ends. 2. Act of twisting, condition of being twisted; manner or degree in which thing is twisted; peculiar tendency of mind, character, etc.; twisting strain, torque; angle through which thing is twisted.

twĭs'ter *n.* (esp.) Liar, dishonest person, crook; twisting ball in cricket or billiards; girder.

twĭt *v.t.* Reproach, upbraid, taunt.

twĭtch[1] *v.* Pull with light jerk, pull at, jerk at, esp. to call attention; (of features, muscles, etc.) move or contract spasmodically. ~ *n.* 1. Sudden sharp pull or tug, jerk; sudden involuntary, usu. slight, contraction. 2. Noose tightened by stick, used to compress horse's lip or muzzle to keep him quiet during operation etc. **twĭtch'y** *adj.*

twĭtch[2] *n.* ~ (*grass*), COUCH[2]-grass.

twīte *n.* Kind of linnet (*Linota flavirostris*) of N. Britain and Scandinavia; mountain linnet.

twĭtt'er *v.* (Of bird) utter succession of light tremulous notes, chirp continuously (freq. fig., of person); utter, express, thus. ~ *n.* State of tremulous excitement; twittering, light tremulous chirping.

'twixt *prep.* Betwixt, between.

two (tōō) *adj.* & *n.* One more than one (2, ii, or II); *one or ~, ~ or three*, a few, a small number; *put ~ and ~ together*, draw inference from facts; *in ~ ~s*, (colloq.) in a very short time, immediately; *~-edged*, having 2 cutting edges; (fig.) cutting both ways, ambiguous; *~-faced*, having 2 faces; deceitful, insincere; *twofold*, double, doubly; *~-handed*, wielded with both hands; worked or wielded by hands of 2 persons; (of card-game etc.) for 2 persons; *~-line*, (printing) having depth of 2 lines of size of type specified; *twopence* (tŭp'ens), sum of 2 pence (2*d.*); *twopenny* (tŭp'enĭ), worth, costing, twopence; paltry, trumpery, trifling; *Twopenny Tube*, (hist.) Central London (underground) Railway, on which fare for any distance was orig. twopence; *twopenny-halfpenny* (tŭp'nihā'pnĭ), (usu., fig.) petty, cheap, worthless; *~-piece* (*suit*), coat and skirt or coat and dress meant to be worn together; *~-ply*, of 2 strands, layers, or thicknesses; *~-step*, ballroom dance with sliding steps in march or polka time; *~-stroke*, (internal combustion engine) in which power stroke occurs on each revolution of crank-shaft (ill. COMBUSTION); *T~ Thousand Guineas*, annual race for 3-year-olds run at Newmarket; *~-way*, (esp.) allowing passage of fluid in either of 2 directions; *~-way switch*, device by which electric current can be switched on or off at either of 2 points.

Tȳb'urn. Place of public execution for Middlesex (until 1783) near what is now Marble Arch, London; *~ tree*, the gallows. [orig. *Teobernan*, = 'boundary stream', name of former small tributary of Thames]

T.Y.C. *abbrev.* Thames Yacht Club.

Tȳchōn'ĭan, Tȳchŏn'ĭc (-k-) *adjs.* Of (astronomical system of) Tycho BRAHE.

tȳcōōn' *n.* Business magnate. [Jap. *taikun* great lord, title applied by foreigners to shogun of Japan 1854–68 (Chin. *ta* great, *kuin* prince)]

tȳke *n.* Dog, cur; low fellow; (*Yorkshire*) ~, Yorkshireman.

Tȳl'er[1], John (1790–1862). 10th president of U.S., 1841–5.

Tȳl'er[2], Wat (d. 1381). English rebel, led Peasants' Revolt 1381.

tȳm'pan *n.* 1. Appliance in printing-press interposed between platen etc. and sheet to be printed to equalize pressure, in hand-presses usu. double frame covered with sheets of parchment or strong linen, with packing of blanket, rubber, etc., between. 2. (archit.) TYMPANUM.

tȳmpăn'ĭc *adj.* Of the or a tympanum; resonant when struck; *~ bone*, in mammals, bone supporting tympanic membrane; *~ membrane*, thin membrane closing middle ear and serving to transmit vibrations from air to inner ear.

tȳmpanī'tēs (-z) *n.* Distension of abdomen caused by gas or air in intestine or peritoneal cavity. **tȳmpanĭt'ic** *adj.*

tȳm'panum *n.* 1. (anat.) Ear-drum, middle ear, cavity in temporal bone filled with air, closed externally by tympanic membrane and containing chain of small bones by which sound vibrations are conveyed to inner ear (ill. EAR); tympanic membrane; similar membrane in insects covering organ of hearing in leg etc.; (ornith.) bony labyrinth at base of trachea in some ducks with resonant membranes in walls. 2. (archit.) Vertical recessed face (usu. triangular) of pediment; space between lintel and arch of door etc., carving etc. on this (ill. DOOR).

Tȳn'dale (-*a*l), William (d. 1536). English reformer and martyr, translator of the Bible.

TYPE: A. PIECE OF TYPE. B. PARTS OF LETTERS. C. TYPE FACES, PRINTERS' FLOWERS, AND ORNAMENTAL RULES

A. 1. Stem or shank. 2. Body size. 3. Feet. 4. Face or printing surface. 5. Bevel. 6. Shoulder. 7. Set. 8. Nick. 9. Type-height. B. 10. Ascender. 11. x-height. 12. Beard. 13. Counter. 14. Serif. 15. Kern. 16. Descender. 17. Hair-line

Tȳne. River of NE. England, flowing into the North Sea near Newcastle.

Tȳn'wald (-wŏ-). In Isle of Man, assembly of governor, council acting as upper house, and House of Keys, to proclaim enacted laws to the people.

tȳpe *n.* 1. Person, thing, event, serving as illustration, symbol, or characteristic specimen, of another thing or of a class. 2. General form, character, etc., distinguishing particular class or group; kind, class, as distinguished by particular character. 3. (biol.) Species or genus regarded as most complete example of essential characteristics of genus, family, etc., and from which family etc. is named. 4. Biblical event regarded as symbolic or as foreshadowing a later one (its *antitype*). 5. Object, conception, work of art, serving as model for later artists. 6. Device on either side of medal or coin. 7. Small block, usu. of metal or wood, with raised letter, figure, etc., on its upper surface for use in printing; (collect.) set, supply, kind, of these. 8. *~-metal*, alloy of lead, antimony, and tin from which printing-types are cast; *~-script*, (matter) written with typewriter; *~-setter*, compositor; composing-machine; *type-write* (*v.*) write with typewriter; *type'writer*, machine for writing in characters similar to those of print, the characters being produced by striking the paper through an inked ribbon by steel types arranged on separate rods or on a wheel and actuated by striking corresponding keys on a keyboard; the paper is clipped to a paten on a carriage, which is automatically moved when a key is struck; (also, chiefly U.S.) typist.

~ *v.* 1. Be a type of, typify. 2. Determine type or group of, classify acc. to type. 3. Write with typewriter.

tȳph'oid *adj.* & *n.* ~ (*fever*), infectious eruptive febrile disease (formerly supposed to be variety of typhus) caused by ~ *bacillus* (*Bacillus typhosis*) and characterized by catarrhal inflammation of intestines. **tȳphoid'al** *adj.*

tȳphōō n' *n.* Violent cyclonic storm, esp. one occurring in the China seas and adjacent regions. **tȳphŏn'ĭc** *adj.* [f. Chin. *tai fung*, dial. forms of *ta* big, *feng* wind]

tȳph'us *n.* Acute contagious fever transmitted to man by body-lice or rat-fleas infected by *Rickettsia prowazekii*, and characterized by eruption of rose-coloured spots, extreme prostration, and usu. delirium. **tȳph'ous** *adj.*

tȳp'ĭcal *adj.* Serving as type, symbol, or representative specimen, symbolical, emblematic; distinctive, characteristic. **tȳp'ĭcally** *adv.*

tȳp'ĭfȳ *v.t.* Represent by type or symbol, foreshadow; serve as type or example of.

tȳp'ist *n.* One who uses a typewriter.

tȳpŏg'raphy *n.* Art, practice, of printing from types; style, appearance, of printed matter. **tȳpŏg'rapher** *n.* **tȳpogrăph'ĭc(al)** *adjs.*

tȳpŏl'ogy *n.* 1. Classification of archaeological remains etc. according to type. 2. Doctrine, interpretation, of biblical types and antitypes, study of these. **tȳpolŏ'gical** *adj.* **tȳpolŏ'gically** *adv.*

Tyr (tēr). (Scand. myth.) God of battle, equated with the Roman Mars.

tȳrănn'ĭc(al) *adjs.* (*-ic* rare). Acting like, characteristic of, a tyrant; despotic, arbitrary, oppressive, cruel. **tȳrănn'ĭcally** *adv.*

tȳrănn'ĭcīde *n.* Killer, killing, of tyrant. **tȳrănnĭcīd'al** *adj.*

tȳ'rannīze *v.* Play the tyrant; rule despotically or cruelly (*over*).

tȳrannosaur'us *n.* Fossil dinosaur, the largest known carnivore, remains of which have been found in N. America.

tȳ'rannous *adj.* Ruling or acting tyrannically; oppressive, unjustly severe or cruel. **tȳ'rannously** *adv.*

tȳ'ranny *n.* 1. Government of, State ruled by, tyrant or absolute ruler. 2. Oppressive or despotic government; arbitrary or oppressive exercise of power; tyrannical act or behaviour.

tȳr'ant *n.* 1. (Gk hist.) Absolute ruler who seized sovereign power without legal right; (despotic) usurper. 2. Oppressive, unjust, or cruel ruler, despot; person exercising power or authority arbitrarily or cruelly. 3. ~ (*-bird*, *-flycatcher*), bird of American passerine family *Tyrannidae*.

tȳre[1], **tīre** *ns.* 1. (usu. *tire*) Metal rim or hoop round wheel (ill. WAGON). 2. (U.S. usu. *tire*, in English usu. *tyre*) Endless rubber cushion, solid or tubular with air-inflated inner tube inside, fitted on rim of wheel of bicycle, motor-car; etc.; *tubeless* ~, air-inflated tyre without inner tube.

Tȳre[2]. Ancient seaport of the Phoenicians (mod. *Sur*) on Lebanon coast; ~ *and Sidon*, (N.T.) towns referred to as instances of sinfulness (Matt. xi. 21, 22; Luke x. 13, 14). **Tȳ'rĭan** *adj.* & *n.* ~ *purple*, purple dye made from shell-fish by the Tyrians and exported by them to ancient Greece and Rome.

tȳr'o, tīr'o *n.* Beginner or learner. in anything, novice.

Tȳ'rol, Tĭ'rol (*or* tĭrōl'). Alpine province of W. Austria, the S. part of which was ceded to Italy in 1919. **Tȳrolēse', Tĭrolēse'** (-z) *adj.* & *n.*

Tȳrōne'. County of Northern Ireland.

Tȳ'rrhēne, Tȳrrhēn'ĭan *adjs.* & *ns.* ETRUSCAN.

tzar etc.: see TSAR etc.

Tzigane (tsĭgahn') *adj.* Of the Hungarian gipsies or their music. ~ *n.* Hungarian gipsy.

U

U, u (yōō). 21st letter of modern English and 20th of ancient Roman alphabet, where it was identical in form and origin with *v*. *U*, *u*, now always represents a vowel sound except after *g*, where it is freq. silent (*guard*, *plague*), in final *-que*, where it is always silent (*grotesque*), and after *q* in other positions, where it has the value of *w* (*quick*, *inquest*), as also in various words after *s* and *g* (*persuade*, *anguish*).

U *abbrev.* Universal (i.e. for everyone, referring to cinema picture).

U.A.B. *abbrev.* Unemployment Assistance Board.

ūbī'ety *n.* Being in definite place, local relation.

ūbĭq'uĭty *n.* Omnipresence; being everywhere or in many places at the same time. **ūbĭq'uĭtous** *adj.* **ūbĭq'uĭtously** *adv.* **ūbĭq'uĭtousnėss** *n.*

U-boat *n.* German submarine. [Ger. *U-Boot*, abbrev. f. *Unterseeboot* submarine]

u.c. *abbrev.* Upper case (of print).

ūd'al *n.* Kind of freehold right based on uninterrupted possession prevailing in N. Europe before the establishment of the feudal system and still existing in Orkney and Shetland.

U.D.C. *abbrev.* Urban District Council.

ŭdd'er *n.* Pendulous baggy organ, provided with two or more teats, by which milk is secreted in cows and certain other female animals.

Ugăn'da. Former Brit. Protectorate in Central Africa, N. of Lake Victoria; republic since 1963; capital, Kampala.

ugh (ŭ(h), ŏŏ(h)) *int.* Expressing disgust etc.

ŭg'ly *adj.* Unpleasing or repulsive to sight or hearing; morally repulsive, vile; disquieting, threatening; extremely awkward or unpromising (task, situation); ~ *customer*, unpleasantly formidable person; ~ *duckling*, dull or plain child who becomes brilliant adult (w. ref. to cygnet in a brood of ducklings in Hans Andersen's tale). **ŭg'lĭfȳ** *v.t.* **ŭg'lĭly** *adv.* **ŭg'lĭnėss** *n.* **ŭg'ly** *n.* 1. Head-dress of silk on wire frame, worn in mid-19th c. as protection to bonnet. 2. Mottled green citrus fruit produced by crossing grape-fruit with tangerine.

Ug'rĭan, Ug'rĭc (ū-) *adjs.* & *ns.* (Language, member) of the E. branch of the Finno-Ugrian or Finnic peoples, specif. the Hungarians and Magyars. [*Ugra*, name of the country on both sides of the Ural mountains]

uh'lan (ōō-, ū-) *n.* Cavalryman armed with lance in some European armies, esp. former German army. [Fr., Ger., f. Polish (*h*)*ulan*, f. Turk. *oghlān* son, youth, servant]

Uh'land (ōō-), Johann Ludwig (1787–1862). German poet and ballad-writer.

Uitlander (āt'lŏnd*er*) *n.* Outlander; British resident in former S. African republics (Orange Free State, Transvaal). [(Cape) Du., f. *uit* out, *land* land]

U.K. *abbrev.* United Kingdom.

ūkāse' *n.* Decree or edict, with force of law, of former Russian emperor or government; any arbitrary order. [Russ. *ukaz'* command]

Ukraine (ūkrān', ōōkrīn'). 'Little Russia', a constituent republic of U.S.S.R., to the N. of the Black Sea; capital, Kiev. **Ukrain'ian** *adj.* & *n.*

ukulele, ukelale (ūkelāl'ĕ) *n.* Small 4-stringed guitar of Portuguese origin which became popular in Hawaii and subsequently in U.S. and Europe. [Hawaiian, = 'jumping flea']

ŭl'cer *n.* Open sore on external or internal surface of body, secreting pus; (fig.) corroding or corrupting influence, plague-spot. **ŭl'cerous** *adj.* **ŭl'cerously** *adv.*

ŭl'cerāte *v.* Form ulcer(s), form ulcer(s) in or on, fester. **ŭlcerā'tion** *n.*

U'lėma (ōō-) *n.* Moslem doctors of sacred law and theology esp. in the former Turkish Empire. [Arab. *'ulema*, pl. of *'alim* learned]

Ulfilas = WULFILA.

ūlī'ginōse, ūlī'ginous *adjs.* Waterlogged, muddy, swampy; (bot.) growing in muddy places.

ŭll'age *n.* Amount by which cask or bottle falls short of being quite full.

ŭl'na *n.* (pl. *-ae*). Large inner bone of forearm, extending from elbow to wrist (ill. SKELETON); corresponding bone of foreleg in quadrupeds and of wing in birds. **ŭl'nar** *adj.*

Ul'ster[1] (ŭ-). Former province of Ireland, comprising the 'six counties' which now form Northern Ireland (Antrim, Armagh, Down, Fermanagh, Londonderry, Tyrone) and 3 others which are part of Eire (Cavan, Donegal, Monaghan); (loosely) Northern Ireland.

ŭl'ster[2] *n.* Long loose freq. belted overcoat, orig. of Ulster frieze. [f. ULSTER[1]]

ult. *abbrev.* *Ultimo* (of last month).

ŭltēr'ior *adj.* Situated beyond; more remote; in the background, beyond what is seen or avowed. **ŭltēr'iorly** *adv.*

ŭl'timate *adj.* Last, final; beyond which there is no advance, progress, etc.; fundamental, elemental. **ŭl'timately** *adv.*

Ultima Thule: see THULE.

ŭltimāt'um *n.* (pl. *-tums, -ta*). Final statement of terms, rejection of which by opposite party may lead to rupture, declaration of war, etc.

ŭl'timō (abbrev. ult.) *adv.* Of last month.

ŭl'tra *adj.* & *n.* (Person) holding extreme views, esp. in religion or politics. [orig. as abbrev. of Fr. *ultra-royaliste*]

ultra- *prefix.* Lying beyond or on the other side of; (with adjs.) going beyond, surpassing; having (the quality etc. expressed by the adj.) in extreme or excessive degree.

ŭltramarine' (-ēn) *adj.* Situated beyond the sea. ~ *n.* Brilliant deep-blue pigment got from lapis lazuli; various imitations of this. [L *ultra* beyond, *mare* sea (w. ref. to foreign origin of lapis lazuli)]

ŭltramicroscŏp'ic *adj.* Too small to be seen with microscope.

ŭltramŏn'tāne *adj.* Situated S. of the Alps; Italian; favourable to the absolute authority of the pope in matters of faith and discipline. ~ *n.* One who resides S. of the Alps; person holding ultramontane views. **ŭltramŏn'tānism, ŭltramŏn'tānist** *ns.* [L *ultra* beyond, *mons* mountain]

ŭltramŭn'dāne *adj.* (Of or pertaining to things) lying outside the world or beyond the limits of the solar system.

ŭltra-shôrt *adj.* (of radio wave) Having a wave-length below 10 metres.

ŭltrasŏn'ic *adj.* (of sound) So high-pitched as to be beyond the range of human hearing; ~ *frequency*, sound-wave frequency higher than *c* 15 kilocycles per sec.

ŭltra-vī'olėt *adj.* (of light-rays) Lying beyond the violet end of the visible spectrum.

ŭlt'ra vīr'ēs (-z) *predic. adj.* Beyond one's powers; exceeding the powers granted by law.

ŭl'ūlāte *v.i.* Howl, wail. **ūlūlā'tion** *n.*

Uly'sses: see ODYSSEUS.

ŭm'bel *n.* (bot.) Inflorescence with pedicels of nearly equal length springing from common centre (ill. INFLORESCENCE). **ŭm'bellate, ŭmbellĭf'erous, ŭmbĕll'ifôrm** *adjs.* [L *umbella* sunshade, dim. of *umbra* shadow]

ŭm'ber *n.* Brown earth (iron and manganese) used as pigment; *burnt* ~, slightly redder preparation of this. ~ *adj.* Of the colour of umber. [Fr. (*terre d'*)*ombre* or It. (*terra di*) *ombra*, either = 'shadow' (L *umbra*) or f. fem. of L *Umber* Umbrian]

ŭmbĭl'ical *adj.* Of, affecting, situated near, forming, umbilicus; ~ *cord*, flexible tube attaching foetus to placenta, navel-string. **ŭmbĭl'icate, -āted** *adjs.* Resembling a navel.

ŭmbilīc'us *n.* Central depression in abdomen, marking point of attachment of umbilical cord, navel; small depression or hollow suggesting this; (geom.) point in surface through which all its lines of curvature pass.

ŭm'bō *n.* Boss of shield (ill. SHIELD); any round or conical projection, esp. most protuberant point of univalve shell or of each valve of bivalve shell. **ŭm'bonal, ŭm'bonate** *adjs.*

ŭm'bra *n.* (pl. *-ae*). The earth's or moon's shadow in an eclipse, esp. the complete shadow as dist. f. the *penumbra* (ill. ECLIPSE); dark central part of a sun-spot. **ŭm'bral** *adj.* [L, = 'shade']

ŭm'brage *n.* 1. Sense of slight or injury, offence. 2. (chiefly poet.) Shade. **ŭmbrā'geous** (-jus) *adj.*

ŭmbrĕll'a *n.* Light portable screen usu. circular and supported on central stick, used in hot countries as protection against sun, and in some Oriental and African countries as symbol of rank or state; portable protection against rain etc., made of silk or similar material fastened on slender ribs which are attached radially to stick and can be readily raised to form an arched circular canopy; structure resembling an umbrella, esp. (zool.) gelatinous disc or bell-shaped structure of jelly-fish, (conch.) umbrella-shell; the part of its shell like an open umbrella; screen of fighter-aircraft or (in full ~ *barrage*) a curtain of fire put up as protection against hostile aircraft; ~*-bird*, S. or Central Amer. bird of genus *Cephalopterus*, esp. Brazilian *C. ornatus*, with black plumage and large crest curving forward from the back of the head; ~*-pine*, parasol pine (*Sciadopitys verticillata*), Japanese evergreen tree with symmetrical branches and needle-shaped leaves in umbrella-like whorls; ~*-shell*, limpet-like marine gastropod of genus *Umbrella*.

Um'bria (ŭ-). Province of central Italy.

Um'brian *adj.* & *n.* (Language, native) of (ancient) Umbria; ~ *school*, Renaissance school of painting to which Raphael and Perugino belonged.

umiak (ōōm'yăk) *n.* Long open Eskimo boat of skins over wooden framework, paddled by women.

umlaut (ōōm'lowt) *n.* (In Germanic languages) vowel change due to *i* or *u* (now usu. lost or altered) in following syllable, e.g. Ger. *mann männer*, *fuss füsse*, Engl. *man men*, *foot feet*; the diacritical sign (¨) indicating this. [Ger. *um* about, *laut* sound]

ŭm'pīre *n.* One who decides between disputants or contending parties and whose decision is usu. accepted as final; (law) third person called upon to settle question submitted to arbitrators who cannot agree; person chosen to enforce rules of games or contest and settle disputes or doubtful points. ~ *v.* Act as umpire; act as umpire in (game etc.). [OF *nomper* peerless, in sense 'odd man' (*non* not, *per* PEER)]

ŭmp'teen' *adj.* & *n.* (slang) An indeterminate but large number (of). [joc. formation, on analogy of *thirteen* etc.]

'un *pron.* (colloq.) One.

un-[1] *prefix*, used with verbs and verbal derivatives and in forming new verbs from adjectives, nouns, etc., to signify contrary or reverse action to that of simple verb (or, rarely, intensification of negative force of verb, as in *unloose*), or deprivation or removal of some quality or property.

un-[2] *prefix*, freely and extensively used with adjectives (esp. past participles), adverbs, and nouns to express negation; = *not*, *in-*, *non-*. The number of words with this and the preceding prefix is almost limitless, and as the meaning usu. presents no difficulties, few such words are listed in this dictionary.

U.N. *abbrev.* UNITED NATIONS.

ūnadŏpt'ėd *adj.* (of road) Not taken over for maintenance by local authority.

ūnăn'ĭmous *adj.* All of one mind, agreeing in opinion; (of opinion, vote, etc.) formed, held, given, etc., with general agreement or consent. **ūnăn'ĭmously** *adv.* **ūnanĭm'ity, ūnăn'ĭmousnėss** *ns.*

unawares (ŭnawārz') *adv.* Unexpectedly, unconsciously; by surprise.

ŭnbeknownst' (-bĭnōn-) *adj.* & *adv.* (colloq. or dial.) Without the knowledge (of).

ŭnbo'som (-bŏŏz-) *v.* Disclose, reveal; ~ *oneself*, disclose one's secrets, thoughts, etc.

ŭncănn'y *adj.* Supernatural, mysterious, uncomfortably strange or unfamiliar. **ŭncănn'ĭly** *adv.* **ŭncănn'ĭnėss** *n.*

ŭn'cial (-shl) *adj.* Of, written in, a form of majuscule script resembling capitals but with some ascending and descending strokes, used in Greek and Latin MSS. of the 4th–8th centuries (ill. SCRIPT); *half-~*, intermediate between uncial and minuscule. ~ *n.* Uncial letter; uncial MS. [L *uncialis* in LL sense 'inch-high', 'large', f. *uncia* twelfth part of foot, inch]

ŭn'cifôrm *adj.* & *n.* Hook-shaped (bone, process).

ŭn'cinate *adj.* Hooked, furnished with hooks.

uncle (ŭng'kl) *adj.* 1. Father's or mother's brother, aunt's husband; (U.S.) familiar form of address to elderly man, esp. (in southern U.S.) Negro, (*talk* etc.) *like a Dutch ~*, with kindly severity; *U~ Sam*, Government (or people) of U.S. (perh. facetious expansion of initials *U.S.*). 2. (slang) Pawnbroker.

ŭnc'ō *adj.* & *adv.* (Sc. & north. dial.) Extreme(ly), unusual(ly); *the ~ guid*, those professedly strict in morals and religion. ~ *n.* Stranger. [shortening of *uncouth*]

ŭncŏn'scious (-shus) *adj.* Not conscious; ~ *mind*, (psychol.) those mental processes whose existence is inferred from their effects. ~ *n.* Unconscious mind; *collective ~*, (Jungian psychol.) alleged unconscious mental processes common to all mankind.

ŭncouth' (-ōōth) *adj.* Odd, uncomely, awkward, clumsy, in shape, sound, bearing, etc. **ŭncouth'ly** *adv.* **ŭncouth'nėss** *n.* [OE *uncuth* = 'unknown', 'unfamiliar']

ŭnc'tion *n.* 1. Anointing with oil etc. as religious rite or symbol (esp. of investiture with kingship or other office); unguent; *extreme ~*; see EXTREME. 2. (Manner suggesting) deep spiritual or religious feeling; simulation of this, affected enthusiasm, gush; manner showing keen appreciation or enjoyment of situation etc.

ŭnc'tūous *adj.* 1. Of the nature or quality of an unguent, oily, greasy in feel, appearance, etc. 2. Full of (esp. simulated) unction; complacently agreeable or self-satisfied. **ŭnc'tuously** *adv.* **ŭnc'tūousnėss** *n.*

ŭn'der *prep.* In or to position lower than, below, at the foot of; within, on the inside, of; inferior to, less than; supporting or sustaining; subjected to, undergoing, liable to, on condition of, subject to; governed, controlled, or bound by; in accordance with; in the form of; in the time of; (*speak* etc.) ~ *one's breath*, in a whisper; ~ *a cloud*: see CLOUD; ~ *the rose*, SUB-ROSA; ~ *the sun*, anywhere on earth; ~ *way*: see WAY. ~ *adv.* In a lower place or subordinate condition. ~ *adj.* Lower. **ŭn'dermōst** *adj.*

under- *prefix.* Below; beneath, lower than; insufficiently, incompletely; situated beneath, subordinate.

ŭnderăct' *v.* Act (part) with too much restraint.

ŭnder-āge' *adj.* Not of full age, of less than age fixed as lowest in particular.

ŭn'der-ârm *adj.* & *adv.* (of bowling in cricket, service in lawn tennis) (Performed) with arm lower than the shoulder.

ŭn'dercărriage *n.* The lower framework of a vehicle which supports the superstructure; the landing-gear of an aeroplane.

ŭn'derclothes (-ōz, -ōdhz), **ŭn'derclōthing** (-dh-) *ns.* Clothing worn below outer garments, esp. next to the skin.

ŭn'der-cover *adj.* Acting, done, surreptitiously or secretly.

ŭn'dercrŏft *n.* Crypt.

ŭn'dercŭrrent *n.* Current flowing below surface or upper current; (fig.) suppressed or underlying activity, force, etc.

ŭn'dercŭt *n.* (esp.) Under-side of sirloin of beef; (U.S.) joint of beef from under shoulder-blade. **ŭndercŭt'** *v.t.* Cut (away) below or beneath, esp. in carving; supplant by working for lower payment or selling at lower prices; offer goods etc. at (such prices).

ŭn'derdŏg *n.* (fig.) Overcome or worsted party to contest, inferior or subjected person.

ŭnderdraw' *v.t.* (esp.) Cover (inside of roof or under-side of floor) with boards or lath and plaster.

ŭn'derfŏŏt, ŭn'der fŏŏt *adj.* & *adv.* Lying under, beneath, the foot or feet; in(to) state of subjection or inferiority; inferior, abject.

ŭndergō' *v.t.* (past t. *-went*, past part. *-gone*). Be subjected to, suffer, endure.

ŭndergrăd'ūate *n.* Member of university who has not yet taken a degree (freq. attrib.).

ŭnderground' *adv.* Below the surface of the ground; in(to) secrecy or concealment. **ŭn'derground** *adj.* & *n.* (Railway) situated underground; (political movement etc.) conducted or existing in secret, hidden.

ŭn'dergrowth (-ōth) *n.* Growth of plants or shrubs under trees etc.

ŭnderhănd' (*or* ŭn'-) *adj.* & *adv.* Clandestine(ly), secret(ly), not above-board; (cricket, of bowling) under-arm.

ŭnderhŭng' *adj.* (Of lower jaw) projecting beyond upper jaw; (of person, animal) having underhung jaw.

ŭnderlīe' *v.t.* Lie, be situated, under; (fig.) be the basis or foundation of, lie under surface aspect of.

ŭnderlīne' *v.t.* Draw line(s) beneath (words etc.) for emphasis, emphasize.

ŭn'derling *n.* (usu. contempt.) Subordinate.

ŭndermīne' *v.t.* Make mine or excavation under; wear away base or foundation of; injure, wear out, etc., insidiously, secretly, or imperceptibly.

ŭnderneath' *adv.* & *prep.* At or to a lower place (than), below. **ŭn'derneath** *adj.* & *n.* Lower (surface, part).

ŭnderpin' *v.t.* Support or strengthen (building etc.) from beneath.

ŭn'derplŏt *n.* (Dramatic or literary) plot subordinate to main plot.

ŭnderrāte' *v.t.* Form too low an estimate of.

ŭndershŏŏt' *v.* (Of aircraft) land short of the runway.

ŭn'dershŏt *adj.* (Of wheel) turned by water flowing under it (ill. WATER).

ŭnderstănd' *v.* (past t. and past part. *-stŏŏd*). Perceive the meaning of; know how to deal with; infer, esp. from information received; take for granted. **ŭnderstănd'ing** *n.* (esp.) Intelligence; agreement; convention, thing agreed upon. ~ *adj.* Intelligent, having understanding. **ŭnderstănd'ingly** *adv.*

ŭn'derstrăpper *n.* Underling.

ŭn'derstŭdy *n.* Actor who studies part in order to play it at short notice in absence of usual performer. ~ *v.t.* Study (part) thus, act as understudy to (principal performer).

ŭndertāke' *v.* Bind oneself to perform; engage in, enter upon (work, enterprise, etc.); promise (*to* do); guarantee; (colloq.) manage funerals. **ŭn'dertāker** *n.* (esp.) One whose business is to carry out arrangements for funerals. **ŭndertāk'ing** *n.* (esp.) Work etc. undertaken, enterprise; business of funeral undertaker.

ŭn'dertōne *n.* Low or subdued, underlying or subordinate, tone.

ŭn'dertow (-tō) *n.* Current below sea-surface moving in contrary direction to surface current.

ŭn'derwear (-wār) *n.* Underclothes.

ŭn'derwood *n.* Small trees or shrubs, brushwood, growing beneath trees.

ŭn'derworld (-wẽr-) *n.* (esp.) Infernal regions; lowest social stratum.

ŭnderwrīte' *v.* (past t. *-wrōte*, past part. *-writt'en*). (esp.) Subscribe (insurance policy), thereby accepting risk of insurance; undertake esp. marine insurance; agree to take up stock not bought by public in (new company or new issue). **ŭn'derwrīter** *n.*

ŭn'dies (-dĭz) *n.pl.* (colloq.) Women's underclothes.

ŭndine' (-ēn) *n.* Female water-sprite who by marrying a mortal and bearing a child might receive a soul. [invented by Paracelsus, f. L *unda* wave]

ŭndrĕss' *v.* Take off clothes. **ŭn'drĕss** *n.* (esp., mil. etc.) Uniform for ordinary occasions, as dist. from *full* or *service dress* (freq. attrib.).

ŭn'dūlant *adj.* Undulating, rising and falling like waves; ~ *fever*, persistent remittent fever with profuse perspiration, swollen joints, and enlarged spleen, transmitted through milk esp. of cows with contagious abortion.

ŭn'dūlate *adj.* With wave-like markings; having waved surface or outline, arranged in wave-like curves. **ŭn'dūlately** *adv.* **ŭn'dūlāte** *v.i.* Have wavy motion or look. **ŭn'dūlāting** *adj.*

ŭndūlā'tion *n.* Wavy motion or form, gentle rise and fall, each wave of this; set of wavy lines.

ŭn'dūlatory *adj.* Undulating, wavy; of, due to, undulation.

ŭndūl'y *adv.* Unrightfully, improperly; excessively.

ŭn'dy, -dee *adj.* (her.) Wavy (ill. HERALDRY). [Fr. *ondi*, f. L *unda* wave]

unearth' (-ẽrth) *v.t.* Dig up, disinter; force out of hole or burrow; (fig.) bring to light, disclose, find by searching.

ŭnearth'ly (-ẽrth-) *adj.* Celestial, not of this earth; supernatural, ghostly; (colloq.) not appropriate, absurdly early or inconvenient.

ŭnėmployed' (-oid) *adj.* Not employed or occupied; not in use. **ŭnėmploy'ment** *n.*; ~ *benefit*, payment made by State to unemployed person under Insurance Act.

U.N.E.S.C.O., Unesco (ūnĕs'kō) *abbrevs.* United Nations Educational, Scientific, & Cultural Organization.

ŭngain'ly *adj.* Awkward, clumsy, ungraceful. **ŭngain'lĭnėss** *n.*

ŭng'ual (-nggw-) *adj.* Of, like, bearing, a nail, claw, or hoof.

ŭng'uent (-nggw-) *n.* Ointment, salve.

ŭnguĭc'ūlate (-nggw-) *adj.* Having, furnished with, unguis, nail(s) or claw(s); (zool.) of the group of mammals *Unguiculata.*

ŭng'uĭs (-nggw-) *n.* (pl. *-gues*, pr. -gwēz). (zool.) Nail, claw.

ŭng'ūla (-ngg-) *n.* (pl. *-ae*). 1. Hoof, claw, talon. 2. (math.) Cone, cylinder, with top cut off by plane oblique to base (ill. CONE).

ŭng'ūlate (-ngg-) *adj.* Hoof-shaped; (of mammals) having hoofs.

ŭnhĭnge' (-nj) *v.t.* (chiefly in past part.). Derange, disorder (mind).

uni- *prefix.* One; having, composed or consisting of, characterized by, etc., one (thing specified by second element).

Un'iat(e) (ū-) *adj.* & *n.* (Member) of any of those Christian Churches (in E. Europe and the Near East) which accept the Catholic faith and acknowledge the pope's supremacy but retain their own organization and liturgy. [Russ. *uniyat* f. *uniya* union (L *unus* one)]

ūnĭcăm'eral *adj.* Having one (legislative) chamber.

U.N.I.C.E.F., Unicef (ūn'ĭsĕf) *abbrevs.* United Nations International Children's Emergency Fund.

ūnĭcĕll'ūlar *adj.* (esp. of living organism) Having, composed of, a single cell.

ūn'ĭcorn *n.* Fabulous animal represented as having the body of a horse with a single horn projecting from its forehead; heraldic representation of this, usu. with legs of deer, lion's tail, and straight spirally twisted horn, esp. as supporter of royal arms of Gt Britain or Scotland; ~ (*-shell*), marine gasteropod with horn-like lip projecting from shell.

ūn'ĭform *adj.* Being or remaining the same in different places, at different times, etc., unvarying, consistent; plain, unbroken, undiversified; conforming to one standard, rule, or pattern, alike, similar. **ūn'ĭformly** *adv.* **ūn'ĭform** *n.* Distinctive dress of uniform cut, material, and colour worn by all members of particular military or other organization. ~ *v.* Make uniform; dress in uniform.

ūnĭform'ĭty *n.* Being uniform, sameness, consistency, conformity; *Act of U~*, (hist.) any of 3 Acts (passed in 1549, 1559, 1662), regulating public worship in Gt Britain and prescribing use of a particular Book of Common Prayer.

ūn'ĭfȳ *v.t.* Reduce to unity or uniformity. **ūnĭfĭcā'tion** *n.*

ūnĭlăt'eral *adj.* One-sided; of, affecting, etc., one side (only); made by, binding on, affecting, one party only. **ūnĭlăt'erally** *adv.*

ūn'ion (-yon) *n.* Uniting, joining, being united, coalition, junction; marriage; concord, agreement; whole resulting from combination of parts or members; TRADE union; (formerly) two or more parishes consolidated for administration of poor laws, workhouse erected by such union; kinds of joint or coupling for pipes etc.; union cloth; Union Jack; Union Society; *the U~*, (hist.) uniting of Scottish and English crowns (1603) or parliaments (1707); uniting of parliaments of Gt Britain and Ireland (1801); (formation of) the UNITED STATES OF AMERICA; ~ *cloth*, textile fabric of different yarns woven together, esp. cotton and linen or cotton and wool; *U~ flag, Jack*, national flag of Gt Britain, combining red cross of St. George and white saltire cross of St. Andrew surmounted by red saltire cross of St. Patrick, and retaining blue ground of banner of St. Andrew (ill. FLAG); *U~ Society*, at Oxford, Cambridge, and some other universities, (premises of) general club and debating society open to all members, or all undergraduates, of university; ~ *suit* (U.S.), undergarment combining vest and drawers, combinations.

ūn'ionist (-nyo-) *n.* 1. Member of a trade union; advocate of trade unions. 2. One who desires or advocates union, esp. of particular legislative or political union, as (U.S.) supporter of Federal Union of U.S., esp. (in Civil War of 1861–5) as opp. Secessionist; (British politics) supporter of maintenance of parliamentary union between Gt Britain and Ireland (now freq. simply = Conservative). ~ *adj.* Of, supporting, belonging to, union, unionism, or unionists. **ūn'ionĭsm** *n.*

Union of South Africa: see SOUTH AFRICA.

Union of Soviet Socialist Republics: see SOVIET UNION.

unique (ūnēk') *adj.* Of which there is only one; unmatched, unequalled; having no like, equal, or parallel. **ūnique'ly** *adv.* **ūnique'nėss** *n.*

ūn'ĭson *n.* (mus.) Coincidence in pitch; sound or note of same pitch as another; combination of voices or instruments at same pitch; *in* ~, at same pitch; in concord, agreement or harmony. **ūnĭs'onant** *adj.* **ūnĭs'onance** *n.*

ūn'ĭt *n.* Single magnitude or number regarded as undivided whole, esp. the numeral 'one'; any determinate quantity, magnitude, etc., as basis or standard of measurement for other quantities of same kind; each of the individuals or groups into which a complex whole may be analysed; that part of collective body or whole regarded as lowest or least to have separate existence. ~ *adj.* Of, being, forming, a unit, individual.

Unitār'ian (ū-) *n.* One who maintains that the Godhead is one person, not a Trinity; member of Christian body which originated in England in 17th c. and maintains this doctrine. ~ *adj.* Of Unitarians or their doctrine. **Unitār'ianism** *n.*

ūn'ĭtary *adj.* Of, based on, proceeding from, etc., a unit or unity; individual, simple, that is a unit.

ūnīte' *v.* Join together, make or become one, combine, consolidate, amalgamate; agree, combine, cooperate (*in*). **ūnīt'ĕd** *adj.*; *U~ Brethren*, MORAVIANS; *U~ Irishman*, member of the Society of United Irishmen, a political association which was formed 1791 by Wolfe Tone, originally to promote union between Catholics and Protestants, and helped to organize the rebellion of 1798. **ūnīt'ĕdly** *adv.*

United Kingdom. Great Britain and Ireland (from 1801 to 1922); Great Britain and Northern Ireland (from 1922).

United Nations. (orig.) The nations at war with the Axis, 1939–45; hence, international organization of these and other States established as successor to the League of Nations by the ~ *Charter* signed at San Francisco on 26 June 1945; its main object is the maintenance of peace and its 6 principal organs are the General Assembly, Security Council, Secretariat (at New York), International Court (at The Hague), Economic and Social Council, and Trusteeship Council; abbrev. U.N.

United Provinces. The 7 northern provinces of the Netherlands, which formed a union in 1579 that led to the formation of a Dutch Republic and later to the Kingdom of the NETHERLANDS.

United Provinces (of Agra and Oudh). Former province of British India; since 1947 a State of the Republic of India, known officially as Uttar Pradesh.

United States of America (abbrev. U.S.A. or U.S.). Republic of N. America, bounded on N. by Canada and on S. by Mexico; a federation of 50 States with federal capital at Washington in District of Columbia; governs also various island territories. The country was colonized in 17th c. by several European nations, esp. Spanish and French in S., Dutch in N., and British in E., who gained ascendancy over the rest; the colonies were ruled by Britain until 1775 when they revolted (War of American Independence, 1775–83); the 13 orig. States agreed on a constitution (1787–8), and chose George Washington as first president (for U.S. presidents see Appendix VI and separate entries; see also AMERICA).

ūn'ĭty *n.* Oneness, being one or single or individual; being formed of parts that constitute a whole; due interconnexion and coherence of parts; thing showing such unity, thing forming complex whole; (math.) the numeral one as basis of number; harmony, concord, between persons etc.; any of the 3 Aristotelian principles of dramatic composition as adapted by French classical dramatists, by which a play should consist of one main action, represented as occurring at one time and in one place.

Univ. *abbrev.* University.

ūnĭvāl'ent (*or* -ĭv'*a*l-) *adj.* (chem.) Having a VALENCY of 1.

ūn'ĭvălve *adj.* (zool., of shell) Composed of a single valve, (of mollusc) having such shell.

ūnĭvẽrs'al *adj.* Of, belonging to, done, or used by, etc., all persons or things in the world or in the class concerned; applicable to all cases; ~ *donor*, person whose blood-group is such that his blood may be transfused into any other person irrespective of the latter's grouping; ~ *joint*, joint or coupling permitting of free movement in any direction of the parts joined, esp. one in which one connected part conveys rotary action to other;

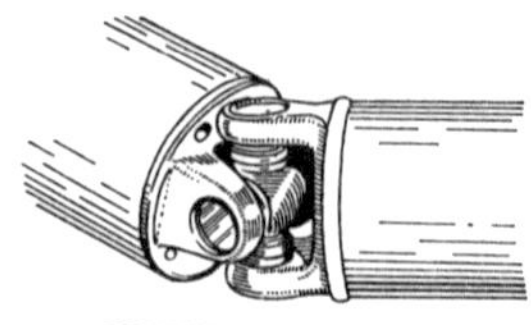

UNIVERSAL JOINT

~ *proposition*, (logic) proposition in which the predicate is affirmed or denied of the entire subject; ~ *suffrage*, suffrage extending to all persons, or all male persons, over a specified age, except lunatics, criminals, and aliens. **ūnĭvẽrs'ally** *adv.* **ūnĭvẽrsăl'ĭty** *n.* **ūnĭvẽrs'alīze** *v.t.* **ūnĭvẽrs'al** *n.* (logic) Universal proposition; (philos.) general notion or idea, thing that by its nature may be predicated of many.

ūnĭvẽrs'alism *n.* (theol.) Doctrine that all mankind will eventually be saved. **ūnĭvẽrs'alist** *n.* One who holds this doctrine, esp. (*U~*) member of an organized sect chiefly in U.S.

ūn'ĭvẽrse *n.* All created or existing things, the whole creation, the cosmos; the world or earth; all mankind.

ūnĭvẽrs'ĭty *n.* Whole body of teachers and scholars engaged at particular place in giving and receiving instruction in higher branches of learning; such persons as corporate body with definite organization and powers (esp. of conferring degrees), forming institution for promotion of higher education; colleges, buildings, etc., of such a body.

Univẽr'sity College. (esp.) 1. A college of the University of Oxford, founded 1280. 2. A college of the University of London, founded 1827 by Dr George Birkbeck (abbrev. U.C.L.).

ŭnkĕmpt' *adj.* Uncombed, dishevelled; untidy, neglected-looking.

ŭnlĕss' *conj.* If . . . not, except when.

U.N.O., UNO, Un'ō (ū-)*abbrevs.* United Nations Organization.

ŭn'quōte. Direction used in dictation to indicate the end of a quotation.

ŭnrăv'el *v.* Take out of tangled or intertwined condition (freq. fig.); undo, pull out (woven or esp. knitted fabric); come undone, become unknit or disentangled.

U.N.R.R.A., Unrra (ŭn'rah) *abbrevs.* United Nations Relief and Rehabilitation Administration.

ŭnrul'y (-rōō-) *adj.* Not amenable to rule or discipline; turbulent. **ŭnrul'inėss** *n.*

ŭnsight'ly (-sīt-) *adj.* Unpleasing to the eye, ugly.

ŭntĭl' *prep.* & *conj.* = TILL[4].

ŭn'to (-ōō) *prep.* (archaic) To.

ŭntouch'able (-tŭ-) *n.* Non-caste Hindu (whom a caste man may not touch).

ŭntō'ward (*or* ŭntowŏrd') *adj.* Perverse, refractory; awkward; unlucky; unseemly. **ŭntō'wardly** *adv.* **ŭntō'wardnėss** *n.*

ŭnwiel'dy *adj.* Slow or clumsy of movement, awkward to handle, wield, or manage, by reason of size, shape, or weight. **ŭnwiel'dinėss** *n.*

ŭp *adv.* To, in, a high or higher place, position, degree, amount, value, etc.; to or in a capital or university, to or in place farther north or otherwise conventionally regarded as higher; to or in the place in question or where the speaker etc. is; to or in erect or vertical position esp. as favourable to activity, out of bed, out of lying or sitting or kneeling posture, in(to) condition of efficiency or activity; (with verbs, in many special uses which should be sought under the verb concerned, but usu.) expressing complete or effectual result etc.; ~ *against*, in(to) contact or collision with; (colloq.) faced or confronted by; *up in*, (colloq.) expert, well-informed, in subject etc.; *up to*, as high or far as, up towards, so as to reach or arrive at; until; as many or much as; fit or qualified for, capable of, able to deal with, ready for; on a level with; engaged in, occupying oneself with; (colloq.) obligatory or incumbent on; *up with*, so as to overtake; on a level with. ~ *prep.* To a higher point of, on or along in ascending direction; at or in a higher part of. ~ *adj.* Moving, sloping, going, towards a higher point or to the capital. ~ *n.* *Ups and downs*, rises and falls; undulating ground; alternately good and bad fortune. ~ *v.* 1. Drive up (swans) for marking. 2. (colloq.) Begin abruptly or boldly (to do something), *he ups and says . . .*

u.p. *abbrev.* Under proof.

U.P. *abbrev.* United Presbyterian; United Press.

Upăn'ishăd (ū-). Any of various treatises forming part of the VEDIC literature of the Hindus and dealing chiefly with deity, creation, and existence.

ūp'as *n.* ~ (*-tree*), fabulous Javanese tree poisoning all animal and vegetable life for miles around; (bot.) the Javanese tree *Antiaris toxicaria*, yielding poisonous juice; poison obtained from this.

ŭp'-beat *n.* (mus.) Unaccented beat, esp. last beat in bar.

ŭpbraid' *v.t.* Chide, reproach.

ŭp'bringing *n.* Bringing up of young persons, early rearing and training.

ŭp'cast (-ah-) *n.* (esp.) 1. (mining & geol.) (Fault caused by) upward dislocation of seam. 2. (mining) ~ *shaft*, shaft through which air passes out of mine (ill. MINE).

ŭp'-coun'try (-kŭn-) *n.*, *adj.*, & *adv.* (To, in, of) inland part of country.

ŭp-ĕnd' *v.* Set, rise up, on end.

ŭp'-grāde *n.* (U.S.) Upward slope; *on the* ~, ascending, improving. **ŭp-grāde'** *v.* Promote, raise to higher scale of salary.

ŭpheave' *v.* Lift up, raise; throw up with violence, esp. by volcanic action; rise up. **ŭpheav'al** *n.*

ŭp'hill *adj.* Sloping upwards; (fig.) arduous, difficult, laborious. ~ *adv.* With upward slope on hill, with slope in upward direction.

ŭphōld' *v.t.* (past t. and past part. *-hĕld*). Hold up, keep erect, support; give support or countenance to; maintain, confirm (decision etc.).

ŭphōl'ster *v.t.* Furnish (room etc.) with hangings, carpets, etc.; provide (chair etc.) with textile covering, padding, etc., cover chair (*with*, *in*). **ŭphōl'sterer, ŭphōl'stery** *ns.* [*n.* f. obs. *upholster*, *upholder* one who upholds, i.e. keeps in repair; *v.* back-formation]

ŭp'keep *n.* (Cost of) maintenance in good condition or repair.

ŭp'land *n.* Piece of high ground, stretch of hilly or mountainous country. ~ *adj.* Living, growing, situated, etc., on high ground.

ŭplift' *v.t.* Raise up, elevate (esp. fig.). **ŭp'lift** *n.* (colloq.) Elevating or edifying effect, moral inspiration.

upŏn' *prep.* = ON.

ŭpp'er *adj.* Higher in place, situated above; superior in rank, authority, dignity, etc.; ~ *crust*, (colloq.) aristocracy, highest social circles; ~*-cut*, (boxing) short-arm upward blow; ~ *deck*, highest continuous deck of ship; ~ *hand*, mastery, control, or advantage (*of*, *over*); ~ *house*, higher legislative assembly, esp. House of Lords; ~ *ten*, upper classes, aristocracy. ~ *n.* Upper part of boot or shoe (ill. SHOE); *on one's* ~*s*, (colloq.) poor, having hard luck.

ŭpp'ermōst *adj.* Highest in place or rank. ~ *adv.* On or to the top.

ŭpp'ish *adj.* Self-assertive, pert, putting on airs. **ŭpp'ishly** *adv.* **ŭpp'ishnėss** *n.*

ŭpraise' (-z) *v.t.* Raise up, elevate, rear.

ŭp'right (-rīt) *adj.* & *adv.* Erect, vertical; righteous, strictly honourable or honest. **ŭp'rightly** *adv.* **ŭp'rightnėss** *n.* **ŭp'right** *n.* Upright PIANOFORTE; post or rod fixed upright esp. as support to some structure.

ŭprīs'ing (-z-) *n.* (esp.) Insurrection, popular rising against authority etc.

ŭp'roar (-ōr) *n.* Tumult, violent disturbance, clamour. **ŭproar'ious** *adj.* **ŭproar'iously** *adv.* **ŭproar'iousnėss** *n.*

ŭproot' *v.t.* Tear up by the roots; eradicate, destroy.

ŭpsĕt'[1] *v.* (past t. and past part. *upsĕt'*). Overturn, be overturned; disturb the peace, composure, temper, digestion, etc., of. ~ *n.* Upsetting, being upset.

ŭp'sĕt[2] *adj.* ~ *price*, price fixed as lowest for which property offered at auction will be sold.

ŭp'shŏt *n.* Final issue, conclusion.

ŭp'sīde-down' *adv.* & *adj.* With the upper part under, inverted, in(to) total disorder. [altered from ME *up so down* up as if down]

ŭpsīdes' (-dz) *adv.* (colloq., orig. Sc.) ~ *with*, even or quits with, avenged on.

ūpsīl'on (*or* ū'psĭ-) *n.* Greek letter Υ, υ (= *u*; freq. transliterated *y*).

ŭp'stairs (-z) *adj.* **ŭpstairs'** *adv.* On, to, an upper storey.

ŭpstănd'ing *adj.* Well set up, erect.

ŭp'start *n.* One who has newly or suddenly risen in position or importance (freq. attrib.).

ŭp-stream' *adv.* **ŭp'-stream** *adj.* (Moving, done) against the current.

ŭp'strōke *n.* Upward line made in writing.

ŭp'tāke' *n.* (Sc. and colloq.) Understanding, apprehension.

ŭp'thrŭst *n.* (geol.) Thrusting, being thrust, up, esp. by volcanic action.

ŭp to dāte, up'-to-dāte' *adv. phr.* & *adj.* (Extending) right up to the present time; abreast of the times in style, fashion, information, knowledge, etc.

ŭp'ward *adj.* Directed, moving, towards a higher place (lit. and fig.). **ŭp'ward(s)** *adv.* In upward direction; *upwards of*, (rather) more than.

Ur (ẽr). Ancient city of Mesopotamia (at Tell Muqayyar in S. Iraq), a centre of Sumerian civilization *c* 2000 B.C.; identified, since its excavation, with the 'Ur of the Chaldees' whence Abraham migrated to Haran (Gen. xi. 28, 31); laid waste by Babylonians *c* 1800 B.C.; partially rebuilt by Nebuchadnezzar of Babylon in 6th c. B.C.

ūraem'ia *n.* (path.) Presence in blood of urinary matter normally eliminated by kidneys; condition caused by failure of kidneys to function. **ūraem'ic** *adj.*

ūrae'us *n.* (Egyptian antiq.) Representation of (head and neck of) sacred asp or serpent, as emblem of supreme power, esp. in head-dress of ancient Egyptian divinities and sovereigns. [modern latinization of Gk *ouraios*, supposed to be ancient Egyptian for cobra]

Ur'al-Altā'ic (ūr-) *adj.* Of (the people of) the Urals and Altaic mountain ranges of central Asia; of a family of Finnic, Mongolian, Turkic, and other agglutinative languages of N. Europe and Asia.

Ur'als (ūr-). Mountain range in Russia, forming a natural boundary between Europe and Asia.

Urān'ia (ūr-). The muse of astronomy; epithet of Aphrodite (Venus).

ūrān'ium *n.* Heavy greyish metallic radio-active element, found in pitchblende and minerals, capable of nuclear fission and hence used in the production of atomic energy and atomic bombs; symbol U, at. no. 92, at. wt 238·03. **ūrăn'ic, ūrān'ous** *adjs.* [f. URANUS]

ūranŏg'raphy *n.* Descriptive astronomy.

ūranŏm'ėtry *n.* Measurement of stellar distances; map showing positions and magnitudes of stars.

Ur'anus (ūr-; *or* ūrān'-). 1. (Gk myth.) The personification of the sky, the most ancient of the Greek gods and the first ruler of the universe. 2. (astron.) The 7th of the major planets, farthest from the sun except Neptune and Pluto; discovered in 1781 by Sir W. Herschel (ill. PLANET).

ûrb'an[1] *adj.* Of, living or situated in, a city or town.

Urb'an[2] (ẽr-). Name of 8 popes: *Urban II*, pope 1088–99, inaugurated the first crusade; *Urban VIII*, pope 1623–44, Florentine scholar and poet.

ûrbāne' *adj.* Courteous, civil; bland, suave. **ûrbāne'ly** *adv.* **ûrbăn'ity** *n.* [L *urbanus* of the city, refined, polished (*urbs* city)]

ûrb'anīze *v.t.* Render urban; remove rural character of (district or population). **ûrbanīzā'tion** *n.*

ûrch'in *n.* 1. Hedgehog (archaic or dial.); *sea-*~: see SEA. 2. Roguish or mischievous boy; little fellow, boy. [ME *hurcheon* hedgehog, f. L *ericius*]

Urdu (oor'dōō). A form of Hindustani, spoken chiefly by the Moslem races in India. [Hind., lit. = 'camp language']

ūr'ėa (*or* ūrē'a) *n.* (chem.) *Carbamide*, $CO(NH_2)_2$, soluble nitrogenous crystalline compound present in urine of mammals, birds, and some reptiles, and also in blood, milk, etc.

ūrēt'er *n.* Either of two ducts conveying urine from kidney to bladder or cloaca (ill. KIDNEY).

ūrēth'ra *n.* Duct through which urine is discharged from bladder (ill. PELVIS). **ūrēth'ral** *adj.*

ûrge *v.t.* Drive forcibly, impel, hasten; entreat, exhort, earnestly or persistently; ply with argument or entreaty; advocate pressingly. ~ *n.* Impelling motive, force, pressure, etc.

ûr'gent *adj.* Pressing, calling for immediate action or attention; importunate, earnest and persistent in demand. **ûr'gently** *adv.* **ûr'gency** *n.*

Urī'ah (ū-). (O.T.) An officer in David's army, the husband of Bathsheba, whom David caused to be killed in battle (2 Sam. xi).

ūr'ic *adj.* Of urine; ~ *acid*, white crystalline acid found in urine of mammals, birds, etc.

Ur'iel (ūr-). One of the 7 archangels enumerated in the 'Book of Enoch'.

ūr'im and thŭmm'im *ns.* Two objects of unknown nature, mentioned in the Bible as being kept in the breastplate of the High Priest (Exod. xxviii. 30). [Heb. = 'light' and 'perfection']

ūrin'al (*or* ūr'ĭ-) *n.* Vessel for receiving urine; building or erection for use of persons requiring to pass urine.

ūr'inary *adj.* Of urine.

ūr'ināte *v.i.* Pass urine. **ūrinā'tion** *n.*

ūr'ine *n.* Fluid excreted by kidneys in man and other mammals, stored in bladder and voided at intervals through urethra; similar fluid in other vertebrates. **ūr'inous** *adj.*

ûrn *n.* Vessel or vase with foot and usu. with rounded body, esp. as used for storing ashes of the dead, or as vessel or measure; large vessel with tap in which water is kept hot or tea made. ~ *v.t.* Deposit (ashes etc.) in urn.

ūr'odēle *n.* (zool.) Member of the amphibian order *Urodela*, comprising newts and salamanders.

ūrŏl'ogy *n.* Study of diseases of urinary system. **ūrŏl'ogist** *n.*

Urs'a (êr-). Name of two Northern constellations, ~ *Major*, the Great Bear or the Plough, and ~ *Minor*, the Little Bear, which contains the Pole Star. [L, = 'she-bear']

ûrs'ine *adj.* Of, like, a bear.

Urs'ūla (êr-) *n.* British saint and martyr, who, acc. to legend, was put to death with 11,000 virgins, having been captured by Huns near Cologne when on a pilgrimage.

Urs'ūline (êr-) *adj.* & *n.* (Nun) of an order founded by St. Angela Merici at Brescia in 1537 for nursing the sick and teaching girls. [named after St. URSULA, patron saint of the foundress]

ûrticār'ia *n.* NETTLE-rash.

urubu (ōō'rōōbōō) *n.* Black vulture (*Coragyps atratus*) of S. America and southern U.S.

Uruguay (ūrōōgwī'). 1. River of S. America, flowing southwards from Brazil and joining the Plata river. 2. S. Amer. republic, lying to the E. of the Uruguay river, inaugurated in 1830; capital, Montevideo. **Uruguay'an** *adj.* & *n.*

us (ŭs, *us*) *pers. pron.* Objective case of WE.

U.S. *abbrev.* United States (of America).

U.S.A. *abbrev.* United States of America; United States Army.

U.S.(A.)A.F. *abbrev.* United States (Army) Air Force.

ūs'age (-z-) *n.* Manner of using or treating, treatment; habitual or customary practice, established use (esp. of word); quantity used; (law) habitual but not necessarily immemorial practice.

ūs'ance (-z-) *n.* Time allowed by commercial usage for payment of esp. foreign bill of exchange etc.

use (ūz) *v.* 1. Employ for a purpose or as instrument or material; exercise, put into operation, avail oneself of; ~ *up*, use the whole of, find a use for what remains of; exhaust, wear out. 2. Treat in specified manner. 3. (now only in past. t. *used* (ūst)) Be accustomed, have as constant or frequent practice; (past part.) accustomed. **ūs'able** (-z-) *adj.* **use** (ūs) *n.* 1. Using, employment, application to a purpose; right or power of using; availability, utility, purpose for which thing can be used, occasion for using. 2. Ritual and liturgy of a church, diocese, etc. 3. (law) Benefit or profit of lands etc. held by another solely for the beneficiary.

ūse'ful (-sf-) *adj.* Of use, serviceable; suitable for use, advantageous, profitable. **ūse'fully** *adv.* **ūse'fulnėss** *n.*

ūse'lėss (-sl-) *adj.* Serving no useful purpose, unavailing; of inadequate or insufficient capacity, inefficient. **ūse'lėssly** *adv.* **ūse'lėssnėss** *n.*

ūs'er (-z-) *n.* (law) Continued use or exercise of right etc.; presumptive right arising from use.

ŭsh'er *n.* Official or servant who acts as doorkeeper or shows people to seats in church, law-court, etc.; official at court who walks before person of rank; under-teacher, assistant schoolmaster (now only as a traditional title, or contempt.). **ŭsherĕtte'** *n.* Female usher esp. in cinema. **ŭsh'er** *v.t.* Act as usher to; precede (person) as usher, announce, show *in*, *out* (freq. fig.). [OF *uissier* f. L *ostiarius* doorkeeper (*ostium* door)]

U.S.N. *abbrev.* United States Navy.

ūs'quėbaugh (-baw) *n.* Whisky. [Ir. & Sc. Gaelic *uisge beatha* water of life]

U.S.S. *abbrev.* United States Senate; United States Ship (or Steamer).

U.S.S.C. *abbrev.* United States Supreme Court.

U.S.S.R. *abbrev.* Union of Soviet Socialist Republics (see SOVIET UNION).

ū'sual (-zhōōal) *adj.* Commonly or ordinarily observed, practised, used, happening, to be found, etc.; current, ordinary, customary, wonted. **ū'sually** *adv.* **ū'sualnėss** *n.*

ūs'ūfrŭct (ūz-) *n.* (law) Right of enjoying use and advantages of another's property, short of causing damage or prejudice to this; use, enjoyment (*of* something). **ūsūfrŭc'tūary** *adj.* & *n.* Of usufruct, (person) enjoying usufruct.

ū'surer (-zh*u*-) *n.* One who lends money at exorbitant or illegal rates of interest.

usûrp' (ūz-) *v.* Seize, assume, (power, right, etc.) wrongfully. **ūsurpā'tion** (-z*er*-), **ūsûrp'er** *ns.*

ū'sury (-zh*u*-) *n.* Practice of lending money at exorbitant interest, esp. at higher interest than is allowed by law; such interest. **ūsūr'ious** (-z-) *adj.* **ūsūr'iously** *adv.* **ūsūr'iousnėss** *n.*

ut (ōōt, ŭt) *n.* 1. (hist.) First note of the hexachord. 2. First note of octave in solmization, now usu. called DOH. [named, with the other 5 notes of the hexachord, after syllables from a Latin hymn: *Ut* queant laxis *re*sonare fibris *Mi*ra gestorum *fa*muli tuorum, *Sol*ve polluti *la*bii reatum; because in this hymn the notes of the hexachord fell on these syllables]

Ut. *abbrev.* Utah.

Ut'ah (ū-). Mountain State of U.S., admitted to the Union in 1896; capital, Salt Lake City.

ūtĕn'sil *n.* Instrument, implement, vessel, esp. in domestic use.

ūt'erine *adj.* 1. Having the same mother but different fathers. 2. Of, situated in, connected with, the uterus.

ūt'erus *n.* (pl. *-ī*). Womb, organ in which the young of mammals are conceived, develop, and are protected till birth (ill. PELVIS).

Uth'er Pĕndrăg'on (ū-). In the Arthurian legend, king of the Britons and father of ARTHUR.

ūtilitār'ian *adj.* Of, consisting in, based on, utility, esp., regarding the greatest good of the greatest number as the chief consideration of morality; holding utilitarian views or principles. ~ *n.* One who holds or supports utilitarian views; one devoted to mere utility or material interests.

Ūtilitār'ianism *n.* Utilitarian principles, doctrines, etc., esp. as expounded by BENTHAM and J. S. MILL.

ūtil'ity *n.* 1. Usefulness, fitness for some desirable end or useful purpose, profitableness; power to satisfy human wants; useful thing; (*public*) *utilities*, (organizations supplying) gas, water, electricity, transport services, means of communication, etc., provided for some or all members of the community and regarded as so essential to the life of the community that they are subject to various forms of public control. 2. (*attrib.*) Reared, kept, made, etc., for useful ends as opp. to display or show purposes; (hist.) applied to clothes, furniture, etc., made in standardized form in accordance with the official allowance of material **1942**; **~ *actor, man***, actor of small parts.

ūt'ilize *v.t.* Make use of, turn to account, use. **ūtilizā'tion** *n.*

ŭt'mōst *adj.* Furthest, extreme; that is such in the highest degree. **~** *n.* The utmost point, degree, limit, extent, etc.; the best of one's ability, power, etc.

Utōp'ia (ū-). Name of the imaginary island governed on a perfect political and social system, which forms the title of a book by Sir Thomas More published in 1516; any ideally perfect social and political system. **Utōp'ian** *adj.* & *n.* (Inhabitant) of Utopia; (characteristic of) an ardent but unpractical reformer. **ūtōp'ianism** *n.*

Utrecht (ūt'rĕχt, ōōtrĕχt'). City and province of the Netherlands; *Peace of* **~**, the peace concluded in 1713, which terminated the War of the Spanish Succession; **~ *velvet***, kind of mohair plush.

ūt'ricle *n.* (bot., zool.) Small cell, sac, or bladder-like part or process, esp. one of two sacs in membranous labyrinth of the inner ear. **ūtric'ūlar** *adj.*

Uttar Pradesh (ōō-, -āsh *or* -ĕsh). State in N. India (formerly United Provinces), bordering on Tibet and Nepal; capital, Lucknow.

ŭtt'er[1] *adj.* Complete, total, unqualified. **ŭtt'erly** *adv.* **ŭtt'ernėss** *n.* **ŭtt'ermōst** *adj.*

ŭtt'er[2] *v.t.* 1. Emit audibly; express in spoken or written words. 2. Put (notes, base coin, etc.) into circulation. **ŭtt'erance** *n.* Uttering; power of speech; spoken words.

ūv'ūla *n.* (pl. *-ae*). Conical fleshy prolongation hanging from middle of pendent margin of soft palate (ill. HEAD). **ūv'ūlar** *adj.*

ŭxōr'ious *adj.* Excessively fond of one's wife; marked by such fondness. **ŭxōr'iously** *adv.* **ŭxōr'iousnėss** *n.*

Uz'bĕk, Uz'bĕg (ōōz-, ŭz-) *adj.* & *n.* Member of a Turkish race inhabiting **Uzbĕkistan'** (-ahn), area S. and SE. of the Aral Sea, a constituent republic of the Soviet Union (capital, Tashkent).

V

V, v. 22nd letter of modern English and 20th of ancient Roman alphabet, adopted in form from early Greek vowel-symbol V, and in English representing a labio-dental voiced spirant. 1. V, v, Roman numeral symbol for five. 2. *V day* or *VJ day*, 15th Aug. 1945, day fixed for the official celebration of the end of the war of 1939–45; *VE day*, 8th May 1945, day fixed for the official celebration of the end of hostilities in Europe; *V-formation*, formation of aircraft in flight in shape of letter V; *V-sign*, in the war of 1939–45, first two fingers held apart in shape of letter V, the initial letter of *victory*; *V-weapon*, [abbrev. f. Ger. *Vergeltung* retribution] flying bomb (also known as *V1*) or rocket projectile (also known as *V2*) of type devised by Germans and used towards end of war of 1939–45.

v. *abbrev.* Verse; versus; *vide.*

V *abbrev.* Volt.

Va *abbrev.* Virginia.

V.A. *abbrev.* Vice-Admiral; (Order of) Victoria and Albert.

Vaal (vahl). River of S. Africa, rising in Transvaal and flowing SW. into Orange River.

vāc'ancy *n.* Being vacant; vacant space, breach, gap; lack of intelligence, inanity; unoccupied office, post, or dignity.

vāc'ant *adj.* Empty, not filled or occupied; (of the mind) unoccupied with thought; without intelligence; **~** *possession*, legal and auctioneer's term implying that immediate occupation and possession of a house etc. is offered. **vāc'antly** *adv.*

vacāte' (*or*, esp. U.S., vā'kāt) *v.t.* Leave (office, position) vacant; give up possession or occupancy of (house etc.); (law) make void, annul, cancel.

vacā'tion (*or*, esp. U.S., vā-) *n.* Vacating; time during which law-courts, schools, or universities are closed; (chiefly U.S.) holiday.

văc'cināte (-ks-) *v.t.* Inoculate with virus of cow-pox (*vaccinia*) to procure immunity from smallpox, or with a preparation of micro-organisms to protect against infectious disease. **văccinā'tion** *n.*

văc'cine (-ksēn, -ĭn) *n.* Preparation of cow-pox virus used for inoculation against smallpox; any preparation of micro-organisms used as an immunizing agent.

văccin'ia (-ks-) *n.* Cow-pox.

vă'cillāte *v.i.* Swing or sway unsteadily; hover doubtfully; waver between different opinions, etc. **văcillā'tion** *n.*

vacū'ity *n.* Empty space; absolute emptiness; vacuousness, vacancy.

văcūolā'tion *n.* (bot.) Formation of vacuoles during development of living cells.

văc'ūole *n.* Space within protoplasm usu. filled with liquid (ill. CELL).

văc'ūous *adj.* Empty; void; unintelligent, vacant. **văc'ūously** *adv.* **văc'ūousnėss** *n.*

văc'ūum *n.* Space entirely empty of matter; empty space; space, vessel, empty of air, esp. one from which air has been artificially withdrawn; **~ *bottle, flask, jar, jug***, vessel with double wall enclosing vacuum, used for keeping liquids etc. hot or cold; **~ *brake***, brake operated by (partial) vacuum, used esp. on railway-trains; **~ *cleaner***, apparatus for removing dust etc. from carpets, upholstery, etc., by suction; **~ *pump***, pump for producing a vacuum; **~ *tube***, sealed glass or metal tube or bulb from which almost all the air has been removed, so that electrical current can flow between electrodes inside without disturbance by a gaseous atmosphere; wireless valve. **~** *v.t.* (colloq.) Clean with vacuum cleaner.

V.A.D. *abbrev.* (Member of) Voluntary Aid Detachment.

vād'ė-mēc'um *n.* Book or other thing carried constantly about the person, esp. handbook or manual. [L, = 'go with me']

văg'abŏnd *adj.* Wandering, having no settled habitation or home; straying; (as) of a vagabond. **~** *n.* Vagabond person, esp. idle and worthless wanderer, vagrant; (colloq.) scamp, rascal. **văg'abŏndage, văg'abŏndism** *ns.* **văg'abŏndish** *adj.* **văgabŏndize** *v.i.*

vagār'y *n.* Capricious or extravagant action, notion, etc.; freak, caprice.

vagīn'a *n.* Sheath-like covering, organ, or part; membranous canal leading from vulva to uterus in female mammals (ill. PELVIS); analogous structure in some other animals. **vagīn'al** *adj.*

vāg'rant *n.* One without settled home or regular work, wandering from place to place, tramp, wanderer; (law) idle and disorderly person liable to term of imprisonment. **~** *adj.* That is a vagrant;

(as) of a vagrant; roving, itinerant. **vāg'rantly** *adv.* **vāg'rancy** *n.*

vāgue (-g) *adj.* Indistinct, not clearly expressed or perceived, of uncertain or ill-defined meaning or character or appearance; forgetful, unbusinesslike. **vāgue'ly** (-gl-) *adv.* **vāgue'nėss** *n.*

vāg'us *n.* (anat., zool.) Pneumogastric nerve, either of 10th pair of cranial nerves, with branches to thoracic and abdominal viscera etc.

vain *adj.* Unsubstantial, empty, of no effect, unavailing; having excessively high opinion (*of* one's own appearance, qualities, possessions, etc.); *in* ~, to no effect or purpose, vainly; *take in* ~, utter, use (name, esp. of God), needlessly, casually, or idly. **vain'ly** *adv.*

vainglōr'y *n.* Boastfulness, extreme vanity. **vainglōr'ious** *adj.* **vainglōr'iously** *adv.* **vainglōr'iousnėss** *n.*

vair *n.* Kind of grey-and-white squirrel-skin much used in 13th–14th centuries as lining or trimming (archaic); (her.) representation of this with small shield-shaped spaces of two tinctures, usu. azure and argent, arranged alternately (ill. HERALDRY).

Vaisya (vī'sya) *n.* (Member of) the 3rd of the 4 great Hindu castes, comprising merchants and agriculturists. [Sansk. *vaisya* peasant, labourer]

Vălais' (-ĕ). Canton of Switzerland.

văl'ance *n.* Short curtain round frame or canopy of bedstead (ill. BED), above window or under shelf.

vāle[1] *n.* Valley (now chiefly poet.).

vāl'ė[2] *int.* & *n.* Farewell. [L, = 'be well!']

vălėdĭc'tion *n.* (Words used in) bidding farewell.

vălėdictōr'ian *n.* (U.S.) Farewell oration delivered by senior scholar on graduation etc.; speaker of this.

vălėdĭc'tory *adj.* & *n.* (Speech, oration) bidding farewell.

valence: see VALENCY.

Valĕn'cia (-sha). Town and province of E. Spain; variety of almond, raisin, orange, and other fruits, produced there.

Valenciennes (vălahṅsyĕn'). Town in NE. France, formerly Flemish; ~ *(lace)*, (in Engl. usu. pr. vălensēnz'), fine bobbin-lace made at Valenciennes in 17th and 18th centuries.

vāl'ency, vāl'ence *ns.* (chem.) 1. The power which atoms possess of combining with one another to form molecules; ~ *bond*, linkage between two atoms in a molecule, formed either by the transfer of an electron from one atom to the other (*electrovalent bond*) or by the sharing of electrons, two to each link, between the atoms (*covalent bond*). 2. A number indicating the number of atoms of hydrogen with which a single atom of a given element can combine; an element with a valency of 1 is *univalent* or *monovalent*, of 2 *bivalent* or *divalent*, of 3 *tervalent* or *trivalent*, of 4 *quadrivalent* or *tetravalent*, etc.

Văl'entīne[1], St. Name of several saints of whom most celebrated are two martyrs whose festivals fall on 14th Feb., both belonging to reign of the emperor Claudius.

văl'entīne[2] *n.* 1. *St. Valentine's day*, 14th Feb., on which birds were believed to mate and sweethearts were chosen. 2. Sweetheart chosen on St. Valentine's day; gift given on this occasion (archaic); letter or card, of sentimental or comic nature, sent, usu. anonymously, to person of opposite sex on St. Valentine's day.

Valera, Eamon de: see DE VALERA.

valēr'ian *n.* Any species of widely distributed herbaceous genus *Valeriana*, esp. *V. officinalis* with small pink or white flowers and strong odour esteemed by cats; dried roots etc. of species of valerian used as carminative etc., or in scents etc.

valĕ'rĭc (*or* -ēr-), **valērĭăn'ĭc** *adjs.* Derived from valerian; ~ *acid*, any of 4 strong-smelling isomeric fatty acids.

Val'éry (vălā-), Paul (1871–1945). French poet.

văl'ėt (*or* -lā) *n.* (also ~ *de chambre*, pr. vălā de shahṅbr). Manservant attending on man's person and having charge of clothes etc.; one who cleans, presses, and mends clothes. ~ *v.t.* Wait on, act, as valet.

vălėtūdĭnār'ian *adj.* & *n.* (Person) of infirm health, esp. unduly solicitous or anxiously concerned about health. **vălėtūdĭnār'ianĭsm** *n.* **vălėtūd'ĭnary** *adj.*

văl'gus *n.* (path.) Deformity in which the legs are knock-kneed, i.e. the distal parts are bent outward; knock-kneed person.

Vălhăll'a. (Northern myth.) Hall assigned to heroes who have died in battle, in which they feast with Odin.

văl'iant (-ya-) *adj.* Brave, courageous. **văl'iantly** *adv.*

văl'id *adj.* (Of reason, argument, etc.) sound, defensible, well-grounded; (law) sound and sufficient, executed with proper formalities. **văl'idly** *adv.* **valĭd'ĭty** *n.*

văl'idāte *v.t.* Make valid, ratify, confirm. **văl'idā'tion** *n.*

vălise' (-ēz) *n.* Kind of travelling-bag carried by hand (chiefly U.S.); large waterproof case for an officer's bedding and spare clothing, rolled up from one end and secured by straps.

vălkȳ'rie (*or* -ĭr'ĭ) *n.* (Northern myth.) Each of 12 war-maidens supposed to hover over battle-fields selecting those to be slain and conducting them to Valhalla.

Val(l)ĕtt'a. Capital city and port of Malta.

văll'ey *n.* Long depression or hollow between hills, freq. with stream or river along bottom; stretch of country drained or watered by river-system; any depression or hollow resembling valley, esp. trough between waves; angle formed by intersection of two roofs or roof and wall (ill. ROOF); ~ *of the shadow of death*, experience of being near to death (Ps. xxiii. 4).

Văll'ey Forge. Valley near Philadelphia where George Washington and Amer. Revolutionary army passed winter of 1777–8 in conditions of great hardship.

văl(l)ōn'ĭa *n.* Dried acorn cups of the ~ *oak* (*Quercus aegilops*), a Levantine evergreen oak; used in tanning, dyeing, etc.

văll'um *n.* (Rom. antiq.) Rampart surmounted by stockade, or wall, of earth, sods, or stone, as means of defence.

Valois (văl'wah). Medieval duchy of France; *House of* ~, French royal line 1328–1589.

văl'orize *v.t.* Fix or raise price of (commodity) by artificial means, esp. by centrally organized scheme. **vălorizā'tion** *n.*

văl'our (-ler) *n.* (now chiefly poet. and rhet.) Courage, esp. as shown in war or conflict. **văl'orous** *adj.* **văl'orously** *adv.*

Vălparais'o (-āzō, -īzō). Seaport and city of Aconcagua province, Chile.

valse (vahls, vawls) *n.* Waltz.

văl'ūable *adj.* Of great value, price, or worth. ~ *n.* (usu. pl.) Valuable thing or possession esp. small article.

vălūā'tion *n.* Estimation (esp. by professional valuer) of thing's worth; worth so estimated, price set on thing.

văl'ūe *n.* 1. Amount of commodity, money, etc., considered equivalent for something else; material or monetary worth of thing; worth, desirability, utility, qualities on which these depend; (econ.) amount of commodity, money, etc., for which something else is readily available; FACE, SURPLUS, SURRENDER, ~: see these words. 2. (math. etc.) Precise number or amount represented by figure, quantity, etc. 3. (mus.) Relative duration of tone signified by note. 4. (painting) Relation of part of picture to others in respect of light and shade, part characterized by particular tone. ~ *v.t.* Estimate value of, appraise, esp. professionally; have high or specified opinion of, prize, esteem, appreciate.

văl'ūelėss *adj.* Worthless. **văl'ūelėssnėss** *n.*

văl'ūer *n.* (esp.) One who estimates or assesses values professionally.

valūt'a *n.* Agreed value of currency, its exchange value with other currencies; currency with respect to these values.

văl′vate, vălved (-vd) *adjs.* Having valve(s).

vălve *n.* 1. Door controlling flow of water in sluice; device for controlling flow of any fluid, usu. acting by yielding to pressure in one direction only. 2. (anat.) Membranous fold or other device in organ or passage of body closing automatically to prevent reflux of blood or other fluid (ill. HEART). 3. (pop.) A thermionic or wireless valve (see VACUUM tube; ill. THERMIONIC). 4. (mus.) Device for varying length of tube in instruments of horn or trumpet kind (ill. BRASS). 5. (conch.) Each half of hinged shell, single shell of same form; (bot.) each half or section of dehiscent pod, capsule, etc.

văl′vūlar *adj.* Of, like, acting as, furnished with, valve(s).

văm′brāce *n.* (hist.) Defensive armour for forearm (ill. ARMOUR).

vamōōse′ (-s) *v.i.* (slang) Make off, decamp (from). [Span. *vamos* let us go]

vămp[1] *n.* 1. Upper front part of boot or shoe (ill. SHOE). 2. Something vamped up or patched; (mus.) improvised accompaniment, introducing bars of song etc. ~ *v.* 1. Put new vamp to (boot, shoe); repair, patch *up*. 2. Make *up*, produce (as) by patching; compose, put together (book etc.) out of old materials; serve up (something old) as new by addition or alteration; (mus.) improvise (accompaniment etc.), improvise accompaniments.

vămp[2] *n.* Adventuress, woman who exploits men. ~ *v.t.* Attract as vamp, allure, entice. [abbrev. of *vampire*]

văm′pīre *n.* 1. Reanimated corpse supposed in parts of central and E. Europe to leave grave at night and renew its life by sucking blood of sleeping persons; hence, person preying on others; vamp. 2. Stage trap-door allowing demon etc. to appear or disappear suddenly. 3. ~ (*bat*), various small bats of S. America which suck blood of animals (genera *Desmodus*, *Diaemus*, and *Diphylla*); various other bats, chiefly S. American, which do not suck blood, esp. the large *false* ~ (*Vampyrus spectrum*). **vămpī′rĭc, văm′pīrĭsh** *adjs.* **văm′pīrĭsm** *n.*

văn[1] *n.* (archaic) Winnowing-machine or shovel; (poet.) wing, esp. of bird.

văn[2] *n.* Front part, foremost division, of army, fleet, etc., moving forward or onward; (fig.) leaders of movement etc. [abbrev. of *vanguard*]

văn[3] *n.* Covered vehicle for carrying goods; railway-truck for goods, luggage, mails, or for use of guard. [abbrev. of *caravan*]

văn[4] *n.* (lawn tennis) Advantage; esp. in ~ *in*, ~ *out*. [abbrev. of *vantage*]

văn′adate *n.* Salt of vanadium.

vanā′dium *n.* Extremely hard, steel-white metallic element found in small quantities in combination in many minerals; symbol V, at. no. 23, at. wt 50·942; ~ *steel*, steel alloyed with vanadium (and sometimes other elements). **vanăd′ĭc, văn′adous** *adjs.* [ON *Vanadis*, a name of FREYJA]

Văn′brugh (-brŏ), Sir John (1664–1726). English playwright and architect.

Văn Būr′en, Martin (1782–1862). 8th president of U.S., 1836–40.

Văncouv′er (-kōō-). City and seaport of British Columbia, Canada; ~ *Island*, large island off Pacific coast, opposite Vancouver. [George *Vancouver* (1758–98), Engl. navigator and explorer of W. coast of N. America]

Văn′dal *n.* 1. One of an ancient Germanic people who invaded W. Europe, and settled in Gaul, Spain, etc., in 4th and 5th centuries and finally (428–9) migrated to N. Africa; in 455 they sacked Rome in a marauding expedition; their kingdom in N. Africa was overthrown by Belisarius in 533. 2. (*v*~) Wilful or ignorant destroyer of anything beautiful, venerable, or worthy of preservation. **văn′dalĭsm** *n.* **văndalĭs′tĭc** *adj.*

Văn de Vĕl′de (-dĕ). Dutch family of artists; the best-known are Willem the younger (1633–1707), marine painter, and his brother Adriaen (1636–72), landscape-painter.

Văn Diem′en's Land. Old name of Tasmania. [named by Tasman after Anthony *Van Diemen* (1593–1645), Du. governor of Java, who sent him on his voyage]

Văn Dyck (-dīk), **Văndȳke′**, Sir Anthony (1599–1641). Flemish portrait-painter who worked for some years, and died, in England; *vandyke beard*, neat pointed beard of kind freq. found in his paintings; *vandyke brown*, a deep-brown pigment; *vandyke collar*, broad lace or linen collar with deeply indented edge, seen in portraits by Van Dyck. **văndȳke′** *n.* Each of deep points forming border of vandyke collar. ~ *v.t.* Cut (cloth etc.) in vandykes.

vāne *n.* Weathercock; windmill-sail; blade, wing, or other projection attached to axis etc. so as to be acted on by current of air or liquid; the barbs of a feather (ill. FEATHER); sight of surveying instrument.

Vanĕss′a. Genus of butterflies, including peacock, red admiral, etc.

Văn Eyck (īk), Jan (1390?–1440). Flemish artist; pioneer, together with his brother Huibrecht or Hubert (1366?–1426), in use of oils in painting.

Văn Gogh (gŏχ), Vincent (1853–90). Dutch Post-Impressionist painter, active chiefly in France.

văn′guard (-gârd) *n.* Van, forefront.

vanĭll′a *n.* (Long slender pod-like capsule of) the climbing orchid *Vanilla planifolia* or other species of this tropical American genus; aromatic extract of this used as flavouring or perfume.

vanĭll′ĭn *n.* (chem.) The fragrant principle of vanilla, a derivative of *benzaldehyde*, C_6H_5CHO.

văn′ĭsh *v.i.* Disappear from sight, esp. suddenly and mysteriously; pass, fade, away; cease to exist; (math.) become zero; *vanishing cream*, face cream which is quickly absorbed by skin; *vanishing point*, in perspective, point at which receding parallel lines appear to meet.

văn′ĭty *n.* What is vain or worthless; futility, worthlessness, emptiness; empty pride, self-conceit and desire for admiration; ~ (*-bag*, *-case*), woman's small handbag or case containing mirror, face powder, etc.; *V*~ *Fair*, (from Bunyan's 'Pilgrim's Progress') the world as scene of idle amusement and vain display; fashionable world of society.

vănq′uĭsh *v.t.* (now chiefly rhet.) Conquer, overcome.

va′ntage (vah-) *n.* Advantage (esp. in lawn tennis); ~*-ground*, *coign of* ~, position giving superiority in defence or attack.

văp′ĭd *adj.* Insipid, flat. **văp′ĭdly** *adv.* **vapĭd′ĭty, văp′ĭdnėss** *ns.*

vāp′orīze *v.* Convert, be converted, into vapour. **vāp′orīzer** *n.* (esp.) Apparatus for vaporizing liquid, fine spray. **vāporīzā′tion** *n.*

vāp′our (-*er*) *n.* Matter diffused or suspended in air, as mist, steam, etc., esp. form into which liquids are converted by action of heat; (physics) gaseous form of normally liquid or solid substance; vaporized substance; (pl., archaic) depression, spleen. ~ *v.i.* Emit vapour; talk fantastically or boastingly. **vāporĭf′ĭc, vāp′orous, vāp′oury** *adjs.* **vāp′orously** *adv.* **vāp′orousnėss** *n.*

văquero (-kār′ō) *n.* (In Spanish America and south-western U.S.) herdsman, cowboy.

Varăn′gian (-j-) *adj.* & *n.* (One) of the Scandinavian rovers who in 9th and 10th centuries traded, through Russia, with Constantinople, where they served as a bodyguard to the Byzantine emperors (~ *Guard*); ~ *kings*, the 'Rus' dynasty of Russia, founded 862 at Novgorod by the Varangian Rurik.

vār′ĭable *adj.* Apt, liable, to vary or change, capable of variation; modifiable, alterable, changeable, shifting, inconstant; (of star) varying periodically in brightness or magnitude; (math. etc., of quantity etc.) that may assume a succession of values, having different values under different conditions. **vārĭabĭl′ĭty, vār′ĭablenėss** *ns.* **vār′ĭably** *adv.*

vār′iable *n.* Variable quantity, star, or other thing; shifting wind, (pl.) parts of sea where steady wind is not expected.

vār′iance *n.* Disagreement, difference of opinion, lack of harmony (esp. in *at* ~); (law) discrepancy between two documents, statements, etc., that should agree.

vār′iant *adj.* Differing *from* something or from standard, type, etc. ~ *n.* Variant form, spelling, reading, etc.

vāriā′tion *n.* 1. Varying, undergoing or making modification or alteration, esp. from normal condition, action, or amount, or from standard or type; extent of this. 2. (astron.) Deviation of heavenly body from mean orbit or motion. 3. (Of magnetic needle) deviation from true north-and-south line, declination. 4. (math.) Change in function(s) of equation due to indefinitely small change of value of constants; ~ *of curve*, change of curve into neighbouring curve; *calculus of* ~*s*, branch of calculus dealing with variations of curves. 5. (mus.) One of series of repetitions of theme or tune with changes which do not disguise its identity.

văricĕll′a *n.* Chicken-pox. **văricĕll′ous** *adj.*

vă′ricocēle *n.* Varicose swelling of spermatic veins.

vār′icoloured (-kŭlerd) *adj.* Of various colours, variegated in colour.

vă′ricōse *adj.* (Of veins) having permanent abnormal local dilatation; affected with, resembling, of, a varix or varices; designed for treatment of varicose veins. **văricŏs′ity** *n.*

vār′iegāte (-rig- *or* -riig-) *v.t.* Diversify in appearance, esp. in colour. **vār′iegātėd** *adj.* **vārieगā′tion** *n.* Being variegated, esp. (bot.) presence of two or more colours in leaves, petals, etc.; defective or special development leading to such colouring; variegated marking.

varī′ety *n.* 1. Being varied, diversity, absence of monotony, sameness, or uniformity; collection of different things. 2. Different form *of* some thing, quality, or condition; kind, sort; (biol.) (plant, animal, belonging to) group distinguished by characteristics considered too trivial to allow of its classification as distinct species. 3. (freq. pl.) Entertainment such as is provided in music-halls, consisting of a number of different independent 'turns' or performances; ~ *theatre*, theatre in which such performances are given.

vār′ifōrm *adj.* Of various forms.

varī′ola *n.* Smallpox. **varī′olar, văriŏl′ic, varī′olous** *adjs.*

vār′iōle *n.* Something resembling smallpox mark, as spherule of variolite.

vār′iolīte *n.* Rock with whitish spherules embedded in it. **vāriolit′ic** *adj.*

vāriōr′um *n.* & *adj.* (Edition, esp. of classical author or text) with notes of various editors or commentators. [L, gen. pl. of *varius* various]

vār′ious *adj.* Different, diverse; separate, several. **vār′iously** *adv.* **vār′iousnėss** *n.*

vār′ix *n.* 1. Permanent abnormal dilatation of vein or artery, usu. with tortuous development. 2. Prominent longitudinal ridge on surface of shell.

vârl′ėt *n.* (hist.) Knight's attendant or page; (archaic) menial, low fellow, scoundrel.

vârm′int *n.* (U.S. and dial.) Vermin; mischievous or discreditable person or animal.

vârn′ish *n.* Resinous matter dissolved in oil or spirit, used for spreading over surface to produce a translucent and usu. glossy protective coating; preparations of other substances, e.g. wax, cellulose, for same purpose; surface so formed; gloss; superficial polish of manner; external appearance or display without underlying reality. ~ *v.t.* Coat with varnish; gloss (*over*), disguise; *varnishing day*, day before opening of exhibition of paintings on which exhibitors may retouch and varnish their work.

Vă′rrō, Marcus Terentius (116–27 B.C.). Roman antiquarian and prolific author of books of history, biography, grammar, geography, and of 'De Re Rustica', a treatise on agriculture.

vârs′ity *n.* (colloq.) University (now chiefly in reference to sport, as ~ *boat, match*).

vârsovienne′ (-vyĕn) *n.* (Music for) dance resembling mazurka. [Fr., = ('dance) of Warsaw']

Vâr′una. In Hindu religion, supreme cosmic deity, creator, and ruler.

vār′y *v.* Change, make different, modify, diversify; suffer change; be or become different in degree or quality; be of different kinds; ~ (*inversely*) *as*, change in quantity or value in (inverse) proportion to.

Vasâr′i, Giorgio (1511–74). Italian painter, architect, and author of 'Lives' of Italian painters, sculptors, and architects.

Vasco da Gama: see GAMA.

văs′cūlar *adj.* (biol., anat.) Of tubular vessels; containing, supplied with, these; ~ *system*, system of tubes within an organism for conveying fluid, esp. blood, sap.

vase (vahz; U.S. vās, vāz) *n.* Vessel, usu. of greater height than width, used as ornament, for holding flowers, etc.

văs′ėline (-ēn, -in) *n.* Proprietary name of an unctuous substance got from petroleum and used for ointments etc. [Ger. *wasser* water, Gk *elaion* oil]

vās′ifōrm *adj.* Duct-shaped, tubular.

vāso-mōt or *adj.* (Of nerves) acting on walls of blood-vessels so as to constrict or dilate these and thus regulate flow of blood.

văss′al *n.* (hist.) In feudal system, one holding lands on condition of homage and allegiance to superior; (transf.) humble servant or subordinate, slave. **văss′alage** *n.* (hist.) Condition, obligations, service, of vassal; servitude, dependence; fief.

Văss′ar Cŏll′ege. College for women in State of New York, founded 1861 by Matthew Vassar, an Amer. brewer.

vast (vah-) *adj.* Immense, huge, very great. **vast′ly** *adv.* **vast′nėss** *n.*

văt *n.* 1. Large tub, cask, cistern, or other vessel for holding or storing liquids. 2. Dyeing liquor, esp. liquor containing dye in soluble non-dyeing form, which oxidizes and is deposited in fibres when textile steeped in the liquor is exposed to air; ~-*dye*, dye so used. ~ *v.* Place, treat, mature, in vat.

Văt′ican. Pope's palace and official residence on Vatican Hill in Rome; the papal government; ~ *City*, independent papal state in Rome, including Vatican and St. Peter's, established 1929 by Lateran Council; ~ *Council*, council of 1869–70 which proclaimed papal infallibility; ~ *Hill*, hill in Rome on W. bank of Tiber, opposite ancient Rome.

vatĭ′cināte *v.* Prophesy, foretell. **vaticinā′tion** *n.*

Vauban (vōbahn′), Sébastian le Prestre de (1633–1707). Marshal of France and constructor of fortifications.

vaudeville (vō′dvĭl) *n.* (orig.) French popular e.g. topical song with refrain; comedy enlivened by such songs; now, music-hall variety entertainment. [Fr., prob. f. earlier (*chanson du*) *Vau de Vire* (song of) valley of the Vire, Normandy]

Vaughan (vawn), Henry (1622–95). English metaphysical poet

GREEK VASE SHAPES

1. Amphora. 2. Crater. 3. Lecythus. 4. Hydria. 5. Cylix

and mystic, of Welsh birth and parentage.

Vaughan Will'iams (vawn), Ralph (1872–1958). English composer of symphonies, choral works, etc.

vault[1] *n.* Arched structure of masonry usu. supported by walls or pillars and serving as roof or carrying other parts of building; any arched surface resembling this, esp. apparently concave surface of sky; room or other part of building covered by vault, esp. when subterranean and used as cellar for storing food, wine, etc.; room of this kind without arched roof, underground room, strongroom; (partly) underground burial chamber in cemetery or under church. ~ *v.t.* Construct with, cover (as) with vault; form vault over; make in form of vault.

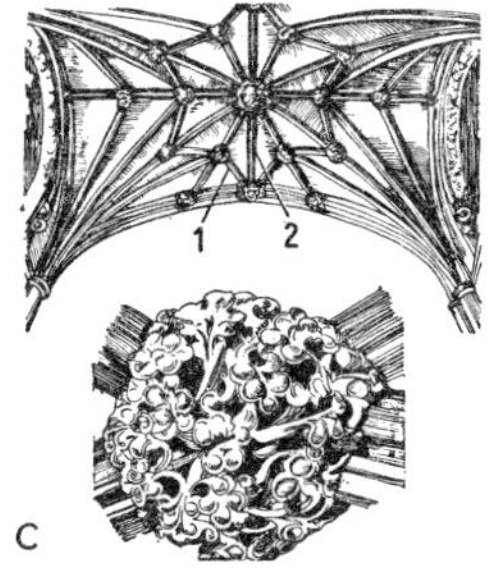

A B C D

MEDIEVAL VAULTS: A. BARREL VAULT. B. GROINED CROSS-VAULT. C. RIBBED VAULT AND DETAIL OF BOSS. D. FAN VAULT

1. Lierne. 2. Ridge rib

vault[2] *n.* Leap, spring, performed by vaulting. ~ *v.* Leap, spring, esp. while resting on the hand(s) or with help of pole; spring over thus; *vaulting-horse*, (gymnastics) wooden figure of horse for practice in vaulting.

vaunt *n.* (archaic or rhet.) Boast. ~ *v.* Boast, brag, (of). **vaunt'ingly** *adv.*

Vaux'hall (vŏx-hawl). District of London on S. bank of Thames, site of a famous pleasure garden 1661–1859. [orig. *Falkes' Hall*, f. 13th-c. owner *Falkes* de Breauté]

V.C. *abbrev.* Vice-Chancellor; Victoria Cross.

v.d. *abbrev.* Various dates.

V.D. *abbrev.* Venereal disease; Volunteer Decoration.

v. dep. *abbrev.* Verb deponent.

V.D.H. *abbrev.* Valvular disease of the heart.

veal *n.* Flesh of calf as food.

vĕc'tor *n.* 1. (math.) (Representation by line of appropriate length and having suitable direction of) quantity having both magnitude and direction. 2. (path.) Carrier of disease, esp. insect which conveys pathogenic organisms from one host to another. ~ *v.t.* (orig. U.S.) Direct (aircraft) on a course.

Ve'da (vā-). One of the Sanskrit books forming the oldest sacred literature of the Hindus; esp. any of the 4 collections of hymns, prayers, charms, etc., the RIG-VEDA and the *Yajur-*, *Sāma-*, and *Atharva-Vedas*. **Ve'dic** *adj.* [Sansk. *vēda* (sacred) knowledge]

Vedăn'ta (vā-). The older Upanishads and other Vedic books; system of philosophy based on these. **Vedăn'tic** *adj.* [Sansk. VEDA, *anta* end]

veer *v.* Change direction, esp. (of wind) in direction of sun's course; (of ship) turn with head away from wind, cause to turn thus; (fig.) change from one state, tendency, etc., to another, be variable.

Vēg'a. Brightest star in N. hemisphere, in constellation Lyra. [Arab. (*al nasr*) *al wākis* 'the falling (vulture)', meaning the constellation Lyra]

Ve'ga Carp'iō (vā-), Lope Felix de (1562–1635). Spanish poet and playwright.

Vēg'an *n.* Vegetarian who eats no butter, eggs, cheese, or milk. ~ *adj.* Of Vegans or their diet.

vĕ'gėtable *n.* Living organism belonging to plant kingdom, plant; (esp.) herbaceous plant cultivated for food. ~ *adj.* Of (the nature of), derived from, concerned with, comprising, plants; ~ *kingdom*, that division of organic nature to which plants belong; ~ *marrow*, kind of gourd (*Cucurbita pepo*), used as vegetable or for jam.

vĕ'gėtal *adj.* Of (the nature of) plants; exhibiting, producing, phenomena of physical life and growth (usu. contrasted with *animal*).

vĕgėtār'ian *n.* One who eats no animal food, or none that is obtained by destruction of animal life. ~ *adj.* Of vegetarian(s); living on vegetables; consisting of vegetables. **vĕgėtār'ianism** *n.*

vĕ'gėtāte *v.i.* Grow as or like plant(s); (fig.) lead dull monotonous life without intellectual activity or social intercourse.

vĕ'gėtative *adj.* **vĕ'gėtatively** *adv.* **vĕ'gėtativenėss** *n.*

vĕgėtā'tion *n.* 1. Vegetating; plants collectively, vegetable growths. 2. (path.) Morbid growth or excrescence on part of body.

ve'hement (vēĭ-) *adj.* Intense, violent, acting with great force; exhibiting, caused by, strong feeling or excitement. **ve'hemently** *adv.* **ve'hemence** *n.*

ve'hicle (vēĭ-) *n.* 1. Carriage or conveyance for persons or goods, any means of transport, esp. by land. 2. Substance, esp. liquid, used as medium for application, administration, etc., of another substance, as drug; liquid in which pigment is suspended. 3. Thing, person, as means, channel, or instrument of expression, communication, etc. **vehic'ular** (vĭhĭ-) *adj.*

Vehmgericht (fām'gerĭχt). One of the secret tribunals having great power in Westphalia and elsewhere in Germany from end of 12th to middle of 16th c.

veil (vāl) *n.* 1. Piece of linen or other material as part of nun's head-dress, falling over head and shoulders; *take the* ~, become nun. 2. Piece of thin, usu. more or less transparent, material worn over head or face as part of head-dress or to conceal the face or protect it from sun, dust, etc.; curtain; (fig.) disguise, cloak, mask, anything which conceals or covers; *beyond the* ~, in(to) the next world; *draw a* ~ *over*, conceal, avoid discussing or dealing with. 3. Velum. ~ *v.t.* Cover (as) with veil; (fig.) conceal, disguise, mask. **veil'ing** *n.* (esp.) Material for veils, net.

vein (vān) *n.* 1. Each of the tubular vessels in which blood is conveyed from all parts of body back to heart (ill. BLOOD); (pop.) any blood-vessel. 2. (bot.) One of the slender bundles of tissue forming framework of leaf (ill. LEAF). 3. (entom.) Nervure of insect's wing (ill. INSECT). 4. Anything suggesting or resembling vein, esp. streak of different colour in wood, marble, etc., channel of water in ice etc.; (geol.) crack or fissure in rock, freq. filled with mineral matter; (min.) fissure containing metallic ore (ill. MINE). 5. Distinctive character or tendency, cast of mind or disposition, mood. **vein'lėss, vein'y** *adjs.* **vein** *v.t.* Fill or cover (as) with vein(s). **vein'ĭng** *n.*

vēl'ar *adj.* Of a velum, esp. velum of palate; (phon., of sound) formed with back of tongue near or touching soft palate.

Vėlă'zquez (-skwĭz *or* -skĭs), Diego Rodriguez de Silva y (1599–1660). Spanish artist, court painter to Philip IV.

veld (fĕlt) *n.* In S. Africa, fenced or unfenced grassland. [Afrikaans (formerly Du. *veldt*, = 'field')]

vĕllē'ĭty *n.* Low degree of volition not prompting to action.

vĕll'ĭcāte *v.* Twitch, move convulsively. **vĕllĭcā'tion** *n.*

vĕll'um *n.* Skin (strictly calfskin) dressed and prepared for writing, painting, etc.; imitations of this, esp. (commerc.) smooth-surfaced writing-paper.

vėlŏ'cĭpēde *n.* Various light vehicles propelled by riders, esp. early forms of bicycle and tricycle.

vėlŏ'cĭty *n.* Rapidity of motion, operation, or action; (physics, eng., etc.) speed of motion in a particular direction; *actual* ~, speed at which a body moving on a curve actually moves as distinct from its *circular* ~ (speed at which it is moving round a point) and its *radial* ~ (speed at which it is moving away from or towards that point).

vėlour(s) (-oor') *n.* Woven fabric with plush-like or velvety pile; felt with similar surface, used for hats; hat of this.

velskoen (fĕl'skōōn) *n.* Shoe of untanned hide, without nails, as used in S. Africa (Engl. *veldtschoe*). [Du. *vel* skin]

vēl'um *n.* (pl. *-la*). (anat., bot., zool.) Membrane or membranous partition; esp. the soft palate, a membranous septum extending backwards from the hard palate (ill. HEAD).

vĕl'vėt *n.* Textile fabric, wholly or partly of silk, having a dense smooth pile on one side formed by loops of additional weft-threads, the loops being usu. cut through during the weaving (ill. WEAVE); surface, substance, resembling this in softness or rich appearance, e.g. soft downy skin covering newly grown antlers of deer; *on* ~, in easy or advantageous position. ~ *adj.* Of, soft as, velvet; ~ *glove*, outward gentleness cloaking inflexibility. **vĕl'vėty** *adj.*

vĕlvėteen' *n.* & *adj.* (Of) a cotton fabric resembling velvet with a pile formed usu. by weft-threads; (pl.) velveteen trousers.

Ven. *abbrev.* Venerable.

vēn'a cāv'a *n.* Each of two veins (*inferior* ~ and *superior* ~) conveying blood to right atrium of heart (ill. HEART).

vēn'al *adj.* (Of person) that may be bribed, willing to lend support, exert influence, or sacrifice principles, from mercenary motive; (of action etc.) characteristic of venal person. **vēn'ally** *adv.* **vėnăl'ĭty** *n.*

vėnā'tion *n.* Arrangement of veins in a leaf or leaf-like organ.

vĕnd *v.* Sell (now rare exc. law); offer (esp. small articles) for sale, hawk; *vending machine*, (orig. U.S.) slot-machine. **vĕn'dor** *n.*

vĕn'dāce *n.* Kinds of small delicate freshwater fish (*Coregonus vandesius* and *C. gracilior*) of some Scottish and English lakes.

Vend'ée, La (vahṅdā). Maritime department of W. France; *Wars of the* ~ (1793–6), insurrection of people of La Vendée against Republic. **Vĕndē'an** *adj.* & *n.* (Inhabitant) of La Vendée; of the insurrection of 1793.

Vendémiaire (vahṅdāmyār'). 1st month of French revolutionary calendar, 22nd Sept.–22nd Oct. [L *vindemia* vintage]

vĕndĕtt'a *n.* Blood-feud, esp. one practised through generations, as in Corsica and parts of Italy.

vėneer' *v.t.* Cover, overlay, (furniture etc.) with thin sheet of finer wood or other more beautiful or valuable material; (fig.) give merely specious or superficial appearance of some good quality to, gloss over. ~ *n.* Thin outer sheet used in veneering; (fig.) superficial appearance.

vĕn'erable *adj.* Entitled to veneration on account of age, character, etc.; (in C. of E.) as title of archdeacons; (in R.C. Ch.) as title of one who has attained lowest of 3 degrees of sanctity but is not yet beatified or canonized; *V~ Bede*: see BEDE. **vĕnerabĭl'ĭty, vĕn'erablenėss** *ns.* **vĕn'erably** *adv.*

vĕn'erāte *v.t.* Regard with feelings of respect and reverence; consider as exalted or sacred. **vĕnerā'tion** *n.*

vėnēr'ėal *adj.* Of, connected with, sexual desire or intercourse; (of disease) communicated by sexual intercourse with infected person; infected with venereal disease, as e.g. gonorrhoea or syphilis. [f. VENUS]

Vėnē'tian (-shn) *adj.* & *n.* (Inhabitant) of Venice; ~ *blind*, window blind of horizontal slats that may be turned so as to admit or exclude light; ~ *glass*, decorative glassware made at Murano near Venice since 15th c., freq. very elaborate and sometimes fusing clear glass with opaque or with glass of various colours; ~ *lace*, one of several varieties of point lace; ~ *pearl*, imitation pearl made of solid glass; ~ *red*, reddish pigment consisting of ferric oxides; ~ *School*, school of painting centred in Venice in the 15th and 16th centuries, culminating in the work of Giorgione, Titian, Veronese, and Tintoretto; revival of this in 18th c.; ~ *window*: see ill. WINDOW.

Vĕnėzue'la (-zwā'la). S. Amer. republic on Caribbean Sea, formed 1830 after secession from the Republic of Colombia; capital, Caracas. **Vĕnėzue'lan** *adj.* & *n.* (Native, inhabitant) of Venezuela.

vĕn'geance (-jans) *n.* Avenging oneself on another, retributive or vindictive punishment, hurt or harm inflicted in revenge; *with a* ~, in an extreme degree, with great force or violence.

vĕnge'ful (-jf-) *adj.* Seeking vengeance, disposed to revenge, vindictive. **vĕnge'fully** *adv.* **vĕnge'fulnėss** *n.*

vēn'ial *adj.* (Of sin or fault) pardonable, excusable, not grave or heinous, (theol.) not MORTAL. **vēn'ially** *adv.* **vēn'ialnėss, vēniăl'ĭty** *ns.*

Vĕn'ice (Ital. *Venezia*). Seaport of NE. Italy built on numerous islands in a lagoon of the Adriatic; formerly the chief European port for trade with the East, famous esp. for its beauty and (from 15th to 18th c.) as a centre of art; ~ *glass*, VENETIAN glass; ~ *treacle*, old antidote to poisonous bites compounded of many drugs mixed with honey, theriac; ~ *turpentine*, larch resin, used in painting.

vĕn'ison (-nzn, -nĭzn) *n.* Deer's flesh as food.

Vĕnizelos (-zā'los), Eleutherios (1864–1936). Greek statesman, born in Crete; several times prime minister of Greece between 1910 and 1933; supported Allied cause in the war of 1914–18 in opposition to king of Greece.

vĕn'om *n.* Poisonous fluid secreted by certain snakes etc. and injected by biting or stinging; (fig.) bitter or virulent feeling, language, etc. **vĕn'omous** *adj.* **vĕn'omously** *adv.* **vĕn'omousnėss** *n.*

vēn'ous *adj.* Of veins; veined; (of blood) having given up oxygen in capillaries and hence of dark-red colour, like blood contained in veins (opp. ARTERIAL). **vēn'ōse** *adj.* (esp.) Having many or very marked veins. **vėnŏs'ĭty** *n.* (esp., med.) Condition in which arteries contain venous blood.

vĕnt[1] *n.* Opening or slit in garment, esp. slit in back of coat.

vĕnt[2] *n.* Hole or opening allowing passage out of or into confined space, as hole in top of barrel to admit air while liquid is drawn out, finger-hole in musical instrument etc.; anus, esp. of lower animals; (fig.) outlet, free passage, free play; ~*-hole*, vent. ~ *v.t.* Make vent in; give vent or free expression to.

vĕn'ter *n.* (anat.) Belly; protuberance or concave part of muscle or bone; (law) womb, mother.

vĕn'tĭlāte *v.t.* Expose to fresh air, purify by air, oxygenate; cause air to circulate freely in (enclosed space); make public, discuss freely. **vĕntĭlā'tion** *n.*,

vĕnt'ilātor *n.* (esp.) Contrivance, e.g. revolving fan, for ventilating building, ship, mine, etc.; opening in wall, freq. with grid, for same purpose.

Ventose (vahṅtōz'). 6th month of French revolutionary calendar, 19th Feb.–20th Mar. [L *ventus* wind]

vĕn'tral *adj.* Of the abdomen, abdominal; of the anterior or lower surface (opp. DORSAL). **ventrally** *adv.*

vĕn'tricle *n.* (anat., zool.) Cavity of body, esp. cavity of heart from which blood is pumped into arteries (in mammals and birds, either of two such cavities; ill. HEART); one of series of communicating cavities in brain formed by enlargements of neural canal (ill. BRAIN). **vĕntric'ūlar, vĕntri'cūlous** *adjs.*

vĕntril'oquism, vĕntril'oquy *ns.* Practice of speaking etc. without visible movement of the lips and in such a manner that the voice appears to come from some other person or object. **vĕntrilō'quial, vĕntriloquis'tic, vĕntril'oquous** *adjs.* **vĕntril'oquist** *n.* **vĕntril'oquize** *v.i.* [L *venter* belly, *loqui* speak]

vĕn'ture *n.* Undertaking of a risk, risky undertaking; (archaic) property at stake, thing risked; *at a* ~, at random. ~ *v.* Dare; not be afraid, make bold *to* do, hazard (opinion etc.). **vĕn'turesome** (-chers-) *adj.* **vĕn'turesomely** *adv.* **vĕn'turesomenėss** *n.*

vĕn'ūe *n.* (law) County, district, where jury is summoned to come for trial of case; (pop.) rendezvous, meeting-place.

vēn'ūle *n.* (anat.) Minute vein.

Vēn'us. 1. Roman goddess of beauty and (esp. sensual) love, identified with Greek Aphrodite; ~ *of Milo*, Hellenistic marble statue of Aphrodite found on island of Melos in 1820 and now in the Louvre; *Mount of* ~, (palmistry) protuberance at base of the thumb; ~*'s comb*, annual of parsley family with comb-like fruit; marine snail (*Murex tenuisspina*) having rows of long spines on shell; ~*'s fly-trap*, N. Amer. insectivorous plant (*Dionaea muscipula*); ~*'s hair*, delicate maidenhair fern; ~*'s slipper*, 'lady's slipper'; wild orchid (*Cypripedium*). 2. 2nd planet in order of distance from sun, in orbit between Mercury and the earth; the morning or evening star (ill. PLANET).

Vēn'usbĕrg. Mountain, identified with Hörselberg in Thuringia, in the caverns of which, according to the Tannhäuser legend, Venus held her court.

verā'cious (-shus) *adj.* Speaking, disposed to speak, truth; true, accurate. **verā'ciously** *adv.* **verā'city** *n.*

verăn'da(h) (-da) *n.* Open roofed portico or gallery along side of house. [Hindi, f. Port. or Span. *varanda* railing]

vĕrb *n.* (gram.) Part of speech which expresses action, occurrence, or being.

vĕrb'al *adj.* 1. Of, concerned with, words; oral, not written; verbatim; ~ *note*, (diplomacy) unsigned note or memorandum as reminder of matter not of immediate importance. 2. Of (the nature of) a verb; ~ *noun*, noun derived from verb-stem and having some verbal constructions (as English nouns ending in *-ing*). **vĕrb'ally** *adv.*

vĕrb'alism *n.* Verbal expression; predominance of merely verbal over real significance. **vĕrb'alist** *n.* One concerned with words only, apart from reality or meaning.

vĕrb'alize *v.t.* Make (noun etc.) into verb. **vĕrbalizā'tion** *n.*

verbāt'im *adv.* &-*adj.* Word for word, in the exact words.

verbēn'a *n.* Vervain, (plant of) large genus of chiefly Amer. herbs with flowers in clusters; garden variety of this with blue, white, or crimson flowers.

vĕrb'iage *n.* Needless abundance of words.

verbōse' *adj.* Prolix, wordy; using, expressed in, too many words. **verbōse'ly** *adv.* **verbōse'nėss, verbŏs'ity** *ns.*

vĕrb. săp. Phrase implying that further explanation or statement is unnecessary. [abbrev. of L *verbum sat est sapienti* a word to the wise is sufficient]

Vĕrcingĕt'orix. Gallic chief of the Arverni (occupants of the district now called Auvergne) in 52 B.C. in their war against Julius Caesar.

vĕrd'ant *adj.* Green. **vĕrd'antly** *adv.* **vĕrd'ancy** *n.*

vĕrd-ăntique' (-ēk) *n.* Ornamental green serpentine marble; green patina on bronzes, verdigris; (*Oriental*) ~, green porphyry. [OF, = 'antique green']

vĕrd'erer *n.* (hist.) Judicial officer of royal forest, keeping forest assizes, etc.

Verdi (vărd'ē), Giuseppe Fortunino Francesco (1813–1901). Italian composer of operas and church music.

vĕrd'ict *n.* Decision of jury in civil or criminal cause on issue submitted to them; decision, judgement.

vĕrd'igris (*or* -ēs) *n.* Green or greenish-blue deposit forming on copper or brass as a rust; copper acetate, obtained by action of dilute acetic acid on copper and used as pigment and mordant in dyeing. [OF *vert de Grece* green of Greece]

Verdun (vărdŭṅ'). Town and fortress on Meuse, NE. France, successfully held against the Germans in 1916.

vĕrd'ure (-dyer) *n.* Fresh green colour of flourishing vegetation; green vegetation. **vĕrd'ūrous** *adj.*

vĕrge[1] *n.* 1. Extreme edge, brink, border; grass edging of path, flower-bed, etc. 2. (hist.) Area of 12 miles round king's court subject to jurisdiction of Lord High Steward (with ref. to his wand of office, see 3); (18th c.) precincts of Whitehall as place of sanctuary; (archit.) edge of tiles projecting over gable. 3. Wand, rod, carried before bishop, dean, etc., as emblem of office; shaft or spindle in various mechanisms, esp. of watch balance in old vertical escapement; (archit.) shaft of column. ~ *v.i.* Border (*up*)*on*.

vĕrge[2] *v.i.* Incline downwards or in specified direction.

vĕr'ger *n.* Official carrying rod or other symbol of office before dignitaries of cathedral, church, or university; one who takes care of interior of church and acts as attendant.

Vergil: see VIRGIL.

Verhaeren (-hăr'en), Émile (1855–1916). Belgian poet.

vėrid'ical *adj.* Truthful, veracious. **vėrid'ically** *adv.*

vĕ'rify *v.t.* Establish the truth or correctness of, examine for this purpose; (pass.) be proved true or correct by result, be borne out. **vĕ'rifiable** *adj.* **vĕrifiabil'ity, vĕrificā'tion** *ns.*

vĕ'rily *adv.* (archaic) Really, in truth.

vĕrisimil'itūde *n.* Appearance of truth or reality; probability; apparent truth.

vĕ'ritable *adj.* Real, properly or correctly so called. **vĕr'itably** *adv.*

vĕ'rity *n.* Truth; true statement; reality, fact.

vĕr'juice (-ōōs) *n.* Acid juice of crab-apples, unripe grapes, etc., used in cooking.

Verlaine (vărlĕn'), Paul (1844–96). French lyric poet belonging to the Symbolist movement.

Vermeer', Jan (1632–75). Dutch painter, of Delft.

vĕrm'eil (-mil) *n.* Silver gilt; red varnish used to give lustre to gilding; orange-red garnet; (poet.) vermilion. ~ *adj.* (poet.) Vermilion.

vĕrmicĕll'i *n.* Slender worm-like threads made from glutinous wheaten paste (orig. in Italy); cf. MACARONI, SPAGHETTI. [It., = 'little worms' (L *vermis* worm)]

vĕrm'icide *n.* Substance used to kill worms, esp. intestinal worms.

vermic'ūlar *adj.* Worm-like in form or movements; of worm-eaten appearance; marked with close wavy lines; (med.) of, caused by, intestinal worms.

vermic'ūlātėd *adj.* Covered or ornamented with close wavy markings like those made by gnawing of worms or their sinuous movements (ill. MASONRY). **vermicūlā'tion** *n.*

vĕrm'iform *adj.* Worm-shaped; ~ *appendix*, small worm-like blind tube extending from caecum in man and some other mammals.

vẽrm'ifūge *n.* Substance that expels worms from intestines.

vermil'ion (-yon) *n.* Cinnabar, red crystalline mercuric sulphide or similar earth, used as pigment etc.; brilliant scarlet colour of this. ~ *adj.* Of this colour. ~ *v.t.* Colour (as) with vermilion.

vẽrm'in *n.* (usu. collect.) Animals and birds injurious to game, crops, etc.; creeping or wingless insects etc. of noxious or offensive kind, esp. those infesting or parasitic on living beings or plants; noxious, vile, or offensive persons. **vẽr'minous** *adj.* (esp.) Infested with, full of, vermin; caused by vermin. **vẽrm'inously** *adv.* **vẽrm'inousness** *n.*

Vermŏnt'. New England State of U.S., admitted to Union in 1791; capital, Montpelier.

vẽrm'outh (-ōōth; *or* vārm'-ōōt) *n.* White wine flavoured with wormwood or other aromatic herbs, made esp. in France and Italy. [Fr., f. Ger. *wermuth* wormwood]

vernăc'ūlar *adj.* (Of language, idiom, word) of one's own native country, native, indigenous, not of foreign origin or of learned formation; (of disease) = ENDEMIC. ~ *n.* The language or dialect of the country. **vernăc'ūlarly** *adv.* **vernăc'ūlarīze** *v.t.*

vẽrn'al *adj.* Of, appropriate to, coming or happening in, spring; ~ *equinox*: see EQUINOX; ~ *grass*, kind of European grass (*Anthoxanthum odoratum*), sweet-smelling when dry and freq. grown for hay. **vẽrn'ally** *adv.*

vẽrn'alīze *v.t.* Accelerate flowering by treatment of seed or seedlings. **vẽrnalīzā'tion** *n.*

vernā'tion *n.* (bot.) Arrangement of leaves in bud.

Verne (vārn), Jules (1828–1905). French novelist, who achieved popularity by combination of adventure with popular science in his 'Twenty Thousand Leagues under the Sea' etc.

vẽrn'ier *n.* Short graduated scale sliding along fixed scale, for measuring fractional parts of divisions of larger scale. [after

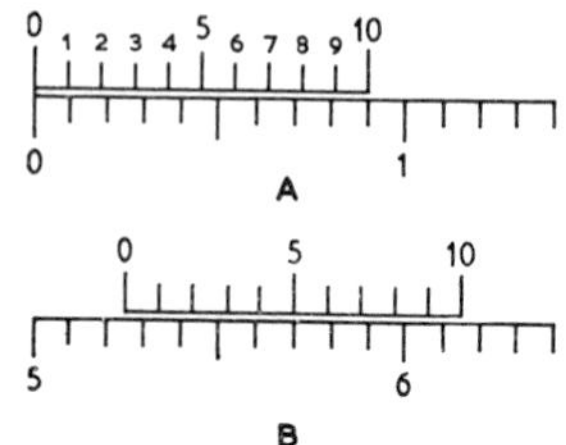

VERNIER SCALE

A. Main scale (lower) in units and tenths, with vernier (above) to read hundredths. B. Showing a reading of 5·25

Pierre *Vernier* (1580–1637), French mathematician]

Verōn'a. City of N. Italy.

vĕ'ronal *n.* Hypnotic drug (*diethylbarbituric acid*) in form of white slightly bitter powder. [Ger. trade-name]

Vĕronēse'[1] (-z) *adj.* & *n.* (Native, inhabitant) of Verona.

Vĕrone'se[2] (-nāzĕ). Paolo Cagliari (1528–88). Italian painter.

Verŏn'ica[1], St. A woman who, acc. to legend, wiped the sweat from the face of Christ on the way to Calvary with a handkerchief (preserved at St. Peter's, Rome) on which His features were miraculously impressed.

verŏn'ica[2] *n.* (Any of) large genus of herbs or shrubs with leafy stems and blue (occas. pink or white) flowers in racemes or spikes, speedwell. [app. f. name of St. VERONICA[1]]

vĕrruc'a (-ōō-) *n.* Wart, wart-like formation or growth. **vĕ'rrucōse, vĕrruc'ous** *adjs.*

Versailles (vārsī'). Town SW. of Paris, which contains the royal palace built by Louis XIII and XIV; *Treaty of* ~, treaty which terminated the Amer. War of Independence in 1783; treaty signed on 28th June 1919 between Germany and the Allies which terminated the war of 1914–18.

vẽrs'atīle *adj.* Turning easily or readily from one subject, occupation, etc., to another, showing facility in varied subjects, many-sided; (bot., zool.) turning, moving freely (as) on pivot or hinge. **vẽrs'atīlely** *adv.* **vẽrsatĭl'ĭty** *n.*

vẽrse *n.* 1. Words arranged according to rules of prosody and forming complete metrical line (now chiefly in ref. to Gk and Latin poetry). 2. Small number of metrical or rhythmical lines forming either a whole in themselves or a unit in a longer composition, stanza. 3. Metrical composition or structure; poetry esp. with ref. to metrical form as dist. from PROSE. 4. Each of the short sections into which the chapters of the Bible are divided. 5. Short sentence as part of liturgy; solo passage in anthem etc.

vẽrsed[1] (-st) *adj.* ~ *sine*, quantity obtained by subtracting cosine from unity.

vẽrsed[2] (-st) *adj.* Experienced, practised, skilled (*in* subject etc.).

vẽrs'icle *n.* Each of a series of short sentences said or sung in liturgy, esp. sentence said by the minister or priest and followed by another (RESPONSE) from the people; (pl.) versicles and responses collectively.

vẽrs'ĭfȳ *v.* Make verses; turn into, narrate in, verse. **vẽrsĭfĭcā'tion** *n.*

vẽr'sion (-shn) *n.* 1. Rendering of work, passage, etc., into another language; particular form of statement, account, etc., given by one person or party. 2. (obstetrics) Turning of foetus in womb to facilitate delivery.

vers libre (vār lēbr) *n.* Free verse, verse with no regular metrical system and arranged in lines of irregular length, freq. unrhymed, but having certain rhythms. **versli'brĭst** (vārlē-) *n.*

vẽrs'ō *n.* Back of leaf in manuscript or printed book, left-hand page of book (abbrev. v; opp. RECTO); reverse of coin or medal.

vẽrs'or *n.* (math.) In quaternions, factor expressing direction and amount of turning of vector.

vẽrst *n.* Obsolete Russian measure of length, about ⅔ of English mile.

vẽrs'us *prep.* (abbrev. v.). Against.

vẽrt *n.* (her.) The tincture green (ill. HERALDRY).

vẽrt'ėbra *n.* (pl. -*ae*). Each of the bony segments composing the spinal column (ill. SPINE); (pl., loosely) the backbone; *cervical vertebrae*, those of neck; *thoracic*, of ribs; *lumbar*, of loins; *sacral*, of hips; *caudal*, of tail. **vẽrt'ėbral** *adj.* **vẽrt'ėbrally** *adv.*

vẽrt'ėbrate *adj.* & *n.* (Animal) belonging to the *Vertebrata*, the division containing all animals having a cranium and a spinal column or a notochord and including mammals, birds, reptiles, amphibians, and fishes.

vẽrtėbrā'tion *n.* Formation of, division into, vertebrae or similar segments.

vẽrt'ĕx *n.* (pl. usu. -*ĭcēs*). Top, highest part or point; top of the head; (math.) point opposite base of (plane or solid) figure, point where axis meets curve or surface, or where lines forming angle meet.

vẽrt'ĭcal *adj.* Of, at, passing through, vertex or zenith, having position in heavens directly above given place or point; placed, moving, at right angles to plane of horizon, perpendicular, upright; of, at, affecting, vertex of the head; ~ *combine, trust*, one operating successive processes of manufacture or distribution of a product, as dist. from HORIZONTAL combine, trust. **vẽrt'ĭcally** *adv.* **vẽrtĭcăl'ĭty** *n.*, **vẽrt'ĭcal** *n.* Vertical line, plane, or circle.

vẽrt'ĭcĭl *n.* (bot.) Number of similar organs or parts arranged in circle round axis. **vẽrtĭ'cĭllate** *adj.* **vẽrtĭ'cĭllately** *adv.*

vẽrt'ĭgo (*or* vertī'-, -tē'-) *n.* Dizziness, condition with sensation of whirling and tendency to lose equilibrium. **vertĭ'gĭnous** *adj.* Of vertigo; causing, tending to cause, giddiness. **vertĭ'gĭnously** *adv.* **vertĭ'gĭnousnėss** *n.*

Vertŭm'nus. Ancient-Italian deity, worshipped as god of the changing year, and the giver of fruits.

Vĕ'rulam (-rōō-), **Vĕrulām'ium.** Romano-British town whose modern name is St. Albans (Hertfordshire).

vẽrv'ain *n.* Common European herbaceous plant (*Verbena* *officinalis*), and other species of *Verbena*.

vẽrve *n.* Vigour, enthusiasm, energy, esp. in literary work.

vẽr′vėt *n.* (also ~ *guenon*) Small greyish African monkey (*Cercopithecus pygerythrus*).

vĕ′ry *adj.* Real, true, genuine, properly so called or designated; *the* ~, used to emphasize identity, significance, extreme degree, etc. ~ *adv.* (used with adjs., advs., adjectival participles, but not other parts of verbs) In a high degree, to a great extent, extremely; ~ *well*, formula of consent or approval.

Vĕ′ry light *n.* Coloured flare fired from *Very pistol* esp. for night signalling or to provide temporary illumination in night-fighting. [invented by Lt S. W. *Very*, 1877]

vėsĭc′a *n.* 1. (anat.) Bladder. 2. ~ (*piscis* or *piscium* = fish's or fishes'), the pointed oval (0) used as an aureole in medieval sculpture and painting. **vĕs′ical** *adj.*

vĕs′icāte *v.t.* Raise blisters on (skin etc.). **vĕs′icant, vĕs′icatory** *adjs.* & *ns.* (Substance) causing formation of blisters. **vĕsicā′tion** *n.*

vĕs′icle *n.* Small bladder-like vessel, cavity, sac; (path.) small, usu. round, elevation of cuticle containing clear watery fluid. **vėsĭc′ūlar, vėsĭc′ūlate, -ātėd** *adjs.*

Vĕspā′sian (-zhn). Titus Flavius Vespasianus (A.D. 9–79), Roman emperor A.D. 70–79; began building the Colosseum.

vĕs′per *n.* 1. *V*~, the evening star, Hesperus (i.e. the planet Venus). 2. (pl.) 6th of canonical hours of breviary, said or sung towards evening, evensong; ~ *bell*, bell that calls to vespers; *Sicilian V*~*s*: see SICILIAN.

vĕs′pertine *adj.* Of, taking place in, evening; (of animals etc.) appearing, active, (of flowers) blooming, in evening; (of star etc.) setting at or just after sunset.

Vĕspu′cci (-ōōchē), Amerigo (1451–1512). Florentine merchant who settled in Spain; he claimed to have made a voyage in 1497 in which he discovered the mainland of S. America; in virtue of this claim, which has not been proved, his name was given to the continent of America.

vĕss′el *n.* 1. Hollow receptacle for liquid etc., esp. domestic utensil, freq. of circular section, used for preparing, storing, or serving of food or drink; (bibl.) person regarded as containing or receiving some spiritual quality. 2. (anat., zool.) Membranous canal, duct, etc., in which body-fluids are contained or circulated, esp. artery or vein (*blood*-~); (bot.) woody duct carrying or containing sap etc., (rare) seed-vessel. 3. Any craft or ship, now usu. one larger than rowing-boat.

vĕst[1] *n.* Waistcoat (now chiefly shop term and U.S.); knitted or woven undergarment for upper part of body; (also *vestee′*) part of front of woman's bodice etc., usu. piece of lace etc., filling opening at neck; ~-*pocket*, waistcoat pocket (chiefly attrib. of articles etc., as cameras) of small size.

vĕs′tĭge (-j) *n.* Trace, track, evidence (of something no longer existing or present); (biol.) organ or part which is small or degenerate in descendants but in ancestors was fully developed. **vĕstĭ′gial** *adj.*

vĕst′ment *n.* Garment, esp. worn by king or official on ceremonial occasion; any of official garments of priests, choristers, etc., during divine service etc., esp. chasuble.

ANGLICAN VESTMENTS: A, B. BISHOP. C, D. PRIEST

1. Mitre. 2. Orphrey. 3. Morse. 4. Cope. 5. Crosier. 6. Chimere. 7. Rochet. 8. Surplice. 9. Tippet. 10. Cassock. 11. Hood. 12. Chasuble. 13. Alb. 14. Amice. 15. Maniple. 16. Stole

vĕst[2] *v.* 1. (chiefly passive) Invest (person) *with* power, authority, etc.; put in full or legal possession of something, place or secure (something, freq. power or authority) in possession of person(s). 2. Become vested (*in* person), pass into possession of. **vĕs′tėd** *adj.* (esp. with *right, interest*) Established or secured in hands or under authority of certain person(s).

Vĕs′ta[1]. 1. Roman goddess of hearth and household, daughter of Saturn, with temple in Rome whose sacred fire was tended by 4 (later 6) *Vestal virgins*, vowed to chastity. 2. One of minor planets or asteroids with orbit between Mars and Jupiter.

vĕs′ta[2] *n.* Kind of short match, esp. with wax shaft. [f. VESTA[1]]

vĕs′tal *adj.* Of the goddess Vesta or the vestal virgins; chaste, virgin, marked by chastity or purity; ~ *virgin*: see VESTA[1], sense 1; hence, woman of spotless chastity. ~ *n.* Vestal virgin, nun.

vĕs′tĭbūle *n.* 1. Ante-chamber, hall, lobby, between entrance door and interior of house or other building; porch of church etc. 2. (Gk and Rom. antiq.) Enclosed or partially enclosed space in front of main entrance of house. 3. (chiefly U.S.) Enclosed and covered-in entrance at end of railway coach giving access to carriage and usu. communicating with other coaches. 4. (anat.) Dilated entrance to a canal or cavity in the body; ~ *of inner ear*, cavity between middle ear and cochlea (ill. EAR); ~ *of mouth*, space between the lips and cheeks and the gums. **vĕstĭb′ūlar** *adj.*

vĕs′trȳ *n.* Room or part of church used for keeping vestments, vessels, records, etc., for robing of clergy and choir, for parish meetings, etc.; (in English parishes) ratepayers of parish, representatives of these, assembled (freq. in vestry of parish church) for dispatch of parochial business; ~-*clerk*, clerk of such vestry; *vestryman*, member of parochial vestry.

Vėsū′vĭus. Active volcano near Naples, Italy. **Vėsū′vĭan** *adj.* Of Vesuvius.

vĕt *n.* (colloq.) Veterinary surgeon. ~ *v.t.* Examine, treat (beast, person) medically; submit (scheme, work, etc.) to careful examination.

vĕtch *n.* Leguminous plant of *Vicia* (esp. *V. sativa*, common tare) or related genera, many of which are valuable for fodder; *kidney*-~, leguminous herb, *Anthyllis vulneraria*. **vĕtch′lĭng** *n.* Any small plant of genus *Lathyrus*.

vĕt′eran *adj.* Grown old in service; experienced by long practice; (of army) composed of veteran troops; (of service) long-continued. ~ *n.* Veteran person, esp. soldier; (U.S.) ex-service man.

vĕt′erĭnary *adj.* Of, for, concerned with (treatment of) diseases and injuries of cattle and other animals. **vĕt′erĭnary, vĕt′erĭnār′ĭan** *ns.* (abbrev. vet) Veterinary surgeon.

vē′tō *n.* Prohibition of proposed or intended act; (exercise of) constitutional right to prohibit passing or putting in force of an enactment or measure. ~ *v.t.* Exercise veto against. [L, = 'I forbid']

vĕx *v.t.* Anger by slight or petty annoyance, irritate; (archaic) grieve, afflict; (chiefly poet.) agitate, toss about, put into state of commotion; *vexed question*, one much discussed or contested.
vĕxā'tion *n.* Being vexed, irritation; vexing thing. **vĕxā'tious** (-sh*u*s) *adj.* **vĕxā'tiously** *adv.* **vĕxā'tiousnėss** *n.*
vĕxĭll'um *n.* (pl. *-illa*). 1.

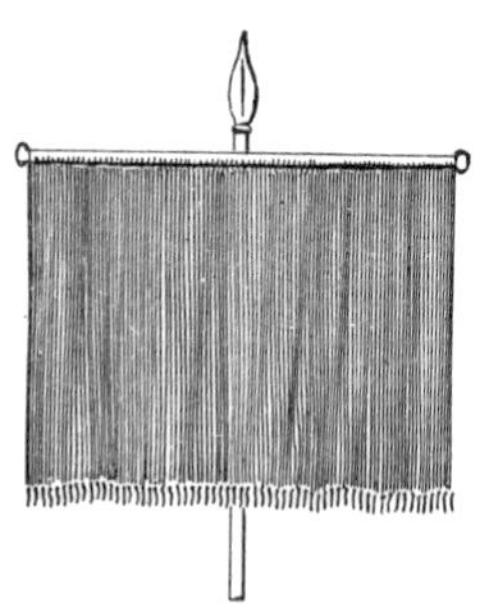

VEXILLUM

Banner of Roman troops; body of troops under this. 2. (eccles.) Small piece of linen or silk wound round upper part of crosier. 3. (bot.) Large upper petal (*standard*) of papilionaceous flower (ill. FLOWER). 4. (ornith.) Vane of feather. **vĕx'ĭllary** *adj.*
v.f. *abbrev.* Very fair.
v.g. *abbrev.* Very good.
V.G. *abbrev.* Vicar-General.
V.H.F. *abbrev.* Very high FREQUENCY.
vī'a *prep.* By way of, through (specified place).
vī'able *adj.* Capable of maintaining separate existence (of child at birth etc.); able to live in particular environment; (bot., of seeds) having ability to germinate. **vīabĭl'ĭty** *n.* [Fr., f. *vie* life]
vī'adŭct *n.* Bridge-like structure carrying railway or road over valley, river, etc.
vī'al *n.* Small vessel for liquid medicines, now esp. small glass bottle.
vī'a mĕd'ĭa. Intermediate course between extremes. [L, = 'middle way']
vī'and *n.* (usu. pl.) Article(s) of food, provision(s), victual(s).
viăt'ĭcum *n.* 1. Eucharist as administered to one (in danger of) dying. 2. (rare) Sum of money for travelling expenses, provisions for journey. [L, = 'travelling-money', f. *via* way]
vībrăc'ūlum *n.* (pl. -l*a*). (zool.) Slender whip-like movable individual in some polyzoan colonies serving e.g. to prevent noxious material from settling.
vīb'rant *adj.* Vibrating, thrilling, resonant. **vīb'rantly** *adv.* **vīb'rancy** *n.*
vīb'raphōne *n.* Percussion instrument with lids of resonators kept in constant motion by an electric current so as to produce a pulsating effect.
vībrāte' *v.* (Cause to) swing to and fro periodically, oscillate, quiver; set, be, in state of vibration; thrill; (of sound) strike ear with quivering or pulsating effect; (of pendulum) measure (seconds etc.) by vibration.
vīb'ratĭle *adj.* Of vibration, vibratory; (of cilia etc.) capable of vibrating.
vībrā'tion *n.* (esp., physics) Rapid reciprocating motion to and fro, up and down, etc., of particles of elastic body produced by disturbance of its equilibrium. **vībrā'tional** (-sh*o*-) *adj.*

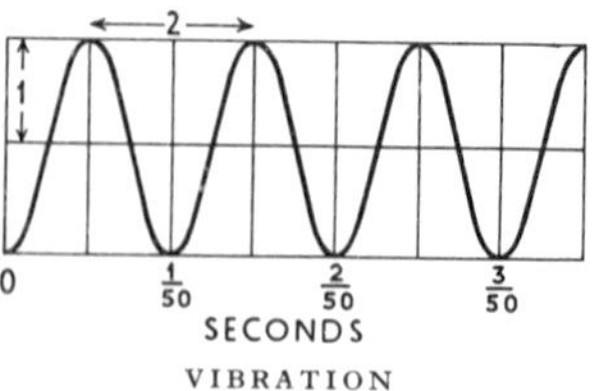

VIBRATION

1. Amplitude. 2. Wave-length or cycle. The frequency is 50 cycles per second. The wave traces a sine curve

vĭbra'tō (-ah-) *n.* (mus.) Pulsating effect in singing etc. produced by variation of emphasis on some tone, throb, 'wobble'.
vībrāt'or *n.* Thing, person, that vibrates. **vīb'ratory** *adj.* Characterized by, causing, connected with, vibration; capable of vibrating.
vībrĭss'ae *n.pl.* (anat., zool.) Stiff hairs about mouth of many animals (e.g. those in human nostrils, or 'whiskers' of cat) freq. serving as organs of touch; bristle-like feathers about beak of some birds.
vībûr'num *n.* Plant of widely distributed genus (*V*~) of shrubs including guelder-rose, laurustinus, wayfaring-tree, etc.
vĭc *n.* V-shaped formation of aircraft in flight. [name of the letter V in the phonetic alphabet]
Vic. *abbrev.* Victoria.
vĭc'ar *n.* Earthly representative of God or Christ; esp. the pope (*V*~ *of Christ*); (in England) incumbent of parish who receives only part of the tithe rent charge or none (cf. RECTOR); (R.C. Ch.) one who represents another in ecclesiastical or religious matters, esp. bishop's deputy; ~ *choral* (Ch. of Engl.) clerical or lay assistant in some (esp. musical) parts of cathedral service; ~ *general*, (R.C. Ch.) bishop's representative in jurisdictional or administrative matters; (Ch. of Engl.) lay official assisting (arch)bishop in ecclesiastical causes etc.; (hist.) title given to Thomas Cromwell (1535) as king's representative in ecclesiastical affairs; *V*~ *of Bray*: see BRAY[3].
vĭc'arage *n.* Benefice, residence, of vicar.
vĭcar'ĭal *adj.* Of, serving as, a vicar.
vĭcar'ĭous *adj.* Deputed, delegated; acting, done, endured, for another; **vĭcar'ĭously** *adv.* **vĭcar'ĭousnėss** *n.*
vĭc'arshĭp *n.* Office of vicar.
vīce[1] *n.* Evil, esp. grossly immoral, habit or conduct; depravity, serious fault; defect, blemish; fault, bad trick (of horse etc.).
vīce[2] *n.* Tool attached to bench with two jaws worked by screw for gripping firmly and holding thing being worked upon by metalworker, carpenter, etc.

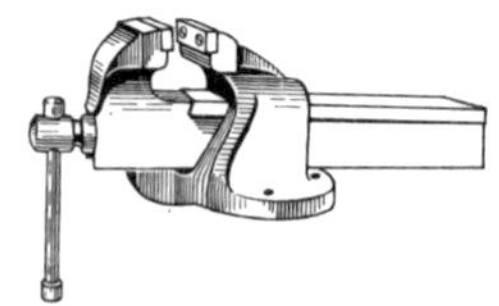

VICE

vīce[3] *n.* (colloq.) Vice-president, -chairman, -chancellor, etc., substitute, deputy.
vī'cė[4] *prep.* In the place of, in succession to.
vice-[5] *prefix.* With the sense 'person acting or qualified to act in place of, or as assistant or next in rank to'.
vīce-ăd'miral *n.* Naval officer ranking next below admiral; civil officer exercising admiralty jurisdiction in British colonial possessions etc. **vīce-ăd'miralty** *n.* Office or jurisdiction, area under jurisdiction, of civil vice-admiral.
vīce-chan'cellor (-ah-) *n.* (esp., in universities) Acting representative of Chancellor, discharging most administrative duties. **vīce-chan'cellorshĭp** *n.*
vicegē'rent (vīsjĕ'- *or* -jēr-) *n.* & *adj.* (Person) exercising delegated power, deputy. **vicegē'rency** *n.*
vīcĕnn'ĭal *adj.* Lasting, happening every, 20 years.
Vicen'te (vīsĕn't*e*), Gil (*c* 1465–1536). Portuguese poet and playwright, sometimes called the Portuguese Shakespeare.
vice-rē'gent (vīsr-) *n.* One acting in place of regent.
vicereine (vīs'rān) *n.* Wife of viceroy.
vice'roy (vīsr-) *n.* 1. Person acting as governor of country, province, etc., in name and by authority of supreme ruler; (hist.) representative of British Crown in India. 2. Handsome red-and-black Amer. butterfly, *Basilarchia archippus.* **vicerē'gal, viceroy'al** *adjs.* **vīceroy'alty** *n.*
vī'cė vêr'sa *adv. phr.* The other way round, conversely.
Vichy (vēsh'ē). Town in central France noted for mineral waters; ~ *Government*, French Government, with headquarters at Vichy,

which administered S. part of France (~ *France*) and collaborated with Germans after Franco-German armistice of 1940; ~ *water*, effervescent mineral water from Vichy, freq. bottled.

vi'cinage *n.* Neighbourhood, surrounding district; being or living near others, relation of neighbours.

vicin'ity *n.* Surrounding district; nearness in place; close relationship; *in the* ~ (*of*), in the neighbourhood (of).

vi'cious (-shus) *adj.* Of the nature of, addicted to, vice; evil; depraved; (of language, reasoning, etc.) incorrect, faulty, unsound, corrupt; (of horses etc.) having vices; bad-tempered, spiteful; ~ *circle*: see CIRCLE. **vi'ciously** *adv.* **vi'ciousness** *n.*

viciss'itūde *n.* Change of circumstances, esp. of condition or fortune.

Vicks'burg. Town in Mississippi, on the Mississippi River, where, in 1863, the Federal forces under Grant besieged the Confederates, who surrendered on 4th July; this victory and Gettysburg marked the turning-point in the Amer. Civil War.

Vico (vēk'ō), Giovanni Battista (1668–1744). Italian philosopher, jurist, and historian.

vic'tim *n.* Living creature sacrificed to a deity or in performance of religious rite; person who is killed or made to suffer by cruel or oppressive treatment; (loosely) one who suffers injury, hardship, loss, etc.

vic'timize *v.t.* Cause to suffer inconvenience, discomfort, annoyance, etc.; cheat, defraud; treat unjustly or with undue harshness, esp. by dismissal as result of strike. **victimizā'tion** *n.*

vic'tor *n.* (rhet.) Conqueror in battle or contest.

Vic'tor Emmăn'ūel. Name of 3 kings of Sardinia, 2 of whom became kings of Italy; *Victor Emmanuel I* (1759–1824), king of Sardinia 1802–21; *Victor Emmanuel II* (1820–78), first king of Italy 1861–78; *Victor Emmanuel III* (1869–1947), king of Italy 1900–46.

Victōr'ia[1] (1819–1901). Daughter of Edward, Duke of Kent, 4th son of George III; queen of Great Britain and Ireland 1837–1901; empress of India 1877–1901; married Prince Albert of Saxe-Coburg-Gotha, 1840.

Victōr'ia[2]. State of Commonwealth of Australia, in the extreme SE. of the continent, capital, Melbourne.

Victōr'ia[3]. Capital of British Columbia, Canada, and principal city of Vancouver Island.

Victōr'ia[4], Lake. Largest lake in Africa and chief reservoir of Nile.

victōr'ia[5] *n.* 1. Light low 4-wheeled carriage with collapsible hood, seats for (usu.) 2 passengers and raised driver's seat. 2.

VICTORIA

(Plant of) S. Amer. genus of gigantic water-lilies, with leaves sometimes 5 feet in diameter. 3. Variety of large red luscious plum. [f. name of Queen VICTORIA[1]]

Victōr'ia and Albert Museum. A British national museum founded 1852 as a 'Museum of Ornamental Art'; renamed by Queen Victoria after herself and her consort when she laid the foundation stone of its new building in South Kensington in 1899.

Victōr'ia Cross. (abbrev. V.C.). Decoration awarded for conspicuous bravery to members of British and British Commonwealth armed forces, first instituted by Queen Victoria in 1856 and struck from metal of guns captured at Sebastopol during the Crimean War; it consists of a cross paty of bronze with the Royal Crown surmounted by a lion in the centre, and, beneath, the inscription 'For Valour' (ill. MEDAL).

Victōr'ia Falls. Famous waterfalls on the course of the ZAMBEZI, discovered by David Livingstone in 1855.

Victōr'ian *adj.* & *n.* Of, (person) living in, the reign of Queen VICTORIA[1]; characteristic of the ethics, culture, etc., of that period; ~ *Order*, order founded in 1896 by Queen Victoria and awarded for personal service to the sovereign.

vic'torine (-ēn) *n.* (hist.) Woman's fur tippet fastening in front with two loose ends hanging down.

victōr'ious *adj.* Triumphant, successful in contest or struggle; marked by, producing, victory. **victōr'iously** *adv.* **victōr'iousness** *n.*

vic'tory *n.* Supremacy achieved by battle or in war, defeat of enemy; triumph or ultimate success in any contest or enterprise.

victual (vi'tl) *n.* (usu. pl.) Food, provisions. ~ *v.* Supply with victuals; lay in supply of victuals; eat.

victualler (vit'ler) *n.* Purveyor of victuals or provisions, esp. (*licensed* ~), keeper of public house, licensed to sell food and esp. drink for consumption on the premises; ship employed to carry stores for other ships.

vicugna, -uña (-ōō'nya) *n.* S. Amer. mammal (*Lama vicugna*) of N. Andes, related to llama and alpaca, and with fine silky wool used for textiles; soft cloth made of this, imitation of it.

vīd'ē (*or* -ē) *v.imp.* (as direction to reader) Refer to, consult.

vidēl'icĕt *adv.* (abbrev. *viz.*, usu. spoken as *namely*). That is to say, namely, to wit.

vie *v.i.* (pres. part. *vȳ'ing*). Contend or compete for superiority in some respect (*with*), be rivals.

Viĕnn'a. (Ger. *Wien*). Capital of Austria; *Congress of* ~, (1814–15) conference of European statesmen which readjusted territories and governments throughout Europe after the Napoleonic Wars. **Viennēse'** (-z) *adj.* & *n.* (Native, inhabitant) of Vienna.

Vienne (vēĕn'). Town in SE. France. *Council of* ~, 15th Oecumenical Council held 1311–12 when Pope Clement V suppressed the Knights TEMPLAR.

Viĕtnăm'. Independent republic, formed 1946 from the Tongking, Annam, and Cochin-China provinces of Fr. Indo-China; since 1954 divided into *N.* ~, capital Hanoi, and *S.* ~, capital Saigon. **Viĕtnamēse'** (-z) *adj.* & *n.*

view (vū) *n.* Inspection by eye or mind; inspection by jury of place, property, etc., concerned in case; power of seeing, range of physical or mental vision; what is seen, scene, prospect; picture etc. representing this; mental survey, mental attitude; *in* ~ *of*, having regard to, considering; *on* ~, open to inspection; *with a* ~ *to*, for the purpose of, as a step towards; with an eye to, in the hope of getting; *point of* ~, position from which thing is viewed, way of looking at a matter; *private* ~, view of exhibition open only to invited guests, usu. on day before public opening; ~*-finder*, attachment to camera showing view in range of camera lens; similar device used by painters; ~*-halloo'*, shout of huntsman on seeing fox break cover; ~*-point*, point of view. ~ *v.t.* Survey with eyes or mind, form impression or judgement of.

view'er (vū'er) *n.* (esp.) Spectator of television broadcast.

vi'gil *n.* Keeping awake during usual time for sleep; eve of a festival, esp. eve that is a fast; watch kept on this; nocturnal service; (pl.) prayers at such service, esp. for the dead; *keep* ~, keep watch.

vi'gilance *n.* Watchfulness against danger or action of others, caution, circumspection; ~ *committee*, (U.S.) self-appointed committee for maintenance of justice and order, esp. for summary punishment of crime when processes of law are considered inadequate. **vi'gilant** *adj.* **vi'gilantly** *adv.*

vigilăn'tē *n.* (orig. U.S.) Member of vigilance committee.

vignette (vēnyĕt') *n.* Decorative design, usu. small, on blank space in book, having edges shading off into surrounding paper; photograph with edges shading off into background; (fig.) character sketch or short description. ~ *v.t.* Make vignette of esp. by shading off or softening away edges. [Fr., = 'little vine', ornamental design at end of chapter]

Vigny (vēn'yē), Alfred de (1797–1863). French lyric poet, dramatist, and novelist, early leader of the Romantic movement.

Vig'ō. Seaport in NW. Spain.

vig'our (-*er*) *n.* Active physical strength or energy; flourishing physical condition, vitality; mental or moral strength, force, or energy. **vig'orous** *adj.* **vig'orously** *adv.* **vig'orousness** *n.*

Vik'ing *adj.* & *n.* (One) of the Scandinavians during the period (8th–11th centuries) when they became active as traders esp. between Russia and W. Europe, and also took to piracy, plundering and temporarily occupying many of the coastal districts and river valleys of N. and W. Europe.

vila'yĕt (-lah-) *n.* A chief administrative division or province of Turkey.

vile *adj.* Despicable on moral grounds, base, depraved, degraded; worthless, paltry, of poor or bad quality; disgusting, filthy; shameful, ignominious. **vile'ly** *adv.* **vile'ness** *n.*

vil'ify̆ *v.t.* Defame, traduce, speak evil of.

vil'ipĕnd *v.t.* (literary) Disparage, vilify.

vill'a *n.* 1. Country house or residence, with farm etc. (obs.); Italian country house. 2. Small house, detached or semi-detached, in suburban or residential district. **vill'adom** *n.* Suburban villas or their residents; the comfortable or smug middle-class world. [L *villa* farmhouse]

vill'age *n.* Assemblage of houses etc. in country district, larger than hamlet and smaller than town; (U.S.) small municipality with limited corporate powers. **vill'ager** *n.* Inhabitant of village (usu. implying rusticity).

vill'ain (-*a*n) *n.* Person guilty or capable of great wickedness, scoundrel; character in play, novel, etc., whose evil motives or actions are important element of plot; (colloq., playful) rascal, scamp. **vill'ainy** *n.*

vill'ainous (-*a*n-) *adj.* Worthy of a villain, wicked, vile; (colloq.) abominably bad. **vill'ainously** *adv.* **vill'ainousness** *n.*

villanĕlle' *n.* Poem usu. of 5 three-line stanzas and final quatrain, with two rhymes throughout, the 1st and 3rd lines of the 1st stanza being repeated alternately as refrain in other stanzas and as final couplet in the quatrain.

villĕggiatur'a (-jatoor*a*) *n.* Stay, retirement, in the country (in Italy), holiday spent thus.

vill'ein (-in) *n.* (hist.) In feudal system, peasant cultivator entirely subject to a lord or attached to a manor. **vill'einage** *n.* Tenure of villein; being a villein, serfdom.

Villiers de l'Isle-Adam (vēlyā' *de* lēl-ahdahń'), Philippe August Mathia, Comte de (1838–89). French Symbolist poet, dramatist, and novelist.

Villon (vē'yawń), François (1431–*c* 1463). French lyric poet, writer of ballades and rondeaux.

vill'ōse, vill'ous *adjs.* Covered with (numerous close slender projections resembling) thick-set hairs.

vill'us *n.* (pl. *villī*). (bot.) Long slender soft hair; (anat., zool.) slender hair-like projection, esp. of small intestine.

Vil'na, Wil'nō (v-). City of Lithuania (also *Vilnius*); area surrounding this, occupied by Poland 1920, incorporated in U.S.S.R. 1945.

vim *n.* (colloq., orig. U.S.) Vigour, energy, 'go'.

vimin'ėous *adj.* Made of pliable twigs or wickerwork; (bot.) producing long flexible shoots or twigs.

vinaigrĕtte' (-nig-) *n.* 1. Small ornamental bottle holding aromatic salts etc., smelling-bottle.

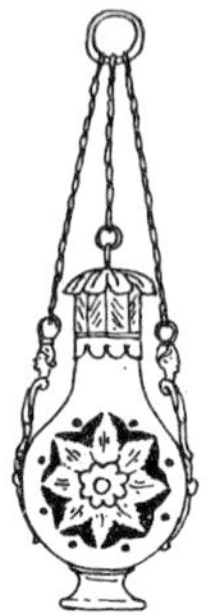

SILVER VINAIGRETTE

2. ~ (*sauce*), sauce of oil, vinegar, etc., used esp. with cold meat.

Vin'cent de Paul, St. (1576–1660). French Roman Catholic reformer, founder of 'Congregation of Priests of the Mission', a missionary society now usu. known as the Lazarists, and of a society of 'Sisters of Charity'. **Vincĕn'tian** (-shn) *adj.* & *n.* (Member) of one of these societies.

Vinci: see LEONARDO DA VINCI.

vinc'ūlum *n.* (math.) Straight line drawn over two or more terms denoting that these are subject to the same operations of multiplication, division, etc., by another term; (anat.) ligament, frenum. [L, = 'bond']

vin'dicāte *v.t.* Maintain the cause of (person, religion, etc.) successfully; establish the existence or merits or justice of (one's veracity, courage, conduct, character, assertion). **vindicā'tion** *n.*

vin'dicatory *adj.* Tending to vindicate; (of laws) punitive.

vindic'tive *adj.* Revengeful, avenging, given to revenge; ~ *damages*, damages awarded not only to compensate plaintiff but also to punish defendant. **vindic'tively** *adv.* **vindic'tiveness** *n.*

vine *n.* Trailing or climbing woody-stemmed plant (*Vitis*, esp. *V. vinifera*, from the fruit of which wine is made) bearing grapes, grape-vine; any trailing or climbing plant.

vin'ėgar *n.* Sour liquid (dilute acetic acid) produced by acetous fermentation of wine, malt liquors, etc., and used as condiment, preservative, etc. ~ *v.t.* Season, treat, with vinegar. **vin'ėgary** *adj.* Sour like vinegar, acid. [OF *vin* wine, *aigre* sour]

vin'ery *n.* Glass-house for growing grapes.

vine'yard (-ny-) *n.* Plantation of grape-vines, esp. for wine-making.

vingt-et-un (vănt ā ŭń) *n.* Card-game in which players' object is to obtain from dealer cards with values adding up to 21. [Fr., = 'twenty-one']

Vin'land. Region of N. America, probably near Cape Cod, where a settlement was made in the 11th c. by Norsemen under Leif Ericsson. [f. legend that grape-vines were found there]

vi'nō de pās'tō (vē-) *n.* Moderately sweet type of sherry. [Span., = 'wine for a meal']

vin ordinaire' (văń; -ār) *n.* Cheap usu. red wine for ordinary use in France, usu. drunk when young.

vin'ous *adj.* Of, like, due to, addicted to, wine. **vin'ously** *adv.* **vin'ousness** *n.*

vin'tage *n.* (Season of) grape-harvest; wine, esp. of good quality; wine made from grapes of particular district (freq. used with ref. to the age of a wine or the year when it was made; also used *attrib.* and *transf.*). **vin'tager** *n.* Grape-harvester.

vint'ner *n.* Wine-merchant.

vi'ol *n.* Late-medieval stringed musical instrument, similar in shape to violin, but usu. with 6 strings and held downwards on or between the knees; ~ *da gamba*, later name for bass viol, predecessor of violoncello; ~ *d'amore*, tenor viol, instrument like violin but with wire 'sympathetic strings' under finger-board, having very sweet and affecting tone (*illustration*, *p.* 919).

vi'ola[1] *n.* Genus (*V*~) of herbaceous plants including violets and pansies; hybrid garden-plant of this genus, more uniformly and delicately coloured than pansy. [L, = 'violet']

viōl'a[2] *n.* Tenor member of violin family of musical instruments, slightly larger than violin, of lower pitch (its lowest note being C below middle C) and with less bright quality of tone (ill. STRING); ~ *da gamba*, ~ *d'amore*: see VIOL.

violā'ceous (-shus) *adj.* (bot.) Of the violet family (*Violaceae*).

vī'olāte *v.t.* Transgress requirements of (law, oath, treaty, conscience, etc.); treat profanely, break in upon (sanctuary, privacy, etc.); commit rape upon. **violā'tion** *n.*

vī'olence *n.* Violent treatment or conduct, outrage, injury; violent feeling or language, vehemence; intensity (*of*); (law) (intimidation by threat of) unlawful exercise of physical force.

vī'olent *adj.* Marked by, caused by, acting with, great physical force or unlawful exercise of force; intense, vehement, passionate, furious, impetuous. **vī'olently** *adv.*

vī'olėt *n.* 1. Plant of genus *Viola*, esp. the sweet-scented *V. odorata*, with purplish-blue, mauve, or white flowers; various similar plants of other genera. 2. The purplish-blue colour of the violet, colour at opposite end of spectrum from red. ~ *adj.* Of this colour.

violin' *n.* Stringed musical instrument held under chin with left hand and played with bow or occas. by plucking (ill. STRING); it has a resonant curvilinear soundbox of polished wood over which are stretched 4 strings tuned in fifths, the lowest note being G below middle C; part for violin in instrumental composition, player of this; *first* ~, leading instrument or part in orchestra or other instrumental ensemble; *second* ~, subsidiary violin part below first; ~ *family*, group of instruments including violin, viola, violoncello, and double bass. **violin'ist** *n.* Player of violin. [It. *violino* little VIOLA[2]]

vī'olist *n.* Player on the viol.

violoncell'o (-chĕlō) *n.* (usu. abbrev. *cello*) Large instrument of violin family played supported on floor between performer's knees,

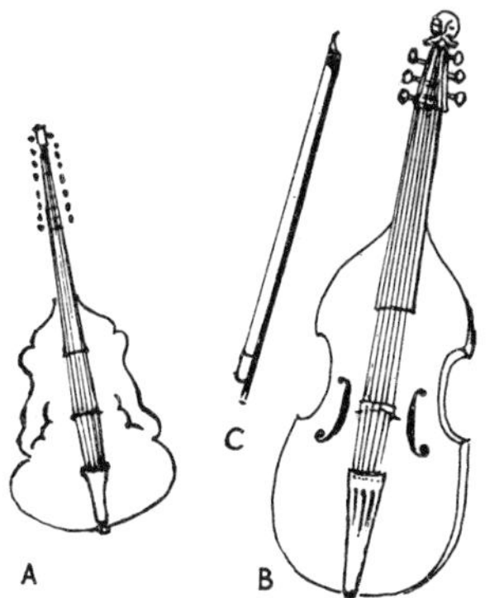

VIOL: A. VIOL D'AMORE. B. VIOL DA GAMBA. C. BOW

normally taking bass part in string ensembles but having very wide range (ill. STRING). **violoncĕll'ist** *n.* (usu. abbrev. *cellist*) Player of this. [It., dim. of *violone* double bass, f. VIOLA[2]]

V.I.P. *abbrev.* Very important person.

vip'er *n.* Small venomous snake, adder (*Vipera berus*), abundant in Europe and parts of Asia, the only venomous snake found in Britain (ill. ADDER); any snake of the genus *Vipera* or family *Viperidae*; (fig.) malignant or treacherous person; ~'*s bugloss*, coarse prickly European weed (*Echium vulgare*) with handsome blue flowers; ~'*s grass*, arrow-leaved yellow-flowered perennial herb (*Scorzonera hispanica*) with long thick edible root. **vip'erine, vip'erish, vip'erous** *adjs.*

virāg'ō *n.* (pl. *-s*). Turbulent woman, termagant. [L, = 'female warrior', f. *vir* man]

vīr'al *adj.* (Of disease) caused by a VIRUS.

Virchow (fērk'ō), Rudolf (1821–1902). German pathologist and anthropologist; author of 'Cellular Pathology' (1858).

vī'rėlay *n.* (hist.) Short lyric poem of a kind which originated (14th c.) in France, consisting of short lines arranged in stanzas with only two rhymes, the end-rhyme of one stanza being the chief rhyme of the next.

virĕs'cence *n.* Greenness, esp. (bot.) in petals etc. normally of some other colour. **virĕs'cent** *adj.*

vir̄g'ate *n.* (hist.) English land-measure, usu. ¼ of a hide.

Vir̄'gil. Publius Vergilius Maro (70–19 B.C.), Roman poet, whose chief works were the 'Aeneid', the epic poem of the Roman people, recounting the adventures of Aeneas and his Trojans; the 'Georgics', a didactic poem on agriculture and rearing of cattle and bees; the 'Eclogues' or 'Bucolics', pastoral poems. **Virgil'ian** *adj.* Of, in the style of, Virgil.

vir̄'gin *n.* Person, esp. woman, who has had no sexual intercourse; (eccles.) in early Christian times, unmarried or chaste woman distinguished for piety and steadfastness in religion; *The* (*Blessed*) *V*~ (*Mary*), mother of Christ; image or picture representing her; ~'*s bower*, travellers' joy or other species of *Clematis*. ~ *adj.* That is a virgin; of, befitting, a virgin; undefiled; spotless, not yet or not previously touched, handled, or employed; ~ *forest*, forest as yet untouched by man; *V*~ *Queen*, Elizabeth I of England; ~ *rock*, rock not yet cut into or quarried; ~ *soil*, soil not yet brought into cultivation. **vir̄gin'ity** *n.* Condition or quality of a virgin.

vir̄'ginal *adj.* Being, befitting, belonging to, a virgin. **vir̄'ginally** *adv.* **vir̄'ginal** *n* (freq. pl.) Keyboard instrument, earliest (16th and 17th centuries) and simplest form of harpsichord, with one string

VIRGINALS

to a note, in box or case, usu. without legs

Virgin'ia. S. Atlantic State of U.S., one of the original 13 States of North Amer. Union, and site of first English settlement (1607) in America; capital, Richmond; ~ *creeper*, N. Amer. climbing plants (*Ampelopsis hederacea* and *quinquefolia*) cultivated for ornament; ~ *reel*, (U.S.) a country-dance, called in England 'Sir Roger de Coverley'; ~ (*tobacco*), variety of tobacco grown in Virginia; any American tobacco. **Virgin'ian** *adj.* & *n.* [named in honour of Elizabeth I of England (VIRGIN Queen)]

Vir̄'gin Islands. Group of about 100 small islands in W. Indies, mostly uninhabited; divided between Britain and U.S.

Vir̄g'ō. Zodiacal constellation lying between Leo and Libra; 6th sign (♍) of zodiac, which sun enters towards end of August.

viridĕs'cent *adj.* Greenish, somewhat green. **viridĕs'cence** *n.*

virid'ian *n.* & *adj.* 1. (Of) yellowish-green colour. 2. Chromium oxide, an emerald-green pigment.

virid'ity *n.* Greenness, esp. of foliage or grass; mental or bodily freshness.

vi'rile (*or* vir̄-) *adj.* Of, characteristic of, a man, manly, masculine; capable of procreation; having masculine vigour or strength. **viril'ity** *n.*

vir̄ŏl'ogy *n.* Study of viruses. **vir̄ŏl'ogist** *n.*

vir̄tu', vĕr̄tu' (-ōō) *n.* (archaic) Love or knowledge of, taste for, the fine arts; *article*, *object*, *of* ~, curio, antique, or other product of the fine arts.

vir̄t'ūal *adj.* That is so in essence or effect, although not formally or actually; ~ *focus*, (optics) apparent focus of reflected or refracted rays of light. **vir̄t'ually** *adv.* **vir̄tūăl'ity** *n.*

vir̄t'ūe *n.* Moral excellence, uprightness, goodness; a particular moral excellence, moral quality regarded as of special excellence or importance; chastity, esp. of women; good quality or influence, efficacy; *by*, *in*, ~ *of*, on the strength or ground of; (pl.) 7th order of angels. [L *virtus* worth, valour, f. *vir* man]

vir̄tūŏs'ō (-z-) *n.* (pl. *-si* pr. -sē). Person with special interest in or knowledge of works of art or virtu; person skilled in technique of an art, esp. of performance on musical instrument. **vīrtūŏs'ity** *n.* [It. *virtuoso* learned, skilled, f. L *virtus* (see VIRTUE)]

vīrt'ūous *adj.* Possessing, showing, moral rectitude; chaste. **vīrt'ūously** *adv.* **vīrt'ūousnėss** *n.*

vi'rūlent (*or* -rōō-; *also* vĭr'-) *adj.* Poisonous; malignant, bitter; (of disease) extremely violent. **vi'rūlently** *adv.* **vi'rūlence** *n.*

vīr'us *n.* 1. Organic particle, much smaller than bacteria or other classifiable micro-organisms, existing only within cells of animal and plant bodies and capable of producing various diseases. 2. Poisonous substance, the product of disease, found in the tissues and body-fluids. 3. (fig.) Moral poison, malignity, acrimony. [L, = 'poison']

vĭs *n.* Force, strength; ~ *inĕr'tiae* (-shĭē), inertia, tendency to remain inactive.

Vis., Visct *abbrevs.* Viscount.

visa (vēz'a) *n.* Endorsement on passport etc. signifying that it has been examined and found correct; written permission to enter country whose government regards passport alone as insufficient. ~ *v.t.* Mark with visa.

vĭs'age (-z-) *n.* (now chiefly literary) Face.

vis-à-vis (vēzahvē') *n.* Either of two persons or things facing or situated opposite each other. ~ *prep.* & *adv.* Over against, in comparison with; facing, face-to-face (with).

viscacha: see VIZCACHA.

vĭs'cera *n.pl.* Internal organs of principal cavities of animal body, as intestines, heart, liver, etc. **vĭs'ceral** *adj.*

vĭs'cid *adj.* Glutinous, sticky. **viscĭd'ity** *n.*

vĭs'cōse *n.* Highly viscous solution of cellulose compound obtained by treating wood-pulp or cotton fibre with caustic soda and carbon disulphide, used in manufacture of rayon, 'Cellophane', etc.

viscŏs'ity *n.* Quality, degree, of being viscous; (physics) body's property of resisting alteration in position of its parts relative to each other.

visc'ount (vīk-) *n.* Member of 4th order of British peerage, between earl and baron; courtesy title of earl's eldest son. **visc'ountcy, visc'ountėss, visc'ounty** *ns.*

vĭs'cous *adj.* Glutinous, gluey, sticky; having viscosity; intermediate between solid and fluid, adhesively soft. **vĭs'cously** *adv.* **vĭs'cousnėss** *n.*

vĭs'cus *n.* (anat.) Internal organ (sing. of VISCERA).

visé (vēz'ā) *n.* & *v.t.* = VISA.

Vĭsh'nu (-ōō). One of the principal Hindu deities, identified by his worshippers with the supreme deity and regarded as saviour of the world. **Vĭsh'nuism** *n.*

vĭs'ĭble (-z-) *adj.* Capable of being seen; that can be seen at particular time, under certain conditions, etc.; in sight; that can be perceived or observed, apparent, open, obvious. **visĭbĭl'ity** *n.* (esp.) Conditions of light, atmosphere, etc., as regards distinguishing of objects by sight; possibility of seeing, range of vision, under such conditions. **vĭs'ĭbly** *adv.*

Vĭs'ĭgŏth (-z-) *n.* West Goth, one of that branch of Goths which entered Roman territory towards end of 4th c. and subsequently established in Spain a kingdom overthrown by the Moors in 711–12. **Visĭgŏth'ĭc** *adj.*

vĭ'sion (-zhn) *n.* 1. Act or faculty of seeing, sight; perception of things by means of the light coming from them which enters the eye. 2. Power of discerning future conditions, sagacity in planning, foresight. 3. Thing, person, seen in dream or trance; supernatural apparition, phantom; thing, esp. of attractive or fantastic character, seen vividly in the imagination; person, sight, of unusual beauty.

vĭs'ionary (-zho-) *adj.* Given to seeing visions or indulging in fanciful theories; seen (only) in a vision, existing only in imagination; unreal, fantastic, unpractical. ~ *n.* Visionary person.

vĭs'ĭt (-z-) *v.t.* Go, come, to see (person, place, etc.) as act of friendship or social ceremony, on business, from curiosity, for official inspection, etc.; (of disease, calamity, etc.) come upon, attack; (bibl.) punish (person, sin), avenge (sins etc.) *upon* person, comfort, bless, (person *with* salvation etc.); *visiting-card*, small card with one's name, address, etc., left in making call etc. ~ *n.* Call on a person or at a place; temporary residence with a person or at a place; occasion of going *to* doctor, dentist, etc., for examination or treatment, doctor's professional call on patient; formal or official call for purpose of inspection etc.

vĭs'ĭtant (-z-) *n.* 1. Migratory bird, as temporarily frequenting particular locality. 2. (poet., rhet.) Visitor. 3. *V*~, member of an order of nuns (Sisters of the Visitation) concerned with education of young girls.

visĭtā'tion (-z-) *n.* 1. Official visit of inspection etc., esp. bishop's inspection of churches of his diocese. 2. (colloq.) Unduly protracted visit or social call. 3. Boarding of vessel belonging to another State to learn her character and purpose (*right of* ~, right to do this, not including right of search). 4. Divine dispensation of punishment or reward, notable experience, esp. affliction, compared to this. 5. *V*~ (*of Our Lady*), visit of Virgin Mary to Elizabeth (Luke i. 39); day, 2nd July, commemorating this; *Nuns of the V*~: see VISITANT. 6. *V*~ *of the Sick*, an office of the Anglican Church. 7. (zool.) Unusual or large migration of animals.

vĭs'ĭtor (-z-) *n.* One who visits; esp., one with right or duty of supervision (usu. exercised periodically) over university, college, school, or the like; *visitors' book*, book in which visitors to a place enter their names.

vĭs'or (-z-), **vĭz'or** *n.* (hist.) Movable front part of helmet, covering face, and with openings for seeing and breathing (ill. ARMOUR); (U.S.) peak of cap; (hist.) mask.

vĭs'ta *n.* View, prospect, esp. through avenue of trees or other long narrow opening; such an opening; (fig.) mental view of extensive period of time or series of events etc.

Vĭs'tūla. River of Poland flowing from the Carpathians to the Baltic at Danzig.

vĭs'ūal (-z- *or* -zh-) *adj.* Of, concerned with, seeing; used in seeing, received through sight; ~ *angle*, angle formed by two straight lines from extreme points of object to centre of eye; ~ *purple*, purple-red pigment present in retinal rods of eyes, abundant in eyes of nocturnal animals. **vĭs'ūally** *adv.*

vĭs'ūalīze (-z-, -zh-) *v.t.* Make mental vision or image of (something not present or not visible), make visible to imagination. **visūalīzā'tion** *n.*

vīt'a glass *n.* Trade-name for special kind of glass for windows etc., which does not exclude ultra-violet or actinic rays of sunlight. [L *vita* life]

vīt'al *adj.* Of, concerned with, essential to, organic life; essential to existence or to the matter in hand; affecting life, fatal to life or to success, etc.; ~ *capacity*, (physiol.) volume of air that can be expelled from lungs after strongest possible inspiration; ~ *parts*, parts of body essential to life, as lungs, heart, brain, etc.; ~ *statistics*, those relating to births, deaths, health, disease, etc. **vīt'ally** *adv.* **vīt'als** *n.pl.* Vital parts of body.

vīt'alism *n.* Doctrine that life originates in a vital principle distinct from chemical and other physical forces. **vīt'alist** *n.* **vītalĭs'tĭc** *adj.*

vītăl'ity *n.* Vital power, ability to sustain life; (fig.) active force or power, activity, animation, liveliness.

vīt'alīze *v.t.* Put life or animation into, infuse with vitality or vigour. **vītalīzā'tion** *n.*

vĭt'amĭn *n.* Any of a number of substances existing in small quantities in certain foodstuffs, the presence of which in the diet is considered essential for promotion of normal growth and nutrition and the prevention of 'deficiency diseases'; ~ *A*, present in liver-oils, butter-fat, green leaves, etc., is essential to growth, and its absence causes a characteristic eye-disease, xerophthalmia; the ~ *B group*, present in yeast products, pulses etc., comprises a number of separate substances concerned esp. with the formation and functioning of important enzymes in the body; ~ *C*, ascorbic acid, is present in green leaves esp. of cabbage kind, black currants, and the juice of citrus fruits, and deficiency leads to scurvy; ~ *D*, present in fish-liver oils and egg-yolk, is apparently concerned in the deposition of calcium phosphate in bones, and deficiency causes rickets; ~ *E* is present in germ-layer of wheat and green leaves and its absence from diet causes sterility; ~ *K* [f. initial of its discoverer, Koch, Danish chemist] present in various foodstuffs, esp. green leaves, facilitates clotting of blood in post-operational jaundice and similar conditions. **vīt'amin, vītamĭn'ĭc, vītăm'ĭnous** *adjs.* **vīt'amĭnīze** *v.t.* Introduce vitamin(s) into (food). [orig. named *vitamine* f. L *vita* life and Engl. AMINE, in the belief that an amino-acid was present]

vītĕll'ĭn *n.* (biochemistry) Chief protein of yolk of egg. **vītĕll'ĭne** *adj.* Of the vitellus; ~ *membrane*, membrane enclosing vitellus. **vītĕll'us** *n.* (embryol.) Yolk of an egg.

Vitĕll'ius, Aulus (A.D. 15–69). Roman emperor after the death of Otho (A.D. 69), defeated in the same year by Vespasian and murdered.

vĭ'tiāte (-shĭ-) *v.t.* Impair the quality of, corrupt, debase; make invalid or ineffectual. **vĭtiā'tion** *n.*

vĭt'ĭcŭlture *n.* Cultivation of the vine.

Vĭt(t)ôr'ĭa. Town in NE. Spain, where in 1813 Wellington defeated the French under Joseph Bonaparte and thus freed Spain from French domination.

vĭt'rėous *adj.* Of, of the nature of, glass; resembling glass in composition, brittleness, hardness, lustre, transparency, etc.; ~ *body, humour*, transparent colourless gelatinous substance filling posterior part of eyeball. **vĭt'rėously** *adv.* **vĭtrėŏs'ĭty** *n.*

vĭt'rĭfȳ *v.* Convert, be converted, into glass or glass-like substance; render, become, vitreous. **vĭtrĭfăc'tion, vĭtrĭfĭcā'tion** *ns.*

vĭt'rĭŏl *n.* Various metallic sulphates used in the arts or medicinally, esp. iron sulphate; (*oil of*) ~, concentrated sulphuric acid; (fig.) causticity, acrimony, of feeling or utterance. **vĭtrĭŏl'ĭc** *adj.* (esp., fig.) Extremely caustic, scathing, bitter, or malignant.

Vĭtruv'ĭus (-rōō-). Marcus. Vitruvius Pollio (1st c. A.D.), Roman architect, whose book 'De architectura' had much influence on Renaissance building. **Vĭtruv'ĭan** *adj.* Of, in the style of, Vitruvius; ~ *scroll*, convoluted scroll-pattern as architectural ornament.

vĭtt'a *n.* (pl. *-ae*). 1. (Rom. antiq.) Fillet, garland. 2. Lappet of mitre. 3. (bot.) One of a number of oil-tubes in pericarp of fruit of most umbelliferous plants. **vĭtt'āte** *adj.*

Vĭttôr'ĭō Vĕn'ĕtō. Town in N. Italy, scene of a series of battles in which the Austrians were decisively and finally defeated by the Allies in Oct. 1918.

vītūp'erāte *v.t.* Revile, abuse. **vītūperā'tion** *n.* **vītūp'erative** *adj.* **vītūp'eratively** *adv.*

Vīt'us, St. (*c* 300). Child martyr of the DIOCLETIAN persecution; *St. Vitus's dance*, popular name of chorea, disease characterized by involuntary movement of the muscles.

viv'a[1] (vē-) *n.* & *int.* (Salute, greeting, cry, of) 'long live . . .'. [It., 3rd pers. imperat. of *vivere* live]

vīv'a[2] *n.* = VIVA VOCE.

vivace (vēvah'chā) *adv.* & *n.* (mus.) (Passage, performance) in brisk and lively manner.

vĭvā'cious (-shus) *adj.* Lively, sprightly, animated. **vĭvā'ciously** *adv.* **vĭvă'city** *n.*

vivandière (vēvahṅdyār') *n.* Formerly, in French and other continental armies, woman following troops and selling provisions and liquor.

vīvār'ĭum *n.* (pl. *-ia*). Place or enclosure for keeping living animals etc. as far as possible under natural conditions, for interest or scientific study.

vīv'a vō'cė *adv. phr.* & *adj.* Oral(ly). ~ *n.* Oral examination. [L, = 'with the living voice']

vive (vēv) *int.* Long live, as ~ *le roi*, long live the king. [Fr., 3rd pers. sing. imperat. of *vivre* live]

vīvĕ'rrīne *adj.* Of the *Viverridae* or civet family, Asiatic and African family of cat-like carnivores.

vĭv'ĭd *adj.* (Of colour, light, etc.) brilliant, intense, glaring; clearly or distinctly perceived or perceptible, intensely or strongly felt or expressed, (capable of) presenting subjects or ideas in clear and striking manner. **vĭv'ĭdly** *adv.* **vĭv'ĭdnėss** *n.*

vĭv'ĭfȳ *v.t.* (chiefly fig.) Give life to, animate.

vīvĭp'arous *adj.* 1. (zool.) Bringing forth young in developed state, not hatching from egg (cf. OVIPAROUS). 2. (bot.) Germinating while still attached to the parent plant; having such seeds. **vīvĭp'arously** *adv.* **vīvĭp'arousnėss, vīvĭpă'rĭty** *ns.* **vīvĭp'ary** *n.* (bot. only).

vĭv'ĭsĕct *v.t.* Perform vivisection upon. **vĭvĭsĕc'tion** *n.* Performance of surgical experiments on living animals in laboratory for the advancement of (esp. medical) knowledge. **vĭvĭsĕc'tionist** (-sho-) *n.* One who approves of or advocates this practice.

vīx'en *n.* She-fox; ill-tempered quarrelsome woman, shrew. **vīx'enish** *adj.*

viz. (usu. read 'namely') *adv.* Abbrev. of VIDELICET.

vĭz'ard *n.* (archaic) Mask; visor.

vĭzcăch'a (-s-), **vĭs-** *n.* Large burrowing S. Amer. rodent (*Lagostomus trichodactylus*) with long soft fur, grey on back and yellowish-white beneath.

vizier (vĭzēr', vĭz'ĭer) *n.* In various Mohammedan countries, high administrative official, esp. (*grand* ~) chief minister of former Turkish Empire. [Arab. *wazīr* king's minister, orig. porter (*wazara* carry)]

v.l. *abbrev. Varia lectio* (variant reading).

Vlach (vlăk) *n.* Wallachian, one of the Latin-speaking people, of Roman colonial origin, occupying parts of SE. Europe. [Slav, ult. f. Germanic *Walh* foreigner]

Vlăd'ĭmĭr (-mēr), St. (*c* 956–1015). Grand duke of Kiev and prince of Russia; he was baptized in 988 and introduced the Orthodox Church into Russia.

Vlădĭvŏs'tŏk. Far Eastern seaport and naval base of Soviet Russia, terminus of Trans-Siberian railway.

V.O. *abbrev.* Victorian Order.

vōc'able *n.* Word, esp. with ref. to form rather than meaning.

vocăb'ūlary *n.* List of words with their meanings, glossary; sum of words used in a language, or in a particular book or branch of science etc., or by a particular person, class, profession, etc.

vōc'al *adj.* Of, concerned with, uttered by, the voice; (poet.) endowed (as) with a voice; expressive, eloquent; (of music) composed for voice(s) with or without accompaniment; (phonet.) of a vowel, vocalic; ~ *cords* or *folds*, the voice-producing organs, two strap-like membranes stretched across the larynx, each having a medial edge which is free to vibrate in the air-stream (ill. HEAD); the pitch of voice is determined by the frequency of vibration and the length of the cords, women's being shorter than men's; ~ *score*, musical score showing voice parts in full. **vōc'ally** *adv.* **vōc'al** *n.* 1. Vowel. 2. (R.C. Ch.) Person entitled to vote in certain elections.

vocăl'ĭc *adj.* Of, concerning, vowel(s); of the nature of a vowel; rich in vowels.

vōc'alism *n.* Use of voice in speech or singing; system of vowels in a language. **vōc'alist** *n.* Singer.

vōc'alīze *v.* Utter, make vocal;

convert into, use as, vowel; furnish with vowels or vowel-points; sing, esp. on vowel-sound(s). **vōcalizā'tion** *n.*

vocā'tion *n.* Divine call to, sense of fitness for, a career or occupation; employment, trade, profession. **vocā'tional** (-sho-) *adj.* **vocā'tionally** *adv.*

vŏc'atĭve *adj.* & *n.* (Case in inflected languages) used in address or invocation.

vocĭf'erāte *v.* Utter, cry out, noisily; shout, bawl. **vocĭferā'tion** *n.*

vocĭf'erous *adj.* Clamorous, noisy. **vocĭf'erously** *adv.* **vocĭf'erousnėss** *n.*

vŏd'ka *n.* Alcoholic spirit made esp. in Russia by distillation of rye etc. [Russ., dim of *voda* water]

Vogler (fōg'ler), Georg Joseph (1749–1814). German musical composer and organist, known as *Abt* ~, i.e. Abbé.

vōgue (-g) *n.* Popularity, general acceptance or currency; prevailing fashion; *in* ~, in fashion, generally current.

voice *n.* 1. Sound uttered by the mouth, esp. human utterance in speaking, shouting, or singing; use of the voice esp. in spoken or (fig.) written words; opinion so expressed; right to express opinion; vote; (phonet.) sound uttered with vibration or resonance of vocal cords (dist. from *breath* or *whisper*); (mus.) singing voice, quality of

APPROXIMATE COMPASS OF SINGING VOICES

1. Soprano. 2. Contralto. 3. Alto. 4. Tenor. 5. Baritone. 6. Bass

this. 2. (gram.) Set of forms of a verb showing relation of the subject to the action (ACTIVE, PASSIVE, MIDDLE, etc.). ~ *v.t.* Give utterance to, express; (phonet.) utter with voice, change from voiceless to voiced; (mus.) regulate tone-quality of organ pipes. **voiced** (-st) *adj.* (esp., phonet.) Uttered with voice, sonant.

voice'lėss (-sl-) *adj.* Speechless, dumb, mute; (phonet.) not voiced. **voice'lėssly** *adv.* **voice'lėssnėss** *n.*

void *adj.* Empty, vacant; invalid, not binding; (poet., rhet.) ineffectual, useless; ~ *of*, lacking, free from. ~ *n.* Empty space. ~ *v.t.* Render void or invalid; emit (excrement etc.).

void'ance *n.* (esp., eccles.) Fact of benefice etc. being or becoming void or vacant.

void'ėd *adj.* (esp., of heraldic bearing) Having central area cut away, so as to show the field; (of velvet) having no pile in some parts, the pile-thread being buried in the foundation fabric.

voile (vwahl, voil) *n.* Thin semi-transparent cotton, wool, or silk dress-material. [Fr., = 'veil']

vol. *abbrev.* Volume.

vōl'ant *adj.* Flying, capable of flight; (her.) represented as flying; (poet.) nimble, rapid.

vōl'ar *adj.* (anat.) Of palm of hand or sole of foot.

vŏl'atīle *adj.* Readily evaporating at ordinary temperatures; (fig.) changeable, flighty, lively, gay; evanescent, transient; ~ *oil*, essential oil. **vŏlatĭl'ĭty** *n.*

volăt'ĭlīze (*or* vŏl'*a*-) *v.* (Cause to) evaporate; make, become, volatile. **volătĭlīzā'tion** *n.*

vŏl-au-vent (-ōvahṅ) *n.* Pie, usu. for one person, of light puff pastry filled with sauce containing meat, fish, etc. [Fr., lit. 'flight in the wind']

vŏlcăn'ĭc *adj.* Of, produced by, a volcano; characterized by volcanoes; ~ *glass*, obsidian. **vŏlcăn'ĭcally** *adv.*

vŏlcān'ō *n.* Hill or mountain, more or less conical, composed partly or wholly of discharged matter, with crater(s) or other opening(s) in earth's crust through

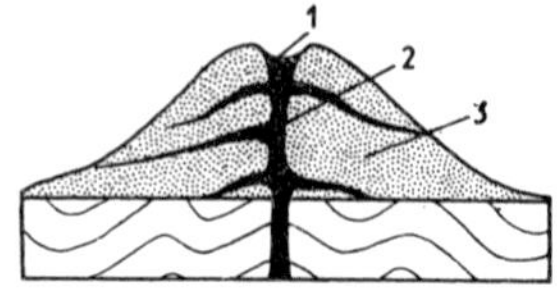

SECTION OF A VOLCANO

1. Crater. 2. Lava. 3. Tuff

which steam, gases, ashes, rocks, and freq. streams of molten material are or have been periodically ejected; (fig.) violent, esp. suppressed, feeling, passion, etc. **vŏl'canism** *n.* Volcanic activity. [It., f. L. *Volcanus* VULCAN]

vōle *n.* Small rodent with short ears and tail, rounded snout, and herbivorous teeth; Br. species: *bank* ~ (*Evotomys glareolus*), *field*-~ (*Microtus agrestis*) and *water*-~ (*Arvicola amphibius*).

Vŏl'ga. Longest river of Europe, rising in NW. Russia and flowing E., then S. to the Caspian Sea.

Vŏl'gogrăd : see STALINGRAD.

volĭ'tion *n.* Act, power, of willing or resolving, exercise of the will. **volĭ'tional** (-sho-) *adj.* **volĭ'tionally** *adv.*

vŏl'ley *n.* Salvo, simultaneous discharge, shower, of missiles (or fig. of oaths etc.); (tennis, lawn tennis, etc.) return stroke at ball before it touches ground, (cricket) full pitch; ~-*ball*, game in which large inflated ball is struck with hands from alternate sides of high net without touching ground. ~ *v.* Discharge (missiles etc.), return, hit, bowl, (ball), in volley; fly in volley; make sound like volleys of artillery.

Vŏl'scī *n.pl.* Ancient warlike people of E. Latium, subdued by Romans in 4th c. B.C. **Vŏl'scian** *adj.* & *n.* (Language, member) of this people.

Vŏl'sungs. In Scand. legend, family descending from Odin whose history is related in the 'Volsunga Saga'.

vōlt[1] *n.* Unit of electromotive force, the electrical pressure that if steadily applied to a conductor whose resistance is 1 ohm will produce a current of 1 ampere. [f. VOLTA]

volt[2]: see VOLTE.

Vŏl'ta, Alessandro (1745–1827). Italian physicist, a pioneer of electrical science; first devised apparatus for chemically developing electric currents.

vŏl'tage *n.* Electromotive force expressed in volts.

vŏltā'ĭc *adj.* Producing electricity, (of electricity) generated, by chemical action, after the method discovered by VOLTA; (consisting) of, caused by, connected with, such electricity.

Vŏltaire' (-ār), François Marie Arouet de (1694–1778). French deist philosopher, historian, dramatist, and writer of historical and satirical poems and tales; famous for his anti-clericalism, his witty scepticism, and his influence on the leaders of the French Revolution.

vŏltăm'ėter *n.* Instrument for measuring electricity by amount of electrolysis produced.

vōlte, vōlt *n.* (manège) Horse's sideways gait in circle; (fencing) quick movement to escape thrust. ~ *v.* Make a volte.

vŏlte-face (-tfahs) *n.* Complete change of front in argument, politics, etc.

vŏlt'mēter *n.* Any instrument for measuring voltage.

vŏl'ūble *adj.* Fluent, glib; speaking, spoken, with great readiness or fluency. **vŏlūbĭl'ĭty, vŏl'ūblenėss** *ns.* **vŏl'ūbly** *adv.*

vŏl'ūme *n.* 1. Collection of written or esp. printed sheets bound together to form a book; division of work (intended to be) separately bound. 2. Bulk, mass, quantity, esp. large quantity; space occupied by anything, esp. as measured in cubic units; size, dimensions, amount, *of*. 3. (usu. pl.) Wreath, coil, rounded mass, of smoke etc. 4. (mus. etc.) Quantity, power, fullness, of tone or sound.

vŏlūmĕt'rĭc *adj.* Of, pertaining to, measurement of volume. **vŏlūmĕt'rĭcally** *adv.*

volūm'ĭnous *adj.* 1. Containing, consisting of, many coils or convolutions. 2. Consisting of many volumes; (of writer) producing many books etc. 3. Of great volume, bulky, ample. **volūm'ĭnously** *adv.* **volūm'ĭnousnėss, volūmĭnŏs'ĭty** *ns.*

vŏl'untary *adj.* Done, acting, able to act, of one's own free will;

purposed, intentional, not constrained; (of bodily action etc.) controlled by the will; brought about, produced, maintained, etc., by voluntary action; *V~ Aid Detachment*, group of men or women organized by the Order of St. John, the St. Andrew's Ambulance Association, or the British Red Cross Society, undertaking first aid and nursing duties; ~ *hospital*, one maintained by voluntary contributions. **vŏl'untarĭly** *adv.* **vŏl'untarinėss** *n.* **vŏl'untary** *n.* (orig.) Extempore performance, esp. as prelude to other music; (now) organ solo played before, during, or after any church service; music composed for this.

vŏlunteer' *n.* One who voluntarily offers his services or enrols himself for any enterprise, esp. for service in any of the armed forces; (hist.) member of British military company or force formed by voluntary enlistment and distinct from regular army; *V~ State*, popular name of Tennessee, so called because of its remarkable record in furnishing volunteers in the Civil War. ~ *v.* Undertake, offer, voluntarily; make voluntary offer of one's services; be a volunteer.

volŭp'tūary *n.* & *adj.* Of, concerned with, (person) given up to, indulgence in luxury and gratification of the senses.

volŭp'tūous *adj.* Of, derived from, marked by, addicted to, gratification of the senses. **volŭp'tūously** *adv.* **volŭp'tūousnėss** *n.*

volūte' *n.* Spiral scroll forming chief ornament of Ionic capital and used also in Corinthian and Composite capitals (ill. ORDER); spiral conformation, convolution, esp. of spiral shell; marine gastropod of genus *Voluta* and allied genera, chiefly tropical, and freq. with very handsome shell. ~ *adj.* Having the form of a volute, forming spiral curve(s).

volū'tion *n.* Convolution, spiral turn, whorl of spiral shell; rolling or revolving movement.

vŏl'va *n.* (bot.) Membranous covering enclosing many fungi in early stages of growth (ill. FUNGUS).

vŏm'it *v.* Eject contents of stomach through mouth; bring up, eject, (as) by vomiting, belch forth, spew out. ~ *n.* Matter ejected from stomach; emetic; *black ~*, (blackish matter vomited in severe cases of) yellow fever.

vorā'cious (-sh*us*) *adj.* Greedy in eating; gluttonous, ravenous. **vorā'ciously** *adv.* **vorā'ciousnėss, vorā'city** *ns.*

vôrt'ĕx *n.* (pl. *-ĭcēs*, *-ĕxes*). 1. Mass of fluid, esp. liquid, with rapid circular movement round axis and tendency to form vacuum or cavity in centre towards which bodies are attracted, whirlpool; anything likened to this, esp. by reason of rush or excitement, rapid change, or absorbing effect. 2. Trail of vapour, often of a whirling form, left in the sky by the exhaust of an aeroplane. 3. In older theories of the universe, esp. that of Descartes, (cosmic matter carried round in) rapid rotatory movement round centre or axis, supposed to account for origin and phenomena of terrestrial and other systems. **vôrt'ical** *adj.* **vôrt'ically** *adv.*

vôrt'icism *n.* 1. Philosophical theory of vortices (see prec.). 2. Theory of a group of futurist painters etc., first expounded 1913 by Wyndham Lewis, that art should express the 'seething vortex of modern life'. **vôrt'icist** *n.*

Vôrt'igern. Legendary British prince supposed to have invited the Jutes to Britain and to have married the daughter of Hengist.

Vosges (vōzh). Mountain system of E. France.

vōt'ary *n.* One bound by vow(s), esp. to religious life; devotee, devoted or zealous worshipper, ardent follower (*of*). **vōt'arėss** *n.* Female votary.

vōte *n.* Expression of one's acceptance or rejection signified by ballot, show of hands, voice, or otherwise; right to vote; opinion expressed, resolution or decision carried, by voting; votes collectively. ~ *v.* Give a vote, express choice or preference by ballot, show of hands, etc.; choose, elect, establish, ratify, grant, confer, by vote; pronounce, declare, by general consent; (colloq.) propose, suggest; *voting-paper*, slip of paper used in voting by ballot.

vōt'ive *adj.* Dedicated, offered, consecrated, etc., in fulfilment of a vow.

vouch *v.* Confirm, uphold, (statement) by evidence or assertion; answer, be surety, *for*.

vouch'er *n.* Document, receipt, etc., to attest correctness of accounts or monetary transactions, authorize or establish payment, etc.; esp. document which can be exchanged for goods or services as token of payment made or promised.

vouchsāfe' *v.t.* Give, grant, bestow, in condescending or gracious manner; deign to give, condescend (*to* do).

voussoir (vōō'swâr) *n.* Each of the wedge-shaped or tapered stones forming an arch (ill. ARCH).

vow *v.t.* Promise, or undertake solemnly, esp. by a vow; make solemn resolve to exact (vengeance), harbour (hatred), etc. ~ *n.* Solemn promise or engagement, esp. to God or to any deity or saint.

vow'ėl *n.* Speech-sound produced by vibrations of vocal cords, modified or characterized by form of vocal cavities, but without audible friction (opp. to, but not sharply divided from, CONSONANT); letter representing this, as a, e, i, o, u; *~-point*, sign used to indicate vowel in certain alphabets, as Hebrew etc.

vŏx ăngĕl'ĭca. Organ-stop of soft pleasant tone, freq. with slight 'wave' produced by two pipes not tuned exactly together.

vŏx hūma'na (-mā-, -mah-). Organ reed-stop, quality and tone of which resembles human voice.

vŏx pŏp'ūlī. Voice of the people; public opinion, popular belief, general verdict.

voy'age *n.* Journey, esp. to distant place or country, by sea or water. ~ *v.* Travel by water; traverse, travel over. **voy'ager** *n.*

voyeur (vwahyêr') *n.* One who derives gratification from looking at sexual organs of others.

V.R. *abbrev.* *Victoria Regina* (= Queen Victoria); Volunteer Reserve.

V.S. *abbrev.* Veterinary Surgeon.

Vt *abbrev.* Vermont.

Vŭl'can. Roman equivalent of the Greek god Hephaestus, god of fire and patron of workers in metal.

Vŭl'canist *n.* (geol.) One who holds *plutonic theory*, i.e. that most geological phenomena are due to action of internal heat (opp. NEPTUNIST).

vŭl'canīte *n.* Ebonite, black variety of rubber hardened by treatment with sulphur at high temperatures.

vŭl'canīze *v.t.* Harden and make (rubber etc.) more durable by chemical means, esp. by combining it with sulphur, either by subjection to great heat or at ordinary temperatures. **vŭlcanīzā'tion** *n.*

Vulg. *abbrev.* Vulgate.

vŭl'gar *adj.* Of, characteristic of, the common people, plebeian, coarse, low; in common use, generally prevalent; ~ *fraction*: see FRACTION; ~ *tongue*, vernacular, popular or native language, esp. as opposed to Latin. **vŭl'garly** *adv.* **vŭl'garism, vŭlgă'rity** *ns.*

vŭlgâr'ian *n.* Vulgar (esp. rich) person.

vŭl'garīze *v.t.* Make vulgar or commonplace; reduce to level of something usual or ordinary. **vŭlgarīzā'tion** *n.*

Vŭl'gate. Latin version of Bible prepared (in the main) by St. Jerome, 383–405; recension of this published 1592 by order of Pope Clement VIII, official text of R.C. Church. [L *vulgare* make public]

vŭl'nerable *adj.* That may be wounded, open to attack, injury, or assault, not proof against weapon, criticism, etc.; (in contract bridge) that has won one game towards rubber, and therefore liable to double penalties. **vŭlnerabĭl'ĭty** *n.*

vŭl'nerary *adj.* & *n.* (Drug, preparation, etc.) useful in or used for healing wounds.

vŭl'pīne *adj.* Of fox(es); characteristic of, like, fox; crafty, cunning.

vŭl'ture *n.* Any of various large raptorial birds feeding largely on carrion and often with head and neck almost naked; (fig.) rapacious person. **vŭl'turīne** (-cher-) *adj.*

vŭl'va *n.* External female genital organ, esp. external opening of vagina.

vv. *abbrev.* Verses.

W

W, w (dŭb'*e*lyōō). 23rd letter of modern English alphabet, originally a ligatured doubling of the Roman letter represented by *u* and *v* of modern alphabets, pronounced as a voiced bilabial spirant and, after vowels, as a *u*-glide, the second element of a diphthong.

w. *abbrev.* Watt; wicket; wide; wife; with.

W. *abbrev.* (Air-Raid) Warden; Welsh; West (as compass point, and as London postal district).

W.A.A.C. *abbrev.* Women's Army Auxiliary Corps (in 1914–18 war). **Waac** (wăk) *n.* (colloq.) Member of this.

W.A.A.F. *abbrev.* Women's Auxiliary Air Force, an auxiliary of the R.A.F., formed 1939; now called Women's Royal Air Force (W.R.A.F.). **Waaf** (wăf) *n.* (colloq.) Member of W.A.A.F.

wad (wŏd) *n.* Small bundle or mass of soft flexible material used as pad etc., esp. plug or disc of felt, cardboard, etc., keeping powder and shot compact in cartridge to prevent gas passing between shot and barrel when the cartridge is fired; (U.S.) tight roll, esp. of bank-notes, (colloq.) wealth, money. ~ *v.t.* Press, compress, roll into wad; line, pad, with wadding; furnish, plug, with wad.

wadd'ĭng (wŏd-) *n.* (Soft pliable material for making) wads; loose, soft, fibrous material for padding, stuffing, packing, quilting, etc.

wadd'le (wŏ-) *v.i.* Walk with short steps and swaying motion natural to stout short-legged person or to bird with short legs set far apart, as duck. ~ *n.* Waddling gait.

wadd'y (wŏ-) *n.* Wooden war-club of Australian aborigines.

wāde[1] *v.* Walk through water or any soft substance which impedes motion; walk through (stream etc.); (fig.) progress slowly or with difficulty (*through* book etc.); *wading bird*: see WADER. ~ *n.* Act of wading.

Wāde[2], George (1673–1741). British field-marshal; served in Marlborough's army; was sent (1724) to the Highlands of Scotland, where he built numerous bridges and metalled roads.

wād'er *n.* (esp.) Long-legged bird, as crane, heron, sandpiper, that wades in shallow water; (pl.) long waterproof garments covering feet and legs and coming up above waist, worn by fishermen etc.

Wadham College (wŏd'*a*m). College of the University of Oxford, founded 1612 by Nicholas Wadham and Dorothy his wife, of Somerset.

wa'dĭ, wa'dy (wah-) *n.* In N. Africa etc., rocky ravine or watercourse, dry except in rainy season.

w.a.f. *abbrev.* With all faults.

Wafd (-ah-). Nationalist party in Egypt. **Waf'dist** *n.* Adherent of this party.

wāf'er *n.* Very thin light sweet crisp biscuit or cake now chiefly eaten with ices; thin disc of unleavened bread used at Eucharist; small disc of gelatine, flour and gum, etc., formerly used for sealing letters; disc of red paper stuck on legal document instead of seal. ~ *v.t.* Attach or seal with wafer. **wāf'ery** *adj.*

wa'ffle[1] (wŏ-) *n.* Small soft crisp batter-cake with honeycomb surface; ~*-iron*, utensil, usu. of two shallow metal pans hinged together, between which waffle is baked or fried.

wa'ffle[2] (wŏ-) *v.i.* & *n.* (slang) (Utter) wordy nonsense; twaddle.

waft (wah-) *n.* Act of waving, waving movement; whiff of odour, breath of wind; (naut., also *w(h)eft*), flag or some substitute, usu. knotted, hoisted as signal, etc. ~ *v.t.* Convey (as) through air or over water, sweep smoothly and lightly along.

wăg[1] *v.* Shake or move briskly to and fro, oscillate; *wag'tail*, small bird of genus *Motacilla* with slender body and long tail which is freq. in wagging motion; various Amer. or Australian birds resembling these. ~ *n.* Single wagging motion.

wăg[2] *n.* Facetious person, habitual joker. **wăgg'ery** *n.* Drollery, jesting, joking. **wăgg'ĭsh** *adj.* **wăgg'ishly** *adv.* **wăgg'ĭshnėss** *n.*

wāge[1] *n.* Amount paid periodically, esp. by day or week or month, for work or service of employee or servant (usu. pl.); requital, reward (usu. pl.); (pl., econ.) that part of total production of community which is the reward of all forms of labour (as dist. from remuneration received by capital); *wages council*, board composed of representatives of employers and employees with some neutral members and neutral chairman, appointed by Ministry of Labour to determine or recommend rates of wages, hours of work, etc., in certain industries.

wāge[2] *v.t.* Carry on (war etc.).

wā'ger *n.* & *v.t.* Bet, stake; ~ *of battle*, (hist.) challenge by defendant to decide his guilt or innocence by single combat.

wăgg'le *v.* Move (something held or fixed at one end), be moved, to and fro with short quick motions. ~ *n.* Act of waggling; esp. (golf) preliminary swinging of club-head over ball before stroke.

wăg(g)'on *n.* 4-wheeled vehicle for drawing heavy loads, often with removable semicylindrical tilt or cover, usu. drawn by 2 or more horses; open railway truck; vehicle for carrying water, whence *on the* ~, (slang) abstaining from alcohol; ~*-boiler*, *-ceiling*, *-roof*, *-vault*, one shaped like wagon-tilt.

WAGON

1. Tilt. 2. Dished wheel. 3. Tire. 4. Spring. 5. Axle-tree. 6. Shaft

wăg(g)'oner *n.* Driver of wagon; *the W*~, the N. constellation Auriga.

wăg(g)onĕtte' *n.* 4-wheeled horse-drawn vehicle, open or with removable cover, with facing side-seats and transverse seat(s) at front (*illustration, p. 925*).

Wagner (vahg'-), Wilhelm Richard (1813–83). German composer of operas ("The Ring of the

Nibelungen', 'Tristan and Isolde', 'The Mastersingers', 'Parsifal', etc.); revolutionized opera by his 'music-dramas' for which he wrote both text and music, dispensing with set arias and choruses; spent his last years at Bayreuth where his tradition is carried on. **Wag-nēr'ian** *adj.* & *n.* **Wagnerĕsque'** (-k) *adj.*

wagon-lit (vahg'awṅ lē) *n.* Sleeping-car on continental railway. [Fr. *wagon* wagon, *lit* bed]

Wăg'ram (v-). Place near Vienna where Napoleon defeated the Austrians in 1809.

wagtail: see WAG¹ *v.*

Waha'bi (-hah-). Follower of Abd-el-Wahhab (1691–1787), Mohammedan reformer; the sect acquired considerable political power throughout Arabia in the 20th c.

waif *n.* (law) Any object or animal found ownerless; homeless and helpless person, esp. unowned or abandoned child; *~s and strays,* odds and ends; homeless or neglected children.

wail *n.* Prolonged plaintive inarticulate cry of pain, grief, etc.; bitter lamentation; sound resembling cry of pain. ~ *v.* Utter wails or persistent and bitter lamentations or complaints; bewail, lament; *Wailing Wall,* high wall in Jerusalem, supposed to contain some stones of Solomon's temple, to which Jews resort on Fridays to pray and lament. **wail'ful** *adj.* (chiefly poet.).

wain *n.* Wagon; (*Charles's*) *W~,* group of 7 bright stars in Great Bear constellation.

wain'scot *n.* Wooden panelling or boarding on room-wall; (hist.) fine quality of imported oak. ~ *v.t.* Line with wainscot. **wain'scoting** *n.* Wainscot or material for it.

waist *n.* Part of human body between ribs and hip-bones, normally slenderer than parts above and below it; middle narrower part of anything; part of garment covering waist, narrowed part of garment corresponding to waist (but sometimes worn higher or lower than position of this); (chiefly U.S.) bodice, blouse; (naut.) middle part of upper deck of ship, between quarter-deck and forecastle; *~-band,* band going round waist, esp. one forming upper part of lower garment; *~-cloth,* loin-cloth; *waist'coat* (*or* wĕs'kot), garment, usu. sleeveless, covering upper part of body usu. down to waist, worn under outer garment (ill. COAT); *~-line,* line of waist, esp. of garment.

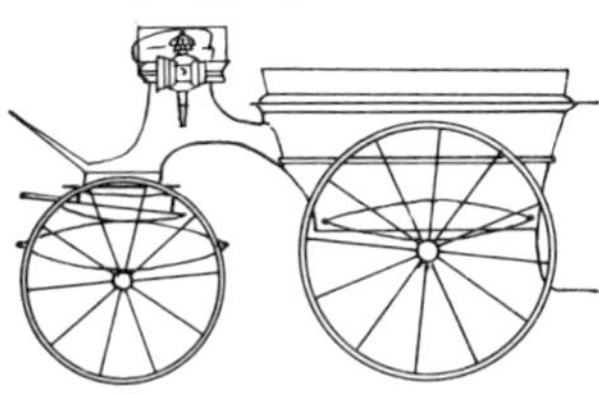

WAGONETTE

wait *v.* 1. Abstain from action or departure till some expected event occurs; pause, tarry; be expectant or on the watch. 2. Await, bide. 3. Act as attendant *on* person; serve food and drink, shift plates at table; ~ *(up)on,* pay respectful visit to. 4. Defer (meal) till someone arrives. 5. *~-a-bit,* (f. Afrikaans *wag-'n-bietje*) various plants and shrubs, esp. species of *Mimosa,* with hooked and clinging thorns. ~ *n.* 1. Act or time of waiting; *lie in ~,* lurk in ambush. 2. (pl.) Street singers of Christmas carols; (hist.) official bands of musicians maintained by a town or city.

wait'er *n.* (esp.) Man employed at hotel, restaurant, etc., (or, U.S., in private house) to wait upon guests, take orders for meals, etc.; tray, salver (see DUMB waiter). **wait'rĕss** *n.* Woman so employed.

wait'ing *n.* (esp.) (Period of) official attendance at court; *in ~,* on duty, in attendance; ~ *game,* abstention from attempting to secure advantages in early part of game etc. in order to act more effectively at later stage; *~-list,* list of persons waiting for appointment, next chance of obtaining something etc.; *~-room,* room provided for persons to wait in, esp. at railway-station or house of consultant.

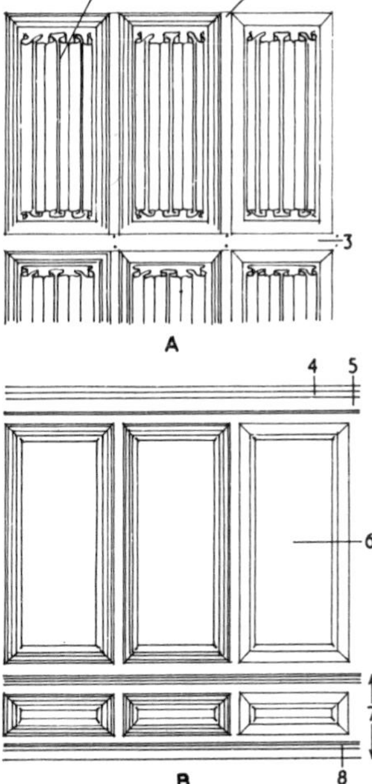

WAINSCOT: A. 16TH C. B. LATE 17TH C.

1. Linenfold. 2. Stile. 3. Rail. 4. Cornice. 5. Frieze. 6. Panel. 7. Dado. 8. Skirting

waive *v.t.* Relinquish, refrain from insisting on, refuse to avail oneself of (advantage, privilege, claim, opportunity, etc.). **waiv'er** *n.* (law) Waiving.

wāke¹ *v.* (past t. *wōke, wāked;* past part. *wāked, wōken*). Cease to sleep, rouse from sleep, (freq. ~ *up*); be awake (archaic except in pres. part.); cease, rouse, from sloth, torpidity, inactivity, etc.; rise, raise, from the dead; arouse, excite (feeling, activity, etc.), evoke (sound, echo, etc.); (chiefly Ir.) hold wake over; *~-robin,* the plant *Arum maculatum,* cuckoo-pint, lords-and-ladies; (U.S.) various liliaceous plants of genus *Trillium,* and certain plants of the Arum family, esp. the *arrow-arum, Arum virginicum.*

wāke² *n.* (Vigil of) festival in commemoration of dedication of church (hist.); (usu. pl.) annual holiday in N. England; (chiefly with ref. to Irish custom) watch by corpse before burial; drinking, lamentation, feasting, etc., associated with this.

wāke³ *n.* Track left on water's surface by ship or other moving object; *in the ~ of,* following close behind; in imitation of; following as a result or consequence.

wāke'ful (-kf-) *adj.* Keeping awake, esp. while others sleep; unable to sleep; marked by absence or want of sleep. **wāke'fully** *adv.* **wāke'fulnĕss** *n.*

Wāke Island. N. Pacific island under the sovereignty of U.S.

wāk'en *v.* Cause to be, become, awake; wake up.

Walbûrg'a (wŏ-), St. (*c* 780). English missionary to Germany, abbess of Heidenheim; commemorated 1st May (see WALPURGIS).

Walcheren (văl'keren). Island of the province of Zeeland in the Netherlands.

Waldĕn'sēs (wŏ-, -z). Adherents of a puritanical religious sect originating in S. France *c* 1170 through preaching of a rich Lyons merchant, Peter Waldo; excommunicated 1184, and scattered by persecution into Germany and Bohemia, they became a separately organized Church, which associated itself with the Protestant Reformation of the 16th c. and still exists, chiefly in N. Italy and in N. and S. America. **Waldĕn'sian** *adj.* & *n.* (Member) of the Waldenses.

Waldo, Peter: see WALDENSES.

wāle *n.* 1. Weal. 2. One of horizontal timbers connecting and bracing piles of trench, dam, etc.; (naut.) one of the broader thicker timbers extending along ship's sides at different heights. ~ *v.t.* Mark, furnish, with wales.

Wāl'er *n.* (colloq., orig. Anglo-Ind.) Horse, esp. cavalry-horse, imported from Australia, esp. New South Wales.

Wales (wālz). Principality occupying extreme W. of central southern portion of Gt Britain; orig. independent; was conquered by Edward I and united with England by the *Statute of* ~ (1284); *Prince of* ~, title usu. conferred (since 1301) on eldest son of reigning sovereign of England.

Wălhăll'a (v-): see VALHALLA.

walk (wawk) *v.* Travel, go, on foot; perambulate, tread floor or surface of, go over or along on foot; (of bipeds) progress by alternate movements of legs so that one foot is always on the ground, (of quadrupeds) go at gait in which there are always 2, and during part of step 3, feet on ground (opp. to *run*, *trot*, *gallop*, etc.); (of ghost etc.) appear; cause to walk with one; take charge of (hound-puppy at walk); (archaic) live with specified principle or in specified manner, conduct oneself; ~ *about*, stroll; ~ *away from*, outdistance with ease; ~ *off*, depart, esp. abruptly; ~ *off with*, carry away, steal; ~ *on*, play non-speaking part on stage; ~ *out*, (esp., colloq.) strike; hence ~-*out* (*n.*); ~ *out with*, (colloq.) court; ~ *over*, (of horse) win race in which there is no other starter by going over (course) at walking pace; win a race or other contest with little or no effort; ~-*over* (*n.*) race in which winner walks over; ~ *the boards*, be actor; ~ *the hospitals*, be medical student; ~ *the plank*: see PLANK; ~ *the streets*, (esp.) be a prostitute; ~-*up*, (U.S. colloq.) block of flats in which there is no lift; *walking delegate*, trade-union official who visits sick members, interviews employers, etc.; *walking-stick*, stick carried when walking and normally designed to give additional support to the body; *walking-stick* (*insect*), STICK insect; *walking-stick palm*, Australian palm (*Bacularia monostachya*) with stems suitable for making walking-sticks; *walking-tour*, pleasure journey on foot. **walk'er** *n.* **walk** *n.* 1. Walking gait, walking pace; manner of walking, spell of walking, esp. short journey on foot for exercise or pleasure. 2. Place for walking, tree-bordered avenue, broad path in garden or pleasure-ground, sidewalk, footpath; beat or round of forest official, hawker, etc.; course or circuit for walking; sheepwalk; place where hound-puppy is sent to accustom it to variety of surroundings (esp. in *at* ~, *put to* ~); place where game-cock is kept; *cock of the* ~, person whose supremacy in his own circle is undisputed. 3. Department of action, calling, profession, occupation (usu. ~ *of life*).

walk'ie-talk'ie (wawkĭ, tawkĭ) *n.* Radio transmitting and receiving set carried on the person.

Wălkȳ'rĭe (v-): *see* VALKYRIE.

wall (wawl) *n.* Structure of stone, bricks, earth, etc., of some height, serving as rampart, embankment, defensive enclosure of city, castle, etc., or to enclose or divide off house, room, field, garden, etc.; something resembling wall in appearance or function; (anat., zool., bot.) investment or lining tissue (of organ or cavity of body, cell, vesicle, tumour, etc.); *wall'flower*, plant of genus *Cheiranthus*, esp. *C. cheiri*, with yellow or orange-brown fragrant flowers, growing wild on old walls, rocks, etc., and cultivated in gardens; (colloq.) woman sitting out dances for lack of partners; *Siberian wallflower*, small plant resembling wallflower, with bright orange flowers, called by horticulturists *Cheiranthus* × *Allionii*, but more probably an *Erysimum*; ~-*fruit*, fruit of trees grown against a wall; ~ *game*, kind of football peculiar to Eton, played against a wall; *wall'-paper*, paper-hangings, paper for covering interior walls of rooms; ~-*plate*, timber or other horizontal member laid on or in wall to support rafters, distribute pressure, etc. (ill. ROOF). ~ *v.t.* Provide or protect with wall; close (*up*, *in*) block, shut *up*, with wall(s).

wall'aby (wŏ-) *n.* Any of various smaller species of kangaroo.

Wall'ace[1] (wŏ-), Alfred Russel (1822–1913). English naturalist and traveller.

Wall'ace[2] (wŏ-), Sir William (1270?–1305). National hero of Scotland; resisted the English under Edward I, was captured by treachery and executed in London.

Wall'ace Collection (wŏ-). Collection of art treasures made by Sir Richard Wallace (1818–90) and left to the nation in 1897, now housed in Manchester Sq., London.

Wal(l)achia (wŏlăk'ĭa). Former principality of SE. Europe, constituting after union (1859) with Moldavia part of the kingdom of Rumania. **Wal(l)ăch'ian** *adj.* & *n.* (Inhabitant, language) of Wallachia, VLACH.

wall'a(h) (wŏ-) *n.* (orig. Anglo-Ind.) Person employed about or concerned with something; (colloq.) man, person. [Hind. *-wālā*, suffix equivalent in some uses to English *-er*]

Wallenstein (văl'enshtīn), Albrecht Eusebius von, Duke of Friedland (1583–1634). Bohemian general; led the Imperial troops in the Thirty Years War; was defeated by Gustavus Adolphus at Lützen (1632) and assassinated by some of his own officers on account of suspected treason.

wall'ĕt (wŏ-) *n.* Bag, esp. pilgrim's or beggar's, for holding provisions etc. on journey; flat, usu. leather, bag, closed by flap or opening like book, for holding paper money, documents, etc.; bag for holding small tools, items of equipment, etc.

wall-eye (wawl'-ī) *n.* Eye with iris whitish (or occas. streaked, particoloured, or different in colour from other eye) or with divergent squint. **wall-eyed** *adj.* Having wall-eye; (U.S., of fishes) with large prominent eyes.

Walloon' *adj.* & *n.* (Member, language) of people, of Gaulish origin and speaking a French dialect, forming chief part of population of SE. Belgium.

wall'op (wŏ-) *n.* (colloq.) Heavy resounding blow, whack. ~ *v.t.* Thrash, beat. **wall'oping** *n.* ~ *adj.* Big, strapping, thumping.

wall'ow (wŏl'ō) *v.i.* Roll about in mud, sand, water, etc.; (of ship) roll helplessly; (fig.) take delight in gross pleasures etc. ~ *n.* Act of wallowing; place where buffalo, elephant, etc., goes to wallow; depression, mud-hole, dust-hole, formed by this.

Wall'sĕnd (wawlz-). Town (at end of Roman Wall) in Northumberland; fine grade of household coal.

Wall Street (wawl). Street in New York City, on or near which are concentrated chief financial institutions of U.S.; the American money-market.

wa'lnut (wawl-) *n.* Fruit, consisting of two-lobed seed enclosed in spheroidal shell covered with green fleshy husk, of various trees of genus *Juglans*, esp. *J. regia*; any tree of *Juglans* or some related genera; wood of walnut-tree, used in cabinet-making.

Wal'pōle (wŏl-), Sir Robert, 1st Earl of Orford (1676–1745). English statesman, leader of WHIG party and first prime minister of England. ~, Horace, 4th Earl (1717–97). His son; author of a novel 'The Castle of Otranto', writings on art, and a famous series of letters.

Walpurgis Night (vălpoorg'ĭs). Eve of 1st May, on which, acc. to German legend, a witches' Sabbath took place on the Brocken, a peak of the Harz mountains; named after St. WALBURGA, who was believed to have power of protection against the black arts.

wa'lrus (waw-) *n.* Large carnivorous amphibious mammal. *Odobenus rosmarus*) of Arctic seas, allied to seals and sea-lions, and chiefly distinguished by two long tusks; ~ *moustache*, man's long thick moustache hanging down over mouth.

Wal'singham (wŏ-), Sir Francis (*c* 1530–90). English statesman under Queen Elizabeth I.

Wal'ter (wŏ-), John (1738/9–1812). Founder of 'The Times' newspaper, London.

Walther von der Vogelweide (văl'ter; fōg'elvīde). Early 13th-c. German lyric poet, a minnesinger.

Wal'ton (wŏ-), Izaak (1593–1683). English writer, remembered for his 'Compleat Angler' (1653) and 'Lives' of several contemporary writers.

waltz (wawls, wŏls) *n.* Dance performed to music in triple time by couples who progress at the same time as they swing round and round with smooth sliding steps; music for this, or in its characteristic time and rhythm. ~ *v.* Dance waltz; move lightly, trippingly, etc.; move (person) as in waltz.

wam'pum (wŏ-) *n.* Cylindrical white and mauve beads of polished ends of shells threaded to form broad belts and formerly greatly used by N. Amer. Indians of the E. coast as currency, as ornaments, or (as substitute for writing, through the figures and patterns used) for mnemonic or symbolic purposes, recording treaties, etc.

wan (wŏn) *adj.* Pale, pallid, colourless, sickly. **wan'ly** *adv.* **wan'nėss** *n.*

wand (wŏ-) *n.* Slender rod or staff carried as sign of office by verger, beadle, usher, etc.; staff used in enchantments by fairy or magician.

wa'nder (wŏ-) *v.* Roam, ramble, move idly or restlessly or casually about, stroll, saunter; go from country to country or place to place without settled route or destination; stray, diverge from right way, get lost; wind, meander; be unsettled or incoherent in mind, purpose, talk, etc., be inattentive or delirious, rave; traverse in wandering. **wa'nderer, wa'ndering** *ns.* **wa'ndering** *adj.* *Wandering Jew*, person of medieval legend condemned to wander the earth without rest until Day of Judgement, as punishment for insulting Christ on way to crucifixion.

wan'derlust (vahn'derlo͞ost) *n.* Strong desire to wander or travel.

wanderōō' (wŏ-) *n.* Purple-faced langur of Ceylon (*Kasi senex*).

wāne *v.i.* Decrease in brilliance, size, or splendour, decline; lose power, vigour, importance, intensity, etc.; (of moon) undergo periodical decrease in extent of visible illuminated portion during second half of lunation. ~ *n.* (Period of) waning, decline.

wăng'le (-nggl) *v.t.* (slang) Accomplish, obtain, bring about, by scheming or contrivance; manipulate, fake, (account, report, etc.). ~ *n.* Act of wangling.

want (wŏ-) *n.* Lack, absence, deficiency, *of*; lack of necessaries of life, penury, destitution; need, condition marked by lack of necessary or desirable thing; (chiefly pl.) something needed or desired. ~ *v.* Be without or have too little of, fall short (by specified amount) *of*; be in want; require; desire, wish for possession or presence of; *wanted*, (esp.) sought for by police; *wanting*, (esp.) lacking *in*, unequal *to*; lacking, minus, without.

wa'nton (wŏ-) *adj.* Sportive, playful, frisky; licentious, lewd; (of cruelty, insult, neglect, etc.) unprovoked, reckless, arbitrary. **wa'ntonly** *adv.* **wa'ntonnėss** *n.* **wa'nton** *n.* Unchaste woman. ~ *v.i.* (chiefly archaic and poet.) Gambol, frolic; luxuriate, revel, *in*; sport amorously or lewdly.

wa'pentāke (wŏ-, wă-) *n.* (hist.) In some eastern and midland English shires (where Danish element in population was large), subdivision corresponding to HUNDRED of other counties.

wa'pitĭ (wŏ-) *n.* N. Amer. stag or elk (*Cervus canadensis*), resembling European red deer but larger.

war (wor̂) *n.* Quarrel usu. between nations conducted by force, state of open hostility and suspension of ordinary international law prevalent during such quarrel, attack or series of attacks by army or navy or air force or all three; fighting as profession; (fig.) hostility between persons; *civil* ~, war between parts of one nation for supremacy; *cold* ~, unfriendly relations between nations characterized by hostile propaganda, attempted economic sabotage, and threat of actual war; *holy* ~, war waged in support of some religious cause; *private* ~, feud between persons or families carried on in defiance of laws of murder etc.; (also) armed attack made by members of one State without government sanction upon another; *declare* ~, announce that hostilities may be expected (also fig.); *go to* ~, begin hostilities, *be at, make, wage*, ~, carry them on; *~-cloud*, position in international affairs that threatens war; ~ *correspondent*, newspaper correspondent reporting on war; *~-cry*, phrase or name shouted in charging or rallying to attack; party catchword; *~-dance*, savages' dance before warlike excursion or after victory; *W~ Department*, department of U.S. Government responsible for army and air force; *~-god*, god worshipped as giving victory in war, esp. the Gk Ares or Roman Mars; *~-head*, explosive head of torpedo or similar weapon; *~-horse*, charger (now chiefly fig. in *old war-~*, person excited by memories of past combats or controversies); *~-lord*, military commander (transl. of Ger. *Kriegsherr*, used esp. of William II of Germany and of Chinese civil-war generals); *war'monger*, one who seeks to bring about a war; *W~ Office*, department of British Government responsible for army; ~ *of nerves*, attempt to wear down opponent by gradual destruction of morale; *~-paint*, paint applied to face and body by savages before battle; (colloq.) one's best clothes and finery, ceremonial costume; *~-path*, (route taken by) warlike expedition of N. Amer. Indians; *on the ~-path*, (fig.) engaged in, preparing for, any conflict; *~-plane*, military aircraft; *warship*, ship armed and manned for war; *~-song*, song inciting to war or celebrating martial deeds; *~-whoop*, yell esp. of N. Amer. Indians in charging; *~-worn*, experienced or damaged in or exhausted by war. ~ *v.* (chiefly literary) Make war, be at war; *warring*, contending, discordant.

War. *abbrev.* Warwickshire.

Warb'ĕck (wor̂-), Perkin (1474–99). The 2nd of two pretenders to the English Crown in the reign of Henry VII (cf. SIMNEL); he claimed to be Richard, Duke of York, and led an insurrection in 1497, but was captured and hanged.

war'ble[1] (wor̂-) *v.* Sing softly and sweetly, sing with trills and quavers; (of small stream) make melody as it flows. ~ *n.* Warbling sound.

war'ble[2] (wor̂-) *n.* Small hard tumour produced by pressure of saddle on horse's back; swelling on back of cattle etc. produced by larvae of warble-fly; larva, living under skin of cattle etc., of *~-fly*, any of various dipterous insects causing warbles (e.g. *Hypoderma bovis*).

warb'ler (wor̂-) *n.* (esp.) Various small Old World plain-coloured singing birds of family *Silviidae*, including blackcap, whitethroat, etc.; various small Amer. usu. bright-coloured birds; various small birds of Australia and New Zealand.

ward[1] (wor̂d) *n.* 1. Act of guarding or defending (now only in *keep watch and* ~); confinement, custody (archaic); guardianship of minor or other person legally incapable of conducting his affairs. 2. Minor under care of guardian or Court of Chancery. 3. Separate room or division of prison or hospital or (hist.) workhouse. 4. Administrative division of borough or city, or of Cumberland, Northumberland, and some Scottish counties. 5. Each ridge projecting from inside plate of lock, preventing passage of any key not having corresponding incisions; each incision in bit of key corresponding to ward of lock (ill. LOCK). 6. BAILEY. 7. *~-maid*, maidservant in hospital ward; *ward'mote*, meeting of citizens of ward, esp. in City of London of liverymen of ward under presidency of alderman; *~-room*, mess-room or living-space of naval commissioned officers below commanding officer. ~ *v.t.* Have in keeping, protect (chiefly now of God); parry (*off* blow), keep *off* (danger etc.).

Ward[2] (wor̂d), Mary Augusta, better known as Mrs Humphry Ward (1851–1920). English novelist.

ward'en[1] (wor̂-) *n.* 1. President, governor (*of* certain colleges, schools, hospitals, the CINQUE

PORTS, etc.); governor of prison (esp. in old title *W~ of the Fleet*); *W~ of the Standards*, officer of the Board of Trade having custody of the standards of weight and measure; *W~ of the Stannaries*, Duke of Cornwall's officer presiding over mining parliaments of Cornwall. 2. CHURCHwarden. 3. (in war of 1939–45) Member of civil organization for assistance of civilian population in air-raids. **ward'enship** *n.*

ward'en[2] (wŏr-) *n.* Variety of cooking-pear.

ward'er (wŏr-) *n.* Sentinel, watchman on tower (archaic); official in charge of prisoners in jail. **ward'ress** *n.*

Wardour Street (wŏrd'*er*). Street in Soho, London, formerly occupied by dealers in antique and imitation-antique furniture (whence ~ *English*, pseudo-archaic diction in historical novels etc.) and now by the offices of film companies.

ward'rōbe (wŏr-) *n.* Place where clothes are kept, esp. large cupboard with hangers, movable trays, drawers, etc.; room where theatrical costumes and properties are kept; in royal or noble household, department charged with care of wearing apparel (chiefly in titles); person's stock of clothes; ~ *dealer*, dealer in second-hand clothes; ~ *mistress*, woman in charge of professional wardrobe of actor, actress, or theatrical company; ~ *trunk*, upright trunk in which dresses, coats, etc., are hung, and other clothes packed in separate drawers, etc.

wāre[1] *n.* Articles made for sale, goods; esp., vessels etc. of baked clay (usu. with defining word, as *Staffordshire* ~, *Wedgwood* ~); (pl.) things that person has for sale.

wāre[2] *pred. adj.* (poet.) Aware.

ware[3] (wŏr, wār) *v.t.* (usu. imper., esp. in hunting-field) Beware of, look out for.

ware'house (wār-h-) *n.* (Part of) building used for storage of merchandise, wholesaler's goods for sale, furniture or other property temporarily stored for owner; large retail shop; government building (*bonded* ~) where dutiable or excisable goods are kept until the duty is paid. ~ (-z) *v.t.* Store in warehouse.

war'fāre (wŏr-) *n.* State of war, being engaged in war, conflict.

war'līke (wŏr-) *adj.* Martial; skilled in, fond of, war; of, for use in, war; bellicose, threatening war.

war'lŏck (wŏr-) *n.* (archaic) Wizard, sorcerer.

warm (wŏr-) *adj.* 1. Of, at, rather high temperature, giving out considerable degree of heat (but less than that indicated by *hot*); (of persons etc.) glowing with exercise, excitement, eating and drinking, etc.; (of clothes etc.) serving to keep one warm. 2. (Of feelings etc.) sympathetic, emotional, tender, cordial; ardent, zealous, eager, excited, heated; indignant, angry; (of position etc.) difficult or dangerous to meet or maintain; (of conflict) vigorous, harassing; (of scent or trail) fresh, strong; (of person seeking or guessing in children's games) near object sought, on verge of finding or guessing. 3. (Of colour) suggesting warmth; esp., of, containing, rich reds and yellows. 4. (colloq., now rare) Comfortably off, well-to-do. 5. *~-blooded*, of birds and mammals, having constant body-temperature normally higher than that of surrounding medium; (fig.) passionate, amorous, emotional; ~ *front*, (meteor.) line between cold air and advancing warm air (ill. WEATHER); *~-hearted*, of, showing, proceeding from, generous and affectionate disposition. ~ *n.* Warming, being warmed; *British* ~, short warm overcoat worn esp. by army officers. **warm'ly** *adv.* **warm'nėss, warmth** *ns.* **warm** *v.* Make warm; excite; become warm, animated, or sympathetic; *warm'ing-pan*, long-handled covered metal (usu. brass) pan for holding live coals etc., formerly used for warming beds.

warn (wŏrn) *v.t.* Give timely notice to (person etc.) of impending danger or misfortune, put on guard, caution *against*; admonish; notify of something requiring attention, give previous notice to; ~ *off*, give notice to person to keep at distance, *off* private ground, etc.; ~ *off* (*the course, the Turf*), prohibit (offender against Jockey Club rules) from riding or running horses at its meetings.

warn'ĭng (wŏr-) *n.* (esp.) Thing that serves to warn; notice of, or caution against, possible danger; notice of termination of business relation, esp. by landlord to tenant, employer to employee, master to servant, or vice versa.

warp (wŏrp) *v.* 1. Make, become, crooked or perverted, bias, change from straight or right or natural state. 2. (naut.) Move (ship) by hauling on rope attached to fixed point; (of ship etc.) progress thus. 3. Choke, be choked, *up* with alluvial deposit; cover (land) with deposit of alluvial soil by natural or artificial flooding. ~ *n.* 1. Threads stretched lengthwise in loom to be crossed by weft (ill. WEAVE). 2. Rope used in towing or warping. 3. Crooked state produced in timber etc. by uneven shrinking or expansion; (fig.) perversion or perverse inclination of mind. 4. Sediment or alluvial deposit, esp. that left by turbid water kept standing on poor land.

wa'rrant (wŏ-) *n.* 1. Act, token, of authorization, sanction; justifying reason or ground for action, belief, etc.; proof, authoritative witness. 2. Document conveying authority or security; esp. written authorization to pay or receive money; executive authority's writ or order empowering officer to make arrest or search, execute judicial sentence, etc.; writing issued by sovereign, officer of State, etc., authorizing performance of some act; (mil., naval) official certificate of rank issued to officer lower than commissioned officer; ~ *officer*, officer holding office by warrant (in British armed forces now intermediate in rank between commissioned and non-commissioned officers). ~ *v.t.* Serve as warrant for, justify; guarantee. **wa'rranter,** (law) **wa'rrantor** *ns.*

wa'rranty (wŏ-) *n.* Authority, justification (*for*); (esp., law) express or implied undertaking by vendor that his title is secure or that thing sold fulfils specified conditions; in insurance contract, engagement by insured that certain statements are true or certain conditions shall be fulfilled.

wa'rren (wŏ-) *n.* Piece of land where rabbits breed or abound; (fig.) densely populated building or district; (hist.) piece of land enclosed and preserved for breeding game.

wa'rrior (wŏ-) *n.* Fighting man, valiant or experienced soldier (now poet. or rhet.); fighting man of past ages or uncivilized peoples; ~ *ant*, reddish European and American species of ant (*Formica sanguinea*) capturing and enslaving other ants.

War'saw (wŏr-). Capital city of Poland (*Warszawa*).

wart (wŏrt) *n.* Small round dry tough excrescence on skin caused by abnormal growth of papillae and thickening of epidermis over them; rounded excrescence or protuberance on skin of animal, surface of plant, etc.; *~-hog*, African wild hog of genus (*Phacochoevus aethiopicus*), with large warty excrescences on face and large protruding tusks. **wart'y** *adj.*

Warwick[1] (wŏ'rĭk). County town of WARWICKSHIRE.

Warwick[2] (wŏ'rĭk), Richard Neville, Earl of (1428–71). 'The Kingmaker'; instrumental in placing Edward IV on the throne in 1461 and in restoring Henry VI in 1470; killed at the Battle of Barnet.

Warwickshire (wŏ'rĭk-). Midland county of England.

wār'y *adj.* (Habitually) on one's guard, circumspect, cautious, careful. **wār'ĭly** *adv.* **wār'ĭnėss** *n.*

wash (wŏ-) *v.* 1. Cleanse with liquid; take (stain, dirt, etc.) *out, off, away*, by washing; wash oneself or esp. one's hands (and face); wash clothes; (of textile material, dye, etc.) bear washing without deterioration; (fig.) purify; ~ one's *hands of*, decline responsibility for; ~ *up*, wash (table utensils etc.)

after use; *washed out*, (fig.) enfeebled, limp, exhausted. 2. Moisten; (of sea, river, etc.) flow past, beat upon (shore, walls, etc.), sweep *over*, surge *against*; make (channel etc.) thus. 3. Sift (ore), sift ore, sand, etc. (*for* gold etc.), by action of water; brush thin coating of watery colour over (wall, drawing, etc.); coat (inferior metal) thinly with gold etc. **wash'able** *adj.* **wash** *n.* 1. Washing, being washed; process of being laundered (esp. *in, at, the* ~); quantity of clothes etc. (to be) washed. 2. Lotion; liquid applied to hair esp. to cleanse it. 3. Thin even layer of transparent water-colour or diluted ink; coating of wall-colouring. 4. Solution applied to metal to give effect of gold or silver. 5. Visible or audible motion of agitated water, esp. waves caused by passage of vessel; disturbance in air caused by passage of aircraft. 6. Sandbank, tract of land, alternately covered and exposed by sea; low-lying often-flooded ground with shallow pools and marshes; shallow pool, backwater, etc.; (U.S.) dry bed of winter torrent; *the W*~, shallow-water bay of North Sea between Lincolnshire and Norfolk, forming estuary of several rivers. 7. Kitchen swill or brewery refuse as food for pigs, liquid food for other animals. 8. Solid particles carried away or deposited by running water; soil from which gold or diamonds may be washed out. 9. Malt or other substance(s) steeped in water to ferment before distillation; washy or vapid liquor or (fig.) writing etc. **wash-** *prefix.* ~*-ball*, ball of soap for washing, shaving, etc.; ~*-basin*, bowl for washing hands etc.; ~*-board*, corrugated board on which clothes etc. may be scrubbed; ~*-bottle*, (chem.) bottle containing liquid through which gases may be passed for purification; ~*-day*, day on which clothes are washed; ~*-drawing*, (drawing produced by) method of using washes of colour or ink; ~*-hand-stand*, piece of furniture for holding wash-basin, ewer, soap-dish, etc.; ~*-house*, outbuilding for washing clothes; ~*-leather*, soft kind of leather (usu. split sheepskin) dressed to resemble chamois, used for dusting, cleaning, etc.; leather treated with alum (or buff leather) for soldiers' belts; ~*-out*, (esp.) (site of) removal by flood of part of hill-side, road, track, railway, etc.; the washing out of a cavity of the body, result of this; (slang) disappointing failure, fiasco; ~*-room*, (U.S.) room with toilet facilities, lavatory; ~*-stand*, wash-hand-stand; ~*-tub*, tub for washing clothes etc.

Wash. *abbrev.* Washington.

wash'er[1] (wŏ-) *n.* Person, thing, that washes; ~*-man*, *-woman*, man (esp. Chinese or other Asiatic), woman, whose occupation is washing clothes.

wash'er[2] (wŏ-) *n.* Disc or flattened ring of metal, leather, rubber, fibre, etc., placed between two surfaces to relieve rotative friction or prevent lateral motion, under plunger of screw-down water-tap etc. to prevent leakage, under nut of bolt or tie-rod etc. (ill. COCK).

wash'ery (wŏ-) *n.* Place where the washing of coal, ore, wool, etc., is carried on.

wash'ing (wŏ-) *n.* (esp.) Clothes, linen sent to the wash; ~*-day*, wash-day; ~*-machine*, machine, hand- or power-driven, used for washing clothes etc.; ~*-soda*, form of sodium carbonate used in washing clothes etc.

Wash'ington[1] (wŏ-), George (1732–99). Commander-in-chief of the Continental Forces in the War of American Independence and first president of U.S., 1789–97.

Wash'ington[2] (wŏ-). Administrative capital of U.S., conterminous with the District of Columbia on the NE. bank of the Potomac River; founded during presidency of George Washington and named after him; ~ *Conference*, conference of world powers held in 1921 to discuss limitation of naval armaments.

Wash'ington[3] (wŏ-). Most northerly of the Pacific States of U.S., admitted to the Union 1889; capital, Olympia.

wash'y (wŏ-) *adj.* (Of food etc.) too much diluted, weak, sloppy, thin; (of colour) faded-looking, weak, pale; (of style, utterance, etc.) feeble, diffuse, wanting force or vigour. **wash'ily** *adv.* **wash'iness** *n.*

wasp (wŏ-) *n.* Any of a large family (*Vespoidea*) of hymenopterous insects, often carnivorous, with slender body, abdomen attached to thorax by narrow stalk, usu. two pairs of fully-developed wings and often formidable sting; esp. the common wasp (*Vespa vulgaris*) and similar species, with alternate rings of black and yellow on abdomen and marked taste for fruits and sweet things; ~ *waist*, very slender waist, esp. one produced by tight lacing; ~*-waisted*, having such a waist.

wasp'ish (wŏ-) *adj.* Irritable, petulantly spiteful, ill-tempered, irascible. **wasp'ishly** *adv.* **wasp'ishness** *n.*

wasp'y (wŏ-) *adj.* Wasp-like; abounding in wasps.

wassail (wŏsl, wăsl, wasāl') *n.* (archaic) Salutation in presenting cup of wine to guest; festive occasion, drinking-bout; liquor in which healths were drunk, esp. spiced ale drunk on Twelfth Night and Christmas Eve; ~*-bowl*, large bowl for this. ~ *v.i.* Make merry; sit carousing and drinking healths. **wass'ailer** *n.* [ON *ves heill* 'be in good health', form of salutation]

Wass'ermann (vahs-). ~ *test*, blood test employed in diagnosis of syphilis. [August *Wassermann*, Ger. pathologist (1866–1925)].

wās'tage *n.* Loss or diminution by use, wear, decay, leakage, etc.; amount wasted.

wāste[1] *n.* 1. Desert, waste region; dreary scene or expanse. 2. Consumption, loss or diminution from use, wear and tear, etc.; wasting, useless or extravagant expenditure or consumption, squandering (*of*); *run to* ~, (of liquid) flow away so as to be wasted; (fig.) be expended uselessly. 3. Waste matter; useless remains (esp. of manufacturing process), scraps, shreds; esp. scraps, remnants, from manufacture of cotton, woollen, etc., yarn or textiles, used for cleaning machinery, absorbing oil, etc.; ~*-pipe*, pipe for carrying off used or superfluous water. **waste** *adj.* 1. (of land, region, etc.) Desert, uninhabited, desolate, barren; uncultivated; (fig.) monotonous, without features of interest; not built upon; *lay* ~, ravage; ~ *land*, land not utilized for cultivation or building. 2. Superfluous, refuse, left over; no longer serving a purpose; ~ *paper*, paper thrown away as spoiled, superfluous, useless, etc.; ~*-paper basket*, basket for this; ~ *product*, useless by-product of manufacture or physiological process; ~ *steam*, superfluous steam discharged from boiler, spent steam discharged from cylinder, of steam-engine.

wāste[2] *v.* 1. Lay waste; (law) bring (estate) into bad condition by damage or neglect. 2. Expend to no purpose or for inadequate result, use extravagantly, squander; run to waste. 3. Wear gradually away, be used up, lose substance or volume by gradual loss, decay, etc.; wither; reduce one's weight by training etc.

wāste'ful (-tf-) *adj.* Given to, exhibiting, waste; extravagant. **wāste'fully** *adv.* **wāste'fulness** *n.*

wās'ter *n.* (esp., colloq.) Dissolute or good-for-nothing person.

wās'trel *n.* Good-for-nothing, worthless, disreputable person; neglected street-child; wasteful person, spendthrift.

watch (wŏ-) *v.* Remain awake for devotion or other purpose, keep vigil; be on the alert *for*, keep watch, be vigilant; exercise protecting care *over*; keep eyes fixed on, keep under observation, follow observantly. **watch'er** *n.* **watch** *n.* 1. Watching, keeping awake and vigilant at night for guarding, attending, etc.; (hist.) each of (3, 4, or 5) periods into which night was anciently divided; (naut.) period of time (usu. 4 hours) for which each division of ship's company remains on duty, sailor's turn of duty; part, usu. one-half, of officers and crew who together work ship during a watch; ~ *and* ~, arrangement by which 2 halves of ship's crew take duty alternately every 4 hours. 2. Watching, observing, with continuous attention, continued look-out, guard; one who watches, look-out man; (hist.) man, body of men, charged with patrolling and guarding streets at night, proclaiming the hour, etc.; early 18th-c. name of irregular Highland troops; *Black W~*, (from their dark-coloured tartan) some of these troops embodied (1739–40) as 42nd Regiment. 3. Small timepiece with spring-driven movement, for carrying on person (ill. CLOCK). 4. *~-chain*, chain attaching timepiece to one's person; *W~ Committee*, committee of borough or county council responsible for security and police administration; *~-dog*, dog kept to guard house, property, etc.; *~-fire*, fire burning at night as signal or for use of sentinel or other person(s) on watch; *~-glass*, thin piece of glass, usu. concavo-convex, fitted over dial-plate of watch or used as receptacle for material under observation etc.; *~-guard*, chain, cord, ribbon, etc., for securing watch on person; *~-gun*, gun fired at changing of watch; *watch'man*, formerly, one who patrolled streets at night to safeguard life and property; now esp. man employed to guard building etc., esp. at night; *~-night*, (religious service lasting till after midnight held on) New Year's Eve; *~-pocket*, small pocket, usu. in waistcoat, for holding a watch; *~-spring*, mainspring of watch; *~-tower*, tower from which observation is kept of approach of danger; *watch'word*, (hist.) military. password; word or phrase expressing guiding principle or rule of action of party or individual.

watch'ful (wŏ-) *adj.* Wakeful (archaic); accustomed to, engaged in, watching, vigilant; showing vigilance. **watch'fully** *adv.* **watch'fulness** *n.*

wa'ter (waw-) *n.* 1. Transparent, colourless, tasteless, inodorous liquid (H_2O) composing seas, lakes, and rivers, falling as rain, issuing from springs, etc., and convertible into steam by heat and into ice by cold; this as supplied for domestic needs, esp. through pipes; sheet or body of water, (now chiefly Sc.) stream, river; liquid resembling (and usu. containing) water, as tears, saliva, urine, etc.; aqueous decoction, infusion, etc., used in medicine or as cosmetic or perfume; (freq. pl.) water of mineral spring(s) used medicinally for bathing or drinking; state of tide (in *high*, *low*, ~); *heavy* ~: see HEAVY; *strong* ~*s* (archaic), distilled alcoholic liquors; ~ *on the brain*, hydrocephalus; ~ *on the knee*, accumulation of inflammatory exudate in knee-joint. 2. Characteristic transparency and lustre of diamond or pearl; *of the first* ~, of the finest quality. 3. *~-bath*, (esp., chem.) vessel containing water in or over which vessels containing chemical preparations etc. are placed for cooling, evaporating, etc.; *~-bear*: see TARDIGRADE; *~-biscuit*, unsweetened biscuit made with flour and water; *~-boatman*, aquatic insect (*Notonecta*) with boat-shaped body and oar-like legs which swims upside-down over surface of water; ~ *bok*, *-buck*, S. African antelope of genus *Kobus*, frequenting river-banks; *~-borne*, (esp., of diseases) communicated by use of contaminated drinking-water etc.; (of sea-plane) having landed on water; *~-bottle*, bottle to hold drinking-water, esp. kind of flask carried by soldiers and travellers; *~-buck*, water-bok; *~-buffalo*, common domestic buffalo; *W~-carrier*, constellation of Aquarius; *~-cart*, cart carrying water, esp. for sprinkling streets; *~-clock*, water-operated machine for measuring time; *~-closet*, private place for the evacuation of bowels and urination with pan flushed out by water (abbrev. W.C.); *~-colour*, artists' paint made of pigment mixed usu. with gum and diluted with water; esp., transparent variety of this, aquarelle; picture painted, art or method of painting, with such colours; *~-cooled*, (of internal combustion engine) cooled by means of circulating water; *~-cooler* (esp.) small tank containing cooled drinking-water; *watercourse*, (bed or channel of) stream of water, river, brook; *watercress*, hardy perennial cress (*Nasturtium officinale*) growing in springs and clear running streams, and with pungent leaves used as a salad; *~-cure*, hydropathy, medical treatment by application of water; *~-diviner*, *-finder*, one who finds subterranean water with a dowsing-rod; *waterfall*, more or less perpendicular descent of water from a height, cascade; *~-flag*, yellow iris; *waterfowl*, bird(s) frequenting water, esp. swimming game-bird(s); *~-front*, (U.S.) land or buildings abutting on river, lake, sea, etc.; *~-gas*, gas (mixture of hydrogen and carbon monoxide), made by forcing steam over red-hot coke and used as fuel etc.; *~-gilding*, gilding by application of liquid amalgam and subsequent evaporation of mercury; *~-glass*, tube with glass bottom for observing objects under water; aqueous solution of sodium or potassium silicate, solidifying on exposure to air and used as cement, fire-proof paint, for preserving eggs, etc.; *~-hammer*, concussion of water made when its flow through pipe is suddenly checked; *~-hen*, any of various ralline birds, esp. moorhen and Amer. coot; *~-hole*, hole or hollow containing water, esp. in desert or dry bed of stream; *~-ice*, frozen confection of flavoured water and sugar; *~-jacket*, casing holding water, esp. casing through which water circulates in water-cooled engines, guns, etc.; *~-jump*, place where horse must jump over water in steeplechase etc.; *~-level*, (height of) surface of water; upward limit of saturation by water; *~-lily*, aquatic plant of *Nymphaea* and related genera, and similar plants with broad floating leaves and showy fragrant flowers; *~-line*, line on ship's side corresponding to surface of water when she is afloat, esp. proper line of floatation when ship is fully loaded; linear watermark in paper; *waterlogged*, filled or saturated with water so as to be unbuoyant, heavy and unmanageable; (of ground etc.) made useless by saturation with water; *~-main*, chief pipe in system of water-supply; *wa'terman*, (esp.) boatman plying for hire on river etc.; *wa'termark*, distinguishing mark or design in paper visible when it is held up to light; *high-* (*low-*) *water mark*, line to which water of tide, flood, etc. rises (recedes); *~-meadow*, meadow periodically inundated by stream; *~-melon*, large fruit with smooth hard rind, soft pink or red pulp, and abundant sweet watery juice, of *Citrullus vulgaris*; plant, native of tropical Africa and widely cultivated, bearing this; *~-mill*, mill driven by water; *~-mint*, aquatic plant of labiate genus *Mentha*; *~-nymph*, nymph inhabiting or presiding over water, naiad; *~-ouzel*, any small bird of genus *Cinclus*, related to thrushes, but with habit of diving and walking in swift streams; *~-plantain*, plant of genus *Alisma*, with plantain-like leaves, growing in ditches etc.; *W~ Poet*, title adopted by the poet John TAYLOR; ~ *polo*, game played by teams of swimmers with ball like football; *~-power*, mechanical force derived from weight or motion of water; *wa'terproof* (*adj.*) impervious to water; (*n.*) waterproof garment or material; (*v.t.*) make waterproof; *~-rat*, aquatic rodent of genus *Arvicola*, water-vole; (U.S.) musk-rat; (Austral.) aquatic mouse of genus *Hydromys*; *~-rate*, charge made for use of public water-supply; *wa'tershed*, summit or boundary line separating waters flowing into different rivers or river basins; whole catchment area of river system; *~-snake*, any snake inhabiting or frequenting water, esp. various non-poisonous fresh-water snakes of *Natrix* and related genera; *~-splash*, shallow stream or ford across road; (colloq.) water-jump; *wa'terspout*, (esp.) gyrating column of mist, spray, and water produced by action of whirlwind on part of sea and clouds above it; sudden and violent fall of rain, cloud-burst; ~-*table*, level at which porous rock etc. is saturated by underground water, height to which such water naturally rises in well etc.; (archit.) projecting horizontal course in wall to throw off rainfall; *wa'tertight*, so closely constructed or fitted that water cannot leak through; (of argument etc.) unassailable; *watertight compartment*, each of compartments with watertight partitions into which interior of ship is divided for safety; (fig.) division of anything regarded as kept entirely separate from rest; ~-*tower*, structure supporting elevated tank to secure necessary pressure for water-supply; fire-fighting apparatus for delivering water at considerable height; ~-*vole*: see VOLE; ~-*wagon*, wagon for carrying water; *on the* ~-*wagon*, (slang) abstaining from alcoholic liquor; ~-*wagtail*, common pied wagtail; ~-*wave*, wave made when hair is damp; ~-*way*, navigable channel; (naut.) channel round ship's deck to drain off water; ~-*weed*, any aquatic plant with inconspicuous flowers; ~-*wheel*, wheel rotated by action of water and driving machinery; wheel for raising water

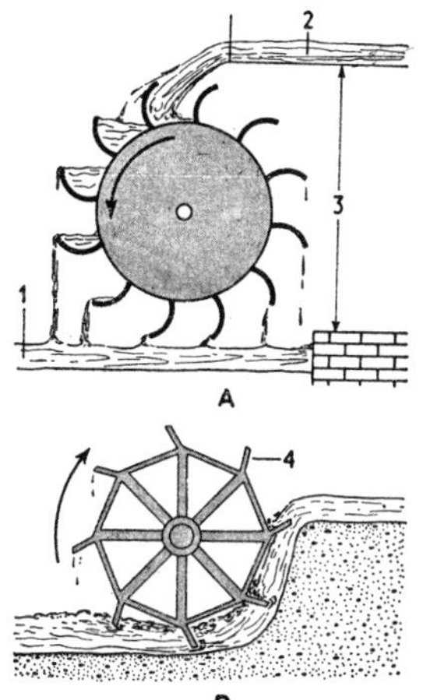

WATER-WHEEL: A. OVERSHOT. B. UNDERSHOT BREAST-WHEEL

1. Tail-race. 2. Mill-race. 3. Head of water. 4. Float

for irrigation etc. in boxes or buckets fitted on its circumference; ~-*wings*, inflated floats used as supports by persons learning to swim; *wa'terworks*, assemblage of machinery, buildings, engineering constructions, etc., for supplying town, ornamental fountain, etc., with water through pipes; (slang) tears. **wa'terless** *adj.* **wa'ter** *v.* Give (animal) water to drink, (of animals) go to pool, etc., to drink; furnish (ship etc.) with, take in, supply of water; supply water to (plant, crop, etc.), esp. by pouring or sprinkling; add water to (drink, etc.), dilute (freq. ~ *down*); (of eyes) fill and run with moisture, (of mouth) secrete abundant saliva in anticipation of appetizing food etc.; (commerc.) increase nominal amount of (company's stock or capital) by issue of new shares without corresponding addition to assets; (chiefly in past part.) produce wavy lustrous finish on (silk or other textiles) by sprinkling with water and passing through calender; *watering-can*, portable vessel for watering plants, with long tubular spout freq. ending with rose; *watering-cart*, water-cart; *watering-place*, pool, trough, etc., where animals obtain water; place where supply of water is obtained; spa; seaside place frequented by holiday visitors and invalids.

Wa'terford (waw-). Maritime county and city of Munster, Eire; ~ *glass*, glassware produced at a factory at Waterford.

Waterlōō' (waw-). Village S. of Brussels, Belgium, where on 18th June 1815 Napoleon was finally defeated by the British under the Duke of Wellington and the Prussians; hence, *meet one's* ~, suffer final defeat.

wa'tery (waw-) *adj.* Of, consisting of, water (esp. in ~ *grave*, place in which person lies drowned); full of, covered with, containing too much, water, suffused or running with, water; resembling water in colour, pale; washed out; (of liquids) too thin, diluted, having little or no taste; (fig.) vapid, insipid, feeble.

Wat'ling Street (wŏ-). Roman road running NW. across England from Richborough in Kent through London and St. Albans to Wroxeter in Shropshire.

Wat'son[1] (wŏ-), Dr. (In stories by Sir A. Conan Doyle) a stolid medical man, companion and assistant of the detective Sherlock Holmes; his qualities serve as a foil to his friend's brilliance.

Wat'son[2] (wŏ-), Sir William (1858–1935). English poet.

Watt[1] (wŏt), James (1736–1819). Scottish inventor of the steam-engine.

watt[2] (wŏt) *n.* The practical unit of (esp. electric) power, work done per second when 1 ampere flows under a potential difference of 1 volt; equivalent to rate of work of 1 joule per second; 746 watts = 1 h.p.; ~-*meter*, instrument for measuring electric power in terms of watts. [f. WATT[1]]

watt'age (wŏ-) *n.* Amount of electric power expressed in watts.

Watteau (wŏt'ō), Antoine (1684–1721). French genre-painter, whose pictures of shepherds and shepherdesses in the costumes of the 18th c. have caused his name to be given to various kinds of female dress, as ~ *bodice*, *hat*, *dress*, etc.

watt'le[1] (wŏ-) *n.* 1. Interlaced rods and twigs or branches used for fences and walls and roofs of buildings; ~ *and daub*, this plastered with clay or mud as building material for huts etc. (ill. HALF-timber). 2. (from use of its long pliant branches for making wattle fences etc.) Various Australian species of *Acacia* with fragrant golden-yellow flowers (adopted as Austral. national emblem), and bark used in tanning. ~ *v.t.* Construct of wattle; interlace (twigs etc.) to form wattle; enclose, fill up, with wattle-work.

watt'le[2] (wŏ-) *n.* Fleshy, usu. bright-coloured, lobe pendent from head or neck of turkey, domestic fowl, and other birds; barb, fleshy appendage on mouth of some fishes.

Watts[1] (wŏ-), George Frederick (1817–1904). English painter of portraits and allegorical pictures.

Watts[2] (wŏ-), Isaac (1674–1748). English writer of hymns and poems for children.

wāve *n.* 1. Moving ridge or swell of water between two troughs; movement of sea etc. in which such waves are formed. 2. Undulating configuration or line in or on surface, as hair etc. 3. Something resembling or supposed to resemble a wave, esp. temporary heightening of emotion, influence, etc.; *heat*, *cold*, ~, spell of hot or cold weather. 4. (physics) Oscillatory condition which is propagated from place to place, such that the same type of vibration occurs all along the path with a difference of PHASE (i.e. slightly delayed in time; ill. VIBRATION); *light*, *heat*, *radio*, ~*s*, electromagnetic waves propagated through space; *sound*-~, wave of compression propagated through gases, liquids, or solids; *water*-~, series of vertical vibrations, controlled by force of gravity, traversing surface of water; ~-*form*, shape of wave, graphical or arithmetical specification of this; ~-*length*, distance between successive points of equal phase in the direction of propagation of a wave; electromagnetic wave used by radio station; ~ *mechanics*, system of wave equations used to calculate the behaviour of atoms and subatomic particles when Newtonian mechanics no longer suffices. 5. Act or gesture of waving. ~ *v.* 1. Move in waves, undulate; move to and fro, shake, sway; impart waving movement to; wave hand in greeting or as signal; motion (person) *away*, *back*, *in*, etc., by movement of hand. 2. Give undulating surface, course, or appearance to, make wavy; (of hair, lines, etc.) have such appearance, be wavy.

wāve'lėt (-vl-) *n.* Small wave, ripple.

wāv'er *v.i.* Change, vary, fluctuate, shake, tremble; be irresolute, show doubt or indecision; falter, show signs of giving way. **wāv'erer** *n.* **wāv'eringly** *adv.*

wāv'y̆ *adj.* Undulating; forming undulating line or series of wave-like curves; *W~ Navy*, (colloq.) the Royal Naval Volunteer Reserve (from the wavy gold-lace stripes or rings formerly worn on sleeves). **wāv'ily** *adv.* **wāv'inėss** *n.*

wăx[1] *n.* 1. Bees-wax, sticky plastic yellowish substance of low melting-point secreted by bees from special abdominal glands, used as material of honeycomb; white brittle translucent odourless tasteless substance got from this by purifying and bleaching and used for candles, as plastic material for modelling, as basis of polishes, as air-excluding protective coating, etc. 2. Any of class of natural substances of plant or animal origin resembling bees-wax in general properties and in being composed of fatty acids and alcohols; various mineral substances (hydrocarbons) resembling bees-wax. 3. Compound, chiefly of lac, used to receive impression of seal, sealing-wax. 4. Thick resinous composition used by shoemakers for rubbing thread, cobblers'-wax. 5. Cerumen, ear-wax. 6. *wax'berry*, (fruit of) wax myrtle; *~-bill*, any of numerous small birds of weaver-bird family with waxy-looking pink, red, or white beaks; *~ candle*, candle of bees-wax, paraffin wax, etc.; *~ casting*, casting by making a wax model, laying a fire-proof mould round it, melting out the wax, and pouring molten metal in its place; *~ doll*, doll with head etc. of wax; person with pretty but unexpressive face; *~-end*, thread coated with wax and usu. pointed with bristle, used by shoemakers; *~ insect*, various wax-secreting insects, esp. a Chinese scale-insect (*Ericerus*); *~-light*, taper or candle of wax; *~ myrtle*, plant of genus *Myrica*, esp. two eastern N. Amer. species with aromatic foliage and small hard berries thickly coated with a white wax; *~ paper*, paper coated with wax used as waterproof and airtight wrapping etc.; *wax'wing*, various Amer. and Asiatic passerine birds of genus *Bombycilla*, esp. *B. garrulus*, with showy crest and red wax-like tips on wing-feathers; *wax'work*, modelling in wax; object modelled in wax, esp. life-size figure of person with wax head, hands, etc., coloured and clothed to look like life; (pl.) exhibition of such figures. *~ v.t.* Smear, coat, polish, treat, with wax.

wăx[2] *n.* (slang) Fit of anger. **wăx'y**[1] *adj.* Angry; quick-tempered.

wăx[3] *v.i.* (Of moon) undergo periodical increase in extent of visible illuminated portion in first part of lunation, before full moon (opp. WANE); (archaic and poet.) grow, increase; change by growth or increase, become (*fat, merry*, etc.).

wăx'en *adj.* Made of, coated with, wax; resembling wax, esp. in smooth and lustrous surface, pallor, or softness and impressibility.

wăx'y[2] *adj.* Resembling wax, esp. easily moulded, or presenting smooth pale translucent surface; (of tissue) affected with amyloid degeneration. **wăx'inėss** *n.*

way *n.* 1. Road, track, path, street (esp. in phrases *across, over, the ~*, etc.); place of passage through door, crowd, etc.; (pl.) inclined structure, usu. of timber, on which ship is built and down which it is slid at launch (ill. LAUNCH); (pl.) parallel sills forming track for carriage or table of lathe or other machine; (pl.) inclined plane of parallel wooden rails or planks for sliding down heavy loads. 2. Route, line or course of travel for reaching place; opportunity for passage or advance, (fig.) freedom of action, scope, opportunity; travel or motion in particular direction, direction of motion, relative position, aspect; distance (to be) travelled, distance between places or to a place; (naut.) progress, rate of progress, through water, impetus gained by vessel in motion; *lead the ~*, act as guide or leader; *out-of-the-~* (*adj.*) uncommon, remarkable; remote, inaccessible; *the other ~ about, round*, conversely, vice versa. 3. Path or course of life or conduct, (pl.) habits of life, esp. with regard to moral conduct; course of action, device, method, means; customary or usual, habitual or characteristic, manner of acting, behaving, speaking, etc., (pl.) habits; condition regarded as hopeful or the contrary; kind, sort (now only in *in the ~ of* and similar phrases), kind *of business*; *~s and means*, methods, esp. of providing money. 4. *make ~*, open a passage (*for*), move to allow person to pass; leave place vacant *for* (successor etc.); *make one's ~*, proceed in certain direction or to certain place; make progress in career, advance in wealth, reputation, etc.; *pay one's ~*, pay expenses as they arise, without incurring debts; (of business etc.) be carried on at least without loss; *see one's ~*, (esp., fig.) feel justified in deciding *to do* something; *by the ~*, by the road-side; while going along; (fig.) incidentally, in passing; *by ~ of*, via; in capacity or function of, as something equivalent to; in the habit of (do*ing*), making a profession of, having a reputation for (be*ing*, do*ing*, something); *under ~*, (of vessel) having begun to move through water (also freq. fig.); *~-bill*, list of passengers or goods on conveyance; *way'farer*, traveller, esp. on foot; *way'faring*, travelling, itinerant; *way'faring tree*, European and Asiatic shrub (*Viburnum Lantana*), growing wild in hedges etc., with broad leaves downy beneath, dense cymes of white flowers, and green berries turning red and then black; the closely related Amer. *V. alnifolium* hobble-bush; *waylay'*, lie in wait for; wait for and accost or stop (person) to rob or interview him; *~ leave* (rent or charge for) permission to convey minerals etc. across person's land, telephone wires over buildings, water-pipes or drains across private lands, etc.; *wayside*, (land bordering) side of road or path; (*adj.*) situated on, growing at, lying near, etc., wayside; *~-worn*, wearied by travel. *~ adv.* (U.S. and dial.) Away; (esp.) at or to a great distance, far; *~ back*, (colloq.) long ago; the distant past; a remote or rural district.

Way'land (the) Smith. Hero of Teutonic myth, a smith with supernatural powers; in English legend, supposed to have his forge in a dolmen near the White Horse on the Berkshire Downs.

way'ward *adj.* Childishly or capriciously self-willed or perverse, erratic, freakish, unaccountable. **way'wardly** *adv.* **way'wardnėss** *n.*

wayz'gōōse *n.* Annual festivity of printing-house.

W. by N., W by N, W. by S., W by S *abbrevs.* West by North, by South.

w.c. *abbrev.* Water-closet.

W.C. *abbrev.* West Central (London postal district).

W.C.A. *abbrev.* Women's Christian Association.

W/Cdr *abbrev.* Wing Commander.

W.D. *abbrev.* War Department.

W.D.A., W.D.C. *abbrevs.* War Damage Act, Contribution.

wē *pron.* 1st person plural nom. pron., denoting speaker and other person(s) associated with him as subject of sentence; used by sovereign or ruler, by newspaper writer or editor etc., instead of *I*.

W.E.A. *abbrev.* Workers' Educational Association.

weak *adj.* Wanting in strength, power or number; fragile, easily broken, bent, or defeated; wanting in vigour, feeble, sickly; wanting in resolution or power of resisting temptation, easily led; (of action etc.) not effective, showing weakness; (of argument etc.) unconvincing, logically deficient; (of liquid, esp. infusion) watery, thin; (of stress, a speech-sound, etc.) having relatively little force etc., (of word or syllable, esp. final syllable of verse) unstressed; (gram., of Germanic verbs) forming past tense by addition of suffix, (of Germanic nouns or adjs.) belonging to any declension in which Old Teut. stem ended in *-n*; ~ *ending*, (in verse) occurrence of unstressed monosyllable in normally stressed place at end of line; *~-kneed*, (esp., fig.) wanting in resolution or determination; *~-minded*, lacking strength of purpose; mentally deficient. **weak'ly**[1] *adv.*

weak'en *v.* Make, become, weak or weaker.

weak'lĭng *n.* Weak or feeble person or animal.

weak'ly[2] *adj.* Sickly, not robust, ailing.

weak'nĕss *n.* (esp.) Weak point, failing, defect, foolish or self-indulgent liking *for*.

weal[1] *n.* Welfare, well-being, prosperity (now chiefly in ~ *and woe*), (archaic) *common~* = commonwealth.

weal[2] *n.* Ridge or mark raised on flesh by stroke of rod, lash, etc. ~ *v.t.* Raise weal(s) on.

weald *n.* Tract of country, formerly wooded, between N. and S. Downs of SE. England, including parts of Kent, Surrey, Hampshire, and Sussex; *~-clay*, beds of clay, sandstone, limestone, and ironstone, forming top of weald strata, with abundant fossil remains.

weal'den *adj.* Of the weald. ~ *n.* Series of lower-cretaceous freshwater strata above oolite and below chalk, best exemplified in the weald.

wealth (wĕl-) *n.* Riches, large possessions, opulence, being rich; the rich; abundance, *a* profusion or lavish display *of*. **weal'thy** *adj.* **weal'thĭly** *adv.* **weal'thĭnĕss** *n.*

wean *v.t.* Accustom (child or other young mammal) to food other than its mother's milk; (fig.) detach, alienate *from* accustomed object of pursuit or enjoyment, reconcile gradually to privation of something.

wean'lĭng *n.* Newly weaned child or other young mammal.

weap'on (wĕp-) *n.* Instrument used in war or combat as means of attack or defence; any part of body (esp. of bird or beast) used for similar purpose, as claw, horn, etc.; any action or means used against another in conflict.

wear[1] (wār) *v.* (past t. *wōre*, past part. *wōrn*). 1. Be dressed in (habitually or on specific occasion); have on, be covered or decked with; dress (hair, beard, etc.), allow to grow, in specific fashion, or as opposed to shaving or wearing wig; (of ship etc.) fly (flag, colours); (transf. and fig.) bear, carry, exhibit, present (scar, appearance, title, etc.), carry in one's heart, mind, or memory. 2. Waste and impair, damage, deteriorate, gradually by use or attrition; suffer such waste, damage, or deterioration; come or bring into specified state by use, rub *off*, *out*, *away*, *down*, etc.; make (hole, groove, etc.) by attrition; exhaust, tire or be tired *out*; put *down* by persistence; endure continued use *well*, *badly*, etc., remain specified time in working order or presentable state, last long; ~ *out*, use, be used, until usable no longer. 3. (Of time) go slowly and tediously *on*, pass (time), be passed, gradually *away*. **wear'able** *adj.* **wear'er** *n.* **wear** *n.* 1. Wearing or being worn on person, use as clothes; thing to wear, fashionable or suitable apparel. 2. Damage or deterioration due to ordinary use (freq. ~ *and tear*); capacity for resisting wear and tear.

wear[2] (wār) *v.* (past t. and past part. *wōre*). (naut.) Put (ship) about, (of ship) come about, by turning head away from wind.

wear'isome (wēr-) *adj.* Causing weariness, monotonous, fatiguing. **wear'ĭsomely** *adv.* **wear'ĭsomenĕss** *n.*

weary (wēr'i) *adj.* 1. Tired, worn out with exertion, endurance, wakefulness, etc., intensely fatigued; sick or impatient *of*; dispirited, depressed. 2. Tiring, toilsome, tedious, irksome. **wear'ĭly** *adv.* **wear'ĭnĕss** *n.* **wear'y** *v.* Make, grow, weary.

weas'and (wēz-) *n.* (archaic) Windpipe; oesophagus and throat generally.

weasel (wēzl) *n.* 1. Small slender-bodied reddish-brown carnivorous mammal (*Putorius vulgaris*) closely allied to stoats and polecats and remarkable for ferocity and bloodthirstiness; *~-faced*, having thin sharp features. 2. Tracked motor vehicle for use on snow in arctic conditions.

weath'er (wĕdh-) *n.* Atmospheric conditions prevailing at a specified time or place with respect to heat or cold, quantity of sunshine, presence or absence of rain, snow, fog, etc., strength of wind; adverse, unpleasant, or hurtful condition of atmosphere, rain, frost, wind, etc., as destructive agents; (naut.) direction in which wind is blowing; *make heavy ~ of*, find trying or difficult; *under the ~*, (orig. U.S.) indisposed, not very well; in adversity; *~-beaten*, worn, defaced, damaged, bronzed, hardened, etc., by exposure to weather; *~-board*, one of series of overlapping horizontal boards covering outside of wall(s); sloping board over window or other opening to throw off rain; *~-boarded*, *-boarding*; *~-bound*, detained by bad weather; *~-chart*, diagram showing details of weather over wide area; *weathercock*, weather-vane esp. in form of cock turning with head to wind; (fig.) changeable or inconstant person; *~-eye*; *keep one's ~-eye open*, be watchful and alert; *~-forecast*, forecast of weather to be expected in an ensuing period; *~-gauge*, (naut.) position of a ship to windward of another; hence, position of advantage; *~-glass*, barometer; *~-house*, toy hygroscope in form of small house with figures of man and woman emerging from porches in wet and dry weather; *~-map*, = weather-chart; *~-proof*, impervious to weather; *~-ship*, one acting as a meteorological station; *~-station*, meteorological observation post. ~ *adj.* (naut.) Windward. ~ *v.* 1. Expose to atmospheric changes; wear away, be worn away, disintegrate, discolour, by exposure to weather. 2. (naut.) Pass, sail to windward of; withstand or come safely through (storm etc.); (fig.) come safely through (trouble, adversity, etc.).

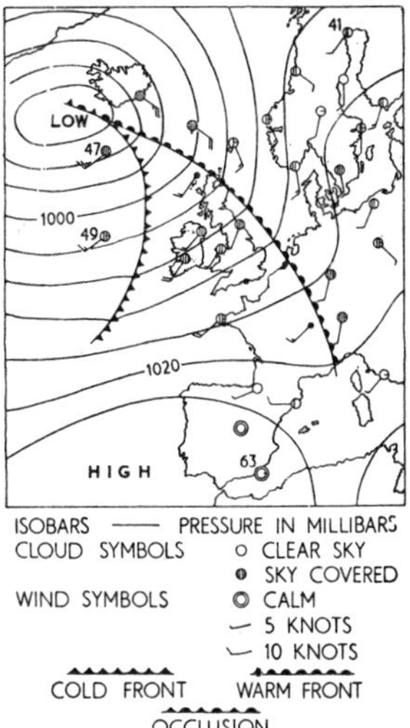

METEOROLOGICAL CHART

The system at the top left is a cyclone, and the one at the bottom left is an anticyclone. Wind-arrows point down wind. Numbers beside wind symbols give temperature in degrees F.

weave *v.* (past t. *wōve*, past part. *wōv'en* and, chiefly in some trade phrases, *wōve*). Form fabric by carrying a continuous thread or threads (the *weft*) back and forth across a set of lengthwise threads (the *warp*) so that warp and weft are interlaced; operate loom; make (thread etc.) into fabric, (fabric) out of thread etc., thus; (fig.) intermingle as if by weaving, form or introduce *into* connected whole thus; (cause to) move from side to side or in devious or intricate course; (R.A.F. slang) manœuvre aircraft thus, dodge, take evasive action; *wove paper*, paper with uniform unlined surface given by making in frame of crossed-wire gauze. ~ *n.* Style, method, of weaving (*illustration p.* 934).

weav'er *n.* (esp.) 1. One who weaves fabrics. 2. ~ (*-bird*), any of numerous Asiatic or African tropical birds (family *Ploceidae*) building elaborately interwoven nests.

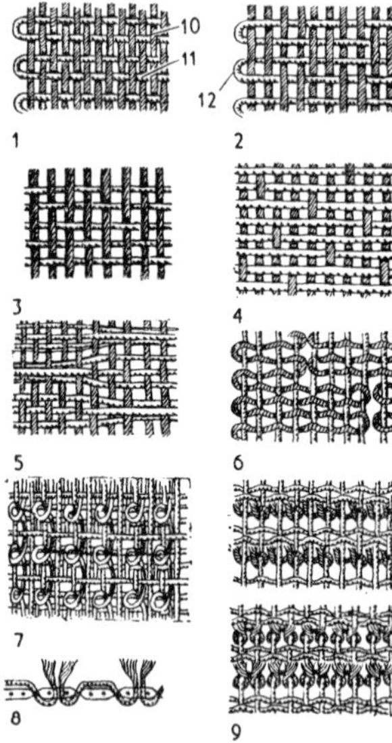

WEAVES

1. Plain (tabby). 2. Hopsack. 3. Twill. 4. Satin. 5. Huckaback. 6. Tapestry. 7. Terry. 8. Velvet (section). 9. Pile carpet weaves, Persian knots above and Turkish below. 10. Warp. 11. Weft. 12. Selvedge

weaz'en(ed) (-zn, -znd) *adj.* = WIZEN(ED).

wĕb *n.* 1. Woven fabric, esp. whole piece in process of weaving or after coming from loom; (fig.) thing of complicated structure or workmanship, tissue. 2. Cobweb (freq. fig.); filmy texture spun by some caterpillars etc. 3. Tissue or membrane in animal body or plant; membrane or fold of skin connecting digits, esp. that between toes of aquatic bird or beast, forming palmate foot; vane of feather (ill. FEATHER); thin flat plate or part connecting more solid parts in machinery; centre part of girder between flanges (ill. GIRDER); (paper-making) (large roll of paper made on) endless wire-cloth on rollers carrying the pulp. 4. *~-fingered*, having fingers united by fold of skin; *~-foot*, foot with webbed toes; (U.S.) nickname for native of Oregon; *~-footed*; *~-worm*, (U.S.) various more or less gregarious caterpillars spinning large webs in which they feed or rest. ~ *v.t.* Cover with web or fine network; stretch threads of spider's web across (micrometer etc.); connect (fingers, toes) with web or membrane.

wĕbb'ĭng *n.* (esp.) Stout strong closely woven material in form of narrow bands, used by upholsterers etc.

Weber[1] (vāb'*er*), Carl Maria von (1786–1826). German composer of romantic operas, as 'Der Freischütz', 'Oberon', etc.

Weber[2] (vāb'*er*), Wilhelm Eduard (1804–91). German physicist; devised the centimetre-gram-second system of measurement of electrical quantities now in general use.

Wĕb'ster[1], John (*c* 1580–*c* 1625). English writer of comedies and tragedies.

Wĕb'ster[2], Noah (1758–1843). Amer. lexicographer, advocate of reform of English spelling.

wĕd *v.* (past t. *wĕdd'ed*, past part. *wĕdd'ĕd* or, rarely and not in adj. use, *wĕd*). Marry; unite, join, or couple intimately *with*; *be wedded to* pursuit etc., be obstinately attached to it.

Wed. *abbrev.* Wednesday.

wĕdd'ĭng *n.* Marriage ceremony with its attendant festivities; *~-breakfast*, entertainment usual between ceremony and departure for honeymoon; *~-cake*, large rich iced and decorated cake usu. cut by bride and distributed to guests at wedding and sent in small portions to absent friends etc.; *~-card(s)*, cards with names of pair sent to friends as announcement of wedding; *~-day*, (anniversary of) day of wedding; *~-march*, march (esp. Mendelssohn's) for performance at wedding; *~-ring*, ring, usu. of plain gold or platinum, placed by bridegroom on third finger of bride's left hand as part of wedding ceremony, and usu. worn constantly afterwards.

wĕdge *n.* Piece of wood, metal, etc., thick at one end and tapering to thin edge at the other, used as tool operated by percussion or pressure on thick end for splitting wood, stone, etc., forcing things apart, widening opening, rendering separate parts immovable, etc.; (mech.) type of simple machine (a variety of inclined plane); anything shaped like wedge; American golf-club, a heavy lofted iron used for pitching; *thin end of the ~*, small beginning which it is hoped or feared may lead to something greater. ~ *v.* Tighten, fasten tightly, by driving in wedge(s); split *off*, force *apart*, with wedge; drive, push, squeeze (object) into position where it is held fast; pack or crowd (*together*) in close formation or limited space.

Wĕdg'wŏŏd, Josiah (1730–95). Founder of pottery works at Etruria, village (built for his workmen) near Stoke on Trent, England; ~ (*ware*), ware made at this factory, esp. fine porcelain with small cameo reliefs in white paste on a tinted matt ground; ~ *blue*, shade of blue of the variety called 'jasper'.

wĕd'lŏck *n.* Married state (esp. in *born in*, *out of*, ~, legitimate, illegitimate).

Wednesday (wĕn'zdā *or* -dĭ). 4th day of the week; *Ash ~*: see ASH. [OE *wódnes dæg* day of WODEN; transl. of LL *Mercurii dies* day of Mercury]

wee *adj.* Little, very small, tiny (chiefly Sc. and in nursery use); *~ folk*, fairies; *Wee Free Kirk*, *Wee Frees*, nickname of minority of Free Church of Scotland that refused to enter union with United Presbyterian Church by which United Free Church was formed in 1900.

weed *n.* Herbaceous plant not valued for use or beauty, growing wild or rank and regarded as cumbering ground or hindering growth of more valued plants; (colloq.) tobacco, *a* cigar; lanky and weakly horse or person. **weed'lĕss, weed'y** *adjs.* **weed** *v.* Clear ground of weeds; free (land, a crop, etc.) from weeds, remove (weeds); eradicate, remove, clear *out* (faults, inferior or superfluous individuals, etc.).

weeds *n.pl.* Deep mourning worn by widow (usu. *widow's ~*).

week *n.* Cycle of 7 days beginning (in the calendar of Christian countries) with Sunday; period of any 7 successive days; the 6 working days as opp. to Sunday; *week'day*, any day other than Sunday; *~-end*, holiday period at end of week, usu. from Saturday noon or Friday night to Monday; (*v.i.*) make week-end visit, &c.

week'ly *adj.* & *adv.* (Occurring, issuing, done, etc.) once a week, every week; of, for, lasting, a week. ~ *n.* Weekly newspaper or periodical.

ween *v.t.* (archaic & poet.) Think, consider, deem.

ween'y *adj.* (colloq.) Tiny.

weep *v.* (past t. and past part. *wĕpt*). Shed tears; shed tears over, shed (tears), lament, utter, with tears; shed moisture in drops, exude drop of water, exude (water or other liquid); *weeping-gas*, tear gas; *weeping willow*, large Asiatic species of willow (*Salix babylonica*), with long slender branches drooping towards ground, cultivated in Europe as ornamental tree and regarded as symbolical of mourning.

weep'er *n.* (esp.) 1. Capuchin monkey of S. America. 2. (pl.) Conventional sign of mourning, esp. hat-band or scarf of black crape worn at funeral. 3. (pl., slang) Long flowing side-whiskers 4. Small attendant figure on tomb.

weev'er *n.* Marine fish of genus *Trachinus* with many strong sharp venomous dorsal spines.

weev'il *n.* Beetle of the large family *Curculionidae*, usu. of small size, with head elongated into kind of snout; many larvae, and freq. the beetles themselves, are very destructive, boring into grain, fruit, nuts, bark of trees, etc.; any insect damaging stored grain. **weev'il(l)ed** (-vld), **wee'villy** (-vlĭ) *adjs.* Infested with weevils.

wĕft *n.* Threads crossing from side to side of web and interwoven with warp (ill. WEAVE); any one of these; yarn for weft-threads.

Wehrmacht (vār′măχt) *n.* The German armed forces.

weigh (wā) *v.* 1. Heave up (ship's anchor) before sailing; ~ *anchor*, sail; raise (sunk ship etc.) from bottom of water. 2. Find weight of with scales or other machine; balance in hands (as if) to guess weight of; take definite weight of, take specified weight from larger quantity (freq. ~ *out*); be equal to or balance (specified weight) in scales; (fig.) estimate relative value or importance of (*with, against*), consider, ponder, balance in the mind; have specified importance or value, be of account, have influence (*with*); ~ *one's words*, speak deliberately and in calculated terms; ~ *down*, draw, bend, force, down by pressure of weight; depress, oppress, lie heavy on; ~ *in with*, (colloq.) introduce, produce; ~ *out, in*, (of jockey) be weighed before, after, race; ~ (*up*)*on*, be burdensome, heavy, oppressive, on; ~ *up*, (colloq.) appraise, form estimate of; ~*-bridge*, platform scale, flush with road, for weighing vehicles etc.; ~*-house*, public building in which goods can be weighed officially; *weigh′man*, man employed to weigh goods etc., esp., in colliery, one who weighs tubs of coal at pit-mouth; *weighing-machine*, contrivance for weighing, esp. one for heavy loads, of more complicated mechanism than simple balance. ~ *n.* Process or occasion of weighing; *under* ~, corruption (from association with phrase *weigh anchor*) of *under way* (see WAY, *n.*).

weight (wāt) *n.* 1. Force with which body is attracted to earth; product of mass of any body and the average force of terrestrial gravitation; mass or relative heaviness as property of material substances; amount that thing etc. weighs, expressed in units of some recognized scale; portion or quantity weighing definite amount; heavy mass, burden, load; heavy burden *of* care, responsibility, etc.; importance, influence, authority; persuasive or convincing power (of argument etc.), preponderance (*of* evidence, authority) on one side of question. 2. Any of various systems, with series of units in fixed arithmetical relations, used for stating weight of anything; piece of metal etc. of known weight, used in scales for weighing articles; heavy piece of metal etc. used to pull or press down something, give impulse to machinery (e.g. in clock), act as counterpoise, etc.; heavy stone thrown from one hand close to shoulder in athletic sport of *putting the* ~. **weight′lèss** *adj.* **weight′lèssnèss** *n.* **weight** *v.t.* Attach a weight to, hold down with weight(s); impede or burden with load; add weight to (textiles or other commodities) by addition of adulterant etc.; (statistics) multiply components of (average) by compensating factors.

weight′y (wāt-) *adj.* Heavy, weighing much; momentous, important; requiring or giving evidence of earnest thought, consideration, or application; influential, authoritative. **weight′ily** *adv.* **weight′inèss** *n.*

Weil (vīl), Adolf (1848–1916). German physician; ~*'s disease*, infectious febrile disease with severe jaundice, caused by a spirochaete.

Wei′mar (vī-). Town in Thuringia, Germany, famous as the residence of Goethe and Schiller and as the seat of the National Assembly of Germany (1919–33); ~ *Constitution*, Republican constitution of Germany drawn up in 1919.

weir (wēr) *n.* Dam or barrier across river etc. to retain water and regulate its flow; fence or enclosure of stakes etc. in river, harbour, etc., to catch or preserve fish.

weird[1] (wērd) *n.* Fate, destiny (archaic or Sc.).

weird[2] (wērd) *adj.* Connected with fate; uncanny, unearthly, supernatural; (colloq.) queer, strange, fantastic. **weird′ly** *adv.* **weird′nèss** *n.* [f. WEIRD[1], f. phrase ~ *sisters* the Fates, the witches, in Shakespeare's 'Macbeth']

Weis′mann (vīs-), August (1834–1914). German biologist. **Weis′mannism** *n.* Theory of heredity, which assumes the continuity of the germ-plasm and the non-transmission of acquired characteristics.

Wĕlch *adj.* Old spelling of WELSH retained in names of ~ *Regiment* and *Royal* ~ *Fusiliers*.

wĕl′come *int.* Hail, know that your coming gives pleasure (often in phrases as ~ *home*, ~ *to Brighton*). ~ *n.* Saying 'welcome' to person; kind or glad reception or entertainment of person or acceptance of offer. ~ *v.t.* Say 'welcome' to, receive gladly. ~ *adj.* Gladly received; acceptable as visitor; ungrudgingly permitted *to* do something or given right *to* thing. [OE *wilcuma* (*wil-* desire, pleasure, and *cuma* comer) one whose coming is pleasing, later changed to *wel-* (= WELL[2]) after OF *bien venu*]

wĕld[1] *n.* Plant *Reseda lutea*, dyer's-weed; yellow dye yielded by this.

wĕld[2] *v.* Unite (pieces of metal) into solid mass by hammering or pressure, usu. when metal is soft but not melted; (of metal) admit of being welded; (fig.) unite intimately or inseparably; *arc-welding*: see ARC. **wĕld′er** *n.* **wĕld** *n.* Joint made by welding.

wĕl′fāre *n.* Good fortune, happiness, or well-being (of person, community, etc.); *W~ State*, one having highly developed social services (e.g. health, insurance) controlled or financed by government; ~ *work*, organized effort for welfare of class or group, esp. of employees of factory etc.; ~ *worker*, one employed in welfare work.

wĕl′kin *n.* (literary, chiefly poet.) Sky, firmament.

wĕll[1] *n.* 1. (archaic and poet.) Spring, fountain; (fig.) source, origin. 2. Pit, esp. circular vertical excavation, usu. lined with masonry, sunk in ground to obtain supply of water; shaft sunk in ground for obtaining oil, gas, brine, etc., for storage of ice, etc. 3. Enclosed space more or less resembling well-shaft, esp. central open space of winding or spiral staircase, lift-shaft, deep narrow space between surrounding walls of building(s) for light and ventilation, space on floor of law-court where solicitors sit, deep receptacle in piece of furniture, body of vehicle, etc.; (naut.) vertical shaft protecting pump in ship's hold; receptacle for liquid, esp. for ink in inkstand. 4. ~*-deck*, (naut.) space on main deck of ship enclosed by bulwarks and higher decks (ill. SHIP); ~*-head*, (esp. fig.) chief source, fountain-head; ~*-room*, building where water from mineral spring is dispensed; ~*-spring*, head-spring of stream etc.; (fig.) fountain-head, source of perennial emanation or supply. ~ *v.i.* Spring (*up, out, forth*), from or as from fountain.

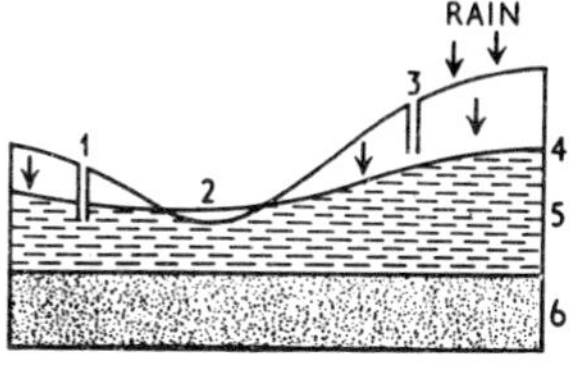

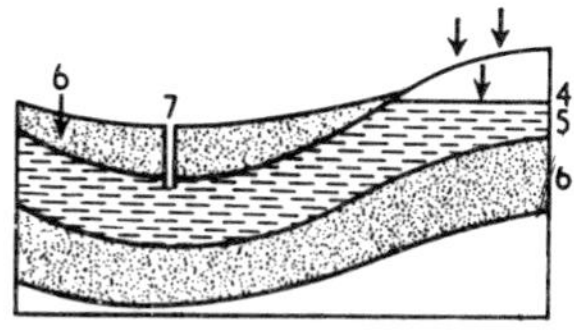

WELLS

1. Permanent well. 2. River. 3. Intermittent well. 4. Water-table. 5. Pervious rock. 6. Impervious rock. 7. Artesian well

wĕll[2] *adj.* (chiefly predic.) In good health; in satisfactory state or position, satisfactory; advisable, right and proper. ~ *adv.* 1. In good manner or style, satisfactorily, rightly. 2. Thoroughly, carefully, completely, sufficiently; to a considerable distance, degree, or extent, quite. 3. Heartily, kindly, approvingly, laudatorily, on good terms. 4. Probably, easily, with reason, wisely, advisably. 5. *as* ~, with equal reason; preferably; in addition, also; *as* ~ *as*, (esp.) to the same extent, in the same degree, as much . . . as; in addition to, both . . . and, not only . . . but also. ~ *int.* Introducing remark or statement, to express astonishment, relief, concession, resumption of talk or subject, qualified recognition of point, expectation, resignation, etc.; *very* ~, denoting agreement, approval, or acquiescence. *well-* is freq. used in combination esp. with past and present participles of vbs., and with adjs. ending in *-ed*; *~-advised'*, (esp.) prudent, wary, wise; *~-affec'ted*, favourably disposed, inclined to be friendly (*towards*), loyal; *~-appoin'ted*, properly equipped or fitted out; *~'-being*, happy, healthy, or prosperous condition, moral or physical welfare; *~-born'*, of noble or distinguished family; *~-bred'*, having or displaying good breeding or manners, courteous, refined; (of animals) of good breed or stock; *~-condi'tioned*, of good disposition, morals, or behaviour; sound, healthy, in good physical condition; *~-conduc'ted*, properly directed or managed; well-behaved; *~-connec'ted*, (esp.) of good family and connexions; *~-disposed'*, (esp.) disposed to be friendly or favourable (*towards*, *to*); *~'-doing*, virtuous life and behaviour; *~'(-)done'*, skilfully or rightly done (freq. as exclamation); (of meat etc.) thoroughly cooked; *~-fav'oured*, good-looking; *~-found*, fully furnished and equipped; *~-foun'ded*, (esp.) having foundation in fact, based on good grounds or reason; *~-groomed'*, (esp., of persons) with hair, skin, etc., carefully tended; *~-groun'ded*, well-founded; well-trained in rudiments; *~-informed'*, having well-stored mind, fully furnished with general or special knowledge; *~-inten'tioned*, having, showing, based on, good intentions; *~-knit*, (esp., of person, his frame) strongly and compactly built, not loosely made; *~-made*, (esp. of person or animal) of good build, well-proportioned; *~-marked*, clearly defined, easy to distinguish or recognize; *~-mean'ing*, well-intentioned (freq. with implication of inefficiency or unwisdom); *well'(-)nigh'*, very nearly, almost wholly; *~'(-)off'*, fortunately situated; fairly or sufficiently rich; *~-preserved'*, (freq., of elderly person) carrying his years well; *~-read*, well-informed by reading, learned (*in*), versed or skilled (*in*); *~-roun'ded*, symmetrical, (of sentence etc.) full and well-turned; *~-spok'en*, (esp.) having good or ready speech, refined in speech; *~-timed'*, timely, opportune; *~-to-do'*, prosperous, in easy circumstances, sufficiently rich; *~-tried'*, often tried or tested with good result; *~-turned'*, (esp., of speech) neatly finished, happily expressed; *~'-wisher*, one who wishes well to another, a cause, etc.; *~-worn'*, (esp.) trite, hackneyed.

wĕlladay', wĕllaway' *ints.* of grief (archaic).

Wĕll'ĭngton¹, Arthur Wellesley, first Duke of (1769–1852). British general and statesman; led the British forces in the Peninsular War, defeated Napoleon at Waterloo (1815); prime minister 1828–30; ~ (*boot*), orig. a military boot reaching to the knee in front and cut away behind; now (esp. in pl. *wellingtons*) waterproof rubber boot sometimes reaching to the knee.

Wĕll'ĭngton². Capital of New Zealand, in the North Island.

Wĕllingtōn'ĭa. Genus of large Californian pines. [named after the Duke of WELLINGTON¹]

Wĕlls (-lz), Herbert George (1866–1946). English writer of Utopian and sociological novels. **Wĕll'sĭan** *adj.* After the manner of Wells.

wĕlsh¹ *v.* (Of bookmaker etc.) Decamp without paying (winner of bet at race-meeting etc.). **wĕl'sher** *n.*

Wĕlsh² *adj.* & *n.* (People) of Wales; language of Wales, one of the Celtic group of languages; ~ *dresser*, open oak kind orig. made in Wales; ~ *flannel*, heavy variety with a bluish tinge made from Welsh fleeces; ~ *Guards*, one of the British regiments of Household troops; ~ *harp*, large triple-strung harp. orig. used in Wales; *Welshman*, male native of Wales; ~ *mutton*, mutton obtained from small breed of sheep pastured in Wales; ~ *rabbit*, dish consisting of melted or toasted cheese, with seasoning, poured over buttered toast, sometimes incorrectly called ~ *rarebit*; *Welshwoman*, female native of Wales.

wĕlt *n.* 1. Strip of leather sewn between edge of sole and turned-in edge of upper in soling boot or shoe (ill. SHOE); ribbed or reinforced border of knitted garment. 2. Ridge on flesh, esp. mark of heavy blow or healed wound, weal. ~ *v.t.* 1. Provide with welt. 2. Raise weals on, beat, flog.

wĕl'ter¹ *v.i.* Roll, wallow; be tossed or tumbled about; lie prostrate *in* (blood or gore); (fig.) be sunk or deeply involved *in*. ~ *n.* State of turmoil or upheaval; surging or confused mass.

wĕl'ter² *adj.* (Of races etc.) for heavy-weight riders; ~ *weight*, (horse-racing) heavy-weight rider; extra weight (28 lb.) sometimes imposed in addition to weight for age; (boxer with) weight of 10 st. 7 lb. or less, between light- and middle-weight.

wĕn *n.* More or less permanent benign tumour on scalp or other part of body; (fig.) abnormally large or congested city (*the great W* ~, London).

Wĕn'cĕslas, St., Duke of Bohemia, (early 10th c.). National saint of Bohemia, commemorated 28th Sept.

wĕnch *n.* Girl, young woman (now dial.); girl of rustic or working class; (in parts of U.S.) coloured woman, esp. one employed as maidservant; (archaic) strumpet. ~ *v.i.* Associate with whores.

wĕnd¹ *v.* Direct one's *way*; (archaic) go.

Wĕnd² *n.* One of a Slavonic people of E. Germany, now chiefly peasants of Lusatia, E. Saxony, but formerly extending over N. Germany. **Wĕn'dĭsh** *adj.* & *n.* Of the Wends; (of) the W. Slavonic language of the Wends.

Wĕn'sleydāle. District of N. Riding of Yorkshire, upper part of Ure valley; breed of long-woolled sheep originating here; kind of cheese made in the valley.

wĕn'tletrăp (-lt-) *n.* Any marine shell of genus *Scalaria*, usu. white, with many convolutions. [Du. *wenteltrap* winding stair, spiral shell]

wer(e)wolf (wēr'wŏŏlf) *n.* In folk-lore, human being who changes into a wolf.

Wer'fel (vār-), Franz (1890–1945). Austrian expressionist poet, dramatist, and novelist.

Werther (vār'ter). Hero of Goethe's sentimental novel 'Die Leiden des jungen Werthers' (Sorrows of young Werther, 1774). **Werthēr'ĭan** *adj.* Morbidly sentimental. **Wer'therĭsm** *n.*

Weser (vāz'er). One of the principal rivers of Germany, flowing into the North Sea.

Wesley (wĕs'lĭ *or* wĕz'lĭ). John ~ (1703–91), religious teacher and founder of METHODISM; Charles ~ (1707–88), his brother, author of many hymns; Samuel Sebastian ~ (1810–76) grandson of Charles, organist and composer of church music. **Wĕs'leyan** (*or* -lē'an) *adj.* & *n.* (Follower) of John Wesley or his teaching. **Wĕs'leyanĭsm** *n.*

Wĕss'ĕx. 1. Kingdom of WEST SAXONS. 2. Those counties of SW. England, principally Dorset, which are the scene of Thomas Hardy's novels.

wĕst¹ *n.* (abbrev. W.) Cardinal point lying opposite east and at right angles to north and south, point in heavens where sun sets on equator at equinox, corresponding point on earth; western part of world, or of country, region, or area, esp. Europe and America as dist. from Asia; the western hemisphere; the western States of U.S. (now, those lying west of Mississippi River), West End of London; west wind. ~ *adj.* Lying towards, situated in, of, the west; ~ *country*, (esp.) south-western counties (Somerset, Devon, etc.) of England; *W~ End*, (esp.) part of London lying west of Charing Cross and Regent St., and including fashionable shopping district, Mayfair, and the Parks; fashionable or aristocratic quarter of any town; *~ wall* [f. Ger. *Westwall*] the line of defences erected by the Germans for the protection of their western borders; *~ wind*, wind blowing from west. *~ adv.* Towards, in direction of, in region of, west; *go ~*, (esp.) go to America or the Western States; (fig.) die, perish, be destroyed. **wĕst'ward** *adv.*, *adj.*, & *n.* **wĕst'wards** *adv.*

Wĕst², Benjamin (1738–1820). American painter, active chiefly in England.

wĕs'terĭng *adj.* & *part.* Tending, declining, towards the west (usu. of sun).

wĕs'terly *adj.* & *adv.* 1. Towards the west. 2. (of wind) Coming from the west.

wĕs'tern *adj.* Living or situated in, coming from, the west; of Western countries or races as dist. from Oriental; of, constituting, the West of the U.S.; *W~ Australia*, a State of Australia; *W~ Church*, Latin or Roman Catholic Church (occas., including also Anglican Church or all churches of western Christendom) as dist. from Greek or Eastern Church; *W~ Empire*, more westerly of two parts into which Roman Empire was divided by Theodosius in 395, with Rome as its capital; *W~ Hemisphere*: see HEMISPHERE; *W~ Union*, proposed union of the Western democracies as a counterpoise to the Soviet Union. *~ n.* 1. Westerner. 2. Film or novel about adventures of cowboys, rustlers, etc., in western parts of N. America. **wĕs'terner** *n.* Inhabitant or native of west, esp. of Western States of U.S.

wĕs'ternīze *v.t.* Make Western, esp. make (Eastern country or people) more Western in institutions, ideas, etc.

West India *attrib.* Of the WEST INDIES; *West-Indiaman*, vessel engaged in West India trade.

West Indies. Chain of islands extending from coast of Florida to Venezuela and enclosing Caribbean Sea; inhabited largely by black and coloured people whose ancestors were brought there from Africa by European settlers to work on the plantations. **West Indian** *adj.* & *n.* (Native, inhabitant) of West Indies.

wĕst'ĭng *n.* Westward progress or deviation, esp. in sailing.

Wĕst'ĭnghouse, George (1846–1914). American inventor; *~ brake*, kind worked by compressed air on railway trains.

Wĕst Lōth'ĭan (-dh-). County in mid-Scotland S. of the Firth of Forth, formerly called *Linlithgow(shire)*.

Wĕstmeath' (-dh). County of Leinster, Eire.

Wĕst'mĭnster. City in the administrative county of London, containing the Houses of Parliament (*Palace of ~*) and many government offices etc.; hence, British parliamentary life or politics; *Statute of ~*, a declaration issued by the Imperial Conference of 1931 defining the mutual relations of Great Britain and the Dominions and recognizing the equality of status of the Dominions as autonomous communities within the British Empire; *~ Abbey*, collegiate church of St. Peter in the City of Westminster, several times reconstructed from a church orig. built by Edward the Confessor in the 10th c., scene of the coronation of English kings and burial-place of many kings, statesmen, soldiers, poets, etc.; *~ Hall*, part of the old Westminster Palace, built by William II and rebuilt, substantially in its present form, by Richard II; meeting-place of early parliaments and principal seat of justice from the time of Henry III until the 19th c.; *~ School*, public school, founded by Queen Elizabeth in 1560, adjoining Westminster Abbey.

Wĕst'morland. County in NW. England.

West North Central States. A geographical division of the U.S., made by the U.S. Census Bureau, comprising Minnesota, Iowa, Missouri, North Dakota, South Dakota, Nebraska, and Kansas.

Wĕstphāl'ĭa (Ger. *Westfalen*). Former province of NW. Germany which from 1815 formed part of Prussia; now part of the province North Rhine–Westphalia (capital, Düsseldorf); *Peace of ~* (1648), peace which ended the Thirty Years War. **Wĕstphāl'ĭan** *adj.* & *n.* (Native) of Westphalia; *~ ham*, kind made by smoking with juniper twigs and berries over a beechwood fire.

Wĕst Point. U.S. military academy at West Point on W. bank of Hudson River, N.Y. State.

Wĕst Rīd'ĭng. Administrative division comprising S. and W. part of Yorkshire.

Wĕst Săx'on *adj.* & *n.* (Of) the Old English dialect spoken by any of divisions of Saxons in England occupying area S. of Thames and westward from Surrey and Sussex; (one) of these people.

West South Central States. A geographical division of the U.S., made by the U.S. Census Bureau, comprising Arkansas, Louisiana, Oklahoma, and Texas.

Wĕst Virgĭn'ĭa. South-Atlantic State of U.S., admitted to the Union 1863; capital, Charleston.

wĕt *adj.* Liquid; rainy; moist, damp, soaked, etc., with (or *with*) liquid; employing, done by means of, water or other liquid; (naut., of vessel) liable to ship much water over bows or gunwale; addicted to, concerned with, supplying, alcoholic drinks; (U.S.) favouring sale of alcoholic liquors; (U.S. slang) wrong, misguided, wrong-headed; (slang) lacking vitality, feeble; *~ blanket*, (esp., fig.) person or thing serving to damp or discourage activity, enthusiasm, or cheerfulness; *~- bob*, boy at Eton who goes in for rowing; *~-bulb thermometer*, one having its bulb covered with wet muslin so that the difference between its reading and that of a dry-bulb thermometer indicates the amount of water vapour in the air; *~ dock*, dock containing enough water for ship to float; *~-fly*, (angling) artificial fly allowed to sink below surface of water; *~-nurse*, woman employed to suckle another's child; *~-nurse* (*v.*) act as wet-nurse to; *~ pack*, (med.) form of bath, in which patient is wrapped in wet sheets, esp. to reduce fever; *~ plate*, (photog.) sensitized collodion plate exposed in camera while collodion is moist. **wĕt'ly** *adv.* **wĕt'nėss** *n.* **wĕtt'ish** *adj.* **wĕt** *v.* Make wet. *~ n.* Moisture, liquid that wets something, rainy weather; (slang) a drink; (U.S.) one opposed to prohibition or in favour of allowing sale of alcoholic drinks.

wĕth'er (-dh-) *n.* Castrated male sheep; *grey ~s*, hard sandstone boulders lying on surface of downs in Devonshire and Wiltshire.

Wĕx'ford. Maritime county and city of Leinster, Eire.

w.f. *abbrev.* (print.) Wrong fount (of type).

W.F.T.U. *abbrev.* World Federation of Trade Unions.

wh- initially is usually pronounced *w-* in modern standard southern English, but the sound *hw-* is general in Scotland, Ireland, northern England, and America.

whăck *n.* Heavy resounding blow, esp. with stick; (colloq.) portion, share, esp. large or full share. *~ v.t.* Beat or strike vigorously.

whăck'er *n.* (slang) Unusually large thing or person.

whăck'ĭng *adj.* (slang) Abnormally large, 'whopping'.

whāle¹ *n.* Any fish-like marine mammal of order *Cetacea*, with short fore-limbs like fins and tail with horizontal flukes; esp. one of the larger of these, hunted for oil, whalebone, etc. (*illustration, p.* 938); *Blue ~*: see RORQUAL; *right ~*, a whalebone-whale, esp. of genus *Balaena*; (colloq., chiefly U.S.) something impressive in size or amount, or superlative in quality; *~- back*, anything shaped like back of whale, esp. arched structure over deck of ship, kind of steam-vessel, much used on the Amer. Great Lakes, with spoon bow and main decks covered in and rounded over; ~-*boat*, long narrow rowing-boat, sharp at both ends, used in whale-fishing or carried as life-boat; *whale′bone*, elastic horny substance growing in series of thin parallel plates in upper jaw of some whales and used in feeding, baleen; strip of this, used as stiffening in clothes etc.; ~-*oil*, oil obtained from blubber of whales. ~ *v.i.* Engage in fishing for whales.

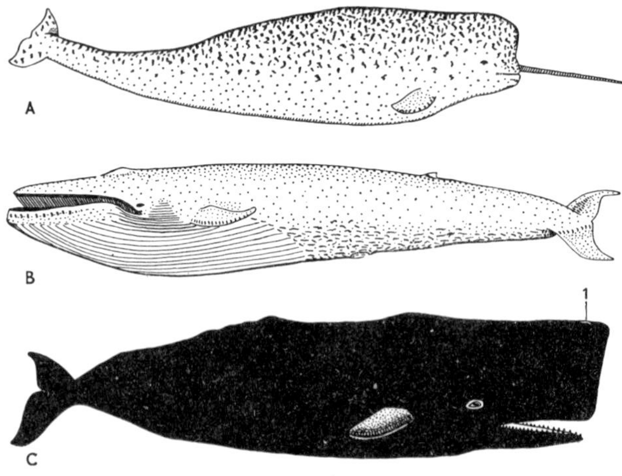

A. NARWHAL. B. SIBBALD'S RORQUAL. C. SPERM WHALE

1. Blowhole. Sibbald's rorqual (or blue whale) is the largest known living animal (100 ft long)

whāle[2] *v.* (chiefly U.S. colloq.) Beat, flog, thrash; perform some (implied or specified) action vigorously or vehemently.

whāl′er *n.* Ship, man, engaged in whale-fishing.

whăng *v.* (colloq.) Strike heavily and loudly; (of drum etc.) sound (as) under heavy blow. ~ Whanging sound or blow.

whăngee′ (-nggē) *n.* (Cane made from) various Chinese and Japanese bamboos of genus *Phyllostachys.* [Chin. *huang* kind of bamboo]

wharf (-ôrf) *n.* Substantial structure of stone, timber, etc., at water's edge for loading or unloading of ships lying alongside. ~ *v.t.* Discharge (cargo), accommodate (ships), at wharf. **whar′fage** *n.* Provision of accommodation at wharf; charge made for this; wharfs collectively.

wharf′inger (-ôrfĭnj-) *n.* Owner or keeper of wharf.

Whart′on (wôr-), Edith (1862–1937). American novelist.

what (wŏt) *adj.* & *pron.* 1. *interrog. adj.* Asking for selection from indefinite number or for specification of amount, number, or kind. 2. *exclam.* How great, how strange, how remarkable in some way; before adjs., how. 3. *relative adj.* The . . . that, any . . . that, as much or many . . . as. 4. *interrog. pron.* What thing(s)?; what did you say?; ~ *not*, other things of the same kind, anything; ~-*not*, a something, some indefinite or trivial thing; (19th c.) piece of furniture with shelves for knick-knacks; *know what's* ~, have good judgement or apprehension; know the matter in hand, know what is fitting or profitable. 5. *exclam.* What thing(s)!, how much! 6. *rel. pron.* That or those which; the thing(s) that; anything that; a thing that.

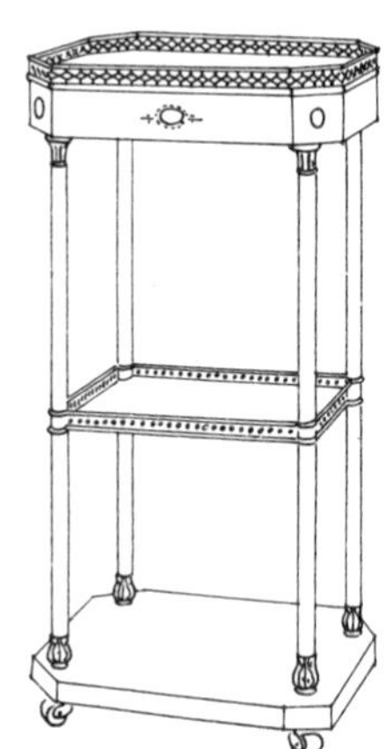

WHAT-NOT

whatĕv′er (-ŏt-), (poet.) **whate′er** (-ār) *pron.* & *adj.* Anything at all, anything that; any . . . at all that; no matter what; (colloq.) as emphatic extension of 'what' implying perplexity or surprise.

whatsōĕv′er (-ŏt-), (poet.) **whatsōe′er** (wŏtsōār′) *pron.* & *adj.* (More emphatic for) whatever.

whaup *n.* (Sc.) Curlew.

wheal *n.* & *v.* Weal.

wheat *n.* Cereal plant, *Triticum*, esp. *T. vulgare*, closely related to barley and rye; its grain, furnishing meal or flour, the chief breadstuff in temperate countries; ~-*belt*, region in which wheat is chief agricultural product, e.g. prairie provinces of Canada; ~-*grass*, couch-grass; *wheat′meal*, meal of wheat, esp. wholemeal. **wheat′en** *adj.* Of wheat, of grain or flour of wheat.

wheat′ear (-ēr) *n.* Various small passerine birds of genus *Oenanthe*, of N. parts of Europe, Asia, and America, esp. *O. oenanthe*, cock of which has bluish-grey back, blackish wings, and white rump and upper tail-feathers. [prob. *whit eeres* white arse]

Wheat′stone, Sir Charles (1802–75). English physicist and inventor; ~ *bridge*, device utilizing galvanometer for comparison of electrical resistances.

whee′dle *v.* Entice or persuade by soft words or flattery; obtain by such action; use soft words or flattery.

wheel *n.* 1. Circular frame or disc arranged to revolve on axis and used to facilitate motion of vehicle or for various mechanical purposes; wheel-like structure or thing; instrument or appliance with wheel as essential part, e.g. bicycle; revolving firework in form of spiral; ancient instrument of torture. 2. Motion as of wheel, circular motion, motion of line as on pivoted end esp. as military evolution; *right, left,* ~, words of command to troops in line to swing round on right, left, flank as pivot. 3. *on wheels*, (fig.) with rapid easy motion; *wheels within wheels*, intricate machinery, indirect or secret agencies; ~-*animal(cule)*, rotifer; ~-*back*, (chair with) wheel-like back characteristic of those made by Hepplewhite *c* 1775; (also) traditional Windsor chair with wheel design in centre-piece of back (ill. CHAIR); *wheel′barrow*, shallow open box

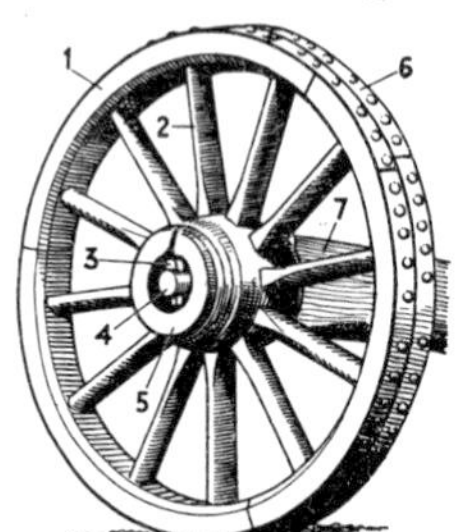

WHEEL

1. Felloe, 2. Spoke. 3. Linchpin. 4. Axle or arbor. 5. Hub or nave. 6. Strake. 7. Axle-tree

with shafts and one wheel for carrying small loads on; ~*-base*, distance between points of contact with ground or rail of front and back wheels of vehicle; ~*-chair*, invalid's chair on wheels; ~*-horse*: WHEELER; ~*-house*, structure enclosing large wheel, esp. (naut.) superstructure containing steering-wheel; ~*-load*, part of load of vehicle borne by single wheel; ~*-lock* (gun with) lock in which powder was fired by friction of small wheel against flint (ill. MUSKET); ~*-race*, part of mill-race where mill-wheel is fixed; ~*-spin*, rotation of wheels of (esp. motor) vehicle without traction, as on mud or ice; ~*-tread*, part of tyre or rim that touches ground; *wheel'wright*, one who makes or mends wooden wheels of farm vehicles. ~ *v.* 1. Turn on axis or pivot, (cause to) move in circle or spiral; change direction, face another way, turn *round* or *about*. 2. Push or pull (wheel-chair, bicycle, etc.).

wheel'er *n.* (esp.) Pole- or shaft-horse in four-in-hand, tandem, etc.; WHEELWRIGHT; (in comb.) vehicle etc. having specif. no. of wheels, e.g. *3-*~.

wheeze *v.* Breathe hard with audible whistling or piping sound from dryness or obstruction in throat; utter with wheezing. ~ *n.* 1. Sound of wheezing. 2. (orig., theatr. slang) Gag, esp. one frequently repeated; (slang) catch-phrase, trick or dodge. **wheez'y** *adj.* **wheez'ily** *adv.* **wheez'iness** *n.*

whĕlk[1] *n.* Marine gastropod mollusc of *Buccinum* and allied genera, with spiral shell, esp. *B. undatum*, common in Europe and N. America and much used for food; various similar molluscs.

whĕlk[2] *n.* Pimple.

whĕlm *v.t.* (poet., rhet.) Submerge, engulf, overwhelm.

whĕlp *n.* Young dog, puppy; young of lion, tiger, bear, and wolf (archaic); disagreeable or ill-bred child or youth. ~ *v.* Bring forth (whelp(s)), bring forth whelps.

whĕn *adv.* & *conj.* At what time, on what occasion, in what case or circumstances; at the time that, on the occasion that; at any time at which; at which time, on which occasion, and (just) then; what time, which time, (*day* etc.) at or on which; in the circumstances in which; seeing that, considering that, since; while on the contrary, whereas; (as n.) time, date, occasion; *say* ~, (in pouring drink etc.) tell me when to stop.

whĕnce *adv.* & *conj.* (archaic) From where, from what or which place or source; (with *place* etc.) from which; (as n.) place of origin, source.

whĕnĕv'er, (poet.) **whĕne'er** (-nār), (emphat., archaic) **whĕnsōĕv'er** *advs.* At whatever time, on whatever occasion; as soon as, every time that.

where (wār) *adv.* & *conj.* At or in what place, position, or circumstances; in what respect, in what, from what source, etc.; to what place; in, at, to, the or a place in or at which; (*place* etc.) in or at which; in or at which (place), and there; (as n.) place, locality. **where-** in combination with preps. forms advs. etc. (now chiefly archaic or formal) with the general meaning of the prep. followed by *what* or *which*; so **whereaf'ter, whereat', wherebȳ', wherefor', wherein', whereof', whereon', wherethrough', whereto', whereupon', wherewith'**, etc. **whereabouts'** *adv.* About where, in or near what place or position? **where'abouts** *n.* (Approximate) position or situation (of), place in or near which person or thing is. **whereas'** *conj.* In view or consideration of the fact that, inasmuch as (chiefly in preamble of legal or other formal document); while on the contrary, but on the other hand. **where'fōre** *adv.* For what; for what purpose, reason, cause, or end, why; on which account, for which reason, and therefore; (archaic) because of which, in consequence or as a result of which. **wherĕv'er**, (poet.) **where'er'** (-rār), (emphat.) **wheresōĕv'er** *advs.* At or to whatever place etc. **wherewithal'** (-dhawl) *n.* (colloq.) Means, esp. pecuniary means, *to* do or for the purpose in view.

whĕ'rry *n.* Light rowing-boat for carrying passengers and goods, esp. formerly on rivers; large light type of barge or lighter, esp. with single sail. **whĕ'rryman** *n.*

whĕt *n.* Sharpening; something that whets the appetite, esp. small draught of liquor as appetizer. ~ *v.t.* Sharpen; make (interest, wits, appetite, etc.) (more) acute, keen, or eager; *whet'stone*, shaped stone, natural or artificial, for giving sharp edge to cutting tools; any hard fine-grained rock from which whetstones are made.

whĕth'er (-dh-) *conj.* Introducing dependent question or its equivalent expressing doubt, choice, etc., between alternations, or, freq. as ordinary sign of indirect interrogation (*if*). ~ *pron.* & *adj.* (archaic) Which of the two.

whew (hwū *or* whistle-like sound) *int.* Expressing astonishment, consternation, etc.

whey (wā) *n.* Serum or watery part remaining after separation of curd from milk, esp. in cheese-making.

whĭch *adj.* & *pron.* 1. *interrog.* What one(s) of a stated or implied set of persons, things, or alternatives. 2. *rel.* The ordinary relative adj. and pron. (archaic of persons), introducing additional statement about the antecedent, = 'and that (it, they, etc.)', 'that'.

whĭchĕv'er, (emphat., archaic) **whĭchsōĕ'ver** *adjs.* & *prons.* Any or either (of definite set of persons or things) that . . .; no matter which.

whĭd'ah, whȳ- (-da) *n.* (also ~*-bird*) Various African weaver-birds of genus *Vidua*, males of which have prevailingly black plumage with white or buff markings, and very long drooping tail-feathers. [orig. *widow*-bird, f. colour of plumage, altered by assoc. with *Whidah* (now Ouidah), town in Dahomey]

whĭff *n.* 1. Puff, waft, of air, smoke, odour, etc. 2. Light narrow outrigged boat for one sculler, used on Thames. ~ *v.* Blow or puff lightly.

whĭf'fle *v.* 1. Puff lightly; move as if blown by puff of air. 2. Make light whistling sound. ~ *n.* Slight movement of air.

Whĭg *adj.* & *n.* (Member) of the political party in Great Britain that, after the Revolution of 1688, aimed at subordinating the power of the Crown to that of Parliament and the upper classes, passed the Reform Bill, and in the 19th c. was succeeded by the Liberal party (opp. TORY). **Whĭgg'ery, Whĭgg'ism** *ns.* **Whĭgg'ish** *adj.* **Whĭgg'ishly** *adv.* **Whĭgg'ishnėss** *n.* [used earlier of Scotch Covenanters, prob. short for *whiggamer*, *-more*, of uncertain origin]

whīle *n.* Space of time, esp. time spent in doing something (now only in *worth* (one's) ~, worth doing, advantageous); *a* ~, (colloq.) a considerable time, some time; *all the, this*, ~, during the whole time (that); *once in a* ~, occasionally, at long intervals; *at* ~*s*, sometimes, at intervals. ~ *conj.* During the time that, for as long as, at the same time as; when on the contrary, whereas, although; and at the same time, besides that. ~ *v.t.* Pass (time etc.) *away* in leisurely manner or without wearisomeness. **whīles** (-lz) *conj.* (archaic) While.

whīl'om *adv.* & *adj.* (archaic) (That existed, or was such) at some past time; former(ly).

whīlst *adv.* & *conj.* = WHILE.

whĭm *n.* Sudden fancy, caprice, freakish notion.

whĭm'brel *n.* Various small species of curlew, esp. the European *Numenius phaeopus*.

whĭm'per *n.* Feeble, whining, broken cry (as) of child about to burst into tears. ~ *v.* Make whimper(s), cry and whine softly; utter whimperingly.

whĭm'sĭcal (-z-) *adj.* Capricious, fantastic, characterized by whims. **whim'sically** *adv.* **whĭmsĭcăl'ĭty** *n.*

whĭm'sy (-zĭ) *n.* Crotchet, whim.

whĭn[1] *n.* Gorse, furze; *whin'-chat*, small European bird, *Pratincola rubetra*, allied to stonechat, with brownish mottled plumage and sweet song.

whĭn[2], whĭn′sĭll, whĭn′stone *ns.* (Boulder or slab of) various very hard dark-coloured esp. basaltic rocks or stones, used for road-metal and in building.

whĭn′berry *n.* Bilberry or whortleberry.

whīne *n.* Long-drawn complaining cry (as) of dog; suppressed nasal tone; feeble, mean or undignified complaint. ~ *v.* Utter whine(s); utter, complain, whiningly.

whinn′y *v.i.* Neigh gently or joyfully. ~ *n.* Whinnying sound.

whĭp *n.* 1. Instrument for flogging or beating, or for urging on horse etc., consisting usu. of lash attached to short or long stick. 2. (also *whipper-in*) Official responsible to huntsman for managing hounds and seeing that they do not stray from pack; hence, in British and some other Parliaments, official appointed to maintain discipline among members of his party in House of Parliament, give them necessary information, and secure their attendance esp. at divisions; also, written notice issued by him requesting attendance on particular occasion; *three-line* ~, such notice underlined 3 times to indicate its importance. 3. Whipping or lashing motion, esp. slight bending movement produced by sudden strain. 4. Simple kind of tackle for hoisting light objects, consisting of block with rope rove through it (*single* ~) or of standing block and running block with fall of former attached to latter (*double* ~, ~ *on* ~). 5. *whip′cord*, thin tough kind of hempen cord for whip-lashes etc.; close-woven worsted fabric with fine close diagonal ribs, used for riding-breeches etc.; ~*-hand*, hand in which whip is held; (fig.) upper hand, control (*of*), advantage; ~*-lash*, lash of whip; object resembling this; ~*-saw*, saw with very long narrow tapering blade; ~*-scorpion*, kinds of arachnid resembling scorpion but without sting and usu. with lash-like organ at end of body; ~*-snake*, various slender snakes; ~*-stitch*, (sew with) whipping stitch. ~ *v.* 1. Move suddenly or briskly, snatch, dart; make *up* quickly or hastily. 2. Beat, drive or urge on, (as) with whip; lash, flog; beat up (eggs, cream, etc.) into froth with fork or other instrument; (angling) throw line or bait on water with movement like stroke of whip; (colloq.) overcome, defeat, 'lick'; ~ *in*, drive (hounds) with whip back into pack. 3. Bind round (rope, stick, etc.) with close covering of twine, thread, etc.; sew over and over, overcast, esp. hem, or gather (fabric) by overcasting rolled edge with fine stitches. ~*-graft*, (make) graft with slit in end of both scion and stock, tongue of each being inserted in slit of the other; *whipping-boy*, (hist.) boy educated with young prince and chastised in his stead (also fig.); *whipping-post*, post to which offenders were tied to be whipped; *whip(ping)-top*, top kept spinning by strokes of lash; ~*-round*, appeal to number of persons for contribution to fund etc.

whĭpp′er *n.* ~*-in*: see WHIP *n.* 2; ~*-snapper*, small child; young and insignificant but impertinent person.

whĭpp′ėt *n.* 1. Small dog like greyhound used for racing and coursing, and orig. bred (19th c.) in north of England from cross between greyhound and terrier or spaniel. 2. (mil.) Kind of fast light tank.

whĭp′poorwĭll *n.* Nocturnal bird (*Antrostromus vociferus*) allied to nightjar, of eastern U.S. and Canada. [f. its cry]

Whĭp′snāde. Park in the Chiltern Hills, Bedfordshire, a reserve for the breeding and exhibition of wild animals, maintained by the Zoological Society of London.

whĭrl *v.* Swing round and round, revolve rapidly; send, travel, swiftly in orbit or curve; convey, go, rapidly in wheeled conveyance; (of brain, senses, etc.) be giddy, seem to spin round; *whirl′pool*, part of river, sea, etc., where water is in constant and usu. rapid circular motion; *whirl′wind*, mass of air whirling rapidly round and round and moving progressively over surface of land or water (also fig. of violent motion). ~ *n.* Whirling, swift, or violent movement; disturbance, commotion; distracted or dizzy state.

whĭrl′ĭgĭg (-g-) *n.* Spinning toy like sails of windmill revolving on stick; merry-go-round; revolving motion.

whĭrr *n.* & *v.i.* (Make) continuous buzzing or vibratory sound, as of bird's rapidly fluttering wings, swiftly turning wheel, etc.

whĭsk *n.* 1. Bunch of twigs, grass, hair, bristles, etc., for brushing or dusting; instrument, freq. bundle of wires, for beating up eggs, cream, etc., into a froth; slender hair-like part or appendage, as on tails of certain insects etc.; panicle of certain plants, esp. common millet. 2. Quick sweeping movement (as) of whisk, animal's tail, etc. ~ *v.* Convey, go, move with light rapid sweeping motion; brush or sweep lightly and rapidly from surface; beat up (eggs, cream, etc.), esp. with whisk.

whĭs′ker *n.* Hair on cheeks or sides of face of adult man; each of set of projecting hairs or bristles on upper lip or about mouth of cat or other animals, birds, etc.; star-shaped contrivance fitted to nose of a torpedo to ensure that the torpedo explodes without glancing off the target. **whĭs′kered** (-*erd*), **whĭs′kery** *adjs.*

whĭs′ky, whĭs′key *ns.* (the spelling *whiskey* is now used to distinguish the Irish kind). Spirit distilled, orig. in Scotland and Ireland, but now also in U.S., Canada, and Australia, from malted barley, rye, maize, potatoes, or other cereals; ~*-toddy*, hot water and whisky usu. flavoured with lemon and sugar [Gael. *uisge*(*beatha*) water (of life)]

whĭs′per *n.* Speech or vocal sound without vibration of vocal cords; remark uttered thus; soft rustling sound; insinuation, rumour, hint. ~ *v.* Utter in whisper, esp. for sake of secrecy; communicate etc. quietly or confidentially; (of leaves etc.) make soft rustling sound; *Whispering Gallery*, circular gallery below dome of St. Paul's Cathedral, London, where a whisper can be heard from one side to the other; similar galleries elsewhere.

whĭst *n.* Game of cards played (usu.) by 2 pairs of opponents with pack of 52 cards; one suit, usu. determined by turning up last card dealt, is trumps, and tricks are taken by highest card of suit led or highest trump, if any; *progressive* ~, number of games of whist played simultaneously at different tables, one or more players from each passing periodically to the next; ~*-drive*, social function at which progressive whist is played, usu. for prizes.

whĭs′tle (-sl) *n.* 1. Tubular wind instrument of wood, metal, etc., producing shrill tone by forcing air or steam against a sharp edge or into a bell and causing it to vibrate, used (blown by mouth) by policemen, boatswains, etc., or (blown by steam) on railway engines, steamships, etc., for giving signal or alarm; also as musical toy, usu. of tin and pierced with six holes; (joc., colloq.) mouth or throat (esp. in *wet one's* ~, take a drink); ~ *stop*, (U.S.) pause of train at station to allow electioneer to make speech (from practice of announcing stop at country place by sounding train-whistle). 2. Whistling, clear shrill sound produced by forcing breath through lips contracted to narrow opening; similar sound made by whistle or pipe; clear shrill note of bird; any similar sound, as of wind blowing through trees or missile flying through air. ~ *v.* Make sound of whistle with mouth, esp. as call or signal, expression of derision, contempt, astonishment, etc.; utter, produce, clear shrill sound or note; blow whistle; produce, utter, by whistling; call, send, (*away*, *off*, *up*) by whistling; ~ *for*, (colloq.) seek or expect in vain, go without.

whĭs′tler[1] (-sl-) *n.* One who whistles; (local) various whistling birds; large marmot of mountainous parts of N. America.

Whis'tler[2] (-sl-), James Abbott McNeill (1834–1903). American-born painter and etcher, active chiefly in England.

whit[1] *n.* (chiefly with neg.) Particle, least possible amount.

Whit[2], **Whit'sun** *adjs.* Connected with, belonging to, following, *Whit Sunday* (= *white Sunday*), the 7th Sunday after Easter, commemorating the descent of the Holy Spirit on the day of Pentecost, so called because white robes were worn on it; *Whit Monday*, *Tuesday*, those following Whit Sunday; *Whit week*, that containing Whit Sunday; *Whit'suntide*, the week-end or week including Whit Sunday.

white *adj.* Of the colour of snow or milk, of colour produced by reflection or transmission of all kinds of light in proportions in which they exist in complete visible spectrum, without sensible absorption; of some colour approaching this, pale, less dark than other things of the same kind; (fig.) innocent, unstained, harmless; (politics) of royalist, counter-revolutionary, or reactionary tendency (opp. RED); ~ *ant*, termite; *white'bait*, small silvery-white fish (fry of various fishes, chiefly herring and sprat) caught in large number in Thames Estuary and elsewhere, and esteemed as delicacy; other small fishes resembling this and used as food; *white'beam*, small tree (*Sorbus aria*) with large leaves having white silky hairs on underside; ~ *bear*, polar bear; *white'cap*, various birds with light-coloured patch on head, esp. male redstart; white-crested wave; ~-*collar*, engaged in, being, non-manual work; ~ *corpuscle*, leucocyte; ~ *currant*, variety of *Ribes* with white berries; ~ *dwarf*, one of class of small stars of great density radiating white light; ~ *elephant*, Indian elephant with pale-coloured skin, venerated as rarity in Siam etc.; (fig.) burdensome or useless possession; ~ *ensign*, ensign with St. George's cross on white ground, flag of the British Navy, also flown by Royal Yacht Squadron; ~ *feather*, symbol or emblem of cowardice (from white feather in game-cock's tail, held to show that he is not pure-bred); *white'fish*, any light-coloured or silvery fish, as cod, haddock, whiting, etc.; lake-fish of *Coregonus* and allied genera, resembling salmon and valued as food; ~ *flag*, flag of plain white used as flag of truce and in token of surrender; *W~ Friar*, Carmelite; ~ *frost*, hoar-frost, frozen dew; ~ *gold*, white-coloured alloy of gold, esp. alloy with nickel and zinc, resembling platinum; ~-*heart* (*cherry*), yellowish-white cultivated cherry; ~ *heat*, degree of temperature (higher than *red heat*) at which body radiates white light (freq. fig. of passions etc.); *W~ Horse*, figure of a horse cut on the face of the chalk downs near Wantage, Berkshire, pop. supposed to be the national symbol of the Saxons; similar figures elsewhere; ~ *horses*, white-crested waves; ~-*hot*, at white heat; *W~ House*, official residence of U.S. President, at Washington, D.C.; ~ *lead*, basic lead carbonate, a heavy white powder, used as white pigment; ~ *lie*, innocent, harmless, or trivial lie, fib; ~-*livered*, cowardly, dastardly; ~ *man*, member of race with light-coloured skin or complexion, esp. of European extraction; (colloq.) honourable, trustworthy, person; ~ *meat*, light-coloured meat, as poultry, veal, pork; ~ *metal*, various white or silver-coloured alloys, esp. one which is easily fusible and so suitable for lining high-speed bearings; *W~ Monk*, Cistercian; ~-*paper*, (esp. English) government report, usu. less extensive than BLUE *book*; ~ *sapphire*, colourless variety of sapphire; ~ *sauce*, sauce of flour or cornflour, milk, and butter, variously flavoured; ~ *slave*, woman held unwillingly for purpose of prostitution, esp. one transported from one State or country to another; ~ *slaver*, *slavery*; *white'smith*, tinsmith; polisher or finisher of metal goods (dist. from forger); ~ *staff*, white rod or wand carried as symbol of office by Lord High Treasurer of England, Lord Steward of Household, etc.; *white'thorn*, hawthorn; *white'throat*, various species of warbler, esp. (*common whitethroat*) *Sylvia cinerea*; also, N. Amer. ~-*throated sparrow*, brown sparrow (*Zonotrichia albicollis*) with white patch on throat; *white'wash*, liquid composition of lime and water or whiting, size, and water, for whitening walls, ceilings, etc.; (fig.) glossing over person's faults; *white'wash* (*v.*) apply whitewash to (lit. and fig.); ~ *wine*, any light-coloured wine (of colour ranging from pale yellow to amber; dist. from *red wine*). **white'ly** *adv.* **white'ness** *n.* **whit'ish** *adj.* **white** *n.* White or light-coloured part of anything; white or nearly white colour; kinds of white pigment; white clothes or material; translucent viscid fluid surrounding yolk of egg, becoming white when coagulated; sclerotic coat, white part of eyeball surrounding coloured iris; white man; white butterfly, pigeon, pig, etc.; member of political party called 'white', reactionary, legitimist, extreme conservative; player having white (or light-coloured) pieces in chess etc.

White'chăpel (-t-ch-). District of London, E. of the City; ~ *cart*, light two-wheeled spring-cart.

White'field (-tf-), George (1714–70). English religious reformer, one of the founders of METHODISM, who engaged in evangelical preaching in N. America, adopted Calvinistic views, and formed a party of Calvinistic Methodists.

White'hall (-t-hawl). Thoroughfare in the City of Westminster, London, bordered by government offices; hence, British Government or its policy. [f. *White Hall*, palace built by Wolsey which stood N. of Westminster Abbey]

whit'en *v.* Make, become, white or whiter. **whit'ening** *n.* = WHITING[1].

White Russia = BELORUSSIA. **White Russian** *adj.* & *n.* (Inhabitant, language) of White Russia.

White Sea. Gulf of the Arctic Ocean, in N. Russia.

whith'er (-dh-) *adv.* (archaic) To where.

whit'ing[1] *n.* Preparation of finely powdered chalk used for whitewashing, cleaning plate, etc.

whit'ing[2] *n.* Common European small gadoid fish (*Gadus merlangus*) with pearly white flesh, used as food; various other fishes resembling this.

whit'leather (-lĕdh-) *n.* Tawed leather; light-coloured soft pliant leather dressed with alum and salt.

Whit'ley Council. One of a number of boards representing both employers and staff, set up (first in 1917) to settle wages, conditions of work, etc., in certain industries (where they are usu. known as Joint Industrial Councils) and in the civil service and local government service. [J. H. *Whitley*, chairman of committee recommending the councils]

whit'low (-ō) *n.* Inflammation, usu. with suppuration, on finger or toe, esp. about nail.

Whit'man, Walt (1819–92). American poet, author of poems on moral, social, and political questions, written in an unconventional form between rhythmical prose and verse.

Whitt'ier, John Greenleaf (1807–92). American poet, the 'Quaker poet'.

Whitt'ington, Dick. Sir Richard Whittington, 3 times Lord Mayor of London (1397, 1406, 1419), hero of the popular legend of Whittington and his cat.

whitt'le *v.* Dress, pare, with knife; cut thin slices or shavings from surface of, make or shape thus; (fig.) reduce amount or effect of by successive abstractions, pare *down*, take *away* by degrees.

whit'y *adj.* Whitish (chiefly in ~-*brown*).

whiz(z) *v.* (Cause to) make sound as of body rushing through air; move swiftly (as) with such sound; ~-*bang*, (slang) kind of small high-velocity shell whose passing through the air can be heard before the report of the gun that fired it. ~ *n.* Act, sound, of whizzing.

W.H.O. *abbrev.* World Health Organization.

who (hōō) *pron.* 1. *interrog.* What or which person(s)?; what sort of person(s) in regard to origin, position, authority, etc.?; *Who's Who,* title of reference book of contemporary biography (first issued 1849) and of similar works. 2. *rel.* (Person or persons) that; and or but he (she, they); (archaic) the or any person(s) that.

whoa (wō'*a*) *int.* Word of command to horse etc. to stop or stand still.

whodŭn(n)'it (hōō-) *n.* (slang) Detective or mystery story.

whoĕv'er (hōō-), (poet.) **whoe'er** (hōōār') *prons.* Whatever person(s), any(one) who; no matter who.

whole (hōl) *adj.* In sound condition, uninjured, not broken or divided, intact; integral, without fractions; undiminished, without subtraction; all, all of; *with* one's ~ *heart,* heartily, with concentrated effort, etc., whence ~-*hearted, -heartedly, -heartedness*; *go the* ~ *hog,* go to the utmost limit; act etc. without reservation; ~-*hogger,* one who goes the whole hog; *wholemeal,* meal or flour made from whole grain of wheat (sometimes including bran); ~ *plate,* (photographic plate or film) of the size 6½ × 8½ in. ~ *n.* Full, complete, or total amount (*of*); complete thing; organic unity, complex system, total made up of parts.

whole'sāle (hōls-) *n.* Selling of articles in large quantities to be retailed by others. ~ *adj.* Selling by wholesale; pertaining to sale in gross; unlimited, indiscriminate; doing, done, largely or profusely. ~ *adv.* In large quantities, in gross; in abundance, extensively, indiscriminately. **whōle'sāler** *n.* One who sells wholesale.

whole'some (hōls-) *adj.* Promoting, conducive to, health or well-being; beneficial, salutary, salubrious; not morbid, healthy. **whōle'somely** *adv.* **whōle'someness** *n.*

whōlly (hōl'-lĭ) *adv.* Entirely, completely, to the full extent, altogether; exclusively.

whom (hōōm) *pron.* Objective case of WHO.

whoop (hōōp) *n.* & *int.* (Cry of) whoop!, expressing excitement, exultation, etc. (used esp. in hunting by N. Amer. Indians as signal or war-cry); characteristic drawing-in of breath after coughing in whooping-cough. ~ *v.i.* Utter whoop; *whoop'ing-cough,* infectious disease, esp. of children, with violent convulsive cough followed by whoop, caused by a bacillus, *Haemophilus pertussis.*

whoopee' (hōō-, wōō-) *n.* (orig. U.S. slang) *Make* ~, rejoice noisily or hilariously, have a good time.

whŏp *v.t.* (slang) Thrash, defeat, overcome. **whŏpp'ĭng** *adj.* Abnormally large or great. **whŏpp'er** *n.* Very large thing; monstrous falsehood.

whore (hōr) *n.* Prostitute, strumpet; ~ *of Babylon,* (see Rev. xvii. 1, 5, etc.) abusively applied to Church of Rome, esp. in 17th c. ~ *v.i.* Have to do with whore(s), fornicate; (fig., archaic, after Deut. xxxi. 16; *go a-whoring after strange gods* etc., practise idolatry or iniquity. **whōre'dom** *n.* Fornication. **whōre'monger** *n.* Fornicator.

whōrl *n.* Small fly-wheel or pulley on spindle to steady its motion (ill. SPINNING); convolution, coil, something suggesting whirling movement, esp. (of finger-print) complete circle formed by central papillary ridges; each turn of spiral shell or any spiral structure; (bot.) ring of leaves, flowers, etc., springing from stem or axis at same level.

whor'tleberry (wẽrtlb-) *n.* (Blue-black fruit of) dwarf shrub *Vaccinium myrtillus,* bilberry.

whose (hōōz) *pron.* Possessive case of WHO.

whȳ *adv.* 1. *interrog.* On what ground?, for what reason?, with what purpose?. 2. *rel.* On account of which. ~ *n.* Reason, cause, explanation, esp. in *why(s) and wherefore(s).* ~ *int.* As expression of (esp. mild or slight) surprise, slight protest, etc., or emphasizing or calling attention to following statement, in opposition to possible doubt or objection.

W.I. *abbrev.* West Indies; Women's Institute.

wĭbb'le *v.t.* (eng.) = END-mill.

wick[1] *n.* Bundle of fibre, now usu. loosely twisted or woven cotton, immersed at one end in oil or grease of lamp, candle, etc., and drawing it up to maintain flame at other end.

wick[2] *n.* (obs. except in place-names or other compounds) Town, village, hamlet.

wĭck'ĕd *adj.* Sinful, iniquitous, vicious, morally depraved; (colloq., usu. joc.) very or excessively bad, malicious, mischievous, roguish; *W~ Bible,* English edition of 1632 with 'not' omitted in 7th commandment. **wĭck'ĕdly** *adv.* **wĭck'ĕdnĕss** *n.*

wick'er *n.* Plaited pliant twigs or osiers as material of baskets, chairs, mats, etc.; *wickerwork,* things made of wicker; craft of making them.

wĭck'ĕt *n.* 1. (also ~-*gate*) Small gate or door, esp. one made in or placed beside large one. 2. (cricket) Set of three stumps fixed upright in ground and surmounted by two bails, forming structure (27 × 8 in.) to be defended by batsman from balls aimed by bowler (ill. CRICKET); time during which batsman is or might be in; ground between and about wickets, pitch; ~ *falls,* batsman is out; *keep* ~, be wicket-keeper; *take a* ~, (of bowler) put batsman out; *win by 4* (etc.) ~*s,* win having lost only 6 wickets in the last innings; ~-*keeper,* fieldsman stationed behind wicket to stop ball if it passes by, and if possible get batsman out by stumping or catching.

Wĭck'low (-ō). Maritime county and city of Leinster, Eire.

wĭdd'ershĭns (-nz), **wĭth-** (-dh-) *adv.* (*dial.*) In direction contrary to apparent course of sun (considered as unlucky or disastrous). [MLG *wider-* against, *sin* direction]

wīde *adj.* 1. Measuring much from side to side; broad, not narrow; having specified measurement from side to side (as *road 20 ft* ~). 2. Extending far, embracing much, of great extent; not tight, close, or restricted; loose, free, liberal, unprejudiced, general. 3. Open to full extent. 4. At considerable distance from point or mark, not within reasonable distance *of.* 5. ~-*angle,* (of lens) having short focus and field extending through wide angle; ~ *ball,* = wide (*n.*); ~-*eyed,* with eyes wide open, gazing intently; (fig.) wondering, naïve. **wīde'ly** *adv.* **wīde** *adv.* Over or through large space or region, far abroad (now only in *far and* ~); at wide interval(s), far apart; with wide opening, to full extent, at a distance to one side, so as to miss mark or way, astray, esp. (cricket) out of reach of batsman; ~ *awake,* fully awake; (colloq.) on the alert, fully aware of what is going on, sharp-witted, knowing; ~-*awake* (*n.*) soft wide-brimmed felt hat; *widespread,* widely disseminated or diffused. ~ *n.* (cricket) Ball bowled wide of wicket out of batsman's range and counting one run to his side.

wīd'en *v.* Make, become, wide or wider.

widgeon: see WIGEON.

wĭd'ow (-ō) *n.* Woman who has lost her husband by death and not married again; ~-*bird,* WHIDAH; ~*'s cruse,* small supply that seems inexhaustible (see 1 Kings xvii. 10–16, 2 Kings iv. 1–7); ~*'s mite*: see Mark xii. 42; ~*'s peak,* V-shaped growth of hair in centre of forehead; ~*'s weeds,* heavy mourning, including long black veil, formerly worn by widows. ~ *v.t.* Make widow or widower of (usu. in past part.); bereave, deprive *of.* **wĭd'owhŏŏd** *n.*

wĭd'ower (-ōer) *n.* Man who has lost his wife by death and not married again.

wĭdth *n.* Distance or measurement from side to side; large extent; piece of material of same width as when woven, esp. one of such pieces sewn together to make garment etc.

Wie'land (vē-), Christoph Martin (1733–1813). German poet and writer of verse romances; translated some of Shakespeare's plays into German.

wield *v.t.* Control, sway, hold and use, manage.

wīfe *n.* (pl. *wives*). 1. Married woman esp. in relation to her husband. 2. Woman, esp. one who is old and rustic or uneducated (now rare exc. in *old wives' tale*, foolish or superstitious tradition). **wīfe'hŏŏd** *n.* **wīfe'lėss, wīfe'ly** *adjs.*

wĭg *n.* Artificial head of hair worn to conceal baldness, or as disguise, or as part of professional,

WIGS. A. PERIWIG OR PERUKE, *c* 1680. B. RAMILLIES, EARLY 18TH C. C. FULL-BOTTOMED, 1766. D. BAG-WIG, *c* 1725

1. Cravat. 2. Cocked Hat. 3. Queue

ceremonial, or (formerly) fashionable costume; coarse hair on shoulders of full-grown male fur-seal; *~s on the green*, (colloq., orig. Irish) coming to blows, sharp altercation.

wi'geon, widg- (-jon) *n.* Wild duck, esp. *Anas penelope* of Europe and N. Asia and *A. americana* of N. America.

wigg'ing (-g-) *n.* (colloq.) Severe rebuke, scolding.

wigg'le *v.t.* (colloq. or dial.) Cause (something) to move from side to side; scull (boat) with single oar over stern.

wight[1] (wīt) *n.* (archaic) Person.

Wight[2] (wīt), Isle of. Island off the S. coast of England.

Wigorn. *abbrev.* (Bishop) of Worcester, replacing surname in his signature.

Wig'townshire (-tun-). County of SW. Scotland.

wĭg'wăg *v.* (colloq.) Wag, esp. wave flag or other object to and fro in signalling.

wĭg'wăm (*or* -ŏm) *n.* Tent or cabin of N. Amer. Indian tribes of region of Great Lakes and eastward, formed of bark, matting, or hides stretched over frame of converging poles.

Wĭl'berfōrce, William (1759–1833). English M.P.; devoted himself to the cause of the abolition of the slave-trade and slavery. Samuel ~ (1805–73), his son, successively bishop of Oxford and Winchester, and initiator of revision of A.V.

Wĭl'cŏx, Mrs Ella Wheeler (1850–1919). American poet and journalist.

wīld *adj.* Living or growing in state of nature, not domesticated, tame, or cultivated; uncultivated, uninhabited, waste; uncivilized, savage; rebellious; not under control or restraint; fierce, violent, tempestuous; violently excited or agitated; passionately desirous (*to do*), elated, enthusiastic; haphazard, reckless, extravagant; ~ *cat*, European wild species (*Felis catus*), larger and stronger than domestic cat and similar in colour and marking to tabby; (orig. U.S. colloq.) unsound or risky enterprise (freq. attrib.); *~-cat strike*, unofficial strike; *wild'fire*, highly inflammable composition very difficult to extinguish, formerly used in warfare etc. (now chiefly in *spread like wildfire*, spread with immense rapidity); phosphorescent light; *~-fowl*, wild birds, esp. wild game; *~ goose*, any undomesticated goose, in England usu. greylag (*Anser anser*), in N. Amer. the Canada goose (*Bernicha canadensis*); *~ goose chase*, foolish, fruitless, or hopeless quest; *~ man*, savage; *~ man* (*of the woods*), orang-outan; *~ oats*, wild grass of genus *Avena*; youthful indiscretions and escapades (esp. in *sow* one's *~ oats*); *W~ West*, western States of U.S. at period when they were lawless frontier districts; *wild'wood*, (chiefly poet.) uncultivated or unfrequented wood. **wīld'ly** *adv.* **wīld'nėss** *n.* **wīld** *n.* (usu. pl.) Desert, wild tract.

Wilde, Oscar Fingal O'Flahertie Wills (1854–1900). Irish-born writer of comedies, novels, and verse, a wit and aesthete.

wildebeest (vĭl'debāst) *n.* Gnu. [S. Afr. Du., = 'wild beast']

wild'ernėss *n.* Desert, uncultivated and uninhabited land or tract; part of garden left looking uncultivated; mingled, confused, or vast assemblage *of*; *in the ~*, (of political party, with ref. to Num. xiv. 33) out of office.

wīld'ing *n.* Wild plant, esp. wild crab-apple; fruit of such plant.

wīle *n.* Trick, cunning procedure, artifice. ~ *v.t.* Lure, entice.

Wĭl'frĭd or **Wĭl'frĭth,** St. (634–700). Bishop of York, instrumental in winning over King Oswy of Northumbria to the Roman, as opposed to the Columban, Church.

wĭl'ful *adj.* Asserting or disposed to assert one's own will against persuasion, instruction, or command, obstinately self-willed; done on purpose, deliberate, intentional, due to perversity or self-will. **wĭl'fully** *adv.* **wĭl'fulnėss** *n.*

Wĭlhĕlmsha'ven (vĭ-; -hahfen). German North Sea port and naval base on Jade Bay in Lower Saxony.

Wilhelmstrasse (vĭl'hĕlm-shtrahse). Street in Berlin where Foreign Ministry and other government buildings were situated; hence, (hist.) German Foreign Ministry.

Wĭlkes (-ks), John (1727–97). English Radical M.P., journalist, and agitator, several times expelled from the House of Commons.

Wĭl'kĭe, Sir David (1785–1841). Scottish painter.

wĭll[1] *n.* 1. Faculty or function which is directed to conscious and intentional action; act, action, of willing; intention or determination that something shall be done or happen; desire, wish, inclination (*to* do); (archaic or poet.) what one desires; *against one's ~*, unwillingly; *at ~*, according to one's volition or choice, as one will; at the command or disposal (*of*); (of estate etc.) held during owner's pleasure, (of tenant) that may be ousted at any time; *of one's own free ~*, of one's own accord, voluntarily; *with a ~*, resolutely, determinedly, energetically; *~-power*, (strength of) will, esp. power to control one's own actions etc. 2. Person's formal declaration, usu. in writing, of his intention as to disposal of his property etc. after his death; document in which this is expressed. ~ *v.* 1. Determine by the will, choose or decide to do something or that something shall be done; exercise the will; bring, get, (*into* etc.) by exercise of will; control (person), induce (another) *to do*, by exercise of one's will. 2. Direct by will or testament; dispose of by will, bequeath.

wĭll[2] *v.t.* & *aux.* (pres. *I, he, we, you, they, ~*; past and conditional *would* pr. wŏŏd; neg. *~ not, won't; would not, wouldn't*). 1. *v.t.* Desire (thing; archaic); want, desire, choose, to; wish that; consent, be prevailed on, to; intend unconditionally; be accustomed, be observed from time to time, to; be likely to. 2. *v. aux.* (in 2nd and 3rd pers.) forming plain future or conditional statement or question; (in 1st pers.) to form future or conditional statement expressing speaker's will or intention.

wĭll'ėt *n.* Large N. Amer. shore-bird of snipe family (*Symphemia semipalmata*).

Wĭll'iam[1]. Name of 4 kings of England: *William I* (*c* 1027–87), 'The Conqueror', Duke of Normandy, claimed the English throne, invaded England and defeated Harold at the Battle of Hastings (1066), king of England 1066–87; *William II* (1056–1100), 'Rufus', the Conqueror's son, king of England 1087–1100; *William III* (1650–1702), Prince of Orange, married Mary, daughter of James II, and reigned jointly with her 1689–94, and alone (after her death) until 1702; *William IV* (1765–1837), 3rd son of George III, succeeded his brother, George IV in 1830.

Wĭll'ĭam². Anglicized form of name (*Wilhelm*) of two German emperors and kings of Prussia; *William I* (1797–1888), king of Prussia 1861–, first German emperor 1871–; *William II* (1859–1941), 'The Kaiser', grandson of William I, succeeded his father, Frederick III, 1888, abdicated 1918 after the defeat of Germany, and fled to Holland.

Wĭll'ĭam³. Anglicized form of name (*Willem*) of 3 kings of the Netherlands: *William I* (1772–1843) became 1st king of the Netherlands after the defeat of Napoleon, 1815, abdicated 1840 in favour of his son, *William II* (1792–1849), 2nd king of the Netherlands 1840–9; *William III* (1817–90), son of William II, whom he succeeded 1849.

Wĭll'ĭam and Mār'y Cŏll'ége. College at Williamsburg, Virginia, founded 1693 by Dr James Blair.

Wĭll'ĭam(s) (pear). Very juicy September-ripening variety of Bon Chrétien pear. [prop. *Williams's*, from name of first distributor in England]

Wĭll'ĭam the Silent (1533–84). Prince of Orange and count of Nassau; led the insurrection of the Netherlands against Spain and became (1580) the first stadholder of the United Provinces of the Netherlands.

wĭll'ĭng *adj.* Not reluctant (*to* do), ready to be of use or service; given, rendered, performed, etc., willingly. **wĭll'ĭngly** *adv.* **wĭll'ĭngnĕss** *n.*

wĭll-o'-the-wĭsp *n.* = IGNIS FATUUS; (fig.) person or thing that deludes or misleads by fugitive appearances. [orig. *Will with the wisp* (= handful of lighted tow etc.)]

Wĭll'oughby (-lobĭ), Sir Hugh (d. 1553). English navigator; perished on the way to Russia, which was reached, via the White Sea, by other members of his expedition.

wĭll'ow (-ō) *n.* Tree or shrub of genus *Salix*, widely distributed in temperate and cold regions, usu. growing by water and with pliant branches and long narrow drooping leaves, grown for ornament or as furnishing osiers, light smooth soft wood, or medicinal astringent bark; cricket- or baseball-bat (made of willow-wood); *wear the (green)* ~, grieve for loss of loved one; *~-herb*, plant of *Epilobium* and related genera, esp. *E. angustifolium*, with narrow willow-like leaves and showy purplish-pink flowers, a common weed in all parts of North Temperate zone; *~ pattern*, blue pattern, of Chinese origin, on white china, introduced

WILLOW PATTERN

into England in late 18th c. by Thomas Turner, and including willow-tree etc.; *~-tree*, willow; *~-warbler*, *-wren*, small European song-bird, *Phylloscopus trochilus*, and other birds of this and related genera. **wĭll'owy** *adj.* 1. Abounding in willows, bordered or shaded with willows. 2. Lithe and slender.

Wĭll Scârl'ĕt. One of the companions of Robin Hood.

Will's (coffee-house). Coffee-house formerly at corner of Bow St. and Russell St., London, frequented by wits, poets, and gamesters in Queen Anne's reign.

wĭll'y-nĭll'y *adv.* & *adj.* With or against the will of the persons concerned, whether one will or no, willing(ly) or unwilling(ly).

Wilno: see VILNA.

Wĭl'son¹, (James) Harold (1916–), British labour politician; prime minister 1964– .

Wĭl'son², John (1785–1854). 'Christopher North', professor at Edinburgh University and notable literary critic.

Wĭl'son³, Thomas Woodrow (1856–1924). 28th president of U.S., 1913–21; U.S. representative at the peace treaty negotiations after the war of 1914–18 and sponsor of the Covenant of the League of Nations.

wĭlt *v.* (Cause to) fade, droop, become limp.

Wĭl'ton. Town in S. Wiltshire, noted since 16th c. for manufacture of carpets; ~ (*carpet*), woollen or worsted carpet with short thick pile, resembling Brussels carpet, first made at Wilton.

Wilts. *abbrev.* Wiltshire.

Wĭlt'shire. County of SW. England; breed of sheep, kind of smoked bacon, variety of Cheddar cheese, as produced in Wiltshire.

wīl'ȳ *adj.* Full of wiles, crafty, cunning. **wīl'ĭly** *adv.* **wīl'ĭnĕss** *n.*

Wĭm'bledon (-bld-). Suburb of London, in Surrey, scene of international lawn tennis championships and matches.

wĭm'ple *n.* Cloth of linen or silk so folded as to cover head, chin, sides of face, and neck, formerly worn by women and retained in dress of nuns (ill. KIRTLE). ~ *v.* Envelop in wimple, veil; fall in folds.

wĭn *v.* (past t. and past part. *won* pr. wŭn). Be victorious in (game, battle, race, law action, etc.); be victorious, gain victory; get, gain, secure, esp. by effort or competition, as price or reward, by merit, or in gaming or betting; gain affection or allegiance of, bring *over* to one's party or cause; make one's way to, make one's way *to, through*, etc.; get (coal, stone, or other mineral) from mine, pit, etc.; ~ *out* (colloq.), *through*, gain one's end, be successful; *winning*, (as adj.) charming, attractive; *winning hazard*: see HAZARD; *winning-post*, post marking end of race-course; *winnings*, money won by gaming or betting. **wĭnn'er** *n.* **wĭn** *n.* (colloq.) Victory in game or contest; (pl.) winnings, gains.

wince *v.i.* Make involuntary shrinking movement, start, with pain, in alarm, etc., flinch. ~ *n.* Such movement.

wĭn'cey *n.* Durable fabric with usu. linen warp and woollen weft. **wĭnceyĕtte'** *n.* Similar fabric with cotton warp.

wĭnch *n.* Crank of wheel or axle; hoisting or hauling apparatus consisting essentially of revolving horizontal drum worked by a crank.

Wĭn'chĕster. Cathedral city in Hampshire; once the capital of Wessex and later of the Anglo-Saxon kingdom; ~ (*College*), public school situated there, founded 1382 by William of Wykeham; ~ (*quart*), (bottle containing) half a gallon, so called because standard measures were formerly deposited at Winchester.

Win'ckelmann (vĭngkl-), Johann Joachim (1717–68). German writer on Greek art and antiquities.

wĭnd¹ (*poet. also* wīnd) *n.* 1. Air in motion, current of air of any degree of force perceptible to senses occurring naturally in atmosphere; this in reference to direction from which it blows or (naut.) its direction or position in relation to ship; air artificially put in motion by passage of missile, action of bellows, etc.; scent, esp. of person or animal in hunting etc., conveyed on wind; *raise the* ~, (fig., colloq.) obtain money needed; *sail* etc. *close to the* ~, (fig.) come very near indecency or dishonesty; *take* ~ *out of person's sails*, (fig.) put him at a disadvantage, esp. by anticipating his arguments etc.; *get* ~ *of*, (fig.) begin to suspect, hear rumour of; *in the* ~, happening or ready to happen, astir, afoot; *like the* ~, swiftly. 2. Gas in stomach or intestines; *break* ~, release it by anus; *get, have, put, the* ~ *up*, (slang) be in, put into, state of alarm or 'funk'. 3. Breath as needed in exertion, power of fetching breath without difficulty

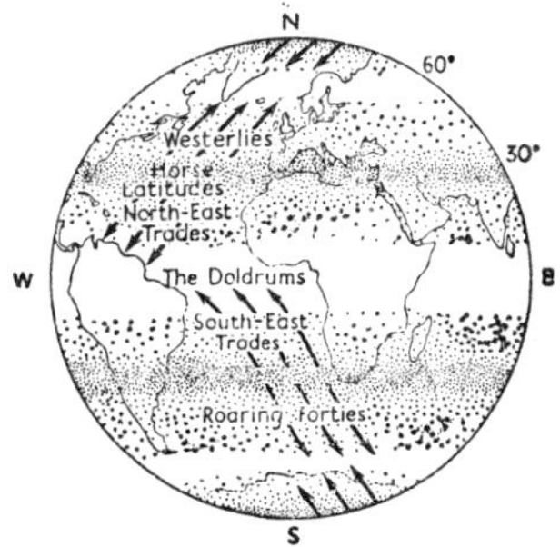

THE DIRECTIONS OF THE PREVAILING WINDS IN THE ATLANTIC

while running etc.; part of body in front of stomach, blow on which checks action of diaphragm and takes away breath; *second* ~, regular breathing regained after breathlessness during continued exertion. 4. Breath as used in speaking, esp. (fig.) empty talk. 5. Breath or air as used for sounding musical instrument, as horn, flute, organ-pipe; (players of) wind-instruments of orchestra collectively. 6. ~*-bag*, wordy talker; ~*-bound*, kept from sailing by adverse winds; ~ *brace*, strengthening timber of roof (ill. ROOF); ~*-break*, something, esp. row of trees, used to break force of wind or as protection against it; ~*-cheater*, windproof jacket fitting closely at waist and wrists; ~*-chest*, chest in organ etc. filled with wind from bellows and admitting it to pipes or reeds (ill. ORGAN); ~*-cone*, piece of cloth shaped like truncated cone, held open at larger end by ring of wire and used to indicate direction of wind, drogue; ~*-egg*, imperfect or unfertilized egg, esp. with soft shell; *wind'fall*, something blown down by wind, esp. fruit; (fig.) unexpected good fortune, esp. legacy; *wind'flower*, anemone; *wind'gall*, soft tumour on horse's leg just above fetlock; fragment of rainbow or prismatic halo, supposed to presage windy weather; *wind'hover*, kestrel; ~ *instrument*, musical instrument in which sound is produced by current of air, esp. by breath; *wind'jammer*, (colloq.) sailing-ship; ~ *machine*, machine used in theatre etc. for producing blast of air or sound of wind; *wind'mill*, mill for grinding corn, pumping water, etc., worked by action of wind on sails; *wind'pipe*, air passage between throat and bronchi or lungs, trachea; *wind'-proof*, affording protection from wind; *wind'row*, row of mown grass or hay raked up to dry before being made into cocks, similar row of peats, corn-sheaves, etc.; *wind'-screen*, screen to keep off wind, esp. sheet of glass, etc., in front of motor-car driver, etc. (ill. MOTOR); ~*-shake*, flaw or crack in timber supposed to be caused by wind; ~*-shield*, (U.S.) windscreen; ~*-sleeve*, *-sock*, = wind-cone; ~*-swept*, swept by winds, exposed; ~*-tight*, constructed so as to keep out wind; ~ *tunnel*, enclosed chamber through which wind may be blown at known velocities, for testing (models of) aircraft etc.; *wind'ward*, (region) lying in direction from which wind blows, facing the wind. **wind'lèss** *adj.* **wind** *v.* 1. (wī-) Sound (horn or bugle) by blowing; blow (note, call, etc.) on horn etc. 2. (wĭ-) Detect presence of by scent. 3. (wĭ-) Deprive of breath, make out of breath.

wīnd² *v.* (past t. and past part. *wound*). Move, traverse, in curved or sinuous course; coil, wrap closely, around something or upon itself, encircle or enclose thus; haul or hoist by turning windlass, etc.; tighten (*up*) coiled spring of (clock etc.), or (fig.) tension, intensity, or efficiency of; ~ *up*, bring or come to conclusion, conclude; arrange and adjust affairs of (company, business concern) on its dissolution; *winding-up*, such dissolution; *winding-sheet*, shroud; drippings of candle-grease clinging to side of candle. **wīnd'er** *n.* Person, thing, that winds; winding step in staircase (ill. STAIR).

Wĭn'dermēre. Largest lake in England, in the Lake District; town situated above its E. shore.

Windhoek (vĭnt'hŏŏk). Capital of SW. Africa.

wĭnd'lass *n.* Mechanical contrivance for hauling or hoisting, consisting essentially of horizontal roller or beam on supports, with rope or chain wound round. ~ *v.t.* Hoist or haul with windlass.

WINDLASS

1. Pawl. 2. Ratchet

wĭn'dow (-ō) *n.* Opening, usu. filled with glass, in wall or roof of building, ship, carriage, etc., to admit light or air and afford view of what is outside or inside; window space or opening, esp. used for display of goods, advertisements, etc., in shop etc.; any opening resembling window in shape or function; ~*-box*, box placed outside window for cultivating (esp. ornamental) plants; ~*-dresser*, one who arranges display in shop window etc.; ~*-dressing*, art of arranging such display, (fig.) adroit presentation of facts etc. to give falsely favourable impression; ~*-envelope*, envelope with opening or transparent panel in front through which address is visible; ~*-seat*, seat below window, usu. in recess or bay; ~*-sill*, SILL. (*Illustration, p. 946.*)

Wĭnd'sor (-nz*er*). Town in Berkshire on right bank of Thames,

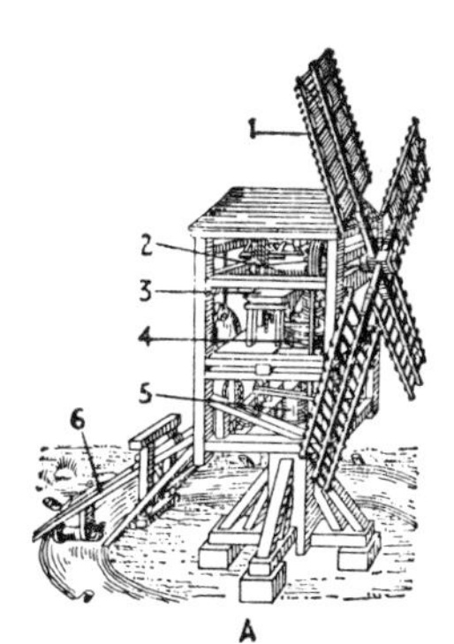

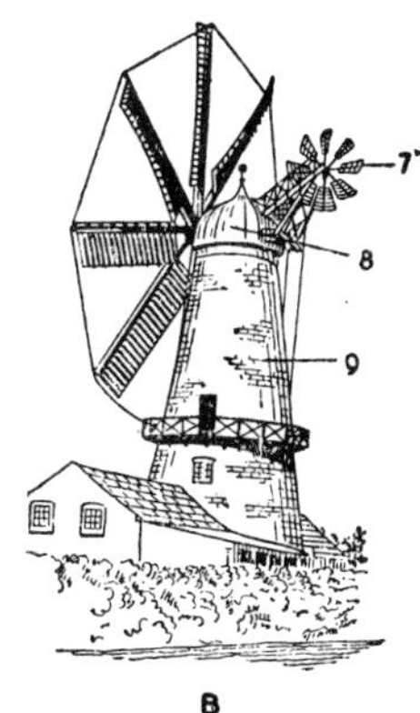

WINDMILLS. A. POST MILL FOR GRINDING CORN. B. TOWER MILL FOR RAISING WATER

1. Sails. 2. Shaft on which sails are mounted. 3. Hopper. 4. Millstones. 5. Post on which mill turns. 6. Tail-pole for turning mill into the wind. 7. Fan. 8. Movable cap. 9. Fixed tower

site of royal residence ~ *Castle*; *House of* ~, surname assumed by British Royal Family in 1917; *Knights of* ~, small body of military officers who have pensions and apartments in Windsor Castle; *Duke of* ~, title conferred on Edward VIII on his abdication in 1936; ~ *chair*, kind of wooden chair with back formed of upright rod-like pieces surmounted by freq. curved or hoop-shaped cross-piece (ill. CHAIR); ~ (*soap*), kind of usu. brown or white scented toilet soap.

WINDOWS: A. LANCET, EARLY 13TH C. (INTERIOR). B. PLATE TRACERY, EARLY 13TH C. C. GEOMETRIC BAR TRACERY, LATE 13TH C. D. DECORATED CURVILINEAR TRACERY WITH OGEE ARCH, 14TH C. E. PERPENDICULAR TRACERY, 15TH C. F. ROSE-WINDOW, 14TH C. G. ORIEL WINDOW, 15TH C. H. BAY-WINDOW, 15TH C. I. MULLION WINDOW, 16TH C. J. DORMER WINDOW. K. VENETIAN OR PALLADIAN WINDOW, 18TH C. L. SASH-WINDOW, 18TH C. M. SASH-WINDOW, 18TH C. (INTERIOR). N. FRENCH WINDOW, EARLY 19TH C.

1. Embrasure or splay. 2. Rear-arch. 3. Rear-vault. 4. Hood-mould, label, or dripstone. 5. Quatrefoil. 6. Iron stanchion. 7. Cusp. 8. Foil. 9. Mullion. 10. Transom. 11. Light. 12. Casement window with leaded quarries. 13. Lintel. 14. Architrave. 15. Glazing bar. 16. Pane. 17. Sill. 18. Pelmet. 19. Curtain. 20. Window-seat. 21. Shutter in reveal. 22. Balcony

Wĭnd'ward Islands. Group of islands, consisting of Grenada, St. Vincent, the Grenadines, St. Lucia, and Dominica and forming part of the British W. Indian possessions.

wĭnd'y *adj.* Wind-swept; exposed to, blown upon or through, by wind; in which wind is frequent or prevalent, accompanied by (much) wind; generating, characterized by, flatulence; wordy, verbose, empty; (slang) frightened. **wĭnd'ĭly** *adv.* **wĭnd'inėss** *n.*

wīne *n.* 1. Fermented grape-juice for drinking; kinds of this, varying in colour from *red* (usu. a purplish crimson) to *white* (pale gold); *dessert* ~, wine for drinking with dessert or after meal; *fortified* ~, wine to which spirit has been added during manufacture; *table* ~, wine for drinking at meal. 2. Various fermented drinks more or less resembling wine, made from juice of other fruits or flowers or root vegetables. 3. (pharmacy, obs.) Solution of specified medicinal substance in wine. 4. Colour of red wine. 5. *spirit(s) of* ~, (archaic) alcohol; *~-apple*, large red apple with winy flavour; *~-bibber*, tippler, drunkard; *~-biscuit*, light usu. sweet biscuit served with wine; biscuit flavoured with wine; *~-cellar*, cellar used for storing wine; contents of this; *~-cooler*, vessel in which bottles of wine are cooled with ice; *~-glass*, small drinking-glass, usu. with stem and foot, for wine; (as measure) usu. = sherry-glass, about 4 tablespoons; *~-press*, press in which grape-juice is extracted for making wine; *~ red*: see 4 above; *~-sap*, large red Amer. winter apple; *~-skin*, skin of goat etc. sewn together to make primitive wine-vessel; *~-sour*, small acid variety of plum; *~-stone*, deposit of crude tartar in wine-casks; *~-vault*, cellar for storing wine; bar, shop, etc., where wine is retailed. **wīn'y** *adj.* **wīne** *v.* Drink wine; entertain to wine.

wĭng *n.* 1. Organ of flight of any flying animal, in birds a specially modified fore-limb, in bats, extension of skin attached to modified parts of fore-limb, in insects membranous expansions attached to thorax in addition to limbs. 2. Power or means of flight, flying. 3. Anything resembling wing in form or function, esp. one of the main supporting surfaces (planes) of aircraft. 4. Lateral part or appendage, esp. curved side-piece over wheel of motor-car etc. as protection against mud. 5. Either of two divisions on each side of main body of army or fleet in battle. 6. (football, hockey, etc.) (Player occupying) position of forwards on either side of centre. 7. Section of political party etc. holding views deviating from centre: see RIGHT ~, LEFT ~. 8. Subordinate part of building on one side of main or central part. 9. Each of side-scenes on stage, (usu. pl.) space at side of stage where these stand (ill. THEATRE). 10. (anat., bot.) Lateral part or projection of some organ or structure, as lateral cartilage of nose, thin membranous appendage of seed or fruit serving for its dispersal by wind, etc. 11. Division of military air-force, in R.A.F. usu. comprising three squadrons, in U.S., three groups. 12. (pl.) Representation of pair of bird's wings worn as badge by those who have passed flying tests. 13. *~-case*, horny covering of functional wings in certain insects; *~-chair*, chair with side-pieces projecting forwards at top of high back, for protection from draughts (ill. CHAIR); *~-collar*, man's stiff collar with upper corners turned down; *W~ Commander*, officer of R.A.F. of rank between Group Captain and Squadron Leader; *~-covert*, each of small feathers overlying flight-feathers of bird's wing; *~-flap*, FLAP of aeroplane; *~-flutter*, vibration of wings of aircraft; *~-load(ing)*, total weight of loaded aircraft divided by area of supporting surfaces; *~-nut*, nut with projections for thumb and fingers to turn it by (ill. SCREW); *~-rib*, end rib of loin of beef; *~-span*, *-spread*, extreme measurement between tips of wings of bird or aircraft; *~-tip*, outer end or tip of wing of bird, aircraft, etc. ~ *v.* Equip with wings; enable to fly or mount; send in flight, lend speed to; travel, traverse, on wings; wound (esp. game bird) in the wing.

wĭnged (-ngd, -ng'ĭd) *adj.* Having wings; swift, rapid, 'flying', (of speech) conveying its message swiftly and effectively; ~ *elm*, small N. Amer. elm (*Ulmus alata*) with corky winged branches; *W~ Horse*, Pegasus; ~ *pea*, S. European annual herb (*Lotus Tetragonolobus*) with 4-winged pods; *W~ Victory*, statue of (Greek) goddess of victory with wings, esp. Nike of Samothrace, preserved in Louvre.

wĭng'less *adj.* Having no wings; (of birds) having rudimentary wings not used for flight.

wĭnk *v.* Blink; close one eye momentarily in flippant or frivolous manner; close (an eye, eyes) for a moment; move swiftly, (cause to) flicker like an eyelid, twinkle; give (signal, message, etc.) by flashing lights; ~ *at*, shut one's eyes to, connive at; *like wink'ing*, in a flash, in a twinkling. ~ *n.* Act of winking, esp. as signal; *not a ~ of sleep*, no sleep at all; *forty winks*, short sleep, nap; *tip, give the* ~, give signal or intimation.

wĭnk'le *n.* Periwinkle, edible sea snail. ~ *v.t.* ~ *out*, extract or eject (as a winkle from its shell with a pin).

Wĭnn'ĭpĕg. Capital city of Manitoba, Canada; *Lake* ~, lake in Manitoba.

wĭnn'ow (-ō) *v.t.* Fan (grain) free of chaff etc., fan (chaff) *away, out, from*; sift, separate, clear of worthless or inferior element, extract, select (*out*) thus.

wĭn'some *adj.* Attractive, charming, winning, pleasing. **wĭn'somely** *adv.* **wĭn'somenėss** *n.*

wĭn'ter *n.* 1. Coldest season of year, popularly reckoned in N. hemisphere as comprising December, January, and February, but astronomically as lasting from winter solstice (21st or 22nd Dec.) to vernal equinox (20th or 21st Mar.); (opp. SUMMER) colder half of year. 2. *attrib.* or *adj.* Of, characteristic of, winter; occurring, used, etc., in, lasting for, winter; (of fruit) ripening late or keeping well until or during winter; ~ *aconite*, small perennial herb (*Eranthis hyemalis*) producing bright-yellow starry flowers in winter; *~-fallow*, (land) lying fallow during winter; ~ *garden*, conservatory in which plants are kept flourishing in winter; *win'tergreen*, various creeping or low shrubby plants with leaves remaining green in winter, esp. N. Amer. *Gaultheria procumbens*, with drooping white flowers, edible scarlet berries, and aromatic leaves yielding oil used in medicine and for flavouring; *W~ Palace*, former royal residence on River Neva in Leningrad (St. Petersburg), later used as museum and art gallery; ~ *quarters*, quarters used in winter, esp. by troops between campaigns or by members of expedition; ~ *solstice*, time at which sun reaches winter tropic (in N. hemisphere tropic of Capricorn, in S. hemisphere tropic of Cancer); ~ *sports*, open-air sports, as skiing, skating, practised in Switzerland etc. in winter; ~ *wheat* (*oats* etc.), wheat (oats etc.) sown in autumn and remaining in ground all winter. ~ *v.* Spend winter (*at, in*); keep, feed, during winter.

Winton. *abbrev.* (Bishop) of Winchester, replacing surname in his signature.

wĭn'try *adj.* Characteristic of winter, having the temperature, storminess, etc., appropriate to winter, cold, windy, cheerless; (of smile, greeting, etc.) devoid of warmth, dreary, chilly. **wĭn'trĭnėss** *n.*

wīpe *v.* Clean or dry surface of by rubbing with cloth etc.; clear away (moisture, dust, etc.) thus; apply soft or liquid substance over surface by rubbing it on, esp., (plumbing) apply solder to (joint) thus; ~ *out*, destroy, annihilate, exterminate; ~ *the floor with*, (slang) humiliate (person) by defeat or correction. ~ *n.* Act of wiping; (slang) handkerchief.

wīre *n.* (Piece of) metal drawn into slender flexible rod or thread;

length or line of this used for various purposes, esp. for fencing, as conductor of electric current, etc.; wire-netting, framework of wire; snare for rabbits etc.; (pl.) lines by which puppets are worked (chiefly fig., in *pull (the) ~s*); (colloq.) telegram; *~ cloth*, fabric woven from wire; *~-cutter*, tool for cutting wire; *wire'draw* (*v.*) draw out into wire; elongate, attenuate; *~-drawn* (*adj.*) fine-spun, elaborately subtle or refined; *~-edge*, turned-over strip of metal sometimes produced on edge of tool etc. by faulty sharpening; *~ entanglement*, entanglement of barbed wire stretched over ground to impede enemy's advance; *~ gauge*, gauge for measuring diameter of wire etc.; standard series of sizes to which wire etc. is made; *~-gauze*, gauze-like fabric of wire; *~-haired*, (of dogs, esp. terriers) having rough hard wiry coat; *~-mark*, faint line in paper made by wires of mould; *~ nail*, nail of circular section, pointed but not tapering; *~-netting*, netting made of wire; *~-puller*, politician etc. who privately influences others by 'pulling the wires'; *~-walker*, acrobat performing feats on wire rope; *wire'-worm*, slender yellow larva of any click beetle destructive to plants; (also) millepede which destroys plant roots; *~-wove paper*, fine smooth paper made in wire-gauze frame, used esp. for letter-writing. ~ *v.* Furnish, support, stiffen, secure, with wires; snare with wire; (colloq.) telegraph.

wīre'lĕss (-īrl-) *adj.* Without wire(s), esp. (of telegraphy, telephony) with no connecting wire between transmitting and receiving stations, signals or intelligence being carried through space by electromagnetic waves; = RADIO; *~ set*, radio receiver. ~ *n.* RADIO receiver or transmitter; RADIOTELEPHONY; RADIOTELEGRAPHY. ~ *v.* Send (message etc.), inform (person) by radiotelegraphy or radiotelephony.

wīr'y *adj.* Made of wire; tough and flexible like wire; (of persons) tough, sinewy, untiring. **wīr'ĭly** *adv.* **wīr'ĭnĕss** *n.*

Wisc. *abbrev.* Wisconsin.

Wiscŏn'sin. East North Central State of U.S., admitted to Union 1848; capital, Madison.

Wisd. *abbrev.* Wisdom (of Solomon; Apocr.).

wis'dom (-z-) *n.* Being wise; soundness of judgement in matters relating to life and conduct; knowledge, enlightenment, learning; *W~ (of Solomon)*, *Book of ~*, a book of the Apocrypha; *~ of Jesus the son of Sirach*, the Apocryphal book *Ecclesiasticus*; *W~ literature*, the biblical books of Job, Proverbs, Ecclesiastes, Wisdom of Solomon, Ecclesiasticus, and Epistle of James; *~ tooth*, hindmost molar tooth on each side of upper and lower jaws in humans, usu. appearing about age of twenty (ill. TOOTH).

wīse[1] (-z) *n.* 1. (archaic) Way, manner, guise. 2. As *suffix* forming advs. from ns. or adjs., with the meaning 'in such-and-such a manner, way, or respect'.

wīse[2] (-z) *adj.* Having, exercising, proceeding from, indicating, sound judgement resulting from experience and knowledge; sagacious, prudent, sensible, discreet; having knowledge (*of*); (archaic) skilled in magic or occult arts; *be, get, ~ to*, (U.S. colloq.) be, become, aware of; *put ~ (to)*, inform (of); *wise'crack*, smart remark, witticism; (*v.i.*) make wisecracks; *~ man*, man of good judgement or discernment; (archaic) one skilled in magic, wizard, esp. one of the 3 MAGI who came from the East to worship the infant Jesus; *~ woman*, witch, female soothsayer, esp. harmless or beneficent one. **wīse'ly** (-zl-) *adv.*

wīse'acre (-zāk*er*) *n.* Sententious dullard. [MDu. *wijsseggher* soothsayer]

wish *n.* (Expression of) desire or aspiration; request; (pl.) expression of desire for another's welfare, success, etc.; *~-bone*, forked bone between neck and breast of cooked bird, merrythought (because when two persons have pulled it apart the holder of the larger piece is entitled to the magical fulfilment of a wish); *~-fulfilment*, (psychoanal.) alleged tendency of wishes, esp. when unconscious, to seek gratification in reality or fantasy. ~ *v.* Have, feel, express, a wish for; express desire or aspiration *for*; want (*to* do, person *to* do); request; (esp. in expressions of goodwill, greeting, etc.) desire (something, esp. something good) for a person etc.; *wish'ing-cap, -gate, -well*, etc., cap, well, etc., supposed to assure fulfilment of wishes.

wĭsh'ful *adj.* Wishing, desirous; *~ thinking*, believing a thing to be so because it is desired or desirable. **wĭsh'fully** *adv.* **wĭsh'fulnĕss** *n.*

wĭsh'y-wash'y (-wŏ-) *adj.* Thin, sloppy; feeble or poor in quality or character.

wisp *n.* Small bundle or twist of straw, hay, etc.; thin, narrow, filmy, or slight piece or scrap (*of*). **wĭsp'y** *adj.*

wistār'ia, -ēr'ia *n.* Plant of leguminous genus *Wistaria* of N. Amer., Japanese and Chinese hardy climbing deciduous shrubs with pendulous racemes of blue-lilac, purple, or white papilionaceous flowers. [Caspar *Wistar* or *Wister*, Amer. anatomist (1761–1818)]

wĭst'ful *adj.* Yearningly or mournfully expectant, eager, or watchful. **wĭst'fully** *adv.* **wĭst'fulnĕss** *n.*

wĭt[1] *n.* 1. (sing. or pl.) Intelligence, understanding; *five ~s*, the five senses; *have one's ~s about one*, be mentally alert; *out of one's ~s*, mad, distracted; *at one's ~'s end*, utterly perplexed; *live by one's ~s*, subsist by ingenious hand-to-mouth shifts. 2. Unexpected combining or contrasting of previously unconnected ideas or expressions; power of causing surprise and delight by this; capacity for making brilliant observations in an amusing way. 3. Person with this capacity; (archaic) person of great mental ability, man of talent. **wĭt'lĕss** *adj.* (literary and archaic) Foolish, unintelligent; lacking wit.

wĭt[2] *v.* (archaic) Know; *to ~*, that is to say, namely. **wĭtt'ĭng** *adj.* Not unconscious or unintentional. **wĭtt'ĭngly** *adv.*

wĭtch[1] *n.* Sorceress, woman supposed to have dealings with devil or evil spirits; (fig.) fascinating or bewitching woman; *old ~*, malevolent or ugly old woman, hag; *white ~*, sorceress whose purposes are beneficent; *~ ball*, coloured glass ball of kind formerly hung up to keep away witches; *witch'craft*, sorcery, use of magic; *~-doctor*, MEDICINE-man; *witches' Sabbath*, midnight meeting of demons, sorcerers, and witches, presided over by the Devil, supposed in medieval times to have been held annually as orgy or festival. ~ *v.t.* Bewitch; (fig.) fascinate, charm; *witching time (of night)*, (after 'Hamlet', III. ii. 406) time when witches are active, midnight. **wĭtch'ery** *n.*

wĭtch[2] *n.* Flat-fish (*Glyptocephalus cynoglossus*) resembling lemon sole, used for food. [prob. f. WITCH[1], from its uncanny appearance]

wĭtch[3], **wȳch** *ns.* In names of various trees with pliant branches; *~-alder*, shrub of genus *Fothergilla*, with alder-like leaves; *~-elm*, species of elm (*Ulmus glabra*) with broader leaves and more spreading branches than common elm; *~-hazel*, N. Amer. shrub (*Hamamelis virginica*) with hazel-like leaves and yellow flowers; astringent extract of bark of this used as remedy for bruises, sprains, etc., and in cosmetics.

wĭt'ĕnagĕmōt' (-g-) *n.* (hist.) National assembly of the Anglo-Saxons. [OE, = 'assembly of wise men' (*wita* wise man, *gemot* meeting, moot)]

with (-dh, -th) *prep.* 1. (Of conflict, rivalry, etc.) against, in opposition to. 2. In or into company of or relation to, among, beside. 3. Agreeably or in harmonious relations to. 4. Having, carrying, possessed of, characterized by. 5. In the care, charge, or possession of. 6. By use of as instrument or means, by addition or supply of, by operation of, owing to. 7. In same way, direction, degree, at same time, as. 8. In regard to, concerning, in the mind or view of. 9. So as to be separated from. 10. Despite, notwithstanding, the presence of.

withal′ (-dhawl) *adv.* & *prep.* (archaic) With (it); in addition, moreover, as well, at the same time.

withdraw′ (*or* widh-) *v.* 1. Pull aside or back; take away, remove; retract. 2. Retire from presence or place, go aside or apart. **withdraw′al** *n.*

with′e (-dhĭ *or* widh), **with′y** (-dhĭ) *ns.* (pl. *-thes* pr. -dhĭz, or *-ths*). Tough flexible twig or branch esp. of willow or osier used for binding bundles, making baskets, etc.

with′er (-dh-) *v.* Make, become, dry or shrivelled (*up*); deprive of or lose vigour, vitality, freshness, importance; decline, languish, decay; blight, paralyse (*with* look of scorn etc.). **with′ering** *adj.* **with′eringly** *adv.*

with′ers (-dherz) *n.pl.* Ridge between shoulder-blades of horse and some other animals (ill. HORSE); *my ~ are unwrung*, imputation does not touch me. [named as part that takes strain of collar, f. OE *wither* against]

withershins: see WIDDERSHINS.

withhōld′ (-dh-h-, -th-h-) *v.t.* Hold back, restrain; refuse to give, grant, or allow.

within′ (-dh-) *adv.* Inside, internally, inwardly; indoors; (theatr.) behind the scenes. ~ *prep.* To, on, in, the inside of; enclosed by; in the limits of; not beyond, above, outside, or farther than the extent of; in the scope or sphere of action of.

without′ (-dh-) *adv.* (literary or archaic) Outside, externally. ~ *prep.* 1. (archaic) Outside of. 2. Not having, not with; devoid of; lacking; free from. ~ *conj.* (now archaic or illiterate) Unless.

withstănd′ (-dh-, -th-) *v.t.* Resist, oppose.

with′y: see WITHE.

wit′nėss *n.* 1. Testimony, evidence; confirmation. 2. Person giving sworn testimony in law-court or for legal purpose; person attesting execution of document by adding his signature; thing or person whose existence, position, etc., is testimony *to* or proof *of*; person present as spectator or auditor; *hostile ~*, witness in court etc. giving evidence adverse to party by whom he is called; *~-box*, enclosed space from which witness gives evidence; *~-stand*, (U.S.) stand from which witness gives evidence. ~ *v.* State in evidence (archaic); give evidence, serve as evidence; indicate, serve as evidence of; see, be spectator of; sign (document) as witness.

Witt′elsbach (v-, -ăχ). Line of Bavarian princes to which belonged, from 1806 to 1918, the kings of Bavaria.

Witt′enběrg (v-). German university town on the Elbe, famous as the place where Luther taught.

witt′icism *n.* Witty saying, piece of wit; esp. joke at another's expense, jeer, witty sarcasm. [coined by Dryden from WITTY, after *criticism*]

witt′ingly *adv.*: see WIT[2] *v.*

witt′y *adj.* Capable of, given to, saying or writing brilliantly or sparklingly amusing things; full of wit.

wiz′ard *n.* Magician, sorcerer, male witch; person who effects seeming impossibilities. ~ *adj.* (colloq.) Marvellous, wonderful. **wiz′ardry** *n.*

wiz′en(ed) (-zn, -znd) *adjs.* Of shrivelled or dried-up appearance.

W/L *abbrev.* Wave-length.

W.L.A. *abbrev.* Women's Land Army.

W. long. *abbrev.* West longitude.

Wm *abbrev.* William.

WNW., WNW *abbrevs.* West-north-west.

wō *int.* Stop.

W.O. *abbrev.* War Office; Warrant Officer.

woad *n.* European biennial plant, *Isatis tinctoria*; blue, black, or green dye-stuff obtained from this, used before the introduction of indigo and afterwards in conjunction with it.

wŏbb′le *v.i.* Move unsteadily or with uncertain direction from side to side or backwards and forwards; shake, rock, quiver; (fig.) vacillate, hesitate, waver. ~ *n.* Wobbling motion. **wŏbb′ly** *adj.*

Wōd′an: see ODIN.

woe (wō) *n.* (chiefly poet. or joc.) Affliction, bitter grief, distress; (pl.) calamities, troubles; *~ is me!* alas!; *~ be to, betide*, a curse upon; *~ betide you if*, you will be in trouble if; *woe′begone* (-ŏn), dismal-looking. **woe′ful** *adj.* **woe′fully** *adv.*

wōld *n.* Elevated tract of open uncultivated country or moorland; rolling uplands.

wolf[1] (wo͝o-) *n.* (pl. *-ves*). 1. Various largish mammals of dog tribe (*Canis*) of Europe, Asia, and N. America, with harsh grey or brownish-grey fur, erect pointed ears, and bushy tail, noted for fierceness and rapacity; rapacious or greedy person; *cry ~*, raise false alarm; *keep ~ from the door*, ward off hunger or starvation; *~ in sheep's clothing*, person concealing malicious intentions under guise of friendliness etc. 2. (mus.) Harsh howling sound of certain chords on keyed instruments, esp. organ, tuned by unequal temperament. 3. *~-cub*, young wolf; member of junior division of Boy Scouts (from 8 to 11 years old); *~-dog, -hound*, various large varieties of dog kept for hunting wolves, esp. Irish greyhound and Russian borzoi; cross between domestic dog and wolf, esp. *Alsatian ~-dog, ~-hound*, cross of German sheep-dog with strain of wolf; *~'s-bane*, aconite, esp. European *Aconitum vulparia*, with dull-yellow flowers. **wolf′ish** *adj.* **wolf′ishly** *adv.* **wolf′ishnėss** *n.* **wolf** *v.t.* Devour ravenously.

Wolf[2] (vŏlf), Hugo (1860–1903). Austrian composer, esp. of songs.

Wolfe (wo͝olf), James (1727–59). English general; commanded the British forces at the siege of Quebec, in which he was killed.

Wolff[1] (vŏlf), Christian (1679–1754). German rationalist philosopher.

Wolff[2] (vŏlf), Kaspar Friedrich (1733–94). German embryologist; *Wolffian body*, one of two renal organs of vertebrate embryos, becoming the kidneys in fishes and amphibians.

wol′fram (wo͝o-) *n.* Ore (*ferrous tungstate*, $FeWO_4$) yielding tungsten; (rare) tungsten.

Wol′fram von Esch′enbach (vŏl-, ĕshenbăχ) (early 13th c.). German epic poet, whose chief work was 'Parzival'.

Woll′aston (wo͝o-), William Hyde (1766–1822). English chemist, discoverer of palladium and rhodium.

Wolsey (wo͝ol′zĭ), Thomas (*c* 1475–1530). Archbishop of York, cardinal and statesman; chancellor under Henry VIII 1515–29.

wolverene, -ine (wo͝ol′verēn) *n.* The glutton, *Gulo luscus*, a carnivorous mammal of N. America with blackish shaggy fur; the related *G. gulo* of N. Europe and Asia; *W~*, (nickname for) inhabitant of the *W~ State*, Michigan.

wo′man (wo͝o-) *n.* (pl. *women* pr. wĭm′ĭn). Adult human female; female servant or attendant; (without article) the average or typical woman, the female sex; (attrib.) female, as *~ doctor, ~ friend*; *womankind, womenfolk*, women in general (one's *womenkind, womenfolk*, the women of one's family); *women's rights*, rights claimed for women of equal privileges and opportunities with men; *Women's Voluntary Service(s)*, organization formed in 1938 to give help with A.R.P. (later Civil Defence). ~ *v.* Cause to behave like a woman, cause to weep etc. (rare); address as 'woman' (not 'lady'). **wo′manhood** *n.* Being a (grown) woman; womankind; character or qualities natural to a woman.

wo′manish (wo͝o-) *adj.* (usu. contempt., of man, his feelings, etc.) Like women or their ways, effeminate. **wo′manishly** *adv.* **wo′manishnėss** *n.*

wo′manize (wo͝o-) *v.* Make womanish; (of men) consort illicitly with women.

wo′manly (wo͝o-) *adj.* Having, showing, the qualities befitting a (grown) woman; not masculine or girlish. **wo′manlinėss** *n.*

womb (wo͞om) *n.* Organ in female mammal in which child or young is conceived and nourished till birth, uterus (ill. PELVIS); (fig.) place where anything is generated or produced.

wŏm'băt *n.* Burrowing herbivorous marsupial of genus *Phascolomys*, native to S. Australia and Tasmania, with thick heavy body, short legs, rudimentary tail, and general resemblance to small bear.

WOMBAT

wo'nder (wŭ-) *n.* 1. Marvel, miracle, prodigy; astonishing thing, deed, event, occurrence, etc.; *Seven W~s of the World*, 7 monuments regarded as most remarkable structures of ancient times: see SEVEN; *for a ~*, as instance of surprising or exceptional fact or happening; *no ~*, (it is) not surprising. 2. Emotion excited by something novel and unexpected, or inexplicable; astonishment mixed with perplexity, bewildered curiosity, or admiration. 3. *wonderland*, imaginary realm of wonders, fairyland; *W~ State*, popular name of Arkansas, so called because of its remarkable natural resources; *~-worker*, one who performs wonders or miracles. ~ *v.* 1. Be affected with wonder, marvel; *I shouldn't ~*, (colloq.) I should not be surprised. 2. Feel some doubt or curiosity, be desirous to know or learn.

wo'nderful (wŭ-) *adj.* Marvellous, surprising; surprisingly large, fine, excellent, etc. **wo'nderfully** *adv.* **wo'nderfulness** *n.*

wo'ndrous (wŭ-) *adj.* & *adv.* poet., rhet.) Wonderful(ly). **wo'ndrously** *adv.*

wŏnk'y *adj.* (slang) Shaky, trembling, unsound.

wōnt *predic. adj.* (usu. with verb 'to be') Accustomed, used (*to* do). ~ *v.i.* (archaic) Be accustomed (*to*); *wonted*, accustomed, usual, habitual; (archaic or U.S.) used, wont; (U.S.) made familiar with environment. ~ *n.* Habitual or customary usage.

wōn't: see WILL².

wōō *v.* Pay court (to), ask or seek the love of, make love (to); pursue, seek to win; coax, court, invite, tempt. **wōō'er** *n.*

wŏŏd¹ *n.* 1. Collection of trees growing more or less thickly together, of considerable extent; piece of ground covered with trees; (now rare) wooded country, woodland; *out of the wood(s)*, clear of a difficulty, danger, etc. 2. Hard compact fibrous substance making up trunks and branches of trees and shrubs between bark and pith, whether growing or cut down ready for use in arts and crafts, for fuel, etc.; a particular kind of wood; (gardening) branch-wood. 3. Something made of wood, esp. *the* cask in which wine etc. is stored, each bowl in the game of bowls, (mus.) wooden wind-instruments, wood-wind. 4. ~ *alcohol*, kind of spirit, methyl alcohol, obtained by dry distillation of wood; ~ *anemone*, various common wild anemones, abundant in woods and flowering in early spring; *wood'bine*, *wood'bind*, various climbing plants, now esp. common wild fragrant yellow-flowered honeysuckle (*Lonicera periclymenum*), (U.S.) Virginia creeper; *~-block*, block of wood, e.g. for paving or esp. with design for printing from; *wood'cock*, common European migratory bird, *Scolopax rusticola*, allied to snipe, with long bill, large eyes, and mottled plumage, esteemed as food; similar but smaller N. Amer. *Philohela minor*; *woodcraft*, knowledge of and skill in forest conditions applied to hunting, maintaining oneself, making one's way, etc.; *wood'cut*, print obtained from design cut in relief on block of wood (usu. sawn along the grain); this art; *wood'cutter*, one who fells or lops trees for timber or fuel; ~ *engraving*, print obtained from design engraved on block of wood (usu. sawn across grain); this art; *wood'land*, wooded country, woods; (attrib.) of, in, growing or dwelling in, consisting of, etc., woodland; *wood'lark*, small European species of lark (*Lulullа arborea*) which perches on trees, with shorter tail and more variegated plumage than skylark and different song; *~-louse*, small terrestrial isopod crustacean of *Oniscus* or related genera, esp. *O. asellus*, found in old wood, under stones, etc.; *wood'man*, forester, wood-cutter; *~-nymph*, nymph of the woods, dryad; *wood'pecker*, any bird of numerous genera and species of family *Picidae*, found in most parts of world, with plumage usu. bright-coloured and variegated, characterized by habit of pecking holes in trunks and branches of trees to find insect food or make cavities for laying eggs; *~-pigeon*, ring-dove, *Columba palumbus*; *~-pulp*, pulp made by mechanical or chemical disintegration of wood-fibre, used for making paper etc.; *wood'ruff*, low-growing European woodland herb (*Asperula odorata*) with clusters of small white flowers and whorls of strongly sweet-scented leaves; *wood'sman*, (chiefly U.S.) man living in or frequenting woods, one skilled in woodcraft; *~-sorrel*, low-growing spring-flowering woodland plant (*Oxalis acetosella*) with delicate trifoliate leaves and small white flowers streaked with purple; various other species of *Oxalis*; *~-tar*, tar obtained in dry distillation of wood; *~-wind*, wooden wind instruments of orchestra; *wood'work*, work done in wood, as carpentry; work in wood, wooden part *of* anything, esp. wooden interior parts of building. **wŏŏd'ėd** *adj.* Covered with growing trees; abounding in woods.

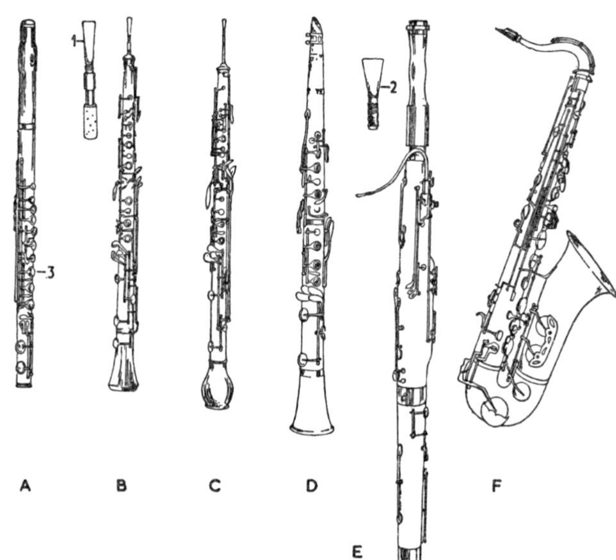

WOOD-WIND INSTRUMENTS. A. FLUTE. B. OBOE. C. COR ANGLAIS. D. CLARINET. E. BASSOON. F. SAXOPHONE

1. Double-reed mouth-piece of oboe. 2. Double-reed mouth-piece of bassoon. 3. Key

Wŏŏd², Sir Henry Joseph (1869–1944). English musical composer and conductor of promenade concerts at Queen's Hall, London.

Wŏŏd'bŭry, Walter Bentley (1834–85). English photographer and inventor; *~-type*, process in which a design on a film of gelatine, obtained from a photographic negative, is transferred by heavy pressure to a metal plate from which it may be printed; print thus produced.

wŏŏd'chŭck *n.* Thick-bodied reddish-brown marmot (*Marmota monax*) of north-eastern U.S. and Canada. [f. Amer. Ind. name, cf. Cree *wuchak, otchock*]

wŏŏd'en *adj.* Made, consisting, of wood; resembling wood, dull or dead like sound of wood when struck, dull and inert, stiff and lifeless, inexpressive; *~ head*, blockhead; *~-headed*; *~ horse*, Trojan horse, wooden figure of horse, in which Greek invaders were hidden, introduced into besieged Troy by stratagem; *~ spoon*, (esp.) spoon made of wood traditionally presented at Cambridge to candidate placed lowest in Mathematical Tripos; (person taking) this position; *~ walls*, ships, shipping, as defensive force. **wŏŏd'enly** *adv.* **wŏŏd'ennĕss** *n.*

wŏŏd'y *adj.* Covered with trees, abounding in woods, well-wooded; of the nature of, consisting of, wood; resembling (that of) wood; (of plant) forming wood, having woody stems and branches; *~ nightshade*, plant of nightshade kind (*Solanum dulcamara*), with purple flowers and bright-red berries, bittersweet.

wŏŏf *n.* (archaic and poet.) Weft.

wŏŏl *n.* Fine soft curly hair forming fleecy coat of domesticated sheep and similar animals, characterized by imbricated surface of the filaments, to which is due its property of felting, and used chiefly in prepared state for making cloth; twisted woollen yarn used for knitting etc.; woollen garment or cloth; short soft under-hair or down of some animals; something resembling wool, esp. downy substance found on some plants, Negro's short crisp curly hair; any fine fibrous substance naturally or artificially produced; *dyed in the ~*, dyed before spinning; (fig.) thoroughgoing, out-and-out; *pull the ~ over one's eyes*, hoodwink, deceive; *~-gathering*, gathering fragments of wool torn from sheep by bushes etc.; absent-minded(ness), indulging or indulgence in idle imagining; *~-pack*, (bag holding) large quantity of wool or fleeces; rounded cumulus cloud with horizontal base; *wool'-sack*, large package or bale of wool; large wool-stuffed cushion forming usual seat of Lord Chancellor in House of Lords (said to have been adopted in Edward III's reign as reminder to lords of importance of wool trade; ill. PARLIAMENT); hence, lord chancellorship; *~-staple*, market appointed for sale of wool; *wool'work*, wool embroidery, esp. on canvas. *~ adj.* (commerc.) Made of wool throughout (cf. WOOLLEN).

wŏŏll'en, (U.S.) **wŏŏl'en** *adj.* & *n.* (Fabric, esp. coarse or loosely woven) made of wool or (commerc.) made of yarns which contain wool fibres.

wŏŏll'y *adj.* Bearing, naturally covered with, wool or wool-like hair; resembling or suggesting wool in softness, texture, etc.; confused, blurred, hazy, 'fuzzy'; (of plants) pubescent, downy; *wild and ~*, resembling West of U.S. in frontier days, uncivilized, barbarous, lawless; *~ bear*, (colloq.) large hairy caterpillar, esp. larva of tiger-moth. *~ n.* Woollen, esp. knitted, garment.

Wŏŏ'lwich (-lĭj). Metropolitan borough of London, site of the Royal Arsenal, and formerly of the Royal Military Academy (see SANDHURST).

wŏp *n.* (slang, usu. contempt.) Italian or other S. European, esp. immigrant into U.S.

Worcester¹ (wŏŏs'ter). City and county town of WORCESTERSHIRE; *Battle of ~* (1651), in which Cromwell defeated the Scottish army with Charles II; *~ china* or *Royal ~*, porcelain made at Worcester in factory founded 1751; *~ sauce*, pungent condiment consisting of soy, vinegar, etc., first made at Worcester.

Worcester² (wŏŏs'ter). City of Massachusetts (U.S.).

Worcester College (wŏŏs'ter). College of the University of Oxford; orig. a 13th-c. Benedictine foundation called Gloucester College; refounded 1714 by a Worcestershire man, Sir Thomas Cookes.

Worcestershire (wŏŏs't-). W. midland county of England.

Worcs. *abbrev.* Worcestershire.

word (wẽrd) *n.* 1. Vocal sound or combination of sounds, or written or printed symbols of these, constituting minimal element of speech having a meaning as such and capable of independent grammatical use; *~ for ~*, verbatim, exact(ly); *last ~*, final utterance in conversation or esp. dispute; (pl.) last utterance before death; final or conclusive statement, *the* latest thing. 2. Thing(s) said, speech, utterance (usu. pl.); (pl.) text of song, actor's part, etc.; verbal expression contrasted with action or thought; (pl.) contentious or violent talk, altercation; (with negative etc.) anything at all (said or written); watchword, password; report, tidings, information; command, order; promise, undertaking; declaration, assurance; *the W~ (of God)*, the Bible or some part of it; *man of his ~*, one who keeps his promises. 3. *~-blind*, unable as result of brain injury or disease to understand written or printed words; so *~-deaf*, unable to understand speech though capable of hearing the sounds; *~-painting*, vivid descriptive writing; *~-perfect*, knowing perfectly every word of lesson, theatrical part, etc.; *~-square*, series of words so arranged as to read the same vertically and horizontally, puzzle of which solution is such a series. *~ v.t.* Put into words, phrase, select words to express. **word'ing** *n.* (esp.) Form of words used, phrasing. **word'lĕss** *adj.*

Wordsworth (wẽrdz'werth), William (1770–1850). English Romantic lyric poet, one of the 'Lake School' of poets; poet laureate from 1843.

word'y (wẽr-) *adj.* Verbose, using or containing (too) many words; in, consisting of, words. **word'ĭly** *adv.* **word'ĭnĕss** *n.*

work (wẽrk) *n.* 1. Action involving effort or exertion, esp. as means of gaining livelihood; labour done in making something, as dist. from materials used; (physics etc.) operation of a force in producing movement or other physical change, esp. as measurable quantity; something to do or to be done, employment, business, function; act, deed, proceeding, (pl.) doings; (theol., pl.) moral action considered in relation to justification; *the ~ of* . . ., a proceeding occupying (a stated time); *at ~*, engaged in work, working, operating; *in ~*, in regular occupation, gainfully employed; *out of ~*, without work to do, unemployed; *set to ~*, set (person), apply oneself, to a task, or to do something. 2. Product of labour, thing(s) made; result of action; (pl.) architectural or engineering operations; (mil.) fortified building, defensive structure, fortification; literary or musical composition, product of any fine art, as statue, picture, etc., (pl. or collect. sing.) person's writings, compositions, paintings, etc., as a whole; sewing, embroidery, knitting, etc., esp. as distinctively feminine employments. 3. (pl.) Establishment, building with machinery, etc., where industrial process, esp. manufacture, is carried on; (pl.) internal mechanism, moving parts, of piece of machinery, etc., esp. clock or watch. 4. *~-bag, -basket, -box*, bag etc. holding materials and implements for needlework; *work'day*, day on which work is ordinarily performed, weekday; *work'hardened*, (of some metals) rendered brittle or otherwise altered by repeated bending, hammering, etc.; *workhouse*, (term not now in official use) public institution for maintenance of paupers, in which able-bodied are set to work; *work'man*, man hired to do work or (usu.) manual labour, esp. skilled labour; craftsman; one who works in specified manner; *work'manlike*, characteristic of a good workman, efficient; *work'-manship*, skill as a workman, craftsmanship exhibited in piece of work; *work'people*, people employed in manual or industrial labour for wages; *works committee, council*, committee of workers in factory etc. or their representatives; *work'shop*, room or building in which manual or industrial work is carried on; *work'shy*, disinclined for work, lazy; *~-table*, table for holding working-implements; *work'woman*, female worker or operative, esp. one employed in needlework. **work'lėss** *adj.* & *n.*

work *v.* 1. Engage, be engaged, in bodily or mental work; carry on, operations; make efforts; be craftsman (*in* some material); (of machine, plan, etc.) operate, act, (of person) put or keep (machine etc.) in operation; keep (person, machine, etc.) at work or going, exact toil from; purchase (one's *passage* etc.) with labour instead of money. 2. Carry on, manage, control; have influence or effect, exercise influence on; bring about, effect, accomplish, produce as result. 3. Be in motion, be agitated; cause agitation; ferment. 4. (Cause to) make way, make (way etc.), slowly or with difficulty or by shifting motions; gradually become (tight, free, etc.) by motion. 5. Knead, hammer, fashion, into shape or desired consistency; artificially and gradually excite (one*self*, others) *into* (a rage etc.). 6. Do, make by, needlework or the like. 7. Solve (sum) by mathematical processes. 8. *~ off*, get rid of, free oneself from; finish working at; pass off, palm off; *~ out*, find (amount etc.), solve (sum) by calculation, (of amount etc.) be calculated (*at*); exhaust (mine etc.) by working; accomplish, attain, with difficulty; develop, elaborate, plan or provide for details of; discharge (debt, obligation), pay for, by labour instead of money; (of athlete, team, etc.) box, play, etc., for practice not in contest; *~-out*, practice game, bout, run, etc.; *~ up*, bring gradually to efficient state; elaborate in description; advance gradually *to* (climax); excite, incite, stir up, arouse (*to*); stir up, make up (materials), compose, produce, construct; study (subject) carefully and in detail.

work'able (wẽr-) *adj.* That can be worked, fashioned, manipulated, managed, conducted, etc. **work'ably** *adv.* **workabil'ity** *n.*

work'aday (wẽr-) *adj.* Of, characteristic of, workday or its occupations; of ordinary humdrum everyday life.

work er (wẽr-) *n.* (esp.) 1. One employed for a wage, esp. in manual or industrial work; one who works either with hand or brain, 'producer of wealth' as opp. to capitalist. 2. Neuter or undeveloped female of certain social hymenopterous and other insects, as ants and bees, which supplies food and performs other services for community (ill. BEE).

work'ing (wẽr-) *n.* (esp.) Way thing works, result of its working; action, operation; (chiefly pl.) place in which mineral is or has been extracted, excavation(s) made in quarrying, mining, tunnelling, etc.; *~ capital*, capital used in actual conduct of business, not invested in buildings, machinery, etc.; *~-day*, workday, number of hours of work entitling workman to day's pay, portion of day devoted to work; *~ drawing(s)*, scale drawing(s) from which workmen carry out construction; *~ order*, condition in which machine, system, etc., works (well, badly, etc.). *~ adj.* (esp.) Engaged in manual or industrial work; *~ class(es)*, grade(s) of society comprising those employed for wages, esp. in manual or industrial occupations; *~-class*, of, for, the working class; *~-man*, man of working class; *~ model*, model of machine etc. capable of doing work on small scale, or of being operated; *~ party*, (1) (mil.) party of men detailed for special work outside usual duties; (2) committee (orig. representing workers and management) appointed by government to report on the policies necessary to secure efficiency in any industry; any committee appointed to investigate and report on a question.

world (wẽr-) *n.* 1. Human existence, *this* present life; pursuits and interests, affairs and conditions of (this present) life; secular or lay life and interests; *the other, the next, a better, ~*, the future state, life after death; *~ without end*, endlessly, eternally. 2. Earth and all created things upon it; planet or other heavenly body, esp. one viewed as inhabited; material universe as ordered system, system of created things; everything, all phenomena; countries of the earth and their inhabitants, all people; human society; particular section of this, esp. high or fashionable society; sphere of interest, action, or thought; (freq. pl.) a great quantity, vast or infinite amount or extent; *the ~'s end*, farthest attainable limit; *not . . . for (all) the ~, for ~s*, not on any account; *for all the ~*, in every respect (like); *New W~*, part(s) of world discovered at comparatively late period, esp. the Americas, the Western Hemisphere, as dist. from the *Old W~*, the Eastern Hemisphere, esp. Europe and Asia; *~-history*, history embracing events of whole world; *~-language*, artificial language intended for universal use; *~ politics*, international politics, politics based upon considerations affecting whole world; *~-power*, any of powers (nations, empires) dominating world politics; *~ war*, war affecting (most of) the world; *1st W~ War*, that of 1914–18, *2nd*, 1939–45; *~-weary*, weary of (the life of) the world; *~-wide*, spread over the world, known or found everywhere, universal.

world'ling (wẽr-) *n.* Worldly person.

world'ly (wẽr-) *adj.* Temporal, earthly; exclusively or predominantly concerned with or devoted to affairs of this life, esp. to pursuit of wealth or pleasure; *~ goods*, property; *~-minded*, intent on worldly things; *~ wisdom*, esp. prudence in advancing one's own interests; *~-wise*, having worldly wisdom. **world'linėss** *n.*

worm (wẽrm) *n.* 1. Slender burrowing invertebrate animal esp. of genus *Lumbricus*, usu. brown or reddish with soft body divided into segments, earthworm (ill. EARTHworm); any annelid (*ringed* or *segmented ~*), nematode (*round-~*), or platyhelminth (*flatworm*); platyhelminth or nematode living as parasite in intestine of man or other animal, (pl.) disorder characterized by presence of these; larva of insect, maggot, grub, esp. one feeding on or destructive to fruit, leaves, timber, flesh, etc.; maggot supposed to eat dead bodies in the grave; long slender marine mollusc (*teredo ~*) destroying timber by boring. 2. Abject, miserable, or contemptible person. 3. (fig.) Grief or passion that preys stealthily on the heart or torments the conscience. 4. Natural or artificial object resembling earthworm; small worm-shaped ligament in dog's tongue; various spiral implements, esp. spiral of male or female screw, endless or tangent screw whose thread gears with teeth of toothed wheel etc. (ill. GEAR); long spiral or coiled tube connected to head of still, in which vapour is condensed. 5. *~-cast*, convoluted mass of mould voided by earthworm and left on surface of ground; *~-eaten*, eaten into by worm(s), full of worm-holes; decayed, decrepit, antiquated; *~-gear*, worm-wheel (and worm); *~-hole*, hole in wood, fruit, book, etc., made by burrowing insect larva; *~-wheel*, toothed wheel gearing with worm. **worm'y** *adj.* **worm** *v.* 1. Hunt for worms; rid (plants etc.) of worms or grubs; extract 'worm' from tongue of (dog) as supposed safeguard against madness. 2. Progress or move sinuously; make one's way insidiously, insinuate one*self*, *into* (person's confidence, secrets, etc.); *~ out*, extract (secret etc.) by insidious questioning.

worm'wŏŏd (wẽr-) *n.* European woody herb (*Artemisia absinthium*) with bitter aromatic taste, yielding dark-green oil, and formerly used as tonic and vermifuge, as protection against moths and fleas, etc., and now for making vermouth and absinthe; (fig.) bitter humiliation or its cause.

wǒrn *adj.* (past part. of WEAR *v.*) Impaired by use, exposure, or wear; enfeebled, exhausted, by toil, age, anxiety, etc.; *~-out*, no longer of use or service; utterly wasted in strength or vitality; stale, trite.

wo'rry (wŭ-) *n.* Harassing anxiety or solicitude; cause of this, matter for anxiety, (pl.) cares, troubles. ~ *v.* 1. Seize by throat with teeth and tear or lacerate, kill or injure by biting and shaking (of dog etc.); (fig.) harass, work at, get *along* or *through* with persistent aggression or dogged effort or struggle; vex or distress by inconsiderate or importunate behaviour, pester with repeated demands, requests, etc. 2. Make anxious and ill at ease; give way to anxiety or mental disquietude.

worse (wě̃rs) *adj.* & *adv.* Used as comparative of *bad, evil, ill, badly*; or as opposite of *better*. ~ *n.* Worse thing(s); worse condition. **wors'en** *v.* Make or become worse, deteriorate.

wor'shĭp (wě̃r-) *n.* 1. Reverence paid to being or power regarded as divine; acts, rites, or ceremonies displaying this; adoration or devotion comparable to this felt or shown to person or principle; *public ~*, church service. 2. *his, your, W~*, used to or of certain magistrates in court, and formerly to show respect to other persons. ~ *v.* Adore as divine, pay religious homage to; idolize, regard with adoration; attend public worship; be full of adoration. **wor'shipper** *n.*

wor'shĭpful (wě̃r-) *adj.* 1. Entitled to honour or respect (archaic); as honorific title, now restricted to justices of the peace, aldermen, recorders, London City companies, and freemasons' lodges and their masters; *right ~*, title applied to mayors and the sheriffs, aldermen, and recorder of London. 2. (archaic) Imbued with spirit of veneration; worthy of worship. **wor'shĭpfully** *adv.* **wor'shĭpfulnėss** *n.*

worst (wě̃r-) *adj.* & *adv.* Used as superlative of *bad, evil, ill, badly*; least good or well. ~ *n.* Worst part, feature, state, event, possible issue, action, etc.; *if the ~ come(s) to the ~*, if things fall out as badly as possible or conceivable; *at (the) ~*, in the most evil or undesirable possible state; even on the most unfavourable view or surmise; *do one's ~*, do the utmost evil or harm possible; *get* (etc.) *the ~ of*, be worsted in. ~ *v.t.* Get the better of, defeat, outdo, best.

wor'stėd (wŏŏs-) *n.* Fine smooth-surfaced yarn spun from long-staple wool which has been combed so that fibres lie parallel; fabric woven from this. ~ *adj.* Made of worsted. [f. *Worste(a)d* in Norfolk]

wort[1] (wě̃rt) *n.* Plant or herb used for food or medicine (archaic exc. as second element of plant-names).

wort[2] (wě̃rt) *n.* Infusion of malt or other grain which after fermentation becomes beer.

worth (wě̃rth) *predic. adj.* Of the value of (a specified amount or sum); of specified or certain value in other than material respects; sufficiently valuable or important to be equivalent or good return for (something); possessed of, owning; deserving or worthy of (something); ~ *while*, worth the time or effort spent; *~-while*, that is worth time or effort expended. **worth'less** *adj.* **worth'lėssly** *adv.* **worth'lėssnėss** *n.* **worth** *n.* What a thing is worth, value; equivalent *of* specified sum or amount.

worthy (wě̃r'dhĭ) *adj.* Estimable; having high moral standard; of sufficient worth, value, desert, or merit (*to*), deserving (*of*). ~ *n.* Distinguished, eminent, or famous person, esp. hero of antiquity; *the Nine Worthies*, famous personages of ancient and medieval history and legend, 3 Jews (Joshua, David, Judas Maccabaeus), 3 Gentiles (Hector, Alexander, Julius Caesar), and 3 Christians (Arthur, Charlemagne, Godfrey of Bouillon).

would (wŏŏd), past tense and conditional of WILL (*v.*); *would'-be* (*adj.*). desiring or professing to be, posing as.

wound[1] (wōō-) *n.* Injury done by cutting, stabbing, lacerating, etc., animal or vegetable tissues with hard or sharp instrument, bullet, etc. (freq. fig.); *~-wort*, various plants used for healing or dressing wounds, esp. species of *Stachys*, golden-rod, comfrey, kidney-vetch, etc. ~ *v.* Inflict wound (on); inflict pain or hurt on, pain, grieve deeply.

wound[2], past part. of WIND[2].

wōve *adj.* (var. of WOVEN). (esp., of paper) Made on mould of closely woven wire.

wōv'en *adj.* (past part. of *weave*). Made by weaving, that has been subjected to weaving; interlaced, intertwined.

wow[1] *n.* (U.S. slang) A striking or 'howling' success.

wow[2] *n.* (sound engineering) Waver, tremolo, in reproduced sound, due to fluctuations in record-speed.

wows'er (-z-) *n.* (Austral.) Puritanical fanatic.

W.P. *abbrev.* Weather permitting.

W.P.B. *abbrev.* Waste-paper basket.

W.R. *abbrev.* West Riding (of Yorkshire).

W.R.A.C. *abbrev.* Women's Royal Army Corps.

wrăck (r-) *n.* Seaweed or other marine vegetation cast up or growing on tidal seashore, and used for manure etc.

W.R.A.F. *abbrev.* Women's Royal Air Force.

wraith (r-) *n.* Apparition, ghost, of dead person; spectral appearance of living person supposed to portend his death.

wrangle (răng'gl) *n.* & *v.i.* Brawl; (engage in) noisy, vehement, or contentious argument or quarrel.

wrăng'ler (rängg-) *n.* One who wrangles, quarrelsome person; (at Univ. of Cambridge) candidate placed in first class in mathematical tripos (f. obs. sense of person who disputes publicly on a thesis); *senior ~*, first in first class when it was arranged in order of merit. **wrăn'glership** *n.*

wrăp (r-) *v.* Enfold, enclose, pack, swathe, (freq. *up*) in garment or folded or soft encircling material; form wrap or covering for; involve, enfold, *in* something obscuring or disguising; fold, wind, draw (covering, garment, etc.) *round, about*, etc.; ~ *over*, overlap; ~ *up*, put on wraps; *wrapped up*, (esp.) engrossed, centred, absorbed, *in*; bound up with, involved *in*. ~ *n.* Wrapper, covering; blanket, rug, etc., (usu. pl.) additional outer garment worn as defence against wind and weather; woman's shawl, scarf, or the like.

wrăpp'er (r-) *n.* (esp.) Protective covering for parcel etc.; paper enclosing newspaper etc. for posting; paper cover of pamphlet or periodical; detachable outer paper cover of book; loose enveloping robe or gown; tobacco-leaf of superior grade used for outer cover of cigar.

wrăpp'ing (r-) *n.* (esp., pl.) Wraps, enveloping garments; *~-paper*, strong paper for packing or wrapping up parcels.

wrasse (răs) *n.* Any species of family *Labridae* of spiny-finned, usu. brilliant-coloured, edible marine fishes, esp. the 'ballan' or 'old wife' (*Labrus maculatus*) and the striped or red wrasse (*L. mixtus*), of Atlantic coasts of Europe.

wrath (rawth, U.S. rahth) *n.* (chiefly poet. or rhet.) Anger, indignation. **wrath'ful** *adj.* **wrath'fully** *adv.* **wrath'fulnėss** *n.*

wreak (rēk) *v.t.* Give vent or expression to, gratify (anger etc.), *upon*; avenge (person); take vengeance, inflict retributive punishment, for (injury etc.); inflict (vengeance) *on, upon*; cause (harm, damage, etc.).

wreath (rēth) *n.* (pl. pr. -dhz). Flowers or leaves strung or woven or wound together into ring for wearing on head or for decorating statue, building, coffin, etc.; carved imitation of this; similar ring of soft twisted material, as silk; curl *of* smoke, circular or curved band of cloud, light drifting mass of sand, snow, etc.

wreathe (-dh) *v.* Encircle as (or with, or as with) a wreath; form into wreath; entwine; wind, turn (flexible object) round or over something; (of smoke etc.) move in wreath-like shape.

wreck (rĕk) *n.* Disabling, destruction, ruin, overthrow, esp. of ship; ship that has suffered wreck; what remains *of* thing or person that has suffered ruin, waste, disablement, dilapidation, etc., anything broken down or ruined, person of undermined or shattered constitution; (law) goods etc. cast up by sea, piece of wreckage. ~ *v.* Cause wreck of (ship, train, person's constitution, undertaking, etc.); suffer wreck.

wrĕck'age (r-) *n.* Fragments or remains of wrecked or shattered vessel, structure, etc.; (fig.) act or process of wrecking.

wrĕck'er (r-) *n.* (esp.) One who tries from shore to bring about shipwreck in order to plunder or profit by wreckage; one who steals wreckage; person employed in recovering wrecked ship or its contents; one who obstructs undertaking etc.

wren[1] (rĕn) *n.* Any of numerous species of genus *Troglodytes* of small, usu. brown, passerine song-birds, esp. the common European wren (Jenny-W~), *T. troglodytes*, a very small dark-brown mottled bird with short erect tail; various other small birds of similar appearance or habits.

Wren[2] (rĕn) *n.* Member of Women's Royal Naval Service, an auxiliary of British Royal Navy first formed in war of 1914–18 and revived in 1939. [f. initials]

Wren[3] (rĕn), Sir Christopher (1632–1723). English architect; designer of St. Paul's Cathedral and many other London churches and buildings after Great Fire of 1666.

wrĕnch (r-) *n.* 1. Violent twist, turn, or pull; (fig.) pain or anguish caused by parting. 2. Instrument or tool of various forms for gripping or turning bolt-head, nut, etc., consisting essentially of metal bars with (freq. adjustable) jaws; spanner (ill. SPANNER). ~ *v.* Twist, turn; pull round or sideways, violently or with effort; pull *off*, *away*, *out*, thus; injure, pain, by straining or stretching.

wrĕst (r-) *v.* Twist, deflect, distort, pervert; force or wrench away from person's grasp. ~ *n.* Tuning-key of wire-stringed instrument, as harp, piano; ~*-block*, part of piano holding ~*-pins* to which strings are attached.

wrestle (rĕs'l) *n.* Wrestling-match; hard struggle. ~ *v.* Strive to overpower and throw to the ground another, esp. in contest governed by fixed rules, by grappling with him and tripping or overbalancing him; have wrestling-match with; contend, grapple, struggle, *with* thing, difficulties, feelings, forces, etc.; (western U.S.) throw (cattle) for branding. **wrĕstler** (-sl-), **wrĕstling** *ns.*

wrĕtch (r-) *n.* Miserable, unhappy, unfortunate, or hapless, person; contemptible, vile, or despicable person, one without conscience or shame (freq. as term of playful abuse).

wrĕtch'ėd (r-) *adj.* Miserable, unhappy, afflicted; inferior, of poor quality, of no merit; contemptible; unsatisfactory; causing discontent, discomfort, or nuisance. **wrĕtch'edly** *adv.* **wrĕtch'ėdnėss** *n.*

wrĭgg'le (r-) *n.* Wriggling movement. ~ *v.* Twist or turn body about with short writhing movements; (fig.) be slippery, practise evasion; move (one*self*, part of body, etc.) with wriggling motion, make (*way*) by wriggling.

wright[1] (rīt) *n.* Artificer, handicraftsman, maker (now rare exc. in compounds).

Wright[2] (rīt), Orville (1871–1948) and Wilbur (1867–1912). Two brothers, American technicians, who built and flew (1903) the first heavier-than-air motor-driven flying machine.

wrĭng (r-) *v.t.* (past t. and past part. *wrŭng*). Press, squeeze, or twist, with hands or machine, esp. so as to drain or make dry, strain (moisture etc.) by squeezing or torsion from moist or wet thing; twist forcibly, break by twisting, torture, distress, rack; extort, get (money, concession, etc.) *out of* or *from* by exaction or importunity; press or clasp (person's *hand*) forcibly or with emotion; ~ *one's hands*, clasp and twist them together in distress or pain; *wring'ing (wet)*, so wet that moisture may be wrung out. ~ *n.* Squeeze, act of wringing.

wrĭng'er (r-) *n.* (esp.) Device for wringing water from laundered clothes etc., usu. consisting essentially of two rollers between which article is squeezed.

wrĭnk'le (r-). *n.* 1. Furrow-like crease, depression or ridge in skin (esp. of kind produced by age, care, etc.) or other flexible surface. 2. (colloq.) Useful hint, tip; clever expedient or device. **wrĭnk'ly** *adj.* **wrĭnk'le** *v.* Acquire or assume wrinkles; produce wrinkles in.

wrĭst (r-) *n.* Joint in man connecting hand with forearm, carpus (ill. HAND); analogous joint in other animals; part of garment covering wrist; ~*-band*, band of sleeve covering or fastening about wrist; wristlet; ~*-bone*, a carpal bone; ~*-watch*, small watch worn on wristlet or strap round wrist.

wrĭst'lėt (r-) *n.* Band, bracelet, strap, worn on wrist to strengthen or guard it, as ornament, to hold watch, etc.; handcuff.

wrĭt (r-) *n.* 1. *Holy, sacred,* ~, the Bible. 2. Formal written order issued by court in name of sovereign, State, etc., directing person(s) to whom it is addressed to do or refrain from doing specified act; document issued by Crown summoning spiritual or temporal lord to attend Parliament or directing sheriff to hold election of member(s) of Parliament.

wrīte (r-) *v.* (past t. *wrōte*, past part. *writt'en*). Form symbols representing letter(s) or word(s) esp. on paper, parchment, etc., with pen, pencil, brush, etc., form (such symbols), set (words etc.) down in writing, express in writing; chronicle, make record or account of; convey (message, information, etc) by letter; engage in writing or authorship; produce writing; ~ *down*, set down in writing; write in disparagement or depreciation of; reduce (total, assets, etc.) to lower amount; ~ *off*, record cancelling of (bad debt, depreciated stock, etc.); reckon as lost; ~*-off (n.)* something that must be regarded as total loss; ~ *out*, make written copy of; transcribe in full or detail; ~ *up*, write full account or record of; give full or elaborate description of; commend by appreciative writing, praise in writing.

wrīt'er (r-) *n.* One who writes; author; clerk, esp. in government offices, Royal Navy, etc., (hist.) clerk in service of former East India Company; (Sc.) law-clerk, legal practitioner; *W~ to the Signet*, (abbrev. W.S.), one of ancient Scottish society of law-agents conducting cases before Court of Session and having exclusive privilege of preparing Crown writs, charters, etc.; Scots solicitor; ~*'s cramp*, painful spasmodic cramp affecting muscles of hand and fingers used in writing, and resulting from excessive writing. **wrīt'ership** *n.*

writhe (rīdh) *v.* Twist or roll oneself about (as) in acute pain, squirm; twist (*body* etc.) about, contort. ~ *n.* Act of writhing.

wrīt'ing (r-) *n.* (esp.) Written document; (piece of) literary work; personal script, handwriting; *put in* ~, write down; ~*-case*, case holding writing-materials; ~*-desk*, desk; ~*-master*, instructor in penmanship; the yellow-hammer (from marks like scribbling on eggs); ~*-paper*, paper for writing on with ink, esp. note-paper; ~*-table*, desk.

wrĭtt'en (r-) *adj.* (past part. of WRITE). That is in writing, esp. as opp. to *oral* or *printed*.

W.R.N.S. *abbrev.* Women's Royal Naval Service.

wrŏng (r-) *adj.* 1. Not morally right or equitable, unjust; doing or prone to do evil; not correct or proper; not true, incorrect, false, mistaken; judging, acting, etc., contrary to facts, in error; ~-

headed, perversely or obstinately wrong, characterized by perversity of judgement; ~*-headedness*. 2. Not in good order or condition, amiss; not what is required or intended, unsuitable, inappropriate; (of way etc.) leading in, tending to, direction other than what is intended, desired, or expected; ~ *end*, end or limit less adapted or suitable for particular purpose; *get hold of the* ~ *end of the stick*, (fig.) be mistaken in judgement etc.; ~ *side*, side of fabric etc. not meant to be shown; disadvantageous, undesirable, etc., side *of* some place, object, etc.; *on the* ~ *side of*, older than (specified age); *get up, out of bed, on the* ~ *side*, be in irritable mood; ~ *side out*, (fig.) in bad temper, irritable, peevish; (the) ~ *way*, in contrary or opposite way to proper or usual one. **wrŏng'ly** *adv.* **wrŏng'nĕss** *n.* **wrŏng** *adv.* Amiss, in wrong course or direction; mistakenly, erroneously; in improper or unfitting manner; *go* ~, go astray; happen amiss or unfortunately; get out of gear or working order; take to evil courses, esp. (of woman) fall from virtue. ~ *n.* What is morally wrong; wrong action; unjust action or treatment; being wrong in attitude, procedure, or belief (freq. *in the* ~); ~*-doing*, transgression against moral or established law. ~ *v.t.* Treat unjustly, do wrong to; do injustice to by statement, opinion, etc.; dishonour by word or thought.

wrŏng'ful (r-) *adj.* Marked by wrong, unfairness, injustice, etc.; contrary to law, etc., unlawful, illegal; (of persons) holding office, possession, etc., unlawfully or without legitimacy or right. **wrŏng'fully** *adv.* **wrŏng'fulnĕss** *n.*

wroth (rōth, rŏ-) *predic. adj.* (rhet., poet., etc.) Angry, stirred to wrath.

wrought (rawt) *adj.* Worked, processed, manufactured, worked into shape: (of metals) beaten out or shaped with hammer etc.; ~ *iron*: see IRON; ~*-up*, stirred up, excited or agitated.

wry (rī) *adj.* Distorted, turned to one side; temporarily twisted or contorted in disgust, disrelish, etc.; ~*-bill*, New Zealand shorebird (*Anarhynchus frontalis*), allied to plovers, with bill deflected to one side; ~*-mouth*, numerous large fish of family *Cryptacanthodidae*, of blenny kind, the ghost-fish of northern Atlantic coasts of N. America; *wry'neck*, deformity with contortion of neck and face and lateral inclination of head, torticollis; species of genus *Jynx* of small migratory birds allied to woodpeckers, esp. common *J. torquilla* of Europe and Asia, with peculiar manner of writhing neck and head. **wrȳ'ly** *adv.* **wrȳ'nĕss** *n.*

W.S. *abbrev.* Writer to the Signet.

W.S.W., WSW *abbrevs.* West-south-west.

W/T *abbrev.* Wireless telegraphy, telephony.

wt *abbrev.* Weight.

Wul'fila (wŏŏ-) (*c* 311–83). Gothic bishop who translated the New Testament into Gothic.

Wundt (vŏŏnt), Wilhelm (1832–1920). German philosopher and psychologist.

Wür'ttemberg. Former State of SW. Germany, now divided between provinces of Baden-Württemberg (capital, Stuttgart) and Württemberg-Hohenzollern (capital, Tübingen).

W. Va. *abbrev.* West Virginia.

W.V.S. *abbrev.* Women's Voluntary Service(s).

Wȳandŏtte'. Name of tribe of N. Amer. Indians; (orig. Amer.) breed of medium-sized domestic fowl, orig. white laced with black but now bred in various colours.

wȳch-elm etc.: see WITCH[3].

Wȳch'erley, William (1640–1716). English writer of 'Restoration' comedies.

Wȳc'lif or **Wȳcliffe,** John (*c* 1320–84). English religious reformer; attacked the papacy and asserted the right of every man to examine the Bible for himself; instituted the first translation into English of the whole Bible, himself translating the Gospels and probably other parts; his doctrines were taken up by the LOLLARDS.

Wykeham (wĭk'*a*m), William of (1324–1408). Bishop of Winchester and founder of Winchester College (1382) and New College, Oxford (1379). **Wykehamist** *n.* (Former) pupil of Winchester College.

wȳnd *n.* (Sc.) Narrow street or passage off main thoroughfare; narrow cross-street, lane, or alley.

Wyo. *abbrev.* Wyoming.

Wȳōm'ĭng. Mountain State of U.S., admitted to the Union 1890; capital, Cheyenne.

wȳv'ern *n.* (her.) Winged dragon with two feet like eagle's and barbed tail. [OF *wyvre* viper]

X

X, x (ĕks). 24th letter of modern English and 21st of ancient Roman alphabet, adopted from the Greek alphabet introduced into Italy, with the value (ks) which it usually has in modern English. Initially *x*, pronounced as *z*, is used in English words nearly all of which are of Greek origin. 1. X is the Roman numeral symbol for ten; so xx, 20, xc, 90, etc. 2. (U.S. colloq.) x = ten-dollar note. 3. In algebra etc. *x* is symbol of unknown or variable quantity, or the first of such quantities; hence, incalculable or unknown factor or influence. 4. In designation of brands of ale etc. XX or double X = medium quality, XXX or treble X, strongest quality. 5. In abbreviations X = Christ (from Greek ΧΡΙΣΤΟΣ); Xmas = Christmas. 6. (chem.) X = xenon. 7. *x-height*, height of an x, height of body of letter (ill. TYPE).

xăn'thāte (z-) *n.* (chem.) Salt of xanthic acid.

xăn'thēin (z-) *n.* (chem.) Yellow colouring matter found in plants.

Xăn'thĭan Marbles (z-, -th-). A collection of sculptures, now in the British Museum, discovered (1838) by Sir Charles Fellows in the ruins of Xanthus, an ancient city of Asia Minor.

xăn'thĭc (z-) *adj.* (chem. etc.) Yellow; of xanthin; ~ *acid*, a complex acid ($C_3H_6OS_2$), many of whose salts (*xanthates*) are yellow.

xăn'thĭn(e) (z-) *n.* (chem.) Substance related to uric acid and found in animal secretions.

Xanthipp'ē (zăntĭ-). Wife of Socrates, reputed to be a shrew; shrewish woman or wife.

xănthōm'a (z-) *n.* (path.) Skin disease characterized by irregular yellowish patches on eyelids, neck, etc.

xăn'thophȳll (z-) *n.* Dark-brown crystalline compound found in plants, usu. associated with chlorophyll, and forming yellow colouring-matter of autumn leaves.

xăn'thous (z-) *adj.* (Of races) having yellow(ish) or red(dish) hair; having yellow skin.

Xăv'ĭer (z-), St. Francis (1506–52). Spanish Jesuit, one of the founders of the Society of Jesus, and a famous missionary in the Far East, commemorated 3rd Dec.

x-cp. *abbrev.* Ex coupon.

xd, x-d., x-div. *abbrevs.* Ex dividend.

xēb'ĕc (z-) *n.* Small three-masted Mediterranean vessel, usu. lateen rigged with some square sails, formerly used as ship of war.

Xĕnŏc'rătēs (z-, -z). Greek Platonic philosopher (396–314 B.C.).

xĕn'olĭth (z-) *n.* (geol.) Stone or rock occurring in a system to which it does not belong.

xĕn'on (z-) *n.* (chem.) Heavy inert gaseous element present in minute quantity in atmosphere; symbol Xe, at. no. 54, at. wt 131·30. [Gk *xenos* strange]

Xĕnŏph'ănēs (z-, -z) (*c* 576–480 B.C.). Greek philosopher and poet, formerly thought to have been the founder of the ELEATIC School of philosophy.

xĕnophōb'ĭa (z-) *n.* Morbid dislike or fear of foreigners, foreign customs, etc. **xĕn'ophōbe** *n.* Person showing xenophobia.

Xĕn'ophon (z-). Athenian historian and philosopher (*c* 430–*c* 355 B.C.); pupil of Socrates; joined the expedition of Cyrus against Artaxerxes, and was elected one of the generals of the Greek force, which was left in a dangerous situation between the Tigris and Euphrates; after the treacherous murder of its generals by Artaxerxes he led it in the Retreat of the Ten Thousand to the Black Sea; his principal works include the 'Anabasis' and 'Hellenica', histories of Greece, the 'Memorabilia' of Socrates and the 'Symposium', in which he expounds the doctrines and defends the character of Socrates.

Xeres. Old spelling of JEREZ (DE LA FRONTERA).

xērŏph'agy (z-) *n.* Strictest form of fast, practised in Eastern Church esp. during Lent or Holy Week, and forbidding meat, fish, cheese, milk, butter, oil, wine, and all seasonings except salt.

xērŏph'ĭlous (z-) *adj.* (bot.) Adapted to extremely dry conditions.

xērophthăl'mĭa (z-) *n.* (path.) Inflammation of the conjunctiva with abnormal dryness and corrugation.

xēr'ophȳte (z-) *n.* Plant adapted to very dry conditions, desert plant.

Xērx'ēs (z-, -z). King of Persia 485–465 B.C., son of Darius; invaded Greece and overcame the resistance of Leonidas and the Spartans at Thermopylae, but was defeated at Salamis 480 B.C.; called Ahasuerus in the Book of Esther.

x-i. *abbrev.* Ex interest.

Xĭph'ĭăs (z-) *n.* 1. (zool.) Genus of fishes, comprising the common swordfish (~ *gladius*). 2. (astron.) Southern constellation, also called Dorado. [Gk *xiphos* sword]

xĭph'oid (z-) *adj.* Sword-shaped; ~ *process*, cartilaginous or bony process at lower or posterior end of sternum in man and other animals, the *xiphisternum* (ill. SKELETON).

Xmas. Abbrev. (in writing only) of Christmas (see X, sense 5).

xō'anon (z-) *n.* (Gk antiq.; pl. *-ana*). Primitive usu. wooden image of deity, supposed to have fallen from heaven.

X-rays (ĕks-) *n.pl.* Electromagnetic radiations of very short wave-length emitted by electrons whose velocity is suddenly reduced; they are capable of passing through an extensive thickness of any body, whether transparent or not, of acting on photographic plates, and of ionizing gases; *X-ray* (*photograph*), shadow-photograph, esp. of bodies impervious to light, made with X-rays. **X-ray** *v.t.* Photograph, examine, with X-rays; treat (disease, patient) with X-rays. [Ger. *X-strahlen*, name given by their discoverer, RÖNTGEN, to indicate that their essential nature was unknown]

Xt(ian). Abbrev. (in writing only) of Christ(ian) (prop. X = Gk letter chi, formed like English X).

xȳl'ĕm (z-) *n.* (bot.) Woody tissue including vessels and fibres forming harder part of fibrovascular tissues of plant (opp. PHLOEM; ill. STEM).

xȳl'ēne (z-) *n.* (chem.) One of 3 colourless, oily, isomeric hydrocarbons, derivatives of benzene, obtained from wood, tar, etc.

xȳl'ograph (z-, -ahf) *n.* Woodcut, esp. of early period.

xȳ'lonīte (z-) *n.* = CELLULOID.

xȳlŏph'agous (z-) *adj.* (of insects) Feeding on, boring into, wood.

xȳl'ophōne (z-) *n.* Musical instrument consisting of a series of flat wooden bars, graduated in length to sound the musical scale, resting on strips of straw or felt, and played by striking with small wooden hammer(s).

Y

Y, y (wī). 25th letter of modern English and 23rd of ancient Roman alphabet, representing ultimately Υ, Y, of Greek alphabet, a differentiated form of primitive V (see U, V); first adopted in Latin alphabet as V, and later re-adopted in form Y to represented Y of borrowed Greek words. As a vowel, *y* in modern English may represent all the sounds (except ĕ) commonly spelt with *i*, and it is used as the normal spelling (*a*) for final *i*-sounds, (*b*) in Greek words, representing υ, (*c*) before *i* in inflexional forms of verbs ending in *-y* or *-ie*, (*d*) in plural of nouns ending in *-y* preceded by another vowel. As a consonant, *y* represents a voiced palatal spirant. 1. The letter or its shape, figure, marking, object, etc., of this shape; *Y-branch*, piece of piping with branch at acute angle to main. 2. (math.) Denoting 2nd of series of unknown or variable quantities (cf. *x*).

Y. *abbrev.* Yeomanry.

y- *prefix* esp. of past participles, still found in a few archaic forms, as *yclad* clad, *yclept* called, *ywis* surely.

yacht (yŏt) *n.* Light sailing-

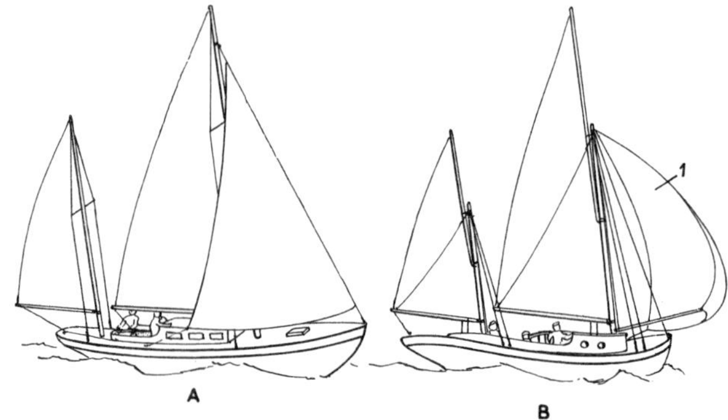

YACHTS: A. BERMUDAN-RIGGED YAWL. B. GUNTER-RIGGED KETCH

1. Spinnaker

vessel kept, and usu. specially built, for racing; vessel propelled by sails, steam, or any motive power other than oars, and used for private pleasure excursions, cruising, travel, etc.; ~ *club*, club esp. for yacht-racing; *yacht'sman*, person who yachts. ~ *v.i.* Race or cruise in yacht. [early mod. Du. *jaght(e)*, = *jaghtschip* (*jagen* to hunt); named f. its speed]

yăff'le *n.* (dial.) Green woodpecker. [imit. of bird's laughing cry]

yah *int.* of disgust, defiance, or derision.

yahōō' *n.* In Swift's 'Gulliver's Travels', race of brutes in human shape; hence, degraded or bestial human being.

Yah'veh, Yah'weh (-vā). Modern transliteration of the characters of the Hebrew word which is translated in the Bible as JEHOVAH.

yăk *n.* Large humped bovine mammal with long silky hair on sides, tail, etc., found wild and domesticated in Tibet and other high regions of central Asia; used as a beast of burden. [Tibetan *gyag*]

Yakutsk' (yahkōō-). Autonomous republic of Asiatic Russia (part of R.S.F.S.R.) formed in 1922.

Yāle lŏck *n.* Trade-name applied to certain cylinder locks for doors etc. [Linus *Yale* (1821–68), Amer. locksmith]

Yāle (University). Orig. founded (1701) as a school at Saybrook, Connecticut; transferred to New Haven, Connecticut, 1718, and called Yale College in consequence of benefactions received from Elihu Yale (1648–1721), a native of Boston, Massachusetts, who entered the service of the East India Company and became governor of Madras. It received a charter 1745, and assumed the name of Yale University 1887.

yăm *n.* Starchy tuberous root, largely replacing potato as a staple food in many tropical and subtropical countries, of various species of *Dioscorea*, twining herbs or shrubs with spikes of small inconspicuous flowers; any of these plants.

Ya'ma (yah-). (Hindu myth.) The ruler of the world of the dead.

Yăng'tzė (Kiăng) (ky-). Principal river of China; rises in Tibet and flows through central China to E. China Sea.

yănk[1] *n.* & *v.* (U.S. and slang) (Pull with) sudden sharp tug or jerk.

Yănk[2]. Colloq. abbrev. of YANKEE.

Yănk'ee *n.* Native or inhabitant of New England or of northern States of U.S. generally; (applied by non-Americans to) any inhabitant of U.S.; (*attrib.*) of Yankees; that is a Yankee; ~ *Doodle*, popular U.S. song considered characteristically national; a Yankee. [perh. f. Du. *Janke* dim. of *Jan* John used derisively; or f. *Jengees* Indian pronunciation of *English*]

ya'ourt (yah-ûrt) *n.* YOG(H)URT.

yăp *n.* & *v.i.* (Utter) shrill or fussy bark, yelp. [imit.]

yăpp *n.* Kind of bookbinding in limp leather with overlapping edges or flaps (ill. BOOK). [name of London bookseller for whom this style of binding was first made *c* 1860]

yar̄b'orough (-b*oro*) *n.* (cards) Whist- or bridge-hand with no card above a 9. [from an Earl of Yarborough who used to bet against its occurrence]

yar̄d[1] *n.* Piece of enclosed ground, esp. one surrounded by or attached to building(s) or used for some manufacturing or other purpose; prison-yard, shipyard, dockyard, stockyard, etc.; (now chiefly U.S.) garden; farm-yard; ground near railway station where rolling-stock is kept, trains made up, etc.; *the Y~*, SCOTLAND YARD; *~-master*, manager of railway-yard. ~ *v.t.* Enclose (cattle etc.) in yard. **yar̄d'age**[1] *n.* Fees payable for use of stockyard.

yar̄d[2] *n.* 1. Unit of British and Amer. long measure, equal to 3 feet or 36 inches (see Appendix X); also measure of area (sq.~), or of solidity (cu. ~), as in ~ *of gravel, lime*, etc.; yard-length of material; *~-measure*, rod, tape, etc., a yard long, usu. marked in feet and inches; ~ *of clay*, long clay pipe; ~ *of tin*, coachman's horn; *yardstick*, stick as yard-measure; (fig.) standard, criterion. 2. (naut.) Long usu. cylindrical spar, tapering to each end, slung (usu. at its centre for square sail) from mast, to support and extend sail (ill. SAIL[1]); *~-arm*, either end of yard of square-rigged vessel. **yar̄d'age**[2] *n.* Number of yards of material etc.

Yar̄m'outh (-m*u*th). Fishing-town on coast of Norfolk, England; ~ *bloater*, slightly salted and smoked herring.

yar̄n *n.* 1. Fibre, as of cotton, wool, silk, flax, spun and prepared for use in weaving, knitting, etc. 2. (colloq., orig. naut.) Story, tale; *spin a* ~, tell (usu. long) tale. ~ *v.i.* (colloq.) Tell yarn(s).

yă'rrow (-rō) *n.* Herb (*Achillea millefolium*), common on roadsides, dry meadows, and waste ground, with tough greyish stem, finely divided bipinnate leaves, and dull-white or pinkish flower-heads in close flat clusters; various other species of *Achillea*.

yăsh'măk *n.* Double veil concealing face below eyes, worn by Mohammedan women in public.

yăt'aghan (-găn) *n.* Short sword of Moslem countries with slight reverse curve (ill. SWORD).

yaw *v.i.* (naut. and aeronautics) Deviate from straight course owing to action of heavy sea or strong winds. ~ *n.* Such deviation.

yawl *n.* Ship's boat like small pinnace, with 4 or 6 oars; 2-masted fore-and-aft sailing-boat with after mast much smaller than main mast and placed far aft (ill. YACHT); small sailing-boat with stem and stern alike used for fishing etc.

yawn *v.* Breathe in involuntarily with mouth wide open, as from drowsiness, fatigue, boredom, etc.; utter or say with yawn; (of chasm etc.) gape, have wide opening. ~ *n.* Act of yawning.

yaws (-z) *n.pl.* Framboesia, contagious skin disease with raspberry-like tubercles or excrescences on skin, prevalent among tropical native populations and having many analogies with syphilis.

y̆clĕpt' *adj.* (archaic or joc.) Called (so-and-so).

yd *abbrev.* Yard.

yē[1] *pers. pron.*, 2nd pers. nom. pl. (archaic, dial. or poet.) You.

y[e], **ye**[2] *abbrev.* (pr. yē). The (now only pseudo-archaic or joc.; the *y* is a survival of the obs. letter þ, = *th*).

yea (yā) *adv.* & *n.* (archaic) Yes.

yean *v.* (archaic) Bring forth (lamb, kid, etc.), bring forth young, as sheep, goat, etc.

yean'lĭng *n.* (archaic) Young lamb or kid.

year *n.* 1. Time occupied by the earth in one revolution round the sun (also *astronomical, equinoctial, natural, solar, tropical*, ~; = 365 days, 5 hours, 48 minutes, 46 seconds) or by the sun in recovering its previous apparent relation to the fixed stars (*astral* or *sidereal* year, longer by 20 minutes, 23 seconds). 2. Period of days (esp. *common* ~ of 365 days reckoned from 1st Jan. or *leap-* or *bissextile*~ of 366) used by community for dating or other purposes commencing on a certain day, usu. divided into 12 months, and corresponding more or less exactly in length to the astronomical year (also called *civil, calendar*, or *legal*~). 3. Such space of time with limits not necessarily coinciding with those of civil year, used in reckoning age, period of office, occupation, etc., or for special purpose, as taxation, payment of dividends, etc. 4. (pl.) Age (of person); (pl.) period, times, a very long time. 5. ~ *in*, ~ *out*, right through the year, continuously; *~-book*, annual publication containing information for the year.

year'lĭng *n.* & *adj.* (Animal, esp. sheep, calf, or foal) a year old; (racing) colt one year old from 1st Jan. of year of foaling.

year'ly *adj.* & *adv.* (Occurring, observed, done, etc.) once a year or every year; annual(ly).

yearn (yẽrn) *v.i.* Long; be moved with compassion or tender feelings. **yearn'ing** *n.*

yeast *n.* Greyish-yellow substance produced as froth or sediment during alcoholic fermentation of malt worts and other saccharine fluids, consisting of aggregated cells of minute fungi of family *Saccharomycetaceae*, and used in manufacture of beer, to leaven bread, etc., and in medicine; ~ *cell*, minute unicellular fungus of this family. **yeast'y** *adj.* Frothy like yeast; in a ferment, working like yeast; made with yeast. **yeast'inèss** *n.*

Yeats (yāts), William Butler (1865–1939). Irish lyric poet and dramatist; assisted in the creation of an Irish national theatre.

yĕgg *n.* (also *yegg'man*) Burglar, esp. one who breaks open safes (U.S. slang). [said to be name of Amer. safe-breaker]

yĕll *n.* Sharp loud outcry of strong and sudden emotion, as rage, horror, agony; (U.S.) set of words or syllables shouted as an organized cheer, as by Amer. college students. ~ *v.* Make, utter with, yell.

yĕll'ow (-ō) *adj.* Of the colour of buttercup or lemon or sulphur or gold, most luminous of the primary colours, occurring in spectrum between green and orange; having a yellow skin or complexion, as the Mongolian peoples; (orig. U.S., of newspaper etc.) recklessly or unscrupulously sensational; (orig. U.S.) cowardly, craven; *yell'owback*, cheap (esp. French) novel in yellow paper cover or yellow paper boards; ~ *belly*, (contempt.) Mexican; half-caste; *Y~ Book*, English illustrated quarterly (1894–7), with contributions from Aubrey Beardsley, Max Beerbohm, Henry James, Walter Sickert, and many other distinguished writers and artists; ~ *fever*, highly fatal febrile disease of hot climates, characterized by jaundice, vomiting, haemorrhages, etc., and transmitted by a mosquito; ~*-hammer*, common European species of bunting (*Emberiza citrinella*), with bright-yellow head, throat, and under-parts; ~ *jack*, yellow fever; quarantine flag; ~ *ochre*: see OCHRE; ~ *peril*, danger that the yellow races may overwhelm the white or dominate the world; ~ *soap*, common household soap of tallow, rosin, and soda; ~ *spot*, point of acutest vision in retina. ~ *n.* Yellow colour, pigment, fabric, etc.; yellow species or variety of bird, butterfly, moth, flower, etc. ~ *v.* Turn yellow.

Yĕll'ow River. Most northerly of China's great rivers, known as 'China's Sorrow', because of its uncontrollable floods. [trans. Chinese *Hwang Ho*]

Yĕll'ow Sea. The sea between the province of Shantung and Korea, into which the Yellow River formerly flowed. [trans. Chinese *Hwang Hai*]

Yĕll'owstōne National Park. An area of about 3,438 sq. miles in the State of Wyoming, U.S., reserved (since 1872) for public uses, named after the *Yellowstone River*, a tributary of the Missouri, which rises in the Park.

yĕlp *n.* & *v.i.* (Utter) sharp shrill bark or cry (as) of dog in pain, excitement, etc.

Ye'mĕn (yā-). Republic since 1962 (kingdom 1934–62) of SW. Arabia, the *Arabia Felix* of the ancients, freed from Turkish rule in 1918; capital, Taiz.

yĕn[1] *n.* (pl. same). Principal monetary unit of Japan, = 100 sen; ~ *min piao*, People's Currency, principal monetary unit of China. [Jap., f. Chin. *yüan* round, dollar]

yĕn[2] *n.* (U.S. slang) Passionate or impelling desire or longing. [Chin. *yen* smoke, opium]

Yeo(m). *abbrev.* Yeomanry.

yeo'man (yō-) *n.* (pl. *-men*). 1. Small landowner, person of middle class engaged in agriculture (esp. *attrib.*, as ~ *farmer*); (hist.) person qualified by possessing free land of 40*s.* annual value to serve on juries, vote for knight of shire, etc. 2. (hist.) Servant and attendant in royal or noble household of rank between sergeant and groom or squire and page; *Y~ of the Guard*, member of bodyguard of English sovereign, first appointed by Henry VII, and now acting chiefly as warders of Tower of London. 3. (U.S. navy) Petty officer performing clerical duties on board ship; ~ *of the signals*, (Royal Navy) petty officer in branch concerned with visual signalling. 4. Member of yeomanry force; ~*('s) service*, help in need; efficient service. **yeo'manly** *adj.* Of, befitting, a yeoman or yeomen.

yeo'manry (yō-) *n.* Yeomen collectively; volunteer cavalry force in Brit. army, orig. formed as home defence force in 1766; *Imperial Y~*, title of corps recruited for service in South African War (1899–1902), afterwards extended to original yeomanry, and retained until (1908) the corps became part of Territorial Army.

yĕp. Dial. (esp. U.S.) pronunciation of YES.

yĕrb'a (maté) (mätā') *n.* Paraguay tea, MATÉ. [Span., f. L *herba* grass, herb, and native *mati*]

yĕs *adv.* & *n.* (Utterance of) word expressing affirmative reply to question, statement, command, etc.; ~*-man*, (colloq.) person who agrees with everything that is said to him, esp. one who endorses and supports the opinion or proposals of a superior.

yĕs'terday *n.* & *adv.* (On) the day immediately preceding today; (in) time not long past.

yĕs'ter-year *n.* Last year (poet.). [coined by D. G. Rossetti to translate Fr. *antan*, f. L *ante annum*]

yĕt *adv.* 1. In addition or continuation, besides, also (archaic); (with comparative) even, still; *nor* ~, and also not. 2. Up to this or that time, till now, till then; at some time in the future, hereafter (though not hitherto), henceforth, even now (though not till now); *not* ~, still not, not by this (or that) time; *as* ~, hitherto. ~ *adj.* That is still such, still continuing. ~ *conj.* In spite of that, nevertheless, notwithstanding.

yĕt'ĭ *n.* Either of 2 unidentified animals occas. seen on high slopes of Himalayas, the one being prob. the Himalayan red bear (*Ursus arctos isabellinus*) and the other possibly the Himalayan langur monkey (*Presbytis entellus achilles*). [Tibetan *yeh* rocky area, *teh* animal]

yew *n.* Tree (also ~*-tree*) of coniferous genus *Taxus*, widely distributed in North Temperate Zone, esp. common European *T. baccata*, with heavy elastic wood

YEW
1. Fruit. 2. Aril

and dense dark-green foliage, freq. planted in churchyards and regarded as symbol of sadness; wood of this, formerly used for making bows.

Ygerne: see IGRAINE.

Yg̃g'drasĭl (ĭg-). (Scand. myth.) The world tree, an ash; its roots and branches connect heaven, earth, and hell, and the NORNS sit beneath it. [ON, app. f. *Yggr* name of Odin + *drasill* horse]

Y.H.A. *abbrev.* Youth Hostels Association.

Yid *n.* (slang, contempt.) Jew.

Yidd'ish *adj.* & *n.* (Of) the language used by Jews in Europe and America, a German dialect (orig. from Middle Rhine area) with an admixture of Hebrew elements and of words borrowed from several modern languages. [Ger. *jūdisch* Jewish]

yield *v.* 1. Give as due or of right, render (service, obedience, thanks, etc.) (archaic); grant, allow, accord, bestow; give forth. 2. Produce, bear, furnish (crop, fruit, minerals, etc.); give to supply need or serve purpose, supply for use; produce as profit, bring in. 3. Give up, deliver over, surrender, resign; comply with demand for, concede; make submission (*to*); give way *to* persuasion, entreaty, etc., comply with demand; be inferior *to*; ~ *to*, give way under, be affected by, physical action or agent, as pressure, heat, etc. ~ *n.* Amount yielded or produced, output, return.

yl'ăng-yl'ăng (ēl-, -ēl-) *n.* Tree (*Cananga odorata*) of Malaya, Philippines, etc., with fragrant greenish-yellow flowers; perfume distilled from these.

Y.L.I. *abbrev.* Yorkshire Light Infantry.

Y.M.C.A. *abbrev.* YOUNG Men's Christian Association.

Ym'ir (ē-). (Scand. myth.) Primeval giant from whose body the gods created the world.

yōd'el *v.* Sing or warble with interchange of ordinary and falsetto voice in manner of Swiss and Tyrolese mountaineers. ~ *n.* Yodelling cry; yodelling-match.

Yōg'a *n.* Hindu system of ascetic practice, abstract meditation, and mental concentration as means of attaining union with Supreme Spirit. [Sansk. *yoga* union]

yŏg'(h)urt (-gert), **yaourt** (yah'-oort) *n.* Semi-solid junket-like or curd-like food prepared from milk fermented by addition of *Lactobacillus bulgaricus*. [Turk. *yōghurt*]

yōg'i (-g-) *n.* Devotee of YOGA.

yō-heave-hō *int.* Used by sailors hauling at rope or capstan, heaving up anchor, etc.

yō-hō *int.* (orig. naut.) Used to call attention, or in heaving together etc.

yoicks *int.* Used in fox-hunting to urge on hounds.

yōke *n.* 1. Contrivance, usu. curved or hollowed piece of wood over animals' necks, fastened at centre to chain or trace by which plough or vehicle is drawn, used from ancient times for coupling two animals, esp. oxen, for drawing vehicle etc. 2. Pair *of* oxen etc. 3. Piece of wood shaped to fit person's shoulders and support pail etc. at each end. 4. (Rom. hist.) Uplifted yoke, or arch of 3 spears symbolizing it, under which defeated enemy was made to march; (fig.) sway, dominion, servitude; (fig.) bond of union, esp. marriage tie. 5. Part of garment fitting shoulders (or hips) and supporting depending part. 6. Object resembling a yoke in shape, esp. cross-bar on which bell swings; cross-bar of rudder to whose ends steering lines are fastened, coupling-piece of two pipes discharging into one; kinds of coupling or controlling piece in machinery. ~ *v.t.* Put yoke upon; harness (draught-animal) *to* vehicle or plough; (fig.) couple, unite, join, link (*together*).

yōk'el *n.* (contempt.) Country bumpkin, (stupid or ignorant) countryman.

Yōkoha'ma (-hah-). Seaport of Tokyo, Japan.

yolk (yōk) *n.* Yellow(ish) internal part of egg, containing vitellin and other proteins, surrounded by white and serving as nourishment for young before hatching; (biol.) corresponding part in any animal ovum, serving for nutrition of embryo; substance from which embryo is developed ill. EMBRYO). **yolked** (yōkt) *adj.*

Yōm Kĭpp'ur. (Jewish religion) The Day of Atonement, falling on the 10th day of the month Tishri (approx. October) and observed as a solemn fast day acc. to the rites described in Lev. xvi.

yŏn, yŏn'der *adjs.* & *advs.* (archaic or dial.) (Situated) over there, at some distance (but within sight).

yōre *n.* (Only in) *of* ~, in or of time long past, former(ly).

yōrk[1] *v.t.* Bowl with yorker.

Yōrk[2]. City and county borough of Yorkshire and seat of the archbishop and primate of England.

Yōrk[3], House of. English royal dynasty, descending from Edmund of Langley (1341–1402), 5th son of Edward III and (from 1385) 1st Duke of York. The rivalry between Richard, Duke of York (1411–60) and the LANCASTRIANS led to the Wars of the Roses, in which the Yorkists were the 'white rose' party. Edward IV, Edward V, and Richard III were reigning monarchs of this line, which was united with the dynasty of Lancaster when Henry VII married the eldest daughter of Edward IV (1486).

yōrk'er *n.* (cricket) Ball so bowled as to pitch inside crease or just beneath bat. [prob. f. YORK[2]]

Yōrk'ist *n.* & *adj.* (Adherent) of the house of YORK[3], esp. in the Wars of the ROSES.

Yorks. *abbrev.* Yorkshire.

Yōrk'shire. County of NE. England, subdivided into N., E., and W. Ridings; ~ *pudding*, baked batter, usu. eaten with meat, esp. roast beef; ~ *terrier*, small, long-haired terrier.

Yōrk'town. Town on the shore of Chesapeake Bay, where, in 1781, the British army under Lord Cornwallis was blockaded by the American army and the French fleet.

Yōsĕm'ĭtē (National Park). Area reserved for public use in California (U.S.) containing the ~ *Valley* and ~ *Falls*, named after the ~ *River*, which traverses it.

you (yōō, yŏŏ) *pers. pron.* 2nd pers. sing. (with pl. verb) and pl. The person(s) or thing(s) addressed; (in general statements freq. =) one, anyone, everyone, a person.

young[1] (yŭ-) *adj.* That has lived, existed, etc., a relatively short time; lately begun, formed, introduced, etc., recent, new; of young person(s) or youth; youthful, esp. having freshness or vigour of youth; *Y~ Chevalier, Y~ Pretender*: see PRETENDER; *Y~ Men's Christian Association*, association (founded 1844 in England) for promoting spiritual, intellectual, and physical welfare of young men (abbrev. Y.M.C.A.; *Y~ Women's Christian Association*, abbrev. Y.W.C.A., similar association founded 1855); *Y~ Turks*, Turkish party which in 1908 forced Sultan Abdul Hamid II to proclaim liberal constitution and in 1909 deposed him in favour of his brother, Mohammed V. ~ *n.* Young people; young ones, offspring, of animals; *with* ~, pregnant.

Young[2] (yŭ-), Arthur (1741–1820). Writer of a large number of works on agricultural subjects and travel books, esp. famous for his 'Travels in France' (1792).

Young[3] (yŭ-), Brigham (1801–77). MORMON leader; headed the Mormon migration to Utah (1847), founded Salt Lake City, and was appointed governor of Utah (1851).

Young[4] (yŭ-), Edward (1683–1765). English poet, chiefly remembered for his didactic poem, 'Night Thoughts on Life, Death, and Immortality' (1742–5).

young'ster (yŭ-) *n.* Young person, esp. young man; child, esp. boy.

your (ūr, yōr) *poss. pron.* & *adj.* Of, belonging to, spoken of by, done to or by, you; (vaguely, archaic) that you know of, familiar.

yours (ūrz, yōrz) *poss. pron.* The one(s) belonging to or of you; (*predic.*) belonging to you, at your service.

yoursĕlf', yoursĕlves' *prons.* Emphatic and reflexive pronouns corresponding to *you*.

youth (yōō-) *n.* 1. Being young; early part of life, esp. adolescence; quality or condition characteristic of the young. 2. The young collectively; ~ *hostel*, cheap lodging, usu. provided by an association (in Britain, the *Y~ Hostels Association*) where young holiday-makers put up for the night. 3. Young person, esp. young man between boyhood and maturity. **youth'ful** *adj.* **youth'fully** *adv.* **youth'fulnĕss** *n.*

yowl *n.* & *v.* (Utter) loud wailing cry (as) of dog in distress, pain, etc., howl.

Ypres (ēpr). Belgian cloth-manufacturing town in W. Flanders, completely destroyed during the war of 1914–18 and subsequently rebuilt; *1st battle of* ~, allied defence against German attack, 21st–29th Oct. 1914; *2nd*, 22nd Apr.–24th May 1915, first in which poison gas was used on large scale; *3rd*, allied offensive of July–Nov. 1917, also called Passchendaele.

yr(s) *abbrevs.* Year(s); your(s).

y[t] (pr. as that) *abbrev.* That (conj.): see Y[E].

ytterb'ium *n.* Metallic element of rare-earth group; symbol Yb, at. no. 70, at. wt 173·04. [f. *Ytterby* in Sweden]

ytt'rium *n.* Metallic element closely resembling ytterbium and found with it in gadolinite and other minerals; symbol Y, at. no. 39, at. wt 88·905.

Yucatan (ūk*a*tahn'). Mexican State on the ~ *Peninsula* between the Gulf of Mexico and the Gulf of Honduras, separated from Cuba by the ~ *Strait.*

yŭcc'a *n.* (Plant or flower of) liliaceous genus, native to Central America, Mexico, etc., with woody stem, a crown of usu. rigid narrow pointed leaves, and upright cluster of white bell-shaped flowers.

Yugoslav (ūg'*o*slahv) *adj.* & *n.* (Native, inhabitant) of Yugoslavia; (one) of the South Slavs, comprising Serbs, Croats, and Slovenes; the Serbo-Croatian language.

Yugosla'via (-slahv*ĭa*). Balkan country, formed under a monarchy in Dec. 1918 by the union of Bosnia, Croatia, Dalmatia, Montenegro, Serbia, and Slovenia, proclaimed a republic in Nov. 1945; capital, Belgrade. [f. Serbian, = 'South Slav']

Yukon (ūk'ŏn). A Territory of NW. Canada, constituted a separate political unit in 1898 with its capital at Dawson; river of Canada flowing into the Bering Sea.

yule (ūl) *n.* (also *~-tide*) The Christmas festival; *~-log,* large log burnt on hearth at Christmas.

Yŭn'năn. Town and province of SW. China.

Yves, St.: see IVES.

Y.W.C.A. *abbrev.* YOUNG Women's Christian Association.

Z

Z, z (zĕd, U.S. zē). 26th and last letter of modern English and 23rd of later Roman alphabet, derived through Latin and Greek from Phoenician and ancient Hebrew, I, Z, Z, and representing the voiced form of *s*, especially in loan-words. 1. The letter or its sound; something shaped like the letter z; *from A to Z,* from beginning to end, all through. 2. Third of set of unknown or variable quantities (cf. *x, y*).

Zămbēz'ĭ, bēs'ĭ(-z-). African river, rising in N. Rhodesia and flowing into the Indian Ocean; on its course are the Victoria Falls.

zān'y *n.* Buffoon, simpleton; (hist.) attendant on clown or acrobat awkwardly imitating his master's acts. [Fr. or It. *zani* servants acting as clowns in 'Commedia dell' Arte' (Venetian form of *Gianni* = *Giovanni* John)]

Zănzibâr'. Former sultanate and British protectorate of E. Africa, consisting of the islands of Zanzibar and Pemba and some adjacent islets lying between 5° and 6° S. about 20 miles from the mainland; since 1964, republic with Tanganyika. **Zănzibar'i** *n.* Native of Zanzibar.

Zărathŭs'tra. Old Iranian form of ZOROASTER.

zarēb'a, -rī'ba (-rē-) *n.* Fence, stockade, usu. of thorn-bushes, for defence of camp, village, etc., in Sudan etc. [Arab. *zarība(h)* cattle-pen]

zeal *n.* Ardour, eagerness, enthusiasm, in pursuit of some end or in favour of person or cause. **zeal'ous** (zĕl-) *adj.* **zeal'ously** *adv.*

Zeal'and (zēl-) (Dan. *Sjoelland*). Group of islands in E. Denmark; largest island of this group, on which Copenhagen is situated.

zeal'ot (zĕl-) *n.* 1. Zealous person, fanatical enthusiast. 2. *Z~,* (hist.) member of Jewish sect which aimed at Jewish theocracy over the world and fiercely resisted Romans until fall of Jerusalem in A.D. 70. **zeal'otry** *n.*

Zĕb'ėdee. (N.T.) Father of the Apostles James and John.

zĕb'ra *n.* African equine mammal (*Equus zebra*), related to horse and ass, covered with black or brownish stripes on whitish or buff ground; *Burchell's, Grévy's, ~,* other species; *~ crossing,* striped street-crossing where pedestrians have precedence over other traffic; *~-wood,* (ornamentally striped wood of) various trees and shrubs.

zēb'ū *n.* Humped species of ox (*Bos indicus*), domesticated in India, China, Japan, and parts of Africa.

Zech. *abbrev.* Zechariah (O.T.).

Zĕcharī'ah (-k, *-a*). The 11th of the minor prophets of the O.T.; the O.T. book containing his prophecy.

zĕd *n.* The letter z.

Zĕdėkī'ah (*-a*). Son of Josiah, and the last king of Judah; he rebelled against Nebuchadnezzar and was carried off to Babylon into captivity (2 Kings xxiv–xxv, 2 Chron. xxvi).

zee *n.* (chiefly U.S.) The letter z.

Zeel'and (zēl-, zāl-). Maritime province of the Netherlands, consisting of 6 islands in the Scheldt estuary.

zeitgeist (tsīt'gīst) *n.* Spirit of the times; characteristic trend of thought, culture, etc., of period. [Ger. *zeit* time, *geist* spirit]

zėmin'dâr *n.* (hist., in India, esp. Bengal) Person holding land for which he paid land-tax to British Government. [Hind. f. Pers. *zemīndār* landholder]

zĕm'stvō *n.* (hist.) Russian elective district or provincial council for local government, established by Alexander II (1864), and superseded after 1917 by SOVIETS. [Russ. *zemlya* land]

zėna'na (-ahn-) *n.* 1. Part of dwelling-house in which women of family are or were secluded in India and Persia. 2. ~ (*-cloth*), light thin striped dress-fabric. [Hind., f. Pers. *zanāna* (*zan* woman)]

Zĕnd. Old Iranian, language of the Avesta, forming with Old Persian the Iranian group of Indo-European languages. [f. ZEND-AVESTA, because Zend was erron. thought to denote the language of the books]

Zĕnd-Avĕs'ta. Sacred writings of the Zoroastrians (cf. ZOROASTER, PARSEE). [properly *Avesta-va-Zend,* text with interpretation]

zĕn'ĭth *n.* Point of sky directly overhead (ill. CELESTIAL); (fig.) highest point or state, culmination, acme. **zĕn'ĭthal** *adj.* *~-projection,* projection of a portion of the globe upon a plane tangent to it at its centre, ensuring that all points have their true compass directions from the centre of the map (ill. PROJECTION). [Arab. *samt* (*ar-rās*) way (over the head)]

Zēn'ō¹ of Citium (*c* 300 B.C.). Greek philosopher, founder of STOIC School.

Zēn'ō² of Elea (*c* 450 B.C.). Disciple of PARMENIDES.

Zeph. *abbrev.* Zephaniah (O.T.).

Zĕphanī'ah (*-a*). 9th of the minor prophets of the O.T.; the O.T. book containing his prophecy.

zĕph'yr (*-er*) *n.* 1. The west wind, esp. personified; soft mild gentle wind or breeze. 2. (Undergarment made from) fine very thin woollen material.

Zĕpp'ėlin *n.* Cigar-shaped rigid dirigible airship of the type constructed by Count Ferdinand von Zeppelin in 1900, used in air raids against Britain in the war of 1914–18.

zēr'ō *n.* Figure 0, cipher (now chiefly U.S.); point or line marked 0 on graduated scale, esp. in thermometer or other measuring instrument; temperature corresponding to zero of thermometer, degree of heat reckoned as 0° (in Centigrade and Réaumur scales, freezing-point of water; in Fahrenheit scale, 32° below this); (fig.) lowest point, bottom of scale, nullity, nonentity; *absolute* ~, lowest possible temperature; *at* ~, (fly) below 500 ft; ~ (*-hour*), (orig. and esp. mil.) hour at which any planned operation is timed to begin. [Arab *çifr* cipher]

zĕst *n.* Piquancy, stimulating flavour; keen enjoyment or interest, relish, gusto. [Fr. *zeste* orange- or lemon-peel]

zēt'a *n.* 6th letter (Ζ, ζ) of Greek alphabet.

Zĕt'land. Old name of the SHETLAND Islands.

zeug'ma (zū-) *n.* (gram., rhet.) Figure of speech by which single word is made to refer to two or more words in sentence, esp. when properly applying only to one of them, or applying to them in different senses, e.g. *with weeping eyes and hearts*; freq. used = SYLLEPSIS [Gk, = 'yoking']

Zeus (zūs). In Gk myth., son of Cronos, whom he overthrew and succeeded as supreme god. Zeus and his brothers divided the universe by casting lots, Zeus obtaining heaven, Poseidon the sea, and Hades the underworld. He was regarded as the king and father of gods and men, with powers over all other deities save the Fates, as the dispenser of good and evil, giver of laws and defender of house and hearth. He is represented in various legends as the consort of a number of goddesses and as assuming various disguises in his amours with mortals, but, the Greeks being monogamous, the idea finally prevailed that he had but one legitimate spouse, Hera. He corresponds to the Roman JUPITER.

Zeuxis (zūk'sĭs). Greek painter (5th c. B.C.); his most famous work was a picture of Helen of Troy.

zĭb'ĕt *n.* Asiatic or Indian civet cat (*Vivena zibetha*).

zĭg'zăg *n.* Series of short lines inclined at angles in alternate directions; something having such lines or sharp turns. ~ *adj.* Having form of zigzag; with abrupt alternate left and right turns. ~ *adv.* In zigzag manner or course. ~ *v.i.* Move in zigzag course.

zĭnc *n.* Hard bluish-white metallic element, brittle at subnormal temperatures and above 200° C., but malleable between 100° and 150° C., used for roofing, coating or 'galvanizing' sheet-iron, to make alloys, esp. brass, and in voltaic cells etc.; symbol Zn, at. no. 30, at. wt 65·37; ~ *ointment*, white unguent made from zinc oxide; ~ *oxide*, antiseptic astringent powder used for skin affections. ~ *v.t.* Treat, coat, with zinc.

Zĭng'arō (-ngg-) *n.* (pl. *-rĭ*). Gipsy.

zĭnn'ĭa *n.* Genus of tropical Amer. composite plants with showy flowers, esp. *Z~ elegans*, the common garden species. [J. G. *Zinn* (1727–59), German professor of medicine]

Zī'on. One of the hills of Jerusalem, on which the city of David was built, and which became the centre of Jewish life and worship; hence, the house of God, the Jewish religion, the Christian Church, the Heavenly Jerusalem or kingdom of God, a Christian (esp. nonconformist) place of worship. **Zī'onĭsm** *n.* Movement among modern Jews founded 1897 by an Austrian, Theodor Herzl, which resulted in the re-establishment of a Jewish nation in the land of Israel. **Zī'onĭst** *n.* & *adj.* (Adherent) of Zionism. [Heb. *Tsīyōn* hill]

zĭp *n.* (colloq.) (Movement accompanied by) light sharp sound as of tearing canvas, flying bullet, etc.; (fig.) energy, force, impetus; ~ (*-fastener*), zipper. [imit.]

zĭpp'er *n.* Slide fastener, device consisting of two flexible strips with interlocking metal or plastic projections which can be closed or opened by a sliding clip pulled along them. [orig., proprietary name for kind of boot with slide fastener]

zîr'con *n.* Native silicate of zirconium, occurring usu. in variously coloured tetragonal crystals, of which translucent varieties are used as gems, esp. red or brownish kinds called HYACINTH. [Arab. *zarqūn*]

zîrcōn'ium *n.* Metallic element obtained from zircon etc. as black powder or greyish crystalline substance; symbol Zr, at. no. 40, at. wt 91·22.

Ziska (zĭs'ka *or* shĭsh'ka), Jan (1360–1424). Bohemian nobleman who became leader of the HUSSITES and gained many victories over the Imperialists.

zĭth'er *n.* Musical instrument somewhat like dulcimer with flat sound-box and numerous strings (up to 40), held horizontally and played with fingers and plectrum.

zlōt'y *n.* (pl. same). Principal monetary unit of Poland, = 100 groszy. [Pol., = 'golden']

zōd'ĭăc *n.* 1. A belt of the heavens limited by lines about 8° from the ecliptic on each side, including all apparent positions of the sun and planets as known to the ancient astronomers, and divided into 12 equal parts called *signs of the* ~ (ARIES, TAURUS, GEMINI, CANCER, LEO, VIRGO, LIBRA, SCORPIO, SAGITTARIUS, CAPRICORNUS, AQUARIUS, PISCES) each formerly containing the similarly named *zodiacal constellation* but now by precession of equinoxes coinciding with the constellation that bears the name of the preceding sign (e.g. the constellation Aries is now in Taurus). 2. (now rare) Complete course, circuit, or compass. [Gk *zōdiakos* (*kuklos*) (circle) of figures, f. *zōdion* dim. of *zōon* animal]

zōdī'acal *adj.* Of, in, the zodiac; ~ *light*, luminous tract of sky shaped like tall triangle occas. seen in east before sunrise or in west after sunset esp. in tropics.

zō'ĕtrōpe *n.* Mechanical toy with series of images representing successive positions of moving object, so arranged on inner surface of cylinder that when it is rapidly rotated the object appears to be in motion. [Gk *zoē* life, *tropos* turn]

Zŏff'any, John (1733–1810). German painter who came to England in 1758; famous for his pictures of stage scenes.

Zōl'a, Émile (1840–1902). French naturalistic novelist, author of 'Thérèse Raquin' (1867) and the Rougon-Macquart series of novels dealing with 19th-c. French life.

Zō'laism *n.* Excessively realistic treatment of the grosser sides of human nature, as in Zola's novels.

Zöll'ner's Lines (tsêr-) *n.pl.* Parallel lines made to appear to converge or diverge by series of short lines parallel to each other and intersecting each of them obliquely. [J. K. F. *Zöllner*, German physicist]

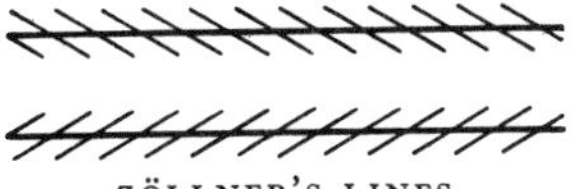
ZÖLLNER'S LINES

zollverein (tsŏl'ferīn) *n.* Union of States having common customs tariff against outsiders and usu. free trade with each other; specif., customs union formed (1834) among the German States under the leadership of Prussia.

zŏm'bĭ(e) *n.* A corpse said to be revived by witchcraft.

zōne *n.* 1. (chiefly poet.) Girdle, belt; circumscribing or enclosing band or ring, esp. one of series of concentric or alternate stripes of colour, light or shade, etc., extending round something or over surface. 2. Each of 5 encircling regions, distinguished by differences of climate, and named the *torrid* ~, (north and south) *temperate* ~*s*, and (arctic and antarctic) *frigid* ~*s*, into which surface of earth is divided by tropics of Cancer and Capricorn and polar circles (ill. EARTH). 3. Area enclosed between two concentric circles; any well-defined tract or region of more or less belt-like form. 4. Any of 24 areas each bounded by two lines of longitude 15 degrees apart, the first of which extends 7½ degrees E. and W. of the meridian of Greenwich, and within each of which the standard (*zone*) time is the same and differs from that of the adjacent areas by one hour. 5. Any part of a town or region divided off from other parts for a particular purpose (esp. in town and country planning). 6. (math.) Part of surface of sphere enclosed between two parallel planes, or of surface of any solid of revolution contained between two planes perpendicular to the axis. 7. (crystall.) Series of faces in crystal having their lines of intersection parallel. **zōn'al** *adj.* **zōn'ally** *adv.* **zōne** *v.t.* Mark, encircle, with a zone, divide into zones (esp. in town and country planning). [f. L *zona*, f. Gr. *zōnē* girdle]

zōō *n.* ZOOLOGICAL Gardens.

zōogėŏg'raphy *n.* (Study of) the geographical distribution of animals. **zōogėŏg'rapher** *n.* **zōogēogrăph'ical** *adj.*

zōŏg'raphy *n.* Descriptive zoology. **zōŏg'rapher** *n.* **zōogrăph'ical** *adj.*

zō'oid *n.* Individual member of a colony of animals joined together.

zōŏl'atry *n.* Worship of animals.

zōŏl'ogy *n.* Branch of biology dealing with the animal kingdom and the physiology, classification, habits, etc., of its members. **zōŏl'ogist** *n.* **zōolŏ'gical** *adj.* *Z~ Gardens*, orig. gardens of London Zoological Society in Regent's Park, housing the society's collection of wild animals; any garden or park in which wild animals are kept for public exhibition.

zōōm *v.* Make loud low-pitched buzzing sound; (of aircraft) climb for short time at high speed and very steep angle; make (aircraft) climb thus. [imit.]

zōomōrph'ic *adj.* Representing or imitating animal forms; having form of an animal; attributing form or nature of animal to something, esp. deity.

zō'ophȳte *n.* Any of various animals of low organization, usu. fixed, and freq. resembling plants or flowers in having branched or radiating structure, as crinoids, sea-anemones, corals, sponges, etc. **zōophȳt'ic** *adj.*

zō'ospōre. Spore occurring in certain algae, fungi, etc., having power of locomotion.

Zōrn'dōrf (ts-). Place in Brandenburg where Frederick the Great defeated the Russians in 1758.

Zŏrōăs'ter. (also *Zerduscht*, *Zarathustra*). A Persian believed to have lived in the 6th c. B.C., founder of the dualistic religious system of the Magi and ancient Persia which survives among the PARSEES of India; its scriptures, the ZEND-AVESTA, teach that Ormazd, lord of goodness and light and creator of mankind, is ceaselessly at war with Ahriman and the evil spirits of darkness. **Zŏrōăs'trian** *adj.* & *n.* **Zŏrōăs'trianism** *n.*

Zouave (zōō'ahv) *n.* Member of corps of light infantry orig. recruited from Zouaoua tribe of Algiers but now chiefly French soldiers distinguished for physique and dash, wearing uniform of bright-coloured baggy trousers, short open-fronted embroidered jacket, wide sash, and turban or tasselled cap.

zounds (zōō-) *int.* (archaic) Used in oaths and asseverations, colloquial shortening of *by God's wounds*.

zucchetto (tsōōkĕt'ō) *n.* Small round skull-cap worn by R.C. ecclesiastics. The pope's is white; a cardinal's, red; a bishop's, violet; that of others, black.

Zuider (*or* Zuyder) Zee (zīd'*er* *or* zoid'*er* zē). Large shallow inlet of the North Sea in the Netherlands, the reclamation of which was begun in 1924 for the purpose of forming a new province. [Du., = 'southern sea']

Zu'lu (zōōl'ōō) *n.* & *adj.* (Member, language) of a South African Bantu people inhabiting NE. part of Natal. **Zul'ulănd.** African province annexed to Natal in 1897.

Zurich (zūrĭk). (Ger. *Zürich*) Canton of E. Switzerland; the capital of the canton, situated on *Lake ~*.

Zwĭng'lĭ (-ngg-), Ulrich (1484–1531). Swiss religious reformer; his doctrines, which contain elements of Reformed as distinguished from Lutheran doctrine, led to civil war between the Swiss cantons, in which he was killed. **Zwĭnglĭan** *adj.* & *n.* (Follower) of Zwingli. **Zwĭnglĭanĭsm** *n.*

zȳgodăc'tȳl *adj.* & *n.* (Bird) with toes arranged in pairs, two before and two behind, e.g. parrot.

zȳgōm'a *n.* Bony arch on each side of skull of vertebrates, joining cranial and facial bones, and consisting of cheek-bone and its connexions (ill. HEAD). **zȳgomăt'ic** *adj.*

zȳgomōrph'ic *adj.* Having one plane of symmetry (esp. of flowers).

zȳg'ospōre *n.* (In some algae and fungi) spore or germ-cell arising from fusion of two similar cells.

zȳg'ōte *n.* (biol.) Cell arising from union of two reproductive cells or gametes, fertilized ovum (ill. ALGA). **zȳgŏt'ic** *adj.*

zȳ'mase *n.* (biochem.) Any of a group of enzymes converting glucose and a few other carbohydrates, in the presence of oxygen, into carbon dioxide and water, or, in the absence of oxygen, into alcohol and carbon dioxide, or into lactic acid.

zȳmŏl'ysĭs *n.* Action of enzymes, changes produced by this. **zȳmolȳt'ic** *adj.*

zȳmōs'ĭs *n.* Fermentation; zymotic disease. **zȳmŏt'ic** *adj.* Of fermentation; (med., of disease, now rare) infectious or contagious.

zȳm'ūrgy *n.* Branch of applied chemistry dealing with science of wine-making, brewing, and distilling.

ADDENDA

ă'cronȳm *n.* Word formed from initial letters of other words (e.g. *Anzac*, *Nato*, *radar*).

A.L.A. *abbrev.* American Library Association.

ălfăl'fa *n.* Lucerne.

ăn'orăk *n.* Long hooded jacket of skin or cloth, worn esp. in Arctic regions; weather-proof jacket of similar style for sports wear. [Eskimo *anoraq*]

ăpotropā'ic *adj.* Having or reputed to have the power of averting evil influence or ill luck.

avant-garde (ăvŏng-gārd) *n.* The pioneers or innovators in any art in a particular period (freq. attrib.). [F]

aweigh (*a*wā') *adv.* (Of anchor) just raised from bottom in weighing.

Bahrein, Bahrain (-rān). An independent sheikhdom consisting of a group of islands, the largest being Bahrein, in the Persian Gulf.

beat'nĭk *n.* (also *beat*) One of the *beat generation* (post 1939–45 war), who disclaims social responsibility, and by dress and behaviour shows indifference to or contempt for conventional society.

Bĕnn'ėtt, Enoch Arnold (1867–1931). English novelist; author of novels of life in the Potteries, including 'The Old Wives' Tale' (1908), 'Clayhanger' (1910), 'Riceyman Steps' (1923), etc.

booth. *telephone* ~, compartment containing a telephone.

Bornholm disease (-hōm) *n.* Epidemic pleurodynia, a virus disease characterized by acute pain and a short febrile period. [*Bornholm*, Dan. island in Baltic]

Bŏtswan'a (-ahn-). Republic of E. Africa, formerly British protectorate of BECHUANALAND; independent 1966; capital, Gaberones.

bouclé (bo͞o'klā). *n.* Yarn of looped or curled ply; fabric of this.

brief[1]. ~*-case*, flat, rectangular, usu. leather, case for carrying documents etc.

Burundi (bo͝orŭn'di). Republic on E. side of Lake Tanganyika; formerly a Belgian trusteeship under the UNITED NATIONS; became an independent state in 1962; capital, Bujumbura (formerly Usumbura).

capsule. 6. Detachable nosecone of rocket or space missile for carrying astronaut, instruments for recording and transmitting scientific data, etc.

Central African Republic. Formerly the French colony of Ubanghi Shari lying just N. of the Equator; became fully independent 1960; capital, Bangui.

chrōmatŏg'raphy (k-) *n.* Procedure for separation and purification of the components of a mixture by various methods of partition, adsorption, ion exchange, electrophoresis, etc. The name was originally applied to the separation of substances which appeared as a series of coloured bands (a *chromatogram*), but the method is now used to isolate and identify colourless compounds also.

clamp[2] *n.* Compact mound or pile, esp. of bricks for burning in the open air, or of potatoes etc. for storing within a cover of straw and earth.

C.M.B. *abbrev.* (certificated by) Central Midwives' Board; coastal motor-boat.

C.N.D., CND *abbrev.* Campaign for Nuclear Disarmament.

C.O.I. *abbrev.* Central Office of Information.

commercial. *n.* (also) Radio or television advertising announcement or programme.

consôr'tium (-shĭ-) *n.* (pl. *-ia*). 1. Temporary co-operation of a number of powers, large banks, etc., for a common purpose (e.g. to give financial help to a State). 2. (law) The right of either spouse to conjugal companionship etc. of the other.

co-operative. ~ *n.* Co-operative factory, farm, or other enterprise.

count[1]. (n. 1.) ~*-down*, audible reverse counting, usu. in seconds, from a given number to zero, marking the lapse of time before an event, esp. the launching of a missile etc.

C.R.O. *abbrev.* Commonwealth Relations Office.

cross-. ~*staff*, (obs.) navigational instrument for measuring altitudes (superseded by quadrant); surveying instrument for setting out right angles.

Day-Lewis, Cecil (1904–). English poet (also detective novelist, pseudonym 'Nicholas Blake'); poet laureate 1968– .

dĭdjerĭdo͞o' *n.* Australian aboriginal wind musical instrument of tubular shape.

dîrn'dl *n.* Dress with tight bodice and full skirt; full skirt with tight waist-band.

dĭs'cothèque (-tĕk) *n.* Dance-hall or night-club where dancing takes place to the accompaniment of music on records.

DNA *abbrev.* Deoxyribonucleic acid, generic term for polymers made up of different kinds of *nucleotide units* which are compounds of the pentose sugar *deoxyribose* attached to a nitrogenous base and linked by phosphate. DNA occurs in the chromosomes of cell nuclei and controls the passing on of hereditary characters.

Dŏpp'ler effect *n.* (phys.) The observed change in frequency of electro-magnetic and sound waves, caused by relative motion between observer and source (e.g. the apparent change of pitch of sound produced by a body when approaching, passing, and receding at speed). [C. J. *Doppler* (1803–53), Austrian physicist]

drogue. 3. Cone similar to 2. towed by life-boats etc. to reduce speed.

drosŏph'ĭla *n.* Fly of genus *D*~, used in genetic research; common fruit-fly.

E.F.T.A., Ef'ta *abbrev.* European Free Trade Association.

ėlĕctrophorēs'is *n.* The migration of colloidal particles under the influence of an electric field; combined with chromatography constitutes a technique for the separation and purification of compounds. **ėlĕctrophorĕt'ic** *adj.*

El'iot (ĕl-), Thomas Stearns (1888–1965). Poet and critic, born in St. Louis, Missouri; naturalized British citizen 1927; author of 'The Waste Land' (1922), 'Murder in the Cathedral' (1935), 'Four Quartets' (1944), etc.

Ern'ie (ẽr-) *n.* Device for drawing prize-winning numbers of premium bonds. [*e*lectronic *r*andom *n*umber *i*ndicator *e*quipment]

ĕs'calāte *v.i.* Increase or expand by degrees. **ĕscalā'tion** *n.*

fĕnn'ėc *n.* Large-eared fox (*Fennecus zerda*) of African and Asian deserts; the smallest known fox (2 ft long).

fissi- comb. form of L *fissus* cleft, divided.

fĭssĭdăc'tȳl *adj.* With digits divided.

fĭssĭp'arous *adj.* Reproducing by fission.

flu'orĭdā'tion (-o͞o-) *n.* (esp.) Addition of traces of fluoride to public water-supply with the object of reducing the incidence of dental caries.

foundation. 3. ~ *garment*, woman's supporting undergarment, e.g. corset.

fruit. 5. ~ *machine*, coin-operated gambling machine.

găng'lĭng (-ngg-) *adj.* Loosely built, lanky.

G.A.T.T. *abbrev.* General Agreement on Tariffs and Trade.

gĭbberĕll'ic acid *n.* A white crystalline solid isolated from a soil-borne pathogenic fungus (*Gibberella fujikuroi*). Its presence in minute traces induces the breaking of dormancy, early flowering and accelerated vegetative growth in a wide variety of plants, though many of its effects are due mainly to cell elongation.

gĭmm'ĭck (g-) *n.* (sl., orig. U.S.) Tricky device, device adopted for the purpose of attracting attention or publicity.

grăd *n.* Unit of angular measure, $^1/_{1000}$ part of a right angle.

Guyăn'a (gī-). The former colony of British Guiana, situated on NE. coast of S. America; independent State and member of the British Commonwealth 1966; capital, Georgetown.

Home (hŭm), Sir Alexander Frederick Douglas-, formerly 14th Earl of Home (1903–). British Conservative politician; foreign secretary 1957–63; prime minister 1963–4.

Hŏv'ercraft (-ahft) *n.* Vehicle that travels low over land or water on a cushion of compressed air provided by a downward blast. [trade-mark]

I.C.B.M. *abbrev.* Inter-continental ballistic missile.

I.R.B.M. *abbrev.* Intermediate-range ballistic missile.

I.R.O. *abbrev.* International Refugee Organization.

I.T.A. *abbrev.* Independent Television Authority.

Jĭn'nah, Mohammed Ali (1876–1948). Moslem lawyer; first governor-general of Pakistan (1947–8).

juke-box (jo͞ok-) *n.* Machine that automatically plays selected gramophone records when coin is inserted.

kĭbbutz' (-o͞o-) *n.* (pl. *-im*). Communal (esp. agricultural) settlement in Israel. [mod. Heb.]

lās'er (-z-) *n.* = *optical* MASER. [*l*ight *a*mplification by *s*timulated *e*mission of *r*adiation]

launderĕtte' *n.* Self-service laundry. [trade-mark]

L.E.A. *abbrev.* Local Education Authority.

Leeuwenhoek (lā'venho͝ok), Anton van (1632–1723). Dutch microscopist and naturalist; using single-lens microscopes of his own making he was the first to observe bacteria, protozoa, and other minute forms of life.

Lĕsōth'ō. State in S. Africa, independent since 1966 (formerly Basutoland); capital, Maseru.

Mala'wi (-lah-). State of central Africa, W. and S. of Lake Nyasa; formerly the British protectorate of Nyasaland; independent 1964; capital, Zomba.

Mal'i (-ah-), Inland State in NW. Africa, formerly the French colony of Soudan (see SUDAN); since 1958 an autonomous republic within the French Community; capital, Bamako.

măn'ĭc *adj.* Of, affected with, mania.

măn'ĭc-deprĕss'ĭve *adj.* Characterized by alternating mania and depression. ~ *n.* Person suffering from manic-depressive psychosis.

mās'er (-z-) *n.* Device for amplifying microwaves; *optical* ~ (for amplifying light waves). [*m*icrowave *a*mplification by *s*timulated *e*mission of *r*adiation]

mayday *n.* International radio-telephonic distress signal from aircraft or ship. [pron. of Fr. *m' aidez* help me]

may'hĕm *n.* Crime of causing malicious personal injury; also fig.

mĭl *n.* Unit of length, = $^1/_{1000}$ in., used in measuring diameter of wire etc.

M.O.W.B. *abbrev.* Ministry of Works and Public Buildings.

M.P.N.I. *abbrev.* Ministry of Pensions and National Insurance.

M.R.B.M. *abbrev.* Medium-range ballistic missile.

M.S.A. *abbrev.* Mutual Security Agency (replacing E.C.A.).

Nass'er (nah-), Gamel Abdel (1918–). Egyptian army officer and politician; president of Egypt 1954; president of United Arab Republic 1958– .

N.C.U. *abbrev.* National Cyclists' Union.

N.E.D.C. *abbrev.* National Economic Development Council (colloq. Nĕdd'y).

New'lands, John Alexander Reina (1837–98). English chemist who formulated (1863–6) what he called the Law of Octaves, according to which, if the chemical elements be arranged in order of their atomic weights, similarity in chemical and physical properties will be seen to occur at regular intervals: the eighth element resembling the first, the ninth the second, and so on. The periodic classification of the elements was independently carried much further by Mendeleev (1869) and Lothar Meyer (1870): see PERIODIC *law*.

N.I.C. *abbrev.* National Incomes Commission (colloq. Nĭck'y).

Nĭx'on, Richard Milhous (1913–). Vice-president of the U.S. 1953–61; 37th president 1969– .

non-U *abbrev.* Not upper-class.

O.E.C.D. *abbrev.* Organization for European Co-operation and Development (formerly O.E.E.C.)

ŏm'budsman (-bŏŏd-) *n.* Person appointed to investigate private individuals' grievances against governmental or local authorities.

out'băck *adj.* & *n.* (Austral.) (Of) the more remote settlements.

P.D.S.A. *abbrev.* People's Dispensary for Sick Animals.

pẽrm'afrŏst *n.* Permanently frozen subsoil in arctic regions. [f. *perma*(nent) *frost*]

premium. 1. ~ (*savings*) *bond*, government security with cash prizes drawn weekly in place of regular interest.

prōg'răm(me). (also) Series of operations to be performed by computer. ~ *v.t.* Prepare programme for (computer).

psychėdĕl'ĭc (sīk-) *adj.* (Of drug) hallucinatory, giving illusion of freedom from limitations of reality; suggesting experience or effect of such drugs.

quadrant. (also) Surveying instrument with mirrors for measuring altitudes up to 90° with a graduated arc of 8th part of circle; octant, superseded by sextant.

R.A.V.C. *abbrev.* Royal Army Veterinary Corp.

revenant (rĕvenahṅ, rĕv'enant) *n.* One who returns, esp. after long absence or from the dead; a ghost.

RNA *abbrev.* Ribonucleic acid, generic term for polymers made up of different kinds of *nucleotide units* which are compounds of the pentose sugar *ribose* attached to a nitrogenous base and linked by phosphate. RNA is present in the nucleoli and cytoplasm of living cells and associated with the ability of the cell to synthesize proteins. Cf. DNA.

R.S.D., R.S.E. *abbrevs.* Royal Society of Dublin, of Edinburgh.

Ruăn'da (rōō-). Small State in N. Central Africa, between Tanganyika and the Congolese Republic; independent republic 1962; capital, Kigali.

Rŭth'erford, Ernest, 1st Baron Rutherford of Nelson (1871–1937). Physicist, born in New Zealand; professor at Montreal, Manchester, and, from 1919, Cavendish Professor of Physics at Cambridge; his study of radioactivity led to the discovery of nuclear fission and atomic energy.

scrŭff'y *adj.* Despicable, mean, shabby.

S.C.C. *abbrev.* Sea Cadet Corps.

semĕs'ter *n.* Half-year course or term in German and other universities.

S.E.N. *abbrev.* State Enrolled Nurse.

Southern Ye'mĕn (sŭthn; yā-). Peoples' Republic of S. Yemen set up in 1967; consisting of former Federation of S. Arabia and E. Aden Protectorate; capital, Aden.

Stalingrad. Since 1962 renamed Volgograd.

S.T.D. *abbrev.* Subscriber trunk dialling (telephony).

Tănzān'ia (*or* -zanē'*a*). Name of United Republic of Tanganyika and Zanzibar, formed in 1964; capital, Dar es Salaam.

teach'-ĭn *n.* (colloq.) Kind of oral symposium on subject of topical interest.

thermodynamics. *1st law of* ~: during transformation of heat into another form of energy there is a constant relation between the amount of heat expended and the energy gained; the same is true of the reverse process. *2nd law of* ~: heat cannot pass of its own accord from a colder to a hotter body.

thẽrmonūc'lėar *adj.* Of or concerned with reactions involving the fusion of atomic nuclei at very high temperatures, as in a hydrogen bomb.

touché (tōō'shā) *adj.* (lit.) Touched, esp. (fencing) by opponent's foil; (as *int.*) acknowledgement of home thrust in argument. [F]

trăm'polĭn(e) *n.* Elastic contrivance resembling spring-mattress used in physical training and by acrobats etc.

trănsdū'cer *n.* Device that accepts power from one part of a system and emits power in a different form to another part, as between electrical, mechanical, or acoustic parts.

trănsĭs'tor *n.* Small electronic device using the flow of electrons in a solid to perform most of the functions of a thermionic valve; used in portable radio sets, hearing aids, and other kinds of electronic apparatus; also attrib., as ~ *radio*.

trănsĭs'torīzed *adj.* Fitted with transistors instead of valves.

U *abbrev.* Upper-class.

U.A.R. *abbrev.* United Arab Republic.

Upper Vŏl'ta. Inland republic of W. Africa, formerly part of the French Colony of the Ivory Coast; independent since 1960; capital, Ouagadougou.

Vŏl'gogrăd. New name of STALINGRAD.

V.T.O.L. *abbrev.* Vertical take-off and landing (aircraft).

W.R.I. *abbrev.* War Risk Insurance; Women's Rural Institute.

Zăm'bia. Republic of Central Africa; formerly the British protectorate of N. Rhodesia; independent 1964; capital, Lusaka.

APPENDIXES

APPENDIX I

ROMAN EMPERORS

Augustus	27 B.C.–A.D. 14
Tiberius	14–37
Gaius (Caligula)	37–41
Claudius	41–54
Nero	54–68
Galba	68–69
Otho	69
Vitellius	69
Vespasian	69–79
Titus	79–81
Domitian	81–96
Nerva	96–98
Trajan	98–117
Hadrian	117–138
Antoninus Pius	138–161
Marcus Aurelius and Lucius Verus	161–169
Marcus Aurelius alone	169–177
Marcus Aurelius and Commodus	177–180
Commodus alone	180–192
Pertinax	193
Didius Julianus	193
Septimius Severus alone	193–198
Septimius Severus and Antoninus (Caracalla)	198–209
Septimius Severus, Antoninus (Caracalla), and Geta	209–211
Antoninus (Caracalla) and Geta	211–212
Antoninus (Caracalla) alone	212–217
Macrinus alone	217–218
Macrinus and Diadumenianus	218
Antoninus (Elagabalus)	218–222
Severus Alexander	222–235
Maximinus Thrax	235–238
Gordian I and Gordian II	238
Pupienus and Balbinus	238
Gordian III	238–244
Philip the Arabian alone	244–247
Philip the Arabian and Philip	247–249
Decius	249–251
Trebonianus Gallus and Volusianus	251–253
Aemilianus	253
Valerian and Gallienus	253–260
Gallienus alone	260–268
Claudius II (Gothicus)	268–270
Quintillus	270
Aurelian	270–275
Tacitus	275–276
Florian	276
Probus	276–282
Carus	282–283
Carinus and Numerianus	283–284
Diocletian alone	284–286
Diocletian and Maximian	286–305
Constantius I and Galerius	305–306
Galerius, Severus, and Constantine I	306–307
Galerius, Licinius, and Constantine I	307–310
Galerius, Licinius, Constantine I, and Maximinus Daia	310–311
Licinius and Constantine I	311–324
Constantine I alone	324–337
Constantine II, Constantius II, and Constans	337–340
Constantius II and Constans	340–350
Constantius II alone	350–361
Julian (the Apostate)	361–363
Jovian	363–364
Valentinian I and Valens	364–367
Valentinian I, Valens, and Gratian	367–375
Valens, Gratian, and Valentinian II	375–378
Gratian, Valentinian II, and Theodosius I	379–383
Valentinian II, Theodosius I, and Arcadius	383–392
Theodosius I and Arcadius	392–393
Theodosius I, Arcadius, and Honorius	393–395

Western Emperors

Honorius	395–423
Constantius III	421
Valentinian III	425–455
Petronius Maximus	455
Avitus	455–456
Majorian	457–461
Libius Severus	461–465
Anthemius	467–472
Olybrius	472
Glycerius	473
Julius Nepos	473–475
Romulus Augustulus	475–476

Eastern Emperors

Arcadius	395–408
Theodosius II	408–450
Marcian	450–457
Leo I	457–474
Leo II	473–474
Zeno	474–491
Anastasius I	491–518
Justin I	518–527
Justinian I	527–565
Tiberius II, Constantinus	578–582
Maurice	582–602
Phocas	602–610
Heraclius Constantinus and Heracleonas	641–642
Constans II	642–668
Constantine IV	668–685
Justinian II	705–711
Philippicus	711–713

Anastasius II, Artemius	713–715	Leo IV	775–779
Theodosius III	715–717	Constantine VI	779–797
Leo III, the Isaurian	717–740	Irene	797–802
Constantine V, Copronymus	740–775		

APPENDIX II

EMPERORS OF THE WESTERN (OR HOLY ROMAN) EMPIRE

• Indicates those medieval emperors who were never crowned at Rome.

Frankish Emperors

Charles the Great	800–814
Louis the Pious	814–840
Lothar I	840–855
Louis II	(in Italy) 855–875
Charles (II) the Bald	875–877
Charles (III) the Fat	881–887
Guy of Spoleto	(in Italy) 891–894
Lambert of Spoleto	(in Italy) 894–898
Arnulf of Carinthia	896–899

Saxon Emperors

Otto I	962–973
Otto II	973–983
Otto III	983–1002
Henry II	1002–1024

Franconian or Salian Emperors

Conrad II	1024–1039
Henry III	1039–1056
Henry IV	1056–1106
Henry V	1106–1125
Lothar II	1125–1137

Hohenstaufen Emperors

Conrad III•	1138–1152
Frederick I Barbarossa	1152–1190
Henry VI	1190–1197
Philip•	1198–1208
Otto IV	1198–1212
Frederick II	1212–1250
Conrad IV•	1250–1254

Interregnum

Rudolph I of Habsburg•	1273–1291
Adolf of Nassau•	1292–1298
Albert I of Habsburg•	1298–1308
Henry VII of Luxemburg	1308–1313
Louis IV of Bavaria	1314–1347

Luxemburg Emperors

Charles IV	1347–1378
Wenzel or Wenceslas•	1378–1400
Rupert of the Palatinate•	1400–1410
Sigismund	1410–1437

Habsburg Emperors

Albert II•	1438–1439
Frederick III	1440–1493
Maximilian I	1493–1519
Charles V	1519–1556
Ferdinand I	1556–1564
Maximilian II	1564–1576
Rudolph II	1576–1612
Matthias	1612–1619
Ferdinand II	1619–1637
Ferdinand III	1637–1657
Leopold I	1658–1705
Joseph I	1705–1711
Charles VI	1711–1740
Charles VII (Bavaria)	1742–1745
Francis I (Lorraine)	1745–1765
Joseph II	1765–1790
Leopold II	1790–1792
Francis II	1792–1806

APPENDIX III

THE POPES SINCE THE SEVENTH CENTURY

Gregory I	590–604	John IV	640–642
Sabinian	604–606	Theodore I	642–649
Boniface III	607	Martin I	649–653
Boniface IV	608–615	Eugenius I	654–657
Deusdedit I	615–618	Vitalian	657–672
Boniface V	619–625	Deusdedit II (Adeodatus)	672–676
Honorius I	625–638	Donus	676–678
Severinus	640	Agatho	678–681

Leo II	682–683
Benedict II	684–685
John V	685–686
Conon	686–687
[Theodore and Paschal, 687, antipopes]	
Sergius I	687–701
John VI	701–705
John VII	705–707
Sisinnius	708
Constantine	708–715
Gregory II	715–731
Gregory III	731–741
Zachary	741–752
Stephen II	752
Stephen III	752–757
Paul I	757–767
[Constantine, 767–768; Philip 768; antipopes]	
Stephen IV	768–772
Adrian I	772–795
Leo III	795–816
Stephen V	816–817
Paschal I	817–824
Eugenius II	824–827
Valentine	827
Gregory IV	827–844
[John, antipope]	
Sergius II	844–847
Leo IV	847–855
Benedict III	855–858
[Anastasius, 855, antipope]	
Nicholas I	858–867
Adrian II	867–872
John VIII	872–882
Marinus (Martin) I	882–884
Adrian III	884–885
Stephen VI	885–891
Formosus	891–896
Boniface VI	896
Stephen VII	896
Romanus	897
Theodore II	897
John IX	898–900
Benedict IV	900–903
Leo V	903
[Christopher, 903, antipope]	
Sergius III	904–911
Anastasius III	911–913
Lando	913–914
John X	914–928
Leo VI	928
Stephen VIII	929–931
John XI	931–936
Leo VII	936–939
Stephen IX	939–942
Marinus II (Martin III)	942–946
Agapitus II	946–955
John XII	955–963
Leo VIII	963–965
Benedict V	964
John XIII	965–972
Benedict VI	973–974
[Boniface VII, antipope, 974]	
Benedict VII	974–983
John XIV	983–984
John XV	985–996
Gregory V	996–999
[John XVI, 997–998, antipope]	
Sylvester II	999–1003
John XVII	1003
John XVIII	1004–1009
Sergius IV	1009–1112
Benedict VIII	1012–1024
John XIX	1024–1032
Benedict IX	1032–1046
[Sylvester III, 1045, antipope]	
Gregory VI	1045–1046
Clement II	1046–1047
Benedict IX again	1047–1048
Damasus II	1048
Leo IX	1049–1054
Victor II	1055–1057
Stephen X	1057–1058
[Benedict X, 1058–1059, antipope]	
Nicholas II	1059–1061
Alexander II	1061–1073
[Honorius II, 1061–1072, antipope]	
Gregory VII	1073–1085
[Clement III, 1084–1100, antipope]	
Victor III	1086–1087
Urban II	1088–1099
Paschal II	1099–1118
[Theodoric, 1100; Albert, 1102; Sylvester IV, 1105–1111; antipopes]	
Gelasius II	1118–1119
[Gregory VIII, 1118–1121, antipope]	
Calixtus II	1119–1124
Honorius II	1124–1130
Innocent II	1130–1143
[Anacletus IV, 1130–1138, antipope]	
Celestine II	1143–1144
Lucius II	1144–1145
Eugenius III	1145–1153
Anastasius IV	1153–1154
Adrian IV	1154–1159
Alexander III	1159–1181
[Victor IV, 1159–1164; Paschal III, 1164–1168; Calixtus III, 1168–1178; Innocent III, 1179–1180; antipopes]	
Lucius III	1181–1185
Urban III	1185–1187
Gregory VIII	1187
Clement III	1187–1191
Celestine III	1191–1198
Innocent III	1198–1216
Honorius III	1216–1227
Gregory IX	1227–1241
Celestine IV	1241
Innocent IV	1243–1254
Alexander IV	1254–1261
Urban IV	1261–1264
Clement IV	1265–1268
Gregory X	1271–1276
Innocent V	1276
Adrian V	1276
John XXI	1276–1277
Nicholas III	1277–1280
Martin IV	1281–1285
Honorius IV	1285–1287
Nicholas IV	1288–1292
Celestine V	1294
Boniface VIII	1294–1303
Benedict XI	1303–1304
Clement V	1305–1314
John XXII	1316–1334
[Nicholas V, 1328–1330, antipope]	
Benedict XII	1334–1342
Clement VI	1342–1352

Innocent VI	1352–1362
Urban V	1362–1370
Gregory XI	1370–1378
Urban VI	1378–1389
[Clement VII, 1378–1394, antipope]	
Boniface IX	1389–1404
[Benedict XIII, 1394–1417, antipope]	
Innocent VII	1404–1406
Gregory XII	1406–1415
[Alexander V, 1409–1410; John XXIII, 1410–1419; antipopes]	
Martin V	1417–1431
Eugenius IV	1431–1447
[Felix V, 1439–1449, antipope]	
Nicholas V	1447–1455
Calixtus III	1455–1458
Pius II	1458–1464
Paul II	1464–1471
Sixtus IV	1471–1484
Innocent VIII	1484–1492
Alexander VI	1492–1503
Pius III	1503
Julius II	1503–1513
Leo X	1513–1521
Adrian VI	1522–1523
Clement VII	1523–1534
Paul III	1534–1549
Julius III	1550–1555
Marcellus II	1555
Paul IV	1555–1559
Pius IV	1559–1565
Pius V	1566–1572
Gregory XIII	1572–1585
Sixtus V	1585–1590
Urban VII	1590
Gregory XIV	1590–1591
Innocent IX	1591
Clement VIII	1592–1605
Leo XI	1605
Paul V	1605–1621
Gregory XV	1621–1623
Urban VIII	1623–1644
Innocent X	1644–1655
Alexander VII	1655–1667
Clement IX	1667–1669
Clement X	1670–1676
Innocent XI	1676–1689
Alexander VIII	1689–1691
Innocent XII	1691–1700
Clement XI	1700–1721
Innocent XIII	1721–1724
Benedict XIII	1724–1730
Clement XII	1730–1740
Benedict XIV	1740–1758
Clement XIII	1758–1769
Clement XIV	1769–1774
Pius VI	1775–1799
Pius VII	1800–1823
Leo XII	1823–1829
Pius VIII	1829–1830
Gregory XVI	1831–1846
Pius IX	1846–1878
Leo XIII	1878–1903
Pius X	1903–1914
Benedict XV	1914–1922
Pius XI	1922–1939
Pius XII	1939–1958
John XXIII	1958–1963
Paul VI	1963–

APPENDIX IV

RULERS OF ENGLAND AND OF THE UNITED KINGDOM

Saxon Line

Edwy	955–959
Edgar	959–975
Edward the Martyr	975–979
Ethelred the Unready	979–1016
Edmund Ironside	1016

Danish Line

Canute (Cnut)	1016–1035
Harold I	1035–1040
Hardicanute (Harthacnut)	1040–1042

Saxon Line

Edward the Confessor	1042–1066
Harold II (Godwinson)	1066

House of Normandy

William I (the Conqueror)	1066–1087
William II	1087–1100
Henry I	1100–1135
Stephen	1135–1154

House of Plantagenet

Henry II	1154–1189
Richard I	1189–1199
John	1199–1216
Henry III	1216–1272
Edward I	1272–1307
Edward II	1307–1327
Edward III	1327–1377
Richard II	1377–1399

House of Lancaster

Henry IV	1399–1413
Henry V	1413–1422
Henry VI	1422–1461

House of York

Edward IV	1461–1483
Edward V	1483
Richard III	1483–1485

House of Tudor

Henry VII	1485–1509
Henry VIII	1509–1547

Edward VI	1547–1553
Mary I	1553–1558
Elizabeth I	1558–1603

House of Stuart

James I of England and VI of Scotland	1603–1625
Charles I	1625–1649

Commonwealth (declared 1649)

Oliver Cromwell, Lord Protector	1653–1658
Richard Cromwell	1658–1659

House of Stuart

Charles II	1660–1685
James II	1685–1688
William III and Mary II (Mary d. 1694)	1689–1702
Anne	1702–1714

House of Hanover

George I	1714–1727
George II	1727–1760
George III	1760–1820
George IV	1820–1830
William IV	1830–1837
Victoria	1837–1901

House of Saxe-Coburg

Edward VII	1901–1910

House of Windsor

George V	1910–1936
Edward VIII	1936
George VI	1936–1952
Elizabeth II	1952–

APPENDIX V

PRIME MINISTERS OF GREAT BRITAIN

Sir Robert Walpole	1730–1741
Earl of Wilmington	1741–1743
Henry Pelham	1743–1754
Duke of Newcastle	1754–1756
Duke of Devonshire	1756–1757
Duke of Newcastle	1757–1762
Earl of Bute	1762–1763
George Grenville	1763–1765
Marquis of Rockingham	1765–1766
Earl of Chatham	1766–1768
Duke of Grafton	1768–1770
Lord North	1770–1782
Marquis of Rockingham	1782
Earl of Shelburne	1782–1783
Duke of Portland	1783
William Pitt	1783–1801
Henry Addington	1801–1804
William Pitt	1804–1806
Lord William Grenville	1806–1807
Duke of Portland	1807–1809
Spencer Perceval	1809–1812
Earl of Liverpool	1812–1827
George Canning	1827
Viscount Goderich	1827–1828
Duke of Wellington	1828–1830
Earl Grey	1830–1834
Viscount Melbourne	1834
Duke of Wellington	1834
Sir Robert Peel	1834–1835
Viscount Melbourne	1835–1841
Sir Robert Peel	1841–1846
Lord John Russell	1846–1852
Earl of Derby	1852
Earl of Aberdeen	1852–1855
Viscount Palmerston	1855–1858
Earl of Derby	1858–1859
Viscount Palmerston	1859–1865
Earl Russell	1865–1866
Earl of Derby	1866–1868
Benjamin Disraeli	1868
William Ewart Gladstone	1868–1874
Benjamin Disraeli, Earl of Beaconsfield	1874–1880
William Ewart Gladstone	1880–1885
Marquis of Salisbury	1885–1886
William Ewart Gladstone	1886
Marquis of Salisbury	1886–1892
William Ewart Gladstone	1892–1894
Earl of Rosebery	1894–1895
Marquis of Salisbury	1895–1902
Arthur James Balfour	1902–1905
Sir Henry Campbell-Bannerman	1905–1908
Herbert Henry Asquith	1908–1916
David Lloyd George	1916–1922
Andrew Bonar Law	1922–1923
Stanley Baldwin	1923–1924
James Ramsay MacDonald	1924
Stanley Baldwin	1924–1929
James Ramsay MacDonald	1929–1935
Stanley Baldwin	1935–1937
Neville Chamberlain	1937–1940
Winston Spencer Churchill	1940–1945
Clement Richard Attlee	1945–1951
Sir Winston Spencer Churchill	1951–1955
Sir Anthony Eden	1955–1957
Harold Macmillan	1957–1963
Sir Alexander Douglas-Home	1963–1964
Harold Wilson	1964–

APPENDIX VI

PRESIDENTS OF THE UNITED STATES OF AMERICA

1. George Washington	1789	13. Millard Fillmore	1850	25. William McKinley	1897
2. John Adams	1797	14. Franklin Pierce	1853	26. Theodore Roosevelt	1901
3. Thomas Jefferson	1801	15. James Buchanan	1857	27. William H. Taft	1909
4. James Madison	1809	16. Abraham Lincoln	1861	28. T. Woodrow Wilson	1913
5. James Monroe	1817	17. Andrew Johnson	1865	29. Warren G. Harding	1921
6. John Quincy Adams	1825	18. Ulysses S. Grant	1869	30. Calvin Coolidge	1923
7. Andrew Jackson	1829	19. Rutherford B. Hayes	1877	31. Herbert C. Hoover	1929
8. Martin Van Buren	1837	20. James A. Garfield	1881	32. Franklin D. Roosevelt	1933
9. William H. Harrison	1841	21. Chester A. Arthur	1881	33. Harry S. Truman	1945
10. John Tyler	1841	22. Grover Cleveland	1885	34. Dwight D. Eisenhower	1953
11. James K. Polk	1845	23. Benjamin Harrison	1889	35. John F. Kennedy	1961
12. Zachary Taylor	1849	24. Grover Cleveland	1893	36. Lyndon B. Johnson	1963

APPENDIX VII

STATES OF THE UNITED STATES OF AMERICA WITH THEIR CAPITALS

Alabama: Montgomery.
Alaska: Juneau.
Arizona: Phoenix.
Arkansas: Little Rock.
California: Sacramento.
Colorado: Denver.
Connecticut: Hartford.
Delaware: Dover.
Florida: Tallahassee.
Georgia: Atlanta.
Hawaii: Honolulu.
Idaho: Boise.
Illinois: Springfield.
Indiana: Indianapolis.
Iowa: Des Moines.
Kansas: Topeka.
Kentucky: Frankfort.
Louisiana: Baton Rouge.
Maine: Augusta.
Maryland: Annapolis.
Massachusetts: Boston.
Michigan: Lansing.
Minnesota: St. Paul.
Mississippi: Jackson.
Missouri: Jefferson City.
Montana: Helena.
Nebraska: Lincoln.
Nevada: Carson City.
New Hampshire: Concord.
New Jersey: Trenton.
New Mexico: Santa Fé.
New York: Albany.
North Carolina: Raleigh.
North Dakota: Bismarck.
Ohio: Columbus.
Oklahoma: Oklahoma City.
Oregon: Salem.
Pennsylvania: Harrisburg.
Rhode Island: Providence.
South Carolina: Columbia.
South Dakota: Pierre.
Tennessee: Nashville.
Texas: Austin.
Utah: Salt Lake City.
Vermont: Montpelier.
Virginia: Richmond.
Washington: Olympia.
West Virginia: Charleston.
Wisconsin: Madison.
Wyoming: Cheyenne.

APPENDIX VIII

COUNTIES AND COUNTY TOWNS OF THE UNITED KINGDOM

England

County	*County Town*	*County Council Offices*
Bedfordshire	Bedford	Bedford
Berkshire	Reading	Reading
Buckinghamshire	Aylesbury	Aylesbury
Cambridgeshire	Cambridge	
Co. of Cambridge		Cambridge
Isle of Ely		March
Cheshire	Chester	Chester
Cornwall	Bodmin	Truro
Cumberland	Carlisle	Carlisle

County	County Town	County Council Offices
Derbyshire	Derby	Derby
Devonshire	Exeter	Exeter
Dorset	Dorchester	Dorchester
Durham	Durham	Durham
Essex	Chelmsford	Chelmsford
Gloucestershire	Gloucester	Gloucester
Hampshire	Winchester	
Co. of Southampton		Winchester
Isle of Wight		Newport
Herefordshire	Hereford	Hereford
Hertfordshire	Hertford	Hertford
Huntingdonshire	Huntingdon	Huntingdon
Kent	Maidstone	Maidstone
Lancashire	Lancaster (Assize towns Lancaster, Liverpool, and Manchester)	Preston
Leicestershire	Leicester	Leicester
Lincolnshire	Lincoln	
Holland		Boston
Kesteven		Sleaford
Lindsey		Lincoln
Middlesex	Brentford (Assizes in Old Bailey, City of London)	Westminster
Monmouthshire	Monmouth (Assize town Newport)	Newport
Norfolk	Norwich	Norwich
Northamptonshire	Northampton	
Co. of Northampton		Northampton
Soke of Peterborough		Peterborough
Northumberland	Newcastle upon Tyne	Newcastle upon Tyne
Nottinghamshire	Nottingham	Nottingham
Oxfordshire	Oxford	Oxford
Rutland	Oakham	Oakham
Shropshire	Shrewsbury	Shrewsbury
Somerset	Taunton (Assize towns Taunton and Wells)	Taunton
Staffordshire	Stafford	Stafford
Suffolk	Ipswich (Assize towns Ipswich and Bury St. Edmunds)	
East Suffolk		Ipswich
West Suffolk		Bury St. Edmunds
Surrey	Kingston upon Thames	Kingston upon Thames
Sussex	Lewes	
East Sussex		Lewes
West Sussex		Chichester
Warwickshire	Warwick (Assize towns Warwick and Birmingham)	Warwick
Westmorland	Appleby	Kendal
Wiltshire	Salisbury (Assize towns Salisbury and Devizes)	Trowbridge
Worcestershire	Worcester	Worcester
Yorkshire	York (Assize towns York and Leeds)	
East Riding		Beverley
North Riding		Northallerton
West Riding		Wakefield

Scotland

County	County Town	County Council Offices
Aberdeenshire	Aberdeen	Aberdeen
Angus	Forfar (Circuit town Dundee)	Forfar
Argyllshire and islands	Inveraray	Lochgilphead
Ayrshire	Ayr	Ayr
Banffshire	Banff (Circuit town Aberdeen)	Banff
Berwickshire	Duns (Circuit town Jedburgh)	Duns
Buteshire and Isle of Arran	Rothesay (Circuit town Glasgow)	Rothesay
Caithness	Wick (Circuit town Inverness)	Wick
Clackmannanshire	Alloa (Circuit town Stirling)	Alloa
Dumfriesshire	Dumfries	Dumfries
Dunbartonshire	Dumbarton (Circuit town Stirling)	Dumbarton

County	County Town	County Council Offices
East Lothian	Haddington (Circuit town Edinburgh)	Haddington
Fife	Cupar (Circuit town Perth)	Cupar
Inverness-shire and islands	Inverness	Inverness
Kincardineshire	Stonehaven (Circuit town Aberdeen)	Stonehaven
Kinross-shire	Kinross (Circuit town Stirling)	Kinross
Kirkcudbrightshire	Kirkcudbright (Circuit town Dumfries)	Kirkcudbright
Lanarkshire	Lanark (Circuit town Glasgow)	Glasgow
Midlothian	Edinburgh	Edinburgh
Morayshire	Elgin (Circuit town Inverness)	Elgin
Nairnshire	Nairn (Circuit town Inverness)	Nairn
Orkney Islands	Kirkwall (Circuit town Inverness)	Kirkwall
Peeblesshire	Peebles (Circuit town Edinburgh)	Peebles
Perthshire	Perth	Perth
Renfrewshire	Renfrew (Circuit town Glasgow)	Paisley
Ross and Cromarty and Isle of Lewis	Dingwall (Circuit town Inverness)	Dingwall
Roxburghshire	Jedburgh	Newtown St. Boswells
Selkirkshire	Selkirk (Circuit town Jedburgh)	Selkirk
Shetland Islands	Lerwick (Circuit town Inverness)	Inverness
Stirlingshire	Stirling	Stirling
Sutherland	Dornoch (Circuit town Inverness)	Golspie
West Lothian	Linlithgow (Circuit town Edinburgh)	Linlithgow
Wigtownshire	Wigtown (Circuit town Dumfries)	Stranraer

Wales

County	County Town	County Council Offices
Anglesey	Beaumaris	Llangefni
Brecknockshire	Brecon	Brecon
Caernarvonshire	Caernarvon	Caernarvon
Cardiganshire	Cardigan (Assize town Lampeter)	Aberystwyth and Aberayron
Carmarthenshire	Carmarthen	Carmarthen
Denbighshire	Ruthin	Ruthin
Flintshire	Mold	Mold
Glamorgan	Cardiff	Cardiff
Merionethshire	Dolgelley	Dolgelley
Montgomeryshire	Welshpool (Assize towns Welshpool and Newtown)	Welshpool
Pembrokeshire	Haverfordwest	Haverfordwest
Radnorshire	Presteigne (Assize towns Presteigne and Newtown)	Llandrindod Wells

Northern Ireland

County	County Town	County Council Offices
Antrim	Belfast	Belfast
Armagh	Armagh	Armagh
Down	Downpatrick	Downpatrick
Fermanagh	Enniskillen	Enniskillen
Londonderry	Londonderry	Londonderry and Coleraine
Tyrone	Omagh	Omagh

APPENDIX IX

THE CHEMICAL ELEMENTS

Atomic number		*Atomic weight*	*Symbol*	*Atomic number*		*Atomic weight*	*Symbol*
1	Hydrogen	1·00797	H	4	Beryllium	9·0122	Be
2	Helium	4·0026	He	5	Boron	10·811	B
3	Lithium	6·939	Li	6	Carbon	12·01115	C

Atomic number		*Atomic weight*	*Symbol*	*Atomic number*		*Atomic weight*	*Symbol*
7	Nitrogen	14·0067	N	50	Tin	118·69	Sn
8	Oxygen	15·9994	O	51	Antimony	121·75	Sb
9	Fluorine	18·9984	F	52	Tellurium	127·60	Te
10	Neon	20·183	Ne	53	Iodine	126·9044	I
11	Sodium	22·9898	Na	54	Xenon	131·30	Xe
12	Magnesium	24·312	Mg	55	Caesium	132·905	Cs
13	Aluminium	26·9815	Al	56	Barium	137·34	Ba
14	Silicon	28·086	Si	57	Lanthanum	138·91	La
15	Phosphorus	30·9738	P	58	Cerium	140·12	Ce
16	Sulphur	32·064	S	59	Praseodymium	140·907	Pr
17	Chlorine	35·453	Cl	60	Neodymium	144·24	Nd
18	Argon	39·948	A	61	Promethium	147*	Pm
19	Potassium	39·102	K	62	Samarium	150·35	Sm
20	Calcium	40·08	Ca	63	Europium	151·96	Eu
21	Scandium	44·956	Sc	64	Gadolinium	157·25	Gd
22	Titanium	47·90	Ti	65	Terbium	158·924	Tb
23	Vanadium	50·942	V	66	Dysprosium	162·50	Dy
24	Chromium	51·996	Cr	67	Holmium	164·930	Ho
25	Manganese	54·9381	Mn	68	Erbium	167·26	Er
26	Iron	55·847	Fe	69	Thulium	168·934	Tm
27	Cobalt	58·9332	Co	70	Ytterbium	173·04	Yb
28	Nickel	58·71	Ni	71	Lutecium	174·97	Lu
29	Copper	63·54	Cu	72	Hafnium	178·49	Hf
30	Zinc	65·37	Zn	73	Tantalum	180·948	Ta
31	Gallium	69·72	Ga	74	Tungsten	183·85	W
32	Germanium	72·59	Ge	75	Rhenium	186·2	Re
33	Arsenic	74·9216	As	76	Osmium	190·2	Os
34	Selenium	78·96	Se	77	Iridium	192·2	Ir
35	Bromine	79·909	Br	78	Platinum	195·09	Pt
36	Krypton	83·80	Kr	79	Gold	196·967	Au
37	Rubidium	85·47	Rb	80	Mercury	200·59	Hg
38	Strontium	87·62	Sr	81	Thallium	204·37	Tl
39	Yttrium	88·905	Y	82	Lead	207·19	Pb
40	Zirconium	91·22	Zr	83	Bismuth	208·980	Bi
41	Niobium	92·906	Nb	84	Polonium	210*	Po
42	Molybdenum	95·94	Mo	85	Astatine	211*	At
43	Technetium	99*	Tc	86	Radon	222*	Rn
44	Ruthenium	101·07	Ru	87	Francium	223*	Fr
45	Rhodium	102·905	Rh	88	Radium	226·05	Ra
46	Palladium	106·4	Pd	89	Actinium	227*	Ac
47	Silver	107·870	Ag	90	Thorium	232·038	Th
48	Cadmium	112·40	Cd	91	Protactinium	231*	Pa
49	Indium	114·82	In	92	Uranium	238·03	U

TRANSURANIC ELEMENTS

Atomic number		*Atomic weight*	*Symbol*	*Atomic number*		*Atomic weight*	*Symbol*
93	Neptunium	237*	Np	98	Californium	244*	Cf
94	Plutonium	239*	Pu	99	Einsteinium	253*	E
95	Americium	241*	Am	100	Fermium	256*	Fm
96	Curium	242*	Cm	101	Mendelevium†		Mv
97	Berkelium	243*	Bk	102	Nobelium†		No

* Principal isotope. † Isotopic weight not yet known.

APPENDIX X

WEIGHTS AND MEASURES

BRITISH AND AMERICAN MEASURES OF WEIGHT

Avoirdupois weight

	grain	0·0648 gram
	dram	1·772 grams
16 drams	ounce (oz.)	28·35 grams
16 ounces or 7,000 grains	POUND (lb.)	0·454 kilogram
14 pounds	stone	6·35 kilograms
28 pounds	quarter	12·7 kilograms
25 pounds	U.S. quarter	11·34 kilograms
4 quarters or 112 pounds	hundredweight (cwt.)	50·80 kilograms
4 quarters or 100 pounds	U.S. hundredweight (cwt.)	45·36 kilograms
20 hundredweight or 2,240 pounds	long ton	1,016·05 kilograms
20 hundredweight or 2,000 pounds	U.S. short ton	907·19 kilograms

Troy weight

	grain	0·0648 gram
24 grains	pennyweight (dwt.)	1·555 grams
20 pennyweights or 480 grains	ounce	31·1035 grams
12 ounces or 5,760 grains	pound (not a legal measure but used for convenience)	373·27 grams

Apothecaries' weight

	grain	0·0648 gram
20 grains	scruple (℈)	1·296 grams
3 scruples or 60 grains	drachm or (U.S.) dram (ʒ)	3·888 grams
8 drachms or 480 grains	ounce (℥) (= troy ounce)	31·1035 grams

Apothecaries' fluid measure

	minim (min., ♏)	0·0059 centilitre
60 minims	fluid drachm (f. ʒ)	0·355 centilitre
8 fluid drachms	fluid ounce (f. ℥ or fl. oz.)	0·284 decilitre
20 fluid ounces	pint (O.)	0·568 litre
8 pints	gallon (C.)	4·546 litres

BRITISH MEASURES OF CAPACITY

	fluid ounce	0·284 decilitre
	gill	1·42 decilitres
4 gills or 20 fluid ounces	pint	0·568 litre
2 pints	quart	1·136 litre
4 quarts	GALLON (imperial gallon, 277·274 cubic inches)	4·546 litres
2 gallons	peck	9·092 litres
4 pecks or 8 gallons	bushel	0·364 hectolitre
8 bushels	quarter	2·909 hectolitres

AMERICAN MEASURES OF CAPACITY

Liquid measure

	minim	0·059 millilitre
60 minims	fluid dram	3·6966 millilitres
8 fluid drams	fluid ounce	0·296 decilitre
16 fluid ounces	pint	0·473 litre

2 pints	quart	0·946 litre
4 quarts	GALLON (Winchester or wine gallon, 231 cubic inches)	3·785 litres

Dry measure

	pint	0·551 litre
2 pints	quart	1·101 litre
8 quarts	peck	8·809 litres
4 pecks	bushel	35·328 litres

BRITISH AND AMERICAN LINEAR MEASURES

	inch	2·54 centimetres (4 in. = approx. 10 cm.)
7·92 inches	link	0·201 metre
12 inches	foot	0·3048 metre
3 feet	yard	0·9144 metre
6 feet	fathom	1·8288 metres
5½ yards	rod, pole, or perch	5·0292 metres
22 yards or 4 rods or 100 links	chain	20·11678 metres
10 chains or 220 yards	furlong	201·1678 metres
8 furlongs or 1,760 yards or 5,280 feet	statute mile	1·60934 kilometres (5 miles = approx. 8 km.)
6,080 feet	nautical mile	1·8533 kilometres

BRITISH AND AMERICAN SQUARE MEASURES

	square inch	6·452 square centimetres
144 square inches	square foot	0·0929 square metre
9 square feet	square yard	0·8361 square metre
30¼ square yards	square rod, pole, or perch	25·29 square metres
40 square rods	rood	0·101 hectare
4 roods or 10 square chains or 4,840 square yards	acre	0·405 hectare
640 acres or 3,097,600 square yards	square mile	2·59 square kilometres

BRITISH AND AMERICAN CUBIC MEASURES

	cubic inch	16·387 cubic centimetres
1,728 cubic inches	cubic foot	0·0283 cubic metre
27 cubic feet	cubic yard	0·765 cubic metre
100 cubic feet	register ton	2·832 cubic metres

METRIC SYSTEM

Measures of length

1,000 microns	millimetre	0·039 inch
10 millimetres	centimetre	0·3937 inch
10 centimetres	decimetre	3·937 inches
10 decimetres	METRE	39·37 inches
10 metres	decametre	32 feet 10 inches (nearly 11 yards)
10 decametres	hectometre	328 feet 1 inch (about $\frac{1}{16}$ mile)
10 hectometres or 1,000 metres	kilometre	0·621 mile (roughly $\frac{5}{8}$), or 3,280 feet 10 inches

Square measures

100 square millimetres	square centimetre	0·155 square inch
100 square centimetres	square decimetre	15·50 square inches
100 square decimetres	square metre or centiare	1·196 square yards or 1,550 square inches
100 square metres	are	119·6 square yards, approx $\frac{1}{40}$ acre
100 ares	hectare	2·4711 acres

Cubic measures

1,000 cubic millimetres	cubic centimetre	0·061 cubic inch
1,000 cubic centimetres	cubic decimetre	61·024 cubic inches
1,000 cubic decimetres	cubic metre or stere	35·31 cubic feet or 1·308 cubic yards
100 cubic metres	hectostere	130·8 cubic yards

Measures of capacity

	millilitre	16·894 minims
10 millilitres	centilitre	2 fluid drachms 49 minims
10 centilitres	decilitre	3 fluid ounces, 4 drachms, 10·4 minims (about 3½ fluid ounces)
10 decilitres	LITRE	1·7598 pints or about 35 fluid ounces
10 litres	decalitre	2·2 imperial gallons
10 decalitres	hectolitre	22 imperial gallons

Measures of weight

	milligram	0·015 grain
10 milligrams	centigram	0·154 grain (about ⅐)
10 centigrams	decigram	1·543 grains
10 decigrams	gram	15·432 grains or 0·035 ounce
10 grams	decagram	0·353 ounce (about ⅓)
10 decagrams	hectogram	3·527 ounces
10 hectograms or 1,000 grams	KILOGRAM	2·205 pounds (5 kilograms = approx. 11 pounds)
100 kilograms	quintal	220·46 pounds or 1·968 hundredweight
1,000 kilograms	metric ton	2,204·6 pounds

ANGULAR MEASURES

	second (″)
60 seconds	minute (′)
60 minutes	degree (°)
90 degrees	right angle or quadrant
4 quadrants or 360 degrees	circle

TEMPERATURES—CENTIGRADE AND FAHRENHEIT

Centigrade	*Fahrenheit*
−17·8°	0°
−10°	14°
0°	32°
10°	50°
20°	68°
30°	86°
40°	104°
50°	122°
60°	140°
70°	158°
80°	176°
90°	194°
100°	212°

To convert Centigrade into Fahrenheit: multiply by 9, divide by 5, and add 32.
To convert Fahrenheit into Centigrade: subtract 32, multiply by 5, and divide by 9.

PRINTED IN GREAT BRITAIN AT THE UNIVERSITY PRESS, OXFORD
BY VIVIAN RIDLER, PRINTER TO THE UNIVERSITY